The Asian Databook

First Edition

The Asian Databook

Detailed Statistics and Rankings on the Asian and Pacific Islander Population, including 23 Ethnic Backgrounds from Bangladeshi to Vietnamese, for 1,883 U.S. Counties and Cities.

A Universal Reference Book

Grey House Publishing

PUBLISHER: Leslie Mackenzie
EDITOR: David Garoogian
EDITORIAL DIRECTOR: Laura Mars-Proietti

PRODUCTION MANAGER: Robert Oakes

MARKETING DIRECTOR: Jessica Moody

A Universal Reference Book
Grey House Publishing, Inc.
185 Millerton Road
Millerton, NY 12546
518.789.8700
FAX 518.789.0545
www.greyhouse.com
e-mail: books @greyhouse.com

First edition

Printed in the USA

Publishers Cataloging-In-Publication Data
(Prepared by The Donohue Group, Inc.)

The Asian databook : detailed statistics and rankings on the Asian population, including ethnic backgrounds from U.S. counties and cities / Editor: David Garoogian.-- 1st ed. --

p. ; cm.
ISBN: 1-59237-044-6

1. Asian Americans--Population--Statistics. I. Garoogian, David.

E184.O6 A853 2004
305.895073

Table of Contents

Introduction

Welcome to the first edition of *The Asian Databook*, produced by Universal Reference Publications, an imprint of Grey House Publishing. Developed in the same format as our successful *Hispanic Databook*, published earlier this year, *The Asian Databook* responds to requests by librarians and researchers for statistical information on this growing segment of the US population. According to the US Census Bureau, the Asian population increased faster between 1990 and 2000 than the total US population – a 48% increase for Asians versus a 13% increase for the total population.

The Asian Databook takes a detailed look at this growing group and offers statistics on 14 topics for 23 Asian, Native Hawaiian and other Pacific Islander groups. Raw data comes from Census 2000, Summary File 4 (SF4). Our editors spent countless hours working with the Census files to present dozens of comparisons and configurations.

In more than 2,000 pages, researchers will find data for 1,833 places in the US. In all, 50 States and DC, 786 Counties and 1,045 Cities are represented. County criteria is population over 49,999; City and Town criteria is population over 9,999 and having Asian, Native Hawaiian and other Pacific Islander population greater than the national average. This dual criteria allows inclusion of many smaller places with high percentages of Asians and Pacific Islanders.

Section One – Statistical Tables
The tables in this section are organized into 14 topics. They are arranged alphabetically by State, then County, then City. Topics include: Overall Population; Median Age; Average Household Size; Language Spoken at Home (English Only); Foreign Born (and Naturalized Citizens); Educational Attainment (High School, College); Income (Median Household, Per Capita, Poverty Status); Housing (Homeownership, Home Value, Rent).

We isolated data for all 23 Asian and Pacific Islander groups per Census 2000 (SF4). Asian groups are Asian Indian, Bangladeshi, Cambodian, Chinese, Filipino, Hmong, Indonesian, Japanese, Korean, Laotian, Malaysian, Pakistani, Sri Lankan, Taiwanese; Thai and Vietnamese. Native Hawaiian and Other Pacific Islander groups are Fijian, Guamanian or Chamorro, Native Hawaiian, Samoan and Tongan. Data is also calculated for the total Asian and Pacific Islander populations.

Charts for all topics present the data as a number. For example, *Median Household Income* among Taiwanese in the US is $54,928. *Median Home Value* for Japanese in the US is $238,300. Many charts offer a number and a percentage, plus several additional comparisons – percentage of total population, percentage of total Asian population, and percentage of the chart's population parameters. See the User's Guide following this Introduction for a complete explanation of data.

Section Two – Rankings
This section offers 547 tables that rank all the states, the top 75 counties and the top 75 cities for all ethnic origins in 14 different topics. The top 75 are from the entire universe of US places with these population groups whether or not they meet the criteria to be in Section One.

You will, therefore, find rankings for cities with a population under 50,000 that are not included in Section One data because they are too small, or the population percentages are less than the national average. Our editors feel that by ranking the top 75 places regardless of size, we provide the user with not only another approach to the data, but also additional important community comparisons.

All topics are ranked by number and many also by percentage. Users will learn that: 31.38 percent of the population in Hamtramck, Michigan is Bangladeshi; Oklahoma has the highest percent of Hmongs who speak English only at home; and Salt Lake City has the most Tongans who are four-year college graduates.

Added Features:
City Finder List – this is an alphabetical list of all 1,045 cities profiled in Section One in *The Asian Databook,* with its county and state. It makes easy work of finding a city without knowing its county.

The Asian Databook CD-ROM – this companion CD-ROM is available at no additional charge to purchasers of the print book who return the coupon in the back of the book. It includes the same topics as the print product, but for 3,426 places with Asian and Pacific Islander population – thousands more than the print. It includes all states, counties and cities with Asian or Native Hawaiian and other Pacific Islander residents.

User's Guide

Places Covered in Print Version

United States

All 50 states plus the District of Columbia.

786 counties and county-equivalents with populations over 49,999. County-equivalents include boroughs in Alaska, parishes in Louisiana, the independent cities of Baltimore (MD), Carson City (NV), St. Louis (MO), and 16 independent cities in Virginia.

616 incorporated municipalities with populations over 9,999 whose Asian and/or Native Hawaiian and other Pacific Islander population rates are greater than the national average. Depending on the state, municipalities are incorporated as either cities, towns, villages, or boroughs. A few municipalities have a form of government combined with another entity (e.g. county) and are listed as "special cities."

259 census designated places (CDP) with populations over 9,999 whose Asian and/or Native Hawaiian and other Pacific Islander population rates are greater than the national average. The U.S. Bureau of the Census defines a CDP as "a statistical entity, defined for each decennial census according to Census Bureau guidelines, comprising a densely settled concentration of population that is not within an incorporated place, but is locally identified by a name. CDPs are delineated cooperatively by state and local officials and the Census Bureau, following Census Bureau guidelines. Beginning with Census 2000 there are no size limits."

170 minor civil divisions with populations over 9,999 whose Asian and/or Native Hawaiian and other Pacific Islander population rates are greater than the national average. Called towns, townships, districts, gores, locations, and plantations for the states where the Census Bureau has determined that they serve as general-purpose governments. Those states are Connecticut, Maine, Massachusetts, Michigan, Minnesota, New Hampshire, New Jersey, New York, Pennsylvania, Rhode Island, Vermont, and Wisconsin. In some states incorporated municipalities are part of minor civil divisions and in some states they are independent of them.

Places Covered in CD-ROM Version

United States

All 50 states plus the District of Columbia.

916 counties and county-equivalents. County-equivalents include census areas and boroughs in Alaska, parishes in Louisiana, the independent cities of Baltimore (MD), Carson City (NV), St. Louis (MO), and 19 independent cities in Virginia.

1,456 incorporated municipalities. Depending on the state, municipalities are incorporated as either cities, towns, villages, or boroughs. A few municipalities have a form of government combined with another entity (e.g. county) and are listed as "special cities."

627 census designated places (CDP). The U.S. Bureau of the Census defines a CDP as "a statistical entity, defined for each decennial census according to Census Bureau guidelines, comprising a densely settled concentration of population that is not within an incorporated place, but is locally identified by a name. CDPs are delineated cooperatively by state and local officials and the Census Bureau, following Census Bureau guidelines. Beginning with Census 2000 there are no size limits."

375 minor civil divisions. Called towns, townships, districts, gores, locations, and plantations) for the states where the Census Bureau has determined that they serve as general-purpose governments. Those states are Connecticut, Maine, Massachusetts, Michigan, Minnesota, New Hampshire, New Jersey, New York, Pennsylvania, Rhode Island, Vermont, and Wisconsin. In some states incorporated municipalities are part of minor civil divisions and in some states they are independent of them.

Note: *Ranking tables in both the print and CD-ROM versions include all places with Asian and/or Native Hawaiian and other Pacific Islander residents. Places with no Asian/Native Hawaiian and Other Pacific Islander residents have been excluded from both versions.*

Source of Data

CENSUS 2000

Data for this publication was derived from following source: *U.S. Bureau of the Census, Census of Population and Housing, 2000: Summary File 4.* Summary File 4 (SF 4) contains sample data, which is the information compiled from the questions asked of a sample (generally 1-in-6) of all people and housing units. Summary File 4 is repeated or iterated for the total population and 335 additional population groups. This publication focuses on the following 23 population groups:

- Asian
  - Asian Indian
  - Bangladeshi
  - Cambodian
  - Chinese (except Taiwanese)
  - Filipino
  - Hmong
  - Indonesian
  - Japanese
  - Korean
  - Laotian
  - Malaysian
  - Pakistani
  - Sri Lankan
  - Taiwanese
  - Thai
  - Vietnamese
- Native Hawaiian and Other Pacific Islander
  - Fijian
  - Guamanian or Chamorro
  - Hawaiian, Native
  - Samoan
  - Tongan

Please note that this book only includes people who responded to the question on race by indicating only one race. These people are classified by the Census Bureau as the race *alone* population. For example, respondents reporting a single detailed Asian group, such as Korean or Filipino, would be included in the Asian *alone* population. Respondents reporting more than one detailed Asian group, such as Chinese and Japanese or Asian Indian and Chinese and Vietnamese would also be included in the Asian *alone* population. This is because all of the detailed groups in these example combinations are part of the larger Asian race category. The same criteria apply to the Native Hawaiian and Other Pacific Islander groups.

In order for any of the tables for a specific group to be shown in Summary File 4, the data must meet a minimum population threshold. For Summary File 4, all tables are repeated for each race group, American Indian and Alaska Native tribe, and Hispanic or Latino group if the 100-percent count of people of that specific group in a particular geographic area is 100 or more. There also must be 50 or more unweighted people of that specific group in a particular geographic area. For example, if there are 100 or more 100-percent people tabulated as Korean in County A, and there are 50 or more unweighted people, then all matrices for Korean are shown in SF 4 for County A.

To maintain confidentiality, the Census Bureau applies statistical procedures that introduce some uncertainty into data for small geographic areas with small population groups. Therefore, tables may contain both sampling and nonsampling error.

In an iterated file such as SF 4, the universes *households, families,* and *occupied housing units* are classified by the race or ethnic group of the householder. In any population table where there is no note, the universe classification is always based on the race or ethnicity of the person. In all housing tables, the universe classification is based on the race or ethnicity of the householder.

Comparing SF 4 Estimates with Corresponding Values in SF 1 and SF 2

As in earlier censuses, the responses from the sample of households reporting on long forms must be weighted to reflect the entire population. Specifically, each responding household represents, on average, six or seven other households who reported using short forms. One consequence of the weighting procedures is that each estimate based on the long form responses has an associated confidence interval. These confidence intervals are wider (as a percentage of the estimate) for geographic areas with smaller populations and for characteristics that occur less frequently in the area being examined (such as the proportion of people in poverty in a middle-income neighborhood). In order to release as much useful information as possible, statisticians must balance a number of factors. In particular, for Census 2000, the Bureau of the Census created weighting areas—geographic areas from which about two hundred or more long forms were completed—which are large enough to produce good quality estimates. If smaller weighting areas had been used, the confidence intervals around the estimates would have been significantly wider, rendering many estimates less useful due to their lower reliability. The disadvantage of using weighting areas this large is that, for smaller geographic areas within them, the estimates of characteristics that are also reported on the short form will not match the counts reported in SF 1 or SF 2. Examples of these characteristics are the total number of people, the number of people reporting specific racial categories, and the number of housing units. The official values for items reported on the short form come from SF 1 and SF 2. The differences between the long form estimates in SF 4 and values in SF 1 or SF 2 are particularly noticeable for the smallest places, tracts, and block groups. The long form estimates of total population and total housing units in SF 4 will, however, match the SF 1 and SF 2 counts for larger geographic areas such as counties and states, and will be essentially the same for medium and large cities. This phenomenon also occurred for the 1990 Census, although in that case, the weighting areas included relatively small places. As a result, the long form estimates matched the short form counts for those places, but the confidence intervals around the estimates of characteristics collected only on the long form were often significantly wider (as a percentage of the estimate). SF 1 gives exact numbers even for very small groups and areas; whereas, SF 4 gives estimates for small groups and areas such as tracts and small places that are less exact. The goal of SF 4 is to identify large differences among areas or large changes over time. Estimates for small areas and small population groups often do exhibit large changes from one census to the next, so having the capability to measure them is worthwhile.

Topics

POPULATION

Total Population: Sample count of total population of all races.

Asian Population: A person having origins in any of the original peoples of the Far East, Southeast Asia, or the Indian subcontinent including, for example, Cambodia, China, India, Japan, Korea, Malaysia, Pakistan, the Philippine Islands, Thailand, and Vietnam. It includes Asian Indian, Bangladeshi, Cambodian, Chinese (except Taiwanese), Filipino, Hmong, Indonesian, Japanese, Korean, Laotian, Malaysian, Pakistani, Sri Lankan, Taiwanese, Thai, and Vietnamese.

Native Hawaiian or Other Pacific Islander (NHPI) Population: A person having origins in any of the original peoples of Hawaii, Guam, Samoa, or other Pacific Islands. It includes people who indicate their race as Fijian, Guamanian or Chamorro, Native Hawaiian, Samoan, and Tongan.

The data on race, which was asked of all people, were derived from answers to long-form questionnaire Item 6 and short-form questionnaire Item 8. The concept of race, as used by the Census Bureau, reflects self-identification by people according to the race or races with which they most closely identify. These categories are socio-political constructs and should not be interpreted as being scientific or anthropological in nature. Furthermore, the race categories include both racial and national-origin groups.

If an individual did not provide a race response, the race or races of the householder or other household members were assigned using specific rules of precedence of household relationship. For example, if race was missing for a natural-born child in the household, then either the race or races of the householder, another natural-born child, or the spouse of the householder were assigned. If race was not reported for anyone in the household, the race or races of a householder in a previously processed household were assigned.

AGE

Median Age: Divides the age distribution into two equal parts: one-half of the cases falling below the median age and one-half above the median. Median age is computed on the basis of a single year of age standard distribution.

The data on age, which was asked of all people, were derived from answers to the long-form questionnaire Item 4 and short-form questionnaire Item 6. The age classification is based on the age of the person in complete years as of April 1, 2000. The age of the person usually was derived from their date of birth information. Their reported age was used only when date of birth information was unavailable.

HOUSEHOLD SIZE

Average Household Size: A measure obtained by dividing the number of people in households by the total number of households (or householders). In cases where household members are tabulated by race or Hispanic origin, household members are classified by the race or Hispanic origin of the householder rather than the race or Hispanic origin of each individual. Average household size is rounded to the nearest hundredth.

LANGUAGE SPOKEN AT HOME

English Only: Number and percentage of population 5 years and over who report speaking English-only at home.

Language spoken at home data were derived from answers to long-form questionnaire Items 11a and 11b, which were asked of a sample of the population. Data were edited to include in tabulations only the population 5 years old and over. Questions 11a and 11b referred to languages spoken at home in an effort to measure the current use of languages other than English. People who knew languages other than English but did not use them at home or who only used them elsewhere were excluded. Most people who reported speaking a language other than English at home also speak English. The questions did not permit determination of the primary or dominant language of people who spoke both English and another language.

FOREIGN-BORN

Foreign Born: Number and percentage of population who were not U.S. citizens at birth. Foreign-born people are those who indicated they were either a U.S. citizen by naturalization or they were not a citizen of the United States.

Foreign-Born Naturalized Citizens: Number and percentage of population who were not U.S. citizens at birth but became U.S. citizens by naturalization.

The data on place of birth were derived from answers to long-form questionnaire Item 12 which was asked of a sample of the population. Respondents were asked to report the U.S. state, Puerto Rico, U.S. Island Area, or foreign country where they were born. People not reporting a place of birth were assigned the state or country of birth of another family member or their residence 5 years earlier, or were imputed the response of another person with similar characteristics. People born outside the United States were asked to report their place of birth according to current international boundaries. Since numerous changes in boundaries of foreign countries have occurred in the last century, some people may have reported their place of birth in terms of boundaries that existed at the time of their birth or emigration, or in accordance with their own national preference.

EDUCATIONAL ATTAINMENT

High School Graduates: Number and percentage of the population age 25 and over who have a high school diploma or higher. This category includes people whose highest degree was a high school diploma or its equivalent, people who attended college but did not receive a degree, and people who received a college, university, or professional degree. People who reported completing the 12th grade but not receiving a diploma are not high school graduates.

Four-Year College Graduates: Number and percentage of the population age 25 and over who have a 4-year college, university, or professional degree.

Data on educational attainment were derived from answers to long-form questionnaire Item 9, which was asked of a sample of the population. Data on attainment are tabulated for the population 25 years old and over.

The order in which degrees were listed on the questionnaire suggested that doctorate degrees were "higher" than professional school degrees, which were "higher" than master's degrees. The question included instructions for people currently enrolled in school to report the level of the previous grade attended or the highest degree received. Respondents who did not report educational attainment or enrollment level were assigned the attainment of a person of the same age, race, Hispanic or Latino origin, occupation and sex, where possible, who resided in the same or a nearby area. Respondents who filled more than one box were edited to the highest level or degree reported.

The question included a response category that allowed respondents to report completing the 12th grade without receiving a high school diploma. It allowed people who received either a high school diploma or the equivalent (Test of General Educational Development—G.E.D.) and did not attend college, to be reported as "high school graduate(s)." The category "Associate degree" included people whose highest degree is an associate degree, which generally requires 2 years of college level work and is either in an occupational program that prepares them for a specific occupation, or an academic program primarily in the arts and sciences. The course work may or may not be transferable to a bachelor's degree. Master's degrees include the traditional MA and MS degrees and field-specific degrees, such as MSW, MEd, MBA, MLS, and MEng. Some examples of professional degrees include medicine, dentistry, chiropractic, optometry, osteopathic medicine, pharmacy, podiatry, veterinary medicine, law, and theology. Vocational and technical training such as barber school training; business, trade, technical, and vocational schools; or other training for a specific trade, are specifically excluded.

INCOME AND POVERTY

Median Household Income (in dollars): Includes the income of the householder and all other individuals 15 years old and over in the household, whether they are related to the householder or not. The median divides the income distribution into two equal parts: one-half of the cases falling below the median income and one-half above the median. For households, the median income is based on the distribution of the total number of households including those with no income. Median income for households is computed on the basis of a standard distribution and is rounded to the nearest whole dollar.

Per Capita Income (in dollars): Per capita income is the mean income computed for every man, woman, and child in a particular group. It is derived by dividing the total income of a particular group by the total population in that group. Per capita income is rounded to the nearest whole dollar.

The data on income in 1999 were derived from answers to long-form questionnaire Items 31 and 32, which were asked of a sample of the population 15 years old and over. "Total income" is the sum of the amounts reported separately for wage or salary income; net self-employment income; interest, dividends, or net rental or royalty income or income from estates and trusts; social security or railroad retirement income; Supplemental Security Income (SSI); public assistance or welfare payments; retirement, survivor, or disability pensions; and all other income.

Receipts from the following sources are not included as income: capital gains, money received from the sale of property (unless the recipient was engaged in the business of selling such property); the value of income "in kind" from food stamps, public housing subsidies, medical care, employer contributions for individuals, etc.; withdrawal of bank deposits; money borrowed; tax refunds; exchange of money between relatives living in the same household; and gifts and lump-sum inheritances, insurance payments, and other types of lump-sum receipts.

The eight types of income reported in the census are defined as follows:

Wage or salary income. Wage or salary income includes total money earnings received for work performed as an employee during the calendar year 1999. It includes wages, salary, armed forces pay, commissions, tips, piece-rate payments, and cash bonuses earned before deductions were made for taxes, bonds, pensions, union dues, etc.

Self-employment income. Self-employment income includes both farm and nonfarm self-employment income. Nonfarm self-employment income includes net money income (gross receipts minus expenses) from one's own business, professional enterprise, or partnership. Gross receipts include the value of all goods sold and services rendered. Expenses include costs of goods purchased, rent, heat, light, power, depreciation charges, wages and salaries paid, business taxes (not personal income taxes), etc. Farm self-employment income includes net money income (gross receipts minus operating expenses) from the operation of a farm by a person on his or her own account, as an owner, renter, or sharecropper. Gross receipts include the value of all products sold, government farm programs, money received from the rental of farm equipment to others, and incidental receipts from the sale of wood, sand, gravel, etc. Operating expenses include cost of feed, fertilizer, seed, and other farming supplies, cash wages paid to farmhands, depreciation charges, cash rent, interest on farm mortgages, farm building repairs, farm taxes (not state and federal personal income taxes), etc. The value of fuel, food, or other farm products used for family living is not included as part of net income.

Interest, dividends, or net rental income. Interest, dividends, or net rental income includes interest on savings or bonds, dividends from stockholdings or membership in associations, net income from rental of property to others and receipts from boarders or lodgers, net royalties, and periodic payments from an estate or trust fund.

Social Security income. Social security income includes social security pensions and survivors benefits, permanent disability insurance payments made by the Social Security Administration prior to deductions for medical insurance, and railroad retirement insurance checks from the U.S. government. Medicare reimbursements are not included.

Supplemental Security Income (SSI). Supplemental Security Income (SSI) is a nationwide U.S. assistance program administered by the Social Security Administration that guarantees a minimum level of income for needy aged, blind, or disabled individuals. The census questionnaire for Puerto Rico asked about the receipt of SSI; however, SSI is not a federally administered program in Puerto Rico. Therefore, it is probably not being interpreted by most respondents as the same as SSI in the United States. The only way a resident of Puerto Rico could have appropriately reported SSI would have been if they lived in the United States at any time during calendar year 1999 and received SSI.

Public assistance income. Public assistance income includes general assistance and Temporary Assistance to Needy Families (TANF). Separate payments received for hospital or other medical care (vendor payments) are excluded. This does not include Supplemental Security Income (SSI).

Retirement income. Retirement income includes: (1) retirement pensions and survivor benefits from a former employer; labor union; or federal, state, or local government; and the U.S. military; (2) income from workers' compensation; disability income from companies or unions; federal, state, or local government; and the U.S. military; (3) periodic receipts from annuities and insurance; and (4) regular income from IRA and KEOGH plans. This does not include social security income.

All other income. All other income includes unemployment compensation, Veterans' Administration (VA) payments, alimony and child support, contributions received periodically from people not living in the household, military family allotments, and other kinds of periodic income other than earnings.

Poverty Status: Number and percentage of population with income in 1999 below the poverty level. Based on individuals for whom poverty status is determined. Poverty status was determined for all people except institutionalized people, people in military group quarters, people in college dormitories, and unrelated individuals under 15 years old.

The poverty status of families and unrelated individuals in 1999 was determined using 48 thresholds (income cutoffs) arranged in a two dimensional matrix. The matrix consists of family size (from 1 person to 9 or more people) cross-classified by presence and number of family members under 18 years old (from no children present to 8 or more children present). Unrelated individuals and 2-person families were further differentiated by the age of the reference person (RP) (under 65 years old and 65 years old and over).

To determine a person's poverty status, one compares the person's total family income with the poverty threshold appropriate for that person's family size and composition. If the total income of that person's family is less than the threshold appropriate for that family, then the person is considered poor, together with every member of his or her family. If a person is not living with anyone related by birth, marriage, or adoption, then the person's own income is compared with his or her poverty threshold.

HOUSING

Homeownership: Number and percentage of housing units that are owner-occupied.

The data on tenure, which was asked at all occupied housing units, were obtained from answers to long-form questionnaire Item 33, and short-form questionnaire Item 2. All occupied housing units are classified as either owner occupied or renter occupied.

A housing unit is owner occupied if the owner or co-owner lives in the unit even if it is mortgaged or not fully paid for. The owner or co-owner must live in the unit and usually is Person 1 on the questionnaire. The unit is "Owned by you or someone in this household with a mortgage or loan" if it is being purchased with a mortgage or some other debt arrangement, such as a deed of trust, trust deed, contract to purchase, land contract, or purchase agreement. The unit is also considered owned with a mortgage if it is built on leased land and there is a mortgage on the unit. Mobile homes occupied by owners with installment loans balances are also included in this category.

Median Gross Rent (in dollars): Median monthly gross rent on specified renter-occupied and specified vacant-for-rent units. Specified renter-occupied and specified vacant-for-rent units exclude 1-family houses on 10 acres or more.

The data on gross rent were obtained from answers to long-form questionnaire Items 45a-d, which were asked on a sample basis. Gross rent is the contract rent plus the estimated average monthly cost of utilities (electricity, gas, water and sewer) and fuels (oil, coal, kerosene, wood, etc.) if these are paid by the renter (or paid for the renter by someone else). Gross rent is intended to eliminate differentials that result from varying practices with respect to the inclusion of utilities and fuels as part of the rental payment. The estimated costs of utilities and fuels are reported on an annual basis but are converted to monthly figures for the tabulations. Renter units occupied without payment of cash rent are shown separately as ''No cash rent'' in the tabulations.

Housing units that are renter occupied without payment of cash rent are shown separately as "No cash rent" in census data products. The unit may be owned by friends or relatives who live elsewhere and who allow occupancy without charge. Rent-free houses or apartments may be provided to compensate caretakers, ministers, tenant farmers, sharecroppers, or others.

Contract rent is the monthly rent agreed to or contracted for, regardless of any furnishings, utilities, fees, meals, or services that may be included. For vacant units, it is the monthly rent asked for the rental unit at the time of enumeration.

If the contract rent includes rent for a business unit or for living quarters occupied by another household, only that part of the rent estimated to be for the respondent's unit was included. Excluded was any rent paid for additional units or for business premises.

If a renter pays rent to the owner of a condominium or cooperative, and the condominium fee or cooperative carrying charge also is paid by the renter to the owner, the condominium fee or carrying charge was included as rent.

If a renter receives payments from lodgers or roomers who are listed as members of the household, the rent without deduction for any payments received from the lodgers or roomers was to be reported. The respondent was to report the rent agreed to or contracted for even if paid by someone else such as friends or relatives living elsewhere, a church or welfare agency, or the government through subsidies or vouchers.

The median divides the rent distribution into two equal parts: one-half of the cases falling below the median contract rent and one-half above the median. Median contract rents are computed on the basis of a standard distribution and are rounded to the nearest whole dollar. Units reported as "No cash rent" are excluded.

Median Home Value (in dollars): Reported by the owner of specified owner-occupied or specified vacant-for-sale housing units. Specified owner-occupied and specified vacant-for-sale housing units include only 1-family houses on less than 10 acres without a business or medical office on the property. The data for "specified units" exclude mobile homes, houses with a business or medical office, houses on 10 or more acres, and housing units in multi-unit buildings.

The data on value (also referred to as "price asked" for vacant units) were obtained from answers to long-form questionnaire Item 51, which was asked on a sample basis at owner-occupied housing units and units that were being bought, or vacant for sale at the time of enumeration. Value is the respondent's estimate of how much the property (house and lot, mobile home and lot, or condominium unit) would sell for if it were for sale. If the house or mobile home was owned or being bought, but the land on which it sits was not, the respondent was asked to estimate the combined value of the house or mobile home and the land. For vacant units, value was the price asked for the property. Value was tabulated separately for all owner-occupied and vacant-for-sale housing units, owner-occupied and vacant-for-sale mobile homes, and specified owner-occupied and specified vacant-for-sale housing units.

The median divides the value distribution into two equal parts: one-half of the cases falling below the median value of the property (house and lot, mobile home and lot, or condominium unit) and one-half above the median. Median values are computed on the basis of a standard distribution and are rounded to the nearest hundred dollars.

How to Read the Tables

There are three types of tables located in Section I.

Type I (1 line per entry). Six tables fall into this category: Median Age; Average Household Size; Median Household Income; Per Capita Income; Median Gross Rent; Median Home Value.

Place	All households	Asian households	NHPI[1] households	Asian Indian
UNITED STATES	41,994	51,908	42,717	63,669
ALABAMA	34,135	42,007	37,583	54,113
Baldwin County	40,250	53,864	-	-
Calhoun County	31,768	35,179	-	-
Etowah County	31,170	55,500	-	-
Houston County	34,431	32,083	-	-

Each line represents a number (eg. median household income, median age, etc.)

For example:
The median household income of Asian Indians in the U.S. is $63,669

Type II (3 lines per entry). One table falls into this category: Population.

Place	Total population	① Total Asian population	② Total NHPI[1] population	③ Asian Indian
UNITED STATES	281,421,906	10,171,820 3.61	378,782 0.13	1,645,510 16.18 0.58
ALABAMA	4,447,100	29,908 0.67	1,187 0.03	6,686 22.36 0.15
Baldwin County	140,415	535 0.38	-	-

The first line shows the number of persons.
The second line shows the number as a percentage of column 2 for Asian groups and as a percentage of column 3 for Native Hawaiian and Other Pacific Islander groups.
The third line shows the number as a percentage of the total population (column 1)

For example:
There are 1,645,510 Asian Indians in the U.S.
Asian Indians make up 16.18% of the total Asian population in the U.S.
Asian Indians make up 0.58% of the total population of the U.S.

Type III (5 lines per entry). Seven tables fall into this category: Language Spoken at Home: English Only; Foreign Born; Foreign-Born Naturalized Citizens; Educational Attainment: High School Graduates; Educational Attainment: Four-Year College Graduates; Poverty Status; Homeownership

Place	① Total population 25 years and over who are 4-year college graduates	② Asian population 25 years and over	③ Asians 25 years and over who are 4-year college graduates	④ NHPI[1] population 25 years and over	⑤ NHPIs[1] 25 years and over who are 4-year college graduates	Asian Indian
UNITED STATES	44,462,605 24.40	6,640,671	2,925,743 44.06 44.06 6.58	206,675	28,498 13.79 13.79 0.06	668,029 63.89 22.83 10.06 1.50
ALABAMA	549,608 19.03	18,999	9,173 48.28 48.28 1.67	639	101 15.81 15.81 0.02	2,961 71.59 32.28 15.59 0.54

The first line shows the number of persons
The second line shows the number as a percentage rate
The third line shows the number as a percentage of column 3 for Asian groups and as a percentage of column 5 for Native Hawaiian and Other Pacific Islander groups
The fourth line shows the number as a percentage of column 2 for Asian groups and as a percentage of column 4 for Native Hawaiian and Other Pacific Islander groups
The fifth line shows the number as a percentage of column 1

EXAMPLE
There are 668,029 Asian Indian 4-year college graduates in the U.S.
The Asian Indian 4-year college graduation rate is 63.89% in the U.S.
22.83% of Asian 4-year college graduates in the U.S. are Asian Indian
10.06% of Asians in the U.S. are Asian Indian 4-year college graduates
1.50% of all 4-year college graduates in the U.S. are Asian Indian

General Note: A dash indicates that data for that specific population group within the associated geographic area is less than the threshold(s). The population threshold on Summary File 4 is 100. In addition, there must be at least 50 or more unweighted cases of the population group. However, numbers less than 100 (including 0) may appear because the thresholds apply to the entire universe (e.g. Population 5 years and over), not the specific data element (e.g. Speak only English). In addition, numbers may not add up to totals and percentages may not add up to 100% within the same row.

Asian, Native Hawaiian and Other Pacific Islander Population

(Universe: Total Population)

Place	Total population	Total Asian population	Total NHPI[1] population	Asian Indian	Bangladeshi	Cambodian	Chinese[2]	Fijian	Filipino	Guamanian[3]	Hawaiian, Native	Hmong	Indonesian	Japanese	Korean	Laotian	Malaysian	Pakistani	Samoan	Sri Lankan	Taiwanese	Thai	Tongan	Vietnamese
UNITED STATES	281,421,906	10,171,820 3.61	378,782 0.13	1,645,510 16.18 0.58	41,428 0.41 0.01	178,043 1.75 0.06	2,300,219 22.61 0.82	10,265 2.71 <0.01	1,864,120 18.33 0.66	55,130 14.55 0.02	139,495 36.83 0.05	170,049 1.67 0.06	37,167 0.37 0.01	795,051 7.82 0.28	1,072,682 10.55 0.38	167,792 1.65 0.06	10,711 0.11 <0.01	155,909 1.53 0.06	85,243 22.50 0.03	19,078 0.19 0.01	122,751 1.21 0.04	110,851 1.09 0.04	27,686 7.31 0.01	1,110,207 10.91 0.39
ALABAMA	4,447,100	29,908 0.67	1,187 0.03	6,686 22.36 0.15	-	565 1.89 0.01	5,709 19.09 0.13	-	2,441 8.16 0.05	424 35.72 0.01	-	-	-	1,892 6.33 0.04	4,024 13.45 0.09	829 2.77 0.02	-	385 1.29 0.01	-	-	-	621 2.08 0.01	-	4,631 15.48 0.10
Baldwin County	140,415	535 0.38	-	-	-	-	-	-	-	-	-	-	-	-	-	-	-	-	-	-	-	-	-	-
Calhoun County	112,249	671 0.60	-	-	-	-	-	-	-	-	-	-	-	-	-	-	-	-	-	-	-	-	-	-
Etowah County	103,459	361 0.35	-	-	-	-	-	-	-	-	-	-	-	-	-	-	-	-	-	-	-	-	-	-
Houston County	88,787	500 0.56	-	-	-	-	-	-	-	-	-	-	-	-	-	-	-	-	-	-	-	-	-	-
Jefferson County	662,047	5,793 0.88	-	1,401 24.18 0.21	-	-	1,892 32.66 0.29	-	-	-	-	-	-	-	464 8.01 0.07	-	-	-	-	-	-	-	-	868 14.98 0.13
Lee County	115,092	1,834 1.59	-	-	-	-	629 34.30 0.55	-	-	-	-	-	-	-	-	-	-	-	-	-	-	-	-	-
Madison County	276,700	4,706 1.70	-	1,480 31.45 0.53	-	-	690 14.66 0.25	-	-	-	-	-	-	-	968 20.57 0.35	-	-	-	-	-	-	-	-	377 8.01 0.14
Mobile County	399,843	5,256 1.31	-	580 11.04 0.15	-	389 7.40 0.10	669 12.73 0.17	-	369 7.02 0.09	-	-	-	-	-	-	314 5.97 0.08	-	-	-	-	-	-	-	2,053 39.06 0.51
Montgomery County	223,510	1,779 0.80	-	-	-	-	-	-	-	-	-	-	-	-	-	-	-	-	-	-	-	-	-	-
Morgan County	111,064	571 0.51	-	-	-	-	-	-	-	-	-	-	-	-	-	-	-	-	-	-	-	-	-	-
Shelby County	143,293	1,006 0.70	-	387 38.47 0.27	-	-	-	-	-	-	-	-	-	-	-	-	-	-	-	-	-	-	-	-
Tuscaloosa County	164,875	1,533 0.93	-	-	-	-	-	-	-	-	-	-	-	-	-	-	-	-	-	-	-	-	-	-
ALASKA	626,932	25,496 4.07	3,122 0.50	546 2.14 0.09	-	-	1,564 6.13 0.25	-	12,488 48.98 1.99	-	499 15.98 0.08	522 2.05 0.08	-	1,425 5.59 0.23	4,554 17.86 0.73	1,368 5.37 0.22	-	-	1,534 49.14 0.24	-	-	782 3.07 0.12	419 13.42 0.07	969 3.80 0.15

Notes: Please refer to the User's Guide for an explanation of data; data is arranged alphabetically by state, then county, then city within each county; table includes counties with populations greater than 49,999 unless noted and cities with populations greater than 9,999 whose Asian and/or NHPI population rates are greater than the national average; (1) Native Hawaiian and other Pacific Islander; (2) excludes Taiwanese; (3) includes Chamorro; (4) county does not meet population threshold but is shown in order to allow inclusion of city

Place	Total population	Total Asian population	Total NHPI[1] population	Asian Indian	Bangladeshi	Cambodian	Chinese[2]	Fijian	Filipino	Guamanian[3]	Hawaiian, Native	Hmong	Indonesian	Japanese	Korean	Laotian	Malaysian	Pakistani	Samoan	Sri Lankan	Taiwanese	Thai	Tongan	Vietnamese
Anchorage Borough	260,283	14,266 5.48	2,027 0.78	316 2.22 0.12	-	-	864 6.06 0.33	-	5,036 35.30 1.93	-	-	522 3.66 0.20	-	885 6.20 0.34	3,448 24.17 1.32	1,265 8.87 0.49	-	-	1,208 59.60 0.46	-	-	577 4.04 0.22	-	484 3.39 0.19
Fairbanks North Star Borough	82,840	2,001 2.42	-	-	-	-	354 17.69 0.43	-	570 28.49 0.69	-	-	-	-	-	548 27.39 0.66	-	-	-	-	-	-	-	-	-
Juneau City and Borough	30,711	1,396 4.55	-	-	-	-	-	-	1,042 74.64 3.39	-	-	-	-	-	-	-	-	-	-	-	-	-	-	-
Matanuska-Susitna Borough	59,322	385 0.65	-	-	-	-	-	-	-	-	-	-	-	-	-	-	-	-	-	-	-	-	-	-
ARIZONA	5,130,632	91,223 1.78	6,166 0.12	14,510 15.91 0.28	-	1,240 1.36 0.02	21,069 23.10 0.41	-	16,205 17.76 0.32	1,265 20.52 0.02	1,985 32.19 0.04	-	573 0.63 0.01	7,446 8.16 0.15	9,936 10.89 0.19	891 0.98 0.02	-	672 0.74 0.01	850 13.79 0.02	-	794 0.87 0.02	1,631 1.79 0.03	634 10.28 0.01	11,704 12.83 0.23
Cochise County	117,755	1,960 1.66	-	-	-	-	-	-	429 21.89 0.36	-	-	-	-	-	767 39.13 0.65	-	-	-	-	-	-	-	-	-
Coconino County	116,320	894 0.77	-	-	-	-	-	-	-	-	-	-	-	-	-	-	-	-	-	-	-	-	-	-
Maricopa County	3,072,149	66,294 2.16	3,811 0.12	11,289 17.03 0.37	-	1,186 1.79 0.04	15,505 23.39 0.50	-	11,901 17.95 0.39	647 16.98 0.02	1,109 29.10 0.04	-	412 0.62 0.01	4,875 7.35 0.16	6,047 9.12 0.20	601 0.91 0.02	-	520 0.78 0.02	553 14.51 0.02	-	642 0.97 0.02	1,146 1.73 0.04	527 13.83 0.02	8,914 13.45 0.29
Chandler (city)	176,338	7,460 4.23	-	1,552 20.80 0.88	-	-	2,028 27.18 1.15	-	1,163 15.59 0.66	-	-	-	-	-	-	-	-	-	-	-	-	-	-	954 12.79 0.54
Gilbert (town)	109,936	4,016 3.65	-	746 18.58 0.68	-	-	1,184 29.48 1.08	-	736 18.33 0.67	-	-	-	-	-	-	-	-	-	-	-	-	-	-	-
Mesa (city)	397,215	6,022 1.52	647 0.16	591 9.81 0.15	-	-	1,015 16.85 0.26	-	1,472 24.44 0.37	-	-	-	-	586 9.73 0.15	718 11.92 0.18	-	-	-	-	-	-	-	-	754 12.52 0.19
Phoenix (city)	1,320,994	25,613 1.94	1,745 0.13	4,433 17.31 0.34	-	553 2.16 0.04	5,568 21.74 0.42	-	5,033 19.65 0.38	-	503 28.83 0.04	-	-	1,582 6.18 0.12	1,977 7.72 0.15	-	-	-	-	-	-	-	-	4,433 17.31 0.34
Tempe (city)	158,426	7,920 5.00	-	1,888 23.84 1.19	-	-	1,940 24.49 1.22	-	591 7.46 0.37	-	-	-	-	639 8.07 0.40	690 8.71 0.44	-	-	-	-	-	-	-	-	800 10.10 0.50
Mohave County	155,032	921 0.59	-	-	-	-	-	-	-	-	-	-	-	-	-	-	-	-	-	-	-	-	-	-
Pima County	843,746	16,907 2.00	1,084 0.13	1,993 11.79 0.24	-	-	4,692 27.75 0.56	-	2,401 14.20 0.28	-	466 42.99 0.06	-	-	1,494 8.84 0.18	2,234 13.21 0.26	-	-	-	-	-	-	-	-	2,267 13.41 0.27
Tucson (city)	486,591	11,641 2.39	734 0.15	1,343 11.54 0.28	-	-	3,176 27.28 0.65	-	1,751 15.04 0.36	-	-	-	-	996 8.56 0.20	1,276 10.96 0.26	-	-	-	-	-	-	-	-	1,858 15.96 0.38
Pinal County	179,727	993 0.55	-	-	-	-	-	-	-	-	-	-	-	-	-	-	-	-	-	-	-	-	-	-

Notes: Please refer to the User's Guide for an explanation of data; data is arranged alphabetically by state, then county, then city within each county; table includes counties with populations greater than 49,999 unless noted and cities with populations greater than 9,999 whose Asian and/or NHPI population rates are greater than the national average; (1) Native Hawaiian and other Pacific Islander; (2) excludes Taiwanese; (3) includes Chamorro; (4) county does not meet population threshold but is shown in order to allow inclusion of city

Place	Total population	Total Asian population	Total NHPI[1] population	Asian Indian	Bangladeshi	Cambodian	Chinese[2]	Fijian	Filipino	Guamanian[3]	Hawaiian, Native	Hmong	Indonesian	Japanese	Korean	Laotian	Malaysian	Pakistani	Samoan	Sri Lankan	Taiwanese	Thai	Tongan	Vietnamese
Yavapai County	167,517	847 0.51	-	-	-	-	-	-	-	-	-	-	-	-	-	-	-	-	-	-	-	-	-	-
Yuma County	160,026	1,345 0.84	-	-	-	-	-	-	446 33.16 0.28	-	-	-	-	-	-	-	-	-	-	-	-	-	-	-
ARKANSAS	2,673,400	19,081 0.71	1,534 0.06	2,694 14.12 0.10	-	-	2,956 15.49 0.11	-	2,303 12.07 0.09	-	298 19.43 0.01	-	-	1,094 5.73 0.04	1,496 7.84 0.06	2,712 14.21 0.10	-	-	-	-	-	292 1.53 0.01	-	3,864 20.25 0.14
Benton County	153,406	1,495 0.97	-	419 28.03 0.27	-	-	-	-	-	-	-	-	-	-	-	-	-	-	-	-	-	-	-	384 25.69 0.25
Craighead County	82,148	517 0.63	-	-	-	-	-	-	-	-	-	-	-	-	-	-	-	-	-	-	-	-	-	-
Crawford County	53,247	631 1.19	-	-	-	-	-	-	-	-	-	-	-	-	-	-	-	-	-	-	-	-	-	-
Faulkner County	86,014	526 0.61	-	-	-	-	-	-	-	-	-	-	-	-	-	-	-	-	-	-	-	-	-	-
Jefferson County	84,278	443 0.53	-	-	-	-	-	-	-	-	-	-	-	-	-	-	-	-	-	-	-	-	-	-
Pulaski County	361,474	4,335 1.20	-	967 22.31 0.27	-	-	870 20.07 0.24	-	668 15.41 0.18	-	-	-	-	-	-	-	-	-	-	-	-	-	-	-
Saline County	83,529	454 0.54	-	-	-	-	-	-	-	-	-	-	-	-	-	-	-	-	-	-	-	-	-	-
Sebastian County	115,071	3,581 3.11	-	-	-	-	-	-	-	-	-	-	-	-	-	1,154 32.23 1.00	-	-	-	-	-	-	-	1,794 50.10 1.56
Fort Smith (city)	80,414	3,277 4.08	-	-	-	-	-	-	-	-	-	-	-	-	-	1,123 34.27 1.40	-	-	-	-	-	-	-	1,713 52.27 2.13
Washington County	157,715	2,607 1.65	756 0.48	-	-	-	785 30.11 0.50	-	-	-	-	-	-	-	-	551 21.14 0.35	-	-	-	-	-	-	-	-
Springdale (city)	46,060	739 1.60	694 1.51	-	-	-	-	-	-	-	-	-	-	-	-	421 56.97 0.91	-	-	-	-	-	-	-	-
CALIFORNIA	33,871,648	3,682,975 10.87	113,858 0.34	307,105 8.34 0.91	2,748 0.07 0.01	71,266 1.94 0.21	914,033 24.82 2.70	8,410 7.39 0.02	920,052 24.98 2.72	20,472 17.98 0.06	19,661 17.27 0.06	68,706 1.87 0.20	16,388 0.44 0.05	289,155 7.85 0.85	343,742 9.33 1.01	56,896 1.54 0.17	1,761 0.05 0.01	19,837 0.54 0.06	38,906 34.17 0.11	5,416 0.15 0.02	63,580 1.73 0.19	36,155 0.98 0.11	12,167 10.69 0.04	446,475 12.12 1.32
Alameda County	1,443,741	293,807 20.35	9,188 0.64	41,824 14.24 2.90	-	3,903 1.33 0.27	106,960 36.40 7.41	1,463 15.92 0.10	69,680 23.72 4.83	1,311 14.27 0.09	1,283 13.96 0.09	-	643 0.22 0.04	12,424 4.23 0.86	14,530 4.95 1.01	3,162 1.08 0.22	-	1,979 0.67 0.14	2,406 26.19 0.17	-	3,935 1.34 0.27	1,453 0.49 0.10	1,832 19.94 0.13	23,530 8.01 1.63
Alameda (city)	72,259	18,698 25.88	796 1.10	1,072 5.73 1.48	-	-	7,434 39.76 10.29	-	6,047 32.34 8.37	-	-	-	-	702 3.75 0.97	1,231 6.58 1.70	-	-	-	-	-	-	-	-	1,303 6.97 1.80

Notes: Please refer to the User's Guide for an explanation of data; data is arranged alphabetically by state, then county, then city within each county; table includes counties with populations greater than 49,999 unless noted and cities with populations greater than 9,999 whose Asian and/or NHPI population rates are greater than the national average; (1) Native Hawaiian and other Pacific Islander; (2) excludes Taiwanese; (3) includes Chamorro; (4) county does not meet population threshold but is shown in order to allow inclusion of city

Place	Total population	Total Asian population	Total NHPI[1] population	Asian Indian	Bangladeshi	Cambodian	Chinese[2]	Fijian	Filipino	Guamanian[3]	Hawaiian, Native	Hmong	Indonesian	Japanese	Korean	Laotian	Malaysian	Pakistani	Samoan	Sri Lankan	Taiwanese	Thai	Tongan	Vietnamese
Albany (city)	16,444	4,246 25.82	-	331 7.80 2.01	-	-	2,058 48.47 12.52	-	-	-	-	-	-	643 15.14 3.91	520 12.25 3.16	-	-	-	-	-	-	-	-	-
Ashland (cdp)	20,766	3,127 15.06	-	-	-	-	965 30.86 4.65	-	1,326 42.40 6.39	-	-	-	-	-	-	-	-	-	-	-	-	-	-	-
Berkeley (city)	102,743	16,660 16.22	-	1,769 10.62 1.72	-	-	7,227 43.38 7.03	-	1,165 6.99 1.13	-	-	-	-	2,164 12.99 2.11	1,621 9.73 1.58	-	-	-	-	-	408 2.45 0.40	-	-	932 5.59 0.91
Castro Valley (cdp)	57,410	7,317 12.75	-	835 11.41 1.45	-	-	3,451 47.16 6.01	-	1,185 16.20 2.06	-	-	-	-	622 8.50 1.08	748 10.22 1.30	-	-	-	-	-	-	-	-	-
Cherryland (cdp)	13,782	1,182 8.58	-	-	-	-	-	-	625 52.88 4.53	-	-	-	-	-	-	-	-	-	-	-	-	-	-	-
Dublin (city)	30,036	2,965 9.87	-	572 19.29 1.90	-	-	909 30.66 3.03	-	788 26.58 2.62	-	-	-	-	-	-	-	-	-	-	-	-	-	-	-
Fremont (city)	203,413	74,753 36.75	670 0.33	20,690 27.68 10.17	-	-	26,292 35.17 12.93	-	11,400 15.25 5.60	-	-	-	-	1,554 2.08 0.76	3,981 5.33 1.96	-	-	1,102 1.47 0.54	-	-	2,452 3.28 1.21	-	-	4,345 5.81 2.14
Hayward (city)	139,895	26,106 18.66	2,357 1.68	3,566 13.66 2.55	-	-	3,674 14.07 2.63	843 35.77 0.60	12,560 48.11 8.98	-	-	-	-	1,271 4.87 0.91	818 3.13 0.58	-	-	-	582 24.69 0.42	-	-	-	-	2,607 9.99 1.86
Livermore (city)	73,436	4,261 5.80	-	605 14.20 0.82	-	-	761 17.86 1.04	-	1,624 38.11 2.21	-	-	-	-	-	-	-	-	-	-	-	-	-	-	470 11.03 0.64
Newark (city)	42,471	9,249 21.78	-	1,609 17.40 3.79	-	-	1,694 18.32 3.99	-	3,475 37.57 8.18	-	-	-	-	-	545 5.89 1.28	-	-	-	-	-	-	-	-	736 7.96 1.73
Oakland (city)	399,477	60,110 15.05	2,581 0.65	1,720 2.86 0.43	-	2,935 4.88 0.73	31,523 52.44 7.89	-	6,677 11.11 1.67	-	-	-	-	2,102 3.50 0.53	1,766 2.94 0.44	2,389 3.97 0.60	-	-	-	-	-	-	1,312 50.83 0.33	8,216 13.67 2.06
Piedmont (city)	10,952	1,805 16.48	-	-	-	-	1,360 75.35 12.42	-	-	-	-	-	-	-	-	-	-	-	-	-	-	-	-	-
Pleasanton (city)	63,569	7,392 11.63	-	1,581 21.39 2.49	-	-	2,616 35.39 4.12	-	836 11.31 1.32	-	-	-	-	691 9.35 1.09	644 8.71 1.01	-	-	-	-	-	-	-	-	-
San Leandro (city)	79,286	18,317 23.10	608 0.77	702 3.83 0.89	-	-	8,221 44.88 10.37	-	6,212 33.91 7.83	-	-	-	-	529 2.89 0.67	458 2.50 0.58	-	-	-	-	-	-	-	-	1,290 7.04 1.63
San Lorenzo (cdp)	21,947	3,479 15.85	-	-	-	-	975 28.03 4.44	-	1,380 39.67 6.29	-	-	-	-	-	-	-	-	-	-	-	-	-	-	301 8.65 1.37
Union City (city)	66,861	29,442 44.03	634 0.95	5,377 18.26 8.04	-	-	5,959 20.24 8.91	-	13,128 44.59 19.63	-	-	-	-	487 1.65 0.73	943 3.20 1.41	-	-	-	-	-	-	-	-	2,047 6.95 3.06
Butte County	203,171	6,553 3.23	-	432 6.59 0.21	-	-	713 10.88 0.35	-	361 5.51 0.18	-	-	2,824 43.09 1.39	-	626 9.55 0.31	-	551 8.41 0.27	-	-	-	-	-	-	-	-

Notes: Please refer to the User's Guide for an explanation of data; data is arranged alphabetically by state, then county, then city within each county; table includes counties with populations greater than 49,999 unless noted and cities with populations greater than 9,999 whose Asian and/or NHPI population rates are greater than the national average; (1) Native Hawaiian and other Pacific Islander; (2) excludes Taiwanese; (3) includes Chamorro; (4) county does not meet population threshold but is shown in order to allow inclusion of city

Place	Total population	Total Asian population	Total NHPI[1] population	Asian Indian	Bangladeshi	Cambodian	Chinese[2]	Fijian	Filipino	Guamanian[3]	Hawaiian, Native	Hmong	Indonesian	Japanese	Korean	Laotian	Malaysian	Pakistani	Samoan	Sri Lankan	Taiwanese	Thai	Tongan	Vietnamese
Chico (city)	59,444	2,278 3.83	-	-	-	-	409 17.95 0.69	-	-	-	-	729 32.00 1.23	-	-	-	-	-	-	-	-	-	-	-	-
Oroville (city)	12,969	729 5.62	-	-	-	-	-	-	-	-	-	483 66.26 3.72	-	-	-	-	-	-	-	-	-	-	-	-
Contra Costa County	948,816	103,198 10.88	3,391 0.36	11,198 10.85 1.18	-	-	27,686 26.83 2.92	538 15.87 0.06	34,436 33.37 3.63	544 16.04 0.06	595 17.55 0.06	-	473 0.46 0.05	8,295 8.04 0.87	4,492 4.35 0.47	4,275 4.14 0.45	-	708 0.69 0.07	759 22.38 0.08	-	1,261 1.22 0.13	635 0.62 0.07	451 13.30 0.05	5,432 5.26 0.57
Alamo (cdp)	15,142	863 5.70	-	-	-	-	-	-	-	-	-	-	-	-	-	-	-	-	-	-	-	-	-	-
Antioch (city)	90,814	6,674 7.35	408 0.45	353 5.29 0.39	-	-	1,120 16.78 1.23	-	3,517 52.70 3.87	-	-	-	-	-	-	-	-	-	-	-	-	-	-	475 7.12 0.52
Bay Point (cdp)	21,415	2,471 11.54	-	-	-	-	-	-	1,218 49.29 5.69	-	-	-	-	-	-	-	-	-	-	-	-	-	-	-
Blackhawk-Camino-Tass. (cdp)	9,966	1,682 16.88	-	-	-	-	963 57.25 9.66	-	-	-	-	-	-	-	-	-	-	-	-	-	-	-	-	-
Clayton (city)	10,792	596 5.52	-	-	-	-	-	-	-	-	-	-	-	-	-	-	-	-	-	-	-	-	-	-
Concord (city)	121,710	11,117 9.13	468 0.38	1,538 13.83 1.26	-	-	2,608 23.46 2.14	-	4,140 37.24 3.40	-	-	-	-	854 7.68 0.70	458 4.12 0.38	-	-	-	-	-	-	-	-	659 5.93 0.54
Danville (town)	42,127	3,588 8.52	-	459 12.79 1.09	-	-	1,555 43.34 3.69	-	460 12.82 1.09	-	-	-	-	-	-	-	-	-	-	-	-	-	-	-
El Cerrito (city)	23,179	5,634 24.31	-	375 6.66 1.62	-	-	2,467 43.79 10.64	-	478 8.48 2.06	-	-	-	-	1,232 21.87 5.32	-	-	-	-	-	-	-	-	-	-
El Sobrante (cdp)	11,605	1,349 11.62	-	361 26.76 3.11	-	-	-	-	-	-	-	-	-	-	-	-	-	-	-	-	-	-	-	-
Hercules (city)	19,299	8,291 42.96	-	676 8.15 3.50	-	-	1,603 19.33 8.31	-	4,936 59.53 25.58	-	-	-	-	-	-	-	-	-	-	-	-	-	-	-
Lafayette (city)	23,463	1,660 7.07	-	-	-	-	814 49.04 3.47	-	-	-	-	-	-	-	-	-	-	-	-	-	-	-	-	-
Martinez (city)	36,167	2,319 6.41	-	-	-	-	483 20.83 1.34	-	974 42.00 2.69	-	-	-	-	-	-	-	-	-	-	-	-	-	-	-
Moraga (town)	16,642	2,163 13.00	-	-	-	-	1,230 56.87 7.39	-	-	-	-	-	-	-	-	-	-	-	-	-	-	-	-	-
Orinda (city)	17,446	1,524 8.74	-	-	-	-	893 58.60 5.12	-	-	-	-	-	-	-	-	-	-	-	-	-	-	-	-	-

Notes: Please refer to the User's Guide for an explanation of data; data is arranged alphabetically by state, then county, then city within each county; table includes counties with populations greater than 49,999 unless noted and cities with populations greater than 9,999 whose Asian and/or NHPI population rates are greater than the national average; (1) Native Hawaiian and other Pacific Islander; (2) excludes Taiwanese; (3) includes Chamorro; (4) county does not meet population threshold but is shown in order to allow inclusion of city

Place	Total population	Total Asian population	Total NHPI[1] population	Asian Indian	Bangladeshi	Cambodian	Chinese[2]	Fijian	Filipino	Guamanian[3]	Hawaiian, Native	Hmong	Indonesian	Japanese	Korean	Laotian	Malaysian	Pakistani	Samoan	Sri Lankan	Taiwanese	Thai	Tongan	Vietnamese
Pinole (city)	19,394	4,095 21.11	-	-	-	-	880 21.49 4.54	-	2,013 49.16 10.38	-	-	-	-	-	-	-	-	-	-	-	-	-	-	-
Pittsburg (city)	56,820	7,248 12.76	554 0.98	955 13.18 1.68	-	-	450 6.21 0.79	-	4,774 65.87 8.40	-	-	-	-	-	-	-	-	-	-	-	-	-	-	-
Pleasant Hill (city)	32,847	3,286 10.00	-	-	-	-	918 27.94 2.79	-	839 25.53 2.55	-	-	-	-	-	522 15.89 1.59	-	-	-	-	-	-	-	-	-
Richmond (city)	99,716	12,088 12.12	401 0.40	1,112 9.20 1.12	-	-	3,113 25.75 3.12	-	2,776 22.96 2.78	-	-	-	-	883 7.30 0.89	462 3.82 0.46	2,379 19.68 2.39	-	-	-	-	-	-	-	463 3.83 0.46
San Pablo (city)	30,121	4,912 16.31	-	605 12.32 2.01	-	-	-	-	1,739 35.40 5.77	-	-	-	-	-	-	1,116 22.72 3.71	-	-	-	-	-	-	-	710 14.45 2.36
San Ramon (city)	44,477	6,804 15.30	-	1,393 20.47 3.13	-	-	2,691 39.55 6.05	-	939 13.80 2.11	-	-	-	-	451 6.63 1.01	-	-	-	-	-	-	-	-	-	-
Walnut Creek (city)	64,583	6,201 9.60	-	559 9.01 0.87	-	-	2,646 42.67 4.10	-	1,216 19.61 1.88	-	-	-	-	833 13.43 1.29	491 7.92 0.76	-	-	-	-	-	-	-	-	-
El Dorado County	156,299	3,055 1.95	-	-	-	-	-	-	1,359 44.48 0.87	-	-	-	-	506 16.56 0.32	-	-	-	-	-	-	-	-	-	-
El Dorado Hills (cdp)	18,083	658 3.64	-	-	-	-	-	-	-	-	-	-	-	-	-	-	-	-	-	-	-	-	-	-
South Lake Tahoe (city)	23,720	1,415 5.97	-	-	-	-	-	-	983 69.47 4.14	-	-	-	-	-	-	-	-	-	-	-	-	-	-	-
Fresno County	799,407	63,895 7.99	652 0.08	6,965 10.90 0.87	-	3,933 6.16 0.49	4,846 7.58 0.61	-	6,209 9.72 0.78	-	-	24,045 37.63 3.01	-	5,719 8.95 0.72	1,334 2.09 0.17	6,270 9.81 0.78	-	-	-	-	-	-	-	2,125 3.33 0.27
Clovis (city)	68,197	4,429 6.49	-	-	-	-	-	-	680 15.35 1.00	-	-	1,799 40.62 2.64	-	548 12.37 0.80	-	-	-	-	-	-	-	-	-	-
Fresno (city)	427,224	48,485 11.35	-	3,719 7.67 0.87	-	3,611 7.45 0.85	3,722 7.68 0.87	-	4,424 9.12 1.04	-	-	20,344 41.96 4.76	-	2,661 5.49 0.62	938 1.93 0.22	5,482 11.31 1.28	-	-	-	-	-	-	-	1,728 3.56 0.40
Reedley (city)	20,776	782 3.76	-	-	-	-	-	-	-	-	-	-	-	-	-	-	-	-	-	-	-	-	-	-
Humboldt County	126,518	1,859 1.47	-	-	-	-	-	-	-	-	-	-	-	286 15.38 0.23	-	-	-	-	-	-	-	-	-	-
Imperial County	142,361	2,819 1.98	-	-	-	-	593 21.04 0.42	-	881 31.25 0.62	-	-	-	-	-	493 17.49 0.35	-	-	-	-	-	-	-	-	-
Kern County	661,645	21,562 3.26	778 0.12	4,154 19.27 0.63	-	431 2.00 0.07	2,077 9.63 0.31	-	10,551 48.93 1.59	-	-	-	-	1,043 4.84 0.16	1,263 5.86 0.19	-	-	-	-	-	-	-	-	649 3.01 0.10

Notes: Please refer to the User's Guide for an explanation of data; data is arranged alphabetically by state, then county, then city within each county; table includes counties with populations greater than 49,999 unless noted and cities with populations greater than 9,999 whose Asian and/or NHPI population rates are greater than the national average; (1) Native Hawaiian and other Pacific Islander; (2) excludes Taiwanese; (3) includes Chamorro; (4) county does not meet population threshold but is shown in order to allow inclusion of city

Place	Total population	Total Asian population	Total NHPI[1] population	Asian Indian	Bangladeshi	Cambodian	Chinese[2]	Fijian	Filipino	Guamanian[3]	Hawaiian, Native	Hmong	Indonesian	Japanese	Korean	Laotian	Malaysian	Pakistani	Samoan	Sri Lankan	Taiwanese	Thai	Tongan	Vietnamese
Bakersfield (city)	247,385	10,499 4.24	468 0.19	3,149 29.99 1.27	-	-	1,506 14.34 0.61	-	2,739 26.09 1.11	-	-	-	-	649 6.18 0.26	966 9.20 0.39	-	-	-	-	-	-	-	-	439 4.18 0.18
Delano (city)	38,981	6,027 15.46	-	-	-	-	-	-	5,619 93.23 14.41	-	-	-	-	-	-	-	-	-	-	-	-	-	-	-
Ridgecrest (city)	25,195	1,036 4.11	-	-	-	-	-	-	489 47.20 1.94	-	-	-	-	-	-	-	-	-	-	-	-	-	-	-
Kings County	129,461	3,771 2.91	-	-	-	-	-	-	2,461 65.26 1.90	-	-	-	-	-	-	-	-	-	-	-	-	-	-	-
Lemoore (city)	19,524	1,434 7.34	-	-	-	-	-	-	1,072 74.76 5.49	-	-	-	-	-	-	-	-	-	-	-	-	-	-	-
Lake County	58,309	529 0.91	-	-	-	-	-	-	-	-	-	-	-	-	-	-	-	-	-	-	-	-	-	-
Los Angeles County	9,519,338	1,134,263 11.92	27,221 0.29	58,987 5.20 0.62	1,325 0.12 0.01	30,052 2.65 0.32	291,347 25.69 3.06	493 1.81 0.01	262,020 23.10 2.75	3,139 11.53 0.03	4,398 16.16 0.05	440 0.04 <0.01	5,626 0.50 0.06	112,548 9.92 1.18	185,440 16.35 1.95	3,152 0.28 0.03	534 0.05 0.01	4,729 0.42 0.05	13,553 49.79 0.14	2,441 0.22 0.03	34,746 3.06 0.37	19,564 1.72 0.21	2,276 8.36 0.02	78,258 6.90 0.82
Agoura Hills (city)	20,324	1,242 6.11	-	-	-	-	-	-	-	-	-	-	-	-	-	-	-	-	-	-	-	-	-	-
Alhambra (city)	85,961	40,563 47.19	-	514 1.27 0.60	-	-	26,345 64.95 30.65	-	1,909 4.71 2.22	-	-	-	-	1,502 3.70 1.75	882 2.17 1.03	-	-	-	-	-	1,558 3.84 1.81	-	-	4,395 10.83 5.11
Altadena (cdp)	42,550	1,758 4.13	-	-	-	-	-	-	314 17.86 0.74	-	-	-	-	627 35.67 1.47	-	-	-	-	-	-	-	-	-	-
Arcadia (city)	52,951	23,996 45.32	-	657 2.74 1.24	-	-	13,992 58.31 26.42	-	804 3.35 1.52	-	-	-	-	1,148 4.78 2.17	1,933 8.06 3.65	-	-	-	-	-	3,753 15.64 7.09	-	-	-
Artesia (city)	16,380	4,524 27.62	-	479 10.59 2.92	-	-	637 14.08 3.89	-	1,789 39.54 10.92	-	-	-	-	-	875 19.34 5.34	-	-	-	-	-	-	-	-	-
Avocado Heights (cdp)	15,140	1,362 9.00	-	-	-	-	-	-	-	-	-	-	-	-	-	-	-	-	-	-	-	-	-	-
Azusa (city)	44,371	2,430 5.48	-	-	-	-	-	-	1,193 49.09 2.69	-	-	-	-	-	-	-	-	-	-	-	-	-	-	-
Baldwin Park (city)	75,753	9,017 11.90	-	-	-	-	2,795 31.00 3.69	-	4,067 45.10 5.37	-	-	-	-	-	-	-	-	-	-	-	-	-	-	950 10.54 1.25
Bellflower (city)	72,829	7,181 9.86	-	-	-	534 7.44 0.73	-	-	3,653 50.87 5.02	-	-	-	-	-	929 12.94 1.28	-	-	-	-	-	-	389 5.42 0.53	-	-
Beverly Hills (city)	33,829	2,570 7.60	-	-	-	-	513 19.96 1.52	-	-	-	-	-	-	-	912 35.49 2.70	-	-	-	-	-	-	-	-	-

Notes: Please refer to the User's Guide for an explanation of data; data is arranged alphabetically by state, then county, then city within each county; table includes counties with populations greater than 49,999 unless noted and cities with populations greater than 9,999 whose Asian and/or NHPI population rates are greater than the national average; (1) Native Hawaiian and other Pacific Islander; (2) excludes Taiwanese; (3) includes Chamorro; (4) county does not meet population threshold but is shown in order to allow inclusion of city

Place	Total population	Total Asian population	Total NHPI[1] population	Asian Indian	Bangladeshi	Cambodian	Chinese[2]	Fijian	Filipino	Guamanian[3]	Hawaiian, Native	Hmong	Indonesian	Japanese	Korean	Laotian	Malaysian	Pakistani	Samoan	Sri Lankan	Taiwanese	Thai	Tongan	Vietnamese
Burbank (city)	100,316	9,089 9.06	-	953 10.49 0.95	-	-	900 9.90 0.90	-	3,301 36.32 3.29	-	-	-	-	626 6.89 0.62	1,980 21.78 1.97	-	-	-	-	-	-	-	-	524 5.77 0.52
Calabasas (city)	20,100	1,652 8.22	-	-	-	-	508 30.75 2.53	-	-	-	-	-	-	-	-	-	-	-	-	-	-	-	-	-
Carson (city)	89,549	20,156 22.51	1,929 2.15	-	-	-	501 2.49 0.56	-	17,331 85.98 19.35	-	-	-	-	631 3.13 0.70	-	-	-	-	1,438 74.55 1.61	-	-	-	-	321 1.59 0.36
Cerritos (city)	51,507	30,185 58.60	-	2,946 9.76 5.72	-	-	5,791 19.19 11.24	-	5,725 18.97 11.11	-	-	-	-	2,007 6.65 3.90	8,829 29.25 17.14	-	-	-	-	-	1,791 5.93 3.48	466 1.54 0.90	-	1,260 4.17 2.45
Citrus (cdp)	10,648	784 7.36	-	-	-	-	-	-	-	-	-	-	-	-	-	-	-	-	-	-	-	-	-	-
Claremont (city)	33,978	3,983 11.72	-	536 13.46 1.58	-	-	1,068 26.81 3.14	-	-	-	-	-	-	-	611 15.34 1.80	-	-	-	-	-	-	-	-	-
Compton (city)	93,226	420 0.45	1,028 1.10	-	-	-	-	-	-	-	-	-	-	-	-	-	-	-	981 95.43 1.05	-	-	-	-	-
Covina (city)	47,144	4,565 9.68	-	-	-	-	1,167 25.56 2.48	-	1,353 29.64 2.87	-	-	-	-	399 8.74 0.85	-	-	-	-	-	-	-	-	-	442 9.68 0.94
Culver City (city)	38,816	4,738 12.21	-	621 13.11 1.60	-	-	773 16.31 1.99	-	998 21.06 2.57	-	-	-	-	1,374 29.00 3.54	-	-	-	-	-	-	-	-	-	-
Diamond Bar (city)	56,349	23,831 42.29	-	2,482 10.42 4.40	-	-	7,669 32.18 13.61	-	3,138 13.17 5.57	-	-	-	-	689 2.89 1.22	5,597 23.49 9.93	-	-	-	-	-	2,099 8.81 3.72	-	-	696 2.92 1.24
Downey (city)	107,323	7,814 7.28	-	451 5.77 0.42	-	-	513 6.57 0.48	-	1,925 24.64 1.79	-	-	-	-	377 4.82 0.35	3,179 40.68 2.96	-	-	-	-	-	-	-	-	412 5.27 0.38
Duarte (city)	21,486	2,730 12.71	-	-	-	-	439 16.08 2.04	-	1,411 51.68 6.57	-	-	-	-	-	-	-	-	-	-	-	-	-	-	-
East San Gabriel (cdp)	14,588	6,104 41.84	-	-	-	-	3,504 57.40 24.02	-	-	-	-	-	-	559 9.16 3.83	-	-	-	-	-	-	641 10.50 4.39	-	-	-
El Monte (city)	116,249	21,529 18.52	-	-	-	-	11,701 54.35 10.07	-	969 4.50 0.83	-	-	-	-	-	-	-	-	-	-	-	401 1.86 0.34	-	-	6,369 29.58 5.48
El Segundo (city)	15,970	1,063 6.66	-	-	-	-	-	-	-	-	-	-	-	-	-	-	-	-	-	-	-	-	-	-
Gardena (city)	57,818	15,458 26.74	-	-	-	-	881 5.70 1.52	-	1,767 11.43 3.06	-	-	-	-	6,685 43.25 11.56	3,745 24.23 6.48	-	-	-	-	-	-	-	-	1,291 8.35 2.23
Glendale (city)	195,047	31,944 16.38	-	970 3.04 0.50	-	-	2,712 8.49 1.39	-	11,559 36.19 5.93	-	-	-	-	1,682 5.27 0.86	12,475 39.05 6.40	-	-	-	-	-	-	420 1.31 0.22	-	952 2.98 0.49

Notes: Please refer to the User's Guide for an explanation of data; data is arranged alphabetically by state, then county, then city within each county; table includes counties with populations greater than 49,999 unless noted and cities with populations greater than 9,999 whose Asian and/or NHPI population rates are greater than the national average; (1) Native Hawaiian and other Pacific Islander; (2) excludes Taiwanese; (3) includes Chamorro; (4) county does not meet population threshold but is shown in order to allow inclusion of city

Place	Total population	Total Asian population	Total NHPI[1] population	Asian Indian	Bangladeshi	Cambodian	Chinese[2]	Fijian	Filipino	Guamanian[3]	Hawaiian, Native	Hmong	Indonesian	Japanese	Korean	Laotian	Malaysian	Pakistani	Samoan	Sri Lankan	Taiwanese	Thai	Tongan	Vietnamese
Glendora (city)	49,719	3,254 6.54	-	533 16.38 1.07	-	-	868 26.67 1.75	-	827 25.41 1.66	-	-	-	-	-	-	-	-	-	-	-	-	-	-	-
Hacienda Heights (cdp)	53,112	19,225 36.20	-	-	-	-	9,122 47.45 17.18	-	1,342 6.98 2.53	-	-	-	-	1,330 6.92 2.50	2,571 13.37 4.84	-	-	-	-	-	2,875 14.95 5.41	-	-	482 2.51 0.91
Hawaiian Gardens (city)	14,915	1,292 8.66	-	-	-	-	-	-	-	-	-	-	-	-	755 58.44 5.06	-	-	-	-	-	-	-	-	-
Hawthorne (city)	83,963	5,948 7.08	546 0.65	481 8.09 0.57	-	-	544 9.15 0.65	-	2,226 37.42 2.65	-	-	-	-	449 7.55 0.53	-	-	-	-	-	-	-	-	-	1,477 24.83 1.76
Hermosa Beach (city)	18,442	864 4.68	-	-	-	-	-	-	-	-	-	-	-	-	-	-	-	-	-	-	-	-	-	-
La Canada Flintridge (city)	20,381	3,981 19.53	-	-	-	-	769 19.32 3.77	-	-	-	-	-	-	381 9.57 1.87	2,230 56.02 10.94	-	-	-	-	-	-	-	-	-
La Crescenta-Montrose (cdp)	18,408	3,524 19.14	-	-	-	-	-	-	348 9.88 1.89	-	-	-	-	-	2,501 70.97 13.59	-	-	-	-	-	-	-	-	-
La Mirada (city)	46,782	6,968 14.89	-	519 7.45 1.11	-	-	706 10.13 1.51	-	2,200 31.57 4.70	-	-	-	-	390 5.60 0.83	2,314 33.21 4.95	-	-	-	-	-	-	-	-	-
La Puente (city)	41,009	2,883 7.03	-	-	-	-	882 30.59 2.15	-	1,002 34.76 2.44	-	-	-	-	-	-	-	-	-	-	-	-	-	-	-
La Verne (city)	31,845	2,372 7.45	-	-	-	-	-	-	875 36.89 2.75	-	-	-	-	-	-	-	-	-	-	-	-	-	-	-
Lakewood (city)	79,412	10,432 13.14	762 0.96	431 4.13 0.54	-	732 7.02 0.92	1,014 9.72 1.28	-	4,776 45.78 6.01	-	-	-	-	724 6.94 0.91	1,444 13.84 1.82	-	-	-	598 78.48 0.75	-	-	-	-	442 4.24 0.56
Lancaster (city)	118,783	4,596 3.87	-	638 13.88 0.54	-	-	498 10.84 0.42	-	2,080 45.26 1.75	-	-	-	-	-	-	-	-	-	-	-	-	-	-	-
Lawndale (city)	31,729	2,928 9.23	463 1.46	-	-	-	-	-	656 22.40 2.07	-	-	-	-	-	-	-	-	-	-	-	-	-	-	1,317 44.98 4.15
Lomita (city)	19,984	2,265 11.33	-	-	-	-	-	-	458 20.22 2.29	-	-	-	-	621 27.42 3.11	535 23.62 2.68	-	-	-	-	-	-	-	-	-
Long Beach (city)	461,381	55,040 11.93	5,145 1.12	1,192 2.17 0.26	-	17,711 32.18 3.84	3,136 5.70 0.68	-	17,962 32.63 3.89	-	-	-	-	3,586 6.52 0.78	1,736 3.15 0.38	742 1.35 0.16	-	-	3,733 72.56 0.81	-	-	604 1.10 0.13	-	5,073 9.22 1.10
Los Angeles (city)	3,694,834	368,644 9.98	6,445 0.17	24,129 6.55 0.65	831 0.23 0.02	4,208 1.14 0.11	60,066 16.29 1.63	-	102,003 27.67 2.76	1,149 17.83 0.03	1,613 25.03 0.04	-	1,790 0.49 0.05	36,755 9.97 0.99	91,291 24.76 2.47	689 0.19 0.02	-	1,676 0.45 0.05	2,055 31.89 0.06	1,208 0.33 0.03	3,326 0.90 0.09	9,083 2.46 0.25	342 5.31 0.01	19,508 5.29 0.53
Manhattan Beach (city)	34,039	2,023 5.94	-	-	-	-	558 27.58 1.64	-	-	-	-	-	-	610 30.15 1.79	-	-	-	-	-	-	-	-	-	-

Notes: Please refer to the User's Guide for an explanation of data; data is arranged alphabetically by state, then county, then city within each county; table includes counties with populations greater than 49,999 unless noted and cities with populations greater than 9,999 whose Asian and/or NHPI population rates are greater than the national average; (1) Native Hawaiian and other Pacific Islander; (2) excludes Taiwanese; (3) includes Chamorro; (4) county does not meet population threshold but is shown in order to allow inclusion of city

Place	Total population	Total Asian population	Total NHPI[1] population	Asian Indian	Bangladeshi	Cambodian	Chinese[2]	Fijian	Filipino	Guamanian[3]	Hawaiian, Native	Hmong	Indonesian	Japanese	Korean	Laotian	Malaysian	Pakistani	Samoan	Sri Lankan	Taiwanese	Thai	Tongan	Vietnamese
Monrovia (city)	36,817	2,480 6.74	-	-	-	-	702 28.31 1.91	-	921 37.14 2.50	-	-	-	-	-	-	-	-	-	-	-	-	-	-	-
Montebello (city)	61,960	7,022 11.33	-	-	-	-	2,525 35.96 4.08	-	870 12.39 1.40	-	-	-	-	1,790 25.49 2.89	628 8.94 1.01	-	-	-	-	-	-	-	-	-
Monterey Park (city)	59,933	36,674 61.19	-	-	-	413 1.13 0.69	22,725 61.96 37.92	-	844 2.30 1.41	-	-	-	-	4,813 13.12 8.03	859 2.34 1.43	-	-	-	-	-	1,051 2.87 1.75	-	-	3,239 8.83 5.40
Norwalk (city)	103,223	12,174 11.79	-	1,341 11.02 1.30	-	503 4.13 0.49	930 7.64 0.90	-	4,478 36.78 4.34	-	-	-	-	478 3.93 0.46	2,517 20.68 2.44	-	-	-	-	-	-	-	-	858 7.05 0.83
Palmdale (city)	116,573	4,308 3.70	-	425 9.87 0.36	-	-	-	-	2,193 50.91 1.88	-	-	-	-	-	-	-	-	-	-	-	-	-	-	-
Palos Verdes Estates (city)	13,340	2,317 17.37	-	-	-	-	549 23.69 4.12	-	-	-	-	-	-	667 28.79 5.00	289 12.47 2.17	-	-	-	-	-	-	-	-	-
Pasadena (city)	133,871	13,378 9.99	-	853 6.38 0.64	-	-	4,179 31.24 3.12	-	2,598 19.42 1.94	-	-	-	-	2,247 16.80 1.68	1,393 10.41 1.04	-	-	-	-	-	-	-	-	769 5.75 0.57
Pomona (city)	149,644	10,733 7.17	-	635 5.92 0.42	-	757 7.05 0.51	2,000 18.63 1.34	-	2,851 26.56 1.91	-	-	-	-	516 4.81 0.34	-	533 4.97 0.36	-	-	-	-	-	-	-	1,747 16.28 1.17
Rancho Palos Verdes (city)	41,301	10,372 25.11	-	566 5.46 1.37	-	-	2,645 25.50 6.40	-	586 5.65 1.42	-	-	-	-	3,056 29.46 7.40	2,430 23.43 5.88	-	-	-	-	-	540 5.21 1.31	-	-	-
Redondo Beach (city)	63,261	5,896 9.32	-	503 8.53 0.80	-	-	1,208 20.49 1.91	-	795 13.48 1.26	-	-	-	-	1,995 33.84 3.15	669 11.35 1.06	-	-	-	-	-	-	-	-	-
Rosemead (city)	53,280	25,917 48.64	-	-	-	775 2.99 1.45	14,970 57.76 28.10	-	718 2.77 1.35	-	-	-	-	781 3.01 1.47	-	-	-	-	-	-	-	-	-	5,938 22.91 11.14
Rowland Heights (cdp)	48,329	24,773 51.26	-	1,044 4.21 2.16	-	-	11,422 46.11 23.63	-	3,276 13.22 6.78	-	-	-	-	658 2.66 1.36	3,725 15.04 7.71	-	-	-	-	-	2,593 10.47 5.37	-	-	624 2.52 1.29
San Dimas (city)	35,064	3,172 9.05	-	-	-	-	1,196 37.70 3.41	-	770 24.27 2.20	-	-	-	-	-	-	-	-	-	-	-	-	-	-	-
San Gabriel (city)	39,306	19,190 48.82	-	-	-	-	11,716 61.05 29.81	-	1,162 6.06 2.96	-	-	-	-	627 3.27 1.60	-	-	-	-	-	-	763 3.98 1.94	-	-	2,667 13.90 6.79
San Marino (city)	12,973	6,071 46.80	-	-	-	-	3,915 64.49 30.18	-	-	-	-	-	-	-	-	-	-	-	-	-	1,526 25.14 11.76	-	-	-
Santa Clarita (city)	151,381	7,586 5.01	-	760 10.02 0.50	-	-	860 11.34 0.57	-	2,489 32.81 1.64	-	-	-	-	1,119 14.75 0.74	808 10.65 0.53	-	-	-	-	-	-	-	-	506 6.67 0.33
Santa Monica (city)	84,084	5,986 7.12	-	629 10.51 0.75	-	-	1,590 26.56 1.89	-	488 8.15 0.58	-	-	-	-	1,834 30.64 2.18	743 12.41 0.88	-	-	-	-	-	-	-	-	-

Notes: Please refer to the User's Guide for an explanation of data; data is arranged alphabetically by state, then county, then city within each county; table includes counties with populations greater than 49,999 unless noted and cities with populations greater than 9,999 whose Asian and/or NHPI population rates are greater than the national average; (1) Native Hawaiian and other Pacific Islander; (2) excludes Taiwanese; (3) includes Chamorro; (4) county does not meet population threshold but is shown in order to allow inclusion of city

Place	Total population	Total Asian population	Total NHPI[1] population	Asian Indian	Bangladeshi	Cambodian	Chinese[2]	Fijian	Filipino	Guamanian[3]	Hawaiian, Native	Hmong	Indonesian	Japanese	Korean	Laotian	Malaysian	Pakistani	Samoan	Sri Lankan	Taiwanese	Thai	Tongan	Vietnamese
Sierra Madre (city)	10,578	566 5.35	-	-	-	-	-	-	-	-	-	-	-	-	-	-	-	-	-	-	-	-	-	-
South El Monte (city)	20,935	1,597 7.63	-	-	-	-	691 43.27 3.30	-	-	-	-	-	-	-	-	-	-	-	-	-	-	-	-	632 39.57 3.02
South Pasadena (city)	24,303	6,249 25.71	-	-	-	-	3,340 53.45 13.74	-	-	-	-	-	-	996 15.94 4.10	679 10.87 2.79	-	-	-	-	-	-	-	-	-
South San Jose Hills (cdp)	20,190	1,241 6.15	-	-	-	-	-	-	729 58.74 3.61	-	-	-	-	-	-	-	-	-	-	-	-	-	-	-
Temple City (city)	33,296	12,936 38.85	-	-	-	-	7,912 61.16 23.76	-	649 5.02 1.95	-	-	-	-	576 4.45 1.73	502 3.88 1.51	-	-	-	-	-	1,532 11.84 4.60	-	-	847 6.55 2.54
Torrance (city)	137,933	39,445 28.60	-	2,204 5.59 1.60	-	-	5,904 14.97 4.28	-	3,549 9.00 2.57	-	-	-	-	13,508 34.25 9.79	8,532 21.63 6.19	-	-	656 1.66 0.48	-	-	1,290 3.27 0.94	-	-	1,837 4.66 1.33
Valinda (cdp)	21,789	1,936 8.89	-	-	-	-	-	-	1,009 52.12 4.63	-	-	-	-	-	-	-	-	-	-	-	-	-	-	474 24.48 2.18
Vincent (cdp)	15,094	1,093 7.24	-	-	-	-	-	-	620 56.72 4.11	-	-	-	-	-	-	-	-	-	-	-	-	-	-	-
Walnut (city)	30,004	16,880 56.26	-	800 4.74 2.67	-	-	6,312 37.39 21.04	-	3,452 20.45 11.51	-	-	-	-	436 2.58 1.45	1,892 11.21 6.31	-	-	-	-	-	1,926 11.41 6.42	-	-	575 3.41 1.92
West Carson (cdp)	21,138	5,067 23.97	-	-	-	-	-	-	2,121 41.86 10.03	-	-	-	-	1,118 22.06 5.29	860 16.97 4.07	-	-	-	-	-	-	-	-	-
West Covina (city)	104,893	23,749 22.64	449 0.43	501 2.11 0.48	-	-	6,611 27.84 6.30	-	10,043 42.29 9.57	-	-	-	-	724 3.05 0.69	917 3.86 0.87	-	-	-	-	-	948 3.99 0.90	-	-	2,160 9.10 2.06
West Hollywood (city)	35,716	1,412 3.95	-	-	-	-	-	-	-	-	-	-	-	-	-	-	-	-	-	-	-	-	-	-
West Puente Valley (cdp)	22,943	1,733 7.55	-	-	-	-	-	-	730 42.12 3.18	-	-	-	-	-	-	-	-	-	-	-	-	-	-	462 26.66 2.01
Whittier (city)	83,838	3,270 3.90	-	-	-	-	1,198 36.64 1.43	-	658 20.12 0.78	-	-	-	-	433 13.24 0.52	351 10.73 0.42	-	-	-	-	-	-	-	-	-
Madera County	123,109	1,544 1.25	-	576 37.31 0.47	-	-	-	-	439 28.43 0.36	-	-	-	-	-	-	-	-	-	-	-	-	-	-	-
Marin County	247,289	10,961 4.43	-	1,443 13.16 0.58	-	-	3,181 29.02 1.29	-	1,244 11.35 0.50	-	-	-	-	1,613 14.72 0.65	1,175 10.72 0.48	-	-	-	-	-	-	-	-	1,272 11.60 0.51
Larkspur (city)	12,002	440 3.67	-	-	-	-	-	-	-	-	-	-	-	-	-	-	-	-	-	-	-	-	-	-

Notes: Please refer to the User's Guide for an explanation of data; data is arranged alphabetically by state, then county, then city within each county; table includes counties with populations greater than 49,999 unless noted and cities with populations greater than 9,999 whose Asian and/or NHPI population rates are greater than the national average; (1) Native Hawaiian and other Pacific Islander; (2) excludes Taiwanese; (3) includes Chamorro; (4) county does not meet population threshold but is shown in order to allow inclusion of city

Place	Total population	Total Asian population	Total NHPI[1] population	Asian Indian	Bangladeshi	Cambodian	Chinese[2]	Fijian	Filipino	Guamanian[3]	Hawaiian, Native	Hmong	Indonesian	Japanese	Korean	Laotian	Malaysian	Pakistani	Samoan	Sri Lankan	Taiwanese	Thai	Tongan	Vietnamese
Novato (city)	47,795	2,515 5.26	-	-	-	-	648 25.77 1.36	-	469 18.65 0.98	-	-	-	-	-	-	-	-	-	-	-	-	-	-	-
San Rafael (city)	56,132	3,163 5.63	-	519 16.41 0.92	-	-	1,004 31.74 1.79	-	-	-	-	-	-	-	-	-	-	-	-	-	-	-	-	673 21.28 1.20
Tamalpais-Homestead (cdp)	10,596	508 4.79	-	-	-	-	-	-	-	-	-	-	-	-	-	-	-	-	-	-	-	-	-	-
Mendocino County	86,265	826 0.96	-	-	-	-	-	-	-	-	-	-	-	-	-	-	-	-	-	-	-	-	-	-
Merced County	210,554	14,464 6.87	-	2,138 14.78 1.02	-	-	451 3.12 0.21	-	1,515 10.47 0.72	-	-	6,585 45.53 3.13	-	541 3.74 0.26	-	1,723 11.91 0.82	-	-	-	-	-	-	-	-
Atwater (city)	22,896	1,238 5.41	-	-	-	-	-	-	-	-	-	393 31.74 1.72	-	-	-	-	-	-	-	-	-	-	-	-
Livingston (city)	10,350	1,553 15.00	-	1,245 80.17 12.03	-	-	-	-	-	-	-	-	-	-	-	-	-	-	-	-	-	-	-	-
Merced (city)	63,991	7,099 11.09	-	-	-	-	-	-	-	-	-	4,228 59.56 6.61	-	-	-	1,394 19.64 2.18	-	-	-	-	-	-	-	-
Monterey County	401,762	24,221 6.03	1,823 0.45	1,290 5.33 0.32	-	-	2,145 8.86 0.53	-	11,517 47.55 2.87	674 36.97 0.17	-	-	-	3,332 13.76 0.83	2,850 11.77 0.71	-	-	-	-	-	-	-	-	1,952 8.06 0.49
Marina (city)	25,052	4,223 16.86	504 2.01	-	-	-	-	-	1,266 29.98 5.05	-	-	-	-	374 8.86 1.49	1,252 29.65 5.00	-	-	-	-	-	-	-	-	735 17.40 2.93
Monterey (city)	29,773	2,342 7.87	-	-	-	-	438 18.70 1.47	-	441 18.83 1.48	-	-	-	-	732 31.26 2.46	-	-	-	-	-	-	-	-	-	-
Pacific Grove (city)	15,459	660 4.27	-	-	-	-	-	-	-	-	-	-	-	-	-	-	-	-	-	-	-	-	-	-
Salinas (city)	150,724	9,091 6.03	547 0.36	578 6.36 0.38	-	-	575 6.32 0.38	-	5,941 65.35 3.94	-	-	-	-	786 8.65 0.52	470 5.17 0.31	-	-	-	-	-	-	-	-	477 5.25 0.32
Seaside (city)	31,786	3,347 10.53	-	-	-	-	-	-	1,979 59.13 6.23	-	-	-	-	418 12.49 1.32	-	-	-	-	-	-	-	-	-	469 14.01 1.48
Napa County	124,279	3,936 3.17	-	-	-	-	555 14.10 0.45	-	1,996 50.71 1.61	-	-	-	-	415 10.54 0.33	-	-	-	-	-	-	-	-	-	-
Nevada County	92,033	593 0.64	-	-	-	-	-	-	-	-	-	-	-	-	-	-	-	-	-	-	-	-	-	-
Orange County	2,846,289	386,344 13.57	8,530 0.30	26,910 6.97 0.95	-	4,468 1.16 0.16	49,820 12.90 1.75	-	48,920 12.66 1.72	1,103 12.93 0.04	1,701 19.94 0.06	1,055 0.27 0.04	1,908 0.49 0.07	29,970 7.76 1.05	57,487 14.88 2.02	2,914 0.75 0.10	-	2,632 0.68 0.09	3,721 43.62 0.13	677 0.18 0.02	9,243 2.39 0.32	3,159 0.82 0.11	581 6.81 0.02	136,197 35.25 4.79

Notes: Please refer to the User's Guide for an explanation of data; data is arranged alphabetically by state, then county, then city within each county; table includes counties with populations greater than 49,999 unless noted and cities with populations greater than 9,999 whose Asian and/or NHPI population rates are greater than the national average; (1) Native Hawaiian and other Pacific Islander; (2) excludes Taiwanese; (3) includes Chamorro; (4) county does not meet population threshold but is shown in order to allow inclusion of city

Place	Total population	Total Asian population	Total NHPI[1] population	Asian Indian	Bangladeshi	Cambodian	Chinese[2]	Fijian	Filipino	Guamanian[3]	Hawaiian, Native	Hmong	Indonesian	Japanese	Korean	Laotian	Malaysian	Pakistani	Samoan	Sri Lankan	Taiwanese	Thai	Tongan	Vietnamese
Aliso Viejo (cdp)	40,225	4,377 10.88	-	543 12.41 1.35	-	-	700 15.99 1.74	-	865 19.76 2.15	-	-	-	-	584 13.34 1.45	482 11.01 1.20	-	-	-	-	-	-	-	-	513 11.72 1.28
Anaheim (city)	327,357	39,590 12.09	1,094 0.33	4,125 10.42 1.26	-	-	3,888 9.82 1.19	-	7,741 19.55 2.36	-	-	-	-	2,203 5.56 0.67	6,640 16.77 2.03	796 2.01 0.24	-	424 1.07 0.13	555 50.73 0.17	-	669 1.69 0.20	456 1.15 0.14	-	10,568 26.69 3.23
Brea (city)	35,122	3,155 8.98	-	457 14.48 1.30	-	-	488 15.47 1.39	-	503 15.94 1.43	-	-	-	-	-	821 26.02 2.34	-	-	-	-	-	-	-	-	-
Buena Park (city)	78,358	16,914 21.59	-	1,741 10.29 2.22	-	-	1,373 8.12 1.75	-	5,092 30.11 6.50	-	-	-	-	746 4.41 0.95	5,324 31.48 6.79	-	-	-	-	-	-	-	-	994 5.88 1.27
Costa Mesa (city)	108,785	7,878 7.24	652 0.60	429 5.45 0.39	-	-	957 12.15 0.88	-	1,333 16.92 1.23	-	-	-	-	1,509 19.15 1.39	590 7.49 0.54	-	-	-	-	-	-	-	-	2,241 28.45 2.06
Cypress (city)	46,534	9,470 20.35	-	694 7.33 1.49	-	-	1,473 15.55 3.17	-	1,742 18.39 3.74	-	-	-	-	942 9.95 2.02	2,573 27.17 5.53	-	-	-	-	-	744 7.86 1.60	-	-	766 8.09 1.65
Foothill Ranch (cdp)	10,907	1,713 15.71	-	-	-	-	-	-	-	-	-	-	-	-	-	-	-	-	-	-	-	-	-	-
Fountain Valley (city)	54,995	14,421 26.22	-	739 5.12 1.34	-	-	2,435 16.89 4.43	-	593 4.11 1.08	-	-	-	-	1,416 9.82 2.57	1,065 7.39 1.94	-	-	-	-	-	397 2.75 0.72	-	-	7,117 49.35 12.94
Fullerton (city)	126,246	20,248 16.04	-	1,835 9.06 1.45	-	-	2,789 13.77 2.21	-	2,201 10.87 1.74	-	-	-	-	1,132 5.59 0.90	8,988 44.39 7.12	-	-	-	-	-	-	-	-	1,580 7.80 1.25
Garden Grove (city)	165,710	51,029 30.79	1,266 0.76	724 1.42 0.44	-	500 0.98 0.30	2,573 5.04 1.55	-	2,942 5.77 1.78	-	-	-	-	1,044 2.05 0.63	6,062 11.88 3.66	-	-	-	773 61.06 0.47	-	-	-	-	35,023 68.63 21.14
Huntington Beach (city)	189,940	17,636 9.29	359 0.19	1,011 5.73 0.53	-	-	2,957 16.77 1.56	-	1,670 9.47 0.88	-	-	-	-	2,857 16.20 1.50	1,672 9.48 0.88	-	-	-	-	-	577 3.27 0.30	-	-	5,876 33.32 3.09
Irvine (city)	143,034	42,386 29.63	-	4,652 10.98 3.25	-	-	11,425 26.95 7.99	-	3,332 7.86 2.33	-	-	-	-	5,135 12.11 3.59	7,984 18.84 5.58	-	-	-	-	-	2,622 6.19 1.83	-	-	4,852 11.45 3.39
La Habra (city)	59,191	3,397 5.74	-	-	-	-	477 14.04 0.81	-	592 17.43 1.00	-	-	-	-	-	1,218 35.86 2.06	-	-	-	-	-	-	-	-	-
La Palma (city)	15,131	6,574 43.45	-	600 9.13 3.97	-	-	932 14.18 6.16	-	1,232 18.74 8.14	-	-	-	-	719 10.94 4.75	2,401 36.52 15.87	-	-	-	-	-	-	-	-	-
Laguna Hills (city)	31,277	3,259 10.42	-	-	-	-	570 17.49 1.82	-	625 19.18 2.00	-	-	-	-	-	-	-	-	-	-	-	-	-	-	570 17.49 1.82
Laguna Niguel (city)	61,963	4,689 7.57	-	-	-	-	1,003 21.39 1.62	-	846 18.04 1.37	-	-	-	-	854 18.21 1.38	676 14.42 1.09	-	-	-	-	-	-	-	-	464 9.90 0.75
Lake Forest (city)	58,806	5,447 9.26	-	738 13.55 1.25	-	-	677 12.43 1.15	-	1,043 19.15 1.77	-	-	-	-	574 10.54 0.98	577 10.59 0.98	-	-	-	-	-	-	-	-	1,390 25.52 2.36

Notes: Please refer to the User's Guide for an explanation of data; data is arranged alphabetically by state, then county, then city within each county; table includes counties with populations greater than 49,999 unless noted and cities with populations greater than 9,999 whose Asian and/or NHPI population rates are greater than the national average; (1) Native Hawaiian and other Pacific Islander; (2) excludes Taiwanese; (3) includes Chamorro; (4) county does not meet population threshold but is shown in order to allow inclusion of city

Place	Total population	Total Asian population	Total NHPI[1] population	Asian Indian	Bangladeshi	Cambodian	Chinese[2]	Fijian	Filipino	Guamanian[3]	Hawaiian, Native	Hmong	Indonesian	Japanese	Korean	Laotian	Malaysian	Pakistani	Samoan	Sri Lankan	Taiwanese	Thai	Tongan	Vietnamese
Los Alamitos (city)	11,260	1,050 9.33	-	-	-	-	-	-	-	-	-	-	-	-	-	-	-	-	-	-	-	-	-	-
Mission Viejo (city)	92,780	7,380 7.95	-	620 8.40 0.67	-	-	1,285 17.41 1.38	-	1,497 20.28 1.61	-	-	-	-	1,080 14.63 1.16	801 10.85 0.86	-	-	-	-	-	-	-	-	1,320 17.89 1.42
Newport Beach (city)	70,022	2,762 3.94	-	-	-	-	709 25.67 1.01	-	-	-	-	-	-	491 17.78 0.70	-	-	-	-	-	-	-	-	-	-
Orange (city)	128,438	11,711 9.12	-	856 7.31 0.67	-	-	1,305 11.14 1.02	-	2,029 17.33 1.58	-	-	-	-	777 6.63 0.60	1,614 13.78 1.26	-	-	-	-	-	462 3.95 0.36	-	-	3,832 32.72 2.98
Placentia (city)	47,099	5,254 11.16	-	524 9.97 1.11	-	-	1,142 21.74 2.42	-	767 14.60 1.63	-	-	-	-	472 8.98 1.00	696 13.25 1.48	-	-	-	-	-	-	-	-	935 17.80 1.99
Rancho Santa Margarita (city)	47,718	3,836 8.04	-	-	-	-	601 15.67 1.26	-	1,094 28.52 2.29	-	-	-	-	-	-	-	-	-	-	-	-	-	-	528 13.76 1.11
Rossmoor (cdp)	10,252	514 5.01	-	-	-	-	-	-	-	-	-	-	-	-	-	-	-	-	-	-	-	-	-	-
Santa Ana (city)	337,512	29,802 8.83	1,276 0.38	583 1.96 0.17	-	1,736 5.83 0.51	2,031 6.81 0.60	-	2,244 7.53 0.66	-	-	528 1.77 0.16	-	833 2.80 0.25	686 2.30 0.20	967 3.24 0.29	-	-	700 54.86 0.21	-	-	-	-	19,211 64.46 5.69
Seal Beach (city)	24,283	1,255 5.17	-	-	-	-	-	-	-	-	-	-	-	367 29.24 1.51	-	-	-	-	-	-	-	-	-	-
Stanton (city)	36,934	5,727 15.51	-	-	-	-	-	-	1,195 20.87 3.24	-	-	-	-	-	787 13.74 2.13	-	-	-	-	-	-	-	-	2,735 47.76 7.41
Tustin (city)	67,551	9,359 13.85	-	1,292 13.80 1.91	-	-	1,317 14.07 1.95	-	1,723 18.41 2.55	-	-	-	-	690 7.37 1.02	1,170 12.50 1.73	-	-	-	-	-	467 4.99 0.69	-	-	1,723 18.41 2.55
Tustin Foothills (cdp)	24,018	1,707 7.11	-	-	-	-	487 28.53 2.03	-	-	-	-	-	-	-	-	-	-	-	-	-	-	-	-	-
Westminster (city)	87,884	33,351 37.95	435 0.49	420 1.26 0.48	-	-	1,553 4.66 1.77	-	1,404 4.21 1.60	-	-	-	-	1,025 3.07 1.17	703 2.11 0.80	-	-	-	376 86.44 0.43	-	-	-	-	27,121 81.32 30.86
Yorba Linda (city)	58,595	6,403 10.93	-	695 10.85 1.19	-	-	1,615 25.22 2.76	-	923 14.42 1.58	-	-	-	-	838 13.09 1.43	883 13.79 1.51	-	-	-	-	-	-	-	-	643 10.04 1.10
Placer County	248,399	7,256 2.92	-	859 11.84 0.35	-	-	1,331 18.34 0.54	-	1,961 27.03 0.79	-	-	-	-	1,815 25.01 0.73	497 6.85 0.20	-	-	-	-	-	-	-	-	445 6.13 0.18
Rocklin (city)	36,563	1,314 3.59	-	-	-	-	-	-	-	-	-	-	-	441 33.56 1.21	-	-	-	-	-	-	-	-	-	-
Roseville (city)	80,092	3,358 4.19	-	638 19.00 0.80	-	-	688 20.49 0.86	-	988 29.42 1.23	-	-	-	-	505 15.04 0.63	-	-	-	-	-	-	-	-	-	-

Notes: Please refer to the User's Guide for an explanation of data; data is arranged alphabetically by state, then county, then city within each county; table includes counties with populations greater than 49,999 unless noted and cities with populations greater than 9,999 whose Asian and/or NHPI population rates are greater than the national average; (1) Native Hawaiian and other Pacific Islander; (2) excludes Taiwanese; (3) includes Chamorro; (4) county does not meet population threshold but is shown in order to allow inclusion of city

Place	Total population	Total Asian population	Total NHPI[1] population	Asian Indian	Bangladeshi	Cambodian	Chinese[2]	Fijian	Filipino	Guamanian[3]	Hawaiian, Native	Hmong	Indonesian	Japanese	Korean	Laotian	Malaysian	Pakistani	Samoan	Sri Lankan	Taiwanese	Thai	Tongan	Vietnamese
Riverside County	1,545,387	54,648	3,719	5,630	-	600	5,993	-	19,627	942	809	487	-	4,447	5,736	1,488	-	444	943	-	498	876	-	6,156
				10.30		1.10	10.97		35.92	25.33	21.75	0.89		8.14	10.50	2.72		0.81	25.36		0.91	1.60		11.26
		3.54	0.24	0.36		0.04	0.39		1.27	0.06	0.05	0.03		0.29	0.37	0.10		0.03	0.06		0.03	0.06		0.40
Banning (city)	23,443	1,057	-	-	-	-	-	-	-	-	-	-	-	-	-	341	-	-	-	-	-	-	-	-
																32.26								
		4.51														1.45								
Corona (city)	124,935	9,285	-	1,506	-	-	887	-	3,046	-	-	-	-	598	1,228	-	-	-	-	-	-	-	-	1,427
				16.22			9.55		32.81					6.44	13.23									15.37
		7.43		1.21			0.71		2.44					0.48	0.98									1.14
Moreno Valley (city)	142,548	7,995	-	-	-	-	469	-	3,974	-	-	-	-	499	676	488	-	-	-	-	-	-	-	602
							5.87		49.71					6.24	8.46	6.10								7.53
		5.61					0.33		2.79					0.35	0.47	0.34								0.42
Palm Springs (city)	42,848	1,756	-	-	-	-	-	-	1,149	-	-	-	-	-	-	-	-	-	-	-	-	-	-	-
									65.43															
		4.10							2.68															
Pedley (cdp)	11,076	459	-	-	-	-	-	-	-	-	-	-	-	-	-	-	-	-	-	-	-	-	-	-
		4.14																						
Riverside (city)	255,093	14,185	1,061	1,474	-	-	2,345	-	3,176	-	-	-	-	1,129	1,853	344	-	-	-	-	-	-	-	2,290
				10.39			16.53		22.39					7.96	13.06	2.43								16.14
		5.56	0.42	0.58			0.92		1.25					0.44	0.73	0.13								0.90
Temecula (city)	57,425	2,668	-	-	-	-	383	-	1,377	-	-	-	-	-	-	-	-	-	-	-	-	-	-	-
							14.36		51.61															
		4.65					0.67		2.40															
Sacramento County	1,223,499	134,881	6,269	12,742	-	1,117	28,723	1,751	24,045	875	654	17,314	-	12,307	4,674	9,648	-	1,436	1,239	-	406	739	741	16,557
				9.45		0.83	21.30	27.93	17.83	13.96	10.43	12.84		9.12	3.47	7.15		1.06	19.76		0.30	0.55	11.82	12.28
		11.02	0.51	1.04		0.09	2.35	0.14	1.97	0.07	0.05	1.42		1.01	0.38	0.79		0.12	0.10		0.03	0.06	0.06	1.35
Arden-Arcade (cdp)	96,004	4,766	-	718	-	-	895	-	1,096	-	-	351	-	507	-	-	-	-	-	-	-	-	-	399
				15.07			18.78		23.00			7.36		10.64										8.37
		4.96		0.75			0.93		1.14			0.37		0.53										0.42
Elk Grove (cdp)	60,255	10,532	-	1,445	-	-	1,476	-	3,387	-	-	-	-	455	-	-	-	-	-	-	-	-	-	2,174
				13.72			14.01		32.16					4.32										20.64
		17.48		2.40			2.45		5.62					0.76										3.61
Fair Oaks (cdp)	28,008	1,200	-	-	-	-	-	-	-	-	-	-	-	-	-	-	-	-	-	-	-	-	-	-
		4.28																						
Florin (cdp)	27,577	5,500	-	305	-	-	671	-	943	-	-	1,061	-	-	-	-	-	-	-	-	-	-	-	1,302
				5.55			12.20		17.15			19.29												23.67
		19.94		1.11			2.43		3.42			3.85												4.72
Folsom (city)	51,912	3,626	-	1,385	-	-	601	-	634	-	-	-	-	-	-	-	-	-	-	-	-	-	-	-
				38.20			16.57		17.48															
		6.98		2.67			1.16		1.22															
Foothill Farms (cdp)	17,393	798	-	-	-	-	-	-	-	-	-	-	-	-	-	-	-	-	-	-	-	-	-	-
		4.59																						
La Riviera (cdp)	10,273	883	-	-	-	-	-	-	-	-	-	-	-	-	-	-	-	-	-	-	-	-	-	-
		8.60																						
Laguna (cdp)	34,404	6,259	-	710	-	-	1,949	-	1,822	-	-	-	-	559	-	-	-	-	-	-	-	-	-	505
				11.34			31.14		29.11					8.93										8.07
		18.19		2.06			5.67		5.30					1.62										1.47

Notes: Please refer to the User's Guide for an explanation of data; data is arranged alphabetically by state, then county, then city within each county; table includes counties with populations greater than 49,999 unless noted and cities with populations greater than 9,999 whose Asian and/or NHPI population rates are greater than the national average; (1) Native Hawaiian and other Pacific Islander; (2) excludes Taiwanese; (3) includes Chamorro; (4) county does not meet population threshold but is shown in order to allow inclusion of city

Place	Total population	Total Asian population	Total NHPI[1] population	Asian Indian	Bangladeshi	Cambodian	Chinese[2]	Fijian	Filipino	Guamanian[3]	Hawaiian, Native	Hmong	Indonesian	Japanese	Korean	Laotian	Malaysian	Pakistani	Samoan	Sri Lankan	Taiwanese	Thai	Tongan	Vietnamese
North Highlands (cdp)	44,079	2,463 5.59	-	-	-	-	-	-	824 33.46 1.87	-	-	-	-	-	-	-	-	-	-	-	-	-	-	641 26.03 1.45
Parkway-S. Sacramento (cdp)	36,490	6,735 18.46	-	-	-	-	526 7.81 1.44	-	-	-	-	2,750 40.83 7.54	-	-	-	1,392 20.67 3.81	-	-	-	-	-	-	-	1,110 16.48 3.04
Rancho Cordova (cdp)	54,586	4,375 8.01	-	598 13.67 1.10	-	-	485 11.09 0.89	-	1,013 23.15 1.86	-	-	-	-	-	428 9.78 0.78	-	-	-	-	-	-	-	-	840 19.20 1.54
Rosemont (cdp)	22,830	2,698 11.82	-	-	-	-	-	-	435 16.12 1.91	-	-	-	-	-	478 17.72 2.09	-	-	-	-	-	-	-	-	540 20.01 2.37
Sacramento (city)	407,075	67,400 16.56	3,692 0.91	4,053 6.01 1.00	-	483 0.72 0.12	18,984 28.17 4.66	1,240 33.59 0.30	8,185 12.14 2.01	-	-	12,070 17.91 2.97	-	6,716 9.96 1.65	698 1.04 0.17	6,305 9.35 1.55	-	779 1.16 0.19	733 19.85 0.18	-	-	-	574 15.55 0.14	6,497 9.64 1.60
Vineyard (cdp)	10,007	1,629 16.28	-	-	-	-	-	-	709 43.52 7.09	-	-	-	-	-	-	-	-	-	-	-	-	-	-	-
San Benito County	53,234	1,033 1.94	-	-	-	-	-	-	536 51.89 1.01	-	-	-	-	-	-	-	-	-	-	-	-	-	-	-
San Bernardino County	1,709,434	79,103 4.63	5,019 0.29	7,965 10.07 0.47	-	1,742 2.20 0.10	10,667 13.48 0.62	-	25,621 32.39 1.50	1,042 20.76 0.06	610 12.15 0.04	-	3,301 4.17 0.19	4,313 5.45 0.25	7,171 9.07 0.42	475 0.60 0.03	-	683 0.86 0.04	2,036 40.57 0.12	-	2,039 2.58 0.12	1,705 2.16 0.10	810 16.14 0.05	10,306 13.03 0.60
Chino (city)	67,600	3,351 4.96	-	-	-	-	-	-	1,572 46.91 2.33	-	-	-	-	-	-	-	-	-	-	-	-	-	-	468 13.97 0.69
Chino Hills (city)	66,716	14,256 21.37	-	1,178 8.26 1.77	-	-	3,487 24.46 5.23	-	5,566 39.04 8.34	-	-	-	-	552 3.87 0.83	1,047 7.34 1.57	-	-	-	-	-	634 4.45 0.95	-	-	794 5.57 1.19
Colton (city)	48,011	2,440 5.08	-	-	-	-	-	-	589 24.14 1.23	-	-	-	-	-	-	-	-	-	-	-	-	-	-	-
Fontana (city)	128,174	5,898 4.60	604 0.47	658 11.16 0.51	-	-	-	-	2,976 50.46 2.32	-	-	-	-	-	-	-	-	-	-	-	-	-	-	-
Grand Terrace (city)	11,793	602 5.10	-	-	-	-	-	-	-	-	-	-	-	-	-	-	-	-	-	-	-	-	-	-
Highland (city)	44,629	2,832 6.35	-	-	-	-	-	-	960 33.90 2.15	-	-	-	-	-	-	-	-	-	-	-	-	-	-	605 21.36 1.36
Loma Linda (city)	18,582	4,351 23.42	-	404 9.29 2.17	-	-	720 16.55 3.87	-	1,042 23.95 5.61	-	-	-	522 12.00 2.81	-	810 18.62 4.36	-	-	-	-	-	-	-	-	-
Montclair (city)	33,119	2,645 7.99	-	-	-	-	-	-	-	-	-	-	-	-	-	-	-	-	-	-	-	-	-	1,223 46.24 3.69
Ontario (city)	157,339	6,130 3.90	544 0.35	509 8.30 0.32	-	-	469 7.65 0.30	-	2,314 37.75 1.47	-	-	-	-	-	-	-	-	-	-	-	-	-	-	1,608 26.23 1.02

Notes: Please refer to the User's Guide for an explanation of data; data is arranged alphabetically by state, then county, then city within each county; table includes counties with populations greater than 49,999 unless noted and cities with populations greater than 9,999 whose Asian and/or NHPI population rates are greater than the national average; (1) Native Hawaiian and other Pacific Islander; (2) excludes Taiwanese; (3) includes Chamorro; (4) county does not meet population threshold but is shown in order to allow inclusion of city

Place	Total population	Total Asian population	Total NHPI[1] population	Asian Indian	Bangladeshi	Cambodian	Chinese[2]	Fijian	Filipino	Guamanian[3]	Hawaiian, Native	Hmong	Indonesian	Japanese	Korean	Laotian	Malaysian	Pakistani	Samoan	Sri Lankan	Taiwanese	Thai	Tongan	Vietnamese
Rancho Cucamonga (city)	128,161	7,360 5.74	-	983 13.36 0.77	-	-	1,338 18.18 1.04	-	2,174 29.54 1.70	-	-	-	-	527 7.16 0.41	759 10.31 0.59	-	-	-	-	-	-	-	-	527 7.16 0.41
Redlands (city)	63,672	3,292 5.17	-	398 12.09 0.63	-	-	489 14.85 0.77	-	643 19.53 1.01	-	-	-	-	-	552 16.77 0.87	-	-	-	-	-	-	-	-	-
Rialto (city)	91,711	1,748 1.91	532 0.58	-	-	-	-	-	497 28.43 0.54	-	-	-	-	-	-	-	-	-	-	-	-	-	-	-
San Bernardino (city)	185,388	7,501 4.05	748 0.40	890 11.87 0.48	-	446 5.95 0.24	601 8.01 0.32	-	1,789 23.85 0.97	-	-	-	449 5.99 0.24	-	394 5.25 0.21	-	-	-	478 63.90 0.26	-	-	-	-	1,514 20.18 0.82
Upland (city)	68,427	4,996 7.30	-	582 11.65 0.85	-	-	702 14.05 1.03	-	567 11.35 0.83	-	-	-	-	-	965 19.32 1.41	-	-	-	-	-	468 9.37 0.68	-	-	849 16.99 1.24
Victorville (city)	64,516	2,398 3.72	-	-	-	-	-	-	1,221 50.92 1.89	-	-	-	-	-	-	-	-	-	-	-	-	-	-	-
San Diego County	2,813,833	248,653 8.84	13,482 0.48	9,626 3.87 0.34	-	4,369 1.76 0.16	28,936 11.64 1.03	-	120,655 48.52 4.29	4,629 34.33 0.16	2,217 16.44 0.08	1,375 0.55 0.05	490 0.20 0.02	18,760 7.54 0.67	11,378 4.58 0.40	7,117 2.86 0.25	-	540 0.22 0.02	4,954 36.75 0.18	-	2,362 0.95 0.08	1,309 0.53 0.05	435 3.23 0.02	34,496 13.87 1.23
Bonita (cdp)	12,018	994 8.27	-	-	-	-	-	-	540 54.33 4.49	-	-	-	-	-	-	-	-	-	-	-	-	-	-	-
Carlsbad (city)	77,998	3,177 4.07	-	-	-	-	713 22.44 0.91	-	619 19.48 0.79	-	-	-	-	477 15.01 0.61	-	-	-	-	-	-	-	-	-	-
Chula Vista (city)	173,860	18,851 10.84	752 0.43	-	-	-	1,066 5.65 0.61	-	13,076 69.37 7.52	425 56.52 0.24	-	-	-	2,022 10.73 1.16	1,408 7.47 0.81	-	-	-	-	-	-	-	-	-
Coronado (city)	24,226	907 3.74	-	-	-	-	-	-	465 51.27 1.92	-	-	-	-	-	-	-	-	-	-	-	-	-	-	-
Escondido (city)	133,528	5,552 4.16	-	-	-	-	433 7.80 0.32	-	2,039 36.73 1.53	-	-	-	-	-	-	479 8.63 0.36	-	-	-	-	-	-	-	1,283 23.11 0.96
Imperial Beach (city)	26,980	1,826 6.77	-	-	-	-	-	-	1,511 82.75 5.60	-	-	-	-	-	-	-	-	-	-	-	-	-	-	-
La Mesa (city)	54,751	2,255 4.12	-	-	-	-	-	-	573 25.41 1.05	-	-	-	-	-	-	-	-	-	-	-	-	-	-	-
La Presa (cdp)	32,854	3,397 10.34	-	-	-	-	-	-	3,068 90.31 9.34	-	-	-	-	-	-	-	-	-	-	-	-	-	-	-
Lemon Grove (city)	24,954	1,447 5.80	-	-	-	-	-	-	715 49.41 2.87	-	-	-	-	-	-	-	-	-	-	-	-	-	-	365 25.22 1.46
National City (city)	54,405	9,966 18.32	-	-	-	-	-	-	9,061 90.92 16.65	-	-	-	-	-	-	-	-	-	-	-	-	-	-	-

Notes: Please refer to the User's Guide for an explanation of data; data is arranged alphabetically by state, then county, then city within each county; table includes counties with populations greater than 49,999 unless noted and cities with populations greater than 9,999 whose Asian and/or NHPI population rates are greater than the national average; (1) Native Hawaiian and other Pacific Islander; (2) excludes Taiwanese; (3) includes Chamorro; (4) county does not meet population threshold but is shown in order to allow inclusion of city

Place	Total population	Total Asian population	Total NHPI[1] population	Asian Indian	Bangladeshi	Cambodian	Chinese[2]	Fijian	Filipino	Guamanian[3]	Hawaiian, Native	Hmong	Indonesian	Japanese	Korean	Laotian	Malaysian	Pakistani	Samoan	Sri Lankan	Taiwanese	Thai	Tongan	Vietnamese
Oceanside (city)	160,905	8,991 5.59	2,274 1.41	-	-	-	500 5.56 0.31	-	5,255 58.45 3.27	-	-	-	-	1,189 13.22 0.74	-	-	-	-	1,532 67.37 0.95	-	-	-	-	869 9.67 0.54
Poway (city)	48,295	3,458 7.16	-	-	-	-	693 20.04 1.43	-	1,371 39.65 2.84	-	-	-	-	-	-	-	-	-	-	-	-	-	-	-
Rancho San Diego (cdp)	20,043	1,010 5.04	-	-	-	-	-	-	546 54.06 2.72	-	-	-	-	-	-	-	-	-	-	-	-	-	-	-
San Diego (city)	1,223,341	166,326 13.60	6,216 0.51	6,519 3.92 0.53	-	3,916 2.35 0.32	21,962 13.20 1.80	-	73,785 44.36 6.03	2,077 33.41 0.17	1,125 18.10 0.09	1,092 0.66 0.09	-	10,195 6.13 0.83	6,804 4.09 0.56	6,037 3.63 0.49	-	-	2,171 34.93 0.18	-	1,587 0.95 0.13	823 0.49 0.07	-	28,549 17.16 2.33
San Marcos (city)	55,160	2,463 4.47	-	-	-	-	424 17.21 0.77	-	1,252 50.83 2.27	-	-	-	-	-	-	-	-	-	-	-	-	-	-	-
Solana Beach (city)	12,887	529 4.10	-	-	-	-	-	-	-	-	-	-	-	-	-	-	-	-	-	-	-	-	-	-
Spring Valley (cdp)	26,643	1,361 5.11	-	-	-	-	-	-	629 46.22 2.36	-	-	-	-	-	-	-	-	-	-	-	-	-	-	-
Vista (city)	90,131	3,160 3.51	582 0.65	-	-	-	-	-	1,185 37.50 1.31	-	-	-	-	589 18.64 0.65	-	-	-	-	-	-	-	-	-	-
San Francisco County	776,733	239,938 30.89	3,581 0.46	4,834 2.01 0.62	-	646 0.27 0.08	154,490 64.39 19.89	-	40,072 16.70 5.16	-	-	-	873 0.36 0.11	10,818 4.51 1.39	7,134 2.97 0.92	-	-	556 0.23 0.07	2,279 63.64 0.29	-	771 0.32 0.10	1,461 0.61 0.19	-	10,430 4.35 1.34
San Francisco (city)	776,733	239,938 30.89	3,581 0.46	4,834 2.01 0.62	-	646 0.27 0.08	154,490 64.39 19.89	-	40,072 16.70 5.16	-	-	-	873 0.36 0.11	10,818 4.51 1.39	7,134 2.97 0.92	-	-	556 0.23 0.07	2,279 63.64 0.29	-	771 0.32 0.10	1,461 0.61 0.19	-	10,430 4.35 1.34
San Joaquin County	563,598	65,065 11.54	1,785 0.32	5,205 8.00 0.92	-	9,469 14.55 1.68	5,648 8.68 1.00	-	21,167 32.53 3.76	-	415 23.25 0.07	5,948 9.14 1.06	-	3,565 5.48 0.63	834 1.28 0.15	3,080 4.73 0.55	-	1,337 2.05 0.24	360 20.17 0.06	-	-	-	-	6,320 9.71 1.12
Lathrop (city)	10,334	1,463 14.16	-	-	-	-	-	-	1,063 72.66 10.29	-	-	-	-	-	-	-	-	-	-	-	-	-	-	-
Lodi (city)	57,037	3,114 5.46	-	768 24.66 1.35	-	-	-	-	638 20.49 1.12	-	-	-	-	662 21.26 1.16	-	-	-	-	-	-	-	-	-	-
Stockton (city)	242,714	48,681 20.06	1,036 0.43	2,138 4.39 0.88	-	9,101 18.70 3.75	4,285 8.80 1.77	-	15,033 30.88 6.19	-	-	4,953 10.17 2.04	-	1,617 3.32 0.67	-	2,968 6.10 1.22	-	702 1.44 0.29	-	-	-	-	-	5,751 11.81 2.37
Tracy (city)	56,839	4,763 8.38	-	1,137 23.87 2.00	-	-	369 7.75 0.65	-	2,012 42.24 3.54	-	-	-	-	-	-	-	-	-	-	-	-	-	-	-
San Luis Obispo County	246,681	6,850 2.78	-	622 9.08 0.25	-	-	1,116 16.29 0.45	-	2,455 35.84 1.00	-	-	-	-	1,014 14.80 0.41	739 10.79 0.30	-	-	-	-	-	-	-	-	-
Baywood-Los Osos (cdp)	14,154	845 5.97	-	-	-	-	-	-	585 69.23 4.13	-	-	-	-	-	-	-	-	-	-	-	-	-	-	-

Notes: Please refer to the User's Guide for an explanation of data; data is arranged alphabetically by state, then county, then city within each county; table includes counties with populations greater than 49,999 unless noted and cities with populations greater than 9,999 whose Asian and/or NHPI population rates are greater than the national average; (1) Native Hawaiian and other Pacific Islander; (2) excludes Taiwanese; (3) includes Chamorro; (4) county does not meet population threshold but is shown in order to allow inclusion of city

Place	Total population	Total Asian population	Total NHPI[1] population	Asian Indian	Bangladeshi	Cambodian	Chinese[2]	Fijian	Filipino	Guamanian[3]	Hawaiian, Native	Hmong	Indonesian	Japanese	Korean	Laotian	Malaysian	Pakistani	Samoan	Sri Lankan	Taiwanese	Thai	Tongan	Vietnamese
Grover Beach (city)	13,006	501 3.85	-	-	-	-	-	-	-	-	-	-	-	-	-	-	-	-	-	-	-	-	-	-
San Luis Obispo (city)	44,148	2,273 5.15	-	-	-	-	558 24.55 1.26	-	536 23.58 1.21	-	-	-	-	-	-	-	-	-	-	-	-	-	-	-
San Mateo County	707,161	142,162 20.10	8,533 1.21	11,093 7.80 1.57	-	-	47,417 33.35 6.71	1,157 13.56 0.16	60,114 42.29 8.50	402 4.71 0.06	805 9.43 0.11	-	756 0.53 0.11	9,467 6.66 1.34	4,358 3.07 0.62	-	-	-	1,451 17.00 0.21	-	779 0.55 0.11	701 0.49 0.10	3,654 42.82 0.52	2,800 1.97 0.40
Belmont (city)	25,138	3,923 15.61	-	723 18.43 2.88	-	-	1,692 43.13 6.73	-	642 16.37 2.55	-	-	-	-	443 11.29 1.76	-	-	-	-	-	-	-	-	-	-
Burlingame (city)	27,975	3,739 13.37	-	-	-	-	1,834 49.05 6.56	-	571 15.27 2.04	-	-	-	-	387 10.35 1.38	-	-	-	-	-	-	-	-	-	-
Daly City (city)	103,549	52,289 50.50	866 0.84	1,058 2.02 1.02	-	-	13,756 26.31 13.28	-	32,923 62.96 31.79	-	-	-	-	821 1.57 0.79	797 1.52 0.77	-	-	-	-	-	-	-	-	925 1.77 0.89
East Palo Alto (city)	29,450	563 1.91	2,211 7.51	-	-	-	-	-	-	-	-	-	-	-	-	-	-	-	-	-	-	-	1,494 67.57 5.07	-
Foster City (city)	28,803	9,377 32.56	-	1,778 18.96 6.17	-	-	4,231 45.12 14.69	-	800 8.53 2.78	-	-	-	-	1,496 15.95 5.19	390 4.16 1.35	-	-	-	-	-	-	-	-	-
Hillsborough (town)	10,823	2,702 24.97	-	-	-	-	1,995 73.83 18.43	-	-	-	-	-	-	-	-	-	-	-	-	-	-	-	-	-
Menlo Park (city)	30,786	2,154 7.00	-	-	-	-	860 39.93 2.79	-	-	-	-	-	-	453 21.03 1.47	-	-	-	-	-	-	-	-	-	-
Millbrae (city)	20,727	5,898 28.46	-	373 6.32 1.80	-	-	3,826 64.87 18.46	-	676 11.46 3.26	-	-	-	-	406 6.88 1.96	320 5.43 1.54	-	-	-	-	-	-	-	-	-
Pacifica (city)	38,413	5,897 15.35	-	-	-	-	1,523 25.83 3.96	-	3,259 55.27 8.48	-	-	-	-	362 6.14 0.94	-	-	-	-	-	-	-	-	-	-
Redwood City (city)	75,447	6,932 9.19	566 0.75	1,265 18.25 1.68	-	-	2,540 36.64 3.37	-	1,445 20.85 1.92	-	-	-	-	595 8.58 0.79	-	-	-	-	-	-	-	-	-	-
San Bruno (city)	40,164	7,496 18.66	1,017 2.53	1,052 14.03 2.62	-	-	2,164 28.87 5.39	-	3,060 40.82 7.62	-	-	-	-	483 6.44 1.20	-	-	-	-	-	-	-	-	533 52.41 1.33	-
San Carlos (city)	27,697	1,841 6.65	-	-	-	-	702 38.13 2.53	-	-	-	-	-	-	-	-	-	-	-	-	-	-	-	-	-
San Mateo (city)	92,372	14,221 15.40	1,369 1.48	2,180 15.33 2.36	-	-	5,293 37.22 5.73	-	2,944 20.70 3.19	-	-	-	-	2,014 14.16 2.18	575 4.04 0.62	-	-	-	-	-	-	-	638 46.60 0.69	403 2.83 0.44
South San Francisco (city)	60,727	17,618 29.01	874 1.44	733 4.16 1.21	-	-	4,621 26.23 7.61	-	10,358 58.79 17.06	-	-	-	-	525 2.98 0.86	-	-	-	-	-	-	-	-	-	-

Notes: Please refer to the User's Guide for an explanation of data; data is arranged alphabetically by state, then county, then city within each county; table includes counties with populations greater than 49,999 unless noted and cities with populations greater than 9,999 whose Asian and/or NHPI population rates are greater than the national average; (1) Native Hawaiian and other Pacific Islander; (2) excludes Taiwanese; (3) includes Chamorro; (4) county does not meet population threshold but is shown in order to allow inclusion of city

Place	Total population	Total Asian population	Total NHPI[1] population	Asian Indian	Bangladeshi	Cambodian	Chinese[2]	Fijian	Filipino	Guamanian[3]	Hawaiian, Native	Hmong	Indonesian	Japanese	Korean	Laotian	Malaysian	Pakistani	Samoan	Sri Lankan	Taiwanese	Thai	Tongan	Vietnamese
Santa Barbara County	399,347	15,630 3.91	905 0.23	875 5.60 0.22	-	-	2,603 16.65 0.65	-	4,880 31.22 1.22	-	-	355 2.27 0.09	-	2,301 14.72 0.58	1,616 10.34 0.40	-	-	-	-	-	-	-	-	1,224 7.83 0.31
Goleta (cdp)	55,367	3,247 5.86	-	-	-	-	776 23.90 1.40	-	530 16.32 0.96	-	-	-	-	455 14.01 0.82	-	-	-	-	-	-	-	-	-	493 15.18 0.89
Isla Vista (cdp)	18,381	1,973 10.73	-	-	-	-	674 34.16 3.67	-	-	-	-	-	-	-	426 21.59 2.32	-	-	-	-	-	-	-	-	-
Lompoc (city)	41,078	1,539 3.75	-	-	-	-	-	-	357 23.20 0.87	-	-	-	-	-	-	-	-	-	-	-	-	-	-	-
Orcutt (cdp)	28,846	1,056 3.66	-	-	-	-	-	-	-	-	-	-	-	-	-	-	-	-	-	-	-	-	-	-
Santa Maria (city)	77,113	3,639 4.72	-	-	-	-	-	-	2,403 66.03 3.12	-	-	-	-	444 12.20 0.58	-	-	-	-	-	-	-	-	-	-
Santa Clara County	1,682,585	430,201 25.57	5,793 0.34	65,087 15.13 3.87	484 0.11 0.03	4,399 1.02 0.26	112,600 26.17 6.69	511 8.82 0.03	77,815 18.09 4.62	1,390 23.99 0.08	1,146 19.78 0.07	-	687 0.16 0.04	26,980 6.27 1.60	21,673 5.04 1.29	2,062 0.48 0.12	-	2,751 0.64 0.16	1,719 29.67 0.10	-	5,298 1.23 0.31	1,334 0.31 0.08	-	97,419 22.64 5.79
Alum Rock (cdp)	13,779	1,258 9.13	-	-	-	-	-	-	-	-	-	-	-	-	-	-	-	-	-	-	-	-	-	557 44.28 4.04
Campbell (city)	38,187	5,641 14.77	-	769 13.63 2.01	-	-	1,472 26.09 3.85	-	626 11.10 1.64	-	-	-	-	792 14.04 2.07	854 15.14 2.24	-	-	-	-	-			-	910 16.13 2.38
Cupertino (city)	50,657	22,599 44.61	-	4,771 21.11 9.42	-	-	10,519 46.55 20.77	-	409 1.81 0.81	-	-	-	-	2,417 10.70 4.77	2,235 9.89 4.41	-	-	-	-	-	792 3.50 1.56	-	-	734 3.25 1.45
Gilroy (city)	41,587	1,912 4.60	-	-	-	-	384 20.08 0.92	-	657 34.36 1.58	-	-	-	-	-	-	-	-	-	-	-	-	-	-	-
Los Altos (city)	27,585	4,177 15.14	-	522 12.50 1.89	-	-	2,047 49.01 7.42	-	-	-	-	-	-	685 16.40 2.48	-	-	-	-	-	-	-	-	-	-
Los Gatos (town)	28,683	2,338 8.15	-	-	-	-	902 38.58 3.14	-	-	-	-	-	-	490 20.96 1.71	-	-	-	-	-	-	-	-	-	-
Milpitas (city)	62,714	32,766 52.25	631 1.01	4,727 14.43 7.54	-	-	8,104 24.73 12.92	-	9,018 27.52 14.38	-	-	-	-	588 1.79 0.94	850 2.59 1.36	-	-	-	-	-	-	-	-	7,922 24.18 12.63
Morgan Hill (city)	33,635	2,113 6.28	-	-	-	-	419 19.83 1.25	-	-	-	-	-	-	466 22.05 1.39	-	-	-	-	-	-	-	-	-	-
Mountain View (city)	70,467	14,561 20.66	-	2,906 19.96 4.12	-	-	5,488 37.69 7.79	-	2,100 14.42 2.98	-	-	-	-	1,668 11.46 2.37	696 4.78 0.99	-	-	-	-	-	-	-	-	863 5.93 1.22
Palo Alto (city)	58,783	10,307 17.53	-	1,453 14.10 2.47	-	-	5,457 52.94 9.28	-	417 4.05 0.71	-	-	-	-	1,195 11.59 2.03	983 9.54 1.67	-	-	-	-	-	-	-	-	-

Notes: Please refer to the User's Guide for an explanation of data; data is arranged alphabetically by state, then county, then city within each county; table includes counties with populations greater than 49,999 unless noted and cities with populations greater than 9,999 whose Asian and/or NHPI population rates are greater than the national average; (1) Native Hawaiian and other Pacific Islander; (2) excludes Taiwanese; (3) includes Chamorro; (4) county does not meet population threshold but is shown in order to allow inclusion of city

Place	Total population	Total Asian population	Total NHPI[1] population	Asian Indian	Bangladeshi	Cambodian	Chinese[2]	Fijian	Filipino	Guamanian[3]	Hawaiian, Native	Hmong	Indonesian	Japanese	Korean	Laotian	Malaysian	Pakistani	Samoan	Sri Lankan	Taiwanese	Thai	Tongan	Vietnamese
San Jose (city)	893,889	239,465 26.79	3,234 0.36	25,079 10.47 2.81	-	3,989 1.67 0.45	50,905 21.26 5.69	-	49,606 20.72 5.55	732 22.63 0.08	535 16.54 0.06	-	-	11,199 4.68 1.25	9,378 3.92 1.05	1,893 0.79 0.21	-	1,319 0.55 0.15	1,218 37.66 0.14	-	2,053 0.86 0.23	631 0.26 0.07	-	75,956 31.72 8.50
Santa Clara (city)	102,104	29,195 28.59	382 0.37	8,870 30.38 8.69	-	-	4,694 16.08 4.60	-	5,934 20.33 5.81	-	-	-	-	1,447 4.96 1.42	2,065 7.07 2.02	-	-	469 1.61 0.46	-	-	-	-	-	4,638 15.89 4.54
Saratoga (city)	29,855	8,531 28.57	-	1,238 14.51 4.15	-	-	4,991 58.50 16.72	-	-	-	-	-	-	536 6.28 1.80	552 6.47 1.85	-	-	-	-	-	332 3.89 1.11	-	-	-
Stanford (cdp)	13,307	3,460 26.00	-	656 18.96 4.93	-	-	1,589 45.92 11.94	-	-	-	-	-	-	-	368 10.64 2.77	-	-	-	-	-	-	-	-	-
Sunnyvale (city)	131,905	42,604 32.30	536 0.41	12,211 28.66 9.26	-	-	12,306 28.88 9.33	-	6,567 15.41 4.98	-	-	-	-	3,445 8.09 2.61	2,697 6.33 2.04	-	-	-	-	-	671 1.57 0.51	-	-	3,176 7.45 2.41
Santa Cruz County	255,602	8,390 3.28	-	978 11.66 0.38	-	-	2,026 24.15 0.79	-	2,044 24.36 0.80	-	-	-	-	1,749 20.85 0.68	483 5.76 0.19	-	-	-	-	-	-	-	-	428 5.10 0.17
Capitola (city)	10,204	484 4.74	-	-	-	-	-	-	-	-	-	-	-	-	-	-	-	-	-	-	-	-	-	-
Santa Cruz (city)	54,364	2,795 5.14	-	426 15.24 0.78	-	-	913 32.67 1.68	-	528 18.89 0.97	-	-	-	-	429 15.35 0.79	-	-	-	-	-	-	-	-	-	-
Scotts Valley (city)	11,518	655 5.69	-	-	-	-	-	-	-	-	-	-	-	-	-	-	-	-	-	-	-	-	-	-
Shasta County	163,256	3,219 1.97	-	-	-	-	-	-	449 13.95 0.28	-	-	-	-	-	-	1,745 54.21 1.07	-	-	-	-	-	-	-	-
Solano County	394,542	49,899 12.65	3,189 0.81	2,833 5.68 0.72	-	-	3,140 6.29 0.80	-	35,862 71.87 9.09	1,351 42.36 0.34	654 20.51 0.17	411 0.82 0.10	-	1,993 3.99 0.51	968 1.94 0.25	754 1.51 0.19	-	-	625 19.60 0.16	-	-	-	-	1,404 2.81 0.36
Benicia (city)	26,967	1,941 7.20	-	-	-	-	461 23.75 1.71	-	1,051 54.15 3.90	-	-	-	-	-	-	-	-	-	-	-	-	-	-	-
Fairfield (city)	96,168	10,596 11.02	1,037 1.08	943 8.90 0.98	-	-	933 8.81 0.97	-	6,058 57.17 6.30	541 52.17 0.56	-	-	-	700 6.61 0.73	390 3.68 0.41	389 3.67 0.40	-	-	-	-	-	-	-	-
Suisun City (city)	26,050	4,803 18.44	-	421 8.77 1.62	-	-	-	-	3,099 64.52 11.90	-	-	-	-	-	-	-	-	-	-	-	-	-	-	-
Vacaville (city)	88,644	3,700 4.17	-	-	-	-	-	-	1,913 51.70 2.16	-	-	-	-	-	-	-	-	-	-	-	-	-	-	-
Vallejo (city)	116,351	27,632 23.75	1,396 1.20	921 3.33 0.79	-	-	901 3.26 0.77	-	23,274 84.23 20.00	572 40.97 0.49	-	-	-	367 1.33 0.32	-	-	-	-	-	-	-	-	-	634 2.29 0.54
Sonoma County	458,614	14,070 3.07	750 0.16	1,739 12.36 0.38	-	850 6.04 0.19	2,769 19.68 0.60	-	2,496 17.74 0.54	-	-	-	-	1,559 11.08 0.34	891 6.33 0.19	1,082 7.69 0.24	-	-	-	-	-	-	-	1,353 9.62 0.30

Notes: Please refer to the User's Guide for an explanation of data; data is arranged alphabetically by state, then county, then city within each county; table includes counties with populations greater than 49,999 unless noted and cities with populations greater than 9,999 whose Asian and/or NHPI population rates are greater than the national average; (1) Native Hawaiian and other Pacific Islander; (2) excludes Taiwanese; (3) includes Chamorro; (4) county does not meet population threshold but is shown in order to allow inclusion of city

Place	Total population	Total Asian population	Total NHPI[1] population	Asian Indian	Bangladeshi	Cambodian	Chinese[2]	Fijian	Filipino	Guamanian[3]	Hawaiian, Native	Hmong	Indonesian	Japanese	Korean	Laotian	Malaysian	Pakistani	Samoan	Sri Lankan	Taiwanese	Thai	Tongan	Vietnamese
Petaluma (city)	54,538	2,232 4.09	-	-	-	-	686 30.73 1.26	-	-	-	-	-	-	-	-	-	-	-	-	-	-	-	-	-
Rohnert Park (city)	42,388	2,473 5.83	-	-	-	-	453 18.32 1.07	-	716 28.95 1.69	-	-	-	-	-	-	-	-	-	-	-	-	-	-	-
Santa Rosa (city)	147,532	5,607 3.80	-	706 12.59 0.48	-	646 11.52 0.44	810 14.45 0.55	-	735 13.11 0.50	-	-	-	-	407 7.26 0.28	-	633 11.29 0.43	-	-	-	-	-	-	-	776 13.84 0.53
Stanislaus County	446,997	18,392 4.11	1,804 0.40	4,349 23.65 0.97	-	3,230 17.56 0.72	1,853 10.08 0.41	698 38.69 0.16	2,765 15.03 0.62	-	-	969 5.27 0.22	-	814 4.43 0.18	-	1,589 8.64 0.36	-	-	-	-	-	-	-	1,393 7.57 0.31
Ceres (city)	34,534	1,759 5.09	-	851 48.38 2.46	-	-	-	-	-	-	-	-	-	-	-	-	-	-	-	-	-	-	-	-
Modesto (city)	189,460	11,219 5.92	1,217 0.64	1,958 17.45 1.03	-	2,538 22.62 1.34	1,141 10.17 0.60	494 40.59 0.26	1,543 13.75 0.81	-	-	406 3.62 0.21	-	388 3.46 0.20	-	1,141 10.17 0.60	-	-	-	-	-	-	-	1,141 10.17 0.60
Salida (cdp)	12,560	487 3.88	-	-	-	-	-	-	-	-	-	-	-	-	-	-	-	-	-	-	-	-	-	-
Turlock (city)	55,488	2,410 4.34	-	1,068 44.32 1.92	-	-	-	-	-	-	-	-	-	-	-	-	-	-	-	-	-	-	-	-
Sutter County	78,930	8,869 11.24	-	7,281 82.09 9.22	-	-	-	-	411 4.63 0.52	-	-	-	-	364 4.10 0.46	-	-	-	-	-	-	-	-	-	-
South Yuba City (cdp)	12,885	2,922 22.68	-	2,672 91.44 20.74	-	-	-	-	-	-	-	-	-	-	-	-	-	-	-	-	-	-	-	-
Yuba City (city)	36,586	3,087 8.44	-	2,222 71.98 6.07	-	-	-	-	-	-	-	-	-	-	-	-	-	-	-	-	-	-	-	-
Tehama County	56,039	415 0.74	-	-	-	-	-	-	-	-	-	-	-	-	-	-	-	-	-	-	-	-	-	-
Tulare County	368,021	12,336 3.35	-	1,033 8.37 0.28	-	-	722 5.85 0.20	-	4,572 37.06 1.24	-	-	1,087 8.81 0.30	-	593 4.81 0.16	370 3.00 0.10	3,142 25.47 0.85	-	-	-	-	-	-	-	-
Porterville (city)	40,025	2,100 5.25	-	-	-	-	-	-	994 47.33 2.48	-	-	-	-	-	-	-	-	-	-	-	-	-	-	-
Visalia (city)	91,513	5,077 5.55	-	-	-	-	-	-	801 15.78 0.88	-	-	541 10.66 0.59	-	-	-	2,154 42.43 2.35	-	-	-	-	-	-	-	-
Tuolumne County	54,501	451 0.83	-	-	-	-	-	-	-	-	-	-	-	-	-	-	-	-	-	-	-	-	-	-
Ventura County	753,197	39,182 5.20	1,669 0.22	4,246 10.84 0.56	-	-	5,096 13.01 0.68	-	15,255 38.93 2.03	-	575 34.45 0.08	-	-	5,214 13.31 0.69	2,589 6.61 0.34	-	-	-	612 36.67 0.08	-	797 2.03 0.11	-	-	3,233 8.25 0.43

Notes: Please refer to the User's Guide for an explanation of data; data is arranged alphabetically by state, then county, then city within each county; table includes counties with populations greater than 49,999 unless noted and cities with populations greater than 9,999 whose Asian and/or NHPI population rates are greater than the national average; (1) Native Hawaiian and other Pacific Islander; (2) excludes Taiwanese; (3) includes Chamorro; (4) county does not meet population threshold but is shown in order to allow inclusion of city

Place	Total population	Total Asian population	Total NHPI[1] population	Asian Indian	Bangladeshi	Cambodian	Chinese[2]	Fijian	Filipino	Guamanian[3]	Hawaiian, Native	Hmong	Indonesian	Japanese	Korean	Laotian	Malaysian	Pakistani	Samoan	Sri Lankan	Taiwanese	Thai	Tongan	Vietnamese
Camarillo (city)	57,122	4,014 7.03	-	-	-	-	481 11.98 0.84	-	1,366 34.03 2.39	-	-	-	-	703 17.51 1.23	443 11.04 0.78	-	-	-	-	-	-	-	-	434 10.81 0.76
Moorpark (city)	31,274	1,353 4.33	-	-	-	-	-	-	-	-	-	-	-	-	-	-	-	-	-	-	-	-	-	-
Oxnard (city)	170,595	12,641 7.41	869 0.51	468 3.70 0.27	-	-	366 2.90 0.21	-	9,005 71.24 5.28	-	-	-	-	1,196 9.46 0.70	423 3.35 0.25	-	-	-	541 62.26 0.32	-	-	-	-	779 6.16 0.46
Port Hueneme (city)	21,846	1,314 6.01	-	-	-	-	-	-	987 75.11 4.52	-	-	-	-	-	-	-	-	-	-	-	-	-	-	-
Simi Valley (city)	111,547	6,710 6.02	-	1,376 20.51 1.23	-	-	1,033 15.39 0.93	-	1,277 19.03 1.14	-	-	-	-	788 11.74 0.71	587 8.75 0.53	-	-	-	-	-	-	-	-	966 14.40 0.87
Thousand Oaks (city)	116,725	6,378 5.46	-	1,138 17.84 0.97	-	-	1,845 28.93 1.58	-	560 8.78 0.48	-	-	-	-	857 13.44 0.73	482 7.56 0.41	-	-	-	-	-	-	-	-	476 7.46 0.41
Yolo County	168,660	15,792 9.36	715 0.42	1,792 11.35 1.06	-	-	5,630 35.65 3.34	526 73.57 0.31	1,689 10.70 1.00	-	-	665 4.21 0.39	-	1,484 9.40 0.88	1,106 7.00 0.66	524 3.32 0.31	-	-	-	-	-	-	-	1,395 8.83 0.83
Davis (city)	60,341	9,963 16.51	-	778 7.81 1.29	-	-	4,444 44.61 7.36	-	1,106 11.10 1.83	-	-	-	-	860 8.63 1.43	810 8.13 1.34	-	-	-	-	-	-	-	-	1,036 10.40 1.72
West Sacramento (city)	31,604	2,251 7.12	-	467 20.75 1.48	-	-	-	-	-	-	-	579 25.72 1.83	-	-	-	-	-	-	-	-	-	-	-	-
Woodland (city)	49,132	1,781 3.62	-	421 23.64 0.86	-	-	-	-	-	-	-	-	-	-	-	-	-	-	-	-	-	-	-	-
Yuba County	60,219	4,551 7.56	-	-	-	-	-	-	532 11.69 0.88	-	-	2,700 59.33 4.48	-	-	-	-	-	-	-	-	-	-	-	-
Linda (cdp)	13,415	2,539 18.93	-	-	-	-	-	-	-	-	-	2,031 79.99 15.14	-	-	-	-	-	-	-	-	-	-	-	-
Marysville (city)	12,298	767 6.24	-	-	-	-	-	-	-	-	-	-	-	-	-	-	-	-	-	-	-	-	-	-
Olivehurst (cdp)	11,093	547 4.93	-	-	-	-	-	-	-	-	-	-	-	-	-	-	-	-	-	-	-	-	-	-
COLORADO	4,301,261	93,306 2.17	4,298 0.10	11,826 12.67 0.27	-	1,478 1.58 0.03	14,825 15.89 0.34	-	9,320 9.99 0.22	1,012 23.55 0.02	1,454 33.83 0.03	3,014 3.23 0.07	770 0.83 0.02	11,894 12.75 0.28	15,293 16.39 0.36	2,315 2.48 0.05	-	813 0.87 0.02	916 21.31 0.02	-	680 0.73 0.02	1,947 2.09 0.05	-	13,666 14.65 0.32
Adams County	363,857	11,508 3.16	-	644 5.60 0.18	-	-	1,126 9.78 0.31	-	846 7.35 0.23	-	-	2,144 18.63 0.59	-	957 8.32 0.26	921 8.00 0.25	1,067 9.27 0.29	-	-	-	-	-	-	-	2,239 19.46 0.62
Berkley (cdp)	10,600	419 3.95	-	-	-	-	-	-	-	-	-	-	-	-	-	-	-	-	-	-	-	-	-	-

Notes: Please refer to the User's Guide for an explanation of data; data is arranged alphabetically by state, then county, then city within each county; table includes counties with populations greater than 49,999 unless noted and cities with populations greater than 9,999 whose Asian and/or NHPI population rates are greater than the national average; (1) Native Hawaiian and other Pacific Islander; (2) excludes Taiwanese; (3) includes Chamorro; (4) county does not meet population threshold but is shown in order to allow inclusion of city

Place	Total population	Total Asian population	Total NHPI[1] population	Asian Indian	Bangladeshi	Cambodian	Chinese[2]	Fijian	Filipino	Guamanian[3]	Hawaiian, Native	Hmong	Indonesian	Japanese	Korean	Laotian	Malaysian	Pakistani	Samoan	Sri Lankan	Taiwanese	Thai	Tongan	Vietnamese
Federal Heights (city)	12,064	748 6.20	-	-	-	-	-	-	-	-	-	-	-	-	-	-	-	-	-	-	-	-	-	-
Westminster (city)	101,197	5,460 5.40	-	469 8.59 0.46	-	-	641 11.74 0.63	-	-	-	-	1,015 18.59 1.00	-	-	553 10.13 0.55	676 12.38 0.67	-	-	-	-	-	-	-	823 15.07 0.81
Arapahoe County	487,967	18,693 3.83	554 0.11	2,374 12.70 0.49	-	-	3,060 16.37 0.63	-	2,180 11.66 0.45	-	-	-	-	1,729 9.25 0.35	4,486 24.00 0.92	-	-	-	-	-	-	-	-	2,738 14.65 0.56
Aurora (city)	275,936	11,335 4.11	387 0.14	1,041 9.18 0.38	-	441 3.89 0.16	1,622 14.31 0.59	-	1,472 12.99 0.53	-	-	-	-	1,022 9.02 0.37	2,509 22.13 0.91	-	-	-	-	-	-	-	-	1,915 16.89 0.69
Boulder County	291,288	9,175 3.15	-	1,171 12.76 0.40	-	-	2,488 27.12 0.85	-	405 4.41 0.14	-	-	-	-	1,325 14.44 0.45	1,230 13.41 0.42	-	-	-	-	-	-	-	-	729 7.95 0.25
Boulder (city)	94,510	3,604 3.81	-	415 11.51 0.44	-	-	943 26.17 1.00	-	-	-	-	-	-	520 14.43 0.55	772 21.42 0.82	-	-	-	-	-	-	-	-	-
Broomfield (city)	38,297	1,648 4.30	-	-	-	-	337 20.45 0.88	-	-	-	-	-	-	-	-	-	-	-	-	-	-	-	-	-
Lafayette (city)	23,349	892 3.82	-	-	-	-	-	-	-	-	-	-	-	-	-	-	-	-	-	-	-	-	-	-
Denver County	554,636	15,172 2.74	447 0.08	2,043 13.47 0.37	-	398 2.62 0.07	2,141 14.11 0.39	-	963 6.35 0.17	-	-	-	-	1,974 13.01 0.36	1,276 8.41 0.23	-	-	-	-	-	-	406 2.68 0.07	-	4,449 29.32 0.80
Douglas County	175,766	4,303 2.45	-	853 19.82 0.49	-	-	1,285 29.86 0.73	-	-	-	-	-	-	-	608 14.13 0.35	-	-	-	-	-	-	-	-	-
Highlands Ranch (cdp)	70,864	2,913 4.11	-	650 22.31 0.92	-	-	929 31.89 1.31	-	-	-	-	-	-	-	-	-	-	-	-	-	-	-	-	-
El Paso County	516,929	13,154 2.54	1,291 0.25	1,942 14.76 0.38	-	-	1,023 7.78 0.20	-	2,548 19.37 0.49	492 38.11 0.10	-	-	-	1,467 11.15 0.28	3,936 29.92 0.76	-	-	-	-	-	-	-	-	909 6.91 0.18
Colorado Springs (city)	360,798	10,295 2.85	798 0.22	1,882 18.28 0.52	-	-	844 8.20 0.23	-	1,737 16.87 0.48	-	-	-	-	1,029 10.00 0.29	3,005 29.19 0.83	-	-	-	-	-	-	-	-	757 7.35 0.21
Jefferson County	527,056	11,752 2.23	437 0.08	1,446 12.30 0.27	-	-	1,915 16.30 0.36	-	945 8.04 0.18	-	-	412 3.51 0.08	-	1,897 16.14 0.36	1,484 12.63 0.28	920 7.83 0.17	-	-	-	-	-	-	-	1,726 14.69 0.33
Larimer County	251,494	3,616 1.44	-	626 17.31 0.25	-	-	866 23.95 0.34	-	-	-	-	-	-	576 15.93 0.23	598 16.54 0.24	-	-	-	-	-	-	-	-	-
Mesa County	116,255	424 0.36	-	-	-	-	-	-	-	-	-	-	-	-	-	-	-	-	-	-	-	-	-	-
Pueblo County	141,472	761 0.54	-	-	-	-	-	-	-	-	-	-	-	-	-	-	-	-	-	-	-	-	-	-

Notes: Please refer to the User's Guide for an explanation of data; data is arranged alphabetically by state, then county, then city within each county; table includes counties with populations greater than 49,999 unless noted and cities with populations greater than 9,999 whose Asian and/or NHPI population rates are greater than the national average; (1) Native Hawaiian and other Pacific Islander; (2) excludes Taiwanese; (3) includes Chamorro; (4) county does not meet population threshold but is shown in order to allow inclusion of city

Place	Total population	Total Asian population	Total NHPI[1] population	Asian Indian	Bangladeshi	Cambodian	Chinese[2]	Fijian	Filipino	Guamanian[3]	Hawaiian, Native	Hmong	Indonesian	Japanese	Korean	Laotian	Malaysian	Pakistani	Samoan	Sri Lankan	Taiwanese	Thai	Tongan	Vietnamese
Weld County	180,936	1,533 0.85	-	-	-	-	-	-	-	-	-	-	-	495 32.29 0.27	-	-	-	-	-	-	-	-	-	-
CONNECTICUT	3,405,565	82,277 2.42	1,357 0.04	23,905 29.05 0.70	348 0.42 0.01	2,161 2.63 0.06	18,776 22.82 0.55	-	7,511 9.13 0.22	419 30.88 0.01	-	-	-	4,552 5.53 0.13	6,726 8.17 0.20	3,107 3.78 0.09	-	2,112 2.57 0.06	-	-	819 1.00 0.02	784 0.95 0.02	-	7,399 8.99 0.22
Fairfield County	882,567	28,452 3.22	-	8,345 29.33 0.95	-	1,442 5.07 0.16	5,800 20.39 0.66	-	2,435 8.56 0.28	-	-	-	-	2,641 9.28 0.30	1,932 6.79 0.22	1,031 3.62 0.12	-	543 1.91 0.06	-	-	-	-	-	2,396 8.42 0.27
Danbury (city)	74,848	3,671 4.90	-	1,198 32.63 1.60	-	572 15.58 0.76	478 13.02 0.64	-	-	-	-	-	-	-	-	-	-	-	-	-	-	-	-	-
Greenwich (town)	61,101	3,259 5.33	-	398 12.21 0.65	-	-	639 19.61 1.05	-	-	-	-	-	-	1,383 42.44 2.26	-	-	-	-	-	-	-	-	-	-
Stamford (city)	117,083	5,735 4.90	-	2,871 50.06 2.45	-	-	1,150 20.05 0.98	-	805 14.04 0.69	-	-	-	-	-	-	-	-	-	-	-	-	-	-	-
Hartford County	857,183	21,058 2.46	-	6,726 31.94 0.78	-	-	3,856 18.31 0.45	-	1,761 8.36 0.21	-	-	-	-	541 2.57 0.06	1,445 6.86 0.17	1,215 5.77 0.14	-	668 3.17 0.08	-	-	-	-	-	3,201 15.20 0.37
East Hartford (town)	49,575	2,091 4.22	-	622 29.75 1.25	-	-	-	-	-	-	-	-	-	-	-	-	-	-	-	-	-	-	-	553 26.45 1.12
Farmington (town)	23,641	972 4.11	-	-	-	-	-	-	-	-	-	-	-	-	-	-	-	-	-	-	-	-	-	-
Glastonbury (town)	31,876	1,212 3.80	-	501 41.34 1.57	-	-	-	-	-	-	-	-	-	-	-	-	-	-	-	-	-	-	-	-
Rocky Hill (town)	17,942	711 3.96	-	-	-	-	-	-	-	-	-	-	-	-	-	-	-	-	-	-	-	-	-	-
South Windsor (town)	24,471	965 3.94	-	-	-	-	-	-	-	-	-	-	-	-	-	-	-	-	-	-	-	-	-	-
West Hartford (town)	63,589	3,063 4.82	-	772 25.20 1.21	-	-	824 26.90 1.30	-	-	-	-	-	-	-	-	-	-	-	-	-	-	-	-	670 21.87 1.05
Litchfield County	182,193	2,278 1.25	-	460 20.19 0.25	-	-	410 18.00 0.23	-	-	-	-	-	-	-	368 16.15 0.20	-	-	-	-	-	-	-	-	265 11.63 0.15
Middlesex County	155,071	2,272 1.47	-	651 28.65 0.42	-	-	545 23.99 0.35	-	-	-	-	-	-	-	-	-	-	-	-	-	-	-	-	-
New Haven County	824,008	19,615 2.38	-	5,916 30.16 0.72	-	-	5,361 27.33 0.65	-	1,616 8.24 0.20	-	-	-	-	890 4.54 0.11	2,054 10.47 0.25	504 2.57 0.06	-	653 3.33 0.08	-	-	-	-	-	890 4.54 0.11
New Haven (city)	123,626	4,623 3.74	-	807 17.46 0.65	-	-	1,777 38.44 1.44	-	-	-	-	-	-	-	540 11.68 0.44	-	-	-	-	-	-	-	-	-

Notes: Please refer to the User's Guide for an explanation of data; data is arranged alphabetically by state, then county, then city within each county; table includes counties with populations greater than 49,999 unless noted and cities with populations greater than 9,999 whose Asian and/or NHPI population rates are greater than the national average; (1) Native Hawaiian and other Pacific Islander; (2) excludes Taiwanese; (3) includes Chamorro; (4) county does not meet population threshold but is shown in order to allow inclusion of city

Place	Total population	Total Asian population	Total NHPI[1] population	Asian Indian	Bangladeshi	Cambodian	Chinese[2]	Fijian	Filipino	Guamanian[3]	Hawaiian, Native	Hmong	Indonesian	Japanese	Korean	Laotian	Malaysian	Pakistani	Samoan	Sri Lankan	Taiwanese	Thai	Tongan	Vietnamese
New London County	259,088	4,806 1.85	-	919 19.12 0.35	-	-	1,554 32.33 0.60	-	1,032 21.47 0.40	-	-	-	-	-	-	-	-	-	-	-	-	-	-	-
Tolland County	136,364	3,123 2.29	-	855 27.38 0.63	-	-	1,073 34.36 0.79	-	-	-	-	-	-	-	-	-	-	-	-	-	-	-	-	-
Mansfield (town)	20,720	1,487 7.18	-	442 29.72 2.13	-	-	606 40.75 2.92	-	-	-	-	-	-	-	-	-	-	-	-	-	-	-	-	-
Storrs (cdp)	11,175	1,064 9.52	-	-	-	-	545 51.22 4.88	-	-	-	-	-	-	-	-	-	-	-	-	-	-	-	-	-
Windham County	109,091	673 0.62	-	-	-	-	-	-	-	-	-	-	-	-	-	-	-	-	-	-	-	-	-	-
DELAWARE	783,600	16,053 2.05	335 0.04	5,231 32.59 0.67	-	-	4,102 25.55 0.52	-	1,825 11.37 0.23	-	-	-	-	605 3.77 0.08	1,850 11.52 0.24	-	-	379 2.36 0.05	-	-	-	-	-	686 4.27 0.09
Kent County	126,697	2,083 1.64	-	419 20.12 0.33	-	-	-	-	499 23.96 0.39	-	-	-	-	-	-	-	-	-	-	-	-	-	-	-
New Castle County	500,265	13,182 2.64	-	4,648 35.26 0.93	-	-	3,752 28.46 0.75	-	1,113 8.44 0.22	-	-	-	-	386 2.93 0.08	1,405 10.66 0.28	-	-	-	-	-	-	-	-	536 4.07 0.11
Hockessin (cdp)	12,896	837 6.49	-	-	-	-	-	-	-	-	-	-	-	-	-	-	-	-	-	-	-	-	-	-
Newark (city)	28,570	1,219 4.27	-	-	-	-	541 44.38 1.89	-	-	-	-	-	-	-	-	-	-	-	-	-	-	-	-	-
Pike Creek (cdp)	19,748	1,085 5.49	-	-	-	-	-	-	-	-	-	-	-	-	-	-	-	-	-	-	-	-	-	-
Sussex County	156,638	788 0.50	-	-	-	-	-	-	-	-	-	-	-	-	-	-	-	-	-	-	-	-	-	-
DISTRICT OF COLUMBIA	572,059	14,762 2.58	-	2,415 16.36 0.42	-	-	3,843 26.03 0.67	-	2,119 14.35 0.37	-	-	-	-	1,037 7.02 0.18	1,168 7.91 0.20	-	-	-	-	-	-	-	-	1,789 12.12 0.31
FLORIDA	15,982,378	264,377 1.65	6,812 0.04	67,790 25.64 0.42	1,260 0.48 0.01	2,762 1.04 0.02	44,867 16.97 0.28	-	54,332 20.55 0.34	2,020 29.65 0.01	1,971 28.93 0.01	-	894 0.34 0.01	11,346 4.29 0.07	19,077 7.22 0.12	4,031 1.52 0.03	-	5,446 2.06 0.03	849 12.46 0.01	402 0.15 <0.01	2,027 0.77 0.01	6,572 2.49 0.04	-	33,391 12.63 0.21
Alachua County	217,955	7,858 3.61	-	1,949 24.80 0.89	-	-	2,135 27.17 0.98	-	1,046 13.31 0.48	-	-	-	-	433 5.51 0.20	1,005 12.79 0.46	-	-	-	-	-	-	-	-	617 7.85 0.28
Gainesville (city)	95,605	4,399 4.60	-	1,056 24.01 1.10	-	-	1,456 33.10 1.52	-	-	-	-	-	-	-	501 11.39 0.52	-	-	-	-	-	-	-	-	-
Bay County	148,217	2,369 1.60	-	-	-	-	-	-	484 20.43 0.33	-	-	-	-	-	-	-	-	-	-	-	-	-	-	666 28.11 0.45

Notes: Please refer to the User's Guide for an explanation of data; data is arranged alphabetically by state, then county, then city within each county; table includes counties with populations greater than 49,999 unless noted and cities with populations greater than 9,999 whose Asian and/or NHPI population rates are greater than the national average; (1) Native Hawaiian and other Pacific Islander; (2) excludes Taiwanese; (3) includes Chamorro; (4) county does not meet population threshold but is shown in order to allow inclusion of city

Place	Total population	Total Asian population	Total NHPI[1] population	Asian Indian	Bangladeshi	Cambodian	Chinese[2]	Fijian	Filipino	Guamanian[3]	Hawaiian, Native	Hmong	Indonesian	Japanese	Korean	Laotian	Malaysian	Pakistani	Samoan	Sri Lankan	Taiwanese	Thai	Tongan	Vietnamese
Callaway (city)	14,253	530 3.72	-	-	-	-	-	-	-	-	-	-	-	-	-	-	-	-	-	-	-	-	-	-
Brevard County	476,230	7,122 1.50	-	1,971 27.67 0.41	-	-	892 12.52 0.19	-	1,537 21.58 0.32	-	-	-	-	525 7.37 0.11	621 8.72 0.13	-	-	-	-	-	-	-	-	763 10.71 0.16
Broward County	1,623,018	36,505 2.25	645 0.04	13,009 35.64 0.80	-	-	8,556 23.44 0.53	-	4,870 13.34 0.30	-	-	-	-	1,045 2.86 0.06	2,260 6.19 0.14	-	-	1,097 3.01 0.07	-	-	-	599 1.64 0.04	-	2,867 7.85 0.18
Cooper City (city)	27,685	1,241 4.48	-	593 47.78 2.14	-	-	-	-	-	-	-	-	-	-	-	-	-	-	-	-	-	-	-	-
Pembroke Pines (city)	137,112	5,004 3.65	-	1,752 35.01 1.28	-	-	1,153 23.04 0.84	-	927 18.53 0.68	-	-	-	-	-	-	-	-	-	-	-	-	-	-	-
Charlotte County	141,627	872 0.62	-	-	-	-	-	-	-	-	-	-	-	-	-	-	-	-	-	-	-	-	-	-
Citrus County	118,085	1,145 0.97	-	-	-	-	-	-	-	-	-	-	-	-	-	-	-	-	-	-	-	-	-	-
Clay County	140,814	2,901 2.06	-	-	-	-	-	-	1,724 59.43 1.22	-	-	-	-	-	-	-	-	-	-	-	-	-	-	-
Bellair-Meadowbrook Ter. (cdp)	16,565	635 3.83	-	-	-	-	-	-	-	-	-	-	-	-	-	-	-	-	-	-	-	-	-	-
Collier County	251,377	1,200 0.48	-	-	-	-	-	-	-	-	-	-	-	-	-	-	-	-	-	-	-	-	-	-
Columbia County	56,513	386 0.68	-	-	-	-	-	-	-	-	-	-	-	-	-	-	-	-	-	-	-	-	-	-
Duval County	778,879	20,554 2.64	507 0.07	2,767 13.46 0.36	-	1,001 4.87 0.13	1,642 7.99 0.21	-	10,206 49.65 1.31	-	-	-	-	550 2.68 0.07	967 4.70 0.12	-	-	-	-	-	-	-	-	2,112 10.28 0.27
Escambia County	294,410	6,565 2.23	-	516 7.86 0.18	-	-	587 8.94 0.20	-	2,717 41.39 0.92	-	-	-	-	-	-	-	-	-	-	-	-	-	-	1,597 24.33 0.54
Bellview (cdp)	21,067	787 3.74	-	-	-	-	-	-	412 52.35 1.96	-	-	-	-	-	-	-	-	-	-	-	-	-	-	-
Myrtle Grove (cdp)	17,307	812 4.69	-	-	-	-	-	-	471 58.00 2.72	-	-	-	-	-	-	-	-	-	-	-	-	-	-	-
Hernando County	130,802	773 0.59	-	-	-	-	-	-	-	-	-	-	-	-	-	-	-	-	-	-	-	-	-	-
Highlands County	87,366	964 1.10	-	-	-	-	-	-	447 46.37 0.51	-	-	-	-	-	-	-	-	-	-	-	-	-	-	-

Notes: Please refer to the User's Guide for an explanation of data; data is arranged alphabetically by state, then county, then city within each county; table includes counties with populations greater than 49,999 unless noted and cities with populations greater than 9,999 whose Asian and/or NHPI population rates are greater than the national average; (1) Native Hawaiian and other Pacific Islander; (2) excludes Taiwanese; (3) includes Chamorro; (4) county does not meet population threshold but is shown in order to allow inclusion of city

Place	Total population	Total Asian population	Total NHPI[1] population	Asian Indian	Bangladeshi	Cambodian	Chinese[2]	Fijian	Filipino	Guamanian[3]	Hawaiian, Native	Hmong	Indonesian	Japanese	Korean	Laotian	Malaysian	Pakistani	Samoan	Sri Lankan	Taiwanese	Thai	Tongan	Vietnamese
Hillsborough County	998,948	21,571 2.16	540 0.05	5,901 27.36 0.59	-	-	2,679 12.42 0.27	-	3,203 14.85 0.32	-	-	-	-	863 4.00 0.09	2,718 12.60 0.27	-	-	-	-	-	-	676 3.13 0.07	-	3,993 18.51 0.40
Westchase (cdp)	11,116	508 4.57	-	-	-	-	-	-	-	-	-	-	-	-	-	-	-	-	-	-	-	-	-	-
Indian River County	112,947	864 0.76	-	-	-	-	-	-	-	-	-	-	-	-	-	-	-	-	-	-	-	-	-	-
Lake County	210,528	1,422 0.68	-	-	-	-	-	-	-	-	-	-	-	-	-	-	-	-	-	-	-	-	-	-
Lee County	440,888	3,159 0.72	-	669 21.18 0.15	-	-	596 18.87 0.14	-	1,104 34.95 0.25	-	-	-	-	-	-	-	-	-	-	-	-	-	-	-
Leon County	239,452	4,858 2.03	-	1,508 31.04 0.63	-	-	1,085 22.33 0.45	-	526 10.83 0.22	-	-	-	-	-	446 9.18 0.19	-	-	-	-	-	-	-	-	-
Manatee County	264,002	2,237 0.85	-	-	-	-	-	-	538 24.05 0.20	-	-	-	-	-	-	-	-	-	-	-	-	-	-	-
Marion County	258,916	2,221 0.86	-	949 42.73 0.37	-	-	-	-	-	-	-	-	-	-	-	-	-	-	-	-	-	-	-	-
Martin County	126,731	701 0.55	-	-	-	-	-	-	-	-	-	-	-	-	-	-	-	-	-	-	-	-	-	-
Miami-Dade County	2,253,362	30,692 1.36	605 0.03	8,938 29.12 0.40	-	-	8,889 28.96 0.39	-	4,521 14.73 0.20	-	-	-	-	1,404 4.57 0.06	1,336 4.35 0.06	-	-	794 2.59 0.04	-	-	-	882 2.87 0.04	-	1,595 5.20 0.07
Doral (cdp)	20,513	1,186 5.78	-	-	-	-	-	-	-	-	-	-	-	-	-	-	-	-	-	-	-	-	-	-
Ives Estates (cdp)	17,417	831 4.77	-	-	-	-	-	-	-	-	-	-	-	-	-	-	-	-	-	-	-	-	-	-
North Miami Beach (city)	40,673	1,706 4.19	-	396 23.21 0.97	-	-	741 43.43 1.82	-	-	-	-	-	-	-	-	-	-	-	-	-	-	-	-	-
Pinecrest (village)	19,181	884 4.61	-	-	-	-	-	-	-	-	-	-	-	-	-	-	-	-	-	-	-	-	-	-
Monroe County	79,589	566 0.71	-	-	-	-	-	-	-	-	-	-	-	-	-	-	-	-	-	-	-	-	-	-
Nassau County	57,663	422 0.73	-	-	-	-	-	-	-	-	-	-	-	-	-	-	-	-	-	-	-	-	-	-
Okaloosa County	170,498	4,432 2.60	-	-	-	-	-	-	1,742 39.31 1.02	-	-	-	-	-	720 16.25 0.42	-	-	-	-	-	-	624 14.08 0.37	-	400 9.03 0.23

Notes: Please refer to the User's Guide for an explanation of data; data is arranged alphabetically by state, then county, then city within each county; table includes counties with populations greater than 49,999 unless noted and cities with populations greater than 9,999 whose Asian and/or NHPI population rates are greater than the national average; (1) Native Hawaiian and other Pacific Islander; (2) excludes Taiwanese; (3) includes Chamorro; (4) county does not meet population threshold but is shown in order to allow inclusion of city

Place	Total population	Total Asian population	Total NHPI[1] population	Asian Indian	Bangladeshi	Cambodian	Chinese[2]	Fijian	Filipino	Guamanian[3]	Hawaiian, Native	Hmong	Indonesian	Japanese	Korean	Laotian	Malaysian	Pakistani	Samoan	Sri Lankan	Taiwanese	Thai	Tongan	Vietnamese
Wright (cdp)	21,553	825 3.83	-	-	-	-	-	-	-	-	-	-	-	-	-	-	-	-	-	-	-	-	-	-
Orange County	896,344	28,748 3.21	853 0.10	7,651 26.61 0.85	-	-	3,992 13.89 0.45	-	4,524 15.74 0.50	-	-	-	-	1,200 4.17 0.13	2,145 7.46 0.24	-	-	901 3.13 0.10	-	-	-	-	-	6,357 22.11 0.71
Oak Ridge (cdp)	22,407	1,306 5.83	-	-	-	-	-	-	-	-	-	-	-	-	-	-	-	-	-	-	-	-	-	527 40.35 2.35
Osceola County	172,493	3,642 2.11	-	966 26.52 0.56	-	-	584 16.04 0.34	-	883 24.24 0.51	-	-	-	-	-	-	-	-	-	-	-	-	-	-	-
Palm Beach County	1,131,184	16,895 1.49	423 0.04	5,098 30.17 0.45	-	-	3,641 21.55 0.32	-	2,238 13.25 0.20	-	-	-	-	574 3.40 0.05	932 5.52 0.08	-	-	-	-	-	-	760 4.50 0.07	-	1,994 11.80 0.18
Pasco County	344,765	3,489 1.01	-	993 28.46 0.29	-	-	504 14.45 0.15	-	994 28.49 0.29	-	-	-	-	-	-	-	-	-	-	-	-	-	-	-
Pinellas County	921,482	18,783 2.04	-	3,648 19.42 0.40	-	718 3.82 0.08	2,085 11.10 0.23	-	3,034 16.15 0.33	-	-	-	-	568 3.02 0.06	854 4.55 0.09	1,855 9.88 0.20	-	-	-	-	-	488 2.60 0.05	-	4,234 22.54 0.46
Pinellas Park (city)	45,414	1,811 3.99	-	-	-	-	-	-	-	-	-	-	-	-	-	-	-	-	-	-	-	-	-	526 29.04 1.16
Polk County	483,924	5,805 1.20	-	1,717 29.58 0.35	-	-	595 10.25 0.12	-	902 15.54 0.19	-	-	-	-	-	-	401 6.91 0.08	-	-	-	-	-	-	-	872 15.02 0.18
Putnam County	70,423	291 0.41	-	-	-	-	-	-	-	-	-	-	-	-	-	-	-	-	-	-	-	-	-	-
St. Johns County	123,135	1,244 1.01	-	-	-	-	-	-	-	-	-	-	-	-	-	-	-	-	-	-	-	-	-	-
St. Lucie County	192,695	1,885 0.98	-	-	-	-	-	-	-	-	-	-	-	-	-	-	-	-	-	-	-	-	-	-
Santa Rosa County	117,743	1,608 1.37	-	-	-	-	-	-	707 43.97 0.60	-	-	-	-	-	-	-	-	-	-	-	-	-	-	-
Sarasota County	325,957	2,624 0.81	-	-	-	-	426 16.23 0.13	-	540 20.58 0.17	-	-	-	-	-	-	-	-	-	-	-	-	-	-	683 26.03 0.21
Seminole County	365,196	8,682 2.38	-	2,781 32.03 0.76	-	-	1,385 15.95 0.38	-	1,313 15.12 0.36	-	-	-	-	-	976 11.24 0.27	-	-	-	-	-	-	-	-	1,064 12.26 0.29
Volusia County	443,343	4,812 1.09	-	1,590 33.04 0.36	-	-	658 13.67 0.15	-	881 18.31 0.20	-	-	-	-	-	462 9.60 0.10	-	-	-	-	-	-	-	-	-
GEORGIA	8,186,453	171,463 2.09	3,866 0.05	44,732 26.09 0.55	1,257 0.73 0.02	3,479 2.03 0.04	25,436 14.83 0.31	-	10,436 6.09 0.13	1,443 37.33 0.02	814 21.06 0.01	1,200 0.70 0.01	550 0.32 0.01	7,511 4.38 0.09	27,708 16.16 0.34	4,730 2.76 0.06	-	3,906 2.28 0.05	762 19.71 0.01	-	1,844 1.08 0.02	2,250 1.31 0.03	-	29,494 17.20 0.36

Notes: Please refer to the User's Guide for an explanation of data; data is arranged alphabetically by state, then county, then city within each county; table includes counties with populations greater than 49,999 unless noted and cities with populations greater than 9,999 whose Asian and/or NHPI population rates are greater than the national average; (1) Native Hawaiian and other Pacific Islander; (2) excludes Taiwanese; (3) includes Chamorro; (4) county does not meet population threshold but is shown in order to allow inclusion of city

Place	Total population	Total Asian population	Total NHPI[1] population	Asian Indian	Bangladeshi	Cambodian	Chinese[2]	Fijian	Filipino	Guamanian[3]	Hawaiian, Native	Hmong	Indonesian	Japanese	Korean	Laotian	Malaysian	Pakistani	Samoan	Sri Lankan	Taiwanese	Thai	Tongan	Vietnamese
Bartow County	76,019	616 0.81	-	-	-	-	-	-	-	-	-	-	-	-	-	-	-	-	-	-	-	-	-	-
Bibb County	153,887	1,593 1.04	-	-	-	-	-	-	-	-	-	-	-	-	-	-	-	-	-	-	-	-	-	-
Bulloch County	55,983	591 1.06	-	-	-	-	-	-	-	-	-	-	-	-	-	-	-	-	-	-	-	-	-	-
Carroll County	87,268	471 0.54	-	-	-	-	-	-	-	-	-	-	-	-	-	-	-	-	-	-	-	-	-	-
Catoosa County	53,282	419 0.79	-	-	-	-	-	-	-	-	-	-	-	-	-	-	-	-	-	-	-	-	-	-
Chatham County	232,048	4,048 1.74	-	758 18.73 0.33	-	-	767 18.95 0.33	-	-	-	-	-	-	-	459 11.34 0.20	-	-	-	-	-	-	-	-	1,014 25.05 0.44
Cherokee County	141,903	1,428 1.01	-	339 23.74 0.24	-	-	-	-	-	-	-	-	-	-	-	-	-	-	-	-	-	-	-	-
Clarke County	101,489	3,250 3.20	-	738 22.71 0.73	-	-	957 29.45 0.94	-	-	-	-	-	-	-	548 16.86 0.54	-	-	-	-	-	-	-	-	-
Clayton County	236,517	10,344 4.37	-	1,301 12.58 0.55	-	1,048 10.13 0.44	549 5.31 0.23	-	-	-	-	-	-	-	-	1,258 12.16 0.53	-	419 4.05 0.18	-	-	-	-	-	4,391 42.45 1.86
Forest Park (city)	21,293	1,297 6.09	-	-	-	-	-	-	-	-	-	-	-	-	-	-	-	-	-	-	-	-	-	958 73.86 4.50
Riverdale (city)	12,453	1,030 8.27	-	-	-	-	-	-	-	-	-	-	-	-	-	-	-	-	-	-	-	-	-	470 45.63 3.77
Cobb County	607,751	18,486 3.04	-	5,389 29.15 0.89	-	-	3,444 18.63 0.57	-	1,186 6.42 0.20	-	-	-	-	994 5.38 0.16	2,997 16.21 0.49	-	-	647 3.50 0.11	-	-	-	-	-	1,671 9.04 0.27
Smyrna (city)	40,780	1,619 3.97	-	570 35.21 1.40	-	-	-	-	-	-	-	-	-	-	-	-	-	-	-	-	-	-	-	-
Columbia County	89,288	2,878 3.22	-	913 31.72 1.02	-	-	548 19.04 0.61	-	-	-	-	-	-	-	436 15.15 0.49	-	-	-	-	-	-	-	-	-
Martinez (cdp)	27,553	1,409 5.11	-	484 34.35 1.76	-	-	-	-	-	-	-	-	-	-	-	-	-	-	-	-	-	-	-	-
Coweta County	89,215	584 0.65	-	-	-	-	-	-	-	-	-	-	-	-	-	-	-	-	-	-	-	-	-	-
DeKalb County	665,865	26,537 3.99	-	7,341 27.66 1.10	550 2.07 0.08	610 2.30 0.09	3,907 14.72 0.59	-	655 2.47 0.10	-	-	-	-	892 3.36 0.13	3,300 12.44 0.50	-	-	-	-	-	-	-	-	6,516 24.55 0.98

Notes: Please refer to the User's Guide for an explanation of data; data is arranged alphabetically by state, then county, then city within each county; table includes counties with populations greater than 49,999 unless noted and cities with populations greater than 9,999 whose Asian and/or NHPI population rates are greater than the national average; (1) Native Hawaiian and other Pacific Islander; (2) excludes Taiwanese; (3) includes Chamorro; (4) county does not meet population threshold but is shown in order to allow inclusion of city

Place	Total population	Total Asian population	Total NHPI[1] population	Asian Indian	Bangladeshi	Cambodian	Chinese[2]	Fijian	Filipino	Guamanian[3]	Hawaiian, Native	Hmong	Indonesian	Japanese	Korean	Laotian	Malaysian	Pakistani	Samoan	Sri Lankan	Taiwanese	Thai	Tongan	Vietnamese
Druid Hills (cdp)	12,686	867 6.83	-	-	-	-	-	-	-	-	-	-	-	-	-	-	-	-	-	-	-	-	-	-
Dunwoody (cdp)	32,808	2,480 7.56	-	1,081 43.59 3.29	-	-	-	-	-	-	-	-	-	-	447 18.02 1.36	-	-	-	-	-	-	-	-	-
North Atlanta (cdp)	38,403	1,710 4.45	-	-	-	-	-	-	-	-	-	-	-	-	-	-	-	-	-	-	-	-	-	-
North Decatur (cdp)	15,156	847 5.59	-	-	-	-	-	-	-	-	-	-	-	-	-	-	-	-	-	-	-	-	-	-
North Druid Hills (cdp)	18,852	1,268 6.73	-	575 45.35 3.05	-	-	-	-	-	-	-	-	-	-	-	-	-	-	-	-	-	-	-	-
Tucker (cdp)	26,616	1,987 7.47	-	-	-	-	-	-	-	-	-	-	-	-	-	-	-	-	-	-	-	-	-	326 16.41 1.22
Dougherty County	96,065	696 0.72	-	-	-	-	-	-	-	-	-	-	-	-	-	-	-	-	-	-	-	-	-	-
Douglas County	92,174	897 0.97	-	-	-	-	-	-	-	-	-	-	-	-	-	-	-	-	-	-	-	-	-	-
Fayette County	91,263	2,071 2.27	-	-	-	-	-	-	-	-	-	-	-	631 30.47 0.69	-	-	-	-	-	-	-	-	-	-
Peachtree City (city)	31,896	1,263 3.96	-	-	-	-	-	-	-	-	-	-	-	604 47.82 1.89	-	-	-	-	-	-	-	-	-	-
Floyd County	90,565	1,212 1.34	-	472 38.94 0.52	-	-	-	-	-	-	-	-	-	-	-	-	-	-	-	-	-	-	-	-
Forsyth County	98,407	756 0.77	-	-	-	-	-	-	-	-	-	-	-	-	-	-	-	-	-	-	-	-	-	-
Fulton County	816,006	23,763 2.91	-	7,223 30.40 0.89	-	-	5,398 22.72 0.66	-	866 3.64 0.11	-	-	-	-	936 3.94 0.11	4,076 17.15 0.50	-	-	-	-	-	-	-	-	2,983 12.55 0.37
Alpharetta (city)	34,611	1,709 4.94	-	631 36.92 1.82	-	-	468 27.38 1.35	-	-	-	-	-	-	-	-	-	-	-	-	-	-	-	-	-
Roswell (city)	79,844	2,963 3.71	-	829 27.98 1.04	-	-	586 19.78 0.73	-	-	-	-	-	-	-	857 28.92 1.07	-	-	-	-	-	-	-	-	-
Glynn County	67,568	553 0.82	-	-	-	-	-	-	-	-	-	-	-	-	-	-	-	-	-	-	-	-	-	-
Gwinnett County	588,448	41,021 6.97	506 0.09	11,002 26.82 1.87	-	902 2.20 0.15	5,075 12.37 0.86	-	1,224 2.98 0.21	-	-	-	-	866 2.11 0.15	9,260 22.57 1.57	1,093 2.66 0.19	-	1,142 2.78 0.19	-	-	474 1.16 0.08	-	-	7,468 18.21 1.27

Notes: Please refer to the User's Guide for an explanation of data; data is arranged alphabetically by state, then county, then city within each county; table includes counties with populations greater than 49,999 unless noted and cities with populations greater than 9,999 whose Asian and/or NHPI population rates are greater than the national average; (1) Native Hawaiian and other Pacific Islander; (2) excludes Taiwanese; (3) includes Chamorro; (4) county does not meet population threshold but is shown in order to allow inclusion of city

Place	Total population	Total Asian population	Total NHPI[1] population	Asian Indian	Bangladeshi	Cambodian	Chinese[2]	Fijian	Filipino	Guamanian[3]	Hawaiian, Native	Hmong	Indonesian	Japanese	Korean	Laotian	Malaysian	Pakistani	Samoan	Sri Lankan	Taiwanese	Thai	Tongan	Vietnamese
Duluth (city)	22,388	2,725 12.17	-	912 33.47 4.07	-	-	525 19.27 2.35	-	-	-	-	-	-	-	688 25.25 3.07	-	-	-	-	-	-	-	-	-
Lilburn (city)	11,350	1,466 12.92	-	388 26.47 3.42	-	-	-	-	-	-	-	-	-	-	-	-	-	-	-	-	-	-	-	462 31.51 4.07
Mountain Park (cdp)	11,485	1,055 9.19	-	690 65.40 6.01	-	-	-	-	-	-	-	-	-	-	-	-	-	-	-	-	-	-	-	-
Hall County	139,277	1,817 1.30	-	-	-	-	-	-	-	-	-	-	-	-	-	-	-	-	-	-	-	-	-	1,204 66.26 0.86
Henry County	119,341	2,134 1.79	-	820 38.43 0.69	-	-	-	-	-	-	-	-	-	-	-	-	-	-	-	-	-	-	-	-
Houston County	110,765	1,777 1.60	-	-	-	-	-	-	550 30.95 0.50	-	-	-	-	-	-	-	-	-	-	-	-	-	-	-
Liberty County	61,610	957 1.55	-	-	-	-	-	-	-	-	-	-	-	-	377 39.39 0.61	-	-	-	-	-	-	-	-	-
Lowndes County	92,115	852 0.92	-	-	-	-	-	-	-	-	-	-	-	-	-	-	-	-	-	-	-	-	-	-
Muscogee County	186,291	2,983 1.60	385 0.21	556 18.64 0.30	-	-	366 12.27 0.20	-	451 15.12 0.24	-	-	-	-	-	780 26.15 0.42	-	-	-	-	-	-	-	-	-
Columbus (sp. city)	185,797	2,983 1.61	385 0.21	556 18.64 0.30	-	-	366 12.27 0.20	-	451 15.12 0.24	-	-	-	-	-	780 26.15 0.42	-	-	-	-	-	-	-	-	-
Newton County	62,001	442 0.71	-	-	-	-	-	-	-	-	-	-	-	-	-	-	-	-	-	-	-	-	-	-
Richmond County	199,775	3,023 1.51	-	677 22.39 0.34	-	-	529 17.50 0.26	-	-	-	-	-	-	-	870 28.78 0.44	-	-	-	-	-	-	-	-	-
Rockdale County	70,111	1,140 1.63	-	-	-	-	-	-	-	-	-	-	-	-	-	-	-	-	-	-	-	-	-	-
Spalding County	58,417	418 0.72	-	-	-	-	-	-	-	-	-	-	-	-	-	-	-	-	-	-	-	-	-	-
Troup County	58,779	415 0.71	-	-	-	-	-	-	-	-	-	-	-	-	-	-	-	-	-	-	-	-	-	-
Walton County	60,687	478 0.79	-	-	-	-	-	-	-	-	-	-	-	-	-	-	-	-	-	-	-	-	-	-
Whitfield County	83,525	864 1.03	-	-	-	-	-	-	-	-	-	-	-	-	-	-	-	-	-	-	-	-	-	-

Notes: Please refer to the User's Guide for an explanation of data; data is arranged alphabetically by state, then county, then city within each county; table includes counties with populations greater than 49,999 unless noted and cities with populations greater than 9,999 whose Asian and/or NHPI population rates are greater than the national average; (1) Native Hawaiian and other Pacific Islander; (2) excludes Taiwanese; (3) includes Chamorro; (4) county does not meet population threshold but is shown in order to allow inclusion of city

Place	Total population	Total Asian population	Total NHPI[1] population	Asian Indian	Bangladeshi	Cambodian	Chinese[2]	Fijian	Filipino	Guamanian[3]	Hawaiian, Native	Hmong	Indonesian	Japanese	Korean	Laotian	Malaysian	Pakistani	Samoan	Sri Lankan	Taiwanese	Thai	Tongan	Vietnamese
HAWAII	1,211,537	503,950 41.60	112,561 9.29	1,244 0.25 0.10	-	211 0.04 0.02	55,726 11.06 4.60	-	171,678 34.07 14.17	1,491 1.32 0.12	80,965 71.93 6.68	-	-	200,364 39.76 16.54	23,708 4.70 1.96	1,686 0.33 0.14	-	-	14,359 12.76 1.19	-	821 0.16 0.07	1,398 0.28 0.12	4,181 3.71 0.35	8,345 1.66 0.69
Hawaii County	148,677	39,708 26.71	16,227 10.91	-	-	-	1,344 3.38 0.90	-	13,101 32.99 8.81	-	13,947 85.95 9.38	-	-	20,628 51.95 13.87	874 2.20 0.59	-	-	-	296 1.82 0.20	-	-	-	-	-
Hilo (cdp)	40,798	15,349 37.62	4,969 12.18	-	-	-	497 3.24 1.22	-	2,053 13.38 5.03	-	4,177 84.06 10.24	-	-	11,092 72.27 27.19	396 2.58 0.97	-	-	-	-	-	-	-	-	-
Honolulu County	876,156	404,493 46.17	77,175 8.81	1,004 0.25 0.11	-	-	52,871 13.07 6.03	-	125,893 31.12 14.37	1,328 1.72 0.15	50,284 65.16 5.74	-	-	159,611 39.46 18.22	21,709 5.37 2.48	1,645 0.41 0.19	-	-	13,847 17.94 1.58	-	791 0.20 0.09	1,149 0.28 0.13	3,082 3.99 0.35	7,775 1.92 0.89
Ewa Beach (cdp)	14,650	7,204 49.17	1,456 9.94	-	-	-	-	-	5,618 77.98 38.35	-	948 65.11 6.47	-	-	820 11.38 5.60	-	-	-	-	421 28.91 2.87	-	-	-	-	-
Halawa (cdp)	13,955	7,231 51.82	1,512 10.83	-	-	-	732 10.12 5.25	-	2,856 39.50 20.47	-	708 46.83 5.07	-	-	2,498 34.55 17.90	-	-	-	-	661 43.72 4.74	-	-	-	-	-
Honolulu (cdp)	371,619	208,028 55.98	25,856 6.96	614 0.30 0.17	-	-	38,918 18.71 10.47	-	43,653 20.98 11.75	677 2.62 0.18	14,400 55.69 3.87	-	-	85,585 41.14 23.03	15,451 7.43 4.16	984 0.47 0.26	-	-	4,452 17.22 1.20	-	702 0.34 0.19	535 0.26 0.14	1,558 6.03 0.42	6,565 3.16 1.77
Kailua (cdp)	36,585	7,872 21.52	2,743 7.50	-	-	-	1,204 15.29 3.29	-	978 12.42 2.67	-	2,525 92.05 6.90	-	-	4,324 54.93 11.82	376 4.78 1.03	-	-	-	-	-	-	-	-	-
Kaneohe (cdp)	34,976	13,801 39.46	4,046 11.57	-	-	-	1,434 10.39 4.10	-	1,675 12.14 4.79	-	3,388 83.74 9.69	-	-	8,412 60.95 24.05	449 3.25 1.28	-	-	-	-	-	-	-	-	-
Kaneohe Station (cdp)	11,827	629 5.32	-	-	-	-	-	-	-	-	-	-	-	-	-	-	-	-	-	-	-	-	-	-
Makakilo City (cdp)	13,158	4,415 33.55	1,355 10.30	-	-	-	-	-	2,364 53.54 17.97	-	991 73.14 7.53	-	-	971 21.99 7.38	-	-	-	-	-	-	-	-	-	-
Mililani Town (cdp)	28,565	13,195 46.19	1,173 4.11	-	-	-	973 7.37 3.41	-	3,146 23.84 11.01	-	874 74.51 3.06	-	-	7,043 53.38 24.66	497 3.77 1.74	-	-	-	-	-	-	-	-	-
Nanakuli (cdp)	10,698	1,059 9.90	4,104 38.36	-	-	-	-	-	646 61.00 6.04	-	3,086 75.19 28.85	-	-	-	-	-	-	-	753 18.35 7.04	-	-	-	-	-
Pearl City (cdp)	30,818	16,882 54.78	1,791 5.81	-	-	-	1,264 7.49 4.10	-	4,268 25.28 13.85	-	1,358 75.82 4.41	-	-	9,453 55.99 30.67	378 2.24 1.23	-	-	-	-	-	-	-	-	-
Schofield Barracks (cdp)	14,434	525 3.64	-	-	-	-	-	-	-	-	-	-	-	-	-	-	-	-	-	-	-	-	-	-
Wahiawa (cdp)	16,151	7,193 44.54	1,734 10.74	-	-	-	-	-	2,921 40.61 18.09	-	937 54.04 5.80	-	-	3,240 45.04 20.06	-	-	-	-	-	-	-	-	-	-
Waianae (cdp)	10,649	1,928 18.10	2,793 26.23	-	-	-	-	-	1,016 52.70 9.54	-	2,388 85.50 22.42	-	-	552 28.63 5.18	-	-	-	-	-	-	-	-	-	-

Notes: Please refer to the User's Guide for an explanation of data; data is arranged alphabetically by state, then county, then city within each county; table includes counties with populations greater than 49,999 unless noted and cities with populations greater than 9,999 whose Asian and/or NHPI population rates are greater than the national average; (1) Native Hawaiian and other Pacific Islander; (2) excludes Taiwanese; (3) includes Chamorro; (4) county does not meet population threshold but is shown in order to allow inclusion of city

Place	Total population	Total Asian population	Total NHPI[1] population	Asian Indian	Bangladeshi	Cambodian	Chinese[2]	Fijian	Filipino	Guamanian[3]	Hawaiian, Native	Hmong	Indonesian	Japanese	Korean	Laotian	Malaysian	Pakistani	Samoan	Sri Lankan	Taiwanese	Thai	Tongan	Vietnamese
Waimalu (cdp)	29,504	15,849 53.72	1,564 5.30	-	-	-	1,276 8.05 4.32	-	3,335 21.04 11.30	-	1,003 64.13 3.40	-	-	7,933 50.05 26.89	1,251 7.89 4.24	-	-	-	-	-	-	-	-	-
Waipahu (cdp)	33,109	21,657 65.41	4,026 12.16	-	-	-	582 2.69 1.76	-	16,540 76.37 49.96	-	973 24.17 2.94	-	-	3,342 15.43 10.09	-	-	-	-	2,120 52.66 6.40	-	-	-	-	-
Waipio (cdp)	11,641	6,544 56.22	627 5.39	-	-	-	-	-	2,432 37.16 20.89	-	436 69.54 3.75	-	-	2,873 43.90 24.68	-	-	-	-	-	-	-	-	-	-
Kauai County	58,463	20,929 35.80	5,314 9.09	-	-	-	421 2.01 0.72	-	11,117 53.12 19.02	-	4,927 92.72 8.43	-	-	7,591 36.27 12.98	-	-	-	-	-	-	-	-	-	-
Maui County	128,094	38,790 30.28	13,757 10.74	-	-	-	1,090 2.81 0.85	-	21,552 55.56 16.83	-	11,719 85.19 9.15	-	-	12,519 32.27 9.77	943 2.43 0.74	-	-	-	-	-	-	-	794 5.77 0.62	-
Kahului (cdp)	20,020	10,796 53.93	1,834 9.16	-	-	-	-	-	6,417 59.44 32.05	-	1,454 79.28 7.26	-	-	3,441 31.87 17.19	-	-	-	-	-	-	-	-	-	-
Kihei (cdp)	16,832	4,134 24.56	1,137 6.75	-	-	-	-	-	3,174 76.78 18.86	-	798 70.18 4.74	-	-	465 11.25 2.76	-	-	-	-	-	-	-	-	-	-
Wailuku (cdp)	12,419	5,045 40.62	1,378 11.10	-	-	-	-	-	1,584 31.40 12.75	-	1,287 93.40 10.36	-	-	2,657 52.67 21.39	-	-	-	-	-	-	-	-	-	-
IDAHO	1,293,953	11,321 0.87	1,232 0.10	1,142 10.09 0.09	-	-	1,804 15.93 0.14	-	1,640 14.49 0.13	-	362 29.38 0.03	-	-	2,651 23.42 0.20	1,273 11.24 0.10	508 4.49 0.04	-	-	-	-	-	-	-	1,360 12.01 0.11
Ada County	300,904	4,738 1.57	413 0.14	619 13.06 0.21	-	-	700 14.77 0.23	-	501 10.57 0.17	-	-	-	-	717 15.13 0.24	502 10.60 0.17	-	-	-	-	-	-	-	-	967 20.41 0.32
Bannock County	75,565	785 1.04	-	-	-	-	-	-	-	-	-	-	-	-	-	-	-	-	-	-	-	-	-	-
Bonneville County	82,522	486 0.59	-	-	-	-	-	-	-	-	-	-	-	-	-	-	-	-	-	-	-	-	-	-
Canyon County	131,441	1,090 0.83	-	-	-	-	-	-	-	-	-	-	-	307 28.17 0.23	-	-	-	-	-	-	-	-	-	-
Kootenai County	108,685	581 0.53	-	-	-	-	-	-	-	-	-	-	-	-	-	-	-	-	-	-	-	-	-	-
Twin Falls County	64,284	384 0.60	-	-	-	-	-	-	-	-	-	-	-	-	-	-	-	-	-	-	-	-	-	-
ILLINOIS	12,419,293	423,440 3.41	3,811 0.03	123,275 29.11 0.99	805 0.19 0.01	3,503 0.83 0.03	73,587 17.38 0.59	-	86,245 20.37 0.69	815 21.39 0.01	914 23.98 0.01	-	956 0.23 0.01	20,835 4.92 0.17	52,079 12.30 0.42	4,915 1.16 0.04	567 0.13 <0.01	15,588 3.68 0.13	874 22.93 0.01	554 0.13 <0.01	3,570 0.84 0.03	5,848 1.38 0.05	-	18,420 4.35 0.15
Champaign County	179,669	11,602 6.46	-	2,415 20.82 1.34	-	-	3,278 28.25 1.82	-	722 6.22 0.40	-	-	-	-	593 5.11 0.33	2,546 21.94 1.42	-	-	-	-	-	-	-	-	668 5.76 0.37

Notes: Please refer to the User's Guide for an explanation of data; data is arranged alphabetically by state, then county, then city within each county; table includes counties with populations greater than 49,999 unless noted and cities with populations greater than 9,999 whose Asian and/or NHPI population rates are greater than the national average; (1) Native Hawaiian and other Pacific Islander; (2) excludes Taiwanese; (3) includes Chamorro; (4) county does not meet population threshold but is shown in order to allow inclusion of city

Place	Total population	Total Asian population	Total NHPI[1] population	Asian Indian	Bangladeshi	Cambodian	Chinese[2]	Fijian	Filipino	Guamanian[3]	Hawaiian, Native	Hmong	Indonesian	Japanese	Korean	Laotian	Malaysian	Pakistani	Samoan	Sri Lankan	Taiwanese	Thai	Tongan	Vietnamese
Champaign (city)	67,873	4,602 6.78	-	1,118 24.29 1.65	-	-	1,063 23.10 1.57	-	-	-	-	-	-	-	881 19.14 1.30	-	-	-	-	-	-	-	-	430 9.34 0.63
Urbana (city)	36,196	5,283 14.60	-	981 18.57 2.71	-	-	1,803 34.13 4.98	-	-	-	-	-	-	-	1,157 21.90 3.20	-	-	-	-	-	-	-	-	-
Coles County	53,196	364 0.68	-	-	-	-	-	-	-	-	-	-	-	-	-	-	-	-	-	-	-	-	-	-
Cook County	5,376,741	260,996 4.85	1,596 0.03	69,489 26.62 1.29	-	2,227 0.85 0.04	47,189 18.08 0.88	-	54,595 20.92 1.02	-	-	-	494 0.19 0.01	14,263 5.46 0.27	35,589 13.64 0.66	1,253 0.48 0.02	-	10,612 4.07 0.20	-	-	1,752 0.67 0.03	4,002 1.53 0.07	-	11,010 4.22 0.20
Arlington Heights (village)	76,098	4,671 6.14	-	1,229 26.31 1.62	-	-	546 11.69 0.72	-	689 14.75 0.91	-	-	-	-	994 21.28 1.31	796 17.04 1.05	-	-	-	-	-	-	-	-	-
Chicago (city)	2,895,964	127,052 4.39	1,065 0.04	24,208 19.05 0.84	-	1,911 1.50 0.07	31,416 24.73 1.08	-	27,874 21.94 0.96	-	-	-	-	6,043 4.76 0.21	12,576 9.90 0.43	-	-	6,437 5.07 0.22	-	-	776 0.61 0.03	2,144 1.69 0.07	-	8,179 6.44 0.28
Des Plaines (city)	58,695	4,382 7.47	-	1,953 44.57 3.33	-	-	507 11.57 0.86	-	947 21.61 1.61	-	-	-	-	-	-	-	-	-	-	-	-	-	-	-
Elk Grove Village (village)	34,758	3,311 9.53	-	1,068 32.26 3.07	-	-	419 12.65 1.21	-	591 17.85 1.70	-	-	-	-	610 18.42 1.75	-	-	-	-	-	-	-	-	-	-
Evanston (city)	74,239	4,493 6.05	-	1,204 26.80 1.62	-	-	1,196 26.62 1.61	-	523 11.64 0.70	-	-	-	-	376 8.37 0.51	662 14.73 0.89	-	-	-	-	-	-	-	-	-
Forest Park (village)	15,688	1,048 6.68	-	-	-	-	-	-	-	-	-	-	-	-	-	-	-	-	-	-	-	-	-	-
Glenview (village)	41,679	4,212 10.11	-	622 14.77 1.49	-	-	700 16.62 1.68	-	580 13.77 1.39	-	-	-	-	314 7.45 0.75	1,597 37.92 3.83	-	-	-	-	-	-	-	-	-
Hanover Park (village)	38,366	4,249 11.07	-	1,895 44.60 4.94	-	-	-	-	1,163 27.37 3.03	-	-	-	-	-	-	-	-	-	-	-	-	-	-	-
Hoffman Estates (village)	50,352	7,480 14.86	-	2,740 36.63 5.44	-	-	821 10.98 1.63	-	865 11.56 1.72	-	-	-	-	836 11.18 1.66	1,426 19.06 2.83	-	-	-	-	-	-	-	-	-
Lincolnwood (village)	12,359	2,641 21.37	-	792 29.99 6.41	-	-	-	-	493 18.67 3.99	-	-	-	-	-	650 24.61 5.26	-	-	-	-	-	-	-	-	-
Morton Grove (village)	22,452	4,931 21.96	-	1,532 31.07 6.82	-	-	-	-	1,786 36.22 7.95	-	-	-	-	-	870 17.64 3.87	-	-	-	-	-	-	-	-	-
Mount Prospect (village)	56,706	6,482 11.43	-	3,155 48.67 5.56	-	-	587 9.06 1.04	-	481 7.42 0.85	-	-	-	-	445 6.87 0.78	1,446 22.31 2.55	-	-	-	-	-	-	-	-	-
Niles (village)	30,144	3,381 11.22	-	1,366 40.40 4.53	-	-	-	-	628 18.57 2.08	-	-	-	-	-	1,005 29.72 3.33	-	-	-	-	-	-	-	-	-

Notes: Please refer to the User's Guide for an explanation of data; data is arranged alphabetically by state, then county, then city within each county; table includes counties with populations greater than 49,999 unless noted and cities with populations greater than 9,999 whose Asian and/or NHPI population rates are greater than the national average; (1) Native Hawaiian and other Pacific Islander; (2) excludes Taiwanese; (3) includes Chamorro; (4) county does not meet population threshold but is shown in order to allow inclusion of city

Place	Total population	Total Asian population	Total NHPI[1] population	Asian Indian	Bangladeshi	Cambodian	Chinese[2]	Fijian	Filipino	Guamanian[3]	Hawaiian, Native	Hmong	Indonesian	Japanese	Korean	Laotian	Malaysian	Pakistani	Samoan	Sri Lankan	Taiwanese	Thai	Tongan	Vietnamese
Northbrook (village)	33,425	2,920 8.74	-	-	-	-	501 17.16 1.50	-	-	-	-	-	-	-	1,548 53.01 4.63	-	-	-	-	-	-	-	-	-
Oak Park (village)	52,524	2,267 4.32	-	772 34.05 1.47	-	-	489 21.57 0.93	-	-	-	-	-	-	-	-	-	-	-	-	-	-	-	-	-
Orland Park (village)	51,103	2,132 4.17	-	647 30.35 1.27	-	-	-	-	678 31.80 1.33	-	-	-	-	-	-	-	-	-	-	-	-	-	-	-
Palatine (village)	65,156	5,225 8.02	-	2,210 42.30 3.39	-	-	687 13.15 1.05	-	710 13.59 1.09	-	-	-	-	-	601 11.50 0.92	-	-	-	-	-	-	-	-	-
Prospect Heights (city)	17,541	630 3.59	-	-	-	-	-	-	-	-	-	-	-	-	-	-	-	-	-	-	-	-	-	-
Rolling Meadows (city)	24,618	1,478 6.00	-	457 30.92 1.86	-	-	-	-	-	-	-	-	-	-	-	-	-	-	-	-	-	-	-	-
Schaumburg (village)	74,511	10,285 13.80	-	4,529 44.04 6.08	-	-	1,336 12.99 1.79	-	926 9.00 1.24	-	-	-	-	940 9.14 1.26	1,775 17.26 2.38	-	-	-	-	-	-	-	-	-
Schiller Park (village)	11,784	715 6.07	-	-	-	-	-	-	-	-	-	-	-	-	-	-	-	-	-	-	-	-	-	-
Skokie (village)	63,320	13,321 21.04	-	3,845 28.86 6.07	-	-	1,657 12.44 2.62	-	3,090 23.20 4.88	-	-	-	-	-	2,524 18.95 3.99	-	-	495 3.72 0.78	-	-	-	-	-	-
Streamwood (village)	36,732	3,314 9.02	-	1,236 37.30 3.36	-	-	-	-	1,183 35.70 3.22	-	-	-	-	-	-	-	-	-	-	-	-	-	-	-
Wheeling (village)	34,411	2,968 8.63	-	1,398 47.10 4.06	-	-	-	-	585 19.71 1.70	-	-	-	-	-	-	-	-	-	-	-	-	-	-	-
Wilmette (village)	27,684	2,214 8.00	-	-	-	-	412 18.61 1.49	-	-	-	-	-	-	346 15.63 1.25	776 35.05 2.80	-	-	-	-	-	-	-	-	-
DeKalb County	88,969	2,089 2.35	-	641 30.68 0.72	-	-	-	-	-	-	-	-	-	-	-	-	-	-	-	-	-	-	-	-
DeKalb (city)	38,840	1,778 4.58	-	566 31.83 1.46	-	-	-	-	-	-	-	-	-	-	-	-	-	-	-	-	-	-	-	-
DuPage County	904,161	71,389 7.90	-	31,875 44.65 3.53	-	-	10,103 14.15 1.12	-	14,111 19.77 1.56	-	-	-	-	1,462 2.05 0.16	4,218 5.91 0.47	-	-	2,815 3.94 0.31	-	-	840 1.18 0.09	418 0.59 0.05	-	2,827 3.96 0.31
Addison (village)	35,709	2,954 8.27	-	1,652 55.92 4.63	-	-	-	-	502 16.99 1.41	-	-	-	-	-	-	-	-	-	-	-	-	-	-	-
Bartlett (village)	36,840	2,934 7.96	-	1,495 50.95 4.06	-	-	-	-	659 22.46 1.79	-	-	-	-	-	-	-	-	-	-	-	-	-	-	-

Notes: Please refer to the User's Guide for an explanation of data; data is arranged alphabetically by state, then county, then city within each county; table includes counties with populations greater than 49,999 unless noted and cities with populations greater than 9,999 whose Asian and/or NHPI population rates are greater than the national average; (1) Native Hawaiian and other Pacific Islander; (2) excludes Taiwanese; (3) includes Chamorro; (4) county does not meet population threshold but is shown in order to allow inclusion of city

Place	Total population	Total Asian population	Total NHPI[1] population	Asian Indian	Bangladeshi	Cambodian	Chinese[2]	Fijian	Filipino	Guamanian[3]	Hawaiian, Native	Hmong	Indonesian	Japanese	Korean	Laotian	Malaysian	Pakistani	Samoan	Sri Lankan	Taiwanese	Thai	Tongan	Vietnamese
Bensenville (village)	20,507	1,242 6.06	-	755 60.79 3.68	-	-	-	-	-	-	-	-	-	-	-	-	-	-	-	-	-	-	-	-
Bloomingdale (village)	21,582	1,932 8.95	-	916 47.41 4.24	-	-	-	-	-	-	-	-	-	-	-	-	-	-	-	-	-	-	-	-
Burr Ridge (village)	10,328	1,032 9.99	-	637 61.72 6.17	-	-	-	-	-	-	-	-	-	-	-	-	-	-	-	-	-	-	-	-
Carol Stream (village)	39,790	4,071 10.23	-	1,823 44.78 4.58	-	-	-	-	1,074 26.38 2.70	-	-	-	-	-	-	-	-	-	-	-	-	-	-	472 11.59 1.19
Darien (city)	22,966	2,909 12.67	-	1,494 51.36 6.51	-	-	-	-	787 27.05 3.43	-	-	-	-	-	-	-	-	-	-	-	-	-	-	-
Downers Grove (village)	48,638	2,976 6.12	-	1,341 45.06 2.76	-	-	582 19.56 1.20	-	539 18.11 1.11	-	-	-	-	-	-	-	-	-	-	-	-	-	-	-
Glen Ellyn (village)	27,040	1,318 4.87	-	510 38.69 1.89	-	-	-	-	-	-	-	-	-	-	-	-	-	-	-	-	-	-	-	-
Glendale Heights (village)	31,676	6,298 19.88	-	2,780 44.14 8.78	-	-	-	-	1,744 27.69 5.51	-	-	-	-	-	-	-	-	-	-	-	-	-	-	799 12.69 2.52
Hinsdale (village)	17,482	866 4.95	-	-	-	-	-	-	-	-	-	-	-	-	-	-	-	-	-	-	-	-	-	-
Lisle (village)	21,119	2,175 10.30	-	770 35.40 3.65	-	-	666 30.62 3.15	-	-	-	-	-	-	-	-	-	-	-	-	-	-	-	-	-
Lombard (village)	41,859	2,912 6.96	-	1,304 44.78 3.12	-	-	-	-	667 22.91 1.59	-	-	-	-	-	-	-	-	-	-	-	-	-	-	-
Naperville (city)	128,300	11,700 9.12	-	4,674 39.95 3.64	-	-	4,044 34.56 3.15	-	690 5.90 0.54	-	-	-	-	-	870 7.44 0.68	-	-	-	-	-	431 3.68 0.34	-	-	-
Roselle (village)	23,280	1,816 7.80	-	855 47.08 3.67	-	-	-	-	-	-	-	-	-	-	-	-	-	-	-	-	-	-	-	-
Villa Park (village)	22,291	896 4.02	-	-	-	-	-	-	-	-	-	-	-	-	-	-	-	-	-	-	-	-	-	-
Warrenville (city)	13,194	521 3.95	-	-	-	-	-	-	-	-	-	-	-	-	-	-	-	-	-	-	-	-	-	-
Westmont (village)	24,343	2,900 11.91	-	1,352 46.62 5.55	-	-	479 16.52 1.97	-	503 17.34 2.07	-	-	-	-	-	-	-	-	-	-	-	-	-	-	-
Wheaton (city)	55,439	2,711 4.89	-	950 35.04 1.71	-	-	-	-	-	-	-	-	-	-	-	-	-	-	-	-	-	-	-	382 14.09 0.69

Notes: Please refer to the User's Guide for an explanation of data; data is arranged alphabetically by state, then county, then city within each county; table includes counties with populations greater than 49,999 unless noted and cities with populations greater than 9,999 whose Asian and/or NHPI population rates are greater than the national average; (1) Native Hawaiian and other Pacific Islander; (2) excludes Taiwanese; (3) includes Chamorro; (4) county does not meet population threshold but is shown in order to allow inclusion of city

Place	Total population	Total Asian population	Total NHPI[1] population	Asian Indian	Bangladeshi	Cambodian	Chinese[2]	Fijian	Filipino	Guamanian[3]	Hawaiian, Native	Hmong	Indonesian	Japanese	Korean	Laotian	Malaysian	Pakistani	Samoan	Sri Lankan	Taiwanese	Thai	Tongan	Vietnamese
Woodridge (village)	31,075	3,503 11.27	-	1,644 46.93 5.29	-	-	-	-	1,162 33.17 3.74	-	-	-	-	-	-	-	-	-	-	-	-	-	-	-
Jackson County	59,612	1,931 3.24	-	-	-	-	416 21.54 0.70	-	-	-	-	-	-	-	-	-	-	-	-	-	-	-	-	-
Carbondale (city)	20,700	1,429 6.90	-	-	-	-	-	-	-	-	-	-	-	-	-	-	-	-	-	-	-	-	-	-
Kane County	404,119	7,056 1.75	-	1,613 22.86 0.40	-	-	855 12.12 0.21	-	1,326 18.79 0.33	-	-	-	-	-	479 6.79 0.12	1,046 14.82 0.26	-	-	-	-	-	-	-	478 6.77 0.12
South Elgin (village)	15,673	842 5.37	-	-	-	-	-	-	-	-	-	-	-	-	-	-	-	-	-	-	-	-	-	-
Kankakee County	103,833	730 0.70	-	-	-	-	-	-	-	-	-	-	-	-	-	-	-	-	-	-	-	-	-	-
Kendall County	54,544	671 1.23	-	-	-	-	-	-	-	-	-	-	-	-	-	-	-	-	-	-	-	-	-	-
Knox County	55,836	448 0.80	-	-	-	-	-	-	-	-	-	-	-	-	-	-	-	-	-	-	-	-	-	-
La Salle County	111,509	506 0.45	-	-	-	-	-	-	-	-	-	-	-	-	-	-	-	-	-	-	-	-	-	-
Lake County	644,356	25,305 3.93	-	5,669 22.40 0.88	-	-	4,851 19.17 0.75	-	6,988 27.62 1.08	-	-	-	-	1,488 5.88 0.23	3,910 15.45 0.61	-	-	519 2.05 0.08	-	-	-	-	-	585 2.31 0.09
Buffalo Grove (village)	42,591	3,687 8.66	-	758 20.56 1.78	-	-	607 16.46 1.43	-	434 11.77 1.02	-	-	-	-	611 16.57 1.43	1,095 29.70 2.57	-	-	-	-	-	-	-	-	-
Gages Lake (cdp)	10,459	411 3.93	-	-	-	-	-	-	-	-	-	-	-	-	-	-	-	-	-	-	-	-	-	-
Grayslake (village)	18,479	905 4.90	-	-	-	-	-	-	-	-	-	-	-	-	-	-	-	-	-	-	-	-	-	-
Gurnee (village)	28,615	2,361 8.25	-	733 31.05 2.56	-	-	367 15.54 1.28	-	767 32.49 2.68	-	-	-	-	-	-	-	-	-	-	-	-	-	-	-
Lake Zurich (village)	18,144	691 3.81	-	-	-	-	-	-	-	-	-	-	-	-	-	-	-	-	-	-	-	-	-	-
Libertyville (village)	20,696	986 4.76	-	-	-	-	-	-	-	-	-	-	-	-	-	-	-	-	-	-	-	-	-	-
Mundelein (village)	30,588	2,054 6.72	-	-	-	-	542 26.39 1.77	-	617 30.04 2.02	-	-	-	-	-	-	-	-	-	-	-	-	-	-	-

Notes: Please refer to the User's Guide for an explanation of data; data is arranged alphabetically by state, then county, then city within each county; table includes counties with populations greater than 49,999 unless noted and cities with populations greater than 9,999 whose Asian and/or NHPI population rates are greater than the national average; (1) Native Hawaiian and other Pacific Islander; (2) excludes Taiwanese; (3) includes Chamorro; (4) county does not meet population threshold but is shown in order to allow inclusion of city

Place	Total population	Total Asian population	Total NHPI[1] population	Asian Indian	Bangladeshi	Cambodian	Chinese[2]	Fijian	Filipino	Guamanian[3]	Hawaiian, Native	Hmong	Indonesian	Japanese	Korean	Laotian	Malaysian	Pakistani	Samoan	Sri Lankan	Taiwanese	Thai	Tongan	Vietnamese
Vernon Hills (village)	20,606	2,316 11.24	-	538 23.23 2.61	-	-	679 29.32 3.30	-	-	-	-	-	-	-	643 27.76 3.12	-	-	-	-	-	-	-	-	-
Macon County	114,706	745 0.65	-	-	-	-	-	-	-	-	-	-	-	-	-	-	-	-	-	-	-	-	-	-
Madison County	258,941	1,264 0.49	-	356 28.16 0.14	-	-	-	-	-	-	-	-	-	-	-	-	-	-	-	-	-	-	-	-
McHenry County	260,077	3,408 1.31	-	954 27.99 0.37	-	-	547 16.05 0.21	-	978 28.70 0.38	-	-	-	-	-	-	-	-	-	-	-	-	-	-	-
McLean County	150,433	3,117 2.07	-	1,243 39.88 0.83	-	-	682 21.88 0.45	-	-	-	-	-	-	-	-	-	-	-	-	-	-	-	-	-
Peoria County	183,433	3,159 1.72	-	1,060 33.55 0.58	-	-	897 28.40 0.49	-	-	-	-	-	-	-	-	-	-	-	-	-	-	-	-	310 9.81 0.17
Rock Island County	149,374	1,469 0.98	-	597 40.64 0.40	-	-	-	-	-	-	-	-	-	-	-	-	-	-	-	-	-	-	-	-
St. Clair County	256,082	2,269 0.89	-	-	-	-	-	-	638 28.12 0.25	-	-	-	-	-	404 17.81 0.16	-	-	-	-	-	-	-	-	-
Sangamon County	188,951	1,988 1.05	-	685 34.46 0.36	-	-	362 18.21 0.19	-	-	-	-	-	-	-	-	-	-	-	-	-	-	-	-	-
Tazewell County	128,485	572 0.45	-	-	-	-	-	-	-	-	-	-	-	-	-	-	-	-	-	-	-	-	-	-
Vermilion County	83,919	512 0.61	-	-	-	-	-	-	-	-	-	-	-	-	-	-	-	-	-	-	-	-	-	-
Will County	502,266	11,282 2.25	-	2,915 25.84 0.58	-	-	1,548 13.72 0.31	-	3,036 26.91 0.60	-	-	-	-	-	938 8.31 0.19	-	-	437 3.87 0.09	-	-	-	-	-	619 5.49 0.12
Bolingbrook (village)	56,454	3,786 6.71	-	1,091 28.82 1.93	-	-	-	-	1,166 30.80 2.07	-	-	-	-	-	-	-	-	-	-	-	-	-	-	-
Winnebago County	278,418	4,448 1.60	-	648 14.57 0.23	-	-	-	-	544 12.23 0.20	-	-	-	-	-	458 10.30 0.16	1,299 29.20 0.47	-	-	-	-	-	-	-	579 13.02 0.21
INDIANA	6,080,485	57,193 0.94	1,762 0.03	14,159 24.76 0.23	-	583 1.02 0.01	11,537 20.17 0.19	-	6,892 12.05 0.11	526 29.85 0.01	664 37.68 0.01	-	-	4,812 8.41 0.08	7,099 12.41 0.12	983 1.72 0.02	-	713 1.25 0.01	-	-	733 1.28 0.01	904 1.58 0.01	-	4,714 8.24 0.08
Allen County	331,849	4,452 1.34	-	1,020 22.91 0.31	-	-	524 11.77 0.16	-	484 10.87 0.15	-	-	-	-	-	-	-	-	-	-	-	-	-	-	809 18.17 0.24
Bartholomew County	71,435	1,182 1.65	-	426 36.04 0.60	-	-	-	-	-	-	-	-	-	-	-	-	-	-	-	-	-	-	-	-

Notes: Please refer to the User's Guide for an explanation of data; data is arranged alphabetically by state, then county, then city within each county; table includes counties with populations greater than 49,999 unless noted and cities with populations greater than 9,999 whose Asian and/or NHPI population rates are greater than the national average; (1) Native Hawaiian and other Pacific Islander; (2) excludes Taiwanese; (3) includes Chamorro; (4) county does not meet population threshold but is shown in order to allow inclusion of city

Place	Total population	Total Asian population	Total NHPI[1] population	Asian Indian	Bangladeshi	Cambodian	Chinese[2]	Fijian	Filipino	Guamanian[3]	Hawaiian, Native	Hmong	Indonesian	Japanese	Korean	Laotian	Malaysian	Pakistani	Samoan	Sri Lankan	Taiwanese	Thai	Tongan	Vietnamese
Clark County	96,472	428 0.44	-	-	-	-	-	-	-	-	-	-	-	-	-	-	-	-	-	-	-	-	-	-
Delaware County	118,769	752 0.63	-	-	-	-	-	-	-	-	-	-	-	-	-	-	-	-	-	-	-	-	-	-
Elkhart County	182,791	1,606 0.88	-	-	-	-	-	-	-	-	-	-	-	-	-	-	-	-	-	-	-	-	-	-
Grant County	73,403	469 0.64	-	-	-	-	-	-	-	-	-	-	-	-	-	-	-	-	-	-	-	-	-	-
Hamilton County	182,740	4,119 2.25	-	1,083 26.29 0.59	-	-	850 20.64 0.47	-	-	-	-	-	-	-	-	-	-	-	-	-	-	-	-	-
Carmel (city)	37,802	1,636 4.33	-	-	-	-	-	-	-	-	-	-	-	-	-	-	-	-	-	-	-	-	-	-
Hendricks County	104,093	673 0.65	-	-	-	-	-	-	-	-	-	-	-	-	-	-	-	-	-	-	-	-	-	-
Howard County	84,964	682 0.80	-	-	-	-	-	-	-	-	-	-	-	-	-	-	-	-	-	-	-	-	-	-
Johnson County	115,209	955 0.83	-	-	-	-	-	-	-	-	-	-	-	-	-	-	-	-	-	-	-	-	-	-
Kosciusko County	74,057	378 0.51	-	-	-	-	-	-	-	-	-	-	-	-	-	-	-	-	-	-	-	-	-	-
Lake County	484,564	3,940 0.81	-	1,436 36.45 0.30	-	-	629 15.96 0.13	-	786 19.95 0.16	-	-	-	-	-	542 13.76 0.11	-	-	-	-	-	-	-	-	-
Munster (town)	21,511	952 4.43	-	419 44.01 1.95	-	-	-	-	-	-	-	-	-	-	-	-	-	-	-	-	-	-	-	-
LaPorte County	110,106	361 0.33	-	-	-	-	-	-	-	-	-	-	-	-	-	-	-	-	-	-	-	-	-	-
Madison County	133,358	502 0.38	-	-	-	-	-	-	-	-	-	-	-	-	-	-	-	-	-	-	-	-	-	-
Marion County	860,454	11,505 1.34	-	3,369 29.28 0.39	-	-	2,265 19.69 0.26	-	1,456 12.66 0.17	-	-	-	-	508 4.42 0.06	1,204 10.47 0.14	-	-	-	-	-	-	-	-	1,276 11.09 0.15
Monroe County	120,563	3,912 3.24	-	699 17.87 0.58	-	-	811 20.73 0.67	-	-	-	-	-	-	-	1,070 27.35 0.89	-	-	-	-	-	-	-	-	-
Bloomington (city)	69,229	3,458 5.00	-	572 16.54 0.83	-	-	758 21.92 1.09	-	-	-	-	-	-	-	971 28.08 1.40	-	-	-	-	-	-	-	-	-

Notes: Please refer to the User's Guide for an explanation of data; data is arranged alphabetically by state, then county, then city within each county; table includes counties with populations greater than 49,999 unless noted and cities with populations greater than 9,999 whose Asian and/or NHPI population rates are greater than the national average; (1) Native Hawaiian and other Pacific Islander; (2) excludes Taiwanese; (3) includes Chamorro; (4) county does not meet population threshold but is shown in order to allow inclusion of city

Place	Total population	Total Asian population	Total NHPI[1] population	Asian Indian	Bangladeshi	Cambodian	Chinese[2]	Fijian	Filipino	Guamanian[3]	Hawaiian, Native	Hmong	Indonesian	Japanese	Korean	Laotian	Malaysian	Pakistani	Samoan	Sri Lankan	Taiwanese	Thai	Tongan	Vietnamese
Porter County	146,798	1,053 0.72	-	-	-	-	-	-	-	-	-	-	-	-	-	-	-	-	-	-	-	-	-	-
St. Joseph County	265,559	3,464 1.30	-	678 19.57 0.26	-	-	847 24.45 0.32	-	-	-	-	-	-	-	459 13.25 0.17	-	-	-	-	-	-	-	-	-
Tippecanoe County	148,955	6,760 4.54	-	1,656 24.50 1.11	-	-	2,156 31.89 1.45	-	-	-	-	-	-	390 5.77 0.26	1,033 15.28 0.69	-	-	-	-	-	-	-	-	-
West Lafayette (city)	28,949	3,159 10.91	-	978 30.96 3.38	-	-	955 30.23 3.30	-	-	-	-	-	-	-	-	-	-	-	-	-	-	-	-	-
Vanderburgh County	171,922	1,589 0.92	-	-	-	-	-	-	-	-	-	-	-	-	-	-	-	-	-	-	-	-	-	-
Vigo County	105,848	1,096 1.04	-	-	-	-	-	-	-	-	-	-	-	-	-	-	-	-	-	-	-	-	-	-
Wayne County	71,097	476 0.67	-	-	-	-	-	-	-	-	-	-	-	-	-	-	-	-	-	-	-	-	-	-
IOWA	2,926,324	35,023 1.20	955 0.03	5,407 15.44 0.18	-	824 2.35 0.03	5,604 16.00 0.19	-	2,249 6.42 0.08	-	-	-	-	1,285 3.67 0.04	4,882 13.94 0.17	3,968 11.33 0.14	-	390 1.11 0.01	-	-	446 1.27 0.02	930 2.66 0.03	-	6,771 19.33 0.23
Black Hawk County	128,012	1,316 1.03	-	-	-	-	-	-	-	-	-	-	-	-	-	-	-	-	-	-	-	-	-	-
Buena Vista County[4]	20,411	885 4.34	-	-	-	-	-	-	-	-	-	-	-	-	-	578 65.31 2.83	-	-	-	-	-	-	-	-
Storm Lake (city)	10,150	769 7.58	-	-	-	-	-	-	-	-	-	-	-	-	-	527 68.53 5.19	-	-	-	-	-	-	-	-
Johnson County	111,006	4,406 3.97	-	806 18.29 0.73	-	-	1,491 33.84 1.34	-	-	-	-	-	-	-	751 17.04 0.68	-	-	-	-	-	-	-	-	-
Coralville (city)	15,143	647 4.27	-	-	-	-	-	-	-	-	-	-	-	-	-	-	-	-	-	-	-	-	-	-
Iowa City (city)	62,381	3,495 5.60	-	595 17.02 0.95	-	-	1,320 37.77 2.12	-	-	-	-	-	-	-	523 14.96 0.84	-	-	-	-	-	-	-	-	-
Linn County	191,701	2,647 1.38	-	832 31.43 0.43	-	-	-	-	-	-	-	-	-	-	331 12.50 0.17	-	-	-	-	-	-	-	-	-
Polk County	374,601	9,173 2.45	-	1,298 14.15 0.35	-	419 4.57 0.11	1,056 11.51 0.28	-	-	-	-	-	-	-	736 8.02 0.20	1,654 18.03 0.44	-	-	-	-	-	358 3.90 0.10	-	2,508 27.34 0.67
Pottawattamie County	87,704	548 0.62	-	-	-	-	-	-	-	-	-	-	-	-	-	-	-	-	-	-	-	-	-	-

Notes: Please refer to the User's Guide for an explanation of data; data is arranged alphabetically by state, then county, then city within each county; table includes counties with populations greater than 49,999 unless noted and cities with populations greater than 9,999 whose Asian and/or NHPI population rates are greater than the national average; (1) Native Hawaiian and other Pacific Islander; (2) excludes Taiwanese; (3) includes Chamorro; (4) county does not meet population threshold but is shown in order to allow inclusion of city

Place	Total population	Total Asian population	Total NHPI[1] population	Asian Indian	Bangladeshi	Cambodian	Chinese[2]	Fijian	Filipino	Guamanian[3]	Hawaiian, Native	Hmong	Indonesian	Japanese	Korean	Laotian	Malaysian	Pakistani	Samoan	Sri Lankan	Taiwanese	Thai	Tongan	Vietnamese
Scott County	158,668	2,274 1.43	-	-	-	-	-	-	-	-	-	-	-	-	-	-	-	-	-	-	-	-	-	998 43.89 0.63
Story County	79,981	3,620 4.53	-	700 19.34 0.88	-	-	1,167 32.24 1.46	-	-	-	-	-	-	-	761 21.02 0.95	-	-	-	-	-	-	-	-	-
Ames (city)	50,656	3,471 6.85	-	660 19.01 1.30	-	-	1,137 32.76 2.24	-	-	-	-	-	-	-	732 21.09 1.45	-	-	-	-	-	-	-	-	-
Woodbury County	103,877	2,386 2.30	-	-	-	-	-	-	-	-	-	-	-	-	-	-	-	-	-	-	-	-	-	1,434 60.10 1.38
KANSAS	2,688,418	44,772 1.67	1,208 0.04	7,681 17.16 0.29	-	707 1.58 0.03	7,055 15.76 0.26	-	3,381 7.55 0.13	-	404 33.44 0.02	931 2.08 0.03	-	1,833 4.09 0.07	4,361 9.74 0.16	2,842 6.35 0.11	-	779 1.74 0.03	-	-	518 1.16 0.02	650 1.45 0.02	-	11,293 25.22 0.42
Cowley County[4]	36,291	552 1.52	-	-	-	-	-	-	-	-	-	-	-	-	-	348 63.04 0.96	-	-	-	-	-	-	-	-
Winfield (city)	12,228	485 3.97	-	-	-	-	-	-	-	-	-	-	-	-	-	344 70.93 2.81	-	-	-	-	-	-	-	-
Douglas County	99,962	3,335 3.34	-	491 14.72 0.49	-	-	967 29.00 0.97	-	-	-	-	-	-	-	526 15.77 0.53	-	-	-	-	-	-	-	-	-
Lawrence (city)	80,083	3,296 4.12	-	475 14.41 0.59	-	-	967 29.34 1.21	-	-	-	-	-	-	-	522 15.84 0.65	-	-	-	-	-	-	-	-	-
Johnson County	451,086	12,582 2.79	-	4,054 32.22 0.90	-	-	2,591 20.59 0.57	-	944 7.50 0.21	-	-	-	-	445 3.54 0.10	1,331 10.58 0.30	640 5.09 0.14	-	-	-	-	-	-	-	1,335 10.61 0.30
Overland Park (city)	148,848	5,672 3.81	-	1,981 34.93 1.33	-	-	1,293 22.80 0.87	-	-	-	-	-	-	-	601 10.60 0.40	-	-	-	-	-	-	-	-	589 10.38 0.40
Leavenworth County	68,691	747 1.09	-	-	-	-	-	-	-	-	-	-	-	-	-	-	-	-	-	-	-	-	-	-
Riley County	62,843	1,992 3.17	-	-	-	-	674 33.84 1.07	-	-	-	-	-	-	-	424 21.29 0.67	-	-	-	-	-	-	-	-	-
Manhattan (city)	44,823	1,712 3.82	-	-	-	-	645 37.68 1.44	-	-	-	-	-	-	-	-	-	-	-	-	-	-	-	-	-
Saline County	53,597	861 1.61	-	-	-	-	-	-	-	-	-	-	-	-	-	-	-	-	-	-	-	-	-	372 43.21 0.69
Sedgwick County	452,869	14,175 3.13	431 0.10	1,301 9.18 0.29	-	461 3.25 0.10	1,456 10.27 0.32	-	690 4.87 0.15	-	-	-	-	-	558 3.94 0.12	1,053 7.43 0.23	-	-	-	-	-	-	-	6,733 47.50 1.49
Wichita (city)	343,997	12,682 3.69	-	1,249 9.85 0.36	-	-	1,357 10.70 0.39	-	537 4.23 0.16	-	-	-	-	-	480 3.78 0.14	694 5.47 0.20	-	-	-	-	-	-	-	6,412 50.56 1.86

Notes: Please refer to the User's Guide for an explanation of data; data is arranged alphabetically by state, then county, then city within each county; table includes counties with populations greater than 49,999 unless noted and cities with populations greater than 9,999 whose Asian and/or NHPI population rates are greater than the national average; (1) Native Hawaiian and other Pacific Islander; (2) excludes Taiwanese; (3) includes Chamorro; (4) county does not meet population threshold but is shown in order to allow inclusion of city

Place	Total population	Total Asian population	Total NHPI[1] population	Asian Indian	Bangladeshi	Cambodian	Chinese[2]	Fijian	Filipino	Guamanian[3]	Hawaiian, Native	Hmong	Indonesian	Japanese	Korean	Laotian	Malaysian	Pakistani	Samoan	Sri Lankan	Taiwanese	Thai	Tongan	Vietnamese
Shawnee County	169,871	1,478 0.87	-	-	-	-	-	-	-	-	-	-	-	-	-	-	-	-	-	-	-	-	-	-
Wyandotte County	157,882	2,225 1.41	-	-	-	-	-	-	-	-	-	779 35.01 0.49	-	-	-	-	-	-	-	-	-	-	-	-
KENTUCKY	4,041,769	28,994 0.72	1,155 0.03	6,734 23.23 0.17	-	-	5,234 18.05 0.13	-	3,129 10.79 0.08	368 31.86 0.01	-	-	-	3,177 10.96 0.08	4,041 13.94 0.10	-	-	563 1.94 0.01	-	-	-	422 1.46 0.01	-	3,206 11.06 0.08
Boone County	85,991	1,014 1.18	-	-	-	-	-	-	-	-	-	-	-	459 45.27 0.53	-	-	-	-	-	-	-	-	-	-
Campbell County	88,616	580 0.65	-	-	-	-	-	-	-	-	-	-	-	-	-	-	-	-	-	-	-	-	-	-
Christian County	72,265	617 0.85	-	-	-	-	-	-	-	-	-	-	-	-	-	-	-	-	-	-	-	-	-	-
Fayette County	260,512	5,824 2.24	-	1,374 23.59 0.53	-	-	1,739 29.86 0.67	-	-	-	-	-	-	908 15.59 0.35	-	-	-	-	-	-	-	-	-	-
Hardin County	94,174	1,892 2.01	-	-	-	-	-	-	-	-	-	-	-	-	750 39.64 0.80	-	-	-	-	-	-	-	-	-
Radcliff (city)	21,850	939 4.30	-	-	-	-	-	-	-	-	-	-	-	-	-	-	-	-	-	-	-	-	-	-
Jefferson County	693,604	9,043 1.30	-	2,475 27.37 0.36	-	-	1,424 15.75 0.21	-	925 10.23 0.13	-	-	-	-	355 3.93 0.05	1,053 11.64 0.15	-	-	-	-	-	-	-	-	1,784 19.73 0.26
Kenton County	151,464	866 0.57	-	-	-	-	-	-	-	-	-	-	-	-	-	-	-	-	-	-	-	-	-	-
Madison County	70,872	567 0.80	-	-	-	-	-	-	-	-	-	-	-	-	-	-	-	-	-	-	-	-	-	-
Warren County	92,522	1,102 1.19	-	-	-	-	-	-	-	-	-	-	-	-	-	-	-	-	-	-	-	-	-	-
LOUISIANA	4,468,976	55,492 1.24	1,379 0.03	8,641 15.57 0.19	-	-	6,792 12.24 0.15	-	4,727 8.52 0.11	467 33.87 0.01	406 29.44 0.01	-	-	1,425 2.57 0.03	2,735 4.93 0.06	1,294 2.33 0.03	-	975 1.76 0.02	-	-	494 0.89 0.01	645 1.16 0.01	-	25,049 45.14 0.56
Ascension Parish	76,627	320 0.42	-	-	-	-	-	-	-	-	-	-	-	-	-	-	-	-	-	-	-	-	-	-
Bossier Parish	98,310	1,151 1.17	-	-	-	-	-	-	-	-	-	-	-	-	-	-	-	-	-	-	-	-	-	-
Caddo Parish	252,161	1,914 0.76	-	494 25.81 0.20	-	-	-	-	-	-	-	-	-	-	-	-	-	-	-	-	-	-	-	-

Notes: Please refer to the User's Guide for an explanation of data; data is arranged alphabetically by state, then county, then city within each county; table includes counties with populations greater than 49,999 unless noted and cities with populations greater than 9,999 whose Asian and/or NHPI population rates are greater than the national average; (1) Native Hawaiian and other Pacific Islander; (2) excludes Taiwanese; (3) includes Chamorro; (4) county does not meet population threshold but is shown in order to allow inclusion of city

Place	Total population	Total Asian population	Total NHPI[1] population	Asian Indian	Bangladeshi	Cambodian	Chinese[2]	Fijian	Filipino	Guamanian[3]	Hawaiian, Native	Hmong	Indonesian	Japanese	Korean	Laotian	Malaysian	Pakistani	Samoan	Sri Lankan	Taiwanese	Thai	Tongan	Vietnamese
Calcasieu Parish	183,577	1,096 0.60	-	-	-	-	-	-	-	-	-	-	-	-	-	-	-	-	-	-	-	-	-	-
East Baton Rouge Parish	412,852	8,729 2.11	-	1,891 21.66 0.46	-	-	1,700 19.48 0.41	-	463 5.30 0.11	-	-	-	-	-	-	-	-	-	-	-	-	-	-	3,515 40.27 0.85
Iberia Parish	73,266	1,474 2.01	-	-	-	-	-	-	-	-	-	-	-	-	-	900 61.06 1.23	-	-	-	-	-	-	-	391 26.53 0.53
Jefferson Parish	455,466	13,790 3.03	-	1,739 12.61 0.38	-	-	1,936 14.04 0.43	-	979 7.10 0.21	-	-	-	-	-	606 4.39 0.13	-	-	445 3.23 0.10	-	-	-	-	-	6,909 50.10 1.52
Gretna (city)	17,338	642 3.70	-	-	-	-	-	-	-	-	-	-	-	-	-	-	-	-	-	-	-	-	-	371 57.79 2.14
Harvey (cdp)	22,259	1,147 5.15	-	-	-	-	-	-	-	-	-	-	-	-	-	-	-	-	-	-	-	-	-	854 74.46 3.84
Timberlane (cdp)	11,460	638 5.57	-	-	-	-	-	-	-	-	-	-	-	-	-	-	-	-	-	-	-	-	-	568 89.03 4.96
Woodmere (cdp)	13,102	711 5.43	-	-	-	-	-	-	-	-	-	-	-	-	-	-	-	-	-	-	-	-	-	503 70.75 3.84
Lafayette Parish	190,503	2,142 1.12	-	625 29.18 0.33	-	-	-	-	-	-	-	-	-	-	-	-	-	-	-	-	-	-	-	739 34.50 0.39
Lafourche Parish	89,974	525 0.58	-	-	-	-	-	-	-	-	-	-	-	-	-	-	-	-	-	-	-	-	-	-
Orleans Parish	484,674	10,503 2.17	-	1,248 11.88 0.26	-	-	806 7.67 0.17	-	468 4.46 0.10	-	-	-	-	-	-	-	-	-	-	-	-	-	-	6,962 66.29 1.44
Ouachita Parish	147,250	784 0.53	-	-	-	-	-	-	-	-	-	-	-	-	-	-	-	-	-	-	-	-	-	-
Rapides Parish	126,337	1,090 0.86	-	-	-	-	-	-	-	-	-	-	-	-	-	-	-	-	-	-	-	-	-	-
St. Bernard Parish	67,229	1,079 1.60	-	-	-	-	-	-	-	-	-	-	-	-	-	-	-	-	-	-	-	-	-	496 45.97 0.74
St. Mary Parish	53,500	979 1.83	-	-	-	-	-	-	-	-	-	-	-	-	-	-	-	-	-	-	-	-	-	883 90.19 1.65
St. Tammany Parish	191,268	1,456 0.76	-	-	-	-	-	-	-	-	-	-	-	-	-	-	-	-	-	-	-	-	-	309 21.22 0.16
Terrebonne Parish	104,503	868 0.83	-	-	-	-	-	-	-	-	-	-	-	-	-	-	-	-	-	-	-	-	-	389 44.82 0.37

Notes: Please refer to the User's Guide for an explanation of data; data is arranged alphabetically by state, then county, then city within each county; table includes counties with populations greater than 49,999 unless noted and cities with populations greater than 9,999 whose Asian and/or NHPI population rates are greater than the national average; (1) Native Hawaiian and other Pacific Islander; (2) excludes Taiwanese; (3) includes Chamorro; (4) county does not meet population threshold but is shown in order to allow inclusion of city

Place	Total population	Total Asian population	Total NHPI[1] population	Asian Indian	Bangladeshi	Cambodian	Chinese[2]	Fijian	Filipino	Guamanian[3]	Hawaiian, Native	Hmong	Indonesian	Japanese	Korean	Laotian	Malaysian	Pakistani	Samoan	Sri Lankan	Taiwanese	Thai	Tongan	Vietnamese
Vermilion Parish	53,807	1,045 1.94	-	-	-	-	-	-	-	-	-	-	-	-	-	-	-	-	-	-	-	-	-	934 89.38 1.74
Abbeville (city)	11,932	684 5.73	-	-	-	-	-	-	-	-	-	-	-	-	-	-	-	-	-	-	-	-	-	654 95.61 5.48
Vernon Parish	52,531	1,125 2.14	-	-	-	-	-	-	-	-	-	-	-	-	347 30.84 0.66	-	-	-	-	-	-	-	-	-
MAINE	1,274,923	8,259 0.65	301 0.02	978 11.84 0.08	-	1,010 12.23 0.08	1,632 19.76 0.13	-	1,170 14.17 0.09	-	-	-	-	592 7.17 0.05	735 8.90 0.06	-	-	-	-	-	-	-	-	1,115 13.50 0.09
Androscoggin County	103,793	533 0.51	-	-	-	-	-	-	-	-	-	-	-	-	-	-	-	-	-	-	-	-	-	-
Aroostook County	73,938	404 0.55	-	-	-	-	-	-	-	-	-	-	-	-	-	-	-	-	-	-	-	-	-	-
Cumberland County	265,612	3,325 1.25	-	-	-	661 19.88 0.25	441 13.26 0.17	-	325 9.77 0.12	-	-	-	-	-	-	-	-	-	-	-	-	-	-	652 19.61 0.25
Hancock County	51,791	194 0.37	-	-	-	-	-	-	-	-	-	-	-	-	-	-	-	-	-	-	-	-	-	-
Kennebec County	117,114	654 0.56	-	-	-	-	-	-	-	-	-	-	-	-	-	-	-	-	-	-	-	-	-	-
Oxford County	54,755	253 0.46	-	-	-	-	-	-	-	-	-	-	-	-	-	-	-	-	-	-	-	-	-	-
Penobscot County	144,919	998 0.69	-	-	-	-	294 29.46 0.20	-	-	-	-	-	-	-	-	-	-	-	-	-	-	-	-	-
York County	186,742	946 0.51	-	-	-	-	-	-	-	-	-	-	-	-	-	-	-	-	-	-	-	-	-	-
MARYLAND	5,296,486	209,713 3.96	2,030 0.04	49,766 23.73 0.94	1,204 0.57 0.02	1,708 0.81 0.03	47,202 22.51 0.89	-	26,672 12.72 0.50	701 34.53 0.01	515 25.37 0.01	-	1,108 0.53 0.02	6,921 3.30 0.13	39,113 18.65 0.74	736 0.35 0.01	-	5,094 2.43 0.10	-	1,122 0.54 0.02	2,377 1.13 0.04	2,854 1.36 0.05	-	16,683 7.96 0.31
Allegany County	74,930	454 0.61	-	-	-	-	-	-	-	-	-	-	-	-	-	-	-	-	-	-	-	-	-	-
Anne Arundel County	489,656	11,380 2.32	-	1,693 14.88 0.35	-	-	1,493 13.12 0.30	-	2,479 21.78 0.51	-	-	-	-	683 6.00 0.14	3,686 32.39 0.75	-	-	-	-	-	-	-	-	-
Severn (cdp)	35,179	1,624 4.62	-	-	-	-	-	-	-	-	-	-	-	-	770 47.41 2.19	-	-	-	-	-	-	-	-	-
South Gate (cdp)	28,732	1,436 5.00	-	-	-	-	-	-	-	-	-	-	-	-	854 59.47 2.97	-	-	-	-	-	-	-	-	-

Notes: Please refer to the User's Guide for an explanation of data; data is arranged alphabetically by state, then county, then city within each county; table includes counties with populations greater than 49,999 unless noted and cities with populations greater than 9,999 whose Asian and/or NHPI population rates are greater than the national average; (1) Native Hawaiian and other Pacific Islander; (2) excludes Taiwanese; (3) includes Chamorro; (4) county does not meet population threshold but is shown in order to allow inclusion of city

Place	Total population	Total Asian population	Total NHPI[1] population	Asian Indian	Bangladeshi	Cambodian	Chinese[2]	Fijian	Filipino	Guamanian[3]	Hawaiian, Native	Hmong	Indonesian	Japanese	Korean	Laotian	Malaysian	Pakistani	Samoan	Sri Lankan	Taiwanese	Thai	Tongan	Vietnamese
Baltimore Independent City	651,154	10,256 1.58	-	2,115 20.62 0.32	-	-	2,273 22.16 0.35	-	1,398 13.63 0.21	-	-	-	-	-	1,770 17.26 0.27	-	-	-	-	-	-	-	-	810 7.90 0.12
Baltimore County	754,292	23,723 3.15	-	6,188 26.08 0.82	-	-	4,515 19.03 0.60	-	3,270 13.78 0.43	-	-	-	-	676 2.85 0.09	5,114 21.56 0.68	-	-	1,003 4.23 0.13	-	-	-	-	-	1,243 5.24 0.16
Arbutus (cdp)	20,116	970 4.82	-	-	-	-	-	-	-	-	-	-	-	-	-	-	-	-	-	-	-	-	-	-
Carney (cdp)	28,357	1,589 5.60	-	-	-	-	351 22.09 1.24	-	-	-	-	-	-	-	768 48.33 2.71	-	-	-	-	-	-	-	-	-
Cockeysville (cdp)	19,571	1,741 8.90	-	-	-	-	-	-	-	-	-	-	-	-	668 38.37 3.41	-	-	-	-	-	-	-	-	-
Lutherville-Timonium (cdp)	15,590	662 4.25	-	-	-	-	-	-	-	-	-	-	-	-	-	-	-	-	-	-	-	-	-	-
Mays Chapel (cdp)	11,422	821 7.19	-	-	-	-	-	-	-	-	-	-	-	-	-	-	-	-	-	-	-	-	-	-
Owings Mills (cdp)	20,212	775 3.83	-	-	-	-	-	-	-	-	-	-	-	-	-	-	-	-	-	-	-	-	-	-
Perry Hall (cdp)	28,601	1,497 5.23	-	-	-	-	-	-	-	-	-	-	-	-	525 35.07 1.84	-	-	-	-	-	-	-	-	-
Reisterstown (cdp)	22,484	1,030 4.58	-	564 54.76 2.51	-	-	-	-	-	-	-	-	-	-	-	-	-	-	-	-	-	-	-	-
Rossville (cdp)	11,655	556 4.77	-	-	-	-	-	-	-	-	-	-	-	-	-	-	-	-	-	-	-	-	-	-
Towson (cdp)	51,838	1,938 3.74	-	-	-	-	846 43.65 1.63	-	-	-	-	-	-	-	-	-	-	-	-	-	-	-	-	-
Woodlawn (cdp)	36,125	2,170 6.01	-	883 40.69 2.44	-	-	-	-	-	-	-	-	-	-	-	-	-	-	-	-	-	-	-	-
Calvert County	74,563	655 0.88	-	-	-	-	-	-	-	-	-	-	-	-	-	-	-	-	-	-	-	-	-	-
Carroll County	150,897	1,299 0.86	-	-	-	-	-	-	-	-	-	-	-	-	-	-	-	-	-	-	-	-	-	-
Cecil County	85,951	564 0.66	-	-	-	-	-	-	-	-	-	-	-	-	-	-	-	-	-	-	-	-	-	-
Charles County	120,546	1,884 1.56	-	-	-	-	-	-	472 25.05 0.39	-	-	-	-	-	-	-	-	-	-	-	-	-	-	-

Notes: Please refer to the User's Guide for an explanation of data; data is arranged alphabetically by state, then county, then city within each county; table includes counties with populations greater than 49,999 unless noted and cities with populations greater than 9,999 whose Asian and/or NHPI population rates are greater than the national average; (1) Native Hawaiian and other Pacific Islander; (2) excludes Taiwanese; (3) includes Chamorro; (4) county does not meet population threshold but is shown in order to allow inclusion of city

Place	Total population	Total Asian population	Total NHPI[1] population	Asian Indian	Bangladeshi	Cambodian	Chinese[2]	Fijian	Filipino	Guamanian[3]	Hawaiian, Native	Hmong	Indonesian	Japanese	Korean	Laotian	Malaysian	Pakistani	Samoan	Sri Lankan	Taiwanese	Thai	Tongan	Vietnamese
Frederick County	195,277	3,327 1.70	-	623 18.73 0.32	-	-	787 23.65 0.40	-	-	-	-	-	-	-	527 15.84 0.27	-	-	-	-	-	-	-	-	-
Harford County	218,590	3,169 1.45	-	640 20.20 0.29	-	-	-	-	561 17.70 0.26	-	-	-	-	-	761 24.01 0.35	-	-	-	-	-	-	-	-	-
Howard County	247,842	18,712 7.55	-	4,758 25.43 1.92	-	-	3,701 19.78 1.49	-	1,380 7.37 0.56	-	-	-	-	-	6,013 32.13 2.43	-	-	652 3.48 0.26	-	-	-	-	-	727 3.89 0.29
Columbia (cdp)	88,391	6,274 7.10	-	1,801 28.71 2.04	-	-	1,570 25.02 1.78	-	509 8.11 0.58	-	-	-	-	-	1,446 23.05 1.64	-	-	-	-	-	-	-	-	-
Elkridge (cdp)	22,011	1,406 6.39	-	-	-	-	-	-	-	-	-	-	-	-	374 26.60 1.70	-	-	-	-	-	-	-	-	-
Ellicott City (cdp)	56,309	6,661 11.83	-	1,130 16.96 2.01	-	-	1,263 18.96 2.24	-	405 6.08 0.72	-	-	-	-	-	2,868 43.06 5.09	-	-	395 5.93 0.70	-	-	-	-	-	-
North Laurel (cdp)	20,633	1,390 6.74	-	416 29.93 2.02	-	-	-	-	-	-	-	-	-	-	422 30.36 2.05	-	-	-	-	-	-	-	-	-
Savage-Guilford (cdp)	12,609	730 5.79	-	-	-	-	-	-	-	-	-	-	-	-	-	-	-	-	-	-	-	-	-	-
Montgomery County	873,341	97,994 11.22	489 0.06	24,411 24.91 2.80	826 0.84 0.09	1,161 1.18 0.13	27,384 27.94 3.14	-	6,898 7.04 0.79	-	-	-	928 0.95 0.11	3,159 3.22 0.36	15,458 15.77 1.77	-	-	1,830 1.87 0.21	-	748 0.76 0.09	1,144 1.17 0.13	1,327 1.35 0.15	-	9,384 9.58 1.07
Aspen Hill (cdp)	50,223	5,557 11.06	-	694 12.49 1.38	-	-	1,798 32.36 3.58	-	679 12.22 1.35	-	-	-	-	-	1,000 18.00 1.99	-	-	-	-	-	-	-	-	431 7.76 0.86
Bethesda (cdp)	55,300	4,261 7.71	-	1,009 23.68 1.82	-	-	1,252 29.38 2.26	-	393 9.22 0.71	-	-	-	-	442 10.37 0.80	608 14.27 1.10	-	-	-	-	-	-	-	-	-
Calverton (cdp)	12,608	2,095 16.62	-	702 33.51 5.57	-	-	-	-	-	-	-	-	-	-	568 27.11 4.51	-	-	-	-	-	-	-	-	-
Colesville (cdp)	19,863	3,390 17.07	-	733 21.62 3.69	-	-	724 21.36 3.64	-	-	-	-	-	-	-	1,156 34.10 5.82	-	-	-	-	-	-	-	-	331 9.76 1.67
Fairland (cdp)	21,581	3,328 15.42	-	816 24.52 3.78	-	-	612 18.39 2.84	-	-	-	-	-	-	-	1,262 37.92 5.85	-	-	-	-	-	-	-	-	-
Gaithersburg (city)	52,780	6,935 13.14	-	1,690 24.37 3.20	-	-	2,442 35.21 4.63	-	438 6.32 0.83	-	-	-	-	-	915 13.19 1.73	-	-	-	-	-	-	-	-	577 8.32 1.09
Germantown (cdp)	55,152	5,283 9.58	-	2,100 39.75 3.81	-	-	1,012 19.16 1.83	-	-	-	-	-	-	-	392 7.42 0.71	-	-	-	-	-	-	-	-	509 9.63 0.92
Montgomery Village (cdp)	37,889	4,276 11.29	-	1,758 41.11 4.64	-	-	701 16.39 1.85	-	571 13.35 1.51	-	-	-	-	-	-	-	-	-	-	-	-	-	-	403 9.42 1.06

Notes: Please refer to the User's Guide for an explanation of data; data is arranged alphabetically by state, then county, then city within each county; table includes counties with populations greater than 49,999 unless noted and cities with populations greater than 9,999 whose Asian and/or NHPI population rates are greater than the national average; (1) Native Hawaiian and other Pacific Islander; (2) excludes Taiwanese; (3) includes Chamorro; (4) county does not meet population threshold but is shown in order to allow inclusion of city

Place	Total population	Total Asian population	Total NHPI[1] population	Asian Indian	Bangladeshi	Cambodian	Chinese[2]	Fijian	Filipino	Guamanian[3]	Hawaiian, Native	Hmong	Indonesian	Japanese	Korean	Laotian	Malaysian	Pakistani	Samoan	Sri Lankan	Taiwanese	Thai	Tongan	Vietnamese
North Bethesda (cdp)	38,643	4,536 11.74	-	1,045 23.04 2.70	-	-	1,445 31.86 3.74	-	376 8.29 0.97	-	-	-	-	522 11.51 1.35	678 14.95 1.75	-	-	-	-	-	-	-	-	-
North Potomac (cdp)	22,945	6,183 26.95	-	1,165 18.84 5.08	-	-	3,244 52.47 14.14	-	-	-	-	-	-	-	1,050 16.98 4.58	-	-	-	-	-	-	-	-	-
Olney (cdp)	31,651	2,585 8.17	-	697 26.96 2.20	-	-	635 24.56 2.01	-	-	-	-	-	-	-	651 25.18 2.06	-	-	-	-	-	-	-	-	-
Potomac (cdp)	44,821	5,819 12.98	-	1,484 25.50 3.31	-	-	1,946 33.44 4.34	-	372 6.39 0.83	-	-	-	-	-	1,116 19.18 2.49	-	-	-	-	-	-	-	-	-
Redland (cdp)	17,251	2,930 16.98	-	748 25.53 4.34	-	-	798 27.24 4.63	-	309 10.55 1.79	-	-	-	-	-	411 14.03 2.38	-	-	-	-	-	-	-	-	-
Rockville (city)	47,257	6,677 14.13	-	997 14.93 2.11	-	-	2,679 40.12 5.67	-	429 6.43 0.91	-	-	-	-	444 6.65 0.94	909 13.61 1.92	-	-	-	-	-	-	-	-	445 6.66 0.94
Silver Spring (cdp)	76,725	6,302 8.21	-	1,421 22.55 1.85	-	326 5.17 0.42	746 11.84 0.97	-	469 7.44 0.61	-	-	-	-	-	450 7.14 0.59	-	-	-	-	-	-	-	-	1,771 28.10 2.31
Takoma Park (city)	17,180	714 4.16	-	-	-	-	-	-	-	-	-	-	-	-	-	-	-	-	-	-	-	-	-	-
Wheaton-Glenmont (cdp)	57,723	7,096 12.29	-	1,197 16.87 2.07	-	-	1,867 26.31 3.23	-	682 9.61 1.18	-	-	-	-	-	835 11.77 1.45	-	-	-	-	-	-	-	-	1,167 16.45 2.02
White Oak (cdp)	20,897	2,508 12.00	-	542 21.61 2.59	-	-	447 17.82 2.14	-	-	-	-	-	-	-	639 25.48 3.06	-	-	-	-	-	-	-	-	656 26.16 3.14
Prince George's County	801,515	30,390 3.79	-	7,129 23.46 0.89	-	-	4,918 16.18 0.61	-	8,239 27.11 1.03	-	-	-	-	636 2.09 0.08	3,691 12.15 0.46	-	-	680 2.24 0.08	-	-	-	334 1.10 0.04	-	2,625 8.64 0.33
Adelphi (cdp)	15,016	1,400 9.32	-	-	-	-	-	-	-	-	-	-	-	-	-	-	-	-	-	-	-	-	-	-
Beltsville (cdp)	15,725	1,706 10.85	-	517 30.30 3.29	-	-	-	-	-	-	-	-	-	-	284 16.65 1.81	-	-	-	-	-	-	-	-	-
College Park (city)	24,590	2,236 9.09	-	638 28.53 2.59	-	-	703 31.44 2.86	-	-	-	-	-	-	-	-	-	-	-	-	-	-	-	-	-
Fort Washington (cdp)	24,184	2,413 9.98	-	-	-	-	-	-	1,932 80.07 7.99	-	-	-	-	-	-	-	-	-	-	-	-	-	-	-
Friendly (cdp)	10,973	657 5.99	-	-	-	-	-	-	523 79.60 4.77	-	-	-	-	-	-	-	-	-	-	-	-	-	-	-
Glenn Dale (cdp)	12,816	1,008 7.87	-	-	-	-	-	-	-	-	-	-	-	-	-	-	-	-	-	-	-	-	-	-

Notes: Please refer to the User's Guide for an explanation of data; data is arranged alphabetically by state, then county, then city within each county; table includes counties with populations greater than 49,999 unless noted and cities with populations greater than 9,999 whose Asian and/or NHPI population rates are greater than the national average; (1) Native Hawaiian and other Pacific Islander; (2) excludes Taiwanese; (3) includes Chamorro; (4) county does not meet population threshold but is shown in order to allow inclusion of city

Place	Total population	Total Asian population	Total NHPI[1] population	Asian Indian	Bangladeshi	Cambodian	Chinese[2]	Fijian	Filipino	Guamanian[3]	Hawaiian, Native	Hmong	Indonesian	Japanese	Korean	Laotian	Malaysian	Pakistani	Samoan	Sri Lankan	Taiwanese	Thai	Tongan	Vietnamese
Greenbelt (city)	21,391	2,577 12.05	-	726 28.17 3.39	-	-	594 23.05 2.78	-	-	-	-	-	-	-	603 23.40 2.82	-	-	-	-	-	-	-	-	-
Hyattsville (city)	14,833	695 4.69	-	-	-	-	-	-	-	-	-	-	-	-	-	-	-	-	-	-	-	-	-	-
Lanham-Seabrook (cdp)	18,087	916 5.06	-	-	-	-	-	-	-	-	-	-	-	-	-	-	-	-	-	-	-	-	-	-
Laurel (city)	20,054	1,215 6.06	-	-	-	-	-	-	-	-	-	-	-	-	-	-	-	-	-	-	-	-	-	-
New Carrollton (city)	12,845	517 4.02	-	-	-	-	-	-	-	-	-	-	-	-	-	-	-	-	-	-	-	-	-	-
South Laurel (cdp)	20,790	1,164 5.60	-	-	-	-	-	-	-	-	-	-	-	-	-	-	-	-	-	-	-	-	-	-
St. Mary's County	86,211	1,623 1.88	-	279 17.19 0.32	-	-	-	-	654 40.30 0.76	-	-	-	-	-	-	-	-	-	-	-	-	-	-	-
Lexington Park (cdp)	10,845	436 4.02	-	-	-	-	-	-	-	-	-	-	-	-	-	-	-	-	-	-	-	-	-	-
Washington County	131,923	1,000 0.76	-	-	-	-	-	-	-	-	-	-	-	-	-	-	-	-	-	-	-	-	-	-
Wicomico County	84,644	1,746 2.06	-	440 25.20 0.52	-	-	-	-	-	-	-	-	-	-	590 33.79 0.70	-	-	-	-	-	-	-	-	-
Salisbury (city)	24,159	997 4.13	-	-	-	-	-	-	-	-	-	-	-	-	-	-	-	-	-	-	-	-	-	-
MASSACHUSETTS	6,349,097	238,246 3.75	1,835 0.03	41,935 17.60 0.66	561 0.24 0.01	20,370 8.55 0.32	82,051 34.44 1.29	-	9,287 3.90 0.15	445 24.25 0.01	507 27.63 0.01	993 0.42 0.02	710 0.30 0.01	10,958 4.60 0.17	17,400 7.30 0.27	3,647 1.53 0.06	-	2,356 0.99 0.04	-	469 0.20 0.01	2,536 1.06 0.04	2,255 0.95 0.04	-	34,376 14.43 0.54
Barnstable County	222,230	1,372 0.62	-	-	-	-	432 31.49 0.19	-	-	-	-	-	-	-	-	-	-	-	-	-	-	-	-	-
Berkshire County	134,953	1,259 0.93	-	345 27.40 0.26	-	-	-	-	-	-	-	-	-	-	-	-	-	-	-	-	-	-	-	-
Bristol County	534,678	7,292 1.36	-	1,519 20.83 0.28	-	2,173 29.80 0.41	1,399 19.19 0.26	-	414 5.68 0.08	-	-	-	-	-	562 7.71 0.11	-	-	-	-	-	-	-	-	452 6.20 0.08
Essex County	723,419	17,261 2.39	-	2,466 14.29 0.34	-	3,754 21.75 0.52	3,288 19.05 0.45	-	675 3.91 0.09	-	-	-	-	1,020 5.91 0.14	1,546 8.96 0.21	387 2.24 0.05	-	-	-	-	-	-	-	3,037 17.59 0.42
Andover (town)	31,247	2,078 6.65	-	503 24.21 1.61	-	-	819 39.41 2.62	-	-	-	-	-	-	-	-	-	-	-	-	-	-	-	-	-

Notes: Please refer to the User's Guide for an explanation of data; data is arranged alphabetically by state, then county, then city within each county; table includes counties with populations greater than 49,999 unless noted and cities with populations greater than 9,999 whose Asian and/or NHPI population rates are greater than the national average; (1) Native Hawaiian and other Pacific Islander; (2) excludes Taiwanese; (3) includes Chamorro; (4) county does not meet population threshold but is shown in order to allow inclusion of city

Place	Total population	Total Asian population	Total NHPI[1] population	Asian Indian	Bangladeshi	Cambodian	Chinese[2]	Fijian	Filipino	Guamanian[3]	Hawaiian, Native	Hmong	Indonesian	Japanese	Korean	Laotian	Malaysian	Pakistani	Samoan	Sri Lankan	Taiwanese	Thai	Tongan	Vietnamese
Lynn (city)	89,122	5,899 6.62	-	411 6.97 0.46	-	2,999 50.84 3.37	-	-	-	-	-	-	-	-	-	-	-	-	-	-	-	-	-	1,179 19.99 1.32
North Andover (town)	27,202	1,084 3.99	-	-	-	-	344 31.73 1.26	-	-	-	-	-	-	-	-	-	-	-	-	-	-	-	-	-
Franklin County	71,535	641 0.90	-	-	-	-	-	-	-	-	-	-	-	-	-	-	-	-	-	-	-	-	-	-
Hampden County	456,228	6,054 1.33	-	717 11.84 0.16	-	455 7.52 0.10	1,195 19.74 0.26	-	-	-	-	-	-	-	454 7.50 0.10	-	-	-	-	-	-	-	-	1,939 32.03 0.43
Hampshire County	152,251	4,811 3.16	-	846 17.58 0.56	-	-	1,599 33.24 1.05	-	-	-	-	-	-	-	760 15.80 0.50	-	-	-	-	-	-	-	-	-
Amherst Center (cdp)	17,155	1,356 7.90	-	-	-	-	-	-	-	-	-	-	-	-	-	-	-	-	-	-	-	-	-	-
Amherst (town)	34,873	2,992 8.58	-	-	-	-	1,069 35.73 3.07	-	-	-	-	-	-	-	-	-	-	-	-	-	-	-	-	-
Middlesex County	1,465,396	91,645 6.25	-	21,930 23.93 1.50	-	10,974 11.97 0.75	29,963 32.69 2.04	-	2,550 2.78 0.17	-	-	-	-	3,876 4.23 0.26	7,100 7.75 0.48	1,807 1.97 0.12	-	593 0.65 0.04	-	-	1,272 1.39 0.09	901 0.98 0.06	-	6,736 7.35 0.46
Acton (town)	20,331	1,813 8.92	-	652 35.96 3.21	-	-	811 44.73 3.99	-	-	-	-	-	-	-	-	-	-	-	-	-	-	-	-	-
Arlington (town)	42,389	2,006 4.73	-	-	-	-	729 36.34 1.72	-	-	-	-	-	-	-	-	-	-	-	-	-	-	-	-	-
Bedford (town)	12,595	789 6.26	-	-	-	-	-	-	-	-	-	-	-	-	-	-	-	-	-	-	-	-	-	-
Belmont (cdp)	24,194	1,297 5.36	-	-	-	-	561 43.25 2.32	-	-	-	-	-	-	-	-	-	-	-	-	-	-	-	-	-
Belmont (town)	24,194	1,297 5.36	-	-	-	-	561 43.25 2.32	-	-	-	-	-	-	-	-	-	-	-	-	-	-	-	-	-
Burlington (town)	22,876	2,314 10.12	-	1,512 65.34 6.61	-	-	-	-	-	-	-	-	-	-	-	-	-	-	-	-	-	-	-	-
Cambridge (city)	101,355	12,112 11.95	-	2,768 22.85 2.73	-	-	4,340 35.83 4.28	-	-	-	-	-	-	1,063 8.78 1.05	1,931 15.94 1.91	-	-	-	-	-	-	-	-	-
Chelmsford (town)	33,858	1,550 4.58	-	369 23.81 1.09	-	-	573 36.97 1.69	-	-	-	-	-	-	-	-	-	-	-	-	-	-	-	-	-
Framingham (town)	66,910	3,446 5.15	-	1,377 39.96 2.06	-	-	1,050 30.47 1.57	-	-	-	-	-	-	-	-	-	-	-	-	-	-	-	-	-

Notes: Please refer to the User's Guide for an explanation of data; data is arranged alphabetically by state, then county, then city within each county; table includes counties with populations greater than 49,999 unless noted and cities with populations greater than 9,999 whose Asian and/or NHPI population rates are greater than the national average; (1) Native Hawaiian and other Pacific Islander; (2) excludes Taiwanese; (3) includes Chamorro; (4) county does not meet population threshold but is shown in order to allow inclusion of city

Place	Total population	Total Asian population	Total NHPI[1] population	Asian Indian	Bangladeshi	Cambodian	Chinese[2]	Fijian	Filipino	Guamanian[3]	Hawaiian, Native	Hmong	Indonesian	Japanese	Korean	Laotian	Malaysian	Pakistani	Samoan	Sri Lankan	Taiwanese	Thai	Tongan	Vietnamese
Lexington (town)	30,355	3,251 10.71	-	840 25.84 2.77	-	-	1,339 41.19 4.41	-	-	-	-	-	-	-	452 13.90 1.49	-	-	-	-	-	-	-	-	-
Lowell (city)	105,167	17,161 16.32	-	2,594 15.12 2.47	-	9,521 55.48 9.05	759 4.42 0.72	-	-	-	-	-	-	-	-	1,467 8.55 1.39	-	-	-	-	-	-	-	1,490 8.68 1.42
Malden (city)	56,340	7,879 13.98	-	1,046 13.28 1.86	-	-	4,107 52.13 7.29	-	-	-	-	-	-	-	-	-	-	-	-	-	-	-	-	1,339 16.99 2.38
Marlborough (city)	36,255	1,601 4.42	-	696 43.47 1.92	-	-	-	-	-	-	-	-	-	-	-	-	-	-	-	-	-	-	-	-
Medford (city)	55,765	2,338 4.19	-	403 17.24 0.72	-	-	870 37.21 1.56	-	-	-	-	-	-	-	-	-	-	-	-	-	-	-	-	363 15.53 0.65
Natick (town)	32,170	1,294 4.02	-	-	-	-	655 50.62 2.04	-	-	-	-	-	-	-	-	-	-	-	-	-	-	-	-	-
Newton (city)	83,829	6,323 7.54	-	578 9.14 0.69	-	-	3,948 62.44 4.71	-	-	-	-	-	-	-	669 10.58 0.80	-	-	-	-	-	-	-	-	-
Somerville (city)	77,478	5,013 6.47	-	1,291 25.75 1.67	-	-	2,042 40.73 2.64	-	-	-	-	-	-	-	453 9.04 0.58	-	-	-	-	-	-	-	-	-
Sudbury (town)	16,841	615 3.65	-	-	-	-	-	-	-	-	-	-	-	-	-	-	-	-	-	-	-	-	-	-
Waltham (city)	59,226	4,638 7.83	-	1,963 42.32 3.31	-	-	1,488 32.08 2.51	-	-	-	-	-	-	-	-	-	-	-	-	-	-	-	-	-
Wayland (town)	13,100	682 5.21	-	-	-	-	-	-	-	-	-	-	-	-	-	-	-	-	-	-	-	-	-	-
Westford (town)	20,754	951 4.58	-	-	-	-	370 38.91 1.78	-	-	-	-	-	-	-	-	-	-	-	-	-	-	-	-	-
Weston (town)	11,469	910 7.93	-	-	-	-	385 42.31 3.36	-	-	-	-	-	-	-	-	-	-	-	-	-	-	-	-	-
Winchester (town)	20,810	794 3.82	-	-	-	-	-	-	-	-	-	-	-	-	-	-	-	-	-	-	-	-	-	-
Woburn (city)	37,258	1,827 4.90	-	1,002 54.84 2.69	-	-	-	-	-	-	-	-	-	-	-	-	-	-	-	-	-	-	-	-
Norfolk County	650,308	36,121 5.55	-	5,066 14.03 0.78	-	-	19,185 53.11 2.95	-	1,888 5.23 0.29	-	-	-	-	2,080 5.76 0.32	2,249 6.23 0.35	-	-	-	-	-	423 1.17 0.07	-	-	2,818 7.80 0.43
Brookline (town)	57,061	7,787 13.65	-	1,084 13.92 1.90	-	-	3,585 46.04 6.28	-	-	-	-	-	-	1,325 17.02 2.32	992 12.74 1.74	-	-	-	-	-	-	-	-	-

Notes: Please refer to the User's Guide for an explanation of data; data is arranged alphabetically by state, then county, then city within each county; table includes counties with populations greater than 49,999 unless noted and cities with populations greater than 9,999 whose Asian and/or NHPI population rates are greater than the national average; (1) Native Hawaiian and other Pacific Islander; (2) excludes Taiwanese; (3) includes Chamorro; (4) county does not meet population threshold but is shown in order to allow inclusion of city

Place	Total population	Total Asian population	Total NHPI[1] population	Asian Indian	Bangladeshi	Cambodian	Chinese[2]	Fijian	Filipino	Guamanian[3]	Hawaiian, Native	Hmong	Indonesian	Japanese	Korean	Laotian	Malaysian	Pakistani	Samoan	Sri Lankan	Taiwanese	Thai	Tongan	Vietnamese
Needham (town)	28,911	1,062 3.67	-	-	-	-	606 57.06 2.10	-	-	-	-	-	-	-	-	-	-	-	-	-	-	-	-	-
Norwood (town)	28,587	1,384 4.84	-	758 54.77 2.65	-	-	-	-	-	-	-	-	-	-	-	-	-	-	-	-	-	-	-	-
Quincy (city)	88,025	14,007 15.91	-	969 6.92 1.10	-	-	9,442 67.41 10.73	-	859 6.13 0.98	-	-	-	-	-	-	-	-	-	-	-	-	-	-	1,463 10.44 1.66
Randolph (town)	30,997	3,152 10.17	-	-	-	-	1,526 48.41 4.92	-	-	-	-	-	-	-	-	-	-	-	-	-	-	-	-	659 20.91 2.13
Sharon (town)	17,408	694 3.99	-	-	-	-	-	-	-	-	-	-	-	-	-	-	-	-	-	-	-	-	-	-
Wellesley (town)	26,613	1,784 6.70	-	-	-	-	905 50.73 3.40	-	-	-	-	-	-	-	-	-	-	-	-	-	-	-	-	-
Plymouth County	472,822	4,491 0.95	-	626 13.94 0.13	-	-	1,053 23.45 0.22	-	537 11.96 0.11	-	-	-	-	-	-	-	-	-	-	-	-	-	-	710 15.81 0.15
Suffolk County	689,807	48,115 6.98	-	4,353 9.05 0.63	-	1,718 3.57 0.25	19,925 41.41 2.89	-	1,856 3.86 0.27	-	-	-	-	2,269 4.72 0.33	2,590 5.38 0.38	-	-	-	-	-	465 0.97 0.07	-	-	12,459 25.89 1.81
Boston (city)	589,141	44,345 7.53	-	4,051 9.14 0.69	-	626 1.41 0.11	19,420 43.79 3.30	-	1,741 3.93 0.30	-	-	-	-	2,235 5.04 0.38	2,423 5.46 0.41	-	-	-	-	-	465 1.05 0.08	-	-	11,126 25.09 1.89
Chelsea (city)	35,080	1,455 4.15	-	-	-	-	-	-	-	-	-	-	-	-	-	-	-	-	-	-	-	-	-	739 50.79 2.11
Revere (city)	47,283	2,161 4.57	-	-	-	810 37.48 1.71	-	-	-	-	-	-	-	-	-	-	-	-	-	-	-	-	-	575 26.61 1.22
Worcester County	750,963	18,965 2.53	-	3,895 20.54 0.52	-	395 2.08 0.05	3,458 18.23 0.46	-	478 2.52 0.06	-	-	663 3.50 0.09	-	391 2.06 0.05	1,199 6.32 0.16	1,013 5.34 0.13	-	397 2.09 0.05	-	-	-	-	-	5,645 29.77 0.75
Fitchburg (city)	39,102	1,748 4.47	-	-	-	-	-	-	-	-	-	608 34.78 1.55	-	-	-	390 22.31 1.00	-	-	-	-	-	-	-	-
Northborough (town)	14,013	762 5.44	-	-	-	-	-	-	-	-	-	-	-	-	-	-	-	-	-	-	-	-	-	-
Shrewsbury (town)	31,640	2,574 8.14	-	1,139 44.25 3.60	-	-	654 25.41 2.07	-	-	-	-	-	-	-	-	-	-	-	-	-	-	-	-	516 20.05 1.63
Westborough (town)	17,997	1,429 7.94	-	601 42.06 3.34	-	-	482 33.73 2.68	-	-	-	-	-	-	-	-	-	-	-	-	-	-	-	-	-
Worcester (city)	172,648	7,893 4.57	-	1,058 13.40 0.61	-	-	960 12.16 0.56	-	-	-	-	-	-	-	-	-	-	-	-	-	-	-	-	4,287 54.31 2.48

Notes: Please refer to the User's Guide for an explanation of data; data is arranged alphabetically by state, then county, then city within each county; table includes counties with populations greater than 49,999 unless noted and cities with populations greater than 9,999 whose Asian and/or NHPI population rates are greater than the national average; (1) Native Hawaiian and other Pacific Islander; (2) excludes Taiwanese; (3) includes Chamorro; (4) county does not meet population threshold but is shown in order to allow inclusion of city

Place	Total population	Total Asian population	Total NHPI[1] population	Asian Indian	Bangladeshi	Cambodian	Chinese[2]	Fijian	Filipino	Guamanian[3]	Hawaiian, Native	Hmong	Indonesian	Japanese	Korean	Laotian	Malaysian	Pakistani	Samoan	Sri Lankan	Taiwanese	Thai	Tongan	Vietnamese
MICHIGAN	9,938,444	174,824 1.76	2,669 0.03	54,464 31.15 0.55	1,683 0.96 0.02	1,594 0.91 0.02	29,443 16.84 0.30	-	17,590 10.06 0.18	685 25.67 0.01	792 29.67 0.01	5,657 3.24 0.06	652 0.37 0.01	10,646 6.09 0.11	21,014 12.02 0.21	2,787 1.59 0.03	457 0.26 <0.01	4,978 2.85 0.05	474 17.76 <0.01	356 0.20 <0.01	2,284 1.31 0.02	1,604 0.92 0.02	-	12,974 7.42 0.13
Allegan County	105,665	592 0.56	-	-	-	-	-	-	-	-	-	-	-	-	-	-	-	-	-	-	-	-	-	-
Bay County	110,157	617 0.56	-	-	-	-	-	-	-	-	-	-	-	-	-	-	-	-	-	-	-	-	-	-
Berrien County	162,453	1,671 1.03	-	473 28.31 0.29	-	-	-	-	318 19.03 0.20	-	-	-	-	-	391 23.40 0.24	-	-	-	-	-	-	-	-	-
Calhoun County	137,985	1,473 1.07	-	-	-	-	-	-	-	-	-	-	-	446 30.28 0.32	-	-	-	-	-	-	-	-	-	-
Cass County	51,104	324 0.63	-	-	-	-	-	-	-	-	-	-	-	-	-	143 44.14 0.28	-	-	-	-	-	-	-	-
Clinton County	64,753	358 0.55	-	-	-	-	-	-	-	-	-	-	-	-	-	-	-	-	-	-	-	-	-	-
Eaton County	103,655	1,222 1.18	-	361 29.54 0.35	-	-	-	-	-	-	-	-	-	-	-	-	-	-	-	-	-	-	-	294 24.06 0.28
Genesee County	436,141	3,161 0.72	-	1,168 36.95 0.27	-	-	398 12.59 0.09	-	423 13.38 0.10	-	-	-	-	-	454 14.36 0.10	-	-	-	-	-	-	-	-	-
Ingham County	279,320	9,991 3.58	-	2,020 20.22 0.72	-	-	1,780 17.82 0.64	-	621 6.22 0.22	-	-	595 5.96 0.21	-	522 5.22 0.19	1,747 17.49 0.63	-	-	-	-	-	-	-	-	1,336 13.37 0.48
East Lansing (city)	46,704	3,836 8.21	-	758 19.76 1.62	-	-	861 22.45 1.84	-	-	-	-	-	-	-	990 25.81 2.12	-	-	-	-	-	-	-	-	-
Meridian charter (township)	38,987	2,453 6.29	-	903 36.81 2.32	-	-	532 21.69 1.36	-	-	-	-	-	-	-	380 15.49 0.97	-	-	-	-	-	-	-	-	-
Okemos (cdp)	22,686	1,916 8.45	-	754 39.35 3.32	-	-	372 19.42 1.64	-	-	-	-	-	-	-	-	-	-	-	-	-	-	-	-	-
Ionia County	61,518	219 0.36	-	-	-	-	-	-	-	-	-	-	-	-	-	-	-	-	-	-	-	-	-	-
Isabella County	63,351	799 1.26	-	-	-	-	-	-	-	-	-	-	-	-	-	-	-	-	-	-	-	-	-	-
Jackson County	158,422	732 0.46	-	-	-	-	-	-	-	-	-	-	-	-	-	-	-	-	-	-	-	-	-	-
Kalamazoo County	238,603	4,315 1.81	-	1,281 29.69 0.54	-	-	859 19.91 0.36	-	-	-	-	-	-	-	709 16.43 0.30	-	-	-	-	-	-	-	-	-

Notes: Please refer to the User's Guide for an explanation of data; data is arranged alphabetically by state, then county, then city within each county; table includes counties with populations greater than 49,999 unless noted and cities with populations greater than 9,999 whose Asian and/or NHPI population rates are greater than the national average; (1) Native Hawaiian and other Pacific Islander; (2) excludes Taiwanese; (3) includes Chamorro; (4) county does not meet population threshold but is shown in order to allow inclusion of city

Place	Total population	Total Asian population	Total NHPI[1] population	Asian Indian	Bangladeshi	Cambodian	Chinese[2]	Fijian	Filipino	Guamanian[3]	Hawaiian, Native	Hmong	Indonesian	Japanese	Korean	Laotian	Malaysian	Pakistani	Samoan	Sri Lankan	Taiwanese	Thai	Tongan	Vietnamese
Kent County	574,335	10,515 1.83	-	1,385 13.17 0.24	-	-	1,050 9.99 0.18	-	632 6.01 0.11	-	-	-	-	-	1,895 18.02 0.33	-	-	-	-	-	-	-	-	4,315 41.04 0.75
Kentwood (city)	45,239	2,504 5.54	-	-	-	-	-	-	-	-	-	-	-	-	445 17.77 0.98	-	-	-	-	-	-	-	-	1,223 48.84 2.70
Lenawee County	98,890	533 0.54	-	-	-	-	-	-	-	-	-	-	-	-	-	-	-	-	-	-	-	-	-	-
Livingston County	156,951	1,059 0.67	-	-	-	-	-	-	-	-	-	-	-	-	-	-	-	-	-	-	-	-	-	-
Macomb County	788,149	17,378 2.20	-	5,545 31.91 0.70	-	-	2,393 13.77 0.30	-	3,410 19.62 0.43	-	-	1,082 6.23 0.14	-	-	1,515 8.72 0.19	-	-	530 3.05 0.07	-	-	-	-	-	1,424 8.19 0.18
Sterling Heights (city)	124,471	6,510 5.23	-	2,420 37.17 1.94	-	-	981 15.07 0.79	-	1,332 20.46 1.07	-	-	-	-	-	631 9.69 0.51	-	-	-	-	-	-	-	-	448 6.88 0.36
Marquette County	64,634	306 0.47	-	-	-	-	-	-	-	-	-	-	-	-	-	-	-	-	-	-	-	-	-	-
Midland County	82,874	1,165 1.41	-	380 32.62 0.46	-	-	389 33.39 0.47	-	-	-	-	-	-	-	-	-	-	-	-	-	-	-	-	-
Monroe County	145,945	944 0.65	-	-	-	-	-	-	-	-	-	-	-	-	-	-	-	-	-	-	-	-	-	-
Muskegon County	170,200	745 0.44	-	-	-	-	-	-	-	-	-	-	-	-	-	-	-	-	-	-	-	-	-	-
Oakland County	1,194,156	48,378 4.05	-	19,155 39.59 1.60	-	-	8,697 17.98 0.73	-	4,002 8.27 0.34	-	-	1,081 2.23 0.09	-	4,282 8.85 0.36	4,826 9.98 0.40	-	-	973 2.01 0.08	-	-	1,259 2.60 0.11	-	-	1,647 3.40 0.14
Auburn Hills (city)	19,801	1,229 6.21	-	676 55.00 3.41	-	-	-	-	-	-	-	-	-	-	-	-	-	-	-	-	-	-	-	-
Bloomfield (township)	43,027	2,717 6.31	-	1,176 43.28 2.73	-	-	-	-	-	-	-	-	-	-	577 21.24 1.34	-	-	-	-	-	-	-	-	-
Farmington (city)	10,423	1,065 10.22	-	823 77.28 7.90	-	-	-	-	-	-	-	-	-	-	-	-	-	-	-	-	-	-	-	-
Farmington Hills (city)	82,111	5,722 6.97	-	3,421 59.79 4.17	-	-	880 15.38 1.07	-	375 6.55 0.46	-	-	-	-	-	-	-	-	-	-	-	-	-	-	-
Madison Heights (city)	31,101	1,595 5.13	-	-	-	-	547 34.29 1.76	-	-	-	-	-	-	-	-	-	-	-	-	-	-	-	-	-
Novi (city)	47,459	3,991 8.41	-	1,117 27.99 2.35	-	-	813 20.37 1.71	-	-	-	-	-	-	1,148 28.76 2.42	-	-	-	-	-	-	-	-	-	-

Notes: Please refer to the User's Guide for an explanation of data; data is arranged alphabetically by state, then county, then city within each county; table includes counties with populations greater than 49,999 unless noted and cities with populations greater than 9,999 whose Asian and/or NHPI population rates are greater than the national average; (1) Native Hawaiian and other Pacific Islander; (2) excludes Taiwanese; (3) includes Chamorro; (4) county does not meet population threshold but is shown in order to allow inclusion of city

Place	Total population	Total Asian population	Total NHPI[1] population	Asian Indian	Bangladeshi	Cambodian	Chinese[2]	Fijian	Filipino	Guamanian[3]	Hawaiian, Native	Hmong	Indonesian	Japanese	Korean	Laotian	Malaysian	Pakistani	Samoan	Sri Lankan	Taiwanese	Thai	Tongan	Vietnamese
Rochester (city)	10,467	549 5.25	-	-	-	-	-	-	-	-	-	-	-	-	-	-	-	-	-	-	-	-	-	-
Rochester Hills (city)	68,840	4,596 6.68	-	1,951 42.45 2.83	-	-	1,016 22.11 1.48	-	-	-	-	-	-	-	372 8.09 0.54	-	-	-	-	-	-	-	-	-
Troy (city)	80,959	10,378 12.82	-	4,656 44.86 5.75	-	-	2,284 22.01 2.82	-	751 7.24 0.93	-	-	-	-	-	1,232 11.87 1.52	-	-	-	-	-	558 5.38 0.69	-	-	-
West Bloomfield (township)	64,804	4,994 7.71	-	1,691 33.86 2.61	-	-	596 11.93 0.92	-	428 8.57 0.66	-	-	-	-	1,272 25.47 1.96	499 9.99 0.77	-	-	-	-	-	-	-	-	-
Ottawa County	238,314	5,180 2.17	-	469 9.05 0.20	-	1,083 20.91 0.45	424 8.19 0.18	-	-	-	-	-	-	-	535 10.33 0.22	1,147 22.14 0.48	-	-	-	-	-	-	-	737 14.23 0.31
Holland (city)	35,211	1,271 3.61	-	-	-	-	-	-	-	-	-	-	-	-	-	-	-	-	-	-	-	-	-	-
Saginaw County	210,039	1,747 0.83	-	339 19.40 0.16	-	-	-	-	375 21.47 0.18	-	-	-	-	-	338 19.35 0.16	-	-	-	-	-	-	-	-	-
St. Clair County	164,235	424 0.26	-	-	-	-	-	-	-	-	-	-	-	-	-	-	-	-	-	-	-	-	-	-
St. Joseph County	62,422	297 0.48	-	-	-	-	-	-	-	-	-	-	-	-	-	-	-	-	-	-	-	-	-	-
Washtenaw County	322,895	20,021 6.20	-	4,740 23.68 1.47	-	-	6,061 30.27 1.88	-	946 4.73 0.29	-	-	-	-	1,709 8.54 0.53	3,690 18.43 1.14	-	-	465 2.32 0.14	-	-	520 2.60 0.16	-	-	458 2.29 0.14
Ann Arbor (city)	114,110	13,389 11.73	-	3,245 24.24 2.84	-	-	4,207 31.42 3.69	-	529 3.95 0.46	-	-	-	-	1,273 9.51 1.12	2,525 18.86 2.21	-	-	-	-	-	441 3.29 0.39	-	-	-
Pittsfield charter (township)	30,126	2,769 9.19	-	660 23.84 2.19	-	-	784 28.31 2.60	-	-	-	-	-	-	-	566 20.44 1.88	-	-	-	-	-	-	-	-	-
Scio (township)	15,674	611 3.90	-	-	-	-	-	-	-	-	-	-	-	-	-	-	-	-	-	-	-	-	-	-
Wayne County	2,061,162	35,273 1.71	495 0.02	14,502 41.11 0.70	1,163 3.30 0.06	-	4,985 14.13 0.24	-	4,298 12.18 0.21	-	-	1,833 5.20 0.09	-	1,047 2.97 0.05	1,803 5.11 0.09	-	-	2,178 6.17 0.11	-	-	-	-	-	1,213 3.44 0.06
Brownstown (township)	22,989	925 4.02	-	-	-	-	-	-	-	-	-	-	-	-	-	-	-	-	-	-	-	-	-	-
Canton (township)	76,310	6,569 8.61	-	3,556 54.13 4.66	-	-	1,244 18.94 1.63	-	613 9.33 0.80	-	-	-	-	-	299 4.55 0.39	-	-	-	-	-	-	-	-	-
Hamtramck (city)	22,976	2,358 10.26	-	1,130 47.92 4.92	740 31.38 3.22	-	-	-	-	-	-	-	-	-	-	-	-	-	-	-	-	-	-	-

Notes: Please refer to the User's Guide for an explanation of data; data is arranged alphabetically by state, then county, then city within each county; table includes counties with populations greater than 49,999 unless noted and cities with populations greater than 9,999 whose Asian and/or NHPI population rates are greater than the national average; (1) Native Hawaiian and other Pacific Islander; (2) excludes Taiwanese; (3) includes Chamorro; (4) county does not meet population threshold but is shown in order to allow inclusion of city

Place	Total population	Total Asian population	Total NHPI[1] population	Asian Indian	Bangladeshi	Cambodian	Chinese[2]	Fijian	Filipino	Guamanian[3]	Hawaiian, Native	Hmong	Indonesian	Japanese	Korean	Laotian	Malaysian	Pakistani	Samoan	Sri Lankan	Taiwanese	Thai	Tongan	Vietnamese
Inkster (city)	30,115	1,140 3.79	-	742 65.09 2.46	-	-	-	-	-	-	-	-	-	-	-	-	-	-	-	-	-	-	-	-
Northville (township)	21,036	922 4.38	-	429 46.53 2.04	-	-	-	-	-	-	-	-	-	-	-	-	-	-	-	-	-	-	-	-
MINNESOTA	4,919,479	139,245 2.83	1,724 0.04	16,278 11.69 0.33	-	5,128 3.68 0.10	14,917 10.71 0.30	-	5,900 4.24 0.12	427 24.77 0.01	579 33.58 0.01	43,156 30.99 0.88	-	4,183 3.00 0.09	12,853 9.23 0.26	8,997 6.46 0.18	-	1,098 0.79 0.02	-	-	463 0.33 0.01	920 0.66 0.02	-	18,384 13.20 0.37
Anoka County	298,084	4,992 1.67	-	909 18.21 0.30	-	-	440 8.81 0.15	-	380 7.61 0.13	-	-	571 11.44 0.19	-	-	708 14.18 0.24	-	-	-	-	-	-	-	-	948 18.99 0.32
Columbia Heights (city)	18,512	672 3.63	-	-	-	-	-	-	-	-	-	-	-	-	-	-	-	-	-	-	-	-	-	-
Blue Earth County	55,941	883 1.58	-	-	-	-	-	-	-	-	-	-	-	-	-	-	-	-	-	-	-	-	-	-
Carver County	70,205	1,039 1.48	-	-	-	-	-	-	-	-	-	-	-	-	-	-	-	-	-	-	-	-	-	-
Clay County	51,229	394 0.77	-	-	-	-	-	-	-	-	-	-	-	-	-	-	-	-	-	-	-	-	-	-
Crow Wing County	55,099	218 0.40	-	-	-	-	-	-	-	-	-	-	-	-	-	-	-	-	-	-	-	-	-	-
Dakota County	355,904	9,152 2.57	-	1,695 18.52 0.48	-	451 4.93 0.13	1,381 15.09 0.39	-	817 8.93 0.23	-	-	-	-	-	1,113 12.16 0.31	729 7.97 0.20	-	-	-	-	-	-	-	1,755 19.18 0.49
Eagan (city)	63,629	3,087 4.85	-	668 21.64 1.05	-	-	500 16.20 0.79	-	-	-	-	-	-	-	-	-	-	-	-	-	-	-	-	570 18.46 0.90
Hennepin County	1,116,200	53,136 4.76	583 0.05	7,805 14.69 0.70	-	1,788 3.36 0.16	6,042 11.37 0.54	-	1,875 3.53 0.17	-	-	13,324 25.08 1.19	-	1,683 3.17 0.15	4,729 8.90 0.42	4,409 8.30 0.40	-	408 0.77 0.04	-	-	-	-	-	8,150 15.34 0.73
Bloomington (city)	85,202	4,254 4.99	-	541 12.72 0.63	-	489 11.50 0.57	796 18.71 0.93	-	-	-	-	-	-	-	504 11.85 0.59	-	-	-	-	-	-	-	-	1,171 27.53 1.37
Brooklyn Center (city)	29,061	2,606 8.97	-	-	-	-	-	-	-	-	-	1,452 55.72 5.00	-	-	-	320 12.28 1.10	-	-	-	-	-	-	-	-
Brooklyn Park (city)	67,388	6,200 9.20	-	914 14.74 1.36	-	-	-	-	-	-	-	1,100 17.74 1.63	-	-	-	1,445 23.31 2.14	-	-	-	-	-	-	-	1,486 23.97 2.21
Eden Prairie (city)	54,901	2,793 5.09	-	586 20.98 1.07	-	-	673 24.10 1.23	-	-	-	-	-	-	-	-	-	-	-	-	-	-	-	-	530 18.98 0.97
Hopkins (city)	17,061	964 5.65	-	460 47.72 2.70	-	-	-	-	-	-	-	-	-	-	-	-	-	-	-	-	-	-	-	-

Notes: Please refer to the User's Guide for an explanation of data; data is arranged alphabetically by state, then county, then city within each county; table includes counties with populations greater than 49,999 unless noted and cities with populations greater than 9,999 whose Asian and/or NHPI population rates are greater than the national average; (1) Native Hawaiian and other Pacific Islander; (2) excludes Taiwanese; (3) includes Chamorro; (4) county does not meet population threshold but is shown in order to allow inclusion of city

Place	Total population	Total Asian population	Total NHPI[1] population	Asian Indian	Bangladeshi	Cambodian	Chinese[2]	Fijian	Filipino	Guamanian[3]	Hawaiian, Native	Hmong	Indonesian	Japanese	Korean	Laotian	Malaysian	Pakistani	Samoan	Sri Lankan	Taiwanese	Thai	Tongan	Vietnamese
Minneapolis (city)	382,452	23,912 6.25	-	2,094 8.76 0.55	-	498 2.08 0.13	2,064 8.63 0.54	-	727 3.04 0.19	-	-	10,266 42.93 2.68	-	762 3.19 0.20	1,623 6.79 0.42	1,627 6.80 0.43	-	-	-	-	-	-	-	2,804 11.73 0.73
Plymouth (city)	65,903	2,463 3.74	-	919 37.31 1.39	-	-	427 17.34 0.65	-	-	-	-	-	-	-	361 14.66 0.55	-	-	-	-	-	-	-	-	-
Richfield (city)	34,441	1,760 5.11	-	-	-	-	-	-	-	-	-	-	-	-	-	-	-	-	-	-	-	-	-	421 23.92 1.22
Nobles County[4]	20,832	774 3.72	-	-	-	-	-	-	-	-	-	-	-	-	-	404 52.20 1.94	-	-	-	-	-	-	-	-
Worthington (city)	11,288	706 6.25	-	-	-	-	-	-	-	-	-	-	-	-	-	371 52.55 3.29	-	-	-	-	-	-	-	-
Olmsted County	124,277	5,329 4.29	-	1,014 19.03 0.82	-	722 13.55 0.58	589 11.05 0.47	-	-	-	-	400 7.51 0.32	-	429 8.05 0.35	492 9.23 0.40	440 8.26 0.35	-	-	-	-	-	-	-	726 13.62 0.58
Rochester (city)	85,392	4,806 5.63	-	958 19.93 1.12	-	559 11.63 0.65	551 11.46 0.65	-	-	-	-	400 8.32 0.47	-	-	379 7.89 0.44	438 9.11 0.51	-	-	-	-	-	-	-	695 14.46 0.81
Otter Tail County	57,159	171 0.30	-	-	-	-	-	-	-	-	-	-	-	-	-	-	-	-	-	-	-	-	-	-
Ramsey County	511,035	44,030 8.62	-	2,319 5.27 0.45	-	1,110 2.52 0.22	3,460 7.86 0.68	-	896 2.03 0.18	-	-	26,620 60.46 5.21	-	542 1.23 0.11	1,989 4.52 0.39	933 2.12 0.18	-	-	-	-	-	-	-	3,601 8.18 0.70
Maplewood (city)	34,942	1,358 3.89	-	-	-	-	307 22.61 0.88	-	-	-	-	396 29.16 1.13	-	-	-	-	-	-	-	-	-	-	-	-
New Brighton (city)	22,249	916 4.12	-	-	-	-	-	-	-	-	-	-	-	-	-	-	-	-	-	-	-	-	-	-
Roseville (city)	33,757	1,624 4.81	-	-	-	-	679 41.81 2.01	-	-	-	-	-	-	-	-	-	-	-	-	-	-	-	-	-
St. Paul (city)	287,151	35,316 12.30	-	849 2.40 0.30	-	928 2.63 0.32	984 2.79 0.34	-	538 1.52 0.19	-	-	25,482 72.15 8.87	-	-	913 2.59 0.32	861 2.44 0.30	-	-	-	-	-	-	-	2,553 7.23 0.89
Vadnais Heights (city)	13,062	567 4.34	-	-	-	-	-	-	-	-	-	-	-	-	-	-	-	-	-	-	-	-	-	-
Rice County	56,665	885 1.56	-	-	-	-	-	-	-	-	-	-	-	-	-	-	-	-	-	-	-	-	-	-
St. Louis County	200,528	1,504 0.75	-	-	-	-	-	-	-	-	-	-	-	-	361 24.00 0.18	-	-	-	-	-	-	-	-	-
Scott County	89,498	1,867 2.09	-	-	-	362 19.39 0.40	-	-	-	-	-	-	-	-	-	-	-	-	-	-	-	-	-	394 21.10 0.44

Notes: Please refer to the User's Guide for an explanation of data; data is arranged alphabetically by state, then county, then city within each county; table includes counties with populations greater than 49,999 unless noted and cities with populations greater than 9,999 whose Asian and/or NHPI population rates are greater than the national average; (1) Native Hawaiian and other Pacific Islander; (2) excludes Taiwanese; (3) includes Chamorro; (4) county does not meet population threshold but is shown in order to allow inclusion of city

Place	Total population	Total Asian population	Total NHPI[1] population	Asian Indian	Bangladeshi	Cambodian	Chinese[2]	Fijian	Filipino	Guamanian[3]	Hawaiian, Native	Hmong	Indonesian	Japanese	Korean	Laotian	Malaysian	Pakistani	Samoan	Sri Lankan	Taiwanese	Thai	Tongan	Vietnamese
Savage (city)	21,184	1,101 5.20	-	-	-	-	-	-	-	-	-	-	-	-	-	-	-	-	-	-	-	-	-	-
Sherburne County	64,417	374 0.58	-	-	-	-	-	-	-	-	-	-	-	-	-	-	-	-	-	-	-	-	-	-
Stearns County	133,166	1,796 1.35	-	-	-	-	-	-	-	-	-	-	-	-	-	-	-	-	-	-	-	-	-	610 33.96 0.46
Washington County	201,130	4,362 2.17	-	569 13.04 0.28	-	-	706 16.19 0.35	-	-	-	-	771 17.68 0.38	-	-	680 15.59 0.34	-	-	-	-	-	-	-	-	529 12.13 0.26
Woodbury (city)	46,464	2,382 5.13	-	427 17.93 0.92	-	-	377 15.83 0.81	-	-	-	-	353 14.82 0.76	-	-	-	-	-	-	-	-	-	-	-	-
Wright County	89,986	196 0.22	-	-	-	-	-	-	-	-	-	-	-	-	-	-	-	-	-	-	-	-	-	-
MISSISSIPPI	2,844,658	17,709 0.62	677 0.02	3,325 18.78 0.12	-	-	2,666 15.05 0.09	-	2,619 14.79 0.09	-	-	-	-	538 3.04 0.02	1,378 7.78 0.05	-	-	-	-	-	-	-	-	5,337 30.14 0.19
DeSoto County	107,199	676 0.63	-	-	-	-	-	-	-	-	-	-	-	-	-	-	-	-	-	-	-	-	-	-
Forrest County	72,604	626 0.86	-	-	-	-	-	-	-	-	-	-	-	-	-	-	-	-	-	-	-	-	-	-
Harrison County	189,601	4,976 2.62	-	-	-	-	-	-	814 16.36 0.43	-	-	-	-	-	-	-	-	-	-	-	-	-	-	2,797 56.21 1.48
Biloxi (city)	50,713	2,451 4.83	-	-	-	-	-	-	430 17.54 0.85	-	-	-	-	-	-	-	-	-	-	-	-	-	-	1,483 60.51 2.92
Hinds County	250,800	1,315 0.52	-	580 44.11 0.23	-	-	-	-	-	-	-	-	-	-	-	-	-	-	-	-	-	-	-	-
Jackson County	131,420	1,945 1.48	-	-	-	-	-	-	-	-	-	-	-	-	-	-	-	-	-	-	-	-	-	1,060 54.50 0.81
Madison County	74,674	585 0.78	-	-	-	-	-	-	-	-	-	-	-	-	-	-	-	-	-	-	-	-	-	-
Oktibbeha County[4]	42,902	1,077 2.51	-	-	-	-	-	-	-	-	-	-	-	-	-	-	-	-	-	-	-	-	-	-
Starkville (city)	22,037	798 3.62	-	-	-	-	-	-	-	-	-	-	-	-	-	-	-	-	-	-	-	-	-	-
Rankin County	115,327	554 0.48	-	-	-	-	-	-	-	-	-	-	-	-	-	-	-	-	-	-	-	-	-	-

Notes: Please refer to the User's Guide for an explanation of data; data is arranged alphabetically by state, then county, then city within each county; table includes counties with populations greater than 49,999 unless noted and cities with populations greater than 9,999 whose Asian and/or NHPI population rates are greater than the national average; (1) Native Hawaiian and other Pacific Islander; (2) excludes Taiwanese; (3) includes Chamorro; (4) county does not meet population threshold but is shown in order to allow inclusion of city

Place	Total population	Total Asian population	Total NHPI[1] population	Asian Indian	Bangladeshi	Cambodian	Chinese[2]	Fijian	Filipino	Guamanian[3]	Hawaiian, Native	Hmong	Indonesian	Japanese	Korean	Laotian	Malaysian	Pakistani	Samoan	Sri Lankan	Taiwanese	Thai	Tongan	Vietnamese
MISSOURI	5,595,211	60,429 1.08	3,071 0.05	11,845 19.60 0.21	-	879 1.45 0.02	12,766 21.13 0.23	-	7,254 12.00 0.13	612 19.93 0.01	695 22.63 0.01	-	-	3,425 5.67 0.06	6,507 10.77 0.12	716 1.18 0.01	-	1,053 1.74 0.02	1,004 32.69 0.02	-	972 1.61 0.02	1,372 2.27 0.02	-	10,506 17.39 0.19
Boone County	135,454	3,865 2.85	-	808 20.91 0.60	-	-	1,202 31.10 0.89	-	-	-	-	-	-	-	513 13.27 0.38	-	-	-	-	-	-	-	-	-
Columbia (city)	84,780	3,574 4.22	-	781 21.85 0.92	-	-	1,152 32.23 1.36	-	-	-	-	-	-	-	425 11.89 0.50	-	-	-	-	-	-	-	-	-
Cape Girardeau County	68,693	446 0.65	-	-	-	-	-	-	-	-	-	-	-	-	-	-	-	-	-	-	-	-	-	-
Cass County	82,092	346 0.42	-	-	-	-	-	-	-	-	-	-	-	-	-	-	-	-	-	-	-	-	-	-
Clay County	184,006	2,165 1.18	-	405 18.71 0.22	-	-	-	-	-	-	-	-	-	-	-	-	-	-	-	-	-	-	-	617 28.50 0.34
Cole County	71,397	661 0.93	-	-	-	-	-	-	-	-	-	-	-	-	-	-	-	-	-	-	-	-	-	-
Franklin County	93,807	326 0.35	-	-	-	-	-	-	-	-	-	-	-	-	-	-	-	-	-	-	-	-	-	-
Greene County	240,391	2,207 0.92	-	-	-	-	364 16.49 0.15	-	-	-	-	-	-	-	359 16.27 0.15	-	-	-	-	-	-	-	-	417 18.89 0.17
Jackson County	654,880	8,646 1.32	926 0.14	1,070 12.38 0.16	-	-	1,277 14.77 0.19	-	1,277 14.77 0.19	-	-	-	-	408 4.72 0.06	568 6.57 0.09	-	-	-	470 50.76 0.07	-	-	-	-	2,880 33.31 0.44
Independence (city)	113,207	1,022 0.90	405 0.36	-	-	-	-	-	-	-	-	-	-	-	-	-	-	-	-	-	-	-	-	-
Jasper County	104,686	598 0.57	-	-	-	-	-	-	-	-	-	-	-	-	-	-	-	-	-	-	-	-	-	-
Jefferson County	198,099	745 0.38	-	-	-	-	-	-	-	-	-	-	-	-	-	-	-	-	-	-	-	-	-	-
Newton County	52,636	177 0.34	-	-	-	-	-	-	-	-	-	-	-	-	-	-	-	-	-	-	-	-	-	-
Phelps County[4]	39,825	836 2.10	-	325 38.88 0.82	-	-	-	-	-	-	-	-	-	-	-	-	-	-	-	-	-	-	-	-
Rolla (city)	16,540	684 4.14	-	-	-	-	-	-	-	-	-	-	-	-	-	-	-	-	-	-	-	-	-	-
Platte County	73,781	1,115 1.51	-	-	-	-	-	-	-	-	-	-	-	-	-	-	-	-	-	-	-	-	-	-

Notes: Please refer to the User's Guide for an explanation of data; data is arranged alphabetically by state, then county, then city within each county; table includes counties with populations greater than 49,999 unless noted and cities with populations greater than 9,999 whose Asian and/or NHPI population rates are greater than the national average; (1) Native Hawaiian and other Pacific Islander; (2) excludes Taiwanese; (3) includes Chamorro; (4) county does not meet population threshold but is shown in order to allow inclusion of city

Place	Total population	Total Asian population	Total NHPI[1] population	Asian Indian	Bangladeshi	Cambodian	Chinese[2]	Fijian	Filipino	Guamanian[3]	Hawaiian, Native	Hmong	Indonesian	Japanese	Korean	Laotian	Malaysian	Pakistani	Samoan	Sri Lankan	Taiwanese	Thai	Tongan	Vietnamese
St. Charles County	283,883	2,392 0.84	-	577 24.12 0.20	-	-	415 17.35 0.15	-	403 16.85 0.14	-	-	-	-	-	-	-	-	-	-	-	-	-	-	-
Saint Louis Independent City	348,189	7,075 2.03	-	737 10.42 0.21	-	-	1,128 15.94 0.32	-	548 7.75 0.16	-	-	-	-	-	-	-	-	-	-	-	-	-	-	3,219 45.50 0.92
St. Louis County	1,016,315	21,534 2.12	437 0.04	5,699 26.47 0.56	-	-	6,003 27.88 0.59	-	2,012 9.34 0.20	-	-	-	-	1,211 5.62 0.12	2,546 11.82 0.25	-	-	569 2.64 0.06	-	-	648 3.01 0.06	378 1.76 0.04	-	1,468 6.82 0.14
Chesterfield (city)	46,973	2,442 5.20	-	663 27.15 1.41	-	-	793 32.47 1.69	-	-	-	-	-	-	-	-	-	-	-	-	-	-	-	-	-
Clayton (city)	12,826	788 6.14	-	-	-	-	-	-	-	-	-	-	-	-	-	-	-	-	-	-	-	-	-	-
Creve Coeur (city)	16,291	872 5.35	-	-	-	-	-	-	-	-	-	-	-	-	-	-	-	-	-	-	-	-	-	-
Manchester (city)	19,080	935 4.90	-	-	-	-	-	-	-	-	-	-	-	-	-	-	-	-	-	-	-	-	-	-
Maryland Heights (city)	25,937	1,788 6.89	-	696 38.93 2.68	-	-	512 28.64 1.97	-	-	-	-	-	-	-	-	-	-	-	-	-	-	-	-	-
Town and Country (city)	10,879	829 7.62	-	381 45.96 3.50	-	-	-	-	-	-	-	-	-	-	-	-	-	-	-	-	-	-	-	-
MONTANA	902,195	4,363 0.48	447 0.05	450 10.31 0.05	-	-	650 14.90 0.07	-	785 17.99 0.09	-	264 59.06 0.03	-	-	850 19.48 0.09	839 19.23 0.09	-	-	-	-	-	-	-	-	-
Cascade County	80,357	498 0.62	-	-	-	-	-	-	-	-	-	-	-	-	-	-	-	-	-	-	-	-	-	-
Flathead County	74,471	251 0.34	-	-	-	-	-	-	-	-	-	-	-	-	-	-	-	-	-	-	-	-	-	-
Gallatin County	67,831	693 1.02	-	-	-	-	-	-	-	-	-	-	-	-	-	-	-	-	-	-	-	-	-	-
Missoula County	95,802	919 0.96	-	-	-	-	-	-	-	-	-	-	-	-	-	-	-	-	-	-	-	-	-	-
Yellowstone County	129,352	666 0.51	-	-	-	-	-	-	-	-	-	-	-	-	-	-	-	-	-	-	-	-	-	-
NEBRASKA	1,711,263	21,126 1.23	673 0.04	3,199 15.14 0.19	-	-	2,847 13.48 0.17	-	2,065 9.77 0.12	-	-	-	-	1,383 6.55 0.08	2,229 10.55 0.13	816 3.86 0.05	-	-	-	-	-	461 2.18 0.03	-	6,680 31.62 0.39
Douglas County	463,585	7,912 1.71	-	2,039 25.77 0.44	-	-	1,389 17.56 0.30	-	885 11.19 0.19	-	-	-	-	695 8.78 0.15	818 10.34 0.18	-	-	-	-	-	-	-	-	1,282 16.20 0.28

Notes: Please refer to the User's Guide for an explanation of data; data is arranged alphabetically by state, then county, then city within each county; table includes counties with populations greater than 49,999 unless noted and cities with populations greater than 9,999 whose Asian and/or NHPI population rates are greater than the national average; (1) Native Hawaiian and other Pacific Islander; (2) excludes Taiwanese; (3) includes Chamorro; (4) county does not meet population threshold but is shown in order to allow inclusion of city

Place	Total population	Total Asian population	Total NHPI[1] population	Asian Indian	Bangladeshi	Cambodian	Chinese[2]	Fijian	Filipino	Guamanian[3]	Hawaiian, Native	Hmong	Indonesian	Japanese	Korean	Laotian	Malaysian	Pakistani	Samoan	Sri Lankan	Taiwanese	Thai	Tongan	Vietnamese
Hall County	53,534	544 1.02	-	-	-	-	-	-	-	-	-	-	-	-	-	-	-	-	-	-	-	-	-	-
Lancaster County	250,291	6,700 2.68	-	650 9.70 0.26	-	-	967 14.43 0.39	-	-	-	-	-	-	-	363 5.42 0.15	-	-	-	-	-	-	-	-	3,776 56.36 1.51
Sarpy County	122,595	2,230 1.82	-	-	-	-	-	-	493 22.11 0.40	-	-	-	-	-	458 20.54 0.37	-	-	-	-	-	-	-	-	422 18.92 0.34
NEVADA	1,998,257	89,121 4.46	7,806 0.39	4,860 5.45 0.24	-	738 0.83 0.04	13,540 15.19 0.68	-	40,527 45.47 2.03	1,139 14.59 0.06	3,405 43.62 0.17	-	-	8,395 9.42 0.42	7,582 8.51 0.38	1,189 1.33 0.06	-	532 0.60 0.03	1,567 20.07 0.08	-	597 0.67 0.03	2,977 3.34 0.15	790 10.12 0.04	4,095 4.59 0.20
Carson City Independent City	52,457	1,070 2.04	-	-	-	-	-	-	276 25.79 0.53	-	-	-	-	-	-	-	-	-	-	-	-	-	-	-
Clark County	1,375,765	71,495 5.20	5,918 0.43	2,920 4.08 0.21	-	718 1.00 0.05	10,730 15.01 0.78	-	32,626 45.63 2.37	958 16.19 0.07	3,080 52.04 0.22	-	-	6,694 9.36 0.49	6,527 9.13 0.47	1,177 1.65 0.09	-	-	1,116 18.86 0.08	-	429 0.60 0.03	2,620 3.66 0.19	-	3,292 4.60 0.24
Enterprise (cdp)	14,437	701 4.86	-	-	-	-	-	-	-	-	-	-	-	-	-	-	-	-	-	-	-	-	-	-
Henderson (city)	176,048	6,683 3.80	758 0.43	466 6.97 0.26	-	-	803 12.02 0.46	-	2,733 40.89 1.55	-	443 58.44 0.25	-	-	777 11.63 0.44	821 12.28 0.47	-	-	-	-	-	-	-	-	-
Las Vegas (city)	478,868	21,634 4.52	1,673 0.35	1,007 4.65 0.21	-	-	2,720 12.57 0.57	-	10,791 49.88 2.25	-	781 46.68 0.16	-	-	2,453 11.34 0.51	1,435 6.63 0.30	-	-	-	-	-	-	700 3.24 0.15	-	610 2.82 0.13
North Las Vegas (city)	115,489	3,845 3.33	747 0.65	-	-	-	-	-	2,195 57.09 1.90	-	-	-	-	-	-	-	-	-	-	-	-	-	-	-
Paradise (cdp)	185,832	12,628 6.80	841 0.45	642 5.08 0.35	-	-	1,835 14.53 0.99	-	5,692 45.07 3.06	-	599 71.22 0.32	-	-	1,408 11.15 0.76	1,362 10.79 0.73	-	-	-	-	-	-	-	-	584 4.62 0.31
Spring Valley (cdp)	117,649	12,944 11.00	657 0.56	-	-	-	4,222 32.62 3.59	-	3,910 30.21 3.32	-	-	-	-	720 5.56 0.61	1,353 10.45 1.15	-	-	-	-	-	-	497 3.84 0.42	-	975 7.53 0.83
Sunrise Manor (cdp)	155,683	8,644 5.55	429 0.28	-	-	-	482 5.58 0.31	-	4,830 55.88 3.10	-	-	-	-	601 6.95 0.39	731 8.46 0.47	-	-	-	-	-	-	-	-	-
Winchester (cdp)	26,802	1,480 5.52	-	-	-	-	-	-	449 30.34 1.68	-	-	-	-	-	-	-	-	-	-	-	-	-	-	-
Washoe County	339,486	14,327 4.22	1,502 0.44	1,603 11.19 0.47	-	-	2,373 16.56 0.70	-	6,422 44.82 1.89	-	-	-	-	1,284 8.96 0.38	753 5.26 0.22	-	-	-	-	-	-	-	577 38.42 0.17	712 4.97 0.21
Reno (city)	180,658	9,438 5.22	952 0.53	950 10.07 0.53	-	-	1,487 15.76 0.82	-	4,272 45.26 2.36	-	-	-	-	934 9.90 0.52	451 4.78 0.25	-	-	-	-	-	-	-	-	459 4.86 0.25
Sparks (city)	66,532	3,133 4.71	-	-	-	-	655 20.91 0.98	-	1,454 46.41 2.19	-	-	-	-	-	-	-	-	-	-	-	-	-	-	-

Notes: Please refer to the User's Guide for an explanation of data; data is arranged alphabetically by state, then county, then city within each county; table includes counties with populations greater than 49,999 unless noted and cities with populations greater than 9,999 whose Asian and/or NHPI population rates are greater than the national average; (1) Native Hawaiian and other Pacific Islander; (2) excludes Taiwanese; (3) includes Chamorro; (4) county does not meet population threshold but is shown in order to allow inclusion of city

Place	Total population	Total Asian population	Total NHPI[1] population	Asian Indian	Bangladeshi	Cambodian	Chinese[2]	Fijian	Filipino	Guamanian[3]	Hawaiian, Native	Hmong	Indonesian	Japanese	Korean	Laotian	Malaysian	Pakistani	Samoan	Sri Lankan	Taiwanese	Thai	Tongan	Vietnamese
NEW HAMPSHIRE	1,235,786	15,422 1.25	-	3,579 23.21 0.29	-	-	3,873 25.11 0.31	-	1,272 8.25 0.10	-	-	-	-	936 6.07 0.08	1,950 12.64 0.16	371 2.41 0.03	-	-	-	-	-	-	-	1,682 10.91 0.14
Belknap County	56,325	347 0.62	-	-	-	-	-	-	-	-	-	-	-	-	-	-	-	-	-	-	-	-	-	-
Cheshire County	73,825	486 0.66	-	-	-	-	-	-	-	-	-	-	-	-	-	-	-	-	-	-	-	-	-	-
Grafton County	81,743	1,251 1.53	-	-	-	-	422 33.73 0.52	-	-	-	-	-	-	-	-	-	-	-	-	-	-	-	-	-
Hanover (town)	10,850	653 6.02	-	-	-	-	-	-	-	-	-	-	-	-	-	-	-	-	-	-	-	-	-	-
Hillsborough County	380,841	7,366 1.93	-	2,169 29.45 0.57	-	-	1,882 25.55 0.49	-	397 5.39 0.10	-	-	-	-	-	607 8.24 0.16	-	-	-	-	-	-	-	-	1,089 14.78 0.29
Nashua (city)	86,605	3,387 3.91	-	1,449 42.78 1.67	-	-	792 23.38 0.91	-	-	-	-	-	-	-	-	-	-	-	-	-	-	-	-	-
Merrimack County	136,225	1,134 0.83	-	-	-	-	-	-	-	-	-	-	-	-	-	-	-	-	-	-	-	-	-	-
Rockingham County	277,359	2,946 1.06	-	478 16.23 0.17	-	-	841 28.55 0.30	-	414 14.05 0.15	-	-	-	-	-	423 14.36 0.15	-	-	-	-	-	-	-	-	-
Strafford County	112,233	1,477 1.32	-	-	-	-	345 23.36 0.31	-	-	-	-	-	-	-	-	-	-	-	-	-	-	-	-	-
NEW JERSEY	8,414,350	481,794 5.73	2,709 0.03	169,209 35.12 2.01	2,256 0.47 0.03	658 0.14 0.01	94,444 19.60 1.12	-	88,408 18.35 1.05	602 22.22 0.01	652 24.07 0.01	-	1,020 0.21 0.01	13,780 2.86 0.16	64,328 13.35 0.76	480 0.10 0.01	-	12,450 2.58 0.15	639 23.59 0.01	1,335 0.28 0.02	5,851 1.21 0.07	1,845 0.38 0.02	-	14,979 3.11 0.18
Atlantic County	252,552	12,952 5.13	-	4,033 31.14 1.60	407 3.14 0.16	-	2,061 15.91 0.82	-	2,172 16.77 0.86	-	-	-	-	-	627 4.84 0.25	-	-	503 3.88 0.20	-	-	-	-	-	2,060 15.90 0.82
Atlantic City (city)	40,517	4,131 10.20	-	905 21.91 2.23	-	-	720 17.43 1.78	-	511 12.37 1.26	-	-	-	-	-	-	-	-	-	-	-	-	-	-	1,187 28.73 2.93
Brigantine (city)	12,594	780 6.19	-	-	-	-	-	-	-	-	-	-	-	-	-	-	-	-	-	-	-	-	-	-
Egg Harbor (township)	30,619	1,704 5.57	-	-	-	-	-	-	-	-	-	-	-	-	-	-	-	-	-	-	-	-	-	-
Galloway (township)	31,159	2,657 8.53	-	1,292 48.63 4.15	-	-	-	-	-	-	-	-	-	-	-	-	-	-	-	-	-	-	-	-
Ventnor City (city)	12,910	1,048 8.12	-	-	-	-	-	-	-	-	-	-	-	-	-	-	-	-	-	-	-	-	-	-

Notes: Please refer to the User's Guide for an explanation of data; data is arranged alphabetically by state, then county, then city within each county; table includes counties with populations greater than 49,999 unless noted and cities with populations greater than 9,999 whose Asian and/or NHPI population rates are greater than the national average; (1) Native Hawaiian and other Pacific Islander; (2) excludes Taiwanese; (3) includes Chamorro; (4) county does not meet population threshold but is shown in order to allow inclusion of city

Place	Total population	Total Asian population	Total NHPI[1] population	Asian Indian	Bangladeshi	Cambodian	Chinese[2]	Fijian	Filipino	Guamanian[3]	Hawaiian, Native	Hmong	Indonesian	Japanese	Korean	Laotian	Malaysian	Pakistani	Samoan	Sri Lankan	Taiwanese	Thai	Tongan	Vietnamese
Bergen County	884,118	94,124 10.65	-	17,398 18.48 1.97	-	-	13,057 13.87 1.48	-	14,898 15.83 1.69	-	-	-	-	6,997 7.43 0.79	36,102 38.36 4.08	-	-	1,501 1.59 0.17	-	-	829 0.88 0.09	503 0.53 0.06	-	526 0.56 0.06
Bergenfield (borough)	26,247	5,347 20.37	-	1,510 28.24 5.75	-	-	-	-	3,228 60.37 12.30	-	-	-	-	-	-	-	-	-	-	-	-	-	-	-
Cliffside Park (borough)	23,007	2,650 11.52	-	-	-	-	-	-	-	-	-	-	-	446 16.83 1.94	1,482 55.92 6.44	-	-	-	-	-	-	-	-	-
Dumont (borough)	17,503	1,927 11.01	-	541 28.07 3.09	-	-	-	-	605 31.40 3.46	-	-	-	-	-	-	-	-	-	-	-	-	-	-	-
Elmwood Park (borough)	18,925	1,638 8.66	-	1,016 62.03 5.37	-	-	-	-	-	-	-	-	-	-	-	-	-	-	-	-	-	-	-	-
Englewood (city)	26,203	1,388 5.30	-	-	-	-	-	-	419 30.19 1.60	-	-	-	-	-	-	-	-	-	-	-	-	-	-	-
Fair Lawn (borough)	31,637	1,829 5.78	-	653 35.70 2.06	-	-	-	-	536 29.31 1.69	-	-	-	-	-	-	-	-	-	-	-	-	-	-	-
Fairview (borough)	13,255	679 5.12	-	-	-	-	-	-	-	-	-	-	-	-	-	-	-	-	-	-	-	-	-	-
Fort Lee (borough)	35,461	11,004 31.03	-	606 5.51 1.71	-	-	1,724 15.67 4.86	-	-	-	-	-	-	2,008 18.25 5.66	5,911 53.72 16.67	-	-	-	-	-	-	-	-	-
Franklin Lakes (borough)	10,422	713 6.84	-	-	-	-	-	-	-	-	-	-	-	-	-	-	-	-	-	-	-	-	-	-
Glen Rock (borough)	11,546	722 6.25	-	-	-	-	-	-	-	-	-	-	-	-	-	-	-	-	-	-	-	-	-	-
Hackensack (city)	42,677	3,192 7.48	-	968 30.33 2.27	-	-	-	-	713 22.34 1.67	-	-	-	-	-	639 20.02 1.50	-	-	-	-	-	-	-	-	-
Hasbrouck Heights (borough)	11,662	626 5.37	-	-	-	-	-	-	-	-	-	-	-	-	-	-	-	-	-	-	-	-	-	-
Hillsdale (borough)	10,087	515 5.11	-	-	-	-	-	-	-	-	-	-	-	-	-	-	-	-	-	-	-	-	-	-
Little Ferry (borough)	10,800	1,845 17.08	-	432 23.41 4.00	-	-	-	-	384 20.81 3.56	-	-	-	-	-	738 40.00 6.83	-	-	-	-	-	-	-	-	-
Lodi (borough)	23,971	2,036 8.49	-	1,080 53.05 4.51	-	-	-	-	565 27.75 2.36	-	-	-	-	-	-	-	-	-	-	-	-	-	-	-
Lyndhurst (township)	19,383	1,160 5.98	-	-	-	-	-	-	-	-	-	-	-	-	-	-	-	-	-	-	-	-	-	-

Notes: Please refer to the User's Guide for an explanation of data; data is arranged alphabetically by state, then county, then city within each county; table includes counties with populations greater than 49,999 unless noted and cities with populations greater than 9,999 whose Asian and/or NHPI population rates are greater than the national average; (1) Native Hawaiian and other Pacific Islander; (2) excludes Taiwanese; (3) includes Chamorro; (4) county does not meet population threshold but is shown in order to allow inclusion of city

Place	Total population	Total Asian population	Total NHPI[1] population	Asian Indian	Bangladeshi	Cambodian	Chinese[2]	Fijian	Filipino	Guamanian[3]	Hawaiian, Native	Hmong	Indonesian	Japanese	Korean	Laotian	Malaysian	Pakistani	Samoan	Sri Lankan	Taiwanese	Thai	Tongan	Vietnamese
Mahwah (township)	24,062	1,551 6.45	-	513 33.08 2.13	-	-	-	-	-	-	-	-	-	-	-	-	-	-	-	-	-	-	-	-
New Milford (borough)	16,400	2,311 14.09	-	621 26.87 3.79	-	-	-	-	953 41.24 5.81	-	-	-	-	-	-	-	-	-	-	-	-	-	-	-
North Arlington (borough)	15,181	828 5.45	-	-	-	-	-	-	-	-	-	-	-	-	-	-	-	-	-	-	-	-	-	-
Palisades Park (borough)	17,073	7,002 41.01	-	-	-	-	-	-	-	-	-	-	-	-	5,902 84.29 34.57	-	-	-	-	-	-	-	-	-
Paramus (borough)	25,737	4,413 17.15	-	1,307 29.62 5.08	-	-	459 10.40 1.78	-	826 18.72 3.21	-	-	-	-	-	1,390 31.50 5.40	-	-	-	-	-	-	-	-	-
Ramsey (borough)	14,351	825 5.75	-	-	-	-	-	-	-	-	-	-	-	-	-	-	-	-	-	-	-	-	-	-
Ridgefield (borough)	10,830	1,776 16.40	-	-	-	-	-	-	-	-	-	-	-	-	1,341 75.51 12.38	-	-	-	-	-	-	-	-	-
Ridgefield Park (village)	12,873	1,104 8.58	-	-	-	-	-	-	-	-	-	-	-	-	451 40.85 3.50	-	-	-	-	-	-	-	-	-
Ridgewood (village)	24,936	2,111 8.47	-	-	-	-	-	-	-	-	-	-	-	447 21.17 1.79	570 27.00 2.29	-	-	-	-	-	-	-	-	-
River Edge (borough)	10,946	1,350 12.33	-	-	-	-	-	-	-	-	-	-	-	-	473 35.04 4.32	-	-	-	-	-	-	-	-	-
Rutherford (borough)	18,110	2,079 11.48	-	348 16.74 1.92	-	-	-	-	-	-	-	-	-	-	904 43.48 4.99	-	-	-	-	-	-	-	-	-
Saddle Brook (township)	13,155	728 5.53	-	-	-	-	-	-	-	-	-	-	-	-	-	-	-	-	-	-	-	-	-	-
Teaneck (township)	39,260	2,829 7.21	-	809 28.60 2.06	-	-	-	-	868 30.68 2.21	-	-	-	-	-	-	-	-	-	-	-	-	-	-	-
Tenafly (borough)	13,806	2,587 18.74	-	-	-	-	745 28.80 5.40	-	-	-	-	-	-	-	1,179 45.57 8.54	-	-	-	-	-	-	-	-	-
Wallington (borough)	11,583	546 4.71	-	-	-	-	-	-	-	-	-	-	-	-	-	-	-	-	-	-	-	-	-	-
Westwood (borough)	10,999	527 4.79	-	-	-	-	-	-	-	-	-	-	-	-	-	-	-	-	-	-	-	-	-	-
Wyckoff (township)	16,508	641 3.88	-	-	-	-	-	-	-	-	-	-	-	-	-	-	-	-	-	-	-	-	-	-

Notes: Please refer to the User's Guide for an explanation of data; data is arranged alphabetically by state, then county, then city within each county; table includes counties with populations greater than 49,999 unless noted and cities with populations greater than 9,999 whose Asian and/or NHPI population rates are greater than the national average; (1) Native Hawaiian and other Pacific Islander; (2) excludes Taiwanese; (3) includes Chamorro; (4) county does not meet population threshold but is shown in order to allow inclusion of city

Place	Total population	Total Asian population	Total NHPI[1] population	Asian Indian	Bangladeshi	Cambodian	Chinese[2]	Fijian	Filipino	Guamanian[3]	Hawaiian, Native	Hmong	Indonesian	Japanese	Korean	Laotian	Malaysian	Pakistani	Samoan	Sri Lankan	Taiwanese	Thai	Tongan	Vietnamese
Burlington County	423,394	11,170 2.64	-	3,741 33.49 0.88	-	-	1,569 14.05 0.37	-	2,039 18.25 0.48	-	-	-	-	489 4.38 0.12	1,971 17.65 0.47	-	-	-		-	-	-	-	540 4.83 0.13
Browns Mills (cdp)	11,352	478 4.21	-	-	-	-	-	-	-	-	-	-	-	-	350 73.22 3.08	-	-	-	-	-	-	-	-	-
Evesham (township)	42,428	1,597 3.76	-	359 22.48 0.85	-	-	448 28.05 1.06	-	-	-	-	-	-	-	-	-	-	-	-	-	-	-	-	-
Maple Shade (township)	19,079	1,083 5.68	-	651 60.11 3.41	-	-	-	-	-	-	-	-	-	-	-	-	-	-	-	-	-	-	-	-
Marlton (cdp)	10,249	392 3.82	-	-	-	-	-	-	-	-	-	-	-	-	-	-	-	-	-	-	-	-	-	-
Mount Laurel (township)	40,221	1,722 4.28	-	570 33.10 1.42	-	-	492 28.57 1.22	-	-	-	-	-	-	-	-	-	-	-	-	-	-	-	-	-
Camden County	508,932	19,842 3.90	-	5,038 25.39 0.99	-	313 1.58 0.06	3,918 19.75 0.77	-	3,783 19.07 0.74	-	-	-	-	-	1,734 8.74 0.34	-	-	376 1.89 0.07	-	-	-	-	-	3,165 15.95 0.62
Barclay-Kingston (cdp)	10,778	883 8.19	-	-	-	-	-	-	-	-	-	-	-	-	-	-	-	-	-	-	-	-	-	-
Bellmawr (borough)	11,262	450 4.00	-	-	-	-	-	-	-	-	-	-	-	-	-	-	-	-	-	-	-	-	-	-
Cherry Hill Mall (cdp)	13,469	1,291 9.58	-	-	-	-	-	-	-	-	-	-	-	-	-	-	-	-	-	-	-	-	-	-
Cherry Hill (township)	69,965	6,595 9.43	-	1,381 20.94 1.97	-	-	1,833 27.79 2.62	-	1,479 22.43 2.11	-	-	-	-	-	1,017 15.42 1.45	-	-	-	-	-	-	-	-	-
Echelon (cdp)	10,389	1,347 12.97	-	809 60.06 7.79	-	-	-	-	-	-	-	-	-	-	-	-	-	-	-	-	-	-	-	-
Greentree (cdp)	11,496	1,925 16.74	-	588 30.55 5.11	-	-	771 40.05 6.71	-	-	-	-	-	-	-	-	-	-	-	-	-	-	-	-	-
Pennsauken (township)	35,703	1,556 4.36	-	-	-	-	-	-	-	-	-	-	-	-	-	-	-	-	-	-	-	-	-	692 44.47 1.94
Springdale (cdp)	14,412	1,196 8.30	-	-	-	-	467 39.05 3.24	-	-	-	-	-	-	-	-	-	-	-	-	-	-	-	-	-
Voorhees (township)	28,126	3,077 10.94	-	1,769 57.49 6.29	-	-	618 20.08 2.20	-	409 13.29 1.45	-	-	-	-	-	-	-	-	-	-	-	-	-	-	-
Cape May County	102,326	615 0.60	-	-	-	-	-	-	-	-	-	-	-	-	-	-	-	-	-	-	-	-	-	-

Notes: Please refer to the User's Guide for an explanation of data; data is arranged alphabetically by state, then county, then city within each county; table includes counties with populations greater than 49,999 unless noted and cities with populations greater than 9,999 whose Asian and/or NHPI population rates are greater than the national average; (1) Native Hawaiian and other Pacific Islander; (2) excludes Taiwanese; (3) includes Chamorro; (4) county does not meet population threshold but is shown in order to allow inclusion of city

Place	Total population	Total Asian population	Total NHPI[1] population	Asian Indian	Bangladeshi	Cambodian	Chinese[2]	Fijian	Filipino	Guamanian[3]	Hawaiian, Native	Hmong	Indonesian	Japanese	Korean	Laotian	Malaysian	Pakistani	Samoan	Sri Lankan	Taiwanese	Thai	Tongan	Vietnamese
Cumberland County	146,438	1,171 0.80	-	414 35.35 0.28	-	-	-	-	-	-	-	-	-	-	-	-	-	-	-	-	-	-	-	-
Essex County	793,633	29,468 3.71	458 0.06	8,695 29.51 1.10	-	-	6,118 20.76 0.77	-	7,941 26.95 1.00	-	-	-	-	600 2.04 0.08	2,791 9.47 0.35	-	-	609 2.07 0.08	-	-	477 1.62 0.06	-	-	1,053 3.57 0.13
Belleville (township)	35,928	4,228 11.77	-	890 21.05 2.48	-	-	-	-	2,129 50.35 5.93	-	-	-	-	-	-	-	-	-	-	-	-	-	-	424 10.03 1.18
Bloomfield (township)	47,683	4,056 8.51	-	1,504 37.08 3.15	-	-	495 12.20 1.04	-	1,589 39.18 3.33	-	-	-	-	-	-	-	-	-	-	-	-	-	-	-
Cedar Grove (township)	12,300	605 4.92	-	-	-	-	-	-	-	-	-	-	-	-	-	-	-	-	-	-	-	-	-	-
Livingston (township)	27,391	3,990 14.57	-	745 18.67 2.72	-	-	1,574 39.45 5.75	-	576 14.44 2.10	-	-	-	-	-	795 19.92 2.90	-	-	-	-	-	-	-	-	-
Millburn (township)	19,765	1,508 7.63	-	-	-	-	653 43.30 3.30	-	-	-	-	-	-	-	-	-	-	-	-	-	-	-	-	-
Nutley (township)	27,362	1,995 7.29	-	735 36.84 2.69	-	-	-	-	487 24.41 1.78	-	-	-	-	-	-	-	-	-	-	-	-	-	-	-
Verona (township)	13,533	612 4.52	-	-	-	-	-	-	-	-	-	-	-	-	-	-	-	-	-	-	-	-	-	-
West Caldwell (township)	11,233	413 3.68	-	-	-	-	-	-	-	-	-	-	-	-	-	-	-	-	-	-	-	-	-	-
West Orange (township)	44,852	3,756 8.37	-	1,032 27.48 2.30	-	-	788 20.98 1.76	-	962 25.61 2.14	-	-	-	-	-	631 16.80 1.41	-	-	-	-	-	-	-	-	-
Gloucester County	254,673	4,162 1.63	-	993 23.86 0.39	-	-	750 18.02 0.29	-	1,366 32.82 0.54	-	-	-	-	-	434 10.43 0.17	-	-	-	-	-	-	-	-	-
Hudson County	608,975	57,191 9.39	-	20,604 36.03 3.38	-	-	6,734 11.77 1.11	-	19,877 34.76 3.26	-	-	-	-	936 1.64 0.15	3,206 5.61 0.53	-	-	2,320 4.06 0.38	-	-	-	-	-	1,640 2.87 0.27
Bayonne (city)	61,842	2,599 4.20	-	534 20.55 0.86	-	-	-	-	1,329 51.14 2.15	-	-	-	-	-	295 11.35 0.48	-	-	-	-	-	-	-	-	-
Guttenberg (town)	10,693	743 6.95	-	-	-	-	-	-	-	-	-	-	-	-	-	-	-	-	-	-	-	-	-	-
Harrison (town)	14,424	1,759 12.19	-	-	-	-	1,314 74.70 9.11	-	-	-	-	-	-	-	-	-	-	-	-	-	-	-	-	-
Hoboken (city)	38,669	1,694 4.38	-	652 38.49 1.69	-	-	491 28.98 1.27	-	-	-	-	-	-	-	-	-	-	-	-	-	-	-	-	-

Notes: Please refer to the User's Guide for an explanation of data; data is arranged alphabetically by state, then county, then city within each county; table includes counties with populations greater than 49,999 unless noted and cities with populations greater than 9,999 whose Asian and/or NHPI population rates are greater than the national average; (1) Native Hawaiian and other Pacific Islander; (2) excludes Taiwanese; (3) includes Chamorro; (4) county does not meet population threshold but is shown in order to allow inclusion of city

Place	Total population	Total Asian population	Total NHPI[1] population	Asian Indian	Bangladeshi	Cambodian	Chinese[2]	Fijian	Filipino	Guamanian[3]	Hawaiian, Native	Hmong	Indonesian	Japanese	Korean	Laotian	Malaysian	Pakistani	Samoan	Sri Lankan	Taiwanese	Thai	Tongan	Vietnamese
Jersey City (city)	240,055	39,070 16.28	-	13,384 34.26 5.58	-	-	2,907 7.44 1.21	-	16,459 42.13 6.86	-	-	-	-	-	1,481 3.79 0.62	-	-	1,878 4.81 0.78	-	-	-	-	-	1,394 3.57 0.58
Kearny (town)	40,513	2,280 5.63	-	815 35.75 2.01	-	-	917 40.22 2.26	-	-	-	-	-	-	-	-	-	-	-	-	-	-	-	-	-
North Bergen (township)	58,206	3,516 6.04	-	2,364 67.24 4.06	-	-	319 9.07 0.55	-	-	-	-	-	-	-	-	-	-	-	-	-	-	-	-	-
Secaucus (town)	15,839	1,853 11.70	-	533 28.76 3.37	-	-	-	-	635 34.27 4.01	-	-	-	-	-	-	-	-	-	-	-	-	-	-	-
Weehawken (township)	13,501	608 4.50	-	-	-	-	-	-	-	-	-	-	-	-	-	-	-	-	-	-	-	-	-	-
Hunterdon County	121,989	2,595 2.13	-	1,060 40.85 0.87	-	-	707 27.24 0.58	-	-	-	-	-	-	-	-	-	-	-	-	-	-	-	-	-
Mercer County	350,761	17,429 4.97	-	6,836 39.22 1.95	-	-	4,616 26.48 1.32	-	1,154 6.62 0.33	-	-	-	-	620 3.56 0.18	1,981 11.37 0.56	-	-	660 3.79 0.19	-	-	488 2.80 0.14	-	-	-
East Windsor (township)	24,919	2,363 9.48	-	1,492 63.14 5.99	-	-	-	-	-	-	-	-	-	-	-	-	-	-	-	-	-	-	-	-
Hopewell (township)	16,105	668 4.15	-	-	-	-	-	-	-	-	-	-	-	-	-	-	-	-	-	-	-	-	-	-
Lawrence (township)	29,159	2,291 7.86	-	1,169 51.03 4.01	-	-	653 28.50 2.24	-	-	-	-	-	-	-	-	-	-	-	-	-	-	-	-	-
Princeton (borough)	14,203	931 6.55	-	-	-	-	-	-	-	-	-	-	-	-	-	-	-	-	-	-	-	-	-	-
Princeton (township)	16,027	1,684 10.51	-	421 25.00 2.63	-	-	722 42.87 4.50	-	-	-	-	-	-	-	-	-	-	-	-	-	-	-	-	-
West Windsor (township)	21,907	4,798 21.90	-	1,613 33.62 7.36	-	-	1,816 37.85 8.29	-	-	-	-	-	-	-	429 8.94 1.96	-	-	-	-	-	-	-	-	-
Middlesex County	750,162	104,114 13.88	-	54,163 52.02 7.22	387 0.37 0.05	-	21,277 20.44 2.84	-	12,499 12.01 1.67	-	-	-	488 0.47 0.07	662 0.64 0.09	5,351 5.14 0.71	-	-	3,174 3.05 0.42	-	497 0.48 0.07	1,360 1.31 0.18	-	-	2,250 2.16 0.30
Avenel (cdp)	17,552	3,296 18.78	-	2,183 66.23 12.44	-	-	-	-	-	-	-	-	-	-	-	-	-	-	-	-	-	-	-	-
Carteret (borough)	20,709	1,656 8.00	-	1,102 66.55 5.32	-	-	-	-	-	-	-	-	-	-	-	-	-	-	-	-	-	-	-	-
Colonia (cdp)	17,756	1,263 7.11	-	625 49.49 3.52	-	-	-	-	330 26.13 1.86	-	-	-	-	-	-	-	-	-	-	-	-	-	-	-

Notes: Please refer to the User's Guide for an explanation of data; data is arranged alphabetically by state, then county, then city within each county; table includes counties with populations greater than 49,999 unless noted and cities with populations greater than 9,999 whose Asian and/or NHPI population rates are greater than the national average; (1) Native Hawaiian and other Pacific Islander; (2) excludes Taiwanese; (3) includes Chamorro; (4) county does not meet population threshold but is shown in order to allow inclusion of city

Place	Total population	Total Asian population	Total NHPI[1] population	Asian Indian	Bangladeshi	Cambodian	Chinese[2]	Fijian	Filipino	Guamanian[3]	Hawaiian, Native	Hmong	Indonesian	Japanese	Korean	Laotian	Malaysian	Pakistani	Samoan	Sri Lankan	Taiwanese	Thai	Tongan	Vietnamese
East Brunswick (township)	46,756	7,634 16.33	-	2,619 34.31 5.60	-	-	3,100 40.61 6.63	-	565 7.40 1.21	-	-	-	-	-	439 5.75 0.94	-	-	-	-	-	-	-	-	-
Edison (township)	97,687	28,438 29.11	-	16,349 57.49 16.74	-	-	5,826 20.49 5.96	-	2,572 9.04 2.63	-	-	-	-	-	1,261 4.43 1.29	-	-	674 2.37 0.69	-	-	663 2.33 0.68	-	-	-
Fords (cdp)	15,136	2,383 15.74	-	1,148 48.17 7.58	-	-	-	-	659 27.65 4.35	-	-	-	-	-	-	-	-	-	-	-	-	-	-	-
Highland Park (borough)	13,999	1,926 13.76	-	627 32.55 4.48	-	-	862 44.76 6.16	-	-	-	-	-	-	-	-	-	-	-	-	-	-	-	-	-
Iselin (cdp)	16,595	3,982 24.00	-	2,817 70.74 16.97	-	-	511 12.83 3.08	-	-	-	-	-	-	-	-	-	-	-	-	-	-	-	-	-
Metuchen (borough)	12,840	941 7.33	-	-	-	-	-	-	-	-	-	-	-	-	-	-	-	-	-	-	-	-	-	-
Middlesex (borough)	13,717	609 4.44	-	-	-	-	-	-	-	-	-	-	-	-	-	-	-	-	-	-	-	-	-	-
New Brunswick (city)	48,573	2,719 5.60	-	1,122 41.27 2.31	-	-	444 16.33 0.91	-	-	-	-	-	-	-	-	-	-	-	-	-	-	-	-	-
North Brunswick (township)	36,287	5,148 14.19	-	3,010 58.47 8.29	-	-	833 16.18 2.30	-	440 8.55 1.21	-	-	-	-	-	465 9.03 1.28	-	-	-	-	-	-	-	-	-
Old Bridge (township)	60,456	6,489 10.73	-	2,827 43.57 4.68	-	-	1,204 18.55 1.99	-	1,275 19.65 2.11	-	-	-	-	-	-	-	-	526 8.11 0.87	-	-	-	-	-	-
Piscataway (township)	50,482	12,562 24.88	-	5,941 47.29 11.77	-	-	2,495 19.86 4.94	-	2,153 17.14 4.26	-	-	-	-	-	792 6.30 1.57	-	-	-	-	-	-	-	-	-
Plainsboro (township)	20,215	6,164 30.49	-	3,266 52.99 16.16	-	-	1,674 27.16 8.28	-	-	-	-	-	-	-	-	-	-	-	-	-	-	-	-	-
Princeton Meadows (cdp)	13,244	3,875 29.26	-	2,179 56.23 16.45	-	-	890 22.97 6.72	-	-	-	-	-	-	-	-	-	-	-	-	-	-	-	-	-
Sayreville (borough)	40,377	4,184 10.36	-	2,502 59.80 6.20	-	-	664 15.87 1.64	-	659 15.75 1.63	-	-	-	-	-	-	-	-	-	-	-	-	-	-	-
South Brunswick (township)	37,734	6,888 18.25	-	3,861 56.05 10.23	-	-	1,414 20.53 3.75	-	540 7.84 1.43	-	-	-	-	-	-	-	-	-	-	-	-	-	-	-
South Plainfield (borough)	21,810	1,761 8.07	-	726 41.23 3.33	-	-	-	-	388 22.03 1.78	-	-	-	-	-	-	-	-	-	-	-	-	-	-	366 20.78 1.68
Woodbridge (township)	97,203	13,949 14.35	-	8,806 63.13 9.06	-	-	1,345 9.64 1.38	-	1,939 13.90 1.99	-	-	-	-	-	642 4.60 0.66	-	-	467 3.35 0.48	-	-	-	-	-	-

Notes: Please refer to the User's Guide for an explanation of data; data is arranged alphabetically by state, then county, then city within each county; table includes counties with populations greater than 49,999 unless noted and cities with populations greater than 9,999 whose Asian and/or NHPI population rates are greater than the national average; (1) Native Hawaiian and other Pacific Islander; (2) excludes Taiwanese; (3) includes Chamorro; (4) county does not meet population threshold but is shown in order to allow inclusion of city

Place	Total population	Total Asian population	Total NHPI[1] population	Asian Indian	Bangladeshi	Cambodian	Chinese[2]	Fijian	Filipino	Guamanian[3]	Hawaiian, Native	Hmong	Indonesian	Japanese	Korean	Laotian	Malaysian	Pakistani	Samoan	Sri Lankan	Taiwanese	Thai	Tongan	Vietnamese
Monmouth County	615,301	24,047 3.91	-	6,832 28.41 1.11	-	-	9,293 38.65 1.51	-	3,340 13.89 0.54	-	-	-	-	361 1.50 0.06	1,985 8.25 0.32	-	-	411 1.71 0.07	-	-	-	-	-	724 3.01 0.12
Aberdeen (township)	17,387	943 5.42	-	394 41.78 2.27	-	-	390 41.36 2.24	-	-	-	-	-	-	-	-	-	-	-	-	-	-	-	-	-
Colts Neck (township)	12,331	519 4.21	-	-	-	-	-	-	-	-	-	-	-	-	-	-	-	-	-	-	-	-	-	-
Eatontown (borough)	13,998	1,262 9.02	-	-	-	-	-	-	-	-	-	-	-	-	-	-	-	-	-	-	-	-	-	-
Freehold (township)	31,537	1,711 5.43	-	482 28.17 1.53	-	-	545 31.85 1.73	-	391 22.85 1.24	-	-	-	-	-	-	-	-	-	-	-	-	-	-	-
Holmdel (township)	15,781	2,610 16.54	-	455 17.43 2.88	-	-	1,617 61.95 10.25	-	-	-	-	-	-	-	-	-	-	-	-	-	-	-	-	-
Howell (township)	48,903	1,849 3.78	-	650 35.15 1.33	-	-	-	-	482 26.07 0.99	-	-	-	-	-	-	-	-	-	-	-	-	-	-	-
Manalapan (township)	33,423	1,528 4.57	-	611 39.99 1.83	-	-	514 33.64 1.54	-	-	-	-	-	-	-	-	-	-	-	-	-	-	-	-	-
Marlboro (township)	36,403	4,550 12.50	-	1,038 22.81 2.85	-	-	2,627 57.74 7.22	-	-	-	-	-	-	-	-	-	-	-	-	-	-	-	-	-
Morganville (cdp)	11,135	1,058 9.50	-	-	-	-	647 61.15 5.81	-	-	-	-	-	-	-	-	-	-	-	-	-	-	-	-	-
Ocean (township)	26,959	1,525 5.66	-	576 37.77 2.14	-	-	-	-	-	-	-	-	-	-	-	-	-	-	-	-	-	-	-	-
Tinton Falls (borough)	15,055	797 5.29	-	-	-	-	-	-	-	-	-	-	-	-	-	-	-	-	-	-	-	-	-	-
West Freehold (cdp)	12,534	581 4.64	-	-	-	-	-	-	-	-	-	-	-	-	-	-	-	-	-	-	-	-	-	-
Morris County	470,212	30,070 6.39	-	10,579 35.18 2.25	-	-	9,306 30.95 1.98	-	3,221 10.71 0.69	-	-	-	-	755 2.51 0.16	2,682 8.92 0.57	-	-	758 2.52 0.16	-	-	702 2.33 0.15	-	-	755 2.51 0.16
Chatham (township)	10,086	565 5.60	-	-	-	-	-	-	-	-	-	-	-	-	-	-	-	-	-	-	-	-	-	-
Denville (township)	15,824	810 5.12	-	-	-	-	-	-	-	-	-	-	-	-	-	-	-	-	-	-	-	-	-	-
East Hanover (township)	11,393	1,245 10.93	-	-	-	-	616 49.48 5.41	-	-	-	-	-	-	-	-	-	-	-	-	-	-	-	-	-

Notes: Please refer to the User's Guide for an explanation of data; data is arranged alphabetically by state, then county, then city within each county; table includes counties with populations greater than 49,999 unless noted and cities with populations greater than 9,999 whose Asian and/or NHPI population rates are greater than the national average; (1) Native Hawaiian and other Pacific Islander; (2) excludes Taiwanese; (3) includes Chamorro; (4) county does not meet population threshold but is shown in order to allow inclusion of city

Place	Total population	Total Asian population	Total NHPI[1] population	Asian Indian	Bangladeshi	Cambodian	Chinese[2]	Fijian	Filipino	Guamanian[3]	Hawaiian, Native	Hmong	Indonesian	Japanese	Korean	Laotian	Malaysian	Pakistani	Samoan	Sri Lankan	Taiwanese	Thai	Tongan	Vietnamese
Hanover (township)	12,898	1,237 9.59	-	392 31.69 3.04	-	-	563 45.51 4.37	-	-	-	-	-	-	-	-	-	-	-	-	-	-	-	-	-
Lincoln Park (borough)	10,930	617 5.65	-	-	-	-	-	-	-	-	-	-	-	-	-	-	-	-	-	-	-	-	-	-
Montville (township)	20,839	2,652 12.73	-	998 37.63 4.79	-	-	949 35.78 4.55	-	-	-	-	-	-	-	-	-	-	-	-	-	-	-	-	-
Morris (township)	21,796	911 4.18	-	-	-	-	-	-	-	-	-	-	-	-	-	-	-	-	-	-	-	-	-	-
Mount Olive (township)	24,193	1,639 6.77	-	680 41.49 2.81	-	-	-	-	-	-	-	-	-	-	-	-	-	-	-	-	-	-	-	-
Parsippany-Troy Hills (twp)	50,649	9,048 17.86	-	4,120 45.53 8.13	-	-	2,616 28.91 5.16	-	762 8.42 1.50	-	-	-	-	-	471 5.21 0.93	-	-	-	-	-	-	-	-	-
Randolph (township)	24,847	2,495 10.04	-	913 36.59 3.67	-	-	773 30.98 3.11	-	-	-	-	-	-	-	-	-	-	-	-	-	-	-	-	-
Rockaway (township)	22,930	1,317 5.74	-	631 47.91 2.75	-	-	-	-	-	-	-	-	-	-	-	-	-	-	-	-	-	-	-	-
Roxbury (township)	23,883	874 3.66	-	-	-	-	-	-	-	-	-	-	-	-	-	-	-	-	-	-	-	-	-	-
Succasunna-Kenvil (cdp)	12,530	521 4.16	-	-	-	-	-	-	-	-	-	-	-	-	-	-	-	-	-	-	-	-	-	-
Ocean County	510,916	6,657 1.30	-	1,614 24.25 0.32	-	-	1,152 17.31 0.23	-	2,459 36.94 0.48	-	-	-	-	-	538 8.08 0.11	-	-	-	-	-	-	-	-	-
Passaic County	489,049	18,458 3.77	-	9,015 48.84 1.84	545 2.95 0.11	-	1,938 10.50 0.40	-	3,480 18.85 0.71	-	-	-	-	-	1,633 8.85 0.33	-	-	-	-	-	-	-	-	-
Clifton (city)	78,672	5,425 6.90	-	2,925 53.92 3.72	-	-	408 7.52 0.52	-	1,245 22.95 1.58	-	-	-	-	-	322 5.94 0.41	-	-	-	-	-	-	-	-	-
Little Falls (township)	10,855	459 4.23	-	-	-	-	-	-	-	-	-	-	-	-	-	-	-	-	-	-	-	-	-	-
Passaic (city)	67,861	3,830 5.64	-	2,522 65.85 3.72	-	-	-	-	756 19.74 1.11	-	-	-	-	-	-	-	-	-	-	-	-	-	-	-
Wayne (township)	54,115	3,245 6.00	-	1,085 33.44 2.00	-	-	687 21.17 1.27	-	356 10.97 0.66	-	-	-	-	-	872 26.87 1.61	-	-	-	-	-	-	-	-	-
Salem County	64,285	370 0.58	-	-	-	-	-	-	-	-	-	-	-	-	-	-	-	-	-	-	-	-	-	-

Notes: Please refer to the User's Guide for an explanation of data; data is arranged alphabetically by state, then county, then city within each county; table includes counties with populations greater than 49,999 unless noted and cities with populations greater than 9,999 whose Asian and/or NHPI population rates are greater than the national average; (1) Native Hawaiian and other Pacific Islander; (2) excludes Taiwanese; (3) includes Chamorro; (4) county does not meet population threshold but is shown in order to allow inclusion of city

Place	Total population	Total Asian population	Total NHPI[1] population	Asian Indian	Bangladeshi	Cambodian	Chinese[2]	Fijian	Filipino	Guamanian[3]	Hawaiian, Native	Hmong	Indonesian	Japanese	Korean	Laotian	Malaysian	Pakistani	Samoan	Sri Lankan	Taiwanese	Thai	Tongan	Vietnamese
Somerset County	297,490	25,117 8.44	-	10,208 40.64 3.43	-	-	7,365 29.32 2.48	-	3,079 12.26 1.03	-	-	-	-	595 2.37 0.20	1,398 5.57 0.47	-	-	814 3.24 0.27	-	-	549 2.19 0.18	-	-	493 1.96 0.17
Bernards (township)	24,575	1,926 7.84	-	547 28.40 2.23	-	-	939 48.75 3.82	-	-	-	-	-	-	-	-	-	-	-	-	-	-	-	-	-
Branchburg (township)	14,562	1,065 7.31	-	590 55.40 4.05	-	-	-	-	-	-	-	-	-	-	-	-	-	-	-	-	-	-	-	-
Bridgewater (township)	42,882	4,723 11.01	-	1,957 41.44 4.56	-	-	1,609 34.07 3.75	-	-	-	-	-	-	-	-	-	-	-	-	-	-	-	-	-
Franklin (township)	50,903	6,404 12.58	-	3,311 51.70 6.50	-	-	1,317 20.57 2.59	-	832 12.99 1.63	-	-	-	-	-	-	-	-	-	-	-	-	-	-	-
Hillsborough (township)	36,654	2,548 6.95	-	958 37.60 2.61	-	-	720 28.26 1.96	-	-	-	-	-	-	-	-	-	-	-	-	-	-	-	-	-
Montgomery (township)	17,465	1,971 11.29	-	594 30.14 3.40	-	-	920 46.68 5.27	-	-	-	-	-	-	-	-	-	-	-	-	-	-	-	-	-
North Plainfield (borough)	21,103	1,059 5.02	-	-	-	-	-	-	-	-	-	-	-	-	-	-	-	-	-	-	-	-	-	-
Somerset (cdp)	23,053	1,831 7.94	-	715 39.05 3.10	-	-	413 22.56 1.79	-	555 30.31 2.41	-	-	-	-	-	-	-	-	-	-	-	-	-	-	-
Somerville (borough)	12,481	868 6.95	-	-	-	-	-	-	-	-	-	-	-	-	-	-	-	-	-	-	-	-	-	-
Warren (township)	14,259	1,602 11.24	-	520 32.46 3.65	-	-	625 39.01 4.38	-	-	-	-	-	-	-	-	-	-	-	-	-	-	-	-	-
Sussex County	144,166	1,628 1.13	-	409 25.12 0.28	-	-	-	-	499 30.65 0.35	-	-	-	-	-	-	-	-	-	-	-	-	-	-	-
Union County	522,541	19,393 3.71	-	6,826 35.20 1.31	-	-	3,789 19.54 0.73	-	5,731 29.55 1.10	-	-	-	-	-	1,119 5.77 0.21	-	-	360 1.86 0.07	-	-	-	-	-	442 2.28 0.08
Berkeley Heights (township)	13,407	1,050 7.83	-	-	-	-	418 39.81 3.12	-	-	-	-	-	-	-	-	-	-	-	-	-	-	-	-	-
New Providence (borough)	11,907	896 7.52	-	-	-	-	373 41.63 3.13	-	-	-	-	-	-	-	-	-	-	-	-	-	-	-	-	-
Rahway (city)	26,500	1,149 4.34	-	-	-	-	-	-	516 44.91 1.95	-	-	-	-	-	-	-	-	-	-	-	-	-	-	-
Roselle Park (borough)	13,281	1,243 9.36	-	878 70.64 6.61	-	-	-	-	-	-	-	-	-	-	-	-	-	-	-	-	-	-	-	-

Notes: Please refer to the User's Guide for an explanation of data; data is arranged alphabetically by state, then county, then city within each county; table includes counties with populations greater than 49,999 unless noted and cities with populations greater than 9,999 whose Asian and/or NHPI population rates are greater than the national average; (1) Native Hawaiian and other Pacific Islander; (2) excludes Taiwanese; (3) includes Chamorro; (4) county does not meet population threshold but is shown in order to allow inclusion of city

Place	Total population	Total Asian population	Total NHPI[1] population	Asian Indian	Bangladeshi	Cambodian	Chinese[2]	Fijian	Filipino	Guamanian[3]	Hawaiian, Native	Hmong	Indonesian	Japanese	Korean	Laotian	Malaysian	Pakistani	Samoan	Sri Lankan	Taiwanese	Thai	Tongan	Vietnamese
Scotch Plains (township)	22,732	1,593 7.01	-	633 39.74 2.78	-	-	460 28.88 2.02	-	-	-	-	-	-	-	-	-	-	-	-	-	-	-	-	-
Springfield (township)	14,429	559 3.87	-	-	-	-	-	-	-	-	-	-	-	-	-	-	-	-	-	-	-	-	-	-
Summit (city)	21,131	812 3.84	-	390 48.03 1.85	-	-	-	-	-	-	-	-	-	-	-	-	-	-	-	-	-	-	-	-
Union (township)	54,405	4,258 7.83	-	1,032 24.24 1.90	-	-	513 12.05 0.94	-	2,131 50.05 3.92	-	-	-	-	-	-	-	-	-	-	-	-	-	-	-
Westfield (town)	29,644	1,109 3.74	-	-	-	-	-	-	-	-	-	-	-	-	-	-	-	-	-	-	-	-	-	-
Warren County	102,437	1,221 1.19	-	543 44.47 0.53	-	-	-	-	-	-	-	-	-	-	-	-	-	-	-	-	-	-	-	-
NEW MEXICO	1,819,046	18,286 1.01	1,248 0.07	2,424 13.26 0.13	-	-	3,992 21.83 0.22	-	2,942 16.09 0.16	365 29.25 0.02	394 31.57 0.02	-	-	2,065 11.29 0.11	1,737 9.50 0.10	-	-	-	-	-	-	401 2.19 0.02	-	2,797 15.30 0.15
Bernalillo County	556,678	9,864 1.77	532 0.10	1,155 11.71 0.21	-	-	2,041 20.69 0.37	-	1,052 10.67 0.19	-	-	-	-	1,119 11.34 0.20	864 8.76 0.16	-	-	-	-	-	-	-	-	2,479 25.13 0.45
Chaves County	61,382	387 0.63	-	-	-	-	-	-	-	-	-	-	-	-	-	-	-	-	-	-	-	-	-	-
Dona Ana County	174,682	1,386 0.79	-	-	-	-	397 28.64 0.23	-	-	-	-	-	-	-	-	-	-	-	-	-	-	-	-	-
Los Alamos County[4]	18,343	798 4.35	-	-	-	-	-	-	-	-	-	-	-	-	-	-	-	-	-	-	-	-	-	-
Los Alamos (cdp)	11,902	609 5.12	-	-	-	-	-	-	-	-	-	-	-	-	-	-	-	-	-	-	-	-	-	-
Otero County	62,298	714 1.15	-	-	-	-	-	-	-	-	-	-	-	-	-	-	-	-	-	-	-	-	-	-
Sandoval County	89,908	748 0.83	-	-	-	-	-	-	332 44.39 0.37	-	-	-	-	-	-	-	-	-	-	-	-	-	-	-
Santa Fe County	129,292	944 0.73	-	-	-	-	-	-	-	-	-	-	-	-	-	-	-	-	-	-	-	-	-	-
NEW YORK	18,976,457	1,044,423 5.50	7,903 0.04	250,027 23.94 1.32	20,087 1.92 0.11	2,910 0.28 0.02	416,955 39.92 2.20	-	86,722 8.30 0.46	1,759 22.26 0.01	1,442 18.25 0.01	-	2,433 0.23 0.01	37,594 3.60 0.20	120,775 11.56 0.64	3,216 0.31 0.02	1,402 0.13 0.01	32,123 3.08 0.17	1,439 18.21 0.01	2,689 0.26 0.01	7,790 0.75 0.04	6,597 0.63 0.03	-	23,176 2.22 0.12
Albany County	294,565	7,887 2.68	-	2,452 31.09 0.83	-	-	1,965 24.91 0.67	-	701 8.89 0.24	-	-	-	-	-	976 12.37 0.33	-	-	-	-	-	-	-	-	533 6.76 0.18

Notes: Please refer to the User's Guide for an explanation of data; data is arranged alphabetically by state, then county, then city within each county; table includes counties with populations greater than 49,999 unless noted and cities with populations greater than 9,999 whose Asian and/or NHPI population rates are greater than the national average; (1) Native Hawaiian and other Pacific Islander; (2) excludes Taiwanese; (3) includes Chamorro; (4) county does not meet population threshold but is shown in order to allow inclusion of city

Place	Total population	Total Asian population	Total NHPI[1] population	Asian Indian	Bangladeshi	Cambodian	Chinese[2]	Fijian	Filipino	Guamanian[3]	Hawaiian, Native	Hmong	Indonesian	Japanese	Korean	Laotian	Malaysian	Pakistani	Samoan	Sri Lankan	Taiwanese	Thai	Tongan	Vietnamese
Colonie (town)	79,258	2,919 3.68	-	1,219 41.76 1.54	-	-	612 20.97 0.77	-	-	-	-	-	-	-	-	-	-	-	-	-	-	-	-	-
Guilderland (town)	32,688	1,238 3.79	-	414 33.44 1.27	-	-	-	-	-	-	-	-	-	-	-	-	-	-	-	-	-	-	-	-
Bronx County (Bronx)	1,332,650	39,076 2.93	1,099 0.08	14,743 37.73 1.11	1,992 5.10 0.15	810 2.07 0.06	6,346 16.24 0.48	-	4,934 12.63 0.37	-	-	-	-	519 1.33 0.04	3,462 8.86 0.26	-	-	1,124 2.88 0.08	-	-	-	-	-	2,995 7.66 0.22
Broome County	200,536	5,321 2.65	-	938 17.63 0.47	-	-	1,557 29.26 0.78	-	-	-	-	-	-	-	783 14.72 0.39	517 9.72 0.26	-	-	-	-	-	-	-	513 9.64 0.26
Johnson City (village)	15,541	826 5.31	-	-	-	-	-	-	-	-	-	-	-	-	-	-	-	-	-	-	-	-	-	-
Vestal (town)	26,535	2,105 7.93	-	-	-	-	850 40.38 3.20	-	-	-	-	-	-	-	-	-	-	-	-	-	-	-	-	-
Cattaraugus County	83,955	441 0.53	-	-	-	-	-	-	-	-	-	-	-	-	-	-	-	-	-	-	-	-	-	-
Cayuga County	81,963	343 0.42	-	-	-	-	-	-	-	-	-	-	-	-	-	-	-	-	-	-	-	-	-	-
Chautauqua County	139,750	462 0.33	-	-	-	-	-	-	-	-	-	-	-	-	-	-	-	-	-	-	-	-	-	-
Chemung County	91,070	796 0.87	-	-	-	-	-	-	-	-	-	-	-	-	-	-	-	-	-	-	-	-	-	-
Chenango County	51,401	171 0.33	-	-	-	-	-	-	-	-	-	-	-	-	-	-	-	-	-	-	-	-	-	-
Clinton County	79,894	714 0.89	-	-	-	-	-	-	-	-	-	-	-	-	-	-	-	-	-	-	-	-	-	-
Columbia County	63,094	461 0.73	-	-	-	-	-	-	-	-	-	-	-	-	-	-	-	-	-	-	-	-	-	-
Dutchess County	280,150	7,091 2.53	-	2,862 40.36 1.02	-	-	2,064 29.11 0.74	-	-	-	-	-	-	-	755 10.65 0.27	-	-	-	-	-	-	-	-	-
Arlington (cdp)	12,439	766 6.16	-	-	-	-	-	-	-	-	-	-	-	-	-	-	-	-	-	-	-	-	-	-
Poughkeepsie (town)	42,743	1,835 4.29	-	967 52.70 2.26	-	-	406 22.13 0.95	-	-	-	-	-	-	-	-	-	-	-	-	-	-	-	-	-
Wappinger (town)	26,308	1,180 4.49	-	452 38.31 1.72	-	-	-	-	-	-	-	-	-	-	-	-	-	-	-	-	-	-	-	-

Notes: Please refer to the User's Guide for an explanation of data; data is arranged alphabetically by state, then county, then city within each county; table includes counties with populations greater than 49,999 unless noted and cities with populations greater than 9,999 whose Asian and/or NHPI population rates are greater than the national average; (1) Native Hawaiian and other Pacific Islander; (2) excludes Taiwanese; (3) includes Chamorro; (4) county does not meet population threshold but is shown in order to allow inclusion of city

Place	Total population	Total Asian population	Total NHPI[1] population	Asian Indian	Bangladeshi	Cambodian	Chinese[2]	Fijian	Filipino	Guamanian[3]	Hawaiian, Native	Hmong	Indonesian	Japanese	Korean	Laotian	Malaysian	Pakistani	Samoan	Sri Lankan	Taiwanese	Thai	Tongan	Vietnamese
Erie County	950,265	12,893 1.36	-	3,420 26.53 0.36	-	-	3,057 23.71 0.32	-	675 5.24 0.07	-	-	-	-	496 3.85 0.05	1,988 15.42 0.21	-	-	-	-	-	-	-	-	1,519 11.78 0.16
Amherst (town)	116,510	5,559 4.77	-	1,805 32.47 1.55	-	-	1,683 30.28 1.44	-	-	-	-	-	-	-	939 16.89 0.81	-	-	-	-	-	-	-	-	-
Herkimer County	64,427	255 0.40	-	-	-	-	-	-	-	-	-	-	-	-	-	-	-	-	-	-	-	-	-	-
Jefferson County	111,738	1,171 1.05	-	-	-	-	-	-	310 26.47 0.28	-	-	-	-	-	358 30.57 0.32	-	-	-	-	-	-	-	-	-
Kings County (Brooklyn)	2,465,326	185,814 7.54	1,549 0.06	24,795 13.34 1.01	3,928 2.11 0.16	501 0.27 0.02	120,803 65.01 4.90	-	7,149 3.85 0.29	489 31.57 0.02	-	-	-	2,176 1.17 0.09	6,761 3.64 0.27	-	-	9,621 5.18 0.39	-	-	-	-	-	3,830 2.06 0.16
Livingston County	64,328	685 1.06	-	-	-	-	-	-	-	-	-	-	-	-	-	-	-	-	-	-	-	-	-	-
Madison County	69,441	478 0.69	-	-	-	-	-	-	-	-	-	-	-	-	-	-	-	-	-	-	-	-	-	-
Monroe County	735,343	17,744 2.41	-	4,495 25.33 0.61	-	381 2.15 0.05	3,976 22.41 0.54	-	612 3.45 0.08	-	-	-	-	583 3.29 0.08	2,505 14.12 0.34	1,355 7.64 0.18	-	462 2.60 0.06	-	-	-	-	-	2,267 12.78 0.31
Brighton (town)	35,588	2,811 7.90	-	1,005 35.75 2.82	-	-	640 22.77 1.80	-	-	-	-	-	-	-	-	-	-	-	-	-	-	-	-	-
Henrietta (town)	39,028	2,028 5.20	-	472 23.27 1.21	-	-	504 24.85 1.29	-	-	-	-	-	-	-	-	-	-	-	-	-	-	-	-	-
Pittsford (town)	27,222	1,274 4.68	-	577 45.29 2.12	-	-	-	-	-	-	-	-	-	-	-	-	-	-	-	-	-	-	-	-
Nassau County	1,334,544	62,536 4.69	410 0.03	23,475 37.54 1.76	-	-	14,934 23.88 1.12	-	7,168 11.46 0.54	-	-	-	-	1,787 2.86 0.13	9,085 14.53 0.68	-	-	2,348 3.75 0.18	-	-	604 0.97 0.05	376 0.60 0.03	-	450 0.72 0.03
East Meadow (cdp)	37,501	2,418 6.45	-	1,129 46.69 3.01	-	-	-	-	348 14.39 0.93	-	-	-	-	-	-	-	-	-	-	-	-	-	-	-
Elmont (cdp)	32,657	3,178 9.73	-	1,910 60.10 5.85	-	-	-	-	550 17.31 1.68	-	-	-	-	-	-	-	-	-	-	-	-	-	-	-
Franklin Square (cdp)	29,342	1,173 4.00	-	454 38.70 1.55	-	-	-	-	-	-	-	-	-	-	-	-	-	-	-	-	-	-	-	-
Glen Cove (city)	26,622	1,053 3.96	-	325 30.86 1.22	-	-	-	-	-	-	-	-	-	-	398 37.80 1.50	-	-	-	-	-	-	-	-	-
Hicksville (cdp)	41,260	3,689 8.94	-	1,854 50.26 4.49	-	-	746 20.22 1.81	-	517 14.01 1.25	-	-	-	-	-	-	-	-	-	-	-	-	-	-	-

Notes: Please refer to the User's Guide for an explanation of data; data is arranged alphabetically by state, then county, then city within each county; table includes counties with populations greater than 49,999 unless noted and cities with populations greater than 9,999 whose Asian and/or NHPI population rates are greater than the national average; (1) Native Hawaiian and other Pacific Islander; (2) excludes Taiwanese; (3) includes Chamorro; (4) county does not meet population threshold but is shown in order to allow inclusion of city

Place	Total population	Total Asian population	Total NHPI[1] population	Asian Indian	Bangladeshi	Cambodian	Chinese[2]	Fijian	Filipino	Guamanian[3]	Hawaiian, Native	Hmong	Indonesian	Japanese	Korean	Laotian	Malaysian	Pakistani	Samoan	Sri Lankan	Taiwanese	Thai	Tongan	Vietnamese
Jericho (cdp)	12,984	1,483 11.42	-	-	-	-	-	-	-	-	-	-	-	-	717 48.35 5.52	-	-	-	-	-	-	-	-	-
Mineola (village)	19,240	903 4.69	-	345 38.21 1.79	-	-	-	-	-	-	-	-	-	-	-	-	-	-	-	-	-	-	-	-
North Hempstead (town)	222,611	20,579 9.24	-	7,642 37.13 3.43	-	-	5,598 27.20 2.51	-	1,357 6.59 0.61	-	-	-	-	955 4.64 0.43	3,248 15.78 1.46	-	-	618 3.00 0.28	-	-	283 1.38 0.13	-	-	-
North Merrick (cdp)	11,844	479 4.04	-	-	-	-	-	-	-	-	-	-	-	-	-	-	-	-	-	-	-	-	-	-
North New Hyde Park (cdp)	14,542	2,141 14.72	-	1,197 55.91 8.23	-	-	720 33.63 4.95	-	-	-	-	-	-	-	-	-	-	-	-	-	-	-	-	-
North Valley Stream (cdp)	15,789	1,469 9.30	-	633 43.09 4.01	-	-	-	-	-	-	-	-	-	-	-	-	-	-	-	-	-	-	-	-
Oyster Bay (town)	293,925	13,857 4.71	-	5,141 37.10 1.75	-	-	3,674 26.51 1.25	-	1,283 9.26 0.44	-	-	-	-	374 2.70 0.13	2,472 17.84 0.84	-	-	-	-	-	-	-	-	-
Plainview (cdp)	25,637	1,250 4.88	-	342 27.36 1.33	-	-	351 28.08 1.37	-	-	-	-	-	-	-	387 30.96 1.51	-	-	-	-	-	-	-	-	-
Port Washington (cdp)	15,194	962 6.33	-	256 26.61 1.68	-	-	-	-	-	-	-	-	-	-	-	-	-	-	-	-	-	-	-	-
Salisbury (cdp)	12,301	1,089 8.85	-	378 34.71 3.07	-	-	-	-	-	-	-	-	-	-	-	-	-	-	-	-	-	-	-	-
Syosset (cdp)	18,544	2,327 12.55	-	729 31.33 3.93	-	-	779 33.48 4.20	-	-	-	-	-	-	-	560 24.07 3.02	-	-	-	-	-	-	-	-	-
Valley Stream (village)	36,394	2,553 7.01	-	-	-	-	796 31.18 2.19	-	612 23.97 1.68	-	-	-	-	-	-	-	-	-	-	-	-	-	-	-
West Hempstead (cdp)	18,707	994 5.31	-	346 34.81 1.85	-	-	-	-	-	-	-	-	-	-	-	-	-	-	-	-	-	-	-	-
Westbury (village)	14,263	694 4.87	-	-	-	-	-	-	-	-	-	-	-	-	-	-	-	-	-	-	-	-	-	-
Woodmere (cdp)	16,447	607 3.69	-	-	-	-	-	-	-	-	-	-	-	-	-	-	-	-	-	-	-	-	-	-
New York City	8,008,278	788,110 9.84	4,870 0.06	170,182 21.59 2.13	19,149 2.43 0.24	1,619 0.21 0.02	357,540 45.37 4.46	-	58,946 7.48 0.74	1,176 24.15 0.01	776 15.93 0.01	-	1,816 0.23 0.02	22,302 2.83 0.28	87,139 11.06 1.09	-	1,197 0.15 0.01	23,855 3.03 0.30	729 14.97 0.01	2,004 0.25 0.03	4,907 0.62 0.06	3,823 0.49 0.05	-	12,310 1.56 0.15
New York County (Manhattan)	1,537,195	144,368 9.39	612 0.04	14,273 9.89 0.93	783 0.54 0.05	-	85,330 59.11 5.55	-	8,831 6.12 0.57	-	-	-	-	14,137 9.79 0.92	11,419 7.91 0.74	-	-	1,086 0.75 0.07	-	-	1,051 0.73 0.07	835 0.58 0.05	-	1,569 1.09 0.10

Notes: Please refer to the User's Guide for an explanation of data; data is arranged alphabetically by state, then county, then city within each county; table includes counties with populations greater than 49,999 unless noted and cities with populations greater than 9,999 whose Asian and/or NHPI population rates are greater than the national average; (1) Native Hawaiian and other Pacific Islander; (2) excludes Taiwanese; (3) includes Chamorro; (4) county does not meet population threshold but is shown in order to allow inclusion of city

Place	Total population	Total Asian population	Total NHPI[1] population	Asian Indian	Bangladeshi	Cambodian	Chinese[2]	Fijian	Filipino	Guamanian[3]	Hawaiian, Native	Hmong	Indonesian	Japanese	Korean	Laotian	Malaysian	Pakistani	Samoan	Sri Lankan	Taiwanese	Thai	Tongan	Vietnamese
Niagara County	219,846	1,148 0.52	-	431 37.54 0.20	-	-	-	-	-	-	-	-	-	-	-	-	-	-	-	-	-	-	-	-
Oneida County	235,469	2,740 1.16	-	575 20.99 0.24	-	-	294 10.73 0.12	-	-	-	-	-	-	-	-	-	-	-	-	-	-	-	-	1,091 39.82 0.46
Onondaga County	458,336	9,593 2.09	-	1,983 20.67 0.43	-	-	1,696 17.68 0.37	-	759 7.91 0.17	-	-	-	-	351 3.66 0.08	1,305 13.60 0.28	-	-	-	-	-	-	-	-	1,723 17.96 0.38
Ontario County	100,224	696 0.69	-	-	-	-	-	-	-	-	-	-	-	-	-	-	-	-	-	-	-	-	-	-
Orange County	341,367	5,476 1.60	-	1,721 31.43 0.50	-	-	1,289 23.54 0.38	-	775 14.15 0.23	-	-	-	-	-	814 14.86 0.24	-	-	-	-	-	-	-	-	-
Oswego County	122,377	540 0.44	-	-	-	-	-	-	-	-	-	-	-	-	-	-	-	-	-	-	-	-	-	-
Otsego County	61,676	304 0.49	-	-	-	-	-	-	-	-	-	-	-	-	-	-	-	-	-	-	-	-	-	-
Putnam County	95,745	1,213 1.27	-	415 34.21 0.43	-	-	424 34.95 0.44	-	-	-	-	-	-	-	-	-	-	-	-	-	-	-	-	-
Queens County (Queens)	2,229,379	394,314 17.69	1,394 0.06	109,933 27.88 4.93	12,402 3.15 0.56	-	137,739 34.93 6.18	-	32,843 8.33 1.47	-	-	-	1,243 0.32 0.06	5,283 1.34 0.24	62,255 15.79 2.79	-	567 0.14 0.03	11,252 2.85 0.50	-	937 0.24 0.04	3,463 0.88 0.16	2,364 0.60 0.11	-	3,739 0.95 0.17
Rensselaer County	152,538	2,430 1.59	-	436 17.94 0.29	-	-	1,084 44.61 0.71	-	-	-	-	-	-	-	373 15.35 0.24	-	-	-	-	-	-	-	-	-
Richmond Co. (Staten Island)	443,728	24,538 5.53	-	6,438 26.24 1.45	-	-	7,322 29.84 1.65	-	5,189 21.15 1.17	-	-	-	-	-	3,242 13.21 0.73	-	-	772 3.15 0.17	-	527 2.15 0.12	-	-	-	-
Rockland County	286,753	16,130 5.63	-	5,582 34.61 1.95	-	-	2,000 12.40 0.70	-	4,505 27.93 1.57	-	-	-	-	-	1,911 11.85 0.67	-	-	-	-	-	-	-	-	-
Clarkstown (town)	82,082	6,705 8.17	-	2,394 35.70 2.92	-	-	794 11.84 0.97	-	2,182 32.54 2.66	-	-	-	-	-	721 10.75 0.88	-	-	-	-	-	-	-	-	-
Nanuet (cdp)	16,709	1,559 9.33	-	579 37.14 3.47	-	-	-	-	-	-	-	-	-	-	-	-	-	-	-	-	-	-	-	-
New City (cdp)	34,137	2,583 7.57	-	1,067 41.31 3.13	-	-	-	-	590 22.84 1.73	-	-	-	-	-	-	-	-	-	-	-	-	-	-	-
Orangetown (town)	47,801	3,001 6.28	-	681 22.69 1.42	-	-	581 19.36 1.22	-	712 23.73 1.49	-	-	-	-	-	568 18.93 1.19	-	-	-	-	-	-	-	-	-
Ramapo (town)	108,905	5,131 4.71	-	2,015 39.27 1.85	-	-	473 9.22 0.43	-	1,356 26.43 1.25	-	-	-	-	-	539 10.50 0.49	-	-	-	-	-	-	-	-	-

Notes: Please refer to the User's Guide for an explanation of data; data is arranged alphabetically by state, then county, then city within each county; table includes counties with populations greater than 49,999 unless noted and cities with populations greater than 9,999 whose Asian and/or NHPI population rates are greater than the national average; (1) Native Hawaiian and other Pacific Islander; (2) excludes Taiwanese; (3) includes Chamorro; (4) county does not meet population threshold but is shown in order to allow inclusion of city

Place	Total population	Total Asian population	Total NHPI[1] population	Asian Indian	Bangladeshi	Cambodian	Chinese[2]	Fijian	Filipino	Guamanian[3]	Hawaiian, Native	Hmong	Indonesian	Japanese	Korean	Laotian	Malaysian	Pakistani	Samoan	Sri Lankan	Taiwanese	Thai	Tongan	Vietnamese
Spring Valley (village)	25,374	1,479 5.83	-	774 52.33 3.05	-	-	-	-	-	-	-	-	-	-	-	-	-	-	-	-	-	-	-	-
St. Lawrence County	111,931	657 0.59	-	-	-	-	-	-	-	-	-	-	-	-	-	-	-	-	-	-	-	-	-	-
Saratoga County	200,635	2,179 1.09	-	694 31.85 0.35	-	-	394 18.08 0.20	-	-	-	-	-	-	-	446 20.47 0.22	-	-	-	-	-	-	-	-	-
Schenectady County	146,555	2,850 1.94	-	1,147 40.25 0.78	-	-	842 29.54 0.57	-	-	-	-	-	-	-	-	-	-	-	-	-	-	-	-	-
Niskayuna (town)	20,259	1,175 5.80	-	519 44.17 2.56	-	-	-	-	-	-	-	-	-	-	-	-	-	-	-	-	-	-	-	-
Steuben County	98,726	799 0.81	-	-	-	-	-	-	-	-	-	-	-	-	-	-	-	-	-	-	-	-	-	-
Suffolk County	1,419,369	34,143 2.41	427 0.03	10,260 30.05 0.72	-	-	9,744 28.54 0.69	-	4,055 11.88 0.29	-	-	-	-	1,044 3.06 0.07	3,909 11.45 0.28	-	-	2,007 5.88 0.14	-	-	428 1.25 0.03	387 1.13 0.03	-	704 2.06 0.05
Coram (cdp)	34,979	1,284 3.67	-	-	-	-	428 33.33 1.22	-	-	-	-	-	-	-	-	-	-	-	-	-	-	-	-	-
Dix Hills (cdp)	26,096	1,955 7.49	-	831 42.51 3.18	-	-	446 22.81 1.71	-	-	-	-	-	-	-	-	-	-	-	-	-	-	-	-	-
Elwood (cdp)	10,845	712 6.57	-	-	-	-	-	-	-	-	-	-	-	-	-	-	-	-	-	-	-	-	-	-
Lake Grove (village)	10,397	554 5.33	-	-	-	-	-	-	-	-	-	-	-	-	-	-	-	-	-	-	-	-	-	-
Melville (cdp)	14,538	637 4.38	-	-	-	-	-	-	-	-	-	-	-	-	-	-	-	-	-	-	-	-	-	-
Setauket-East Setauket (cdp)	15,952	1,477 9.26	-	-	-	-	676 45.77 4.24	-	-	-	-	-	-	-	-	-	-	-	-	-	-	-	-	-
Stony Brook (cdp)	13,683	802 5.86	-	-	-	-	421 52.49 3.08	-	-	-	-	-	-	-	-	-	-	-	-	-	-	-	-	-
Sullivan County	73,966	855 1.16	-	-	-	-	-	-	-	-	-	-	-	-	-	-	-	-	-	-	-	-	-	-
Tioga County	51,784	349 0.67	-	-	-	-	-	-	-	-	-	-	-	-	-	-	-	-	-	-	-	-	-	-
Tompkins County	96,501	7,146 7.41	-	1,050 14.69 1.09	-	-	3,111 43.53 3.22	-	-	-	-	-	-	582 8.14 0.60	1,203 16.83 1.25	-	-	-	-	-	-	-	-	-

Notes: Please refer to the User's Guide for an explanation of data; data is arranged alphabetically by state, then county, then city within each county; table includes counties with populations greater than 49,999 unless noted and cities with populations greater than 9,999 whose Asian and/or NHPI population rates are greater than the national average; (1) Native Hawaiian and other Pacific Islander; (2) excludes Taiwanese; (3) includes Chamorro; (4) county does not meet population threshold but is shown in order to allow inclusion of city

Place	Total population	Total Asian population	Total NHPI[1] population	Asian Indian	Bangladeshi	Cambodian	Chinese[2]	Fijian	Filipino	Guamanian[3]	Hawaiian, Native	Hmong	Indonesian	Japanese	Korean	Laotian	Malaysian	Pakistani	Samoan	Sri Lankan	Taiwanese	Thai	Tongan	Vietnamese
Ithaca (city)	29,006	4,039 13.92	-	527 13.05 1.82	-	-	1,994 49.37 6.87	-	-	-	-	-	-	-	475 11.76 1.64	-	-	-	-	-	-	-	-	-
Lansing (town)	10,300	1,071 10.40	-	-	-	-	-	-	-	-	-	-	-	-	-	-	-	-	-	-	-	-	-	-
Ulster County	177,749	1,815 1.02	-	-	-	-	538 29.64 0.30	-	-	-	-	-	-	-	-	-	-	-	-	-	-	-	-	-
New Paltz (town)	12,830	576 4.49	-	-	-	-	-	-	-	-	-	-	-	-	-	-	-	-	-	-	-	-	-	-
Warren County	63,303	504 0.80	-	-	-	-	-	-	-	-	-	-	-	-	-	-	-	-	-	-	-	-	-	-
Wayne County	93,765	394 0.42	-	-	-	-	-	-	-	-	-	-	-	-	-	-	-	-	-	-	-	-	-	-
Westchester County	923,459	41,751 4.52	-	14,496 34.72 1.57	-	-	7,087 16.97 0.77	-	4,956 11.87 0.54	-	-	-	-	7,502 17.97 0.81	4,228 10.13 0.46	-	-	842 2.02 0.09	-	-	338 0.81 0.04	594 1.42 0.06	-	-
Dobbs Ferry (village)	10,622	750 7.06	-	-	-	-	-	-	-	-	-	-	-	-	-	-	-	-	-	-	-	-	-	-
Eastchester (cdp)	18,564	1,293 6.97	-	-	-	-	-	-	-	-	-	-	-	549 42.46 2.96	-	-	-	-	-	-	-	-	-	-
Eastchester (town)	31,318	2,265 7.23	-	-	-	-	-	-	-	-	-	-	-	1,210 53.42 3.86	-	-	-	-	-	-	-	-	-	-
Greenburgh (town)	86,764	7,818 9.01	-	2,586 33.08 2.98	-	-	1,275 16.31 1.47	-	579 7.41 0.67	-	-	-	-	1,957 25.03 2.26	1,000 12.79 1.15	-	-	-	-	-	-	-	-	-
Harrison (village)	24,143	1,336 5.53	-	-	-	-	-	-	-	-	-	-	-	693 51.87 2.87	-	-	-	-	-	-	-	-	-	-
New Castle (town)	17,491	1,014 5.80	-	404 39.84 2.31	-	-	308 30.37 1.76	-	-	-	-	-	-	-	-	-	-	-	-	-	-	-	-	-
New Rochelle (city)	72,182	2,686 3.72	-	1,175 43.75 1.63	-	-	541 20.14 0.75	-	-	-	-	-	-	-	-	-	-	-	-	-	-	-	-	-
North Castle (town)	10,849	471 4.34	-	-	-	-	-	-	-	-	-	-	-	-	-	-	-	-	-	-	-	-	-	-
Ossining (town)	36,534	1,510 4.13	-	696 46.09 1.91	-	-	-	-	-	-	-	-	-	-	-	-	-	-	-	-	-	-	-	-
Ossining (village)	24,010	937 3.90	-	305 32.55 1.27	-	-	-	-	-	-	-	-	-	-	-	-	-	-	-	-	-	-	-	-

Notes: Please refer to the User's Guide for an explanation of data; data is arranged alphabetically by state, then county, then city within each county; table includes counties with populations greater than 49,999 unless noted and cities with populations greater than 9,999 whose Asian and/or NHPI population rates are greater than the national average; (1) Native Hawaiian and other Pacific Islander; (2) excludes Taiwanese; (3) includes Chamorro; (4) county does not meet population threshold but is shown in order to allow inclusion of city

Place	Total population	Total Asian population	Total NHPI[1] population	Asian Indian	Bangladeshi	Cambodian	Chinese[2]	Fijian	Filipino	Guamanian[3]	Hawaiian, Native	Hmong	Indonesian	Japanese	Korean	Laotian	Malaysian	Pakistani	Samoan	Sri Lankan	Taiwanese	Thai	Tongan	Vietnamese
Pelham (town)	11,866	454 3.83	-	-	-	-	-	-	-	-	-	-	-	-	-	-	-	-	-	-	-	-	-	-
Rye (city)	14,955	1,075 7.19	-	-	-	-	-	-	-	-	-	-	-	645 60.00 4.31	-	-	-	-	-	-	-	-	-	-
Scarsdale (village)	17,823	2,225 12.48	-	415 18.65 2.33	-	-	376 16.90 2.11	-	-	-	-	-	-	784 35.24 4.40	383 17.21 2.15	-	-	-	-	-	-	-	-	-
Tarrytown (village)	11,090	638 5.75	-	-	-	-	-	-	-	-	-	-	-	-	-	-	-	-	-	-	-	-	-	-
White Plains (city)	53,077	2,199 4.14	-	787 35.79 1.48	-	-	562 25.56 1.06	-	-	-	-	-	-	-	-	-	-	-	-	-	-	-	-	-
Yonkers (city)	196,086	9,564 4.88	-	4,689 49.03 2.39	-	-	874 9.14 0.45	-	1,817 19.00 0.93	-	-	-	-	-	1,063 11.11 0.54	-	-	-	-	-	-	-	-	-
NORTH CAROLINA	8,049,313	111,292 1.38	3,699 0.05	25,350 22.78 0.31	-	2,370 2.13 0.03	17,502 15.73 0.22	-	10,194 9.16 0.13	1,197 32.36 0.01	1,146 30.98 0.01	6,819 6.13 0.08	-	6,037 5.42 0.08	12,403 11.14 0.15	4,966 4.46 0.06	-	1,874 1.68 0.02	495 13.38 0.01	-	971 0.87 0.01	1,625 1.46 0.02	-	15,604 14.02 0.19
Alamance County	130,800	1,155 0.88	-	-	-	-	-	-	-	-	-	-	-	-	-	-	-	-	-	-	-	-	-	-
Buncombe County	206,330	1,849 0.90	-	552 29.85 0.27	-	-	-	-	-	-	-	-	-	-	-	-	-	-	-	-	-	-	-	-
Burke County	89,148	3,023 3.39	-	-	-	-	-	-	-	-	-	2,005 66.32 2.25	-	-	-	496 16.41 0.56	-	-	-	-	-	-	-	-
Cabarrus County	131,063	1,072 0.82	-	-	-	-	-	-	-	-	-	-	-	-	-	-	-	-	-	-	-	-	-	-
Catawba County	141,685	3,792 2.68	-	-	-	-	-	-	-	-	-	1,794 47.31 1.27	-	-	-	650 17.14 0.46	-	-	-	-	-	-	-	503 13.26 0.36
Hickory (city)	37,511	1,616 4.31	-	-	-	-	-	-	-	-	-	543 33.60 1.45	-	-	-	-	-	-	-	-	-	-	-	-
Cleveland County	96,287	785 0.82	-	-	-	-	-	-	-	-	-	-	-	-	-	-	-	-	-	-	-	-	-	-
Craven County	91,436	1,148 1.26	-	-	-	-	-	-	477 41.55 0.52	-	-	-	-	-	-	-	-	-	-	-	-	-	-	-
Cumberland County	302,963	6,126 2.02	503 0.17	664 10.84 0.22	-	-	-	-	982 16.03 0.32	-	-	-	-	451 7.36 0.15	2,100 34.28 0.69	-	-	-	-	-	-	-	-	721 11.77 0.24
Davidson County	147,246	1,267 0.86	-	-	-	517 40.81 0.35	-	-	-	-	-	-	-	-	-	-	-	-	-	-	-	-	-	-

Notes: Please refer to the User's Guide for an explanation of data; data is arranged alphabetically by state, then county, then city within each county; table includes counties with populations greater than 49,999 unless noted and cities with populations greater than 9,999 whose Asian and/or NHPI population rates are greater than the national average; (1) Native Hawaiian and other Pacific Islander; (2) excludes Taiwanese; (3) includes Chamorro; (4) county does not meet population threshold but is shown in order to allow inclusion of city

Place	Total population	Total Asian population	Total NHPI[1] population	Asian Indian	Bangladeshi	Cambodian	Chinese[2]	Fijian	Filipino	Guamanian[3]	Hawaiian, Native	Hmong	Indonesian	Japanese	Korean	Laotian	Malaysian	Pakistani	Samoan	Sri Lankan	Taiwanese	Thai	Tongan	Vietnamese
Durham County	223,314	7,052 3.16	-	2,709 38.41 1.21	-	-	1,618 22.94 0.72	-	584 8.28 0.26	-	-	-	-	386 5.47 0.17	602 8.54 0.27	-	-	-	-	-	-	-	-	-
Forsyth County	306,067	3,227 1.05	-	607 18.81 0.20	-	-	919 28.48 0.30	-	283 8.77 0.09	-	-	-	-	-	-	-	-	-	-	-	-	-	-	520 16.11 0.17
Gaston County	190,365	1,508 0.79	-	-	-	-	-	-	-	-	-	-	-	-	-	-	-	-	-	-	-	-	-	505 33.49 0.27
Guilford County	421,048	9,341 2.22	-	1,747 18.70 0.41	-	-	1,017 10.89 0.24	-	541 5.79 0.13	-	-	-	-	-	964 10.32 0.23	488 5.22 0.12	-	409 4.38 0.10	-	-	-	-	-	2,966 31.75 0.70
Halifax County	57,370	375 0.65	-	-	-	-	-	-	-	-	-	-	-	-	-	-	-	-	-	-	-	-	-	-
Harnett County	91,025	639 0.70	-	-	-	-	-	-	-	-	-	-	-	-	-	-	-	-	-	-	-	-	-	-
Henderson County	89,173	440 0.49	-	-	-	-	-	-	-	-	-	-	-	-	-	-	-	-	-	-	-	-	-	-
Iredell County	122,660	1,110 0.90	-	-	-	-	-	-	-	-	-	-	-	-	-	-	-	-	-	-	-	-	-	-
Johnston County	121,965	579 0.47	-	-	-	-	-	-	-	-	-	-	-	-	-	-	-	-	-	-	-	-	-	-
Lenoir County	59,648	392 0.66	-	-	-	-	-	-	-	-	-	-	-	-	-	-	-	-	-	-	-	-	-	-
Mecklenburg County	695,454	20,819 2.99	-	5,165 24.81 0.74	-	767 3.68 0.11	2,926 14.05 0.42	-	1,155 5.55 0.17	-	-	569 2.73 0.08	-	834 4.01 0.12	2,443 11.73 0.35	876 4.21 0.13	-	-	-	-	-	-	-	4,652 22.34 0.67
Nash County	87,420	413 0.47	-	-	-	-	-	-	-	-	-	-	-	-	-	-	-	-	-	-	-	-	-	-
New Hanover County	160,307	1,381 0.86	-	-	-	-	-	-	-	-	-	-	-	-	-	-	-	-	-	-	-	-	-	-
Onslow County	150,355	2,566 1.71	400 0.27	-	-	-	-	-	1,144 44.58 0.76	-	-	-	-	487 18.98 0.32	-	-	-	-	-	-	-	-	-	-
Orange County	118,227	4,646 3.93	-	708 15.24 0.60	-	-	1,682 36.20 1.42	-	-	-	-	-	-	521 11.21 0.44	784 16.87 0.66	-	-	-	-	-	-	-	-	-
Carrboro (town)	16,704	802 4.80	-	-	-	-	-	-	-	-	-	-	-	-	-	-	-	-	-	-	-	-	-	-
Chapel Hill (town)	48,796	3,327 6.82	-	573 17.22 1.17	-	-	1,213 36.46 2.49	-	-	-	-	-	-	-	558 16.77 1.14	-	-	-	-	-	-	-	-	-

Notes: Please refer to the User's Guide for an explanation of data; data is arranged alphabetically by state, then county, then city within each county; table includes counties with populations greater than 49,999 unless noted and cities with populations greater than 9,999 whose Asian and/or NHPI population rates are greater than the national average; (1) Native Hawaiian and other Pacific Islander; (2) excludes Taiwanese; (3) includes Chamorro; (4) county does not meet population threshold but is shown in order to allow inclusion of city

Place	Total population	Total Asian population	Total NHPI[1] population	Asian Indian	Bangladeshi	Cambodian	Chinese[2]	Fijian	Filipino	Guamanian[3]	Hawaiian, Native	Hmong	Indonesian	Japanese	Korean	Laotian	Malaysian	Pakistani	Samoan	Sri Lankan	Taiwanese	Thai	Tongan	Vietnamese
Pitt County	133,798	1,245 0.93	-	-	-	-	-	-	-	-	-	-	-	-	-	-	-	-	-	-	-	-	-	-
Randolph County	130,454	785 0.60	-	-	-	-	-	-	-	-	-	-	-	-	-	-	-	-	-	-	-	-	-	-
Robeson County	123,339	936 0.76	-	-	-	-	-	-	-	-	-	-	-	-	-	-	-	-	-	-	-	-	-	-
Rowan County	130,340	808 0.62	-	-	-	-	-	-	-	-	-	-	-	-	-	-	-	-	-	-	-	-	-	-
Stanly County	58,100	752 1.29	-	-	-	-	-	-	-	-	-	318 42.29 0.55	-	-	-	-	-	-	-	-	-	-	-	-
Surry County	71,219	478 0.67	-	-	-	-	-	-	-	-	-	-	-	-	-	-	-	-	-	-	-	-	-	-
Union County	123,677	586 0.47	-	-	-	-	-	-	-	-	-	-	-	-	-	-	-	-	-	-	-	-	-	-
Wake County	627,846	20,722 3.30	-	6,941 33.50 1.11	-	-	4,929 23.79 0.79	-	1,212 5.85 0.19	-	-	-	-	831 4.01 0.13	2,197 10.60 0.35	-	-	445 2.15 0.07	-	-	-	-	-	2,333 11.26 0.37
Apex (town)	20,072	761 3.79	-	-	-	-	-	-	-	-	-	-	-	-	-	-	-	-	-	-	-	-	-	-
Cary (town)	94,530	7,521 7.96	-	3,381 44.95 3.58	-	-	1,908 25.37 2.02	-	-	-	-	-	-	358 4.76 0.38	514 6.83 0.54	-	-	-	-	-	-	-	-	454 6.04 0.48
Wayne County	113,329	1,078 0.95	-	-	-	-	-	-	-	-	-	-	-	-	-	-	-	-	-	-	-	-	-	-
Wilkes County	65,632	332 0.51	-	-	-	-	-	-	-	-	-	-	-	-	-	-	-	-	-	-	-	-	-	-
NORTH DAKOTA	642,200	3,342 0.52	-	1,042 31.18 0.16	-	-	429 12.84 0.07	-	577 17.27 0.09	-	-	-	-	-	365 10.92 0.06	-	-	-	-	-	-	-	-	-
Cass County	123,138	1,422 1.15	-	414 29.11 0.34	-	-	-	-	-	-	-	-	-	-	-	-	-	-	-	-	-	-	-	-
Grand Forks County	66,109	632 0.96	-	-	-	-	-	-	-	-	-	-	-	-	-	-	-	-	-	-	-	-	-	-
Ward County	58,795	307 0.52	-	-	-	-	-	-	-	-	-	-	-	-	-	-	-	-	-	-	-	-	-	-
OHIO	11,353,140	132,131 1.16	2,641 0.02	37,624 28.47 0.33	648 0.49 0.01	2,615 1.98 0.02	27,676 20.95 0.24	-	13,179 9.97 0.12	666 25.22 0.01	791 29.95 0.01	-	1,061 0.80 0.01	10,291 7.79 0.09	13,886 10.51 0.12	2,998 2.27 0.03	348 0.26 <0.01	1,641 1.24 0.01	491 18.59 <0.01	514 0.39 <0.01	2,213 1.67 0.02	1,900 1.44 0.02	-	10,357 7.84 0.09

Notes: Please refer to the User's Guide for an explanation of data; data is arranged alphabetically by state, then county, then city within each county; table includes counties with populations greater than 49,999 unless noted and cities with populations greater than 9,999 whose Asian and/or NHPI population rates are greater than the national average; (1) Native Hawaiian and other Pacific Islander; (2) excludes Taiwanese; (3) includes Chamorro; (4) county does not meet population threshold but is shown in order to allow inclusion of city

Place	Total population	Total Asian population	Total NHPI[1] population	Asian Indian	Bangladeshi	Cambodian	Chinese[2]	Fijian	Filipino	Guamanian[3]	Hawaiian, Native	Hmong	Indonesian	Japanese	Korean	Laotian	Malaysian	Pakistani	Samoan	Sri Lankan	Taiwanese	Thai	Tongan	Vietnamese
Allen County	108,473	534 0.49	-	-	-	-	-	-	-	-	-	-	-	-	-	-	-	-	-	-	-	-	-	-
Ashtabula County	102,728	287 0.28	-	-	-	-	-	-	-	-	-	-	-	-	-	-	-	-	-	-	-	-	-	-
Athens County	62,223	1,116 1.79	-	-	-	-	-	-	-	-	-	-	-	-	-	-	-	-	-	-	-	-	-	-
Athens (city)	21,192	876 4.13	-	-	-	-	-	-	-	-	-	-	-	-	-	-	-	-	-	-	-	-	-	-
Butler County	332,807	5,077 1.53	-	1,789 35.24 0.54	-	-	1,007 19.83 0.30	-	450 8.86 0.14	-	-	-	-	-	471 9.28 0.14	-	-	-	-	-	-	-	-	650 12.80 0.20
Clark County	144,742	671 0.46	-	-	-	-	-	-	-	-	-	-	-	-	-	-	-	-	-	-	-	-	-	-
Clermont County	177,977	1,078 0.61	-	382 35.44 0.21	-	-	-	-	-	-	-	-	-	-	-	-	-	-	-	-	-	-	-	-
Columbiana County	112,075	325 0.29	-	-	-	-	-	-	-	-	-	-	-	-	-	-	-	-	-	-	-	-	-	-
Cuyahoga County	1,393,978	25,831 1.85	-	9,055 35.05 0.65	-	484 1.87 0.03	6,073 23.51 0.44	-	2,789 10.80 0.20	-	-	-	-	1,266 4.90 0.09	1,835 7.10 0.13	-	-	-	-	-	-	-	-	2,085 8.07 0.15
Mayfield Heights (city)	19,386	798 4.12	-	388 48.62 2.00	-	-	-	-	-	-	-	-	-	-	-	-	-	-	-	-	-	-	-	-
Richmond Heights (city)	10,944	515 4.71	-	-	-	-	-	-	-	-	-	-	-	-	-	-	-	-	-	-	-	-	-	-
Solon (city)	21,802	1,070 4.91	-	470 43.93 2.16	-	-	346 32.34 1.59	-	-	-	-	-	-	-	-	-	-	-	-	-	-	-	-	-
Westlake (city)	31,856	1,354 4.25	-	541 39.96 1.70	-	-	-	-	-	-	-	-	-	-	-	-	-	-	-	-	-	-	-	-
Delaware County	109,989	1,755 1.60	-	435 24.79 0.40	-	-	554 31.57 0.50	-	-	-	-	-	-	-	-	-	-	-	-	-	-	-	-	-
Fairfield County	122,759	874 0.71	-	-	-	-	-	-	-	-	-	-	-	-	-	-	-	-	-	-	-	-	-	-
Franklin County	1,068,978	32,912 3.08	362 0.03	8,240 25.04 0.77	-	1,309 3.98 0.12	7,261 22.06 0.68	-	1,794 5.45 0.17	-	-	-	530 1.61 0.05	3,227 9.80 0.30	3,334 10.13 0.31	1,136 3.45 0.11	-	513 1.56 0.05	-	-	756 2.30 0.07	428 1.30 0.04	-	2,443 7.42 0.23
Dublin (city)	31,478	2,497 7.93	-	666 26.67 2.12	-	-	510 20.42 1.62	-	-	-	-	-	-	820 32.84 2.60	-	-	-	-	-	-	-	-	-	-

Notes: Please refer to the User's Guide for an explanation of data; data is arranged alphabetically by state, then county, then city within each county; table includes counties with populations greater than 49,999 unless noted and cities with populations greater than 9,999 whose Asian and/or NHPI population rates are greater than the national average; (1) Native Hawaiian and other Pacific Islander; (2) excludes Taiwanese; (3) includes Chamorro; (4) county does not meet population threshold but is shown in order to allow inclusion of city

Place	Total population	Total Asian population	Total NHPI[1] population	Asian Indian	Bangladeshi	Cambodian	Chinese[2]	Fijian	Filipino	Guamanian[3]	Hawaiian, Native	Hmong	Indonesian	Japanese	Korean	Laotian	Malaysian	Pakistani	Samoan	Sri Lankan	Taiwanese	Thai	Tongan	Vietnamese
Hilliard (city)	24,186	1,006 4.16	-	-	-	-	-	-	-	-	-	-	-	-	-	-	-	-	-	-	-	-	-	-
Geauga County	90,895	370 0.41	-	-	-	-	-	-	-	-	-	-	-	-	-	-	-	-	-	-	-	-	-	-
Greene County	147,886	2,883 1.95	-	875 30.35 0.59	-	-	428 14.85 0.29	-	-	-	-	-	-	-	570 19.77 0.39	-	-	-	-	-	-	-	-	-
Hamilton County	845,303	12,652 1.50	-	3,969 31.37 0.47	-	351 2.77 0.04	2,999 23.70 0.35	-	1,315 10.39 0.16	-	-	-	-	609 4.81 0.07	1,144 9.04 0.14	-	-	-	-	-	-	-	-	1,056 8.35 0.12
Blue Ash (city)	12,755	898 7.04	-	405 45.10 3.18	-	-	-	-	-	-	-	-	-	-	-	-	-	-	-	-	-	-	-	-
Sharonville (city)	13,702	556 4.06	-	393 70.68 2.87	-	-	-	-	-	-	-	-	-	-	-	-	-	-	-	-	-	-	-	-
Hancock County	71,295	764 1.07	-	-	-	-	-	-	-	-	-	-	-	-	-	-	-	-	-	-	-	-	-	-
Lake County	227,511	2,234 0.98	-	679 30.39 0.30	-	-	533 23.86 0.23	-	-	-	-	-	-	-	-	-	-	-	-	-	-	-	-	-
Licking County	145,491	687 0.47	-	-	-	-	-	-	-	-	-	-	-	-	-	-	-	-	-	-	-	-	-	-
Lorain County	284,664	1,715 0.60	-	394 22.97 0.14	-	-	-	-	433 25.25 0.15	-	-	-	-	-	-	-	-	-	-	-	-	-	-	-
Lucas County	455,054	5,326 1.17	-	1,618 30.38 0.36	-	-	1,422 26.70 0.31	-	598 11.23 0.13	-	-	-	-	-	515 9.67 0.11	-	-	-	-	-	-	-	-	-
Mahoning County	257,555	1,018 0.40	-	-	-	-	-	-	-	-	-	-	-	-	-	-	-	-	-	-	-	-	-	-
Marion County	66,217	364 0.55	-	-	-	-	-	-	-	-	-	-	-	-	-	-	-	-	-	-	-	-	-	-
Medina County	151,095	1,153 0.76	-	442 38.33 0.29	-	-	-	-	-	-	-	-	-	-	-	-	-	-	-	-	-	-	-	-
Miami County	98,868	845 0.85	-	-	-	-	-	-	-	-	-	-	-	-	-	-	-	-	-	-	-	-	-	-
Montgomery County	559,062	7,190 1.29	-	2,118 29.46 0.38	-	-	1,129 15.70 0.20	-	716 9.96 0.13	-	-	-	-	640 8.90 0.11	792 11.02 0.14	-	-	-	-	-	-	-	-	1,037 14.42 0.19
Portage County	152,061	1,156 0.76	-	-	-	-	-	-	-	-	-	-	-	-	-	-	-	-	-	-	-	-	-	-

Notes: Please refer to the User's Guide for an explanation of data; data is arranged alphabetically by state, then county, then city within each county; table includes counties with populations greater than 49,999 unless noted and cities with populations greater than 9,999 whose Asian and/or NHPI population rates are greater than the national average; (1) Native Hawaiian and other Pacific Islander; (2) excludes Taiwanese; (3) includes Chamorro; (4) county does not meet population threshold but is shown in order to allow inclusion of city

Place	Total population	Total Asian population	Total NHPI[1] population	Asian Indian	Bangladeshi	Cambodian	Chinese[2]	Fijian	Filipino	Guamanian[3]	Hawaiian, Native	Hmong	Indonesian	Japanese	Korean	Laotian	Malaysian	Pakistani	Samoan	Sri Lankan	Taiwanese	Thai	Tongan	Vietnamese
Richland County	128,852	709 0.55	-	-	-	-	-	-	-	-	-	-	-	-	-	-	-	-	-	-	-	-	-	-
Stark County	378,098	1,811 0.48	-	447 24.68 0.12	-	-	388 21.42 0.10	-	-	-	-	-	-	-	-	-	-	-	-	-	-	-	-	-
Summit County	542,899	7,735 1.42	-	2,042 26.40 0.38	-	-	1,723 22.28 0.32	-	495 6.40 0.09	-	-	-	-	431 5.57 0.08	924 11.95 0.17	763 9.86 0.14	-	-	-	-	-	-	-	677 8.75 0.12
Trumbull County	225,116	1,009 0.45	-	-	-	-	-	-	-	-	-	-	-	-	-	-	-	-	-	-	-	-	-	-
Warren County	158,383	2,167 1.37	-	671 30.96 0.42	-	-	518 23.90 0.33	-	-	-	-	-	-	-	-	-	-	-	-	-	-	-	-	-
Wayne County	111,564	767 0.69	-	-	-	-	-	-	-	-	-	-	-	-	-	-	-	-	-	-	-	-	-	-
Wood County	121,065	1,170 0.97	-	-	-	-	-	-	-	-	-	-	-	-	-	-	-	-	-	-	-	-	-	-
OKLAHOMA	3,450,654	45,546 1.32	1,840 0.05	8,302 18.23 0.24	-	329 0.72 0.01	6,642 14.58 0.19	-	4,184 9.19 0.12	400 21.74 0.01	676 36.74 0.02	335 0.74 0.01	-	2,790 6.13 0.08	4,626 10.16 0.13	881 1.93 0.03	514 1.13 0.01	1,122 2.46 0.03	-	-	354 0.78 0.01	823 1.81 0.02	-	12,221 26.83 0.35
Canadian County	87,697	2,180 2.49	-	1,209 55.46 1.38	-	-	-	-	-	-	-	-	-	-	-	-	-	-	-	-	-	-	-	591 27.11 0.67
Cleveland County	208,016	5,879 2.83	-	895 15.22 0.43	-	-	1,085 18.46 0.52	-	560 9.53 0.27	-	-	-	-	-	708 12.04 0.34	-	-	-	-	-	-	-	-	1,700 28.92 0.82
Comanche County	114,996	2,430 2.11	-	-	-	-	-	-	548 22.55 0.48	-	-	-	-	-	836 34.40 0.73	-	-	-	-	-	-	-	-	-
Garfield County	57,813	499 0.86	-	-	-	-	-	-	-	-	-	-	-	-	-	-	-	-	-	-	-	-	-	-
Muskogee County	69,451	351 0.51	-	-	-	-	-	-	-	-	-	-	-	-	-	-	-	-	-	-	-	-	-	-
Oklahoma County	660,448	18,171 2.75	-	2,857 15.72 0.43	-	-	2,199 12.10 0.33	-	1,257 6.92 0.19	-	-	-	-	1,005 5.53 0.15	1,214 6.68 0.18	493 2.71 0.07	-	-	-	-	-	397 2.18 0.06	-	6,842 37.65 1.04
Payne County	68,190	1,906 2.80	-	-	-	-	667 34.99 0.98	-	-	-	-	-	-	-	-	-	-	-	-	-	-	-	-	-
Stillwater (city)	38,968	1,869 4.80	-	-	-	-	663 35.47 1.70	-	-	-	-	-	-	-	-	-	-	-	-	-	-	-	-	-
Pottawatomie County	65,521	372 0.57	-	-	-	-	-	-	-	-	-	-	-	-	-	-	-	-	-	-	-	-	-	-

Notes: Please refer to the User's Guide for an explanation of data; data is arranged alphabetically by state, then county, then city within each county; table includes counties with populations greater than 49,999 unless noted and cities with populations greater than 9,999 whose Asian and/or NHPI population rates are greater than the national average; (1) Native Hawaiian and other Pacific Islander; (2) excludes Taiwanese; (3) includes Chamorro; (4) county does not meet population threshold but is shown in order to allow inclusion of city

Place	Total population	Total Asian population	Total NHPI[1] population	Asian Indian	Bangladeshi	Cambodian	Chinese[2]	Fijian	Filipino	Guamanian[3]	Hawaiian, Native	Hmong	Indonesian	Japanese	Korean	Laotian	Malaysian	Pakistani	Samoan	Sri Lankan	Taiwanese	Thai	Tongan	Vietnamese
Tulsa County	563,299	8,601 1.53	-	1,947 22.64 0.35	-	-	1,546 17.97 0.27	-	468 5.44 0.08	-	-	-	-	-	893 10.38 0.16	-	-	544 6.32 0.10	-	-	-	-	-	2,048 23.81 0.36
Wagoner County	57,491	489 0.85	-	-	-	-	-	-	-	-	-	-	-	-	-	-	-	-	-	-	-	-	-	-
OREGON	3,421,399	99,136 2.90	7,583 0.22	10,188 10.28 0.30	-	2,749 2.77 0.08	18,514 18.68 0.54	373 4.92 0.01	10,675 10.77 0.31	1,110 14.64 0.03	1,977 26.07 0.06	1,367 1.38 0.04	641 0.65 0.02	11,652 11.75 0.34	12,815 12.93 0.37	3,701 3.73 0.11	-	390 0.39 0.01	773 10.19 0.02	-	800 0.81 0.02	1,496 1.51 0.04	445 5.87 0.01	19,040 19.21 0.56
Benton County	78,153	3,331 4.26	-	-	-	-	943 28.31 1.21	-	-	-	-	-	-	432 12.97 0.55	731 21.95 0.94	-	-	-	-	-	-	-	-	-
Corvallis (city)	49,184	3,031 6.16	-	-	-	-	906 29.89 1.84	-	-	-	-	-	-	-	632 20.85 1.28	-	-	-	-	-	-	-	-	-
Clackamas County	338,391	8,114 2.40	616 0.18	701 8.64 0.21	-	-	1,847 22.76 0.55	-	970 11.95 0.29	-	-	-	-	1,003 12.36 0.30	1,690 20.83 0.50	-	-	-	-	-	-	-	-	949 11.70 0.28
Lake Oswego (city)	35,222	1,494 4.24	-	-	-	-	422 28.25 1.20	-	-	-	-	-	-	-	-	-	-	-	-	-	-	-	-	-
Coos County	62,779	345 0.55	-	-	-	-	-	-	-	-	-	-	-	-	-	-	-	-	-	-	-	-	-	-
Deschutes County	115,367	615 0.53	-	-	-	-	-	-	-	-	-	-	-	-	-	-	-	-	-	-	-	-	-	-
Douglas County	100,399	593 0.59	-	-	-	-	-	-	-	-	-	-	-	-	-	-	-	-	-	-	-	-	-	-
Jackson County	181,269	1,398 0.77	-	-	-	-	-	-	-	-	-	-	-	-	-	-	-	-	-	-	-	-	-	-
Josephine County	75,726	396 0.52	-	-	-	-	-	-	-	-	-	-	-	-	-	-	-	-	-	-	-	-	-	-
Klamath County	63,775	474 0.74	-	-	-	-	-	-	-	-	-	-	-	-	-	-	-	-	-	-	-	-	-	-
Lane County	322,959	6,103 1.89	588 0.18	603 9.88 0.19	-	-	1,185 19.42 0.37	-	571 9.36 0.18	-	-	-	-	1,281 20.99 0.40	1,225 20.07 0.38	-	-	-	-	-	-	-	-	-
Linn County	103,069	780 0.76	-	-	-	-	-	-	-	-	-	-	-	-	-	-	-	-	-	-	-	-	-	-
Marion County	284,834	4,801 1.69	761 0.27	360 7.50 0.13	-	-	785 16.35 0.28	-	657 13.68 0.23	-	-	-	-	608 12.66 0.21	620 12.91 0.22	-	-	-	-	-	-	-	-	830 17.29 0.29
Salem (city)	136,694	3,310 2.42	382 0.28	-	-	-	656 19.82 0.48	-	381 11.51 0.28	-	-	-	-	388 11.72 0.28	-	-	-	-	-	-	-	-	-	492 14.86 0.36

Notes: Please refer to the User's Guide for an explanation of data; data is arranged alphabetically by state, then county, then city within each county; table includes counties with populations greater than 49,999 unless noted and cities with populations greater than 9,999 whose Asian and/or NHPI population rates are greater than the national average; (1) Native Hawaiian and other Pacific Islander; (2) excludes Taiwanese; (3) includes Chamorro; (4) county does not meet population threshold but is shown in order to allow inclusion of city

Place	Total population	Total Asian population	Total NHPI[1] population	Asian Indian	Bangladeshi	Cambodian	Chinese[2]	Fijian	Filipino	Guamanian[3]	Hawaiian, Native	Hmong	Indonesian	Japanese	Korean	Laotian	Malaysian	Pakistani	Samoan	Sri Lankan	Taiwanese	Thai	Tongan	Vietnamese
Multnomah County	660,486	37,280 5.64	2,511 0.38	1,825 4.90 0.28	-	1,067 2.86 0.16	7,014 18.81 1.06	-	3,324 8.92 0.50	-	468 18.64 0.07	1,057 2.84 0.16	-	3,551 9.53 0.54	2,582 6.93 0.39	2,602 6.98 0.39	-	-	-	-	-	492 1.32 0.07	359 14.30 0.05	11,460 30.74 1.74
Portland (city)	529,025	33,683 6.37	2,010 0.38	1,520 4.51 0.29	-	1,039 3.08 0.20	6,471 19.21 1.22	-	2,743 8.14 0.52	-	348 17.31 0.07	931 2.76 0.18	-	3,054 9.07 0.58	2,194 6.51 0.41	2,302 6.83 0.44	-	-	-	-	-	450 1.34 0.09	352 17.51 0.07	10,874 32.28 2.06
Polk County	62,380	773 1.24	-	-	-	-	-	-	-	-	-	-	-	-	-	-	-	-	-	-	-	-	-	-
Umatilla County	70,548	492 0.70	-	-	-	-	-	-	-	-	-	-	-	-	-	-	-	-	-	-	-	-	-	-
Washington County	445,342	29,946 6.72	1,399 0.31	5,568 18.59 1.25	-	1,104 3.69 0.25	4,906 16.38 1.10	-	3,130 10.45 0.70	-	425 30.38 0.10	-	-	2,695 9.00 0.61	4,298 14.35 0.97	622 2.08 0.14	-	-	-	-	-	-	-	5,019 16.76 1.13
Aloha (cdp)	42,097	3,122 7.42	-	-	-	-	-	-	416 13.32 0.99	-	-	-	-	-	-	-	-	-	-	-	-	-	-	1,118 35.81 2.66
Beaverton (city)	75,918	7,449 9.81	-	1,742 23.39 2.29	-	357 4.79 0.47	1,026 13.77 1.35	-	726 9.75 0.96	-	-	-	-	678 9.10 0.89	1,235 16.58 1.63	-	-	-	-	-	-	-	-	916 12.30 1.21
Cedar Mill (cdp)	12,776	982 7.69	-	-	-	-	-	-	-	-	-	-	-	-	-	-	-	-	-	-	-	-	-	-
Hillsboro (city)	69,883	4,366 6.25	-	1,317 30.16 1.88	-	-	597 13.67 0.85	-	-	-	-	-	-	-	527 12.07 0.75	-	-	-	-	-	-	-	-	745 17.06 1.07
Tigard (city)	41,261	2,458 5.96	-	-	-	-	622 25.31 1.51	-	-	-	-	-	-	-	-	-	-	-	-	-	-	-	-	444 18.06 1.08
Tualatin (city)	22,587	1,007 4.46	-	-	-	-	-	-	-	-	-	-	-	-	-	-	-	-	-	-	-	-	-	-
Yamhill County	84,992	872 1.03	-	-	-	-	-	-	-	-	-	-	-	-	-	-	-	-	-	-	-	-	-	-
PENNSYLVANIA	12,281,054	216,631 1.76	3,721 0.03	56,233 25.96 0.46	706 0.33 0.01	8,696 4.01 0.07	48,041 22.18 0.39	-	14,713 6.79 0.12	805 21.63 0.01	1,004 26.98 0.01	788 0.36 0.01	536 0.25 <0.01	7,186 3.32 0.06	32,880 15.18 0.27	2,268 1.05 0.02	-	3,026 1.40 0.02	844 22.68 0.01	330 0.15 <0.01	2,277 1.05 0.02	1,798 0.83 0.01	-	28,625 13.21 0.23
Adams County	91,292	639 0.70	-	-	-	-	-	-	-	-	-	-	-	-	-	-	-	-	-	-	-	-	-	-
Allegheny County	1,281,666	20,851 1.63	650 0.05	7,534 36.13 0.59	-	-	4,957 23.77 0.39	-	1,118 5.36 0.09	-	-	-	-	1,217 5.84 0.09	2,257 10.82 0.18	-	-	-	-	-	451 2.16 0.04	-	-	1,287 6.17 0.10
Muni. of Monroeville (borough)	29,349	1,165 3.97	-	683 58.63 2.33	-	-	-	-	-	-	-	-	-	-	-	-	-	-	-	-	-	-	-	-
Scott (township)	17,288	1,000 5.78	-	832 83.20 4.81	-	-	-	-	-	-	-	-	-	-	-	-	-	-	-	-	-	-	-	-

Notes: Please refer to the User's Guide for an explanation of data; data is arranged alphabetically by state, then county, then city within each county; table includes counties with populations greater than 49,999 unless noted and cities with populations greater than 9,999 whose Asian and/or NHPI population rates are greater than the national average; (1) Native Hawaiian and other Pacific Islander; (2) excludes Taiwanese; (3) includes Chamorro; (4) county does not meet population threshold but is shown in order to allow inclusion of city

Place	Total population	Total Asian population	Total NHPI[1] population	Asian Indian	Bangladeshi	Cambodian	Chinese[2]	Fijian	Filipino	Guamanian[3]	Hawaiian, Native	Hmong	Indonesian	Japanese	Korean	Laotian	Malaysian	Pakistani	Samoan	Sri Lankan	Taiwanese	Thai	Tongan	Vietnamese
Scott Township (cdp)	17,288	1,000 5.78	-	832 83.20 4.81	-	-	-	-	-	-	-	-	-	-	-	-	-	-	-	-	-	-	-	-
Upper St. Clair (township)	20,053	779 3.88	-	520 66.75 2.59	-	-	-	-	-	-	-	-	-	-	-	-	-	-	-	-	-	-	-	-
Beaver County	181,412	451 0.25	-	-	-	-	-	-	-	-	-	-	-	-	-	-	-	-	-	-	-	-	-	-
Berks County	373,638	3,621 0.97	-	781 21.57 0.21	-	-	625 17.26 0.17	-	-	-	-	-	-	-	314 8.67 0.08	-	-	-	-	-	-	-	-	1,163 32.12 0.31
Blair County	129,144	562 0.44	-	-	-	-	-	-	-	-	-	-	-	-	-	-	-	-	-	-	-	-	-	-
Bradford County	62,761	198 0.32	-	-	-	-	-	-	-	-	-	-	-	-	-	-	-	-	-	-	-	-	-	-
Bucks County	597,635	14,171 2.37	-	5,887 41.54 0.99	-	-	2,136 15.07 0.36	-	1,561 11.02 0.26	-	-	-	-	-	2,208 15.58 0.37	-	-	-	-	-	-	-	-	559 3.94 0.09
Bensalem (township)	58,434	3,807 6.52	-	1,884 49.49 3.22	-	-	-	-	-	-	-	-	-	-	686 18.02 1.17	-	-	-	-	-	-	-	-	-
Lower Makefield (township)	32,681	1,351 4.13	-	562 41.60 1.72	-	-	-	-	-	-	-	-	-	-	-	-	-	-	-	-	-	-	-	-
Newtown (township)	18,245	899 4.93	-	-	-	-	-	-	-	-	-	-	-	-	-	-	-	-	-	-	-	-	-	-
Butler County	174,083	942 0.54	-	448 47.56 0.26	-	-	-	-	-	-	-	-	-	-	-	-	-	-	-	-	-	-	-	-
Cambria County	152,598	560 0.37	-	-	-	-	-	-	-	-	-	-	-	-	-	-	-	-	-	-	-	-	-	-
Centre County	135,758	5,369 3.95	-	1,259 23.45 0.93	-	-	1,746 32.52 1.29	-	-	-	-	-	-	-	1,032 19.22 0.76	-	-	-	-	-	-	-	-	-
Ferguson (township)	14,063	1,012 7.20	-	-	-	-	-	-	-	-	-	-	-	-	-	-	-	-	-	-	-	-	-	-
Patton (township)	11,420	516 4.52	-	-	-	-	-	-	-	-	-	-	-	-	-	-	-	-	-	-	-	-	-	-
State College (borough)	38,420	3,462 9.01	-	768 22.18 2.00	-	-	1,165 33.65 3.03	-	-	-	-	-	-	-	590 17.04 1.54	-	-	-	-	-	-	-	-	-
Chester County	433,501	8,755 2.02	-	2,785 31.81 0.64	-	-	2,342 26.75 0.54	-	567 6.48 0.13	-	-	-	-	400 4.57 0.09	1,082 12.36 0.25	-	-	-	-	-	-	-	-	834 9.53 0.19

Notes: Please refer to the User's Guide for an explanation of data; data is arranged alphabetically by state, then county, then city within each county; table includes counties with populations greater than 49,999 unless noted and cities with populations greater than 9,999 whose Asian and/or NHPI population rates are greater than the national average; (1) Native Hawaiian and other Pacific Islander; (2) excludes Taiwanese; (3) includes Chamorro; (4) county does not meet population threshold but is shown in order to allow inclusion of city

Place	Total population	Total Asian population	Total NHPI[1] population	Asian Indian	Bangladeshi	Cambodian	Chinese[2]	Fijian	Filipino	Guamanian[3]	Hawaiian, Native	Hmong	Indonesian	Japanese	Korean	Laotian	Malaysian	Pakistani	Samoan	Sri Lankan	Taiwanese	Thai	Tongan	Vietnamese
Tredyffrin (township)	29,062	1,694 5.83	-	649 38.31 2.23	-	-	613 36.19 2.11	-	-	-	-	-	-	-	-	-	-	-	-	-	-	-	-	-
West Goshen (township)	20,495	777 3.79	-	-	-	-	-	-	-	-	-	-	-	-	-	-	-	-	-	-	-	-	-	-
West Whiteland (township)	16,499	608 3.69	-	-	-	-	-	-	-	-	-	-	-	-	-	-	-	-	-	-	-	-	-	-
Clearfield County	83,382	268 0.32	-	-	-	-	-	-	-	-	-	-	-	-	-	-	-	-	-	-	-	-	-	-
Columbia County	64,151	295 0.46	-	-	-	-	-	-	-	-	-	-	-	-	-	-	-	-	-	-	-	-	-	-
Crawford County	90,366	288 0.32	-	-	-	-	-	-	-	-	-	-	-	-	-	-	-	-	-	-	-	-	-	-
Cumberland County	213,674	3,444 1.61	-	1,040 30.20 0.49	-	-	512 14.87 0.24	-	-	-	-	-	-	-	691 20.06 0.32	-	-	-	-	-	-	-	-	606 17.60 0.28
Hampden (township)	24,193	889 3.67	-	-	-	-	-	-	-	-	-	-	-	-	-	-	-	-	-	-	-	-	-	-
Dauphin County	251,798	5,028 2.00	-	1,066 21.20 0.42	-	-	832 16.55 0.33	-	-	-	-	-	-	-	427 8.49 0.17	-	-	-	-	-	-	-	-	1,754 34.88 0.70
Derry (township)	21,273	886 4.16	-	-	-	-	-	-	-	-	-	-	-	-	-	-	-	-	-	-	-	-	-	-
Hershey (cdp)	12,777	547 4.28	-	-	-	-	-	-	-	-	-	-	-	-	-	-	-	-	-	-	-	-	-	-
Delaware County	550,864	18,290 3.32	-	5,188 28.37 0.94	-	-	3,533 19.32 0.64	-	1,199 6.56 0.22	-	-	-	-	708 3.87 0.13	3,455 18.89 0.63	-	-	645 3.53 0.12	-	-	-	-	-	1,943 10.62 0.35
Broomall (cdp)	11,175	777 6.95	-	-	-	-	-	-	-	-	-	-	-	-	466 59.97 4.17	-	-	-	-	-	-	-	-	-
Drexel Hill (cdp)	29,301	1,138 3.88	-	-	-	-	355 31.20 1.21	-	-	-	-	-	-	-	-	-	-	-	-	-	-	-	-	-
Marple (township)	23,737	1,265 5.33	-	-	-	-	-	-	-	-	-	-	-	-	665 52.57 2.80	-	-	-	-	-	-	-	-	-
Radnor (township)	30,878	1,600 5.18	-	-	-	-	394 24.63 1.28	-	-	-	-	-	-	-	-	-	-	-	-	-	-	-	-	-
Upper Darby (township)	81,821	7,107 8.69	-	2,028 28.54 2.48	-	-	1,523 21.43 1.86	-	-	-	-	-	-	-	995 14.00 1.22	-	-	-	-	-	-	-	-	1,179 16.59 1.44

Notes: Please refer to the User's Guide for an explanation of data; data is arranged alphabetically by state, then county, then city within each county; table includes counties with populations greater than 49,999 unless noted and cities with populations greater than 9,999 whose Asian and/or NHPI population rates are greater than the national average; (1) Native Hawaiian and other Pacific Islander; (2) excludes Taiwanese; (3) includes Chamorro; (4) county does not meet population threshold but is shown in order to allow inclusion of city

Place	Total population	Total Asian population	Total NHPI[1] population	Asian Indian	Bangladeshi	Cambodian	Chinese[2]	Fijian	Filipino	Guamanian[3]	Hawaiian, Native	Hmong	Indonesian	Japanese	Korean	Laotian	Malaysian	Pakistani	Samoan	Sri Lankan	Taiwanese	Thai	Tongan	Vietnamese
Erie County	280,843	1,811 0.64	-	523 28.88 0.19	-	-	-	-	-	-	-	-	-	-	-	-	-	-	-	-	-	-	-	-
Franklin County	129,313	909 0.70	-	-	-	-	-	-	-	-	-	-	-	-	-	-	-	-	-	-	-	-	-	-
Indiana County	89,605	663 0.74	-	-	-	-	-	-	-	-	-	-	-	-	-	-	-	-	-	-	-	-	-	-
Lackawanna County	213,295	1,806 0.85	-	670 37.10 0.31	-	-	-	-	-	-	-	-	-	-	-	-	-	-	-	-	-	-	-	-
Lancaster County	470,658	6,563 1.39	-	779 11.87 0.17	-	-	1,295 19.73 0.28	-	-	-	-	458 6.98 0.10	-	-	568 8.65 0.12	-	-	-	-	-	-	-	-	2,063 31.43 0.44
Lawrence County	94,643	293 0.31	-	-	-	-	-	-	-	-	-	-	-	-	-	-	-	-	-	-	-	-	-	-
Lebanon County	120,327	1,108 0.92	-	-	-	-	-	-	-	-	-	-	-	-	-	-	-	-	-	-	-	-	-	-
Lehigh County	312,090	6,841 2.19	-	2,158 31.55 0.69	-	-	1,637 23.93 0.52	-	-	-	-	-	-	-	714 10.44 0.23	-	-	-	-	-	-	-	-	1,454 21.25 0.47
Fullerton (cdp)	14,213	687 4.83	-	-	-	-	-	-	-	-	-	-	-	-	-	-	-	-	-	-	-	-	-	-
Lower Macungie (township)	19,220	874 4.55	-	-	-	-	409 46.80 2.13	-	-	-	-	-	-	-	-	-	-	-	-	-	-	-	-	-
Upper Macungie (township)	13,895	627 4.51	-	-	-	-	-	-	-	-	-	-	-	-	-	-	-	-	-	-	-	-	-	-
Luzerne County	319,250	1,534 0.48	-	411 26.79 0.13	-	-	-	-	-	-	-	-	-	-	-	-	-	-	-	-	-	-	-	-
Lycoming County	120,044	490 0.41	-	-	-	-	-	-	-	-	-	-	-	-	-	-	-	-	-	-	-	-	-	-
Mercer County	120,293	671 0.56	-	-	-	-	-	-	-	-	-	-	-	-	-	-	-	-	-	-	-	-	-	-
Monroe County	138,687	1,395 1.01	-	420 30.11 0.30	-	-	-	-	-	-	-	-	-	-	-	-	-	-	-	-	-	-	-	-
Montgomery County	750,097	29,431 3.92	-	7,433 25.26 0.99	-	-	5,497 18.68 0.73	-	1,960 6.66 0.26	-	-	-	-	715 2.43 0.10	9,203 31.27 1.23	-	-	-	-	-	-	-	-	2,429 8.25 0.32
Cheltenham (township)	36,875	2,391 6.48	-	-	-	-	-	-	-	-	-	-	-	-	1,119 46.80 3.03	-	-	-	-	-	-	-	-	-

Notes: Please refer to the User's Guide for an explanation of data; data is arranged alphabetically by state, then county, then city within each county; table includes counties with populations greater than 49,999 unless noted and cities with populations greater than 9,999 whose Asian and/or NHPI population rates are greater than the national average; (1) Native Hawaiian and other Pacific Islander; (2) excludes Taiwanese; (3) includes Chamorro; (4) county does not meet population threshold but is shown in order to allow inclusion of city

Place	Total population	Total Asian population	Total NHPI[1] population	Asian Indian	Bangladeshi	Cambodian	Chinese[2]	Fijian	Filipino	Guamanian[3]	Hawaiian, Native	Hmong	Indonesian	Japanese	Korean	Laotian	Malaysian	Pakistani	Samoan	Sri Lankan	Taiwanese	Thai	Tongan	Vietnamese
East Norriton (township)	13,140	538 4.09	-	-	-	-	-	-	-	-	-	-	-	-	-	-	-	-	-	-	-	-	-	-
Hatfield (township)	16,640	1,819 10.93	-	973 53.49 5.85	-	-	-	-	-	-	-	-	-	-	-	-	-	-	-	-	-	-	-	-
Horsham (township)	24,232	1,150 4.75	-	-	-	-	-	-	-	-	-	-	-	-	512 44.52 2.11	-	-	-	-	-	-	-	-	-
King of Prussia (cdp)	18,539	1,895 10.22	-	768 40.53 4.14	-	-	406 21.42 2.19	-	-	-	-	-	-	-	-	-	-	-	-	-	-	-	-	-
Lansdale (borough)	16,071	1,329 8.27	-	450 33.86 2.80	-	-	-	-	-	-	-	-	-	-	-	-	-	-	-	-	-	-	-	-
Lower Gwynedd (township)	10,422	403 3.87	-	-	-	-	-	-	-	-	-	-	-	-	-	-	-	-	-	-	-	-	-	-
Lower Providence (township)	22,409	1,014 4.52	-	-	-	-	474 46.75 2.12	-	-	-	-	-	-	-	-	-	-	-	-	-	-	-	-	-
Montgomery (township)	22,025	1,827 8.30	-	577 31.58 2.62	-	-	-	-	-	-	-	-	-	-	723 39.57 3.28	-	-	-	-	-	-	-	-	-
Montgomeryville (cdp)	11,958	820 6.86	-	-	-	-	-	-	-	-	-	-	-	-	-	-	-	-	-	-	-	-	-	-
Plymouth (township)	16,045	832 5.19	-	-	-	-	-	-	-	-	-	-	-	-	332 39.90 2.07	-	-	-	-	-	-	-	-	-
Towamencin (township)	17,601	1,043 5.93	-	-	-	-	-	-	-	-	-	-	-	-	-	-	-	-	-	-	-	-	-	-
Upper Dublin (township)	25,878	1,514 5.85	-	-	-	-	-	-	-	-	-	-	-	-	830 54.82 3.21	-	-	-	-	-	-	-	-	-
Upper Gwynedd (township)	14,243	1,144 8.03	-	-	-	-	319 27.88 2.24	-	-	-	-	-	-	-	-	-	-	-	-	-	-	-	-	-
Upper Merion (township)	26,844	2,161 8.05	-	910 42.11 3.39	-	-	444 20.55 1.65	-	-	-	-	-	-	-	-	-	-	-	-	-	-	-	-	-
Whitpain (township)	18,703	1,247 6.67	-	-	-	-	-	-	-	-	-	-	-	-	586 46.99 3.13	-	-	-	-	-	-	-	-	-
Northampton County	267,066	3,756 1.41	-	1,241 33.04 0.46	-	-	757 20.15 0.28	-	-	-	-	-	-	-	461 12.27 0.17	-	-	-	-	-	-	-	-	473 12.59 0.18
Northumberland County	94,556	373 0.39	-	-	-	-	-	-	-	-	-	-	-	-	-	-	-	-	-	-	-	-	-	-

Notes: Please refer to the User's Guide for an explanation of data; data is arranged alphabetically by state, then county, then city within each county; table includes counties with populations greater than 49,999 unless noted and cities with populations greater than 9,999 whose Asian and/or NHPI population rates are greater than the national average; (1) Native Hawaiian and other Pacific Islander; (2) excludes Taiwanese; (3) includes Chamorro; (4) county does not meet population threshold but is shown in order to allow inclusion of city

Place	Total population	Total Asian population	Total NHPI[1] population	Asian Indian	Bangladeshi	Cambodian	Chinese[2]	Fijian	Filipino	Guamanian[3]	Hawaiian, Native	Hmong	Indonesian	Japanese	Korean	Laotian	Malaysian	Pakistani	Samoan	Sri Lankan	Taiwanese	Thai	Tongan	Vietnamese
Philadelphia County	1,517,550	65,171 4.29	790 0.05	12,541 19.24 0.83	-	6,407 9.83 0.42	17,807 27.32 1.17	-	3,824 5.87 0.25	-	-	-	-	1,105 1.70 0.07	6,529 10.02 0.43	1,214 1.86 0.08	-	629 0.97 0.04	-	-	-	-	-	11,074 16.99 0.73
Philadelphia (city)	1,517,550	65,171 4.29	790 0.05	12,541 19.24 0.83	-	6,407 9.83 0.42	17,807 27.32 1.17	-	3,824 5.87 0.25	-	-	-	-	1,105 1.70 0.07	6,529 10.02 0.43	1,214 1.86 0.08	-	629 0.97 0.04	-	-	-	-	-	11,074 16.99 0.73
Schuylkill County	150,336	553 0.37	-	-	-	-	-	-	-	-	-	-	-	-	-	-	-	-	-	-	-	-	-	-
Washington County	202,897	631 0.31	-	-	-	-	-	-	-	-	-	-	-	-	-	-	-	-	-	-	-	-	-	-
Westmoreland County	369,993	1,724 0.47	-	447 25.93 0.12	-	-	-	-	-	-	-	-	-	-	-	-	-	-	-	-	-	-	-	-
York County	381,751	3,150 0.83	-	527 16.73 0.14	-	-	677 21.49 0.18	-	-	-	-	-	-	-	625 19.84 0.16	-	-	-	-	-	-	-	-	584 18.54 0.15
RHODE ISLAND	1,048,319	23,825 2.27	441 0.04	2,548 10.69 0.24	-	5,105 21.43 0.49	4,562 19.15 0.44	-	2,126 8.92 0.20	-	-	961 4.03 0.09	-	785 3.29 0.07	1,923 8.07 0.18	2,889 12.13 0.28	-	-	-	-	-	-	-	1,028 4.31 0.10
Bristol County	50,648	420 0.83	-	-	-	-	-	-	-	-	-	-	-	-	-	-	-	-	-	-	-	-	-	-
Kent County	167,090	2,187 1.31	-	-	-	-	369 16.87 0.22	-	-	-	-	-	-	-	418 19.11 0.25	-	-	-	-	-	-	-	-	-
Newport County	85,433	982 1.15	-	-	-	-	-	-	461 46.95 0.54	-	-	-	-	-	-	-	-	-	-	-	-	-	-	-
Providence County	621,602	18,319 2.95	-	1,863 10.17 0.30	-	4,825 26.34 0.78	3,184 17.38 0.51	-	1,101 6.01 0.18	-	-	831 4.54 0.13	-	-	1,178 6.43 0.19	2,750 15.01 0.44	-	-	-	-	-	-	-	808 4.41 0.13
Providence (city)	173,618	10,707 6.17	-	912 8.52 0.53	-	3,582 33.45 2.06	1,499 14.00 0.86	-	517 4.83 0.30	-	-	674 6.29 0.39	-	-	714 6.67 0.41	1,326 12.38 0.76	-	-	-	-	-	-	-	-
Woonsocket (city)	43,224	1,646 3.81	-	-	-	-	-	-	-	-	-	-	-	-	-	912 55.41 2.11	-	-	-	-	-	-	-	-
Washington County	123,546	1,917 1.55	-	-	-	-	574 29.94 0.46	-	-	-	-	-	-	-	-	-	-	-	-	-	-	-	-	-
SOUTH CAROLINA	4,012,012	36,505 0.91	1,384 0.03	8,215 22.50 0.20	-	341 0.93 0.01	6,262 17.15 0.16	-	6,953 19.05 0.17	359 25.94 0.01	496 35.84 0.01	860 2.36 0.02	-	2,282 6.25 0.06	3,546 9.71 0.09	1,324 3.63 0.03	-	-	-	-	-	688 1.88 0.02	-	3,814 10.45 0.10
Aiken County	142,552	940 0.66	-	-	-	-	-	-	-	-	-	-	-	-	-	-	-	-	-	-	-	-	-	-
Anderson County	165,740	836 0.50	-	-	-	-	-	-	-	-	-	-	-	-	-	-	-	-	-	-	-	-	-	-

Notes: Please refer to the User's Guide for an explanation of data; data is arranged alphabetically by state, then county, then city within each county; table includes counties with populations greater than 49,999 unless noted and cities with populations greater than 9,999 whose Asian and/or NHPI population rates are greater than the national average; (1) Native Hawaiian and other Pacific Islander; (2) excludes Taiwanese; (3) includes Chamorro; (4) county does not meet population threshold but is shown in order to allow inclusion of city

Place	Total population	Total Asian population	Total NHPI[1] population	Asian Indian	Bangladeshi	Cambodian	Chinese[2]	Fijian	Filipino	Guamanian[3]	Hawaiian, Native	Hmong	Indonesian	Japanese	Korean	Laotian	Malaysian	Pakistani	Samoan	Sri Lankan	Taiwanese	Thai	Tongan	Vietnamese
Beaufort County	120,937	1,014 0.84	-	-	-	-	-	-	-	-	-	-	-	-	-	-	-	-	-	-	-	-	-	-
Berkeley County	142,651	2,933 2.06	-	-	-	-	-	-	1,811 61.75 1.27	-	-	-	-	-	-	-	-	-	-	-	-	-	-	-
Charleston County	309,969	3,502 1.13	-	633 18.08 0.20	-	-	701 20.02 0.23	-	997 28.47 0.32	-	-	-	-	-	-	-	-	-	-	-	-	-	-	-
Dorchester County	96,413	1,254 1.30	-	-	-	-	-	-	638 50.88 0.66	-	-	-	-	-	-	-	-	-	-	-	-	-	-	-
Florence County	125,761	1,026 0.82	-	-	-	-	-	-	-	-	-	-	-	-	-	-	-	-	-	-	-	-	-	-
Greenville County	379,616	4,893 1.29	-	1,430 29.23 0.38	-	-	717 14.65 0.19	-	533 10.89 0.14	-	-	-	-	-	-	-	-	-	-	-	-	-	-	1,139 23.28 0.30
Greenwood County	66,271	422 0.64	-	-	-	-	-	-	-	-	-	-	-	-	-	-	-	-	-	-	-	-	-	-
Horry County	196,629	1,548 0.79	-	-	-	-	-	-	-	-	-	-	-	-	-	-	-	-	-	-	-	-	-	-
Lexington County	216,014	1,945 0.90	-	602 30.95 0.28	-	-	566 29.10 0.26	-	-	-	-	-	-	-	-	-	-	-	-	-	-	-	-	-
Oconee County	66,215	264 0.40	-	-	-	-	-	-	-	-	-	-	-	-	-	-	-	-	-	-	-	-	-	-
Pickens County	110,757	1,316 1.19	-	518 39.36 0.47	-	-	383 29.10 0.35	-	-	-	-	-	-	-	-	-	-	-	-	-	-	-	-	-
Clemson (city)	12,111	598 4.94	-	-	-	-	-	-	-	-	-	-	-	-	-	-	-	-	-	-	-	-	-	-
Richland County	320,677	5,611 1.75	-	1,494 26.63 0.47	-	-	1,104 19.68 0.34	-	522 9.30 0.16	-	-	-	-	-	1,261 22.47 0.39	-	-	-	-	-	-	-	-	528 9.41 0.16
Spartanburg County	253,791	4,152 1.64	-	764 18.40 0.30	-	-	-	-	-	-	-	750 18.06 0.30	-	-	-	678 16.33 0.27	-	-	-	-	-	-	-	-
Sumter County	104,646	932 0.89	-	-	-	-	-	-	-	-	-	-	-	-	-	-	-	-	-	-	-	-	-	-
York County	164,614	1,312 0.80	-	-	-	-	-	-	-	-	-	-	-	-	-	-	-	-	-	-	-	-	-	445 33.92 0.27
SOUTH DAKOTA	754,844	4,729 0.63	-	581 12.29 0.08	-	-	679 14.36 0.09	-	704 14.89 0.09	-	-	-	-	412 8.71 0.05	745 15.75 0.10	218 4.61 0.03	-	-	-	-	-	-	-	715 15.12 0.09

Notes: Please refer to the User's Guide for an explanation of data; data is arranged alphabetically by state, then county, then city within each county; table includes counties with populations greater than 49,999 unless noted and cities with populations greater than 9,999 whose Asian and/or NHPI population rates are greater than the national average; (1) Native Hawaiian and other Pacific Islander; (2) excludes Taiwanese; (3) includes Chamorro; (4) county does not meet population threshold but is shown in order to allow inclusion of city

Place	Total population	Total Asian population	Total NHPI[1] population	Asian Indian	Bangladeshi	Cambodian	Chinese[2]	Fijian	Filipino	Guamanian[3]	Hawaiian, Native	Hmong	Indonesian	Japanese	Korean	Laotian	Malaysian	Pakistani	Samoan	Sri Lankan	Taiwanese	Thai	Tongan	Vietnamese
Minnehaha County	148,281	1,585 1.07	-	-	-	-	-	-	-	-	-	-	-	-	-	-	-	-	-	-	-	-	-	523 33.00 0.35
Pennington County	88,565	914 1.03	-	-	-	-	-	-	-	-	-	-	-	-	-	-	-	-	-	-	-	-	-	-
TENNESSEE	5,689,283	54,132 0.95	2,159 0.04	11,956 22.09 0.21	-	1,190 2.20 0.02	8,303 15.34 0.15	-	5,282 9.76 0.09	619 28.67 0.01	560 25.94 0.01	-	-	3,868 7.15 0.07	6,902 12.75 0.12	4,015 7.42 0.07	-	764 1.41 0.01	540 25.01 0.01	-	580 1.07 0.01	995 1.84 0.02	-	7,061 13.04 0.12
Anderson County	71,330	513 0.72	-	-	-	-	-	-	-	-	-	-	-	-	-	-	-	-	-	-	-	-	-	-
Blount County	105,823	638 0.60	-	-	-	-	-	-	-	-	-	-	-	-	-	-	-	-	-	-	-	-	-	-
Bradley County	87,965	480 0.55	-	-	-	-	-	-	-	-	-	-	-	-	-	-	-	-	-	-	-	-	-	-
Davidson County	569,891	11,691 2.05	400 0.07	2,528 21.62 0.44	-	-	1,518 12.98 0.27	-	801 6.85 0.14	-	-	-	-	859 7.35 0.15	1,300 11.12 0.23	1,311 11.21 0.23	-	-	-	-	-	-	-	1,686 14.42 0.30
Hamilton County	307,896	3,852 1.25	-	1,140 29.60 0.37	-	-	-	-	415 10.77 0.13	-	-	-	-	-	524 13.60 0.17	-	-	-	-	-	-	-	-	436 11.32 0.14
Knox County	382,032	4,548 1.19	-	1,340 29.46 0.35	-	-	927 20.38 0.24	-	-	-	-	-	-	-	533 11.72 0.14	-	-	-	-	-	-	-	-	473 10.40 0.12
Madison County	91,837	557 0.61	-	-	-	-	-	-	-	-	-	-	-	-	-	-	-	-	-	-	-	-	-	-
Montgomery County	134,768	2,448 1.82	-	-	-	-	-	-	-	-	-	-	-	-	1,111 45.38 0.82	-	-	-	-	-	-	-	-	-
Putnam County	62,315	581 0.93	-	-	-	-	-	-	-	-	-	-	-	-	-	-	-	-	-	-	-	-	-	-
Rutherford County	182,023	3,253 1.79	-	-	-	-	-	-	-	-	-	-	-	-	-	1,565 48.11 0.86	-	-	-	-	-	-	-	-
Shelby County	897,472	14,925 1.66	493 0.05	3,582 24.00 0.40	-	516 3.46 0.06	2,800 18.76 0.31	-	1,362 9.13 0.15	-	-	-	-	515 3.45 0.06	1,233 8.26 0.14	-	-	-	-	-	-	-	-	3,342 22.39 0.37
Germantown (city)	37,281	1,380 3.70	-	531 38.48 1.42	-	-	421 30.51 1.13	-	-	-	-	-	-	-	-	-	-	-	-	-	-	-	-	-
Sullivan County	153,048	585 0.38	-	-	-	-	-	-	-	-	-	-	-	-	-	-	-	-	-	-	-	-	-	-
Sumner County	130,449	877 0.67	-	-	-	-	-	-	-	-	-	-	-	-	-	-	-	-	-	-	-	-	-	-

Notes: Please refer to the User's Guide for an explanation of data; data is arranged alphabetically by state, then county, then city within each county; table includes counties with populations greater than 49,999 unless noted and cities with populations greater than 9,999 whose Asian and/or NHPI population rates are greater than the national average; (1) Native Hawaiian and other Pacific Islander; (2) excludes Taiwanese; (3) includes Chamorro; (4) county does not meet population threshold but is shown in order to allow inclusion of city

Place	Total population	Total Asian population	Total NHPI[1] population	Asian Indian	Bangladeshi	Cambodian	Chinese[2]	Fijian	Filipino	Guamanian[3]	Hawaiian, Native	Hmong	Indonesian	Japanese	Korean	Laotian	Malaysian	Pakistani	Samoan	Sri Lankan	Taiwanese	Thai	Tongan	Vietnamese
Washington County	107,198	729 0.68	-	-	-	-	-	-	-	-	-	-	-	-	-	-	-	-	-	-	-	-	-	-
Weakley County[4]	34,895	467 1.34	-	-	-	-	-	-	-	-	-	-	-	-	-	-	-	-	-	-	-	-	-	-
Martin (city)	10,544	430 4.08	-	-	-	-	-	-	-	-	-	-	-	-	-	-	-	-	-	-	-	-	-	-
Williamson County	126,638	1,497 1.18	-	-	-	-	-	-	-	-	-	-	-	-	-	-	-	-	-	-	-	-	-	-
Wilson County	88,809	303 0.34	-	-	-	-	-	-	-	-	-	-	-	-	-	-	-	-	-	-	-	-	-	-
TEXAS	20,851,820	555,928 2.67	12,464 0.06	127,256 22.89 0.61	2,574 0.46 0.01	7,603 1.37 0.04	98,330 17.69 0.47	-	58,615 10.54 0.28	3,304 26.51 0.02	3,655 29.32 0.02	-	1,771 0.32 0.01	16,114 2.90 0.08	44,374 7.98 0.21	9,862 1.77 0.05	670 0.12 <0.01	18,872 3.39 0.09	2,033 16.31 0.01	976 0.18 <0.01	7,859 1.41 0.04	7,114 1.28 0.03	501 4.02 <0.01	134,145 24.13 0.64
Anderson County	55,109	406 0.74	-	-	-	-	-	-	-	-	-	-	-	-	-	-	-	-	-	-	-	-	-	-
Angelina County	80,130	539 0.67	-	-	-	-	-	-	-	-	-	-	-	-	-	-	-	-	-	-	-	-	-	-
Bell County	237,974	6,114 2.57	1,264 0.53	583 9.54 0.24	-	-	-	-	1,634 26.73 0.69	596 47.15 0.25	-	-	-	382 6.25 0.16	2,368 38.73 1.00	-	-	-	-	-	-	-	-	-
Killeen (city)	86,822	3,805 4.38	1,046 1.20	-	-	-	-	-	1,100 28.91 1.27	500 47.80 0.58	-	-	-	-	1,570 41.26 1.81	-	-	-	-	-	-	-	-	-
Bexar County	1,392,931	22,586 1.62	1,130 0.08	3,738 16.55 0.27	-	-	3,705 16.40 0.27	-	5,208 23.06 0.37	-	420 37.17 0.03	-	-	1,715 7.59 0.12	2,578 11.41 0.19	385 1.70 0.03	-	-	-	-	-	814 3.60 0.06	-	2,879 12.75 0.21
Bowie County	89,306	448 0.50	-	-	-	-	-	-	-	-	-	-	-	-	-	-	-	-	-	-	-	-	-	-
Brazoria County	241,767	4,720 1.95	-	907 19.22 0.38	-	383 8.11 0.16	641 13.58 0.27	-	681 14.43 0.28	-	-	-	-	-	-	-	-	-	-	-	-	-	-	1,324 28.05 0.55
Brazos County	152,415	6,238 4.09	-	1,776 28.47 1.17	-	-	1,650 26.45 1.08	-	-	-	-	-	-	-	908 14.56 0.60	-	-	-	-	-	-	-	-	468 7.50 0.31
College Station (city)	67,900	5,160 7.60	-	1,312 25.43 1.93	-	-	1,452 28.14 2.14	-	-	-	-	-	-	-	778 15.08 1.15	-	-	-	-	-	-	-	-	-
Calhoun County[4]	20,647	683 3.31	-	-	-	-	-	-	-	-	-	-	-	-	-	-	-	-	-	-	-	-	-	165 24.16 0.80
Port Lavaca (city)	12,014	493 4.10	-	-	-	-	-	-	-	-	-	-	-	-	-	-	-	-	-	-	-	-	-	-

Notes: Please refer to the User's Guide for an explanation of data; data is arranged alphabetically by state, then county, then city within each county; table includes counties with populations greater than 49,999 unless noted and cities with populations greater than 9,999 whose Asian and/or NHPI population rates are greater than the national average; (1) Native Hawaiian and other Pacific Islander; (2) excludes Taiwanese; (3) includes Chamorro; (4) county does not meet population threshold but is shown in order to allow inclusion of city

Place	Total population	Total Asian population	Total NHPI[1] population	Asian Indian	Bangladeshi	Cambodian	Chinese[2]	Fijian	Filipino	Guamanian[3]	Hawaiian, Native	Hmong	Indonesian	Japanese	Korean	Laotian	Malaysian	Pakistani	Samoan	Sri Lankan	Taiwanese	Thai	Tongan	Vietnamese
Cameron County	335,227	1,509 0.45	-	-	-	-	-	-	584 38.70 0.17	-	-	-	-	-	-	-	-	-	-	-	-	-	-	-
Collin County	491,675	33,606 6.84	-	8,746 26.03 1.78	-	-	12,526 37.27 2.55	-	1,451 4.32 0.30	-	-	-	-	914 2.72 0.19	2,841 8.45 0.58	-	-	958 2.85 0.19	-	-	850 2.53 0.17	454 1.35 0.09	-	3,493 10.39 0.71
Allen (city)	43,457	1,639 3.77	-	451 27.52 1.04	-	-	-	-	-	-	-	-	-	-	-	-	-	-	-	-	-	-	-	396 24.16 0.91
Plano (city)	222,301	22,465 10.11	-	5,680 25.28 2.56	-	-	9,305 41.42 4.19	-	780 3.47 0.35	-	-	-	-	499 2.22 0.22	2,139 9.52 0.96	-	-	604 2.69 0.27	-	-	564 2.51 0.25	-	-	1,804 8.03 0.81
Comal County	78,021	443 0.57	-	-	-	-	-	-	-	-	-	-	-	-	-	-	-	-	-	-	-	-	-	-
Coryell County	74,978	1,380 1.84	433 0.58	-	-	-	-	-	-	-	-	-	-	-	495 35.87 0.66	-	-	-	-	-	-	-	-	-
Dallas County	2,218,899	87,446 3.94	987 0.04	23,736 27.14 1.07	673 0.77 0.03	2,357 2.70 0.11	11,734 13.42 0.53	-	5,994 6.85 0.27	-	-	-	-	2,224 2.54 0.10	9,340 10.68 0.42	2,337 2.67 0.11	-	3,713 4.25 0.17	-	-	804 0.92 0.04	1,105 1.26 0.05	-	19,878 22.73 0.90
Addison (town)	13,800	1,104 8.00	-	606 54.89 4.39	-	-	-	-	-	-	-	-	-	-	-	-	-	-	-	-	-	-	-	-
Coppell (city)	35,955	3,444 9.58	-	1,140 33.10 3.17	-	-	776 22.53 2.16	-	-	-	-	-	-	-	680 19.74 1.89	-	-	-	-	-	-	-	-	-
Farmers Branch (city)	28,325	1,051 3.71	-	-	-	-	-	-	-	-	-	-	-	-	-	-	-	-	-	-	-	-	-	-
Garland (city)	215,991	15,646 7.24	-	3,102 19.83 1.44	-	-	1,675 10.71 0.78	-	1,113 7.11 0.52	-	-	-	-	-	1,138 7.27 0.53	-	-	831 5.31 0.38	-	-	-	-	-	6,301 40.27 2.92
Grand Prairie (city)	127,049	5,295 4.17	-	733 13.84 0.58	-	-	-	-	704 13.30 0.55	-	-	-	-	-	-	391 7.38 0.31	-	-	-	-	-	-	-	2,383 45.00 1.88
Irving (city)	191,611	15,637 8.16	-	6,093 38.97 3.18	-	-	1,547 9.89 0.81	-	774 4.95 0.40	-	-	-	-	678 4.34 0.35	2,480 15.86 1.29	479 3.06 0.25	-	429 2.74 0.22	-	-	-	-	-	1,574 10.07 0.82
Mesquite (city)	124,578	4,557 3.66	-	2,293 50.32 1.84	-	-	-	-	920 20.19 0.74	-	-	-	-	-	-	-	-	-	-	-	-	-	-	-
Richardson (city)	91,635	10,196 11.13	-	2,422 23.75 2.64	-	-	3,055 29.96 3.33	-	375 3.68 0.41	-	-	-	-	-	1,031 10.11 1.13	-	-	423 4.15 0.46	-	-	-	-	-	1,741 17.08 1.90
Rowlett (city)	44,326	1,681 3.79	-	568 33.79 1.28	-	-	-	-	-	-	-	-	-	-	-	-	-	-	-	-	-	-	-	-
Denton County	432,976	17,110 3.95	-	6,031 35.25 1.39	-	726 4.24 0.17	2,012 11.76 0.46	-	852 4.98 0.20	-	-	-	-	478 2.79 0.11	2,261 13.21 0.52	-	-	840 4.91 0.19	-	-	-	-	-	2,606 15.23 0.60

Notes: Please refer to the User's Guide for an explanation of data; data is arranged alphabetically by state, then county, then city within each county; table includes counties with populations greater than 49,999 unless noted and cities with populations greater than 9,999 whose Asian and/or NHPI population rates are greater than the national average; (1) Native Hawaiian and other Pacific Islander; (2) excludes Taiwanese; (3) includes Chamorro; (4) county does not meet population threshold but is shown in order to allow inclusion of city

Place	Total population	Total Asian population	Total NHPI[1] population	Asian Indian	Bangladeshi	Cambodian	Chinese[2]	Fijian	Filipino	Guamanian[3]	Hawaiian, Native	Hmong	Indonesian	Japanese	Korean	Laotian	Malaysian	Pakistani	Samoan	Sri Lankan	Taiwanese	Thai	Tongan	Vietnamese
Carrollton (city)	109,215	11,415 10.45	-	4,384 38.41 4.01	-	818 7.17 0.75	676 5.92 0.62	-	-	-	-	-	-	-	1,053 9.22 0.96	-	-	1,166 10.21 1.07	-	-	-	-	-	2,404 21.06 2.20
Lewisville (city)	77,514	3,043 3.93	-	1,224 40.22 1.58	-	-	-	-	-	-	-	-	-	-	-	-	-	-	-	-	-	-	-	452 14.85 0.58
Ector County	121,123	880 0.73	-	-	-	-	-	-	-	-	-	-	-	-	-	-	-	-	-	-	-	-	-	-
El Paso County	679,622	6,956 1.02	554 0.08	1,014 14.58 0.15	-	-	812 11.67 0.12	-	1,796 25.82 0.26	-	-	-	-	797 11.46 0.12	1,713 24.63 0.25	-	-	-	-	-	-	-	-	-
Ellis County	111,360	441 0.40	-	-	-	-	-	-	-	-	-	-	-	-	-	-	-	-	-	-	-	-	-	-
Fort Bend County	354,452	38,774 10.94	-	12,788 32.98 3.61	-	-	9,849 25.40 2.78	-	4,395 11.33 1.24	-	-	-	-	-	1,146 2.96 0.32	-	-	2,441 6.30 0.69	-	-	1,216 3.14 0.34	-	-	5,208 13.43 1.47
Cinco Ranch (cdp)	11,237	690 6.14	-	-	-	-	-	-	-	-	-	-	-	-	-	-	-	-	-	-	-	-	-	-
Mission Bend (cdp)	30,900	5,175 16.75	-	1,310 25.31 4.24	-	-	687 13.28 2.22	-	921 17.80 2.98	-	-	-	-	-	-	-	-	480 9.28 1.55	-	-	-	-	-	1,263 24.41 4.09
Missouri City (city)	52,477	5,746 10.95	-	1,923 33.47 3.66	-	-	1,385 24.10 2.64	-	1,035 18.01 1.97	-	-	-	-	-	-	-	-	-	-	-	-	-	-	585 10.18 1.11
New Territory (cdp)	13,886	3,250 23.40	-	1,569 48.28 11.30	-	-	698 21.48 5.03	-	-	-	-	-	-	-	-	-	-	-	-	-	-	-	-	-
Stafford (city)	15,620	3,312 21.20	-	1,280 38.65 8.19	-	-	534 16.12 3.42	-	518 15.64 3.32	-	-	-	-	-	-	-	-	-	-	-	-	-	-	605 18.27 3.87
Sugar Land (city)	63,507	14,417 22.70	-	4,338 30.09 6.83	-	-	5,287 36.67 8.33	-	996 6.91 1.57	-	-	-	-	-	440 3.05 0.69	-	-	618 4.29 0.97	-	-	937 6.50 1.48	-	-	1,276 8.85 2.01
Galveston County	250,158	5,275 2.11	-	968 18.35 0.39	-	-	883 16.74 0.35	-	814 15.43 0.33	-	-	-	-	-	-	-	-	-	-	-	-	-	-	1,712 32.45 0.68
Grayson County	110,595	647 0.59	-	-	-	-	-	-	-	-	-	-	-	-	-	-	-	-	-	-	-	-	-	-
Gregg County	111,379	644 0.58	-	-	-	-	-	-	-	-	-	-	-	-	-	-	-	-	-	-	-	-	-	-
Guadalupe County	89,023	896 1.01	-	-	-	-	-	-	-	-	-	-	-	-	-	-	-	-	-	-	-	-	-	-
Harris County	3,400,578	171,977 5.06	1,514 0.04	35,997 20.93 1.06	688 0.40 0.02	2,012 1.17 0.06	31,418 18.27 0.92	-	15,774 9.17 0.46	639 42.21 0.02	-	-	690 0.40 0.02	3,679 2.14 0.11	8,114 4.72 0.24	1,182 0.69 0.03	-	7,332 4.26 0.22	-	-	2,223 1.29 0.07	1,333 0.78 0.04	-	55,445 32.24 1.63

Notes: Please refer to the User's Guide for an explanation of data; data is arranged alphabetically by state, then county, then city within each county; table includes counties with populations greater than 49,999 unless noted and cities with populations greater than 9,999 whose Asian and/or NHPI population rates are greater than the national average; (1) Native Hawaiian and other Pacific Islander; (2) excludes Taiwanese; (3) includes Chamorro; (4) county does not meet population threshold but is shown in order to allow inclusion of city

Place	Total population	Total Asian population	Total NHPI[1] population	Asian Indian	Bangladeshi	Cambodian	Chinese[2]	Fijian	Filipino	Guamanian[3]	Hawaiian, Native	Hmong	Indonesian	Japanese	Korean	Laotian	Malaysian	Pakistani	Samoan	Sri Lankan	Taiwanese	Thai	Tongan	Vietnamese
Bellaire (city)	15,581	1,052 6.75	-	-	-	-	454 43.16 2.91	-	-	-	-	-	-	-	-	-	-	-	-	-	-	-	-	-
Houston (city)	1,954,848	102,484 5.24	876 0.04	20,476 19.98 1.05	-	723 0.71 0.04	21,856 21.33 1.12	-	7,686 7.50 0.39	442 50.46 0.02	-	-	517 0.50 0.03	2,407 2.35 0.12	5,190 5.06 0.27	-	-	4,997 4.88 0.26	-	-	1,492 1.46 0.08	881 0.86 0.05	-	31,820 31.05 1.63
West University Place (city)	14,211	745 5.24	-	-	-	-	-	-	-	-	-	-	-	-	-	-	-	-	-	-	-	-	-	-
Hays County	97,589	851 0.87	-	-	-	-	-	-	-	-	-	-	-	-	-	-	-	-	-	-	-	-	-	-
Hidalgo County	569,463	3,156 0.55	-	630 19.96 0.11	-	-	-	-	1,508 47.78 0.26	-	-	-	-	-	-	-	-	-	-	-	-	-	-	-
Hunt County	76,596	557 0.73	-	-	-	-	-	-	-	-	-	-	-	-	-	-	-	-	-	-	-	-	-	-
Jefferson County	252,051	7,033 2.79	-	901 12.81 0.36	-	-	486 6.91 0.19	-	954 13.56 0.38	-	-	-	-	-	-	-	-	-	-	-	-	-	-	4,095 58.23 1.62
Port Arthur (city)	57,756	3,388 5.87	-	-	-	-	-	-	-	-	-	-	-	-	-	-	-	-	-	-	-	-	-	2,829 83.50 4.90
Johnson County	126,811	650 0.51	-	-	-	-	-	-	-	-	-	-	-	-	-	-	-	-	-	-	-	-	-	-
Kaufman County	71,313	487 0.68	-	-	-	-	-	-	-	-	-	-	-	-	-	-	-	-	-	-	-	-	-	-
Lubbock County	242,628	2,971 1.22	-	763 25.68 0.31	-	-	597 20.09 0.25	-	-	-	-	-	-	-	-	-	-	-	-	-	-	-	-	368 12.39 0.15
McLennan County	213,517	2,134 1.00	-	394 18.46 0.18	-	-	-	-	-	-	-	-	-	-	-	-	-	-	-	-	-	-	-	-
Midland County	116,009	1,065 0.92	-	398 37.37 0.34	-	-	-	-	-	-	-	-	-	-	-	-	-	-	-	-	-	-	-	-
Montgomery County	293,768	3,133 1.07	-	974 31.09 0.33	-	-	691 22.06 0.24	-	466 14.87 0.16	-	-	-	-	-	-	-	-	-	-	-	-	-	-	-
Nacogdoches County	59,203	383 0.65	-	-	-	-	-	-	-	-	-	-	-	-	-	-	-	-	-	-	-	-	-	-
Nueces County	313,645	3,507 1.12	-	625 17.82 0.20	-	-	-	-	1,614 46.02 0.51	-	-	-	-	-	-	-	-	-	-	-	-	-	-	-
Orange County	84,966	697 0.82	-	-	-	-	-	-	-	-	-	-	-	-	-	-	-	-	-	-	-	-	-	377 54.09 0.44

Notes: Please refer to the User's Guide for an explanation of data; data is arranged alphabetically by state, then county, then city within each county; table includes counties with populations greater than 49,999 unless noted and cities with populations greater than 9,999 whose Asian and/or NHPI population rates are greater than the national average; (1) Native Hawaiian and other Pacific Islander; (2) excludes Taiwanese; (3) includes Chamorro; (4) county does not meet population threshold but is shown in order to allow inclusion of city

Place	Total population	Total Asian population	Total NHPI[1] population	Asian Indian	Bangladeshi	Cambodian	Chinese[2]	Fijian	Filipino	Guamanian[3]	Hawaiian, Native	Hmong	Indonesian	Japanese	Korean	Laotian	Malaysian	Pakistani	Samoan	Sri Lankan	Taiwanese	Thai	Tongan	Vietnamese
Potter County	113,546	2,990 2.63	-	-	-	-	-	-	-	-	-	-	-	-	-	1,059 35.42 0.93	-	-	-	-	-	-	-	1,063 35.55 0.94
Randall County	104,312	1,131 1.08	-	-	-	-	-	-	-	-	-	-	-	-	-	-	-	-	-	-	-	-	-	-
San Patricio County	67,138	451 0.67	-	-	-	-	-	-	-	-	-	-	-	-	-	-	-	-	-	-	-	-	-	-
Smith County	174,706	1,105 0.63	-	-	-	-	-	-	-	-	-	-	-	-	-	-	-	-	-	-	-	-	-	-
Tarrant County	1,446,219	51,202 3.54	1,646 0.11	9,474 18.50 0.66	-	778 1.52 0.05	5,550 10.84 0.38	-	3,480 6.80 0.24	-	-	-	-	1,033 2.02 0.07	3,190 6.23 0.22	3,193 6.24 0.22	-	986 1.93 0.07	-	-	672 1.31 0.05	775 1.51 0.05	365 22.17 0.03	19,171 37.44 1.33
Arlington (city)	332,695	19,271 5.79	-	3,007 15.60 0.90	-	-	2,763 14.34 0.83	-	1,192 6.19 0.36	-	-	-	-	-	906 4.70 0.27	-	-	-	-	-	415 2.15 0.12	-	-	9,023 46.82 2.71
Euless (city)	46,088	3,232 7.01	-	1,244 38.49 2.70	-	-	-	-	-	-	-	-	-	-	-	-	-	-	-	-	-	-	-	-
Haltom City (city)	39,229	3,106 7.92	-	-	-	-	-	-	-	-	-	-	-	-	-	812 26.14 2.07	-	-	-	-	-	-	-	1,576 50.74 4.02
Taylor County	126,555	1,678 1.33	-	-	-	-	-	-	597 35.58 0.47	-	-	-	-	-	-	-	-	-	-	-	-	-	-	-
Tom Green County	104,010	724 0.70	-	-	-	-	-	-	-	-	-	-	-	-	-	-	-	-	-	-	-	-	-	-
Travis County	812,280	36,119 4.45	676 0.08	8,431 23.34 1.04	-	-	8,798 24.36 1.08	-	2,218 6.14 0.27	-	-	-	-	1,215 3.36 0.15	4,154 11.50 0.51	-	-	724 2.00 0.09	-	-	840 2.33 0.10	402 1.11 0.05	-	7,386 20.45 0.91
Austin (city)	656,302	30,866 4.70	445 0.07	7,336 23.77 1.12	-	-	8,022 25.99 1.22	-	1,732 5.61 0.26	-	-	-	-	1,135 3.68 0.17	3,632 11.77 0.55	-	-	526 1.70 0.08	-	-	748 2.42 0.11	-	-	5,789 18.76 0.88
Pflugerville (city)	16,366	728 4.45	-	-	-	-	-	-	-	-	-	-	-	-	-	-	-	-	-	-	-	-	-	-
Wells Branch (cdp)	11,249	1,077 9.57	-	-	-	-	-	-	-	-	-	-	-	-	-	-	-	-	-	-	-	-	-	-
Victoria County	84,088	492 0.59	-	-	-	-	-	-	-	-	-	-	-	-	-	-	-	-	-	-	-	-	-	-
Webb County	193,117	801 0.41	-	-	-	-	-	-	-	-	-	-	-	-	-	-	-	-	-	-	-	-	-	-
Wichita County	131,664	2,538 1.93	-	-	-	-	-	-	581 22.89 0.44	-	-	-	-	-	-	-	-	-	-	-	-	-	-	798 31.44 0.61

Notes: Please refer to the User's Guide for an explanation of data; data is arranged alphabetically by state, then county, then city within each county; table includes counties with populations greater than 49,999 unless noted and cities with populations greater than 9,999 whose Asian and/or NHPI population rates are greater than the national average; (1) Native Hawaiian and other Pacific Islander; (2) excludes Taiwanese; (3) includes Chamorro; (4) county does not meet population threshold but is shown in order to allow inclusion of city

Place	Total population	Total Asian population	Total NHPI[1] population	Asian Indian	Bangladeshi	Cambodian	Chinese[2]	Fijian	Filipino	Guamanian[3]	Hawaiian, Native	Hmong	Indonesian	Japanese	Korean	Laotian	Malaysian	Pakistani	Samoan	Sri Lankan	Taiwanese	Thai	Tongan	Vietnamese
Williamson County	249,967	6,457 2.58	-	1,672 25.89 0.67	-	-	1,438 22.27 0.58	-	-	-	-	-	-	-	701 10.86 0.28	-	-	-	-	-	-	-	-	1,098 17.00 0.44
Brushy Creek (cdp)	15,898	933 5.87	-	-	-	-	-	-	-	-	-	-	-	-	-	-	-	-	-	-	-	-	-	-
Jollyville (cdp)	15,466	1,181 7.64	-	-	-	-	-	-	-	-	-	-	-	-	-	-	-	-	-	-	-	-	-	-
UTAH	2,233,169	36,878 1.65	14,366 0.64	3,157 8.56 0.14	-	1,457 3.95 0.07	7,245 19.65 0.32	-	3,705 10.05 0.17	-	1,341 9.33 0.06	-	-	5,980 16.22 0.27	3,582 9.71 0.16	2,204 5.98 0.10	-	401 1.09 0.02	3,760 26.17 0.17	-	370 1.00 0.02	707 1.92 0.03	6,795 47.30 0.30	5,553 15.06 0.25
Cache County	91,391	1,733 1.90	-	-	-	-	570 32.89 0.62	-	-	-	-	-	-	-	-	-	-	-	-	-	-	-	-	-
Davis County	238,994	3,497 1.46	928 0.39	-	-	-	-	-	827 23.65 0.35	-	-	-	-	795 22.73 0.33	377 10.78 0.16	-	-	-	-	-	-	-	-	-
Salt Lake County	898,387	23,211 2.58	10,334 1.15	2,199 9.47 0.24	-	1,109 4.78 0.12	4,543 19.57 0.51	-	1,768 7.62 0.20	-	480 4.64 0.05	-	-	3,126 13.47 0.35	1,808 7.79 0.20	1,789 7.71 0.20	-	-	2,586 25.02 0.29	-	-	-	5,938 57.46 0.66	4,668 20.11 0.52
Kearns (cdp)	33,619	862 2.56	406 1.21	-	-	-	-	-	-	-	-	-	-	-	-	-	-	-	-	-	-	-	-	-
Salt Lake City (city)	181,456	6,484 3.57	3,315 1.83	669 10.32 0.37	-	-	1,575 24.29 0.87	-	522 8.05 0.29	-	-	-	-	962 14.84 0.53	509 7.85 0.28	-	-	-	454 13.70 0.25	-	-	-	2,447 73.82 1.35	1,351 20.84 0.74
Sandy (city)	88,259	1,544 1.75	383 0.43	-	-	-	408 26.42 0.46	-	-	-	-	-	-	-	-	-	-	-	-	-	-	-	-	-
Taylorsville (city)	57,878	1,736 3.00	713 1.23	-	-	-	-	-	-	-	-	-	-	-	-	-	-	-	-	-	-	-	-	593 34.16 1.02
West Jordan (city)	68,216	1,198 1.76	699 1.02	-	-	-	-	-	-	-	-	-	-	-	-	-	-	-	-	-	-	-	470 67.24 0.69	-
West Valley City (city)	108,823	4,764 4.38	3,126 2.87	-	-	660 13.85 0.61	686 14.40 0.63	-	-	-	-	-	-	-	-	461 9.68 0.42	-	-	861 27.54 0.79	-	-	-	1,806 57.77 1.66	1,502 31.53 1.38
Utah County	368,536	3,959 1.07	1,805 0.49	-	-	-	1,222 30.87 0.33	-	409 10.33 0.11	-	387 21.44 0.11	-	-	761 19.22 0.21	522 13.19 0.14	-	-	-	549 30.42 0.15	-	-	-	462 25.60 0.13	-
Orem (city)	84,333	1,233 1.46	700 0.83	-	-	-	-	-	-	-	-	-	-	-	-	-	-	-	-	-	-	-	-	-
Provo (city)	105,258	1,972 1.87	668 0.63	-	-	-	765 38.79 0.73	-	-	-	-	-	-	433 21.96 0.41	-	-	-	-	-	-	-	-	-	-
Washington County	90,354	459 0.51	462 0.51	-	-	-	-	-	-	-	-	-	-	-	-	-	-	-	-	-	-	-	-	-

Notes: Please refer to the User's Guide for an explanation of data; data is arranged alphabetically by state, then county, then city within each county; table includes counties with populations greater than 49,999 unless noted and cities with populations greater than 9,999 whose Asian and/or NHPI population rates are greater than the national average; (1) Native Hawaiian and other Pacific Islander; (2) excludes Taiwanese; (3) includes Chamorro; (4) county does not meet population threshold but is shown in order to allow inclusion of city

Place	Total population	Total Asian population	Total NHPI[1] population	Asian Indian	Bangladeshi	Cambodian	Chinese[2]	Fijian	Filipino	Guamanian[3]	Hawaiian, Native	Hmong	Indonesian	Japanese	Korean	Laotian	Malaysian	Pakistani	Samoan	Sri Lankan	Taiwanese	Thai	Tongan	Vietnamese
St. George (city)	49,621	388 0.78	418 0.84	-	-	-	-	-	-	-	-	-	-	-	-	-	-	-	-	-	-	-	-	-
Weber County	196,533	2,352 1.20	-	-	-	-	-	-	-	-	-	-	-	635 27.00 0.32	-	-	-	-	-	-	-	-	-	-
VERMONT	608,827	4,851 0.80	-	697 14.37 0.11	-	-	1,136 23.42 0.19	-	314 6.47 0.05	-	-	-	-	376 7.75 0.06	680 14.02 0.11	-	-	-	-	-	-	-	-	1,072 22.10 0.18
Chittenden County	146,571	2,732 1.86	-	370 13.54 0.25	-	-	669 24.49 0.46	-	-	-	-	-	-	-	-	-	-	-	-	-	-	-	-	837 30.64 0.57
Rutland County	63,400	213 0.34	-	-	-	-	-	-	-	-	-	-	-	-	-	-	-	-	-	-	-	-	-	-
Washington County	58,039	262 0.45	-	-	-	-	-	-	-	-	-	-	-	-	-	-	-	-	-	-	-	-	-	-
Windsor County	57,418	446 0.78	-	-	-	-	-	-	-	-	-	-	-	-	-	-	-	-	-	-	-	-	-	-
VIRGINIA	7,078,515	256,355 3.62	3,617 0.05	47,578 18.56 0.67	1,808 0.71 0.03	4,968 1.94 0.07	34,252 13.36 0.48	-	48,016 18.73 0.68	1,015 28.06 0.01	924 25.55 0.01	-	1,095 0.43 0.02	8,854 3.45 0.13	45,059 17.58 0.64	3,001 1.17 0.04	-	10,459 4.08 0.15	520 14.38 0.01	636 0.25 0.01	1,315 0.51 0.02	3,581 1.40 0.05	-	35,444 13.83 0.50
Albemarle County	79,236	2,458 3.10	-	720 29.29 0.91	-	-	899 36.57 1.13	-	-	-	-	-	-	-	-	-	-	-	-	-	-	-	-	-
Alexandria Independent City	128,283	6,985 5.44	-	1,581 22.63 1.23	-	-	803 11.50 0.63	-	1,083 15.50 0.84	-	-	-	-	-	1,245 17.82 0.97	-	-	574 8.22 0.45	-	-	-	-	-	484 6.93 0.38
Arlington County	189,453	15,761 8.32	-	3,481 22.09 1.84	-	353 2.24 0.19	2,347 14.89 1.24	-	2,049 13.00 1.08	-	-	-	-	1,136 7.21 0.60	1,392 8.83 0.73	-	-	801 5.08 0.42	-	-	-	-	-	2,189 13.89 1.16
Arlington (cdp)	189,453	15,761 8.32	-	3,481 22.09 1.84	-	353 2.24 0.19	2,347 14.89 1.24	-	2,049 13.00 1.08	-	-	-	-	1,136 7.21 0.60	1,392 8.83 0.73	-	-	801 5.08 0.42	-	-	-	-	-	2,189 13.89 1.16
Bedford County	60,371	581 0.96	-	-	-	-	-	-	-	-	-	-	-	-	-	-	-	-	-	-	-	-	-	-
Charlottesville Independent City	45,049	2,172 4.82	-	494 22.74 1.10	-	-	701 32.27 1.56	-	-	-	-	-	-	-	-	-	-	-	-	-	-	-	-	-
Chesapeake Independent City	199,184	3,440 1.73	-	-	-	-	-	-	1,801 52.35 0.90	-	-	-	-	-	-	-	-	-	-	-	-	-	-	-
Chesterfield County	259,903	6,363 2.45	-	1,041 16.36 0.40	-	666 10.47 0.26	945 14.85 0.36	-	701 11.02 0.27	-	-	-	-	-	1,516 23.83 0.58	-	-	-	-	-	-	-	-	744 11.69 0.29
Fairfax Independent City	21,498	2,530 11.77	-	506 20.00 2.35	-	-	514 20.32 2.39	-	-	-	-	-	-	-	549 21.70 2.55	-	-	-	-	-	-	-	-	432 17.08 2.01

Notes: Please refer to the User's Guide for an explanation of data; data is arranged alphabetically by state, then county, then city within each county; table includes counties with populations greater than 49,999 unless noted and cities with populations greater than 9,999 whose Asian and/or NHPI population rates are greater than the national average; (1) Native Hawaiian and other Pacific Islander; (2) excludes Taiwanese; (3) includes Chamorro; (4) county does not meet population threshold but is shown in order to allow inclusion of city

Place	Total population	Total Asian population	Total NHPI[1] population	Asian Indian	Bangladeshi	Cambodian	Chinese[2]	Fijian	Filipino	Guamanian[3]	Hawaiian, Native	Hmong	Indonesian	Japanese	Korean	Laotian	Malaysian	Pakistani	Samoan	Sri Lankan	Taiwanese	Thai	Tongan	Vietnamese
Fairfax County	969,749	123,612 12.75	884 0.09	24,955 20.19 2.57	902 0.73 0.09	1,845 1.49 0.19	16,185 13.09 1.67	-	12,727 10.30 1.31	-	-	-	595 0.48 0.06	2,907 2.35 0.30	27,684 22.40 2.85	1,516 1.23 0.16	-	6,289 5.09 0.65	-	-	738 0.60 0.08	1,492 1.21 0.15	-	21,292 17.22 2.20
Annandale (cdp)	55,041	10,446 18.98	-	1,146 10.97 2.08	-	-	972 9.30 1.77	-	640 6.13 1.16	-	-	-	-	-	3,356 32.13 6.10	-	-	-	-	-	-	-	-	3,349 32.06 6.08
Bailey's Crossroads (cdp)	22,860	2,502 10.94	-	-	-	-	-	-	-	-	-	-	-	-	-	-	-	359 14.35 1.57	-	-	-	-	-	575 22.98 2.52
Burke (cdp)	57,651	8,266 14.34	-	1,423 17.22 2.47	-	-	755 9.13 1.31	-	1,074 12.99 1.86	-	-	-	-	-	3,114 37.67 5.40	-	-	-	-	-	-	-	-	1,136 13.74 1.97
Centreville (cdp)	48,537	6,337 13.06	-	1,651 26.05 3.40	-	-	949 14.98 1.96	-	914 14.42 1.88	-	-	-	-	-	1,621 25.58 3.34	-	-	-	-	-	-	-	-	420 6.63 0.87
Chantilly (cdp)	41,089	6,492 15.80	-	2,090 32.19 5.09	-	-	964 14.85 2.35	-	-	-	-	-	-	-	1,168 17.99 2.84	-	-	-	-	-	-	-	-	990 15.25 2.41
Franconia (cdp)	31,968	3,142 9.83	-	414 13.18 1.30	-	-	-	-	587 18.68 1.84	-	-	-	-	-	594 18.91 1.86	-	-	-	-	-	-	-	-	525 16.71 1.64
Groveton (cdp)	21,263	1,628 7.66	-	-	-	-	-	-	-	-	-	-	-	-	-	-	-	-	-	-	-	-	-	-
Herndon (town)	21,662	3,199 14.77	-	1,056 33.01 4.87	-	-	-	-	-	-	-	-	-	-	-	-	-	-	-	-	-	-	-	424 13.25 1.96
Hybla Valley (cdp)	16,817	1,281 7.62	-	-	-	-	-	-	-	-	-	-	-	-	-	-	-	-	-	-	-	-	-	-
Idylwood (cdp)	16,055	3,183 19.83	-	997 31.32 6.21	-	-	572 17.97 3.56	-	-	-	-	-	-	-	-	-	-	-	-	-	-	-	-	650 20.42 4.05
Jefferson (cdp)	27,339	5,249 19.20	-	844 16.08 3.09	-	-	547 10.42 2.00	-	504 9.60 1.84	-	-	-	-	-	-	-	-	-	-	-	-	-	-	2,289 43.61 8.37
Lincolnia (cdp)	15,867	2,337 14.73	-	-	-	-	-	-	-	-	-	-	-	-	-	-	-	517 22.12 3.26	-	-	-	-	-	502 21.48 3.16
Lorton (cdp)	17,760	1,425 8.02	-	-	-	-	-	-	-	-	-	-	-	-	-	-	-	-	-	-	-	-	-	-
McLean (cdp)	39,003	4,229 10.84	-	953 22.53 2.44	-	-	771 18.23 1.98	-	507 11.99 1.30	-	-	-	-	551 13.03 1.41	825 19.51 2.12	-	-	-	-	-	-	-	-	-
Merrifield (cdp)	11,080	3,156 28.48	-	850 26.93 7.67	-	-	-	-	-	-	-	-	-	-	849 26.90 7.66	-	-	-	-	-	-	-	-	703 22.28 6.34
Mount Vernon (cdp)	28,582	1,856 6.49	-	-	-	-	-	-	-	-	-	-	-	-	462 24.89 1.62	-	-	-	-	-	-	-	-	-

Notes: Please refer to the User's Guide for an explanation of data; data is arranged alphabetically by state, then county, then city within each county; table includes counties with populations greater than 49,999 unless noted and cities with populations greater than 9,999 whose Asian and/or NHPI population rates are greater than the national average; (1) Native Hawaiian and other Pacific Islander; (2) excludes Taiwanese; (3) includes Chamorro; (4) county does not meet population threshold but is shown in order to allow inclusion of city

Place	Total population	Total Asian population	Total NHPI[1] population	Asian Indian	Bangladeshi	Cambodian	Chinese[2]	Fijian	Filipino	Guamanian[3]	Hawaiian, Native	Hmong	Indonesian	Japanese	Korean	Laotian	Malaysian	Pakistani	Samoan	Sri Lankan	Taiwanese	Thai	Tongan	Vietnamese
Newington (cdp)	19,704	2,141 10.87	-	374 17.47 1.90	-	-	-	-	479 22.37 2.43	-	-	-	-	-	481 22.47 2.44	-	-	-	-	-	-	-	-	-
Oakton (cdp)	29,385	4,123 14.03	-	944 22.90 3.21	-	-	1,002 24.30 3.41	-	-	-	-	-	-	-	1,126 27.31 3.83	-	-	-	-	-	-	-	-	458 11.11 1.56
Reston (cdp)	56,447	5,237 9.28	-	1,906 36.39 3.38	-	-	714 13.63 1.26	-	581 11.09 1.03	-	-	-	-	-	680 12.98 1.20	-	-	-	-	-	-	-	-	-
Rose Hill (cdp)	14,948	1,223 8.18	-	-	-	-	-	-	-	-	-	-	-	-	-	-	-	-	-	-	-	-	-	-
Springfield (cdp)	30,262	6,589 21.77	-	963 14.62 3.18	-	-	426 6.47 1.41	-	1,028 15.60 3.40	-	-	-	-	-	799 12.13 2.64	398 6.04 1.32	-	-	-	-	-	-	-	1,848 28.05 6.11
Tysons Corner (cdp)	18,501	3,155 17.05	-	736 23.33 3.98	-	-	654 20.73 3.53	-	-	-	-	-	-	-	786 24.91 4.25	-	-	-	-	-	-	-	-	-
Vienna (town)	14,549	1,207 8.30	-	-	-	-	-	-	-	-	-	-	-	-	-	-	-	-	-	-	-	-	-	-
West Springfield (cdp)	28,605	3,917 13.69	-	445 11.36 1.56	-	-	336 8.58 1.17	-	-	-	-	-	-	-	1,364 34.82 4.77	-	-	-	-	-	-	-	-	902 23.03 3.15
Wolf Trap (cdp)	13,879	1,254 9.04	-	361 28.79 2.60	-	-	271 21.61 1.95	-	-	-	-	-	-	-	-	-	-	-	-	-	-	-	-	-
Falls Church Independent City	10,377	674 6.50	-	-	-	-	-	-	-	-	-	-	-	-	-	-	-	-	-	-	-	-	-	-
Fauquier County	55,139	471 0.85	-	-	-	-	-	-	-	-	-	-	-	-	-	-	-	-	-	-	-	-	-	-
Frederick County	59,209	515 0.87	-	-	-	-	-	-	-	-	-	-	-	-	-	-	-	-	-	-	-	-	-	-
Hampton Independent City	146,437	2,570 1.76	-	-	-	-	-	-	671 26.11 0.46	-	-	-	-	-	-	-	-	-	-	-	-	-	-	527 20.51 0.36
Hanover County	86,320	539 0.62	-	-	-	-	-	-	-	-	-	-	-	-	-	-	-	-	-	-	-	-	-	-
Henrico County	262,300	9,273 3.54	-	2,693 29.04 1.03	-	814 8.78 0.31	1,642 17.71 0.63	-	695 7.49 0.26	-	-	-	-	-	921 9.93 0.35	-	-	-	-	-	-	-	-	1,482 15.98 0.57
Glen Allen (cdp)	12,770	467 3.66	-	-	-	-	-	-	-	-	-	-	-	-	-	-	-	-	-	-	-	-	-	-
Laurel (cdp)	14,602	775 5.31	-	-	-	-	-	-	-	-	-	-	-	-	-	-	-	-	-	-	-	-	-	-

Notes: Please refer to the User's Guide for an explanation of data; data is arranged alphabetically by state, then county, then city within each county; table includes counties with populations greater than 49,999 unless noted and cities with populations greater than 9,999 whose Asian and/or NHPI population rates are greater than the national average; (1) Native Hawaiian and other Pacific Islander; (2) excludes Taiwanese; (3) includes Chamorro; (4) county does not meet population threshold but is shown in order to allow inclusion of city

Place	Total population	Total Asian population	Total NHPI[1] population	Asian Indian	Bangladeshi	Cambodian	Chinese[2]	Fijian	Filipino	Guamanian[3]	Hawaiian, Native	Hmong	Indonesian	Japanese	Korean	Laotian	Malaysian	Pakistani	Samoan	Sri Lankan	Taiwanese	Thai	Tongan	Vietnamese
Loudoun County	169,599	8,927 5.26	-	1,901 21.29 1.12	-	-	1,148 12.86 0.68	-	1,170 13.11 0.69	-	-	-	-	-	1,093 12.24 0.64	-	-	627 7.02 0.37	-	-	-	-	-	1,745 19.55 1.03
Lynchburg Independent City	65,269	960 1.47	-	-	-	-	-	-	-	-	-	-	-	-	-	-	-	-	-	-	-	-	-	-
Manassas Park Indep. City	10,290	385 3.74	-	-	-	-	-	-	-	-	-	-	-	-	-	-	-	-	-	-	-	-	-	-
Montgomery County	83,629	3,132 3.75	-	641 20.47 0.77	-	-	875 27.94 1.05	-	-	-	-	-	-	-	771 24.62 0.92	-	-	-	-	-	-	-	-	-
Blacksburg (town)	39,393	2,885 7.32	-	593 20.55 1.51	-	-	837 29.01 2.12	-	-	-	-	-	-	-	701 24.30 1.78	-	-	-	-	-	-	-	-	-
Newport News Independent City	180,150	4,212 2.34	-	-	-	-	441 10.47 0.24	-	756 17.95 0.42	-	-	-	-	-	1,121 26.61 0.62	-	-	-	-	-	-	-	-	708 16.81 0.39
Norfolk Independent City	234,403	7,007 2.99	-	406 5.79 0.17	-	-	750 10.70 0.32	-	4,274 61.00 1.82	-	-	-	-	-	-	-	-	-	-	-	-	-	-	359 5.12 0.15
Portsmouth Independent City	100,565	815 0.81	-	-	-	-	-	-	473 58.04 0.47	-	-	-	-	-	-	-	-	-	-	-	-	-	-	-
Prince William County	280,813	10,436 3.72	-	2,030 19.45 0.72	-	-	941 9.02 0.34	-	2,194 21.02 0.78	-	-	-	-	456 4.37 0.16	1,683 16.13 0.60	-	-	813 7.79 0.29	-	-	-	-	-	959 9.19 0.34
Bull Run (cdp)	11,399	598 5.25	-	-	-	-	-	-	-	-	-	-	-	-	-	-	-	-	-	-	-	-	-	-
Dale City (cdp)	56,053	2,864 5.11	-	629 21.96 1.12	-	-	-	-	683 23.85 1.22	-	-	-	-	-	-	-	-	324 11.31 0.58	-	-	-	-	-	-
Lake Ridge (cdp)	30,579	1,116 3.65	-	-	-	-	-	-	-	-	-	-	-	-	-	-	-	-	-	-	-	-	-	-
Woodbridge (cdp)	31,858	1,512 4.75	-	-	-	-	-	-	-	-	-	-	-	-	-	-	-	-	-	-	-	-	-	-
Richmond Independent City	197,790	2,438 1.23	-	515 21.12 0.26	-	-	-	-	423 17.35 0.21	-	-	-	-	-	-	-	-	-	-	-	-	-	-	-
Roanoke Independent City	94,911	1,004 1.06	-	-	-	-	-	-	-	-	-	-	-	-	-	-	-	-	-	-	-	-	-	-
Roanoke County	85,778	999 1.16	-	-	-	-	-	-	-	-	-	-	-	-	-	-	-	-	-	-	-	-	-	-
Spotsylvania County	90,395	1,281 1.42	-	-	-	-	-	-	-	-	-	-	-	-	-	-	-	-	-	-	-	-	-	-

Notes: Please refer to the User's Guide for an explanation of data; data is arranged alphabetically by state, then county, then city within each county; table includes counties with populations greater than 49,999 unless noted and cities with populations greater than 9,999 whose Asian and/or NHPI population rates are greater than the national average; (1) Native Hawaiian and other Pacific Islander; (2) excludes Taiwanese; (3) includes Chamorro; (4) county does not meet population threshold but is shown in order to allow inclusion of city

Place	Total population	Total Asian population	Total NHPI[1] population	Asian Indian	Bangladeshi	Cambodian	Chinese[2]	Fijian	Filipino	Guamanian[3]	Hawaiian, Native	Hmong	Indonesian	Japanese	Korean	Laotian	Malaysian	Pakistani	Samoan	Sri Lankan	Taiwanese	Thai	Tongan	Vietnamese
Stafford County	92,446	1,497 1.62	-	-	-	-	-	-	378 25.25 0.41	-	-	-	-	-	-	-	-	-	-	-	-	-	-	-
Suffolk Independent City	63,677	533 0.84	-	-	-	-	-	-	-	-	-	-	-	-	-	-	-	-	-	-	-	-	-	-
Virginia Beach Independent City	425,257	20,207 4.75	-	1,224 6.06 0.29	-	-	1,624 8.04 0.38	-	13,532 66.97 3.18	-	-	-	-	746 3.69 0.18	783 3.87 0.18	-	-	-	-	-	-	-	-	1,189 5.88 0.28
Williamsburg Independent City	11,998	521 4.34	-	-	-	-	-	-	-	-	-	-	-	-	-	-	-	-	-	-	-	-	-	-
York County	56,297	1,836 3.26	-	261 14.22 0.46	-	-	-	-	-	-	-	-	-	-	552 30.07 0.98	-	-	-	-	-	-	-	-	-
WASHINGTON	5,894,121	320,979 5.45	21,738 0.37	22,489 7.01 0.38	-	14,766 4.60 0.25	57,273 17.84 0.97	709 3.26 0.01	65,057 20.27 1.10	5,380 24.75 0.09	4,511 20.75 0.08	1,494 0.47 0.03	1,242 0.39 0.02	37,296 11.62 0.63	46,494 14.49 0.79	8,097 2.52 0.14	-	1,259 0.39 0.02	7,072 32.53 0.12	422 0.13 0.01	3,788 1.18 0.06	3,892 1.21 0.07	844 3.88 0.01	44,658 13.91 0.76
Benton County	142,475	2,934 2.06	-	404 13.77 0.28	-	-	533 18.17 0.37	-	-	-	-	-	-	-	409 13.94 0.29	-	-	-	-	-	-	-	-	503 17.14 0.35
Richland (city)	38,653	1,566 4.05	-	-	-	-	410 26.18 1.06	-	-	-	-	-	-	-	-	-	-	-	-	-	-	-	-	-
Chelan County	66,616	417 0.63	-	-	-	-	-	-	-	-	-	-	-	-	-	-	-	-	-	-	-	-	-	-
Clallam County	64,525	870 1.35	-	-	-	-	-	-	-	-	-	-	-	-	-	-	-	-	-	-	-	-	-	-
Clark County	345,238	10,622 3.08	1,329 0.38	745 7.01 0.22	-	427 4.02 0.12	1,650 15.53 0.48	-	1,747 16.45 0.51	-	-	-	-	1,282 12.07 0.37	1,302 12.26 0.38	413 3.89 0.12	-	-	-	-	-	-	-	2,353 22.15 0.68
Five Corners (cdp)	12,119	585 4.83	-	-	-	-	-	-	-	-	-	-	-	-	-	-	-	-	-	-	-	-	-	-
Orchards (cdp)	17,924	768 4.28	-	-	-	-	-	-	-	-	-	-	-	-	-	-	-	-	-	-	-	-	-	-
Vancouver (city)	143,226	6,155 4.30	943 0.66	-	-	-	1,017 16.52 0.71	-	902 14.65 0.63	-	-	-	-	801 13.01 0.56	687 11.16 0.48	-	-	-	-	-	-	-	-	1,503 24.42 1.05
Cowlitz County	92,948	1,259 1.35	-	-	-	354 28.12 0.38	-	-	-	-	-	-	-	-	-	-	-	-	-	-	-	-	-	396 31.45 0.43
Grant County	74,698	569 0.76	-	-	-	-	-	-	-	-	-	-	-	-	-	-	-	-	-	-	-	-	-	-
Grays Harbor County	67,194	640 0.95	-	-	-	-	-	-	-	-	-	-	-	-	-	-	-	-	-	-	-	-	-	-

Notes: Please refer to the User's Guide for an explanation of data; data is arranged alphabetically by state, then county, then city within each county; table includes counties with populations greater than 49,999 unless noted and cities with populations greater than 9,999 whose Asian and/or NHPI population rates are greater than the national average; (1) Native Hawaiian and other Pacific Islander; (2) excludes Taiwanese; (3) includes Chamorro; (4) county does not meet population threshold but is shown in order to allow inclusion of city

Place	Total population	Total Asian population	Total NHPI[1] population	Asian Indian	Bangladeshi	Cambodian	Chinese[2]	Fijian	Filipino	Guamanian[3]	Hawaiian, Native	Hmong	Indonesian	Japanese	Korean	Laotian	Malaysian	Pakistani	Samoan	Sri Lankan	Taiwanese	Thai	Tongan	Vietnamese
Island County	71,558	2,847 3.98	-	-	-	-	-	-	1,894 66.53 2.65	-	-	-	-	388 13.63 0.54	-	-	-	-	-	-	-	-	-	-
Oak Harbor (city)	19,905	1,739 8.74	-	-	-	-	-	-	1,360 78.21 6.83	-	-	-	-	-	-	-	-	-	-	-	-	-	-	-
King County	1,737,034	187,788 10.81	8,270 0.48	14,033 7.47 0.81	-	6,623 3.53 0.38	43,786 23.32 2.52	543 6.57 0.03	33,778 17.99 1.94	834 10.08 0.05	1,377 16.65 0.08	889 0.47 0.05	830 0.44 0.05	22,416 11.94 1.29	20,185 10.75 1.16	5,040 2.68 0.29	-	526 0.28 0.03	3,921 47.41 0.23	-	3,024 1.61 0.17	1,950 1.04 0.11	502 6.07 0.03	27,041 14.40 1.56
Auburn (city)	40,279	1,565 3.89	-	-	-	-	-	-	-	-	-	-	-	-	-	-	-	-	-	-	-	-	-	-
Bellevue (city)	109,189	18,828 17.24	-	2,421 12.86 2.22	-	-	5,819 30.91 5.33	-	1,068 5.67 0.98	-	-	-	-	2,986 15.86 2.73	2,431 12.91 2.23	464 2.46 0.42	-	-	-	-	929 4.93 0.85	-	-	1,340 7.12 1.23
Bothell (city)	29,869	2,317 7.76	-	-	-	-	583 25.16 1.95	-	-	-	-	-	-	-	-	-	-	-	-	-	-	-	-	-
Bryn Mawr-Skyway (cdp)	14,050	3,055 21.74	-	-	-	-	-	-	874 28.61 6.22	-	-	-	-	613 20.07 4.36	-	-	-	-	-	-	-	-	-	425 13.91 3.02
Burien (city)	31,744	2,138 6.74	-	-	-	-	-	-	512 23.95 1.61	-	-	-	-	-	-	-	-	-	-	-	-	-	-	403 18.85 1.27
Cascade-Fairwood (cdp)	34,433	4,647 13.50	-	-	-	-	903 19.43 2.62	-	1,231 26.49 3.58	-	-	-	-	527 11.34 1.53	-	-	-	-	-	-	-	-	-	748 16.10 2.17
Cottage Lake (cdp)	24,299	1,051 4.33	-	-	-	-	-	-	-	-	-	-	-	-	-	-	-	-	-	-	-	-	-	-
Des Moines (city)	29,409	2,465 8.38	390 1.33	-	-	-	-	-	465 18.86 1.58	-	-	-	-	-	-	-	-	-	-	-	-	-	-	540 21.91 1.84
East Hill-Meridian (cdp)	29,620	3,905 13.18	-	757 19.39 2.56	-	-	796 20.38 2.69	-	688 17.62 2.32	-	-	-	-	-	-	-	-	-	-	-	-	-	-	562 14.39 1.90
Federal Way (city)	83,233	10,162 12.21	895 1.08	-	-	-	855 8.41 1.03	-	1,899 18.69 2.28	-	-	-	-	620 6.10 0.74	4,435 43.64 5.33	-	-	-	491 54.86 0.59	-	-	-	-	1,135 11.17 1.36
Inglewood-Finn Hill (cdp)	22,652	1,679 7.41	-	-	-	-	411 24.48 1.81	-	-	-	-	-	-	-	-	-	-	-	-	-	-	-	-	-
Issaquah (city)	11,205	704 6.28	-	-	-	-	-	-	-	-	-	-	-	-	-	-	-	-	-	-	-	-	-	-
Kenmore (city)	18,540	1,226 6.61	-	-	-	-	-	-	-	-	-	-	-	-	-	-	-	-	-	-	-	-	-	-
Kent (city)	79,325	7,720 9.73	-	1,481 19.18 1.87	-	-	1,001 12.97 1.26	-	1,620 20.98 2.04	-	-	-	-	554 7.18 0.70	831 10.76 1.05	-	-	-	-	-	-	-	-	1,446 18.73 1.82

Notes: Please refer to the User's Guide for an explanation of data; data is arranged alphabetically by state, then county, then city within each county; table includes counties with populations greater than 49,999 unless noted and cities with populations greater than 9,999 whose Asian and/or NHPI population rates are greater than the national average; (1) Native Hawaiian and other Pacific Islander; (2) excludes Taiwanese; (3) includes Chamorro; (4) county does not meet population threshold but is shown in order to allow inclusion of city

Place	Total population	Total Asian population	Total NHPI[1] population	Asian Indian	Bangladeshi	Cambodian	Chinese[2]	Fijian	Filipino	Guamanian[3]	Hawaiian, Native	Hmong	Indonesian	Japanese	Korean	Laotian	Malaysian	Pakistani	Samoan	Sri Lankan	Taiwanese	Thai	Tongan	Vietnamese
Kingsgate (cdp)	12,028	1,503 12.50	-	-	-	-	362 24.09 3.01	-	-	-	-	-	-	-	-	-	-	-	-	-	-	-	-	-
Kirkland (city)	44,986	3,476 7.73	-	-	-	-	801 23.04 1.78	-	-	-	-	-	-	522 15.02 1.16	-	-	-	-	-	-	-	-	-	534 15.36 1.19
Lake Forest Park (city)	13,443	1,157 8.61	-	-	-	-	-	-	-	-	-	-	-	-	-	-	-	-	-	-	-	-	-	-
Lakeland North (cdp)	15,146	941 6.21	-	-	-	-	-	-	-	-	-	-	-	-	-	-	-	-	-	-	-	-	-	-
Lakeland South (cdp)	11,499	665 5.78	-	-	-	-	-	-	-	-	-	-	-	-	-	-	-	-	-	-	-	-	-	-
Lea Hill (cdp)	10,669	519 4.86	-	-	-	-	-	-	-	-	-	-	-	-	-	-	-	-	-	-	-	-	-	-
Mercer Island (city)	22,036	2,436 11.05	-	-	-	-	1,040 42.69 4.72	-	-	-	-	-	-	568 23.32 2.58	-	-	-	-	-	-	-	-	-	-
Redmond (city)	45,389	6,028 13.28	-	1,251 20.75 2.76	-	-	1,932 32.05 4.26	-	-	-	-	-	-	774 12.84 1.71	486 8.06 1.07	-	-	-	-	-	-	-	-	-
Renton (city)	49,894	6,648 13.32	-	-	-	-	1,215 18.28 2.44	-	1,562 23.50 3.13	-	-	-	-	630 9.48 1.26	-	-	-	-	-	-	-	-	-	1,777 26.73 3.56
Riverton-Boulevard Park (cdp)	11,389	1,524 13.38	-	-	-	-	-	-	-	-	-	-	-	-	-	-	-	-	-	-	-	-	-	-
Sammamish (city)	34,119	2,530 7.42	-	-	-	-	1,111 43.91 3.26	-	-	-	-	-	-	-	-	-	-	-	-	-	-	-	-	-
SeaTac (city)	25,523	2,945 11.54	614 2.41	576 19.56 2.26	-	-	-	-	725 24.62 2.84	-	-	-	-	-	-	-	-	-	-	-	-	-	-	546 18.54 2.14
Seattle (city)	563,375	73,849 13.11	2,514 0.45	2,730 3.70 0.48	-	2,524 3.42 0.45	18,871 25.55 3.35	-	16,226 21.97 2.88	-	-	-	378 0.51 0.07	9,321 12.62 1.65	4,960 6.72 0.88	2,647 3.58 0.47	-	-	1,344 53.46 0.24	-	977 1.32 0.17	878 1.19 0.16	-	11,443 15.50 2.03
Shoreline (city)	52,954	6,613 12.49	-	384 5.81 0.73	-	-	1,755 26.54 3.31	-	1,174 17.75 2.22	-	-	-	-	405 6.12 0.76	1,361 20.58 2.57	-	-	-	-	-	-	-	-	888 13.43 1.68
Tukwila (city)	17,204	1,788 10.39	332 1.93	-	-	-	-	-	606 33.89 3.52	-	-	-	-	-	-	-	-	-	-	-	-	-	-	-
Union Hill-Novelty Hill (cdp)	11,179	528 4.72	-	-	-	-	-	-	-	-	-	-	-	-	-	-	-	-	-	-	-	-	-	-
White Center (cdp)	20,848	4,478 21.48	-	-	-	1,186 26.49 5.69	-	-	474 10.59 2.27	-	-	-	-	-	-	-	-	-	-	-	-	-	-	2,041 45.58 9.79

Notes: Please refer to the User's Guide for an explanation of data; data is arranged alphabetically by state, then county, then city within each county; table includes counties with populations greater than 49,999 unless noted and cities with populations greater than 9,999 whose Asian and/or NHPI population rates are greater than the national average; (1) Native Hawaiian and other Pacific Islander; (2) excludes Taiwanese; (3) includes Chamorro; (4) county does not meet population threshold but is shown in order to allow inclusion of city

Place	Total population	Total Asian population	Total NHPI[1] population	Asian Indian	Bangladeshi	Cambodian	Chinese[2]	Fijian	Filipino	Guamanian[3]	Hawaiian, Native	Hmong	Indonesian	Japanese	Korean	Laotian	Malaysian	Pakistani	Samoan	Sri Lankan	Taiwanese	Thai	Tongan	Vietnamese
Kitsap County	231,969	10,465 4.51	1,698 0.73	-	-	-	471 4.50 0.20	-	6,972 66.62 3.01	1,043 61.43 0.45	-	-	-	1,195 11.42 0.52	609 5.82 0.26	-	-	-	-	-	-	-	-	440 4.20 0.19
Bremerton (city)	37,054	2,074 5.60	-	-	-	-	-	-	1,468 70.78 3.96	-	-	-	-	-	-	-	-	-	-	-	-	-	-	-
Silverdale (cdp)	15,768	1,751 11.10	-	-	-	-	-	-	1,477 84.35 9.37	-	-	-	-	-	-	-	-	-	-	-	-	-	-	-
Lewis County	68,600	380 0.55	-	-	-	-	-	-	-	-	-	-	-	-	-	-	-	-	-	-	-	-	-	-
Pierce County	700,820	34,671 4.95	5,075 0.72	788 2.27 0.11	-	4,058 11.70 0.58	1,755 5.06 0.25	-	6,774 19.54 0.97	1,825 35.96 0.26	895 17.64 0.13	-	-	3,521 10.16 0.50	11,122 32.08 1.59	427 1.23 0.06	-	-	1,729 34.07 0.25	-	-	396 1.14 0.06	-	4,286 12.36 0.61
Elk Plain (cdp)	15,687	627 4.00	-	-	-	-	-	-	-	-	-	-	-	-	-	-	-	-	-	-	-	-	-	-
Fort Lewis (cdp)	19,026	659 3.46	317 1.67	-	-	-	-	-	390 59.18 2.05	-	-	-	-	-	-	-	-	-	-	-	-	-	-	-
Lakewood (city)	58,317	5,181 8.88	746 1.28	-	-	-	-	-	1,222 23.59 2.10	-	-	-	-	641 12.37 1.10	2,337 45.11 4.01	-	-	-	293 39.28 0.50	-	-	-	-	-
Parkland (cdp)	23,908	1,589 6.65	415 1.74	-	-	-	-	-	-	-	-	-	-	-	801 50.41 3.35	-	-	-	-	-	-	-	-	-
Spanaway (cdp)	21,447	1,275 5.94	578 2.70	-	-	-	-	-	526 41.25 2.45	-	-	-	-	-	583 45.73 2.72	-	-	-	-	-	-	-	-	-
Tacoma (city)	193,177	14,336 7.42	1,347 0.70	-	-	3,157 22.02 1.63	744 5.19 0.39	-	1,987 13.86 1.03	436 32.37 0.23	-	-	-	950 6.63 0.49	3,075 21.45 1.59	310 2.16 0.16	-	-	627 46.55 0.32	-	-	-	-	3,120 21.76 1.62
University Place (city)	30,120	2,311 7.67	-	-	-	-	-	-	-	-	-	-	-	-	1,237 53.53 4.11	-	-	-	-	-	-	-	-	-
Skagit County	102,979	1,459 1.42	-	-	-	-	-	-	484 33.17 0.47	-	-	-	-	-	-	-	-	-	-	-	-	-	-	-
Snohomish County	606,024	35,534 5.86	1,250 0.21	2,682 7.55 0.44	-	1,998 5.62 0.33	4,427 12.46 0.73	-	7,633 21.48 1.26	-	509 40.72 0.08	-	-	2,454 6.91 0.40	7,428 20.90 1.23	764 2.15 0.13	-	432 1.22 0.07	-	-	-	-	-	5,250 14.77 0.87
Alderwood Manor (cdp)	15,254	1,245 8.16	-	-	-	-	-	-	-	-	-	-	-	-	-	-	-	-	-	-	-	-	-	-
Edmonds (city)	39,610	2,187 5.52	-	-	-	-	-	-	364 16.64 0.92	-	-	-	-	-	575 26.29 1.45	-	-	-	-	-	-	-	-	-
Everett (city)	91,290	6,057 6.63	-	589 9.72 0.65	-	638 10.53 0.70	-	-	1,813 29.93 1.99	-	-	-	-	-	-	-	-	-	-	-	-	-	-	1,189 19.63 1.30

Notes: Please refer to the User's Guide for an explanation of data; data is arranged alphabetically by state, then county, then city within each county; table includes counties with populations greater than 49,999 unless noted and cities with populations greater than 9,999 whose Asian and/or NHPI population rates are greater than the national average; (1) Native Hawaiian and other Pacific Islander; (2) excludes Taiwanese; (3) includes Chamorro; (4) county does not meet population threshold but is shown in order to allow inclusion of city

Place	Total population	Total Asian population	Total NHPI[1] population	Asian Indian	Bangladeshi	Cambodian	Chinese[2]	Fijian	Filipino	Guamanian[3]	Hawaiian, Native	Hmong	Indonesian	Japanese	Korean	Laotian	Malaysian	Pakistani	Samoan	Sri Lankan	Taiwanese	Thai	Tongan	Vietnamese
Lynnwood (city)	33,730	4,706 13.95	-	-	-	-	624 13.26 1.85	-	915 19.44 2.71	-	-	-	-	-	1,037 22.04 3.07	-	-	-	-	-	-	-	-	979 20.80 2.90
Martha Lake (cdp)	12,640	1,171 9.26	-	-	-	-	-	-	-	-	-	-	-	-	-	-	-	-	-	-	-	-	-	-
Marysville (city)	25,221	953 3.78	-	-	-	-	-	-	-	-	-	-	-	-	-	-	-	-	-	-	-	-	-	-
Mill Creek (city)	11,444	1,187 10.37	-	-	-	-	-	-	-	-	-	-	-	-	444 37.41 3.88	-	-	-	-	-	-	-	-	-
Mountlake Terrace (city)	20,300	2,347 11.56	-	-	-	-	-	-	554 23.60 2.73	-	-	-	-	-	600 25.56 2.96	-	-	-	-	-	-	-	-	-
Mukilteo (city)	18,042	2,092 11.60	-	-	-	-	-	-	-	-	-	-	-	-	1,006 48.09 5.58	-	-	-	-	-	-	-	-	-
North Creek (cdp)	25,979	1,537 5.92	-	-	-	-	-	-	-	-	-	-	-	-	-	-	-	-	-	-	-	-	-	-
Paine Field-Lk. Stickney (cdp)	24,249	1,572 6.48	-	-	-	-	-	-	-	-	-	-	-	-	-	-	-	-	-	-	-	-	-	-
Picnic Pt.-N. Lynnwood (cdp)	22,824	2,482 10.87	-	-	-	-	-	-	404 16.28 1.77	-	-	-	-	-	871 35.09 3.82	-	-	-	-	-	-	-	-	-
Seattle Hill-Silver Firs (cdp)	35,551	2,755 7.75	-	-	-	-	-	-	593 21.52 1.67	-	-	-	-	-	618 22.43 1.74	-	-	-	-	-	-	-	-	457 16.59 1.29
Spokane County	417,939	7,444 1.78	695 0.17	626 8.41 0.15	-	-	913 12.26 0.22	-	975 13.10 0.23	-	-	533 7.16 0.13	-	1,668 22.41 0.40	672 9.03 0.16	-	-	-	-	-	-	-	-	1,244 16.71 0.30
Spokane (city)	196,143	4,379 2.23	422 0.22	-	-	-	546 12.47 0.28	-	475 10.85 0.24	-	-	411 9.39 0.21	-	1,018 23.25 0.52	374 8.54 0.19	-	-	-	-	-	-	-	-	789 18.02 0.40
Thurston County	207,355	9,424 4.54	1,205 0.58	484 5.14 0.23	-	837 8.88 0.40	885 9.39 0.43	-	1,621 17.20 0.78	730 60.58 0.35	-	-	-	787 8.35 0.38	2,154 22.86 1.04	-	-	-	-	-	-	-	-	1,762 18.70 0.85
Lacey (city)	31,107	2,517 8.09	-	-	-	-	-	-	470 18.67 1.51	-	-	-	-	-	612 24.31 1.97	-	-	-	-	-	-	-	-	587 23.32 1.89
Olympia (city)	42,345	2,326 5.49	-	-	-	-	-	-	-	-	-	-	-	-	-	-	-	-	-	-	-	-	-	708 30.44 1.67
Tumwater (city)	12,646	479 3.79	-	-	-	-	-	-	-	-	-	-	-	-	-	-	-	-	-	-	-	-	-	-
Walla Walla County	55,180	772 1.40	-	-	-	-	-	-	-	-	-	-	-	-	-	-	-	-	-	-	-	-	-	-

Notes: Please refer to the User's Guide for an explanation of data; data is arranged alphabetically by state, then county, then city within each county; table includes counties with populations greater than 49,999 unless noted and cities with populations greater than 9,999 whose Asian and/or NHPI population rates are greater than the national average; (1) Native Hawaiian and other Pacific Islander; (2) excludes Taiwanese; (3) includes Chamorro; (4) county does not meet population threshold but is shown in order to allow inclusion of city

Place	Total population	Total Asian population	Total NHPI[1] population	Asian Indian	Bangladeshi	Cambodian	Chinese[2]	Fijian	Filipino	Guamanian[3]	Hawaiian, Native	Hmong	Indonesian	Japanese	Korean	Laotian	Malaysian	Pakistani	Samoan	Sri Lankan	Taiwanese	Thai	Tongan	Vietnamese
Whatcom County	166,814	4,416 2.65	-	1,240 28.08 0.74	-	-	526 11.91 0.32	-	512 11.59 0.31	-	-	-	-	499 11.30 0.30	453 10.26 0.27	-	-	-	-	-	-	-	-	623 14.11 0.37
Bellingham (city)	66,815	2,680 4.01	-	610 22.76 0.91	-	-	-	-	-	-	-	-	-	-	-	-	-	-	-	-	-	-	-	472 17.61 0.71
Whitman County[4]	40,740	2,230 5.47	-	-	-	-	685 30.72 1.68	-	-	-	-	-	-	610 27.35 1.50	-	-	-	-	-	-	-	-	-	-
Pullman (city)	24,740	1,992 8.05	-	-	-	-	582 29.22 2.35	-	-	-	-	-	-	562 28.21 2.27	-	-	-	-	-	-	-	-	-	-
Yakima County	222,581	2,180 0.98	-	-	-	-	-	-	930 42.66 0.42	-	-	-	-	-	-	-	-	-	-	-	-	-	-	-
WEST VIRGINIA	1,808,344	9,445 0.52	405 0.02	2,529 26.78 0.14	-	-	1,651 17.48 0.09	-	1,658 17.55 0.09	-	-	-	-	879 9.31 0.05	894 9.47 0.05	-	-	324 3.43 0.02	-	-	-	-	-	442 4.68 0.02
Cabell County	96,784	748 0.77	-	-	-	-	-	-	-	-	-	-	-	-	-	-	-	-	-	-	-	-	-	-
Harrison County	68,652	398 0.58	-	-	-	-	-	-	-	-	-	-	-	-	-	-	-	-	-	-	-	-	-	-
Kanawha County	200,073	1,670 0.83	-	571 34.19 0.29	-	-	-	-	-	-	-	-	-	-	-	-	-	-	-	-	-	-	-	-
Monongalia County	81,866	1,910 2.33	-	554 29.01 0.68	-	-	614 32.15 0.75	-	-	-	-	-	-	-	-	-	-	-	-	-	-	-	-	-
Putnam County	51,589	300 0.58	-	-	-	-	-	-	-	-	-	-	-	-	-	-	-	-	-	-	-	-	-	-
Raleigh County	79,220	663 0.84	-	-	-	-	-	-	-	-	-	-	-	-	-	-	-	-	-	-	-	-	-	-
Wood County	87,986	395 0.45	-	-	-	-	-	-	-	-	-	-	-	-	-	-	-	-	-	-	-	-	-	-
WISCONSIN	5,363,675	83,077 1.55	1,577 0.03	11,280 13.58 0.21	-	627 0.75 0.01	9,610 11.57 0.18	-	5,459 6.57 0.10	425 26.95 0.01	433 27.46 0.01	31,010 37.33 0.58	406 0.49 0.01	2,986 3.59 0.06	6,846 8.24 0.13	4,135 4.98 0.08	-	927 1.12 0.02	-	-	673 0.81 0.01	870 1.05 0.02	-	3,871 4.66 0.07
Brown County	226,778	4,596 2.03	-	306 6.66 0.13	-	-	-	-	-	-	-	2,417 52.59 1.07	-	-	-	440 9.57 0.19	-	-	-	-	-	-	-	-
Chippewa County	55,195	469 0.85	-	-	-	-	-	-	-	-	-	359 76.55 0.65	-	-	-	-	-	-	-	-	-	-	-	-
Columbia County	52,468	177 0.34	-	-	-	-	-	-	-	-	-	-	-	-	-	-	-	-	-	-	-	-	-	-

Notes: Please refer to the User's Guide for an explanation of data; data is arranged alphabetically by state, then county, then city within each county; table includes counties with populations greater than 49,999 unless noted and cities with populations greater than 9,999 whose Asian and/or NHPI population rates are greater than the national average; (1) Native Hawaiian and other Pacific Islander; (2) excludes Taiwanese; (3) includes Chamorro; (4) county does not meet population threshold but is shown in order to allow inclusion of city

Place	Total population	Total Asian population	Total NHPI[1] population	Asian Indian	Bangladeshi	Cambodian	Chinese[2]	Fijian	Filipino	Guamanian[3]	Hawaiian, Native	Hmong	Indonesian	Japanese	Korean	Laotian	Malaysian	Pakistani	Samoan	Sri Lankan	Taiwanese	Thai	Tongan	Vietnamese
Dane County	426,526	14,296 3.35	-	2,170 15.18 0.51	-	-	3,169 22.17 0.74	-	668 4.67 0.16	-	-	2,297 16.07 0.54	-	799 5.59 0.19	1,906 13.33 0.45	344 2.41 0.08	-	-	-	-	426 2.98 0.10	-	-	735 5.14 0.17
Madison (city)	207,525	11,641 5.61	-	1,431 12.29 0.69	-	-	2,784 23.92 1.34	-	447 3.84 0.22	-	-	1,819 15.63 0.88	-	689 5.92 0.33	1,694 14.55 0.82	-	-	-	-	-	423 3.63 0.20	-	-	635 5.45 0.31
Dodge County	85,897	268 0.31	-	-	-	-	-	-	-	-	-	-	-	-	-	-	-	-	-	-	-	-	-	-
Eau Claire County	93,142	2,323 2.49	-	-	-	-	-	-	-	-	-	1,384 59.58 1.49	-	-	-	-	-	-	-	-	-	-	-	-
Fond du Lac County	97,296	588 0.60	-	-	-	-	-	-	-	-	-	265 45.07 0.27	-	-	-	-	-	-	-	-	-	-	-	-
Jefferson County	74,021	215 0.29	-	-	-	-	-	-	-	-	-	-	-	-	-	-	-	-	-	-	-	-	-	-
Kenosha County	149,577	1,381 0.92	-	-	-	-	-	-	-	-	-	-	-	-	-	-	-	-	-	-	-	-	-	-
La Crosse County	107,120	2,855 2.67	-	-	-	-	-	-	-	-	-	1,941 67.99 1.81	-	-	-	-	-	-	-	-	-	-	-	-
La Crosse (city)	51,638	1,943 3.76	-	-	-	-	-	-	-	-	-	1,342 69.07 2.60	-	-	-	-	-	-	-	-	-	-	-	-
Manitowoc County	82,887	1,471 1.77	-	-	-	-	-	-	-	-	-	939 63.83 1.13	-	-	-	-	-	-	-	-	-	-	-	-
Marathon County	125,834	5,156 4.10	-	-	-	-	-	-	-	-	-	4,107 79.65 3.26	-	-	-	-	-	-	-	-	-	-	-	-
Wausau (city)	38,404	4,168 10.85	-	-	-	-	-	-	-	-	-	3,434 82.39 8.94	-	-	-	-	-	-	-	-	-	-	-	-
Milwaukee County	940,164	22,356 2.38	520 0.06	3,800 17.00 0.40	-	-	2,248 10.06 0.24	-	1,623 7.26 0.17	-	-	7,484 33.48 0.80	-	743 3.32 0.08	1,281 5.73 0.14	1,718 7.68 0.18	-	355 1.59 0.04	-	-	-	-	-	1,307 5.85 0.14
Outagamie County	160,971	3,635 2.26	-	444 12.21 0.28	-	-	-	-	-	-	-	2,328 64.04 1.45	-	-	-	-	-	-	-	-	-	-	-	-
Appleton (city)	70,124	3,192 4.55	-	-	-	-	-	-	-	-	-	2,331 73.03 3.32	-	-	-	-	-	-	-	-	-	-	-	-
Ozaukee County	82,317	670 0.81	-	-	-	-	-	-	-	-	-	-	-	-	-	-	-	-	-	-	-	-	-	-
Portage County	67,182	1,295 1.93	-	-	-	-	-	-	-	-	-	869 67.10 1.29	-	-	-	-	-	-	-	-	-	-	-	-

Notes: Please refer to the User's Guide for an explanation of data; data is arranged alphabetically by state, then county, then city within each county; table includes counties with populations greater than 49,999 unless noted and cities with populations greater than 9,999 whose Asian and/or NHPI population rates are greater than the national average; (1) Native Hawaiian and other Pacific Islander; (2) excludes Taiwanese; (3) includes Chamorro; (4) county does not meet population threshold but is shown in order to allow inclusion of city

Place	Total population	Total Asian population	Total NHPI[1] population	Asian Indian	Bangladeshi	Cambodian	Chinese[2]	Fijian	Filipino	Guamanian[3]	Hawaiian, Native	Hmong	Indonesian	Japanese	Korean	Laotian	Malaysian	Pakistani	Samoan	Sri Lankan	Taiwanese	Thai	Tongan	Vietnamese
Stevens Point (city)	24,492	1,035 4.23	-	-	-	-	-	-	-	-	-	757 73.14 3.09	-	-	-	-	-	-	-	-	-	-	-	-
Racine County	188,831	1,277 0.68	-	-	-	-	-	-	-	-	-	-	-	-	-	-	-	-	-	-	-	-	-	-
Rock County	152,307	1,338 0.88	-	-	-	-	-	-	-	-	-	-	-	-	-	-	-	-	-	-	-	-	-	-
St. Croix County	63,155	263 0.42	-	-	-	-	-	-	-	-	-	-	-	-	-	-	-	-	-	-	-	-	-	-
Sauk County	55,225	209 0.38	-	-	-	-	-	-	-	-	-	-	-	-	-	-	-	-	-	-	-	-	-	-
Sheboygan County	112,646	3,575 3.17	-	-	-	-	-	-	-	-	-	2,492 69.71 2.21	-	-	-	-	-	-	-	-	-	-	-	-
Sheboygan (city)	50,801	3,289 6.47	-	-	-	-	-	-	-	-	-	2,387 72.58 4.70	-	-	-	-	-	-	-	-	-	-	-	-
Walworth County	93,759	567 0.60	-	-	-	-	-	-	-	-	-	-	-	-	-	-	-	-	-	-	-	-	-	-
Washington County	117,493	513 0.44	-	-	-	-	-	-	-	-	-	-	-	-	-	-	-	-	-	-	-	-	-	-
Waukesha County	360,767	5,005 1.39	-	1,652 33.01 0.46	-	-	1,145 22.88 0.32	-	403 8.05 0.11	-	-	-	-	-	592 11.83 0.16	-	-	-	-	-	-	-	-	-
Winnebago County	156,763	2,456 1.57	-	-	-	-	-	-	-	-	-	1,493 60.79 0.95	-	-	-	-	-	-	-	-	-	-	-	-
Wood County	75,555	1,160 1.54	-	-	-	-	-	-	-	-	-	591 50.95 0.78	-	-	-	-	-	-	-	-	-	-	-	-
WYOMING	493,782	2,972 0.60	-	423 14.23 0.09	-	-	615 20.69 0.12	-	523 17.60 0.11	-	-	-	-	523 17.60 0.11	470 15.81 0.10	-	-	-	-	-	-	-	-	-
Laramie County	81,607	817 1.00	-	-	-	-	-	-	-	-	-	-	-	-	-	-	-	-	-	-	-	-	-	-
Natrona County	66,533	409 0.61	-	-	-	-	-	-	-	-	-	-	-	-	-	-	-	-	-	-	-	-	-	-

Notes: Please refer to the User's Guide for an explanation of data; data is arranged alphabetically by state, then county, then city within each county; table includes counties with populations greater than 49,999 unless noted and cities with populations greater than 9,999 whose Asian and/or NHPI population rates are greater than the national average; (1) Native Hawaiian and other Pacific Islander; (2) excludes Taiwanese; (3) includes Chamorro; (4) county does not meet population threshold but is shown in order to allow inclusion of city

Median Age

(Universe: Total Population)

Place	Total population	Total Asian population	Total NHPI[1] population	Asian Indian	Bangladeshi	Cambodian	Chinese[2]	Fijian	Filipino	Guamanian[3]	Hawaiian, Native	Hmong	Indonesian	Japanese	Korean	Laotian	Malaysian	Pakistani	Samoan	Sri Lankan	Taiwanese	Thai	Tongan	Vietnamese
UNITED STATES	35.4	33.0	27.6	30.3	29.7	23.8	35.6	29.3	35.5	29.3	31.8	16.3	30.1	42.6	32.7	26.1	29.2	28.7	24.4	35.8	32.8	34.7	23.2	30.5
ALABAMA	36.0	30.9	28.0	28.9	-	20.5	30.5	-	37.2	24.3	-	-	-	39.8	33.3	33.0	-	28.4	-	-	-	34.8	-	27.2
Baldwin County	39.1	32.1	-	-	-	-	-	-	-	-	-	-	-	-	-	-	-	-	-	-	-	-	-	-
Calhoun County	37.3	37.7	-	-	-	-	-	-	-	-	-	-	-	-	-	-	-	-	-	-	-	-	-	-
Etowah County	38.2	35.7	-	-	-	-	-	-	-	-	-	-	-	-	-	-	-	-	-	-	-	-	-	-
Houston County	36.8	36.3	-	-	-	-	-	-	-	-	-	-	-	-	-	-	-	-	-	-	-	-	-	-
Jefferson County	36.1	30.1	-	27.4	-	-	31.5	-	-	-	-	-	-	-	29.3	-	-	-	-	-	-	-	-	24.7
Lee County	27.6	29.9	-	-	-	-	30.6	-	-	-	-	-	-	-	-	-	-	-	-	-	-	-	-	-
Madison County	35.9	33.4	-	32.8	-	-	32.0	-	-	-	-	-	-	-	37.2	-	-	-	-	-	-	-	-	38.7
Mobile County	34.6	26.4	-	25.0	-	17.5	26.1	-	41.5	-	-	-	-	-	-	27.3	-	-	-	-	-	-	-	25.6
Montgomery County	33.9	34.6	-	-	-	-	-	-	-	-	-	-	-	-	-	-	-	-	-	-	-	-	-	-
Morgan County	36.7	31.1	-	-	-	-	-	-	-	-	-	-	-	-	-	-	-	-	-	-	-	-	-	-
Shelby County	34.8	29.3	-	29.3	-	-	-	-	-	-	-	-	-	-	-	-	-	-	-	-	-	-	-	-
Tuscaloosa County	31.9	27.5	-	-	-	-	-	-	-	-	-	-	-	-	-	-	-	-	-	-	-	-	-	-
ALASKA	32.5	35.0	21.8	29.4	-	-	36.8	-	35.1	-	29.8	13.7	-	43.6	38.5	21.1	-	-	19.4	-	-	31.5	15.1	28.2
Anchorage Borough	32.4	33.8	22.1	34.8	-	-	38.6	-	32.6	-	-	13.7	-	44.4	38.8	20.3	-	-	19.2	-	-	29.8	-	27.1
Fairbanks North Star Borough	29.6	34.9	-	-	-	-	34.2	-	31.5	-	-	-	-	-	38.5	-	-	-	-	-	-	-	-	-
Juneau City and Borough	35.3	34.2	-	-	-	-	-	-	35.2	-	-	-	-	-	-	-	-	-	-	-	-	-	-	-
Matanuska-Susitna Borough	34.1	42.0	-	-	-	-	-	-	-	-	-	-	-	-	-	-	-	-	-	-	-	-	-	-
ARIZONA	34.3	32.3	24.9	29.5	-	24.7	34.2	-	33.1	27.5	25.5	-	34.0	40.9	32.1	30.9	-	30.6	27.3	-	29.6	31.2	18.7	30.7
Cochise County	36.9	41.9	-	-	-	-	-	-	39.7	-	-	-	-	-	42.5	-	-	-	-	-	-	-	-	-
Coconino County	29.5	30.2	-	-	-	-	-	-	-	-	-	-	-	-	-	-	-	-	-	-	-	-	-	-
Maricopa County	33.1	32.0	25.3	29.6	-	24.2	34.3	-	32.7	28.7	23.6	-	35.2	41.0	32.0	28.1	-	30.4	27.0	-	33.4	30.1	24.4	30.4
Chandler (city)	31.2	32.2	-	30.6	-	-	32.7	-	35.4	-	-	-	-	-	-	-	-	-	-	-	-	-	-	30.8
Gilbert (town)	30.3	32.6	-	31.0	-	-	34.9	-	32.6	-	-	-	-	-	-	-	-	-	-	-	-	-	-	-
Mesa (city)	32.0	33.0	20.7	33.8	-	-	32.9	-	33.0	-	-	-	-	43.5	33.5	-	-	-	-	-	-	-	-	31.5
Phoenix (city)	30.8	32.2	25.8	30.3	-	26.5	37.6	-	32.5	-	25.6	-	-	41.1	29.8	-	-	-	-	-	-	-	-	29.9
Tempe (city)	28.8	27.6	-	26.2	-	-	28.2	-	30.5	-	-	-	-	31.1	31.1	-	-	-	-	-	-	-	-	27.4
Mohave County	42.8	39.5	-	-	-	-	-	-	-	-	-	-	-	-	-	-	-	-	-	-	-	-	-	-
Pima County	35.9	31.1	26.2	27.0	-	-	32.5	-	30.9	-	26.2	-	-	36.1	28.6	-	-	-	-	-	-	-	-	31.8
Tucson (city)	32.3	29.8	24.7	25.2	-	-	30.4	-	30.2	-	-	-	-	34.7	28.8	-	-	-	-	-	-	-	-	31.1
Pinal County	37.1	35.1	-	-	-	-	-	-	-	-	-	-	-	-	-	-	-	-	-	-	-	-	-	-
Yavapai County	44.4	39.2	-	-	-	-	-	-	-	-	-	-	-	-	-	-	-	-	-	-	-	-	-	-
Yuma County	34.1	40.1	-	-	-	-	-	-	38.5	-	-	-	-	-	-	-	-	-	-	-	-	-	-	-
ARKANSAS	36.2	31.4	21.6	29.9	-	-	33.4	-	34.8	-	25.9	-	-	47.8	34.3	25.8	-	-	-	-	-	33.5	-	29.5
Benton County	35.5	29.6	-	28.1	-	-	-	-	-	-	-	-	-	-	-	-	-	-	-	-	-	-	-	36.0
Craighead County	33.3	23.5	-	-	-	-	-	-	-	-	-	-	-	-	-	-	-	-	-	-	-	-	-	-
Crawford County	35.3	29.9	-	-	-	-	-	-	-	-	-	-	-	-	-	-	-	-	-	-	-	-	-	-

Notes: Please refer to the User's Guide for an explanation of data; data is arranged alphabetically by state, then county, then city within each county; table includes counties with populations greater than 49,999 unless noted and cities with populations greater than 9,999 whose Asian and/or NHPI population rates are greater than the national average; (1) Native Hawaiian and other Pacific Islander; (2) excludes Taiwanese; (3) includes Chamorro; (4) county does not meet population threshold but is shown in order to allow inclusion of city

Place	Total population	Total Asian population	Total NHPI[1] population	Asian Indian	Bangladeshi	Cambodian	Chinese[2]	Fijian	Filipino	Guamanian[3]	Hawaiian, Native	Hmong	Indonesian	Japanese	Korean	Laotian	Malaysian	Pakistani	Samoan	Sri Lankan	Taiwanese	Thai	Tongan	Vietnamese
Faulkner County	31.1	23.9	-	-	-	-	-	-	-	-	-	-	-	-	-	-	-	-	-	-	-	-	-	-
Jefferson County	35.1	36.3	-	-	-	-	-	-	-	-	-	-	-	-	-	-	-	-	-	-	-	-	-	-
Pulaski County	35.1	33.4	-	27.9	-	-	35.1	-	39.3	-	-	-	-	-	-	-	-	-	-	-	-	-	-	-
Saline County	36.8	30.6	-	-	-	-	-	-	-	-	-	-	-	-	-	-	-	-	-	-	-	-	-	-
Sebastian County	35.8	32.4	-	-	-	-	-	-	-	-	-	-	-	-	-	29.5	-	-	-	-	-	-	-	33.5
Fort Smith (city)	35.6	32.0	-	-	-	-	-	-	-	-	-	-	-	-	-	29.8	-	-	-	-	-	-	-	33.1
Washington County	30.9	27.4	20.0	-	-	-	28.4	-	-	-	-	-	-	-	-	23.8	-	-	-	-	-	-	-	-
Springdale (city)	30.8	29.1	19.4	-	-	-	-	-	-	-	-	-	-	-	-	26.5	-	-	-	-	-	-	-	-
CALIFORNIA	33.5	34.5	28.3	30.3	30.7	21.8	37.1	28.7	35.7	31.7	35.0	16.0	31.8	43.4	34.9	23.3	33.3	28.3	23.8	36.7	33.8	36.6	24.8	31.6
Alameda County	34.7	33.6	27.0	29.8	-	19.5	36.5	25.7	35.2	30.8	36.9	-	30.3	42.8	31.5	22.7	-	30.0	20.7	-	31.4	29.6	19.8	29.9
Alameda (city)	38.4	36.4	29.7	30.0	-	-	37.1	-	37.7	-	-	-	-	49.2	35.8	-	-	-	-	-	-	-	-	29.4
Albany (city)	36.7	32.6	-	30.0	-	-	33.0	-	-	-	-	-	-	38.8	30.5	-	-	-	-	-	-	-	-	-
Ashland (cdp)	31.1	35.4	-	-	-	-	37.5	-	35.0	-	-	-	-	-	-	-	-	-	-	-	-	-	-	-
Berkeley (city)	32.6	23.8	-	22.8	-	-	22.7	-	30.1	-	-	-	-	40.6	23.0	-	-	-	-	-	23.0	-	-	22.4
Castro Valley (cdp)	39.3	37.7	-	34.0	-	-	37.7	-	38.4	-	-	-	-	45.6	38.3	-	-	-	-	-	-	-	-	-
Cherryland (cdp)	31.8	31.3	-	-	-	-	-	-	30.1	-	-	-	-	-	-	-	-	-	-	-	-	-	-	-
Dublin (city)	34.6	33.9	-	31.5	-	-	33.7	-	38.5	-	-	-	-	-	-	-	-	-	-	-	-	-	-	-
Fremont (city)	34.8	32.9	33.3	29.7	-	-	35.7	-	36.6	-	-	-	-	41.6	32.4	-	-	31.0	-	-	33.7	-	-	31.9
Hayward (city)	32.0	32.9	27.4	29.2	-	-	38.3	24.8	34.7	-	-	-	-	35.3	33.5	-	-	-	28.0	-	-	-	-	28.3
Livermore (city)	35.1	34.6	-	31.6	-	-	37.7	-	34.2	-	-	-	-	-	-	-	-	-	-	-	-	-	-	34.0
Newark (city)	33.0	34.1	-	30.1	-	-	40.8	-	32.9	-	-	-	-	-	41.0	-	-	-	-	-	-	-	-	29.6
Oakland (city)	33.7	35.9	21.1	32.6	-	18.4	40.0	-	37.0	-	-	-	-	44.1	34.5	20.5	-	-	-	-	-	-	16.5	29.7
Piedmont (city)	43.9	42.9	-	-	-	-	42.3	-	-	-	-	-	-	-	-	-	-	-	-	-	-	-	-	-
Pleasanton (city)	36.9	34.1	-	31.7	-	-	36.2	-	35.6	-	-	-	-	39.2	32.8	-	-	-	-	-	-	-	-	-
San Leandro (city)	38.3	35.8	18.5	28.1	-	-	38.4	-	33.4	-	-	-	-	53.1	34.5	-	-	-	-	-	-	-	-	32.0
San Lorenzo (cdp)	38.6	37.5	-	-	-	-	39.5	-	36.9	-	-	-	-	-	-	-	-	-	-	-	-	-	-	31.7
Union City (city)	33.0	33.2	35.2	29.7	-	-	36.3	-	34.5	-	-	-	-	48.5	38.5	-	-	-	-	-	-	-	-	29.5
Butte County	35.8	22.1	-	25.8	-	-	34.9	-	37.2	-	-	15.0	-	29.9	-	15.4	-	-	-	-	-	-	-	-
Chico (city)	26.0	22.9	-	-	-	-	32.4	-	-	-	-	15.8	-	-	-	-	-	-	-	-	-	-	-	-
Oroville (city)	32.5	14.8	-	-	-	-	-	-	-	-	-	11.3	-	-	-	-	-	-	-	-	-	-	-	-
Contra Costa County	36.6	36.5	27.6	32.3	-	-	39.7	22.3	35.7	31.5	36.9	-	39.1	44.6	34.6	24.4	-	29.1	23.7	-	42.4	35.7	20.3	31.3
Alamo (cdp)	42.8	40.5	-	-	-	-	-	-	-	-	-	-	-	-	-	-	-	-	-	-	-	-	-	-
Antioch (city)	32.4	34.8	20.3	34.1	-	-	37.6	-	33.0	-	-	-	-	-	-	-	-	-	-	-	-	-	-	31.8
Bay Point (cdp)	29.8	32.7	-	-	-	-	-	-	33.6	-	-	-	-	-	-	-	-	-	-	-	-	-	-	-
Blackhawk-Camino-Tass. (cdp)	41.3	38.9	-	-	-	-	39.4	-	-	-	-	-	-	-	-	-	-	-	-	-	-	-	-	-
Clayton (city)	40.0	43.0	-	-	-	-	-	-	-	-	-	-	-	-	-	-	-	-	-	-	-	-	-	-
Concord (city)	35.3	37.4	19.3	38.5	-	-	38.9	-	34.7	-	-	-	-	47.0	33.8	-	-	-	-	-	-	-	-	38.2
Danville (town)	39.8	37.7	-	32.7	-	-	39.2	-	38.9	-	-	-	-	-	-	-	-	-	-	-	-	-	-	-
El Cerrito (city)	43.1	39.4	-	31.6	-	-	41.9	-	36.5	-	-	-	-	47.4	-	-	-	-	-	-	-	-	-	-
El Sobrante (cdp)	38.1	37.6	-	28.3	-	-	-	-	-	-	-	-	-	-	-	-	-	-	-	-	-	-	-	-
Hercules (city)	37.3	37.4	-	31.8	-	-	41.3	-	36.4	-	-	-	-	-	-	-	-	-	-	-	-	-	-	-

Notes: Please refer to the User's Guide for an explanation of data; data is arranged alphabetically by state, then county, then city within each county; table includes counties with populations greater than 49,999 unless noted and cities with populations greater than 9,999 whose Asian and/or NHPI population rates are greater than the national average; (1) Native Hawaiian and other Pacific Islander; (2) excludes Taiwanese; (3) includes Chamorro; (4) county does not meet population threshold but is shown in order to allow inclusion of city

Place	Total population	Total Asian population	Total NHPI[1] population	Asian Indian	Bangladeshi	Cambodian	Chinese[2]	Fijian	Filipino	Guamanian[3]	Hawaiian, Native	Hmong	Indonesian	Japanese	Korean	Laotian	Malaysian	Pakistani	Samoan	Sri Lankan	Taiwanese	Thai	Tongan	Vietnamese
Lafayette (city)	42.8	41.4	-	-	-	-	41.8	-	-	-	-	-	-	-	-	-	-	-	-	-	-	-	-	-
Martinez (city)	38.4	39.7	-	-	-	-	45.7	-	39.8	-	-	-	-	-	-	-	-	-	-	-	-	-	-	-
Moraga (town)	41.5	39.1	-	-	-	-	43.3	-	-	-	-	-	-	-	-	-	-	-	-	-	-	-	-	-
Orinda (city)	45.4	41.3	-	-	-	-	43.7	-	-	-	-	-	-	-	-	-	-	-	-	-	-	-	-	-
Pinole (city)	38.6	37.2	-	-	-	-	38.3	-	37.7	-	-	-	-	-	-	-	-	-	-	-	-	-	-	-
Pittsburg (city)	31.3	34.5	23.4	30.3	-	-	37.5	-	36.5	-	-	-	-	-	-	-	-	-	-	-	-	-	-	-
Pleasant Hill (city)	38.9	34.4	-	-	-	-	36.5	-	33.3	-	-	-	-	-	30.0	-	-	-	-	-	-	-	-	-
Richmond (city)	33.0	33.8	30.4	31.8	-	-	38.7	-	37.3	-	-	-	-	48.8	28.9	23.7	-	-	-	-	-	-	-	26.9
San Pablo (city)	29.8	33.2	-	34.6	-	-	-	-	35.8	-	-	-	-	-	-	28.6	-	-	-	-	-	-	-	30.5
San Ramon (city)	36.8	35.5	-	30.5	-	-	36.9	-	39.3	-	-	-	-	41.3	-	-	-	-	-	-	-	-	-	-
Walnut Creek (city)	44.8	38.2	-	32.7	-	-	42.7	-	32.4	-	-	-	-	45.1	35.8	-	-	-	-	-	-	-	-	-
El Dorado County	39.6	38.4	-	-	-	-	-	-	34.5	-	-	-	-	44.8	-	-	-	-	-	-	-	-	-	-
El Dorado Hills (cdp)	38.1	34.9	-	-	-	-	-	-	-	-	-	-	-	-	-	-	-	-	-	-	-	-	-	-
South Lake Tahoe (city)	33.4	38.3	-	-	-	-	-	-	36.0	-	-	-	-	-	-	-	-	-	-	-	-	-	-	-
Fresno County	30.1	24.2	24.2	31.4	-	18.7	38.9	-	36.5	-	-	15.8	-	49.0	30.8	20.4	-	-	-	-	-	-	-	27.7
Clovis (city)	33.1	26.5	-	-	-	-	-	-	31.4	-	-	16.5	-	46.6	-	-	-	-	-	-	-	-	-	-
Fresno (city)	28.6	21.8	-	30.4	-	18.4	38.3	-	35.4	-	-	15.7	-	43.2	30.8	20.6	-	-	-	-	-	-	-	26.8
Reedley (city)	29.2	46.0	-	-	-	-	-	-	-	-	-	-	-	-	-	-	-	-	-	-	-	-	-	-
Humboldt County	36.4	26.1	-	-	-	-	-	-	-	-	-	-	-	30.5	-	-	-	-	-	-	-	-	-	-
Imperial County	31.3	33.6	-	-	-	-	37.9	-	31.5	-	-	-	-	-	32.6	-	-	-	-	-	-	-	-	-
Kern County	30.8	34.6	25.4	33.2	-	20.3	41.3	-	35.3	-	-	-	-	41.5	36.1	-	-	-	-	-	-	-	-	28.7
Bakersfield (city)	30.3	33.1	21.3	32.4	-	-	39.1	-	32.7	-	-	-	-	41.1	33.4	-	-	-	-	-	-	-	-	31.6
Delano (city)	28.4	35.7	-	-	-	-	-	-	36.4	-	-	-	-	-	-	-	-	-	-	-	-	-	-	-
Ridgecrest (city)	35.3	35.8	-	-	-	-	-	-	40.3	-	-	-	-	-	-	-	-	-	-	-	-	-	-	-
Kings County	30.4	35.7	-	-	-	-	-	-	37.1	-	-	-	-	-	-	-	-	-	-	-	-	-	-	-
Lemoore (city)	27.3	40.9	-	-	-	-	-	-	41.8	-	-	-	-	-	-	-	-	-	-	-	-	-	-	-
Lake County	43.0	43.4	-	-	-	-	-	-	-	-	-	-	-	-	-	-	-	-	-	-	-	-	-	-
Los Angeles County	32.2	36.2	27.2	31.9	31.6	24.1	37.1	37.4	36.6	31.0	34.4	19.9	31.5	43.8	35.9	26.9	33.4	30.3	23.9	36.1	34.5	38.7	22.3	32.4
Agoura Hills (city)	38.2	39.1	-	-	-	-	-	-	-	-	-	-	-	-	-	-	-	-	-	-	-	-	-	-
Alhambra (city)	35.1	36.0	-	33.4	-	-	36.7	-	36.4	-	-	-	-	42.9	35.9	-	-	-	-	-	37.3	-	-	32.3
Altadena (cdp)	38.2	42.9	-	-	-	-	-	-	38.8	-	-	-	-	49.1	-	-	-	-	-	-	-	-	-	-
Arcadia (city)	40.4	36.8	-	34.9	-	-	37.4	-	37.2	-	-	-	-	38.9	35.9	-	-	-	-	-	34.1	-	-	-
Artesia (city)	33.8	35.4	-	31.5	-	-	39.3	-	34.5	-	-	-	-	-	35.2	-	-	-	-	-	-	-	-	-
Avocado Heights (cdp)	30.4	39.9	-	-	-	-	-	-	-	-	-	-	-	-	-	-	-	-	-	-	-	-	-	-
Azusa (city)	27.0	31.9	-	-	-	-	-	-	35.1	-	-	-	-	-	-	-	-	-	-	-	-	-	-	-
Baldwin Park (city)	27.1	37.8	-	-	-	-	38.0	-	38.9	-	-	-	-	-	-	-	-	-	-	-	-	-	-	33.8
Bellflower (city)	30.1	35.2	-	-	-	34.2	-	-	32.8	-	-	-	-	-	36.5	-	-	-	-	-	-	40.6	-	-
Beverly Hills (city)	41.5	36.6	-	-	-	-	40.8	-	-	-	-	-	-	-	37.8	-	-	-	-	-	-	-	-	-
Burbank (city)	36.6	34.7	-	32.3	-	-	36.6	-	34.5	-	-	-	-	40.5	35.0	-	-	-	-	-	-	-	-	27.6
Calabasas (city)	38.6	41.1	-	-	-	-	41.8	-	-	-	-	-	-	-	-	-	-	-	-	-	-	-	-	-
Carson (city)	34.0	38.8	23.6	-	-	-	35.9	-	38.2	-	-	-	-	68.1	-	-	-	-	23.2	-	-	-	-	44.6

Notes: Please refer to the User's Guide for an explanation of data; data is arranged alphabetically by state, then county, then city within each county; table includes counties with populations greater than 49,999 unless noted and cities with populations greater than 9,999 whose Asian and/or NHPI population rates are greater than the national average; (1) Native Hawaiian and other Pacific Islander; (2) excludes Taiwanese; (3) includes Chamorro; (4) county does not meet population threshold but is shown in order to allow inclusion of city

Place	Total population	Total Asian population	Total NHPI[1] population	Asian Indian	Bangladeshi	Cambodian	Chinese[2]	Fijian	Filipino	Guamanian[3]	Hawaiian, Native	Hmong	Indonesian	Japanese	Korean	Laotian	Malaysian	Pakistani	Samoan	Sri Lankan	Taiwanese	Thai	Tongan	Vietnamese
Cerritos (city)	39.2	38.1	-	35.0	-	-	40.7	-	40.2	-	-	-	-	42.3	36.4	-	-	-	-	-	38.0	46.9	-	33.8
Citrus (cdp)	28.3	30.2	-	-	-	-	-	-	-	-	-	-	-	-	-	-	-	-	-	-	-	-	-	-
Claremont (city)	36.8	28.9	-	34.3	-	-	34.6	-	-	-	-	-	-	-	23.4	-	-	-	-	-	-	-	-	-
Compton (city)	25.0	46.6	17.5	-	-	-	-	-	-	-	-	-	-	-	-	-	-	-	17.1	-	-	-	-	-
Covina (city)	33.7	35.9	-	-	-	-	39.9	-	31.7	-	-	-	-	45.0	-	-	-	-	-	-	-	-	-	28.4
Culver City (city)	39.7	39.1	-	32.1	-	-	39.1	-	40.7	-	-	-	-	47.7	-	-	-	-	-	-	-	-	-	-
Diamond Bar (city)	36.4	35.6	-	34.3	-	-	36.2	-	35.8	-	-	-	-	41.9	35.7	-	-	-	-	-	32.9	-	-	32.7
Downey (city)	31.8	38.0	-	31.1	-	-	43.8	-	36.9	-	-	-	-	47.2	36.2	-	-	-	-	-	-	-	-	40.4
Duarte (city)	34.7	38.0	-	-	-	-	42.6	-	34.5	-	-	-	-	-	-	-	-	-	-	-	-	-	-	-
East San Gabriel (cdp)	37.1	36.5	-	-	-	-	37.5	-	-	-	-	-	-	46.1	-	-	-	-	-	-	29.4	-	-	-
El Monte (city)	27.1	34.8	-	-	-	-	36.3	-	35.6	-	-	-	-	-	-	-	-	-	-	-	47.5	-	-	30.7
El Segundo (city)	36.5	36.3	-	-	-	-	-	-	-	-	-	-	-	-	-	-	-	-	-	-	-	-	-	-
Gardena (city)	34.5	42.6	-	-	-	-	45.3	-	38.0	-	-	-	-	52.8	37.3	-	-	-	-	-	-	-	-	32.0
Glendale (city)	37.6	35.9	-	31.8	-	-	39.6	-	36.5	-	-	-	-	38.9	34.3	-	-	-	-	-	-	48.6	-	38.0
Glendora (city)	37.2	39.2	-	39.8	-	-	41.8	-	34.6	-	-	-	-	-	-	-	-	-	-	-	-	-	-	-
Hacienda Heights (cdp)	36.7	38.4	-	-	-	-	39.1	-	35.2	-	-	-	-	51.3	36.9	-	-	-	-	-	35.3	-	-	37.8
Hawaiian Gardens (city)	25.8	38.8	-	-	-	-	-	-	-	-	-	-	-	-	44.3	-	-	-	-	-	-	-	-	-
Hawthorne (city)	28.9	34.9	30.5	36.6	-	-	43.1	-	37.1	-	-	-	-	41.2	-	-	-	-	-	-	-	-	-	30.5
Hermosa Beach (city)	34.3	33.2	-	-	-	-	-	-	-	-	-	-	-	-	-	-	-	-	-	-	-	-	-	-
La Canada Flintridge (city)	41.8	38.1	-	-	-	-	37.3	-	-	-	-	-	-	49.5	36.6	-	-	-	-	-	-	-	-	-
La Crescenta-Montrose (cdp)	39.3	37.0	-	-	-	-	-	-	37.8	-	-	-	-	-	35.8	-	-	-	-	-	-	-	-	-
La Mirada (city)	35.7	36.2	-	35.6	-	-	34.9	-	34.7	-	-	-	-	65.1	36.5	-	-	-	-	-	-	-	-	-
La Puente (city)	27.7	40.1	-	-	-	-	38.6	-	42.3	-	-	-	-	-	-	-	-	-	-	-	-	-	-	-
La Verne (city)	37.5	36.6	-	-	-	-	-	-	33.7	-	-	-	-	-	-	-	-	-	-	-	-	-	-	-
Lakewood (city)	35.5	34.2	25.4	30.7	-	28.6	35.3	-	32.9	-	-	-	-	39.8	35.8	-	-	-	25.5	-	-	-	-	31.7
Lancaster (city)	31.1	36.4	-	33.6	-	-	33.3	-	38.4	-	-	-	-	-	-	-	-	-	-	-	-	-	-	-
Lawndale (city)	29.4	34.5	24.4	-	-	-	-	-	38.8	-	-	-	-	-	-	-	-	-	-	-	-	-	-	32.3
Lomita (city)	35.5	41.8	-	-	-	-	-	-	38.5	-	-	-	-	46.2	37.7	-	-	-	-	-	-	-	-	-
Long Beach (city)	30.9	30.9	22.9	31.0	-	20.4	34.4	-	34.9	-	-	-	-	43.5	36.5	20.4	-	-	21.8	-	-	36.2	-	33.0
Los Angeles (city)	31.8	35.8	31.8	30.1	31.4	27.0	35.9	-	36.9	32.1	36.6	-	34.1	44.5	35.8	29.3	-	30.1	28.4	35.7	29.9	38.0	21.5	31.0
Manhattan Beach (city)	37.6	39.3	-	-	-	-	37.8	-	-	-	-	-	-	45.6	-	-	-	-	-	-	-	-	-	-
Monrovia (city)	33.8	37.3	-	-	-	-	36.6	-	36.3	-	-	-	-	-	-	-	-	-	-	-	-	-	-	-
Montebello (city)	31.4	44.0	-	-	-	-	46.2	-	42.4	-	-	-	-	51.9	39.7	-	-	-	-	-	-	-	-	-
Monterey Park (city)	38.7	40.7	-	-	-	25.4	40.7	-	39.4	-	-	-	-	55.4	38.3	-	-	-	-	-	39.1	-	-	31.8
Norwalk (city)	30.0	35.1	-	29.0	-	30.2	39.4	-	37.1	-	-	-	-	53.7	32.2	-	-	-	-	-	-	-	-	34.8
Palmdale (city)	29.0	38.8	-	35.8	-	-	-	-	37.8	-	-	-	-	-	-	-	-	-	-	-	-	-	-	-
Palos Verdes Estates (city)	46.7	42.3	-	-	-	-	42.5	-	-	-	-	-	-	44.2	43.4	-	-	-	-	-	-	-	-	-
Pasadena (city)	34.6	34.5	-	32.4	-	-	33.6	-	37.1	-	-	-	-	43.9	30.3	-	-	-	-	-	-	-	-	37.9
Pomona (city)	26.6	27.4	-	29.3	-	18.6	30.1	-	28.9	-	-	-	-	31.5	-	23.9	-	-	-	-	-	-	-	29.4
Rancho Palos Verdes (city)	44.6	40.3	-	37.6	-	-	43.7	-	42.1	-	-	-	-	39.8	39.8	-	-	-	-	-	40.0	-	-	-
Redondo Beach (city)	36.9	35.2	-	33.0	-	-	36.7	-	34.5	-	-	-	-	37.1	34.0	-	-	-	-	-	-	-	-	-

Notes: Please refer to the User's Guide for an explanation of data; data is arranged alphabetically by state, then county, then city within each county; table includes counties with populations greater than 49,999 unless noted and cities with populations greater than 9,999 whose Asian and/or NHPI population rates are greater than the national average; (1) Native Hawaiian and other Pacific Islander; (2) excludes Taiwanese; (3) includes Chamorro; (4) county does not meet population threshold but is shown in order to allow inclusion of city

Place	Total population	Total Asian population	Total NHPI[1] population	Asian Indian	Bangladeshi	Cambodian	Chinese[2]	Fijian	Filipino	Guamanian[3]	Hawaiian, Native	Hmong	Indonesian	Japanese	Korean	Laotian	Malaysian	Pakistani	Samoan	Sri Lankan	Taiwanese	Thai	Tongan	Vietnamese
Rosemead (city)	32.5	34.5	-	-	-	31.6	34.9	-	43.1	-	-	-	-	49.5	-	-	-	-	-	-	-	-	-	32.4
Rowland Heights (cdp)	35.2	36.7	-	33.4	-	-	37.0	-	39.4	-	-	-	-	46.5	37.1	-	-	-	-	-	34.2	-	-	34.3
San Dimas (city)	37.6	38.5	-	-	-	-	39.0	-	30.6	-	-	-	-	-	-	-	-	-	-	-	-	-	-	-
San Gabriel (city)	35.8	35.4	-	-	-	-	36.4	-	33.3	-	-	-	-	43.9	-	-	-	-	-	-	33.1	-	-	32.0
San Marino (city)	42.3	37.0	-	-	-	-	36.1	-	-	-	-	-	-	-	-	-	-	-	-	-	39.4	-	-	-
Santa Clarita (city)	33.6	35.6	-	35.6	-	-	37.8	-	36.2	-	-	-	-	38.7	34.5	-	-	-	-	-	-	-	-	32.5
Santa Monica (city)	39.2	35.4	-	35.7	-	-	34.8	-	36.0	-	-	-	-	39.5	31.1	-	-	-	-	-	-	-	-	-
Sierra Madre (city)	42.8	43.5	-	-	-	-	-	-	-	-	-	-	-	-	-	-	-	-	-	-	-	-	-	-
South El Monte (city)	26.9	34.3	-	-	-	-	35.1	-	-	-	-	-	-	-	-	-	-	-	-	-	-	-	-	33.0
South Pasadena (city)	37.6	38.9	-	-	-	-	40.9	-	-	-	-	-	-	39.4	35.6	-	-	-	-	-	-	-	-	-
South San Jose Hills (cdp)	26.8	35.3	-	-	-	-	-	-	40.9	-	-	-	-	-	-	-	-	-	-	-	-	-	-	-
Temple City (city)	38.5	37.4	-	-	-	-	36.7	-	42.2	-	-	-	-	50.6	39.7	-	-	-	-	-	35.0	-	-	37.7
Torrance (city)	38.6	37.0	-	30.5	-	-	37.9	-	36.6	-	-	-	-	39.5	36.7	-	-	28.9	-	-	35.9	-	-	33.2
Valinda (cdp)	27.9	39.5	-	-	-	-	-	-	40.0	-	-	-	-	-	-	-	-	-	-	-	-	-	-	35.6
Vincent (cdp)	29.9	34.4	-	-	-	-	-	-	34.6	-	-	-	-	-	-	-	-	-	-	-	-	-	-	-
Walnut (city)	37.3	36.5	-	36.9	-	-	36.6	-	40.4	-	-	-	-	44.3	37.0	-	-	-	-	-	36.2	-	-	34.2
West Carson (cdp)	38.6	38.6	-	-	-	-	-	-	35.8	-	-	-	-	44.6	36.1	-	-	-	-	-	-	-	-	-
West Covina (city)	33.1	34.8	21.3	36.8	-	-	34.8	-	35.4	-	-	-	-	41.8	35.9	-	-	-	-	-	34.2	-	-	31.8
West Hollywood (city)	39.5	34.1	-	-	-	-	-	-	-	-	-	-	-	-	-	-	-	-	-	-	-	-	-	-
West Puente Valley (cdp)	29.1	39.3	-	-	-	-	-	-	40.4	-	-	-	-	-	-	-	-	-	-	-	-	-	-	35.5
Whittier (city)	33.0	37.3	-	-	-	-	37.0	-	36.5	-	-	-	-	49.7	31.9	-	-	-	-	-	-	-	-	-
Madera County	32.9	39.3	-	39.7	-	-	-	-	35.0	-	-	-	-	-	-	-	-	-	-	-	-	-	-	-
Marin County	41.4	38.4	-	31.7	-	-	40.5	-	40.5	-	-	-	-	46.1	36.5	-	-	-	-	-	-	-	-	32.4
Larkspur (city)	46.9	39.1	-	-	-	-	-	-	-	-	-	-	-	-	-	-	-	-	-	-	-	-	-	-
Novato (city)	39.6	38.5	-	-	-	-	42.8	-	37.2	-	-	-	-	-	-	-	-	-	-	-	-	-	-	-
San Rafael (city)	38.7	34.8	-	29.4	-	-	37.9	-	-	-	-	-	-	-	-	-	-	-	-	-	-	-	-	29.6
Tamalpais-Homestead (cdp)	42.8	42.7	-	-	-	-	-	-	-	-	-	-	-	-	-	-	-	-	-	-	-	-	-	-
Mendocino County	38.9	41.0	-	-	-	-	-	-	-	-	-	-	-	-	-	-	-	-	-	-	-	-	-	-
Merced County	29.2	20.4	-	31.5	-	-	47.2	-	40.0	-	-	15.0	-	61.4	-	19.7	-	-	-	-	-	-	-	-
Atwater (city)	28.4	31.2	-	-	-	-	-	-	-	-	-	15.1	-	-	-	-	-	-	-	-	-	-	-	-
Livingston (city)	25.4	31.2	-	31.0	-	-	-	-	-	-	-	-	-	-	-	-	-	-	-	-	-	-	-	-
Merced (city)	27.9	17.3	-	-	-	-	-	-	-	-	-	14.6	-	-	-	20.6	-	-	-	-	-	-	-	-
Monterey County	31.9	37.6	30.3	31.7	-	-	43.2	-	35.8	27.4	-	-	-	52.6	39.7	-	-	-	-	-	-	-	-	30.8
Marina (city)	32.6	37.5	33.2	-	-	-	-	-	34.5	-	-	-	-	54.8	40.0	-	-	-	-	-	-	-	-	30.1
Monterey (city)	35.9	32.7	-	-	-	-	32.1	-	29.9	-	-	-	-	36.3	-	-	-	-	-	-	-	-	-	-
Pacific Grove (city)	44.6	45.1	-	-	-	-	-	-	-	-	-	-	-	-	-	-	-	-	-	-	-	-	-	-
Salinas (city)	28.6	36.4	16.0	35.6	-	-	43.1	-	35.5	-	-	-	-	45.0	36.0	-	-	-	-	-	-	-	-	33.2
Seaside (city)	29.8	36.7	-	-	-	-	-	-	35.4	-	-	-	-	66.5	-	-	-	-	-	-	-	-	-	28.8
Napa County	38.3	35.4	-	-	-	-	36.0	-	36.1	-	-	-	-	36.7	-	-	-	-	-	-	-	-	-	-
Nevada County	43.2	45.8	-	-	-	-	-	-	-	-	-	-	-	-	-	-	-	-	-	-	-	-	-	-
Orange County	33.5	33.9	28.6	31.9	-	30.1	36.1	-	34.2	35.4	35.1	22.3	34.7	40.9	34.8	29.2	-	28.9	25.1	36.5	34.3	35.1	21.8	32.2

Notes: Please refer to the User's Guide for an explanation of data; data is arranged alphabetically by state, then county, then city within each county; table includes counties with populations greater than 49,999 unless noted and cities with populations greater than 9,999 whose Asian and/or NHPI population rates are greater than the national average; (1) Native Hawaiian and other Pacific Islander; (2) excludes Taiwanese; (3) includes Chamorro; (4) county does not meet population threshold but is shown in order to allow inclusion of city

Place	Total population	Total Asian population	Total NHPI[1] population	Asian Indian	Bangladeshi	Cambodian	Chinese[2]	Fijian	Filipino	Guamanian[3]	Hawaiian, Native	Hmong	Indonesian	Japanese	Korean	Laotian	Malaysian	Pakistani	Samoan	Sri Lankan	Taiwanese	Thai	Tongan	Vietnamese
Aliso Viejo (cdp)	32.6	34.2	-	31.4	-	-	34.8	-	32.4	-	-	-	-	35.0	34.1	-	-	-	-	-	-	-	-	34.1
Anaheim (city)	30.4	34.1	26.5	34.3	-	-	39.2	-	34.3	-	-	-	-	46.5	34.4	28.6	-	26.3	28.2	-	28.2	38.3	-	31.9
Brea (city)	37.2	35.9	-	29.5	-	-	40.3	-	35.1	-	-	-	-	-	35.5	-	-	-	-	-	-	-	-	-
Buena Park (city)	32.2	33.7	-	32.8	-	-	38.9	-	33.2	-	-	-	-	42.5	33.7	-	-	-	-	-	-	-	-	33.4
Costa Mesa (city)	32.2	30.9	25.3	27.8	-	-	33.7	-	30.9	-	-	-	-	31.1	30.6	-	-	-	-	-	-	-	-	30.3
Cypress (city)	36.6	35.9	-	32.4	-	-	39.4	-	36.4	-	-	-	-	48.3	32.7	-	-	-	-	-	32.6	-	-	34.9
Foothill Ranch (cdp)	32.3	36.0	-	-	-	-	-	-	-	-	-	-	-	-	-	-	-	-	-	-	-	-	-	-
Fountain Valley (city)	38.1	35.3	-	32.7	-	-	38.6	-	34.9	-	-	-	-	46.2	39.2	-	-	-	-	-	37.3	-	-	32.9
Fullerton (city)	33.1	33.4	-	33.0	-	-	34.3	-	32.7	-	-	-	-	44.9	33.5	-	-	-	-	-	-	-	-	32.6
Garden Grove (city)	32.4	33.1	23.8	34.5	-	31.6	36.2	-	35.6	-	-	-	-	53.3	39.2	-	-	-	23.1	-	-	-	-	31.6
Huntington Beach (city)	36.2	37.1	30.9	34.8	-	-	41.0	-	35.3	-	-	-	-	42.7	39.8	-	-	-	-	-	42.8	-	-	34.4
Irvine (city)	33.3	28.6	-	27.3	-	-	29.0	-	23.8	-	-	-	-	33.6	28.4	-	-	-	-	-	33.7	-	-	28.7
La Habra (city)	31.9	36.3	-	-	-	-	37.5	-	39.9	-	-	-	-	-	31.7	-	-	-	-	-	-	-	-	-
La Palma (city)	38.6	36.6	-	31.1	-	-	37.1	-	37.3	-	-	-	-	52.3	35.6	-	-	-	-	-	-	-	-	-
Laguna Hills (city)	38.4	39.2	-	-	-	-	43.0	-	38.6	-	-	-	-	-	-	-	-	-	-	-	-	-	-	33.5
Laguna Niguel (city)	37.7	39.2	-	-	-	-	40.6	-	40.4	-	-	-	-	41.9	36.5	-	-	-	-	-	-	-	-	35.4
Lake Forest (city)	35.2	36.2	-	30.2	-	-	38.5	-	36.5	-	-	-	-	41.0	42.4	-	-	-	-	-	-	-	-	33.7
Los Alamitos (city)	36.8	36.3	-	-	-	-	-	-	-	-	-	-	-	-	-	-	-	-	-	-	-	-	-	-
Mission Viejo (city)	37.4	37.0	-	32.3	-	-	38.0	-	35.7	-	-	-	-	39.9	42.5	-	-	-	-	-	-	-	-	33.6
Newport Beach (city)	41.6	34.1	-	-	-	-	33.9	-	-	-	-	-	-	40.2	-	-	-	-	-	-	-	-	-	-
Orange (city)	33.3	35.4	-	35.6	-	-	35.9	-	36.0	-	-	-	-	39.6	40.8	-	-	-	-	-	45.7	-	-	31.9
Placentia (city)	33.4	33.6	-	29.7	-	-	30.8	-	36.9	-	-	-	-	42.9	34.2	-	-	-	-	-	-	-	-	33.2
Rancho Santa Margarita (city)	31.7	34.4	-	-	-	-	36.8	-	35.5	-	-	-	-	-	-	-	-	-	-	-	-	-	-	34.0
Rossmoor (cdp)	42.8	40.0	-	-	-	-	-	-	-	-	-	-	-	-	-	-	-	-	-	-	-	-	-	-
Santa Ana (city)	26.5	33.2	28.6	29.6	-	29.7	36.7	-	34.6	-	-	22.6	-	48.9	40.8	26.0	-	-	28.0	-	-	-	-	33.1
Seal Beach (city)	53.7	38.8	-	-	-	-	-	-	-	-	-	-	-	45.6	-	-	-	-	-	-	-	-	-	-
Stanton (city)	30.4	33.1	-	-	-	-	-	-	39.0	-	-	-	-	-	40.7	-	-	-	-	-	-	-	-	31.0
Tustin (city)	31.8	32.9	-	33.1	-	-	34.2	-	32.6	-	-	-	-	36.1	35.2	-	-	-	-	-	33.3	-	-	32.0
Tustin Foothills (cdp)	42.3	40.8	-	-	-	-	46.9	-	-	-	-	-	-	-	-	-	-	-	-	-	-	-	-	-
Westminster (city)	34.3	33.0	22.5	29.8	-	-	38.0	-	35.2	-	-	-	-	52.6	41.2	-	-	-	23.5	-	-	-	-	32.1
Yorba Linda (city)	37.5	38.5	-	39.0	-	-	40.3	-	34.6	-	-	-	-	43.5	35.0	-	-	-	-	-	-	-	-	35.6
Placer County	38.2	38.0	-	28.3	-	-	39.5	-	37.8	-	-	-	-	46.2	30.5	-	-	-	-	-	-	-	-	30.4
Rocklin (city)	34.5	37.0	-	-	-	-	-	-	-	-	-	-	-	37.9	-	-	-	-	-	-	-	-	-	-
Roseville (city)	36.8	35.0	-	27.4	-	-	38.1	-	38.0	-	-	-	-	39.0	-	-	-	-	-	-	-	-	-	-
Riverside County	33.3	33.8	28.1	31.4	-	26.5	29.7	-	35.7	32.4	36.9	15.6	-	44.2	33.9	28.9	-	30.1	21.7	-	23.6	42.4	-	30.3
Banning (city)	40.1	22.1	-	-	-	-	-	-	-	-	-	-	-	-	-	27.5	-	-	-	-	-	-	-	-
Corona (city)	29.9	34.0	-	31.9	-	-	33.4	-	36.5	-	-	-	-	40.6	32.9	-	-	-	-	-	-	-	-	32.2
Moreno Valley (city)	27.3	36.0	-	-	-	-	31.4	-	36.8	-	-	-	-	47.9	40.0	28.4	-	-	-	-	-	-	-	31.9
Palm Springs (city)	47.0	39.8	-	-	-	-	-	-	38.3	-	-	-	-	-	-	-	-	-	-	-	-	-	-	-
Pedley (cdp)	31.9	34.4	-	-	-	-	-	-	-	-	-	-	-	-	-	-	-	-	-	-	-	-	-	-
Riverside (city)	30.1	25.9	28.7	28.9	-	-	22.5	-	30.1	-	-	-	-	36.8	25.2	29.6	-	-	-	-	-	-	-	29.7

Notes: Please refer to the User's Guide for an explanation of data; data is arranged alphabetically by state, then county, then city within each county; table includes counties with populations greater than 49,999 unless noted and cities with populations greater than 9,999 whose Asian and/or NHPI population rates are greater than the national average; (1) Native Hawaiian and other Pacific Islander; (2) excludes Taiwanese; (3) includes Chamorro; (4) county does not meet population threshold but is shown in order to allow inclusion of city

Place	Total population	Total Asian population	Total NHPI[1] population	Asian Indian	Bangladeshi	Cambodian	Chinese[2]	Fijian	Filipino	Guamanian[3]	Hawaiian, Native	Hmong	Indonesian	Japanese	Korean	Laotian	Malaysian	Pakistani	Samoan	Sri Lankan	Taiwanese	Thai	Tongan	Vietnamese
Temecula (city)	31.1	35.5	-	-	-	-	37.2	-	34.3	-	-	-	-	-	-	-	-	-	-	-	-	-	-	-
Sacramento County	34.1	31.5	26.7	29.7	-	24.3	37.8	28.1	35.7	29.6	32.3	16.0	-	46.8	34.9	19.4	-	26.0	20.8	-	42.1	34.3	25.4	29.4
Arden-Arcade (cdp)	37.6	32.1	-	32.7	-	-	37.2	-	32.8	-	-	22.1	-	46.6	-	-	-	-	-	-	-	-	-	29.4
Elk Grove (cdp)	32.0	31.6	-	29.7	-	-	29.9	-	37.2	-	-	-	-	42.3	-	-	-	-	-	-	-	-	-	30.9
Fair Oaks (cdp)	40.8	33.8	-	-	-	-	-	-	-	-	-	-	-	-	-	-	-	-	-	-	-	-	-	-
Florin (cdp)	31.9	26.0	-	33.1	-	-	29.6	-	43.6	-	-	13.4	-	-	-	-	-	-	-	-	-	-	-	26.7
Folsom (city)	35.9	32.9	-	30.7	-	-	36.1	-	34.4	-	-	-	-	-	-	-	-	-	-	-	-	-	-	-
Foothill Farms (cdp)	30.6	32.1	-	-	-	-	-	-	-	-	-	-	-	-	-	-	-	-	-	-	-	-	-	-
La Riviera (cdp)	34.8	36.8	-	-	-	-	-	-	-	-	-	-	-	-	-	-	-	-	-	-	-	-	-	-
Laguna (cdp)	32.8	34.7	-	30.9	-	-	34.8	-	36.2	-	-	-	-	39.6	-	-	-	-	-	-	-	-	-	30.5
North Highlands (cdp)	30.4	32.3	-	-	-	-	-	-	34.0	-	-	-	-	-	-	-	-	-	-	-	-	-	-	31.5
Parkway-S. Sacramento (cdp)	27.2	20.3	-	-	-	-	26.6	-	-	-	-	14.9	-	-	-	18.9	-	-	-	-	-	-	-	31.4
Rancho Cordova (cdp)	32.3	30.8	-	26.9	-	-	29.2	-	36.0	-	-	-	-	-	37.2	-	-	-	-	-	-	-	-	28.8
Rosemont (cdp)	31.6	34.8	-	-	-	-	-	-	34.0	-	-	-	-	-	42.0	-	-	-	-	-	-	-	-	33.1
Sacramento (city)	33.2	30.6	26.0	28.9	-	25.4	41.0	27.9	35.0	-	-	15.8	-	48.4	33.0	18.9	-	24.6	20.3	-	-	-	21.0	26.4
Vineyard (cdp)	34.8	35.5	-	-	-	-	-	-	36.3	-	-	-	-	-	-	-	-	-	-	-	-	-	-	-
San Benito County	31.5	38.0	-	-	-	-	-	-	38.0	-	-	-	-	-	-	-	-	-	-	-	-	-	-	-
San Bernardino County	30.6	34.3	26.9	30.5	-	20.9	35.6	-	35.9	30.6	33.5	-	30.1	42.0	34.8	25.4	-	35.6	20.1	-	36.3	40.7	23.1	30.9
Chino (city)	31.1	32.8	-	-	-	-	-	-	31.5	-	-	-	-	-	-	-	-	-	-	-	-	-	-	33.2
Chino Hills (city)	32.9	34.4	-	31.3	-	-	33.6	-	34.1	-	-	-	-	38.1	37.4	-	-	-	-	-	32.7	-	-	36.6
Colton (city)	27.2	33.5	-	-	-	-	-	-	36.7	-	-	-	-	-	-	-	-	-	-	-	-	-	-	-
Fontana (city)	26.4	32.5	26.0	26.7	-	-	-	-	34.9	-	-	-	-	-	-	-	-	-	-	-	-	-	-	-
Grand Terrace (city)	36.5	31.2	-	-	-	-	-	-	-	-	-	-	-	-	-	-	-	-	-	-	-	-	-	-
Highland (city)	29.5	35.3	-	-	-	-	-	-	36.5	-	-	-	-	-	-	-	-	-	-	-	-	-	-	27.5
Loma Linda (city)	34.2	33.2	-	37.3	-	-	34.6	-	38.0	-	-	-	27.3	-	30.0	-	-	-	-	-	-	-	-	-
Montclair (city)	29.5	33.9	-	-	-	-	-	-	-	-	-	-	-	-	-	-	-	-	-	-	-	-	-	30.2
Ontario (city)	27.7	35.0	18.1	27.4	-	-	35.7	-	38.2	-	-	-	-	-	-	-	-	-	-	-	-	-	-	31.6
Rancho Cucamonga (city)	32.4	36.2	-	31.0	-	-	38.8	-	33.7	-	-	-	-	41.2	38.2	-	-	-	-	-	-	-	-	31.7
Redlands (city)	35.0	33.7	-	27.7	-	-	37.1	-	41.2	-	-	-	-	-	30.3	-	-	-	-	-	-	-	-	-
Rialto (city)	26.7	30.9	28.4	-	-	-	-	-	36.9	-	-	-	-	-	-	-	-	-	-	-	-	-	-	-
San Bernardino (city)	27.6	29.5	22.6	25.9	-	19.7	32.0	-	36.9	-	-	-	19.3	-	31.2	-	-	-	15.7	-	-	-	-	27.8
Upland (city)	34.7	35.3	-	30.7	-	-	39.5	-	50.9	-	-	-	-	-	30.1	-	-	-	-	-	41.5	-	-	32.0
Victorville (city)	30.8	36.0	-	-	-	-	-	-	34.2	-	-	-	-	-	-	-	-	-	-	-	-	-	-	-
San Diego County	33.4	33.4	29.6	29.4	-	20.5	34.2	-	35.1	32.7	35.2	19.4	31.2	40.4	30.2	26.6	-	25.3	25.5	-	31.5	31.5	23.2	31.1
Bonita (cdp)	40.9	44.5	-	-	-	-	-	-	53.1	-	-	-	-	-	-	-	-	-	-	-	-	-	-	-
Carlsbad (city)	38.9	36.9	-	-	-	-	35.1	-	37.0	-	-	-	-	44.4	-	-	-	-	-	-	-	-	-	-
Chula Vista (city)	33.2	36.1	33.4	-	-	-	36.9	-	35.1	34.6	-	-	-	43.2	36.5	-	-	-	-	-	-	-	-	-
Coronado (city)	33.9	29.8	-	-	-	-	-	-	30.7	-	-	-	-	-	-	-	-	-	-	-	-	-	-	-
Escondido (city)	31.2	34.3	-	-	-	-	45.5	-	32.1	-	-	-	-	-	-	23.7	-	-	-	-	-	-	-	32.6
Imperial Beach (city)	28.4	37.4	-	-	-	-	-	-	37.6	-	-	-	-	-	-	-	-	-	-	-	-	-	-	-
La Mesa (city)	37.6	30.6	-	-	-	-	-	-	32.1	-	-	-	-	-	-	-	-	-	-	-	-	-	-	-

Notes: Please refer to the User's Guide for an explanation of data; data is arranged alphabetically by state, then county, then city within each county; table includes counties with populations greater than 49,999 unless noted and cities with populations greater than 9,999 whose Asian and/or NHPI population rates are greater than the national average; (1) Native Hawaiian and other Pacific Islander; (2) excludes Taiwanese; (3) includes Chamorro; (4) county does not meet population threshold but is shown in order to allow inclusion of city

Place	Total population	Total Asian population	Total NHPI[1] population	Asian Indian	Bangladeshi	Cambodian	Chinese[2]	Fijian	Filipino	Guamanian[3]	Hawaiian, Native	Hmong	Indonesian	Japanese	Korean	Laotian	Malaysian	Pakistani	Samoan	Sri Lankan	Taiwanese	Thai	Tongan	Vietnamese
La Presa (cdp)	32.3	39.1	-	-	-	-	-	-	38.0	-	-	-	-	-	-	-	-	-	-	-	-	-	-	-
Lemon Grove (city)	34.9	35.2	-	-	-	-	-	-	35.8	-	-	-	-	-	-	-	-	-	-	-	-	-	-	28.1
National City (city)	28.9	38.8	-	-	-	-	-	-	39.1	-	-	-	-	-	-	-	-	-	-	-	-	-	-	-
Oceanside (city)	33.6	37.4	26.9	-	-	-	38.7	-	35.4	-	-	-	-	51.3	-	-	-	-	26.6	-	-	-	-	33.1
Poway (city)	37.0	35.5	-	-	-	-	40.8	-	31.6	-	-	-	-	-	-	-	-	-	-	-	-	-	-	-
Rancho San Diego (cdp)	36.4	37.5	-	-	-	-	-	-	39.3	-	-	-	-	-	-	-	-	-	-	-	-	-	-	-
San Diego (city)	32.7	32.1	28.8	28.4	-	19.7	33.1	-	34.7	31.8	34.3	19.0	-	36.2	28.5	26.7	-	-	21.8	-	30.6	30.1	-	30.9
San Marcos (city)	32.4	35.8	-	-	-	-	33.7	-	36.5	-	-	-	-	-	-	-	-	-	-	-	-	-	-	-
Solana Beach (city)	42.4	38.9	-	-	-	-	-	-	-	-	-	-	-	-	-	-	-	-	-	-	-	-	-	-
Spring Valley (cdp)	33.0	36.4	-	-	-	-	-	-	37.8	-	-	-	-	-	-	-	-	-	-	-	-	-	-	-
Vista (city)	30.5	36.0	23.6	-	-	-	-	-	36.3	-	-	-	-	36.9	-	-	-	-	-	-	-	-	-	-
San Francisco County	36.6	38.6	28.8	30.0	-	28.5	40.6	-	38.2	-	-	-	26.1	42.4	32.5	-	-	24.0	22.7	-	30.2	31.0	-	32.9
San Francisco (city)	36.6	38.6	28.8	30.0	-	28.5	40.6	-	38.2	-	-	-	26.1	42.4	32.5	-	-	24.0	22.7	-	30.2	31.0	-	32.9
San Joaquin County	32.1	28.6	27.3	29.3	-	18.3	42.0	-	35.4	-	29.9	15.9	-	50.5	37.0	21.8	-	21.3	29.2	-	-	-	-	22.6
Lathrop (city)	30.2	31.4	-	-	-	-	-	-	32.9	-	-	-	-	-	-	-	-	-	-	-	-	-	-	-
Lodi (city)	33.9	34.1	-	31.1	-	-	-	-	29.2	-	-	-	-	56.7	-	-	-	-	-	-	-	-	-	-
Stockton (city)	30.2	27.0	26.5	29.3	-	18.4	42.5	-	35.7	-	-	15.7	-	50.2	-	21.8	-	21.8	-	-	-	-	-	22.0
Tracy (city)	31.1	31.6	-	28.5	-	-	36.8	-	33.2	-	-	-	-	-	-	-	-	-	-	-	-	-	-	-
San Luis Obispo County	37.3	29.2	-	29.5	-	-	23.5	-	32.0	-	-	-	-	42.0	35.7	-	-	-	-	-	-	-	-	-
Baywood-Los Osos (cdp)	43.5	37.7	-	-	-	-	-	-	35.5	-	-	-	-	-	-	-	-	-	-	-	-	-	-	-
Grover Beach (city)	34.8	32.2	-	-	-	-	-	-	-	-	-	-	-	-	-	-	-	-	-	-	-	-	-	-
San Luis Obispo (city)	26.9	23.1	-	-	-	-	22.2	-	21.9	-	-	-	-	-	-	-	-	-	-	-	-	-	-	-
San Mateo County	37.0	35.5	30.0	30.3	-	-	37.9	31.2	35.0	39.8	39.9	-	25.9	41.7	34.0	-	-	-	26.5	-	31.2	35.3	27.5	31.3
Belmont (city)	38.7	35.1	-	28.0	-	-	37.5	-	37.1	-	-	-	-	43.4	-	-	-	-	-	-	-	-	-	-
Burlingame (city)	38.0	34.1	-	-	-	-	35.9	-	36.3	-	-	-	-	38.3	-	-	-	-	-	-	-	-	-	-
Daly City (city)	35.4	34.8	37.1	31.9	-	-	37.2	-	34.3	-	-	-	-	44.5	30.6	-	-	-	-	-	-	-	-	32.5
East Palo Alto (city)	25.6	36.6	25.7	-	-	-	-	-	-	-	-	-	-	-	-	-	-	-	-	-	-	-	25.3	-
Foster City (city)	38.6	34.4	-	30.0	-	-	39.3	-	36.9	-	-	-	-	36.3	32.9	-	-	-	-	-	-	-	-	-
Hillsborough (town)	45.1	41.4	-	-	-	-	41.8	-	-	-	-	-	-	-	-	-	-	-	-	-	-	-	-	-
Menlo Park (city)	37.8	34.0	-	-	-	-	37.0	-	-	-	-	-	-	35.0	-	-	-	-	-	-	-	-	-	-
Millbrae (city)	41.9	36.2	-	32.5	-	-	38.1	-	39.1	-	-	-	-	34.3	37.2	-	-	-	-	-	-	-	-	-
Pacifica (city)	37.7	34.8	-	-	-	-	38.6	-	33.4	-	-	-	-	50.1	-	-	-	-	-	-	-	-	-	-
Redwood City (city)	35.0	33.7	29.5	28.0	-	-	35.7	-	34.5	-	-	-	-	46.9	-	-	-	-	-	-	-	-	-	-
San Bruno (city)	36.7	35.4	26.2	30.1	-	-	38.0	-	34.3	-	-	-	-	40.0	-	-	-	-	-	-	-	-	22.4	-
San Carlos (city)	40.0	38.0	-	-	-	-	37.0	-	-	-	-	-	-	-	-	-	-	-	-	-	-	-	-	-
San Mateo (city)	37.4	36.6	32.1	30.4	-	-	38.9	-	37.0	-	-	-	-	43.9	33.4	-	-	-	-	-	-	-	31.5	31.2
South San Francisco (city)	35.9	36.3	28.7	36.5	-	-	37.2	-	35.7	-	-	-	-	48.0	-	-	-	-	-	-	-	-	-	-
Santa Barbara County	33.6	31.3	31.5	27.6	-	-	27.9	-	34.8	-	-	13.6	-	43.5	25.7	-	-	-	-	-	-	-	-	25.9
Goleta (cdp)	38.6	31.7	-	-	-	-	35.3	-	27.9	-	-	-	-	37.3	-	-	-	-	-	-	-	-	-	28.6
Isla Vista (cdp)	21.1	21.8	-	-	-	-	21.9	-	-	-	-	-	-	-	22.0	-	-	-	-	-	-	-	-	-
Lompoc (city)	32.2	34.1	-	-	-	-	-	-	39.0	-	-	-	-	-	-	-	-	-	-	-	-	-	-	-

Notes: Please refer to the User's Guide for an explanation of data; data is arranged alphabetically by state, then county, then city within each county; table includes counties with populations greater than 49,999 unless noted and cities with populations greater than 9,999 whose Asian and/or NHPI population rates are greater than the national average; (1) Native Hawaiian and other Pacific Islander; (2) excludes Taiwanese; (3) includes Chamorro; (4) county does not meet population threshold but is shown in order to allow inclusion of city

Place	Total population	Total Asian population	Total NHPI[1] population	Asian Indian	Bangladeshi	Cambodian	Chinese[2]	Fijian	Filipino	Guamanian[3]	Hawaiian, Native	Hmong	Indonesian	Japanese	Korean	Laotian	Malaysian	Pakistani	Samoan	Sri Lankan	Taiwanese	Thai	Tongan	Vietnamese
Orcutt (cdp)	39.7	42.0	-	-	-	-	-	-	-	-	-	-	-	-	-	-	-	-	-	-	-	-	-	-
Santa Maria (city)	29.4	37.8	-	-	-	-	-	-	37.6	-	-	-	-	57.5	-	-	-	-	-	-	-	-	-	-
Santa Clara County	34.1	32.7	29.3	29.3	31.5	24.7	35.0	28.2	34.2	30.1	31.9	-	34.3	41.2	33.2	24.7	-	28.6	27.5	-	33.4	28.7	-	32.1
Alum Rock (cdp)	31.0	37.0	-	-	-	-	-	-	-	-	-	-	-	-	-	-	-	-	-	-	-	-	-	37.5
Campbell (city)	35.4	33.5	-	28.7	-	-	33.5	-	31.2	-	-	-	-	49.0	37.1	-	-	-	-	-	-	-	-	33.1
Cupertino (city)	38.0	34.7	-	31.9	-	-	36.5	-	42.2	-	-	-	-	37.6	33.7	-	-	-	-	-	34.1	-	-	37.8
Gilroy (city)	30.2	35.2	-	-	-	-	41.4	-	35.5	-	-	-	-	-	-	-	-	-	-	-	-	-	-	-
Los Altos (city)	44.5	41.4	-	38.8	-	-	41.7	-	-	-	-	-	-	46.0	-	-	-	-	-	-	-	-	-	-
Los Gatos (town)	41.4	37.5	-	-	-	-	38.6	-	-	-	-	-	-	40.0	-	-	-	-	-	-	-	-	-	-
Milpitas (city)	33.3	33.4	23.1	28.9	-	-	35.1	-	34.3	-	-	-	-	43.8	35.9	-	-	-	-	-	-	-	-	34.1
Morgan Hill (city)	34.0	36.7	-	-	-	-	35.8	-	-	-	-	-	-	41.1	-	-	-	-	-	-	-	-	-	-
Mountain View (city)	34.7	32.5	-	29.1	-	-	33.4	-	35.9	-	-	-	-	42.9	30.7	-	-	-	-	-	-	-	-	32.1
Palo Alto (city)	40.4	36.4	-	32.7	-	-	37.4	-	39.0	-	-	-	-	42.2	31.2	-	-	-	-	-	-	-	-	-
San Jose (city)	32.7	32.7	28.0	29.9	-	24.5	34.7	-	33.6	33.6	28.9	-	-	42.9	33.2	24.3	-	28.4	26.3	-	34.7	27.8	-	31.8
Santa Clara (city)	33.5	30.7	35.3	28.3	-	-	33.0	-	34.1	-	-	-	-	38.7	32.4	-	-	26.3	-	-	-	-	-	33.2
Saratoga (city)	43.3	38.5	-	37.0	-	-	38.3	-	-	-	-	-	-	42.8	41.0	-	-	-	-	-	30.0	-	-	-
Stanford (cdp)	22.1	22.4	-	21.9	-	-	22.8	-	-	-	-	-	-	-	22.1	-	-	-	-	-	-	-	-	-
Sunnyvale (city)	34.4	31.4	33.1	28.6	-	-	34.5	-	33.9	-	-	-	-	35.9	33.9	-	-	-	-	-	33.7	-	-	33.3
Santa Cruz County	35.2	34.4	-	32.5	-	-	31.0	-	32.3	-	-	-	-	46.1	27.9	-	-	-	-	-	-	-	-	22.6
Capitola (city)	39.1	35.7	-	-	-	-	-	-	-	-	-	-	-	-	-	-	-	-	-	-	-	-	-	-
Santa Cruz (city)	31.8	25.7	-	29.6	-	-	22.9	-	28.1	-	-	-	-	31.8	-	-	-	-	-	-	-	-	-	-
Scotts Valley (city)	37.7	34.9	-	-	-	-	-	-	-	-	-	-	-	-	-	-	-	-	-	-	-	-	-	-
Shasta County	39.1	28.7	-	-	-	-	-	-	40.6	-	-	-	-	-	-	18.4	-	-	-	-	-	-	-	-
Solano County	34.1	36.2	30.9	30.4	-	-	41.3	-	36.5	37.4	36.9	17.4	-	53.0	40.2	26.1	-	-	25.0	-	-	-	-	30.4
Benicia (city)	39.1	40.1	-	-	-	-	45.0	-	40.7	-	-	-	-	-	-	-	-	-	-	-	-	-	-	-
Fairfield (city)	31.5	35.1	37.8	34.0	-	-	38.6	-	34.2	41.1	-	-	-	59.6	42.1	24.8	-	-	-	-	-	-	-	-
Suisun City (city)	32.1	35.1	-	27.6	-	-	-	-	35.4	-	-	-	-	-	-	-	-	-	-	-	-	-	-	-
Vacaville (city)	34.0	36.8	-	-	-	-	-	-	36.6	-	-	-	-	-	-	-	-	-	-	-	-	-	-	-
Vallejo (city)	35.3	36.3	30.2	29.7	-	-	41.3	-	37.0	35.6	-	-	-	47.8	-	-	-	-	-	-	-	-	-	25.5
Sonoma County	37.6	35.0	30.0	29.9	-	20.2	37.4	-	35.4	-	-	-	-	46.4	39.6	27.1	-	-	-	-	-	-	-	34.0
Petaluma (city)	37.3	36.0	-	-	-	-	40.1	-	-	-	-	-	-	-	-	-	-	-	-	-	-	-	-	-
Rohnert Park (city)	31.5	30.1	-	-	-	-	31.3	-	33.4	-	-	-	-	-	-	-	-	-	-	-	-	-	-	-
Santa Rosa (city)	36.4	33.5	-	31.7	-	19.9	39.3	-	36.3	-	-	-	-	42.6	-	27.4	-	-	-	-	-	-	-	34.6
Stanislaus County	31.9	29.2	26.1	30.7	-	18.2	36.4	23.7	37.4	-	-	16.6	-	45.3	-	24.8	-	-	-	-	-	-	-	27.2
Ceres (city)	29.6	29.8	-	27.2	-	-	-	-	-	-	-	-	-	-	-	-	-	-	-	-	-	-	-	-
Modesto (city)	33.0	27.6	25.4	35.1	-	18.6	35.3	24.0	36.5	-	-	15.7	-	40.5	-	24.9	-	-	-	-	-	-	-	26.0
Salida (cdp)	29.1	33.4	-	-	-	-	-	-	-	-	-	-	-	-	-	-	-	-	-	-	-	-	-	-
Turlock (city)	31.3	31.2	-	31.4	-	-	-	-	-	-	-	-	-	-	-	-	-	-	-	-	-	-	-	-
Sutter County	34.4	32.5	-	30.5	-	-	-	-	38.4	-	-	-	-	50.9	-	-	-	-	-	-	-	-	-	-
South Yuba City (cdp)	36.2	29.3	-	28.5	-	-	-	-	-	-	-	-	-	-	-	-	-	-	-	-	-	-	-	-
Yuba City (city)	32.1	35.0	-	32.2	-	-	-	-	-	-	-	-	-	-	-	-	-	-	-	-	-	-	-	-

Notes: Please refer to the User's Guide for an explanation of data; data is arranged alphabetically by state, then county, then city within each county; table includes counties with populations greater than 49,999 unless noted and cities with populations greater than 9,999 whose Asian and/or NHPI population rates are greater than the national average; (1) Native Hawaiian and other Pacific Islander; (2) excludes Taiwanese; (3) includes Chamorro; (4) county does not meet population threshold but is shown in order to allow inclusion of city

Place	Total population	Total Asian population	Total NHPI[1] population	Asian Indian	Bangladeshi	Cambodian	Chinese[2]	Fijian	Filipino	Guamanian[3]	Hawaiian, Native	Hmong	Indonesian	Japanese	Korean	Laotian	Malaysian	Pakistani	Samoan	Sri Lankan	Taiwanese	Thai	Tongan	Vietnamese
Tehama County	37.8	31.2	-	-	-	-	-	-	-	-	-	-	-	-	-	-	-	-	-	-	-	-	-	-
Tulare County	29.2	29.7	-	26.5	-	-	44.2	-	35.7	-	-	16.1	-	59.1	38.5	18.8	-	-	-	-	-	-	-	-
Porterville (city)	28.5	30.6	-	-	-	-	-	-	32.3	-	-	-	-	-	-	-	-	-	-	-	-	-	-	-
Visalia (city)	31.5	24.3	-	-	-	-	-	-	33.3	-	-	13.3	-	-	-	18.8	-	-	-	-	-	-	-	-
Tuolumne County	42.8	35.1	-	-	-	-	-	-	-	-	-	-	-	-	-	-	-	-	-	-	-	-	-	-
Ventura County	34.4	37.3	34.7	33.1	-	-	39.3	-	37.9	-	37.2	-	-	43.1	34.9	-	-	-	25.6	-	38.4	-	-	34.2
Camarillo (city)	38.6	36.5	-	-	-	-	36.5	-	40.3	-	-	-	-	43.1	30.9	-	-	-	-	-	-	-	-	31.1
Moorpark (city)	31.7	36.6	-	-	-	-	-	-	-	-	-	-	-	-	-	-	-	-	-	-	-	-	-	-
Oxnard (city)	29.0	38.4	35.3	26.6	-	-	39.0	-	37.8	-	-	-	-	51.8	44.7	-	-	-	24.9	-	-	-	-	29.9
Port Hueneme (city)	30.5	35.9	-	-	-	-	-	-	34.9	-	-	-	-	-	-	-	-	-	-	-	-	-	-	-
Simi Valley (city)	34.9	36.3	-	33.3	-	-	37.6	-	41.7	-	-	-	-	39.1	32.4	-	-	-	-	-	-	-	-	34.6
Thousand Oaks (city)	37.7	37.8	-	33.0	-	-	39.2	-	44.1	-	-	-	-	40.7	36.0	-	-	-	-	-	-	-	-	33.8
Yolo County	29.5	22.6	29.1	23.8	-	-	22.2	22.5	23.1	-	-	13.1	-	33.4	22.9	17.6	-	-	-	-	-	-	-	22.0
Davis (city)	25.2	22.4	-	23.5	-	-	21.8	-	22.4	-	-	-	-	29.8	22.7	-	-	-	-	-	-	-	-	22.1
West Sacramento (city)	34.0	24.7	-	28.5	-	-	-	-	-	-	-	12.2	-	-	-	-	-	-	-	-	-	-	-	-
Woodland (city)	32.6	32.1	-	32.1	-	-	-	-	-	-	-	-	-	-	-	-	-	-	-	-	-	-	-	-
Yuba County	31.5	19.0	-	-	-	-	-	-	30.9	-	-	15.4	-	-	-	-	-	-	-	-	-	-	-	-
Linda (cdp)	26.0	15.8	-	-	-	-	-	-	-	-	-	14.9	-	-	-	-	-	-	-	-	-	-	-	-
Marysville (city)	32.9	28.8	-	-	-	-	-	-	-	-	-	-	-	-	-	-	-	-	-	-	-	-	-	-
Olivehurst (cdp)	31.4	26.1	-	-	-	-	-	-	-	-	-	-	-	-	-	-	-	-	-	-	-	-	-	-
COLORADO	34.4	31.3	28.1	28.5	-	24.5	34.1	-	33.4	34.0	31.2	19.0	28.5	43.0	32.7	25.7	-	28.0	21.9	-	32.1	31.4	-	29.5
Adams County	31.5	29.4	-	27.3	-	-	34.2	-	30.9	-	-	19.4	-	52.9	37.2	25.4	-	-	-	-	-	-	-	30.9
Berkley (cdp)	33.0	24.0	-	-	-	-	-	-	-	-	-	-	-	-	-	-	-	-	-	-	-	-	-	-
Federal Heights (city)	31.3	29.1	-	-	-	-	-	-	-	-	-	-	-	-	-	-	-	-	-	-	-	-	-	-
Westminster (city)	32.7	28.4	-	28.7	-	-	34.1	-	-	-	-	18.8	-	-	34.7	29.8	-	-	-	-	-	-	-	29.5
Arapahoe County	34.7	33.4	33.3	29.4	-	-	37.3	-	36.4	-	-	-	-	43.8	35.4	-	-	-	-	-	-	-	-	30.5
Aurora (city)	31.9	35.4	34.0	29.6	-	23.2	37.5	-	37.5	-	-	-	-	45.2	38.8	-	-	-	-	-	-	-	-	29.8
Boulder County	33.5	29.8	-	28.0	-	-	33.2	-	30.7	-	-	-	-	34.1	25.7	-	-	-	-	-	-	-	-	27.3
Boulder (city)	29.1	27.4	-	26.2	-	-	30.0	-	-	-	-	-	-	31.5	25.8	-	-	-	-	-	-	-	-	-
Broomfield (city)	33.8	31.0	-	-	-	-	31.7	-	-	-	-	-	-	-	-	-	-	-	-	-	-	-	-	-
Lafayette (city)	33.6	32.2	-	-	-	-	-	-	-	-	-	-	-	-	-	-	-	-	-	-	-	-	-	-
Denver County	33.3	29.9	25.0	27.3	-	27.1	33.6	-	32.2	-	-	-	-	40.5	29.7	-	-	-	-	-	-	27.3	-	29.3
Douglas County	33.8	34.0	-	29.4	-	-	35.1	-	-	-	-	-	-	-	36.6	-	-	-	-	-	-	-	-	-
Highlands Ranch (cdp)	32.3	34.2	-	28.8	-	-	35.5	-	-	-	-	-	-	-	-	-	-	-	-	-	-	-	-	-
El Paso County	33.0	33.2	26.4	28.3	-	-	31.2	-	33.8	32.1	-	-	-	47.1	38.8	-	-	-	-	-	-	-	-	30.4
Colorado Springs (city)	33.6	31.9	25.7	28.3	-	-	29.9	-	31.9	-	-	-	-	45.7	37.0	-	-	-	-	-	-	-	-	29.9
Jefferson County	36.9	31.3	27.5	30.7	-	-	32.3	-	35.0	-	-	19.1	-	45.7	32.7	26.5	-	-	-	-	-	-	-	28.0
Larimer County	33.4	29.2	-	26.2	-	-	33.4	-	-	-	-	-	-	32.9	20.6	-	-	-	-	-	-	-	-	-
Mesa County	38.1	31.6	-	-	-	-	-	-	-	-	-	-	-	-	-	-	-	-	-	-	-	-	-	-
Pueblo County	36.9	33.8	-	-	-	-	-	-	-	-	-	-	-	-	-	-	-	-	-	-	-	-	-	-
Weld County	31.1	27.9	-	-	-	-	-	-	-	-	-	-	-	36.7	-	-	-	-	-	-	-	-	-	-

Notes: Please refer to the User's Guide for an explanation of data; data is arranged alphabetically by state, then county, then city within each county; table includes counties with populations greater than 49,999 unless noted and cities with populations greater than 9,999 whose Asian and/or NHPI population rates are greater than the national average; (1) Native Hawaiian and other Pacific Islander; (2) excludes Taiwanese; (3) includes Chamorro; (4) county does not meet population threshold but is shown in order to allow inclusion of city

Place	Total population	Total Asian population	Total NHPI[1] population	Asian Indian	Bangladeshi	Cambodian	Chinese[2]	Fijian	Filipino	Guamanian[3]	Hawaiian, Native	Hmong	Indonesian	Japanese	Korean	Laotian	Malaysian	Pakistani	Samoan	Sri Lankan	Taiwanese	Thai	Tongan	Vietnamese
CONNECTICUT	37.5	30.8	25.8	30.5	33.0	27.5	32.2	-	34.8	33.0	-	-	-	34.5	27.2	29.8	-	29.3	-	-	24.3	30.2	-	30.5
Fairfield County	37.4	32.3	-	31.5	-	26.6	35.2	-	35.8	-	-	-	-	35.0	27.6	29.2	-	29.3	-	-	-	-	-	31.3
Danbury (city)	35.4	31.6	-	31.6	-	24.5	36.8	-	-	-	-	-	-	-	-	-	-	-	-	-	-	-	-	-
Greenwich (town)	40.3	35.2	-	38.5	-	-	38.7	-	-	-	-	-	-	32.6	-	-	-	-	-	-	-	-	-	-
Stamford (city)	36.6	31.5	-	29.2	-	-	34.2	-	36.3	-	-	-	-	-	-	-	-	-	-	-	-	-	-	-
Hartford County	37.7	31.1	-	30.8	-	-	33.9	-	33.1	-	-	-	-	32.3	31.6	30.8	-	29.3	-	-	-	-	-	30.3
East Hartford (town)	37.5	31.4	-	31.6	-	-	-	-	-	-	-	-	-	-	-	-	-	-	-	-	-	-	-	29.4
Farmington (town)	40.0	35.5	-	-	-	-	-	-	-	-	-	-	-	-	-	-	-	-	-	-	-	-	-	-
Glastonbury (town)	39.8	35.9	-	37.8	-	-	-	-	-	-	-	-	-	-	-	-	-	-	-	-	-	-	-	-
Rocky Hill (town)	40.7	29.2	-	-	-	-	-	-	-	-	-	-	-	-	-	-	-	-	-	-	-	-	-	-
South Windsor (town)	39.0	33.6	-	-	-	-	-	-	-	-	-	-	-	-	-	-	-	-	-	-	-	-	-	-
West Hartford (town)	40.2	33.7	-	34.4	-	-	36.7	-	-	-	-	-	-	-	-	-	-	-	-	-	-	-	-	29.8
Litchfield County	39.7	30.0	-	36.8	-	-	30.8	-	-	-	-	-	-	-	20.7	-	-	-	-	-	-	-	-	30.2
Middlesex County	38.7	28.8	-	27.7	-	-	31.3	-	-	-	-	-	-	-	-	-	-	-	-	-	-	-	-	-
New Haven County	37.1	29.5	-	29.5	-	-	29.8	-	35.2	-	-	-	-	32.0	26.6	30.4	-	28.9	-	-	-	-	-	31.4
New Haven (city)	29.5	27.0	-	26.9	-	-	27.4	-	-	-	-	-	-	-	24.6	-	-	-	-	-	-	-	-	-
New London County	37.1	32.0	-	31.9	-	-	30.3	-	37.3	-	-	-	-	-	-	-	-	-	-	-	-	-	-	-
Tolland County	35.7	28.1	-	25.5	-	-	29.4	-	-	-	-	-	-	-	-	-	-	-	-	-	-	-	-	-
Mansfield (town)	21.9	24.7	-	21.6	-	-	27.5	-	-	-	-	-	-	-	-	-	-	-	-	-	-	-	-	-
Storrs (cdp)	20.7	23.9	-	-	-	-	26.9	-	-	-	-	-	-	-	-	-	-	-	-	-	-	-	-	-
Windham County	36.3	26.7	-	-	-	-	-	-	-	-	-	-	-	-	-	-	-	-	-	-	-	-	-	-
DELAWARE	36.1	32.6	23.0	30.3	-	-	33.0	-	38.6	-	-	-	-	45.1	34.3	-	-	33.3	-	-	-	-	-	32.3
Kent County	34.6	36.5	-	33.8	-	-	-	-	41.9	-	-	-	-	-	-	-	-	-	-	-	-	-	-	-
New Castle County	35.1	32.0	-	30.0	-	-	32.9	-	35.3	-	-	-	-	39.5	32.9	-	-	-	-	-	-	-	-	31.8
Hockessin (cdp)	41.4	37.6	-	-	-	-	-	-	-	-	-	-	-	-	-	-	-	-	-	-	-	-	-	-
Newark (city)	22.7	27.2	-	-	-	-	28.5	-	-	-	-	-	-	-	-	-	-	-	-	-	-	-	-	-
Pike Creek (cdp)	36.1	33.6	-	-	-	-	-	-	-	-	-	-	-	-	-	-	-	-	-	-	-	-	-	-
Sussex County	41.0	34.5	-	-	-	-	-	-	-	-	-	-	-	-	-	-	-	-	-	-	-	-	-	-
DISTRICT OF COLUMBIA	34.7	29.8	-	30.0	-	-	31.8	-	36.3	-	-	-	-	32.2	28.2	-	-	-	-	-	-	-	-	28.2
FLORIDA	38.8	34.1	29.6	32.1	33.0	29.5	36.4	-	36.3	29.1	33.6	-	40.0	41.0	35.8	29.5	-	32.4	28.9	39.4	36.2	39.1	-	30.5
Alachua County	29.0	25.9	-	23.9	-	-	27.4	-	30.1	-	-	-	-	32.1	28.8	-	-	-	-	-	-	-	-	25.3
Gainesville (city)	26.5	25.7	-	23.2	-	-	27.5	-	-	-	-	-	-	-	28.8	-	-	-	-	-	-	-	-	-
Bay County	37.5	35.2	-	-	-	-	-	-	35.1	-	-	-	-	-	-	-	-	-	-	-	-	-	-	27.5
Callaway (city)	33.2	35.9	-	-	-	-	-	-	-	-	-	-	-	-	-	-	-	-	-	-	-	-	-	-
Brevard County	41.6	38.3	-	34.9	-	-	38.4	-	38.4	-	-	-	-	45.0	43.2	-	-	-	-	-	-	-	-	36.3
Broward County	37.9	35.0	35.5	33.5	-	-	37.3	-	37.6	-	-	-	-	39.7	32.7	-	-	31.0	-	-	-	36.9	-	30.0
Cooper City (city)	37.2	38.0	-	38.5	-	-	-	-	-	-	-	-	-	-	-	-	-	-	-	-	-	-	-	-
Pembroke Pines (city)	36.7	35.9	-	31.8	-	-	37.7	-	39.9	-	-	-	-	-	-	-	-	-	-	-	-	-	-	-
Charlotte County	54.2	40.9	-	-	-	-	-	-	-	-	-	-	-	-	-	-	-	-	-	-	-	-	-	-
Citrus County	52.6	39.2	-	-	-	-	-	-	-	-	-	-	-	-	-	-	-	-	-	-	-	-	-	-
Clay County	35.9	38.2	-	-	-	-	-	-	41.2	-	-	-	-	-	-	-	-	-	-	-	-	-	-	-

Notes: Please refer to the User's Guide for an explanation of data; data is arranged alphabetically by state, then county, then city within each county; table includes counties with populations greater than 49,999 unless noted and cities with populations greater than 9,999 whose Asian and/or NHPI population rates are greater than the national average; (1) Native Hawaiian and other Pacific Islander; (2) excludes Taiwanese; (3) includes Chamorro; (4) county does not meet population threshold but is shown in order to allow inclusion of city

Place	Total population	Total Asian population	Total NHPI[1] population	Asian Indian	Bangladeshi	Cambodian	Chinese[2]	Fijian	Filipino	Guamanian[3]	Hawaiian, Native	Hmong	Indonesian	Japanese	Korean	Laotian	Malaysian	Pakistani	Samoan	Sri Lankan	Taiwanese	Thai	Tongan	Vietnamese
Bellair-Meadowbrook Ter. (cdp)	32.9	39.5	-	-	-	-	-	-	-	-	-	-	-	-	-	-	-	-	-	-	-	-	-	-
Collier County	44.1	31.8	-	-	-	-	-	-	-	-	-	-	-	-	-	-	-	-	-	-	-	-	-	-
Columbia County	37.4	31.9	-	-	-	-	-	-	-	-	-	-	-	-	-	-	-	-	-	-	-	-	-	-
Duval County	34.2	33.1	25.8	30.8	-	28.9	36.2	-	35.2	-	-	-	-	36.7	36.5	-	-	-	-	-	-	-	-	29.3
Escambia County	35.5	32.2	-	29.0	-	-	34.5	-	34.8	-	-	-	-	-	-	-	-	-	-	-	-	-	-	24.3
Bellview (cdp)	36.2	34.8	-	-	-	-	-	-	41.6	-	-	-	-	-	-	-	-	-	-	-	-	-	-	-
Myrtle Grove (cdp)	32.3	32.8	-	-	-	-	-	-	36.9	-	-	-	-	-	-	-	-	-	-	-	-	-	-	-
Hernando County	49.2	40.0	-	-	-	-	-	-	-	-	-	-	-	-	-	-	-	-	-	-	-	-	-	-
Highlands County	50.0	36.9	-	-	-	-	-	-	40.2	-	-	-	-	-	-	-	-	-	-	-	-	-	-	-
Hillsborough County	35.2	32.4	27.9	29.7	-	-	34.3	-	31.8	-	-	-	-	43.5	37.2	-	-	-	-	-	-	35.4	-	31.1
Westchase (cdp)	34.0	32.0	-	-	-	-	-	-	-	-	-	-	-	-	-	-	-	-	-	-	-	-	-	-
Indian River County	46.9	33.9	-	-	-	-	-	-	-	-	-	-	-	-	-	-	-	-	-	-	-	-	-	-
Lake County	44.9	33.8	-	-	-	-	-	-	-	-	-	-	-	-	-	-	-	-	-	-	-	-	-	-
Lee County	45.1	37.2	-	33.6	-	-	35.3	-	39.4	-	-	-	-	-	-	-	-	-	-	-	-	-	-	-
Leon County	29.6	30.9	-	29.4	-	-	31.6	-	30.2	-	-	-	-	-	32.6	-	-	-	-	-	-	-	-	-
Manatee County	43.6	36.4	-	-	-	-	-	-	35.3	-	-	-	-	-	-	-	-	-	-	-	-	-	-	-
Marion County	43.8	37.9	-	32.9	-	-	-	-	-	-	-	-	-	-	-	-	-	-	-	-	-	-	-	-
Martin County	47.3	36.6	-	-	-	-	-	-	-	-	-	-	-	-	-	-	-	-	-	-	-	-	-	-
Miami-Dade County	35.8	34.9	31.6	31.4	-	-	38.2	-	38.5	-	-	-	-	38.4	37.0	-	-	36.3	-	-	-	37.6	-	27.5
Doral (cdp)	32.8	32.3	-	-	-	-	-	-	-	-	-	-	-	-	-	-	-	-	-	-	-	-	-	-
Ives Estates (cdp)	34.6	32.4	-	-	-	-	-	-	-	-	-	-	-	-	-	-	-	-	-	-	-	-	-	-
North Miami Beach (city)	35.1	37.0	-	32.7	-	-	41.0	-	-	-	-	-	-	-	-	-	-	-	-	-	-	-	-	-
Pinecrest (village)	38.3	38.6	-	-	-	-	-	-	-	-	-	-	-	-	-	-	-	-	-	-	-	-	-	-
Monroe County	42.6	38.1	-	-	-	-	-	-	-	-	-	-	-	-	-	-	-	-	-	-	-	-	-	-
Nassau County	38.3	36.2	-	-	-	-	-	-	-	-	-	-	-	-	-	-	-	-	-	-	-	-	-	-
Okaloosa County	36.2	38.0	-	-	-	-	-	-	34.6	-	-	-	-	-	38.4	-	-	-	-	-	-	48.7	-	30.3
Wright (cdp)	34.0	40.9	-	-	-	-	-	-	-	-	-	-	-	-	-	-	-	-	-	-	-	-	-	-
Orange County	33.6	33.0	24.7	32.8	-	-	36.2	-	33.5	-	-	-	-	35.3	35.2	-	-	32.6	-	-	-	-	-	30.4
Oak Ridge (cdp)	29.1	31.9	-	-	-	-	-	-	-	-	-	-	-	-	-	-	-	-	-	-	-	-	-	31.2
Osceola County	34.7	37.3	-	29.4	-	-	44.1	-	40.8	-	-	-	-	-	-	-	-	-	-	-	-	-	-	-
Palm Beach County	41.8	35.4	33.2	33.6	-	-	36.4	-	36.5	-	-	-	-	47.1	39.3	-	-	-	-	-	-	38.3	-	32.9
Pasco County	44.8	37.2	-	33.4	-	-	39.0	-	38.5	-	-	-	-	-	-	-	-	-	-	-	-	-	-	-
Pinellas County	43.1	33.7	-	34.0	-	25.4	38.5	-	35.3	-	-	-	-	39.8	38.8	29.5	-	-	-	-	-	37.2	-	31.9
Pinellas Park (city)	40.2	34.4	-	-	-	-	-	-	-	-	-	-	-	-	-	-	-	-	-	-	-	-	-	30.8
Polk County	38.6	33.0	-	34.2	-	-	34.3	-	38.3	-	-	-	-	-	-	27.7	-	-	-	-	-	-	-	27.7
Putnam County	40.5	39.4	-	-	-	-	-	-	-	-	-	-	-	-	-	-	-	-	-	-	-	-	-	-
St. Johns County	40.9	36.6	-	-	-	-	-	-	-	-	-	-	-	-	-	-	-	-	-	-	-	-	-	-
St. Lucie County	42.1	38.4	-	-	-	-	-	-	-	-	-	-	-	-	-	-	-	-	-	-	-	-	-	-
Santa Rosa County	36.8	38.2	-	-	-	-	-	-	39.9	-	-	-	-	-	-	-	-	-	-	-	-	-	-	-
Sarasota County	50.4	35.8	-	-	-	-	26.8	-	41.1	-	-	-	-	-	-	-	-	-	-	-	-	-	-	32.9
Seminole County	36.3	34.8	-	34.6	-	-	36.6	-	33.9	-	-	-	-	-	34.0	-	-	-	-	-	-	-	-	33.5

Notes: Please refer to the User's Guide for an explanation of data; data is arranged alphabetically by state, then county, then city within each county; table includes counties with populations greater than 49,999 unless noted and cities with populations greater than 9,999 whose Asian and/or NHPI population rates are greater than the national average; (1) Native Hawaiian and other Pacific Islander; (2) excludes Taiwanese; (3) includes Chamorro; (4) county does not meet population threshold but is shown in order to allow inclusion of city

Place	Total population	Total Asian population	Total NHPI[1] population	Asian Indian	Bangladeshi	Cambodian	Chinese[2]	Fijian	Filipino	Guamanian[3]	Hawaiian, Native	Hmong	Indonesian	Japanese	Korean	Laotian	Malaysian	Pakistani	Samoan	Sri Lankan	Taiwanese	Thai	Tongan	Vietnamese
Volusia County	42.4	35.4	-	35.6	-	-	36.3	-	37.4	-	-	-	-	-	29.7	-	-	-	-	-	-	-	-	-
GEORGIA	33.5	31.1	27.4	29.8	30.5	28.5	33.3	-	34.1	27.8	33.9	19.6	28.8	36.0	33.8	28.1	-	30.4	26.5	-	33.2	32.4	-	29.5
Bartow County	33.9	25.4	-	-	-	-	-	-	-	-	-	-	-	-	-	-	-	-	-	-	-	-	-	-
Bibb County	34.8	29.6	-	-	-	-	-	-	-	-	-	-	-	-	-	-	-	-	-	-	-	-	-	-
Bulloch County	26.1	25.0	-	-	-	-	-	-	-	-	-	-	-	-	-	-	-	-	-	-	-	-	-	-
Carroll County	32.6	26.9	-	-	-	-	-	-	-	-	-	-	-	-	-	-	-	-	-	-	-	-	-	-
Catoosa County	35.8	31.0	-	-	-	-	-	-	-	-	-	-	-	-	-	-	-	-	-	-	-	-	-	-
Chatham County	34.6	32.4	-	28.5	-	-	45.0	-	-	-	-	-	-	-	25.8	-	-	-	-	-	-	-	-	34.4
Cherokee County	33.9	31.4	-	30.0	-	-	-	-	-	-	-	-	-	-	-	-	-	-	-	-	-	-	-	-
Clarke County	25.5	27.2	-	23.6	-	-	30.4	-	-	-	-	-	-	-	23.7	-	-	-	-	-	-	-	-	-
Clayton County	30.3	30.3	-	34.6	-	23.5	33.3	-	-	-	-	-	-	-	-	29.5	-	27.8	-	-	-	-	-	29.8
Forest Park (city)	29.6	29.0	-	-	-	-	-	-	-	-	-	-	-	-	-	-	-	-	-	-	-	-	-	28.7
Riverdale (city)	29.2	29.2	-	-	-	-	-	-	-	-	-	-	-	-	-	-	-	-	-	-	-	-	-	29.2
Cobb County	33.3	31.7	-	29.5	-	-	34.7	-	32.7	-	-	-	-	36.1	35.9	-	-	34.2	-	-	-	-	-	27.9
Smyrna (city)	32.4	30.9	-	27.3	-	-	-	-	-	-	-	-	-	-	-	-	-	-	-	-	-	-	-	-
Columbia County	35.5	36.9	-	41.4	-	-	38.4	-	-	-	-	-	-	-	37.3	-	-	-	-	-	-	-	-	-
Martinez (cdp)	35.8	39.0	-	44.1	-	-	-	-	-	-	-	-	-	-	-	-	-	-	-	-	-	-	-	-
Coweta County	33.6	34.5	-	-	-	-	-	-	-	-	-	-	-	-	-	-	-	-	-	-	-	-	-	-
DeKalb County	32.3	30.6	-	29.4	30.5	31.6	31.8	-	35.9	-	-	-	-	32.8	33.9	-	-	-	-	-	-	-	-	29.4
Druid Hills (cdp)	28.1	21.7	-	-	-	-	-	-	-	-	-	-	-	-	-	-	-	-	-	-	-	-	-	-
Dunwoody (cdp)	38.4	30.7	-	28.8	-	-	-	-	-	-	-	-	-	-	33.5	-	-	-	-	-	-	-	-	-
North Atlanta (cdp)	31.1	31.1	-	-	-	-	-	-	-	-	-	-	-	-	-	-	-	-	-	-	-	-	-	-
North Decatur (cdp)	40.3	29.1	-	-	-	-	-	-	-	-	-	-	-	-	-	-	-	-	-	-	-	-	-	-
North Druid Hills (cdp)	33.0	29.3	-	29.0	-	-	-	-	-	-	-	-	-	-	-	-	-	-	-	-	-	-	-	-
Tucker (cdp)	39.8	36.1	-	-	-	-	-	-	-	-	-	-	-	-	-	-	-	-	-	-	-	-	-	31.1
Dougherty County	32.4	34.0	-	-	-	-	-	-	-	-	-	-	-	-	-	-	-	-	-	-	-	-	-	-
Douglas County	33.9	32.2	-	-	-	-	-	-	-	-	-	-	-	-	-	-	-	-	-	-	-	-	-	-
Fayette County	38.4	34.5	-	-	-	-	-	-	-	-	-	-	-	35.0	-	-	-	-	-	-	-	-	-	-
Peachtree City (city)	37.8	35.1	-	-	-	-	-	-	-	-	-	-	-	34.6	-	-	-	-	-	-	-	-	-	-
Floyd County	35.8	30.6	-	31.2	-	-	-	-	-	-	-	-	-	-	-	-	-	-	-	-	-	-	-	-
Forsyth County	34.7	34.2	-	-	-	-	-	-	-	-	-	-	-	-	-	-	-	-	-	-	-	-	-	-
Fulton County	32.8	29.5	-	27.6	-	-	30.1	-	31.7	-	-	-	-	34.5	31.2	-	-	-	-	-	-	-	-	29.6
Alpharetta (city)	33.4	30.5	-	28.2	-	-	36.4	-	-	-	-	-	-	-	-	-	-	-	-	-	-	-	-	-
Roswell (city)	35.4	33.2	-	31.8	-	-	34.8	-	-	-	-	-	-	-	37.1	-	-	-	-	-	-	-	-	-
Glynn County	38.0	30.9	-	-	-	-	-	-	-	-	-	-	-	-	-	-	-	-	-	-	-	-	-	-
Gwinnett County	32.7	31.8	27.6	31.0	-	22.4	36.5	-	36.7	-	-	-	-	36.9	33.7	30.7	-	29.4	-	-	34.4	-	-	29.6
Duluth (city)	32.6	31.6	-	29.9	-	-	36.8	-	-	-	-	-	-	-	35.2	-	-	-	-	-	-	-	-	-
Lilburn (city)	34.4	29.3	-	30.1	-	-	-	-	-	-	-	-	-	-	-	-	-	-	-	-	-	-	-	28.4
Mountain Park (cdp)	41.1	35.1	-	29.8	-	-	-	-	-	-	-	-	-	-	-	-	-	-	-	-	-	-	-	-
Hall County	32.2	28.8	-	-	-	-	-	-	-	-	-	-	-	-	-	-	-	-	-	-	-	-	-	28.0
Henry County	33.5	34.7	-	34.3	-	-	-	-	-	-	-	-	-	-	-	-	-	-	-	-	-	-	-	-

Notes: Please refer to the User's Guide for an explanation of data; data is arranged alphabetically by state, then county, then city within each county; table includes counties with populations greater than 49,999 unless noted and cities with populations greater than 9,999 whose Asian and/or NHPI population rates are greater than the national average; (1) Native Hawaiian and other Pacific Islander; (2) excludes Taiwanese; (3) includes Chamorro; (4) county does not meet population threshold but is shown in order to allow inclusion of city

Place	Total population	Total Asian population	Total NHPI[1] population	Asian Indian	Bangladeshi	Cambodian	Chinese[2]	Fijian	Filipino	Guamanian[3]	Hawaiian, Native	Hmong	Indonesian	Japanese	Korean	Laotian	Malaysian	Pakistani	Samoan	Sri Lankan	Taiwanese	Thai	Tongan	Vietnamese
Houston County	34.0	35.0	-	-	-	-	-	-	34.3	-	-	-	-	-	-	-	-	-	-	-	-	-	-	-
Liberty County	25.0	31.8	-	-	-	-	-	-	-	-	-	-	-	-	37.5	-	-	-	-	-	-	-	-	-
Lowndes County	30.4	33.3	-	-	-	-	-	-	-	-	-	-	-	-	-	-	-	-	-	-	-	-	-	-
Muscogee County	32.7	33.5	22.3	30.8	-	-	33.5	-	30.9	-	-	-	-	-	38.3	-	-	-	-	-	-	-	-	-
Columbus (sp. city)	32.7	33.5	22.3	30.8	-	-	33.5	-	30.9	-	-	-	-	-	38.3	-	-	-	-	-	-	-	-	-
Newton County	33.5	22.7	-	-	-	-	-	-	-	-	-	-	-	-	-	-	-	-	-	-	-	-	-	-
Richmond County	32.6	33.0	-	28.8	-	-	32.9	-	-	-	-	-	-	-	39.7	-	-	-	-	-	-	-	-	-
Rockdale County	35.7	34.5	-	-	-	-	-	-	-	-	-	-	-	-	-	-	-	-	-	-	-	-	-	-
Spalding County	34.8	30.7	-	-	-	-	-	-	-	-	-	-	-	-	-	-	-	-	-	-	-	-	-	-
Troup County	34.6	35.7	-	-	-	-	-	-	-	-	-	-	-	-	-	-	-	-	-	-	-	-	-	-
Walton County	34.0	23.8	-	-	-	-	-	-	-	-	-	-	-	-	-	-	-	-	-	-	-	-	-	-
Whitfield County	33.1	29.5	-	-	-	-	-	-	-	-	-	-	-	-	-	-	-	-	-	-	-	-	-	-
HAWAII	36.5	42.7	28.6	36.0	-	16.9	46.2	-	36.2	29.3	31.3	-	-	50.4	41.9	28.5	-	-	24.6	-	42.2	35.5	27.0	33.6
Hawaii County	38.8	45.8	28.7	-	-	-	47.7	-	39.4	-	30.3	-	-	52.0	41.9	-	-	-	36.3	-	-	-	-	-
Hilo (cdp)	39.1	48.6	27.0	-	-	-	50.9	-	42.3	-	28.1	-	-	51.9	44.3	-	-	-	-	-	-	-	-	-
Honolulu County	35.9	42.3	28.5	35.9	-	-	46.1	-	35.8	29.1	31.9	-	-	49.8	42.0	28.3	-	-	24.2	-	41.4	35.3	27.2	33.8
Ewa Beach (cdp)	32.5	36.5	29.4	-	-	-	-	-	34.0	-	29.2	-	-	55.5	-	-	-	-	23.4	-	-	-	-	-
Halawa (cdp)	37.4	43.9	32.1	-	-	-	44.3	-	37.7	-	42.1	-	-	50.0	-	-	-	-	19.4	-	-	-	-	-
Honolulu (cdp)	40.0	44.0	29.7	33.4	-	-	46.6	-	36.0	25.6	36.2	-	-	51.3	41.7	32.1	-	-	24.9	-	42.2	35.2	28.3	32.4
Kailua (cdp)	39.4	46.6	36.2	-	-	-	47.8	-	40.3	-	36.2	-	-	51.4	54.6	-	-	-	-	-	-	-	-	-
Kaneohe (cdp)	38.7	45.0	30.4	-	-	-	51.8	-	39.5	-	31.4	-	-	48.2	48.3	-	-	-	-	-	-	-	-	-
Kaneohe Station (cdp)	22.1	28.1	-	-	-	-	-	-	-	-	-	-	-	-	-	-	-	-	-	-	-	-	-	-
Makakilo City (cdp)	33.0	37.8	27.9	-	-	-	-	-	34.3	-	27.3	-	-	43.9	-	-	-	-	-	-	-	-	-	-
Mililani Town (cdp)	36.7	43.3	32.3	-	-	-	49.5	-	39.0	-	32.9	-	-	46.8	48.8	-	-	-	-	-	-	-	-	-
Nanakuli (cdp)	26.5	36.4	26.1	-	-	-	-	-	35.3	-	32.1	-	-	-	-	-	-	-	22.3	-	-	-	-	-
Pearl City (cdp)	37.6	50.0	31.4	-	-	-	55.6	-	40.5	-	30.6	-	-	56.0	41.7	-	-	-	-	-	-	-	-	-
Schofield Barracks (cdp)	22.0	26.1	-	-	-	-	-	-	-	-	-	-	-	-	-	-	-	-	-	-	-	-	-	-
Wahiawa (cdp)	37.3	48.9	23.9	-	-	-	-	-	37.5	-	34.7	-	-	61.8	-	-	-	-	-	-	-	-	-	-
Waianae (cdp)	29.7	42.2	26.8	-	-	-	-	-	36.9	-	28.3	-	-	53.5	-	-	-	-	-	-	-	-	-	-
Waimalu (cdp)	37.8	43.4	28.4	-	-	-	47.7	-	38.9	-	28.8	-	-	48.7	41.2	-	-	-	-	-	-	-	-	-
Waipahu (cdp)	35.6	41.1	21.4	-	-	-	44.9	-	37.0	-	31.8	-	-	61.6	-	-	-	-	19.9	-	-	-	-	-
Waipio (cdp)	33.7	39.0	29.0	-	-	-	-	-	33.4	-	28.2	-	-	42.6	-	-	-	-	-	-	-	-	-	-
Kauai County	38.4	43.9	28.8	-	-	-	48.3	-	37.8	-	28.9	-	-	55.0	-	-	-	-	-	-	-	-	-	-
Maui County	36.9	42.2	29.2	-	-	-	48.6	-	36.0	-	30.1	-	-	53.3	37.9	-	-	-	-	-	-	-	26.6	-
Kahului (cdp)	36.4	43.8	27.5	-	-	-	-	-	36.6	-	29.8	-	-	60.5	-	-	-	-	-	-	-	-	-	-
Kihei (cdp)	35.6	34.5	32.0	-	-	-	-	-	32.2	-	31.8	-	-	46.1	-	-	-	-	-	-	-	-	-	-
Wailuku (cdp)	38.1	46.4	26.5	-	-	-	-	-	35.7	-	27.3	-	-	55.2	-	-	-	-	-	-	-	-	-	-
IDAHO	33.3	33.2	23.8	27.1	-	-	32.9	-	35.2	-	26.3	-	-	43.1	28.3	32.7	-	-	-	-	-	-	-	31.0
Ada County	32.9	32.8	24.3	28.8	-	-	32.5	-	34.7	-	-	-	-	38.5	27.8	-	-	-	-	-	-	-	-	31.7
Bannock County	29.8	34.0	-	-	-	-	-	-	-	-	-	-	-	-	-	-	-	-	-	-	-	-	-	-
Bonneville County	32.0	38.7	-	-	-	-	-	-	-	-	-	-	-	-	-	-	-	-	-	-	-	-	-	-

Notes: Please refer to the User's Guide for an explanation of data; data is arranged alphabetically by state, then county, then city within each county; table includes counties with populations greater than 49,999 unless noted and cities with populations greater than 9,999 whose Asian and/or NHPI population rates are greater than the national average; (1) Native Hawaiian and other Pacific Islander; (2) excludes Taiwanese; (3) includes Chamorro; (4) county does not meet population threshold but is shown in order to allow inclusion of city

Place	Total population	Total Asian population	Total NHPI[1] population	Asian Indian	Bangladeshi	Cambodian	Chinese[2]	Fijian	Filipino	Guamanian[3]	Hawaiian, Native	Hmong	Indonesian	Japanese	Korean	Laotian	Malaysian	Pakistani	Samoan	Sri Lankan	Taiwanese	Thai	Tongan	Vietnamese
Canyon County	30.5	32.4	-	-	-	-	-	-	-	-	-	-	-	44.5	-	-	-	-	-	-	-	-	-	-
Kootenai County	36.2	33.3	-	-	-	-	-	-	-	-	-	-	-	-	-	-	-	-	-	-	-	-	-	-
Twin Falls County	34.9	34.1	-	-	-	-	-	-	-	-	-	-	-	-	-	-	-	-	-	-	-	-	-	-
ILLINOIS	34.8	32.0	28.3	30.0	28.2	26.8	34.2	-	34.6	32.4	33.6	-	31.2	39.3	32.0	28.2	25.8	29.8	24.9	34.8	30.7	32.1	-	29.0
Champaign County	28.7	24.0	-	22.6	-	-	25.2	-	22.6	-	-	-	-	28.2	24.3	-	-	-	-	-	-	-	-	27.6
Champaign (city)	25.4	24.2	-	23.0	-	-	24.8	-	-	-	-	-	-	-	24.3	-	-	-	-	-	-	-	-	28.9
Urbana (city)	24.7	23.2	-	21.8	-	-	25.5	-	-	-	-	-	-	-	23.0	-	-	-	-	-	-	-	-	-
Coles County	31.0	29.3	-	-	-	-	-	-	-	-	-	-	-	-	-	-	-	-	-	-	-	-	-	-
Cook County	33.8	32.4	28.5	29.8	-	27.2	34.7	-	35.3	-	-	-	31.3	39.9	33.3	30.8	-	29.9	-	-	29.8	33.6	-	28.9
Arlington Heights (village)	39.7	31.6	-	28.7	-	-	37.0	-	34.0	-	-	-	-	36.4	30.6	-	-	-	-	-	-	-	-	-
Chicago (city)	31.7	32.0	28.3	28.9	-	27.6	34.6	-	35.3	-	-	-	-	45.1	32.2	-	-	30.5	-	-	26.4	30.8	-	28.8
Des Plaines (city)	39.8	33.2	-	30.9	-	-	38.5	-	33.5	-	-	-	-	-	-	-	-	-	-	-	-	-	-	-
Elk Grove Village (village)	38.2	34.5	-	32.8	-	-	40.6	-	35.8	-	-	-	-	34.6	-	-	-	-	-	-	-	-	-	-
Evanston (city)	32.8	25.4	-	24.4	-	-	23.9	-	30.5	-	-	-	-	32.5	25.6	-	-	-	-	-	-	-	-	-
Forest Park (village)	35.8	35.1	-	-	-	-	-	-	-	-	-	-	-	-	-	-	-	-	-	-	-	-	-	-
Glenview (village)	41.3	38.1	-	39.0	-	-	44.4	-	36.4	-	-	-	-	36.9	35.1	-	-	-	-	-	-	-	-	-
Hanover Park (village)	29.9	32.1	-	30.8	-	-	-	-	33.1	-	-	-	-	-	-	-	-	-	-	-	-	-	-	-
Hoffman Estates (village)	33.2	32.1	-	31.3	-	-	33.6	-	35.4	-	-	-	-	32.9	32.2	-	-	-	-	-	-	-	-	-
Lincolnwood (village)	45.4	37.1	-	35.3	-	-	-	-	42.9	-	-	-	-	-	42.3	-	-	-	-	-	-	-	-	-
Morton Grove (village)	44.6	37.5	-	31.7	-	-	-	-	37.8	-	-	-	-	-	40.8	-	-	-	-	-	-	-	-	-
Mount Prospect (village)	37.4	32.6	-	31.4	-	-	31.4	-	34.5	-	-	-	-	40.6	35.5	-	-	-	-	-	-	-	-	-
Niles (village)	46.2	35.9	-	31.5	-	-	-	-	35.9	-	-	-	-	-	42.0	-	-	-	-	-	-	-	-	-
Northbrook (village)	44.2	41.4	-	-	-	-	42.3	-	-	-	-	-	-	-	41.7	-	-	-	-	-	-	-	-	-
Oak Park (village)	35.9	30.5	-	30.0	-	-	32.8	-	-	-	-	-	-	-	-	-	-	-	-	-	-	-	-	-
Orland Park (village)	41.2	36.2	-	40.7	-	-	-	-	31.7	-	-	-	-	-	-	-	-	-	-	-	-	-	-	-
Palatine (village)	34.4	31.2	-	28.4	-	-	32.8	-	33.5	-	-	-	-	-	33.7	-	-	-	-	-	-	-	-	-
Prospect Heights (city)	33.8	27.9	-	-	-	-	-	-	-	-	-	-	-	-	-	-	-	-	-	-	-	-	-	-
Rolling Meadows (city)	34.9	31.6	-	29.2	-	-	-	-	-	-	-	-	-	-	-	-	-	-	-	-	-	-	-	-
Schaumburg (village)	35.5	30.6	-	29.5	-	-	32.9	-	37.0	-	-	-	-	31.5	32.9	-	-	-	-	-	-	-	-	-
Schiller Park (village)	33.6	33.0	-	-	-	-	-	-	-	-	-	-	-	-	-	-	-	-	-	-	-	-	-	-
Skokie (village)	41.9	35.2	-	32.3	-	-	36.9	-	35.4	-	-	-	-	-	37.4	-	-	30.6	-	-	-	-	-	-
Streamwood (village)	32.7	34.0	-	31.1	-	-	-	-	37.0	-	-	-	-	-	-	-	-	-	-	-	-	-	-	-
Wheeling (village)	34.2	31.3	-	29.4	-	-	-	-	35.4	-	-	-	-	-	-	-	-	-	-	-	-	-	-	-
Wilmette (village)	42.1	36.9	-	-	-	-	36.6	-	-	-	-	-	-	37.7	38.9	-	-	-	-	-	-	-	-	-
DeKalb County	28.4	22.4	-	22.5	-	-	-	-	-	-	-	-	-	-	-	-	-	-	-	-	-	-	-	-
DeKalb (city)	23.0	22.2	-	22.6	-	-	-	-	-	-	-	-	-	-	-	-	-	-	-	-	-	-	-	-
DuPage County	35.4	32.7	-	31.1	-	-	35.7	-	35.5	-	-	-	-	40.3	34.4	-	-	29.7	-	-	43.5	31.1	-	30.5
Addison (village)	32.2	31.5	-	31.2	-	-	-	-	39.6	-	-	-	-	-	-	-	-	-	-	-	-	-	-	-
Bartlett (village)	33.4	32.1	-	30.7	-	-	-	-	34.7	-	-	-	-	-	-	-	-	-	-	-	-	-	-	-
Bensenville (village)	32.0	31.3	-	28.8	-	-	-	-	-	-	-	-	-	-	-	-	-	-	-	-	-	-	-	-
Bloomingdale (village)	37.8	32.8	-	32.3	-	-	-	-	-	-	-	-	-	-	-	-	-	-	-	-	-	-	-	-

Notes: Please refer to the User's Guide for an explanation of data; data is arranged alphabetically by state, then county, then city within each county; table includes counties with populations greater than 49,999 unless noted and cities with populations greater than 9,999 whose Asian and/or NHPI population rates are greater than the national average; (1) Native Hawaiian and other Pacific Islander; (2) excludes Taiwanese; (3) includes Chamorro; (4) county does not meet population threshold but is shown in order to allow inclusion of city

Place	Total population	Total Asian population	Total NHPI[1] population	Asian Indian	Bangladeshi	Cambodian	Chinese[2]	Fijian	Filipino	Guamanian[3]	Hawaiian, Native	Hmong	Indonesian	Japanese	Korean	Laotian	Malaysian	Pakistani	Samoan	Sri Lankan	Taiwanese	Thai	Tongan	Vietnamese
Burr Ridge (village)	43.1	44.0	-	38.0	-	-	-	-	-	-	-	-	-	-	-	-	-	-	-	-	-	-	-	-
Carol Stream (village)	31.9	32.0	-	31.3	-	-	-	-	34.8	-	-	-	-	-	-	-	-	-	-	-	-	-	-	28.6
Darien (city)	40.4	37.2	-	35.2	-	-	-	-	39.1	-	-	-	-	-	-	-	-	-	-	-	-	-	-	-
Downers Grove (village)	39.2	35.7	-	34.2	-	-	37.6	-	41.3	-	-	-	-	-	-	-	-	-	-	-	-	-	-	-
Glen Ellyn (village)	36.6	31.2	-	29.9	-	-	-	-	-	-	-	-	-	-	-	-	-	-	-	-	-	-	-	-
Glendale Heights (village)	30.6	31.3	-	29.8	-	-	-	-	32.7	-	-	-	-	-	-	-	-	-	-	-	-	-	-	31.4
Hinsdale (village)	38.7	38.5	-	-	-	-	-	-	-	-	-	-	-	-	-	-	-	-	-	-	-	-	-	-
Lisle (village)	35.4	30.6	-	27.6	-	-	35.8	-	-	-	-	-	-	-	-	-	-	-	-	-	-	-	-	-
Lombard (village)	37.2	30.5	-	28.8	-	-	-	-	33.9	-	-	-	-	-	-	-	-	-	-	-	-	-	-	-
Naperville (city)	34.3	33.4	-	31.7	-	-	34.8	-	33.1	-	-	-	-	-	36.6	-	-	-	-	-	40.5	-	-	-
Roselle (village)	35.4	34.9	-	33.8	-	-	-	-	-	-	-	-	-	-	-	-	-	-	-	-	-	-	-	-
Villa Park (village)	34.8	29.1	-	-	-	-	-	-	-	-	-	-	-	-	-	-	-	-	-	-	-	-	-	-
Warrenville (city)	33.7	34.7	-	-	-	-	-	-	-	-	-	-	-	-	-	-	-	-	-	-	-	-	-	-
Westmont (village)	36.3	33.5	-	29.4	-	-	44.2	-	43.1	-	-	-	-	-	-	-	-	-	-	-	-	-	-	-
Wheaton (city)	36.0	31.3	-	32.5	-	-	-	-	-	-	-	-	-	-	-	-	-	-	-	-	-	-	-	-
Woodridge (village)	33.4	32.5	-	31.1	-	-	-	-	36.4	-	-	-	-	-	-	-	-	-	-	-	-	-	-	27.2
Jackson County	27.8	26.3	-	-	-	-	26.4	-	-	-	-	-	-	-	-	-	-	-	-	-	-	-	-	-
Carbondale (city)	24.8	26.1	-	-	-	-	-	-	-	-	-	-	-	-	-	-	-	-	-	-	-	-	-	-
Kane County	32.4	31.6	-	29.5	-	-	35.0	-	34.2	-	-	-	-	-	32.9	26.1	-	-	-	-	-	-	-	28.9
South Elgin (village)	30.9	32.0	-	-	-	-	-	-	-	-	-	-	-	-	-	-	-	-	-	-	-	-	-	-
Kankakee County	35.4	36.1	-	-	-	-	-	-	-	-	-	-	-	-	-	-	-	-	-	-	-	-	-	-
Kendall County	34.1	27.6	-	-	-	-	-	-	-	-	-	-	-	-	-	-	-	-	-	-	-	-	-	-
Knox County	39.4	20.8	-	-	-	-	-	-	-	-	-	-	-	-	-	-	-	-	-	-	-	-	-	-
La Salle County	38.1	36.0	-	-	-	-	-	-	-	-	-	-	-	-	-	-	-	-	-	-	-	-	-	-
Lake County	33.9	34.4	-	32.9	-	-	36.2	-	34.0	-	-	-	-	39.1	34.0	-	-	29.6	-	-	-	-	-	31.6
Buffalo Grove (village)	37.7	34.4	-	31.6	-	-	38.2	-	37.3	-	-	-	-	36.2	34.1	-	-	-	-	-	-	-	-	-
Gages Lake (cdp)	35.2	37.5	-	-	-	-	-	-	-	-	-	-	-	-	-	-	-	-	-	-	-	-	-	-
Grayslake (village)	32.9	33.7	-	-	-	-	-	-	-	-	-	-	-	-	-	-	-	-	-	-	-	-	-	-
Gurnee (village)	34.3	35.5	-	34.9	-	-	35.8	-	33.8	-	-	-	-	-	-	-	-	-	-	-	-	-	-	-
Lake Zurich (village)	34.8	35.9	-	-	-	-	-	-	-	-	-	-	-	-	-	-	-	-	-	-	-	-	-	-
Libertyville (village)	38.8	37.0	-	-	-	-	-	-	-	-	-	-	-	-	-	-	-	-	-	-	-	-	-	-
Mundelein (village)	31.9	31.8	-	-	-	-	35.1	-	31.8	-	-	-	-	-	-	-	-	-	-	-	-	-	-	-
Vernon Hills (village)	34.0	35.1	-	34.1	-	-	35.8	-	-	-	-	-	-	-	34.2	-	-	-	-	-	-	-	-	-
Macon County	38.0	30.1	-	-	-	-	-	-	-	-	-	-	-	-	-	-	-	-	-	-	-	-	-	-
Madison County	36.8	31.3	-	40.1	-	-	-	-	-	-	-	-	-	-	-	-	-	-	-	-	-	-	-	-
McHenry County	34.3	32.5	-	29.7	-	-	33.7	-	32.0	-	-	-	-	-	-	-	-	-	-	-	-	-	-	-
McLean County	30.6	28.7	-	27.5	-	-	32.9	-	-	-	-	-	-	-	-	-	-	-	-	-	-	-	-	-
Peoria County	36.1	31.2	-	28.9	-	-	34.7	-	-	-	-	-	-	-	-	-	-	-	-	-	-	-	-	31.7
Rock Island County	37.8	27.8	-	27.2	-	-	-	-	-	-	-	-	-	-	-	-	-	-	-	-	-	-	-	-
St. Clair County	35.5	36.3	-	-	-	-	-	-	36.6	-	-	-	-	-	39.6	-	-	-	-	-	-	-	-	-
Sangamon County	37.4	33.0	-	29.6	-	-	42.3	-	-	-	-	-	-	-	-	-	-	-	-	-	-	-	-	-

Notes: Please refer to the User's Guide for an explanation of data; data is arranged alphabetically by state, then county, then city within each county; table includes counties with populations greater than 49,999 unless noted and cities with populations greater than 9,999 whose Asian and/or NHPI population rates are greater than the national average; (1) Native Hawaiian and other Pacific Islander; (2) excludes Taiwanese; (3) includes Chamorro; (4) county does not meet population threshold but is shown in order to allow inclusion of city

Place	Total population	Total Asian population	Total NHPI[1] population	Asian Indian	Bangladeshi	Cambodian	Chinese[2]	Fijian	Filipino	Guamanian[3]	Hawaiian, Native	Hmong	Indonesian	Japanese	Korean	Laotian	Malaysian	Pakistani	Samoan	Sri Lankan	Taiwanese	Thai	Tongan	Vietnamese
Tazewell County	38.1	33.1	-	-	-	-	-	-	-	-	-	-	-	-	-	-	-	-	-	-	-	-	-	-
Vermilion County	38.1	35.8	-	-	-	-	-	-	-	-	-	-	-	-	-	-	-	-	-	-	-	-	-	-
Will County	33.4	31.7	-	32.3	-	-	34.3	-	31.8	-	-	-	-	-	29.4	-	-	23.5	-	-	-	-	-	28.6
Bolingbrook (village)	31.3	32.7	-	31.4	-	-	-	-	35.5	-	-	-	-	-	-	-	-	-	-	-	-	-	-	-
Winnebago County	36.0	29.2	-	34.7	-	-	-	-	32.0	-	-	-	-	-	27.5	29.3	-	-	-	-	-	-	-	28.7
INDIANA	35.3	30.1	26.5	28.7	-	22.8	30.7	-	33.6	24.4	29.4	-	-	32.8	29.3	29.2	-	27.8	-	-	31.4	31.3	-	29.0
Allen County	34.2	31.1	-	31.7	-	-	36.3	-	32.9	-	-	-	-	-	-	-	-	-	-	-	-	-	-	30.3
Bartholomew County	36.2	31.1	-	28.5	-	-	-	-	-	-	-	-	-	-	-	-	-	-	-	-	-	-	-	-
Clark County	36.6	32.5	-	-	-	-	-	-	-	-	-	-	-	-	-	-	-	-	-	-	-	-	-	-
Delaware County	33.8	25.5	-	-	-	-	-	-	-	-	-	-	-	-	-	-	-	-	-	-	-	-	-	-
Elkhart County	33.2	29.9	-	-	-	-	-	-	-	-	-	-	-	-	-	-	-	-	-	-	-	-	-	-
Grant County	37.4	30.4	-	-	-	-	-	-	-	-	-	-	-	-	-	-	-	-	-	-	-	-	-	-
Hamilton County	34.2	33.6	-	31.7	-	-	34.6	-	-	-	-	-	-	-	-	-	-	-	-	-	-	-	-	-
Carmel (city)	37.3	34.2	-	-	-	-	-	-	-	-	-	-	-	-	-	-	-	-	-	-	-	-	-	-
Hendricks County	35.7	37.9	-	-	-	-	-	-	-	-	-	-	-	-	-	-	-	-	-	-	-	-	-	-
Howard County	37.1	29.9	-	-	-	-	-	-	-	-	-	-	-	-	-	-	-	-	-	-	-	-	-	-
Johnson County	35.0	34.1	-	-	-	-	-	-	-	-	-	-	-	-	-	-	-	-	-	-	-	-	-	-
Kosciusko County	35.2	33.6	-	-	-	-	-	-	-	-	-	-	-	-	-	-	-	-	-	-	-	-	-	-
Lake County	36.1	36.1	-	31.7	-	-	36.2	-	39.5	-	-	-	-	-	48.3	-	-	-	-	-	-	-	-	-
Munster (town)	43.0	42.7	-	36.9	-	-	-	-	-	-	-	-	-	-	-	-	-	-	-	-	-	-	-	-
LaPorte County	37.1	35.7	-	-	-	-	-	-	-	-	-	-	-	-	-	-	-	-	-	-	-	-	-	-
Madison County	37.6	32.7	-	-	-	-	-	-	-	-	-	-	-	-	-	-	-	-	-	-	-	-	-	-
Marion County	33.7	31.8	-	30.3	-	-	35.0	-	33.2	-	-	-	-	42.7	30.2	-	-	-	-	-	-	-	-	29.6
Monroe County	27.5	25.6	-	25.0	-	-	26.5	-	-	-	-	-	-	-	26.1	-	-	-	-	-	-	-	-	-
Bloomington (city)	23.5	25.3	-	23.2	-	-	26.3	-	-	-	-	-	-	-	26.3	-	-	-	-	-	-	-	-	-
Porter County	36.5	32.7	-	-	-	-	-	-	-	-	-	-	-	-	-	-	-	-	-	-	-	-	-	-
St. Joseph County	34.6	30.7	-	29.6	-	-	30.0	-	-	-	-	-	-	-	32.7	-	-	-	-	-	-	-	-	-
Tippecanoe County	27.2	25.0	-	22.6	-	-	26.9	-	-	-	-	-	-	30.8	28.3	-	-	-	-	-	-	-	-	-
West Lafayette (city)	22.3	23.0	-	22.4	-	-	23.0	-	-	-	-	-	-	-	-	-	-	-	-	-	-	-	-	-
Vanderburgh County	37.0	29.8	-	-	-	-	-	-	-	-	-	-	-	-	-	-	-	-	-	-	-	-	-	-
Vigo County	35.0	28.5	-	-	-	-	-	-	-	-	-	-	-	-	-	-	-	-	-	-	-	-	-	-
Wayne County	37.8	33.1	-	-	-	-	-	-	-	-	-	-	-	-	-	-	-	-	-	-	-	-	-	-
IOWA	36.7	27.9	23.8	28.1	-	23.3	28.5	-	35.9	-	-	-	-	30.5	21.0	27.4	-	24.3	-	-	32.7	32.9	-	29.6
Black Hawk County	34.4	29.5	-	-	-	-	-	-	-	-	-	-	-	-	-	-	-	-	-	-	-	-	-	-
Buena Vista County[4]	36.6	26.2	-	-	-	-	-	-	-	-	-	-	-	-	-	25.3	-	-	-	-	-	-	-	-
Storm Lake (city)	32.6	26.0	-	-	-	-	-	-	-	-	-	-	-	-	-	25.6	-	-	-	-	-	-	-	-
Johnson County	28.6	27.8	-	28.4	-	-	28.6	-	-	-	-	-	-	-	24.9	-	-	-	-	-	-	-	-	-
Coralville (city)	29.7	29.6	-	-	-	-	-	-	-	-	-	-	-	-	-	-	-	-	-	-	-	-	-	-
Iowa City (city)	25.5	27.2	-	29.2	-	-	28.2	-	-	-	-	-	-	-	24.0	-	-	-	-	-	-	-	-	-
Linn County	35.3	28.1	-	28.2	-	-	-	-	-	-	-	-	-	-	18.2	-	-	-	-	-	-	-	-	-
Polk County	34.4	29.7	-	29.6	-	24.0	33.8	-	-	-	-	-	-	-	25.8	28.6	-	-	-	-	-	33.5	-	29.7

Notes: Please refer to the User's Guide for an explanation of data; data is arranged alphabetically by state, then county, then city within each county; table includes counties with populations greater than 49,999 unless noted and cities with populations greater than 9,999 whose Asian and/or NHPI population rates are greater than the national average; (1) Native Hawaiian and other Pacific Islander; (2) excludes Taiwanese; (3) includes Chamorro; (4) county does not meet population threshold but is shown in order to allow inclusion of city

Place	Total population	Total Asian population	Total NHPI[1] population	Asian Indian	Bangladeshi	Cambodian	Chinese[2]	Fijian	Filipino	Guamanian[3]	Hawaiian, Native	Hmong	Indonesian	Japanese	Korean	Laotian	Malaysian	Pakistani	Samoan	Sri Lankan	Taiwanese	Thai	Tongan	Vietnamese
Pottawattamie County	36.5	30.2	-	-	-	-	-	-	-	-	-	-	-	-	-	-	-	-	-	-	-	-	-	-
Scott County	35.5	28.7	-	-	-	-	-	-	-	-	-	-	-	-	-	-	-	-	-	-	-	-	-	28.1
Story County	26.5	26.0	-	24.7	-	-	27.0	-	-	-	-	-	-	-	25.2	-	-	-	-	-	-	-	-	-
Ames (city)	23.6	26.0	-	24.7	-	-	27.0	-	-	-	-	-	-	-	25.7	-	-	-	-	-	-	-	-	-
Woodbury County	34.5	28.1	-	-	-	-	-	-	-	-	-	-	-	-	-	-	-	-	-	-	-	-	-	29.7
KANSAS	35.3	29.3	30.5	28.2	-	26.6	31.3	-	35.1	-	35.1	17.0	-	35.8	31.8	27.7	-	28.3	-	-	32.3	29.5	-	28.5
Cowley County[4]	37.0	27.8	-	-	-	-	-	-	-	-	-	-	-	-	-	29.5	-	-	-	-	-	-	-	-
Winfield (city)	34.9	27.7	-	-	-	-	-	-	-	-	-	-	-	-	-	29.6	-	-	-	-	-	-	-	-
Douglas County	26.7	25.4	-	24.6	-	-	27.6	-	-	-	-	-	-	-	25.3	-	-	-	-	-	-	-	-	-
Lawrence (city)	25.4	25.4	-	24.6	-	-	27.6	-	-	-	-	-	-	-	25.3	-	-	-	-	-	-	-	-	-
Johnson County	35.3	30.8	-	28.8	-	-	35.2	-	36.5	-	-	-	-	36.9	35.8	28.8	-	-	-	-	-	-	-	28.6
Overland Park (city)	36.5	30.3	-	28.6	-	-	35.2	-	-	-	-	-	-	-	38.4	-	-	-	-	-	-	-	-	27.3
Leavenworth County	35.6	35.8	-	-	-	-	-	-	-	-	-	-	-	-	-	-	-	-	-	-	-	-	-	-
Riley County	23.8	28.3	-	-	-	-	30.6	-	-	-	-	-	-	-	28.5	-	-	-	-	-	-	-	-	-
Manhattan (city)	23.5	28.5	-	-	-	-	30.6	-	-	-	-	-	-	-	-	-	-	-	-	-	-	-	-	-
Saline County	36.0	34.0	-	-	-	-	-	-	-	-	-	-	-	-	-	-	-	-	-	-	-	-	-	29.5
Sedgwick County	33.8	28.9	26.1	27.6	-	27.1	30.9	-	39.5	-	-	-	-	-	30.1	24.2	-	-	-	-	-	-	-	28.6
Wichita (city)	33.6	28.7	-	27.3	-	-	30.6	-	37.5	-	-	-	-	-	29.6	24.4	-	-	-	-	-	-	-	28.5
Shawnee County	37.2	33.1	-	-	-	-	-	-	-	-	-	-	-	-	-	-	-	-	-	-	-	-	-	-
Wyandotte County	32.9	24.4	-	-	-	-	-	-	-	-	-	15.5	-	-	-	-	-	-	-	-	-	-	-	-
KENTUCKY	35.9	30.9	26.7	29.9	-	-	31.4	-	34.9	26.4	-	-	-	34.9	32.6	-	-	29.1	-	-	-	31.2	-	28.6
Boone County	33.5	32.2	-	-	-	-	-	-	-	-	-	-	-	33.0	-	-	-	-	-	-	-	-	-	-
Campbell County	35.3	28.5	-	-	-	-	-	-	-	-	-	-	-	-	-	-	-	-	-	-	-	-	-	-
Christian County	27.9	24.7	-	-	-	-	-	-	-	-	-	-	-	-	-	-	-	-	-	-	-	-	-	-
Fayette County	33.1	30.3	-	27.8	-	-	30.6	-	-	-	-	-	-	28.9	-	-	-	-	-	-	-	-	-	-
Hardin County	33.5	36.0	-	-	-	-	-	-	-	-	-	-	-	-	41.9	-	-	-	-	-	-	-	-	-
Radcliff (city)	33.7	38.4	-	-	-	-	-	-	-	-	-	-	-	-	-	-	-	-	-	-	-	-	-	-
Jefferson County	36.7	30.9	-	29.0	-	-	35.1	-	39.0	-	-	-	-	38.6	31.8	-	-	-	-	-	-	-	-	28.3
Kenton County	34.6	29.4	-	-	-	-	-	-	-	-	-	-	-	-	-	-	-	-	-	-	-	-	-	-
Madison County	30.8	27.1	-	-	-	-	-	-	-	-	-	-	-	-	-	-	-	-	-	-	-	-	-	-
Warren County	32.4	25.8	-	-	-	-	-	-	-	-	-	-	-	-	-	-	-	-	-	-	-	-	-	-
LOUISIANA	34.2	30.5	29.2	30.2	-	-	32.8	-	35.1	30.8	31.1	-	-	41.1	33.3	27.7	-	30.5	-	-	44.0	36.7	-	27.6
Ascension Parish	32.1	33.1	-	-	-	-	-	-	-	-	-	-	-	-	-	-	-	-	-	-	-	-	-	-
Bossier Parish	33.8	35.4	-	-	-	-	-	-	-	-	-	-	-	-	-	-	-	-	-	-	-	-	-	-
Caddo Parish	35.3	32.1	-	31.6	-	-	-	-	-	-	-	-	-	-	-	-	-	-	-	-	-	-	-	-
Calcasieu Parish	34.6	35.0	-	-	-	-	-	-	-	-	-	-	-	-	-	-	-	-	-	-	-	-	-	-
East Baton Rouge Parish	31.8	27.7	-	27.7	-	-	31.9	-	27.8	-	-	-	-	-	-	-	-	-	-	-	-	-	-	25.2
Iberia Parish	33.3	25.6	-	-	-	-	-	-	-	-	-	-	-	-	-	25.6	-	-	-	-	-	-	-	20.4
Jefferson Parish	36.0	32.7	-	32.2	-	-	36.0	-	38.6	-	-	-	-	-	41.5	-	-	35.4	-	-	-	-	-	29.8
Gretna (city)	35.7	33.5	-	-	-	-	-	-	-	-	-	-	-	-	-	-	-	-	-	-	-	-	-	26.8
Harvey (cdp)	32.1	32.6	-	-	-	-	-	-	-	-	-	-	-	-	-	-	-	-	-	-	-	-	-	28.8

Notes: Please refer to the User's Guide for an explanation of data; data is arranged alphabetically by state, then county, then city within each county; table includes counties with populations greater than 49,999 unless noted and cities with populations greater than 9,999 whose Asian and/or NHPI population rates are greater than the national average; (1) Native Hawaiian and other Pacific Islander; (2) excludes Taiwanese; (3) includes Chamorro; (4) county does not meet population threshold but is shown in order to allow inclusion of city

Place	Total population	Total Asian population	Total NHPI[1] population	Asian Indian	Bangladeshi	Cambodian	Chinese[2]	Fijian	Filipino	Guamanian[3]	Hawaiian, Native	Hmong	Indonesian	Japanese	Korean	Laotian	Malaysian	Pakistani	Samoan	Sri Lankan	Taiwanese	Thai	Tongan	Vietnamese
Timberlane (cdp)	37.1	34.8	-	-	-	-	-	-	-	-	-	-	-	-	-	-	-	-	-	-	-	-	-	35.5
Woodmere (cdp)	29.1	34.2	-	-	-	-	-	-	-	-	-	-	-	-	-	-	-	-	-	-	-	-	-	32.1
Lafayette Parish	32.5	27.9	-	26.1	-	-	-	-	-	-	-	-	-	-	-	-	-	-	-	-	-	-	-	25.6
Lafourche Parish	34.1	35.4	-	-	-	-	-	-	-	-	-	-	-	-	-	-	-	-	-	-	-	-	-	-
Orleans Parish	33.3	29.5	-	29.0	-	-	29.6	-	36.2	-	-	-	-	-	-	-	-	-	-	-	-	-	-	28.1
Ouachita Parish	32.5	30.3	-	-	-	-	-	-	-	-	-	-	-	-	-	-	-	-	-	-	-	-	-	-
Rapides Parish	35.5	31.3	-	-	-	-	-	-	-	-	-	-	-	-	-	-	-	-	-	-	-	-	-	-
St. Bernard Parish	36.8	29.7	-	-	-	-	-	-	-	-	-	-	-	-	-	-	-	-	-	-	-	-	-	19.6
St. Mary Parish	34.6	18.2	-	-	-	-	-	-	-	-	-	-	-	-	-	-	-	-	-	-	-	-	-	17.5
St. Tammany Parish	36.4	33.3	-	-	-	-	-	-	-	-	-	-	-	-	-	-	-	-	-	-	-	-	-	27.8
Terrebonne Parish	33.2	25.4	-	-	-	-	-	-	-	-	-	-	-	-	-	-	-	-	-	-	-	-	-	22.2
Vermilion Parish	35.1	25.8	-	-	-	-	-	-	-	-	-	-	-	-	-	-	-	-	-	-	-	-	-	23.3
Abbeville (city)	34.6	21.9	-	-	-	-	-	-	-	-	-	-	-	-	-	-	-	-	-	-	-	-	-	22.6
Vernon Parish	28.2	30.3	-	-	-	-	-	-	-	-	-	-	-	-	38.9	-	-	-	-	-	-	-	-	-
MAINE	38.7	27.9	33.9	26.2	-	19.9	30.2	-	33.7	-	-	-	-	43.6	24.9	-	-	-	-	-	-	-	-	27.6
Androscoggin County	37.4	24.7	-	-	-	-	-	-	-	-	-	-	-	-	-	-	-	-	-	-	-	-	-	-
Aroostook County	40.7	26.5	-	-	-	-	-	-	-	-	-	-	-	-	-	-	-	-	-	-	-	-	-	-
Cumberland County	37.7	26.5	-	-	-	18.9	20.6	-	29.7	-	-	-	-	-	-	-	-	-	-	-	-	-	-	29.3
Hancock County	41.0	33.5	-	-	-	-	-	-	-	-	-	-	-	-	-	-	-	-	-	-	-	-	-	-
Kennebec County	38.6	32.1	-	-	-	-	-	-	-	-	-	-	-	-	-	-	-	-	-	-	-	-	-	-
Oxford County	40.1	23.9	-	-	-	-	-	-	-	-	-	-	-	-	-	-	-	-	-	-	-	-	-	-
Penobscot County	37.4	25.4	-	-	-	-	33.2	-	-	-	-	-	-	-	-	-	-	-	-	-	-	-	-	-
York County	38.5	27.9	-	-	-	-	-	-	-	-	-	-	-	-	-	-	-	-	-	-	-	-	-	-
MARYLAND	36.1	33.9	30.9	32.5	31.8	30.6	35.7	-	36.1	29.5	35.4	-	30.8	38.4	33.8	32.0	-	29.3	-	38.6	31.3	36.7	-	31.0
Allegany County	39.2	29.7	-	-	-	-	-	-	-	-	-	-	-	-	-	-	-	-	-	-	-	-	-	-
Anne Arundel County	36.1	34.0	-	29.7	-	-	31.3	-	36.7	-	-	-	-	47.3	34.8	-	-	-	-	-	-	-	-	-
Severn (cdp)	33.1	35.5	-	-	-	-	-	-	-	-	-	-	-	-	35.9	-	-	-	-	-	-	-	-	-
South Gate (cdp)	32.0	35.3	-	-	-	-	-	-	-	-	-	-	-	-	34.6	-	-	-	-	-	-	-	-	-
Baltimore Independent City	35.0	27.4	-	26.6	-	-	27.8	-	26.5	-	-	-	-	-	28.5	-	-	-	-	-	-	-	-	27.6
Baltimore County	37.9	33.1	-	31.6	-	-	35.7	-	38.5	-	-	-	-	36.1	32.4	-	-	28.6	-	-	-	-	-	28.3
Arbutus (cdp)	36.9	30.4	-	-	-	-	-	-	-	-	-	-	-	-	-	-	-	-	-	-	-	-	-	-
Carney (cdp)	39.0	34.2	-	-	-	-	33.8	-	-	-	-	-	-	-	31.7	-	-	-	-	-	-	-	-	-
Cockeysville (cdp)	33.2	32.9	-	-	-	-	-	-	-	-	-	-	-	-	32.1	-	-	-	-	-	-	-	-	-
Lutherville-Timonium (cdp)	45.3	44.2	-	-	-	-	-	-	-	-	-	-	-	-	-	-	-	-	-	-	-	-	-	-
Mays Chapel (cdp)	41.6	39.0	-	-	-	-	-	-	-	-	-	-	-	-	-	-	-	-	-	-	-	-	-	-
Owings Mills (cdp)	31.5	30.8	-	-	-	-	-	-	-	-	-	-	-	-	-	-	-	-	-	-	-	-	-	-
Perry Hall (cdp)	37.6	36.4	-	-	-	-	-	-	-	-	-	-	-	-	31.8	-	-	-	-	-	-	-	-	-
Reisterstown (cdp)	34.5	29.1	-	29.1	-	-	-	-	-	-	-	-	-	-	-	-	-	-	-	-	-	-	-	-
Rossville (cdp)	32.7	31.8	-	-	-	-	-	-	-	-	-	-	-	-	-	-	-	-	-	-	-	-	-	-
Towson (cdp)	38.2	31.7	-	-	-	-	36.8	-	-	-	-	-	-	-	-	-	-	-	-	-	-	-	-	-
Woodlawn (cdp)	35.4	29.5	-	28.4	-	-	-	-	-	-	-	-	-	-	-	-	-	-	-	-	-	-	-	-

Notes: Please refer to the User's Guide for an explanation of data; data is arranged alphabetically by state, then county, then city within each county; table includes counties with populations greater than 49,999 unless noted and cities with populations greater than 9,999 whose Asian and/or NHPI population rates are greater than the national average; (1) Native Hawaiian and other Pacific Islander; (2) excludes Taiwanese; (3) includes Chamorro; (4) county does not meet population threshold but is shown in order to allow inclusion of city

Place	Total population	Total Asian population	Total NHPI[1] population	Asian Indian	Bangladeshi	Cambodian	Chinese[2]	Fijian	Filipino	Guamanian[3]	Hawaiian, Native	Hmong	Indonesian	Japanese	Korean	Laotian	Malaysian	Pakistani	Samoan	Sri Lankan	Taiwanese	Thai	Tongan	Vietnamese
Calvert County	35.9	37.4	-	-	-	-	-	-	-	-	-	-	-	-	-	-	-	-	-	-	-	-	-	-
Carroll County	36.9	31.6	-	-	-	-	-	-	-	-	-	-	-	-	-	-	-	-	-	-	-	-	-	-
Cecil County	35.7	33.6	-	-	-	-	-	-	-	-	-	-	-	-	-	-	-	-	-	-	-	-	-	-
Charles County	34.7	36.1	-	-	-	-	-	-	34.9	-	-	-	-	-	-	-	-	-	-	-	-	-	-	-
Frederick County	35.7	31.9	-	32.1	-	-	33.3	-	-	-	-	-	-	-	36.9	-	-	-	-	-	-	-	-	-
Harford County	36.2	33.8	-	35.0	-	-	-	-	33.1	-	-	-	-	-	35.5	-	-	-	-	-	-	-	-	-
Howard County	35.5	34.2	-	34.2	-	-	36.3	-	34.3	-	-	-	-	-	33.6	-	-	28.7	-	-	-	-	-	32.7
Columbia (cdp)	35.7	34.0	-	34.2	-	-	37.3	-	33.2	-	-	-	-	-	32.7	-	-	-	-	-	-	-	-	-
Elkridge (cdp)	31.8	31.6	-	-	-	-	-	-	-	-	-	-	-	-	30.1	-	-	-	-	-	-	-	-	-
Ellicott City (cdp)	37.4	35.9	-	35.8	-	-	37.0	-	36.4	-	-	-	-	-	35.7	-	-	19.8	-	-	-	-	-	-
North Laurel (cdp)	33.3	34.7	-	32.9	-	-	-	-	-	-	-	-	-	-	34.6	-	-	-	-	-	-	-	-	-
Savage-Guilford (cdp)	32.4	33.3	-	-	-	-	-	-	-	-	-	-	-	-	-	-	-	-	-	-	-	-	-	-
Montgomery County	36.9	35.5	31.0	33.9	34.3	30.8	37.4	-	36.6	-	-	-	31.8	38.0	35.1	-	-	31.3	-	40.1	36.1	39.4	-	32.4
Aspen Hill (cdp)	37.4	36.7	-	34.7	-	-	39.8	-	36.4	-	-	-	-	-	36.8	-	-	-	-	-	-	-	-	35.1
Bethesda (cdp)	41.5	37.8	-	35.9	-	-	38.9	-	35.8	-	-	-	-	43.6	31.9	-	-	-	-	-	-	-	-	-
Calverton (cdp)	36.5	33.3	-	32.3	-	-	-	-	-	-	-	-	-	-	30.9	-	-	-	-	-	-	-	-	-
Colesville (cdp)	42.4	38.3	-	44.0	-	-	41.1	-	-	-	-	-	-	-	35.6	-	-	-	-	-	-	-	-	35.4
Fairland (cdp)	32.3	32.9	-	31.3	-	-	33.5	-	-	-	-	-	-	-	35.0	-	-	-	-	-	-	-	-	-
Gaithersburg (city)	33.3	33.5	-	31.6	-	-	36.3	-	33.8	-	-	-	-	-	34.2	-	-	-	-	-	-	-	-	32.1
Germantown (cdp)	31.7	32.3	-	30.9	-	-	34.6	-	-	-	-	-	-	-	35.6	-	-	-	-	-	-	-	-	29.9
Montgomery Village (cdp)	34.7	31.6	-	29.4	-	-	38.3	-	36.7	-	-	-	-	-	-	-	-	-	-	-	-	-	-	34.4
North Bethesda (cdp)	39.7	34.3	-	32.0	-	-	36.5	-	37.4	-	-	-	-	34.1	31.8	-	-	-	-	-	-	-	-	-
North Potomac (cdp)	36.5	37.3	-	37.7	-	-	37.4	-	-	-	-	-	-	-	35.7	-	-	-	-	-	-	-	-	-
Olney (cdp)	36.8	35.9	-	35.9	-	-	35.2	-	-	-	-	-	-	-	31.8	-	-	-	-	-	-	-	-	-
Potomac (cdp)	43.8	41.5	-	40.2	-	-	41.8	-	42.8	-	-	-	-	-	41.3	-	-	-	-	-	-	-	-	-
Redland (cdp)	35.7	36.4	-	38.2	-	-	36.1	-	35.2	-	-	-	-	-	31.5	-	-	-	-	-	-	-	-	-
Rockville (city)	37.8	35.1	-	33.5	-	-	36.3	-	32.6	-	-	-	-	31.6	33.9	-	-	-	-	-	-	-	-	32.8
Silver Spring (cdp)	34.5	33.5	-	31.2	-	28.7	36.3	-	34.8	-	-	-	-	-	32.9	-	-	-	-	-	-	-	-	32.7
Takoma Park (city)	36.2	36.5	-	-	-	-	-	-	-	-	-	-	-	-	-	-	-	-	-	-	-	-	-	-
Wheaton-Glenmont (cdp)	35.8	36.0	-	35.8	-	-	40.0	-	37.3	-	-	-	-	-	36.4	-	-	-	-	-	-	-	-	33.1
White Oak (cdp)	34.0	31.4	-	32.1	-	-	33.9	-	-	-	-	-	-	-	33.5	-	-	-	-	-	-	-	-	28.0
Prince George's County	33.4	32.1	-	31.0	-	-	30.6	-	36.8	-	-	-	-	44.8	33.4	-	-	30.7	-	-	-	26.5	-	29.7
Adelphi (cdp)	32.2	32.8	-	-	-	-	-	-	-	-	-	-	-	-	-	-	-	-	-	-	-	-	-	-
Beltsville (cdp)	35.1	31.7	-	28.5	-	-	-	-	-	-	-	-	-	-	37.3	-	-	-	-	-	-	-	-	-
College Park (city)	21.5	22.7	-	24.0	-	-	22.0	-	-	-	-	-	-	-	-	-	-	-	-	-	-	-	-	-
Fort Washington (cdp)	40.1	40.4	-	-	-	-	-	-	40.8	-	-	-	-	-	-	-	-	-	-	-	-	-	-	-
Friendly (cdp)	38.0	32.7	-	-	-	-	-	-	32.3	-	-	-	-	-	-	-	-	-	-	-	-	-	-	-
Glenn Dale (cdp)	34.6	38.7	-	-	-	-	-	-	-	-	-	-	-	-	-	-	-	-	-	-	-	-	-	-
Greenbelt (city)	31.8	29.9	-	30.0	-	-	29.6	-	-	-	-	-	-	-	31.0	-	-	-	-	-	-	-	-	-
Hyattsville (city)	34.6	31.6	-	-	-	-	-	-	-	-	-	-	-	-	-	-	-	-	-	-	-	-	-	-
Lanham-Seabrook (cdp)	35.9	32.9	-	-	-	-	-	-	-	-	-	-	-	-	-	-	-	-	-	-	-	-	-	-

Notes: Please refer to the User's Guide for an explanation of data; data is arranged alphabetically by state, then county, then city within each county; table includes counties with populations greater than 49,999 unless noted and cities with populations greater than 9,999 whose Asian and/or NHPI population rates are greater than the national average; (1) Native Hawaiian and other Pacific Islander; (2) excludes Taiwanese; (3) includes Chamorro; (4) county does not meet population threshold but is shown in order to allow inclusion of city

Place	Total population	Total Asian population	Total NHPI[1] population	Asian Indian	Bangladeshi	Cambodian	Chinese[2]	Fijian	Filipino	Guamanian[3]	Hawaiian, Native	Hmong	Indonesian	Japanese	Korean	Laotian	Malaysian	Pakistani	Samoan	Sri Lankan	Taiwanese	Thai	Tongan	Vietnamese
Laurel (city)	33.9	31.8	-	-	-	-	-	-	-	-	-	-	-	-	-	-	-	-	-	-	-	-	-	-
New Carrollton (city)	32.4	32.7	-	-	-	-	-	-	-	-	-	-	-	-	-	-	-	-	-	-	-	-	-	-
South Laurel (cdp)	31.1	35.0	-	-	-	-	-	-	-	-	-	-	-	-	-	-	-	-	-	-	-	-	-	-
St. Mary's County	34.3	35.0	-	41.1	-	-	-	-	34.8	-	-	-	-	-	-	-	-	-	-	-	-	-	-	-
Lexington Park (cdp)	27.1	32.1	-	-	-	-	-	-	-	-	-	-	-	-	-	-	-	-	-	-	-	-	-	-
Washington County	37.3	34.2	-	-	-	-	-	-	-	-	-	-	-	-	-	-	-	-	-	-	-	-	-	-
Wicomico County	36.0	35.1	-	31.8	-	-	-	-	-	-	-	-	-	-	36.2	-	-	-	-	-	-	-	-	-
Salisbury (city)	29.4	29.5	-	-	-	-	-	-	-	-	-	-	-	-	-	-	-	-	-	-	-	-	-	-
MASSACHUSETTS	36.6	29.6	28.5	28.7	29.6	21.0	33.7	-	34.2	28.3	24.1	16.3	25.5	30.6	26.5	25.9	-	25.4	-	39.5	27.3	31.0	-	28.7
Barnstable County	44.6	30.6	-	-	-	-	33.3	-	-	-	-	-	-	-	-	-	-	-	-	-	-	-	-	-
Berkshire County	40.6	24.6	-	25.8	-	-	-	-	-	-	-	-	-	-	-	-	-	-	-	-	-	-	-	-
Bristol County	36.8	30.1	-	31.3	-	18.7	34.1	-	40.6	-	-	-	-	-	21.2	-	-	-	-	-	-	-	-	35.4
Essex County	37.6	30.2	-	30.3	-	21.6	35.5	-	37.4	-	-	-	-	32.8	31.3	34.3	-	-	-	-	-	-	-	29.5
Andover (town)	39.5	36.0	-	31.5	-	-	36.5	-	-	-	-	-	-	-	-	-	-	-	-	-	-	-	-	-
Lynn (city)	34.6	23.9	-	30.5	-	21.3	-	-	-	-	-	-	-	-	-	-	-	-	-	-	-	-	-	27.5
North Andover (town)	37.3	36.0	-	-	-	-	39.5	-	-	-	-	-	-	-	-	-	-	-	-	-	-	-	-	-
Franklin County	39.7	31.1	-	-	-	-	-	-	-	-	-	-	-	-	-	-	-	-	-	-	-	-	-	-
Hampden County	36.5	29.4	-	31.7	-	24.6	33.2	-	-	-	-	-	-	-	26.7	-	-	-	-	-	-	-	-	27.4
Hampshire County	34.5	22.5	-	22.5	-	-	23.9	-	-	-	-	-	-	-	21.2	-	-	-	-	-	-	-	-	-
Amherst Center (cdp)	20.8	20.9	-	-	-	-	-	-	-	-	-	-	-	-	-	-	-	-	-	-	-	-	-	-
Amherst (town)	21.8	22.1	-	-	-	-	23.6	-	-	-	-	-	-	-	-	-	-	-	-	-	-	-	-	-
Middlesex County	36.4	29.4	-	29.0	-	20.8	32.5	-	33.9	-	-	-	-	33.4	27.0	25.0	-	24.1	-	-	28.7	30.0	-	28.9
Acton (town)	38.0	35.5	-	28.8	-	-	37.6	-	-	-	-	-	-	-	-	-	-	-	-	-	-	-	-	-
Arlington (town)	39.7	31.8	-	-	-	-	33.4	-	-	-	-	-	-	-	-	-	-	-	-	-	-	-	-	-
Bedford (town)	42.4	36.8	-	-	-	-	-	-	-	-	-	-	-	-	-	-	-	-	-	-	-	-	-	-
Belmont (cdp)	40.5	35.0	-	-	-	-	36.8	-	-	-	-	-	-	-	-	-	-	-	-	-	-	-	-	-
Belmont (town)	40.5	35.0	-	-	-	-	36.8	-	-	-	-	-	-	-	-	-	-	-	-	-	-	-	-	-
Burlington (town)	38.1	30.8	-	30.0	-	-	-	-	-	-	-	-	-	-	-	-	-	-	-	-	-	-	-	-
Cambridge (city)	30.5	26.3	-	26.3	-	-	25.9	-	-	-	-	-	-	30.7	26.4	-	-	-	-	-	-	-	-	-
Chelmsford (town)	39.0	34.5	-	32.0	-	-	38.4	-	-	-	-	-	-	-	-	-	-	-	-	-	-	-	-	-
Framingham (town)	36.3	30.9	-	30.0	-	-	34.2	-	-	-	-	-	-	-	-	-	-	-	-	-	-	-	-	-
Lexington (town)	43.6	36.8	-	35.2	-	-	39.0	-	-	-	-	-	-	-	26.8	-	-	-	-	-	-	-	-	-
Lowell (city)	31.6	25.4	-	28.1	-	20.3	34.3	-	-	-	-	-	-	-	-	25.2	-	-	-	-	-	-	-	28.5
Malden (city)	36.0	30.7	-	28.0	-	-	32.9	-	-	-	-	-	-	-	-	-	-	-	-	-	-	-	-	28.5
Marlborough (city)	36.4	30.4	-	29.2	-	-	-	-	-	-	-	-	-	-	-	-	-	-	-	-	-	-	-	-
Medford (city)	37.6	30.0	-	31.9	-	-	33.0	-	-	-	-	-	-	-	-	-	-	-	-	-	-	-	-	29.3
Natick (town)	38.6	32.6	-	-	-	-	34.4	-	-	-	-	-	-	-	-	-	-	-	-	-	-	-	-	-
Newton (city)	39.0	33.6	-	35.4	-	-	35.1	-	-	-	-	-	-	-	23.8	-	-	-	-	-	-	-	-	-
Somerville (city)	31.1	28.0	-	28.0	-	-	28.5	-	-	-	-	-	-	-	23.4	-	-	-	-	-	-	-	-	-
Sudbury (town)	39.0	37.6	-	-	-	-	-	-	-	-	-	-	-	-	-	-	-	-	-	-	-	-	-	-
Waltham (city)	34.3	28.2	-	27.1	-	-	31.3	-	-	-	-	-	-	-	-	-	-	-	-	-	-	-	-	-

Notes: Please refer to the User's Guide for an explanation of data; data is arranged alphabetically by state, then county, then city within each county; table includes counties with populations greater than 49,999 unless noted and cities with populations greater than 9,999 whose Asian and/or NHPI population rates are greater than the national average; (1) Native Hawaiian and other Pacific Islander; (2) excludes Taiwanese; (3) includes Chamorro; (4) county does not meet population threshold but is shown in order to allow inclusion of city

Place	Total population	Total Asian population	Total NHPI[1] population	Asian Indian	Bangladeshi	Cambodian	Chinese[2]	Fijian	Filipino	Guamanian[3]	Hawaiian, Native	Hmong	Indonesian	Japanese	Korean	Laotian	Malaysian	Pakistani	Samoan	Sri Lankan	Taiwanese	Thai	Tongan	Vietnamese
Wayland (town)	41.2	36.3	-	-	-	-	-	-	-	-	-	-	-	-	-	-	-	-	-	-	-	-	-	-
Westford (town)	36.9	33.7	-	-	-	-	34.4	-	-	-	-	-	-	-	-	-	-	-	-	-	-	-	-	-
Weston (town)	41.6	35.2	-	-	-	-	38.8	-	-	-	-	-	-	-	-	-	-	-	-	-	-	-	-	-
Winchester (town)	41.1	38.0	-	-	-	-	-	-	-	-	-	-	-	-	-	-	-	-	-	-	-	-	-	-
Woburn (city)	38.3	29.4	-	27.7	-	-	-	-	-	-	-	-	-	-	-	-	-	-	-	-	-	-	-	-
Norfolk County	38.1	32.2	-	29.5	-	-	35.3	-	35.1	-	-	-	-	31.5	27.5	-	-	-	-	-	24.0	-	-	29.5
Brookline (town)	34.8	31.4	-	27.6	-	-	36.1	-	-	-	-	-	-	30.3	28.6	-	-	-	-	-	-	-	-	-
Needham (town)	40.7	34.9	-	-	-	-	37.3	-	-	-	-	-	-	-	-	-	-	-	-	-	-	-	-	-
Norwood (town)	38.2	30.6	-	28.8	-	-	-	-	-	-	-	-	-	-	-	-	-	-	-	-	-	-	-	-
Quincy (city)	37.7	32.5	-	28.4	-	-	34.4	-	33.7	-	-	-	-	-	-	-	-	-	-	-	-	-	-	30.1
Randolph (town)	38.5	34.0	-	-	-	-	36.3	-	-	-	-	-	-	-	-	-	-	-	-	-	-	-	-	31.5
Sharon (town)	40.1	39.8	-	-	-	-	-	-	-	-	-	-	-	-	-	-	-	-	-	-	-	-	-	-
Wellesley (town)	37.6	20.9	-	-	-	-	21.3	-	-	-	-	-	-	-	-	-	-	-	-	-	-	-	-	-
Plymouth County	36.9	31.9	-	31.0	-	-	32.8	-	38.8	-	-	-	-	-	-	-	-	-	-	-	-	-	-	29.2
Suffolk County	31.8	28.8	-	25.6	-	20.8	35.4	-	28.3	-	-	-	-	25.6	26.3	-	-	-	-	-	26.1	-	-	28.1
Boston (city)	31.2	28.8	-	25.3	-	25.1	35.3	-	27.8	-	-	-	-	25.5	26.3	-	-	-	-	-	26.1	-	-	28.3
Chelsea (city)	31.6	27.7	-	-	-	-	-	-	-	-	-	-	-	-	-	-	-	-	-	-	-	-	-	27.7
Revere (city)	38.0	27.8	-	-	-	19.5	-	-	-	-	-	-	-	-	-	-	-	-	-	-	-	-	-	26.6
Worcester County	36.4	29.5	-	29.7	-	24.8	33.2	-	36.8	-	-	14.7	-	28.1	32.9	26.1	-	27.8	-	-	-	-	-	29.5
Fitchburg (city)	34.5	19.3	-	-	-	-	-	-	-	-	-	14.1	-	-	-	23.5	-	-	-	-	-	-	-	-
Northborough (town)	37.5	35.3	-	-	-	-	-	-	-	-	-	-	-	-	-	-	-	-	-	-	-	-	-	-
Shrewsbury (town)	37.3	31.5	-	30.2	-	-	33.9	-	-	-	-	-	-	-	-	-	-	-	-	-	-	-	-	30.9
Westborough (town)	36.8	32.1	-	29.6	-	-	34.2	-	-	-	-	-	-	-	-	-	-	-	-	-	-	-	-	-
Worcester (city)	33.6	28.5	-	28.3	-	-	28.7	-	-	-	-	-	-	-	-	-	-	-	-	-	-	-	-	29.2
MICHIGAN	35.6	29.7	25.4	29.7	29.1	27.4	32.3	-	34.5	23.9	26.9	17.5	25.7	34.0	24.4	24.4	23.5	28.7	28.1	34.8	33.6	30.6	-	28.6
Allegan County	35.2	25.7	-	-	-	-	-	-	-	-	-	-	-	-	-	-	-	-	-	-	-	-	-	-
Bay County	38.3	28.9	-	-	-	-	-	-	-	-	-	-	-	-	-	-	-	-	-	-	-	-	-	-
Berrien County	37.5	30.3	-	28.2	-	-	-	-	38.4	-	-	-	-	-	22.8	-	-	-	-	-	-	-	-	-
Calhoun County	36.5	32.6	-	-	-	-	-	-	-	-	-	-	-	32.9	-	-	-	-	-	-	-	-	-	-
Cass County	38.3	35.8	-	-	-	-	-	-	-	-	-	-	-	-	-	32.6	-	-	-	-	-	-	-	-
Clinton County	36.7	21.3	-	-	-	-	-	-	-	-	-	-	-	-	-	-	-	-	-	-	-	-	-	-
Eaton County	36.6	28.3	-	27.2	-	-	-	-	-	-	-	-	-	-	-	-	-	-	-	-	-	-	-	29.4
Genesee County	35.1	31.7	-	30.5	-	-	34.6	-	43.0	-	-	-	-	-	23.7	-	-	-	-	-	-	-	-	-
Ingham County	30.5	26.9	-	28.0	-	-	29.3	-	28.6	-	-	13.9	-	29.6	25.4	-	-	-	-	-	-	-	-	26.6
East Lansing (city)	21.7	25.3	-	25.3	-	-	27.9	-	-	-	-	-	-	-	25.6	-	-	-	-	-	-	-	-	-
Meridian charter (township)	35.9	30.9	-	31.0	-	-	36.1	-	-	-	-	-	-	-	25.8	-	-	-	-	-	-	-	-	-
Okemos (cdp)	35.7	28.9	-	27.5	-	-	36.0	-	-	-	-	-	-	-	-	-	-	-	-	-	-	-	-	-
Ionia County	32.8	25.9	-	-	-	-	-	-	-	-	-	-	-	-	-	-	-	-	-	-	-	-	-	-
Isabella County	25.0	25.9	-	-	-	-	-	-	-	-	-	-	-	-	-	-	-	-	-	-	-	-	-	-
Jackson County	36.6	31.7	-	-	-	-	-	-	-	-	-	-	-	-	-	-	-	-	-	-	-	-	-	-
Kalamazoo County	32.7	26.8	-	28.2	-	-	27.4	-	-	-	-	-	-	-	18.7	-	-	-	-	-	-	-	-	-

Notes: Please refer to the User's Guide for an explanation of data; data is arranged alphabetically by state, then county, then city within each county; table includes counties with populations greater than 49,999 unless noted and cities with populations greater than 9,999 whose Asian and/or NHPI population rates are greater than the national average; (1) Native Hawaiian and other Pacific Islander; (2) excludes Taiwanese; (3) includes Chamorro; (4) county does not meet population threshold but is shown in order to allow inclusion of city

Place	Total population	Total Asian population	Total NHPI[1] population	Asian Indian	Bangladeshi	Cambodian	Chinese[2]	Fijian	Filipino	Guamanian[3]	Hawaiian, Native	Hmong	Indonesian	Japanese	Korean	Laotian	Malaysian	Pakistani	Samoan	Sri Lankan	Taiwanese	Thai	Tongan	Vietnamese
Kent County	32.6	28.3	-	28.7	-	-	30.1	-	35.2	-	-	-	-	-	18.9	-	-	-	-	-	-	-	-	29.0
Kentwood (city)	32.7	29.4	-	-	-	-	-	-	-	-	-	-	-	-	28.3	-	-	-	-	-	-	-	-	28.6
Lenawee County	36.4	34.2	-	-	-	-	-	-	-	-	-	-	-	-	-	-	-	-	-	-	-	-	-	-
Livingston County	36.3	31.1	-	-	-	-	-	-	-	-	-	-	-	-	-	-	-	-	-	-	-	-	-	-
Macomb County	36.9	30.4	-	30.6	-	-	34.8	-	33.6	-	-	21.2	-	-	25.2	-	-	30.5	-	-	-	-	-	29.2
Sterling Heights (city)	36.9	31.6	-	31.3	-	-	35.8	-	33.0	-	-	-	-	-	28.8	-	-	-	-	-	-	-	-	30.5
Marquette County	37.6	34.9	-	-	-	-	-	-	-	-	-	-	-	-	-	-	-	-	-	-	-	-	-	-
Midland County	36.3	33.9	-	32.0	-	-	39.9	-	-	-	-	-	-	-	-	-	-	-	-	-	-	-	-	-
Monroe County	36.1	27.5	-	-	-	-	-	-	-	-	-	-	-	-	-	-	-	-	-	-	-	-	-	-
Muskegon County	35.6	27.0	-	-	-	-	-	-	-	-	-	-	-	-	-	-	-	-	-	-	-	-	-	-
Oakland County	36.7	31.8	-	30.6	-	-	36.1	-	36.6	-	-	18.3	-	34.0	31.3	-	-	29.9	-	-	37.0	-	-	27.1
Auburn Hills (city)	30.9	28.9	-	27.7	-	-	-	-	-	-	-	-	-	-	-	-	-	-	-	-	-	-	-	-
Bloomfield (township)	45.2	43.1	-	40.7	-	-	-	-	-	-	-	-	-	-	39.8	-	-	-	-	-	-	-	-	-
Farmington (city)	39.9	29.5	-	29.1	-	-	-	-	-	-	-	-	-	-	-	-	-	-	-	-	-	-	-	-
Farmington Hills (city)	38.9	31.1	-	30.3	-	-	37.3	-	33.3	-	-	-	-	-	-	-	-	-	-	-	-	-	-	-
Madison Heights (city)	35.8	31.0	-	-	-	-	35.6	-	-	-	-	-	-	-	-	-	-	-	-	-	-	-	-	-
Novi (city)	35.2	32.8	-	32.2	-	-	37.5	-	-	-	-	-	-	33.3	-	-	-	-	-	-	-	-	-	-
Rochester (city)	35.8	31.1	-	-	-	-	-	-	-	-	-	-	-	-	-	-	-	-	-	-	-	-	-	-
Rochester Hills (city)	38.0	32.7	-	31.8	-	-	34.0	-	-	-	-	-	-	-	27.5	-	-	-	-	-	-	-	-	-
Troy (city)	38.1	32.9	-	31.2	-	-	34.5	-	38.8	-	-	-	-	-	35.4	-	-	-	-	-	37.2	-	-	-
West Bloomfield (township)	40.2	33.9	-	34.4	-	-	42.4	-	33.7	-	-	-	-	31.7	37.2	-	-	-	-	-	-	-	-	-
Ottawa County	32.3	24.7	-	19.7	-	24.7	30.4	-	-	-	-	-	-	-	15.4	25.7	-	-	-	-	-	-	-	27.9
Holland (city)	29.2	27.8	-	-	-	-	-	-	-	-	-	-	-	-	-	-	-	-	-	-	-	-	-	-
Saginaw County	36.4	28.8	-	32.4	-	-	-	-	31.4	-	-	-	-	-	25.6	-	-	-	-	-	-	-	-	-
St. Clair County	36.5	32.9	-	-	-	-	-	-	-	-	-	-	-	-	-	-	-	-	-	-	-	-	-	-
St. Joseph County	35.6	37.6	-	-	-	-	-	-	-	-	-	-	-	-	-	-	-	-	-	-	-	-	-	-
Washtenaw County	31.4	27.6	-	26.1	-	-	28.5	-	31.5	-	-	-	-	30.4	26.9	-	-	29.1	-	-	28.5	-	-	23.9
Ann Arbor (city)	28.2	26.1	-	24.8	-	-	26.8	-	26.5	-	-	-	-	30.1	25.4	-	-	-	-	-	27.8	-	-	-
Pittsfield charter (township)	31.4	30.1	-	30.0	-	-	31.9	-	-	-	-	-	-	-	28.8	-	-	-	-	-	-	-	-	-
Scio (township)	37.7	34.9	-	-	-	-	-	-	-	-	-	-	-	-	-	-	-	-	-	-	-	-	-	-
Wayne County	34.1	30.1	30.5	29.5	27.6	-	34.4	-	34.8	-	-	15.2	-	36.5	27.4	-	-	27.6	-	-	-	-	-	29.3
Brownstown (township)	32.8	29.3	-	-	-	-	-	-	-	-	-	-	-	-	-	-	-	-	-	-	-	-	-	-
Canton (township)	33.4	32.0	-	31.0	-	-	34.4	-	35.7	-	-	-	-	-	29.0	-	-	-	-	-	-	-	-	-
Hamtramck (city)	32.0	24.5	-	22.4	23.9	-	-	-	-	-	-	-	-	-	-	-	-	-	-	-	-	-	-	-
Inkster (city)	32.1	28.2	-	28.1	-	-	-	-	-	-	-	-	-	-	-	-	-	-	-	-	-	-	-	-
Northville (township)	41.3	32.9	-	32.2	-	-	-	-	-	-	-	-	-	-	-	-	-	-	-	-	-	-	-	-
MINNESOTA	35.4	24.8	30.0	28.6	-	24.6	31.7	-	33.6	33.8	31.5	16.1	-	35.4	20.5	25.1	-	29.2	-	-	39.2	30.4	-	29.7
Anoka County	33.9	27.6	-	30.4	-	-	36.1	-	35.8	-	-	17.0	-	-	20.7	-	-	-	-	-	-	-	-	29.1
Columbia Heights (city)	39.5	29.0	-	-	-	-	-	-	-	-	-	-	-	-	-	-	-	-	-	-	-	-	-	-
Blue Earth County	30.2	23.9	-	-	-	-	-	-	-	-	-	-	-	-	-	-	-	-	-	-	-	-	-	-
Carver County	33.8	28.8	-	-	-	-	-	-	-	-	-	-	-	-	-	-	-	-	-	-	-	-	-	-

Notes: Please refer to the User's Guide for an explanation of data; data is arranged alphabetically by state, then county, then city within each county; table includes counties with populations greater than 49,999 unless noted and cities with populations greater than 9,999 whose Asian and/or NHPI population rates are greater than the national average; (1) Native Hawaiian and other Pacific Islander; (2) excludes Taiwanese; (3) includes Chamorro; (4) county does not meet population threshold but is shown in order to allow inclusion of city

Place	Total population	Total Asian population	Total NHPI[1] population	Asian Indian	Bangladeshi	Cambodian	Chinese[2]	Fijian	Filipino	Guamanian[3]	Hawaiian, Native	Hmong	Indonesian	Japanese	Korean	Laotian	Malaysian	Pakistani	Samoan	Sri Lankan	Taiwanese	Thai	Tongan	Vietnamese
Clay County	32.6	23.9	-	-	-	-	-	-	-	-	-	-	-	-	-	-	-	-	-	-	-	-	-	-
Crow Wing County	39.5	24.2	-	-	-	-	-	-	-	-	-	-	-	-	-	-	-	-	-	-	-	-	-	-
Dakota County	33.8	28.9	-	28.8	-	26.2	35.1	-	29.8	-	-	-	-	-	19.2	26.2	-	-	-	-	-	-	-	30.1
Eagan (city)	33.0	29.5	-	29.0	-	-	34.3	-	-	-	-	-	-	-	-	-	-	-	-	-	-	-	-	29.7
Hennepin County	34.9	26.2	29.9	28.6	-	25.0	31.2	-	33.1	-	-	15.6	-	35.3	24.1	26.5	-	29.5	-	-	-	-	-	29.6
Bloomington (city)	40.0	30.5	-	30.3	-	26.3	33.8	-	-	-	-	-	-	-	20.7	-	-	-	-	-	-	-	-	30.6
Brooklyn Center (city)	35.5	19.9	-	-	-	-	-	-	-	-	-	17.4	-	-	-	32.0	-	-	-	-	-	-	-	-
Brooklyn Park (city)	32.0	26.5	-	29.1	-	-	-	-	-	-	-	19.0	-	-	-	25.9	-	-	-	-	-	-	-	30.1
Eden Prairie (city)	34.4	30.5	-	29.4	-	-	32.6	-	-	-	-	-	-	-	-	-	-	-	-	-	-	-	-	35.5
Hopkins (city)	34.3	27.9	-	28.2	-	-	-	-	-	-	-	-	-	-	-	-	-	-	-	-	-	-	-	-
Minneapolis (city)	31.3	23.4	-	26.9	-	18.0	28.4	-	32.7	-	-	14.9	-	33.5	26.6	24.4	-	-	-	-	-	-	-	27.6
Plymouth (city)	36.0	29.9	-	29.4	-	-	34.7	-	-	-	-	-	-	-	30.2	-	-	-	-	-	-	-	-	-
Richfield (city)	36.8	29.0	-	-	-	-	-	-	-	-	-	-	-	-	-	-	-	-	-	-	-	-	-	28.8
Nobles County[4]	37.5	28.8	-	-	-	-	-	-	-	-	-	-	-	-	-	26.6	-	-	-	-	-	-	-	-
Worthington (city)	36.3	30.0	-	-	-	-	-	-	-	-	-	-	-	-	-	26.9	-	-	-	-	-	-	-	-
Olmsted County	35.1	27.6	-	28.3	-	18.6	33.2	-	-	-	-	17.6	-	34.5	17.0	21.1	-	-	-	-	-	-	-	32.1
Rochester (city)	34.2	27.6	-	28.3	-	17.9	32.6	-	-	-	-	17.6	-	-	17.2	21.1	-	-	-	-	-	-	-	31.4
Otter Tail County	41.1	30.3	-	-	-	-	-	-	-	-	-	-	-	-	-	-	-	-	-	-	-	-	-	-
Ramsey County	33.7	19.9	-	29.7	-	25.8	32.3	-	33.2	-	-	16.2	-	35.3	20.5	17.4	-	-	-	-	-	-	-	29.5
Maplewood (city)	38.1	30.3	-	-	-	-	33.0	-	-	-	-	14.6	-	-	-	-	-	-	-	-	-	-	-	-
New Brighton (city)	37.1	32.6	-	-	-	-	-	-	-	-	-	-	-	-	-	-	-	-	-	-	-	-	-	-
Roseville (city)	40.8	29.1	-	-	-	-	32.3	-	-	-	-	-	-	-	-	-	-	-	-	-	-	-	-	-
St. Paul (city)	31.1	18.0	-	27.3	-	25.8	30.8	-	32.1	-	-	16.2	-	-	21.1	16.3	-	-	-	-	-	-	-	28.5
Vadnais Heights (city)	35.6	25.6	-	-	-	-	-	-	-	-	-	-	-	-	-	-	-	-	-	-	-	-	-	-
Rice County	32.8	22.6	-	-	-	-	-	-	-	-	-	-	-	-	-	-	-	-	-	-	-	-	-	-
St. Louis County	39.1	22.3	-	-	-	-	-	-	-	-	-	-	-	-	17.9	-	-	-	-	-	-	-	-	-
Scott County	32.8	30.1	-	-	-	28.7	-	-	-	-	-	-	-	-	-	-	-	-	-	-	-	-	-	31.1
Savage (city)	31.9	32.2	-	-	-	-	-	-	-	-	-	-	-	-	-	-	-	-	-	-	-	-	-	-
Sherburne County	31.6	22.8	-	-	-	-	-	-	-	-	-	-	-	-	-	-	-	-	-	-	-	-	-	-
Stearns County	31.5	23.6	-	-	-	-	-	-	-	-	-	-	-	-	-	-	-	-	-	-	-	-	-	29.0
Washington County	35.2	27.5	-	31.0	-	-	35.2	-	-	-	-	15.1	-	-	15.3	-	-	-	-	-	-	-	-	31.2
Woodbury (city)	33.6	31.2	-	31.0	-	-	35.6	-	-	-	-	15.5	-	-	-	-	-	-	-	-	-	-	-	-
Wright County	33.0	20.8	-	-	-	-	-	-	-	-	-	-	-	-	-	-	-	-	-	-	-	-	-	-
MISSISSIPPI	34.0	30.8	26.8	30.6	-	-	35.6	-	33.4	-	-	-	-	42.5	32.6	-	-	-	-	-	-	-	-	24.9
DeSoto County	34.0	30.9	-	-	-	-	-	-	-	-	-	-	-	-	-	-	-	-	-	-	-	-	-	-
Forrest County	29.7	24.3	-	-	-	-	-	-	-	-	-	-	-	-	-	-	-	-	-	-	-	-	-	-
Harrison County	34.0	30.3	-	-	-	-	-	-	30.9	-	-	-	-	-	-	-	-	-	-	-	-	-	-	24.8
Biloxi (city)	32.3	28.7	-	-	-	-	-	-	29.7	-	-	-	-	-	-	-	-	-	-	-	-	-	-	24.2
Hinds County	32.0	30.7	-	30.2	-	-	-	-	-	-	-	-	-	-	-	-	-	-	-	-	-	-	-	-
Jackson County	34.8	30.7	-	-	-	-	-	-	-	-	-	-	-	-	-	-	-	-	-	-	-	-	-	24.7
Madison County	33.5	42.9	-	-	-	-	-	-	-	-	-	-	-	-	-	-	-	-	-	-	-	-	-	-

Notes: Please refer to the User's Guide for an explanation of data; data is arranged alphabetically by state, then county, then city within each county; table includes counties with populations greater than 49,999 unless noted and cities with populations greater than 9,999 whose Asian and/or NHPI population rates are greater than the national average; (1) Native Hawaiian and other Pacific Islander; (2) excludes Taiwanese; (3) includes Chamorro; (4) county does not meet population threshold but is shown in order to allow inclusion of city

Place	Total population	Total Asian population	Total NHPI[1] population	Asian Indian	Bangladeshi	Cambodian	Chinese[2]	Fijian	Filipino	Guamanian[3]	Hawaiian, Native	Hmong	Indonesian	Japanese	Korean	Laotian	Malaysian	Pakistani	Samoan	Sri Lankan	Taiwanese	Thai	Tongan	Vietnamese
Oktibbeha County[4]	24.8	25.5	-	-	-	-	-	-	-	-	-	-	-	-	-	-	-	-	-	-	-	-	-	-
Starkville (city)	25.1	26.7	-	-	-	-	-	-	-	-	-	-	-	-	-	-	-	-	-	-	-	-	-	-
Rankin County	34.8	33.6	-	-	-	-	-	-	-	-	-	-	-	-	-	-	-	-	-	-	-	-	-	-
MISSOURI	36.2	30.5	26.5	29.0	-	20.1	31.1	-	34.8	31.2	32.1	-	-	38.1	30.0	32.3	-	30.0	24.4	-	33.2	30.4	-	28.9
Boone County	29.5	28.9	-	29.2	-	-	30.7	-	-	-	-	-	-	-	25.6	-	-	-	-	-	-	-	-	-
Columbia (city)	27.0	28.7	-	29.0	-	-	30.5	-	-	-	-	-	-	-	26.3	-	-	-	-	-	-	-	-	-
Cape Girardeau County	35.2	22.9	-	-	-	-	-	-	-	-	-	-	-	-	-	-	-	-	-	-	-	-	-	-
Cass County	36.0	35.8	-	-	-	-	-	-	-	-	-	-	-	-	-	-	-	-	-	-	-	-	-	-
Clay County	35.0	28.5	-	26.8	-	-	-	-	-	-	-	-	-	-	-	-	-	-	-	-	-	-	-	28.0
Cole County	35.6	30.3	-	-	-	-	-	-	-	-	-	-	-	-	-	-	-	-	-	-	-	-	-	-
Franklin County	35.8	29.5	-	-	-	-	-	-	-	-	-	-	-	-	-	-	-	-	-	-	-	-	-	-
Greene County	35.2	28.2	-	-	-	-	25.0	-	-	-	-	-	-	-	25.9	-	-	-	-	-	-	-	-	28.9
Jackson County	35.3	29.6	26.6	28.5	-	-	31.2	-	33.9	-	-	-	-	45.9	29.8	-	-	-	24.2	-	-	-	-	27.9
Independence (city)	37.9	34.6	22.7	-	-	-	-	-	-	-	-	-	-	-	-	-	-	-	-	-	-	-	-	-
Jasper County	34.9	29.7	-	-	-	-	-	-	-	-	-	-	-	-	-	-	-	-	-	-	-	-	-	-
Jefferson County	34.9	31.9	-	-	-	-	-	-	-	-	-	-	-	-	-	-	-	-	-	-	-	-	-	-
Newton County	37.1	39.8	-	-	-	-	-	-	-	-	-	-	-	-	-	-	-	-	-	-	-	-	-	-
Phelps County[4]	35.0	28.9	-	26.0	-	-	-	-	-	-	-	-	-	-	-	-	-	-	-	-	-	-	-	-
Rolla (city)	28.7	28.6	-	-	-	-	-	-	-	-	-	-	-	-	-	-	-	-	-	-	-	-	-	-
Platte County	36.1	34.2	-	-	-	-	-	-	-	-	-	-	-	-	-	-	-	-	-	-	-	-	-	-
St. Charles County	34.3	32.2	-	31.7	-	-	28.9	-	38.5	-	-	-	-	-	-	-	-	-	-	-	-	-	-	-
Saint Louis Independent City	33.8	29.6	-	27.9	-	-	30.4	-	34.6	-	-	-	-	-	-	-	-	-	-	-	-	-	-	28.8
St. Louis County	37.6	32.1	24.8	29.9	-	-	33.1	-	39.4	-	-	-	-	36.5	29.0	-	-	30.7	-	-	35.6	33.8	-	34.2
Chesterfield (city)	41.7	34.8	-	31.3	-	-	39.3	-	-	-	-	-	-	-	-	-	-	-	-	-	-	-	-	-
Clayton (city)	36.1	33.9	-	-	-	-	-	-	-	-	-	-	-	-	-	-	-	-	-	-	-	-	-	-
Creve Coeur (city)	43.6	39.8	-	-	-	-	-	-	-	-	-	-	-	-	-	-	-	-	-	-	-	-	-	-
Manchester (city)	36.3	32.0	-	-	-	-	-	-	-	-	-	-	-	-	-	-	-	-	-	-	-	-	-	-
Maryland Heights (city)	34.1	28.9	-	27.8	-	-	33.5	-	-	-	-	-	-	-	-	-	-	-	-	-	-	-	-	-
Town and Country (city)	46.0	45.6	-	46.3	-	-	-	-	-	-	-	-	-	-	-	-	-	-	-	-	-	-	-	-
MONTANA	37.6	30.4	31.4	28.6	-	-	29.4	-	36.9	-	26.8	-	-	43.0	17.6	-	-	-	-	-	-	-	-	-
Cascade County	36.9	40.1	-	-	-	-	-	-	-	-	-	-	-	-	-	-	-	-	-	-	-	-	-	-
Flathead County	38.9	35.6	-	-	-	-	-	-	-	-	-	-	-	-	-	-	-	-	-	-	-	-	-	-
Gallatin County	30.7	22.6	-	-	-	-	-	-	-	-	-	-	-	-	-	-	-	-	-	-	-	-	-	-
Missoula County	33.4	26.0	-	-	-	-	-	-	-	-	-	-	-	-	-	-	-	-	-	-	-	-	-	-
Yellowstone County	36.8	27.3	-	-	-	-	-	-	-	-	-	-	-	-	-	-	-	-	-	-	-	-	-	-
NEBRASKA	35.4	28.3	25.2	27.6	-	-	30.5	-	37.4	-	-	-	-	38.7	22.4	28.8	-	-	-	-	-	28.8	-	27.2
Douglas County	33.7	27.7	-	27.3	-	-	30.6	-	39.3	-	-	-	-	28.1	23.9	-	-	-	-	-	-	-	-	26.0
Hall County	35.9	29.5	-	-	-	-	-	-	-	-	-	-	-	-	-	-	-	-	-	-	-	-	-	-
Lancaster County	32.1	27.6	-	29.2	-	-	30.1	-	-	-	-	-	-	-	25.7	-	-	-	-	-	-	-	-	26.8
Sarpy County	31.6	31.3	-	-	-	-	-	-	39.9	-	-	-	-	-	32.3	-	-	-	-	-	-	-	-	27.7
NEVADA	35.2	36.2	29.2	33.7	-	30.6	37.0	-	35.2	29.7	32.1	-	-	48.0	37.6	31.8	-	28.4	25.1	-	43.5	38.3	24.8	33.9

Notes: Please refer to the User's Guide for an explanation of data; data is arranged alphabetically by state, then county, then city within each county; table includes counties with populations greater than 49,999 unless noted and cities with populations greater than 9,999 whose Asian and/or NHPI population rates are greater than the national average; (1) Native Hawaiian and other Pacific Islander; (2) excludes Taiwanese; (3) includes Chamorro; (4) county does not meet population threshold but is shown in order to allow inclusion of city

Place	Total population	Total Asian population	Total NHPI[1] population	Asian Indian	Bangladeshi	Cambodian	Chinese[2]	Fijian	Filipino	Guamanian[3]	Hawaiian, Native	Hmong	Indonesian	Japanese	Korean	Laotian	Malaysian	Pakistani	Samoan	Sri Lankan	Taiwanese	Thai	Tongan	Vietnamese
Carson City Independent City	39.0	34.7	-	-	-	-	-	-	34.9	-	-	-	-	-	-	-	-	-	-	-	-	-	-	-
Clark County	34.5	36.4	29.9	36.0	-	30.4	37.1	-	35.4	30.4	31.6	-	-	48.6	37.3	32.2	-	-	24.6	-	44.0	38.5	-	34.1
Enterprise (cdp)	38.6	33.9	-	-	-	-	-	-	-	-	-	-	-	-	-	-	-	-	-	-	-	-	-	-
Henderson (city)	36.0	36.7	31.3	36.7	-	-	40.6	-	35.0	-	31.7	-	-	42.8	35.5	-	-	-	-	-	-	-	-	-
Las Vegas (city)	34.5	37.4	30.0	35.2	-	-	39.6	-	35.9	-	33.3	-	-	48.6	39.7	-	-	-	-	-	-	36.2	-	40.1
North Las Vegas (city)	28.9	35.1	28.8	-	-	-	-	-	32.5	-	-	-	-	-	-	-	-	-	-	-	-	-	-	-
Paradise (cdp)	35.5	35.4	29.0	35.4	-	-	39.6	-	34.5	-	26.7	-	-	41.0	31.8	-	-	-	-	-	-	-	-	34.4
Spring Valley (cdp)	36.3	35.6	27.1	-	-	-	33.2	-	36.5	-	-	-	-	48.9	38.1	-	-	-	-	-	-	36.5	-	30.7
Sunrise Manor (cdp)	31.7	37.0	33.5	-	-	-	37.8	-	35.9	-	-	-	-	59.3	42.3	-	-	-	-	-	-	-	-	-
Winchester (cdp)	40.8	41.4	-	-	-	-	-	-	46.3	-	-	-	-	-	-	-	-	-	-	-	-	-	-	-
Washoe County	35.8	34.5	24.0	30.6	-	-	36.5	-	33.5	-	-	-	-	42.2	40.8	-	-	-	-	-	-	-	21.4	33.5
Reno (city)	34.7	33.6	24.4	30.7	-	-	39.1	-	32.8	-	-	-	-	37.0	40.8	-	-	-	-	-	-	-	-	28.1
Sparks (city)	34.7	34.7	-	-	-	-	30.8	-	35.2	-	-	-	-	-	-	-	-	-	-	-	-	-	-	-
NEW HAMPSHIRE	37.2	29.9	-	28.3	-	-	31.8	-	34.5	-	-	-	-	34.5	25.0	28.0	-	-	-	-	-	-	-	30.4
Belknap County	39.9	32.8	-	-	-	-	-	-	-	-	-	-	-	-	-	-	-	-	-	-	-	-	-	-
Cheshire County	37.5	26.9	-	-	-	-	-	-	-	-	-	-	-	-	-	-	-	-	-	-	-	-	-	-
Grafton County	37.4	22.6	-	-	-	-	23.3	-	-	-	-	-	-	-	-	-	-	-	-	-	-	-	-	-
Hanover (town)	22.9	21.7	-	-	-	-	-	-	-	-	-	-	-	-	-	-	-	-	-	-	-	-	-	-
Hillsborough County	36.0	30.4	-	29.0	-	-	33.7	-	34.3	-	-	-	-	-	27.7	-	-	-	-	-	-	-	-	30.8
Nashua (city)	35.9	30.6	-	30.0	-	-	35.4	-	-	-	-	-	-	-	-	-	-	-	-	-	-	-	-	-
Merrimack County	37.7	29.2	-	-	-	-	-	-	-	-	-	-	-	-	-	-	-	-	-	-	-	-	-	-
Rockingham County	37.3	31.5	-	28.2	-	-	36.3	-	34.9	-	-	-	-	-	28.4	-	-	-	-	-	-	-	-	-
Strafford County	34.4	29.7	-	-	-	-	29.6	-	-	-	-	-	-	-	-	-	-	-	-	-	-	-	-	-
NEW JERSEY	36.9	33.0	30.5	31.0	30.1	30.6	35.7	-	35.5	26.4	31.4	-	33.0	37.3	32.4	26.5	-	28.7	34.6	35.0	37.3	33.8	-	30.5
Atlantic County	37.0	33.4	-	32.4	28.8	-	37.5	-	35.5	-	-	-	-	-	33.9	-	-	35.4	-	-	-	-	-	32.2
Atlantic City (city)	35.1	34.2	-	35.1	-	-	41.5	-	39.5	-	-	-	-	-	-	-	-	-	-	-	-	-	-	31.4
Brigantine (city)	40.6	29.1	-	-	-	-	-	-	-	-	-	-	-	-	-	-	-	-	-	-	-	-	-	-
Egg Harbor (township)	36.1	33.9	-	-	-	-	-	-	-	-	-	-	-	-	-	-	-	-	-	-	-	-	-	-
Galloway (township)	33.8	31.7	-	32.0	-	-	-	-	-	-	-	-	-	-	-	-	-	-	-	-	-	-	-	-
Ventnor City (city)	39.9	30.3	-	-	-	-	-	-	-	-	-	-	-	-	-	-	-	-	-	-	-	-	-	-
Bergen County	39.1	34.1	-	32.9	-	-	36.6	-	35.5	-	-	-	-	35.1	33.5	-	-	32.2	-	-	37.2	32.5	-	30.1
Bergenfield (borough)	37.7	33.5	-	31.7	-	-	-	-	33.6	-	-	-	-	-	-	-	-	-	-	-	-	-	-	-
Cliffside Park (borough)	39.8	34.2	-	-	-	-	-	-	-	-	-	-	-	31.8	33.6	-	-	-	-	-	-	-	-	-
Dumont (borough)	38.7	36.5	-	31.9	-	-	-	-	36.6	-	-	-	-	-	-	-	-	-	-	-	-	-	-	-
Elmwood Park (borough)	38.2	33.3	-	33.5	-	-	-	-	-	-	-	-	-	-	-	-	-	-	-	-	-	-	-	-
Englewood (city)	37.4	35.1	-	-	-	-	-	-	35.8	-	-	-	-	-	-	-	-	-	-	-	-	-	-	-
Fair Lawn (borough)	41.8	33.3	-	31.4	-	-	-	-	39.2	-	-	-	-	-	-	-	-	-	-	-	-	-	-	-
Fairview (borough)	34.5	32.0	-	-	-	-	-	-	-	-	-	-	-	-	-	-	-	-	-	-	-	-	-	-
Fort Lee (borough)	41.2	33.6	-	33.3	-	-	34.1	-	-	-	-	-	-	33.4	33.2	-	-	-	-	-	-	-	-	-
Franklin Lakes (borough)	40.6	36.4	-	-	-	-	-	-	-	-	-	-	-	-	-	-	-	-	-	-	-	-	-	-
Glen Rock (borough)	39.5	37.9	-	-	-	-	-	-	-	-	-	-	-	-	-	-	-	-	-	-	-	-	-	-

Notes: Please refer to the User's Guide for an explanation of data; data is arranged alphabetically by state, then county, then city within each county; table includes counties with populations greater than 49,999 unless noted and cities with populations greater than 9,999 whose Asian and/or NHPI population rates are greater than the national average; (1) Native Hawaiian and other Pacific Islander; (2) excludes Taiwanese; (3) includes Chamorro; (4) county does not meet population threshold but is shown in order to allow inclusion of city

Place	Total population	Total Asian population	Total NHPI[1] population	Asian Indian	Bangladeshi	Cambodian	Chinese[2]	Fijian	Filipino	Guamanian[3]	Hawaiian, Native	Hmong	Indonesian	Japanese	Korean	Laotian	Malaysian	Pakistani	Samoan	Sri Lankan	Taiwanese	Thai	Tongan	Vietnamese
Hackensack (city)	36.4	31.2	-	29.5	-	-	-	-	34.2	-	-	-	-	-	32.3	-	-	-	-	-	-	-	-	-
Hasbrouck Heights (borough)	39.7	35.6	-	-	-	-	-	-	-	-	-	-	-	-	-	-	-	-	-	-	-	-	-	-
Hillsdale (borough)	39.8	35.7	-	-	-	-	-	-	-	-	-	-	-	-	-	-	-	-	-	-	-	-	-	-
Little Ferry (borough)	37.4	31.8	-	32.3	-	-	-	-	34.2	-	-	-	-	-	31.4	-	-	-	-	-	-	-	-	-
Lodi (borough)	36.3	31.6	-	32.0	-	-	-	-	27.9	-	-	-	-	-	-	-	-	-	-	-	-	-	-	-
Lyndhurst (township)	39.6	30.8	-	-	-	-	-	-	-	-	-	-	-	-	-	-	-	-	-	-	-	-	-	-
Mahwah (township)	37.1	32.5	-	31.5	-	-	-	-	-	-	-	-	-	-	-	-	-	-	-	-	-	-	-	-
New Milford (borough)	40.1	34.3	-	33.8	-	-	-	-	33.1	-	-	-	-	-	-	-	-	-	-	-	-	-	-	-
North Arlington (borough)	40.6	30.9	-	-	-	-	-	-	-	-	-	-	-	-	-	-	-	-	-	-	-	-	-	-
Palisades Park (borough)	35.4	32.8	-	-	-	-	-	-	-	-	-	-	-	-	32.8	-	-	-	-	-	-	-	-	-
Paramus (borough)	42.9	36.2	-	34.5	-	-	39.4	-	38.5	-	-	-	-	-	34.9	-	-	-	-	-	-	-	-	-
Ramsey (borough)	39.0	37.0	-	-	-	-	-	-	-	-	-	-	-	-	-	-	-	-	-	-	-	-	-	-
Ridgefield (borough)	39.8	32.9	-	-	-	-	-	-	-	-	-	-	-	-	32.1	-	-	-	-	-	-	-	-	-
Ridgefield Park (village)	37.3	32.6	-	-	-	-	-	-	-	-	-	-	-	-	33.3	-	-	-	-	-	-	-	-	-
Ridgewood (village)	39.1	36.9	-	-	-	-	-	-	-	-	-	-	-	39.7	22.9	-	-	-	-	-	-	-	-	-
River Edge (borough)	40.8	36.4	-	-	-	-	-	-	-	-	-	-	-	-	35.0	-	-	-	-	-	-	-	-	-
Rutherford (borough)	38.5	33.2	-	36.5	-	-	-	-	-	-	-	-	-	-	31.8	-	-	-	-	-	-	-	-	-
Saddle Brook (township)	40.0	35.1	-	-	-	-	-	-	-	-	-	-	-	-	-	-	-	-	-	-	-	-	-	-
Teaneck (township)	38.7	35.5	-	38.2	-	-	-	-	37.5	-	-	-	-	-	-	-	-	-	-	-	-	-	-	-
Tenafly (borough)	40.8	35.1	-	-	-	-	40.3	-	-	-	-	-	-	-	28.2	-	-	-	-	-	-	-	-	-
Wallington (borough)	37.5	31.3	-	-	-	-	-	-	-	-	-	-	-	-	-	-	-	-	-	-	-	-	-	-
Westwood (borough)	39.4	36.8	-	-	-	-	-	-	-	-	-	-	-	-	-	-	-	-	-	-	-	-	-	-
Wyckoff (township)	40.9	40.1	-	-	-	-	-	-	-	-	-	-	-	-	-	-	-	-	-	-	-	-	-	-
Burlington County	37.2	35.3	-	31.0	-	-	35.1	-	37.1	-	-	-	-	67.1	36.0	-	-	-	-	-	-	-	-	37.4
Browns Mills (cdp)	34.9	45.1	-	-	-	-	-	-	-	-	-	-	-	-	40.4	-	-	-	-	-	-	-	-	-
Evesham (township)	36.4	34.7	-	31.6	-	-	36.4	-	-	-	-	-	-	-	-	-	-	-	-	-	-	-	-	-
Maple Shade (township)	36.5	28.8	-	27.0	-	-	-	-	-	-	-	-	-	-	-	-	-	-	-	-	-	-	-	-
Marlton (cdp)	37.2	32.4	-	-	-	-	-	-	-	-	-	-	-	-	-	-	-	-	-	-	-	-	-	-
Mount Laurel (township)	38.9	34.1	-	32.2	-	-	35.7	-	-	-	-	-	-	-	-	-	-	-	-	-	-	-	-	-
Camden County	35.9	32.7	-	33.4	-	28.8	35.4	-	34.6	-	-	-	-	-	31.6	-	-	28.8	-	-	-	-	-	30.3
Barclay-Kingston (cdp)	41.4	32.5	-	-	-	-	-	-	-	-	-	-	-	-	-	-	-	-	-	-	-	-	-	-
Bellmawr (borough)	40.3	32.2	-	-	-	-	-	-	-	-	-	-	-	-	-	-	-	-	-	-	-	-	-	-
Cherry Hill Mall (cdp)	41.6	33.4	-	-	-	-	-	-	-	-	-	-	-	-	-	-	-	-	-	-	-	-	-	-
Cherry Hill (township)	41.6	35.1	-	36.2	-	-	39.1	-	34.2	-	-	-	-	-	29.5	-	-	-	-	-	-	-	-	-
Echelon (cdp)	35.6	31.0	-	30.6	-	-	-	-	-	-	-	-	-	-	-	-	-	-	-	-	-	-	-	-
Greentree (cdp)	39.7	38.7	-	35.4	-	-	39.6	-	-	-	-	-	-	-	-	-	-	-	-	-	-	-	-	-
Pennsauken (township)	36.4	30.6	-	-	-	-	-	-	-	-	-	-	-	-	-	-	-	-	-	-	-	-	-	29.8
Springdale (cdp)	44.2	38.4	-	-	-	-	39.9	-	-	-	-	-	-	-	-	-	-	-	-	-	-	-	-	-
Voorhees (township)	37.3	34.3	-	34.4	-	-	34.6	-	28.0	-	-	-	-	-	-	-	-	-	-	-	-	-	-	-
Cape May County	42.6	38.8	-	-	-	-	-	-	-	-	-	-	-	-	-	-	-	-	-	-	-	-	-	-
Cumberland County	35.7	37.4	-	33.3	-	-	-	-	-	-	-	-	-	-	-	-	-	-	-	-	-	-	-	-

Notes: Please refer to the User's Guide for an explanation of data; data is arranged alphabetically by state, then county, then city within each county; table includes counties with populations greater than 49,999 unless noted and cities with populations greater than 9,999 whose Asian and/or NHPI population rates are greater than the national average; (1) Native Hawaiian and other Pacific Islander; (2) excludes Taiwanese; (3) includes Chamorro; (4) county does not meet population threshold but is shown in order to allow inclusion of city

Place	Total population	Total Asian population	Total NHPI[1] population	Asian Indian	Bangladeshi	Cambodian	Chinese[2]	Fijian	Filipino	Guamanian[3]	Hawaiian, Native	Hmong	Indonesian	Japanese	Korean	Laotian	Malaysian	Pakistani	Samoan	Sri Lankan	Taiwanese	Thai	Tongan	Vietnamese
Essex County	34.9	34.5	30.8	32.8	-	-	36.5	-	36.1	-	-	-	-	40.7	33.8	-	-	31.2	-	-	41.7	-	-	29.5
Belleville (township)	36.6	31.5	-	31.5	-	-	-	-	32.7	-	-	-	-	-	-	-	-	-	-	-	-	-	-	29.0
Bloomfield (township)	37.8	35.5	-	33.6	-	-	35.8	-	38.0	-	-	-	-	-	-	-	-	-	-	-	-	-	-	-
Cedar Grove (township)	43.5	40.2	-	-	-	-	-	-	-	-	-	-	-	-	-	-	-	-	-	-	-	-	-	-
Livingston (township)	40.8	36.5	-	38.3	-	-	36.3	-	31.2	-	-	-	-	-	38.9	-	-	-	-	-	-	-	-	-
Millburn (township)	39.7	36.6	-	-	-	-	34.0	-	-	-	-	-	-	-	-	-	-	-	-	-	-	-	-	-
Nutley (township)	40.0	33.8	-	30.6	-	-	-	-	38.2	-	-	-	-	-	-	-	-	-	-	-	-	-	-	-
Verona (township)	41.1	34.5	-	-	-	-	-	-	-	-	-	-	-	-	-	-	-	-	-	-	-	-	-	-
West Caldwell (township)	41.3	42.1	-	-	-	-	-	-	-	-	-	-	-	-	-	-	-	-	-	-	-	-	-	-
West Orange (township)	40.0	36.6	-	34.1	-	-	39.3	-	40.4	-	-	-	-	-	31.0	-	-	-	-	-	-	-	-	-
Gloucester County	36.3	32.7	-	32.8	-	-	31.8	-	40.6	-	-	-	-	-	20.5	-	-	-	-	-	-	-	-	-
Hudson County	33.9	32.1	-	30.6	-	-	32.6	-	35.4	-	-	-	-	32.8	31.5	-	-	28.9	-	-	-	-	-	29.1
Bayonne (city)	38.2	32.7	-	31.7	-	-	-	-	33.4	-	-	-	-	-	38.3	-	-	-	-	-	-	-	-	-
Guttenberg (town)	35.2	32.5	-	-	-	-	-	-	-	-	-	-	-	-	-	-	-	-	-	-	-	-	-	-
Harrison (town)	34.5	31.5	-	-	-	-	31.6	-	-	-	-	-	-	-	-	-	-	-	-	-	-	-	-	-
Hoboken (city)	30.5	27.6	-	25.5	-	-	29.0	-	-	-	-	-	-	-	-	-	-	-	-	-	-	-	-	-
Jersey City (city)	32.7	32.5	-	30.6	-	-	33.2	-	35.7	-	-	-	-	-	30.8	-	-	28.9	-	-	-	-	-	29.6
Kearny (town)	35.0	30.8	-	26.8	-	-	33.0	-	-	-	-	-	-	-	-	-	-	-	-	-	-	-	-	-
North Bergen (township)	36.1	34.9	-	35.0	-	-	32.7	-	-	-	-	-	-	-	-	-	-	-	-	-	-	-	-	-
Secaucus (town)	39.4	30.9	-	30.0	-	-	-	-	28.8	-	-	-	-	-	-	-	-	-	-	-	-	-	-	-
Weehawken (township)	35.3	32.2	-	-	-	-	-	-	-	-	-	-	-	-	-	-	-	-	-	-	-	-	-	-
Hunterdon County	38.9	33.0	-	33.3	-	-	35.2	-	-	-	-	-	-	-	-	-	-	-	-	-	-	-	-	-
Mercer County	36.2	32.6	-	31.7	-	-	33.8	-	37.2	-	-	-	-	36.3	30.3	-	-	25.4	-	-	41.5	-	-	-
East Windsor (township)	35.6	32.6	-	32.5	-	-	-	-	-	-	-	-	-	-	-	-	-	-	-	-	-	-	-	-
Hopewell (township)	39.2	36.8	-	-	-	-	-	-	-	-	-	-	-	-	-	-	-	-	-	-	-	-	-	-
Lawrence (township)	36.8	34.0	-	32.6	-	-	35.0	-	-	-	-	-	-	-	-	-	-	-	-	-	-	-	-	-
Princeton (borough)	25.1	24.9	-	-	-	-	-	-	-	-	-	-	-	-	-	-	-	-	-	-	-	-	-	-
Princeton (township)	40.7	31.7	-	38.6	-	-	30.5	-	-	-	-	-	-	-	-	-	-	-	-	-	-	-	-	-
West Windsor (township)	37.5	36.9	-	34.7	-	-	36.9	-	-	-	-	-	-	-	36.2	-	-	-	-	-	-	-	-	-
Middlesex County	35.8	30.9	-	29.9	29.7	-	34.4	-	33.5	-	-	-	33.4	34.0	29.9	-	-	26.6	-	36.4	34.9	-	-	28.6
Avenel (cdp)	35.6	29.2	-	28.9	-	-	-	-	-	-	-	-	-	-	-	-	-	-	-	-	-	-	-	-
Carteret (borough)	36.8	31.5	-	32.0	-	-	-	-	-	-	-	-	-	-	-	-	-	-	-	-	-	-	-	-
Colonia (cdp)	40.1	36.2	-	33.2	-	-	-	-	39.9	-	-	-	-	-	-	-	-	-	-	-	-	-	-	-
East Brunswick (township)	39.2	35.6	-	34.9	-	-	37.1	-	27.8	-	-	-	-	-	31.9	-	-	-	-	-	-	-	-	-
Edison (township)	36.4	30.8	-	29.9	-	-	34.7	-	34.7	-	-	-	-	-	32.2	-	-	27.2	-	-	37.2	-	-	-
Fords (cdp)	37.5	30.6	-	29.3	-	-	-	-	36.9	-	-	-	-	-	-	-	-	-	-	-	-	-	-	-
Highland Park (borough)	34.8	29.9	-	28.6	-	-	33.9	-	-	-	-	-	-	-	-	-	-	-	-	-	-	-	-	-
Iselin (cdp)	37.7	30.3	-	29.3	-	-	34.7	-	-	-	-	-	-	-	-	-	-	-	-	-	-	-	-	-
Metuchen (borough)	39.8	32.9	-	-	-	-	-	-	-	-	-	-	-	-	-	-	-	-	-	-	-	-	-	-
Middlesex (borough)	38.3	31.5	-	-	-	-	-	-	-	-	-	-	-	-	-	-	-	-	-	-	-	-	-	-
New Brunswick (city)	23.4	22.9	-	23.2	-	-	23.5	-	-	-	-	-	-	-	-	-	-	-	-	-	-	-	-	-

Notes: Please refer to the User's Guide for an explanation of data; data is arranged alphabetically by state, then county, then city within each county; table includes counties with populations greater than 49,999 unless noted and cities with populations greater than 9,999 whose Asian and/or NHPI population rates are greater than the national average; (1) Native Hawaiian and other Pacific Islander; (2) excludes Taiwanese; (3) includes Chamorro; (4) county does not meet population threshold but is shown in order to allow inclusion of city

Place	Total population	Total Asian population	Total NHPI[1] population	Asian Indian	Bangladeshi	Cambodian	Chinese[2]	Fijian	Filipino	Guamanian[3]	Hawaiian, Native	Hmong	Indonesian	Japanese	Korean	Laotian	Malaysian	Pakistani	Samoan	Sri Lankan	Taiwanese	Thai	Tongan	Vietnamese
North Brunswick (township)	35.9	32.1	-	31.4	-	-	37.2	-	38.5	-	-	-	-	-	29.9	-	-	-	-	-	-	-	-	-
Old Bridge (township)	36.4	33.0	-	31.9	-	-	33.4	-	33.7	-	-	-	-	-	-	-	-	32.4	-	-	-	-	-	-
Piscataway (township)	33.6	29.3	-	29.4	-	-	29.7	-	34.1	-	-	-	-	-	22.3	-	-	-	-	-	-	-	-	-
Plainsboro (township)	33.0	31.1	-	29.6	-	-	33.4	-	-	-	-	-	-	-	-	-	-	-	-	-	-	-	-	-
Princeton Meadows (cdp)	31.8	30.3	-	28.9	-	-	32.9	-	-	-	-	-	-	-	-	-	-	-	-	-	-	-	-	-
Sayreville (borough)	36.6	30.1	-	28.7	-	-	33.6	-	31.3	-	-	-	-	-	-	-	-	-	-	-	-	-	-	-
South Brunswick (township)	35.2	33.2	-	31.5	-	-	35.9	-	41.1	-	-	-	-	-	-	-	-	-	-	-	-	-	-	-
South Plainfield (borough)	38.1	33.3	-	34.5	-	-	-	-	39.9	-	-	-	-	-	-	-	-	-	-	-	-	-	-	28.3
Woodbridge (township)	37.4	30.1	-	29.4	-	-	34.9	-	32.7	-	-	-	-	-	34.8	-	-	23.9	-	-	-	-	-	-
Monmouth County	37.8	35.7	-	32.5	-	-	36.8	-	38.3	-	-	-	-	53.1	33.2	-	-	27.4	-	-	-	-	-	33.1
Aberdeen (township)	37.5	33.8	-	29.6	-	-	36.4	-	-	-	-	-	-	-	-	-	-	-	-	-	-	-	-	-
Colts Neck (township)	32.6	34.4	-	-	-	-	-	-	-	-	-	-	-	-	-	-	-	-	-	-	-	-	-	-
Eatontown (borough)	36.5	30.8	-	-	-	-	-	-	-	-	-	-	-	-	-	-	-	-	-	-	-	-	-	-
Freehold (township)	38.3	39.3	-	36.4	-	-	38.4	-	49.6	-	-	-	-	-	-	-	-	-	-	-	-	-	-	-
Holmdel (township)	41.2	38.8	-	39.3	-	-	37.7	-	-	-	-	-	-	-	-	-	-	-	-	-	-	-	-	-
Howell (township)	35.8	38.3	-	31.7	-	-	-	-	36.9	-	-	-	-	-	-	-	-	-	-	-	-	-	-	-
Manalapan (township)	38.0	34.4	-	34.8	-	-	37.8	-	-	-	-	-	-	-	-	-	-	-	-	-	-	-	-	-
Marlboro (township)	38.1	35.9	-	31.7	-	-	36.3	-	-	-	-	-	-	-	-	-	-	-	-	-	-	-	-	-
Morganville (cdp)	39.9	35.4	-	-	-	-	36.5	-	-	-	-	-	-	-	-	-	-	-	-	-	-	-	-	-
Ocean (township)	38.5	35.6	-	31.5	-	-	-	-	-	-	-	-	-	-	-	-	-	-	-	-	-	-	-	-
Tinton Falls (borough)	36.6	31.5	-	-	-	-	-	-	-	-	-	-	-	-	-	-	-	-	-	-	-	-	-	-
West Freehold (cdp)	40.4	42.1	-	-	-	-	-	-	-	-	-	-	-	-	-	-	-	-	-	-	-	-	-	-
Morris County	38.0	34.2	-	32.3	-	-	36.7	-	37.3	-	-	-	-	41.2	29.7	-	-	27.8	-	-	38.5	-	-	29.3
Chatham (township)	40.1	33.9	-	-	-	-	-	-	-	-	-	-	-	-	-	-	-	-	-	-	-	-	-	-
Denville (township)	39.7	34.1	-	-	-	-	-	-	-	-	-	-	-	-	-	-	-	-	-	-	-	-	-	-
East Hanover (township)	41.3	38.2	-	-	-	-	38.5	-	-	-	-	-	-	-	-	-	-	-	-	-	-	-	-	-
Hanover (township)	40.4	34.2	-	29.8	-	-	36.7	-	-	-	-	-	-	-	-	-	-	-	-	-	-	-	-	-
Lincoln Park (borough)	40.1	34.5	-	-	-	-	-	-	-	-	-	-	-	-	-	-	-	-	-	-	-	-	-	-
Montville (township)	39.2	36.4	-	36.7	-	-	36.7	-	-	-	-	-	-	-	-	-	-	-	-	-	-	-	-	-
Morris (township)	40.9	36.9	-	-	-	-	-	-	-	-	-	-	-	-	-	-	-	-	-	-	-	-	-	-
Mount Olive (township)	34.2	29.8	-	29.2	-	-	-	-	-	-	-	-	-	-	-	-	-	-	-	-	-	-	-	-
Parsippany-Troy Hills (twp)	37.9	34.2	-	32.1	-	-	36.8	-	41.4	-	-	-	-	-	35.4	-	-	-	-	-	-	-	-	-
Randolph (township)	36.9	31.5	-	29.0	-	-	34.3	-	-	-	-	-	-	-	-	-	-	-	-	-	-	-	-	-
Rockaway (township)	37.6	35.6	-	37.1	-	-	-	-	-	-	-	-	-	-	-	-	-	-	-	-	-	-	-	-
Roxbury (township)	37.6	33.1	-	-	-	-	-	-	-	-	-	-	-	-	-	-	-	-	-	-	-	-	-	-
Succasunna-Kenvil (cdp)	37.6	32.2	-	-	-	-	-	-	-	-	-	-	-	-	-	-	-	-	-	-	-	-	-	-
Ocean County	41.1	35.0	-	32.7	-	-	39.8	-	35.2	-	-	-	-	-	17.3	-	-	-	-	-	-	-	-	-
Passaic County	35.0	32.8	-	30.9	26.7	-	35.6	-	37.5	-	-	-	-	-	34.4	-	-	-	-	-	-	-	-	-
Clifton (city)	39.3	34.6	-	32.4	-	-	35.1	-	37.1	-	-	-	-	-	33.5	-	-	-	-	-	-	-	-	-
Little Falls (township)	41.0	31.1	-	-	-	-	-	-	-	-	-	-	-	-	-	-	-	-	-	-	-	-	-	-
Passaic (city)	28.7	32.8	-	31.0	-	-	-	-	39.8	-	-	-	-	-	-	-	-	-	-	-	-	-	-	-

Notes: Please refer to the User's Guide for an explanation of data; data is arranged alphabetically by state, then county, then city within each county; table includes counties with populations greater than 49,999 unless noted and cities with populations greater than 9,999 whose Asian and/or NHPI population rates are greater than the national average; (1) Native Hawaiian and other Pacific Islander; (2) excludes Taiwanese; (3) includes Chamorro; (4) county does not meet population threshold but is shown in order to allow inclusion of city

Place	Total population	Total Asian population	Total NHPI[1] population	Asian Indian	Bangladeshi	Cambodian	Chinese[2]	Fijian	Filipino	Guamanian[3]	Hawaiian, Native	Hmong	Indonesian	Japanese	Korean	Laotian	Malaysian	Pakistani	Samoan	Sri Lankan	Taiwanese	Thai	Tongan	Vietnamese
Wayne (township)	40.0	34.5	-	32.0	-	-	37.1	-	33.4	-	-	-	-	-	39.1	-	-	-	-	-	-	-	-	-
Salem County	38.2	34.3	-	-	-	-	-	-	-	-	-	-	-	-	-	-	-	-	-	-	-	-	-	-
Somerset County	37.2	33.2	-	31.5	-	-	36.4	-	32.9	-	-	-	-	37.8	30.3	-	-	29.6	-	-	37.0	-	-	31.2
Bernards (township)	39.1	35.7	-	34.0	-	-	39.1	-	-	-	-	-	-	-	-	-	-	-	-	-	-	-	-	-
Branchburg (township)	37.6	35.0	-	33.1	-	-	-	-	-	-	-	-	-	-	-	-	-	-	-	-	-	-	-	-
Bridgewater (township)	37.9	33.2	-	32.6	-	-	36.0	-	-	-	-	-	-	-	-	-	-	-	-	-	-	-	-	-
Franklin (township)	36.5	31.8	-	29.2	-	-	35.2	-	38.1	-	-	-	-	-	-	-	-	-	-	-	-	-	-	-
Hillsborough (township)	35.4	32.0	-	32.4	-	-	36.1	-	-	-	-	-	-	-	-	-	-	-	-	-	-	-	-	-
Montgomery (township)	36.4	34.1	-	33.8	-	-	35.5	-	-	-	-	-	-	-	-	-	-	-	-	-	-	-	-	-
North Plainfield (borough)	34.4	30.8	-	-	-	-	-	-	-	-	-	-	-	-	-	-	-	-	-	-	-	-	-	-
Somerset (cdp)	36.0	31.2	-	27.8	-	-	35.1	-	36.5	-	-	-	-	-	-	-	-	-	-	-	-	-	-	-
Somerville (borough)	35.2	30.7	-	-	-	-	-	-	-	-	-	-	-	-	-	-	-	-	-	-	-	-	-	-
Warren (township)	39.7	40.1	-	41.4	-	-	38.8	-	-	-	-	-	-	-	-	-	-	-	-	-	-	-	-	-
Sussex County	37.1	33.0	-	37.9	-	-	-	-	32.8	-	-	-	-	-	-	-	-	-	-	-	-	-	-	-
Union County	36.7	34.0	-	32.0	-	-	37.3	-	35.1	-	-	-	-	-	31.9	-	-	22.7	-	-	-	-	-	33.0
Berkeley Heights (township)	40.2	36.7	-	-	-	-	38.2	-	-	-	-	-	-	-	-	-	-	-	-	-	-	-	-	-
New Providence (borough)	38.7	34.7	-	-	-	-	38.1	-	-	-	-	-	-	-	-	-	-	-	-	-	-	-	-	-
Rahway (city)	37.7	37.0	-	-	-	-	-	-	39.0	-	-	-	-	-	-	-	-	-	-	-	-	-	-	-
Roselle Park (borough)	37.0	34.3	-	33.9	-	-	-	-	-	-	-	-	-	-	-	-	-	-	-	-	-	-	-	-
Scotch Plains (township)	38.7	33.8	-	30.2	-	-	37.8	-	-	-	-	-	-	-	-	-	-	-	-	-	-	-	-	-
Springfield (township)	42.2	33.2	-	-	-	-	-	-	-	-	-	-	-	-	-	-	-	-	-	-	-	-	-	-
Summit (city)	37.3	33.1	-	31.5	-	-	-	-	-	-	-	-	-	-	-	-	-	-	-	-	-	-	-	-
Union (township)	38.8	33.2	-	35.2	-	-	35.4	-	32.7	-	-	-	-	-	-	-	-	-	-	-	-	-	-	-
Westfield (town)	38.3	35.3	-	-	-	-	-	-	-	-	-	-	-	-	-	-	-	-	-	-	-	-	-	-
Warren County	37.9	30.4	-	30.1	-	-	-	-	-	-	-	-	-	-	-	-	-	-	-	-	-	-	-	-
NEW MEXICO	34.7	33.3	32.6	32.0	-	-	32.7	-	32.8	26.0	35.8	-	-	44.8	32.8	-	-	-	-	-	-	45.4	-	31.3
Bernalillo County	35.2	32.6	31.4	30.9	-	-	30.9	-	33.2	-	-	-	-	45.3	32.2	-	-	-	-	-	-	-	-	31.1
Chaves County	35.6	40.5	-	-	-	-	-	-	-	-	-	-	-	-	-	-	-	-	-	-	-	-	-	-
Dona Ana County	30.4	32.9	-	-	-	-	33.7	-	-	-	-	-	-	-	-	-	-	-	-	-	-	-	-	-
Los Alamos County[4]	40.5	32.9	-	-	-	-	-	-	-	-	-	-	-	-	-	-	-	-	-	-	-	-	-	-
Los Alamos (cdp)	40.1	32.9	-	-	-	-	-	-	-	-	-	-	-	-	-	-	-	-	-	-	-	-	-	-
Otero County	33.7	33.4	-	-	-	-	-	-	-	-	-	-	-	-	-	-	-	-	-	-	-	-	-	-
Sandoval County	35.4	34.7	-	-	-	-	-	-	32.2	-	-	-	-	-	-	-	-	-	-	-	-	-	-	-
Santa Fe County	38.4	34.3	-	-	-	-	-	-	-	-	-	-	-	-	-	-	-	-	-	-	-	-	-	-
NEW YORK	36.0	33.3	29.1	31.4	29.6	21.9	35.6	-	37.2	26.5	34.0	-	32.0	33.8	31.9	27.5	36.6	28.1	28.4	36.0	31.0	35.1	-	29.6
Albany County	36.9	28.6	-	30.5	-	-	28.6	-	33.9	-	-	-	-	-	20.8	-	-	-	-	-	-	-	-	30.0
Colonie (town)	39.8	33.5	-	34.3	-	-	38.1	-	-	-	-	-	-	-	-	-	-	-	-	-	-	-	-	-
Guilderland (town)	39.1	30.9	-	30.4	-	-	-	-	-	-	-	-	-	-	-	-	-	-	-	-	-	-	-	-
Bronx County (Bronx)	31.5	32.3	25.7	31.2	29.2	19.0	36.4	-	35.3	-	-	-	-	35.3	35.4	-	-	31.1	-	-	-	-	-	27.9
Broome County	38.2	22.4	-	26.4	-	-	21.4	-	-	-	-	-	-	-	22.3	22.7	-	-	-	-	-	-	-	28.8
Johnson City (village)	39.7	24.9	-	-	-	-	-	-	-	-	-	-	-	-	-	-	-	-	-	-	-	-	-	-

Notes: Please refer to the User's Guide for an explanation of data; data is arranged alphabetically by state, then county, then city within each county; table includes counties with populations greater than 49,999 unless noted and cities with populations greater than 9,999 whose Asian and/or NHPI population rates are greater than the national average; (1) Native Hawaiian and other Pacific Islander; (2) excludes Taiwanese; (3) includes Chamorro; (4) county does not meet population threshold but is shown in order to allow inclusion of city

Place	Total population	Total Asian population	Total NHPI[1] population	Asian Indian	Bangladeshi	Cambodian	Chinese[2]	Fijian	Filipino	Guamanian[3]	Hawaiian, Native	Hmong	Indonesian	Japanese	Korean	Laotian	Malaysian	Pakistani	Samoan	Sri Lankan	Taiwanese	Thai	Tongan	Vietnamese
Vestal (town)	34.8	20.8	-	-	-	-	20.7	-	-	-	-	-	-	-	-	-	-	-	-	-	-	-	-	-
Cattaraugus County	37.4	31.5	-	-	-	-	-	-	-	-	-	-	-	-	-	-	-	-	-	-	-	-	-	-
Cayuga County	37.5	37.8	-	-	-	-	-	-	-	-	-	-	-	-	-	-	-	-	-	-	-	-	-	-
Chautauqua County	38.1	22.8	-	-	-	-	-	-	-	-	-	-	-	-	-	-	-	-	-	-	-	-	-	-
Chemung County	37.9	34.6	-	-	-	-	-	-	-	-	-	-	-	-	-	-	-	-	-	-	-	-	-	-
Chenango County	38.4	44.3	-	-	-	-	-	-	-	-	-	-	-	-	-	-	-	-	-	-	-	-	-	-
Clinton County	35.7	29.0	-	-	-	-	-	-	-	-	-	-	-	-	-	-	-	-	-	-	-	-	-	-
Columbia County	40.7	28.9	-	-	-	-	-	-	-	-	-	-	-	-	-	-	-	-	-	-	-	-	-	-
Dutchess County	36.8	32.3	-	31.3	-	-	33.4	-	-	-	-	-	-	-	29.4	-	-	-	-	-	-	-	-	-
Arlington (cdp)	31.3	23.9	-	-	-	-	-	-	-	-	-	-	-	-	-	-	-	-	-	-	-	-	-	-
Poughkeepsie (town)	35.2	31.0	-	29.7	-	-	31.7	-	-	-	-	-	-	-	-	-	-	-	-	-	-	-	-	-
Wappinger (town)	36.6	30.9	-	32.1	-	-	-	-	-	-	-	-	-	-	-	-	-	-	-	-	-	-	-	-
Erie County	38.1	28.6	-	29.6	-	-	29.3	-	34.4	-	-	-	-	29.1	24.3	-	-	-	-	-	-	-	-	28.0
Amherst (town)	39.5	28.8	-	33.3	-	-	28.3	-	-	-	-	-	-	-	24.3	-	-	-	-	-	-	-	-	-
Herkimer County	39.1	31.0	-	-	-	-	-	-	-	-	-	-	-	-	-	-	-	-	-	-	-	-	-	-
Jefferson County	32.6	28.8	-	-	-	-	-	-	29.2	-	-	-	-	-	33.0	-	-	-	-	-	-	-	-	-
Kings County (Brooklyn)	33.3	33.2	24.8	30.6	29.2	30.7	34.9	-	34.8	20.4	-	-	-	31.2	31.3	-	-	27.2	-	-	-	-	-	30.1
Livingston County	35.4	21.5	-	-	-	-	-	-	-	-	-	-	-	-	-	-	-	-	-	-	-	-	-	-
Madison County	36.1	21.7	-	-	-	-	-	-	-	-	-	-	-	-	-	-	-	-	-	-	-	-	-	-
Monroe County	36.2	28.6	-	29.7	-	19.9	29.8	-	32.1	-	-	-	-	35.9	19.8	28.1	-	32.4	-	-	-	-	-	30.8
Brighton (town)	40.2	30.5	-	30.8	-	-	28.9	-	-	-	-	-	-	-	-	-	-	-	-	-	-	-	-	-
Henrietta (town)	29.9	24.4	-	22.9	-	-	25.1	-	-	-	-	-	-	-	-	-	-	-	-	-	-	-	-	-
Pittsford (town)	40.7	32.1	-	40.2	-	-	-	-	-	-	-	-	-	-	-	-	-	-	-	-	-	-	-	-
Nassau County	38.7	35.3	30.6	33.7	-	-	38.0	-	36.1	-	-	-	-	36.4	34.9	-	-	26.6	-	-	39.7	34.5	-	31.2
East Meadow (cdp)	39.1	33.1	-	32.1	-	-	-	-	32.7	-	-	-	-	-	-	-	-	-	-	-	-	-	-	-
Elmont (cdp)	36.7	33.3	-	35.0	-	-	-	-	33.9	-	-	-	-	-	-	-	-	-	-	-	-	-	-	-
Franklin Square (cdp)	39.1	34.5	-	30.9	-	-	-	-	-	-	-	-	-	-	-	-	-	-	-	-	-	-	-	-
Glen Cove (city)	39.0	33.7	-	28.4	-	-	-	-	-	-	-	-	-	-	39.0	-	-	-	-	-	-	-	-	-
Hicksville (cdp)	39.0	31.9	-	32.0	-	-	35.1	-	30.5	-	-	-	-	-	-	-	-	-	-	-	-	-	-	-
Jericho (cdp)	42.0	35.8	-	-	-	-	-	-	-	-	-	-	-	-	39.2	-	-	-	-	-	-	-	-	-
Mineola (village)	38.6	31.7	-	32.0	-	-	-	-	-	-	-	-	-	-	-	-	-	-	-	-	-	-	-	-
North Hempstead (town)	40.0	35.7	-	34.8	-	-	37.6	-	36.9	-	-	-	-	35.3	35.6	-	-	25.3	-	-	40.8	-	-	-
North Merrick (cdp)	39.8	32.4	-	-	-	-	-	-	-	-	-	-	-	-	-	-	-	-	-	-	-	-	-	-
North New Hyde Park (cdp)	42.0	34.6	-	32.2	-	-	37.5	-	-	-	-	-	-	-	-	-	-	-	-	-	-	-	-	-
North Valley Stream (cdp)	37.2	30.9	-	34.1	-	-	-	-	-	-	-	-	-	-	-	-	-	-	-	-	-	-	-	-
Oyster Bay (town)	39.9	35.7	-	34.6	-	-	37.9	-	35.2	-	-	-	-	37.0	36.4	-	-	-	-	-	-	-	-	-
Plainview (cdp)	40.8	37.2	-	30.8	-	-	39.2	-	-	-	-	-	-	-	38.1	-	-	-	-	-	-	-	-	-
Port Washington (cdp)	40.2	38.3	-	31.5	-	-	-	-	-	-	-	-	-	-	-	-	-	-	-	-	-	-	-	-
Salisbury (cdp)	39.2	32.9	-	37.2	-	-	-	-	-	-	-	-	-	-	-	-	-	-	-	-	-	-	-	-
Syosset (cdp)	40.7	37.6	-	33.8	-	-	37.9	-	-	-	-	-	-	-	42.3	-	-	-	-	-	-	-	-	-
Valley Stream (village)	38.8	35.9	-	-	-	-	38.1	-	33.4	-	-	-	-	-	-	-	-	-	-	-	-	-	-	-

Notes: Please refer to the User's Guide for an explanation of data; data is arranged alphabetically by state, then county, then city within each county; table includes counties with populations greater than 49,999 unless noted and cities with populations greater than 9,999 whose Asian and/or NHPI population rates are greater than the national average; (1) Native Hawaiian and other Pacific Islander; (2) excludes Taiwanese; (3) includes Chamorro; (4) county does not meet population threshold but is shown in order to allow inclusion of city

Place	Total population	Total Asian population	Total NHPI[1] population	Asian Indian	Bangladeshi	Cambodian	Chinese[2]	Fijian	Filipino	Guamanian[3]	Hawaiian, Native	Hmong	Indonesian	Japanese	Korean	Laotian	Malaysian	Pakistani	Samoan	Sri Lankan	Taiwanese	Thai	Tongan	Vietnamese
West Hempstead (cdp)	37.5	36.5	-	32.7	-	-	-	-	-	-	-	-	-	-	-	-	-	-	-	-	-	-	-	-
Westbury (village)	37.1	36.2	-	-	-	-	-	-	-	-	-	-	-	-	-	-	-	-	-	-	-	-	-	-
Woodmere (cdp)	40.3	31.2	-	-	-	-	-	-	-	-	-	-	-	-	-	-	-	-	-	-	-	-	-	-
New York City	34.4	33.9	27.5	31.1	29.5	25.8	36.2	-	38.1	24.8	30.6	-	32.2	33.0	33.3	-	38.0	28.0	22.8	35.2	31.2	36.1	-	29.8
New York County (Manhattan)	35.8	33.7	28.3	29.0	26.6	-	36.5	-	39.1	-	-	-	-	33.8	29.2	-	-	28.9	-	-	26.6	34.7	-	30.0
Niagara County	38.3	30.7	-	32.7	-	-	-	-	-	-	-	-	-	-	-	-	-	-	-	-	-	-	-	-
Oneida County	38.2	29.9	-	23.6	-	-	34.9	-	-	-	-	-	-	-	-	-	-	-	-	-	-	-	-	29.2
Onondaga County	36.3	28.6	-	30.3	-	-	29.1	-	34.8	-	-	-	-	35.4	24.2	-	-	-	-	-	-	-	-	29.3
Ontario County	37.9	26.5	-	-	-	-	-	-	-	-	-	-	-	-	-	-	-	-	-	-	-	-	-	-
Orange County	34.9	33.7	-	32.3	-	-	34.1	-	36.6	-	-	-	-	-	28.9	-	-	-	-	-	-	-	-	-
Oswego County	35.0	28.6	-	-	-	-	-	-	-	-	-	-	-	-	-	-	-	-	-	-	-	-	-	-
Otsego County	37.1	22.4	-	-	-	-	-	-	-	-	-	-	-	-	-	-	-	-	-	-	-	-	-	-
Putnam County	37.5	37.6	-	34.5	-	-	41.1	-	-	-	-	-	-	-	-	-	-	-	-	-	-	-	-	-
Queens County (Queens)	35.7	34.4	30.4	31.8	29.9	-	37.0	-	38.8	-	-	-	31.6	31.5	35.3	-	38.1	28.2	-	32.3	36.1	36.5	-	30.4
Rensselaer County	36.8	25.0	-	25.6	-	-	25.8	-	-	-	-	-	-	-	16.6	-	-	-	-	-	-	-	-	-
Richmond Co. (Staten Island)	36.2	36.1	-	32.9	-	-	37.3	-	38.1	-	-	-	-	-	41.3	-	-	26.0	-	42.9	-	-	-	-
Rockland County	36.2	35.5	-	34.2	-	-	35.0	-	38.5	-	-	-	-	-	37.5	-	-	-	-	-	-	-	-	-
Clarkstown (town)	39.1	35.5	-	34.2	-	-	35.4	-	37.7	-	-	-	-	-	36.0	-	-	-	-	-	-	-	-	-
Nanuet (cdp)	37.7	34.6	-	31.1	-	-	-	-	-	-	-	-	-	-	-	-	-	-	-	-	-	-	-	-
New City (cdp)	39.7	35.2	-	35.1	-	-	-	-	34.8	-	-	-	-	-	-	-	-	-	-	-	-	-	-	-
Orangetown (town)	39.1	38.0	-	34.9	-	-	34.1	-	47.4	-	-	-	-	-	38.3	-	-	-	-	-	-	-	-	-
Ramapo (town)	31.7	34.5	-	32.2	-	-	33.9	-	36.4	-	-	-	-	-	35.1	-	-	-	-	-	-	-	-	-
Spring Valley (village)	29.3	32.0	-	30.2	-	-	-	-	-	-	-	-	-	-	-	-	-	-	-	-	-	-	-	-
St. Lawrence County	35.3	24.9	-	-	-	-	-	-	-	-	-	-	-	-	-	-	-	-	-	-	-	-	-	-
Saratoga County	36.8	32.5	-	38.5	-	-	36.5	-	-	-	-	-	-	-	17.6	-	-	-	-	-	-	-	-	-
Schenectady County	38.4	28.6	-	26.8	-	-	35.0	-	-	-	-	-	-	-	-	-	-	-	-	-	-	-	-	-
Niskayuna (town)	42.3	33.8	-	30.7	-	-	-	-	-	-	-	-	-	-	-	-	-	-	-	-	-	-	-	-
Steuben County	38.3	30.6	-	-	-	-	-	-	-	-	-	-	-	-	-	-	-	-	-	-	-	-	-	-
Suffolk County	36.6	31.9	32.8	32.0	-	-	31.3	-	36.6	-	-	-	-	46.5	27.6	-	-	27.1	-	-	39.8	31.3	-	32.5
Coram (cdp)	35.4	33.7	-	-	-	-	34.1	-	-	-	-	-	-	-	-	-	-	-	-	-	-	-	-	-
Dix Hills (cdp)	39.5	38.7	-	35.9	-	-	41.4	-	-	-	-	-	-	-	-	-	-	-	-	-	-	-	-	-
Elwood (cdp)	39.6	39.5	-	-	-	-	-	-	-	-	-	-	-	-	-	-	-	-	-	-	-	-	-	-
Lake Grove (village)	34.8	30.4	-	-	-	-	-	-	-	-	-	-	-	-	-	-	-	-	-	-	-	-	-	-
Melville (cdp)	39.3	38.5	-	-	-	-	-	-	-	-	-	-	-	-	-	-	-	-	-	-	-	-	-	-
Setauket-East Setauket (cdp)	37.1	28.2	-	-	-	-	27.5	-	-	-	-	-	-	-	-	-	-	-	-	-	-	-	-	-
Stony Brook (cdp)	39.0	35.1	-	-	-	-	34.1	-	-	-	-	-	-	-	-	-	-	-	-	-	-	-	-	-
Sullivan County	38.9	37.8	-	-	-	-	-	-	-	-	-	-	-	-	-	-	-	-	-	-	-	-	-	-
Tioga County	38.0	33.8	-	-	-	-	-	-	-	-	-	-	-	-	-	-	-	-	-	-	-	-	-	-
Tompkins County	28.4	22.5	-	23.8	-	-	21.8	-	-	-	-	-	-	25.1	22.5	-	-	-	-	-	-	-	-	-
Ithaca (city)	22.0	21.1	-	21.8	-	-	20.8	-	-	-	-	-	-	-	21.1	-	-	-	-	-	-	-	-	-
Lansing (town)	35.0	30.1	-	-	-	-	-	-	-	-	-	-	-	-	-	-	-	-	-	-	-	-	-	-

Notes: Please refer to the User's Guide for an explanation of data; data is arranged alphabetically by state, then county, then city within each county; table includes counties with populations greater than 49,999 unless noted and cities with populations greater than 9,999 whose Asian and/or NHPI population rates are greater than the national average; (1) Native Hawaiian and other Pacific Islander; (2) excludes Taiwanese; (3) includes Chamorro; (4) county does not meet population threshold but is shown in order to allow inclusion of city

Place	Total population	Total Asian population	Total NHPI[1] population	Asian Indian	Bangladeshi	Cambodian	Chinese[2]	Fijian	Filipino	Guamanian[3]	Hawaiian, Native	Hmong	Indonesian	Japanese	Korean	Laotian	Malaysian	Pakistani	Samoan	Sri Lankan	Taiwanese	Thai	Tongan	Vietnamese
Ulster County	38.2	28.5	-	-	-	-	25.4	-	-	-	-	-	-	-	-	-	-	-	-	-	-	-	-	-
New Paltz (town)	26.5	22.2	-	-	-	-	-	-	-	-	-	-	-	-	-	-	-	-	-	-	-	-	-	-
Warren County	39.0	35.3	-	-	-	-	-	-	-	-	-	-	-	-	-	-	-	-	-	-	-	-	-	-
Wayne County	37.0	27.4	-	-	-	-	-	-	-	-	-	-	-	-	-	-	-	-	-	-	-	-	-	-
Westchester County	37.8	34.8	-	32.6	-	-	37.5	-	35.5	-	-	-	-	35.1	35.8	-	-	28.2	-	-	37.4	43.7	-	-
Dobbs Ferry (village)	38.9	33.5	-	-	-	-	-	-	-	-	-	-	-	-	-	-	-	-	-	-	-	-	-	-
Eastchester (cdp)	42.1	34.9	-	-	-	-	-	-	-	-	-	-	-	33.3	-	-	-	-	-	-	-	-	-	-
Eastchester (town)	40.1	33.0	-	-	-	-	-	-	-	-	-	-	-	32.0	-	-	-	-	-	-	-	-	-	-
Greenburgh (town)	39.9	35.8	-	32.1	-	-	38.1	-	35.6	-	-	-	-	36.4	38.2	-	-	-	-	-	-	-	-	-
Harrison (village)	37.1	32.8	-	-	-	-	-	-	-	-	-	-	-	33.3	-	-	-	-	-	-	-	-	-	-
New Castle (town)	39.4	37.8	-	37.2	-	-	44.5	-	-	-	-	-	-	-	-	-	-	-	-	-	-	-	-	-
New Rochelle (city)	37.3	34.1	-	31.3	-	-	34.8	-	-	-	-	-	-	-	-	-	-	-	-	-	-	-	-	-
North Castle (town)	39.5	37.2	-	-	-	-	-	-	-	-	-	-	-	-	-	-	-	-	-	-	-	-	-	-
Ossining (town)	37.6	33.9	-	33.3	-	-	-	-	-	-	-	-	-	-	-	-	-	-	-	-	-	-	-	-
Ossining (village)	35.8	32.1	-	28.6	-	-	-	-	-	-	-	-	-	-	-	-	-	-	-	-	-	-	-	-
Pelham (town)	38.6	37.8	-	-	-	-	-	-	-	-	-	-	-	-	-	-	-	-	-	-	-	-	-	-
Rye (city)	38.4	37.5	-	-	-	-	-	-	-	-	-	-	-	37.5	-	-	-	-	-	-	-	-	-	-
Scarsdale (village)	39.6	36.2	-	36.1	-	-	42.8	-	-	-	-	-	-	33.2	38.0	-	-	-	-	-	-	-	-	-
Tarrytown (village)	37.4	30.4	-	-	-	-	-	-	-	-	-	-	-	-	-	-	-	-	-	-	-	-	-	-
White Plains (city)	38.0	31.6	-	30.5	-	-	31.8	-	-	-	-	-	-	-	-	-	-	-	-	-	-	-	-	-
Yonkers (city)	36.2	33.8	-	31.8	-	-	41.2	-	35.0	-	-	-	-	-	35.6	-	-	-	-	-	-	-	-	-
NORTH CAROLINA	35.4	30.1	26.3	29.7	-	25.0	32.7	-	32.5	28.0	25.7	16.3	-	37.0	33.4	25.2	-	27.7	25.9	-	36.5	34.7	-	29.2
Alamance County	36.4	30.2	-	-	-	-	-	-	-	-	-	-	-	-	-	-	-	-	-	-	-	-	-	-
Buncombe County	39.0	30.7	-	30.9	-	-	-	-	-	-	-	-	-	-	-	-	-	-	-	-	-	-	-	-
Burke County	36.9	16.4	-	-	-	-	-	-	-	-	-	14.7	-	-	-	18.2	-	-	-	-	-	-	-	-
Cabarrus County	35.5	25.9	-	-	-	-	-	-	-	-	-	-	-	-	-	-	-	-	-	-	-	-	-	-
Catawba County	36.2	21.3	-	-	-	-	-	-	-	-	-	18.0	-	-	-	11.9	-	-	-	-	-	-	-	26.6
Hickory (city)	34.5	21.7	-	-	-	-	-	-	-	-	-	17.9	-	-	-	-	-	-	-	-	-	-	-	-
Cleveland County	36.7	23.6	-	-	-	-	-	-	-	-	-	-	-	-	-	-	-	-	-	-	-	-	-	-
Craven County	34.7	31.9	-	-	-	-	-	-	34.2	-	-	-	-	-	-	-	-	-	-	-	-	-	-	-
Cumberland County	29.7	35.0	25.8	29.9	-	-	-	-	31.9	-	-	-	-	56.1	36.5	-	-	-	-	-	-	-	-	32.7
Davidson County	36.9	26.5	-	-	-	22.6	-	-	-	-	-	-	-	-	-	-	-	-	-	-	-	-	-	-
Durham County	32.3	28.8	-	27.0	-	-	29.4	-	31.7	-	-	-	-	33.0	26.2	-	-	-	-	-	-	-	-	-
Forsyth County	36.0	31.5	-	29.3	-	-	35.2	-	30.6	-	-	-	-	-	-	-	-	-	-	-	-	-	-	30.7
Gaston County	36.4	34.1	-	-	-	-	-	-	-	-	-	-	-	-	-	-	-	-	-	-	-	-	-	29.6
Guilford County	35.1	29.5	-	30.3	-	-	31.3	-	31.1	-	-	-	-	-	36.0	29.0	-	25.3	-	-	-	-	-	27.9
Halifax County	37.2	32.1	-	-	-	-	-	-	-	-	-	-	-	-	-	-	-	-	-	-	-	-	-	-
Harnett County	32.6	33.1	-	-	-	-	-	-	-	-	-	-	-	-	-	-	-	-	-	-	-	-	-	-
Henderson County	42.7	40.5	-	-	-	-	-	-	-	-	-	-	-	-	-	-	-	-	-	-	-	-	-	-
Iredell County	36.7	31.0	-	-	-	-	-	-	-	-	-	-	-	-	-	-	-	-	-	-	-	-	-	-
Johnston County	34.4	23.0	-	-	-	-	-	-	-	-	-	-	-	-	-	-	-	-	-	-	-	-	-	-

Notes: Please refer to the User's Guide for an explanation of data; data is arranged alphabetically by state, then county, then city within each county; table includes counties with populations greater than 49,999 unless noted and cities with populations greater than 9,999 whose Asian and/or NHPI population rates are greater than the national average; (1) Native Hawaiian and other Pacific Islander; (2) excludes Taiwanese; (3) includes Chamorro; (4) county does not meet population threshold but is shown in order to allow inclusion of city

Place	Total population	Total Asian population	Total NHPI[1] population	Asian Indian	Bangladeshi	Cambodian	Chinese[2]	Fijian	Filipino	Guamanian[3]	Hawaiian, Native	Hmong	Indonesian	Japanese	Korean	Laotian	Malaysian	Pakistani	Samoan	Sri Lankan	Taiwanese	Thai	Tongan	Vietnamese
Lenoir County	38.4	29.7	-	-	-	-	-	-	-	-	-	-	-	-	-	-	-	-	-	-	-	-	-	-
Mecklenburg County	33.1	30.8	-	30.8	-	23.3	33.1	-	32.4	-	-	19.4	-	32.0	33.3	32.2	-	-	-	-	-	-	-	30.2
Nash County	36.7	39.1	-	-	-	-	-	-	-	-	-	-	-	-	-	-	-	-	-	-	-	-	-	-
New Hanover County	36.2	31.1	-	-	-	-	-	-	-	-	-	-	-	-	-	-	-	-	-	-	-	-	-	-
Onslow County	25.0	32.6	23.4	-	-	-	-	-	31.4	-	-	-	-	44.5	-	-	-	-	-	-	-	-	-	-
Orange County	30.5	28.2	-	25.1	-	-	33.1	-	-	-	-	-	-	35.5	22.9	-	-	-	-	-	-	-	-	-
Carrboro (town)	27.8	27.9	-	-	-	-	-	-	-	-	-	-	-	-	-	-	-	-	-	-	-	-	-	-
Chapel Hill (town)	24.2	27.4	-	23.6	-	-	32.1	-	-	-	-	-	-	-	22.6	-	-	-	-	-	-	-	-	-
Pitt County	30.5	29.4	-	-	-	-	-	-	-	-	-	-	-	-	-	-	-	-	-	-	-	-	-	-
Randolph County	36.2	32.3	-	-	-	-	-	-	-	-	-	-	-	-	-	-	-	-	-	-	-	-	-	-
Robeson County	32.2	33.8	-	-	-	-	-	-	-	-	-	-	-	-	-	-	-	-	-	-	-	-	-	-
Rowan County	36.4	27.2	-	-	-	-	-	-	-	-	-	-	-	-	-	-	-	-	-	-	-	-	-	-
Stanly County	37.2	17.2	-	-	-	-	-	-	-	-	-	15.9	-	-	-	-	-	-	-	-	-	-	-	-
Surry County	38.1	13.8	-	-	-	-	-	-	-	-	-	-	-	-	-	-	-	-	-	-	-	-	-	-
Union County	34.3	28.6	-	-	-	-	-	-	-	-	-	-	-	-	-	-	-	-	-	-	-	-	-	-
Wake County	32.9	30.7	-	29.7	-	-	33.3	-	32.4	-	-	-	-	33.2	29.4	-	-	26.9	-	-	-	-	-	29.6
Apex (town)	31.6	31.9	-	-	-	-	-	-	-	-	-	-	-	-	-	-	-	-	-	-	-	-	-	-
Cary (town)	33.7	31.6	-	30.4	-	-	35.8	-	-	-	-	-	-	32.6	30.6	-	-	-	-	-	-	-	-	31.6
Wayne County	35.0	36.9	-	-	-	-	-	-	-	-	-	-	-	-	-	-	-	-	-	-	-	-	-	-
Wilkes County	38.4	25.6	-	-	-	-	-	-	-	-	-	-	-	-	-	-	-	-	-	-	-	-	-	-
NORTH DAKOTA	36.2	29.6	-	28.8	-	-	31.1	-	31.2	-	-	-	-	-	29.4	-	-	-	-	-	-	-	-	-
Cass County	31.3	27.2	-	28.8	-	-	-	-	-	-	-	-	-	-	-	-	-	-	-	-	-	-	-	-
Grand Forks County	29.1	31.5	-	-	-	-	-	-	-	-	-	-	-	-	-	-	-	-	-	-	-	-	-	-
Ward County	32.7	32.0	-	-	-	-	-	-	-	-	-	-	-	-	-	-	-	-	-	-	-	-	-	-
OHIO	36.3	30.9	25.8	30.1	30.9	23.7	32.2	-	35.8	27.8	28.3	-	23.1	36.1	30.1	26.3	26.0	27.8	27.8	36.4	30.4	30.1	-	29.0
Allen County	36.3	31.4	-	-	-	-	-	-	-	-	-	-	-	-	-	-	-	-	-	-	-	-	-	-
Ashtabula County	37.4	35.4	-	-	-	-	-	-	-	-	-	-	-	-	-	-	-	-	-	-	-	-	-	-
Athens County	25.5	26.5	-	-	-	-	-	-	-	-	-	-	-	-	-	-	-	-	-	-	-	-	-	-
Athens (city)	21.4	25.0	-	-	-	-	-	-	-	-	-	-	-	-	-	-	-	-	-	-	-	-	-	-
Butler County	34.2	30.1	-	29.3	-	-	30.8	-	35.6	-	-	-	-	-	27.7	-	-	-	-	-	-	-	-	29.0
Clark County	37.6	30.9	-	-	-	-	-	-	-	-	-	-	-	-	-	-	-	-	-	-	-	-	-	-
Clermont County	34.8	33.4	-	33.5	-	-	-	-	-	-	-	-	-	-	-	-	-	-	-	-	-	-	-	-
Columbiana County	38.4	38.5	-	-	-	-	-	-	-	-	-	-	-	-	-	-	-	-	-	-	-	-	-	-
Cuyahoga County	37.3	32.2	-	30.7	-	28.3	33.7	-	38.4	-	-	-	-	37.3	32.8	-	-	-	-	-	-	-	-	30.7
Mayfield Heights (city)	43.9	30.2	-	29.8	-	-	-	-	-	-	-	-	-	-	-	-	-	-	-	-	-	-	-	-
Richmond Heights (city)	40.2	34.1	-	-	-	-	-	-	-	-	-	-	-	-	-	-	-	-	-	-	-	-	-	-
Solon (city)	39.4	39.7	-	41.0	-	-	37.4	-	-	-	-	-	-	-	-	-	-	-	-	-	-	-	-	-
Westlake (city)	41.9	43.2	-	41.2	-	-	-	-	-	-	-	-	-	-	-	-	-	-	-	-	-	-	-	-
Delaware County	35.3	32.2	-	30.6	-	-	35.3	-	-	-	-	-	-	-	-	-	-	-	-	-	-	-	-	-
Fairfield County	36.2	29.7	-	-	-	-	-	-	-	-	-	-	-	-	-	-	-	-	-	-	-	-	-	-
Franklin County	32.6	28.9	24.6	28.6	-	23.7	30.9	-	34.1	-	-	-	22.0	32.4	28.5	27.6	-	25.3	-	-	28.4	29.8	-	28.2

Notes: Please refer to the User's Guide for an explanation of data; data is arranged alphabetically by state, then county, then city within each county; table includes counties with populations greater than 49,999 unless noted and cities with populations greater than 9,999 whose Asian and/or NHPI population rates are greater than the national average; (1) Native Hawaiian and other Pacific Islander; (2) excludes Taiwanese; (3) includes Chamorro; (4) county does not meet population threshold but is shown in order to allow inclusion of city

Place	Total population	Total Asian population	Total NHPI[1] population	Asian Indian	Bangladeshi	Cambodian	Chinese[2]	Fijian	Filipino	Guamanian[3]	Hawaiian, Native	Hmong	Indonesian	Japanese	Korean	Laotian	Malaysian	Pakistani	Samoan	Sri Lankan	Taiwanese	Thai	Tongan	Vietnamese
Dublin (city)	35.4	32.2	-	29.3	-	-	35.1	-	-	-	-	-	-	33.4	-	-	-	-	-	-	-	-	-	-
Hilliard (city)	33.1	34.3	-	-	-	-	-	-	-	-	-	-	-	-	-	-	-	-	-	-	-	-	-	-
Geauga County	38.6	42.6	-	-	-	-	-	-	-	-	-	-	-	-	-	-	-	-	-	-	-	-	-	-
Greene County	35.6	34.4	-	32.9	-	-	31.1	-	-	-	-	-	-	-	37.9	-	-	-	-	-	-	-	-	-
Hamilton County	35.6	30.8	-	29.6	-	26.8	32.9	-	32.3	-	-	-	-	42.4	29.3	-	-	-	-	-	-	-	-	29.2
Blue Ash (city)	39.8	30.3	-	29.4	-	-	-	-	-	-	-	-	-	-	-	-	-	-	-	-	-	-	-	-
Sharonville (city)	39.5	30.5	-	28.6	-	-	-	-	-	-	-	-	-	-	-	-	-	-	-	-	-	-	-	-
Hancock County	35.9	29.3	-	-	-	-	-	-	-	-	-	-	-	-	-	-	-	-	-	-	-	-	-	-
Lake County	38.6	33.2	-	30.4	-	-	33.4	-	-	-	-	-	-	-	-	-	-	-	-	-	-	-	-	-
Licking County	36.7	34.1	-	-	-	-	-	-	-	-	-	-	-	-	-	-	-	-	-	-	-	-	-	-
Lorain County	36.5	33.3	-	35.5	-	-	-	-	38.1	-	-	-	-	-	-	-	-	-	-	-	-	-	-	-
Lucas County	35.2	32.0	-	28.1	-	-	33.6	-	38.3	-	-	-	-	-	33.5	-	-	-	-	-	-	-	-	-
Mahoning County	39.8	31.1	-	-	-	-	-	-	-	-	-	-	-	-	-	-	-	-	-	-	-	-	-	-
Marion County	37.2	33.3	-	-	-	-	-	-	-	-	-	-	-	-	-	-	-	-	-	-	-	-	-	-
Medina County	36.7	31.4	-	32.7	-	-	-	-	-	-	-	-	-	-	-	-	-	-	-	-	-	-	-	-
Miami County	37.8	37.8	-	-	-	-	-	-	-	-	-	-	-	-	-	-	-	-	-	-	-	-	-	-
Montgomery County	36.5	32.7	-	31.5	-	-	35.6	-	37.7	-	-	-	-	40.2	34.6	-	-	-	-	-	-	-	-	29.6
Portage County	34.4	27.7	-	-	-	-	-	-	-	-	-	-	-	-	-	-	-	-	-	-	-	-	-	-
Richland County	37.7	31.6	-	-	-	-	-	-	-	-	-	-	-	-	-	-	-	-	-	-	-	-	-	-
Stark County	38.3	36.9	-	35.1	-	-	31.7	-	-	-	-	-	-	-	-	-	-	-	-	-	-	-	-	-
Summit County	37.1	30.3	-	29.9	-	-	32.9	-	38.4	-	-	-	-	35.9	29.9	22.4	-	-	-	-	-	-	-	27.0
Trumbull County	39.0	37.7	-	-	-	-	-	-	-	-	-	-	-	-	-	-	-	-	-	-	-	-	-	-
Warren County	35.2	30.6	-	29.9	-	-	33.7	-	-	-	-	-	-	-	-	-	-	-	-	-	-	-	-	-
Wayne County	35.5	28.8	-	-	-	-	-	-	-	-	-	-	-	-	-	-	-	-	-	-	-	-	-	-
Wood County	32.7	33.7	-	-	-	-	-	-	-	-	-	-	-	-	-	-	-	-	-	-	-	-	-	-
OKLAHOMA	35.6	30.0	27.3	28.9	-	29.0	30.4	-	34.4	34.9	32.8	17.0	-	33.2	34.3	26.1	23.5	26.3	-	-	30.1	35.4	-	30.1
Canadian County	35.6	30.3	-	30.1	-	-	-	-	-	-	-	-	-	-	-	-	-	-	-	-	-	-	-	28.4
Cleveland County	32.4	27.8	-	23.8	-	-	29.3	-	28.5	-	-	-	-	-	28.9	-	-	-	-	-	-	-	-	28.6
Comanche County	30.2	39.1	-	-	-	-	-	-	32.5	-	-	-	-	-	43.1	-	-	-	-	-	-	-	-	-
Garfield County	37.8	35.8	-	-	-	-	-	-	-	-	-	-	-	-	-	-	-	-	-	-	-	-	-	-
Muskogee County	36.8	33.2	-	-	-	-	-	-	-	-	-	-	-	-	-	-	-	-	-	-	-	-	-	-
Oklahoma County	34.3	30.1	-	30.5	-	-	29.6	-	34.6	-	-	-	-	27.0	34.6	29.3	-	-	-	-	-	35.4	-	31.1
Payne County	27.6	24.8	-	-	-	-	24.5	-	-	-	-	-	-	-	-	-	-	-	-	-	-	-	-	-
Stillwater (city)	24.1	24.8	-	-	-	-	24.5	-	-	-	-	-	-	-	-	-	-	-	-	-	-	-	-	-
Pottawatomie County	35.8	26.4	-	-	-	-	-	-	-	-	-	-	-	-	-	-	-	-	-	-	-	-	-	-
Tulsa County	34.5	30.4	-	29.3	-	-	34.5	-	31.9	-	-	-	-	-	30.8	-	-	24.2	-	-	-	-	-	29.8
Wagoner County	36.4	27.0	-	-	-	-	-	-	-	-	-	-	-	-	-	-	-	-	-	-	-	-	-	-
OREGON	36.4	31.4	27.4	28.8	-	28.4	35.2	31.2	35.2	27.4	32.2	19.1	25.1	37.9	30.0	26.6	-	28.1	24.2	-	28.8	31.5	17.6	30.8
Benton County	31.4	25.7	-	-	-	-	26.5	-	-	-	-	-	-	26.2	22.8	-	-	-	-	-	-	-	-	-
Corvallis (city)	27.2	25.3	-	-	-	-	26.4	-	-	-	-	-	-	-	24.3	-	-	-	-	-	-	-	-	-
Clackamas County	37.6	36.2	28.0	33.9	-	-	38.0	-	33.3	-	-	-	-	45.9	35.5	-	-	-	-	-	-	-	-	30.5

Notes: Please refer to the User's Guide for an explanation of data; data is arranged alphabetically by state, then county, then city within each county; table includes counties with populations greater than 49,999 unless noted and cities with populations greater than 9,999 whose Asian and/or NHPI population rates are greater than the national average; (1) Native Hawaiian and other Pacific Islander; (2) excludes Taiwanese; (3) includes Chamorro; (4) county does not meet population threshold but is shown in order to allow inclusion of city

Place	Total population	Total Asian population	Total NHPI[1] population	Asian Indian	Bangladeshi	Cambodian	Chinese[2]	Fijian	Filipino	Guamanian[3]	Hawaiian, Native	Hmong	Indonesian	Japanese	Korean	Laotian	Malaysian	Pakistani	Samoan	Sri Lankan	Taiwanese	Thai	Tongan	Vietnamese
Lake Oswego (city)	41.3	35.8	-	-	-	-	42.4	-	-	-	-	-	-	-	-	-	-	-	-	-	-	-	-	-
Coos County	43.1	33.1	-	-	-	-	-	-	-	-	-	-	-	-	-	-	-	-	-	-	-	-	-	-
Deschutes County	38.4	32.4	-	-	-	-	-	-	-	-	-	-	-	-	-	-	-	-	-	-	-	-	-	-
Douglas County	41.4	36.8	-	-	-	-	-	-	-	-	-	-	-	-	-	-	-	-	-	-	-	-	-	-
Jackson County	39.3	32.5	-	-	-	-	-	-	-	-	-	-	-	-	-	-	-	-	-	-	-	-	-	-
Josephine County	43.0	36.5	-	-	-	-	-	-	-	-	-	-	-	-	-	-	-	-	-	-	-	-	-	-
Klamath County	38.0	30.8	-	-	-	-	-	-	-	-	-	-	-	-	-	-	-	-	-	-	-	-	-	-
Lane County	36.8	26.4	26.3	24.9	-	-	26.2	-	33.0	-	-	-	-	28.9	25.2	-	-	-	-	-	-	-	-	-
Linn County	37.5	29.8	-	-	-	-	-	-	-	-	-	-	-	-	-	-	-	-	-	-	-	-	-	-
Marion County	33.8	33.9	25.8	28.8	-	-	40.1	-	43.6	-	-	-	-	26.5	27.7	-	-	-	-	-	-	-	-	33.1
Salem (city)	33.9	31.6	26.8	-	-	-	38.6	-	43.7	-	-	-	-	24.2	-	-	-	-	-	-	-	-	-	33.4
Multnomah County	35.0	31.4	25.0	28.5	-	25.4	35.9	-	35.9	-	28.9	19.4	-	38.0	31.9	26.1	-	-	-	-	-	29.7	16.1	30.8
Portland (city)	35.2	31.3	24.8	28.7	-	24.6	35.7	-	35.8	-	28.4	19.6	-	36.7	32.2	26.6	-	-	-	-	-	29.2	15.8	30.8
Polk County	36.5	28.3	-	-	-	-	-	-	-	-	-	-	-	-	-	-	-	-	-	-	-	-	-	-
Umatilla County	34.9	27.6	-	-	-	-	-	-	-	-	-	-	-	-	-	-	-	-	-	-	-	-	-	-
Washington County	33.1	31.2	29.1	28.8	-	30.1	34.2	-	33.5	-	29.9	-	-	35.6	35.0	28.4	-	-	-	-	-	-	-	31.0
Aloha (cdp)	31.4	31.3	-	-	-	-	-	-	33.5	-	-	-	-	-	-	-	-	-	-	-	-	-	-	30.6
Beaverton (city)	32.7	31.5	-	28.5	-	30.0	37.5	-	33.9	-	-	-	-	37.1	37.8	-	-	-	-	-	-	-	-	32.8
Cedar Mill (cdp)	35.9	36.8	-	-	-	-	-	-	-	-	-	-	-	-	-	-	-	-	-	-	-	-	-	-
Hillsboro (city)	29.8	28.9	-	28.1	-	-	30.1	-	-	-	-	-	-	-	30.6	-	-	-	-	-	-	-	-	31.2
Tigard (city)	34.5	32.2	-	-	-	-	34.9	-	-	-	-	-	-	-	-	-	-	-	-	-	-	-	-	31.3
Tualatin (city)	32.1	27.8	-	-	-	-	-	-	-	-	-	-	-	-	-	-	-	-	-	-	-	-	-	-
Yamhill County	33.9	32.7	-	-	-	-	-	-	-	-	-	-	-	-	-	-	-	-	-	-	-	-	-	-
PENNSYLVANIA	38.0	30.1	27.6	29.7	28.7	22.8	31.1	-	34.4	24.1	30.4	19.8	29.6	33.9	29.9	27.8	-	28.6	30.3	36.7	29.0	30.0	-	29.9
Adams County	37.1	30.9	-	-	-	-	-	-	-	-	-	-	-	-	-	-	-	-	-	-	-	-	-	-
Allegheny County	39.7	29.2	33.2	29.4	-	-	31.0	-	33.3	-	-	-	-	30.8	27.4	-	-	-	-	-	27.1	-	-	29.1
Muni. of Monroeville (borough)	42.4	32.8	-	31.1	-	-	-	-	-	-	-	-	-	-	-	-	-	-	-	-	-	-	-	-
Scott (township)	41.7	27.9	-	28.0	-	-	-	-	-	-	-	-	-	-	-	-	-	-	-	-	-	-	-	-
Scott Township (cdp)	41.7	27.9	-	28.0	-	-	-	-	-	-	-	-	-	-	-	-	-	-	-	-	-	-	-	-
Upper St. Clair (township)	41.6	38.6	-	37.7	-	-	-	-	-	-	-	-	-	-	-	-	-	-	-	-	-	-	-	-
Beaver County	40.6	34.8	-	-	-	-	-	-	-	-	-	-	-	-	-	-	-	-	-	-	-	-	-	-
Berks County	37.5	32.0	-	37.8	-	-	30.3	-	-	-	-	-	-	-	32.5	-	-	-	-	-	-	-	-	27.8
Blair County	39.5	32.2	-	-	-	-	-	-	-	-	-	-	-	-	-	-	-	-	-	-	-	-	-	-
Bradford County	39.0	32.4	-	-	-	-	-	-	-	-	-	-	-	-	-	-	-	-	-	-	-	-	-	-
Bucks County	37.7	32.5	-	31.7	-	-	34.7	-	35.9	-	-	-	-	-	31.9	-	-	-	-	-	-	-	-	33.0
Bensalem (township)	36.5	31.4	-	31.5	-	-	-	-	-	-	-	-	-	-	30.9	-	-	-	-	-	-	-	-	-
Lower Makefield (township)	39.2	33.5	-	37.9	-	-	-	-	-	-	-	-	-	-	-	-	-	-	-	-	-	-	-	-
Newtown (township)	36.8	32.8	-	-	-	-	-	-	-	-	-	-	-	-	-	-	-	-	-	-	-	-	-	-
Butler County	37.7	34.1	-	33.5	-	-	-	-	-	-	-	-	-	-	-	-	-	-	-	-	-	-	-	-
Cambria County	41.2	35.7	-	-	-	-	-	-	-	-	-	-	-	-	-	-	-	-	-	-	-	-	-	-
Centre County	28.6	25.6	-	24.4	-	-	26.7	-	-	-	-	-	-	-	25.6	-	-	-	-	-	-	-	-	-

Notes: Please refer to the User's Guide for an explanation of data; data is arranged alphabetically by state, then county, then city within each county; table includes counties with populations greater than 49,999 unless noted and cities with populations greater than 9,999 whose Asian and/or NHPI population rates are greater than the national average; (1) Native Hawaiian and other Pacific Islander; (2) excludes Taiwanese; (3) includes Chamorro; (4) county does not meet population threshold but is shown in order to allow inclusion of city

Place	Total population	Total Asian population	Total NHPI[1] population	Asian Indian	Bangladeshi	Cambodian	Chinese[2]	Fijian	Filipino	Guamanian[3]	Hawaiian, Native	Hmong	Indonesian	Japanese	Korean	Laotian	Malaysian	Pakistani	Samoan	Sri Lankan	Taiwanese	Thai	Tongan	Vietnamese
Ferguson (township)	31.6	30.3	-	-	-	-	-	-	-	-	-	-	-	-	-	-	-	-	-	-	-	-	-	-
Patton (township)	28.2	29.5	-	-	-	-	-	-	-	-	-	-	-	-	-	-	-	-	-	-	-	-	-	-
State College (borough)	21.8	23.9	-	23.4	-	-	26.0	-	-	-	-	-	-	-	22.7	-	-	-	-	-	-	-	-	-
Chester County	37.0	32.7	-	30.6	-	-	36.1	-	34.2	-	-	-	-	39.8	29.1	-	-	-	-	-	-	-	-	34.1
Tredyffrin (township)	40.0	33.4	-	27.8	-	-	36.2	-	-	-	-	-	-	-	-	-	-	-	-	-	-	-	-	-
West Goshen (township)	36.5	32.0	-	-	-	-	-	-	-	-	-	-	-	-	-	-	-	-	-	-	-	-	-	-
West Whiteland (township)	35.1	32.9	-	-	-	-	-	-	-	-	-	-	-	-	-	-	-	-	-	-	-	-	-	-
Clearfield County	39.3	39.6	-	-	-	-	-	-	-	-	-	-	-	-	-	-	-	-	-	-	-	-	-	-
Columbia County	37.5	30.6	-	-	-	-	-	-	-	-	-	-	-	-	-	-	-	-	-	-	-	-	-	-
Crawford County	37.9	37.7	-	-	-	-	-	-	-	-	-	-	-	-	-	-	-	-	-	-	-	-	-	-
Cumberland County	38.1	33.8	-	33.7	-	-	37.3	-	-	-	-	-	-	-	36.8	-	-	-	-	-	-	-	-	32.2
Hampden (township)	40.5	36.2	-	-	-	-	-	-	-	-	-	-	-	-	-	-	-	-	-	-	-	-	-	-
Dauphin County	37.9	30.9	-	30.9	-	-	31.7	-	-	-	-	-	-	-	27.6	-	-	-	-	-	-	-	-	30.6
Derry (township)	40.6	32.6	-	-	-	-	-	-	-	-	-	-	-	-	-	-	-	-	-	-	-	-	-	-
Hershey (cdp)	42.9	33.1	-	-	-	-	-	-	-	-	-	-	-	-	-	-	-	-	-	-	-	-	-	-
Delaware County	37.4	31.6	-	30.9	-	-	33.7	-	31.1	-	-	-	-	30.9	34.0	-	-	29.0	-	-	-	-	-	30.0
Broomall (cdp)	42.4	38.0	-	-	-	-	-	-	-	-	-	-	-	-	38.6	-	-	-	-	-	-	-	-	-
Drexel Hill (cdp)	36.7	31.2	-	-	-	-	33.6	-	-	-	-	-	-	-	-	-	-	-	-	-	-	-	-	-
Marple (township)	43.5	39.4	-	-	-	-	-	-	-	-	-	-	-	-	40.0	-	-	-	-	-	-	-	-	-
Radnor (township)	31.7	32.1	-	-	-	-	37.9	-	-	-	-	-	-	-	-	-	-	-	-	-	-	-	-	-
Upper Darby (township)	35.3	31.1	-	28.8	-	-	33.3	-	-	-	-	-	-	-	33.1	-	-	-	-	-	-	-	-	30.2
Erie County	36.3	28.3	-	26.9	-	-	-	-	-	-	-	-	-	-	-	-	-	-	-	-	-	-	-	-
Franklin County	38.2	25.3	-	-	-	-	-	-	-	-	-	-	-	-	-	-	-	-	-	-	-	-	-	-
Indiana County	36.4	28.9	-	-	-	-	-	-	-	-	-	-	-	-	-	-	-	-	-	-	-	-	-	-
Lackawanna County	40.4	30.8	-	30.4	-	-	-	-	-	-	-	-	-	-	-	-	-	-	-	-	-	-	-	-
Lancaster County	36.1	29.2	-	29.4	-	-	32.8	-	-	-	-	18.2	-	-	20.5	-	-	-	-	-	-	-	-	30.3
Lawrence County	40.4	30.2	-	-	-	-	-	-	-	-	-	-	-	-	-	-	-	-	-	-	-	-	-	-
Lebanon County	38.5	36.0	-	-	-	-	-	-	-	-	-	-	-	-	-	-	-	-	-	-	-	-	-	-
Lehigh County	38.3	31.2	-	31.1	-	-	31.9	-	-	-	-	-	-	-	27.6	-	-	-	-	-	-	-	-	29.0
Fullerton (cdp)	39.4	31.9	-	-	-	-	-	-	-	-	-	-	-	-	-	-	-	-	-	-	-	-	-	-
Lower Macungie (township)	41.3	38.5	-	-	-	-	36.6	-	-	-	-	-	-	-	-	-	-	-	-	-	-	-	-	-
Upper Macungie (township)	38.7	36.7	-	-	-	-	-	-	-	-	-	-	-	-	-	-	-	-	-	-	-	-	-	-
Luzerne County	40.9	30.2	-	35.6	-	-	-	-	-	-	-	-	-	-	-	-	-	-	-	-	-	-	-	-
Lycoming County	38.2	31.1	-	-	-	-	-	-	-	-	-	-	-	-	-	-	-	-	-	-	-	-	-	-
Mercer County	39.6	30.9	-	-	-	-	-	-	-	-	-	-	-	-	-	-	-	-	-	-	-	-	-	-
Monroe County	37.3	32.6	-	29.3	-	-	-	-	-	-	-	-	-	-	-	-	-	-	-	-	-	-	-	-
Montgomery County	38.1	32.5	-	29.8	-	-	35.3	-	33.1	-	-	-	-	39.8	34.3	-	-	-	-	-	-	-	-	30.3
Cheltenham (township)	40.1	32.7	-	-	-	-	-	-	-	-	-	-	-	-	32.8	-	-	-	-	-	-	-	-	-
East Norriton (township)	42.3	31.6	-	-	-	-	-	-	-	-	-	-	-	-	-	-	-	-	-	-	-	-	-	-
Hatfield (township)	36.6	31.9	-	32.7	-	-	-	-	-	-	-	-	-	-	-	-	-	-	-	-	-	-	-	-
Horsham (township)	35.6	33.5	-	-	-	-	-	-	-	-	-	-	-	-	34.7	-	-	-	-	-	-	-	-	-

Notes: Please refer to the User's Guide for an explanation of data; data is arranged alphabetically by state, then county, then city within each county; table includes counties with populations greater than 49,999 unless noted and cities with populations greater than 9,999 whose Asian and/or NHPI population rates are greater than the national average; (1) Native Hawaiian and other Pacific Islander; (2) excludes Taiwanese; (3) includes Chamorro; (4) county does not meet population threshold but is shown in order to allow inclusion of city

Place	Total population	Total Asian population	Total NHPI[1] population	Asian Indian	Bangladeshi	Cambodian	Chinese[2]	Fijian	Filipino	Guamanian[3]	Hawaiian, Native	Hmong	Indonesian	Japanese	Korean	Laotian	Malaysian	Pakistani	Samoan	Sri Lankan	Taiwanese	Thai	Tongan	Vietnamese
King of Prussia (cdp)	37.1	30.7	-	29.3	-	-	31.6	-	-	-	-	-	-	-	-	-	-	-	-	-	-	-	-	-
Lansdale (borough)	36.7	30.4	-	30.2	-	-	-	-	-	-	-	-	-	-	-	-	-	-	-	-	-	-	-	-
Lower Gwynedd (township)	44.2	40.2	-	-	-	-	-	-	-	-	-	-	-	-	-	-	-	-	-	-	-	-	-	-
Lower Providence (township)	36.6	33.0	-	-	-	-	34.0	-	-	-	-	-	-	-	-	-	-	-	-	-	-	-	-	-
Montgomery (township)	37.2	37.8	-	31.7	-	-	-	-	-	-	-	-	-	-	40.1	-	-	-	-	-	-	-	-	-
Montgomeryville (cdp)	36.8	34.4	-	-	-	-	-	-	-	-	-	-	-	-	-	-	-	-	-	-	-	-	-	-
Plymouth (township)	41.1	36.6	-	-	-	-	-	-	-	-	-	-	-	-	39.0	-	-	-	-	-	-	-	-	-
Towamencin (township)	37.3	31.9	-	-	-	-	-	-	-	-	-	-	-	-	-	-	-	-	-	-	-	-	-	-
Upper Dublin (township)	40.8	37.8	-	-	-	-	-	-	-	-	-	-	-	-	32.5	-	-	-	-	-	-	-	-	-
Upper Gwynedd (township)	39.6	33.6	-	-	-	-	33.8	-	-	-	-	-	-	-	-	-	-	-	-	-	-	-	-	-
Upper Merion (township)	38.0	30.8	-	29.0	-	-	32.3	-	-	-	-	-	-	-	-	-	-	-	-	-	-	-	-	-
Whitpain (township)	40.9	38.3	-	-	-	-	-	-	-	-	-	-	-	-	40.0	-	-	-	-	-	-	-	-	-
Northampton County	38.5	29.6	-	31.3	-	-	26.5	-	-	-	-	-	-	-	23.0	-	-	-	-	-	-	-	-	26.1
Northumberland County	40.6	33.8	-	-	-	-	-	-	-	-	-	-	-	-	-	-	-	-	-	-	-	-	-	-
Philadelphia County	34.3	28.5	24.7	27.1	-	21.1	29.4	-	34.8	-	-	-	-	30.8	28.9	27.5	-	31.3	-	-	-	-	-	29.7
Philadelphia (city)	34.3	28.5	24.7	27.1	-	21.1	29.4	-	34.8	-	-	-	-	30.8	28.9	27.5	-	31.3	-	-	-	-	-	29.7
Schuylkill County	40.8	35.6	-	-	-	-	-	-	-	-	-	-	-	-	-	-	-	-	-	-	-	-	-	-
Washington County	40.8	28.9	-	-	-	-	-	-	-	-	-	-	-	-	-	-	-	-	-	-	-	-	-	-
Westmoreland County	41.3	32.1	-	30.1	-	-	-	-	-	-	-	-	-	-	-	-	-	-	-	-	-	-	-	-
York County	37.8	31.0	-	31.7	-	-	30.3	-	-	-	-	-	-	-	21.5	-	-	-	-	-	-	-	-	31.5
RHODE ISLAND	36.8	27.2	24.4	27.9	-	21.4	28.4	-	36.0	-	-	17.8	-	40.0	24.7	27.8	-	-	-	-	-	-	-	26.6
Bristol County	39.2	24.7	-	-	-	-	-	-	-	-	-	-	-	-	-	-	-	-	-	-	-	-	-	-
Kent County	38.9	32.3	-	-	-	-	31.7	-	-	-	-	-	-	-	25.3	-	-	-	-	-	-	-	-	-
Newport County	38.5	31.9	-	-	-	-	-	-	31.8	-	-	-	-	-	-	-	-	-	-	-	-	-	-	-
Providence County	35.6	26.3	-	26.6	-	21.8	27.2	-	35.2	-	-	16.4	-	-	24.9	28.0	-	-	-	-	-	-	-	27.0
Providence (city)	28.4	23.2	-	24.0	-	20.7	23.1	-	35.0	-	-	12.6	-	-	22.6	28.6	-	-	-	-	-	-	-	-
Woonsocket (city)	34.8	27.5	-	-	-	-	-	-	-	-	-	-	-	-	-	29.7	-	-	-	-	-	-	-	-
Washington County	37.4	31.3	-	-	-	-	32.3	-	-	-	-	-	-	-	-	-	-	-	-	-	-	-	-	-
SOUTH CAROLINA	35.6	31.7	31.7	29.6	-	25.4	32.1	-	34.7	31.7	35.2	14.9	-	39.2	34.8	25.7	-	-	-	-	-	45.6	-	30.0
Aiken County	36.6	38.5	-	-	-	-	-	-	-	-	-	-	-	-	-	-	-	-	-	-	-	-	-	-
Anderson County	37.4	29.9	-	-	-	-	-	-	-	-	-	-	-	-	-	-	-	-	-	-	-	-	-	-
Beaufort County	36.0	28.7	-	-	-	-	-	-	-	-	-	-	-	-	-	-	-	-	-	-	-	-	-	-
Berkeley County	32.0	38.6	-	-	-	-	-	-	40.5	-	-	-	-	-	-	-	-	-	-	-	-	-	-	-
Charleston County	34.7	30.9	-	26.4	-	-	33.0	-	28.6	-	-	-	-	-	-	-	-	-	-	-	-	-	-	-
Dorchester County	34.9	36.6	-	-	-	-	-	-	44.0	-	-	-	-	-	-	-	-	-	-	-	-	-	-	-
Florence County	35.7	35.3	-	-	-	-	-	-	-	-	-	-	-	-	-	-	-	-	-	-	-	-	-	-
Greenville County	35.6	31.2	-	29.4	-	-	30.6	-	31.7	-	-	-	-	-	-	-	-	-	-	-	-	-	-	30.8
Greenwood County	35.4	31.1	-	-	-	-	-	-	-	-	-	-	-	-	-	-	-	-	-	-	-	-	-	-
Horry County	38.5	35.0	-	-	-	-	-	-	-	-	-	-	-	-	-	-	-	-	-	-	-	-	-	-
Lexington County	35.8	32.0	-	32.2	-	-	28.6	-	-	-	-	-	-	-	-	-	-	-	-	-	-	-	-	-
Oconee County	39.2	36.0	-	-	-	-	-	-	-	-	-	-	-	-	-	-	-	-	-	-	-	-	-	-

Notes: Please refer to the User's Guide for an explanation of data; data is arranged alphabetically by state, then county, then city within each county; table includes counties with populations greater than 49,999 unless noted and cities with populations greater than 9,999 whose Asian and/or NHPI population rates are greater than the national average; (1) Native Hawaiian and other Pacific Islander; (2) excludes Taiwanese; (3) includes Chamorro; (4) county does not meet population threshold but is shown in order to allow inclusion of city

Place	Total population	Total Asian population	Total NHPI[1] population	Asian Indian	Bangladeshi	Cambodian	Chinese[2]	Fijian	Filipino	Guamanian[3]	Hawaiian, Native	Hmong	Indonesian	Japanese	Korean	Laotian	Malaysian	Pakistani	Samoan	Sri Lankan	Taiwanese	Thai	Tongan	Vietnamese
Pickens County	32.8	26.0	-	23.6	-	-	30.6	-	-	-	-	-	-	-	-	-	-	-	-	-	-	-	-	-
Clemson (city)	24.6	24.3	-	-	-	-	-	-	-	-	-	-	-	-	-	-	-	-	-	-	-	-	-	-
Richland County	32.7	29.6	-	25.5	-	-	31.2	-	28.8	-	-	-	-	-	33.6	-	-	-	-	-	-	-	-	25.9
Spartanburg County	36.0	28.4	-	37.3	-	-	-	-	-	-	-	14.7	-	-	-	24.9	-	-	-	-	-	-	-	-
Sumter County	33.6	34.2	-	-	-	-	-	-	-	-	-	-	-	-	-	-	-	-	-	-	-	-	-	-
York County	34.9	30.2	-	-	-	-	-	-	-	-	-	-	-	-	-	-	-	-	-	-	-	-	-	28.8
SOUTH DAKOTA	35.6	27.6	-	25.6	-	-	31.0	-	34.9	-	-	-	-	28.0	16.1	24.5	-	-	-	-	-	-	-	27.3
Minnehaha County	33.5	25.5	-	-	-	-	-	-	-	-	-	-	-	-	-	-	-	-	-	-	-	-	-	27.1
Pennington County	35.1	26.9	-	-	-	-	-	-	-	-	-	-	-	-	-	-	-	-	-	-	-	-	-	-
TENNESSEE	36.0	30.5	28.7	29.7	-	25.5	33.0	-	33.0	25.2	33.9	-	-	33.1	33.5	29.8	-	23.5	29.3	-	30.5	29.9	-	28.1
Anderson County	39.9	36.1	-	-	-	-	-	-	-	-	-	-	-	-	-	-	-	-	-	-	-	-	-	-
Blount County	38.3	29.8	-	-	-	-	-	-	-	-	-	-	-	-	-	-	-	-	-	-	-	-	-	-
Bradley County	35.6	37.7	-	-	-	-	-	-	-	-	-	-	-	-	-	-	-	-	-	-	-	-	-	-
Davidson County	34.2	29.3	21.5	29.6	-	-	28.8	-	32.5	-	-	-	-	30.5	31.6	27.7	-	-	-	-	-	-	-	28.0
Hamilton County	37.5	31.4	-	31.7	-	-	-	-	39.2	-	-	-	-	-	29.3	-	-	-	-	-	-	-	-	30.1
Knox County	36.1	29.6	-	29.6	-	-	32.8	-	-	-	-	-	-	-	27.2	-	-	-	-	-	-	-	-	26.2
Madison County	34.8	29.8	-	-	-	-	-	-	-	-	-	-	-	-	-	-	-	-	-	-	-	-	-	-
Montgomery County	29.9	35.7	-	-	-	-	-	-	-	-	-	-	-	-	41.4	-	-	-	-	-	-	-	-	-
Putnam County	34.4	25.9	-	-	-	-	-	-	-	-	-	-	-	-	-	-	-	-	-	-	-	-	-	-
Rutherford County	31.4	32.6	-	-	-	-	-	-	-	-	-	-	-	-	-	30.9	-	-	-	-	-	-	-	-
Shelby County	33.1	30.2	33.0	28.0	-	34.9	35.1	-	33.9	-	-	-	-	34.5	32.1	-	-	-	-	-	-	-	-	27.5
Germantown (city)	41.4	36.9	-	34.4	-	-	41.5	-	-	-	-	-	-	-	-	-	-	-	-	-	-	-	-	-
Sullivan County	39.9	29.8	-	-	-	-	-	-	-	-	-	-	-	-	-	-	-	-	-	-	-	-	-	-
Sumner County	36.3	41.5	-	-	-	-	-	-	-	-	-	-	-	-	-	-	-	-	-	-	-	-	-	-
Washington County	37.0	29.8	-	-	-	-	-	-	-	-	-	-	-	-	-	-	-	-	-	-	-	-	-	-
Weakley County[4]	34.9	26.7	-	-	-	-	-	-	-	-	-	-	-	-	-	-	-	-	-	-	-	-	-	-
Martin (city)	26.7	26.6	-	-	-	-	-	-	-	-	-	-	-	-	-	-	-	-	-	-	-	-	-	-
Williamson County	36.4	30.9	-	-	-	-	-	-	-	-	-	-	-	-	-	-	-	-	-	-	-	-	-	-
Wilson County	36.3	32.9	-	-	-	-	-	-	-	-	-	-	-	-	-	-	-	-	-	-	-	-	-	-
TEXAS	32.5	31.5	27.1	30.1	30.1	27.2	33.9	-	34.2	28.9	30.1	-	28.5	37.2	33.4	29.0	32.6	29.2	22.2	35.1	32.7	34.8	24.7	30.5
Anderson County	35.8	31.4	-	-	-	-	-	-	-	-	-	-	-	-	-	-	-	-	-	-	-	-	-	-
Angelina County	34.4	30.1	-	-	-	-	-	-	-	-	-	-	-	-	-	-	-	-	-	-	-	-	-	-
Bell County	29.2	36.2	25.7	34.2	-	-	-	-	31.3	35.6	-	-	-	52.5	41.7	-	-	-	-	-	-	-	-	-
Killeen (city)	26.6	36.6	25.4	-	-	-	-	-	32.1	39.2	-	-	-	-	41.6	-	-	-	-	-	-	-	-	-
Bexar County	32.3	34.9	28.4	31.4	-	-	36.0	-	34.1	-	37.9	-	-	42.1	39.1	29.7	-	-	-	-	-	39.4	-	35.2
Bowie County	36.3	43.1	-	-	-	-	-	-	-	-	-	-	-	-	-	-	-	-	-	-	-	-	-	-
Brazoria County	34.2	32.5	-	34.2	-	25.8	31.8	-	38.2	-	-	-	-	-	-	-	-	-	-	-	-	-	-	30.1
Brazos County	23.6	26.0	-	24.2	-	-	28.1	-	-	-	-	-	-	-	28.8	-	-	-	-	-	-	-	-	23.5
College Station (city)	21.9	25.9	-	24.2	-	-	27.7	-	-	-	-	-	-	-	28.6	-	-	-	-	-	-	-	-	-
Calhoun County[4]	35.6	33.9	-	-	-	-	-	-	-	-	-	-	-	-	-	-	-	-	-	-	-	-	-	29.5
Port Lavaca (city)	31.8	34.3	-	-	-	-	-	-	-	-	-	-	-	-	-	-	-	-	-	-	-	-	-	-

Notes: Please refer to the User's Guide for an explanation of data; data is arranged alphabetically by state, then county, then city within each county; table includes counties with populations greater than 49,999 unless noted and cities with populations greater than 9,999 whose Asian and/or NHPI population rates are greater than the national average; (1) Native Hawaiian and other Pacific Islander; (2) excludes Taiwanese; (3) includes Chamorro; (4) county does not meet population threshold but is shown in order to allow inclusion of city

Place	Total population	Total Asian population	Total NHPI[1] population	Asian Indian	Bangladeshi	Cambodian	Chinese[2]	Fijian	Filipino	Guamanian[3]	Hawaiian, Native	Hmong	Indonesian	Japanese	Korean	Laotian	Malaysian	Pakistani	Samoan	Sri Lankan	Taiwanese	Thai	Tongan	Vietnamese
Cameron County	29.2	34.8	-	-	-	-	-	-	33.3	-	-	-	-	-	-	-	-	-	-	-	-	-	-	-
Collin County	33.1	32.2	-	29.8	-	-	35.0	-	32.9	-	-	-	-	36.0	31.7	-	-	29.7	-	-	34.1	36.4	-	31.2
Allen (city)	31.4	31.5	-	29.0	-	-	-	-	-	-	-	-	-	-	-	-	-	-	-	-	-	-	-	32.3
Plano (city)	34.3	32.9	-	31.2	-	-	34.9	-	33.3	-	-	-	-	35.7	33.3	-	-	29.1	-	-	34.8	-	-	31.2
Comal County	38.8	35.5	-	-	-	-	-	-	-	-	-	-	-	-	-	-	-	-	-	-	-	-	-	-
Coryell County	27.6	33.2	24.1	-	-	-	-	-	-	-	-	-	-	-	42.1	-	-	-	-	-	-	-	-	-
Dallas County	31.3	31.0	27.4	29.6	29.0	24.9	32.8	-	36.7	-	-	-	-	36.4	35.3	27.0	-	28.9	-	-	31.2	36.8	-	30.2
Addison (town)	31.5	30.6	-	29.9	-	-	-	-	-	-	-	-	-	-	-	-	-	-	-	-	-	-	-	-
Coppell (city)	33.4	32.5	-	31.4	-	-	37.3	-	-	-	-	-	-	-	35.8	-	-	-	-	-	-	-	-	-
Farmers Branch (city)	34.2	30.6	-	-	-	-	-	-	-	-	-	-	-	-	-	-	-	-	-	-	-	-	-	-
Garland (city)	31.9	31.8	-	31.7	-	-	35.5	-	39.4	-	-	-	-	-	35.2	-	-	27.0	-	-	-	-	-	30.5
Grand Prairie (city)	30.7	31.1	-	32.4	-	-	-	-	31.1	-	-	-	-	-	-	20.4	-	-	-	-	-	-	-	29.5
Irving (city)	30.3	29.8	-	28.2	-	-	31.2	-	40.1	-	-	-	-	33.9	32.3	27.2	-	29.7	-	-	-	-	-	30.5
Mesquite (city)	32.2	33.2	-	32.3	-	-	-	-	35.5	-	-	-	-	-	-	-	-	-	-	-	-	-	-	-
Richardson (city)	36.0	32.5	-	28.0	-	-	35.7	-	39.3	-	-	-	-	-	39.3	-	-	32.1	-	-	-	-	-	31.4
Rowlett (city)	33.2	34.2	-	31.2	-	-	-	-	-	-	-	-	-	-	-	-	-	-	-	-	-	-	-	-
Denton County	31.2	30.0	-	29.3	-	28.8	30.8	-	34.9	-	-	-	-	30.7	30.1	-	-	24.5	-	-	-	-	-	29.9
Carrollton (city)	33.3	32.1	-	32.1	-	25.2	32.6	-	-	-	-	-	-	-	33.9	-	-	24.5	-	-	-	-	-	31.7
Lewisville (city)	29.9	30.6	-	30.0	-	-	-	-	-	-	-	-	-	-	-	-	-	-	-	-	-	-	-	30.5
Ector County	32.3	30.8	-	-	-	-	-	-	-	-	-	-	-	-	-	-	-	-	-	-	-	-	-	-
El Paso County	30.2	35.1	28.5	33.0	-	-	31.7	-	33.3	-	-	-	-	51.7	38.2	-	-	-	-	-	-	-	-	-
Ellis County	33.4	35.6	-	-	-	-	-	-	-	-	-	-	-	-	-	-	-	-	-	-	-	-	-	-
Fort Bend County	33.6	34.8	-	33.7	-	-	37.7	-	34.3	-	-	-	-	-	33.7	-	-	30.1	-	-	37.3	-	-	32.8
Cinco Ranch (cdp)	36.0	33.9	-	-	-	-	-	-	-	-	-	-	-	-	-	-	-	-	-	-	-	-	-	-
Mission Bend (cdp)	32.0	34.4	-	37.5	-	-	37.8	-	32.9	-	-	-	-	-	-	-	-	31.1	-	-	-	-	-	33.2
Missouri City (city)	35.8	36.1	-	36.8	-	-	36.0	-	39.9	-	-	-	-	-	-	-	-	-	-	-	-	-	-	34.0
New Territory (cdp)	30.8	32.6	-	30.1	-	-	36.9	-	-	-	-	-	-	-	-	-	-	-	-	-	-	-	-	-
Stafford (city)	31.4	31.1	-	27.2	-	-	38.2	-	23.7	-	-	-	-	-	-	-	-	-	-	-	-	-	-	32.5
Sugar Land (city)	37.6	37.0	-	35.3	-	-	39.8	-	37.5	-	-	-	-	-	39.9	-	-	28.2	-	-	39.9	-	-	33.6
Galveston County	35.9	32.6	-	31.7	-	-	36.8	-	41.1	-	-	-	-	-	-	-	-	-	-	-	-	-	-	29.5
Grayson County	37.5	34.0	-	-	-	-	-	-	-	-	-	-	-	-	-	-	-	-	-	-	-	-	-	-
Gregg County	35.2	28.4	-	-	-	-	-	-	-	-	-	-	-	-	-	-	-	-	-	-	-	-	-	-
Guadalupe County	35.3	33.5	-	-	-	-	-	-	-	-	-	-	-	-	-	-	-	-	-	-	-	-	-	-
Harris County	31.4	32.4	28.3	30.8	31.2	31.3	35.8	-	34.8	28.9	-	-	30.3	34.9	34.6	30.2	-	29.5	-	-	41.6	30.4	-	31.6
Bellaire (city)	40.0	37.8	-	-	-	-	40.8	-	-	-	-	-	-	-	-	-	-	-	-	-	-	-	-	-
Houston (city)	31.0	32.1	28.8	30.4	-	33.3	35.2	-	34.6	28.9	-	-	29.1	32.9	33.5	-	-	29.0	-	-	39.1	31.1	-	31.2
West University Place (city)	39.0	38.3	-	-	-	-	-	-	-	-	-	-	-	-	-	-	-	-	-	-	-	-	-	-
Hays County	28.4	25.0	-	-	-	-	-	-	-	-	-	-	-	-	-	-	-	-	-	-	-	-	-	-
Hidalgo County	27.3	34.9	-	32.9	-	-	-	-	32.9	-	-	-	-	-	-	-	-	-	-	-	-	-	-	-
Hunt County	35.6	25.8	-	-	-	-	-	-	-	-	-	-	-	-	-	-	-	-	-	-	-	-	-	-
Jefferson County	35.5	27.1	-	31.8	-	-	31.4	-	34.2	-	-	-	-	-	-	-	-	-	-	-	-	-	-	23.9

Notes: Please refer to the User's Guide for an explanation of data; data is arranged alphabetically by state, then county, then city within each county; table includes counties with populations greater than 49,999 unless noted and cities with populations greater than 9,999 whose Asian and/or NHPI population rates are greater than the national average; (1) Native Hawaiian and other Pacific Islander; (2) excludes Taiwanese; (3) includes Chamorro; (4) county does not meet population threshold but is shown in order to allow inclusion of city

Place	Total population	Total Asian population	Total NHPI[1] population	Asian Indian	Bangladeshi	Cambodian	Chinese[2]	Fijian	Filipino	Guamanian[3]	Hawaiian, Native	Hmong	Indonesian	Japanese	Korean	Laotian	Malaysian	Pakistani	Samoan	Sri Lankan	Taiwanese	Thai	Tongan	Vietnamese
Port Arthur (city)	35.1	25.0	-	-	-	-	-	-	-	-	-	-	-	-	-	-	-	-	-	-	-	-	-	23.5
Johnson County	34.4	27.9	-	-	-	-	-	-	-	-	-	-	-	-	-	-	-	-	-	-	-	-	-	-
Kaufman County	35.1	43.0	-	-	-	-	-	-	-	-	-	-	-	-	-	-	-	-	-	-	-	-	-	-
Lubbock County	30.7	29.3	-	24.6	-	-	30.8	-	-	-	-	-	-	-	-	-	-	-	-	-	-	-	-	27.1
McLennan County	32.2	25.8	-	23.2	-	-	-	-	-	-	-	-	-	-	-	-	-	-	-	-	-	-	-	-
Midland County	34.5	34.1	-	31.1	-	-	-	-	-	-	-	-	-	-	-	-	-	-	-	-	-	-	-	-
Montgomery County	34.5	34.7	-	33.1	-	-	36.6	-	37.8	-	-	-	-	-	-	-	-	-	-	-	-	-	-	-
Nacogdoches County	29.8	32.9	-	-	-	-	-	-	-	-	-	-	-	-	-	-	-	-	-	-	-	-	-	-
Nueces County	33.6	35.7	-	35.9	-	-	-	-	35.9	-	-	-	-	-	-	-	-	-	-	-	-	-	-	-
Orange County	36.1	34.6	-	-	-	-	-	-	-	-	-	-	-	-	-	-	-	-	-	-	-	-	-	31.8
Potter County	32.3	31.0	-	-	-	-	-	-	-	-	-	-	-	-	-	26.6	-	-	-	-	-	-	-	30.7
Randall County	35.0	31.8	-	-	-	-	-	-	-	-	-	-	-	-	-	-	-	-	-	-	-	-	-	-
San Patricio County	32.1	34.3	-	-	-	-	-	-	-	-	-	-	-	-	-	-	-	-	-	-	-	-	-	-
Smith County	35.7	31.3	-	-	-	-	-	-	-	-	-	-	-	-	-	-	-	-	-	-	-	-	-	-
Tarrant County	32.5	30.4	26.1	29.8	-	21.8	32.0	-	34.2	-	-	-	-	41.1	32.7	30.5	-	31.6	-	-	32.0	31.0	24.4	29.5
Arlington (city)	30.9	29.6	-	27.9	-	-	32.0	-	35.4	-	-	-	-	-	32.6	-	-	-	-	-	30.1	-	-	29.2
Euless (city)	32.4	31.8	-	32.1	-	-	-	-	-	-	-	-	-	-	-	-	-	-	-	-	-	-	-	-
Haltom City (city)	32.5	29.5	-	-	-	-	-	-	-	-	-	-	-	-	-	27.5	-	-	-	-	-	-	-	28.8
Taylor County	32.4	31.1	-	-	-	-	-	-	30.8	-	-	-	-	-	-	-	-	-	-	-	-	-	-	-
Tom Green County	34.0	33.5	-	-	-	-	-	-	-	-	-	-	-	-	-	-	-	-	-	-	-	-	-	-
Travis County	30.5	27.6	25.7	26.2	-	-	28.3	-	29.7	-	-	-	-	33.1	26.8	-	-	25.4	-	-	24.4	28.7	-	28.8
Austin (city)	29.7	27.1	26.2	26.0	-	-	27.8	-	28.5	-	-	-	-	31.9	26.2	-	-	25.2	-	-	23.8	-	-	28.4
Pflugerville (city)	31.3	36.5	-	-	-	-	-	-	-	-	-	-	-	-	-	-	-	-	-	-	-	-	-	-
Wells Branch (cdp)	30.2	29.7	-	-	-	-	-	-	-	-	-	-	-	-	-	-	-	-	-	-	-	-	-	-
Victoria County	34.3	34.9	-	-	-	-	-	-	-	-	-	-	-	-	-	-	-	-	-	-	-	-	-	-
Webb County	26.5	31.9	-	-	-	-	-	-	-	-	-	-	-	-	-	-	-	-	-	-	-	-	-	-
Wichita County	33.3	30.5	-	-	-	-	-	-	26.8	-	-	-	-	-	-	-	-	-	-	-	-	-	-	32.5
Williamson County	32.4	31.4	-	31.9	-	-	32.8	-	-	-	-	-	-	-	31.1	-	-	-	-	-	-	-	-	29.8
Brushy Creek (cdp)	31.9	32.3	-	-	-	-	-	-	-	-	-	-	-	-	-	-	-	-	-	-	-	-	-	-
Jollyville (cdp)	31.5	33.5	-	-	-	-	-	-	-	-	-	-	-	-	-	-	-	-	-	-	-	-	-	-
UTAH	27.2	29.5	22.0	26.7	-	22.5	31.0	-	31.2	-	25.9	-	-	39.0	26.7	25.5	-	26.0	21.8	-	28.7	30.9	20.0	29.0
Cache County	23.9	24.7	-	-	-	-	25.7	-	-	-	-	-	-	-	-	-	-	-	-	-	-	-	-	-
Davis County	26.8	33.4	23.7	-	-	-	-	-	33.1	-	-	-	-	44.5	25.9	-	-	-	-	-	-	-	-	-
Salt Lake County	28.9	30.0	21.5	27.9	-	21.4	32.0	-	32.1	-	28.5	-	-	41.3	28.7	24.9	-	-	22.4	-	-	-	19.8	29.1
Kearns (cdp)	26.4	26.3	19.3	-	-	-	-	-	-	-	-	-	-	-	-	-	-	-	-	-	-	-	-	-
Salt Lake City (city)	30.0	30.8	21.3	26.7	-	-	29.9	-	33.5	-	-	-	-	46.1	29.4	-	-	-	25.3	-	-	-	17.8	30.2
Sandy (city)	29.2	32.9	21.1	-	-	-	35.8	-	-	-	-	-	-	-	-	-	-	-	-	-	-	-	-	-
Taylorsville (city)	27.6	27.4	22.8	-	-	-	-	-	-	-	-	-	-	-	-	-	-	-	-	-	-	-	-	28.8
West Jordan (city)	25.0	29.6	19.9	-	-	-	-	-	-	-	-	-	-	-	-	-	-	-	-	-	-	-	19.7	-
West Valley City (city)	26.9	27.8	20.7	-	-	18.9	30.6	-	-	-	-	-	-	-	-	24.9	-	-	21.9	-	-	-	17.5	29.4
Utah County	23.3	25.3	22.3	-	-	-	27.3	-	25.7	-	23.5	-	-	24.8	24.7	-	-	-	21.3	-	-	-	20.0	-

Notes: Please refer to the User's Guide for an explanation of data; data is arranged alphabetically by state, then county, then city within each county; table includes counties with populations greater than 49,999 unless noted and cities with populations greater than 9,999 whose Asian and/or NHPI population rates are greater than the national average; (1) Native Hawaiian and other Pacific Islander; (2) excludes Taiwanese; (3) includes Chamorro; (4) county does not meet population threshold but is shown in order to allow inclusion of city

Place	Total population	Total Asian population	Total NHPI[1] population	Asian Indian	Bangladeshi	Cambodian	Chinese[2]	Fijian	Filipino	Guamanian[3]	Hawaiian, Native	Hmong	Indonesian	Japanese	Korean	Laotian	Malaysian	Pakistani	Samoan	Sri Lankan	Taiwanese	Thai	Tongan	Vietnamese
Orem (city)	24.0	30.5	22.1	-	-	-	-	-	-	-	-	-	-	-	-	-	-	-	-	-	-	-	-	-
Provo (city)	22.9	24.4	22.9	-	-	-	26.6	-	-	-	-	-	-	23.0	-	-	-	-	-	-	-	-	-	-
Washington County	31.3	27.4	18.3	-	-	-	-	-	-	-	-	-	-	-	-	-	-	-	-	-	-	-	-	-
St. George (city)	31.8	27.7	18.2	-	-	-	-	-	-	-	-	-	-	-	-	-	-	-	-	-	-	-	-	-
Weber County	29.4	33.1	-	-	-	-	-	-	-	-	-	-	-	49.6	-	-	-	-	-	-	-	-	-	-
VERMONT	37.6	24.9	-	24.3	-	-	26.5	-	30.4	-	-	-	-	31.6	20.3	-	-	-	-	-	-	-	-	23.3
Chittenden County	34.2	25.2	-	24.7	-	-	25.7	-	-	-	-	-	-	-	-	-	-	-	-	-	-	-	-	25.4
Rutland County	39.5	25.4	-	-	-	-	-	-	-	-	-	-	-	-	-	-	-	-	-	-	-	-	-	-
Washington County	38.4	28.2	-	-	-	-	-	-	-	-	-	-	-	-	-	-	-	-	-	-	-	-	-	-
Windsor County	41.1	28.1	-	-	-	-	-	-	-	-	-	-	-	-	-	-	-	-	-	-	-	-	-	-
VIRGINIA	35.8	32.6	27.8	29.7	29.6	27.4	34.1	-	35.6	27.0	32.6	-	28.9	38.6	34.5	30.8	-	26.7	27.3	35.6	33.7	35.9	-	32.8
Albemarle County	37.5	31.5	-	30.1	-	-	33.3	-	-	-	-	-	-	-	-	-	-	-	-	-	-	-	-	-
Alexandria Independent City	34.5	31.2	-	27.7	-	-	33.9	-	32.8	-	-	-	-	-	31.9	-	-	27.6	-	-	-	-	-	34.6
Arlington County	34.0	31.4	-	29.8	-	24.1	31.3	-	35.4	-	-	-	-	33.0	30.3	-	-	26.1	-	-	-	-	-	34.8
Arlington (cdp)	34.0	31.4	-	29.8	-	24.1	31.3	-	35.4	-	-	-	-	33.0	30.3	-	-	26.1	-	-	-	-	-	34.8
Bedford County	39.9	33.7	-	-	-	-	-	-	-	-	-	-	-	-	-	-	-	-	-	-	-	-	-	-
Charlottesville Independent City	25.4	21.5	-	20.9	-	-	22.8	-	-	-	-	-	-	-	-	-	-	-	-	-	-	-	-	-
Chesapeake Independent City	34.8	35.8	-	-	-	-	-	-	38.4	-	-	-	-	-	-	-	-	-	-	-	-	-	-	-
Chesterfield County	35.9	33.9	-	39.1	-	23.2	32.0	-	40.9	-	-	-	-	-	36.2	-	-	-	-	-	-	-	-	30.3
Fairfax Independent City	37.4	33.3	-	27.0	-	-	36.3	-	-	-	-	-	-	-	36.9	-	-	-	-	-	-	-	-	36.7
Fairfax County	36.1	33.7	28.7	30.3	28.9	28.8	36.4	-	37.1	-	-	-	27.6	38.9	35.7	32.3	-	26.9	-	-	40.9	40.1	-	34.0
Annandale (cdp)	37.5	34.0	-	30.6	-	-	32.4	-	36.9	-	-	-	-	-	34.6	-	-	-	-	-	-	-	-	34.4
Bailey's Crossroads (cdp)	33.3	33.5	-	-	-	-	-	-	-	-	-	-	-	-	-	-	-	26.3	-	-	-	-	-	37.3
Burke (cdp)	37.8	36.9	-	35.5	-	-	41.2	-	39.7	-	-	-	-	-	36.4	-	-	-	-	-	-	-	-	35.1
Centreville (cdp)	31.2	31.5	-	29.5	-	-	38.5	-	31.0	-	-	-	-	-	33.5	-	-	-	-	-	-	-	-	35.0
Chantilly (cdp)	33.7	31.1	-	28.6	-	-	31.9	-	-	-	-	-	-	-	34.4	-	-	-	-	-	-	-	-	32.3
Franconia (cdp)	35.4	35.1	-	30.7	-	-	-	-	36.2	-	-	-	-	-	36.5	-	-	-	-	-	-	-	-	35.6
Groveton (cdp)	34.7	33.5	-	-	-	-	-	-	-	-	-	-	-	-	-	-	-	-	-	-	-	-	-	-
Herndon (town)	31.5	31.6	-	29.7	-	-	-	-	-	-	-	-	-	-	-	-	-	-	-	-	-	-	-	31.8
Hybla Valley (cdp)	34.1	36.3	-	-	-	-	-	-	-	-	-	-	-	-	-	-	-	-	-	-	-	-	-	-
Idylwood (cdp)	33.4	30.5	-	28.3	-	-	31.0	-	-	-	-	-	-	-	-	-	-	-	-	-	-	-	-	36.0
Jefferson (cdp)	35.2	32.0	-	29.0	-	-	30.9	-	38.5	-	-	-	-	-	-	-	-	-	-	-	-	-	-	32.4
Lincolnia (cdp)	34.4	34.5	-	-	-	-	-	-	-	-	-	-	-	-	-	-	-	25.3	-	-	-	-	-	34.3
Lorton (cdp)	33.4	36.8	-	-	-	-	-	-	-	-	-	-	-	-	-	-	-	-	-	-	-	-	-	-
McLean (cdp)	43.2	40.6	-	39.6	-	-	45.3	-	40.9	-	-	-	-	35.7	38.5	-	-	-	-	-	-	-	-	-
Merrifield (cdp)	32.7	30.7	-	30.3	-	-	-	-	-	-	-	-	-	-	30.0	-	-	-	-	-	-	-	-	29.5
Mount Vernon (cdp)	36.0	35.9	-	-	-	-	-	-	-	-	-	-	-	-	39.7	-	-	-	-	-	-	-	-	-
Newington (cdp)	36.4	35.7	-	30.0	-	-	-	-	37.0	-	-	-	-	-	35.9	-	-	-	-	-	-	-	-	-
Oakton (cdp)	36.9	32.1	-	31.3	-	-	35.0	-	-	-	-	-	-	-	31.8	-	-	-	-	-	-	-	-	32.3
Reston (cdp)	36.3	31.5	-	28.8	-	-	36.8	-	35.8	-	-	-	-	-	34.7	-	-	-	-	-	-	-	-	-
Rose Hill (cdp)	38.3	33.0	-	-	-	-	-	-	-	-	-	-	-	-	-	-	-	-	-	-	-	-	-	-

Notes: Please refer to the User's Guide for an explanation of data; data is arranged alphabetically by state, then county, then city within each county; table includes counties with populations greater than 49,999 unless noted and cities with populations greater than 9,999 whose Asian and/or NHPI population rates are greater than the national average; (1) Native Hawaiian and other Pacific Islander; (2) excludes Taiwanese; (3) includes Chamorro; (4) county does not meet population threshold but is shown in order to allow inclusion of city

Place	Total population	Total Asian population	Total NHPI[1] population	Asian Indian	Bangladeshi	Cambodian	Chinese[2]	Fijian	Filipino	Guamanian[3]	Hawaiian, Native	Hmong	Indonesian	Japanese	Korean	Laotian	Malaysian	Pakistani	Samoan	Sri Lankan	Taiwanese	Thai	Tongan	Vietnamese
Springfield (cdp)	36.0	32.8	-	32.6	-	-	30.5	-	34.7	-	-	-	-	-	35.2	30.9	-	-	-	-	-	-	-	33.4
Tysons Corner (cdp)	36.4	31.7	-	29.4	-	-	37.5	-	-	-	-	-	-	-	35.1	-	-	-	-	-	-	-	-	-
Vienna (town)	39.5	41.2	-	-	-	-	-	-	-	-	-	-	-	-	-	-	-	-	-	-	-	-	-	-
West Springfield (cdp)	38.7	33.2	-	32.3	-	-	35.1	-	-	-	-	-	-	-	38.6	-	-	-	-	-	-	-	-	28.0
Wolf Trap (cdp)	41.3	41.8	-	37.6	-	-	42.2	-	-	-	-	-	-	-	-	-	-	-	-	-	-	-	-	-
Falls Church Independent City	40.0	36.0	-	-	-	-	-	-	-	-	-	-	-	-	-	-	-	-	-	-	-	-	-	-
Fauquier County	37.7	32.4	-	-	-	-	-	-	-	-	-	-	-	-	-	-	-	-	-	-	-	-	-	-
Frederick County	36.6	36.6	-	-	-	-	-	-	-	-	-	-	-	-	-	-	-	-	-	-	-	-	-	-
Hampton Independent City	34.1	36.1	-	-	-	-	-	-	35.0	-	-	-	-	-	-	-	-	-	-	-	-	-	-	36.0
Hanover County	37.5	37.5	-	-	-	-	-	-	-	-	-	-	-	-	-	-	-	-	-	-	-	-	-	-
Henrico County	36.2	31.0	-	30.4	-	22.3	33.9	-	29.1	-	-	-	-	-	31.5	-	-	-	-	-	-	-	-	30.8
Glen Allen (cdp)	35.0	34.5	-	-	-	-	-	-	-	-	-	-	-	-	-	-	-	-	-	-	-	-	-	-
Laurel (cdp)	34.6	30.3	-	-	-	-	-	-	-	-	-	-	-	-	-	-	-	-	-	-	-	-	-	-
Loudoun County	33.6	31.6	-	30.8	-	-	32.7	-	33.5	-	-	-	-	-	31.1	-	-	30.8	-	-	-	-	-	31.6
Lynchburg Independent City	35.3	27.6	-	-	-	-	-	-	-	-	-	-	-	-	-	-	-	-	-	-	-	-	-	-
Manassas Park Indep. City	30.3	31.0	-	-	-	-	-	-	-	-	-	-	-	-	-	-	-	-	-	-	-	-	-	-
Montgomery County	25.9	23.3	-	23.5	-	-	25.9	-	-	-	-	-	-	-	22.3	-	-	-	-	-	-	-	-	-
Blacksburg (town)	21.9	22.9	-	23.1	-	-	25.6	-	-	-	-	-	-	-	22.0	-	-	-	-	-	-	-	-	-
Newport News Independent City	31.9	35.6	-	-	-	-	35.0	-	31.1	-	-	-	-	-	42.1	-	-	-	-	-	-	-	-	32.6
Norfolk Independent City	29.6	30.8	-	25.7	-	-	30.4	-	34.9	-	-	-	-	-	-	-	-	-	-	-	-	-	-	29.1
Portsmouth Independent City	34.6	27.6	-	-	-	-	-	-	30.6	-	-	-	-	-	-	-	-	-	-	-	-	-	-	-
Prince William County	32.1	32.8	-	28.3	-	-	39.4	-	35.5	-	-	-	-	43.1	36.6	-	-	25.0	-	-	-	-	-	31.3
Bull Run (cdp)	28.9	33.4	-	-	-	-	-	-	-	-	-	-	-	-	-	-	-	-	-	-	-	-	-	-
Dale City (cdp)	31.5	34.4	-	32.8	-	-	-	-	36.8	-	-	-	-	-	-	-	-	29.4	-	-	-	-	-	-
Lake Ridge (cdp)	34.0	32.6	-	-	-	-	-	-	-	-	-	-	-	-	-	-	-	-	-	-	-	-	-	-
Woodbridge (cdp)	30.4	31.2	-	-	-	-	-	-	-	-	-	-	-	-	-	-	-	-	-	-	-	-	-	-
Richmond Independent City	33.9	25.5	-	24.5	-	-	-	-	26.1	-	-	-	-	-	-	-	-	-	-	-	-	-	-	-
Roanoke Independent City	37.9	29.9	-	-	-	-	-	-	-	-	-	-	-	-	-	-	-	-	-	-	-	-	-	-
Roanoke County	40.9	33.3	-	-	-	-	-	-	-	-	-	-	-	-	-	-	-	-	-	-	-	-	-	-
Spotsylvania County	34.5	37.3	-	-	-	-	-	-	-	-	-	-	-	-	-	-	-	-	-	-	-	-	-	-
Stafford County	33.2	37.8	-	-	-	-	-	-	40.3	-	-	-	-	-	-	-	-	-	-	-	-	-	-	-
Suffolk Independent City	36.3	39.6	-	-	-	-	-	-	-	-	-	-	-	-	-	-	-	-	-	-	-	-	-	-
Virginia Beach Independent City	32.9	35.6	-	33.4	-	-	39.2	-	36.2	-	-	-	-	38.8	42.0	-	-	-	-	-	-	-	-	30.9
Williamsburg Independent City	22.6	20.8	-	-	-	-	-	-	-	-	-	-	-	-	-	-	-	-	-	-	-	-	-	-
York County	36.7	35.9	-	37.5	-	-	-	-	-	-	-	-	-	-	36.9	-	-	-	-	-	-	-	-	-
WASHINGTON	35.4	33.2	26.5	29.8	-	24.6	35.5	29.2	34.9	26.9	30.8	15.9	27.1	41.6	34.2	26.7	-	28.1	23.8	32.7	30.1	31.8	26.4	30.5
Benton County	34.7	37.9	-	41.1	-	-	36.9	-	-	-	-	-	-	-	31.3	-	-	-	-	-	-	-	-	36.4
Richland (city)	37.7	38.5	-	-	-	-	38.1	-	-	-	-	-	-	-	-	-	-	-	-	-	-	-	-	-
Chelan County	36.5	33.2	-	-	-	-	-	-	-	-	-	-	-	-	-	-	-	-	-	-	-	-	-	-
Clallam County	43.7	36.7	-	-	-	-	-	-	-	-	-	-	-	-	-	-	-	-	-	-	-	-	-	-
Clark County	34.2	33.3	22.7	28.2	-	31.4	34.9	-	37.3	-	-	-	-	38.3	35.5	29.4	-	-	-	-	-	-	-	29.4

Notes: Please refer to the User's Guide for an explanation of data; data is arranged alphabetically by state, then county, then city within each county; table includes counties with populations greater than 49,999 unless noted and cities with populations greater than 9,999 whose Asian and/or NHPI population rates are greater than the national average; (1) Native Hawaiian and other Pacific Islander; (2) excludes Taiwanese; (3) includes Chamorro; (4) county does not meet population threshold but is shown in order to allow inclusion of city

Place	Total population	Total Asian population	Total NHPI[1] population	Asian Indian	Bangladeshi	Cambodian	Chinese[2]	Fijian	Filipino	Guamanian[3]	Hawaiian, Native	Hmong	Indonesian	Japanese	Korean	Laotian	Malaysian	Pakistani	Samoan	Sri Lankan	Taiwanese	Thai	Tongan	Vietnamese
Five Corners (cdp)	33.2	29.6	-	-	-	-	-	-	-	-	-	-	-	-	-	-	-	-	-	-	-	-	-	-
Orchards (cdp)	29.6	29.8	-	-	-	-	-	-	-	-	-	-	-	-	-	-	-	-	-	-	-	-	-	-
Vancouver (city)	33.1	33.7	21.1	-	-	-	35.9	-	41.1	-	-	-	-	37.1	37.7	-	-	-	-	-	-	-	-	29.7
Cowlitz County	36.7	34.7	-	-	-	19.6	-	-	-	-	-	-	-	-	-	-	-	-	-	-	-	-	-	33.6
Grant County	31.1	37.3	-	-	-	-	-	-	-	-	-	-	-	-	-	-	-	-	-	-	-	-	-	-
Grays Harbor County	38.7	32.3	-	-	-	-	-	-	-	-	-	-	-	-	-	-	-	-	-	-	-	-	-	-
Island County	37.0	33.6	-	-	-	-	-	-	35.0	-	-	-	-	40.5	-	-	-	-	-	-	-	-	-	-
Oak Harbor (city)	28.1	32.0	-	-	-	-	-	-	33.4	-	-	-	-	-	-	-	-	-	-	-	-	-	-	-
King County	35.8	32.9	26.7	29.5	-	24.5	35.8	30.1	34.6	25.3	31.8	12.3	26.6	41.3	31.5	25.9	-	28.2	24.0	-	30.0	30.5	34.3	30.2
Auburn (city)	33.8	31.2	-	-	-	-	-	-	-	-	-	-	-	-	-	-	-	-	-	-	-	-	-	-
Bellevue (city)	38.3	32.8	-	28.1	-	-	35.6	-	38.1	-	-	-	-	38.6	31.8	28.4	-	-	-	-	30.8	-	-	33.3
Bothell (city)	36.5	30.8	-	-	-	-	30.9	-	-	-	-	-	-	-	-	-	-	-	-	-	-	-	-	-
Bryn Mawr-Skyway (cdp)	38.0	35.5	-	-	-	-	-	-	34.1	-	-	-	-	51.7	-	-	-	-	-	-	-	-	-	28.9
Burien (city)	38.8	31.3	-	-	-	-	-	-	32.5	-	-	-	-	-	-	-	-	-	-	-	-	-	-	27.9
Cascade-Fairwood (cdp)	34.8	34.4	-	-	-	-	37.6	-	38.0	-	-	-	-	39.5	-	-	-	-	-	-	-	-	-	29.4
Cottage Lake (cdp)	37.6	37.1	-	-	-	-	-	-	-	-	-	-	-	-	-	-	-	-	-	-	-	-	-	-
Des Moines (city)	36.9	29.9	22.0	-	-	-	-	-	31.7	-	-	-	-	-	-	-	-	-	-	-	-	-	-	30.2
East Hill-Meridian (cdp)	34.8	34.3	-	31.9	-	-	35.2	-	33.1	-	-	-	-	-	-	-	-	-	-	-	-	-	-	30.2
Federal Way (city)	32.6	33.6	25.3	-	-	-	38.4	-	32.5	-	-	-	-	40.5	35.4	-	-	-	20.4	-	-	-	-	28.6
Inglewood-Finn Hill (cdp)	35.9	34.3	-	-	-	-	37.2	-	-	-	-	-	-	-	-	-	-	-	-	-	-	-	-	-
Issaquah (city)	36.9	34.3	-	-	-	-	-	-	-	-	-	-	-	-	-	-	-	-	-	-	-	-	-	-
Kenmore (city)	37.6	32.6	-	-	-	-	-	-	-	-	-	-	-	-	-	-	-	-	-	-	-	-	-	-
Kent (city)	32.0	31.7	-	30.5	-	-	33.9	-	31.0	-	-	-	-	44.0	31.0	-	-	-	-	-	-	-	-	29.4
Kingsgate (cdp)	33.9	30.2	-	-	-	-	32.4	-	-	-	-	-	-	-	-	-	-	-	-	-	-	-	-	-
Kirkland (city)	36.2	32.8	-	-	-	-	31.7	-	-	-	-	-	-	39.0	-	-	-	-	-	-	-	-	-	36.5
Lake Forest Park (city)	42.3	40.6	-	-	-	-	-	-	-	-	-	-	-	-	-	-	-	-	-	-	-	-	-	-
Lakeland North (cdp)	35.4	35.0	-	-	-	-	-	-	-	-	-	-	-	-	-	-	-	-	-	-	-	-	-	-
Lakeland South (cdp)	36.8	39.8	-	-	-	-	-	-	-	-	-	-	-	-	-	-	-	-	-	-	-	-	-	-
Lea Hill (cdp)	33.3	22.2	-	-	-	-	-	-	-	-	-	-	-	-	-	-	-	-	-	-	-	-	-	-
Mercer Island (city)	43.9	41.0	-	-	-	-	41.4	-	-	-	-	-	-	51.3	-	-	-	-	-	-	-	-	-	-
Redmond (city)	34.2	30.5	-	27.0	-	-	32.3	-	-	-	-	-	-	36.5	41.2	-	-	-	-	-	-	-	-	-
Renton (city)	34.4	33.5	-	-	-	-	39.0	-	37.5	-	-	-	-	43.3	-	-	-	-	-	-	-	-	-	30.9
Riverton-Boulevard Park (cdp)	33.1	30.1	-	-	-	-	-	-	-	-	-	-	-	-	-	-	-	-	-	-	-	-	-	-
Sammamish (city)	35.6	34.1	-	-	-	-	36.3	-	-	-	-	-	-	-	-	-	-	-	-	-	-	-	-	-
SeaTac (city)	34.4	32.0	26.8	36.5	-	-	-	-	32.9	-	-	-	-	-	-	-	-	-	-	-	-	-	-	28.3
Seattle (city)	35.5	33.0	26.3	31.2	-	23.8	36.6	-	35.0	-	-	-	24.7	41.8	27.9	25.5	-	-	23.6	-	29.0	26.9	-	30.1
Shoreline (city)	39.1	35.1	-	36.9	-	-	36.9	-	37.9	-	-	-	-	40.5	34.4	-	-	-	-	-	-	-	-	29.0
Tukwila (city)	33.6	32.6	20.5	-	-	-	-	-	32.0	-	-	-	-	-	-	-	-	-	-	-	-	-	-	-
Union Hill-Novelty Hill (cdp)	36.0	34.4	-	-	-	-	-	-	-	-	-	-	-	-	-	-	-	-	-	-	-	-	-	-
White Center (cdp)	34.5	29.7	-	-	-	19.8	-	-	39.8	-	-	-	-	-	-	-	-	-	-	-	-	-	-	30.2
Kitsap County	35.8	37.0	26.8	-	-	-	38.5	-	36.4	26.0	-	-	-	46.1	37.0	-	-	-	-	-	-	-	-	29.0

Notes: Please refer to the User's Guide for an explanation of data; data is arranged alphabetically by state, then county, then city within each county; table includes counties with populations greater than 49,999 unless noted and cities with populations greater than 9,999 whose Asian and/or NHPI population rates are greater than the national average; (1) Native Hawaiian and other Pacific Islander; (2) excludes Taiwanese; (3) includes Chamorro; (4) county does not meet population threshold but is shown in order to allow inclusion of city

Place	Total population	Total Asian population	Total NHPI[1] population	Asian Indian	Bangladeshi	Cambodian	Chinese[2]	Fijian	Filipino	Guamanian[3]	Hawaiian, Native	Hmong	Indonesian	Japanese	Korean	Laotian	Malaysian	Pakistani	Samoan	Sri Lankan	Taiwanese	Thai	Tongan	Vietnamese
Bremerton (city)	30.5	33.3	-	-	-	-	-	-	33.7	-	-	-	-	-	-	-	-	-	-	-	-	-	-	-
Silverdale (cdp)	32.6	37.3	-	-	-	-	-	-	35.3	-	-	-	-	-	-	-	-	-	-	-	-	-	-	-
Lewis County	38.6	37.0	-	-	-	-	-	-	-	-	-	-	-	-	-	-	-	-	-	-	-	-	-	-
Pierce County	34.2	36.5	26.3	28.7	-	20.9	39.9	-	35.1	26.1	29.8	-	-	50.8	39.4	30.9	-	-	23.0	-	-	40.4	-	31.0
Elk Plain (cdp)	32.3	34.1	-	-	-	-	-	-	-	-	-	-	-	-	-	-	-	-	-	-	-	-	-	-
Fort Lewis (cdp)	22.3	27.1	22.9	-	-	-	-	-	27.5	-	-	-	-	-	-	-	-	-	-	-	-	-	-	-
Lakewood (city)	35.4	41.8	26.4	-	-	-	-	-	36.6	-	-	-	-	69.1	42.8	-	-	-	21.8	-	-	-	-	-
Parkland (cdp)	31.8	40.6	22.9	-	-	-	-	-	-	-	-	-	-	-	40.6	-	-	-	-	-	-	-	-	-
Spanaway (cdp)	33.1	41.5	19.9	-	-	-	-	-	31.1	-	-	-	-	-	44.9	-	-	-	-	-	-	-	-	-
Tacoma (city)	34.2	33.7	27.0	-	-	20.1	34.9	-	37.6	26.5	-	-	-	41.8	39.5	32.9	-	-	21.1	-	-	-	-	30.1
University Place (city)	36.9	33.8	-	-	-	-	-	-	-	-	-	-	-	-	35.3	-	-	-	-	-	-	-	-	-
Skagit County	37.2	29.5	-	-	-	-	-	-	31.8	-	-	-	-	-	-	-	-	-	-	-	-	-	-	-
Snohomish County	34.7	32.7	28.7	31.5	-	26.7	33.5	-	33.7	-	31.4	-	-	39.0	35.8	29.5	-	27.4	-	-	-	-	-	31.2
Alderwood Manor (cdp)	34.9	34.2	-	-	-	-	-	-	-	-	-	-	-	-	-	-	-	-	-	-	-	-	-	-
Edmonds (city)	41.9	33.4	-	-	-	-	-	-	30.9	-	-	-	-	-	37.8	-	-	-	-	-	-	-	-	-
Everett (city)	32.4	31.5	-	30.7	-	22.7	-	-	33.6	-	-	-	-	-	-	-	-	-	-	-	-	-	-	31.2
Lynnwood (city)	35.0	32.6	-	-	-	-	32.4	-	32.2	-	-	-	-	-	36.3	-	-	-	-	-	-	-	-	31.3
Martha Lake (cdp)	33.7	31.4	-	-	-	-	-	-	-	-	-	-	-	-	-	-	-	-	-	-	-	-	-	-
Marysville (city)	32.9	35.0	-	-	-	-	-	-	-	-	-	-	-	-	-	-	-	-	-	-	-	-	-	-
Mill Creek (city)	38.3	35.6	-	-	-	-	-	-	-	-	-	-	-	-	34.4	-	-	-	-	-	-	-	-	-
Mountlake Terrace (city)	33.6	33.1	-	-	-	-	-	-	30.9	-	-	-	-	-	34.9	-	-	-	-	-	-	-	-	-
Mukilteo (city)	37.1	36.7	-	-	-	-	-	-	-	-	-	-	-	-	35.3	-	-	-	-	-	-	-	-	-
North Creek (cdp)	32.7	32.1	-	-	-	-	-	-	-	-	-	-	-	-	-	-	-	-	-	-	-	-	-	-
Paine Field-Lk. Stickney (cdp)	31.2	31.2	-	-	-	-	-	-	-	-	-	-	-	-	-	-	-	-	-	-	-	-	-	-
Picnic Pt.-N. Lynnwood (cdp)	33.2	31.8	-	-	-	-	-	-	32.6	-	-	-	-	-	34.3	-	-	-	-	-	-	-	-	-
Seattle Hill-Silver Firs (cdp)	34.4	33.7	-	-	-	-	-	-	27.0	-	-	-	-	-	35.6	-	-	-	-	-	-	-	-	33.0
Spokane County	35.5	29.5	27.6	28.3	-	-	29.8	-	33.2	-	-	16.9	-	35.2	24.9	-	-	-	-	-	-	-	-	34.4
Spokane (city)	34.8	29.0	27.6	-	-	-	35.7	-	33.9	-	-	14.6	-	39.9	21.5	-	-	-	-	-	-	-	-	31.5
Thurston County	36.7	34.7	28.7	28.1	-	24.2	37.0	-	37.5	33.1	-	-	-	38.9	40.9	-	-	-	-	-	-	-	-	32.9
Lacey (city)	35.0	34.1	-	-	-	-	-	-	29.9	-	-	-	-	-	40.9	-	-	-	-	-	-	-	-	31.1
Olympia (city)	35.7	35.5	-	-	-	-	-	-	-	-	-	-	-	-	-	-	-	-	-	-	-	-	-	37.5
Tumwater (city)	36.4	31.7	-	-	-	-	-	-	-	-	-	-	-	-	-	-	-	-	-	-	-	-	-	-
Walla Walla County	35.0	23.8	-	-	-	-	-	-	-	-	-	-	-	-	-	-	-	-	-	-	-	-	-	-
Whatcom County	34.1	26.7	-	29.7	-	-	32.3	-	26.4	-	-	-	-	29.3	22.4	-	-	-	-	-	-	-	-	28.7
Bellingham (city)	30.6	24.5	-	25.8	-	-	-	-	-	-	-	-	-	-	-	-	-	-	-	-	-	-	-	28.3
Whitman County[4]	24.7	24.7	-	-	-	-	26.9	-	-	-	-	-	-	23.8	-	-	-	-	-	-	-	-	-	-
Pullman (city)	22.5	24.6	-	-	-	-	28.0	-	-	-	-	-	-	24.0	-	-	-	-	-	-	-	-	-	-
Yakima County	31.5	34.7	-	-	-	-	-	-	42.5	-	-	-	-	-	-	-	-	-	-	-	-	-	-	-
WEST VIRGINIA	38.9	31.0	22.4	30.9	-	-	30.5	-	39.5	-	-	-	-	27.4	27.0	-	-	29.7	-	-	-	-	-	34.1
Cabell County	37.7	29.4	-	-	-	-	-	-	-	-	-	-	-	-	-	-	-	-	-	-	-	-	-	-
Harrison County	39.0	23.4	-	-	-	-	-	-	-	-	-	-	-	-	-	-	-	-	-	-	-	-	-	-

Notes: Please refer to the User's Guide for an explanation of data; data is arranged alphabetically by state, then county, then city within each county; table includes counties with populations greater than 49,999 unless noted and cities with populations greater than 9,999 whose Asian and/or NHPI population rates are greater than the national average; (1) Native Hawaiian and other Pacific Islander; (2) excludes Taiwanese; (3) includes Chamorro; (4) county does not meet population threshold but is shown in order to allow inclusion of city

Place	Total population	Total Asian population	Total NHPI[1] population	Asian Indian	Bangladeshi	Cambodian	Chinese[2]	Fijian	Filipino	Guamanian[3]	Hawaiian, Native	Hmong	Indonesian	Japanese	Korean	Laotian	Malaysian	Pakistani	Samoan	Sri Lankan	Taiwanese	Thai	Tongan	Vietnamese
Kanawha County	40.3	32.6	-	40.6	-	-	-	-	-	-	-	-	-	-	-	-	-	-	-	-	-	-	-	-
Monongalia County	30.5	28.0	-	25.2	-	-	32.1	-	-	-	-	-	-	-	-	-	-	-	-	-	-	-	-	-
Putnam County	37.7	29.4	-	-	-	-	-	-	-	-	-	-	-	-	-	-	-	-	-	-	-	-	-	-
Raleigh County	39.6	37.1	-	-	-	-	-	-	-	-	-	-	-	-	-	-	-	-	-	-	-	-	-	-
Wood County	39.3	38.2	-	-	-	-	-	-	-	-	-	-	-	-	-	-	-	-	-	-	-	-	-	-
WISCONSIN	36.1	23.7	25.3	28.4	-	21.6	29.8	-	33.5	23.3	28.8	15.9	24.7	37.9	24.1	21.1	-	25.6	-	-	29.6	27.2	-	28.8
Brown County	34.2	18.6	-	26.5	-	-	-	-	-	-	-	16.8	-	-	-	15.3	-	-	-	-	-	-	-	-
Chippewa County	37.6	18.0	-	-	-	-	-	-	-	-	-	15.9	-	-	-	-	-	-	-	-	-	-	-	-
Columbia County	37.9	39.4	-	-	-	-	-	-	-	-	-	-	-	-	-	-	-	-	-	-	-	-	-	-
Dane County	33.3	26.0	-	27.0	-	-	26.9	-	31.6	-	-	17.4	-	33.7	27.1	24.8	-	-	-	-	29.7	-	-	29.4
Madison (city)	30.9	25.6	-	26.6	-	-	26.1	-	31.9	-	-	17.0	-	31.9	27.3	-	-	-	-	-	29.6	-	-	29.2
Dodge County	37.0	25.9	-	-	-	-	-	-	-	-	-	-	-	-	-	-	-	-	-	-	-	-	-	-
Eau Claire County	32.3	18.1	-	-	-	-	-	-	-	-	-	15.7	-	-	-	-	-	-	-	-	-	-	-	-
Fond du Lac County	37.0	17.9	-	-	-	-	-	-	-	-	-	14.6	-	-	-	-	-	-	-	-	-	-	-	-
Jefferson County	36.6	33.1	-	-	-	-	-	-	-	-	-	-	-	-	-	-	-	-	-	-	-	-	-	-
Kenosha County	34.9	32.4	-	-	-	-	-	-	-	-	-	-	-	-	-	-	-	-	-	-	-	-	-	-
La Crosse County	33.6	16.9	-	-	-	-	-	-	-	-	-	15.3	-	-	-	-	-	-	-	-	-	-	-	-
La Crosse (city)	30.3	17.5	-	-	-	-	-	-	-	-	-	15.5	-	-	-	-	-	-	-	-	-	-	-	-
Manitowoc County	38.3	18.2	-	-	-	-	-	-	-	-	-	17.0	-	-	-	-	-	-	-	-	-	-	-	-
Marathon County	36.3	15.7	-	-	-	-	-	-	-	-	-	14.8	-	-	-	-	-	-	-	-	-	-	-	-
Wausau (city)	36.7	15.4	-	-	-	-	-	-	-	-	-	14.6	-	-	-	-	-	-	-	-	-	-	-	-
Milwaukee County	33.8	26.2	25.9	29.3	-	-	32.8	-	31.4	-	-	16.6	-	41.9	28.0	23.8	-	29.4	-	-	-	-	-	29.3
Outagamie County	34.4	18.2	-	20.4	-	-	-	-	-	-	-	16.0	-	-	-	-	-	-	-	-	-	-	-	-
Appleton (city)	33.8	16.1	-	-	-	-	-	-	-	-	-	15.0	-	-	-	-	-	-	-	-	-	-	-	-
Ozaukee County	38.9	33.7	-	-	-	-	-	-	-	-	-	-	-	-	-	-	-	-	-	-	-	-	-	-
Portage County	32.9	17.0	-	-	-	-	-	-	-	-	-	14.7	-	-	-	-	-	-	-	-	-	-	-	-
Stevens Point (city)	25.7	17.6	-	-	-	-	-	-	-	-	-	14.5	-	-	-	-	-	-	-	-	-	-	-	-
Racine County	36.2	30.8	-	-	-	-	-	-	-	-	-	-	-	-	-	-	-	-	-	-	-	-	-	-
Rock County	36.0	29.5	-	-	-	-	-	-	-	-	-	-	-	-	-	-	-	-	-	-	-	-	-	-
St. Croix County	34.9	26.9	-	-	-	-	-	-	-	-	-	-	-	-	-	-	-	-	-	-	-	-	-	-
Sauk County	37.2	27.8	-	-	-	-	-	-	-	-	-	-	-	-	-	-	-	-	-	-	-	-	-	-
Sheboygan County	37.0	17.0	-	-	-	-	-	-	-	-	-	14.8	-	-	-	-	-	-	-	-	-	-	-	-
Sheboygan (city)	35.5	16.4	-	-	-	-	-	-	-	-	-	14.7	-	-	-	-	-	-	-	-	-	-	-	-
Walworth County	35.3	29.7	-	-	-	-	-	-	-	-	-	-	-	-	-	-	-	-	-	-	-	-	-	-
Washington County	36.6	30.4	-	-	-	-	-	-	-	-	-	-	-	-	-	-	-	-	-	-	-	-	-	-
Waukesha County	38.2	30.8	-	28.7	-	-	36.4	-	36.7	-	-	-	-	-	24.2	-	-	-	-	-	-	-	-	-
Winnebago County	35.5	20.3	-	-	-	-	-	-	-	-	-	14.9	-	-	-	-	-	-	-	-	-	-	-	-
Wood County	38.1	17.4	-	-	-	-	-	-	-	-	-	15.3	-	-	-	-	-	-	-	-	-	-	-	-
WYOMING	36.4	32.6	-	31.2	-	-	33.3	-	36.0	-	-	-	-	40.6	27.4	-	-	-	-	-	-	-	-	-
Laramie County	35.3	31.9	-	-	-	-	-	-	-	-	-	-	-	-	-	-	-	-	-	-	-	-	-	-
Natrona County	36.9	38.2	-	-	-	-	-	-	-	-	-	-	-	-	-	-	-	-	-	-	-	-	-	-

Notes: Please refer to the User's Guide for an explanation of data; data is arranged alphabetically by state, then county, then city within each county; table includes counties with populations greater than 49,999 unless noted and cities with populations greater than 9,999 whose Asian and/or NHPI population rates are greater than the national average; (1) Native Hawaiian and other Pacific Islander; (2) excludes Taiwanese; (3) includes Chamorro; (4) county does not meet population threshold but is shown in order to allow inclusion of city

Average Household Size

(Universe: Households)

Place	All households	Asian households	NHPI[1] households	Asian Indian	Bangladeshi	Cambodian	Chinese[2]	Fijian	Filipino	Guamanian[3]	Hawaiian, Native	Hmong	Indonesian	Japanese	Korean	Laotian	Malaysian	Pakistani	Samoan	Sri Lankan	Taiwanese	Thai	Tongan	Vietnamese
UNITED STATES	2.59	3.08	3.60	3.06	3.67	4.41	2.91	3.72	3.41	3.31	3.21	6.14	2.67	2.25	2.76	4.23	2.61	3.80	4.33	2.86	2.85	2.64	5.31	3.70
ALABAMA	2.49	2.77	3.62	2.87	-	4.20	2.51	-	2.45	3.48	-	-	-	2.05	2.61	3.70	-	3.25	-	-	-	2.45	-	3.40
Baldwin County	2.50	3.05	-	-	-	-	-	-	-	-	-	-	-	-	-	-	-	-	-	-	-	-	-	-
Calhoun County	2.42	2.25	-	-	-	-	-	-	-	-	-	-	-	-	-	-	-	-	-	-	-	-	-	-
Etowah County	2.44	2.43	-	-	-	-	-	-	-	-	-	-	-	-	-	-	-	-	-	-	-	-	-	-
Houston County	2.44	2.88	-	-	-	-	-	-	-	-	-	-	-	-	-	-	-	-	-	-	-	-	-	-
Jefferson County	2.45	2.70	-	2.72	-	-	2.75	-	-	-	-	-	-	-	2.10	-	-	-	-	-	-	-	-	3.89
Lee County	2.42	2.43	-	-	-	-	2.12	-	-	-	-	-	-	-	-	-	-	-	-	-	-	-	-	-
Madison County	2.45	2.77	-	3.04	-	-	2.51	-	-	-	-	-	-	-	2.66	-	-	-	-	-	-	-	-	2.87
Mobile County	2.61	3.39	-	3.54	-	4.91	2.69	-	2.75	-	-	-	-	-	-	4.01	-	-	-	-	-	-	-	3.76
Montgomery County	2.46	2.49	-	-	-	-	-	-	-	-	-	-	-	-	-	-	-	-	-	-	-	-	-	-
Morgan County	2.51	3.15	-	-	-	-	-	-	-	-	-	-	-	-	-	-	-	-	-	-	-	-	-	-
Shelby County	2.59	2.40	-	2.38	-	-	-	-	-	-	-	-	-	-	-	-	-	-	-	-	-	-	-	-
Tuscaloosa County	2.42	2.51	-	-	-	-	-	-	-	-	-	-	-	-	-	-	-	-	-	-	-	-	-	-
ALASKA	2.74	3.30	4.13	2.97	-	-	2.61	-	3.74	-	3.53	6.03	-	2.15	2.63	4.36	-	-	4.90	-	-	3.50	5.20	3.33
Anchorage Borough	2.66	3.17	4.36	2.90	-	-	2.50	-	3.38	-	-	6.03	-	2.09	2.69	4.56	-	-	5.05	-	-	3.34	-	3.45
Fairbanks North Star Borough	2.68	2.70	-	-	-	-	2.87	-	3.61	-	-	-	-	-	2.32	-	-	-	-	-	-	-	-	-
Juneau City and Borough	2.60	3.75	-	-	-	-	-	-	4.08	-	-	-	-	-	-	-	-	-	-	-	-	-	-	-
Matanuska-Susitna Borough	2.84	3.32	-	-	-	-	-	-	-	-	-	-	-	-	-	-	-	-	-	-	-	-	-	-
ARIZONA	2.64	2.73	3.33	2.81	-	4.00	2.61	-	2.95	3.37	3.09	-	2.44	2.07	2.51	3.35	-	3.26	3.74	-	2.56	2.17	4.77	3.36
Cochise County	2.55	2.47	-	-	-	-	-	-	2.58	-	-	-	-	-	1.97	-	-	-	-	-	-	-	-	-
Coconino County	2.80	2.32	-	-	-	-	-	-	-	-	-	-	-	-	-	-	-	-	-	-	-	-	-	-
Maricopa County	2.67	2.81	3.54	2.82	-	4.17	2.66	-	3.08	3.34	3.44	-	2.33	2.13	2.59	3.54	-	3.75	4.12	-	2.67	2.23	4.77	3.41
Chandler (city)	2.82	2.90	-	2.92	-	-	2.63	-	3.30	-	-	-	-	-	-	-	-	-	-	-	-	-	-	3.03
Gilbert (town)	3.09	3.38	-	3.35	-	-	3.11	-	4.11	-	-	-	-	-	-	-	-	-	-	-	-	-	-	-
Mesa (city)	2.68	2.80	4.89	2.72	-	-	2.83	-	3.12	-	-	-	-	2.19	2.35	-	-	-	-	-	-	-	-	3.61
Phoenix (city)	2.79	2.91	3.11	2.90	-	4.10	2.68	-	3.05	-	3.06	-	-	2.10	2.78	-	-	-	-	-	-	-	-	3.75
Tempe (city)	2.41	2.38	-	2.36	-	-	2.37	-	3.28	-	-	-	-	1.56	1.83	-	-	-	-	-	-	-	-	3.14
Mohave County	2.45	2.44	-	-	-	-	-	-	-	-	-	-	-	-	-	-	-	-	-	-	-	-	-	-
Pima County	2.47	2.49	2.80	2.53	-	-	2.52	-	2.51	-	2.61	-	-	1.83	2.33	-	-	-	-	-	-	-	-	3.35
Tucson (city)	2.42	2.39	2.74	2.36	-	-	2.37	-	2.60	-	-	-	-	1.60	1.99	-	-	-	-	-	-	-	-	3.31
Pinal County	2.68	2.72	-	-	-	-	-	-	-	-	-	-	-	-	-	-	-	-	-	-	-	-	-	-
Yavapai County	2.34	2.36	-	-	-	-	-	-	-	-	-	-	-	-	-	-	-	-	-	-	-	-	-	-
Yuma County	2.86	2.56	-	-	-	-	-	-	3.31	-	-	-	-	-	-	-	-	-	-	-	-	-	-	-
ARKANSAS	2.49	2.90	4.26	2.63	-	-	2.71	-	2.71	-	2.57	-	-	1.78	2.37	3.72	-	-	-	-	-	2.94	-	3.38
Benton County	2.60	2.94	-	2.45	-	-	-	-	-	-	-	-	-	-	-	-	-	-	-	-	-	-	-	3.54
Craighead County	2.46	4.31	-	-	-	-	-	-	-	-	-	-	-	-	-	-	-	-	-	-	-	-	-	-
Crawford County	2.68	4.39	-	-	-	-	-	-	-	-	-	-	-	-	-	-	-	-	-	-	-	-	-	-

Notes: Please refer to the User's Guide for an explanation of data; data is arranged alphabetically by state, then county, then city within each county; table includes counties with populations greater than 49,999 unless noted and cities with populations greater than 9,999 whose Asian and/or NHPI population rates are greater than the national average; (1) Native Hawaiian and other Pacific Islander; (2) excludes Taiwanese; (3) includes Chamorro; (4) county does not meet population threshold but is shown in order to allow inclusion of city

Place	All households	Asian households	NHPI[1] households	Asian Indian	Bangladeshi	Cambodian	Chinese[2]	Fijian	Filipino	Guamanian[3]	Hawaiian, Native	Hmong	Indonesian	Japanese	Korean	Laotian	Malaysian	Pakistani	Samoan	Sri Lankan	Taiwanese	Thai	Tongan	Vietnamese
Faulkner County	2.57	2.69	-	-	-	-	-	-	-	-	-	-	-	-	-	-	-	-	-	-	-	-	-	-
Jefferson County	2.58	3.03	-	-	-	-	-	-	-	-	-	-	-	-	-	-	-	-	-	-	-	-	-	-
Pulaski County	2.39	2.54	-	2.50	-	-	2.68	-	2.93	-	-	-	-	-	-	-	-	-	-	-	-	-	-	-
Saline County	2.57	4.27	-	-	-	-	-	-	-	-	-	-	-	-	-	-	-	-	-	-	-	-	-	-
Sebastian County	2.49	3.19	-	-	-	-	-	-	-	-	-	-	-	-	-	3.55	-	-	-	-	-	-	-	3.35
Fort Smith (city)	2.42	3.29	-	-	-	-	-	-	-	-	-	-	-	-	-	3.57	-	-	-	-	-	-	-	3.46
Washington County	2.52	2.80	5.70	-	-	-	2.71	-	-	-	-	-	-	-	-	3.32	-	-	-	-	-	-	-	-
Springdale (city)	2.79	3.64	5.85	-	-	-	-	-	-	-	-	-	-	-	-	3.63	-	-	-	-	-	-	-	-
CALIFORNIA	2.87	3.23	3.87	3.17	3.13	4.72	2.98	3.92	3.59	3.36	2.85	6.64	2.99	2.24	2.87	4.90	2.89	3.83	4.78	3.10	3.14	3.09	5.72	3.97
Alameda County	2.70	3.18	3.89	3.14	-	4.78	2.97	3.78	3.72	2.80	2.69	-	3.55	2.23	2.72	4.87	-	3.69	5.36	-	3.07	2.58	6.10	3.70
Alameda (city)	2.35	3.12	3.25	2.94	-	-	3.07	-	3.39	-	-	-	-	2.18	2.86	-	-	-	-	-	-	-	-	3.70
Albany (city)	2.33	2.68	-	2.50	-	-	2.66	-	-	-	-	-	-	2.52	2.93	-	-	-	-	-	-	-	-	-
Ashland (cdp)	2.83	3.34	-	-	-	-	3.41	-	3.55	-	-	-	-	-	-	-	-	-	-	-	-	-	-	-
Berkeley (city)	2.15	2.06	-	2.32	-	-	2.04	-	2.21	-	-	-	-	1.85	1.87	-	-	-	-	-	2.46	-	-	2.50
Castro Valley (cdp)	2.58	3.13	-	3.32	-	-	3.23	-	2.96	-	-	-	-	2.62	2.95	-	-	-	-	-	-	-	-	-
Cherryland (cdp)	2.86	3.16	-	-	-	-	-	-	3.81	-	-	-	-	-	-	-	-	-	-	-	-	-	-	-
Dublin (city)	2.66	3.05	-	3.12	-	-	2.85	-	3.39	-	-	-	-	-	-	-	-	-	-	-	-	-	-	-
Fremont (city)	2.95	3.28	3.23	3.14	-	-	3.12	-	3.71	-	-	-	-	2.35	3.55	-	-	3.99	-	-	3.46	-	-	3.85
Hayward (city)	3.07	3.45	3.75	3.22	-	-	2.83	3.73	3.91	-	-	-	-	2.34	2.64	-	-	-	5.26	-	-	-	-	3.80
Livermore (city)	2.80	2.95	-	3.16	-	-	2.04	-	3.43	-	-	-	-	-	-	-	-	-	-	-	-	-	-	4.02
Newark (city)	3.25	3.40	-	3.15	-	-	2.63	-	4.02	-	-	-	-	-	3.93	-	-	-	-	-	-	-	-	4.19
Oakland (city)	2.60	3.02	5.39	2.68	-	4.96	2.95	-	3.02	-	-	-	-	1.99	1.85	5.35	-	-	-	-	-	-	7.25	3.55
Piedmont (city)	2.90	3.02	-	-	-	-	3.19	-	-	-	-	-	-	-	-	-	-	-	-	-	-	-	-	-
Pleasanton (city)	2.72	3.18	-	2.95	-	-	3.19	-	3.20	-	-	-	-	2.87	3.38	-	-	-	-	-	-	-	-	-
San Leandro (city)	2.56	3.52	4.27	2.61	-	-	3.56	-	3.86	-	-	-	-	2.37	2.85	-	-	-	-	-	-	-	-	3.75
San Lorenzo (cdp)	2.90	3.87	-	-	-	-	3.53	-	3.94	-	-	-	-	-	-	-	-	-	-	-	-	-	-	4.84
Union City (city)	3.57	4.06	3.65	3.88	-	-	3.50	-	4.55	-	-	-	-	2.91	3.36	-	-	-	-	-	-	-	-	4.33
Butte County	2.48	3.98	-	2.98	-	-	2.35	-	2.66	-	-	7.19	-	2.09	-	5.41	-	-	-	-	-	-	-	-
Chico (city)	2.41	2.89	-	-	-	-	2.17	-	-	-	-	5.36	-	-	-	-	-	-	-	-	-	-	-	-
Oroville (city)	2.49	6.29	-	-	-	-	-	-	-	-	-	7.69	-	-	-	-	-	-	-	-	-	-	-	-
Contra Costa County	2.72	3.21	3.80	3.24	-	-	2.92	5.21	3.60	3.24	2.97	-	2.43	2.38	2.84	5.02	-	4.01	4.44	-	2.87	3.92	5.77	3.72
Alamo (cdp)	2.89	3.21	-	-	-	-	-	-	-	-	-	-	-	-	-	-	-	-	-	-	-	-	-	-
Antioch (city)	3.08	3.78	3.44	4.01	-	-	3.40	-	4.16	-	-	-	-	-	-	-	-	-	-	-	-	-	-	4.28
Bay Point (cdp)	3.25	4.06	-	-	-	-	-	-	4.32	-	-	-	-	-	-	-	-	-	-	-	-	-	-	-
Blackhawk-Camino-Tass. (cdp)	3.00	3.50	-	-	-	-	3.43	-	-	-	-	-	-	-	-	-	-	-	-	-	-	-	-	-
Clayton (city)	2.74	3.08	-	-	-	-	-	-	-	-	-	-	-	-	-	-	-	-	-	-	-	-	-	-
Concord (city)	2.73	2.96	4.81	2.98	-	-	2.64	-	3.32	-	-	-	-	2.46	2.48	-	-	-	-	-	-	-	-	2.69
Danville (town)	2.77	3.34	-	3.67	-	-	3.53	-	2.93	-	-	-	-	-	-	-	-	-	-	-	-	-	-	-
El Cerrito (city)	2.25	2.66	-	2.75	-	-	2.56	-	3.37	-	-	-	-	2.32	-	-	-	-	-	-	-	-	-	-
El Sobrante (cdp)	2.54	3.12	-	3.34	-	-	-	-	-	-	-	-	-	-	-	-	-	-	-	-	-	-	-	-
Hercules (city)	3.02	3.68	-	4.11	-	-	3.04	-	3.99	-	-	-	-	-	-	-	-	-	-	-	-	-	-	-

Notes: Please refer to the User's Guide for an explanation of data; data is arranged alphabetically by state, then county, then city within each county; table includes counties with populations greater than 49,999 unless noted and cities with populations greater than 9,999 whose Asian and/or NHPI population rates are greater than the national average; (1) Native Hawaiian and other Pacific Islander; (2) excludes Taiwanese; (3) includes Chamorro; (4) county does not meet population threshold but is shown in order to allow inclusion of city

Place	All households	Asian households	NHPI[1] households	Asian Indian	Bangladeshi	Cambodian	Chinese[2]	Fijian	Filipino	Guamanian[3]	Hawaiian, Native	Hmong	Indonesian	Japanese	Korean	Laotian	Malaysian	Pakistani	Samoan	Sri Lankan	Taiwanese	Thai	Tongan	Vietnamese
Lafayette (city)	2.60	2.71	-	-	-	-	2.89	-	-	-	-	-	-	-	-	-	-	-	-	-	-	-	-	-
Martinez (city)	2.43	3.24	-	-	-	-	3.40	-	3.51	-	-	-	-	-	-	-	-	-	-	-	-	-	-	-
Moraga (town)	2.60	3.13	-	-	-	-	3.22	-	-	-	-	-	-	-	-	-	-	-	-	-	-	-	-	-
Orinda (city)	2.65	2.90	-	-	-	-	2.96	-	-	-	-	-	-	-	-	-	-	-	-	-	-	-	-	-
Pinole (city)	2.80	3.54	-	-	-	-	2.99	-	3.92	-	-	-	-	-	-	-	-	-	-	-	-	-	-	-
Pittsburg (city)	3.16	3.69	4.38	3.57	-	-	2.82	-	3.80	-	-	-	-	-	-	-	-	-	-	-	-	-	-	-
Pleasant Hill (city)	2.37	2.77	-	-	-	-	2.73	-	2.86	-	-	-	-	-	2.91	-	-	-	-	-	-	-	-	-
Richmond (city)	2.82	3.12	4.54	3.32	-	-	2.69	-	3.33	-	-	-	-	1.92	2.78	5.08	-	-	-	-	-	-	-	3.31
San Pablo (city)	3.26	3.74	-	3.47	-	-	-	-	3.46	-	-	-	-	-	-	4.66	-	-	-	-	-	-	-	4.10
San Ramon (city)	2.63	3.25	-	3.11	-	-	3.46	-	3.27	-	-	-	-	2.61	-	-	-	-	-	-	-	-	-	-
Walnut Creek (city)	2.08	2.51	-	2.32	-	-	2.63	-	2.39	-	-	-	-	2.23	2.75	-	-	-	-	-	-	-	-	-
El Dorado County	2.63	2.99	-	-	-	-	-	-	3.28	-	-	-	-	2.17	-	-	-	-	-	-	-	-	-	-
El Dorado Hills (cdp)	3.04	2.71	-	-	-	-	-	-	-	-	-	-	-	-	-	-	-	-	-	-	-	-	-	-
South Lake Tahoe (city)	2.50	3.20	-	-	-	-	-	-	3.54	-	-	-	-	-	-	-	-	-	-	-	-	-	-	-
Fresno County	3.09	4.23	3.86	4.21	-	5.60	2.84	-	3.36	-	-	6.89	-	2.22	2.73	4.87	-	-	-	-	-	-	-	3.79
Clovis (city)	2.80	3.84	-	-	-	-	-	-	3.99	-	-	6.27	-	2.29	-	-	-	-	-	-	-	-	-	-
Fresno (city)	2.99	4.46	-	3.94	-	5.75	2.89	-	3.31	-	-	6.91	-	2.18	2.80	4.73	-	-	-	-	-	-	-	3.82
Reedley (city)	3.55	2.56	-	-	-	-	-	-	-	-	-	-	-	-	-	-	-	-	-	-	-	-	-	-
Humboldt County	2.39	3.11	-	-	-	-	-	-	-	-	-	-	-	2.12	-	-	-	-	-	-	-	-	-	-
Imperial County	3.33	2.82	-	-	-	-	2.99	-	2.94	-	-	-	-	-	3.20	-	-	-	-	-	-	-	-	-
Kern County	3.03	3.44	3.42	4.27	-	5.15	2.73	-	3.53	-	-	-	-	2.46	2.70	-	-	-	-	-	-	-	-	3.74
Bakersfield (city)	2.91	3.24	3.71	4.25	-	-	2.76	-	2.82	-	-	-	-	2.81	2.85	-	-	-	-	-	-	-	-	3.31
Delano (city)	4.00	4.24	-	-	-	-	-	-	4.24	-	-	-	-	-	-	-	-	-	-	-	-	-	-	-
Ridgecrest (city)	2.52	2.95	-	-	-	-	-	-	3.06	-	-	-	-	-	-	-	-	-	-	-	-	-	-	-
Kings County	3.18	3.11	-	-	-	-	-	-	3.10	-	-	-	-	-	-	-	-	-	-	-	-	-	-	-
Lemoore (city)	3.05	3.11	-	-	-	-	-	-	2.94	-	-	-	-	-	-	-	-	-	-	-	-	-	-	-
Lake County	2.39	2.49	-	-	-	-	-	-	-	-	-	-	-	-	-	-	-	-	-	-	-	-	-	-
Los Angeles County	2.98	3.05	4.06	3.06	3.29	4.65	3.04	2.86	3.42	3.59	2.93	4.12	2.91	2.20	2.81	4.28	2.59	3.54	4.75	3.19	3.21	3.28	6.09	3.84
Agoura Hills (city)	2.98	2.88	-	-	-	-	-	-	-	-	-	-	-	-	-	-	-	-	-	-	-	-	-	-
Alhambra (city)	2.89	3.11	-	2.82	-	-	3.08	-	3.47	-	-	-	-	2.21	2.86	-	-	-	-	-	2.88	-	-	3.51
Altadena (cdp)	2.81	2.58	-	-	-	-	-	-	2.81	-	-	-	-	2.23	-	-	-	-	-	-	-	-	-	-
Arcadia (city)	2.75	3.34	-	3.44	-	-	3.27	-	3.31	-	-	-	-	2.99	3.59	-	-	-	-	-	3.73	-	-	-
Artesia (city)	3.54	3.79	-	3.52	-	-	3.63	-	4.33	-	-	-	-	-	3.44	-	-	-	-	-	-	-	-	-
Avocado Heights (cdp)	3.98	3.23	-	-	-	-	-	-	-	-	-	-	-	-	-	-	-	-	-	-	-	-	-	-
Azusa (city)	3.42	3.20	-	-	-	-	-	-	3.36	-	-	-	-	-	-	-	-	-	-	-	-	-	-	-
Baldwin Park (city)	4.43	3.95	-	-	-	-	3.47	-	4.51	-	-	-	-	-	-	-	-	-	-	-	-	-	-	4.57
Bellflower (city)	3.09	3.55	-	-	-	4.28	-	-	3.72	-	-	-	-	-	3.07	-	-	-	-	-	-	3.22	-	-
Beverly Hills (city)	2.25	2.79	-	-	-	-	2.40	-	-	-	-	-	-	-	3.29	-	-	-	-	-	-	-	-	-
Burbank (city)	2.39	2.89	-	3.29	-	-	2.12	-	3.04	-	-	-	-	1.64	3.27	-	-	-	-	-	-	-	-	3.31
Calabasas (city)	2.73	3.05	-	-	-	-	3.45	-	-	-	-	-	-	-	-	-	-	-	-	-	-	-	-	-
Carson (city)	3.59	4.04	5.18	-	-	-	3.87	-	4.23	-	-	-	-	2.22	-	-	-	-	5.73	-	-	-	-	4.15

Notes: Please refer to the User's Guide for an explanation of data; data is arranged alphabetically by state, then county, then city within each county; table includes counties with populations greater than 49,999 unless noted and cities with populations greater than 9,999 whose Asian and/or NHPI population rates are greater than the national average; (1) Native Hawaiian and other Pacific Islander; (2) excludes Taiwanese; (3) includes Chamorro; (4) county does not meet population threshold but is shown in order to allow inclusion of city

Place	All households	Asian households	NHPI[1] households	Asian Indian	Bangladeshi	Cambodian	Chinese[2]	Fijian	Filipino	Guamanian[3]	Hawaiian, Native	Hmong	Indonesian	Japanese	Korean	Laotian	Malaysian	Pakistani	Samoan	Sri Lankan	Taiwanese	Thai	Tongan	Vietnamese
Cerritos (city)	3.34	3.68	-	3.88	-	-	3.50	-	3.68	-	-	-	-	3.06	3.76	-	-	-	-	-	3.58	3.83	-	4.46
Citrus (cdp)	3.99	3.40	-	-	-	-	-	-	-	-	-	-	-	-	-	-	-	-	-	-	-	-	-	-
Claremont (city)	2.54	3.08	-	2.99	-	-	2.67	-	-	-	-	-	-	-	3.15	-	-	-	-	-	-	-	-	-
Compton (city)	4.16	3.76	5.95	-	-	-	-	-	-	-	-	-	-	-	-	-	-	-	6.24	-	-	-	-	-
Covina (city)	2.92	3.36	-	-	-	-	2.90	-	4.02	-	-	-	-	2.92	-	-	-	-	-	-	-	-	-	4.92
Culver City (city)	2.30	2.66	-	3.23	-	-	2.45	-	3.46	-	-	-	-	2.32	-	-	-	-	-	-	-	-	-	-
Diamond Bar (city)	3.17	3.48	-	3.89	-	-	3.42	-	3.81	-	-	-	-	2.63	3.48	-	-	-	-	-	3.37	-	-	4.02
Downey (city)	3.10	3.35	-	2.96	-	-	2.84	-	3.29	-	-	-	-	2.86	3.49	-	-	-	-	-	-	-	-	3.54
Duarte (city)	3.17	3.58	-	-	-	-	2.84	-	4.23	-	-	-	-	-	-	-	-	-	-	-	-	-	-	-
East San Gabriel (cdp)	2.79	3.21	-	-	-	-	3.03	-	-	-	-	-	-	3.15	-	-	-	-	-	-	3.26	-	-	-
El Monte (city)	4.24	4.04	-	-	-	-	3.86	-	4.35	-	-	-	-	-	-	-	-	-	-	-	2.25	-	-	4.62
El Segundo (city)	2.26	2.29	-	-	-	-	-	-	-	-	-	-	-	-	-	-	-	-	-	-	-	-	-	-
Gardena (city)	2.79	2.43	-	-	-	-	2.84	-	3.06	-	-	-	-	1.99	2.74	-	-	-	-	-	-	-	-	4.27
Glendale (city)	2.67	2.95	-	2.79	-	-	2.66	-	3.02	-	-	-	-	2.03	3.15	-	-	-	-	-	-	2.81	-	3.10
Glendora (city)	2.88	3.26	-	3.58	-	-	3.37	-	3.26	-	-	-	-	-	-	-	-	-	-	-	-	-	-	-
Hacienda Heights (cdp)	3.32	3.40	-	-	-	-	3.25	-	4.02	-	-	-	-	2.68	3.39	-	-	-	-	-	3.91	-	-	7.36
Hawaiian Gardens (city)	4.07	2.78	-	-	-	-	-	-	-	-	-	-	-	-	2.60	-	-	-	-	-	-	-	-	-
Hawthorne (city)	2.93	3.12	4.62	3.14	-	-	3.02	-	3.30	-	-	-	-	1.97	-	-	-	-	-	-	-	-	-	3.55
Hermosa Beach (city)	1.94	1.61	-	-	-	-	-	-	-	-	-	-	-	-	-	-	-	-	-	-	-	-	-	-
La Canada Flintridge (city)	2.93	3.68	-	-	-	-	3.73	-	-	-	-	-	-	2.71	3.89	-	-	-	-	-	-	-	-	-
La Crescenta-Montrose (cdp)	2.65	3.18	-	-	-	-	-	-	2.54	-	-	-	-	-	3.52	-	-	-	-	-	-	-	-	-
La Mirada (city)	3.10	3.40	-	3.35	-	-	2.96	-	4.20	-	-	-	-	2.41	3.14	-	-	-	-	-	-	-	-	-
La Puente (city)	4.34	3.32	-	-	-	-	3.21	-	3.04	-	-	-	-	-	-	-	-	-	-	-	-	-	-	-
La Verne (city)	2.81	3.19	-	-	-	-	-	-	3.71	-	-	-	-	-	-	-	-	-	-	-	-	-	-	-
Lakewood (city)	2.96	3.54	4.58	3.25	-	4.46	3.20	-	3.92	-	-	-	-	2.56	3.22	-	-	-	4.95	-	-	-	-	3.32
Lancaster (city)	2.93	2.96	-	3.31	-	-	2.79	-	3.14	-	-	-	-	-	-	-	-	-	-	-	-	-	-	-
Lawndale (city)	3.31	3.35	4.85	-	-	-	-	-	2.94	-	-	-	-	-	-	-	-	-	-	-	-	-	-	4.05
Lomita (city)	2.49	2.49	-	-	-	-	-	-	2.38	-	-	-	-	2.06	3.20	-	-	-	-	-	-	-	-	-
Long Beach (city)	2.76	3.45	4.71	2.78	-	4.74	2.55	-	3.46	-	-	-	-	1.92	2.01	4.25	-	-	5.03	-	-	2.72	-	3.54
Los Angeles (city)	2.83	2.70	3.41	2.88	3.24	4.33	2.57	-	3.19	3.09	2.97	-	2.40	1.92	2.51	3.78	-	3.38	3.92	2.97	2.25	3.14	5.20	3.44
Manhattan Beach (city)	2.35	2.47	-	-	-	-	2.60	-	-	-	-	-	-	2.29	-	-	-	-	-	-	-	-	-	-
Monrovia (city)	2.72	2.78	-	-	-	-	2.60	-	3.38	-	-	-	-	-	-	-	-	-	-	-	-	-	-	-
Montebello (city)	3.27	2.76	-	-	-	-	2.64	-	3.23	-	-	-	-	2.31	3.31	-	-	-	-	-	-	-	-	-
Monterey Park (city)	3.05	3.13	-	-	-	4.85	3.12	-	3.27	-	-	-	-	2.57	3.11	-	-	-	-	-	3.00	-	-	4.24
Norwalk (city)	3.78	3.67	-	4.17	-	3.94	2.90	-	4.21	-	-	-	-	2.86	3.05	-	-	-	-	-	-	-	-	3.77
Palmdale (city)	3.39	3.48	-	4.23	-	-	-	-	3.67	-	-	-	-	-	-	-	-	-	-	-	-	-	-	-
Palos Verdes Estates (city)	2.67	3.42	-	-	-	-	3.37	-	-	-	-	-	-	3.01	3.48	-	-	-	-	-	-	-	-	-
Pasadena (city)	2.52	2.26	-	2.30	-	-	2.00	-	2.83	-	-	-	-	2.01	2.14	-	-	-	-	-	-	-	-	3.34
Pomona (city)	3.81	3.64	-	3.46	-	5.90	3.34	-	3.95	-	-	-	-	2.35	-	5.01	-	-	-	-	-	-	-	4.21
Rancho Palos Verdes (city)	2.66	3.17	-	3.26	-	-	2.95	-	3.16	-	-	-	-	3.00	3.56	-	-	-	-	-	3.09	-	-	-
Redondo Beach (city)	2.21	2.48	-	2.28	-	-	2.70	-	2.59	-	-	-	-	2.30	2.75	-	-	-	-	-	-	-	-	-

Notes: Please refer to the User's Guide for an explanation of data; data is arranged alphabetically by state, then county, then city within each county; table includes counties with populations greater than 49,999 unless noted and cities with populations greater than 9,999 whose Asian and/or NHPI population rates are greater than the national average; (1) Native Hawaiian and other Pacific Islander; (2) excludes Taiwanese; (3) includes Chamorro; (4) county does not meet population threshold but is shown in order to allow inclusion of city

Place	All households	Asian households	NHPI[1] households	Asian Indian	Bangladeshi	Cambodian	Chinese[2]	Fijian	Filipino	Guamanian[3]	Hawaiian, Native	Hmong	Indonesian	Japanese	Korean	Laotian	Malaysian	Pakistani	Samoan	Sri Lankan	Taiwanese	Thai	Tongan	Vietnamese
Rosemead (city)	3.78	4.08	-	-	-	4.14	4.26	-	3.55	-	-	-	-	2.13	-	-	-	-	-	-	-	-	-	4.39
Rowland Heights (cdp)	3.39	3.43	-	4.17	-	-	3.33	-	3.78	-	-	-	-	2.78	3.46	-	-	-	-	-	3.26	-	-	4.33
San Dimas (city)	2.77	3.09	-	-	-	-	3.23	-	3.50	-	-	-	-	-	-	-	-	-	-	-	-	-	-	-
San Gabriel (city)	3.07	3.44	-	-	-	-	3.35	-	3.75	-	-	-	-	2.36	-	-	-	-	-	-	2.98	-	-	3.93
San Marino (city)	3.03	3.65	-	-	-	-	3.76	-	-	-	-	-	-	-	-	-	-	-	-	-	3.44	-	-	-
Santa Clarita (city)	2.96	3.17	-	2.98	-	-	3.49	-	3.26	-	-	-	-	2.50	3.07	-	-	-	-	-	-	-	-	3.61
Santa Monica (city)	1.84	1.94	-	2.29	-	-	1.78	-	1.78	-	-	-	-	1.96	2.13	-	-	-	-	-	-	-	-	-
Sierra Madre (city)	2.20	2.53	-	-	-	-	-	-	-	-	-	-	-	-	-	-	-	-	-	-	-	-	-	-
South El Monte (city)	4.64	4.43	-	-	-	-	4.59	-	-	-	-	-	-	-	-	-	-	-	-	-	-	-	-	4.50
South Pasadena (city)	2.30	2.66	-	-	-	-	2.76	-	-	-	-	-	-	2.11	2.79	-	-	-	-	-	-	-	-	-
South San Jose Hills (cdp)	5.13	4.23	-	-	-	-	-	-	4.53	-	-	-	-	-	-	-	-	-	-	-	-	-	-	-
Temple City (city)	2.88	3.45	-	-	-	-	3.42	-	4.39	-	-	-	-	2.79	3.54	-	-	-	-	-	3.56	-	-	4.08
Torrance (city)	2.51	2.85	-	2.88	-	-	2.79	-	3.24	-	-	-	-	2.50	3.13	-	-	4.00	-	-	3.35	-	-	3.66
Valinda (cdp)	4.55	4.23	-	-	-	-	-	-	4.63	-	-	-	-	-	-	-	-	-	-	-	-	-	-	5.15
Vincent (cdp)	3.90	4.21	-	-	-	-	-	-	4.32	-	-	-	-	-	-	-	-	-	-	-	-	-	-	-
Walnut (city)	3.63	3.78	-	3.79	-	-	3.52	-	4.12	-	-	-	-	2.56	3.89	-	-	-	-	-	4.04	-	-	5.59
West Carson (cdp)	2.85	2.96	-	-	-	-	-	-	3.19	-	-	-	-	2.35	3.10	-	-	-	-	-	-	-	-	-
West Covina (city)	3.31	3.68	3.92	3.05	-	-	3.37	-	4.02	-	-	-	-	2.60	2.78	-	-	-	-	-	3.67	-	-	4.58
West Hollywood (city)	1.54	1.69	-	-	-	-	-	-	-	-	-	-	-	-	-	-	-	-	-	-	-	-	-	-
West Puente Valley (cdp)	4.71	4.34	-	-	-	-	-	-	4.26	-	-	-	-	-	-	-	-	-	-	-	-	-	-	5.56
Whittier (city)	2.88	3.02	-	-	-	-	3.32	-	2.70	-	-	-	-	2.82	3.05	-	-	-	-	-	-	-	-	-
Madera County	3.18	3.83	-	4.79	-	-	-	-	3.71	-	-	-	-	-	-	-	-	-	-	-	-	-	-	-
Marin County	2.34	2.66	-	2.63	-	-	2.64	-	2.59	-	-	-	-	1.96	3.07	-	-	-	-	-	-	-	-	3.54
Larkspur (city)	1.92	1.98	-	-	-	-	-	-	-	-	-	-	-	-	-	-	-	-	-	-	-	-	-	-
Novato (city)	2.52	3.03	-	-	-	-	3.20	-	3.31	-	-	-	-	-	-	-	-	-	-	-	-	-	-	-
San Rafael (city)	2.41	2.75	-	2.85	-	-	2.55	-	-	-	-	-	-	-	-	-	-	-	-	-	-	-	-	3.80
Tamalpais-Homestead (cdp)	2.34	2.96	-	-	-	-	-	-	-	-	-	-	-	-	-	-	-	-	-	-	-	-	-	-
Mendocino County	2.52	2.47	-	-	-	-	-	-	-	-	-	-	-	-	-	-	-	-	-	-	-	-	-	-
Merced County	3.25	4.82	-	4.61	-	-	2.41	-	2.93	-	-	6.76	-	2.16	-	5.18	-	-	-	-	-	-	-	-
Atwater (city)	3.13	4.90	-	-	-	-	-	-	-	-	-	7.20	-	-	-	-	-	-	-	-	-	-	-	-
Livingston (city)	4.30	4.35	-	4.74	-	-	-	-	-	-	-	-	-	-	-	-	-	-	-	-	-	-	-	-
Merced (city)	3.06	5.36	-	-	-	-	-	-	-	-	-	6.45	-	-	-	5.24	-	-	-	-	-	-	-	-
Monterey County	3.14	3.05	3.33	3.23	-	-	2.47	-	3.58	3.31	-	-	-	2.23	2.81	-	-	-	-	-	-	-	-	3.68
Marina (city)	2.78	3.21	3.03	-	-	-	-	-	3.47	-	-	-	-	2.40	3.28	-	-	-	-	-	-	-	-	4.18
Monterey (city)	2.13	2.32	-	-	-	-	2.23	-	2.82	-	-	-	-	2.28	-	-	-	-	-	-	-	-	-	-
Pacific Grove (city)	2.10	1.88	-	-	-	-	-	-	-	-	-	-	-	-	-	-	-	-	-	-	-	-	-	-
Salinas (city)	3.67	3.28	4.45	3.63	-	-	2.64	-	3.65	-	-	-	-	2.24	2.87	-	-	-	-	-	-	-	-	3.53
Seaside (city)	3.20	3.56	-	-	-	-	-	-	4.10	-	-	-	-	2.19	-	-	-	-	-	-	-	-	-	3.88
Napa County	2.62	3.43	-	-	-	-	2.70	-	4.04	-	-	-	-	2.57	-	-	-	-	-	-	-	-	-	-
Nevada County	2.47	2.33	-	-	-	-	-	-	-	-	-	-	-	-	-	-	-	-	-	-	-	-	-	-
Orange County	3.00	3.44	3.95	3.31	-	4.48	2.93	-	3.49	2.71	2.59	6.13	3.01	2.40	3.19	5.12	-	3.92	5.46	3.35	3.25	3.21	4.24	4.20

Notes: Please refer to the User's Guide for an explanation of data; data is arranged alphabetically by state, then county, then city within each county; table includes counties with populations greater than 49,999 unless noted and cities with populations greater than 9,999 whose Asian and/or NHPI population rates are greater than the national average; (1) Native Hawaiian and other Pacific Islander; (2) excludes Taiwanese; (3) includes Chamorro; (4) county does not meet population threshold but is shown in order to allow inclusion of city

Place	All households	Asian households	NHPI[1] households	Asian Indian	Bangladeshi	Cambodian	Chinese[2]	Fijian	Filipino	Guamanian[3]	Hawaiian, Native	Hmong	Indonesian	Japanese	Korean	Laotian	Malaysian	Pakistani	Samoan	Sri Lankan	Taiwanese	Thai	Tongan	Vietnamese
Aliso Viejo (cdp)	2.48	2.94	-	2.89	-	-	2.53	-	3.21	-	-	-	-	2.47	2.82	-	-	-	-	-	-	-	-	3.05
Anaheim (city)	3.34	3.44	4.59	3.39	-	-	2.92	-	3.52	-	-	-	-	2.20	3.21	4.94	-	4.19	6.09	-	3.28	3.43	-	4.17
Brea (city)	2.69	3.14	-	3.44	-	-	3.22	-	3.25	-	-	-	-	-	3.10	-	-	-	-	-	-	-	-	-
Buena Park (city)	3.30	3.66	-	3.93	-	-	3.24	-	3.99	-	-	-	-	2.46	3.46	-	-	-	-	-	-	-	-	4.06
Costa Mesa (city)	2.69	2.70	4.25	2.35	-	-	2.25	-	2.67	-	-	-	-	2.17	2.38	-	-	-	-	-	-	-	-	3.75
Cypress (city)	2.94	3.36	-	3.46	-	-	3.33	-	3.36	-	-	-	-	2.47	3.60	-	-	-	-	-	3.91	-	-	3.50
Foothill Ranch (cdp)	2.86	3.25	-	-	-	-	-	-	-	-	-	-	-	-	-	-	-	-	-	-	-	-	-	-
Fountain Valley (city)	3.00	3.68	-	3.59	-	-	3.27	-	3.10	-	-	-	-	2.83	3.21	-	-	-	-	-	3.38	-	-	4.34
Fullerton (city)	2.83	3.14	-	3.13	-	-	2.84	-	3.38	-	-	-	-	2.05	3.40	-	-	-	-	-	-	-	-	3.31
Garden Grove (city)	3.56	4.08	4.96	3.92	-	3.83	3.67	-	4.46	-	-	-	-	2.06	3.04	-	-	-	6.49	-	-	-	-	4.46
Huntington Beach (city)	2.56	2.95	3.09	3.15	-	-	2.58	-	2.72	-	-	-	-	2.35	2.77	-	-	-	-	-	3.11	-	-	3.86
Irvine (city)	2.66	3.08	-	3.11	-	-	2.89	-	3.45	-	-	-	-	2.65	3.21	-	-	-	-	-	3.14	-	-	3.55
La Habra (city)	3.08	3.15	-	-	-	-	2.73	-	3.28	-	-	-	-	-	3.19	-	-	-	-	-	-	-	-	-
La Palma (city)	3.05	3.49	-	3.94	-	-	3.02	-	4.11	-	-	-	-	2.71	3.48	-	-	-	-	-	-	-	-	-
Laguna Hills (city)	2.80	3.33	-	-	-	-	2.82	-	3.98	-	-	-	-	-	-	-	-	-	-	-	-	-	-	3.92
Laguna Niguel (city)	2.65	2.76	-	-	-	-	2.66	-	3.05	-	-	-	-	2.27	3.42	-	-	-	-	-	-	-	-	3.10
Lake Forest (city)	2.89	3.21	-	3.28	-	-	2.81	-	3.65	-	-	-	-	1.94	3.14	-	-	-	-	-	-	-	-	4.02
Los Alamitos (city)	2.60	2.94	-	-	-	-	-	-	-	-	-	-	-	-	-	-	-	-	-	-	-	-	-	-
Mission Viejo (city)	2.83	3.30	-	3.52	-	-	3.04	-	3.84	-	-	-	-	2.76	3.18	-	-	-	-	-	-	-	-	4.01
Newport Beach (city)	2.08	2.36	-	-	-	-	2.50	-	-	-	-	-	-	2.00	-	-	-	-	-	-	-	-	-	-
Orange (city)	3.00	3.37	-	3.18	-	-	2.96	-	3.59	-	-	-	-	2.41	2.78	-	-	-	-	-	3.02	-	-	4.28
Placentia (city)	3.09	3.34	-	4.00	-	-	3.09	-	3.07	-	-	-	-	2.26	3.54	-	-	-	-	-	-	-	-	3.98
Rancho Santa Margarita (city)	2.90	3.23	-	-	-	-	3.05	-	3.24	-	-	-	-	-	-	-	-	-	-	-	-	-	-	3.69
Rossmoor (cdp)	2.77	3.02	-	-	-	-	-	-	-	-	-	-	-	-	-	-	-	-	-	-	-	-	-	-
Santa Ana (city)	4.55	3.97	4.36	2.88	-	5.41	3.11	-	3.31	-	-	6.95	-	2.00	2.30	5.51	-	-	5.62	-	-	-	-	4.33
Seal Beach (city)	1.84	2.60	-	-	-	-	-	-	-	-	-	-	-	2.48	-	-	-	-	-	-	-	-	-	-
Stanton (city)	3.38	3.51	-	-	-	-	-	-	3.62	-	-	-	-	-	2.89	-	-	-	-	-	-	-	-	3.96
Tustin (city)	2.81	3.19	-	3.61	-	-	2.66	-	3.36	-	-	-	-	2.36	3.19	-	-	-	-	-	2.81	-	-	3.67
Tustin Foothills (cdp)	2.90	3.42	-	-	-	-	3.38	-	-	-	-	-	-	-	-	-	-	-	-	-	-	-	-	-
Westminster (city)	3.31	3.99	5.11	3.45	-	-	3.34	-	3.36	-	-	-	-	2.44	2.87	-	-	-	5.94	-	-	-	-	4.25
Yorba Linda (city)	3.05	3.38	-	3.49	-	-	3.26	-	3.90	-	-	-	-	2.95	3.51	-	-	-	-	-	-	-	-	3.63
Placer County	2.63	2.91	-	3.11	-	-	2.71	-	3.51	-	-	-	-	2.32	3.85	-	-	-	-	-	-	-	-	3.14
Rocklin (city)	2.75	2.94	-	-	-	-	-	-	-	-	-	-	-	2.82	-	-	-	-	-	-	-	-	-	-
Roseville (city)	2.57	3.20	-	2.99	-	-	2.70	-	4.03	-	-	-	-	2.54	-	-	-	-	-	-	-	-	-	-
Riverside County	2.98	3.28	3.77	3.44	-	4.31	2.75	-	3.62	4.02	3.04	5.72	-	2.29	3.14	4.05	-	3.53	3.92	-	3.05	3.09	-	3.77
Banning (city)	2.59	4.51	-	-	-	-	-	-	-	-	-	-	-	-	-	4.42	-	-	-	-	-	-	-	-
Corona (city)	3.28	3.54	-	3.84	-	-	2.83	-	3.67	-	-	-	-	2.59	4.13	-	-	-	-	-	-	-	-	3.60
Moreno Valley (city)	3.61	3.78	-	-	-	-	3.34	-	4.15	-	-	-	-	2.51	3.17	4.18	-	-	-	-	-	-	-	4.47
Palm Springs (city)	2.06	3.37	-	-	-	-	-	-	3.99	-	-	-	-	-	-	-	-	-	-	-	-	-	-	-
Pedley (cdp)	3.43	4.75	-	-	-	-	-	-	-	-	-	-	-	-	-	-	-	-	-	-	-	-	-	-
Riverside (city)	3.01	2.90	3.37	3.15	-	-	2.44	-	3.11	-	-	-	-	2.29	2.73	3.77	-	-	-	-	-	-	-	3.49

Notes: Please refer to the User's Guide for an explanation of data; data is arranged alphabetically by state, then county, then city within each county; table includes counties with populations greater than 49,999 unless noted and cities with populations greater than 9,999 whose Asian and/or NHPI population rates are greater than the national average; (1) Native Hawaiian and other Pacific Islander; (2) excludes Taiwanese; (3) includes Chamorro; (4) county does not meet population threshold but is shown in order to allow inclusion of city

Place	All households	Asian households	NHPI[1] households	Asian Indian	Bangladeshi	Cambodian	Chinese[2]	Fijian	Filipino	Guamanian[3]	Hawaiian, Native	Hmong	Indonesian	Japanese	Korean	Laotian	Malaysian	Pakistani	Samoan	Sri Lankan	Taiwanese	Thai	Tongan	Vietnamese
Temecula (city)	3.15	3.21	-	-	-	-	3.02	-	3.49	-	-	-	-	-	-	-	-	-	-	-	-	-	-	-
Sacramento County	2.64	3.37	3.45	3.37	-	4.12	2.86	3.66	3.18	2.76	2.40	6.63	-	2.24	2.73	5.57	-	4.91	3.82	-	2.34	2.44	6.11	3.78
Arden-Arcade (cdp)	2.20	2.35	-	2.87	-	-	2.12	-	2.25	-	-	3.98	-	1.98	-	-	-	-	-	-	-	-	-	2.20
Elk Grove (cdp)	3.22	4.01	-	4.33	-	-	3.56	-	3.96	-	-	-	-	2.83	-	-	-	-	-	-	-	-	-	4.37
Fair Oaks (cdp)	2.47	2.97	-	-	-	-	-	-	-	-	-	-	-	-	-	-	-	-	-	-	-	-	-	-
Florin (cdp)	2.98	4.02	-	3.67	-	-	2.99	-	3.23	-	-	6.14	-	-	-	-	-	-	-	-	-	-	-	4.62
Folsom (city)	2.61	2.92	-	3.03	-	-	2.82	-	3.30	-	-	-	-	-	-	-	-	-	-	-	-	-	-	-
Foothill Farms (cdp)	2.69	3.10	-	-	-	-	-	-	-	-	-	-	-	-	-	-	-	-	-	-	-	-	-	-
La Riviera (cdp)	2.36	2.45	-	-	-	-	-	-	-	-	-	-	-	-	-	-	-	-	-	-	-	-	-	-
Laguna (cdp)	3.04	3.52	-	4.53	-	-	3.30	-	3.83	-	-	-	-	2.92	-	-	-	-	-	-	-	-	-	3.29
North Highlands (cdp)	2.83	3.56	-	-	-	-	-	-	3.03	-	-	-	-	-	-	-	-	-	-	-	-	-	-	3.79
Parkway-S. Sacramento (cdp)	3.24	4.52	-	-	-	-	3.43	-	-	-	-	6.46	-	-	-	4.94	-	-	-	-	-	-	-	3.62
Rancho Cordova (cdp)	2.66	2.85	-	2.47	-	-	2.62	-	2.80	-	-	-	-	-	2.64	-	-	-	-	-	-	-	-	3.20
Rosemont (cdp)	2.66	2.86	-	-	-	-	-	-	2.40	-	-	-	-	-	2.81	-	-	-	-	-	-	-	-	3.19
Sacramento (city)	2.57	3.43	3.80	3.34	-	4.16	2.84	3.72	3.03	-	-	6.94	-	2.09	2.10	5.60	-	5.61	4.03	-	-	-	6.99	4.00
Vineyard (cdp)	3.06	3.47	-	-	-	-	-	-	3.93	-	-	-	-	-	-	-	-	-	-	-	-	-	-	-
San Benito County	3.31	2.73	-	-	-	-	-	-	3.01	-	-	-	-	-	-	-	-	-	-	-	-	-	-	-
San Bernardino County	3.15	3.43	4.20	3.60	-	4.44	3.14	-	3.60	3.55	2.71	-	3.75	2.49	2.95	4.23	-	3.28	5.10	-	3.50	3.06	5.32	4.02
Chino (city)	3.43	3.66	-	-	-	-	-	-	4.08	-	-	-	-	-	-	-	-	-	-	-	-	-	-	4.54
Chino Hills (city)	3.33	3.67	-	3.48	-	-	3.44	-	3.94	-	-	-	-	3.04	3.55	-	-	-	-	-	3.81	-	-	4.34
Colton (city)	3.24	3.37	-	-	-	-	-	-	3.71	-	-	-	-	-	-	-	-	-	-	-	-	-	-	-
Fontana (city)	3.76	4.07	4.16	4.19	-	-	-	-	4.07	-	-	-	-	-	-	-	-	-	-	-	-	-	-	-
Grand Terrace (city)	2.76	2.91	-	-	-	-	-	-	-	-	-	-	-	-	-	-	-	-	-	-	-	-	-	-
Highland (city)	3.31	3.65	-	-	-	-	-	-	3.57	-	-	-	-	-	-	-	-	-	-	-	-	-	-	4.10
Loma Linda (city)	2.43	2.96	-	3.09	-	-	3.24	-	3.19	-	-	-	4.01	-	2.40	-	-	-	-	-	-	-	-	-
Montclair (city)	3.68	3.68	-	-	-	-	-	-	-	-	-	-	-	-	-	-	-	-	-	-	-	-	-	4.13
Ontario (city)	3.60	3.52	5.16	4.17	-	-	2.47	-	3.65	-	-	-	-	-	-	-	-	-	-	-	-	-	-	4.41
Rancho Cucamonga (city)	3.03	3.19	-	3.59	-	-	2.85	-	3.48	-	-	-	-	2.68	3.09	-	-	-	-	-	-	-	-	3.29
Redlands (city)	2.62	2.85	-	3.69	-	-	2.99	-	2.42	-	-	-	-	-	2.85	-	-	-	-	-	-	-	-	-
Rialto (city)	3.70	4.16	5.50	-	-	-	-	-	4.18	-	-	-	-	-	-	-	-	-	-	-	-	-	-	-
San Bernardino (city)	3.18	3.61	4.07	4.02	-	4.67	3.27	-	3.57	-	-	-	4.82	-	2.43	-	-	-	5.02	-	-	-	-	4.12
Upland (city)	2.76	3.06	-	3.29	-	-	2.81	-	2.40	-	-	-	-	-	3.44	-	-	-	-	-	3.40	-	-	3.62
Victorville (city)	3.03	3.53	-	-	-	-	-	-	3.73	-	-	-	-	-	-	-	-	-	-	-	-	-	-	-
San Diego County	2.73	3.32	3.61	2.79	-	4.64	2.82	-	3.68	3.47	2.83	7.41	2.68	2.19	2.79	4.49	-	2.61	4.48	-	3.00	2.43	5.36	3.71
Bonita (cdp)	2.85	2.76	-	-	-	-	-	-	2.70	-	-	-	-	-	-	-	-	-	-	-	-	-	-	-
Carlsbad (city)	2.46	2.65	-	-	-	-	2.79	-	2.63	-	-	-	-	2.16	-	-	-	-	-	-	-	-	-	-
Chula Vista (city)	3.00	3.32	3.15	-	-	-	2.86	-	3.60	3.56	-	-	-	2.39	3.17	-	-	-	-	-	-	-	-	-
Coronado (city)	2.28	2.65	-	-	-	-	-	-	2.56	-	-	-	-	-	-	-	-	-	-	-	-	-	-	-
Escondido (city)	3.00	3.44	-	-	-	-	2.39	-	3.57	-	-	-	-	-	-	5.78	-	-	-	-	-	-	-	3.77
Imperial Beach (city)	2.84	3.05	-	-	-	-	-	-	3.08	-	-	-	-	-	-	-	-	-	-	-	-	-	-	-
La Mesa (city)	2.23	2.64	-	-	-	-	-	-	2.88	-	-	-	-	-	-	-	-	-	-	-	-	-	-	-

Notes: Please refer to the User's Guide for an explanation of data; data is arranged alphabetically by state, then county, then city within each county; table includes counties with populations greater than 49,999 unless noted and cities with populations greater than 9,999 whose Asian and/or NHPI population rates are greater than the national average; (1) Native Hawaiian and other Pacific Islander; (2) excludes Taiwanese; (3) includes Chamorro; (4) county does not meet population threshold but is shown in order to allow inclusion of city

Place	All households	Asian households	NHPI[1] households	Asian Indian	Bangladeshi	Cambodian	Chinese[2]	Fijian	Filipino	Guamanian[3]	Hawaiian, Native	Hmong	Indonesian	Japanese	Korean	Laotian	Malaysian	Pakistani	Samoan	Sri Lankan	Taiwanese	Thai	Tongan	Vietnamese
La Presa (cdp)	3.27	4.10	-	-	-	-	-	-	4.25	-	-	-	-	-	-	-	-	-	-	-	-	-	-	-
Lemon Grove (city)	2.85	3.71	-	-	-	-	-	-	3.95	-	-	-	-	-	-	-	-	-	-	-	-	-	-	4.68
National City (city)	3.37	3.22	-	-	-	-	-	-	3.22	-	-	-	-	-	-	-	-	-	-	-	-	-	-	-
Oceanside (city)	2.82	3.21	4.70	-	-	-	2.39	-	3.73	-	-	-	-	2.34	-	-	-	-	5.18	-	-	-	-	3.67
Poway (city)	3.07	3.75	-	-	-	-	3.17	-	4.34	-	-	-	-	-	-	-	-	-	-	-	-	-	-	-
Rancho San Diego (cdp)	2.87	3.29	-	-	-	-	-	-	3.48	-	-	-	-	-	-	-	-	-	-	-	-	-	-	-
San Diego (city)	2.61	3.39	3.76	2.62	-	4.69	2.85	-	3.84	3.59	2.65	7.01	-	2.11	2.74	4.38	-	-	5.12	-	2.81	2.38	-	3.72
San Marcos (city)	3.02	3.37	-	-	-	-	3.20	-	4.18	-	-	-	-	-	-	-	-	-	-	-	-	-	-	-
Solana Beach (city)	2.24	2.25	-	-	-	-	-	-	-	-	-	-	-	-	-	-	-	-	-	-	-	-	-	-
Spring Valley (cdp)	2.88	2.97	-	-	-	-	-	-	2.82	-	-	-	-	-	-	-	-	-	-	-	-	-	-	-
Vista (city)	3.04	2.63	3.16	-	-	-	-	-	3.15	-	-	-	-	1.81	-	-	-	-	-	-	-	-	-	-
San Francisco County	2.29	2.99	3.90	2.23	-	3.31	3.06	-	3.43	-	-	-	2.35	1.80	2.24	-	-	4.32	5.31	-	2.34	2.27	-	3.49
San Francisco (city)	2.29	2.99	3.90	2.23	-	3.31	3.06	-	3.43	-	-	-	2.35	1.80	2.24	-	-	4.32	5.31	-	2.34	2.27	-	3.49
San Joaquin County	3.00	3.78	3.93	4.06	-	5.06	2.67	-	3.52	-	3.54	6.22	-	2.26	2.25	4.65	-	4.64	5.07	-	-	-	-	4.39
Lathrop (city)	3.63	3.95	-	-	-	-	-	-	3.84	-	-	-	-	-	-	-	-	-	-	-	-	-	-	-
Lodi (city)	2.72	2.94	-	4.00	-	-	-	-	2.84	-	-	-	-	2.00	-	-	-	-	-	-	-	-	-	-
Stockton (city)	3.02	3.87	3.90	3.75	-	5.06	2.66	-	3.45	-	-	6.34	-	2.26	-	4.72	-	4.32	-	-	-	-	-	4.54
Tracy (city)	3.22	3.86	-	4.60	-	-	2.89	-	4.16	-	-	-	-	-	-	-	-	-	-	-	-	-	-	-
San Luis Obispo County	2.49	2.74	-	2.80	-	-	2.39	-	3.33	-	-	-	-	2.26	2.67	-	-	-	-	-	-	-	-	-
Baywood-Los Osos (cdp)	2.38	4.06	-	-	-	-	-	-	4.98	-	-	-	-	-	-	-	-	-	-	-	-	-	-	-
Grover Beach (city)	2.58	3.49	-	-	-	-	-	-	-	-	-	-	-	-	-	-	-	-	-	-	-	-	-	-
San Luis Obispo (city)	2.27	2.29	-	-	-	-	2.26	-	2.44	-	-	-	-	-	-	-	-	-	-	-	-	-	-	-
San Mateo County	2.74	3.22	4.68	2.71	-	-	2.95	3.87	4.00	3.26	2.55	-	2.99	2.29	2.71	-	-	-	5.58	-	2.69	3.46	6.13	3.35
Belmont (city)	2.36	2.45	-	2.37	-	-	2.49	-	2.71	-	-	-	-	2.04	-	-	-	-	-	-	-	-	-	-
Burlingame (city)	2.20	2.40	-	-	-	-	2.51	-	2.09	-	-	-	-	1.86	-	-	-	-	-	-	-	-	-	-
Daly City (city)	3.34	3.94	3.95	2.73	-	-	3.44	-	4.44	-	-	-	-	2.46	2.55	-	-	-	-	-	-	-	-	4.17
East Palo Alto (city)	4.21	2.59	6.50	-	-	-	-	-	-	-	-	-	-	-	-	-	-	-	-	-	-	-	6.81	-
Foster City (city)	2.47	2.73	-	2.32	-	-	2.68	-	3.55	-	-	-	-	2.88	2.92	-	-	-	-	-	-	-	-	-
Hillsborough (town)	2.91	3.37	-	-	-	-	3.37	-	-	-	-	-	-	-	-	-	-	-	-	-	-	-	-	-
Menlo Park (city)	2.39	2.41	-	-	-	-	2.62	-	-	-	-	-	-	2.05	-	-	-	-	-	-	-	-	-	-
Millbrae (city)	2.57	3.47	-	3.50	-	-	3.57	-	3.51	-	-	-	-	3.10	3.27	-	-	-	-	-	-	-	-	-
Pacifica (city)	2.74	3.45	-	-	-	-	3.07	-	3.90	-	-	-	-	2.51	-	-	-	-	-	-	-	-	-	-
Redwood City (city)	2.61	2.50	3.98	2.50	-	-	2.45	-	3.18	-	-	-	-	1.84	-	-	-	-	-	-	-	-	-	-
San Bruno (city)	2.74	3.00	4.93	3.24	-	-	2.63	-	3.56	-	-	-	-	2.49	-	-	-	-	-	-	-	-	6.22	-
San Carlos (city)	2.42	2.61	-	-	-	-	2.71	-	-	-	-	-	-	-	-	-	-	-	-	-	-	-	-	-
San Mateo (city)	2.44	2.58	4.89	2.72	-	-	2.50	-	3.12	-	-	-	-	2.09	2.50	-	-	-	-	-	-	-	6.05	3.60
South San Francisco (city)	3.05	3.46	4.08	3.35	-	-	3.02	-	3.91	-	-	-	-	2.10	-	-	-	-	-	-	-	-	-	-
Santa Barbara County	2.80	2.92	3.41	2.36	-	-	2.65	-	3.63	-	-	5.87	-	2.12	2.53	-	-	-	-	-	-	-	-	3.47
Goleta (cdp)	2.73	3.01	-	-	-	-	2.58	-	3.78	-	-	-	-	2.49	-	-	-	-	-	-	-	-	-	3.71
Isla Vista (cdp)	2.97	2.11	-	-	-	-	2.25	-	-	-	-	-	-	-	2.32	-	-	-	-	-	-	-	-	-
Lompoc (city)	2.88	3.38	-	-	-	-	-	-	3.23	-	-	-	-	-	-	-	-	-	-	-	-	-	-	-

Notes: Please refer to the User's Guide for an explanation of data; data is arranged alphabetically by state, then county, then city within each county; table includes counties with populations greater than 49,999 unless noted and cities with populations greater than 9,999 whose Asian and/or NHPI population rates are greater than the national average; (1) Native Hawaiian and other Pacific Islander; (2) excludes Taiwanese; (3) includes Chamorro; (4) county does not meet population threshold but is shown in order to allow inclusion of city

Place	All households	Asian households	NHPI[1] households	Asian Indian	Bangladeshi	Cambodian	Chinese[2]	Fijian	Filipino	Guamanian[3]	Hawaiian, Native	Hmong	Indonesian	Japanese	Korean	Laotian	Malaysian	Pakistani	Samoan	Sri Lankan	Taiwanese	Thai	Tongan	Vietnamese
Orcutt (cdp)	2.75	2.94	-	-	-	-	-	-	-	-	-	-	-	-	-	-	-	-	-	-	-	-	-	-
Santa Maria (city)	3.39	3.64	-	-	-	-	-	-	4.05	-	-	-	-	2.40	-	-	-	-	-	-	-	-	-	-
Santa Clara County	2.92	3.34	3.91	2.98	2.88	5.00	2.98	4.00	4.12	3.68	2.85	-	2.57	2.37	3.03	5.39	-	4.02	5.00	-	2.95	2.92	-	4.11
Alum Rock (cdp)	4.02	4.45	-	-	-	-	-	-	-	-	-	-	-	-	-	-	-	-	-	-	-	-	-	4.53
Campbell (city)	2.37	2.85	-	3.00	-	-	2.61	-	3.16	-	-	-	-	2.19	3.25	-	-	-	-	-	-	-	-	3.55
Cupertino (city)	2.76	3.25	-	3.40	-	-	3.23	-	3.01	-	-	-	-	2.81	3.69	-	-	-	-	-	3.14	-	-	3.49
Gilroy (city)	3.45	3.35	-	-	-	-	3.09	-	3.47	-	-	-	-	-	-	-	-	-	-	-	-	-	-	-
Los Altos (city)	2.60	2.93	-	3.00	-	-	3.16	-	-	-	-	-	-	2.49	-	-	-	-	-	-	-	-	-	-
Los Gatos (town)	2.33	2.93	-	-	-	-	3.02	-	-	-	-	-	-	2.53	-	-	-	-	-	-	-	-	-	-
Milpitas (city)	3.47	3.77	5.41	3.54	-	-	3.39	-	4.34	-	-	-	-	2.30	2.73	-	-	-	-	-	-	-	-	4.18
Morgan Hill (city)	3.06	2.94	-	-	-	-	2.68	-	-	-	-	-	-	2.90	-	-	-	-	-	-	-	-	-	-
Mountain View (city)	2.24	2.41	-	2.37	-	-	2.36	-	2.90	-	-	-	-	1.96	2.25	-	-	-	-	-	-	-	-	3.23
Palo Alto (city)	2.30	2.68	-	2.63	-	-	2.89	-	2.65	-	-	-	-	2.06	2.52	-	-	-	-	-	-	-	-	-
San Jose (city)	3.19	3.66	4.01	3.24	-	5.12	3.14	-	4.32	3.46	3.05	-	-	2.40	3.12	5.56	-	4.07	4.93	-	2.95	3.47	-	4.21
Santa Clara (city)	2.58	2.95	4.41	2.74	-	-	2.41	-	3.90	-	-	-	-	1.96	3.01	-	-	4.78	-	-	-	-	-	3.58
Saratoga (city)	2.82	3.53	-	3.77	-	-	3.58	-	-	-	-	-	-	2.65	3.46	-	-	-	-	-	3.56	-	-	-
Stanford (cdp)	2.25	2.16	-	2.35	-	-	2.07	-	-	-	-	-	-	-	2.26	-	-	-	-	-	-	-	-	-
Sunnyvale (city)	2.49	2.71	3.21	2.55	-	-	2.49	-	3.69	-	-	-	-	2.27	2.85	-	-	-	-	-	2.58	-	-	3.55
Santa Cruz County	2.70	2.67	-	2.48	-	-	2.55	-	3.36	-	-	-	-	2.26	2.75	-	-	-	-	-	-	-	-	3.64
Capitola (city)	2.12	3.40	-	-	-	-	-	-	-	-	-	-	-	-	-	-	-	-	-	-	-	-	-	-
Santa Cruz (city)	2.44	2.44	-	2.14	-	-	2.58	-	2.97	-	-	-	-	2.03	-	-	-	-	-	-	-	-	-	-
Scotts Valley (city)	2.59	3.11	-	-	-	-	-	-	-	-	-	-	-	-	-	-	-	-	-	-	-	-	-	-
Shasta County	2.52	3.96	-	-	-	-	-	-	3.22	-	-	-	-	-	-	5.23	-	-	-	-	-	-	-	-
Solano County	2.90	3.55	3.74	3.77	-	-	2.91	-	3.67	3.67	2.95	7.08	-	2.12	3.28	4.66	-	-	5.16	-	-	-	-	3.79
Benicia (city)	2.60	3.06	-	-	-	-	4.15	-	2.77	-	-	-	-	-	-	-	-	-	-	-	-	-	-	-
Fairfield (city)	2.97	3.33	3.59	3.98	-	-	3.02	-	3.42	3.91	-	-	-	1.78	2.92	4.35	-	-	-	-	-	-	-	-
Suisun City (city)	3.27	4.03	-	4.69	-	-	-	-	4.09	-	-	-	-	-	-	-	-	-	-	-	-	-	-	-
Vacaville (city)	2.83	2.98	-	-	-	-	-	-	3.34	-	-	-	-	-	-	-	-	-	-	-	-	-	-	-
Vallejo (city)	2.89	3.72	3.87	3.49	-	-	2.72	-	3.81	3.59	-	-	-	2.22	-	-	-	-	-	-	-	-	-	4.50
Sonoma County	2.59	3.23	3.87	3.94	-	4.79	2.84	-	3.09	-	-	-	-	2.12	2.98	5.12	-	-	-	-	-	-	-	3.76
Petaluma (city)	2.70	3.54	-	-	-	-	2.98	-	-	-	-	-	-	-	-	-	-	-	-	-	-	-	-	-
Rohnert Park (city)	2.64	3.33	-	-	-	-	3.48	-	3.73	-	-	-	-	-	-	-	-	-	-	-	-	-	-	-
Santa Rosa (city)	2.56	3.25	-	4.19	-	5.55	2.41	-	2.63	-	-	-	-	1.67	-	5.18	-	-	-	-	-	-	-	3.82
Stanislaus County	3.03	3.90	3.64	4.06	-	5.55	3.04	4.17	3.30	-	-	5.45	-	2.56	-	5.06	-	-	-	-	-	-	-	3.77
Ceres (city)	3.31	4.66	-	4.43	-	-	-	-	-	-	-	-	-	-	-	-	-	-	-	-	-	-	-	-
Modesto (city)	2.86	4.05	4.06	4.07	-	5.28	3.15	4.55	3.44	-	-	6.96	-	2.62	-	5.09	-	-	-	-	-	-	-	4.15
Salida (cdp)	3.50	4.31	-	-	-	-	-	-	-	-	-	-	-	-	-	-	-	-	-	-	-	-	-	-
Turlock (city)	2.91	3.31	-	3.89	-	-	-	-	-	-	-	-	-	-	-	-	-	-	-	-	-	-	-	-
Sutter County	2.86	3.92	-	4.45	-	-	-	-	2.36	-	-	-	-	1.74	-	-	-	-	-	-	-	-	-	-
South Yuba City (cdp)	3.09	4.64	-	5.03	-	-	-	-	-	-	-	-	-	-	-	-	-	-	-	-	-	-	-	-
Yuba City (city)	2.67	3.15	-	3.66	-	-	-	-	-	-	-	-	-	-	-	-	-	-	-	-	-	-	-	-

Notes: Please refer to the User's Guide for an explanation of data; data is arranged alphabetically by state, then county, then city within each county; table includes counties with populations greater than 49,999 unless noted and cities with populations greater than 9,999 whose Asian and/or NHPI population rates are greater than the national average; (1) Native Hawaiian and other Pacific Islander; (2) excludes Taiwanese; (3) includes Chamorro; (4) county does not meet population threshold but is shown in order to allow inclusion of city

Place	All households	Asian households	NHPI[1] households	Asian Indian	Bangladeshi	Cambodian	Chinese[2]	Fijian	Filipino	Guamanian[3]	Hawaiian, Native	Hmong	Indonesian	Japanese	Korean	Laotian	Malaysian	Pakistani	Samoan	Sri Lankan	Taiwanese	Thai	Tongan	Vietnamese
Tehama County	2.61	3.80	-	-	-	-	-	-	-	-	-	-	-	-	-	-	-	-	-	-	-	-	-	-
Tulare County	3.28	4.04	-	4.37	-	-	3.17	-	3.68	-	-	6.34	-	1.96	2.92	5.94	-	-	-	-	-	-	-	-
Porterville (city)	3.21	4.26	-	-	-	-	-	-	4.54	-	-	-	-	-	-	-	-	-	-	-	-	-	-	-
Visalia (city)	2.91	4.35	-	-	-	-	-	-	3.06	-	-	6.42	-	-	-	5.67	-	-	-	-	-	-	-	-
Tuolumne County	2.37	2.38	-	-	-	-	-	-	-	-	-	-	-	-	-	-	-	-	-	-	-	-	-	-
Ventura County	3.04	3.30	3.55	3.32	-	-	2.94	-	3.80	-	3.08	-	-	2.62	3.01	-	-	-	5.07	-	3.38	-	-	3.90
Camarillo (city)	2.62	3.23	-	-	-	-	3.11	-	3.58	-	-	-	-	2.70	2.64	-	-	-	-	-	-	-	-	4.71
Moorpark (city)	3.48	3.31	-	-	-	-	-	-	-	-	-	-	-	-	-	-	-	-	-	-	-	-	-	-
Oxnard (city)	3.85	3.66	4.36	3.83	-	-	2.68	-	4.14	-	-	-	-	2.29	2.68	-	-	-	5.71	-	-	-	-	4.41
Port Hueneme (city)	2.87	3.14	-	-	-	-	-	-	3.67	-	-	-	-	-	-	-	-	-	-	-	-	-	-	-
Simi Valley (city)	3.03	3.41	-	3.67	-	-	2.90	-	3.39	-	-	-	-	2.65	3.69	-	-	-	-	-	-	-	-	4.34
Thousand Oaks (city)	2.75	2.98	-	3.06	-	-	2.87	-	2.61	-	-	-	-	2.94	3.03	-	-	-	-	-	-	-	-	3.26
Yolo County	2.72	2.76	4.09	2.86	-	-	2.63	5.27	2.72	-	-	7.10	-	2.10	2.57	4.12	-	-	-	-	-	-	-	3.00
Davis (city)	2.50	2.52	-	2.17	-	-	2.64	-	2.61	-	-	-	-	2.22	2.37	-	-	-	-	-	-	-	-	2.89
West Sacramento (city)	2.75	3.91	-	4.13	-	-	-	-	-	-	-	7.23	-	-	-	-	-	-	-	-	-	-	-	-
Woodland (city)	2.89	3.09	-	3.81	-	-	-	-	-	-	-	-	-	-	-	-	-	-	-	-	-	-	-	-
Yuba County	2.87	5.10	-	-	-	-	-	-	2.51	-	-	7.23	-	-	-	-	-	-	-	-	-	-	-	-
Linda (cdp)	3.29	6.77	-	-	-	-	-	-	-	-	-	7.64	-	-	-	-	-	-	-	-	-	-	-	-
Marysville (city)	2.50	3.41	-	-	-	-	-	-	-	-	-	-	-	-	-	-	-	-	-	-	-	-	-	-
Olivehurst (cdp)	3.16	6.08	-	-	-	-	-	-	-	-	-	-	-	-	-	-	-	-	-	-	-	-	-	-
COLORADO	2.53	2.81	2.86	2.60	-	4.34	2.71	-	2.82	3.05	2.52	5.24	2.75	2.09	2.66	4.70	-	3.40	3.62	-	2.22	2.46	-	3.58
Adams County	2.81	3.53	-	3.18	-	-	3.06	-	2.85	-	-	5.31	-	2.05	2.71	4.75	-	-	-	-	-	-	-	3.70
Berkley (cdp)	2.85	5.07	-	-	-	-	-	-	-	-	-	-	-	-	-	-	-	-	-	-	-	-	-	-
Federal Heights (city)	2.38	3.90	-	-	-	-	-	-	-	-	-	-	-	-	-	-	-	-	-	-	-	-	-	-
Westminster (city)	2.62	3.54	-	3.07	-	-	3.28	-	-	-	-	5.90	-	-	2.63	4.07	-	-	-	-	-	-	-	4.51
Arapahoe County	2.53	2.94	2.72	2.72	-	-	2.93	-	3.17	-	-	-	-	2.36	2.88	-	-	-	-	-	-	-	-	3.67
Aurora (city)	2.60	2.98	2.47	2.96	-	4.84	3.01	-	3.02	-	-	-	-	2.30	2.67	-	-	-	-	-	-	-	-	3.44
Boulder County	2.46	2.66	-	2.30	-	-	2.69	-	2.50	-	-	-	-	2.29	2.43	-	-	-	-	-	-	-	-	2.87
Boulder (city)	2.20	2.32	-	2.10	-	-	2.32	-	-	-	-	-	-	1.90	2.36	-	-	-	-	-	-	-	-	-
Broomfield (city)	2.77	3.69	-	-	-	-	3.18	-	-	-	-	-	-	-	-	-	-	-	-	-	-	-	-	-
Lafayette (city)	2.61	2.78	-	-	-	-	-	-	-	-	-	-	-	-	-	-	-	-	-	-	-	-	-	-
Denver County	2.26	2.44	2.27	2.26	-	4.06	2.10	-	2.22	-	-	-	-	1.72	2.22	-	-	-	-	-	-	2.09	-	3.59
Douglas County	2.87	3.01	-	2.81	-	-	3.24	-	-	-	-	-	-	-	2.81	-	-	-	-	-	-	-	-	-
Highlands Ranch (cdp)	2.88	3.09	-	2.91	-	-	3.28	-	-	-	-	-	-	-	-	-	-	-	-	-	-	-	-	-
El Paso County	2.60	2.66	3.36	2.44	-	-	2.70	-	2.96	3.17	-	-	-	2.03	2.75	-	-	-	-	-	-	-	-	3.30
Colorado Springs (city)	2.49	2.63	2.98	2.44	-	-	2.75	-	2.75	-	-	-	-	1.97	2.74	-	-	-	-	-	-	-	-	3.46
Jefferson County	2.52	3.06	2.72	2.64	-	-	3.00	-	2.92	-	-	6.66	-	2.29	2.71	4.99	-	-	-	-	-	-	-	3.90
Larimer County	2.52	2.50	-	2.97	-	-	2.41	-	-	-	-	-	-	2.25	2.47	-	-	-	-	-	-	-	-	-
Mesa County	2.46	3.43	-	-	-	-	-	-	-	-	-	-	-	-	-	-	-	-	-	-	-	-	-	-
Pueblo County	2.51	2.45	-	-	-	-	-	-	-	-	-	-	-	-	-	-	-	-	-	-	-	-	-	-
Weld County	2.78	2.57	-	-	-	-	-	-	-	-	-	-	-	2.03	-	-	-	-	-	-	-	-	-	-

Notes: Please refer to the User's Guide for an explanation of data; data is arranged alphabetically by state, then county, then city within each county; table includes counties with populations greater than 49,999 unless noted and cities with populations greater than 9,999 whose Asian and/or NHPI population rates are greater than the national average; (1) Native Hawaiian and other Pacific Islander; (2) excludes Taiwanese; (3) includes Chamorro; (4) county does not meet population threshold but is shown in order to allow inclusion of city

Place	All households	Asian households	NHPI[1] households	Asian Indian	Bangladeshi	Cambodian	Chinese[2]	Fijian	Filipino	Guamanian[3]	Hawaiian, Native	Hmong	Indonesian	Japanese	Korean	Laotian	Malaysian	Pakistani	Samoan	Sri Lankan	Taiwanese	Thai	Tongan	Vietnamese
CONNECTICUT	2.53	2.91	3.56	2.85	3.36	4.47	2.75	-	2.73	3.77	-	-	-	2.66	2.58	3.71	-	3.63	-	-	2.68	2.58	-	3.53
Fairfield County	2.66	3.08	-	2.80	-	5.16	2.76	-	2.88	-	-	-	-	3.37	2.80	4.00	-	3.96	-	-	-	-	-	3.92
Danbury (city)	2.64	3.17	-	2.84	-	5.00	2.44	-	-	-	-	-	-	-	-	-	-	-	-	-	-	-	-	-
Greenwich (town)	2.60	3.27	-	3.18	-	-	2.83	-	-	-	-	-	-	3.74	-	-	-	-	-	-	-	-	-	-
Stamford (city)	2.54	2.57	-	2.48	-	-	2.40	-	2.87	-	-	-	-	-	-	-	-	-	-	-	-	-	-	-
Hartford County	2.48	3.05	-	3.05	-	-	2.86	-	2.79	-	-	-	-	2.23	2.63	3.74	-	3.74	-	-	-	-	-	3.51
East Hartford (town)	2.42	3.20	-	3.44	-	-	-	-	-	-	-	-	-	-	-	-	-	-	-	-	-	-	-	3.51
Farmington (town)	2.46	3.12	-	-	-	-	-	-	-	-	-	-	-	-	-	-	-	-	-	-	-	-	-	-
Glastonbury (town)	2.58	3.63	-	3.88	-	-	-	-	-	-	-	-	-	-	-	-	-	-	-	-	-	-	-	-
Rocky Hill (town)	2.26	2.53	-	-	-	-	-	-	-	-	-	-	-	-	-	-	-	-	-	-	-	-	-	-
South Windsor (town)	2.71	4.12	-	-	-	-	-	-	-	-	-	-	-	-	-	-	-	-	-	-	-	-	-	-
West Hartford (town)	2.39	3.39	-	3.33	-	-	3.18	-	-	-	-	-	-	-	-	-	-	-	-	-	-	-	-	3.74
Litchfield County	2.51	3.24	-	2.92	-	-	3.55	-	-	-	-	-	-	-	3.64	-	-	-	-	-	-	-	-	3.66
Middlesex County	2.43	2.80	-	2.67	-	-	2.84	-	-	-	-	-	-	-	-	-	-	-	-	-	-	-	-	-
New Haven County	2.49	2.63	-	2.73	-	-	2.55	-	2.73	-	-	-	-	1.99	2.51	3.37	-	3.49	-	-	-	-	-	2.97
New Haven (city)	2.39	2.03	-	2.15	-	-	2.06	-	-	-	-	-	-	-	1.90	-	-	-	-	-	-	-	-	-
New London County	2.48	2.69	-	2.67	-	-	3.08	-	2.39	-	-	-	-	-	-	-	-	-	-	-	-	-	-	-
Tolland County	2.53	2.64	-	2.94	-	-	2.72	-	-	-	-	-	-	-	-	-	-	-	-	-	-	-	-	-
Mansfield (town)	2.41	2.44	-	2.93	-	-	2.39	-	-	-	-	-	-	-	-	-	-	-	-	-	-	-	-	-
Storrs (cdp)	2.25	2.41	-	-	-	-	2.51	-	-	-	-	-	-	-	-	-	-	-	-	-	-	-	-	-
Windham County	2.56	2.37	-	-	-	-	-	-	-	-	-	-	-	-	-	-	-	-	-	-	-	-	-	-
DELAWARE	2.54	2.77	3.25	2.83	-	-	2.71	-	2.79	-	-	-	-	2.13	2.72	-	-	3.35	-	-	-	-	-	3.49
Kent County	2.61	2.63	-	2.86	-	-	-	-	2.62	-	-	-	-	-	-	-	-	-	-	-	-	-	-	-
New Castle County	2.55	2.81	-	2.82	-	-	2.72	-	2.95	-	-	-	-	2.21	2.78	-	-	-	-	-	-	-	-	3.55
Hockessin (cdp)	2.85	2.74	-	-	-	-	-	-	-	-	-	-	-	-	-	-	-	-	-	-	-	-	-	-
Newark (city)	2.44	2.76	-	-	-	-	3.02	-	-	-	-	-	-	-	-	-	-	-	-	-	-	-	-	-
Pike Creek (cdp)	2.38	2.89	-	-	-	-	-	-	-	-	-	-	-	-	-	-	-	-	-	-	-	-	-	-
Sussex County	2.45	2.45	-	-	-	-	-	-	-	-	-	-	-	-	-	-	-	-	-	-	-	-	-	-
DISTRICT OF COLUMBIA	2.16	1.96	-	1.71	-	-	2.02	-	2.18	-	-	-	-	1.49	1.54	-	-	-	-	-	-	-	-	2.70
FLORIDA	2.46	2.91	2.91	2.97	3.40	3.82	2.71	-	2.93	3.41	2.54	-	2.29	2.10	2.59	3.62	-	3.74	2.60	2.23	2.60	2.51	-	3.42
Alachua County	2.34	2.23	-	2.33	-	-	2.17	-	2.72	-	-	-	-	1.71	2.32	-	-	-	-	-	-	-	-	2.11
Gainesville (city)	2.25	2.07	-	2.08	-	-	2.04	-	-	-	-	-	-	-	2.15	-	-	-	-	-	-	-	-	-
Bay County	2.43	2.68	-	-	-	-	-	-	2.54	-	-	-	-	-	-	-	-	-	-	-	-	-	-	3.46
Callaway (city)	2.58	3.09	-	-	-	-	-	-	-	-	-	-	-	-	-	-	-	-	-	-	-	-	-	-
Brevard County	2.35	2.72	-	3.13	-	-	2.40	-	3.03	-	-	-	-	1.85	2.23	-	-	-	-	-	-	-	-	2.85
Broward County	2.45	2.96	2.25	3.00	-	-	2.87	-	3.20	-	-	-	-	2.15	2.69	-	-	3.48	-	-	-	3.01	-	3.14
Cooper City (city)	3.06	3.58	-	3.41	-	-	-	-	-	-	-	-	-	-	-	-	-	-	-	-	-	-	-	-
Pembroke Pines (city)	2.61	2.93	-	3.05	-	-	2.89	-	3.17	-	-	-	-	-	-	-	-	-	-	-	-	-	-	-
Charlotte County	2.17	2.80	-	-	-	-	-	-	-	-	-	-	-	-	-	-	-	-	-	-	-	-	-	-
Citrus County	2.20	2.73	-	-	-	-	-	-	-	-	-	-	-	-	-	-	-	-	-	-	-	-	-	-
Clay County	2.76	3.20	-	-	-	-	-	-	3.17	-	-	-	-	-	-	-	-	-	-	-	-	-	-	-

Notes: Please refer to the User's Guide for an explanation of data; data is arranged alphabetically by state, then county, then city within each county; table includes counties with populations greater than 49,999 unless noted and cities with populations greater than 9,999 whose Asian and/or NHPI population rates are greater than the national average; (1) Native Hawaiian and other Pacific Islander; (2) excludes Taiwanese; (3) includes Chamorro; (4) county does not meet population threshold but is shown in order to allow inclusion of city

Place	All households	Asian households	NHPI[1] households	Asian Indian	Bangladeshi	Cambodian	Chinese[2]	Fijian	Filipino	Guamanian[3]	Hawaiian, Native	Hmong	Indonesian	Japanese	Korean	Laotian	Malaysian	Pakistani	Samoan	Sri Lankan	Taiwanese	Thai	Tongan	Vietnamese
Bellair-Meadowbrook Ter. (cdp)	2.53	3.05	-	-	-	-	-	-	-	-	-	-	-	-	-	-	-	-	-	-	-	-	-	-
Collier County	2.39	2.45	-	-	-	-	-	-	-	-	-	-	-	-	-	-	-	-	-	-	-	-	-	-
Columbia County	2.56	2.34	-	-	-	-	-	-	-	-	-	-	-	-	-	-	-	-	-	-	-	-	-	-
Duval County	2.51	3.01	3.10	2.64	-	4.11	2.66	-	3.18	-	-	-	-	1.90	2.74	-	-	-	-	-	-	-	-	3.27
Escambia County	2.45	3.15	-	3.94	-	-	2.80	-	2.89	-	-	-	-	-	-	-	-	-	-	-	-	-	-	3.82
Bellview (cdp)	2.61	3.35	-	-	-	-	-	-	3.13	-	-	-	-	-	-	-	-	-	-	-	-	-	-	-
Myrtle Grove (cdp)	2.49	2.83	-	-	-	-	-	-	2.56	-	-	-	-	-	-	-	-	-	-	-	-	-	-	-
Hernando County	2.32	3.00	-	-	-	-	-	-	-	-	-	-	-	-	-	-	-	-	-	-	-	-	-	-
Highlands County	2.29	3.17	-	-	-	-	-	-	3.53	-	-	-	-	-	-	-	-	-	-	-	-	-	-	-
Hillsborough County	2.51	2.88	3.23	2.86	-	-	2.67	-	2.53	-	-	-	-	1.85	2.95	-	-	-	-	-	-	2.62	-	3.76
Westchase (cdp)	2.66	3.07	-	-	-	-	-	-	-	-	-	-	-	-	-	-	-	-	-	-	-	-	-	-
Indian River County	2.25	3.04	-	-	-	-	-	-	-	-	-	-	-	-	-	-	-	-	-	-	-	-	-	-
Lake County	2.34	2.94	-	-	-	-	-	-	-	-	-	-	-	-	-	-	-	-	-	-	-	-	-	-
Lee County	2.31	2.60	-	2.99	-	-	2.62	-	2.57	-	-	-	-	-	-	-	-	-	-	-	-	-	-	-
Leon County	2.34	2.48	-	2.60	-	-	2.36	-	2.76	-	-	-	-	-	2.00	-	-	-	-	-	-	-	-	-
Manatee County	2.29	2.83	-	-	-	-	-	-	2.10	-	-	-	-	-	-	-	-	-	-	-	-	-	-	-
Marion County	2.36	3.02	-	3.30	-	-	-	-	-	-	-	-	-	-	-	-	-	-	-	-	-	-	-	-
Martin County	2.23	2.23	-	-	-	-	-	-	-	-	-	-	-	-	-	-	-	-	-	-	-	-	-	-
Miami-Dade County	2.84	2.79	3.07	2.85	-	-	2.69	-	2.77	-	-	-	-	2.20	2.78	-	-	3.64	-	-	-	2.72	-	3.24
Doral (cdp)	2.65	2.54	-	-	-	-	-	-	-	-	-	-	-	-	-	-	-	-	-	-	-	-	-	-
Ives Estates (cdp)	2.55	2.66	-	-	-	-	-	-	-	-	-	-	-	-	-	-	-	-	-	-	-	-	-	-
North Miami Beach (city)	2.87	3.11	-	2.67	-	-	3.29	-	-	-	-	-	-	-	-	-	-	-	-	-	-	-	-	-
Pinecrest (village)	3.06	3.21	-	-	-	-	-	-	-	-	-	-	-	-	-	-	-	-	-	-	-	-	-	-
Monroe County	2.23	2.52	-	-	-	-	-	-	-	-	-	-	-	-	-	-	-	-	-	-	-	-	-	-
Nassau County	2.60	2.91	-	-	-	-	-	-	-	-	-	-	-	-	-	-	-	-	-	-	-	-	-	-
Okaloosa County	2.49	2.51	-	-	-	-	-	-	2.68	-	-	-	-	-	2.35	-	-	-	-	-	-	2.00	-	3.61
Wright (cdp)	2.32	2.60	-	-	-	-	-	-	-	-	-	-	-	-	-	-	-	-	-	-	-	-	-	-
Orange County	2.61	3.05	3.04	2.99	-	-	2.91	-	3.07	-	-	-	-	2.24	2.73	-	-	4.09	-	-	-	-	-	3.50
Oak Ridge (cdp)	3.01	3.30	-	-	-	-	-	-	-	-	-	-	-	-	-	-	-	-	-	-	-	-	-	3.65
Osceola County	2.79	3.20	-	3.96	-	-	2.66	-	3.31	-	-	-	-	-	-	-	-	-	-	-	-	-	-	-
Palm Beach County	2.34	2.92	3.16	2.96	-	-	2.77	-	2.85	-	-	-	-	2.02	2.34	-	-	-	-	-	-	2.89	-	3.39
Pasco County	2.30	3.14	-	3.73	-	-	2.81	-	2.75	-	-	-	-	-	-	-	-	-	-	-	-	-	-	-
Pinellas County	2.16	3.08	-	3.13	-	3.91	2.64	-	2.79	-	-	-	-	2.08	2.35	3.99	-	-	-	-	-	3.24	-	3.49
Pinellas Park (city)	2.30	3.37	-	-	-	-	-	-	-	-	-	-	-	-	-	-	-	-	-	-	-	-	-	3.23
Polk County	2.52	3.25	-	3.33	-	-	2.98	-	3.29	-	-	-	-	-	-	3.98	-	-	-	-	-	-	-	4.00
Putnam County	2.48	3.37	-	-	-	-	-	-	-	-	-	-	-	-	-	-	-	-	-	-	-	-	-	-
St. Johns County	2.44	2.68	-	-	-	-	-	-	-	-	-	-	-	-	-	-	-	-	-	-	-	-	-	-
St. Lucie County	2.47	3.22	-	-	-	-	-	-	-	-	-	-	-	-	-	-	-	-	-	-	-	-	-	-
Santa Rosa County	2.63	3.08	-	-	-	-	-	-	2.76	-	-	-	-	-	-	-	-	-	-	-	-	-	-	-
Sarasota County	2.13	2.94	-	-	-	-	2.62	-	2.76	-	-	-	-	-	-	-	-	-	-	-	-	-	-	3.99
Seminole County	2.59	3.06	-	3.22	-	-	2.99	-	2.83	-	-	-	-	-	2.88	-	-	-	-	-	-	-	-	3.88

Notes: Please refer to the User's Guide for an explanation of data; data is arranged alphabetically by state, then county, then city within each county; table includes counties with populations greater than 49,999 unless noted and cities with populations greater than 9,999 whose Asian and/or NHPI population rates are greater than the national average; (1) Native Hawaiian and other Pacific Islander; (2) excludes Taiwanese; (3) includes Chamorro; (4) county does not meet population threshold but is shown in order to allow inclusion of city

Place	All households	Asian households	NHPI[1] households	Asian Indian	Bangladeshi	Cambodian	Chinese[2]	Fijian	Filipino	Guamanian[3]	Hawaiian, Native	Hmong	Indonesian	Japanese	Korean	Laotian	Malaysian	Pakistani	Samoan	Sri Lankan	Taiwanese	Thai	Tongan	Vietnamese
Volusia County	2.32	2.67	-	3.18	-	-	2.16	-	3.05	-	-	-	-	-	2.20	-	-	-	-	-	-	-	-	-
GEORGIA	2.64	3.18	3.10	3.11	3.99	4.41	2.84	-	2.87	3.23	2.74	5.56	2.49	2.29	2.93	3.95	-	3.85	3.24	-	2.97	2.65	-	4.11
Bartow County	2.76	4.13	-	-	-	-	-	-	-	-	-	-	-	-	-	-	-	-	-	-	-	-	-	-
Bibb County	2.49	2.99	-	-	-	-	-	-	-	-	-	-	-	-	-	-	-	-	-	-	-	-	-	-
Bulloch County	2.52	2.45	-	-	-	-	-	-	-	-	-	-	-	-	-	-	-	-	-	-	-	-	-	-
Carroll County	2.66	3.27	-	-	-	-	-	-	-	-	-	-	-	-	-	-	-	-	-	-	-	-	-	-
Catoosa County	2.59	3.13	-	-	-	-	-	-	-	-	-	-	-	-	-	-	-	-	-	-	-	-	-	-
Chatham County	2.49	3.05	-	3.73	-	-	2.54	-	-	-	-	-	-	-	2.75	-	-	-	-	-	-	-	-	3.58
Cherokee County	2.84	3.31	-	3.59	-	-	-	-	-	-	-	-	-	-	-	-	-	-	-	-	-	-	-	-
Clarke County	2.35	2.48	-	2.93	-	-	2.42	-	-	-	-	-	-	-	2.26	-	-	-	-	-	-	-	-	-
Clayton County	2.84	3.94	-	3.07	-	4.55	3.73	-	-	-	-	-	-	-	-	4.34	-	3.37	-	-	-	-	-	4.44
Forest Park (city)	2.95	3.87	-	-	-	-	-	-	-	-	-	-	-	-	-	-	-	-	-	-	-	-	-	3.94
Riverdale (city)	2.82	4.16	-	-	-	-	-	-	-	-	-	-	-	-	-	-	-	-	-	-	-	-	-	5.13
Cobb County	2.64	3.00	-	2.86	-	-	2.94	-	2.77	-	-	-	-	2.64	2.92	-	-	3.99	-	-	-	-	-	3.98
Smyrna (city)	2.17	2.23	-	2.20	-	-	-	-	-	-	-	-	-	-	-	-	-	-	-	-	-	-	-	-
Columbia County	2.85	3.30	-	3.45	-	-	3.50	-	-	-	-	-	-	-	3.02	-	-	-	-	-	-	-	-	-
Martinez (cdp)	2.78	3.39	-	3.56	-	-	-	-	-	-	-	-	-	-	-	-	-	-	-	-	-	-	-	-
Coweta County	2.81	3.15	-	-	-	-	-	-	-	-	-	-	-	-	-	-	-	-	-	-	-	-	-	-
DeKalb County	2.61	3.04	-	2.80	4.50	4.82	2.63	-	2.18	-	-	-	-	1.87	2.44	-	-	-	-	-	-	-	-	4.32
Druid Hills (cdp)	2.07	1.99	-	-	-	-	-	-	-	-	-	-	-	-	-	-	-	-	-	-	-	-	-	-
Dunwoody (cdp)	2.35	2.72	-	2.46	-	-	-	-	-	-	-	-	-	-	2.82	-	-	-	-	-	-	-	-	-
North Atlanta (cdp)	2.34	2.34	-	-	-	-	-	-	-	-	-	-	-	-	-	-	-	-	-	-	-	-	-	-
North Decatur (cdp)	1.85	2.31	-	-	-	-	-	-	-	-	-	-	-	-	-	-	-	-	-	-	-	-	-	-
North Druid Hills (cdp)	1.84	2.30	-	2.28	-	-	-	-	-	-	-	-	-	-	-	-	-	-	-	-	-	-	-	-
Tucker (cdp)	2.53	3.33	-	-	-	-	-	-	-	-	-	-	-	-	-	-	-	-	-	-	-	-	-	3.66
Dougherty County	2.57	3.45	-	-	-	-	-	-	-	-	-	-	-	-	-	-	-	-	-	-	-	-	-	-
Douglas County	2.78	3.06	-	-	-	-	-	-	-	-	-	-	-	-	-	-	-	-	-	-	-	-	-	-
Fayette County	2.88	3.37	-	-	-	-	-	-	-	-	-	-	-	3.15	-	-	-	-	-	-	-	-	-	-
Peachtree City (city)	2.89	3.27	-	-	-	-	-	-	-	-	-	-	-	3.15	-	-	-	-	-	-	-	-	-	-
Floyd County	2.55	3.54	-	3.98	-	-	-	-	-	-	-	-	-	-	-	-	-	-	-	-	-	-	-	-
Forsyth County	2.82	2.98	-	-	-	-	-	-	-	-	-	-	-	-	-	-	-	-	-	-	-	-	-	-
Fulton County	2.44	2.88	-	2.85	-	-	2.69	-	2.27	-	-	-	-	2.00	3.02	-	-	-	-	-	-	-	-	4.02
Alpharetta (city)	2.52	2.86	-	2.66	-	-	2.65	-	-	-	-	-	-	-	-	-	-	-	-	-	-	-	-	-
Roswell (city)	2.61	3.09	-	2.91	-	-	2.71	-	-	-	-	-	-	-	3.51	-	-	-	-	-	-	-	-	-
Glynn County	2.43	2.72	-	-	-	-	-	-	-	-	-	-	-	-	-	-	-	-	-	-	-	-	-	-
Gwinnett County	2.87	3.41	4.09	3.41	-	4.47	2.90	-	2.65	-	-	-	-	2.29	3.26	3.83	-	4.32	-	-	2.82	-	-	4.24
Duluth (city)	2.53	3.21	-	3.43	-	-	2.94	-	-	-	-	-	-	-	3.14	-	-	-	-	-	-	-	-	-
Lilburn (city)	2.80	3.99	-	4.40	-	-	-	-	-	-	-	-	-	-	-	-	-	-	-	-	-	-	-	4.16
Mountain Park (cdp)	2.72	3.76	-	3.90	-	-	-	-	-	-	-	-	-	-	-	-	-	-	-	-	-	-	-	-
Hall County	2.89	4.32	-	-	-	-	-	-	-	-	-	-	-	-	-	-	-	-	-	-	-	-	-	5.53
Henry County	2.87	3.79	-	3.87	-	-	-	-	-	-	-	-	-	-	-	-	-	-	-	-	-	-	-	-

Notes: Please refer to the User's Guide for an explanation of data; data is arranged alphabetically by state, then county, then city within each county; table includes counties with populations greater than 49,999 unless noted and cities with populations greater than 9,999 whose Asian and/or NHPI population rates are greater than the national average; (1) Native Hawaiian and other Pacific Islander; (2) excludes Taiwanese; (3) includes Chamorro; (4) county does not meet population threshold but is shown in order to allow inclusion of city

Place	All households	Asian households	NHPI[1] households	Asian Indian	Bangladeshi	Cambodian	Chinese[2]	Fijian	Filipino	Guamanian[3]	Hawaiian, Native	Hmong	Indonesian	Japanese	Korean	Laotian	Malaysian	Pakistani	Samoan	Sri Lankan	Taiwanese	Thai	Tongan	Vietnamese
Houston County	2.65	3.08	-	-	-	-	-	-	3.54	-	-	-	-	-	-	-	-	-	-	-	-	-	-	-
Liberty County	2.92	2.86	-	-	-	-	-	-	-	-	-	-	-	-	2.57	-	-	-	-	-	-	-	-	-
Lowndes County	2.61	3.31	-	-	-	-	-	-	-	-	-	-	-	-	-	-	-	-	-	-	-	-	-	-
Muscogee County	2.54	2.91	3.50	3.32	-	-	2.84	-	3.40	-	-	-	-	-	2.80	-	-	-	-	-	-	-	-	-
Columbus (sp. city)	2.54	2.91	3.50	3.32	-	-	2.84	-	3.40	-	-	-	-	-	2.80	-	-	-	-	-	-	-	-	-
Newton County	2.77	3.16	-	-	-	-	-	-	-	-	-	-	-	-	-	-	-	-	-	-	-	-	-	-
Richmond County	2.55	2.69	-	2.99	-	-	3.76	-	-	-	-	-	-	-	2.00	-	-	-	-	-	-	-	-	-
Rockdale County	2.87	3.48	-	-	-	-	-	-	-	-	-	-	-	-	-	-	-	-	-	-	-	-	-	-
Spalding County	2.67	3.20	-	-	-	-	-	-	-	-	-	-	-	-	-	-	-	-	-	-	-	-	-	-
Troup County	2.61	3.39	-	-	-	-	-	-	-	-	-	-	-	-	-	-	-	-	-	-	-	-	-	-
Walton County	2.82	5.10	-	-	-	-	-	-	-	-	-	-	-	-	-	-	-	-	-	-	-	-	-	-
Whitfield County	2.82	3.30	-	-	-	-	-	-	-	-	-	-	-	-	-	-	-	-	-	-	-	-	-	-
HAWAII	2.91	3.00	3.73	2.78	-	2.87	2.78	-	4.25	3.33	3.53	-	-	2.48	2.42	3.97	-	-	4.54	-	3.06	2.54	5.06	3.04
Hawaii County	2.76	2.76	3.46	-	-	-	2.96	-	3.55	-	3.34	-	-	2.38	2.53	-	-	-	4.31	-	-	-	-	-
Hilo (cdp)	2.70	2.49	3.39	-	-	-	2.41	-	2.92	-	3.27	-	-	2.40	2.65	-	-	-	-	-	-	-	-	-
Honolulu County	2.95	3.00	3.86	2.82	-	-	2.77	-	4.35	3.30	3.62	-	-	2.51	2.41	3.98	-	-	4.56	-	3.09	2.50	5.35	3.02
Ewa Beach (cdp)	4.39	4.75	5.08	-	-	-	-	-	5.37	-	4.95	-	-	2.86	-	-	-	-	6.13	-	-	-	-	-
Halawa (cdp)	3.27	3.42	4.02	-	-	-	3.56	-	4.66	-	3.26	-	-	2.65	-	-	-	-	5.74	-	-	-	-	-
Honolulu (cdp)	2.57	2.68	3.37	2.40	-	-	2.62	-	4.18	3.13	3.07	-	-	2.31	2.29	3.78	-	-	3.73	-	3.14	1.81	5.00	2.95
Kailua (cdp)	2.98	3.06	3.51	-	-	-	3.49	-	3.79	-	3.54	-	-	2.77	2.48	-	-	-	-	-	-	-	-	-
Kaneohe (cdp)	3.14	3.21	3.86	-	-	-	3.39	-	4.81	-	3.74	-	-	2.98	2.71	-	-	-	-	-	-	-	-	-
Kaneohe Station (cdp)	3.23	3.43	-	-	-	-	-	-	-	-	-	-	-	-	-	-	-	-	-	-	-	-	-	-
Makakilo City (cdp)	3.36	3.62	4.37	-	-	-	-	-	4.23	-	3.96	-	-	2.64	-	-	-	-	-	-	-	-	-	-
Mililani Town (cdp)	3.16	3.16	3.84	-	-	-	2.91	-	3.63	-	3.59	-	-	2.99	3.28	-	-	-	-	-	-	-	-	-
Nanakuli (cdp)	4.75	4.60	4.92	-	-	-	-	-	5.08	-	4.53	-	-	-	-	-	-	-	7.26	-	-	-	-	-
Pearl City (cdp)	3.16	3.12	4.26	-	-	-	3.00	-	4.41	-	3.88	-	-	2.72	2.86	-	-	-	-	-	-	-	-	-
Schofield Barracks (cdp)	3.49	2.85	-	-	-	-	-	-	-	-	-	-	-	-	-	-	-	-	-	-	-	-	-	-
Wahiawa (cdp)	2.98	2.93	3.63	-	-	-	-	-	4.04	-	2.92	-	-	2.52	-	-	-	-	-	-	-	-	-	-
Waianae (cdp)	4.07	3.78	4.62	-	-	-	-	-	4.03	-	4.63	-	-	2.99	-	-	-	-	-	-	-	-	-	-
Waimalu (cdp)	2.78	2.97	3.45	-	-	-	2.86	-	3.96	-	3.08	-	-	2.63	3.49	-	-	-	-	-	-	-	-	-
Waipahu (cdp)	4.22	4.37	4.76	-	-	-	4.36	-	4.94	-	4.00	-	-	2.92	-	-	-	-	4.95	-	-	-	-	-
Waipio (cdp)	2.91	3.15	2.70	-	-	-	-	-	4.44	-	2.61	-	-	2.74	-	-	-	-	-	-	-	-	-	-
Kauai County	2.86	3.06	3.44	-	-	-	2.81	-	3.80	-	3.40	-	-	2.37	-	-	-	-	-	-	-	-	-	-
Maui County	2.91	3.26	3.58	-	-	-	2.84	-	4.39	-	3.51	-	-	2.35	2.56	-	-	-	-	-	-	-	4.42	-
Kahului (cdp)	3.27	3.43	3.35	-	-	-	-	-	4.61	-	3.16	-	-	2.38	-	-	-	-	-	-	-	-	-	-
Kihei (cdp)	2.71	3.79	3.35	-	-	-	-	-	4.46	-	3.12	-	-	2.22	-	-	-	-	-	-	-	-	-	-
Wailuku (cdp)	2.75	2.59	3.80	-	-	-	-	-	3.95	-	3.79	-	-	2.22	-	-	-	-	-	-	-	-	-	-
IDAHO	2.69	2.56	3.33	2.47	-	-	2.67	-	2.42	-	3.01	-	-	2.23	2.75	3.63	-	-	-	-	-	-	-	3.17
Ada County	2.59	2.47	3.61	2.20	-	-	2.54	-	1.99	-	-	-	-	2.06	2.41	-	-	-	-	-	-	-	-	3.10
Bannock County	2.69	2.30	-	-	-	-	-	-	-	-	-	-	-	-	-	-	-	-	-	-	-	-	-	-
Bonneville County	2.83	2.31	-	-	-	-	-	-	-	-	-	-	-	-	-	-	-	-	-	-	-	-	-	-

Notes: Please refer to the User's Guide for an explanation of data; data is arranged alphabetically by state, then county, then city within each county; table includes counties with populations greater than 49,999 unless noted and cities with populations greater than 9,999 whose Asian and/or NHPI population rates are greater than the national average; (1) Native Hawaiian and other Pacific Islander; (2) excludes Taiwanese; (3) includes Chamorro; (4) county does not meet population threshold but is shown in order to allow inclusion of city

Place	All households	Asian households	NHPI[1] households	Asian Indian	Bangladeshi	Cambodian	Chinese[2]	Fijian	Filipino	Guamanian[3]	Hawaiian, Native	Hmong	Indonesian	Japanese	Korean	Laotian	Malaysian	Pakistani	Samoan	Sri Lankan	Taiwanese	Thai	Tongan	Vietnamese
Canyon County	2.85	2.92	-	-	-	-	-	-	-	-	-	-	-	2.49	-	-	-	-	-	-	-	-	-	-
Kootenai County	2.59	2.77	-	-	-	-	-	-	-	-	-	-	-	-	-	-	-	-	-	-	-	-	-	-
Twin Falls County	2.64	3.29	-	-	-	-	-	-	-	-	-	-	-	-	-	-	-	-	-	-	-	-	-	-
ILLINOIS	2.63	2.96	3.23	3.17	2.87	4.33	2.72	-	3.13	2.87	2.49	-	2.49	2.16	2.63	3.89	2.24	3.78	3.35	2.83	2.32	2.59	-	3.50
Champaign County	2.33	2.24	-	2.33	-	-	2.22	-	2.08	-	-	-	-	1.69	2.16	-	-	-	-	-	-	-	-	3.15
Champaign (city)	2.23	2.06	-	2.08	-	-	1.94	-	-	-	-	-	-	-	1.84	-	-	-	-	-	-	-	-	3.32
Urbana (city)	2.14	2.24	-	2.36	-	-	2.30	-	-	-	-	-	-	-	2.13	-	-	-	-	-	-	-	-	-
Coles County	2.31	2.63	-	-	-	-	-	-	-	-	-	-	-	-	-	-	-	-	-	-	-	-	-	-
Cook County	2.68	2.89	3.28	3.11	-	4.47	2.67	-	3.04	-	-	-	2.17	2.14	2.61	4.16	-	3.76	-	-	2.00	2.60	-	3.52
Arlington Heights (village)	2.44	2.50	-	2.22	-	-	2.64	-	2.99	-	-	-	-	2.02	3.30	-	-	-	-	-	-	-	-	-
Chicago (city)	2.67	2.65	3.32	2.72	-	4.54	2.66	-	2.83	-	-	-	-	1.85	1.99	-	-	3.57	-	-	1.60	2.30	-	3.49
Des Plaines (city)	2.58	3.83	-	4.66	-	-	3.01	-	3.91	-	-	-	-	-	-	-	-	-	-	-	-	-	-	-
Elk Grove Village (village)	2.60	3.14	-	3.58	-	-	2.59	-	3.49	-	-	-	-	3.13	-	-	-	-	-	-	-	-	-	-
Evanston (city)	2.27	2.14	-	2.04	-	-	1.85	-	3.07	-	-	-	-	2.20	1.98	-	-	-	-	-	-	-	-	-
Forest Park (village)	2.03	2.58	-	-	-	-	-	-	-	-	-	-	-	-	-	-	-	-	-	-	-	-	-	-
Glenview (village)	2.67	3.31	-	3.93	-	-	2.79	-	3.31	-	-	-	-	2.41	3.48	-	-	-	-	-	-	-	-	-
Hanover Park (village)	3.40	3.68	-	3.67	-	-	-	-	3.63	-	-	-	-	-	-	-	-	-	-	-	-	-	-	-
Hoffman Estates (village)	2.93	3.42	-	3.60	-	-	3.02	-	3.21	-	-	-	-	3.00	3.47	-	-	-	-	-	-	-	-	-
Lincolnwood (village)	2.75	3.99	-	4.37	-	-	-	-	4.14	-	-	-	-	-	3.67	-	-	-	-	-	-	-	-	-
Morton Grove (village)	2.70	3.65	-	4.30	-	-	-	-	3.63	-	-	-	-	-	3.39	-	-	-	-	-	-	-	-	-
Mount Prospect (village)	2.62	3.09	-	3.14	-	-	2.83	-	2.90	-	-	-	-	2.68	3.29	-	-	-	-	-	-	-	-	-
Niles (village)	2.40	3.24	-	4.13	-	-	-	-	3.38	-	-	-	-	-	2.93	-	-	-	-	-	-	-	-	-
Northbrook (village)	2.65	3.28	-	-	-	-	3.18	-	-	-	-	-	-	-	3.36	-	-	-	-	-	-	-	-	-
Oak Park (village)	2.26	2.31	-	2.38	-	-	2.88	-	-	-	-	-	-	-	-	-	-	-	-	-	-	-	-	-
Orland Park (village)	2.72	3.74	-	4.09	-	-	-	-	4.12	-	-	-	-	-	-	-	-	-	-	-	-	-	-	-
Palatine (village)	2.56	2.79	-	2.98	-	-	2.32	-	2.83	-	-	-	-	-	2.78	-	-	-	-	-	-	-	-	-
Prospect Heights (city)	2.70	2.61	-	-	-	-	-	-	-	-	-	-	-	-	-	-	-	-	-	-	-	-	-	-
Rolling Meadows (city)	2.69	2.96	-	3.46	-	-	-	-	-	-	-	-	-	-	-	-	-	-	-	-	-	-	-	-
Schaumburg (village)	2.35	2.74	-	2.76	-	-	2.76	-	2.31	-	-	-	-	2.46	3.01	-	-	-	-	-	-	-	-	-
Schiller Park (village)	2.82	3.92	-	-	-	-	-	-	-	-	-	-	-	-	-	-	-	-	-	-	-	-	-	-
Skokie (village)	2.68	3.49	-	3.82	-	-	2.92	-	3.84	-	-	-	-	-	3.19	-	-	4.04	-	-	-	-	-	-
Streamwood (village)	3.01	3.39	-	3.42	-	-	-	-	3.78	-	-	-	-	-	-	-	-	-	-	-	-	-	-	-
Wheeling (village)	2.57	2.97	-	3.21	-	-	-	-	3.47	-	-	-	-	-	-	-	-	-	-	-	-	-	-	-
Wilmette (village)	2.75	3.34	-	-	-	-	3.11	-	-	-	-	-	-	2.95	3.31	-	-	-	-	-	-	-	-	-
DeKalb County	2.56	2.55	-	2.66	-	-	-	-	-	-	-	-	-	-	-	-	-	-	-	-	-	-	-	-
DeKalb (city)	2.42	2.60	-	2.73	-	-	-	-	-	-	-	-	-	-	-	-	-	-	-	-	-	-	-	-
DuPage County	2.73	3.28	-	3.43	-	-	2.94	-	3.40	-	-	-	-	2.02	2.85	-	-	3.98	-	-	3.12	2.44	-	3.59
Addison (village)	3.05	3.39	-	3.48	-	-	-	-	4.12	-	-	-	-	-	-	-	-	-	-	-	-	-	-	-
Bartlett (village)	3.02	3.75	-	4.28	-	-	-	-	3.34	-	-	-	-	-	-	-	-	-	-	-	-	-	-	-
Bensenville (village)	2.93	2.89	-	3.25	-	-	-	-	-	-	-	-	-	-	-	-	-	-	-	-	-	-	-	-
Bloomingdale (village)	2.53	3.42	-	4.33	-	-	-	-	-	-	-	-	-	-	-	-	-	-	-	-	-	-	-	-

Notes: Please refer to the User's Guide for an explanation of data; data is arranged alphabetically by state, then county, then city within each county; table includes counties with populations greater than 49,999 unless noted and cities with populations greater than 9,999 whose Asian and/or NHPI population rates are greater than the national average; (1) Native Hawaiian and other Pacific Islander; (2) excludes Taiwanese; (3) includes Chamorro; (4) county does not meet population threshold but is shown in order to allow inclusion of city

Place	All households	Asian households	NHPI[1] households	Asian Indian	Bangladeshi	Cambodian	Chinese[2]	Fijian	Filipino	Guamanian[3]	Hawaiian, Native	Hmong	Indonesian	Japanese	Korean	Laotian	Malaysian	Pakistani	Samoan	Sri Lankan	Taiwanese	Thai	Tongan	Vietnamese
Burr Ridge (village)	2.94	3.62	-	4.10	-	-	-	-	-	-	-	-	-	-	-	-	-	-	-	-	-	-	-	-
Carol Stream (village)	2.88	3.65	-	3.54	-	-	-	-	3.97	-	-	-	-	-	-	-	-	-	-	-	-	-	-	4.22
Darien (city)	2.60	3.65	-	4.02	-	-	-	-	3.41	-	-	-	-	-	-	-	-	-	-	-	-	-	-	-
Downers Grove (village)	2.52	3.11	-	3.15	-	-	2.96	-	3.53	-	-	-	-	-	-	-	-	-	-	-	-	-	-	-
Glen Ellyn (village)	2.64	3.22	-	3.35	-	-	-	-	-	-	-	-	-	-	-	-	-	-	-	-	-	-	-	-
Glendale Heights (village)	2.91	3.56	-	4.03	-	-	-	-	3.53	-	-	-	-	-	-	-	-	-	-	-	-	-	-	3.47
Hinsdale (village)	2.84	2.83	-	-	-	-	-	-	-	-	-	-	-	-	-	-	-	-	-	-	-	-	-	-
Lisle (village)	2.41	3.11	-	3.05	-	-	3.22	-	-	-	-	-	-	-	-	-	-	-	-	-	-	-	-	-
Lombard (village)	2.47	2.93	-	3.03	-	-	-	-	3.14	-	-	-	-	-	-	-	-	-	-	-	-	-	-	-
Naperville (city)	2.89	3.40	-	3.45	-	-	3.39	-	3.47	-	-	-	-	-	3.55	-	-	-	-	-	3.36	-	-	-
Roselle (village)	2.76	2.95	-	3.25	-	-	-	-	-	-	-	-	-	-	-	-	-	-	-	-	-	-	-	-
Villa Park (village)	2.85	4.24	-	-	-	-	-	-	-	-	-	-	-	-	-	-	-	-	-	-	-	-	-	-
Warrenville (city)	2.68	3.31	-	-	-	-	-	-	-	-	-	-	-	-	-	-	-	-	-	-	-	-	-	-
Westmont (village)	2.38	2.72	-	2.88	-	-	2.39	-	3.01	-	-	-	-	-	-	-	-	-	-	-	-	-	-	-
Wheaton (city)	2.64	3.04	-	2.97	-	-	-	-	-	-	-	-	-	-	-	-	-	-	-	-	-	-	-	3.73
Woodridge (village)	2.70	3.22	-	3.07	-	-	-	-	3.83	-	-	-	-	-	-	-	-	-	-	-	-	-	-	-
Jackson County	2.20	1.93	-	-	-	-	1.77	-	-	-	-	-	-	-	-	-	-	-	-	-	-	-	-	-
Carbondale (city)	2.00	1.79	-	-	-	-	-	-	-	-	-	-	-	-	-	-	-	-	-	-	-	-	-	-
Kane County	2.97	3.53	-	3.88	-	-	2.89	-	3.18	-	-	-	-	-	3.24	4.18	-	-	-	-	-	-	-	3.59
South Elgin (village)	2.81	4.77	-	-	-	-	-	-	-	-	-	-	-	-	-	-	-	-	-	-	-	-	-	-
Kankakee County	2.61	3.22	-	-	-	-	-	-	-	-	-	-	-	-	-	-	-	-	-	-	-	-	-	-
Kendall County	2.89	3.87	-	-	-	-	-	-	-	-	-	-	-	-	-	-	-	-	-	-	-	-	-	-
Knox County	2.33	3.22	-	-	-	-	-	-	-	-	-	-	-	-	-	-	-	-	-	-	-	-	-	-
La Salle County	2.50	2.29	-	-	-	-	-	-	-	-	-	-	-	-	-	-	-	-	-	-	-	-	-	-
Lake County	2.88	3.27	-	3.26	-	-	3.06	-	3.57	-	-	-	-	3.01	3.23	-	-	4.26	-	-	-	-	-	3.22
Buffalo Grove (village)	2.72	3.20	-	3.33	-	-	2.81	-	2.72	-	-	-	-	3.16	3.73	-	-	-	-	-	-	-	-	-
Gages Lake (cdp)	2.76	3.16	-	-	-	-	-	-	-	-	-	-	-	-	-	-	-	-	-	-	-	-	-	-
Grayslake (village)	2.85	3.55	-	-	-	-	-	-	-	-	-	-	-	-	-	-	-	-	-	-	-	-	-	-
Gurnee (village)	2.71	3.55	-	3.45	-	-	2.87	-	4.32	-	-	-	-	-	-	-	-	-	-	-	-	-	-	-
Lake Zurich (village)	3.17	3.51	-	-	-	-	-	-	-	-	-	-	-	-	-	-	-	-	-	-	-	-	-	-
Libertyville (village)	2.74	2.92	-	-	-	-	-	-	-	-	-	-	-	-	-	-	-	-	-	-	-	-	-	-
Mundelein (village)	3.11	3.59	-	-	-	-	3.53	-	3.83	-	-	-	-	-	-	-	-	-	-	-	-	-	-	-
Vernon Hills (village)	2.68	3.15	-	3.22	-	-	3.21	-	-	-	-	-	-	-	3.11	-	-	-	-	-	-	-	-	-
Macon County	2.39	2.67	-	-	-	-	-	-	-	-	-	-	-	-	-	-	-	-	-	-	-	-	-	-
Madison County	2.48	2.41	-	2.61	-	-	-	-	-	-	-	-	-	-	-	-	-	-	-	-	-	-	-	-
McHenry County	2.89	3.22	-	4.05	-	-	2.61	-	3.36	-	-	-	-	-	-	-	-	-	-	-	-	-	-	-
McLean County	2.45	2.40	-	2.40	-	-	2.67	-	-	-	-	-	-	-	-	-	-	-	-	-	-	-	-	-
Peoria County	2.43	2.43	-	2.40	-	-	2.52	-	-	-	-	-	-	-	-	-	-	-	-	-	-	-	-	2.90
Rock Island County	2.38	3.10	-	3.10	-	-	-	-	-	-	-	-	-	-	-	-	-	-	-	-	-	-	-	-
St. Clair County	2.60	2.88	-	-	-	-	-	-	3.15	-	-	-	-	-	2.14	-	-	-	-	-	-	-	-	-
Sangamon County	2.36	2.61	-	2.64	-	-	2.87	-	-	-	-	-	-	-	-	-	-	-	-	-	-	-	-	-

Notes: Please refer to the User's Guide for an explanation of data; data is arranged alphabetically by state, then county, then city within each county; table includes counties with populations greater than 49,999 unless noted and cities with populations greater than 9,999 whose Asian and/or NHPI population rates are greater than the national average; (1) Native Hawaiian and other Pacific Islander; (2) excludes Taiwanese; (3) includes Chamorro; (4) county does not meet population threshold but is shown in order to allow inclusion of city

Place	All households	Asian households	NHPI[1] households	Asian Indian	Bangladeshi	Cambodian	Chinese[2]	Fijian	Filipino	Guamanian[3]	Hawaiian, Native	Hmong	Indonesian	Japanese	Korean	Laotian	Malaysian	Pakistani	Samoan	Sri Lankan	Taiwanese	Thai	Tongan	Vietnamese
Tazewell County	2.48	3.28	-	-	-	-	-	-	-	-	-	-	-	-	-	-	-	-	-	-	-	-	-	-
Vermilion County	2.42	2.96	-	-	-	-	-	-	-	-	-	-	-	-	-	-	-	-	-	-	-	-	-	-
Will County	2.94	3.49	-	3.76	-	-	3.13	-	3.30	-	-	-	-	-	3.29	-	-	5.59	-	-	-	-	-	3.84
Bolingbrook (village)	3.23	3.76	-	4.07	-	-	-	-	3.62	-	-	-	-	-	-	-	-	-	-	-	-	-	-	-
Winnebago County	2.53	3.16	-	2.93	-	-	-	-	2.60	-	-	-	-	-	2.55	3.74	-	-	-	-	-	-	-	3.55
INDIANA	2.53	2.58	2.94	2.76	-	3.80	2.50	-	2.62	3.03	2.93	-	-	2.06	2.22	3.41	-	3.69	-	-	1.80	2.19	-	3.03
Allen County	2.53	2.91	-	2.87	-	-	2.79	-	2.72	-	-	-	-	-	-	-	-	-	-	-	-	-	-	3.65
Bartholomew County	2.52	2.48	-	2.21	-	-	-	-	-	-	-	-	-	-	-	-	-	-	-	-	-	-	-	-
Clark County	2.45	2.09	-	-	-	-	-	-	-	-	-	-	-	-	-	-	-	-	-	-	-	-	-	-
Delaware County	2.37	2.28	-	-	-	-	-	-	-	-	-	-	-	-	-	-	-	-	-	-	-	-	-	-
Elkhart County	2.72	3.12	-	-	-	-	-	-	-	-	-	-	-	-	-	-	-	-	-	-	-	-	-	-
Grant County	2.43	2.39	-	-	-	-	-	-	-	-	-	-	-	-	-	-	-	-	-	-	-	-	-	-
Hamilton County	2.74	3.03	-	3.52	-	-	2.88	-	-	-	-	-	-	-	-	-	-	-	-	-	-	-	-	-
Carmel (city)	2.72	3.11	-	-	-	-	-	-	-	-	-	-	-	-	-	-	-	-	-	-	-	-	-	-
Hendricks County	2.70	3.18	-	-	-	-	-	-	-	-	-	-	-	-	-	-	-	-	-	-	-	-	-	-
Howard County	2.40	2.81	-	-	-	-	-	-	-	-	-	-	-	-	-	-	-	-	-	-	-	-	-	-
Johnson County	2.63	2.69	-	-	-	-	-	-	-	-	-	-	-	-	-	-	-	-	-	-	-	-	-	-
Kosciusko County	2.66	3.26	-	-	-	-	-	-	-	-	-	-	-	-	-	-	-	-	-	-	-	-	-	-
Lake County	2.64	2.98	-	3.47	-	-	3.57	-	2.93	-	-	-	-	-	2.26	-	-	-	-	-	-	-	-	-
Munster (town)	2.61	3.31	-	4.33	-	-	-	-	-	-	-	-	-	-	-	-	-	-	-	-	-	-	-	-
LaPorte County	2.52	2.55	-	-	-	-	-	-	-	-	-	-	-	-	-	-	-	-	-	-	-	-	-	-
Madison County	2.42	2.02	-	-	-	-	-	-	-	-	-	-	-	-	-	-	-	-	-	-	-	-	-	-
Marion County	2.39	2.54	-	2.47	-	-	2.58	-	2.66	-	-	-	-	1.65	2.18	-	-	-	-	-	-	-	-	2.81
Monroe County	2.26	1.86	-	2.14	-	-	1.91	-	-	-	-	-	-	-	1.88	-	-	-	-	-	-	-	-	-
Bloomington (city)	2.09	1.79	-	2.04	-	-	1.86	-	-	-	-	-	-	-	1.86	-	-	-	-	-	-	-	-	-
Porter County	2.62	2.98	-	-	-	-	-	-	-	-	-	-	-	-	-	-	-	-	-	-	-	-	-	-
St. Joseph County	2.51	2.51	-	2.36	-	-	2.40	-	-	-	-	-	-	-	2.17	-	-	-	-	-	-	-	-	-
Tippecanoe County	2.42	2.20	-	2.51	-	-	1.91	-	-	-	-	-	-	2.08	2.32	-	-	-	-	-	-	-	-	-
West Lafayette (city)	2.26	2.09	-	2.52	-	-	1.75	-	-	-	-	-	-	-	-	-	-	-	-	-	-	-	-	-
Vanderburgh County	2.34	2.46	-	-	-	-	-	-	-	-	-	-	-	-	-	-	-	-	-	-	-	-	-	-
Vigo County	2.38	2.15	-	-	-	-	-	-	-	-	-	-	-	-	-	-	-	-	-	-	-	-	-	-
Wayne County	2.42	3.33	-	-	-	-	-	-	-	-	-	-	-	-	-	-	-	-	-	-	-	-	-	-
IOWA	2.45	2.88	2.95	2.52	-	4.71	2.55	-	2.61	-	-	-	-	1.90	2.32	3.89	-	3.21	-	-	2.35	2.64	-	3.71
Black Hawk County	2.44	2.71	-	-	-	-	-	-	-	-	-	-	-	-	-	-	-	-	-	-	-	-	-	-
Buena Vista County[4]	2.53	3.70	-	-	-	-	-	-	-	-	-	-	-	-	-	4.11	-	-	-	-	-	-	-	-
Storm Lake (city)	2.55	3.69	-	-	-	-	-	-	-	-	-	-	-	-	-	4.06	-	-	-	-	-	-	-	-
Johnson County	2.34	2.24	-	2.32	-	-	2.25	-	-	-	-	-	-	-	2.15	-	-	-	-	-	-	-	-	-
Coralville (city)	2.21	2.20	-	-	-	-	-	-	-	-	-	-	-	-	-	-	-	-	-	-	-	-	-	-
Iowa City (city)	2.23	2.25	-	2.42	-	-	2.25	-	-	-	-	-	-	-	1.92	-	-	-	-	-	-	-	-	-
Linn County	2.43	2.72	-	2.42	-	-	-	-	-	-	-	-	-	-	1.97	-	-	-	-	-	-	-	-	-
Polk County	2.45	3.36	-	2.69	-	5.13	2.77	-	-	-	-	-	-	-	2.90	4.18	-	-	-	-	-	3.26	-	3.73

Notes: Please refer to the User's Guide for an explanation of data; data is arranged alphabetically by state, then county, then city within each county; table includes counties with populations greater than 49,999 unless noted and cities with populations greater than 9,999 whose Asian and/or NHPI population rates are greater than the national average; (1) Native Hawaiian and other Pacific Islander; (2) excludes Taiwanese; (3) includes Chamorro; (4) county does not meet population threshold but is shown in order to allow inclusion of city

Place	All households	Asian households	NHPI[1] households	Asian Indian	Bangladeshi	Cambodian	Chinese[2]	Fijian	Filipino	Guamanian[3]	Hawaiian, Native	Hmong	Indonesian	Japanese	Korean	Laotian	Malaysian	Pakistani	Samoan	Sri Lankan	Taiwanese	Thai	Tongan	Vietnamese
Pottawattamie County	2.54	2.17	-	-	-	-	-	-	-	-	-	-	-	-	-	-	-	-	-	-	-	-	-	-
Scott County	2.49	3.06	-	-	-	-	-	-	-	-	-	-	-	-	-	-	-	-	-	-	-	-	-	4.57
Story County	2.39	2.36	-	2.71	-	-	2.30	-	-	-	-	-	-	-	2.39	-	-	-	-	-	-	-	-	-
Ames (city)	2.30	2.35	-	2.67	-	-	2.26	-	-	-	-	-	-	-	2.43	-	-	-	-	-	-	-	-	-
Woodbury County	2.58	3.92	-	-	-	-	-	-	-	-	-	-	-	-	-	-	-	-	-	-	-	-	-	4.13
KANSAS	2.51	2.93	2.79	2.73	-	3.64	2.66	-	2.58	-	2.56	5.84	-	1.84	2.58	3.64	-	3.10	-	-	2.05	2.02	-	3.71
Cowley County[4]	2.45	4.21	-	-	-	-	-	-	-	-	-	-	-	-	-	4.71	-	-	-	-	-	-	-	-
Winfield (city)	2.36	4.33	-	-	-	-	-	-	-	-	-	-	-	-	-	4.75	-	-	-	-	-	-	-	-
Douglas County	2.37	2.27	-	2.48	-	-	2.31	-	-	-	-	-	-	-	2.63	-	-	-	-	-	-	-	-	-
Lawrence (city)	2.29	2.28	-	2.48	-	-	2.31	-	-	-	-	-	-	-	2.65	-	-	-	-	-	-	-	-	-
Johnson County	2.55	2.87	-	2.77	-	-	2.80	-	2.90	-	-	-	-	2.39	2.91	3.26	-	-	-	-	-	-	-	3.79
Overland Park (city)	2.46	2.80	-	2.59	-	-	2.55	-	-	-	-	-	-	-	3.01	-	-	-	-	-	-	-	-	4.37
Leavenworth County	2.69	2.62	-	-	-	-	-	-	-	-	-	-	-	-	-	-	-	-	-	-	-	-	-	-
Riley County	2.42	2.75	-	-	-	-	2.58	-	-	-	-	-	-	-	2.97	-	-	-	-	-	-	-	-	-
Manhattan (city)	2.30	2.67	-	-	-	-	2.56	-	-	-	-	-	-	-	-	-	-	-	-	-	-	-	-	-
Saline County	2.43	3.24	-	-	-	-	-	-	-	-	-	-	-	-	-	-	-	-	-	-	-	-	-	3.74
Sedgwick County	2.53	3.08	2.82	2.57	-	3.48	2.67	-	2.18	-	-	-	-	-	2.33	3.79	-	-	-	-	-	-	-	3.62
Wichita (city)	2.44	3.06	-	2.64	-	-	2.61	-	2.17	-	-	-	-	-	2.44	3.64	-	-	-	-	-	-	-	3.64
Shawnee County	2.39	2.57	-	-	-	-	-	-	-	-	-	-	-	-	-	-	-	-	-	-	-	-	-	-
Wyandotte County	2.62	3.46	-	-	-	-	-	-	-	-	-	6.53	-	-	-	-	-	-	-	-	-	-	-	-
KENTUCKY	2.47	2.68	2.74	2.73	-	-	2.60	-	2.69	3.17	-	-	-	2.12	2.48	-	-	3.11	-	-	-	2.03	-	3.72
Boone County	2.73	3.01	-	-	-	-	-	-	-	-	-	-	-	2.77	-	-	-	-	-	-	-	-	-	-
Campbell County	2.49	2.82	-	-	-	-	-	-	-	-	-	-	-	-	-	-	-	-	-	-	-	-	-	-
Christian County	2.66	3.01	-	-	-	-	-	-	-	-	-	-	-	-	-	-	-	-	-	-	-	-	-	-
Fayette County	2.29	2.39	-	2.41	-	-	2.38	-	-	-	-	-	-	2.33	-	-	-	-	-	-	-	-	-	-
Hardin County	2.62	2.82	-	-	-	-	-	-	-	-	-	-	-	-	2.45	-	-	-	-	-	-	-	-	-
Radcliff (city)	2.55	2.82	-	-	-	-	-	-	-	-	-	-	-	-	-	-	-	-	-	-	-	-	-	-
Jefferson County	2.37	2.75	-	2.53	-	-	2.63	-	2.54	-	-	-	-	1.54	2.52	-	-	-	-	-	-	-	-	4.05
Kenton County	2.52	2.47	-	-	-	-	-	-	-	-	-	-	-	-	-	-	-	-	-	-	-	-	-	-
Madison County	2.41	3.15	-	-	-	-	-	-	-	-	-	-	-	-	-	-	-	-	-	-	-	-	-	-
Warren County	2.46	2.77	-	-	-	-	-	-	-	-	-	-	-	-	-	-	-	-	-	-	-	-	-	-
LOUISIANA	2.61	3.17	3.08	2.79	-	-	2.56	-	2.81	3.07	2.95	-	-	2.03	2.74	4.44	-	3.30	-	-	2.49	2.73	-	3.76
Ascension Parish	2.84	3.32	-	-	-	-	-	-	-	-	-	-	-	-	-	-	-	-	-	-	-	-	-	-
Bossier Parish	2.62	2.92	-	-	-	-	-	-	-	-	-	-	-	-	-	-	-	-	-	-	-	-	-	-
Caddo Parish	2.51	3.01	-	2.83	-	-	-	-	-	-	-	-	-	-	-	-	-	-	-	-	-	-	-	-
Calcasieu Parish	2.60	2.84	-	-	-	-	-	-	-	-	-	-	-	-	-	-	-	-	-	-	-	-	-	-
East Baton Rouge Parish	2.54	3.02	-	2.84	-	-	2.59	-	3.32	-	-	-	-	-	-	-	-	-	-	-	-	-	-	3.59
Iberia Parish	2.83	4.78	-	-	-	-	-	-	-	-	-	-	-	-	-	5.04	-	-	-	-	-	-	-	5.13
Jefferson Parish	2.56	3.11	-	2.50	-	-	2.65	-	3.00	-	-	-	-	-	3.25	-	-	3.02	-	-	-	-	-	3.64
Gretna (city)	2.38	3.22	-	-	-	-	-	-	-	-	-	-	-	-	-	-	-	-	-	-	-	-	-	3.61
Harvey (cdp)	2.79	3.51	-	-	-	-	-	-	-	-	-	-	-	-	-	-	-	-	-	-	-	-	-	3.98

Notes: Please refer to the User's Guide for an explanation of data; data is arranged alphabetically by state, then county, then city within each county; table includes counties with populations greater than 49,999 unless noted and cities with populations greater than 9,999 whose Asian and/or NHPI population rates are greater than the national average; (1) Native Hawaiian and other Pacific Islander; (2) excludes Taiwanese; (3) includes Chamorro; (4) county does not meet population threshold but is shown in order to allow inclusion of city

Place	All households	Asian households	NHPI[1] households	Asian Indian	Bangladeshi	Cambodian	Chinese[2]	Fijian	Filipino	Guamanian[3]	Hawaiian, Native	Hmong	Indonesian	Japanese	Korean	Laotian	Malaysian	Pakistani	Samoan	Sri Lankan	Taiwanese	Thai	Tongan	Vietnamese
Timberlane (cdp)	2.82	4.12	-	-	-	-	-	-	-	-	-	-	-	-	-	-	-	-	-	-	-	-	-	4.29
Woodmere (cdp)	3.50	4.13	-	-	-	-	-	-	-	-	-	-	-	-	-	-	-	-	-	-	-	-	-	4.48
Lafayette Parish	2.56	2.94	-	2.90	-	-	-	-	-	-	-	-	-	-	-	-	-	-	-	-	-	-	-	3.79
Lafourche Parish	2.75	2.87	-	-	-	-	-	-	-	-	-	-	-	-	-	-	-	-	-	-	-	-	-	-
Orleans Parish	2.48	3.14	-	2.72	-	-	2.06	-	1.97	-	-	-	-	-	-	-	-	-	-	-	-	-	-	3.80
Ouachita Parish	2.57	2.39	-	-	-	-	-	-	-	-	-	-	-	-	-	-	-	-	-	-	-	-	-	-
Rapides Parish	2.56	3.31	-	-	-	-	-	-	-	-	-	-	-	-	-	-	-	-	-	-	-	-	-	-
St. Bernard Parish	2.65	3.75	-	-	-	-	-	-	-	-	-	-	-	-	-	-	-	-	-	-	-	-	-	4.60
St. Mary Parish	2.74	4.27	-	-	-	-	-	-	-	-	-	-	-	-	-	-	-	-	-	-	-	-	-	4.52
St. Tammany Parish	2.73	3.62	-	-	-	-	-	-	-	-	-	-	-	-	-	-	-	-	-	-	-	-	-	3.97
Terrebonne Parish	2.86	3.72	-	-	-	-	-	-	-	-	-	-	-	-	-	-	-	-	-	-	-	-	-	3.94
Vermilion Parish	2.67	4.34	-	-	-	-	-	-	-	-	-	-	-	-	-	-	-	-	-	-	-	-	-	4.53
Abbeville (city)	2.56	4.54	-	-	-	-	-	-	-	-	-	-	-	-	-	-	-	-	-	-	-	-	-	4.56
Vernon Parish	2.69	2.91	-	-	-	-	-	-	-	-	-	-	-	-	2.39	-	-	-	-	-	-	-	-	-
MAINE	2.39	2.92	2.95	2.49	-	3.90	3.17	-	2.73	-	-	-	-	2.10	2.15	-	-	-	-	-	-	-	-	3.13
Androscoggin County	2.38	3.65	-	-	-	-	-	-	-	-	-	-	-	-	-	-	-	-	-	-	-	-	-	-
Aroostook County	2.36	2.99	-	-	-	-	-	-	-	-	-	-	-	-	-	-	-	-	-	-	-	-	-	-
Cumberland County	2.38	3.04	-	-	-	4.10	2.81	-	2.41	-	-	-	-	-	-	-	-	-	-	-	-	-	-	3.26
Hancock County	2.31	2.77	-	-	-	-	-	-	-	-	-	-	-	-	-	-	-	-	-	-	-	-	-	-
Kennebec County	2.38	2.67	-	-	-	-	-	-	-	-	-	-	-	-	-	-	-	-	-	-	-	-	-	-
Oxford County	2.42	2.62	-	-	-	-	-	-	-	-	-	-	-	-	-	-	-	-	-	-	-	-	-	-
Penobscot County	2.38	2.88	-	-	-	-	3.19	-	-	-	-	-	-	-	-	-	-	-	-	-	-	-	-	-
York County	2.47	3.03	-	-	-	-	-	-	-	-	-	-	-	-	-	-	-	-	-	-	-	-	-	-
MARYLAND	2.60	3.05	2.93	3.08	3.72	4.13	2.90	-	3.11	2.61	3.25	-	3.53	2.09	2.98	4.58	-	3.89	-	2.83	2.72	2.79	-	3.75
Allegany County	2.34	3.26	-	-	-	-	-	-	-	-	-	-	-	-	-	-	-	-	-	-	-	-	-	-
Anne Arundel County	2.65	2.84	-	2.85	-	-	2.80	-	2.96	-	-	-	-	2.18	2.98	-	-	-	-	-	-	-	-	-
Severn (cdp)	2.91	3.05	-	-	-	-	-	-	-	-	-	-	-	-	3.31	-	-	-	-	-	-	-	-	-
South Gate (cdp)	2.53	2.75	-	-	-	-	-	-	-	-	-	-	-	-	3.06	-	-	-	-	-	-	-	-	-
Baltimore Independent City	2.43	2.07	-	1.94	-	-	1.88	-	2.77	-	-	-	-	-	1.77	-	-	-	-	-	-	-	-	3.45
Baltimore County	2.46	2.93	-	2.95	-	-	2.82	-	2.79	-	-	-	-	2.18	3.05	-	-	3.22	-	-	-	-	-	3.85
Arbutus (cdp)	2.44	2.42	-	-	-	-	-	-	-	-	-	-	-	-	-	-	-	-	-	-	-	-	-	-
Carney (cdp)	2.29	3.08	-	-	-	-	3.02	-	-	-	-	-	-	-	3.51	-	-	-	-	-	-	-	-	-
Cockeysville (cdp)	2.12	2.51	-	-	-	-	-	-	-	-	-	-	-	-	2.74	-	-	-	-	-	-	-	-	-
Lutherville-Timonium (cdp)	2.32	2.53	-	-	-	-	-	-	-	-	-	-	-	-	-	-	-	-	-	-	-	-	-	-
Mays Chapel (cdp)	2.44	3.19	-	-	-	-	-	-	-	-	-	-	-	-	-	-	-	-	-	-	-	-	-	-
Owings Mills (cdp)	2.25	2.78	-	-	-	-	-	-	-	-	-	-	-	-	-	-	-	-	-	-	-	-	-	-
Perry Hall (cdp)	2.54	3.28	-	-	-	-	-	-	-	-	-	-	-	-	3.32	-	-	-	-	-	-	-	-	-
Reisterstown (cdp)	2.55	3.10	-	3.09	-	-	-	-	-	-	-	-	-	-	-	-	-	-	-	-	-	-	-	-
Rossville (cdp)	2.33	2.55	-	-	-	-	-	-	-	-	-	-	-	-	-	-	-	-	-	-	-	-	-	-
Towson (cdp)	2.16	2.74	-	-	-	-	2.83	-	-	-	-	-	-	-	-	-	-	-	-	-	-	-	-	-
Woodlawn (cdp)	2.57	3.63	-	3.24	-	-	-	-	-	-	-	-	-	-	-	-	-	-	-	-	-	-	-	-

Notes: Please refer to the User's Guide for an explanation of data; data is arranged alphabetically by state, then county, then city within each county; table includes counties with populations greater than 49,999 unless noted and cities with populations greater than 9,999 whose Asian and/or NHPI population rates are greater than the national average; (1) Native Hawaiian and other Pacific Islander; (2) excludes Taiwanese; (3) includes Chamorro; (4) county does not meet population threshold but is shown in order to allow inclusion of city

Place	All households	Asian households	NHPI[1] households	Asian Indian	Bangladeshi	Cambodian	Chinese[2]	Fijian	Filipino	Guamanian[3]	Hawaiian, Native	Hmong	Indonesian	Japanese	Korean	Laotian	Malaysian	Pakistani	Samoan	Sri Lankan	Taiwanese	Thai	Tongan	Vietnamese
Calvert County	2.91	2.97	-	-	-	-	-	-	-	-	-	-	-	-	-	-	-	-	-	-	-	-	-	-
Carroll County	2.80	3.21	-	-	-	-	-	-	-	-	-	-	-	-	-	-	-	-	-	-	-	-	-	-
Cecil County	2.71	2.95	-	-	-	-	-	-	-	-	-	-	-	-	-	-	-	-	-	-	-	-	-	-
Charles County	2.86	3.27	-	-	-	-	-	-	3.13	-	-	-	-	-	-	-	-	-	-	-	-	-	-	-
Frederick County	2.72	3.10	-	2.85	-	-	2.62	-	-	-	-	-	-	-	3.20	-	-	-	-	-	-	-	-	-
Harford County	2.72	3.10	-	3.57	-	-	-	-	2.98	-	-	-	-	-	2.62	-	-	-	-	-	-	-	-	-
Howard County	2.71	3.25	-	3.35	-	-	3.10	-	2.92	-	-	-	-	-	3.37	-	-	4.35	-	-	-	-	-	3.24
Columbia (cdp)	2.54	2.98	-	3.10	-	-	2.86	-	2.57	-	-	-	-	-	3.10	-	-	-	-	-	-	-	-	-
Elkridge (cdp)	2.64	3.28	-	-	-	-	-	-	-	-	-	-	-	-	3.37	-	-	-	-	-	-	-	-	-
Ellicott City (cdp)	2.76	3.39	-	3.45	-	-	3.33	-	3.18	-	-	-	-	-	3.37	-	-	4.57	-	-	-	-	-	-
North Laurel (cdp)	2.82	3.03	-	2.99	-	-	-	-	-	-	-	-	-	-	3.33	-	-	-	-	-	-	-	-	-
Savage-Guilford (cdp)	2.64	3.73	-	-	-	-	-	-	-	-	-	-	-	-	-	-	-	-	-	-	-	-	-	-
Montgomery County	2.66	3.12	3.38	3.12	3.58	4.34	2.98	-	3.07	-	-	-	3.90	2.13	3.10	-	-	4.29	-	3.11	3.19	2.82	-	3.75
Aspen Hill (cdp)	2.73	3.28	-	3.07	-	-	3.28	-	3.63	-	-	-	-	-	2.67	-	-	-	-	-	-	-	-	3.75
Bethesda (cdp)	2.30	2.53	-	2.85	-	-	2.44	-	3.08	-	-	-	-	2.27	2.30	-	-	-	-	-	-	-	-	-
Calverton (cdp)	2.72	3.26	-	2.84	-	-	-	-	-	-	-	-	-	-	3.24	-	-	-	-	-	-	-	-	-
Colesville (cdp)	3.00	3.82	-	3.65	-	-	4.17	-	-	-	-	-	-	-	3.66	-	-	-	-	-	-	-	-	3.67
Fairland (cdp)	2.47	3.29	-	3.26	-	-	2.98	-	-	-	-	-	-	-	3.41	-	-	-	-	-	-	-	-	-
Gaithersburg (city)	2.65	2.90	-	2.67	-	-	2.92	-	3.03	-	-	-	-	-	2.75	-	-	-	-	-	-	-	-	3.84
Germantown (cdp)	2.65	2.97	-	2.88	-	-	2.60	-	-	-	-	-	-	-	3.10	-	-	-	-	-	-	-	-	3.37
Montgomery Village (cdp)	2.68	3.08	-	2.97	-	-	2.48	-	3.34	-	-	-	-	-	-	-	-	-	-	-	-	-	-	3.75
North Bethesda (cdp)	2.17	2.31	-	2.30	-	-	2.25	-	2.28	-	-	-	-	1.99	2.67	-	-	-	-	-	-	-	-	-
North Potomac (cdp)	3.32	3.52	-	3.37	-	-	3.56	-	-	-	-	-	-	-	3.67	-	-	-	-	-	-	-	-	-
Olney (cdp)	3.05	3.37	-	3.83	-	-	2.96	-	-	-	-	-	-	-	4.24	-	-	-	-	-	-	-	-	-
Potomac (cdp)	2.85	3.22	-	3.41	-	-	3.02	-	3.68	-	-	-	-	-	3.34	-	-	-	-	-	-	-	-	-
Redland (cdp)	3.23	3.56	-	3.33	-	-	3.70	-	3.91	-	-	-	-	-	3.22	-	-	-	-	-	-	-	-	-
Rockville (city)	2.65	3.04	-	2.88	-	-	2.85	-	3.15	-	-	-	-	2.38	3.07	-	-	-	-	-	-	-	-	3.70
Silver Spring (cdp)	2.50	2.88	-	2.90	-	4.90	2.36	-	2.37	-	-	-	-	-	1.65	-	-	-	-	-	-	-	-	4.22
Takoma Park (city)	2.43	2.27	-	-	-	-	-	-	-	-	-	-	-	-	-	-	-	-	-	-	-	-	-	-
Wheaton-Glenmont (cdp)	2.93	3.41	-	3.13	-	-	3.30	-	4.02	-	-	-	-	-	3.37	-	-	-	-	-	-	-	-	3.64
White Oak (cdp)	2.63	3.16	-	3.35	-	-	2.76	-	-	-	-	-	-	-	3.08	-	-	-	-	-	-	-	-	3.67
Prince George's County	2.74	3.30	-	3.34	-	-	3.05	-	3.56	-	-	-	-	1.68	2.79	-	-	3.81	-	-	-	3.28	-	4.42
Adelphi (cdp)	2.74	2.84	-	-	-	-	-	-	-	-	-	-	-	-	-	-	-	-	-	-	-	-	-	-
Beltsville (cdp)	2.74	3.61	-	4.21	-	-	-	-	-	-	-	-	-	-	2.59	-	-	-	-	-	-	-	-	-
College Park (city)	2.64	3.13	-	3.50	-	-	3.49	-	-	-	-	-	-	-	-	-	-	-	-	-	-	-	-	-
Fort Washington (cdp)	2.91	3.64	-	-	-	-	-	-	3.56	-	-	-	-	-	-	-	-	-	-	-	-	-	-	-
Friendly (cdp)	3.15	4.37	-	-	-	-	-	-	4.74	-	-	-	-	-	-	-	-	-	-	-	-	-	-	-
Glenn Dale (cdp)	3.13	4.03	-	-	-	-	-	-	-	-	-	-	-	-	-	-	-	-	-	-	-	-	-	-
Greenbelt (city)	2.30	3.10	-	3.00	-	-	3.18	-	-	-	-	-	-	-	3.04	-	-	-	-	-	-	-	-	-
Hyattsville (city)	2.64	3.54	-	-	-	-	-	-	-	-	-	-	-	-	-	-	-	-	-	-	-	-	-	-
Lanham-Seabrook (cdp)	2.87	4.50	-	-	-	-	-	-	-	-	-	-	-	-	-	-	-	-	-	-	-	-	-	-

Notes: Please refer to the User's Guide for an explanation of data; data is arranged alphabetically by state, then county, then city within each county; table includes counties with populations greater than 49,999 unless noted and cities with populations greater than 9,999 whose Asian and/or NHPI population rates are greater than the national average; (1) Native Hawaiian and other Pacific Islander; (2) excludes Taiwanese; (3) includes Chamorro; (4) county does not meet population threshold but is shown in order to allow inclusion of city

Place	All households	Asian households	NHPI[1] households	Asian Indian	Bangladeshi	Cambodian	Chinese[2]	Fijian	Filipino	Guamanian[3]	Hawaiian, Native	Hmong	Indonesian	Japanese	Korean	Laotian	Malaysian	Pakistani	Samoan	Sri Lankan	Taiwanese	Thai	Tongan	Vietnamese
Laurel (city)	2.20	2.84	-	-	-	-	-	-	-	-	-	-	-	-	-	-	-	-	-	-	-	-	-	-
New Carrollton (city)	2.79	2.52	-	-	-	-	-	-	-	-	-	-	-	-	-	-	-	-	-	-	-	-	-	-
South Laurel (cdp)	2.48	3.07	-	-	-	-	-	-	-	-	-	-	-	-	-	-	-	-	-	-	-	-	-	-
St. Mary's County	2.71	3.02	-	4.02	-	-	-	-	3.10	-	-	-	-	-	-	-	-	-	-	-	-	-	-	-
Lexington Park (cdp)	2.58	3.68	-	-	-	-	-	-	-	-	-	-	-	-	-	-	-	-	-	-	-	-	-	-
Washington County	2.47	2.89	-	-	-	-	-	-	-	-	-	-	-	-	-	-	-	-	-	-	-	-	-	-
Wicomico County	2.53	3.11	-	3.27	-	-	-	-	-	-	-	-	-	-	3.08	-	-	-	-	-	-	-	-	-
Salisbury (city)	2.36	3.53	-	-	-	-	-	-	-	-	-	-	-	-	-	-	-	-	-	-	-	-	-	-
MASSACHUSETTS	2.51	2.98	2.62	2.68	2.82	4.55	2.88	-	2.64	3.54	2.62	6.07	2.26	2.04	2.39	4.32	-	3.84	-	2.86	2.43	2.35	-	3.86
Barnstable County	2.28	2.61	-	-	-	-	2.48	-	-	-	-	-	-	-	-	-	-	-	-	-	-	-	-	-
Berkshire County	2.31	2.71	-	2.33	-	-	-	-	-	-	-	-	-	-	-	-	-	-	-	-	-	-	-	-
Bristol County	2.53	3.15	-	2.96	-	4.26	2.90	-	2.82	-	-	-	-	-	2.08	-	-	-	-	-	-	-	-	3.65
Essex County	2.57	3.40	-	2.87	-	4.54	3.06	-	2.53	-	-	-	-	2.45	2.64	5.57	-	-	-	-	-	-	-	4.10
Andover (town)	2.73	3.09	-	2.88	-	-	3.62	-	-	-	-	-	-	-	-	-	-	-	-	-	-	-	-	-
Lynn (city)	2.61	4.32	-	4.38	-	4.58	-	-	-	-	-	-	-	-	-	-	-	-	-	-	-	-	-	4.53
North Andover (town)	2.61	3.31	-	-	-	-	3.17	-	-	-	-	-	-	-	-	-	-	-	-	-	-	-	-	-
Franklin County	2.38	2.93	-	-	-	-	-	-	-	-	-	-	-	-	-	-	-	-	-	-	-	-	-	-
Hampden County	2.52	3.36	-	3.33	-	3.94	3.50	-	-	-	-	-	-	-	2.66	-	-	-	-	-	-	-	-	4.08
Hampshire County	2.39	2.51	-	2.31	-	-	2.63	-	-	-	-	-	-	-	2.29	-	-	-	-	-	-	-	-	-
Amherst Center (cdp)	2.20	2.29	-	-	-	-	-	-	-	-	-	-	-	-	-	-	-	-	-	-	-	-	-	-
Amherst (town)	2.45	2.60	-	-	-	-	2.61	-	-	-	-	-	-	-	-	-	-	-	-	-	-	-	-	-
Middlesex County	2.52	3.01	-	2.80	-	4.77	2.87	-	2.67	-	-	-	-	2.16	2.60	4.60	-	3.23	-	-	2.60	2.32	-	3.61
Acton (town)	2.70	2.87	-	2.74	-	-	2.97	-	-	-	-	-	-	-	-	-	-	-	-	-	-	-	-	-
Arlington (town)	2.22	2.37	-	-	-	-	2.22	-	-	-	-	-	-	-	-	-	-	-	-	-	-	-	-	-
Bedford (town)	2.60	3.77	-	-	-	-	-	-	-	-	-	-	-	-	-	-	-	-	-	-	-	-	-	-
Belmont (cdp)	2.46	3.14	-	-	-	-	3.16	-	-	-	-	-	-	-	-	-	-	-	-	-	-	-	-	-
Belmont (town)	2.46	3.14	-	-	-	-	3.16	-	-	-	-	-	-	-	-	-	-	-	-	-	-	-	-	-
Burlington (town)	2.75	2.84	-	2.86	-	-	-	-	-	-	-	-	-	-	-	-	-	-	-	-	-	-	-	-
Cambridge (city)	2.03	2.17	-	2.29	-	-	2.07	-	-	-	-	-	-	1.81	2.29	-	-	-	-	-	-	-	-	-
Chelmsford (town)	2.60	3.35	-	2.69	-	-	3.41	-	-	-	-	-	-	-	-	-	-	-	-	-	-	-	-	-
Framingham (town)	2.43	2.48	-	2.54	-	-	2.45	-	-	-	-	-	-	-	-	-	-	-	-	-	-	-	-	-
Lexington (town)	2.66	3.44	-	3.50	-	-	3.20	-	-	-	-	-	-	-	4.24	-	-	-	-	-	-	-	-	-
Lowell (city)	2.67	4.01	-	2.97	-	4.79	2.13	-	-	-	-	-	-	-	-	4.48	-	-	-	-	-	-	-	3.66
Malden (city)	2.42	3.23	-	2.49	-	-	3.52	-	-	-	-	-	-	-	-	-	-	-	-	-	-	-	-	3.88
Marlborough (city)	2.46	2.50	-	2.63	-	-	-	-	-	-	-	-	-	-	-	-	-	-	-	-	-	-	-	-
Medford (city)	2.43	2.81	-	2.56	-	-	2.82	-	-	-	-	-	-	-	-	-	-	-	-	-	-	-	-	3.85
Natick (town)	2.41	3.18	-	-	-	-	3.21	-	-	-	-	-	-	-	-	-	-	-	-	-	-	-	-	-
Newton (city)	2.51	3.19	-	3.21	-	-	3.26	-	-	-	-	-	-	-	3.47	-	-	-	-	-	-	-	-	-
Somerville (city)	2.38	2.65	-	2.85	-	-	2.78	-	-	-	-	-	-	-	2.06	-	-	-	-	-	-	-	-	-
Sudbury (town)	3.01	3.00	-	-	-	-	-	-	-	-	-	-	-	-	-	-	-	-	-	-	-	-	-	-
Waltham (city)	2.30	2.64	-	2.87	-	-	2.44	-	-	-	-	-	-	-	-	-	-	-	-	-	-	-	-	-

Notes: Please refer to the User's Guide for an explanation of data; data is arranged alphabetically by state, then county, then city within each county; table includes counties with populations greater than 49,999 unless noted and cities with populations greater than 9,999 whose Asian and/or NHPI population rates are greater than the national average; (1) Native Hawaiian and other Pacific Islander; (2) excludes Taiwanese; (3) includes Chamorro; (4) county does not meet population threshold but is shown in order to allow inclusion of city

Place	All households	Asian households	NHPI[1] households	Asian Indian	Bangladeshi	Cambodian	Chinese[2]	Fijian	Filipino	Guamanian[3]	Hawaiian, Native	Hmong	Indonesian	Japanese	Korean	Laotian	Malaysian	Pakistani	Samoan	Sri Lankan	Taiwanese	Thai	Tongan	Vietnamese
Wayland (town)	2.80	3.08	-	-	-	-	-	-	-	-	-	-	-	-	-	-	-	-	-	-	-	-	-	-
Westford (town)	3.02	3.33	-	-	-	-	3.30	-	-	-	-	-	-	-	-	-	-	-	-	-	-	-	-	-
Weston (town)	2.87	3.85	-	-	-	-	3.53	-	-	-	-	-	-	-	-	-	-	-	-	-	-	-	-	-
Winchester (town)	2.64	3.05	-	-	-	-	-	-	-	-	-	-	-	-	-	-	-	-	-	-	-	-	-	-
Woburn (city)	2.46	2.61	-	2.60	-	-	-	-	-	-	-	-	-	-	-	-	-	-	-	-	-	-	-	-
Norfolk County	2.54	3.07	-	2.54	-	-	3.29	-	2.96	-	-	-	-	2.32	2.59	-	-	-	-	-	3.10	-	-	3.98
Brookline (town)	2.18	2.52	-	2.15	-	-	2.74	-	-	-	-	-	-	2.25	2.56	-	-	-	-	-	-	-	-	-
Needham (town)	2.64	3.24	-	-	-	-	3.61	-	-	-	-	-	-	-	-	-	-	-	-	-	-	-	-	-
Norwood (town)	2.41	2.69	-	2.67	-	-	-	-	-	-	-	-	-	-	-	-	-	-	-	-	-	-	-	-
Quincy (city)	2.22	3.32	-	2.05	-	-	3.58	-	2.99	-	-	-	-	-	-	-	-	-	-	-	-	-	-	3.81
Randolph (town)	2.71	3.99	-	-	-	-	3.88	-	-	-	-	-	-	-	-	-	-	-	-	-	-	-	-	4.53
Sharon (town)	2.91	3.47	-	-	-	-	-	-	-	-	-	-	-	-	-	-	-	-	-	-	-	-	-	-
Wellesley (town)	2.69	3.20	-	-	-	-	3.44	-	-	-	-	-	-	-	-	-	-	-	-	-	-	-	-	-
Plymouth County	2.74	3.69	-	3.45	-	-	3.56	-	3.23	-	-	-	-	-	-	-	-	-	-	-	-	-	-	4.56
Suffolk County	2.34	2.60	-	2.02	-	4.09	2.49	-	2.37	-	-	-	-	1.53	1.65	-	-	-	-	-	1.92	-	-	3.96
Boston (city)	2.31	2.54	-	2.01	-	3.77	2.49	-	2.34	-	-	-	-	1.53	1.62	-	-	-	-	-	1.92	-	-	3.90
Chelsea (city)	2.87	3.88	-	-	-	-	-	-	-	-	-	-	-	-	-	-	-	-	-	-	-	-	-	4.73
Revere (city)	2.42	3.36	-	-	-	4.50	-	-	-	-	-	-	-	-	-	-	-	-	-	-	-	-	-	4.34
Worcester County	2.55	3.28	-	2.83	-	4.95	3.14	-	2.31	-	-	6.60	-	2.68	2.62	4.08	-	4.28	-	-	-	-	-	3.67
Fitchburg (city)	2.49	5.00	-	-	-	-	-	-	-	-	-	7.36	-	-	-	4.61	-	-	-	-	-	-	-	-
Northborough (town)	2.81	3.50	-	-	-	-	-	-	-	-	-	-	-	-	-	-	-	-	-	-	-	-	-	-
Shrewsbury (town)	2.53	3.05	-	2.82	-	-	3.04	-	-	-	-	-	-	-	-	-	-	-	-	-	-	-	-	4.37
Westborough (town)	2.63	3.15	-	2.99	-	-	3.26	-	-	-	-	-	-	-	-	-	-	-	-	-	-	-	-	-
Worcester (city)	2.41	3.24	-	2.65	-	-	3.00	-	-	-	-	-	-	-	-	-	-	-	-	-	-	-	-	3.61
MICHIGAN	2.56	2.88	3.05	2.88	3.88	3.97	2.61	-	2.80	3.78	2.78	5.58	2.38	2.36	2.48	4.02	2.68	3.81	2.48	3.52	2.64	1.92	-	3.54
Allegan County	2.71	2.10	-	-	-	-	-	-	-	-	-	-	-	-	-	-	-	-	-	-	-	-	-	-
Bay County	2.46	3.07	-	-	-	-	-	-	-	-	-	-	-	-	-	-	-	-	-	-	-	-	-	-
Berrien County	2.48	2.84	-	2.94	-	-	-	-	2.48	-	-	-	-	-	3.05	-	-	-	-	-	-	-	-	-
Calhoun County	2.47	2.47	-	-	-	-	-	-	-	-	-	-	-	2.45	-	-	-	-	-	-	-	-	-	-
Cass County	2.57	3.94	-	-	-	-	-	-	-	-	-	-	-	-	-	4.90	-	-	-	-	-	-	-	-
Clinton County	2.70	3.48	-	-	-	-	-	-	-	-	-	-	-	-	-	-	-	-	-	-	-	-	-	-
Eaton County	2.53	3.07	-	2.75	-	-	-	-	-	-	-	-	-	-	-	-	-	-	-	-	-	-	-	4.43
Genesee County	2.53	2.62	-	2.76	-	-	2.07	-	2.46	-	-	-	-	-	1.93	-	-	-	-	-	-	-	-	-
Ingham County	2.42	2.61	-	2.57	-	-	2.32	-	2.75	-	-	5.50	-	1.79	2.05	-	-	-	-	-	-	-	-	3.86
East Lansing (city)	2.23	2.04	-	2.15	-	-	1.90	-	-	-	-	-	-	-	2.02	-	-	-	-	-	-	-	-	-
Meridian charter (township)	2.35	2.59	-	2.92	-	-	3.06	-	-	-	-	-	-	-	1.95	-	-	-	-	-	-	-	-	-
Okemos (cdp)	2.43	2.61	-	3.12	-	-	3.23	-	-	-	-	-	-	-	-	-	-	-	-	-	-	-	-	-
Ionia County	2.70	1.66	-	-	-	-	-	-	-	-	-	-	-	-	-	-	-	-	-	-	-	-	-	-
Isabella County	2.55	2.31	-	-	-	-	-	-	-	-	-	-	-	-	-	-	-	-	-	-	-	-	-	-
Jackson County	2.54	2.06	-	-	-	-	-	-	-	-	-	-	-	-	-	-	-	-	-	-	-	-	-	-
Kalamazoo County	2.43	2.42	-	2.69	-	-	2.14	-	-	-	-	-	-	-	2.35	-	-	-	-	-	-	-	-	-

Notes: Please refer to the User's Guide for an explanation of data; data is arranged alphabetically by state, then county, then city within each county; table includes counties with populations greater than 49,999 unless noted and cities with populations greater than 9,999 whose Asian and/or NHPI population rates are greater than the national average; (1) Native Hawaiian and other Pacific Islander; (2) excludes Taiwanese; (3) includes Chamorro; (4) county does not meet population threshold but is shown in order to allow inclusion of city

Place	All households	Asian households	NHPI[1] households	Asian Indian	Bangladeshi	Cambodian	Chinese[2]	Fijian	Filipino	Guamanian[3]	Hawaiian, Native	Hmong	Indonesian	Japanese	Korean	Laotian	Malaysian	Pakistani	Samoan	Sri Lankan	Taiwanese	Thai	Tongan	Vietnamese
Kent County	2.63	3.31	-	3.03	-	-	3.06	-	2.47	-	-	-	-	-	2.73	-	-	-	-	-	-	-	-	3.81
Kentwood (city)	2.43	3.65	-	-	-	-	-	-	-	-	-	-	-	-	3.16	-	-	-	-	-	-	-	-	4.17
Lenawee County	2.61	2.56	-	-	-	-	-	-	-	-	-	-	-	-	-	-	-	-	-	-	-	-	-	-
Livingston County	2.81	2.78	-	-	-	-	-	-	-	-	-	-	-	-	-	-	-	-	-	-	-	-	-	-
Macomb County	2.52	3.18	-	3.17	-	-	2.67	-	3.06	-	-	5.26	-	-	2.78	-	-	4.56	-	-	-	-	-	3.50
Sterling Heights (city)	2.66	3.22	-	3.53	-	-	2.83	-	2.84	-	-	-	-	-	2.74	-	-	-	-	-	-	-	-	3.56
Marquette County	2.35	2.10	-	-	-	-	-	-	-	-	-	-	-	-	-	-	-	-	-	-	-	-	-	-
Midland County	2.56	2.94	-	2.63	-	-	3.12	-	-	-	-	-	-	-	-	-	-	-	-	-	-	-	-	-
Monroe County	2.68	3.06	-	-	-	-	-	-	-	-	-	-	-	-	-	-	-	-	-	-	-	-	-	-
Muskegon County	2.59	2.61	-	-	-	-	-	-	-	-	-	-	-	-	-	-	-	-	-	-	-	-	-	-
Oakland County	2.50	2.92	-	2.87	-	-	2.83	-	2.86	-	-	5.64	-	2.60	2.83	-	-	3.78	-	-	3.11	-	-	3.41
Auburn Hills (city)	2.24	2.78	-	2.76	-	-	-	-	-	-	-	-	-	-	-	-	-	-	-	-	-	-	-	-
Bloomfield (township)	2.52	3.01	-	3.14	-	-	-	-	-	-	-	-	-	-	2.89	-	-	-	-	-	-	-	-	-
Farmington (city)	2.14	2.41	-	2.35	-	-	-	-	-	-	-	-	-	-	-	-	-	-	-	-	-	-	-	-
Farmington Hills (city)	2.41	2.64	-	2.60	-	-	2.74	-	3.86	-	-	-	-	-	-	-	-	-	-	-	-	-	-	-
Madison Heights (city)	2.33	2.25	-	-	-	-	2.46	-	-	-	-	-	-	-	-	-	-	-	-	-	-	-	-	-
Novi (city)	2.52	3.04	-	3.30	-	-	3.11	-	-	-	-	-	-	2.58	-	-	-	-	-	-	-	-	-	-
Rochester (city)	2.23	2.45	-	-	-	-	-	-	-	-	-	-	-	-	-	-	-	-	-	-	-	-	-	-
Rochester Hills (city)	2.58	3.08	-	3.08	-	-	3.22	-	-	-	-	-	-	-	3.32	-	-	-	-	-	-	-	-	-
Troy (city)	2.69	3.07	-	3.03	-	-	2.98	-	2.79	-	-	-	-	-	3.40	-	-	-	-	-	3.28	-	-	-
West Bloomfield (township)	2.74	3.40	-	3.68	-	-	3.24	-	3.32	-	-	-	-	3.21	2.87	-	-	-	-	-	-	-	-	-
Ottawa County	2.80	3.57	-	3.54	-	4.11	4.14	-	-	-	-	-	-	-	1.86	3.77	-	-	-	-	-	-	-	3.42
Holland (city)	2.66	3.35	-	-	-	-	-	-	-	-	-	-	-	-	-	-	-	-	-	-	-	-	-	-
Saginaw County	2.54	2.76	-	3.16	-	-	-	-	3.63	-	-	-	-	-	2.20	-	-	-	-	-	-	-	-	-
St. Clair County	2.61	2.89	-	-	-	-	-	-	-	-	-	-	-	-	-	-	-	-	-	-	-	-	-	-
St. Joseph County	2.62	2.34	-	-	-	-	-	-	-	-	-	-	-	-	-	-	-	-	-	-	-	-	-	-
Washtenaw County	2.40	2.34	-	2.24	-	-	2.28	-	2.16	-	-	-	-	2.25	2.39	-	-	3.97	-	-	2.15	-	-	2.96
Ann Arbor (city)	2.22	2.25	-	2.13	-	-	2.23	-	1.89	-	-	-	-	2.31	2.42	-	-	-	-	-	2.13	-	-	-
Pittsfield charter (township)	2.42	2.52	-	2.39	-	-	2.43	-	-	-	-	-	-	-	2.27	-	-	-	-	-	-	-	-	-
Scio (township)	2.60	3.10	-	-	-	-	-	-	-	-	-	-	-	-	-	-	-	-	-	-	-	-	-	-
Wayne County	2.64	3.10	3.30	3.16	3.96	-	2.69	-	2.88	-	-	6.82	-	1.97	2.16	-	-	3.81	-	-	-	-	-	3.07
Brownstown (township)	2.76	3.56	-	-	-	-	-	-	-	-	-	-	-	-	-	-	-	-	-	-	-	-	-	-
Canton (township)	2.78	3.27	-	3.38	-	-	3.04	-	3.19	-	-	-	-	-	3.14	-	-	-	-	-	-	-	-	-
Hamtramck (city)	2.74	4.60	-	4.45	4.66	-	-	-	-	-	-	-	-	-	-	-	-	-	-	-	-	-	-	-
Inkster (city)	2.67	2.43	-	2.30	-	-	-	-	-	-	-	-	-	-	-	-	-	-	-	-	-	-	-	-
Northville (township)	2.38	2.76	-	3.10	-	-	-	-	-	-	-	-	-	-	-	-	-	-	-	-	-	-	-	-
MINNESOTA	2.52	3.62	3.11	2.73	-	4.01	2.72	-	2.83	3.66	3.34	6.05	-	2.14	2.35	4.16	-	3.44	-	-	2.83	2.45	-	3.39
Anoka County	2.77	3.68	-	3.21	-	-	3.09	-	3.52	-	-	6.05	-	-	1.94	-	-	-	-	-	-	-	-	4.36
Columbia Heights (city)	2.29	3.77	-	-	-	-	-	-	-	-	-	-	-	-	-	-	-	-	-	-	-	-	-	-
Blue Earth County	2.45	2.54	-	-	-	-	-	-	-	-	-	-	-	-	-	-	-	-	-	-	-	-	-	-
Carver County	2.84	3.55	-	-	-	-	-	-	-	-	-	-	-	-	-	-	-	-	-	-	-	-	-	-

Notes: Please refer to the User's Guide for an explanation of data; data is arranged alphabetically by state, then county, then city within each county; table includes counties with populations greater than 49,999 unless noted and cities with populations greater than 9,999 whose Asian and/or NHPI population rates are greater than the national average; (1) Native Hawaiian and other Pacific Islander; (2) excludes Taiwanese; (3) includes Chamorro; (4) county does not meet population threshold but is shown in order to allow inclusion of city

Place	All households	Asian households	NHPI[1] households	Asian Indian	Bangladeshi	Cambodian	Chinese[2]	Fijian	Filipino	Guamanian[3]	Hawaiian, Native	Hmong	Indonesian	Japanese	Korean	Laotian	Malaysian	Pakistani	Samoan	Sri Lankan	Taiwanese	Thai	Tongan	Vietnamese
Clay County	2.53	2.85	-	-	-	-	-	-	-	-	-	-	-	-	-	-	-	-	-	-	-	-	-	-
Crow Wing County	2.42	2.48	-	-	-	-	-	-	-	-	-	-	-	-	-	-	-	-	-	-	-	-	-	-
Dakota County	2.69	3.28	-	2.98	-	3.59	2.90	-	4.12	-	-	-	-	-	2.90	4.15	-	-	-	-	-	-	-	3.83
Eagan (city)	2.65	3.08	-	2.65	-	-	2.48	-	-	-	-	-	-	-	-	-	-	-	-	-	-	-	-	4.48
Hennepin County	2.38	3.37	2.85	2.59	-	3.96	2.63	-	2.46	-	-	6.50	-	2.06	2.03	4.21	-	3.75	-	-	-	-	-	3.33
Bloomington (city)	2.30	3.20	-	2.62	-	4.01	3.06	-	-	-	-	-	-	-	2.61	-	-	-	-	-	-	-	-	3.69
Brooklyn Center (city)	2.51	5.51	-	-	-	-	-	-	-	-	-	6.93	-	-	-	4.43	-	-	-	-	-	-	-	-
Brooklyn Park (city)	2.75	4.19	-	3.36	-	-	-	-	-	-	-	7.32	-	-	-	4.51	-	-	-	-	-	-	-	4.22
Eden Prairie (city)	2.67	3.02	-	2.37	-	-	3.33	-	-	-	-	-	-	-	-	-	-	-	-	-	-	-	-	2.86
Hopkins (city)	2.03	2.55	-	2.52	-	-	-	-	-	-	-	-	-	-	-	-	-	-	-	-	-	-	-	-
Minneapolis (city)	2.24	3.46	-	2.35	-	4.12	2.22	-	2.13	-	-	6.46	-	1.78	1.89	3.84	-	-	-	-	-	-	-	2.80
Plymouth (city)	2.59	2.99	-	2.91	-	-	2.48	-	-	-	-	-	-	-	2.94	-	-	-	-	-	-	-	-	-
Richfield (city)	2.25	3.27	-	-	-	-	-	-	-	-	-	-	-	-	-	-	-	-	-	-	-	-	-	3.20
Nobles County[4]	2.57	3.40	-	-	-	-	-	-	-	-	-	-	-	-	-	4.24	-	-	-	-	-	-	-	-
Worthington (city)	2.54	3.32	-	-	-	-	-	-	-	-	-	-	-	-	-	4.25	-	-	-	-	-	-	-	-
Olmsted County	2.53	3.08	-	2.57	-	4.49	2.26	-	-	-	-	6.93	-	2.56	3.03	4.01	-	-	-	-	-	-	-	2.98
Rochester (city)	2.43	3.06	-	2.58	-	4.61	2.28	-	-	-	-	6.93	-	-	3.03	4.01	-	-	-	-	-	-	-	2.97
Otter Tail County	2.46	2.58	-	-	-	-	-	-	-	-	-	-	-	-	-	-	-	-	-	-	-	-	-	-
Ramsey County	2.45	4.38	-	2.77	-	3.87	2.82	-	2.64	-	-	5.87	-	2.13	2.41	4.80	-	-	-	-	-	-	-	3.21
Maplewood (city)	2.47	3.84	-	-	-	-	3.29	-	-	-	-	5.29	-	-	-	-	-	-	-	-	-	-	-	-
New Brighton (city)	2.39	2.51	-	-	-	-	-	-	-	-	-	-	-	-	-	-	-	-	-	-	-	-	-	-
Roseville (city)	2.20	3.18	-	-	-	-	3.51	-	-	-	-	-	-	-	-	-	-	-	-	-	-	-	-	-
St. Paul (city)	2.46	4.87	-	3.07	-	3.95	2.23	-	2.68	-	-	5.94	-	-	2.13	4.97	-	-	-	-	-	-	-	3.15
Vadnais Heights (city)	2.56	3.91	-	-	-	-	-	-	-	-	-	-	-	-	-	-	-	-	-	-	-	-	-	-
Rice County	2.64	3.41	-	-	-	-	-	-	-	-	-	-	-	-	-	-	-	-	-	-	-	-	-	-
St. Louis County	2.32	2.71	-	-	-	-	-	-	-	-	-	-	-	-	2.23	-	-	-	-	-	-	-	-	-
Scott County	2.88	3.48	-	-	-	4.02	-	-	-	-	-	-	-	-	-	-	-	-	-	-	-	-	-	3.66
Savage (city)	3.10	3.50	-	-	-	-	-	-	-	-	-	-	-	-	-	-	-	-	-	-	-	-	-	-
Sherburne County	2.90	3.09	-	-	-	-	-	-	-	-	-	-	-	-	-	-	-	-	-	-	-	-	-	-
Stearns County	2.64	2.76	-	-	-	-	-	-	-	-	-	-	-	-	-	-	-	-	-	-	-	-	-	3.87
Washington County	2.77	3.95	-	3.11	-	-	3.48	-	-	-	-	5.28	-	-	4.31	-	-	-	-	-	-	-	-	4.38
Woodbury (city)	2.76	3.87	-	3.35	-	-	3.21	-	-	-	-	5.63	-	-	-	-	-	-	-	-	-	-	-	-
Wright County	2.84	1.65	-	-	-	-	-	-	-	-	-	-	-	-	-	-	-	-	-	-	-	-	-	-
MISSISSIPPI	2.62	2.98	3.39	2.92	-	-	2.53	-	2.71	-	-	-	-	1.72	2.66	-	-	-	-	-	-	-	-	3.67
DeSoto County	2.75	3.46	-	-	-	-	-	-	-	-	-	-	-	-	-	-	-	-	-	-	-	-	-	-
Forrest County	2.47	2.14	-	-	-	-	-	-	-	-	-	-	-	-	-	-	-	-	-	-	-	-	-	-
Harrison County	2.55	3.22	-	-	-	-	-	-	2.68	-	-	-	-	-	-	-	-	-	-	-	-	-	-	3.92
Biloxi (city)	2.42	3.49	-	-	-	-	-	-	3.05	-	-	-	-	-	-	-	-	-	-	-	-	-	-	3.97
Hinds County	2.64	2.60	-	2.47	-	-	-	-	-	-	-	-	-	-	-	-	-	-	-	-	-	-	-	-
Jackson County	2.71	3.10	-	-	-	-	-	-	-	-	-	-	-	-	-	-	-	-	-	-	-	-	-	3.48
Madison County	2.66	2.58	-	-	-	-	-	-	-	-	-	-	-	-	-	-	-	-	-	-	-	-	-	-

Notes: Please refer to the User's Guide for an explanation of data; data is arranged alphabetically by state, then county, then city within each county; table includes counties with populations greater than 49,999 unless noted and cities with populations greater than 9,999 whose Asian and/or NHPI population rates are greater than the national average; (1) Native Hawaiian and other Pacific Islander; (2) excludes Taiwanese; (3) includes Chamorro; (4) county does not meet population threshold but is shown in order to allow inclusion of city

Place	All households	Asian households	NHPI[1] households	Asian Indian	Bangladeshi	Cambodian	Chinese[2]	Fijian	Filipino	Guamanian[3]	Hawaiian, Native	Hmong	Indonesian	Japanese	Korean	Laotian	Malaysian	Pakistani	Samoan	Sri Lankan	Taiwanese	Thai	Tongan	Vietnamese
Oktibbeha County[4]	2.41	2.62	-	-	-	-	-	-	-	-	-	-	-	-	-	-	-	-	-	-	-	-	-	-
Starkville (city)	2.23	2.43	-	-	-	-	-	-	-	-	-	-	-	-	-	-	-	-	-	-	-	-	-	-
Rankin County	2.62	3.12	-	-	-	-	-	-	-	-	-	-	-	-	-	-	-	-	-	-	-	-	-	-
MISSOURI	2.47	2.64	3.24	2.63	-	4.49	2.53	-	2.57	2.97	2.73	-	-	1.98	2.39	3.42	-	3.18	4.07	-	2.17	2.30	-	3.37
Boone County	2.38	2.47	-	2.67	-	-	2.79	-	-	-	-	-	-	-	2.11	-	-	-	-	-	-	-	-	-
Columbia (city)	2.26	2.43	-	2.65	-	-	2.78	-	-	-	-	-	-	-	2.07	-	-	-	-	-	-	-	-	-
Cape Girardeau County	2.42	2.10	-	-	-	-	-	-	-	-	-	-	-	-	-	-	-	-	-	-	-	-	-	-
Cass County	2.68	4.30	-	-	-	-	-	-	-	-	-	-	-	-	-	-	-	-	-	-	-	-	-	-
Clay County	2.49	2.79	-	2.75	-	-	-	-	-	-	-	-	-	-	-	-	-	-	-	-	-	-	-	3.55
Cole County	2.43	2.22	-	-	-	-	-	-	-	-	-	-	-	-	-	-	-	-	-	-	-	-	-	-
Franklin County	2.65	3.11	-	-	-	-	-	-	-	-	-	-	-	-	-	-	-	-	-	-	-	-	-	-
Greene County	2.33	2.73	-	-	-	-	2.84	-	-	-	-	-	-	-	2.60	-	-	-	-	-	-	-	-	4.18
Jackson County	2.41	2.84	3.89	2.90	-	-	2.14	-	2.96	-	-	-	-	1.92	2.19	-	-	-	4.65	-	-	-	-	3.49
Independence (city)	2.36	2.91	5.67	-	-	-	-	-	-	-	-	-	-	-	-	-	-	-	-	-	-	-	-	-
Jasper County	2.46	2.43	-	-	-	-	-	-	-	-	-	-	-	-	-	-	-	-	-	-	-	-	-	-
Jefferson County	2.74	3.06	-	-	-	-	-	-	-	-	-	-	-	-	-	-	-	-	-	-	-	-	-	-
Newton County	2.56	2.53	-	-	-	-	-	-	-	-	-	-	-	-	-	-	-	-	-	-	-	-	-	-
Phelps County[4]	2.38	2.08	-	2.51	-	-	-	-	-	-	-	-	-	-	-	-	-	-	-	-	-	-	-	-
Rolla (city)	2.22	1.93	-	-	-	-	-	-	-	-	-	-	-	-	-	-	-	-	-	-	-	-	-	-
Platte County	2.49	2.84	-	-	-	-	-	-	-	-	-	-	-	-	-	-	-	-	-	-	-	-	-	-
St. Charles County	2.75	2.86	-	3.51	-	-	2.28	-	2.66	-	-	-	-	-	-	-	-	-	-	-	-	-	-	-
Saint Louis Independent City	2.29	2.43	-	1.83	-	-	2.04	-	1.88	-	-	-	-	-	-	-	-	-	-	-	-	-	-	3.27
St. Louis County	2.46	2.66	2.67	2.74	-	-	2.68	-	2.59	-	-	-	-	2.05	2.70	-	-	3.11	-	-	2.46	2.55	-	3.17
Chesterfield (city)	2.53	3.24	-	3.24	-	-	3.34	-	-	-	-	-	-	-	-	-	-	-	-	-	-	-	-	-
Clayton (city)	2.12	2.46	-	-	-	-	-	-	-	-	-	-	-	-	-	-	-	-	-	-	-	-	-	-
Creve Coeur (city)	2.28	2.44	-	-	-	-	-	-	-	-	-	-	-	-	-	-	-	-	-	-	-	-	-	-
Manchester (city)	2.64	3.00	-	-	-	-	-	-	-	-	-	-	-	-	-	-	-	-	-	-	-	-	-	-
Maryland Heights (city)	2.24	2.38	-	2.15	-	-	2.52	-	-	-	-	-	-	-	-	-	-	-	-	-	-	-	-	-
Town and Country (city)	2.72	3.29	-	3.07	-	-	-	-	-	-	-	-	-	-	-	-	-	-	-	-	-	-	-	-
MONTANA	2.44	2.42	3.55	2.62	-	-	2.65	-	2.55	-	3.85	-	-	1.82	2.59	-	-	-	-	-	-	-	-	-
Cascade County	2.40	2.23	-	-	-	-	-	-	-	-	-	-	-	-	-	-	-	-	-	-	-	-	-	-
Flathead County	2.47	3.20	-	-	-	-	-	-	-	-	-	-	-	-	-	-	-	-	-	-	-	-	-	-
Gallatin County	2.46	2.46	-	-	-	-	-	-	-	-	-	-	-	-	-	-	-	-	-	-	-	-	-	-
Missoula County	2.39	2.52	-	-	-	-	-	-	-	-	-	-	-	-	-	-	-	-	-	-	-	-	-	-
Yellowstone County	2.43	2.34	-	-	-	-	-	-	-	-	-	-	-	-	-	-	-	-	-	-	-	-	-	-
NEBRASKA	2.49	2.87	2.78	2.54	-	-	2.38	-	2.44	-	-	-	-	1.95	2.09	3.64	-	-	-	-	-	2.28	-	4.24
Douglas County	2.48	2.53	-	2.51	-	-	2.40	-	2.32	-	-	-	-	1.81	2.04	-	-	-	-	-	-	-	-	3.94
Hall County	2.57	3.43	-	-	-	-	-	-	-	-	-	-	-	-	-	-	-	-	-	-	-	-	-	-
Lancaster County	2.40	3.28	-	2.69	-	-	2.33	-	-	-	-	-	-	-	1.88	-	-	-	-	-	-	-	-	4.43
Sarpy County	2.79	2.83	-	-	-	-	-	-	3.06	-	-	-	-	-	2.48	-	-	-	-	-	-	-	-	4.29
NEVADA	2.61	2.88	3.42	3.01	-	3.59	2.73	-	3.23	3.63	2.89	-	-	2.02	2.53	3.33	-	3.60	4.32	-	2.72	2.65	4.71	2.97

Notes: Please refer to the User's Guide for an explanation of data; data is arranged alphabetically by state, then county, then city within each county; table includes counties with populations greater than 49,999 unless noted and cities with populations greater than 9,999 whose Asian and/or NHPI population rates are greater than the national average; (1) Native Hawaiian and other Pacific Islander; (2) excludes Taiwanese; (3) includes Chamorro; (4) county does not meet population threshold but is shown in order to allow inclusion of city

Place	All households	Asian households	NHPI[1] households	Asian Indian	Bangladeshi	Cambodian	Chinese[2]	Fijian	Filipino	Guamanian[3]	Hawaiian, Native	Hmong	Indonesian	Japanese	Korean	Laotian	Malaysian	Pakistani	Samoan	Sri Lankan	Taiwanese	Thai	Tongan	Vietnamese
Carson City Independent City	2.43	3.05	-	-	-	-	-	-	3.85	-	-	-	-	-	-	-	-	-	-	-	-	-	-	-
Clark County	2.65	2.85	3.31	2.67	-	3.72	2.72	-	3.20	3.70	2.99	-	-	2.05	2.57	3.33	-	-	4.26	-	2.46	2.52	-	2.89
Enterprise (cdp)	2.46	2.90	-	-	-	-	-	-	-	-	-	-	-	-	-	-	-	-	-	-	-	-	-	-
Henderson (city)	2.63	2.96	3.27	2.97	-	-	2.86	-	3.27	-	3.42	-	-	2.11	2.99	-	-	-	-	-	-	-	-	-
Las Vegas (city)	2.66	2.77	3.12	2.86	-	-	2.56	-	3.08	-	2.52	-	-	2.04	2.62	-	-	-	-	-	-	2.41	-	2.61
North Las Vegas (city)	3.35	3.40	4.69	-	-	-	-	-	3.86	-	-	-	-	-	-	-	-	-	-	-	-	-	-	-
Paradise (cdp)	2.38	2.52	2.73	2.29	-	-	2.24	-	2.86	-	3.11	-	-	2.25	2.20	-	-	-	-	-	-	-	-	2.52
Spring Valley (cdp)	2.45	3.01	3.33	-	-	-	3.11	-	3.30	-	-	-	-	2.00	2.70	-	-	-	-	-	-	2.84	-	3.19
Sunrise Manor (cdp)	2.89	3.24	4.38	-	-	-	2.74	-	3.57	-	-	-	-	2.01	2.80	-	-	-	-	-	-	-	-	-
Winchester (cdp)	2.22	2.53	-	-	-	-	-	-	2.74	-	-	-	-	-	-	-	-	-	-	-	-	-	-	-
Washoe County	2.53	3.01	4.26	3.70	-	-	2.76	-	3.40	-	-	-	-	1.93	2.24	-	-	-	-	-	-	-	5.59	3.71
Reno (city)	2.38	2.84	3.78	3.29	-	-	2.53	-	3.30	-	-	-	-	1.68	2.16	-	-	-	-	-	-	-	-	3.47
Sparks (city)	2.67	3.43	-	-	-	-	3.32	-	3.60	-	-	-	-	-	-	-	-	-	-	-	-	-	-	-
NEW HAMPSHIRE	2.53	2.87	-	2.77	-	-	2.73	-	2.80	-	-	-	-	2.34	2.90	3.81	-	-	-	-	-	-	-	3.71
Belknap County	2.46	2.98	-	-	-	-	-	-	-	-	-	-	-	-	-	-	-	-	-	-	-	-	-	-
Cheshire County	2.46	3.43	-	-	-	-	-	-	-	-	-	-	-	-	-	-	-	-	-	-	-	-	-	-
Grafton County	2.38	2.78	-	-	-	-	2.51	-	-	-	-	-	-	-	-	-	-	-	-	-	-	-	-	-
Hanover (town)	2.47	3.62	-	-	-	-	-	-	-	-	-	-	-	-	-	-	-	-	-	-	-	-	-	-
Hillsborough County	2.58	2.79	-	2.76	-	-	2.57	-	2.15	-	-	-	-	-	2.52	-	-	-	-	-	-	-	-	3.84
Nashua (city)	2.46	2.69	-	2.84	-	-	2.25	-	-	-	-	-	-	-	-	-	-	-	-	-	-	-	-	-
Merrimack County	2.50	2.67	-	-	-	-	-	-	-	-	-	-	-	-	-	-	-	-	-	-	-	-	-	-
Rockingham County	2.63	3.05	-	2.55	-	-	3.12	-	4.03	-	-	-	-	-	2.51	-	-	-	-	-	-	-	-	-
Strafford County	2.50	3.15	-	-	-	-	3.81	-	-	-	-	-	-	-	-	-	-	-	-	-	-	-	-	-
NEW JERSEY	2.68	3.22	3.00	3.28	3.68	3.92	2.99	-	3.46	3.61	2.86	-	3.09	2.37	3.09	4.45	-	4.07	3.39	3.45	3.07	2.72	-	3.78
Atlantic County	2.59	3.47	-	3.73	3.87	-	3.12	-	3.44	-	-	-	-	-	3.18	-	-	3.72	-	-	-	-	-	3.69
Atlantic City (city)	2.46	3.15	-	2.83	-	-	3.06	-	3.11	-	-	-	-	-	-	-	-	-	-	-	-	-	-	3.66
Brigantine (city)	2.30	3.90	-	-	-	-	-	-	-	-	-	-	-	-	-	-	-	-	-	-	-	-	-	-
Egg Harbor (township)	2.75	3.62	-	-	-	-	-	-	-	-	-	-	-	-	-	-	-	-	-	-	-	-	-	-
Galloway (township)	2.70	3.75	-	4.29	-	-	-	-	-	-	-	-	-	-	-	-	-	-	-	-	-	-	-	-
Ventnor City (city)	2.35	3.57	-	-	-	-	-	-	-	-	-	-	-	-	-	-	-	-	-	-	-	-	-	-
Bergen County	2.64	3.19	-	3.39	-	-	2.89	-	3.55	-	-	-	-	2.59	3.20	-	-	4.04	-	-	3.29	2.71	-	3.72
Bergenfield (borough)	2.92	4.15	-	4.41	-	-	-	-	4.44	-	-	-	-	-	-	-	-	-	-	-	-	-	-	-
Cliffside Park (borough)	2.29	2.45	-	-	-	-	-	-	-	-	-	-	-	2.09	2.72	-	-	-	-	-	-	-	-	-
Dumont (borough)	2.75	3.79	-	5.16	-	-	-	-	3.44	-	-	-	-	-	-	-	-	-	-	-	-	-	-	-
Elmwood Park (borough)	2.66	3.28	-	3.30	-	-	-	-	-	-	-	-	-	-	-	-	-	-	-	-	-	-	-	-
Englewood (city)	2.79	3.19	-	-	-	-	-	-	3.60	-	-	-	-	-	-	-	-	-	-	-	-	-	-	-
Fair Lawn (borough)	2.66	4.18	-	4.25	-	-	-	-	4.29	-	-	-	-	-	-	-	-	-	-	-	-	-	-	-
Fairview (borough)	2.72	3.13	-	-	-	-	-	-	-	-	-	-	-	-	-	-	-	-	-	-	-	-	-	-
Fort Lee (borough)	2.14	2.71	-	2.94	-	-	2.63	-	-	-	-	-	-	2.49	2.88	-	-	-	-	-	-	-	-	-
Franklin Lakes (borough)	3.16	3.77	-	-	-	-	-	-	-	-	-	-	-	-	-	-	-	-	-	-	-	-	-	-
Glen Rock (borough)	2.90	3.44	-	-	-	-	-	-	-	-	-	-	-	-	-	-	-	-	-	-	-	-	-	-

Notes: Please refer to the User's Guide for an explanation of data; data is arranged alphabetically by state, then county, then city within each county; table includes counties with populations greater than 49,999 unless noted and cities with populations greater than 9,999 whose Asian and/or NHPI population rates are greater than the national average; (1) Native Hawaiian and other Pacific Islander; (2) excludes Taiwanese; (3) includes Chamorro; (4) county does not meet population threshold but is shown in order to allow inclusion of city

Place	All households	Asian households	NHPI[1] households	Asian Indian	Bangladeshi	Cambodian	Chinese[2]	Fijian	Filipino	Guamanian[3]	Hawaiian, Native	Hmong	Indonesian	Japanese	Korean	Laotian	Malaysian	Pakistani	Samoan	Sri Lankan	Taiwanese	Thai	Tongan	Vietnamese
Hackensack (city)	2.26	2.41	-	2.16	-	-	-	-	3.06	-	-	-	-	-	2.41	-	-	-	-	-	-	-	-	-
Hasbrouck Heights (borough)	2.57	2.92	-	-	-	-	-	-	-	-	-	-	-	-	-	-	-	-	-	-	-	-	-	-
Hillsdale (borough)	2.88	3.21	-	-	-	-	-	-	-	-	-	-	-	-	-	-	-	-	-	-	-	-	-	-
Little Ferry (borough)	2.48	2.89	-	3.29	-	-	-	-	3.52	-	-	-	-	-	2.49	-	-	-	-	-	-	-	-	-
Lodi (borough)	2.50	3.29	-	3.06	-	-	-	-	3.43	-	-	-	-	-	-	-	-	-	-	-	-	-	-	-
Lyndhurst (township)	2.45	3.07	-	-	-	-	-	-	-	-	-	-	-	-	-	-	-	-	-	-	-	-	-	-
Mahwah (township)	2.42	3.03	-	3.27	-	-	-	-	-	-	-	-	-	-	-	-	-	-	-	-	-	-	-	-
New Milford (borough)	2.54	3.15	-	3.16	-	-	-	-	3.51	-	-	-	-	-	-	-	-	-	-	-	-	-	-	-
North Arlington (borough)	2.37	2.76	-	-	-	-	-	-	-	-	-	-	-	-	-	-	-	-	-	-	-	-	-	-
Palisades Park (borough)	2.73	3.07	-	-	-	-	-	-	-	-	-	-	-	-	3.10	-	-	-	-	-	-	-	-	-
Paramus (borough)	3.00	4.01	-	4.58	-	-	3.29	-	3.93	-	-	-	-	-	4.16	-	-	-	-	-	-	-	-	-
Ramsey (borough)	2.68	2.94	-	-	-	-	-	-	-	-	-	-	-	-	-	-	-	-	-	-	-	-	-	-
Ridgefield (borough)	2.69	3.46	-	-	-	-	-	-	-	-	-	-	-	-	3.61	-	-	-	-	-	-	-	-	-
Ridgefield Park (village)	2.56	2.92	-	-	-	-	-	-	-	-	-	-	-	-	3.14	-	-	-	-	-	-	-	-	-
Ridgewood (village)	2.88	3.51	-	-	-	-	-	-	-	-	-	-	-	3.11	4.02	-	-	-	-	-	-	-	-	-
River Edge (borough)	2.61	3.06	-	-	-	-	-	-	-	-	-	-	-	-	3.48	-	-	-	-	-	-	-	-	-
Rutherford (borough)	2.53	3.18	-	2.71	-	-	-	-	-	-	-	-	-	-	3.31	-	-	-	-	-	-	-	-	-
Saddle Brook (township)	2.57	3.54	-	-	-	-	-	-	-	-	-	-	-	-	-	-	-	-	-	-	-	-	-	-
Teaneck (township)	2.86	3.46	-	3.93	-	-	-	-	3.61	-	-	-	-	-	-	-	-	-	-	-	-	-	-	-
Tenafly (borough)	2.86	3.23	-	-	-	-	3.13	-	-	-	-	-	-	-	3.54	-	-	-	-	-	-	-	-	-
Wallington (borough)	2.44	2.83	-	-	-	-	-	-	-	-	-	-	-	-	-	-	-	-	-	-	-	-	-	-
Westwood (borough)	2.42	2.88	-	-	-	-	-	-	-	-	-	-	-	-	-	-	-	-	-	-	-	-	-	-
Wyckoff (township)	2.89	3.36	-	-	-	-	-	-	-	-	-	-	-	-	-	-	-	-	-	-	-	-	-	-
Burlington County	2.65	2.94	-	3.05	-	-	3.05	-	3.31	-	-	-	-	1.62	2.99	-	-	-	-	-	-	-	-	3.27
Browns Mills (cdp)	2.80	3.36	-	-	-	-	-	-	-	-	-	-	-	-	3.99	-	-	-	-	-	-	-	-	-
Evesham (township)	2.65	3.05	-	2.77	-	-	3.44	-	-	-	-	-	-	-	-	-	-	-	-	-	-	-	-	-
Maple Shade (township)	2.23	2.36	-	2.62	-	-	-	-	-	-	-	-	-	-	-	-	-	-	-	-	-	-	-	-
Marlton (cdp)	2.49	3.05	-	-	-	-	-	-	-	-	-	-	-	-	-	-	-	-	-	-	-	-	-	-
Mount Laurel (township)	2.40	2.88	-	3.13	-	-	2.98	-	-	-	-	-	-	-	-	-	-	-	-	-	-	-	-	-
Camden County	2.68	3.48	-	3.29	-	4.95	3.20	-	3.68	-	-	-	-	-	3.17	-	-	3.50	-	-	-	-	-	4.27
Barclay-Kingston (cdp)	2.61	3.77	-	-	-	-	-	-	-	-	-	-	-	-	-	-	-	-	-	-	-	-	-	-
Bellmawr (borough)	2.53	3.36	-	-	-	-	-	-	-	-	-	-	-	-	-	-	-	-	-	-	-	-	-	-
Cherry Hill Mall (cdp)	2.57	3.66	-	-	-	-	-	-	-	-	-	-	-	-	-	-	-	-	-	-	-	-	-	-
Cherry Hill (township)	2.61	3.62	-	3.41	-	-	3.57	-	3.76	-	-	-	-	-	3.58	-	-	-	-	-	-	-	-	-
Echelon (cdp)	2.07	3.11	-	3.27	-	-	-	-	-	-	-	-	-	-	-	-	-	-	-	-	-	-	-	-
Greentree (cdp)	2.99	3.65	-	3.91	-	-	3.47	-	-	-	-	-	-	-	-	-	-	-	-	-	-	-	-	-
Pennsauken (township)	2.83	4.08	-	-	-	-	-	-	-	-	-	-	-	-	-	-	-	-	-	-	-	-	-	4.36
Springdale (cdp)	2.68	3.99	-	-	-	-	4.57	-	-	-	-	-	-	-	-	-	-	-	-	-	-	-	-	-
Voorhees (township)	2.59	3.35	-	3.39	-	-	3.09	-	4.08	-	-	-	-	-	-	-	-	-	-	-	-	-	-	-
Cape May County	2.37	2.78	-	-	-	-	-	-	-	-	-	-	-	-	-	-	-	-	-	-	-	-	-	-
Cumberland County	2.73	2.94	-	4.14	-	-	-	-	-	-	-	-	-	-	-	-	-	-	-	-	-	-	-	-

Notes: Please refer to the User's Guide for an explanation of data; data is arranged alphabetically by state, then county, then city within each county; table includes counties with populations greater than 49,999 unless noted and cities with populations greater than 9,999 whose Asian and/or NHPI population rates are greater than the national average; (1) Native Hawaiian and other Pacific Islander; (2) excludes Taiwanese; (3) includes Chamorro; (4) county does not meet population threshold but is shown in order to allow inclusion of city

Place	All households	Asian households	NHPI[1] households	Asian Indian	Bangladeshi	Cambodian	Chinese[2]	Fijian	Filipino	Guamanian[3]	Hawaiian, Native	Hmong	Indonesian	Japanese	Korean	Laotian	Malaysian	Pakistani	Samoan	Sri Lankan	Taiwanese	Thai	Tongan	Vietnamese
Essex County	2.72	3.23	2.92	3.14	-	-	3.01	-	3.48	-	-	-	-	2.78	3.08	-	-	3.64	-	-	3.50	-	-	3.62
Belleville (township)	2.61	3.52	-	3.01	-	-	-	-	4.07	-	-	-	-	-	-	-	-	-	-	-	-	-	-	3.96
Bloomfield (township)	2.48	3.27	-	3.12	-	-	3.30	-	3.44	-	-	-	-	-	-	-	-	-	-	-	-	-	-	-
Cedar Grove (township)	2.57	2.98	-	-	-	-	-	-	-	-	-	-	-	-	-	-	-	-	-	-	-	-	-	-
Livingston (township)	2.93	3.63	-	3.99	-	-	3.37	-	3.90	-	-	-	-	-	3.58	-	-	-	-	-	-	-	-	-
Millburn (township)	2.81	3.25	-	-	-	-	3.48	-	-	-	-	-	-	-	-	-	-	-	-	-	-	-	-	-
Nutley (township)	2.51	3.35	-	3.58	-	-	-	-	3.19	-	-	-	-	-	-	-	-	-	-	-	-	-	-	-
Verona (township)	2.41	3.50	-	-	-	-	-	-	-	-	-	-	-	-	-	-	-	-	-	-	-	-	-	-
West Caldwell (township)	2.74	3.17	-	-	-	-	-	-	-	-	-	-	-	-	-	-	-	-	-	-	-	-	-	-
West Orange (township)	2.67	3.28	-	2.83	-	-	3.23	-	3.64	-	-	-	-	-	3.50	-	-	-	-	-	-	-	-	-
Gloucester County	2.75	3.42	-	3.46	-	-	3.54	-	3.47	-	-	-	-	-	2.86	-	-	-	-	-	-	-	-	-
Hudson County	2.60	2.99	-	3.17	-	-	2.40	-	3.23	-	-	-	-	1.86	2.15	-	-	4.35	-	-	-	-	-	3.41
Bayonne (city)	2.41	3.35	-	3.40	-	-	-	-	3.39	-	-	-	-	-	2.86	-	-	-	-	-	-	-	-	-
Guttenberg (town)	2.37	2.01	-	-	-	-	-	-	-	-	-	-	-	-	-	-	-	-	-	-	-	-	-	-
Harrison (town)	2.81	2.85	-	-	-	-	3.02	-	-	-	-	-	-	-	-	-	-	-	-	-	-	-	-	-
Hoboken (city)	1.92	2.14	-	2.51	-	-	2.20	-	-	-	-	-	-	-	-	-	-	-	-	-	-	-	-	-
Jersey City (city)	2.67	3.08	-	3.23	-	-	2.19	-	3.25	-	-	-	-	-	1.94	-	-	4.45	-	-	-	-	-	3.47
Kearny (town)	2.80	2.94	-	3.39	-	-	2.69	-	-	-	-	-	-	-	-	-	-	-	-	-	-	-	-	-
North Bergen (township)	2.71	3.27	-	3.49	-	-	3.26	-	-	-	-	-	-	-	-	-	-	-	-	-	-	-	-	-
Secaucus (town)	2.40	3.32	-	3.24	-	-	-	-	3.95	-	-	-	-	-	-	-	-	-	-	-	-	-	-	-
Weehawken (township)	2.25	2.20	-	-	-	-	-	-	-	-	-	-	-	-	-	-	-	-	-	-	-	-	-	-
Hunterdon County	2.69	2.96	-	3.09	-	-	2.87	-	-	-	-	-	-	-	-	-	-	-	-	-	-	-	-	-
Mercer County	2.62	3.17	-	3.34	-	-	2.93	-	3.01	-	-	-	-	2.25	3.26	-	-	3.89	-	-	3.60	-	-	-
East Windsor (township)	2.60	2.75	-	3.01	-	-	-	-	-	-	-	-	-	-	-	-	-	-	-	-	-	-	-	-
Hopewell (township)	2.76	3.51	-	-	-	-	-	-	-	-	-	-	-	-	-	-	-	-	-	-	-	-	-	-
Lawrence (township)	2.48	3.48	-	3.96	-	-	3.00	-	-	-	-	-	-	-	-	-	-	-	-	-	-	-	-	-
Princeton (borough)	2.19	1.88	-	-	-	-	-	-	-	-	-	-	-	-	-	-	-	-	-	-	-	-	-	-
Princeton (township)	2.57	2.88	-	3.30	-	-	2.60	-	-	-	-	-	-	-	-	-	-	-	-	-	-	-	-	-
West Windsor (township)	2.98	3.46	-	3.56	-	-	3.54	-	-	-	-	-	-	-	3.22	-	-	-	-	-	-	-	-	-
Middlesex County	2.74	3.25	-	3.19	3.40	-	3.04	-	3.75	-	-	-	3.72	2.03	3.16	-	-	4.09	-	3.57	3.10	-	-	4.26
Avenel (cdp)	2.75	3.21	-	3.02	-	-	-	-	-	-	-	-	-	-	-	-	-	-	-	-	-	-	-	-
Carteret (borough)	2.87	3.93	-	3.70	-	-	-	-	-	-	-	-	-	-	-	-	-	-	-	-	-	-	-	-
Colonia (cdp)	2.87	3.78	-	3.84	-	-	-	-	3.65	-	-	-	-	-	-	-	-	-	-	-	-	-	-	-
East Brunswick (township)	2.84	3.46	-	3.48	-	-	3.28	-	4.21	-	-	-	-	-	3.57	-	-	-	-	-	-	-	-	-
Edison (township)	2.72	3.32	-	3.24	-	-	3.18	-	4.03	-	-	-	-	-	3.29	-	-	4.03	-	-	4.02	-	-	-
Fords (cdp)	2.71	3.00	-	2.65	-	-	-	-	3.50	-	-	-	-	-	-	-	-	-	-	-	-	-	-	-
Highland Park (borough)	2.37	2.41	-	2.28	-	-	2.41	-	-	-	-	-	-	-	-	-	-	-	-	-	-	-	-	-
Iselin (cdp)	2.77	3.34	-	3.37	-	-	3.03	-	-	-	-	-	-	-	-	-	-	-	-	-	-	-	-	-
Metuchen (borough)	2.57	3.88	-	-	-	-	-	-	-	-	-	-	-	-	-	-	-	-	-	-	-	-	-	-
Middlesex (borough)	2.71	4.13	-	-	-	-	-	-	-	-	-	-	-	-	-	-	-	-	-	-	-	-	-	-
New Brunswick (city)	3.22	2.43	-	2.57	-	-	1.81	-	-	-	-	-	-	-	-	-	-	-	-	-	-	-	-	-

Notes: Please refer to the User's Guide for an explanation of data; data is arranged alphabetically by state, then county, then city within each county; table includes counties with populations greater than 49,999 unless noted and cities with populations greater than 9,999 whose Asian and/or NHPI population rates are greater than the national average; (1) Native Hawaiian and other Pacific Islander; (2) excludes Taiwanese; (3) includes Chamorro; (4) county does not meet population threshold but is shown in order to allow inclusion of city

Place	All households	Asian households	NHPI[1] households	Asian Indian	Bangladeshi	Cambodian	Chinese[2]	Fijian	Filipino	Guamanian[3]	Hawaiian, Native	Hmong	Indonesian	Japanese	Korean	Laotian	Malaysian	Pakistani	Samoan	Sri Lankan	Taiwanese	Thai	Tongan	Vietnamese
North Brunswick (township)	2.58	3.05	-	3.05	-	-	2.53	-	3.82	-	-	-	-	-	3.27	-	-	-	-	-	-	-	-	-
Old Bridge (township)	2.79	3.49	-	3.51	-	-	3.08	-	3.62	-	-	-	-	-	-	-	-	4.24	-	-	-	-	-	-
Piscataway (township)	2.84	3.34	-	3.26	-	-	2.84	-	4.16	-	-	-	-	-	3.74	-	-	-	-	-	-	-	-	-
Plainsboro (township)	2.30	2.84	-	2.91	-	-	3.00	-	-	-	-	-	-	-	-	-	-	-	-	-	-	-	-	-
Princeton Meadows (cdp)	2.23	2.79	-	2.97	-	-	2.74	-	-	-	-	-	-	-	-	-	-	-	-	-	-	-	-	-
Sayreville (borough)	2.68	3.06	-	2.91	-	-	3.18	-	3.47	-	-	-	-	-	-	-	-	-	-	-	-	-	-	-
South Brunswick (township)	2.80	3.23	-	3.39	-	-	2.85	-	3.45	-	-	-	-	-	-	-	-	-	-	-	-	-	-	-
South Plainfield (borough)	3.01	4.51	-	4.89	-	-	-	-	4.32	-	-	-	-	-	-	-	-	-	-	-	-	-	-	4.40
Woodbridge (township)	2.72	3.12	-	2.99	-	-	3.06	-	3.47	-	-	-	-	-	3.31	-	-	4.56	-	-	-	-	-	-
Monmouth County	2.70	3.27	-	3.34	-	-	3.23	-	3.50	-	-	-	-	1.81	3.02	-	-	4.19	-	-	-	-	-	3.59
Aberdeen (township)	2.67	2.65	-	2.38	-	-	2.65	-	-	-	-	-	-	-	-	-	-	-	-	-	-	-	-	-
Colts Neck (township)	3.16	3.38	-	-	-	-	-	-	-	-	-	-	-	-	-	-	-	-	-	-	-	-	-	-
Eatontown (borough)	2.34	2.41	-	-	-	-	-	-	-	-	-	-	-	-	-	-	-	-	-	-	-	-	-	-
Freehold (township)	2.76	3.43	-	3.79	-	-	3.29	-	3.26	-	-	-	-	-	-	-	-	-	-	-	-	-	-	-
Holmdel (township)	3.09	3.48	-	3.30	-	-	3.53	-	-	-	-	-	-	-	-	-	-	-	-	-	-	-	-	-
Howell (township)	3.04	3.51	-	3.84	-	-	-	-	3.97	-	-	-	-	-	-	-	-	-	-	-	-	-	-	-
Manalapan (township)	3.09	3.82	-	3.84	-	-	3.50	-	-	-	-	-	-	-	-	-	-	-	-	-	-	-	-	-
Marlboro (township)	3.14	3.73	-	3.96	-	-	3.62	-	-	-	-	-	-	-	-	-	-	-	-	-	-	-	-	-
Morganville (cdp)	3.09	3.80	-	-	-	-	3.56	-	-	-	-	-	-	-	-	-	-	-	-	-	-	-	-	-
Ocean (township)	2.62	3.06	-	3.17	-	-	-	-	-	-	-	-	-	-	-	-	-	-	-	-	-	-	-	-
Tinton Falls (borough)	2.51	3.38	-	-	-	-	-	-	-	-	-	-	-	-	-	-	-	-	-	-	-	-	-	-
West Freehold (cdp)	2.59	3.08	-	-	-	-	-	-	-	-	-	-	-	-	-	-	-	-	-	-	-	-	-	-
Morris County	2.72	3.26	-	3.28	-	-	3.13	-	3.56	-	-	-	-	2.48	3.48	-	-	4.29	-	-	3.00	-	-	3.68
Chatham (township)	2.53	2.31	-	-	-	-	-	-	-	-	-	-	-	-	-	-	-	-	-	-	-	-	-	-
Denville (township)	2.59	3.78	-	-	-	-	-	-	-	-	-	-	-	-	-	-	-	-	-	-	-	-	-	-
East Hanover (township)	2.96	3.73	-	-	-	-	3.50	-	-	-	-	-	-	-	-	-	-	-	-	-	-	-	-	-
Hanover (township)	2.70	3.29	-	3.79	-	-	3.21	-	-	-	-	-	-	-	-	-	-	-	-	-	-	-	-	-
Lincoln Park (borough)	2.53	3.19	-	-	-	-	-	-	-	-	-	-	-	-	-	-	-	-	-	-	-	-	-	-
Montville (township)	2.80	3.09	-	2.77	-	-	3.18	-	-	-	-	-	-	-	-	-	-	-	-	-	-	-	-	-
Morris (township)	2.56	2.90	-	-	-	-	-	-	-	-	-	-	-	-	-	-	-	-	-	-	-	-	-	-
Mount Olive (township)	2.67	3.05	-	2.79	-	-	-	-	-	-	-	-	-	-	-	-	-	-	-	-	-	-	-	-
Parsippany-Troy Hills (twp)	2.53	3.33	-	3.46	-	-	3.14	-	3.34	-	-	-	-	-	3.17	-	-	-	-	-	-	-	-	-
Randolph (township)	2.86	3.28	-	2.70	-	-	3.53	-	-	-	-	-	-	-	-	-	-	-	-	-	-	-	-	-
Rockaway (township)	2.82	3.48	-	4.01	-	-	-	-	-	-	-	-	-	-	-	-	-	-	-	-	-	-	-	-
Roxbury (township)	2.85	3.85	-	-	-	-	-	-	-	-	-	-	-	-	-	-	-	-	-	-	-	-	-	-
Succasunna-Kenvil (cdp)	3.06	4.35	-	-	-	-	-	-	-	-	-	-	-	-	-	-	-	-	-	-	-	-	-	-
Ocean County	2.51	3.13	-	3.19	-	-	2.93	-	3.44	-	-	-	-	-	2.06	-	-	-	-	-	-	-	-	-
Passaic County	2.92	3.60	-	4.00	4.79	-	3.01	-	3.34	-	-	-	-	-	2.83	-	-	-	-	-	-	-	-	-
Clifton (city)	2.59	3.70	-	4.15	-	-	3.00	-	3.60	-	-	-	-	-	2.31	-	-	-	-	-	-	-	-	-
Little Falls (township)	2.32	3.27	-	-	-	-	-	-	-	-	-	-	-	-	-	-	-	-	-	-	-	-	-	-
Passaic (city)	3.45	3.78	-	3.89	-	-	-	-	3.36	-	-	-	-	-	-	-	-	-	-	-	-	-	-	-

Notes: Please refer to the User's Guide for an explanation of data; data is arranged alphabetically by state, then county, then city within each county; table includes counties with populations greater than 49,999 unless noted and cities with populations greater than 9,999 whose Asian and/or NHPI population rates are greater than the national average; (1) Native Hawaiian and other Pacific Islander; (2) excludes Taiwanese; (3) includes Chamorro; (4) county does not meet population threshold but is shown in order to allow inclusion of city

Place	All households	Asian households	NHPI[1] households	Asian Indian	Bangladeshi	Cambodian	Chinese[2]	Fijian	Filipino	Guamanian[3]	Hawaiian, Native	Hmong	Indonesian	Japanese	Korean	Laotian	Malaysian	Pakistani	Samoan	Sri Lankan	Taiwanese	Thai	Tongan	Vietnamese
Wayne (township)	2.74	3.07	-	3.15	-	-	2.90	-	3.70	-	-	-	-	-	3.00	-	-	-	-	-	-	-	-	-
Salem County	2.59	3.38	-	-	-	-	-	-	-	-	-	-	-	-	-	-	-	-	-	-	-	-	-	-
Somerset County	2.69	3.26	-	3.29	-	-	3.16	-	3.40	-	-	-	-	2.17	3.28	-	-	4.22	-	-	3.16	-	-	3.71
Bernards (township)	2.59	3.15	-	2.87	-	-	3.36	-	-	-	-	-	-	-	-	-	-	-	-	-	-	-	-	-
Branchburg (township)	2.74	3.72	-	3.84	-	-	-	-	-	-	-	-	-	-	-	-	-	-	-	-	-	-	-	-
Bridgewater (township)	2.71	3.31	-	3.38	-	-	3.26	-	-	-	-	-	-	-	-	-	-	-	-	-	-	-	-	-
Franklin (township)	2.58	2.97	-	3.00	-	-	2.74	-	3.26	-	-	-	-	-	-	-	-	-	-	-	-	-	-	-
Hillsborough (township)	2.87	3.49	-	3.56	-	-	3.19	-	-	-	-	-	-	-	-	-	-	-	-	-	-	-	-	-
Montgomery (township)	2.99	3.31	-	3.41	-	-	3.58	-	-	-	-	-	-	-	-	-	-	-	-	-	-	-	-	-
North Plainfield (borough)	2.89	3.23	-	-	-	-	-	-	-	-	-	-	-	-	-	-	-	-	-	-	-	-	-	-
Somerset (cdp)	2.76	2.64	-	2.47	-	-	2.24	-	3.88	-	-	-	-	-	-	-	-	-	-	-	-	-	-	-
Somerville (borough)	2.47	2.88	-	-	-	-	-	-	-	-	-	-	-	-	-	-	-	-	-	-	-	-	-	-
Warren (township)	3.05	3.78	-	3.66	-	-	3.66	-	-	-	-	-	-	-	-	-	-	-	-	-	-	-	-	-
Sussex County	2.81	3.25	-	3.24	-	-	-	-	3.23	-	-	-	-	-	-	-	-	-	-	-	-	-	-	-
Union County	2.77	3.24	-	3.29	-	-	2.80	-	3.65	-	-	-	-	-	2.86	-	-	4.91	-	-	-	-	-	3.14
Berkeley Heights (township)	2.90	3.18	-	-	-	-	2.98	-	-	-	-	-	-	-	-	-	-	-	-	-	-	-	-	-
New Providence (borough)	2.67	2.80	-	-	-	-	2.57	-	-	-	-	-	-	-	-	-	-	-	-	-	-	-	-	-
Rahway (city)	2.63	3.22	-	-	-	-	-	-	3.67	-	-	-	-	-	-	-	-	-	-	-	-	-	-	-
Roselle Park (borough)	2.58	3.69	-	3.82	-	-	-	-	-	-	-	-	-	-	-	-	-	-	-	-	-	-	-	-
Scotch Plains (township)	2.71	2.93	-	2.67	-	-	3.16	-	-	-	-	-	-	-	-	-	-	-	-	-	-	-	-	-
Springfield (township)	2.40	2.93	-	-	-	-	-	-	-	-	-	-	-	-	-	-	-	-	-	-	-	-	-	-
Summit (city)	2.68	2.60	-	2.80	-	-	-	-	-	-	-	-	-	-	-	-	-	-	-	-	-	-	-	-
Union (township)	2.71	3.87	-	3.72	-	-	3.17	-	4.24	-	-	-	-	-	-	-	-	-	-	-	-	-	-	-
Westfield (town)	2.76	3.32	-	-	-	-	-	-	-	-	-	-	-	-	-	-	-	-	-	-	-	-	-	-
Warren County	2.61	3.81	-	4.13	-	-	-	-	-	-	-	-	-	-	-	-	-	-	-	-	-	-	-	-
NEW MEXICO	2.63	2.66	2.78	2.58	-	-	2.74	-	2.71	2.96	2.39	-	-	2.11	2.55	-	-	-	-	-	-	2.34	-	3.12
Bernalillo County	2.47	2.64	2.49	2.46	-	-	2.84	-	2.56	-	-	-	-	2.05	2.30	-	-	-	-	-	-	-	-	3.10
Chaves County	2.66	2.93	-	-	-	-	-	-	-	-	-	-	-	-	-	-	-	-	-	-	-	-	-	-
Dona Ana County	2.85	2.90	-	-	-	-	2.61	-	-	-	-	-	-	-	-	-	-	-	-	-	-	-	-	-
Los Alamos County[4]	2.44	2.93	-	-	-	-	-	-	-	-	-	-	-	-	-	-	-	-	-	-	-	-	-	-
Los Alamos (cdp)	2.33	3.03	-	-	-	-	-	-	-	-	-	-	-	-	-	-	-	-	-	-	-	-	-	-
Otero County	2.66	2.24	-	-	-	-	-	-	-	-	-	-	-	-	-	-	-	-	-	-	-	-	-	-
Sandoval County	2.84	3.13	-	-	-	-	-	-	3.84	-	-	-	-	-	-	-	-	-	-	-	-	-	-	-
Santa Fe County	2.42	2.39	-	-	-	-	-	-	-	-	-	-	-	-	-	-	-	-	-	-	-	-	-	-
NEW YORK	2.61	3.11	2.94	3.36	4.23	3.90	3.15	-	3.01	3.19	2.58	-	2.68	1.93	2.79	3.76	2.58	4.11	3.25	3.12	2.52	2.52	-	3.40
Albany County	2.31	2.61	-	2.50	-	-	2.54	-	2.87	-	-	-	-	-	2.25	-	-	-	-	-	-	-	-	3.42
Colonie (town)	2.42	2.93	-	2.70	-	-	3.14	-	-	-	-	-	-	-	-	-	-	-	-	-	-	-	-	-
Guilderland (town)	2.40	2.69	-	2.63	-	-	-	-	-	-	-	-	-	-	-	-	-	-	-	-	-	-	-	-
Bronx County (Bronx)	2.78	3.21	3.13	3.24	4.06	4.94	3.04	-	2.95	-	-	-	-	1.66	2.80	-	-	3.69	-	-	-	-	-	4.22
Broome County	2.37	2.62	-	2.77	-	-	2.24	-	-	-	-	-	-	-	2.24	4.22	-	-	-	-	-	-	-	2.86
Johnson City (village)	2.12	3.06	-	-	-	-	-	-	-	-	-	-	-	-	-	-	-	-	-	-	-	-	-	-

Notes: Please refer to the User's Guide for an explanation of data; data is arranged alphabetically by state, then county, then city within each county; table includes counties with populations greater than 49,999 unless noted and cities with populations greater than 9,999 whose Asian and/or NHPI population rates are greater than the national average; (1) Native Hawaiian and other Pacific Islander; (2) excludes Taiwanese; (3) includes Chamorro; (4) county does not meet population threshold but is shown in order to allow inclusion of city

Place	All households	Asian households	NHPI[1] households	Asian Indian	Bangladeshi	Cambodian	Chinese[2]	Fijian	Filipino	Guamanian[3]	Hawaiian, Native	Hmong	Indonesian	Japanese	Korean	Laotian	Malaysian	Pakistani	Samoan	Sri Lankan	Taiwanese	Thai	Tongan	Vietnamese
Vestal (town)	2.45	2.31	-	-	-	-	2.07	-	-	-	-	-	-	-	-	-	-	-	-	-	-	-	-	-
Cattaraugus County	2.52	3.01	-	-	-	-	-	-	-	-	-	-	-	-	-	-	-	-	-	-	-	-	-	-
Cayuga County	2.52	2.83	-	-	-	-	-	-	-	-	-	-	-	-	-	-	-	-	-	-	-	-	-	-
Chautauqua County	2.45	3.20	-	-	-	-	-	-	-	-	-	-	-	-	-	-	-	-	-	-	-	-	-	-
Chemung County	2.44	3.32	-	-	-	-	-	-	-	-	-	-	-	-	-	-	-	-	-	-	-	-	-	-
Chenango County	2.52	2.07	-	-	-	-	-	-	-	-	-	-	-	-	-	-	-	-	-	-	-	-	-	-
Clinton County	2.47	2.52	-	-	-	-	-	-	-	-	-	-	-	-	-	-	-	-	-	-	-	-	-	-
Columbia County	2.43	3.21	-	-	-	-	-	-	-	-	-	-	-	-	-	-	-	-	-	-	-	-	-	-
Dutchess County	2.63	2.85	-	3.08	-	-	2.61	-	-	-	-	-	-	-	2.72	-	-	-	-	-	-	-	-	-
Arlington (cdp)	2.30	2.73	-	-	-	-	-	-	-	-	-	-	-	-	-	-	-	-	-	-	-	-	-	-
Poughkeepsie (town)	2.57	2.70	-	3.12	-	-	1.97	-	-	-	-	-	-	-	-	-	-	-	-	-	-	-	-	-
Wappinger (town)	2.66	2.71	-	2.81	-	-	-	-	-	-	-	-	-	-	-	-	-	-	-	-	-	-	-	-
Erie County	2.41	2.67	-	2.84	-	-	2.40	-	2.97	-	-	-	-	1.79	2.17	-	-	-	-	-	-	-	-	3.51
Amherst (town)	2.42	2.88	-	3.34	-	-	2.56	-	-	-	-	-	-	-	2.37	-	-	-	-	-	-	-	-	-
Herkimer County	2.46	2.14	-	-	-	-	-	-	-	-	-	-	-	-	-	-	-	-	-	-	-	-	-	-
Jefferson County	2.58	3.02	-	-	-	-	-	-	3.48	-	-	-	-	-	2.92	-	-	-	-	-	-	-	-	-
Kings County (Brooklyn)	2.75	3.52	3.44	3.34	4.41	3.49	3.66	-	2.84	4.77	-	-	-	1.80	2.66	-	-	4.28	-	-	-	-	-	3.58
Livingston County	2.60	2.75	-	-	-	-	-	-	-	-	-	-	-	-	-	-	-	-	-	-	-	-	-	-
Madison County	2.55	2.10	-	-	-	-	-	-	-	-	-	-	-	-	-	-	-	-	-	-	-	-	-	-
Monroe County	2.47	2.86	-	2.72	-	4.31	2.69	-	2.67	-	-	-	-	1.97	2.44	3.72	-	3.56	-	-	-	-	-	3.66
Brighton (town)	2.14	2.53	-	2.38	-	-	2.77	-	-	-	-	-	-	-	-	-	-	-	-	-	-	-	-	-
Henrietta (town)	2.60	2.69	-	2.48	-	-	3.10	-	-	-	-	-	-	-	-	-	-	-	-	-	-	-	-	-
Pittsford (town)	2.65	3.87	-	3.80	-	-	-	-	-	-	-	-	-	-	-	-	-	-	-	-	-	-	-	-
Nassau County	2.93	3.67	3.51	3.84	-	-	3.45	-	3.73	-	-	-	-	2.36	3.69	-	-	4.92	-	-	3.42	3.12	-	4.62
East Meadow (cdp)	2.95	3.89	-	4.19	-	-	-	-	3.35	-	-	-	-	-	-	-	-	-	-	-	-	-	-	-
Elmont (cdp)	3.28	3.93	-	4.01	-	-	-	-	3.93	-	-	-	-	-	-	-	-	-	-	-	-	-	-	-
Franklin Square (cdp)	2.87	3.96	-	4.51	-	-	-	-	-	-	-	-	-	-	-	-	-	-	-	-	-	-	-	-
Glen Cove (city)	2.72	3.44	-	3.77	-	-	-	-	-	-	-	-	-	-	3.68	-	-	-	-	-	-	-	-	-
Hicksville (cdp)	3.00	3.95	-	4.11	-	-	3.31	-	4.50	-	-	-	-	-	-	-	-	-	-	-	-	-	-	-
Jericho (cdp)	2.78	3.67	-	-	-	-	-	-	-	-	-	-	-	-	3.73	-	-	-	-	-	-	-	-	-
Mineola (village)	2.57	2.98	-	2.95	-	-	-	-	-	-	-	-	-	-	-	-	-	-	-	-	-	-	-	-
North Hempstead (town)	2.84	3.62	-	3.78	-	-	3.64	-	3.60	-	-	-	-	2.44	3.62	-	-	4.52	-	-	3.28	-	-	-
North Merrick (cdp)	2.97	3.98	-	-	-	-	-	-	-	-	-	-	-	-	-	-	-	-	-	-	-	-	-	-
North New Hyde Park (cdp)	2.88	4.07	-	4.51	-	-	3.66	-	-	-	-	-	-	-	-	-	-	-	-	-	-	-	-	-
North Valley Stream (cdp)	3.20	4.56	-	4.78	-	-	-	-	-	-	-	-	-	-	-	-	-	-	-	-	-	-	-	-
Oyster Bay (town)	2.93	3.66	-	3.88	-	-	3.42	-	3.83	-	-	-	-	2.19	3.71	-	-	-	-	-	-	-	-	-
Plainview (cdp)	2.94	3.49	-	3.52	-	-	3.15	-	-	-	-	-	-	-	4.16	-	-	-	-	-	-	-	-	-
Port Washington (cdp)	2.73	2.95	-	3.51	-	-	-	-	-	-	-	-	-	-	-	-	-	-	-	-	-	-	-	-
Salisbury (cdp)	3.05	3.57	-	3.09	-	-	-	-	-	-	-	-	-	-	-	-	-	-	-	-	-	-	-	-
Syosset (cdp)	2.92	3.48	-	4.11	-	-	3.27	-	-	-	-	-	-	-	3.32	-	-	-	-	-	-	-	-	-
Valley Stream (village)	2.91	3.94	-	-	-	-	3.54	-	4.29	-	-	-	-	-	-	-	-	-	-	-	-	-	-	-

Notes: Please refer to the User's Guide for an explanation of data; data is arranged alphabetically by state, then county, then city within each county; table includes counties with populations greater than 49,999 unless noted and cities with populations greater than 9,999 whose Asian and/or NHPI population rates are greater than the national average; (1) Native Hawaiian and other Pacific Islander; (2) excludes Taiwanese; (3) includes Chamorro; (4) county does not meet population threshold but is shown in order to allow inclusion of city

Place	All households	Asian households	NHPI[1] households	Asian Indian	Bangladeshi	Cambodian	Chinese[2]	Fijian	Filipino	Guamanian[3]	Hawaiian, Native	Hmong	Indonesian	Japanese	Korean	Laotian	Malaysian	Pakistani	Samoan	Sri Lankan	Taiwanese	Thai	Tongan	Vietnamese
West Hempstead (cdp)	3.08	3.82	-	3.80	-	-	-	-	-	-	-	-	-	-	-	-	-	-	-	-	-	-	-	-
Westbury (village)	3.06	3.84	-	-	-	-	-	-	-	-	-	-	-	-	-	-	-	-	-	-	-	-	-	-
Woodmere (cdp)	3.00	4.77	-	-	-	-	-	-	-	-	-	-	-	-	-	-	-	-	-	-	-	-	-	-
New York City	2.59	3.11	2.97	3.38	4.25	4.01	3.18	-	2.90	3.31	2.65	-	2.82	1.67	2.75	-	2.54	4.09	3.41	3.23	2.52	2.57	-	3.42
New York County (Manhattan)	2.00	2.25	1.82	2.04	4.18	-	2.65	-	1.81	-	-	-	-	1.58	1.69	-	-	2.52	-	-	1.50	1.84	-	1.85
Niagara County	2.45	2.97	-	3.72	-	-	-	-	-	-	-	-	-	-	-	-	-	-	-	-	-	-	-	-
Oneida County	2.43	2.98	-	3.63	-	-	2.31	-	-	-	-	-	-	-	-	-	-	-	-	-	-	-	-	3.51
Onondaga County	2.45	2.58	-	2.55	-	-	2.24	-	2.71	-	-	-	-	2.28	1.88	-	-	-	-	-	-	-	-	3.26
Ontario County	2.53	2.17	-	-	-	-	-	-	-	-	-	-	-	-	-	-	-	-	-	-	-	-	-	-
Orange County	2.85	3.08	-	3.22	-	-	3.51	-	2.73	-	-	-	-	-	2.79	-	-	-	-	-	-	-	-	-
Oswego County	2.60	2.35	-	-	-	-	-	-	-	-	-	-	-	-	-	-	-	-	-	-	-	-	-	-
Otsego County	2.43	1.90	-	-	-	-	-	-	-	-	-	-	-	-	-	-	-	-	-	-	-	-	-	-
Putnam County	2.86	3.05	-	3.43	-	-	2.60	-	-	-	-	-	-	-	-	-	-	-	-	-	-	-	-	-
Queens County (Queens)	2.81	3.34	3.06	3.68	4.23	-	3.21	-	3.30	-	-	-	2.86	1.88	3.06	-	2.62	4.21	-	3.82	3.10	3.05	-	3.73
Rensselaer County	2.46	2.73	-	2.54	-	-	2.85	-	-	-	-	-	-	-	2.57	-	-	-	-	-	-	-	-	-
Richmond Co. (Staten Island)	2.78	3.40	-	3.72	-	-	3.33	-	3.44	-	-	-	-	-	2.90	-	-	4.40	-	3.96	-	-	-	-
Rockland County	3.01	3.60	-	3.65	-	-	3.53	-	3.61	-	-	-	-	-	3.44	-	-	-	-	-	-	-	-	-
Clarkstown (town)	2.90	3.76	-	3.92	-	-	3.15	-	3.80	-	-	-	-	-	3.97	-	-	-	-	-	-	-	-	-
Nanuet (cdp)	2.72	3.50	-	4.11	-	-	-	-	-	-	-	-	-	-	-	-	-	-	-	-	-	-	-	-
New City (cdp)	3.02	3.87	-	4.00	-	-	-	-	3.78	-	-	-	-	-	-	-	-	-	-	-	-	-	-	-
Orangetown (town)	2.62	3.26	-	3.17	-	-	3.72	-	3.01	-	-	-	-	-	3.02	-	-	-	-	-	-	-	-	-
Ramapo (town)	3.36	3.67	-	3.66	-	-	4.49	-	3.61	-	-	-	-	-	3.27	-	-	-	-	-	-	-	-	-
Spring Valley (village)	3.32	3.22	-	3.25	-	-	-	-	-	-	-	-	-	-	-	-	-	-	-	-	-	-	-	-
St. Lawrence County	2.49	2.35	-	-	-	-	-	-	-	-	-	-	-	-	-	-	-	-	-	-	-	-	-	-
Saratoga County	2.51	2.74	-	2.82	-	-	3.05	-	-	-	-	-	-	-	2.21	-	-	-	-	-	-	-	-	-
Schenectady County	2.38	2.91	-	3.08	-	-	2.71	-	-	-	-	-	-	-	-	-	-	-	-	-	-	-	-	-
Niskayuna (town)	2.56	3.11	-	2.98	-	-	-	-	-	-	-	-	-	-	-	-	-	-	-	-	-	-	-	-
Steuben County	2.49	2.52	-	-	-	-	-	-	-	-	-	-	-	-	-	-	-	-	-	-	-	-	-	-
Suffolk County	2.96	3.31	3.91	3.40	-	-	3.09	-	3.37	-	-	-	-	2.26	3.02	-	-	4.61	-	-	2.92	3.16	-	3.72
Coram (cdp)	2.74	2.81	-	-	-	-	2.65	-	-	-	-	-	-	-	-	-	-	-	-	-	-	-	-	-
Dix Hills (cdp)	3.23	3.73	-	3.70	-	-	3.73	-	-	-	-	-	-	-	-	-	-	-	-	-	-	-	-	-
Elwood (cdp)	3.13	3.64	-	-	-	-	-	-	-	-	-	-	-	-	-	-	-	-	-	-	-	-	-	-
Lake Grove (village)	3.00	3.58	-	-	-	-	-	-	-	-	-	-	-	-	-	-	-	-	-	-	-	-	-	-
Melville (cdp)	2.89	3.14	-	-	-	-	-	-	-	-	-	-	-	-	-	-	-	-	-	-	-	-	-	-
Setauket-East Setauket (cdp)	2.87	2.49	-	-	-	-	2.09	-	-	-	-	-	-	-	-	-	-	-	-	-	-	-	-	-
Stony Brook (cdp)	2.87	3.45	-	-	-	-	3.32	-	-	-	-	-	-	-	-	-	-	-	-	-	-	-	-	-
Sullivan County	2.50	3.15	-	-	-	-	-	-	-	-	-	-	-	-	-	-	-	-	-	-	-	-	-	-
Tioga County	2.59	3.27	-	-	-	-	-	-	-	-	-	-	-	-	-	-	-	-	-	-	-	-	-	-
Tompkins County	2.32	2.23	-	2.42	-	-	2.16	-	-	-	-	-	-	1.66	2.46	-	-	-	-	-	-	-	-	-
Ithaca (city)	2.11	2.11	-	2.23	-	-	2.15	-	-	-	-	-	-	-	2.28	-	-	-	-	-	-	-	-	-
Lansing (town)	2.33	2.30	-	-	-	-	-	-	-	-	-	-	-	-	-	-	-	-	-	-	-	-	-	-

Notes: Please refer to the User's Guide for an explanation of data; data is arranged alphabetically by state, then county, then city within each county; table includes counties with populations greater than 49,999 unless noted and cities with populations greater than 9,999 whose Asian and/or NHPI population rates are greater than the national average; (1) Native Hawaiian and other Pacific Islander; (2) excludes Taiwanese; (3) includes Chamorro; (4) county does not meet population threshold but is shown in order to allow inclusion of city

Place	All households	Asian households	NHPI[1] households	Asian Indian	Bangladeshi	Cambodian	Chinese[2]	Fijian	Filipino	Guamanian[3]	Hawaiian, Native	Hmong	Indonesian	Japanese	Korean	Laotian	Malaysian	Pakistani	Samoan	Sri Lankan	Taiwanese	Thai	Tongan	Vietnamese
Ulster County	2.47	2.52	-	-	-	-	2.38	-	-	-	-	-	-	-	-	-	-	-	-	-	-	-	-	-
New Paltz (town)	2.36	2.16	-	-	-	-	-	-	-	-	-	-	-	-	-	-	-	-	-	-	-	-	-	-
Warren County	2.41	3.26	-	-	-	-	-	-	-	-	-	-	-	-	-	-	-	-	-	-	-	-	-	-
Wayne County	2.63	3.22	-	-	-	-	-	-	-	-	-	-	-	-	-	-	-	-	-	-	-	-	-	-
Westchester County	2.67	3.10	-	3.30	-	-	2.75	-	3.20	-	-	-	-	2.99	3.11	-	-	3.97	-	-	2.34	2.85	-	-
Dobbs Ferry (village)	2.54	3.26	-	-	-	-	-	-	-	-	-	-	-	-	-	-	-	-	-	-	-	-	-	-
Eastchester (cdp)	2.42	2.80	-	-	-	-	-	-	-	-	-	-	-	2.76	-	-	-	-	-	-	-	-	-	-
Eastchester (town)	2.46	2.83	-	-	-	-	-	-	-	-	-	-	-	3.07	-	-	-	-	-	-	-	-	-	-
Greenburgh (town)	2.57	3.01	-	2.98	-	-	2.85	-	3.07	-	-	-	-	2.86	3.54	-	-	-	-	-	-	-	-	-
Harrison (village)	2.72	3.09	-	-	-	-	-	-	-	-	-	-	-	3.20	-	-	-	-	-	-	-	-	-	-
New Castle (town)	3.02	3.26	-	3.39	-	-	3.00	-	-	-	-	-	-	-	-	-	-	-	-	-	-	-	-	-
New Rochelle (city)	2.67	2.97	-	3.18	-	-	2.63	-	-	-	-	-	-	-	-	-	-	-	-	-	-	-	-	-
North Castle (town)	2.99	3.68	-	-	-	-	-	-	-	-	-	-	-	-	-	-	-	-	-	-	-	-	-	-
Ossining (town)	2.63	3.21	-	3.10	-	-	-	-	-	-	-	-	-	-	-	-	-	-	-	-	-	-	-	-
Ossining (village)	2.61	3.25	-	3.19	-	-	-	-	-	-	-	-	-	-	-	-	-	-	-	-	-	-	-	-
Pelham (town)	2.86	3.89	-	-	-	-	-	-	-	-	-	-	-	-	-	-	-	-	-	-	-	-	-	-
Rye (city)	2.78	3.21	-	-	-	-	-	-	-	-	-	-	-	3.18	-	-	-	-	-	-	-	-	-	-
Scarsdale (village)	3.15	3.87	-	4.63	-	-	3.20	-	-	-	-	-	-	3.83	4.04	-	-	-	-	-	-	-	-	-
Tarrytown (village)	2.33	2.84	-	-	-	-	-	-	-	-	-	-	-	-	-	-	-	-	-	-	-	-	-	-
White Plains (city)	2.47	2.25	-	2.31	-	-	2.51	-	-	-	-	-	-	-	-	-	-	-	-	-	-	-	-	-
Yonkers (city)	2.61	3.44	-	3.92	-	-	2.50	-	3.31	-	-	-	-	-	2.94	-	-	-	-	-	-	-	-	-
NORTH CAROLINA	2.49	3.04	3.36	2.88	-	4.30	2.75	-	2.71	3.38	2.99	5.74	-	2.28	2.59	4.38	-	3.48	3.38	-	2.73	2.52	-	3.55
Alamance County	2.46	3.86	-	-	-	-	-	-	-	-	-	-	-	-	-	-	-	-	-	-	-	-	-	-
Buncombe County	2.33	3.17	-	3.46	-	-	-	-	-	-	-	-	-	-	-	-	-	-	-	-	-	-	-	-
Burke County	2.47	5.51	-	-	-	-	-	-	-	-	-	6.49	-	-	-	6.01	-	-	-	-	-	-	-	-
Cabarrus County	2.60	3.55	-	-	-	-	-	-	-	-	-	-	-	-	-	-	-	-	-	-	-	-	-	-
Catawba County	2.51	4.52	-	-	-	-	-	-	-	-	-	5.44	-	-	-	5.96	-	-	-	-	-	-	-	3.72
Hickory (city)	2.34	4.25	-	-	-	-	-	-	-	-	-	5.04	-	-	-	-	-	-	-	-	-	-	-	-
Cleveland County	2.53	3.88	-	-	-	-	-	-	-	-	-	-	-	-	-	-	-	-	-	-	-	-	-	-
Craven County	2.49	2.75	-	-	-	-	-	-	3.66	-	-	-	-	-	-	-	-	-	-	-	-	-	-	-
Cumberland County	2.65	2.81	2.85	2.89	-	-	-	-	2.92	-	-	-	-	2.14	2.52	-	-	-	-	-	-	-	-	3.37
Davidson County	2.50	3.87	-	-	-	4.71	-	-	-	-	-	-	-	-	-	-	-	-	-	-	-	-	-	-
Durham County	2.40	2.29	-	2.42	-	-	1.99	-	2.37	-	-	-	-	1.89	1.84	-	-	-	-	-	-	-	-	-
Forsyth County	2.39	2.59	-	2.16	-	-	2.57	-	2.45	-	-	-	-	-	-	-	-	-	-	-	-	-	-	3.26
Gaston County	2.54	3.36	-	-	-	-	-	-	-	-	-	-	-	-	-	-	-	-	-	-	-	-	-	3.88
Guilford County	2.41	3.40	-	2.97	-	-	3.32	-	2.42	-	-	-	-	-	3.00	3.86	-	5.10	-	-	-	-	-	3.94
Halifax County	2.51	3.55	-	-	-	-	-	-	-	-	-	-	-	-	-	-	-	-	-	-	-	-	-	-
Harnett County	2.60	2.72	-	-	-	-	-	-	-	-	-	-	-	-	-	-	-	-	-	-	-	-	-	-
Henderson County	2.33	2.94	-	-	-	-	-	-	-	-	-	-	-	-	-	-	-	-	-	-	-	-	-	-
Iredell County	2.56	3.50	-	-	-	-	-	-	-	-	-	-	-	-	-	-	-	-	-	-	-	-	-	-
Johnston County	2.57	3.16	-	-	-	-	-	-	-	-	-	-	-	-	-	-	-	-	-	-	-	-	-	-

Notes: Please refer to the User's Guide for an explanation of data; data is arranged alphabetically by state, then county, then city within each county; table includes counties with populations greater than 49,999 unless noted and cities with populations greater than 9,999 whose Asian and/or NHPI population rates are greater than the national average; (1) Native Hawaiian and other Pacific Islander; (2) excludes Taiwanese; (3) includes Chamorro; (4) county does not meet population threshold but is shown in order to allow inclusion of city

Place	All households	Asian households	NHPI[1] households	Asian Indian	Bangladeshi	Cambodian	Chinese[2]	Fijian	Filipino	Guamanian[3]	Hawaiian, Native	Hmong	Indonesian	Japanese	Korean	Laotian	Malaysian	Pakistani	Samoan	Sri Lankan	Taiwanese	Thai	Tongan	Vietnamese
Lenoir County	2.42	3.63	-	-	-	-	-	-	-	-	-	-	-	-	-	-	-	-	-	-	-	-	-	-
Mecklenburg County	2.49	3.08	-	2.89	-	4.32	2.81	-	2.75	-	-	5.35	-	2.39	2.85	3.39	-	-	-	-	-	-	-	3.58
Nash County	2.54	2.87	-	-	-	-	-	-	-	-	-	-	-	-	-	-	-	-	-	-	-	-	-	-
New Hanover County	2.29	2.43	-	-	-	-	-	-	-	-	-	-	-	-	-	-	-	-	-	-	-	-	-	-
Onslow County	2.72	2.34	3.87	-	-	-	-	-	2.47	-	-	-	-	1.70	-	-	-	-	-	-	-	-	-	-
Orange County	2.36	2.46	-	2.30	-	-	2.70	-	-	-	-	-	-	2.35	2.30	-	-	-	-	-	-	-	-	-
Carrboro (town)	2.17	2.29	-	-	-	-	-	-	-	-	-	-	-	-	-	-	-	-	-	-	-	-	-	-
Chapel Hill (town)	2.20	2.46	-	2.26	-	-	2.63	-	-	-	-	-	-	-	2.30	-	-	-	-	-	-	-	-	-
Pitt County	2.42	2.27	-	-	-	-	-	-	-	-	-	-	-	-	-	-	-	-	-	-	-	-	-	-
Randolph County	2.55	3.53	-	-	-	-	-	-	-	-	-	-	-	-	-	-	-	-	-	-	-	-	-	-
Robeson County	2.75	3.77	-	-	-	-	-	-	-	-	-	-	-	-	-	-	-	-	-	-	-	-	-	-
Rowan County	2.51	3.96	-	-	-	-	-	-	-	-	-	-	-	-	-	-	-	-	-	-	-	-	-	-
Stanly County	2.54	4.84	-	-	-	-	-	-	-	-	-	6.00	-	-	-	-	-	-	-	-	-	-	-	-
Surry County	2.46	7.38	-	-	-	-	-	-	-	-	-	-	-	-	-	-	-	-	-	-	-	-	-	-
Union County	2.81	2.94	-	-	-	-	-	-	-	-	-	-	-	-	-	-	-	-	-	-	-	-	-	-
Wake County	2.51	2.86	-	2.89	-	-	2.83	-	2.55	-	-	-	-	2.72	2.77	-	-	3.10	-	-	-	-	-	3.25
Apex (town)	2.71	3.12	-	-	-	-	-	-	-	-	-	-	-	-	-	-	-	-	-	-	-	-	-	-
Cary (town)	2.69	3.00	-	3.11	-	-	3.06	-	-	-	-	-	-	2.94	2.62	-	-	-	-	-	-	-	-	3.03
Wayne County	2.56	2.72	-	-	-	-	-	-	-	-	-	-	-	-	-	-	-	-	-	-	-	-	-	-
Wilkes County	2.43	3.37	-	-	-	-	-	-	-	-	-	-	-	-	-	-	-	-	-	-	-	-	-	-
NORTH DAKOTA	2.40	2.63	-	2.83	-	-	2.65	-	2.74	-	-	-	-	-	2.04	-	-	-	-	-	-	-	-	-
Cass County	2.32	2.53	-	2.41	-	-	-	-	-	-	-	-	-	-	-	-	-	-	-	-	-	-	-	-
Grand Forks County	2.42	2.53	-	-	-	-	-	-	-	-	-	-	-	-	-	-	-	-	-	-	-	-	-	-
Ward County	2.46	2.65	-	-	-	-	-	-	-	-	-	-	-	-	-	-	-	-	-	-	-	-	-	-
OHIO	2.49	2.68	2.99	2.71	2.92	3.98	2.55	-	2.66	3.72	2.70	-	2.25	2.31	2.39	3.99	2.62	3.23	3.19	2.52	2.61	2.39	-	3.20
Allen County	2.52	2.94	-	-	-	-	-	-	-	-	-	-	-	-	-	-	-	-	-	-	-	-	-	-
Ashtabula County	2.56	2.67	-	-	-	-	-	-	-	-	-	-	-	-	-	-	-	-	-	-	-	-	-	-
Athens County	2.40	2.08	-	-	-	-	-	-	-	-	-	-	-	-	-	-	-	-	-	-	-	-	-	-
Athens (city)	2.21	2.12	-	-	-	-	-	-	-	-	-	-	-	-	-	-	-	-	-	-	-	-	-	-
Butler County	2.61	3.11	-	3.15	-	-	2.76	-	3.05	-	-	-	-	-	3.35	-	-	-	-	-	-	-	-	3.11
Clark County	2.48	3.01	-	-	-	-	-	-	-	-	-	-	-	-	-	-	-	-	-	-	-	-	-	-
Clermont County	2.68	2.43	-	2.57	-	-	-	-	-	-	-	-	-	-	-	-	-	-	-	-	-	-	-	-
Columbiana County	2.52	2.87	-	-	-	-	-	-	-	-	-	-	-	-	-	-	-	-	-	-	-	-	-	-
Cuyahoga County	2.39	2.72	-	2.87	-	4.26	2.68	-	2.55	-	-	-	-	2.15	2.19	-	-	-	-	-	-	-	-	3.30
Mayfield Heights (city)	1.95	2.69	-	2.57	-	-	-	-	-	-	-	-	-	-	-	-	-	-	-	-	-	-	-	-
Richmond Heights (city)	2.21	2.19	-	-	-	-	-	-	-	-	-	-	-	-	-	-	-	-	-	-	-	-	-	-
Solon (city)	2.88	3.18	-	3.21	-	-	3.02	-	-	-	-	-	-	-	-	-	-	-	-	-	-	-	-	-
Westlake (city)	2.38	3.03	-	2.69	-	-	-	-	-	-	-	-	-	-	-	-	-	-	-	-	-	-	-	-
Delaware County	2.70	3.03	-	2.81	-	-	3.01	-	-	-	-	-	-	-	-	-	-	-	-	-	-	-	-	-
Fairfield County	2.64	3.69	-	-	-	-	-	-	-	-	-	-	-	-	-	-	-	-	-	-	-	-	-	-
Franklin County	2.39	2.55	2.66	2.35	-	3.88	2.50	-	2.31	-	-	-	2.08	2.48	2.15	3.61	-	3.73	-	-	2.59	2.78	-	3.07

Notes: Please refer to the User's Guide for an explanation of data; data is arranged alphabetically by state, then county, then city within each county; table includes counties with populations greater than 49,999 unless noted and cities with populations greater than 9,999 whose Asian and/or NHPI population rates are greater than the national average; (1) Native Hawaiian and other Pacific Islander; (2) excludes Taiwanese; (3) includes Chamorro; (4) county does not meet population threshold but is shown in order to allow inclusion of city

Place	All households	Asian households	NHPI[1] households	Asian Indian	Bangladeshi	Cambodian	Chinese[2]	Fijian	Filipino	Guamanian[3]	Hawaiian, Native	Hmong	Indonesian	Japanese	Korean	Laotian	Malaysian	Pakistani	Samoan	Sri Lankan	Taiwanese	Thai	Tongan	Vietnamese
Dublin (city)	2.80	3.14	-	3.14	-	-	3.24	-	-	-	-	-	-	3.20	-	-	-	-	-	-	-	-	-	-
Hilliard (city)	2.80	2.84	-	-	-	-	-	-	-	-	-	-	-	-	-	-	-	-	-	-	-	-	-	-
Geauga County	2.84	2.87	-	-	-	-	-	-	-	-	-	-	-	-	-	-	-	-	-	-	-	-	-	-
Greene County	2.53	2.71	-	2.93	-	-	2.62	-	-	-	-	-	-	-	2.83	-	-	-	-	-	-	-	-	-
Hamilton County	2.38	2.50	-	2.42	-	3.60	2.40	-	2.84	-	-	-	-	1.82	2.36	-	-	-	-	-	-	-	-	3.53
Blue Ash (city)	2.48	3.06	-	3.12	-	-	-	-	-	-	-	-	-	-	-	-	-	-	-	-	-	-	-	-
Sharonville (city)	2.16	2.54	-	2.73	-	-	-	-	-	-	-	-	-	-	-	-	-	-	-	-	-	-	-	-
Hancock County	2.49	2.36	-	-	-	-	-	-	-	-	-	-	-	-	-	-	-	-	-	-	-	-	-	-
Lake County	2.50	2.83	-	3.04	-	-	3.27	-	-	-	-	-	-	-	-	-	-	-	-	-	-	-	-	-
Licking County	2.56	2.22	-	-	-	-	-	-	-	-	-	-	-	-	-	-	-	-	-	-	-	-	-	-
Lorain County	2.61	2.68	-	2.89	-	-	-	-	3.42	-	-	-	-	-	-	-	-	-	-	-	-	-	-	-
Lucas County	2.44	2.51	-	2.75	-	-	2.21	-	2.62	-	-	-	-	-	2.74	-	-	-	-	-	-	-	-	-
Mahoning County	2.44	2.82	-	-	-	-	-	-	-	-	-	-	-	-	-	-	-	-	-	-	-	-	-	-
Marion County	2.50	2.76	-	-	-	-	-	-	-	-	-	-	-	-	-	-	-	-	-	-	-	-	-	-
Medina County	2.74	3.30	-	3.77	-	-	-	-	-	-	-	-	-	-	-	-	-	-	-	-	-	-	-	-
Miami County	2.53	2.30	-	-	-	-	-	-	-	-	-	-	-	-	-	-	-	-	-	-	-	-	-	-
Montgomery County	2.37	2.73	-	2.91	-	-	2.52	-	2.38	-	-	-	-	2.16	2.85	-	-	-	-	-	-	-	-	3.08
Portage County	2.56	2.01	-	-	-	-	-	-	-	-	-	-	-	-	-	-	-	-	-	-	-	-	-	-
Richland County	2.47	2.77	-	-	-	-	-	-	-	-	-	-	-	-	-	-	-	-	-	-	-	-	-	-
Stark County	2.49	2.63	-	3.29	-	-	2.73	-	-	-	-	-	-	-	-	-	-	-	-	-	-	-	-	-
Summit County	2.45	3.05	-	2.77	-	-	2.76	-	2.84	-	-	-	-	2.57	3.14	4.53	-	-	-	-	-	-	-	3.84
Trumbull County	2.48	2.36	-	-	-	-	-	-	-	-	-	-	-	-	-	-	-	-	-	-	-	-	-	-
Warren County	2.71	3.17	-	3.09	-	-	2.70	-	-	-	-	-	-	-	-	-	-	-	-	-	-	-	-	-
Wayne County	2.67	3.13	-	-	-	-	-	-	-	-	-	-	-	-	-	-	-	-	-	-	-	-	-	-
Wood County	2.51	2.70	-	-	-	-	-	-	-	-	-	-	-	-	-	-	-	-	-	-	-	-	-	-
OKLAHOMA	2.48	2.79	3.16	2.83	-	4.21	2.35	-	2.72	2.32	3.06	6.14	-	1.93	2.36	3.90	2.72	3.52	-	-	1.75	2.07	-	3.35
Canadian County	2.70	3.90	-	4.04	-	-	-	-	-	-	-	-	-	-	-	-	-	-	-	-	-	-	-	3.68
Cleveland County	2.51	2.66	-	3.00	-	-	2.21	-	2.72	-	-	-	-	-	2.36	-	-	-	-	-	-	-	-	3.50
Comanche County	2.62	2.62	-	-	-	-	-	-	2.49	-	-	-	-	-	2.46	-	-	-	-	-	-	-	-	-
Garfield County	2.42	2.07	-	-	-	-	-	-	-	-	-	-	-	-	-	-	-	-	-	-	-	-	-	-
Muskogee County	2.51	3.04	-	-	-	-	-	-	-	-	-	-	-	-	-	-	-	-	-	-	-	-	-	-
Oklahoma County	2.41	2.79	-	2.66	-	-	2.24	-	2.87	-	-	-	-	1.99	2.01	3.86	-	-	-	-	-	2.28	-	3.33
Payne County	2.29	2.03	-	-	-	-	2.23	-	-	-	-	-	-	-	-	-	-	-	-	-	-	-	-	-
Stillwater (city)	2.12	2.02	-	-	-	-	2.23	-	-	-	-	-	-	-	-	-	-	-	-	-	-	-	-	-
Pottawatomie County	2.55	2.20	-	-	-	-	-	-	-	-	-	-	-	-	-	-	-	-	-	-	-	-	-	-
Tulsa County	2.43	2.89	-	2.53	-	-	2.55	-	2.94	-	-	-	-	-	2.93	-	-	3.75	-	-	-	-	-	3.42
Wagoner County	2.72	4.58	-	-	-	-	-	-	-	-	-	-	-	-	-	-	-	-	-	-	-	-	-	-
OREGON	2.50	2.87	3.06	2.61	-	3.63	2.77	2.97	3.10	3.14	2.68	4.88	2.26	2.08	2.64	4.10	-	3.50	3.12	-	2.45	2.41	4.17	3.67
Benton County	2.42	2.28	-	-	-	-	2.49	-	-	-	-	-	-	1.86	2.27	-	-	-	-	-	-	-	-	-
Corvallis (city)	2.26	2.23	-	-	-	-	2.46	-	-	-	-	-	-	-	2.30	-	-	-	-	-	-	-	-	-
Clackamas County	2.61	2.88	3.35	3.02	-	-	2.84	-	3.18	-	-	-	-	2.43	2.75	-	-	-	-	-	-	-	-	3.88

Notes: Please refer to the User's Guide for an explanation of data; data is arranged alphabetically by state, then county, then city within each county; table includes counties with populations greater than 49,999 unless noted and cities with populations greater than 9,999 whose Asian and/or NHPI population rates are greater than the national average; (1) Native Hawaiian and other Pacific Islander; (2) excludes Taiwanese; (3) includes Chamorro; (4) county does not meet population threshold but is shown in order to allow inclusion of city

Place	All households	Asian households	NHPI[1] households	Asian Indian	Bangladeshi	Cambodian	Chinese[2]	Fijian	Filipino	Guamanian[3]	Hawaiian, Native	Hmong	Indonesian	Japanese	Korean	Laotian	Malaysian	Pakistani	Samoan	Sri Lankan	Taiwanese	Thai	Tongan	Vietnamese
Lake Oswego (city)	2.37	2.89	-	-	-	-	3.14	-	-	-	-	-	-	-	-	-	-	-	-	-	-	-	-	-
Coos County	2.34	2.24	-	-	-	-	-	-	-	-	-	-	-	-	-	-	-	-	-	-	-	-	-	-
Deschutes County	2.50	1.70	-	-	-	-	-	-	-	-	-	-	-	-	-	-	-	-	-	-	-	-	-	-
Douglas County	2.48	2.35	-	-	-	-	-	-	-	-	-	-	-	-	-	-	-	-	-	-	-	-	-	-
Jackson County	2.48	2.59	-	-	-	-	-	-	-	-	-	-	-	-	-	-	-	-	-	-	-	-	-	-
Josephine County	2.41	2.61	-	-	-	-	-	-	-	-	-	-	-	-	-	-	-	-	-	-	-	-	-	-
Klamath County	2.49	2.24	-	-	-	-	-	-	-	-	-	-	-	-	-	-	-	-	-	-	-	-	-	-
Lane County	2.42	2.15	3.33	2.34	-	-	2.18	-	2.99	-	-	-	-	1.52	2.72	-	-	-	-	-	-	-	-	-
Linn County	2.58	2.53	-	-	-	-	-	-	-	-	-	-	-	-	-	-	-	-	-	-	-	-	-	-
Marion County	2.69	2.98	3.74	3.05	-	-	2.72	-	3.11	-	-	-	-	2.10	2.65	-	-	-	-	-	-	-	-	3.44
Salem (city)	2.53	3.06	3.55	-	-	-	2.89	-	2.94	-	-	-	-	1.82	-	-	-	-	-	-	-	-	-	3.24
Multnomah County	2.36	3.09	3.26	2.55	-	4.02	2.94	-	3.05	-	2.61	4.93	-	2.02	2.14	4.31	-	-	-	-	-	2.64	4.98	3.82
Portland (city)	2.29	3.09	3.09	2.39	-	4.13	2.93	-	3.00	-	2.19	4.70	-	1.92	2.11	4.32	-	-	-	-	-	2.60	4.98	3.82
Polk County	2.61	3.14	-	-	-	-	-	-	-	-	-	-	-	-	-	-	-	-	-	-	-	-	-	-
Umatilla County	2.66	3.61	-	-	-	-	-	-	-	-	-	-	-	-	-	-	-	-	-	-	-	-	-	-
Washington County	2.61	2.90	2.68	2.61	-	3.49	2.68	-	3.25	-	2.98	-	-	2.40	2.96	3.50	-	-	-	-	-	-	-	3.52
Aloha (cdp)	2.94	3.44	-	-	-	-	-	-	3.79	-	-	-	-	-	-	-	-	-	-	-	-	-	-	4.04
Beaverton (city)	2.43	2.79	-	2.43	-	2.82	2.65	-	3.01	-	-	-	-	2.75	2.93	-	-	-	-	-	-	-	-	3.23
Cedar Mill (cdp)	2.67	3.14	-	-	-	-	-	-	-	-	-	-	-	-	-	-	-	-	-	-	-	-	-	-
Hillsboro (city)	2.75	2.54	-	2.29	-	-	2.11	-	-	-	-	-	-	-	2.83	-	-	-	-	-	-	-	-	-
Tigard (city)	2.49	3.14	-	-	-	-	3.16	-	-	-	-	-	-	-	-	-	-	-	-	-	-	-	-	3.40
Tualatin (city)	2.61	2.86	-	-	-	-	-	-	-	-	-	-	-	-	-	-	-	-	-	-	-	-	-	3.99
Yamhill County	2.79	3.61	-	-	-	-	-	-	-	-	-	-	-	-	-	-	-	-	-	-	-	-	-	-
PENNSYLVANIA	2.48	2.92	3.51	2.91	2.82	4.47	2.73	-	2.80	3.48	3.30	6.19	2.79	1.98	2.71	4.05	-	3.45	4.09	2.52	2.06	2.07	-	3.52
Adams County	2.60	2.79	-	-	-	-	-	-	-	-	-	-	-	-	-	-	-	-	-	-	-	-	-	-
Allegheny County	2.31	2.37	3.45	2.52	-	-	2.25	-	2.41	-	-	-	-	1.71	2.23	-	-	-	-	-	1.82	-	-	3.39
Muni. of Monroeville (borough)	2.29	2.79	-	2.97	-	-	-	-	-	-	-	-	-	-	-	-	-	-	-	-	-	-	-	-
Scott (township)	2.14	2.19	-	2.20	-	-	-	-	-	-	-	-	-	-	-	-	-	-	-	-	-	-	-	-
Scott Township (cdp)	2.14	2.19	-	2.20	-	-	-	-	-	-	-	-	-	-	-	-	-	-	-	-	-	-	-	-
Upper St. Clair (township)	2.81	3.34	-	3.50	-	-	-	-	-	-	-	-	-	-	-	-	-	-	-	-	-	-	-	-
Beaver County	2.44	2.56	-	-	-	-	-	-	-	-	-	-	-	-	-	-	-	-	-	-	-	-	-	-
Berks County	2.55	3.11	-	3.00	-	-	3.10	-	-	-	-	-	-	-	1.96	-	-	-	-	-	-	-	-	3.77
Blair County	2.42	3.27	-	-	-	-	-	-	-	-	-	-	-	-	-	-	-	-	-	-	-	-	-	-
Bradford County	2.53	2.06	-	-	-	-	-	-	-	-	-	-	-	-	-	-	-	-	-	-	-	-	-	-
Bucks County	2.69	3.15	-	3.27	-	-	2.65	-	3.27	-	-	-	-	-	3.21	-	-	-	-	-	-	-	-	2.80
Bensalem (township)	2.56	3.03	-	2.86	-	-	-	-	-	-	-	-	-	-	3.27	-	-	-	-	-	-	-	-	-
Lower Makefield (township)	2.77	3.36	-	3.53	-	-	-	-	-	-	-	-	-	-	-	-	-	-	-	-	-	-	-	-
Newtown (township)	2.68	3.09	-	-	-	-	-	-	-	-	-	-	-	-	-	-	-	-	-	-	-	-	-	-
Butler County	2.54	2.45	-	2.80	-	-	-	-	-	-	-	-	-	-	-	-	-	-	-	-	-	-	-	-
Cambria County	2.38	2.52	-	-	-	-	-	-	-	-	-	-	-	-	-	-	-	-	-	-	-	-	-	-
Centre County	2.45	2.26	-	2.70	-	-	2.19	-	-	-	-	-	-	-	2.03	-	-	-	-	-	-	-	-	-

Notes: Please refer to the User's Guide for an explanation of data; data is arranged alphabetically by state, then county, then city within each county; table includes counties with populations greater than 49,999 unless noted and cities with populations greater than 9,999 whose Asian and/or NHPI population rates are greater than the national average; (1) Native Hawaiian and other Pacific Islander; (2) excludes Taiwanese; (3) includes Chamorro; (4) county does not meet population threshold but is shown in order to allow inclusion of city

Place	All households	Asian households	NHPI[1] households	Asian Indian	Bangladeshi	Cambodian	Chinese[2]	Fijian	Filipino	Guamanian[3]	Hawaiian, Native	Hmong	Indonesian	Japanese	Korean	Laotian	Malaysian	Pakistani	Samoan	Sri Lankan	Taiwanese	Thai	Tongan	Vietnamese
Ferguson (township)	2.54	2.56	-	-	-	-	-	-	-	-	-	-	-	-	-	-	-	-	-	-	-	-	-	-
Patton (township)	2.39	2.51	-	-	-	-	-	-	-	-	-	-	-	-	-	-	-	-	-	-	-	-	-	-
State College (borough)	2.30	2.12	-	2.46	-	-	2.13	-	-	-	-	-	-	-	1.89	-	-	-	-	-	-	-	-	-
Chester County	2.65	3.02	-	2.77	-	-	2.93	-	2.99	-	-	-	-	2.52	3.38	-	-	-	-	-	-	-	-	3.97
Tredyffrin (township)	2.36	2.80	-	2.67	-	-	2.81	-	-	-	-	-	-	-	-	-	-	-	-	-	-	-	-	-
West Goshen (township)	2.68	3.02	-	-	-	-	-	-	-	-	-	-	-	-	-	-	-	-	-	-	-	-	-	-
West Whiteland (township)	2.44	2.81	-	-	-	-	-	-	-	-	-	-	-	-	-	-	-	-	-	-	-	-	-	-
Clearfield County	2.44	2.82	-	-	-	-	-	-	-	-	-	-	-	-	-	-	-	-	-	-	-	-	-	-
Columbia County	2.42	2.29	-	-	-	-	-	-	-	-	-	-	-	-	-	-	-	-	-	-	-	-	-	-
Crawford County	2.50	2.68	-	-	-	-	-	-	-	-	-	-	-	-	-	-	-	-	-	-	-	-	-	-
Cumberland County	2.40	2.99	-	3.29	-	-	2.80	-	-	-	-	-	-	-	2.61	-	-	-	-	-	-	-	-	3.99
Hampden (township)	2.48	3.11	-	-	-	-	-	-	-	-	-	-	-	-	-	-	-	-	-	-	-	-	-	-
Dauphin County	2.39	2.85	-	2.56	-	-	2.50	-	-	-	-	-	-	-	2.87	-	-	-	-	-	-	-	-	3.25
Derry (township)	2.32	2.48	-	-	-	-	-	-	-	-	-	-	-	-	-	-	-	-	-	-	-	-	-	-
Hershey (cdp)	2.21	2.74	-	-	-	-	-	-	-	-	-	-	-	-	-	-	-	-	-	-	-	-	-	-
Delaware County	2.56	3.09	-	3.05	-	-	2.90	-	2.69	-	-	-	-	2.32	3.21	-	-	4.13	-	-	-	-	-	3.44
Broomall (cdp)	2.62	3.37	-	-	-	-	-	-	-	-	-	-	-	-	3.46	-	-	-	-	-	-	-	-	-
Drexel Hill (cdp)	2.46	2.66	-	-	-	-	2.60	-	-	-	-	-	-	-	-	-	-	-	-	-	-	-	-	-
Marple (township)	2.64	3.36	-	-	-	-	-	-	-	-	-	-	-	-	3.62	-	-	-	-	-	-	-	-	-
Radnor (township)	2.38	2.77	-	-	-	-	2.75	-	-	-	-	-	-	-	-	-	-	-	-	-	-	-	-	-
Upper Darby (township)	2.50	3.24	-	3.12	-	-	3.28	-	-	-	-	-	-	-	3.14	-	-	-	-	-	-	-	-	3.59
Erie County	2.51	2.64	-	2.72	-	-	-	-	-	-	-	-	-	-	-	-	-	-	-	-	-	-	-	-
Franklin County	2.50	3.15	-	-	-	-	-	-	-	-	-	-	-	-	-	-	-	-	-	-	-	-	-	-
Indiana County	2.47	2.51	-	-	-	-	-	-	-	-	-	-	-	-	-	-	-	-	-	-	-	-	-	-
Lackawanna County	2.38	3.17	-	3.34	-	-	-	-	-	-	-	-	-	-	-	-	-	-	-	-	-	-	-	-
Lancaster County	2.64	3.37	-	2.96	-	-	3.31	-	-	-	-	6.72	-	-	2.38	-	-	-	-	-	-	-	-	3.36
Lawrence County	2.47	2.37	-	-	-	-	-	-	-	-	-	-	-	-	-	-	-	-	-	-	-	-	-	-
Lebanon County	2.49	3.20	-	-	-	-	-	-	-	-	-	-	-	-	-	-	-	-	-	-	-	-	-	-
Lehigh County	2.48	2.80	-	2.76	-	-	2.63	-	-	-	-	-	-	-	2.41	-	-	-	-	-	-	-	-	3.52
Fullerton (cdp)	2.27	2.46	-	-	-	-	-	-	-	-	-	-	-	-	-	-	-	-	-	-	-	-	-	-
Lower Macungie (township)	2.65	3.30	-	-	-	-	3.44	-	-	-	-	-	-	-	-	-	-	-	-	-	-	-	-	-
Upper Macungie (township)	2.66	3.00	-	-	-	-	-	-	-	-	-	-	-	-	-	-	-	-	-	-	-	-	-	-
Luzerne County	2.34	2.92	-	3.14	-	-	-	-	-	-	-	-	-	-	-	-	-	-	-	-	-	-	-	-
Lycoming County	2.44	2.10	-	-	-	-	-	-	-	-	-	-	-	-	-	-	-	-	-	-	-	-	-	-
Mercer County	2.44	2.94	-	-	-	-	-	-	-	-	-	-	-	-	-	-	-	-	-	-	-	-	-	-
Monroe County	2.72	3.47	-	4.05	-	-	-	-	-	-	-	-	-	-	-	-	-	-	-	-	-	-	-	-
Montgomery County	2.54	3.03	-	2.94	-	-	2.75	-	2.81	-	-	-	-	2.21	3.21	-	-	-	-	-	-	-	-	3.57
Cheltenham (township)	2.47	3.02	-	-	-	-	-	-	-	-	-	-	-	-	3.00	-	-	-	-	-	-	-	-	-
East Norriton (township)	2.46	2.55	-	-	-	-	-	-	-	-	-	-	-	-	-	-	-	-	-	-	-	-	-	-
Hatfield (township)	2.64	3.55	-	3.64	-	-	-	-	-	-	-	-	-	-	-	-	-	-	-	-	-	-	-	-
Horsham (township)	2.64	2.70	-	-	-	-	-	-	-	-	-	-	-	-	2.91	-	-	-	-	-	-	-	-	-

Notes: Please refer to the User's Guide for an explanation of data; data is arranged alphabetically by state, then county, then city within each county; table includes counties with populations greater than 49,999 unless noted and cities with populations greater than 9,999 whose Asian and/or NHPI population rates are greater than the national average; (1) Native Hawaiian and other Pacific Islander; (2) excludes Taiwanese; (3) includes Chamorro; (4) county does not meet population threshold but is shown in order to allow inclusion of city

Place	All households	Asian households	NHPI[1] households	Asian Indian	Bangladeshi	Cambodian	Chinese[2]	Fijian	Filipino	Guamanian[3]	Hawaiian, Native	Hmong	Indonesian	Japanese	Korean	Laotian	Malaysian	Pakistani	Samoan	Sri Lankan	Taiwanese	Thai	Tongan	Vietnamese
King of Prussia (cdp)	2.23	2.37	-	2.48	-	-	2.18	-	-	-	-	-	-	-	-	-	-	-	-	-	-	-	-	-
Lansdale (borough)	2.36	3.16	-	2.93	-	-	-	-	-	-	-	-	-	-	-	-	-	-	-	-	-	-	-	-
Lower Gwynedd (township)	2.38	3.02	-	-	-	-	-	-	-	-	-	-	-	-	-	-	-	-	-	-	-	-	-	-
Lower Providence (township)	2.72	2.87	-	-	-	-	3.02	-	-	-	-	-	-	-	-	-	-	-	-	-	-	-	-	-
Montgomery (township)	2.75	3.74	-	4.13	-	-	-	-	-	-	-	-	-	-	3.38	-	-	-	-	-	-	-	-	-
Montgomeryville (cdp)	2.85	4.02	-	-	-	-	-	-	-	-	-	-	-	-	-	-	-	-	-	-	-	-	-	-
Plymouth (township)	2.43	2.88	-	-	-	-	-	-	-	-	-	-	-	-	3.25	-	-	-	-	-	-	-	-	-
Towamencin (township)	2.55	3.41	-	-	-	-	-	-	-	-	-	-	-	-	-	-	-	-	-	-	-	-	-	-
Upper Dublin (township)	2.78	3.36	-	-	-	-	-	-	-	-	-	-	-	-	3.87	-	-	-	-	-	-	-	-	-
Upper Gwynedd (township)	2.62	3.05	-	-	-	-	3.31	-	-	-	-	-	-	-	-	-	-	-	-	-	-	-	-	-
Upper Merion (township)	2.32	2.49	-	2.71	-	-	2.21	-	-	-	-	-	-	-	-	-	-	-	-	-	-	-	-	-
Whitpain (township)	2.62	3.39	-	-	-	-	-	-	-	-	-	-	-	-	3.43	-	-	-	-	-	-	-	-	-
Northampton County	2.52	3.30	-	3.80	-	-	3.01	-	-	-	-	-	-	-	2.31	-	-	-	-	-	-	-	-	4.14
Northumberland County	2.34	3.32	-	-	-	-	-	-	-	-	-	-	-	-	-	-	-	-	-	-	-	-	-	-
Philadelphia County	2.48	2.98	3.94	2.88	-	4.54	2.81	-	2.80	-	-	-	-	1.50	2.27	4.22	-	3.54	-	-	-	-	-	3.67
Philadelphia (city)	2.48	2.98	3.94	2.88	-	4.54	2.81	-	2.80	-	-	-	-	1.50	2.27	4.22	-	3.54	-	-	-	-	-	3.67
Schuylkill County	2.37	2.57	-	-	-	-	-	-	-	-	-	-	-	-	-	-	-	-	-	-	-	-	-	-
Washington County	2.44	2.89	-	-	-	-	-	-	-	-	-	-	-	-	-	-	-	-	-	-	-	-	-	-
Westmoreland County	2.41	3.25	-	3.85	-	-	-	-	-	-	-	-	-	-	-	-	-	-	-	-	-	-	-	-
York County	2.52	3.39	-	3.50	-	-	3.24	-	-	-	-	-	-	-	3.37	-	-	-	-	-	-	-	-	3.43
RHODE ISLAND	2.47	3.11	3.13	2.57	-	4.13	2.71	-	2.77	-	-	6.80	-	2.77	2.18	3.58	-	-	-	-	-	-	-	3.73
Bristol County	2.51	3.40	-	-	-	-	-	-	-	-	-	-	-	-	-	-	-	-	-	-	-	-	-	-
Kent County	2.45	3.16	-	-	-	-	2.65	-	-	-	-	-	-	-	3.88	-	-	-	-	-	-	-	-	-
Newport County	2.36	2.50	-	-	-	-	-	-	2.46	-	-	-	-	-	-	-	-	-	-	-	-	-	-	-
Providence County	2.48	3.14	-	2.47	-	4.09	2.61	-	2.99	-	-	7.20	-	-	1.79	3.58	-	-	-	-	-	-	-	3.65
Providence (city)	2.57	3.05	-	2.11	-	4.02	2.24	-	2.81	-	-	8.13	-	-	1.55	3.66	-	-	-	-	-	-	-	-
Woonsocket (city)	2.37	3.41	-	-	-	-	-	-	-	-	-	-	-	-	-	3.46	-	-	-	-	-	-	-	-
Washington County	2.52	2.92	-	-	-	-	3.23	-	-	-	-	-	-	-	-	-	-	-	-	-	-	-	-	-
SOUTH CAROLINA	2.53	2.87	2.80	2.97	-	3.60	2.81	-	2.84	3.24	2.72	6.84	-	2.02	2.40	4.18	-	-	-	-	-	1.87	-	3.06
Aiken County	2.53	2.98	-	-	-	-	-	-	-	-	-	-	-	-	-	-	-	-	-	-	-	-	-	-
Anderson County	2.48	3.31	-	-	-	-	-	-	-	-	-	-	-	-	-	-	-	-	-	-	-	-	-	-
Beaufort County	2.51	2.80	-	-	-	-	-	-	-	-	-	-	-	-	-	-	-	-	-	-	-	-	-	-
Berkeley County	2.75	2.92	-	-	-	-	-	-	2.83	-	-	-	-	-	-	-	-	-	-	-	-	-	-	-
Charleston County	2.42	2.47	-	2.34	-	-	2.55	-	2.66	-	-	-	-	-	-	-	-	-	-	-	-	-	-	-
Dorchester County	2.72	2.94	-	-	-	-	-	-	3.19	-	-	-	-	-	-	-	-	-	-	-	-	-	-	-
Florence County	2.59	2.92	-	-	-	-	-	-	-	-	-	-	-	-	-	-	-	-	-	-	-	-	-	-
Greenville County	2.46	2.84	-	2.96	-	-	2.90	-	2.97	-	-	-	-	-	-	-	-	-	-	-	-	-	-	2.84
Greenwood County	2.48	2.93	-	-	-	-	-	-	-	-	-	-	-	-	-	-	-	-	-	-	-	-	-	-
Horry County	2.37	3.07	-	-	-	-	-	-	-	-	-	-	-	-	-	-	-	-	-	-	-	-	-	-
Lexington County	2.56	2.95	-	3.24	-	-	2.75	-	-	-	-	-	-	-	-	-	-	-	-	-	-	-	-	-
Oconee County	2.40	2.68	-	-	-	-	-	-	-	-	-	-	-	-	-	-	-	-	-	-	-	-	-	-

Notes: Please refer to the User's Guide for an explanation of data; data is arranged alphabetically by state, then county, then city within each county; table includes counties with populations greater than 49,999 unless noted and cities with populations greater than 9,999 whose Asian and/or NHPI population rates are greater than the national average; (1) Native Hawaiian and other Pacific Islander; (2) excludes Taiwanese; (3) includes Chamorro; (4) county does not meet population threshold but is shown in order to allow inclusion of city

Place	All households	Asian households	NHPI[1] households	Asian Indian	Bangladeshi	Cambodian	Chinese[2]	Fijian	Filipino	Guamanian[3]	Hawaiian, Native	Hmong	Indonesian	Japanese	Korean	Laotian	Malaysian	Pakistani	Samoan	Sri Lankan	Taiwanese	Thai	Tongan	Vietnamese
Pickens County	2.50	2.51	-	2.99	-	-	2.28	-	-	-	-	-	-	-	-	-	-	-	-	-	-	-	-	-
Clemson (city)	2.31	2.65	-	-	-	-	-	-	-	-	-	-	-	-	-	-	-	-	-	-	-	-	-	-
Richland County	2.44	2.57	-	2.78	-	-	2.62	-	2.58	-	-	-	-	-	2.33	-	-	-	-	-	-	-	-	3.31
Spartanburg County	2.52	3.69	-	3.05	-	-	-	-	-	-	-	6.94	-	-	-	3.99	-	-	-	-	-	-	-	-
Sumter County	2.68	2.53	-	-	-	-	-	-	-	-	-	-	-	-	-	-	-	-	-	-	-	-	-	-
York County	2.63	3.35	-	-	-	-	-	-	-	-	-	-	-	-	-	-	-	-	-	-	-	-	-	3.13
SOUTH DAKOTA	2.50	2.76	-	2.56	-	-	2.30	-	3.31	-	-	-	-	1.92	2.01	4.75	-	-	-	-	-	-	-	3.68
Minnehaha County	2.46	3.28	-	-	-	-	-	-	-	-	-	-	-	-	-	-	-	-	-	-	-	-	-	4.51
Pennington County	2.48	2.95	-	-	-	-	-	-	-	-	-	-	-	-	-	-	-	-	-	-	-	-	-	-
TENNESSEE	2.48	2.85	2.86	2.74	-	4.14	2.67	-	2.83	3.39	2.66	-	-	2.15	2.50	3.70	-	3.68	2.34	-	2.12	2.29	-	3.58
Anderson County	2.37	2.59	-	-	-	-	-	-	-	-	-	-	-	-	-	-	-	-	-	-	-	-	-	-
Blount County	2.42	2.94	-	-	-	-	-	-	-	-	-	-	-	-	-	-	-	-	-	-	-	-	-	-
Bradley County	2.50	2.96	-	-	-	-	-	-	-	-	-	-	-	-	-	-	-	-	-	-	-	-	-	-
Davidson County	2.30	2.70	1.79	2.34	-	-	2.46	-	2.61	-	-	-	-	2.03	2.51	3.65	-	-	-	-	-	-	-	3.58
Hamilton County	2.41	2.74	-	2.90	-	-	-	-	2.67	-	-	-	-	-	2.25	-	-	-	-	-	-	-	-	3.11
Knox County	2.34	2.52	-	2.74	-	-	2.21	-	-	-	-	-	-	-	2.31	-	-	-	-	-	-	-	-	3.59
Madison County	2.49	3.87	-	-	-	-	-	-	-	-	-	-	-	-	-	-	-	-	-	-	-	-	-	-
Montgomery County	2.70	2.60	-	-	-	-	-	-	-	-	-	-	-	-	2.25	-	-	-	-	-	-	-	-	-
Putnam County	2.40	2.96	-	-	-	-	-	-	-	-	-	-	-	-	-	-	-	-	-	-	-	-	-	-
Rutherford County	2.65	3.33	-	-	-	-	-	-	-	-	-	-	-	-	-	3.60	-	-	-	-	-	-	-	-
Shelby County	2.59	2.95	2.68	2.74	-	3.85	2.73	-	2.74	-	-	-	-	2.42	2.46	-	-	-	-	-	-	-	-	3.83
Germantown (city)	2.82	3.49	-	3.84	-	-	3.46	-	-	-	-	-	-	-	-	-	-	-	-	-	-	-	-	-
Sullivan County	2.36	2.64	-	-	-	-	-	-	-	-	-	-	-	-	-	-	-	-	-	-	-	-	-	-
Sumner County	2.64	2.71	-	-	-	-	-	-	-	-	-	-	-	-	-	-	-	-	-	-	-	-	-	-
Washington County	2.33	3.06	-	-	-	-	-	-	-	-	-	-	-	-	-	-	-	-	-	-	-	-	-	-
Weakley County[4]	2.38	2.27	-	-	-	-	-	-	-	-	-	-	-	-	-	-	-	-	-	-	-	-	-	-
Martin (city)	2.16	2.26	-	-	-	-	-	-	-	-	-	-	-	-	-	-	-	-	-	-	-	-	-	-
Williamson County	2.80	3.49	-	-	-	-	-	-	-	-	-	-	-	-	-	-	-	-	-	-	-	-	-	-
Wilson County	2.67	2.94	-	-	-	-	-	-	-	-	-	-	-	-	-	-	-	-	-	-	-	-	-	-
TEXAS	2.74	3.01	3.34	3.01	2.88	4.07	2.68	-	2.91	3.35	2.89	-	2.42	2.14	2.68	3.81	2.31	3.65	3.84	2.54	2.75	2.40	4.19	3.51
Anderson County	2.58	3.06	-	-	-	-	-	-	-	-	-	-	-	-	-	-	-	-	-	-	-	-	-	-
Angelina County	2.69	3.54	-	-	-	-	-	-	-	-	-	-	-	-	-	-	-	-	-	-	-	-	-	-
Bell County	2.68	2.71	3.88	3.20	-	-	-	-	2.91	3.50	-	-	-	1.66	2.70	-	-	-	-	-	-	-	-	-
Killeen (city)	2.66	2.72	4.06	-	-	-	-	-	3.05	3.57	-	-	-	-	2.71	-	-	-	-	-	-	-	-	-
Bexar County	2.78	2.65	3.08	2.95	-	-	2.53	-	2.66	-	2.57	-	-	2.12	2.18	3.65	-	-	-	-	-	2.50	-	2.97
Bowie County	2.50	2.56	-	-	-	-	-	-	-	-	-	-	-	-	-	-	-	-	-	-	-	-	-	-
Brazoria County	2.81	3.48	-	3.32	-	4.44	3.54	-	3.48	-	-	-	-	-	-	-	-	-	-	-	-	-	-	3.66
Brazos County	2.52	2.34	-	2.79	-	-	2.21	-	-	-	-	-	-	-	2.00	-	-	-	-	-	-	-	-	2.74
College Station (city)	2.33	2.39	-	2.95	-	-	2.26	-	-	-	-	-	-	-	2.07	-	-	-	-	-	-	-	-	-
Calhoun County[4]	2.75	3.38	-	-	-	-	-	-	-	-	-	-	-	-	-	-	-	-	-	-	-	-	-	4.17
Port Lavaca (city)	2.86	3.23	-	-	-	-	-	-	-	-	-	-	-	-	-	-	-	-	-	-	-	-	-	-

Notes: Please refer to the User's Guide for an explanation of data; data is arranged alphabetically by state, then county, then city within each county; table includes counties with populations greater than 49,999 unless noted and cities with populations greater than 9,999 whose Asian and/or NHPI population rates are greater than the national average; (1) Native Hawaiian and other Pacific Islander; (2) excludes Taiwanese; (3) includes Chamorro; (4) county does not meet population threshold but is shown in order to allow inclusion of city

Place	All households	Asian households	NHPI[1] households	Asian Indian	Bangladeshi	Cambodian	Chinese[2]	Fijian	Filipino	Guamanian[3]	Hawaiian, Native	Hmong	Indonesian	Japanese	Korean	Laotian	Malaysian	Pakistani	Samoan	Sri Lankan	Taiwanese	Thai	Tongan	Vietnamese
Cameron County	3.41	2.71	-	-	-	-	-	-	2.75	-	-	-	-	-	-	-	-	-	-	-	-	-	-	-
Collin County	2.68	3.02	-	2.85	-	-	3.03	-	2.93	-	-	-	-	2.44	3.28	-	-	3.49	-	-	3.19	3.75	-	3.27
Allen (city)	3.06	3.58	-	3.79	-	-	-	-	-	-	-	-	-	-	-	-	-	-	-	-	-	-	-	3.41
Plano (city)	2.72	3.26	-	3.09	-	-	3.28	-	3.17	-	-	-	-	2.61	3.46	-	-	3.78	-	-	3.22	-	-	3.53
Comal County	2.64	2.96	-	-	-	-	-	-	-	-	-	-	-	-	-	-	-	-	-	-	-	-	-	-
Coryell County	2.91	2.06	4.59	-	-	-	-	-	-	-	-	-	-	-	2.18	-	-	-	-	-	-	-	-	-
Dallas County	2.70	2.98	3.18	2.91	2.72	4.14	2.67	-	2.70	-	-	-	-	2.16	2.84	3.76	-	3.41	-	-	2.70	2.34	-	3.38
Addison (town)	1.83	2.15	-	2.36	-	-	-	-	-	-	-	-	-	-	-	-	-	-	-	-	-	-	-	-
Coppell (city)	2.94	3.58	-	3.42	-	-	3.38	-	-	-	-	-	-	-	3.75	-	-	-	-	-	-	-	-	-
Farmers Branch (city)	2.85	2.58	-	-	-	-	-	-	-	-	-	-	-	-	-	-	-	-	-	-	-	-	-	-
Garland (city)	2.93	3.60	-	3.80	-	-	3.37	-	3.01	-	-	-	-	-	3.35	-	-	3.89	-	-	-	-	-	3.69
Grand Prairie (city)	2.91	3.64	-	4.20	-	-	-	-	3.15	-	-	-	-	-	-	4.96	-	-	-	-	-	-	-	3.71
Irving (city)	2.49	2.54	-	2.45	-	-	2.32	-	2.45	-	-	-	-	2.17	2.68	3.45	-	3.05	-	-	-	-	-	2.79
Mesquite (city)	2.82	3.66	-	3.68	-	-	-	-	3.89	-	-	-	-	-	-	-	-	-	-	-	-	-	-	-
Richardson (city)	2.59	3.06	-	2.94	-	-	2.92	-	2.83	-	-	-	-	-	3.41	-	-	3.52	-	-	-	-	-	3.20
Rowlett (city)	3.08	3.95	-	4.33	-	-	-	-	-	-	-	-	-	-	-	-	-	-	-	-	-	-	-	-
Denton County	2.66	3.05	-	3.31	-	5.07	2.25	-	2.78	-	-	-	-	1.99	2.66	-	-	4.37	-	-	-	-	-	3.68
Carrollton (city)	2.77	3.76	-	3.66	-	4.57	2.99	-	-	-	-	-	-	-	3.53	-	-	4.05	-	-	-	-	-	3.92
Lewisville (city)	2.56	3.19	-	3.23	-	-	-	-	-	-	-	-	-	-	-	-	-	-	-	-	-	-	-	4.39
Ector County	2.73	3.39	-	-	-	-	-	-	-	-	-	-	-	-	-	-	-	-	-	-	-	-	-	-
El Paso County	3.18	2.56	4.49	2.60	-	-	2.50	-	2.92	-	-	-	-	1.90	2.62	-	-	-	-	-	-	-	-	-
Ellis County	2.95	4.25	-	-	-	-	-	-	-	-	-	-	-	-	-	-	-	-	-	-	-	-	-	-
Fort Bend County	3.13	3.65	-	3.73	-	-	3.41	-	3.70	-	-	-	-	-	3.76	-	-	4.44	-	-	3.64	-	-	3.59
Cinco Ranch (cdp)	3.33	3.60	-	-	-	-	-	-	-	-	-	-	-	-	-	-	-	-	-	-	-	-	-	-
Mission Bend (cdp)	3.42	3.83	-	3.50	-	-	3.39	-	4.38	-	-	-	-	-	-	-	-	5.26	-	-	-	-	-	3.55
Missouri City (city)	3.08	3.53	-	3.35	-	-	3.84	-	3.57	-	-	-	-	-	-	-	-	-	-	-	-	-	-	2.94
New Territory (cdp)	3.49	3.86	-	4.09	-	-	3.57	-	-	-	-	-	-	-	-	-	-	-	-	-	-	-	-	-
Stafford (city)	2.67	3.39	-	3.63	-	-	2.85	-	3.58	-	-	-	-	-	-	-	-	-	-	-	-	-	-	3.35
Sugar Land (city)	3.06	3.66	-	3.81	-	-	3.46	-	3.68	-	-	-	-	-	3.32	-	-	4.58	-	-	3.72	-	-	3.73
Galveston County	2.59	2.84	-	2.62	-	-	2.34	-	2.91	-	-	-	-	-	-	-	-	-	-	-	-	-	-	3.65
Grayson County	2.51	2.74	-	-	-	-	-	-	-	-	-	-	-	-	-	-	-	-	-	-	-	-	-	-
Gregg County	2.54	2.91	-	-	-	-	-	-	-	-	-	-	-	-	-	-	-	-	-	-	-	-	-	-
Guadalupe County	2.82	2.89	-	-	-	-	-	-	-	-	-	-	-	-	-	-	-	-	-	-	-	-	-	-
Harris County	2.78	3.06	3.30	3.09	3.18	3.60	2.60	-	3.05	3.44	-	-	2.56	2.28	2.69	3.42	-	3.62	-	-	2.55	2.71	-	3.48
Bellaire (city)	2.60	3.44	-	-	-	-	3.49	-	-	-	-	-	-	-	-	-	-	-	-	-	-	-	-	-
Houston (city)	2.67	2.80	3.11	2.78	-	3.33	2.41	-	2.71	3.17	-	-	2.66	2.23	2.49	-	-	3.50	-	-	2.41	2.63	-	3.22
West University Place (city)	2.69	2.70	-	-	-	-	-	-	-	-	-	-	-	-	-	-	-	-	-	-	-	-	-	-
Hays County	2.69	2.64	-	-	-	-	-	-	-	-	-	-	-	-	-	-	-	-	-	-	-	-	-	-
Hidalgo County	3.60	2.91	-	3.11	-	-	-	-	2.98	-	-	-	-	-	-	-	-	-	-	-	-	-	-	-
Hunt County	2.60	2.40	-	-	-	-	-	-	-	-	-	-	-	-	-	-	-	-	-	-	-	-	-	-
Jefferson County	2.55	3.66	-	3.32	-	-	2.87	-	3.23	-	-	-	-	-	-	-	-	-	-	-	-	-	-	4.15

Notes: Please refer to the User's Guide for an explanation of data; data is arranged alphabetically by state, then county, then city within each county; table includes counties with populations greater than 49,999 unless noted and cities with populations greater than 9,999 whose Asian and/or NHPI population rates are greater than the national average; (1) Native Hawaiian and other Pacific Islander; (2) excludes Taiwanese; (3) includes Chamorro; (4) county does not meet population threshold but is shown in order to allow inclusion of city

Place	All households	Asian households	NHPI[1] households	Asian Indian	Bangladeshi	Cambodian	Chinese[2]	Fijian	Filipino	Guamanian[3]	Hawaiian, Native	Hmong	Indonesian	Japanese	Korean	Laotian	Malaysian	Pakistani	Samoan	Sri Lankan	Taiwanese	Thai	Tongan	Vietnamese
Port Arthur (city)	2.61	4.00	-	-	-	-	-	-	-	-	-	-	-	-	-	-	-	-	-	-	-	-	-	4.40
Johnson County	2.85	3.48	-	-	-	-	-	-	-	-	-	-	-	-	-	-	-	-	-	-	-	-	-	-
Kaufman County	2.87	3.51	-	-	-	-	-	-	-	-	-	-	-	-	-	-	-	-	-	-	-	-	-	-
Lubbock County	2.51	2.35	-	2.79	-	-	2.12	-	-	-	-	-	-	-	-	-	-	-	-	-	-	-	-	3.43
McLennan County	2.59	2.28	-	2.79	-	-	-	-	-	-	-	-	-	-	-	-	-	-	-	-	-	-	-	-
Midland County	2.68	3.37	-	3.46	-	-	-	-	-	-	-	-	-	-	-	-	-	-	-	-	-	-	-	-
Montgomery County	2.82	2.99	-	2.75	-	-	3.12	-	3.28	-	-	-	-	-	-	-	-	-	-	-	-	-	-	-
Nacogdoches County	2.48	3.25	-	-	-	-	-	-	-	-	-	-	-	-	-	-	-	-	-	-	-	-	-	-
Nueces County	2.79	3.00	-	3.35	-	-	-	-	3.20	-	-	-	-	-	-	-	-	-	-	-	-	-	-	-
Orange County	2.65	3.44	-	-	-	-	-	-	-	-	-	-	-	-	-	-	-	-	-	-	-	-	-	3.93
Potter County	2.61	3.56	-	-	-	-	-	-	-	-	-	-	-	-	-	4.00	-	-	-	-	-	-	-	3.84
Randall County	2.49	2.22	-	-	-	-	-	-	-	-	-	-	-	-	-	-	-	-	-	-	-	-	-	-
San Patricio County	2.98	2.51	-	-	-	-	-	-	-	-	-	-	-	-	-	-	-	-	-	-	-	-	-	-
Smith County	2.59	3.14	-	-	-	-	-	-	-	-	-	-	-	-	-	-	-	-	-	-	-	-	-	-
Tarrant County	2.67	3.23	3.28	2.86	-	4.36	2.69	-	2.76	-	-	-	-	2.12	2.86	4.12	-	3.52	-	-	2.85	2.27	4.18	3.79
Arlington (city)	2.65	3.26	-	2.85	-	-	2.94	-	2.34	-	-	-	-	-	2.72	-	-	-	-	-	2.68	-	-	3.92
Euless (city)	2.39	3.03	-	2.82	-	-	-	-	-	-	-	-	-	-	-	-	-	-	-	-	-	-	-	-
Haltom City (city)	2.60	3.48	-	-	-	-	-	-	-	-	-	-	-	-	-	4.13	-	-	-	-	-	-	-	3.73
Taylor County	2.54	2.40	-	-	-	-	-	-	2.17	-	-	-	-	-	-	-	-	-	-	-	-	-	-	-
Tom Green County	2.52	2.34	-	-	-	-	-	-	-	-	-	-	-	-	-	-	-	-	-	-	-	-	-	-
Travis County	2.47	2.49	3.10	2.35	-	-	2.18	-	2.53	-	-	-	-	1.98	2.36	-	-	3.18	-	-	2.50	2.53	-	3.34
Austin (city)	2.40	2.39	2.41	2.27	-	-	2.14	-	2.45	-	-	-	-	1.94	2.30	-	-	2.94	-	-	2.44	-	-	3.21
Pflugerville (city)	3.13	3.93	-	-	-	-	-	-	-	-	-	-	-	-	-	-	-	-	-	-	-	-	-	-
Wells Branch (cdp)	2.03	2.86	-	-	-	-	-	-	-	-	-	-	-	-	-	-	-	-	-	-	-	-	-	-
Victoria County	2.75	2.85	-	-	-	-	-	-	-	-	-	-	-	-	-	-	-	-	-	-	-	-	-	-
Webb County	3.75	3.14	-	-	-	-	-	-	-	-	-	-	-	-	-	-	-	-	-	-	-	-	-	-
Wichita County	2.49	2.87	-	-	-	-	-	-	2.96	-	-	-	-	-	-	-	-	-	-	-	-	-	-	3.68
Williamson County	2.82	3.16	-	3.18	-	-	3.15	-	-	-	-	-	-	-	3.05	-	-	-	-	-	-	-	-	3.59
Brushy Creek (cdp)	3.22	3.21	-	-	-	-	-	-	-	-	-	-	-	-	-	-	-	-	-	-	-	-	-	-
Jollyville (cdp)	2.68	3.16	-	-	-	-	-	-	-	-	-	-	-	-	-	-	-	-	-	-	-	-	-	-
UTAH	3.12	3.13	4.73	3.20	-	5.11	2.92	-	3.35	-	3.43	-	-	2.43	2.57	4.37	-	4.75	4.69	-	2.52	2.66	5.57	3.96
Cache County	3.23	2.84	-	-	-	-	2.43	-	-	-	-	-	-	-	-	-	-	-	-	-	-	-	-	-
Davis County	3.31	2.92	4.03	-	-	-	-	-	3.31	-	-	-	-	2.39	3.37	-	-	-	-	-	-	-	-	-
Salt Lake County	2.99	3.22	5.03	3.33	-	5.19	2.95	-	3.53	-	3.01	-	-	2.35	2.37	4.76	-	-	4.84	-	-	-	5.79	3.99
Kearns (cdp)	3.66	4.82	6.62	-	-	-	-	-	-	-	-	-	-	-	-	-	-	-	-	-	-	-	-	-
Salt Lake City (city)	2.47	2.48	5.25	3.16	-	-	2.34	-	2.57	-	-	-	-	1.80	1.91	-	-	-	4.16	-	-	-	6.34	3.09
Sandy (city)	3.42	3.76	6.23	-	-	-	4.15	-	-	-	-	-	-	-	-	-	-	-	-	-	-	-	-	-
Taylorsville (city)	3.12	4.06	4.13	-	-	-	-	-	-	-	-	-	-	-	-	-	-	-	-	-	-	-	-	4.85
West Jordan (city)	3.58	3.78	5.89	-	-	-	-	-	-	-	-	-	-	-	-	-	-	-	-	-	-	-	5.48	-
West Valley City (city)	3.36	4.38	5.48	-	-	5.10	4.69	-	-	-	-	-	-	-	-	4.39	-	-	5.28	-	-	-	6.24	4.63
Utah County	3.58	3.22	4.22	-	-	-	3.28	-	3.30	-	3.65	-	-	3.28	3.43	-	-	-	4.87	-	-	-	4.13	-

Notes: Please refer to the User's Guide for an explanation of data; data is arranged alphabetically by state, then county, then city within each county; table includes counties with populations greater than 49,999 unless noted and cities with populations greater than 9,999 whose Asian and/or NHPI population rates are greater than the national average; (1) Native Hawaiian and other Pacific Islander; (2) excludes Taiwanese; (3) includes Chamorro; (4) county does not meet population threshold but is shown in order to allow inclusion of city

Place	All households	Asian households	NHPI[1] households	Asian Indian	Bangladeshi	Cambodian	Chinese[2]	Fijian	Filipino	Guamanian[3]	Hawaiian, Native	Hmong	Indonesian	Japanese	Korean	Laotian	Malaysian	Pakistani	Samoan	Sri Lankan	Taiwanese	Thai	Tongan	Vietnamese
Orem (city)	3.56	3.01	4.51	-	-	-	-	-	-	-	-	-	-	-	-	-	-	-	-	-	-	-	-	-
Provo (city)	3.34	3.12	3.55	-	-	-	3.28	-	-	-	-	-	-	2.97	-	-	-	-	-	-	-	-	-	-
Washington County	2.97	2.94	5.24	-	-	-	-	-	-	-	-	-	-	-	-	-	-	-	-	-	-	-	-	-
St. George (city)	2.81	2.78	5.23	-	-	-	-	-	-	-	-	-	-	-	-	-	-	-	-	-	-	-	-	-
Weber County	2.95	2.95	-	-	-	-	-	-	-	-	-	-	-	2.45	-	-	-	-	-	-	-	-	-	-
VERMONT	2.44	2.90	-	2.61	-	-	2.99	-	2.74	-	-	-	-	2.50	1.78	-	-	-	-	-	-	-	-	3.84
Chittenden County	2.46	2.92	-	2.47	-	-	3.00	-	-	-	-	-	-	-	-	-	-	-	-	-	-	-	-	3.66
Rutland County	2.39	2.12	-	-	-	-	-	-	-	-	-	-	-	-	-	-	-	-	-	-	-	-	-	-
Washington County	2.36	2.37	-	-	-	-	-	-	-	-	-	-	-	-	-	-	-	-	-	-	-	-	-	-
Windsor County	2.35	3.76	-	-	-	-	-	-	-	-	-	-	-	-	-	-	-	-	-	-	-	-	-	-
VIRGINIA	2.54	3.05	2.93	2.96	3.69	4.29	2.79	-	3.14	3.24	2.49	-	2.62	2.14	2.88	3.82	-	4.17	2.98	2.85	2.38	2.47	-	3.49
Albemarle County	2.43	2.57	-	2.89	-	-	2.49	-	-	-	-	-	-	-	-	-	-	-	-	-	-	-	-	-
Alexandria Independent City	2.04	2.24	-	2.41	-	-	2.25	-	2.21	-	-	-	-	-	1.67	-	-	3.51	-	-	-	-	-	2.14
Arlington County	2.14	2.22	-	2.19	-	3.82	1.89	-	2.41	-	-	-	-	1.54	1.83	-	-	4.12	-	-	-	-	-	2.68
Arlington (cdp)	2.14	2.22	-	2.19	-	3.82	1.89	-	2.41	-	-	-	-	1.54	1.83	-	-	4.12	-	-	-	-	-	2.68
Bedford County	2.52	3.33	-	-	-	-	-	-	-	-	-	-	-	-	-	-	-	-	-	-	-	-	-	-
Charlottesville Independent City	2.27	2.30	-	2.53	-	-	2.16	-	-	-	-	-	-	-	-	-	-	-	-	-	-	-	-	-
Chesapeake Independent City	2.79	3.08	-	-	-	-	-	-	3.26	-	-	-	-	-	-	-	-	-	-	-	-	-	-	-
Chesterfield County	2.73	3.40	-	3.21	-	5.33	3.22	-	2.99	-	-	-	-	-	3.33	-	-	-	-	-	-	-	-	3.85
Fairfax Independent City	2.62	3.24	-	2.98	-	-	3.44	-	-	-	-	-	-	-	3.08	-	-	-	-	-	-	-	-	3.34
Fairfax County	2.73	3.31	3.50	3.17	3.81	4.18	3.03	-	3.28	-	-	-	3.09	2.75	3.13	4.21	-	4.32	-	-	2.83	2.87	-	3.75
Annandale (cdp)	2.74	3.32	-	2.68	-	-	3.22	-	3.14	-	-	-	-	-	2.97	-	-	-	-	-	-	-	-	4.08
Bailey's Crossroads (cdp)	2.66	2.98	-	-	-	-	-	-	-	-	-	-	-	-	-	-	-	4.07	-	-	-	-	-	3.06
Burke (cdp)	2.97	3.60	-	3.75	-	-	3.48	-	3.46	-	-	-	-	-	3.55	-	-	-	-	-	-	-	-	3.86
Centreville (cdp)	2.76	3.32	-	3.44	-	-	3.27	-	3.52	-	-	-	-	-	3.27	-	-	-	-	-	-	-	-	3.12
Chantilly (cdp)	2.74	3.20	-	3.29	-	-	3.32	-	-	-	-	-	-	-	2.69	-	-	-	-	-	-	-	-	3.79
Franconia (cdp)	2.39	3.03	-	2.81	-	-	-	-	2.65	-	-	-	-	-	2.88	-	-	-	-	-	-	-	-	3.18
Groveton (cdp)	2.63	3.07	-	-	-	-	-	-	-	-	-	-	-	-	-	-	-	-	-	-	-	-	-	-
Herndon (town)	3.11	4.13	-	4.03	-	-	-	-	-	-	-	-	-	-	-	-	-	-	-	-	-	-	-	4.59
Hybla Valley (cdp)	2.61	3.12	-	-	-	-	-	-	-	-	-	-	-	-	-	-	-	-	-	-	-	-	-	-
Idylwood (cdp)	2.43	2.80	-	2.67	-	-	2.82	-	-	-	-	-	-	-	-	-	-	-	-	-	-	-	-	3.14
Jefferson (cdp)	2.71	3.23	-	2.77	-	-	2.62	-	3.56	-	-	-	-	-	-	-	-	-	-	-	-	-	-	3.58
Lincolnia (cdp)	3.04	3.70	-	-	-	-	-	-	-	-	-	-	-	-	-	-	-	4.24	-	-	-	-	-	4.67
Lorton (cdp)	2.66	3.34	-	-	-	-	-	-	-	-	-	-	-	-	-	-	-	-	-	-	-	-	-	-
McLean (cdp)	2.70	3.03	-	2.98	-	-	2.98	-	3.61	-	-	-	-	3.28	2.82	-	-	-	-	-	-	-	-	-
Merrifield (cdp)	2.58	3.31	-	3.14	-	-	-	-	-	-	-	-	-	-	3.41	-	-	-	-	-	-	-	-	4.16
Mount Vernon (cdp)	2.70	3.42	-	-	-	-	-	-	-	-	-	-	-	-	2.96	-	-	-	-	-	-	-	-	-
Newington (cdp)	2.95	3.77	-	4.29	-	-	-	-	3.91	-	-	-	-	-	3.72	-	-	-	-	-	-	-	-	-
Oakton (cdp)	2.60	3.03	-	3.07	-	-	2.98	-	-	-	-	-	-	-	2.83	-	-	-	-	-	-	-	-	3.88
Reston (cdp)	2.40	2.72	-	2.60	-	-	2.35	-	3.28	-	-	-	-	-	2.53	-	-	-	-	-	-	-	-	-
Rose Hill (cdp)	2.66	3.46	-	-	-	-	-	-	-	-	-	-	-	-	-	-	-	-	-	-	-	-	-	-

Notes: Please refer to the User's Guide for an explanation of data; data is arranged alphabetically by state, then county, then city within each county; table includes counties with populations greater than 49,999 unless noted and cities with populations greater than 9,999 whose Asian and/or NHPI population rates are greater than the national average; (1) Native Hawaiian and other Pacific Islander; (2) excludes Taiwanese; (3) includes Chamorro; (4) county does not meet population threshold but is shown in order to allow inclusion of city

Place	All households	Asian households	NHPI[1] households	Asian Indian	Bangladeshi	Cambodian	Chinese[2]	Fijian	Filipino	Guamanian[3]	Hawaiian, Native	Hmong	Indonesian	Japanese	Korean	Laotian	Malaysian	Pakistani	Samoan	Sri Lankan	Taiwanese	Thai	Tongan	Vietnamese
Springfield (cdp)	2.86	4.09	-	3.97	-	-	3.49	-	4.50	-	-	-	-	-	3.23	4.41	-	-	-	-	-	-	-	4.23
Tysons Corner (cdp)	2.08	2.57	-	2.52	-	-	2.56	-	-	-	-	-	-	-	2.53	-	-	-	-	-	-	-	-	-
Vienna (town)	2.72	3.59	-	-	-	-	-	-	-	-	-	-	-	-	-	-	-	-	-	-	-	-	-	-
West Springfield (cdp)	2.77	3.92	-	4.69	-	-	3.30	-	-	-	-	-	-	-	3.51	-	-	-	-	-	-	-	-	5.01
Wolf Trap (cdp)	3.03	3.54	-	4.03	-	-	3.33	-	-	-	-	-	-	-	-	-	-	-	-	-	-	-	-	-
Falls Church Independent City	2.31	2.24	-	-	-	-	-	-	-	-	-	-	-	-	-	-	-	-	-	-	-	-	-	-
Fauquier County	2.74	3.46	-	-	-	-	-	-	-	-	-	-	-	-	-	-	-	-	-	-	-	-	-	-
Frederick County	2.64	3.49	-	-	-	-	-	-	-	-	-	-	-	-	-	-	-	-	-	-	-	-	-	-
Hampton Independent City	2.48	2.53	-	-	-	-	-	-	2.48	-	-	-	-	-	-	-	-	-	-	-	-	-	-	3.13
Hanover County	2.71	3.13	-	-	-	-	-	-	-	-	-	-	-	-	-	-	-	-	-	-	-	-	-	-
Henrico County	2.39	2.85	-	2.61	-	5.38	2.77	-	2.39	-	-	-	-	-	2.60	-	-	-	-	-	-	-	-	3.42
Glen Allen (cdp)	2.48	3.06	-	-	-	-	-	-	-	-	-	-	-	-	-	-	-	-	-	-	-	-	-	-
Laurel (cdp)	2.22	2.89	-	-	-	-	-	-	-	-	-	-	-	-	-	-	-	-	-	-	-	-	-	-
Loudoun County	2.82	3.46	-	3.36	-	-	2.87	-	3.46	-	-	-	-	-	3.69	-	-	4.40	-	-	-	-	-	3.82
Lynchburg Independent City	2.31	2.40	-	-	-	-	-	-	-	-	-	-	-	-	-	-	-	-	-	-	-	-	-	-
Manassas Park Indep. City	3.16	3.64	-	-	-	-	-	-	-	-	-	-	-	-	-	-	-	-	-	-	-	-	-	-
Montgomery County	2.40	2.32	-	2.83	-	-	2.22	-	-	-	-	-	-	-	2.56	-	-	-	-	-	-	-	-	-
Blacksburg (town)	2.35	2.34	-	2.81	-	-	2.24	-	-	-	-	-	-	-	2.64	-	-	-	-	-	-	-	-	-
Newport News Independent City	2.50	2.78	-	-	-	-	2.38	-	2.91	-	-	-	-	-	2.52	-	-	-	-	-	-	-	-	3.69
Norfolk Independent City	2.45	2.77	-	2.55	-	-	2.36	-	2.97	-	-	-	-	-	-	-	-	-	-	-	-	-	-	2.88
Portsmouth Independent City	2.51	3.17	-	-	-	-	-	-	3.13	-	-	-	-	-	-	-	-	-	-	-	-	-	-	-
Prince William County	2.94	3.33	-	3.77	-	-	2.84	-	3.07	-	-	-	-	1.97	3.23	-	-	4.47	-	-	-	-	-	3.36
Bull Run (cdp)	2.41	2.53	-	-	-	-	-	-	-	-	-	-	-	-	-	-	-	-	-	-	-	-	-	-
Dale City (cdp)	3.18	4.04	-	4.82	-	-	-	-	4.13	-	-	-	-	-	-	-	-	4.91	-	-	-	-	-	-
Lake Ridge (cdp)	2.74	2.73	-	-	-	-	-	-	-	-	-	-	-	-	-	-	-	-	-	-	-	-	-	-
Woodbridge (cdp)	2.94	3.18	-	-	-	-	-	-	-	-	-	-	-	-	-	-	-	-	-	-	-	-	-	-
Richmond Independent City	2.21	2.06	-	1.84	-	-	-	-	2.42	-	-	-	-	-	-	-	-	-	-	-	-	-	-	-
Roanoke Independent City	2.20	3.06	-	-	-	-	-	-	-	-	-	-	-	-	-	-	-	-	-	-	-	-	-	-
Roanoke County	2.40	2.97	-	-	-	-	-	-	-	-	-	-	-	-	-	-	-	-	-	-	-	-	-	-
Spotsylvania County	2.87	2.93	-	-	-	-	-	-	-	-	-	-	-	-	-	-	-	-	-	-	-	-	-	-
Stafford County	3.02	2.54	-	-	-	-	-	-	2.52	-	-	-	-	-	-	-	-	-	-	-	-	-	-	-
Suffolk Independent City	2.69	2.79	-	-	-	-	-	-	-	-	-	-	-	-	-	-	-	-	-	-	-	-	-	-
Virginia Beach Independent City	2.70	3.40	-	3.00	-	-	3.60	-	3.56	-	-	-	-	2.30	2.40	-	-	-	-	-	-	-	-	3.33
Williamsburg Independent City	2.07	2.78	-	-	-	-	-	-	-	-	-	-	-	-	-	-	-	-	-	-	-	-	-	-
York County	2.80	3.36	-	4.13	-	-	-	-	-	-	-	-	-	-	3.45	-	-	-	-	-	-	-	-	-
WASHINGTON	2.53	2.92	3.44	2.84	-	4.25	2.76	3.53	3.22	3.39	2.77	5.43	2.12	2.09	2.77	4.14	-	3.16	4.08	3.13	3.01	2.39	4.73	3.44
Benton County	2.68	2.65	-	2.54	-	-	2.78	-	-	-	-	-	-	-	2.48	-	-	-	-	-	-	-	-	3.78
Richland (city)	2.49	2.83	-	-	-	-	2.78	-	-	-	-	-	-	-	-	-	-	-	-	-	-	-	-	-
Chelan County	2.63	2.49	-	-	-	-	-	-	-	-	-	-	-	-	-	-	-	-	-	-	-	-	-	-
Clallam County	2.30	2.60	-	-	-	-	-	-	-	-	-	-	-	-	-	-	-	-	-	-	-	-	-	-
Clark County	2.69	3.04	3.68	3.24	-	3.26	2.79	-	3.10	-	-	-	-	2.40	2.69	3.94	-	-	-	-	-	-	-	3.65

Notes: Please refer to the User's Guide for an explanation of data; data is arranged alphabetically by state, then county, then city within each county; table includes counties with populations greater than 49,999 unless noted and cities with populations greater than 9,999 whose Asian and/or NHPI population rates are greater than the national average; (1) Native Hawaiian and other Pacific Islander; (2) excludes Taiwanese; (3) includes Chamorro; (4) county does not meet population threshold but is shown in order to allow inclusion of city

Place	All households	Asian households	NHPI[1] households	Asian Indian	Bangladeshi	Cambodian	Chinese[2]	Fijian	Filipino	Guamanian[3]	Hawaiian, Native	Hmong	Indonesian	Japanese	Korean	Laotian	Malaysian	Pakistani	Samoan	Sri Lankan	Taiwanese	Thai	Tongan	Vietnamese
Five Corners (cdp)	2.95	4.39	-	-	-	-	-	-	-	-	-	-	-	-	-	-	-	-	-	-	-	-	-	-
Orchards (cdp)	3.02	3.88	-	-	-	-	-	-	-	-	-	-	-	-	-	-	-	-	-	-	-	-	-	-
Vancouver (city)	2.49	2.81	3.88	-	-	-	2.61	-	2.80	-	-	-	-	2.32	2.50	-	-	-	-	-	-	-	-	3.36
Cowlitz County	2.55	3.53	-	-	-	5.11	-	-	-	-	-	-	-	-	-	-	-	-	-	-	-	-	-	3.10
Grant County	2.92	2.13	-	-	-	-	-	-	-	-	-	-	-	-	-	-	-	-	-	-	-	-	-	-
Grays Harbor County	2.48	2.55	-	-	-	-	-	-	-	-	-	-	-	-	-	-	-	-	-	-	-	-	-	-
Island County	2.52	2.81	-	-	-	-	-	-	3.08	-	-	-	-	2.03	-	-	-	-	-	-	-	-	-	-
Oak Harbor (city)	2.69	3.20	-	-	-	-	-	-	3.29	-	-	-	-	-	-	-	-	-	-	-	-	-	-	-
King County	2.39	2.87	3.47	2.66	-	4.05	2.78	3.52	3.21	2.62	2.64	5.44	1.92	2.09	2.72	4.20	-	2.88	4.17	-	2.98	2.25	4.34	3.49
Auburn (city)	2.47	3.42	-	-	-	-	-	-	-	-	-	-	-	-	-	-	-	-	-	-	-	-	-	-
Bellevue (city)	2.37	2.69	-	2.21	-	-	2.73	-	2.72	-	-	-	-	2.31	3.09	4.34	-	-	-	-	3.38	-	-	3.23
Bothell (city)	2.50	3.22	-	-	-	-	2.65	-	-	-	-	-	-	-	-	-	-	-	-	-	-	-	-	-
Bryn Mawr-Skyway (cdp)	2.47	3.30	-	-	-	-	-	-	3.36	-	-	-	-	2.86	-	-	-	-	-	-	-	-	-	3.74
Burien (city)	2.36	3.37	-	-	-	-	-	-	3.90	-	-	-	-	-	-	-	-	-	-	-	-	-	-	3.71
Cascade-Fairwood (cdp)	2.66	3.12	-	-	-	-	3.06	-	3.20	-	-	-	-	2.33	-	-	-	-	-	-	-	-	-	3.85
Cottage Lake (cdp)	3.10	3.26	-	-	-	-	-	-	-	-	-	-	-	-	-	-	-	-	-	-	-	-	-	-
Des Moines (city)	2.49	3.03	3.84	-	-	-	-	-	3.12	-	-	-	-	-	-	-	-	-	-	-	-	-	-	3.65
East Hill-Meridian (cdp)	2.97	3.32	-	3.34	-	-	3.17	-	4.27	-	-	-	-	-	-	-	-	-	-	-	-	-	-	2.92
Federal Way (city)	2.63	3.02	3.81	-	-	-	2.79	-	3.20	-	-	-	-	2.09	3.05	-	-	-	4.04	-	-	-	-	3.42
Inglewood-Finn Hill (cdp)	2.73	2.93	-	-	-	-	2.76	-	-	-	-	-	-	-	-	-	-	-	-	-	-	-	-	-
Issaquah (city)	2.26	2.59	-	-	-	-	-	-	-	-	-	-	-	-	-	-	-	-	-	-	-	-	-	-
Kenmore (city)	2.51	2.80	-	-	-	-	-	-	-	-	-	-	-	-	-	-	-	-	-	-	-	-	-	-
Kent (city)	2.53	3.32	-	3.59	-	-	2.77	-	3.46	-	-	-	-	2.13	3.63	-	-	-	-	-	-	-	-	3.90
Kingsgate (cdp)	2.74	3.53	-	-	-	-	2.91	-	-	-	-	-	-	-	-	-	-	-	-	-	-	-	-	-
Kirkland (city)	2.14	2.51	-	-	-	-	2.53	-	-	-	-	-	-	2.14	-	-	-	-	-	-	-	-	-	3.72
Lake Forest Park (city)	2.58	3.01	-	-	-	-	-	-	-	-	-	-	-	-	-	-	-	-	-	-	-	-	-	-
Lakeland North (cdp)	3.02	3.65	-	-	-	-	-	-	-	-	-	-	-	-	-	-	-	-	-	-	-	-	-	-
Lakeland South (cdp)	2.74	3.01	-	-	-	-	-	-	-	-	-	-	-	-	-	-	-	-	-	-	-	-	-	-
Lea Hill (cdp)	2.96	4.25	-	-	-	-	-	-	-	-	-	-	-	-	-	-	-	-	-	-	-	-	-	-
Mercer Island (city)	2.58	3.06	-	-	-	-	3.16	-	-	-	-	-	-	2.72	-	-	-	-	-	-	-	-	-	-
Redmond (city)	2.32	2.55	-	2.20	-	-	2.53	-	-	-	-	-	-	2.51	2.75	-	-	-	-	-	-	-	-	-
Renton (city)	2.29	2.83	-	-	-	-	2.75	-	3.03	-	-	-	-	1.97	-	-	-	-	-	-	-	-	-	3.48
Riverton-Boulevard Park (cdp)	2.53	3.21	-	-	-	-	-	-	-	-	-	-	-	-	-	-	-	-	-	-	-	-	-	-
Sammamish (city)	3.05	2.92	-	-	-	-	3.24	-	-	-	-	-	-	-	-	-	-	-	-	-	-	-	-	-
SeaTac (city)	2.52	3.38	3.86	3.26	-	-	-	-	3.40	-	-	-	-	-	-	-	-	-	-	-	-	-	-	5.39
Seattle (city)	2.08	2.65	3.20	2.23	-	3.98	2.61	-	3.15	-	-	-	1.87	1.78	1.99	4.23	-	-	4.80	-	2.48	2.13	-	3.33
Shoreline (city)	2.49	3.36	-	3.41	-	-	3.76	-	3.40	-	-	-	-	2.48	3.03	-	-	-	-	-	-	-	-	3.62
Tukwila (city)	2.39	2.67	4.29	-	-	-	-	-	3.29	-	-	-	-	-	-	-	-	-	-	-	-	-	-	-
Union Hill-Novelty Hill (cdp)	3.15	3.25	-	-	-	-	-	-	-	-	-	-	-	-	-	-	-	-	-	-	-	-	-	-
White Center (cdp)	2.75	4.01	-	-	-	4.53	-	-	3.76	-	-	-	-	-	-	-	-	-	-	-	-	-	-	3.86
Kitsap County	2.60	3.00	2.95	-	-	-	2.40	-	3.19	3.44	-	-	-	2.16	2.61	-	-	-	-	-	-	-	-	2.94

Notes: Please refer to the User's Guide for an explanation of data; data is arranged alphabetically by state, then county, then city within each county; table includes counties with populations greater than 49,999 unless noted and cities with populations greater than 9,999 whose Asian and/or NHPI population rates are greater than the national average; (1) Native Hawaiian and other Pacific Islander; (2) excludes Taiwanese; (3) includes Chamorro; (4) county does not meet population threshold but is shown in order to allow inclusion of city

Place	All households	Asian households	NHPI[1] households	Asian Indian	Bangladeshi	Cambodian	Chinese[2]	Fijian	Filipino	Guamanian[3]	Hawaiian, Native	Hmong	Indonesian	Japanese	Korean	Laotian	Malaysian	Pakistani	Samoan	Sri Lankan	Taiwanese	Thai	Tongan	Vietnamese
Bremerton (city)	2.29	2.71	-	-	-	-	-	-	2.77	-	-	-	-	-	-	-	-	-	-	-	-	-	-	-
Silverdale (cdp)	2.64	3.72	-	-	-	-	-	-	3.86	-	-	-	-	-	-	-	-	-	-	-	-	-	-	-
Lewis County	2.56	3.07	-	-	-	-	-	-	-	-	-	-	-	-	-	-	-	-	-	-	-	-	-	-
Pierce County	2.60	2.97	3.64	3.34	-	4.67	2.58	-	3.27	3.82	2.64	-	-	2.04	2.68	3.64	-	-	4.25	-	-	2.98	-	3.43
Elk Plain (cdp)	3.08	3.77	-	-	-	-	-	-	-	-	-	-	-	-	-	-	-	-	-	-	-	-	-	-
Fort Lewis (cdp)	3.74	3.88	4.63	-	-	-	-	-	3.99	-	-	-	-	-	-	-	-	-	-	-	-	-	-	-
Lakewood (city)	2.38	2.60	3.55	-	-	-	-	-	3.02	-	-	-	-	1.82	2.48	-	-	-	4.62	-	-	-	-	-
Parkland (cdp)	2.54	2.59	3.33	-	-	-	-	-	-	-	-	-	-	-	2.41	-	-	-	-	-	-	-	-	-
Spanaway (cdp)	2.83	3.41	5.17	-	-	-	-	-	3.99	-	-	-	-	-	3.83	-	-	-	-	-	-	-	-	-
Tacoma (city)	2.45	3.13	3.28	-	-	4.70	2.42	-	3.25	3.41	-	-	-	1.80	2.52	3.70	-	-	4.18	-	-	-	-	3.57
University Place (city)	2.46	2.93	-	-	-	-	-	-	-	-	-	-	-	-	3.00	-	-	-	-	-	-	-	-	-
Skagit County	2.61	2.85	-	-	-	-	-	-	3.40	-	-	-	-	-	-	-	-	-	-	-	-	-	-	-
Snohomish County	2.65	3.30	3.10	3.37	-	4.33	2.96	-	3.50	-	3.32	-	-	2.44	3.33	4.43	-	3.69	-	-	-	-	-	3.37
Alderwood Manor (cdp)	2.74	3.57	-	-	-	-	-	-	-	-	-	-	-	-	-	-	-	-	-	-	-	-	-	-
Edmonds (city)	2.32	2.64	-	-	-	-	-	-	2.84	-	-	-	-	-	2.67	-	-	-	-	-	-	-	-	-
Everett (city)	2.40	3.21	-	3.05	-	3.73	-	-	3.58	-	-	-	-	-	-	-	-	-	-	-	-	-	-	3.28
Lynnwood (city)	2.50	3.45	-	-	-	-	3.06	-	3.67	-	-	-	-	-	3.66	-	-	-	-	-	-	-	-	3.24
Martha Lake (cdp)	2.75	3.91	-	-	-	-	-	-	-	-	-	-	-	-	-	-	-	-	-	-	-	-	-	-
Marysville (city)	2.67	3.00	-	-	-	-	-	-	-	-	-	-	-	-	-	-	-	-	-	-	-	-	-	-
Mill Creek (city)	2.45	3.37	-	-	-	-	-	-	-	-	-	-	-	-	3.60	-	-	-	-	-	-	-	-	-
Mountlake Terrace (city)	2.55	3.52	-	-	-	-	-	-	4.30	-	-	-	-	-	3.09	-	-	-	-	-	-	-	-	-
Mukilteo (city)	2.67	3.70	-	-	-	-	-	-	-	-	-	-	-	-	4.32	-	-	-	-	-	-	-	-	-
North Creek (cdp)	2.83	2.89	-	-	-	-	-	-	-	-	-	-	-	-	-	-	-	-	-	-	-	-	-	-
Paine Field-Lk. Stickney (cdp)	2.39	2.92	-	-	-	-	-	-	-	-	-	-	-	-	-	-	-	-	-	-	-	-	-	-
Picnic Pt.-N. Lynnwood (cdp)	2.62	3.00	-	-	-	-	-	-	3.21	-	-	-	-	-	3.32	-	-	-	-	-	-	-	-	-
Seattle Hill-Silver Firs (cdp)	3.04	3.61	-	-	-	-	-	-	4.45	-	-	-	-	-	3.17	-	-	-	-	-	-	-	-	3.27
Spokane County	2.46	2.65	2.95	2.70	-	-	2.49	-	2.81	-	-	5.27	-	1.81	1.66	-	-	-	-	-	-	-	-	3.53
Spokane (city)	2.32	2.62	3.10	-	-	-	2.35	-	2.72	-	-	5.78	-	1.84	1.65	-	-	-	-	-	-	-	-	3.36
Thurston County	2.50	3.10	4.20	2.87	-	4.21	2.75	-	3.49	4.43	-	-	-	2.17	2.79	-	-	-	-	-	-	-	-	3.20
Lacey (city)	2.48	3.44	-	-	-	-	-	-	4.18	-	-	-	-	-	2.72	-	-	-	-	-	-	-	-	3.48
Olympia (city)	2.20	2.56	-	-	-	-	-	-	-	-	-	-	-	-	-	-	-	-	-	-	-	-	-	2.88
Tumwater (city)	2.22	2.47	-	-	-	-	-	-	-	-	-	-	-	-	-	-	-	-	-	-	-	-	-	-
Walla Walla County	2.54	2.54	-	-	-	-	-	-	-	-	-	-	-	-	-	-	-	-	-	-	-	-	-	-
Whatcom County	2.51	2.95	-	4.06	-	-	2.26	-	3.12	-	-	-	-	1.70	2.56	-	-	-	-	-	-	-	-	3.01
Bellingham (city)	2.22	2.62	-	3.91	-	-	-	-	-	-	-	-	-	-	-	-	-	-	-	-	-	-	-	3.17
Whitman County[4]	2.31	2.06	-	-	-	-	2.25	-	-	-	-	-	-	1.50	-	-	-	-	-	-	-	-	-	-
Pullman (city)	2.23	1.93	-	-	-	-	2.07	-	-	-	-	-	-	1.46	-	-	-	-	-	-	-	-	-	-
Yakima County	2.96	2.80	-	-	-	-	-	-	2.95	-	-	-	-	-	-	-	-	-	-	-	-	-	-	-
WEST VIRGINIA	2.39	2.55	4.73	2.66	-	-	2.90	-	2.63	-	-	-	-	1.73	1.94	-	-	2.55	-	-	-	-	-	3.09
Cabell County	2.26	2.12	-	-	-	-	-	-	-	-	-	-	-	-	-	-	-	-	-	-	-	-	-	-
Harrison County	2.42	1.77	-	-	-	-	-	-	-	-	-	-	-	-	-	-	-	-	-	-	-	-	-	-

Notes: Please refer to the User's Guide for an explanation of data; data is arranged alphabetically by state, then county, then city within each county; table includes counties with populations greater than 49,999 unless noted and cities with populations greater than 9,999 whose Asian and/or NHPI population rates are greater than the national average; (1) Native Hawaiian and other Pacific Islander; (2) excludes Taiwanese; (3) includes Chamorro; (4) county does not meet population threshold but is shown in order to allow inclusion of city

Place	All households	Asian households	NHPI[1] households	Asian Indian	Bangladeshi	Cambodian	Chinese[2]	Fijian	Filipino	Guamanian[3]	Hawaiian, Native	Hmong	Indonesian	Japanese	Korean	Laotian	Malaysian	Pakistani	Samoan	Sri Lankan	Taiwanese	Thai	Tongan	Vietnamese
Kanawha County	2.28	2.87	-	2.74	-	-	-	-	-	-	-	-	-	-	-	-	-	-	-	-	-	-	-	-
Monongalia County	2.28	2.41	-	2.34	-	-	2.55	-	-	-	-	-	-	-	-	-	-	-	-	-	-	-	-	-
Putnam County	2.56	3.37	-	-	-	-	-	-	-	-	-	-	-	-	-	-	-	-	-	-	-	-	-	-
Raleigh County	2.37	3.36	-	-	-	-	-	-	-	-	-	-	-	-	-	-	-	-	-	-	-	-	-	-
Wood County	2.39	2.33	-	-	-	-	-	-	-	-	-	-	-	-	-	-	-	-	-	-	-	-	-	-
WISCONSIN	2.50	3.49	3.01	2.74	-	3.19	2.50	-	2.72	2.99	2.53	5.86	1.65	1.91	2.37	4.57	-	2.81	-	-	1.91	1.80	-	3.00
Brown County	2.51	4.47	-	2.57	-	-	-	-	-	-	-	5.22	-	-	-	6.01	-	-	-	-	-	-	-	-
Chippewa County	2.53	5.29	-	-	-	-	-	-	-	-	-	6.59	-	-	-	-	-	-	-	-	-	-	-	-
Columbia County	2.49	2.96	-	-	-	-	-	-	-	-	-	-	-	-	-	-	-	-	-	-	-	-	-	-
Dane County	2.36	2.51	-	2.35	-	-	2.20	-	2.78	-	-	4.76	-	1.79	2.18	3.79	-	-	-	-	1.75	-	-	3.12
Madison (city)	2.18	2.41	-	2.10	-	-	2.17	-	2.92	-	-	4.81	-	1.71	2.20	-	-	-	-	-	1.75	-	-	3.02
Dodge County	2.55	2.35	-	-	-	-	-	-	-	-	-	-	-	-	-	-	-	-	-	-	-	-	-	-
Eau Claire County	2.45	5.09	-	-	-	-	-	-	-	-	-	6.59	-	-	-	-	-	-	-	-	-	-	-	-
Fond du Lac County	2.52	3.28	-	-	-	-	-	-	-	-	-	5.32	-	-	-	-	-	-	-	-	-	-	-	-
Jefferson County	2.55	3.54	-	-	-	-	-	-	-	-	-	-	-	-	-	-	-	-	-	-	-	-	-	-
Kenosha County	2.59	2.81	-	-	-	-	-	-	-	-	-	-	-	-	-	-	-	-	-	-	-	-	-	-
La Crosse County	2.44	5.15	-	-	-	-	-	-	-	-	-	6.87	-	-	-	-	-	-	-	-	-	-	-	-
La Crosse (city)	2.23	5.10	-	-	-	-	-	-	-	-	-	7.03	-	-	-	-	-	-	-	-	-	-	-	-
Manitowoc County	2.49	5.16	-	-	-	-	-	-	-	-	-	6.02	-	-	-	-	-	-	-	-	-	-	-	-
Marathon County	2.60	5.98	-	-	-	-	-	-	-	-	-	6.58	-	-	-	-	-	-	-	-	-	-	-	-
Wausau (city)	2.36	5.93	-	-	-	-	-	-	-	-	-	6.49	-	-	-	-	-	-	-	-	-	-	-	-
Milwaukee County	2.42	3.30	2.56	2.67	-	-	2.22	-	2.78	-	-	6.02	-	2.01	2.04	4.10	-	2.54	-	-	-	-	-	2.73
Outagamie County	2.60	4.68	-	3.63	-	-	-	-	-	-	-	5.59	-	-	-	-	-	-	-	-	-	-	-	-
Appleton (city)	2.52	5.24	-	-	-	-	-	-	-	-	-	6.13	-	-	-	-	-	-	-	-	-	-	-	-
Ozaukee County	2.61	3.49	-	-	-	-	-	-	-	-	-	-	-	-	-	-	-	-	-	-	-	-	-	-
Portage County	2.53	5.65	-	-	-	-	-	-	-	-	-	7.06	-	-	-	-	-	-	-	-	-	-	-	-
Stevens Point (city)	2.29	5.57	-	-	-	-	-	-	-	-	-	6.73	-	-	-	-	-	-	-	-	-	-	-	-
Racine County	2.59	2.54	-	-	-	-	-	-	-	-	-	-	-	-	-	-	-	-	-	-	-	-	-	-
Rock County	2.54	2.53	-	-	-	-	-	-	-	-	-	-	-	-	-	-	-	-	-	-	-	-	-	-
St. Croix County	2.66	3.01	-	-	-	-	-	-	-	-	-	-	-	-	-	-	-	-	-	-	-	-	-	-
Sauk County	2.51	3.61	-	-	-	-	-	-	-	-	-	-	-	-	-	-	-	-	-	-	-	-	-	-
Sheboygan County	2.50	5.14	-	-	-	-	-	-	-	-	-	5.61	-	-	-	-	-	-	-	-	-	-	-	-
Sheboygan (city)	2.38	5.27	-	-	-	-	-	-	-	-	-	5.58	-	-	-	-	-	-	-	-	-	-	-	-
Walworth County	2.57	2.17	-	-	-	-	-	-	-	-	-	-	-	-	-	-	-	-	-	-	-	-	-	-
Washington County	2.65	4.69	-	-	-	-	-	-	-	-	-	-	-	-	-	-	-	-	-	-	-	-	-	-
Waukesha County	2.62	2.99	-	3.08	-	-	3.12	-	2.59	-	-	-	-	-	3.07	-	-	-	-	-	-	-	-	-
Winnebago County	2.43	4.19	-	-	-	-	-	-	-	-	-	5.89	-	-	-	-	-	-	-	-	-	-	-	-
Wood County	2.47	5.06	-	-	-	-	-	-	-	-	-	6.86	-	-	-	-	-	-	-	-	-	-	-	-
WYOMING	2.47	2.55	-	2.79	-	-	3.39	-	2.85	-	-	-	-	1.79	2.32	-	-	-	-	-	-	-	-	-
Laramie County	2.44	2.26	-	-	-	-	-	-	-	-	-	-	-	-	-	-	-	-	-	-	-	-	-	-
Natrona County	2.42	2.47	-	-	-	-	-	-	-	-	-	-	-	-	-	-	-	-	-	-	-	-	-	-

Notes: Please refer to the User's Guide for an explanation of data; data is arranged alphabetically by state, then county, then city within each county; table includes counties with populations greater than 49,999 unless noted and cities with populations greater than 9,999 whose Asian and/or NHPI population rates are greater than the national average; (1) Native Hawaiian and other Pacific Islander; (2) excludes Taiwanese; (3) includes Chamorro; (4) county does not meet population threshold but is shown in order to allow inclusion of city

Language Spoken at Home: English Only

(Universe: Population 5 Years and Over)

Place	Total population 5 years and over who speak English-only at home	Asian population 5 years and over	Asians 5 years and over who speak English-only at home	NHPI[1] population 5 years and over	NHPIs[1] 5 years and over who speak English-only at home	Asian Indian	Bangladeshi	Cambodian	Chinese[2]	Fijian	Filipino	Guamanian[3]	Hawaiian, Native	Hmong	Indonesian	Japanese	Korean	Laotian	Malaysian	Pakistani	Samoan	Sri Lankan	Taiwanese	Thai	Tongan	Vietnamese
UNITED STATES	215,423,557 82.11	9,520,205	2,003,642 21.05 21.05 0.93	347,400	195,395 56.24 56.24 0.09	292,374 19.30 14.59 3.07 0.14	1,536 4.09 0.08 0.02 <0.01	13,874 8.43 0.69 0.15 0.01	322,586 14.95 16.10 3.39 0.15	1,565 16.31 0.80 0.45 <0.01	517,234 29.31 25.81 5.43 0.24	28,796 56.44 14.74 8.29 0.01	108,611 83.03 55.59 31.26 0.05	6,566 4.39 0.33 0.07 <0.01	5,855 16.71 0.29 0.06 <0.01	405,791 52.73 20.25 4.26 0.19	183,215 18.06 9.14 1.92 0.09	11,151 7.18 0.56 0.12 0.01	1,960 19.18 0.10 0.02 <0.01	10,887 7.73 0.54 0.11 0.01	27,622 35.88 14.14 7.95 0.01	4,553 25.34 0.23 0.05 <0.01	9,368 7.99 0.47 0.10 <0.01	20,712 19.23 1.03 0.22 0.01	4,175 17.04 2.14 1.20 <0.01	71,438 6.94 3.57 0.75 0.03
ALABAMA	3,989,795 96.09	27,708	5,650 20.39 20.39 0.14	1,112	667 59.98 59.98 0.02	1,157 18.91 20.48 4.18 0.03	-	54 10.74 0.96 0.19 <0.01	633 12.55 11.20 2.28 0.02	-	909 38.83 16.09 3.28 0.02	173 47.27 25.94 15.56 <0.01	-	-	-	525 29.02 9.29 1.89 0.01	1,115 29.06 19.73 4.02 0.03	68 8.85 1.20 0.25 <0.01	-	42 12.00 0.74 0.15 <0.01	-	-	-	152 25.85 2.69 0.55 <0.01	-	404 9.27 7.15 1.46 0.01
Baldwin County	126,636 96.04	489	161 32.92 32.92 0.13	-	-	-	-	-	-	-	-	-	-	-	-	-	-	-	-	-	-	-	-	-	-	-
Calhoun County	101,661 96.53	622	160 25.72 25.72 0.16	-	-	-	-	-	-	-	-	-	-	-	-	-	-	-	-	-	-	-	-	-	-	-
Etowah County	93,845 96.97	344	191 55.52 55.52 0.20	-	-	-	-	-	-	-	-	-	-	-	-	-	-	-	-	-	-	-	-	-	-	-
Houston County	80,378 97.04	461	49 10.63 10.63 0.06	-	-	-	-	-	-	-	-	-	-	-	-	-	-	-	-	-	-	-	-	-	-	-
Jefferson County	590,312 95.37	5,317	1,038 19.52 19.52 0.18	-	-	219 16.79 21.10 4.12 0.04	-	-	167 10.23 16.09 3.14 0.03	-	-	-	-	-	-	-	192 43.15 18.50 3.61 0.03	-	-	-	-	-	-	-	-	65 8.05 6.26 1.22 0.01
Lee County	102,448 94.89	1,742	235 13.49 13.49 0.23	-	-	-	-	-	39 6.67 16.60 2.24 0.04	-	-	-	-	-	-	-	-	-	-	-	-	-	-	-	-	-
Madison County	243,863 94.52	4,350	1,081 24.85 24.85 0.44	-	-	290 21.17 26.83 6.67 0.12	-	-	119 19.90 11.01 2.74 0.05	-	-	-	-	-	-	-	280 30.63 25.90 6.44 0.11	-	-	-	-	-	-	-	-	52 14.29 4.81 1.20 0.02

Notes: Please refer to the User's Guide for an explanation of data; data is arranged alphabetically by state, then county, then city within each county; table includes counties with populations greater than 49,999 unless noted and cities with populations greater than 9,999 whose Asian and/or NHPI population rates are greater than the national average; (1) Native Hawaiian and other Pacific Islander; (2) excludes Taiwanese; (3) includes Chamorro; (4) county does not meet population threshold but is shown in order to allow inclusion of city

Place	Total population 5 years and over who speak English-only at home	Asian population 5 years and over	Asians 5 years and over who speak English-only at home	NHPI[1] population 5 years and over	NHPIs[1] 5 years and over who speak English-only at home	Asian Indian	Bangladeshi	Cambodian	Chinese[2]	Fijian	Filipino	Guamanian[3]	Hawaiian, Native	Hmong	Indonesian	Japanese	Korean	Laotian	Malaysian	Pakistani	Samoan	Sri Lankan	Taiwanese	Thai	Tongan	Vietnamese
Mobile County	353,594 95.42	4,798	555 11.57 11.57 0.16	-	-	37 6.98 6.67 0.77 0.01	-	21 6.42 3.78 0.44 0.01	54 8.78 9.73 1.13 0.02	-	159 45.43 28.65 3.31 0.04	-	-	-	-	-	-	61 21.63 10.99 1.27 0.02	-	-	-	-	-	-	-	122 6.30 21.98 2.54 0.03
Montgomery County	199,832 96.00	1,695	308 18.17 18.17 0.15	-	-	-	-	-	-	-	-	-	-	-	-	-	-	-	-	-	-	-	-	-	-	-
Morgan County	99,165 95.61	516	75 14.53 14.53 0.08	-	-	-	-	-	-	-	-	-	-	-	-	-	-	-	-	-	-	-	-	-	-	-
Shelby County	126,979 95.80	901	320 35.52 35.52 0.25	-	-	104 27.51 32.50 11.54 0.08	-	-	-	-	-	-	-	-	-	-	-	-	-	-	-	-	-	-	-	-
Tuscaloosa County	147,682 95.58	1,507	207 13.74 13.74 0.14	-	-	-	-	-	-	-	-	-	-	-	-	-	-	-	-	-	-	-	-	-	-	-
ALASKA	496,982 85.72	23,825	5,530 23.21 23.21 1.11	2,741	1,110 40.50 40.50 0.22	206 41.28 3.73 0.86 0.04	-	-	320 23.39 5.79 1.34 0.06	-	2,667 22.70 48.23 11.19 0.54	-	356 77.56 32.07 12.99 0.07	15 3.30 0.27 0.06 <0.01	-	817 58.15 14.77 3.43 0.16	678 15.69 12.26 2.85 0.14	76 6.07 1.37 0.32 0.02	-	-	370 27.86 33.33 13.50 0.07	-	-	163 23.02 2.95 0.68 0.03	42 12.00 3.78 1.53 0.01	165 18.19 2.98 0.69 0.03
Anchorage Borough	207,818 86.37	13,215	2,931 22.18 22.18 1.41	1,781	696 39.08 39.08 0.33	119 40.75 4.06 0.90 0.06	-	-	188 26.22 6.41 1.42 0.09	-	1,233 26.04 42.07 9.33 0.59	-	-	15 3.30 0.51 0.11 0.01	-	466 53.69 15.90 3.53 0.22	377 11.55 12.86 2.85 0.18	69 6.00 2.35 0.52 0.03	-	-	297 28.59 42.67 16.68 0.14	-	-	103 20.44 3.51 0.78 0.05	-	135 30.07 4.61 1.02 0.06
Fairbanks North Star Borough	70,244 92.18	1,911	569 29.77 29.77 0.81	-	-	-	-	-	44 13.21 7.73 2.30 0.06	-	175 31.93 30.76 9.16 0.25	-	-	-	-	-	143 27.39 25.13 7.48 0.20	-	-	-	-	-	-	-	-	-
Juneau City and Borough	25,983 90.50	1,294	344 26.58 26.58 1.32	-	-	-	-	-	-	-	204 21.34 59.30 15.77 0.79	-	-	-	-	-	-	-	-	-	-	-	-	-	-	-
Matanuska-Susitna Borough	52,357 94.90	368	195 52.99 52.99 0.37	-	-	-	-	-	-	-	-	-	-	-	-	-	-	-	-	-	-	-	-	-	-	-

Notes: Please refer to the User's Guide for an explanation of data; data is arranged alphabetically by state, then county, then city within each county; table includes counties with populations greater than 49,999 unless noted and cities with populations greater than 9,999 whose Asian and/or NHPI population rates are greater than the national average; (1) Native Hawaiian and other Pacific Islander; (2) excludes Taiwanese; (3) includes Chamorro; (4) county does not meet population threshold but is shown in order to allow inclusion of city

Place	Total population 5 years and over who speak English-only at home	Asian population 5 years and over	Asians 5 years and over who speak English-only at home	NHPI[1] population 5 years and over	NHPIs[1] 5 years and over who speak English-only at home	Asian Indian	Bangladeshi	Cambodian	Chinese[2]	Fijian	Filipino	Guamanian[3]	Hawaiian, Native	Hmong	Indonesian	Japanese	Korean	Laotian	Malaysian	Pakistani	Samoan	Sri Lankan	Taiwanese	Thai	Tongan	Vietnamese
ARIZONA	3,523,487	85,047	22,474	5,668	3,251	2,617	-	194	4,022	-	5,792	858	1,360	-	116	3,481	2,772	168	-	65	366	-	107	529	142	1,025
	74.14		26.43		57.36	19.51		17.77	20.46		37.90	73.71	73.51		21.76	48.57	29.66	19.88		10.45	45.98		14.02	33.31	23.36	9.55
						11.64		0.86	17.90		25.77	26.39	41.83		0.52	15.49	12.33	0.75		0.29	11.26		0.48	2.35	4.37	4.56
			26.43		57.36	3.08		0.23	4.73		6.81	15.14	23.99		0.14	4.09	3.26	0.20		0.08	6.46		0.13	0.62	2.51	1.21
			0.64		0.09	0.07		0.01	0.11		0.16	0.02	0.04		<0.01	0.10	0.08	<0.01		<0.01	0.01		<0.01	0.02	<0.01	0.03
Cochise County	77,529	1,935	648	-	-	-	-	-	-	-	177	-	-	-	-	-	192	-	-	-	-	-	-	-	-	-
	70.45		33.49								41.75						25.03									
											27.31						29.63									
			33.49								9.15						9.92									
			0.84								0.23						0.25									
Coconino County	77,374	879	257	-	-	-	-	-	-	-	-	-	-	-	-	-	-	-	-	-	-	-	-	-	-	-
	71.79		29.24																							
			29.24																							
			0.33																							
Maricopa County	2,148,696	61,506	15,583	3,507	1,773	1,960	-	169	2,691	-	4,045	440	774	-	81	2,424	1,712	116	-	62	172	-	68	329	41	758
	75.85		25.34		50.56	18.89		16.17	18.59		36.25	72.85	72.27		20.51	51.86	30.30	20.07		13.00	33.66		11.13	29.56	8.18	9.34
						12.58		1.08	17.27		25.96	24.82	43.65		0.52	15.56	10.99	0.74		0.40	9.70		0.44	2.11	2.31	4.86
			25.34		50.56	3.19		0.27	4.38		6.58	12.55	22.07		0.13	3.94	2.78	0.19		0.10	4.90		0.11	0.53	1.17	1.23
			0.73		0.08	0.09		0.01	0.13		0.19	0.02	0.04		<0.01	0.11	0.08	0.01		<0.01	0.01		<0.01	0.02	<0.01	0.04
Chandler (city)	125,190	6,776	1,396	-	-	193	-	-	263	-	437	-	-	-	-	-	-	-	-	-	-	-	-	-	-	86
	77.98		20.60			14.38			14.33		39.80															9.72
						13.83			18.84		31.30															6.16
			20.60			2.85			3.88		6.45															1.27
			1.12			0.15			0.21		0.35															0.07
Gilbert (town)	86,140	3,568	934	-	-	75	-	-	209	-	253	-	-	-	-	-	-	-	-	-	-	-	-	-	-	-
	87.57		26.18			12.02			18.95		36.72															
						8.03			22.38		27.09															
			26.18			2.10			5.86		7.09															
			1.08			0.09			0.24		0.29															
Mesa (city)	296,298	5,589	1,548	634	358	66	-	-	158	-	492	-	-	-	-	343	205	-	-	-	-	-	-	-	-	63
	81.19		27.70		56.47	11.28			16.63		36.63					60.92	31.20									8.76
						4.26			10.21		31.78					22.16	13.24									4.07
			27.70		56.47	1.18			2.83		8.80					6.14	3.67									1.13
			0.52		0.12	0.02			0.05		0.17					0.12	0.07									0.02
Phoenix (city)	818,864	23,798	5,775	1,620	755	771	-	91	1,059	-	1,592	-	322	-	-	675	597	-	-	-	-	-	-	-	-	346
	67.83		24.27		46.60	18.64		18.57	20.42		33.18		64.79			45.61	32.78									8.64
						13.35		1.58	18.34		27.57		42.65			11.69	10.34									5.99
			24.27		46.60	3.24		0.38	4.45		6.69		19.88			2.84	2.51									1.45
			0.71		0.09	0.09		0.01	0.13		0.19		0.04			0.08	0.07									0.04
Tempe (city)	117,627	7,530	1,616	-	-	307	-	-	293	-	224	-	-	-	-	372	151	-	-	-	-	-	-	-	-	81
	78.57		21.46			16.77			15.79		40.80					58.95	22.78									10.86
						19.00			18.13		13.86					23.02	9.34									5.01
			21.46			4.08			3.89		2.97					4.94	2.01									1.08
			1.37			0.26			0.25		0.19					0.32	0.13									0.07
Mohave County	130,214	864	289	-	-	-	-	-	-	-	-	-	-	-	-	-	-	-	-	-	-	-	-	-	-	-
	89.31		33.45																							
			33.45																							
			0.22																							

Notes: Please refer to the User's Guide for an explanation of data; data is arranged alphabetically by state, then county, then city within each county; table includes counties with populations greater than 49,999 unless noted and cities with populations greater than 9,999 whose Asian and/or NHPI population rates are greater than the national average; (1) Native Hawaiian and other Pacific Islander; (2) excludes Taiwanese; (3) includes Chamorro; (4) county does not meet population threshold but is shown in order to allow inclusion of city

Place	Total population 5 years and over who speak English-only at home	Asian population 5 years and over	Asians 5 years and over who speak English-only at home	NHPI[1] population 5 years and over	NHPIs[1] 5 years and over who speak English-only at home	Asian Indian	Bangladeshi	Cambodian	Chinese[2]	Fijian	Filipino	Guamanian[3]	Hawaiian, Native	Hmong	Indonesian	Japanese	Korean	Laotian	Malaysian	Pakistani	Samoan	Sri Lankan	Taiwanese	Thai	Tongan	Vietnamese
Pima County	572,101	15,888	4,446	994	695	369	-	-	1,098	-	1,037	-	300	-	-	639	666	-	-	-	-	-	-	-	-	174
	72.52		27.98		69.92	19.43			25.20		45.46		74.07			44.19	31.93									8.13
						8.30			24.70		23.32		43.17			14.37	14.98									3.91
			27.98		69.92	2.32			6.91		6.53		30.18			4.02	4.19									1.10
			0.78		0.12	0.06			0.19		0.18		0.05			0.11	0.12									0.03
Tucson (city)	304,940	10,995	2,637	661	431	170	-	-	624	-	694	-	-	-	-	381	357	-	-	-	-	-	-	-	-	115
	67.43		23.98		65.20	13.41			21.08		41.38					38.76	29.77									6.61
						6.45			23.66		26.32					14.45	13.54									4.36
			23.98		65.20	1.55			5.68		6.31					3.47	3.25									1.05
			0.86		0.14	0.06			0.20		0.23					0.12	0.12									0.04
Pinal County	125,420	901	232	-	-	-	-	-	-	-	-	-	-	-	-	-	-	-	-	-	-	-	-	-	-	-
	74.82		25.75																							
			25.75																							
			0.18																							
Yavapai County	143,456	811	289	-	-	-	-	-	-	-	-	-	-	-	-	-	-	-	-	-	-	-	-	-	-	-
	90.26		35.64																							
			35.64																							
			0.20																							
Yuma County	80,375	1,246	375	-	-	-	-	-	-	-	214	-	-	-	-	-	-	-	-	-	-	-	-	-	-	-
	54.49		30.10								49.88															
											57.07															
			30.10								17.17															
			0.47								0.27															
ARKANSAS	2,368,450	17,764	3,788	1,284	469	450	-	-	502	-	836	-	253	-	-	399	425	197	-	-	-	-	-	95	-	461
	95.03		21.32		36.53	18.63			18.19		38.65		86.94			36.51	29.29	7.96						34.05		12.87
						11.88			13.25		22.07		53.94			10.53	11.22	5.20						2.51		12.17
			21.32		36.53	2.53			2.83		4.71		19.70			2.25	2.39	1.11						0.53		2.60
			0.16		0.02	0.02			0.02		0.04		0.01			0.02	0.02	0.01						<0.01		0.02
Benton County	127,380	1,339	211	-	-	37	-	-	-	-	-	-	-	-	-	-	-	-	-	-	-	-	-	-	-	9
	89.77		15.76			10.54																				2.59
						17.54																				4.27
			15.76			2.76																				0.67
			0.17			0.03																				0.01
Craighead County	73,647	468	96	-	-	-	-	-	-	-	-	-	-	-	-	-	-	-	-	-	-	-	-	-	-	-
	96.16		20.51																							
			20.51																							
			0.13																							
Crawford County	47,012	591	186	-	-	-	-	-	-	-	-	-	-	-	-	-	-	-	-	-	-	-	-	-	-	-
	95.45		31.47																							
			31.47																							
			0.40																							
Faulkner County	76,937	512	141	-	-	-	-	-	-	-	-	-	-	-	-	-	-	-	-	-	-	-	-	-	-	-
	95.99		27.54																							
			27.54																							
			0.18																							

Notes: Please refer to the User's Guide for an explanation of data; data is arranged alphabetically by state, then county, then city within each county; table includes counties with populations greater than 49,999 unless noted and cities with populations greater than 9,999 whose Asian and/or NHPI population rates are greater than the national average; (1) Native Hawaiian and other Pacific Islander; (2) excludes Taiwanese; (3) includes Chamorro; (4) county does not meet population threshold but is shown in order to allow inclusion of city

Place	Total population 5 years and over who speak English-only at home	Asian population 5 years and over	Asians 5 years and over who speak English-only at home	NHPI[1] population 5 years and over	NHPIs[1] 5 years and over who speak English-only at home	Asian Indian	Bangladeshi	Cambodian	Chinese[2]	Fijian	Filipino	Guamanian[3]	Hawaiian, Native	Hmong	Indonesian	Japanese	Korean	Laotian	Malaysian	Pakistani	Samoan	Sri Lankan	Taiwanese	Thai	Tongan	Vietnamese
Jefferson County	75,800 96.60	427	79 18.50 18.50 0.10	-	-	-	-	-	-	-	-	-	-	-	-	-	-	-	-	-	-	-	-	-	-	-
Pulaski County	317,025 94.47	4,018	987 24.56 24.56 0.31	-	-	182 21.46 18.44 4.53 0.06	-	-	163 20.22 16.51 4.06 0.05	-	179 28.55 18.14 4.45 0.06	-	-	-	-	-	-	-	-	-	-	-	-	-	-	-
Saline County	75,749 96.94	429	77 17.95 17.95 0.10	-	-	-	-	-	-	-	-	-	-	-	-	-	-	-	-	-	-	-	-	-	-	-
Sebastian County	96,611 90.64	3,286	459 13.97 13.97 0.48	-	-	-	-	-	-	-	-	-	-	-	-	-	-	104 9.96 22.66 3.16 0.11	-	-	-	-	-	-	-	151 9.18 32.90 4.60 0.16
Fort Smith (city)	65,305 87.98	3,002	343 11.43 11.43 0.53	-	-	-	-	-	-	-	-	-	-	-	-	-	-	104 10.13 30.32 3.46 0.16	-	-	-	-	-	-	-	129 8.25 37.61 4.30 0.20
Washington County	130,592 89.49	2,452	419 17.09 17.09 0.32	575	41 7.13 7.13 0.03	-	-	-	137 18.56 32.70 5.59 0.10	-	-	-	-	-	-	-	-	15 2.94 3.58 0.61 0.01	-	-	-	-	-	-	-	-
Springdale (city)	32,955 78.96	678	93 13.72 13.72 0.28	524	27 5.15 5.15 0.08	-	-	-	-	-	-	-	-	-	-	-	-	0 0.00 0.00 0.00 0.00	-	-	-	-	-	-	-	-
CALIFORNIA	19,014,873 60.52	3,468,292	690,135 19.90 19.90 3.63	104,505	46,002 44.02 44.02 0.24	43,853 15.58 6.35 1.26 0.23	116 4.70 0.02 <0.01 <0.01	4,957 7.48 0.72 0.14 0.03	134,723 15.55 19.52 3.88 0.71	1,163 14.83 2.53 1.11 0.01	240,320 27.60 34.82 6.93 1.26	11,488 60.01 24.97 10.99 0.06	15,552 82.99 33.81 14.88 0.08	3,332 5.48 0.48 0.10 0.02	2,653 17.28 0.38 0.08 0.01	148,375 52.88 21.50 4.28 0.78	37,891 11.60 5.49 1.09 0.20	3,524 6.68 0.51 0.10 0.02	472 27.91 0.07 0.01 <0.01	1,957 10.93 0.28 0.06 0.01	10,730 30.72 23.33 10.27 0.06	1,318 25.63 0.19 0.04 0.01	3,388 5.60 0.49 0.10 0.02	4,439 12.57 0.64 0.13 0.02	1,411 13.05 3.07 1.35 0.01	24,519 5.88 3.55 0.71 0.13
Alameda County	850,906 63.19	274,487	51,624 18.81 18.81 6.07	8,434	3,139 37.22 37.22 0.37	4,545 12.03 8.80 1.66 0.53	-	291 7.98 0.56 0.11 0.03	15,101 15.02 29.25 5.50 1.77	201 14.77 6.40 2.38 0.02	17,993 27.36 34.85 6.56 2.11	792 64.29 25.23 9.39 0.09	981 78.99 31.25 11.63 0.12	-	120 21.13 0.23 0.04 0.01	6,821 56.66 13.21 2.48 0.80	1,988 14.43 3.85 0.72 0.23	160 5.48 0.31 0.06 0.02	-	181 10.08 0.35 0.07 0.02	600 27.75 19.11 7.11 0.07	-	216 5.95 0.42 0.08 0.03	269 18.80 0.52 0.10 0.03	243 15.02 7.74 2.88 0.03	1,317 6.02 2.55 0.48 0.15
Alameda (city)	45,140 66.15	17,661	3,551 20.11 20.11 7.87	730	408 55.89 55.89 0.90	169 17.21 4.76 0.96 0.37	-	-	1,263 17.95 35.57 7.15 2.80	-	1,372 23.97 38.64 7.77 3.04	-	-	-	-	358 51.22 10.08 2.03 0.79	110 9.35 3.10 0.62 0.24	-	-	-	-	-	-	-	-	57 4.64 1.61 0.32 0.13

Notes: Please refer to the User's Guide for an explanation of data; data is arranged alphabetically by state, then county, then city within each county; table includes counties with populations greater than 49,999 unless noted and cities with populations greater than 9,999 whose Asian and/or NHPI population rates are greater than the national average; (1) Native Hawaiian and other Pacific Islander; (2) excludes Taiwanese; (3) includes Chamorro; (4) county does not meet population threshold but is shown in order to allow inclusion of city

Place	Total population 5 years and over who speak English-only at home	Asian population 5 years and over	Asians 5 years and over who speak English-only at home	NHPI[1] population 5 years and over	NHPIs[1] 5 years and over who speak English-only at home	Asian Indian	Bangladeshi	Cambodian	Chinese[2]	Fijian	Filipino	Guamanian[3]	Hawaiian, Native	Hmong	Indonesian	Japanese	Korean	Laotian	Malaysian	Pakistani	Samoan	Sri Lankan	Taiwanese	Thai	Tongan	Vietnamese
	9,854	3,999	773	-	-	52	-	-	234	-	-	-	-	-	-	257	38	-	-	-	-	-	-	-	-	-
	63.85		19.33			16.56			12.11							41.92	8.09									
Albany (city)						6.73			30.27							33.25	4.92									
			19.33			1.30			5.85							6.43	0.95									
			7.84			0.53			2.37							2.61	0.39									
	11,023	2,972	483	-	-	-	-	-	96	-	229	-	-	-	-	-	-	-	-	-	-	-	-	-	-	-
	57.97		16.25						10.45		17.78															
Ashland (cdp)									19.88		47.41															
			16.25						3.23		7.71															
			4.38						0.87		2.08															
	71,676	16,365	5,331	-	-	607	-	-	1,869	-	582	-	-	-	-	1,156	407	-	-	-	-	-	76	-	-	172
	72.48		32.58			35.62			26.28		51.23					54.22	25.19						18.63			18.70
Berkeley (city)						11.39			35.06		10.92					21.68	7.63						1.43			3.23
			32.58			3.71			11.42		3.56					7.06	2.49						0.46			1.05
			7.44			0.85			2.61		0.81					1.61	0.57						0.11			0.24
	41,758	6,892	1,905	-	-	93	-	-	887	-	373	-	-	-	-	378	65	-	-	-	-	-	-	-	-	-
	76.98		27.64			12.22			27.53		32.75					64.51	8.86									
Castro Valley (cdp)						4.88			46.56		19.58					19.84	3.41									
			27.64			1.35			12.87		5.41					5.48	0.94									
			4.56			0.22			2.12		0.89					0.91	0.16									
	7,002	1,078	203	-	-	-	-	-	-	-	103	-	-	-	-	-	-	-	-	-	-	-	-	-	-	-
	55.57		18.83								17.55															
Cherryland (cdp)											50.74															
			18.83								9.55															
			2.90								1.47															
	22,895	2,766	790	-	-	17	-	-	233	-	293	-	-	-	-	-	-	-	-	-	-	-	-	-	-	-
	81.03		28.56			3.39			27.03		38.30															
Dublin (city)						2.15			29.49		37.09															
			28.56			0.61			8.42		10.59															
			3.45			0.07			1.02		1.28															
	99,965	68,344	10,017	636	392	1,831	-	-	2,485	-	3,390	-	-	-	-	1,009	341	-	-	68	-	-	61	-	-	256
	53.06		14.66		61.64	9.95			10.27		31.55					67.27	9.26			6.99			2.73			6.40
Fremont (city)						18.28			24.81		33.84					10.07	3.40			0.68			0.61			2.56
			14.66		61.64	2.68			3.64		4.96					1.48	0.50			0.10			0.09			0.37
			10.02		0.39	1.83			2.49		3.39					1.01	0.34			0.07			0.06			0.26
	65,909	24,367	4,789	2,223	586	280	-	-	517	113	2,995	-	-	-	-	575	128	-	-	-	39	-	-	-	-	95
	51.10		19.65		26.36	8.60			15.17	14.29	25.33					45.93	16.37				7.21					3.87
Hayward (city)						5.85			10.80	19.28	62.54					12.01	2.67				6.66					1.98
			19.65		26.36	1.15			2.12	5.08	12.29					2.36	0.53				1.75					0.39
			7.27		0.89	0.42			0.78	0.17	4.54					0.87	0.19				0.06					0.14
	56,918	3,890	1,279	-	-	107	-	-	194	-	567	-	-	-	-	-	-	-	-	-	-	-	-	-	-	44
	83.91		32.88			20.23			26.80		38.03															9.98
Livermore (city)						8.37			15.17		44.33															3.44
			32.88			2.75			4.99		14.58															1.13
			2.25			0.19			0.34		1.00															0.08
	21,809	8,620	1,993	-	-	148	-	-	403	-	1,033	-	-	-	-	-	37	-	-	-	-	-	-	-	-	19
	55.16		23.12			9.99			25.33		31.77						7.07									2.83
Newark (city)						7.43			20.22		51.83						1.86									0.95
			23.12			1.72			4.68		11.98						0.43									0.22
			9.14			0.68			1.85		4.74						0.17									0.09

Notes: Please refer to the User's Guide for an explanation of data; data is arranged alphabetically by state, then county, then city within each county; table includes counties with populations greater than 49,999 unless noted and cities with populations greater than 9,999 whose Asian and/or NHPI population rates are greater than the national average; (1) Native Hawaiian and other Pacific Islander; (2) excludes Taiwanese; (3) includes Chamorro; (4) county does not meet population threshold but is shown in order to allow inclusion of city

Place	Total population 5 years and over who speak English-only at home	Asian population 5 years and over	Asians 5 years and over who speak English-only at home	NHPI[1] population 5 years and over	NHPIs[1] 5 years and over who speak English-only at home	Asian Indian	Bangladeshi	Cambodian	Chinese[2]	Fijian	Filipino	Guamanian[3]	Hawaiian, Native	Hmong	Indonesian	Japanese	Korean	Laotian	Malaysian	Pakistani	Samoan	Sri Lankan	Taiwanese	Thai	Tongan	Vietnamese
Oakland (city)	234,737 63.18	56,978	8,587 15.07 15.07 3.66	2,319	558 24.06 24.06 0.24	325 19.98 3.78 0.57 0.14	-	151 5.55 1.76 0.27 0.06	3,692 12.30 43.00 6.48 1.57	-	1,699 26.44 19.79 2.98 0.72	-	-	-	-	1,174 57.49 13.67 2.06 0.50	447 26.19 5.21 0.78 0.19	111 5.00 1.29 0.19 0.05	-	-	-	-	-	-	117 10.33 20.97 5.05 0.05	385 5.01 4.48 0.68 0.16
Piedmont (city)	8,539 82.30	1,736	600 34.56 34.56 7.03	-	-	-	-	-	400 30.56 66.67 23.04 4.68	-	-	-	-	-	-	-	-	-	-	-	-	-	-	-	-	-
Pleasanton (city)	48,899 82.56	6,721	1,907 28.37 28.37 3.90	-	-	224 15.34 11.75 3.33 0.46	-	-	583 24.31 30.57 8.67 1.19	-	358 44.92 18.77 5.33 0.73	-	-	-	-	446 69.04 23.39 6.64 0.91	78 13.95 4.09 1.16 0.16	-	-	-	-	-	-	-	-	-
San Leandro (city)	45,584 61.23	17,075	2,844 16.66 16.66 6.24	523	243 46.46 46.46 0.53	73 11.48 2.57 0.43 0.16	-	-	895 11.62 31.47 5.24 1.96	-	1,260 21.96 44.30 7.38 2.76	-	-	-	-	310 60.67 10.90 1.82 0.68	22 5.35 0.77 0.13 0.05	-	-	-	-	-	-	-	-	103 8.53 3.62 0.60 0.23
San Lorenzo (cdp)	14,342 69.60	3,261	743 22.78 22.78 5.18	-	-	-	-	-	230 25.08 30.96 7.05 1.60	-	305 23.64 41.05 9.35 2.13	-	-	-	-	-	-	-	-	-	-	-	-	-	-	30 10.31 4.04 0.92 0.21
Union City (city)	25,204 40.75	27,283	4,557 16.70 16.70 18.08	629	242 38.47 38.47 0.96	445 9.20 9.77 1.63 1.77	-	-	611 11.02 13.41 2.24 2.42	-	2,964 23.97 65.04 10.86 11.76	-	-	-	-	195 41.05 4.28 0.71 0.77	39 4.26 0.86 0.14 0.15	-	-	-	-	-	-	-	-	53 2.95 1.16 0.19 0.21
Butte County	167,598 87.52	6,002	1,157 19.28 19.28 0.69	-	-	42 10.40 3.63 0.70 0.03	-	-	156 22.41 13.48 2.60 0.09	-	169 48.56 14.61 2.82 0.10	-	-	117 4.75 10.11 1.95 0.07	-	296 51.84 25.58 4.93 0.18	-	47 9.09 4.06 0.78 0.03	-	-	-	-	-	-	-	-
Chico (city)	48,017 85.93	2,089	434 20.78 20.78 0.90	-	-	-	-	-	89 22.08 20.51 4.26 0.19	-	-	-	-	0 0.00 0.00 0.00 0.00	-	-	-	-	-	-	-	-	-	-	-	-
Oroville (city)	10,315 87.11	647	10 1.55 1.55 0.10	-	-	-	-	-	-	-	-	-	-	5 1.21 50.00 0.77 0.05	-	-	-	-	-	-	-	-	-	-	-	-
Contra Costa County	654,278 74.03	97,403	27,177 27.90 27.90 4.15	3,123	1,365 43.71 43.71 0.21	1,576 15.22 5.80 1.62 0.24	-	-	7,201 27.16 26.50 7.39 1.10	101 19.20 7.40 3.23 0.02	9,681 29.86 35.62 9.94 1.48	324 64.03 23.74 10.37 0.05	518 87.95 37.95 16.59 0.08	-	132 29.07 0.49 0.14 0.02	5,140 63.45 18.91 5.28 0.79	928 21.74 3.41 0.95 0.14	225 5.69 0.83 0.23 0.03	-	16 2.57 0.06 0.02 <0.01	197 28.59 14.43 6.31 0.03	-	102 8.38 0.38 0.10 0.02	97 16.55 0.36 0.10 0.01	56 15.43 4.10 1.79 0.01	506 9.86 1.86 0.52 0.08

Notes: Please refer to the User's Guide for an explanation of data; data is arranged alphabetically by state, then county, then city within each county; table includes counties with populations greater than 49,999 unless noted and cities with populations greater than 9,999 whose Asian and/or NHPI population rates are greater than the national average; (1) Native Hawaiian and other Pacific Islander; (2) excludes Taiwanese; (3) includes Chamorro; (4) county does not meet population threshold but is shown in order to allow inclusion of city

Place	Total population 5 years and over who speak English-only at home	Asian population 5 years and over	Asians 5 years and over who speak English-only at home	NHPI[1] population 5 years and over	NHPIs[1] 5 years and over who speak English-only at home	Asian Indian	Bangladeshi	Cambodian	Chinese[2]	Fijian	Filipino	Guamanian[3]	Hawaiian, Native	Hmong	Indonesian	Japanese	Korean	Laotian	Malaysian	Pakistani	Samoan	Sri Lankan	Taiwanese	Thai	Tongan	Vietnamese
Alamo (cdp)	12,629 89.73	841	502 59.69 59.69 3.97	-	-	-	-	-	-	-	-	-	-	-	-	-	-	-	-	-	-	-	-	-	-	-
Antioch (city)	64,785 77.94	6,238	1,953 31.31 31.31 3.01	377	158 41.91 41.91 0.24	40 12.08 2.05 0.64 0.06	-	-	254 23.74 13.01 4.07 0.39	-	1,213 37.45 62.11 19.45 1.87	-	-	-	-	-	-	-	-	-	-	-	-	-	-	99 21.66 5.07 1.59 0.15
Bay Point (cdp)	10,495 54.32	2,308	336 14.56 14.56 3.20	-	-	-	-	-	-	-	218 19.17 64.88 9.45 2.08	-	-	-	-	-	-	-	-	-	-	-	-	-	-	-
Blackhawk-Camino-Tass. (cdp)	7,355 78.19	1,592	474 29.77 29.77 6.44	-	-	-	-	-	273 30.37 57.59 17.15 3.71	-	-	-	-	-	-	-	-	-	-	-	-	-	-	-	-	-
Clayton (city)	9,109 90.19	567	324 57.14 57.14 3.56	-	-	-	-	-	-	-	-	-	-	-	-	-	-	-	-	-	-	-	-	-	-	-
Concord (city)	78,953 69.74	10,544	2,785 26.41 26.41 3.53	409	99 24.21 24.21 0.13	246 17.01 8.83 2.33 0.31	-	-	593 23.21 21.29 5.62 0.75	-	1,123 29.37 40.32 10.65 1.42	-	-	-	-	452 54.46 16.23 4.29 0.57	92 20.86 3.30 0.87 0.12	-	-	-	-	-	-	-	-	86 13.48 3.09 0.82 0.11
Danville (town)	34,074 86.83	3,390	1,298 38.29 38.29 3.81	-	-	108 25.41 8.32 3.19 0.32	-	-	567 38.28 43.68 16.73 1.66	-	176 40.46 13.56 5.19 0.52	-	-	-	-	-	-	-	-	-	-	-	-	-	-	-
El Cerrito (city)	15,245 68.73	5,410	1,542 28.50 28.50 10.11	-	-	93 25.34 6.03 1.72 0.61	-	-	424 17.79 27.50 7.84 2.78	-	158 35.51 10.25 2.92 1.04	-	-	-	-	673 54.94 43.64 12.44 4.41	-	-	-	-	-	-	-	-	-	-
El Sobrante (cdp)	8,206 75.40	1,237	237 19.16 19.16 2.89	-	-	17 5.20 7.17 1.37 0.21	-	-	-	-	-	-	-	-	-	-	-	-	-	-	-	-	-	-	-	-
Hercules (city)	10,414 57.26	7,895	2,303 29.17 29.17 22.11	-	-	84 13.53 3.65 1.06 0.81	-	-	288 18.70 12.51 3.65 2.77	-	1,614 34.07 70.08 20.44 15.50	-	-	-	-	-	-	-	-	-	-	-	-	-	-	-

Notes: Please refer to the User's Guide for an explanation of data; data is arranged alphabetically by state, then county, then city within each county; table includes counties with populations greater than 49,999 unless noted and cities with populations greater than 9,999 whose Asian and/or NHPI population rates are greater than the national average; (1) Native Hawaiian and other Pacific Islander; (2) excludes Taiwanese; (3) includes Chamorro; (4) county does not meet population threshold but is shown in order to allow inclusion of city

Place	Total population 5 years and over who speak English-only at home	Asian population 5 years and over	Asians 5 years and over who speak English-only at home	NHPI[1] population 5 years and over	NHPIs[1] 5 years and over who speak English-only at home	Asian Indian	Bangladeshi	Cambodian	Chinese[2]	Fijian	Filipino	Guamanian[3]	Hawaiian, Native	Hmong	Indonesian	Japanese	Korean	Laotian	Malaysian	Pakistani	Samoan	Sri Lankan	Taiwanese	Thai	Tongan	Vietnamese
Lafayette (city)	19,247 86.96	1,601	532 33.23 33.23 2.76	-	-	-	-	-	184 23.35 34.59 11.49 0.96	-	-	-	-	-	-	-	-	-	-	-	-	-	-	-	-	-
Martinez (city)	29,360 86.07	2,179	733 33.64 33.64 2.50	-	-	-	-	-	195 42.03 26.60 8.95 0.66	-	237 25.76 32.33 10.88 0.81	-	-	-	-	-	-	-	-	-	-	-	-	-	-	-
Moraga (town)	12,998 81.63	2,079	769 36.99 36.99 5.92	-	-	-	-	-	385 32.11 50.07 18.52 2.96	-	-	-	-	-	-	-	-	-	-	-	-	-	-	-	-	-
Orinda (city)	14,340 86.76	1,457	705 48.39 48.39 4.92	-	-	-	-	-	389 45.55 55.18 26.70 2.71	-	-	-	-	-	-	-	-	-	-	-	-	-	-	-	-	-
Pinole (city)	12,948 70.48	3,924	1,108 28.24 28.24 8.56	-	-	-	-	-	236 27.93 21.30 6.01 1.82	-	548 28.12 49.46 13.97 4.23	-	-	-	-	-	-	-	-	-	-	-	-	-	-	-
Pittsburg (city)	32,157 61.50	6,858	1,683 24.54 24.54 5.23	472	173 36.65 36.65 0.54	100 11.33 5.94 1.46 0.31	-	-	112 25.99 6.65 1.63 0.35	-	1,132 25.11 67.26 16.51 3.52	-	-	-	-	-	-	-	-	-	-	-	-	-	-	-
Pleasant Hill (city)	25,358 82.25	3,148	1,053 33.45 33.45 4.15	-	-	-	-	-	285 32.31 27.07 9.05 1.12	-	314 38.43 29.82 9.97 1.24	-	-	-	-	-	82 16.50 7.79 2.60 0.32	-	-	-	-	-	-	-	-	-
Richmond (city)	58,702 63.76	11,322	2,390 21.11 21.11 4.07	372	164 44.09 44.09 0.28	92 9.16 3.85 0.81 0.16	-	-	664 22.18 27.78 5.86 1.13	-	715 27.54 29.92 6.32 1.22	-	-	-	-	542 64.91 22.68 4.79 0.92	85 19.27 3.56 0.75 0.14	119 5.40 4.98 1.05 0.20	-	-	-	-	-	-	-	34 8.11 1.42 0.30 0.06
San Pablo (city)	11,438 41.48	4,643	356 7.67 7.67 3.11	-	-	41 7.07 11.52 0.88 0.36	-	-	-	-	180 11.16 50.56 3.88 1.57	-	-	-	-	-	-	75 7.12 21.07 1.62 0.66	-	-	-	-	-	-	-	0 0.00 0.00 0.00 0.00
San Ramon (city)	32,926 79.81	6,228	1,984 31.86 31.86 6.03	-	-	220 17.68 11.09 3.53 0.67	-	-	773 30.80 38.96 12.41 2.35	-	384 41.97 19.35 6.17 1.17	-	-	-	-	361 82.99 18.20 5.80 1.10	-	-	-	-	-	-	-	-	-	-

Notes: Please refer to the User's Guide for an explanation of data; data is arranged alphabetically by state, then county, then city within each county; table includes counties with populations greater than 49,999 unless noted and cities with populations greater than 9,999 whose Asian and/or NHPI population rates are greater than the national average; (1) Native Hawaiian and other Pacific Islander; (2) excludes Taiwanese; (3) includes Chamorro; (4) county does not meet population threshold but is shown in order to allow inclusion of city

Place	Total population 5 years and over who speak English-only at home	Asian population 5 years and over	Asians 5 years and over who speak English-only at home	NHPI[1] population 5 years and over	NHPIs[1] 5 years and over who speak English-only at home	Asian Indian	Bangladeshi	Cambodian	Chinese[2]	Fijian	Filipino	Guamanian[3]	Hawaiian, Native	Hmong	Indonesian	Japanese	Korean	Laotian	Malaysian	Pakistani	Samoan	Sri Lankan	Taiwanese	Thai	Tongan	Vietnamese
Walnut Creek (city)	49,626	5,898	1,759	-	-	112	-	-	630	-	293	-	-	-	-	485	101	-	-	-	-	-	-	-	-	-
	80.59		29.82			20.55			24.80		25.63					60.10	21.54									
						6.37			35.82		16.66					27.57	5.74									
			29.82			1.90			10.68		4.97					8.22	1.71									
			3.54			0.23			1.27		0.59					0.98	0.20									
El Dorado County	132,474	2,796	1,093	-	-	-	-	-	-	-	254	-	-	-	-	371	-	-	-	-	-	-	-	-	-	-
	89.89		39.09								20.68					73.32										
											23.24					33.94										
			39.09								9.08					13.27										
			0.83								0.19					0.28										
El Dorado Hills (cdp)	15,728	571	270	-	-	-	-	-	-	-	-	-	-	-	-	-	-	-	-	-	-	-	-	-	-	-
	93.41		47.29																							
			47.29																							
			1.72																							
South Lake Tahoe (city)	15,484	1,307	241	-	-	-	-	-	-	-	87	-	-	-	-	-	-	-	-	-	-	-	-	-	-	-
	69.90		18.44								9.70															
											36.10															
			18.44								6.66															
			1.56								0.56															
Fresno County	433,491	58,845	10,718	585	354	451	-	260	1,356	-	2,140	-	-	1,087	-	3,877	391	468	-	-	-	-	-	-	-	97
	59.19		18.21		60.51	7.13		7.11	29.44		36.23			5.08		69.05	30.50	8.05								4.87
						4.21		2.43	12.65		19.97			10.14		36.17	3.65	4.37								0.91
			18.21		60.51	0.77		0.44	2.30		3.64			1.85		6.59	0.66	0.80								0.16
			2.47		0.08	0.10		0.06	0.31		0.49			0.25		0.89	0.09	0.11								0.02
Clovis (city)	52,389	4,157	1,204	-	-	-	-	-	-	-	410	-	-	68	-	423	-	-	-	-	-	-	-	-	-	-
	82.91		28.96								63.47			4.16		77.19										
											34.05			5.65		35.13										
			28.96								9.86			1.64		10.18										
			2.30								0.78			0.13		0.81										
Fresno (city)	235,220	44,364	6,573	-	-	254	-	241	885	-	1,373	-	-	897	-	1,722	226	451	-	-	-	-	-	-	-	74
	60.51		14.82			7.58		7.21	24.99		32.78			4.97		66.85	24.73	8.90								4.53
						3.86		3.67	13.46		20.89			13.65		26.20	3.44	6.86								1.13
			14.82			0.57		0.54	1.99		3.09			2.02		3.88	0.51	1.02								0.17
			2.79			0.11		0.10	0.38		0.58			0.38		0.73	0.10	0.19								0.03
Reedley (city)	7,770	750	352	-	-	-	-	-	-	-	-	-	-	-	-	-	-	-	-	-	-	-	-	-	-	-
	41.16		46.93																							
			46.93																							
			4.53																							
Humboldt County	109,493	1,701	569	-	-	-	-	-	-	-	-	-	-	-	-	199	-	-	-	-	-	-	-	-	-	-
	91.69		33.45													70.07										
																34.97										
			33.45													11.70										
			0.52													0.18										
Imperial County	42,305	2,637	547	-	-	-	-	-	33	-	288	-	-	-	-	-	14	-	-	-	-	-	-	-	-	-
	32.16		20.74						5.91		34.20						3.22									
									6.03		52.65						2.56									
			20.74						1.25		10.92						0.53									
			1.29						0.08		0.68						0.03									

Notes: Please refer to the User's Guide for an explanation of data; data is arranged alphabetically by state, then county, then city within each county; table includes counties with populations greater than 49,999 unless noted and cities with populations greater than 9,999 whose Asian and/or NHPI population rates are greater than the national average; (1) Native Hawaiian and other Pacific Islander; (2) excludes Taiwanese; (3) includes Chamorro; (4) county does not meet population threshold but is shown in order to allow inclusion of city

Place	Total population 5 years and over who speak English-only at home	Asian population 5 years and over	Asians 5 years and over who speak English-only at home	NHPI[1] population 5 years and over	NHPIs[1] 5 years and over who speak English-only at home	Asian Indian	Bangladeshi	Cambodian	Chinese[2]	Fijian	Filipino	Guamanian[3]	Hawaiian, Native	Hmong	Indonesian	Japanese	Korean	Laotian	Malaysian	Pakistani	Samoan	Sri Lankan	Taiwanese	Thai	Tongan	Vietnamese
Kern County	404,239	20,021	5,104	705	485	491	-	11	629	-	2,541	-	-	-	-	708	268	-	-	-	-	-	-	-	-	116
	66.64		25.49		68.79	13.01		2.83	32.04		25.85					70.03	22.35									19.63
						9.62		0.22	12.32		49.78					13.87	5.25									2.27
			25.49		68.79	2.45		0.05	3.14		12.69					3.54	1.34									0.58
			1.26		0.12	0.12		<0.01	0.16		0.63					0.18	0.07									0.03
Bakersfield (city)	164,979	9,680	2,439	419	238	313	-	-	401	-	869	-	-	-	-	456	209	-	-	-	-	-	-	-	-	43
	72.94		25.20		56.80	11.03			28.28		34.69					71.81	22.67									10.72
						12.83			16.44		35.63					18.70	8.57									1.76
			25.20		56.80	3.23			4.14		8.98					4.71	2.16									0.44
			1.48		0.14	0.19			0.24		0.53					0.28	0.13									0.03
Delano (city)	9,724	5,596	897	-	-	-	-	-	-	-	821	-	-	-	-	-	-	-	-	-	-	-	-	-	-	-
	27.47		16.03								15.71															
											91.53															
			16.03								14.67															
			9.22								8.44															
Ridgecrest (city)	20,496	968	369	-	-	-	-	-	-	-	154	-	-	-	-	-	-	-	-	-	-	-	-	-	-	-
	87.46		38.12								32.98															
											41.73															
			38.12								15.91															
			1.80								0.75															
Kings County	75,441	3,569	1,039	-	-	-	-	-	-	-	653	-	-	-	-	-	-	-	-	-	-	-	-	-	-	-
	63.26		29.11								27.70															
											62.85															
			29.11								18.30															
			1.38								0.87															
Lemoore (city)	12,541	1,352	312	-	-	-	-	-	-	-	264	-	-	-	-	-	-	-	-	-	-	-	-	-	-	-
	71.10		23.08								25.68															
											84.62															
			23.08								19.53															
			2.49								2.11															
Lake County	49,641	517	208	-	-	-	-	-	-	-	-	-	-	-	-	-	-	-	-	-	-	-	-	-	-	-
	89.84		40.23																							
			40.23																							
			0.42																							
Los Angeles County	4,032,614	1,076,167	190,202	24,840	9,757	10,682	68	2,048	33,062	144	55,111	1,524	3,366	0	821	54,840	14,884	189	83	393	3,262	496	1,144	1,672	258	4,466
	45.87		17.67		39.28	19.32	5.77	7.34	11.96	30.64	22.20	53.27	80.28	0.00	15.43	50.16	8.42	6.40	15.78	9.20	26.95	21.74	3.45	8.74	12.27	6.06
						5.62	0.04	1.08	17.38	1.48	28.97	15.62	34.50	0.00	0.43	28.83	7.83	0.10	0.04	0.21	33.43	0.26	0.60	0.88	2.64	2.35
			17.67		39.28	0.99	0.01	0.19	3.07	0.58	5.12	6.14	13.55	0.00	0.08	5.10	1.38	0.02	0.01	0.04	13.13	0.05	0.11	0.16	1.04	0.41
			4.72		0.24	0.26	<0.01	0.05	0.82	<0.01	1.37	0.04	0.08	0.00	0.02	1.36	0.37	<0.01	<0.01	0.01	0.08	0.01	0.03	0.04	0.01	0.11
Agoura Hills (city)	15,704	1,203	437	-	-	-	-	-	-	-	-	-	-	-	-	-	-	-	-	-	-	-	-	-	-	-
	81.50		36.33																							
			36.33																							
			2.78																							
Alhambra (city)	22,404	38,488	3,095	-	-	95	-	-	1,420	-	422	-	-	-	-	683	63	-	-	-	-	-	31	-	-	164
	27.73		8.04			19.39			5.68		22.77					45.99	7.36						2.03			3.96
						3.07			45.88		13.63					22.07	2.04						1.00			5.30
			8.04			0.25			3.69		1.10					1.77	0.16						0.08			0.43
			13.81			0.42			6.34		1.88					3.05	0.28						0.14			0.73

Notes: Please refer to the User's Guide for an explanation of data; data is arranged alphabetically by state, then county, then city within each county; table includes counties with populations greater than 49,999 unless noted and cities with populations greater than 9,999 whose Asian and/or NHPI population rates are greater than the national average; (1) Native Hawaiian and other Pacific Islander; (2) excludes Taiwanese; (3) includes Chamorro; (4) county does not meet population threshold but is shown in order to allow inclusion of city

Place	Total population 5 years and over who speak English-only at home	Asian population 5 years and over	Asians 5 years and over who speak English-only at home	NHPI[1] population 5 years and over	NHPIs[1] 5 years and over who speak English-only at home	Asian Indian	Bangladeshi	Cambodian	Chinese[2]	Fijian	Filipino	Guamanian[3]	Hawaiian, Native	Hmong	Indonesian	Japanese	Korean	Laotian	Malaysian	Pakistani	Samoan	Sri Lankan	Taiwanese	Thai	Tongan	Vietnamese
Altadena (cdp)	28,854 72.47	1,707	733 42.94 42.94 2.54	-	-	-	-	-	-	-	78 25.83 10.64 4.57 0.27	-	-	-	-	420 66.99 57.30 24.60 1.46	-	-	-	-	-	-	-	-	-	-
Arcadia (city)	23,081 45.59	22,724	1,892 8.33 8.33 8.20	-	-	134 21.30 7.08 0.59 0.58	-	-	835 6.35 44.13 3.67 3.62	-	207 26.92 10.94 0.91 0.90	-	-	-	-	305 26.92 16.12 1.34 1.32	136 7.23 7.19 0.60 0.59	-	-	-	-	-	86 2.40 4.55 0.38 0.37	-	-	-
Artesia (city)	5,360 35.25	4,240	526 12.41 12.41 9.81	-	-	82 18.64 15.59 1.93 1.53	-	-	24 3.90 4.56 0.57 0.45	-	282 16.90 53.61 6.65 5.26	-	-	-	-	-	46 5.54 8.75 1.08 0.86	-	-	-	-	-	-	-	-	-
Avocado Heights (cdp)	4,035 28.97	1,302	313 24.04 24.04 7.76	-	-	-	-	-	-	-	-	-	-	-	-	-	-	-	-	-	-	-	-	-	-	-
Azusa (city)	17,680 43.87	2,295	379 16.51 16.51 2.14	-	-	-	-	-	-	-	275 24.47 72.56 11.98 1.56	-	-	-	-	-	-	-	-	-	-	-	-	-	-	-
Baldwin Park (city)	14,537 21.26	8,395	1,041 12.40 12.40 7.16	-	-	-	-	-	134 5.23 12.87 1.60 0.92	-	689 18.36 66.19 8.21 4.74	-	-	-	-	-	-	-	-	-	-	-	-	-	-	27 2.97 2.59 0.32 0.19
Bellflower (city)	35,511 53.71	6,768	1,033 15.26 15.26 2.91	-	-	-	-	30 5.69 2.90 0.44 0.08	-	-	706 20.94 68.34 10.43 1.99	-	-	-	-	-	30 3.42 2.90 0.44 0.08	-	-	-	-	-	-	34 8.88 3.29 0.50 0.10	-	-
Beverly Hills (city)	18,213 55.76	2,504	419 16.73 16.73 2.30	-	-	-	-	-	88 17.67 21.00 3.51 0.48	-	-	-	-	-	-	-	93 10.25 22.20 3.71 0.51	-	-	-	-	-	-	-	-	-
Burbank (city)	54,479 57.43	8,582	1,621 18.89 18.89 2.98	-	-	80 9.31 4.94 0.93 0.15	-	-	189 21.90 11.66 2.20 0.35	-	743 23.88 45.84 8.66 1.36	-	-	-	-	301 50.33 18.57 3.51 0.55	53 2.83 3.27 0.62 0.10	-	-	-	-	-	-	-	-	70 14.46 4.32 0.82 0.13
Calabasas (city)	14,634 77.43	1,610	433 26.89 26.89 2.96	-	-	-	-	-	68 13.55 15.70 4.22 0.46	-	-	-	-	-	-	-	-	-	-	-	-	-	-	-	-	-

Notes: Please refer to the User's Guide for an explanation of data; data is arranged alphabetically by state, then county, then city within each county; table includes counties with populations greater than 49,999 unless noted and cities with populations greater than 9,999 whose Asian and/or NHPI population rates are greater than the national average; (1) Native Hawaiian and other Pacific Islander; (2) excludes Taiwanese; (3) includes Chamorro; (4) county does not meet population threshold but is shown in order to allow inclusion of city

Place	Total population 5 years and over who speak English-only at home	Asian population 5 years and over	Asians 5 years and over who speak English-only at home	NHPI[1] population 5 years and over	NHPIs[1] 5 years and over who speak English-only at home	Asian Indian	Bangladeshi	Cambodian	Chinese[2]	Fijian	Filipino	Guamanian[3]	Hawaiian, Native	Hmong	Indonesian	Japanese	Korean	Laotian	Malaysian	Pakistani	Samoan	Sri Lankan	Taiwanese	Thai	Tongan	Vietnamese
Carson (city)	41,858 50.13	19,141	4,269 22.30 22.30 10.20	1,676	586 34.96 34.96 1.40	-	-	-	166 36.01 3.89 0.87 0.40	-	3,327 20.28 77.93 17.38 7.95	-	-	-	-	437 69.70 10.24 2.28 1.04	-	-	-	-	272 22.15 46.42 16.23 0.65	-	-	-	-	16 4.98 0.37 0.08 0.04
Cerritos (city)	19,663 40.02	28,872	4,922 17.05 17.05 25.03	-	-	370 13.43 7.52 1.28 1.88	-	-	760 13.70 15.44 2.63 3.87	-	1,509 27.61 30.66 5.23 7.67	-	-	-	-	1,285 67.74 26.11 4.45 6.54	540 6.31 10.97 1.87 2.75	-	-	-	-	-	67 3.88 1.36 0.23 0.34	88 18.88 1.79 0.30 0.45	-	102 8.50 2.07 0.35 0.52
Citrus (cdp)	4,233 43.68	696	150 21.55 21.55 3.54	-	-	-	-	-	-	-	-	-	-	-	-	-	-	-	-	-	-	-	-	-	-	-
Claremont (city)	24,691 75.47	3,836	1,012 26.38 26.38 4.10	-	-	182 35.76 17.98 4.74 0.74	-	-	218 21.50 21.54 5.68 0.88	-	-	-	-	-	-	-	94 15.46 9.29 2.45 0.38	-	-	-	-	-	-	-	-	-
Compton (city)	37,485 44.83	382	55 14.40 14.40 0.15	919	171 18.61 18.61 0.46	-	-	-	-	-	-	-	-	-	-	-	-	-	-	-	160 18.29 93.57 17.41 0.43	-	-	-	-	-
Covina (city)	28,067 64.40	4,311	963 22.34 22.34 3.43	-	-	-	-	-	62 5.71 6.44 1.44 0.22	-	399 30.25 41.43 9.26 1.42	-	-	-	-	229 60.26 23.78 5.31 0.82	-	-	-	-	-	-	-	-	-	11 2.77 1.14 0.26 0.04
Culver City (city)	23,869 64.78	4,597	1,623 35.31 35.31 6.80	-	-	93 16.01 5.73 2.02 0.39	-	-	261 33.76 16.08 5.68 1.09	-	249 25.49 15.34 5.42 1.04	-	-	-	-	786 57.75 48.43 17.10 3.29	-	-	-	-	-	-	-	-	-	-
Diamond Bar (city)	24,526 46.12	22,516	2,803 12.45 12.45 11.43	-	-	285 12.18 10.17 1.27 1.16	-	-	683 9.61 24.37 3.03 2.78	-	926 30.87 33.04 4.11 3.78	-	-	-	-	320 47.13 11.42 1.42 1.30	293 5.47 10.45 1.30 1.19	-	-	-	-	-	40 1.98 1.43 0.18 0.16	-	-	48 7.07 1.71 0.21 0.20
Downey (city)	39,224 39.70	7,398	1,077 14.56 14.56 2.75	-	-	79 19.75 7.34 1.07 0.20	-	-	128 25.50 11.88 1.73 0.33	-	383 21.07 35.56 5.18 0.98	-	-	-	-	262 77.06 24.33 3.54 0.67	85 2.80 7.89 1.15 0.22	-	-	-	-	-	-	-	-	41 10.07 3.81 0.55 0.10
Duarte (city)	9,858 49.80	2,562	538 21.00 21.00 5.46	-	-	-	-	-	81 19.80 15.06 3.16 0.82	-	283 21.42 52.60 11.05 2.87	-	-	-	-	-	-	-	-	-	-	-	-	-	-	-

Notes: Please refer to the User's Guide for an explanation of data; data is arranged alphabetically by state, then county, then city within each county; table includes counties with populations greater than 49,999 unless noted and cities with populations greater than 9,999 whose Asian and/or NHPI population rates are greater than the national average; (1) Native Hawaiian and other Pacific Islander; (2) excludes Taiwanese; (3) includes Chamorro; (4) county does not meet population threshold but is shown in order to allow inclusion of city

Place	Total population 5 years and over who speak English-only at home	Asian population 5 years and over	Asians 5 years and over who speak English-only at home	NHPI[1] population 5 years and over	NHPIs[1] 5 years and over who speak English-only at home	Asian Indian	Bangladeshi	Cambodian	Chinese[2]	Fijian	Filipino	Guamanian[3]	Hawaiian, Native	Hmong	Indonesian	Japanese	Korean	Laotian	Malaysian	Pakistani	Samoan	Sri Lankan	Taiwanese	Thai	Tongan	Vietnamese
East San Gabriel (cdp)	5,957 43.66	5,667	694 12.25 12.25 11.65	-	-	-	-	-	209 6.47 30.12 3.69 3.51	-	-	-	-	-	-	289 51.70 41.64 5.10 4.85	-	-	-	-	-	-	31 5.19 4.47 0.55 0.52	-	-	-
El Monte (city)	20,243 19.26	20,233	1,281 6.33 6.33 6.33	-	-	-	-	-	633 5.72 49.41 3.13 3.13	-	134 14.41 10.46 0.66 0.66	-	-	-	-	-	-	-	-	-	-	-	6 1.57 0.47 0.03 0.03	-	-	196 3.33 15.30 0.97 0.97
El Segundo (city)	12,952 86.35	1,016	446 43.90 43.90 3.44	-	-	-	-	-	-	-	-	-	-	-	-	-	-	-	-	-	-	-	-	-	-	-
Gardena (city)	27,691 51.86	14,805	4,766 32.19 32.19 17.21	-	-	-	-	-	217 25.12 4.55 1.47 0.78	-	442 26.53 9.27 2.99 1.60	-	-	-	-	3,506 53.54 73.56 23.68 12.66	205 5.92 4.30 1.38 0.74	-	-	-	-	-	-	-	-	84 6.95 1.76 0.57 0.30
Glendale (city)	60,773 33.03	30,233	4,418 14.61 14.61 7.27	-	-	223 25.23 5.05 0.74 0.37	-	-	564 21.60 12.77 1.87 0.93	-	1,986 18.22 44.95 6.57 3.27	-	-	-	-	742 46.00 16.79 2.45 1.22	537 4.54 12.15 1.78 0.88	-	-	-	-	-	-	13 3.10 0.29 0.04 0.02	-	90 9.70 2.04 0.30 0.15
Glendora (city)	35,545 76.21	3,149	696 22.10 22.10 1.96	-	-	67 12.81 9.63 2.13 0.19	-	-	166 19.44 23.85 5.27 0.47	-	207 26.44 29.74 6.57 0.58	-	-	-	-	-	-	-	-	-	-	-	-	-	-	-
Hacienda Heights (cdp)	19,208 38.35	18,400	2,120 11.52 11.52 11.04	-	-	-	-	-	620 7.13 29.25 3.37 3.23	-	390 29.84 18.40 2.12 2.03	-	-	-	-	684 52.86 32.26 3.72 3.56	166 6.71 7.83 0.90 0.86	-	-	-	-	-	50 1.81 2.36 0.27 0.26	-	-	14 3.08 0.66 0.08 0.07
Hawaiian Gardens (city)	3,863 28.86	1,223	107 8.75 8.75 2.77	-	-	-	-	-	-	-	-	-	-	-	-	-	31 4.25 28.97 2.53 0.80	-	-	-	-	-	-	-	-	-
Hawthorne (city)	37,391 49.40	5,566	905 16.26 16.26 2.42	496	173 34.88 34.88 0.46	106 22.89 11.71 1.90 0.28	-	-	89 16.36 9.83 1.60 0.24	-	296 14.11 32.71 5.32 0.79	-	-	-	-	296 69.81 32.71 5.32 0.79	-	-	-	-	-	-	-	-	-	41 3.00 4.53 0.74 0.11
Hermosa Beach (city)	15,875 89.37	852	476 55.87 55.87 3.00	-	-	-	-	-	-	-	-	-	-	-	-	-	-	-	-	-	-	-	-	-	-	-

Notes: Please refer to the User's Guide for an explanation of data; data is arranged alphabetically by state, then county, then city within each county; table includes counties with populations greater than 49,999 unless noted and cities with populations greater than 9,999 whose Asian and/or NHPI population rates are greater than the national average; (1) Native Hawaiian and other Pacific Islander; (2) excludes Taiwanese; (3) includes Chamorro; (4) county does not meet population threshold but is shown in order to allow inclusion of city

Place	Total population 5 years and over who speak English-only at home	Asian population 5 years and over	Asians 5 years and over who speak English-only at home	NHPI[1] population 5 years and over	NHPIs[1] 5 years and over who speak English-only at home	Asian Indian	Bangladeshi	Cambodian	Chinese[2]	Fijian	Filipino	Guamanian[3]	Hawaiian, Native	Hmong	Indonesian	Japanese	Korean	Laotian	Malaysian	Pakistani	Samoan	Sri Lankan	Taiwanese	Thai	Tongan	Vietnamese
La Canada Flintridge (city)	13,933 72.04	3,814	774 20.29 20.29 5.56	-	-	-	-	-	198 28.05 25.58 5.19 1.42	-	-	-	-	-	-	211 55.97 27.26 5.53 1.51	123 5.72 15.89 3.22 0.88	-	-	-	-	-	-	-	-	-
La Crescenta-Montrose (cdp)	11,162 64.35	3,323	450 13.54 13.54 4.03	-	-	-	-	-	-	-	105 31.53 23.33 3.16 0.94	-	-	-	-	-	86 3.67 19.11 2.59 0.77	-	-	-	-	-	-	-	-	-
La Mirada (city)	27,794 63.07	6,571	1,165 17.73 17.73 4.19	-	-	86 17.52 7.38 1.31 0.31	-	-	145 22.14 12.45 2.21 0.52	-	574 27.57 49.27 8.74 2.07	-	-	-	-	206 55.98 17.68 3.13 0.74	83 3.80 7.12 1.26 0.30	-	-	-	-	-	-	-	-	-
La Puente (city)	8,935 23.95	2,740	316 11.53 11.53 3.54	-	-	-	-	-	76 9.13 24.05 2.77 0.85	-	108 11.48 34.18 3.94 1.21	-	-	-	-	-	-	-	-	-	-	-	-	-	-	-
La Verne (city)	22,943 76.28	2,264	612 27.03 27.03 2.67	-	-	-	-	-	-	-	181 22.77 29.58 7.99 0.79	-	-	-	-	-	-	-	-	-	-	-	-	-	-	-
Lakewood (city)	52,375 70.89	9,796	2,164 22.09 22.09 4.13	656	245 37.35 37.35 0.47	44 11.17 2.03 0.45 0.08	-	96 13.79 4.44 0.98 0.18	162 16.91 7.49 1.65 0.31	-	1,095 24.40 50.60 11.18 2.09	-	-	-	-	496 70.86 22.92 5.06 0.95	79 5.72 3.65 0.81 0.15	-	-	-	185 35.85 75.51 28.20 0.35	-	-	-	-	33 8.11 1.52 0.34 0.06
Lancaster (city)	85,597 78.34	4,404	1,450 32.92 32.92 1.69	-	-	121 20.27 8.34 2.75 0.14	-	-	166 35.39 11.45 3.77 0.19	-	679 33.73 46.83 15.42 0.79	-	-	-	-	-	-	-	-	-	-	-	-	-	-	-
Lawndale (city)	12,263 42.50	2,773	383 13.81 13.81 3.12	387	130 33.59 33.59 1.06	-	-	-	-	-	142 24.03 37.08 5.12 1.16	-	-	-	-	-	-	-	-	-	-	-	-	-	-	28 2.25 7.31 1.01 0.23
Lomita (city)	12,883 69.97	2,158	554 25.67 25.67 4.30	-	-	-	-	-	-	-	134 29.26 24.19 6.21 1.04	-	-	-	-	285 47.82 51.44 13.21 2.21	38 7.45 6.86 1.76 0.29	-	-	-	-	-	-	-	-	-
Long Beach (city)	236,221 55.77	51,846	9,468 18.26 18.26 4.01	4,673	1,284 27.48 27.48 0.54	306 26.20 3.23 0.59 0.13	-	1,115 6.81 11.78 2.15 0.47	652 21.41 6.89 1.26 0.28	-	3,942 23.18 41.63 7.60 1.67	-	-	-	-	2,073 58.38 21.89 4.00 0.88	377 23.02 3.98 0.73 0.16	79 11.99 0.83 0.15 0.03	-	-	722 21.66 56.23 15.45 0.31	-	-	67 11.17 0.71 0.13 0.03	-	307 6.38 3.24 0.59 0.13

Notes: Please refer to the User's Guide for an explanation of data; data is arranged alphabetically by state, then county, then city within each county; table includes counties with populations greater than 49,999 unless noted and cities with populations greater than 9,999 whose Asian and/or NHPI population rates are greater than the national average; (1) Native Hawaiian and other Pacific Islander; (2) excludes Taiwanese; (3) includes Chamorro; (4) county does not meet population threshold but is shown in order to allow inclusion of city

Place	Total population 5 years and over who speak English-only at home	Asian population 5 years and over	Asians 5 years and over who speak English-only at home	NHPI[1] population 5 years and over	NHPIs[1] 5 years and over who speak English-only at home	Asian Indian	Bangladeshi	Cambodian	Chinese[2]	Fijian	Filipino	Guamanian[3]	Hawaiian, Native	Hmong	Indonesian	Japanese	Korean	Laotian	Malaysian	Pakistani	Samoan	Sri Lankan	Taiwanese	Thai	Tongan	Vietnamese
Los Angeles (city)	1,438,573 42.15	351,407	63,722 18.13 18.13 4.43	5,991	2,772 46.27 46.27 0.19	4,302 19.09 6.75 1.22 0.30	40 5.48 0.06 0.01 <0.01	311 7.83 0.49 0.09 0.02	9,756 16.85 15.31 2.78 0.68	-	19,701 20.39 30.92 5.61 1.37	482 46.26 17.39 8.05 0.03	1,156 75.11 41.70 19.30 0.08	-	244 14.55 0.38 0.07 0.02	16,046 44.59 25.18 4.57 1.12	7,362 8.46 11.55 2.10 0.51	35 5.25 0.05 0.01 <0.01	-	142 9.31 0.22 0.04 0.01	667 34.90 24.06 11.13 0.05	278 25.05 0.44 0.08 0.02	183 5.65 0.29 0.05 0.01	648 7.34 1.02 0.18 0.05	53 16.99 1.91 0.88 <0.01	1,314 7.14 2.06 0.37 0.09
Manhattan Beach (city)	28,100 88.31	1,914	1,096 57.26 57.26 3.90	-	-	-	-	-	289 56.23 26.37 15.10 1.03	-	-	-	-	-	-	436 73.65 39.78 22.78 1.55	-	-	-	-	-	-	-	-	-	-
Monrovia (city)	21,953 64.69	2,323	458 19.72 19.72 2.09	-	-	-	-	-	93 14.26 20.31 4.00 0.42	-	165 19.21 36.03 7.10 0.75	-	-	-	-	-	-	-	-	-	-	-	-	-	-	-
Montebello (city)	15,633 27.48	6,770	1,972 29.13 29.13 12.61	-	-	-	-	-	512 20.92 25.96 7.56 3.28	-	206 23.98 10.45 3.04 1.32	-	-	-	-	1,142 65.07 57.91 16.87 7.31	17 2.78 0.86 0.25 0.11	-	-	-	-	-	-	-	-	-
Monterey Park (city)	13,685 24.14	35,003	4,739 13.54 13.54 34.63	-	-	-	-	24 6.25 0.51 0.07 0.18	1,595 7.34 33.66 4.56 11.66	-	123 15.00 2.60 0.35 0.90	-	-	-	-	2,434 51.15 51.36 6.95 17.79	87 10.73 1.84 0.25 0.64	-	-	-	-	-	12 1.23 0.25 0.03 0.09	-	-	100 3.36 2.11 0.29 0.73
Norwalk (city)	36,265 38.42	11,501	1,920 16.69 16.69 5.29	-	-	184 14.89 9.58 1.60 0.51	-	31 6.92 1.61 0.27 0.09	104 11.70 5.42 0.90 0.29	-	846 19.95 44.06 7.36 2.33	-	-	-	-	379 80.13 19.74 3.30 1.05	164 6.87 8.54 1.43 0.45	-	-	-	-	-	-	-	-	66 8.28 3.44 0.57 0.18
Palmdale (city)	69,173 65.33	4,070	1,080 26.54 26.54 1.56	-	-	126 35.80 11.67 3.10 0.18	-	-	-	-	539 25.69 49.91 13.24 0.78	-	-	-	-	-	-	-	-	-	-	-	-	-	-	-
Palos Verdes Estates (city)	9,884 78.36	2,173	574 26.42 26.42 5.81	-	-	-	-	-	120 24.34 20.91 5.52 1.21	-	-	-	-	-	-	232 35.47 40.42 10.68 2.35	24 8.30 4.18 1.10 0.24	-	-	-	-	-	-	-	-	-
Pasadena (city)	68,587 55.01	12,743	3,361 26.38 26.38 4.90	-	-	171 20.96 5.09 1.34 0.25	-	-	851 21.39 25.32 6.68 1.24	-	429 17.17 12.76 3.37 0.63	-	-	-	-	1,228 56.51 36.54 9.64 1.79	351 27.23 10.44 2.75 0.51	-	-	-	-	-	-	-	-	88 11.64 2.62 0.69 0.13
Pomona (city)	50,419 37.20	10,104	1,986 19.66 19.66 3.94	-	-	129 21.04 6.50 1.28 0.26	-	71 10.38 3.58 0.70 0.14	320 17.41 16.11 3.17 0.63	-	754 27.44 37.97 7.46 1.50	-	-	-	-	272 54.29 13.70 2.69 0.54	-	11 2.24 0.55 0.11 0.02	-	-	-	-	-	-	-	173 10.12 8.71 1.71 0.34

Notes: Please refer to the User's Guide for an explanation of data; data is arranged alphabetically by state, then county, then city within each county; table includes counties with populations greater than 49,999 unless noted and cities with populations greater than 9,999 whose Asian and/or NHPI population rates are greater than the national average; (1) Native Hawaiian and other Pacific Islander; (2) excludes Taiwanese; (3) includes Chamorro; (4) county does not meet population threshold but is shown in order to allow inclusion of city

Place	Total population 5 years and over who speak English-only at home	Asian population 5 years and over	Asians 5 years and over who speak English-only at home	NHPI[1] population 5 years and over	NHPIs[1] 5 years and over who speak English-only at home	Asian Indian	Bangladeshi	Cambodian	Chinese[2]	Fijian	Filipino	Guamanian[3]	Hawaiian, Native	Hmong	Indonesian	Japanese	Korean	Laotian	Malaysian	Pakistani	Samoan	Sri Lankan	Taiwanese	Thai	Tongan	Vietnamese
Rancho Palos Verdes (city)	26,809	9,916	2,138	-	-	133	-	-	535	-	150	-	-	-	-	962	168	-	-	-	-	-	16	-	-	-
	67.86		21.56			24.91			20.62		26.64					33.83	7.15						3.01			
						6.22			25.02		7.02					45.00	7.86						0.75			
			21.56			1.34			5.40		1.51					9.70	1.69						0.16			
			7.97			0.50			2.00		0.56					3.59	0.63						0.06			
Redondo Beach (city)	46,879	5,545	2,449	-	-	146	-	-	457	-	437	-	-	-	-	1,019	184	-	-	-	-	-	-	-	-	-
	78.69		44.17			31.06			40.41		57.05					54.55	28.89									
						5.96			18.66		17.84					41.61	7.51									
			44.17			2.63			8.24		7.88					18.38	3.32									
			5.22			0.31			0.97		0.93					2.17	0.39									
Rosemead (city)	9,869	24,305	1,535	-	-	-	-	89	588	-	115	-	-	-	-	430	-	-	-	-	-	-	-	-	-	204
	19.99		6.32					12.73	4.17		16.72					55.48										3.73
								5.80	38.31		7.49					28.01										13.29
			6.32					0.37	2.42		0.47					1.77										0.84
			15.55					0.90	5.96		1.17					4.36										2.07
Rowland Heights (cdp)	12,936	23,270	1,866	-	-	138	-	-	505	-	612	-	-	-	-	276	158	-	-	-	-	-	91	-	-	0
	28.72		8.02			14.35			4.73		19.45					42.53	4.50						3.70			0.00
						7.40			27.06		32.80					14.79	8.47						4.88			0.00
			8.02			0.59			2.17		2.63					1.19	0.68						0.39			0.00
			14.42			1.07			3.90		4.73					2.13	1.22						0.70			0.00
San Dimas (city)	24,266	2,984	687	-	-	-	-	-	198	-	171	-	-	-	-	-	-	-	-	-	-	-	-	-	-	-
	73.49		23.02						17.43		24.68															
									28.82		24.89															
			23.02						6.64		5.73															
			2.83						0.82		0.70															
San Gabriel (city)	10,968	18,040	1,689	-	-	-	-	-	574	-	276	-	-	-	-	335	-	-	-	-	-	-	5	-	-	263
	29.78		9.36						5.23		24.58					54.92							0.73			10.34
									33.98		16.34					19.83							0.30			15.57
			9.36						3.18		1.53					1.86							0.03			1.46
			15.40						5.23		2.52					3.05							0.05			2.40
San Marino (city)	6,170	5,774	782	-	-	-	-	-	520	-	-	-	-	-	-	-	-	-	-	-	-	-	71	-	-	-
	50.06		13.54						14.09														4.82			
									66.50														9.08			
			13.54						9.01														1.23			
			12.67						8.43														1.15			
Santa Clarita (city)	107,110	7,062	2,213	-	-	165	-	-	146	-	641	-	-	-	-	664	145	-	-	-	-	-	-	-	-	79
	76.85		31.34			23.88			18.48		27.23					62.29	19.18									16.77
						7.46			6.60		28.97					30.00	6.55									3.57
			31.34			2.34			2.07		9.08					9.40	2.05									1.12
			2.07			0.15			0.14		0.60					0.62	0.14									0.07
Santa Monica (city)	57,174	5,828	2,021	-	-	185	-	-	499	-	150	-	-	-	-	730	184	-	-	-	-	-	-	-	-	-
	70.84		34.68			30.48			33.00		31.19					40.51	25.14									
						9.15			24.69		7.42					36.12	9.10									
			34.68			3.17			8.56		2.57					12.53	3.16									
			3.53			0.32			0.87		0.26					1.28	0.32									
Sierra Madre (city)	8,734	552	313	-	-	-	-	-	-	-	-	-	-	-	-	-	-	-	-	-	-	-	-	-	-	-
	87.17		56.70																							
			56.70																							
			3.58																							

Notes: Please refer to the User's Guide for an explanation of data; data is arranged alphabetically by state, then county, then city within each county; table includes counties with populations greater than 49,999 unless noted and cities with populations greater than 9,999 whose Asian and/or NHPI population rates are greater than the national average; (1) Native Hawaiian and other Pacific Islander; (2) excludes Taiwanese; (3) includes Chamorro; (4) county does not meet population threshold but is shown in order to allow inclusion of city

Place	Total population 5 years and over who speak English-only at home	Asian population 5 years and over	Asians 5 years and over who speak English-only at home	NHPI[1] population 5 years and over	NHPIs[1] 5 years and over who speak English-only at home	Asian Indian	Bangladeshi	Cambodian	Chinese[2]	Fijian	Filipino	Guamanian[3]	Hawaiian, Native	Hmong	Indonesian	Japanese	Korean	Laotian	Malaysian	Pakistani	Samoan	Sri Lankan	Taiwanese	Thai	Tongan	Vietnamese
South El Monte (city)	3,217	1,466	81	-	-	-	-	-	35	-	-	-	-	-	-	-	-	-	-	-	-	-	-	-	-	17
	17.13		5.53						5.74																	2.83
									43.21																	20.99
			5.53						2.39																	1.16
			2.52						1.09																	0.53
South Pasadena (city)	15,454	6,031	1,663	-	-	-	-	-	748	-	-	-	-	-	-	515	63	-	-	-	-	-	-	-	-	-
	66.85		27.57						23.10							51.97	9.49									
									44.98							30.97	3.79									
			27.57						12.40							8.54	1.04									
			10.76						4.84							3.33	0.41									
South San Jose Hills (cdp)	3,548	1,213	228	-	-	-	-	-	-	-	128	-	-	-	-	-	-	-	-	-	-	-	-	-	-	-
	19.23		18.80								17.83															
											56.14															
			18.80								10.55															
			6.43								3.61															
Temple City (city)	15,136	12,139	1,260	-	-	-	-	-	466	-	158	-	-	-	-	360	56	-	-	-	-	-	75	-	-	38
	48.28		10.38						6.39		24.35					63.38	11.43						5.05			4.76
									36.98		12.54					28.57	4.44						5.95			3.02
			10.38						3.84		1.30					2.97	0.46						0.62			0.31
			8.32						3.08		1.04					2.38	0.37						0.50			0.25
Torrance (city)	84,117	37,326	10,339	-	-	401	-	-	1,097	-	1,056	-	-	-	-	6,276	728	-	-	22	-	-	31	-	-	102
	64.57		27.70			19.43			19.50		31.10					49.07	8.84			4.02			2.52			5.85
						3.88			10.61		10.21					60.70	7.04			0.21			0.30			0.99
			27.70			1.07			2.94		2.83					16.81	1.95			0.06			0.08			0.27
			12.29			0.48			1.30		1.26					7.46	0.87			0.03			0.04			0.12
Valinda (cdp)	6,079	1,877	297	-	-	-	-	-	-	-	158	-	-	-	-	-	-	-	-	-	-	-	-	-	-	31
	30.62		15.82								16.41															6.60
											53.20															10.44
			15.82								8.42															1.65
			4.89								2.60															0.51
Vincent (cdp)	6,393	988	147	-	-	-	-	-	-	-	54	-	-	-	-	-	-	-	-	-	-	-	-	-	-	-
	46.34		14.88								9.76															
											36.73															
			14.88								5.47															
			2.30								0.84															
Walnut (city)	10,307	15,975	2,000	-	-	58	-	-	468	-	906	-	-	-	-	212	149	-	-	-	-	-	30	-	-	0
	36.03		12.52			7.69			7.92		27.05					51.71	8.26						1.66			0.00
						2.90			23.40		45.30					10.60	7.45						1.50			0.00
			12.52			0.36			2.93		5.67					1.33	0.93						0.19			0.00
			19.40			0.56			4.54		8.79					2.06	1.45						0.29			0.00
West Carson (cdp)	10,481	4,772	1,306	-	-	-	-	-	-	-	350	-	-	-	-	690	56	-	-	-	-	-	-	-	-	-
	52.89		27.37								17.38					63.95	7.10									
											26.80					52.83	4.29									
			27.37								7.33					14.46	1.17									
			12.46								3.34					6.58	0.53									
West Covina (city)	45,563	22,237	3,429	411	172	58	-	-	534	-	1,924	-	-	-	-	506	110	-	-	-	-	-	0	-	-	46
	46.97		15.42		41.85	12.34			8.59		20.57					70.67	12.49						0.00			2.30
						1.69			15.57		56.11					14.76	3.21						0.00			1.34
			15.42		41.85	0.26			2.40		8.65					2.28	0.49						0.00			0.21
			7.53		0.38	0.13			1.17		4.22					1.11	0.24						0.00			0.10

Notes: Please refer to the User's Guide for an explanation of data; data is arranged alphabetically by state, then county, then city within each county; table includes counties with populations greater than 49,999 unless noted and cities with populations greater than 9,999 whose Asian and/or NHPI population rates are greater than the national average; (1) Native Hawaiian and other Pacific Islander; (2) excludes Taiwanese; (3) includes Chamorro; (4) county does not meet population threshold but is shown in order to allow inclusion of city

Place	Total population 5 years and over who speak English-only at home	Asian population 5 years and over	Asians 5 years and over who speak English-only at home	NHPI[1] population 5 years and over	NHPIs[1] 5 years and over who speak English-only at home	Asian Indian	Bangladeshi	Cambodian	Chinese[2]	Fijian	Filipino	Guamanian[3]	Hawaiian, Native	Hmong	Indonesian	Japanese	Korean	Laotian	Malaysian	Pakistani	Samoan	Sri Lankan	Taiwanese	Thai	Tongan	Vietnamese
West Hollywood (city)	21,790 61.98	1,391	621 44.64 44.64 2.85	-	-	-	-	-	-	-	-	-	-	-	-	-	-	-	-	-	-	-	-	-	-	-
West Puente Valley (cdp)	5,587 26.46	1,671	245 14.66 14.66 4.39	-	-	-	-	-	-	-	146 21.10 59.59 8.74 2.61	-	-	-	-	-	-	-	-	-	-	-	-	-	-	24 5.25 9.80 1.44 0.43
Whittier (city)	46,937 60.70	3,091	1,045 33.81 33.81 2.23	-	-	-	-	-	299 26.44 28.61 9.67 0.64	-	213 34.75 20.38 6.89 0.45	-	-	-	-	249 58.87 23.83 8.06 0.53	118 35.98 11.29 3.82 0.25	-	-	-	-	-	-	-	-	-
Madera County	71,693 63.04	1,414	432 30.55 30.55 0.60	-	-	52 9.87 12.04 3.68 0.07	-	-	-	-	141 37.40 32.64 9.97 0.20	-	-	-	-	-	-	-	-	-	-	-	-	-	-	-
Marin County	188,413 80.52	10,514	3,538 33.65 33.65 1.88	-	-	302 21.90 8.54 2.87 0.16	-	-	1,179 39.23 33.32 11.21 0.63	-	586 47.41 16.56 5.57 0.31	-	-	-	-	821 52.87 23.21 7.81 0.44	269 23.98 7.60 2.56 0.14	-	-	-	-	-	-	-	-	75 6.10 2.12 0.71 0.04
Larkspur (city)	9,691 84.77	427	215 50.35 50.35 2.22	-	-	-	-	-	-	-	-	-	-	-	-	-	-	-	-	-	-	-	-	-	-	-
Novato (city)	35,438 78.83	2,420	662 27.36 27.36 1.87	-	-	-	-	-	205 33.88 30.97 8.47 0.58	-	158 34.27 23.87 6.53 0.45	-	-	-	-	-	-	-	-	-	-	-	-	-	-	-
San Rafael (city)	35,417 67.08	2,995	736 24.57 24.57 2.08	-	-	145 29.65 19.70 4.84 0.41	-	-	239 25.87 32.47 7.98 0.67	-	-	-	-	-	-	-	-	-	-	-	-	-	-	-	-	22 3.31 2.99 0.73 0.06
Tamalpais-Homestead (cdp)	8,805 87.91	485	280 57.73 57.73 3.18	-	-	-	-	-	-	-	-	-	-	-	-	-	-	-	-	-	-	-	-	-	-	-
Mendocino County	67,987 83.86	797	327 41.03 41.03 0.48	-	-	-	-	-	-	-	-	-	-	-	-	-	-	-	-	-	-	-	-	-	-	-

Notes: Please refer to the User's Guide for an explanation of data; data is arranged alphabetically by state, then county, then city within each county; table includes counties with populations greater than 49,999 unless noted and cities with populations greater than 9,999 whose Asian and/or NHPI population rates are greater than the national average; (1) Native Hawaiian and other Pacific Islander; (2) excludes Taiwanese; (3) includes Chamorro; (4) county does not meet population threshold but is shown in order to allow inclusion of city

Place	Total population 5 years and over who speak English-only at home	Asian population 5 years and over	Asians 5 years and over who speak English-only at home	NHPI[1] population 5 years and over	NHPIs[1] 5 years and over who speak English-only at home	Asian Indian	Bangladeshi	Cambodian	Chinese[2]	Fijian	Filipino	Guamanian[3]	Hawaiian, Native	Hmong	Indonesian	Japanese	Korean	Laotian	Malaysian	Pakistani	Samoan	Sri Lankan	Taiwanese	Thai	Tongan	Vietnamese
Merced County	105,364 54.80	13,222	2,274 17.20 17.20 2.16	-	-	169 8.86 7.43 1.28 0.16	-	-	158 37.71 6.95 1.19 0.15	-	531 37.06 23.35 4.02 0.50	-	-	589 10.09 25.90 4.45 0.56	-	379 70.06 16.67 2.87 0.36	-	105 6.42 4.62 0.79 0.10	-	-	-	-	-	-	-	-
Atwater (city)	12,542 60.23	1,178	234 19.86 19.86 1.87	-	-	-	-	-	-	-	-	-	-	8 2.15 3.42 0.68 0.06	-	-	-	-	-	-	-	-	-	-	-	-
Livingston (city)	1,724 18.49	1,394	122 8.75 8.75 7.08	-	-	49 4.46 40.16 3.52 2.84	-	-	-	-	-	-	-	-	-	-	-	-	-	-	-	-	-	-	-	-
Merced (city)	34,058 58.45	6,396	832 13.01 13.01 2.44	-	-	-	-	-	-	-	-	-	-	360 9.74 43.27 5.63 1.06	-	-	-	96 7.22 11.54 1.50 0.28	-	-	-	-	-	-	-	-
Monterey County	195,650 52.74	22,855	7,331 32.08 32.08 3.75	1,687	1,144 67.81 67.81 0.58	233 19.71 3.18 1.02 0.12	-	-	610 29.80 8.32 2.67 0.31	-	3,816 35.46 52.05 16.70 1.95	420 66.56 36.71 24.90 0.21	-	-	-	1,590 48.53 21.69 6.96 0.81	394 14.14 5.37 1.72 0.20	-	-	-	-	-	-	-	-	247 13.65 3.37 1.08 0.13
Marina (city)	15,346 64.74	4,011	993 24.76 24.76 6.47	475	351 73.89 73.89 2.29	-	-	-	-	-	399 33.36 40.18 9.95 2.60	-	-	-	-	190 51.63 19.13 4.74 1.24	160 13.09 16.11 3.99 1.04	-	-	-	-	-	-	-	-	96 14.26 9.67 2.39 0.63
Monterey (city)	21,220 75.04	2,210	813 36.79 36.79 3.83	-	-	-	-	-	68 17.13 8.36 3.08 0.32	-	221 52.87 27.18 10.00 1.04	-	-	-	-	319 44.62 39.24 14.43 1.50	-	-	-	-	-	-	-	-	-	-
Pacific Grove (city)	12,674 84.86	638	212 33.23 33.23 1.67	-	-	-	-	-	-	-	-	-	-	-	-	-	-	-	-	-	-	-	-	-	-	-
Salinas (city)	54,276 39.64	8,521	2,908 34.13 34.13 5.36	472	249 52.75 52.75 0.46	54 10.67 1.86 0.63 0.10	-	-	209 38.00 7.19 2.45 0.39	-	1,962 35.40 67.47 23.03 3.61	-	-	-	-	422 55.38 14.51 4.95 0.78	96 20.92 3.30 1.13 0.18	-	-	-	-	-	-	-	-	92 19.78 3.16 1.08 0.17
Seaside (city)	16,239 56.39	3,158	827 26.19 26.19 5.09	-	-	-	-	-	-	-	562 30.33 67.96 17.80 3.46	-	-	-	-	158 38.63 19.11 5.00 0.97	-	-	-	-	-	-	-	-	-	23 5.30 2.78 0.73 0.14

Notes: Please refer to the User's Guide for an explanation of data; data is arranged alphabetically by state, then county, then city within each county; table includes counties with populations greater than 49,999 unless noted and cities with populations greater than 9,999 whose Asian and/or NHPI population rates are greater than the national average; (1) Native Hawaiian and other Pacific Islander; (2) excludes Taiwanese; (3) includes Chamorro; (4) county does not meet population threshold but is shown in order to allow inclusion of city

Place	Total population 5 years and over who speak English-only at home	Asian population 5 years and over	Asians 5 years and over who speak English-only at home	NHPI[1] population 5 years and over	NHPIs[1] 5 years and over who speak English-only at home	Asian Indian	Bangladeshi	Cambodian	Chinese[2]	Fijian	Filipino	Guamanian[3]	Hawaiian, Native	Hmong	Indonesian	Japanese	Korean	Laotian	Malaysian	Pakistani	Samoan	Sri Lankan	Taiwanese	Thai	Tongan	Vietnamese
Napa County	87,307 74.75	3,704	1,155 31.18 31.18 1.32	-	-	-	-	-	174 33.98 15.06 4.70 0.20	-	598 32.22 51.77 16.14 0.68	-	-	-	-	172 43.22 14.89 4.64 0.20	-	-	-	-	-	-	-	-	-	-
Nevada County	82,188 93.59	569	356 62.57 62.57 0.43	-	-	-	-	-	-	-	-	-	-	-	-	-	-	-	-	-	-	-	-	-	-	-
Orange County	1,542,698 58.60	363,154	58,819 16.20 16.20 3.81	8,021	3,812 47.53 47.53 0.25	4,480 17.98 7.62 1.23 0.29	-	386 9.24 0.66 0.11 0.03	8,809 18.54 14.98 2.43 0.57	-	14,124 30.32 24.01 3.89 0.92	683 64.56 17.92 8.52 0.04	1,282 79.68 33.63 15.98 0.08	90 9.23 0.15 0.02 0.01	300 16.55 0.51 0.08 0.02	15,605 53.84 26.53 4.30 1.01	4,908 9.05 8.34 1.35 0.32	157 5.85 0.27 0.04 0.01	-	298 12.53 0.51 0.08 0.02	1,148 33.16 30.12 14.31 0.07	141 22.27 0.24 0.04 0.01	515 5.86 0.88 0.14 0.03	294 9.49 0.50 0.08 0.02	133 23.71 3.49 1.66 0.01	5,946 4.70 10.11 1.64 0.39
Aliso Viejo (cdp)	27,219 74.99	4,003	1,117 27.90 27.90 4.10	-	-	59 12.50 5.28 1.47 0.22	-	-	185 28.86 16.56 4.62 0.68	-	319 39.73 28.56 7.97 1.17	-	-	-	-	290 52.16 25.96 7.24 1.07	100 22.73 8.95 2.50 0.37	-	-	-	-	-	-	-	-	85 17.93 7.61 2.12 0.31
Anaheim (city)	134,266 45.17	36,906	5,095 13.81 13.81 3.79	976	432 44.26 44.26 0.32	559 14.65 10.97 1.51 0.42	-	-	573 15.39 11.25 1.55 0.43	-	1,449 19.96 28.44 3.93 1.08	-	-	-	-	1,279 59.54 25.10 3.47 0.95	454 7.32 8.91 1.23 0.34	9 1.19 0.18 0.02 0.01	-	25 6.58 0.49 0.07 0.02	283 55.27 65.51 29.00 0.21	-	0 0.00 0.00 0.00 0.00	17 3.91 0.33 0.05 0.01	-	467 4.82 9.17 1.27 0.35
Brea (city)	25,026 75.63	2,961	599 20.23 20.23 2.39	-	-	93 22.04 15.53 3.14 0.37	-	-	79 16.92 13.19 2.67 0.32	-	88 18.88 14.69 2.97 0.35	-	-	-	-	-	55 7.10 9.18 1.86 0.22	-	-	-	-	-	-	-	-	-
Buena Park (city)	37,272 51.67	15,853	2,082 13.13 13.13 5.59	-	-	111 7.04 5.33 0.70 0.30	-	-	121 9.33 5.81 0.76 0.32	-	900 18.84 43.23 5.68 2.41	-	-	-	-	409 56.65 19.64 2.58 1.10	218 4.33 10.47 1.38 0.58	-	-	-	-	-	-	-	-	69 7.56 3.31 0.44 0.19
Costa Mesa (city)	63,219 62.47	7,614	1,802 23.67 23.67 2.85	597	205 34.34 34.34 0.32	90 22.11 4.99 1.18 0.14	-	-	242 26.19 13.43 3.18 0.38	-	505 38.73 28.02 6.63 0.80	-	-	-	-	604 41.40 33.52 7.93 0.96	87 15.03 4.83 1.14 0.14	-	-	-	-	-	-	-	-	173 8.11 9.60 2.27 0.27
Cypress (city)	30,769 70.19	8,916	1,771 19.86 19.86 5.76	-	-	139 21.42 7.85 1.56 0.45	-	-	181 12.66 10.22 2.03 0.59	-	469 28.58 26.48 5.26 1.52	-	-	-	-	565 61.48 31.90 6.34 1.84	155 6.55 8.75 1.74 0.50	-	-	-	-	-	46 6.65 2.60 0.52 0.15	-	-	84 11.43 4.74 0.94 0.27
Foothill Ranch (cdp)	7,262 75.42	1,624	390 24.01 24.01 5.37	-	-	-	-	-	-	-	-	-	-	-	-	-	-	-	-	-	-	-	-	-	-	-

Notes: Please refer to the User's Guide for an explanation of data; data is arranged alphabetically by state, then county, then city within each county; table includes counties with populations greater than 49,999 unless noted and cities with populations greater than 9,999 whose Asian and/or NHPI population rates are greater than the national average; (1) Native Hawaiian and other Pacific Islander; (2) excludes Taiwanese; (3) includes Chamorro; (4) county does not meet population threshold but is shown in order to allow inclusion of city

Place	Total population 5 years and over who speak English-only at home	Asian population 5 years and over	Asians 5 years and over who speak English-only at home	NHPI[1] population 5 years and over	NHPIs[1] 5 years and over who speak English-only at home	Asian Indian	Bangladeshi	Cambodian	Chinese[2]	Fijian	Filipino	Guamanian[3]	Hawaiian, Native	Hmong	Indonesian	Japanese	Korean	Laotian	Malaysian	Pakistani	Samoan	Sri Lankan	Taiwanese	Thai	Tongan	Vietnamese
Fountain Valley (city)	33,348	13,474	2,113	-	-	62	-	-	440	-	255	-	-	-	-	829	122	-	-	-	-	-	29	-	-	255
	64.56		15.68			9.23			18.88		43.81					61.32	11.90						7.61			3.89
						2.93			20.82		12.07					39.23	5.77						1.37			12.07
			15.68			0.46			3.27		1.89					6.15	0.91						0.22			1.89
			6.34			0.19			1.32		0.76					2.49	0.37						0.09			0.76
Fullerton (city)	68,948	19,130	2,913	-	-	254	-	-	443	-	760	-	-	-	-	649	466	-	-	-	-	-	-	-	-	148
	58.85		15.23			14.71			16.67		36.40					58.00	5.54									9.80
						8.72			15.21		26.09					22.28	16.00									5.08
			15.23			1.33			2.32		3.97					3.39	2.44									0.77
			4.22			0.37			0.64		1.10					0.94	0.68									0.21
Garden Grove (city)	62,198	47,368	3,171	1,172	259	89	-	23	220	-	635	-	-	-	-	597	323	-	-	-	100	-	-	-	-	1,132
	40.75		6.69		22.10	12.88		4.78	9.24		22.77					57.46	5.70				14.49					3.49
						2.81		0.73	6.94		20.03					18.83	10.19				38.61					35.70
			6.69		22.10	0.19		0.05	0.46		1.34					1.26	0.68				8.53					2.39
			5.10		0.42	0.14		0.04	0.35		1.02					0.96	0.52				0.16					1.82
Huntington Beach (city)	139,239	16,782	4,454	340	285	225	-	-	711	-	759	-	-	-	-	1,856	269	-	-	-	-	-	8	-	-	334
	78.07		26.54		83.82	22.91			25.20		46.91					67.15	16.31						1.47			6.11
						5.05			15.96		17.04					41.67	6.04						0.18			7.50
			26.54		83.82	1.34			4.24		4.52					11.06	1.60						0.05			1.99
			3.20		0.20	0.16			0.51		0.55					1.33	0.19						0.01			0.24
Irvine (city)	81,501	40,064	7,575	-	-	1,031	-	-	1,582	-	1,660	-	-	-	-	1,326	741	-	-	-	-	-	146	-	-	527
	60.34		18.91			24.06			14.60		51.30					27.31	9.79						5.69			11.60
						13.61			20.88		21.91					17.50	9.78						1.93			6.96
			18.91			2.57			3.95		4.14					3.31	1.85						0.36			1.32
			9.29			1.27			1.94		2.04					1.63	0.91						0.18			0.65
La Habra (city)	30,610	3,197	722	-	-	-	-	-	149	-	142	-	-	-	-	-	93	-	-	-	-	-	-	-	-	-
	56.20		22.58						32.89		24.74						8.27									
									20.64		19.67						12.88									
			22.58						4.66		4.44						2.91									
			2.36						0.49		0.46						0.30									
La Palma (city)	7,387	6,191	1,171	-	-	109	-	-	116	-	306	-	-	-	-	487	88	-	-	-	-	-	-	-	-	-
	51.43		18.91			19.93			13.12		26.06					70.58	3.88									
						9.31			9.91		26.13					41.59	7.51									
			18.91			1.76			1.87		4.94					7.87	1.42									
			15.85			1.48			1.57		4.14					6.59	1.19									
Laguna Hills (city)	21,156	3,153	797	-	-	-	-	-	183	-	191	-	-	-	-	-	-	-	-	-	-	-	-	-	-	75
	71.95		25.28						32.11		31.83															14.79
									22.96		23.96															9.41
			25.28						5.80		6.06															2.38
			3.77						0.87		0.90															0.35
Laguna Niguel (city)	45,129	4,512	1,596	-	-	-	-	-	306	-	299	-	-	-	-	548	167	-	-	-	-	-	-	-	-	78
	78.65		35.37						32.28		35.94					66.42	25.42									16.81
									19.17		18.73					34.34	10.46									4.89
			35.37						6.78		6.63					12.15	3.70									1.73
			3.54						0.68		0.66					1.21	0.37									0.17
Lake Forest (city)	39,918	5,212	1,151	-	-	137	-	-	159	-	306	-	-	-	-	264	64	-	-	-	-	-	-	-	-	146
	72.93		22.08			21.11			24.27		29.80					47.23	11.47									10.99
						11.90			13.81		26.59					22.94	5.56									12.68
			22.08			2.63			3.05		5.87					5.07	1.23									2.80
			2.88			0.34			0.40		0.77					0.66	0.16									0.37

Notes: Please refer to the User's Guide for an explanation of data; data is arranged alphabetically by state, then county, then city within each county; table includes counties with populations greater than 49,999 unless noted and cities with populations greater than 9,999 whose Asian and/or NHPI population rates are greater than the national average; (1) Native Hawaiian and other Pacific Islander; (2) excludes Taiwanese; (3) includes Chamorro; (4) county does not meet population threshold but is shown in order to allow inclusion of city

Place	Total population 5 years and over who speak English-only at home	Asian population 5 years and over	Asians 5 years and over who speak English-only at home	NHPI[1] population 5 years and over	NHPIs[1] 5 years and over who speak English-only at home	Asian Indian	Bangladeshi	Cambodian	Chinese[2]	Fijian	Filipino	Guamanian[3]	Hawaiian, Native	Hmong	Indonesian	Japanese	Korean	Laotian	Malaysian	Pakistani	Samoan	Sri Lankan	Taiwanese	Thai	Tongan	Vietnamese
Los Alamitos (city)	8,503 80.02	1,004	340 33.86 33.86 4.00	-	-	-	-	-	-	-	-	-	-	-	-	-	-	-	-	-	-	-	-	-	-	-
Mission Viejo (city)	68,215 78.85	6,912	1,867 27.01 27.01 2.74	-	-	118 20.21 6.32 1.71 0.17	-	-	300 25.19 16.07 4.34 0.44	-	499 35.19 26.73 7.22 0.73	-	-	-	-	596 57.75 31.92 8.62 0.87	94 11.91 5.03 1.36 0.14	-	-	-	-	-	-	-	-	65 5.35 3.48 0.94 0.10
Newport Beach (city)	58,578 87.32	2,657	929 34.96 34.96 1.59	-	-	-	-	-	215 31.02 23.14 8.09 0.37	-	-	-	-	-	-	268 55.60 28.85 10.09 0.46	-	-	-	-	-	-	-	-	-	-
Orange (city)	75,327 63.33	10,989	2,062 18.76 18.76 2.74	-	-	139 17.91 6.74 1.26 0.18	-	-	240 19.05 11.64 2.18 0.32	-	570 29.16 27.64 5.19 0.76	-	-	-	-	504 67.02 24.44 4.59 0.67	170 11.41 8.24 1.55 0.23	-	-	-	-	-	90 19.82 4.36 0.82 0.12	-	-	215 6.05 10.43 1.96 0.29
Placentia (city)	28,177 64.45	4,961	1,226 24.71 24.71 4.35	-	-	68 14.02 5.55 1.37 0.24	-	-	229 21.13 18.68 4.62 0.81	-	197 27.02 16.07 3.97 0.70	-	-	-	-	328 71.15 26.75 6.61 1.16	165 25.27 13.46 3.33 0.59	-	-	-	-	-	-	-	-	116 13.29 9.46 2.34 0.41
Rancho Santa Margarita (city)	34,976 81.72	3,541	1,165 32.90 32.90 3.33	-	-	-	-	-	113 20.96 9.70 3.19 0.32	-	412 38.76 35.36 11.64 1.18	-	-	-	-	-	-	-	-	-	-	-	-	-	-	54 11.84 4.64 1.52 0.15
Rossmoor (cdp)	8,802 90.29	507	219 43.20 43.20 2.49	-	-	-	-	-	-	-	-	-	-	-	-	-	-	-	-	-	-	-	-	-	-	-
Santa Ana (city)	61,679 20.36	28,064	2,307 8.22 8.22 3.74	1,237	562 45.43 45.43 0.91	80 15.27 3.47 0.29 0.13	-	120 7.22 5.20 0.43 0.19	337 16.82 14.61 1.20 0.55	-	549 25.70 23.80 1.96 0.89	-	-	29 6.17 1.26 0.10 0.05	-	326 39.85 14.13 1.16 0.53	120 17.73 5.20 0.43 0.19	58 6.74 2.51 0.21 0.09	-	-	230 33.97 40.93 18.59 0.37	-	-	-	-	615 3.42 26.66 2.19 1.00
Seal Beach (city)	20,658 88.11	1,204	611 50.75 50.75 2.96	-	-	-	-	-	-	-	-	-	-	-	-	263 76.23 43.04 21.84 1.27	-	-	-	-	-	-	-	-	-	-
Stanton (city)	13,923 41.52	5,340	606 11.35 11.35 4.35	-	-	-	-	-	-	-	291 25.53 48.02 5.45 2.09	-	-	-	-	-	63 8.32 10.40 1.18 0.45	-	-	-	-	-	-	-	-	66 2.61 10.89 1.24 0.47

Notes: Please refer to the User's Guide for an explanation of data; data is arranged alphabetically by state, then county, then city within each county; table includes counties with populations greater than 49,999 unless noted and cities with populations greater than 9,999 whose Asian and/or NHPI population rates are greater than the national average; (1) Native Hawaiian and other Pacific Islander; (2) excludes Taiwanese; (3) includes Chamorro; (4) county does not meet population threshold but is shown in order to allow inclusion of city

Place	Total population 5 years and over who speak English-only at home	Asian population 5 years and over	Asians 5 years and over who speak English-only at home	NHPI[1] population 5 years and over	NHPIs[1] 5 years and over who speak English-only at home	Asian Indian	Bangladeshi	Cambodian	Chinese[2]	Fijian	Filipino	Guamanian[3]	Hawaiian, Native	Hmong	Indonesian	Japanese	Korean	Laotian	Malaysian	Pakistani	Samoan	Sri Lankan	Taiwanese	Thai	Tongan	Vietnamese
Tustin (city)	33,196 53.44	8,887	1,441 16.21 16.21 4.34	-	-	103 8.70 7.15 1.16 0.31	-	-	189 14.67 13.12 2.13 0.57	-	475 29.14 32.96 5.34 1.43	-	-	-	-	239 35.41 16.59 2.69 0.72	163 14.42 11.31 1.83 0.49	-	-	-	-	-	22 5.13 1.53 0.25 0.07	-	-	112 6.81 7.77 1.26 0.34
Tustin Foothills (cdp)	19,030 84.18	1,643	431 26.23 26.23 2.26	-	-	-	-	-	84 17.87 19.49 5.11 0.44	-	-	-	-	-	-	-	-	-	-	-	-	-	-	-	-	-
Westminster (city)	35,375 43.35	31,191	2,306 7.39 7.39 6.52	419	93 22.20 22.20 0.26	79 21.47 3.43 0.25 0.22	-	-	212 14.30 9.19 0.68 0.60	-	535 38.97 23.20 1.72 1.51	-	-	-	-	573 56.79 24.85 1.84 1.62	72 10.62 3.12 0.23 0.20	-	-	-	42 11.67 45.16 10.02 0.12	-	-	-	-	733 2.91 31.79 2.35 2.07
Yorba Linda (city)	44,660 80.89	6,114	1,725 28.21 28.21 3.86	-	-	115 17.06 6.67 1.88 0.26	-	-	314 20.08 18.20 5.14 0.70	-	323 37.38 18.72 5.28 0.72	-	-	-	-	639 76.80 37.04 10.45 1.43	131 15.27 7.59 2.14 0.29	-	-	-	-	-	-	-	-	87 14.15 5.04 1.42 0.19
Placer County	208,034 89.41	6,820	2,950 43.26 43.26 1.42	-	-	68 9.08 2.31 1.00 0.03	-	-	565 46.58 19.15 8.28 0.27	-	689 37.24 23.36 10.10 0.33	-	-	-	-	1,184 66.07 40.14 17.36 0.57	210 45.26 7.12 3.08 0.10	-	-	-	-	-	-	-	-	53 12.93 1.80 0.78 0.03
Rocklin (city)	31,226 92.59	1,254	595 47.45 47.45 1.91	-	-	-	-	-	-	-	-	-	-	-	-	253 58.70 42.52 20.18 0.81	-	-	-	-	-	-	-	-	-	-
Roseville (city)	64,362 86.60	3,087	1,160 37.58 37.58 1.80	-	-	26 4.69 2.24 0.84 0.04	-	-	297 49.67 25.60 9.62 0.46	-	339 36.41 29.22 10.98 0.53	-	-	-	-	346 68.51 29.83 11.21 0.54	-	-	-	-	-	-	-	-	-	-
Riverside County	957,094 67.12	51,744	13,490 26.07 26.07 1.41	3,344	1,760 52.63 52.63 0.18	881 16.89 6.53 1.70 0.09	-	86 15.55 0.64 0.17 0.01	1,204 21.00 8.93 2.33 0.13	-	6,299 33.80 46.69 12.17 0.66	448 51.14 25.45 13.40 0.05	661 84.74 37.56 19.77 0.07	28 6.70 0.21 0.05 <0.01	-	2,315 53.90 17.16 4.47 0.24	741 13.65 5.49 1.43 0.08	76 5.31 0.56 0.15 0.01	-	91 22.47 0.67 0.18 0.01	332 40.59 18.86 9.93 0.03	-	40 8.15 0.30 0.08 <0.01	222 25.90 1.65 0.43 0.02	-	525 8.96 3.89 1.01 0.05
Banning (city)	16,226 74.29	942	171 18.15 18.15 1.05	-	-	-	-	-	-	-	-	-	-	-	-	-	-	42 13.55 24.56 4.46 0.26	-	-	-	-	-	-	-	-
Corona (city)	72,436 64.17	8,577	1,851 21.58 21.58 2.56	-	-	187 13.88 10.10 2.18 0.26	-	-	98 11.71 5.29 1.14 0.14	-	895 31.18 48.35 10.43 1.24	-	-	-	-	306 54.16 16.53 3.57 0.42	67 6.12 3.62 0.78 0.09	-	-	-	-	-	-	-	-	138 10.39 7.46 1.61 0.19

Notes: Please refer to the User's Guide for an explanation of data; data is arranged alphabetically by state, then county, then city within each county; table includes counties with populations greater than 49,999 unless noted and cities with populations greater than 9,999 whose Asian and/or NHPI population rates are greater than the national average; (1) Native Hawaiian and other Pacific Islander; (2) excludes Taiwanese; (3) includes Chamorro; (4) county does not meet population threshold but is shown in order to allow inclusion of city

Place	Total population 5 years and over who speak English-only at home	Asian population 5 years and over	Asians 5 years and over who speak English-only at home	NHPI[1] population 5 years and over	NHPIs[1] 5 years and over who speak English-only at home	Asian Indian	Bangladeshi	Cambodian	Chinese[2]	Fijian	Filipino	Guamanian[3]	Hawaiian, Native	Hmong	Indonesian	Japanese	Korean	Laotian	Malaysian	Pakistani	Samoan	Sri Lankan	Taiwanese	Thai	Tongan	Vietnamese
Moreno Valley (city)	84,681 65.05	7,652	1,988 25.98 25.98 2.35	-	-	-	-	-	139 31.38 6.99 1.82 0.16	-	1,135 29.78 57.09 14.83 1.34	-	-	-	-	276 57.74 13.88 3.61 0.33	46 6.97 2.31 0.60 0.05	0 0.00 0.00 0.00 0.00	-	-	-	-	-	-	-	28 4.72 1.41 0.37 0.03
Palm Springs (city)	29,508 72.36	1,672	434 25.96 25.96 1.47	-	-	-	-	-	-	-	281 26.07 64.75 16.81 0.95	-	-	-	-	-	-	-	-	-	-	-	-	-	-	-
Pedley (cdp)	7,116 69.11	423	58 13.71 13.71 0.82	-	-	-	-	-	-	-	-	-	-	-	-	-	-	-	-	-	-	-	-	-	-	-
Riverside (city)	152,238 64.68	13,670	3,261 23.86 23.86 2.14	915	450 49.18 49.18 0.30	285 20.21 8.74 2.08 0.19	-	-	404 17.77 12.39 2.96 0.27	-	1,151 37.55 35.30 8.42 0.76	-	-	-	-	649 59.82 19.90 4.75 0.43	303 16.83 9.29 2.22 0.20	34 10.12 1.04 0.25 0.02	-	-	-	-	-	-	-	124 5.67 3.80 0.91 0.08
Temecula (city)	42,092 80.63	2,538	734 28.92 28.92 1.74	-	-	-	-	-	124 33.88 16.89 4.89 0.29	-	442 33.46 60.22 17.42 1.05	-	-	-	-	-	-	-	-	-	-	-	-	-	-	-
Sacramento County	859,305 75.64	125,447	30,174 24.05 24.05 3.51	5,769	1,868 32.38 32.38 0.22	1,605 13.72 5.32 1.28 0.19	-	93 8.90 0.31 0.07 0.01	6,401 23.48 21.21 5.10 0.74	192 11.55 10.28 3.33 0.02	8,515 37.32 28.22 6.79 0.99	554 67.40 29.66 9.60 0.06	588 93.48 31.48 10.19 0.07	693 4.59 2.30 0.55 0.08	-	7,928 65.96 26.27 6.32 0.92	921 20.79 3.05 0.73 0.11	636 7.23 2.11 0.51 0.07	-	220 17.21 0.73 0.18 0.03	284 25.94 15.20 4.92 0.03	-	69 17.60 0.23 0.06 0.01	164 22.87 0.54 0.13 0.02	56 8.59 3.00 0.97 0.01	1,131 7.35 3.75 0.90 0.13
Arden-Arcade (cdp)	73,165 81.15	4,534	1,224 27.00 27.00 1.67	-	-	101 15.14 8.25 2.23 0.14	-	-	201 24.39 16.42 4.43 0.27	-	352 32.99 28.76 7.76 0.48	-	-	37 12.37 3.02 0.82 0.05	-	282 56.06 23.04 6.22 0.39	-	-	-	-	-	-	-	-	-	19 4.99 1.55 0.42 0.03
Elk Grove (cdp)	41,388 74.50	9,824	2,078 21.15 21.15 5.02	-	-	133 10.25 6.40 1.35 0.32	-	-	165 11.90 7.94 1.68 0.40	-	1,086 33.62 52.26 11.05 2.62	-	-	-	-	337 75.73 16.22 3.43 0.81	-	-	-	-	-	-	-	-	-	167 7.94 8.04 1.70 0.40
Fair Oaks (cdp)	22,906 86.48	1,126	405 35.97 35.97 1.77	-	-	-	-	-	-	-	-	-	-	-	-	-	-	-	-	-	-	-	-	-	-	-
Florin (cdp)	16,206 64.02	5,032	756 15.02 15.02 4.66	-	-	37 13.60 4.89 0.74 0.23	-	-	80 12.82 10.58 1.59 0.49	-	295 32.60 39.02 5.86 1.82	-	-	20 2.15 2.65 0.40 0.12	-	-	-	-	-	-	-	-	-	-	-	64 5.31 8.47 1.27 0.39

Notes: Please refer to the User's Guide for an explanation of data; data is arranged alphabetically by state, then county, then city within each county; table includes counties with populations greater than 49,999 unless noted and cities with populations greater than 9,999 whose Asian and/or NHPI population rates are greater than the national average; (1) Native Hawaiian and other Pacific Islander; (2) excludes Taiwanese; (3) includes Chamorro; (4) county does not meet population threshold but is shown in order to allow inclusion of city

Place	Total population 5 years and over who speak English-only at home	Asian population 5 years and over	Asians 5 years and over who speak English-only at home	NHPI[1] population 5 years and over	NHPIs[1] 5 years and over who speak English-only at home	Asian Indian	Bangladeshi	Cambodian	Chinese[2]	Fijian	Filipino	Guamanian[3]	Hawaiian, Native	Hmong	Indonesian	Japanese	Korean	Laotian	Malaysian	Pakistani	Samoan	Sri Lankan	Taiwanese	Thai	Tongan	Vietnamese
Folsom (city)	41,976 86.65	3,285	1,106 33.67 33.67 2.63	-	-	198 16.42 17.90 6.03 0.47	-	-	161 29.87 14.56 4.90 0.38	-	360 61.02 32.55 10.96 0.86	-	-	-	-	-	-	-	-	-	-	-	-	-	-	-
Foothill Farms (cdp)	13,379 84.40	689	151 21.92 21.92 1.13	-	-	-	-	-	-	-	-	-	-	-	-	-	-	-	-	-	-	-	-	-	-	-
La Riviera (cdp)	7,940 81.33	860	246 28.60 28.60 3.10	-	-	-	-	-	-	-	-	-	-	-	-	-	-	-	-	-	-	-	-	-	-	-
Laguna (cdp)	23,957 76.60	5,745	1,865 32.46 32.46 7.78	-	-	85 12.84 4.56 1.48 0.35	-	-	395 22.43 21.18 6.88 1.65	-	627 37.21 33.62 10.91 2.62	-	-	-	-	476 88.81 25.52 8.29 1.99	-	-	-	-	-	-	-	-	-	0 0.00 0.00 0.00 0.00
North Highlands (cdp)	30,560 75.83	2,287	506 22.13 22.13 1.66	-	-	-	-	-	-	-	317 41.28 62.65 13.86 1.04	-	-	-	-	-	-	-	-	-	-	-	-	-	-	11 1.79 2.17 0.48 0.04
Parkway-S. Sacramento (cdp)	18,139 55.05	6,051	453 7.49 7.49 2.50	-	-	-	-	-	73 15.05 16.11 1.21 0.40	-	-	-	-	71 2.95 15.67 1.17 0.39	-	-	-	55 4.31 12.14 0.91 0.30	-	-	-	-	-	-	-	9 0.90 1.99 0.15 0.05
Rancho Cordova (cdp)	37,363 74.53	3,980	893 22.44 22.44 2.39	-	-	73 14.51 8.17 1.83 0.20	-	-	126 26.92 14.11 3.17 0.34	-	350 37.43 39.19 8.79 0.94	-	-	-	-	-	50 12.32 5.60 1.26 0.13	-	-	-	-	-	-	-	-	67 8.77 7.50 1.68 0.18
Rosemont (cdp)	16,291 76.42	2,545	700 27.50 27.50 4.30	-	-	-	-	-	-	-	242 60.05 34.57 9.51 1.49	-	-	-	-	-	75 16.38 10.71 2.95 0.46	-	-	-	-	-	-	-	-	12 2.29 1.71 0.47 0.07
Sacramento (city)	255,173 67.39	62,927	14,448 22.96 22.96 5.66	3,354	866 25.82 25.82 0.34	420 11.04 2.91 0.67 0.16	-	28 6.01 0.19 0.04 0.01	4,334 23.76 30.00 6.89 1.70	137 11.58 15.82 4.08 0.05	2,730 34.80 18.90 4.34 1.07	-	-	522 4.95 3.61 0.83 0.20	-	4,447 67.50 30.78 7.07 1.74	220 32.84 1.52 0.35 0.09	428 7.35 2.96 0.68 0.17	-	114 16.91 0.79 0.18 0.04	202 31.37 23.33 6.02 0.08	-	-	-	23 4.65 2.66 0.69 0.01	441 7.41 3.05 0.70 0.17
Vineyard (cdp)	7,293 79.02	1,540	441 28.64 28.64 6.05	-	-	-	-	-	-	-	257 37.14 58.28 16.69 3.52	-	-	-	-	-	-	-	-	-	-	-	-	-	-	-

Notes: Please refer to the User's Guide for an explanation of data; data is arranged alphabetically by state, then county, then city within each county; table includes counties with populations greater than 49,999 unless noted and cities with populations greater than 9,999 whose Asian and/or NHPI population rates are greater than the national average; (1) Native Hawaiian and other Pacific Islander; (2) excludes Taiwanese; (3) includes Chamorro; (4) county does not meet population threshold but is shown in order to allow inclusion of city

Place	Total population 5 years and over who speak English-only at home	Asian population 5 years and over	Asians 5 years and over who speak English-only at home	NHPI[1] population 5 years and over	NHPIs[1] 5 years and over who speak English-only at home	Asian Indian	Bangladeshi	Cambodian	Chinese[2]	Fijian	Filipino	Guamanian[3]	Hawaiian, Native	Hmong	Indonesian	Japanese	Korean	Laotian	Malaysian	Pakistani	Samoan	Sri Lankan	Taiwanese	Thai	Tongan	Vietnamese
San Benito County	30,248 62.21	1,011	494 48.86 48.86 1.63	-	-	-	-	-	-	-	305 57.66 61.74 30.17 1.01	-	-	-	-	-	-	-	-	-	-	-	-	-	-	-
San Bernardino County	1,035,292 66.00	74,410	16,911 22.73 22.73 1.63	4,457	1,566 35.14 35.14 0.15	1,383 18.74 8.18 1.86 0.13	-	210 12.79 1.24 0.28 0.02	1,842 18.37 10.89 2.48 0.18	-	7,665 31.56 45.33 10.30 0.74	433 43.83 27.65 9.72 0.04	466 82.04 29.76 10.46 0.05	-	255 8.76 1.51 0.34 0.02	2,553 60.80 15.10 3.43 0.25	1,197 17.55 7.08 1.61 0.12	27 6.47 0.16 0.04 <0.01	-	112 17.10 0.66 0.15 0.01	406 23.69 25.93 9.11 0.04	-	91 4.74 0.54 0.12 0.01	193 11.49 1.14 0.26 0.02	97 14.00 6.19 2.18 0.01	495 5.13 2.93 0.67 0.05
Chino (city)	38,733 61.62	3,177	784 24.68 24.68 2.02	-	-	-	-	-	-	-	439 29.66 55.99 13.82 1.13	-	-	-	-	-	-	-	-	-	-	-	-	-	-	22 4.98 2.81 0.69 0.06
Chino Hills (city)	39,333 64.38	13,126	2,986 22.75 22.75 7.59	-	-	159 14.83 5.32 1.21 0.40	-	-	394 12.65 13.19 3.00 1.00	-	1,719 33.03 57.57 13.10 4.37	-	-	-	-	383 72.95 12.83 2.92 0.97	86 8.65 2.88 0.66 0.22	-	-	-	-	-	12 2.19 0.40 0.09 0.03	-	-	72 9.41 2.41 0.55 0.18
Colton (city)	22,326 51.51	2,264	573 25.31 25.31 2.57	-	-	-	-	-	-	-	183 33.76 31.94 8.08 0.82	-	-	-	-	-	-	-	-	-	-	-	-	-	-	-
Fontana (city)	57,265 49.63	5,529	1,553 28.09 28.09 2.71	567	191 33.69 33.69 0.33	158 25.04 10.17 2.86 0.28	-	-	-	-	979 34.48 63.04 17.71 1.71	-	-	-	-	-	-	-	-	-	-	-	-	-	-	-
Grand Terrace (city)	8,816 79.89	515	172 33.40 33.40 1.95	-	-	-	-	-	-	-	-	-	-	-	-	-	-	-	-	-	-	-	-	-	-	-
Highland (city)	27,227 66.91	2,745	646 23.53 23.53 2.37	-	-	-	-	-	-	-	268 28.51 41.49 9.76 0.98	-	-	-	-	-	-	-	-	-	-	-	-	-	-	6 1.04 0.93 0.22 0.02
Loma Linda (city)	10,919 62.53	4,108	930 22.64 22.64 8.52	-	-	121 30.87 13.01 2.95 1.11	-	-	137 19.35 14.73 3.33 1.25	-	294 30.31 31.61 7.16 2.69	-	-	-	51 10.43 5.48 1.24 0.47	-	141 18.31 15.16 3.43 1.29	-	-	-	-	-	-	-	-	-
Montclair (city)	12,993 42.90	2,522	213 8.45 8.45 1.64	-	-	-	-	-	-	-	-	-	-	-	-	-	-	-	-	-	-	-	-	-	-	21 1.79 9.86 0.83 0.16

Notes: Please refer to the User's Guide for an explanation of data; data is arranged alphabetically by state, then county, then city within each county; table includes counties with populations greater than 49,999 unless noted and cities with populations greater than 9,999 whose Asian and/or NHPI population rates are greater than the national average; (1) Native Hawaiian and other Pacific Islander; (2) excludes Taiwanese; (3) includes Chamorro; (4) county does not meet population threshold but is shown in order to allow inclusion of city

Place	Total population 5 years and over who speak English-only at home	Asian population 5 years and over	Asians 5 years and over who speak English-only at home	NHPI[1] population 5 years and over	NHPIs[1] 5 years and over who speak English-only at home	Asian Indian	Bangladeshi	Cambodian	Chinese[2]	Fijian	Filipino	Guamanian[3]	Hawaiian, Native	Hmong	Indonesian	Japanese	Korean	Laotian	Malaysian	Pakistani	Samoan	Sri Lankan	Taiwanese	Thai	Tongan	Vietnamese
Ontario (city)	66,780 46.98	5,781	1,021 17.66 17.66 1.53	494	65 13.16 13.16 0.10	36 7.88 3.53 0.62 0.05	-	-	89 19.26 8.72 1.54 0.13	-	522 23.55 51.13 9.03 0.78	-	-	-	-	-	-	-	-	-	-	-	-	-	-	38 2.55 3.72 0.66 0.06
Rancho Cucamonga (city)	89,562 75.02	7,029	1,644 23.39 23.39 1.84	-	-	171 18.43 10.40 2.43 0.19	-	-	239 18.36 14.54 3.40 0.27	-	579 27.96 35.22 8.24 0.65	-	-	-	-	385 75.34 23.42 5.48 0.43	26 3.54 1.58 0.37 0.03	-	-	-	-	-	-	-	-	45 9.57 2.74 0.64 0.05
Redlands (city)	46,520 77.93	3,136	840 26.79 26.79 1.81	-	-	60 16.13 7.14 1.91 0.13	-	-	197 41.04 23.45 6.28 0.42	-	231 36.67 27.50 7.37 0.50	-	-	-	-	-	122 23.24 14.52 3.89 0.26	-	-	-	-	-	-	-	-	-
Rialto (city)	47,417 57.04	1,587	351 22.12 22.12 0.74	480	122 25.42 25.42 0.26	-	-	-	-	-	137 30.31 39.03 8.63 0.29	-	-	-	-	-	-	-	-	-	-	-	-	-	-	-
San Bernardino (city)	99,631 59.56	7,084	1,066 15.05 15.05 1.07	639	204 31.92 31.92 0.20	119 14.34 11.16 1.68 0.12	-	20 4.59 1.88 0.28 0.02	46 8.26 4.32 0.65 0.05	-	410 23.96 38.46 5.79 0.41	-	-	-	61 15.21 5.72 0.86 0.06	-	78 23.01 7.32 1.10 0.08	-	-	-	52 13.90 25.49 8.14 0.05	-	-	-	-	79 5.43 7.41 1.12 0.08
Upland (city)	46,681 73.24	4,737	738 15.58 15.58 1.58	-	-	103 19.47 13.96 2.17 0.22	-	-	91 13.58 12.33 1.92 0.19	-	171 30.65 23.17 3.61 0.37	-	-	-	-	-	102 11.31 13.82 2.15 0.22	-	-	-	-	-	0 0.00 0.00 0.00 0.00	-	-	22 2.67 2.98 0.46 0.05
Victorville (city)	44,368 75.36	2,286	894 39.11 39.11 2.01	-	-	-	-	-	-	-	575 49.23 64.32 25.15 1.30	-	-	-	-	-	-	-	-	-	-	-	-	-	-	-
San Diego County	1,752,737 66.96	234,358	57,934 24.72 24.72 3.31	12,444	7,227 58.08 58.08 0.41	1,949 21.79 3.36 0.83 0.11	-	273 6.83 0.47 0.12 0.02	5,536 20.45 9.56 2.36 0.32	-	34,179 29.91 59.00 14.58 1.95	2,801 63.27 38.76 22.51 0.16	1,955 92.13 27.05 15.71 0.11	43 3.39 0.07 0.02 <0.01	88 19.38 0.15 0.04 0.01	7,774 42.61 13.42 3.32 0.44	2,364 21.92 4.08 1.01 0.13	439 6.66 0.76 0.19 0.03	-	76 15.48 0.13 0.03 <0.01	1,760 39.50 24.35 14.14 0.10	-	224 10.25 0.39 0.10 0.01	394 30.95 0.68 0.17 0.02	68 20.99 0.94 0.55 <0.01	2,151 6.65 3.71 0.92 0.12
Bonita (cdp)	7,881 67.90	967	389 40.23 40.23 4.94	-	-	-	-	-	-	-	221 40.93 56.81 22.85 2.80	-	-	-	-	-	-	-	-	-	-	-	-	-	-	-
Carlsbad (city)	60,608 83.00	2,974	974 32.75 32.75 1.61	-	-	-	-	-	155 25.12 15.91 5.21 0.26	-	237 39.43 24.33 7.97 0.39	-	-	-	-	309 65.61 31.72 10.39 0.51	-	-	-	-	-	-	-	-	-	-

Notes: Please refer to the User's Guide for an explanation of data; data is arranged alphabetically by state, then county, then city within each county; table includes counties with populations greater than 49,999 unless noted and cities with populations greater than 9,999 whose Asian and/or NHPI population rates are greater than the national average; (1) Native Hawaiian and other Pacific Islander; (2) excludes Taiwanese; (3) includes Chamorro; (4) county does not meet population threshold but is shown in order to allow inclusion of city

Place	Total population 5 years and over who speak English-only at home	Asian population 5 years and over	Asians 5 years and over who speak English-only at home	NHPI[1] population 5 years and over	NHPIs[1] 5 years and over who speak English-only at home	Asian Indian	Bangladeshi	Cambodian	Chinese[2]	Fijian	Filipino	Guamanian[3]	Hawaiian, Native	Hmong	Indonesian	Japanese	Korean	Laotian	Malaysian	Pakistani	Samoan	Sri Lankan	Taiwanese	Thai	Tongan	Vietnamese
Chula Vista (city)	76,109 47.42	17,669	5,532 31.31 31.31 7.27	700	415 59.29 59.29 0.55	-	-	-	190 18.59 3.43 1.08 0.25	-	4,229 34.53 76.45 23.93 5.56	216 52.68 52.05 30.86 0.28	-	-	-	607 30.95 10.97 3.44 0.80	136 10.20 2.46 0.77 0.18	-	-	-	-	-	-	-	-	-
Coronado (city)	19,606 84.35	901	332 36.85 36.85 1.69	-	-	-	-	-	-	-	133 28.60 40.06 14.76 0.68	-	-	-	-	-	-	-	-	-	-	-	-	-	-	-
Escondido (city)	75,357 61.88	5,245	1,357 25.87 25.87 1.80	-	-	-	-	-	75 17.73 5.53 1.43 0.10	-	755 39.14 55.64 14.39 1.00	-	-	-	-	-	-	0 0.00 0.00 0.00 0.00	-	-	-	-	-	-	-	185 15.49 13.63 3.53 0.25
Imperial Beach (city)	15,070 60.84	1,712	461 26.93 26.93 3.06	-	-	-	-	-	-	-	319 22.48 69.20 18.63 2.12	-	-	-	-	-	-	-	-	-	-	-	-	-	-	-
La Mesa (city)	42,773 82.78	2,116	668 31.57 31.57 1.56	-	-	-	-	-	-	-	271 50.28 40.57 12.81 0.63	-	-	-	-	-	-	-	-	-	-	-	-	-	-	-
La Presa (cdp)	19,455 63.64	3,238	851 26.28 26.28 4.37	-	-	-	-	-	-	-	763 26.23 89.66 23.56 3.92	-	-	-	-	-	-	-	-	-	-	-	-	-	-	-
Lemon Grove (city)	16,920 72.76	1,366	470 34.41 34.41 2.78	-	-	-	-	-	-	-	352 51.31 74.89 25.77 2.08	-	-	-	-	-	-	-	-	-	-	-	-	-	-	16 4.80 3.40 1.17 0.09
National City (city)	14,929 29.78	9,368	1,529 16.32 16.32 10.24	-	-	-	-	-	-	-	1,347 15.82 88.10 14.38 9.02	-	-	-	-	-	-	-	-	-	-	-	-	-	-	-
Oceanside (city)	100,853 67.83	8,504	2,460 28.93 28.93 2.44	2,042	764 37.41 37.41 0.76	-	-	-	118 25.71 4.80 1.39 0.12	-	1,391 28.02 56.54 16.36 1.38	-	-	-	-	629 53.85 25.57 7.40 0.62	-	-	-	-	372 27.05 48.69 18.22 0.37	-	-	-	-	50 6.40 2.03 0.59 0.05
Poway (city)	38,690 85.20	3,276	1,136 34.68 34.68 2.94	-	-	-	-	-	199 29.35 17.52 6.07 0.51	-	572 44.93 50.35 17.46 1.48	-	-	-	-	-	-	-	-	-	-	-	-	-	-	-

Notes: Please refer to the User's Guide for an explanation of data; data is arranged alphabetically by state, then county, then city within each county; table includes counties with populations greater than 49,999 unless noted and cities with populations greater than 9,999 whose Asian and/or NHPI population rates are greater than the national average; (1) Native Hawaiian and other Pacific Islander; (2) excludes Taiwanese; (3) includes Chamorro; (4) county does not meet population threshold but is shown in order to allow inclusion of city

Place	Total population 5 years and over who speak English-only at home	Asian population 5 years and over	Asians 5 years and over who speak English-only at home	NHPI[1] population 5 years and over	NHPIs[1] 5 years and over who speak English-only at home	Asian Indian	Bangladeshi	Cambodian	Chinese[2]	Fijian	Filipino	Guamanian[3]	Hawaiian, Native	Hmong	Indonesian	Japanese	Korean	Laotian	Malaysian	Pakistani	Samoan	Sri Lankan	Taiwanese	Thai	Tongan	Vietnamese
Rancho San Diego (cdp)	15,110 80.19	973	412 42.34 42.34 2.73	-	-	-	-	-	-	-	189 36.00 45.87 19.42 1.25	-	-	-	-	-	-	-	-	-	-	-	-	-	-	-
San Diego (city)	714,484 62.58	156,492	34,354 21.95 21.95 4.81	5,727	3,512 61.32 61.32 0.49	1,116 18.30 3.25 0.71 0.16	-	210 5.85 0.61 0.13 0.03	3,721 18.14 10.83 2.38 0.52	-	20,457 29.24 59.55 13.07 2.86	1,361 68.36 38.75 23.76 0.19	1,003 94.98 28.56 17.51 0.14	32 3.21 0.09 0.02 <0.01	-	3,783 38.47 11.01 2.42 0.53	1,350 21.06 3.93 0.86 0.19	385 6.91 1.12 0.25 0.05	-	-	849 43.63 24.17 14.82 0.12	-	106 7.24 0.31 0.07 0.01	252 31.07 0.73 0.16 0.04	-	1,494 5.58 4.35 0.95 0.21
San Marcos (city)	31,967 63.35	2,323	678 29.19 29.19 2.12	-	-	-	-	-	93 23.37 13.72 4.00 0.29	-	360 30.28 53.10 15.50 1.13	-	-	-	-	-	-	-	-	-	-	-	-	-	-	-
Solana Beach (city)	9,875 79.76	507	219 43.20 43.20 2.22	-	-	-	-	-	-	-	-	-	-	-	-	-	-	-	-	-	-	-	-	-	-	-
Spring Valley (cdp)	18,891 76.68	1,275	492 38.59 38.59 2.60	-	-	-	-	-	-	-	288 47.45 58.54 22.59 1.52	-	-	-	-	-	-	-	-	-	-	-	-	-	-	-
Vista (city)	52,000 63.15	3,040	945 31.09 31.09 1.82	508	359 70.67 70.67 0.69	-	-	-	-	-	429 37.76 45.40 14.11 0.83	-	-	-	-	210 35.65 22.22 6.91 0.40	-	-	-	-	-	-	-	-	-	-
San Francisco County	404,571 54.26	230,295	38,722 16.81 16.81 9.57	3,266	1,079 33.04 33.04 0.27	1,604 34.58 4.14 0.70 0.40	-	25 3.96 0.06 0.01 0.01	17,978 12.13 46.43 7.81 4.44	-	9,450 24.56 24.40 4.10 2.34	-	-	-	139 16.35 0.36 0.06 0.03	4,587 43.11 11.85 1.99 1.13	1,848 26.67 4.77 0.80 0.46	-	-	28 5.32 0.07 0.01 0.01	428 20.88 39.67 13.10 0.11	-	71 9.38 0.18 0.03 0.02	240 16.76 0.62 0.10 0.06	-	884 8.91 2.28 0.38 0.22
San Francisco (city)	404,571 54.26	230,295	38,722 16.81 16.81 9.57	3,266	1,079 33.04 33.04 0.27	1,604 34.58 4.14 0.70 0.40	-	25 3.96 0.06 0.01 0.01	17,978 12.13 46.43 7.81 4.44	-	9,450 24.56 24.40 4.10 2.34	-	-	-	139 16.35 0.36 0.06 0.03	4,587 43.11 11.85 1.99 1.13	1,848 26.67 4.77 0.80 0.46	-	-	28 5.32 0.07 0.01 0.01	428 20.88 39.67 13.10 0.11	-	71 9.38 0.18 0.03 0.02	240 16.76 0.62 0.10 0.06	-	884 8.91 2.28 0.38 0.22
San Joaquin County	344,240 66.27	60,284	12,915 21.42 21.42 3.75	1,662	853 51.32 51.32 0.25	501 10.67 3.88 0.83 0.15	-	288 3.30 2.23 0.48 0.08	1,046 19.68 8.10 1.74 0.30	-	6,879 34.60 53.26 11.41 2.00	-	303 80.59 35.52 18.23 0.09	162 3.08 1.25 0.27 0.05	-	2,267 66.66 17.55 3.76 0.66	208 26.40 1.61 0.35 0.06	228 8.20 1.77 0.38 0.07	-	123 10.21 0.95 0.20 0.04	122 34.86 14.30 7.34 0.04	-	-	-	-	361 6.11 2.80 0.60 0.10
Lathrop (city)	5,786 61.46	1,375	416 30.25 30.25 7.19	-	-	-	-	-	-	-	251 25.02 60.34 18.25 4.34	-	-	-	-	-	-	-	-	-	-	-	-	-	-	-

Notes: Please refer to the User's Guide for an explanation of data; data is arranged alphabetically by state, then county, then city within each county; table includes counties with populations greater than 49,999 unless noted and cities with populations greater than 9,999 whose Asian and/or NHPI population rates are greater than the national average; (1) Native Hawaiian and other Pacific Islander; (2) excludes Taiwanese; (3) includes Chamorro; (4) county does not meet population threshold but is shown in order to allow inclusion of city

Place	Total population 5 years and over who speak English-only at home	Asian population 5 years and over	Asians 5 years and over who speak English-only at home	NHPI[1] population 5 years and over	NHPIs[1] 5 years and over who speak English-only at home	Asian Indian	Bangladeshi	Cambodian	Chinese[2]	Fijian	Filipino	Guamanian[3]	Hawaiian, Native	Hmong	Indonesian	Japanese	Korean	Laotian	Malaysian	Pakistani	Samoan	Sri Lankan	Taiwanese	Thai	Tongan	Vietnamese
Lodi (city)	36,942	2,835	887	-	-	56	-	-	-	-	301	-	-	-	-	441	-	-	-	-	-	-	-	-	-	-
	70.25		31.29			8.07					49.02					74.24										
						6.31					33.93					49.72										
			31.29			1.98					10.62					15.56										
			2.40			0.15					0.81					1.19										
Stockton (city)	130,099	45,188	7,753	922	536	220	-	277	647	-	4,440	-	-	120	-	955	-	228	-	33	-	-	-	-	-	262
	58.46		17.16		58.13	11.29		3.30	15.85		31.45			2.75		60.37		8.52		5.08						4.85
						2.84		3.57	8.35		57.27			1.55		12.32		2.94		0.43						3.38
			17.16		58.13	0.49		0.61	1.43		9.83			0.27		2.11		0.50		0.07						0.58
			5.96		0.41	0.17		0.21	0.50		3.41			0.09		0.73		0.18		0.03						0.20
Tracy (city)	37,647	4,339	1,320	-	-	77	-	-	83	-	759	-	-	-	-	-	-	-	-	-	-	-	-	-	-	-
	72.82		30.42			7.44			26.95		41.09															
						5.83			6.29		57.50															
			30.42			1.77			1.91		17.49															
			3.51			0.20			0.22		2.02															
San Luis Obispo County	200,112	6,693	2,591	-	-	127	-	-	339	-	1,024	-	-	-	-	601	152	-	-	-	-	-	-	-	-	-
	85.33		38.71			20.96			30.38		42.76					59.80	21.35									
						4.90			13.08		39.52					23.20	5.87									
			38.71			1.90			5.06		15.30					8.98	2.27									
			1.29			0.06			0.17		0.51					0.30	0.08									
Baywood-Los Osos (cdp)	11,927	777	178	-	-	-	-	-	-	-	100	-	-	-	-	-	-	-	-	-	-	-	-	-	-	-
	88.76		22.91								18.05															
											56.18															
			22.91								12.87															
			1.49								0.84															
Grover Beach (city)	9,609	463	114	-	-	-	-	-	-	-	-	-	-	-	-	-	-	-	-	-	-	-	-	-	-	-
	79.58		24.62																							
			24.62																							
			1.19																							
San Luis Obispo (city)	36,637	2,264	813	-	-	-	-	-	175	-	323	-	-	-	-	-	-	-	-	-	-	-	-	-	-	-
	86.10		35.91						31.36		60.26															
									21.53		39.73															
			35.91						7.73		14.27															
			2.22						0.48		0.88															
San Mateo County	387,594	134,081	32,677	7,848	1,970	1,724	-	-	9,078	103	14,586	248	634	-	160	4,163	737	-	-	-	344	-	96	130	274	409
	58.50		24.37		25.10	17.03			20.15	9.80	25.71	62.31	83.31		21.86	46.09	17.81				24.98		12.83	18.68	8.37	15.52
						5.28			27.78	5.23	44.64	12.59	32.18		0.49	12.74	2.26				17.46		0.29	0.40	13.91	1.25
			24.37		25.10	1.29			6.77	1.31	10.88	3.16	8.08		0.12	3.10	0.55				4.38		0.07	0.10	3.49	0.31
			8.43		0.51	0.44			2.34	0.03	3.76	0.06	0.16		0.04	1.07	0.19				0.09		0.02	0.03	0.07	0.11
Belmont (city)	17,439	3,623	1,179	-	-	49	-	-	481	-	250	-	-	-	-	252	-	-	-	-	-	-	-	-	-	-
	73.68		32.54			7.38			30.70		42.02					61.17										
						4.16			40.80		21.20					21.37										
			32.54			1.35			13.28		6.90					6.96										
			6.76			0.28			2.76		1.43					1.45										
Burlingame (city)	18,985	3,587	905	-	-	-	-	-	263	-	254	-	-	-	-	166	-	-	-	-	-	-	-	-	-	-
	71.52		25.23						14.81		46.27					42.89										
									29.06		28.07					18.34										
			25.23						7.33		7.08					4.63										
			4.77						1.39		1.34					0.87										

Notes: Please refer to the User's Guide for an explanation of data; data is arranged alphabetically by state, then county, then city within each county; table includes counties with populations greater than 49,999 unless noted and cities with populations greater than 9,999 whose Asian and/or NHPI population rates are greater than the national average; (1) Native Hawaiian and other Pacific Islander; (2) excludes Taiwanese; (3) includes Chamorro; (4) county does not meet population threshold but is shown in order to allow inclusion of city

Place	Total population 5 years and over who speak English-only at home	Asian population 5 years and over	Asians 5 years and over who speak English-only at home	NHPI[1] population 5 years and over	NHPIs[1] 5 years and over who speak English-only at home	Asian Indian	Bangladeshi	Cambodian	Chinese[2]	Fijian	Filipino	Guamanian[3]	Hawaiian, Native	Hmong	Indonesian	Japanese	Korean	Laotian	Malaysian	Pakistani	Samoan	Sri Lankan	Taiwanese	Thai	Tongan	Vietnamese
Daly City (city)	32,653	49,257	9,662	813	276	208	-	-	1,700	-	6,692	-	-	-	-	368	132	-	-	-	-	-	-	-	-	135
	33.56		19.62		33.95	21.12			13.04		21.65					45.54	17.62									15.15
						2.15			17.59		69.26					3.81	1.37									1.40
			19.62		33.95	0.42			3.45		13.59					0.75	0.27									0.27
			29.59		0.85	0.64			5.21		20.49					1.13	0.40									0.41
East Palo Alto (city)	9,372	553	155	2,013	263	-	-	-	-	-	-	-	-	-	-	-	-	-	-	-	-	-	-	-	26	-
	35.21		28.03		13.07																				1.95	
																									9.89	
			28.03		13.07																				1.29	
			1.65		2.81																				0.28	
Foster City (city)	16,380	8,785	2,015	-	-	134	-	-	931	-	224	-	-	-	-	463	67	-	-	-	-	-	-	-	-	-
	60.33		22.94			8.67			22.76		29.28					34.07	17.96									
						6.65			46.20		11.12					22.98	3.33									
			22.94			1.53			10.60		2.55					5.27	0.76									
			12.30			0.82			5.68		1.37					2.83	0.41									
Hillsborough (town)	7,159	2,554	472	-	-	-	-	-	346	-	-	-	-	-	-	-	-	-	-	-	-	-	-	-	-	-
	69.82		18.48						18.14																	
									73.31																	
			18.48						13.55																	
			6.59						4.83																	
Menlo Park (city)	20,977	1,991	659	-	-	-	-	-	291	-	-	-	-	-	-	122	-	-	-	-	-	-	-	-	-	-
	72.75		33.10						37.07							29.33										
									44.16							18.51										
			33.10						14.62							6.13										
			3.14						1.39							0.58										
Millbrae (city)	11,213	5,566	1,103	-	-	50	-	-	619	-	261	-	-	-	-	100	24	-	-	-	-	-	-	-	-	-
	56.80		19.82			14.71			17.09		40.34					27.93	7.77									
						4.53			56.12		23.66					9.07	2.18									
			19.82			0.90			11.12		4.69					1.80	0.43									
			9.84			0.45			5.52		2.33					0.89	0.21									
Pacifica (city)	27,550	5,579	1,693	-	-	-	-	-	428	-	857	-	-	-	-	204	-	-	-	-	-	-	-	-	-	-
	75.60		30.35						29.72		27.82					57.30										
									25.28		50.62					12.05										
			30.35						7.67		15.36					3.66										
			6.15						1.55		3.11					0.74										
Redwood City (city)	42,306	6,378	1,934	506	204	231	-	-	554	-	522	-	-	-	-	343	-	-	-	-	-	-	-	-	-	-
	60.59		30.32		40.32	20.94			23.72		37.83					58.04										
						11.94			28.65		26.99					17.74										
			30.32		40.32	3.62			8.69		8.18					5.38										
			4.57		0.48	0.55			1.31		1.23					0.81										
San Bruno (city)	21,838	7,081	2,049	961	135	110	-	-	555	-	988	-	-	-	-	247	-	-	-	-	-	-	-	-	40	-
	57.78		28.94		14.05	11.55			26.94		33.89					54.05									8.39	
						5.37			27.09		48.22					12.05									29.63	
			28.94		14.05	1.55			7.84		13.95					3.49									4.16	
			9.38		0.62	0.50			2.54		4.52					1.13									0.18	
San Carlos (city)	20,817	1,750	755	-	-	-	-	-	277	-	-	-	-	-	-	-	-	-	-	-	-	-	-	-	-	-
	80.81		43.14						42.35																	
									36.69																	
			43.14						15.83																	
			3.63						1.33																	

Notes: Please refer to the User's Guide for an explanation of data; data is arranged alphabetically by state, then county, then city within each county; table includes counties with populations greater than 49,999 unless noted and cities with populations greater than 9,999 whose Asian and/or NHPI population rates are greater than the national average; (1) Native Hawaiian and other Pacific Islander; (2) excludes Taiwanese; (3) includes Chamorro; (4) county does not meet population threshold but is shown in order to allow inclusion of city

Place	Total population 5 years and over who speak English-only at home	Asian population 5 years and over	Asians 5 years and over who speak English-only at home	NHPI[1] population 5 years and over	NHPIs[1] 5 years and over who speak English-only at home	Asian Indian	Bangladeshi	Cambodian	Chinese[2]	Fijian	Filipino	Guamanian[3]	Hawaiian, Native	Hmong	Indonesian	Japanese	Korean	Laotian	Malaysian	Pakistani	Samoan	Sri Lankan	Taiwanese	Thai	Tongan	Vietnamese
San Mateo (city)	54,174	13,526	3,564	1,263	321	294	-	-	1,006	-	936	-	-	-	-	912	101	-	-	-	-	-	-	-	70	48
	62.39		26.35		25.42	14.33			19.69		33.71					47.08	18.84								12.24	13.22
						8.25			28.23		26.26					25.59	2.83								21.81	1.35
			26.35		25.42	2.17			7.44		6.92					6.74	0.75								5.54	0.35
			6.58		0.59	0.54			1.86		1.73					1.68	0.19								0.13	0.09
South San Francisco (city)	25,716	16,623	4,202	787	292	71	-	-	942	-	2,681	-	-	-	-	296	-	-	-	-	-	-	-	-	-	-
	45.35		25.28		37.10	10.13			21.50		27.40					57.93										
						1.69			22.42		63.80					7.04										
			25.28		37.10	0.43			5.67		16.13					1.78										
			16.34		1.14	0.28			3.66		10.43					1.15										
Santa Barbara County	251,390	14,802	5,280	881	547	239	-	-	736	-	1,761	-	-	11	-	1,328	392	-	-	-	-	-	-	-	-	185
	67.24		35.67		62.09	31.28			29.86		38.17			3.75		58.94	25.41									15.93
						4.53			13.94		33.35			0.21		25.15	7.42									3.50
			35.67		62.09	1.61			4.97		11.90			0.07		8.97	2.65									1.25
			2.10		0.22	0.10			0.29		0.70			<0.01		0.53	0.16									0.07
Goleta (cdp)	38,720	3,076	1,045	-	-	-	-	-	236	-	181	-	-	-	-	299	-	-	-	-	-	-	-	-	-	55
	73.93		33.97						31.64		35.49					67.65										11.96
									22.58		17.32					28.61										5.26
			33.97						7.67		5.88					9.72										1.79
			2.70						0.61		0.47					0.77										0.14
Isla Vista (cdp)	12,647	1,941	691	-	-	-	-	-	156	-	-	-	-	-	-	-	91	-	-	-	-	-	-	-	-	-
	70.46		35.60						23.71								22.20									
									22.58								13.17									
			35.60						8.04								4.69									
			5.46						1.23								0.72									
Lompoc (city)	25,866	1,429	450	-	-	-	-	-	-	-	163	-	-	-	-	-	-	-	-	-	-	-	-	-	-	-
	68.15		31.49								48.51															
											36.22															
			31.49								11.41															
			1.74								0.63															
Orcutt (cdp)	23,704	1,010	424	-	-	-	-	-	-	-	-	-	-	-	-	-	-	-	-	-	-	-	-	-	-	-
	87.12		41.98																							
			41.98																							
			1.79																							
Santa Maria (city)	34,040	3,390	978	-	-	-	-	-	-	-	660	-	-	-	-	190	-	-	-	-	-	-	-	-	-	-
	48.40		28.85								29.24					45.24										
											67.48					19.43										
			28.85								19.47					5.60										
			2.87								1.94					0.56										
Santa Clara County	854,337	398,975	66,873	5,297	2,694	7,248	28	323	14,746	75	19,439	839	939	-	117	14,020	2,599	236	-	152	395	-	421	177	-	4,462
	54.62		16.76		50.86	12.43	6.70	7.75	14.04	15.24	26.58	67.39	84.75		17.23	54.14	12.83	12.51		6.26	26.02		8.40	13.58		4.94
						10.84	0.04	0.48	22.05	2.78	29.07	31.14	34.86		0.17	20.97	3.89	0.35		0.23	14.66		0.63	0.26		6.67
			16.76		50.86	1.82	0.01	0.08	3.70	1.42	4.87	15.84	17.73		0.03	3.51	0.65	0.06		0.04	7.46		0.11	0.04		1.12
			7.83		0.32	0.85	<0.01	0.04	1.73	0.01	2.28	0.10	0.11		0.01	1.64	0.30	0.03		0.02	0.05		0.05	0.02		0.52
Alum Rock (cdp)	4,856	1,191	200	-	-	-	-	-	-	-	-	-	-	-	-	-	-	-	-	-	-	-	-	-	-	0
	38.20		16.79																							0.00
																										0.00
			16.79																							0.00
			4.12																							0.00

Notes: Please refer to the User's Guide for an explanation of data; data is arranged alphabetically by state, then county, then city within each county; table includes counties with populations greater than 49,999 unless noted and cities with populations greater than 9,999 whose Asian and/or NHPI population rates are greater than the national average; (1) Native Hawaiian and other Pacific Islander; (2) excludes Taiwanese; (3) includes Chamorro; (4) county does not meet population threshold but is shown in order to allow inclusion of city

Place	Total population 5 years and over who speak English-only at home	Asian population 5 years and over	Asians 5 years and over who speak English-only at home	NHPI[1] population 5 years and over	NHPIs[1] 5 years and over who speak English-only at home	Asian Indian	Bangladeshi	Cambodian	Chinese[2]	Fijian	Filipino	Guamanian[3]	Hawaiian, Native	Hmong	Indonesian	Japanese	Korean	Laotian	Malaysian	Pakistani	Samoan	Sri Lankan	Taiwanese	Thai	Tongan	Vietnamese
Campbell (city)	26,366	5,229	1,616	-	-	84	-	-	429	-	262	-	-	-	-	575	105	-	-	-	-	-	-	-	-	93
	73.34		30.90			12.52			32.21		43.67					74.58	12.74									10.85
						5.20			26.55		16.21					35.58	6.50									5.75
			30.90			1.61			8.20		5.01					11.00	2.01									1.78
			6.13			0.32			1.63		0.99					2.18	0.40									0.35
Cupertino (city)	23,785	20,977	3,013	-	-	575	-	-	1,301	-	93	-	-	-	-	605	161	-	-	-	-	-	17	-	-	66
	50.04		14.36			13.44			13.16		23.54					27.23	7.67						2.31			9.39
						19.08			43.18		3.09					20.08	5.34						0.56			2.19
			14.36			2.74			6.20		0.44					2.88	0.77						0.08			0.31
			12.67			2.42			5.47		0.39					2.54	0.68						0.07			0.28
Gilroy (city)	21,318	1,777	830	-	-	-	-	-	100	-	370	-	-	-	-	-	-	-	-	-	-	-	-	-	-	-
	56.44		46.71						28.57		57.99															
									12.05		44.58															
			46.71						5.63		20.82															
			3.89						0.47		1.74															
Los Altos (city)	20,760	3,979	1,172	-	-	111	-	-	548	-	-	-	-	-	-	328	-	-	-	-	-	-	-	-	-	-
	79.78		29.45			23.92			27.68							48.38										
						9.47			46.76							27.99										
			29.45			2.79			13.77							8.24										
			5.65			0.53			2.64							1.58										
Los Gatos (town)	22,404	2,169	582	-	-	-	-	-	121	-	-	-	-	-	-	187	-	-	-	-	-	-	-	-	-	-
	82.60		26.83						14.76							41.83										
									20.79							32.13										
			26.83						5.58							8.62										
			2.60						0.54							0.83										
Milpitas (city)	23,281	30,205	4,014	512	273	388	-	-	779	-	2,050	-	-	-	-	262	69	-	-	-	-	-	-	-	-	258
	39.99		13.29		53.32	9.46			10.41		24.25					44.56	8.44									3.52
						9.67			19.41		51.07					6.53	1.72									6.43
			13.29		53.32	1.28			2.58		6.79					0.87	0.23									0.85
			17.24		1.17	1.67			3.35		8.81					1.13	0.30									1.11
Morgan Hill (city)	22,922	1,943	731	-	-	-	-	-	85	-	-	-	-	-	-	342	-	-	-	-	-	-	-	-	-	-
	74.40		37.62						22.37							77.20										
									11.63							46.79										
			37.62						4.37							17.60										
			3.19						0.37							1.49										
Mountain View (city)	39,790	13,657	3,376	-	-	380	-	-	1,050	-	742	-	-	-	-	852	180	-	-	-	-	-	-	-	-	27
	60.08		24.72			14.15			20.67		36.32					51.98	26.95									3.30
						11.26			31.10		21.98					25.24	5.33									0.80
			24.72			2.78			7.69		5.43					6.24	1.32									0.20
			8.48			0.96			2.64		1.86					2.14	0.45									0.07
Palo Alto (city)	39,839	9,711	2,430	-	-	292	-	-	1,096	-	147	-	-	-	-	491	210	-	-	-	-	-	-	-	-	-
	71.37		25.02			21.53			21.29		36.57					42.00	22.68									
						12.02			45.10		6.05					20.21	8.64									
			25.02			3.01			11.29		1.51					5.06	2.16									
			6.10			0.73			2.75		0.37					1.23	0.53									
San Jose (city)	402,804	221,799	32,844	2,972	1,334	2,574	-	261	5,213	-	11,786	445	420	-	-	6,607	1,164	217	-	80	226	-	118	91	-	3,210
	48.77		14.81		44.89	11.46		6.88	11.03		25.36	66.82	79.70			61.12	13.30	12.52		6.88	20.56		6.09	14.51		4.57
						7.84		0.79	15.87		35.88	33.36	31.48			20.12	3.54	0.66		0.24	16.94		0.36	0.28		9.77
			14.81		44.89	1.16		0.12	2.35		5.31	14.97	14.13			2.98	0.52	0.10		0.04	7.60		0.05	0.04		1.45
			8.15		0.33	0.64		0.06	1.29		2.93	0.11	0.10			1.64	0.29	0.05		0.02	0.06		0.03	0.02		0.80

Notes: Please refer to the User's Guide for an explanation of data; data is arranged alphabetically by state, then county, then city within each county; table includes counties with populations greater than 49,999 unless noted and cities with populations greater than 9,999 whose Asian and/or NHPI population rates are greater than the national average; (1) Native Hawaiian and other Pacific Islander; (2) excludes Taiwanese; (3) includes Chamorro; (4) county does not meet population threshold but is shown in order to allow inclusion of city

Place	Total population 5 years and over who speak English-only at home	Asian population 5 years and over	Asians 5 years and over who speak English-only at home	NHPI[1] population 5 years and over	NHPIs[1] 5 years and over who speak English-only at home	Asian Indian	Bangladeshi	Cambodian	Chinese[2]	Fijian	Filipino	Guamanian[3]	Hawaiian, Native	Hmong	Indonesian	Japanese	Korean	Laotian	Malaysian	Pakistani	Samoan	Sri Lankan	Taiwanese	Thai	Tongan	Vietnamese
Santa Clara (city)	55,086	26,973	4,722	370	188	725	-	-	701	-	1,538	-	-	-	-	944	177	-	-	9	-	-	-	-	-	341
	57.63		17.51		50.81	9.10			15.96		27.50					66.57	9.36			2.27						7.86
						15.35			14.85		32.57					19.99	3.75			0.19						7.22
			17.51		50.81	2.69			2.60		5.70					3.50	0.66			0.03						1.26
			8.57		0.34	1.32			1.27		2.79					1.71	0.32			0.02						0.62
Saratoga (city)	19,046	8,027	1,598	-	-	439	-	-	557	-	-	-	-	-	-	252	38	-	-	-	-	-	13	-	-	-
	67.35		19.91			37.65			11.89							49.32	7.00						4.14			
						27.47			34.86							15.77	2.38						0.81			
			19.91			5.47			6.94							3.14	0.47						0.16			
			8.39			2.30			2.92							1.32	0.20						0.07			
Stanford (cdp)	8,634	3,381	915	-	-	228	-	-	377	-	-	-	-	-	-	-	55	-	-	-	-	-	-	-	-	-
	66.96		27.06			35.57			24.04								15.49									
						24.92			41.20								6.01									
			27.06			6.74			11.15								1.63									
			10.60			2.64			4.37								0.64									
Sunnyvale (city)	66,572	39,167	6,479	510	270	1,006	-	-	1,741	-	1,648	-	-	-	-	1,267	264	-	-	-	-	-	56	-	-	209
	54.24		16.54		52.94	9.31			15.22		26.68					39.54	10.80						8.56			6.80
						15.53			26.87		25.44					19.56	4.07						0.86			3.23
			16.54		52.94	2.57			4.45		4.21					3.23	0.67						0.14			0.53
			9.73		0.41	1.51			2.62		2.48					1.90	0.40						0.08			0.31
Santa Cruz County	173,472	8,051	3,296	-	-	338	-	-	601	-	883	-	-	-	-	1,093	74	-	-	-	-	-	-	-	-	80
	72.21		40.94			37.31			31.19		45.10					63.73	15.81									18.96
						10.25			18.23		26.79					33.16	2.25									2.43
			40.94			4.20			7.46		10.97					13.58	0.92									0.99
			1.90			0.19			0.35		0.51					0.63	0.04									0.05
Capitola (city)	8,044	469	81	-	-	-	-	-	-	-	-	-	-	-	-	-	-	-	-	-	-	-	-	-	-	-
	82.40		17.27																							
			17.27																							
			1.01																							
Santa Cruz (city)	40,149	2,680	1,162	-	-	137	-	-	292	-	277	-	-	-	-	323	-	-	-	-	-	-	-	-	-	-
	77.69		43.36			34.42			33.80		54.00					76.00										
						11.79			25.13		23.84					27.80										
			43.36			5.11			10.90		10.34					12.05										
			2.89			0.34			0.73		0.69					0.80										
Scotts Valley (city)	9,372	607	196	-	-	-	-	-	-	-	-	-	-	-	-	-	-	-	-	-	-	-	-	-	-	-
	87.78		32.29																							
			32.29																							
			2.09																							
Shasta County	143,595	3,053	573	-	-	-	-	-	-	-	207	-	-	-	-	-	-	61	-	-	-	-	-	-	-	-
	93.50		18.77								46.10							3.71								
											36.13							10.65								
			18.77								6.78							2.00								
			0.40								0.14							0.04								
Solano County	276,347	47,148	14,309	2,968	1,623	485	-	-	987	-	10,377	688	526	39	-	961	274	29	-	-	225	-	-	-	-	164
	75.44		30.35		54.68	18.39			32.08		30.64	53.13	82.45	10.21		50.63	29.15	4.05			41.21					12.06
						3.39			6.90		72.52	42.39	32.41	0.27		6.72	1.91	0.20			13.86					1.15
			30.35		54.68	1.03			2.09		22.01	23.18	17.72	0.08		2.04	0.58	0.06			7.58					0.35
			5.18		0.59	0.18			0.36		3.76	0.25	0.19	0.01		0.35	0.10	0.01			0.08					0.06

Notes: Please refer to the User's Guide for an explanation of data; data is arranged alphabetically by state, then county, then city within each county; table includes counties with populations greater than 49,999 unless noted and cities with populations greater than 9,999 whose Asian and/or NHPI population rates are greater than the national average; (1) Native Hawaiian and other Pacific Islander; (2) excludes Taiwanese; (3) includes Chamorro; (4) county does not meet population threshold but is shown in order to allow inclusion of city

Place	Total population 5 years and over who speak English-only at home	Asian population 5 years and over	Asians 5 years and over who speak English-only at home	NHPI[1] population 5 years and over	NHPIs[1] 5 years and over who speak English-only at home	Asian Indian	Bangladeshi	Cambodian	Chinese[2]	Fijian	Filipino	Guamanian[3]	Hawaiian, Native	Hmong	Indonesian	Japanese	Korean	Laotian	Malaysian	Pakistani	Samoan	Sri Lankan	Taiwanese	Thai	Tongan	Vietnamese
Benicia (city)	22,393 87.38	1,915	813 42.45 42.45 3.63	-	-	-	-	-	113 24.51 13.90 5.90 0.50	-	478 46.01 58.79 24.96 2.13	-	-	-	-	-	-	-	-	-	-	-	-	-	-	-
Fairfield (city)	66,828 75.65	9,983	3,156 31.61 31.61 4.72	992	508 51.21 51.21 0.76	141 15.74 4.47 1.41 0.21	-	-	292 31.77 9.25 2.92 0.44	-	1,989 35.04 63.02 19.92 2.98	294 55.58 57.87 29.64 0.44	-	-	-	280 42.68 8.87 2.80 0.42	93 24.35 2.95 0.93 0.14	20 5.45 0.63 0.20 0.03	-	-	-	-	-	-	-	-
Suisun City (city)	17,108 71.12	4,570	1,405 30.74 30.74 8.21	-	-	108 27.62 7.69 2.36 0.63	-	-	-	-	1,008 33.99 71.74 22.06 5.89	-	-	-	-	-	-	-	-	-	-	-	-	-	-	-
Vacaville (city)	69,861 84.63	3,468	1,471 42.42 42.42 2.11	-	-	-	-	-	-	-	835 46.91 56.76 24.08 1.20	-	-	-	-	-	-	-	-	-	-	-	-	-	-	-
Vallejo (city)	72,356 66.77	26,054	6,994 26.84 26.84 9.67	1,261	565 44.81 44.81 0.78	106 12.27 1.52 0.41 0.15	-	-	241 27.45 3.45 0.93 0.33	-	5,923 26.99 84.69 22.73 8.19	269 48.21 47.61 21.33 0.37	-	-	-	217 61.13 3.10 0.83 0.30	-	-	-	-	-	-	-	-	-	38 6.38 0.54 0.15 0.05
Sonoma County	345,971 80.16	13,229	3,768 28.48 28.48 1.09	653	325 49.77 49.77 0.09	224 14.14 5.94 1.69 0.06	-	72 9.18 1.91 0.54 0.02	747 28.83 19.82 5.65 0.22	-	1,062 44.58 28.18 8.03 0.31	-	-	-	-	945 60.62 25.08 7.14 0.27	264 30.41 7.01 2.00 0.08	60 5.79 1.59 0.45 0.02	-	-	-	-	-	-	-	69 5.65 1.83 0.52 0.02
Petaluma (city)	41,636 81.72	2,041	601 29.45 29.45 1.44	-	-	-	-	-	179 28.19 29.78 8.77 0.43	-	-	-	-	-	-	-	-	-	-	-	-	-	-	-	-	-
Rohnert Park (city)	32,934 83.08	2,271	638 28.09 28.09 1.94	-	-	-	-	-	51 13.21 7.99 2.25 0.15	-	281 41.26 44.04 12.37 0.85	-	-	-	-	-	-	-	-	-	-	-	-	-	-	-
Santa Rosa (city)	107,677 77.84	5,343	1,090 20.40 20.40 1.01	-	-	56 8.32 5.14 1.05 0.05	-	60 10.08 5.50 1.12 0.06	231 28.91 21.19 4.32 0.21	-	259 37.11 23.76 4.85 0.24	-	-	-	-	211 51.84 19.36 3.95 0.20	-	31 5.08 2.84 0.58 0.03	-	-	-	-	-	-	-	14 1.99 1.28 0.26 0.01
Stanislaus County	278,370 67.59	17,224	3,314 19.24 19.24 1.19	1,679	464 27.64 27.64 0.17	189 4.69 5.70 1.10 0.07	-	348 11.71 10.50 2.02 0.13	403 23.36 12.16 2.34 0.14	35 5.48 7.54 2.08 0.01	1,233 46.23 37.21 7.16 0.44	-	-	72 7.87 2.17 0.42 0.03	-	526 66.75 15.87 3.05 0.19	-	79 5.28 2.38 0.46 0.03	-	-	-	-	-	-	-	55 4.26 1.66 0.32 0.02

Notes: Please refer to the User's Guide for an explanation of data; data is arranged alphabetically by state, then county, then city within each county; table includes counties with populations greater than 49,999 unless noted and cities with populations greater than 9,999 whose Asian and/or NHPI population rates are greater than the national average; (1) Native Hawaiian and other Pacific Islander; (2) excludes Taiwanese; (3) includes Chamorro; (4) county does not meet population threshold but is shown in order to allow inclusion of city

Place	Total population 5 years and over who speak English-only at home	Asian population 5 years and over	Asians 5 years and over who speak English-only at home	NHPI[1] population 5 years and over	NHPIs[1] 5 years and over who speak English-only at home	Asian Indian	Bangladeshi	Cambodian	Chinese[2]	Fijian	Filipino	Guamanian[3]	Hawaiian, Native	Hmong	Indonesian	Japanese	Korean	Laotian	Malaysian	Pakistani	Samoan	Sri Lankan	Taiwanese	Thai	Tongan	Vietnamese
	20,025	1,600	267	-	-	4	-	-	-	-	-	-	-	-	-	-	-	-	-	-	-	-	-	-	-	-
	63.86		16.69			0.53																				
Ceres (city)						1.50																				
			16.69			0.25																				
			1.33			0.02																				
	126,058	10,508	1,842	1,110	225	119	-	307	190	0	653	-	-	49	-	230	-	44	-	-	-	-	-	-	-	29
	71.86		17.53		20.27	6.51		12.94	17.92	0.00	43.74			13.42		62.33		4.09								2.75
Modesto (city)						6.46		16.67	10.31	0.00	35.45			2.66		12.49		2.39								1.57
			17.53		20.27	1.13		2.92	1.81	0.00	6.21			0.47		2.19		0.42								0.28
			1.46		0.18	0.09		0.24	0.15	0.00	0.52			0.04		0.18		0.03								0.02
	8,190	456	187	-	-	-	-	-	-	-	-	-	-	-	-	-	-	-	-	-	-	-	-	-	-	-
	72.83		41.01																							
Salida (cdp)																										
			41.01																							
			2.28																							
	32,169	2,285	490	-	-	33	-	-	-	-	-	-	-	-	-	-	-	-	-	-	-	-	-	-	-	-
	62.92		21.44			3.24																				
Turlock (city)						6.73																				
			21.44			1.44																				
			1.52			0.10																				
	51,048	8,067	822	-	-	374	-	-	-	-	94	-	-	-	-	226	-	-	-	-	-	-	-	-	-	-
	69.67		10.19			5.64					25.41					64.39										
Sutter County						45.50					11.44					27.49										
			10.19			4.64					1.17					2.80										
			1.61			0.73					0.18					0.44										
	8,163	2,659	191	-	-	135	-	-	-	-	-	-	-	-	-	-	-	-	-	-	-	-	-	-	-	-
	68.80		7.18			5.58																				
South Yuba City (cdp)						70.68																				
			7.18			5.08																				
			2.34			1.65																				
	23,949	2,821	341	-	-	100	-	-	-	-	-	-	-	-	-	-	-	-	-	-	-	-	-	-	-	-
	70.90		12.09			4.93																				
Yuba City (city)						29.33																				
			12.09			3.54																				
			1.42			0.42																				
	44,908	381	182	-	-	-	-	-	-	-	-	-	-	-	-	-	-	-	-	-	-	-	-	-	-	-
	85.56		47.77																							
Tehama County																										
			47.77																							
			0.41																							
	188,536	11,570	2,104	-	-	89	-	-	204	-	1,080	-	-	67	-	366	61	57	-	-	-	-	-	-	-	-
	56.21		18.18			9.20			29.23		25.28			7.03		61.72	16.80	1.92								
Tulare County						4.23			9.70		51.33			3.18		17.40	2.90	2.71								
			18.18			0.77			1.76		9.33			0.58		3.16	0.53	0.49								
			1.12			0.05			0.11		0.57			0.04		0.19	0.03	0.03								
	20,517	1,951	320	-	-	-	-	-	-	-	176	-	-	-	-	-	-	-	-	-	-	-	-	-	-	-
	56.72		16.40								19.71															
Porterville (city)											55.00															
			16.40								9.02															
			1.56								0.86															

Notes: Please refer to the User's Guide for an explanation of data; data is arranged alphabetically by state, then county, then city within each county; table includes counties with populations greater than 49,999 unless noted and cities with populations greater than 9,999 whose Asian and/or NHPI population rates are greater than the national average; (1) Native Hawaiian and other Pacific Islander; (2) excludes Taiwanese; (3) includes Chamorro; (4) county does not meet population threshold but is shown in order to allow inclusion of city

Place	Total population 5 years and over who speak English-only at home	Asian population 5 years and over	Asians 5 years and over who speak English-only at home	NHPI[1] population 5 years and over	NHPIs[1] 5 years and over who speak English-only at home	Asian Indian	Bangladeshi	Cambodian	Chinese[2]	Fijian	Filipino	Guamanian[3]	Hawaiian, Native	Hmong	Indonesian	Japanese	Korean	Laotian	Malaysian	Pakistani	Samoan	Sri Lankan	Taiwanese	Thai	Tongan	Vietnamese
Visalia (city)	59,541 70.88	4,759	780 16.39 16.39 1.31	-	-	-	-	-	-	-	284 37.32 36.41 5.97 0.48	-	-	23 5.10 2.95 0.48 0.04	-	-	-	57 2.84 7.31 1.20 0.10	-	-	-	-	-	-	-	-
Tuolumne County	48,955 94.21	416	199 47.84 47.84 0.41	-	-	-	-	-	-	-	-	-	-	-	-	-	-	-	-	-	-	-	-	-	-	-
Ventura County	467,351 67.02	36,857	10,713 29.07 29.07 2.29	1,542	824 53.44 53.44 0.18	1,108 28.66 10.34 3.01 0.24	-	-	1,254 26.31 11.71 3.40 0.27	-	3,946 27.40 36.83 10.71 0.84	-	391 74.90 47.45 25.36 0.08	-	-	2,690 53.43 25.11 7.30 0.58	524 21.46 4.89 1.42 0.11	-	-	-	182 32.97 22.09 11.80 0.04	-	48 6.18 0.45 0.13 0.01	-	-	320 10.59 2.99 0.87 0.07
Camarillo (city)	42,681 80.17	3,620	1,175 32.46 32.46 2.75	-	-	-	-	-	182 40.27 15.49 5.03 0.43	-	373 30.25 31.74 10.30 0.87	-	-	-	-	374 56.75 31.83 10.33 0.88	103 25.88 8.77 2.85 0.24	-	-	-	-	-	-	-	-	30 8.11 2.55 0.83 0.07
Moorpark (city)	20,646 71.66	1,293	592 45.78 45.78 2.87	-	-	-	-	-	-	-	-	-	-	-	-	-	-	-	-	-	-	-	-	-	-	-
Oxnard (city)	58,856 37.86	11,918	2,985 25.05 25.05 5.07	810	329 40.62 40.62 0.56	251 57.57 8.41 2.11 0.43	-	-	54 16.56 1.81 0.45 0.09	-	2,028 23.91 67.94 17.02 3.45	-	-	-	-	420 35.32 14.07 3.52 0.71	46 11.17 1.54 0.39 0.08	-	-	-	153 31.35 46.50 18.89 0.26	-	-	-	-	67 9.52 2.24 0.56 0.11
Port Hueneme (city)	12,191 61.23	1,231	320 26.00 26.00 2.62	-	-	-	-	-	-	-	197 21.51 61.56 16.00 1.62	-	-	-	-	-	-	-	-	-	-	-	-	-	-	-
Simi Valley (city)	81,698 79.04	6,304	1,486 23.57 23.57 1.82	-	-	131 10.40 8.82 2.08 0.16	-	-	203 21.66 13.66 3.22 0.25	-	423 33.89 28.47 6.71 0.52	-	-	-	-	358 48.44 24.09 5.68 0.44	140 25.32 9.42 2.22 0.17	-	-	-	-	-	-	-	-	90 9.74 6.06 1.43 0.11
Thousand Oaks (city)	88,321 80.94	6,027	2,049 34.00 34.00 2.32	-	-	393 40.06 19.18 6.52 0.44	-	-	467 26.72 22.79 7.75 0.53	-	222 40.81 10.83 3.68 0.25	-	-	-	-	570 67.94 27.82 9.46 0.65	93 20.31 4.54 1.54 0.11	-	-	-	-	-	-	-	-	74 16.02 3.61 1.23 0.08
Yolo County	107,131 67.89	15,251	4,303 28.21 28.21 4.02	620	173 27.90 27.90 0.16	256 14.81 5.95 1.68 0.24	-	-	1,433 26.14 33.30 9.40 1.34	31 7.19 17.92 5.00 0.03	1,000 60.98 23.24 6.56 0.93	-	-	82 13.46 1.91 0.54 0.08	-	701 49.23 16.29 4.60 0.65	270 25.12 6.27 1.77 0.25	18 4.02 0.42 0.12 0.02	-	-	-	-	-	-	-	165 11.89 3.83 1.08 0.15

Notes: Please refer to the User's Guide for an explanation of data; data is arranged alphabetically by state, then county, then city within each county; table includes counties with populations greater than 49,999 unless noted and cities with populations greater than 9,999 whose Asian and/or NHPI population rates are greater than the national average; (1) Native Hawaiian and other Pacific Islander; (2) excludes Taiwanese; (3) includes Chamorro; (4) county does not meet population threshold but is shown in order to allow inclusion of city

Place	Total population 5 years and over who speak English-only at home	Asian population 5 years and over	Asians 5 years and over who speak English-only at home	NHPI[1] population 5 years and over	NHPIs[1] 5 years and over who speak English-only at home	Asian Indian	Bangladeshi	Cambodian	Chinese[2]	Fijian	Filipino	Guamanian[3]	Hawaiian, Native	Hmong	Indonesian	Japanese	Korean	Laotian	Malaysian	Pakistani	Samoan	Sri Lankan	Taiwanese	Thai	Tongan	Vietnamese
Davis (city)	43,542 75.63	9,751	3,189 32.70 32.70 7.32	-	-	175 23.27 5.49 1.79 0.40	-	-	1,217 28.00 38.16 12.48 2.80	-	720 67.10 22.58 7.38 1.65	-	-	-	-	428 51.75 13.42 4.39 0.98	214 26.42 6.71 2.19 0.49	-	-	-	-	-	-	-	-	147 14.29 4.61 1.51 0.34
West Sacramento (city)	17,973 61.58	2,073	352 16.98 16.98 1.96	-	-	28 6.41 7.95 1.35 0.16	-	-	-	-	-	-	-	82 15.50 23.30 3.96 0.46	-	-	-	-	-	-	-	-	-	-	-	-
Woodland (city)	29,300 64.82	1,701	368 21.63 21.63 1.26	-	-	21 5.07 5.71 1.23 0.07	-	-	-	-	-	-	-	-	-	-	-	-	-	-	-	-	-	-	-	-
Yuba County	43,268 78.11	4,209	723 17.18 17.18 1.67	-	-	-	-	-	-	-	260 50.49 35.96 6.18 0.60	-	-	183 7.54 25.31 4.35 0.42	-	-	-	-	-	-	-	-	-	-	-	-
Linda (cdp)	7,791 64.45	2,272	290 12.76 12.76 3.72	-	-	-	-	-	-	-	-	-	-	140 7.86 48.28 6.16 1.80	-	-	-	-	-	-	-	-	-	-	-	-
Marysville (city)	9,200 80.03	730	133 18.22 18.22 1.45	-	-	-	-	-	-	-	-	-	-	-	-	-	-	-	-	-	-	-	-	-	-	-
Olivehurst (cdp)	7,480 73.72	536	71 13.25 13.25 0.95	-	-	-	-	-	-	-	-	-	-	-	-	-	-	-	-	-	-	-	-	-	-	-
COLORADO	3,402,266 84.92	86,601	24,492 28.28 28.28 0.72	3,983	2,821 70.83 70.83 0.08	2,613 24.46 10.67 3.02 0.08	-	144 10.71 0.59 0.17 <0.01	2,928 22.09 11.95 3.38 0.09	-	4,251 47.71 17.36 4.91 0.12	665 68.28 23.57 16.70 0.02	1,136 82.44 40.27 28.52 0.03	75 2.76 0.31 0.09 <0.01	96 13.79 0.39 0.11 <0.01	7,050 60.52 28.78 8.14 0.21	3,784 26.15 15.45 4.37 0.11	121 5.61 0.49 0.14 <0.01	-	143 19.22 0.58 0.17 <0.01	528 64.39 18.72 13.26 0.02	-	134 20.40 0.55 0.15 <0.01	387 20.98 1.58 0.45 0.01	-	1,011 8.07 4.13 1.17 0.03
Adams County	261,523 78.36	10,633	1,996 18.77 18.77 0.76	-	-	142 24.03 7.11 1.34 0.05	-	-	145 14.37 7.26 1.36 0.06	-	439 53.34 21.99 4.13 0.17	-	-	75 3.86 3.76 0.71 0.03	-	628 65.83 31.46 5.91 0.24	141 16.53 7.06 1.33 0.05	52 5.23 2.61 0.49 0.02	-	-	-	-	-	-	-	112 5.40 5.61 1.05 0.04
Berkley (cdp)	6,575 67.42	369	12 3.25 3.25 0.18	-	-	-	-	-	-	-	-	-	-	-	-	-	-	-	-	-	-	-	-	-	-	-

Notes: Please refer to the User's Guide for an explanation of data; data is arranged alphabetically by state, then county, then city within each county; table includes counties with populations greater than 49,999 unless noted and cities with populations greater than 9,999 whose Asian and/or NHPI population rates are greater than the national average; (1) Native Hawaiian and other Pacific Islander; (2) excludes Taiwanese; (3) includes Chamorro; (4) county does not meet population threshold but is shown in order to allow inclusion of city

Place	Total population 5 years and over who speak English-only at home	Asian population 5 years and over	Asians 5 years and over who speak English-only at home	NHPI[1] population 5 years and over	NHPIs[1] 5 years and over who speak English-only at home	Asian Indian	Bangladeshi	Cambodian	Chinese[2]	Fijian	Filipino	Guamanian[3]	Hawaiian, Native	Hmong	Indonesian	Japanese	Korean	Laotian	Malaysian	Pakistani	Samoan	Sri Lankan	Taiwanese	Thai	Tongan	Vietnamese
Federal Heights (city)	8,947 80.78	698	122 17.48 17.48 1.36	-	-	-	-	-	-	-	-	-	-	-	-	-	-	-	-	-	-	-	-	-	-	-
Westminster (city)	80,403 85.50	4,983	926 18.58 18.58 1.15	-	-	42 9.91 4.54 0.84 0.05	-	-	90 15.82 9.72 1.81 0.11	-	-	-	-	4 0.44 0.43 0.08 <0.01	-	-	120 23.39 12.96 2.41 0.15	17 2.58 1.84 0.34 0.02	-	-	-	-	-	-	-	85 11.49 9.18 1.71 0.11
Arapahoe County	384,272 84.49	17,470	4,004 22.92 22.92 1.04	537	303 56.42 56.42 0.08	507 23.96 12.66 2.90 0.13	-	-	577 20.59 14.41 3.30 0.15	-	669 32.32 16.71 3.83 0.17	-	-	-	-	1,018 60.38 25.42 5.83 0.26	736 17.21 18.38 4.21 0.19	-	-	-	-	-	-	-	-	97 3.83 2.42 0.56 0.03
Aurora (city)	196,319 77.29	10,603	2,222 20.96 20.96 1.13	349	152 43.55 43.55 0.08	236 26.08 10.62 2.23 0.12	-	41 10.17 1.85 0.39 0.02	272 18.38 12.24 2.57 0.14	-	428 30.08 19.26 4.04 0.22	-	-	-	-	614 60.73 27.63 5.79 0.31	320 13.42 14.40 3.02 0.16	-	-	-	-	-	-	-	-	60 3.42 2.70 0.57 0.03
Boulder County	236,441 86.38	8,362	2,518 30.11 30.11 1.06	-	-	230 21.62 9.13 2.75 0.10	-	-	402 18.64 15.97 4.81 0.17	-	257 66.07 10.21 3.07 0.11	-	-	-	-	794 62.82 31.53 9.50 0.34	390 34.64 15.49 4.66 0.16	-	-	-	-	-	-	-	-	72 11.16 2.86 0.86 0.03
Boulder (city)	77,198 85.04	3,349	962 28.72 28.72 1.25	-	-	92 23.35 9.56 2.75 0.12	-	-	198 23.21 20.58 5.91 0.26	-	-	-	-	-	-	254 49.90 26.40 7.58 0.33	206 28.97 21.41 6.15 0.27	-	-	-	-	-	-	-	-	-
Broomfield (city)	31,803 89.92	1,475	376 25.49 25.49 1.18	-	-	-	-	-	30 10.27 7.98 2.03 0.09	-	-	-	-	-	-	-	-	-	-	-	-	-	-	-	-	-
Lafayette (city)	17,722 82.50	809	213 26.33 26.33 1.20	-	-	-	-	-	-	-	-	-	-	-	-	-	-	-	-	-	-	-	-	-	-	-
Denver County	377,881 73.04	14,078	3,565 25.32 25.32 0.94	426	322 75.59 75.59 0.09	522 27.80 14.64 3.71 0.14	-	20 5.60 0.56 0.14 0.01	472 24.49 13.24 3.35 0.12	-	478 51.56 13.41 3.40 0.13	-	-	-	-	1,074 55.05 30.13 7.63 0.28	398 33.31 11.16 2.83 0.11	-	-	-	-	-	-	37 9.37 1.04 0.26 0.01	-	265 6.50 7.43 1.88 0.07
Douglas County	147,338 92.80	3,863	1,062 27.49 27.49 0.72	-	-	156 21.64 14.69 4.04 0.11	-	-	165 14.56 15.54 4.27 0.11	-	-	-	-	-	-	-	148 25.30 13.94 3.83 0.10	-	-	-	-	-	-	-	-	-

Notes: Please refer to the User's Guide for an explanation of data; data is arranged alphabetically by state, then county, then city within each county; table includes counties with populations greater than 49,999 unless noted and cities with populations greater than 9,999 whose Asian and/or NHPI population rates are greater than the national average; (1) Native Hawaiian and other Pacific Islander; (2) excludes Taiwanese; (3) includes Chamorro; (4) county does not meet population threshold but is shown in order to allow inclusion of city

Place	Total population 5 years and over who speak English-only at home	Asian population 5 years and over	Asians 5 years and over who speak English-only at home	NHPI[1] population 5 years and over	NHPIs[1] 5 years and over who speak English-only at home	Asian Indian	Bangladeshi	Cambodian	Chinese[2]	Fijian	Filipino	Guamanian[3]	Hawaiian, Native	Hmong	Indonesian	Japanese	Korean	Laotian	Malaysian	Pakistani	Samoan	Sri Lankan	Taiwanese	Thai	Tongan	Vietnamese
Highlands Ranch (cdp)	57,519 91.10	2,612	608 23.28 23.28 1.06	-	-	113 21.00 18.59 4.33 0.20	-	-	115 13.82 18.91 4.40 0.20	-	-	-	-	-	-	-	-	-	-	-	-	-	-	-	-	-
El Paso County	423,609 88.64	12,342	3,833 31.06 31.06 0.90	1,220	840 68.85 68.85 0.20	291 16.86 7.59 2.36 0.07	-	-	343 36.57 8.95 2.78 0.08	-	1,109 45.86 28.93 8.99 0.26	322 67.22 38.33 26.39 0.08	-	-	-	678 47.41 17.69 5.49 0.16	846 22.48 22.07 6.85 0.20	-	-	-	-	-	-	-	-	124 14.90 3.24 1.00 0.03
Colorado Springs (city)	294,745 88.27	9,581	2,814 29.37 29.37 0.95	750	541 72.13 72.13 0.18	262 15.66 9.31 2.73 0.09	-	-	270 34.75 9.59 2.82 0.09	-	712 43.65 25.30 7.43 0.24	-	-	-	-	499 49.31 17.73 5.21 0.17	633 22.18 22.49 6.61 0.21	-	-	-	-	-	-	-	-	111 16.32 3.94 1.16 0.04
Jefferson County	448,457 90.77	10,872	3,272 30.10 30.10 0.73	383	311 81.20 81.20 0.07	352 26.41 10.76 3.24 0.08	-	-	379 22.29 11.58 3.49 0.08	-	439 48.72 13.42 4.04 0.10	-	-	0 0.00 0.00 0.00 0.00	-	1,261 68.13 38.54 11.60 0.28	469 33.84 14.33 4.31 0.10	24 2.87 0.73 0.22 0.01	-	-	-	-	-	-	-	161 10.31 4.92 1.48 0.04
Larimer County	216,318 91.53	3,327	1,250 37.57 37.57 0.58	-	-	78 13.38 6.24 2.34 0.04	-	-	197 26.48 15.76 5.92 0.09	-	-	-	-	-	-	355 62.39 28.40 10.67 0.16	292 53.78 23.36 8.78 0.13	-	-	-	-	-	-	-	-	-
Mesa County	100,424 92.03	405	169 41.73 41.73 0.17	-	-	-	-	-	-	-	-	-	-	-	-	-	-	-	-	-	-	-	-	-	-	-
Pueblo County	110,841 83.87	710	173 24.37 24.37 0.16	-	-	-	-	-	-	-	-	-	-	-	-	-	-	-	-	-	-	-	-	-	-	-
Weld County	133,144 79.75	1,473	784 53.22 53.22 0.59	-	-	-	-	-	-	-	-	-	-	-	-	396 80.00 50.51 26.88 0.30	-	-	-	-	-	-	-	-	-	-
CONNECTICUT	2,600,601 81.66	75,777	15,354 20.26 20.26 0.59	1,246	840 67.42 67.42 0.03	4,838 21.84 31.51 6.38 0.19	20 6.13 0.13 0.03 <0.01	216 11.08 1.41 0.29 0.01	3,086 17.92 20.10 4.07 0.12	-	2,106 29.86 13.72 2.78 0.08	292 75.06 34.76 23.43 0.01	-	-	-	959 23.63 6.25 1.27 0.04	1,834 29.22 11.94 2.42 0.07	243 8.53 1.58 0.32 0.01	-	162 8.34 1.06 0.21 0.01	-	-	99 12.69 0.64 0.13 <0.01	179 23.99 1.17 0.24 0.01	-	477 7.06 3.11 0.63 0.02
Fairfield County	623,417 76.10	26,135	5,205 19.92 19.92 0.83	-	-	1,670 21.62 32.08 6.39 0.27	-	146 11.01 2.80 0.56 0.02	1,306 24.35 25.09 5.00 0.21	-	643 27.73 12.35 2.46 0.10	-	-	-	-	381 16.19 7.32 1.46 0.06	465 25.85 8.93 1.78 0.07	61 6.38 1.17 0.23 0.01	-	49 9.78 0.94 0.19 0.01	-	-	-	-	-	119 5.57 2.29 0.46 0.02

Notes: Please refer to the User's Guide for an explanation of data; data is arranged alphabetically by state, then county, then city within each county; table includes counties with populations greater than 49,999 unless noted and cities with populations greater than 9,999 whose Asian and/or NHPI population rates are greater than the national average; (1) Native Hawaiian and other Pacific Islander; (2) excludes Taiwanese; (3) includes Chamorro; (4) county does not meet population threshold but is shown in order to allow inclusion of city

Place	Total population 5 years and over who speak English-only at home	Asian population 5 years and over	Asians 5 years and over who speak English-only at home	NHPI[1] population 5 years and over	NHPIs[1] 5 years and over who speak English-only at home	Asian Indian	Bangladeshi	Cambodian	Chinese[2]	Fijian	Filipino	Guamanian[3]	Hawaiian, Native	Hmong	Indonesian	Japanese	Korean	Laotian	Malaysian	Pakistani	Samoan	Sri Lankan	Taiwanese	Thai	Tongan	Vietnamese
Danbury (city)	45,674	3,374	473	-	-	155	-	88	70	-	-	-	-	-	-	-	-	-	-	-	-	-	-	-	-	-
	65.30		14.02			14.07		16.51	15.35																	
						32.77		18.60	14.80																	
			14.02			4.59		2.61	2.07																	
			1.04			0.34		0.19	0.15																	
Greenwich (town)	44,982	2,941	436	-	-	112	-	-	157	-	-	-	-	-	-	24	-	-	-	-	-	-	-	-	-	-
	79.09		14.82			28.94			25.08							2.04										
						25.69			36.01							5.50										
			14.82			3.81			5.34							0.82										
			0.97			0.25			0.35							0.05										
Stamford (city)	71,104	5,332	1,279	-	-	580	-	-	255	-	243	-	-	-	-	-	-	-	-	-	-	-	-	-	-	-
	65.11		23.99			21.52			24.06		31.89															
						45.35			19.94		19.00															
			23.99			10.88			4.78		4.56															
			1.80			0.82			0.36		0.34															
Hartford County	628,513	19,349	3,526	-	-	1,394	-	-	511	-	456	-	-	-	-	153	289	86	-	37	-	-	-	-	-	209
	78.30		18.22			22.06			14.58		28.25					31.94	21.86	7.90		6.31						7.10
						39.53			14.49		12.93					4.34	8.20	2.44		1.05						5.93
			18.22			7.20			2.64		2.36					0.79	1.49	0.44		0.19						1.08
			0.56			0.22			0.08		0.07					0.02	0.05	0.01		0.01						0.03
East Hartford (town)	34,366	1,917	396	-	-	173	-	-	-	-	-	-	-	-	-	-	-	-	-	-	-	-	-	-	-	27
	73.96		20.66			29.67																				5.49
						43.69																				6.82
			20.66			9.02																				1.41
			1.15			0.50																				0.08
Farmington (town)	18,481	902	141	-	-	-	-	-	-	-	-	-	-	-	-	-	-	-	-	-	-	-	-	-	-	-
	82.93		15.63																							
			15.63																							
			0.76																							
Glastonbury (town)	26,368	1,118	192	-	-	65	-	-	-	-	-	-	-	-	-	-	-	-	-	-	-	-	-	-	-	-
	89.01		17.17			13.54																				
						33.85																				
			17.17			5.81																				
			0.73			0.25																				
Rocky Hill (town)	14,087	669	93	-	-	-	-	-	-	-	-	-	-	-	-	-	-	-	-	-	-	-	-	-	-	-
	82.57		13.90																							
			13.90																							
			0.66																							
South Windsor (town)	19,801	882	65	-	-	-	-	-	-	-	-	-	-	-	-	-	-	-	-	-	-	-	-	-	-	-
	86.43		7.37																							
			7.37																							
			0.33																							
West Hartford (town)	46,919	2,855	441	-	-	169	-	-	80	-	-	-	-	-	-	-	-	-	-	-	-	-	-	-	-	48
	78.37		15.45			23.37			10.44																	7.58
						38.32			18.14																	10.88
			15.45			5.92			2.80																	1.68
			0.94			0.36			0.17																	0.10

Notes: Please refer to the User's Guide for an explanation of data; data is arranged alphabetically by state, then county, then city within each county; table includes counties with populations greater than 49,999 unless noted and cities with populations greater than 9,999 whose Asian and/or NHPI population rates are greater than the national average; (1) Native Hawaiian and other Pacific Islander; (2) excludes Taiwanese; (3) includes Chamorro; (4) county does not meet population threshold but is shown in order to allow inclusion of city

Place	Total population 5 years and over who speak English-only at home	Asian population 5 years and over	Asians 5 years and over who speak English-only at home	NHPI[1] population 5 years and over	NHPIs[1] 5 years and over who speak English-only at home	Asian Indian	Bangladeshi	Cambodian	Chinese[2]	Fijian	Filipino	Guamanian[3]	Hawaiian, Native	Hmong	Indonesian	Japanese	Korean	Laotian	Malaysian	Pakistani	Samoan	Sri Lankan	Taiwanese	Thai	Tongan	Vietnamese
Litchfield County	157,582	2,103	580	-	-	119	-	-	69	-	-	-	-	-	-	-	184	-	-	-	-	-	-	-	-	9
	91.85		27.58			27.05			19.55								50.83									3.83
						20.52			11.90								31.72									1.55
			27.58			5.66			3.28								8.75									0.43
			0.37			0.08			0.04								0.12									0.01
Middlesex County	131,757	2,108	630	-	-	156	-	-	122	-	-	-	-	-	-	-	-	-	-	-	-	-	-	-	-	-
	90.53		29.89			25.28			24.95																	
						24.76			19.37																	
			29.89			7.40			5.79																	
			0.48			0.12			0.09																	
New Haven County	635,369	18,090	3,447	-	-	1,094	-	-	729	-	324	-	-	-	-	188	516	69	-	59	-	-	-	-	-	58
	82.33		19.05			20.43			14.70		21.08					24.54	26.72	14.97		9.41						6.79
						31.74			21.15		9.40					5.45	14.97	2.00		1.71						1.68
			19.05			6.05			4.03		1.79					1.04	2.85	0.38		0.33						0.32
			0.54			0.17			0.11		0.05					0.03	0.08	0.01		0.01						0.01
New Haven (city)	82,434	4,382	956	-	-	223	-	-	221	-	-	-	-	-	-	-	101	-	-	-	-	-	-	-	-	-
	71.62		21.82			30.30			13.04								19.31									
						23.33			23.12								10.56									
			21.82			5.09			5.04								2.30									
			1.16			0.27			0.27								0.12									
New London County	218,025	4,445	1,214	-	-	162	-	-	268	-	386	-	-	-	-	-	-	-	-	-	-	-	-	-	-	-
	89.75		27.31			19.01			19.05		40.25															
						13.34			22.08		31.80															
			27.31			3.64			6.03		8.68															
			0.56			0.07			0.12		0.18															
Tolland County	115,455	2,904	569	-	-	230	-	-	64	-	-	-	-	-	-	-	-	-	-	-	-	-	-	-	-	-
	89.98		19.59			28.47			6.52																	
						40.42			11.25																	
			19.59			7.92			2.20																	
			0.49			0.20			0.06																	
Mansfield (town)	16,550	1,421	179	-	-	108	-	-	22	-	-	-	-	-	-	-	-	-	-	-	-	-	-	-	-	-
	82.08		12.60			25.12			3.89																	
						60.34			12.29																	
			12.60			7.60			1.55																	
			1.08			0.65			0.13																	
Storrs (cdp)	8,664	1,010	101	-	-	-	-	-	14	-	-	-	-	-	-	-	-	-	-	-	-	-	-	-	-	-
	78.34		10.00						2.78																	
									13.86																	
			10.00						1.39																	
			1.17						0.16																	
Windham County	90,483	643	183	-	-	-	-	-	-	-	-	-	-	-	-	-	-	-	-	-	-	-	-	-	-	-
	88.32		28.46																							
			28.46																							
			0.20																							
DELAWARE	662,845	14,848	3,037	335	161	812	-	-	416	-	544	-	-	-	-	320	388	-	-	93	-	-	-	-	-	91
	90.51		20.45		48.06	17.00			11.03		31.32					53.51	22.03			28.01						14.65
						26.74			13.70		17.91					10.54	12.78			3.06						3.00
			20.45		48.06	5.47			2.80		3.66					2.16	2.61			0.63						0.61
			0.46		0.02	0.12			0.06		0.08					0.05	0.06			0.01						0.01

Notes: Please refer to the User's Guide for an explanation of data; data is arranged alphabetically by state, then county, then city within each county; table includes counties with populations greater than 49,999 unless noted and cities with populations greater than 9,999 whose Asian and/or NHPI population rates are greater than the national average; (1) Native Hawaiian and other Pacific Islander; (2) excludes Taiwanese; (3) includes Chamorro; (4) county does not meet population threshold but is shown in order to allow inclusion of city

Place	Total population 5 years and over who speak English-only at home	Asian population 5 years and over	Asians 5 years and over who speak English-only at home	NHPI[1] population 5 years and over	NHPIs[1] 5 years and over who speak English-only at home	Asian Indian	Bangladeshi	Cambodian	Chinese[2]	Fijian	Filipino	Guamanian[3]	Hawaiian, Native	Hmong	Indonesian	Japanese	Korean	Laotian	Malaysian	Pakistani	Samoan	Sri Lankan	Taiwanese	Thai	Tongan	Vietnamese
Kent County	108,274 92.10	1,948	495 25.41 25.41 0.46	-	-	53 13.35 10.71 2.72 0.05	-	-	-	-	130 27.84 26.26 6.67 0.12	-	-	-	-	-	-	-	-	-	-	-	-	-	-	-
New Castle County	417,425 89.35	12,180	2,280 18.72 18.72 0.55	-	-	685 16.15 30.04 5.62 0.16	-	-	380 10.97 16.67 3.12 0.09	-	316 29.90 13.86 2.59 0.08	-	-	-	-	210 55.41 9.21 1.72 0.05	318 23.84 13.95 2.61 0.08	-	-	-	-	-	-	-	-	64 13.06 2.81 0.53 0.02
Hockessin (cdp)	10,599 87.71	781	108 13.83 13.83 1.02	-	-	-	-	-	-	-	-	-	-	-	-	-	-	-	-	-	-	-	-	-	-	-
Newark (city)	24,599 88.84	1,179	229 19.42 19.42 0.93	-	-	-	-	-	49 9.12 21.40 4.16 0.20	-	-	-	-	-	-	-	-	-	-	-	-	-	-	-	-	-
Pike Creek (cdp)	16,475 89.07	1,014	240 23.67 23.67 1.46	-	-	-	-	-	-	-	-	-	-	-	-	-	-	-	-	-	-	-	-	-	-	-
Sussex County	137,146 92.91	720	262 36.39 36.39 0.19	-	-	-	-	-	-	-	-	-	-	-	-	-	-	-	-	-	-	-	-	-	-	-
DISTRICT OF COLUMBIA	449,241 83.25	14,056	4,267 30.36 30.36 0.95	-	-	1,139 48.00 26.69 8.10 0.25	-	-	847 23.81 19.85 6.03 0.19	-	656 32.05 15.37 4.67 0.15	-	-	-	-	263 25.58 6.16 1.87 0.06	414 37.33 9.70 2.95 0.09	-	-	-	-	-	-	-	-	119 7.13 2.79 0.85 0.03
FLORIDA	11,569,739 76.91	248,294	65,032 26.19 26.19 0.56	6,416	3,558 55.46 55.46 0.03	21,428 34.05 32.95 8.63 0.19	32 2.80 0.05 0.01 <0.01	351 13.36 0.54 0.14 <0.01	9,153 21.90 14.07 3.69 0.08	-	16,338 31.41 25.12 6.58 0.14	829 43.86 23.30 12.92 0.01	1,519 81.54 42.69 23.68 0.01	-	126 14.96 0.19 0.05 <0.01	4,185 38.08 6.44 1.69 0.04	4,264 23.55 6.56 1.72 0.04	382 10.07 0.59 0.15 <0.01	-	483 9.69 0.74 0.19 <0.01	359 45.79 10.09 5.60 <0.01	114 29.84 0.18 0.05 <0.01	393 20.01 0.60 0.16 <0.01	1,593 25.02 2.45 0.64 0.01	-	2,713 8.73 4.17 1.09 0.02
Alachua County	183,049 88.49	7,539	1,753 23.25 23.25 0.96	-	-	544 28.44 31.03 7.22 0.30	-	-	177 8.77 10.10 2.35 0.10	-	505 49.90 28.81 6.70 0.28	-	-	-	-	147 36.12 8.39 1.95 0.08	95 10.17 5.42 1.26 0.05	-	-	-	-	-	-	-	-	114 18.87 6.50 1.51 0.06
Gainesville (city)	78,746 86.29	4,202	854 20.32 20.32 1.08	-	-	290 27.94 33.96 6.90 0.37	-	-	110 7.99 12.88 2.62 0.14	-	-	-	-	-	-		48 10.55 5.62 1.14 0.06	-	-	-	-	-	-	-	-	-

Notes: Please refer to the User's Guide for an explanation of data; data is arranged alphabetically by state, then county, then city within each county; table includes counties with populations greater than 49,999 unless noted and cities with populations greater than 9,999 whose Asian and/or NHPI population rates are greater than the national average; (1) Native Hawaiian and other Pacific Islander; (2) excludes Taiwanese; (3) includes Chamorro; (4) county does not meet population threshold but is shown in order to allow inclusion of city

Place	Total population 5 years and over who speak English-only at home	Asian population 5 years and over	Asians 5 years and over who speak English-only at home	NHPI[1] population 5 years and over	NHPIs[1] 5 years and over who speak English-only at home	Asian Indian	Bangladeshi	Cambodian	Chinese[2]	Fijian	Filipino	Guamanian[3]	Hawaiian, Native	Hmong	Indonesian	Japanese	Korean	Laotian	Malaysian	Pakistani	Samoan	Sri Lankan	Taiwanese	Thai	Tongan	Vietnamese
Bay County	130,288 93.59	2,236	582 26.03 26.03 0.45	-	-	-	-	-	-	-	150 32.61 25.77 6.71 0.12	-	-	-	-	-	-	-	-	-	-	-	-	-	-	80 13.31 13.75 3.58 0.06
Callaway (city)	12,151 92.05	485	156 32.16 32.16 1.28	-	-	-	-	-	-	-	-	-	-	-	-	-	-	-	-	-	-	-	-	-	-	-
Brevard County	412,102 91.26	6,768	1,937 28.62 28.62 0.47	-	-	515 28.31 26.59 7.61 0.12	-	-	225 27.08 11.62 3.32 0.05	-	494 33.86 25.50 7.30 0.12	-	-	-	-	275 52.38 14.20 4.06 0.07	121 19.64 6.25 1.79 0.03	-	-	-	-	-	-	-	-	116 15.68 5.99 1.71 0.03
Broward County	1,083,041 71.21	33,911	11,197 33.02 33.02 1.03	602	390 64.78 64.78 0.04	5,904 48.99 52.73 17.41 0.55	-	-	1,848 23.34 16.50 5.45 0.17	-	1,494 31.98 13.34 4.41 0.14	-	-	-	-	396 38.56 3.54 1.17 0.04	523 24.94 4.67 1.54 0.05	-	-	85 8.23 0.76 0.25 0.01	-	-	-	170 29.57 1.52 0.50 0.02	-	262 10.16 2.34 0.77 0.02
Cooper City (city)	19,666 75.27	1,204	249 20.68 20.68 1.27	-	-	126 22.66 50.60 10.47 0.64	-	-	-	-	-	-	-	-	-	-	-	-	-	-	-	-	-	-	-	-
Pembroke Pines (city)	79,783 62.55	4,512	1,377 30.52 30.52 1.73	-	-	665 42.63 48.29 14.74 0.83	-	-	288 27.88 20.92 6.38 0.36	-	216 24.41 15.69 4.79 0.27	-	-	-	-	-	-	-	-	-	-	-	-	-	-	-
Charlotte County	125,400 91.76	855	138 16.14 16.14 0.11	-	-	-	-	-	-	-	-	-	-	-	-	-	-	-	-	-	-	-	-	-	-	-
Citrus County	106,153 93.41	1,086	275 25.32 25.32 0.26	-	-	-	-	-	-	-	-	-	-	-	-	-	-	-	-	-	-	-	-	-	-	-
Clay County	121,540 92.27	2,731	829 30.36 30.36 0.68	-	-	-	-	-	-	-	465 27.91 56.09 17.03 0.38	-	-	-	-	-	-	-	-	-	-	-	-	-	-	-
Bellair-Meadowbrook Ter. (cdp)	13,670 88.27	608	137 22.53 22.53 1.00	-	-	-	-	-	-	-	-	-	-	-	-	-	-	-	-	-	-	-	-	-	-	-

Notes: Please refer to the User's Guide for an explanation of data; data is arranged alphabetically by state, then county, then city within each county; table includes counties with populations greater than 49,999 unless noted and cities with populations greater than 9,999 whose Asian and/or NHPI population rates are greater than the national average; (1) Native Hawaiian and other Pacific Islander; (2) excludes Taiwanese; (3) includes Chamorro; (4) county does not meet population threshold but is shown in order to allow inclusion of city

Place	Total population 5 years and over who speak English-only at home	Asian population 5 years and over	Asians 5 years and over who speak English-only at home	NHPI[1] population 5 years and over	NHPIs[1] 5 years and over who speak English-only at home	Asian Indian	Bangladeshi	Cambodian	Chinese[2]	Fijian	Filipino	Guamanian[3]	Hawaiian, Native	Hmong	Indonesian	Japanese	Korean	Laotian	Malaysian	Pakistani	Samoan	Sri Lankan	Taiwanese	Thai	Tongan	Vietnamese
	178,413	1,093	471	-	-	-	-	-	-	-	-	-	-	-	-	-	-	-	-	-	-	-	-	-	-	-
	74.94		43.09																							
Collier County																										
			43.09																							
			0.26																							
	50,221	373	91	-	-	-	-	-	-	-	-	-	-	-	-	-	-	-	-	-	-	-	-	-	-	-
	94.93		24.40																							
Columbia County																										
			24.40																							
			0.18																							
	654,825	19,316	4,871	427	260	438	-	106	217	-	3,303	-	-	-	-	224	147	-	-	-	-	-	-	-	-	126
	90.55		25.22		60.89	17.77		11.22	14.11		33.84					41.79	16.33									6.54
Duval County						8.99		2.18	4.45		67.81					4.60	3.02									2.59
			25.22		60.89	2.27		0.55	1.12		17.10					1.16	0.76									0.65
			0.74		0.04	0.07		0.02	0.03		0.50					0.03	0.02									0.02
	257,796	6,215	1,704	-	-	111	-	-	75	-	1,011	-	-	-	-	-	-	-	-	-	-	-	-	-	-	123
	93.19		27.42			24.61			13.49		37.96															8.52
Escambia County						6.51			4.40		59.33															7.22
			27.42			1.79			1.21		16.27															1.98
			0.66			0.04			0.03		0.39															0.05
	18,455	747	266	-	-	-	-	-	-	-	155	-	-	-	-	-	-	-	-	-	-	-	-	-	-	-
	93.50		35.61								38.37															
Bellview (cdp)											58.27															
			35.61								20.75															
			1.44								0.84															
	14,689	775	237	-	-	-	-	-	-	-	175	-	-	-	-	-	-	-	-	-	-	-	-	-	-	-
	90.63		30.58								37.88															
Myrtle Grove (cdp)											73.84															
			30.58								22.58															
			1.61								1.19															
	113,262	704	200	-	-	-	-	-	-	-	-	-	-	-	-	-	-	-	-	-	-	-	-	-	-	-
	90.67		28.41																							
Hernando County																										
			28.41																							
			0.18																							
	71,297	892	143	-	-	-	-	-	-	-	87	-	-	-	-	-	-	-	-	-	-	-	-	-	-	-
	86.12		16.03								20.76															
Highlands County											60.84															
			16.03								9.75															
			0.20								0.12															
	736,750	20,228	4,820	523	433	1,358	-	-	607	-	1,013	-	-	-	-	382	537	-	-	-	-	-	-	156	-	299
	79.11		23.83		82.79	25.15			24.48		33.12					45.42	20.77							23.93		7.90
Hillsborough County						28.17			12.59		21.02					7.93	11.14							3.24		6.20
			23.83		82.79	6.71			3.00		5.01					1.89	2.65							0.77		1.48
			0.65		0.06	0.18			0.08		0.14					0.05	0.07							0.02		0.04
	8,301	475	170	-	-	-	-	-	-	-	-	-	-	-	-	-	-	-	-	-	-	-	-	-	-	-
	83.51		35.79																							
Westchase (cdp)																										
			35.79																							
			2.05																							

Notes: Please refer to the User's Guide for an explanation of data; data is arranged alphabetically by state, then county, then city within each county; table includes counties with populations greater than 49,999 unless noted and cities with populations greater than 9,999 whose Asian and/or NHPI population rates are greater than the national average; (1) Native Hawaiian and other Pacific Islander; (2) excludes Taiwanese; (3) includes Chamorro; (4) county does not meet population threshold but is shown in order to allow inclusion of city

Place	Total population 5 years and over who speak English-only at home	Asian population 5 years and over	Asians 5 years and over who speak English-only at home	NHPI[1] population 5 years and over	NHPIs[1] 5 years and over who speak English-only at home	Asian Indian	Bangladeshi	Cambodian	Chinese[2]	Fijian	Filipino	Guamanian[3]	Hawaiian, Native	Hmong	Indonesian	Japanese	Korean	Laotian	Malaysian	Pakistani	Samoan	Sri Lankan	Taiwanese	Thai	Tongan	Vietnamese
Indian River County	96,498 89.56	806	213 26.43 26.43 0.22	-	-	-	-	-	-	-	-	-	-	-	-	-	-	-	-	-	-	-	-	-	-	-
Lake County	182,724 91.56	1,308	329 25.15 25.15 0.18	-	-	-	-	-	-	-	-	-	-	-	-	-	-	-	-	-	-	-	-	-	-	-
Lee County	361,208 86.46	2,970	878 29.56 29.56 0.24	-	-	138 23.27 15.72 4.65 0.04	-	-	216 38.85 24.60 7.27 0.06	-	278 26.55 31.66 9.36 0.08	-	-	-	-	-	-	-	-	-	-	-	-	-	-	-
Leon County	208,570 92.40	4,470	1,343 30.04 30.04 0.64	-	-	576 41.26 42.89 12.89 0.28	-	-	188 19.85 14.00 4.21 0.09	-	189 38.10 14.07 4.23 0.09	-	-	-	-	-	75 18.89 5.58 1.68 0.04	-	-	-	-	-	-	-	-	-
Manatee County	218,481 87.74	2,173	524 24.11 24.11 0.24	-	-	-	-	-	-	-	121 22.49 23.09 5.57 0.06	-	-	-	-	-	-	-	-	-	-	-	-	-	-	-
Marion County	224,174 91.19	2,044	710 34.74 34.74 0.32	-	-	342 39.63 48.17 16.73 0.15	-	-	-	-	-	-	-	-	-	-	-	-	-	-	-	-	-	-	-	-
Martin County	107,584 88.71	690	286 41.45 41.45 0.27	-	-	-	-	-	-	-	-	-	-	-	-	-	-	-	-	-	-	-	-	-	-	-
Miami-Dade County	676,347 32.08	28,911	7,409 25.63 25.63 1.10	599	264 44.07 44.07 0.04	3,346 39.94 45.16 11.57 0.49	-	-	1,993 23.81 26.90 6.89 0.29	-	746 17.36 10.07 2.58 0.11	-	-	-	-	231 17.04 3.12 0.80 0.03	210 16.50 2.83 0.73 0.03	-	-	23 3.16 0.31 0.08 <0.01	-	-	-	168 19.47 2.27 0.58 0.02	-	191 13.19 2.58 0.66 0.03
Doral (cdp)	2,898 15.64	1,047	74 7.07 7.07 2.55	-	-	-	-	-	-	-	-	-	-	-	-	-	-	-	-	-	-	-	-	-	-	-
Ives Estates (cdp)	8,535 52.60	756	131 17.33 17.33 1.53	-	-	-	-	-	-	-	-	-	-	-	-	-	-	-	-	-	-	-	-	-	-	-

Notes: Please refer to the User's Guide for an explanation of data; data is arranged alphabetically by state, then county, then city within each county; table includes counties with populations greater than 49,999 unless noted and cities with populations greater than 9,999 whose Asian and/or NHPI population rates are greater than the national average; (1) Native Hawaiian and other Pacific Islander; (2) excludes Taiwanese; (3) includes Chamorro; (4) county does not meet population threshold but is shown in order to allow inclusion of city

Place	Total population 5 years and over who speak English-only at home	Asian population 5 years and over	Asians 5 years and over who speak English-only at home	NHPI[1] population 5 years and over	NHPIs[1] 5 years and over who speak English-only at home	Asian Indian	Bangladeshi	Cambodian	Chinese[2]	Fijian	Filipino	Guamanian[3]	Hawaiian, Native	Hmong	Indonesian	Japanese	Korean	Laotian	Malaysian	Pakistani	Samoan	Sri Lankan	Taiwanese	Thai	Tongan	Vietnamese
North Miami Beach (city)	14,349	1,632	292	-	-	159	-	-	67	-	-	-	-	-	-	-	-	-	-	-	-	-	-	-	-	-
	37.82		17.89			44.29			9.12																	
						54.45			22.95																	
			17.89			9.74			4.11																	
			2.03			1.11			0.47																	
Pinecrest (village)	10,057	818	127	-	-	-	-	-	-	-	-	-	-	-	-	-	-	-	-	-	-	-	-	-	-	-
	56.03		15.53																							
			15.53																							
			1.26																							
Monroe County	59,964	528	165	-	-	-	-	-	-	-	-	-	-	-	-	-	-	-	-	-	-	-	-	-	-	-
	78.59		31.25																							
			31.25																							
			0.28																							
Nassau County	52,061	401	203	-	-	-	-	-	-	-	-	-	-	-	-	-	-	-	-	-	-	-	-	-	-	-
	96.15		50.62																							
			50.62																							
			0.39																							
Okaloosa County	147,138	4,218	1,330	-	-	-	-	-	-	-	588	-	-	-	-	-	126	-	-	-	-	-	-	183	-	66
	92.11		31.53								36.18						18.42							29.66		17.28
											44.21						9.47							13.76		4.96
			31.53								13.94						2.99							4.34		1.56
			0.90								0.40						0.09							0.12		0.04
Wright (cdp)	18,487	786	230	-	-	-	-	-	-	-	-	-	-	-	-	-	-	-	-	-	-	-	-	-	-	-
	91.42		29.26																							
			29.26																							
			1.24																							
Orange County	622,997	27,026	6,439	784	315	2,591	-	-	646	-	1,529	-	-	-	-	349	332	-	-	93	-	-	-	-	-	421
	74.58		23.83		40.18	35.89			17.42		35.30					30.80	16.14			11.51						7.09
						40.24			10.03		23.75					5.42	5.16			1.44						6.54
			23.83		40.18	9.59			2.39		5.66					1.29	1.23			0.34						1.56
			1.03		0.05	0.42			0.10		0.25					0.06	0.05			0.01						0.07
Oak Ridge (cdp)	8,435	1,169	138	-	-	-	-	-	-	-	-	-	-	-	-	-	-	-	-	-	-	-	-	-	-	7
	41.16		11.80																							1.51
																										5.07
			11.80																							0.60
			1.64																							0.08
Osceola County	107,397	3,401	744	-	-	246	-	-	76	-	248	-	-	-	-	-	-	-	-	-	-	-	-	-	-	-
	66.70		21.88			28.47			13.36		28.94															
						33.06			10.22		33.33															
			21.88			7.23			2.23		7.29															
			0.69			0.23			0.07		0.23															
Palm Beach County	837,066	15,958	4,085	396	215	1,549	-	-	701	-	593	-	-	-	-	179	309	-	-	-	-	-	-	159	-	209
	78.28		25.60		54.29	32.26			20.44		27.74					32.78	33.99							22.08		11.02
						37.92			17.16		14.52					4.38	7.56							3.89		5.12
			25.60		54.29	9.71			4.39		3.72					1.12	1.94							1.00		1.31
			0.49		0.03	0.19			0.08		0.07					0.02	0.04							0.02		0.02

Notes: Please refer to the User's Guide for an explanation of data; data is arranged alphabetically by state, then county, then city within each county; table includes counties with populations greater than 49,999 unless noted and cities with populations greater than 9,999 whose Asian and/or NHPI population rates are greater than the national average; (1) Native Hawaiian and other Pacific Islander; (2) excludes Taiwanese; (3) includes Chamorro; (4) county does not meet population threshold but is shown in order to allow inclusion of city

Place	Total population 5 years and over who speak English-only at home	Asian population 5 years and over	Asians 5 years and over who speak English-only at home	NHPI[1] population 5 years and over	NHPIs[1] 5 years and over who speak English-only at home	Asian Indian	Bangladeshi	Cambodian	Chinese[2]	Fijian	Filipino	Guamanian[3]	Hawaiian, Native	Hmong	Indonesian	Japanese	Korean	Laotian	Malaysian	Pakistani	Samoan	Sri Lankan	Taiwanese	Thai	Tongan	Vietnamese
Pasco County	293,294 89.72	3,260	854 26.20 26.20 0.29	-	-	196 21.63 22.95 6.01 0.07	-	-	66 14.35 7.73 2.02 0.02	-	316 32.58 37.00 9.69 0.11	-	-	-	-	-	-	-	-	-	-	-	-	-	-	-
Pinellas County	771,726 88.04	17,689	3,363 19.01 19.01 0.44	-	-	894 26.03 26.58 5.05 0.12	-	49 7.18 1.46 0.28 0.01	384 19.82 11.42 2.17 0.05	-	761 26.77 22.63 4.30 0.10	-	-	-	-	157 27.94 4.67 0.89 0.02	280 34.57 8.33 1.58 0.04	108 6.17 3.21 0.61 0.01	-	-	-	-	-	168 35.74 5.00 0.95 0.02	-	238 5.97 7.08 1.35 0.03
Pinellas Park (city)	37,192 87.10	1,680	200 11.90 11.90 0.54	-	-	-	-	-	-	-	-	-	-	-	-	-	-	-	-	-	-	-	-	-	-	26 5.32 13.00 1.55 0.07
Polk County	398,332 87.90	5,315	1,074 20.21 20.21 0.27	-	-	212 13.70 19.74 3.99 0.05	-	-	148 27.61 13.78 2.78 0.04	-	175 20.11 16.29 3.29 0.04	-	-	-	-	-	-	71 19.19 6.61 1.34 0.02	-	-	-	-	-	-	-	94 12.45 8.75 1.77 0.02
Putnam County	61,253 92.75	284	99 34.86 34.86 0.16	-	-	-	-	-	-	-	-	-	-	-	-	-	-	-	-	-	-	-	-	-	-	-
St. Johns County	108,870 93.28	1,168	411 35.19 35.19 0.38	-	-	-	-	-	-	-	-	-	-	-	-	-	-	-	-	-	-	-	-	-	-	-
St. Lucie County	156,941 86.22	1,758	366 20.82 20.82 0.23	-	-	-	-	-	-	-	-	-	-	-	-	-	-	-	-	-	-	-	-	-	-	-
Santa Rosa County	104,132 94.69	1,537	417 27.13 27.13 0.40	-	-	-	-	-	-	-	220 32.21 52.76 14.31 0.21	-	-	-	-	-	-	-	-	-	-	-	-	-	-	-
Sarasota County	280,340 89.47	2,502	698 27.90 27.90 0.25	-	-	-	-	-	87 23.97 12.46 3.48 0.03	-	230 42.59 32.95 9.19 0.08	-	-	-	-	-	-	-	-	-	-	-	-	-	-	55 8.38 7.88 2.20 0.02
Seminole County	288,646 84.41	8,122	1,965 24.19 24.19 0.68	-	-	743 28.47 37.81 9.15 0.26	-	-	313 24.40 15.93 3.85 0.11	-	426 34.47 21.68 5.25 0.15	-	-	-	-	-	123 13.53 6.26 1.51 0.04	-	-	-	-	-	-	-	-	83 8.38 4.22 1.02 0.03

Notes: Please refer to the User's Guide for an explanation of data; data is arranged alphabetically by state, then county, then city within each county; table includes counties with populations greater than 49,999 unless noted and cities with populations greater than 9,999 whose Asian and/or NHPI population rates are greater than the national average; (1) Native Hawaiian and other Pacific Islander; (2) excludes Taiwanese; (3) includes Chamorro; (4) county does not meet population threshold but is shown in order to allow inclusion of city

Place	Total population 5 years and over who speak English-only at home	Asian population 5 years and over	Asians 5 years and over who speak English-only at home	NHPI[1] population 5 years and over	NHPIs[1] 5 years and over who speak English-only at home	Asian Indian	Bangladeshi	Cambodian	Chinese[2]	Fijian	Filipino	Guamanian[3]	Hawaiian, Native	Hmong	Indonesian	Japanese	Korean	Laotian	Malaysian	Pakistani	Samoan	Sri Lankan	Taiwanese	Thai	Tongan	Vietnamese
Volusia County	376,145 89.23	4,589	1,337 29.13 29.13 0.36	-	-	432 28.37 32.31 9.41 0.11	-	-	136 22.19 10.17 2.96 0.04	-	263 32.00 19.67 5.73 0.07	-	-	-	-	-	127 28.93 9.50 2.77 0.03	-	-	-	-	-	-	-	-	-
GEORGIA	6,843,038 90.11	159,664	22,532 14.11 14.11 0.33	3,521	1,781 50.58 50.58 0.03	6,087 14.75 27.01 3.81 0.09	40 3.56 0.18 0.03 <0.01	341 10.52 1.51 0.21 <0.01	3,113 13.26 13.82 1.95 0.05	-	3,437 34.59 15.25 2.15 0.05	377 29.99 21.17 10.71 0.01	637 80.23 35.77 18.09 0.01	13 1.15 0.06 0.01 <0.01	68 13.26 0.30 0.04 <0.01	1,818 25.35 8.07 1.14 0.03	3,464 13.22 15.37 2.17 0.05	174 3.93 0.77 0.11 <0.01	-	294 8.26 1.30 0.18 <0.01	342 48.65 19.20 9.71 <0.01	-	54 3.08 0.24 0.03 <0.01	487 22.37 2.16 0.31 0.01	-	1,425 5.17 6.32 0.89 0.02
Bartow County	66,274 94.46	556	207 37.23 37.23 0.31	-	-	-	-	-	-	-	-	-	-	-	-	-	-	-	-	-	-	-	-	-	-	-
Bibb County	136,787 95.98	1,481	286 19.31 19.31 0.21	-	-	-	-	-	-	-	-	-	-	-	-	-	-	-	-	-	-	-	-	-	-	-
Bulloch County	49,849 94.48	591	144 24.37 24.37 0.29	-	-	-	-	-	-	-	-	-	-	-	-	-	-	-	-	-	-	-	-	-	-	-
Carroll County	77,147 95.16	413	41 9.93 9.93 0.05	-	-	-	-	-	-	-	-	-	-	-	-	-	-	-	-	-	-	-	-	-	-	-
Catoosa County	47,926 96.52	401	167 41.65 41.65 0.35	-	-	-	-	-	-	-	-	-	-	-	-	-	-	-	-	-	-	-	-	-	-	-
Chatham County	202,148 93.33	3,815	752 19.71 19.71 0.37	-	-	99 13.58 13.16 2.60 0.05	-	-	102 14.15 13.56 2.67 0.05	-	-	-	-	-	-	-	129 29.05 17.15 3.38 0.06	-	-	-	-	-	-	-	-	68 7.12 9.04 1.78 0.03
Cherokee County	119,438 91.95	1,264	225 17.80 17.80 0.19	-	-	31 11.83 13.78 2.45 0.03	-	-	-	-	-	-	-	-	-	-	-	-	-	-	-	-	-	-	-	-
Clarke County	84,683 88.16	3,029	383 12.64 12.64 0.45	-	-	98 14.69 25.59 3.24 0.12	-	-	50 5.52 13.05 1.65 0.06	-	-	-	-	-	-	-	32 6.34 8.36 1.06 0.04	-	-	-	-	-	-	-	-	-

Notes: Please refer to the User's Guide for an explanation of data; data is arranged alphabetically by state, then county, then city within each county; table includes counties with populations greater than 49,999 unless noted and cities with populations greater than 9,999 whose Asian and/or NHPI population rates are greater than the national average; (1) Native Hawaiian and other Pacific Islander; (2) excludes Taiwanese; (3) includes Chamorro; (4) county does not meet population threshold but is shown in order to allow inclusion of city

Place	Total population 5 years and over who speak English-only at home	Asian population 5 years and over	Asians 5 years and over who speak English-only at home	NHPI[1] population 5 years and over	NHPIs[1] 5 years and over who speak English-only at home	Asian Indian	Bangladeshi	Cambodian	Chinese[2]	Fijian	Filipino	Guamanian[3]	Hawaiian, Native	Hmong	Indonesian	Japanese	Korean	Laotian	Malaysian	Pakistani	Samoan	Sri Lankan	Taiwanese	Thai	Tongan	Vietnamese
Clayton County	184,297 85.05	9,608	606 6.31 6.31 0.33	-	-	131 10.60 21.62 1.36 0.07	-	74 7.66 12.21 0.77 0.04	92 19.29 15.18 0.96 0.05	-	-	-	-	-	-	-	-	22 1.89 3.63 0.23 0.01	-	10 2.81 1.65 0.10 0.01	-	-	-	-	-	125 3.04 20.63 1.30 0.07
Forest Park (city)	14,345 73.66	1,255	33 2.63 2.63 0.23	-	-	-	-	-	-	-	-	-	-	-	-	-	-	-	-	-	-	-	-	-	-	9 0.98 27.27 0.72 0.06
Riverdale (city)	9,096 81.26	918	45 4.90 4.90 0.49	-	-	-	-	-	-	-	-	-	-	-	-	-	-	-	-	-	-	-	-	-	-	10 2.33 22.22 1.09 0.11
Cobb County	481,572 85.30	17,235	2,707 15.71 15.71 0.56	-	-	780 15.69 28.81 4.53 0.16	-	-	339 10.83 12.52 1.97 0.07	-	386 33.74 14.26 2.24 0.08	-	-	-	-	151 15.86 5.58 0.88 0.03	407 14.35 15.04 2.36 0.08	-	-	84 14.17 3.10 0.49 0.02	-	-	-	-	-	170 10.89 6.28 0.99 0.04
Smyrna (city)	30,088 78.63	1,480	193 13.04 13.04 0.64	-	-	37 7.39 19.17 2.50 0.12	-	-	-	-	-	-	-	-	-	-	-	-	-	-	-	-	-	-	-	-
Columbia County	76,346 91.83	2,698	415 15.38 15.38 0.54	-	-	138 15.88 33.25 5.11 0.18	-	-	59 11.68 14.22 2.19 0.08	-	-	-	-	-	-	-	73 17.46 17.59 2.71 0.10	-	-	-	-	-	-	-	-	-
Martinez (cdp)	23,152 89.73	1,345	202 15.02 15.02 0.87	-	-	71 15.14 35.15 5.28 0.31	-	-	-	-	-	-	-	-	-	-	-	-	-	-	-	-	-	-	-	-
Coweta County	77,496 94.37	544	197 36.21 36.21 0.25	-	-	-	-	-	-	-	-	-	-	-	-	-	-	-	-	-	-	-	-	-	-	-
DeKalb County	511,239 82.59	24,905	3,056 12.27 12.27 0.60	-	-	1,103 16.07 36.09 4.43 0.22	8 1.57 0.26 0.03 <0.01	33 5.74 1.08 0.13 0.01	572 15.93 18.72 2.30 0.11	-	282 43.79 9.23 1.13 0.06	-	-	-	-	130 15.53 4.25 0.52 0.03	343 10.86 11.22 1.38 0.07	-	-	-	-	-	-	-	-	222 3.65 7.26 0.89 0.04
Druid Hills (cdp)	10,352 84.46	854	212 24.82 24.82 2.05	-	-	-	-	-	-	-	-	-	-	-	-	-	-	-	-	-	-	-	-	-	-	-

Notes: Please refer to the User's Guide for an explanation of data; data is arranged alphabetically by state, then county, then city within each county; table includes counties with populations greater than 49,999 unless noted and cities with populations greater than 9,999 whose Asian and/or NHPI population rates are greater than the national average; (1) Native Hawaiian and other Pacific Islander; (2) excludes Taiwanese; (3) includes Chamorro; (4) county does not meet population threshold but is shown in order to allow inclusion of city

Place	Total population 5 years and over who speak English-only at home	Asian population 5 years and over	Asians 5 years and over who speak English-only at home	NHPI[1] population 5 years and over	NHPIs[1] 5 years and over who speak English-only at home	Asian Indian	Bangladeshi	Cambodian	Chinese[2]	Fijian	Filipino	Guamanian[3]	Hawaiian, Native	Hmong	Indonesian	Japanese	Korean	Laotian	Malaysian	Pakistani	Samoan	Sri Lankan	Taiwanese	Thai	Tongan	Vietnamese
Dunwoody (cdp)	25,392 82.85	2,276	242 10.63 10.63 0.95	-	-	103 10.63 42.56 4.53 0.41	-	-	-	-	-	-	-	-	-	-	40 9.07 16.53 1.76 0.16	-	-	-	-	-	-	-	-	-
North Atlanta (cdp)	22,068 61.27	1,552	278 17.91 17.91 1.26	-	-	-	-	-	-	-	-	-	-	-	-	-	-	-	-	-	-	-	-	-	-	-
North Decatur (cdp)	12,648 87.15	800	175 21.88 21.88 1.38	-	-	-	-	-	-	-	-	-	-	-	-	-	-	-	-	-	-	-	-	-	-	-
North Druid Hills (cdp)	15,207 83.60	1,197	294 24.56 24.56 1.93	-	-	167 31.27 56.80 13.95 1.10	-	-	-	-	-	-	-	-	-	-	-	-	-	-	-	-	-	-	-	-
Tucker (cdp)	20,027 79.96	1,865	241 12.92 12.92 1.20	-	-	-	-	-	-	-	-	-	-	-	-	-	-	-	-	-	-	-	-	-	-	7 2.32 2.90 0.38 0.03
Dougherty County	84,829 95.60	696	42 6.03 6.03 0.05	-	-	-	-	-	-	-	-	-	-	-	-	-	-	-	-	-	-	-	-	-	-	-
Douglas County	80,181 93.82	854	177 20.73 20.73 0.22	-	-	-	-	-	-	-	-	-	-	-	-	-	-	-	-	-	-	-	-	-	-	-
Fayette County	79,981 92.99	1,951	467 23.94 23.94 0.58	-	-	-	-	-	-	-	-	-	-	-	-	89 14.78 19.06 4.56 0.11	-	-	-	-	-	-	-	-	-	-
Peachtree City (city)	27,033 90.34	1,197	358 29.91 29.91 1.32	-	-	-	-	-	-	-	-	-	-	-	-	89 15.48 24.86 7.44 0.33	-	-	-	-	-	-	-	-	-	-
Floyd County	77,950 92.22	1,129	177 15.68 15.68 0.23	-	-	31 6.94 17.51 2.75 0.04	-	-	-	-	-	-	-	-	-	-	-	-	-	-	-	-	-	-	-	-

Notes: Please refer to the User's Guide for an explanation of data; data is arranged alphabetically by state, then county, then city within each county; table includes counties with populations greater than 49,999 unless noted and cities with populations greater than 9,999 whose Asian and/or NHPI population rates are greater than the national average; (1) Native Hawaiian and other Pacific Islander; (2) excludes Taiwanese; (3) includes Chamorro; (4) county does not meet population threshold but is shown in order to allow inclusion of city

Place	Total population 5 years and over who speak English-only at home	Asian population 5 years and over	Asians 5 years and over who speak English-only at home	NHPI[1] population 5 years and over	NHPIs[1] 5 years and over who speak English-only at home	Asian Indian	Bangladeshi	Cambodian	Chinese[2]	Fijian	Filipino	Guamanian[3]	Hawaiian, Native	Hmong	Indonesian	Japanese	Korean	Laotian	Malaysian	Pakistani	Samoan	Sri Lankan	Taiwanese	Thai	Tongan	Vietnamese
Forsyth County	81,312 91.37	664	112 16.87 16.87 0.14	-	-	-	-	-	-	-	-	-	-	-	-	-	-	-	-	-	-	-	-	-	-	-
Fulton County	658,421 86.73	22,205	3,321 14.96 14.96 0.50	-	-	1,044 15.54 31.44 4.70 0.16	-	-	712 14.41 21.44 3.21 0.11	-	370 44.00 11.14 1.67 0.06	-	-	-	-	207 22.80 6.23 0.93 0.03	444 11.42 13.37 2.00 0.07	-	-	-	-	-	-	-	-	132 4.71 3.97 0.59 0.02
Alpharetta (city)	27,124 85.97	1,561	218 13.97 13.97 0.80	-	-	56 9.52 25.69 3.59 0.21	-	-	104 23.85 47.71 6.66 0.38	-	-	-	-	-	-	-	-	-	-	-	-	-	-	-	-	-
Roswell (city)	60,314 80.92	2,740	371 13.54 13.54 0.62	-	-	99 13.36 26.68 3.61 0.16	-	-	113 22.20 30.46 4.12 0.19	-	-	-	-	-	-	-	31 3.65 8.36 1.13 0.05	-	-	-	-	-	-	-	-	-
Glynn County	59,571 94.22	493	129 26.17 26.17 0.22	-	-	-	-	-	-	-	-	-	-	-	-	-	-	-	-	-	-	-	-	-	-	-
Gwinnett County	426,736 78.77	37,882	3,829 10.11 10.11 0.90	469	227 48.40 48.40 0.05	1,313 13.24 34.29 3.47 0.31	-	149 17.57 3.89 0.39 0.03	431 9.02 11.26 1.14 0.10	-	353 29.97 9.22 0.93 0.08	-	-	-	-	260 32.10 6.79 0.69 0.06	720 8.30 18.80 1.90 0.17	0 0.00 0.00 0.00 0.00	-	51 4.80 1.33 0.13 0.01	-	-	14 3.20 0.37 0.04 <0.01	-	-	309 4.49 8.07 0.82 0.07
Duluth (city)	15,502 74.94	2,490	198 7.95 7.95 1.28	-	-	69 8.76 34.85 2.77 0.45	-	-	18 3.61 9.09 0.72 0.12	-	-	-	-	-	-	-	46 6.84 23.23 1.85 0.30	-	-	-	-	-	-	-	-	-
Lilburn (city)	7,723 72.33	1,394	181 12.98 12.98 2.34	-	-	74 19.53 40.88 5.31 0.96	-	-	-	-	-	-	-	-	-	-	-	-	-	-	-	-	-	-	-	50 11.85 27.62 3.59 0.65
Mountain Park (cdp)	9,293 85.36	980	83 8.47 8.47 0.89	-	-	24 3.90 28.92 2.45 0.26	-	-	-	-	-	-	-	-	-	-	-	-	-	-	-	-	-	-	-	-
Hall County	101,506 79.28	1,702	244 14.34 14.34 0.24	-	-	-	-	-	-	-	-	-	-	-	-	-	-	-	-	-	-	-	-	-	-	35 3.10 14.34 2.06 0.03

Notes: Please refer to the User's Guide for an explanation of data; data is arranged alphabetically by state, then county, then city within each county; table includes counties with populations greater than 49,999 unless noted and cities with populations greater than 9,999 whose Asian and/or NHPI population rates are greater than the national average; (1) Native Hawaiian and other Pacific Islander; (2) excludes Taiwanese; (3) includes Chamorro; (4) county does not meet population threshold but is shown in order to allow inclusion of city

Place	Total population 5 years and over who speak English-only at home	Asian population 5 years and over	Asians 5 years and over who speak English-only at home	NHPI population 5 years and over	NHPIs[1] 5 years and over who speak English-only at home	Asian Indian	Bangladeshi	Cambodian	Chinese[2]	Fijian	Filipino	Guamanian[3]	Hawaiian, Native	Hmong	Indonesian	Japanese	Korean	Laotian	Malaysian	Pakistani	Samoan	Sri Lankan	Taiwanese	Thai	Tongan	Vietnamese
Henry County	103,560 94.38	2,002	268 13.39 13.39 0.26	-	-	51 6.51 19.03 2.55 0.05	-	-	-	-	-	-	-	-	-	-	-	-	-	-	-	-	-	-	-	-
Houston County	96,792 93.94	1,649	406 24.62 24.62 0.42	-	-	-	-	-	-	-	110 21.57 27.09 6.67 0.11	-	-	-	-	-	-	-	-	-	-	-	-	-	-	-
Liberty County	48,106 87.13	914	207 22.65 22.65 0.43	-	-	-	-	-	-	-	-	-	-	-	-	-	49 13.80 23.67 5.36 0.10	-	-	-	-	-	-	-	-	-
Lowndes County	81,522 95.09	848	294 34.67 34.67 0.36	-	-	-	-	-	-	-	-	-	-	-	-	-	-	-	-	-	-	-	-	-	-	-
Muscogee County	158,649 91.88	2,794	663 23.73 23.73 0.42	310	167 53.87 53.87 0.11	58 11.11 8.75 2.08 0.04	-	-	95 27.94 14.33 3.40 0.06	-	159 38.41 23.98 5.69 0.10	-	-	-	-	-	180 24.06 27.15 6.44 0.11	-	-	-	-	-	-	-	-	-
Columbus (sp. city)	158,232 91.89	2,794	663 23.73 23.73 0.42	310	167 53.87 53.87 0.11	58 11.11 8.75 2.08 0.04	-	-	95 27.94 14.33 3.40 0.06	-	159 38.41 23.98 5.69 0.10	-	-	-	-	-	180 24.06 27.15 6.44 0.11	-	-	-	-	-	-	-	-	-
Newton County	54,981 96.10	369	57 15.45 15.45 0.10	-	-	-	-	-	-	-	-	-	-	-	-	-	-	-	-	-	-	-	-	-	-	-
Richmond County	173,207 93.42	2,854	675 23.65 23.65 0.39	-	-	76 12.10 11.26 2.66 0.04	-	-	84 16.57 12.44 2.94 0.05	-	-	-	-	-	-	-	172 20.40 25.48 6.03 0.10	-	-	-	-	-	-	-	-	-
Rockdale County	59,122 90.29	1,043	130 12.46 12.46 0.22	-	-	-	-	-	-	-	-	-	-	-	-	-	-	-	-	-	-	-	-	-	-	-
Spalding County	51,946 95.94	412	32 7.77 7.77 0.06	-	-	-	-	-	-	-	-	-	-	-	-	-	-	-	-	-	-	-	-	-	-	-

Notes: Please refer to the User's Guide for an explanation of data; data is arranged alphabetically by state, then county, then city within each county; table includes counties with populations greater than 49,999 unless noted and cities with populations greater than 9,999 whose Asian and/or NHPI population rates are greater than the national average; (1) Native Hawaiian and other Pacific Islander; (2) excludes Taiwanese; (3) includes Chamorro; (4) county does not meet population threshold but is shown in order to allow inclusion of city

Place	Total population 5 years and over who speak English-only at home	Asian population 5 years and over	Asians 5 years and over who speak English-only at home	NHPI[1] population 5 years and over	NHPIs[1] 5 years and over who speak English-only at home	Asian Indian	Bangladeshi	Cambodian	Chinese[2]	Fijian	Filipino	Guamanian[3]	Hawaiian, Native	Hmong	Indonesian	Japanese	Korean	Laotian	Malaysian	Pakistani	Samoan	Sri Lankan	Taiwanese	Thai	Tongan	Vietnamese
Troup County	52,459 96.16	386	55 14.25 14.25 0.10	-	-	-	-	-	-	-	-	-	-	-	-	-	-	-	-	-	-	-	-	-	-	-
Walton County	53,401 95.70	416	34 8.17 8.17 0.06	-	-	-	-	-	-	-	-	-	-	-	-	-	-	-	-	-	-	-	-	-	-	-
Whitfield County	59,886 77.81	768	140 18.23 18.23 0.23	-	-	-	-	-	-	-	-	-	-	-	-	-	-	-	-	-	-	-	-	-	-	-
HAWAII	832,226 73.37	483,570	271,577 56.16 56.16 32.63	103,416	72,432 70.04 70.04 8.70	552 45.54 0.20 0.11 0.07	-	45 29.22 0.02 0.01 0.01	25,717 47.72 9.47 5.32 3.09	-	60,376 37.21 22.23 12.49 7.25	714 50.46 0.99 0.69 0.09	63,416 84.41 87.55 61.32 7.62	-	-	148,182 75.53 54.56 30.64 17.81	6,127 26.55 2.26 1.27 0.74	115 6.99 0.04 0.02 0.01	-	-	4,096 31.17 5.65 3.96 0.49	-	75 9.31 0.03 0.02 0.01	349 25.61 0.13 0.07 0.04	502 13.43 0.69 0.49 0.06	697 8.87 0.26 0.14 0.08
Hawaii County	114,032 81.57	38,325	24,399 63.66 63.66 21.40	14,989	10,949 73.05 73.05 9.60	-	-	-	830 63.99 3.40 2.17 0.73	-	5,109 40.88 20.94 13.33 4.48	-	10,323 79.60 94.28 68.87 9.05	-	-	15,324 75.93 62.81 39.98 13.44	434 50.58 1.78 1.13 0.38	-	-	-	78 26.99 0.71 0.52 0.07	-	-	-	-	-
Hilo (cdp)	31,756 82.46	14,884	11,169 75.04 75.04 35.17	4,603	3,289 71.45 71.45 10.36	-	-	-	346 72.38 3.10 2.32 1.09	-	1,059 53.57 9.48 7.12 3.33	-	3,098 79.19 94.19 67.30 9.76	-	-	8,469 78.21 75.83 56.90 26.67	228 59.07 2.04 1.53 0.72	-	-	-	-	-	-	-	-	-
Honolulu County	583,116 71.12	387,964	215,686 55.59 55.59 36.99	70,976	48,066 67.72 67.72 8.24	432 43.86 0.20 0.11 0.07	-	-	23,812 46.56 11.04 6.14 4.08	-	44,123 37.13 20.46 11.37 7.57	664 52.45 1.38 0.94 0.11	40,408 86.31 84.07 56.93 6.93	-	-	116,985 74.93 54.24 30.15 20.06	5,268 24.93 2.44 1.36 0.90	99 6.17 0.05 0.03 0.02	-	-	3,960 31.34 8.24 5.58 0.68	-	75 9.66 0.03 0.02 0.01	333 29.55 0.15 0.09 0.06	368 13.11 0.77 0.52 0.06	597 8.16 0.28 0.15 0.10
Ewa Beach (cdp)	8,816 64.50	6,801	2,825 41.54 41.54 32.04	1,394	1,071 76.83 76.83 12.15	-	-	-	-	-	1,612 30.69 57.06 23.70 18.28	-	885 96.09 82.63 63.49 10.04	-	-	622 76.41 22.02 9.15 7.06	-	-	-	-	178 46.11 16.62 12.77 2.02	-	-	-	-	-
Halawa (cdp)	9,173 69.58	6,929	4,029 58.15 58.15 43.92	1,406	881 62.66 62.66 9.60	-	-	-	375 52.30 9.31 5.41 4.09	-	989 37.38 24.55 14.27 10.78	-	556 80.81 63.11 39.54 6.06	-	-	2,041 82.73 50.66 29.46 22.25	-	-	-	-	264 45.44 29.97 18.78 2.88	-	-	-	-	-
Honolulu (cdp)	226,630 64.20	200,487	101,064 50.41 50.41 44.59	23,733	13,980 58.91 58.91 6.17	216 36.06 0.21 0.11 0.10	-	-	15,280 40.47 15.12 7.62 6.74	-	13,245 32.11 13.11 6.61 5.84	281 43.70 2.01 1.18 0.12	11,554 85.45 82.65 48.68 5.10	-	-	58,460 69.59 57.84 29.16 25.80	2,951 19.66 2.92 1.47 1.30	33 3.47 0.03 0.02 0.01	-	-	877 21.60 6.27 3.70 0.39	-	40 5.78 0.04 0.02 0.02	114 21.76 0.11 0.06 0.05	136 9.65 0.97 0.57 0.06	414 6.72 0.41 0.21 0.18

Notes: Please refer to the User's Guide for an explanation of data; data is arranged alphabetically by state, then county, then city within each county; table includes counties with populations greater than 49,999 unless noted and cities with populations greater than 9,999 whose Asian and/or NHPI population rates are greater than the national average; (1) Native Hawaiian and other Pacific Islander; (2) excludes Taiwanese; (3) includes Chamorro; (4) county does not meet population threshold but is shown in order to allow inclusion of city

Place	Total population 5 years and over who speak English-only at home	Asian population 5 years and over	Asians 5 years and over who speak English-only at home	NHPI[1] population 5 years and over	NHPIs[1] 5 years and over who speak English-only at home	Asian Indian	Bangladeshi	Cambodian	Chinese[2]	Fijian	Filipino	Guamanian[3]	Hawaiian, Native	Hmong	Indonesian	Japanese	Korean	Laotian	Malaysian	Pakistani	Samoan	Sri Lankan	Taiwanese	Thai	Tongan	Vietnamese
Kailua (cdp)	30,248	7,617	5,733	2,559	2,070	-	-	-	848	-	491	-	1,959	-	-	3,429	243	-	-	-	-	-	-	-	-	-
	87.54		75.27		80.89				73.17		51.36		83.11			81.29	64.63									
									14.79		8.56		94.64			59.81	4.24									
			75.27		80.89				11.13		6.45		76.55			45.02	3.19									
			18.95		6.84				2.80		1.62		6.48			11.34	0.80									
Kaneohe (cdp)	28,215	13,421	10,525	3,776	2,976	-	-	-	1,145	-	831	-	2,668	-	-	6,794	216	-	-	-	-	-	-	-	-	-
	85.14		78.42		78.81				81.49		51.94		84.64			82.64	49.09									
									10.88		7.90		89.65			64.55	2.05									
			78.42		78.81				8.53		6.19		70.66			50.62	1.61									
			37.30		10.55				4.06		2.95		9.46			24.08	0.77									
Kaneohe Station (cdp)	8,580	560	196	-	-	-	-	-	-	-	-	-	-	-	-	-	-	-	-	-	-	-	-	-	-	-
	81.67		35.00																							
			35.00																							
			2.28																							
Makakilo City (cdp)	9,399	4,223	2,591	1,260	951	-	-	-	-	-	1,219	-	838	-	-	661	-	-	-	-	-	-	-	-	-	-
	78.47		61.35		75.48						54.91		92.49			70.10										
											47.05		88.12			25.51										
			61.35		75.48						28.87		66.51			15.65										
			27.57		10.12						12.97		8.92			7.03										
Mililani Town (cdp)	22,405	12,750	9,694	1,114	842	-	-	-	563	-	1,760	-	731	-	-	5,924	240	-	-	-	-	-	-	-	-	-
	83.68		76.03		75.58				59.45		57.93		88.61			86.23	48.78									
									5.81		18.16		86.82			61.11	2.48									
			76.03		75.58				4.42		13.80		65.62			46.46	1.88									
			43.27		3.76				2.51		7.86		3.26			26.44	1.07									
Nanakuli (cdp)	7,721	1,006	626	3,696	2,677	-	-	-	-	-	323	-	2,407	-	-	-	-	-	-	-	122	-	-	-	-	-
	79.87		62.23		72.43						52.86		85.63								17.48					
											51.60		89.91								4.56					
			62.23		72.43						32.11		65.12								3.30					
			8.11		34.67						4.18		31.17								1.58					
Pearl City (cdp)	22,058	16,391	10,997	1,698	1,193	-	-	-	715	-	1,669	-	992	-	-	7,392	129	-	-	-	-	-	-	-	-	-
	75.23		67.09		70.26				58.04		41.20		77.56			79.18	34.58									
									6.50		15.18		83.15			67.22	1.17									
			67.09		70.26				4.36		10.18		58.42			45.10	0.79									
			49.85		5.41				3.24		7.57		4.50			33.51	0.58									
Schofield Barracks (cdp)	10,358	481	158	-	-	-	-	-	-	-	-	-	-	-	-	-	-	-	-	-	-	-	-	-	-	-
	83.00		32.85																							
			32.85																							
			1.53																							
Wahiawa (cdp)	11,073	6,972	4,180	1,631	1,020	-	-	-	-	-	1,140	-	785	-	-	2,272	-	-	-	-	-	-	-	-	-	-
	73.12		59.95		62.54						41.26		87.71			70.93										
											27.27		76.96			54.35										
			59.95		62.54						16.35		48.13			32.59										
			37.75		9.21						10.30		7.09			20.52										
Waianae (cdp)	7,744	1,873	1,013	2,497	1,968	-	-	-	-	-	478	-	1,825	-	-	359	-	-	-	-	-	-	-	-	-	-
	79.92		54.08		78.81						48.88		84.49			65.04										
											47.19		92.73			35.44										
			54.08		78.81						25.52		73.09			19.17										
			13.08		25.41						6.17		23.57			4.64										

Notes: Please refer to the User's Guide for an explanation of data; data is arranged alphabetically by state, then county, then city within each county; table includes counties with populations greater than 49,999 unless noted and cities with populations greater than 9,999 whose Asian and/or NHPI population rates are greater than the national average; (1) Native Hawaiian and other Pacific Islander; (2) excludes Taiwanese; (3) includes Chamorro; (4) county does not meet population threshold but is shown in order to allow inclusion of city

Place	Total population 5 years and over who speak English-only at home	Asian population 5 years and over	Asians 5 years and over who speak English-only at home	NHPI[1] population 5 years and over	NHPIs[1] 5 years and over who speak English-only at home	Asian Indian	Bangladeshi	Cambodian	Chinese[2]	Fijian	Filipino	Guamanian[3]	Hawaiian, Native	Hmong	Indonesian	Japanese	Korean	Laotian	Malaysian	Pakistani	Samoan	Sri Lankan	Taiwanese	Thai	Tongan	Vietnamese
Waimalu (cdp)	21,586	15,287	10,717	1,474	1,041	-	-	-	711	-	1,424	-	857	-	-	6,743	252	-	-	-	-	-	-	-	-	-
	77.50		70.11		70.62				56.83		44.42		90.78			86.69	20.98									
									6.63		13.29		82.32			62.92	2.35									
			70.11		70.62				4.65		9.32		58.14			44.11	1.65									
			49.65		4.82				3.29		6.60		3.97			31.24	1.17									
Waipahu (cdp)	15,516	20,571	8,208	3,589	1,651	-	-	-	437	-	4,645	-	805	-	-	2,333	-	-	-	-	597	-	-	-	-	-
	50.22		39.90		46.00				79.17		29.79		89.05			69.98					31.59					
									5.32		56.59		48.76			28.42					36.16					
			39.90		46.00				2.12		22.58		22.43			11.34					16.63					
			52.90		10.64				2.82		29.94		5.19			15.04					3.85					
Waipio (cdp)	8,329	6,234	4,195	555	402	-	-	-	-	-	1,054	-	358	-	-	2,283	-	-	-	-	-	-	-	-	-	-
	76.33		67.29		72.43						46.09		92.27			81.51										
											25.13		89.05			54.42										
			67.29		72.43						16.91		64.50			36.62										
			50.37		4.83						12.65		4.30			27.41										
Kauai County	44,111	20,159	12,804	4,906	3,890	-	-	-	296	-	4,744	-	3,679	-	-	6,364	-	-	-	-	-	-	-	-	-	-
	80.46		63.52		79.29				73.63		44.85		80.89			84.72										
									2.31		37.05		94.58			49.70										
			63.52		79.29				1.47		23.53		74.99			31.57										
			29.03		8.82				0.67		10.75		8.34			14.43										
Maui County	90,879	37,092	18,673	12,457	9,468	-	-	-	779	-	6,400	-	8,947	-	-	9,494	317	-	-	-	-	-	-	-	69	-
	75.94		50.34		76.01				74.55		31.47		83.57			76.79	34.76								10.27	
									4.17		34.27		94.50			50.84	1.70								0.73	
			50.34		76.01				2.10		17.25		71.82			25.60	0.85								0.55	
			20.55		10.42				0.86		7.04		9.84			10.45	0.35								0.08	
Kahului (cdp)	11,622	10,337	4,815	1,678	1,197	-	-	-	-	-	1,684	-	1,097	-	-	2,556	-	-	-	-	-	-	-	-	-	-
	62.62		46.58		71.33						27.81		78.86			74.93										
											34.97		91.65			53.08										
			46.58		71.33						16.29		65.38			24.73										
			41.43		10.30						14.49		9.44			21.99										
Kihei (cdp)	11,801	3,865	1,550	1,057	742	-	-	-	-	-	970	-	618	-	-	321	-	-	-	-	-	-	-	-	-	-
	75.39		40.10		70.20						32.89		82.95			69.03										
											62.58		83.29			20.71										
			40.10		70.20						25.10		58.47			8.31										
			13.13		6.29						8.22		5.24			2.72										
Wailuku (cdp)	9,340	4,872	3,225	1,229	1,087	-	-	-	-	-	604	-	1,028	-	-	2,145	-	-	-	-	-	-	-	-	-	-
	80.39		66.19		88.45						40.43		88.93			81.07										
											18.73		94.57			66.51										
			66.19		88.45						12.40		83.65			44.03										
			34.53		11.64						6.47		11.01			22.97										
IDAHO	1,084,914	10,655	4,254	1,135	774	261	-	-	381	-	712	-	319	-	-	1,808	503	51	-	-	-	-	-	-	-	145
	90.65		39.92		68.19	24.53			23.66		45.03		93.82			70.21	41.16	10.67								11.57
						6.14			8.96		16.74		41.21			42.50	11.82	1.20								3.41
			39.92		68.19	2.45			3.58		6.68		28.11			16.97	4.72	0.48								1.36
			0.39		0.07	0.02			0.04		0.07		0.03			0.17	0.05	<0.01								0.01
Ada County	256,116	4,384	1,476	381	204	94	-	-	192	-	214	-	-	-	-	465	191	-	-	-	-	-	-	-	-	84
	92.16		33.67		53.54	16.76			31.74		43.50					67.39	39.30									9.41
						6.37			13.01		14.50					31.50	12.94									5.69
			33.67		53.54	2.14			4.38		4.88					10.61	4.36									1.92
			0.58		0.08	0.04			0.07		0.08					0.18	0.07									0.03

Notes: Please refer to the User's Guide for an explanation of data; data is arranged alphabetically by state, then county, then city within each county; table includes counties with populations greater than 49,999 unless noted and cities with populations greater than 9,999 whose Asian and/or NHPI population rates are greater than the national average; (1) Native Hawaiian and other Pacific Islander; (2) excludes Taiwanese; (3) includes Chamorro; (4) county does not meet population threshold but is shown in order to allow inclusion of city

Place	Total population 5 years and over who speak English-only at home	Asian population 5 years and over	Asians 5 years and over who speak English-only at home	NHPI[1] population 5 years and over	NHPIs[1] 5 years and over who speak English-only at home	Asian Indian	Bangladeshi	Cambodian	Chinese[2]	Fijian	Filipino	Guamanian[3]	Hawaiian, Native	Hmong	Indonesian	Japanese	Korean	Laotian	Malaysian	Pakistani	Samoan	Sri Lankan	Taiwanese	Thai	Tongan	Vietnamese
Bannock County	65,058	753	243	-	-	-	-	-	-	-	-	-	-	-	-	-	-	-	-	-	-	-	-	-	-	-
	93.67		32.27																							
			32.27																							
			0.37																							
Bonneville County	69,784	457	250	-	-	-	-	-	-	-	-	-	-	-	-	-	-	-	-	-	-	-	-	-	-	-
	92.13		54.70																							
			54.70																							
			0.36																							
Canyon County	98,451	997	383	-	-	-	-	-	-	-	-	-	-	-	-	202	-	-	-	-	-	-	-	-	-	-
	82.37		38.42													69.66										
																52.74										
			38.42													20.26										
			0.39													0.21										
Kootenai County	97,526	530	289	-	-	-	-	-	-	-	-	-	-	-	-	-	-	-	-	-	-	-	-	-	-	-
	96.31		54.53																							
			54.53																							
			0.30																							
Twin Falls County	52,656	370	98	-	-	-	-	-	-	-	-	-	-	-	-	-	-	-	-	-	-	-	-	-	-	-
	88.46		26.49																							
			26.49																							
			0.19																							
ILLINOIS	9,326,786	394,950	69,142	3,547	1,950	15,677	66	363	8,605	-	21,009	312	718	-	116	7,895	7,930	291	100	1,027	409	119	418	872	-	1,459
	80.77		17.51		54.98	13.77	8.92	11.28	12.64		25.68	40.15	81.96		13.68	39.50	16.12	6.39	18.98	7.21	49.88	22.12	12.04	15.39		8.64
						22.67	0.10	0.53	12.45		30.39	16.00	36.82		0.17	11.42	11.47	0.42	0.14	1.49	20.97	0.17	0.60	1.26		2.11
			17.51		54.98	3.97	0.02	0.09	2.18		5.32	8.80	20.24		0.03	2.00	2.01	0.07	0.03	0.26	11.53	0.03	0.11	0.22		0.37
			0.74		0.02	0.17	<0.01	<0.01	0.09		0.23	<0.01	0.01		<0.01	0.08	0.09	<0.01	<0.01	0.01	<0.01	<0.01	<0.01	0.01		0.02
Champaign County	149,387	11,014	2,025	-	-	537	-	-	308	-	383	-	-	-	-	175	328	-	-	-	-	-	-	-	-	28
	88.24		18.39			23.76			9.97		53.79					30.22	13.59									4.33
						26.52			15.21		18.91					8.64	16.20									1.38
			18.39			4.88			2.80		3.48					1.59	2.98									0.25
			1.36			0.36			0.21		0.26					0.12	0.22									0.02
Champaign (city)	56,151	4,381	910	-	-	229	-	-	170	-	-	-	-	-	-	-	176	-	-	-	-	-	-	-	-	14
	86.93		20.77			22.39			16.54								20.71									3.43
						25.16			18.68								19.34									1.54
			20.77			5.23			3.88								4.02									0.32
			1.62			0.41			0.30								0.31									0.02
Urbana (city)	26,994	5,089	810	-	-	235	-	-	113	-	-	-	-	-	-	-	120	-	-	-	-	-	-	-	-	-
	78.03		15.92			24.33			6.65								10.75									
						29.01			13.95								14.81									
			15.92			4.62			2.22								2.36									
			3.00			0.87			0.42								0.44									
Coles County	48,336	338	71	-	-	-	-	-	-	-	-	-	-	-	-	-	-	-	-	-	-	-	-	-	-	-
	95.94		21.01																							
			21.01																							
			0.15																							

Notes: Please refer to the User's Guide for an explanation of data; data is arranged alphabetically by state, then county, then city within each county; table includes counties with populations greater than 49,999 unless noted and cities with populations greater than 9,999 whose Asian and/or NHPI population rates are greater than the national average; (1) Native Hawaiian and other Pacific Islander; (2) excludes Taiwanese; (3) includes Chamorro; (4) county does not meet population threshold but is shown in order to allow inclusion of city

Place	Total population 5 years and over who speak English-only at home	Asian population 5 years and over	Asians 5 years and over who speak English-only at home	NHPI[1] population 5 years and over	NHPIs[1] 5 years and over who speak English-only at home	Asian Indian	Bangladeshi	Cambodian	Chinese[2]	Fijian	Filipino	Guamanian[3]	Hawaiian, Native	Hmong	Indonesian	Japanese	Korean	Laotian	Malaysian	Pakistani	Samoan	Sri Lankan	Taiwanese	Thai	Tongan	Vietnamese
Cook County	3,453,547	245,061	39,337	1,471	585	8,044	-	184	5,312	-	12,228	-	-	-	51	5,433	4,343	60	-	542	-	-	291	419	-	704
	69.19		16.05		39.77	12.51		8.92	11.98		23.49				11.31	39.57	12.84	4.86		5.62			16.97	10.80		6.91
						20.45		0.47	13.50		31.09				0.13	13.81	11.04	0.15		1.38			0.74	1.07		1.79
			16.05		39.77	3.28		0.08	2.17		4.99				0.02	2.22	1.77	0.02		0.22			0.12	0.17		0.29
			1.14		0.02	0.23		0.01	0.15		0.35				<0.01	0.16	0.13	<0.01		0.02			0.01	0.01		0.02
Arlington Heights (village)	58,797	4,325	880	-	-	217	-	-	117	-	184	-	-	-	-	175	107	-	-	-	-	-	-	-	-	-
	82.33		20.35			19.00			24.02		28.40					18.82	14.70									
						24.66			13.30		20.91					19.89	12.16									
			20.35			5.02			2.71		4.25					4.05	2.47									
			1.50			0.37			0.20		0.31					0.30	0.18									
Chicago (city)	1,726,905	120,178	20,070	992	293	3,627	-	175	2,929	-	6,039	-	-	-	-	3,129	2,166	-	-	268	-	-	162	216	-	467
	64.46		16.70		29.54	16.07		9.74	9.85		22.58					52.48	17.86			4.53			20.88	10.47		6.22
						18.07		0.87	14.59		30.09					15.59	10.79			1.34			0.81	1.08		2.33
			16.70		29.54	3.02		0.15	2.44		5.03					2.60	1.80			0.22			0.13	0.18		0.39
			1.16		0.02	0.21		0.01	0.17		0.35					0.18	0.13			0.02			0.01	0.01		0.03
Des Plaines (city)	37,429	4,113	698	-	-	76	-	-	76	-	292	-	-	-	-	-	-	-	-	-	-	-	-	-	-	-
	67.58		16.97			4.18			16.45		32.27															
						10.89			10.89		41.83															
			16.97			1.85			1.85		7.10															
			1.86			0.20			0.20		0.78															
Elk Grove Village (village)	26,057	3,033	466	-	-	88	-	-	81	-	162	-	-	-	-	49	-	-	-	-	-	-	-	-	-	-
	79.99		15.36			9.01			20.77		28.57					9.04										
						18.88			17.38		34.76					10.52										
			15.36			2.90			2.67		5.34					1.62										
			1.79			0.34			0.31		0.62					0.19										
Evanston (city)	57,304	4,293	1,110	-	-	408	-	-	170	-	173	-	-	-	-	137	155	-	-	-	-	-	-	-	-	-
	81.81		25.86			35.76			14.96		34.95					38.16	24.60									
						36.76			15.32		15.59					12.34	13.96									
			25.86			9.50			3.96		4.03					3.19	3.61									
			1.94			0.71			0.30		0.30					0.24	0.27									
Forest Park (village)	11,731	943	108	-	-	-	-	-	-	-	-	-	-	-	-	-	-	-	-	-	-	-	-	-	-	-
	80.59		11.45																							
			11.45																							
			0.92																							
Glenview (village)	28,583	4,027	730	-	-	37	-	-	149	-	178	-	-	-	-	102	155	-	-	-	-	-	-	-	-	-
	73.52		18.13			6.18			21.75		31.45					34.00	10.29									
						5.07			20.41		24.38					13.97	21.23									
			18.13			0.92			3.70		4.42					2.53	3.85									
			2.55			0.13			0.52		0.62					0.36	0.54									
Hanover Park (village)	21,679	3,891	689	-	-	237	-	-	-	-	278	-	-	-	-		-	-	-	-	-	-	-	-	-	-
	62.09		17.71			13.88					25.55															
						34.40					40.35															
			17.71			6.09					7.14															
			3.18			1.09					1.28															
Hoffman Estates (village)	32,634	6,892	643	-	-	218	-	-	57	-	176	-	-	-	-	36	67	-	-	-	-	-	-	-	-	-
	69.86		9.33			8.52			7.82		22.19					4.74	5.08									
						33.90			8.86		27.37					5.60	10.42									
			9.33			3.16			0.83		2.55					0.52	0.97									
			1.97			0.67			0.17		0.54					0.11	0.21									

Notes: Please refer to the User's Guide for an explanation of data; data is arranged alphabetically by state, then county, then city within each county; table includes counties with populations greater than 49,999 unless noted and cities with populations greater than 9,999 whose Asian and/or NHPI population rates are greater than the national average; (1) Native Hawaiian and other Pacific Islander; (2) excludes Taiwanese; (3) includes Chamorro; (4) county does not meet population threshold but is shown in order to allow inclusion of city

Place	Total population 5 years and over who speak English-only at home	Asian population 5 years and over	Asians 5 years and over who speak English-only at home	NHPI[1] population 5 years and over	NHPIs[1] 5 years and over who speak English-only at home	Asian Indian	Bangladeshi	Cambodian	Chinese[2]	Fijian	Filipino	Guamanian[3]	Hawaiian, Native	Hmong	Indonesian	Japanese	Korean	Laotian	Malaysian	Pakistani	Samoan	Sri Lankan	Taiwanese	Thai	Tongan	Vietnamese
Lincolnwood (village)	6,247	2,516	552	-	-	79	-	-	-	-	143	-	-	-	-	-	71	-	-	-	-	-	-	-	-	-
	53.25		21.94			10.81					29.01						11.40									
						14.31					25.91						12.86									
			21.94			3.14					5.68						2.82									
			8.84			1.26					2.29						1.14									
Morton Grove (village)	12,304	4,646	801	-	-	152	-	-	-	-	420	-	-	-	-	-	78	-	-	-	-	-	-	-	-	-
	57.49		17.24			10.96					25.04						9.11									
						18.98					52.43						9.74									
			17.24			3.27					9.04						1.68									
			6.51			1.24					3.41						0.63									
Mount Prospect (village)	34,513	6,100	524	-	-	160	-	-	27	-	122	-	-	-	-	112	95	-	-	-	-	-	-	-	-	-
	65.06		8.59			5.42			5.02		25.90					26.73	6.87									
						30.53			5.15		23.28					21.37	18.13									
			8.59			2.62			0.44		2.00					1.84	1.56									
			1.52			0.46			0.08		0.35					0.32	0.28									
Niles (village)	16,216	3,215	397	-	-	123	-	-	-	-	96	-	-	-	-	-	79	-	-	-	-	-	-	-	-	-
	55.97		12.35			9.85					15.41						8.19									
						30.98					24.18						19.90									
			12.35			3.83					2.99						2.46									
			2.45			0.76					0.59						0.49									
Northbrook (village)	25,278	2,825	325	-	-	-	-	-	74	-	-	-	-	-	-	-	72	-	-	-	-	-	-	-	-	-
	80.18		11.50						15.68								4.75									
									22.77								22.15									
			11.50						2.62								2.55									
			1.29						0.29								0.28									
Oak Park (village)	42,570	2,064	582	-	-	146	-	-	134	-	-	-	-	-	-	-	-	-	-	-	-	-	-	-	-	-
	87.04		28.20			19.76			34.81																	
						25.09			23.02																	
			28.20			7.07			6.49																	
			1.37			0.34			0.31																	
Orland Park (village)	40,756	2,014	603	-	-	155	-	-	-	-	288	-	-	-	-	-	-	-	-	-	-	-	-	-	-	-
	84.14		29.94			25.62					44.72															
						25.70					47.76															
			29.94			7.70					14.30															
			1.48			0.38					0.71															
Palatine (village)	43,517	4,762	568	-	-	193	-	-	72	-	114	-	-	-	-	-	44	-	-	-	-	-	-	-	-	-
	72.03		11.93			9.59			12.39		17.09						7.99									
						33.98			12.68		20.07						7.75									
			11.93			4.05			1.51		2.39						0.92									
			1.31			0.44			0.17		0.26						0.10									
Prospect Heights (city)	8,916	604	107	-	-	-	-	-	-	-	-	-	-	-	-	-	-	-	-	-	-	-	-	-	-	-
	54.84		17.72																							
			17.72																							
			1.20																							
Rolling Meadows (city)	16,608	1,341	265	-	-	8	-	-	-	-	-	-	-	-	-	-	-	-	-	-	-	-	-	-	-	-
	72.71		19.76			2.07																				
						3.02																				
			19.76			0.60																				
			1.60			0.05																				

Notes: Please refer to the User's Guide for an explanation of data; data is arranged alphabetically by state, then county, then city within each county; table includes counties with populations greater than 49,999 unless noted and cities with populations greater than 9,999 whose Asian and/or NHPI population rates are greater than the national average; (1) Native Hawaiian and other Pacific Islander; (2) excludes Taiwanese; (3) includes Chamorro; (4) county does not meet population threshold but is shown in order to allow inclusion of city

Place	Total population 5 years and over who speak English-only at home	Asian population 5 years and over	Asians 5 years and over who speak English-only at home	NHPI[1] population 5 years and over	NHPIs[1] 5 years and over who speak English-only at home	Asian Indian	Bangladeshi	Cambodian	Chinese[2]	Fijian	Filipino	Guamanian[3]	Hawaiian, Native	Hmong	Indonesian	Japanese	Korean	Laotian	Malaysian	Pakistani	Samoan	Sri Lankan	Taiwanese	Thai	Tongan	Vietnamese
Schaumburg (village)	52,695 75.08	9,432	817 8.66 8.66 1.55	-	-	289 6.96 35.37 3.06 0.55	-	-	64 5.19 7.83 0.68 0.12	-	203 22.73 24.85 2.15 0.39	-	-	-	-	105 12.50 12.85 1.11 0.20	102 6.30 12.48 1.08 0.19	-	-	-	-	-	-	-	-	-
Schiller Park (village)	4,888 44.43	662	34 5.14 5.14 0.70	-	-	-	-	-	-	-	-	-	-	-	-	-	-	-	-	-	-	-	-	-	-	-
Skokie (village)	32,890 54.75	12,585	1,870 14.86 14.86 5.69	-	-	466 13.01 24.92 3.70 1.42	-	-	220 14.35 11.76 1.75 0.67	-	627 21.06 33.53 4.98 1.91	-	-	-	-	-	168 6.92 8.98 1.33 0.51	-	-	52 11.61 2.78 0.41 0.16	-	-	-	-	-	-
Streamwood (village)	23,737 70.37	2,989	364 12.18 12.18 1.53	-	-	30 2.71 8.24 1.00 0.13	-	-	-	-	188 17.54 51.65 6.29 0.79	-	-	-	-	-	-	-	-	-	-	-	-	-	-	-
Wheeling (village)	19,329 60.36	2,753	297 10.79 10.79 1.54	-	-	94 7.37 31.65 3.41 0.49	-	-	-	-	100 18.90 33.67 3.63 0.52	-	-	-	-	-	-	-	-	-	-	-	-	-	-	-
Wilmette (village)	21,563 83.86	2,118	331 15.63 15.63 1.54	-	-	-	-	-	32 8.14 9.67 1.51 0.15	-	-	-	-	-	-	99 29.73 29.91 4.67 0.46	59 7.73 17.82 2.79 0.27	-	-	-	-	-	-	-	-	-
DeKalb County	75,010 89.97	1,973	676 34.26 34.26 0.90	-	-	216 34.45 31.95 10.95 0.29	-	-	-	-	-	-	-	-	-	-	-	-	-	-	-	-	-	-	-	-
DeKalb (city)	31,198 84.94	1,712	559 32.65 32.65 1.79	-	-	196 35.19 35.06 11.45 0.63	-	-	-	-	-	-	-	-	-	-	-	-	-	-	-	-	-	-	-	-
DuPage County	664,523 79.24	65,895	11,113 16.86 16.86 1.67	-	-	3,667 12.57 33.00 5.56 0.55	-	-	1,198 13.11 10.78 1.82 0.18	-	3,757 28.11 33.81 5.70 0.57	-	-	-	-	605 43.49 5.44 0.92 0.09	786 19.73 7.07 1.19 0.12	-	-	303 11.43 2.73 0.46 0.05	-	-	28 3.45 0.25 0.04 <0.01	104 26.13 0.94 0.16 0.02	-	185 7.35 1.66 0.28 0.03
Addison (village)	17,500 53.10	2,709	342 12.62 12.62 1.95	-	-	193 12.57 56.43 7.12 1.10	-	-	-	-	86 17.70 25.15 3.17 0.49	-	-	-	-	-	-	-	-	-	-	-	-	-	-	-

Notes: Please refer to the User's Guide for an explanation of data; data is arranged alphabetically by state, then county, then city within each county; table includes counties with populations greater than 49,999 unless noted and cities with populations greater than 9,999 whose Asian and/or NHPI population rates are greater than the national average; (1) Native Hawaiian and other Pacific Islander; (2) excludes Taiwanese; (3) includes Chamorro; (4) county does not meet population threshold but is shown in order to allow inclusion of city

Place	Total population 5 years and over who speak English-only at home	Asian population 5 years and over	Asians 5 years and over who speak English-only at home	NHPI[1] population 5 years and over	NHPIs[1] 5 years and over who speak English-only at home	Asian Indian	Bangladeshi	Cambodian	Chinese[2]	Fijian	Filipino	Guamanian[3]	Hawaiian, Native	Hmong	Indonesian	Japanese	Korean	Laotian	Malaysian	Pakistani	Samoan	Sri Lankan	Taiwanese	Thai	Tongan	Vietnamese
Bartlett (village)	27,194 82.80	2,619	367 14.01 14.01 1.35	-	-	101 7.64 27.52 3.86 0.37	-	-	-	-	157 26.21 42.78 5.99 0.58	-	-	-	-	-	-	-	-	-	-	-	-	-	-	-
Bensenville (village)	10,622 55.77	1,131	143 12.64 12.64 1.35	-	-	35 5.30 24.48 3.09 0.33	-	-	-	-	-	-	-	-	-	-	-	-	-	-	-	-	-	-	-	-
Bloomingdale (village)	16,522 80.95	1,832	322 17.58 17.58 1.95	-	-	55 6.41 17.08 3.00 0.33	-	-	-	-	-	-	-	-	-	-	-	-	-	-	-	-	-	-	-	-
Burr Ridge (village)	8,063 82.45	1,011	233 23.05 23.05 2.89	-	-	133 21.42 57.08 13.16 1.65	-	-	-	-	-	-	-	-	-	-	-	-	-	-	-	-	-	-	-	-
Carol Stream (village)	28,613 77.73	3,756	642 17.09 17.09 2.24	-	-	152 8.90 23.68 4.05 0.53	-	-	-	-	354 34.20 55.14 9.42 1.24	-	-	-	-	-	-	-	-	-	-	-	-	-	-	67 17.49 10.44 1.78 0.23
Darien (city)	16,988 78.47	2,719	400 14.71 14.71 2.35	-	-	162 11.87 40.50 5.96 0.95	-	-	-	-	166 21.45 41.50 6.11 0.98	-	-	-	-	-	-	-	-	-	-	-	-	-	-	-
Downers Grove (village)	39,725 87.08	2,778	609 21.92 21.92 1.53	-	-	267 21.55 43.84 9.61 0.67	-	-	38 6.67 6.24 1.37 0.10	-	179 33.84 29.39 6.44 0.45	-	-	-	-	-	-	-	-	-	-	-	-	-	-	-
Glen Ellyn (village)	21,381 86.22	1,191	195 16.37 16.37 0.91	-	-	22 4.72 11.28 1.85 0.10	-	-	-	-	-	-	-	-	-	-	-	-	-	-	-	-	-	-	-	-
Glendale Heights (village)	17,214 59.07	5,755	707 12.28 12.28 4.11	-	-	228 9.23 32.25 3.96 1.32	-	-	-	-	352 21.60 49.79 6.12 2.04	-	-	-	-	-	-	-	-	-	-	-	-	-	-	7 0.95 0.99 0.12 0.04
Hinsdale (village)	14,323 89.45	772	159 20.60 20.60 1.11	-	-	-	-	-	-	-	-	-	-	-	-	-	-	-	-	-	-	-	-	-	-	-

Notes: Please refer to the User's Guide for an explanation of data; data is arranged alphabetically by state, then county, then city within each county; table includes counties with populations greater than 49,999 unless noted and cities with populations greater than 9,999 whose Asian and/or NHPI population rates are greater than the national average; (1) Native Hawaiian and other Pacific Islander; (2) excludes Taiwanese; (3) includes Chamorro; (4) county does not meet population threshold but is shown in order to allow inclusion of city

Place	Total population 5 years and over who speak English-only at home	Asian population 5 years and over	Asians 5 years and over who speak English-only at home	NHPI[1] population 5 years and over	NHPIs[1] 5 years and over who speak English-only at home	Asian Indian	Bangladeshi	Cambodian	Chinese[2]	Fijian	Filipino	Guamanian[3]	Hawaiian, Native	Hmong	Indonesian	Japanese	Korean	Laotian	Malaysian	Pakistani	Samoan	Sri Lankan	Taiwanese	Thai	Tongan	Vietnamese
Lisle (village)	16,023 81.70	1,952	302 15.47 15.47 1.88	-	-	62 9.06 20.53 3.18 0.39	-	-	31 5.16 10.26 1.59 0.19	-	-	-	-	-	-	-	-	-	-	-	-	-	-	-	-	-
Lombard (village)	33,425 84.99	2,682	522 19.46 19.46 1.56	-	-	124 10.18 23.75 4.62 0.37	-	-	-	-	183 31.18 35.06 6.82 0.55	-	-	-	-	-	-	-	-	-	-	-	-	-	-	-
Naperville (city)	99,729 84.78	10,661	1,570 14.73 14.73 1.57	-	-	621 14.54 39.55 5.82 0.62	-	-	383 10.63 24.39 3.59 0.38	-	246 39.61 15.67 2.31 0.25	-	-	-	-	-	144 17.50 9.17 1.35 0.14	-	-	-	-	-	28 6.67 1.78 0.26 0.03	-	-	-
Roselle (village)	17,246 79.58	1,717	287 16.72 16.72 1.66	-	-	98 12.13 34.15 5.71 0.57	-	-	-	-	-	-	-	-	-	-	-	-	-	-	-	-	-	-	-	-
Villa Park (village)	16,599 80.31	832	73 8.77 8.77 0.44	-	-	-	-	-	-	-	-	-	-	-	-	-	-	-	-	-	-	-	-	-	-	-
Warrenville (city)	10,578 86.66	482	85 17.63 17.63 0.80	-	-	-	-	-	-	-	-	-	-	-	-	-	-	-	-	-	-	-	-	-	-	-
Westmont (village)	16,945 74.80	2,684	370 13.79 13.79 2.18	-	-	135 11.28 36.49 5.03 0.80	-	-	60 13.33 16.22 2.24 0.35	-	98 20.16 26.49 3.65 0.58	-	-	-	-	-	-	-	-	-	-	-	-	-	-	-
Wheaton (city)	45,862 88.37	2,522	499 19.79 19.79 1.09	-	-	108 12.19 21.64 4.28 0.24	-	-	-	-	-	-	-	-	-	-	-	-	-	-	-	-	-	-	-	5 1.48 1.00 0.20 0.01
Woodridge (village)	22,307 77.36	3,272	524 16.01 16.01 2.35	-	-	116 7.77 22.14 3.55 0.52	-	-	-	-	317 28.61 60.50 9.69 1.42	-	-	-	-	-	-	-	-	-	-	-	-	-	-	-
Jackson County	51,896 91.64	1,807	290 16.05 16.05 0.56	-	-	-	-	-	50 13.89 17.24 2.77 0.10	-	-	-	-	-	-	-	-	-	-	-	-	-	-	-	-	-

Notes: Please refer to the User's Guide for an explanation of data; data is arranged alphabetically by state, then county, then city within each county; table includes counties with populations greater than 49,999 unless noted and cities with populations greater than 9,999 whose Asian and/or NHPI population rates are greater than the national average; (1) Native Hawaiian and other Pacific Islander; (2) excludes Taiwanese; (3) includes Chamorro; (4) county does not meet population threshold but is shown in order to allow inclusion of city

Place	Total population 5 years and over who speak English-only at home	Asian population 5 years and over	Asians 5 years and over who speak English-only at home	NHPI[1] population 5 years and over	NHPIs[1] 5 years and over who speak English-only at home	Asian Indian	Bangladeshi	Cambodian	Chinese[2]	Fijian	Filipino	Guamanian[3]	Hawaiian, Native	Hmong	Indonesian	Japanese	Korean	Laotian	Malaysian	Pakistani	Samoan	Sri Lankan	Taiwanese	Thai	Tongan	Vietnamese
Carbondale (city)	16,893 85.92	1,325	172 12.98 12.98 1.02	-	-	-	-	-	-	-	-	-	-	-	-	-	-	-	-	-	-	-	-	-	-	-
Kane County	276,235 74.88	6,343	1,221 19.25 19.25 0.44	-	-	144 9.74 11.79 2.27 0.05	-	-	199 26.50 16.30 3.14 0.07	-	368 31.40 30.14 5.80 0.13	-	-	-	-	-	132 31.65 10.81 2.08 0.05	72 7.89 5.90 1.14 0.03	-	-	-	-	-	-	-	25 5.71 2.05 0.39 0.01
South Elgin (village)	11,525 83.38	743	87 11.71 11.71 0.75	-	-	-	-	-	-	-	-	-	-	-	-	-	-	-	-	-	-	-	-	-	-	-
Kankakee County	90,472 93.58	682	99 14.52 14.52 0.11	-	-	-	-	-	-	-	-	-	-	-	-	-	-	-	-	-	-	-	-	-	-	-
Kendall County	45,461 90.57	590	249 42.20 42.20 0.55	-	-	-	-	-	-	-	-	-	-	-	-	-	-	-	-	-	-	-	-	-	-	-
Knox County	50,384 95.76	427	105 24.59 24.59 0.21	-	-	-	-	-	-	-	-	-	-	-	-	-	-	-	-	-	-	-	-	-	-	-
La Salle County	98,752 94.44	470	131 27.87 27.87 0.13	-	-	-	-	-	-	-	-	-	-	-	-	-	-	-	-	-	-	-	-	-	-	-
Lake County	464,971 78.61	23,331	4,783 20.50 20.50 1.03	-	-	953 18.14 19.92 4.08 0.20	-	-	630 14.76 13.17 2.70 0.14	-	1,753 26.57 36.65 7.51 0.38	-	-	-	-	379 27.44 7.92 1.62 0.08	512 13.94 10.70 2.19 0.11	-	-	37 7.86 0.77 0.16 0.01	-	-	-	-	-	106 21.59 2.22 0.45 0.02
Buffalo Grove (village)	30,091 75.53	3,422	622 18.18 18.18 2.07	-	-	134 20.49 21.54 3.92 0.45	-	-	105 19.09 16.88 3.07 0.35	-	176 40.84 28.30 5.14 0.58	-	-	-	-	73 12.46 11.74 2.13 0.24	102 9.76 16.40 2.98 0.34	-	-	-	-	-	-	-	-	-
Gages Lake (cdp)	8,598 89.33	362	66 18.23 18.23 0.77	-	-	-	-	-	-	-	-	-	-	-	-	-	-	-	-	-	-	-	-	-	-	-

Notes: Please refer to the User's Guide for an explanation of data; data is arranged alphabetically by state, then county, then city within each county; table includes counties with populations greater than 49,999 unless noted and cities with populations greater than 9,999 whose Asian and/or NHPI population rates are greater than the national average; (1) Native Hawaiian and other Pacific Islander; (2) excludes Taiwanese; (3) includes Chamorro; (4) county does not meet population threshold but is shown in order to allow inclusion of city

Place	Total population 5 years and over who speak English-only at home	Asian population 5 years and over	Asians 5 years and over who speak English-only at home	NHPI[1] population 5 years and over	NHPIs[1] 5 years and over who speak English-only at home	Asian Indian	Bangladeshi	Cambodian	Chinese[2]	Fijian	Filipino	Guamanian[3]	Hawaiian, Native	Hmong	Indonesian	Japanese	Korean	Laotian	Malaysian	Pakistani	Samoan	Sri Lankan	Taiwanese	Thai	Tongan	Vietnamese
Grayslake (village)	14,529 89.07	785	175 22.29 22.29 1.20	-	-	-	-	-	-	-	-	-	-	-	-	-	-	-	-	-	-	-	-	-	-	-
Gurnee (village)	21,536 83.16	2,171	484 22.29 22.29 2.25	-	-	131 19.49 27.07 6.03 0.61	-	-	54 16.62 11.16 2.49 0.25	-	166 23.18 34.30 7.65 0.77	-	-	-	-	-	-	-	-	-	-	-	-	-	-	-
Lake Zurich (village)	14,054 84.79	595	125 21.01 21.01 0.89	-	-	-	-	-	-	-	-	-	-	-	-	-	-	-	-	-	-	-	-	-	-	-
Libertyville (village)	16,776 86.97	960	185 19.27 19.27 1.10	-	-	-	-	-	-	-	-	-	-	-	-	-	-	-	-	-	-	-	-	-	-	-
Mundelein (village)	18,950 68.24	1,840	393 21.36 21.36 2.07	-	-	-	-	-	49 11.72 12.47 2.66 0.26	-	183 30.30 46.56 9.95 0.97	-	-	-	-	-	-	-	-	-	-	-	-	-	-	-
Vernon Hills (village)	13,597 71.82	2,113	232 10.98 10.98 1.71	-	-	45 8.62 19.40 2.13 0.33	-	-	36 5.99 15.52 1.70 0.26	-	-	-	-	-	-	-	61 10.45 26.29 2.89 0.45	-	-	-	-	-	-	-	-	-
Macon County	103,871 96.72	681	219 32.16 32.16 0.21	-	-	-	-	-	-	-	-	-	-	-	-	-	-	-	-	-	-	-	-	-	-	-
Madison County	234,608 96.70	1,142	435 38.09 38.09 0.19	-	-	84 24.00 19.31 7.36 0.04	-	-	-	-	-	-	-	-	-	-	-	-	-	-	-	-	-	-	-	-
McHenry County	213,070 89.11	3,094	811 26.21 26.21 0.38	-	-	81 9.40 9.99 2.62 0.04	-	-	81 17.05 9.99 2.62 0.04	-	280 31.53 34.53 9.05 0.13	-	-	-	-	-	-	-	-	-	-	-	-	-	-	-
McLean County	132,245 93.96	2,887	654 22.65 22.65 0.49	-	-	248 21.53 37.92 8.59 0.19	-	-	52 8.55 7.95 1.80 0.04	-	-	-	-	-	-	-	-	-	-	-	-	-	-	-	-	-

Notes: Please refer to the User's Guide for an explanation of data; data is arranged alphabetically by state, then county, then city within each county; table includes counties with populations greater than 49,999 unless noted and cities with populations greater than 9,999 whose Asian and/or NHPI population rates are greater than the national average; (1) Native Hawaiian and other Pacific Islander; (2) excludes Taiwanese; (3) includes Chamorro; (4) county does not meet population threshold but is shown in order to allow inclusion of city

Place	Total population 5 years and over who speak English-only at home	Asian population 5 years and over	Asians 5 years and over who speak English-only at home	NHPI[1] population 5 years and over	NHPIs[1] 5 years and over who speak English-only at home	Asian Indian	Bangladeshi	Cambodian	Chinese[2]	Fijian	Filipino	Guamanian[3]	Hawaiian, Native	Hmong	Indonesian	Japanese	Korean	Laotian	Malaysian	Pakistani	Samoan	Sri Lankan	Taiwanese	Thai	Tongan	Vietnamese
Peoria County	160,741 94.04	2,868	620 21.62 21.62 0.39	-	-	156 16.00 25.16 5.44 0.10	-	-	115 14.23 18.55 4.01 0.07	-	-	-	-	-	-	-	-	-	-	-	-	-	-	-	-	47 17.60 7.58 1.64 0.03
Rock Island County	128,092 91.59	1,353	319 23.58 23.58 0.25	-	-	55 10.22 17.24 4.07 0.04	-	-	-	-	-	-	-	-	-	-	-	-	-	-	-	-	-	-	-	-
St. Clair County	227,785 95.50	2,132	559 26.22 26.22 0.25	-	-	-	-	-	-	-	215 34.79 38.46 10.08 0.09	-	-	-	-	-	57 14.62 10.20 2.67 0.03	-	-	-	-	-	-	-	-	-
Sangamon County	170,568 96.39	1,859	496 26.68 26.68 0.29	-	-	146 23.14 29.44 7.85 0.09	-	-	27 8.36 5.44 1.45 0.02	-	-	-	-	-	-	-	-	-	-	-	-	-	-	-	-	-
Tazewell County	117,249 97.36	522	184 35.25 35.25 0.16	-	-	-	-	-	-	-	-	-	-	-	-	-	-	-	-	-	-	-	-	-	-	-
Vermilion County	74,986 95.69	465	158 33.98 33.98 0.21	-	-	-	-	-	-	-	-	-	-	-	-	-	-	-	-	-	-	-	-	-	-	-
Will County	405,351 88.03	10,250	2,048 19.98 19.98 0.51	-	-	498 18.42 24.32 4.86 0.12	-	-	138 10.15 6.74 1.35 0.03	-	637 22.91 31.10 6.21 0.16	-	-	-	-	-	234 26.93 11.43 2.28 0.06	-	-	11 2.94 0.54 0.11 <0.01	-	-	-	-	-	79 15.55 3.86 0.77 0.02
Bolingbrook (village)	40,519 79.42	3,481	538 15.46 15.46 1.33	-	-	114 11.37 21.19 3.27 0.28	-	-	-	-	152 13.66 28.25 4.37 0.38	-	-	-	-	-	-	-	-	-	-	-	-	-	-	-
Winnebago County	233,038 90.04	4,106	758 18.46 18.46 0.33	-	-	163 25.63 21.50 3.97 0.07	-	-	-	-	128 26.07 16.89 3.12 0.05	-	-	-	-	-	184 42.69 24.27 4.48 0.08	22 1.85 2.90 0.54 0.01	-	-	-	-	-	-	-	34 6.00 4.49 0.83 0.01
INDIANA	5,295,736 93.60	53,023	12,639 23.84 23.84 0.24	1,652	1,159 70.16 70.16 0.02	2,408 18.26 19.05 4.54 0.05	-	120 21.47 0.95 0.23 <0.01	1,853 17.55 14.66 3.49 0.03	-	2,591 40.40 20.50 4.89 0.05	287 58.10 24.76 17.37 0.01	537 85.78 46.33 32.51 0.01	-	-	1,407 30.92 11.13 2.65 0.03	2,012 30.77 15.92 3.79 0.04	178 18.90 1.41 0.34 <0.01	-	86 13.59 0.68 0.16 <0.01	-	-	95 13.65 0.75 0.18 <0.01	246 28.41 1.95 0.46 <0.01	-	523 11.88 4.14 0.99 0.01

Notes: Please refer to the User's Guide for an explanation of data; data is arranged alphabetically by state, then county, then city within each county; table includes counties with populations greater than 49,999 unless noted and cities with populations greater than 9,999 whose Asian and/or NHPI population rates are greater than the national average; (1) Native Hawaiian and other Pacific Islander; (2) excludes Taiwanese; (3) includes Chamorro; (4) county does not meet population threshold but is shown in order to allow inclusion of city

Place	Total population 5 years and over who speak English-only at home	Asian population 5 years and over	Asians 5 years and over who speak English-only at home	NHPI[1] population 5 years and over	NHPIs[1] 5 years and over who speak English-only at home	Asian Indian	Bangladeshi	Cambodian	Chinese[2]	Fijian	Filipino	Guamanian[3]	Hawaiian, Native	Hmong	Indonesian	Japanese	Korean	Laotian	Malaysian	Pakistani	Samoan	Sri Lankan	Taiwanese	Thai	Tongan	Vietnamese
Allen County	283,447 92.48	4,167	1,028 24.67 24.67 0.36	-	-	243 24.92 23.64 5.83 0.09	-	-	136 29.50 13.23 3.26 0.05	-	258 55.36 25.10 6.19 0.09	-	-	-	-	-	-	-	-	-	-	-	-	-	-	78 10.09 7.59 1.87 0.03
Bartholomew County	62,650 94.66	1,044	155 14.85 14.85 0.25	-	-	49 13.54 31.61 4.69 0.08	-	-	-	-	-	-	-	-	-	-	-	-	-	-	-	-	-	-	-	-
Clark County	87,087 96.86	416	145 34.86 34.86 0.17	-	-	-	-	-	-	-	-	-	-	-	-	-	-	-	-	-	-	-	-	-	-	-
Delaware County	107,865 96.52	709	221 31.17 31.17 0.20	-	-	-	-	-	-	-	-	-	-	-	-	-	-	-	-	-	-	-	-	-	-	-
Elkhart County	143,855 85.60	1,498	301 20.09 20.09 0.21	-	-	-	-	-	-	-	-	-	-	-	-	-	-	-	-	-	-	-	-	-	-	-
Grant County	66,272 96.10	444	102 22.97 22.97 0.15	-	-	-	-	-	-	-	-	-	-	-	-	-	-	-	-	-	-	-	-	-	-	-
Hamilton County	156,275 94.15	3,714	938 25.26 25.26 0.60	-	-	129 13.58 13.75 3.47 0.08	-	-	144 19.51 15.35 3.88 0.09	-	-	-	-	-	-	-	-	-	-	-	-	-	-	-	-	-
Carmel (city)	31,848 91.47	1,522	290 19.05 19.05 0.91	-	-	-	-	-	-	-	-	-	-	-	-	-	-	-	-	-	-	-	-	-	-	-
Hendricks County	93,702 97.07	652	187 28.68 28.68 0.20	-	-	-	-	-	-	-	-	-	-	-	-	-	-	-	-	-	-	-	-	-	-	-
Howard County	75,866 96.10	596	112 18.79 18.79 0.15	-	-	-	-	-	-	-	-	-	-	-	-	-	-	-	-	-	-	-	-	-	-	-

Notes: Please refer to the User's Guide for an explanation of data; data is arranged alphabetically by state, then county, then city within each county; table includes counties with populations greater than 49,999 unless noted and cities with populations greater than 9,999 whose Asian and/or NHPI population rates are greater than the national average; (1) Native Hawaiian and other Pacific Islander; (2) excludes Taiwanese; (3) includes Chamorro; (4) county does not meet population threshold but is shown in order to allow inclusion of city

Place	Total population 5 years and over who speak English-only at home	Asian population 5 years and over	Asians 5 years and over who speak English-only at home	NHPI[1] population 5 years and over	NHPIs[1] 5 years and over who speak English-only at home	Asian Indian	Bangladeshi	Cambodian	Chinese[2]	Fijian	Filipino	Guamanian[3]	Hawaiian, Native	Hmong	Indonesian	Japanese	Korean	Laotian	Malaysian	Pakistani	Samoan	Sri Lankan	Taiwanese	Thai	Tongan	Vietnamese
Johnson County	102,881 96.49	848	275 32.43 32.43 0.27	-	-	-	-	-	-	-	-	-	-	-	-	-	-	-	-	-	-	-	-	-	-	-
Kosciusko County	62,828 91.58	354	105 29.66 29.66 0.17	-	-	-	-	-	-	-	-	-	-	-	-	-	-	-	-	-	-	-	-	-	-	-
Lake County	389,523 86.54	3,676	825 22.44 22.44 0.21	-	-	183 13.55 22.18 4.98 0.05	-	-	100 17.89 12.12 2.72 0.03	-	270 36.73 32.73 7.34 0.07	-	-	-	-	-	92 17.36 11.15 2.50 0.02	-	-	-	-	-	-	-	-	-
Munster (town)	17,579 85.75	917	204 22.25 22.25 1.16	-	-	55 14.07 26.96 6.00 0.31	-	-	-	-	-	-	-	-	-	-	-	-	-	-	-	-	-	-	-	-
LaPorte County	96,957 94.08	349	153 43.84 43.84 0.16	-	-	-	-	-	-	-	-	-	-	-	-	-	-	-	-	-	-	-	-	-	-	-
Madison County	121,119 96.92	485	207 42.68 42.68 0.17	-	-	-	-	-	-	-	-	-	-	-	-	-	-	-	-	-	-	-	-	-	-	-
Marion County	738,672 92.70	10,653	2,204 20.69 20.69 0.30	-	-	503 16.32 22.82 4.72 0.07	-	-	276 13.48 12.52 2.59 0.04	-	363 26.38 16.47 3.41 0.05	-	-	-	-	231 48.02 10.48 2.17 0.03	385 33.54 17.47 3.61 0.05	-	-	-	-	-	-	-	-	86 7.06 3.90 0.81 0.01
Monroe County	105,258 91.92	3,796	855 22.52 22.52 0.81	-	-	186 26.84 21.75 4.90 0.18	-	-	129 16.37 15.09 3.40 0.12	-	-	-	-	-	-	-	113 11.17 13.22 2.98 0.11	-	-	-	-	-	-	-	-	-
Bloomington (city)	58,783 88.35	3,375	673 19.94 19.94 1.14	-	-	155 27.39 23.03 4.59 0.26	-	-	129 17.15 19.17 3.82 0.22	-	-	-	-	-	-	-	64 6.98 9.51 1.90 0.11	-	-	-	-	-	-	-	-	-
Porter County	128,741 93.78	964	289 29.98 29.98 0.22	-	-	-	-	-	-	-	-	-	-	-	-	-	-	-	-	-	-	-	-	-	-	-

Notes: Please refer to the User's Guide for an explanation of data; data is arranged alphabetically by state, then county, then city within each county; table includes counties with populations greater than 49,999 unless noted and cities with populations greater than 9,999 whose Asian and/or NHPI population rates are greater than the national average; (1) Native Hawaiian and other Pacific Islander; (2) excludes Taiwanese; (3) includes Chamorro; (4) county does not meet population threshold but is shown in order to allow inclusion of city

Place	Total population 5 years and over who speak English-only at home	Asian population 5 years and over	Asians 5 years and over who speak English-only at home	NHPI[1] population 5 years and over	NHPIs[1] 5 years and over who speak English-only at home	Asian Indian	Bangladeshi	Cambodian	Chinese[2]	Fijian	Filipino	Guamanian[3]	Hawaiian, Native	Hmong	Indonesian	Japanese	Korean	Laotian	Malaysian	Pakistani	Samoan	Sri Lankan	Taiwanese	Thai	Tongan	Vietnamese
St. Joseph County	225,726 91.44	3,248	844 25.99 25.99 0.37	-	-	205 32.44 24.29 6.31 0.09	-	-	145 18.01 17.18 4.46 0.06	-	-	-	-	-	-	-	127 29.74 15.05 3.91 0.06	-	-	-	-	-	-	-	-	-
Tippecanoe County	124,060 88.56	6,358	1,281 20.15 20.15 1.03	-	-	259 16.22 20.22 4.07 0.21	-	-	347 16.67 27.09 5.46 0.28	-	-	-	-	-	-	81 21.20 6.32 1.27 0.07	136 15.80 10.62 2.14 0.11	-	-	-	-	-	-	-	-	-
West Lafayette (city)	23,515 83.32	3,077	644 20.93 20.93 2.74	-	-	158 16.44 24.53 5.13 0.67	-	-	243 25.61 37.73 7.90 1.03	-	-	-	-	-	-	-	-	-	-	-	-	-	-	-	-	-
Vanderburgh County	155,085 96.16	1,445	356 24.64 24.64 0.23	-	-	-	-	-	-	-	-	-	-	-	-	-	-	-	-	-	-	-	-	-	-	-
Vigo County	95,485 96.07	1,002	146 14.57 14.57 0.15	-	-	-	-	-	-	-	-	-	-	-	-	-	-	-	-	-	-	-	-	-	-	-
Wayne County	64,057 95.99	455	72 15.82 15.82 0.11	-	-	-	-	-	-	-	-	-	-	-	-	-	-	-	-	-	-	-	-	-	-	-
IOWA	2,578,477 94.16	32,245	6,741 20.91 20.91 0.26	897	581 64.77 64.77 0.02	1,166 23.37 17.30 3.62 0.05	-	67 9.13 0.99 0.21 <0.01	624 12.26 9.26 1.94 0.02	-	823 37.80 12.21 2.55 0.03	-	-	-	-	440 34.98 6.53 1.36 0.02	2,260 50.79 33.53 7.01 0.09	200 5.51 2.97 0.62 0.01	-	30 8.96 0.45 0.09 <0.01	-	-	23 5.25 0.34 0.07 <0.01	160 18.10 2.37 0.50 0.01	-	374 6.01 5.55 1.16 0.01
Black Hawk County	112,431 93.50	1,239	318 25.67 25.67 0.28	-	-	-	-	-	-	-	-	-	-	-	-	-	-	-	-	-	-	-	-	-	-	-
Buena Vista County[4]	16,025 83.35	805	66 8.20 8.20 0.41	-	-	-	-	-	-	-	-	-	-	-	-	-	-	29 5.35 43.94 3.60 0.18	-	-	-	-	-	-	-	-
Storm Lake (city)	6,931 72.84	698	54 7.74 7.74 0.78	-	-	-	-	-	-	-	-	-	-	-	-	-	-	20 4.07 37.04 2.87 0.29	-	-	-	-	-	-	-	-

Notes: Please refer to the User's Guide for an explanation of data; data is arranged alphabetically by state, then county, then city within each county; table includes counties with populations greater than 49,999 unless noted and cities with populations greater than 9,999 whose Asian and/or NHPI population rates are greater than the national average; (1) Native Hawaiian and other Pacific Islander; (2) excludes Taiwanese; (3) includes Chamorro; (4) county does not meet population threshold but is shown in order to allow inclusion of city

Place	Total population 5 years and over who speak English-only at home	Asian population 5 years and over	Asians 5 years and over who speak English-only at home	NHPI[1] population 5 years and over	NHPIs[1] 5 years and over who speak English-only at home	Asian Indian	Bangladeshi	Cambodian	Chinese[2]	Fijian	Filipino	Guamanian[3]	Hawaiian, Native	Hmong	Indonesian	Japanese	Korean	Laotian	Malaysian	Pakistani	Samoan	Sri Lankan	Taiwanese	Thai	Tongan	Vietnamese
Johnson County	93,749 89.49	4,120	795 19.30 19.30 0.85	-	-	209 28.83 26.29 5.07 0.22	-	-	125 9.18 15.72 3.03 0.13	-	-	-	-	-	-	-	143 20.08 17.99 3.47 0.15	-	-	-	-	-	-	-	-	-
Coralville (city)	12,408 88.45	623	38 6.10 6.10 0.31	-	-	-	-	-	-	-	-	-	-	-	-	-	-	-	-	-	-	-	-	-	-	-
Iowa City (city)	52,421 87.91	3,242	630 19.43 19.43 1.20	-	-	136 26.36 21.59 4.19 0.26	-	-	112 9.19 17.78 3.45 0.21	-	-	-	-	-	-	-	129 26.65 20.48 3.98 0.25	-	-	-	-	-	-	-	-	-
Linn County	169,838 95.17	2,380	680 28.57 28.57 0.40	-	-	134 17.87 19.71 5.63 0.08	-	-	-	-	-	-	-	-	-	-	217 74.32 31.91 9.12 0.13	-	-	-	-	-	-	-	-	-
Polk County	315,689 91.13	8,436	1,100 13.04 13.04 0.35	-	-	138 11.35 12.55 1.64 0.04	-	13 3.60 1.18 0.15 <0.01	120 12.26 10.91 1.42 0.04	-	-	-	-	-	-	-	333 49.55 30.27 3.95 0.11	37 2.52 3.36 0.44 0.01	-	-	-	-	-	35 9.89 3.18 0.41 0.01	-	151 6.49 13.73 1.79 0.05
Pottawattamie County	78,283 95.47	496	169 34.07 34.07 0.22	-	-	-	-	-	-	-	-	-	-	-	-	-	-	-	-	-	-	-	-	-	-	-
Scott County	139,307 94.39	2,010	357 17.76 17.76 0.26	-	-	-	-	-	-	-	-	-	-	-	-	-	-	-	-	-	-	-	-	-	-	33 3.67 9.24 1.64 0.02
Story County	68,719 90.65	3,422	464 13.56 13.56 0.68	-	-	134 20.15 28.88 3.92 0.19	-	-	54 4.87 11.64 1.58 0.08	-	-	-	-	-	-	-	126 18.31 27.16 3.68 0.18	-	-	-	-	-	-	-	-	-
Ames (city)	42,167 87.15	3,289	410 12.47 12.47 0.97	-	-	124 19.62 30.24 3.77 0.29	-	-	47 4.33 11.46 1.43 0.11	-	-	-	-	-	-	-	100 15.17 24.39 3.04 0.24	-	-	-	-	-	-	-	-	-
Woodbury County	84,839 88.23	2,133	208 9.75 9.75 0.25	-	-	-	-	-	-	-	-	-	-	-	-	-	-	-	-	-	-	-	-	-	-	17 1.31 8.17 0.80 0.02

Notes: Please refer to the User's Guide for an explanation of data; data is arranged alphabetically by state, then county, then city within each county; table includes counties with populations greater than 49,999 unless noted and cities with populations greater than 9,999 whose Asian and/or NHPI population rates are greater than the national average; (1) Native Hawaiian and other Pacific Islander; (2) excludes Taiwanese; (3) includes Chamorro; (4) county does not meet population threshold but is shown in order to allow inclusion of city

Place	Total population 5 years and over who speak English-only at home	Asian population 5 years and over	Asians 5 years and over who speak English-only at home	NHPI[1] population 5 years and over	NHPIs[1] 5 years and over who speak English-only at home	Asian Indian	Bangladeshi	Cambodian	Chinese[2]	Fijian	Filipino	Guamanian[3]	Hawaiian, Native	Hmong	Indonesian	Japanese	Korean	Laotian	Malaysian	Pakistani	Samoan	Sri Lankan	Taiwanese	Thai	Tongan	Vietnamese
KANSAS	2,281,705	41,330	6,875	1,147	715	1,071	-	83	792	-	1,174	-	358	32	-	707	1,093	130	-	120	-	-	105	149	-	683
	91.26		16.63		62.34	15.16		13.52	12.26		36.79		92.75	3.76		39.70	26.61	5.01		17.05			20.75	23.84		6.60
						15.58		1.21	11.52		17.08		50.07	0.47		10.28	15.90	1.89		1.75			1.53	2.17		9.93
			16.63		62.34	2.59		0.20	1.92		2.84		31.21	0.08		1.71	2.64	0.31		0.29			0.25	0.36		1.65
			0.30		0.03	0.05		<0.01	0.03		0.05		0.02	<0.01		0.03	0.05	0.01		0.01			<0.01	0.01		0.03
Cowley County[4]	32,356	490	56	-	-	-	-	-	-	-	-	-	-	-	-	-	-	0	-	-	-	-	-	-	-	-
	95.27		11.43															0.00								
																		0.00								
			11.43															0.00								
			0.17															0.00								
Winfield (city)	10,559	425	36	-	-	-	-	-	-	-	-	-	-	-	-	-	-	0	-	-	-	-	-	-	-	-
	92.29		8.47															0.00								
																		0.00								
			8.47															0.00								
			0.34															0.00								
Douglas County	86,424	3,180	738	-	-	134	-	-	123	-	-	-	-	-	-	-	141	-	-	-	-	-	-	-	-	-
	91.54		23.21			27.40			13.37								29.31									
						18.16			16.67								19.11									
			23.21			4.21			3.87								4.43									
			0.85			0.16			0.14								0.16									
Lawrence (city)	68,244	3,143	708	-	-	120	-	-	123	-	-	-	-	-	-	-	137	-	-	-	-	-	-	-	-	-
	90.09		22.53			25.26			13.37								28.72									
						16.95			17.37								19.35									
			22.53			3.82			3.91								4.36									
			1.04			0.18			0.18								0.20									
Johnson County	383,228	11,478	1,888	-	-	447	-	-	321	-	321	-	-	-	-	150	235	31	-	-	-	-	-	-	-	109
	91.80		16.45			12.23			13.75		36.27					35.63	18.77	5.14								8.96
						23.68			17.00		17.00					7.94	12.45	1.64								5.77
			16.45			3.89			2.80		2.80					1.31	2.05	0.27								0.95
			0.49			0.12			0.08		0.08					0.04	0.06	0.01								0.03
Overland Park (city)	124,321	5,209	746	-	-	208	-	-	113	-	-	-	-	-	-	-	99	-	-	-	-	-	-	-	-	0
	89.93		14.32			11.51			9.50								17.22									0.00
						27.88			15.15								13.27									0.00
			14.32			3.99			2.17								1.90									0.00
			0.60			0.17			0.09								0.08									0.00
Leavenworth County	59,846	686	221	-	-	-	-	-	-	-	-	-	-	-	-	-	-	-	-	-	-	-	-	-	-	-
	93.69		32.22																							
			32.22																							
			0.37																							
Riley County	53,564	1,873	312	-	-	-	-	-	45	-	-	-	-	-	-	-	105	-	-	-	-	-	-	-	-	-
	90.25		16.66						7.18								27.63									
									14.42								33.65									
			16.66						2.40								5.61									
			0.58						0.08								0.20									
Manhattan (city)	38,886	1,621	220	-	-	-	-	-	37	-	-	-	-	-	-	-	-	-	-	-	-	-	-	-	-	-
	90.56		13.57						6.19																	
									16.82																	
			13.57						2.28																	
			0.57						0.10																	

Notes: Please refer to the User's Guide for an explanation of data; data is arranged alphabetically by state, then county, then city within each county; table includes counties with populations greater than 49,999 unless noted and cities with populations greater than 9,999 whose Asian and/or NHPI population rates are greater than the national average; (1) Native Hawaiian and other Pacific Islander; (2) excludes Taiwanese; (3) includes Chamorro; (4) county does not meet population threshold but is shown in order to allow inclusion of city

Place	Total population 5 years and over who speak English-only at home	Asian population 5 years and over	Asians 5 years and over who speak English-only at home	NHPI[1] population 5 years and over	NHPIs[1] 5 years and over who speak English-only at home	Asian Indian	Bangladeshi	Cambodian	Chinese[2]	Fijian	Filipino	Guamanian[3]	Hawaiian, Native	Hmong	Indonesian	Japanese	Korean	Laotian	Malaysian	Pakistani	Samoan	Sri Lankan	Taiwanese	Thai	Tongan	Vietnamese
Saline County	46,450 92.99	810	121 14.94 14.94 0.26	-	-	-	-	-	-	-	-	-	-	-	-	-	-	-	-	-	-	-	-	-	-	6 1.81 4.96 0.74 0.01
Sedgwick County	372,640 89.24	13,019	1,622 12.46 12.46 0.44	399	243 60.90 60.90 0.07	175 14.23 10.79 1.34 0.05	-	35 8.79 2.16 0.27 0.01	131 9.77 8.08 1.01 0.04	-	219 32.44 13.50 1.68 0.06	-	-	-	-	-	189 36.56 11.65 1.45 0.05	25 2.64 1.54 0.19 0.01	-	-	-	-	-	-	-	367 5.95 22.63 2.82 0.10
Wichita (city)	276,098 87.12	11,617	1,318 11.35 11.35 0.48	-	-	168 14.24 12.75 1.45 0.06	-	-	108 8.70 8.19 0.93 0.04	-	177 33.91 13.43 1.52 0.06	-	-	-	-	-	132 30.07 10.02 1.14 0.05	13 2.08 0.99 0.11 <0.01	-	-	-	-	-	-	-	339 5.78 25.72 2.92 0.12
Shawnee County	148,702 93.95	1,407	314 22.32 22.32 0.21	-	-	-	-	-	-	-	-	-	-	-	-	-	-	-	-	-	-	-	-	-	-	-
Wyandotte County	122,532 84.38	1,999	285 14.26 14.26 0.23	-	-	-	-	-	-	-	-	-	-	23 3.23 8.07 1.15 0.02	-	-	-	-	-	-	-	-	-	-	-	-
KENTUCKY	3,627,757 96.07	26,795	5,294 19.76 19.76 0.15	1,064	589 55.36 55.36 0.02	1,180 18.94 22.29 4.40 0.03	-	-	502 10.61 9.48 1.87 0.01	-	1,093 36.71 20.65 4.08 0.03	152 43.18 25.81 14.29 <0.01	-	-	-	484 16.22 9.14 1.81 0.01	1,108 29.44 20.93 4.14 0.03	-	-	55 10.98 1.04 0.21 <0.01	-	-	-	88 21.46 1.66 0.33 <0.01	-	311 10.55 5.87 1.16 0.01
Boone County	75,062 94.81	919	187 20.35 20.35 0.25	-	-	-	-	-	-	-	-	-	-	-	-	38 8.98 20.32 4.13 0.05	-	-	-	-	-	-	-	-	-	-
Campbell County	79,921 96.83	514	143 27.82 27.82 0.18	-	-	-	-	-	-	-	-	-	-	-	-	-	-	-	-	-	-	-	-	-	-	-
Christian County	60,273 92.57	554	154 27.80 27.80 0.26	-	-	-	-	-	-	-	-	-	-	-	-	-	-	-	-	-	-	-	-	-	-	-
Fayette County	224,074 91.66	5,404	831 15.38 15.38 0.37	-	-	253 19.86 30.45 4.68 0.11	-	-	92 5.77 11.07 1.70 0.04	-	-	-	-	-	-	73 8.99 8.78 1.35 0.03	-	-	-	-	-	-	-	-	-	-

Notes: Please refer to the User's Guide for an explanation of data; data is arranged alphabetically by state, then county, then city within each county; table includes counties with populations greater than 49,999 unless noted and cities with populations greater than 9,999 whose Asian and/or NHPI population rates are greater than the national average; (1) Native Hawaiian and other Pacific Islander; (2) excludes Taiwanese; (3) includes Chamorro; (4) county does not meet population threshold but is shown in order to allow inclusion of city

Place	Total population 5 years and over who speak English-only at home	Asian population 5 years and over	Asians 5 years and over who speak English-only at home	NHPI[1] population 5 years and over	NHPIs[1] 5 years and over who speak English-only at home	Asian Indian	Bangladeshi	Cambodian	Chinese[2]	Fijian	Filipino	Guamanian[3]	Hawaiian, Native	Hmong	Indonesian	Japanese	Korean	Laotian	Malaysian	Pakistani	Samoan	Sri Lankan	Taiwanese	Thai	Tongan	Vietnamese
Hardin County	80,554 92.15	1,778	348 19.57 19.57 0.43	-	-	-	-	-	-	-	-	-	-	-	-	-	95 13.09 27.30 5.34 0.12	-	-	-	-	-	-	-	-	-
Radcliff (city)	17,390 86.18	873	72 8.25 8.25 0.41	-	-	-	-	-	-	-	-	-	-	-	-	-	-	-	-	-	-	-	-	-	-	-
Jefferson County	611,664 94.54	8,337	1,549 18.58 18.58 0.25	-	-	422 18.47 27.24 5.06 0.07	-	-	121 9.61 7.81 1.45 0.02	-	314 35.84 20.27 3.77 0.05	-	-	-	-	121 35.38 7.81 1.45 0.02	256 25.86 16.53 3.07 0.04	-	-	-	-	-	-	-	-	133 8.17 8.59 1.60 0.02
Kenton County	135,407 96.47	814	246 30.22 30.22 0.18	-	-	-	-	-	-	-	-	-	-	-	-	-	-	-	-	-	-	-	-	-	-	-
Madison County	64,023 96.46	523	106 20.27 20.27 0.17	-	-	-	-	-	-	-	-	-	-	-	-	-	-	-	-	-	-	-	-	-	-	-
Warren County	80,933 93.34	1,012	107 10.57 10.57 0.13	-	-	-	-	-	-	-	-	-	-	-	-	-	-	-	-	-	-	-	-	-	-	-
LOUISIANA	3,771,003 90.79	51,417	7,835 15.24 15.24 0.21	1,276	870 68.18 68.18 0.02	1,693 20.70 21.61 3.29 0.04	-	-	1,321 21.01 16.86 2.57 0.04	-	1,517 34.02 19.36 2.95 0.04	322 73.68 37.01 25.24 0.01	316 86.58 36.32 24.76 0.01	-	-	445 32.96 5.68 0.87 0.01	693 27.06 8.84 1.35 0.02	69 5.75 0.88 0.13 <0.01	-	45 5.29 0.57 0.09 <0.01	-	-	26 5.33 0.33 0.05 <0.01	190 30.06 2.43 0.37 0.01	-	1,080 4.70 13.78 2.10 0.03
Ascension Parish	66,289 94.16	309	106 34.30 34.30 0.16	-	-	-	-	-	-	-	-	-	-	-	-	-	-	-	-	-	-	-	-	-	-	-
Bossier Parish	85,893 94.39	1,064	253 23.78 23.78 0.29	-	-	-	-	-	-	-	-	-	-	-	-	-	-	-	-	-	-	-	-	-	-	-
Caddo Parish	225,710 96.16	1,804	323 17.90 17.90 0.14	-	-	103 22.79 31.89 5.71 0.05	-	-	-	-	-	-	-	-	-	-	-	-	-	-	-	-	-	-	-	-

Notes: Please refer to the User's Guide for an explanation of data; data is arranged alphabetically by state, then county, then city within each county; table includes counties with populations greater than 49,999 unless noted and cities with populations greater than 9,999 whose Asian and/or NHPI population rates are greater than the national average; (1) Native Hawaiian and other Pacific Islander; (2) excludes Taiwanese; (3) includes Chamorro; (4) county does not meet population threshold but is shown in order to allow inclusion of city

Place	Total population 5 years and over who speak English-only at home	Asian population 5 years and over	Asians 5 years and over who speak English-only at home	NHPI[1] population 5 years and over	NHPIs[1] 5 years and over who speak English-only at home	Asian Indian	Bangladeshi	Cambodian	Chinese[2]	Fijian	Filipino	Guamanian[3]	Hawaiian, Native	Hmong	Indonesian	Japanese	Korean	Laotian	Malaysian	Pakistani	Samoan	Sri Lankan	Taiwanese	Thai	Tongan	Vietnamese
Calcasieu Parish	155,360 91.26	991	249 25.13 25.13 0.16	-	-	-	-	-	-	-	-	-	-	-	-	-	-	-	-	-	-	-	-	-	-	-
East Baton Rouge Parish	354,079 92.25	8,183	1,073 13.11 13.11 0.30	-	-	320 17.54 29.82 3.91 0.09	-	-	230 15.02 21.44 2.81 0.06	-	152 35.51 14.17 1.86 0.04	-	-	-	-	-	-	-	-	-	-	-	-	-	-	110 3.31 10.25 1.34 0.03
Iberia Parish	56,791 84.18	1,352	91 6.73 6.73 0.16	-	-	-	-	-	-	-	-	-	-	-	-	-	-	9 1.09 9.89 0.67 0.02	-	-	-	-	-	-	-	10 2.79 10.99 0.74 0.02
Jefferson Parish	370,259 87.01	12,685	1,311 10.34 10.34 0.35	-	-	222 13.75 16.93 1.75 0.06	-	-	361 19.88 27.54 2.85 0.10	-	311 33.12 23.72 2.45 0.08	-	-	-	-	-	45 7.67 3.43 0.35 0.01	-	-	8 1.98 0.61 0.06 <0.01	-	-	-	-	-	238 3.82 18.15 1.88 0.06
Gretna (city)	14,139 87.50	577	80 13.86 13.86 0.57	-	-	-	-	-	-	-	-	-	-	-	-	-	-	-	-	-	-	-	-	-	-	7 2.23 8.75 1.21 0.05
Harvey (cdp)	17,634 86.79	1,057	56 5.30 5.30 0.32	-	-	-	-	-	-	-	-	-	-	-	-	-	-	-	-	-	-	-	-	-	-	7 0.89 12.50 0.66 0.04
Timberlane (cdp)	9,253 86.34	578	54 9.34 9.34 0.58	-	-	-	-	-	-	-	-	-	-	-	-	-	-	-	-	-	-	-	-	-	-	34 6.69 62.96 5.88 0.37
Woodmere (cdp)	10,551 87.10	651	35 5.38 5.38 0.33	-	-	-	-	-	-	-	-	-	-	-	-	-	-	-	-	-	-	-	-	-	-	0 0.00 0.00 0.00 0.00
Lafayette Parish	144,399 81.69	1,997	246 12.32 12.32 0.17	-	-	122 20.30 49.59 6.11 0.08	-	-	-	-	-	-	-	-	-	-	-	-	-	-	-	-	-	-	-	31 4.61 12.60 1.55 0.02
Lafourche Parish	65,775 78.53	506	135 26.68 26.68 0.21	-	-	-	-	-	-	-	-	-	-	-	-	-	-	-	-	-	-	-	-	-	-	-

Notes: Please refer to the User's Guide for an explanation of data; data is arranged alphabetically by state, then county, then city within each county; table includes counties with populations greater than 49,999 unless noted and cities with populations greater than 9,999 whose Asian and/or NHPI population rates are greater than the national average; (1) Native Hawaiian and other Pacific Islander; (2) excludes Taiwanese; (3) includes Chamorro; (4) county does not meet population threshold but is shown in order to allow inclusion of city

Place	Total population 5 years and over who speak English-only at home	Asian population 5 years and over	Asians 5 years and over who speak English-only at home	NHPI[1] population 5 years and over	NHPIs[1] 5 years and over who speak English-only at home	Asian Indian	Bangladeshi	Cambodian	Chinese[2]	Fijian	Filipino	Guamanian[3]	Hawaiian, Native	Hmong	Indonesian	Japanese	Korean	Laotian	Malaysian	Pakistani	Samoan	Sri Lankan	Taiwanese	Thai	Tongan	Vietnamese
	414,214	9,881	1,183	-	-	343	-	-	211	-	194	-	-	-	-	-	-	-	-	-	-	-	-	-	-	169
	91.69		11.97			28.44			27.65		42.45															2.60
Orleans Parish						28.99			17.84		16.40															14.29
			11.97			3.47			2.14		1.96															1.71
			0.29			0.08			0.05		0.05															0.04
	132,516	776	168	-	-	-	-	-	-	-	-	-	-	-	-	-	-	-	-	-	-	-	-	-	-	-
	96.98		21.65																							
Ouachita Parish																										
			21.65																							
			0.13																							
	111,804	1,024	255	-	-	-	-	-	-	-	-	-	-	-	-	-	-	-	-	-	-	-	-	-	-	-
	95.14		24.90																							
Rapides Parish																										
			24.90																							
			0.23																							
	58,473	1,012	150	-	-	-	-	-	-	-	-	-	-	-	-	-	-	-	-	-	-	-	-	-	-	11
	92.71		14.82																							2.38
St. Bernard Parish																										7.33
			14.82																							1.09
			0.26																							0.02
	44,582	904	109	-	-	-	-	-	-	-	-	-	-	-	-	-	-	-	-	-	-	-	-	-	-	37
	89.98		12.06																							4.58
St. Mary Parish																										33.94
			12.06																							4.09
			0.24																							0.08
	168,403	1,343	489	-	-	-	-	-	-	-	-	-	-	-	-	-	-	-	-	-	-	-	-	-	-	48
	94.70		36.41																							17.14
St. Tammany Parish																										9.82
			36.41																							3.57
			0.29																							0.03
	83,960	771	97	-	-	-	-	-	-	-	-	-	-	-	-	-	-	-	-	-	-	-	-	-	-	27
	86.80		12.58																							7.87
Terrebonne Parish																										27.84
			12.58																							3.50
			0.12																							0.03
	36,012	927	58	-	-	-	-	-	-	-	-	-	-	-	-	-	-	-	-	-	-	-	-	-	-	36
	72.10		6.26																							4.36
Vermilion Parish																										62.07
			6.26																							3.88
			0.16																							0.10
	8,357	607	16	-	-	-	-	-	-	-	-	-	-	-	-	-	-	-	-	-	-	-	-	-	-	16
	75.74		2.64																							2.74
Abbeville (city)																										100.00
			2.64																							2.64
			0.19																							0.19
	43,246	1,015	327	-	-	-	-	-	-	-	-	-	-	-	-	-	106	-	-	-	-	-	-	-	-	-
	90.96		32.22														32.12									
Vernon Parish																	32.42									
			32.22														10.44									
			0.76														0.25									

Notes: Please refer to the User's Guide for an explanation of data; data is arranged alphabetically by state, then county, then city within each county; table includes counties with populations greater than 49,999 unless noted and cities with populations greater than 9,999 whose Asian and/or NHPI population rates are greater than the national average; (1) Native Hawaiian and other Pacific Islander; (2) excludes Taiwanese; (3) includes Chamorro; (4) county does not meet population threshold but is shown in order to allow inclusion of city

Place	Total population 5 years and over who speak English-only at home	Asian population 5 years and over	Asians 5 years and over who speak English-only at home	NHPI[1] population 5 years and over	NHPIs[1] 5 years and over who speak English-only at home	Asian Indian	Bangladeshi	Cambodian	Chinese[2]	Fijian	Filipino	Guamanian[3]	Hawaiian, Native	Hmong	Indonesian	Japanese	Korean	Laotian	Malaysian	Pakistani	Samoan	Sri Lankan	Taiwanese	Thai	Tongan	Vietnamese
MAINE	1,110,198 92.20	7,548	2,484 32.91 32.91 0.22	276	161 58.33 58.33 0.01	390 42.95 15.70 5.17 0.04	-	185 20.37 7.45 2.45 0.02	298 21.39 12.00 3.95 0.03	-	521 46.39 20.97 6.90 0.05	-	-	-	-	279 47.13 11.23 3.70 0.03	374 53.13 15.06 4.95 0.03	-	-	-	-	-	-	-	-	219 21.68 8.82 2.90 0.02
Androscoggin County	81,607 83.58	508	147 28.94 28.94 0.18	-	-	-	-	-	-	-	-	-	-	-	-	-	-	-	-	-	-	-	-	-	-	-
Aroostook County	53,303 75.95	355	101 28.45 28.45 0.19	-	-	-	-	-	-	-	-	-	-	-	-	-	-	-	-	-	-	-	-	-	-	-
Cumberland County	235,349 94.05	3,016	701 23.24 23.24 0.30	-	-	-	-	57 9.81 8.13 1.89 0.02	111 30.75 15.83 3.68 0.05	-	164 51.57 23.40 5.44 0.07	-	-	-	-	-	-	-	-	-	-	-	-	-	-	43 7.43 6.13 1.43 0.02
Hancock County	47,524 96.42	168	66 39.29 39.29 0.14	-	-	-	-	-	-	-	-	-	-	-	-	-	-	-	-	-	-	-	-	-	-	-
Kennebec County	102,051 92.18	618	203 32.85 32.85 0.20	-	-	-	-	-	-	-	-	-	-	-	-	-	-	-	-	-	-	-	-	-	-	-
Oxford County	49,529 95.45	237	142 59.92 59.92 0.29	-	-	-	-	-	-	-	-	-	-	-	-	-	-	-	-	-	-	-	-	-	-	-
Penobscot County	130,938 95.44	940	432 45.96 45.96 0.33	-	-	-	-	-	62 22.79 14.35 6.60 0.05	-	-	-	-	-	-	-	-	-	-	-	-	-	-	-	-	-
York County	159,073 90.56	850	321 37.76 37.76 0.20	-	-	-	-	-	-	-	-	-	-	-	-	-	-	-	-	-	-	-	-	-	-	-
MARYLAND	4,322,329 87.41	196,052	36,143 18.44 18.44 0.84	1,905	1,202 63.10 63.10 0.03	9,705 20.88 26.85 4.95 0.22	50 4.43 0.14 0.03 <0.01	199 12.25 0.55 0.10 <0.01	5,815 13.27 16.09 2.97 0.13	-	7,494 29.38 20.73 3.82 0.17	377 57.82 31.36 19.79 0.01	431 87.96 35.86 22.62 0.01	-	86 8.50 0.24 0.04 <0.01	2,378 36.31 6.58 1.21 0.06	5,626 15.32 15.57 2.87 0.13	48 6.69 0.13 0.02 <0.01	-	441 9.60 1.22 0.22 0.01	-	217 20.45 0.60 0.11 0.01	168 7.60 0.46 0.09 <0.01	498 17.88 1.38 0.25 0.01	-	1,343 8.69 3.72 0.69 0.03

Notes: Please refer to the User's Guide for an explanation of data; data is arranged alphabetically by state, then county, then city within each county; table includes counties with populations greater than 49,999 unless noted and cities with populations greater than 9,999 whose Asian and/or NHPI population rates are greater than the national average; (1) Native Hawaiian and other Pacific Islander; (2) excludes Taiwanese; (3) includes Chamorro; (4) county does not meet population threshold but is shown in order to allow inclusion of city

Place	Total population 5 years and over who speak English-only at home	Asian population 5 years and over	Asians 5 years and over who speak English-only at home	NHPI[1] population 5 years and over	NHPIs[1] 5 years and over who speak English-only at home	Asian Indian	Bangladeshi	Cambodian	Chinese[2]	Fijian	Filipino	Guamanian[3]	Hawaiian, Native	Hmong	Indonesian	Japanese	Korean	Laotian	Malaysian	Pakistani	Samoan	Sri Lankan	Taiwanese	Thai	Tongan	Vietnamese
Allegany County	69,246 97.24	414	135 32.61 32.61 0.19	-	-	-	-	-	-	-	-	-	-	-	-	-	-	-	-	-	-	-	-	-	-	-
Anne Arundel County	423,447 92.66	10,650	2,807 26.36 26.36 0.66	-	-	273 16.99 9.73 2.56 0.06	-	-	351 25.23 12.50 3.30 0.08	-	996 42.35 35.48 9.35 0.24	-	-	-	-	337 50.37 12.01 3.16 0.08	485 14.29 17.28 4.55 0.11	-	-	-	-	-	-	-	-	-
Severn (cdp)	28,907 89.25	1,519	452 29.76 29.76 1.56	-	-	-	-	-	-	-	-	-	-	-	-	-	95 13.53 21.02 6.25 0.33	-	-	-	-	-	-	-	-	-
South Gate (cdp)	23,780 88.95	1,380	185 13.41 13.41 0.78	-	-	-	-	-	-	-	-	-	-	-	-	-	66 8.07 35.68 4.78 0.28	-	-	-	-	-	-	-	-	-
Baltimore Independent City	562,065 92.24	9,696	2,799 28.87 28.87 0.50	-	-	796 39.41 28.44 8.21 0.14	-	-	386 17.71 13.79 3.98 0.07	-	545 41.10 19.47 5.62 0.10	-	-	-	-	-	431 25.29 15.40 4.45 0.08	-	-	-	-	-	-	-	-	69 9.32 2.47 0.71 0.01
Baltimore County	641,282 90.38	22,175	4,266 19.24 19.24 0.67	-	-	1,238 21.18 29.02 5.58 0.19	-	-	488 11.55 11.44 2.20 0.08	-	1,035 32.87 24.26 4.67 0.16	-	-	-	-	175 26.48 4.10 0.79 0.03	866 18.37 20.30 3.91 0.14	-	-	57 6.18 1.34 0.26 0.01	-	-	-	-	-	107 9.71 2.51 0.48 0.02
Arbutus (cdp)	17,144 90.14	922	185 20.07 20.07 1.08	-	-	-	-	-	-	-	-	-	-	-	-	-	-	-	-	-	-	-	-	-	-	-
Carney (cdp)	24,008 89.13	1,517	284 18.72 18.72 1.18	-	-	-	-	-	27 8.33 9.51 1.78 0.11	-	-	-	-	-	-	-	114 15.77 40.14 7.51 0.47	-	-	-	-	-	-	-	-	-
Cockeysville (cdp)	15,485 83.48	1,647	284 17.24 17.24 1.83	-	-	-	-	-	-	-	-	-	-	-	-	-	108 16.77 38.03 6.56 0.70	-	-	-	-	-	-	-	-	-
Lutherville-Timonium (cdp)	13,057 87.68	645	71 11.01 11.01 0.54	-	-	-	-	-	-	-	-	-	-	-	-	-	-	-	-	-	-	-	-	-	-	-

Notes: Please refer to the User's Guide for an explanation of data; data is arranged alphabetically by state, then county, then city within each county; table includes counties with populations greater than 49,999 unless noted and cities with populations greater than 9,999 whose Asian and/or NHPI population rates are greater than the national average; (1) Native Hawaiian and other Pacific Islander; (2) excludes Taiwanese; (3) includes Chamorro; (4) county does not meet population threshold but is shown in order to allow inclusion of city

Place	Total population 5 years and over who speak English-only at home	Asian population 5 years and over	Asians 5 years and over who speak English-only at home	NHPI[1] population 5 years and over	NHPIs[1] 5 years and over who speak English-only at home	Asian Indian	Bangladeshi	Cambodian	Chinese[2]	Fijian	Filipino	Guamanian[3]	Hawaiian, Native	Hmong	Indonesian	Japanese	Korean	Laotian	Malaysian	Pakistani	Samoan	Sri Lankan	Taiwanese	Thai	Tongan	Vietnamese
Mays Chapel (cdp)	9,471 88.41	777	178 22.91 22.91 1.88	-	-	-	-	-	-	-	-	-	-	-	-	-	-	-	-	-	-	-	-	-	-	-
Owings Mills (cdp)	16,132 86.66	726	175 24.10 24.10 1.08	-	-	-	-	-	-	-	-	-	-	-	-	-	-	-	-	-	-	-	-	-	-	-
Perry Hall (cdp)	24,432 90.79	1,352	170 12.57 12.57 0.70	-	-	-	-	-	-	-	-	-	-	-	-	-	37 7.86 21.76 2.74 0.15	-	-	-	-	-	-	-	-	-
Reisterstown (cdp)	17,405 82.89	981	197 20.08 20.08 1.13	-	-	63 11.50 31.98 6.42 0.36	-	-	-	-	-	-	-	-	-	-	-	-	-	-	-	-	-	-	-	-
Rossville (cdp)	9,542 88.07	535	123 22.99 22.99 1.29	-	-	-	-	-	-	-	-	-	-	-	-	-	-	-	-	-	-	-	-	-	-	-
Towson (cdp)	44,601 90.05	1,845	355 19.24 19.24 0.80	-	-	-	-	-	49 6.10 13.80 2.66 0.11	-	-	-	-	-	-	-	-	-	-	-	-	-	-	-	-	-
Woodlawn (cdp)	29,604 88.49	1,941	166 8.55 8.55 0.56	-	-	98 12.61 59.04 5.05 0.33	-	-	-	-	-	-	-	-	-	-	-	-	-	-	-	-	-	-	-	-
Calvert County	66,690 95.84	622	217 34.89 34.89 0.33	-	-	-	-	-	-	-	-	-	-	-	-	-	-	-	-	-	-	-	-	-	-	-
Carroll County	134,858 95.80	1,199	434 36.20 36.20 0.32	-	-	-	-	-	-	-	-	-	-	-	-	-	-	-	-	-	-	-	-	-	-	-
Cecil County	76,738 95.88	525	170 32.38 32.38 0.22	-	-	-	-	-	-	-	-	-	-	-	-	-	-	-	-	-	-	-	-	-	-	-

Notes: Please refer to the User's Guide for an explanation of data; data is arranged alphabetically by state, then county, then city within each county; table includes counties with populations greater than 49,999 unless noted and cities with populations greater than 9,999 whose Asian and/or NHPI population rates are greater than the national average; (1) Native Hawaiian and other Pacific Islander; (2) excludes Taiwanese; (3) includes Chamorro; (4) county does not meet population threshold but is shown in order to allow inclusion of city

Place	Total population 5 years and over who speak English-only at home	Asian population 5 years and over	Asians 5 years and over who speak English-only at home	NHPI[1] population 5 years and over	NHPIs[1] 5 years and over who speak English-only at home	Asian Indian	Bangladeshi	Cambodian	Chinese[2]	Fijian	Filipino	Guamanian[3]	Hawaiian, Native	Hmong	Indonesian	Japanese	Korean	Laotian	Malaysian	Pakistani	Samoan	Sri Lankan	Taiwanese	Thai	Tongan	Vietnamese
Charles County	106,185 94.88	1,707	540 31.63 31.63 0.51	-	-	-	-	-	-	-	215 51.68 39.81 12.60 0.20	-	-	-	-	-	-	-	-	-	-	-	-	-	-	-
Frederick County	170,995 94.36	3,047	756 24.81 24.81 0.44	-	-	120 21.86 15.87 3.94 0.07	-	-	147 19.89 19.44 4.82 0.09	-	-	-	-	-	-	-	155 32.98 20.50 5.09 0.09	-	-	-	-	-	-	-	-	-
Harford County	191,302 94.25	2,908	996 34.25 34.25 0.52	-	-	159 27.18 15.96 5.47 0.08	-	-	-	-	191 34.92 19.18 6.57 0.10	-	-	-	-	-	263 36.28 26.41 9.04 0.14	-	-	-	-	-	-	-	-	-
Howard County	197,631 86.00	17,319	3,264 18.85 18.85 1.65	-	-	949 21.41 29.07 5.48 0.48	-	-	358 10.83 10.97 2.07 0.18	-	501 37.73 15.35 2.89 0.25	-	-	-	-	-	783 13.96 23.99 4.52 0.40	-	-	44 6.98 1.35 0.25 0.02	-	-	-	-	-	88 12.50 2.70 0.51 0.04
Columbia (cdp)	69,728 84.62	5,870	1,406 23.95 23.95 2.02	-	-	464 27.93 33.00 7.90 0.67	-	-	178 12.21 12.66 3.03 0.26	-	162 33.82 11.52 2.76 0.23	-	-	-	-	-	313 22.93 22.26 5.33 0.45	-	-	-	-	-	-	-	-	-
Elkridge (cdp)	17,349 87.51	1,241	165 13.30 13.30 0.95	-	-	-	-	-	-	-	-	-	-	-	-	-	33 10.31 20.00 2.66 0.19	-	-	-	-	-	-	-	-	-
Ellicott City (cdp)	43,853 83.25	6,261	865 13.82 13.82 1.97	-	-	178 17.37 20.58 2.84 0.41	-	-	109 9.32 12.60 1.74 0.25	-	139 36.29 16.07 2.22 0.32	-	-	-	-	-	257 9.30 29.71 4.10 0.59	-	-	16 4.21 1.85 0.26 0.04	-	-	-	-	-	-
North Laurel (cdp)	16,422 86.57	1,274	316 24.80 24.80 1.92	-	-	116 29.15 36.71 9.11 0.71	-	-	-	-	-	-	-	-	-	-	58 16.20 18.35 4.55 0.35	-	-	-	-	-	-	-	-	-
Savage-Guilford (cdp)	9,961 87.59	647	102 15.77 15.77 1.02	-	-	-	-	-	-	-	-	-	-	-	-	-	-	-	-	-	-	-	-	-	-	-
Montgomery County	556,682 68.43	91,510	13,208 14.43 14.43 2.37	464	204 43.97 43.97 0.04	4,391 19.35 33.25 4.80 0.79	26 3.34 0.20 0.03 <0.01	94 8.59 0.71 0.10 0.02	3,100 12.20 23.47 3.39 0.56	-	1,390 21.16 10.52 1.52 0.25	-	-	-	51 6.03 0.39 0.06 0.01	842 28.60 6.37 0.92 0.15	1,543 10.53 11.68 1.69 0.28	-	-	197 11.70 1.49 0.22 0.04	-	126 18.10 0.95 0.14 0.02	35 3.31 0.26 0.04 0.01	200 15.36 1.51 0.22 0.04	-	511 5.84 3.87 0.56 0.09

Notes: Please refer to the User's Guide for an explanation of data; data is arranged alphabetically by state, then county, then city within each county; table includes counties with populations greater than 49,999 unless noted and cities with populations greater than 9,999 whose Asian and/or NHPI population rates are greater than the national average; (1) Native Hawaiian and other Pacific Islander; (2) excludes Taiwanese; (3) includes Chamorro; (4) county does not meet population threshold but is shown in order to allow inclusion of city

Place	Total population 5 years and over who speak English-only at home	Asian population 5 years and over	Asians 5 years and over who speak English-only at home	NHPI[1] population 5 years and over	NHPIs[1] 5 years and over who speak English-only at home	Asian Indian	Bangladeshi	Cambodian	Chinese[2]	Fijian	Filipino	Guamanian[3]	Hawaiian, Native	Hmong	Indonesian	Japanese	Korean	Laotian	Malaysian	Pakistani	Samoan	Sri Lankan	Taiwanese	Thai	Tongan	Vietnamese
Aspen Hill (cdp)	29,745 63.49	5,229	809 15.47 15.47 2.72	-	-	143 22.59 17.68 2.73 0.48	-	-	246 14.91 30.41 4.70 0.83	-	90 13.74 11.12 1.72 0.30	-	-	-	-	-	126 13.06 15.57 2.41 0.42	-	-	-	-	-	-	-	-	33 7.88 4.08 0.63 0.11
Bethesda (cdp)	39,970 76.51	4,087	918 22.46 22.46 2.30	-	-	208 20.61 22.66 5.09 0.52	-	-	202 17.63 22.00 4.94 0.51	-	140 37.33 15.25 3.43 0.35	-	-	-	-	89 20.14 9.69 2.18 0.22	170 29.88 18.52 4.16 0.43	-	-	-	-	-	-	-	-	-
Calverton (cdp)	8,423 71.86	1,944	368 18.93 18.93 4.37	-	-	196 30.02 53.26 10.08 2.33	-	-	-	-	-	-	-	-	-	-	38 7.45 10.33 1.95 0.45	-	-	-	-	-	-	-	-	-
Colesville (cdp)	13,470 71.00	3,250	435 13.38 13.38 3.23	-	-	153 21.19 35.17 4.71 1.14	-	-	101 14.77 23.22 3.11 0.75	-	-	-	-	-	-	-	59 5.28 13.56 1.82 0.44	-	-	-	-	-	-	-	-	33 10.12 7.59 1.02 0.24
Fairland (cdp)	13,587 68.01	3,051	316 10.36 10.36 2.33	-	-	116 16.48 36.71 3.80 0.85	-	-	50 8.77 15.82 1.64 0.37	-	-	-	-	-	-	-	94 7.76 29.75 3.08 0.69	-	-	-	-	-	-	-	-	-
Gaithersburg (city)	28,482 58.96	6,397	507 7.93 7.93 1.78	-	-	142 9.44 28.01 2.22 0.50	-	-	171 7.57 33.73 2.67 0.60	-	59 14.68 11.64 0.92 0.21	-	-	-	-	-	36 4.03 7.10 0.56 0.13	-	-	-	-	-	-	-	-	56 10.67 11.05 0.88 0.20
Germantown (cdp)	37,406 74.62	4,780	659 13.79 13.79 1.76	-	-	272 14.16 41.27 5.69 0.73	-	-	115 12.58 17.45 2.41 0.31	-	-	-	-	-	-	-	64 18.03 9.71 1.34 0.17	-	-	-	-	-	-	-	-	30 6.48 4.55 0.63 0.08
Montgomery Village (cdp)	23,405 66.94	3,898	563 14.44 14.44 2.41	-	-	239 15.56 42.45 6.13 1.02	-	-	57 8.72 10.12 1.46 0.24	-	103 18.59 18.29 2.64 0.44	-	-	-	-	-	-	-	-	-	-	-	-	-	-	10 2.71 1.78 0.26 0.04
North Bethesda (cdp)	23,858 65.06	4,236	755 17.82 17.82 3.16	-	-	198 20.00 26.23 4.67 0.83	-	-	200 14.72 26.49 4.72 0.84	-	84 22.34 11.13 1.98 0.35	-	-	-	-	103 22.64 13.64 2.43 0.43	81 12.84 10.73 1.91 0.34	-	-	-	-	-	-	-	-	-
North Potomac (cdp)	13,448 62.91	5,839	543 9.30 9.30 4.04	-	-	203 18.19 37.38 3.48 1.51	-	-	142 4.69 26.15 2.43 1.06	-	-	-	-	-	-	-	104 10.18 19.15 1.78 0.77	-	-	-	-	-	-	-	-	-

Notes: Please refer to the User's Guide for an explanation of data; data is arranged alphabetically by state, then county, then city within each county; table includes counties with populations greater than 49,999 unless noted and cities with populations greater than 9,999 whose Asian and/or NHPI population rates are greater than the national average; (1) Native Hawaiian and other Pacific Islander; (2) excludes Taiwanese; (3) includes Chamorro; (4) county does not meet population threshold but is shown in order to allow inclusion of city

Place	Total population 5 years and over who speak English-only at home	Asian population 5 years and over	Asians 5 years and over who speak English-only at home	NHPI[1] population 5 years and over	NHPIs[1] 5 years and over who speak English-only at home	Asian Indian	Bangladeshi	Cambodian	Chinese[2]	Fijian	Filipino	Guamanian[3]	Hawaiian, Native	Hmong	Indonesian	Japanese	Korean	Laotian	Malaysian	Pakistani	Samoan	Sri Lankan	Taiwanese	Thai	Tongan	Vietnamese
Olney (cdp)	23,912 81.45	2,440	391 16.02 16.02 1.64	-	-	94 14.01 24.04 3.85 0.39	-	-	131 22.43 33.50 5.37 0.55	-	-	-	-	-	-	-	48 7.74 12.28 1.97 0.20	-	-	-	-	-	-	-	-	-
Potomac (cdp)	30,125 71.12	5,493	972 17.70 17.70 3.23	-	-	320 22.99 32.92 5.83 1.06	-	-	283 15.59 29.12 5.15 0.94	-	85 23.88 8.74 1.55 0.28	-	-	-	-	-	171 16.12 17.59 3.11 0.57	-	-	-	-	-	-	-	-	-
Redland (cdp)	9,749 60.95	2,727	251 9.20 9.20 2.57	-	-	56 7.73 22.31 2.05 0.57	-	-	47 6.71 18.73 1.72 0.48	-	32 11.19 12.75 1.17 0.33	-	-	-	-	-	39 10.08 15.54 1.43 0.40	-	-	-	-	-	-	-	-	-
Rockville (city)	27,962 63.10	6,186	709 11.46 11.46 2.54	-	-	231 24.95 32.58 3.73 0.83	-	-	264 10.51 37.24 4.27 0.94	-	45 10.98 6.35 0.73 0.16	-	-	-	-	29 8.38 4.09 0.47 0.10	75 8.94 10.58 1.21 0.27	-	-	-	-	-	-	-	-	9 2.18 1.27 0.15 0.03
Silver Spring (cdp)	41,763 58.60	5,961	905 15.18 15.18 2.17	-	-	340 24.71 37.57 5.70 0.81	-	5 1.65 0.55 0.08 0.01	75 10.78 8.29 1.26 0.18	-	95 21.21 10.50 1.59 0.23	-	-	-	-	-	110 24.66 12.15 1.85 0.26	-	-	-	-	-	-	-	-	92 5.67 10.17 1.54 0.22
Takoma Park (city)	10,896 68.40	692	200 28.90 28.90 1.84	-	-	-	-	-	-	-	-	-	-	-	-	-	-	-	-	-	-	-	-	-	-	-
Wheaton-Glenmont (cdp)	28,019 52.19	6,653	1,009 15.17 15.17 3.60	-	-	357 31.56 35.38 5.37 1.27	-	-	242 13.73 23.98 3.64 0.86	-	104 16.40 10.31 1.56 0.37	-	-	-	-	-	29 3.68 2.87 0.44 0.10	-	-	-	-	-	-	-	-	36 3.31 3.57 0.54 0.13
White Oak (cdp)	11,705 60.33	2,350	248 10.55 10.55 2.12	-	-	67 12.98 27.02 2.85 0.57	-	-	36 8.76 14.52 1.53 0.31	-	-	-	-	-	-	-	53 8.66 21.37 2.26 0.45	-	-	-	-	-	-	-	-	36 6.00 14.52 1.53 0.31
Prince George's County	625,419 84.08	28,741	5,445 18.95 18.95 0.87	-	-	1,476 22.12 27.11 5.14 0.24	-	-	581 12.48 10.67 2.02 0.09	-	1,992 25.18 36.58 6.93 0.32	-	-	-	-	225 36.00 4.13 0.78 0.04	528 15.12 9.70 1.84 0.08	-	-	18 3.00 0.33 0.06 <0.01	-	-	-	58 17.85 1.07 0.20 0.01	-	168 6.90 3.09 0.58 0.03
Adelphi (cdp)	7,844 56.38	1,319	304 23.05 23.05 3.88	-	-	-	-	-	-	-	-	-	-	-	-	-	-	-	-	-	-	-	-	-	-	-

Notes: Please refer to the User's Guide for an explanation of data; data is arranged alphabetically by state, then county, then city within each county; table includes counties with populations greater than 49,999 unless noted and cities with populations greater than 9,999 whose Asian and/or NHPI population rates are greater than the national average; (1) Native Hawaiian and other Pacific Islander; (2) excludes Taiwanese; (3) includes Chamorro; (4) county does not meet population threshold but is shown in order to allow inclusion of city

Place	Total population 5 years and over who speak English-only at home	Asian population 5 years and over	Asians 5 years and over who speak English-only at home	NHPI[1] population 5 years and over	NHPIs[1] 5 years and over who speak English-only at home	Asian Indian	Bangladeshi	Cambodian	Chinese[2]	Fijian	Filipino	Guamanian[3]	Hawaiian, Native	Hmong	Indonesian	Japanese	Korean	Laotian	Malaysian	Pakistani	Samoan	Sri Lankan	Taiwanese	Thai	Tongan	Vietnamese
Beltsville (cdp)	10,551 71.95	1,580	253 16.01 16.01 2.40	-	-	113 24.62 44.66 7.15 1.07	-	-	-	-	-	-	-	-	-	-	28 10.07 11.07 1.77 0.27	-	-	-	-	-	-	-	-	-
College Park (city)	19,647 82.13	2,139	512 23.94 23.94 2.61	-	-	109 18.05 21.29 5.10 0.55	-	-	114 17.17 22.27 5.33 0.58	-	-	-	-	-	-	-	-	-	-	-	-	-	-	-	-	-
Fort Washington (cdp)	19,326 84.34	2,316	581 25.09 25.09 3.01	-	-	-	-	-	-	-	468 25.12 80.55 20.21 2.42	-	-	-	-	-	-	-	-	-	-	-	-	-	-	-
Friendly (cdp)	9,335 90.53	645	184 28.53 28.53 1.97	-	-	-	-	-	-	-	164 32.09 89.13 25.43 1.76	-	-	-	-	-	-	-	-	-	-	-	-	-	-	-
Glenn Dale (cdp)	9,596 81.12	965	184 19.07 19.07 1.92	-	-	-	-	-	-	-	-	-	-	-	-	-	-	-	-	-	-	-	-	-	-	-
Greenbelt (city)	14,081 70.57	2,440	171 7.01 7.01 1.21	-	-	60 9.02 35.09 2.46 0.43	-	-	34 6.16 19.88 1.39 0.24	-	-	-	-	-	-	-	46 8.01 26.90 1.89 0.33	-	-	-	-	-	-	-	-	-
Hyattsville (city)	10,170 73.45	650	188 28.92 28.92 1.85	-	-	-	-	-	-	-	-	-	-	-	-	-	-	-	-	-	-	-	-	-	-	-
Lanham-Seabrook (cdp)	13,993 82.47	850	27 3.18 3.18 0.19	-	-	-	-	-	-	-	-	-	-	-	-	-	-	-	-	-	-	-	-	-	-	-
Laurel (city)	15,400 82.18	1,190	201 16.89 16.89 1.31	-	-	-	-	-	-	-	-	-	-	-	-	-	-	-	-	-	-	-	-	-	-	-
New Carrollton (city)	9,601 80.79	490	129 26.33 26.33 1.34	-	-	-	-	-	-	-	-	-	-	-	-	-	-	-	-	-	-	-	-	-	-	-

Notes: Please refer to the User's Guide for an explanation of data; data is arranged alphabetically by state, then county, then city within each county; table includes counties with populations greater than 49,999 unless noted and cities with populations greater than 9,999 whose Asian and/or NHPI population rates are greater than the national average; (1) Native Hawaiian and other Pacific Islander; (2) excludes Taiwanese; (3) includes Chamorro; (4) county does not meet population threshold but is shown in order to allow inclusion of city

Place	Total population 5 years and over who speak English-only at home	Asian population 5 years and over	Asians 5 years and over who speak English-only at home	NHPI[1] population 5 years and over	NHPIs[1] 5 years and over who speak English-only at home	Asian Indian	Bangladeshi	Cambodian	Chinese[2]	Fijian	Filipino	Guamanian[3]	Hawaiian, Native	Hmong	Indonesian	Japanese	Korean	Laotian	Malaysian	Pakistani	Samoan	Sri Lankan	Taiwanese	Thai	Tongan	Vietnamese
South Laurel (cdp)	15,330 80.43	1,110	96 8.65 8.65 0.63	-	-	-	-	-	-	-	-	-	-	-	-	-	-	-	-	-	-	-	-	-	-	-
St. Mary's County	75,056 93.83	1,517	459 30.26 30.26 0.61	-	-	24 9.13 5.23 1.58 0.03	-	-	-	-	240 38.46 52.29 15.82 0.32	-	-	-	-	-	-	-	-	-	-	-	-	-	-	-
Lexington Park (cdp)	8,861 90.15	403	114 28.29 28.29 1.29	-	-	-	-	-	-	-	-	-	-	-	-	-	-	-	-	-	-	-	-	-	-	-
Washington County	119,772 96.76	938	187 19.94 19.94 0.16	-	-	-	-	-	-	-	-	-	-	-	-	-	-	-	-	-	-	-	-	-	-	-
Wicomico County	74,842 94.21	1,655	157 9.49 9.49 0.21	-	-	41 10.00 26.11 2.48 0.05	-	-	-	-	-	-	-	-	-	-	72 12.41 45.86 4.35 0.10	-	-	-	-	-	-	-	-	-
Salisbury (city)	20,580 90.31	937	54 5.76 5.76 0.26	-	-	-	-	-	-	-	-	-	-	-	-	-	-	-	-	-	-	-	-	-	-	-
MASSACHUSETTS	4,838,679 81.26	221,108	35,268 15.95 15.95 0.73	1,740	911 52.36 52.36 0.02	7,571 19.59 21.47 3.42 0.16	37 7.52 0.10 0.02 <0.01	1,043 5.63 2.96 0.47 0.02	10,322 13.50 29.27 4.67 0.21	-	3,405 38.15 9.65 1.54 0.07	122 29.05 13.39 7.01 <0.01	351 74.52 38.53 20.17 0.01	19 2.17 0.05 0.01 <0.01	167 24.49 0.47 0.08 <0.01	2,531 24.31 7.18 1.14 0.05	4,597 28.40 13.03 2.08 0.10	286 8.43 0.81 0.13 0.01	-	122 5.68 0.35 0.06 <0.01	-	156 35.45 0.44 0.07 <0.01	363 15.19 1.03 0.16 0.01	385 17.91 1.09 0.17 0.01	-	2,243 7.05 6.36 1.01 0.05
Barnstable County	197,334 93.23	1,225	385 31.43 31.43 0.20	-	-	-	-	-	95 27.94 24.68 7.76 0.05	-	-	-	-	-	-	-	-	-	-	-	-	-	-	-	-	-
Berkshire County	119,754 93.59	1,161	299 25.75 25.75 0.25	-	-	44 14.10 14.72 3.79 0.04	-	-	-	-	-	-	-	-	-	-	-	-	-	-	-	-	-	-	-	-
Bristol County	395,282 78.93	6,727	1,425 21.18 21.18 0.36	-	-	209 14.93 14.67 3.11 0.05	-	176 8.68 12.35 2.62 0.04	216 17.16 15.16 3.21 0.05	-	211 51.46 14.81 3.14 0.05	-	-	-	-	-	309 66.45 21.68 4.59 0.08	-	-	-	-	-	-	-	-	64 14.16 4.49 0.95 0.02

Notes: Please refer to the User's Guide for an explanation of data; data is arranged alphabetically by state, then county, then city within each county; table includes counties with populations greater than 49,999 unless noted and cities with populations greater than 9,999 whose Asian and/or NHPI population rates are greater than the national average; (1) Native Hawaiian and other Pacific Islander; (2) excludes Taiwanese; (3) includes Chamorro; (4) county does not meet population threshold but is shown in order to allow inclusion of city

Place	Total population 5 years and over who speak English-only at home	Asian population 5 years and over	Asians 5 years and over who speak English-only at home	NHPI[1] population 5 years and over	NHPIs[1] 5 years and over who speak English-only at home	Asian Indian	Bangladeshi	Cambodian	Chinese[2]	Fijian	Filipino	Guamanian[3]	Hawaiian, Native	Hmong	Indonesian	Japanese	Korean	Laotian	Malaysian	Pakistani	Samoan	Sri Lankan	Taiwanese	Thai	Tongan	Vietnamese
Essex County	544,872 80.65	15,798	2,340 14.81 14.81 0.43	-	-	410 17.93 17.52 2.60 0.08	-	70 2.08 2.99 0.44 0.01	568 19.10 24.27 3.60 0.10	-	263 40.71 11.24 1.66 0.05	-	-	-	-	280 28.84 11.97 1.77 0.05	342 24.69 14.62 2.16 0.06	19 5.18 0.81 0.12 <0.01	-	-	-	-	-	-	-	225 7.90 9.62 1.42 0.04
Andover (town)	25,630 87.88	1,893	435 22.98 22.98 1.70	-	-	133 28.30 30.57 7.03 0.52	-	-	120 16.62 27.59 6.34 0.47	-	-	-	-	-	-	-	-	-	-	-	-	-	-	-	-	-
Lynn (city)	54,356 65.85	5,351	442 8.26 8.26 0.81	-	-	58 15.51 13.12 1.08 0.11	-	70 2.62 15.84 1.31 0.13	-	-	-	-	-	-	-	-	-	-	-	-	-	-	-	-	-	51 4.65 11.54 0.95 0.09
North Andover (town)	22,203 87.61	974	159 16.32 16.32 0.72	-	-	-	-	-	43 14.29 27.04 4.41 0.19	-	-	-	-	-	-	-	-	-	-	-	-	-	-	-	-	-
Franklin County	63,647 93.77	606	161 26.57 26.57 0.25	-	-	-	-	-	-	-	-	-	-	-	-	-	-	-	-	-	-	-	-	-	-	-
Hampden County	331,641 77.75	5,524	932 16.87 16.87 0.28	-	-	135 20.93 14.48 2.44 0.04	-	13 3.45 1.39 0.24 <0.01	130 11.95 13.95 2.35 0.04	-	-	-	-	-	-	-	151 36.47 16.20 2.73 0.05	-	-	-	-	-	-	-	-	213 12.02 22.85 3.86 0.06
Hampshire County	128,539 88.28	4,659	1,042 22.37 22.37 0.81	-	-	168 20.51 16.12 3.61 0.13	-	-	295 19.24 28.31 6.33 0.23	-	-	-	-	-	-	-	251 33.60 24.09 5.39 0.20	-	-	-	-	-	-	-	-	-
Amherst Center (cdp)	13,784 81.56	1,331	319 23.97 23.97 2.31	-	-	-	-	-	-	-	-	-	-	-	-	-	-	-	-	-	-	-	-	-	-	-
Amherst (town)	27,162 79.87	2,908	527 18.12 18.12 1.94	-	-	-	-	-	159 15.57 30.17 5.47 0.59	-	-	-	-	-	-	-	-	-	-	-	-	-	-	-	-	-
Middlesex County	1,093,227 79.58	84,326	13,371 15.86 15.86 1.22	-	-	3,449 17.16 25.79 4.09 0.32	-	588 5.91 4.40 0.70 0.05	4,286 15.56 32.05 5.08 0.39	-	869 35.20 6.50 1.03 0.08	-	-	-	-	876 24.13 6.55 1.04 0.08	1,414 21.39 10.58 1.68 0.13	149 8.83 1.11 0.18 0.01	-	66 12.92 0.49 0.08 0.01	-	-	195 16.25 1.46 0.23 0.02	144 16.86 1.08 0.17 0.01	-	485 7.77 3.63 0.58 0.04

Notes: Please refer to the User's Guide for an explanation of data; data is arranged alphabetically by state, then county, then city within each county; table includes counties with populations greater than 49,999 unless noted and cities with populations greater than 9,999 whose Asian and/or NHPI population rates are greater than the national average; (1) Native Hawaiian and other Pacific Islander; (2) excludes Taiwanese; (3) includes Chamorro; (4) county does not meet population threshold but is shown in order to allow inclusion of city

Place	Total population 5 years and over who speak English-only at home	Asian population 5 years and over	Asians 5 years and over who speak English-only at home	NHPI[1] population 5 years and over	NHPIs[1] 5 years and over who speak English-only at home	Asian Indian	Bangladeshi	Cambodian	Chinese[2]	Fijian	Filipino	Guamanian[3]	Hawaiian, Native	Hmong	Indonesian	Japanese	Korean	Laotian	Malaysian	Pakistani	Samoan	Sri Lankan	Taiwanese	Thai	Tongan	Vietnamese
Acton (town)	16,085 85.35	1,682	221 13.14 13.14 1.37	-	-	67 11.24 30.32 3.98 0.42	-	-	52 6.85 23.53 3.09 0.32	-	-	-	-	-	-	-	-	-	-	-	-	-	-	-	-	-
Arlington (town)	33,041 83.07	1,830	432 23.61 23.61 1.31	-	-	-	-	-	163 24.18 37.73 8.91 0.49	-	-	-	-	-	-	-	-	-	-	-	-	-	-	-	-	-
Bedford (town)	10,318 87.55	733	110 15.01 15.01 1.07	-	-	-	-	-	-	-	-	-	-	-	-	-	-	-	-	-	-	-	-	-	-	-
Belmont (cdp)	18,234 80.04	1,187	212 17.86 17.86 1.16	-	-	-	-	-	114 21.51 53.77 9.60 0.63	-	-	-	-	-	-	-	-	-	-	-	-	-	-	-	-	-
Belmont (town)	18,234 80.04	1,187	212 17.86 17.86 1.16	-	-	-	-	-	114 21.51 53.77 9.60 0.63	-	-	-	-	-	-	-	-	-	-	-	-	-	-	-	-	-
Burlington (town)	17,445 81.91	2,043	231 11.31 11.31 1.32	-	-	169 12.88 73.16 8.27 0.97	-	-	-	-	-	-	-	-	-	-	-	-	-	-	-	-	-	-	-	-
Cambridge (city)	66,834 68.78	11,561	2,776 24.01 24.01 4.15	-	-	837 31.28 30.15 7.24 1.25	-	-	867 20.66 31.23 7.50 1.30	-	-	-	-	-	-	199 20.37 7.17 1.72 0.30	376 20.57 13.54 3.25 0.56	-	-	-	-	-	-	-	-	-
Chelmsford (town)	28,471 90.05	1,429	263 18.40 18.40 0.92	-	-	79 24.69 30.04 5.53 0.28	-	-	65 11.99 24.71 4.55 0.23	-	-	-	-	-	-	-	-	-	-	-	-	-	-	-	-	-
Framingham (town)	44,260 70.82	3,172	486 15.32 15.32 1.10	-	-	263 20.34 54.12 8.29 0.59	-	-	75 8.11 15.43 2.36 0.17	-	-	-	-	-	-	-	-	-	-	-	-	-	-	-	-	-
Lexington (town)	23,275 81.24	3,051	546 17.90 17.90 2.35	-	-	220 27.78 40.29 7.21 0.95	-	-	146 11.92 26.74 4.79 0.63	-	-	-	-	-	-	-	42 9.40 7.69 1.38 0.18	-	-	-	-	-	-	-	-	-

Notes: Please refer to the User's Guide for an explanation of data; data is arranged alphabetically by state, then county, then city within each county; table includes counties with populations greater than 49,999 unless noted and cities with populations greater than 9,999 whose Asian and/or NHPI population rates are greater than the national average; (1) Native Hawaiian and other Pacific Islander; (2) excludes Taiwanese; (3) includes Chamorro; (4) county does not meet population threshold but is shown in order to allow inclusion of city

Place	Total population 5 years and over who speak English-only at home	Asian population 5 years and over	Asians 5 years and over who speak English-only at home	NHPI[1] population 5 years and over	NHPIs[1] 5 years and over who speak English-only at home	Asian Indian	Bangladeshi	Cambodian	Chinese[2]	Fijian	Filipino	Guamanian[3]	Hawaiian, Native	Hmong	Indonesian	Japanese	Korean	Laotian	Malaysian	Pakistani	Samoan	Sri Lankan	Taiwanese	Thai	Tongan	Vietnamese
Lowell (city)	57,792	15,547	1,027	-	-	161	-	485	83	-	-	-	-	-	-	-	-	42	-	-	-	-	-	-	-	78
	59.26		6.61			6.87		5.63	11.98									3.09								5.80
						15.68		47.22	8.08									4.09								7.59
			6.61			1.04		3.12	0.53									0.27								0.50
			1.78			0.28		0.84	0.14									0.07								0.13
Malden (city)	36,461	7,181	644	-	-	95	-	-	238	-	-	-	-	-	-	-	-	-	-	-	-	-	-	-	-	46
	68.72		8.97			10.02			6.34																	3.78
						14.75			36.96																	7.14
			8.97			1.32			3.31																	0.64
			1.77			0.26			0.65																	0.13
Marlborough (city)	27,285	1,433	265	-	-	76	-	-	-	-	-	-	-	-	-	-	-	-	-	-	-	-	-	-	-	-
	80.51		18.49			12.86																				
						28.68																				
			18.49			5.30																				
			0.97			0.28																				
Medford (city)	41,794	2,190	417	-	-	114	-	-	125	-	-	-	-	-	-	-	-	-	-	-	-	-	-	-	-	6
	78.77		19.04			30.56			15.61																	1.79
						27.34			29.98																	1.44
			19.04			5.21			5.71																	0.27
			1.00			0.27			0.30																	0.01
Natick (town)	26,684	1,210	261	-	-	-	-	-	121	-	-	-	-	-	-	-	-	-	-	-	-	-	-	-	-	-
	89.35		21.57						19.61																	
									46.36																	
			21.57						10.00																	
			0.98						0.45																	
Newton (city)	62,464	5,782	1,088	-	-	119	-	-	597	-	-	-	-	-	-	-	90	-	-	-	-	-	-	-	-	-
	78.84		18.82			21.76			16.75								15.10									
						10.94			54.87								8.27									
			18.82			2.06			10.33								1.56									
			1.74			0.19			0.96								0.14									
Somerville (city)	47,653	4,751	1,024	-	-	264	-	-	353	-	-	-	-	-	-	-	91	-	-	-	-	-	-	-	-	-
	64.37		21.55			21.95			18.51								21.11									
						25.78			34.47								8.89									
			21.55			5.56			7.43								1.92									
			2.15			0.55			0.74								0.19									
Sudbury (town)	13,799	567	115	-	-	-	-	-	-	-	-	-	-	-	-	-	-	-	-	-	-	-	-	-	-	-
	89.87		20.28																							
			20.28																							
			0.83																							
Waltham (city)	41,509	4,286	515	-	-	177	-	-	175	-	-	-	-	-	-	-	-	-	-	-	-	-	-	-	-	-
	73.50		12.02			9.73			12.86																	
						34.37			33.98																	
			12.02			4.13			4.08																	
			1.24			0.43			0.42																	
Wayland (town)	10,805	596	69	-	-	-	-	-	-	-	-	-	-	-	-	-	-	-	-	-	-	-	-	-	-	-
	88.63		11.58																							
			11.58																							
			0.64																							

Notes: Please refer to the User's Guide for an explanation of data; data is arranged alphabetically by state, then county, then city within each county; table includes counties with populations greater than 49,999 unless noted and cities with populations greater than 9,999 whose Asian and/or NHPI population rates are greater than the national average; (1) Native Hawaiian and other Pacific Islander; (2) excludes Taiwanese; (3) includes Chamorro; (4) county does not meet population threshold but is shown in order to allow inclusion of city

Place	Total population 5 years and over who speak English-only at home	Asian population 5 years and over	Asians 5 years and over who speak English-only at home	NHPI[1] population 5 years and over	NHPIs[1] 5 years and over who speak English-only at home	Asian Indian	Bangladeshi	Cambodian	Chinese[2]	Fijian	Filipino	Guamanian[3]	Hawaiian, Native	Hmong	Indonesian	Japanese	Korean	Laotian	Malaysian	Pakistani	Samoan	Sri Lankan	Taiwanese	Thai	Tongan	Vietnamese
Westford (town)	17,076 90.18	833	151 18.13 18.13 0.88	-	-	-	-	-	75 23.81 49.67 9.00 0.44	-	-	-	-	-	-	-	-	-	-	-	-	-	-	-	-	-
Weston (town)	9,093 85.40	836	212 25.36 25.36 2.33	-	-	-	-	-	67 18.72 31.60 8.01 0.74	-	-	-	-	-	-	-	-	-	-	-	-	-	-	-	-	-
Winchester (town)	16,714 86.55	740	118 15.95 15.95 0.71	-	-	-	-	-	-	-	-	-	-	-	-	-	-	-	-	-	-	-	-	-	-	-
Woburn (city)	30,308 86.01	1,717	228 13.28 13.28 0.75	-	-	66 7.20 28.95 3.84 0.22	-	-	-	-	-	-	-	-	-	-	-	-	-	-	-	-	-	-	-	-
Norfolk County	520,486 85.54	33,482	5,072 15.15 15.15 0.97	-	-	1,066 22.75 21.02 3.18 0.20	-	-	1,852 10.36 36.51 5.53 0.36	-	484 27.74 9.54 1.45 0.09	-	-	-	-	437 22.49 8.62 1.31 0.08	554 27.22 10.92 1.65 0.11	-	-	-	-	-	24 6.25 0.47 0.07 <0.01	-	-	213 8.38 4.20 0.64 0.04
Brookline (town)	38,652 71.03	7,299	1,631 22.35 22.35 4.22	-	-	440 42.80 26.98 6.03 1.14	-	-	575 16.94 35.25 7.88 1.49	-	-	-	-	-	-	233 19.15 14.29 3.19 0.60	193 21.16 11.83 2.64 0.50	-	-	-	-	-	-	-	-	-
Needham (town)	23,814 89.13	943	273 28.95 28.95 1.15	-	-	-	-	-	125 23.95 45.79 13.26 0.52	-	-	-	-	-	-	-	-	-	-	-	-	-	-	-	-	-
Norwood (town)	22,720 84.69	1,204	120 9.97 9.97 0.53	-	-	18 2.87 15.00 1.50 0.08	-	-	-	-	-	-	-	-	-	-	-	-	-	-	-	-	-	-	-	-
Quincy (city)	63,724 76.23	13,131	962 7.33 7.33 1.51	-	-	107 11.46 11.12 0.81 0.17	-	-	504 5.67 52.39 3.84 0.79	-	121 15.32 12.58 0.92 0.19	-	-	-	-	-	-	-	-	-	-	-	-	-	-	64 4.85 6.65 0.49 0.10
Randolph (town)	21,496 73.77	2,865	198 6.91 6.91 0.92	-	-	-	-	-	63 4.56 31.82 2.20 0.29	-	-	-	-	-	-	-	-	-	-	-	-	-	-	-	-	25 4.36 12.63 0.87 0.12

Notes: Please refer to the User's Guide for an explanation of data; data is arranged alphabetically by state, then county, then city within each county; table includes counties with populations greater than 49,999 unless noted and cities with populations greater than 9,999 whose Asian and/or NHPI population rates are greater than the national average; (1) Native Hawaiian and other Pacific Islander; (2) excludes Taiwanese; (3) includes Chamorro; (4) county does not meet population threshold but is shown in order to allow inclusion of city

Place	Total population 5 years and over who speak English-only at home	Asian population 5 years and over	Asians 5 years and over who speak English-only at home	NHPI[1] population 5 years and over	NHPIs[1] 5 years and over who speak English-only at home	Asian Indian	Bangladeshi	Cambodian	Chinese[2]	Fijian	Filipino	Guamanian[3]	Hawaiian, Native	Hmong	Indonesian	Japanese	Korean	Laotian	Malaysian	Pakistani	Samoan	Sri Lankan	Taiwanese	Thai	Tongan	Vietnamese
Sharon (town)	13,802 85.12	673	156 23.18 23.18 1.13	-	-	-	-	-	-	-	-	-	-	-	-	-	-	-	-	-	-	-	-	-	-	-
Wellesley (town)	21,189 85.77	1,716	328 19.11 19.11 1.55	-	-	-	-	-	124 14.64 37.80 7.23 0.59	-	-	-	-	-	-	-	-	-	-	-	-	-	-	-	-	-
Plymouth County	395,467 89.89	4,148	1,012 24.40 24.40 0.26	-	-	114 19.06 11.26 2.75 0.03	-	-	222 23.27 21.94 5.35 0.06	-	176 35.20 17.39 4.24 0.04	-	-	-	-	-	-	-	-	-	-	-	-	-	-	31 4.74 3.06 0.75 0.01
Suffolk County	431,448 66.20	45,928	7,009 15.26 15.26 1.62	-	-	1,509 36.13 21.53 3.29 0.35	-	138 8.41 1.97 0.30 0.03	2,133 11.11 30.43 4.64 0.49	-	876 48.03 12.50 1.91 0.20	-	-	-	-	417 18.92 5.95 0.91 0.10	788 31.41 11.24 1.72 0.18	-	-	-	-	-	86 19.20 1.23 0.19 0.02	-	-	627 5.42 8.95 1.37 0.15
Boston (city)	371,185 66.60	42,426	6,601 15.56 15.56 1.78	-	-	1,493 38.34 22.62 3.52 0.40	-	72 11.76 1.09 0.17 0.02	2,026 10.82 30.69 4.78 0.55	-	859 50.26 13.01 2.02 0.23	-	-	-	-	412 18.93 6.24 0.97 0.11	754 31.91 11.42 1.78 0.20	-	-	-	-	-	86 19.20 1.30 0.20 0.02	-	-	496 4.80 7.51 1.17 0.13
Chelsea (city)	13,453 41.63	1,352	123 9.10 9.10 0.91	-	-	-	-	-	-	-	-	-	-	-	-	-	-	-	-	-	-	-	-	-	-	74 10.71 60.16 5.47 0.55
Revere (city)	31,658 70.95	2,008	264 13.15 13.15 0.83	-	-	-	-	66 8.55 25.00 3.29 0.21	-	-	-	-	-	-	-	-	-	-	-	-	-	-	-	-	-	57 10.96 21.59 2.84 0.18
Worcester County	595,964 85.00	17,326	2,160 12.47 12.47 0.36	-	-	434 12.54 20.09 2.50 0.07	-	11 3.31 0.51 0.06 <0.01	349 11.07 16.16 2.01 0.06	-	210 45.85 9.72 1.21 0.04	-	-	0 0.00 0.00 0.00 0.00	-	110 30.30 5.09 0.63 0.02	345 30.21 15.97 1.99 0.06	68 7.35 3.15 0.39 0.01	-	17 4.66 0.79 0.10 <0.01	-	-	-	-	-	316 6.04 14.63 1.82 0.05
Fitchburg (city)	28,003 76.29	1,533	120 7.83 7.83 0.43	-	-	-	-	-	-	-	-	-	-	0 0.00 0.00 0.00 0.00	-	-	-	54 15.17 45.00 3.52 0.19	-	-	-	-	-	-	-	-
Northborough (town)	11,887 91.45	707	134 18.95 18.95 1.13	-	-	-	-	-	-	-	-	-	-	-	-	-	-	-	-	-	-	-	-	-	-	-

Notes: Please refer to the User's Guide for an explanation of data; data is arranged alphabetically by state, then county, then city within each county; table includes counties with populations greater than 49,999 unless noted and cities with populations greater than 9,999 whose Asian and/or NHPI population rates are greater than the national average; (1) Native Hawaiian and other Pacific Islander; (2) excludes Taiwanese; (3) includes Chamorro; (4) county does not meet population threshold but is shown in order to allow inclusion of city

Place	Total population 5 years and over who speak English-only at home	Asian population 5 years and over	Asians 5 years and over who speak English-only at home	NHPI[1] population 5 years and over	NHPIs[1] 5 years and over who speak English-only at home	Asian Indian	Bangladeshi	Cambodian	Chinese[2]	Fijian	Filipino	Guamanian[3]	Hawaiian, Native	Hmong	Indonesian	Japanese	Korean	Laotian	Malaysian	Pakistani	Samoan	Sri Lankan	Taiwanese	Thai	Tongan	Vietnamese
Shrewsbury (town)	25,068 85.98	2,323	287 12.35 12.35 1.14	-	-	85 8.61 29.62 3.66 0.34	-	-	78 13.13 27.18 3.36 0.31	-	-	-	-	-	-	-	-	-	-	-	-	-	-	-	-	50 10.33 17.42 2.15 0.20
Westborough (town)	13,842 82.73	1,320	158 11.97 11.97 1.14	-	-	51 9.50 32.28 3.86 0.37	-	-	58 12.98 36.71 4.39 0.42	-	-	-	-	-	-	-	-	-	-	-	-	-	-	-	-	-
Worcester (city)	116,145 71.89	7,293	626 8.58 8.58 0.54	-	-	123 13.03 19.65 1.69 0.11	-	-	60 6.80 9.58 0.82 0.05	-	-	-	-	-	-	-	-	-	-	-	-	-	-	-	-	192 4.78 30.67 2.63 0.17
MICHIGAN	8,487,401 91.57	160,722	31,322 19.49 19.49 0.37	2,459	1,529 62.18 62.18 0.02	7,579 15.26 24.20 4.72 0.09	41 2.76 0.13 0.03 <0.01	173 11.74 0.55 0.11 <0.01	3,884 14.30 12.40 2.42 0.05	-	5,229 31.38 16.69 3.25 0.06	246 40.26 16.09 10.00 <0.01	666 86.61 43.56 27.08 0.01	250 5.00 0.80 0.16 <0.01	84 13.73 0.27 0.05 <0.01	2,441 24.67 7.79 1.52 0.03	7,530 38.74 24.04 4.69 0.09	137 5.49 0.44 0.09 <0.01	77 17.95 0.25 0.05 <0.01	250 5.74 0.80 0.16 <0.01	225 53.83 14.72 9.15 <0.01	112 34.04 0.36 0.07 <0.01	211 9.59 0.67 0.13 <0.01	363 23.15 1.16 0.23 <0.01	-	1,167 9.80 3.73 0.73 0.01
Allegan County	91,396 93.22	553	229 41.41 41.41 0.25	-	-	-	-	-	-	-	-	-	-	-	-	-	-	-	-	-	-	-	-	-	-	-
Bay County	98,294 95.00	536	106 19.78 19.78 0.11	-	-	-	-	-	-	-	-	-	-	-	-	-	-	-	-	-	-	-	-	-	-	-
Berrien County	141,013 92.88	1,578	402 25.48 25.48 0.29	-	-	120 26.55 29.85 7.60 0.09	-	-	-	-	127 42.05 31.59 8.05 0.09	-	-	-	-	-	61 17.23 15.17 3.87 0.04	-	-	-	-	-	-	-	-	-
Calhoun County	122,810 95.18	1,346	357 26.52 26.52 0.29	-	-	-	-	-	-	-	-	-	-	-	-	65 15.97 18.21 4.83 0.05	-	-	-	-	-	-	-	-	-	-
Cass County	45,973 95.79	303	57 18.81 18.81 0.12	-	-	-	-	-	-	-	-	-	-	-	-	-	-	7 5.19 12.28 2.31 0.02	-	-	-	-	-	-	-	-
Clinton County	57,876 96.01	336	140 41.67 41.67 0.24	-	-	-	-	-	-	-	-	-	-	-	-	-	-	-	-	-	-	-	-	-	-	-

Notes: Please refer to the User's Guide for an explanation of data; data is arranged alphabetically by state, then county, then city within each county; table includes counties with populations greater than 49,999 unless noted and cities with populations greater than 9,999 whose Asian and/or NHPI population rates are greater than the national average; (1) Native Hawaiian and other Pacific Islander; (2) excludes Taiwanese; (3) includes Chamorro; (4) county does not meet population threshold but is shown in order to allow inclusion of city

Place	Total population 5 years and over who speak English-only at home	Asian population 5 years and over	Asians 5 years and over who speak English-only at home	NHPI[1] population 5 years and over	NHPIs[1] 5 years and over who speak English-only at home	Asian Indian	Bangladeshi	Cambodian	Chinese[2]	Fijian	Filipino	Guamanian[3]	Hawaiian, Native	Hmong	Indonesian	Japanese	Korean	Laotian	Malaysian	Pakistani	Samoan	Sri Lankan	Taiwanese	Thai	Tongan	Vietnamese
Eaton County	92,353 95.06	1,132	178 15.72 15.72 0.19	-	-	58 17.96 32.58 5.12 0.06	-	-	-	-	-	-	-	-	-	-	-	-	-	-	-	-	-	-	-	0 0.00 0.00 0.00 0.00
Genesee County	386,259 95.47	2,926	914 31.24 31.24 0.24	-	-	288 26.94 31.51 9.84 0.07	-	-	57 15.36 6.24 1.95 0.01	-	147 35.85 16.08 5.02 0.04	-	-	-	-	-	235 54.91 25.71 8.03 0.06	-	-	-	-	-	-	-	-	-
Ingham County	234,888 89.72	9,395	1,561 16.62 16.62 0.66	-	-	399 20.75 25.56 4.25 0.17	-	-	206 12.27 13.20 2.19 0.09	-	253 42.52 16.21 2.69 0.11	-	-	15 2.82 0.96 0.16 0.01	-	152 29.46 9.74 1.62 0.06	371 22.94 23.77 3.95 0.16	-	-	-	-	-	-	-	-	37 3.01 2.37 0.39 0.02
East Lansing (city)	38,537 84.60	3,632	623 17.15 17.15 1.62	-	-	211 28.94 33.87 5.81 0.55	-	-	78 9.55 12.52 2.15 0.20	-	-	-	-	-	-	-	156 16.94 25.04 4.30 0.40	-	-	-	-	-	-	-	-	-
Meridian charter (township)	32,646 88.61	2,348	414 17.63 17.63 1.27	-	-	118 13.90 28.50 5.03 0.36	-	-	90 17.21 21.74 3.83 0.28	-	-	-	-	-	-	-	84 23.93 20.29 3.58 0.26	-	-	-	-	-	-	-	-	-
Okemos (cdp)	18,672 86.94	1,839	329 17.89 17.89 1.76	-	-	88 12.24 26.75 4.79 0.47	-	-	74 20.27 22.49 4.02 0.40	-	-	-	-	-	-	-	-	-	-	-	-	-	-	-	-	-
Ionia County	54,963 95.90	210	114 54.29 54.29 0.21	-	-	-	-	-	-	-	-	-	-	-	-	-	-	-	-	-	-	-	-	-	-	-
Isabella County	57,098 95.17	779	156 20.03 20.03 0.27	-	-	-	-	-	-	-	-	-	-	-	-	-	-	-	-	-	-	-	-	-	-	-
Jackson County	141,475 95.61	680	185 27.21 27.21 0.13	-	-	-	-	-	-	-	-	-	-	-	-	-	-	-	-	-	-	-	-	-	-	-
Kalamazoo County	208,262 93.30	4,090	1,168 28.56 28.56 0.56	-	-	322 26.39 27.57 7.87 0.15	-	-	147 17.73 12.59 3.59 0.07	-	-	-	-	-	-	-	310 48.29 26.54 7.58 0.15	-	-	-	-	-	-	-	-	-

Notes: Please refer to the User's Guide for an explanation of data; data is arranged alphabetically by state, then county, then city within each county; table includes counties with populations greater than 49,999 unless noted and cities with populations greater than 9,999 whose Asian and/or NHPI population rates are greater than the national average; (1) Native Hawaiian and other Pacific Islander; (2) excludes Taiwanese; (3) includes Chamorro; (4) county does not meet population threshold but is shown in order to allow inclusion of city

Place	Total population 5 years and over who speak English-only at home	Asian population 5 years and over	Asians 5 years and over who speak English-only at home	NHPI[1] population 5 years and over	NHPIs[1] 5 years and over who speak English-only at home	Asian Indian	Bangladeshi	Cambodian	Chinese[2]	Fijian	Filipino	Guamanian[3]	Hawaiian, Native	Hmong	Indonesian	Japanese	Korean	Laotian	Malaysian	Pakistani	Samoan	Sri Lankan	Taiwanese	Thai	Tongan	Vietnamese
Kent County	476,293 89.83	9,537	2,163 22.68 22.68 0.45	-	-	266 21.09 12.30 2.79 0.06	-	-	131 13.95 6.06 1.37 0.03	-	275 44.72 12.71 2.88 0.06	-	-	-	-	-	878 53.83 40.59 9.21 0.18	-	-	-	-	-	-	-	-	280 7.09 12.94 2.94 0.06
Kentwood (city)	36,506 87.27	2,238	299 13.36 13.36 0.82	-	-	-	-	-	-	-	-	-	-	-	-	-	101 27.30 33.78 4.51 0.28	-	-	-	-	-	-	-	-	93 8.50 31.10 4.16 0.25
Lenawee County	87,445 94.33	475	177 37.26 37.26 0.20	-	-	-	-	-	-	-	-	-	-	-	-	-	-	-	-	-	-	-	-	-	-	-
Livingston County	140,291 96.31	982	372 37.88 37.88 0.27	-	-	-	-	-	-	-	-	-	-	-	-	-	-	-	-	-	-	-	-	-	-	-
Macomb County	645,489 87.56	16,021	3,070 19.16 19.16 0.48	-	-	690 13.57 22.48 4.31 0.11	-	-	326 14.57 10.62 2.03 0.05	-	893 27.85 29.09 5.57 0.14	-	-	86 8.81 2.80 0.54 0.01	-	-	574 41.27 18.70 3.58 0.09	-	-	20 4.21 0.65 0.12 <0.01	-	-	-	-	-	122 9.30 3.97 0.76 0.02
Sterling Heights (city)	89,680 76.87	5,959	1,022 17.15 17.15 1.14	-	-	314 14.34 30.72 5.27 0.35	-	-	142 15.60 13.89 2.38 0.16	-	324 25.27 31.70 5.44 0.36	-	-	-	-	-	126 22.22 12.33 2.11 0.14	-	-	-	-	-	-	-	-	57 13.67 5.58 0.96 0.06
Marquette County	58,686 95.57	306	157 51.31 51.31 0.27	-	-	-	-	-	-	-	-	-	-	-	-	-	-	-	-	-	-	-	-	-	-	-
Midland County	74,250 95.75	1,068	325 30.43 30.43 0.44	-	-	63 20.26 19.38 5.90 0.08	-	-	93 25.41 28.62 8.71 0.13	-	-	-	-	-	-	-	-	-	-	-	-	-	-	-	-	-
Monroe County	130,864 96.02	850	263 30.94 30.94 0.20	-	-	-	-	-	-	-	-	-	-	-	-	-	-	-	-	-	-	-	-	-	-	-
Muskegon County	151,625 95.56	689	302 43.83 43.83 0.20	-	-	-	-	-	-	-	-	-	-	-	-	-	-	-	-	-	-	-	-	-	-	-

Notes: Please refer to the User's Guide for an explanation of data; data is arranged alphabetically by state, then county, then city within each county; table includes counties with populations greater than 49,999 unless noted and cities with populations greater than 9,999 whose Asian and/or NHPI population rates are greater than the national average; (1) Native Hawaiian and other Pacific Islander; (2) excludes Taiwanese; (3) includes Chamorro; (4) county does not meet population threshold but is shown in order to allow inclusion of city

Place	Total population 5 years and over who speak English-only at home	Asian population 5 years and over	Asians 5 years and over who speak English-only at home	NHPI[1] population 5 years and over	NHPIs[1] 5 years and over who speak English-only at home	Asian Indian	Bangladeshi	Cambodian	Chinese[2]	Fijian	Filipino	Guamanian[3]	Hawaiian, Native	Hmong	Indonesian	Japanese	Korean	Laotian	Malaysian	Pakistani	Samoan	Sri Lankan	Taiwanese	Thai	Tongan	Vietnamese
Oakland County	973,064 87.33	44,398	7,118 16.03 16.03 0.73	-	-	2,112 12.22 29.67 4.76 0.22	-	-	1,107 13.83 15.55 2.49 0.11	-	1,182 31.19 16.61 2.66 0.12	-	-	23 2.34 0.32 0.05 <0.01	-	603 15.67 8.47 1.36 0.06	1,164 25.48 16.35 2.62 0.12	-	-	97 11.01 1.36 0.22 0.01	-	-	65 5.44 0.91 0.15 0.01	-	-	168 10.69 2.36 0.38 0.02
Auburn Hills (city)	15,857 86.05	1,124	88 7.83 7.83 0.55	-	-	43 7.00 48.86 3.83 0.27	-	-	-	-	-	-	-	-	-	-	-	-	-	-	-	-	-	-	-	-
Bloomfield (township)	34,231 83.77	2,615	506 19.35 19.35 1.48	-	-	207 18.55 40.91 7.92 0.60	-	-	-	-	-	-	-	-	-	-	47 8.38 9.29 1.80 0.14	-	-	-	-	-	-	-	-	-
Farmington (city)	8,221 84.01	912	68 7.46 7.46 0.83	-	-	19 2.71 27.94 2.08 0.23	-	-	-	-	-	-	-	-	-	-	-	-	-	-	-	-	-	-	-	-
Farmington Hills (city)	62,994 81.46	5,250	693 13.20 13.20 1.10	-	-	303 9.75 43.72 5.77 0.48	-	-	125 15.61 18.04 2.38 0.20	-	141 38.63 20.35 2.69 0.22	-	-	-	-	-	-	-	-	-	-	-	-	-	-	-
Madison Heights (city)	24,265 83.23	1,490	202 13.56 13.56 0.83	-	-	-	-	-	66 13.69 32.67 4.43 0.27	-	-	-	-	-	-	-	-	-	-	-	-	-	-	-	-	-
Novi (city)	37,686 85.62	3,569	519 14.54 14.54 1.38	-	-	125 12.98 24.08 3.50 0.33	-	-	100 13.07 19.27 2.80 0.27	-	-	-	-	-	-	87 8.95 16.76 2.44 0.23	-	-	-	-	-	-	-	-	-	-
Rochester (city)	8,649 89.51	511	94 18.40 18.40 1.09	-	-	-	-	-	-	-	-	-	-	-	-	-	-	-	-	-	-	-	-	-	-	-
Rochester Hills (city)	55,355 85.95	4,163	659 15.83 15.83 1.19	-	-	229 13.35 34.75 5.50 0.41	-	-	104 11.39 15.78 2.50 0.19	-	-	-	-	-	-	-	90 26.24 13.66 2.16 0.16	-	-	-	-	-	-	-	-	-
Troy (city)	57,823 76.08	9,498	981 10.33 10.33 1.70	-	-	374 8.93 38.12 3.94 0.65	-	-	195 9.35 19.88 2.05 0.34	-	194 26.54 19.78 2.04 0.34	-	-	-	-	-	98 8.44 9.99 1.03 0.17	-	-	-	-	-	20 3.88 2.04 0.21 0.03	-	-	-

Notes: Please refer to the User's Guide for an explanation of data; data is arranged alphabetically by state, then county, then city within each county; table includes counties with populations greater than 49,999 unless noted and cities with populations greater than 9,999 whose Asian and/or NHPI population rates are greater than the national average; (1) Native Hawaiian and other Pacific Islander; (2) excludes Taiwanese; (3) includes Chamorro; (4) county does not meet population threshold but is shown in order to allow inclusion of city

Place	Total population 5 years and over who speak English-only at home	Asian population 5 years and over	Asians 5 years and over who speak English-only at home	NHPI[1] population 5 years and over	NHPIs[1] 5 years and over who speak English-only at home	Asian Indian	Bangladeshi	Cambodian	Chinese[2]	Fijian	Filipino	Guamanian[3]	Hawaiian, Native	Hmong	Indonesian	Japanese	Korean	Laotian	Malaysian	Pakistani	Samoan	Sri Lankan	Taiwanese	Thai	Tongan	Vietnamese
West Bloomfield (township)	45,767 75.52	4,597	711 15.47 15.47 1.55	-	-	236 15.23 33.19 5.13 0.52	-	-	80 13.77 11.25 1.74 0.17	-	184 48.55 25.88 4.00 0.40	-	-	-	-	20 1.73 2.81 0.44 0.04	137 28.13 19.27 2.98 0.30	-	-	-	-	-	-	-	-	-
Ottawa County	200,820 91.14	4,591	999 21.76 21.76 0.50	-	-	141 33.25 14.11 3.07 0.07	-	83 8.36 8.31 1.81 0.04	14 4.59 1.40 0.30 0.01	-	-	-	-	-	-	-	394 81.57 39.44 8.58 0.20	58 5.74 5.81 1.26 0.03	-	-	-	-	-	-	-	38 5.60 3.80 0.83 0.02
Holland (city)	25,159 77.46	1,133	213 18.80 18.80 0.85	-	-	-	-	-	-	-	-	-	-	-	-	-	-	-	-	-	-	-	-	-	-	-
Saginaw County	183,338 93.61	1,602	401 25.03 25.03 0.22	-	-	126 41.58 31.42 7.87 0.07	-	-	-	-	74 21.89 18.45 4.62 0.04	-	-	-	-	-	102 32.59 25.44 6.37 0.06	-	-	-	-	-	-	-	-	-
St. Clair County	146,860 95.92	389	135 34.70 34.70 0.09	-	-	-	-	-	-	-	-	-	-	-	-	-	-	-	-	-	-	-	-	-	-	-
St. Joseph County	53,534 92.42	276	91 32.97 32.97 0.17	-	-	-	-	-	-	-	-	-	-	-	-	-	-	-	-	-	-	-	-	-	-	-
Washtenaw County	262,763 86.78	18,643	3,549 19.04 19.04 1.35	-	-	1,076 24.32 30.32 5.77 0.41	-	-	765 13.49 21.56 4.10 0.29	-	424 44.82 11.95 2.27 0.16	-	-	-	-	238 15.24 6.71 1.28 0.09	721 20.82 20.32 3.87 0.27	-	-	12 3.18 0.34 0.06 <0.01	-	-	82 16.17 2.31 0.44 0.03	-	-	59 14.05 1.66 0.32 0.02
Ann Arbor (city)	86,565 79.92	12,537	2,345 18.70 18.70 2.71	-	-	764 24.83 32.58 6.09 0.88	-	-	522 13.11 22.26 4.16 0.60	-	309 58.41 13.18 2.46 0.36	-	-	-	-	145 12.53 6.18 1.16 0.17	409 17.34 17.44 3.26 0.47	-	-	-	-	-	64 14.51 2.73 0.51 0.07	-	-	-
Pittsfield charter (township)	22,292 79.91	2,575	432 16.78 16.78 1.94	-	-	126 21.25 29.17 4.89 0.57	-	-	103 14.11 23.84 4.00 0.46	-	-	-	-	-	-	-	92 16.91 21.30 3.57 0.41	-	-	-	-	-	-	-	-	-
Scio (township)	13,715 93.90	554	192 34.66 34.66 1.40	-	-	-	-	-	-	-	-	-	-	-	-	-	-	-	-	-	-	-	-	-	-	-

Notes: Please refer to the User's Guide for an explanation of data; data is arranged alphabetically by state, then county, then city within each county; table includes counties with populations greater than 49,999 unless noted and cities with populations greater than 9,999 whose Asian and/or NHPI population rates are greater than the national average; (1) Native Hawaiian and other Pacific Islander; (2) excludes Taiwanese; (3) includes Chamorro; (4) county does not meet population threshold but is shown in order to allow inclusion of city

Place	Total population 5 years and over who speak English-only at home	Asian population 5 years and over	Asians 5 years and over who speak English-only at home	NHPI[1] population 5 years and over	NHPIs[1] 5 years and over who speak English-only at home	Asian Indian	Bangladeshi	Cambodian	Chinese[2]	Fijian	Filipino	Guamanian[3]	Hawaiian, Native	Hmong	Indonesian	Japanese	Korean	Laotian	Malaysian	Pakistani	Samoan	Sri Lankan	Taiwanese	Thai	Tongan	Vietnamese
Wayne County	1,703,518 89.22	32,059	4,584 14.30 14.30 0.27	455	268 58.90 58.90 0.02	1,305 9.93 28.47 4.07 0.08	17 1.67 0.37 0.05 <0.01	-	558 12.26 12.17 1.74 0.03	-	900 22.15 19.63 2.81 0.05	-		100 6.33 2.18 0.31 0.01	-	346 34.43 7.55 1.08 0.02	757 45.33 16.51 2.36 0.04	-	-	62 3.29 1.35 0.19 <0.01	-	-	-	-	-	149 13.76 3.25 0.46 0.01
Brownstown (township)	19,218 90.72	861	46 5.34 5.34 0.24	-	-	-	-	-	-	-	-	-	-	-	-	-	-	-	-	-	-	-	-	-	-	-
Canton (township)	60,314 86.52	5,802	650 11.20 11.20 1.08	-	-	279 8.82 42.92 4.81 0.46	-	-	78 7.51 12.00 1.34 0.13	-	174 29.10 26.77 3.00 0.29	-	-	-	-	-	53 19.78 8.15 0.91 0.09	-	-	-	-	-	-	-	-	-
Hamtramck (city)	9,680 45.57	2,131	81 3.80 3.80 0.84	-	-	60 6.05 74.07 2.82 0.62	7 1.06 8.64 0.33 0.07	-	-	-	-	-	-	-	-	-	-	-	-	-	-	-	-	-	-	-
Inkster (city)	25,522 92.13	1,010	53 5.25 5.25 0.21	-	-	5 0.75 9.43 0.50 0.02	-	-	-	-	-	-	-	-	-	-	-	-	-	-	-	-	-	-	-	-
Northville (township)	17,686 88.25	853	139 16.30 16.30 0.79	-	-	96 25.13 69.06 11.25 0.54	-	-	-	-	-	-	-	-	-	-	-	-	-	-	-	-	-	-	-	-
MINNESOTA	4,201,503 91.51	125,708	22,211 17.67 17.67 0.53	1,665	981 58.92 58.92 0.02	4,142 27.95 18.65 3.29 0.10	-	392 8.24 1.76 0.31 0.01	1,859 13.76 8.37 1.48 0.04	-	2,079 36.76 9.36 1.65 0.05	202 48.21 20.59 12.13 <0.01	374 67.03 38.12 22.46 0.01	1,240 3.30 5.58 0.99 0.03	-	1,624 40.65 7.31 1.29 0.04	7,643 64.63 34.41 6.08 0.18	554 6.81 2.49 0.44 0.01	-	55 5.56 0.25 0.04 <0.01	-	-	76 17.08 0.34 0.06 <0.01	178 20.27 0.80 0.14 <0.01	-	1,274 7.55 5.74 1.01 0.03
Anoka County	260,104 94.34	4,460	1,228 27.53 27.53 0.47	-	-	224 27.48 18.24 5.02 0.09	-	-	105 26.99 8.55 2.35 0.04	-	165 45.83 13.44 3.70 0.06	-	-	12 2.53 0.98 0.27 <0.01	-	-	455 69.25 37.05 10.20 0.17	-	-	-	-	-	-	-	-	51 6.34 4.15 1.14 0.02
Columbia Heights (city)	15,526 88.52	616	84 13.64 13.64 0.54	-	-	-	-	-	-	-	-	-	-	-	-	-	-	-	-	-	-	-	-	-	-	-
Blue Earth County	50,039 94.77	867	176 20.30 20.30 0.35	-	-	-	-	-	-	-	-	-	-	-	-	-	-	-	-	-	-	-	-	-	-	-

Notes: Please refer to the User's Guide for an explanation of data; data is arranged alphabetically by state, then county, then city within each county; table includes counties with populations greater than 49,999 unless noted and cities with populations greater than 9,999 whose Asian and/or NHPI population rates are greater than the national average; (1) Native Hawaiian and other Pacific Islander; (2) excludes Taiwanese; (3) includes Chamorro; (4) county does not meet population threshold but is shown in order to allow inclusion of city

Place	Total population 5 years and over who speak English-only at home	Asian population 5 years and over	Asians 5 years and over who speak English-only at home	NHPI[1] population 5 years and over	NHPIs[1] 5 years and over who speak English-only at home	Asian Indian	Bangladeshi	Cambodian	Chinese[2]	Fijian	Filipino	Guamanian[3]	Hawaiian, Native	Hmong	Indonesian	Japanese	Korean	Laotian	Malaysian	Pakistani	Samoan	Sri Lankan	Taiwanese	Thai	Tongan	Vietnamese
Carver County	60,072 93.79	993	341 34.34 34.34 0.57	-	-	-	-	-	-	-	-	-	-	-	-	-	-	-	-	-	-	-	-	-	-	-
Clay County	44,383 92.31	364	120 32.97 32.97 0.27	-	-	-	-	-	-	-	-	-	-	-	-	-	-	-	-	-	-	-	-	-	-	-
Crow Wing County	50,178 96.86	200	98 49.00 49.00 0.20	-	-	-	-	-	-	-	-	-	-	-	-	-	-	-	-	-	-	-	-	-	-	-
Dakota County	303,539 92.41	8,345	1,858 22.26 22.26 0.61	-	-	382 25.76 20.56 4.58 0.13	-	20 4.91 1.08 0.24 0.01	152 12.23 8.18 1.82 0.05	-	204 27.20 10.98 2.44 0.07	-	-	-	-	-	690 67.12 37.14 8.27 0.23	68 10.45 3.66 0.81 0.02	-	-	-	-	-	-	-	78 4.85 4.20 0.93 0.03
Eagan (city)	52,529 89.84	2,801	434 15.49 15.49 0.83	-	-	58 10.25 13.36 2.07 0.11	-	-	97 20.73 22.35 3.46 0.18	-	-	-	-	-	-	-	-	-	-	-	-	-	-	-	-	5 0.94 1.15 0.18 0.01
Hennepin County	909,793 87.16	48,554	8,889 18.31 18.31 0.98	553	242 43.76 43.76 0.03	2,038 28.27 22.93 4.20 0.22	-	113 6.74 1.27 0.23 0.01	803 14.62 9.03 1.65 0.09	-	753 40.68 8.47 1.55 0.08	-	-	444 3.80 4.99 0.91 0.05	-	676 42.78 7.60 1.39 0.07	2,654 60.15 29.86 5.47 0.29	260 6.52 2.92 0.54 0.03	-	21 5.68 0.24 0.04 <0.01	-	-	-	-	-	594 7.82 6.68 1.22 0.07
Bloomington (city)	72,755 90.14	3,918	750 19.14 19.14 1.03	-	-	104 21.31 13.87 2.65 0.14	-	22 4.82 2.93 0.56 0.03	41 5.53 5.47 1.05 0.06	-	-	-	-	-	-	-	261 56.13 34.80 6.66 0.36	-	-	-	-	-	-	-	-	30 2.71 4.00 0.77 0.04
Brooklyn Center (city)	22,830 84.10	2,376	232 9.76 9.76 1.02	-	-	-	-	-	-	-	-	-	-	61 4.67 26.29 2.57 0.27	-	-	-	8 2.74 3.45 0.34 0.04	-	-	-	-	-	-	-	-
Brooklyn Park (city)	52,439 84.64	5,597	894 15.97 15.97 1.70	-	-	296 36.82 33.11 5.29 0.56	-	-	-	-	-	-	-	75 7.57 8.39 1.34 0.14	-	-	-	70 5.34 7.83 1.25 0.13	-	-	-	-	-	-	-	99 7.63 11.07 1.77 0.19
Eden Prairie (city)	45,163 89.32	2,506	477 19.03 19.03 1.06	-	-	121 21.57 25.37 4.83 0.27	-	-	64 11.74 13.42 2.55 0.14	-	-	-	-	-	-	-	-	-	-	-	-	-	-	-	-	7 1.46 1.47 0.28 0.02

Notes: Please refer to the User's Guide for an explanation of data; data is arranged alphabetically by state, then county, then city within each county; table includes counties with populations greater than 49,999 unless noted and cities with populations greater than 9,999 whose Asian and/or NHPI population rates are greater than the national average; (1) Native Hawaiian and other Pacific Islander; (2) excludes Taiwanese; (3) includes Chamorro; (4) county does not meet population threshold but is shown in order to allow inclusion of city

Place	Total population 5 years and over who speak English-only at home	Asian population 5 years and over	Asians 5 years and over who speak English-only at home	NHPI[1] population 5 years and over	NHPIs[1] 5 years and over who speak English-only at home	Asian Indian	Bangladeshi	Cambodian	Chinese[2]	Fijian	Filipino	Guamanian[3]	Hawaiian, Native	Hmong	Indonesian	Japanese	Korean	Laotian	Malaysian	Pakistani	Samoan	Sri Lankan	Taiwanese	Thai	Tongan	Vietnamese
Hopkins (city)	13,605 84.10	921	161 17.48 17.48 1.18	-	-	79 18.68 49.07 8.58 0.58	-	-	-	-	-	-	-	-	-	-	-	-	-	-	-	-	-	-	-	-
Minneapolis (city)	288,932 80.74	21,822	3,284 15.05 15.05 1.14	-	-	780 39.14 23.75 3.57 0.27	-	43 8.83 1.31 0.20 0.01	295 15.20 8.98 1.35 0.10	-	265 37.11 8.07 1.21 0.09	-	-	291 3.26 8.86 1.33 0.10	-	239 32.17 7.28 1.10 0.08	846 54.13 25.76 3.88 0.29	93 6.44 2.83 0.43 0.03	-	-	-	-	-	-	-	257 9.69 7.83 1.18 0.09
Plymouth (city)	55,753 90.82	2,252	472 20.96 20.96 0.85	-	-	180 21.66 38.14 7.99 0.32	-	-	101 26.86 21.40 4.48 0.18	-	-	-	-	-	-	-	101 28.77 21.40 4.48 0.18	-	-	-	-	-	-	-	-	-
Richfield (city)	27,906 86.47	1,639	279 17.02 17.02 1.00	-	-	-	-	-	-	-	-	-	-	-	-	-	-	-	-	-	-	-	-	-	-	51 12.56 18.28 3.11 0.18
Nobles County[4]	16,428 84.64	698	100 14.33 14.33 0.61	-	-	-	-	-	-	-	-	-	-	-	-	-	-	17 4.67 17.00 2.44 0.10	-	-	-	-	-	-	-	-
Worthington (city)	7,841 75.03	636	88 13.84 13.84 1.12	-	-	-	-	-	-	-	-	-	-	-	-	-	-	17 5.09 19.32 2.67 0.22	-	-	-	-	-	-	-	-
Olmsted County	104,163 90.22	4,745	842 17.74 17.74 0.81	-	-	246 29.67 29.22 5.18 0.24	-	13 1.98 1.54 0.27 0.01	79 14.71 9.38 1.66 0.08	-	-	-	-	0 0.00 0.00 0.00 0.00	-	85 22.02 10.10 1.79 0.08	278 58.40 33.02 5.86 0.27	39 10.16 4.63 0.82 0.04	-	-	-	-	-	-	-	40 5.87 4.75 0.84 0.04
Rochester (city)	69,332 87.77	4,267	636 14.91 14.91 0.92	-	-	213 27.13 33.49 4.99 0.31	-	4 0.78 0.63 0.09 0.01	63 12.63 9.91 1.48 0.09	-	-	-	-	0 0.00 0.00 0.00 0.00	-	-	194 52.29 30.50 4.55 0.28	39 10.21 6.13 0.91 0.06	-	-	-	-	-	-	-	28 4.31 4.40 0.66 0.04
Otter Tail County	51,138 94.74	145	50 34.48 34.48 0.10	-	-	-	-	-	-	-	-	-	-	-	-	-	-	-	-	-	-	-	-	-	-	-
Ramsey County	400,823 84.20	38,964	3,726 9.56 9.56 0.93	-	-	509 23.91 13.66 1.31 0.13	-	112 10.81 3.01 0.29 0.03	321 10.22 8.62 0.82 0.08	-	286 33.61 7.68 0.73 0.07	-	-	724 3.13 19.43 1.86 0.18	-	253 48.47 6.79 0.65 0.06	1,114 62.69 29.90 2.86 0.28	42 5.04 1.13 0.11 0.01	-	-	-	-	-	-	-	179 5.42 4.80 0.46 0.04

Notes: Please refer to the User's Guide for an explanation of data; data is arranged alphabetically by state, then county, then city within each county; table includes counties with populations greater than 49,999 unless noted and cities with populations greater than 9,999 whose Asian and/or NHPI population rates are greater than the national average; (1) Native Hawaiian and other Pacific Islander; (2) excludes Taiwanese; (3) includes Chamorro; (4) county does not meet population threshold but is shown in order to allow inclusion of city

Place	Total population 5 years and over who speak English-only at home	Asian population 5 years and over	Asians 5 years and over who speak English-only at home	NHPI[1] population 5 years and over	NHPIs[1] 5 years and over who speak English-only at home	Asian Indian	Bangladeshi	Cambodian	Chinese[2]	Fijian	Filipino	Guamanian[3]	Hawaiian, Native	Hmong	Indonesian	Japanese	Korean	Laotian	Malaysian	Pakistani	Samoan	Sri Lankan	Taiwanese	Thai	Tongan	Vietnamese
Maplewood (city)	29,981	1,238	194	-	-	-	-	-	11	-	-	-	-	16	-	-	-	-	-	-	-	-	-	-	-	-
	91.74		15.67						4.03					4.56												
									5.67					8.25												
			15.67						0.89					1.29												
			0.65						0.04					0.05												
New Brighton (city)	19,016	855	144	-	-	-	-	-	-	-	-	-	-	-	-	-	-	-	-	-	-	-	-	-	-	-
	90.92		16.84																							
			16.84																							
			0.76																							
Roseville (city)	29,119	1,474	202	-	-	-	-	-	35	-	-	-	-	-	-	-	-	-	-	-	-	-	-	-	-	-
	90.61		13.70						5.80																	
									17.33																	
			13.70						2.37																	
			0.69						0.12																	
St. Paul (city)	207,592	31,090	2,352	-	-	240	-	97	195	-	175	-	-	674	-	-	529	42	-	-	-	-	-	-	-	110
	78.18		7.57			31.58		11.25	21.48		34.79			3.05			64.36	5.52								4.66
						10.20		4.12	8.29		7.44			28.66			22.49	1.79								4.68
			7.57			0.77		0.31	0.63		0.56			2.17			1.70	0.14								0.35
			1.13			0.12		0.05	0.09		0.08			0.32			0.25	0.02								0.05
Vadnais Heights (city)	11,411	477	69	-	-	-	-	-	-	-	-	-	-	-	-	-	-	-	-	-	-	-	-	-	-	-
	93.74		14.47																							
			14.47																							
			0.60																							
Rice County	48,188	862	245	-	-	-	-	-	-	-	-	-	-	-	-	-	-	-	-	-	-	-	-	-	-	-
	90.57		28.42																							
			28.42																							
			0.51																							
St. Louis County	180,649	1,345	490	-	-	-	-	-	-	-	-	-	-	-	-	-	251	-	-	-	-	-	-	-	-	-
	95.03		36.43														82.84									
																	51.22									
			36.43														18.66									
			0.27														0.14									
Scott County	75,736	1,662	358	-	-	-	-	42	-	-	-	-	-	-	-	-	-	-	-	-	-	-	-	-	-	63
	93.14		21.54					12.92																		19.87
								11.73																		17.60
			21.54					2.53																		3.79
			0.47					0.06																		0.08
Savage (city)	17,087	996	177	-	-	-	-	-	-	-	-	-	-	-	-	-	-	-	-	-	-	-	-	-	-	-
	91.51		17.77																							
			17.77																							
			1.04																							
Sherburne County	56,558	352	150	-	-	-	-	-	-	-	-	-	-	-	-	-	-	-	-	-	-	-	-	-	-	-
	95.74		42.61																							
			42.61																							
			0.27																							

Notes: Please refer to the User's Guide for an explanation of data; data is arranged alphabetically by state, then county, then city within each county; table includes counties with populations greater than 49,999 unless noted and cities with populations greater than 9,999 whose Asian and/or NHPI population rates are greater than the national average; (1) Native Hawaiian and other Pacific Islander; (2) excludes Taiwanese; (3) includes Chamorro; (4) county does not meet population threshold but is shown in order to allow inclusion of city

Place	Total population 5 years and over who speak English-only at home	Asian population 5 years and over	Asians 5 years and over who speak English-only at home	NHPI[1] population 5 years and over	NHPIs[1] 5 years and over who speak English-only at home	Asian Indian	Bangladeshi	Cambodian	Chinese[2]	Fijian	Filipino	Guamanian[3]	Hawaiian, Native	Hmong	Indonesian	Japanese	Korean	Laotian	Malaysian	Pakistani	Samoan	Sri Lankan	Taiwanese	Thai	Tongan	Vietnamese
Stearns County	116,753 93.72	1,675	289 17.25 17.25 0.25	-	-	-	-	-	-	-	-	-	-	-	-	-	-	-	-	-	-	-	-	-	-	8 1.40 2.77 0.48 0.01
Washington County	175,194 94.31	3,811	769 20.18 20.18 0.44	-	-	119 24.64 15.47 3.12 0.07	-	-	122 19.74 15.86 3.20 0.07	-	-	-	-	8 1.27 1.04 0.21 <0.01	-	-	280 47.78 36.41 7.35 0.16	-	-	-	-	-	-	-	-	35 7.80 4.55 0.92 0.02
Woodbury (city)	38,045 90.55	2,133	342 16.03 16.03 0.90	-	-	61 17.18 17.84 2.86 0.16	-	-	69 20.35 20.18 3.23 0.18	-	-	-	-	8 2.61 2.34 0.38 0.02	-	-	-	-	-	-	-	-	-	-	-	-
Wright County	79,842 96.80	181	139 76.80 76.80 0.17	-	-	-	-	-	-	-	-	-	-	-	-	-	-	-	-	-	-	-	-	-	-	-
MISSISSIPPI	2,545,931 96.38	16,542	3,095 18.71 18.71 0.12	629	496 78.86 78.86 0.02	625 20.12 20.19 3.78 0.02	-	-	419 16.86 13.54 2.53 0.02	-	788 31.88 25.46 4.76 0.03	-	-	-	-	177 32.90 5.72 1.07 0.01	379 29.29 12.25 2.29 0.01	-	-	-	-	-	-	-	-	310 6.29 10.02 1.87 0.01
DeSoto County	95,270 96.36	632	207 32.75 32.75 0.22	-	-	-	-	-	-	-	-	-	-	-	-	-	-	-	-	-	-	-	-	-	-	-
Forrest County	65,069 95.92	584	96 16.44 16.44 0.15	-	-	-	-	-	-	-	-	-	-	-	-	-	-	-	-	-	-	-	-	-	-	-
Harrison County	164,142 93.33	4,583	646 14.10 14.10 0.39	-	-	-	-	-	-	-	253 33.96 39.16 5.52 0.15	-	-	-	-	-	-	-	-	-	-	-	-	-	-	34 1.33 5.26 0.74 0.02
Biloxi (city)	42,224 89.89	2,231	261 11.70 11.70 0.62	-	-	-	-	-	-	-	123 32.54 47.13 5.51 0.29	-	-	-	-	-	-	-	-	-	-	-	-	-	-	11 0.81 4.21 0.49 0.03
Hinds County	224,324 96.54	1,236	293 23.71 23.71 0.13	-	-	68 11.97 23.21 5.50 0.03	-	-	-	-	-	-	-	-	-	-	-	-	-	-	-	-	-	-	-	-

Notes: Please refer to the User's Guide for an explanation of data; data is arranged alphabetically by state, then county, then city within each county; table includes counties with populations greater than 49,999 unless noted and cities with populations greater than 9,999 whose Asian and/or NHPI population rates are greater than the national average; (1) Native Hawaiian and other Pacific Islander; (2) excludes Taiwanese; (3) includes Chamorro; (4) county does not meet population threshold but is shown in order to allow inclusion of city

Place	Total population 5 years and over who speak English-only at home	Asian population 5 years and over	Asians 5 years and over who speak English-only at home	NHPI[1] population 5 years and over	NHPIs[1] 5 years and over who speak English-only at home	Asian Indian	Bangladeshi	Cambodian	Chinese[2]	Fijian	Filipino	Guamanian[3]	Hawaiian, Native	Hmong	Indonesian	Japanese	Korean	Laotian	Malaysian	Pakistani	Samoan	Sri Lankan	Taiwanese	Thai	Tongan	Vietnamese
Jackson County	115,957	1,875	391	-	-	-	-	-	-	-	-	-	-	-	-	-	-	-	-	-	-	-	-	-	-	165
	94.90		20.85																							16.34
																										42.20
			20.85																							8.80
			0.34																							0.14
Madison County	66,047	570	77	-	-	-	-	-	-	-	-	-	-	-	-	-	-	-	-	-	-	-	-	-	-	-
	95.92		13.51																							
			13.51																							
			0.12																							
Oktibbeha County[4]	38,218	1,006	140	-	-	-	-	-	-	-	-	-	-	-	-	-	-	-	-	-	-	-	-	-	-	-
	94.71		13.92																							
			13.92																							
			0.37																							
Starkville (city)	19,319	733	51	-	-	-	-	-	-	-	-	-	-	-	-	-	-	-	-	-	-	-	-	-	-	-
	93.29		6.96																							
			6.96																							
			0.26																							
Rankin County	103,357	510	52	-	-	-	-	-	-	-	-	-	-	-	-	-	-	-	-	-	-	-	-	-	-	-
	96.36		10.20																							
			10.20																							
			0.05																							
MISSOURI	4,961,741	55,928	12,766	2,834	1,758	2,446	-	74	1,657	-	2,312	368	587	-	-	1,477	2,269	44	-	133	466	-	76	392	-	902
	94.94		22.83		62.03	22.45		9.15	14.33		34.14	64.11	87.61			44.70	37.37	6.64		13.87	52.18		8.15	29.50		9.31
						19.16		0.58	12.98		18.11	20.93	33.39			11.57	17.77	0.34		1.04	26.51		0.60	3.07		7.07
			22.83		62.03	4.37		0.13	2.96		4.13	12.99	20.71			2.64	4.06	0.08		0.24	16.44		0.14	0.70		1.61
			0.26		0.04	0.05		<0.01	0.03		0.05	0.01	0.01			0.03	0.05	<0.01		<0.01	0.01		<0.01	0.01		0.02
Boone County	118,117	3,555	749	-	-	189	-	-	123	-	-	-	-	-	-	-	148	-	-	-	-	-	-	-	-	-
	92.90		21.07			25.51			10.95								32.39									
						25.23			16.42								19.76									
			21.07			5.32			3.46								4.16									
			0.63			0.16			0.10								0.13									
Columbia (city)	72,450	3,304	676	-	-	189	-	-	116	-	-	-	-	-	-	-	108	-	-	-	-	-	-	-	-	-
	90.72		20.46			26.21			10.81								27.55									
						27.96			17.16								15.98									
			20.46			5.72			3.51								3.27									
			0.93			0.26			0.16								0.15									
Cape Girardeau County	62,540	446	157	-	-	-	-	-	-	-	-	-	-	-	-	-	-	-	-	-	-	-	-	-	-	-
	96.69		35.20																							
			35.20																							
			0.25																							
Cass County	73,604	322	90	-	-	-	-	-	-	-	-	-	-	-	-	-	-	-	-	-	-	-	-	-	-	-
	96.80		27.95																							
			27.95																							
			0.12																							

Notes: Please refer to the User's Guide for an explanation of data; data is arranged alphabetically by state, then county, then city within each county; table includes counties with populations greater than 49,999 unless noted and cities with populations greater than 9,999 whose Asian and/or NHPI population rates are greater than the national average; (1) Native Hawaiian and other Pacific Islander; (2) excludes Taiwanese; (3) includes Chamorro; (4) county does not meet population threshold but is shown in order to allow inclusion of city

Place	Total population 5 years and over who speak English-only at home	Asian population 5 years and over	Asians 5 years and over who speak English-only at home	NHPI[1] population 5 years and over	NHPIs[1] 5 years and over who speak English-only at home	Asian Indian	Bangladeshi	Cambodian	Chinese[2]	Fijian	Filipino	Guamanian[3]	Hawaiian, Native	Hmong	Indonesian	Japanese	Korean	Laotian	Malaysian	Pakistani	Samoan	Sri Lankan	Taiwanese	Thai	Tongan	Vietnamese
Clay County	161,928 94.82	2,030	443 21.82 21.82 0.27	-	-	97 25.59 21.90 4.78 0.06	-	-	-	-	-	-	-	-	-	-	-	-	-	-	-	-	-	-	-	23 3.83 5.19 1.13 0.01
Cole County	63,611 95.45	599	152 25.38 25.38 0.24	-	-	-	-	-	-	-	-	-	-	-	-	-	-	-	-	-	-	-	-	-	-	-
Franklin County	85,120 97.44	316	127 40.19 40.19 0.15	-	-	-	-	-	-	-	-	-	-	-	-	-	-	-	-	-	-	-	-	-	-	-
Greene County	216,725 96.01	2,053	474 23.09 23.09 0.22	-	-	-	-	-	29 8.98 6.12 1.41 0.01	-	-	-	-	-	-	-	113 32.47 23.84 5.50 0.05	-	-	-	-	-	-	-	-	25 6.53 5.27 1.22 0.01
Jackson County	562,686 92.36	8,021	1,641 20.46 20.46 0.29	876	482 55.02 55.02 0.09	99 9.96 6.03 1.23 0.02	-	-	210 18.18 12.80 2.62 0.04	-	372 31.10 22.67 4.64 0.07	-	-	-	-	175 43.42 10.66 2.18 0.03	240 44.12 14.63 2.99 0.04	-	-	-	195 45.03 40.46 22.26 0.03	-	-	-	-	258 9.84 15.72 3.22 0.05
Independence (city)	100,518 95.05	924	290 31.39 31.39 0.29	372	148 39.78 39.78 0.15	-	-	-	-	-	-	-	-	-	-	-	-	-	-	-	-	-	-	-	-	-
Jasper County	92,051 94.77	568	104 18.31 18.31 0.11	-	-	-	-	-	-	-	-	-	-	-	-	-	-	-	-	-	-	-	-	-	-	-
Jefferson County	178,446 97.08	680	238 35.00 35.00 0.13	-	-	-	-	-	-	-	-	-	-	-	-	-	-	-	-	-	-	-	-	-	-	-
Newton County	47,221 96.40	167	53 31.74 31.74 0.11	-	-	-	-	-	-	-	-	-	-	-	-	-	-	-	-	-	-	-	-	-	-	-
Phelps County[4]	35,416 94.34	796	95 11.93 11.93 0.27	-	-	24 7.72 25.26 3.02 0.07	-	-	-	-	-	-	-	-	-	-	-	-	-	-	-	-	-	-	-	-

Notes: Please refer to the User's Guide for an explanation of data; data is arranged alphabetically by state, then county, then city within each county; table includes counties with populations greater than 49,999 unless noted and cities with populations greater than 9,999 whose Asian and/or NHPI population rates are greater than the national average; (1) Native Hawaiian and other Pacific Islander; (2) excludes Taiwanese; (3) includes Chamorro; (4) county does not meet population threshold but is shown in order to allow inclusion of city

Place	Total population 5 years and over who speak English-only at home	Asian population 5 years and over	Asians 5 years and over who speak English-only at home	NHPI[1] population 5 years and over	NHPIs[1] 5 years and over who speak English-only at home	Asian Indian	Bangladeshi	Cambodian	Chinese[2]	Fijian	Filipino	Guamanian[3]	Hawaiian, Native	Hmong	Indonesian	Japanese	Korean	Laotian	Malaysian	Pakistani	Samoan	Sri Lankan	Taiwanese	Thai	Tongan	Vietnamese
Rolla (city)	13,975 89.70	650	55 8.46 8.46 0.39	-	-	-	-	-	-	-	-	-	-	-	-	-	-	-	-	-	-	-	-	-	-	-
Platte County	64,895 94.44	1,010	179 17.72 17.72 0.28	-	-	-	-	-	-	-	-	-	-	-	-	-	-	-	-	-	-	-	-	-	-	-
St. Charles County	251,800 96.01	2,140	752 35.14 35.14 0.30	-	-	95 17.40 12.63 4.44 0.04	-	-	61 19.06 8.11 2.85 0.02	-	149 39.21 19.81 6.96 0.06	-	-	-	-	-	-	-	-	-	-	-	-	-	-	-
Saint Louis Independent City	296,924 91.43	6,649	1,320 19.85 19.85 0.44	-	-	270 36.99 20.45 4.06 0.09	-	-	255 23.99 19.32 3.84 0.09	-	165 33.00 12.50 2.48 0.06	-	-	-	-	-	-	-	-	-	-	-	-	-	-	243 8.11 18.41 3.65 0.08
St. Louis County	891,645 93.62	19,808	4,112 20.76 20.76 0.46	371	237 63.88 63.88 0.03	1,146 22.20 27.87 5.79 0.13	-	-	611 11.23 14.86 3.08 0.07	-	601 31.82 14.62 3.03 0.07	-	-	-	-	419 36.40 10.19 2.12 0.05	905 38.45 22.01 4.57 0.10	-	-	43 8.13 1.05 0.22 <0.01	-	-	41 6.65 1.00 0.21 <0.01	36 9.52 0.88 0.18 <0.01	-	89 6.64 2.16 0.45 0.01
Chesterfield (city)	39,897 90.01	2,272	315 13.86 13.86 0.79	-	-	109 17.96 34.60 4.80 0.27	-	-	41 5.48 13.02 1.80 0.10	-	-	-	-	-	-	-	-	-	-	-	-	-	-	-	-	-
Clayton (city)	10,851 88.71	748	152 20.32 20.32 1.40	-	-	-	-	-	-	-	-	-	-	-	-	-	-	-	-	-	-	-	-	-	-	-
Creve Coeur (city)	13,557 87.40	835	117 14.01 14.01 0.86	-	-	-	-	-	-	-	-	-	-	-	-	-	-	-	-	-	-	-	-	-	-	-
Manchester (city)	15,846 89.76	817	194 23.75 23.75 1.22	-	-	-	-	-	-	-	-	-	-	-	-	-	-	-	-	-	-	-	-	-	-	-
Maryland Heights (city)	21,510 87.99	1,688	191 11.32 11.32 0.89	-	-	73 11.16 38.22 4.32 0.34	-	-	55 11.48 28.80 3.26 0.26	-	-	-	-	-	-	-	-	-	-	-	-	-	-	-	-	-

Notes: Please refer to the User's Guide for an explanation of data; data is arranged alphabetically by state, then county, then city within each county; table includes counties with populations greater than 49,999 unless noted and cities with populations greater than 9,999 whose Asian and/or NHPI population rates are greater than the national average; (1) Native Hawaiian and other Pacific Islander; (2) excludes Taiwanese; (3) includes Chamorro; (4) county does not meet population threshold but is shown in order to allow inclusion of city

Place	Total population 5 years and over who speak English-only at home	Asian population 5 years and over	Asians 5 years and over who speak English-only at home	NHPI[1] population 5 years and over	NHPIs[1] 5 years and over who speak English-only at home	Asian Indian	Bangladeshi	Cambodian	Chinese[2]	Fijian	Filipino	Guamanian[3]	Hawaiian, Native	Hmong	Indonesian	Japanese	Korean	Laotian	Malaysian	Pakistani	Samoan	Sri Lankan	Taiwanese	Thai	Tongan	Vietnamese
	8,860	821	169	-	-	64	-	-	-	-	-	-	-	-	-	-	-	-	-	-	-	-	-	-	-	-
	84.86		20.58			16.84																				
Town and Country (city)						37.87																				
			20.58			7.80																				
			1.91			0.72																				
	803,031	4,111	2,058	402	290	202	-	-	146	-	375	-	215	-	-	489	523	-	-	-	-	-	-	-	-	-
	94.77		50.06		72.14	47.31			26.59		49.73		89.21			58.15	64.41									
MONTANA						9.82			7.09		18.22		74.14			23.76	25.41									
			50.06		72.14	4.91			3.55		9.12		53.48			11.89	12.72									
			0.26		0.04	0.03			0.02		0.05		0.03			0.06	0.07									
	71,193	486	207	-	-	-	-	-	-	-	-	-	-	-	-	-	-	-	-	-	-	-	-	-	-	-
	94.92		42.59																							
Cascade County																										
			42.59																							
			0.29																							
	67,603	225	129	-	-	-	-	-	-	-	-	-	-	-	-	-	-	-	-	-	-	-	-	-	-	-
	96.52		57.33																							
Flathead County																										
			57.33																							
			0.19																							
	60,700	662	311	-	-	-	-	-	-	-	-	-	-	-	-	-	-	-	-	-	-	-	-	-	-	-
	94.98		46.98																							
Gallatin County																										
			46.98																							
			0.51																							
	86,082	838	285	-	-	-	-	-	-	-	-	-	-	-	-	-	-	-	-	-	-	-	-	-	-	-
	95.16		34.01																							
Missoula County																										
			34.01																							
			0.33																							
	115,107	637	409	-	-	-	-	-	-	-	-	-	-	-	-	-	-	-	-	-	-	-	-	-	-	-
	95.20		64.21																							
Yellowstone County																										
			64.21																							
			0.36																							
	1,469,046	19,534	4,210	606	299	608	-	-	379	-	727	-	-	-	-	610	1,059	50	-	-	-	-	-	166	-	319
	92.12		21.55		49.34	20.30			14.74		37.13					45.35	52.50	6.57						36.01		5.26
NEBRASKA						14.44			9.00		17.27					14.49	25.15	1.19						3.94		7.58
			21.55		49.34	3.11			1.94		3.72					3.12	5.42	0.26						0.85		1.63
			0.29		0.02	0.04			0.03		0.05					0.04	0.07	<0.01						0.01		0.02
	388,742	7,347	1,786	-	-	419	-	-	189	-	313	-	-	-	-	274	381	-	-	-	-	-	-	-	-	100
	90.50		24.31			21.94			15.06		36.95					41.02	51.91									8.52
Douglas County						23.46			10.58		17.53					15.34	21.33									5.60
			24.31			5.70			2.57		4.26					3.73	5.19									1.36
			0.46			0.11			0.05		0.08					0.07	0.10									0.03
	42,738	477	58	-	-	-	-	-	-	-	-	-	-	-	-	-	-	-	-	-	-	-	-	-	-	-
	86.41		12.16																							
Hall County																										
			12.16																							
			0.14																							

Notes: Please refer to the User's Guide for an explanation of data; data is arranged alphabetically by state, then county, then city within each county; table includes counties with populations greater than 49,999 unless noted and cities with populations greater than 9,999 whose Asian and/or NHPI population rates are greater than the national average; (1) Native Hawaiian and other Pacific Islander; (2) excludes Taiwanese; (3) includes Chamorro; (4) county does not meet population threshold but is shown in order to allow inclusion of city

Place	Total population 5 years and over who speak English-only at home	Asian population 5 years and over	Asians 5 years and over who speak English-only at home	NHPI[1] population 5 years and over	NHPIs[1] 5 years and over who speak English-only at home	Asian Indian	Bangladeshi	Cambodian	Chinese[2]	Fijian	Filipino	Guamanian[3]	Hawaiian, Native	Hmong	Indonesian	Japanese	Korean	Laotian	Malaysian	Pakistani	Samoan	Sri Lankan	Taiwanese	Thai	Tongan	Vietnamese
Lancaster County	213,189 91.23	6,156	655 10.64 10.64 0.31	-	-	105 17.10 16.03 1.71 0.05	-	-	83 9.33 12.67 1.35 0.04	-	-	-	-	-	-	-	140 43.08 21.37 2.27 0.07	-	-	-	-	-	-	-	-	70 2.05 10.69 1.14 0.03
Sarpy County	105,654 93.85	2,103	642 30.53 30.53 0.61	-	-	-	-	-	-	-	130 27.54 20.25 6.18 0.12	-	-	-	-	-	158 35.35 24.61 7.51 0.15	-	-	-	-	-	-	-	-	80 20.05 12.46 3.80 0.08
NEVADA	1,425,748 76.91	84,339	21,862 25.92 25.92 1.53	7,216	4,553 63.10 63.10 0.32	986 21.96 4.51 1.17 0.07	-	48 6.86 0.22 0.06 <0.01	2,153 16.89 9.85 2.55 0.15	-	9,762 25.62 44.65 11.57 0.68	576 53.68 12.65 7.98 0.04	2,641 82.04 58.01 36.60 0.19	-	-	4,510 54.40 20.63 5.35 0.32	1,667 22.91 7.63 1.98 0.12	65 5.82 0.30 0.08 <0.01	-	100 20.16 0.46 0.12 0.01	745 52.65 16.36 10.32 0.05	-	39 6.57 0.18 0.05 <0.01	521 18.02 2.38 0.62 0.04	114 16.40 2.50 1.58 0.01	452 11.85 2.07 0.54 0.03
Carson City Independent City	41,896 85.14	981	288 29.36 29.36 0.69	-	-	-	-	-	-	-	61 22.93 21.18 6.22 0.15	-	-	-	-	-	-	-	-	-	-	-	-	-	-	-
Clark County	942,435 74.04	67,709	17,278 25.52 25.52 1.83	5,474	3,796 69.35 69.35 0.40	706 26.20 4.09 1.04 0.07	-	45 6.56 0.26 0.07 <0.01	1,638 16.19 9.48 2.42 0.17	-	7,812 25.47 45.21 11.54 0.83	471 52.80 12.41 8.60 0.05	2,367 81.23 62.36 43.24 0.25	-	-	3,540 53.72 20.49 5.23 0.38	1,286 20.53 7.44 1.90 0.14	65 5.89 0.38 0.10 0.01	-	-	583 58.53 15.36 10.65 0.06	-	39 9.15 0.23 0.06 <0.01	445 17.40 2.58 0.66 0.05	-	326 10.54 1.89 0.48 0.03
Enterprise (cdp)	11,185 82.72	651	164 25.19 25.19 1.47	-	-	-	-	-	-	-	-	-	-	-	-	-	-	-	-	-	-	-	-	-	-	-
Henderson (city)	142,399 86.77	6,436	2,123 32.99 32.99 1.49	688	540 78.49 78.49 0.38	100 21.46 4.71 1.55 0.07	-	-	188 25.51 8.86 2.92 0.13	-	869 32.85 40.93 13.50 0.61	-	368 89.54 68.15 53.49 0.26	-	-	427 54.95 20.11 6.63 0.30	201 26.62 9.47 3.12 0.14	-	-	-	-	-	-	-	-	-
Las Vegas (city)	323,798 73.21	20,506	5,847 28.51 28.51 1.81	1,561	1,026 65.73 65.73 0.32	245 26.12 4.19 1.19 0.08	-	-	546 21.32 9.34 2.66 0.17	-	2,655 26.26 45.41 12.95 0.82	-	591 78.59 57.60 37.86 0.18	-	-	1,248 52.48 21.34 6.09 0.39	410 29.12 7.01 2.00 0.13	-	-	-	-	-	-	137 20.15 2.34 0.67 0.04	-	102 16.83 1.74 0.50 0.03
North Las Vegas (city)	65,113 62.84	3,625	1,150 31.72 31.72 1.77	686	407 59.33 59.33 0.63	-	-	-	-	-	603 29.52 52.43 16.63 0.93	-	-	-	-	-	-	-	-	-	-	-	-	-	-	-
Paradise (cdp)	120,738 69.49	12,111	3,003 24.80 24.80 2.49	776	530 68.30 68.30 0.44	116 19.80 3.86 0.96 0.10	-	-	314 17.70 10.46 2.59 0.26	-	1,279 23.65 42.59 10.56 1.06	-	395 71.30 74.53 50.90 0.33	-	-	766 54.87 25.51 6.32 0.63	204 15.25 6.79 1.68 0.17	-	-	-	-	-	-	-	-	34 6.06 1.13 0.28 0.03

Notes: Please refer to the User's Guide for an explanation of data; data is arranged alphabetically by state, then county, then city within each county; table includes counties with populations greater than 49,999 unless noted and cities with populations greater than 9,999 whose Asian and/or NHPI population rates are greater than the national average; (1) Native Hawaiian and other Pacific Islander; (2) excludes Taiwanese; (3) includes Chamorro; (4) county does not meet population threshold but is shown in order to allow inclusion of city

Place	Total population 5 years and over who speak English-only at home	Asian population 5 years and over	Asians 5 years and over who speak English-only at home	NHPI[1] population 5 years and over	NHPIs[1] 5 years and over who speak English-only at home	Asian Indian	Bangladeshi	Cambodian	Chinese[2]	Fijian	Filipino	Guamanian[3]	Hawaiian, Native	Hmong	Indonesian	Japanese	Korean	Laotian	Malaysian	Pakistani	Samoan	Sri Lankan	Taiwanese	Thai	Tongan	Vietnamese
Spring Valley (cdp)	81,702	12,069	2,062	588	406	-	-	-	384	-	830	-	-	-	-	317	145	-	-	-	-	-	-	11	-	52
	73.93		17.09		69.05				9.74		22.85					44.27	11.40							2.30		6.05
									18.62		40.25					15.37	7.03							0.53		2.52
			17.09		69.05				3.18		6.88					2.63	1.20							0.09		0.43
			2.52		0.50				0.47		1.02					0.39	0.18							0.01		0.06
Sunrise Manor (cdp)	101,008	8,127	1,915	404	247	-	-	-	76	-	976	-	-	-	-	351	170	-	-	-	-	-	-	-	-	-
	71.29		23.56		61.14				16.24		21.67					59.19	23.78									
									3.97		50.97					18.33	8.88									
			23.56		61.14				0.94		12.01					4.32	2.09									
			1.90		0.24				0.08		0.97					0.35	0.17									
Winchester (cdp)	16,441	1,417	247	-	-	-	-	-	-	-	94	-	-	-	-	-	-	-	-	-	-	-	-	-	-	-
	64.90		17.43								21.36															
											38.06															
			17.43								6.63															
			1.50								0.57															
Washoe County	253,447	13,506	3,295	1,382	493	216	-	-	427	-	1,405	-	-	-	-	712	211	-	-	-	-	-	-	-	46	92
	80.10		24.40		35.67	14.57			19.11		23.25					55.45	28.59								9.27	14.56
						6.56			12.96		42.64					21.61	6.40								9.33	2.79
			24.40		35.67	1.60			3.16		10.40					5.27	1.56								3.33	0.68
			1.30		0.19	0.09			0.17		0.55					0.28	0.08								0.02	0.04
Reno (city)	128,788	8,960	1,961	865	229	110	-	-	253	-	840	-	-	-	-	462	98	-	-	-	-	-	-	-	-	74
	76.39		21.89		26.47	12.56			17.51		20.83					49.46	22.17									17.75
						5.61			12.90		42.84					23.56	5.00									3.77
			21.89		26.47	1.23			2.82		9.38					5.16	1.09									0.83
			1.52		0.18	0.09			0.20		0.65					0.36	0.08									0.06
Sparks (city)	48,025	2,928	764	-	-	-	-	-	102	-	341	-	-	-	-	-	-	-	-	-	-	-	-	-	-	-
	77.80		26.09						17.38		25.22															
									13.35		44.63															
			26.09						3.48		11.65															
			1.59						0.21		0.71															
NEW HAMPSHIRE	1,064,252	14,178	3,371	-	-	542	-	-	689	-	447	-	-	-	-	341	646	23	-	-	-	-	-	-	-	196
	91.72		23.78			16.94			19.29		36.52					38.02	36.54	7.03								12.20
						16.08			20.44		13.26					10.12	19.16	0.68								5.81
			23.78			3.82			4.86		3.15					2.41	4.56	0.16								1.38
			0.32			0.05			0.06		0.04					0.03	0.06	<0.01								0.02
Belknap County	50,244	314	70	-	-	-	-	-	-	-	-	-	-	-	-	-	-	-	-	-	-	-	-	-	-	-
	94.22		22.29																							
			22.29																							
			0.14																							
Cheshire County	66,541	441	140	-	-	-	-	-	-	-	-	-	-	-	-	-	-	-	-	-	-	-	-	-	-	-
	95.03		31.75																							
			31.75																							
			0.21																							
Grafton County	73,184	1,178	353	-	-	-	-	-	97	-	-	-	-	-	-	-	-	-	-	-	-	-	-	-	-	-
	94.40		29.97						25.26																	
									27.48																	
			29.97						8.23																	
			0.48						0.13																	

Notes: Please refer to the User's Guide for an explanation of data; data is arranged alphabetically by state, then county, then city within each county; table includes counties with populations greater than 49,999 unless noted and cities with populations greater than 9,999 whose Asian and/or NHPI population rates are greater than the national average; (1) Native Hawaiian and other Pacific Islander; (2) excludes Taiwanese; (3) includes Chamorro; (4) county does not meet population threshold but is shown in order to allow inclusion of city

Place	Total population 5 years and over who speak English-only at home	Asian population 5 years and over	Asians 5 years and over who speak English-only at home	NHPI[1] population 5 years and over	NHPIs[1] 5 years and over who speak English-only at home	Asian Indian	Bangladeshi	Cambodian	Chinese[2]	Fijian	Filipino	Guamanian[3]	Hawaiian, Native	Hmong	Indonesian	Japanese	Korean	Laotian	Malaysian	Pakistani	Samoan	Sri Lankan	Taiwanese	Thai	Tongan	Vietnamese
Hanover (town)	9,221 87.58	635	136 21.42 21.42 1.47	-	-	-	-	-	-	-	-	-	-	-	-	-	-	-	-	-	-	-	-	-	-	-
Hillsborough County	310,121 87.33	6,759	1,369 20.25 20.25 0.44	-	-	254 13.31 18.55 3.76 0.08	-	-	292 16.43 21.33 4.32 0.09	-	139 36.01 10.15 2.06 0.04	-	-	-	-	-	204 39.38 14.90 3.02 0.07	-	-	-	-	-	-	-	-	94 8.94 6.87 1.39 0.03
Nashua (city)	67,413 83.15	3,132	473 15.10 15.10 0.70	-	-	92 7.30 19.45 2.94 0.14	-	-	128 16.49 27.06 4.09 0.19	-	-	-	-	-	-	-	-	-	-	-	-	-	-	-	-	-
Merrimack County	119,976 93.56	1,092	305 27.93 27.93 0.25	-	-	-	-	-	-	-	-	-	-	-	-	-	-	-	-	-	-	-	-	-	-	-
Rockingham County	243,626 93.97	2,636	722 27.39 27.39 0.30	-	-	79 19.32 10.94 3.00 0.03	-	-	168 22.22 23.27 6.37 0.07	-	132 33.42 18.28 5.01 0.05	-	-	-	-	-	171 44.53 23.68 6.49 0.07	-	-	-	-	-	-	-	-	-
Strafford County	98,282 93.05	1,378	317 23.00 23.00 0.32	-	-	-	-	-	51 16.45 16.09 3.70 0.05	-	-	-	-	-	-	-	-	-	-	-	-	-	-	-	-	-
NEW JERSEY	5,854,578 74.52	445,318	63,808 14.33 14.33 1.09	2,531	1,216 48.04 48.04 0.02	19,789 12.81 31.01 4.44 0.34	54 2.63 0.08 0.01 <0.01	63 10.03 0.10 0.01 <0.01	11,064 12.68 17.34 2.48 0.19	-	18,059 21.72 28.30 4.06 0.31	186 36.19 15.30 7.35 <0.01	464 74.00 38.16 18.33 0.01	-	184 19.13 0.29 0.04 <0.01	2,311 18.00 3.62 0.52 0.04	6,823 11.35 10.69 1.53 0.12	116 24.42 0.18 0.03 <0.01	-	782 6.86 1.23 0.18 0.01	276 44.16 22.70 10.90 <0.01	323 26.05 0.51 0.07 0.01	306 5.54 0.48 0.07 0.01	279 15.93 0.44 0.06 <0.01	-	1,324 9.59 2.07 0.30 0.02
Atlantic County	188,376 79.68	12,043	1,148 9.53 9.53 0.61	-	-	245 6.64 21.34 2.03 0.13	0 0.00 0.00 0.00 0.00	-	131 6.78 11.41 1.09 0.07	-	317 15.36 27.61 2.63 0.17	-	-	-	-	-	74 13.01 6.45 0.61 0.04	-	-	19 3.92 1.66 0.16 0.01	-	-	-	-	-	123 6.56 10.71 1.02 0.07
Atlantic City (city)	23,119 61.58	3,817	134 3.51 3.51 0.58	-	-	13 1.54 9.70 0.34 0.06	-	-	41 5.84 30.60 1.07 0.18	-	32 6.72 23.88 0.84 0.14	-	-	-	-	-	-	-	-	-	-	-	-	-	-	0 0.00 0.00 0.00 0.00
Brigantine (city)	9,388 78.59	737	92 12.48 12.48 0.98	-	-	-	-	-	-	-	-	-	-	-	-	-	-	-	-	-	-	-	-	-	-	-

Notes: Please refer to the User's Guide for an explanation of data; data is arranged alphabetically by state, then county, then city within each county; table includes counties with populations greater than 49,999 unless noted and cities with populations greater than 9,999 whose Asian and/or NHPI population rates are greater than the national average; (1) Native Hawaiian and other Pacific Islander; (2) excludes Taiwanese; (3) includes Chamorro; (4) county does not meet population threshold but is shown in order to allow inclusion of city

Place	Total population 5 years and over who speak English-only at home	Asian population 5 years and over	Asians 5 years and over who speak English-only at home	NHPI[1] population 5 years and over	NHPIs[1] 5 years and over who speak English-only at home	Asian Indian	Bangladeshi	Cambodian	Chinese[2]	Fijian	Filipino	Guamanian[3]	Hawaiian, Native	Hmong	Indonesian	Japanese	Korean	Laotian	Malaysian	Pakistani	Samoan	Sri Lankan	Taiwanese	Thai	Tongan	Vietnamese
Egg Harbor (township)	24,237 85.38	1,586	205 12.93 12.93 0.85	-	-	-	-	-	-	-	-	-	-	-	-	-	-	-	-	-	-	-	-	-	-	-
Galloway (township)	24,240 82.97	2,490	311 12.49 12.49 1.28	-	-	79 6.50 25.40 3.17 0.33	-	-	-	-	-	-	-	-	-	-	-	-	-	-	-	-	-	-	-	-
Ventnor City (city)	8,400 68.81	944	67 7.10 7.10 0.80	-	-	-	-	-	-	-	-	-	-	-	-	-	-	-	-	-	-	-	-	-	-	-
Bergen County	560,343 67.56	87,184	9,041 10.37 10.37 1.61	-	-	2,069 12.97 22.88 2.37 0.37	-	-	1,728 14.16 19.11 1.98 0.31	-	2,586 18.61 28.60 2.97 0.46	-	-	-	-	494 7.73 5.46 0.57 0.09	1,594 4.75 17.63 1.83 0.28	-	-	117 8.52 1.29 0.13 0.02	-	-	7 0.91 0.08 0.01 <0.01	32 6.63 0.35 0.04 0.01	-	42 8.97 0.46 0.05 0.01
Bergenfield (borough)	14,788 60.54	4,938	825 16.71 16.71 5.58	-	-	315 23.03 38.18 6.38 2.13	-	-	-	-	443 14.81 53.70 8.97 3.00	-	-	-	-	-	-	-	-	-	-	-	-	-	-	-
Cliffside Park (borough)	9,570 43.76	2,433	208 8.55 8.55 2.17	-	-	-	-	-	-	-	-	-	-	-	-	27 6.46 12.98 1.11 0.28	43 3.24 20.67 1.77 0.45	-	-	-	-	-	-	-	-	-
Dumont (borough)	12,681 77.82	1,775	330 18.59 18.59 2.60	-	-	83 17.51 25.15 4.68 0.65	-	-	-	-	103 18.20 31.21 5.80 0.81	-	-	-	-	-	-	-	-	-	-	-	-	-	-	-
Elmwood Park (borough)	10,420 57.95	1,549	134 8.65 8.65 1.29	-	-	68 7.06 50.75 4.39 0.65	-	-	-	-	-	-	-	-	-	-	-	-	-	-	-	-	-	-	-	-
Englewood (city)	16,313 67.09	1,272	270 21.23 21.23 1.66	-	-	-	-	-	-	-	80 21.00 29.63 6.29 0.49	-	-	-	-	-	-	-	-	-	-	-	-	-	-	-
Fair Lawn (borough)	20,256 67.67	1,662	230 13.84 13.84 1.14	-	-	24 4.21 10.43 1.44 0.12	-	-	-	-	147 27.63 63.91 8.84 0.73	-	-	-	-	-	-	-	-	-	-	-	-	-	-	-

Notes: Please refer to the User's Guide for an explanation of data; data is arranged alphabetically by state, then county, then city within each county; table includes counties with populations greater than 49,999 unless noted and cities with populations greater than 9,999 whose Asian and/or NHPI population rates are greater than the national average; (1) Native Hawaiian and other Pacific Islander; (2) excludes Taiwanese; (3) includes Chamorro; (4) county does not meet population threshold but is shown in order to allow inclusion of city

Place	Total population 5 years and over who speak English-only at home	Asian population 5 years and over	Asians 5 years and over who speak English-only at home	NHPI[1] population 5 years and over	NHPIs[1] 5 years and over who speak English-only at home	Asian Indian	Bangladeshi	Cambodian	Chinese[2]	Fijian	Filipino	Guamanian[3]	Hawaiian, Native	Hmong	Indonesian	Japanese	Korean	Laotian	Malaysian	Pakistani	Samoan	Sri Lankan	Taiwanese	Thai	Tongan	Vietnamese
Fairview (borough)	4,321	575	41	-	-	-	-	-	-	-	-	-	-	-	-	-	-	-	-	-	-	-	-	-	-	-
	34.99		7.13																							
			7.13																							
			0.95																							
Fort Lee (borough)	15,129	10,045	656	-	-	88	-	-	127	-	-	-	-	-	-	79	278	-	-	-	-	-	-	-	-	-
	44.99		6.53			15.83			7.85							4.57	5.14									
						13.41			19.36							12.04	42.38									
			6.53			0.88			1.26							0.79	2.77									
			4.34			0.58			0.84							0.52	1.84									
Franklin Lakes (borough)	8,016	692	108	-	-	-	-	-	-	-	-	-	-	-	-	-	-	-	-	-	-	-	-	-	-	-
	82.34		15.61																							
			15.61																							
			1.35																							
Glen Rock (borough)	9,188	666	85	-	-	-	-	-	-	-	-	-	-	-	-	-	-	-	-	-	-	-	-	-	-	-
	86.70		12.76																							
			12.76																							
			0.93																							
Hackensack (city)	24,093	2,926	294	-	-	90	-	-	-	-	109	-	-	-	-	-	14	-	-	-	-	-	-	-	-	-
	59.99		10.05			10.24					17.36						2.36									
						30.61					37.07						4.76									
			10.05			3.08					3.73						0.48									
			1.22			0.37					0.45						0.06									
Hasbrouck Heights (borough)	8,384	576	102	-	-	-	-	-	-	-	-	-	-	-	-	-	-	-	-	-	-	-	-	-	-	-
	76.42		17.71																							
			17.71																							
			1.22																							
Hillsdale (borough)	7,959	476	93	-	-	-	-	-	-	-	-	-	-	-	-	-	-	-	-	-	-	-	-	-	-	-
	85.09		19.54																							
			19.54																							
			1.17																							
Little Ferry (borough)	5,835	1,670	137	-	-	56	-	-	-	-	61	-	-	-	-	-	15	-	-	-	-	-	-	-	-	-
	57.49		8.20			13.46					17.33						2.37									
						40.88					44.53						10.95									
			8.20			3.35					3.65						0.90									
			2.35			0.96					1.05						0.26									
Lodi (borough)	13,009	1,823	135	-	-	42	-	-	-	-	74	-	-	-	-	-	-	-	-	-	-	-	-	-	-	-
	58.00		7.41			4.22					15.64															
						31.11					54.81															
			7.41			2.30					4.06															
			1.04			0.32					0.57															
Lyndhurst (township)	13,612	1,071	119	-	-	-	-	-	-	-	-	-	-	-	-	-	-	-	-	-	-	-	-	-	-	-
	73.57		11.11																							
			11.11																							
			0.87																							

Notes: Please refer to the User's Guide for an explanation of data; data is arranged alphabetically by state, then county, then city within each county; table includes counties with populations greater than 49,999 unless noted and cities with populations greater than 9,999 whose Asian and/or NHPI population rates are greater than the national average; (1) Native Hawaiian and other Pacific Islander; (2) excludes Taiwanese; (3) includes Chamorro; (4) county does not meet population threshold but is shown in order to allow inclusion of city

Place	Total population 5 years and over who speak English-only at home	Asian population 5 years and over	Asians 5 years and over who speak English-only at home	NHPI[1] population 5 years and over	NHPIs[1] 5 years and over who speak English-only at home	Asian Indian	Bangladeshi	Cambodian	Chinese[2]	Fijian	Filipino	Guamanian[3]	Hawaiian, Native	Hmong	Indonesian	Japanese	Korean	Laotian	Malaysian	Pakistani	Samoan	Sri Lankan	Taiwanese	Thai	Tongan	Vietnamese
Mahwah (township)	18,110 81.05	1,374	220 16.01 16.01 1.21	-	-	56 12.56 25.45 4.08 0.31	-	-	-	-	-	-	-	-	-	-	-	-	-	-	-	-	-	-	-	-
New Milford (borough)	10,506 68.15	2,156	262 12.15 12.15 2.49	-	-	57 9.98 21.76 2.64 0.54	-	-	-	-	150 16.63 57.25 6.96 1.43	-	-	-	-	-	-	-	-	-	-	-	-	-	-	-
North Arlington (borough)	10,238 70.57	752	54 7.18 7.18 0.53	-	-	-	-	-	-	-	-	-	-	-	-	-	-	-	-	-	-	-	-	-	-	-
Palisades Park (borough)	4,409 27.71	6,418	250 3.90 3.90 5.67	-	-	-	-	-	-	-	-	-	-	-	-	-	177 3.28 70.80 2.76 4.01	-	-	-	-	-	-	-	-	-
Paramus (borough)	16,438 67.36	4,112	348 8.46 8.46 2.12	-	-	131 10.75 37.64 3.19 0.80	-	-	35 8.29 10.06 0.85 0.21	-	104 13.77 29.89 2.53 0.63	-	-	-	-	-	50 3.79 14.37 1.22 0.30	-	-	-	-	-	-	-	-	-
Ramsey (borough)	11,484 86.60	763	117 15.33 15.33 1.02	-	-	-	-	-	-	-	-	-	-	-	-	-	-	-	-	-	-	-	-	-	-	-
Ridgefield (borough)	5,496 53.18	1,688	82 4.86 4.86 1.49	-	-	-	-	-	-	-	-	-	-	-	-	-	0 0.00 0.00 0.00 0.00	-	-	-	-	-	-	-	-	-
Ridgefield Park (village)	7,865 64.89	1,029	167 16.23 16.23 2.12	-	-	-	-	-	-	-	-	-	-	-	-	-	25 6.25 14.97 2.43 0.32	-	-	-	-	-	-	-	-	-
Ridgewood (village)	18,734 81.00	2,046	313 15.30 15.30 1.67	-	-	-	-	-	-	-	-	-	-	-	-	25 5.71 7.99 1.22 0.13	33 5.97 10.54 1.61 0.18	-	-	-	-	-	-	-	-	-
River Edge (borough)	7,335 71.84	1,257	93 7.40 7.40 1.27	-	-	-	-	-	-	-	-	-	-	-	-	-	12 2.72 12.90 0.95 0.16	-	-	-	-	-	-	-	-	-

Notes: Please refer to the User's Guide for an explanation of data; data is arranged alphabetically by state, then county, then city within each county; table includes counties with populations greater than 49,999 unless noted and cities with populations greater than 9,999 whose Asian and/or NHPI population rates are greater than the national average; (1) Native Hawaiian and other Pacific Islander; (2) excludes Taiwanese; (3) includes Chamorro; (4) county does not meet population threshold but is shown in order to allow inclusion of city

Place	Total population 5 years and over who speak English-only at home	Asian population 5 years and over	Asians 5 years and over who speak English-only at home	NHPI[1] population 5 years and over	NHPIs[1] 5 years and over who speak English-only at home	Asian Indian	Bangladeshi	Cambodian	Chinese[2]	Fijian	Filipino	Guamanian[3]	Hawaiian, Native	Hmong	Indonesian	Japanese	Korean	Laotian	Malaysian	Pakistani	Samoan	Sri Lankan	Taiwanese	Thai	Tongan	Vietnamese
Rutherford (borough)	12,652 73.42	1,921	183 9.53 9.53 1.45	-	-	60 18.58 32.79 3.12 0.47	-	-	-	-	-	-	-	-	-	-	43 5.08 23.50 2.24 0.34	-	-	-	-	-	-	-	-	-
Saddle Brook (township)	9,433 75.92	680	104 15.29 15.29 1.10	-	-	-	-	-	-	-	-	-	-	-	-	-	-	-	-	-	-	-	-	-	-	-
Teaneck (township)	26,776 72.57	2,708	359 13.26 13.26 1.34	-	-	75 9.43 20.89 2.77 0.28	-	-	-	-	195 23.33 54.32 7.20 0.73	-	-	-	-	-	-	-	-	-	-	-	-	-	-	-
Tenafly (borough)	8,272 63.96	2,455	285 11.61 11.61 3.45	-	-	-	-	-	165 23.01 57.89 6.72 1.99	-	-	-	-	-	-	-	13 1.15 4.56 0.53 0.16	-	-	-	-	-	-	-	-	-
Wallington (borough)	4,937 45.07	478	14 2.93 2.93 0.28	-	-	-	-	-	-	-	-	-	-	-	-	-	-	-	-	-	-	-	-	-	-	-
Westwood (borough)	8,275 80.95	494	28 5.67 5.67 0.34	-	-	-	-	-	-	-	-	-	-	-	-	-	-	-	-	-	-	-	-	-	-	-
Wyckoff (township)	13,372 87.35	603	95 15.75 15.75 0.71	-	-	-	-	-	-	-	-	-	-	-	-	-	-	-	-	-	-	-	-	-	-	-
Burlington County	355,616 89.66	10,394	2,085 20.06 20.06 0.59	-	-	487 13.99 23.36 4.69 0.14	-	-	235 16.75 11.27 2.26 0.07	-	554 29.23 26.57 5.33 0.16	-	-	-	-	149 30.72 7.15 1.43 0.04	383 20.47 18.37 3.68 0.11	-	-	-	-	-	-	-	-	76 14.84 3.65 0.73 0.02
Browns Mills (cdp)	9,008 84.53	458	57 12.45 12.45 0.63	-	-	-	-	-	-	-	-	-	-	-	-	-	8 2.37 14.04 1.75 0.09	-	-	-	-	-	-	-	-	-
Evesham (township)	35,942 91.27	1,471	293 19.92 19.92 0.82	-	-	50 14.62 17.06 3.40 0.14	-	-	65 15.05 22.18 4.42 0.18	-	-	-	-	-	-	-	-	-	-	-	-	-	-	-	-	-

Notes: Please refer to the User's Guide for an explanation of data; data is arranged alphabetically by state, then county, then city within each county; table includes counties with populations greater than 49,999 unless noted and cities with populations greater than 9,999 whose Asian and/or NHPI population rates are greater than the national average; (1) Native Hawaiian and other Pacific Islander; (2) excludes Taiwanese; (3) includes Chamorro; (4) county does not meet population threshold but is shown in order to allow inclusion of city

Place	Total population 5 years and over who speak English-only at home	Asian population 5 years and over	Asians 5 years and over who speak English-only at home	NHPI[1] population 5 years and over	NHPIs[1] 5 years and over who speak English-only at home	Asian Indian	Bangladeshi	Cambodian	Chinese[2]	Fijian	Filipino	Guamanian[3]	Hawaiian, Native	Hmong	Indonesian	Japanese	Korean	Laotian	Malaysian	Pakistani	Samoan	Sri Lankan	Taiwanese	Thai	Tongan	Vietnamese
Maple Shade (township)	15,648 86.76	968	50 5.17 5.17 0.32	-	-	6 1.08 12.00 0.62 0.04	-	-	-	-	-	-	-	-	-	-	-	-	-	-	-	-	-	-	-	-
Marlton (cdp)	8,554 89.11	362	32 8.84 8.84 0.37	-	-	-	-	-	-	-	-	-	-	-	-	-	-	-	-	-	-	-	-	-	-	-
Mount Laurel (township)	34,297 90.52	1,609	412 25.61 25.61 1.20	-	-	116 21.64 28.16 7.21 0.34	-	-	59 13.98 14.32 3.67 0.17	-	-	-	-	-	-	-	-	-	-	-	-	-	-	-	-	-
Camden County	400,711 84.42	18,499	2,933 15.85 15.85 0.73	-	-	590 12.62 20.12 3.19 0.15	-	5 1.66 0.17 0.03 <0.01	438 11.90 14.93 2.37 0.11	-	1,006 27.76 34.30 5.44 0.25	-	-	-	-	-	311 18.77 10.60 1.68 0.08	-	-	56 16.87 1.91 0.30 0.01	-	-	-	-	-	182 6.33 6.21 0.98 0.05
Barclay-Kingston (cdp)	8,987 88.32	825	211 25.58 25.58 2.35	-	-	-	-	-	-	-	-	-	-	-	-	-	-	-	-	-	-	-	-	-	-	-
Bellmawr (borough)	9,468 88.16	433	2 0.46 0.46 0.02	-	-	-	-	-	-	-	-	-	-	-	-	-	-	-	-	-	-	-	-	-	-	-
Cherry Hill Mall (cdp)	10,263 80.58	1,204	170 14.12 14.12 1.66	-	-	-	-	-	-	-	-	-	-	-	-	-	-	-	-	-	-	-	-	-	-	-
Cherry Hill (township)	54,852 82.93	6,233	947 15.19 15.19 1.73	-	-	175 13.13 18.48 2.81 0.32	-	-	98 5.64 10.35 1.57 0.18	-	464 33.02 49.00 7.44 0.85	-	-	-	-	-	55 5.60 5.81 0.88 0.10	-	-	-	-	-	-	-	-	-
Echelon (cdp)	7,940 80.77	1,237	101 8.16 8.16 1.27	-	-	41 5.68 40.59 3.31 0.52	-	-	-	-	-	-	-	-	-	-	-	-	-	-	-	-	-	-	-	-
Greentree (cdp)	8,319 76.92	1,847	211 11.42 11.42 2.54	-	-	71 12.50 33.65 3.84 0.85	-	-	42 5.74 19.91 2.27 0.50	-	-	-	-	-	-	-	-	-	-	-	-	-	-	-	-	-

Notes: Please refer to the User's Guide for an explanation of data; data is arranged alphabetically by state, then county, then city within each county; table includes counties with populations greater than 49,999 unless noted and cities with populations greater than 9,999 whose Asian and/or NHPI population rates are greater than the national average; (1) Native Hawaiian and other Pacific Islander; (2) excludes Taiwanese; (3) includes Chamorro; (4) county does not meet population threshold but is shown in order to allow inclusion of city

Place	Total population 5 years and over who speak English-only at home	Asian population 5 years and over	Asians 5 years and over who speak English-only at home	NHPI[1] population 5 years and over	NHPIs[1] 5 years and over who speak English-only at home	Asian Indian	Bangladeshi	Cambodian	Chinese[2]	Fijian	Filipino	Guamanian[3]	Hawaiian, Native	Hmong	Indonesian	Japanese	Korean	Laotian	Malaysian	Pakistani	Samoan	Sri Lankan	Taiwanese	Thai	Tongan	Vietnamese
Pennsauken (township)	26,804 79.92	1,455	158 10.86 10.86 0.59	-	-	-	-	-	-	-	-	-	-	-	-	-	-	-	-	-	-	-	-	-	-	56 8.89 35.44 3.85 0.21
Springdale (cdp)	11,459 83.62	1,162	143 12.31 12.31 1.25	-	-	-	-	-	5 1.12 3.50 0.43 0.04	-	-	-	-	-	-	-	-	-	-	-	-	-	-	-	-	-
Voorhees (township)	21,572 81.74	2,887	469 16.25 16.25 2.17	-	-	209 12.64 44.56 7.24 0.97	-	-	118 20.38 25.16 4.09 0.55	-	110 27.50 23.45 3.81 0.51	-	-	-	-	-	-	-	-	-	-	-	-	-	-	-
Cape May County	90,696 93.36	580	143 24.66 24.66 0.16	-	-	-	-	-	-	-	-	-	-	-	-	-	-	-	-	-	-	-	-	-	-	-
Cumberland County	109,457 79.55	1,098	319 29.05 29.05 0.29	-	-	20 5.25 6.27 1.82 0.02	-	-	-	-	-	-	-	-	-	-	-	-	-	-	-	-	-	-	-	-
Essex County	517,923 70.32	27,628	5,800 20.99 20.99 1.12	443	257 58.01 58.01 0.05	2,318 28.52 39.97 8.39 0.45	-	-	849 14.79 14.64 3.07 0.16	-	1,633 21.80 28.16 5.91 0.32	-	-	-	-	148 27.51 2.55 0.54 0.03	467 17.83 8.05 1.69 0.09	-	-	41 7.44 0.71 0.15 0.01	-	-	0 0.00 0.00 0.00 0.00	-	-	64 6.77 1.10 0.23 0.01
Belleville (township)	19,493 57.44	3,888	533 13.71 13.71 2.73	-	-	100 11.92 18.76 2.57 0.51	-	-	-	-	371 18.90 69.61 9.54 1.90	-	-	-	-	-	-	-	-	-	-	-	-	-	-	22 5.99 4.13 0.57 0.11
Bloomfield (township)	31,259 69.48	3,814	771 20.21 20.21 2.47	-	-	364 26.26 47.21 9.54 1.16	-	-	52 11.11 6.74 1.36 0.17	-	308 20.28 39.95 8.08 0.99	-	-	-	-	-	-	-	-	-	-	-	-	-	-	-
Cedar Grove (township)	9,892 85.00	594	65 10.94 10.94 0.66	-	-	-	-	-	-	-	-	-	-	-	-	-	-	-	-	-	-	-	-	-	-	-
Livingston (township)	19,230 75.40	3,765	503 13.36 13.36 2.62	-	-	194 26.65 38.57 5.15 1.01	-	-	91 6.22 18.09 2.42 0.47	-	158 28.42 31.41 4.20 0.82	-	-	-	-	-	60 7.89 11.93 1.59 0.31	-	-	-	-	-	-	-	-	-

Notes: Please refer to the User's Guide for an explanation of data; data is arranged alphabetically by state, then county, then city within each county; table includes counties with populations greater than 49,999 unless noted and cities with populations greater than 9,999 whose Asian and/or NHPI population rates are greater than the national average; (1) Native Hawaiian and other Pacific Islander; (2) excludes Taiwanese; (3) includes Chamorro; (4) county does not meet population threshold but is shown in order to allow inclusion of city

Place	Total population 5 years and over who speak English-only at home	Asian population 5 years and over	Asians 5 years and over who speak English-only at home	NHPI[1] population 5 years and over	NHPIs[1] 5 years and over who speak English-only at home	Asian Indian	Bangladeshi	Cambodian	Chinese[2]	Fijian	Filipino	Guamanian[3]	Hawaiian, Native	Hmong	Indonesian	Japanese	Korean	Laotian	Malaysian	Pakistani	Samoan	Sri Lankan	Taiwanese	Thai	Tongan	Vietnamese
Millburn (township)	14,886 82.60	1,373	189 13.77 13.77 1.27	-	-	-	-	-	53 9.09 28.04 3.86 0.36	-	-	-	-	-	-	-	-	-	-	-	-	-	-	-	-	-
Nutley (township)	20,538 79.15	1,908	282 14.78 14.78 1.37	-	-	102 14.51 36.17 5.35 0.50	-	-	-	-	91 19.49 32.27 4.77 0.44	-	-	-	-	-	-	-	-	-	-	-	-	-	-	-
Verona (township)	10,956 86.74	584	101 17.29 17.29 0.92	-	-	-	-	-	-	-	-	-	-	-	-	-	-	-	-	-	-	-	-	-	-	-
West Caldwell (township)	9,058 87.12	366	72 19.67 19.67 0.79	-	-	-	-	-	-	-	-	-	-	-	-	-	-	-	-	-	-	-	-	-	-	-
West Orange (township)	28,490 68.01	3,518	690 19.61 19.61 2.42	-	-	248 26.44 35.94 7.05 0.87	-	-	105 14.21 15.22 2.98 0.37	-	218 23.98 31.59 6.20 0.77	-	-	-	-	-	97 16.14 14.06 2.76 0.34	-	-	-	-	-	-	-	-	-
Gloucester County	222,858 93.55	3,883	951 24.49 24.49 0.43	-	-	129 13.68 13.56 3.32 0.06	-	-	104 14.96 10.94 2.68 0.05	-	401 30.80 42.17 10.33 0.18	-	-	-	-	-	137 38.81 14.41 3.53 0.06	-	-	-	-	-	-	-	-	-
Hudson County	250,459 43.86	53,577	7,195 13.43 13.43 2.87	-	-	2,103 11.05 29.23 3.93 0.84	-	-	651 10.43 9.05 1.22 0.26	-	3,286 17.44 45.67 6.13 1.31	-	-	-	-	103 11.84 1.43 0.19 0.04	517 16.53 7.19 0.96 0.21	-	-	77 3.66 1.07 0.14 0.03	-	-	-	-	-	143 9.06 1.99 0.27 0.06
Bayonne (city)	39,571 67.99	2,324	378 16.27 16.27 0.96	-	-	87 18.59 23.02 3.74 0.22	-	-	-	-	269 22.00 71.16 11.57 0.68	-	-	-	-	-	0 0.00 0.00 0.00 0.00	-	-	-	-	-	-	-	-	-
Guttenberg (town)	3,202 32.01	699	99 14.16 14.16 3.09	-	-	-	-	-	-	-	-	-	-	-	-	-	-	-	-	-	-	-	-	-	-	-
Harrison (town)	3,786 27.98	1,547	90 5.82 5.82 2.38	-	-	-	-	-	66 5.80 73.33 4.27 1.74	-	-	-	-	-	-	-	-	-	-	-	-	-	-	-	-	-

Notes: Please refer to the User's Guide for an explanation of data; data is arranged alphabetically by state, then county, then city within each county; table includes counties with populations greater than 49,999 unless noted and cities with populations greater than 9,999 whose Asian and/or NHPI population rates are greater than the national average; (1) Native Hawaiian and other Pacific Islander; (2) excludes Taiwanese; (3) includes Chamorro; (4) county does not meet population threshold but is shown in order to allow inclusion of city

Place	Total population 5 years and over who speak English-only at home	Asian population 5 years and over	Asians 5 years and over who speak English-only at home	NHPI[1] population 5 years and over	NHPIs[1] 5 years and over who speak English-only at home	Asian Indian	Bangladeshi	Cambodian	Chinese[2]	Fijian	Filipino	Guamanian[3]	Hawaiian, Native	Hmong	Indonesian	Japanese	Korean	Laotian	Malaysian	Pakistani	Samoan	Sri Lankan	Taiwanese	Thai	Tongan	Vietnamese
Hoboken (city)	26,712 71.33	1,659	533 32.13 32.13 2.00	-	-	149 23.21 27.95 8.98 0.56	-	-	143 30.17 26.83 8.62 0.54	-	-	-	-	-	-	-	-	-	-	-	-	-	-	-	-	-
Jersey City (city)	112,059 50.04	36,746	4,788 13.03 13.03 4.27	-	-	1,351 10.90 28.22 3.68 1.21	-	-	317 11.62 6.62 0.86 0.28	-	2,497 15.98 52.15 6.80 2.23	-	-	-	-	-	235 16.12 4.91 0.64 0.21	-	-	58 3.39 1.21 0.16 0.05	-	-	-	-	-	110 8.11 2.30 0.30 0.10
Kearny (town)	17,931 46.93	2,104	181 8.60 8.60 1.01	-	-	74 10.29 40.88 3.52 0.41	-	-	17 1.98 9.39 0.81 0.09	-	-	-	-	-	-	-	-	-	-	-	-	-	-	-	-	-
North Bergen (township)	15,168 27.79	3,326	264 7.94 7.94 1.74	-	-	146 6.58 55.30 4.39 0.96	-	-	15 4.98 5.68 0.45 0.10	-	-	-	-	-	-	-	-	-	-	-	-	-	-	-	-	-
Secaucus (town)	10,461 69.44	1,723	328 19.04 19.04 3.14	-	-	66 13.98 20.12 3.83 0.63	-	-	-	-	176 29.78 53.66 10.21 1.68	-	-	-	-	-	-	-	-	-	-	-	-	-	-	-
Weehawken (township)	5,844 45.42	577	100 17.33 17.33 1.71	-	-	-	-	-	-	-	-	-	-	-	-	-	-	-	-	-	-	-	-	-	-	-
Hunterdon County	104,053 91.38	2,361	693 29.35 29.35 0.67	-	-	234 23.66 33.77 9.91 0.22	-	-	213 35.38 30.74 9.02 0.20	-	-	-	-	-	-	-	-	-	-	-	-	-	-	-	-	-
Mercer County	262,336 79.84	16,190	3,152 19.47 19.47 1.20	-	-	1,243 19.98 39.44 7.68 0.47	-	-	550 12.99 17.45 3.40 0.21	-	343 31.18 10.88 2.12 0.13	-	-	-	-	167 27.97 5.30 1.03 0.06	487 25.52 15.45 3.01 0.19	-	-	58 9.37 1.84 0.36 0.02	-	-	79 16.70 2.51 0.49 0.03	-	-	-
East Windsor (township)	16,337 71.29	2,091	293 14.01 14.01 1.79	-	-	160 12.36 54.61 7.65 0.98	-	-	-	-	-	-	-	-	-	-	-	-	-	-	-	-	-	-	-	-
Hopewell (township)	13,450 89.19	607	135 22.24 22.24 1.00	-	-	-	-	-	-	-	-	-	-	-	-	-	-	-	-	-	-	-	-	-	-	-

Notes: Please refer to the User's Guide for an explanation of data; data is arranged alphabetically by state, then county, then city within each county; table includes counties with populations greater than 49,999 unless noted and cities with populations greater than 9,999 whose Asian and/or NHPI population rates are greater than the national average; (1) Native Hawaiian and other Pacific Islander; (2) excludes Taiwanese; (3) includes Chamorro; (4) county does not meet population threshold but is shown in order to allow inclusion of city

Place	Total population 5 years and over who speak English-only at home	Asian population 5 years and over	Asians 5 years and over who speak English-only at home	NHPI[1] population 5 years and over	NHPIs[1] 5 years and over who speak English-only at home	Asian Indian	Bangladeshi	Cambodian	Chinese[2]	Fijian	Filipino	Guamanian[3]	Hawaiian, Native	Hmong	Indonesian	Japanese	Korean	Laotian	Malaysian	Pakistani	Samoan	Sri Lankan	Taiwanese	Thai	Tongan	Vietnamese
Lawrence (township)	22,077 80.18	2,073	437 21.08 21.08 1.98	-	-	262 25.00 59.95 12.64 1.19	-	-	113 19.09 25.86 5.45 0.51	-	-	-	-	-	-	-	-	-	-	-	-	-	-	-	-	-
Princeton (borough)	11,437 83.27	931	245 26.32 26.32 2.14	-	-	-	-	-	-	-	-	-	-	-	-	-	-	-	-	-	-	-	-	-	-	-
Princeton (township)	11,384 74.88	1,606	319 19.86 19.86 2.80	-	-	73 19.21 22.88 4.55 0.64	-	-	105 15.15 32.92 6.54 0.92	-	-	-	-	-	-	-	-	-	-	-	-	-	-	-	-	-
West Windsor (township)	14,437 70.61	4,506	723 16.05 16.05 5.01	-	-	259 17.08 35.82 5.75 1.79	-	-	193 11.67 26.69 4.28 1.34	-	-	-	-	-	-	-	86 20.05 11.89 1.91 0.60	-	-	-	-	-	-	-	-	-
Middlesex County	467,470 66.65	95,149	10,985 11.55 11.55 2.35	-	-	4,366 8.93 39.75 4.59 0.93	18 4.85 0.16 0.02 <0.01	-	2,001 10.21 18.22 2.10 0.43	-	2,897 24.86 26.37 3.04 0.62	-	-	-	44 9.57 0.40 0.05 0.01	125 19.87 1.14 0.13 0.03	657 13.16 5.98 0.69 0.14	-	-	203 6.96 1.85 0.21 0.04	-	152 33.55 1.38 0.16 0.03	62 4.82 0.56 0.07 0.01	-	-	118 5.54 1.07 0.12 0.03
Avenel (cdp)	10,263 62.51	2,922	175 5.99 5.99 1.71	-	-	90 4.60 51.43 3.08 0.88	-	-	-	-	-	-	-	-	-	-	-	-	-	-	-	-	-	-	-	-
Carteret (borough)	11,988 61.75	1,542	122 7.91 7.91 1.02	-	-	36 3.55 29.51 2.33 0.30	-	-	-	-	-	-	-	-	-	-	-	-	-	-	-	-	-	-	-	-
Colonia (cdp)	12,915 77.60	1,152	239 20.75 20.75 1.85	-	-	73 13.27 30.54 6.34 0.57	-	-	-	-	110 34.27 46.03 9.55 0.85	-	-	-	-	-	-	-	-	-	-	-	-	-	-	-
East Brunswick (township)	30,946 70.26	7,205	930 12.91 12.91 3.01	-	-	310 12.45 33.33 4.30 1.00	-	-	304 10.33 32.69 4.22 0.98	-	215 40.57 23.12 2.98 0.69	-	-	-	-	-	53 13.02 5.70 0.74 0.17	-	-	-	-	-	-	-	-	-
Edison (township)	54,951 60.04	25,803	2,360 9.15 9.15 4.29	-	-	1,180 7.98 50.00 4.57 2.15	-	-	407 7.70 17.25 1.58 0.74	-	491 21.05 20.81 1.90 0.89	-	-	-	-	-	85 7.17 3.60 0.33 0.15	-	-	55 9.24 2.33 0.21 0.10	-	-	6 0.97 0.25 0.02 0.01	-	-	-

Notes: Please refer to the User's Guide for an explanation of data; data is arranged alphabetically by state, then county, then city within each county; table includes counties with populations greater than 49,999 unless noted and cities with populations greater than 9,999 whose Asian and/or NHPI population rates are greater than the national average; (1) Native Hawaiian and other Pacific Islander; (2) excludes Taiwanese; (3) includes Chamorro; (4) county does not meet population threshold but is shown in order to allow inclusion of city

Place	Total population 5 years and over who speak English-only at home	Asian population 5 years and over	Asians 5 years and over who speak English-only at home	NHPI[1] population 5 years and over	NHPIs[1] 5 years and over who speak English-only at home	Asian Indian	Bangladeshi	Cambodian	Chinese[2]	Fijian	Filipino	Guamanian[3]	Hawaiian, Native	Hmong	Indonesian	Japanese	Korean	Laotian	Malaysian	Pakistani	Samoan	Sri Lankan	Taiwanese	Thai	Tongan	Vietnamese
Fords (cdp)	9,809 69.17	2,135	130 6.09 6.09 1.33	-	-	44 4.25 33.85 2.06 0.45	-	-	-	-	76 12.97 58.46 3.56 0.77	-	-	-	-	-	-	-	-	-	-	-	-	-	-	-
Highland Park (borough)	8,735 66.21	1,787	123 6.88 6.88 1.41	-	-	62 10.95 50.41 3.47 0.71	-	-	31 3.86 25.20 1.73 0.35	-	-	-	-	-	-	-	-	-	-	-	-	-	-	-	-	-
Iselin (cdp)	10,368 66.68	3,612	390 10.80 10.80 3.76	-	-	184 7.36 47.18 5.09 1.77	-	-	21 4.41 5.38 0.58 0.20	-	-	-	-	-	-	-	-	-	-	-	-	-	-	-	-	-
Metuchen (borough)	9,892 82.18	876	142 16.21 16.21 1.44	-	-	-	-	-	-	-	-	-	-	-	-	-	-	-	-	-	-	-	-	-	-	-
Middlesex (borough)	10,670 83.16	558	86 15.41 15.41 0.81	-	-	-	-	-	-	-	-	-	-	-	-	-	-	-	-	-	-	-	-	-	-	-
New Brunswick (city)	24,357 53.83	2,661	859 32.28 32.28 3.53	-	-	305 28.27 35.51 11.46 1.25	-	-	152 34.23 17.69 5.71 0.62	-	-	-	-	-	-	-	-	-	-	-	-	-	-	-	-	-
North Brunswick (township)	22,693 67.03	4,683	456 9.74 9.74 2.01	-	-	207 7.65 45.39 4.42 0.91	-	-	56 7.19 12.28 1.20 0.25	-	107 26.95 23.46 2.28 0.47	-	-	-	-	-	57 13.51 12.50 1.22 0.25	-	-	-	-	-	-	-	-	-
Old Bridge (township)	41,777 74.31	6,026	941 15.62 15.62 2.25	-	-	305 11.65 32.41 5.06 0.73	-	-	144 13.25 15.30 2.39 0.34	-	359 29.97 38.15 5.96 0.86	-	-	-	-	-	-	-	-	34 6.73 3.61 0.56 0.08	-	-	-	-	-	-
Piscataway (township)	30,314 63.74	11,653	1,289 11.06 11.06 4.25	-	-	437 8.15 33.90 3.75 1.44	-	-	192 8.16 14.90 1.65 0.63	-	515 24.80 39.95 4.42 1.70	-	-	-	-	-	28 3.93 2.17 0.24 0.09	-	-	-	-	-	-	-	-	-
Plainsboro (township)	11,228 59.93	5,555	585 10.53 10.53 5.21	-	-	244 8.37 41.71 4.39 2.17	-	-	124 8.45 21.20 2.23 1.10	-	-	-	-	-	-	-	-	-	-	-	-	-	-	-	-	-

Notes: Please refer to the User's Guide for an explanation of data; data is arranged alphabetically by state, then county, then city within each county; table includes counties with populations greater than 49,999 unless noted and cities with populations greater than 9,999 whose Asian and/or NHPI population rates are greater than the national average; (1) Native Hawaiian and other Pacific Islander; (2) excludes Taiwanese; (3) includes Chamorro; (4) county does not meet population threshold but is shown in order to allow inclusion of city

Place	Total population 5 years and over who speak English-only at home	Asian population 5 years and over	Asians 5 years and over who speak English-only at home	NHPI[1] population 5 years and over	NHPIs[1] 5 years and over who speak English-only at home	Asian Indian	Bangladeshi	Cambodian	Chinese[2]	Fijian	Filipino	Guamanian[3]	Hawaiian, Native	Hmong	Indonesian	Japanese	Korean	Laotian	Malaysian	Pakistani	Samoan	Sri Lankan	Taiwanese	Thai	Tongan	Vietnamese
Princeton Meadows (cdp)	7,457 60.72	3,508	406 11.57 11.57 5.44	-	-	225 11.62 55.42 6.41 3.02	-	-	41 5.17 10.10 1.17 0.55	-	-	-	-	-	-	-	-	-	-	-	-	-	-	-	-	-
Sayreville (borough)	27,555 73.16	3,714	358 9.64 9.64 1.30	-	-	164 7.53 45.81 4.42 0.60	-	-	40 6.80 11.17 1.08 0.15	-	109 17.81 30.45 2.93 0.40	-	-	-	-	-	-	-	-	-	-	-	-	-	-	-
South Brunswick (township)	25,162 72.16	6,222	747 12.01 12.01 2.97	-	-	284 8.37 38.02 4.56 1.13	-	-	191 14.40 25.57 3.07 0.76	-	129 24.90 17.27 2.07 0.51	-	-	-	-	-	-	-	-	-	-	-	-	-	-	-
South Plainfield (borough)	16,505 80.42	1,604	313 19.51 19.51 1.90	-	-	190 29.46 60.70 11.85 1.15	-	-	-	-	62 16.49 19.81 3.87 0.38	-	-	-	-	-	-	-	-	-	-	-	-	-	-	4 1.19 1.28 0.25 0.02
Woodbridge (township)	63,332 69.74	12,469	1,178 9.45 9.45 1.86	-	-	543 6.93 46.10 4.35 0.86	-	-	96 7.88 8.15 0.77 0.15	-	380 21.71 32.26 3.05 0.60	-	-	-	-	-	49 8.35 4.16 0.39 0.08	-	-	20 4.72 1.70 0.16 0.03	-	-	-	-	-	-
Monmouth County	488,958 85.29	22,380	4,387 19.60 19.60 0.90	-	-	1,202 18.86 27.40 5.37 0.25	-	-	1,259 14.52 28.70 5.63 0.26	-	854 27.25 19.47 3.82 0.17	-	-	-	-	190 52.63 4.33 0.85 0.04	433 23.73 9.87 1.93 0.09	-	-	29 8.38 0.66 0.13 0.01	-	-	-	-	-	83 12.91 1.89 0.37 0.02
Aberdeen (township)	13,692 84.62	878	189 21.53 21.53 1.38	-	-	77 20.92 40.74 8.77 0.56	-	-	71 19.61 37.57 8.09 0.52	-	-	-	-	-	-	-	-	-	-	-	-	-	-	-	-	-
Colts Neck (township)	9,935 87.97	486	152 31.28 31.28 1.53	-	-	-	-	-	-	-	-	-	-	-	-	-	-	-	-	-	-	-	-	-	-	-
Eatontown (borough)	10,445 80.24	1,138	190 16.70 16.70 1.82	-	-	-	-	-		-	-	-	-	-	-	-	-	-	-	-	-	-	-	-	-	-
Freehold (township)	25,074 85.27	1,588	447 28.15 28.15 1.78	-	-	135 30.75 30.20 8.50 0.54	-	-	90 17.65 20.13 5.67 0.36	-	106 28.19 23.71 6.68 0.42	-	-	-	-	-	-	-	-	-	-	-	-	-	-	-

Notes: Please refer to the User's Guide for an explanation of data; data is arranged alphabetically by state, then county, then city within each county; table includes counties with populations greater than 49,999 unless noted and cities with populations greater than 9,999 whose Asian and/or NHPI population rates are greater than the national average; (1) Native Hawaiian and other Pacific Islander; (2) excludes Taiwanese; (3) includes Chamorro; (4) county does not meet population threshold but is shown in order to allow inclusion of city

Place	Total population 5 years and over who speak English-only at home	Asian population 5 years and over	Asians 5 years and over who speak English-only at home	NHPI[1] population 5 years and over	NHPIs[1] 5 years and over who speak English-only at home	Asian Indian	Bangladeshi	Cambodian	Chinese[2]	Fijian	Filipino	Guamanian[3]	Hawaiian, Native	Hmong	Indonesian	Japanese	Korean	Laotian	Malaysian	Pakistani	Samoan	Sri Lankan	Taiwanese	Thai	Tongan	Vietnamese
Holmdel (township)	11,176 75.07	2,535	386 15.23 15.23 3.45	-	-	103 23.57 26.68 4.06 0.92	-	-	203 12.95 52.59 8.01 1.82	-	-	-	-	-	-	-	-	-	-	-	-	-	-	-	-	-
Howell (township)	38,607 85.93	1,738	385 22.15 22.15 1.00	-	-	124 20.70 32.21 7.13 0.32	-	-	-	-	126 28.70 32.73 7.25 0.33	-	-	-	-	-	-	-	-	-	-	-	-	-	-	-
Manalapan (township)	26,775 85.82	1,414	331 23.41 23.41 1.24	-	-	115 20.32 34.74 8.13 0.43	-	-	114 23.75 34.44 8.06 0.43	-	-	-	-	-	-	-	-	-	-	-	-	-	-	-	-	-
Marlboro (township)	26,298 77.95	4,085	418 10.23 10.23 1.59	-	-	146 15.19 34.93 3.57 0.56	-	-	161 6.87 38.52 3.94 0.61	-	-	-	-	-	-	-	-	-	-	-	-	-	-	-	-	-
Morganville (cdp)	8,438 81.00	927	74 7.98 7.98 0.88	-	-	-	-	-	29 5.27 39.19 3.13 0.34	-	-	-	-	-	-	-	-	-	-	-	-	-	-	-	-	-
Ocean (township)	20,213 80.05	1,435	147 10.24 10.24 0.73	-	-	16 2.95 10.88 1.11 0.08	-	-	-	-	-	-	-	-	-	-	-	-	-	-	-	-	-	-	-	-
Tinton Falls (borough)	11,723 84.59	732	97 13.25 13.25 0.83	-	-	-	-	-	-	-	-	-	-	-	-	-	-	-	-	-	-	-	-	-	-	-
West Freehold (cdp)	10,181 86.05	551	143 25.95 25.95 1.40	-	-	-	-	-	-	-	-	-	-	-	-	-	-	-	-	-	-	-	-	-	-	-
Morris County	351,459 80.29	27,722	4,222 15.23 15.23 1.20	-	-	1,352 13.95 32.02 4.88 0.38	-	-	948 11.23 22.45 3.42 0.27	-	814 26.17 19.28 2.94 0.23	-	-	-	-	148 21.08 3.51 0.53 0.04	576 22.44 13.64 2.08 0.16	-	-	27 3.90 0.64 0.10 0.01	-	-	18 2.83 0.43 0.06 0.01	-	-	106 15.41 2.51 0.38 0.03
Chatham (township)	8,260 88.50	537	149 27.75 27.75 1.80	-	-	-	-	-	-	-	-	-	-	-	-	-	-	-	-	-	-	-	-	-	-	-

Notes: Please refer to the User's Guide for an explanation of data; data is arranged alphabetically by state, then county, then city within each county; table includes counties with populations greater than 49,999 unless noted and cities with populations greater than 9,999 whose Asian and/or NHPI population rates are greater than the national average; (1) Native Hawaiian and other Pacific Islander; (2) excludes Taiwanese; (3) includes Chamorro; (4) county does not meet population threshold but is shown in order to allow inclusion of city

Place	Total population 5 years and over who speak English-only at home	Asian population 5 years and over	Asians 5 years and over who speak English-only at home	NHPI[1] population 5 years and over	NHPIs[1] 5 years and over who speak English-only at home	Asian Indian	Bangladeshi	Cambodian	Chinese[2]	Fijian	Filipino	Guamanian[3]	Hawaiian, Native	Hmong	Indonesian	Japanese	Korean	Laotian	Malaysian	Pakistani	Samoan	Sri Lankan	Taiwanese	Thai	Tongan	Vietnamese
Denville (township)	12,697 86.49	709	179 25.25 25.25 1.41	-	-	-	-	-	-	-	-	-	-	-	-	-	-	-	-	-	-	-	-	-	-	-
East Hanover (township)	7,831 73.25	1,170	176 15.04 15.04 2.25	-	-	-	-	-	26 4.29 14.77 2.22 0.33	-	-	-	-	-	-	-	-	-	-	-	-	-	-	-	-	-
Hanover (township)	9,569 79.20	1,146	167 14.57 14.57 1.75	-	-	54 15.21 32.34 4.71 0.56	-	-	65 12.45 38.92 5.67 0.68	-	-	-	-	-	-	-	-	-	-	-	-	-	-	-	-	-
Lincoln Park (borough)	8,180 79.28	592	128 21.62 21.62 1.56	-	-	-	-	-	-	-	-	-	-	-	-	-	-	-	-	-	-	-	-	-	-	-
Montville (township)	14,991 77.25	2,496	338 13.54 13.54 2.25	-	-	154 16.38 45.56 6.17 1.03	-	-	78 8.94 23.08 3.13 0.52	-	-	-	-	-	-	-	-	-	-	-	-	-	-	-	-	-
Morris (township)	17,568 86.64	876	190 21.69 21.69 1.08	-	-	-	-	-	-	-	-	-	-	-	-	-	-	-	-	-	-	-	-	-	-	-
Mount Olive (township)	18,625 84.34	1,430	237 16.57 16.57 1.27	-	-	73 12.03 30.80 5.10 0.39	-	-	-	-	-	-	-	-	-	-	-	-	-	-	-	-	-	-	-	-
Parsippany-Troy Hills (twp)	32,329 67.67	8,339	754 9.04 9.04 2.33	-	-	249 6.64 33.02 2.99 0.77	-	-	117 4.90 15.52 1.40 0.36	-	220 29.33 29.18 2.64 0.68	-	-	-	-	-	84 18.58 11.14 1.01 0.26	-	-	-	-	-	-	-	-	-
Randolph (township)	18,715 81.49	2,262	390 17.24 17.24 2.08	-	-	120 14.71 30.77 5.31 0.64	-	-	165 24.92 42.31 7.29 0.88	-	-	-	-	-	-	-	-	-	-	-	-	-	-	-	-	-
Rockaway (township)	17,425 82.21	1,236	125 10.11 10.11 0.72	-	-	31 5.14 24.80 2.51 0.18	-	-	-	-	-	-	-	-	-	-	-	-	-	-	-	-	-	-	-	-

Notes: Please refer to the User's Guide for an explanation of data; data is arranged alphabetically by state, then county, then city within each county; table includes counties with populations greater than 49,999 unless noted and cities with populations greater than 9,999 whose Asian and/or NHPI population rates are greater than the national average; (1) Native Hawaiian and other Pacific Islander; (2) excludes Taiwanese; (3) includes Chamorro; (4) county does not meet population threshold but is shown in order to allow inclusion of city

Place	Total population 5 years and over who speak English-only at home	Asian population 5 years and over	Asians 5 years and over who speak English-only at home	NHPI[1] population 5 years and over	NHPIs[1] 5 years and over who speak English-only at home	Asian Indian	Bangladeshi	Cambodian	Chinese[2]	Fijian	Filipino	Guamanian[3]	Hawaiian, Native	Hmong	Indonesian	Japanese	Korean	Laotian	Malaysian	Pakistani	Samoan	Sri Lankan	Taiwanese	Thai	Tongan	Vietnamese
Roxbury (township)	19,438 87.62	797	155 19.45 19.45 0.80	-	-	-	-	-	-	-	-	-	-	-	-	-	-	-	-	-	-	-	-	-	-	-
Succasunna-Kenvil (cdp)	10,071 86.74	471	59 12.53 12.53 0.59	-	-	-	-	-	-	-	-	-	-	-	-	-	-	-	-	-	-	-	-	-	-	-
Ocean County	426,432 89.06	6,128	1,664 27.15 27.15 0.39	-	-	437 29.17 26.26 7.13 0.10	-	-	203 19.08 12.20 3.31 0.05	-	571 25.17 34.31 9.32 0.13	-	-	-	-	-	300 63.69 18.03 4.90 0.07	-	-	-	-	-	-	-	-	-
Passaic County	263,028 58.10	16,870	1,858 11.01 11.01 0.71	-	-	672 8.25 36.17 3.98 0.26	9 1.88 0.48 0.05 <0.01	-	195 11.02 10.50 1.16 0.07	-	637 19.62 34.28 3.78 0.24	-	-	-	-	-	147 9.58 7.91 0.87 0.06	-	-	-	-	-	-	-	-	-
Clifton (city)	42,138 56.92	5,077	638 12.57 12.57 1.51	-	-	207 7.65 32.45 4.08 0.49	-	-	31 7.99 4.86 0.61 0.07	-	339 28.90 53.13 6.68 0.80	-	-	-	-	-	6 1.93 0.94 0.12 0.01	-	-	-	-	-	-	-	-	-
Little Falls (township)	8,259 79.96	431	75 17.40 17.40 0.91	-	-	-	-	-	-	-	-	-	-	-	-	-	-	-	-	-	-	-	-	-	-	-
Passaic (city)	17,630 28.86	3,532	278 7.87 7.87 1.58	-	-	118 5.14 42.45 3.34 0.67	-	-	-	-	140 19.50 50.36 3.96 0.79	-	-	-	-	-	-	-	-	-	-	-	-	-	-	-
Wayne (township)	39,325 77.50	2,971	260 8.75 8.75 0.66	-	-	135 13.61 51.92 4.54 0.34	-	-	64 10.36 24.62 2.15 0.16	-	10 3.26 3.85 0.34 0.03	-	-	-	-	-	21 2.56 8.08 0.71 0.05	-	-	-	-	-	-	-	-	-
Salem County	56,603 93.67	346	121 34.97 34.97 0.21	-	-	-	-	-	-	-	-	-	-	-	-	-	-	-	-	-	-	-	-	-	-	-
Somerset County	212,271 77.05	22,714	3,320 14.62 14.62 1.56	-	-	1,217 13.25 36.66 5.36 0.57	-	-	876 13.16 26.39 3.86 0.41	-	671 23.56 20.21 2.95 0.32	-	-	-	-	148 27.31 4.46 0.65 0.07	166 13.33 5.00 0.73 0.08	-	-	80 10.67 2.41 0.35 0.04	-	-	51 9.90 1.54 0.22 0.02	-	-	42 9.81 1.27 0.18 0.02

Notes: Please refer to the User's Guide for an explanation of data; data is arranged alphabetically by state, then county, then city within each county; table includes counties with populations greater than 49,999 unless noted and cities with populations greater than 9,999 whose Asian and/or NHPI population rates are greater than the national average; (1) Native Hawaiian and other Pacific Islander; (2) excludes Taiwanese; (3) includes Chamorro; (4) county does not meet population threshold but is shown in order to allow inclusion of city

Place	Total population 5 years and over who speak English-only at home	Asian population 5 years and over	Asians 5 years and over who speak English-only at home	NHPI[1] population 5 years and over	NHPIs[1] 5 years and over who speak English-only at home	Asian Indian	Bangladeshi	Cambodian	Chinese[2]	Fijian	Filipino	Guamanian[3]	Hawaiian, Native	Hmong	Indonesian	Japanese	Korean	Laotian	Malaysian	Pakistani	Samoan	Sri Lankan	Taiwanese	Thai	Tongan	Vietnamese
Bernards (township)	19,219 85.05	1,741	404 23.21 23.21 2.10	-	-	133 28.00 32.92 7.64 0.69	-	-	163 19.20 40.35 9.36 0.85	-	-	-	-	-	-	-	-	-	-	-	-	-	-	-	-	-
Branchburg (township)	11,702 87.37	996	190 19.08 19.08 1.62	-	-	88 15.52 46.32 8.84 0.75	-	-	-	-	-	-	-	-	-	-	-	-	-	-	-	-	-	-	-	-
Bridgewater (township)	31,489 79.49	4,196	509 12.13 12.13 1.62	-	-	163 9.31 32.02 3.88 0.52	-	-	164 11.48 32.22 3.91 0.52	-	-	-	-	-	-	-	-	-	-	-	-	-	-	-	-	-
Franklin (township)	34,129 72.30	5,703	610 10.70 10.70 1.79	-	-	328 11.22 53.77 5.75 0.96	-	-	105 8.95 17.21 1.84 0.31	-	129 16.56 21.15 2.26 0.38	-	-	-	-	-	-	-	-	-	-	-	-	-	-	-
Hillsborough (township)	28,163 83.54	2,284	343 15.02 15.02 1.22	-	-	129 15.34 37.61 5.65 0.46	-	-	92 14.26 26.82 4.03 0.33	-	-	-	-	-	-	-	-	-	-	-	-	-	-	-	-	-
Montgomery (township)	13,152 82.34	1,768	316 17.87 17.87 2.40	-	-	66 13.39 20.89 3.73 0.50	-	-	129 15.36 40.82 7.30 0.98	-	-	-	-	-	-	-	-	-	-	-	-	-	-	-	-	-
North Plainfield (borough)	11,266 57.70	1,021	145 14.20 14.20 1.29	-	-	-	-	-	-	-	-	-	-	-	-	-	-	-	-	-	-	-	-	-	-	-
Somerset (cdp)	15,784 73.35	1,663	264 15.87 15.87 1.67	-	-	117 18.11 44.32 7.04 0.74	-	-	49 12.73 18.56 2.95 0.31	-	82 16.05 31.06 4.93 0.52	-	-	-	-	-	-	-	-	-	-	-	-	-	-	-
Somerville (borough)	8,345 71.80	807	113 14.00 14.00 1.35	-	-	-	-	-	-	-	-	-	-	-	-	-	-	-	-	-	-	-	-	-	-	-
Warren (township)	10,303 77.74	1,523	279 18.32 18.32 2.71	-	-	159 30.99 56.99 10.44 1.54	-	-	59 10.12 21.15 3.87 0.57	-	-	-	-	-	-	-	-	-	-	-	-	-	-	-	-	-

Notes: Please refer to the User's Guide for an explanation of data; data is arranged alphabetically by state, then county, then city within each county; table includes counties with populations greater than 49,999 unless noted and cities with populations greater than 9,999 whose Asian and/or NHPI population rates are greater than the national average; (1) Native Hawaiian and other Pacific Islander; (2) excludes Taiwanese; (3) includes Chamorro; (4) county does not meet population threshold but is shown in order to allow inclusion of city

Place	Total population 5 years and over who speak English-only at home	Asian population 5 years and over	Asians 5 years and over who speak English-only at home	NHPI[1] population 5 years and over	NHPIs[1] 5 years and over who speak English-only at home	Asian Indian	Bangladeshi	Cambodian	Chinese[2]	Fijian	Filipino	Guamanian[3]	Hawaiian, Native	Hmong	Indonesian	Japanese	Korean	Laotian	Malaysian	Pakistani	Samoan	Sri Lankan	Taiwanese	Thai	Tongan	Vietnamese
Sussex County	123,162 91.65	1,502	554 36.88 36.88 0.45	-	-	127 34.14 22.92 8.46 0.10	-	-	-	-	196 41.35 35.38 13.05 0.16	-	-	-	-	-	-	-	-	-	-	-	-	-	-	-
Union County	315,019 64.77	17,997	3,048 16.94 16.94 0.97	-	-	909 14.72 29.82 5.05 0.29	-	-	568 15.76 18.64 3.16 0.18	-	1,070 19.94 35.10 5.95 0.34	-	-	-	-	-	174 16.45 5.71 0.97 0.06	-	-	0 0.00 0.00 0.00 0.00	-	-	-	-	-	81 18.54 2.66 0.45 0.03
Berkeley Heights (township)	10,159 82.21	960	150 15.63 15.63 1.48	-	-	-	-	-	68 17.53 45.33 7.08 0.67	-	-	-	-	-	-	-	-	-	-	-	-	-	-	-	-	-
New Providence (borough)	8,916 81.21	838	161 19.21 19.21 1.81	-	-	-	-	-	63 18.37 39.13 7.52 0.71	-	-	-	-	-	-	-	-	-	-	-	-	-	-	-	-	-
Rahway (city)	18,636 74.99	1,086	295 27.16 27.16 1.58	-	-	-	-	-	-	-	139 28.08 47.12 12.80 0.75	-	-	-	-	-	-	-	-	-	-	-	-	-	-	-
Roselle Park (borough)	8,195 65.98	1,159	55 4.75 4.75 0.67	-	-	17 2.06 30.91 1.47 0.21	-	-	-	-	-	-	-	-	-	-	-	-	-	-	-	-	-	-	-	-
Scotch Plains (township)	17,220 81.93	1,455	233 16.01 16.01 1.35	-	-	89 15.98 38.20 6.12 0.52	-	-	68 15.28 29.18 4.67 0.39	-	-	-	-	-	-	-	-	-	-	-	-	-	-	-	-	-
Springfield (township)	10,342 76.24	498	77 15.46 15.46 0.74	-	-	-	-	-	-	-	-	-	-	-	-	-	-	-	-	-	-	-	-	-	-	-
Summit (city)	15,314 79.04	769	163 21.20 21.20 1.06	-	-	49 13.80 30.06 6.37 0.32	-	-	-	-	-	-	-	-	-	-	-	-	-	-	-	-	-	-	-	-
Union (township)	34,304 66.72	3,907	573 14.67 14.67 1.67	-	-	137 14.57 23.91 3.51 0.40	-	-	24 4.83 4.19 0.61 0.07	-	352 18.29 61.43 9.01 1.03	-	-	-	-	-	-	-	-	-	-	-	-	-	-	-

Notes: Please refer to the User's Guide for an explanation of data; data is arranged alphabetically by state, then county, then city within each county; table includes counties with populations greater than 49,999 unless noted and cities with populations greater than 9,999 whose Asian and/or NHPI population rates are greater than the national average; (1) Native Hawaiian and other Pacific Islander; (2) excludes Taiwanese; (3) includes Chamorro; (4) county does not meet population threshold but is shown in order to allow inclusion of city

Place	Total population 5 years and over who speak English-only at home	Asian population 5 years and over	Asians 5 years and over who speak English-only at home	NHPI[1] population 5 years and over	NHPIs[1] 5 years and over who speak English-only at home	Asian Indian	Bangladeshi	Cambodian	Chinese[2]	Fijian	Filipino	Guamanian[3]	Hawaiian, Native	Hmong	Indonesian	Japanese	Korean	Laotian	Malaysian	Pakistani	Samoan	Sri Lankan	Taiwanese	Thai	Tongan	Vietnamese
Westfield (town)	24,221 88.88	1,030	254 24.66 24.66 1.05	-	-	-	-	-	-	-	-	-	-	-	-	-	-	-	-	-	-	-	-	-	-	-
Warren County	87,348 91.57	1,073	189 17.61 17.61 0.22	-	-	57 12.13 30.16 5.31 0.07	-	-	-	-	-	-	-	-	-	-	-	-	-	-	-	-	-	-	-	-
NEW MEXICO	1,072,947 63.49	16,818	5,119 30.44 30.44 0.48	1,151	742 64.47 64.47 0.07	514 22.87 10.04 3.06 0.05	-	-	753 21.35 14.71 4.48 0.07	-	1,156 41.39 22.58 6.87 0.11	203 64.24 27.36 17.64 0.02	276 74.19 37.20 23.98 0.03	-	-	1,183 60.30 23.11 7.03 0.11	638 39.75 12.46 3.79 0.06	-	-	-	-	-	-	113 28.18 2.21 0.67 0.01	-	224 8.82 4.38 1.33 0.02
Bernalillo County	365,331 70.48	9,058	2,564 28.31 28.31 0.70	489	335 68.51 68.51 0.09	251 22.84 9.79 2.77 0.07	-	-	399 22.56 15.56 4.40 0.11	-	443 45.11 17.28 4.89 0.12	-	-	-	-	668 62.96 26.05 7.37 0.18	372 44.71 14.51 4.11 0.10	-	-	-	-	-	-	-	-	183 8.12 7.14 2.02 0.05
Chaves County	37,929 66.57	362	97 26.80 26.80 0.26	-	-	-	-	-	-	-	-	-	-	-	-	-	-	-	-	-	-	-	-	-	-	-
Dona Ana County	73,554 45.63	1,222	420 34.37 34.37 0.57	-	-	-	-	-	91 25.07 21.67 7.45 0.12	-	-	-	-	-	-	-	-	-	-	-	-	-	-	-	-	-
Los Alamos County[4]	15,288 88.50	679	167 24.59 24.59 1.09	-	-	-	-	-	-	-	-	-	-	-	-	-	-	-	-	-	-	-	-	-	-	-
Los Alamos (cdp)	9,725 86.85	518	125 24.13 24.13 1.29	-	-	-	-	-	-	-	-	-	-	-	-	-	-	-	-	-	-	-	-	-	-	-
Otero County	40,670 70.29	682	230 33.72 33.72 0.57	-	-	-	-	-	-	-	-	-	-	-	-	-	-	-	-	-	-	-	-	-	-	-
Sandoval County	56,904 68.24	690	260 37.68 37.68 0.46	-	-	-	-	-	-	-	155 47.11 59.62 22.46 0.27	-	-	-	-	-	-	-	-	-	-	-	-	-	-	-

Notes: Please refer to the User's Guide for an explanation of data; data is arranged alphabetically by state, then county, then city within each county; table includes counties with populations greater than 49,999 unless noted and cities with populations greater than 9,999 whose Asian and/or NHPI population rates are greater than the national average; (1) Native Hawaiian and other Pacific Islander; (2) excludes Taiwanese; (3) includes Chamorro; (4) county does not meet population threshold but is shown in order to allow inclusion of city

Place	Total population 5 years and over who speak English-only at home	Asian population 5 years and over	Asians 5 years and over who speak English-only at home	NHPI[1] population 5 years and over	NHPIs[1] 5 years and over who speak English-only at home	Asian Indian	Bangladeshi	Cambodian	Chinese[2]	Fijian	Filipino	Guamanian[3]	Hawaiian, Native	Hmong	Indonesian	Japanese	Korean	Laotian	Malaysian	Pakistani	Samoan	Sri Lankan	Taiwanese	Thai	Tongan	Vietnamese
Santa Fe County	76,698 63.10	874	274 31.35 31.35 0.36	-	-	-	-	-	-	-	-	-	-	-	-	-	-	-	-	-	-	-	-	-	-	-
NEW YORK	12,786,189 72.04	980,261	156,745 15.99 15.99 1.23	7,256	3,913 53.93 53.93 0.03	67,023 28.98 42.76 6.84 0.52	742 4.04 0.47 0.08 0.01	253 9.43 0.16 0.03 <0.01	35,595 9.04 22.71 3.63 0.28	-	19,000 23.00 12.12 1.94 0.15	791 48.20 20.21 10.90 0.01	814 61.16 20.80 11.22 0.01	-	345 14.77 0.22 0.04 <0.01	6,486 18.14 4.14 0.66 0.05	15,576 13.58 9.94 1.59 0.12	293 9.55 0.19 0.03 <0.01	139 10.15 0.09 0.01 <0.01	1,326 4.57 0.85 0.14 0.01	778 59.34 19.88 10.72 0.01	530 20.67 0.34 0.05 <0.01	736 9.72 0.47 0.08 0.01	958 14.98 0.61 0.10 0.01	-	2,037 9.54 1.30 0.21 0.02
Albany County	250,439 90.08	7,342	1,498 20.40 20.40 0.60	-	-	391 16.95 26.10 5.33 0.16	-	-	228 12.53 15.22 3.11 0.09	-	243 35.42 16.22 3.31 0.10	-	-	-	-	-	355 40.02 23.70 4.84 0.14	-	-	-	-	-	-	-	-	27 5.47 1.80 0.37 0.01
Colonie (town)	67,545 89.74	2,744	530 19.31 19.31 0.78	-	-	180 15.61 33.96 6.56 0.27	-	-	60 10.36 11.32 2.19 0.09	-	-	-	-	-	-	-	-	-	-	-	-	-	-	-	-	-
Guilderland (town)	28,177 90.96	1,120	154 13.75 13.75 0.55	-	-	33 8.35 21.43 2.95 0.12	-	-	-	-	-	-	-	-	-	-	-	-	-	-	-	-	-	-	-	-
Bronx County (Bronx)	578,996 47.26	36,437	9,401 25.80 25.80 1.62	971	380 39.13 39.13 0.07	6,942 51.21 73.84 19.05 1.20	50 2.70 0.53 0.14 0.01	43 5.42 0.46 0.12 0.01	671 11.01 7.14 1.84 0.12	-	724 15.54 7.70 1.99 0.13	-	-	-	-	114 22.62 1.21 0.31 0.02	258 7.80 2.74 0.71 0.04	-	-	54 5.52 0.57 0.15 0.01	-	-	-	-	-	84 3.17 0.89 0.23 0.01
Broome County	172,346 91.08	5,079	862 16.97 16.97 0.50	-	-	177 20.07 20.53 3.48 0.10	-	-	165 10.85 19.14 3.25 0.10	-	-	-	-	-	-	-	148 19.97 17.17 2.91 0.09	94 18.58 10.90 1.85 0.05	-	-	-	-	-	-	-	13 2.73 1.51 0.26 0.01
Johnson City (village)	12,918 88.06	791	189 23.89 23.89 1.46	-	-	-	-	-	-	-	-	-	-	-	-	-	-	-	-	-	-	-	-	-	-	-
Vestal (town)	21,686 85.59	2,052	296 14.42 14.42 1.36	-	-	-	-	-	110 12.94 37.16 5.36 0.51	-	-	-	-	-	-	-	-	-	-	-	-	-	-	-	-	-
Cattaraugus County	74,742 94.87	404	92 22.77 22.77 0.12	-	-	-	-	-	-	-	-	-	-	-	-	-	-	-	-	-	-	-	-	-	-	-

Notes: Please refer to the User's Guide for an explanation of data; data is arranged alphabetically by state, then county, then city within each county; table includes counties with populations greater than 49,999 unless noted and cities with populations greater than 9,999 whose Asian and/or NHPI population rates are greater than the national average; (1) Native Hawaiian and other Pacific Islander; (2) excludes Taiwanese; (3) includes Chamorro; (4) county does not meet population threshold but is shown in order to allow inclusion of city

Place	Total population 5 years and over who speak English-only at home	Asian population 5 years and over	Asians 5 years and over who speak English-only at home	NHPI[1] population 5 years and over	NHPIs[1] 5 years and over who speak English-only at home	Asian Indian	Bangladeshi	Cambodian	Chinese[2]	Fijian	Filipino	Guamanian[3]	Hawaiian, Native	Hmong	Indonesian	Japanese	Korean	Laotian	Malaysian	Pakistani	Samoan	Sri Lankan	Taiwanese	Thai	Tongan	Vietnamese
Cayuga County	72,915 94.48	318	68 21.38 21.38 0.09	-	-	-	-	-	-	-	-	-	-	-	-	-	-	-	-	-	-	-	-	-	-	-
Chautauqua County	122,179 92.79	423	134 31.68 31.68 0.11	-	-	-	-	-	-	-	-	-	-	-	-	-	-	-	-	-	-	-	-	-	-	-
Chemung County	82,002 95.68	723	184 25.45 25.45 0.22	-	-	-	-	-	-	-	-	-	-	-	-	-	-	-	-	-	-	-	-	-	-	-
Chenango County	46,520 96.23	168	76 45.24 45.24 0.16	-	-	-	-	-	-	-	-	-	-	-	-	-	-	-	-	-	-	-	-	-	-	-
Clinton County	71,003 93.68	678	191 28.17 28.17 0.27	-	-	-	-	-	-	-	-	-	-	-	-	-	-	-	-	-	-	-	-	-	-	-
Columbia County	55,726 93.31	419	97 23.15 23.15 0.17	-	-	-	-	-	-	-	-	-	-	-	-	-	-	-	-	-	-	-	-	-	-	-
Dutchess County	231,678 88.08	6,615	1,499 22.66 22.66 0.65	-	-	536 20.57 35.76 8.10 0.23	-	-	463 23.78 30.89 7.00 0.20	-	-	-	-	-	-	-	124 17.17 8.27 1.87 0.05	-	-	-	-	-	-	-	-	-
Arlington (cdp)	9,808 83.56	713	91 12.76 12.76 0.93	-	-	-	-	-	-	-	-	-	-	-	-	-	-	-	-	-	-	-	-	-	-	-
Poughkeepsie (town)	34,932 86.26	1,716	308 17.95 17.95 0.88	-	-	87 10.14 28.25 5.07 0.25	-	-	106 26.57 34.42 6.18 0.30	-	-	-	-	-	-	-	-	-	-	-	-	-	-	-	-	-
Wappinger (town)	20,876 84.67	1,073	333 31.03 31.03 1.60	-	-	147 38.18 44.14 13.70 0.70	-	-	-	-	-	-	-	-	-	-	-	-	-	-	-	-	-	-	-	-

Notes: Please refer to the User's Guide for an explanation of data; data is arranged alphabetically by state, then county, then city within each county; table includes counties with populations greater than 49,999 unless noted and cities with populations greater than 9,999 whose Asian and/or NHPI population rates are greater than the national average; (1) Native Hawaiian and other Pacific Islander; (2) excludes Taiwanese; (3) includes Chamorro; (4) county does not meet population threshold but is shown in order to allow inclusion of city

Place	Total population 5 years and over who speak English-only at home	Asian population 5 years and over	Asians 5 years and over who speak English-only at home	NHPI[1] population 5 years and over	NHPIs[1] 5 years and over who speak English-only at home	Asian Indian	Bangladeshi	Cambodian	Chinese[2]	Fijian	Filipino	Guamanian[3]	Hawaiian, Native	Hmong	Indonesian	Japanese	Korean	Laotian	Malaysian	Pakistani	Samoan	Sri Lankan	Taiwanese	Thai	Tongan	Vietnamese
Erie County	812,588 91.01	11,957	2,469 20.65 20.65 0.30	-	-	716 22.27 29.00 5.99 0.09	-	-	344 12.02 13.93 2.88 0.04	-	220 33.74 8.91 1.84 0.03	-	-	-	-	158 31.85 6.40 1.32 0.02	667 35.94 27.01 5.58 0.08	-	-	-	-	-	-	-	-	177 13.54 7.17 1.48 0.02
Amherst (town)	98,223 89.07	5,215	925 17.74 17.74 0.94	-	-	383 22.46 41.41 7.34 0.39	-	-	218 13.74 23.57 4.18 0.22	-	-	-	-	-	-	-	189 21.82 20.43 3.62 0.19	-	-	-	-	-	-	-	-	-
Herkimer County	57,720 94.84	255	80 31.37 31.37 0.14	-	-	-	-	-	-	-	-	-	-	-	-	-	-	-	-	-	-	-	-	-	-	-
Jefferson County	96,110 92.80	1,097	384 35.00 35.00 0.40	-	-	-	-	-	-	-	140 47.62 36.46 12.76 0.15	-	-	-	-	-	118 34.60 30.73 10.76 0.12	-	-	-	-	-	-	-	-	-
Kings County (Brooklyn)	1,217,121 53.26	173,122	18,266 10.55 10.55 1.50	1,398	569 40.70 40.70 0.05	6,667 29.50 36.50 3.85 0.55	258 7.21 1.41 0.15 0.02	25 5.23 0.14 0.01 <0.01	7,039 6.22 38.54 4.07 0.58	-	1,334 19.89 7.30 0.77 0.11	226 50.45 39.72 16.17 0.02	-	-	-	597 28.48 3.27 0.34 0.05	935 14.47 5.12 0.54 0.08	-	-	316 3.65 1.73 0.18 0.03	-	-	-	-	-	242 6.82 1.32 0.14 0.02
Livingston County	57,909 95.25	655	189 28.85 28.85 0.33	-	-	-	-	-	-	-	-	-	-	-	-	-	-	-	-	-	-	-	-	-	-	-
Madison County	62,076 95.03	451	177 39.25 39.25 0.29	-	-	-	-	-	-	-	-	-	-	-	-	-	-	-	-	-	-	-	-	-	-	-
Monroe County	605,172 87.86	16,510	3,486 21.11 21.11 0.58	-	-	845 20.17 24.24 5.12 0.14	-	13 3.80 0.37 0.08 <0.01	506 13.63 14.52 3.06 0.08	-	240 41.17 6.88 1.45 0.04	-	-	-	-	140 26.07 4.02 0.85 0.02	1,167 49.58 33.48 7.07 0.19	109 8.69 3.13 0.66 0.02	-	16 3.93 0.46 0.10 <0.01	-	-	-	-	-	178 8.55 5.11 1.08 0.03
Brighton (town)	28,111 83.19	2,603	322 12.37 12.37 1.15	-	-	91 9.92 28.26 3.50 0.32	-	-	82 13.33 25.47 3.15 0.29	-	-	-	-	-	-	-	-	-	-	-	-	-	-	-	-	-
Henrietta (town)	33,050 89.11	1,950	558 28.62 28.62 1.69	-	-	120 25.70 21.51 6.15 0.36	-	-	93 19.33 16.67 4.77 0.28	-	-	-	-	-	-	-	-	-	-	-	-	-	-	-	-	-

Notes: Please refer to the User's Guide for an explanation of data; data is arranged alphabetically by state, then county, then city within each county; table includes counties with populations greater than 49,999 unless noted and cities with populations greater than 9,999 whose Asian and/or NHPI population rates are greater than the national average; (1) Native Hawaiian and other Pacific Islander; (2) excludes Taiwanese; (3) includes Chamorro; (4) county does not meet population threshold but is shown in order to allow inclusion of city

Place	Total population 5 years and over who speak English-only at home	Asian population 5 years and over	Asians 5 years and over who speak English-only at home	NHPI[1] population 5 years and over	NHPIs[1] 5 years and over who speak English-only at home	Asian Indian	Bangladeshi	Cambodian	Chinese[2]	Fijian	Filipino	Guamanian[3]	Hawaiian, Native	Hmong	Indonesian	Japanese	Korean	Laotian	Malaysian	Pakistani	Samoan	Sri Lankan	Taiwanese	Thai	Tongan	Vietnamese
Pittsford (town)	23,262 90.81	1,193	232 19.45 19.45 1.00	-	-	93 16.61 40.09 7.80 0.40	-	-	-	-	-	-	-	-	-	-	-	-	-	-	-	-	-	-	-	-
Nassau County	959,465 76.84	58,799	10,684 18.17 18.17 1.11	336	202 60.12 60.12 0.02	4,399 20.10 41.17 7.48 0.46	-	-	2,301 16.37 21.54 3.91 0.24	-	1,779 26.15 16.65 3.03 0.19	-	-	-	-	290 17.42 2.71 0.49 0.03	1,127 12.91 10.55 1.92 0.12	-	-	109 5.10 1.02 0.19 0.01	-	-	46 7.73 0.43 0.08 <0.01	72 20.57 0.67 0.12 0.01	-	65 14.74 0.61 0.11 0.01
East Meadow (cdp)	27,769 78.66	2,152	318 14.78 14.78 1.15	-	-	117 12.04 36.79 5.44 0.42	-	-	-	-	38 12.79 11.95 1.77 0.14	-	-	-	-	-	-	-	-	-	-	-	-	-	-	-
Elmont (cdp)	18,548 60.57	3,029	641 21.16 21.16 3.46	-	-	384 21.27 59.91 12.68 2.07	-	-	-	-	116 21.80 18.10 3.83 0.63	-	-	-	-	-	-	-	-	-	-	-	-	-	-	-
Franklin Square (cdp)	21,004 75.98	1,139	285 25.02 25.02 1.36	-	-	119 26.56 41.75 10.45 0.57	-	-	-	-	-	-	-	-	-	-	-	-	-	-	-	-	-	-	-	-
Glen Cove (city)	15,449 61.47	1,006	137 13.62 13.62 0.89	-	-	62 20.00 45.26 6.16 0.40	-	-	-	-	-	-	-	-	-	-	20 5.17 14.60 1.99 0.13	-	-	-	-	-	-	-	-	-
Hicksville (cdp)	29,156 75.58	3,420	557 16.29 16.29 1.91	-	-	260 15.37 46.68 7.60 0.89	-	-	43 6.03 7.72 1.26 0.15	-	133 26.08 23.88 3.89 0.46	-	-	-	-	-	-	-	-	-	-	-	-	-	-	-
Jericho (cdp)	9,902 81.26	1,403	121 8.62 8.62 1.22	-	-	-	-	-	-	-	-	-	-	-	-	-	9 1.28 7.44 0.64 0.09	-	-	-	-	-	-	-	-	-
Mineola (village)	11,474 63.47	857	173 20.19 20.19 1.51	-	-	82 24.70 47.40 9.57 0.71	-	-	-	-	-	-	-	-	-	-	-	-	-	-	-	-	-	-	-	-
North Hempstead (town)	141,469 67.65	19,397	3,039 15.67 15.67 2.15	-	-	1,274 17.82 41.92 6.57 0.90	-	-	663 12.65 21.82 3.42 0.47	-	411 31.66 13.52 2.12 0.29	-	-	-	-	77 8.78 2.53 0.40 0.05	357 11.34 11.75 1.84 0.25	-	-	32 5.67 1.05 0.16 0.02	-	-	21 7.42 0.69 0.11 0.01	-	-	-

Notes: Please refer to the User's Guide for an explanation of data; data is arranged alphabetically by state, then county, then city within each county; table includes counties with populations greater than 49,999 unless noted and cities with populations greater than 9,999 whose Asian and/or NHPI population rates are greater than the national average; (1) Native Hawaiian and other Pacific Islander; (2) excludes Taiwanese; (3) includes Chamorro; (4) county does not meet population threshold but is shown in order to allow inclusion of city

Place	Total population 5 years and over who speak English-only at home	Asian population 5 years and over	Asians 5 years and over who speak English-only at home	NHPI[1] population 5 years and over	NHPIs[1] 5 years and over who speak English-only at home	Asian Indian	Bangladeshi	Cambodian	Chinese[2]	Fijian	Filipino	Guamanian[3]	Hawaiian, Native	Hmong	Indonesian	Japanese	Korean	Laotian	Malaysian	Pakistani	Samoan	Sri Lankan	Taiwanese	Thai	Tongan	Vietnamese
North Merrick (cdp)	9,704 87.99	452	117 25.88 25.88 1.21	-	-	-	-	-	-	-	-	-	-	-	-	-	-	-	-	-	-	-	-	-	-	-
North New Hyde Park (cdp)	9,858 71.31	1,987	315 15.85 15.85 3.20	-	-	91 8.28 28.89 4.58 0.92	-	-	131 19.44 41.59 6.59 1.33	-	-	-	-	-	-	-	-	-	-	-	-	-	-	-	-	-
North Valley Stream (cdp)	9,836 66.56	1,370	292 21.31 21.31 2.97	-	-	182 29.84 62.33 13.28 1.85	-	-	-	-	-	-	-	-	-	-	-	-	-	-	-	-	-	-	-	-
Oyster Bay (town)	228,112 83.00	13,033	2,136 16.39 16.39 0.94	-	-	809 16.89 37.87 6.21 0.35	-	-	533 15.36 24.95 4.09 0.23	-	339 27.32 15.87 2.60 0.15	-	-	-	-	88 25.36 4.12 0.68 0.04	224 9.51 10.49 1.72 0.10	-	-	-	-	-	-	-	-	-
Plainview (cdp)	19,783 82.66	1,161	100 8.61 8.61 0.51	-	-	22 7.03 22.00 1.89 0.11	-	-	36 11.43 36.00 3.10 0.18	-	-	-	-	-	-	-	5 1.32 5.00 0.43 0.03	-	-	-	-	-	-	-	-	-
Port Washington (cdp)	10,353 73.36	911	134 14.71 14.71 1.29	-	-	58 23.58 43.28 6.37 0.56	-	-	-	-	-	-	-	-	-	-	-	-	-	-	-	-	-	-	-	-
Salisbury (cdp)	8,592 74.96	1,001	77 7.69 7.69 0.90	-	-	5 1.37 6.49 0.50 0.06	-	-	-	-	-	-	-	-	-	-	-	-	-	-	-	-	-	-	-	-
Syosset (cdp)	13,346 77.12	2,194	306 13.95 13.95 2.29	-	-	132 18.99 43.14 6.02 0.99	-	-	113 15.56 36.93 5.15 0.85	-	-	-	-	-	-	-	18 3.29 5.88 0.82 0.13	-	-	-	-	-	-	-	-	-
Valley Stream (village)	25,170 73.37	2,435	484 19.88 19.88 1.92	-	-	-	-	-	175 23.15 36.16 7.19 0.70	-	116 20.24 23.97 4.76 0.46	-	-	-	-	-	-	-	-	-	-	-	-	-	-	-
West Hempstead (cdp)	13,332 76.40	918	203 22.11 22.11 1.52	-	-	77 25.67 37.93 8.39 0.58	-	-	-	-	-	-	-	-	-	-	-	-	-	-	-	-	-	-	-	-

Notes: Please refer to the User's Guide for an explanation of data; data is arranged alphabetically by state, then county, then city within each county; table includes counties with populations greater than 49,999 unless noted and cities with populations greater than 9,999 whose Asian and/or NHPI population rates are greater than the national average; (1) Native Hawaiian and other Pacific Islander; (2) excludes Taiwanese; (3) includes Chamorro; (4) county does not meet population threshold but is shown in order to allow inclusion of city

Place	Total population 5 years and over who speak English-only at home	Asian population 5 years and over	Asians 5 years and over who speak English-only at home	NHPI[1] population 5 years and over	NHPIs[1] 5 years and over who speak English-only at home	Asian Indian	Bangladeshi	Cambodian	Chinese[2]	Fijian	Filipino	Guamanian[3]	Hawaiian, Native	Hmong	Indonesian	Japanese	Korean	Laotian	Malaysian	Pakistani	Samoan	Sri Lankan	Taiwanese	Thai	Tongan	Vietnamese
Westbury (village)	8,394	656	76	-	-	-	-	-	-	-	-	-	-	-	-	-	-	-	-	-	-	-	-	-	-	-
	62.54		11.59																							
			11.59																							
			0.91																							
Woodmere (cdp)	11,684	588	13	-	-	-	-	-	-	-	-	-	-	-	-	-	-	-	-	-	-	-	-	-	-	-
	76.68		2.21																							
			2.21																							
			0.11																							
New York City	3,920,797	740,899	107,879	4,458	2,120	51,139	713	135	26,421	-	11,331	552	282	-	245	3,914	7,397	-	85	754	289	388	430	330	-	960
	52.45		14.56		47.55	32.58	4.07	8.69	7.81		20.19	49.91	40.23		14.10	18.22	8.93		7.25	3.49	43.46	20.43	8.97	8.81		8.41
						47.40	0.66	0.13	24.49		10.50	26.04	13.30		0.23	3.63	6.86		0.08	0.70	13.63	0.36	0.40	0.31		0.89
			14.56		47.55	6.90	0.10	0.02	3.57		1.53	12.38	6.33		0.03	0.53	1.00		0.01	0.10	6.48	0.05	0.06	0.04		0.13
			2.75		0.05	1.30	0.02	<0.01	0.67		0.29	0.01	0.01		0.01	0.10	0.19		<0.01	0.02	0.01	0.01	0.01	0.01		0.02
New York County (Manhattan)	849,603	138,777	24,964	562	242	4,718	30	-	8,896	-	2,650	-	-	-	-	2,601	3,482	-	-	154	-	-	305	170	-	413
	58.11		17.99		43.06	34.20	4.14		10.87		30.62					19.15	31.36			15.37			29.50	20.86		27.68
						18.90	0.12		35.64		10.62					10.42	13.95			0.62			1.22	0.68		1.65
			17.99		43.06	3.40	0.02		6.41		1.91					1.87	2.51			0.11			0.22	0.12		0.30
			2.94		0.03	0.56	<0.01		1.05		0.31					0.31	0.41			0.02			0.04	0.02		0.05
Niagara County	194,596	1,072	328	-	-	146	-	-	-	-	-	-	-	-	-	-	-	-	-	-	-	-	-	-	-	-
	94.13		30.60			36.14																				
						44.51																				
			30.60			13.62																				
			0.17			0.08																				
Oneida County	200,750	2,518	495	-	-	141	-	-	60	-	-	-	-	-	-	-	-	-	-	-	-	-	-	-	-	37
	90.40		19.66			27.59			21.35																	3.81
						28.48			12.12																	7.47
			19.66			5.60			2.38																	1.47
			0.25			0.07			0.03																	0.02
Onondaga County	390,561	8,957	1,733	-	-	362	-	-	219	-	314	-	-	-	-	106	437	-	-	-	-	-	-	-	-	74
	91.14		19.35			19.44			13.90		42.32					32.32	35.10									4.72
						20.89			12.64		18.12					6.12	25.22									4.27
			19.35			4.04			2.45		3.51					1.18	4.88									0.83
			0.44			0.09			0.06		0.08					0.03	0.11									0.02
Ontario County	89,556	603	256	-	-	-	-	-	-	-	-	-	-	-	-	-	-	-	-	-	-	-	-	-	-	-
	95.13		42.45																							
			42.45																							
			0.29																							
Orange County	257,919	5,142	1,413	-	-	396	-	-	196	-	257	-	-	-	-	-	308	-	-	-	-	-	-	-	-	-
	81.77		27.48			24.91			16.21		34.18						40.21									
						28.03			13.87		18.19						21.80									
			27.48			7.70			3.81		5.00						5.99									
			0.55			0.15			0.08		0.10						0.12									
Oswego County	110,027	489	186	-	-	-	-	-	-	-	-	-	-	-	-	-	-	-	-	-	-	-	-	-	-	-
	95.82		38.04																							
			38.04																							
			0.17																							

Notes: Please refer to the User's Guide for an explanation of data; data is arranged alphabetically by state, then county, then city within each county; table includes counties with populations greater than 49,999 unless noted and cities with populations greater than 9,999 whose Asian and/or NHPI population rates are greater than the national average; (1) Native Hawaiian and other Pacific Islander; (2) excludes Taiwanese; (3) includes Chamorro; (4) county does not meet population threshold but is shown in order to allow inclusion of city

Place	Total population 5 years and over who speak English-only at home	Asian population 5 years and over	Asians 5 years and over who speak English-only at home	NHPI[1] population 5 years and over	NHPIs[1] 5 years and over who speak English-only at home	Asian Indian	Bangladeshi	Cambodian	Chinese[2]	Fijian	Filipino	Guamanian[3]	Hawaiian, Native	Hmong	Indonesian	Japanese	Korean	Laotian	Malaysian	Pakistani	Samoan	Sri Lankan	Taiwanese	Thai	Tongan	Vietnamese
Otsego County	55,731	287	90	-	-	-	-	-	-	-	-	-	-	-	-	-	-	-	-	-	-	-	-	-	-	-
	94.86		31.36																							
			31.36																							
			0.16																							
Putnam County	77,373	1,111	417	-	-	153	-	-	93	-	-	-	-	-	-	-	-	-	-	-	-	-	-	-	-	-
	86.80		37.53			40.69			24.41																	
						36.69			22.30																	
			37.53			13.77			8.37																	
			0.54			0.20			0.12																	
Queens County (Queens)	968,415	369,325	51,887	1,322	791	31,745	366	-	9,129	-	5,523	-	-	-	87	555	2,480	-	8	198	-	181	92	77	-	215
	46.36		14.05		59.83	31.41	3.24		7.01		17.73				7.29	10.87	4.22		1.46	1.93		20.52	2.73	3.34		6.06
						61.18	0.71		17.59		10.64				0.17	1.07	4.78		0.02	0.38		0.35	0.18	0.15		0.41
			14.05		59.83	8.60	0.10		2.47		1.50				0.02	0.15	0.67		<0.01	0.05		0.05	0.02	0.02		0.06
			5.36		0.08	3.28	0.04		0.94		0.57				0.01	0.06	0.26		<0.01	0.02		0.02	0.01	0.01		0.02
Rensselaer County	133,070	2,221	403	-	-	108	-	-	86	-	-	-	-	-	-	-	106	-	-	-	-	-	-	-	-	-
	92.90		18.14			25.59			8.94								32.42									
						26.80			21.34								26.30									
			18.14			4.86			3.87								4.77									
			0.30			0.08			0.06								0.08									
Richmond Co. (Staten Island)	306,662	23,238	3,361	-	-	1,067	-	-	686	-	1,100	-	-	-	-	-	242	-	-	32	-	68	-	-	-	-
	74.00		14.46			17.90			9.90		22.16						7.61			4.74		13.26				
						31.75			20.41		32.73						7.20			0.95		2.02				
			14.46			4.59			2.95		4.73						1.04			0.14		0.29				
			1.10			0.35			0.22		0.36						0.08			0.01		0.02				
Rockland County	185,673	14,939	2,844	-	-	1,152	-	-	266	-	908	-	-	-	-	-	172	-	-	-	-	-	-	-	-	-
	70.06		19.04			22.18			15.21		21.42						9.72									
						40.51			9.35		31.93						6.05									
			19.04			7.71			1.78		6.08						1.15									
			1.53			0.62			0.14		0.49						0.09									
Clarkstown (town)	59,444	6,183	1,231	-	-	534	-	-	152	-	428	-	-	-	-	-	32	-	-	-	-	-	-	-	-	-
	77.36		19.91			24.20			21.59		20.87						4.97									
						43.38			12.35		34.77						2.60									
			19.91			8.64			2.46		6.92						0.52									
			2.07			0.90			0.26		0.72						0.05									
Nanuet (cdp)	11,473	1,424	189	-	-	81	-	-	-	-	-	-	-	-	-	-	-	-	-	-	-	-	-	-	-	-
	73.63		13.27			15.79																				
						42.86																				
			13.27			5.69																				
			1.65			0.71																				
New City (cdp)	25,181	2,337	524	-	-	281	-	-	-	-	106	-	-	-	-	-	-	-	-	-	-	-	-	-	-	-
	78.82		22.42			28.76					19.49															
						53.63					20.23															
			22.42			12.02					4.54															
			2.08			1.12					0.42															
Orangetown (town)	36,451	2,783	583	-	-	135	-	-	70	-	179	-	-	-	-	-	95	-	-	-	-	-	-	-	-	-
	81.26		20.95			20.67			14.26		26.02						17.76									
						23.16			12.01		30.70						16.30									
			20.95			4.85			2.52		6.43						3.41									
			1.60			0.37			0.19		0.49						0.26									

Notes: Please refer to the User's Guide for an explanation of data; data is arranged alphabetically by state, then county, then city within each county; table includes counties with populations greater than 49,999 unless noted and cities with populations greater than 9,999 whose Asian and/or NHPI population rates are greater than the national average; (1) Native Hawaiian and other Pacific Islander; (2) excludes Taiwanese; (3) includes Chamorro; (4) county does not meet population threshold but is shown in order to allow inclusion of city

Place	Total population 5 years and over who speak English-only at home	Asian population 5 years and over	Asians 5 years and over who speak English-only at home	NHPI[1] population 5 years and over	NHPIs[1] 5 years and over who speak English-only at home	Asian Indian	Bangladeshi	Cambodian	Chinese[2]	Fijian	Filipino	Guamanian[3]	Hawaiian, Native	Hmong	Indonesian	Japanese	Korean	Laotian	Malaysian	Pakistani	Samoan	Sri Lankan	Taiwanese	Thai	Tongan	Vietnamese
Ramapo (town)	58,317	4,739	760	-	-	348	-	-	31	-	209	-	-	-	-	-	39	-	-	-	-	-	-	-	-	-
	59.12		16.04			18.70			7.45		16.77						7.68									
						45.79			4.08		27.50						5.13									
			16.04			7.34			0.65		4.41						0.82									
			1.30			0.60			0.05		0.36						0.07									
Spring Valley (village)	9,920	1,388	163	-	-	95	-	-	-	-	-	-	-	-	-	-	-	-	-	-	-	-	-	-	-	-
	43.13		11.74			13.23																				
						58.28																				
			11.74			6.84																				
			1.64			0.96																				
St. Lawrence County	100,287	617	186	-	-	-	-	-	-	-	-	-	-	-	-	-	-	-	-	-	-	-	-	-	-	-
	94.65		30.15																							
			30.15																							
			0.19																							
Saratoga County	177,563	2,054	678	-	-	84	-	-	88	-	-	-	-	-	-	-	310	-	-	-	-	-	-	-	-	-
	94.66		33.01			13.75			23.85								69.51									
						12.39			12.98								45.72									
			33.01			4.09			4.28								15.09									
			0.38			0.05			0.05								0.17									
Schenectady County	123,984	2,601	763	-	-	332	-	-	124	-	-	-	-	-	-	-	-	-	-	-	-	-	-	-	-	-
	90.12		29.33			32.42			15.90																	
						43.51			16.25																	
			29.33			12.76			4.77																	
			0.62			0.27			0.10																	
Niskayuna (town)	16,825	1,066	232	-	-	115	-	-	-	-	-	-	-	-	-	-	-	-	-	-	-	-	-	-	-	-
	88.39		21.76			25.00																				
						49.57																				
			21.76			10.79																				
			1.38			0.68																				
Steuben County	89,030	709	163	-	-	-	-	-	-	-	-	-	-	-	-	-	-	-	-	-	-	-	-	-	-	-
	96.04		22.99																							
			22.99																							
			0.18																							
Suffolk County	1,094,244	32,190	6,635	408	277	1,866	-	-	1,425	-	1,296	-	-	-	-	373	1,064	-	-	143	-	-	46	112	-	55
	82.94		20.61		67.89	19.29			15.59		32.90					36.25	28.62			7.90			10.75	30.19		8.70
						28.12			21.48		19.53					5.62	16.04			2.16			0.69	1.69		0.83
			20.61		67.89	5.80			4.43		4.03					1.16	3.31			0.44			0.14	0.35		0.17
			0.61		0.03	0.17			0.13		0.12					0.03	0.10			0.01			<0.01	0.01		0.01
Coram (cdp)	27,191	1,149	234	-	-	-	-	-	80	-	-	-	-	-	-	-	-	-	-	-	-	-	-	-	-	-
	84.00		20.37						19.75																	
									34.19																	
			20.37						6.96																	
			0.86						0.29																	
Dix Hills (cdp)	19,019	1,831	300	-	-	143	-	-	49	-	-	-	-	-	-	-	-	-	-	-	-	-	-	-	-	-
	78.56		16.38			18.82			11.89																	
						47.67			16.33																	
			16.38			7.81			2.68																	
			1.58			0.75			0.26																	

Notes: Please refer to the User's Guide for an explanation of data; data is arranged alphabetically by state, then county, then city within each county; table includes counties with populations greater than 49,999 unless noted and cities with populations greater than 9,999 whose Asian and/or NHPI population rates are greater than the national average; (1) Native Hawaiian and other Pacific Islander; (2) excludes Taiwanese; (3) includes Chamorro; (4) county does not meet population threshold but is shown in order to allow inclusion of city

Place	Total population 5 years and over who speak English-only at home	Asian population 5 years and over	Asians 5 years and over who speak English-only at home	NHPI[1] population 5 years and over	NHPIs[1] 5 years and over who speak English-only at home	Asian Indian	Bangladeshi	Cambodian	Chinese[2]	Fijian	Filipino	Guamanian[3]	Hawaiian, Native	Hmong	Indonesian	Japanese	Korean	Laotian	Malaysian	Pakistani	Samoan	Sri Lankan	Taiwanese	Thai	Tongan	Vietnamese
Elwood (cdp)	8,465 83.50	672	168 25.00 25.00 1.98	-	-	-	-	-	-	-	-	-	-	-	-	-	-	-	-	-	-	-	-	-	-	-
Lake Grove (village)	8,287 86.39	503	108 21.47 21.47 1.30	-	-	-	-	-	-	-	-	-	-	-	-	-	-	-	-	-	-	-	-	-	-	-
Melville (cdp)	11,121 82.61	614	78 12.70 12.70 0.70	-	-	-	-	-	-	-	-	-	-	-	-	-	-	-	-	-	-	-	-	-	-	-
Setauket-East Setauket (cdp)	12,492 83.65	1,427	243 17.03 17.03 1.95	-	-	-	-	-	60 9.49 24.69 4.20 0.48	-	-	-	-	-	-	-	-	-	-	-	-	-	-	-	-	-
Stony Brook (cdp)	10,994 86.59	728	184 25.27 25.27 1.67	-	-	-	-	-	71 18.49 38.59 9.75 0.65	-	-	-	-	-	-	-	-	-	-	-	-	-	-	-	-	-
Sullivan County	59,786 85.77	809	198 24.47 24.47 0.33	-	-	-	-	-	-	-	-	-	-	-	-	-	-	-	-	-	-	-	-	-	-	-
Tioga County	46,696 96.20	326	118 36.20 36.20 0.25	-	-	-	-	-	-	-	-	-	-	-	-	-	-	-	-	-	-	-	-	-	-	-
Tompkins County	79,467 86.10	6,851	1,242 18.13 18.13 1.56	-	-	294 28.41 23.67 4.29 0.37	-	-	451 14.96 36.31 6.58 0.57	-	-	-	-	-	-	124 22.71 9.98 1.81 0.16	104 9.52 8.37 1.52 0.13	-	-	-	-	-	-	-	-	-
Ithaca (city)	21,913 77.37	4,029	785 19.48 19.48 3.58	-	-	169 32.07 21.53 4.19 0.77	-	-	308 15.45 39.24 7.64 1.41	-	-	-	-	-	-	-	59 12.69 7.52 1.46 0.27	-	-	-	-	-	-	-	-	-
Lansing (town)	8,371 86.16	921	139 15.09 15.09 1.66	-	-	-	-	-	-	-	-	-	-	-	-	-	-	-	-	-	-	-	-	-	-	-

Notes: Please refer to the User's Guide for an explanation of data; data is arranged alphabetically by state, then county, then city within each county; table includes counties with populations greater than 49,999 unless noted and cities with populations greater than 9,999 whose Asian and/or NHPI population rates are greater than the national average; (1) Native Hawaiian and other Pacific Islander; (2) excludes Taiwanese; (3) includes Chamorro; (4) county does not meet population threshold but is shown in order to allow inclusion of city

Place	Total population 5 years and over who speak English-only at home	Asian population 5 years and over	Asians 5 years and over who speak English-only at home	NHPI[1] population 5 years and over	NHPIs[1] 5 years and over who speak English-only at home	Asian Indian	Bangladeshi	Cambodian	Chinese[2]	Fijian	Filipino	Guamanian[3]	Hawaiian, Native	Hmong	Indonesian	Japanese	Korean	Laotian	Malaysian	Pakistani	Samoan	Sri Lankan	Taiwanese	Thai	Tongan	Vietnamese
Ulster County	151,064 89.87	1,698	384 22.61 22.61 0.25	-	-	-	-	-	125 24.51 32.55 7.36 0.08	-	-	-	-	-	-	-	-	-	-	-	-	-	-	-	-	-
New Paltz (town)	10,391 84.03	576	163 28.30 28.30 1.57	-	-	-	-	-	-	-	-	-	-	-	-	-	-	-	-	-	-	-	-	-	-	-
Warren County	57,238 95.67	467	204 43.68 43.68 0.36	-	-	-	-	-	-	-	-	-	-	-	-	-	-	-	-	-	-	-	-	-	-	-
Wayne County	83,642 95.33	355	165 46.48 46.48 0.20	-	-	-	-	-	-	-	-	-	-	-	-	-	-	-	-	-	-	-	-	-	-	-
Westchester County	615,323 71.58	38,484	6,856 17.82 17.82 1.11	-	-	2,970 22.41 43.32 7.72 0.48	-	-	1,463 22.42 21.34 3.80 0.24	-	1,000 21.45 14.59 2.60 0.16	-	-	-	-	408 5.98 5.95 1.06 0.07	544 13.49 7.93 1.41 0.09	-	-	41 5.55 0.60 0.11 0.01	-	-	59 17.72 0.86 0.15 0.01	54 9.52 0.79 0.14 0.01	-	-
Dobbs Ferry (village)	7,881 78.38	706	102 14.45 14.45 1.29	-	-	-	-	-	-	-	-	-	-	-	-	-	-	-	-	-	-	-	-	-	-	-
Eastchester (cdp)	13,708 78.74	1,201	174 14.49 14.49 1.27	-	-	-	-	-	-	-	-	-	-	-	-	48 9.60 27.59 4.00 0.35	-	-	-	-	-	-	-	-	-	-
Eastchester (town)	22,721 77.84	2,055	277 13.48 13.48 1.22	-	-	-	-	-	-	-	-	-	-	-	-	60 5.75 21.66 2.92 0.26	-	-	-	-	-	-	-	-	-	-
Greenburgh (town)	60,796 74.87	7,241	1,126 15.55 15.55 1.85	-	-	521 22.03 46.27 7.20 0.86	-	-	219 18.59 19.45 3.02 0.36	-	100 18.59 8.88 1.38 0.16	-	-	-	-	80 4.38 7.10 1.10 0.13	122 12.79 10.83 1.68 0.20	-	-	-	-	-	-	-	-	-
Harrison (village)	16,529 73.32	1,222	136 11.13 11.13 0.82	-	-	-	-	-	-	-	-	-	-	-	-	10 1.63 7.35 0.82 0.06	-	-	-	-	-	-	-	-	-	-

Notes: Please refer to the User's Guide for an explanation of data; data is arranged alphabetically by state, then county, then city within each county; table includes counties with populations greater than 49,999 unless noted and cities with populations greater than 9,999 whose Asian and/or NHPI population rates are greater than the national average; (1) Native Hawaiian and other Pacific Islander; (2) excludes Taiwanese; (3) includes Chamorro; (4) county does not meet population threshold but is shown in order to allow inclusion of city

Place	Total population 5 years and over who speak English-only at home	Asian population 5 years and over	Asians 5 years and over who speak English-only at home	NHPI[1] population 5 years and over	NHPIs[1] 5 years and over who speak English-only at home	Asian Indian	Bangladeshi	Cambodian	Chinese[2]	Fijian	Filipino	Guamanian[3]	Hawaiian, Native	Hmong	Indonesian	Japanese	Korean	Laotian	Malaysian	Pakistani	Samoan	Sri Lankan	Taiwanese	Thai	Tongan	Vietnamese
New Castle (town)	13,640 84.71	933	219 23.47 23.47 1.61	-	-	102 26.91 46.58 10.93 0.75	-	-	78 26.90 35.62 8.36 0.57	-	-	-	-	-	-	-	-	-	-	-	-	-	-	-	-	-
New Rochelle (city)	45,035 66.82	2,485	406 16.34 16.34 0.90	-	-	194 17.85 47.78 7.81 0.43	-	-	67 13.93 16.50 2.70 0.15	-	-	-	-	-	-	-	-	-	-	-	-	-	-	-	-	-
North Castle (town)	8,144 81.16	435	165 37.93 37.93 2.03	-	-	-	-	-	-	-	-	-	-	-	-	-	-	-	-	-	-	-	-	-	-	-
Ossining (town)	23,954 69.94	1,396	226 16.19 16.19 0.94	-	-	84 13.29 37.17 6.02 0.35	-	-	-	-	-	-	-	-	-	-	-	-	-	-	-	-	-	-	-	-
Ossining (village)	14,093 62.60	870	123 14.14 14.14 0.87	-	-	26 9.29 21.14 2.99 0.18	-	-	-	-	-	-	-	-	-	-	-	-	-	-	-	-	-	-	-	-
Pelham (town)	9,212 83.82	431	96 22.27 22.27 1.04	-	-	-	-	-	-	-	-	-	-	-	-	-	-	-	-	-	-	-	-	-	-	-
Rye (city)	10,664 78.02	981	127 12.95 12.95 1.19	-	-	-	-	-	-	-	-	-	-	-	-	9 1.54 7.09 0.92 0.08	-	-	-	-	-	-	-	-	-	-
Scarsdale (village)	12,830 77.89	2,045	356 17.41 17.41 2.77	-	-	182 47.77 51.12 8.90 1.42	-	-	55 15.90 15.45 2.69 0.43	-	-	-	-	-	-	0 0.00 0.00 0.00 0.00	40 10.44 11.24 1.96 0.31	-	-	-	-	-	-	-	-	-
Tarrytown (village)	7,150 69.18	598	49 8.19 8.19 0.69	-	-	-	-	-	-	-	-	-	-	-	-	-	-	-	-	-	-	-	-	-	-	-
White Plains (city)	31,972 64.08	2,002	302 15.08 15.08 0.94	-	-	112 16.74 37.09 5.59 0.35	-	-	75 14.82 24.83 3.75 0.23	-	-	-	-	-	-	-	-	-	-	-	-	-	-	-	-	-

Notes: Please refer to the User's Guide for an explanation of data; data is arranged alphabetically by state, then county, then city within each county; table includes counties with populations greater than 49,999 unless noted and cities with populations greater than 9,999 whose Asian and/or NHPI population rates are greater than the national average; (1) Native Hawaiian and other Pacific Islander; (2) excludes Taiwanese; (3) includes Chamorro; (4) county does not meet population threshold but is shown in order to allow inclusion of city

Place	Total population 5 years and over who speak English-only at home	Asian population 5 years and over	Asians 5 years and over who speak English-only at home	NHPI[1] population 5 years and over	NHPIs[1] 5 years and over who speak English-only at home	Asian Indian	Bangladeshi	Cambodian	Chinese[2]	Fijian	Filipino	Guamanian[3]	Hawaiian, Native	Hmong	Indonesian	Japanese	Korean	Laotian	Malaysian	Pakistani	Samoan	Sri Lankan	Taiwanese	Thai	Tongan	Vietnamese
Yonkers (city)	111,307 60.97	8,801	1,396 15.86 15.86 1.25	-	-	625 14.70 44.77 7.10 0.56	-	-	266 31.29 19.05 3.02 0.24	-	287 16.93 20.56 3.26 0.26	-	-	-	-	-	100 10.07 7.16 1.14 0.09	-	-	-	-	-	-	-	-	-
NORTH CAROLINA	6,909,648 91.97	102,482	19,121 18.66 18.66 0.28	3,399	2,060 60.61 60.61 0.03	4,319 18.59 22.59 4.21 0.06	-	169 7.62 0.88 0.16 <0.01	2,314 14.41 12.10 2.26 0.03	-	3,651 38.09 19.09 3.56 0.05	578 53.67 28.06 17.01 0.01	923 85.30 44.81 27.16 0.01	196 3.33 1.03 0.19 <0.01	-	1,940 34.42 10.15 1.89 0.03	2,534 21.40 13.25 2.47 0.04	293 6.44 1.53 0.29 <0.01	-	138 8.05 0.72 0.13 <0.01	182 39.82 8.83 5.35 <0.01	-	163 17.81 0.85 0.16 <0.01	364 23.50 1.90 0.36 0.01	-	1,282 8.97 6.70 1.25 0.02
Alamance County	110,937 90.65	1,074	120 11.17 11.17 0.11	-	-	-	-	-	-	-	-	-	-	-	-	-	-	-	-	-	-	-	-	-	-	-
Buncombe County	183,265 94.08	1,686	351 20.82 20.82 0.19	-	-	133 25.88 37.89 7.89 0.07	-	-	-	-	-	-	-	-	-	-	-	-	-	-	-	-	-	-	-	-
Burke County	76,903 91.94	2,633	151 5.73 5.73 0.20	-	-	-	-	-	-	-	-	-	-	46 2.68 30.46 1.75 0.06	-	-	-	7 1.57 4.64 0.27 0.01	-	-	-	-	-	-	-	-
Cabarrus County	112,950 92.78	867	151 17.42 17.42 0.13	-	-	-	-	-	-	-	-	-	-	-	-	-	-	-	-	-	-	-	-	-	-	-
Catawba County	119,787 90.53	3,344	343 10.26 10.26 0.29	-	-	-	-	-	-	-	-	-	-	64 4.03 18.66 1.91 0.05	-	-	-	42 7.88 12.24 1.26 0.04	-	-	-	-	-	-	-	36 7.76 10.50 1.08 0.03
Hickory (city)	29,822 85.52	1,386	102 7.36 7.36 0.34	-	-	-	-	-	-	-	-	-	-	0 0.00 0.00 0.00 0.00	-	-	-	-	-	-	-	-	-	-	-	-
Cleveland County	86,302 96.07	754	108 14.32 14.32 0.13	-	-	-	-	-	-	-	-	-	-	-	-	-	-	-	-	-	-	-	-	-	-	-
Craven County	79,360 93.59	1,060	362 34.15 34.15 0.46	-	-	-	-	-	-	-	174 39.82 48.07 16.42 0.22	-	-	-	-	-	-	-	-	-	-	-	-	-	-	-

Notes: Please refer to the User's Guide for an explanation of data; data is arranged alphabetically by state, then county, then city within each county; table includes counties with populations greater than 49,999 unless noted and cities with populations greater than 9,999 whose Asian and/or NHPI population rates are greater than the national average; (1) Native Hawaiian and other Pacific Islander; (2) excludes Taiwanese; (3) includes Chamorro; (4) county does not meet population threshold but is shown in order to allow inclusion of city

Place	Total population 5 years and over who speak English-only at home	Asian population 5 years and over	Asians 5 years and over who speak English-only at home	NHPI[1] population 5 years and over	NHPIs[1] 5 years and over who speak English-only at home	Asian Indian	Bangladeshi	Cambodian	Chinese[2]	Fijian	Filipino	Guamanian[3]	Hawaiian, Native	Hmong	Indonesian	Japanese	Korean	Laotian	Malaysian	Pakistani	Samoan	Sri Lankan	Taiwanese	Thai	Tongan	Vietnamese
Cumberland County	248,238	5,857	1,633	457	309	173	-	-	-	-	439	-	-	-	-	224	419	-	-	-	-	-	-	-	-	69
	89.15		27.88		67.61	27.03					45.30					52.58	20.57									9.77
						10.59					26.88					13.72	25.66									4.23
			27.88		67.61	2.95					7.50					3.82	7.15									1.18
			0.66		0.12	0.07					0.18					0.09	0.17									0.03
Davidson County	129,867	1,179	252	-	-	-	-	51	-	-	-	-	-	-	-	-	-	-	-	-	-	-	-	-	-	-
	94.37		21.37					10.78																		
								20.24																		
			21.37					4.33																		
			0.19					0.04																		
Durham County	179,173	6,589	1,328	-	-	484	-	-	225	-	198	-	-	-	-	76	189	-	-	-	-	-	-	-	-	-
	86.14		20.15			19.18			14.95		36.13					21.41	31.55									
						36.45			16.94		14.91					5.72	14.23									
			20.15			7.35			3.41		3.01					1.15	2.87									
			0.74			0.27			0.13		0.11					0.04	0.11									
Forsyth County	259,565	3,021	685	-	-	197	-	-	136	-	113	-	-	-	-	-	-	-	-	-	-	-	-	-	-	36
	90.83		22.67			34.32			15.91		40.94															7.42
						28.76			19.85		16.50															5.26
			22.67			6.52			4.50		3.74															1.19
			0.26			0.08			0.05		0.04															0.01
Gaston County	167,520	1,373	179	-	-	-	-	-	-	-	-	-	-	-	-	-	-	-	-	-	-	-	-	-	-	4
	94.28		13.04																							0.93
																										2.23
			13.04																							0.29
			0.11																							<0.01
Guilford County	357,623	8,551	1,034	-	-	243	-	-	153	-	161	-	-	-	-	-	66	50	-	10	-	-	-	-	-	181
	90.83		12.09			15.32			16.24		31.76						7.13	10.37		2.75						6.80
						23.50			14.80		15.57						6.38	4.84		0.97						17.50
			12.09			2.84			1.79		1.88						0.77	0.58		0.12						2.12
			0.29			0.07			0.04		0.05						0.02	0.01		<0.01						0.05
Halifax County	52,345	333	68	-	-	-	-	-	-	-	-	-	-	-	-	-	-	-	-	-	-	-	-	-	-	-
	97.24		20.42																							
			20.42																							
			0.13																							
Harnett County	77,608	600	157	-	-	-	-	-	-	-	-	-	-	-	-	-	-	-	-	-	-	-	-	-	-	-
	92.21		26.17																							
			26.17																							
			0.20																							
Henderson County	77,570	439	92	-	-	-	-	-	-	-	-	-	-	-	-	-	-	-	-	-	-	-	-	-	-	-
	92.04		20.96																							
			20.96																							
			0.12																							
Iredell County	107,946	1,011	125	-	-	-	-	-	-	-	-	-	-	-	-	-	-	-	-	-	-	-	-	-	-	-
	94.55		12.36																							
			12.36																							
			0.12																							

Notes: Please refer to the User's Guide for an explanation of data; data is arranged alphabetically by state, then county, then city within each county; table includes counties with populations greater than 49,999 unless noted and cities with populations greater than 9,999 whose Asian and/or NHPI population rates are greater than the national average; (1) Native Hawaiian and other Pacific Islander; (2) excludes Taiwanese; (3) includes Chamorro; (4) county does not meet population threshold but is shown in order to allow inclusion of city

Place	Total population 5 years and over who speak English-only at home	Asian population 5 years and over	Asians 5 years and over who speak English-only at home	NHPI[1] population 5 years and over	NHPIs[1] 5 years and over who speak English-only at home	Asian Indian	Bangladeshi	Cambodian	Chinese[2]	Fijian	Filipino	Guamanian[3]	Hawaiian, Native	Hmong	Indonesian	Japanese	Korean	Laotian	Malaysian	Pakistani	Samoan	Sri Lankan	Taiwanese	Thai	Tongan	Vietnamese
Johnston County	101,914 90.88	577	260 45.06 45.06 0.26	-	-	-	-	-	-	-	-	-	-	-	-	-	-	-	-	-	-	-	-	-	-	-
Lenoir County	52,825 94.66	365	86 23.56 23.56 0.16	-	-	-	-	-	-	-	-	-	-	-	-	-	-	-	-	-	-	-	-	-	-	-
Mecklenburg County	560,787 86.92	19,084	3,013 15.79 15.79 0.54	-	-	764 16.34 25.36 4.00 0.14	-	68 9.48 2.26 0.36 0.01	479 17.99 15.90 2.51 0.09	-	396 35.58 13.14 2.08 0.07	-	-	11 2.12 0.37 0.06 <0.01	-	279 35.95 9.26 1.46 0.05	327 14.37 10.85 1.71 0.06	41 5.13 1.36 0.21 0.01	-	-	-	-	-	-	-	358 8.37 11.88 1.88 0.06
Nash County	76,803 94.05	380	94 24.74 24.74 0.12	-	-	-	-	-	-	-	-	-	-	-	-	-	-	-	-	-	-	-	-	-	-	-
New Hanover County	142,934 94.61	1,267	496 39.15 39.15 0.35	-	-	-	-	-	-	-	-	-	-	-	-	-	-	-	-	-	-	-	-	-	-	-
Onslow County	124,226 90.56	2,496	876 35.10 35.10 0.71	393	218 55.47 55.47 0.18	-	-	-	-	-	414 37.10 47.26 16.59 0.33	-	-	-	-	159 33.90 18.15 6.37 0.13	-	-	-	-	-	-	-	-	-	-
Orange County	99,035 88.07	4,421	808 18.28 18.28 0.82	-	-	168 24.93 20.79 3.80 0.17	-	-	171 10.82 21.16 3.87 0.17	-	-	-	-	-	-	59 12.37 7.30 1.33 0.06	154 20.67 19.06 3.48 0.16	-	-	-	-	-	-	-	-	-
Carrboro (town)	12,495 78.77	756	122 16.14 16.14 0.98	-	-	-	-	-	-	-	-	-	-	-	-	-	-	-	-	-	-	-	-	-	-	-
Chapel Hill (town)	40,418 85.58	3,200	599 18.72 18.72 1.48	-	-	118 21.26 19.70 3.69 0.29	-	-	146 12.58 24.37 4.56 0.36	-	-	-	-	-	-	-	95 17.89 15.86 2.97 0.24	-	-	-	-	-	-	-	-	-
Pitt County	117,685 93.97	1,182	365 30.88 30.88 0.31	-	-	-	-	-	-	-	-	-	-	-	-	-	-	-	-	-	-	-	-	-	-	-

Notes: Please refer to the User's Guide for an explanation of data; data is arranged alphabetically by state, then county, then city within each county; table includes counties with populations greater than 49,999 unless noted and cities with populations greater than 9,999 whose Asian and/or NHPI population rates are greater than the national average; (1) Native Hawaiian and other Pacific Islander; (2) excludes Taiwanese; (3) includes Chamorro; (4) county does not meet population threshold but is shown in order to allow inclusion of city

Place	Total population 5 years and over who speak English-only at home	Asian population 5 years and over	Asians 5 years and over who speak English-only at home	NHPI[1] population 5 years and over	NHPIs[1] 5 years and over who speak English-only at home	Asian Indian	Bangladeshi	Cambodian	Chinese[2]	Fijian	Filipino	Guamanian[3]	Hawaiian, Native	Hmong	Indonesian	Japanese	Korean	Laotian	Malaysian	Pakistani	Samoan	Sri Lankan	Taiwanese	Thai	Tongan	Vietnamese
Randolph County	112,135 92.23	698	86 12.32 12.32 0.08	-	-	-	-	-	-	-	-	-	-	-	-	-	-	-	-	-	-	-	-	-	-	-
Robeson County	105,978 93.22	842	171 20.31 20.31 0.16	-	-	-	-	-	-	-	-	-	-	-	-	-	-	-	-	-	-	-	-	-	-	-
Rowan County	114,644 94.17	678	42 6.19 6.19 0.04	-	-	-	-	-	-	-	-	-	-	-	-	-	-	-	-	-	-	-	-	-	-	-
Stanly County	51,941 95.32	673	35 5.20 5.20 0.07	-	-	-	-	-	-	-	-	-	-	11 3.86 31.43 1.63 0.02	-	-	-	-	-	-	-	-	-	-	-	-
Surry County	61,526 91.91	429	48 11.19 11.19 0.08	-	-	-	-	-	-	-	-	-	-	-	-	-	-	-	-	-	-	-	-	-	-	-
Union County	104,308 91.72	510	142 27.84 27.84 0.14	-	-	-	-	-	-	-	-	-	-	-	-	-	-	-	-	-	-	-	-	-	-	-
Wake County	511,976 87.82	19,070	3,222 16.90 16.90 0.63	-	-	808 12.91 25.08 4.24 0.16	-	-	516 11.49 16.01 2.71 0.10	-	492 43.35 15.27 2.58 0.10	-	-	-	-	252 33.25 7.82 1.32 0.05	380 18.17 11.79 1.99 0.07	-	-	80 18.56 2.48 0.42 0.02	-	-	-	-	-	209 9.68 6.49 1.10 0.04
Apex (town)	16,328 90.57	697	132 18.94 18.94 0.81	-	-	-	-	-	-	-	-	-	-	-	-	-	-	-	-	-	-	-	-	-	-	-
Cary (town)	72,650 83.60	6,828	1,035 15.16 15.16 1.42	-	-	337 11.21 32.56 4.94 0.46	-	-	125 7.37 12.08 1.83 0.17	-	-	-	-	-	-	85 26.40 8.21 1.24 0.12	88 17.64 8.50 1.29 0.12	-	-	-	-	-	-	-	-	51 11.81 4.93 0.75 0.07
Wayne County	97,987 92.77	1,003	212 21.14 21.14 0.22	-	-	-	-	-	-	-	-	-	-	-	-	-	-	-	-	-	-	-	-	-	-	-

Notes: Please refer to the User's Guide for an explanation of data; data is arranged alphabetically by state, then county, then city within each county; table includes counties with populations greater than 49,999 unless noted and cities with populations greater than 9,999 whose Asian and/or NHPI population rates are greater than the national average; (1) Native Hawaiian and other Pacific Islander; (2) excludes Taiwanese; (3) includes Chamorro; (4) county does not meet population threshold but is shown in order to allow inclusion of city

Place	Total population 5 years and over who speak English-only at home	Asian population 5 years and over	Asians 5 years and over who speak English-only at home	NHPI[1] population 5 years and over	NHPIs[1] 5 years and over who speak English-only at home	Asian Indian	Bangladeshi	Cambodian	Chinese[2]	Fijian	Filipino	Guamanian[3]	Hawaiian, Native	Hmong	Indonesian	Japanese	Korean	Laotian	Malaysian	Pakistani	Samoan	Sri Lankan	Taiwanese	Thai	Tongan	Vietnamese
Wilkes County	58,406 94.97	318	54 16.98 16.98 0.09	-	-	-	-	-	-	-	-	-	-	-	-	-	-	-	-	-	-	-	-	-	-	-
NORTH DAKOTA	565,130 93.70	3,148	1,058 33.61 33.61 0.19	-	-	238 24.71 22.50 7.56 0.04	-	-	70 17.20 6.62 2.22 0.01	-	247 45.24 23.35 7.85 0.04	-	-	-	-	-	254 70.17 24.01 8.07 0.04	-	-	-	-	-	-	-	-	-
Cass County	108,743 94.51	1,305	332 25.44 25.44 0.31	-	-	50 13.93 15.06 3.83 0.05	-	-	-	-	-	-	-	-	-	-	-	-	-	-	-	-	-	-	-	-
Grand Forks County	58,145 93.89	627	221 35.25 35.25 0.38	-	-	-	-	-	-	-	-	-	-	-	-	-	-	-	-	-	-	-	-	-	-	-
Ward County	52,015 95.34	300	160 53.33 53.33 0.31	-	-	-	-	-	-	-	-	-	-	-	-	-	-	-	-	-	-	-	-	-	-	-
OHIO	9,951,475 93.88	122,406	25,401 20.75 20.75 0.26	2,358	1,664 70.57 70.57 0.02	6,196 17.88 24.39 5.06 0.06	22 3.76 0.09 0.02 <0.01	225 9.41 0.89 0.18 <0.01	3,429 13.46 13.50 2.80 0.03	-	4,527 36.30 17.82 3.70 0.05	422 71.28 25.36 17.90 <0.01	571 73.96 34.31 24.22 0.01		115 11.88 0.45 0.09 <0.01	2,945 30.10 11.59 2.41 0.03	3,827 29.29 15.07 3.13 0.04	170 6.24 0.67 0.14 <0.01	81 23.68 0.32 0.07 <0.01	191 13.25 0.75 0.16 <0.01	295 68.13 17.73 12.51 <0.01	141 28.20 0.56 0.12 <0.01	180 8.53 0.71 0.15 <0.01	572 31.07 2.25 0.47 0.01	-	1,246 13.15 4.91 1.02 0.01
Allen County	97,817 96.59	506	135 26.68 26.68 0.14	-	-	-	-	-	-	-	-	-	-	-	-	-	-	-	-	-	-	-	-	-	-	-
Ashtabula County	91,085 94.88	282	129 45.74 45.74 0.14	-	-	-	-	-	-	-	-	-	-	-	-	-	-	-	-	-	-	-	-	-	-	-
Athens County	56,027 94.60	1,040	236 22.69 22.69 0.42	-	-	-	-	-	-	-	-	-	-	-	-	-	-	-	-	-	-	-	-	-	-	-
Athens (city)	18,789 90.47	828	161 19.44 19.44 0.86	-	-	-	-	-	-	-	-	-	-	-	-	-	-	-	-	-	-	-	-	-	-	-

Notes: Please refer to the User's Guide for an explanation of data; data is arranged alphabetically by state, then county, then city within each county; table includes counties with populations greater than 49,999 unless noted and cities with populations greater than 9,999 whose Asian and/or NHPI population rates are greater than the national average; (1) Native Hawaiian and other Pacific Islander; (2) excludes Taiwanese; (3) includes Chamorro; (4) county does not meet population threshold but is shown in order to allow inclusion of city

Place	Total population 5 years and over who speak English-only at home	Asian population 5 years and over	Asians 5 years and over who speak English-only at home	NHPI[1] population 5 years and over	NHPIs[1] 5 years and over who speak English-only at home	Asian Indian	Bangladeshi	Cambodian	Chinese[2]	Fijian	Filipino	Guamanian[3]	Hawaiian, Native	Hmong	Indonesian	Japanese	Korean	Laotian	Malaysian	Pakistani	Samoan	Sri Lankan	Taiwanese	Thai	Tongan	Vietnamese
	294,367	4,696	1,023	-	-	326	-	-	169	-	148	-	-	-	-	-	150	-	-	-	-	-	-	-	-	60
	94.99		21.78			19.99			18.23		34.34						35.46									9.85
Butler County						31.87			16.52		14.47						14.66									5.87
			21.78			6.94			3.60		3.15						3.19									1.28
			0.35			0.11			0.06		0.05						0.05									0.02
	131,010	596	227	-	-	-	-	-	-	-	-	-	-	-	-	-	-	-	-	-	-	-	-	-	-	-
	96.97		38.09																							
Clark County																										
			38.09																							
			0.17																							
	159,274	1,005	259	-	-	62	-	-	-	-	-	-	-	-	-	-	-	-	-	-	-	-	-	-	-	-
	96.89		25.77			17.61																				
Clermont County						23.94																				
			25.77			6.17																				
			0.16			0.04																				
	101,711	319	98	-	-	-	-	-	-	-	-	-	-	-	-	-	-	-	-	-	-	-	-	-	-	-
	96.46		30.72																							
Columbiana County																										
			30.72																							
			0.10																							
	1,158,729	23,965	4,405	-	-	1,311	-	30	792	-	719	-	-	-	-	429	539	-	-	-	-	-	-	-	-	228
	88.92		18.38			15.76		6.20	14.25		27.03					35.78	30.45									12.08
Cuyahoga County						29.76		0.68	17.98		16.32					9.74	12.24									5.18
			18.38			5.47		0.13	3.30		3.00					1.79	2.25									0.95
			0.38			0.11		<0.01	0.07		0.06					0.04	0.05									0.02
	14,525	671	125	-	-	29	-	-	-	-	-	-	-	-	-	-	-	-	-	-	-	-	-	-	-	-
	78.46		18.63			9.39																				
Mayfield Heights (city)						23.20																				
			18.63			4.32																				
			0.86			0.20																				
	8,158	490	121	-	-	-	-	-	-	-	-	-	-	-	-	-	-	-	-	-	-	-	-	-	-	-
	78.37		24.69																							
Richmond Heights (city)																										
			24.69																							
			1.48																							
	18,270	1,002	166	-	-	40	-	-	49	-	-	-	-	-	-	-	-	-	-	-	-	-	-	-	-	-
	88.97		16.57			9.09			15.51																	
Solon (city)						24.10			29.52																	
			16.57			3.99			4.89																	
			0.91			0.22			0.27																	
	26,440	1,324	267	-	-	134	-	-	-	-	-	-	-	-	-	-	-	-	-	-	-	-	-	-	-	-
	87.54		20.17			25.82																				
Westlake (city)						50.19																				
			20.17			10.12																				
			1.01			0.51																				
	96,466	1,591	373	-	-	33	-	-	92	-	-	-	-	-	-	-	-	-	-	-	-	-	-	-	-	-
	95.28		23.44			8.85			17.46																	
Delaware County						8.85			24.66																	
			23.44			2.07			5.78																	
			0.39			0.03			0.10																	

Notes: Please refer to the User's Guide for an explanation of data; data is arranged alphabetically by state, then county, then city within each county; table includes counties with populations greater than 49,999 unless noted and cities with populations greater than 9,999 whose Asian and/or NHPI population rates are greater than the national average; (1) Native Hawaiian and other Pacific Islander; (2) excludes Taiwanese; (3) includes Chamorro; (4) county does not meet population threshold but is shown in order to allow inclusion of city

Place	Total population 5 years and over who speak English-only at home	Asian population 5 years and over	Asians 5 years and over who speak English-only at home	NHPI[1] population 5 years and over	NHPIs[1] 5 years and over who speak English-only at home	Asian Indian	Bangladeshi	Cambodian	Chinese[2]	Fijian	Filipino	Guamanian[3]	Hawaiian, Native	Hmong	Indonesian	Japanese	Korean	Laotian	Malaysian	Pakistani	Samoan	Sri Lankan	Taiwanese	Thai	Tongan	Vietnamese
Fairfield County	110,425 96.73	767	251 32.72 32.72 0.23	-	-	-	-	-	-	-	-	-	-	-	-	-	-	-	-	-	-	-	-	-	-	-
Franklin County	902,864 91.01	30,359	5,004 16.48 16.48 0.55	264	174 65.91 65.91 0.02	1,353 17.81 27.04 4.46 0.15	-	132 11.37 2.64 0.43 0.01	663 9.86 13.25 2.18 0.07	-	672 39.32 13.43 2.21 0.07	-	-	-	24 4.64 0.48 0.08 <0.01	470 15.80 9.39 1.55 0.05	735 23.19 14.69 2.42 0.08	46 4.47 0.92 0.15 0.01	-	74 16.37 1.48 0.24 0.01	-	-	57 7.60 1.14 0.19 0.01	89 21.04 1.78 0.29 0.01	-	318 14.33 6.35 1.05 0.04
Dublin (city)	25,516 88.81	2,224	254 11.42 11.42 1.00	-	-	117 19.44 46.06 5.26 0.46	-	-	5 1.14 1.97 0.22 0.02	-	-	-	-	-	-	31 4.30 12.20 1.39 0.12	-	-	-	-	-	-	-	-	-	-
Hilliard (city)	20,371 92.90	927	235 25.35 25.35 1.15	-	-	-	-	-	-	-	-	-	-	-	-	-	-	-	-	-	-	-	-	-	-	-
Geauga County	75,485 88.98	366	181 49.45 49.45 0.24	-	-	-	-	-	-	-	-	-	-	-	-	-	-	-	-	-	-	-	-	-	-	-
Greene County	131,546 94.46	2,778	585 21.06 21.06 0.44	-	-	145 17.22 24.79 5.22 0.11	-	-	16 4.03 2.74 0.58 0.01	-	-	-	-	-	-	-	93 17.16 15.90 3.35 0.07	-	-	-	-	-	-	-	-	-
Hamilton County	744,914 94.42	11,772	2,281 19.38 19.38 0.31	-	-	573 15.41 25.12 4.87 0.08	-	14 4.32 0.61 0.12 <0.01	344 12.46 15.08 2.92 0.05	-	547 44.76 23.98 4.65 0.07	-	-	-	-	238 40.00 10.43 2.02 0.03	297 27.47 13.02 2.52 0.04	-	-	-	-	-	-	-	-	36 3.74 1.58 0.31 <0.01
Blue Ash (city)	10,657 87.75	837	104 12.43 12.43 0.98	-	-	92 24.86 88.46 10.99 0.86	-	-	-	-	-	-	-	-	-	-	-	-	-	-	-	-	-	-	-	-
Sharonville (city)	11,884 91.87	482	34 7.05 7.05 0.29	-	-	17 5.01 50.00 3.53 0.14	-	-	-	-	-	-	-	-	-	-	-	-	-	-	-	-	-	-	-	-
Hancock County	63,454 95.63	703	125 17.78 17.78 0.20	-	-	-	-	-	-	-	-	-	-	-	-	-	-	-	-	-	-	-	-	-	-	-

Notes: Please refer to the User's Guide for an explanation of data; data is arranged alphabetically by state, then county, then city within each county; table includes counties with populations greater than 49,999 unless noted and cities with populations greater than 9,999 whose Asian and/or NHPI population rates are greater than the national average; (1) Native Hawaiian and other Pacific Islander; (2) excludes Taiwanese; (3) includes Chamorro; (4) county does not meet population threshold but is shown in order to allow inclusion of city

Place	Total population 5 years and over who speak English-only at home	Asian population 5 years and over	Asians 5 years and over who speak English-only at home	NHPI[1] population 5 years and over	NHPIs[1] 5 years and over who speak English-only at home	Asian Indian	Bangladeshi	Cambodian	Chinese[2]	Fijian	Filipino	Guamanian[3]	Hawaiian, Native	Hmong	Indonesian	Japanese	Korean	Laotian	Malaysian	Pakistani	Samoan	Sri Lankan	Taiwanese	Thai	Tongan	Vietnamese
Lake County	199,368 93.32	2,035	567 27.86 27.86 0.28	-	-	86 13.98 15.17 4.23 0.04	-	-	112 25.17 19.75 5.50 0.06	-	-	-	-	-	-	-	-	-	-	-	-	-	-	-	-	-
Licking County	131,566 97.03	664	272 40.96 40.96 0.21	-	-	-	-	-	-	-	-	-	-	-	-	-	-	-	-	-	-	-	-	-	-	-
Lorain County	243,568 91.92	1,551	501 32.30 32.30 0.21	-	-	107 29.56 21.36 6.90 0.04	-	-	-	-	85 21.36 16.97 5.48 0.03	-	-	-	-	-	-	-	-	-	-	-	-	-	-	-
Lucas County	395,364 93.24	5,090	990 19.45 19.45 0.25	-	-	348 22.67 35.15 6.84 0.09	-	-	127 9.16 12.83 2.50 0.03	-	202 35.63 20.40 3.97 0.05	-	-	-	-	-	104 21.22 10.51 2.04 0.03	-	-	-	-	-	-	-	-	-
Mahoning County	225,310 93.00	970	243 25.05 25.05 0.11	-	-	-	-	-	-	-	-	-	-	-	-	-	-	-	-	-	-	-	-	-	-	-
Marion County	60,393 96.94	319	89 27.90 27.90 0.15	-	-	-	-	-	-	-	-	-	-	-	-	-	-	-	-	-	-	-	-	-	-	-
Medina County	133,098 94.72	1,079	283 26.23 26.23 0.21	-	-	62 14.98 21.91 5.75 0.05	-	-	-	-	-	-	-	-	-	-	-	-	-	-	-	-	-	-	-	-
Miami County	89,771 97.11	803	230 28.64 28.64 0.26	-	-	-	-	-	-	-	-	-	-	-	-	-	-	-	-	-	-	-	-	-	-	-
Montgomery County	497,979 95.37	6,677	1,404 21.03 21.03 0.28	-	-	372 19.06 26.50 5.57 0.07	-	-	101 9.72 7.19 1.51 0.02	-	243 36.27 17.31 3.64 0.05	-	-	-	-	246 38.80 17.52 3.68 0.05	128 16.98 9.12 1.92 0.03	-	-	-	-	-	-	-	-	123 12.91 8.76 1.84 0.02
Portage County	136,682 95.71	1,122	257 22.91 22.91 0.19	-	-	-	-	-	-	-	-	-	-	-	-	-	-	-	-	-	-	-	-	-	-	-

Notes: Please refer to the User's Guide for an explanation of data; data is arranged alphabetically by state, then county, then city within each county; table includes counties with populations greater than 49,999 unless noted and cities with populations greater than 9,999 whose Asian and/or NHPI population rates are greater than the national average; (1) Native Hawaiian and other Pacific Islander; (2) excludes Taiwanese; (3) includes Chamorro; (4) county does not meet population threshold but is shown in order to allow inclusion of city

Place	Total population 5 years and over who speak English-only at home	Asian population 5 years and over	Asians 5 years and over who speak English-only at home	NHPI[1] population 5 years and over	NHPIs[1] 5 years and over who speak English-only at home	Asian Indian	Bangladeshi	Cambodian	Chinese[2]	Fijian	Filipino	Guamanian[3]	Hawaiian, Native	Hmong	Indonesian	Japanese	Korean	Laotian	Malaysian	Pakistani	Samoan	Sri Lankan	Taiwanese	Thai	Tongan	Vietnamese
Richland County	115,127	680	183	-	-	-	-	-	-	-	-	-	-	-	-	-	-	-	-	-	-	-	-	-	-	-
	95.46		26.91																							
			26.91																							
			0.16																							
Stark County	338,958	1,665	469	-	-	81	-	-	66	-	-	-	-	-	-	-	-	-	-	-	-	-	-	-	-	-
	95.75		28.17			20.35			20.31																	
						17.27			14.07																	
			28.17			4.86			3.96																	
			0.14			0.02			0.02																	
Summit County	478,613	7,002	1,182	-	-	239	-	-	223	-	221	-	-	-	-	157	141	58	-	-	-	-	-	-	-	43
	94.40		16.88			12.92			14.15		47.53					38.39	17.56	8.58								7.05
						20.22			18.87		18.70					13.28	11.93	4.91								3.64
			16.88			3.41			3.18		3.16					2.24	2.01	0.83								0.61
			0.25			0.05			0.05		0.05					0.03	0.03	0.01								0.01
Trumbull County	199,400	949	278	-	-	-	-	-	-	-	-	-	-	-	-	-	-	-	-	-	-	-	-	-	-	-
	94.34		29.29																							
			29.29																							
			0.14																							
Warren County	139,723	1,832	344	-	-	64	-	-	73	-	-	-	-	-	-	-	-	-	-	-	-	-	-	-	-	-
	95.73		18.78			11.49			17.10																	
						18.60			21.22																	
			18.78			3.49			3.98																	
			0.25			0.05			0.05																	
Wayne County	94,390	680	216	-	-	-	-	-	-	-	-	-	-	-	-	-	-	-	-	-	-	-	-	-	-	-
	90.99		31.76																							
			31.76																							
			0.23																							
Wood County	107,445	1,100	239	-	-	-	-	-	-	-	-	-	-	-	-	-	-	-	-	-	-	-	-	-	-	-
	94.23		21.73																							
			21.73																							
			0.22																							
OKLAHOMA	2,977,187	42,656	8,026	1,688	1,055	1,368	-	36	811	-	1,499	214	552	27	-	1,097	1,486	81	32	75	-	-	24	225	-	767
	92.58		18.82		62.50	17.71		11.50	13.07		37.31	57.99	85.45	9.12		41.01	33.48	9.74	6.74	8.14			6.90	27.37		6.76
						17.04		0.45	10.10		18.68	20.28	52.32	0.34		13.67	18.51	1.01	0.40	0.93			0.30	2.80		9.56
			18.82		62.50	3.21		0.08	1.90		3.51	12.68	32.70	0.06		2.57	3.48	0.19	0.08	0.18			0.06	0.53		1.80
			0.27		0.04	0.05		<0.01	0.03		0.05	0.01	0.02	<0.01		0.04	0.05	<0.01	<0.01	<0.01			<0.01	0.01		0.03
Canadian County	76,575	2,020	309	-	-	151	-	-	-	-	-	-	-	-	-	-	-	-	-	-	-	-	-	-	-	19
	93.65		15.30			13.43																				3.46
						48.87																				6.15
			15.30			7.48																				0.94
			0.40			0.20																				0.02
Cleveland County	179,910	5,519	1,097	-	-	169	-	-	145	-	310	-	-	-	-	-	144	-	-	-	-	-	-	-	-	105
	92.42		19.88			20.00			14.13		57.41						21.21									6.81
						15.41			13.22		28.26						13.13									9.57
			19.88			3.06			2.63		5.62						2.61									1.90
			0.61			0.09			0.08		0.17						0.08									0.06

Notes: Please refer to the User's Guide for an explanation of data; data is arranged alphabetically by state, then county, then city within each county; table includes counties with populations greater than 49,999 unless noted and cities with populations greater than 9,999 whose Asian and/or NHPI population rates are greater than the national average; (1) Native Hawaiian and other Pacific Islander; (2) excludes Taiwanese; (3) includes Chamorro; (4) county does not meet population threshold but is shown in order to allow inclusion of city

Place	Total population 5 years and over who speak English-only at home	Asian population 5 years and over	Asians 5 years and over who speak English-only at home	NHPI[1] population 5 years and over	NHPIs[1] 5 years and over who speak English-only at home	Asian Indian	Bangladeshi	Cambodian	Chinese[2]	Fijian	Filipino	Guamanian[3]	Hawaiian, Native	Hmong	Indonesian	Japanese	Korean	Laotian	Malaysian	Pakistani	Samoan	Sri Lankan	Taiwanese	Thai	Tongan	Vietnamese
Comanche County	94,113 88.73	2,347	672 28.63 28.63 0.71	-	-	-	-	-	-	-	184 34.46 27.38 7.84 0.20	-	-	-	-	-	139 16.93 20.68 5.92 0.15	-	-	-	-	-	-	-	-	-
Garfield County	50,863 94.29	473	102 21.56 21.56 0.20	-	-	-	-	-	-	-	-	-	-	-	-	-	-	-	-	-	-	-	-	-	-	-
Muskogee County	61,547 95.30	323	85 26.32 26.32 0.14	-	-	-	-	-	-	-	-	-	-	-	-	-	-	-	-	-	-	-	-	-	-	-
Oklahoma County	541,657 88.39	17,156	2,403 14.01 14.01 0.44	-	-	464 17.09 19.31 2.70 0.09	-	-	191 9.14 7.95 1.11 0.04	-	345 29.06 14.36 2.01 0.06	-	-	-	-	272 27.50 11.32 1.59 0.05	351 29.62 14.61 2.05 0.06	54 11.30 2.25 0.31 0.01	-	-	-	-	-	92 23.17 3.83 0.54 0.02	-	385 6.06 16.02 2.24 0.07
Payne County	60,043 92.89	1,849	181 9.79 9.79 0.30	-	-	-	-	-	55 8.36 30.39 2.97 0.09	-	-	-	-	-	-	-	-	-	-	-	-	-	-	-	-	-
Stillwater (city)	33,460 89.76	1,816	171 9.42 9.42 0.51	-	-	-	-	-	55 8.36 32.16 3.03 0.16	-	-	-	-	-	-	-	-	-	-	-	-	-	-	-	-	-
Pottawatomie County	58,517 95.93	352	118 33.52 33.52 0.20	-	-	-	-	-	-	-	-	-	-	-	-	-	-	-	-	-	-	-	-	-	-	-
Tulsa County	478,283 91.60	7,950	1,604 20.18 20.18 0.34	-	-	361 20.17 22.51 4.54 0.08	-	-	271 19.43 16.90 3.41 0.06	-	190 40.86 11.85 2.39 0.04	-	-	-	-	-	403 48.44 25.12 5.07 0.08	-	-	23 5.44 1.43 0.29 <0.01	-	-	-	-	-	127 6.58 7.92 1.60 0.03
Wagoner County	51,260 95.98	420	76 18.10 18.10 0.15	-	-	-	-	-	-	-	-	-	-	-	-	-	-	-	-	-	-	-	-	-	-	-
OREGON	2,810,654 87.85	92,081	22,860 24.83 24.83 0.81	7,080	3,964 55.99 55.99 0.14	2,271 24.97 9.93 2.47 0.08	-	242 9.54 1.06 0.26 0.01	3,223 18.73 14.10 3.50 0.11	71 19.45 1.79 1.00 <0.01	4,281 42.17 18.73 4.65 0.15	723 67.82 18.24 10.21 0.03	1,621 84.82 40.89 22.90 0.06	16 1.35 0.07 0.02 <0.01	112 18.21 0.49 0.12 <0.01	5,593 49.00 24.47 6.07 0.20	3,552 29.58 15.54 3.86 0.13	270 8.03 1.18 0.29 0.01	-	42 12.84 0.18 0.05 <0.01	354 49.79 8.93 5.00 0.01	-	81 10.80 0.35 0.09 <0.01	316 22.24 1.38 0.34 0.01	151 38.72 3.81 2.13 0.01	1,095 6.25 4.79 1.19 0.04

Notes: Please refer to the User's Guide for an explanation of data; data is arranged alphabetically by state, then county, then city within each county; table includes counties with populations greater than 49,999 unless noted and cities with populations greater than 9,999 whose Asian and/or NHPI population rates are greater than the national average; (1) Native Hawaiian and other Pacific Islander; (2) excludes Taiwanese; (3) includes Chamorro; (4) county does not meet population threshold but is shown in order to allow inclusion of city

Place	Total population 5 years and over who speak English-only at home	Asian population 5 years and over	Asians 5 years and over who speak English-only at home	NHPI[1] population 5 years and over	NHPIs[1] 5 years and over who speak English-only at home	Asian Indian	Bangladeshi	Cambodian	Chinese[2]	Fijian	Filipino	Guamanian[3]	Hawaiian, Native	Hmong	Indonesian	Japanese	Korean	Laotian	Malaysian	Pakistani	Samoan	Sri Lankan	Taiwanese	Thai	Tongan	Vietnamese
Benton County	66,875 90.03	3,081	966 31.35 31.35 1.44	-	-	-	-	-	116 13.44 12.01 3.77 0.17	-	-	-	-	-	-	237 55.50 24.53 7.69 0.35	205 32.18 21.22 6.65 0.31	-	-	-	-	-	-	-	-	-
Corvallis (city)	41,130 87.58	2,822	828 29.34 29.34 2.01	-	-	-	-	-	103 12.32 12.44 3.65 0.25	-	-	-	-	-	-	-	151 27.21 18.24 5.35 0.37	-	-	-	-	-	-	-	-	-
Clackamas County	286,210 90.43	7,665	2,265 29.55 29.55 0.79	561	452 80.57 80.57 0.16	218 32.98 9.62 2.84 0.08	-	-	419 24.43 18.50 5.47 0.15	-	397 43.34 17.53 5.18 0.14	-	-	-	-	595 59.80 26.27 7.76 0.21	301 18.50 13.29 3.93 0.11	-	-	-	-	-	-	-	-	63 7.34 2.78 0.82 0.02
Lake Oswego (city)	30,003 89.53	1,409	369 26.19 26.19 1.23	-	-	-	-	-	81 20.25 21.95 5.75 0.27	-	-	-	-	-	-	-	-	-	-	-	-	-	-	-	-	-
Coos County	57,043 95.50	329	133 40.43 40.43 0.23	-	-	-	-	-	-	-	-	-	-	-	-	-	-	-	-	-	-	-	-	-	-	-
Deschutes County	102,487 94.64	595	238 40.00 40.00 0.23	-	-	-	-	-	-	-	-	-	-	-	-	-	-	-	-	-	-	-	-	-	-	-
Douglas County	91,037 96.08	546	267 48.90 48.90 0.29	-	-	-	-	-	-	-	-	-	-	-	-	-	-	-	-	-	-	-	-	-	-	-
Jackson County	157,236 92.32	1,317	629 47.76 47.76 0.40	-	-	-	-	-	-	-	-	-	-	-	-	-	-	-	-	-	-	-	-	-	-	-
Josephine County	68,300 95.22	393	224 57.00 57.00 0.33	-	-	-	-	-	-	-	-	-	-	-	-	-	-	-	-	-	-	-	-	-	-	-
Klamath County	54,841 91.85	435	239 54.94 54.94 0.44	-	-	-	-	-	-	-	-	-	-	-	-	-	-	-	-	-	-	-	-	-	-	-

Notes: Please refer to the User's Guide for an explanation of data; data is arranged alphabetically by state, then county, then city within each county; table includes counties with populations greater than 49,999 unless noted and cities with populations greater than 9,999 whose Asian and/or NHPI population rates are greater than the national average; (1) Native Hawaiian and other Pacific Islander; (2) excludes Taiwanese; (3) includes Chamorro; (4) county does not meet population threshold but is shown in order to allow inclusion of city

Place	Total population 5 years and over who speak English-only at home	Asian population 5 years and over	Asians 5 years and over who speak English-only at home	NHPI[1] population 5 years and over	NHPIs[1] 5 years and over who speak English-only at home	Asian Indian	Bangladeshi	Cambodian	Chinese[2]	Fijian	Filipino	Guamanian[3]	Hawaiian, Native	Hmong	Indonesian	Japanese	Korean	Laotian	Malaysian	Pakistani	Samoan	Sri Lankan	Taiwanese	Thai	Tongan	Vietnamese
Lane County	280,562 92.15	5,897	1,883 31.93 31.93 0.67	545	269 49.36 49.36 0.10	240 43.01 12.75 4.07 0.09	-	-	213 18.22 11.31 3.61 0.08	-	273 48.75 14.50 4.63 0.10	-	-	-	-	488 38.36 25.92 8.28 0.17	302 26.87 16.04 5.12 0.11	-	-	-	-	-	-	-	-	-
Linn County	90,402 94.15	732	253 34.56 34.56 0.28	-	-	-	-	-	-	-	-	-	-	-	-	-	-	-	-	-	-	-	-	-	-	-
Marion County	211,454 80.46	4,546	1,171 25.76 25.76 0.55	694	265 38.18 38.18 0.13	116 37.30 9.91 2.55 0.05	-	-	159 21.29 13.58 3.50 0.08	-	280 43.75 23.91 6.16 0.13	-	-	-	-	176 29.00 15.03 3.87 0.08	264 44.82 22.54 5.81 0.12	-	-	-	-	-	-	-	-	52 6.52 4.44 1.14 0.02
Salem (city)	104,461 82.63	3,093	720 23.28 23.28 0.69	356	128 35.96 35.96 0.12	-	-	-	125 20.10 17.36 4.04 0.12	-	168 44.56 23.33 5.43 0.16	-	-	-	-	95 24.48 13.19 3.07 0.09	-	-	-	-	-	-	-	-	-	36 7.66 5.00 1.16 0.03
Multnomah County	515,735 83.37	34,403	7,126 20.71 20.71 1.38	2,345	1,080 46.06 46.06 0.21	565 33.65 7.93 1.64 0.11	-	122 12.41 1.71 0.35 0.02	1,118 17.19 15.69 3.25 0.22	-	1,172 37.08 16.45 3.41 0.23	-	424 95.71 39.26 18.08 0.08	9 0.97 0.13 0.03 <0.01	-	1,859 53.82 26.09 5.40 0.36	982 39.66 13.78 2.85 0.19	159 6.75 2.23 0.46 0.03	-	-	-	-	-	65 14.81 0.91 0.19 0.01	112 36.60 10.37 4.78 0.02	523 5.00 7.34 1.52 0.10
Portland (city)	412,928 83.07	31,087	6,043 19.44 19.44 1.46	1,896	827 43.62 43.62 0.20	482 33.64 7.98 1.55 0.12	-	117 12.25 1.94 0.38 0.03	994 16.64 16.45 3.20 0.24	-	953 36.44 15.77 3.07 0.23	-	312 94.26 37.73 16.46 0.08	9 1.11 0.15 0.03 <0.01	-	1,567 52.67 25.93 5.04 0.38	790 37.73 13.07 2.54 0.19	103 4.91 1.70 0.33 0.02	-	-	-	-	-	50 12.59 0.83 0.16 0.01	112 37.46 13.54 5.91 0.03	473 4.76 7.83 1.52 0.11
Polk County	52,480 90.03	716	271 37.85 37.85 0.52	-	-	-	-	-	-	-	-	-	-	-	-	-	-	-	-	-	-	-	-	-	-	-
Umatilla County	54,715 83.77	438	88 20.09 20.09 0.16	-	-	-	-	-	-	-	-	-	-	-	-	-	-	-	-	-	-	-	-	-	-	-
Washington County	334,295 81.41	27,496	5,447 19.81 19.81 1.63	1,338	804 60.09 60.09 0.24	710 14.80 13.03 2.58 0.21	-	100 9.64 1.84 0.36 0.03	824 18.05 15.13 3.00 0.25	-	1,200 40.79 22.03 4.36 0.36	-	334 79.52 41.54 24.96 0.10	-	-	1,062 41.04 19.50 3.86 0.32	596 14.83 10.94 2.17 0.18	52 9.08 0.95 0.19 0.02	-	-	-	-	-	-	-	285 6.10 5.23 1.04 0.09
Aloha (cdp)	30,500 79.45	2,852	456 15.99 15.99 1.50	-	-	-	-	-	-	-	121 31.76 26.54 4.24 0.40	-	-	-	-	-	-	-	-	-	-	-	-	-	-	30 2.89 6.58 1.05 0.10

Notes: Please refer to the User's Guide for an explanation of data; data is arranged alphabetically by state, then county, then city within each county; table includes counties with populations greater than 49,999 unless noted and cities with populations greater than 9,999 whose Asian and/or NHPI population rates are greater than the national average; (1) Native Hawaiian and other Pacific Islander; (2) excludes Taiwanese; (3) includes Chamorro; (4) county does not meet population threshold but is shown in order to allow inclusion of city

Place	Total population 5 years and over who speak English-only at home	Asian population 5 years and over	Asians 5 years and over who speak English-only at home	NHPI[1] population 5 years and over	NHPIs[1] 5 years and over who speak English-only at home	Asian Indian	Bangladeshi	Cambodian	Chinese[2]	Fijian	Filipino	Guamanian[3]	Hawaiian, Native	Hmong	Indonesian	Japanese	Korean	Laotian	Malaysian	Pakistani	Samoan	Sri Lankan	Taiwanese	Thai	Tongan	Vietnamese
Beaverton (city)	54,314 76.98	6,935	1,143 16.48 16.48 2.10	-	-	137 8.90 11.99 1.98 0.25	-	15 4.36 1.31 0.22 0.03	209 20.98 18.29 3.01 0.38	-	288 41.62 25.20 4.15 0.53	-	-	-	-	154 23.26 13.47 2.22 0.28	154 13.18 13.47 2.22 0.28	-	-	-	-	-	-	-	-	64 7.26 5.60 0.92 0.12
Cedar Mill (cdp)	9,989 84.57	918	183 19.93 19.93 1.83	-	-	-	-	-	-	-	-	-	-	-	-	-	-	-	-	-	-	-	-	-	-	-
Hillsboro (city)	48,177 75.92	3,969	815 20.53 20.53 1.69	-	-	173 15.41 21.23 4.36 0.36	-	-	71 13.15 8.71 1.79 0.15	-	-	-	-	-	-	-	65 13.24 7.98 1.64 0.13	-	-	-	-	-	-	-	-	50 7.07 6.13 1.26 0.10
Tigard (city)	31,838 83.72	2,231	465 20.84 20.84 1.46	-	-	-	-	-	154 28.15 33.12 6.90 0.48	-	-	-	-	-	-	-	-	-	-	-	-	-	-	-	-	0 0.00 0.00 0.00 0.00
Tualatin (city)	17,943 85.75	914	378 41.36 41.36 2.11	-	-	-	-	-	-	-	-	-	-	-	-	-	-	-	-	-	-	-	-	-	-	-
Yamhill County	70,367 88.83	835	371 44.43 44.43 0.53	-	-	-	-	-	-	-	-	-	-	-	-	-	-	-	-	-	-	-	-	-	-	-
PENNSYLVANIA	10,583,054 91.58	200,875	34,784 17.32 17.32 0.33	3,369	2,176 64.59 64.59 0.02	8,700 16.67 25.01 4.33 0.08	11 1.75 0.03 0.01 <0.01	631 7.98 1.81 0.31 0.01	5,442 12.35 15.65 2.71 0.05	-	4,953 35.62 14.24 2.47 0.05	435 60.75 19.99 12.91 <0.01	691 71.61 31.76 20.51 0.01	21 2.70 0.06 0.01 <0.01	88 17.85 0.25 0.04 <0.01	2,183 31.71 6.28 1.09 0.02	6,566 21.21 18.88 3.27 0.06	167 7.99 0.48 0.08 <0.01	-	266 9.49 0.76 0.13 <0.01	481 65.44 22.10 14.28 <0.01	72 23.30 0.21 0.04 <0.01	323 14.60 0.93 0.16 <0.01	472 27.10 1.36 0.23 <0.01	-	2,125 8.13 6.11 1.06 0.02
Adams County	81,234 94.55	630	151 23.97 23.97 0.19	-	-	-	-	-	-	-	-	-	-	-	-	-	-	-	-	-	-	-	-	-	-	-
Allegheny County	1,131,112 93.42	19,523	4,214 21.58 21.58 0.37	628	406 64.65 64.65 0.04	1,211 17.17 28.74 6.20 0.11	-	-	557 12.43 13.22 2.85 0.05	-	511 47.67 12.13 2.62 0.05	-	-	-	-	265 22.83 6.29 1.36 0.02	570 26.04 13.53 2.92 0.05	-	-	-	-	-	64 15.17 1.52 0.33 0.01	-	-	141 11.62 3.35 0.72 0.01
Muni. of Monroeville (borough)	25,233 90.23	1,068	154 14.42 14.42 0.61	-	-	89 14.35 57.79 8.33 0.35	-	-	-	-	-	-	-	-	-	-	-	-	-	-	-	-	-	-	-	-

Notes: Please refer to the User's Guide for an explanation of data; data is arranged alphabetically by state, then county, then city within each county; table includes counties with populations greater than 49,999 unless noted and cities with populations greater than 9,999 whose Asian and/or NHPI population rates are greater than the national average; (1) Native Hawaiian and other Pacific Islander; (2) excludes Taiwanese; (3) includes Chamorro; (4) county does not meet population threshold but is shown in order to allow inclusion of city

Place	Total population 5 years and over who speak English-only at home	Asian population 5 years and over	Asians 5 years and over who speak English-only at home	NHPI[1] population 5 years and over	NHPIs[1] 5 years and over who speak English-only at home	Asian Indian	Bangladeshi	Cambodian	Chinese[2]	Fijian	Filipino	Guamanian[3]	Hawaiian, Native	Hmong	Indonesian	Japanese	Korean	Laotian	Malaysian	Pakistani	Samoan	Sri Lankan	Taiwanese	Thai	Tongan	Vietnamese
Scott (township)	14,439 87.98	943	45 4.77 4.77 0.31	-	-	18 2.32 40.00 1.91 0.12	-	-	-	-	-	-	-	-	-	-	-	-	-	-	-	-	-	-	-	-
Scott Township (cdp)	14,439 87.98	943	45 4.77 4.77 0.31	-	-	18 2.32 40.00 1.91 0.12	-	-	-	-	-	-	-	-	-	-	-	-	-	-	-	-	-	-	-	-
Upper St. Clair (township)	17,099 90.80	752	194 25.80 25.80 1.13	-	-	105 20.87 54.12 13.96 0.61	-	-	-	-	-	-	-	-	-	-	-	-	-	-	-	-	-	-	-	-
Beaver County	164,183 95.68	416	140 33.65 33.65 0.09	-	-	-	-	-	-	-	-	-	-	-	-	-	-	-	-	-	-	-	-	-	-	-
Berks County	306,373 87.33	3,348	665 19.86 19.86 0.22	-	-	170 22.34 25.56 5.08 0.06	-	-	97 18.83 14.59 2.90 0.03	-	-	-	-	-	-	-	143 47.19 21.50 4.27 0.05	-	-	-	-	-	-	-	-	52 4.89 7.82 1.55 0.02
Blair County	118,116 96.92	541	157 29.02 29.02 0.13	-	-	-	-	-	-	-	-	-	-	-	-	-	-	-	-	-	-	-	-	-	-	-
Bradford County	57,316 97.24	186	87 46.77 46.77 0.15	-	-	-	-	-	-	-	-	-	-	-	-	-	-	-	-	-	-	-	-	-	-	-
Bucks County	510,814 91.33	12,984	2,434 18.75 18.75 0.48	-	-	751 13.82 30.85 5.78 0.15	-	-	297 16.20 12.20 2.29 0.06	-	545 36.82 22.39 4.20 0.11	-	-	-	-	-	347 17.24 14.26 2.67 0.07	-	-	-	-	-	-	-	-	79 15.31 3.25 0.61 0.02
Bensalem (township)	45,726 82.76	3,604	315 8.74 8.74 0.69	-	-	106 5.94 33.65 2.94 0.23	-	-	-	-	-	-	-	-	-	-	55 8.65 17.46 1.53 0.12	-	-	-	-	-	-	-	-	-
Lower Makefield (township)	27,573 91.15	1,215	406 33.42 33.42 1.47	-	-	161 29.17 39.66 13.25 0.58	-	-	-	-	-	-	-	-	-	-	-	-	-	-	-	-	-	-	-	-

Notes: Please refer to the User's Guide for an explanation of data; data is arranged alphabetically by state, then county, then city within each county; table includes counties with populations greater than 49,999 unless noted and cities with populations greater than 9,999 whose Asian and/or NHPI population rates are greater than the national average; (1) Native Hawaiian and other Pacific Islander; (2) excludes Taiwanese; (3) includes Chamorro; (4) county does not meet population threshold but is shown in order to allow inclusion of city

Place	Total population 5 years and over who speak English-only at home	Asian population 5 years and over	Asians 5 years and over who speak English-only at home	NHPI[1] population 5 years and over	NHPIs[1] 5 years and over who speak English-only at home	Asian Indian	Bangladeshi	Cambodian	Chinese[2]	Fijian	Filipino	Guamanian[3]	Hawaiian, Native	Hmong	Indonesian	Japanese	Korean	Laotian	Malaysian	Pakistani	Samoan	Sri Lankan	Taiwanese	Thai	Tongan	Vietnamese
Newtown (township)	15,253 90.33	790	112 14.18 14.18 0.73	-	-	-	-	-	-	-	-	-	-	-	-	-	-	-	-	-	-	-	-	-	-	-
Butler County	157,969 96.93	882	162 18.37 18.37 0.10	-	-	52 12.04 32.10 5.90 0.03	-	-	-	-	-	-	-	-	-	-	-	-	-	-	-	-	-	-	-	-
Cambria County	138,860 95.86	528	82 15.53 15.53 0.06	-	-	-	-	-	-	-	-	-	-	-	-	-	-	-	-	-	-	-	-	-	-	-
Centre County	118,308 91.35	5,137	1,150 22.39 22.39 0.97	-	-	295 24.22 25.65 5.74 0.25	-	-	261 15.48 22.70 5.08 0.22	-	-	-	-	-	-	-	203 21.01 17.65 3.95 0.17	-	-	-	-	-	-	-	-	-
Ferguson (township)	11,731 88.75	922	206 22.34 22.34 1.76	-	-	-	-	-	-	-	-	-	-	-	-	-	-	-	-	-	-	-	-	-	-	-
Patton (township)	9,916 91.05	495	123 24.85 24.85 1.24	-	-	-	-	-	-	-	-	-	-	-	-	-	-	-	-	-	-	-	-	-	-	-
State College (borough)	32,104 85.24	3,350	751 22.42 22.42 2.34	-	-	163 21.94 21.70 4.87 0.51	-	-	196 17.16 26.10 5.85 0.61	-	-	-	-	-	-	-	100 17.83 13.32 2.99 0.31	-	-	-	-	-	-	-	-	-
Chester County	369,030 91.24	7,941	1,599 20.14 20.14 0.43	-	-	344 13.59 21.51 4.33 0.09	-	-	340 16.11 21.26 4.28 0.09	-	194 34.70 12.13 2.44 0.05	-	-	-	-	147 38.89 9.19 1.85 0.04	323 32.83 20.20 4.07 0.09	-	-	-	-	-	-	-	-	92 12.03 5.75 1.16 0.02
Tredyffrin (township)	24,230 89.03	1,531	215 14.04 14.04 0.89	-	-	56 9.46 26.05 3.66 0.23	-	-	62 10.76 28.84 4.05 0.26	-	-	-	-	-	-	-	-	-	-	-	-	-	-	-	-	-
West Goshen (township)	17,651 92.71	694	66 9.51 9.51 0.37	-	-	-	-	-	-	-	-	-	-	-	-	-	-	-	-	-	-	-	-	-	-	-

Notes: Please refer to the User's Guide for an explanation of data; data is arranged alphabetically by state, then county, then city within each county; table includes counties with populations greater than 49,999 unless noted and cities with populations greater than 9,999 whose Asian and/or NHPI population rates are greater than the national average; (1) Native Hawaiian and other Pacific Islander; (2) excludes Taiwanese; (3) includes Chamorro; (4) county does not meet population threshold but is shown in order to allow inclusion of city

Place	Total population 5 years and over who speak English-only at home	Asian population 5 years and over	Asians 5 years and over who speak English-only at home	NHPI¹ population 5 years and over	NHPIs¹ 5 years and over who speak English-only at home	Asian Indian	Bangladeshi	Cambodian	Chinese²	Fijian	Filipino	Guamanian³	Hawaiian, Native	Hmong	Indonesian	Japanese	Korean	Laotian	Malaysian	Pakistani	Samoan	Sri Lankan	Taiwanese	Thai	Tongan	Vietnamese
West Whiteland (township)	13,917 91.27	544	81 14.89 14.89 0.58	-	-	-	-	-	-	-	-	-	-	-	-	-	-	-	-	-	-	-	-	-	-	-
Clearfield County	76,882 97.47	263	62 23.57 23.57 0.08	-	-	-	-	-	-	-	-	-	-	-	-	-	-	-	-	-	-	-	-	-	-	-
Columbia County	59,087 96.82	291	105 36.08 36.08 0.18	-	-	-	-	-	-	-	-	-	-	-	-	-	-	-	-	-	-	-	-	-	-	-
Crawford County	80,421 94.59	275	110 40.00 40.00 0.14	-	-	-	-	-	-	-	-	-	-	-	-	-	-	-	-	-	-	-	-	-	-	-
Cumberland County	190,515 94.31	3,240	796 24.57 24.57 0.42	-	-	137 14.17 17.21 4.23 0.07	-	-	120 25.26 15.08 3.70 0.06	-	-	-	-	-	-	-	219 33.54 27.51 6.76 0.11	-	-	-	-	-	-	-	-	74 13.05 9.30 2.28 0.04
Hampden (township)	21,408 93.72	840	201 23.93 23.93 0.94	-	-	-	-	-	-	-	-	-	-	-	-	-	-	-	-	-	-	-	-	-	-	-
Dauphin County	216,635 91.48	4,589	778 16.95 16.95 0.36	-	-	186 18.71 23.91 4.05 0.09	-	-	155 20.18 19.92 3.38 0.07	-	-	-	-	-	-	-	122 32.36 15.68 2.66 0.06	-	-	-	-	-	-	-	-	67 4.28 8.61 1.46 0.03
Derry (township)	18,576 91.89	842	267 31.71 31.71 1.44	-	-	-	-	-	-	-	-	-	-	-	-	-	-	-	-	-	-	-	-	-	-	-
Hershey (cdp)	11,000 90.24	530	122 23.02 23.02 1.11	-	-	-	-	-	-	-	-	-	-	-	-	-	-	-	-	-	-	-	-	-	-	-
Delaware County	468,531 90.73	16,864	2,242 13.29 13.29 0.48	-	-	715 14.89 31.89 4.24 0.15	-	-	324 10.02 14.45 1.92 0.07	-	337 30.69 15.03 2.00 0.07	-	-	-	-	181 27.68 8.07 1.07 0.04	436 13.58 19.45 2.59 0.09	-	-	13 2.10 0.58 0.08 <0.01	-	-	-	-	-	57 3.29 2.54 0.34 0.01

Notes: Please refer to the User's Guide for an explanation of data; data is arranged alphabetically by state, then county, then city within each county; table includes counties with populations greater than 49,999 unless noted and cities with populations greater than 9,999 whose Asian and/or NHPI population rates are greater than the national average; (1) Native Hawaiian and other Pacific Islander; (2) excludes Taiwanese; (3) includes Chamorro; (4) county does not meet population threshold but is shown in order to allow inclusion of city

Place	Total population 5 years and over who speak English-only at home	Asian population 5 years and over	Asians 5 years and over who speak English-only at home	NHPI[1] population 5 years and over	NHPIs[1] 5 years and over who speak English-only at home	Asian Indian	Bangladeshi	Cambodian	Chinese[2]	Fijian	Filipino	Guamanian[3]	Hawaiian, Native	Hmong	Indonesian	Japanese	Korean	Laotian	Malaysian	Pakistani	Samoan	Sri Lankan	Taiwanese	Thai	Tongan	Vietnamese
Broomall (cdp)	8,715 82.01	741	92 12.42 12.42 1.06	-	-	-	-	-	-	-	-	-	-	-	-	-	22 5.00 23.91 2.97 0.25	-	-	-	-	-	-	-	-	-
Drexel Hill (cdp)	24,691 90.22	1,027	106 10.32 10.32 0.43	-	-	-	-	-	4 1.27 3.77 0.39 0.02	-	-	-	-	-	-	-	-	-	-	-	-	-	-	-	-	-
Marple (township)	19,055 84.33	1,196	124 10.37 10.37 0.65	-	-	-	-	-	-	-	-	-	-	-	-	-	49 7.67 39.52 4.10 0.26	-	-	-	-	-	-	-	-	-
Radnor (township)	26,111 88.77	1,507	269 17.85 17.85 1.03	-	-	-	-	-	58 15.43 21.56 3.85 0.22	-	-	-	-	-	-	-	-	-	-	-	-	-	-	-	-	-
Upper Darby (township)	63,354 83.00	6,495	539 8.30 8.30 0.85	-	-	219 11.74 40.63 3.37 0.35	-	-	32 2.29 5.94 0.49 0.05	-	-	-	-	-	-	-	108 11.84 20.04 1.66 0.17	-	-	-	-	-	-	-	-	36 3.44 6.68 0.55 0.06
Erie County	248,148 94.11	1,640	417 25.43 25.43 0.17	-	-	69 15.54 16.55 4.21 0.03	-	-	-	-	-	-	-	-	-	-	-	-	-	-	-	-	-	-	-	-
Franklin County	115,639 95.47	825	244 29.58 29.58 0.21	-	-	-	-	-	-	-	-	-	-	-	-	-	-	-	-	-	-	-	-	-	-	-
Indiana County	81,121 95.23	633	128 20.22 20.22 0.16	-	-	-	-	-	-	-	-	-	-	-	-	-	-	-	-	-	-	-	-	-	-	-
Lackawanna County	190,894 94.40	1,689	431 25.52 25.52 0.23	-	-	102 16.35 23.67 6.04 0.05	-	-	-	-	-	-	-	-	-	-	-	-	-	-	-	-	-	-	-	-
Lancaster County	380,622 86.88	6,047	1,277 21.12 21.12 0.34	-	-	204 27.83 15.97 3.37 0.05	-	-	67 5.82 5.25 1.11 0.02	-	-	-	-	14 3.13 1.10 0.23 <0.01	-	-	336 61.54 26.31 5.56 0.09	-	-	-	-	-	-	-	-	200 10.65 15.66 3.31 0.05

Notes: Please refer to the User's Guide for an explanation of data; data is arranged alphabetically by state, then county, then city within each county; table includes counties with populations greater than 49,999 unless noted and cities with populations greater than 9,999 whose Asian and/or NHPI population rates are greater than the national average; (1) Native Hawaiian and other Pacific Islander; (2) excludes Taiwanese; (3) includes Chamorro; (4) county does not meet population threshold but is shown in order to allow inclusion of city

Place	Total population 5 years and over who speak English-only at home	Asian population 5 years and over	Asians 5 years and over who speak English-only at home	NHPI[1] population 5 years and over	NHPIs[1] 5 years and over who speak English-only at home	Asian Indian	Bangladeshi	Cambodian	Chinese[2]	Fijian	Filipino	Guamanian[3]	Hawaiian, Native	Hmong	Indonesian	Japanese	Korean	Laotian	Malaysian	Pakistani	Samoan	Sri Lankan	Taiwanese	Thai	Tongan	Vietnamese
Lawrence County	84,856 94.96	265	95 35.85 35.85 0.11	-	-	-	-	-	-	-	-	-	-	-	-	-	-	-	-	-	-	-	-	-	-	-
Lebanon County	103,954 92.00	1,060	198 18.68 18.68 0.19	-	-	-	-	-	-	-	-	-	-	-	-	-	-	-	-	-	-	-	-	-	-	-
Lehigh County	248,723 84.74	6,213	948 15.26 15.26 0.38	-	-	259 13.07 27.32 4.17 0.10	-	-	244 17.40 25.74 3.93 0.10	-	-	-	-	-	-	-	163 24.26 17.19 2.62 0.07	-	-	-	-	-	-	-	-	80 6.00 8.44 1.29 0.03
Fullerton (cdp)	10,856 80.86	613	47 7.67 7.67 0.43	-	-	-	-	-	-	-	-	-	-	-	-	-	-	-	-	-	-	-	-	-	-	-
Lower Macungie (township)	16,386 90.43	822	82 9.98 9.98 0.50	-	-	-	-	-	61 16.67 74.39 7.42 0.37	-	-	-	-	-	-	-	-	-	-	-	-	-	-	-	-	-
Upper Macungie (township)	11,643 89.66	553	113 20.43 20.43 0.97	-	-	-	-	-	-	-	-	-	-	-	-	-	-	-	-	-	-	-	-	-	-	-
Luzerne County	287,778 94.86	1,435	452 31.50 31.50 0.16	-	-	82 21.75 18.14 5.71 0.03	-	-	-	-	-	-	-	-	-	-	-	-	-	-	-	-	-	-	-	-
Lycoming County	109,699 96.68	430	141 32.79 32.79 0.13	-	-	-	-	-	-	-	-	-	-	-	-	-	-	-	-	-	-	-	-	-	-	-
Mercer County	108,034 95.19	647	201 31.07 31.07 0.19	-	-	-	-	-	-	-	-	-	-	-	-	-	-	-	-	-	-	-	-	-	-	-
Monroe County	117,415 90.03	1,250	406 32.48 32.48 0.35	-	-	104 31.14 25.62 8.32 0.09	-	-	-	-	-	-	-	-	-	-	-	-	-	-	-	-	-	-	-	-

Notes: Please refer to the User's Guide for an explanation of data; data is arranged alphabetically by state, then county, then city within each county; table includes counties with populations greater than 49,999 unless noted and cities with populations greater than 9,999 whose Asian and/or NHPI population rates are greater than the national average; (1) Native Hawaiian and other Pacific Islander; (2) excludes Taiwanese; (3) includes Chamorro; (4) county does not meet population threshold but is shown in order to allow inclusion of city

Place	Total population 5 years and over who speak English-only at home	Asian population 5 years and over	Asians 5 years and over who speak English-only at home	NHPI[1] population 5 years and over	NHPIs[1] 5 years and over who speak English-only at home	Asian Indian	Bangladeshi	Cambodian	Chinese[2]	Fijian	Filipino	Guamanian[3]	Hawaiian, Native	Hmong	Indonesian	Japanese	Korean	Laotian	Malaysian	Pakistani	Samoan	Sri Lankan	Taiwanese	Thai	Tongan	Vietnamese
Montgomery County	635,062 90.38	27,177	3,799 13.98 13.98 0.60	-	-	996 14.54 26.22 3.66 0.16	-	-	632 12.68 16.64 2.33 0.10	-	538 30.02 14.16 1.98 0.08	-	-	-	-	275 40.20 7.24 1.01 0.04	900 10.40 23.69 3.31 0.14	-	-	-	-	-	-	-	-	191 8.74 5.03 0.70 0.03
Cheltenham (township)	30,382 86.77	2,254	229 10.16 10.16 0.75	-	-	-	-	-	-	-	-	-	-	-	-	-	84 7.84 36.68 3.73 0.28	-	-	-	-	-	-	-	-	-
East Norriton (township)	11,148 89.36	520	47 9.04 9.04 0.42	-	-	-	-	-	-	-	-	-	-	-	-	-	-	-	-	-	-	-	-	-	-	-
Hatfield (township)	12,812 82.27	1,648	100 6.07 6.07 0.78	-	-	42 4.86 42.00 2.55 0.33	-	-	-	-	-	-	-	-	-	-	-	-	-	-	-	-	-	-	-	-
Horsham (township)	20,481 90.76	1,067	136 12.75 12.75 0.66	-	-	-	-	-	-	-	-	-	-	-	-	-	33 6.99 24.26 3.09 0.16	-	-	-	-	-	-	-	-	-
King of Prussia (cdp)	14,665 83.60	1,758	233 13.25 13.25 1.59	-	-	82 11.10 35.19 4.66 0.56	-	-	64 17.16 27.47 3.64 0.44	-	-	-	-	-	-	-	-	-	-	-	-	-	-	-	-	-
Lansdale (borough)	12,850 85.21	1,220	163 13.36 13.36 1.27	-	-	21 4.95 12.88 1.72 0.16	-	-	-	-	-	-	-	-	-	-	-	-	-	-	-	-	-	-	-	-
Lower Gwynedd (township)	8,901 90.29	371	35 9.43 9.43 0.39	-	-	-	-	-	-	-	-	-	-	-	-	-	-	-	-	-	-	-	-	-	-	-
Lower Providence (township)	19,297 92.08	874	129 14.76 14.76 0.67	-	-	-	-	-	34 8.40 26.36 3.89 0.18	-	-	-	-	-	-	-	-	-	-	-	-	-	-	-	-	-
Montgomery (township)	17,364 86.75	1,686	136 8.07 8.07 0.78	-	-	33 6.24 24.26 1.96 0.19	-	-	-	-	-	-	-	-	-	-	40 5.84 29.41 2.37 0.23	-	-	-	-	-	-	-	-	-

Notes: Please refer to the User's Guide for an explanation of data; data is arranged alphabetically by state, then county, then city within each county; table includes counties with populations greater than 49,999 unless noted and cities with populations greater than 9,999 whose Asian and/or NHPI population rates are greater than the national average; (1) Native Hawaiian and other Pacific Islander; (2) excludes Taiwanese; (3) includes Chamorro; (4) county does not meet population threshold but is shown in order to allow inclusion of city

Place	Total population 5 years and over who speak English-only at home	Asian population 5 years and over	Asians 5 years and over who speak English-only at home	NHPI[1] population 5 years and over	NHPIs[1] 5 years and over who speak English-only at home	Asian Indian	Bangladeshi	Cambodian	Chinese[2]	Fijian	Filipino	Guamanian[3]	Hawaiian, Native	Hmong	Indonesian	Japanese	Korean	Laotian	Malaysian	Pakistani	Samoan	Sri Lankan	Taiwanese	Thai	Tongan	Vietnamese
Montgomeryville (cdp)	9,623 88.37	761	69 9.07 9.07 0.72	-	-	-	-	-	-	-	-	-	-	-	-	-	-	-	-	-	-	-	-	-	-	-
Plymouth (township)	13,497 88.56	780	53 6.79 6.79 0.39	-	-	-	-	-	-	-	-	-	-	-	-	-	17 5.33 32.08 2.18 0.13	-	-	-	-	-	-	-	-	-
Towamencin (township)	14,858 90.61	896	135 15.07 15.07 0.91	-	-	-	-	-	-	-	-	-	-	-	-	-	-	-	-	-	-	-	-	-	-	-
Upper Dublin (township)	21,563 88.58	1,482	155 10.46 10.46 0.72	-	-	-	-	-	-	-	-	-	-	-	-	-	72 8.82 46.45 4.86 0.33	-	-	-	-	-	-	-	-	-
Upper Gwynedd (township)	11,945 88.40	1,075	232 21.58 21.58 1.94	-	-	-	-	-	58 20.86 25.00 5.40 0.49	-	-	-	-	-	-	-	-	-	-	-	-	-	-	-	-	-
Upper Merion (township)	21,717 85.68	1,998	283 14.16 14.16 1.30	-	-	121 13.89 42.76 6.06 0.56	-	-	68 16.55 24.03 3.40 0.31	-	-	-	-	-	-	-	-	-	-	-	-	-	-	-	-	-
Whitpain (township)	15,391 87.71	1,198	222 18.53 18.53 1.44	-	-	-	-	-	-	-	-	-	-	-	-	-	55 9.39 24.77 4.59 0.36	-	-	-	-	-	-	-	-	-
Northampton County	224,386 89.05	3,385	728 21.51 21.51 0.32	-	-	219 19.48 30.08 6.47 0.10	-	-	52 8.07 7.14 1.54 0.02	-	-	-	-	-	-	-	215 49.20 29.53 6.35 0.10	-	-	-	-	-	-	-	-	37 8.73 5.08 1.09 0.02
Northumberland County	85,743 95.57	340	121 35.59 35.59 0.14	-	-	-	-	-	-	-	-	-	-	-	-	-	-	-	-	-	-	-	-	-	-	-
Philadelphia County	1,168,463 82.29	60,852	7,812 12.84 12.84 0.67	651	360 55.30 55.30 0.03	2,012 17.11 25.76 3.31 0.17	-	378 6.49 4.84 0.62 0.03	1,686 10.04 21.58 2.77 0.14	-	1,117 30.99 14.30 1.84 0.10	-	-	-	-	317 29.30 4.06 0.52 0.03	825 13.26 10.56 1.36 0.07	63 5.71 0.81 0.10 0.01	-	30 5.01 0.38 0.05 <0.01	-	-	-	-	-	560 5.54 7.17 0.92 0.05

Notes: Please refer to the User's Guide for an explanation of data; data is arranged alphabetically by state, then county, then city within each county; table includes counties with populations greater than 49,999 unless noted and cities with populations greater than 9,999 whose Asian and/or NHPI population rates are greater than the national average; (1) Native Hawaiian and other Pacific Islander; (2) excludes Taiwanese; (3) includes Chamorro; (4) county does not meet population threshold but is shown in order to allow inclusion of city

Place	Total population 5 years and over who speak English-only at home	Asian population 5 years and over	Asians 5 years and over who speak English-only at home	NHPI[1] population 5 years and over	NHPIs[1] 5 years and over who speak English-only at home	Asian Indian	Bangladeshi	Cambodian	Chinese[2]	Fijian	Filipino	Guamanian[3]	Hawaiian, Native	Hmong	Indonesian	Japanese	Korean	Laotian	Malaysian	Pakistani	Samoan	Sri Lankan	Taiwanese	Thai	Tongan	Vietnamese
Philadelphia (city)	1,168,463	60,852	7,812	651	360	2,012	-	378	1,686	-	1,117	-	-	-	-	317	825	63	-	30	-	-	-	-	-	560
	82.29		12.84		55.30	17.11		6.49	10.04		30.99					29.30	13.26	5.71		5.01						5.54
						25.76		4.84	21.58		14.30					4.06	10.56	0.81		0.38						7.17
			12.84		55.30	3.31		0.62	2.77		1.84					0.52	1.36	0.10		0.05						0.92
			0.67		0.03	0.17		0.03	0.14		0.10					0.03	0.07	0.01		<0.01						0.05
Schuylkill County	136,615	529	188	-	-	-	-	-	-	-	-	-	-	-	-	-	-	-	-	-	-	-	-	-	-	-
	95.52		35.54																							
			35.54																							
			0.14																							
Washington County	184,746	571	231	-	-	-	-	-	-	-	-	-	-	-	-	-	-	-	-	-	-	-	-	-	-	-
	96.39		40.46																							
			40.46																							
			0.13																							
Westmoreland County	337,767	1,610	286	-	-	63	-	-	-	-	-	-	-	-	-	-	-	-	-	-	-	-	-	-	-	-
	96.26		17.76			15.44																				
						22.03																				
			17.76			3.91																				
			0.08			0.02																				
York County	339,443	2,907	638	-	-	113	-	-	35	-	-	-	-	-	-	-	193	-	-	-	-	-	-	-	-	60
	94.65		21.95			23.16			5.70								32.99									10.97
						17.71			5.49								30.25									9.40
			21.95			3.89			1.20								6.64									2.06
			0.19			0.03			0.01								0.06									0.02
RHODE ISLAND	788,560	22,184	3,135	392	146	469	-	235	653	-	545	-	-	8	-	264	478	61	-	-	-	-	-	-	-	40
	80.04		14.13		37.24	19.53		5.06	15.46		27.10			0.91		35.06	26.02	2.26								4.13
						14.96		7.50	20.83		17.38			0.26		8.42	15.25	1.95								1.28
			14.13		37.24	2.11		1.06	2.94		2.46			0.04		1.19	2.15	0.27								0.18
			0.40		0.02	0.06		0.03	0.08		0.07			<0.01		0.03	0.06	0.01								0.01
Bristol County	40,583	401	108	-	-	-	-	-	-	-	-	-	-	-	-	-	-	-	-	-	-	-	-	-	-	-
	84.61		26.93																							
			26.93																							
			0.27																							
Kent County	143,864	2,017	432	-	-	-	-	-	60	-	-	-	-	-	-	-	78	-	-	-	-	-	-	-	-	-
	91.52		21.42						17.34								20.86									
									13.89								18.06									
			21.42						2.97								3.87									
			0.30						0.04								0.05									
Newport County	73,443	886	275	-	-	-	-	-	-	-	153	-	-	-	-	-	-	-	-	-	-	-	-	-	-	-
	91.35		31.04								37.59															
											55.64															
			31.04								17.27															
			0.37								0.21															
Providence County	423,478	17,061	1,944	-	-	312	-	203	472	-	238	-	-	8	-	-	284	61	-	-	-	-	-	-	-	40
	72.60		11.39			17.93		4.65	15.98		22.22			1.07			24.59	2.38								5.19
						16.05		10.44	24.28		12.24			0.41			14.61	3.14								2.06
			11.39			1.83		1.19	2.77		1.39			0.05			1.66	0.36								0.23
			0.46			0.07		0.05	0.11		0.06			<0.01			0.07	0.01								0.01

Notes: Please refer to the User's Guide for an explanation of data; data is arranged alphabetically by state, then county, then city within each county; table includes counties with populations greater than 49,999 unless noted and cities with populations greater than 9,999 whose Asian and/or NHPI population rates are greater than the national average; (1) Native Hawaiian and other Pacific Islander; (2) excludes Taiwanese; (3) includes Chamorro; (4) county does not meet population threshold but is shown in order to allow inclusion of city

Place	Total population 5 years and over who speak English-only at home	Asian population 5 years and over	Asians 5 years and over who speak English-only at home	NHPI[1] population 5 years and over	NHPIs[1] 5 years and over who speak English-only at home	Asian Indian	Bangladeshi	Cambodian	Chinese[2]	Fijian	Filipino	Guamanian[3]	Hawaiian, Native	Hmong	Indonesian	Japanese	Korean	Laotian	Malaysian	Pakistani	Samoan	Sri Lankan	Taiwanese	Thai	Tongan	Vietnamese
Providence (city)	92,086 56.97	9,990	1,144 11.45 11.45 1.24	-	-	194 22.15 16.96 1.94 0.21	-	138 4.26 12.06 1.38 0.15	278 19.72 24.30 2.78 0.30	-	97 19.36 8.48 0.97 0.11	-	-	0 0.00 0.00 0.00 0.00	-	-	177 25.04 15.47 1.77 0.19	29 2.29 2.53 0.29 0.03	-	-	-	-	-	-	-	-
Woonsocket (city)	29,519 73.89	1,516	141 9.30 9.30 0.48	-	-	-	-	-	-	-	-	-	-	-	-	-	-	25 3.03 17.73 1.65 0.08	-	-	-	-	-	-	-	-
Washington County	107,192 92.12	1,819	376 20.67 20.67 0.35	-	-	-	-	-	51 9.53 13.56 2.80 0.05	-	-	-	-	-	-	-	-	-	-	-	-	-	-	-	-	-
SOUTH CAROLINA	3,552,240 94.76	34,026	7,348 21.60 21.60 0.21	1,340	738 55.07 55.07 0.02	1,492 19.53 20.30 4.38 0.04	-	47 14.92 0.64 0.14 <0.01	699 12.18 9.51 2.05 0.02	-	2,429 36.52 33.06 7.14 0.07	136 40.24 18.43 10.15 <0.01	390 79.27 52.85 29.10 0.01	0 0.00 0.00 0.00 0.00	-	675 31.03 9.19 1.98 0.02	936 27.38 12.74 2.75 0.03	55 4.59 0.75 0.16 <0.01	-	-	-	-	-	159 23.28 2.16 0.47 <0.01	-	327 9.31 4.45 0.96 0.01
Aiken County	127,376 95.67	897	233 25.98 25.98 0.18	-	-	-	-	-	-	-	-	-	-	-	-	-	-	-	-	-	-	-	-	-	-	-
Anderson County	149,583 96.69	759	200 26.35 26.35 0.13	-	-	-	-	-	-	-	-	-	-	-	-	-	-	-	-	-	-	-	-	-	-	-
Beaufort County	101,637 90.12	960	316 32.92 32.92 0.31	-	-	-	-	-	-	-	-	-	-	-	-	-	-	-	-	-	-	-	-	-	-	-
Berkeley County	124,855 94.15	2,781	692 24.88 24.88 0.55	-	-	-	-	-	-	-	464 26.70 67.05 16.68 0.37	-	-	-	-	-	-	-	-	-	-	-	-	-	-	-
Charleston County	271,353 93.59	3,310	1,010 30.51 30.51 0.37	-	-	150 24.71 14.85 4.53 0.06	-	-	59 9.41 5.84 1.78 0.02	-	468 47.76 46.34 14.14 0.17	-	-	-	-	-	-	-	-	-	-	-	-	-	-	-
Dorchester County	85,457 95.02	1,188	462 38.89 38.89 0.54	-	-	-	-	-	-	-	258 41.95 55.84 21.72 0.30	-	-	-	-	-	-	-	-	-	-	-	-	-	-	-

Notes: Please refer to the User's Guide for an explanation of data; data is arranged alphabetically by state, then county, then city within each county; table includes counties with populations greater than 49,999 unless noted and cities with populations greater than 9,999 whose Asian and/or NHPI population rates are greater than the national average; (1) Native Hawaiian and other Pacific Islander; (2) excludes Taiwanese; (3) includes Chamorro; (4) county does not meet population threshold but is shown in order to allow inclusion of city

Place	Total population 5 years and over who speak English-only at home	Asian population 5 years and over	Asians 5 years and over who speak English-only at home	NHPI[1] population 5 years and over	NHPIs[1] 5 years and over who speak English-only at home	Asian Indian	Bangladeshi	Cambodian	Chinese[2]	Fijian	Filipino	Guamanian[3]	Hawaiian, Native	Hmong	Indonesian	Japanese	Korean	Laotian	Malaysian	Pakistani	Samoan	Sri Lankan	Taiwanese	Thai	Tongan	Vietnamese
Florence County	112,856 95.94	917	167 18.21 18.21 0.15	-	-	-	-	-	-	-	-	-	-	-	-	-	-	-	-	-	-	-	-	-	-	-
Greenville County	329,182 92.94	4,567	794 17.39 17.39 0.24	-	-	164 11.95 20.65 3.59 0.05	-	-	150 23.40 18.89 3.28 0.05	-	210 41.34 26.45 4.60 0.06	-	-	-	-	-	-	-	-	-	-	-	-	-	-	43 4.15 5.42 0.94 0.01
Greenwood County	58,673 95.16	362	46 12.71 12.71 0.08	-	-	-	-	-	-	-	-	-	-	-	-	-	-	-	-	-	-	-	-	-	-	-
Horry County	173,936 93.73	1,459	303 20.77 20.77 0.17	-	-	-	-	-	-	-	-	-	-	-	-	-	-	-	-	-	-	-	-	-	-	-
Lexington County	190,705 94.70	1,699	322 18.95 18.95 0.17	-	-	91 18.88 28.26 5.36 0.05	-	-	38 7.71 11.80 2.24 0.02	-	-	-	-	-	-	-	-	-	-	-	-	-	-	-	-	-
Oconee County	59,796 96.17	250	81 32.40 32.40 0.14	-	-	-	-	-	-	-	-	-	-	-	-	-	-	-	-	-	-	-	-	-	-	-
Pickens County	99,013 95.25	1,249	237 18.98 18.98 0.24	-	-	53 11.00 22.36 4.24 0.05	-	-	56 15.30 23.63 4.48 0.06	-	-	-	-	-	-	-	-	-	-	-	-	-	-	-	-	-
Clemson (city)	10,569 90.54	577	54 9.36 9.36 0.51	-	-	-	-	-	-	-	-	-	-	-	-	-	-	-	-	-	-	-	-	-	-	-
Richland County	278,545 92.66	5,294	1,076 20.32 20.32 0.39	-	-	305 22.05 28.35 5.76 0.11	-	-	61 5.88 5.67 1.15 0.02	-	240 48.68 22.30 4.53 0.09	-	-	-	-	-	222 18.33 20.63 4.19 0.08	-	-	-	-	-	-	-	-	64 13.06 5.95 1.21 0.02
Spartanburg County	221,858 93.69	3,741	438 11.71 11.71 0.20	-	-	165 22.60 37.67 4.41 0.07	-	-	-	-	-	-	-	0 0.00 0.00 0.00 0.00	-	-	-	31 5.06 7.08 0.83 0.01	-	-	-	-	-	-	-	-

Notes: Please refer to the User's Guide for an explanation of data; data is arranged alphabetically by state, then county, then city within each county; table includes counties with populations greater than 49,999 unless noted and cities with populations greater than 9,999 whose Asian and/or NHPI population rates are greater than the national average; (1) Native Hawaiian and other Pacific Islander; (2) excludes Taiwanese; (3) includes Chamorro; (4) county does not meet population threshold but is shown in order to allow inclusion of city

Place	Total population 5 years and over who speak English-only at home	Asian population 5 years and over	Asians 5 years and over who speak English-only at home	NHPI[1] population 5 years and over	NHPIs[1] 5 years and over who speak English-only at home	Asian Indian	Bangladeshi	Cambodian	Chinese[2]	Fijian	Filipino	Guamanian[3]	Hawaiian, Native	Hmong	Indonesian	Japanese	Korean	Laotian	Malaysian	Pakistani	Samoan	Sri Lankan	Taiwanese	Thai	Tongan	Vietnamese
Sumter County	92,467 95.44	874	160 18.31 18.31 0.17	-	-	-	-	-	-	-	-	-	-	-	-	-	-	-	-	-	-	-	-	-	-	-
York County	146,479 95.37	1,270	239 18.82 18.82 0.16	-	-	-	-	-	-	-	-	-	-	-	-	-	-	-	-	-	-	-	-	-	-	30 7.16 12.55 2.36 0.02
SOUTH DAKOTA	658,245 93.52	4,245	1,402 33.03 33.03 0.21	-	-	78 15.98 5.56 1.84 0.01	-	-	125 20.13 8.92 2.94 0.02	-	267 39.09 19.04 6.29 0.04	-	-	-	-	189 48.09 13.48 4.45 0.03	392 61.25 27.96 9.23 0.06	28 13.73 2.00 0.66 <0.01	-	-	-	-	-	-	-	70 11.76 4.99 1.65 0.01
Minnehaha County	128,234 93.32	1,344	363 27.01 27.01 0.28	-	-	-	-	-	-	-	-	-	-	-	-	-	-	-	-	-	-	-	-	-	-	36 8.51 9.92 2.68 0.03
Pennington County	78,107 94.92	872	344 39.45 39.45 0.44	-	-	-	-	-	-	-	-	-	-	-	-	-	-	-	-	-	-	-	-	-	-	-
TENNESSEE	5,059,404 95.17	50,128	9,340 18.63 18.63 0.18	1,920	1,159 60.36 60.36 0.02	1,806 16.30 19.34 3.60 0.04	-	75 6.79 0.80 0.15 <0.01	1,155 15.34 12.37 2.30 0.02	-	1,798 36.45 19.25 3.59 0.04	208 42.89 17.95 10.83 <0.01	466 86.30 40.21 24.27 0.01	-	-	930 25.57 9.96 1.86 0.02	1,446 22.15 15.48 2.88 0.03	235 6.29 2.52 0.47 <0.01	-	33 4.73 0.35 0.07 <0.01	276 52.57 23.81 14.37 0.01	-	80 13.79 0.86 0.16 <0.01	219 22.60 2.34 0.44 <0.01	-	552 8.59 5.91 1.10 0.01
Anderson County	64,850 96.40	438	85 19.41 19.41 0.13	-	-	-	-	-	-	-	-	-	-	-	-	-	-	-	-	-	-	-	-	-	-	-
Blount County	96,438 96.77	596	82 13.76 13.76 0.09	-	-	-	-	-	-	-	-	-	-	-	-	-	-	-	-	-	-	-	-	-	-	-
Bradley County	78,630 95.60	451	65 14.41 14.41 0.08	-	-	-	-	-	-	-	-	-	-	-	-	-	-	-	-	-	-	-	-	-	-	-
Davidson County	480,014 90.18	10,847	1,801 16.60 16.60 0.38	378	240 63.49 63.49 0.05	450 19.04 24.99 4.15 0.09	-	-	154 11.28 8.55 1.42 0.03	-	246 31.74 13.66 2.27 0.05	-	-	-	-	233 30.14 12.94 2.15 0.05	178 14.39 9.88 1.64 0.04	102 8.23 5.66 0.94 0.02	-	-	-	-	-	-	-	121 7.86 6.72 1.12 0.03

Notes: Please refer to the User's Guide for an explanation of data; data is arranged alphabetically by state, then county, then city within each county; table includes counties with populations greater than 49,999 unless noted and cities with populations greater than 9,999 whose Asian and/or NHPI population rates are greater than the national average; (1) Native Hawaiian and other Pacific Islander; (2) excludes Taiwanese; (3) includes Chamorro; (4) county does not meet population threshold but is shown in order to allow inclusion of city

Place	Total population 5 years and over who speak English-only at home	Asian population 5 years and over	Asians 5 years and over who speak English-only at home	NHPI[1] population 5 years and over	NHPIs[1] 5 years and over who speak English-only at home	Asian Indian	Bangladeshi	Cambodian	Chinese[2]	Fijian	Filipino	Guamanian[3]	Hawaiian, Native	Hmong	Indonesian	Japanese	Korean	Laotian	Malaysian	Pakistani	Samoan	Sri Lankan	Taiwanese	Thai	Tongan	Vietnamese
Hamilton County	275,038 94.95	3,624	747 20.61 20.61 0.27	-	-	160 14.53 21.42 4.42 0.06	-	-	-	-	154 38.99 20.62 4.25 0.06	-	-	-	-	-	114 23.03 15.26 3.15 0.04	-	-	-	-	-	-	-	-	51 13.28 6.83 1.41 0.02
Knox County	342,926 95.56	4,253	805 18.93 18.93 0.23	-	-	231 18.44 28.70 5.43 0.07	-	-	130 14.94 16.15 3.06 0.04	-	-	-	-	-	-	-	130 27.25 16.15 3.06 0.04	-	-	-	-	-	-	-	-	69 15.10 8.57 1.62 0.02
Madison County	82,156 96.06	487	67 13.76 13.76 0.08	-	-	-	-	-	-	-	-	-	-	-	-	-	-	-	-	-	-	-	-	-	-	-
Montgomery County	113,111 91.56	2,388	707 29.61 29.61 0.63	-	-	-	-	-	-	-	-	-	-	-	-	-	193 17.53 27.30 8.08 0.17	-	-	-	-	-	-	-	-	-
Putnam County	55,460 94.74	568	94 16.55 16.55 0.17	-	-	-	-	-	-	-	-	-	-	-	-	-	-	-	-	-	-	-	-	-	-	-
Rutherford County	158,413 94.12	3,020	257 8.51 8.51 0.16	-	-	-	-	-	-	-	-	-	-	-	-	-	-	71 4.85 27.63 2.35 0.04	-	-	-	-	-	-	-	-
Shelby County	774,966 93.45	13,621	2,054 15.08 15.08 0.27	457	264 57.77 57.77 0.03	342 10.39 16.65 2.51 0.04	-	35 7.00 1.70 0.26 <0.01	377 15.03 18.35 2.77 0.05	-	400 32.44 19.47 2.94 0.05	-	-	-	-	154 32.56 7.50 1.13 0.02	221 19.44 10.76 1.62 0.03	-	-	-	-	-	-	-	-	173 5.69 8.42 1.27 0.02
Germantown (city)	32,563 92.42	1,268	89 7.02 7.02 0.27	-	-	44 8.85 49.44 3.47 0.14	-	-	27 7.38 30.34 2.13 0.08	-	-	-	-	-	-	-	-	-	-	-	-	-	-	-	-	-
Sullivan County	141,222 97.69	548	156 28.47 28.47 0.11	-	-	-	-	-	-	-	-	-	-	-	-	-	-	-	-	-	-	-	-	-	-	-
Sumner County	116,887 95.98	840	203 24.17 24.17 0.17	-	-	-	-	-	-	-	-	-	-	-	-	-	-	-	-	-	-	-	-	-	-	-

Notes: Please refer to the User's Guide for an explanation of data; data is arranged alphabetically by state, then county, then city within each county; table includes counties with populations greater than 49,999 unless noted and cities with populations greater than 9,999 whose Asian and/or NHPI population rates are greater than the national average; (1) Native Hawaiian and other Pacific Islander; (2) excludes Taiwanese; (3) includes Chamorro; (4) county does not meet population threshold but is shown in order to allow inclusion of city

Place	Total population 5 years and over who speak English-only at home	Asian population 5 years and over	Asians 5 years and over who speak English-only at home	NHPI[1] population 5 years and over	NHPIs[1] 5 years and over who speak English-only at home	Asian Indian	Bangladeshi	Cambodian	Chinese[2]	Fijian	Filipino	Guamanian[3]	Hawaiian, Native	Hmong	Indonesian	Japanese	Korean	Laotian	Malaysian	Pakistani	Samoan	Sri Lankan	Taiwanese	Thai	Tongan	Vietnamese
	97,393	658	187	-	-	-	-	-	-	-	-	-	-	-	-	-	-	-	-	-	-	-	-	-	-	-
	96.60		28.42																							
Washington County																										
			28.42																							
			0.19																							
	31,688	451	77	-	-	-	-	-	-	-	-	-	-	-	-	-	-	-	-	-	-	-	-	-	-	-
	96.41		17.07																							
Weakley County[4]																										
			17.07																							
			0.24																							
	9,209	422	65	-	-	-	-	-	-	-	-	-	-	-	-	-	-	-	-	-	-	-	-	-	-	-
	91.32		15.40																							
Martin (city)																										
			15.40																							
			0.71																							
	111,012	1,333	330	-	-	-	-	-	-	-	-	-	-	-	-	-	-	-	-	-	-	-	-	-	-	-
	94.60		24.76																							
Williamson County																										
			24.76																							
			0.30																							
	80,380	286	37	-	-	-	-	-	-	-	-	-	-	-	-	-	-	-	-	-	-	-	-	-	-	-
	97.06		12.94																							
Wilson County																										
			12.94																							
			0.05																							
	13,230,765	515,744	76,530	11,388	5,833	19,020	80	672	11,209	-	15,863	1,599	2,277	-	293	5,614	7,090	681	198	1,147	778	204	530	1,764	126	7,280
	68.76		14.84		51.22	16.25	3.50	9.59	12.25		28.74	52.46	66.52		17.39	36.42	17.15	7.37	30.65	6.76	42.33	22.10	7.06	25.53	28.90	5.85
TEXAS						24.85	0.10	0.88	14.65		20.73	27.41	39.04		0.38	7.34	9.26	0.89	0.26	1.50	13.34	0.27	0.69	2.30	2.16	9.51
			14.84		51.22	3.69	0.02	0.13	2.17		3.08	14.04	19.99		0.06	1.09	1.37	0.13	0.04	0.22	6.83	0.04	0.10	0.34	1.11	1.41
			0.58		0.04	0.14	<0.01	0.01	0.08		0.12	0.01	0.02		<0.01	0.04	0.05	0.01	<0.01	0.01	0.01	<0.01	<0.01	0.01	<0.01	0.06
	48,445	375	90	-	-	-	-	-	-	-	-	-	-	-	-	-	-	-	-	-	-	-	-	-	-	-
	93.17		24.00																							
Anderson County																										
			24.00																							
			0.19																							
	63,796	471	72	-	-	-	-	-	-	-	-	-	-	-	-	-	-	-	-	-	-	-	-	-	-	-
	85.93		15.29																							
Angelina County																										
			15.29																							
			0.11																							
	178,356	5,745	1,586	1,232	680	107	-	-	-	-	497	330	-	-	-	204	451	-	-	-	-	-	-	-	-	-
	82.27		27.61		55.19	20.23					32.46	55.37				54.26	20.08									
Bell County						6.75					31.34	48.53				12.86	28.44									
			27.61		55.19	1.86					8.65	26.79				3.55	7.85									
			0.89		0.38	0.06					0.28	0.19				0.11	0.25									
	60,675	3,572	936	1,023	571	-	-	-	-	-	309	257	-	-	-	-	248	-	-	-	-	-	-	-	-	-
	77.83		26.20		55.82						30.09	51.40					16.60									
Killeen (city)											33.01	45.01					26.50									
			26.20		55.82						8.65	25.12					6.94									
			1.54		0.94						0.51	0.42					0.41									

Notes: Please refer to the User's Guide for an explanation of data; data is arranged alphabetically by state, then county, then city within each county; table includes counties with populations greater than 49,999 unless noted and cities with populations greater than 9,999 whose Asian and/or NHPI population rates are greater than the national average; (1) Native Hawaiian and other Pacific Islander; (2) excludes Taiwanese; (3) includes Chamorro; (4) county does not meet population threshold but is shown in order to allow inclusion of city

Place	Total population 5 years and over who speak English-only at home	Asian population 5 years and over	Asians 5 years and over who speak English-only at home	NHPI[1] population 5 years and over	NHPIs[1] 5 years and over who speak English-only at home	Asian Indian	Bangladeshi	Cambodian	Chinese[2]	Fijian	Filipino	Guamanian[3]	Hawaiian, Native	Hmong	Indonesian	Japanese	Korean	Laotian	Malaysian	Pakistani	Samoan	Sri Lankan	Taiwanese	Thai	Tongan	Vietnamese
Bexar County	729,268 56.81	21,313	5,826 27.34 27.34 0.80	1,039	613 59.00 59.00 0.08	660 19.61 11.33 3.10 0.09	-	-	762 21.54 13.08 3.58 0.10	-	1,847 37.12 31.70 8.67 0.25	-	309 76.87 50.41 29.74 0.04	-	-	797 47.72 13.68 3.74 0.11	557 22.72 9.56 2.61 0.08	28 7.71 0.48 0.13 <0.01	-	-	-	-	-	275 34.12 4.72 1.29 0.04	-	348 12.77 5.97 1.63 0.05
Bowie County	78,919 94.53	396	146 36.87 36.87 0.18	-	-	-	-	-	-	-	-	-	-	-	-	-	-	-	-	-	-	-	-	-	-	-
Brazoria County	175,709 78.68	4,288	613 14.30 14.30 0.35	-	-	182 22.01 29.69 4.24 0.10	-	12 3.34 1.96 0.28 0.01	48 8.73 7.83 1.12 0.03	-	153 23.87 24.96 3.57 0.09	-	-	-	-	-	-	-	-	-	-	-	-	-	-	51 4.15 8.32 1.19 0.03
Brazos County	114,324 80.07	5,761	716 12.43 12.43 0.63	-	-	192 11.63 26.82 3.33 0.17	-	-	119 7.57 16.62 2.07 0.10	-	-	-	-	-	-	-	62 7.82 8.66 1.08 0.05	-	-	-	-	-	-	-	-	57 13.48 7.96 0.99 0.05
College Station (city)	53,589 82.72	4,777	675 14.13 14.13 1.26	-	-	177 14.50 26.22 3.71 0.33	-	-	119 8.59 17.63 2.49 0.22	-	-	-	-	-	-	-	43 6.49 6.37 0.90 0.08	-	-	-	-	-	-	-	-	-
Calhoun County[4]	12,824 67.20	614	11 1.79 1.79 0.09	-	-	-	-	-	-	-	-	-	-	-	-	-	-	-	-	-	-	-	-	-	-	11 7.05 100.00 1.79 0.09
Port Lavaca (city)	6,568 59.68	448	6 1.34 1.34 0.09	-	-	-	-	-	-	-	-	-	-	-	-	-	-	-	-	-	-	-	-	-	-	-
Cameron County	63,824 21.02	1,387	329 23.72 23.72 0.52	-	-	-	-	-	-	-	97 17.51 29.48 6.99 0.15	-	-	-	-	-	-	-	-	-	-	-	-	-	-	-
Collin County	366,248 81.48	30,400	3,718 12.23 12.23 1.02	-	-	1,255 15.97 33.75 4.13 0.34	-	-	883 7.75 23.75 2.90 0.24	-	460 34.30 12.37 1.51 0.13	-	-	-	-	165 19.23 4.44 0.54 0.05	402 15.81 10.81 1.32 0.11	-	-	41 4.82 1.10 0.13 0.01	-	-	11 1.37 0.30 0.04 <0.01	73 17.38 1.96 0.24 0.02	-	211 6.75 5.68 0.69 0.06
Allen (city)	34,097 87.80	1,404	253 18.02 18.02 0.74	-	-	72 18.75 28.46 5.13 0.21	-	-	-	-	-	-	-	-	-	-	-	-	-	-	-	-	-	-	-	38 11.34 15.02 2.71 0.11

Notes: Please refer to the User's Guide for an explanation of data; data is arranged alphabetically by state, then county, then city within each county; table includes counties with populations greater than 49,999 unless noted and cities with populations greater than 9,999 whose Asian and/or NHPI population rates are greater than the national average; (1) Native Hawaiian and other Pacific Islander; (2) excludes Taiwanese; (3) includes Chamorro; (4) county does not meet population threshold but is shown in order to allow inclusion of city

Place	Total population 5 years and over who speak English-only at home	Asian population 5 years and over	Asians 5 years and over who speak English-only at home	NHPI[1] population 5 years and over	NHPIs[1] 5 years and over who speak English-only at home	Asian Indian	Bangladeshi	Cambodian	Chinese[2]	Fijian	Filipino	Guamanian[3]	Hawaiian, Native	Hmong	Indonesian	Japanese	Korean	Laotian	Malaysian	Pakistani	Samoan	Sri Lankan	Taiwanese	Thai	Tongan	Vietnamese
Plano (city)	158,931 77.89	20,263	2,180 10.76 10.76 1.37	-	-	721 14.16 33.07 3.56 0.45	-	-	603 7.22 27.66 2.98 0.38	-	182 26.42 8.35 0.90 0.11	-	-	-	-	89 18.78 4.08 0.44 0.06	292 15.10 13.39 1.44 0.18	-	-	30 5.64 1.38 0.15 0.02	-	-	9 1.65 0.41 0.04 0.01	-	-	85 5.15 3.90 0.42 0.05
Comal County	58,857 80.43	390	121 31.03 31.03 0.21	-	-	-	-	-	-	-	-	-	-	-	-	-	-	-	-	-	-	-	-	-	-	-
Coryell County	58,506 84.73	1,314	432 32.88 32.88 0.74	402	129 32.09 32.09 0.22	-	-	-	-	-	-	-	-	-	-	-	112 23.68 25.93 8.52 0.19	-	-	-	-	-	-	-	-	-
Dallas County	1,375,049 67.46	80,933	10,336 12.77 12.77 0.75	916	426 46.51 46.51 0.03	3,270 14.91 31.64 4.04 0.24	39 6.96 0.38 0.05 <0.01	141 6.61 1.36 0.17 0.01	1,309 11.96 12.66 1.62 0.10	-	1,661 28.63 16.07 2.05 0.12	-	-	-	-	610 29.50 5.90 0.75 0.04	805 9.21 7.79 0.99 0.06	242 11.08 2.34 0.30 0.02	-	294 8.92 2.84 0.36 0.02	-	-	68 8.76 0.66 0.08 <0.01	233 21.28 2.25 0.29 0.02	-	1,060 5.81 10.26 1.31 0.08
Addison (town)	8,674 66.91	1,009	176 17.44 17.44 2.03	-	-	89 15.72 50.57 8.82 1.03	-	-	-	-	-	-	-	-	-	-	-	-	-	-	-	-	-	-	-	-
Coppell (city)	26,873 82.88	3,087	412 13.35 13.35 1.53	-	-	137 13.56 33.25 4.44 0.51	-	-	84 12.14 20.39 2.72 0.31	-	-	-	-	-	-	-	72 11.32 17.48 2.33 0.27	-	-	-	-	-	-	-	-	-
Farmers Branch (city)	16,008 61.13	986	135 13.69 13.69 0.84	-	-	-	-	-	-	-	-	-	-	-	-	-	-	-	-	-	-	-	-	-	-	-
Garland (city)	134,986 68.05	14,457	1,453 10.05 10.05 1.08	-	-	369 13.10 25.40 2.55 0.27	-	-	55 3.45 3.79 0.38 0.04	-	349 31.79 24.02 2.41 0.26	-	-	-	-	-	98 9.09 6.74 0.68 0.07	-	-	71 10.03 4.89 0.49 0.05	-	-	-	-	-	277 4.80 19.06 1.92 0.21
Grand Prairie (city)	78,182 67.40	4,880	605 12.40 12.40 0.77	-	-	115 17.45 19.01 2.36 0.15	-	-	-	-	136 20.99 22.48 2.79 0.17	-	-	-	-	-	-	26 7.22 4.30 0.53 0.03	-	-	-	-	-	-	-	172 7.84 28.43 3.52 0.22
Irving (city)	108,847 61.73	14,342	1,874 13.07 13.07 1.72	-	-	836 14.99 44.61 5.83 0.77	-	-	142 9.91 7.58 0.99 0.13	-	173 23.44 9.23 1.21 0.16	-	-	-	-	89 15.34 4.75 0.62 0.08	155 6.67 8.27 1.08 0.14	94 20.80 5.02 0.66 0.09	-	15 3.77 0.80 0.10 0.01	-	-	-	-	-	143 10.10 7.63 1.00 0.13

Notes: Please refer to the User's Guide for an explanation of data; data is arranged alphabetically by state, then county, then city within each county; table includes counties with populations greater than 49,999 unless noted and cities with populations greater than 9,999 whose Asian and/or NHPI population rates are greater than the national average; (1) Native Hawaiian and other Pacific Islander; (2) excludes Taiwanese; (3) includes Chamorro; (4) county does not meet population threshold but is shown in order to allow inclusion of city

Place	Total population 5 years and over who speak English-only at home	Asian population 5 years and over	Asians 5 years and over who speak English-only at home	NHPI[1] population 5 years and over	NHPIs[1] 5 years and over who speak English-only at home	Asian Indian	Bangladeshi	Cambodian	Chinese[2]	Fijian	Filipino	Guamanian[3]	Hawaiian, Native	Hmong	Indonesian	Japanese	Korean	Laotian	Malaysian	Pakistani	Samoan	Sri Lankan	Taiwanese	Thai	Tongan	Vietnamese
	95,831	4,273	934	-	-	369	-	-	-	-	258	-	-	-	-	-	-	-	-	-	-	-	-	-	-	-
	83.14		21.86			17.08					29.22															
Mesquite (city)						39.51					27.62															
			21.86			8.64					6.04															
			0.97			0.39					0.27															
	64,624	9,527	830	-	-	244	-	-	263	-	125	-	-	-	-	-	25	-	-	5	-	-	-	-	-	61
	75.62		8.71			10.86			9.07		33.78						2.55			1.23						3.86
Richardson (city)						29.40			31.69		15.06						3.01			0.60						7.35
			8.71			2.56			2.76		1.31						0.26			0.05						0.64
			1.28			0.38			0.41		0.19						0.04			0.01						0.09
	35,638	1,582	256	-	-	63	-	-	-	-	-	-	-	-	-	-	-	-	-	-	-	-	-	-	-	-
	88.08		16.18			11.78																				
Rowlett (city)						24.61																				
			16.18			3.98																				
			0.72			0.18																				
	336,049	15,695	2,502	-	-	965	-	75	266	-	289	-	-	-	-	153	277	-	-	79	-	-	-	-	-	161
	84.47		15.94			17.71		11.28	13.99		37.05					33.12	13.35			10.56						6.63
Denton County						38.57		3.00	10.63		11.55					6.12	11.07			3.16						6.43
			15.94			6.15		0.48	1.69		1.84					0.97	1.76			0.50						1.03
			0.74			0.29		0.02	0.08		0.09					0.05	0.08			0.02						0.05
	71,395	10,498	1,081	-	-	506	-	89	85	-	-	-	-	-	-	-	73	-	-	128	-	-	-	-	-	49
	70.92		10.30			12.72		11.59	13.14								7.45			11.87						2.24
Carrollton (city)						46.81		8.23	7.86								6.75			11.84						4.53
			10.30			4.82		0.85	0.81								0.70			1.22						0.47
			1.51			0.71		0.12	0.12								0.10			0.18						0.07
	56,117	2,723	507	-	-	238	-	-	-	-	-	-	-	-	-	-	-	-	-	-	-	-	-	-	-	85
	79.67		18.62			21.77																				20.00
Lewisville (city)						46.94																				16.77
			18.62			8.74																				3.12
			0.90			0.42																				0.15
	70,215	787	151	-	-	-	-	-	-	-	-	-	-	-	-	-	-	-	-	-	-	-	-	-	-	-
	62.95		19.19																							
Ector County																										
			19.19																							
			0.22																							
	165,907	6,580	1,785	520	252	225	-	-	129	-	618	-	-	-	-	204	376	-	-	-	-	-	-	-	-	-
	26.70		27.13		48.46	24.51			16.82		36.01					25.95	23.27									
El Paso County						12.61			7.23		34.62					11.43	21.06									
			27.13		48.46	3.42			1.96		9.39					3.10	5.71									
			1.08		0.15	0.14			0.08		0.37					0.12	0.23									
	85,647	411	113	-	-	-	-	-	-	-	-	-	-	-	-	-	-	-	-	-	-	-	-	-	-	-
	83.23		27.49																							
Ellis County																										
			27.49																							
			0.13																							
	227,070	36,146	4,463	-	-	1,692	-	-	937	-	951	-	-	-	-	-	183	-	-	77	-	-	91	-	-	172
	69.30		12.35			14.24			10.19		22.94						17.51			3.41			7.73			3.55
Fort Bend County						37.91			20.99		21.31						4.10			1.73			2.04			3.85
			12.35			4.68			2.59		2.63						0.51			0.21			0.25			0.48
			1.97			0.75			0.41		0.42						0.08			0.03			0.04			0.08

Notes: Please refer to the User's Guide for an explanation of data; data is arranged alphabetically by state, then county, then city within each county; table includes counties with populations greater than 49,999 unless noted and cities with populations greater than 9,999 whose Asian and/or NHPI population rates are greater than the national average; (1) Native Hawaiian and other Pacific Islander; (2) excludes Taiwanese; (3) includes Chamorro; (4) county does not meet population threshold but is shown in order to allow inclusion of city

Place	Total population 5 years and over who speak English-only at home	Asian population 5 years and over	Asians 5 years and over who speak English-only at home	NHPI[1] population 5 years and over	NHPIs[1] 5 years and over who speak English-only at home	Asian Indian	Bangladeshi	Cambodian	Chinese[2]	Fijian	Filipino	Guamanian[3]	Hawaiian, Native	Hmong	Indonesian	Japanese	Korean	Laotian	Malaysian	Pakistani	Samoan	Sri Lankan	Taiwanese	Thai	Tongan	Vietnamese
Cinco Ranch (cdp)	8,882 84.37	633	85 13.43 13.43 0.96	-	-	-	-	-	-	-	-	-	-	-	-	-	-	-	-	-	-	-	-	-	-	-
Mission Bend (cdp)	15,968 55.86	4,905	628 12.80 12.80 3.93	-	-	234 18.13 37.26 4.77 1.47	-	-	93 14.11 14.81 1.90 0.58	-	146 16.33 23.25 2.98 0.91	-	-	-	-	-	-	-	-	0 0.00 0.00 0.00 0.00	-	-	-	-	-	21 1.80 3.34 0.43 0.13
Missouri City (city)	37,476 77.05	5,298	682 12.87 12.87 1.82	-	-	256 14.35 37.54 4.83 0.68	-	-	107 8.42 15.69 2.02 0.29	-	234 23.80 34.31 4.42 0.62	-	-	-	-	-	-	-	-	-	-	-	-	-	-	27 5.09 3.96 0.51 0.07
New Territory (cdp)	8,422 67.11	2,903	396 13.64 13.64 4.70	-	-	178 12.95 44.95 6.13 2.11	-	-	81 13.02 20.45 2.79 0.96	-	-	-	-	-	-	-	-	-	-	-	-	-	-	-	-	-
Stafford (city)	8,252 56.51	3,075	345 11.22 11.22 4.18	-	-	110 9.71 31.88 3.58 1.33	-	-	33 6.32 9.57 1.07 0.40	-	148 29.13 42.90 4.81 1.79	-	-	-	-	-	-	-	-	-	-	-	-	-	-	27 4.76 7.83 0.88 0.33
Sugar Land (city)	40,505 67.91	13,642	1,660 12.17 12.17 4.10	-	-	673 16.38 40.54 4.93 1.66	-	-	446 8.92 26.87 3.27 1.10	-	230 24.89 13.86 1.69 0.57	-	-	-	-	-	71 16.59 4.28 0.52 0.18	-	-	0 0.00 0.00 0.00 0.00	-	-	76 8.40 4.58 0.56 0.19	-	-	96 7.91 5.78 0.70 0.24
Galveston County	192,779 82.81	4,887	848 17.35 17.35 0.44	-	-	128 13.97 15.09 2.62 0.07	-	-	97 12.19 11.44 1.98 0.05	-	250 32.43 29.48 5.12 0.13	-	-	-	-	-	-	-	-	-	-	-	-	-	-	161 10.39 18.99 3.29 0.08
Grayson County	96,112 92.95	588	134 22.79 22.79 0.14	-	-	-	-	-	-	-	-	-	-	-	-	-	-	-	-	-	-	-	-	-	-	-
Gregg County	93,984 90.66	571	150 26.27 26.27 0.16	-	-	-	-	-	-	-	-	-	-	-	-	-	-	-	-	-	-	-	-	-	-	-
Guadalupe County	60,696 73.24	871	237 27.21 27.21 0.39	-	-	-	-	-	-	-	-	-	-	-	-	-	-	-	-	-	-	-	-	-	-	-

Notes: Please refer to the User's Guide for an explanation of data; data is arranged alphabetically by state, then county, then city within each county; table includes counties with populations greater than 49,999 unless noted and cities with populations greater than 9,999 whose Asian and/or NHPI population rates are greater than the national average; (1) Native Hawaiian and other Pacific Islander; (2) excludes Taiwanese; (3) includes Chamorro; (4) county does not meet population threshold but is shown in order to allow inclusion of city

Place	Total population 5 years and over who speak English-only at home	Asian population 5 years and over	Asians 5 years and over who speak English-only at home	NHPI[1] population 5 years and over	NHPIs[1] 5 years and over who speak English-only at home	Asian Indian	Bangladeshi	Cambodian	Chinese[2]	Fijian	Filipino	Guamanian[3]	Hawaiian, Native	Hmong	Indonesian	Japanese	Korean	Laotian	Malaysian	Pakistani	Samoan	Sri Lankan	Taiwanese	Thai	Tongan	Vietnamese
Harris County	1,992,143 63.81	160,100	18,894 11.80 11.80 0.95	1,343	664 49.44 49.44 0.03	5,164 15.64 27.33 3.23 0.26	18 2.86 0.10 0.01 <0.01	175 9.14 0.93 0.11 0.01	3,365 11.39 17.81 2.10 0.17	-	3,421 23.12 18.11 2.14 0.17	284 52.11 42.77 21.15 0.01	-	-	78 12.52 0.41 0.05 <0.01	1,167 34.04 6.18 0.73 0.06	1,152 14.83 6.10 0.72 0.06	99 8.98 0.52 0.06 <0.01	-	321 4.84 1.70 0.20 0.02	-	-	130 6.01 0.69 0.08 0.01	251 19.61 1.33 0.16 0.01	-	2,437 4.72 12.90 1.52 0.12
Bellaire (city)	12,098 83.57	1,013	286 28.23 28.23 2.36	-	-	-	-	-	122 28.31 42.66 12.04 1.01	-	-	-	-	-	-	-	-	-	-	-	-	-	-	-	-	-
Houston (city)	1,053,207 58.68	95,564	9,852 10.31 10.31 0.94	799	311 38.92 38.92 0.03	2,670 14.25 27.10 2.79 0.25	-	67 9.64 0.68 0.07 0.01	2,072 10.03 21.03 2.17 0.20	-	1,457 20.15 14.79 1.52 0.14	165 42.20 53.05 20.65 0.02	-	-	73 15.57 0.74 0.08 0.01	598 27.11 6.07 0.63 0.06	652 13.04 6.62 0.68 0.06	-	-	183 4.12 1.86 0.19 0.02	-	-	87 5.92 0.88 0.09 0.01	119 14.22 1.21 0.12 0.01	-	1,222 4.11 12.40 1.28 0.12
West University Place (city)	11,242 86.61	681	259 38.03 38.03 2.30	-	-	-	-	-	-	-	-	-	-	-	-	-	-	-	-	-	-	-	-	-	-	-
Hays County	70,395 76.85	803	283 35.24 35.24 0.40	-	-	-	-	-	-	-	-	-	-	-	-	-	-	-	-	-	-	-	-	-	-	-
Hidalgo County	86,361 16.88	2,870	460 16.03 16.03 0.53	-	-	109 18.08 23.70 3.80 0.13	-	-	-	-	216 16.17 46.96 7.53 0.25	-	-	-	-	-	-	-	-	-	-	-	-	-	-	-
Hunt County	65,213 91.16	520	151 29.04 29.04 0.23	-	-	-	-	-	-	-	-	-	-	-	-	-	-	-	-	-	-	-	-	-	-	-
Jefferson County	204,093 86.77	6,401	698 10.90 10.90 0.34	-	-	105 12.61 15.04 1.64 0.05	-	-	120 25.21 17.19 1.87 0.06	-	176 20.80 25.21 2.75 0.09	-	-	-	-	-	-	-	-	-	-	-	-	-	-	165 4.46 23.64 2.58 0.08
Port Arthur (city)	40,937 76.75	3,038	111 3.65 3.65 0.27	-	-	-	-	-	-	-	-	-	-	-	-	-	-	-	-	-	-	-	-	-	-	77 3.01 69.37 2.53 0.19
Johnson County	103,373 87.98	599	145 24.21 24.21 0.14	-	-	-	-	-	-	-	-	-	-	-	-	-	-	-	-	-	-	-	-	-	-	-

Notes: Please refer to the User's Guide for an explanation of data; data is arranged alphabetically by state, then county, then city within each county; table includes counties with populations greater than 49,999 unless noted and cities with populations greater than 9,999 whose Asian and/or NHPI population rates are greater than the national average; (1) Native Hawaiian and other Pacific Islander; (2) excludes Taiwanese; (3) includes Chamorro; (4) county does not meet population threshold but is shown in order to allow inclusion of city

Place	Total population 5 years and over who speak English-only at home	Asian population 5 years and over	Asians 5 years and over who speak English-only at home	NHPI[1] population 5 years and over	NHPIs[1] 5 years and over who speak English-only at home	Asian Indian	Bangladeshi	Cambodian	Chinese[2]	Fijian	Filipino	Guamanian[3]	Hawaiian, Native	Hmong	Indonesian	Japanese	Korean	Laotian	Malaysian	Pakistani	Samoan	Sri Lankan	Taiwanese	Thai	Tongan	Vietnamese
Kaufman County	58,877 88.95	465	54 11.61 11.61 0.09	-	-	-	-	-	-	-	-	-	-	-	-	-	-	-	-	-	-	-	-	-	-	-
Lubbock County	175,195 77.68	2,773	607 21.89 21.89 0.35	-	-	240 31.91 39.54 8.65 0.14	-	-	4 0.75 0.66 0.14 <0.01	-	-	-	-	-	-	-	-	-	-	-	-	-	-	-	-	17 5.15 2.80 0.61 0.01
McLennan County	167,385 84.42	2,056	420 20.43 20.43 0.25	-	-	61 15.64 14.52 2.97 0.04	-	-	-	-	-	-	-	-	-	-	-	-	-	-	-	-	-	-	-	-
Midland County	79,716 74.21	993	231 23.26 23.26 0.29	-	-	80 21.33 34.63 8.06 0.10	-	-	-	-	-	-	-	-	-	-	-	-	-	-	-	-	-	-	-	-
Montgomery County	233,746 86.16	2,979	669 22.46 22.46 0.29	-	-	196 20.83 29.30 6.58 0.08	-	-	87 13.94 13.00 2.92 0.04	-	147 32.59 21.97 4.93 0.06	-	-	-	-	-	-	-	-	-	-	-	-	-	-	-
Nacogdoches County	48,950 88.37	355	82 23.10 23.10 0.17	-	-	-	-	-	-	-	-	-	-	-	-	-	-	-	-	-	-	-	-	-	-	-
Nueces County	165,279 57.06	3,290	707 21.49 21.49 0.43	-	-	80 13.47 11.32 2.43 0.05	-	-	-	-	386 25.60 54.60 11.73 0.23	-	-	-	-	-	-	-	-	-	-	-	-	-	-	-
Orange County	74,704 94.25	682	52 7.62 7.62 0.07	-	-	-	-	-	-	-	-	-	-	-	-	-	-	-	-	-	-	-	-	-	-	8 2.21 15.38 1.17 0.01
Potter County	78,473 75.33	2,759	258 9.35 9.35 0.33	-	-	-	-	-	-	-	-	-	-	-	-	-	-	14 1.46 5.43 0.51 0.02	-	-	-	-	-	-	-	64 6.36 24.81 2.32 0.08
Randall County	88,957 91.59	1,080	230 21.30 21.30 0.26	-	-	-	-	-	-	-	-	-	-	-	-	-	-	-	-	-	-	-	-	-	-	-

Notes: Please refer to the User's Guide for an explanation of data; data is arranged alphabetically by state, then county, then city within each county; table includes counties with populations greater than 49,999 unless noted and cities with populations greater than 9,999 whose Asian and/or NHPI population rates are greater than the national average; (1) Native Hawaiian and other Pacific Islander; (2) excludes Taiwanese; (3) includes Chamorro; (4) county does not meet population threshold but is shown in order to allow inclusion of city

Place	Total population 5 years and over who speak English-only at home	Asian population 5 years and over	Asians 5 years and over who speak English-only at home	NHPI[1] population 5 years and over	NHPIs[1] 5 years and over who speak English-only at home	Asian Indian	Bangladeshi	Cambodian	Chinese[2]	Fijian	Filipino	Guamanian[3]	Hawaiian, Native	Hmong	Indonesian	Japanese	Korean	Laotian	Malaysian	Pakistani	Samoan	Sri Lankan	Taiwanese	Thai	Tongan	Vietnamese
San Patricio County	37,664 60.92	434	136 31.34 31.34 0.36	-	-	-	-	-	-	-	-	-	-	-	-	-	-	-	-	-	-	-	-	-	-	-
Smith County	142,744 87.96	994	256 25.75 25.75 0.18	-	-	-	-	-	-	-	-	-	-	-	-	-	-	-	-	-	-	-	-	-	-	-
Tarrant County	1,040,888 78.14	47,441	6,310 13.30 13.30 0.61	1,403	582 41.48 41.48 0.06	1,312 14.91 20.79 2.77 0.13	-	139 18.76 2.20 0.29 0.01	697 13.66 11.05 1.47 0.07	-	1,071 32.87 16.97 2.26 0.10	-	-	-	-	466 45.51 7.39 0.98 0.04	662 22.66 10.49 1.40 0.06	183 6.07 2.90 0.39 0.02	-	67 7.61 1.06 0.14 0.01	-	-	35 5.56 0.55 0.07 <0.01	211 28.59 3.34 0.44 0.02	71 23.67 12.20 5.06 0.01	1,010 5.69 16.01 2.13 0.10
Arlington (city)	231,505 75.80	17,892	1,834 10.25 10.25 0.79	-	-	336 11.74 18.32 1.88 0.15	-	-	239 9.26 13.03 1.34 0.10	-	381 33.93 20.77 2.13 0.16	-	-	-	-	-	145 17.47 7.91 0.81 0.06	-	-	-	-	-	25 6.31 1.36 0.14 0.01	-	-	369 4.45 20.12 2.06 0.16
Euless (city)	33,429 78.52	2,950	342 11.59 11.59 1.02	-	-	105 9.52 30.70 3.56 0.31	-	-	-	-	-	-	-	-	-	-	-	-	-	-	-	-	-	-	-	-
Haltom City (city)	27,342 75.95	2,812	161 5.73 5.73 0.59	-	-	-	-	-	-	-	-	-	-	-	-	-	-	48 6.54 29.81 1.71 0.18	-	-	-	-	-	-	-	26 1.84 16.15 0.92 0.10
Taylor County	100,846 85.76	1,519	452 29.76 29.76 0.45	-	-	-	-	-	-	-	189 35.80 41.81 12.44 0.19	-	-	-	-	-	-	-	-	-	-	-	-	-	-	-
Tom Green County	71,263 73.45	702	217 30.91 30.91 0.30	-	-	-	-	-	-	-	-	-	-	-	-	-	-	-	-	-	-	-	-	-	-	-
Travis County	537,622 71.32	33,509	6,019 17.96 17.96 1.12	607	310 51.07 51.07 0.06	1,715 22.17 28.49 5.12 0.32	-	-	1,229 14.88 20.42 3.67 0.23	-	896 42.34 14.89 2.67 0.17	-	-	-	-	323 27.05 5.37 0.96 0.06	689 18.13 11.45 2.06 0.13	-	-	30 4.72 0.50 0.09 0.01	-	-	81 10.27 1.35 0.24 0.02	86 21.39 1.43 0.26 0.02	-	520 7.59 8.64 1.55 0.10
Austin (city)	419,884 68.86	28,790	5,237 18.19 18.19 1.25	411	250 60.83 60.83 0.06	1,498 22.14 28.60 5.20 0.36	-	-	1,073 14.19 20.49 3.73 0.26	-	723 44.11 13.81 2.51 0.17	-	-	-	-	300 26.93 5.73 1.04 0.07	606 18.27 11.57 2.10 0.14	-	-	30 6.16 0.57 0.10 0.01	-	-	81 11.62 1.55 0.28 0.02	-	-	429 7.97 8.19 1.49 0.10

Notes: Please refer to the User's Guide for an explanation of data; data is arranged alphabetically by state, then county, then city within each county; table includes counties with populations greater than 49,999 unless noted and cities with populations greater than 9,999 whose Asian and/or NHPI population rates are greater than the national average; (1) Native Hawaiian and other Pacific Islander; (2) excludes Taiwanese; (3) includes Chamorro; (4) county does not meet population threshold but is shown in order to allow inclusion of city

Place	Total population 5 years and over who speak English-only at home	Asian population 5 years and over	Asians 5 years and over who speak English-only at home	NHPI[1] population 5 years and over	NHPIs[1] 5 years and over who speak English-only at home	Asian Indian	Bangladeshi	Cambodian	Chinese[2]	Fijian	Filipino	Guamanian[3]	Hawaiian, Native	Hmong	Indonesian	Japanese	Korean	Laotian	Malaysian	Pakistani	Samoan	Sri Lankan	Taiwanese	Thai	Tongan	Vietnamese
Pflugerville (city)	12,772 85.57	673	83 12.33 12.33 0.65	-	-	-	-	-	-	-	-	-	-	-	-	-	-	-	-	-	-	-	-	-	-	-
Wells Branch (cdp)	8,278 79.06	959	126 13.14 13.14 1.52	-	-	-	-	-	-	-	-	-	-	-	-	-	-	-	-	-	-	-	-	-	-	-
Victoria County	56,776 72.99	431	107 24.83 24.83 0.19	-	-	-	-	-	-	-	-	-	-	-	-	-	-	-	-	-	-	-	-	-	-	-
Webb County	14,046 8.13	757	137 18.10 18.10 0.98	-	-	-	-	-	-	-	-	-	-	-	-	-	-	-	-	-	-	-	-	-	-	-
Wichita County	107,556 87.72	2,434	444 18.24 18.24 0.41	-	-	-	-	-	-	-	165 30.67 37.16 6.78 0.15	-	-	-	-	-	-	-	-	-	-	-	-	-	-	21 2.66 4.73 0.86 0.02
Williamson County	189,447 82.78	5,771	1,219 21.12 21.12 0.64	-	-	270 18.51 22.15 4.68 0.14	-	-	206 16.89 16.90 3.57 0.11	-	-	-	-	-	-	-	156 24.00 12.80 2.70 0.08	-	-	-	-	-	-	-	-	25 2.42 2.05 0.43 0.01
Brushy Creek (cdp)	12,317 86.08	806	232 28.78 28.78 1.88	-	-	-	-	-	-	-	-	-	-	-	-	-	-	-	-	-	-	-	-	-	-	-
Jollyville (cdp)	11,827 82.65	1,077	241 22.38 22.38 2.04	-	-	-	-	-	-	-	-	-	-	-	-	-	-	-	-	-	-	-	-	-	-	-
UTAH	1,770,626 87.49	34,162	9,611 28.13 28.13 0.54	12,535	4,449 35.49 35.49 0.25	756 26.16 7.87 2.21 0.04	-	100 7.19 1.04 0.29 0.01	1,111 16.37 11.56 3.25 0.06	-	1,339 38.83 13.93 3.92 0.08	-	1,149 89.07 25.83 9.17 0.06	-	-	3,575 62.88 37.20 10.46 0.20	1,119 33.03 11.64 3.28 0.06	118 5.89 1.23 0.35 0.01	-	51 14.33 0.53 0.15 <0.01	1,097 33.70 24.66 8.75 0.06	-	112 32.46 1.17 0.33 0.01	161 23.82 1.68 0.47 0.01	1,284 21.54 28.86 10.24 0.07	340 6.78 3.54 1.00 0.02
Cache County	73,418 89.08	1,636	242 14.79 14.79 0.33	-	-	-	-	-	49 8.93 20.25 3.00 0.07	-	-	-	-	-	-	-	-	-	-	-	-	-	-	-	-	-

Notes: Please refer to the User's Guide for an explanation of data; data is arranged alphabetically by state, then county, then city within each county; table includes counties with populations greater than 49,999 unless noted and cities with populations greater than 9,999 whose Asian and/or NHPI population rates are greater than the national average; (1) Native Hawaiian and other Pacific Islander; (2) excludes Taiwanese; (3) includes Chamorro; (4) county does not meet population threshold but is shown in order to allow inclusion of city

Place	Total population 5 years and over who speak English-only at home	Asian population 5 years and over	Asians 5 years and over who speak English-only at home	NHPI[1] population 5 years and over	NHPIs[1] 5 years and over who speak English-only at home	Asian Indian	Bangladeshi	Cambodian	Chinese[2]	Fijian	Filipino	Guamanian[3]	Hawaiian, Native	Hmong	Indonesian	Japanese	Korean	Laotian	Malaysian	Pakistani	Samoan	Sri Lankan	Taiwanese	Thai	Tongan	Vietnamese
Davis County	199,147	3,314	1,385	818	512	-	-	-	-	-	277	-	-	-	-	530	182	-	-	-	-	-	-	-	-	-
	92.42		41.79		62.59						35.60					70.76	48.28									
											20.00					38.27	13.14									
			41.79		62.59						8.36					15.99	5.49									
			0.70		0.26						0.14					0.27	0.09									
Salt Lake County	685,701	21,248	4,979	8,976	2,357	414	-	60	670	-	605	-	386	-	-	1,921	462	98	-	-	608	-	-	-	995	177
	83.80		23.43		26.26	20.73		5.71	15.92		37.55		85.78			65.50	26.99	6.12			27.35				19.12	4.23
						8.31		1.21	13.46		12.15		16.38			38.58	9.28	1.97			25.80				42.21	3.55
			23.43		26.26	1.95		0.28	3.15		2.85		4.30			9.04	2.17	0.46			6.77				11.09	0.83
			0.73		0.34	0.06		0.01	0.10		0.09		0.06			0.28	0.07	0.01			0.09				0.15	0.03
Kearns (cdp)	23,604	789	157	339	82	-	-	-	-	-	-	-	-	-	-	-	-	-	-	-	-	-	-	-	-	-
	78.85		19.90		24.19																					
			19.90		24.19																					
			0.67		0.35																					
Salt Lake City (city)	125,170	6,073	1,442	2,888	641	147	-	-	243	-	204	-	-	-	-	586	52	-	-	-	106	-	-	-	371	14
	74.85		23.74		22.20	23.37			16.62		40.32					62.21	10.90				25.67				17.59	1.16
						10.19			16.85		14.15					40.64	3.61				16.54				57.88	0.97
			23.74		22.20	2.42			4.00		3.36					9.65	0.86				3.67				12.85	0.23
			1.15		0.51	0.12			0.19		0.16					0.47	0.04				0.08				0.30	0.01
Sandy (city)	74,243	1,439	541	350	113	-	-	-	95	-	-	-	-	-	-	-	-	-	-	-	-	-	-	-	-	-
	91.23		37.60		32.29				25.40																	
									17.56																	
			37.60		32.29				6.60																	
			0.73		0.15				0.13																	
Taylorsville (city)	44,572	1,597	177	617	117	-	-	-	-	-	-	-	-	-	-	-	-	-	-	-	-	-	-	-	-	17
	84.13		11.08		18.96																					3.09
																										9.60
			11.08		18.96																					1.06
			0.40		0.26																					0.04
West Jordan (city)	53,650	1,036	191	606	71	-	-	-	-	-	-	-	-	-	-	-	-	-	-	-	-	-	-	-	7	-
	88.61		18.44		11.72																				1.60	
																									9.86	
			18.44		11.72																				1.16	
			0.36		0.13																				0.01	
West Valley City (city)	75,176	4,293	456	2,691	796	-	-	48	62	-	-	-	-	-	-	-	-	7	-	-	286	-	-	-	334	8
	77.46		10.62		29.58			7.86	9.31									1.74			37.48				21.59	0.59
								10.53	13.60									1.54			35.93				41.96	1.75
			10.62		29.58			1.12	1.44									0.16			10.63				12.41	0.19
			0.61		1.06			0.06	0.08									0.01			0.38				0.44	0.01
Utah County	290,564	3,661	1,212	1,578	855	-	-	-	197	-	200	-	341	-	-	306	199	-	-	-	226	-	-	-	124	-
	88.54		33.11		54.18				17.03		54.50		91.67			42.62	40.78				45.84				30.17	
									16.25		16.50		39.88			25.25	16.42				26.43				14.50	
			33.11		54.18				5.38		5.46		21.61			8.36	5.44				14.32				7.86	
			0.42		0.29				0.07		0.07		0.12			0.11	0.07				0.08				0.04	
Orem (city)	65,244	1,180	380	618	322	-	-	-	-	-	-	-	-	-	-	-	-	-	-	-	-	-	-	-	-	-
	86.58		32.20		52.10																					
			32.20		52.10																					
			0.58		0.49																					

Notes: Please refer to the User's Guide for an explanation of data; data is arranged alphabetically by state, then county, then city within each county; table includes counties with populations greater than 49,999 unless noted and cities with populations greater than 9,999 whose Asian and/or NHPI population rates are greater than the national average; (1) Native Hawaiian and other Pacific Islander; (2) excludes Taiwanese; (3) includes Chamorro; (4) county does not meet population threshold but is shown in order to allow inclusion of city

Place	Total population 5 years and over who speak English-only at home	Asian population 5 years and over	Asians 5 years and over who speak English-only at home	NHPI[1] population 5 years and over	NHPIs[1] 5 years and over who speak English-only at home	Asian Indian	Bangladeshi	Cambodian	Chinese[2]	Fijian	Filipino	Guamanian[3]	Hawaiian, Native	Hmong	Indonesian	Japanese	Korean	Laotian	Malaysian	Pakistani	Samoan	Sri Lankan	Taiwanese	Thai	Tongan	Vietnamese
Provo (city)	79,853 83.00	1,871	511 27.31 27.31 0.64	617	394 63.86 63.86 0.49	-	-	-	137 18.49 26.81 7.32 0.17	-	-	-	-	-	-	145 34.69 28.38 7.75 0.18	-	-	-	-	-	-	-	-	-	-
Washington County	75,858 92.37	412	197 47.82 47.82 0.26	407	272 66.83 66.83 0.36	-	-	-	-	-	-	-	-	-	-	-	-	-	-	-	-	-	-	-	-	-
St. George (city)	41,124 90.70	353	170 48.16 48.16 0.41	371	252 67.92 67.92 0.61	-	-	-	-	-	-	-	-	-	-	-	-	-	-	-	-	-	-	-	-	-
Weber County	156,669 87.41	2,275	897 39.43 39.43 0.57	-	-	-	-	-	-	-	-	-	-	-	-	462 72.76 51.51 20.31 0.29	-	-	-	-	-	-	-	-	-	-
VERMONT	540,767 94.07	4,330	1,314 30.35 30.35 0.24	-	-	241 35.65 18.34 5.57 0.04	-	-	198 21.18 15.07 4.57 0.04	-	150 48.08 11.42 3.46 0.03	-	-	-	-	150 44.64 11.42 3.46 0.03	362 59.74 27.55 8.36 0.07	-	-	-	-	-	-	-	-	83 9.08 6.32 1.92 0.02
Chittenden County	127,002 91.98	2,431	592 24.35 24.35 0.47	-	-	108 29.83 18.24 4.44 0.09	-	-	85 15.21 14.36 3.50 0.07	-	-	-	-	-	-	-	-	-	-	-	-	-	-	-	-	59 8.31 9.97 2.43 0.05
Rutland County	57,392 95.35	183	104 56.83 56.83 0.18	-	-	-	-	-	-	-	-	-	-	-	-	-	-	-	-	-	-	-	-	-	-	-
Washington County	51,559 93.89	235	96 40.85 40.85 0.19	-	-	-	-	-	-	-	-	-	-	-	-	-	-	-	-	-	-	-	-	-	-	-
Windsor County	52,268 95.72	422	97 22.99 22.99 0.19	-	-	-	-	-	-	-	-	-	-	-	-	-	-	-	-	-	-	-	-	-	-	-
VIRGINIA	5,884,075 88.89	239,693	44,004 18.36 18.36 0.75	3,335	2,103 63.06 63.06 0.04	7,344 16.80 16.69 3.06 0.12	77 4.79 0.17 0.03 <0.01	567 12.08 1.29 0.24 0.01	4,849 15.14 11.02 2.02 0.08	-	13,768 30.27 31.29 5.74 0.23	533 58.77 25.34 15.98 0.01	801 90.51 38.09 24.02 0.01	-	191 17.97 0.43 0.08 <0.01	3,020 35.45 6.86 1.26 0.05	6,612 15.42 15.03 2.76 0.11	260 9.21 0.59 0.11 <0.01	-	546 5.86 1.24 0.23 0.01	209 46.34 9.94 6.27 <0.01	182 29.35 0.41 0.08 <0.01	164 13.00 0.37 0.07 <0.01	856 24.20 1.95 0.36 0.01	-	2,633 8.02 5.98 1.10 0.04

Notes: Please refer to the User's Guide for an explanation of data; data is arranged alphabetically by state, then county, then city within each county; table includes counties with populations greater than 49,999 unless noted and cities with populations greater than 9,999 whose Asian and/or NHPI population rates are greater than the national average; (1) Native Hawaiian and other Pacific Islander; (2) excludes Taiwanese; (3) includes Chamorro; (4) county does not meet population threshold but is shown in order to allow inclusion of city

Place	Total population 5 years and over who speak English-only at home	Asian population 5 years and over	Asians 5 years and over who speak English-only at home	NHPI[1] population 5 years and over	NHPIs[1] 5 years and over who speak English-only at home	Asian Indian	Bangladeshi	Cambodian	Chinese[2]	Fijian	Filipino	Guamanian[3]	Hawaiian, Native	Hmong	Indonesian	Japanese	Korean	Laotian	Malaysian	Pakistani	Samoan	Sri Lankan	Taiwanese	Thai	Tongan	Vietnamese
Albemarle County	67,834	2,203	388	-	-	112	-	-	50	-	-	-	-	-	-	-	-	-	-	-	-	-	-	-	-	-
	91.36		17.61			19.18			5.94																	
						28.87			12.89																	
			17.61			5.08			2.27																	
			0.57			0.17			0.07																	
Alexandria Independent City	84,234	6,488	1,211	-	-	151	-	-	197	-	278	-	-	-	-	-	220	-	-	24	-	-	-	-	-	80
	70.04		18.67			10.89			26.30		26.94						18.20			4.89						17.17
						12.47			16.27		22.96						18.17			1.98						6.61
			18.67			2.33			3.04		4.28						3.39			0.37						1.23
			1.44			0.18			0.23		0.33						0.26			0.03						0.09
Arlington County	119,812	14,863	3,075	-	-	687	-	26	483	-	527	-	-	-	-	306	480	-	-	37	-	-	-	-	-	214
	66.91		20.69			21.22		7.67	22.11		27.38					27.82	35.96			5.32						10.23
						22.34		0.85	15.71		17.14					9.95	15.61			1.20						6.96
			20.69			4.62		0.17	3.25		3.55					2.06	3.23			0.25						1.44
			2.57			0.57		0.02	0.40		0.44					0.26	0.40			0.03						0.18
Arlington (cdp)	119,812	14,863	3,075	-	-	687	-	26	483	-	527	-	-	-	-	306	480	-	-	37	-	-	-	-	-	214
	66.91		20.69			21.22		7.67	22.11		27.38					27.82	35.96			5.32						10.23
						22.34		0.85	15.71		17.14					9.95	15.61			1.20						6.96
			20.69			4.62		0.17	3.25		3.55					2.06	3.23			0.25						1.44
			2.57			0.57		0.02	0.40		0.44					0.26	0.40			0.03						0.18
Bedford County	55,313	542	136	-	-	-	-	-	-	-	-	-	-	-	-	-	-	-	-	-	-	-	-	-	-	-
	97.24		25.09																							
			25.09																							
			0.25																							
Charlottesville Independent City	38,427	2,135	540	-	-	216	-	-	74	-	-	-	-	-	-	-	-	-	-	-	-	-	-	-	-	-
	89.26		25.29			45.00			10.80																	
						40.00			13.70																	
			25.29			10.12			3.47																	
			1.41			0.56			0.19																	
Chesapeake Independent City	174,633	3,323	1,222	-	-	-	-	-	-	-	687	-	-	-	-	-	-	-	-	-	-	-	-	-	-	-
	94.38		36.77								39.53															
											56.22															
			36.77								20.67															
			0.70								0.39															
Chesterfield County	224,032	5,975	938	-	-	182	-	32	183	-	146	-	-	-	-	-	184	-	-	-	-	-	-	-	-	64
	92.25		15.70			18.33		5.25	21.71		23.25						12.68									8.90
						19.40		3.41	19.51		15.57						19.62									6.82
			15.70			3.05		0.54	3.06		2.44						3.08									1.07
			0.42			0.08		0.01	0.08		0.07						0.08									0.03
Fairfax Independent City	14,043	2,386	196	-	-	25	-	-	13	-	-	-	-	-	-	-	38	-	-	-	-	-	-	-	-	0
	69.40		8.21			5.51			2.69								7.14									0.00
						12.76			6.63								19.39									0.00
			8.21			1.05			0.54								1.59									0.00
			1.40			0.18			0.09								0.27									0.00
Fairfax County	631,768	114,833	14,947	812	400	3,146	61	204	2,077	-	2,963	-	-	-	82	800	2,652	94	-	319	-	-	81	307	-	1,130
	70.03		13.02		49.26	13.84	7.72	11.68	13.68		24.72				14.39	28.94	10.13	6.46		5.71			11.59	20.74		5.75
						21.05	0.41	1.36	13.90		19.82				0.55	5.35	17.74	0.63		2.13			0.54	2.05		7.56
			13.02		49.26	2.74	0.05	0.18	1.81		2.58				0.07	0.70	2.31	0.08		0.28			0.07	0.27		0.98
			2.37		0.06	0.50	0.01	0.03	0.33		0.47				0.01	0.13	0.42	0.01		0.05			0.01	0.05		0.18

Notes: Please refer to the User's Guide for an explanation of data; data is arranged alphabetically by state, then county, then city within each county; table includes counties with populations greater than 49,999 unless noted and cities with populations greater than 9,999 whose Asian and/or NHPI population rates are greater than the national average; (1) Native Hawaiian and other Pacific Islander; (2) excludes Taiwanese; (3) includes Chamorro; (4) county does not meet population threshold but is shown in order to allow inclusion of city

Place	Total population 5 years and over who speak English-only at home	Asian population 5 years and over	Asians 5 years and over who speak English-only at home	NHPI[1] population 5 years and over	NHPIs[1] 5 years and over who speak English-only at home	Asian Indian	Bangladeshi	Cambodian	Chinese[2]	Fijian	Filipino	Guamanian[3]	Hawaiian, Native	Hmong	Indonesian	Japanese	Korean	Laotian	Malaysian	Pakistani	Samoan	Sri Lankan	Taiwanese	Thai	Tongan	Vietnamese
Annandale (cdp)	30,741	9,658	858	-	-	160	-	-	54	-	143	-	-	-	-	-	259	-	-	-	-	-	-	-	-	130
	59.57		8.88			15.67			5.84		23.87						8.21									4.29
						18.65			6.29		16.67						30.19									15.15
			8.88			1.66			0.56		1.48						2.68									1.35
			2.79			0.52			0.18		0.47						0.84									0.42
Bailey's Crossroads (cdp)	7,230	2,371	171	-	-	-	-	-	-	-	-	-	-	-	-	-	-	-	-	0	-	-	-	-	-	30
	34.31		7.21																	0.00						5.41
																				0.00						17.54
			7.21																	0.00						1.27
			2.37																	0.00						0.41
Burke (cdp)	40,041	7,847	1,147	-	-	180	-	-	117	-	289	-	-	-	-	-	271	-	-	-	-	-	-	-	-	41
	73.89		14.62			13.43			15.77		27.82						9.11									3.88
						15.69			10.20		25.20						23.63									3.57
			14.62			2.29			1.49		3.68						3.45									0.52
			2.86			0.45			0.29		0.72						0.68									0.10
Centreville (cdp)	32,411	5,776	880	-	-	141	-	-	103	-	223	-	-	-	-	-	237	-	-	-	-	-	-	-	-	43
	73.59		15.24			9.91			11.22		27.06						15.64									10.75
						16.02			11.70		25.34						26.93									4.89
			15.24			2.44			1.78		3.86						4.10									0.74
			2.72			0.44			0.32		0.69						0.73									0.13
Chantilly (cdp)	27,602	5,987	597	-	-	82	-	-	67	-	-	-	-	-	-	-	119	-	-	-	-	-	-	-	-	99
	72.28		9.97			4.30			7.91								10.35									11.07
						13.74			11.22								19.93									16.58
			9.97			1.37			1.12								1.99									1.65
			2.16			0.30			0.24								0.43									0.36
Franconia (cdp)	22,648	2,911	503	-	-	14	-	-	-	-	164	-	-	-	-	-	95	-	-	-	-	-	-	-	-	71
	76.50		17.28			3.83					30.09						16.24									14.92
						2.78					32.60						18.89									14.12
			17.28			0.48					5.63						3.26									2.44
			2.22			0.06					0.72						0.42									0.31
Groveton (cdp)	13,564	1,470	81	-	-	-	-	-	-	-	-	-	-	-	-	-	-	-	-	-	-	-	-	-	-	-
	68.89		5.51																							
			5.51																							
			0.60																							
Herndon (town)	11,026	2,930	338	-	-	114	-	-	-	-	-	-	-	-	-	-	-	-	-	-	-	-	-	-	-	48
	55.57		11.54			11.66																				12.03
						33.73																				14.20
			11.54			3.89																				1.64
			3.07			1.03																				0.44
Hybla Valley (cdp)	10,245	1,208	186	-	-	-	-	-	-	-	-	-	-	-	-	-	-	-	-	-	-	-	-	-	-	-
	65.88		15.40																							
			15.40																							
			1.82																							
Idylwood (cdp)	8,574	2,954	327	-	-	65	-	-	82	-	-	-	-	-	-	-	-	-	-	-	-	-	-	-	-	23
	57.27		11.07			7.19			15.24																	3.70
						19.88			25.08																	7.03
			11.07			2.20			2.78																	0.78
			3.81			0.76			0.96																	0.27

Notes: Please refer to the User's Guide for an explanation of data; data is arranged alphabetically by state, then county, then city within each county; table includes counties with populations greater than 49,999 unless noted and cities with populations greater than 9,999 whose Asian and/or NHPI population rates are greater than the national average; (1) Native Hawaiian and other Pacific Islander; (2) excludes Taiwanese; (3) includes Chamorro; (4) county does not meet population threshold but is shown in order to allow inclusion of city

Place	Total population 5 years and over who speak English-only at home	Asian population 5 years and over	Asians 5 years and over who speak English-only at home	NHPI[1] population 5 years and over	NHPIs[1] 5 years and over who speak English-only at home	Asian Indian	Bangladeshi	Cambodian	Chinese[2]	Fijian	Filipino	Guamanian[3]	Hawaiian, Native	Hmong	Indonesian	Japanese	Korean	Laotian	Malaysian	Pakistani	Samoan	Sri Lankan	Taiwanese	Thai	Tongan	Vietnamese
Jefferson (cdp)	13,687 53.77	4,842	219 4.52 4.52 1.60	-	-	9 1.22 4.11 0.19 0.07	-	-	62 12.45 28.31 1.28 0.45	-	43 9.56 19.63 0.89 0.31	-	-	-	-	-	-	-	-	-	-	-	-	-	-	27 1.25 12.33 0.56 0.20
Lincolnia (cdp)	6,484 44.28	2,143	194 9.05 9.05 2.99	-	-	-	-	-	-	-	-	-	-	-	-	-	-	-	-	43 9.07 22.16 2.01 0.66	-	-	-	-	-	24 5.52 12.37 1.12 0.37
Lorton (cdp)	12,511 75.81	1,341	176 13.12 13.12 1.41	-	-	-	-	-	-	-	-	-	-	-	-	-	-	-	-	-	-	-	-	-	-	-
McLean (cdp)	27,781 75.73	4,054	757 18.67 18.67 2.72	-	-	176 19.07 23.25 4.34 0.63	-	-	168 22.70 22.19 4.14 0.60	-	154 30.92 20.34 3.80 0.55	-	-	-	-	68 13.82 8.98 1.68 0.24	97 12.00 12.81 2.39 0.35	-	-	-	-	-	-	-	-	-
Merrifield (cdp)	5,235 51.14	2,877	289 10.05 10.05 5.52	-	-	143 18.33 49.48 4.97 2.73	-	-	-	-	-	-	-	-	-	-	30 3.81 10.38 1.04 0.57	-	-	-	-	-	-	-	-	71 11.09 24.57 2.47 1.36
Mount Vernon (cdp)	19,363 73.13	1,725	222 12.87 12.87 1.15	-	-	-	-	-	-	-	-	-	-	-	-	-	69 14.94 31.08 4.00 0.36	-	-	-	-	-	-	-	-	-
Newington (cdp)	13,188 72.05	1,964	243 12.37 12.37 1.84	-	-	30 9.23 12.35 1.53 0.23	-	-	-	-	71 16.17 29.22 3.62 0.54	-	-	-	-	-	61 13.71 25.10 3.11 0.46	-	-	-	-	-	-	-	-	-
Oakton (cdp)	19,058 69.24	3,826	547 14.30 14.30 2.87	-	-	91 10.48 16.64 2.38 0.48	-	-	101 10.79 18.46 2.64 0.53	-	-	-	-	-	-	-	109 10.26 19.93 2.85 0.57	-	-	-	-	-	-	-	-	49 11.19 8.96 1.28 0.26
Reston (cdp)	40,046 76.15	4,830	974 20.17 20.17 2.43	-	-	187 10.81 19.20 3.87 0.47	-	-	208 30.91 21.36 4.31 0.52	-	197 35.12 20.23 4.08 0.49	-	-	-	-	-	148 24.54 15.20 3.06 0.37	-	-	-	-	-	-	-	-	-
Rose Hill (cdp)	10,340 74.61	1,153	198 17.17 17.17 1.91	-	-	-	-	-	-	-	-	-	-	-	-	-	-	-	-	-	-	-	-	-	-	-

Notes: Please refer to the User's Guide for an explanation of data; data is arranged alphabetically by state, then county, then city within each county; table includes counties with populations greater than 49,999 unless noted and cities with populations greater than 9,999 whose Asian and/or NHPI population rates are greater than the national average; (1) Native Hawaiian and other Pacific Islander; (2) excludes Taiwanese; (3) includes Chamorro; (4) county does not meet population threshold but is shown in order to allow inclusion of city

Place	Total population 5 years and over who speak English-only at home	Asian population 5 years and over	Asians 5 years and over who speak English-only at home	NHPI[1] population 5 years and over	NHPIs[1] 5 years and over who speak English-only at home	Asian Indian	Bangladeshi	Cambodian	Chinese[2]	Fijian	Filipino	Guamanian[3]	Hawaiian, Native	Hmong	Indonesian	Japanese	Korean	Laotian	Malaysian	Pakistani	Samoan	Sri Lankan	Taiwanese	Thai	Tongan	Vietnamese
Springfield (cdp)	15,377 54.55	6,026	550 9.13 9.13 3.58	-	-	153 17.79 27.82 2.54 0.99	-	-	87 21.48 15.82 1.44 0.57	-	117 12.47 21.27 1.94 0.76	-	-	-	-	-	65 8.77 11.82 1.08 0.42	35 9.38 6.36 0.58 0.23	-	-	-	-	-	-	-	23 1.33 4.18 0.38 0.15
Tysons Corner (cdp)	10,745 61.48	2,946	418 14.19 14.19 3.89	-	-	107 15.88 25.60 3.63 1.00	-	-	75 11.85 17.94 2.55 0.70	-	-	-	-	-	-	-	102 13.40 24.40 3.46 0.95	-	-	-	-	-	-	-	-	-
Vienna (town)	10,620 78.08	1,102	186 16.88 16.88 1.75	-	-	-	-	-	-	-	-	-	-	-	-	-	-	-	-	-	-	-	-	-	-	-
West Springfield (cdp)	19,985 74.52	3,621	436 12.04 12.04 2.18	-	-	70 16.06 16.06 1.93 0.35	-	-	89 28.62 20.41 2.46 0.45	-	-	-	-	-	-	-	74 5.58 16.97 2.04 0.37	-	-	-	-	-	-	-	-	40 5.44 9.17 1.10 0.20
Wolf Trap (cdp)	10,563 81.72	1,219	275 22.56 22.56 2.60	-	-	98 27.61 35.64 8.04 0.93	-	-	52 20.39 18.91 4.27 0.49	-	-	-	-	-	-	-	-	-	-	-	-	-	-	-	-	-
Falls Church Independent City	7,929 81.31	635	121 19.06 19.06 1.53	-	-	-	-	-	-	-	-	-	-	-	-	-	-	-	-	-	-	-	-	-	-	-
Fauquier County	48,865 94.76	447	121 27.07 27.07 0.25	-	-	-	-	-	-	-	-	-	-	-	-	-	-	-	-	-	-	-	-	-	-	-
Frederick County	52,886 95.51	494	119 24.09 24.09 0.23	-	-	-	-	-	-	-	-	-	-	-	-	-	-	-	-	-	-	-	-	-	-	-
Hampton Independent City	128,122 93.31	2,463	581 23.59 23.59 0.45	-	-	-	-	-	-	-	168 26.17 28.92 6.82 0.13	-	-	-	-	-	-	-	-	-	-	-	-	-	-	107 20.94 18.42 4.34 0.08
Hanover County	77,707 96.36	509	170 33.40 33.40 0.22	-	-	-	-	-	-	-	-	-	-	-	-	-	-	-	-	-	-	-	-	-	-	-

Notes: Please refer to the User's Guide for an explanation of data; data is arranged alphabetically by state, then county, then city within each county; table includes counties with populations greater than 49,999 unless noted and cities with populations greater than 9,999 whose Asian and/or NHPI population rates are greater than the national average; (1) Native Hawaiian and other Pacific Islander; (2) excludes Taiwanese; (3) includes Chamorro; (4) county does not meet population threshold but is shown in order to allow inclusion of city

Place	Total population 5 years and over who speak English-only at home	Asian population 5 years and over	Asians 5 years and over who speak English-only at home	NHPI[1] population 5 years and over	NHPIs[1] 5 years and over who speak English-only at home	Asian Indian	Bangladeshi	Cambodian	Chinese[2]	Fijian	Filipino	Guamanian[3]	Hawaiian, Native	Hmong	Indonesian	Japanese	Korean	Laotian	Malaysian	Pakistani	Samoan	Sri Lankan	Taiwanese	Thai	Tongan	Vietnamese
Henrico County	222,274	8,638	1,443	-	-	355	-	104	261	-	273	-	-	-	-	-	149	-	-	-	-	-	-	-	-	71
	90.96		16.71			14.12		13.42	17.37		41.87						16.67									5.36
						24.60		7.21	18.09		18.92						10.33									4.92
			16.71			4.11		1.20	3.02		3.16						1.72									0.82
			0.65			0.16		0.05	0.12		0.12						0.07									0.03
Glen Allen (cdp)	11,055	417	91	-	-	-	-	-	-	-	-	-	-	-	-	-	-	-	-	-	-	-	-	-	-	-
	93.72		21.82																							
			21.82																							
			0.82																							
Laurel (cdp)	12,170	730	155	-	-	-	-	-	-	-	-	-	-	-	-	-	-	-	-	-	-	-	-	-	-	-
	88.00		21.23																							
			21.23																							
			1.27																							
Loudoun County	130,316	8,128	1,309	-	-	248	-	-	118	-	274	-	-	-	-	-	196	-	-	15	-	-	-	-	-	141
	85.01		16.10			14.35			11.46		25.07						19.60			2.59						8.88
						18.95			9.01		20.93						14.97			1.15						10.77
			16.10			3.05			1.45		3.37						2.41			0.18						1.73
			1.00			0.19			0.09		0.21						0.15			0.01						0.11
Lynchburg Independent City	58,012	906	226	-	-	-	-	-	-	-	-	-	-	-	-	-	-	-	-	-	-	-	-	-	-	-
	94.43		24.94																							
			24.94																							
			0.39																							
Manassas Park Indep. City	7,408	359	66	-	-	-	-	-	-	-	-	-	-	-	-	-	-	-	-	-	-	-	-	-	-	-
	79.96		18.38																							
			18.38																							
			0.89																							
Montgomery County	73,712	2,983	695	-	-	160	-	-	70	-	-	-	-	-	-	-	160	-	-	-	-	-	-	-	-	-
	92.62		23.30			25.76			8.65								21.83									
						23.02			10.07								23.02									
			23.30			5.36			2.35								5.36									
			0.94			0.22			0.09								0.22									
Blacksburg (town)	33,136	2,760	651	-	-	152	-	-	70	-	-	-	-	-	-	-	141	-	-	-	-	-	-	-	-	-
	86.79		23.59			26.53			8.96								21.27									
						23.35			10.75								21.66									
			23.59			5.51			2.54								5.11									
			1.96			0.46			0.21								0.43									
Newport News Independent City	152,149	3,931	960	-	-	-	-	-	89	-	319	-	-	-	-	-	229	-	-	-	-	-	-	-	-	66
	91.71		24.42						21.14		45.64						21.44									10.41
									9.27		33.23						23.85									6.88
			24.42						2.26		8.11						5.83									1.68
			0.63						0.06		0.21						0.15									0.04
Norfolk Independent City	198,440	6,587	1,717	-	-	118	-	-	111	-	1,075	-	-	-	-	-	-	-	-	-	-	-	-	-	-	56
	91.10		26.07			29.28			16.04		26.73															16.57
						6.87			6.46		62.61															3.26
			26.07			1.79			1.69		16.32															0.85
			0.87			0.06			0.06		0.54															0.03

Notes: Please refer to the User's Guide for an explanation of data; data is arranged alphabetically by state, then county, then city within each county; table includes counties with populations greater than 49,999 unless noted and cities with populations greater than 9,999 whose Asian and/or NHPI population rates are greater than the national average; (1) Native Hawaiian and other Pacific Islander; (2) excludes Taiwanese; (3) includes Chamorro; (4) county does not meet population threshold but is shown in order to allow inclusion of city

Place	Total population 5 years and over who speak English-only at home	Asian population 5 years and over	Asians 5 years and over who speak English-only at home	NHPI[1] population 5 years and over	NHPIs[1] 5 years and over who speak English-only at home	Asian Indian	Bangladeshi	Cambodian	Chinese[2]	Fijian	Filipino	Guamanian[3]	Hawaiian, Native	Hmong	Indonesian	Japanese	Korean	Laotian	Malaysian	Pakistani	Samoan	Sri Lankan	Taiwanese	Thai	Tongan	Vietnamese
Portsmouth Independent City	89,221 95.42	770	227 29.48 29.48 0.25	-	-	-	-	-	-	-	167 37.03 73.57 21.69 0.19	-	-	-	-	-	-	-	-	-	-	-	-	-	-	-
Prince William County	215,173 83.71	9,727	2,143 22.03 22.03 1.00	-	-	364 19.45 16.99 3.74 0.17	-	-	210 23.62 9.80 2.16 0.10	-	581 27.56 27.11 5.97 0.27	-	-	-	-	224 50.56 10.45 2.30 0.10	337 21.09 15.73 3.46 0.16	-	-	41 5.66 1.91 0.42 0.02	-	-	-	-	-	134 15.47 6.25 1.38 0.06
Bull Run (cdp)	7,581 74.44	540	79 14.63 14.63 1.04	-	-	-	-	-	-	-	-	-	-	-	-	-	-	-	-	-	-	-	-	-	-	-
Dale City (cdp)	42,073 81.57	2,706	398 14.71 14.71 0.95	-	-	56 9.30 14.07 2.07 0.13	-	-	-	-	131 19.88 32.91 4.84 0.31	-	-	-	-	-	-	-	-	26 8.64 6.53 0.96 0.06	-	-	-	-	-	-
Lake Ridge (cdp)	24,856 87.15	1,047	362 34.57 34.57 1.46	-	-	-	-	-	-	-	-	-	-	-	-	-	-	-	-	-	-	-	-	-	-	-
Woodbridge (cdp)	21,311 73.40	1,464	329 22.47 22.47 1.54	-	-	-	-	-	-	-	-	-	-	-	-	-	-	-	-	-	-	-	-	-	-	-
Richmond Independent City	172,876 93.26	2,337	711 30.42 30.42 0.41	-	-	154 30.80 21.66 6.59 0.09	-	-	-	-	195 48.15 27.43 8.34 0.11	-	-	-	-	-	-	-	-	-	-	-	-	-	-	-
Roanoke Independent City	84,060 94.75	934	176 18.84 18.84 0.21	-	-	-	-	-	-	-	-	-	-	-	-	-	-	-	-	-	-	-	-	-	-	-
Roanoke County	77,166 94.95	912	179 19.63 19.63 0.23	-	-	-	-	-	-	-	-	-	-	-	-	-	-	-	-	-	-	-	-	-	-	-
Spotsylvania County	79,142 94.49	1,227	470 38.30 38.30 0.59	-	-	-	-	-	-	-	-	-	-	-	-	-	-	-	-	-	-	-	-	-	-	-

Notes: Please refer to the User's Guide for an explanation of data; data is arranged alphabetically by state, then county, then city within each county; table includes counties with populations greater than 49,999 unless noted and cities with populations greater than 9,999 whose Asian and/or NHPI population rates are greater than the national average; (1) Native Hawaiian and other Pacific Islander; (2) excludes Taiwanese; (3) includes Chamorro; (4) county does not meet population threshold but is shown in order to allow inclusion of city

Place	Total population 5 years and over who speak English-only at home	Asian population 5 years and over	Asians 5 years and over who speak English-only at home	NHPI[1] population 5 years and over	NHPIs[1] 5 years and over who speak English-only at home	Asian Indian	Bangladeshi	Cambodian	Chinese[2]	Fijian	Filipino	Guamanian[3]	Hawaiian, Native	Hmong	Indonesian	Japanese	Korean	Laotian	Malaysian	Pakistani	Samoan	Sri Lankan	Taiwanese	Thai	Tongan	Vietnamese
Stafford County	79,205 92.72	1,442	417 28.92 28.92 0.53	-	-	-	-	-	-	-	130 34.39 31.18 9.02 0.16	-	-	-	-	-	-	-	-	-	-	-	-	-	-	-
Suffolk Independent City	56,713 95.99	478	89 18.62 18.62 0.16	-	-	-	-	-	-	-	-	-	-	-	-	-	-	-	-	-	-	-	-	-	-	-
Virginia Beach Independent City	354,311 89.72	19,200	5,539 28.85 28.85 1.56	-	-	328 27.70 5.92 1.71 0.09	-	-	212 13.52 3.83 1.10 0.06	-	4,002 31.33 72.25 20.84 1.13	-	-	-	-	247 35.39 4.46 1.29 0.07	223 28.48 4.03 1.16 0.06	-	-	-	-	-	-	-	-	113 9.94 2.04 0.59 0.03
Williamsburg Independent City	10,776 92.30	511	195 38.16 38.16 1.81	-	-	-	-	-	-	-	-	-	-	-	-	-	-	-	-	-	-	-	-	-	-	-
York County	48,762 92.76	1,711	564 32.96 32.96 1.16	-	-	66 29.86 11.70 3.86 0.14	-	-	-	-	-	-	-	-	-	-	147 27.02 26.06 8.59 0.30	-	-	-	-	-	-	-	-	-
WASHINGTON	4,730,512 85.99	301,373	75,843 25.17 25.17 1.60	19,850	10,202 51.40 51.40 0.22	4,170 20.34 5.50 1.38 0.09	-	1,137 8.30 1.50 0.38 0.02	10,987 20.54 14.49 3.65 0.23	108 16.39 1.06 0.54 <0.01	20,358 32.89 26.84 6.76 0.43	2,832 57.18 27.76 14.27 0.06	3,679 85.54 36.06 18.53 0.08	61 4.81 0.08 0.02 <0.01	192 16.33 0.25 0.06 <0.01	19,444 53.50 25.64 6.45 0.41	9,043 20.39 11.92 3.00 0.19	641 8.60 0.85 0.21 0.01	-	139 12.29 0.18 0.05 <0.01	1,979 31.01 19.40 9.97 0.04	150 40.11 0.20 0.05 <0.01	298 8.33 0.39 0.10 0.01	795 20.89 1.05 0.26 0.02	139 19.17 1.36 0.70 <0.01	3,096 7.57 4.08 1.03 0.07
Benton County	113,095 85.81	2,767	894 32.31 32.31 0.79	-	-	28 7.73 3.13 1.01 0.02	-	-	107 21.49 11.97 3.87 0.09	-	-	-	-	-	-	-	245 60.79 27.40 8.85 0.22	-	-	-	-	-	-	-	-	58 12.86 6.49 2.10 0.05
Richland (city)	32,476 89.83	1,467	398 27.13 27.13 1.23	-	-	-	-	-	78 20.31 19.60 5.32 0.24	-	-	-	-	-	-	-	-	-	-	-	-	-	-	-	-	-
Chelan County	49,731 80.37	406	161 39.66 39.66 0.32	-	-	-	-	-	-	-	-	-	-	-	-	-	-	-	-	-	-	-	-	-	-	-
Clallam County	57,381 93.74	831	391 47.05 47.05 0.68	-	-	-	-	-	-	-	-	-	-	-	-	-	-	-	-	-	-	-	-	-	-	-

Notes: Please refer to the User's Guide for an explanation of data; data is arranged alphabetically by state, then county, then city within each county; table includes counties with populations greater than 49,999 unless noted and cities with populations greater than 9,999 whose Asian and/or NHPI population rates are greater than the national average; (1) Native Hawaiian and other Pacific Islander; (2) excludes Taiwanese; (3) includes Chamorro; (4) county does not meet population threshold but is shown in order to allow inclusion of city

Place	Total population 5 years and over who speak English-only at home	Asian population 5 years and over	Asians 5 years and over who speak English-only at home	NHPI[1] population 5 years and over	NHPIs[1] 5 years and over who speak English-only at home	Asian Indian	Bangladeshi	Cambodian	Chinese[2]	Fijian	Filipino	Guamanian[3]	Hawaiian, Native	Hmong	Indonesian	Japanese	Korean	Laotian	Malaysian	Pakistani	Samoan	Sri Lankan	Taiwanese	Thai	Tongan	Vietnamese
Clark County	281,613 88.52	9,789	2,390 24.42 24.42 0.85	1,152	585 50.78 50.78 0.21	200 28.61 8.37 2.04 0.07	-	34 8.56 1.42 0.35 0.01	220 14.78 9.21 2.25 0.08	-	640 39.38 26.78 6.54 0.23	-	-	-	-	587 49.04 24.56 6.00 0.21	354 28.34 14.81 3.62 0.13	30 7.89 1.26 0.31 0.01	-	-	-	-	-	-	-	155 7.34 6.49 1.58 0.06
Five Corners (cdp)	10,108 90.47	542	138 25.46 25.46 1.37	-	-	-	-	-	-	-	-	-	-	-	-	-	-	-	-	-	-	-	-	-	-	-
Orchards (cdp)	13,985 87.37	680	128 18.82 18.82 0.92	-	-	-	-	-	-	-	-	-	-	-	-	-	-	-	-	-	-	-	-	-	-	-
Vancouver (city)	110,695 84.20	5,665	1,292 22.81 22.81 1.17	795	347 43.65 43.65 0.31	-	-	-	153 16.49 11.84 2.70 0.14	-	280 32.04 21.67 4.94 0.25	-	-	-	-	424 57.77 32.82 7.48 0.38	163 24.44 12.62 2.88 0.15	-	-	-	-	-	-	-	-	72 5.45 5.57 1.27 0.07
Cowlitz County	81,312 94.00	1,144	270 23.60 23.60 0.33	-	-	-	-	38 10.92 14.07 3.32 0.05	-	-	-	-	-	-	-	-	-	-	-	-	-	-	-	-	-	18 5.39 6.67 1.57 0.02
Grant County	48,887 71.67	546	309 56.59 56.59 0.63	-	-	-	-	-	-	-	-	-	-	-	-	-	-	-	-	-	-	-	-	-	-	-
Grays Harbor County	58,923 93.60	605	129 21.32 21.32 0.22	-	-	-	-	-	-	-	-	-	-	-	-	-	-	-	-	-	-	-	-	-	-	-
Island County	61,301 91.77	2,707	843 31.14 31.14 1.38	-	-	-	-	-	-	-	474 26.25 56.23 17.51 0.77	-	-	-	-	166 44.62 19.69 6.13 0.27	-	-	-	-	-	-	-	-	-	-
Oak Harbor (city)	15,525 86.91	1,646	471 28.61 28.61 3.03	-	-	-	-	-	-	-	350 26.99 74.31 21.26 2.25	-	-	-	-	-	-	-	-	-	-	-	-	-	-	-
King County	1,332,933 81.65	175,988	42,075 23.91 23.91 3.16	7,549	3,178 42.10 42.10 0.24	2,263 17.66 5.38 1.29 0.17	-	527 8.56 1.25 0.30 0.04	7,939 19.35 18.87 4.51 0.60	61 11.94 1.92 0.81 <0.01	9,633 30.01 22.89 5.47 0.72	478 62.08 15.04 6.33 0.04	1,116 82.48 35.12 14.78 0.08	46 6.27 0.11 0.03 <0.01	141 18.05 0.34 0.08 0.01	11,943 54.67 28.39 6.79 0.90	3,866 20.19 9.19 2.20 0.29	333 7.26 0.79 0.19 0.02	-	52 10.77 0.12 0.03 <0.01	1,055 30.11 33.20 13.98 0.08	-	182 6.38 0.43 0.10 0.01	317 16.66 0.75 0.18 0.02	82 17.48 2.58 1.09 0.01	1,792 7.23 4.26 1.02 0.13

Notes: Please refer to the User's Guide for an explanation of data; data is arranged alphabetically by state, then county, then city within each county; table includes counties with populations greater than 49,999 unless noted and cities with populations greater than 9,999 whose Asian and/or NHPI population rates are greater than the national average; (1) Native Hawaiian and other Pacific Islander; (2) excludes Taiwanese; (3) includes Chamorro; (4) county does not meet population threshold but is shown in order to allow inclusion of city

Place	Total population 5 years and over who speak English-only at home	Asian population 5 years and over	Asians 5 years and over who speak English-only at home	NHPI[1] population 5 years and over	NHPIs[1] 5 years and over who speak English-only at home	Asian Indian	Bangladeshi	Cambodian	Chinese[2]	Fijian	Filipino	Guamanian[3]	Hawaiian, Native	Hmong	Indonesian	Japanese	Korean	Laotian	Malaysian	Pakistani	Samoan	Sri Lankan	Taiwanese	Thai	Tongan	Vietnamese
Auburn (city)	32,055 86.40	1,399	344 24.59 24.59 1.07	-	-	-	-	-	-	-	-	-	-	-	-	-	-	-	-	-	-	-	-	-	-	-
Bellevue (city)	75,405 73.15	17,534	3,482 19.86 19.86 4.62	-	-	290 13.24 8.33 1.65 0.38	-	-	992 18.36 28.49 5.66 1.32	-	329 31.48 9.45 1.88 0.44	-	-	-	-	1,148 39.87 32.97 6.55 1.52	286 12.41 8.21 1.63 0.38	15 3.52 0.43 0.09 0.02	-	-	-	-	8 0.96 0.23 0.05 0.01	-	-	73 5.92 2.10 0.42 0.10
Bothell (city)	24,459 87.63	2,136	650 30.43 30.43 2.66	-	-	-	-	-	164 30.37 25.23 7.68 0.67	-	-	-	-	-	-	-	-	-	-	-	-	-	-	-	-	-
Bryn Mawr-Skyway (cdp)	10,193 77.52	2,892	864 29.88 29.88 8.48	-	-	-	-	-	-	-	163 20.00 18.87 5.64 1.60	-	-	-	-	459 76.63 53.13 15.87 4.50	-	-	-	-	-	-	-	-	-	54 13.67 6.25 1.87 0.53
Burien (city)	24,105 80.47	1,952	410 21.00 21.00 1.70	-	-	-	-	-	-	-	89 19.26 21.71 4.56 0.37	-	-	-	-	-	-	-	-	-	-	-	-	-	-	9 2.38 2.20 0.46 0.04
Cascade-Fairwood (cdp)	26,555 82.96	4,258	1,111 26.09 26.09 4.18	-	-	-	-	-	143 16.49 12.87 3.36 0.54	-	352 29.73 31.68 8.27 1.33	-	-	-	-	384 81.18 34.56 9.02 1.45	-	-	-	-	-	-	-	-	-	38 5.79 3.42 0.89 0.14
Cottage Lake (cdp)	21,103 92.57	983	429 43.64 43.64 2.03	-	-	-	-	-	-	-	-	-	-	-	-	-	-	-	-	-	-	-	-	-	-	-
Des Moines (city)	23,067 83.91	2,252	428 19.01 19.01 1.86	320	153 47.81 47.81 0.66	-	-	-	-	-	115 26.20 26.87 5.11 0.50	-	-	-	-	-	-	-	-	-	-	-	-	-	-	16 3.34 3.74 0.71 0.07
East Hill-Meridian (cdp)	22,300 81.36	3,579	823 23.00 23.00 3.69	-	-	101 15.14 12.27 2.82 0.45	-	-	112 16.16 13.61 3.13 0.50	-	219 33.64 26.61 6.12 0.98	-	-	-	-	-	-	-	-	-	-	-	-	-	-	0 0.00 0.00 0.00 0.00
Federal Way (city)	60,294 78.61	9,604	1,966 20.47 20.47 3.26	764	436 57.07 57.07 0.72	-	-	-	199 24.51 10.12 2.07 0.33	-	653 35.96 33.21 6.80 1.08	-	-	-	-	361 58.60 18.36 3.76 0.60	342 8.16 17.40 3.56 0.57	-	-	-	211 50.48 48.39 27.62 0.35	-	-	-	-	93 9.13 4.73 0.97 0.15

Notes: Please refer to the User's Guide for an explanation of data; data is arranged alphabetically by state, then county, then city within each county; table includes counties with populations greater than 49,999 unless noted and cities with populations greater than 9,999 whose Asian and/or NHPI population rates are greater than the national average; (1) Native Hawaiian and other Pacific Islander; (2) excludes Taiwanese; (3) includes Chamorro; (4) county does not meet population threshold but is shown in order to allow inclusion of city

Place	Total population 5 years and over who speak English-only at home	Asian population 5 years and over	Asians 5 years and over who speak English-only at home	NHPI[1] population 5 years and over	NHPIs[1] 5 years and over who speak English-only at home	Asian Indian	Bangladeshi	Cambodian	Chinese[2]	Fijian	Filipino	Guamanian[3]	Hawaiian, Native	Hmong	Indonesian	Japanese	Korean	Laotian	Malaysian	Pakistani	Samoan	Sri Lankan	Taiwanese	Thai	Tongan	Vietnamese
Inglewood-Finn Hill (cdp)	18,044 85.56	1,593	400 25.11 25.11 2.22	-	-	-	-	-	70 17.03 17.50 4.39 0.39	-	-	-	-	-	-	-	-	-	-	-	-	-	-	-	-	-
Issaquah (city)	9,139 86.98	686	193 28.13 28.13 2.11	-	-	-	-	-	-	-	-	-	-	-	-	-	-	-	-	-	-	-	-	-	-	-
Kenmore (city)	15,218 87.30	1,116	375 33.60 33.60 2.46	-	-	-	-	-	-	-	-	-	-	-	-	-	-	-	-	-	-	-	-	-	-	-
Kent (city)	56,878 78.16	7,072	1,577 22.30 22.30 2.77	-	-	112 8.39 7.10 1.58 0.20	-	-	111 11.43 7.04 1.57 0.20	-	553 36.05 35.07 7.82 0.97	-	-	-	-	411 74.19 26.06 5.81 0.72	140 19.50 8.88 1.98 0.25	-	-	-	-	-	-	-	-	124 9.66 7.86 1.75 0.22
Kingsgate (cdp)	8,958 79.55	1,358	256 18.85 18.85 2.86	-	-	-	-	-	60 18.35 23.44 4.42 0.67	-	-	-	-	-	-	-	-	-	-	-	-	-	-	-	-	-
Kirkland (city)	36,173 85.11	3,259	938 28.78 28.78 2.59	-	-	-	-	-	157 21.87 16.74 4.82 0.43	-	-	-	-	-	-	258 49.43 27.51 7.92 0.71	-	-	-	-	-	-	-	-	-	86 16.48 9.17 2.64 0.24
Lake Forest Park (city)	11,271 88.10	1,113	329 29.56 29.56 2.92	-	-	-	-	-	-	-	-	-	-	-	-	-	-	-	-	-	-	-	-	-	-	-
Lakeland North (cdp)	12,003 85.30	843	253 30.01 30.01 2.11	-	-	-	-	-	-	-	-	-	-	-	-	-	-	-	-	-	-	-	-	-	-	-
Lakeland South (cdp)	9,771 91.78	556	224 40.29 40.29 2.29	-	-	-	-	-	-	-	-	-	-	-	-	-	-	-	-	-	-	-	-	-	-	-
Lea Hill (cdp)	8,846 90.23	477	147 30.82 30.82 1.66	-	-	-	-	-	-	-	-	-	-	-	-	-	-	-	-	-	-	-	-	-	-	-

Notes: Please refer to the User's Guide for an explanation of data; data is arranged alphabetically by state, then county, then city within each county; table includes counties with populations greater than 49,999 unless noted and cities with populations greater than 9,999 whose Asian and/or NHPI population rates are greater than the national average; (1) Native Hawaiian and other Pacific Islander; (2) excludes Taiwanese; (3) includes Chamorro; (4) county does not meet population threshold but is shown in order to allow inclusion of city

Place	Total population 5 years and over who speak English-only at home	Asian population 5 years and over	Asians 5 years and over who speak English-only at home	NHPI[1] population 5 years and over	NHPIs[1] 5 years and over who speak English-only at home	Asian Indian	Bangladeshi	Cambodian	Chinese[2]	Fijian	Filipino	Guamanian[3]	Hawaiian, Native	Hmong	Indonesian	Japanese	Korean	Laotian	Malaysian	Pakistani	Samoan	Sri Lankan	Taiwanese	Thai	Tongan	Vietnamese
Mercer Island (city)	17,931 85.27	2,343	803 34.27 34.27 4.48	-	-	-	-	-	333 33.23 41.47 14.21 1.86	-	-	-	-	-	-	292 51.41 36.36 12.46 1.63	-	-	-	-	-	-	-	-	-	-
Redmond (city)	32,964 77.34	5,534	980 17.71 17.71 2.97	-	-	118 10.33 12.04 2.13 0.36	-	-	207 12.06 21.12 3.74 0.63	-	-	-	-	-	-	258 35.68 26.33 4.66 0.78	75 15.86 7.65 1.36 0.23	-	-	-	-	-	-	-	-	-
Renton (city)	35,958 77.36	6,269	1,519 24.23 24.23 4.22	-	-	-	-	-	145 12.63 9.55 2.31 0.40	-	456 30.52 30.02 7.27 1.27	-	-	-	-	467 74.96 30.74 7.45 1.30	-	-	-	-	-	-	-	-	-	102 6.12 6.71 1.63 0.28
Riverton-Boulevard Park (cdp)	7,453 70.05	1,401	160 11.42 11.42 2.15	-	-	-	-	-	-	-	-	-	-	-	-	-	-	-	-	-	-	-	-	-	-	-
Sammamish (city)	28,307 90.00	2,284	866 37.92 37.92 3.06	-	-	-	-	-	221 22.26 25.52 9.68 0.78	-	-	-	-	-	-	-	-	-	-	-	-	-	-	-	-	-
SeaTac (city)	17,105 71.38	2,755	390 14.16 14.16 2.28	557	147 26.39 26.39 0.86	32 5.78 8.21 1.16 0.19	-	-	-	-	83 12.37 21.28 3.01 0.49	-	-	-	-	-	-	-	-	-	-	-	-	-	-	41 7.88 10.51 1.49 0.24
Seattle (city)	429,105 79.83	70,271	17,555 24.98 24.98 4.09	2,387	935 39.17 39.17 0.22	866 33.50 4.93 1.23 0.20	-	212 9.07 1.21 0.30 0.05	3,412 19.01 19.44 4.86 0.80	-	4,316 27.89 24.59 6.14 1.01	-	-	-	59 15.86 0.34 0.08 0.01	4,913 53.60 27.99 6.99 1.14	1,482 30.47 8.44 2.11 0.35	141 5.76 0.80 0.20 0.03	-	-	223 17.94 23.85 9.34 0.05	-	159 16.39 0.91 0.23 0.04	138 16.22 0.79 0.20 0.03	-	743 7.03 4.23 1.06 0.17
Shoreline (city)	40,543 80.78	6,292	1,164 18.50 18.50 2.87	-	-	40 11.02 3.44 0.64 0.10	-	-	245 14.51 21.05 3.89 0.60	-	398 36.08 34.19 6.33 0.98	-	-	-	-	193 48.86 16.58 3.07 0.48	123 9.48 10.57 1.95 0.30	-	-	-	-	-	-	-	-	38 4.60 3.26 0.60 0.09
Tukwila (city)	10,850 68.00	1,648	298 18.08 18.08 2.75	318	111 34.91 34.91 1.02	-	-	-	-	-	95 16.78 31.88 5.76 0.88	-	-	-	-	-	-	-	-	-	-	-	-	-	-	-
Union Hill-Novelty Hill (cdp)	9,202 88.92	460	165 35.87 35.87 1.79	-	-	-	-	-	-	-	-	-	-	-	-	-	-	-	-	-	-	-	-	-	-	-

Notes: Please refer to the User's Guide for an explanation of data; data is arranged alphabetically by state, then county, then city within each county; table includes counties with populations greater than 49,999 unless noted and cities with populations greater than 9,999 whose Asian and/or NHPI population rates are greater than the national average; (1) Native Hawaiian and other Pacific Islander; (2) excludes Taiwanese; (3) includes Chamorro; (4) county does not meet population threshold but is shown in order to allow inclusion of city

Place	Total population 5 years and over who speak English-only at home	Asian population 5 years and over	Asians 5 years and over who speak English-only at home	NHPI[1] population 5 years and over	NHPIs[1] 5 years and over who speak English-only at home	Asian Indian	Bangladeshi	Cambodian	Chinese[2]	Fijian	Filipino	Guamanian[3]	Hawaiian, Native	Hmong	Indonesian	Japanese	Korean	Laotian	Malaysian	Pakistani	Samoan	Sri Lankan	Taiwanese	Thai	Tongan	Vietnamese
White Center (cdp)	12,450 64.35	4,149	389 9.38 9.38 3.12	-	-	-	-	70 6.16 17.99 1.69 0.56	-	-	94 21.12 24.16 2.27 0.76	-	-	-	-	-	-	-	-	-	-	-	-	-	-	67 3.62 17.22 1.61 0.54
Kitsap County	198,612 91.69	10,009	3,582 35.79 35.79 1.80	1,520	936 61.58 61.58 0.47	-	-	-	146 32.59 4.08 1.46 0.07	-	2,209 33.20 61.67 22.07 1.11	511 55.30 54.59 33.62 0.26	-	-	-	544 46.94 15.19 5.44 0.27	176 29.63 4.91 1.76 0.09	-	-	-	-	-	-	-	-	134 31.46 3.74 1.34 0.07
Bremerton (city)	30,186 88.72	1,961	577 29.42 29.42 1.91	-	-	-	-	-	-	-	359 26.36 62.22 18.31 1.19	-	-	-	-	-	-	-	-	-	-	-	-	-	-	-
Silverdale (cdp)	12,743 86.45	1,721	620 36.03 36.03 4.87	-	-	-	-	-	-	-	553 38.03 89.19 32.13 4.34	-	-	-	-	-	-	-	-	-	-	-	-	-	-	-
Lewis County	60,100 93.64	351	178 50.71 50.71 0.30	-	-	-	-	-	-	-	-	-	-	-	-	-	-	-	-	-	-	-	-	-	-	-
Pierce County	574,433 88.23	32,925	8,042 24.43 24.43 1.40	4,674	2,213 47.35 47.35 0.39	274 37.08 3.41 0.83 0.05	-	301 8.06 3.74 0.91 0.05	578 34.65 7.19 1.76 0.10	-	2,631 41.06 32.72 7.99 0.46	896 54.20 40.49 19.17 0.16	686 83.25 31.00 14.68 0.12	-	-	1,665 47.54 20.70 5.06 0.29	1,563 14.62 19.44 4.75 0.27	50 12.53 0.62 0.15 0.01	-	-	333 20.80 15.05 7.12 0.06	-	-	118 30.26 1.47 0.36 0.02	-	176 4.43 2.19 0.53 0.03
Elk Plain (cdp)	13,228 91.16	589	295 50.08 50.08 2.23	-	-	-	-	-	-	-	-	-	-	-	-	-	-	-	-	-	-	-	-	-	-	-
Fort Lewis (cdp)	13,789 82.94	623	255 40.93 40.93 1.85	294	114 38.78 38.78 0.83	-	-	-	-	-	139 39.27 54.51 22.31 1.01	-	-	-	-	-	-	-	-	-	-	-	-	-	-	-
Lakewood (city)	43,681 80.82	4,993	1,089 21.81 21.81 2.49	661	303 45.84 45.84 0.69	-	-	-	-	-	333 28.63 30.58 6.67 0.76	-	-	-	-	179 27.93 16.44 3.59 0.41	293 13.00 26.91 5.87 0.67	-	-	-	64 23.44 21.12 9.68 0.15	-	-	-	-	-
Parkland (cdp)	19,387 86.63	1,531	375 24.49 24.49 1.93	362	176 48.62 48.62 0.91	-	-	-	-	-	-	-	-	-	-	-	145 18.26 38.67 9.47 0.75	-	-	-	-	-	-	-	-	-

Notes: Please refer to the User's Guide for an explanation of data; data is arranged alphabetically by state, then county, then city within each county; table includes counties with populations greater than 49,999 unless noted and cities with populations greater than 9,999 whose Asian and/or NHPI population rates are greater than the national average; (1) Native Hawaiian and other Pacific Islander; (2) excludes Taiwanese; (3) includes Chamorro; (4) county does not meet population threshold but is shown in order to allow inclusion of city

Place	Total population 5 years and over who speak English-only at home	Asian population 5 years and over	Asians 5 years and over who speak English-only at home	NHPI[1] population 5 years and over	NHPIs[1] 5 years and over who speak English-only at home	Asian Indian	Bangladeshi	Cambodian	Chinese[2]	Fijian	Filipino	Guamanian[3]	Hawaiian, Native	Hmong	Indonesian	Japanese	Korean	Laotian	Malaysian	Pakistani	Samoan	Sri Lankan	Taiwanese	Thai	Tongan	Vietnamese
Spanaway (cdp)	16,966	1,232	289	541	284	-	-	-	-	-	142	-	-	-	-	-	95	-	-	-	-	-	-	-	-	-
	85.91		23.46		52.50						29.28						16.35									
											49.13						32.87									
			23.46		52.50						11.53						7.71									
			1.70		1.67						0.84						0.56									
Tacoma (city)	150,000	13,471	2,466	1,265	568	-	-	252	243	-	769	254	-	-	-	508	237	30	-	-	94	-	-	-	-	90
	83.48		18.31		44.90			8.71	35.68		40.80	63.34				53.59	8.09	9.87			16.10					3.11
								10.22	9.85		31.18	44.72				20.60	9.61	1.22			16.55					3.65
			18.31		44.90			1.87	1.80		5.71	20.08				3.77	1.76	0.22			7.43					0.67
			1.64		0.38			0.17	0.16		0.51	0.17				0.34	0.16	0.02			0.06					0.06
University Place (city)	24,728	2,174	331	-	-	-	-	-	-	-	-	-	-	-	-	-	69	-	-	-	-	-	-	-	-	-
	87.54		15.23														5.84									
																	20.85									
			15.23														3.17									
			1.34														0.28									
Skagit County	85,002	1,366	499	-	-	-	-	-	-	-	182	-	-	-	-	-	-	-	-	-	-	-	-	-	-	-
	88.29		36.53								38.89															
											36.47															
			36.53								13.32															
			0.59								0.21															
Snohomish County	494,203	33,110	7,108	1,174	834	371	-	115	880	-	2,302	-	441	-	-	1,228	1,050	90	-	41	-	-	-	-	-	345
	87.79		21.47		71.04	15.52		6.24	21.42		31.76		92.65			52.19	14.87	12.93		11.02						7.25
						5.22		1.62	12.38		32.39		52.88			17.28	14.77	1.27		0.58						4.85
			21.47		71.04	1.12		0.35	2.66		6.95		37.56			3.71	3.17	0.27		0.12						1.04
			1.44		0.17	0.08		0.02	0.18		0.47		0.09			0.25	0.21	0.02		0.01						0.07
Alderwood Manor (cdp)	12,328	1,167	248	-	-	-	-	-	-	-	-	-	-	-	-	-	-	-	-	-	-	-	-	-	-	-
	86.66		21.25																							
			21.25																							
			2.01																							
Edmonds (city)	33,243	2,055	550	-	-	-	-	-	-	-	92	-	-	-	-	-	89	-	-	-	-	-	-	-	-	-
	88.42		26.76								27.14						16.64									
											16.73						16.18									
			26.76								4.48						4.33									
			1.65								0.28						0.27									
Everett (city)	70,820	5,575	996	-	-	60	-	44	-	-	473	-	-	-	-	-	-	-	-	-	-	-	-	-	-	37
	84.19		17.87			11.83		7.71			27.29															3.50
						6.02		4.42			47.49															3.71
			17.87			1.08		0.79			8.48															0.66
			1.41			0.08		0.06			0.67															0.05
Lynnwood (city)	23,751	4,410	680	-	-	-	-	-	95	-	182	-	-	-	-	-	133	-	-	-	-	-	-	-	-	26
	75.58		15.42						15.75		20.99						13.43									2.87
									13.97		26.76						19.56									3.82
			15.42						2.15		4.13						3.02									0.59
			2.86						0.40		0.77						0.56									0.11
Martha Lake (cdp)	9,684	1,066	117	-	-	-	-	-	-	-	-	-	-	-	-	-	-	-	-	-	-	-	-	-	-	-
	83.10		10.98																							
			10.98																							
			1.21																							

Notes: Please refer to the User's Guide for an explanation of data; data is arranged alphabetically by state, then county, then city within each county; table includes counties with populations greater than 49,999 unless noted and cities with populations greater than 9,999 whose Asian and/or NHPI population rates are greater than the national average; (1) Native Hawaiian and other Pacific Islander; (2) excludes Taiwanese; (3) includes Chamorro; (4) county does not meet population threshold but is shown in order to allow inclusion of city

Place	Total population 5 years and over who speak English-only at home	Asian population 5 years and over	Asians 5 years and over who speak English-only at home	NHPI[1] population 5 years and over	NHPIs[1] 5 years and over who speak English-only at home	Asian Indian	Bangladeshi	Cambodian	Chinese[2]	Fijian	Filipino	Guamanian[3]	Hawaiian, Native	Hmong	Indonesian	Japanese	Korean	Laotian	Malaysian	Pakistani	Samoan	Sri Lankan	Taiwanese	Thai	Tongan	Vietnamese
Marysville (city)	21,116 91.25	892	310 34.75 34.75 1.47	-	-	-	-	-	-	-	-	-	-	-	-	-	-	-	-	-	-	-	-	-	-	-
Mill Creek (city)	8,901 82.25	1,090	139 12.75 12.75 1.56	-	-	-	-	-	-	-	-	-	-	-	-	-	11 2.78 7.91 1.01 0.12	-	-	-	-	-	-	-	-	-
Mountlake Terrace (city)	15,090 79.39	2,204	392 17.79 17.79 2.60	-	-	-	-	-	-	-	176 32.06 44.90 7.99 1.17	-	-	-	-	-	83 14.12 21.17 3.77 0.55	-	-	-	-	-	-	-	-	-
Mukilteo (city)	14,236 83.71	2,003	420 20.97 20.97 2.95	-	-	-	-	-	-	-	-	-	-	-	-	-	114 11.47 27.14 5.69 0.80	-	-	-	-	-	-	-	-	-
North Creek (cdp)	21,568 89.61	1,449	388 26.78 26.78 1.80	-	-	-	-	-	-	-	-	-	-	-	-	-	-	-	-	-	-	-	-	-	-	-
Paine Field-Lk. Stickney (cdp)	18,348 82.69	1,437	204 14.20 14.20 1.11	-	-	-	-	-	-	-	-	-	-	-	-	-	-	-	-	-	-	-	-	-	-	-
Picnic Pt.-N. Lynnwood (cdp)	17,184 80.94	2,342	421 17.98 17.98 2.45	-	-	-	-	-	-	-	122 31.28 28.98 5.21 0.71	-	-	-	-	-	91 10.86 21.62 3.89 0.53	-	-	-	-	-	-	-	-	-
Seattle Hill-Silver Firs (cdp)	29,135 88.94	2,554	713 27.92 27.92 2.45	-	-	-	-	-	-	-	294 51.67 41.23 11.51 1.01	-	-	-	-	-	66 11.38 9.26 2.58 0.23	-	-	-	-	-	-	-	-	55 13.19 7.71 2.15 0.19
Spokane County	364,642 93.41	7,097	2,505 35.30 35.30 0.69	610	405 66.39 66.39 0.11	188 32.58 7.50 2.65 0.05	-	-	193 23.28 7.70 2.72 0.05	-	428 44.58 17.09 6.03 0.12	-	-	15 3.25 0.60 0.21 <0.01	-	975 59.38 38.92 13.74 0.27	374 56.58 14.93 5.27 0.10	-	-	-	-	-	-	-	-	91 7.74 3.63 1.28 0.02
Spokane (city)	168,044 92.12	4,155	1,485 35.74 35.74 0.88	352	207 58.81 58.81 0.12	-	-	-	81 16.46 5.45 1.95 0.05	-	193 41.59 13.00 4.65 0.11	-	-	15 4.41 1.01 0.36 0.01	-	678 67.40 45.66 16.32 0.40	212 57.77 14.28 5.10 0.13	-	-	-	-	-	-	-	-	59 7.87 3.97 1.42 0.04

Notes: Please refer to the User's Guide for an explanation of data; data is arranged alphabetically by state, then county, then city within each county; table includes counties with populations greater than 49,999 unless noted and cities with populations greater than 9,999 whose Asian and/or NHPI population rates are greater than the national average; (1) Native Hawaiian and other Pacific Islander; (2) excludes Taiwanese; (3) includes Chamorro; (4) county does not meet population threshold but is shown in order to allow inclusion of city

Place	Total population 5 years and over who speak English-only at home	Asian population 5 years and over	Asians 5 years and over who speak English-only at home	NHPI[1] population 5 years and over	NHPIs[1] 5 years and over who speak English-only at home	Asian Indian	Bangladeshi	Cambodian	Chinese[2]	Fijian	Filipino	Guamanian[3]	Hawaiian, Native	Hmong	Indonesian	Japanese	Korean	Laotian	Malaysian	Pakistani	Samoan	Sri Lankan	Taiwanese	Thai	Tongan	Vietnamese
Thurston County	176,672 90.76	8,883	2,160 24.32 24.32 1.22	1,121	685 61.11 61.11 0.39	116 27.55 5.37 1.31 0.07	-	58 7.25 2.69 0.65 0.03	275 33.45 12.73 3.10 0.16	-	592 37.59 27.41 6.66 0.34	358 50.64 52.26 31.94 0.20	-	-	-	452 58.40 20.93 5.09 0.26	327 15.88 15.14 3.68 0.19	-	-	-	-	-	-	-	-	94 5.70 4.35 1.06 0.05
Lacey (city)	24,581 85.87	2,413	441 18.28 18.28 1.79	-	-	-	-	-	-	-	155 35.88 35.15 6.42 0.63	-	-	-	-	-	97 16.09 22.00 4.02 0.39	-	-	-	-	-	-	-	-	26 4.68 5.90 1.08 0.11
Olympia (city)	36,068 90.23	2,159	577 26.73 26.73 1.60	-	-	-	-	-	-	-	-	-	-	-	-	-	-	-	-	-	-	-	-	-	-	49 7.31 8.49 2.27 0.14
Tumwater (city)	11,028 92.41	427	114 26.70 26.70 1.03	-	-	-	-	-	-	-	-	-	-	-	-	-	-	-	-	-	-	-	-	-	-	-
Walla Walla County	43,362 83.81	744	295 39.65 39.65 0.68	-	-	-	-	-	-	-	-	-	-	-	-	-	-	-	-	-	-	-	-	-	-	-
Whatcom County	142,022 90.78	4,144	1,378 33.25 33.25 0.97	-	-	224 19.13 16.26 5.41 0.16	-	-	153 32.14 11.10 3.69 0.11	-	222 44.67 16.11 5.36 0.16	-	-	-	-	239 50.21 17.34 5.77 0.17	234 51.66 16.98 5.65 0.16	-	-	-	-	-	-	-	-	102 18.02 7.40 2.46 0.07
Bellingham (city)	57,204 90.24	2,571	815 31.70 31.70 1.42	-	-	86 14.98 10.55 3.35 0.15	-	-	-	-	-	-	-	-	-	-	-	-	-	-	-	-	-	-	-	58 13.52 7.12 2.26 0.10
Whitman County[4]	34,528 89.01	2,137	511 23.91 23.91 1.48	-	-	-	-	-	57 9.09 11.15 2.67 0.17	-	-	-	-	-	-	221 36.23 43.25 10.34 0.64	-	-	-	-	-	-	-	-	-	-
Pullman (city)	20,065 84.77	1,920	445 23.18 23.18 2.22	-	-	-	-	-	54 9.91 12.13 2.81 0.27	-	-	-	-	-	-	173 30.78 38.88 9.01 0.86	-	-	-	-	-	-	-	-	-	-
Yakima County	138,737 68.19	1,989	803 40.37 40.37 0.58	-	-	-	-	-	-	-	368 41.12 45.83 18.50 0.27	-	-	-	-	-	-	-	-	-	-	-	-	-	-	-

Notes: Please refer to the User's Guide for an explanation of data; data is arranged alphabetically by state, then county, then city within each county; table includes counties with populations greater than 49,999 unless noted and cities with populations greater than 9,999 whose Asian and/or NHPI population rates are greater than the national average; (1) Native Hawaiian and other Pacific Islander; (2) excludes Taiwanese; (3) includes Chamorro; (4) county does not meet population threshold but is shown in order to allow inclusion of city

Place	Total population 5 years and over who speak English-only at home	Asian population 5 years and over	Asians 5 years and over who speak English-only at home	NHPI[1] population 5 years and over	NHPIs[1] 5 years and over who speak English-only at home	Asian Indian	Bangladeshi	Cambodian	Chinese[2]	Fijian	Filipino	Guamanian[3]	Hawaiian, Native	Hmong	Indonesian	Japanese	Korean	Laotian	Malaysian	Pakistani	Samoan	Sri Lankan	Taiwanese	Thai	Tongan	Vietnamese
WEST VIRGINIA	1,661,036 97.31	8,829	2,593 29.37 29.37 0.16	366	209 57.10 57.10 0.01	511 21.64 19.71 5.79 0.03	-	-	203 13.29 7.83 2.30 0.01	-	605 38.63 23.33 6.85 0.04	-	-	-	-	211 24.20 8.14 2.39 0.01	491 57.97 18.94 5.56 0.03	-	-	28 9.82 1.08 0.32 <0.01	-	-	-	-	-	103 26.89 3.97 1.17 0.01
Cabell County	88,938 97.25	710	210 29.58 29.58 0.24	-	-	-	-	-	-	-	-	-	-	-	-	-	-	-	-	-	-	-	-	-	-	-
Harrison County	62,816 96.95	388	88 22.68 22.68 0.14	-	-	-	-	-	-	-	-	-	-	-	-	-	-	-	-	-	-	-	-	-	-	-
Kanawha County	182,783 96.88	1,509	368 24.39 24.39 0.20	-	-	50 9.52 13.59 3.31 0.03	-	-	-	-	-	-	-	-	-	-	-	-	-	-	-	-	-	-	-	-
Monongalia County	72,548 93.24	1,813	388 21.40 21.40 0.53	-	-	66 13.10 17.01 3.64 0.09	-	-	67 11.47 17.27 3.70 0.09	-	-	-	-	-	-	-	-	-	-	-	-	-	-	-	-	-
Putnam County	47,151 97.75	245	120 48.98 48.98 0.25	-	-	-	-	-	-	-	-	-	-	-	-	-	-	-	-	-	-	-	-	-	-	-
Raleigh County	72,162 96.36	635	146 22.99 22.99 0.20	-	-	-	-	-	-	-	-	-	-	-	-	-	-	-	-	-	-	-	-	-	-	-
Wood County	81,252 98.06	355	166 46.76 46.76 0.20	-	-	-	-	-	-	-	-	-	-	-	-	-	-	-	-	-	-	-	-	-	-	-
WISCONSIN	4,653,361 92.66	75,007	13,053 17.40 17.40 0.28	1,418	915 64.53 64.53 0.02	1,969 19.41 15.08 2.63 0.04	-	128 21.99 0.98 0.17 <0.01	1,409 16.10 10.79 1.88 0.03	-	2,233 43.64 17.11 2.98 0.05	291 74.62 31.80 20.52 0.01	320 79.40 34.97 22.57 0.01	1,031 3.78 7.90 1.37 0.02	69 17.56 0.53 0.09 <0.01	1,222 42.28 9.36 1.63 0.03	2,752 42.95 21.08 3.67 0.06	361 9.56 2.77 0.48 0.01	-	105 12.08 0.80 0.14 <0.01	-	-	97 15.06 0.74 0.13 <0.01	210 24.91 1.61 0.28 <0.01	-	592 16.43 4.54 0.79 0.01
Brown County	196,085 92.89	4,181	527 12.60 12.60 0.27	-	-	25 9.26 4.74 0.60 0.01	-	-	-	-	-	-	-	66 3.09 12.52 1.58 0.03	-	-	-	69 15.68 13.09 1.65 0.04	-	-	-	-	-	-	-	-

Notes: Please refer to the User's Guide for an explanation of data; data is arranged alphabetically by state, then county, then city within each county; table includes counties with populations greater than 49,999 unless noted and cities with populations greater than 9,999 whose Asian and/or NHPI population rates are greater than the national average; (1) Native Hawaiian and other Pacific Islander; (2) excludes Taiwanese; (3) includes Chamorro; (4) county does not meet population threshold but is shown in order to allow inclusion of city

Place	Total population 5 years and over who speak English-only at home	Asian population 5 years and over	Asians 5 years and over who speak English-only at home	NHPI[1] population 5 years and over	NHPIs[1] 5 years and over who speak English-only at home	Asian Indian	Bangladeshi	Cambodian	Chinese[2]	Fijian	Filipino	Guamanian[3]	Hawaiian, Native	Hmong	Indonesian	Japanese	Korean	Laotian	Malaysian	Pakistani	Samoan	Sri Lankan	Taiwanese	Thai	Tongan	Vietnamese
Chippewa County	50,227 96.96	411	128 31.14 31.14 0.25	-	-	-	-	-	-	-	-	-	-	102 33.22 79.69 24.82 0.20	-	-	-	-	-	-	-	-	-	-	-	-
Columbia County	46,995 95.44	160	54 33.75 33.75 0.11	-	-	-	-	-	-	-	-	-	-	-	-	-	-	-	-	-	-	-	-	-	-	-
Dane County	363,563 90.65	13,245	2,609 19.70 19.70 0.72	-	-	486 23.93 18.63 3.67 0.13	-	-	457 15.14 17.52 3.45 0.13	-	302 46.97 11.58 2.28 0.08	-	-	97 4.88 3.72 0.73 0.03	-	223 28.77 8.55 1.68 0.06	507 28.71 19.43 3.83 0.14	23 7.10 0.88 0.17 0.01	-	-	-	-	43 10.41 1.65 0.32 0.01	-	-	109 15.59 4.18 0.82 0.03
Madison (city)	171,925 87.28	10,921	1,851 16.95 16.95 1.08	-	-	321 23.48 17.34 2.94 0.19	-	-	367 13.60 19.83 3.36 0.21	-	196 43.85 10.59 1.79 0.11	-	-	41 2.59 2.22 0.38 0.02	-	162 24.36 8.75 1.48 0.09	382 24.25 20.64 3.50 0.22	-	-	-	-	-	40 9.76 2.16 0.37 0.02	-	-	95 15.37 5.13 0.87 0.06
Dodge County	77,107 95.44	239	74 30.96 30.96 0.10	-	-	-	-	-	-	-	-	-	-	-	-	-	-	-	-	-	-	-	-	-	-	-
Eau Claire County	82,293 93.85	2,137	295 13.80 13.80 0.36	-	-	-	-	-	-	-	-	-	-	47 3.67 15.93 2.20 0.06	-	-	-	-	-	-	-	-	-	-	-	-
Fond du Lac County	87,199 95.20	543	107 19.71 19.71 0.12	-	-	-	-	-	-	-	-	-	-	4 1.72 3.74 0.74 <0.01	-	-	-	-	-	-	-	-	-	-	-	-
Jefferson County	65,123 93.92	200	73 36.50 36.50 0.11	-	-	-	-	-	-	-	-	-	-	-	-	-	-	-	-	-	-	-	-	-	-	-
Kenosha County	125,839 90.30	1,302	367 28.19 28.19 0.29	-	-	-	-	-	-	-	-	-	-	-	-	-	-	-	-	-	-	-	-	-	-	-
La Crosse County	95,031 94.39	2,419	407 16.83 16.83 0.43	-	-	-	-	-	-	-	-	-	-	55 3.36 13.51 2.27 0.06	-	-	-	-	-	-	-	-	-	-	-	-

Notes: Please refer to the User's Guide for an explanation of data; data is arranged alphabetically by state, then county, then city within each county; table includes counties with populations greater than 49,999 unless noted and cities with populations greater than 9,999 whose Asian and/or NHPI population rates are greater than the national average; (1) Native Hawaiian and other Pacific Islander; (2) excludes Taiwanese; (3) includes Chamorro; (4) county does not meet population threshold but is shown in order to allow inclusion of city

Place	Total population 5 years and over who speak English-only at home	Asian population 5 years and over	Asians 5 years and over who speak English-only at home	NHPI[1] population 5 years and over	NHPIs[1] 5 years and over who speak English-only at home	Asian Indian	Bangladeshi	Cambodian	Chinese[2]	Fijian	Filipino	Guamanian[3]	Hawaiian, Native	Hmong	Indonesian	Japanese	Korean	Laotian	Malaysian	Pakistani	Samoan	Sri Lankan	Taiwanese	Thai	Tongan	Vietnamese
La Crosse (city)	45,645 92.95	1,657	230 13.88 13.88 0.50	-	-	-	-	-	-	-	-	-	-	19 1.68 8.26 1.15 0.04	-	-	-	-	-	-	-	-	-	-	-	-
Manitowoc County	74,004 94.73	1,325	148 11.17 11.17 0.20	-	-	-	-	-	-	-	-	-	-	55 6.48 37.16 4.15 0.07	-	-	-	-	-	-	-	-	-	-	-	-
Marathon County	109,020 92.62	4,572	185 4.05 4.05 0.17	-	-	-	-	-	-	-	-	-	-	64 1.76 34.59 1.40 0.06	-	-	-	-	-	-	-	-	-	-	-	-
Wausau (city)	31,099 86.45	3,691	120 3.25 3.25 0.39	-	-	-	-	-	-	-	-	-	-	64 2.09 53.33 1.73 0.21	-	-	-	-	-	-	-	-	-	-	-	-
Milwaukee County	758,473 86.87	20,232	3,154 15.59 15.59 0.42	444	252 56.76 56.76 0.03	548 16.21 17.37 2.71 0.07	-	-	279 13.55 8.85 1.38 0.04	-	618 41.76 19.59 3.05 0.08	-	-	287 4.36 9.10 1.42 0.04	-	371 51.74 11.76 1.83 0.05	485 39.27 15.38 2.40 0.06	126 7.84 3.99 0.62 0.02	-	11 3.24 0.35 0.05 <0.01	-	-	-	-	-	99 7.91 3.14 0.49 0.01
Outagamie County	140,883 94.04	3,138	342 10.90 10.90 0.24	-	-	101 25.19 29.53 3.22 0.07	-	-	-	-	-	-	-	32 1.59 9.36 1.02 0.02	-	-	-	-	-	-	-	-	-	-	-	-
Appleton (city)	59,752 91.49	2,693	254 9.43 9.43 0.43	-	-	-	-	-	-	-	-	-	-	49 2.49 19.29 1.82 0.08	-	-	-	-	-	-	-	-	-	-	-	-
Ozaukee County	72,795 94.27	609	142 23.32 23.32 0.20	-	-	-	-	-	-	-	-	-	-	-	-	-	-	-	-	-	-	-	-	-	-	-
Portage County	59,193 93.59	1,187	172 14.49 14.49 0.29	-	-	-	-	-	-	-	-	-	-	43 5.40 25.00 3.62 0.07	-	-	-	-	-	-	-	-	-	-	-	-
Stevens Point (city)	21,293 91.35	965	94 9.74 9.74 0.44	-	-	-	-	-	-	-	-	-	-	37 5.32 39.36 3.83 0.17	-	-	-	-	-	-	-	-	-	-	-	-

Notes: Please refer to the User's Guide for an explanation of data; data is arranged alphabetically by state, then county, then city within each county; table includes counties with populations greater than 49,999 unless noted and cities with populations greater than 9,999 whose Asian and/or NHPI population rates are greater than the national average; (1) Native Hawaiian and other Pacific Islander; (2) excludes Taiwanese; (3) includes Chamorro; (4) county does not meet population threshold but is shown in order to allow inclusion of city

Place	Total population 5 years and over who speak English-only at home	Asian population 5 years and over	Asians 5 years and over who speak English-only at home	NHPI[1] population 5 years and over	NHPIs[1] 5 years and over who speak English-only at home	Asian Indian	Bangladeshi	Cambodian
Racine County	160,992 91.63	1,188	308 25.93 25.93 0.19	-	-	-	-	-
Rock County	133,296 93.90	1,201	301 25.06 25.06 0.23	-	-	-	-	-
St. Croix County	56,913 96.91	242	108 44.63 44.63 0.19	-	-	-	-	-
Sauk County	49,062 94.97	191	80 41.88 41.88 0.16	-	-	-	-	-
Sheboygan County	96,241 91.32	3,099	210 6.78 6.78 0.22	-	-	-	-	-
Sheboygan (city)	40,688 86.08	2,819	168 5.96 5.96 0.41	-	-	-	-	-
Walworth County	80,321 90.97	537	99 18.44 18.44 0.12	-	-	-	-	-
Washington County	104,005 94.99	486	222 45.68 45.68 0.21	-	-	-	-	-
Waukesha County	317,650 94.07	4,480	1,127 25.16 25.16 0.35	-	-	174 11.87 15.44 3.88 0.05	-	-
Winnebago County	138,914 94.26	2,156	251 11.64 11.64 0.18	-	-	-	-	-

Place	Chinese[2]	Fijian	Filipino	Guamanian[3]	Hawaiian, Native	Hmong	Indonesian	Japanese	Korean
Racine County	-	-	-	-	-	-	-	-	-
Rock County	-	-	-	-	-	-	-	-	-
St. Croix County	-	-	-	-	-	-	-	-	-
Sauk County	-	-	-	-	-	-	-	-	-
Sheboygan County	-	-	-	-	-	48 2.24 22.86 1.55 0.05	-	-	-
Sheboygan (city)	-	-	-	-	-	47 2.31 27.98 1.67 0.12	-	-	-
Walworth County	-	-	-	-	-	-	-	-	-
Washington County	-	-	-	-	-	-	-	-	-
Waukesha County	263 26.54 23.34 5.87 0.08	-	99 26.68 8.78 2.21 0.03	-	-	-	-	-	245 43.44 21.74 5.47 0.08
Winnebago County	-	-	-	-	-	53 4.16 21.12 2.46 0.04	-	-	-

Place	Laotian	Malaysian	Pakistani	Samoan	Sri Lankan	Taiwanese	Thai	Tongan	Vietnamese
Racine County	-	-	-	-	-	-	-	-	-
Rock County	-	-	-	-	-	-	-	-	-
St. Croix County	-	-	-	-	-	-	-	-	-
Sauk County	-	-	-	-	-	-	-	-	-
Sheboygan County	-	-	-	-	-	-	-	-	-
Sheboygan (city)	-	-	-	-	-	-	-	-	-
Walworth County	-	-	-	-	-	-	-	-	-
Washington County	-	-	-	-	-	-	-	-	-
Waukesha County	-	-	-	-	-	-	-	-	-
Winnebago County	-	-	-	-	-	-	-	-	-

Notes: Please refer to the User's Guide for an explanation of data; data is arranged alphabetically by state, then county, then city within each county; table includes counties with populations greater than 49,999 unless noted and cities with populations greater than 9,999 whose Asian and/or NHPI population rates are greater than the national average; (1) Native Hawaiian and other Pacific Islander; (2) excludes Taiwanese; (3) includes Chamorro; (4) county does not meet population threshold but is shown in order to allow inclusion of city

Place	Total population 5 years and over who speak English-only at home	Asian population 5 years and over	Asians 5 years and over who speak English-only at home	NHPI[1] population 5 years and over	NHPIs[1] 5 years and over who speak English-only at home	Asian Indian	Bangladeshi	Cambodian	Chinese[2]	Fijian	Filipino	Guamanian[3]	Hawaiian, Native	Hmong	Indonesian	Japanese	Korean	Laotian	Malaysian	Pakistani	Samoan	Sri Lankan	Taiwanese	Thai	Tongan	Vietnamese
Wood County	67,693 95.50	1,054	159 15.09 15.09 0.23	-	-	-	-	-	-	-	-	-	-	27 4.82 16.98 2.56 0.04	-	-	-	-	-	-	-	-	-	-	-	-
WYOMING	433,324 93.63	2,808	1,109 39.49 39.49 0.26	-	-	96 24.43 8.66 3.42 0.02	-	-	128 22.03 11.54 4.56 0.03	-	216 44.72 19.48 7.69 0.05	-	-	-	-	252 48.46 22.72 8.97 0.06	170 40.09 15.33 6.05 0.04	-	-	-	-	-	-	-	-	-
Laramie County	70,193 91.96	740	276 37.30 37.30 0.39	-	-	-	-	-	-	-	-	-	-	-	-	-	-	-	-	-	-	-	-	-	-	-
Natrona County	59,107 94.87	401	237 59.10 59.10 0.40	-	-	-	-	-	-	-	-	-	-	-	-	-	-	-	-	-	-	-	-	-	-	-

Notes: Please refer to the User's Guide for an explanation of data; data is arranged alphabetically by state, then county, then city within each county; table includes counties with populations greater than 49,999 unless noted and cities with populations greater than 9,999 whose Asian and/or NHPI population rates are greater than the national average; (1) Native Hawaiian and other Pacific Islander; (2) excludes Taiwanese; (3) includes Chamorro; (4) county does not meet population threshold but is shown in order to allow inclusion of city

Foreign Born

(Universe: Total Population)

Place	Total foreign-born population	Total Asian population	Asians who are foreign born	Total NHPI[1] population	NHPIs[1] who are foreign born	Asian Indian	Bangladeshi	Cambodian	Chinese[2]	Fijian	Filipino	Guamanian[3]	Hawaiian, Native	Hmong	Indonesian	Japanese	Korean	Laotian	Malaysian	Pakistani	Samoan	Sri Lankan	Taiwanese	Thai	Tongan	Vietnamese
	31,107,889	10,171,820	7,012,202	378,782	75,477	1,240,755	34,353	117,164	1,621,997	7,968	1,261,611	6,842	3,019	94,583	30,788	314,178	833,454	114,300	9,510	117,723	17,858	15,767	94,685	86,242	14,221	844,893
	11.05		68.94		19.93	75.40	82.92	65.81	70.51	77.62	67.68	12.41	2.16	55.62	82.84	39.52	77.70	68.12	88.79	75.51	20.95	82.64	77.14	77.80	51.37	76.10
UNITED STATES						17.69	0.49	1.67	23.13	10.56	17.99	9.07	4.00	1.35	0.44	4.48	11.89	1.63	0.14	1.68	23.66	0.22	1.35	1.23	18.84	12.05
			68.94		19.93	12.20	0.34	1.15	15.95	2.10	12.40	1.81	0.80	0.93	0.30	3.09	8.19	1.12	0.09	1.16	4.71	0.16	0.93	0.85	3.75	8.31
			22.54		0.24	3.99	0.11	0.38	5.21	0.03	4.06	0.02	0.01	0.30	0.10	1.01	2.68	0.37	0.03	0.38	0.06	0.05	0.30	0.28	0.05	2.72
	87,772	29,908	21,998	1,187	154	4,929	-	315	4,414	-	1,625	59	-	-	-	1,365	3,272	620	-	313	-	-	-	536	-	3,218
	1.97		73.55		12.97	73.72		55.75	77.32		66.57	13.92				72.15	81.31	74.79		81.30				86.31		69.49
ALABAMA						22.41		1.43	20.07		7.39	38.31				6.21	14.87	2.82		1.42				2.44		14.63
			73.55		12.97	16.48		1.05	14.76		5.43	4.97				4.56	10.94	2.07		1.05				1.79		10.76
			25.06		0.18	5.62		0.36	5.03		1.85	0.07				1.56	3.73	0.71		0.36				0.61		3.67
	2,957	535	341	-	-	-	-	-	-	-	-	-	-	-	-	-	-	-	-	-	-	-	-	-	-	-
	2.11		63.74																							
Baldwin County																										
			63.74																							
			11.53																							
	1,907	671	452	-	-	-	-	-	-	-	-	-	-	-	-	-	-	-	-	-	-	-	-	-	-	-
	1.70		67.36																							
Calhoun County																										
			67.36																							
			23.70																							
	1,687	361	257	-	-	-	-	-	-	-	-	-	-	-	-	-	-	-	-	-	-	-	-	-	-	-
	1.63		71.19																							
Etowah County																										
			71.19																							
			15.23																							
	1,418	500	408	-	-	-	-	-	-	-	-	-	-	-	-	-	-	-	-	-	-	-	-	-	-	-
	1.60		81.60																							
Houston County																										
			81.60																							
			28.77																							
	15,492	5,793	4,219	-	-	1,063	-	-	1,401	-	-	-	-	-	-	-	388	-	-	-	-	-	-	-	-	559
	2.34		72.83			75.87			74.05								83.62									64.40
Jefferson County						25.20			33.21								9.20									13.25
			72.83			18.35			24.18								6.70									9.65
			27.23			6.86			9.04								2.50									3.61
	3,089	1,834	1,402	-	-	-	-	-	525	-	-	-	-	-	-	-	-	-	-	-	-	-	-	-	-	-
	2.68		76.44						83.47																	
Lee County									37.45																	
			76.44						28.63																	
			45.39						17.00																	
	10,976	4,706	3,522	-	-	1,146	-	-	522	-	-	-	-	-	-	-	777	-	-	-	-	-	-	-	-	296
	3.97		74.84			77.43			75.65								80.27									78.51
Madison County						32.54			14.82								22.06									8.40
			74.84			24.35			11.09								16.51									6.29
			32.09			10.44			4.76								7.08									2.70

Notes: Please refer to the User's Guide for an explanation of data; data is arranged alphabetically by state, then county, then city within each county; table includes counties with populations greater than 49,999 unless noted and cities with populations greater than 9,999 whose Asian and/or NHPI population rates are greater than the national average; (1) Native Hawaiian and other Pacific Islander; (2) excludes Taiwanese; (3) includes Chamorro; (4) county does not meet population threshold but is shown in order to allow inclusion of city

Place	Total foreign-born population	Total Asian population	Asians who are foreign born	Total NHPI[1] population	NHPIs[1] who are foreign born	Asian Indian	Bangladeshi	Cambodian	Chinese[2]	Fijian	Filipino	Guamanian[3]	Hawaiian, Native	Hmong	Indonesian	Japanese	Korean	Laotian	Malaysian	Pakistani	Samoan	Sri Lankan	Taiwanese	Thai	Tongan	Vietnamese
Mobile County	9,133	5,256	3,715	-	-	460	-	186	538	-	201	-	-	-	-	-	-	222	-	-	-	-	-	-	-	1,434
	2.28		70.68			79.31		47.81	80.42		54.47							70.70								69.85
						12.38		5.01	14.48		5.41							5.98								38.60
			70.68			8.75		3.54	10.24		3.82							4.22								27.28
			40.68			5.04		2.04	5.89		2.20							2.43								15.70
Montgomery County	4,443	1,779	1,453	-	-	-	-	-	-	-	-	-	-	-	-	-	-	-	-	-	-	-	-	-	-	-
	1.99		81.68																							
			81.68																							
			32.70																							
Morgan County	3,007	571	392	-	-	-	-	-	-	-	-	-	-	-	-	-	-	-	-	-	-	-	-	-	-	-
	2.71		68.65																							
			68.65																							
			13.04																							
Shelby County	3,389	1,006	704	-	-	304	-	-	-	-	-	-	-	-	-	-	-	-	-	-	-	-	-	-	-	-
	2.37		69.98			78.55																				
						43.18																				
			69.98			30.22																				
			20.77			8.97																				
Tuscaloosa County	3,459	1,533	1,228	-	-	-	-	-	-	-	-	-	-	-	-	-	-	-	-	-	-	-	-	-	-	-
	2.10		80.10																							
			80.10																							
			35.50																							
ALASKA	37,170	25,496	17,216	3,122	717	379	-	-	1,157	-	8,444	-	7	242	-	577	3,540	881	-	-	323	-	-	624	183	738
	5.93		67.52		22.97	69.41			73.98		67.62		1.40	46.36		40.49	77.73	64.40			21.06			79.80	43.68	76.16
						2.20			6.72		49.05		0.98	1.41		3.35	20.56	5.12			45.05			3.62	25.52	4.29
			67.52		22.97	1.49			4.54		33.12		0.22	0.95		2.26	13.88	3.46			10.35			2.45	5.86	2.89
			46.32		1.93	1.02			3.11		22.72		0.02	0.65		1.55	9.52	2.37			0.87			1.68	0.49	1.99
Anchorage Borough	21,278	14,266	9,539	2,027	484	202	-	-	649	-	3,361	-	-	242	-	392	2,648	793	-	-	260	-	-	451	-	322
	8.17		66.87		23.88	63.92			75.12		66.74			46.36		44.29	76.80	62.69			21.52			78.16		66.53
						2.12			6.80		35.23			2.54		4.11	27.76	8.31			53.72			4.73		3.38
			66.87		23.88	1.42			4.55		23.56			1.70		2.75	18.56	5.56			12.83			3.16		2.26
			44.83		2.27	0.95			3.05		15.80			1.14		1.84	12.44	3.73			1.22			2.12		1.51
Fairbanks North Star Borough	3,353	2,001	1,500	-	-	-	-	-	285	-	411	-	-	-	-	-	463	-	-	-	-	-	-	-	-	-
	4.05		74.96						80.51		72.11						84.49									
									19.00		27.40						30.87									
			74.96						14.24		20.54						23.14									
			44.74						8.50		12.26						13.81									
Juneau City and Borough	1,760	1,396	929	-	-	-	-	-	-	-	730	-	-	-	-	-	-	-	-	-	-	-	-	-	-	-
	5.73		66.55								70.06															
											78.58															
			66.55								52.29															
			52.78								41.48															
Matanuska-Susitna Borough	1,524	385	274	-	-	-	-	-	-	-	-	-	-	-	-	-	-	-	-	-	-	-	-	-	-	-
	2.57		71.17																							
			71.17																							
			17.98																							

Notes: Please refer to the User's Guide for an explanation of data; data is arranged alphabetically by state, then county, then city within each county; table includes counties with populations greater than 49,999 unless noted and cities with populations greater than 9,999 whose Asian and/or NHPI population rates are greater than the national average; (1) Native Hawaiian and other Pacific Islander; (2) excludes Taiwanese; (3) includes Chamorro; (4) county does not meet population threshold but is shown in order to allow inclusion of city

Place	Total foreign-born population	Total Asian population	Asians who are foreign born	Total NHPI[1] population	NHPIs[1] who are foreign born	Asian Indian	Bangladeshi	Cambodian	Chinese[2]	Fijian	Filipino	Guamanian[3]	Hawaiian, Native	Hmong	Indonesian	Japanese	Korean	Laotian	Malaysian	Pakistani	Samoan	Sri Lankan	Taiwanese	Thai	Tongan	Vietnamese
ARIZONA	656,183	91,223	62,366	6,166	1,406	10,816	-	752	14,047	-	10,546	145	155	-	469	3,841	7,698	599	-	542	204	-	536	1,237	324	8,970
	12.79		68.37		22.80	74.54		60.65	66.67		65.08	11.46	7.81		81.85	51.58	77.48	67.23		80.65	24.00		67.51	75.84	51.10	76.64
						17.34		1.21	22.52		16.91	10.31	11.02		0.75	6.16	12.34	0.96		0.87	14.51		0.86	1.98	23.04	14.38
			68.37		22.80	11.86		0.82	15.40		11.56	2.35	2.51		0.51	4.21	8.44	0.66		0.59	3.31		0.59	1.36	5.25	9.83
			9.50		0.21	1.65		0.11	2.14		1.61	0.02	0.02		0.07	0.59	1.17	0.09		0.08	0.03		0.08	0.19	0.05	1.37
Cochise County	14,438	1,960	1,381	-	-	-	-	-	-	-	254	-	-	-	-	-	661	-	-	-	-	-	-	-	-	-
	12.26		70.46								59.21						86.18									
											18.39						47.86									
			70.46								12.96						33.72									
			9.57								1.76						4.58									
Coconino County	5,051	894	691	-	-	-	-	-	-	-	-	-	-	-	-	-	-	-	-	-	-	-	-	-	-	-
	4.34		77.29																							
			77.29																							
			13.68																							
Maricopa County	441,240	66,294	45,429	3,811	1,066	8,412	-	698	10,598	-	7,747	56	116	-	325	2,327	4,770	423	-	414	162	-	425	892	316	6,753
	14.36		68.53		27.97	74.52		58.85	68.35		65.10	8.66	10.46		78.88	47.73	78.88	70.38		79.62	29.29		66.20	77.84	59.96	75.76
						18.52		1.54	23.33		17.05	5.25	10.88		0.72	5.12	10.50	0.93		0.91	15.20		0.94	1.96	29.64	14.86
			68.53		27.97	12.69		1.05	15.99		11.69	1.47	3.04		0.49	3.51	7.20	0.64		0.62	4.25		0.64	1.35	8.29	10.19
			10.30		0.24	1.91		0.16	2.40		1.76	0.01	0.03		0.07	0.53	1.08	0.10		0.09	0.04		0.10	0.20	0.07	1.53
Chandler (city)	22,785	7,460	4,986	-	-	1,037	-	-	1,400	-	691	-	-	-	-	-	-	-	-	-	-	-	-	-	-	730
	12.92		66.84			66.82			69.03		59.42															76.52
						20.80			28.08		13.86															14.64
			66.84			13.90			18.77		9.26															9.79
			21.88			4.55			6.14		3.03															3.20
Gilbert (town)	7,271	4,016	2,508	-	-	491	-	-	749	-	418	-	-	-	-	-	-	-	-	-	-	-	-	-	-	-
	6.61		62.45			65.82			63.26		56.79															
						19.58			29.86		16.67															
			62.45			12.23			18.65		10.41															
			34.49			6.75			10.30		5.75															
Mesa (city)	44,546	6,022	4,200	647	138	510	-	-	746	-	952	-	-	-	-	270	593	-	-	-	-	-	-	-	-	638
	11.21		69.74		21.33	86.29			73.50		64.67					46.08	82.59									84.62
						12.14			17.76		22.67					6.43	14.12									15.19
			69.74		21.33	8.47			12.39		15.81					4.48	9.85									10.59
			9.43		0.31	1.14			1.67		2.14					0.61	1.33									1.43
Phoenix (city)	257,325	25,613	17,391	1,745	577	3,279	-	345	3,722	-	3,292	-	56	-	-	792	1,496	-	-	-	-	-	-	-	-	3,282
	19.48		67.90		33.07	73.97		62.39	66.85		65.41		11.13			50.06	75.67									74.04
						18.85		1.98	21.40		18.93		9.71			4.55	8.60									18.87
			67.90		33.07	12.80		1.35	14.53		12.85		3.21			3.09	5.84									12.81
			6.76		0.22	1.27		0.13	1.45		1.28		0.02			0.31	0.58									1.28
Tempe (city)	20,422	7,920	5,923	-	-	1,645	-	-	1,462	-	404	-	-	-	-	297	591	-	-	-	-	-	-	-	-	614
	12.89		74.79			87.13			75.36		68.36					46.48	85.65									76.75
						27.77			24.68		6.82					5.01	9.98									10.37
			74.79			20.77			18.46		5.10					3.75	7.46									7.75
			29.00			8.06			7.16		1.98					1.45	2.89									3.01
Mohave County	9,114	921	607	-	-	-	-	-	-	-	-	-	-	-	-	-	-	-	-	-	-	-	-	-	-	-
	5.88		65.91																							
			65.91																							
			6.66																							

Notes: Please refer to the User's Guide for an explanation of data; data is arranged alphabetically by state, then county, then city within each county; table includes counties with populations greater than 49,999 unless noted and cities with populations greater than 9,999 whose Asian and/or NHPI population rates are greater than the national average; (1) Native Hawaiian and other Pacific Islander; (2) excludes Taiwanese; (3) includes Chamorro; (4) county does not meet population threshold but is shown in order to allow inclusion of city

Place	Total foreign-born population	Total Asian population	Asians who are foreign born	Total NHPI[1] population	NHPIs[1] who are foreign born	Asian Indian	Bangladeshi	Cambodian	Chinese[2]	Fijian	Filipino	Guamanian[3]	Hawaiian, Native	Hmong	Indonesian	Japanese	Korean	Laotian	Malaysian	Pakistani	Samoan	Sri Lankan	Taiwanese	Thai	Tongan	Vietnamese
Pima County	100,050 11.86	16,907	11,528 68.18 68.18 11.52	1,084	140 12.92 12.92 0.14	1,532 76.87 13.29 9.06 1.53	-	-	2,926 62.36 25.38 17.31 2.92	-	1,509 62.85 13.09 8.93 1.51	-	35 7.51 25.00 3.23 0.03	-	-	919 61.51 7.97 5.44 0.92	1,668 74.66 14.47 9.87 1.67	-	-	-	-	-	-	-	-	1,797 79.27 15.59 10.63 1.80
Tucson (city)	69,476 14.28	11,641	8,145 69.97 69.97 11.72	734	106 14.44 14.44 0.15	1,044 77.74 12.82 8.97 1.50	-	-	2,089 65.77 25.65 17.95 3.01	-	1,067 60.94 13.10 9.17 1.54	-	-	-	-	671 67.37 8.24 5.76 0.97	1,009 79.08 12.39 8.67 1.45	-	-	-	-	-	-	-	-	1,444 77.72 17.73 12.40 2.08
Pinal County	16,243 9.04	993	667 67.17 67.17 4.11	-	-	-	-	-	-	-	-	-	-	-	-	-	-	-	-	-	-	-	-	-	-	-
Yavapai County	9,945 5.94	847	549 64.82 64.82 5.52	-	-	-	-	-	-	-	-	-	-	-	-	-	-	-	-	-	-	-	-	-	-	-
Yuma County	38,479 24.05	1,345	878 65.28 65.28 2.28	-	-	-	-	-	-	-	232 52.02 26.42 17.25 0.60	-	-	-	-	-	-	-	-	-	-	-	-	-	-	-
ARKANSAS	73,690 2.76	19,081	13,756 72.09 72.09 18.67	1,534	733 47.78 47.78 0.99	1,959 72.72 14.24 10.27 2.66	-	-	2,212 74.83 16.08 11.59 3.00	-	1,535 66.65 11.16 8.04 2.08	-	0 0.00 0.00 0.00 0.00	-	-	787 71.94 5.72 4.12 1.07	1,134 75.80 8.24 5.94 1.54	1,938 71.46 14.09 10.16 2.63	-	-	-	-	-	217 74.32 1.58 1.14 0.29	-	2,800 72.46 20.35 14.67 3.80
Benton County	9,856 6.42	1,495	1,127 75.38 75.38 11.43	-	-	364 86.87 32.30 24.35 3.69	-	-	-	-	-	-	-	-	-	-	-	-	-	-	-	-	-	-	-	283 73.70 25.11 18.93 2.87
Craighead County	1,617 1.97	517	310 59.96 59.96 19.17	-	-	-	-	-	-	-	-	-	-	-	-	-	-	-	-	-	-	-	-	-	-	-
Crawford County	1,264 2.37	631	420 66.56 66.56 33.23	-	-	-	-	-	-	-	-	-	-	-	-	-	-	-	-	-	-	-	-	-	-	-
Faulkner County	1,428 1.66	526	367 69.77 69.77 25.70	-	-	-	-	-	-	-	-	-	-	-	-	-	-	-	-	-	-	-	-	-	-	-

Notes: Please refer to the User's Guide for an explanation of data; data is arranged alphabetically by state, then county, then city within each county; table includes counties with populations greater than 49,999 unless noted and cities with populations greater than 9,999 whose Asian and/or NHPI population rates are greater than the national average; (1) Native Hawaiian and other Pacific Islander; (2) excludes Taiwanese; (3) includes Chamorro; (4) county does not meet population threshold but is shown in order to allow inclusion of city

Place	Total foreign-born population	Total Asian population	Asians who are foreign born	Total NHPI[1] population	NHPIs[1] who are foreign born	Asian Indian	Bangladeshi	Cambodian	Chinese[2]	Fijian	Filipino	Guamanian[3]	Hawaiian, Native	Hmong	Indonesian	Japanese	Korean	Laotian	Malaysian	Pakistani	Samoan	Sri Lankan	Taiwanese	Thai	Tongan	Vietnamese
Jefferson County	950 1.13	443	363 81.94 81.94 38.21	-	-	-	-	-	-	-	-	-	-	-	-	-	-	-	-	-	-	-	-	-	-	-
Pulaski County	10,836 3.00	4,335	3,243 74.81 74.81 29.93	-	-	726 75.08 22.39 16.75 6.70	-	-	718 82.53 22.14 16.56 6.63	-	444 66.47 13.69 10.24 4.10	-	-	-	-	-	-	-	-	-	-	-	-	-	-	-
Saline County	1,119 1.34	454	298 65.64 65.64 26.63	-	-	-	-	-	-	-	-	-	-	-	-	-	-	-	-	-	-	-	-	-	-	-
Sebastian County	7,922 6.88	3,581	2,608 72.83 72.83 32.92	-	-	-	-	-	-	-	-	-	-	-	-	-	-	901 78.08 34.55 25.16 11.37	-	-	-	-	-	-	-	1,324 73.80 50.77 36.97 16.71
Fort Smith (city)	7,420 9.23	3,277	2,438 74.40 74.40 32.86	-	-	-	-	-	-	-	-	-	-	-	-	-	-	889 79.16 36.46 27.13 11.98	-	-	-	-	-	-	-	1,255 73.26 51.48 38.30 16.91
Washington County	11,706 7.42	2,607	1,855 71.15 71.15 15.85	756	537 71.03 71.03 4.59	-	-	-	571 72.74 30.78 21.90 4.88	-	-	-	-	-	-	-	-	357 64.79 19.25 13.69 3.05	-	-	-	-	-	-	-	-
Springdale (city)	7,220 15.68	739	488 66.04 66.04 6.76	694	502 72.33 72.33 6.95	-	-	-	-	-	-	-	-	-	-	-	-	261 62.00 53.48 35.32 3.61	-	-	-	-	-	-	-	-
CALIFORNIA	8,864,255 26.17	3,682,975	2,474,465 67.19 67.19 27.92	113,858	29,763 26.14 26.14 0.34	228,246 74.32 9.22 6.20 2.57	2,273 82.71 0.09 0.06 0.03	45,198 63.42 1.83 1.23 0.51	623,398 68.20 25.19 16.93 7.03	6,518 77.50 21.90 5.72 0.07	621,092 67.51 25.10 16.86 7.01	1,710 8.35 5.75 1.50 0.02	907 4.61 3.05 0.80 0.01	37,725 54.91 1.52 1.02 0.43	12,811 78.17 0.52 0.35 0.14	104,729 36.22 4.23 2.84 1.18	261,782 76.16 10.58 7.11 2.95	37,489 65.89 1.52 1.02 0.42	1,501 85.24 0.06 0.04 0.02	14,016 70.66 0.57 0.38 0.16	8,647 22.23 29.05 7.59 0.10	4,437 81.92 0.18 0.12 0.05	50,582 79.56 2.04 1.37 0.57	27,645 76.46 1.12 0.75 0.31	6,504 53.46 21.85 5.71 0.07	339,401 76.02 13.72 9.22 3.83
Alameda County	392,656 27.20	293,807	198,143 67.44 67.44 50.46	9,188	2,737 29.79 29.79 0.70	32,267 77.15 16.28 10.98 8.22	-	2,422 62.05 1.22 0.82 0.62	71,625 66.96 36.15 24.38 18.24	1,070 73.14 39.09 11.65 0.27	47,048 67.52 23.74 16.01 11.98	77 5.87 2.81 0.84 0.02	47 3.66 1.72 0.51 0.01	-	417 64.85 0.21 0.14 0.11	3,869 31.14 1.95 1.32 0.99	10,584 72.84 5.34 3.60 2.70	1,886 59.65 0.95 0.64 0.48	-	1,523 76.96 0.77 0.52 0.39	276 11.47 10.08 3.00 0.07	-	2,993 76.06 1.51 1.02 0.76	1,107 76.19 0.56 0.38 0.28	900 49.13 32.88 9.80 0.23	17,185 73.03 8.67 5.85 4.38
Alameda (city)	18,830 26.06	18,698	12,298 65.77 65.77 65.31	796	122 15.33 15.33 0.65	819 76.40 6.66 4.38 4.35	-	-	4,550 61.21 37.00 24.33 24.16	-	4,270 70.61 34.72 22.84 22.68	-	-	-	-	225 32.05 1.83 1.20 1.19	952 77.34 7.74 5.09 5.06	-	-	-	-	-	-	-	-	934 71.68 7.59 5.00 4.96

Notes: Please refer to the User's Guide for an explanation of data; data is arranged alphabetically by state, then county, then city within each county; table includes counties with populations greater than 49,999 unless noted and cities with populations greater than 9,999 whose Asian and/or NHPI population rates are greater than the national average; (1) Native Hawaiian and other Pacific Islander; (2) excludes Taiwanese; (3) includes Chamorro; (4) county does not meet population threshold but is shown in order to allow inclusion of city

Place	Total foreign-born population	Total Asian population	Asians who are foreign born	Total NHPI[1] population	NHPIs[1] who are foreign born	Asian Indian	Bangladeshi	Cambodian	Chinese[2]	Fijian	Filipino	Guamanian[3]	Hawaiian, Native	Hmong	Indonesian	Japanese	Korean	Laotian	Malaysian	Pakistani	Samoan	Sri Lankan	Taiwanese	Thai	Tongan	Vietnamese
Albany (city)	4,759	4,246	2,952	-	-	249	-	-	1,506	-	-	-	-	-	-	309	422	-	-	-	-	-	-	-	-	-
	28.94		69.52			75.23			73.18							48.06	81.15									
						8.43			51.02							10.47	14.30									
			69.52			5.86			35.47							7.28	9.94									
			62.03			5.23			31.65							6.49	8.87									
Ashland (cdp)	6,135	3,127	2,326	-	-	-	-	-	749	-	985	-	-	-	-	-	-	-	-	-	-	-	-	-	-	-
	29.54		74.38						77.62		74.28															
									32.20		42.35															
			74.38						23.95		31.50															
			37.91						12.21		16.06															
Berkeley (city)	20,923	16,660	8,809	-	-	975	-	-	3,752	-	652	-	-	-	-	696	1,007	-	-	-	-	-	264	-	-	665
	20.36		52.88			55.12			51.92		55.97					32.16	62.12						64.71			71.35
						11.07			42.59		7.40					7.90	11.43						3.00			7.55
			52.88			5.85			22.52		3.91					4.18	6.04						1.58			3.99
			42.10			4.66			17.93		3.12					3.33	4.81						1.26			3.18
Castro Valley (cdp)	9,450	7,317	4,340	-	-	579	-	-	1,856	-	836	-	-	-	-	173	579	-	-	-	-	-	-	-	-	-
	16.46		59.31			69.34			53.78		70.55					27.81	77.41									
						13.34			42.76		19.26					3.99	13.34									
			59.31			7.91			25.37		11.43					2.36	7.91									
			45.93			6.13			19.64		8.85					1.83	6.13									
Cherryland (cdp)	4,167	1,182	789	-	-	-	-	-	-	-	449	-	-	-	-	-	-	-	-	-	-	-	-	-	-	-
	30.24		66.75								71.84															
											56.91															
			66.75								37.99															
			18.93								10.78															
Dublin (city)	4,070	2,965	1,888	-	-	448	-	-	543	-	556	-	-	-	-	-	-	-	-	-	-	-	-	-	-	-
	13.55		63.68			78.32			59.74		70.56															
						23.73			28.76		29.45															
			63.68			15.11			18.31		18.75															
			46.39			11.01			13.34		13.66															
Fremont (city)	75,494	74,753	53,672	670	173	16,148	-	-	18,898	-	7,617	-	-	-	-	430	2,763	-	-	859	-	-	1,923	-	-	3,110
	37.11		71.80		25.82	78.05			71.88		66.82					27.67	69.40			77.95			78.43			71.58
						30.09			35.21		14.19					0.80	5.15			1.60			3.58			5.79
			71.80		25.82	21.60			25.28		10.19					0.58	3.70			1.15			2.57			4.16
			71.09		0.23	21.39			25.03		10.09					0.57	3.66			1.14			2.55			4.12
Hayward (city)	48,619	26,106	17,960	2,357	885	2,926	-	-	2,577	578	8,360	-	-	-	-	520	648	-	-	-	82	-	-	-	-	1,896
	34.75		68.80		37.55	82.05			70.14	68.56	66.56					40.91	79.22				14.09					72.73
						16.29			14.35	65.31	46.55					2.90	3.61				9.27					10.56
			68.80		37.55	11.21			9.87	24.52	32.02					1.99	2.48				3.48					7.26
			36.94		1.82	6.02			5.30	1.19	17.19					1.07	1.33				0.17					3.90
Livermore (city)	8,952	4,261	2,510	-	-	491	-	-	473	-	883	-	-	-	-	-	-	-	-	-	-	-	-	-	-	312
	12.19		58.91			81.16			62.16		54.37															66.38
						19.56			18.84		35.18															12.43
			58.91			11.52			11.10		20.72															7.32
			28.04			5.48			5.28		9.86															3.49
Newark (city)	13,422	9,249	6,217	-	-	1,262	-	-	1,107	-	2,153	-	-	-	-	-	457	-	-	-	-	-	-	-	-	542
	31.60		67.22			78.43			65.35		61.96						83.85									73.64
						20.30			17.81		34.63						7.35									8.72
			67.22			13.64			11.97		23.28						4.94									5.86
			46.32			9.40			8.25		16.04						3.40									4.04

Notes: Please refer to the User's Guide for an explanation of data; data is arranged alphabetically by state, then county, then city within each county; table includes counties with populations greater than 49,999 unless noted and cities with populations greater than 9,999 whose Asian and/or NHPI population rates are greater than the national average; (1) Native Hawaiian and other Pacific Islander; (2) excludes Taiwanese; (3) includes Chamorro; (4) county does not meet population threshold but is shown in order to allow inclusion of city

Place	Total foreign-born population	Total Asian population	Asians who are foreign born	Total NHPI[1] population	NHPIs[1] who are foreign born	Asian Indian	Bangladeshi	Cambodian	Chinese[2]	Fijian	Filipino	Guamanian[3]	Hawaiian, Native	Hmong	Indonesian	Japanese	Korean	Laotian	Malaysian	Pakistani	Samoan	Sri Lankan	Taiwanese	Thai	Tongan	Vietnamese
Oakland (city)	106,116	60,110	41,156	2,581	854	1,350	-	1,732	22,188	-	4,579	-	-	-	-	634	1,362	1,364	-	-	-	-	-	-	619	6,289
	26.56		68.47		33.09	78.49		59.01	70.39		68.58					30.16	77.12	57.10							47.18	76.55
						3.28		4.21	53.91		11.13					1.54	3.31	3.31							72.48	15.28
			68.47		33.09	2.25		2.88	36.91		7.62					1.05	2.27	2.27							23.98	10.46
			38.78		0.80	1.27		1.63	20.91		4.32					0.60	1.28	1.29							0.58	5.93
Piedmont (city)	1,239	1,805	789	-	-	-	-	-	625	-	-	-	-	-	-	-	-	-	-	-	-	-	-	-	-	-
	11.31		43.71						45.96																	
									79.21																	
			43.71						34.63																	
			63.68						50.44																	
Pleasanton (city)	9,057	7,392	4,286	-	-	1,260	-	-	1,463	-	509	-	-	-	-	95	412	-	-	-	-	-	-	-	-	-
	14.25		57.98			79.70			55.93		60.89					13.75	63.98									
						29.40			34.13		11.88					2.22	9.61									
			57.98			17.05			19.79		6.89					1.29	5.57									
			47.32			13.91			16.15		5.62					1.05	4.55									
San Leandro (city)	21,728	18,317	12,447	608	34	609	-	-	5,505	-	4,365	-	-	-	-	149	307	-	-	-	-	-	-	-	-	917
	27.40		67.95		5.59	86.75			66.96		70.27					28.17	67.03									71.09
						4.89			44.23		35.07					1.20	2.47									7.37
			67.95		5.59	3.32			30.05		23.83					0.81	1.68									5.01
			57.29		0.16	2.80			25.34		20.09					0.69	1.41									4.22
San Lorenzo (cdp)	4,583	3,479	2,255	-	-	-	-	-	586	-	985	-	-	-	-	-	-	-	-	-	-	-	-	-	-	209
	20.88		64.82						60.10		71.38															69.44
									25.99		43.68															9.27
			64.82						16.84		28.31															6.01
			49.20						12.79		21.49															4.56
Union City (city)	29,419	29,442	20,534	634	267	4,044	-	-	4,236	-	9,073	-	-	-	-	194	774	-	-	-	-	-	-	-	-	1,337
	44.00		69.74		42.11	75.21			71.09		69.11					39.84	82.08									65.32
						19.69			20.63		44.19					0.94	3.77									6.51
			69.74		42.11	13.74			14.39		30.82					0.66	2.63									4.54
			69.80		0.91	13.75			14.40		30.84					0.66	2.63									4.54
Butte County	15,668	6,553	4,339	-	-	325	-	-	519	-	200	-	-	1,914	-	271	-	431	-	-	-	-	-	-	-	-
	7.71		66.21			75.23			72.79		55.40			67.78		43.29		78.22								
						7.49			11.96		4.61			44.11		6.25		9.93								
			66.21			4.96			7.92		3.05			29.21		4.14		6.58								
			27.69			2.07			3.31		1.28			12.22		1.73		2.75								
Chico (city)	5,324	2,278	1,593	-	-	-	-	-	306	-	-	-	-	586	-	-	-	-	-	-	-	-	-	-	-	-
	8.96		69.93						74.82					80.38												
									19.21					36.79												
			69.93						13.43					25.72												
			29.92						5.75					11.01												
Oroville (city)	890	729	480	-	-	-	-	-	-	-	-	-	-	290	-	-	-	-	-	-	-	-	-	-	-	-
	6.86		65.84											60.04												
														60.42												
			65.84											39.78												
			53.93											32.58												
Contra Costa County	180,488	103,198	63,111	3,391	990	8,213	-	-	16,136	346	21,949	11	34	-	386	2,336	3,227	2,932	-	560	177	-	1,055	490	202	4,030
	19.02		61.16		29.19	73.34			58.28	64.31	63.74	2.02	5.71		81.61	28.16	71.84	68.58		79.10	23.32		83.66	77.17	44.79	74.19
						13.01			25.57	34.95	34.78	1.11	3.43		0.61	3.70	5.11	4.65		0.89	17.88		1.67	0.78	20.40	6.39
			61.16		29.19	7.96			15.64	10.20	21.27	0.32	1.00		0.37	2.26	3.13	2.84		0.54	5.22		1.02	0.47	5.96	3.91
			34.97		0.55	4.55			8.94	0.19	12.16	0.01	0.02		0.21	1.29	1.79	1.62		0.31	0.10		0.58	0.27	0.11	2.23

Notes: Please refer to the User's Guide for an explanation of data; data is arranged alphabetically by state, then county, then city within each county; table includes counties with populations greater than 49,999 unless noted and cities with populations greater than 9,999 whose Asian and/or NHPI population rates are greater than the national average; (1) Native Hawaiian and other Pacific Islander; (2) excludes Taiwanese; (3) includes Chamorro; (4) county does not meet population threshold but is shown in order to allow inclusion of city

Place	Total foreign-born population	Total Asian population	Asians who are foreign born	Total NHPI[1] population	NHPIs[1] who are foreign born	Asian Indian	Bangladeshi	Cambodian	Chinese[2]	Fijian	Filipino	Guamanian[3]	Hawaiian, Native	Hmong	Indonesian	Japanese	Korean	Laotian	Malaysian	Pakistani	Samoan	Sri Lankan	Taiwanese	Thai	Tongan	Vietnamese
Alamo (cdp)	1,350 8.92	863	333 38.59 38.59 24.67	-	-	-	-	-	-	-	-	-	-	-	-	-	-	-	-	-	-	-	-	-	-	-
Antioch (city)	12,014 13.23	6,674	3,737 55.99 55.99 31.11	408	82 20.10 20.10 0.68	220 62.32 5.89 3.30 1.83	-	-	618 55.18 16.54 9.26 5.14	-	1,962 55.79 52.50 29.40 16.33	-	-	-	-	-	-	-	-	-	-	-	-	-	-	356 74.95 9.53 5.33 2.96
Bay Point (cdp)	6,867 32.07	2,471	1,701 68.84 68.84 24.77	-	-	-	-	-	-	-	855 70.20 50.26 34.60 12.45	-	-	-	-	-	-	-	-	-	-	-	-	-	-	-
Blackhawk-Camino-Tass. (cdp)	1,799 18.05	1,682	917 54.52 54.52 50.97	-	-	-	-	-	465 48.29 50.71 27.65 25.85	-	-	-	-	-	-	-	-	-	-	-	-	-	-	-	-	-
Clayton (city)	887 8.22	596	234 39.26 39.26 26.38	-	-	-	-	-	-	-	-	-	-	-	-	-	-	-	-	-	-	-	-	-	-	-
Concord (city)	28,478 23.40	11,117	7,232 65.05 65.05 25.40	468	209 44.66 44.66 0.73	1,222 79.45 16.90 10.99 4.29	-	-	1,601 61.39 22.14 14.40 5.62	-	2,671 64.52 36.93 24.03 9.38	-	-	-	-	300 35.13 4.15 2.70 1.05	359 78.38 4.96 3.23 1.26	-	-	-	-	-	-	-	-	524 79.51 7.25 4.71 1.84
Danville (town)	4,655 11.05	3,588	1,862 51.90 51.90 40.00	-	-	302 65.80 16.22 8.42 6.49	-	-	704 45.27 37.81 19.62 15.12	-	316 68.70 16.97 8.81 6.79	-	-	-	-	-	-	-	-	-	-	-	-	-	-	-
El Cerrito (city)	5,904 25.47	5,634	3,414 60.60 60.60 57.83	-	-	281 74.93 8.23 4.99 4.76	-	-	1,727 70.00 50.59 30.65 29.25	-	297 62.13 8.70 5.27 5.03	-	-	-	-	349 28.33 10.22 6.19 5.91	-	-	-	-	-	-	-	-	-	-
El Sobrante (cdp)	1,841 15.86	1,349	864 64.05 64.05 46.93	-	-	256 70.91 29.63 18.98 13.91	-	-	-	-	-	-	-	-	-	-	-	-	-	-	-	-	-	-	-	-
Hercules (city)	6,253 32.40	8,291	4,957 59.79 59.79 79.27	-	-	428 63.31 8.63 5.16 6.84	-	-	1,032 64.38 20.82 12.45 16.50	-	2,873 58.21 57.96 34.65 45.95	-	-	-	-	-	-	-	-	-	-	-	-	-	-	-

Notes: Please refer to the User's Guide for an explanation of data; data is arranged alphabetically by state, then county, then city within each county; table includes counties with populations greater than 49,999 unless noted and cities with populations greater than 9,999 whose Asian and/or NHPI population rates are greater than the national average; (1) Native Hawaiian and other Pacific Islander; (2) excludes Taiwanese; (3) includes Chamorro; (4) county does not meet population threshold but is shown in order to allow inclusion of city

Place	Total foreign-born population	Total Asian population	Asians who are foreign born	Total NHPI[1] population	NHPIs[1] who are foreign born	Asian Indian	Bangladeshi	Cambodian	Chinese[2]	Fijian	Filipino	Guamanian[3]	Hawaiian, Native	Hmong	Indonesian	Japanese	Korean	Laotian	Malaysian	Pakistani	Samoan	Sri Lankan	Taiwanese	Thai	Tongan	Vietnamese
Lafayette (city)	2,542	1,660	942	-	-	-	-	-	498	-	-	-	-	-	-	-	-	-	-	-	-	-	-	-	-	-
	10.83		56.75						61.18																	
									52.87																	
			56.75						30.00																	
			37.06						19.59																	
Martinez (city)	3,453	2,319	1,370	-	-	-	-	-	267	-	612	-	-	-	-	-	-	-	-	-	-	-	-	-	-	-
	9.55		59.08						55.28		62.83															
									19.49		44.67															
			59.08						11.51		26.39															
			39.68						7.73		17.72															
Moraga (town)	2,563	2,163	1,209	-	-	-	-	-	687	-	-	-	-	-	-	-	-	-	-	-	-	-	-	-	-	-
	15.40		55.89						55.85																	
									56.82																	
			55.89						31.76																	
			47.17						26.80																	
Orinda (city)	2,120	1,524	634	-	-	-	-	-	346	-	-	-	-	-	-	-	-	-	-	-	-	-	-	-	-	-
	12.15		41.60						38.75																	
									54.57																	
			41.60						22.70																	
			29.91						16.32																	
Pinole (city)	4,201	4,095	2,560	-	-	-	-	-	531	-	1,348	-	-	-	-	-	-	-	-	-	-	-	-	-	-	-
	21.66		62.52						60.34		66.96															
									20.74		52.66															
			62.52						12.97		32.92															
			60.94						12.64		32.09															
Pittsburg (city)	14,105	7,248	4,706	554	160	711	-	-	281	-	3,151	-	-	-	-	-	-	-	-	-	-	-	-	-	-	-
	24.82		64.93		28.88	74.45			62.44		66.00															
						15.11			5.97		66.96															
			64.93		28.88	9.81			3.88		43.47															
			33.36		1.13	5.04			1.99		22.34															
Pleasant Hill (city)	4,608	3,286	1,973	-	-	-	-	-	513	-	507	-	-	-	-	-	375	-	-	-	-	-	-	-	-	-
	14.03		60.04						55.88		60.43						71.84									
									26.00		25.70						19.01									
			60.04						15.61		15.43						11.41									
			42.82						11.13		11.00						8.14									
Richmond (city)	25,751	12,088	7,812	401	136	831	-	-	2,007	-	1,758	-	-	-	-	280	342	1,645	-	-	-	-	-	-	-	338
	25.82		64.63		33.92	74.73			64.47		63.33					31.71	74.03	69.15								73.00
						10.64			25.69		22.50					3.58	4.38	21.06								4.33
			64.63		33.92	6.87			16.60		14.54					2.32	2.83	13.61								2.80
			30.34		0.53	3.23			7.79		6.83					1.09	1.33	6.39								1.31
San Pablo (city)	12,331	4,912	3,547	-	-	441	-	-	-	-	1,297	-	-	-	-	-	-	803	-	-	-	-	-	-	-	506
	40.94		72.21			72.89					74.58							71.95								71.27
						12.43					36.57							22.64								14.27
			72.21			8.98					26.40							16.35								10.30
			28.76			3.58					10.52							6.51								4.10
San Ramon (city)	7,308	6,804	3,967	-	-	1,007	-	-	1,463	-	567	-	-	-	-	70	-	-	-	-	-	-	-	-	-	-
	16.43		58.30			72.29			54.37		60.38					15.52										
						25.38			36.88		14.29					1.76										
			58.30			14.80			21.50		8.33					1.03										
			54.28			13.78			20.02		7.76					0.96										

Notes: Please refer to the User's Guide for an explanation of data; data is arranged alphabetically by state, then county, then city within each county; table includes counties with populations greater than 49,999 unless noted and cities with populations greater than 9,999 whose Asian and/or NHPI population rates are greater than the national average; (1) Native Hawaiian and other Pacific Islander; (2) excludes Taiwanese; (3) includes Chamorro; (4) county does not meet population threshold but is shown in order to allow inclusion of city

Place	Total foreign-born population	Total Asian population	Asians who are foreign born	Total NHPI[1] population	NHPIs[1] who are foreign born	Asian Indian	Bangladeshi	Cambodian	Chinese[2]	Fijian	Filipino	Guamanian[3]	Hawaiian, Native	Hmong	Indonesian	Japanese	Korean	Laotian	Malaysian	Pakistani	Samoan	Sri Lankan	Taiwanese	Thai	Tongan	Vietnamese
	11,747	6,201	3,909	-	-	455	-	-	1,649	-	884	-	-	-	-	271	355	-	-	-	-	-	-	-	-	-
	18.19		63.04			81.40			62.32		72.70					32.53	72.30									
Walnut Creek (city)						11.64			42.18		22.61					6.93	9.08									
			63.04			7.34			26.59		14.26					4.37	5.72									
			33.28			3.87			14.04		7.53					2.31	3.02									
	11,183	3,055	1,631	-	-	-	-	-	-	-	919	-	-	-	-	69	-	-	-	-	-	-	-	-	-	-
	7.15		53.39								67.62					13.64										
El Dorado County											56.35					4.23										
			53.39								30.08					2.26										
			14.58								8.22					0.62										
	904	658	298	-	-	-	-	-	-	-	-	-	-	-	-	-	-	-	-	-	-	-	-	-	-	-
	5.00		45.29																							
El Dorado Hills (cdp)																										
			45.29																							
			32.96																							
	5,314	1,415	940	-	-	-	-	-	-	-	729	-	-	-	-	-	-	-	-	-	-	-	-	-	-	-
	22.40		66.43								74.16															
South Lake Tahoe (city)											77.55															
			66.43								51.52															
			17.69								13.72															
	168,717	63,895	35,757	652	102	4,824	-	2,326	2,713	-	3,817	-	-	13,173	-	956	943	4,037	-	-	-	-	-	-	-	1,492
	21.11		55.96		15.64	69.26		59.14	55.98		61.48			54.78		16.72	70.69	64.39								70.21
Fresno County						13.49		6.51	7.59		10.67			36.84		2.67	2.64	11.29								4.17
			55.96		15.64	7.55		3.64	4.25		5.97			20.62		1.50	1.48	6.32								2.34
			21.19		0.06	2.86		1.38	1.61		2.26			7.81		0.57	0.56	2.39								0.88
	5,463	4,429	2,117	-	-	-	-	-	-	-	332	-	-	808	-	98	-	-	-	-	-	-	-	-	-	-
	8.01		47.80								48.82			44.91		17.88										
Clovis (city)											15.68			38.17		4.63										
			47.80								7.50			18.24		2.21										
			38.75								6.08			14.79		1.79										
	86,937	48,485	28,363	-	-	2,561	-	2,103	2,294	-	2,818	-	-	11,388	-	599	712	3,558	-	-	-	-	-	-	-	1,228
	20.35		58.50			68.86		58.24	61.63		63.70			55.98		22.51	75.91	64.90								71.06
Fresno (city)						9.03		7.41	8.09		9.94			40.15		2.11	2.51	12.54								4.33
			58.50			5.28		4.34	4.73		5.81			23.49		1.24	1.47	7.34								2.53
			32.62			2.95		2.42	2.64		3.24			13.10		0.69	0.82	4.09								1.41
	6,650	782	297	-	-	-	-	-	-	-	-	-	-	-	-	-	-	-	-	-	-	-	-	-	-	-
	32.01		37.98																							
Reedley (city)																										
			37.98																							
			4.47																							
	5,749	1,859	1,015	-	-	-	-	-	-	-	-	-	-	-	-	85	-	-	-	-	-	-	-	-	-	-
	4.54		54.60													29.72										
Humboldt County																8.37										
			54.60													4.57										
			17.66													1.48										
	45,783	2,819	1,762	-	-	-	-	-	372	-	411	-	-	-	-	-	422	-	-	-	-	-	-	-	-	-
	32.16		62.50						62.73		46.65						85.60									
Imperial County									21.11		23.33						23.95									
			62.50						13.20		14.58						14.97									
			3.85						0.81		0.90						0.92									

Notes: Please refer to the User's Guide for an explanation of data; data is arranged alphabetically by state, then county, then city within each county; table includes counties with populations greater than 49,999 unless noted and cities with populations greater than 9,999 whose Asian and/or NHPI population rates are greater than the national average; (1) Native Hawaiian and other Pacific Islander; (2) excludes Taiwanese; (3) includes Chamorro; (4) county does not meet population threshold but is shown in order to allow inclusion of city

Place	Total foreign-born population	Total Asian population	Asians who are foreign born	Total NHPI[1] population	NHPIs[1] who are foreign born	Asian Indian	Bangladeshi	Cambodian	Chinese[2]	Fijian	Filipino	Guamanian[3]	Hawaiian, Native	Hmong	Indonesian	Japanese	Korean	Laotian	Malaysian	Pakistani	Samoan	Sri Lankan	Taiwanese	Thai	Tongan	Vietnamese
Kern County	111,944	21,562	13,838	778	179	3,197	-	270	1,084	-	6,858	-	-	-	-	344	864	-	-	-	-	-	-	-	-	428
	16.92		64.18		23.01	76.96		62.65	52.19		65.00					32.98	68.41									65.95
						23.10		1.95	7.83		49.56					2.49	6.24									3.09
			64.18		23.01	14.83		1.25	5.03		31.81					1.60	4.01									1.98
			12.36		0.16	2.86		0.24	0.97		6.13					0.31	0.77									0.38
Bakersfield (city)	33,631	10,499	6,588	468	161	2,389	-	-	803	-	1,577	-	-	-	-	179	624	-	-	-	-	-	-	-	-	322
	13.59		62.75		34.40	75.87			53.32		57.58					27.58	64.60									73.35
						36.26			12.19		23.94					2.72	9.47									4.89
			62.75		34.40	22.75			7.65		15.02					1.70	5.94									3.07
			19.59		0.48	7.10			2.39		4.69					0.53	1.86									0.96
Delano (city)	14,893	6,027	4,188	-	-	-	-	-	-	-	3,932	-	-	-	-	-	-	-	-	-	-	-	-	-	-	-
	38.21		69.49								69.98															
											93.89															
			69.49								65.24															
			28.12								26.40															
Ridgecrest (city)	1,751	1,036	598	-	-	-	-	-	-	-	322	-	-	-	-	-	-	-	-	-	-	-	-	-	-	-
	6.95		57.72								65.85															
											53.85															
			57.72								31.08															
			34.15								18.39															
Kings County	20,757	3,771	2,375	-	-	-	-	-	-	-	1,699	-	-	-	-	-	-	-	-	-	-	-	-	-	-	-
	16.03		62.98								69.04															
											71.54															
			62.98								45.05															
			11.44								8.19															
Lemoore (city)	2,830	1,434	957	-	-	-	-	-	-	-	701	-	-	-	-	-	-	-	-	-	-	-	-	-	-	-
	14.49		66.74								65.39															
											73.25															
			66.74								48.88															
			33.82								24.77															
Lake County	3,822	529	287	-	-	-	-	-	-	-	-	-	-	-	-	-	-	-	-	-	-	-	-	-	-	-
	6.55		54.25																							
			54.25																							
			7.51																							
Los Angeles County	3,449,444	1,134,263	790,502	27,221	7,042	43,419	1,113	19,526	211,034	380	189,387	576	225	188	4,553	39,898	143,977	2,179	504	3,462	3,399	2,018	28,379	15,010	1,188	61,039
	36.24		69.69		25.87	73.61	84.00	64.97	72.43	77.08	72.28	18.35	5.12	42.73	80.93	35.45	77.64	69.13	94.38	73.21	25.08	82.67	81.68	76.72	52.20	78.00
						5.49	0.14	2.47	26.70	5.40	23.96	8.18	3.20	0.02	0.58	5.05	18.21	0.28	0.06	0.44	48.27	0.26	3.59	1.90	16.87	7.72
			69.69		25.87	3.83	0.10	1.72	18.61	1.40	16.70	2.12	0.83	0.02	0.40	3.52	12.69	0.19	0.04	0.31	12.49	0.18	2.50	1.32	4.36	5.38
			22.92		0.20	1.26	0.03	0.57	6.12	0.01	5.49	0.02	0.01	0.01	0.13	1.16	4.17	0.06	0.01	0.10	0.10	0.06	0.82	0.44	0.03	1.77
Agoura Hills (city)	2,751	1,242	650	-	-	-	-	-	-	-	-	-	-	-	-	-	-	-	-	-	-	-	-	-	-	-
	13.54		52.33																							
			52.33																							
			23.63																							
Alhambra (city)	43,632	40,563	31,813	-	-	408	-	-	21,005	-	1,360	-	-	-	-	629	673	-	-	-	-	-	1,412	-	-	3,580
	50.76		78.43			79.38			79.73		71.24					41.88	76.30						90.63			81.46
						1.28			66.03		4.27					1.98	2.12						4.44			11.25
			78.43			1.01			51.78		3.35					1.55	1.66						3.48			8.83
			72.91			0.94			48.14		3.12					1.44	1.54						3.24			8.20

Notes: Please refer to the User's Guide for an explanation of data; data is arranged alphabetically by state, then county, then city within each county; table includes counties with populations greater than 49,999 unless noted and cities with populations greater than 9,999 whose Asian and/or NHPI population rates are greater than the national average; (1) Native Hawaiian and other Pacific Islander; (2) excludes Taiwanese; (3) includes Chamorro; (4) county does not meet population threshold but is shown in order to allow inclusion of city

Place	Total foreign-born population	Total Asian population	Asians who are foreign born	Total NHPI[1] population	NHPIs[1] who are foreign born	Asian Indian	Bangladeshi	Cambodian	Chinese[2]	Fijian	Filipino	Guamanian[3]	Hawaiian, Native	Hmong	Indonesian	Japanese	Korean	Laotian	Malaysian	Pakistani	Samoan	Sri Lankan	Taiwanese	Thai	Tongan	Vietnamese
Altadena (cdp)	7,966 18.72	1,758	896 50.97 50.97 11.25	-	-	-	-	-	-	-	227 72.29 25.33 12.91 2.85	-	-	-	-	107 17.07 11.94 6.09 1.34	-	-	-	-	-	-	-	-	-	-
Arcadia (city)	23,074 43.58	23,996	18,206 75.87 75.87 78.90	-	-	484 73.67 2.66 2.02 2.10	-	-	10,627 75.95 58.37 44.29 46.06	-	609 75.75 3.35 2.54 2.64	-	-	-	-	688 59.93 3.78 2.87 2.98	1,486 76.88 8.16 6.19 6.44	-	-	-	-	-	3,013 80.28 16.55 12.56 13.06	-	-	-
Artesia (city)	7,508 45.84	4,524	3,511 77.61 77.61 46.76	-	-	425 88.73 12.10 9.39 5.66	-	-	506 79.43 14.41 11.18 6.74	-	1,347 75.29 38.37 29.77 17.94	-	-	-	-	-	726 82.97 20.68 16.05 9.67	-	-	-	-	-	-	-	-	-
Avocado Heights (cdp)	5,571 36.80	1,362	808 59.32 59.32 14.50	-	-	-	-	-	-	-	-	-	-	-	-	-	-	-	-	-	-	-	-	-	-	-
Azusa (city)	15,093 34.02	2,430	1,904 78.35 78.35 12.62	-	-	-	-	-	-	-	960 80.47 50.42 39.51 6.36	-	-	-	-	-	-	-	-	-	-	-	-	-	-	-
Baldwin Park (city)	34,642 45.73	9,017	6,571 72.87 72.87 18.97	-	-	-	-	-	2,160 77.28 32.87 23.95 6.24	-	2,747 67.54 41.80 30.46 7.93	-	-	-	-	-	-	-	-	-	-	-	-	-	-	760 80.00 11.57 8.43 2.19
Bellflower (city)	20,679 28.39	7,181	5,291 73.68 73.68 25.59	-	-	-	-	391 73.22 7.39 5.44 1.89	-	-	2,679 73.34 50.63 37.31 12.96	-	-	-	-	-	727 78.26 13.74 10.12 3.52	-	-	-	-	-	-	277 71.21 5.24 3.86 1.34	-	-
Beverly Hills (city)	12,937 38.24	2,570	1,946 75.72 75.72 15.04	-	-	-	-	-	362 70.57 18.60 14.09 2.80	-	-	-	-	-	-	-	661 72.48 33.97 25.72 5.11	-	-	-	-	-	-	-	-	-
Burbank (city)	31,212 31.11	9,089	6,445 70.91 70.91 20.65	-	-	705 73.98 10.94 7.76 2.26	-	-	637 70.78 9.88 7.01 2.04	-	2,444 74.04 37.92 26.89 7.83	-	-	-	-	250 39.94 3.88 2.75 0.80	1,547 78.13 24.00 17.02 4.96	-	-	-	-	-	-	-	-	340 64.89 5.28 3.74 1.09
Calabasas (city)	3,844 19.12	1,652	1,014 61.38 61.38 26.38	-	-	-	-	-	354 69.69 34.91 21.43 9.21	-	-	-	-	-	-	-	-	-	-	-	-	-	-	-	-	-

Notes: Please refer to the User's Guide for an explanation of data; data is arranged alphabetically by state, then county, then city within each county; table includes counties with populations greater than 49,999 unless noted and cities with populations greater than 9,999 whose Asian and/or NHPI population rates are greater than the national average; (1) Native Hawaiian and other Pacific Islander; (2) excludes Taiwanese; (3) includes Chamorro; (4) county does not meet population threshold but is shown in order to allow inclusion of city

Place	Total foreign-born population	Total Asian population	Asians who are foreign born	Total NHPI[1] population	NHPIs[1] who are foreign born	Asian Indian	Bangladeshi	Cambodian	Chinese[2]	Fijian	Filipino	Guamanian[3]	Hawaiian, Native	Hmong	Indonesian	Japanese	Korean	Laotian	Malaysian	Pakistani	Samoan	Sri Lankan	Taiwanese	Thai	Tongan	Vietnamese
Carson (city)	29,432	20,156	13,898	1,929	212	-	-	-	259	-	12,245	-	-	-	-	99	-	-	-	-	194	-	-	-	-	288
	32.87		68.95		10.99				51.70		70.65					15.69					13.49					89.72
									1.86		88.11					0.71					91.51					2.07
			68.95		10.99				1.28		60.75					0.49					10.06					1.43
			47.22		0.72				0.88		41.60					0.34					0.66					0.98
Cerritos (city)	23,455	30,185	19,998	-	-	2,066	-	-	4,066	-	3,789	-	-	-	-	354	6,200	-	-	-	-	-	1,416	325	-	905
	45.54		66.25			70.13			70.21		66.18					17.64	70.22						79.06	69.74		71.83
						10.33			20.33		18.95					1.77	31.00						7.08	1.63		4.53
			66.25			6.84			13.47		12.55					1.17	20.54						4.69	1.08		3.00
			85.26			8.81			17.34		16.15					1.51	26.43						6.04	1.39		3.86
Citrus (cdp)	3,429	784	601	-	-	-	-	-	-	-	-	-	-	-	-	-	-	-	-	-	-	-	-	-	-	-
	32.20		76.66																							
			76.66																							
			17.53																							
Claremont (city)	5,378	3,983	2,319	-	-	330	-	-	686	-	-	-	-	-	-	-	347	-	-	-	-	-	-	-	-	-
	15.83		58.22			61.57			64.23								56.79									
						14.23			29.58								14.96									
			58.22			8.29			17.22								8.71									
			43.12			6.14			12.76								6.45									
Compton (city)	29,281	420	273	1,028	248	-	-	-	-	-	-	-	-	-	-	-	-	-	-	-	215	-	-	-	-	-
	31.41		65.00		24.12																21.92					
																					86.69					
			65.00		24.12																20.91					
			0.93		0.85																0.73					
Covina (city)	9,451	4,565	3,153	-	-	-	-	-	900	-	955	-	-	-	-	99	-	-	-	-	-	-	-	-	-	326
	20.05		69.07						77.12		70.58					24.81										73.76
									28.54		30.29					3.14										10.34
			69.07						19.72		20.92					2.17										7.14
			33.36						9.52		10.10					1.05										3.45
Culver City (city)	10,329	4,738	2,914	-	-	512	-	-	524	-	800	-	-	-	-	429	-	-	-	-	-	-	-	-	-	-
	26.61		61.50			82.45			67.79		80.16					31.22										
						17.57			17.98		27.45					14.72										
			61.50			10.81			11.06		16.88					9.05										
			28.21			4.96			5.07		7.75					4.15										
Diamond Bar (city)	21,587	23,831	16,449	-	-	1,626	-	-	5,463	-	2,006	-	-	-	-	225	4,080	-	-	-	-	-	1,651	-	-	455
	38.31		69.02			65.51			71.23		63.93					32.66	72.90						78.66			65.37
						9.89			33.21		12.20					1.37	24.80						10.04			2.77
			69.02			6.82			22.92		8.42					0.94	17.12						6.93			1.91
			76.20			7.53			25.31		9.29					1.04	18.90						7.65			2.11
Downey (city)	37,925	7,814	5,512	-	-	285	-	-	385	-	1,388	-	-	-	-	59	2,471	-	-	-	-	-	-	-	-	300
	35.34		70.54			63.19			75.05		72.10					15.65	77.73									72.82
						5.17			6.98		25.18					1.07	44.83									5.44
			70.54			3.65			4.93		17.76					0.76	31.62									3.84
			14.53			0.75			1.02		3.66					0.16	6.52									0.79
Duarte (city)	7,059	2,730	1,896	-	-	-	-	-	293	-	1,031	-	-	-	-	-	-	-	-	-	-	-	-	-	-	-
	32.85		69.45						66.74		73.07															
									15.45		54.38															
			69.45						10.73		37.77															
			26.86						4.15		14.61															

Notes: Please refer to the User's Guide for an explanation of data; data is arranged alphabetically by state, then county, then city within each county; table includes counties with populations greater than 49,999 unless noted and cities with populations greater than 9,999 whose Asian and/or NHPI population rates are greater than the national average; (1) Native Hawaiian and other Pacific Islander; (2) excludes Taiwanese; (3) includes Chamorro; (4) county does not meet population threshold but is shown in order to allow inclusion of city

Place	Total foreign-born population	Total Asian population	Asians who are foreign born	Total NHPI[1] population	NHPIs[1] who are foreign born	Asian Indian	Bangladeshi	Cambodian	Chinese[2]	Fijian	Filipino	Guamanian[3]	Hawaiian, Native	Hmong	Indonesian	Japanese	Korean	Laotian	Malaysian	Pakistani	Samoan	Sri Lankan	Taiwanese	Thai	Tongan	Vietnamese
East San Gabriel (cdp)	6,251 42.85	6,104	4,371 71.61 71.61 69.92	-	-	-	-	-	2,603 74.29 59.55 42.64 41.64	-	-	-	-	-	-	215 38.46 4.92 3.52 3.44	-	-	-	-	-	-	531 82.84 12.15 8.70 8.49	-	-	-
El Monte (city)	59,589 51.26	21,529	16,505 76.66 76.66 27.70	-	-	-	-	-	9,069 77.51 54.95 42.12 15.22	-	707 72.96 4.28 3.28 1.19	-	-	-	-	-	-	-	-	-	-	-	373 93.02 2.26 1.73 0.63	-	-	5,055 79.37 30.63 23.48 8.48
El Segundo (city)	1,973 12.35	1,063	731 68.77 68.77 37.05	-	-	-	-	-	-	-	-	-	-	-	-	-	-	-	-	-	-	-	-	-	-	-
Gardena (city)	18,986 32.84	15,458	8,222 53.19 53.19 43.31	-	-	-	-	-	613 69.58 7.46 3.97 3.23	-	1,215 68.76 14.78 7.86 6.40	-	-	-	-	1,688 25.25 20.53 10.92 8.89	3,045 81.31 37.03 19.70 16.04	-	-	-	-	-	-	-	-	1,043 80.79 12.69 6.75 5.49
Glendale (city)	106,119 54.41	31,944	23,776 74.43 74.43 22.41	-	-	773 79.69 3.25 2.42 0.73	-	-	1,747 64.42 7.35 5.47 1.65	-	8,932 77.27 37.57 27.96 8.42	-	-	-	-	808 48.04 3.40 2.53 0.76	9,626 77.16 40.49 30.13 9.07	-	-	-	-	-	-	361 85.95 1.52 1.13 0.34	-	788 82.77 3.31 2.47 0.74
Glendora (city)	7,034 14.15	3,254	2,146 65.95 65.95 30.51	-	-	384 72.05 17.89 11.80 5.46	-	-	607 69.93 28.29 18.65 8.63	-	562 67.96 26.19 17.27 7.99	-	-	-	-	-	-	-	-	-	-	-	-	-	-	-
Hacienda Heights (cdp)	21,341 40.18	19,225	13,976 72.70 72.70 65.49	-	-	-	-	-	6,845 75.04 48.98 35.60 32.07	-	979 72.95 7.00 5.09 4.59	-	-	-	-	405 30.45 2.90 2.11 1.90	1,889 73.47 13.52 9.83 8.85	-	-	-	-	-	2,409 83.79 17.24 12.53 11.29	-	-	421 87.34 3.01 2.19 1.97
Hawaiian Gardens (city)	6,805 45.63	1,292	988 76.47 76.47 14.52	-	-	-	-	-	-	-	-	-	-	-	-	-	614 81.32 62.15 47.52 9.02	-	-	-	-	-	-	-	-	-
Hawthorne (city)	27,932 33.27	5,948	4,273 71.84 71.84 15.30	546	158 28.94 28.94 0.57	411 85.45 9.62 6.91 1.47	-	-	402 73.90 9.41 6.76 1.44	-	1,741 78.21 40.74 29.27 6.23	-	-	-	-	66 14.70 1.54 1.11 0.24	-	-	-	-	-	-	-	-	-	1,115 75.49 26.09 18.75 3.99
Hermosa Beach (city)	1,490 8.08	864	297 34.38 34.38 19.93	-	-	-	-	-	-	-	-	-	-	-	-	-	-	-	-	-	-	-	-	-	-	-

Notes: Please refer to the User's Guide for an explanation of data; data is arranged alphabetically by state, then county, then city within each county; table includes counties with populations greater than 49,999 unless noted and cities with populations greater than 9,999 whose Asian and/or NHPI population rates are greater than the national average; (1) Native Hawaiian and other Pacific Islander; (2) excludes Taiwanese; (3) includes Chamorro; (4) county does not meet population threshold but is shown in order to allow inclusion of city

Place	Total foreign-born population	Total Asian population	Asians who are foreign born	Total NHPI[1] population	NHPIs[1] who are foreign born	Asian Indian	Bangladeshi	Cambodian	Chinese[2]	Fijian	Filipino	Guamanian[3]	Hawaiian, Native	Hmong	Indonesian	Japanese	Korean	Laotian	Malaysian	Pakistani	Samoan	Sri Lankan	Taiwanese	Thai	Tongan	Vietnamese
La Canada Flintridge (city)	3,973 19.49	3,981	2,384 59.88 59.88 60.01	-	-	-	-	-	416 54.10 17.45 10.45 10.47	-	-	-	-	-	-	148 38.85 6.21 3.72 3.73	1,458 65.38 61.16 36.62 36.70	-	-	-	-	-	-	-	-	-
La Crescenta-Montrose (cdp)	4,977 27.04	3,524	2,411 68.42 68.42 48.44	-	-	-	-	-	-	-	206 59.20 8.54 5.85 4.14	-	-	-	-	-	1,870 74.77 77.56 53.06 37.57	-	-	-	-	-	-	-	-	-
La Mirada (city)	10,626 22.71	6,968	4,847 69.56 69.56 45.61	-	-	369 71.10 7.61 5.30 3.47	-	-	440 62.32 9.08 6.31 4.14	-	1,555 70.68 32.08 22.32 14.63	-	-	-	-	74 18.97 1.53 1.06 0.70	1,819 78.61 37.53 26.11 17.12	-	-	-	-	-	-	-	-	-
La Puente (city)	17,850 43.53	2,883	2,204 76.45 76.45 12.35	-	-	-	-	-	633 71.77 28.72 21.96 3.55	-	799 79.74 36.25 27.71 4.48	-	-	-	-	-	-	-	-	-	-	-	-	-	-	-
La Verne (city)	4,602 14.45	2,372	1,504 63.41 63.41 32.68	-	-	-	-	-	-	-	544 62.17 36.17 22.93 11.82	-	-	-	-	-	-	-	-	-	-	-	-	-	-	-
Lakewood (city)	15,125 19.05	10,432	7,066 67.73 67.73 46.72	762	316 41.47 41.47 2.09	368 85.38 5.21 3.53 2.43	-	469 64.07 6.64 4.50 3.10	749 73.87 10.60 7.18 4.95	-	3,289 68.87 46.55 31.53 21.75	-	-	-	-	148 20.44 2.09 1.42 0.98	1,171 81.09 16.57 11.23 7.74	-	-	-	289 48.33 91.46 37.93 1.91	-	-	-	-	319 72.17 4.51 3.06 2.11
Lancaster (city)	15,476 13.03	4,596	2,977 64.77 64.77 19.24	-	-	461 72.26 15.49 10.03 2.98	-	-	328 65.86 11.02 7.14 2.12	-	1,255 60.34 42.16 27.31 8.11	-	-	-	-	-	-	-	-	-	-	-	-	-	-	-
Lawndale (city)	12,289 38.73	2,928	2,200 75.14 75.14 17.90	463	99 21.38 21.38 0.81	-	-	-	-	-	470 71.65 21.36 16.05 3.82	-	-	-	-	-	-	-	-	-	-	-	-	-	-	1,064 80.79 48.36 36.34 8.66
Lomita (city)	3,936 19.70	2,265	1,354 59.78 59.78 34.40	-	-	-	-	-	-	-	295 64.41 21.79 13.02 7.49	-	-	-	-	190 30.60 14.03 8.39 4.83	439 82.06 32.42 19.38 11.15	-	-	-	-	-	-	-	-	-
Long Beach (city)	132,168 28.65	55,040	35,706 64.87 64.87 27.02	5,145	1,375 26.72 26.72 1.04	851 71.39 2.38 1.55 0.64	-	11,037 62.32 30.91 20.05 8.35	2,000 63.78 5.60 3.63 1.51	-	12,598 70.14 35.28 22.89 9.53	-	-	-	-	1,193 33.27 3.34 2.17 0.90	1,304 75.12 3.65 2.37 0.99	426 57.41 1.19 0.77 0.32	-	-	1,002 26.84 72.87 19.48 0.76	-	-	455 75.33 1.27 0.83 0.34	-	3,877 76.42 10.86 7.04 2.93

Notes: Please refer to the User's Guide for an explanation of data; data is arranged alphabetically by state, then county, then city within each county; table includes counties with populations greater than 49,999 unless noted and cities with populations greater than 9,999 whose Asian and/or NHPI population rates are greater than the national average; (1) Native Hawaiian and other Pacific Islander; (2) excludes Taiwanese; (3) includes Chamorro; (4) county does not meet population threshold but is shown in order to allow inclusion of city

Place	Total foreign-born population	Total Asian population	Asians who are foreign born	Total NHPI[1] population	NHPIs[1] who are foreign born	Asian Indian	Bangladeshi	Cambodian	Chinese[2]	Fijian	Filipino	Guamanian[3]	Hawaiian, Native	Hmong	Indonesian	Japanese	Korean	Laotian	Malaysian	Pakistani	Samoan	Sri Lankan	Taiwanese	Thai	Tongan	Vietnamese
Los Angeles (city)	1,512,720	368,644	262,570	6,445	1,660	17,906	715	2,909	41,487	-	75,891	317	88	-	1,465	14,534	73,077	507	-	1,167	466	948	2,754	7,028	185	15,353
	40.94		71.23		25.76	74.21	86.04	69.13	69.07		74.40	27.59	5.46		81.84	39.54	80.05	73.58		69.63	22.68	78.48	82.80	77.38	54.09	78.70
						6.82	0.27	1.11	15.80		28.90	19.10	5.30		0.56	5.54	27.83	0.19		0.44	28.07	0.36	1.05	2.68	11.14	5.85
			71.23		25.76	4.86	0.19	0.79	11.25		20.59	4.92	1.37		0.40	3.94	19.82	0.14		0.32	7.23	0.26	0.75	1.91	2.87	4.16
			17.36		0.11	1.18	0.05	0.19	2.74		5.02	0.02	0.01		0.10	0.96	4.83	0.03		0.08	0.03	0.06	0.18	0.46	0.01	1.01
Manhattan Beach (city)	3,107	2,023	873	-	-	-	-	-	249	-	-	-	-	-	-	96	-	-	-	-	-	-	-	-	-	-
	9.13		43.15						44.62							15.74										
									28.52							11.00										
			43.15						12.31							4.75										
			28.10						8.01							3.09										
Monrovia (city)	7,916	2,480	1,788	-	-	-	-	-	537	-	678	-	-	-	-	-	-	-	-	-	-	-	-	-	-	-
	21.50		72.10						76.50		73.62															
									30.03		37.92															
			72.10						21.65		27.34															
			22.59						6.78		8.56															
Montebello (city)	23,520	7,022	3,881	-	-	-	-	-	1,497	-	626	-	-	-	-	303	558	-	-	-	-	-	-	-	-	-
	37.96		55.27						59.29		71.95					16.93	88.85									
									38.57		16.13					7.81	14.38									
			55.27						21.32		8.91					4.32	7.95									
			16.50						6.36		2.66					1.29	2.37									
Monterey Park (city)	32,111	36,674	25,665	-	-	-	-	318	17,396	-	684	-	-	-	-	1,128	659	-	-	-	-	-	940	-	-	2,543
	53.58		69.98					77.00	76.55		81.04					23.44	76.72						89.44			78.51
								1.24	67.78		2.67					4.40	2.57						3.66			9.91
			69.98					0.87	47.43		1.87					3.08	1.80						2.56			6.93
			79.93					0.99	54.17		2.13					3.51	2.05						2.93			7.92
Norwalk (city)	37,581	12,174	8,967	-	-	964	-	374	722	-	3,274	-	-	-	-	79	2,069	-	-	-	-	-	-	-	-	648
	36.41		73.66			71.89		74.35	77.63		73.11					16.53	82.20									75.52
						10.75		4.17	8.05		36.51					0.88	23.07									7.23
			73.66			7.92		3.07	5.93		26.89					0.65	17.00									5.32
			23.86			2.57		1.00	1.92		8.71					0.21	5.51									1.72
Palmdale (city)	23,074	4,308	2,904	-	-	267	-	-	-	-	1,509	-	-	-	-	-	-	-	-	-	-	-	-	-	-	-
	19.79		67.41			62.82					68.81															
						9.19					51.96															
			67.41			6.20					35.03															
			12.59			1.16					6.54															
Palos Verdes Estates (city)	2,538	2,317	1,326	-	-	-	-	-	329	-	-	-	-	-	-	277	217	-	-	-	-	-	-	-	-	-
	19.03		57.23						59.93							41.53	75.09									
									24.81							20.89	16.37									
			57.23						14.20							11.96	9.37									
			52.25						12.96							10.91	8.55									
Pasadena (city)	43,277	13,378	9,100	-	-	682	-	-	2,892	-	2,081	-	-	-	-	801	1,041	-	-	-	-	-	-	-	-	661
	32.33		68.02			79.95			69.20		80.10					35.65	74.73									85.96
						7.49			31.78		22.87					8.80	11.44									7.26
			68.02			5.10			21.62		15.56					5.99	7.78									4.94
			21.03			1.58			6.68		4.81					1.85	2.41									1.53
Pomona (city)	54,893	10,733	6,883	-	-	408	-	459	1,233	-	1,850	-	-	-	-	169	-	417	-	-	-	-	-	-	-	1,323
	36.68		64.13			64.25		60.63	61.65		64.89					32.75		78.24								75.73
						5.93		6.67	17.91		26.88					2.46		6.06								19.22
			64.13			3.80		4.28	11.49		17.24					1.57		3.89								12.33
			12.54			0.74		0.84	2.25		3.37					0.31		0.76								2.41

Notes: Please refer to the User's Guide for an explanation of data; data is arranged alphabetically by state, then county, then city within each county; table includes counties with populations greater than 49,999 unless noted and cities with populations greater than 9,999 whose Asian and/or NHPI population rates are greater than the national average; (1) Native Hawaiian and other Pacific Islander; (2) excludes Taiwanese; (3) includes Chamorro; (4) county does not meet population threshold but is shown in order to allow inclusion of city

Place	Total foreign-born population	Total Asian population	Asians who are foreign born	Total NHPI[1] population	NHPIs[1] who are foreign born	Asian Indian	Bangladeshi	Cambodian	Chinese[2]	Fijian	Filipino	Guamanian[3]	Hawaiian, Native	Hmong	Indonesian	Japanese	Korean	Laotian	Malaysian	Pakistani	Samoan	Sri Lankan	Taiwanese	Thai	Tongan	Vietnamese
Rancho Palos Verdes (city)	11,087 26.84	10,372	6,691 64.51 64.51 60.35	-	-	404 71.38 6.04 3.90 3.64	-	-	1,680 63.52 25.11 16.20 15.15	-	405 69.11 6.05 3.90 3.65	-	-	-	-	1,710 55.96 25.56 16.49 15.42	1,814 74.65 27.11 17.49 16.36	-	-	-	-	-	436 80.74 6.52 4.20 3.93	-	-	-
Redondo Beach (city)	10,738 16.97	5,896	3,266 55.39 55.39 30.42	-	-	338 67.20 10.35 5.73 3.15	-	-	705 58.36 21.59 11.96 6.57	-	527 66.29 16.14 8.94 4.91	-	-	-	-	734 36.79 22.47 12.45 6.84	476 71.15 14.57 8.07 4.43	-	-	-	-	-	-	-	-	-
Rosemead (city)	30,024 56.35	25,917	19,359 74.70 74.70 64.48	-	-	-	-	533 68.77 2.75 2.06 1.78	11,151 74.49 57.60 43.03 37.14	-	511 71.17 2.64 1.97 1.70	-	-	-	-	177 22.66 0.91 0.68 0.59	-	-	-	-	-	-	-	-	-	4,760 80.16 24.59 18.37 15.85
Rowland Heights (cdp)	25,534 52.83	24,773	19,029 76.81 76.81 74.52	-	-	712 68.20 3.74 2.87 2.79	-	-	9,002 78.81 47.31 36.34 35.25	-	2,384 72.77 12.53 9.62 9.34	-	-	-	-	277 42.10 1.46 1.12 1.08	2,912 78.17 15.30 11.75 11.40	-	-	-	-	-	2,198 84.77 11.55 8.87 8.61	-	-	478 76.60 2.51 1.93 1.87
San Dimas (city)	5,417 15.45	3,172	1,976 62.30 62.30 36.48	-	-	-	-	-	795 66.47 40.23 25.06 14.68	-	421 54.68 21.31 13.27 7.77	-	-	-	-	-	-	-	-	-	-	-	-	-	-	-
San Gabriel (city)	20,659 52.56	19,190	14,866 77.47 77.47 71.96	-	-	-	-	-	9,350 79.81 62.90 48.72 45.26	-	948 81.58 6.38 4.94 4.59	-	-	-	-	194 30.94 1.30 1.01 0.94	-	-	-	-	-	-	605 79.29 4.07 3.15 2.93	-	-	2,051 76.90 13.80 10.69 9.93
San Marino (city)	4,824 37.18	6,071	4,078 67.17 67.17 84.54	-	-	-	-	-	2,497 63.78 61.23 41.13 51.76	-	-	-	-	-	-	-	-	-	-	-	-	-	1,181 77.39 28.96 19.45 24.48	-	-	-
Santa Clarita (city)	24,727 16.33	7,586	4,762 62.77 62.77 19.26	-	-	510 67.11 10.71 6.72 2.06	-	-	594 69.07 12.47 7.83 2.40	-	1,783 71.64 37.44 23.50 7.21	-	-	-	-	345 30.83 7.24 4.55 1.40	611 75.62 12.83 8.05 2.47	-	-	-	-	-	-	-	-	308 60.87 6.47 4.06 1.25
Santa Monica (city)	20,891 24.85	5,986	3,856 64.42 64.42 18.46	-	-	500 79.49 12.97 8.35 2.39	-	-	1,061 66.73 27.52 17.72 5.08	-	362 74.18 9.39 6.05 1.73	-	-	-	-	931 50.76 24.14 15.55 4.46	494 66.49 12.81 8.25 2.36	-	-	-	-	-	-	-	-	-
Sierra Madre (city)	1,115 10.54	566	264 46.64 46.64 23.68	-	-	-	-	-	-	-	-	-	-	-	-	-	-	-	-	-	-	-	-	-	-	-

Notes: Please refer to the User's Guide for an explanation of data; data is arranged alphabetically by state, then county, then city within each county; table includes counties with populations greater than 49,999 unless noted and cities with populations greater than 9,999 whose Asian and/or NHPI population rates are greater than the national average; (1) Native Hawaiian and other Pacific Islander; (2) excludes Taiwanese; (3) includes Chamorro; (4) county does not meet population threshold but is shown in order to allow inclusion of city

Place	Total foreign-born population	Total Asian population	Asians who are foreign born	Total NHPI[1] population	NHPIs[1] who are foreign born	Asian Indian	Bangladeshi	Cambodian	Chinese[2]	Fijian	Filipino	Guamanian[3]	Hawaiian, Native	Hmong	Indonesian	Japanese	Korean	Laotian	Malaysian	Pakistani	Samoan	Sri Lankan	Taiwanese	Thai	Tongan	Vietnamese
South El Monte (city)	10,861 51.88	1,597	1,208 75.64 75.64 11.12	-	-	-	-	-	489 70.77 40.48 30.62 4.50	-	-	-	-	-	-	-	-	-	-	-	-	-	-	-	-	544 86.08 45.03 34.06 5.01
South Pasadena (city)	5,926 24.38	6,249	3,837 61.40 61.40 64.75	-	-	-	-	-	2,133 63.86 55.59 34.13 35.99	-	-	-	-	-	-	358 35.94 9.33 5.73 6.04	584 86.01 15.22 9.35 9.85	-	-	-	-	-	-	-	-	-
South San Jose Hills (cdp)	9,499 47.05	1,241	902 72.68 72.68 9.50	-	-	-	-	-	-	-	585 80.25 64.86 47.14 6.16	-	-	-	-	-	-	-	-	-	-	-	-	-	-	-
Temple City (city)	12,845 38.58	12,936	9,515 73.55 73.55 74.08	-	-	-	-	-	5,990 75.71 62.95 46.30 46.63	-	491 75.65 5.16 3.80 3.82	-	-	-	-	139 24.13 1.46 1.07 1.08	361 71.91 3.79 2.79 2.81	-	-	-	-	-	1,185 77.35 12.45 9.16 9.23	-	-	639 75.44 6.72 4.94 4.97
Torrance (city)	38,074 27.60	39,445	23,793 60.32 60.32 62.49	-	-	1,810 82.12 7.61 4.59 4.75	-	-	3,946 66.84 16.58 10.00 10.36	-	2,510 70.72 10.55 6.36 6.59	-	-	-	-	5,229 38.71 21.98 13.26 13.73	6,407 75.09 26.93 16.24 16.83	-	-	485 73.93 2.04 1.23 1.27	-	-	1,078 83.57 4.53 2.73 2.83	-	-	1,310 71.31 5.51 3.32 3.44
Valinda (cdp)	8,208 37.67	1,936	1,323 68.34 68.34 16.12	-	-	-	-	-	-	-	727 72.05 54.95 37.55 8.86	-	-	-	-	-	-	-	-	-	-	-	-	-	-	340 71.73 25.70 17.56 4.14
Vincent (cdp)	3,921 25.98	1,093	786 71.91 71.91 20.05	-	-	-	-	-	-	-	477 76.94 60.69 43.64 12.17	-	-	-	-	-	-	-	-	-	-	-	-	-	-	-
Walnut (city)	13,874 46.24	16,880	11,700 69.31 69.31 84.33	-	-	593 74.13 5.07 3.51 4.27	-	-	4,508 71.42 38.53 26.71 32.49	-	2,292 66.40 19.59 13.58 16.52	-	-	-	-	149 34.17 1.27 0.88 1.07	1,300 68.71 11.11 7.70 9.37	-	-	-	-	-	1,445 75.03 12.35 8.56 10.42	-	-	425 73.91 3.63 2.52 3.06
West Carson (cdp)	7,220 34.16	5,067	3,143 62.03 62.03 43.53	-	-	-	-	-	-	-	1,636 77.13 52.05 32.29 22.66	-	-	-	-	228 20.39 7.25 4.50 3.16	635 73.84 20.20 12.53 8.80	-	-	-	-	-	-	-	-	-
West Covina (city)	34,053 32.46	23,749	16,897 71.15 71.15 49.62	449	66 14.70 14.70 0.19	399 79.64 2.36 1.68 1.17	-	-	4,885 73.89 28.91 20.57 14.35	-	7,067 70.37 41.82 29.76 20.75	-	-	-	-	122 16.85 0.72 0.51 0.36	738 80.48 4.37 3.11 2.17	-	-	-	-	-	725 76.48 4.29 3.05 2.13	-	-	1,688 78.15 9.99 7.11 4.96

Notes: Please refer to the User's Guide for an explanation of data; data is arranged alphabetically by state, then county, then city within each county; table includes counties with populations greater than 49,999 unless noted and cities with populations greater than 9,999 whose Asian and/or NHPI population rates are greater than the national average; (1) Native Hawaiian and other Pacific Islander; (2) excludes Taiwanese; (3) includes Chamorro; (4) county does not meet population threshold but is shown in order to allow inclusion of city

Place	Total foreign-born population	Total Asian population	Asians who are foreign born	Total NHPI[1] population	NHPIs[1] who are foreign born	Asian Indian	Bangladeshi	Cambodian	Chinese[2]	Fijian	Filipino	Guamanian[3]	Hawaiian, Native	Hmong	Indonesian	Japanese	Korean	Laotian	Malaysian	Pakistani	Samoan	Sri Lankan	Taiwanese	Thai	Tongan	Vietnamese
West Hollywood (city)	12,809 35.86	1,412	946 67.00 67.00 7.39	-	-	-	-	-	-	-	-	-	-	-	-	-	-	-	-	-	-	-	-	-	-	-
West Puente Valley (cdp)	9,732 42.42	1,733	1,219 70.34 70.34 12.53	-	-	-	-	-	-	-	520 71.23 42.66 30.01 5.34	-	-	-	-	-	-	-	-	-	-	-	-	-	-	330 71.43 27.07 19.04 3.39
Whittier (city)	15,301 18.25	3,270	1,773 54.22 54.22 11.59	-	-	-	-	-	683 57.01 38.52 20.89 4.46	-	392 59.57 22.11 11.99 2.56	-	-	-	-	87 20.09 4.91 2.66 0.57	202 57.55 11.39 6.18 1.32	-	-	-	-	-	-	-	-	-
Madera County	24,753 20.11	1,544	833 53.95 53.95 3.37	-	-	352 61.11 42.26 22.80 1.42	-	-	-	-	234 53.30 28.09 15.16 0.95	-	-	-	-	-	-	-	-	-	-	-	-	-	-	-
Marin County	41,160 16.64	10,961	6,542 59.68 59.68 15.89	-	-	1,160 80.39 17.73 10.58 2.82	-	-	1,575 49.51 24.08 14.37 3.83	-	703 56.51 10.75 6.41 1.71	-	-	-	-	681 42.22 10.41 6.21 1.65	767 65.28 11.72 7.00 1.86	-	-	-	-	-	-	-	-	1,072 84.28 16.39 9.78 2.60
Larkspur (city)	1,588 13.23	440	206 46.82 46.82 12.97	-	-	-	-	-	-	-	-	-	-	-	-	-	-	-	-	-	-	-	-	-	-	-
Novato (city)	8,198 17.15	2,515	1,595 63.42 63.42 19.46	-	-	-	-	-	348 53.70 21.82 13.84 4.24	-	336 71.64 21.07 13.36 4.10	-	-	-	-	-	-	-	-	-	-	-	-	-	-	-
San Rafael (city)	15,746 28.05	3,163	2,225 70.34 70.34 14.13	-	-	465 89.60 20.90 14.70 2.95	-	-	554 55.18 24.90 17.52 3.52	-	-	-	-	-	-	-	-	-	-	-	-	-	-	-	-	568 84.40 25.53 17.96 3.61
Tamalpais-Homestead (cdp)	1,128 10.65	508	187 36.81 36.81 16.58	-	-	-	-	-	-	-	-	-	-	-	-	-	-	-	-	-	-	-	-	-	-	-
Mendocino County	8,833 10.24	826	432 52.30 52.30 4.89	-	-	-	-	-	-	-	-	-	-	-	-	-	-	-	-	-	-	-	-	-	-	-

Notes: Please refer to the User's Guide for an explanation of data; data is arranged alphabetically by state, then county, then city within each county; table includes counties with populations greater than 49,999 unless noted and cities with populations greater than 9,999 whose Asian and/or NHPI population rates are greater than the national average; (1) Native Hawaiian and other Pacific Islander; (2) excludes Taiwanese; (3) includes Chamorro; (4) county does not meet population threshold but is shown in order to allow inclusion of city

Place	Total foreign-born population	Total Asian population	Asians who are foreign born	Total NHPI[1] population	NHPIs[1] who are foreign born	Asian Indian	Bangladeshi	Cambodian	Chinese[2]	Fijian	Filipino	Guamanian[3]	Hawaiian, Native	Hmong	Indonesian	Japanese	Korean	Laotian	Malaysian	Pakistani	Samoan	Sri Lankan	Taiwanese	Thai	Tongan	Vietnamese
Merced County	52,184 24.78	14,464	8,578 59.31 59.31 16.44	-	-	1,490 69.69 17.37 10.30 2.86	-	-	212 47.01 2.47 1.47 0.41	-	838 55.31 9.77 5.79 1.61	-	-	3,820 58.01 44.53 26.41 7.32	-	138 25.51 1.61 0.95 0.26	-	1,161 67.38 13.53 8.03 2.22	-	-	-	-	-	-	-	-
Atwater (city)	4,817 21.04	1,238	737 59.53 59.53 15.30	-	-	-	-	-	-	-	-	-	-	244 62.09 33.11 19.71 5.07	-	-	-	-	-	-	-	-	-	-	-	-
Livingston (city)	5,110 49.37	1,553	1,000 64.39 64.39 19.57	-	-	852 68.43 85.20 54.86 16.67	-	-	-	-	-	-	-	-	-	-	-	-	-	-	-	-	-	-	-	-
Merced (city)	14,152 22.12	7,099	4,289 60.42 60.42 30.31	-	-	-	-	-	-	-	-	-	-	2,493 58.96 58.13 35.12 17.62	-	-	-	977 70.09 22.78 13.76 6.90	-	-	-	-	-	-	-	-
Monterey County	116,559 29.01	24,221	14,282 58.97 58.97 12.25	1,823	301 16.51 16.51 0.26	832 64.50 5.83 3.44 0.71	-	-	1,275 59.44 8.93 5.26 1.09	-	6,673 57.94 46.72 27.55 5.72	26 3.86 8.64 1.43 0.02	-	-	-	1,498 44.96 10.49 6.18 1.29	2,141 75.12 14.99 8.84 1.84	-	-	-	-	-	-	-	-	1,265 64.81 8.86 5.22 1.09
Marina (city)	5,708 22.78	4,223	2,795 66.19 66.19 48.97	504	72 14.29 14.29 1.26	-	-	-	-	-	854 67.46 30.55 20.22 14.96	-	-	-	-	192 51.34 6.87 4.55 3.36	956 76.36 34.20 22.64 16.75	-	-	-	-	-	-	-	-	436 59.32 15.60 10.32 7.64
Monterey (city)	5,307 17.82	2,342	1,432 61.14 61.14 26.98	-	-	-	-	-	336 76.71 23.46 14.35 6.33	-	242 54.88 16.90 10.33 4.56	-	-	-	-	368 50.27 25.70 15.71 6.93	-	-	-	-	-	-	-	-	-	-
Pacific Grove (city)	1,909 12.35	660	456 69.09 69.09 23.89	-	-	-	-	-	-	-	-	-	-	-	-	-	-	-	-	-	-	-	-	-	-	-
Salinas (city)	53,016 35.17	9,091	4,933 54.26 54.26 9.30	547	109 19.93 19.93 0.21	371 64.19 7.52 4.08 0.70	-	-	272 47.30 5.51 2.99 0.51	-	3,216 54.13 65.19 35.38 6.07	-	-	-	-	267 33.97 5.41 2.94 0.50	326 69.36 6.61 3.59 0.61	-	-	-	-	-	-	-	-	330 69.18 6.69 3.63 0.62
Seaside (city)	9,921 31.21	3,347	2,115 63.19 63.19 21.32	-	-	-	-	-	-	-	1,263 63.82 59.72 37.74 12.73	-	-	-	-	242 57.89 11.44 7.23 2.44	-	-	-	-	-	-	-	-	-	306 65.25 14.47 9.14 3.08

Notes: Please refer to the User's Guide for an explanation of data; data is arranged alphabetically by state, then county, then city within each county; table includes counties with populations greater than 49,999 unless noted and cities with populations greater than 9,999 whose Asian and/or NHPI population rates are greater than the national average; (1) Native Hawaiian and other Pacific Islander; (2) excludes Taiwanese; (3) includes Chamorro; (4) county does not meet population threshold but is shown in order to allow inclusion of city

Place	Total foreign-born population	Total Asian population	Asians who are foreign born	Total NHPI[1] population	NHPIs[1] who are foreign born	Asian Indian	Bangladeshi	Cambodian	Chinese[2]	Fijian	Filipino	Guamanian[3]	Hawaiian, Native	Hmong	Indonesian	Japanese	Korean	Laotian	Malaysian	Pakistani	Samoan	Sri Lankan	Taiwanese	Thai	Tongan	Vietnamese
Napa County	22,487	3,936	2,360	-	-	-	-	-	271	-	1,257	-	-	-	-	195	-	-	-	-	-	-	-	-	-	-
	18.09		59.96						48.83		62.98					46.99										
									11.48		53.26					8.26										
			59.96						6.89		31.94					4.95										
			10.49						1.21		5.59					0.87										
Nevada County	4,065	593	216	-	-	-	-	-	-	-	-	-	-	-	-	-	-	-	-	-	-	-	-	-	-	-
	4.42		36.42																							
			36.42																							
			5.31																							
Orange County	849,899	386,344	270,037	8,530	2,026	19,366	-	3,195	33,675	-	32,813	109	69	562	1,500	11,251	43,144	2,054	-	1,855	929	548	7,222	2,380	287	104,353
	29.86		69.90		23.75	71.97		71.51	67.59		67.07	9.88	4.06	53.27	78.62	37.54	75.05	70.49		70.48	24.97	80.95	78.13	75.34	49.40	76.62
						7.17		1.18	12.47		12.15	5.38	3.41	0.21	0.56	4.17	15.98	0.76		0.69	45.85	0.20	2.67	0.88	14.17	38.64
			69.90		23.75	5.01		0.83	8.72		8.49	1.28	0.81	0.15	0.39	2.91	11.17	0.53		0.48	10.89	0.14	1.87	0.62	3.36	27.01
			31.77		0.24	2.28		0.38	3.96		3.86	0.01	0.01	0.07	0.18	1.32	5.08	0.24		0.22	0.11	0.06	0.85	0.28	0.03	12.28
Aliso Viejo (cdp)	7,905	4,377	2,846	-	-	401	-	-	469	-	520	-	-	-	-	212	380	-	-	-	-	-	-	-	-	409
	19.65		65.02			73.85			67.00		60.12					36.30	78.84									79.73
						14.09			16.48		18.27					7.45	13.35									14.37
			65.02			9.16			10.72		11.88					4.84	8.68									9.34
			36.00			5.07			5.93		6.58					2.68	4.81									5.17
Anaheim (city)	123,976	39,590	28,544	1,094	280	3,014	-	-	2,681	-	5,748	-	-	-	-	724	5,117	624	-	294	78	-	556	347	-	8,058
	37.87		72.10		25.59	73.07			68.96		74.25					32.86	77.06	78.39		69.34	14.05		83.11	76.10		76.25
						10.56			9.39		20.14					2.54	17.93	2.19		1.03	27.86		1.95	1.22		28.23
			72.10		25.59	7.61			6.77		14.52					1.83	12.92	1.58		0.74	7.13		1.40	0.88		20.35
			23.02		0.23	2.43			2.16		4.64					0.58	4.13	0.50		0.24	0.06		0.45	0.28		6.50
Brea (city)	6,052	3,155	2,084	-	-	332	-	-	329	-	332	-	-	-	-	-	613	-	-	-	-	-	-	-	-	-
	17.23		66.05			72.65			67.42		66.00						74.67									
						15.93			15.79		15.93						29.41									
			66.05			10.52			10.43		10.52						19.43									
			34.43			5.49			5.44		5.49						10.13									
Buena Park (city)	25,837	16,914	12,325	-	-	1,367	-	-	989	-	3,755	-	-	-	-	245	4,118	-	-	-	-	-	-	-	-	698
	32.97		72.87			78.52			72.03		73.74					32.84	77.35									70.22
						11.09			8.02		30.47					1.99	33.41									5.66
			72.87			8.08			5.85		22.20					1.45	24.35									4.13
			47.70			5.29			3.83		14.53					0.95	15.94									2.70
Costa Mesa (city)	31,722	7,878	5,553	652	313	340	-	-	641	-	916	-	-	-	-	788	503	-	-	-	-	-	-	-	-	1,768
	29.16		70.49		48.01	79.25			66.98		68.72					52.22	85.25									78.89
						6.12			11.54		16.50					14.19	9.06									31.84
			70.49		48.01	4.32			8.14		11.63					10.00	6.38									22.44
			17.51		0.99	1.07			2.02		2.89					2.48	1.59									5.57
Cypress (city)	9,894	9,470	6,262	-	-	527	-	-	990	-	1,127	-	-	-	-	251	1,928	-	-	-	-	-	523	-	-	616
	21.26		66.12			75.94			67.21		64.70					26.65	74.93						70.30			80.42
						8.42			15.81		18.00					4.01	30.79						8.35			9.84
			66.12			5.56			10.45		11.90					2.65	20.36						5.52			6.50
			63.29			5.33			10.01		11.39					2.54	19.49						5.29			6.23
Foothill Ranch (cdp)	1,902	1,713	1,058	-	-	-	-	-	-	-	-	-	-	-	-	-	-	-	-	-	-	-	-	-	-	-
	17.44		61.76																							
			61.76																							
			55.63																							

Notes: Please refer to the User's Guide for an explanation of data; data is arranged alphabetically by state, then county, then city within each county; table includes counties with populations greater than 49,999 unless noted and cities with populations greater than 9,999 whose Asian and/or NHPI population rates are greater than the national average; (1) Native Hawaiian and other Pacific Islander; (2) excludes Taiwanese; (3) includes Chamorro; (4) county does not meet population threshold but is shown in order to allow inclusion of city

Place	Total foreign-born population	Total Asian population	Asians who are foreign born	Total NHPI[1] population	NHPIs[1] who are foreign born	Asian Indian	Bangladeshi	Cambodian	Chinese[2]	Fijian	Filipino	Guamanian[3]	Hawaiian, Native	Hmong	Indonesian	Japanese	Korean	Laotian	Malaysian	Pakistani	Samoan	Sri Lankan	Taiwanese	Thai	Tongan	Vietnamese
Fountain Valley (city)	15,173	14,421	9,767	-	-	581	-	-	1,637	-	348	-	-	-	-	375	781	-	-	-	-	-	322	-	-	5,285
	27.59		67.73			78.62			67.23		58.68					26.48	73.33						81.11			74.26
						5.95			16.76		3.56					3.84	8.00						3.30			54.11
			67.73			4.03			11.35		2.41					2.60	5.42						2.23			36.65
			64.37			3.83			10.79		2.29					2.47	5.15						2.12			34.83
Fullerton (city)	36,431	20,248	13,997	-	-	1,469	-	-	2,010	-	1,273	-	-	-	-	371	6,485	-	-	-	-	-	-	-	-	1,162
	28.86		69.13			80.05			72.07		57.84					32.77	72.15									73.54
						10.50			14.36		9.09					2.65	46.33									8.30
			69.13			7.26			9.93		6.29					1.83	32.03									5.74
			38.42			4.03			5.52		3.49					1.02	17.80									3.19
Garden Grove (city)	71,351	51,029	39,313	1,266	390	547	-	393	1,928	-	2,075	-	-	-	-	293	4,807	-	-	-	214	-	-	-	-	27,844
	43.06		77.04		30.81	75.55		78.60	74.93		70.53					28.07	79.30				27.68					79.50
						1.39		1.00	4.90		5.28					0.75	12.23				54.87					70.83
			77.04		30.81	1.07		0.77	3.78		4.07					0.57	9.42				16.90					54.57
			55.10		0.55	0.77		0.55	2.70		2.91					0.41	6.74				0.30					39.02
Huntington Beach (city)	32,155	17,636	10,916	359	24	775	-	-	1,848	-	1,046	-	-	-	-	847	1,240	-	-	-	-	-	462	-	-	4,145
	16.93		61.90		6.69	76.66			62.50		62.63					29.65	74.16						80.07			70.54
						7.10			16.93		9.58					7.76	11.36						4.23			37.97
			61.90		6.69	4.39			10.48		5.93					4.80	7.03						2.62			23.50
			33.95		0.07	2.41			5.75		3.25					2.63	3.86						1.44			12.89
Irvine (city)	45,877	42,386	28,025	-	-	3,056	-	-	7,626	-	1,628	-	-	-	-	3,219	5,828	-	-	-	-	-	2,072	-	-	3,243
	32.07		66.12			65.69			66.75		48.86					62.69	73.00						79.02			66.84
						10.90			27.21		5.81					11.49	20.80						7.39			11.57
			66.12			7.21			17.99		3.84					7.59	13.75						4.89			7.65
			61.09			6.66			16.62		3.55					7.02	12.70						4.52			7.07
La Habra (city)	15,955	3,397	2,159	-	-	-	-	-	263	-	432	-	-	-	-	-	876	-	-	-	-	-	-	-	-	-
	26.96		63.56						55.14		72.97						71.92									
									12.18		20.01						40.57									
			63.56						7.74		12.72						25.79									
			13.53						1.65		2.71						5.49									
La Palma (city)	5,490	6,574	4,448	-	-	376	-	-	681	-	817	-	-	-	-	130	1,955	-	-	-	-	-	-	-	-	-
	36.28		67.66			62.67			73.07		66.31					18.08	81.42									
						8.45			15.31		18.37					2.92	43.95									
			67.66			5.72			10.36		12.43					1.98	29.74									
			81.02			6.85			12.40		14.88					2.37	35.61									
Laguna Hills (city)	6,985	3,259	2,009	-	-	-	-	-	344	-	413	-	-	-	-	-	-	-	-	-	-	-	-	-	-	351
	22.33		61.64						60.35		66.08															61.58
									17.12		20.56															17.47
			61.64						10.56		12.67															10.77
			28.76						4.92		5.91															5.03
Laguna Niguel (city)	10,869	4,689	2,866	-	-	-	-	-	620	-	566	-	-	-	-	281	447	-	-	-	-	-	-	-	-	346
	17.54		61.12						61.81		66.90					32.90	66.12									74.57
									21.63		19.75					9.80	15.60									12.07
			61.12						13.22		12.07					5.99	9.53									7.38
			26.37						5.70		5.21					2.59	4.11									3.18
Lake Forest (city)	12,423	5,447	3,773	-	-	470	-	-	460	-	733	-	-	-	-	344	471	-	-	-	-	-	-	-	-	969
	21.13		69.27			63.69			67.95		70.28					59.93	81.63									69.71
						12.46			12.19		19.43					9.12	12.48									25.68
			69.27			8.63			8.45		13.46					6.32	8.65									17.79
			30.37			3.78			3.70		5.90					2.77	3.79									7.80

Notes: Please refer to the User's Guide for an explanation of data; data is arranged alphabetically by state, then county, then city within each county; table includes counties with populations greater than 49,999 unless noted and cities with populations greater than 9,999 whose Asian and/or NHPI population rates are greater than the national average; (1) Native Hawaiian and other Pacific Islander; (2) excludes Taiwanese; (3) includes Chamorro; (4) county does not meet population threshold but is shown in order to allow inclusion of city

Place	Total foreign-born population	Total Asian population	Asians who are foreign born	Total NHPI[1] population	NHPIs[1] who are foreign born	Asian Indian	Bangladeshi	Cambodian	Chinese[2]	Fijian	Filipino	Guamanian[3]	Hawaiian, Native	Hmong	Indonesian	Japanese	Korean	Laotian	Malaysian	Pakistani	Samoan	Sri Lankan	Taiwanese	Thai	Tongan	Vietnamese
Los Alamitos (city)	1,618 14.37	1,050	615 58.57 58.57 38.01	-	-	-	-	-	-	-	-	-	-	-	-	-	-	-	-	-	-	-	-	-	-	-
Mission Viejo (city)	15,291 16.48	7,380	4,385 59.42 59.42 28.68	-	-	398 64.19 9.08 5.39 2.60	-	-	768 59.77 17.51 10.41 5.02	-	969 64.73 22.10 13.13 6.34	-	-	-	-	304 28.15 6.93 4.12 1.99	607 75.78 13.84 8.22 3.97	-	-	-	-	-	-	-	-	876 66.36 19.98 11.87 5.73
Newport Beach (city)	7,505 10.72	2,762	1,717 62.17 62.17 22.88	-	-	-	-	-	452 63.75 26.32 16.36 6.02	-	-	-	-	-	-	186 37.88 10.83 6.73 2.48	-	-	-	-	-	-	-	-	-	-
Orange (city)	32,297 25.15	11,711	8,037 68.63 68.63 24.88	-	-	572 66.82 7.12 4.88 1.77	-	-	989 75.79 12.31 8.45 3.06	-	1,413 69.64 17.58 12.07 4.38	-	-	-	-	180 23.17 2.24 1.54 0.56	1,155 71.56 14.37 9.86 3.58	-	-	-	-	-	370 80.09 4.60 3.16 1.15	-	-	2,785 72.68 34.65 23.78 8.62
Placentia (city)	11,554 24.53	5,254	3,446 65.59 65.59 29.83	-	-	393 75.00 11.40 7.48 3.40	-	-	784 68.65 22.75 14.92 6.79	-	533 69.49 15.47 10.14 4.61	-	-	-	-	86 18.22 2.50 1.64 0.74	426 61.21 12.36 8.11 3.69	-	-	-	-	-	-	-	-	652 69.73 18.92 12.41 5.64
Rancho Santa Margarita (city)	6,294 13.19	3,836	2,258 58.86 58.86 35.88	-	-	-	-	-	353 58.74 15.63 9.20 5.61	-	672 61.43 29.76 17.52 10.68	-	-	-	-	-	-	-	-	-	-	-	-	-	-	347 65.72 15.37 9.05 5.51
Rossmoor (cdp)	778 7.59	514	266 51.75 51.75 34.19	-	-	-	-	-	-	-	-	-	-	-	-	-	-	-	-	-	-	-	-	-	-	-
Santa Ana (city)	179,933 53.31	29,802	22,457 75.35 75.35 12.48	1,276	236 18.50 18.50 0.13	443 75.99 1.97 1.49 0.25	-	1,227 70.68 5.46 4.12 0.68	1,551 76.37 6.91 5.20 0.86	-	1,570 69.96 6.99 5.27 0.87	-	-	298 56.44 1.33 1.00 0.17	-	403 48.38 1.79 1.35 0.22	539 78.57 2.40 1.81 0.30	627 64.84 2.79 2.10 0.35	-	-	169 24.14 71.61 13.24 0.09	-	-	-	-	15,094 78.57 67.21 50.65 8.39
Seal Beach (city)	2,812 11.58	1,255	587 46.77 46.77 20.87	-	-	-	-	-	-	-	-	-	-	-	-	85 23.16 14.48 6.77 3.02	-	-	-	-	-	-	-	-	-	-
Stanton (city)	15,243 41.27	5,727	4,383 76.53 76.53 28.75	-	-	-	-	-	-	-	826 69.12 18.85 14.42 5.42	-	-	-	-	-	649 82.47 14.81 11.33 4.26	-	-	-	-	-	-	-	-	2,259 82.60 51.54 39.44 14.82

Notes: Please refer to the User's Guide for an explanation of data; data is arranged alphabetically by state, then county, then city within each county; table includes counties with populations greater than 49,999 unless noted and cities with populations greater than 9,999 whose Asian and/or NHPI population rates are greater than the national average; (1) Native Hawaiian and other Pacific Islander; (2) excludes Taiwanese; (3) includes Chamorro; (4) county does not meet population threshold but is shown in order to allow inclusion of city

Place	Total foreign-born population	Total Asian population	Asians who are foreign born	Total NHPI[1] population	NHPIs[1] who are foreign born	Asian Indian	Bangladeshi	Cambodian	Chinese[2]	Fijian	Filipino	Guamanian[3]	Hawaiian, Native	Hmong	Indonesian	Japanese	Korean	Laotian	Malaysian	Pakistani	Samoan	Sri Lankan	Taiwanese	Thai	Tongan	Vietnamese
Tustin (city)	22,521	9,359	6,907	-	-	1,026	-	-	1,004	-	1,278	-	-	-	-	378	914	-	-	-	-	-	356	-	-	1,173
	33.34		73.80			79.41			76.23		74.17					54.78	78.12						76.23			68.08
						14.85			14.54		18.50					5.47	13.23						5.15			16.98
			73.80			10.96			10.73		13.66					4.04	9.77						3.80			12.53
			30.67			4.56			4.46		5.67					1.68	4.06						1.58			5.21
Tustin Foothills (cdp)	2,929	1,707	1,135	-	-	-	-	-	353	-	-	-	-	-	-	-	-	-	-	-	-	-	-	-	-	-
	12.20		66.49						72.48																	
									31.10																	
			66.49						20.68																	
			38.75						12.05																	
Westminster (city)	37,477	33,351	25,063	435	167	252	-	-	1,101	-	934	-	-	-	-	240	502	-	-	-	167	-	-	-	-	21,185
	42.64		75.15		38.39	60.00			70.90		66.52					23.41	71.41				44.41					78.11
						1.01			4.39		3.73					0.96	2.00				100.00					84.53
			75.15		38.39	0.76			3.30		2.80					0.72	1.51				38.39					63.52
			66.88		0.45	0.67			2.94		2.49					0.64	1.34				0.45					56.53
Yorba Linda (city)	8,128	6,403	3,625	-	-	454	-	-	1,035	-	553	-	-	-	-	126	569	-	-	-	-	-	-	-	-	395
	13.87		56.61			65.32			64.09		59.91					15.04	64.44									61.43
						12.52			28.55		15.26					3.48	15.70									10.90
			56.61			7.09			16.16		8.64					1.97	8.89									6.17
			44.60			5.59			12.73		6.80					1.55	7.00									4.86
Placer County	17,562	7,256	3,644	-	-	591	-	-	664	-	1,117	-	-	-	-	452	327	-	-	-	-	-	-	-	-	304
	7.07		50.22			68.80			49.89		56.96					24.90	65.79									68.31
						16.22			18.22		30.65					12.40	8.97									8.34
			50.22			8.14			9.15		15.39					6.23	4.51									4.19
			20.75			3.37			3.78		6.36					2.57	1.86									1.73
Rocklin (city)	1,911	1,314	641	-	-	-	-	-	-	-	-	-	-	-	-	135	-	-	-	-	-	-	-	-	-	-
	5.23		48.78													30.61										
																21.06										
			48.78													10.27										
			33.54													7.06										
Roseville (city)	7,179	3,358	1,821	-	-	455	-	-	337	-	539	-	-	-	-	146	-	-	-	-	-	-	-	-	-	-
	8.96		54.23			71.32			48.98		54.55					28.91										
						24.99			18.51		29.60					8.02										
			54.23			13.55			10.04		16.05					4.35										
			25.37			6.34			4.69		7.51					2.03										
Riverside County	293,712	54,648	34,243	3,719	706	3,804	-	325	3,805	-	12,427	150	21	203	-	1,842	4,080	1,045	-	281	170	-	418	631	-	4,004
	19.01		62.66		18.98	67.57		54.17	63.49		63.32	15.92	2.60	41.68		41.42	71.13	70.23		63.29	18.03		83.94	72.03		65.04
						11.11		0.95	11.11		36.29	21.25	2.97	0.59		5.38	11.91	3.05		0.82	24.08		1.22	1.84		11.69
			62.66		18.98	6.96		0.59	6.96		22.74	4.03	0.56	0.37		3.37	7.47	1.91		0.51	4.57		0.76	1.15		7.33
			11.66		0.24	1.30		0.11	1.30		4.23	0.05	0.01	0.07		0.63	1.39	0.36		0.10	0.06		0.14	0.21		1.36
Banning (city)	3,343	1,057	574	-	-	-	-	-	-	-	-	-	-	-	-	-	-	203	-	-	-	-	-	-	-	-
	14.26		54.30															59.53								
																		35.37								
			54.30															19.21								
			17.17															6.07								
Corona (city)	26,705	9,285	5,751	-	-	979	-	-	559	-	1,943	-	-	-	-	173	878	-	-	-	-	-	-	-	-	921
	21.38		61.94			65.01			63.02		63.79					28.93	71.50									64.54
						17.02			9.72		33.79					3.01	15.27									16.01
			61.94			10.54			6.02		20.93					1.86	9.46									9.92
			21.54			3.67			2.09		7.28					0.65	3.29									3.45

Notes: Please refer to the User's Guide for an explanation of data; data is arranged alphabetically by state, then county, then city within each county; table includes counties with populations greater than 49,999 unless noted and cities with populations greater than 9,999 whose Asian and/or NHPI population rates are greater than the national average; (1) Native Hawaiian and other Pacific Islander; (2) excludes Taiwanese; (3) includes Chamorro; (4) county does not meet population threshold but is shown in order to allow inclusion of city

Place	Total foreign-born population	Total Asian population	Asians who are foreign born	Total NHPI[1] population	NHPIs[1] who are foreign born	Asian Indian	Bangladeshi	Cambodian	Chinese[2]	Fijian	Filipino	Guamanian[3]	Hawaiian, Native	Hmong	Indonesian	Japanese	Korean	Laotian	Malaysian	Pakistani	Samoan	Sri Lankan	Taiwanese	Thai	Tongan	Vietnamese
Moreno Valley (city)	28,485 19.98	7,995	5,258 65.77 65.77 18.46	-	-	-	-	-	276 58.85 5.25 3.45 0.97	-	2,658 66.88 50.55 33.25 9.33	-	-	-	-	253 50.70 4.81 3.16 0.89	495 73.22 9.41 6.19 1.74	364 74.59 6.92 4.55 1.28	-	-	-	-	-	-	-	454 75.42 8.63 5.68 1.59
Palm Springs (city)	9,166 21.39	1,756	1,228 69.93 69.93 13.40	-	-	-	-	-	-	-	776 67.54 63.19 44.19 8.47	-	-	-	-	-	-	-	-	-	-	-	-	-	-	-
Pedley (cdp)	1,945 17.56	459	337 73.42 73.42 17.33	-	-	-	-	-	-	-	-	-	-	-	-	-	-	-	-	-	-	-	-	-	-	-
Riverside (city)	50,808 19.92	14,185	8,878 62.59 62.59 17.47	1,061	277 26.11 26.11 0.55	1,069 72.52 12.04 7.54 2.10	-	-	1,489 63.50 16.77 10.50 2.93	-	1,858 58.50 20.93 13.10 3.66	-	-	-	-	414 36.67 4.66 2.92 0.81	1,182 63.79 13.31 8.33 2.33	242 70.35 2.73 1.71 0.48	-	-	-	-	-	-	-	1,564 68.30 17.62 11.03 3.08
Temecula (city)	6,897 12.01	2,668	1,713 64.21 64.21 24.84	-	-	-	-	-	232 60.57 13.54 8.70 3.36	-	922 66.96 53.82 34.56 13.37	-	-	-	-	-	-	-	-	-	-	-	-	-	-	-
Sacramento County	197,195 16.12	134,881	78,474 58.18 58.18 39.80	6,269	2,874 45.84 45.84 1.46	9,370 73.54 11.94 6.95 4.75	-	731 65.44 0.93 0.54 0.37	16,293 56.72 20.76 12.08 8.26	1,486 84.87 51.70 23.70 0.75	14,445 60.07 18.41 10.71 7.33	51 5.83 1.77 0.81 0.03	28 4.28 0.97 0.45 0.01	9,678 55.90 12.33 7.18 4.91	-	2,480 20.15 3.16 1.84 1.26	3,447 73.75 4.39 2.56 1.75	5,707 59.15 7.27 4.23 2.89	-	976 67.97 1.24 0.72 0.49	293 23.65 10.19 4.67 0.15	-	300 73.89 0.38 0.22 0.15	551 74.56 0.70 0.41 0.28	429 57.89 14.93 6.84 0.22	11,979 72.35 15.26 8.88 6.07
Arden-Arcade (cdp)	13,688 14.26	4,766	3,210 67.35 67.35 23.45	-	-	589 82.03 18.35 12.36 4.30	-	-	546 61.01 17.01 11.46 3.99	-	785 71.62 24.45 16.47 5.73	-	-	174 49.57 5.42 3.65 1.27	-	212 41.81 6.60 4.45 1.55	-	-	-	-	-	-	-	-	-	327 81.95 10.19 6.86 2.39
Elk Grove (cdp)	9,843 16.34	10,532	6,425 61.00 61.00 65.27	-	-	954 66.02 14.85 9.06 9.69	-	-	945 64.02 14.71 8.97 9.60	-	2,067 61.03 32.17 19.63 21.00	-	-	-	-	44 9.67 0.68 0.42 0.45	-	-	-	-	-	-	-	-	-	1,529 70.33 23.80 14.52 15.53
Fair Oaks (cdp)	2,789 9.96	1,200	686 57.17 57.17 24.60	-	-	-	-	-	-	-	-	-	-	-	-	-	-	-	-	-	-	-	-	-	-	-
Florin (cdp)	6,020 21.83	5,500	3,215 58.45 58.45 53.41	-	-	227 74.43 7.06 4.13 3.77	-	-	402 59.91 12.50 7.31 6.68	-	605 64.16 18.82 11.00 10.05	-	-	508 47.88 15.80 9.24 8.44	-	-	-	-	-	-	-	-	-	-	-	968 74.35 30.11 17.60 16.08

Notes: Please refer to the User's Guide for an explanation of data; data is arranged alphabetically by state, then county, then city within each county; table includes counties with populations greater than 49,999 unless noted and cities with populations greater than 9,999 whose Asian and/or NHPI population rates are greater than the national average; (1) Native Hawaiian and other Pacific Islander; (2) excludes Taiwanese; (3) includes Chamorro; (4) county does not meet population threshold but is shown in order to allow inclusion of city

Place	Total foreign-born population	Total Asian population	Asians who are foreign born	Total NHPI[1] population	NHPIs[1] who are foreign born	Asian Indian	Bangladeshi	Cambodian	Chinese[2]	Fijian	Filipino	Guamanian[3]	Hawaiian, Native	Hmong	Indonesian	Japanese	Korean	Laotian	Malaysian	Pakistani	Samoan	Sri Lankan	Taiwanese	Thai	Tongan	Vietnamese
Folsom (city)	4,577 8.82	3,626	2,199 60.65 60.65 48.04	-	-	1,038 74.95 47.20 28.63 22.68	-	-	357 59.40 16.23 9.85 7.80	-	282 44.48 12.82 7.78 6.16	-	-	-	-	-	-	-	-	-	-	-	-	-	-	-
Foothill Farms (cdp)	2,140 12.30	798	537 67.29 67.29 25.09	-	-	-	-	-	-	-	-	-	-	-	-	-	-	-	-	-	-	-	-	-	-	-
La Riviera (cdp)	1,337 13.01	883	543 61.49 61.49 40.61	-	-	-	-	-	-	-	-	-	-	-	-	-	-	-	-	-	-	-	-	-	-	-
Laguna (cdp)	5,414 15.74	6,259	3,456 55.22 55.22 63.83	-	-	486 68.45 14.06 7.76 8.98	-	-	1,191 61.11 34.46 19.03 22.00	-	1,017 55.82 29.43 16.25 18.78	-	-	-	-	44 7.87 1.27 0.70 0.81	-	-	-	-	-	-	-	-	-	363 71.88 10.50 5.80 6.70
North Highlands (cdp)	7,831 17.77	2,463	1,756 71.30 71.30 22.42	-	-	-	-	-	-	-	464 56.31 26.42 18.84 5.93	-	-	-	-	-	-	-	-	-	-	-	-	-	-	603 94.07 34.34 24.48 7.70
Parkway-S. Sacramento (cdp)	9,990 27.38	6,735	4,154 61.68 61.68 41.58	-	-	-	-	-	340 64.64 8.18 5.05 3.40	-	-	-	-	1,621 58.95 39.02 24.07 16.23	-	-	-	791 56.82 19.04 11.74 7.92	-	-	-	-	-	-	-	912 82.16 21.95 13.54 9.13
Rancho Cordova (cdp)	11,303 20.71	4,375	2,941 67.22 67.22 26.02	-	-	515 86.12 17.51 11.77 4.56	-	-	213 43.92 7.24 4.87 1.88	-	655 64.66 22.27 14.97 5.79	-	-	-	-	-	342 79.91 11.63 7.82 3.03	-	-	-	-	-	-	-	-	567 67.50 19.28 12.96 5.02
Rosemont (cdp)	3,710 16.25	2,698	1,651 61.19 61.19 44.50	-	-	-	-	-	-	-	134 30.80 8.12 4.97 3.61	-	-	-	-	-	349 73.01 21.14 12.94 9.41	-	-	-	-	-	-	-	-	470 87.04 28.47 17.42 12.67
Sacramento (city)	82,616 20.30	67,400	37,237 55.25 55.25 45.07	3,692	1,932 52.33 52.33 2.34	3,054 75.35 8.20 4.53 3.70	-	365 75.57 0.98 0.54 0.44	10,455 55.07 28.08 15.51 12.65	1,063 85.73 55.02 28.79 1.29	5,001 61.10 13.43 7.42 6.05	-	-	6,754 55.96 18.14 10.02 8.18	-	809 12.05 2.17 1.20 0.98	527 75.50 1.42 0.78 0.64	3,734 59.22 10.03 5.54 4.52	-	578 74.20 1.55 0.86 0.70	126 17.19 6.52 3.41 0.15	-	-	-	319 55.57 16.51 8.64 0.39	4,462 68.68 11.98 6.62 5.40
Vineyard (cdp)	1,449 14.48	1,629	1,040 63.84 63.84 71.77	-	-	-	-	-	-	-	439 61.92 42.21 26.95 30.30	-	-	-	-	-	-	-	-	-	-	-	-	-	-	-

Notes: Please refer to the User's Guide for an explanation of data; data is arranged alphabetically by state, then county, then city within each county; table includes counties with populations greater than 49,999 unless noted and cities with populations greater than 9,999 whose Asian and/or NHPI population rates are greater than the national average; (1) Native Hawaiian and other Pacific Islander; (2) excludes Taiwanese; (3) includes Chamorro; (4) county does not meet population threshold but is shown in order to allow inclusion of city

Place	Total foreign-born population	Total Asian population	Asians who are foreign born	Total NHPI[1] population	NHPIs[1] who are foreign born	Asian Indian	Bangladeshi	Cambodian	Chinese[2]	Fijian	Filipino	Guamanian[3]	Hawaiian, Native	Hmong	Indonesian	Japanese	Korean	Laotian	Malaysian	Pakistani	Samoan	Sri Lankan	Taiwanese	Thai	Tongan	Vietnamese
San Benito County	10,026 18.83	1,033	511 49.47 49.47 5.10	-	-	-	-	-	-	-	290 54.10 56.75 28.07 2.89	-	-	-	-	-	-	-	-	-	-	-	-	-	-	-
San Bernardino County	318,647 18.64	79,103	52,507 66.38 66.38 16.48	5,019	1,353 26.96 26.96 0.42	5,571 69.94 10.61 7.04 1.75	-	1,095 62.86 2.09 1.38 0.34	7,222 67.70 13.75 9.13 2.27	-	16,539 64.55 31.50 20.91 5.19	55 5.28 4.07 1.10 0.02	34 5.57 2.51 0.68 0.01	-	2,431 73.64 4.63 3.07 0.76	1,361 31.56 2.59 1.72 0.43	5,033 70.19 9.59 6.36 1.58	332 69.89 0.63 0.42 0.10	-	548 80.23 1.04 0.69 0.17	618 30.35 45.68 12.31 0.19	-	1,609 78.91 3.06 2.03 0.50	1,366 80.12 2.60 1.73 0.43	397 49.01 29.34 7.91 0.12	7,736 75.06 14.73 9.78 2.43
Chino (city)	13,823 20.45	3,351	2,185 65.20 65.20 15.81	-	-	-	-	-	-	-	1,015 64.57 46.45 30.29 7.34	-	-	-	-	-	-	-	-	-	-	-	-	-	-	378 80.77 17.30 11.28 2.73
Chino Hills (city)	15,123 22.67	14,256	9,079 63.69 63.69 60.03	-	-	832 70.63 9.16 5.84 5.50	-	-	2,333 66.91 25.70 16.37 15.43	-	3,437 61.75 37.86 24.11 22.73	-	-	-	-	51 9.24 0.56 0.36 0.34	755 72.11 8.32 5.30 4.99	-	-	-	-	-	428 67.51 4.71 3.00 2.83	-	-	552 69.52 6.08 3.87 3.65
Colton (city)	11,515 23.98	2,440	1,657 67.91 67.91 14.39	-	-	-	-	-	-	-	361 61.29 21.79 14.80 3.14	-	-	-	-	-	-	-	-	-	-	-	-	-	-	-
Fontana (city)	34,490 26.91	5,898	3,676 62.33 62.33 10.66	604	209 34.60 34.60 0.61	475 72.19 12.92 8.05 1.38	-	-	-	-	1,827 61.39 49.70 30.98 5.30	-	-	-	-	-	-	-	-	-	-	-	-	-	-	-
Grand Terrace (city)	1,292 10.96	602	293 48.67 48.67 22.68	-	-	-	-	-	-	-	-	-	-	-	-	-	-	-	-	-	-	-	-	-	-	-
Highland (city)	8,530 19.11	2,832	1,787 63.10 63.10 20.95	-	-	-	-	-	-	-	621 64.69 34.75 21.93 7.28	-	-	-	-	-	-	-	-	-	-	-	-	-	-	471 77.85 26.36 16.63 5.52
Loma Linda (city)	5,528 29.75	4,351	3,002 69.00 69.00 54.31	-	-	295 73.02 9.83 6.78 5.34	-	-	525 72.92 17.49 12.07 9.50	-	640 61.42 21.32 14.71 11.58	-	-	-	405 77.59 13.49 9.31 7.33	-	586 72.35 19.52 13.47 10.60	-	-	-	-	-	-	-	-	-
Montclair (city)	11,295 34.10	2,645	2,149 81.25 81.25 19.03	-	-	-	-	-	-	-	-	-	-	-	-	-	-	-	-	-	-	-	-	-	-	1,077 88.06 50.12 40.72 9.54

Notes: Please refer to the User's Guide for an explanation of data; data is arranged alphabetically by state, then county, then city within each county; table includes counties with populations greater than 49,999 unless noted and cities with populations greater than 9,999 whose Asian and/or NHPI population rates are greater than the national average; (1) Native Hawaiian and other Pacific Islander; (2) excludes Taiwanese; (3) includes Chamorro; (4) county does not meet population threshold but is shown in order to allow inclusion of city

Place	Total foreign-born population	Total Asian population	Asians who are foreign born	Total NHPI[1] population	NHPIs[1] who are foreign born	Asian Indian	Bangladeshi	Cambodian	Chinese[2]	Fijian	Filipino	Guamanian[3]	Hawaiian, Native	Hmong	Indonesian	Japanese	Korean	Laotian	Malaysian	Pakistani	Samoan	Sri Lankan	Taiwanese	Thai	Tongan	Vietnamese
Ontario (city)	48,789 31.01	6,130	4,199 68.50 68.50 8.61	544	206 37.87 37.87 0.42	270 53.05 6.43 4.40 0.55	-	-	329 70.15 7.84 5.37 0.67	-	1,700 73.47 40.49 27.73 3.48	-	-	-	-	-	-	-	-	-	-	-	-	-	-	1,156 71.89 27.53 18.86 2.37
Rancho Cucamonga (city)	17,644 13.77	7,360	5,010 68.07 68.07 28.39	-	-	755 76.81 15.07 10.26 4.28	-	-	963 71.97 19.22 13.08 5.46	-	1,489 68.49 29.72 20.23 8.44	-	-	-	-	131 24.86 2.61 1.78 0.74	535 70.49 10.68 7.27 3.03	-	-	-	-	-	-	-	-	392 74.38 7.82 5.33 2.22
Redlands (city)	8,157 12.81	3,292	2,154 65.43 65.43 26.41	-	-	242 60.80 11.23 7.35 2.97	-	-	388 79.35 18.01 11.79 4.76	-	397 61.74 18.43 12.06 4.87	-	-	-	-	-	342 61.96 15.88 10.39 4.19	-	-	-	-	-	-	-	-	-
Rialto (city)	20,439 22.29	1,748	1,006 57.55 57.55 4.92	532	144 27.07 27.07 0.70	-	-	-	-	-	279 56.14 27.73 15.96 1.37	-	-	-	-	-	-	-	-	-	-	-	-	-	-	-
San Bernardino (city)	38,248 20.63	7,501	5,255 70.06 70.06 13.74	748	199 26.60 26.60 0.52	679 76.29 12.92 9.05 1.78	-	261 58.52 4.97 3.48 0.68	411 68.39 7.82 5.48 1.07	-	1,267 70.82 24.11 16.89 3.31	-	-	-	255 56.79 4.85 3.40 0.67	-	279 70.81 5.31 3.72 0.73	-	-	-	125 26.15 62.81 16.71 0.33	-	-	-	-	1,133 74.83 21.56 15.10 2.96
Upland (city)	11,110 16.24	4,996	3,550 71.06 71.06 31.95	-	-	412 70.79 11.61 8.25 3.71	-	-	508 72.36 14.31 10.17 4.57	-	457 80.60 12.87 9.15 4.11	-	-	-	-	-	608 63.01 17.13 12.17 5.47	-	-	-	-	-	409 87.39 11.52 8.19 3.68	-	-	683 80.45 19.24 13.67 6.15
Victorville (city)	7,937 12.30	2,398	1,400 58.38 58.38 17.64	-	-	-	-	-	-	-	610 49.96 43.57 25.44 7.69	-	-	-	-	-	-	-	-	-	-	-	-	-	-	-
San Diego County	606,254 21.55	248,653	166,843 67.10 67.10 27.52	13,482	1,392 10.32 10.32 0.23	6,967 72.38 4.18 2.80 1.15	-	2,710 62.03 1.62 1.09 0.45	19,240 66.49 11.53 7.74 3.17	-	80,757 66.93 48.40 32.48 13.32	198 4.28 14.22 1.47 0.03	20 0.90 1.44 0.15 <0.01	752 54.69 0.45 0.30 0.12	373 76.12 0.22 0.15 0.06	10,263 54.71 6.15 4.13 1.69	8,397 73.80 5.03 3.38 1.39	5,011 70.41 3.00 2.02 0.83	-	343 63.52 0.21 0.14 0.06	555 11.20 39.87 4.12 0.09	-	1,747 73.96 1.05 0.70 0.29	961 73.41 0.58 0.39 0.16	196 45.06 14.08 1.45 0.03	25,985 75.33 15.57 10.45 4.29
Bonita (cdp)	2,322 19.32	994	641 64.49 64.49 27.61	-	-	-	-	-	-	-	391 72.41 61.00 39.34 16.84	-	-	-	-	-	-	-	-	-	-	-	-	-	-	-
Carlsbad (city)	9,930 12.73	3,177	1,950 61.38 61.38 19.64	-	-	-	-	-	465 65.22 23.85 14.64 4.68	-	323 52.18 16.56 10.17 3.25	-	-	-	-	157 32.91 8.05 4.94 1.58	-	-	-	-	-	-	-	-	-	-

Notes: Please refer to the User's Guide for an explanation of data; data is arranged alphabetically by state, then county, then city within each county; table includes counties with populations greater than 49,999 unless noted and cities with populations greater than 9,999 whose Asian and/or NHPI population rates are greater than the national average; (1) Native Hawaiian and other Pacific Islander; (2) excludes Taiwanese; (3) includes Chamorro; (4) county does not meet population threshold but is shown in order to allow inclusion of city

Place	Total foreign-born population	Total Asian population	Asians who are foreign born	Total NHPI[1] population	NHPIs[1] who are foreign born	Asian Indian	Bangladeshi	Cambodian	Chinese[2]	Fijian	Filipino	Guamanian[3]	Hawaiian, Native	Hmong	Indonesian	Japanese	Korean	Laotian	Malaysian	Pakistani	Samoan	Sri Lankan	Taiwanese	Thai	Tongan	Vietnamese
Chula Vista (city)	49,842 28.67	18,851	11,954 63.41 63.41 23.98	752	52 6.91 6.91 0.10	-	-	-	610 57.22 5.10 3.24 1.22	-	8,203 62.73 68.62 43.51 16.46	21 4.94 40.38 2.79 0.04	-	-	-	1,236 61.13 10.34 6.56 2.48	1,200 85.23 10.04 6.37 2.41	-	-	-	-	-	-	-	-	-
Coronado (city)	2,183 9.01	907	601 66.26 66.26 27.53	-	-	-	-	-	-	-	342 73.55 56.91 37.71 15.67	-	-	-	-	-	-	-	-	-	-	-	-	-	-	-
Escondido (city)	34,005 25.47	5,552	3,747 67.49 67.49 11.02	-	-	-	-	-	342 78.98 9.13 6.16 1.01	-	1,236 60.62 32.99 22.26 3.63	-	-	-	-	-	-	318 66.39 8.49 5.73 0.94	-	-	-	-	-	-	-	925 72.10 24.69 16.66 2.72
Imperial Beach (city)	5,498 20.38	1,826	1,327 72.67 72.67 24.14	-	-	-	-	-	-	-	1,138 75.31 85.76 62.32 20.70	-	-	-	-	-	-	-	-	-	-	-	-	-	-	-
La Mesa (city)	6,373 11.64	2,255	1,533 67.98 67.98 24.05	-	-	-	-	-	-	-	329 57.42 21.46 14.59 5.16	-	-	-	-	-	-	-	-	-	-	-	-	-	-	-
La Presa (cdp)	6,865 20.90	3,397	2,364 69.59 69.59 34.44	-	-	-	-	-	-	-	2,117 69.00 89.55 62.32 30.84	-	-	-	-	-	-	-	-	-	-	-	-	-	-	-
Lemon Grove (city)	3,613 14.48	1,447	846 58.47 58.47 23.42	-	-	-	-	-	-	-	401 56.08 47.40 27.71 11.10	-	-	-	-	-	-	-	-	-	-	-	-	-	-	266 72.88 31.44 18.38 7.36
National City (city)	22,487 41.33	9,966	7,675 77.01 77.01 34.13	-	-	-	-	-	-	-	7,098 78.34 92.48 71.22 31.56	-	-	-	-	-	-	-	-	-	-	-	-	-	-	-
Oceanside (city)	32,965 20.49	8,991	5,771 64.19 64.19 17.51	2,274	345 15.17 15.17 1.05	-	-	-	353 70.60 6.12 3.93 1.07	-	3,506 66.72 60.75 38.99 10.64	-	-	-	-	548 46.09 9.50 6.09 1.66	-	-	-	-	207 13.51 60.00 9.10 0.63	-	-	-	-	567 65.25 9.82 6.31 1.72
Poway (city)	5,136 10.63	3,458	1,985 57.40 57.40 38.65	-	-	-	-	-	416 60.03 20.96 12.03 8.10	-	753 54.92 37.93 21.78 14.66	-	-	-	-	-	-	-	-	-	-	-	-	-	-	-

Notes: Please refer to the User's Guide for an explanation of data; data is arranged alphabetically by state, then county, then city within each county; table includes counties with populations greater than 49,999 unless noted and cities with populations greater than 9,999 whose Asian and/or NHPI population rates are greater than the national average; (1) Native Hawaiian and other Pacific Islander; (2) excludes Taiwanese; (3) includes Chamorro; (4) county does not meet population threshold but is shown in order to allow inclusion of city

Place	Total foreign-born population	Total Asian population	Asians who are foreign born	Total NHPI[1] population	NHPIs[1] who are foreign born	Asian Indian	Bangladeshi	Cambodian	Chinese[2]	Fijian	Filipino	Guamanian[3]	Hawaiian, Native	Hmong	Indonesian	Japanese	Korean	Laotian	Malaysian	Pakistani	Samoan	Sri Lankan	Taiwanese	Thai	Tongan	Vietnamese
Rancho San Diego (cdp)	2,410 12.02	1,010	574 56.83 56.83 23.82	-	-	-	-	-	-	-	320 58.61 55.75 31.68 13.28	-	-	-	-	-	-	-	-	-	-	-	-	-	-	-
San Diego (city)	314,227 25.69	166,326	113,278 68.11 68.11 36.05	6,216	649 10.44 10.44 0.21	4,657 71.44 4.11 2.80 1.48	-	2,427 61.98 2.14 1.46 0.77	14,732 67.08 13.01 8.86 4.69	-	49,609 67.23 43.79 29.83 15.79	35 1.69 5.39 0.56 0.01	0 0.00 0.00 0.00 0.00	576 52.75 0.51 0.35 0.18	-	5,888 57.75 5.20 3.54 1.87	4,997 73.44 4.41 3.00 1.59	4,246 70.33 3.75 2.55 1.35	-	-	236 10.87 36.36 3.80 0.08	-	1,205 75.93 1.06 0.72 0.38	588 71.45 0.52 0.35 0.19	-	21,714 76.06 19.17 13.06 6.91
San Marcos (city)	14,111 25.58	2,463	1,561 63.38 63.38 11.06	-	-	-	-	-	310 73.11 19.86 12.59 2.20	-	750 59.90 48.05 30.45 5.32	-	-	-	-	-	-	-	-	-	-	-	-	-	-	-
Solana Beach (city)	1,893 14.69	529	259 48.96 48.96 13.68	-	-	-	-	-	-	-	-	-	-	-	-	-	-	-	-	-	-	-	-	-	-	-
Spring Valley (cdp)	3,638 13.65	1,361	802 58.93 58.93 22.05	-	-	-	-	-	-	-	414 65.82 51.62 30.42 11.38	-	-	-	-	-	-	-	-	-	-	-	-	-	-	-
Vista (city)	22,030 24.44	3,160	2,178 68.92 68.92 9.89	582	46 7.90 7.90 0.21	-	-	-	-	-	741 62.53 34.02 23.45 3.36	-	-	-	-	381 64.69 17.49 12.06 1.73	-	-	-	-	-	-	-	-	-	-
San Francisco County	285,541 36.76	239,938	166,590 69.43 69.43 58.34	3,581	1,111 31.02 31.02 0.39	3,421 70.77 2.05 1.43 1.20	-	455 70.43 0.27 0.19 0.16	107,744 69.74 64.68 44.90 37.73	-	28,397 70.86 17.05 11.84 9.94	-	-	-	783 89.69 0.47 0.33 0.27	5,085 47.00 3.05 2.12 1.78	5,352 75.02 3.21 2.23 1.87	-	-	335 60.25 0.20 0.14 0.12	654 28.70 58.87 18.26 0.23	-	588 76.26 0.35 0.25 0.21	1,177 80.56 0.71 0.49 0.41	-	8,418 80.71 5.05 3.51 2.95
San Francisco (city)	285,541 36.76	239,938	166,590 69.43 69.43 58.34	3,581	1,111 31.02 31.02 0.39	3,421 70.77 2.05 1.43 1.20	-	455 70.43 0.27 0.19 0.16	107,744 69.74 64.68 44.90 37.73	-	28,397 70.86 17.05 11.84 9.94	-	-	-	783 89.69 0.47 0.33 0.27	5,085 47.00 3.05 2.12 1.78	5,352 75.02 3.21 2.23 1.87	-	-	335 60.25 0.20 0.14 0.12	654 28.70 58.87 18.26 0.23	-	588 76.26 0.35 0.25 0.21	1,177 80.56 0.71 0.49 0.41	-	8,418 80.71 5.05 3.51 2.95
San Joaquin County	109,812 19.48	65,065	36,632 56.30 56.30 33.36	1,785	343 19.22 19.22 0.31	3,485 66.95 9.51 5.36 3.17	-	5,517 58.26 15.06 8.48 5.02	3,365 59.58 9.19 5.17 3.06	-	12,228 57.77 33.38 18.79 11.14	-	22 5.30 6.41 1.23 0.02	3,063 51.50 8.36 4.71 2.79	-	551 15.46 1.50 0.85 0.50	550 65.95 1.50 0.85 0.50	1,903 61.79 5.19 2.92 1.73	-	880 65.82 2.40 1.35 0.80	62 17.22 18.08 3.47 0.06	-	-	-	-	3,915 61.95 10.69 6.02 3.57
Lathrop (city)	2,252 21.79	1,463	905 61.86 61.86 40.19	-	-	-	-	-	-	-	732 68.86 80.88 50.03 32.50	-	-	-	-	-	-	-	-	-	-	-	-	-	-	-

Notes: Please refer to the User's Guide for an explanation of data; data is arranged alphabetically by state, then county, then city within each county; table includes counties with populations greater than 49,999 unless noted and cities with populations greater than 9,999 whose Asian and/or NHPI population rates are greater than the national average; (1) Native Hawaiian and other Pacific Islander; (2) excludes Taiwanese; (3) includes Chamorro; (4) county does not meet population threshold but is shown in order to allow inclusion of city

Place	Total foreign-born population	Total Asian population	Asians who are foreign born	Total NHPI[1] population	NHPIs[1] who are foreign born	Asian Indian	Bangladeshi	Cambodian	Chinese[2]	Fijian	Filipino	Guamanian[3]	Hawaiian, Native	Hmong	Indonesian	Japanese	Korean	Laotian	Malaysian	Pakistani	Samoan	Sri Lankan	Taiwanese	Thai	Tongan	Vietnamese
Lodi (city)	10,741 18.83	3,114	1,611 51.73 51.73 15.00	-	-	545 70.96 33.83 17.50 5.07	-	-	-	-	293 45.92 18.19 9.41 2.73	-	-	-	-	86 12.99 5.34 2.76 0.80	-	-	-	-	-	-	-	-	-	-
Stockton (city)	59,369 24.46	48,681	28,336 58.21 58.21 47.73	1,036	146 14.09 14.09 0.25	1,388 64.92 4.90 2.85 2.34	-	5,362 58.92 18.92 11.01 9.03	2,667 62.24 9.41 5.48 4.49	-	9,031 60.07 31.87 18.55 15.21	-	-	2,589 52.27 9.14 5.32 4.36	-	272 16.82 0.96 0.56 0.46	-	1,840 61.99 6.49 3.78 3.10	-	409 58.26 1.44 0.84 0.69	-	-	-	-	-	3,583 62.30 12.64 7.36 6.04
Tracy (city)	9,564 16.83	4,763	2,597 54.52 54.52 27.15	-	-	749 65.88 28.84 15.73 7.83	-	-	229 62.06 8.82 4.81 2.39	-	1,071 53.23 41.24 22.49 11.20	-	-	-	-	-	-	-	-	-	-	-	-	-	-	-
San Luis Obispo County	22,016 8.92	6,850	3,608 52.67 52.67 16.39	-	-	430 69.13 11.92 6.28 1.95	-	-	649 58.15 17.99 9.47 2.95	-	1,309 53.32 36.28 19.11 5.95	-	-	-	-	345 34.02 9.56 5.04 1.57	519 70.23 14.38 7.58 2.36	-	-	-	-	-	-	-	-	-
Baywood-Los Osos (cdp)	1,166 8.24	845	535 63.31 63.31 45.88	-	-	-	-	-	-	-	389 66.50 72.71 46.04 33.36	-	-	-	-	-	-	-	-	-	-	-	-	-	-	-
Grover Beach (city)	1,514 11.64	501	340 67.86 67.86 22.46	-	-	-	-	-	-	-	-	-	-	-	-	-	-	-	-	-	-	-	-	-	-	-
San Luis Obispo (city)	4,214 9.55	2,273	1,289 56.71 56.71 30.59	-	-	-	-	-	289 51.79 22.42 12.71 6.86	-	226 42.16 17.53 9.94 5.36	-	-	-	-	-	-	-	-	-	-	-	-	-	-	-
San Mateo County	228,118 32.26	142,162	92,912 65.36 65.36 40.73	8,533	3,925 46.00 46.00 1.72	8,752 78.90 9.42 6.16 3.84	-	-	29,976 63.22 32.26 21.09 13.14	779 67.33 19.85 9.13 0.34	40,637 67.60 43.74 28.58 17.81	15 3.73 0.38 0.18 0.01	49 6.09 1.25 0.57 0.02	-	605 80.03 0.65 0.43 0.27	4,043 42.71 4.35 2.84 1.77	3,419 78.45 3.68 2.41 1.50	-	-	-	305 21.02 7.77 3.57 0.13	-	625 80.23 0.67 0.44 0.27	461 65.76 0.50 0.32 0.20	2,208 60.43 56.25 25.88 0.97	2,083 74.39 2.24 1.47 0.91
Belmont (city)	5,673 22.57	3,923	2,258 57.56 57.56 39.80	-	-	585 80.91 25.91 14.91 10.31	-	-	908 53.66 40.21 23.15 16.01	-	343 53.43 15.19 8.74 6.05	-	-	-	-	162 36.57 7.17 4.13 2.86	-	-	-	-	-	-	-	-	-	-
Burlingame (city)	6,875 24.58	3,739	2,659 71.12 71.12 38.68	-	-	-	-	-	1,340 73.06 50.39 35.84 19.49	-	355 62.17 13.35 9.49 5.16	-	-	-	-	224 57.88 8.42 5.99 3.26	-	-	-	-	-	-	-	-	-	-

Notes: Please refer to the User's Guide for an explanation of data; data is arranged alphabetically by state, then county, then city within each county; table includes counties with populations greater than 49,999 unless noted and cities with populations greater than 9,999 whose Asian and/or NHPI population rates are greater than the national average; (1) Native Hawaiian and other Pacific Islander; (2) excludes Taiwanese; (3) includes Chamorro; (4) county does not meet population threshold but is shown in order to allow inclusion of city

Place	Total foreign-born population	Total Asian population	Asians who are foreign born	Total NHPI[1] population	NHPIs[1] who are foreign born	Asian Indian	Bangladeshi	Cambodian	Chinese[2]	Fijian	Filipino	Guamanian[3]	Hawaiian, Native	Hmong	Indonesian	Japanese	Korean	Laotian	Malaysian	Pakistani	Samoan	Sri Lankan	Taiwanese	Thai	Tongan	Vietnamese
Daly City (city)	54,213	52,289	35,710	866	266	813	-	-	9,157	-	22,701	-	-	-	-	363	625	-	-	-	-	-	-	-	-	701
	52.35		68.29		30.72	76.84			66.57		68.95					44.21	78.42									75.78
						2.28			25.64		63.57					1.02	1.75									1.96
			68.29		30.72	1.55			17.51		43.41					0.69	1.20									1.34
			65.87		0.49	1.50			16.89		41.87					0.67	1.15									1.29
East Palo Alto (city)	12,904	563	376	2,211	1,263	-	-	-	-	-	-	-	-	-	-	-	-	-	-	-	-	-	-	-	929	-
	43.82		66.79		57.12																				62.18	
																									73.56	
			66.79		57.12																				42.02	
			2.91		9.79																				7.20	
Foster City (city)	10,141	9,377	6,194	-	-	1,432	-	-	2,804	-	500	-	-	-	-	770	318	-	-	-	-	-	-	-	-	-
	35.21		66.06			80.54			66.27		62.50					51.47	81.54									
						23.12			45.27		8.07					12.43	5.13									
			66.06			15.27			29.90		5.33					8.21	3.39									
			61.08			14.12			27.65		4.93					7.59	3.14									
Hillsborough (town)	2,572	2,702	1,670	-	-	-	-	-	1,188	-	-	-	-	-	-	-	-	-	-	-	-	-	-	-	-	-
	23.76		61.81						59.55																	
									71.14																	
			61.81						43.97																	
			64.93						46.19																	
Menlo Park (city)	7,006	2,154	1,464	-	-	-	-	-	547	-	-	-	-	-	-	281	-	-	-	-	-	-	-	-	-	-
	22.76		67.97						63.60							62.03										
									37.36							19.19										
			67.97						25.39							13.05										
			20.90						7.81							4.01										
Millbrae (city)	7,088	5,898	3,823	-	-	259	-	-	2,506	-	381	-	-	-	-	237	255	-	-	-	-	-	-	-	-	-
	34.20		64.82			69.44			65.50		56.36					58.37	79.69									
						6.77			65.55		9.97					6.20	6.67									
			64.82			4.39			42.49		6.46					4.02	4.32									
			53.94			3.65			35.36		5.38					3.34	3.60									
Pacifica (city)	7,169	5,897	3,506	-	-	-	-	-	798	-	2,068	-	-	-	-	130	-	-	-	-	-	-	-	-	-	-
	18.66		59.45						52.40		63.46					35.91										
									22.76		58.98					3.71										
			59.45						13.53		35.07					2.20										
			48.91						11.13		28.85					1.81										
Redwood City (city)	22,671	6,932	4,551	566	258	1,003	-	-	1,658	-	1,017	-	-	-	-	194	-	-	-	-	-	-	-	-	-	-
	30.05		65.65		45.58	79.29			65.28		70.38					32.61										
						22.04			36.43		22.35					4.26										
			65.65		45.58	14.47			23.92		14.67					2.80										
			20.07		1.14	4.42			7.31		4.49					0.86										
San Bruno (city)	13,021	7,496	4,679	1,017	619	803	-	-	1,300	-	1,969	-	-	-	-	159	-	-	-	-	-	-	-	-	345	-
	32.42		62.42		60.87	76.33			60.07		64.35					32.92									64.73	
						17.16			27.78		42.08					3.40									55.74	
			62.42		60.87	10.71			17.34		26.27					2.12									33.92	
			35.93		4.75	6.17			9.98		15.12					1.22									2.65	
San Carlos (city)	4,332	1,841	1,091	-	-	-	-	-	416	-	-	-	-	-	-	-	-	-	-	-	-	-	-	-	-	-
	15.64		59.26						59.26																	
									38.13																	
			59.26						22.60																	
			25.18						9.60																	

Notes: Please refer to the User's Guide for an explanation of data; data is arranged alphabetically by state, then county, then city within each county; table includes counties with populations greater than 49,999 unless noted and cities with populations greater than 9,999 whose Asian and/or NHPI population rates are greater than the national average; (1) Native Hawaiian and other Pacific Islander; (2) excludes Taiwanese; (3) includes Chamorro; (4) county does not meet population threshold but is shown in order to allow inclusion of city

Place	Total foreign-born population	Total Asian population	Asians who are foreign born	Total NHPI[1] population	NHPIs[1] who are foreign born	Asian Indian	Bangladeshi	Cambodian	Chinese[2]	Fijian	Filipino	Guamanian[3]	Hawaiian, Native	Hmong	Indonesian	Japanese	Korean	Laotian	Malaysian	Pakistani	Samoan	Sri Lankan	Taiwanese	Thai	Tongan	Vietnamese
San Mateo (city)	27,864	14,221	9,099	1,369	637	1,764	-	-	3,503	-	1,861	-	-	-	-	772	446	-	-	-	-	-	-	-	411	281
	30.16		63.98		46.53	80.92			66.18		63.21					38.33	77.57								64.42	69.73
						19.39			38.50		20.45					8.48	4.90								64.52	3.09
			63.98		46.53	12.40			24.63		13.09					5.43	3.14								30.02	1.98
			32.66		2.29	6.33			12.57		6.68					2.77	1.60								1.48	1.01
South San Francisco (city)	23,739	17,618	11,077	874	263	614	-	-	2,475	-	6,905	-	-	-	-	165	-	-	-	-	-	-	-	-	-	-
	39.09		62.87		30.09	83.77			53.56		66.66					31.43										
						5.54			22.34		62.34					1.49										
			62.87		30.09	3.49			14.05		39.19					0.94										
			46.66		1.11	2.59			10.43		29.09					0.70										
Santa Barbara County	84,826	15,630	9,253	905	146	581	-	-	1,638	-	2,908	-	-	154	-	812	1,158	-	-	-	-	-	-	-	-	869
	21.24		59.20		16.13	66.40			62.93		59.59			43.38		35.29	71.66									71.00
						6.28			17.70		31.43			1.66		8.78	12.51									9.39
			59.20		16.13	3.72			10.48		18.61			0.99		5.20	7.41									5.56
			10.91		0.17	0.68			1.93		3.43			0.18		0.96	1.37									1.02
Goleta (cdp)	9,854	3,247	2,042	-	-	-	-	-	548	-	299	-	-	-	-	114	-	-	-	-	-	-	-	-	-	342
	17.80		62.89						70.62		56.42					25.05										69.37
									26.84		14.64					5.58										16.75
			62.89						16.88		9.21					3.51										10.53
			20.72						5.56		3.03					1.16										3.47
Isla Vista (cdp)	3,440	1,973	1,051	-	-	-	-	-	403	-	-	-	-	-	-	-	251	-	-	-	-	-	-	-	-	-
	18.71		53.27						59.79								58.92									
									38.34								23.88									
			53.27						20.43								12.72									
			30.55						11.72								7.30									
Lompoc (city)	7,335	1,539	925	-	-	-	-	-	-	-	190	-	-	-	-	-	-	-	-	-	-	-	-	-	-	-
	17.86		60.10								53.22															
											20.54															
			60.10								12.35															
			12.61								2.59															
Orcutt (cdp)	2,095	1,056	521	-	-	-	-	-	-	-	-	-	-	-	-	-	-	-	-	-	-	-	-	-	-	-
	7.26		49.34																							
			49.34																							
			24.87																							
Santa Maria (city)	24,647	3,639	2,223	-	-	-	-	-	-	-	1,574	-	-	-	-	151	-	-	-	-	-	-	-	-	-	-
	31.96		61.09								65.50					34.01										
											70.81					6.79										
			61.09								43.25					4.15										
			9.02								6.39					0.61										
Santa Clara County	573,130	430,201	304,162	5,793	1,464	51,554	395	2,982	78,399	493	52,877	90	53	-	552	10,203	16,838	1,402	-	1,904	469	-	4,052	1,048	-	75,662
	34.06		70.70		25.27	79.21	81.61	67.79	69.63	96.48	67.95	6.47	4.62		80.35	37.82	77.69	67.99		69.21	27.28		76.48	78.56		77.67
						16.95	0.13	0.98	25.78	33.67	17.38	6.15	3.62		0.18	3.35	5.54	0.46		0.63	32.04		1.33	0.34		24.88
			70.70		25.27	11.98	0.09	0.69	18.22	8.51	12.29	1.55	0.91		0.13	2.37	3.91	0.33		0.44	8.10		0.94	0.24		17.59
			53.07		0.26	9.00	0.07	0.52	13.68	0.09	9.23	0.02	0.01		0.10	1.78	2.94	0.24		0.33	0.08		0.71	0.18		13.20
Alum Rock (cdp)	4,726	1,258	827	-	-	-	-	-	-	-	-	-	-	-	-	-	-	-	-	-	-	-	-	-	-	435
	34.30		65.74																							78.10
																										52.60
			65.74																							34.58
			17.50																							9.20

Notes: Please refer to the User's Guide for an explanation of data; data is arranged alphabetically by state, then county, then city within each county; table includes counties with populations greater than 49,999 unless noted and cities with populations greater than 9,999 whose Asian and/or NHPI population rates are greater than the national average; (1) Native Hawaiian and other Pacific Islander; (2) excludes Taiwanese; (3) includes Chamorro; (4) county does not meet population threshold but is shown in order to allow inclusion of city

Place	Total foreign-born population	Total Asian population	Asians who are foreign born	Total NHPI[1] population	NHPIs[1] who are foreign born	Asian Indian	Bangladeshi	Cambodian	Chinese[2]	Fijian	Filipino	Guamanian[3]	Hawaiian, Native	Hmong	Indonesian	Japanese	Korean	Laotian	Malaysian	Pakistani	Samoan	Sri Lankan	Taiwanese	Thai	Tongan	Vietnamese
Campbell (city)	8,281	5,641	3,605	-	-	647	-	-	873	-	393	-	-	-	-	190	688	-	-	-	-	-	-	-	-	724
	21.69		63.91			84.14			59.31		62.78					23.99	80.56									79.56
						17.95			24.22		10.90					5.27	19.08									20.08
			63.91			11.47			15.48		6.97					3.37	12.20									12.83
			43.53			7.81			10.54		4.75					2.29	8.31									8.74
Cupertino (city)	21,659	22,599	15,916	-	-	3,501	-	-	7,131	-	325	-	-	-	-	1,687	1,707	-	-	-	-	-	619	-	-	569
	42.76		70.43			73.38			67.79		79.46					69.80	76.38						78.16			77.52
						22.00			44.80		2.04					10.60	10.73						3.89			3.58
			70.43			15.49			31.55		1.44					7.46	7.55						2.74			2.52
			73.48			16.16			32.92		1.50					7.79	7.88						2.86			2.63
Gilroy (city)	10,042	1,912	901	-	-	-	-	-	211	-	316	-	-	-	-	-	-	-	-	-	-	-	-	-	-	-
	24.15		47.12						54.95		48.10															
									23.42		35.07															
			47.12						11.04		16.53															
			8.97						2.10		3.15															
Los Altos (city)	4,857	4,177	2,326	-	-	371	-	-	1,090	-	-	-	-	-	-	263	-	-	-	-	-	-	-	-	-	-
	17.61		55.69			71.07			53.25							38.39										
						15.95			46.86							11.31										
			55.69			8.88			26.10							6.30										
			47.89			7.64			22.44							5.41										
Los Gatos (town)	4,260	2,338	1,379	-	-	-	-	-	639	-	-	-	-	-	-	216	-	-	-	-	-	-	-	-	-	-
	14.85		58.98						70.84							44.08										
									46.34							15.66										
			58.98						27.33							9.24										
			32.37						15.00							5.07										
Milpitas (city)	29,646	32,766	24,205	631	139	3,685	-	-	6,076	-	6,296	-	-	-	-	230	723	-	-	-	-	-	-	-	-	6,068
	47.27		73.87		22.03	77.96			74.98		69.82					39.12	85.06									76.60
						15.22			25.10		26.01					0.95	2.99									25.07
			73.87		22.03	11.25			18.54		19.22					0.70	2.21									18.52
			81.65		0.47	12.43			20.50		21.24					0.78	2.44									20.47
Morgan Hill (city)	5,104	2,113	1,091	-	-	-	-	-	249	-	-	-	-	-	-	83	-	-	-	-	-	-	-	-	-	-
	15.17		51.63						59.43							17.81										
									22.82							7.61										
			51.63						11.78							3.93										
			21.38						4.88							1.63										
Mountain View (city)	24,661	14,561	10,235	-	-	2,519	-	-	3,849	-	1,406	-	-	-	-	661	545	-	-	-	-	-	-	-	-	733
	35.00		70.29			86.68			70.13		66.95					39.63	78.30									84.94
						24.61			37.61		13.74					6.46	5.32									7.16
			70.29			17.30			26.43		9.66					4.54	3.74									5.03
			41.50			10.21			15.61		5.70					2.68	2.21									2.97
Palo Alto (city)	15,573	10,307	6,817	-	-	1,094	-	-	3,603	-	297	-	-	-	-	622	710	-	-	-	-	-	-	-	-	-
	26.49		66.14			75.29			66.03		71.22					52.05	72.23									
						16.05			52.85		4.36					9.12	10.42									
			66.14			10.61			34.96		2.88					6.03	6.89									
			43.77			7.02			23.14		1.91					3.99	4.56									
San Jose (city)	329,757	239,465	170,354	3,234	885	19,146	-	2,672	36,192	-	33,966	38	33	-	-	3,223	7,221	1,278	-	916	359	-	1,622	494	-	59,187
	36.89		71.14		27.37	76.34		66.98	71.10		68.47	5.19	6.17			28.78	77.00	67.51		69.45	29.47		79.01	78.29		77.92
						11.24		1.57	21.25		19.94	4.29	3.73			1.89	4.24	0.75		0.54	40.56		0.95	0.29		34.74
			71.14		27.37	8.00		1.12	15.11		14.18	1.18	1.02			1.35	3.02	0.53		0.38	11.10		0.68	0.21		24.72
			51.66		0.27	5.81		0.81	10.98		10.30	0.01	0.01			0.98	2.19	0.39		0.28	0.11		0.49	0.15		17.95

Notes: Please refer to the User's Guide for an explanation of data; data is arranged alphabetically by state, then county, then city within each county; table includes counties with populations greater than 49,999 unless noted and cities with populations greater than 9,999 whose Asian and/or NHPI population rates are greater than the national average; (1) Native Hawaiian and other Pacific Islander; (2) excludes Taiwanese; (3) includes Chamorro; (4) county does not meet population threshold but is shown in order to allow inclusion of city

Place	Total foreign-born population	Total Asian population	Asians who are foreign born	Total NHPI[1] population	NHPIs[1] who are foreign born	Asian Indian	Bangladeshi	Cambodian	Chinese[2]	Fijian	Filipino	Guamanian[3]	Hawaiian, Native	Hmong	Indonesian	Japanese	Korean	Laotian	Malaysian	Pakistani	Samoan	Sri Lankan	Taiwanese	Thai	Tongan	Vietnamese
Santa Clara (city)	35,694	29,195	21,882	382	140	7,586	-	-	3,562	-	3,912	-	-	-	-	430	1,741	-	-	291	-	-	-	-	-	3,621
	34.96		74.95		36.65	85.52			75.88		65.93					29.72	84.31			62.05						78.07
						34.67			16.28		17.88					1.97	7.96			1.33						16.55
			74.95		36.65	25.98			12.20		13.40					1.47	5.96			1.00						12.40
			61.30		0.39	21.25			9.98		10.96					1.20	4.88			0.82						10.14
Saratoga (city)	7,656	8,531	5,132	-	-	762	-	-	3,002	-	-	-	-	-	-	229	404	-	-	-	-	-	222	-	-	-
	25.64		60.16			61.55			60.15							42.72	73.19						66.87			
						14.85			58.50							4.46	7.87						4.33			
			60.16			8.93			35.19							2.68	4.74						2.60			
			67.03			9.95			39.21							2.99	5.28						2.90			
Stanford (cdp)	3,354	3,460	1,942	-	-	357	-	-	898	-	-	-	-	-	-	-	225	-	-	-	-	-	-	-	-	-
	25.20		56.13			54.42			56.51								61.14									
						18.38			46.24								11.59									
			56.13			10.32			25.95								6.50									
			57.90			10.64			26.77								6.71									
Sunnyvale (city)	51,990	42,604	32,192	536	144	10,596	-	-	8,982	-	4,518	-	-	-	-	1,832	2,124	-	-	-	-	-	589	-	-	2,573
	39.41		75.56		26.87	86.77			72.99		68.80					53.18	78.75						87.78			81.01
						32.92			27.90		14.03					5.69	6.60						1.83			7.99
			75.56		26.87	24.87			21.08		10.60					4.30	4.99						1.38			6.04
			61.92		0.28	20.38			17.28		8.69					3.52	4.09						1.13			4.95
Santa Cruz County	46,502	8,390	4,276	-	-	661	-	-	1,137	-	1,069	-	-	-	-	328	350	-	-	-	-	-	-	-	-	299
	18.19		50.97			67.59			56.12		52.30					18.75	72.46									69.86
						15.46			26.59		25.00					7.67	8.19									6.99
			50.97			7.88			13.55		12.74					3.91	4.17									3.56
			9.20			1.42			2.45		2.30					0.71	0.75									0.64
Capitola (city)	1,219	484	349	-	-	-	-	-	-	-	-	-	-	-	-	-	-	-	-	-	-	-	-	-	-	-
	11.95		72.11																							
			72.11																							
			28.63																							
Santa Cruz (city)	8,225	2,795	1,422	-	-	284	-	-	462	-	270	-	-	-	-	108	-	-	-	-	-	-	-	-	-	-
	15.13		50.88			66.67			50.60		51.14					25.17										
						19.97			32.49		18.99					7.59										
			50.88			10.16			16.53		9.66					3.86										
			17.29			3.45			5.62		3.28					1.31										
Scotts Valley (city)	1,206	655	394	-	-	-	-	-	-	-	-	-	-	-	-	-	-	-	-	-	-	-	-	-	-	-
	10.47		60.15																							
			60.15																							
			32.67																							
Shasta County	6,488	3,219	2,155	-	-	-	-	-	-	-	258	-	-	-	-	-	-	1,218	-	-	-	-	-	-	-	-
	3.97		66.95								57.46							69.80								
											11.97							56.52								
			66.95								8.01							37.84								
			33.22								3.98							18.77								
Solano County	66,496	49,899	31,020	3,189	352	1,830	-	-	1,844	-	22,952	16	7	212	-	925	767	440	-	-	87	-	-	-	-	926
	16.85		62.17		11.04	64.60			58.73		64.00	1.18	1.07	51.58		46.41	79.24	58.36			13.92					65.95
						5.90			5.94		73.99	4.55	1.99	0.68		2.98	2.47	1.42			24.72					2.99
			62.17		11.04	3.67			3.70		46.00	0.50	0.22	0.42		1.85	1.54	0.88			2.73					1.86
			46.65		0.53	2.75			2.77		34.52	0.02	0.01	0.32		1.39	1.15	0.66			0.13					1.39

Notes: Please refer to the User's Guide for an explanation of data; data is arranged alphabetically by state, then county, then city within each county; table includes counties with populations greater than 49,999 unless noted and cities with populations greater than 9,999 whose Asian and/or NHPI population rates are greater than the national average; (1) Native Hawaiian and other Pacific Islander; (2) excludes Taiwanese; (3) includes Chamorro; (4) county does not meet population threshold but is shown in order to allow inclusion of city

Place	Total foreign-born population	Total Asian population	Asians who are foreign born	Total NHPI[1] population	NHPIs[1] who are foreign born	Asian Indian	Bangladeshi	Cambodian	Chinese[2]	Fijian	Filipino	Guamanian[3]	Hawaiian, Native	Hmong	Indonesian	Japanese	Korean	Laotian	Malaysian	Pakistani	Samoan	Sri Lankan	Taiwanese	Thai	Tongan	Vietnamese
Benicia (city)	2,530	1,941	1,024	-	-	-	-	-	307	-	511	-	-	-	-	-	-	-	-	-	-	-	-	-	-	-
	9.38		52.76						66.59		48.62															
									29.98		49.90															
			52.76						15.82		26.33															
			40.47						12.13		20.20															
Fairfield (city)	15,647	10,596	6,493	1,037	91	670	-	-	561	-	3,683	0	-	-	-	399	290	255	-	-	-	-	-	-	-	-
	16.27		61.28		8.78	71.05			60.13		60.80	0.00				57.00	74.36	65.55								
						10.32			8.64		56.72	0.00				6.15	4.47	3.93								
			61.28		8.78	6.32			5.29		34.76	0.00				3.77	2.74	2.41								
			41.50		0.58	4.28			3.59		23.54	0.00				2.55	1.85	1.63								
Suisun City (city)	5,166	4,803	3,082	-	-	229	-	-	-	-	2,089	-	-	-	-	-	-	-	-	-	-	-	-	-	-	-
	19.83		64.17			54.39					67.41															
						7.43					67.78															
			64.17			4.77					43.49															
			59.66			4.43					40.44															
Vacaville (city)	7,998	3,700	1,922	-	-	-	-	-	-	-	969	-	-	-	-	-	-	-	-	-	-	-	-	-	-	-
	9.02		51.95								50.65															
											50.42															
			51.95								26.19															
			24.03								12.12															
Vallejo (city)	28,748	27,632	17,906	1,396	228	626	-	-	520	-	15,399	16	-	-	-	164	-	-	-	-	-	-	-	-	-	378
	24.71		64.80		16.33	67.97			57.71		66.16	2.80				44.69										59.62
						3.50			2.90		86.00	7.02				0.92										2.11
			64.80		16.33	2.27			1.88		55.73	1.15				0.59										1.37
			62.29		0.79	2.18			1.81		53.57	0.06				0.57										1.31
Sonoma County	65,726	14,070	8,812	750	143	1,303	-	501	1,651	-	1,416	-	-	-	-	644	688	767	-	-	-	-	-	-	-	1,071
	14.33		62.63		19.07	74.93		58.94	59.62		56.73					41.31	77.22	70.89								79.16
						14.79		5.69	18.74		16.07					7.31	7.81	8.70								12.15
			62.63		19.07	9.26		3.56	11.73		10.06					4.58	4.89	5.45								7.61
			13.41		0.22	1.98		0.76	2.51		2.15					0.98	1.05	1.17								1.63
Petaluma (city)	7,859	2,232	1,413	-	-	-	-	-	445	-	-	-	-	-	-	-	-	-	-	-	-	-	-	-	-	-
	14.41		63.31						64.87																	
									31.49																	
			63.31						19.94																	
			17.98						5.66																	
Rohnert Park (city)	5,208	2,473	1,648	-	-	-	-	-	348	-	391	-	-	-	-	-	-	-	-	-	-	-	-	-	-	-
	12.29		66.64						76.82		54.61															
									21.12		23.73															
			66.64						14.07		15.81															
			31.64						6.68		7.51															
Santa Rosa (city)	24,015	5,607	3,732	-	-	584	-	384	432	-	481	-	-	-	-	201	-	499	-	-	-	-	-	-	-	608
	16.28		66.56			82.72		59.44	53.33		65.44					49.39		78.83								78.35
						15.65		10.29	11.58		12.89					5.39		13.37								16.29
			66.56			10.42		6.85	7.70		8.58					3.58		8.90								10.84
			15.54			2.43		1.60	1.80		2.00					0.84		2.08								2.53
Stanislaus County	81,615	18,392	10,855	1,804	764	3,103	-	1,777	1,003	521	1,421	-	-	369	-	232	-	1,094	-	-	-	-	-	-	-	943
	18.26		59.02		42.35	71.35		55.02	54.13	74.64	51.39			38.08		28.50		68.85								67.70
						28.59		16.37	9.24	68.19	13.09			3.40		2.14		10.08								8.69
			59.02		42.35	16.87		9.66	5.45	28.88	7.73			2.01		1.26		5.95								5.13
			13.30		0.94	3.80		2.18	1.23	0.64	1.74			0.45		0.28		1.34								1.16

Notes: Please refer to the User's Guide for an explanation of data; data is arranged alphabetically by state, then county, then city within each county; table includes counties with populations greater than 49,999 unless noted and cities with populations greater than 9,999 whose Asian and/or NHPI population rates are greater than the national average; (1) Native Hawaiian and other Pacific Islander; (2) excludes Taiwanese; (3) includes Chamorro; (4) county does not meet population threshold but is shown in order to allow inclusion of city

Place	Total foreign-born population	Total Asian population	Asians who are foreign born	Total NHPI[1] population	NHPIs[1] who are foreign born	Asian Indian	Bangladeshi	Cambodian	Chinese[2]	Fijian	Filipino	Guamanian[3]	Hawaiian, Native	Hmong	Indonesian	Japanese	Korean	Laotian	Malaysian	Pakistani	Samoan	Sri Lankan	Taiwanese	Thai	Tongan	Vietnamese
Ceres (city)	6,560 19.00	1,759	1,050 59.69 59.69 16.01	-	-	545 64.04 51.90 30.98 8.31	-	-	-	-	-	-	-	-	-	-	-	-	-	-	-	-	-	-	-	-
Modesto (city)	29,865 15.76	11,219	6,953 61.98 61.98 23.28	1,217	538 44.21 44.21 1.80	1,510 77.12 21.72 13.46 5.06	-	1,465 57.72 21.07 13.06 4.91	658 57.67 9.46 5.87 2.20	369 74.70 68.59 30.32 1.24	843 54.63 12.12 7.51 2.82	-	-	132 32.51 1.90 1.18 0.44	-	160 41.24 2.30 1.43 0.54	-	822 72.04 11.82 7.33 2.75	-	-	-	-	-	-	-	767 67.22 11.03 6.84 2.57
Salida (cdp)	1,853 14.75	487	271 55.65 55.65 14.62	-	-	-	-	-	-	-	-	-	-	-	-	-	-	-	-	-	-	-	-	-	-	-
Turlock (city)	11,916 21.47	2,410	1,310 54.36 54.36 10.99	-	-	759 71.07 57.94 31.49 6.37	-	-	-	-	-	-	-	-	-	-	-	-	-	-	-	-	-	-	-	-
Sutter County	15,228 19.29	8,869	5,604 63.19 63.19 36.80	-	-	4,789 65.77 85.46 54.00 31.45	-	-	-	-	247 60.10 4.41 2.78 1.62	-	-	-	-	91 25.00 1.62 1.03 0.60	-	-	-	-	-	-	-	-	-	-
South Yuba City (cdp)	2,531 19.64	2,922	1,934 66.19 66.19 76.41	-	-	1,763 65.98 91.16 60.34 69.66	-	-	-	-	-	-	-	-	-	-	-	-	-	-	-	-	-	-	-	-
Yuba City (city)	7,134 19.50	3,087	2,060 66.73 66.73 28.88	-	-	1,586 71.38 76.99 51.38 22.23	-	-	-	-	-	-	-	-	-	-	-	-	-	-	-	-	-	-	-	-
Tehama County	4,424 7.89	415	206 49.64 49.64 4.66	-	-	-	-	-	-	-	-	-	-	-	-	-	-	-	-	-	-	-	-	-	-	-
Tulare County	83,124 22.59	12,336	7,625 61.81 61.81 9.17	-	-	736 71.25 9.65 5.97 0.89	-	-	403 55.82 5.29 3.27 0.48	-	2,827 61.83 37.08 22.92 3.40	-	-	581 53.45 7.62 4.71 0.70	-	108 18.21 1.42 0.88 0.13	280 75.68 3.67 2.27 0.34	2,148 68.36 28.17 17.41 2.58	-	-	-	-	-	-	-	-
Porterville (city)	9,041 22.59	2,100	1,462 69.62 69.62 16.17	-	-	-	-	-	-	-	687 69.11 46.99 32.71 7.60	-	-	-	-	-	-	-	-	-	-	-	-	-	-	-

Notes: Please refer to the User's Guide for an explanation of data; data is arranged alphabetically by state, then county, then city within each county; table includes counties with populations greater than 49,999 unless noted and cities with populations greater than 9,999 whose Asian and/or NHPI population rates are greater than the national average; (1) Native Hawaiian and other Pacific Islander; (2) excludes Taiwanese; (3) includes Chamorro; (4) county does not meet population threshold but is shown in order to allow inclusion of city

Place	Total foreign-born population	Total Asian population	Asians who are foreign born	Total NHPI[1] population	NHPIs[1] who are foreign born	Asian Indian	Bangladeshi	Cambodian	Chinese[2]	Fijian	Filipino	Guamanian[3]	Hawaiian, Native	Hmong	Indonesian	Japanese	Korean	Laotian	Malaysian	Pakistani	Samoan	Sri Lankan	Taiwanese	Thai	Tongan	Vietnamese
Visalia (city)	11,733	5,077	3,124	-	-	-	-	-	-	-	444	-	-	250	-	-	-	1,486	-	-	-	-	-	-	-	-
	12.82		61.53								55.43			46.21				68.99								
											14.21			8.00				47.57								
			61.53								8.75			4.92				29.27								
			26.63								3.78			2.13				12.67								
Tuolumne County	1,724	451	234	-	-	-	-	-	-	-	-	-	-	-	-	-	-	-	-	-	-	-	-	-	-	-
	3.16		51.88																							
			51.88																							
			13.57																							
Ventura County	155,913	39,182	25,313	1,669	395	3,086	-	-	3,183	-	10,554	-	78	-	-	1,992	2,044	-	-	-	174	-	560	-	-	2,305
	20.70		64.60		23.67	72.68			62.46		69.18		13.57			38.20	78.95				28.43		70.26			71.30
						12.19			12.57		41.69		19.75			7.87	8.07				44.05		2.21			9.11
			64.60		23.67	7.88			8.12		26.94		4.67			5.08	5.22				10.43		1.43			5.88
			16.24		0.25	1.98			2.04		6.77		0.05			1.28	1.31				0.11		0.36			1.48
Camarillo (city)	7,624	4,014	2,401	-	-	-	-	-	265	-	881	-	-	-	-	226	360	-	-	-	-	-	-	-	-	234
	13.35		59.82						55.09		64.49					32.15	81.26									53.92
									11.04		36.69					9.41	14.99									9.75
			59.82						6.60		21.95					5.63	8.97									5.83
			31.49						3.48		11.56					2.96	4.72									3.07
Moorpark (city)	5,993	1,353	865	-	-	-	-	-	-	-	-	-	-	-	-	-	-	-	-	-	-	-	-	-	-	-
	19.16		63.93																							
			63.93																							
			14.43																							
Oxnard (city)	62,902	12,641	8,548	869	249	299	-	-	234	-	6,342	-	-	-	-	569	328	-	-	-	169	-	-	-	-	516
	36.87		67.62		28.65	63.89			63.93		70.43					47.58	77.54				31.24					66.24
						3.50			2.74		74.19					6.66	3.84				67.87					6.04
			67.62		28.65	2.37			1.85		50.17					4.50	2.59				19.45					4.08
			13.59		0.40	0.48			0.37		10.08					0.90	0.52				0.27					0.82
Port Hueneme (city)	4,561	1,314	963	-	-	-	-	-	-	-	743	-	-	-	-	-	-	-	-	-	-	-	-	-	-	-
	20.88		73.29								75.28															
											77.15															
			73.29								56.54															
			21.11								16.29															
Simi Valley (city)	16,837	6,710	4,511	-	-	1,028	-	-	663	-	870	-	-	-	-	375	397	-	-	-	-	-	-	-	-	737
	15.09		67.23			74.71			64.18		68.13					47.59	67.63									76.29
						22.79			14.70		19.29					8.31	8.80									16.34
			67.23			15.32			9.88		12.97					5.59	5.92									10.98
			26.79			6.11			3.94		5.17					2.23	2.36									4.38
Thousand Oaks (city)	18,165	6,378	3,928	-	-	758	-	-	1,165	-	391	-	-	-	-	230	395	-	-	-	-	-	-	-	-	348
	15.56		61.59			66.61			63.14		69.82					26.84	81.95									73.11
						19.30			29.66		9.95					5.86	10.06									8.86
			61.59			11.88			18.27		6.13					3.61	6.19									5.46
			21.62			4.17			6.41		2.15					1.27	2.17									1.92
Yolo County	34,171	15,792	8,627	715	498	1,089	-	-	3,221	464	656	-	-	317	-	514	699	339	-	-	-	-	-	-	-	911
	20.26		54.63		69.65	60.77			57.21	88.21	38.84			47.67		34.64	63.20	64.69								65.30
						12.62			37.34	93.17	7.60			3.67		5.96	8.10	3.93								10.56
			54.63		69.65	6.90			20.40	64.90	4.15			2.01		3.25	4.43	2.15								5.77
			25.25		1.46	3.19			9.43	1.36	1.92			0.93		1.50	2.05	0.99								2.67

Notes: Please refer to the User's Guide for an explanation of data; data is arranged alphabetically by state, then county, then city within each county; table includes counties with populations greater than 49,999 unless noted and cities with populations greater than 9,999 whose Asian and/or NHPI population rates are greater than the national average; (1) Native Hawaiian and other Pacific Islander; (2) excludes Taiwanese; (3) includes Chamorro; (4) county does not meet population threshold but is shown in order to allow inclusion of city

Place	Total foreign-born population	Total Asian population	Asians who are foreign born	Total NHPI[1] population	NHPIs[1] who are foreign born	Asian Indian	Bangladeshi	Cambodian	Chinese[2]	Fijian	Filipino	Guamanian[3]	Hawaiian, Native	Hmong	Indonesian	Japanese	Korean	Laotian	Malaysian	Pakistani	Samoan	Sri Lankan	Taiwanese	Thai	Tongan	Vietnamese
Davis (city)	10,365 17.18	9,963	5,384 54.04 54.04 51.94	-	-	451 57.97 8.38 4.53 4.35	-	-	2,443 54.97 45.38 24.52 23.57	-	368 33.27 6.84 3.69 3.55	-	-	-	-	336 39.07 6.24 3.37 3.24	499 61.60 9.27 5.01 4.81	-	-	-	-	-	-	-	-	730 70.46 13.56 7.33 7.04
West Sacramento (city)	7,922 25.07	2,251	1,264 56.15 56.15 15.96	-	-	301 64.45 23.81 13.37 3.80	-	-	-	-	-	-	-	269 46.46 21.28 11.95 3.40	-	-	-	-	-	-	-	-	-	-	-	-
Woodland (city)	9,551 19.44	1,781	1,042 58.51 58.51 10.91	-	-	310 73.63 29.75 17.41 3.25	-	-	-	-	-	-	-	-	-	-	-	-	-	-	-	-	-	-	-	-
Yuba County	7,931 13.17	4,551	2,395 52.63 52.63 30.20	-	-	-	-	-	-	-	281 52.82 11.73 6.17 3.54	-	-	1,384 51.26 57.79 30.41 17.45	-	-	-	-	-	-	-	-	-	-	-	-
Linda (cdp)	2,827 21.07	2,539	1,257 49.51 49.51 44.46	-	-	-	-	-	-	-	-	-	-	1,064 52.39 84.65 41.91 37.64	-	-	-	-	-	-	-	-	-	-	-	-
Marysville (city)	1,451 11.80	767	497 64.80 64.80 34.25	-	-	-	-	-	-	-	-	-	-	-	-	-	-	-	-	-	-	-	-	-	-	-
Olivehurst (cdp)	1,692 15.25	547	261 47.71 47.71 15.43	-	-	-	-	-	-	-	-	-	-	-	-	-	-	-	-	-	-	-	-	-	-	-
COLORADO	369,903 8.60	93,306	61,603 66.02 66.02 16.65	4,298	531 12.35 12.35 0.14	8,950 75.68 14.53 9.59 2.42	-	1,075 72.73 1.75 1.15 0.29	10,376 69.99 16.84 11.12 2.81	-	5,694 61.09 9.24 6.10 1.54	57 5.63 10.73 1.33 0.02	23 1.58 4.33 0.54 0.01	1,580 52.42 2.56 1.69 0.43	649 84.29 1.05 0.70 0.18	4,253 35.76 6.90 4.56 1.15	11,780 77.03 19.12 12.63 3.18	1,637 70.71 2.66 1.75 0.44	-	651 80.07 1.06 0.70 0.18	110 12.01 20.72 2.56 0.03	-	509 74.85 0.83 0.55 0.14	1,508 77.45 2.45 1.62 0.41	-	10,134 74.15 16.45 10.86 2.74
Adams County	45,588 12.53	11,508	7,201 62.57 62.57 15.80	-	-	407 63.20 5.65 3.54 0.89	-	-	751 66.70 10.43 6.53 1.65	-	536 63.36 7.44 4.66 1.18	-	-	1,174 54.76 16.30 10.20 2.58	-	217 22.68 3.01 1.89 0.48	753 81.76 10.46 6.54 1.65	752 70.48 10.44 6.53 1.65	-	-	-	-	-	-	-	1,603 71.59 22.26 13.93 3.52
Berkley (cdp)	1,781 16.80	419	267 63.72 63.72 14.99	-	-	-	-	-	-	-	-	-	-	-	-	-	-	-	-	-	-	-	-	-	-	-

Notes: Please refer to the User's Guide for an explanation of data; data is arranged alphabetically by state, then county, then city within each county; table includes counties with populations greater than 49,999 unless noted and cities with populations greater than 9,999 whose Asian and/or NHPI population rates are greater than the national average; (1) Native Hawaiian and other Pacific Islander; (2) excludes Taiwanese; (3) includes Chamorro; (4) county does not meet population threshold but is shown in order to allow inclusion of city

Place	Total foreign-born population	Total Asian population	Asians who are foreign born	Total NHPI[1] population	NHPIs[1] who are foreign born	Asian Indian	Bangladeshi	Cambodian	Chinese[2]	Fijian	Filipino	Guamanian[3]	Hawaiian, Native	Hmong	Indonesian	Japanese	Korean	Laotian	Malaysian	Pakistani	Samoan	Sri Lankan	Taiwanese	Thai	Tongan	Vietnamese
Federal Heights (city)	1,155 9.57	748	452 60.43 60.43 39.13	-	-	-	-	-	-	-	-	-	-	-	-	-	-	-	-	-	-	-	-	-	-	-
Westminster (city)	9,116 9.01	5,460	3,444 63.08 63.08 37.78	-	-	343 73.13 9.96 6.28 3.76	-	-	430 67.08 12.49 7.88 4.72	-	-	-	-	499 49.16 14.49 9.14 5.47	-	-	498 90.05 14.46 9.12 5.46	522 77.22 15.16 9.56 5.73	-	-	-	-	-	-	-	578 70.23 16.78 10.59 6.34
Arapahoe County	53,442 10.95	18,693	13,095 70.05 70.05 24.50	554	139 25.09 25.09 0.26	1,801 75.86 13.75 9.63 3.37	-	-	2,097 68.53 16.01 11.22 3.92	-	1,549 71.06 11.83 8.29 2.90	-	-	-	-	666 38.52 5.09 3.56 1.25	3,326 74.14 25.40 17.79 6.22	-	-	-	-	-	-	-	-	2,132 77.87 16.28 11.41 3.99
Aurora (city)	44,692 16.20	11,335	8,039 70.92 70.92 17.99	387	124 32.04 32.04 0.28	690 66.28 8.58 6.09 1.54	-	355 80.50 4.42 3.13 0.79	1,146 70.65 14.26 10.11 2.56	-	1,090 74.05 13.56 9.62 2.44	-	-	-	-	381 37.28 4.74 3.36 0.85	1,920 76.52 23.88 16.94 4.30	-	-	-	-	-	-	-	-	1,516 79.16 18.86 13.37 3.39
Boulder County	27,279 9.36	9,175	6,093 66.41 66.41 22.34	-	-	873 74.55 14.33 9.51 3.20	-	-	1,846 74.20 30.30 20.12 6.77	-	160 39.51 2.63 1.74 0.59	-	-	-	-	454 34.26 7.45 4.95 1.66	967 78.62 15.87 10.54 3.54	-	-	-	-	-	-	-	-	504 69.14 8.27 5.49 1.85
Boulder (city)	10,829 11.46	3,604	2,428 67.37 67.37 22.42	-	-	306 73.73 12.60 8.49 2.83	-	-	621 65.85 25.58 17.23 5.73	-	-	-	-	-	-	224 43.08 9.23 6.22 2.07	608 78.76 25.04 16.87 5.61	-	-	-	-	-	-	-	-	-
Broomfield (city)	2,531 6.61	1,648	1,082 65.66 65.66 42.75	-	-	-	-	-	260 77.15 24.03 15.78 10.27	-	-	-	-	-	-	-	-	-	-	-	-	-	-	-	-	-
Lafayette (city)	2,282 9.77	892	556 62.33 62.33 24.36	-	-	-	-	-	-	-	-	-	-	-	-	-	-	-	-	-	-	-	-	-	-	-
Denver County	96,601 17.42	15,172	10,573 69.69 69.69 10.95	447	106 23.71 23.71 0.11	1,688 82.62 15.97 11.13 1.75	-	273 68.59 2.58 1.80 0.28	1,526 71.28 14.43 10.06 1.58	-	569 59.09 5.38 3.75 0.59	-	-	-	-	800 40.53 7.57 5.27 0.83	996 78.06 9.42 6.56 1.03	-	-	-	-	-	-	335 82.51 3.17 2.21 0.35	-	3,364 75.61 31.82 22.17 3.48
Douglas County	9,065 5.16	4,303	2,813 65.37 65.37 31.03	-	-	611 71.63 21.72 14.20 6.74	-	-	982 76.42 34.91 22.82 10.83	-	-	-	-	-	-	-	496 81.58 17.63 11.53 5.47	-	-	-	-	-	-	-	-	-

Notes: Please refer to the User's Guide for an explanation of data; data is arranged alphabetically by state, then county, then city within each county; table includes counties with populations greater than 49,999 unless noted and cities with populations greater than 9,999 whose Asian and/or NHPI population rates are greater than the national average; (1) Native Hawaiian and other Pacific Islander; (2) excludes Taiwanese; (3) includes Chamorro; (4) county does not meet population threshold but is shown in order to allow inclusion of city

Place	Total foreign-born population	Total Asian population	Asians who are foreign born	Total NHPI[1] population	NHPIs[1] who are foreign born	Asian Indian	Bangladeshi	Cambodian	Chinese[2]	Fijian	Filipino	Guamanian[3]	Hawaiian, Native	Hmong	Indonesian	Japanese	Korean	Laotian	Malaysian	Pakistani	Samoan	Sri Lankan	Taiwanese	Thai	Tongan	Vietnamese
Highlands Ranch (cdp)	4,717	2,913	1,875	-	-	443	-	-	686	-	-	-	-	-	-	-	-	-	-	-	-	-	-	-	-	-
	6.66		64.37			68.15			73.84																	
						23.63			36.59																	
			64.37			15.21			23.55																	
			39.75			9.39			14.54																	
El Paso County	33,308	13,154	9,159	1,291	110	1,599	-	-	609	-	1,563	11	-	-	-	799	3,056	-	-	-	-	-	-	-	-	727
	6.44		69.63		8.52	82.34			59.53		61.34	2.24				54.46	77.64									79.98
						17.46			6.65		17.07	10.00				8.72	33.37									7.94
			69.63		8.52	12.16			4.63		11.88	0.85				6.07	23.23									5.53
			27.50		0.33	4.80			1.83		4.69	0.03				2.40	9.17									2.18
Colorado Springs (city)	25,264	10,295	7,224	798	97	1,544	-	-	510	-	1,087	-	-	-	-	514	2,320	-	-	-	-	-	-	-	-	602
	7.00		70.17		12.16	82.04			60.43		62.58					49.95	77.20									79.52
						21.37			7.06		15.05					7.12	32.12									8.33
			70.17		12.16	15.00			4.95		10.56					4.99	22.54									5.85
			28.59		0.38	6.11			2.02		4.30					2.03	9.18									2.38
Jefferson County	28,400	11,752	7,273	437	48	1,082	-	-	1,391	-	552	-	-	164	-	522	1,193	612	-	-	-	-	-	-	-	1,144
	5.39		61.89		10.98	74.83			72.64		58.41			39.81		27.52	80.39	66.52								66.28
						14.88			19.13		7.59			2.25		7.18	16.40	8.41								15.73
			61.89		10.98	9.21			11.84		4.70			1.40		4.44	10.15	5.21								9.73
			25.61		0.17	3.81			4.90		1.94			0.58		1.84	4.20	2.15								4.03
Larimer County	10,709	3,616	2,411	-	-	490	-	-	596	-	-	-	-	-	-	188	436	-	-	-	-	-	-	-	-	-
	4.26		66.68			78.27			68.82							32.64	72.91									
						20.32			24.72							7.80	18.08									
			66.68			13.55			16.48							5.20	12.06									
			22.51			4.58			5.57							1.76	4.07									
Mesa County	3,443	424	295	-	-	-	-	-	-	-	-	-	-	-	-	-	-	-	-	-	-	-	-	-	-	-
	2.96		69.58																							
			69.58																							
			8.57																							
Pueblo County	4,194	761	482	-	-	-	-	-	-	-	-	-	-	-	-	-	-	-	-	-	-	-	-	-	-	-
	2.96		63.34																							
			63.34																							
			11.49																							
Weld County	16,752	1,533	677	-	-	-	-	-	-	-	-	-	-	-	-	78	-	-	-	-	-	-	-	-	-	-
	9.26		44.16													15.76										
																11.52										
			44.16													5.09										
			4.04													0.47										
CONNECTICUT	369,967	82,277	60,861	1,357	224	18,347	299	1,456	13,335	-	5,534	47	-	-	-	3,309	5,336	2,314	-	1,741	-	-	459	608	-	5,804
	10.86		73.97		16.51	76.75	85.92	67.38	71.02		73.68	11.22				72.69	79.33	74.48		82.43			56.04	77.55		78.44
						30.15	0.49	2.39	21.91		9.09	20.98				5.44	8.77	3.80		2.86			0.75	1.00		9.54
			73.97		16.51	22.30	0.36	1.77	16.21		6.73	3.46				4.02	6.49	2.81		2.12			0.56	0.74		7.05
			16.45		0.06	4.96	0.08	0.39	3.60		1.50	0.01				0.89	1.44	0.63		0.47			0.12	0.16		1.57
Fairfield County	149,038	28,452	21,217	-	-	6,669	-	938	3,869	-	1,840	-	-	-	-	2,038	1,630	746	-	434	-	-	-	-	-	1,839
	16.89		74.57			79.92		65.05	66.71		75.56					77.17	84.37	72.36		79.93						76.75
						31.43		4.42	18.24		8.67					9.61	7.68	3.52		2.05						8.67
			74.57			23.44		3.30	13.60		6.47					7.16	5.73	2.62		1.53						6.46
			14.24			4.47		0.63	2.60		1.23					1.37	1.09	0.50		0.29						1.23

Notes: Please refer to the User's Guide for an explanation of data; data is arranged alphabetically by state, then county, then city within each county; table includes counties with populations greater than 49,999 unless noted and cities with populations greater than 9,999 whose Asian and/or NHPI population rates are greater than the national average; (1) Native Hawaiian and other Pacific Islander; (2) excludes Taiwanese; (3) includes Chamorro; (4) county does not meet population threshold but is shown in order to allow inclusion of city

Place	Total foreign-born population	Total Asian population	Asians who are foreign born	Total NHPI[1] population	NHPIs[1] who are foreign born	Asian Indian	Bangladeshi	Cambodian	Chinese[2]	Fijian
Danbury (city)	20,241	3,671	2,722	-	-	963	-	321	387	-
	27.04		74.15			80.38		56.12	80.96	
						35.38		11.79	14.22	
			74.15			26.23		8.74	10.54	
			13.45			4.76		1.59	1.91	
Greenwich (town)	11,601	3,259	2,511	-	-	317	-	-	412	-
	18.99		77.05			79.65			64.48	
						12.62			16.41	
			77.05			9.73			12.64	
			21.64			2.73			3.55	
Stamford (city)	34,670	5,735	4,424	-	-	2,431	-	-	796	-
	29.61		77.14			84.67			69.22	
						54.95			17.99	
			77.14			42.39			13.88	
			12.76			7.01			2.30	
Hartford County	100,693	21,058	15,647	-	-	5,034	-	-	2,751	-
	11.75		74.30			74.84			71.34	
						32.17			17.58	
			74.30			23.91			13.06	
			15.54			5.00			2.73	
East Hartford (town)	7,445	2,091	1,572	-	-	493	-	-	-	-
	15.02		75.18			79.26				
						31.36				
			75.18			23.58				
			21.11			6.62				
Farmington (town)	2,807	972	720	-	-	-	-	-	-	-
	11.87		74.07							
			74.07							
			25.65							
Glastonbury (town)	2,396	1,212	852	-	-	333	-	-	-	-
	7.52		70.30			66.47				
						39.08				
			70.30			27.48				
			35.56			13.90				
Rocky Hill (town)	2,197	711	496	-	-	-	-	-	-	-
	12.25		69.76							
			69.76							
			22.58							
South Windsor (town)	2,417	965	663	-	-	-	-	-	-	-
	9.88		68.70							
			68.70							
			27.43							
West Hartford (town)	9,382	3,063	2,243	-	-	512	-	-	599	-
	14.75		73.23			66.32			72.69	
						22.83			26.71	
			73.23			16.72			19.56	
			23.91			5.46			6.38	

Place	Filipino	Guamanian[3]	Hawaiian, Native	Hmong	Indonesian	Japanese	Korean	Laotian	Malaysian	Pakistani	Samoan	Sri Lankan	Taiwanese	Thai	Tongan	Vietnamese
Danbury (city)	-	-	-	-	-	-	-	-	-	-	-	-	-	-	-	-
Greenwich (town)	-	-	-	-	-	1,207	-	-	-	-	-	-	-	-	-	-
						87.27										
						48.07										
						37.04										
						10.40										
Stamford (city)	536	-	-	-	-	-	-	-	-	-	-	-	-	-	-	-
	66.58															
	12.12															
	9.35															
	1.55															
Hartford County	1,267	-	-	-	-	368	1,115	923	-	520	-	-	-	-	-	2,618
	71.95					68.02	77.16	75.97		77.84						81.79
	8.10					2.35	7.13	5.90		3.32						16.73
	6.02					1.75	5.29	4.38		2.47						12.43
	1.26					0.37	1.11	0.92		0.52						2.60
East Hartford (town)	-	-	-	-	-	-	-	-	-	-	-	-	-	-	-	456
																82.46
																29.01
																21.81
																6.12
Farmington (town)	-	-	-	-	-	-	-	-	-	-	-	-	-	-	-	-
Glastonbury (town)	-	-	-	-	-	-	-	-	-	-	-	-	-	-	-	-
Rocky Hill (town)	-	-	-	-	-	-	-	-	-	-	-	-	-	-	-	-
South Windsor (town)	-	-	-	-	-	-	-	-	-	-	-	-	-	-	-	-
West Hartford (town)	-	-	-	-	-	-	-	-	-	-	-	-	-	-	-	567
																84.63
																25.28
																18.51
																6.04

Notes: Please refer to the User's Guide for an explanation of data; data is arranged alphabetically by state, then county, then city within each county; table includes counties with populations greater than 49,999 unless noted and cities with populations greater than 9,999 whose Asian and/or NHPI population rates are greater than the national average; (1) Native Hawaiian and other Pacific Islander; (2) excludes Taiwanese; (3) includes Chamorro; (4) county does not meet population threshold but is shown in order to allow inclusion of city

Place	Total foreign-born population	Total Asian population	Asians who are foreign born	Total NHPI[1] population	NHPIs[1] who are foreign born	Asian Indian	Bangladeshi	Cambodian	Chinese[2]	Fijian	Filipino	Guamanian[3]	Hawaiian, Native	Hmong	Indonesian	Japanese	Korean	Laotian	Malaysian	Pakistani	Samoan	Sri Lankan	Taiwanese	Thai	Tongan	Vietnamese
Litchfield County	9,898 5.43	2,278	1,715 75.29 75.29 17.33	-	-	360 78.26 20.99 15.80 3.64	-	-	313 76.34 18.25 13.74 3.16	-	-	-	-	-	-	-	321 87.23 18.72 14.09 3.24	-	-	-	-	-	-	-	-	202 76.23 11.78 8.87 2.04
Middlesex County	9,230 5.95	2,272	1,517 66.77 66.77 16.44	-	-	454 69.74 29.93 19.98 4.92	-	-	365 66.97 24.06 16.07 3.95	-	-	-	-	-	-	-	-	-	-	-	-	-	-	-	-	-
New Haven County	74,427 9.03	19,615	14,425 73.54 73.54 19.38	-	-	4,452 75.25 30.86 22.70 5.98	-	-	3,859 71.98 26.75 19.67 5.18	-	1,309 81.00 9.07 6.67 1.76	-	-	-	-	616 69.21 4.27 3.14 0.83	1,507 73.37 10.45 7.68 2.02	366 72.62 2.54 1.87 0.49	-	615 94.18 4.26 3.14 0.83	-	-	-	-	-	671 75.39 4.65 3.42 0.90
New Haven (city)	14,350 11.61	4,623	2,959 64.01 64.01 20.62	-	-	502 62.21 16.97 10.86 3.50	-	-	1,246 70.12 42.11 26.95 8.68	-	-	-	-	-	-	-	343 63.52 11.59 7.42 2.39	-	-	-	-	-	-	-	-	-
New London County	14,002 5.40	4,806	3,436 71.49 71.49 24.54	-	-	733 79.76 21.33 15.25 5.23	-	-	1,141 73.42 33.21 23.74 8.15	-	663 64.24 19.30 13.80 4.74	-	-	-	-	-	-	-	-	-	-	-	-	-	-	-
Tolland County	8,011 5.87	3,123	2,439 78.10 78.10 30.45	-	-	612 71.58 25.09 19.60 7.64	-	-	887 82.67 36.37 28.40 11.07	-	-	-	-	-	-	-	-	-	-	-	-	-	-	-	-	-
Mansfield (town)	2,382 11.50	1,487	1,118 75.18 75.18 46.94	-	-	335 75.79 29.96 22.53 14.06	-	-	496 81.85 44.36 33.36 20.82	-	-	-	-	-	-	-	-	-	-	-	-	-	-	-	-	-
Storrs (cdp)	1,623 14.52	1,064	826 77.63 77.63 50.89	-	-	-	-	-	447 82.02 54.12 42.01 27.54	-	-	-	-	-	-	-	-	-	-	-	-	-	-	-	-	-
Windham County	4,668 4.28	673	465 69.09 69.09 9.96	-	-	-	-	-	-	-	-	-	-	-	-	-	-	-	-	-	-	-	-	-	-	-
DELAWARE	44,898 5.73	16,053	12,181 75.88 75.88 27.13	335	119 35.52 35.52 0.27	4,116 78.68 33.79 25.64 9.17	-	-	3,159 77.01 25.93 19.68 7.04	-	1,301 71.29 10.68 8.10 2.90	-	-	-	-	393 64.96 3.23 2.45 0.88	1,536 83.03 12.61 9.57 3.42	-	-	252 66.49 2.07 1.57 0.56	-	-	-	-	-	481 70.12 3.95 3.00 1.07

Notes: Please refer to the User's Guide for an explanation of data; data is arranged alphabetically by state, then county, then city within each county; table includes counties with populations greater than 49,999 unless noted and cities with populations greater than 9,999 whose Asian and/or NHPI population rates are greater than the national average; (1) Native Hawaiian and other Pacific Islander; (2) excludes Taiwanese; (3) includes Chamorro; (4) county does not meet population threshold but is shown in order to allow inclusion of city

Place	Total foreign-born population	Total Asian population	Asians who are foreign born	Total NHPI[1] population	NHPIs[1] who are foreign born	Asian Indian	Bangladeshi	Cambodian	Chinese[2]	Fijian	Filipino	Guamanian[3]	Hawaiian, Native	Hmong	Indonesian	Japanese	Korean	Laotian	Malaysian	Pakistani	Samoan	Sri Lankan	Taiwanese	Thai	Tongan	Vietnamese
Kent County	5,050	2,083	1,510	-	-	289	-	-	-	-	344	-	-	-	-	-	-	-	-	-	-	-	-	-	-	-
	3.99		72.49			68.97					68.94															
						19.14					22.78															
			72.49			13.87					16.51															
			29.90			5.72					6.81															
New Castle County	32,841	13,182	10,085	-	-	3,709	-	-	2,905	-	808	-	-	-	-	226	1,136	-	-	-	-	-	-	-	-	386
	6.56		76.51			79.80			77.43		72.60					58.55	80.85									72.01
						36.78			28.81		8.01					2.24	11.26									3.83
			76.51			28.14			22.04		6.13					1.71	8.62									2.93
			30.71			11.29			8.85		2.46					0.69	3.46									1.18
Hockessin (cdp)	1,406	837	654	-	-	-	-	-	-	-	-	-	-	-	-	-	-	-	-	-	-	-	-	-	-	-
	10.90		78.14																							
			78.14																							
			46.51																							
Newark (city)	2,116	1,219	969	-	-	-	-	-	443	-	-	-	-	-	-	-	-	-	-	-	-	-	-	-	-	-
	7.41		79.49						81.89																	
									45.72																	
			79.49						36.34																	
			45.79						20.94																	
Pike Creek (cdp)	1,598	1,085	736	-	-	-	-	-	-	-	-	-	-	-	-	-	-	-	-	-	-	-	-	-	-	-
	8.09		67.83																							
			67.83																							
			46.06																							
Sussex County	7,007	788	586	-	-	-	-	-	-	-	-	-	-	-	-	-	-	-	-	-	-	-	-	-	-	-
	4.47		74.37																							
			74.37																							
			8.36																							
DISTRICT OF COLUMBIA	73,561	14,762	10,199	-	-	1,601	-	-	2,695	-	1,565	-	-	-	-	718	874	-	-	-	-	-	-	-	-	1,557
	12.86		69.09			66.29			70.13		73.86					69.24	74.83									87.03
						15.70			26.42		15.34					7.04	8.57									15.27
			69.09			10.85			18.26		10.60					4.86	5.92									10.55
			13.86			2.18			3.66		2.13					0.98	1.19									2.12
FLORIDA	2,670,828	264,377	196,638	6,812	1,771	51,515	1,060	2,118	33,776	-	39,071	534	98	-	801	7,916	15,001	2,992	-	3,953	246	326	1,529	5,353	-	25,753
	16.71		74.38		26.00	75.99	84.13	76.68	75.28		71.91	26.44	4.97		89.60	69.77	78.63	74.22		72.59	28.98	81.09	75.43	81.45		77.13
						26.20	0.54	1.08	17.18		19.87	30.15	5.53		0.41	4.03	7.63	1.52		2.01	13.89	0.17	0.78	2.72		13.10
			74.38		26.00	19.49	0.40	0.80	12.78		14.78	7.84	1.44		0.30	2.99	5.67	1.13		1.50	3.61	0.12	0.58	2.02		9.74
			7.36		0.07	1.93	0.04	0.08	1.26		1.46	0.02	<0.01		0.03	0.30	0.56	0.11		0.15	0.01	0.01	0.06	0.20		0.96
Alachua County	15,895	7,858	5,532	-	-	1,264	-	-	1,604	-	640	-	-	-	-	306	833	-	-	-	-	-	-	-	-	453
	7.29		70.40			64.85			75.13		61.19					70.67	82.89									73.42
						22.85			28.99		11.57					5.53	15.06									8.19
			70.40			16.09			20.41		8.14					3.89	10.60									5.76
			34.80			7.95			10.09		4.03					1.93	5.24									2.85
Gainesville (city)	8,320	4,399	3,191	-	-	692	-	-	1,193	-	-	-	-	-	-	-	388	-	-	-	-	-	-	-	-	-
	8.70		72.54			65.53			81.94								77.45									
						21.69			37.39								12.16									
			72.54			15.73			27.12								8.82									
			38.35			8.32			14.34								4.66									

Notes: Please refer to the User's Guide for an explanation of data; data is arranged alphabetically by state, then county, then city within each county; table includes counties with populations greater than 49,999 unless noted and cities with populations greater than 9,999 whose Asian and/or NHPI population rates are greater than the national average; (1) Native Hawaiian and other Pacific Islander; (2) excludes Taiwanese; (3) includes Chamorro; (4) county does not meet population threshold but is shown in order to allow inclusion of city

Place	Total foreign-born population	Total Asian population	Asians who are foreign born	Total NHPI[1] population	NHPIs[1] who are foreign born	Asian Indian	Bangladeshi	Cambodian	Chinese[2]	Fijian	Filipino	Guamanian[3]	Hawaiian, Native	Hmong	Indonesian	Japanese	Korean	Laotian	Malaysian	Pakistani	Samoan	Sri Lankan	Taiwanese	Thai	Tongan	Vietnamese
Bay County	5,382 3.63	2,369	1,615 68.17 68.17 30.01	-	-	-	-	-	-	-	357 73.76 22.11 15.07 6.63	-	-	-	-	-	-	-	-	-	-	-	-	-	-	390 58.56 24.15 16.46 7.25
Callaway (city)	848 5.95	530	318 60.00 60.00 37.50	-	-	-	-	-	-	-	-	-	-	-	-	-	-	-	-	-	-	-	-	-	-	-
Brevard County	31,001 6.51	7,122	5,383 75.58 75.58 17.36	-	-	1,577 80.01 29.30 22.14 5.09	-	-	698 78.25 12.97 9.80 2.25	-	1,088 70.79 20.21 15.28 3.51	-	-	-	-	293 55.81 5.44 4.11 0.95	538 86.63 9.99 7.55 1.74	-	-	-	-	-	-	-	-	561 73.53 10.42 7.88 1.81
Broward County	410,387 25.29	36,505	27,766 76.06 76.06 6.77	645	239 37.05 37.05 0.06	10,283 79.05 37.03 28.17 2.51	-	-	6,404 74.85 23.06 17.54 1.56	-	3,609 74.11 13.00 9.89 0.88	-	-	-	-	725 69.38 2.61 1.99 0.18	1,727 76.42 6.22 4.73 0.42	-	-	837 76.30 3.01 2.29 0.20	-	-	-	470 78.46 1.69 1.29 0.11	-	2,211 77.12 7.96 6.06 0.54
Cooper City (city)	4,684 16.92	1,241	936 75.42 75.42 19.98	-	-	481 81.11 51.39 38.76 10.27	-	-	-	-	-	-	-	-	-	-	-	-	-	-	-	-	-	-	-	-
Pembroke Pines (city)	39,727 28.97	5,004	3,758 75.10 75.10 9.46	-	-	1,346 76.83 35.82 26.90 3.39	-	-	847 73.46 22.54 16.93 2.13	-	754 81.34 20.06 15.07 1.90	-	-	-	-	-	-	-	-	-	-	-	-	-	-	-
Charlotte County	11,292 7.97	872	734 84.17 84.17 6.50	-	-	-	-	-	-	-	-	-	-	-	-	-	-	-	-	-	-	-	-	-	-	-
Citrus County	5,742 4.86	1,145	836 73.01 73.01 14.56	-	-	-	-	-	-	-	-	-	-	-	-	-	-	-	-	-	-	-	-	-	-	-
Clay County	6,356 4.51	2,901	2,198 75.77 75.77 34.58	-	-	-	-	-	-	-	1,356 78.65 61.69 46.74 21.33	-	-	-	-	-	-	-	-	-	-	-	-	-	-	-
Bellair-Meadowbrook Ter. (cdp)	1,063 6.42	635	526 82.83 82.83 49.48	-	-	-	-	-	-	-	-	-	-	-	-	-	-	-	-	-	-	-	-	-	-	-

Notes: Please refer to the User's Guide for an explanation of data; data is arranged alphabetically by state, then county, then city within each county; table includes counties with populations greater than 49,999 unless noted and cities with populations greater than 9,999 whose Asian and/or NHPI population rates are greater than the national average; (1) Native Hawaiian and other Pacific Islander; (2) excludes Taiwanese; (3) includes Chamorro; (4) county does not meet population threshold but is shown in order to allow inclusion of city

Place	Total foreign-born population	Total Asian population	Asians who are foreign born	Total NHPI[1] population	NHPIs[1] who are foreign born	Asian Indian	Bangladeshi	Cambodian	Chinese[2]	Fijian	Filipino	Guamanian[3]	Hawaiian, Native	Hmong	Indonesian	Japanese	Korean	Laotian	Malaysian	Pakistani	Samoan	Sri Lankan	Taiwanese	Thai	Tongan	Vietnamese
Collier County	46,071 18.33	1,200	889 74.08 74.08 1.93	-	-	-	-	-	-	-	-	-	-	-	-	-	-	-	-	-	-	-	-	-	-	-
Columbia County	1,316 2.33	386	277 71.76 71.76 21.05	-	-	-	-	-	-	-	-	-	-	-	-	-	-	-	-	-	-	-	-	-	-	-
Duval County	45,651 5.86	20,554	14,268 69.42 69.42 31.25	507	36 7.10 7.10 0.08	2,086 75.39 14.62 10.15 4.57	-	725 72.43 5.08 3.53 1.59	1,097 66.81 7.69 5.34 2.40	-	6,796 66.59 47.63 33.06 14.89	-	-	-	-	362 65.82 2.54 1.76 0.79	798 82.52 5.59 3.88 1.75	-	-	-	-	-	-	-	-	1,570 74.34 11.00 7.64 3.44
Escambia County	10,821 3.68	6,565	4,291 65.36 65.36 39.65	-	-	356 68.99 8.30 5.42 3.29	-	-	400 68.14 9.32 6.09 3.70	-	1,759 64.74 40.99 26.79 16.26	-	-	-	-	-	-	-	-	-	-	-	-	-	-	1,053 65.94 24.54 16.04 9.73
Bellview (cdp)	874 4.15	787	467 59.34 59.34 53.43	-	-	-	-	-	-	-	266 64.56 56.96 33.80 30.43	-	-	-	-	-	-	-	-	-	-	-	-	-	-	-
Myrtle Grove (cdp)	960 5.55	812	526 64.78 64.78 54.79	-	-	-	-	-	-	-	317 67.30 60.27 39.04 33.02	-	-	-	-	-	-	-	-	-	-	-	-	-	-	-
Hernando County	6,942 5.31	773	623 80.60 80.60 8.97	-	-	-	-	-	-	-	-	-	-	-	-	-	-	-	-	-	-	-	-	-	-	-
Highlands County	7,912 9.06	964	733 76.04 76.04 9.26	-	-	-	-	-	-	-	316 70.69 43.11 32.78 3.99	-	-	-	-	-	-	-	-	-	-	-	-	-	-	-
Hillsborough County	115,151 11.53	21,571	15,847 73.46 73.46 13.76	540	77 14.26 14.26 0.07	4,182 70.87 26.39 19.39 3.63	-	-	1,987 74.17 12.54 9.21 1.73	-	2,268 70.81 14.31 10.51 1.97	-	-	-	-	541 62.69 3.41 2.51 0.47	2,087 76.78 13.17 9.68 1.81	-	-	-	-	-	-	561 82.99 3.54 2.60 0.49	-	3,230 80.89 20.38 14.97 2.81
Westchase (cdp)	1,070 9.63	508	333 65.55 65.55 31.12	-	-	-	-	-	-	-	-	-	-	-	-	-	-	-	-	-	-	-	-	-	-	-

Notes: Please refer to the User's Guide for an explanation of data; data is arranged alphabetically by state, then county, then city within each county; table includes counties with populations greater than 49,999 unless noted and cities with populations greater than 9,999 whose Asian and/or NHPI population rates are greater than the national average; (1) Native Hawaiian and other Pacific Islander; (2) excludes Taiwanese; (3) includes Chamorro; (4) county does not meet population threshold but is shown in order to allow inclusion of city

Place	Total foreign-born population	Total Asian population	Asians who are foreign born	Total NHPI[1] population	NHPIs[1] who are foreign born	Asian Indian	Bangladeshi	Cambodian	Chinese[2]	Fijian	Filipino	Guamanian[3]	Hawaiian, Native	Hmong	Indonesian	Japanese	Korean	Laotian	Malaysian	Pakistani	Samoan	Sri Lankan	Taiwanese	Thai	Tongan	Vietnamese
Indian River County	9,151 8.10	864	635 73.50 73.50 6.94	-	-	-	-	-	-	-	-	-	-	-	-	-	-	-	-	-	-	-	-	-	-	-
Lake County	10,820 5.14	1,422	1,035 72.78 72.78 9.57	-	-	-	-	-	-	-	-	-	-	-	-	-	-	-	-	-	-	-	-	-	-	-
Lee County	40,362 9.15	3,159	2,414 76.42 76.42 5.98	-	-	534 79.82 22.12 16.90 1.32	-	-	418 70.13 17.32 13.23 1.04	-	815 73.82 33.76 25.80 2.02	-	-	-	-	-	-	-	-	-	-	-	-	-	-	-
Leon County	11,345 4.74	4,858	3,578 73.65 73.65 31.54	-	-	1,140 75.60 31.86 23.47 10.05	-	-	816 75.21 22.81 16.80 7.19	-	302 57.41 8.44 6.22 2.66	-	-	-	-	-	354 79.37 9.89 7.29 3.12	-	-	-	-	-	-	-	-	-
Manatee County	22,235 8.42	2,237	1,791 80.06 80.06 8.05	-	-	-	-	-	-	-	472 87.73 26.35 21.10 2.12	-	-	-	-	-	-	-	-	-	-	-	-	-	-	-
Marion County	13,352 5.16	2,221	1,526 68.71 68.71 11.43	-	-	643 67.76 42.14 28.95 4.82	-	-	-	-	-	-	-	-	-	-	-	-	-	-	-	-	-	-	-	-
Martin County	10,318 8.14	701	549 78.32 78.32 5.32	-	-	-	-	-	-	-	-	-	-	-	-	-	-	-	-	-	-	-	-	-	-	-
Miami-Dade County	1,147,765 50.94	30,692	23,901 77.87 77.87 2.08	605	394 65.12 65.12 0.03	6,825 76.36 28.56 22.24 0.59	-	-	6,951 78.20 29.08 22.65 0.61	-	3,586 79.32 15.00 11.68 0.31	-	-	-	-	1,180 84.05 4.94 3.84 0.10	1,008 75.45 4.22 3.28 0.09	-	-	685 86.27 2.87 2.23 0.06	-	-	-	734 83.22 3.07 2.39 0.06	-	1,281 80.31 5.36 4.17 0.11
Doral (cdp)	12,831 62.55	1,186	1,010 85.16 85.16 7.87	-	-	-	-	-	-	-	-	-	-	-	-	-	-	-	-	-	-	-	-	-	-	-
Ives Estates (cdp)	7,092 40.72	831	646 77.74 77.74 9.11	-	-	-	-	-	-	-	-	-	-	-	-	-	-	-	-	-	-	-	-	-	-	-

Notes: Please refer to the User's Guide for an explanation of data; data is arranged alphabetically by state, then county, then city within each county; table includes counties with populations greater than 49,999 unless noted and cities with populations greater than 9,999 whose Asian and/or NHPI population rates are greater than the national average; (1) Native Hawaiian and other Pacific Islander; (2) excludes Taiwanese; (3) includes Chamorro; (4) county does not meet population threshold but is shown in order to allow inclusion of city

Place	Total foreign-born population	Total Asian population	Asians who are foreign born	Total NHPI[1] population	NHPIs[1] who are foreign born	Asian Indian	Bangladeshi	Cambodian	Chinese[2]	Fijian	Filipino	Guamanian[3]	Hawaiian, Native	Hmong	Indonesian	Japanese	Korean	Laotian	Malaysian	Pakistani	Samoan	Sri Lankan	Taiwanese	Thai	Tongan	Vietnamese
North Miami Beach (city)	20,201 49.67	1,706	1,374 80.54 80.54 6.80	-	-	307 77.53 22.34 18.00 1.52	-	-	591 79.76 43.01 34.64 2.93	-	-	-	-	-	-	-	-	-	-	-	-	-	-	-	-	-
Pinecrest (village)	5,302 27.64	884	684 77.38 77.38 12.90	-	-	-	-	-	-	-	-	-	-	-	-	-	-	-	-	-	-	-	-	-	-	-
Monroe County	11,732 14.74	566	407 71.91 71.91 3.47	-	-	-	-	-	-	-	-	-	-	-	-	-	-	-	-	-	-	-	-	-	-	-
Nassau County	1,541 2.67	422	346 81.99 81.99 22.45	-	-	-	-	-	-	-	-	-	-	-	-	-	-	-	-	-	-	-	-	-	-	-
Okaloosa County	8,984 5.27	4,432	3,036 68.50 68.50 33.79	-	-	-	-	-	-	-	1,183 67.91 38.97 26.69 13.17	-	-	-	-	-	581 80.69 19.14 13.11 6.47	-	-	-	-	-	-	518 83.01 17.06 11.69 5.77	-	225 56.25 7.41 5.08 2.50
Wright (cdp)	1,542 7.15	825	580 70.30 70.30 37.61	-	-	-	-	-	-	-	-	-	-	-	-	-	-	-	-	-	-	-	-	-	-	-
Orange County	128,904 14.38	28,748	21,638 75.27 75.27 16.79	853	166 19.46 19.46 0.13	5,793 75.72 26.77 20.15 4.49	-	-	2,976 74.55 13.75 10.35 2.31	-	3,087 68.24 14.27 10.74 2.39	-	-	-	-	911 75.92 4.21 3.17 0.71	1,664 77.58 7.69 5.79 1.29	-	-	614 68.15 2.84 2.14 0.48	-	-	-	-	-	5,267 82.85 24.34 18.32 4.09
Oak Ridge (cdp)	7,957 35.51	1,306	974 74.58 74.58 12.24	-	-	-	-	-	-	-	-	-	-	-	-	-	-	-	-	-	-	-	-	-	-	450 85.39 46.20 34.46 5.66
Osceola County	24,110 13.98	3,642	2,712 74.46 74.46 11.25	-	-	731 75.67 26.95 20.07 3.03	-	-	459 78.60 16.92 12.60 1.90	-	626 70.89 23.08 17.19 2.60	-	-	-	-	-	-	-	-	-	-	-	-	-	-	-
Palm Beach County	196,852 17.40	16,895	12,934 76.56 76.56 6.57	423	94 22.22 22.22 0.05	4,074 79.91 31.50 24.11 2.07	-	-	2,808 77.12 21.71 16.62 1.43	-	1,666 74.44 12.88 9.86 0.85	-	-	-	-	400 69.69 3.09 2.37 0.20	728 78.11 5.63 4.31 0.37	-	-	-	-	-	-	617 81.18 4.77 3.65 0.31	-	1,550 77.73 11.98 9.17 0.79

Notes: Please refer to the User's Guide for an explanation of data; data is arranged alphabetically by state, then county, then city within each county; table includes counties with populations greater than 49,999 unless noted and cities with populations greater than 9,999 whose Asian and/or NHPI population rates are greater than the national average; (1) Native Hawaiian and other Pacific Islander; (2) excludes Taiwanese; (3) includes Chamorro; (4) county does not meet population threshold but is shown in order to allow inclusion of city

Place	Total foreign-born population	Total Asian population	Asians who are foreign born	Total NHPI[1] population	NHPIs[1] who are foreign born	Asian Indian	Bangladeshi	Cambodian	Chinese[2]	Fijian	Filipino	Guamanian[3]	Hawaiian, Native	Hmong	Indonesian	Japanese	Korean	Laotian	Malaysian	Pakistani	Samoan	Sri Lankan	Taiwanese	Thai	Tongan	Vietnamese
Pasco County	24,129	3,489	2,553	-	-	764	-	-	350	-	771	-	-	-	-	-	-	-	-	-	-	-	-	-	-	-
	7.00		73.17			76.94			69.44		77.57															
						29.93			13.71		30.20															
			73.17			21.90			10.03		22.10															
			10.58			3.17			1.45		3.20															
Pinellas County	87,685	18,783	14,421	-	-	2,873	-	532	1,661	-	2,270	-	-	-	-	444	712	1,388	-	-	-	-	-	376	-	3,298
	9.52		76.78			78.76		74.09	79.66		74.82					78.17	83.37	74.82						77.05		77.89
						19.92		3.69	11.52		15.74					3.08	4.94	9.62						2.61		22.87
			76.78			15.30		2.83	8.84		12.09					2.36	3.79	7.39						2.00		17.56
			16.45			3.28		0.61	1.89		2.59					0.51	0.81	1.58						0.43		3.76
Pinellas Park (city)	4,295	1,811	1,425	-	-	-	-	-	-	-	-	-	-	-	-	-	-	-	-	-	-	-	-	-	-	391
	9.46		78.69																							74.33
																										27.44
			78.69																							21.59
			33.18																							9.10
Polk County	33,519	5,805	4,103	-	-	1,243	-	-	433	-	680	-	-	-	-	-	-	273	-	-	-	-	-	-	-	569
	6.93		70.68			72.39			72.77		75.39							68.08								65.25
						30.29			10.55		16.57							6.65								13.87
			70.68			21.41			7.46		11.71							4.70								9.80
			12.24			3.71			1.29		2.03							0.81								1.70
Putnam County	2,371	291	209	-	-	-	-	-	-	-	-	-	-	-	-	-	-	-	-	-	-	-	-	-	-	-
	3.37		71.82																							
			71.82																							
			8.81																							
St. Johns County	6,038	1,244	900	-	-	-	-	-	-	-	-	-	-	-	-	-	-	-	-	-	-	-	-	-	-	-
	4.90		72.35																							
			72.35																							
			14.91																							
St. Lucie County	20,165	1,885	1,348	-	-	-	-	-	-	-	-	-	-	-	-	-	-	-	-	-	-	-	-	-	-	-
	10.46		71.51																							
			71.51																							
			6.68																							
Santa Rosa County	3,549	1,608	1,259	-	-	-	-	-	-	-	585	-	-	-	-	-	-	-	-	-	-	-	-	-	-	-
	3.01		78.30								82.74															
											46.47															
			78.30								36.38															
			35.47								16.48															
Sarasota County	30,416	2,624	1,920	-	-	-	-	-	321	-	412	-	-	-	-	-	-	-	-	-	-	-	-	-	-	511
	9.33		73.17						75.35		76.30															74.82
									16.72		21.46															26.61
			73.17						12.23		15.70															19.47
			6.31						1.06		1.35															1.68
Seminole County	33,285	8,682	6,381	-	-	2,074	-	-	970	-	946	-	-	-	-	-	761	-	-	-	-	-	-	-	-	758
	9.11		73.50			74.58			70.04		72.05						77.97									71.24
						32.50			15.20		14.83						11.93									11.88
			73.50			23.89			11.17		10.90						8.77									8.73
			19.17			6.23			2.91		2.84						2.29									2.28

Notes: Please refer to the User's Guide for an explanation of data; data is arranged alphabetically by state, then county, then city within each county; table includes counties with populations greater than 49,999 unless noted and cities with populations greater than 9,999 whose Asian and/or NHPI population rates are greater than the national average; (1) Native Hawaiian and other Pacific Islander; (2) excludes Taiwanese; (3) includes Chamorro; (4) county does not meet population threshold but is shown in order to allow inclusion of city

Place	Total foreign-born population	Total Asian population	Asians who are foreign born	Total NHPI[1] population	NHPIs[1] who are foreign born	Asian Indian	Bangladeshi	Cambodian	Chinese[2]	Fijian	Filipino	Guamanian[3]	Hawaiian, Native	Hmong	Indonesian	Japanese	Korean	Laotian	Malaysian	Pakistani	Samoan	Sri Lankan	Taiwanese	Thai	Tongan	Vietnamese
	28,353	4,812	3,543	-	-	1,204	-	-	481	-	714	-	-	-	-	-	352	-	-	-	-	-	-	-	-	-
	6.40		73.63			75.72			73.10		81.04						76.19									
Volusia County						33.98			13.58		20.15						9.94									
			73.63			25.02			10.00		14.84						7.32									
			12.50			4.25			1.70		2.52						1.24									
	577,273	171,463	128,879	3,866	855	33,403	951	2,497	18,911	-	7,056	415	25	614	471	5,662	21,859	3,239	-	3,022	113	-	1,342	1,686	-	24,008
	7.05		75.16		22.12	74.67	75.66	71.77	74.35		67.61	28.76	3.07	51.17	85.64	75.38	78.89	68.48		77.37	14.83		72.78	74.93		81.40
GEORGIA						25.92	0.74	1.94	14.67		5.47	48.54	2.92	0.48	0.37	4.39	16.96	2.51		2.34	13.22		1.04	1.31		18.63
			75.16		22.12	19.48	0.55	1.46	11.03		4.12	10.73	0.65	0.36	0.27	3.30	12.75	1.89		1.76	2.92		0.78	0.98		14.00
			22.33		0.15	5.79	0.16	0.43	3.28		1.22	0.07	<0.01	0.11	0.08	0.98	3.79	0.56		0.52	0.02		0.23	0.29		4.16
	1,934	616	291	-	-	-	-	-	-	-	-	-	-	-	-	-	-	-	-	-	-	-	-	-	-	-
	2.54		47.24																							
Bartow County																										
			47.24																							
			15.05																							
	2,897	1,593	1,093	-	-	-	-	-	-	-	-	-	-	-	-	-	-	-	-	-	-	-	-	-	-	-
	1.88		68.61																							
Bibb County																										
			68.61																							
			37.73																							
	1,729	591	419	-	-	-	-	-	-	-	-	-	-	-	-	-	-	-	-	-	-	-	-	-	-	-
	3.09		70.90																							
Bulloch County																										
			70.90																							
			24.23																							
	2,571	471	374	-	-	-	-	-	-	-	-	-	-	-	-	-	-	-	-	-	-	-	-	-	-	-
	2.95		79.41																							
Carroll County																										
			79.41																							
			14.55																							
	897	419	307	-	-	-	-	-	-	-	-	-	-	-	-	-	-	-	-	-	-	-	-	-	-	-
	1.68		73.27																							
Catoosa County																										
			73.27																							
			34.23																							
	9,209	4,048	3,002	-	-	604	-	-	486	-	-	-	-	-	-	-	395	-	-	-	-	-	-	-	-	836
	3.97		74.16			79.68			63.36								86.06									82.45
Chatham County						20.12			16.19								13.16									27.85
			74.16			14.92			12.01								9.76									20.65
			32.60			6.56			5.28								4.29									9.08
	8,273	1,428	1,033	-	-	186	-	-	-	-	-	-	-	-	-	-	-	-	-	-	-	-	-	-	-	-
	5.83		72.34			54.87																				
Cherokee County						18.01																				
			72.34			13.03																				
			12.49			2.25																				
	8,509	3,250	2,314	-	-	469	-	-	827	-	-	-	-	-	-	-	378	-	-	-	-	-	-	-	-	-
	8.38		71.20			63.55			86.42								68.98									
Clarke County						20.27			35.74								16.34									
			71.20			14.43			25.45								11.63									
			27.19			5.51			9.72								4.44									

Notes: Please refer to the User's Guide for an explanation of data; data is arranged alphabetically by state, then county, then city within each county; table includes counties with populations greater than 49,999 unless noted and cities with populations greater than 9,999 whose Asian and/or NHPI population rates are greater than the national average; (1) Native Hawaiian and other Pacific Islander; (2) excludes Taiwanese; (3) includes Chamorro; (4) county does not meet population threshold but is shown in order to allow inclusion of city

Place	Total foreign-born population	Total Asian population	Asians who are foreign born	Total NHPI[1] population	NHPIs[1] who are foreign born	Asian Indian	Bangladeshi	Cambodian	Chinese[2]	Fijian	Filipino	Guamanian[3]	Hawaiian, Native	Hmong	Indonesian	Japanese	Korean	Laotian	Malaysian	Pakistani	Samoan	Sri Lankan	Taiwanese	Thai	Tongan	Vietnamese
Clayton County	25,889 10.95	10,344	8,157 78.86 78.86 31.51	-	-	1,012 77.79 12.41 9.78 3.91	-	754 71.95 9.24 7.29 2.91	346 63.02 4.24 3.34 1.34	-	-	-	-	-	-	-	-	878 69.79 10.76 8.49 3.39	-	339 80.91 4.16 3.28 1.31	-	-	-	-	-	3,847 87.61 47.16 37.19 14.86
Forest Park (city)	4,555 21.39	1,297	1,095 84.43 84.43 24.04	-	-	-	-	-	-	-	-	-	-	-	-	-	-	-	-	-	-	-	-	-	-	857 89.46 78.26 66.08 18.81
Riverdale (city)	1,899 15.25	1,030	857 83.20 83.20 45.13	-	-	-	-	-	-	-	-	-	-	-	-	-	-	-	-	-	-	-	-	-	-	406 86.38 47.37 39.42 21.38
Cobb County	70,439 11.59	18,486	14,352 77.64 77.64 20.38	-	-	4,238 78.64 29.53 22.93 6.02	-	-	2,696 78.28 18.78 14.58 3.83	-	817 68.89 5.69 4.42 1.16	-	-	-	-	817 82.19 5.69 4.42 1.16	2,379 79.38 16.58 12.87 3.38	-	-	516 79.75 3.60 2.79 0.73	-	-	-	-	-	1,317 78.82 9.18 7.12 1.87
Smyrna (city)	7,159 17.56	1,619	1,289 79.62 79.62 18.01	-	-	473 82.98 36.70 29.22 6.61	-	-	-	-	-	-	-	-	-	-	-	-	-	-	-	-	-	-	-	-
Columbia County	4,304 4.82	2,878	1,998 69.42 69.42 46.42	-	-	640 70.10 32.03 22.24 14.87	-	-	360 65.69 18.02 12.51 8.36	-	-	-	-	-	-	-	343 78.67 17.17 11.92 7.97	-	-	-	-	-	-	-	-	-
Martinez (cdp)	1,763 6.40	1,409	1,025 72.75 72.75 58.14	-	-	366 75.62 35.71 25.98 20.76	-	-	-	-	-	-	-	-	-	-	-	-	-	-	-	-	-	-	-	-
Coweta County	3,257 3.65	584	410 70.21 70.21 12.59	-	-	-	-	-	-	-	-	-	-	-	-	-	-	-	-	-	-	-	-	-	-	-
DeKalb County	101,320 15.22	26,537	21,498 81.01 81.01 21.22	-	-	6,035 82.21 28.07 22.74 5.96	470 85.45 2.19 1.77 0.46	476 78.03 2.21 1.79 0.47	3,019 77.27 14.04 11.38 2.98	-	444 67.79 2.07 1.67 0.44	-	-	-	-	754 84.53 3.51 2.84 0.74	2,868 86.91 13.34 10.81 2.83	-	-	-	-	-	-	-	-	5,469 83.93 25.44 20.61 5.40
Druid Hills (cdp)	1,271 10.02	867	471 54.33 54.33 37.06	-	-	-	-	-	-	-	-	-	-	-	-	-	-	-	-	-	-	-	-	-	-	-

Notes: Please refer to the User's Guide for an explanation of data; data is arranged alphabetically by state, then county, then city within each county; table includes counties with populations greater than 49,999 unless noted and cities with populations greater than 9,999 whose Asian and/or NHPI population rates are greater than the national average; (1) Native Hawaiian and other Pacific Islander; (2) excludes Taiwanese; (3) includes Chamorro; (4) county does not meet population threshold but is shown in order to allow inclusion of city

Place	Total foreign-born population	Total Asian population	Asians who are foreign born	Total NHPI[1] population	NHPIs[1] who are foreign born	Asian Indian	Bangladeshi	Cambodian	Chinese[2]	Fijian	Filipino	Guamanian[3]	Hawaiian, Native	Hmong	Indonesian	Japanese	Korean	Laotian	Malaysian	Pakistani	Samoan	Sri Lankan	Taiwanese	Thai	Tongan	Vietnamese
Dunwoody (cdp)	4,893	2,480	2,074	-	-	919	-	-	-	-	-	-	-	-	-	-	428	-	-	-	-	-	-	-	-	-
	14.91		83.63			85.01											95.75									
						44.31											20.64									
			83.63			37.06											17.26									
			42.39			18.78											8.75									
North Atlanta (cdp)	13,400	1,710	1,347	-	-	-	-	-	-	-	-	-	-	-	-	-	-	-	-	-	-	-	-	-	-	-
	34.89		78.77																							
			78.77																							
			10.05																							
North Decatur (cdp)	1,767	847	648	-	-	-	-	-	-	-	-	-	-	-	-	-	-	-	-	-	-	-	-	-	-	-
	11.66		76.51																							
			76.51																							
			36.67																							
North Druid Hills (cdp)	2,788	1,268	934	-	-	401	-	-	-	-	-	-	-	-	-	-	-	-	-	-	-	-	-	-	-	-
	14.79		73.66			69.74																				
						42.93																				
			73.66			31.62																				
			33.50			14.38																				
Tucker (cdp)	4,410	1,987	1,612	-	-	-	-	-	-	-	-	-	-	-	-	-	-	-	-	-	-	-	-	-	-	283
	16.57		81.13																							86.81
																										17.56
			81.13																							14.24
			36.55																							6.42
Dougherty County	1,666	696	596	-	-	-	-	-	-	-	-	-	-	-	-	-	-	-	-	-	-	-	-	-	-	-
	1.73		85.63																							
			85.63																							
			35.77																							
Douglas County	3,550	897	666	-	-	-	-	-	-	-	-	-	-	-	-	-	-	-	-	-	-	-	-	-	-	-
	3.85		74.25																							
			74.25																							
			18.76																							
Fayette County	4,606	2,071	1,519	-	-	-	-	-	-	-	-	-	-	-	-	547	-	-	-	-	-	-	-	-	-	-
	5.05		73.35													86.69										
																36.01										
			73.35													26.41										
			32.98													11.88										
Peachtree City (city)	2,494	1,263	938	-	-	-	-	-	-	-	-	-	-	-	-	526	-	-	-	-	-	-	-	-	-	-
	7.82		74.27													87.09										
																56.08										
			74.27													41.65										
			37.61													21.09										
Floyd County	4,722	1,212	875	-	-	366	-	-	-	-	-	-	-	-	-	-	-	-	-	-	-	-	-	-	-	-
	5.21		72.19			77.54																				
						41.83																				
			72.19			30.20																				
			18.53			7.75																				

Notes: Please refer to the User's Guide for an explanation of data; data is arranged alphabetically by state, then county, then city within each county; table includes counties with populations greater than 49,999 unless noted and cities with populations greater than 9,999 whose Asian and/or NHPI population rates are greater than the national average; (1) Native Hawaiian and other Pacific Islander; (2) excludes Taiwanese; (3) includes Chamorro; (4) county does not meet population threshold but is shown in order to allow inclusion of city

Place	Total foreign-born population	Total Asian population	Asians who are foreign born	Total NHPI[1] population	NHPIs[1] who are foreign born	Asian Indian	Bangladeshi	Cambodian	Chinese[2]	Fijian	Filipino	Guamanian[3]	Hawaiian, Native	Hmong	Indonesian	Japanese	Korean	Laotian	Malaysian	Pakistani	Samoan	Sri Lankan	Taiwanese	Thai	Tongan	Vietnamese
Forsyth County	5,883 5.98	756	532 70.37 70.37 9.04	-	-	-	-	-	-	-	-	-	-	-	-	-	-	-	-	-	-	-	-	-	-	-
Fulton County	78,619 9.63	23,763	16,786 70.64 70.64 21.35	-	-	4,705 65.14 28.03 19.80 5.98	-	-	3,659 67.78 21.80 15.40 4.65	-	530 61.20 3.16 2.23 0.67	-	-	-	-	675 72.12 4.02 2.84 0.86	3,120 76.55 18.59 13.13 3.97	-	-	-	-	-	-	-	-	2,435 81.63 14.51 10.25 3.10
Alpharetta (city)	4,037 11.66	1,709	1,248 73.03 73.03 30.91	-	-	507 80.35 40.63 29.67 12.56	-	-	293 62.61 23.48 17.14 7.26	-	-	-	-	-	-	-	-	-	-	-	-	-	-	-	-	-
Roswell (city)	12,562 15.73	2,963	2,245 75.77 75.77 17.87	-	-	633 76.36 28.20 21.36 5.04	-	-	413 70.48 18.40 13.94 3.29	-	-	-	-	-	-	-	680 79.35 30.29 22.95 5.41	-	-	-	-	-	-	-	-	-
Glynn County	2,244 3.32	553	354 64.01 64.01 15.78	-	-	-	-	-	-	-	-	-	-	-	-	-	-	-	-	-	-	-	-	-	-	-
Gwinnett County	99,518 16.91	41,021	31,278 76.25 76.25 31.43	506	110 21.74 21.74 0.11	8,263 75.10 26.42 20.14 8.30	-	539 59.76 1.72 1.31 0.54	4,016 79.13 12.84 9.79 4.04	-	870 71.08 2.78 2.12 0.87	-	-	-	-	597 68.94 1.91 1.46 0.60	7,313 78.97 23.38 17.83 7.35	758 69.35 2.42 1.85 0.76	-	860 75.31 2.75 2.10 0.86	-	-	352 74.26 1.13 0.86 0.35	-	-	5,969 79.93 19.08 14.55 6.00
Duluth (city)	4,531 20.24	2,725	2,020 74.13 74.13 44.58	-	-	645 70.72 31.93 23.67 14.24	-	-	365 69.52 18.07 13.39 8.06	-	-	-	-	-	-	-	542 78.78 26.83 19.89 11.96	-	-	-	-	-	-	-	-	-
Lilburn (city)	2,432 21.43	1,466	1,029 70.19 70.19 42.31	-	-	260 67.01 25.27 17.74 10.69	-	-	-	-	-	-	-	-	-	-	-	-	-	-	-	-	-	-	-	351 75.97 34.11 23.94 14.43
Mountain Park (cdp)	1,301 11.33	1,055	806 76.40 76.40 61.95	-	-	497 72.03 61.66 47.11 38.20	-	-	-	-	-	-	-	-	-	-	-	-	-	-	-	-	-	-	-	-
Hall County	22,502 16.16	1,817	1,475 81.18 81.18 6.55	-	-	-	-	-	-	-	-	-	-	-	-	-	-	-	-	-	-	-	-	-	-	1,052 87.38 71.32 57.90 4.68

Notes: Please refer to the User's Guide for an explanation of data; data is arranged alphabetically by state, then county, then city within each county; table includes counties with populations greater than 49,999 unless noted and cities with populations greater than 9,999 whose Asian and/or NHPI population rates are greater than the national average; (1) Native Hawaiian and other Pacific Islander; (2) excludes Taiwanese; (3) includes Chamorro; (4) county does not meet population threshold but is shown in order to allow inclusion of city

Place	Total foreign-born population	Total Asian population	Asians who are foreign born	Total NHPI[1] population	NHPIs[1] who are foreign born	Asian Indian	Bangladeshi	Cambodian	Chinese[2]	Fijian	Filipino	Guamanian[3]	Hawaiian, Native	Hmong	Indonesian	Japanese	Korean	Laotian	Malaysian	Pakistani	Samoan	Sri Lankan	Taiwanese	Thai	Tongan	Vietnamese
Henry County	4,045 3.39	2,134	1,503 70.43 70.43 37.16	-	-	576 70.24 38.32 26.99 14.24	-	-	-	-	-	-	-	-	-	-	-	-	-	-	-	-	-	-	-	-
Houston County	3,773 3.41	1,777	1,279 71.98 71.98 33.90	-	-	-	-	-	-	-	399 72.55 31.20 22.45 10.58	-	-	-	-	-	-	-	-	-	-	-	-	-	-	-
Liberty County	3,492 5.67	957	713 74.50 74.50 20.42	-	-	-	-	-	-	-	-	-	-	-	-	-	324 85.94 45.44 33.86 9.28	-	-	-	-	-	-	-	-	-
Lowndes County	2,461 2.67	852	568 66.67 66.67 23.08	-	-	-	-	-	-	-	-	-	-	-	-	-	-	-	-	-	-	-	-	-	-	-
Muscogee County	8,665 4.65	2,983	2,048 68.66 68.66 23.64	385	73 18.96 18.96 0.84	420 75.54 20.51 14.08 4.85	-	-	239 65.30 11.67 8.01 2.76	-	308 68.29 15.04 10.33 3.55	-	-	-	-	-	535 68.59 26.12 17.93 6.17	-	-	-	-	-	-	-	-	-
Columbus (sp. city)	8,632 4.65	2,983	2,048 68.66 68.66 23.73	385	73 18.96 18.96 0.85	420 75.54 20.51 14.08 4.87	-	-	239 65.30 11.67 8.01 2.77	-	308 68.29 15.04 10.33 3.57	-	-	-	-	-	535 68.59 26.12 17.93 6.20	-	-	-	-	-	-	-	-	-
Newton County	1,526 2.46	442	291 65.84 65.84 19.07	-	-	-	-	-	-	-	-	-	-	-	-	-	-	-	-	-	-	-	-	-	-	-
Richmond County	6,791 3.40	3,023	2,094 69.27 69.27 30.83	-	-	495 73.12 23.64 16.37 7.29	-	-	331 62.57 15.81 10.95 4.87	-	-	-	-	-	-	-	690 79.31 32.95 22.83 10.16	-	-	-	-	-	-	-	-	-
Rockdale County	5,361 7.65	1,140	954 83.68 83.68 17.80	-	-	-	-	-	-	-	-	-	-	-	-	-	-	-	-	-	-	-	-	-	-	-
Spalding County	1,272 2.18	418	343 82.06 82.06 26.97	-	-	-	-	-	-	-	-	-	-	-	-	-	-	-	-	-	-	-	-	-	-	-

Notes: Please refer to the User's Guide for an explanation of data; data is arranged alphabetically by state, then county, then city within each county; table includes counties with populations greater than 49,999 unless noted and cities with populations greater than 9,999 whose Asian and/or NHPI population rates are greater than the national average; (1) Native Hawaiian and other Pacific Islander; (2) excludes Taiwanese; (3) includes Chamorro; (4) county does not meet population threshold but is shown in order to allow inclusion of city

Place	Total foreign-born population	Total Asian population	Asians who are foreign born	Total NHPI[1] population	NHPIs[1] who are foreign born	Asian Indian	Bangladeshi	Cambodian	Chinese[2]	Fijian	Filipino	Guamanian[3]	Hawaiian, Native	Hmong	Indonesian	Japanese	Korean	Laotian	Malaysian	Pakistani	Samoan	Sri Lankan	Taiwanese	Thai	Tongan	Vietnamese
Troup County	1,165 1.98	415	345 83.13 83.13 29.61	-	-	-	-	-	-	-	-	-	-	-	-	-	-	-	-	-	-	-	-	-	-	-
Walton County	1,194 1.97	478	312 65.27 65.27 26.13	-	-	-	-	-	-	-	-	-	-	-	-	-	-	-	-	-	-	-	-	-	-	-
Whitfield County	13,895 16.64	864	745 86.23 86.23 5.36	-	-	-	-	-	-	-	-	-	-	-	-	-	-	-	-	-	-	-	-	-	-	-
HAWAII	212,229 17.52	503,950	169,629 33.66 33.66 79.93	112,561	11,353 10.09 10.09 5.35	858 68.97 0.51 0.17 0.40	-	175 82.94 0.10 0.03 0.08	22,813 40.94 13.45 4.53 10.75	-	96,072 55.96 56.64 19.06 45.27	60 4.02 0.53 0.05 0.03	492 0.61 4.33 0.44 0.23	-	-	19,644 9.80 11.58 3.90 9.26	16,655 70.25 9.82 3.30 7.85	1,261 74.79 0.74 0.25 0.59	-	-	2,652 18.47 23.36 2.36 1.25	-	669 81.49 0.39 0.13 0.32	1,193 85.34 0.70 0.24 0.56	2,302 55.06 20.28 2.05 1.08	6,405 76.75 3.78 1.27 3.02
Hawaii County	15,208 10.23	39,708	9,961 25.09 25.09 65.50	16,227	1,250 7.70 7.70 8.22	-	-	-	433 32.22 4.35 1.09 2.85	-	6,841 52.22 68.68 17.23 44.98	-	103 0.74 8.24 0.63 0.68	-	-	1,440 6.98 14.46 3.63 9.47	547 62.59 5.49 1.38 3.60	-	-	-	96 32.43 7.68 0.59 0.63	-	-	-	-	-
Hilo (cdp)	2,937 7.20	15,349	1,874 12.21 12.21 63.81	4,969	454 9.14 9.14 15.46	-	-	-	135 27.16 7.20 0.88 4.60	-	799 38.92 42.64 5.21 27.20	-	17 0.41 3.74 0.34 0.58	-	-	587 5.29 31.32 3.82 19.99	223 56.31 11.90 1.45 7.59	-	-	-	-	-	-	-	-	-
Honolulu County	168,246 19.20	404,493	138,211 34.17 34.17 82.15	77,175	8,950 11.60 11.60 5.32	713 71.02 0.52 0.18 0.42	-	-	21,958 41.53 15.89 5.43 13.05	-	70,751 56.20 51.19 17.49 42.05	60 4.52 0.67 0.08 0.04	336 0.67 3.75 0.44 0.20	-	-	17,257 10.81 12.49 4.27 10.26	15,303 70.49 11.07 3.78 9.10	1,230 74.77 0.89 0.30 0.73	-	-	2,431 17.56 27.16 3.15 1.44	-	658 83.19 0.48 0.16 0.39	956 83.20 0.69 0.24 0.57	1,741 56.49 19.45 2.26 1.03	5,989 77.03 4.33 1.48 3.56
Ewa Beach (cdp)	3,874 26.44	7,204	3,584 49.75 49.75 92.51	1,456	100 6.87 6.87 2.58	-	-	-	-	-	3,347 59.58 93.39 46.46 86.40	-	0 0.00 0.00 0.00 0.00	-	-	70 8.54 1.95 0.97 1.81	-	-	-	-	55 13.06 55.00 3.78 1.42	-	-	-	-	-
Halawa (cdp)	2,811 20.14	7,231	2,402 33.22 33.22 85.45	1,512	123 8.13 8.13 4.38	-	-	-	214 29.23 8.91 2.96 7.61	-	1,553 54.38 64.65 21.48 55.25	-	0 0.00 0.00 0.00 0.00	-	-	225 9.01 9.37 3.11 8.00	-	-	-	-	82 12.41 66.67 5.42 2.92	-	-	-	-	-
Honolulu (cdp)	93,895 25.27	208,028	77,983 37.49 37.49 83.05	25,856	4,837 18.71 18.71 5.15	442 71.99 0.57 0.21 0.47	-	-	17,992 46.23 23.07 8.65 19.16	-	26,747 61.27 34.30 12.86 28.49	22 3.25 0.45 0.09 0.02	131 0.91 2.71 0.51 0.14	-	-	12,356 14.44 15.84 5.94 13.16	11,399 73.78 14.62 5.48 12.14	691 70.22 0.89 0.33 0.74	-	-	882 19.81 18.23 3.41 0.94	-	609 86.75 0.78 0.29 0.65	455 85.05 0.58 0.22 0.48	914 58.66 18.90 3.53 0.97	5,011 76.33 6.43 2.41 5.34

Notes: Please refer to the User's Guide for an explanation of data; data is arranged alphabetically by state, then county, then city within each county; table includes counties with populations greater than 49,999 unless noted and cities with populations greater than 9,999 whose Asian and/or NHPI population rates are greater than the national average; (1) Native Hawaiian and other Pacific Islander; (2) excludes Taiwanese; (3) includes Chamorro; (4) county does not meet population threshold but is shown in order to allow inclusion of city

Place	Total foreign-born population	Total Asian population	Asians who are foreign born	Total NHPI[1] population	NHPIs[1] who are foreign born	Asian Indian	Bangladeshi	Cambodian	Chinese[2]	Fijian	Filipino	Guamanian[3]	Hawaiian, Native	Hmong	Indonesian	Japanese	Korean	Laotian	Malaysian	Pakistani	Samoan	Sri Lankan	Taiwanese	Thai	Tongan	Vietnamese
Kailua (cdp)	2,652	7,872	1,462	2,743	77	-	-	-	254	-	494	-	0	-	-	356	161	-	-	-	-	-	-	-	-	-
	7.25		18.57		2.81				21.10		50.51		0.00			8.23	42.82									
									17.37		33.79		0.00			24.35	11.01									
			18.57		2.81				3.23		6.28		0.00			4.52	2.05									
			55.13		2.90				9.58		18.63		0.00			13.42	6.07									
Kaneohe (cdp)	2,195	13,801	1,593	4,046	104	-	-	-	156	-	689	-	8	-	-	330	261	-	-	-	-	-	-	-	-	-
	6.28		11.54		2.57				10.88		41.13		0.24			3.92	58.13									
									9.79		43.25		7.69			20.72	16.38									
			11.54		2.57				1.13		4.99		0.20			2.39	1.89									
			72.57		4.74				7.11		31.39		0.36			15.03	11.89									
Kaneohe Station (cdp)	909	629	377	-	-	-	-	-	-	-	-	-	-	-	-	-	-	-	-	-	-	-	-	-	-	-
	7.69		59.94																							
			59.94																							
			41.47																							
Makakilo City (cdp)	1,962	4,415	1,619	1,355	77	-	-	-	-	-	1,125	-	0	-	-	148	-	-	-	-	-	-	-	-	-	-
	14.91		36.67		5.68						47.59		0.00			15.24										
											69.49		0.00			9.14										
			36.67		5.68						25.48		0.00			3.35										
			82.52		3.92						57.34		0.00			7.54										
Mililani Town (cdp)	3,111	13,195	2,505	1,173	92	-	-	-	361	-	1,278	-	4	-	-	411	288	-	-	-	-	-	-	-	-	-
	10.89		18.98		7.84				37.10		40.62		0.46			5.84	57.95									
									14.41		51.02		4.35			16.41	11.50									
			18.98		7.84				2.74		9.69		0.34			3.11	2.18									
			80.52		2.96				11.60		41.08		0.13			13.21	9.26									
Nanakuli (cdp)	468	1,059	314	4,104	97	-	-	-	-	-	268	-	6	-	-	-	-	-	-	-	68	-	-	-	-	-
	4.37		29.65		2.36						41.49		0.19								9.03					
											85.35		6.19								70.10					
			29.65		2.36						25.31		0.15								1.66					
			67.09		20.73						57.26		1.28								14.53					
Pearl City (cdp)	4,140	16,882	3,623	1,791	82	-	-	-	375	-	2,152	-	7	-	-	606	251	-	-	-	-	-	-	-	-	-
	13.43		21.46		4.58				29.67		50.42		0.52			6.41	66.40									
									10.35		59.40		8.54			16.73	6.93									
			21.46		4.58				2.22		12.75		0.39			3.59	1.49									
			87.51		1.98				9.06		51.98		0.17			14.64	6.06									
Schofield Barracks (cdp)	808	525	285	-	-	-	-	-	-	-	-	-	-	-	-	-	-	-	-	-	-	-	-	-	-	-
	5.60		54.29																							
			54.29																							
			35.27																							
Wahiawa (cdp)	2,527	7,193	1,934	1,734	372	-	-	-	-	-	1,560	-	6	-	-	196	-	-	-	-	-	-	-	-	-	-
	15.65		26.89		21.45						53.41		0.64			6.05										
											80.66		1.61			10.13										
			26.89		21.45						21.69		0.35			2.72										
			76.53		14.72						61.73		0.24			7.76										
Waianae (cdp)	764	1,928	596	2,793	99	-	-	-	-	-	438	-	10	-	-	41	-	-	-	-	-	-	-	-	-	-
	7.17		30.91		3.54						43.11		0.42			7.43										
											73.49		10.10			6.88										
			30.91		3.54						22.72		0.36			2.13										
			78.01		12.96						57.33		1.31			5.37										

Notes: Please refer to the User's Guide for an explanation of data; data is arranged alphabetically by state, then county, then city within each county; table includes counties with populations greater than 49,999 unless noted and cities with populations greater than 9,999 whose Asian and/or NHPI population rates are greater than the national average; (1) Native Hawaiian and other Pacific Islander; (2) excludes Taiwanese; (3) includes Chamorro; (4) county does not meet population threshold but is shown in order to allow inclusion of city

Place	Total foreign-born population	Total Asian population	Asians who are foreign born	Total NHPI[1] population	NHPIs[1] who are foreign born	Asian Indian	Bangladeshi	Cambodian	Chinese[2]	Fijian	Filipino	Guamanian[3]	Hawaiian, Native	Hmong	Indonesian	Japanese	Korean	Laotian	Malaysian	Pakistani	Samoan	Sri Lankan	Taiwanese	Thai	Tongan	Vietnamese
Waimalu (cdp)	4,320 14.64	15,849	3,658 23.08 23.08 84.68	1,564	199 12.72 12.72 4.61	-	-	-	406 31.82 11.10 2.56 9.40	-	1,588 47.62 43.41 10.02 36.76	-	0 0.00 0.00 0.00 0.00	-	-	496 6.25 13.56 3.13 11.48	906 72.42 24.77 5.72 20.97	-	-	-	-	-	-	-	-	-
Waipahu (cdp)	12,476 37.68	21,657	10,984 50.72 50.72 88.04	4,026	851 21.14 21.14 6.82	-	-	-	122 20.96 1.11 0.56 0.98	-	10,286 62.19 93.65 47.50 82.45	-	0 0.00 0.00 0.00 0.00	-	-	209 6.25 1.90 0.97 1.68	-	-	-	-	382 18.02 44.89 9.49 3.06	-	-	-	-	-
Waipio (cdp)	2,004 17.22	6,544	1,737 26.54 26.54 86.68	627	77 12.28 12.28 3.84	-	-	-	-	-	1,203 49.47 69.26 18.38 60.03	-	22 5.05 28.57 3.51 1.10	-	-	217 7.55 12.49 3.32 10.83	-	-	-	-	-	-	-	-	-	-
Kauai County	7,574 12.96	20,929	6,224 29.74 29.74 82.18	5,314	138 2.60 2.60 1.82	-	-	-	121 28.74 1.94 0.58 1.60	-	5,546 49.89 89.11 26.50 73.22	-	5 0.10 3.62 0.09 0.07	-	-	258 3.40 4.15 1.23 3.41	-	-	-	-	-	-	-	-	-	-
Maui County	21,171 16.53	38,790	15,218 39.23 39.23 71.88	13,757	1,015 7.38 7.38 4.79	-	-	-	301 27.61 1.98 0.78 1.42	-	12,919 59.94 84.89 33.30 61.02	-	48 0.41 4.73 0.35 0.23	-	-	689 5.50 4.53 1.78 3.25	669 70.94 4.40 1.72 3.16	-	-	-	-	-	-	-	404 50.88 39.80 2.94 1.91	-
Kahului (cdp)	5,174 25.84	10,796	4,472 41.42 41.42 86.43	1,834	180 9.81 9.81 3.48	-	-	-	-	-	4,049 63.10 90.54 37.50 78.26	-	0 0.00 0.00 0.00 0.00	-	-	157 4.56 3.51 1.45 3.03	-	-	-	-	-	-	-	-	-	-
Kihei (cdp)	3,285 19.52	4,134	2,138 51.72 51.72 65.08	1,137	199 17.50 17.50 6.06	-	-	-	-	-	1,868 58.85 87.37 45.19 56.86	-	19 2.38 9.55 1.67 0.58	-	-	81 17.42 3.79 1.96 2.47	-	-	-	-	-	-	-	-	-	-
Wailuku (cdp)	1,492 12.01	5,045	1,212 24.02 24.02 81.23	1,378	14 1.02 1.02 0.94	-	-	-	-	-	836 52.78 68.98 16.57 56.03	-	0 0.00 0.00 0.00 0.00	-	-	102 3.84 8.42 2.02 6.84	-	-	-	-	-	-	-	-	-	-
IDAHO	64,080 4.95	11,321	6,864 60.63 60.63 10.71	1,232	144 11.69 11.69 0.22	930 81.44 13.55 8.21 1.45	-	-	1,271 70.45 18.52 11.23 1.98	-	1,056 64.39 15.38 9.33 1.65	-	0 0.00 0.00 0.00 0.00	-	-	728 27.46 10.61 6.43 1.14	993 78.00 14.47 8.77 1.55	393 77.36 5.73 3.47 0.61	-	-	-	-	-	-	-	1,032 75.88 15.03 9.12 1.61
Ada County	12,864 4.28	4,738	3,102 65.47 65.47 24.11	413	20 4.84 4.84 0.16	521 84.17 16.80 11.00 4.05	-	-	450 64.29 14.51 9.50 3.50	-	312 62.28 10.06 6.59 2.43	-	-	-	-	209 29.15 6.74 4.41 1.62	423 84.26 13.64 8.93 3.29	-	-	-	-	-	-	-	-	763 78.90 24.60 16.10 5.93

Notes: Please refer to the User's Guide for an explanation of data; data is arranged alphabetically by state, then county, then city within each county; table includes counties with populations greater than 49,999 unless noted and cities with populations greater than 9,999 whose Asian and/or NHPI population rates are greater than the national average; (1) Native Hawaiian and other Pacific Islander; (2) excludes Taiwanese; (3) includes Chamorro; (4) county does not meet population threshold but is shown in order to allow inclusion of city

Place	Total foreign-born population	Total Asian population	Asians who are foreign born	Total NHPI[1] population	NHPIs[1] who are foreign born	Asian Indian	Bangladeshi	Cambodian	Chinese[2]	Fijian	Filipino	Guamanian[3]	Hawaiian, Native	Hmong	Indonesian	Japanese	Korean	Laotian	Malaysian	Pakistani	Samoan	Sri Lankan	Taiwanese	Thai	Tongan	Vietnamese
Bannock County	1,641 2.17	785	518 65.99 65.99 31.57	-	-	-	-	-	-	-	-	-	-	-	-	-	-	-	-	-	-	-	-	-	-	-
Bonneville County	3,216 3.90	486	241 49.59 49.59 7.49	-	-	-	-	-	-	-	-	-	-	-	-	-	-	-	-	-	-	-	-	-	-	-
Canyon County	11,360 8.64	1,090	584 53.58 53.58 5.14	-	-	-	-	-	-	-	-	-	-	-	-	69 22.48 11.82 6.33 0.61	-	-	-	-	-	-	-	-	-	-
Kootenai County	2,598 2.39	581	321 55.25 55.25 12.36	-	-	-	-	-	-	-	-	-	-	-	-	-	-	-	-	-	-	-	-	-	-	-
Twin Falls County	4,103 6.38	384	288 75.00 75.00 7.02	-	-	-	-	-	-	-	-	-	-	-	-	-	-	-	-	-	-	-	-	-	-	-
ILLINOIS	1,529,058 12.31	423,440	305,563 72.16 72.16 19.98	3,811	938 24.61 24.61 0.06	90,799 73.66 29.72 21.44 5.94	567 70.43 0.19 0.13 0.04	2,479 70.77 0.81 0.59 0.16	53,560 72.78 17.53 12.65 3.50	-	62,050 71.95 20.31 14.65 4.06	262 32.15 27.93 6.87 0.02	68 7.44 7.25 1.78 <0.01	-	852 89.12 0.28 0.20 0.06	11,467 55.04 3.75 2.71 0.75	39,638 76.11 12.97 9.36 2.59	3,464 70.48 1.13 0.82 0.23	461 81.31 0.15 0.11 0.03	12,006 77.02 3.93 2.84 0.79	160 18.31 17.06 4.20 0.01	493 88.99 0.16 0.12 0.03	2,484 69.58 0.81 0.59 0.16	4,443 75.97 1.45 1.05 0.29	-	14,128 76.70 4.62 3.34 0.92
Champaign County	14,389 8.01	11,602	7,768 66.95 66.95 53.99	-	-	1,460 60.46 18.80 12.58 10.15	-	-	2,327 70.99 29.96 20.06 16.17	-	390 54.02 5.02 3.36 2.71	-	-	-	-	363 61.21 4.67 3.13 2.52	1,778 69.84 22.89 15.32 12.36	-	-	-	-	-	-	-	-	540 80.84 6.95 4.65 3.75
Champaign (city)	6,361 9.37	4,602	3,139 68.21 68.21 49.35	-	-	696 62.25 22.17 15.12 10.94	-	-	755 71.03 24.05 16.41 11.87	-	-	-	-	-	-	-	609 69.13 19.40 13.23 9.57	-	-	-	-	-	-	-	-	327 76.05 10.42 7.11 5.14
Urbana (city)	5,732 15.84	5,283	3,446 65.23 65.23 60.12	-	-	566 57.70 16.42 10.71 9.87	-	-	1,295 71.82 37.58 24.51 22.59	-	-	-	-	-	-	-	800 69.14 23.22 15.14 13.96	-	-	-	-	-	-	-	-	-
Coles County	847 1.59	364	301 82.69 82.69 35.54	-	-	-	-	-	-	-	-	-	-	-	-	-	-	-	-	-	-	-	-	-	-	-

Notes: Please refer to the User's Guide for an explanation of data; data is arranged alphabetically by state, then county, then city within each county; table includes counties with populations greater than 49,999 unless noted and cities with populations greater than 9,999 whose Asian and/or NHPI population rates are greater than the national average; (1) Native Hawaiian and other Pacific Islander; (2) excludes Taiwanese; (3) includes Chamorro; (4) county does not meet population threshold but is shown in order to allow inclusion of city

Place	Total foreign-born population	Total Asian population	Asians who are foreign born	Total NHPI[1] population	NHPIs[1] who are foreign born	Asian Indian	Bangladeshi	Cambodian	Chinese[2]	Fijian	Filipino	Guamanian[3]	Hawaiian, Native	Hmong	Indonesian	Japanese	Korean	Laotian	Malaysian	Pakistani	Samoan	Sri Lankan	Taiwanese	Thai	Tongan	Vietnamese
Cook County	1,064,703	260,996	190,926	1,596	552	51,996	-	1,591	34,495	-	40,302	-	-	-	453	7,556	27,100	1,044	-	8,445	-	-	1,237	3,069	-	8,649
	19.80		73.15		34.59	74.83		71.44	73.10		73.82				91.70	52.98	76.15	83.32		79.58			70.61	76.69		78.56
						27.23		0.83	18.07		21.11				0.24	3.96	14.19	0.55		4.42			0.65	1.61		4.53
			73.15		34.59	19.92		0.61	13.22		15.44				0.17	2.90	10.38	0.40		3.24			0.47	1.18		3.31
			17.93		0.05	4.88		0.15	3.24		3.79				0.04	0.71	2.55	0.10		0.79			0.12	0.29		0.81
Arlington Heights (village)	10,546	4,671	3,641	-	-	1,047	-	-	366	-	544	-	-	-	-	764	627	-	-	-	-	-	-	-	-	-
	13.86		77.95			85.19			67.03		78.96					76.86	78.77									
						28.76			10.05		14.94					20.98	17.22									
			77.95			22.41			7.84		11.65					16.36	13.42									
			34.52			9.93			3.47		5.16					7.24	5.95									
Chicago (city)	628,903	127,052	93,435	1,065	463	18,090	-	1,379	23,501	-	20,755	-	-	-	-	2,120	10,011	-	-	5,404	-	-	536	1,637	-	6,533
	21.72		73.54		43.47	74.73		72.16	74.81		74.46					35.08	79.60			83.95			69.07	76.35		79.88
						19.36		1.48	25.15		22.21					2.27	10.71			5.78			0.57	1.75		6.99
			73.54		43.47	14.24		1.09	18.50		16.34					1.67	7.88			4.25			0.42	1.29		5.14
			14.86		0.07	2.88		0.22	3.74		3.30					0.34	1.59			0.86			0.09	0.26		1.04
Des Plaines (city)	14,010	4,382	3,062	-	-	1,524	-	-	296	-	617	-	-	-	-	-	-	-	-	-	-	-	-	-	-	-
	23.87		69.88			78.03			58.38		65.15															
						49.77			9.67		20.15															
			69.88			34.78			6.75		14.08															
			21.86			10.88			2.11		4.40															
Elk Grove Village (village)	4,964	3,311	2,383	-	-	823	-	-	304	-	357	-	-	-	-	505	-	-	-	-	-	-	-	-	-	-
	14.28		71.97			77.06			72.55		60.41					82.79										
						34.54			12.76		14.98					21.19										
			71.97			24.86			9.18		10.78					15.25										
			48.01			16.58			6.12		7.19					10.17										
Evanston (city)	11,448	4,493	2,785	-	-	683	-	-	770	-	375	-	-	-	-	245	342	-	-	-	-	-	-	-	-	-
	15.42		61.99			56.73			64.38		71.70					65.16	51.66									
						24.52			27.65		13.46					8.80	12.28									
			61.99			15.20			17.14		8.35					5.45	7.61									
			24.33			5.97			6.73		3.28					2.14	2.99									
Forest Park (village)	2,329	1,048	909	-	-	-	-	-	-	-	-	-	-	-	-	-	-	-	-	-	-	-	-	-	-	-
	14.85		86.74																							
			86.74																							
			39.03																							
Glenview (village)	8,128	4,212	2,861	-	-	464	-	-	487	-	394	-	-	-	-	200	1,084	-	-	-	-	-	-	-	-	-
	19.50		67.92			74.60			69.57		67.93					63.69	67.88									
						16.22			17.02		13.77					6.99	37.89									
			67.92			11.02			11.56		9.35					4.75	25.74									
			35.20			5.71			5.99		4.85					2.46	13.34									
Hanover Park (village)	10,896	4,249	3,090	-	-	1,385	-	-	-	-	858	-	-	-	-	-	-	-	-	-	-	-	-	-	-	-
	28.40		72.72			73.09					73.77															
						44.82					27.77															
			72.72			32.60					20.19															
			28.36			12.71					7.87															
Hoffman Estates (village)	11,651	7,480	5,715	-	-	2,132	-	-	575	-	658	-	-	-	-	737	1,074	-	-	-	-	-	-	-	-	-
	23.14		76.40			77.81			70.04		76.07					88.16	75.32									
						37.31			10.06		11.51					12.90	18.79									
			76.40			28.50			7.69		8.80					9.85	14.36									
			49.05			18.30			4.94		5.65					6.33	9.22									

Notes: Please refer to the User's Guide for an explanation of data; data is arranged alphabetically by state, then county, then city within each county; table includes counties with populations greater than 49,999 unless noted and cities with populations greater than 9,999 whose Asian and/or NHPI population rates are greater than the national average; (1) Native Hawaiian and other Pacific Islander; (2) excludes Taiwanese; (3) includes Chamorro; (4) county does not meet population threshold but is shown in order to allow inclusion of city

Place	Total foreign-born population	Total Asian population	Asians who are foreign born	Total NHPI[1] population	NHPIs[1] who are foreign born	Asian Indian	Bangladeshi	Cambodian	Chinese[2]	Fijian	Filipino	Guamanian[3]	Hawaiian, Native	Hmong	Indonesian	Japanese	Korean	Laotian	Malaysian	Pakistani	Samoan	Sri Lankan	Taiwanese	Thai	Tongan	Vietnamese
Lincolnwood (village)	4,216 34.11	2,641	1,654 62.63 62.63 39.23	-	-	542 68.43 32.77 20.52 12.86	-	-	-	-	289 58.62 17.47 10.94 6.85	-	-	-	-	-	431 66.31 26.06 16.32 10.22	-	-	-	-	-	-	-	-	-
Morton Grove (village)	7,535 33.56	4,931	3,334 67.61 67.61 44.25	-	-	998 65.14 29.93 20.24 13.24	-	-	-	-	1,271 71.16 38.12 25.78 16.87	-	-	-	-	-	608 69.89 18.24 12.33 8.07	-	-	-	-	-	-	-	-	-
Mount Prospect (village)	15,159 26.73	6,482	4,956 76.46 76.46 32.69	-	-	2,558 81.08 51.61 39.46 16.87	-	-	426 72.57 8.60 6.57 2.81	-	310 64.45 6.26 4.78 2.04	-	-	-	-	286 64.27 5.77 4.41 1.89	1,084 74.97 21.87 16.72 7.15	-	-	-	-	-	-	-	-	-
Niles (village)	10,144 33.65	3,381	2,537 75.04 75.04 25.01	-	-	1,000 73.21 39.42 29.58 9.86	-	-	-	-	419 66.72 16.52 12.39 4.13	-	-	-	-	-	861 85.67 33.94 25.47 8.49	-	-	-	-	-	-	-	-	-
Northbrook (village)	5,089 15.23	2,920	2,056 70.41 70.41 40.40	-	-	-	-	-	329 65.67 16.00 11.27 6.46	-	-	-	-	-	-	-	1,164 75.19 56.61 39.86 22.87	-	-	-	-	-	-	-	-	-
Oak Park (village)	5,165 9.83	2,267	1,665 73.45 73.45 32.24	-	-	595 77.07 35.74 26.25 11.52	-	-	304 62.17 18.26 13.41 5.89	-	-	-	-	-	-	-	-	-	-	-	-	-	-	-	-	-
Orland Park (village)	4,813 9.42	2,132	1,276 59.85 59.85 26.51	-	-	404 62.44 31.66 18.95 8.39	-	-	-	-	379 55.90 29.70 17.78 7.87	-	-	-	-	-	-	-	-	-	-	-	-	-	-	-
Palatine (village)	14,249 21.87	5,225	3,996 76.48 76.48 28.04	-	-	1,767 79.95 44.22 33.82 12.40	-	-	552 80.35 13.81 10.56 3.87	-	564 79.44 14.11 10.79 3.96	-	-	-	-	-	394 65.56 9.86 7.54 2.77	-	-	-	-	-	-	-	-	-
Prospect Heights (city)	6,399 36.48	630	471 74.76 74.76 7.36	-	-	-	-	-	-	-	-	-	-	-	-	-	-	-	-	-	-	-	-	-	-	-
Rolling Meadows (city)	5,245 21.31	1,478	1,090 73.75 73.75 20.78	-	-	325 71.12 29.82 21.99 6.20	-	-	-	-	-	-	-	-	-	-	-	-	-	-	-	-	-	-	-	-

Notes: Please refer to the User's Guide for an explanation of data; data is arranged alphabetically by state, then county, then city within each county; table includes counties with populations greater than 49,999 unless noted and cities with populations greater than 9,999 whose Asian and/or NHPI population rates are greater than the national average; (1) Native Hawaiian and other Pacific Islander; (2) excludes Taiwanese; (3) includes Chamorro; (4) county does not meet population threshold but is shown in order to allow inclusion of city

Place	Total foreign-born population	Total Asian population	Asians who are foreign born	Total NHPI[1] population	NHPIs[1] who are foreign born	Asian Indian	Bangladeshi	Cambodian	Chinese[2]	Fijian	Filipino	Guamanian[3]	Hawaiian, Native	Hmong	Indonesian	Japanese	Korean	Laotian	Malaysian	Pakistani	Samoan	Sri Lankan	Taiwanese	Thai	Tongan	Vietnamese
Schaumburg (village)	14,262 19.14	10,285	7,914 76.95 76.95 55.49	-	-	3,569 78.80 45.10 34.70 25.02	-	-	1,024 76.65 12.94 9.96 7.18	-	721 77.86 9.11 7.01 5.06	-	-	-	-	774 82.34 9.78 7.53 5.43	1,352 76.17 17.08 13.15 9.48	-	-	-	-	-	-	-	-	-
Schiller Park (village)	4,604 39.07	715	560 78.32 78.32 12.16	-	-	-	-	-	-	-	-	-	-	-	-	-	-	-	-	-	-	-	-	-	-	-
Skokie (village)	23,437 37.01	13,321	9,557 71.74 71.74 40.78	-	-	2,628 68.35 27.50 19.73 11.21	-	-	1,156 69.76 12.10 8.68 4.93	-	2,258 73.07 23.63 16.95 9.63	-	-	-	-	-	2,008 79.56 21.01 15.07 8.57	-	-	359 72.53 3.76 2.69 1.53	-	-	-	-	-	-
Streamwood (village)	7,304 19.88	3,314	2,403 72.51 72.51 32.90	-	-	849 68.69 35.33 25.62 11.62	-	-	-	-	929 78.53 38.66 28.03 12.72	-	-	-	-	-	-	-	-	-	-	-	-	-	-	-
Wheeling (village)	10,817 31.43	2,968	2,240 75.47 75.47 20.71	-	-	1,052 75.25 46.96 35.44 9.73	-	-	-	-	424 72.48 18.93 14.29 3.92	-	-	-	-	-	-	-	-	-	-	-	-	-	-	-
Wilmette (village)	3,659 13.22	2,214	1,538 69.47 69.47 42.03	-	-	-	-	-	317 76.94 20.61 14.32 8.66	-	-	-	-	-	-	235 67.92 15.28 10.61 6.42	547 70.49 35.57 24.71 14.95	-	-	-	-	-	-	-	-	-
DeKalb County	5,193 5.84	2,089	1,273 60.94 60.94 24.51	-	-	364 56.79 28.59 17.42 7.01	-	-	-	-	-	-	-	-	-	-	-	-	-	-	-	-	-	-	-	-
DeKalb (city)	3,517 9.06	1,778	1,075 60.46 60.46 30.57	-	-	334 59.01 31.07 18.79 9.50	-	-	-	-	-	-	-	-	-	-	-	-	-	-	-	-	-	-	-	-
DuPage County	138,656 15.34	71,389	51,487 72.12 72.12 37.13	-	-	23,316 73.15 45.29 32.66 16.82	-	-	7,274 72.00 14.13 10.19 5.25	-	9,900 70.16 19.23 13.87 7.14	-	-	-	-	843 57.66 1.64 1.18 0.61	3,251 77.07 6.31 4.55 2.34	-	-	2,032 72.18 3.95 2.85 1.47	-	-	597 71.07 1.16 0.84 0.43	277 66.27 0.54 0.39 0.20	-	2,214 78.32 4.30 3.10 1.60
Addison (village)	12,235 34.26	2,954	2,259 76.47 76.47 18.46	-	-	1,317 79.72 58.30 44.58 10.76	-	-	-	-	382 76.10 16.91 12.93 3.12	-	-	-	-	-	-	-	-	-	-	-	-	-	-	-

Notes: Please refer to the User's Guide for an explanation of data; data is arranged alphabetically by state, then county, then city within each county; table includes counties with populations greater than 49,999 unless noted and cities with populations greater than 9,999 whose Asian and/or NHPI population rates are greater than the national average; (1) Native Hawaiian and other Pacific Islander; (2) excludes Taiwanese; (3) includes Chamorro; (4) county does not meet population threshold but is shown in order to allow inclusion of city

Place	Total foreign-born population	Total Asian population	Asians who are foreign born	Total NHPI[1] population	NHPIs[1] who are foreign born	Asian Indian	Bangladeshi	Cambodian	Chinese[2]	Fijian	Filipino	Guamanian[3]	Hawaiian, Native	Hmong	Indonesian	Japanese	Korean	Laotian	Malaysian	Pakistani	Samoan	Sri Lankan	Taiwanese	Thai	Tongan	Vietnamese
Bartlett (village)	4,032 10.94	2,934	1,947 66.36 66.36 48.29	-	-	964 64.48 49.51 32.86 23.91	-	-	-	-	420 63.73 21.57 14.31 10.42	-	-	-	-	-	-	-	-	-	-	-	-	-	-	-
Bensenville (village)	6,461 31.51	1,242	913 73.51 73.51 14.13	-	-	527 69.80 57.72 42.43 8.16	-	-	-	-	-	-	-	-	-	-	-	-	-	-	-	-	-	-	-	-
Bloomingdale (village)	2,858 13.24	1,932	1,273 65.89 65.89 44.54	-	-	600 65.50 47.13 31.06 20.99	-	-	-	-	-	-	-	-	-	-	-	-	-	-	-	-	-	-	-	-
Burr Ridge (village)	1,359 13.16	1,032	674 65.31 65.31 49.60	-	-	373 58.56 55.34 36.14 27.45	-	-	-	-	-	-	-	-	-	-	-	-	-	-	-	-	-	-	-	-
Carol Stream (village)	6,689 16.81	4,071	2,993 73.52 73.52 44.75	-	-	1,367 74.99 45.67 33.58 20.44	-	-	-	-	694 64.62 23.19 17.05 10.38	-	-	-	-	-	-	-	-	-	-	-	-	-	-	327 69.28 10.93 8.03 4.89
Darien (city)	3,486 15.18	2,909	1,975 67.89 67.89 56.66	-	-	971 64.99 49.16 33.38 27.85	-	-	-	-	590 74.97 29.87 20.28 16.92	-	-	-	-	-	-	-	-	-	-	-	-	-	-	-
Downers Grove (village)	4,752 9.77	2,976	2,066 69.42 69.42 43.48	-	-	989 73.75 47.87 33.23 20.81	-	-	400 68.73 19.36 13.44 8.42	-	368 68.27 17.81 12.37 7.74	-	-	-	-	-	-	-	-	-	-	-	-	-	-	-
Glen Ellyn (village)	2,905 10.74	1,318	1,032 78.30 78.30 35.52	-	-	407 79.80 39.44 30.88 14.01	-	-	-	-	-	-	-	-	-	-	-	-	-	-	-	-	-	-	-	-
Glendale Heights (village)	9,605 30.32	6,298	4,699 74.61 74.61 48.92	-	-	2,042 73.45 43.46 32.42 21.26	-	-	-	-	1,294 74.20 27.54 20.55 13.47	-	-	-	-	-	-	-	-	-	-	-	-	-	-	631 78.97 13.43 10.02 6.57
Hinsdale (village)	1,582 9.05	866	617 71.25 71.25 39.00	-	-	-	-	-	-	-	-	-	-	-	-	-	-	-	-	-	-	-	-	-	-	-

Notes: Please refer to the User's Guide for an explanation of data; data is arranged alphabetically by state, then county, then city within each county; table includes counties with populations greater than 49,999 unless noted and cities with populations greater than 9,999 whose Asian and/or NHPI population rates are greater than the national average; (1) Native Hawaiian and other Pacific Islander; (2) excludes Taiwanese; (3) includes Chamorro; (4) county does not meet population threshold but is shown in order to allow inclusion of city

Place	Total foreign-born population	Total Asian population	Asians who are foreign born	Total NHPI[1] population	NHPIs[1] who are foreign born	Asian Indian	Bangladeshi	Cambodian	Chinese[2]	Fijian	Filipino	Guamanian[3]	Hawaiian, Native	Hmong	Indonesian	Japanese	Korean	Laotian	Malaysian	Pakistani	Samoan	Sri Lankan	Taiwanese	Thai	Tongan	Vietnamese
Lisle (village)	2,757 13.05	2,175	1,500 68.97 68.97 54.41	-	-	546 70.91 36.40 25.10 19.80	-	-	490 73.57 32.67 22.53 17.77	-	-	-	-	-	-	-	-	-	-	-	-	-	-	-	-	-
Lombard (village)	4,850 11.59	2,912	2,180 74.86 74.86 44.95	-	-	1,030 78.99 47.25 35.37 21.24	-	-	-	-	472 70.76 21.65 16.21 9.73	-	-	-	-	-	-	-	-	-	-	-	-	-	-	-
Naperville (city)	14,963 11.66	11,700	8,003 68.40 68.40 53.49	-	-	3,341 71.48 41.75 28.56 22.33	-	-	2,749 67.98 34.35 23.50 18.37	-	390 56.52 4.87 3.33 2.61	-	-	-	-	-	638 73.33 7.97 5.45 4.26	-	-	-	-	-	285 66.13 3.56 2.44 1.90	-	-	-
Roselle (village)	3,516 15.10	1,816	1,363 75.06 75.06 38.77	-	-	666 77.89 48.86 36.67 18.94	-	-	-	-	-	-	-	-	-	-	-	-	-	-	-	-	-	-	-	-
Villa Park (village)	3,203 14.37	896	688 76.79 76.79 21.48	-	-	-	-	-	-	-	-	-	-	-	-	-	-	-	-	-	-	-	-	-	-	-
Warrenville (city)	1,239 9.39	521	370 71.02 71.02 29.86	-	-	-	-	-	-	-	-	-	-	-	-	-	-	-	-	-	-	-	-	-	-	-
Westmont (village)	4,793 19.69	2,900	2,301 79.34 79.34 48.01	-	-	1,085 80.25 47.15 37.41 22.64	-	-	429 89.56 18.64 14.79 8.95	-	348 69.18 15.12 12.00 7.26	-	-	-	-	-	-	-	-	-	-	-	-	-	-	-
Wheaton (city)	5,256 9.48	2,711	2,041 75.29 75.29 38.83	-	-	766 80.63 37.53 28.26 14.57	-	-	-	-	-	-	-	-	-	-	-	-	-	-	-	-	-	-	-	305 79.84 14.94 11.25 5.80
Woodridge (village)	5,387 17.34	3,503	2,567 73.28 73.28 47.65	-	-	1,274 77.49 49.63 36.37 23.65	-	-	-	-	764 65.75 29.76 21.81 14.18	-	-	-	-	-	-	-	-	-	-	-	-	-	-	-
Jackson County	3,129 5.25	1,931	1,550 80.27 80.27 49.54	-	-	-	-	-	352 84.62 22.71 18.23 11.25	-	-	-	-	-	-	-	-	-	-	-	-	-	-	-	-	-

Notes: Please refer to the User's Guide for an explanation of data; data is arranged alphabetically by state, then county, then city within each county; table includes counties with populations greater than 49,999 unless noted and cities with populations greater than 9,999 whose Asian and/or NHPI population rates are greater than the national average; (1) Native Hawaiian and other Pacific Islander; (2) excludes Taiwanese; (3) includes Chamorro; (4) county does not meet population threshold but is shown in order to allow inclusion of city

Place	Total foreign-born population	Total Asian population	Asians who are foreign born	Total NHPI[1] population	NHPIs[1] who are foreign born	Asian Indian	Bangladeshi	Cambodian	Chinese[2]	Fijian	Filipino	Guamanian[3]	Hawaiian, Native	Hmong	Indonesian	Japanese	Korean	Laotian	Malaysian	Pakistani	Samoan	Sri Lankan	Taiwanese	Thai	Tongan	Vietnamese
Carbondale (city)	2,194 10.60	1,429	1,197 83.76 83.76 54.56	-	-	-	-	-	-	-	-	-	-	-	-	-	-	-	-	-	-	-	-	-	-	-
Kane County	63,516 15.72	7,056	4,655 65.97 65.97 7.33	-	-	1,166 72.29 25.05 16.52 1.84	-	-	575 67.25 12.35 8.15 0.91	-	858 64.71 18.43 12.16 1.35	-	-	-	-	-	408 85.18 8.76 5.78 0.64	647 61.85 13.90 9.17 1.02	-	-	-	-	-	-	-	301 62.97 6.47 4.27 0.47
South Elgin (village)	1,419 9.05	842	540 64.13 64.13 38.05	-	-	-	-	-	-	-	-	-	-	-	-	-	-	-	-	-	-	-	-	-	-	-
Kankakee County	3,611 3.48	730	585 80.14 80.14 16.20	-	-	-	-	-	-	-	-	-	-	-	-	-	-	-	-	-	-	-	-	-	-	-
Kendall County	2,899 5.31	671	356 53.06 53.06 12.28	-	-	-	-	-	-	-	-	-	-	-	-	-	-	-	-	-	-	-	-	-	-	-
Knox County	902 1.62	448	213 47.54 47.54 23.61	-	-	-	-	-	-	-	-	-	-	-	-	-	-	-	-	-	-	-	-	-	-	-
La Salle County	3,006 2.70	506	382 75.49 75.49 12.71	-	-	-	-	-	-	-	-	-	-	-	-	-	-	-	-	-	-	-	-	-	-	-
Lake County	95,536 14.83	25,305	17,518 69.23 69.23 18.34	-	-	3,980 70.21 22.72 15.73 4.17	-	-	3,367 69.41 19.22 13.31 3.52	-	4,825 69.05 27.54 19.07 5.05	-	-	-	-	955 64.18 5.45 3.77 1.00	2,839 72.61 16.21 11.22 2.97	-	-	372 71.68 2.12 1.47 0.39	-	-	-	-	-	437 74.70 2.49 1.73 0.46
Buffalo Grove (village)	8,690 20.40	3,687	2,643 71.68 71.68 30.41	-	-	522 68.87 19.75 14.16 6.01	-	-	438 72.16 16.57 11.88 5.04	-	279 64.29 10.56 7.57 3.21	-	-	-	-	536 87.73 20.28 14.54 6.17	742 67.76 28.07 20.12 8.54	-	-	-	-	-	-	-	-	-
Gages Lake (cdp)	863 8.25	411	276 67.15 67.15 31.98	-	-	-	-	-	-	-	-	-	-	-	-	-	-	-	-	-	-	-	-	-	-	-

Notes: Please refer to the User's Guide for an explanation of data; data is arranged alphabetically by state, then county, then city within each county; table includes counties with populations greater than 49,999 unless noted and cities with populations greater than 9,999 whose Asian and/or NHPI population rates are greater than the national average; (1) Native Hawaiian and other Pacific Islander; (2) excludes Taiwanese; (3) includes Chamorro; (4) county does not meet population threshold but is shown in order to allow inclusion of city

Place	Total foreign-born population	Total Asian population	Asians who are foreign born	Total NHPI[1] population	NHPIs[1] who are foreign born	Asian Indian	Bangladeshi	Cambodian	Chinese[2]	Fijian	Filipino	Guamanian[3]	Hawaiian, Native	Hmong	Indonesian	Japanese	Korean	Laotian	Malaysian	Pakistani	Samoan	Sri Lankan	Taiwanese	Thai	Tongan	Vietnamese
Grayslake (village)	1,548	905	618	-	-	-	-	-	-	-	-	-	-	-	-	-	-	-	-	-	-	-	-	-	-	-
	8.38		68.29																							
			68.29																							
			39.92																							
Gurnee (village)	3,362	2,361	1,680	-	-	541	-	-	284	-	491	-	-	-	-	-	-	-	-	-	-	-	-	-	-	-
	11.75		71.16			73.81			77.38		64.02															
						32.20			16.90		29.23															
			71.16			22.91			12.03		20.80															
			49.97			16.09			8.45		14.60															
Lake Zurich (village)	1,589	691	426	-	-	-	-	-	-	-	-	-	-	-	-	-	-	-	-	-	-	-	-	-	-	-
	8.76		61.65																							
			61.65																							
			26.81																							
Libertyville (village)	2,122	986	737	-	-	-	-	-	-	-	-	-	-	-	-	-	-	-	-	-	-	-	-	-	-	-
	10.25		74.75																							
			74.75																							
			34.73																							
Mundelein (village)	7,290	2,054	1,336	-	-	-	-	-	352	-	415	-	-	-	-	-	-	-	-	-	-	-	-	-	-	-
	23.83		65.04						64.94		67.26															
									26.35		31.06															
			65.04						17.14		20.20															
			18.33						4.83		5.69															
Vernon Hills (village)	4,365	2,316	1,623	-	-	377	-	-	442	-	-	-	-	-	-	-	472	-	-	-	-	-	-	-	-	-
	21.18		70.08			70.07			65.10								73.41									
						23.23			27.23								29.08									
			70.08			16.28			19.08								20.38									
			37.18			8.64			10.13								10.81									
Macon County	1,571	745	552	-	-	-	-	-	-	-	-	-	-	-	-	-	-	-	-	-	-	-	-	-	-	-
	1.37		74.09																							
			74.09																							
			35.14																							
Madison County	3,286	1,264	913	-	-	290	-	-	-	-	-	-	-	-	-	-	-	-	-	-	-	-	-	-	-	-
	1.27		72.23			81.46																				
						31.76																				
			72.23			22.94																				
			27.78			8.83																				
McHenry County	18,764	3,408	2,496	-	-	698	-	-	427	-	644	-	-	-	-	-	-	-	-	-	-	-	-	-	-	-
	7.21		73.24			73.17			78.06		65.85															
						27.96			17.11		25.80															
			73.24			20.48			12.53		18.90															
			13.30			3.72			2.28		3.43															
McLean County	4,978	3,117	2,326	-	-	1,025	-	-	522	-	-	-	-	-	-	-	-	-	-	-	-	-	-	-	-	-
	3.31		74.62			82.46			76.54																	
						44.07			22.44																	
			74.62			32.88			16.75																	
			46.73			20.59			10.49																	

Notes: Please refer to the User's Guide for an explanation of data; data is arranged alphabetically by state, then county, then city within each county; table includes counties with populations greater than 49,999 unless noted and cities with populations greater than 9,999 whose Asian and/or NHPI population rates are greater than the national average; (1) Native Hawaiian and other Pacific Islander; (2) excludes Taiwanese; (3) includes Chamorro; (4) county does not meet population threshold but is shown in order to allow inclusion of city

Place	Total foreign-born population	Total Asian population	Asians who are foreign born	Total NHPI[1] population	NHPIs[1] who are foreign born	Asian Indian	Bangladeshi	Cambodian	Chinese[2]	Fijian	Filipino	Guamanian[3]	Hawaiian, Native	Hmong	Indonesian	Japanese	Korean	Laotian	Malaysian	Pakistani	Samoan	Sri Lankan	Taiwanese	Thai	Tongan	Vietnamese
Peoria County	5,825	3,159	2,379	-	-	835	-	-	704	-	-	-	-	-	-	-	-	-	-	-	-	-	-	-	-	234
	3.18		75.31			78.77			78.48																	75.48
						35.10			29.59																	9.84
			75.31			26.43			22.29																	7.41
			40.84			14.33			12.09																	4.02
Rock Island County	6,886	1,469	1,035	-	-	515	-	-	-	-	-	-	-	-	-	-	-	-	-	-	-	-	-	-	-	-
	4.61		70.46			86.26																				
						49.76																				
			70.46			35.06																				
			15.03			7.48																				
St. Clair County	5,443	2,269	1,652	-	-	-	-	-	-	-	443	-	-	-	-	-	397	-	-	-	-	-	-	-	-	-
	2.13		72.81								69.44						98.27									
											26.82						24.03									
			72.81								19.52						17.50									
			30.35								8.14						7.29									
Sangamon County	3,537	1,988	1,374	-	-	421	-	-	298	-	-	-	-	-	-	-	-	-	-	-	-	-	-	-	-	-
	1.87		69.11			61.46			82.32																	
						30.64			21.69																	
			69.11			21.18			14.99																	
			38.85			11.90			8.43																	
Tazewell County	1,455	572	390	-	-	-	-	-	-	-	-	-	-	-	-	-	-	-	-	-	-	-	-	-	-	-
	1.13		68.18																							
			68.18																							
			26.80																							
Vermilion County	1,423	512	298	-	-	-	-	-	-	-	-	-	-	-	-	-	-	-	-	-	-	-	-	-	-	-
	1.70		58.20																							
			58.20																							
			20.94																							
Will County	35,715	11,282	7,622	-	-	2,017	-	-	1,113	-	2,150	-	-	-	-	-	734	-	-	274	-	-	-	-	-	361
	7.11		67.56			69.19			71.90		70.82						78.25			62.70						58.32
						26.46			14.60		28.21						9.63			3.59						4.74
			67.56			17.88			9.87		19.06						6.51			2.43						3.20
			21.34			5.65			3.12		6.02						2.06			0.77						1.01
Bolingbrook (village)	8,108	3,786	2,856	-	-	825	-	-	-	-	966	-	-	-	-	-	-	-	-	-	-	-	-	-	-	-
	14.36		75.44			75.62					82.85															
						28.89					33.82															
			75.44			21.79					25.52															
			35.22			10.18					11.91															
Winnebago County	16,930	4,448	3,144	-	-	437	-	-	-	-	408	-	-	-	-	-	383	923	-	-	-	-	-	-	-	482
	6.08		70.68			67.44					75.00						83.62	71.05								83.25
						13.90					12.98						12.18	29.36								15.33
			70.68			9.82					9.17						8.61	20.75								10.84
			18.57			2.58					2.41						2.26	5.45								2.85
INDIANA	186,534	57,193	42,626	1,762	326	10,497	-	439	8,944	-	4,656	133	17	-	-	3,487	5,798	722	-	491	-	-	590	669	-	3,577
	3.07		74.53		18.50	74.14		75.30	77.52		67.56	25.29	2.56			72.46	81.67	73.45		68.86			80.49	74.00		75.88
						24.63		1.03	20.98		10.92	40.80	5.21			8.18	13.60	1.69		1.15			1.38	1.57		8.39
			74.53		18.50	18.35		0.77	15.64		8.14	7.55	0.96			6.10	10.14	1.26		0.86			1.03	1.17		6.25
			22.85		0.17	5.63		0.24	4.79		2.50	0.07	0.01			1.87	3.11	0.39		0.26			0.32	0.36		1.92

Notes: Please refer to the User's Guide for an explanation of data; data is arranged alphabetically by state, then county, then city within each county; table includes counties with populations greater than 49,999 unless noted and cities with populations greater than 9,999 whose Asian and/or NHPI population rates are greater than the national average; (1) Native Hawaiian and other Pacific Islander; (2) excludes Taiwanese; (3) includes Chamorro; (4) county does not meet population threshold but is shown in order to allow inclusion of city

Place	Total foreign-born population	Total Asian population	Asians who are foreign born	Total NHPI[1] population	NHPIs[1] who are foreign born	Asian Indian	Bangladeshi	Cambodian	Chinese[2]	Fijian	Filipino	Guamanian[3]	Hawaiian, Native	Hmong	Indonesian	Japanese	Korean	Laotian	Malaysian	Pakistani	Samoan	Sri Lankan	Taiwanese	Thai	Tongan	Vietnamese
Allen County	13,394 4.04	4,452	3,309 74.33 74.33 24.71	-	-	724 70.98 21.88 16.26 5.41	-	-	324 61.83 9.79 7.28 2.42	-	317 65.50 9.58 7.12 2.37	-	-	-	-	-	-	-	-	-	-	-	-	-	-	661 81.71 19.98 14.85 4.94
Bartholomew County	2,683 3.76	1,182	940 79.53 79.53 35.04	-	-	370 86.85 39.36 31.30 13.79	-	-	-	-	-	-	-	-	-	-	-	-	-	-	-	-	-	-	-	-
Clark County	1,686 1.75	428	328 76.64 76.64 19.45	-	-	-	-	-	-	-	-	-	-	-	-	-	-	-	-	-	-	-	-	-	-	-
Delaware County	1,754 1.48	752	546 72.61 72.61 31.13	-	-	-	-	-	-	-	-	-	-	-	-	-	-	-	-	-	-	-	-	-	-	-
Elkhart County	12,982 7.10	1,606	1,321 82.25 82.25 10.18	-	-	-	-	-	-	-	-	-	-	-	-	-	-	-	-	-	-	-	-	-	-	-
Grant County	874 1.19	469	317 67.59 67.59 36.27	-	-	-	-	-	-	-	-	-	-	-	-	-	-	-	-	-	-	-	-	-	-	-
Hamilton County	7,283 3.99	4,119	2,765 67.13 67.13 37.97	-	-	740 68.33 26.76 17.97 10.16	-	-	596 70.12 21.56 14.47 8.18	-	-	-	-	-	-	-	-	-	-	-	-	-	-	-	-	-
Carmel (city)	2,756 7.29	1,636	1,151 70.35 70.35 41.76	-	-	-	-	-	-	-	-	-	-	-	-	-	-	-	-	-	-	-	-	-	-	-
Hendricks County	1,663 1.60	673	499 74.15 74.15 30.01	-	-	-	-	-	-	-	-	-	-	-	-	-	-	-	-	-	-	-	-	-	-	-
Howard County	1,487 1.75	682	498 73.02 73.02 33.49	-	-	-	-	-	-	-	-	-	-	-	-	-	-	-	-	-	-	-	-	-	-	-

Notes: Please refer to the User's Guide for an explanation of data; data is arranged alphabetically by state, then county, then city within each county; table includes counties with populations greater than 49,999 unless noted and cities with populations greater than 9,999 whose Asian and/or NHPI population rates are greater than the national average; (1) Native Hawaiian and other Pacific Islander; (2) excludes Taiwanese; (3) includes Chamorro; (4) county does not meet population threshold but is shown in order to allow inclusion of city

Place	Total foreign-born population	Total Asian population	Asians who are foreign born	Total NHPI[1] population	NHPIs[1] who are foreign born	Asian Indian	Bangladeshi	Cambodian	Chinese[2]	Fijian	Filipino	Guamanian[3]	Hawaiian, Native	Hmong	Indonesian	Japanese	Korean	Laotian	Malaysian	Pakistani	Samoan	Sri Lankan	Taiwanese	Thai	Tongan	Vietnamese
Johnson County	1,971 1.71	955	584 61.15 61.15 29.63	-	-	-	-	-	-	-	-	-	-	-	-	-	-	-	-	-	-	-	-	-	-	-
Kosciusko County	2,142 2.89	378	264 69.84 69.84 12.32	-	-	-	-	-	-	-	-	-	-	-	-	-	-	-	-	-	-	-	-	-	-	-
Lake County	25,848 5.33	3,940	2,778 70.51 70.51 10.75	-	-	1,056 73.54 38.01 26.80 4.09	-	-	378 60.10 13.61 9.59 1.46	-	543 69.08 19.55 13.78 2.10	-	-	-	-	-	463 85.42 16.67 11.75 1.79	-	-	-	-	-	-	-	-	-
Munster (town)	1,700 7.90	952	649 68.17 68.17 38.18	-	-	304 72.55 46.84 31.93 17.88	-	-	-	-	-	-	-	-	-	-	-	-	-	-	-	-	-	-	-	-
LaPorte County	2,730 2.48	361	242 67.04 67.04 8.86	-	-	-	-	-	-	-	-	-	-	-	-	-	-	-	-	-	-	-	-	-	-	-
Madison County	1,587 1.19	502	335 66.73 66.73 21.11	-	-	-	-	-	-	-	-	-	-	-	-	-	-	-	-	-	-	-	-	-	-	-
Marion County	39,386 4.58	11,505	8,937 77.68 77.68 22.69	-	-	2,597 77.09 29.06 22.57 6.59	-	-	1,927 85.08 21.56 16.75 4.89	-	1,080 74.18 12.08 9.39 2.74	-	-	-	-	263 51.77 2.94 2.29 0.67	987 81.98 11.04 8.58 2.51	-	-	-	-	-	-	-	-	1,082 84.80 12.11 9.40 2.75
Monroe County	6,566 5.45	3,912	3,130 80.01 80.01 47.67	-	-	525 75.11 16.77 13.42 8.00	-	-	644 79.41 20.58 16.46 9.81	-	-	-	-	-	-	-	928 86.73 29.65 23.72 14.13	-	-	-	-	-	-	-	-	-
Bloomington (city)	5,578 8.06	3,458	2,791 80.71 80.71 50.04	-	-	434 75.87 15.55 12.55 7.78	-	-	601 79.29 21.53 17.38 10.77	-	-	-	-	-	-	-	853 87.85 30.56 24.67 15.29	-	-	-	-	-	-	-	-	-
Porter County	4,359 2.97	1,053	787 74.74 74.74 18.05	-	-	-	-	-	-	-	-	-	-	-	-	-	-	-	-	-	-	-	-	-	-	-

Notes: Please refer to the User's Guide for an explanation of data; data is arranged alphabetically by state, then county, then city within each county; table includes counties with populations greater than 49,999 unless noted and cities with populations greater than 9,999 whose Asian and/or NHPI population rates are greater than the national average; (1) Native Hawaiian and other Pacific Islander; (2) excludes Taiwanese; (3) includes Chamorro; (4) county does not meet population threshold but is shown in order to allow inclusion of city

Place	Total foreign-born population	Total Asian population	Asians who are foreign born	Total NHPI[1] population	NHPIs[1] who are foreign born	Asian Indian	Bangladeshi	Cambodian	Chinese[2]	Fijian	Filipino	Guamanian[3]	Hawaiian, Native	Hmong	Indonesian	Japanese	Korean	Laotian	Malaysian	Pakistani	Samoan	Sri Lankan	Taiwanese	Thai	Tongan	Vietnamese
	12,113	3,464	2,551	-	-	493	-	-	645	-	-	-	-	-	-	-	398	-	-	-	-	-	-	-	-	-
	4.56		73.64			72.71			76.15								86.71									
St. Joseph County						19.33			25.28								15.60									
			73.64			14.23			18.62								11.49									
			21.06			4.07			5.32								3.29									
	12,167	6,760	5,275	-	-	1,325	-	-	1,792	-	-	-	-	-	-	306	810	-	-	-	-	-	-	-	-	-
	8.17		78.03			80.01			83.12							78.46	78.41									
Tippecanoe County						25.12			33.97							5.80	15.36									
			78.03			19.60			26.51							4.53	11.98									
			43.35			10.89			14.73							2.51	6.66									
	3,851	3,159	2,430	-	-	795	-	-	771	-	-	-	-	-	-	-	-	-	-	-	-	-	-	-	-	-
	13.30		76.92			81.29			80.73																	
West Lafayette (city)						32.72			31.73																	
			76.92			25.17			24.41																	
			63.10			20.64			20.02																	
	2,794	1,589	1,223	-	-	-	-	-	-	-	-	-	-	-	-	-	-	-	-	-	-	-	-	-	-	-
	1.63		76.97																							
Vanderburgh County																										
			76.97																							
			43.77																							
	2,119	1,096	808	-	-	-	-	-	-	-	-	-	-	-	-	-	-	-	-	-	-	-	-	-	-	-
	2.00		73.72																							
Vigo County																										
			73.72																							
			38.13																							
	1,086	476	360	-	-	-	-	-	-	-	-	-	-	-	-	-	-	-	-	-	-	-	-	-	-	-
	1.53		75.63																							
Wayne County																										
			75.63																							
			33.15																							
	91,085	35,023	26,674	955	181	4,205	-	514	4,420	-	1,566	-	-	-	-	892	4,007	2,767	-	250	-	-	369	749	-	5,609
	3.11		76.16		18.95	77.77		62.38	78.87		69.63					69.42	82.08	69.73		64.10			82.74	80.54		82.84
IOWA						15.76		1.93	16.57		5.87					3.34	15.02	10.37		0.94			1.38	2.81		21.03
			76.16		18.95	12.01		1.47	12.62		4.47					2.55	11.44	7.90		0.71			1.05	2.14		16.02
			29.28		0.20	4.62		0.56	4.85		1.72					0.98	4.40	3.04		0.27			0.41	0.82		6.16
	4,779	1,316	1,003	-	-	-	-	-	-	-	-	-	-	-	-	-	-	-	-	-	-	-	-	-	-	-
	3.73		76.22																							
Black Hawk County																										
			76.22																							
			20.99																							
	2,541	885	642	-	-	-	-	-	-	-	-	-	-	-	-	-	-	449	-	-	-	-	-	-	-	-
	12.45		72.54															77.68								
Buena Vista County[4]																		69.94								
			72.54															50.73								
			25.27															17.67								
	2,186	769	567	-	-	-	-	-	-	-	-	-	-	-	-	-	-	419	-	-	-	-	-	-	-	-
	21.54		73.73															79.51								
Storm Lake (city)																		73.90								
			73.73															54.49								
			25.94															19.17								

Notes: Please refer to the User's Guide for an explanation of data; data is arranged alphabetically by state, then county, then city within each county; table includes counties with populations greater than 49,999 unless noted and cities with populations greater than 9,999 whose Asian and/or NHPI population rates are greater than the national average; (1) Native Hawaiian and other Pacific Islander; (2) excludes Taiwanese; (3) includes Chamorro; (4) county does not meet population threshold but is shown in order to allow inclusion of city

Place	Total foreign-born population	Total Asian population	Asians who are foreign born	Total NHPI[1] population	NHPIs[1] who are foreign born	Asian Indian	Bangladeshi	Cambodian	Chinese[2]	Fijian	Filipino	Guamanian[3]	Hawaiian, Native	Hmong	Indonesian	Japanese	Korean	Laotian	Malaysian	Pakistani	Samoan	Sri Lankan	Taiwanese	Thai	Tongan	Vietnamese
Johnson County	7,098 6.39	4,406	3,455 78.42 78.42 48.68	-	-	601 74.57 17.40 13.64 8.47	-	-	1,226 82.23 35.48 27.83 17.27	-	-	-	-	-	-	-	636 84.69 18.41 14.43 8.96	-	-	-	-	-	-	-	-	-
Coralville (city)	1,235 8.16	647	572 88.41 88.41 46.32	-	-	-	-	-	-	-	-	-	-	-	-	-	-	-	-	-	-	-	-	-	-	-
Iowa City (city)	5,136 8.23	3,495	2,671 76.42 76.42 52.01	-	-	444 74.62 16.62 12.70 8.64	-	-	1,085 82.20 40.62 31.04 21.13	-	-	-	-	-	-	-	416 79.54 15.57 11.90 8.10	-	-	-	-	-	-	-	-	-
Linn County	4,934 2.57	2,647	1,984 74.95 74.95 40.21	-	-	734 88.22 37.00 27.73 14.88	-	-	-	-	-	-	-	-	-	-	245 74.02 12.35 9.26 4.97	-	-	-	-	-	-	-	-	-
Polk County	22,162 5.92	9,173	6,905 75.28 75.28 31.16	-	-	1,071 82.51 15.51 11.68 4.83	-	268 63.96 3.88 2.92 1.21	731 69.22 10.59 7.97 3.30	-	-	-	-	-	-	-	541 73.51 7.83 5.90 2.44	1,150 69.53 16.65 12.54 5.19	-	-	-	-	-	285 79.61 4.13 3.11 1.29	-	2,122 84.61 30.73 23.13 9.57
Pottawattamie County	1,777 2.03	548	407 74.27 74.27 22.90	-	-	-	-	-	-	-	-	-	-	-	-	-	-	-	-	-	-	-	-	-	-	-
Scott County	4,856 3.06	2,274	1,745 76.74 76.74 35.93	-	-	-	-	-	-	-	-	-	-	-	-	-	-	-	-	-	-	-	-	-	-	831 83.27 47.62 36.54 17.11
Story County	5,537 6.92	3,620	3,059 84.50 84.50 55.25	-	-	536 76.57 17.52 14.81 9.68	-	-	1,053 90.23 34.42 29.09 19.02	-	-	-	-	-	-	-	646 84.89 21.12 17.85 11.67	-	-	-	-	-	-	-	-	-
Ames (city)	5,204 10.27	3,471	2,950 84.99 84.99 56.69	-	-	510 77.27 17.29 14.69 9.80	-	-	1,037 91.20 35.15 29.88 19.93	-	-	-	-	-	-	-	620 84.70 21.02 17.86 11.91	-	-	-	-	-	-	-	-	-
Woodbury County	7,515 7.23	2,386	1,803 75.57 75.57 23.99	-	-	-	-	-	-	-	-	-	-	-	-	-	-	-	-	-	-	-	-	-	-	1,161 80.96 64.39 48.66 15.45

Notes: Please refer to the User's Guide for an explanation of data; data is arranged alphabetically by state, then county, then city within each county; table includes counties with populations greater than 49,999 unless noted and cities with populations greater than 9,999 whose Asian and/or NHPI population rates are greater than the national average; (1) Native Hawaiian and other Pacific Islander; (2) excludes Taiwanese; (3) includes Chamorro; (4) county does not meet population threshold but is shown in order to allow inclusion of city

Place	Total foreign-born population	Total Asian population	Asians who are foreign born	Total NHPI[1] population	NHPIs[1] who are foreign born	Asian Indian	Bangladeshi	Cambodian	Chinese[2]	Fijian	Filipino	Guamanian[3]	Hawaiian, Native	Hmong	Indonesian	Japanese	Korean	Laotian	Malaysian	Pakistani	Samoan	Sri Lankan	Taiwanese	Thai	Tongan	Vietnamese
KANSAS	134,735 5.01	44,772	32,808 73.28 73.28 24.35	1,208	206 17.05 17.05 0.15	5,957 77.56 18.16 13.31 4.42	-	459 64.92 1.40 1.03 0.34	5,508 78.07 16.79 12.30 4.09	-	2,393 70.78 7.29 5.34 1.78	-	0 0.00 0.00 0.00 0.00	380 40.82 1.16 0.85 0.28	-	1,251 68.25 3.81 2.79 0.93	3,324 76.22 10.13 7.42 2.47	2,055 72.31 6.26 4.59 1.53	-	567 72.79 1.73 1.27 0.42	-	-	378 72.97 1.15 0.84 0.28	507 78.00 1.55 1.13 0.38	-	8,343 73.88 25.43 18.63 6.19
Cowley County[4]	902 2.49	552	361 65.40 65.40 40.02	-	-	-	-	-	-	-	-	-	-	-	-	-	-	244 70.11 67.59 44.20 27.05	-	-	-	-	-	-	-	-
Winfield (city)	658 5.38	485	329 67.84 67.84 50.00	-	-	-	-	-	-	-	-	-	-	-	-	-	-	242 70.35 73.56 49.90 36.78	-	-	-	-	-	-	-	-
Douglas County	5,168 5.17	3,335	2,520 75.56 75.56 48.76	-	-	347 70.67 13.77 10.40 6.71	-	-	730 75.49 28.97 21.89 14.13	-	-	-	-	-	-	-	420 79.85 16.67 12.59 8.13	-	-	-	-	-	-	-	-	-
Lawrence (city)	4,964 6.20	3,296	2,487 75.46 75.46 50.10	-	-	331 69.68 13.31 10.04 6.67	-	-	730 75.49 29.35 22.15 14.71	-	-	-	-	-	-	-	416 79.69 16.73 12.62 8.38	-	-	-	-	-	-	-	-	-
Johnson County	25,531 5.66	12,582	9,498 75.49 75.49 37.20	-	-	3,221 79.45 33.91 25.60 12.62	-	-	1,999 77.15 21.05 15.89 7.83	-	685 72.56 7.21 5.44 2.68	-	-	-	-	279 62.70 2.94 2.22 1.09	972 73.03 10.23 7.73 3.81	511 79.84 5.38 4.06 2.00	-	-	-	-	-	-	-	1,014 75.96 10.68 8.06 3.97
Overland Park (city)	11,075 7.44	5,672	4,410 77.75 77.75 39.82	-	-	1,628 82.18 36.92 28.70 14.70	-	-	1,038 80.28 23.54 18.30 9.37	-	-	-	-	-	-	-	415 69.05 9.41 7.32 3.75	-	-	-	-	-	-	-	-	484 82.17 10.98 8.53 4.37
Leavenworth County	1,830 2.66	747	506 67.74 67.74 27.65	-	-	-	-	-	-	-	-	-	-	-	-	-	-	-	-	-	-	-	-	-	-	-
Riley County	3,854 6.13	1,992	1,549 77.76 77.76 40.19	-	-	-	-	-	567 84.12 36.60 28.46 14.71	-	-	-	-	-	-	-	310 73.11 20.01 15.56 8.04	-	-	-	-	-	-	-	-	-
Manhattan (city)	2,899 6.47	1,712	1,366 79.79 79.79 47.12	-	-	-	-	-	546 84.65 39.97 31.89 18.83	-	-	-	-	-	-	-	-	-	-	-	-	-	-	-	-	-

Notes: Please refer to the User's Guide for an explanation of data; data is arranged alphabetically by state, then county, then city within each county; table includes counties with populations greater than 49,999 unless noted and cities with populations greater than 9,999 whose Asian and/or NHPI population rates are greater than the national average; (1) Native Hawaiian and other Pacific Islander; (2) excludes Taiwanese; (3) includes Chamorro; (4) county does not meet population threshold but is shown in order to allow inclusion of city

Place	Total foreign-born population	Total Asian population	Asians who are foreign born	Total NHPI[1] population	NHPIs[1] who are foreign born	Asian Indian	Bangladeshi	Cambodian	Chinese[2]	Fijian	Filipino	Guamanian[3]	Hawaiian, Native	Hmong	Indonesian	Japanese	Korean	Laotian	Malaysian	Pakistani	Samoan	Sri Lankan	Taiwanese	Thai	Tongan	Vietnamese
Saline County	2,161 4.03	861	631 73.29 73.29 29.20	-	-	-	-	-	-	-	-	-	-	-	-	-	-	-	-	-	-	-	-	-	-	290 77.96 45.96 33.68 13.42
Sedgwick County	30,071 6.64	14,175	10,418 73.50 73.50 34.64	431	76 17.63 17.63 0.25	1,112 85.47 10.67 7.84 3.70	-	305 66.16 2.93 2.15 1.01	1,156 79.40 11.10 8.16 3.84	-	597 86.52 5.73 4.21 1.99	-	-	-	-	-	394 70.61 3.78 2.78 1.31	691 65.62 6.63 4.87 2.30	-	-	-	-	-	-	-	4,887 72.58 46.91 34.48 16.25
Wichita (city)	27,938 8.12	12,682	9,453 74.54 74.54 33.84	-	-	1,065 85.27 11.27 8.40 3.81	-	-	1,094 80.62 11.57 8.63 3.92	-	482 89.76 5.10 3.80 1.73	-	-	-	-	-	326 67.92 3.45 2.57 1.17	458 65.99 4.85 3.61 1.64	-	-	-	-	-	-	-	4,650 72.52 49.19 36.67 16.64
Shawnee County	4,554 2.68	1,478	1,049 70.97 70.97 23.03	-	-	-	-	-	-	-	-	-	-	-	-	-	-	-	-	-	-	-	-	-	-	-
Wyandotte County	14,954 9.47	2,225	1,303 58.56 58.56 8.71	-	-	-	-	-	-	-	-	-	-	298 38.25 22.87 13.39 1.99	-	-	-	-	-	-	-	-	-	-	-	-
KENTUCKY	80,271 1.99	28,994	22,404 77.27 77.27 27.91	1,155	165 14.29 14.29 0.21	5,238 77.78 23.38 18.07 6.53	-	-	4,154 79.37 18.54 14.33 5.17	-	2,121 67.79 9.47 7.32 2.64	40 10.87 24.24 3.46 0.05	-	-	-	2,743 86.34 12.24 9.46 3.42	3,276 81.07 14.62 11.30 4.08	-	-	435 77.26 1.94 1.50 0.54	-	-	-	343 81.28 1.53 1.18 0.43	-	2,513 78.38 11.22 8.67 3.13
Boone County	2,584 3.00	1,014	798 78.70 78.70 30.88	-	-	-	-	-	-	-	-	-	-	-	-	434 94.55 54.39 42.80 16.80	-	-	-	-	-	-	-	-	-	-
Campbell County	1,223 1.38	580	424 73.10 73.10 34.67	-	-	-	-	-	-	-	-	-	-	-	-	-	-	-	-	-	-	-	-	-	-	-
Christian County	1,790 2.48	617	395 64.02 64.02 22.07	-	-	-	-	-	-	-	-	-	-	-	-	-	-	-	-	-	-	-	-	-	-	-
Fayette County	15,448 5.93	5,824	4,629 79.48 79.48 29.97	-	-	1,032 75.11 22.29 17.72 6.68	-	-	1,449 83.32 31.30 24.88 9.38	-	-	-	-	-	-	794 87.44 17.15 13.63 5.14	-	-	-	-	-	-	-	-	-	-

Notes: Please refer to the User's Guide for an explanation of data; data is arranged alphabetically by state, then county, then city within each county; table includes counties with populations greater than 49,999 unless noted and cities with populations greater than 9,999 whose Asian and/or NHPI population rates are greater than the national average; (1) Native Hawaiian and other Pacific Islander; (2) excludes Taiwanese; (3) includes Chamorro; (4) county does not meet population threshold but is shown in order to allow inclusion of city

Place	Total foreign-born population	Total Asian population	Asians who are foreign born	Total NHPI[1] population	NHPIs[1] who are foreign born	Asian Indian	Bangladeshi	Cambodian	Chinese[2]	Fijian	Filipino	Guamanian[3]	Hawaiian, Native	Hmong	Indonesian	Japanese	Korean	Laotian	Malaysian	Pakistani	Samoan	Sri Lankan	Taiwanese	Thai	Tongan	Vietnamese
Hardin County	4,267 4.53	1,892	1,415 74.79 74.79 33.16	-	-	-	-	-	-	-	-	-	-	-	-	-	596 79.47 42.12 31.50 13.97	-	-	-	-	-	-	-	-	-
Radcliff (city)	2,001 9.16	939	786 83.71 83.71 39.28	-	-	-	-	-	-	-	-	-	-	-	-	-	-	-	-	-	-	-	-	-	-	-
Jefferson County	23,895 3.45	9,043	7,045 77.91 77.91 29.48	-	-	1,929 77.94 27.38 21.33 8.07	-	-	1,134 79.63 16.10 12.54 4.75	-	660 71.35 9.37 7.30 2.76	-	-	-	-	255 71.83 3.62 2.82 1.07	886 84.14 12.58 9.80 3.71	-	-	-	-	-	-	-	-	1,455 81.56 20.65 16.09 6.09
Kenton County	2,382 1.57	866	599 69.17 69.17 25.15	-	-	-	-	-	-	-	-	-	-	-	-	-	-	-	-	-	-	-	-	-	-	-
Madison County	1,064 1.50	567	436 76.90 76.90 40.98	-	-	-	-	-	-	-	-	-	-	-	-	-	-	-	-	-	-	-	-	-	-	-
Warren County	3,955 4.27	1,102	897 81.40 81.40 22.68	-	-	-	-	-	-	-	-	-	-	-	-	-	-	-	-	-	-	-	-	-	-	-
LOUISIANA	115,885 2.59	55,492	37,072 66.81 66.81 31.99	1,379	178 12.91 12.91 0.15	5,999 69.42 16.18 10.81 5.18	-	-	4,610 67.87 12.44 8.31 3.98	-	3,203 67.76 8.64 5.77 2.76	30 6.42 16.85 2.18 0.03	0 0.00 0.00 0.00 0.00	-	-	997 69.96 2.69 1.80 0.86	2,012 73.56 5.43 3.63 1.74	915 70.71 2.47 1.65 0.79	-	778 79.79 2.10 1.40 0.67	-	-	431 87.25 1.16 0.78 0.37	509 78.91 1.37 0.92 0.44	-	16,138 64.43 43.53 29.08 13.93
Ascension Parish	1,403 1.83	320	224 70.00 70.00 15.97	-	-	-	-	-	-	-	-	-	-	-	-	-	-	-	-	-	-	-	-	-	-	-
Bossier Parish	2,443 2.48	1,151	838 72.81 72.81 34.30	-	-	-	-	-	-	-	-	-	-	-	-	-	-	-	-	-	-	-	-	-	-	-
Caddo Parish	3,781 1.50	1,914	1,295 67.66 67.66 34.25	-	-	319 64.57 24.63 16.67 8.44	-	-	-	-	-	-	-	-	-	-	-	-	-	-	-	-	-	-	-	-

Notes: Please refer to the User's Guide for an explanation of data; data is arranged alphabetically by state, then county, then city within each county; table includes counties with populations greater than 49,999 unless noted and cities with populations greater than 9,999 whose Asian and/or NHPI population rates are greater than the national average; (1) Native Hawaiian and other Pacific Islander; (2) excludes Taiwanese; (3) includes Chamorro; (4) county does not meet population threshold but is shown in order to allow inclusion of city

Place	Total foreign-born population	Total Asian population	Asians who are foreign born	Total NHPI[1] population	NHPIs[1] who are foreign born	Asian Indian	Bangladeshi	Cambodian	Chinese[2]	Fijian	Filipino	Guamanian[3]	Hawaiian, Native	Hmong	Indonesian	Japanese	Korean	Laotian	Malaysian	Pakistani	Samoan	Sri Lankan	Taiwanese	Thai	Tongan	Vietnamese
Calcasieu Parish	2,520 1.37	1,096	726 66.24 66.24 28.81	-	-	-	-	-	-	-	-	-	-	-	-	-	-	-	-	-	-	-	-	-	-	-
East Baton Rouge Parish	15,474 3.75	8,729	6,184 70.84 70.84 39.96	-	-	1,315 69.54 21.26 15.06 8.50	-	-	1,258 74.00 20.34 14.41 8.13	-	286 61.77 4.62 3.28 1.85	-	-	-	-	-	-	-	-	-	-	-	-	-	-	2,517 71.61 40.70 28.83 16.27
Iberia Parish	1,484 2.03	1,474	957 64.93 64.93 64.49	-	-	-	-	-	-	-	-	-	-	-	-	-	-	638 70.89 66.67 43.28 42.99	-	-	-	-	-	-	-	224 57.29 23.41 15.20 15.09
Jefferson Parish	34,062 7.48	13,790	9,512 68.98 68.98 27.93	-	-	1,293 74.35 13.59 9.38 3.80	-	-	1,359 70.20 14.29 9.85 3.99	-	632 64.56 6.64 4.58 1.86	-	-	-	-	-	512 84.49 5.38 3.71 1.50	-	-	392 88.09 4.12 2.84 1.15	-	-	-	-	-	4,468 64.67 46.97 32.40 13.12
Gretna (city)	1,077 6.21	642	438 68.22 68.22 40.67	-	-	-	-	-	-	-	-	-	-	-	-	-	-	-	-	-	-	-	-	-	-	263 70.89 60.05 40.97 24.42
Harvey (cdp)	1,776 7.98	1,147	765 66.70 66.70 43.07	-	-	-	-	-	-	-	-	-	-	-	-	-	-	-	-	-	-	-	-	-	-	560 65.57 73.20 48.82 31.53
Timberlane (cdp)	1,076 9.39	638	483 75.71 75.71 44.89	-	-	-	-	-	-	-	-	-	-	-	-	-	-	-	-	-	-	-	-	-	-	423 74.47 87.58 66.30 39.31
Woodmere (cdp)	867 6.62	711	445 62.59 62.59 51.33	-	-	-	-	-	-	-	-	-	-	-	-	-	-	-	-	-	-	-	-	-	-	336 66.80 75.51 47.26 38.75
Lafayette Parish	4,763 2.50	2,142	1,599 74.65 74.65 33.57	-	-	483 77.28 30.21 22.55 10.14	-	-	-	-	-	-	-	-	-	-	-	-	-	-	-	-	-	-	-	492 66.58 30.77 22.97 10.33
Lafourche Parish	1,336 1.48	525	370 70.48 70.48 27.69	-	-	-	-	-	-	-	-	-	-	-	-	-	-	-	-	-	-	-	-	-	-	-

Notes: Please refer to the User's Guide for an explanation of data; data is arranged alphabetically by state, then county, then city within each county; table includes counties with populations greater than 49,999 unless noted and cities with populations greater than 9,999 whose Asian and/or NHPI population rates are greater than the national average; (1) Native Hawaiian and other Pacific Islander; (2) excludes Taiwanese; (3) includes Chamorro; (4) county does not meet population threshold but is shown in order to allow inclusion of city

Place	Total foreign-born population	Total Asian population	Asians who are foreign born	Total NHPI[1] population	NHPIs[1] who are foreign born	Asian Indian	Bangladeshi	Cambodian	Chinese[2]	Fijian	Filipino	Guamanian[3]	Hawaiian, Native	Hmong	Indonesian	Japanese	Korean	Laotian	Malaysian	Pakistani	Samoan	Sri Lankan	Taiwanese	Thai	Tongan	Vietnamese
Orleans Parish	20,581 4.25	10,503	6,835 65.08 65.08 33.21	-	-	796 63.78 11.65 7.58 3.87	-	-	498 61.79 7.29 4.74 2.42	-	335 71.58 4.90 3.19 1.63	-	-	-	-	-	-	-	-	-	-	-	-	-	-	4,456 64.00 65.19 42.43 21.65
Ouachita Parish	1,487 1.01	784	594 75.77 75.77 39.95	-	-	-	-	-	-	-	-	-	-	-	-	-	-	-	-	-	-	-	-	-	-	-
Rapides Parish	1,969 1.56	1,090	725 66.51 66.51 36.82	-	-	-	-	-	-	-	-	-	-	-	-	-	-	-	-	-	-	-	-	-	-	-
St. Bernard Parish	2,019 3.00	1,079	592 54.87 54.87 29.32	-	-	-	-	-	-	-	-	-	-	-	-	-	-	-	-	-	-	-	-	-	-	244 49.19 41.22 22.61 12.09
St. Mary Parish	1,077 2.01	979	438 44.74 44.74 40.67	-	-	-	-	-	-	-	-	-	-	-	-	-	-	-	-	-	-	-	-	-	-	395 44.73 90.18 40.35 36.68
St. Tammany Parish	4,528 2.37	1,456	832 57.14 57.14 18.37	-	-	-	-	-	-	-	-	-	-	-	-	-	-	-	-	-	-	-	-	-	-	197 63.75 23.68 13.53 4.35
Terrebonne Parish	1,529 1.46	868	553 63.71 63.71 36.17	-	-	-	-	-	-	-	-	-	-	-	-	-	-	-	-	-	-	-	-	-	-	175 44.99 31.65 20.16 11.45
Vermilion Parish	1,081 2.01	1,045	718 68.71 68.71 66.42	-	-	-	-	-	-	-	-	-	-	-	-	-	-	-	-	-	-	-	-	-	-	645 69.06 89.83 61.72 59.67
Abbeville (city)	625 5.24	684	508 74.27 74.27 81.28	-	-	-	-	-	-	-	-	-	-	-	-	-	-	-	-	-	-	-	-	-	-	486 74.31 95.67 71.05 77.76
Vernon Parish	2,169 4.13	1,125	708 62.93 62.93 32.64	-	-	-	-	-	-	-	-	-	-	-	-	-	228 65.71 32.20 20.27 10.51	-	-	-	-	-	-	-	-	-

Notes: Please refer to the User's Guide for an explanation of data; data is arranged alphabetically by state, then county, then city within each county; table includes counties with populations greater than 49,999 unless noted and cities with populations greater than 9,999 whose Asian and/or NHPI population rates are greater than the national average; (1) Native Hawaiian and other Pacific Islander; (2) excludes Taiwanese; (3) includes Chamorro; (4) county does not meet population threshold but is shown in order to allow inclusion of city

Place	Total foreign-born population	Total Asian population	Asians who are foreign born	Total NHPI[1] population	NHPIs[1] who are foreign born	Asian Indian	Bangladeshi	Cambodian	Chinese[2]	Fijian	Filipino	Guamanian[3]	Hawaiian, Native	Hmong	Indonesian	Japanese	Korean	Laotian	Malaysian	Pakistani	Samoan	Sri Lankan	Taiwanese	Thai	Tongan	Vietnamese
MAINE	36,691	8,259	5,863	301	54	709	-	637	1,160	-	869	-	-	-	-	440	524	-	-	-	-	-	-	-	-	820
	2.88		70.99		17.94	72.49		63.07	71.08		74.27					74.32	71.29									73.54
						12.09		10.86	19.79		14.82					7.50	8.94									13.99
			70.99		17.94	8.58		7.71	14.05		10.52					5.33	6.34									9.93
			15.98		0.15	1.93		1.74	3.16		2.37					1.20	1.43									2.23
Androscoggin County	2,658	533	389	-	-	-	-	-	-	-	-	-	-	-	-	-	-	-	-	-	-	-	-	-	-	-
	2.56		72.98																							
			72.98																							
			14.64																							
Aroostook County	4,304	404	269	-	-	-	-	-	-	-	-	-	-	-	-	-	-	-	-	-	-	-	-	-	-	-
	5.82		66.58																							
			66.58																							
			6.25																							
Cumberland County	10,116	3,325	2,415	-	-	-	-	448	299	-	204	-	-	-	-	-	-	-	-	-	-	-	-	-	-	523
	3.81		72.63					67.78	67.80		62.77															80.21
								18.55	12.38		8.45															21.66
			72.63					13.47	8.99		6.14															15.73
			23.87					4.43	2.96		2.02															5.17
Hancock County	1,178	194	133	-	-	-	-	-	-	-	-	-	-	-	-	-	-	-	-	-	-	-	-	-	-	-
	2.27		68.56																							
			68.56																							
			11.29																							
Kennebec County	2,590	654	487	-	-	-	-	-	-	-	-	-	-	-	-	-	-	-	-	-	-	-	-	-	-	-
	2.21		74.46																							
			74.46																							
			18.80																							
Oxford County	993	253	179	-	-	-	-	-	-	-	-	-	-	-	-	-	-	-	-	-	-	-	-	-	-	-
	1.81		70.75																							
			70.75																							
			18.03																							
Penobscot County	3,646	998	693	-	-	-	-	-	217	-	-	-	-	-	-	-	-	-	-	-	-	-	-	-	-	-
	2.52		69.44						73.81																	
									31.31																	
			69.44						21.74																	
			19.01						5.95																	
York County	5,179	946	593	-	-	-	-	-	-	-	-	-	-	-	-	-	-	-	-	-	-	-	-	-	-	-
	2.77		62.68																							
			62.68																							
			11.45																							
MARYLAND	518,315	209,713	156,046	2,030	483	37,464	1,020	1,294	34,319	-	19,434	99	41	-	881	4,625	30,445	549	-	3,917	-	959	1,734	2,259	-	13,121
	9.79		74.41		23.79	75.28	84.72	75.76	72.71		72.86	14.12	7.96		79.51	66.83	77.84	74.59		76.89		85.47	72.95	79.15		78.65
						24.01	0.65	0.83	21.99		12.45	20.50	8.49		0.56	2.96	19.51	0.35		2.51		0.61	1.11	1.45		8.41
			74.41		23.79	17.86	0.49	0.62	16.36		9.27	4.88	2.02		0.42	2.21	14.52	0.26		1.87		0.46	0.83	1.08		6.26
			30.11		0.09	7.23	0.20	0.25	6.62		3.75	0.02	0.01		0.17	0.89	5.87	0.11		0.76		0.19	0.33	0.44		2.53

Notes: Please refer to the User's Guide for an explanation of data; data is arranged alphabetically by state, then county, then city within each county; table includes counties with populations greater than 49,999 unless noted and cities with populations greater than 9,999 whose Asian and/or NHPI population rates are greater than the national average; (1) Native Hawaiian and other Pacific Islander; (2) excludes Taiwanese; (3) includes Chamorro; (4) county does not meet population threshold but is shown in order to allow inclusion of city

Place	Total foreign-born population	Total Asian population	Asians who are foreign born	Total NHPI[1] population	NHPIs[1] who are foreign born	Asian Indian	Bangladeshi	Cambodian	Chinese[2]	Fijian	Filipino	Guamanian[3]	Hawaiian, Native	Hmong	Indonesian	Japanese	Korean	Laotian	Malaysian	Pakistani	Samoan	Sri Lankan	Taiwanese	Thai	Tongan	Vietnamese
Allegany County	924 1.23	454	257 56.61 56.61 27.81	-	-	-	-	-	-	-	-	-	-	-	-	-	-	-	-	-	-	-	-	-	-	-
Anne Arundel County	23,211 4.74	11,380	7,878 69.23 69.23 33.94	-	-	1,308 77.26 16.60 11.49 5.64	-	-	993 66.51 12.60 8.73 4.28	-	1,506 60.75 19.12 13.23 6.49	-	-	-	-	379 55.49 4.81 3.33 1.63	2,819 76.48 35.78 24.77 12.15	-	-	-	-	-	-	-	-	-
Severn (cdp)	2,461 7.00	1,624	1,081 66.56 66.56 43.93	-	-	-	-	-	-	-	-	-	-	-	-	-	556 72.21 51.43 34.24 22.59	-	-	-	-	-	-	-	-	-
South Gate (cdp)	2,184 7.60	1,436	1,121 78.06 78.06 51.33	-	-	-	-	-	-	-	-	-	-	-	-	-	681 79.74 60.75 47.42 31.18	-	-	-	-	-	-	-	-	-
Baltimore Independent City	29,638 4.55	10,256	6,703 65.36 65.36 22.62	-	-	1,314 62.13 19.60 12.81 4.43	-	-	1,622 71.36 24.20 15.82 5.47	-	778 55.65 11.61 7.59 2.63	-	-	-	-	-	1,332 75.25 19.87 12.99 4.49	-	-	-	-	-	-	-	-	590 72.84 8.80 5.75 1.99
Baltimore County	53,784 7.13	23,723	18,099 76.29 76.29 33.65	-	-	4,770 77.08 26.36 20.11 8.87	-	-	3,576 79.20 19.76 15.07 6.65	-	2,339 71.53 12.92 9.86 4.35	-	-	-	-	540 79.88 2.98 2.28 1.00	3,990 78.02 22.05 16.82 7.42	-	-	775 77.27 4.28 3.27 1.44	-	-	-	-	-	899 72.33 4.97 3.79 1.67
Arbutus (cdp)	1,577 7.84	970	793 81.75 81.75 50.29	-	-	-	-	-	-	-	-	-	-	-	-	-	-	-	-	-	-	-	-	-	-	-
Carney (cdp)	2,346 8.27	1,589	1,236 77.78 77.78 52.69	-	-	-	-	-	289 82.34 23.38 18.19 12.32	-	-	-	-	-	-	-	604 78.65 48.87 38.01 25.75	-	-	-	-	-	-	-	-	-
Cockeysville (cdp)	2,815 14.38	1,741	1,366 78.46 78.46 48.53	-	-	-	-	-	-	-	-	-	-	-	-	-	527 78.89 38.58 30.27 18.72	-	-	-	-	-	-	-	-	-
Lutherville-Timonium (cdp)	1,344 8.62	662	519 78.40 78.40 38.62	-	-	-	-	-	-	-	-	-	-	-	-	-	-	-	-	-	-	-	-	-	-	-

Notes: Please refer to the User's Guide for an explanation of data; data is arranged alphabetically by state, then county, then city within each county; table includes counties with populations greater than 49,999 unless noted and cities with populations greater than 9,999 whose Asian and/or NHPI population rates are greater than the national average; (1) Native Hawaiian and other Pacific Islander; (2) excludes Taiwanese; (3) includes Chamorro; (4) county does not meet population threshold but is shown in order to allow inclusion of city

Place	Total foreign-born population	Total Asian population	Asians who are foreign born	Total NHPI[1] population	NHPIs[1] who are foreign born	Asian Indian	Bangladeshi	Cambodian	Chinese[2]	Fijian	Filipino	Guamanian[3]	Hawaiian, Native	Hmong	Indonesian	Japanese	Korean	Laotian	Malaysian	Pakistani	Samoan	Sri Lankan	Taiwanese	Thai	Tongan	Vietnamese
Mays Chapel (cdp)	979 8.57	821	568 69.18 69.18 58.02	-	-	-	-	-	-	-	-	-	-	-	-	-	-	-	-	-	-	-	-	-	-	-
Owings Mills (cdp)	2,111 10.44	775	574 74.06 74.06 27.19	-	-	-	-	-	-	-	-	-	-	-	-	-	-	-	-	-	-	-	-	-	-	-
Perry Hall (cdp)	1,861 6.51	1,497	1,138 76.02 76.02 61.15	-	-	-	-	-	-	-	-	-	-	-	-	-	385 73.33 33.83 25.72 20.69	-	-	-	-	-	-	-	-	-
Reisterstown (cdp)	3,347 14.89	1,030	740 71.84 71.84 22.11	-	-	438 77.66 59.19 42.52 13.09	-	-	-	-	-	-	-	-	-	-	-	-	-	-	-	-	-	-	-	-
Rossville (cdp)	1,103 9.46	556	423 76.08 76.08 38.35	-	-	-	-	-	-	-	-	-	-	-	-	-	-	-	-	-	-	-	-	-	-	-
Towson (cdp)	4,124 7.96	1,938	1,603 82.71 82.71 38.87	-	-	-	-	-	719 84.99 44.85 37.10 17.43	-	-	-	-	-	-	-	-	-	-	-	-	-	-	-	-	-
Woodlawn (cdp)	3,398 9.41	2,170	1,659 76.45 76.45 48.82	-	-	688 77.92 41.47 31.71 20.25	-	-	-	-	-	-	-	-	-	-	-	-	-	-	-	-	-	-	-	-
Calvert County	1,643 2.20	655	420 64.12 64.12 25.56	-	-	-	-	-	-	-	-	-	-	-	-	-	-	-	-	-	-	-	-	-	-	-
Carroll County	3,046 2.02	1,299	842 64.82 64.82 27.64	-	-	-	-	-	-	-	-	-	-	-	-	-	-	-	-	-	-	-	-	-	-	-
Cecil County	1,567 1.82	564	318 56.38 56.38 20.29	-	-	-	-	-	-	-	-	-	-	-	-	-	-	-	-	-	-	-	-	-	-	-

Notes: Please refer to the User's Guide for an explanation of data; data is arranged alphabetically by state, then county, then city within each county; table includes counties with populations greater than 49,999 unless noted and cities with populations greater than 9,999 whose Asian and/or NHPI population rates are greater than the national average; (1) Native Hawaiian and other Pacific Islander; (2) excludes Taiwanese; (3) includes Chamorro; (4) county does not meet population threshold but is shown in order to allow inclusion of city

Place	Total foreign-born population	Total Asian population	Asians who are foreign born	Total NHPI[1] population	NHPIs[1] who are foreign born	Asian Indian	Bangladeshi	Cambodian	Chinese[2]	Fijian	Filipino	Guamanian[3]	Hawaiian, Native	Hmong	Indonesian	Japanese	Korean	Laotian	Malaysian	Pakistani	Samoan	Sri Lankan	Taiwanese	Thai	Tongan	Vietnamese
Charles County	3,470 2.88	1,884	1,218 64.65 64.65 35.10	-	-	-	-	-	-	-	261 55.30 21.43 13.85 7.52	-	-	-	-	-		-	-	-	-	-	-	-	-	-
Frederick County	7,779 3.98	3,327	2,421 72.77 72.77 31.12	-	-	455 73.03 18.79 13.68 5.85	-	-	475 60.36 19.62 14.28 6.11	-	-	-	-	-	-	-	451 85.58 18.63 13.56 5.80	-	-	-	-	-	-	-	-	-
Harford County	7,364 3.37	3,169	2,258 71.25 71.25 30.66	-	-	441 68.91 19.53 13.92 5.99	-	-	-	-	422 75.22 18.69 13.32 5.73	-	-	-	-	-	589 77.40 26.09 18.59 8.00	-	-	-	-	-	-	-	-	-
Howard County	28,113 11.34	18,712	13,566 72.50 72.50 48.26	-	-	3,485 73.25 25.69 18.62 12.40	-	-	2,634 71.17 19.42 14.08 9.37	-	989 71.67 7.29 5.29 3.52	-	-	-	-	-	4,601 76.52 33.92 24.59 16.37	-	-	518 79.45 3.82 2.77 1.84	-	-	-	-	-	543 74.69 4.00 2.90 1.93
Columbia (cdp)	11,665 13.20	6,274	4,613 73.53 73.53 39.55	-	-	1,326 73.63 28.74 21.13 11.37	-	-	1,143 72.80 24.78 18.22 9.80	-	359 70.53 7.78 5.72 3.08	-	-	-	-	-	1,131 78.22 24.52 18.03 9.70	-	-	-	-	-	-	-	-	-
Elkridge (cdp)	2,059 9.35	1,406	1,061 75.46 75.46 51.53	-	-	-	-	-	-	-	-	-	-	-	-	-	284 75.94 26.77 20.20 13.79	-	-	-	-	-	-	-	-	-
Ellicott City (cdp)	7,496 13.31	6,661	4,846 72.75 72.75 64.65	-	-	823 72.83 16.98 12.36 10.98	-	-	881 69.75 18.18 13.23 11.75	-	265 65.43 5.47 3.98 3.54	-	-	-	-	-	2,227 77.65 45.96 33.43 29.71	-	-	305 77.22 6.29 4.58 4.07	-	-	-	-	-	-
North Laurel (cdp)	2,274 11.02	1,390	963 69.28 69.28 42.35	-	-	310 74.52 32.19 22.30 13.63	-	-	-	-	-	-	-	-	-	-	286 67.77 29.70 20.58 12.58	-	-	-	-	-	-	-	-	-
Savage-Guilford (cdp)	1,181 9.37	730	567 77.67 77.67 48.01	-	-	-	-	-	-	-	-	-	-	-	-	-	-	-	-	-	-	-	-	-	-	-
Montgomery County	232,996 26.68	97,994	74,639 76.17 76.17 32.03	489	237 48.47 48.47 0.10	18,521 75.87 24.81 18.90 7.95	692 83.78 0.93 0.71 0.30	846 72.87 1.13 0.86 0.36	19,954 72.87 26.73 20.36 8.56	-	5,656 81.99 7.58 5.77 2.43	-	-	-	726 78.23 0.97 0.74 0.31	2,297 72.71 3.08 2.34 0.99	11,936 77.22 15.99 12.18 5.12	-	-	1,499 81.91 2.01 1.53 0.64	-	645 86.23 0.86 0.66 0.28	825 72.12 1.11 0.84 0.35	1,101 82.97 1.48 1.12 0.47	-	7,704 82.10 10.32 7.86 3.31

Notes: Please refer to the User's Guide for an explanation of data; data is arranged alphabetically by state, then county, then city within each county; table includes counties with populations greater than 49,999 unless noted and cities with populations greater than 9,999 whose Asian and/or NHPI population rates are greater than the national average; (1) Native Hawaiian and other Pacific Islander; (2) excludes Taiwanese; (3) includes Chamorro; (4) county does not meet population threshold but is shown in order to allow inclusion of city

Place	Total foreign-born population	Total Asian population	Asians who are foreign born	Total NHPI[1] population	NHPIs[1] who are foreign born	Asian Indian	Bangladeshi	Cambodian	Chinese[2]	Fijian	Filipino	Guamanian[3]	Hawaiian, Native	Hmong	Indonesian	Japanese	Korean	Laotian	Malaysian	Pakistani	Samoan	Sri Lankan	Taiwanese	Thai	Tongan	Vietnamese
	15,319	5,557	4,211	-	-	516	-	-	1,252	-	575	-	-	-	-	-	779	-	-	-	-	-	-	-	-	412
	30.50		75.78			74.35			69.63		84.68						77.90									95.59
Aspen Hill (cdp)						12.25			29.73		13.65						18.50									9.78
			75.78			9.29			22.53		10.35						14.02									7.41
			27.49			3.37			8.17		3.75						5.09									2.69
	11,830	4,261	3,177	-	-	745	-	-	923	-	296	-	-	-	-	353	445	-	-	-	-	-	-	-	-	-
	21.39		74.56			73.84			73.72		75.32					79.86	73.19									
Bethesda (cdp)						23.45			29.05		9.32					11.11	14.01									
			74.56			17.48			21.66		6.95					8.28	10.44									
			26.86			6.30			7.80		2.50					2.98	3.76									
	3,146	2,095	1,537	-	-	531	-	-	-	-	-	-	-	-	-	-	427	-	-	-	-	-	-	-	-	-
	24.95		73.37			75.64											75.18									
Calverton (cdp)						34.55											27.78									
			73.37			25.35											20.38									
			48.86			16.88											13.57									
	4,717	3,390	2,479	-	-	546	-	-	453	-	-	-	-	-	-	-	911	-	-	-	-	-	-	-	-	258
	23.75		73.13			74.49			62.57								78.81									77.95
Colesville (cdp)						22.03			18.27								36.75									10.41
			73.13			16.11			13.36								26.87									7.61
			52.55			11.58			9.60								19.31									5.47
	6,043	3,328	2,541	-	-	641	-	-	466	-	-	-	-	-	-	-	994	-	-	-	-	-	-	-	-	-
	28.00		76.35			78.55			76.14								78.76									
Fairland (cdp)						25.23			18.34								39.12									
			76.35			19.26			14.00								29.87									
			42.05			10.61			7.71								16.45									
	18,084	6,935	5,463	-	-	1,343	-	-	1,873	-	336	-	-	-	-	-	762	-	-	-	-	-	-	-	-	435
	34.26		78.77			79.47			76.70		76.71						83.28									75.39
Gaithersburg (city)						24.58			34.29		6.15						13.95									7.96
			78.77			19.37			27.01		4.84						10.99									6.27
			30.21			7.43			10.36		1.86						4.21									2.41
	11,134	5,283	4,071	-	-	1,666	-	-	846	-	-	-	-	-	-	-	277	-	-	-	-	-	-	-	-	351
	20.19		77.06			79.33			83.60								70.66									68.96
Germantown (cdp)						40.92			20.78								6.80									8.62
			77.06			31.54			16.01								5.24									6.64
			36.56			14.96			7.60								2.49									3.15
	10,688	4,276	3,314	-	-	1,366	-	-	539	-	487	-	-	-	-	-	-	-	-	-	-	-	-	-	-	306
	28.21		77.50			77.70			76.89		85.29															75.93
Montgomery Village (cdp)						41.22			16.26		14.70															9.23
			77.50			31.95			12.61		11.39															7.16
			31.01			12.78			5.04		4.56															2.86
	12,297	4,536	3,663	-	-	830	-	-	1,163	-	294	-	-	-	-	448	525	-	-	-	-	-	-	-	-	-
	31.82		80.75			79.43			80.48		78.19					85.82	77.43									
North Bethesda (cdp)						22.66			31.75		8.03					12.23	14.33									
			80.75			18.30			25.64		6.48					9.88	11.57									
			29.79			6.75			9.46		2.39					3.64	4.27									
	6,708	6,183	4,514	-	-	789	-	-	2,362	-	-	-	-	-	-	-	819	-	-	-	-	-	-	-	-	-
	29.24		73.01			67.73			72.81								78.00									
North Potomac (cdp)						17.48			52.33								18.14									
			73.01			12.76			38.20								13.25									
			67.29			11.76			35.21								12.21									

Notes: Please refer to the User's Guide for an explanation of data; data is arranged alphabetically by state, then county, then city within each county; table includes counties with populations greater than 49,999 unless noted and cities with populations greater than 9,999 whose Asian and/or NHPI population rates are greater than the national average; (1) Native Hawaiian and other Pacific Islander; (2) excludes Taiwanese; (3) includes Chamorro; (4) county does not meet population threshold but is shown in order to allow inclusion of city

Place	Total foreign-born population	Total Asian population	Asians who are foreign born	Total NHPI[1] population	NHPIs[1] who are foreign born	Asian Indian	Bangladeshi	Cambodian	Chinese[2]	Fijian	Filipino	Guamanian[3]	Hawaiian, Native	Hmong	Indonesian	Japanese	Korean	Laotian	Malaysian	Pakistani	Samoan	Sri Lankan	Taiwanese	Thai	Tongan	Vietnamese
Olney (cdp)	4,428 13.99	2,585	1,632 63.13 63.13 36.86	-	-	528 75.75 32.35 20.43 11.92	-	-	339 53.39 20.77 13.11 7.66	-	-	-	-	-	-	-	361 55.45 22.12 13.97 8.15	-	-	-	-	-	-	-	-	-
Potomac (cdp)	11,078 24.72	5,819	4,140 71.15 71.15 37.37	-	-	1,074 72.37 25.94 18.46 9.69	-	-	1,205 61.92 29.11 20.71 10.88	-	336 90.32 8.12 5.77 3.03	-	-	-	-	-	749 67.11 18.09 12.87 6.76	-	-	-	-	-	-	-	-	-
Redland (cdp)	5,684 32.95	2,930	2,274 77.61 77.61 40.01	-	-	577 77.14 25.37 19.69 10.15	-	-	596 74.69 26.21 20.34 10.49	-	286 92.56 12.58 9.76 5.03	-	-	-	-	-	312 75.91 13.72 10.65 5.49	-	-	-	-	-	-	-	-	-
Rockville (city)	14,644 30.99	6,677	5,515 82.60 82.60 37.66	-	-	734 73.62 13.31 10.99 5.01	-	-	2,189 81.71 39.69 32.78 14.95	-	401 93.47 7.27 6.01 2.74	-	-	-	-	384 86.49 6.96 5.75 2.62	766 84.27 13.89 11.47 5.23	-	-	-	-	-	-	-	-	381 85.62 6.91 5.71 2.60
Silver Spring (cdp)	26,904 35.07	6,302	5,060 80.29 80.29 18.81	-	-	1,232 86.70 24.35 19.55 4.58	-	214 65.64 4.23 3.40 0.80	547 73.32 10.81 8.68 2.03	-	388 82.73 7.67 6.16 1.44	-	-	-	-	-	422 93.78 8.34 6.70 1.57	-	-	-	-	-	-	-	-	1,421 80.24 28.08 22.55 5.28
Takoma Park (city)	4,917 28.62	714	610 85.43 85.43 12.41	-	-	-	-	-	-	-	-	-	-	-	-	-	-	-	-	-	-	-	-	-	-	-
Wheaton-Glenmont (cdp)	22,855 39.59	7,096	5,435 76.59 76.59 23.78	-	-	908 75.86 16.71 12.80 3.97	-	-	1,404 75.20 25.83 19.79 6.14	-	495 72.58 9.11 6.98 2.17	-	-	-	-	-	682 81.68 12.55 9.61 2.98	-	-	-	-	-	-	-	-	997 85.43 18.34 14.05 4.36
White Oak (cdp)	7,307 34.97	2,508	2,049 81.70 81.70 28.04	-	-	457 84.32 22.30 18.22 6.25	-	-	336 75.17 16.40 13.40 4.60	-	-	-	-	-	-	-	543 84.98 26.50 21.65 7.43	-	-	-	-	-	-	-	-	562 85.67 27.43 22.41 7.69
Prince George's County	110,481 13.78	30,390	23,000 75.68 75.68 20.82	-	-	5,610 78.69 24.39 18.46 5.08	-	-	3,685 74.93 16.02 12.13 3.34	-	6,008 72.92 26.12 19.77 5.44	-	-	-	-	433 68.08 1.88 1.42 0.39	2,949 79.90 12.82 9.70 2.67	-	-	546 80.29 2.37 1.80 0.49	-	-	-	228 68.26 0.99 0.75 0.21	-	2,037 77.60 8.86 6.70 1.84
Adelphi (cdp)	6,129 40.82	1,400	1,136 81.14 81.14 18.53	-	-	-	-	-	-	-	-	-	-	-	-	-	-	-	-	-	-	-	-	-	-	-

Notes: Please refer to the User's Guide for an explanation of data; data is arranged alphabetically by state, then county, then city within each county; table includes counties with populations greater than 49,999 unless noted and cities with populations greater than 9,999 whose Asian and/or NHPI population rates are greater than the national average; (1) Native Hawaiian and other Pacific Islander; (2) excludes Taiwanese; (3) includes Chamorro; (4) county does not meet population threshold but is shown in order to allow inclusion of city

Place	Total foreign-born population	Total Asian population	Asians who are foreign born	Total NHPI[1] population	NHPIs[1] who are foreign born	Asian Indian	Bangladeshi	Cambodian	Chinese[2]	Fijian	Filipino	Guamanian[3]	Hawaiian, Native	Hmong	Indonesian	Japanese	Korean	Laotian	Malaysian	Pakistani	Samoan	Sri Lankan	Taiwanese	Thai	Tongan	Vietnamese
Beltsville (cdp)	4,361 27.73	1,706	1,331 78.02 78.02 30.52	-	-	388 75.05 29.15 22.74 8.90	-	-	-	-	-	-	-	-	-	-	246 86.62 18.48 14.42 5.64	-	-	-	-	-	-	-	-	-
College Park (city)	3,159 12.85	2,236	1,393 62.30 62.30 44.10	-	-	431 67.55 30.94 19.28 13.64	-	-	481 68.42 34.53 21.51 15.23	-	-	-	-	-	-	-	-	-	-	-	-	-	-	-	-	-
Fort Washington (cdp)	2,955 12.22	2,413	1,640 67.97 67.97 55.50	-	-	-	-	-	-	-	1,330 68.84 81.10 55.12 45.01	-	-	-	-	-	-	-	-	-	-	-	-	-	-	-
Friendly (cdp)	903 8.23	657	449 68.34 68.34 49.72	-	-	-	-	-	-	-	360 68.83 80.18 54.79 39.87	-	-	-	-	-	-	-	-	-	-	-	-	-	-	-
Glenn Dale (cdp)	1,953 15.24	1,008	732 72.62 72.62 37.48	-	-	-	-	-	-	-	-	-	-	-	-	-	-	-	-	-	-	-	-	-	-	-
Greenbelt (city)	5,822 27.22	2,577	2,197 85.25 85.25 37.74	-	-	605 83.33 27.54 23.48 10.39	-	-	494 83.16 22.49 19.17 8.49	-	-	-	-	-	-	-	507 84.08 23.08 19.67 8.71	-	-	-	-	-	-	-	-	-
Hyattsville (city)	3,635 24.51	695	534 76.83 76.83 14.69	-	-	-	-	-	-	-	-	-	-	-	-	-	-	-	-	-	-	-	-	-	-	-
Lanham-Seabrook (cdp)	3,150 17.42	916	736 80.35 80.35 23.37	-	-	-	-	-	-	-	-	-	-	-	-	-	-	-	-	-	-	-	-	-	-	-
Laurel (city)	3,107 15.49	1,215	1,064 87.57 87.57 34.25	-	-	-	-	-	-	-	-	-	-	-	-	-	-	-	-	-	-	-	-	-	-	-
New Carrollton (city)	2,484 19.34	517	331 64.02 64.02 13.33	-	-	-	-	-	-	-	-	-	-	-	-	-	-	-	-	-	-	-	-	-	-	-

Notes: Please refer to the User's Guide for an explanation of data; data is arranged alphabetically by state, then county, then city within each county; table includes counties with populations greater than 49,999 unless noted and cities with populations greater than 9,999 whose Asian and/or NHPI population rates are greater than the national average; (1) Native Hawaiian and other Pacific Islander; (2) excludes Taiwanese; (3) includes Chamorro; (4) county does not meet population threshold but is shown in order to allow inclusion of city

Place	Total foreign-born population	Total Asian population	Asians who are foreign born	Total NHPI[1] population	NHPIs[1] who are foreign born	Asian Indian	Bangladeshi	Cambodian	Chinese[2]	Fijian	Filipino	Guamanian[3]	Hawaiian, Native	Hmong	Indonesian	Japanese	Korean	Laotian	Malaysian	Pakistani	Samoan	Sri Lankan	Taiwanese	Thai	Tongan	Vietnamese
South Laurel (cdp)	3,480 16.74	1,164	882 75.77 75.77 25.34	-	-	-	-	-	-	-	-	-	-	-	-	-	-	-	-	-	-	-	-	-	-	-
St. Mary's County	2,432 2.82	1,623	1,070 65.93 65.93 44.00	-	-	181 64.87 16.92 11.15 7.44	-	-	-	-	431 65.90 40.28 26.56 17.72	-	-	-	-	-	-	-	-	-	-	-	-	-	-	-
Lexington Park (cdp)	549 5.06	436	317 72.71 72.71 57.74	-	-	-	-	-	-	-	-	-	-	-	-	-	-	-	-	-	-	-	-	-	-	-
Washington County	2,477 1.88	1,000	784 78.40 78.40 31.65	-	-	-	-	-	-	-	-	-	-	-	-	-	-	-	-	-	-	-	-	-	-	-
Wicomico County	3,264 3.86	1,746	1,466 83.96 83.96 44.91	-	-	308 70.00 21.01 17.64 9.44	-	-	-	-	-	-	-	-	-	-	546 92.54 37.24 31.27 16.73	-	-	-	-	-	-	-	-	-
Salisbury (city)	1,608 6.66	997	812 81.44 81.44 50.50	-	-	-	-	-	-	-	-	-	-	-	-	-	-	-	-	-	-	-	-	-	-	-
MASSACHUSETTS	772,983 12.17	238,246	171,034 71.79 71.79 22.13	1,835	428 23.32 23.32 0.06	31,928 76.14 18.67 13.40 4.13	440 78.43 0.26 0.18 0.06	12,944 63.54 7.57 5.43 1.67	57,471 70.04 33.60 24.12 7.43	-	6,384 68.74 3.73 2.68 0.83	177 39.78 41.36 9.65 0.02	0 0.00 0.00 0.00 0.00	481 48.44 0.28 0.20 0.06	568 80.00 0.33 0.24 0.07	8,377 76.45 4.90 3.52 1.08	12,979 74.59 7.59 5.45 1.68	2,467 67.64 1.44 1.04 0.32	-	1,827 77.55 1.07 0.77 0.24	-	384 81.88 0.22 0.16 0.05	1,697 66.92 0.99 0.71 0.22	1,838 81.51 1.07 0.77 0.24	-	26,341 76.63 15.40 11.06 3.41
Barnstable County	10,982 4.94	1,372	928 67.64 67.64 8.45	-	-	-	-	-	280 64.81 30.17 20.41 2.55	-	-	-	-	-	-	-	-	-	-	-	-	-	-	-	-	-
Berkshire County	4,946 3.66	1,259	794 63.07 63.07 16.05	-	-	261 75.65 32.87 20.73 5.28	-	-	-	-	-	-	-	-	-	-	-	-	-	-	-	-	-	-	-	-
Bristol County	62,813 11.75	7,292	5,092 69.83 69.83 8.11	-	-	1,128 74.26 22.15 15.47 1.80	-	1,391 64.01 27.32 19.08 2.21	950 67.91 18.66 13.03 1.51	-	273 65.94 5.36 3.74 0.43	-	-	-	-	-	474 84.34 9.31 6.50 0.75	-	-	-	-	-	-	-	-	368 81.42 7.23 5.05 0.59

Notes: Please refer to the User's Guide for an explanation of data; data is arranged alphabetically by state, then county, then city within each county; table includes counties with populations greater than 49,999 unless noted and cities with populations greater than 9,999 whose Asian and/or NHPI population rates are greater than the national average; (1) Native Hawaiian and other Pacific Islander; (2) excludes Taiwanese; (3) includes Chamorro; (4) county does not meet population threshold but is shown in order to allow inclusion of city

Place	Total foreign-born population	Total Asian population	Asians who are foreign born	Total NHPI[1] population	NHPIs[1] who are foreign born	Asian Indian	Bangladeshi	Cambodian	Chinese[2]	Fijian	Filipino	Guamanian[3]	Hawaiian, Native	Hmong	Indonesian	Japanese	Korean	Laotian	Malaysian	Pakistani	Samoan	Sri Lankan	Taiwanese	Thai	Tongan	Vietnamese
Essex County	82,039 11.34	17,261	12,093 70.06 70.06 14.74	-	-	1,891 76.68 15.64 10.96 2.31	-	2,354 62.71 19.47 13.64 2.87	2,268 68.98 18.75 13.14 2.76	-	473 70.07 3.91 2.74 0.58	-	-	-	-	702 68.82 5.81 4.07 0.86	1,149 74.32 9.50 6.66 1.40	269 69.51 2.22 1.56 0.33	-	-	-	-	-	-	-	2,221 73.13 18.37 12.87 2.71
Andover (town)	3,170 10.14	2,078	1,506 72.47 72.47 47.51	-	-	419 83.30 27.82 20.16 13.22	-	-	522 63.74 34.66 25.12 16.47	-	-	-	-	-	-	-	-	-	-	-	-	-	-	-	-	-
Lynn (city)	20,348 22.83	5,899	3,939 66.77 66.77 19.36	-	-	300 72.99 7.62 5.09 1.47	-	1,893 63.12 48.06 32.09 9.30	-	-	-	-	-	-	-	-	-	-	-	-	-	-	-	-	-	852 72.26 21.63 14.44 4.19
North Andover (town)	2,191 8.05	1,084	809 74.63 74.63 36.92	-	-	-	-	-	245 71.22 30.28 22.60 11.18	-	-	-	-	-	-	-	-	-	-	-	-	-	-	-	-	-
Franklin County	2,610 3.65	641	502 78.32 78.32 19.23	-	-	-	-	-	-	-	-	-	-	-	-	-	-	-	-	-	-	-	-	-	-	-
Hampden County	33,033 7.24	6,054	4,396 72.61 72.61 13.31	-	-	497 69.32 11.31 8.21 1.50	-	282 61.98 6.41 4.66 0.85	764 63.93 17.38 12.62 2.31	-	-	-	-	-	-	-	367 80.84 8.35 6.06 1.11	-	-	-	-	-	-	-	-	1,549 79.89 35.24 25.59 4.69
Hampshire County	9,973 6.55	4,811	3,439 71.48 71.48 34.48	-	-	602 71.16 17.51 12.51 6.04	-	-	1,151 71.98 33.47 23.92 11.54	-	-	-	-	-	-	-	506 66.58 14.71 10.52 5.07	-	-	-	-	-	-	-	-	-
Amherst Center (cdp)	1,868 10.89	1,356	893 65.86 65.86 47.81	-	-	-	-	-	-	-	-	-	-	-	-	-	-	-	-	-	-	-	-	-	-	-
Amherst (town)	4,605 13.21	2,992	2,215 74.03 74.03 48.10	-	-	-	-	-	780 72.97 35.21 26.07 16.94	-	-	-	-	-	-	-	-	-	-	-	-	-	-	-	-	-
Middlesex County	223,465 15.25	91,645	65,617 71.60 71.60 29.36	-	-	17,040 77.70 25.97 18.59 7.63	-	6,821 62.16 10.40 7.44 3.05	20,901 69.76 31.85 22.81 9.35	-	1,884 73.88 2.87 2.06 0.84	-	-	-	-	2,912 75.13 4.44 3.18 1.30	5,193 73.14 7.91 5.67 2.32	1,241 68.68 1.89 1.35 0.56	-	450 75.89 0.69 0.49 0.20	-	-	855 67.22 1.30 0.93 0.38	693 76.91 1.06 0.76 0.31	-	5,141 76.32 7.83 5.61 2.30

Notes: Please refer to the User's Guide for an explanation of data; data is arranged alphabetically by state, then county, then city within each county; table includes counties with populations greater than 49,999 unless noted and cities with populations greater than 9,999 whose Asian and/or NHPI population rates are greater than the national average; (1) Native Hawaiian and other Pacific Islander; (2) excludes Taiwanese; (3) includes Chamorro; (4) county does not meet population threshold but is shown in order to allow inclusion of city

Place	Total foreign-born population	Total Asian population	Asians who are foreign born	Total NHPI[1] population	NHPIs[1] who are foreign born	Asian Indian	Bangladeshi	Cambodian	Chinese[2]	Fijian	Filipino	Guamanian[3]	Hawaiian, Native	Hmong	Indonesian	Japanese	Korean	Laotian	Malaysian	Pakistani	Samoan	Sri Lankan	Taiwanese	Thai	Tongan	Vietnamese
Acton (town)	2,915 14.34	1,813	1,439 79.37 79.37 49.37	-	-	510 78.22 35.44 28.13 17.50	-	-	659 81.26 45.80 36.35 22.61	-	-	-	-	-	-	-	-	-	-	-	-	-	-	-	-	-
Arlington (town)	5,946 14.03	2,006	1,541 76.82 76.82 25.92	-	-	-	-	-	591 81.07 38.35 29.46 9.94	-	-	-	-	-	-	-	-	-	-	-	-	-	-	-	-	-
Bedford (town)	1,216 9.65	789	523 66.29 66.29 43.01	-	-	-	-	-	-	-	-	-	-	-	-	-	-	-	-	-	-	-	-	-	-	-
Belmont (cdp)	3,573 14.77	1,297	966 74.48 74.48 27.04	-	-	-	-	-	382 68.09 39.54 29.45 10.69	-	-	-	-	-	-	-	-	-	-	-	-	-	-	-	-	-
Belmont (town)	3,573 14.77	1,297	966 74.48 74.48 27.04	-	-	-	-	-	382 68.09 39.54 29.45 10.69	-	-	-	-	-	-	-	-	-	-	-	-	-	-	-	-	-
Burlington (town)	3,398 14.85	2,314	1,812 78.31 78.31 53.33	-	-	1,198 79.23 66.11 51.77 35.26	-	-	-	-	-	-	-	-	-	-	-	-	-	-	-	-	-	-	-	-
Cambridge (city)	26,218 25.87	12,112	8,236 68.00 68.00 31.41	-	-	1,912 69.08 23.22 15.79 7.29	-	-	2,847 65.60 34.57 23.51 10.86	-	-	-	-	-	-	885 83.25 10.75 7.31 3.38	1,221 63.23 14.83 10.08 4.66	-	-	-	-	-	-	-	-	-
Chelmsford (town)	2,418 7.14	1,550	1,068 68.90 68.90 44.17	-	-	293 79.40 27.43 18.90 12.12	-	-	363 63.35 33.99 23.42 15.01	-	-	-	-	-	-	-	-	-	-	-	-	-	-	-	-	-
Framingham (town)	14,150 21.15	3,446	2,754 79.92 79.92 19.46	-	-	1,158 84.10 42.05 33.60 8.18	-	-	779 74.19 28.29 22.61 5.51	-	-	-	-	-	-	-	-	-	-	-	-	-	-	-	-	-
Lexington (town)	5,001 16.48	3,251	2,296 70.62 70.62 45.91	-	-	579 68.93 25.22 17.81 11.58	-	-	929 69.38 40.46 28.58 18.58	-	-	-	-	-	-	-	379 83.85 16.51 11.66 7.58	-	-	-	-	-	-	-	-	-

Notes: Please refer to the User's Guide for an explanation of data; data is arranged alphabetically by state, then county, then city within each county; table includes counties with populations greater than 49,999 unless noted and cities with populations greater than 9,999 whose Asian and/or NHPI population rates are greater than the national average; (1) Native Hawaiian and other Pacific Islander; (2) excludes Taiwanese; (3) includes Chamorro; (4) county does not meet population threshold but is shown in order to allow inclusion of city

Place	Total foreign-born population	Total Asian population	Asians who are foreign born	Total NHPI[1] population	NHPIs[1] who are foreign born	Asian Indian	Bangladeshi	Cambodian	Chinese[2]	Fijian	Filipino	Guamanian[3]	Hawaiian, Native	Hmong	Indonesian	Japanese	Korean	Laotian	Malaysian	Pakistani	Samoan	Sri Lankan	Taiwanese	Thai	Tongan	Vietnamese
Lowell (city)	23,267 22.12	17,161	11,754 68.49 68.49 50.52	-	-	2,207 85.08 18.78 12.86 9.49	-	5,799 60.91 49.34 33.79 24.92	656 86.43 5.58 3.82 2.82	-	-	-	-	-	-	-	-	1,036 70.62 8.81 6.04 4.45	-	-	-	-	-	-	-	1,187 79.66 10.10 6.92 5.10
Malden (city)	14,489 25.72	7,879	6,272 79.60 79.60 43.29	-	-	911 87.09 14.52 11.56 6.29	-	-	3,285 79.99 52.38 41.69 22.67	-	-	-	-	-	-	-	-	-	-	-	-	-	-	-	-	1,014 75.73 16.17 12.87 7.00
Marlborough (city)	5,857 16.16	1,601	1,235 77.14 77.14 21.09	-	-	541 77.73 43.81 33.79 9.24	-	-	-	-	-	-	-	-	-	-	-	-	-	-	-	-	-	-	-	-
Medford (city)	9,037 16.21	2,338	1,685 72.07 72.07 18.65	-	-	284 70.47 16.85 12.15 3.14	-	-	603 69.31 35.79 25.79 6.67	-	-	-	-	-	-	-	-	-	-	-	-	-	-	-	-	307 84.57 18.22 13.13 3.40
Natick (town)	3,168 9.85	1,294	892 68.93 68.93 28.16	-	-	-	-	-	403 61.53 45.18 31.14 12.72	-	-	-	-	-	-	-	-	-	-	-	-	-	-	-	-	-
Newton (city)	15,116 18.03	6,323	4,048 64.02 64.02 26.78	-	-	438 75.78 10.82 6.93 2.90	-	-	2,372 60.08 58.60 37.51 15.69	-	-	-	-	-	-	-	422 63.08 10.42 6.67 2.79	-	-	-	-	-	-	-	-	-
Somerville (city)	22,727 29.33	5,013	3,671 73.23 73.23 16.15	-	-	999 77.38 27.21 19.93 4.40	-	-	1,484 72.67 40.42 29.60 6.53	-	-	-	-	-	-	-	279 61.59 7.60 5.57 1.23	-	-	-	-	-	-	-	-	-
Sudbury (town)	1,465 8.70	615	380 61.79 61.79 25.94	-	-	-	-	-	-	-	-	-	-	-	-	-	-	-	-	-	-	-	-	-	-	-
Waltham (city)	11,975 20.22	4,638	3,605 77.73 77.73 30.10	-	-	1,647 83.90 45.69 35.51 13.75	-	-	1,069 71.84 29.65 23.05 8.93	-	-	-	-	-	-	-	-	-	-	-	-	-	-	-	-	-
Wayland (town)	1,161 8.86	682	405 59.38 59.38 34.88	-	-	-	-	-	-	-	-	-	-	-	-	-	-	-	-	-	-	-	-	-	-	-

Notes: Please refer to the User's Guide for an explanation of data; data is arranged alphabetically by state, then county, then city within each county; table includes counties with populations greater than 49,999 unless noted and cities with populations greater than 9,999 whose Asian and/or NHPI population rates are greater than the national average; (1) Native Hawaiian and other Pacific Islander; (2) excludes Taiwanese; (3) includes Chamorro; (4) county does not meet population threshold but is shown in order to allow inclusion of city

Place	Total foreign-born population	Total Asian population	Asians who are foreign born	Total NHPI[1] population	NHPIs[1] who are foreign born	Asian Indian	Bangladeshi	Cambodian	Chinese[2]	Fijian	Filipino	Guamanian[3]	Hawaiian, Native	Hmong	Indonesian	Japanese	Korean	Laotian	Malaysian	Pakistani	Samoan	Sri Lankan	Taiwanese	Thai	Tongan	Vietnamese
Westford (town)	1,312 6.32	951	616 64.77 64.77 46.95	-	-	-	-	-	212 57.30 34.42 22.29 16.16	-	-	-	-	-	-	-	-	-	-	-	-	-	-	-	-	-
Weston (town)	1,449 12.63	910	568 62.42 62.42 39.20	-	-	-	-	-	277 71.95 48.77 30.44 19.12	-	-	-	-	-	-	-	-	-	-	-	-	-	-	-	-	-
Winchester (town)	2,241 10.77	794	587 73.93 73.93 26.19	-	-	-	-	-	-	-	-	-	-	-	-	-	-	-	-	-	-	-	-	-	-	-
Woburn (city)	3,589 9.63	1,827	1,527 83.58 83.58 42.55	-	-	837 83.53 54.81 45.81 23.32	-	-	-	-	-	-	-	-	-	-	-	-	-	-	-	-	-	-	-	-
Norfolk County	76,732 11.80	36,121	25,912 71.74 71.74 33.77	-	-	4,070 80.34 15.71 11.27 5.30	-	-	13,058 68.06 50.39 36.15 17.02	-	1,358 71.93 5.24 3.76 1.77	-	-	-	-	1,632 78.46 6.30 4.52 2.13	1,697 75.46 6.55 4.70 2.21	-	-	-	-	-	246 58.16 0.95 0.68 0.32	-	-	2,124 75.37 8.20 5.88 2.77
Brookline (town)	15,174 26.59	7,787	5,733 73.62 73.62 37.78	-	-	759 70.02 13.24 9.75 5.00	-	-	2,566 71.58 44.76 32.95 16.91	-	-	-	-	-	-	1,082 81.66 18.87 13.89 7.13	758 76.41 13.22 9.73 5.00	-	-	-	-	-	-	-	-	-
Needham (town)	2,765 9.56	1,062	704 66.29 66.29 25.46	-	-	-	-	-	343 56.60 48.72 32.30 12.41	-	-	-	-	-	-	-	-	-	-	-	-	-	-	-	-	-
Norwood (town)	3,361 11.76	1,384	1,124 81.21 81.21 33.44	-	-	646 85.22 57.47 46.68 19.22	-	-	-	-	-	-	-	-	-	-	-	-	-	-	-	-	-	-	-	-
Quincy (city)	17,642 20.04	14,007	10,291 73.47 73.47 58.33	-	-	866 89.37 8.42 6.18 4.91	-	-	6,614 70.05 64.27 47.22 37.49	-	690 80.33 6.70 4.93 3.91	-	-	-	-	-	-	-	-	-	-	-	-	-	-	1,140 77.92 11.08 8.14 6.46
Randolph (town)	6,684 21.56	3,152	2,305 73.13 73.13 34.49	-	-	-	-	-	996 65.27 43.21 31.60 14.90	-	-	-	-	-	-	-	-	-	-	-	-	-	-	-	-	525 79.67 22.78 16.66 7.85

Notes: Please refer to the User's Guide for an explanation of data; data is arranged alphabetically by state, then county, then city within each county; table includes counties with populations greater than 49,999 unless noted and cities with populations greater than 9,999 whose Asian and/or NHPI population rates are greater than the national average; (1) Native Hawaiian and other Pacific Islander; (2) excludes Taiwanese; (3) includes Chamorro; (4) county does not meet population threshold but is shown in order to allow inclusion of city

Place	Total foreign-born population	Total Asian population	Asians who are foreign born	Total NHPI[1] population	NHPIs[1] who are foreign born	Asian Indian	Bangladeshi	Cambodian	Chinese[2]	Fijian	Filipino	Guamanian[3]	Hawaiian, Native	Hmong	Indonesian	Japanese	Korean	Laotian	Malaysian	Pakistani	Samoan	Sri Lankan	Taiwanese	Thai	Tongan	Vietnamese
Sharon (town)	2,111 12.13	694	458 65.99 65.99 21.70	-	-	-	-	-	-	-	-	-	-	-	-	-	-	-	-	-	-	-	-	-	-	-
Wellesley (town)	2,890 10.86	1,784	1,069 59.92 59.92 36.99	-	-	-	-	-	523 57.79 48.92 29.32 18.10	-	-	-	-	-	-	-	-	-	-	-	-	-	-	-	-	-
Plymouth County	29,592 6.26	4,491	2,835 63.13 63.13 9.58	-	-	442 70.61 15.59 9.84 1.49	-	-	603 57.26 21.27 13.43 2.04	-	378 70.39 13.33 8.42 1.28	-	-	-	-	-	-	-	-	-	-	-	-	-	-	461 64.93 16.26 10.26 1.56
Suffolk County	176,031 25.52	48,115	35,573 73.93 73.93 20.21	-	-	2,890 66.39 8.12 6.01 1.64	-	1,170 68.10 3.29 2.43 0.66	14,628 73.42 41.12 30.40 8.31	-	1,049 56.52 2.95 2.18 0.60	-	-	-	-	1,825 80.43 5.13 3.79 1.04	1,970 76.06 5.54 4.09 1.12	-	-	-	-	-	313 67.31 0.88 0.65 0.18	-	-	9,861 79.15 27.72 20.49 5.60
Boston (city)	151,836 25.77	44,345	32,676 73.69 73.69 21.52	-	-	2,618 64.63 8.01 5.90 1.72	-	398 63.58 1.22 0.90 0.26	14,229 73.27 43.55 32.09 9.37	-	934 53.65 2.86 2.11 0.62	-	-	-	-	1,803 80.67 5.52 4.07 1.19	1,822 75.20 5.58 4.11 1.20	-	-	-	-	-	313 67.31 0.96 0.71 0.21	-	-	8,864 79.67 27.13 19.99 5.84
Chelsea (city)	12,674 36.13	1,455	1,135 78.01 78.01 8.96	-	-	-	-	-	-	-	-	-	-	-	-	-	-	-	-	-	-	-	-	-	-	574 77.67 50.57 39.45 4.53
Revere (city)	9,936 21.01	2,161	1,624 75.15 75.15 16.34	-	-	-	-	564 69.63 34.73 26.10 5.68	-	-	-	-	-	-	-	-	-	-	-	-	-	-	-	-	-	414 72.00 25.49 19.16 4.17
Worcester County	59,063 7.86	18,965	13,704 72.26 72.26 23.20	-	-	2,955 75.87 21.56 15.58 5.00	-	268 67.85 1.96 1.41 0.45	2,518 72.82 18.37 13.28 4.26	-	304 63.60 2.22 1.60 0.51	-	-	310 46.76 2.26 1.63 0.52	-	293 74.94 2.14 1.54 0.50	960 80.07 7.01 5.06 1.63	636 62.78 4.64 3.35 1.08	-	335 84.38 2.44 1.77 0.57	-	-	-	-	-	4,207 74.53 30.70 22.18 7.12
Fitchburg (city)	3,227 8.25	1,748	917 52.46 52.46 28.42	-	-	-	-	-	-	-	-	-	-	262 43.09 28.57 14.99 8.12	-	-	-	206 52.82 22.46 11.78 6.38	-	-	-	-	-	-	-	-
Northborough (town)	987 7.04	762	499 65.49 65.49 50.56	-	-	-	-	-	-	-	-	-	-	-	-	-	-	-	-	-	-	-	-	-	-	-

Notes: Please refer to the User's Guide for an explanation of data; data is arranged alphabetically by state, then county, then city within each county; table includes counties with populations greater than 49,999 unless noted and cities with populations greater than 9,999 whose Asian and/or NHPI population rates are greater than the national average; (1) Native Hawaiian and other Pacific Islander; (2) excludes Taiwanese; (3) includes Chamorro; (4) county does not meet population threshold but is shown in order to allow inclusion of city

Place	Total foreign-born population	Total Asian population	Asians who are foreign born	Total NHPI[1] population	NHPIs[1] who are foreign born	Asian Indian	Bangladeshi	Cambodian	Chinese[2]	Fijian	Filipino	Guamanian[3]	Hawaiian, Native	Hmong	Indonesian	Japanese	Korean	Laotian	Malaysian	Pakistani	Samoan	Sri Lankan	Taiwanese	Thai	Tongan	Vietnamese
Shrewsbury (town)	3,407 10.77	2,574	1,888 73.35 73.35 55.42	-	-	874 76.73 46.29 33.95 25.65	-	-	445 68.04 23.57 17.29 13.06	-	-	-	-	-	-	-	-	-	-	-	-	-	-	-	-	380 73.64 20.13 14.76 11.15
Westborough (town)	2,544 14.14	1,429	1,159 81.11 81.11 45.56	-	-	499 83.03 43.05 34.92 19.61	-	-	390 80.91 33.65 27.29 15.33	-	-	-	-	-	-	-	-	-	-	-	-	-	-	-	-	-
Worcester (city)	25,097 14.54	7,893	5,961 75.52 75.52 23.75	-	-	789 74.57 13.24 10.00 3.14	-	-	717 74.69 12.03 9.08 2.86	-	-	-	-	-	-	-	-	-	-	-	-	-	-	-	-	3,241 75.60 54.37 41.06 12.91
MICHIGAN	523,589 5.27	174,824	129,443 74.04 74.04 24.72	2,669	526 19.71 19.71 0.10	41,004 75.29 31.68 23.45 7.83	1,403 83.36 1.08 0.80 0.27	1,112 69.76 0.86 0.64 0.21	21,878 74.31 16.90 12.51 4.18	-	12,391 70.44 9.57 7.09 2.37	217 31.68 41.25 8.13 0.04	41 5.18 7.79 1.54 0.01	3,401 60.12 2.63 1.95 0.65	602 92.33 0.47 0.34 0.11	8,090 75.99 6.25 4.63 1.55	17,107 81.41 13.22 9.79 3.27	1,771 63.55 1.37 1.01 0.34	424 92.78 0.33 0.24 0.08	3,696 74.25 2.86 2.11 0.71	57 12.03 10.84 2.14 0.01	313 87.92 0.24 0.18 0.06	1,627 71.23 1.26 0.93 0.31	1,316 82.04 1.02 0.75 0.25	-	9,651 74.39 7.46 5.52 1.84
Allegan County	3,086 2.92	592	447 75.51 75.51 14.48	-	-	-	-	-	-	-	-	-	-	-	-	-	-	-	-	-	-	-	-	-	-	-
Bay County	1,536 1.39	617	425 68.88 68.88 27.67	-	-	-	-	-	-	-	-	-	-	-	-	-	-	-	-	-	-	-	-	-	-	-
Berrien County	7,891 4.86	1,671	1,287 77.02 77.02 16.31	-	-	384 81.18 29.84 22.98 4.87	-	-	-	-	202 63.52 15.70 12.09 2.56	-	-	-	-	-	314 80.31 24.40 18.79 3.98	-	-	-	-	-	-	-	-	-
Calhoun County	3,258 2.36	1,473	1,130 76.71 76.71 34.68	-	-	-	-	-	-	-	-	-	-	-	-	357 80.04 31.59 24.24 10.96	-	-	-	-	-	-	-	-	-	-
Cass County	979 1.92	324	257 79.32 79.32 26.25	-	-	-	-	-	-	-	-	-	-	-	-	-	-	111 77.62 43.19 34.26 11.34	-	-	-	-	-	-	-	-
Clinton County	783 1.21	358	222 62.01 62.01 28.35	-	-	-	-	-	-	-	-	-	-	-	-	-	-	-	-	-	-	-	-	-	-	-

Notes: Please refer to the User's Guide for an explanation of data; data is arranged alphabetically by state, then county, then city within each county; table includes counties with populations greater than 49,999 unless noted and cities with populations greater than 9,999 whose Asian and/or NHPI population rates are greater than the national average; (1) Native Hawaiian and other Pacific Islander; (2) excludes Taiwanese; (3) includes Chamorro; (4) county does not meet population threshold but is shown in order to allow inclusion of city

Place	Total foreign-born population	Total Asian population	Asians who are foreign born	Total NHPI[1] population	NHPIs[1] who are foreign born	Asian Indian	Bangladeshi	Cambodian	Chinese[2]	Fijian	Filipino	Guamanian[3]	Hawaiian, Native	Hmong	Indonesian	Japanese	Korean	Laotian	Malaysian	Pakistani	Samoan	Sri Lankan	Taiwanese	Thai	Tongan	Vietnamese
Eaton County	2,266 2.19	1,222	917 75.04 75.04 40.47	-	-	320 88.64 34.90 26.19 14.12	-	-	-	-	-	-	-	-	-	-	-	-	-	-	-	-	-	-	-	206 70.07 22.46 16.86 9.09
Genesee County	9,353 2.14	3,161	2,202 69.66 69.66 23.54	-	-	801 68.58 36.38 25.34 8.56	-	-	311 78.14 14.12 9.84 3.33	-	300 70.92 13.62 9.49 3.21	-	-	-	-	-	342 75.33 15.53 10.82 3.66	-	-	-	-	-	-	-	-	-
Ingham County	17,463 6.25	9,991	7,623 76.30 76.30 43.65	-	-	1,525 75.50 20.01 15.26 8.73	-	-	1,370 76.97 17.97 13.71 7.85	-	411 66.18 5.39 4.11 2.35	-	-	365 61.34 4.79 3.65 2.09	-	381 72.99 5.00 3.81 2.18	1,509 86.38 19.80 15.10 8.64	-	-	-	-	-	-	-	-	1,019 76.27 13.37 10.20 5.84
East Lansing (city)	5,483 11.74	3,836	3,056 79.67 79.67 55.74	-	-	585 77.18 19.14 15.25 10.67	-	-	723 83.97 23.66 18.85 13.19	-	-	-	-	-	-	-	876 88.48 28.66 22.84 15.98	-	-	-	-	-	-	-	-	-
Meridian charter (township)	3,378 8.66	2,453	1,844 75.17 75.17 54.59	-	-	693 76.74 37.58 28.25 20.52	-	-	381 71.62 20.66 15.53 11.28	-	-	-	-	-	-	-	300 78.95 16.27 12.23 8.88	-	-	-	-	-	-	-	-	-
Okemos (cdp)	2,332 10.28	1,916	1,385 72.29 72.29 59.39	-	-	562 74.54 40.58 29.33 24.10	-	-	246 66.13 17.76 12.84 10.55	-	-	-	-	-	-	-	-	-	-	-	-	-	-	-	-	-
Ionia County	716 1.16	219	143 65.30 65.30 19.97	-	-	-	-	-	-	-	-	-	-	-	-	-	-	-	-	-	-	-	-	-	-	-
Isabella County	1,467 2.32	799	674 84.36 84.36 45.94	-	-	-	-	-	-	-	-	-	-	-	-	-	-	-	-	-	-	-	-	-	-	-
Jackson County	2,637 1.66	732	607 82.92 82.92 23.02	-	-	-	-	-	-	-	-	-	-	-	-	-	-	-	-	-	-	-	-	-	-	-
Kalamazoo County	9,581 4.02	4,315	3,321 76.96 76.96 34.66	-	-	1,005 78.45 30.26 23.29 10.49	-	-	682 79.39 20.54 15.81 7.12	-	-	-	-	-	-	-	578 81.52 17.40 13.40 6.03	-	-	-	-	-	-	-	-	-

Notes: Please refer to the User's Guide for an explanation of data; data is arranged alphabetically by state, then county, then city within each county; table includes counties with populations greater than 49,999 unless noted and cities with populations greater than 9,999 whose Asian and/or NHPI population rates are greater than the national average; (1) Native Hawaiian and other Pacific Islander; (2) excludes Taiwanese; (3) includes Chamorro; (4) county does not meet population threshold but is shown in order to allow inclusion of city

Place	Total foreign-born population	Total Asian population	Asians who are foreign born	Total NHPI[1] population	NHPIs[1] who are foreign born	Asian Indian	Bangladeshi	Cambodian	Chinese[2]	Fijian	Filipino	Guamanian[3]	Hawaiian, Native	Hmong	Indonesian	Japanese	Korean	Laotian	Malaysian	Pakistani	Samoan	Sri Lankan	Taiwanese	Thai	Tongan	Vietnamese
Kent County	38,154 6.64	10,515	8,118 77.20 77.20 21.28	-	-	1,132 81.73 13.94 10.77 2.97	-	-	748 71.24 9.21 7.11 1.96	-	464 73.42 5.72 4.41 1.22	-	-	-	-	-	1,613 85.12 19.87 15.34 4.23	-	-	-	-	-	-	-	-	3,360 77.87 41.39 31.95 8.81
Kentwood (city)	4,211 9.31	2,504	1,911 76.32 76.32 45.38	-	-	-	-	-	-	-	-	-	-	-	-	-	371 83.37 19.41 14.82 8.81	-	-	-	-	-	-	-	-	921 75.31 48.19 36.78 21.87
Lenawee County	1,631 1.65	533	377 70.73 70.73 23.11	-	-	-	-	-	-	-	-	-	-	-	-	-	-	-	-	-	-	-	-	-	-	-
Livingston County	4,715 3.00	1,059	731 69.03 69.03 15.50	-	-	-	-	-	-	-	-	-	-	-	-	-	-	-	-	-	-	-	-	-	-	-
Macomb County	69,007 8.76	17,378	12,484 71.84 71.84 18.09	-	-	4,287 77.31 34.34 24.67 6.21	-	-	1,760 73.55 14.10 10.13 2.55	-	2,341 68.65 18.75 13.47 3.39	-	-	560 51.76 4.49 3.22 0.81	-	-	1,245 82.18 9.97 7.16 1.80	-	-	430 81.13 3.44 2.47 0.62	-	-	-	-	-	1,050 73.74 8.41 6.04 1.52
Sterling Heights (city)	21,146 16.99	6,510	4,686 71.98 71.98 22.16	-	-	1,751 72.36 37.37 26.90 8.28	-	-	722 73.60 15.41 11.09 3.41	-	937 70.35 20.00 14.39 4.43	-	-	-	-	-	504 79.87 10.76 7.74 2.38	-	-	-	-	-	-	-	-	316 70.54 6.74 4.85 1.49
Marquette County	937 1.45	306	230 75.16 75.16 24.55	-	-	-	-	-	-	-	-	-	-	-	-	-	-	-	-	-	-	-	-	-	-	-
Midland County	2,611 3.15	1,165	818 70.21 70.21 31.33	-	-	286 75.26 34.96 24.55 10.95	-	-	287 73.78 35.09 24.64 10.99	-	-	-	-	-	-	-	-	-	-	-	-	-	-	-	-	-
Monroe County	2,763 1.89	944	585 61.97 61.97 21.17	-	-	-	-	-	-	-	-	-	-	-	-	-	-	-	-	-	-	-	-	-	-	-
Muskegon County	3,159 1.86	745	567 76.11 76.11 17.95	-	-	-	-	-	-	-	-	-	-	-	-	-	-	-	-	-	-	-	-	-	-	-

Notes: Please refer to the User's Guide for an explanation of data; data is arranged alphabetically by state, then county, then city within each county; table includes counties with populations greater than 49,999 unless noted and cities with populations greater than 9,999 whose Asian and/or NHPI population rates are greater than the national average; (1) Native Hawaiian and other Pacific Islander; (2) excludes Taiwanese; (3) includes Chamorro; (4) county does not meet population threshold but is shown in order to allow inclusion of city

Place	Total foreign-born population	Total Asian population	Asians who are foreign born	Total NHPI[1] population	NHPIs[1] who are foreign born	Asian Indian	Bangladeshi	Cambodian	Chinese[2]	Fijian	Filipino	Guamanian[3]	Hawaiian, Native	Hmong	Indonesian	Japanese	Korean	Laotian	Malaysian	Pakistani	Samoan	Sri Lankan	Taiwanese	Thai	Tongan	Vietnamese
Oakland County	119,218 9.98	48,378	35,846 74.10 74.10 30.07	-	-	14,492 75.66 40.43 29.96 12.16	-	-	6,116 70.32 17.06 12.64 5.13	-	2,879 71.94 8.03 5.95 2.41	-	-	665 61.52 1.86 1.37 0.56	-	3,442 80.38 9.60 7.11 2.89	3,835 79.47 10.70 7.93 3.22	-	-	713 73.28 1.99 1.47 0.60	-	-	840 66.72 2.34 1.74 0.70	-	-	1,259 76.44 3.51 2.60 1.06
Auburn Hills (city)	2,058 10.39	1,229	928 75.51 75.51 45.09	-	-	516 76.33 55.60 41.99 25.07	-	-	-	-	-	-	-	-	-	-	-	-	-	-	-	-	-	-	-	-
Bloomfield (township)	6,095 14.17	2,717	2,010 73.98 73.98 32.98	-	-	799 67.94 39.75 29.41 13.11	-	-	-	-	-	-	-	-	-	-	488 84.58 24.28 17.96 8.01	-	-	-	-	-	-	-	-	-
Farmington (city)	1,676 16.08	1,065	926 86.95 86.95 55.25	-	-	726 88.21 78.40 68.17 43.32	-	-	-	-	-	-	-	-	-	-	-	-	-	-	-	-	-	-	-	-
Farmington Hills (city)	12,902 15.71	5,722	4,457 77.89 77.89 34.55	-	-	2,764 80.80 62.01 48.30 21.42	-	-	585 66.48 13.13 10.22 4.53	-	242 64.53 5.43 4.23 1.88	-	-	-	-	-	-	-	-	-	-	-	-	-	-	-
Madison Heights (city)	4,472 14.38	1,595	1,295 81.19 81.19 28.96	-	-	-	-	-	403 73.67 31.12 25.27 9.01	-	-	-	-	-	-	-	-	-	-	-	-	-	-	-	-	-
Novi (city)	6,024 12.69	3,991	2,828 70.86 70.86 46.95	-	-	736 65.89 26.03 18.44 12.22	-	-	529 65.07 18.71 13.25 8.78	-	-	-	-	-	-	971 84.58 34.34 24.33 16.12	-	-	-	-	-	-	-	-	-	-
Rochester (city)	903 8.63	549	353 64.30 64.30 39.09	-	-	-	-	-	-	-	-	-	-	-	-	-	-	-	-	-	-	-	-	-	-	-
Rochester Hills (city)	8,368 12.16	4,596	3,360 73.11 73.11 40.15	-	-	1,401 71.81 41.70 30.48 16.74	-	-	715 70.37 21.28 15.56 8.54	-	-	-	-	-	-	-	324 87.10 9.64 7.05 3.87	-	-	-	-	-	-	-	-	-
Troy (city)	15,851 19.58	10,378	7,668 73.89 73.89 48.38	-	-	3,544 76.12 46.22 34.15 22.36	-	-	1,661 72.72 21.66 16.01 10.48	-	550 73.24 7.17 5.30 3.47	-	-	-	-	-	921 74.76 12.01 8.87 5.81	-	-	-	-	-	338 60.57 4.41 3.26 2.13	-	-	-

Notes: Please refer to the User's Guide for an explanation of data; data is arranged alphabetically by state, then county, then city within each county; table includes counties with populations greater than 49,999 unless noted and cities with populations greater than 9,999 whose Asian and/or NHPI population rates are greater than the national average; (1) Native Hawaiian and other Pacific Islander; (2) excludes Taiwanese; (3) includes Chamorro; (4) county does not meet population threshold but is shown in order to allow inclusion of city

Place	Total foreign-born population	Total Asian population	Asians who are foreign born	Total NHPI[1] population	NHPIs[1] who are foreign born	Asian Indian	Bangladeshi	Cambodian	Chinese[2]	Fijian	Filipino	Guamanian[3]	Hawaiian, Native	Hmong	Indonesian	Japanese	Korean	Laotian	Malaysian	Pakistani	Samoan	Sri Lankan	Taiwanese	Thai	Tongan	Vietnamese
West Bloomfield (township)	12,241 18.89	4,994	3,603 72.15 72.15 29.43	-	-	1,130 66.82 31.36 22.63 9.23	-	-	403 67.62 11.19 8.07 3.29	-	242 56.54 6.72 4.85 1.98	-	-	-	-	1,180 92.77 32.75 23.63 9.64	397 79.56 11.02 7.95 3.24	-	-	-	-	-	-	-	-	-
Ottawa County	11,667 4.90	5,180	3,764 72.66 72.66 32.26	-	-	364 77.61 9.67 7.03 3.12	-	746 68.88 19.82 14.40 6.39	356 83.96 9.46 6.87 3.05	-	-	-	-	-	-	-	512 95.70 13.60 9.88 4.39	745 64.95 19.79 14.38 6.39	-	-	-	-	-	-	-	558 75.71 14.82 10.77 4.78
Holland (city)	3,769 10.70	1,271	937 73.72 73.72 24.86	-	-	-	-	-	-	-	-	-	-	-	-	-	-	-	-	-	-	-	-	-	-	-
Saginaw County	4,290 2.04	1,747	1,274 72.93 72.93 29.70	-	-	218 64.31 17.11 12.48 5.08	-	-	-	-	238 63.47 18.68 13.62 5.55	-	-	-	-	-	306 90.53 24.02 17.52 7.13	-	-	-	-	-	-	-	-	-
St. Clair County	4,453 2.71	424	295 69.58 69.58 6.62	-	-	-	-	-	-	-	-	-	-	-	-	-	-	-	-	-	-	-	-	-	-	-
St. Joseph County	2,131 3.41	297	231 77.78 77.78 10.84	-	-	-	-	-	-	-	-	-	-	-	-	-	-	-	-	-	-	-	-	-	-	-
Washtenaw County	33,164 10.27	20,021	14,544 72.64 72.64 43.85	-	-	3,010 63.50 20.70 15.03 9.08	-	-	4,712 77.74 32.40 23.54 14.21	-	571 60.36 3.93 2.85 1.72	-	-	-	-	1,435 83.97 9.87 7.17 4.33	2,815 76.29 19.36 14.06 8.49	-	-	330 70.97 2.27 1.65 1.00	-	-	409 78.65 2.81 2.04 1.23	-	-	282 61.57 1.94 1.41 0.85
Ann Arbor (city)	18,905 16.57	13,389	9,592 71.64 71.64 50.74	-	-	1,901 58.58 19.82 14.20 10.06	-	-	3,299 78.42 34.39 24.64 17.45	-	271 51.23 2.83 2.02 1.43	-	-	-	-	1,096 86.10 11.43 8.19 5.80	1,902 75.33 19.83 14.21 10.06	-	-	-	-	-	355 80.50 3.70 2.65 1.88	-	-	-
Pittsfield charter (township)	5,036 16.72	2,769	2,100 75.84 75.84 41.70	-	-	515 78.03 24.52 18.60 10.23	-	-	607 77.42 28.90 21.92 12.05	-	-	-	-	-	-	-	420 74.20 20.00 15.17 8.34	-	-	-	-	-	-	-	-	-
Scio (township)	914 5.83	611	419 68.58 68.58 45.84	-	-	-	-	-	-	-	-	-	-	-	-	-	-	-	-	-	-	-	-	-	-	-

Notes: Please refer to the User's Guide for an explanation of data; data is arranged alphabetically by state, then county, then city within each county; table includes counties with populations greater than 49,999 unless noted and cities with populations greater than 9,999 whose Asian and/or NHPI population rates are greater than the national average; (1) Native Hawaiian and other Pacific Islander; (2) excludes Taiwanese; (3) includes Chamorro; (4) county does not meet population threshold but is shown in order to allow inclusion of city

Place	Total foreign-born population	Total Asian population	Asians who are foreign born	Total NHPI[1] population	NHPIs[1] who are foreign born	Asian Indian	Bangladeshi	Cambodian	Chinese[2]	Fijian	Filipino	Guamanian[3]	Hawaiian, Native	Hmong	Indonesian	Japanese	Korean	Laotian	Malaysian	Pakistani	Samoan	Sri Lankan	Taiwanese	Thai	Tongan	Vietnamese
Wayne County	137,769	35,273	26,600	495	72	11,147	1,012	-	3,721	-	3,256	-	-	1,222	-	740	1,487	-	-	1,588	-	-	-	-	-	891
	6.68		75.41		14.55	76.87	87.02		74.64		75.76			66.67		70.68	82.47			72.91						73.45
						41.91	3.80		13.99		12.24			4.59		2.78	5.59			5.97						3.35
			75.41		14.55	31.60	2.87		10.55		9.23			3.46		2.10	4.22			4.50						2.53
			19.31		0.05	8.09	0.73		2.70		2.36			0.89		0.54	1.08			1.15						0.65
Brownstown (township)	1,193	925	533	-	-	-	-	-	-	-	-	-	-	-	-	-	-	-	-	-	-	-	-	-	-	-
	5.19		57.62																							
			57.62																							
			44.68																							
Canton (township)	8,127	6,569	4,839	-	-	2,607	-	-	894	-	448	-	-	-	-	-	272	-	-	-	-	-	-	-	-	-
	10.65		73.66			73.31			71.86		73.08						90.97									
						53.87			18.47		9.26						5.62									
			73.66			39.69			13.61		6.82						4.14									
			59.54			32.08			11.00		5.51						3.35									
Hamtramck (city)	9,432	2,358	1,943	-	-	873	657	-	-	-	-	-	-	-	-	-	-	-	-	-	-	-	-	-	-	-
	41.05		82.40			77.26	88.78																			
						44.93	33.81																			
			82.40			37.02	27.86																			
			20.60			9.26	6.97																			
Inkster (city)	1,628	1,140	930	-	-	673	-	-	-	-	-	-	-	-	-	-	-	-	-	-	-	-	-	-	-	-
	5.41		81.58			90.70																				
						72.37																				
			81.58			59.04																				
			57.13			41.34																				
Northville (township)	2,017	922	709	-	-	296	-	-	-	-	-	-	-	-	-	-	-	-	-	-	-	-	-	-	-	-
	9.59		76.90			69.00																				
						41.75																				
			76.90			32.10																				
			35.15			14.68																				
MINNESOTA	260,463	139,245	96,784	1,724	495	13,036	-	3,543	11,293	-	3,995	113	101	24,551	-	2,473	11,241	5,756	-	872	-	-	349	766	-	14,565
	5.29		69.51		28.71	80.08		69.09	75.71		67.71	26.46	17.44	56.89		59.12	87.46	63.98		79.42			75.38	83.26		79.23
						13.47		3.66	11.67		4.13	22.83	20.40	25.37		2.56	11.61	5.95		0.90			0.36	0.79		15.05
			69.51		28.71	9.36		2.54	8.11		2.87	6.55	5.86	17.63		1.78	8.07	4.13		0.63			0.25	0.55		10.46
			37.16		0.19	5.00		1.36	4.34		1.53	0.04	0.04	9.43		0.95	4.32	2.21		0.33			0.13	0.29		5.59
Anoka County	10,771	4,992	3,456	-	-	693	-	-	309	-	240	-	-	342	-	-	639	-	-	-	-	-	-	-	-	687
	3.61		69.23			76.24			70.23		63.16			59.89			90.25									72.47
						20.05			8.94		6.94			9.90			18.49									19.88
			69.23			13.88			6.19		4.81			6.85			12.80									13.76
			32.09			6.43			2.87		2.23			3.18			5.93									6.38
Columbia Heights (city)	1,547	672	490	-	-	-	-	-	-	-	-	-	-	-	-	-	-	-	-	-	-	-	-	-	-	-
	8.36		72.92																							
			72.92																							
			31.67																							
Blue Earth County	1,628	883	794	-	-	-	-	-	-	-	-	-	-	-	-	-	-	-	-	-	-	-	-	-	-	-
	2.91		89.92																							
			89.92																							
			48.77																							

Notes: Please refer to the User's Guide for an explanation of data; data is arranged alphabetically by state, then county, then city within each county; table includes counties with populations greater than 49,999 unless noted and cities with populations greater than 9,999 whose Asian and/or NHPI population rates are greater than the national average; (1) Native Hawaiian and other Pacific Islander; (2) excludes Taiwanese; (3) includes Chamorro; (4) county does not meet population threshold but is shown in order to allow inclusion of city

Place	Total foreign-born population	Total Asian population	Asians who are foreign born	Total NHPI[1] population	NHPIs[1] who are foreign born	Asian Indian	Bangladeshi	Cambodian	Chinese[2]	Fijian	Filipino	Guamanian[3]	Hawaiian, Native	Hmong	Indonesian	Japanese	Korean	Laotian	Malaysian	Pakistani	Samoan	Sri Lankan	Taiwanese	Thai	Tongan	Vietnamese
Carver County	2,399 3.42	1,039	761 73.24 73.24 31.72	-	-	-	-	-	-	-	-	-	-	-	-	-	-	-	-	-	-	-	-	-	-	-
Clay County	1,339 2.61	394	302 76.65 76.65 22.55	-	-	-	-	-	-	-	-	-	-	-	-	-	-	-	-	-	-	-	-	-	-	-
Crow Wing County	655 1.19	218	171 78.44 78.44 26.11	-	-	-	-	-	-	-	-	-	-	-	-	-	-	-	-	-	-	-	-	-	-	-
Dakota County	18,049 5.07	9,152	6,736 73.60 73.60 37.32	-	-	1,267 74.75 18.81 13.84 7.02	-	296 65.63 4.39 3.23 1.64	1,017 73.64 15.10 11.11 5.63	-	522 63.89 7.75 5.70 2.89	-	-	-	-	-	972 87.33 14.43 10.62 5.39	492 67.49 7.30 5.38 2.73	-	-	-	-	-	-	-	1,368 77.95 20.31 14.95 7.58
Eagan (city)	4,874 7.66	3,087	2,267 73.44 73.44 46.51	-	-	533 79.79 23.51 17.27 10.94	-	-	367 73.40 16.19 11.89 7.53	-	-	-	-	-	-	-	-	-	-	-	-	-	-	-	-	411 72.11 18.13 13.31 8.43
Hennepin County	110,496 9.90	53,136	37,893 71.31 71.31 34.29	583	313 53.69 53.69 0.28	6,466 82.84 17.06 12.17 5.85	-	1,308 73.15 3.45 2.46 1.18	4,629 76.61 12.22 8.71 4.19	-	1,324 70.61 3.49 2.49 1.20	-	-	7,389 55.46 19.50 13.91 6.69	-	946 56.21 2.50 1.78 0.86	4,072 86.11 10.75 7.66 3.69	2,910 66.00 7.68 5.48 2.63	-	325 79.66 0.86 0.61 0.29	-	-	-	-	-	6,612 81.13 17.45 12.44 5.98
Bloomington (city)	6,593 7.74	4,254	3,351 78.77 78.77 50.83	-	-	491 90.76 14.65 11.54 7.45	-	372 76.07 11.10 8.74 5.64	666 83.67 19.87 15.66 10.10	-	-	-	-	-	-	-	398 78.97 11.88 9.36 6.04	-	-	-	-	-	-	-	-	1,029 87.87 30.71 24.19 15.61
Brooklyn Center (city)	3,284 11.30	2,606	1,414 54.26 54.26 43.06	-	-	-	-	-	-	-	-	-	-	664 45.73 46.96 25.48 20.22	-	-	-	211 65.94 14.92 8.10 6.43	-	-	-	-	-	-	-	-
Brooklyn Park (city)	8,951 13.28	6,200	4,258 68.68 68.68 47.57	-	-	637 69.69 14.96 10.27 7.12	-	-	-	-	-	-	-	656 59.64 15.41 10.58 7.33	-	-	-	908 62.84 21.32 14.65 10.14	-	-	-	-	-	-	-	1,121 75.44 26.33 18.08 12.52
Eden Prairie (city)	4,866 8.86	2,793	2,121 75.94 75.94 43.59	-	-	530 90.44 24.99 18.98 10.89	-	-	420 62.41 19.80 15.04 8.63	-	-	-	-	-	-	-	-	-	-	-	-	-	-	-	-	418 78.87 19.71 14.97 8.59

Notes: Please refer to the User's Guide for an explanation of data; data is arranged alphabetically by state, then county, then city within each county; table includes counties with populations greater than 49,999 unless noted and cities with populations greater than 9,999 whose Asian and/or NHPI population rates are greater than the national average; (1) Native Hawaiian and other Pacific Islander; (2) excludes Taiwanese; (3) includes Chamorro; (4) county does not meet population threshold but is shown in order to allow inclusion of city

Place	Total foreign-born population	Total Asian population	Asians who are foreign born	Total NHPI[1] population	NHPIs[1] who are foreign born	Asian Indian	Bangladeshi	Cambodian	Chinese[2]	Fijian	Filipino	Guamanian[3]	Hawaiian, Native	Hmong	Indonesian	Japanese	Korean	Laotian	Malaysian	Pakistani	Samoan	Sri Lankan	Taiwanese	Thai	Tongan	Vietnamese
Hopkins (city)	2,395 14.04	964	873 90.56 90.56 36.45	-	-	429 93.26 49.14 44.50 17.91	-	-	-	-	-	-	-	-	-	-	-	-	-	-	-	-	-	-	-	-
Minneapolis (city)	55,475 14.51	23,912	16,224 67.85 67.85 29.25	-	-	1,736 82.90 10.70 7.26 3.13	-	323 64.86 1.99 1.35 0.58	1,683 81.54 10.37 7.04 3.03	-	483 66.44 2.98 2.02 0.87	-	-	5,770 56.20 35.56 24.13 10.40	-	535 70.21 3.30 2.24 0.96	1,346 82.93 8.30 5.63 2.43	1,045 64.23 6.44 4.37 1.88	-	-	-	-	-	-	-	2,274 81.10 14.02 9.51 4.10
Plymouth (city)	4,856 7.37	2,463	1,823 74.02 74.02 37.54	-	-	751 81.72 41.20 30.49 15.47	-	-	274 64.17 15.03 11.12 5.64	-	-	-	-	-	-	-	285 78.95 15.63 11.57 5.87	-	-	-	-	-	-	-	-	-
Richfield (city)	3,917 11.37	1,760	1,377 78.24 78.24 35.15	-	-	-	-	-	-	-	-	-	-	-	-	-	-	-	-	-	-	-	-	-	-	321 76.25 23.31 18.24 8.20
Nobles County[4]	1,881 9.03	774	484 62.53 62.53 25.73	-	-	-	-	-	-	-	-	-	-	-	-	-	-	246 60.89 50.83 31.78 13.08	-	-	-	-	-	-	-	-
Worthington (city)	1,759 15.58	706	448 63.46 63.46 25.47	-	-	-	-	-	-	-	-	-	-	-	-	-	-	230 61.99 51.34 32.58 13.08	-	-	-	-	-	-	-	-
Olmsted County	9,758 7.85	5,329	3,872 72.66 72.66 39.68	-	-	768 75.74 19.83 14.41 7.87	-	457 63.30 11.80 8.58 4.68	457 77.59 11.80 8.58 4.68	-	-	-	-	226 56.50 5.84 4.24 2.32	-	355 82.75 9.17 6.66 3.64	429 87.20 11.08 8.05 4.40	266 60.45 6.87 4.99 2.73	-	-	-	-	-	-	-	570 78.51 14.72 10.70 5.84
Rochester (city)	8,598 10.07	4,806	3,537 73.60 73.60 41.14	-	-	740 77.24 20.92 15.40 8.61	-	355 63.51 10.04 7.39 4.13	432 78.40 12.21 8.99 5.02	-	-	-	-	226 56.50 6.39 4.70 2.63	-	-	330 87.07 9.33 6.87 3.84	264 60.27 7.46 5.49 3.07	-	-	-	-	-	-	-	539 77.55 15.24 11.22 6.27
Otter Tail County	1,166 2.04	171	113 66.08 66.08 9.69	-	-	-	-	-	-	-	-	-	-	-	-	-	-	-	-	-	-	-	-	-	-	-
Ramsey County	54,263 10.62	44,030	28,335 64.35 64.35 52.22	-	-	1,844 79.52 6.51 4.19 3.40	-	784 70.63 2.77 1.78 1.44	2,587 74.77 9.13 5.88 4.77	-	580 64.73 2.05 1.32 1.07	-	-	15,382 57.78 54.29 34.94 28.35	-	276 50.92 0.97 0.63 0.51	1,767 88.84 6.24 4.01 3.26	597 63.99 2.11 1.36 1.10	-	-	-	-	-	-	-	2,800 77.76 9.88 6.36 5.16

Notes: Please refer to the User's Guide for an explanation of data; data is arranged alphabetically by state, then county, then city within each county; table includes counties with populations greater than 49,999 unless noted and cities with populations greater than 9,999 whose Asian and/or NHPI population rates are greater than the national average; (1) Native Hawaiian and other Pacific Islander; (2) excludes Taiwanese; (3) includes Chamorro; (4) county does not meet population threshold but is shown in order to allow inclusion of city

Place	Total foreign-born population	Total Asian population	Asians who are foreign born	Total NHPI[1] population	NHPIs[1] who are foreign born	Asian Indian	Bangladeshi	Cambodian	Chinese[2]	Fijian	Filipino	Guamanian[3]	Hawaiian, Native	Hmong	Indonesian	Japanese	Korean	Laotian	Malaysian	Pakistani	Samoan	Sri Lankan	Taiwanese	Thai	Tongan	Vietnamese
Maplewood (city)	1,598 4.57	1,358	882 64.95 64.95 55.19	-	-	-	-	-	225 73.29 25.51 16.57 14.08	-	-	-	-	166 41.92 18.82 12.22 10.39	-	-	-	-	-	-	-	-	-	-	-	-
New Brighton (city)	1,515 6.81	916	716 78.17 78.17 47.26	-	-	-	-	-	-	-	-	-	-	-	-	-	-	-	-	-	-	-	-	-	-	-
Roseville (city)	2,197 6.51	1,624	1,195 73.58 73.58 54.39	-	-	-	-	-	487 71.72 40.75 29.99 22.17	-	-	-	-	-	-	-	-	-	-	-	-	-	-	-	-	-
St. Paul (city)	41,138 14.33	35,316	21,860 61.90 61.90 53.14	-	-	574 67.61 2.63 1.63 1.40	-	633 68.21 2.90 1.79 1.54	679 69.00 3.11 1.92 1.65	-	329 61.15 1.51 0.93 0.80	-	-	14,875 58.37 68.05 42.12 36.16	-	-	839 91.89 3.84 2.38 2.04	542 62.95 2.48 1.53 1.32	-	-	-	-	-	-	-	2,012 78.81 9.20 5.70 4.89
Vadnais Heights (city)	661 5.06	567	365 64.37 64.37 55.22	-	-	-	-	-	-	-	-	-	-	-	-	-	-	-	-	-	-	-	-	-	-	-
Rice County	2,697 4.76	885	600 67.80 67.80 22.25	-	-	-	-	-	-	-	-	-	-	-	-	-	-	-	-	-	-	-	-	-	-	-
St. Louis County	3,897 1.94	1,504	1,135 75.47 75.47 29.12	-	-	-	-	-	-	-	-	-	-	-	-	-	311 86.15 27.40 20.68 7.98	-	-	-	-	-	-	-	-	-
Scott County	3,620 4.04	1,867	1,341 71.83 71.83 37.04	-	-	-	-	247 68.23 18.42 13.23 6.82	-	-	-	-	-	-	-	-	-	-	-	-	-	-	-	-	-	241 61.17 17.97 12.91 6.66
Savage (city)	1,282 6.05	1,101	817 74.21 74.21 63.73	-	-	-	-	-	-	-	-	-	-	-	-	-	-	-	-	-	-	-	-	-	-	-
Sherburne County	987 1.53	374	244 65.24 65.24 24.72	-	-	-	-	-	-	-	-	-	-	-	-	-	-	-	-	-	-	-	-	-	-	-

Notes: Please refer to the User's Guide for an explanation of data; data is arranged alphabetically by state, then county, then city within each county; table includes counties with populations greater than 49,999 unless noted and cities with populations greater than 9,999 whose Asian and/or NHPI population rates are greater than the national average; (1) Native Hawaiian and other Pacific Islander; (2) excludes Taiwanese; (3) includes Chamorro; (4) county does not meet population threshold but is shown in order to allow inclusion of city

Place	Total foreign-born population	Total Asian population	Asians who are foreign born	Total NHPI[1] population	NHPIs[1] who are foreign born	Asian Indian	Bangladeshi	Cambodian	Chinese[2]	Fijian	Filipino	Guamanian[3]	Hawaiian, Native	Hmong	Indonesian	Japanese	Korean	Laotian	Malaysian	Pakistani	Samoan	Sri Lankan	Taiwanese	Thai	Tongan	Vietnamese
Stearns County	3,148 2.36	1,796	1,529 85.13 85.13 48.57	-	-	-	-	-	-	-	-	-	-	-	-	-	-	-	-	-	-	-	-	-	-	548 89.84 35.84 30.51 17.41
Washington County	6,860 3.41	4,362	2,886 66.16 66.16 42.07	-	-	414 72.76 14.35 9.49 6.03	-	-	486 68.84 16.84 11.14 7.08	-	-	-	-	371 48.12 12.86 8.51 5.41	-	-	520 76.47 18.02 11.92 7.58	-	-	-	-	-	-	-	-	381 72.02 13.20 8.73 5.55
Woodbury (city)	3,077 6.62	2,382	1,529 64.19 64.19 49.69	-	-	290 67.92 18.97 12.17 9.42	-	-	224 59.42 14.65 9.40 7.28	-	-	-	-	185 52.41 12.10 7.77 6.01	-	-	-	-	-	-	-	-	-	-	-	-
Wright County	960 1.07	196	170 86.73 86.73 17.71	-	-	-	-	-	-	-	-	-	-	-	-	-	-	-	-	-	-	-	-	-	-	-
MISSISSIPPI	39,908 1.40	17,709	12,439 70.24 70.24 31.17	677	32 4.73 4.73 0.08	2,517 75.70 20.23 14.21 6.31	-	-	1,859 69.73 14.94 10.50 4.66	-	1,912 73.00 15.37 10.80 4.79	-	-	-	-	444 82.53 3.57 2.51 1.11	1,120 81.28 9.00 6.32 2.81	-	-	-	-	-	-	-	-	3,308 61.98 26.59 18.68 8.29
DeSoto County	2,051 1.91	676	488 72.19 72.19 23.79	-	-	-	-	-	-	-	-	-	-	-	-	-	-	-	-	-	-	-	-	-	-	-
Forrest County	1,456 2.01	626	515 82.27 82.27 35.37	-	-	-	-	-	-	-	-	-	-	-	-	-	-	-	-	-	-	-	-	-	-	-
Harrison County	6,785 3.58	4,976	3,206 64.43 64.43 47.25	-	-	-	-	-	-	-	536 65.85 16.72 10.77 7.90	-	-	-	-	-	-	-	-	-	-	-	-	-	-	1,635 58.46 51.00 32.86 24.10
Biloxi (city)	2,715 5.35	2,451	1,553 63.36 63.36 57.20	-	-	-	-	-	-	-	268 62.33 17.26 10.93 9.87	-	-	-	-	-	-	-	-	-	-	-	-	-	-	892 60.15 57.44 36.39 32.85
Hinds County	2,682 1.07	1,315	928 70.57 70.57 34.60	-	-	485 83.62 52.26 36.88 18.08	-	-	-	-	-	-	-	-	-	-	-	-	-	-	-	-	-	-	-	-

Notes: Please refer to the User's Guide for an explanation of data; data is arranged alphabetically by state, then county, then city within each county; table includes counties with populations greater than 49,999 unless noted and cities with populations greater than 9,999 whose Asian and/or NHPI population rates are greater than the national average; (1) Native Hawaiian and other Pacific Islander; (2) excludes Taiwanese; (3) includes Chamorro; (4) county does not meet population threshold but is shown in order to allow inclusion of city

Place	Total foreign-born population	Total Asian population	Asians who are foreign born	Total NHPI[1] population	NHPIs[1] who are foreign born	Asian Indian	Bangladeshi	Cambodian	Chinese[2]	Fijian	Filipino	Guamanian[3]	Hawaiian, Native	Hmong	Indonesian	Japanese	Korean	Laotian	Malaysian	Pakistani	Samoan	Sri Lankan	Taiwanese	Thai	Tongan	Vietnamese
	3,484	1,945	1,320	-	-	-	-	-	-	-	-	-	-	-	-	-	-	-	-	-	-	-	-	-	-	614
	2.65		67.87																							57.92
Jackson County																										46.52
			67.87																							31.57
			37.89																							17.62
	1,240	585	478	-	-	-	-	-	-	-	-	-	-	-	-	-	-	-	-	-	-	-	-	-	-	-
	1.66		81.71																							
Madison County																										
			81.71																							
			38.55																							
	1,421	1,077	905	-	-	-	-	-	-	-	-	-	-	-	-	-	-	-	-	-	-	-	-	-	-	-
	3.31		84.03																							
Oktibbeha County[4]																										
			84.03																							
			63.69																							
	1,021	798	661	-	-	-	-	-	-	-	-	-	-	-	-	-	-	-	-	-	-	-	-	-	-	-
	4.63		82.83																							
Starkville (city)																										
			82.83																							
			64.74																							
	1,809	554	480	-	-	-	-	-	-	-	-	-	-	-	-	-	-	-	-	-	-	-	-	-	-	-
	1.57		86.64																							
Rankin County																										
			86.64																							
			26.53																							
	151,196	60,429	44,237	3,071	714	8,491	-	570	9,845	-	5,079	69	27	-	-	2,212	5,021	532	-	824	211	-	762	1,034	-	8,007
	2.70		73.20		23.25	71.68		64.85	77.12		70.02	11.27	3.88			64.58	77.16	74.30		78.25	21.02		78.40	75.36		76.21
MISSOURI						19.19		1.29	22.26		11.48	9.66	3.78			5.00	11.35	1.20		1.86	29.55		1.72	2.34		18.10
			73.20		23.25	14.05		0.94	16.29		8.40	2.25	0.88			3.66	8.31	0.88		1.36	6.87		1.26	1.71		13.25
			29.26		0.47	5.62		0.38	6.51		3.36	0.05	0.02			1.46	3.32	0.35		0.54	0.14		0.50	0.68		5.30
	6,142	3,865	2,804	-	-	547	-	-	931	-	-	-	-	-	-	-	409	-	-	-	-	-	-	-	-	-
	4.53		72.55			67.70			77.45								79.73									
Boone County						19.51			33.20								14.59									
			72.55			14.15			24.09								10.58									
			45.65			8.91			15.16								6.66									
	5,442	3,574	2,595	-	-	527	-	-	895	-	-	-	-	-	-	-	337	-	-	-	-	-	-	-	-	-
	6.42		72.61			67.48			77.69								79.29									
Columbia (city)						20.31			34.49								12.99									
			72.61			14.75			25.04								9.43									
			47.68			9.68			16.45								6.19									
	913	446	349	-	-	-	-	-	-	-	-	-	-	-	-	-	-	-	-	-	-	-	-	-	-	-
	1.33		78.25																							
Cape Girardeau County																										
			78.25																							
			38.23																							
	1,312	346	270	-	-	-	-	-	-	-	-	-	-	-	-	-	-	-	-	-	-	-	-	-	-	-
	1.60		78.03																							
Cass County																										
			78.03																							
			20.58																							

Notes: Please refer to the User's Guide for an explanation of data; data is arranged alphabetically by state, then county, then city within each county; table includes counties with populations greater than 49,999 unless noted and cities with populations greater than 9,999 whose Asian and/or NHPI population rates are greater than the national average; (1) Native Hawaiian and other Pacific Islander; (2) excludes Taiwanese; (3) includes Chamorro; (4) county does not meet population threshold but is shown in order to allow inclusion of city

Place	Total foreign-born population	Total Asian population	Asians who are foreign born	Total NHPI[1] population	NHPIs[1] who are foreign born	Asian Indian	Bangladeshi	Cambodian	Chinese[2]	Fijian	Filipino	Guamanian[3]	Hawaiian, Native	Hmong	Indonesian	Japanese	Korean	Laotian	Malaysian	Pakistani	Samoan	Sri Lankan	Taiwanese	Thai	Tongan	Vietnamese
Clay County	5,261 2.86	2,165	1,530 70.67 70.67 29.08	-	-	270 66.67 17.65 12.47 5.13	-	-	-	-	-	-	-	-	-	-	-	-	-	-	-	-	-	-	-	462 74.88 30.20 21.34 8.78
Cole County	1,570 2.20	661	485 73.37 73.37 30.89	-	-	-	-	-	-	-	-	-	-	-	-	-	-	-	-	-	-	-	-	-	-	-
Franklin County	750 0.80	326	218 66.87 66.87 29.07	-	-	-	-	-	-	-	-	-	-	-	-	-	-	-	-	-	-	-	-	-	-	-
Greene County	4,487 1.87	2,207	1,569 71.09 71.09 34.97	-	-	-	-	-	258 70.88 16.44 11.69 5.75	-	-	-	-	-	-	-	263 73.26 16.76 11.92 5.86	-	-	-	-	-	-	-	-	292 70.02 18.61 13.23 6.51
Jackson County	28,320 4.32	8,646	6,222 71.96 71.96 21.97	926	245 26.46 26.46 0.87	721 67.38 11.59 8.34 2.55	-	-	1,033 80.89 16.60 11.95 3.65	-	931 72.91 14.96 10.77 3.29	-	-	-	-	249 61.03 4.00 2.88 0.88	454 79.93 7.30 5.25 1.60	-	-	-	126 26.81 51.43 13.61 0.44	-	-	-	-	2,134 74.10 34.30 24.68 7.54
Independence (city)	2,953 2.61	1,022	689 67.42 67.42 23.33	405	88 21.73 21.73 2.98	-	-	-	-	-	-	-	-	-	-	-	-	-	-	-	-	-	-	-	-	-
Jasper County	2,747 2.62	598	498 83.28 83.28 18.13	-	-	-	-	-	-	-	-	-	-	-	-	-	-	-	-	-	-	-	-	-	-	-
Jefferson County	1,943 0.98	745	540 72.48 72.48 27.79	-	-	-	-	-	-	-	-	-	-	-	-	-	-	-	-	-	-	-	-	-	-	-
Newton County	748 1.42	177	128 72.32 72.32 17.11	-	-	-	-	-	-	-	-	-	-	-	-	-	-	-	-	-	-	-	-	-	-	-
Phelps County[4]	1,586 3.98	836	696 83.25 83.25 43.88	-	-	261 80.31 37.50 31.22 16.46	-	-	-	-	-	-	-	-	-	-	-	-	-	-	-	-	-	-	-	-

Notes: Please refer to the User's Guide for an explanation of data; data is arranged alphabetically by state, then county, then city within each county; table includes counties with populations greater than 49,999 unless noted and cities with populations greater than 9,999 whose Asian and/or NHPI population rates are greater than the national average; (1) Native Hawaiian and other Pacific Islander; (2) excludes Taiwanese; (3) includes Chamorro; (4) county does not meet population threshold but is shown in order to allow inclusion of city

Place	Total foreign-born population	Total Asian population	Asians who are foreign born	Total NHPI[1] population	NHPIs[1] who are foreign born	Asian Indian	Bangladeshi	Cambodian	Chinese[2]	Fijian	Filipino	Guamanian[3]	Hawaiian, Native	Hmong	Indonesian	Japanese	Korean	Laotian	Malaysian	Pakistani	Samoan	Sri Lankan	Taiwanese	Thai	Tongan	Vietnamese
Rolla (city)	1,257 7.60	684	595 86.99 86.99 47.33	-	-	-	-	-	-	-	-	-	-	-	-	-	-	-	-	-	-	-	-	-	-	-
Platte County	2,742 3.72	1,115	782 70.13 70.13 28.52	-	-	-	-	-	-	-	-	-	-	-	-	-	-	-	-	-	-	-	-	-	-	-
St. Charles County	5,841 2.06	2,392	1,698 70.99 70.99 29.07	-	-	407 70.54 23.97 17.02 6.97	-	-	324 78.07 19.08 13.55 5.55	-	267 66.25 15.72 11.16 4.57	-	-	-	-	-	-	-	-	-	-	-	-	-	-	-
Saint Louis Independent City	19,542 5.61	7,075	5,149 72.78 72.78 26.35	-	-	416 56.45 8.08 5.88 2.13	-	-	822 72.87 15.96 11.62 4.21	-	377 68.80 7.32 5.33 1.93	-	-	-	-	-	-	-	-	-	-	-	-	-	-	2,603 80.86 50.55 36.79 13.32
St. Louis County	42,702 4.20	21,534	16,133 74.92 74.92 37.78	437	55 12.59 12.59 0.13	4,252 74.61 26.36 19.75 9.96	-	-	4,576 76.23 28.36 21.25 10.72	-	1,422 70.68 8.81 6.60 3.33	-	-	-	-	803 66.31 4.98 3.73 1.88	1,976 77.61 12.25 9.18 4.63	-	-	505 88.75 3.13 2.35 1.18	-	-	489 75.46 3.03 2.27 1.15	351 92.86 2.18 1.63 0.82	-	1,097 74.73 6.80 5.09 2.57
Chesterfield (city)	3,736 7.95	2,442	1,767 72.36 72.36 47.30	-	-	432 65.16 24.45 17.69 11.56	-	-	578 72.89 32.71 23.67 15.47	-	-	-	-	-	-	-	-	-	-	-	-	-	-	-	-	-
Clayton (city)	1,061 8.27	788	545 69.16 69.16 51.37	-	-	-	-	-	-	-	-	-	-	-	-	-	-	-	-	-	-	-	-	-	-	-
Creve Coeur (city)	1,476 9.06	872	659 75.57 75.57 44.65	-	-	-	-	-	-	-	-	-	-	-	-	-	-	-	-	-	-	-	-	-	-	-
Manchester (city)	1,383 7.25	935	677 72.41 72.41 48.95	-	-	-	-	-	-	-	-	-	-	-	-	-	-	-	-	-	-	-	-	-	-	-
Maryland Heights (city)	2,656 10.24	1,788	1,564 87.47 87.47 58.89	-	-	617 88.65 39.45 34.51 23.23	-	-	405 79.10 25.90 22.65 15.25	-	-	-	-	-	-	-	-	-	-	-	-	-	-	-	-	-

Notes: Please refer to the User's Guide for an explanation of data; data is arranged alphabetically by state, then county, then city within each county; table includes counties with populations greater than 49,999 unless noted and cities with populations greater than 9,999 whose Asian and/or NHPI population rates are greater than the national average; (1) Native Hawaiian and other Pacific Islander; (2) excludes Taiwanese; (3) includes Chamorro; (4) county does not meet population threshold but is shown in order to allow inclusion of city

Place	Total foreign-born population	Total Asian population	Asians who are foreign born	Total NHPI[1] population	NHPIs[1] who are foreign born	Asian Indian	Bangladeshi	Cambodian	Chinese[2]	Fijian	Filipino	Guamanian[3]	Hawaiian, Native	Hmong	Indonesian	Japanese	Korean	Laotian	Malaysian	Pakistani	Samoan	Sri Lankan	Taiwanese	Thai	Tongan	Vietnamese
Town and Country (city)	1,079 9.92	829	641 77.32 77.32 59.41	-	-	305 80.05 47.58 36.79 28.27	-	-	-	-	-	-	-	-	-	-	-	-	-	-	-	-	-	-	-	-
MONTANA	16,396 1.82	4,363	2,671 61.22 61.22 16.29	447	47 10.51 10.51 0.29	276 61.33 10.33 6.33 1.68	-	-	455 70.00 17.03 10.43 2.78	-	458 58.34 17.15 10.50 2.79	-	0 0.00 0.00 0.00 0.00	-	-	365 42.94 13.67 8.37 2.23	713 84.98 26.69 16.34 4.35	-	-	-	-	-	-	-	-	-
Cascade County	1,903 2.37	498	326 65.46 65.46 17.13	-	-	-	-	-	-	-	-	-	-	-	-	-	-	-	-	-	-	-	-	-	-	-
Flathead County	1,585 2.13	251	188 74.90 74.90 11.86	-	-	-	-	-	-	-	-	-	-	-	-	-	-	-	-	-	-	-	-	-	-	-
Gallatin County	1,838 2.71	693	430 62.05 62.05 23.39	-	-	-	-	-	-	-	-	-	-	-	-	-	-	-	-	-	-	-	-	-	-	-
Missoula County	2,196 2.29	919	544 59.19 59.19 24.77	-	-	-	-	-	-	-	-	-	-	-	-	-	-	-	-	-	-	-	-	-	-	-
Yellowstone County	1,777 1.37	666	426 63.96 63.96 23.97	-	-	-	-	-	-	-	-	-	-	-	-	-	-	-	-	-	-	-	-	-	-	-
NEBRASKA	74,638 4.36	21,126	16,313 77.22 77.22 21.86	673	186 27.64 27.64 0.25	2,667 83.37 16.35 12.62 3.57	-	-	2,317 81.38 14.20 10.97 3.10	-	1,457 70.56 8.93 6.90 1.95	-	-	-	-	761 55.03 4.66 3.60 1.02	1,868 83.80 11.45 8.84 2.50	577 70.71 3.54 2.73 0.77	-	-	-	-	-	382 82.86 2.34 1.81 0.51	-	5,253 78.64 32.20 24.87 7.04
Douglas County	27,418 5.91	7,912	6,044 76.39 76.39 22.04	-	-	1,658 81.31 27.43 20.96 6.05	-	-	1,084 78.04 17.94 13.70 3.95	-	611 69.04 10.11 7.72 2.23	-	-	-	-	425 61.15 7.03 5.37 1.55	672 82.15 11.12 8.49 2.45	-	-	-	-	-	-	-	-	964 75.20 15.95 12.18 3.52
Hall County	4,467 8.34	544	428 78.68 78.68 9.58	-	-	-	-	-	-	-	-	-	-	-	-	-	-	-	-	-	-	-	-	-	-	-

Notes: Please refer to the User's Guide for an explanation of data; data is arranged alphabetically by state, then county, then city within each county; table includes counties with populations greater than 49,999 unless noted and cities with populations greater than 9,999 whose Asian and/or NHPI population rates are greater than the national average; (1) Native Hawaiian and other Pacific Islander; (2) excludes Taiwanese; (3) includes Chamorro; (4) county does not meet population threshold but is shown in order to allow inclusion of city

Place	Total foreign-born population	Total Asian population	Asians who are foreign born	Total NHPI[1] population	NHPIs[1] who are foreign born	Asian Indian	Bangladeshi	Cambodian	Chinese[2]	Fijian	Filipino	Guamanian[3]	Hawaiian, Native	Hmong	Indonesian	Japanese	Korean	Laotian	Malaysian	Pakistani	Samoan	Sri Lankan	Taiwanese	Thai	Tongan	Vietnamese
Lancaster County	13,570	6,700	5,445	-	-	565	-	-	880	-	-	-	-	-	-	-	323	-	-	-	-	-	-	-	-	3,023
	5.42		81.27			86.92			91.00								88.98									80.06
						10.38			16.16								5.93									55.52
			81.27			8.43			13.13								4.82									45.12
			40.13			4.16			6.48								2.38									22.28
Sarpy County	4,495	2,230	1,585	-	-	-	-	-	-	-	379	-	-	-	-	-	327	-	-	-	-	-	-	-	-	256
	3.67		71.08								76.88						71.40									60.66
											23.91						20.63									16.15
			71.08								17.00						14.66									11.48
			35.26								8.43						7.27									5.70
NEVADA	316,593	89,121	61,358	7,806	1,295	3,691	-	581	9,419	-	28,837	149	82	-	-	3,627	5,669	849	-	426	315	-	501	2,314	387	3,253
	15.84		68.85		16.59	75.95		78.73	69.56		71.16	13.08	2.41			43.20	74.77	71.40		80.08	20.10		83.92	77.73	48.99	79.44
						6.02		0.95	15.35		47.00	11.51	6.33			5.91	9.24	1.38		0.69	24.32		0.82	3.77	29.88	5.30
			68.85		16.59	4.14		0.65	10.57		32.36	1.91	1.05			4.07	6.36	0.95		0.48	4.04		0.56	2.60	4.96	3.65
			19.38		0.41	1.17		0.18	2.98		9.11	0.05	0.03			1.15	1.79	0.27		0.13	0.10		0.16	0.73	0.12	1.03
Carson City Independent City	5,205	1,070	702	-	-	-	-	-	-	-	227	-	-	-	-	-	-	-	-	-	-	-	-	-	-	-
	9.92		65.61								82.25															
											32.34															
			65.61								21.21															
			13.49								4.36															
Clark County	247,751	71,495	49,190	5,918	674	2,208	-	561	7,542	-	23,057	138	74	-	-	2,851	4,905	837	-	-	191	-	351	2,076	-	2,658
	18.01		68.80		11.39	75.62		78.13	70.29		70.67	14.41	2.40			42.59	75.15	71.11			17.11		81.82	79.24		80.74
						4.49		1.14	15.33		46.87	20.47	10.98			5.80	9.97	1.70			28.34		0.71	4.22		5.40
			68.80		11.39	3.09		0.78	10.55		32.25	2.33	1.25			3.99	6.86	1.17			3.23		0.49	2.90		3.72
			19.85		0.27	0.89		0.23	3.04		9.31	0.06	0.03			1.15	1.98	0.34			0.08		0.14	0.84		1.07
Enterprise (cdp)	1,551	701	456	-	-	-	-	-	-	-	-	-	-	-	-	-	-	-	-	-	-	-	-	-	-	-
	10.74		65.05																							
			65.05																							
			29.40																							
Henderson (city)	14,678	6,683	4,507	758	46	414	-	-	487	-	1,879	-	10	-	-	378	589	-	-	-	-	-	-	-	-	-
	8.34		67.44		6.07	88.84			60.65		68.75		2.26			48.65	71.74									
						9.19			10.81		41.69		21.74			8.39	13.07									
			67.44		6.07	6.19			7.29		28.12		1.32			5.66	8.81									
			30.71		0.31	2.82			3.32		12.80		0.07			2.58	4.01									
Las Vegas (city)	90,656	21,634	14,413	1,673	249	775	-	-	1,693	-	7,617	-	45	-	-	955	1,011	-	-	-	-	-	-	564	-	552
	18.93		66.62		14.88	76.96			62.24		70.59		5.76			38.93	70.45							80.57		90.49
						5.38			11.75		52.85		18.07			6.63	7.01							3.91		3.83
			66.62		14.88	3.58			7.83		35.21		2.69			4.41	4.67							2.61		2.55
			15.90		0.27	0.85			1.87		8.40		0.05			1.05	1.12							0.62		0.61
North Las Vegas (city)	28,948	3,845	2,567	747	165	-	-	-	-	-	1,511	-	-	-	-	-	-	-	-	-	-	-	-	-	-	-
	25.07		66.76		22.09						68.84															
											58.86															
			66.76		22.09						39.30															
			8.87		0.57						5.22															
Paradise (cdp)	42,050	12,628	9,059	841	77	473	-	-	1,446	-	4,231	-	19	-	-	525	1,121	-	-	-	-	-	-	-	-	484
	22.63		71.74		9.16	73.68			78.80		74.33		3.17			37.29	82.31									82.88
						5.22			15.96		46.70		24.68			5.80	12.37									5.34
			71.74		9.16	3.75			11.45		33.50		2.26			4.16	8.88									3.83
			21.54		0.18	1.12			3.44		10.06		0.05			1.25	2.67									1.15

Notes: Please refer to the User's Guide for an explanation of data; data is arranged alphabetically by state, then county, then city within each county; table includes counties with populations greater than 49,999 unless noted and cities with populations greater than 9,999 whose Asian and/or NHPI population rates are greater than the national average; (1) Native Hawaiian and other Pacific Islander; (2) excludes Taiwanese; (3) includes Chamorro; (4) county does not meet population threshold but is shown in order to allow inclusion of city

Place	Total foreign-born population	Total Asian population	Asians who are foreign born	Total NHPI[1] population	NHPIs[1] who are foreign born	Asian Indian	Bangladeshi	Cambodian	Chinese[2]	Fijian	Filipino	Guamanian[3]	Hawaiian, Native	Hmong	Indonesian	Japanese	Korean	Laotian	Malaysian	Pakistani	Samoan	Sri Lankan	Taiwanese	Thai	Tongan	Vietnamese
	22,316	12,944	9,166	657	35	-	-	-	3,069	-	2,661	-	-	-	-	381	1,051	-	-	-	-	-	-	391	-	733
	18.97		70.81		5.33				72.69		68.06					52.92	77.68							78.67		75.18
Spring Valley (cdp)									33.48		29.03					4.16	11.47							4.27		8.00
			70.81		5.33				23.71		20.56					2.94	8.12							3.02		5.66
			41.07		0.16				13.75		11.92					1.71	4.71							1.75		3.28
	28,380	8,644	5,939	429	53	-	-	-	349	-	3,463	-	-	-	-	305	533	-	-	-	-	-	-	-	-	-
	18.23		68.71		12.35				72.41		71.70					50.75	72.91									
Sunrise Manor (cdp)									5.88		58.31					5.14	8.97									
			68.71		12.35				4.04		40.06					3.53	6.17									
			20.93		0.19				1.23		12.20					1.07	1.88									
	6,832	1,480	1,129	-	-	-	-	-	-	-	330	-	-	-	-	-	-	-	-	-	-	-	-	-	-	-
	25.49		76.28								73.50															
Winchester (cdp)											29.23															
			76.28								22.30															
			16.53								4.83															
	47,993	14,327	10,157	1,502	569	1,220	-	-	1,622	-	4,843	-	-	-	-	582	573	-	-	-	-	-	-	-	284	536
	14.14		70.89		37.88	76.11			68.35		75.41					45.33	76.10								49.22	75.28
Washoe County						12.01			15.97		47.68					5.73	5.64								49.91	5.28
			70.89		37.88	8.52			11.32		33.80					4.06	4.00								18.91	3.74
			21.16		1.19	2.54			3.38		10.09					1.21	1.19								0.59	1.12
	31,185	9,438	6,781	952	354	757	-	-	1,026	-	3,225	-	-	-	-	473	356	-	-	-	-	-	-	-	-	316
	17.26		71.85		37.18	79.68			69.00		75.49					50.64	78.94									68.85
Reno (city)						11.16			15.13		47.56					6.98	5.25									4.66
			71.85		37.18	8.02			10.87		34.17					5.01	3.77									3.35
			21.74		1.14	2.43			3.29		10.34					1.52	1.14									1.01
	10,354	3,133	2,234	-	-	-	-	-	436	-	1,124	-	-	-	-	-	-	-	-	-	-	-	-	-	-	-
	15.56		71.31						66.56		77.30															
Sparks (city)									19.52		50.31															
			71.31						13.92		35.88															
			21.58						4.21		10.86															
	54,154	15,422	11,477	-	-	2,771	-	-	2,777	-	969	-	-	-	-	571	1,557	238	-	-	-	-	-	-	-	1,394
	4.38		74.42			77.42			71.70		76.18					61.00	79.85	64.15								82.88
NEW HAMPSHIRE						24.14			24.20		8.44					4.98	13.57	2.07								12.15
			74.42			17.97			18.01		6.28					3.70	10.10	1.54								9.04
			21.19			5.12			5.13		1.79					1.05	2.88	0.44								2.57
	1,422	347	253	-	-	-	-	-	-	-	-	-	-	-	-	-	-	-	-	-	-	-	-	-	-	-
	2.52		72.91																							
Belknap County																										
			72.91																							
			17.79																							
	1,645	486	390	-	-	-	-	-	-	-	-	-	-	-	-	-	-	-	-	-	-	-	-	-	-	-
	2.23		80.25																							
Cheshire County																										
			80.25																							
			23.71																							
	3,191	1,251	751	-	-	-	-	-	254	-	-	-	-	-	-	-	-	-	-	-	-	-	-	-	-	-
	3.90		60.03						60.19																	
Grafton County									33.82																	
			60.03						20.30																	
			23.53						7.96																	

Notes: Please refer to the User's Guide for an explanation of data; data is arranged alphabetically by state, then county, then city within each county; table includes counties with populations greater than 49,999 unless noted and cities with populations greater than 9,999 whose Asian and/or NHPI population rates are greater than the national average; (1) Native Hawaiian and other Pacific Islander; (2) excludes Taiwanese; (3) includes Chamorro; (4) county does not meet population threshold but is shown in order to allow inclusion of city

Place	Total foreign-born population	Total Asian population	Asians who are foreign born	Total NHPI[1] population	NHPIs[1] who are foreign born	Asian Indian	Bangladeshi	Cambodian	Chinese[2]	Fijian	Filipino	Guamanian[3]	Hawaiian, Native	Hmong	Indonesian	Japanese	Korean	Laotian	Malaysian	Pakistani	Samoan	Sri Lankan	Taiwanese	Thai	Tongan	Vietnamese
Hanover (town)	994	653	327	-	-	-	-	-	-	-	-	-	-	-	-	-	-	-	-	-	-	-	-	-	-	-
	9.16		50.08																							
			50.08																							
			32.90																							
Hillsborough County	25,793	7,366	5,680	-	-	1,692	-	-	1,405	-	340	-	-	-	-	-	507	-	-	-	-	-	-	-	-	923
	6.77		77.11			78.01			74.65		85.64						83.53									84.76
						29.79			24.74		5.99						8.93									16.25
			77.11			22.97			19.07		4.62						6.88									12.53
			22.02			6.56			5.45		1.32						1.97									3.58
Nashua (city)	8,778	3,387	2,671	-	-	1,137	-	-	622	-	-	-	-	-	-	-	-	-	-	-	-	-	-	-	-	-
	10.14		78.86			78.47			78.54																	
						42.57			23.29																	
			78.86			33.57			18.36																	
			30.43			12.95			7.09																	
Merrimack County	4,351	1,134	908	-	-	-	-	-	-	-	-	-	-	-	-	-	-	-	-	-	-	-	-	-	-	-
	3.19		80.07																							
			80.07																							
			20.87																							
Rockingham County	10,390	2,946	2,035	-	-	346	-	-	534	-	314	-	-	-	-	-	326	-	-	-	-	-	-	-	-	-
	3.75		69.08			72.38			63.50		75.85						77.07									
						17.00			26.24		15.43						16.02									
			69.08			11.74			18.13		10.66						11.07									
			19.59			3.33			5.14		3.02						3.14									
Strafford County	3,813	1,477	1,093	-	-	-	-	-	285	-	-	-	-	-	-	-	-	-	-	-	-	-	-	-	-	-
	3.40		74.00						82.61																	
									26.08																	
			74.00						19.30																	
			28.67						7.47																	
NEW JERSEY	1,476,327	481,794	360,165	2,709	795	130,120	1,783	529	65,665	-	65,201	226	66	-	841	10,518	50,953	277	-	9,343	157	1,009	4,360	1,377	-	11,385
	17.55		74.75		29.35	76.90	79.03	80.40	69.53		73.75	37.54	10.12		82.45	76.33	79.21	57.71		75.04	24.57	75.58	74.52	74.63		76.01
						36.13	0.50	0.15	18.23		18.10	28.43	8.30		0.23	2.92	14.15	0.08		2.59	19.75	0.28	1.21	0.38		3.16
			74.75		29.35	27.01	0.37	0.11	13.63		13.53	8.34	2.44		0.17	2.18	10.58	0.06		1.94	5.80	0.21	0.90	0.29		2.36
			24.40		0.05	8.81	0.12	0.04	4.45		4.42	0.02	<0.01		0.06	0.71	3.45	0.02		0.63	0.01	0.07	0.30	0.09		0.77
Atlantic County	29,795	12,952	10,078	-	-	3,190	335	-	1,571	-	1,727	-	-	-	-	-	487	-	-	463	-	-	-	-	-	1,529
	11.80		77.81			79.10	82.31		76.23		79.51						77.67			92.05						74.22
						31.65	3.32		15.59		17.14						4.83			4.59						15.17
			77.81			24.63	2.59		12.13		13.33						3.76			3.57						11.81
			33.82			10.71	1.12		5.27		5.80						1.63			1.55						5.13
Atlantic City (city)	10,009	4,131	3,494	-	-	819	-	-	610	-	434	-	-	-	-	-	-	-	-	-	-	-	-	-	-	932
	24.70		84.58			90.50			84.72		84.93															78.52
						23.44			17.46		12.42															26.67
			84.58			19.83			14.77		10.51															22.56
			34.91			8.18			6.09		4.34															9.31
Brigantine (city)	1,549	780	631	-	-	-	-	-	-	-	-	-	-	-	-	-	-	-	-	-	-	-	-	-	-	-
	12.30		80.90																							
			80.90																							
			40.74																							

Notes: Please refer to the User's Guide for an explanation of data; data is arranged alphabetically by state, then county, then city within each county; table includes counties with populations greater than 49,999 unless noted and cities with populations greater than 9,999 whose Asian and/or NHPI population rates are greater than the national average; (1) Native Hawaiian and other Pacific Islander; (2) excludes Taiwanese; (3) includes Chamorro; (4) county does not meet population threshold but is shown in order to allow inclusion of city

Place	Total foreign-born population	Total Asian population	Asians who are foreign born	Total NHPI[1] population	NHPIs[1] who are foreign born	Asian Indian	Bangladeshi	Cambodian	Chinese[2]	Fijian	Filipino	Guamanian[3]	Hawaiian, Native	Hmong	Indonesian	Japanese	Korean	Laotian	Malaysian	Pakistani	Samoan	Sri Lankan	Taiwanese	Thai	Tongan	Vietnamese
Egg Harbor (township)	2,572 8.40	1,704	1,224 71.83 71.83 47.59	-	-	-	-	-	-	-	-	-	-	-	-	-	-	-	-	-	-	-	-	-	-	-
Galloway (township)	3,494 11.21	2,657	1,883 70.87 70.87 53.89	-	-	1,015 78.56 53.90 38.20 29.05	-	-	-	-	-	-	-	-	-	-	-	-	-	-	-	-	-	-	-	-
Ventnor City (city)	2,972 23.02	1,048	771 73.57 73.57 25.94	-	-	-	-	-	-	-	-	-	-	-	-	-	-	-	-	-	-	-	-	-	-	-
Bergen County	222,301 25.14	94,124	72,553 77.08 77.08 32.64	-	-	13,274 76.30 18.30 14.10 5.97	-	-	9,149 70.07 12.61 9.72 4.12	-	11,079 74.37 15.27 11.77 4.98	-	-	-	-	5,865 83.82 8.08 6.23 2.64	29,122 80.67 40.14 30.94 13.10	-	-	1,075 71.62 1.48 1.14 0.48	-	-	630 76.00 0.87 0.67 0.28	383 76.14 0.53 0.41 0.17	-	374 71.10 0.52 0.40 0.17
Bergenfield (borough)	8,437 32.14	5,347	3,962 74.10 74.10 46.96	-	-	1,080 71.52 27.26 20.20 12.80	-	-	-	-	2,386 73.92 60.22 44.62 28.28	-	-	-	-	-	-	-	-	-	-	-	-	-	-	-
Cliffside Park (borough)	9,953 43.26	2,650	2,163 81.62 81.62 21.73	-	-	-	-	-	-	-	-	-	-	-	-	393 88.12 18.17 14.83 3.95	1,216 82.05 56.22 45.89 12.22	-	-	-	-	-	-	-	-	-
Dumont (borough)	3,253 18.59	1,927	1,391 72.18 72.18 42.76	-	-	432 79.85 31.06 22.42 13.28	-	-	-	-	465 76.86 33.43 24.13 14.29	-	-	-	-	-	-	-	-	-	-	-	-	-	-	-
Elmwood Park (borough)	5,708 30.16	1,638	1,271 77.59 77.59 22.27	-	-	770 75.79 60.58 47.01 13.49	-	-	-	-	-	-	-	-	-	-	-	-	-	-	-	-	-	-	-	-
Englewood (city)	8,079 30.83	1,388	1,020 73.49 73.49 12.63	-	-	-	-	-	-	-	315 75.18 30.88 22.69 3.90	-	-	-	-	-	-	-	-	-	-	-	-	-	-	-
Fair Lawn (borough)	8,476 26.79	1,829	1,377 75.29 75.29 16.25	-	-	488 74.73 35.44 26.68 5.76	-	-	-	-	431 80.41 31.30 23.56 5.08	-	-	-	-	-	-	-	-	-	-	-	-	-	-	-

Notes: Please refer to the User's Guide for an explanation of data; data is arranged alphabetically by state, then county, then city within each county; table includes counties with populations greater than 49,999 unless noted and cities with populations greater than 9,999 whose Asian and/or NHPI population rates are greater than the national average; (1) Native Hawaiian and other Pacific Islander; (2) excludes Taiwanese; (3) includes Chamorro; (4) county does not meet population threshold but is shown in order to allow inclusion of city

Place	Total foreign-born population	Total Asian population	Asians who are foreign born	Total NHPI[1] population	NHPIs[1] who are foreign born	Asian Indian	Bangladeshi	Cambodian	Chinese[2]	Fijian	Filipino	Guamanian[3]	Hawaiian, Native	Hmong	Indonesian	Japanese	Korean	Laotian	Malaysian	Pakistani	Samoan	Sri Lankan	Taiwanese	Thai	Tongan	Vietnamese
Fairview (borough)	6,414 48.39	679	605 89.10 89.10 9.43	-	-	-	-	-	-	-	-	-	-	-	-	-	-	-	-	-	-	-	-	-	-	-
Fort Lee (borough)	15,864 44.74	11,004	8,878 80.68 80.68 55.96	-	-	480 79.21 5.41 4.36 3.03	-	-	1,272 73.78 14.33 11.56 8.02	-	-	-	-	-	-	1,682 83.76 18.95 15.29 10.60	4,834 81.78 54.45 43.93 30.47	-	-	-	-	-	-	-	-	-
Franklin Lakes (borough)	1,231 11.81	713	402 56.38 56.38 32.66	-	-	-	-	-	-	-	-	-	-	-	-	-	-	-	-	-	-	-	-	-	-	-
Glen Rock (borough)	1,276 11.05	722	548 75.90 75.90 42.95	-	-	-	-	-	-	-	-	-	-	-	-	-	-	-	-	-	-	-	-	-	-	-
Hackensack (city)	14,446 33.85	3,192	2,640 82.71 82.71 18.27	-	-	838 86.57 31.74 26.25 5.80	-	-	-	-	515 72.23 19.51 16.13 3.57	-	-	-	-	-	568 88.89 21.52 17.79 3.93	-	-	-	-	-	-	-	-	-
Hasbrouck Heights (borough)	1,977 16.95	626	484 77.32 77.32 24.48	-	-	-	-	-	-	-	-	-	-	-	-	-	-	-	-	-	-	-	-	-	-	-
Hillsdale (borough)	1,343 13.31	515	394 76.50 76.50 29.34	-	-	-	-	-	-	-	-	-	-	-	-	-	-	-	-	-	-	-	-	-	-	-
Little Ferry (borough)	3,357 31.08	1,845	1,482 80.33 80.33 44.15	-	-	337 78.01 22.74 18.27 10.04	-	-	-	-	310 80.73 20.92 16.80 9.23	-	-	-	-	-	614 83.20 41.43 33.28 18.29	-	-	-	-	-	-	-	-	-
Lodi (borough)	7,131 29.75	2,036	1,646 80.84 80.84 23.08	-	-	960 88.89 58.32 47.15 13.46	-	-	-	-	398 70.44 24.18 19.55 5.58	-	-	-	-	-	-	-	-	-	-	-	-	-	-	-
Lyndhurst (township)	3,479 17.95	1,160	847 73.02 73.02 24.35	-	-	-	-	-	-	-	-	-	-	-	-	-	-	-	-	-	-	-	-	-	-	-

Notes: Please refer to the User's Guide for an explanation of data; data is arranged alphabetically by state, then county, then city within each county; table includes counties with populations greater than 49,999 unless noted and cities with populations greater than 9,999 whose Asian and/or NHPI population rates are greater than the national average; (1) Native Hawaiian and other Pacific Islander; (2) excludes Taiwanese; (3) includes Chamorro; (4) county does not meet population threshold but is shown in order to allow inclusion of city

Place	Total foreign-born population	Total Asian population	Asians who are foreign born	Total NHPI[1] population	NHPIs[1] who are foreign born	Asian Indian	Bangladeshi	Cambodian	Chinese[2]	Fijian	Filipino	Guamanian[3]	Hawaiian, Native	Hmong	Indonesian	Japanese	Korean	Laotian	Malaysian	Pakistani	Samoan	Sri Lankan	Taiwanese	Thai	Tongan	Vietnamese
Mahwah (township)	3,194 13.27	1,551	1,021 65.83 65.83 31.97	-	-	365 71.15 35.75 23.53 11.43	-	-	-	-	-	-	-	-	-	-	-	-	-	-	-	-	-	-	-	-
New Milford (borough)	4,066 24.79	2,311	1,788 77.37 77.37 43.97	-	-	506 81.48 28.30 21.90 12.44	-	-	-	-	670 70.30 37.47 28.99 16.48	-	-	-	-	-	-	-	-	-	-	-	-	-	-	-
North Arlington (borough)	3,301 21.74	828	648 78.26 78.26 19.63	-	-	-	-	-	-	-	-	-	-	-	-	-	-	-	-	-	-	-	-	-	-	-
Palisades Park (borough)	9,725 56.96	7,002	5,827 83.22 83.22 59.92	-	-	-	-	-	-	-	-	-	-	-	-	-	4,988 84.51 85.60 71.24 51.29	-	-	-	-	-	-	-	-	-
Paramus (borough)	6,462 25.11	4,413	3,284 74.42 74.42 50.82	-	-	858 65.65 26.13 19.44 13.28	-	-	381 83.01 11.60 8.63 5.90	-	614 74.33 18.70 13.91 9.50	-	-	-	-	-	1,114 80.14 33.92 25.24 17.24	-	-	-	-	-	-	-	-	-
Ramsey (borough)	1,710 11.92	825	597 72.36 72.36 34.91	-	-	-	-	-	-	-	-	-	-	-	-	-	-	-	-	-	-	-	-	-	-	-
Ridgefield (borough)	3,646 33.67	1,776	1,387 78.10 78.10 38.04	-	-	-	-	-	-	-	-	-	-	-	-	-	1,037 77.33 74.77 58.39 28.44	-	-	-	-	-	-	-	-	-
Ridgefield Park (village)	3,081 23.93	1,104	809 73.28 73.28 26.26	-	-	-	-	-	-	-	-	-	-	-	-	-	358 79.38 44.25 32.43 11.62	-	-	-	-	-	-	-	-	-
Ridgewood (village)	4,005 16.06	2,111	1,675 79.35 79.35 41.82	-	-	-	-	-	-	-	-	-	-	-	-	409 91.50 24.42 19.37 10.21	487 85.44 29.07 23.07 12.16	-	-	-	-	-	-	-	-	-
River Edge (borough)	2,344 21.41	1,350	1,036 76.74 76.74 44.20	-	-	-	-	-	-	-	-	-	-	-	-	-	366 77.38 35.33 27.11 15.61	-	-	-	-	-	-	-	-	-

Notes: Please refer to the User's Guide for an explanation of data; data is arranged alphabetically by state, then county, then city within each county; table includes counties with populations greater than 49,999 unless noted and cities with populations greater than 9,999 whose Asian and/or NHPI population rates are greater than the national average; (1) Native Hawaiian and other Pacific Islander; (2) excludes Taiwanese; (3) includes Chamorro; (4) county does not meet population threshold but is shown in order to allow inclusion of city

Place	Total foreign-born population	Total Asian population	Asians who are foreign born	Total NHPI[1] population	NHPIs[1] who are foreign born	Asian Indian	Bangladeshi	Cambodian	Chinese[2]	Fijian	Filipino	Guamanian[3]	Hawaiian, Native	Hmong	Indonesian	Japanese	Korean	Laotian	Malaysian	Pakistani	Samoan	Sri Lankan	Taiwanese	Thai	Tongan	Vietnamese
Rutherford (borough)	3,644 20.12	2,079	1,565 75.28 75.28 42.95	-	-	261 75.00 16.68 12.55 7.16	-	-	-	-	-	-	-	-	-	-	731 80.86 46.71 35.16 20.06	-	-	-	-	-	-	-	-	-
Saddle Brook (township)	2,112 16.05	728	566 77.75 77.75 26.80	-	-	-	-	-	-	-	-	-	-	-	-	-	-	-	-	-	-	-	-	-	-	-
Teaneck (township)	9,435 24.03	2,829	2,189 77.38 77.38 23.20	-	-	676 83.56 30.88 23.90 7.16	-	-	-	-	624 71.89 28.51 22.06 6.61	-	-	-	-	-	-	-	-	-	-	-	-	-	-	-
Tenafly (borough)	3,944 28.57	2,587	1,931 74.64 74.64 48.96	-	-	-	-	-	446 59.87 23.10 17.24 11.31	-	-	-	-	-	-	-	967 82.02 50.08 37.38 24.52	-	-	-	-	-	-	-	-	-
Wallington (borough)	4,734 40.87	546	410 75.09 75.09 8.66	-	-	-	-	-	-	-	-	-	-	-	-	-	-	-	-	-	-	-	-	-	-	-
Westwood (borough)	1,682 15.29	527	413 78.37 78.37 24.55	-	-	-	-	-	-	-	-	-	-	-	-	-	-	-	-	-	-	-	-	-	-	-
Wyckoff (township)	1,530 9.27	641	458 71.45 71.45 29.93	-	-	-	-	-	-	-	-	-	-	-	-	-	-	-	-	-	-	-	-	-	-	-
Burlington County	26,681 6.30	11,170	8,190 73.32 73.32 30.70	-	-	2,890 77.25 35.29 25.87 10.83	-	-	980 62.46 11.97 8.77 3.67	-	1,357 66.55 16.57 12.15 5.09	-	-	-	-	350 71.57 4.27 3.13 1.31	1,606 81.48 19.61 14.38 6.02	-	-	-	-	-	-	-	-	403 74.63 4.92 3.61 1.51
Browns Mills (cdp)	797 7.02	478	358 74.90 74.90 44.92	-	-	-	-	-	-	-	-	-	-	-	-	-	267 76.29 74.58 55.86 33.50	-	-	-	-	-	-	-	-	-
Evesham (township)	2,740 6.46	1,597	1,101 68.94 68.94 40.18	-	-	301 83.84 27.34 18.85 10.99	-	-	224 50.00 20.35 14.03 8.18	-	-	-	-	-	-	-	-	-	-	-	-	-	-	-	-	-

Notes: Please refer to the User's Guide for an explanation of data; data is arranged alphabetically by state, then county, then city within each county; table includes counties with populations greater than 49,999 unless noted and cities with populations greater than 9,999 whose Asian and/or NHPI population rates are greater than the national average; (1) Native Hawaiian and other Pacific Islander; (2) excludes Taiwanese; (3) includes Chamorro; (4) county does not meet population threshold but is shown in order to allow inclusion of city

Place	Total foreign-born population	Total Asian population	Asians who are foreign born	Total NHPI[1] population	NHPIs[1] who are foreign born	Asian Indian	Bangladeshi	Cambodian	Chinese[2]	Fijian	Filipino	Guamanian[3]	Hawaiian, Native	Hmong	Indonesian	Japanese	Korean	Laotian	Malaysian	Pakistani	Samoan	Sri Lankan	Taiwanese	Thai	Tongan	Vietnamese
Maple Shade (township)	1,730 9.07	1,083	947 87.44 87.44 54.74	-	-	573 88.02 60.51 52.91 33.12	-	-	-	-	-	-	-	-	-	-	-	-	-	-	-	-	-	-	-	-
Marlton (cdp)	676 6.60	392	307 78.32 78.32 45.41	-	-	-	-	-	-	-	-	-	-	-	-	-	-	-	-	-	-	-	-	-	-	-
Mount Laurel (township)	2,777 6.90	1,722	1,251 72.65 72.65 45.05	-	-	454 79.65 36.29 26.36 16.35	-	-	337 68.50 26.94 19.57 12.14	-	-	-	-	-	-	-	-	-	-	-	-	-	-	-	-	-
Camden County	35,350 6.95	19,842	14,174 71.43 71.43 40.10	-	-	3,705 73.54 26.14 18.67 10.48	-	256 81.79 1.81 1.29 0.72	2,754 70.29 19.43 13.88 7.79	-	2,638 69.73 18.61 13.30 7.46	-	-	-	-	-	1,244 71.74 8.78 6.27 3.52	-	-	237 63.03 1.67 1.19 0.67	-	-	-	-	-	2,460 77.73 17.36 12.40 6.96
Barclay-Kingston (cdp)	986 9.15	883	576 65.23 65.23 58.42	-	-	-	-	-	-	-	-	-	-	-	-	-	-	-	-	-	-	-	-	-	-	-
Bellmawr (borough)	847 7.52	450	371 82.44 82.44 43.80	-	-	-	-	-	-	-	-	-	-	-	-	-	-	-	-	-	-	-	-	-	-	-
Cherry Hill Mall (cdp)	1,966 14.60	1,291	870 67.39 67.39 44.25	-	-	-	-	-	-	-	-	-	-	-	-	-	-	-	-	-	-	-	-	-	-	-
Cherry Hill (township)	8,720 12.46	6,595	4,529 68.67 68.67 51.94	-	-	1,047 75.81 23.12 15.88 12.01	-	-	1,217 66.39 26.87 18.45 13.96	-	1,027 69.44 22.68 15.57 11.78	-	-	-	-	-	665 65.39 14.68 10.08 7.63	-	-	-	-	-	-	-	-	-
Echelon (cdp)	1,498 14.42	1,347	983 72.98 72.98 65.62	-	-	577 71.32 58.70 42.84 38.52	-	-	-	-	-	-	-	-	-	-	-	-	-	-	-	-	-	-	-	-
Greentree (cdp)	2,041 17.75	1,925	1,372 71.27 71.27 67.22	-	-	391 66.50 28.50 20.31 19.16	-	-	579 75.10 42.20 30.08 28.37	-	-	-	-	-	-	-	-	-	-	-	-	-	-	-	-	-

Notes: Please refer to the User's Guide for an explanation of data; data is arranged alphabetically by state, then county, then city within each county; table includes counties with populations greater than 49,999 unless noted and cities with populations greater than 9,999 whose Asian and/or NHPI population rates are greater than the national average; (1) Native Hawaiian and other Pacific Islander; (2) excludes Taiwanese; (3) includes Chamorro; (4) county does not meet population threshold but is shown in order to allow inclusion of city

Place	Total foreign-born population	Total Asian population	Asians who are foreign born	Total NHPI[1] population	NHPIs[1] who are foreign born	Asian Indian	Bangladeshi	Cambodian	Chinese[2]	Fijian	Filipino	Guamanian[3]	Hawaiian, Native	Hmong	Indonesian	Japanese	Korean	Laotian	Malaysian	Pakistani	Samoan	Sri Lankan	Taiwanese	Thai	Tongan	Vietnamese
Pennsauken (township)	2,822 7.90	1,556	1,271 81.68 81.68 45.04	-	-	-	-	-	-	-	-	-	-	-	-	-	-	-	-	-	-	-	-	-	-	552 79.77 43.43 35.48 19.56
Springdale (cdp)	1,644 11.41	1,196	815 68.14 68.14 49.57	-	-	-	-	-	333 71.31 40.86 27.84 20.26	-	-	-	-	-	-	-	-	-	-	-	-	-	-	-	-	-
Voorhees (township)	3,762 13.38	3,077	2,172 70.59 70.59 57.74	-	-	1,237 69.93 56.95 40.20 32.88	-	-	466 75.40 21.45 15.14 12.39	-	277 67.73 12.75 9.00 7.36	-	-	-	-	-	-	-	-	-	-	-	-	-	-	-
Cape May County	3,288 3.21	615	518 84.23 84.23 15.75	-	-	-	-	-	-	-	-	-	-	-	-	-	-	-	-	-	-	-	-	-	-	-
Cumberland County	9,007 6.15	1,171	677 57.81 57.81 7.52	-	-	263 63.53 38.85 22.46 2.92	-	-	-	-	-	-	-	-	-	-	-	-	-	-	-	-	-	-	-	-
Essex County	168,165 21.19	29,468	21,570 73.20 73.20 12.83	458	130 28.38 28.38 0.08	6,473 74.45 30.01 21.97 3.85	-	-	4,097 66.97 18.99 13.90 2.44	-	5,985 75.37 27.75 20.31 3.56	-	-	-	-	421 70.17 1.95 1.43 0.25	2,036 72.95 9.44 6.91 1.21	-	-	502 82.43 2.33 1.70 0.30	-	-	388 81.34 1.80 1.32 0.23	-	-	813 77.21 3.77 2.76 0.48
Belleville (township)	9,638 26.83	4,228	3,312 78.33 78.33 34.36	-	-	708 79.55 21.38 16.75 7.35	-	-	-	-	1,624 76.28 49.03 38.41 16.85	-	-	-	-	-	-	-	-	-	-	-	-	-	-	356 83.96 10.75 8.42 3.69
Bloomfield (township)	10,892 22.84	4,056	3,053 75.27 75.27 28.03	-	-	1,114 74.07 36.49 27.47 10.23	-	-	331 66.87 10.84 8.16 3.04	-	1,254 78.92 41.07 30.92 11.51	-	-	-	-	-	-	-	-	-	-	-	-	-	-	-
Cedar Grove (township)	1,349 10.97	605	457 75.54 75.54 33.88	-	-	-	-	-	-	-	-	-	-	-	-	-	-	-	-	-	-	-	-	-	-	-
Livingston (township)	5,154 18.82	3,990	2,715 68.05 68.05 52.68	-	-	476 63.89 17.53 11.93 9.24	-	-	1,044 66.33 38.45 26.17 20.26	-	391 67.88 14.40 9.80 7.59	-	-	-	-	-	591 74.34 21.77 14.81 11.47	-	-	-	-	-	-	-	-	-

Notes: Please refer to the User's Guide for an explanation of data; data is arranged alphabetically by state, then county, then city within each county; table includes counties with populations greater than 49,999 unless noted and cities with populations greater than 9,999 whose Asian and/or NHPI population rates are greater than the national average; (1) Native Hawaiian and other Pacific Islander; (2) excludes Taiwanese; (3) includes Chamorro; (4) county does not meet population threshold but is shown in order to allow inclusion of city

Place	Total foreign-born population	Total Asian population	Asians who are foreign born	Total NHPI[1] population	NHPIs[1] who are foreign born	Asian Indian	Bangladeshi	Cambodian	Chinese[2]	Fijian	Filipino	Guamanian[3]	Hawaiian, Native	Hmong	Indonesian	Japanese	Korean	Laotian	Malaysian	Pakistani	Samoan	Sri Lankan	Taiwanese	Thai	Tongan	Vietnamese
Millburn (township)	2,899 14.67	1,508	1,067 70.76 70.76 36.81	-	-	-	-	-	406 62.17 38.05 26.92 14.00	-	-	-	-	-	-	-	-	-	-	-	-	-	-	-	-	-
Nutley (township)	4,012 14.66	1,995	1,505 75.44 75.44 37.51	-	-	565 76.87 37.54 28.32 14.08	-	-	-	-	368 75.56 24.45 18.45 9.17	-	-	-	-	-	-	-	-	-	-	-	-	-	-	-
Verona (township)	1,310 9.68	612	432 70.59 70.59 32.98	-	-	-	-	-	-	-	-	-	-	-	-	-	-	-	-	-	-	-	-	-	-	-
West Caldwell (township)	971 8.64	413	295 71.43 71.43 30.38	-	-	-	-	-	-	-	-	-	-	-	-	-	-	-	-	-	-	-	-	-	-	-
West Orange (township)	11,483 25.60	3,756	2,807 74.73 74.73 24.44	-	-	795 77.03 28.32 21.17 6.92	-	-	570 72.34 20.31 15.18 4.96	-	736 76.51 26.22 19.60 6.41	-	-	-	-	-	433 68.62 15.43 11.53 3.77	-	-	-	-	-	-	-	-	-
Gloucester County	8,566 3.36	4,162	2,943 70.71 70.71 34.36	-	-	789 79.46 26.81 18.96 9.21	-	-	546 72.80 18.55 13.12 6.37	-	858 62.81 29.15 20.62 10.02	-	-	-	-	-	317 73.04 10.77 7.62 3.70	-	-	-	-	-	-	-	-	-
Hudson County	234,597 38.52	57,191	44,974 78.64 78.64 19.17	-	-	16,822 81.64 37.40 29.41 7.17	-	-	5,158 76.60 11.47 9.02 2.20	-	15,066 75.80 33.50 26.34 6.42	-	-	-	-	712 76.07 1.58 1.24 0.30	2,630 82.03 5.85 4.60 1.12	-	-	1,742 75.09 3.87 3.05 0.74	-	-	-	-	-	1,336 81.46 2.97 2.34 0.57
Bayonne (city)	12,470 20.16	2,599	1,944 74.80 74.80 15.59	-	-	425 79.59 21.86 16.35 3.41	-	-	-	-	987 74.27 50.77 37.98 7.91	-	-	-	-	-	246 83.39 12.65 9.47 1.97	-	-	-	-	-	-	-	-	-
Guttenberg (town)	5,259 49.18	743	572 76.99 76.99 10.88	-	-	-	-	-	-	-	-	-	-	-	-	-	-	-	-	-	-	-	-	-	-	-
Harrison (town)	8,078 56.00	1,759	1,455 82.72 82.72 18.01	-	-	-	-	-	1,088 82.80 74.78 61.85 13.47	-	-	-	-	-	-	-	-	-	-	-	-	-	-	-	-	-

Notes: Please refer to the User's Guide for an explanation of data; data is arranged alphabetically by state, then county, then city within each county; table includes counties with populations greater than 49,999 unless noted and cities with populations greater than 9,999 whose Asian and/or NHPI population rates are greater than the national average; (1) Native Hawaiian and other Pacific Islander; (2) excludes Taiwanese; (3) includes Chamorro; (4) county does not meet population threshold but is shown in order to allow inclusion of city

Place	Total foreign-born population	Total Asian population	Asians who are foreign born	Total NHPI[1] population	NHPIs[1] who are foreign born	Asian Indian	Bangladeshi	Cambodian	Chinese[2]	Fijian	Filipino	Guamanian[3]	Hawaiian, Native	Hmong	Indonesian	Japanese	Korean	Laotian	Malaysian	Pakistani	Samoan	Sri Lankan	Taiwanese	Thai	Tongan	Vietnamese
Hoboken (city)	5,588 14.45	1,694	1,058 62.46 62.46 18.93	-	-	434 66.56 41.02 25.62 7.77	-	-	261 53.16 24.67 15.41 4.67	-	-	-	-	-	-	-	-	-	-	-	-	-	-	-	-	-
Jersey City (city)	81,554 33.97	39,070	30,962 79.25 79.25 37.97	-	-	11,080 82.79 35.79 28.36 13.59	-	-	2,279 78.40 7.36 5.83 2.79	-	12,534 76.15 40.48 32.08 15.37	-	-	-	-	-	1,256 84.81 4.06 3.21 1.54	-	-	1,467 78.12 4.74 3.75 1.80	-	-	-	-	-	1,117 80.13 3.61 2.86 1.37
Kearny (town)	15,475 38.20	2,280	1,881 82.50 82.50 12.16	-	-	692 84.91 36.79 30.35 4.47	-	-	774 84.41 41.15 33.95 5.00	-	-	-	-	-	-	-	-	-	-	-	-	-	-	-	-	-
North Bergen (township)	27,216 46.76	3,516	2,784 79.18 79.18 10.23	-	-	1,937 81.94 69.58 55.09 7.12	-	-	174 54.55 6.25 4.95 0.64	-	-	-	-	-	-	-	-	-	-	-	-	-	-	-	-	-
Secaucus (town)	3,246 20.49	1,853	1,380 74.47 74.47 42.51	-	-	396 74.30 28.70 21.37 12.20	-	-	-	-	443 69.76 32.10 23.91 13.65	-	-	-	-	-	-	-	-	-	-	-	-	-	-	-
Weehawken (township)	5,229 38.73	608	435 71.55 71.55 8.32	-	-	-	-	-	-	-	-	-	-	-	-	-	-	-	-	-	-	-	-	-	-	-
Hunterdon County	7,708 6.32	2,595	1,868 71.98 71.98 24.23	-	-	742 70.00 39.72 28.59 9.63	-	-	488 69.02 26.12 18.81 6.33	-	-	-	-	-	-	-	-	-	-	-	-	-	-	-	-	-
Mercer County	48,659 13.87	17,429	11,985 68.76 68.76 24.63	-	-	4,730 69.19 39.47 27.14 9.72	-	-	3,052 66.12 25.47 17.51 6.27	-	821 71.14 6.85 4.71 1.69	-	-	-	-	362 58.39 3.02 2.08 0.74	1,338 67.54 11.16 7.68 2.75	-	-	490 74.24 4.09 2.81 1.01	-	-	333 68.24 2.78 1.91 0.68	-	-	-
East Windsor (township)	5,764 23.13	2,363	1,889 79.94 79.94 32.77	-	-	1,198 80.29 63.42 50.70 20.78	-	-	-	-	-	-	-	-	-	-	-	-	-	-	-	-	-	-	-	-
Hopewell (township)	1,243 7.72	668	488 73.05 73.05 39.26	-	-	-	-	-	-	-	-	-	-	-	-	-	-	-	-	-	-	-	-	-	-	-

Notes: Please refer to the User's Guide for an explanation of data; data is arranged alphabetically by state, then county, then city within each county; table includes counties with populations greater than 49,999 unless noted and cities with populations greater than 9,999 whose Asian and/or NHPI population rates are greater than the national average; (1) Native Hawaiian and other Pacific Islander; (2) excludes Taiwanese; (3) includes Chamorro; (4) county does not meet population threshold but is shown in order to allow inclusion of city

Place	Total foreign-born population	Total Asian population	Asians who are foreign born	Total NHPI[1] population	NHPIs[1] who are foreign born	Asian Indian	Bangladeshi	Cambodian	Chinese[2]	Fijian	Filipino	Guamanian[3]	Hawaiian, Native	Hmong	Indonesian	Japanese	Korean	Laotian	Malaysian	Pakistani	Samoan	Sri Lankan	Taiwanese	Thai	Tongan	Vietnamese
Lawrence (township)	5,097 17.48	2,291	1,740 75.95 75.95 34.14	-	-	912 78.02 52.41 39.81 17.89	-	-	487 74.58 27.99 21.26 9.55	-	-	-	-	-	-	-	-	-	-	-	-	-	-	-	-	-
Princeton (borough)	2,012 14.17	931	263 28.25 28.25 13.07	-	-	-	-	-	-	-	-	-	-	-	-	-	-	-	-	-	-	-	-	-	-	-
Princeton (township)	4,065 25.36	1,684	1,308 77.67 77.67 32.18	-	-	280 66.51 21.41 16.63 6.89	-	-	616 85.32 47.09 36.58 15.15	-	-	-	-	-	-	-	-	-	-	-	-	-	-	-	-	-
West Windsor (township)	4,906 22.39	4,798	3,047 63.51 63.51 62.11	-	-	1,002 62.12 32.88 20.88 20.42	-	-	1,091 60.08 35.81 22.74 22.24	-	-	-	-	-	-	-	306 71.33 10.04 6.38 6.24	-	-	-	-	-	-	-	-	-
Middlesex County	181,761 24.23	104,114	78,566 75.46 75.46 43.22	-	-	42,736 78.90 54.40 41.05 23.51	303 78.29 0.39 0.29 0.17	-	14,873 69.90 18.93 14.29 8.18	-	9,003 72.03 11.46 8.65 4.95	-	-	-	416 85.25 0.53 0.40 0.23	503 75.98 0.64 0.48 0.28	4,076 76.17 5.19 3.91 2.24	-	-	2,355 74.20 3.00 2.26 1.30	-	363 73.04 0.46 0.35 0.20	995 73.16 1.27 0.96 0.55	-	-	1,655 73.56 2.11 1.59 0.91
Avenel (cdp)	4,554 25.95	3,296	2,709 82.19 82.19 59.49	-	-	1,881 86.17 69.44 57.07 41.30	-	-	-	-	-	-	-	-	-	-	-	-	-	-	-	-	-	-	-	-
Carteret (borough)	4,843 23.39	1,656	1,313 79.29 79.29 27.11	-	-	853 77.40 64.97 51.51 17.61	-	-	-	-	-	-	-	-	-	-	-	-	-	-	-	-	-	-	-	-
Colonia (cdp)	2,695 15.18	1,263	870 68.88 68.88 32.28	-	-	450 72.00 51.72 35.63 16.70	-	-	-	-	231 70.00 26.55 18.29 8.57	-	-	-	-	-	-	-	-	-	-	-	-	-	-	-
East Brunswick (township)	10,982 23.49	7,634	5,549 72.69 72.69 50.53	-	-	2,060 78.66 37.12 26.98 18.76	-	-	2,042 65.87 36.80 26.75 18.59	-	406 71.86 7.32 5.32 3.70	-	-	-	-	-	319 72.67 5.75 4.18 2.90	-	-	-	-	-	-	-	-	-
Edison (township)	32,351 33.12	28,438	21,742 76.45 76.45 67.21	-	-	13,119 80.24 60.34 46.13 40.55	-	-	4,094 70.27 18.83 14.40 12.65	-	1,824 70.92 8.39 6.41 5.64	-	-	-	-	-	979 77.64 4.50 3.44 3.03	-	-	452 67.06 2.08 1.59 1.40	-	-	472 71.19 2.17 1.66 1.46	-	-	-

Notes: Please refer to the User's Guide for an explanation of data; data is arranged alphabetically by state, then county, then city within each county; table includes counties with populations greater than 49,999 unless noted and cities with populations greater than 9,999 whose Asian and/or NHPI population rates are greater than the national average; (1) Native Hawaiian and other Pacific Islander; (2) excludes Taiwanese; (3) includes Chamorro; (4) county does not meet population threshold but is shown in order to allow inclusion of city

Place	Total foreign-born population	Total Asian population	Asians who are foreign born	Total NHPI[1] population	NHPIs[1] who are foreign born	Asian Indian	Bangladeshi	Cambodian	Chinese[2]	Fijian	Filipino	Guamanian[3]	Hawaiian, Native	Hmong	Indonesian	Japanese	Korean	Laotian	Malaysian	Pakistani	Samoan	Sri Lankan	Taiwanese	Thai	Tongan	Vietnamese
Fords (cdp)	3,322	2,383	1,799	-	-	934	-	-	-	-	454	-	-	-	-	-	-	-	-	-	-	-	-	-	-	-
	21.95		75.49			81.36					68.89															
						51.92					25.24															
			75.49			39.19					19.05															
			54.15			28.12					13.67															
Highland Park (borough)	4,085	1,926	1,667	-	-	552	-	-	725	-	-	-	-	-	-	-	-	-	-	-	-	-	-	-	-	-
	29.18		86.55			88.04			84.11																	
						33.11			43.49																	
			86.55			28.66			37.64																	
			40.81			13.51			17.75																	
Iselin (cdp)	4,566	3,982	3,165	-	-	2,304	-	-	392	-	-	-	-	-	-	-	-	-	-	-	-	-	-	-	-	-
	27.51		79.48			81.79			76.71																	
						72.80			12.39																	
			79.48			57.86			9.84																	
			69.32			50.46			8.59																	
Metuchen (borough)	1,820	941	705	-	-	-	-	-	-	-	-	-	-	-	-	-	-	-	-	-	-	-	-	-	-	-
	14.17		74.92																							
			74.92																							
			38.74																							
Middlesex (borough)	1,744	609	435	-	-	-	-	-	-	-	-	-	-	-	-	-	-	-	-	-	-	-	-	-	-	-
	12.71		71.43																							
			71.43																							
			24.94																							
New Brunswick (city)	16,215	2,719	1,669	-	-	740	-	-	269	-	-	-	-	-	-	-	-	-	-	-	-	-	-	-	-	-
	33.38		61.38			65.95			60.59																	
						44.34			16.12																	
			61.38			27.22			9.89																	
			10.29			4.56			1.66																	
North Brunswick (township)	8,863	5,148	4,001	-	-	2,391	-	-	656	-	316	-	-	-	-	-	331	-	-	-	-	-	-	-	-	-
	24.42		77.72			79.44			78.75		71.82						71.18									
						59.76			16.40		7.90						8.27									
			77.72			46.45			12.74		6.14						6.43									
			45.14			26.98			7.40		3.57						3.73									
Old Bridge (township)	11,115	6,489	4,580	-	-	2,088	-	-	687	-	868	-	-	-	-	-	-	-	-	409	-	-	-	-	-	-
	18.39		70.58			73.86			57.06		68.08									77.76						
						45.59			15.00		18.95									8.93						
			70.58			32.18			10.59		13.38									6.30						
			41.21			18.79			6.18		7.81									3.68						
Piscataway (township)	15,052	12,562	9,377	-	-	4,604	-	-	1,834	-	1,584	-	-	-	-	-	539	-	-	-	-	-	-	-	-	-
	29.82		74.65			77.50			73.51		73.57						68.06									
						49.10			19.56		16.89						5.75									
			74.65			36.65			14.60		12.61						4.29									
			62.30			30.59			12.18		10.52						3.58									
Plainsboro (township)	6,971	6,164	4,767	-	-	2,705	-	-	1,162	-	-	-	-	-	-	-	-	-	-	-	-	-	-	-	-	-
	34.48		77.34			82.82			69.41																	
						56.74			24.38																	
			77.34			43.88			18.85																	
			68.38			38.80			16.67																	

Notes: Please refer to the User's Guide for an explanation of data; data is arranged alphabetically by state, then county, then city within each county; table includes counties with populations greater than 49,999 unless noted and cities with populations greater than 9,999 whose Asian and/or NHPI population rates are greater than the national average; (1) Native Hawaiian and other Pacific Islander; (2) excludes Taiwanese; (3) includes Chamorro; (4) county does not meet population threshold but is shown in order to allow inclusion of city

Place	Total foreign-born population	Total Asian population	Asians who are foreign born	Total NHPI[1] population	NHPIs[1] who are foreign born	Asian Indian	Bangladeshi	Cambodian	Chinese[2]	Fijian	Filipino	Guamanian[3]	Hawaiian, Native	Hmong	Indonesian	Japanese	Korean	Laotian	Malaysian	Pakistani	Samoan	Sri Lankan	Taiwanese	Thai	Tongan	Vietnamese
Princeton Meadows (cdp)	4,560 34.43	3,875	3,064 79.07 79.07 67.19	-	-	1,807 82.93 58.98 46.63 39.63	-	-	662 74.38 21.61 17.08 14.52	-	-	-	-	-	-	-	-	-	-	-	-	-	-	-	-	-
Sayreville (borough)	8,098 20.06	4,184	3,389 81.00 81.00 41.85	-	-	2,111 84.37 62.29 50.45 26.07	-	-	527 79.37 15.55 12.60 6.51	-	491 74.51 14.49 11.74 6.06	-	-	-	-	-	-	-	-	-	-	-	-	-	-	-
South Brunswick (township)	8,156 21.61	6,888	5,018 72.85 72.85 61.53	-	-	2,746 71.12 54.72 39.87 33.67	-	-	1,002 70.86 19.97 14.55 12.29	-	425 78.70 8.47 6.17 5.21	-	-	-	-	-	-	-	-	-	-	-	-	-	-	-
South Plainfield (borough)	3,221 14.77	1,761	1,282 72.80 72.80 39.80	-	-	523 72.04 40.80 29.70 16.24	-	-	-	-	296 76.29 23.09 16.81 9.19	-	-	-	-	-	-	-	-	-	-	-	-	-	-	277 75.68 21.61 15.73 8.60
Woodbridge (township)	20,871 21.47	13,949	10,927 78.34 78.34 52.35	-	-	7,243 82.25 66.29 51.92 34.70	-	-	926 68.85 8.47 6.64 4.44	-	1,392 71.79 12.74 9.98 6.67	-	-	-	-	-	525 81.78 4.80 3.76 2.52	-	-	373 79.87 3.41 2.67 1.79	-	-	-	-	-	-
Monmouth County	63,807 10.37	24,047	16,772 69.75 69.75 26.29	-	-	4,977 72.85 29.67 20.70 7.80	-	-	6,057 65.18 36.11 25.19 9.49	-	2,381 71.29 14.20 9.90 3.73	-	-	-	-	229 63.43 1.37 0.95 0.36	1,558 78.49 9.29 6.48 2.44	-	-	323 78.59 1.93 1.34 0.51	-	-	-	-	-	571 78.87 3.40 2.37 0.89
Aberdeen (township)	1,995 11.47	943	694 73.59 73.59 34.79	-	-	301 76.40 43.37 31.92 15.09	-	-	261 66.92 37.61 27.68 13.08	-	-	-	-	-	-	-	-	-	-	-	-	-	-	-	-	-
Colts Neck (township)	1,060 8.60	519	310 59.73 59.73 29.25	-	-	-	-	-	-	-	-	-	-	-	-	-	-	-	-	-	-	-	-	-	-	-
Eatontown (borough)	2,307 16.48	1,262	1,014 80.35 80.35 43.95	-	-	-	-	-	-	-	-	-	-	-	-	-	-	-	-	-	-	-	-	-	-	-
Freehold (township)	3,529 11.19	1,711	1,115 65.17 65.17 31.60	-	-	323 67.01 28.97 18.88 9.15	-	-	335 61.47 30.04 19.58 9.49	-	279 71.36 25.02 16.31 7.91	-	-	-	-	-	-	-	-	-	-	-	-	-	-	-

Notes: Please refer to the User's Guide for an explanation of data; data is arranged alphabetically by state, then county, then city within each county; table includes counties with populations greater than 49,999 unless noted and cities with populations greater than 9,999 whose Asian and/or NHPI population rates are greater than the national average; (1) Native Hawaiian and other Pacific Islander; (2) excludes Taiwanese; (3) includes Chamorro; (4) county does not meet population threshold but is shown in order to allow inclusion of city

Place	Total foreign-born population	Total Asian population	Asians who are foreign born	Total NHPI[1] population	NHPIs[1] who are foreign born	Asian Indian	Bangladeshi	Cambodian	Chinese[2]	Fijian	Filipino	Guamanian[3]	Hawaiian, Native	Hmong	Indonesian	Japanese	Korean	Laotian	Malaysian	Pakistani	Samoan	Sri Lankan	Taiwanese	Thai	Tongan	Vietnamese
Holmdel (township)	2,970 18.82	2,610	1,711 65.56 65.56 57.61	-	-	316 69.45 18.47 12.11 10.64	-	-	985 60.92 57.57 37.74 33.16	-	-	-	-	-	-	-	-	-	-	-	-	-	-	-	-	-
Howell (township)	4,360 8.92	1,849	1,318 71.28 71.28 30.23	-	-	446 68.62 33.84 24.12 10.23	-	-	-	-	310 64.32 23.52 16.77 7.11	-	-	-	-	-	-	-	-	-	-	-	-	-	-	-
Manalapan (township)	3,467 10.37	1,528	933 61.06 61.06 26.91	-	-	390 63.83 41.80 25.52 11.25	-	-	287 55.84 30.76 18.78 8.28	-	-	-	-	-	-	-	-	-	-	-	-	-	-	-	-	-
Marlboro (township)	5,621 15.44	4,550	2,884 63.38 63.38 51.31	-	-	690 66.47 23.93 15.16 12.28	-	-	1,577 60.03 54.68 34.66 28.06	-	-	-	-	-	-	-	-	-	-	-	-	-	-	-	-	-
Morganville (cdp)	1,551 13.93	1,058	674 63.71 63.71 43.46	-	-	-	-	-	377 58.27 55.93 35.63 24.31	-	-	-	-	-	-	-	-	-	-	-	-	-	-	-	-	-
Ocean (township)	4,240 15.73	1,525	1,188 77.90 77.90 28.02	-	-	502 87.15 42.26 32.92 11.84	-	-	-	-	-	-	-	-	-	-	-	-	-	-	-	-	-	-	-	-
Tinton Falls (borough)	1,498 9.95	797	578 72.52 72.52 38.58	-	-	-	-	-	-	-	-	-	-	-	-	-	-	-	-	-	-	-	-	-	-	-
West Freehold (cdp)	1,424 11.36	581	380 65.40 65.40 26.69	-	-	-	-	-	-	-	-	-	-	-	-	-	-	-	-	-	-	-	-	-	-	-
Morris County	72,638 15.45	30,070	22,137 73.62 73.62 30.48	-	-	8,112 76.68 36.64 26.98 11.17	-	-	6,579 70.70 29.72 21.88 9.06	-	2,352 73.02 10.62 7.82 3.24	-	-	-	-	594 78.68 2.68 1.98 0.82	2,021 75.35 9.13 6.72 2.78	-	-	526 69.39 2.38 1.75 0.72	-	-	524 74.64 2.37 1.74 0.72	-	-	549 72.72 2.48 1.83 0.76
Chatham (township)	1,212 12.02	565	411 72.74 72.74 33.91	-	-	-	-	-	-	-	-	-	-	-	-	-	-	-	-	-	-	-	-	-	-	-

Notes: Please refer to the User's Guide for an explanation of data; data is arranged alphabetically by state, then county, then city within each county; table includes counties with populations greater than 49,999 unless noted and cities with populations greater than 9,999 whose Asian and/or NHPI population rates are greater than the national average; (1) Native Hawaiian and other Pacific Islander; (2) excludes Taiwanese; (3) includes Chamorro; (4) county does not meet population threshold but is shown in order to allow inclusion of city

Place	Total foreign-born population	Total Asian population	Asians who are foreign born	Total NHPI[1] population	NHPIs[1] who are foreign born	Asian Indian	Bangladeshi	Cambodian	Chinese[2]	Fijian	Filipino	Guamanian[3]	Hawaiian, Native	Hmong	Indonesian	Japanese	Korean	Laotian	Malaysian	Pakistani	Samoan	Sri Lankan	Taiwanese	Thai	Tongan	Vietnamese
Denville (township)	1,673 10.57	810	504 62.22 62.22 30.13	-	-	-	-	-	-	-	-	-	-	-	-	-	-	-	-	-	-	-	-	-	-	-
East Hanover (township)	2,119 18.60	1,245	872 70.04 70.04 41.15	-	-	-	-	-	432 70.13 49.54 34.70 20.39	-	-	-	-	-	-	-	-	-	-	-	-	-	-	-	-	-
Hanover (township)	2,030 15.74	1,237	836 67.58 67.58 41.18	-	-	250 63.78 29.90 20.21 12.32	-	-	368 65.36 44.02 29.75 18.13	-	-	-	-	-	-	-	-	-	-	-	-	-	-	-	-	-
Lincoln Park (borough)	1,481 13.55	617	448 72.61 72.61 30.25	-	-	-	-	-	-	-	-	-	-	-	-	-	-	-	-	-	-	-	-	-	-	-
Montville (township)	3,588 17.22	2,652	1,800 67.87 67.87 50.17	-	-	694 69.54 38.56 26.17 19.34	-	-	671 70.71 37.28 25.30 18.70	-	-	-	-	-	-	-	-	-	-	-	-	-	-	-	-	-
Morris (township)	2,336 10.72	911	644 70.69 70.69 27.57	-	-	-	-	-	-	-	-	-	-	-	-	-	-	-	-	-	-	-	-	-	-	-
Mount Olive (township)	3,134 12.95	1,639	1,216 74.19 74.19 38.80	-	-	552 81.18 45.39 33.68 17.61	-	-	-	-	-	-	-	-	-	-	-	-	-	-	-	-	-	-	-	-
Parsippany-Troy Hills (twp)	13,585 26.82	9,048	6,954 76.86 76.86 51.19	-	-	3,411 82.79 49.05 37.70 25.11	-	-	1,911 73.05 27.48 21.12 14.07	-	522 68.50 7.51 5.77 3.84	-	-	-	-	-	331 70.28 4.76 3.66 2.44	-	-	-	-	-	-	-	-	-
Randolph (township)	3,998 16.09	2,495	1,799 72.10 72.10 45.00	-	-	740 81.05 41.13 29.66 18.51	-	-	443 57.31 24.62 17.76 11.08	-	-	-	-	-	-	-	-	-	-	-	-	-	-	-	-	-
Rockaway (township)	3,038 13.25	1,317	938 71.22 71.22 30.88	-	-	455 72.11 48.51 34.55 14.98	-	-	-	-	-	-	-	-	-	-	-	-	-	-	-	-	-	-	-	-

Notes: Please refer to the User's Guide for an explanation of data; data is arranged alphabetically by state, then county, then city within each county; table includes counties with populations greater than 49,999 unless noted and cities with populations greater than 9,999 whose Asian and/or NHPI population rates are greater than the national average; (1) Native Hawaiian and other Pacific Islander; (2) excludes Taiwanese; (3) includes Chamorro; (4) county does not meet population threshold but is shown in order to allow inclusion of city

Place	Total foreign-born population	Total Asian population	Asians who are foreign born	Total NHPI[1] population	NHPIs[1] who are foreign born	Asian Indian	Bangladeshi	Cambodian	Chinese[2]	Fijian	Filipino	Guamanian[3]	Hawaiian, Native	Hmong	Indonesian	Japanese	Korean	Laotian	Malaysian	Pakistani	Samoan	Sri Lankan	Taiwanese	Thai	Tongan	Vietnamese
Roxbury (township)	2,413 10.10	874	653 74.71 74.71 27.06	-	-	-	-	-	-	-	-	-	-	-	-	-	-	-	-	-	-	-	-	-	-	-
Succasunna-Kenvil (cdp)	1,235 9.86	521	382 73.32 73.32 30.93	-	-	-	-	-	-	-	-	-	-	-	-	-	-	-	-	-	-	-	-	-	-	-
Ocean County	33,152 6.49	6,657	4,907 73.71 73.71 14.80	-	-	1,199 74.29 24.43 18.01 3.62	-	-	860 74.65 17.53 12.92 2.59	-	1,767 71.86 36.01 26.54 5.33	-	-	-	-	-	521 96.84 10.62 7.83 1.57	-	-	-	-	-	-	-	-	-
Passaic County	130,291 26.64	18,458	13,826 74.91 74.91 10.61	-	-	6,751 74.89 48.83 36.57 5.18	435 79.82 3.15 2.36 0.33	-	1,334 68.83 9.65 7.23 1.02	-	2,647 76.06 19.15 14.34 2.03	-	-	-	-	-	1,340 82.06 9.69 7.26 1.03	-	-	-	-	-	-	-	-	-
Clifton (city)	22,992 29.23	5,425	3,842 70.82 70.82 16.71	-	-	2,112 72.21 54.97 38.93 9.19	-	-	286 70.10 7.44 5.27 1.24	-	826 66.35 21.50 15.23 3.59	-	-	-	-	-	259 80.43 6.74 4.77 1.13	-	-	-	-	-	-	-	-	-
Little Falls (township)	1,486 13.69	459	372 81.05 81.05 25.03	-	-	-	-	-	-	-	-	-	-	-	-	-	-	-	-	-	-	-	-	-	-	-
Passaic (city)	31,101 45.83	3,830	3,026 79.01 79.01 9.73	-	-	1,934 76.69 63.91 50.50 6.22	-	-	-	-	618 81.75 20.42 16.14 1.99	-	-	-	-	-	-	-	-	-	-	-	-	-	-	-
Wayne (township)	8,824 16.31	3,245	2,482 76.49 76.49 28.13	-	-	822 75.76 33.12 25.33 9.32	-	-	448 65.21 18.05 13.81 5.08	-	280 78.65 11.28 8.63 3.17	-	-	-	-	-	720 82.57 29.01 22.19 8.16	-	-	-	-	-	-	-	-	-
Salem County	1,620 2.52	370	264 71.35 71.35 16.30	-	-	-	-	-	-	-	-	-	-	-	-	-	-	-	-	-	-	-	-	-	-	-
Somerset County	53,937 18.13	25,117	17,733 70.60 70.60 32.88	-	-	7,466 73.14 42.10 29.72 13.84	-	-	4,873 66.16 27.48 19.40 9.03	-	2,111 68.56 11.90 8.40 3.91	-	-	-	-	388 65.21 2.19 1.54 0.72	1,137 81.33 6.41 4.53 2.11	-	-	637 78.26 3.59 2.54 1.18	-	-	399 72.68 2.25 1.59 0.74	-	-	362 73.43 2.04 1.44 0.67

Notes: Please refer to the User's Guide for an explanation of data; data is arranged alphabetically by state, then county, then city within each county; table includes counties with populations greater than 49,999 unless noted and cities with populations greater than 9,999 whose Asian and/or NHPI population rates are greater than the national average; (1) Native Hawaiian and other Pacific Islander; (2) excludes Taiwanese; (3) includes Chamorro; (4) county does not meet population threshold but is shown in order to allow inclusion of city

Place	Total foreign-born population	Total Asian population	Asians who are foreign born	Total NHPI[1] population	NHPIs[1] who are foreign born	Asian Indian	Bangladeshi	Cambodian	Chinese[2]	Fijian	Filipino	Guamanian[3]	Hawaiian, Native	Hmong	Indonesian	Japanese	Korean	Laotian	Malaysian	Pakistani	Samoan	Sri Lankan	Taiwanese	Thai	Tongan	Vietnamese
Bernards (township)	3,076 12.52	1,926	1,237 64.23 64.23 40.21	-	-	395 72.21 31.93 20.51 12.84	-	-	551 58.68 44.54 28.61 17.91	-	-	-	-	-	-	-	-	-	-	-	-	-	-	-	-	-
Branchburg (township)	1,565 10.75	1,065	705 66.20 66.20 45.05	-	-	388 65.76 55.04 36.43 24.79	-	-	-	-	-	-	-	-	-	-	-	-	-	-	-	-	-	-	-	-
Bridgewater (township)	6,754 15.75	4,723	3,215 68.07 68.07 47.60	-	-	1,324 67.65 41.18 28.03 19.60	-	-	1,076 66.87 33.47 22.78 15.93	-	-	-	-	-	-	-	-	-	-	-	-	-	-	-	-	-
Franklin (township)	11,811 23.20	6,404	4,802 74.98 74.98 40.66	-	-	2,525 76.26 52.58 39.43 21.38	-	-	943 71.60 19.64 14.73 7.98	-	620 74.52 12.91 9.68 5.25	-	-	-	-	-	-	-	-	-	-	-	-	-	-	-
Hillsborough (township)	4,421 12.06	2,548	1,729 67.86 67.86 39.11	-	-	620 64.72 35.86 24.33 14.02	-	-	441 61.25 25.51 17.31 9.98	-	-	-	-	-	-	-	-	-	-	-	-	-	-	-	-	-
Montgomery (township)	2,531 14.49	1,971	1,316 66.77 66.77 52.00	-	-	411 69.19 31.23 20.85 16.24	-	-	587 63.80 44.60 29.78 23.19	-	-	-	-	-	-	-	-	-	-	-	-	-	-	-	-	-
North Plainfield (borough)	6,980 33.08	1,059	815 76.96 76.96 11.68	-	-	-	-	-	-	-	-	-	-	-	-	-	-	-	-	-	-	-	-	-	-	-
Somerset (cdp)	5,264 22.83	1,831	1,374 75.04 75.04 26.10	-	-	552 77.20 40.17 30.15 10.49	-	-	281 68.04 20.45 15.35 5.34	-	428 77.12 31.15 23.38 8.13	-	-	-	-	-	-	-	-	-	-	-	-	-	-	-
Somerville (borough)	2,807 22.49	868	681 78.46 78.46 24.26	-	-	-	-	-	-	-	-	-	-	-	-	-	-	-	-	-	-	-	-	-	-	-
Warren (township)	2,241 15.72	1,602	992 61.92 61.92 44.27	-	-	319 61.35 32.16 19.91 14.23	-	-	392 62.72 39.52 24.47 17.49	-	-	-	-	-	-	-	-	-	-	-	-	-	-	-	-	-

Notes: Please refer to the User's Guide for an explanation of data; data is arranged alphabetically by state, then county, then city within each county; table includes counties with populations greater than 49,999 unless noted and cities with populations greater than 9,999 whose Asian and/or NHPI population rates are greater than the national average; (1) Native Hawaiian and other Pacific Islander; (2) excludes Taiwanese; (3) includes Chamorro; (4) county does not meet population threshold but is shown in order to allow inclusion of city

Place	Total foreign-born population	Total Asian population	Asians who are foreign born	Total NHPI[1] population	NHPIs[1] who are foreign born	Asian Indian	Bangladeshi	Cambodian	Chinese[2]	Fijian	Filipino	Guamanian[3]	Hawaiian, Native	Hmong	Indonesian	Japanese	Korean	Laotian	Malaysian	Pakistani	Samoan	Sri Lankan	Taiwanese	Thai	Tongan	Vietnamese
Sussex County	8,171 5.67	1,628	1,170 71.87 71.87 14.32	-	-	301 73.59 25.73 18.49 3.68	-	-	-	-	334 66.93 28.55 20.52 4.09	-	-	-	-	-	-	-	-	-	-	-	-	-	-	-
Union County	130,916 25.05	19,393	14,360 74.05 74.05 10.97	-	-	5,099 74.70 35.51 26.29 3.89	-	-	2,742 72.37 19.09 14.14 2.09	-	4,347 75.85 30.27 22.42 3.32	-	-	-	-	-	889 79.45 6.19 4.58 0.68	-	-	253 70.28 1.76 1.30 0.19	-	-	-	-	-	403 91.18 2.81 2.08 0.31
Berkeley Heights (township)	1,855 13.84	1,050	708 67.43 67.43 38.17	-	-	-	-	-	291 69.62 41.10 27.71 15.69	-	-	-	-	-	-	-	-	-	-	-	-	-	-	-	-	-
New Providence (borough)	2,133 17.91	896	715 79.80 79.80 33.52	-	-	-	-	-	255 68.36 35.66 28.46 11.95	-	-	-	-	-	-	-	-	-	-	-	-	-	-	-	-	-
Rahway (city)	4,553 17.18	1,149	884 76.94 76.94 19.42	-	-	-	-	-	-	-	378 73.26 42.76 32.90 8.30	-	-	-	-	-	-	-	-	-	-	-	-	-	-	-
Roselle Park (borough)	3,288 24.76	1,243	1,012 81.42 81.42 30.78	-	-	716 81.55 70.75 57.60 21.78	-	-	-	-	-	-	-	-	-	-	-	-	-	-	-	-	-	-	-	-
Scotch Plains (township)	3,577 15.74	1,593	1,201 75.39 75.39 33.58	-	-	473 74.72 39.38 29.69 13.22	-	-	359 78.04 29.89 22.54 10.04	-	-	-	-	-	-	-	-	-	-	-	-	-	-	-	-	-
Springfield (township)	2,937 20.35	559	444 79.43 79.43 15.12	-	-	-	-	-	-	-	-	-	-	-	-	-	-	-	-	-	-	-	-	-	-	-
Summit (city)	3,869 18.31	812	580 71.43 71.43 14.99	-	-	285 73.08 49.14 35.10 7.37	-	-	-	-	-	-	-	-	-	-	-	-	-	-	-	-	-	-	-	-
Union (township)	13,360 24.56	4,258	3,002 70.50 70.50 22.47	-	-	734 71.12 24.45 17.24 5.49	-	-	398 77.58 13.26 9.35 2.98	-	1,490 69.92 49.63 34.99 11.15	-	-	-	-	-	-	-	-	-	-	-	-	-	-	-

Notes: Please refer to the User's Guide for an explanation of data; data is arranged alphabetically by state, then county, then city within each county; table includes counties with populations greater than 49,999 unless noted and cities with populations greater than 9,999 whose Asian and/or NHPI population rates are greater than the national average; (1) Native Hawaiian and other Pacific Islander; (2) excludes Taiwanese; (3) includes Chamorro; (4) county does not meet population threshold but is shown in order to allow inclusion of city

Place	Total foreign-born population	Total Asian population	Asians who are foreign born	Total NHPI[1] population	NHPIs[1] who are foreign born	Asian Indian	Bangladeshi	Cambodian	Chinese[2]	Fijian	Filipino	Guamanian[3]	Hawaiian, Native	Hmong	Indonesian	Japanese	Korean	Laotian	Malaysian	Pakistani	Samoan	Sri Lankan	Taiwanese	Thai	Tongan	Vietnamese
Westfield (town)	2,704 9.12	1,109	783 70.60 70.60 28.96	-	-	-	-	-	-	-	-	-	-	-	-	-	-	-	-	-	-	-	-	-	-	-
Warren County	5,917 5.78	1,221	900 73.71 73.71 15.21	-	-	410 75.51 45.56 33.58 6.93	-	-	-	-	-	-	-	-	-	-	-	-	-	-	-	-	-	-	-	-
NEW MEXICO	149,606 8.22	18,286	11,975 65.49 65.49 8.00	1,248	80 6.41 6.41 0.05	1,743 71.91 14.56 9.53 1.17	-	-	2,774 69.49 23.16 15.17 1.85	-	1,927 65.50 16.09 10.54 1.29	8 2.19 10.00 0.64 0.01	14 3.55 17.50 1.12 0.01	-	-	822 39.81 6.86 4.50 0.55	1,306 75.19 10.91 7.14 0.87	-	-	-	-	-	-	318 79.30 2.66 1.74 0.21	-	2,151 76.90 17.96 11.76 1.44
Bernalillo County	48,073 8.64	9,864	6,471 65.60 65.60 13.46	532	35 6.58 6.58 0.07	787 68.14 12.16 7.98 1.64	-	-	1,323 64.82 20.45 13.41 2.75	-	657 62.45 10.15 6.66 1.37	-	-	-	-	424 37.89 6.55 4.30 0.88	642 74.31 9.92 6.51 1.34	-	-	-	-	-	-	-	-	1,949 78.62 30.12 19.76 4.05
Chaves County	6,891 11.23	387	288 74.42 74.42 4.18	-	-	-	-	-	-	-	-	-	-	-	-	-	-	-	-	-	-	-	-	-	-	-
Dona Ana County	32,623 18.68	1,386	911 65.73 65.73 2.79	-	-	-	-	-	330 83.12 36.22 23.81 1.01	-	-	-	-	-	-	-	-	-	-	-	-	-	-	-	-	-
Los Alamos County[4]	1,232 6.72	798	503 63.03 63.03 40.83	-	-	-	-	-	-	-	-	-	-	-	-	-	-	-	-	-	-	-	-	-	-	-
Los Alamos (cdp)	971 8.16	609	410 67.32 67.32 42.22	-	-	-	-	-	-	-	-	-	-	-	-	-	-	-	-	-	-	-	-	-	-	-
Otero County	6,939 11.14	714	461 64.57 64.57 6.64	-	-	-	-	-	-	-	-	-	-	-	-	-	-	-	-	-	-	-	-	-	-	-
Sandoval County	3,880 4.32	748	565 75.53 75.53 14.56	-	-	-	-	-	-	-	271 81.63 47.96 36.23 6.98	-	-	-	-	-	-	-	-	-	-	-	-	-	-	-

Notes: Please refer to the User's Guide for an explanation of data; data is arranged alphabetically by state, then county, then city within each county; table includes counties with populations greater than 49,999 unless noted and cities with populations greater than 9,999 whose Asian and/or NHPI population rates are greater than the national average; (1) Native Hawaiian and other Pacific Islander; (2) excludes Taiwanese; (3) includes Chamorro; (4) county does not meet population threshold but is shown in order to allow inclusion of city

Place	Total foreign-born population	Total Asian population	Asians who are foreign born	Total NHPI[1] population	NHPIs[1] who are foreign born	Asian Indian	Bangladeshi	Cambodian	Chinese[2]	Fijian	Filipino	Guamanian[3]	Hawaiian, Native	Hmong	Indonesian	Japanese	Korean	Laotian	Malaysian	Pakistani	Samoan	Sri Lankan	Taiwanese	Thai	Tongan	Vietnamese
Santa Fe County	13,075 10.11	944	599 63.45 63.45 4.58	-	-	-	-	-	-	-	-	-	-	-	-	-	-	-	-	-	-	-	-	-	-	-
NEW YORK	3,868,133 20.38	1,044,423	796,943 76.30 76.30 20.60	7,903	2,544 32.19 32.19 0.07	190,604 76.23 23.92 18.25 4.93	16,901 84.14 2.12 1.62 0.44	2,019 69.38 0.25 0.19 0.05	313,366 75.16 39.32 30.00 8.10	-	65,361 75.37 8.20 6.26 1.69	542 30.81 21.31 6.86 0.01	231 16.02 9.08 2.92 0.01	-	1,967 80.85 0.25 0.19 0.05	29,888 79.50 3.75 2.86 0.77	96,184 79.64 12.07 9.21 2.49	2,475 76.96 0.31 0.24 0.06	1,227 87.52 0.15 0.12 0.03	24,909 77.54 3.13 2.38 0.64	239 16.61 9.39 3.02 0.01	2,293 85.27 0.29 0.22 0.06	6,167 79.17 0.77 0.59 0.16	4,900 74.28 0.61 0.47 0.13	-	18,493 79.79 2.32 1.77 0.48
Albany County	19,228 6.53	7,887	5,619 71.24 71.24 29.22	-	-	1,803 73.53 32.09 22.86 9.38	-	-	1,375 69.97 24.47 17.43 7.15	-	479 68.33 8.52 6.07 2.49	-	-	-	-	-	676 69.26 12.03 8.57 3.52	-	-	-	-	-	-	-	-	409 76.74 7.28 5.19 2.13
Colonie (town)	5,414 6.83	2,919	2,165 74.17 74.17 39.99	-	-	905 74.24 41.80 31.00 16.72	-	-	409 66.83 18.89 14.01 7.55	-	-	-	-	-	-	-	-	-	-	-	-	-	-	-	-	-
Guilderland (town)	2,216 6.78	1,238	946 76.41 76.41 42.69	-	-	360 86.96 38.05 29.08 16.25	-	-	-	-	-	-	-	-	-	-	-	-	-	-	-	-	-	-	-	-
Bronx County (Bronx)	385,827 28.95	39,076	30,356 77.68 77.68 7.87	1,099	252 22.93 22.93 0.07	11,542 78.29 38.02 29.54 2.99	1,708 85.74 5.63 4.37 0.44	479 59.14 1.58 1.23 0.12	4,707 74.17 15.51 12.05 1.22	-	3,820 77.42 12.58 9.78 0.99	-	-	-	-	375 72.25 1.24 0.96 0.10	2,945 85.07 9.70 7.54 0.76	-	-	899 79.98 2.96 2.30 0.23	-	-	-	-	-	2,414 80.60 7.95 6.18 0.63
Broome County	10,536 5.25	5,321	3,788 71.19 71.19 35.95	-	-	701 74.73 18.51 13.17 6.65	-	-	1,021 65.57 26.95 19.19 9.69	-	-	-	-	-	-	-	555 70.88 14.65 10.43 5.27	394 76.21 10.40 7.40 3.74	-	-	-	-	-	-	-	444 86.55 11.72 8.34 4.21
Johnson City (village)	1,091 7.02	826	640 77.48 77.48 58.66	-	-	-	-	-	-	-	-	-	-	-	-	-	-	-	-	-	-	-	-	-	-	-
Vestal (town)	2,586 9.75	2,105	1,427 67.79 67.79 55.18	-	-	-	-	-	479 56.35 33.57 22.76 18.52	-	-	-	-	-	-	-	-	-	-	-	-	-	-	-	-	-
Cattaraugus County	1,183 1.41	441	273 61.90 61.90 23.08	-	-	-	-	-	-	-	-	-	-	-	-	-	-	-	-	-	-	-	-	-	-	-

Notes: Please refer to the User's Guide for an explanation of data; data is arranged alphabetically by state, then county, then city within each county; table includes counties with populations greater than 49,999 unless noted and cities with populations greater than 9,999 whose Asian and/or NHPI population rates are greater than the national average; (1) Native Hawaiian and other Pacific Islander; (2) excludes Taiwanese; (3) includes Chamorro; (4) county does not meet population threshold but is shown in order to allow inclusion of city

Place	Total foreign-born population	Total Asian population	Asians who are foreign born	Total NHPI[1] population	NHPIs[1] who are foreign born	Asian Indian	Bangladeshi	Cambodian	Chinese[2]	Fijian	Filipino	Guamanian[3]	Hawaiian, Native	Hmong	Indonesian	Japanese	Korean	Laotian	Malaysian	Pakistani	Samoan	Sri Lankan	Taiwanese	Thai	Tongan	Vietnamese
Cayuga County	1,856 2.26	343	296 86.30 86.30 15.95	-	-	-	-	-	-	-	-	-	-	-	-	-	-	-	-	-	-	-	-	-	-	-
Chautauqua County	2,643 1.89	462	380 82.25 82.25 14.38	-	-	-	-	-	-	-	-	-	-	-	-	-	-	-	-	-	-	-	-	-	-	-
Chemung County	1,972 2.17	796	558 70.10 70.10 28.30	-	-	-	-	-	-	-	-	-	-	-	-	-	-	-	-	-	-	-	-	-	-	-
Chenango County	887 1.73	171	132 77.19 77.19 14.88	-	-	-	-	-	-	-	-	-	-	-	-	-	-	-	-	-	-	-	-	-	-	-
Clinton County	3,628 4.54	714	495 69.33 69.33 13.64	-	-	-	-	-	-	-	-	-	-	-	-	-	-	-	-	-	-	-	-	-	-	-
Columbia County	2,779 4.40	461	368 79.83 79.83 13.24	-	-	-	-	-	-	-	-	-	-	-	-	-	-	-	-	-	-	-	-	-	-	-
Dutchess County	23,600 8.42	7,091	4,785 67.48 67.48 20.28	-	-	1,992 69.60 41.63 28.09 8.44	-	-	1,320 63.95 27.59 18.62 5.59	-	-	-	-	-	-	-	538 71.26 11.24 7.59 2.28	-	-	-	-	-	-	-	-	-
Arlington (cdp)	1,591 12.79	766	495 64.62 64.62 31.11	-	-	-	-	-	-	-	-	-	-	-	-	-	-	-	-	-	-	-	-	-	-	-
Poughkeepsie (town)	4,524 10.58	1,835	1,292 70.41 70.41 28.56	-	-	697 72.08 53.95 37.98 15.41	-	-	294 72.41 22.76 16.02 6.50	-	-	-	-	-	-	-	-	-	-	-	-	-	-	-	-	-
Wappinger (town)	2,734 10.39	1,180	744 63.05 63.05 27.21	-	-	234 51.77 31.45 19.83 8.56	-	-	-	-	-	-	-	-	-	-	-	-	-	-	-	-	-	-	-	-

Notes: Please refer to the User's Guide for an explanation of data; data is arranged alphabetically by state, then county, then city within each county; table includes counties with populations greater than 49,999 unless noted and cities with populations greater than 9,999 whose Asian and/or NHPI population rates are greater than the national average; (1) Native Hawaiian and other Pacific Islander; (2) excludes Taiwanese; (3) includes Chamorro; (4) county does not meet population threshold but is shown in order to allow inclusion of city

Place	Total foreign-born population	Total Asian population	Asians who are foreign born	Total NHPI[1] population	NHPIs[1] who are foreign born	Asian Indian	Bangladeshi	Cambodian	Chinese[2]	Fijian	Filipino	Guamanian[3]	Hawaiian, Native	Hmong	Indonesian	Japanese	Korean	Laotian	Malaysian	Pakistani	Samoan	Sri Lankan	Taiwanese	Thai	Tongan	Vietnamese
Erie County	42,886 4.51	12,893	9,791 75.94 75.94 22.83	-	-	2,644 77.31 27.00 20.51 6.17	-	-	2,238 73.21 22.86 17.36 5.22	-	449 66.52 4.59 3.48 1.05	-	-	-	-	318 64.11 3.25 2.47 0.74	1,569 78.92 16.02 12.17 3.66	-	-	-	-	-	-	-	-	1,234 81.24 12.60 9.57 2.88
Amherst (town)	10,511 9.02	5,559	3,891 69.99 69.99 37.02	-	-	1,327 73.52 34.10 23.87 12.62	-	-	1,086 64.53 27.91 19.54 10.33	-	-	-	-	-	-	-	671 71.46 17.24 12.07 6.38	-	-	-	-	-	-	-	-	-
Herkimer County	1,297 2.01	255	215 84.31 84.31 16.58	-	-	-	-	-	-	-	-	-	-	-	-	-	-	-	-	-	-	-	-	-	-	-
Jefferson County	4,116 3.68	1,171	742 63.36 63.36 18.03	-	-	-	-	-	-	-	193 62.26 26.01 16.48 4.69	-	-	-	-	-	254 70.95 34.23 21.69 6.17	-	-	-	-	-	-	-	-	-
Kings County (Brooklyn)	931,769 37.79	185,814	142,618 76.75 76.75 15.31	1,549	612 39.51 39.51 0.07	19,416 78.31 13.61 10.45 2.08	3,382 86.10 2.37 1.82 0.36	393 78.44 0.28 0.21 0.04	91,569 75.80 64.21 49.28 9.83	-	5,563 77.82 3.90 2.99 0.60	147 30.06 24.02 9.49 0.02	-	-	-	1,582 72.70 1.11 0.85 0.17	5,252 77.68 3.68 2.83 0.56	-	-	7,740 80.45 5.43 4.17 0.83	-	-	-	-	-	2,988 78.02 2.10 1.61 0.32
Livingston County	1,668 2.59	685	472 68.91 68.91 28.30	-	-	-	-	-	-	-	-	-	-	-	-	-	-	-	-	-	-	-	-	-	-	-
Madison County	1,558 2.24	478	292 61.09 61.09 18.74	-	-	-	-	-	-	-	-	-	-	-	-	-	-	-	-	-	-	-	-	-	-	-
Monroe County	53,743 7.31	17,744	13,188 74.32 74.32 24.54	-	-	3,389 75.39 25.70 19.10 6.31	-	273 71.65 2.07 1.54 0.51	2,920 73.44 22.14 16.46 5.43	-	423 69.12 3.21 2.38 0.79	-	-	-	-	368 63.12 2.79 2.07 0.68	2,083 83.15 15.79 11.74 3.88	1,038 76.61 7.87 5.85 1.93	-	287 62.12 2.18 1.62 0.53	-	-	-	-	-	1,704 75.17 12.92 9.60 3.17
Brighton (town)	5,494 15.44	2,811	2,325 82.71 82.71 42.32	-	-	853 84.88 36.69 30.35 15.53	-	-	514 80.31 22.11 18.29 9.36	-	-	-	-	-	-	-	-	-	-	-	-	-	-	-	-	-
Henrietta (town)	3,287 8.42	2,028	1,371 67.60 67.60 41.71	-	-	323 68.43 23.56 15.93 9.83	-	-	322 63.89 23.49 15.88 9.80	-	-	-	-	-	-	-	-	-	-	-	-	-	-	-	-	-

Notes: Please refer to the User's Guide for an explanation of data; data is arranged alphabetically by state, then county, then city within each county; table includes counties with populations greater than 49,999 unless noted and cities with populations greater than 9,999 whose Asian and/or NHPI population rates are greater than the national average; (1) Native Hawaiian and other Pacific Islander; (2) excludes Taiwanese; (3) includes Chamorro; (4) county does not meet population threshold but is shown in order to allow inclusion of city

Place	Total foreign-born population	Total Asian population	Asians who are foreign born	Total NHPI[1] population	NHPIs[1] who are foreign born	Asian Indian	Bangladeshi	Cambodian	Chinese[2]	Fijian	Filipino	Guamanian[3]	Hawaiian, Native	Hmong	Indonesian	Japanese	Korean	Laotian	Malaysian	Pakistani	Samoan	Sri Lankan	Taiwanese	Thai	Tongan	Vietnamese
Pittsford (town)	2,154 7.91	1,274	949 74.49 74.49 44.06	-	-	442 76.60 46.58 34.69 20.52	-	-	-	-	-					-	-	-	-	-	-	-	-	-	-	-
Nassau County	238,414 17.86	62,536	43,566 69.67 69.67 18.27	410	102 24.88 24.88 0.04	16,507 70.32 37.89 26.40 6.92	-	-	9,296 62.25 21.34 14.87 3.90	-	5,297 73.90 12.16 8.47 2.22	-	-	-	-	1,508 84.39 3.46 2.41 0.63	6,659 73.30 15.28 10.65 2.79	-	-	1,696 72.23 3.89 2.71 0.71	-	-	439 72.68 1.01 0.70 0.18	268 71.28 0.62 0.43 0.11	-	418 92.89 0.96 0.67 0.18
East Meadow (cdp)	5,423 14.46	2,418	1,634 67.58 67.58 30.13	-	-	738 65.37 45.17 30.52 13.61	-	-	-	-	265 76.15 16.22 10.96 4.89	-	-	-	-	-	-	-	-	-	-	-	-	-	-	-
Elmont (cdp)	12,039 36.86	3,178	2,288 71.99 71.99 19.00	-	-	1,432 74.97 62.59 45.06 11.89	-	-		-	374 68.00 16.35 11.77 3.11	-	-	-	-	-	-	-	-	-	-	-	-	-	-	-
Franklin Square (cdp)	4,852 16.54	1,173	881 75.11 75.11 18.16	-	-	385 84.80 43.70 32.82 7.93	-	-	-	-		-	-	-	-	-	-	-	-	-	-	-	-	-	-	-
Glen Cove (city)	7,422 27.88	1,053	812 77.11 77.11 10.94	-	-	240 73.85 29.56 22.79 3.23	-	-	-	-	-	-	-	-	-	-	304 76.38 37.44 28.87 4.10	-	-	-	-	-	-	-	-	-
Hicksville (cdp)	7,410 17.96	3,689	2,577 69.86 69.86 34.78	-	-	1,259 67.91 48.86 34.13 16.99	-	-	461 61.80 17.89 12.50 6.22	-	382 73.89 14.82 10.36 5.16	-	-	-	-	-		-	-	-	-	-	-	-	-	-
Jericho (cdp)	1,802 13.88	1,483	1,031 69.52 69.52 57.21	-	-	-	-	-	-	-	-	-	-	-	-	-	522 72.80 50.63 35.20 28.97	-	-	-	-	-	-	-	-	-
Mineola (village)	5,215 27.10	903	709 78.52 78.52 13.60	-	-	264 76.52 37.24 29.24 5.06	-	-	-	-	-	-	-	-	-	-	-	-	-	-	-	-	-	-	-	-
North Hempstead (town)	55,357 24.87	20,579	14,152 68.77 68.77 25.56	-	-	5,310 69.48 37.52 25.80 9.59	-	-	3,538 63.20 25.00 17.19 6.39	-	1,002 73.84 7.08 4.87 1.81	-	-	-	-	830 86.91 5.86 4.03 1.50	2,319 71.40 16.39 11.27 4.19	-	-	388 62.78 2.74 1.89 0.70	-	-	191 67.49 1.35 0.93 0.35	-	-	-

Notes: Please refer to the User's Guide for an explanation of data; data is arranged alphabetically by state, then county, then city within each county; table includes counties with populations greater than 49,999 unless noted and cities with populations greater than 9,999 whose Asian and/or NHPI population rates are greater than the national average; (1) Native Hawaiian and other Pacific Islander; (2) excludes Taiwanese; (3) includes Chamorro; (4) county does not meet population threshold but is shown in order to allow inclusion of city

Place	Total foreign-born population	Total Asian population	Asians who are foreign born	Total NHPI[1] population	NHPIs[1] who are foreign born	Asian Indian	Bangladeshi	Cambodian	Chinese[2]	Fijian	Filipino	Guamanian[3]	Hawaiian, Native	Hmong	Indonesian	Japanese	Korean	Laotian	Malaysian	Pakistani	Samoan	Sri Lankan	Taiwanese	Thai	Tongan	Vietnamese
North Merrick (cdp)	940 7.94	479	323 67.43 67.43 34.36	-	-	-	-	-	-	-	-	-	-	-	-	-	-	-	-	-	-	-	-	-	-	-
North New Hyde Park (cdp)	3,101 21.32	2,141	1,342 62.68 62.68 43.28	-	-	771 64.41 57.45 36.01 24.86	-	-	400 55.56 29.81 18.68 12.90	-	-	-	-	-	-	-	-	-	-	-	-	-	-	-	-	-
North Valley Stream (cdp)	5,408 34.25	1,469	1,023 69.64 69.64 18.92	-	-	401 63.35 39.20 27.30 7.41	-	-	-	-	-	-	-	-	-	-	-	-	-	-	-	-	-	-	-	-
Oyster Bay (town)	35,610 12.12	13,857	9,676 69.83 69.83 27.17	-	-	3,595 69.93 37.15 25.94 10.10	-	-	2,291 62.36 23.68 16.53 6.43	-	974 75.92 10.07 7.03 2.74	-	-	-	-	315 84.22 3.26 2.27 0.88	1,805 73.02 18.65 13.03 5.07	-	-	-	-	-	-	-	-	-
Plainview (cdp)	3,083 12.03	1,250	845 67.60 67.60 27.41	-	-	238 69.59 28.17 19.04 7.72	-	-	217 61.82 25.68 17.36 7.04	-	-	-	-	-	-	-	252 65.12 29.82 20.16 8.17	-	-	-	-	-	-	-	-	-
Port Washington (cdp)	3,231 21.26	962	739 76.82 76.82 22.87	-	-	197 76.95 26.66 20.48 6.10	-	-	-	-	-	-	-	-	-	-	-	-	-	-	-	-	-	-	-	-
Salisbury (cdp)	2,158 17.54	1,089	787 72.27 72.27 36.47	-	-	289 76.46 36.72 26.54 13.39	-	-	-	-	-	-	-	-	-	-	-	-	-	-	-	-	-	-	-	-
Syosset (cdp)	3,261 17.59	2,327	1,579 67.86 67.86 48.42	-	-	519 71.19 32.87 22.30 15.92	-	-	452 58.02 28.63 19.42 13.86	-	-	-	-	-	-	-	411 73.39 26.03 17.66 12.60	-	-	-	-	-	-	-	-	-
Valley Stream (village)	7,129 19.59	2,553	1,796 70.35 70.35 25.19	-	-	-	-	-	472 59.30 26.28 18.49 6.62	-	449 73.37 25.00 17.59 6.30	-	-	-	-	-	-	-	-	-	-	-	-	-	-	-
West Hempstead (cdp)	3,384 18.09	994	726 73.04 73.04 21.45	-	-	242 69.94 33.33 24.35 7.15	-	-	-	-	-	-	-	-	-	-	-	-	-	-	-	-	-	-	-	-

Notes: Please refer to the User's Guide for an explanation of data; data is arranged alphabetically by state, then county, then city within each county; table includes counties with populations greater than 49,999 unless noted and cities with populations greater than 9,999 whose Asian and/or NHPI population rates are greater than the national average; (1) Native Hawaiian and other Pacific Islander; (2) excludes Taiwanese; (3) includes Chamorro; (4) county does not meet population threshold but is shown in order to allow inclusion of city

Place	Total foreign-born population	Total Asian population	Asians who are foreign born	Total NHPI[1] population	NHPIs[1] who are foreign born	Asian Indian	Bangladeshi	Cambodian	Chinese[2]	Fijian	Filipino	Guamanian[3]	Hawaiian, Native	Hmong	Indonesian	Japanese	Korean	Laotian	Malaysian	Pakistani	Samoan	Sri Lankan	Taiwanese	Thai	Tongan	Vietnamese
Westbury (village)	4,471 31.35	694	534 76.95 76.95 11.94	-	-	-	-	-	-	-	-	-	-	-	-	-	-	-	-	-	-	-	-	-	-	-
Woodmere (cdp)	2,505 15.23	607	412 67.87 67.87 16.45	-	-	-	-	-	-	-	-	-	-	-	-	-	-	-	-	-	-	-	-	-	-	-
New York City	2,871,032 35.85	788,110	611,328 77.57 77.57 21.29	4,870	1,904 39.10 39.10 0.07	132,273 77.72 21.64 16.78 4.61	16,146 84.32 2.64 2.05 0.56	1,097 67.76 0.18 0.14 0.04	273,113 76.39 44.68 34.65 9.51	-	45,319 76.88 7.41 5.75 1.58	371 31.55 19.49 7.62 0.01	226 29.12 11.87 4.64 0.01	-	1,412 77.75 0.23 0.18 0.05	18,017 80.79 2.95 2.29 0.63	70,286 80.66 11.50 8.92 2.45	-	1,065 88.97 0.17 0.14 0.04	19,009 79.69 3.11 2.41 0.66	159 21.81 8.35 3.26 0.01	1,722 85.93 0.28 0.22 0.06	4,003 81.58 0.65 0.51 0.14	2,847 74.47 0.47 0.36 0.10	-	9,828 79.84 1.61 1.25 0.34
New York County (Manhattan)	452,440 29.43	144,368	108,329 75.04 75.04 23.94	612	239 39.05 39.05 0.05	9,341 65.45 8.62 6.47 2.06	669 85.44 0.62 0.46 0.15	-	65,914 77.25 60.85 45.66 14.57	-	6,582 74.53 6.08 4.56 1.45	-	-	-	-	11,512 81.43 10.63 7.97 2.54	8,020 70.23 7.40 5.56 1.77	-	-	797 73.39 0.74 0.55 0.18	-	-	652 62.04 0.60 0.45 0.14	599 71.74 0.55 0.41 0.13	-	1,236 78.78 1.14 0.86 0.27
Niagara County	8,495 3.86	1,148	870 75.78 75.78 10.24	-	-	313 72.62 35.98 27.26 3.68	-	-	-	-	-	-	-	-	-	-	-	-	-	-	-	-	-	-	-	-
Oneida County	12,347 5.24	2,740	2,027 73.98 73.98 16.42	-	-	346 60.17 17.07 12.63 2.80	-	-	248 84.35 12.23 9.05 2.01	-	-	-	-	-	-	-	-	-	-	-	-	-	-	-	-	837 76.72 41.29 30.55 6.78
Onondaga County	25,929 5.66	9,593	7,439 77.55 77.55 28.69	-	-	1,483 74.79 19.94 15.46 5.72	-	-	1,412 83.25 18.98 14.72 5.45	-	521 68.64 7.00 5.43 2.01	-	-	-	-	181 51.57 2.43 1.89 0.70	1,146 87.82 15.41 11.95 4.42	-	-	-	-	-	-	-	-	1,467 85.14 19.72 15.29 5.66
Ontario County	2,749 2.74	696	517 74.28 74.28 18.81	-	-	-	-	-	-	-	-	-	-	-	-	-	-	-	-	-	-	-	-	-	-	-
Orange County	28,710 8.41	5,476	3,799 69.38 69.38 13.23	-	-	1,144 66.47 30.11 20.89 3.98	-	-	875 67.88 23.03 15.98 3.05	-	520 67.10 13.69 9.50 1.81	-	-	-	-	-	587 72.11 15.45 10.72 2.04	-	-	-	-	-	-	-	-	-
Oswego County	1,958 1.60	540	362 67.04 67.04 18.49	-	-	-	-	-	-	-	-	-	-	-	-	-	-	-	-	-	-	-	-	-	-	-

Notes: Please refer to the User's Guide for an explanation of data; data is arranged alphabetically by state, then county, then city within each county; table includes counties with populations greater than 49,999 unless noted and cities with populations greater than 9,999 whose Asian and/or NHPI population rates are greater than the national average; (1) Native Hawaiian and other Pacific Islander; (2) excludes Taiwanese; (3) includes Chamorro; (4) county does not meet population threshold but is shown in order to allow inclusion of city

Place	Total foreign-born population	Total Asian population	Asians who are foreign born	Total NHPI[1] population	NHPIs[1] who are foreign born	Asian Indian	Bangladeshi	Cambodian	Chinese[2]	Fijian	Filipino	Guamanian[3]	Hawaiian, Native	Hmong	Indonesian	Japanese	Korean	Laotian	Malaysian	Pakistani	Samoan	Sri Lankan	Taiwanese	Thai	Tongan	Vietnamese
Otsego County	1,416	304	176	-	-	-	-	-	-	-	-	-	-	-	-	-	-	-	-	-	-	-	-	-	-	-
	2.30		57.89																							
			57.89																							
			12.43																							
Putnam County	8,420	1,213	776	-	-	281	-	-	268	-	-	-	-	-	-	-	-	-	-	-	-	-	-	-	-	-
	8.79		63.97			67.71			63.21																	
						36.21			34.54																	
			63.97			23.17			22.09																	
			9.22			3.34			3.18																	
Queens County (Queens)	1,028,339	394,314	312,683	1,394	787	87,280	10,371	-	106,258	-	25,655	-	-	-	1,007	4,419	51,479	-	531	9,082	-	803	3,027	1,779	-	3,082
	46.13		79.30		56.46	79.39	83.62		77.14		78.11				81.01	83.65	82.69		93.65	80.71		85.70	87.41	75.25		82.43
						27.91	3.32		33.98		8.20				0.32	1.41	16.46		0.17	2.90		0.26	0.97	0.57		0.99
			79.30		56.46	22.13	2.63		26.95		6.51				0.26	1.12	13.06		0.13	2.30		0.20	0.77	0.45		0.78
			30.41		0.08	8.49	1.01		10.33		2.49				0.10	0.43	5.01		0.05	0.88		0.08	0.29	0.17		0.30
Rensselaer County	5,709	2,430	1,795	-	-	330	-	-	770	-	-	-	-	-	-	-	337	-	-	-	-	-	-	-	-	-
	3.74		73.87			75.69			71.03								90.35									
						18.38			42.90								18.77									
			73.87			13.58			31.69								13.87									
			31.44			5.78			13.49								5.90									
Richmond Co. (Staten Island)	72,657	24,538	17,342	-	-	4,694	-	-	4,665	-	3,699	-	-	-	-	-	2,590	-	-	491	-	447	-	-	-	-
	16.37		70.67			72.91			63.71		71.29						79.89			63.60		84.82				
						27.07			26.90		21.33						14.93			2.83		2.58				
			70.67			19.13			19.01		15.07						10.56			2.00		1.82				
			23.87			6.46			6.42		5.09						3.56			0.68		0.62				
Rockland County	54,766	16,130	11,729	-	-	4,089	-	-	1,379	-	3,259	-	-	-	-	-	1,488	-	-	-	-	-	-	-	-	-
	19.10		72.72			73.25			68.95		72.34						77.86									
						34.86			11.76		27.79						12.69									
			72.72			25.35			8.55		20.20						9.23									
			21.42			7.47			2.52		5.95						2.72									
Clarkstown (town)	13,683	6,705	4,665	-	-	1,601	-	-	494	-	1,591	-	-	-	-	-	563	-	-	-	-	-	-	-	-	-
	16.67		69.57			66.88			62.22		72.91						78.09									
						34.32			10.59		34.11						12.07									
			69.57			23.88			7.37		23.73						8.40									
			34.09			11.70			3.61		11.63						4.11									
Nanuet (cdp)	3,434	1,559	1,084	-	-	388	-	-	-	-	-	-	-	-	-	-	-	-	-	-	-	-	-	-	-	-
	20.55		69.53			67.01																				
						35.79																				
			69.53			24.89																				
			31.57			11.30																				
New City (cdp)	5,443	2,583	1,746	-	-	687	-	-	-	-	431	-	-	-	-	-	-	-	-	-	-	-	-	-	-	-
	15.94		67.60			64.39					73.05															
						39.35					24.68															
			67.60			26.60					16.69															
			32.08			12.62					7.92															
Orangetown (town)	7,581	3,001	2,283	-	-	543	-	-	418	-	527	-	-	-	-	-	430	-	-	-	-	-	-	-	-	-
	15.86		76.07			79.74			71.94		74.02						75.70									
						23.78			18.31		23.08						18.83									
			76.07			18.09			13.93		17.56						14.33									
			30.11			7.16			5.51		6.95						5.67									

Notes: Please refer to the User's Guide for an explanation of data; data is arranged alphabetically by state, then county, then city within each county; table includes counties with populations greater than 49,999 unless noted and cities with populations greater than 9,999 whose Asian and/or NHPI population rates are greater than the national average; (1) Native Hawaiian and other Pacific Islander; (2) excludes Taiwanese; (3) includes Chamorro; (4) county does not meet population threshold but is shown in order to allow inclusion of city

Place	Total foreign-born population	Total Asian population	Asians who are foreign born	Total NHPI[1] population	NHPIs[1] who are foreign born	Asian Indian	Bangladeshi	Cambodian	Chinese[2]	Fijian	Filipino	Guamanian[3]	Hawaiian, Native	Hmong	Indonesian	Japanese	Korean	Laotian	Malaysian	Pakistani	Samoan	Sri Lankan	Taiwanese	Thai	Tongan	Vietnamese
Ramapo (town)	24,848 22.82	5,131	3,846 74.96 74.96 15.48	-	-	1,555 77.17 40.43 30.31 6.26	-	-	353 74.63 9.18 6.88 1.42	-	960 70.80 24.96 18.71 3.86	-	-	-	-	-	434 80.52 11.28 8.46 1.75	-	-	-	-	-	-	-	-	-
Spring Valley (village)	10,921 43.04	1,479	1,227 82.96 82.96 11.24	-	-	611 78.94 49.80 41.31 5.59	-	-	-	-	-	-	-	-	-	-	-	-	-	-	-	-	-	-	-	-
St. Lawrence County	3,800 3.39	657	506 77.02 77.02 13.32	-	-	-	-	-	-	-	-	-	-	-	-	-	-	-	-	-	-	-	-	-	-	-
Saratoga County	6,188 3.08	2,179	1,647 75.59 75.59 26.62	-	-	500 72.05 30.36 22.95 8.08	-	-	277 70.30 16.82 12.71 4.48	-	-	-	-	-	-	-	391 87.67 23.74 17.94 6.32	-	-	-	-	-	-	-	-	-
Schenectady County	7,811 5.33	2,850	2,077 72.88 72.88 26.59	-	-	907 79.08 43.67 31.82 11.61	-	-	584 69.36 28.12 20.49 7.48	-	-	-	-	-	-	-	-	-	-	-	-	-	-	-	-	-
Niskayuna (town)	1,890 9.33	1,175	847 72.09 72.09 44.81	-	-	410 79.00 48.41 34.89 21.69	-	-	-	-	-	-	-	-	-	-	-	-	-	-	-	-	-	-	-	-
Steuben County	1,845 1.87	799	586 73.34 73.34 31.76	-	-	-	-	-	-	-	-	-	-	-	-	-	-	-	-	-	-	-	-	-	-	-
Suffolk County	158,525 11.17	34,143	24,498 71.75 71.75 15.45	427	93 21.78 21.78 0.06	7,620 74.27 31.10 22.32 4.81	-	-	6,717 68.93 27.42 19.67 4.24	-	2,795 68.93 11.41 8.19 1.76	-	-	-	-	709 67.91 2.89 2.08 0.45	3,083 78.87 12.58 9.03 1.94	-	-	1,406 70.05 5.74 4.12 0.89	-	-	329 76.87 1.34 0.96 0.21	258 66.67 1.05 0.76 0.16	-	557 79.12 2.27 1.63 0.35
Coram (cdp)	3,695 10.56	1,284	866 67.45 67.45 23.44	-	-	-	-	-	287 67.06 33.14 22.35 7.77	-	-	-	-	-	-	-	-	-	-	-	-	-	-	-	-	-
Dix Hills (cdp)	3,717 14.24	1,955	1,251 63.99 63.99 33.66	-	-	529 63.66 42.29 27.06 14.23	-	-	295 66.14 23.58 15.09 7.94	-	-	-	-	-	-	-	-	-	-	-	-	-	-	-	-	-

Notes: Please refer to the User's Guide for an explanation of data; data is arranged alphabetically by state, then county, then city within each county; table includes counties with populations greater than 49,999 unless noted and cities with populations greater than 9,999 whose Asian and/or NHPI population rates are greater than the national average; (1) Native Hawaiian and other Pacific Islander; (2) excludes Taiwanese; (3) includes Chamorro; (4) county does not meet population threshold but is shown in order to allow inclusion of city

Place	Total foreign-born population	Total Asian population	Asians who are foreign born	Total NHPI[1] population	NHPIs[1] who are foreign born	Asian Indian	Bangladeshi	Cambodian	Chinese[2]	Fijian	Filipino	Guamanian[3]	Hawaiian, Native	Hmong	Indonesian	Japanese	Korean	Laotian	Malaysian	Pakistani	Samoan	Sri Lankan	Taiwanese	Thai	Tongan	Vietnamese
Elwood (cdp)	1,239 11.42	712	430 60.39 60.39 34.71	-	-	-	-	-	-	-	-	-	-	-	-	-	-	-	-	-	-	-	-	-	-	-
Lake Grove (village)	914 8.79	554	387 69.86 69.86 42.34	-	-	-	-	-	-	-	-	-	-	-	-	-	-	-	-	-	-	-	-	-	-	-
Melville (cdp)	1,510 10.39	637	436 68.45 68.45 28.87	-	-	-	-	-	-	-	-	-	-	-	-	-	-	-	-	-	-	-	-	-	-	-
Setauket-East Setauket (cdp)	2,185 13.70	1,477	1,180 79.89 79.89 54.00	-	-	-	-	-	574 84.91 48.64 38.86 26.27	-	-	-	-	-	-	-	-	-	-	-	-	-	-	-	-	-
Stony Brook (cdp)	1,464 10.70	802	579 72.19 72.19 39.55	-	-	-	-	-	311 73.87 53.71 38.78 21.24	-	-	-	-	-	-	-	-	-	-	-	-	-	-	-	-	-
Sullivan County	5,875 7.94	855	649 75.91 75.91 11.05	-	-	-	-	-	-	-	-	-	-	-	-	-	-	-	-	-	-	-	-	-	-	-
Tioga County	872 1.68	349	241 69.05 69.05 27.64	-	-	-	-	-	-	-	-	-	-	-	-	-	-	-	-	-	-	-	-	-	-	-
Tompkins County	10,166 10.53	7,146	4,791 67.04 67.04 47.13	-	-	801 76.29 16.72 11.21 7.88	-	-	1,994 64.10 41.62 27.90 19.61	-	-	-	-	-	-	443 76.12 9.25 6.20 4.36	765 63.59 15.97 10.71 7.53	-	-	-	-	-	-	-	-	-
Ithaca (city)	4,650 16.03	4,039	2,406 59.57 59.57 51.74	-	-	356 67.55 14.80 8.81 7.66	-	-	1,175 58.93 48.84 29.09 25.27	-	-	-	-	-	-	-	226 47.58 9.39 5.60 4.86	-	-	-	-	-	-	-	-	-
Lansing (town)	1,305 12.67	1,071	791 73.86 73.86 60.61	-	-	-	-	-	-	-	-	-	-	-	-	-	-	-	-	-	-	-	-	-	-	-

Notes: Please refer to the User's Guide for an explanation of data; data is arranged alphabetically by state, then county, then city within each county; table includes counties with populations greater than 49,999 unless noted and cities with populations greater than 9,999 whose Asian and/or NHPI population rates are greater than the national average; (1) Native Hawaiian and other Pacific Islander; (2) excludes Taiwanese; (3) includes Chamorro; (4) county does not meet population threshold but is shown in order to allow inclusion of city

Place	Total foreign-born population	Total Asian population	Asians who are foreign born	Total NHPI[1] population	NHPIs[1] who are foreign born	Asian Indian	Bangladeshi	Cambodian	Chinese[2]	Fijian	Filipino	Guamanian[3]	Hawaiian, Native	Hmong	Indonesian	Japanese	Korean	Laotian	Malaysian	Pakistani	Samoan	Sri Lankan	Taiwanese	Thai	Tongan	Vietnamese
Ulster County	10,468 5.89	1,815	1,287 70.91 70.91 12.29	-	-	-	-	-	343 63.75 26.65 18.90 3.28	-	-	-	-	-	-	-	-	-	-	-	-	-	-	-	-	-
New Paltz (town)	1,431 11.15	576	336 58.33 58.33 23.48	-	-	-	-	-	-	-	-	-	-	-	-	-	-	-	-	-	-	-	-	-	-	-
Warren County	1,541 2.43	504	333 66.07 66.07 21.61	-	-	-	-	-	-	-	-	-	-	-	-	-	-	-	-	-	-	-	-	-	-	-
Wayne County	2,157 2.30	394	309 78.43 78.43 14.33	-	-	-	-	-	-	-	-	-	-	-	-	-	-	-	-	-	-	-	-	-	-	-
Westchester County	205,429 22.25	41,751	31,862 76.31 76.31 15.51	-	-	10,966 75.65 34.42 26.27 5.34	-	-	4,856 68.52 15.24 11.63 2.36	-	3,928 79.26 12.33 9.41 1.91	-	-	-	-	6,315 84.18 19.82 15.13 3.07	3,307 78.22 10.38 7.92 1.61	-	-	625 74.23 1.96 1.50 0.30	-	-	236 69.82 0.74 0.57 0.11	420 70.71 1.32 1.01 0.20	-	-
Dobbs Ferry (village)	1,897 17.86	750	537 71.60 71.60 28.31	-	-	-	-	-	-	-	-	-	-	-	-	-	-	-	-	-	-	-	-	-	-	-
Eastchester (cdp)	2,957 15.93	1,293	1,035 80.05 80.05 35.00	-	-	-	-	-	-	-	-	-	-	-	-	499 90.89 48.21 38.59 16.88	-	-	-	-	-	-	-	-	-	-
Eastchester (town)	5,239 16.73	2,265	1,833 80.93 80.93 34.99	-	-	-	-	-	-	-	-	-	-	-	-	1,060 87.60 57.83 46.80 20.23	-	-	-	-	-	-	-	-	-	-
Greenburgh (town)	18,195 20.97	7,818	6,042 77.28 77.28 33.21	-	-	2,002 77.42 33.13 25.61 11.00	-	-	913 71.61 15.11 11.68 5.02	-	438 75.65 7.25 5.60 2.41	-	-	-	-	1,685 86.10 27.89 21.55 9.26	740 74.00 12.25 9.47 4.07	-	-	-	-	-	-	-	-	-
Harrison (village)	4,520 18.72	1,336	1,118 83.68 83.68 24.73	-	-	-	-	-	-	-	-	-	-	-	-	648 93.51 57.96 48.50 14.34	-	-	-	-	-	-	-	-	-	-

Notes: Please refer to the User's Guide for an explanation of data; data is arranged alphabetically by state, then county, then city within each county; table includes counties with populations greater than 49,999 unless noted and cities with populations greater than 9,999 whose Asian and/or NHPI population rates are greater than the national average; (1) Native Hawaiian and other Pacific Islander; (2) excludes Taiwanese; (3) includes Chamorro; (4) county does not meet population threshold but is shown in order to allow inclusion of city

Place	Total foreign-born population	Total Asian population	Asians who are foreign born	Total NHPI[1] population	NHPIs[1] who are foreign born	Asian Indian	Bangladeshi	Cambodian	Chinese[2]	Fijian	Filipino	Guamanian[3]	Hawaiian, Native	Hmong	Indonesian	Japanese	Korean	Laotian	Malaysian	Pakistani	Samoan	Sri Lankan	Taiwanese	Thai	Tongan	Vietnamese
New Castle (town)	1,970	1,014	669	-	-	261	-	-	208	-	-	-	-	-	-	-	-	-	-	-	-	-	-	-	-	-
	11.26		65.98			64.60			67.53																	
						39.01			31.09																	
			65.98			25.74			20.51																	
			33.96			13.25			10.56																	
New Rochelle (city)	19,722	2,686	2,131	-	-	920	-	-	402	-	-	-	-	-	-	-	-	-	-	-	-	-	-	-	-	-
	27.32		79.34			78.30			74.31																	
						43.17			18.86																	
			79.34			34.25			14.97																	
			10.81			4.66			2.04																	
North Castle (town)	1,383	471	277	-	-	-	-	-	-	-	-	-	-	-	-	-	-	-	-	-	-	-	-	-	-	-
	12.75		58.81																							
			58.81																							
			20.03																							
Ossining (town)	8,834	1,510	1,219	-	-	548	-	-	-	-	-	-	-	-	-	-	-	-	-	-	-	-	-	-	-	-
	24.18		80.73			78.74																				
						44.95																				
			80.73			36.29																				
			13.80			6.20																				
Ossining (village)	7,311	937	760	-	-	227	-	-	-	-	-	-	-	-	-	-	-	-	-	-	-	-	-	-	-	-
	30.45		81.11			74.43																				
						29.87																				
			81.11			24.23																				
			10.40			3.10																				
Pelham (town)	1,582	454	330	-	-	-	-	-	-	-	-	-	-	-	-	-	-	-	-	-	-	-	-	-	-	-
	13.33		72.69																							
			72.69																							
			20.86																							
Rye (city)	3,214	1,075	842	-	-	-	-	-	-	-	-	-	-	-	-	585	-	-	-	-	-	-	-	-	-	-
	21.49		78.33													90.70										
																69.48										
			78.33													54.42										
			26.20													18.20										
Scarsdale (village)	3,216	2,225	1,529	-	-	278	-	-	225	-	-	-	-	-	-	637	227	-	-	-	-	-	-	-	-	-
	18.04		68.72			66.99			59.84							81.25	59.27									
						18.18			14.72							41.66	14.85									
			68.72			12.49			10.11							28.63	10.20									
			47.54			8.64			7.00							19.81	7.06									
Tarrytown (village)	2,468	638	540	-	-	-	-	-	-	-	-	-	-	-	-	-	-	-	-	-	-	-	-	-	-	-
	22.25		84.64																							
			84.64																							
			21.88																							
White Plains (city)	15,572	2,199	1,731	-	-	615	-	-	401	-	-	-	-	-	-	-	-	-	-	-	-	-	-	-	-	-
	29.34		78.72			78.14			71.35																	
						35.53			23.17																	
			78.72			27.97			18.24																	
			11.12			3.95			2.58																	

Notes: Please refer to the User's Guide for an explanation of data; data is arranged alphabetically by state, then county, then city within each county; table includes counties with populations greater than 49,999 unless noted and cities with populations greater than 9,999 whose Asian and/or NHPI population rates are greater than the national average; (1) Native Hawaiian and other Pacific Islander; (2) excludes Taiwanese; (3) includes Chamorro; (4) county does not meet population threshold but is shown in order to allow inclusion of city

Place	Total foreign-born population	Total Asian population	Asians who are foreign born	Total NHPI[1] population	NHPIs[1] who are foreign born	Asian Indian	Bangladeshi	Cambodian	Chinese[2]	Fijian	Filipino	Guamanian[3]	Hawaiian, Native	Hmong	Indonesian	Japanese	Korean	Laotian	Malaysian	Pakistani	Samoan	Sri Lankan	Taiwanese	Thai	Tongan	Vietnamese
Yonkers (city)	51,687 26.36	9,564	7,313 76.46 76.46 14.15	-	-	3,640 77.63 49.77 38.06 7.04	-	-	591 67.62 8.08 6.18 1.14	-	1,384 76.17 18.93 14.47 2.68	-	-	-	-	-	905 85.14 12.38 9.46 1.75	-	-	-	-	-	-	-	-	-
NORTH CAROLINA	430,000 5.34	111,292	80,098 71.97 71.97 18.63	3,699	699 18.90 18.90 0.16	19,112 75.39 23.86 17.17 4.44	-	1,654 69.79 2.06 1.49 0.38	13,200 75.42 16.48 11.86 3.07	-	7,099 69.64 8.86 6.38 1.65	159 13.28 22.75 4.30 0.04	15 1.31 2.15 0.41 <0.01	3,544 51.97 4.42 3.18 0.82	-	4,078 67.55 5.09 3.66 0.95	9,516 76.72 11.88 8.55 2.21	3,317 66.79 4.14 2.98 0.77	-	1,508 80.47 1.88 1.35 0.35	161 32.53 23.03 4.35 0.04	-	694 71.47 0.87 0.62 0.16	1,257 77.35 1.57 1.13 0.29	-	12,135 77.77 15.15 10.90 2.82
Alamance County	8,281 6.33	1,155	851 73.68 73.68 10.28	-	-	-	-	-	-	-	-	-	-	-	-	-	-	-	-	-	-	-	-	-	-	-
Buncombe County	7,964 3.86	1,849	1,303 70.47 70.47 16.36	-	-	412 74.64 31.62 22.28 5.17	-	-	-	-	-	-	-	-	-	-	-	-	-	-	-	-	-	-	-	-
Burke County	4,292 4.81	3,023	1,768 58.48 58.48 41.19	-	-	-	-	-	-	-	-	-	-	1,055 52.62 59.67 34.90 24.58	-	-	-	336 67.74 19.00 11.11 7.83	-	-	-	-	-	-	-	-
Cabarrus County	6,120 4.67	1,072	742 69.22 69.22 12.12	-	-	-	-	-	-	-	-	-	-	-	-	-	-	-	-	-	-	-	-	-	-	-
Catawba County	9,167 6.47	3,792	2,214 58.39 58.39 24.15	-	-	-	-	-	-	-	-	-	-	952 53.07 43.00 25.11 10.39	-	-	-	307 47.23 13.87 8.10 3.35	-	-	-	-	-	-	-	358 71.17 16.17 9.44 3.91
Hickory (city)	3,704 9.87	1,616	985 60.95 60.95 26.59	-	-	-	-	-	-	-	-	-	-	387 71.27 39.29 23.95 10.45	-	-	-	-	-	-	-	-	-	-	-	-
Cleveland County	1,657 1.72	785	523 66.62 66.62 31.56	-	-	-	-	-	-	-	-	-	-	-	-	-	-	-	-	-	-	-	-	-	-	-
Craven County	3,087 3.38	1,148	775 67.51 67.51 25.11	-	-	-	-	-	-	-	311 65.20 40.13 27.09 10.07	-	-	-	-	-	-	-	-	-	-	-	-	-	-	-

Notes: Please refer to the User's Guide for an explanation of data; data is arranged alphabetically by state, then county, then city within each county; table includes counties with populations greater than 49,999 unless noted and cities with populations greater than 9,999 whose Asian and/or NHPI population rates are greater than the national average; (1) Native Hawaiian and other Pacific Islander; (2) excludes Taiwanese; (3) includes Chamorro; (4) county does not meet population threshold but is shown in order to allow inclusion of city

Place	Total foreign-born population	Total Asian population	Asians who are foreign born	Total NHPI[1] population	NHPIs[1] who are foreign born	Asian Indian	Bangladeshi	Cambodian	Chinese[2]	Fijian	Filipino	Guamanian[3]	Hawaiian, Native	Hmong	Indonesian	Japanese	Korean	Laotian	Malaysian	Pakistani	Samoan	Sri Lankan	Taiwanese	Thai	Tongan	Vietnamese
	15,925	6,126	4,385	503	54	442	-	-	-	-	692	-	-	-	-	270	1,620	-	-	-	-	-	-	-	-	597
	5.26		71.58		10.74	66.57					70.47					59.87	77.14									82.80
Cumberland County						10.08					15.78					6.16	36.94									13.61
			71.58		10.74	7.22					11.30					4.41	26.44									9.75
			27.54		0.34	2.78					4.35					1.70	10.17									3.75
	5,248	1,267	837	-	-	-	-	296	-	-	-	-	-	-	-	-	-	-	-	-	-	-	-	-	-	-
	3.56		66.06					57.25																		
Davidson County								35.36																		
			66.06					23.36																		
			15.95					5.64																		
	24,253	7,052	5,253	-	-	1,972	-	-	1,231	-	451	-	-	-	-	304	438	-	-	-	-	-	-	-	-	-
	10.86		74.49			72.79			76.08		77.23					78.76	72.76									
Durham County						37.54			23.43		8.59					5.79	8.34									
			74.49			27.96			17.46		6.40					4.31	6.21									
			21.66			8.13			5.08		1.86					1.25	1.81									
	19,836	3,227	2,497	-	-	489	-	-	757	-	191	-	-	-	-	-	-	-	-	-	-	-	-	-	-	373
	6.48		77.38			80.56			82.37		67.49															71.73
Forsyth County						19.58			30.32		7.65															14.94
			77.38			15.15			23.46		5.92															11.56
			12.59			2.47			3.82		0.96															1.88
	6,315	1,508	1,093	-	-	-	-	-	-	-	-	-	-	-	-	-	-	-	-	-	-	-	-	-	-	342
	3.32		72.48																							67.72
Gaston County																										31.29
			72.48																							22.68
			17.31																							5.42
	27,317	9,341	7,281	-	-	1,475	-	-	777	-	367	-	-	-	-	-	734	394	-	342	-	-	-	-	-	2,435
	6.49		77.95			84.43			76.40		67.84						76.14	80.74		83.62						82.10
Guilford County						20.26			10.67		5.04						10.08	5.41		4.70						33.44
			77.95			15.79			8.32		3.93						7.86	4.22		3.66						26.07
			26.65			5.40			2.84		1.34						2.69	1.44		1.25						8.91
	644	375	223	-	-	-	-	-	-	-	-	-	-	-	-	-	-	-	-	-	-	-	-	-	-	-
	1.12		59.47																							
Halifax County																										
			59.47																							
			34.63																							
	4,177	639	481	-	-	-	-	-	-	-	-	-	-	-	-	-	-	-	-	-	-	-	-	-	-	-
	4.59		75.27																							
Harnett County																										
			75.27																							
			11.52																							
	5,295	440	363	-	-	-	-	-	-	-	-	-	-	-	-	-	-	-	-	-	-	-	-	-	-	-
	5.94		82.50																							
Henderson County																										
			82.50																							
			6.86																							
	4,472	1,110	780	-	-	-	-	-	-	-	-	-	-	-	-	-	-	-	-	-	-	-	-	-	-	-
	3.65		70.27																							
Iredell County																										
			70.27																							
			17.44																							

Notes: Please refer to the User's Guide for an explanation of data; data is arranged alphabetically by state, then county, then city within each county; table includes counties with populations greater than 49,999 unless noted and cities with populations greater than 9,999 whose Asian and/or NHPI population rates are greater than the national average; (1) Native Hawaiian and other Pacific Islander; (2) excludes Taiwanese; (3) includes Chamorro; (4) county does not meet population threshold but is shown in order to allow inclusion of city

Place	Total foreign-born population	Total Asian population	Asians who are foreign born	Total NHPI[1] population	NHPIs[1] who are foreign born	Asian Indian	Bangladeshi	Cambodian	Chinese[2]	Fijian	Filipino	Guamanian[3]	Hawaiian, Native	Hmong	Indonesian	Japanese	Korean	Laotian	Malaysian	Pakistani	Samoan	Sri Lankan	Taiwanese	Thai	Tongan	Vietnamese
Johnston County	7,236 5.93	579	347 59.93 59.93 4.80	-	-	-	-	-	-	-	-	-	-	-	-	-	-	-	-	-	-	-	-	-	-	-
Lenoir County	1,640 2.75	392	256 65.31 65.31 15.61	-	-	-	-	-	-	-	-	-	-	-	-	-	-	-	-	-	-	-	-	-	-	-
Mecklenburg County	68,349 9.83	20,819	15,296 73.47 73.47 22.38	-	-	3,912 75.74 25.58 18.79 5.72	-	521 67.93 3.41 2.50 0.76	2,031 69.41 13.28 9.76 2.97	-	839 72.64 5.49 4.03 1.23	-	-	319 56.06 2.09 1.53 0.47	-	552 66.19 3.61 2.65 0.81	1,892 77.45 12.37 9.09 2.77	636 72.60 4.16 3.05 0.93	-	-	-	-	-	-	-	3,764 80.91 24.61 18.08 5.51
Nash County	2,607 2.98	413	304 73.61 73.61 11.66	-	-	-	-	-	-	-	-	-	-	-	-	-	-	-	-	-	-	-	-	-	-	-
New Hanover County	5,209 3.25	1,381	879 63.65 63.65 16.87	-	-	-	-	-	-	-	-	-	-	-	-	-	-	-	-	-	-	-	-	-	-	-
Onslow County	6,129 4.08	2,566	1,801 70.19 70.19 29.38	400	44 11.00 11.00 0.72	-	-	-	-	-	833 72.81 46.25 32.46 13.59	-	-	-	-	330 67.76 18.32 12.86 5.38	-	-	-	-	-	-	-	-	-	-
Orange County	10,711 9.06	4,646	3,523 75.83 75.83 32.89	-	-	440 62.15 12.49 9.47 4.11	-	-	1,349 80.20 38.29 29.04 12.59	-	-	-	-	-	-	459 88.10 13.03 9.88 4.29	572 72.96 16.24 12.31 5.34	-	-	-	-	-	-	-	-	-
Carrboro (town)	2,951 17.67	802	630 78.55 78.55 21.35	-	-	-	-	-	-	-	-	-	-	-	-	-	-	-	-	-	-	-	-	-	-	-
Chapel Hill (town)	5,445 11.16	3,327	2,458 73.88 73.88 45.14	-	-	355 61.95 14.44 10.67 6.52	-	-	987 81.37 40.15 29.67 18.13	-	-	-	-	-	-	-	379 67.92 15.42 11.39 6.96	-	-	-	-	-	-	-	-	-
Pitt County	4,879 3.65	1,245	828 66.51 66.51 16.97	-	-	-	-	-	-	-	-	-	-	-	-	-	-	-	-	-	-	-	-	-	-	-

Notes: Please refer to the User's Guide for an explanation of data; data is arranged alphabetically by state, then county, then city within each county; table includes counties with populations greater than 49,999 unless noted and cities with populations greater than 9,999 whose Asian and/or NHPI population rates are greater than the national average; (1) Native Hawaiian and other Pacific Islander; (2) excludes Taiwanese; (3) includes Chamorro; (4) county does not meet population threshold but is shown in order to allow inclusion of city

Place	Total foreign-born population	Total Asian population	Asians who are foreign born	Total NHPI[1] population	NHPIs[1] who are foreign born	Asian Indian	Bangladeshi	Cambodian	Chinese[2]	Fijian	Filipino	Guamanian[3]	Hawaiian, Native	Hmong	Indonesian	Japanese	Korean	Laotian	Malaysian	Pakistani	Samoan	Sri Lankan	Taiwanese	Thai	Tongan	Vietnamese
Randolph County	7,423 5.69	785	581 74.01 74.01 7.83	-	-	-	-	-	-	-	-	-	-	-	-	-	-	-	-	-	-	-	-	-	-	-
Robeson County	5,202 4.22	936	678 72.44 72.44 13.03	-	-	-	-	-	-	-	-	-	-	-	-	-	-	-	-	-	-	-	-	-	-	-
Rowan County	4,872 3.74	808	520 64.36 64.36 10.67	-	-	-	-	-	-	-	-	-	-	-	-	-	-	-	-	-	-	-	-	-	-	-
Stanly County	1,505 2.59	752	397 52.79 52.79 26.38	-	-	-	-	-	-	-	-	-	-	176 55.35 44.33 23.40 11.69	-	-	-	-	-	-	-	-	-	-	-	-
Surry County	3,755 5.27	478	251 52.51 52.51 6.68	-	-	-	-	-	-	-	-	-	-	-	-	-	-	-	-	-	-	-	-	-	-	-
Union County	7,047 5.70	586	423 72.18 72.18 6.00	-	-	-	-	-	-	-	-	-	-	-	-	-	-	-	-	-	-	-	-	-	-	-
Wake County	60,602 9.65	20,722	15,551 75.05 75.05 25.66	-	-	5,445 78.45 35.01 26.28 8.98	-	-	3,761 76.30 24.18 18.15 6.21	-	782 64.52 5.03 3.77 1.29	-	-	-	-	531 63.90 3.41 2.56 0.88	1,594 72.55 10.25 7.69 2.63	-	-	356 80.00 2.29 1.72 0.59	-	-	-	-	-	1,811 77.63 11.65 8.74 2.99
Apex (town)	1,470 7.32	761	549 72.14 72.14 37.35	-	-	-	-	-	-	-	-	-	-	-	-	-	-	-	-	-	-	-	-	-	-	-
Cary (town)	13,203 13.97	7,521	5,624 74.78 74.78 42.60	-	-	2,584 76.43 45.95 34.36 19.57	-	-	1,346 70.55 23.93 17.90 10.19	-	-	-	-	-	-	249 69.55 4.43 3.31 1.89	432 84.05 7.68 5.74 3.27	-	-	-	-	-	-	-	-	381 83.92 6.77 5.07 2.89
Wayne County	4,792 4.23	1,078	784 72.73 72.73 16.36	-	-	-	-	-	-	-	-	-	-	-	-	-	-	-	-	-	-	-	-	-	-	-

Notes: Please refer to the User's Guide for an explanation of data; data is arranged alphabetically by state, then county, then city within each county; table includes counties with populations greater than 49,999 unless noted and cities with populations greater than 9,999 whose Asian and/or NHPI population rates are greater than the national average; (1) Native Hawaiian and other Pacific Islander; (2) excludes Taiwanese; (3) includes Chamorro; (4) county does not meet population threshold but is shown in order to allow inclusion of city

Place	Total foreign-born population	Total Asian population	Asians who are foreign born	Total NHPI[1] population	NHPIs[1] who are foreign born	Asian Indian	Bangladeshi	Cambodian	Chinese[2]	Fijian	Filipino	Guamanian[3]	Hawaiian, Native	Hmong	Indonesian	Japanese	Korean	Laotian	Malaysian	Pakistani	Samoan	Sri Lankan	Taiwanese	Thai	Tongan	Vietnamese
Wilkes County	1,946	332	252	-	-	-	-	-	-	-	-	-	-	-	-	-	-	-	-	-	-	-	-	-	-	-
	2.97		75.90																							
			75.90																							
			12.95																							
NORTH DAKOTA	12,114	3,342	2,408	-	-	809	-	-	358	-	312	-	-	-	-	-	239	-	-	-	-	-	-	-	-	-
	1.89		72.05			77.64			83.45		54.07						65.48									
						33.60			14.87		12.96						9.93									
			72.05			24.21			10.71		9.34						7.15									
			19.88			6.68			2.96		2.58						1.97									
Cass County	3,929	1,422	1,030	-	-	293	-	-	-	-	-	-	-	-	-	-	-	-	-	-	-	-	-	-	-	-
	3.19		72.43			70.77																				
						28.45																				
			72.43			20.60																				
			26.22			7.46																				
Grand Forks County	2,103	632	483	-	-	-	-	-	-	-	-	-	-	-	-	-	-	-	-	-	-	-	-	-	-	-
	3.18		76.42																							
			76.42																							
			22.97																							
Ward County	1,215	307	177	-	-	-	-	-	-	-	-	-	-	-	-	-	-	-	-	-	-	-	-	-	-	-
	2.07		57.65																							
			57.65																							
			14.57																							
OHIO	339,279	132,131	97,818	2,641	311	28,818	507	1,769	20,940	-	8,857	78	7	-	925	7,195	10,873	2,159	296	1,259	50	436	1,643	1,507	-	7,828
	2.99		74.03		11.78	76.59	78.24	67.65	75.66		67.21	11.71	0.88		87.18	69.92	78.30	72.01	85.06	76.72	10.18	84.82	74.24	79.32		75.58
						29.46	0.52	1.81	21.41		9.05	25.08	2.25		0.95	7.36	11.12	2.21	0.30	1.29	16.08	0.45	1.68	1.54		8.00
			74.03		11.78	21.81	0.38	1.34	15.85		6.70	2.95	0.27		0.70	5.45	8.23	1.63	0.22	0.95	1.89	0.33	1.24	1.14		5.92
			28.83		0.09	8.49	0.15	0.52	6.17		2.61	0.02	<0.01		0.27	2.12	3.20	0.64	0.09	0.37	0.01	0.13	0.48	0.44		2.31
Allen County	1,137	534	364	-	-	-	-	-	-	-	-	-	-	-	-	-	-	-	-	-	-	-	-	-	-	-
	1.05		68.16																							
			68.16																							
			32.01																							
Ashtabula County	1,619	287	182	-	-	-	-	-	-	-	-	-	-	-	-	-	-	-	-	-	-	-	-	-	-	-
	1.58		63.41																							
			63.41																							
			11.24																							
Athens County	2,043	1,116	847	-	-	-	-	-	-	-	-	-	-	-	-	-	-	-	-	-	-	-	-	-	-	-
	3.28		75.90																							
			75.90																							
			41.46																							
Athens (city)	1,343	876	694	-	-	-	-	-	-	-	-	-	-	-	-	-	-	-	-	-	-	-	-	-	-	-
	6.34		79.22																							
			79.22																							
			51.68																							

Notes: Please refer to the User's Guide for an explanation of data; data is arranged alphabetically by state, then county, then city within each county; table includes counties with populations greater than 49,999 unless noted and cities with populations greater than 9,999 whose Asian and/or NHPI population rates are greater than the national average; (1) Native Hawaiian and other Pacific Islander; (2) excludes Taiwanese; (3) includes Chamorro; (4) county does not meet population threshold but is shown in order to allow inclusion of city

Place	Total foreign-born population	Total Asian population	Asians who are foreign born	Total NHPI[1] population	NHPIs[1] who are foreign born	Asian Indian	Bangladeshi	Cambodian	Chinese[2]	Fijian	Filipino	Guamanian[3]	Hawaiian, Native	Hmong	Indonesian	Japanese	Korean	Laotian	Malaysian	Pakistani	Samoan	Sri Lankan	Taiwanese	Thai	Tongan	Vietnamese
Butler County	9,147	5,077	3,528	-	-	1,201	-	-	708	-	287	-	-	-	-	-	319	-	-	-	-	-	-	-	-	522
	2.75		69.49			67.13			70.31		63.78						67.73									80.31
						34.04			20.07		8.13						9.04									14.80
			69.49			23.66			13.95		5.65						6.28									10.28
			38.57			13.13			7.74		3.14						3.49									5.71
Clark County	1,724	671	467	-	-	-	-	-	-	-	-	-	-	-	-	-	-	-	-	-	-	-	-	-	-	-
	1.19		69.60																							
			69.60																							
			27.09																							
Clermont County	2,785	1,078	766	-	-	296	-	-	-	-	-	-	-	-	-	-	-	-	-	-	-	-	-	-	-	-
	1.56		71.06			77.49																				
						38.64																				
			71.06			27.46																				
			27.50			10.63																				
Columbiana County	1,599	325	269	-	-	-	-	-	-	-	-	-	-	-	-	-	-	-	-	-	-	-	-	-	-	-
	1.43		82.77																							
			82.77																							
			16.82																							
Cuyahoga County	88,761	25,831	18,942	-	-	6,814	-	385	4,360	-	2,042	-	-	-	-	763	1,375	-	-	-	-	-	-	-	-	1,520
	6.37		73.33			75.25		79.55	71.79		73.22					60.27	74.93									72.90
						35.97		2.03	23.02		10.78					4.03	7.26									8.02
			73.33			26.38		1.49	16.88		7.91					2.95	5.32									5.88
			21.34			7.68		0.43	4.91		2.30					0.86	1.55									1.71
Mayfield Heights (city)	3,506	798	604	-	-	319	-	-	-	-	-	-	-	-	-	-	-	-	-	-	-	-	-	-	-	-
	18.09		75.69			82.22																				
						52.81																				
			75.69			39.97																				
			17.23			9.10																				
Richmond Heights (city)	1,900	515	397	-	-	-	-	-	-	-	-	-	-	-	-	-	-	-	-	-	-	-	-	-	-	-
	17.36		77.09																							
			77.09																							
			20.89																							
Solon (city)	1,879	1,070	754	-	-	350	-	-	247	-	-	-	-	-	-	-	-	-	-	-	-	-	-	-	-	-
	8.62		70.47			74.47			71.39																	
						46.42			32.76																	
			70.47			32.71			23.08																	
			40.13			18.63			13.15																	
Westlake (city)	2,673	1,354	990	-	-	407	-	-	-	-	-	-	-	-	-	-	-	-	-	-	-	-	-	-	-	-
	8.39		73.12			75.23																				
						41.11																				
			73.12			30.06																				
			37.04			15.23																				
Delaware County	2,872	1,755	1,248	-	-	361	-	-	388	-	-	-	-	-	-	-	-	-	-	-	-	-	-	-	-	-
	2.61		71.11			82.99			70.04																	
						28.93			31.09																	
			71.11			20.57			22.11																	
			43.45			12.57			13.51																	

Notes: Please refer to the User's Guide for an explanation of data; data is arranged alphabetically by state, then county, then city within each county; table includes counties with populations greater than 49,999 unless noted and cities with populations greater than 9,999 whose Asian and/or NHPI population rates are greater than the national average; (1) Native Hawaiian and other Pacific Islander; (2) excludes Taiwanese; (3) includes Chamorro; (4) county does not meet population threshold but is shown in order to allow inclusion of city

Place	Total foreign-born population	Total Asian population	Asians who are foreign born	Total NHPI[1] population	NHPIs[1] who are foreign born	Asian Indian	Bangladeshi	Cambodian	Chinese[2]	Fijian	Filipino	Guamanian[3]	Hawaiian, Native	Hmong	Indonesian	Japanese	Korean	Laotian	Malaysian	Pakistani	Samoan	Sri Lankan	Taiwanese	Thai	Tongan	Vietnamese
Fairfield County	1,601 1.30	874	532 60.87 60.87 33.23	-	-	-	-	-	-	-	-	-	-	-	-	-	-	-	-	-	-	-	-	-	-	-
Franklin County	64,487 6.03	32,912	25,016 76.01 76.01 38.79	362	31 8.56 8.56 0.05	6,519 79.11 26.06 19.81 10.11	-	842 64.32 3.37 2.56 1.31	5,639 77.66 22.54 17.13 8.74	-	1,090 60.76 4.36 3.31 1.69	-	-	-	517 97.55 2.07 1.57 0.80	2,554 79.14 10.21 7.76 3.96	2,605 78.13 10.41 7.92 4.04	828 72.89 3.31 2.52 1.28	-	399 77.78 1.59 1.21 0.62	-	-	589 77.91 2.35 1.79 0.91	367 85.75 1.47 1.12 0.57	-	1,882 77.04 7.52 5.72 2.92
Dublin (city)	2,868 9.11	2,497	1,919 76.85 76.85 66.91	-	-	518 77.78 26.99 20.74 18.06	-	-	340 66.67 17.72 13.62 11.85	-	-	-	-	-	-	715 87.20 37.26 28.63 24.93	-	-	-	-	-	-	-	-	-	-
Hilliard (city)	1,026 4.24	1,006	712 70.78 70.78 69.40	-	-	-	-	-	-	-	-	-	-	-	-	-	-	-	-	-	-	-	-	-	-	-
Geauga County	2,553 2.81	370	292 78.92 78.92 11.44	-	-	-	-	-	-	-	-	-	-	-	-	-	-	-	-	-	-	-	-	-	-	-
Greene County	5,098 3.45	2,883	2,293 79.54 79.54 44.98	-	-	708 80.91 30.88 24.56 13.89	-	-	367 85.75 16.01 12.73 7.20	-	-	-	-	-	-	-	490 85.96 21.37 17.00 9.61	-	-	-	-	-	-	-	-	-
Hamilton County	28,579 3.38	12,652	9,708 76.73 76.73 33.97	-	-	3,424 86.27 35.27 27.06 11.98	-	217 61.82 2.24 1.72 0.76	2,376 79.23 24.47 18.78 8.31	-	767 58.33 7.90 6.06 2.68	-	-	-	-	428 70.28 4.41 3.38 1.50	830 72.55 8.55 6.56 2.90	-	-	-	-	-	-	-	-	841 79.64 8.66 6.65 2.94
Blue Ash (city)	1,273 9.98	898	727 80.96 80.96 57.11	-	-	343 84.69 47.18 38.20 26.94	-	-	-	-	-	-	-	-	-	-	-	-	-	-	-	-	-	-	-	-
Sharonville (city)	873 6.37	556	485 87.23 87.23 55.56	-	-	363 92.37 74.85 65.29 41.58	-	-	-	-	-	-	-	-	-	-	-	-	-	-	-	-	-	-	-	-
Hancock County	1,456 2.04	764	636 83.25 83.25 43.68	-	-	-	-	-	-	-	-	-	-	-	-	-	-	-	-	-	-	-	-	-	-	-

Notes: Please refer to the User's Guide for an explanation of data; data is arranged alphabetically by state, then county, then city within each county; table includes counties with populations greater than 49,999 unless noted and cities with populations greater than 9,999 whose Asian and/or NHPI population rates are greater than the national average; (1) Native Hawaiian and other Pacific Islander; (2) excludes Taiwanese; (3) includes Chamorro; (4) county does not meet population threshold but is shown in order to allow inclusion of city

Place	Total foreign-born population	Total Asian population	Asians who are foreign born	Total NHPI[1] population	NHPIs[1] who are foreign born	Asian Indian	Bangladeshi	Cambodian	Chinese[2]	Fijian	Filipino	Guamanian[3]	Hawaiian, Native	Hmong	Indonesian	Japanese	Korean	Laotian	Malaysian	Pakistani	Samoan	Sri Lankan	Taiwanese	Thai	Tongan	Vietnamese
	9,746	2,234	1,582	-	-	520	-	-	364	-	-	-	-	-	-	-	-	-	-	-	-	-	-	-	-	-
	4.28		70.81			76.58			68.29																	
Lake County						32.87			23.01																	
			70.81			23.28			16.29																	
			16.23			5.34			3.73																	
	1,650	687	471	-	-	-	-	-	-	-	-	-	-	-	-	-	-	-	-	-	-	-	-	-	-	-
	1.13		68.56																							
Licking County																										
			68.56																							
			28.55																							
	7,396	1,715	1,190	-	-	283	-	-	-	-	335	-	-	-	-	-	-	-	-	-	-	-	-	-	-	-
	2.60		69.39			71.83					77.37															
Lorain County						23.78					28.15															
			69.39			16.50					19.53															
			16.09			3.83					4.53															
	14,482	5,326	4,049	-	-	1,229	-	-	1,198	-	397	-	-	-	-	-	410	-	-	-	-	-	-	-	-	-
	3.18		76.02			75.96			84.25		66.39						79.61									
Lucas County						30.35			29.59		9.80						10.13									
			76.02			23.08			22.49		7.45						7.70									
			27.96			8.49			8.27		2.74						2.83									
	6,061	1,018	652	-	-	-	-	-	-	-	-	-	-	-	-	-	-	-	-	-	-	-	-	-	-	-
	2.35		64.05																							
Mahoning County																										
			64.05																							
			10.76																							
	735	364	242	-	-	-	-	-	-	-	-	-	-	-	-	-	-	-	-	-	-	-	-	-	-	-
	1.11		66.48																							
Marion County																										
			66.48																							
			32.93																							
	4,550	1,153	780	-	-	315	-	-	-	-	-	-	-	-	-	-	-	-	-	-	-	-	-	-	-	-
	3.01		67.65			71.27																				
Medina County						40.38																				
			67.65			27.32																				
			17.14			6.92																				
	1,467	845	647	-	-	-	-	-	-	-	-	-	-	-	-	-	-	-	-	-	-	-	-	-	-	-
	1.48		76.57																							
Miami County																										
			76.57																							
			44.10																							
	13,807	7,190	5,069	-	-	1,546	-	-	795	-	493	-	-	-	-	389	621	-	-	-	-	-	-	-	-	691
	2.47		70.50			72.99			70.42		68.85					60.78	78.41									66.63
Montgomery County						30.50			15.68		9.73					7.67	12.25									13.63
			70.50			21.50			11.06		6.86					5.41	8.64									9.61
			36.71			11.20			5.76		3.57					2.82	4.50									5.00
	3,043	1,156	939	-	-	-	-	-	-	-	-	-	-	-	-	-	-	-	-	-	-	-	-	-	-	-
	2.00		81.23																							
Portage County																										
			81.23																							
			30.86																							

Notes: Please refer to the User's Guide for an explanation of data; data is arranged alphabetically by state, then county, then city within each county; table includes counties with populations greater than 49,999 unless noted and cities with populations greater than 9,999 whose Asian and/or NHPI population rates are greater than the national average; (1) Native Hawaiian and other Pacific Islander; (2) excludes Taiwanese; (3) includes Chamorro; (4) county does not meet population threshold but is shown in order to allow inclusion of city

Place	Total foreign-born population	Total Asian population	Asians who are foreign born	Total NHPI[1] population	NHPIs[1] who are foreign born	Asian Indian	Bangladeshi	Cambodian	Chinese[2]	Fijian	Filipino	Guamanian[3]	Hawaiian, Native	Hmong	Indonesian	Japanese	Korean	Laotian	Malaysian	Pakistani	Samoan	Sri Lankan	Taiwanese	Thai	Tongan	Vietnamese
Richland County	2,287 1.77	709	596 84.06 84.06 26.06	-	-	-	-	-	-	-	-	-	-	-	-	-	-	-	-	-	-	-	-	-	-	-
Stark County	6,674 1.77	1,811	1,447 79.90 79.90 21.68	-	-	356 79.64 24.60 19.66 5.33	-	-	311 80.15 21.49 17.17 4.66	-	-	-	-	-	-	-	-	-	-	-	-	-	-	-	-	-
Summit County	17,729 3.27	7,735	5,660 73.17 73.17 31.93	-	-	1,502 73.56 26.54 19.42 8.47	-	-	1,225 71.10 21.64 15.84 6.91	-	326 65.86 5.76 4.21 1.84	-	-	-	-	317 73.55 5.60 4.10 1.79	721 78.03 12.74 9.32 4.07	516 67.63 9.12 6.67 2.91	-	-	-	-	-	-	-	547 80.80 9.66 7.07 3.09
Trumbull County	4,089 1.82	1,009	691 68.48 68.48 16.90	-	-	-	-	-	-	-	-	-	-	-	-	-	-	-	-	-	-	-	-	-	-	-
Warren County	3,642 2.30	2,167	1,475 68.07 68.07 40.50	-	-	444 66.17 30.10 20.49 12.19	-	-	375 72.39 25.42 17.31 10.30	-	-	-	-	-	-	-	-	-	-	-	-	-	-	-	-	-
Wayne County	1,885 1.69	767	549 71.58 71.58 29.12	-	-	-	-	-	-	-	-	-	-	-	-	-	-	-	-	-	-	-	-	-	-	-
Wood County	2,925 2.42	1,170	947 80.94 80.94 32.38	-	-	-	-	-	-	-	-	-	-	-	-	-	-	-	-	-	-	-	-	-	-	-
OKLAHOMA	131,747 3.82	45,546	34,148 74.97 74.97 25.92	1,840	381 20.71 20.71 0.29	6,308 75.98 18.47 13.85 4.79	-	198 60.18 0.58 0.43 0.15	5,330 80.25 15.61 11.70 4.05	-	2,768 66.16 8.11 6.08 2.10	25 6.25 6.56 1.36 0.02	27 3.99 7.09 1.47 0.02	176 52.54 0.52 0.39 0.13	-	1,840 65.95 5.39 4.04 1.40	3,778 81.67 11.06 8.29 2.87	689 78.21 2.02 1.51 0.52	453 88.13 1.33 0.99 0.34	799 71.21 2.34 1.75 0.61	-	-	333 94.07 0.98 0.73 0.25	677 82.26 1.98 1.49 0.51	-	9,246 75.66 27.08 20.30 7.02
Canadian County	2,841 3.24	2,180	1,479 67.84 67.84 52.06	-	-	814 67.33 55.04 37.34 28.65	-	-	-	-	-	-	-	-	-	-	-	-	-	-	-	-	-	-	-	413 69.88 27.92 18.94 14.54
Cleveland County	9,206 4.43	5,879	4,303 73.19 73.19 46.74	-	-	679 75.87 15.78 11.55 7.38	-	-	915 84.33 21.26 15.56 9.94	-	294 52.50 6.83 5.00 3.19	-	-	-	-	-	539 76.13 12.53 9.17 5.85	-	-	-	-	-	-	-	-	1,169 68.76 27.17 19.88 12.70

Notes: Please refer to the User's Guide for an explanation of data; data is arranged alphabetically by state, then county, then city within each county; table includes counties with populations greater than 49,999 unless noted and cities with populations greater than 9,999 whose Asian and/or NHPI population rates are greater than the national average; (1) Native Hawaiian and other Pacific Islander; (2) excludes Taiwanese; (3) includes Chamorro; (4) county does not meet population threshold but is shown in order to allow inclusion of city

Place	Total foreign-born population	Total Asian population	Asians who are foreign born	Total NHPI[1] population	NHPIs[1] who are foreign born	Asian Indian	Bangladeshi	Cambodian	Chinese[2]	Fijian	Filipino	Guamanian[3]	Hawaiian, Native	Hmong	Indonesian	Japanese	Korean	Laotian	Malaysian	Pakistani	Samoan	Sri Lankan	Taiwanese	Thai	Tongan	Vietnamese
Comanche County	6,191 5.38	2,430	1,661 68.35 68.35 26.83	-	-	-	-	-	-	-	314 57.30 18.90 12.92 5.07	-	-	-	-	-	692 82.78 41.66 28.48 11.18	-	-	-	-	-	-	-	-	-
Garfield County	1,544 2.67	499	353 70.74 70.74 22.86	-	-	-	-	-	-	-	-	-	-	-	-	-	-	-	-	-	-	-	-	-	-	-
Muskogee County	1,226 1.77	351	258 73.50 73.50 21.04	-	-	-	-	-	-	-	-	-	-	-	-	-	-	-	-	-	-	-	-	-	-	-
Oklahoma County	47,829 7.24	18,171	14,278 78.58 78.58 29.85	-	-	2,286 80.01 16.01 12.58 4.78	-	-	1,834 83.40 12.84 10.09 3.83	-	882 70.17 6.18 4.85 1.84	-	-	-	-	791 78.71 5.54 4.35 1.65	1,046 86.16 7.33 5.76 2.19	429 87.02 3.00 2.36 0.90	-	-	-	-	-	354 89.17 2.48 1.95 0.74	-	5,272 77.05 36.92 29.01 11.02
Payne County	3,115 4.57	1,906	1,686 88.46 88.46 54.13	-	-	-	-	-	593 88.91 35.17 31.11 19.04	-	-	-	-	-	-	-	-	-	-	-	-	-	-	-	-	-
Stillwater (city)	2,848 7.31	1,869	1,656 88.60 88.60 58.15	-	-	-	-	-	589 88.84 35.57 31.51 20.68	-	-	-	-	-	-	-	-	-	-	-	-	-	-	-	-	-
Pottawatomie County	715 1.09	372	233 62.63 62.63 32.59	-	-	-	-	-	-	-	-	-	-	-	-	-	-	-	-	-	-	-	-	-	-	-
Tulsa County	30,230 5.37	8,601	6,426 74.71 74.71 21.26	-	-	1,471 75.55 22.89 17.10 4.87	-	-	1,196 77.36 18.61 13.91 3.96	-	322 68.80 5.01 3.74 1.07	-	-	-	-	-	702 78.61 10.92 8.16 2.32	-	-	329 60.48 5.12 3.83 1.09	-	-	-	-	-	1,614 78.81 25.12 18.77 5.34
Wagoner County	1,062 1.85	489	310 63.39 63.39 29.19	-	-	-	-	-	-	-	-	-	-	-	-	-	-	-	-	-	-	-	-	-	-	-
OREGON	289,702 8.47	99,136	66,927 67.51 67.51 23.10	7,583	2,232 29.43 29.43 0.77	7,724 75.81 11.54 7.79 2.67	-	1,875 68.21 2.80 1.89 0.65	12,564 67.86 18.77 12.67 4.34	269 72.12 12.05 3.55 0.09	6,572 61.56 9.82 6.63 2.27	66 5.95 2.96 0.87 0.02	6 0.30 0.27 0.08 <0.01	645 47.18 0.96 0.65 0.22	528 82.37 0.79 0.53 0.18	5,666 48.63 8.47 5.72 1.96	9,911 77.34 14.81 10.00 3.42	2,412 65.17 3.60 2.43 0.83	-	280 71.79 0.42 0.28 0.10	166 21.47 7.44 2.19 0.06	-	594 74.25 0.89 0.60 0.21	1,256 83.96 1.88 1.27 0.43	240 53.93 10.75 3.16 0.08	14,434 75.81 21.57 14.56 4.98

Notes: Please refer to the User's Guide for an explanation of data; data is arranged alphabetically by state, then county, then city within each county; table includes counties with populations greater than 49,999 unless noted and cities with populations greater than 9,999 whose Asian and/or NHPI population rates are greater than the national average; (1) Native Hawaiian and other Pacific Islander; (2) excludes Taiwanese; (3) includes Chamorro; (4) county does not meet population threshold but is shown in order to allow inclusion of city

Place	Total foreign-born population	Total Asian population	Asians who are foreign born	Total NHPI[1] population	NHPIs[1] who are foreign born	Asian Indian	Bangladeshi	Cambodian	Chinese[2]	Fijian	Filipino	Guamanian[3]	Hawaiian, Native	Hmong	Indonesian	Japanese	Korean	Laotian	Malaysian	Pakistani	Samoan	Sri Lankan	Taiwanese	Thai	Tongan	Vietnamese
Benton County	5,959 7.62	3,331	2,195 65.90 65.90 36.84	-	-	-	-	-	685 72.64 31.21 20.56 11.50	-	-	-	-	-	-	152 35.19 6.92 4.56 2.55	572 78.25 26.06 17.17 9.60	-	-	-	-	-	-	-	-	-
Corvallis (city)	4,772 9.70	3,031	2,025 66.81 66.81 42.44	-	-	-	-	-	662 73.07 32.69 21.84 13.87	-	-	-	-	-	-	-	504 79.75 24.89 16.63 10.56	-	-	-	-	-	-	-	-	-
Clackamas County	24,100 7.12	8,114	5,209 64.20 64.20 21.61	616	88 14.29 14.29 0.37	505 72.04 9.69 6.22 2.10	-	-	1,172 63.45 22.50 14.44 4.86	-	570 58.76 10.94 7.02 2.37	-	-	-	-	431 42.97 8.27 5.31 1.79	1,349 79.82 25.90 16.63 5.60	-	-	-	-	-	-	-	-	590 62.17 11.33 7.27 2.45
Lake Oswego (city)	3,359 9.54	1,494	983 65.80 65.80 29.26	-	-	-	-	-	286 67.77 29.09 19.14 8.51	-	-	-	-	-	-	-	-	-	-	-	-	-	-	-	-	-
Coos County	1,668 2.66	345	274 79.42 79.42 16.43	-	-	-	-	-	-	-	-	-	-	-	-	-	-	-	-	-	-	-	-	-	-	-
Deschutes County	3,189 2.76	615	453 73.66 73.66 14.21	-	-	-	-	-	-	-	-	-	-	-	-	-	-	-	-	-	-	-	-	-	-	-
Douglas County	2,068 2.06	593	347 58.52 58.52 16.78	-	-	-	-	-	-	-	-	-	-	-	-	-	-	-	-	-	-	-	-	-	-	-
Jackson County	8,849 4.88	1,398	880 62.95 62.95 9.94	-	-	-	-	-	-	-	-	-	-	-	-	-	-	-	-	-	-	-	-	-	-	-
Josephine County	2,346 3.10	396	263 66.41 66.41 11.21	-	-	-	-	-	-	-	-	-	-	-	-	-	-	-	-	-	-	-	-	-	-	-
Klamath County	3,085 4.84	474	282 59.49 59.49 9.14	-	-	-	-	-	-	-	-	-	-	-	-	-	-	-	-	-	-	-	-	-	-	-

Notes: Please refer to the User's Guide for an explanation of data; data is arranged alphabetically by state, then county, then city within each county; table includes counties with populations greater than 49,999 unless noted and cities with populations greater than 9,999 whose Asian and/or NHPI population rates are greater than the national average; (1) Native Hawaiian and other Pacific Islander; (2) excludes Taiwanese; (3) includes Chamorro; (4) county does not meet population threshold but is shown in order to allow inclusion of city

Place	Total foreign-born population	Total Asian population	Asians who are foreign born	Total NHPI[1] population	NHPIs[1] who are foreign born	Asian Indian	Bangladeshi	Cambodian	Chinese[2]	Fijian	Filipino	Guamanian[3]	Hawaiian, Native	Hmong	Indonesian	Japanese	Korean	Laotian	Malaysian	Pakistani	Samoan	Sri Lankan	Taiwanese	Thai	Tongan	Vietnamese
Lane County	15,961	6,103	4,395	588	165	424	-	-	849	-	308	-	-	-	-	855	1,050	-	-	-	-	-	-	-	-	-
	4.94		72.01		28.06	70.32			71.65		53.94					66.74	85.71									
						9.65			19.32		7.01					19.45	23.89									
			72.01		28.06	6.95			13.91		5.05					14.01	17.20									
			27.54		1.03	2.66			5.32		1.93					5.36	6.58									
Linn County	3,591	780	513	-	-	-	-	-	-	-	-	-	-	-	-	-	-	-	-	-	-	-	-	-	-	-
	3.48		65.77																							
			65.77																							
			14.29																							
Marion County	35,969	4,801	3,348	761	408	263	-	-	557	-	428	-	-	-	-	430	465	-	-	-	-	-	-	-	-	600
	12.63		69.74		53.61	73.06			70.96		65.14					70.72	75.00									72.29
						7.86			16.64		12.78					12.84	13.89									17.92
			69.74		53.61	5.48			11.60		8.91					8.96	9.69									12.50
			9.31		1.13	0.73			1.55		1.19					1.20	1.29									1.67
Salem (city)	15,968	3,310	2,298	382	231	-	-	-	485	-	231	-	-	-	-	283	-	-	-	-	-	-	-	-	-	392
	11.68		69.43		60.47				73.93		60.63					72.94										79.67
									21.11		10.05					12.32										17.06
			69.43		60.47				14.65		6.98					8.55										11.84
			14.39		1.45				3.04		1.45					1.77										2.45
Multnomah County	83,965	37,280	25,326	2,511	1,019	1,377	-	684	4,739	-	2,232	-	6	520	-	1,526	1,949	1,652	-	-	-	-	-	397	187	8,986
	12.71		67.93		40.58	75.45		64.10	67.56		67.15		1.28	49.20		42.97	75.48	63.49						80.69	52.09	78.41
						5.44		2.70	18.71		8.81		0.59	2.05		6.03	7.70	6.52						1.57	18.35	35.48
			67.93		40.58	3.69		1.83	12.71		5.99		0.24	1.39		4.09	5.23	4.43						1.06	7.45	24.10
			30.16		1.21	1.64		0.81	5.64		2.66		0.01	0.62		1.82	2.32	1.97						0.47	0.22	10.70
Portland (city)	68,976	33,683	23,200	2,010	860	1,159	-	660	4,443	-	1,827	-	6	473	-	1,342	1,677	1,485	-	-	-	-	-	364	180	8,611
	13.04		68.88		42.79	76.25		63.52	68.66		66.61		1.72	50.81		43.94	76.44	64.51						80.89	51.14	79.19
						5.00		2.84	19.15		7.88		0.70	2.04		5.78	7.23	6.40						1.57	20.93	37.12
			68.88		42.79	3.44		1.96	13.19		5.42		0.30	1.40		3.98	4.98	4.41						1.08	8.96	25.56
			33.63		1.25	1.68		0.96	6.44		2.65		0.01	0.69		1.95	2.43	2.15						0.53	0.26	12.48
Polk County	4,024	773	480	-	-	-	-	-	-	-	-	-	-	-	-	-	-	-	-	-	-	-	-	-	-	-
	6.45		62.10																							
			62.10																							
			11.93																							
Umatilla County	5,930	492	308	-	-	-	-	-	-	-	-	-	-	-	-	-	-	-	-	-	-	-	-	-	-	-
	8.41		62.60																							
			62.60																							
			5.19																							
Washington County	63,438	29,946	20,642	1,399	275	4,425	-	751	3,359	-	1,858	-	0	-	-	1,413	3,237	456	-	-	-	-	-	-	-	3,682
	14.24		68.93		19.66	79.47		68.03	68.47		59.36		0.00			52.43	75.31	73.31								73.36
						21.44		3.64	16.27		9.00		0.00			6.85	15.68	2.21								17.84
			68.93		19.66	14.78		2.51	11.22		6.20		0.00			4.72	10.81	1.52								12.30
			32.54		0.43	6.98		1.18	5.29		2.93		0.00			2.23	5.10	0.72								5.80
Aloha (cdp)	6,203	3,122	2,121	-	-	-	-	-	-	-	241	-	-	-	-	-	-	-	-	-	-	-	-	-	-	834
	14.74		67.94								57.93															74.60
											11.36															39.32
			67.94								7.72															26.71
			34.19								3.89															13.45

Notes: Please refer to the User's Guide for an explanation of data; data is arranged alphabetically by state, then county, then city within each county; table includes counties with populations greater than 49,999 unless noted and cities with populations greater than 9,999 whose Asian and/or NHPI population rates are greater than the national average; (1) Native Hawaiian and other Pacific Islander; (2) excludes Taiwanese; (3) includes Chamorro; (4) county does not meet population threshold but is shown in order to allow inclusion of city

Place	Total foreign-born population	Total Asian population	Asians who are foreign born	Total NHPI[1] population	NHPIs[1] who are foreign born	Asian Indian	Bangladeshi	Cambodian	Chinese[2]	Fijian	Filipino	Guamanian[3]	Hawaiian, Native	Hmong	Indonesian	Japanese	Korean	Laotian	Malaysian	Pakistani	Samoan	Sri Lankan	Taiwanese	Thai	Tongan	Vietnamese
Beaverton (city)	14,005 18.45	7,449	5,471 73.45 73.45 39.06	-	-	1,531 87.89 27.98 20.55 10.93	-	253 70.87 4.62 3.40 1.81	674 65.69 12.32 9.05 4.81	-	416 57.30 7.60 5.58 2.97	-	-	-	-	462 68.14 8.44 6.20 3.30	984 79.68 17.99 13.21 7.03	-	-	-	-	-	-	-	-	690 75.33 12.61 9.26 4.93
Cedar Mill (cdp)	1,587 12.42	982	649 66.09 66.09 40.89	-	-	-	-	-	-	-	-	-	-	-	-	-	-	-	-	-	-	-	-	-	-	-
Hillsboro (city)	12,612 18.05	4,366	3,093 70.84 70.84 24.52	-	-	1,107 84.05 35.79 25.36 8.78	-	-	440 73.70 14.23 10.08 3.49	-	-	-	-	-	-	-	377 71.54 12.19 8.63 2.99	-	-	-	-	-	-	-	-	561 75.30 18.14 12.85 4.45
Tigard (city)	5,254 12.73	2,458	1,627 66.19 66.19 30.97	-	-	-	-	-	376 60.45 23.11 15.30 7.16	-	-	-	-	-	-	-	-	-	-	-	-	-	-	-	-	303 68.24 18.62 12.33 5.77
Tualatin (city)	2,816 12.47	1,007	685 68.02 68.02 24.33	-	-	-	-	-	-	-	-	-	-	-	-	-	-	-	-	-	-	-	-	-	-	-
Yamhill County	6,435 7.57	872	439 50.34 50.34 6.82	-	-	-	-	-	-	-	-	-	-	-	-	-	-	-	-	-	-	-	-	-	-	-
PENNSYLVANIA	508,291 4.14	216,631	158,220 73.04 73.04 31.13	3,721	484 13.01 13.01 0.10	41,611 74.00 26.30 19.21 8.19	642 90.93 0.41 0.30 0.13	5,813 66.85 3.67 2.68 1.14	35,283 73.44 22.30 16.29 6.94	-	9,995 67.93 6.32 4.61 1.97	93 11.55 19.21 2.50 0.02	25 2.49 5.17 0.67 <0.01	461 58.50 0.29 0.21 0.09	460 85.82 0.29 0.21 0.09	5,114 71.17 3.23 2.36 1.01	25,590 77.83 16.17 11.81 5.03	1,566 69.05 0.99 0.72 0.31	-	2,356 77.86 1.49 1.09 0.46	94 11.14 19.42 2.53 0.02	287 86.97 0.18 0.13 0.06	1,616 70.97 1.02 0.75 0.32	1,381 76.81 0.87 0.64 0.27	-	22,028 76.95 13.92 10.17 4.33
Adams County	3,130 3.43	639	489 76.53 76.53 15.62	-	-	-	-	-	-	-	-	-	-	-	-	-	-	-	-	-	-	-	-	-	-	-
Allegheny County	48,266 3.77	20,851	15,223 73.01 73.01 31.54	650	126 19.38 19.38 0.26	5,749 76.31 37.77 27.57 11.91	-	-	3,836 77.39 25.20 18.40 7.95	-	665 59.48 4.37 3.19 1.38	-	-	-	-	967 79.46 6.35 4.64 2.00	1,760 77.98 11.56 8.44 3.65	-	-	-	-	-	295 65.41 1.94 1.41 0.61	-	-	961 74.67 6.31 4.61 1.99
Muni. of Monroeville (borough)	1,890 6.44	1,165	921 79.06 79.06 48.73	-	-	547 80.09 59.39 46.95 28.94	-	-	-	-	-	-	-	-	-	-	-	-	-	-	-	-	-	-	-	-

Notes: Please refer to the User's Guide for an explanation of data; data is arranged alphabetically by state, then county, then city within each county; table includes counties with populations greater than 49,999 unless noted and cities with populations greater than 9,999 whose Asian and/or NHPI population rates are greater than the national average; (1) Native Hawaiian and other Pacific Islander; (2) excludes Taiwanese; (3) includes Chamorro; (4) county does not meet population threshold but is shown in order to allow inclusion of city

Place	Total foreign-born population	Total Asian population	Asians who are foreign born	Total NHPI[1] population	NHPIs[1] who are foreign born	Asian Indian	Bangladeshi	Cambodian	Chinese[2]	Fijian	Filipino	Guamanian[3]	Hawaiian, Native	Hmong	Indonesian	Japanese	Korean	Laotian	Malaysian	Pakistani	Samoan	Sri Lankan	Taiwanese	Thai	Tongan	Vietnamese
Scott (township)	1,543 8.93	1,000	889 88.90 88.90 57.62	-	-	808 97.12 90.89 80.80 52.37	-	-	-	-	-	-	-	-	-	-	-	-	-	-	-	-	-	-	-	-
Scott Township (cdp)	1,543 8.93	1,000	889 88.90 88.90 57.62	-	-	808 97.12 90.89 80.80 52.37	-	-	-	-	-	-	-	-	-	-	-	-	-	-	-	-	-	-	-	-
Upper St. Clair (township)	1,384 6.90	779	581 74.58 74.58 41.98	-	-	373 71.73 64.20 47.88 26.95	-	-	-	-	-	-	-	-	-	-	-	-	-	-	-	-	-	-	-	-
Beaver County	2,997 1.65	451	326 72.28 72.28 10.88	-	-	-	-	-	-	-	-	-	-	-	-	-	-	-	-	-	-	-	-	-	-	-
Berks County	16,032 4.29	3,621	2,675 73.87 73.87 16.69	-	-	620 79.39 23.18 17.12 3.87	-	-	475 76.00 17.76 13.12 2.96	-	-	-	-	-	-	-	287 91.40 10.73 7.93 1.79	-	-	-	-	-	-	-	-	789 67.84 29.50 21.79 4.92
Blair County	1,310 1.01	562	393 69.93 69.93 30.00	-	-	-	-	-	-	-	-	-	-	-	-	-	-	-	-	-	-	-	-	-	-	-
Bradford County	607 0.97	198	147 74.24 74.24 24.22	-	-	-	-	-	-	-	-	-	-	-	-	-	-	-	-	-	-	-	-	-	-	-
Bucks County	35,442 5.93	14,171	10,373 73.20 73.20 29.27	-	-	4,429 75.23 42.70 31.25 12.50	-	-	1,523 71.30 14.68 10.75 4.30	-	1,091 69.89 10.52 7.70 3.08	-	-	-	-	-	1,654 74.91 15.95 11.67 4.67	-	-	-	-	-	-	-	-	457 81.75 4.41 3.22 1.29
Bensalem (township)	7,692 13.16	3,807	3,085 81.03 81.03 40.11	-	-	1,565 83.07 50.73 41.11 20.35	-	-	-	-	-	-	-	-	-	-	516 75.22 16.73 13.55 6.71	-	-	-	-	-	-	-	-	-
Lower Makefield (township)	2,347 7.18	1,351	909 67.28 67.28 38.73	-	-	410 72.95 45.10 30.35 17.47	-	-	-	-	-	-	-	-	-	-	-	-	-	-	-	-	-	-	-	-

Notes: Please refer to the User's Guide for an explanation of data; data is arranged alphabetically by state, then county, then city within each county; table includes counties with populations greater than 49,999 unless noted and cities with populations greater than 9,999 whose Asian and/or NHPI population rates are greater than the national average; (1) Native Hawaiian and other Pacific Islander; (2) excludes Taiwanese; (3) includes Chamorro; (4) county does not meet population threshold but is shown in order to allow inclusion of city

Place	Total foreign-born population	Total Asian population	Asians who are foreign born	Total NHPI[1] population	NHPIs[1] who are foreign born	Asian Indian	Bangladeshi	Cambodian	Chinese[2]	Fijian	Filipino	Guamanian[3]	Hawaiian, Native	Hmong	Indonesian	Japanese	Korean	Laotian	Malaysian	Pakistani	Samoan	Sri Lankan	Taiwanese	Thai	Tongan	Vietnamese
Newtown (township)	1,456 7.98	899	638 70.97 70.97 43.82	-	-	-	-	-	-	-	-	-	-	-	-	-	-	-	-	-	-	-	-	-	-	-
Butler County	2,505 1.44	942	734 77.92 77.92 29.30	-	-	343 76.56 46.73 36.41 13.69	-	-	-	-	-	-	-	-	-	-	-	-	-	-	-	-	-	-	-	-
Cambria County	1,935 1.27	560	423 75.54 75.54 21.86	-	-	-	-	-	-	-	-	-	-	-	-	-	-	-	-	-	-	-	-	-	-	-
Centre County	7,829 5.77	5,369	3,964 73.83 73.83 50.63	-	-	932 74.03 23.51 17.36 11.90	-	-	1,287 73.71 32.47 23.97 16.44	-	-	-	-	-	-	-	861 83.43 21.72 16.04 11.00	-	-	-	-	-	-	-	-	-
Ferguson (township)	1,393 9.91	1,012	788 77.87 77.87 56.57	-	-	-	-	-	-	-	-	-	-	-	-	-	-	-	-	-	-	-	-	-	-	-
Patton (township)	869 7.61	516	417 80.81 80.81 47.99	-	-	-	-	-	-	-	-	-	-	-	-	-	-	-	-	-	-	-	-	-	-	-
State College (borough)	4,247 11.05	3,462	2,454 70.88 70.88 57.78	-	-	546 71.09 22.25 15.77 12.86	-	-	836 71.76 34.07 24.15 19.68	-	-	-	-	-	-	-	463 78.47 18.87 13.37 10.90	-	-	-	-	-	-	-	-	-
Chester County	23,770 5.48	8,755	6,274 71.66 71.66 26.39	-	-	2,092 75.12 33.34 23.89 8.80	-	-	1,588 67.81 25.31 18.14 6.68	-	402 70.90 6.41 4.59 1.69	-	-	-	-	269 67.25 4.29 3.07 1.13	850 78.56 13.55 9.71 3.58	-	-	-	-	-	-	-	-	663 79.50 10.57 7.57 2.79
Tredyffrin (township)	2,794 9.61	1,694	1,302 76.86 76.86 46.60	-	-	524 80.74 40.25 30.93 18.75	-	-	455 74.23 34.95 26.86 16.28	-	-	-	-	-	-	-	-	-	-	-	-	-	-	-	-	-
West Goshen (township)	1,201 5.86	777	582 74.90 74.90 48.46	-	-	-	-	-	-	-	-	-	-	-	-	-	-	-	-	-	-	-	-	-	-	-

Notes: Please refer to the User's Guide for an explanation of data; data is arranged alphabetically by state, then county, then city within each county; table includes counties with populations greater than 49,999 unless noted and cities with populations greater than 9,999 whose Asian and/or NHPI population rates are greater than the national average; (1) Native Hawaiian and other Pacific Islander; (2) excludes Taiwanese; (3) includes Chamorro; (4) county does not meet population threshold but is shown in order to allow inclusion of city

Place	Total foreign-born population	Total Asian population	Asians who are foreign born	Total NHPI[1] population	NHPIs[1] who are foreign born	Asian Indian	Bangladeshi	Cambodian	Chinese[2]	Fijian	Filipino	Guamanian[3]	Hawaiian, Native	Hmong	Indonesian	Japanese	Korean	Laotian	Malaysian	Pakistani	Samoan	Sri Lankan	Taiwanese	Thai	Tongan	Vietnamese
West Whiteland (township)	1,038 6.29	608	457 75.16 75.16 44.03	-	-	-	-	-	-	-	-	-	-	-	-	-	-	-	-	-	-	-	-	-	-	-
Clearfield County	560 0.67	268	206 76.87 76.87 36.79	-	-	-	-	-	-	-	-	-	-	-	-	-	-	-	-	-	-	-	-	-	-	-
Columbia County	913 1.42	295	238 80.68 80.68 26.07	-	-	-	-	-	-	-	-	-	-	-	-	-	-	-	-	-	-	-	-	-	-	-
Crawford County	981 1.09	288	188 65.28 65.28 19.16	-	-	-	-	-	-	-	-	-	-	-	-	-	-	-	-	-	-	-	-	-	-	-
Cumberland County	6,923 3.24	3,444	2,649 76.92 76.92 38.26	-	-	826 79.42 31.18 23.98 11.93	-	-	422 82.42 15.93 12.25 6.10	-	-	-	-	-	-	-	559 80.90 21.10 16.23 8.07	-	-	-	-	-	-	-	-	487 80.36 18.38 14.14 7.03
Hampden (township)	1,120 4.63	889	664 74.69 74.69 59.29	-	-	-	-	-	-	-	-	-	-	-	-	-	-	-	-	-	-	-	-	-	-	-
Dauphin County	10,214 4.06	5,028	3,881 77.19 77.19 38.00	-	-	849 79.64 21.88 16.89 8.31	-	-	640 76.92 16.49 12.73 6.27	-	-	-	-	-	-	-	339 79.39 8.73 6.74 3.32	-	-	-	-	-	-	-	-	1,413 80.56 36.41 28.10 13.83
Derry (township)	1,184 5.57	886	632 71.33 71.33 53.38	-	-	-	-	-	-	-	-	-	-	-	-	-	-	-	-	-	-	-	-	-	-	-
Hershey (cdp)	847 6.63	547	417 76.23 76.23 49.23	-	-	-	-	-	-	-	-	-	-	-	-	-	-	-	-	-	-	-	-	-	-	-
Delaware County	36,635 6.65	18,290	13,685 74.82 74.82 37.35	-	-	3,985 76.81 29.12 21.79 10.88	-	-	2,613 73.96 19.09 14.29 7.13	-	862 71.89 6.30 4.71 2.35	-	-	-	-	532 75.14 3.89 2.91 1.45	2,688 77.80 19.64 14.70 7.34	-	-	531 82.33 3.88 2.90 1.45	-	-	-	-	-	1,414 72.77 10.33 7.73 3.86

Notes: Please refer to the User's Guide for an explanation of data; data is arranged alphabetically by state, then county, then city within each county; table includes counties with populations greater than 49,999 unless noted and cities with populations greater than 9,999 whose Asian and/or NHPI population rates are greater than the national average; (1) Native Hawaiian and other Pacific Islander; (2) excludes Taiwanese; (3) includes Chamorro; (4) county does not meet population threshold but is shown in order to allow inclusion of city

Place	Total foreign-born population	Total Asian population	Asians who are foreign born	Total NHPI[1] population	NHPIs[1] who are foreign born	Asian Indian	Bangladeshi	Cambodian	Chinese[2]	Fijian	Filipino	Guamanian[3]	Hawaiian, Native	Hmong	Indonesian	Japanese	Korean	Laotian	Malaysian	Pakistani	Samoan	Sri Lankan	Taiwanese	Thai	Tongan	Vietnamese
Broomall (cdp)	1,460 13.06	777	601 77.35 77.35 41.16	-	-	-	-	-	-	-	-	-	-	-	-	-	371 79.61 61.73 47.75 25.41	-	-	-	-	-	-	-	-	-
Drexel Hill (cdp)	2,157 7.36	1,138	916 80.49 80.49 42.47	-	-	-	-	-	321 90.42 35.04 28.21 14.88	-	-	-	-	-	-	-	-	-	-	-	-	-	-	-	-	-
Marple (township)	2,554 10.76	1,265	949 75.02 75.02 37.16	-	-	-	-	-	-	-	-	-	-	-	-	-	507 76.24 53.42 40.08 19.85	-	-	-	-	-	-	-	-	-
Radnor (township)	2,563 8.30	1,600	1,176 73.50 73.50 45.88	-	-	-	-	-	265 67.26 22.53 16.56 10.34	-	-	-	-	-	-	-	-	-	-	-	-	-	-	-	-	-
Upper Darby (township)	11,369 13.89	7,107	5,552 78.12 78.12 48.83	-	-	1,620 79.88 29.18 22.79 14.25	-	-	1,234 81.02 22.23 17.36 10.85	-	-	-	-	-	-	-	775 77.89 13.96 10.90 6.82	-	-	-	-	-	-	-	-	871 73.88 15.69 12.26 7.66
Erie County	7,706 2.74	1,811	1,272 70.24 70.24 16.51	-	-	342 65.39 26.89 18.88 4.44	-	-	-	-	-	-	-	-	-	-	-	-	-	-	-	-	-	-	-	-
Franklin County	2,632 2.04	909	683 75.14 75.14 25.95	-	-	-	-	-	-	-	-	-	-	-	-	-	-	-	-	-	-	-	-	-	-	-
Indiana County	1,396 1.56	663	501 75.57 75.57 35.89	-	-	-	-	-	-	-	-	-	-	-	-	-	-	-	-	-	-	-	-	-	-	-
Lackawanna County	4,833 2.27	1,806	1,260 69.77 69.77 26.07	-	-	451 67.31 35.79 24.97 9.33	-	-	-	-	-	-	-	-	-	-	-	-	-	-	-	-	-	-	-	-
Lancaster County	15,037 3.19	6,563	4,843 73.79 73.79 32.21	-	-	567 72.79 11.71 8.64 3.77	-	-	1,082 83.55 22.34 16.49 7.20	-	-	-	-	282 61.57 5.82 4.30 1.88	-	-	512 90.14 10.57 7.80 3.40	-	-	-	-	-	-	-	-	1,505 72.95 31.08 22.93 10.01

Notes: Please refer to the User's Guide for an explanation of data; data is arranged alphabetically by state, then county, then city within each county; table includes counties with populations greater than 49,999 unless noted and cities with populations greater than 9,999 whose Asian and/or NHPI population rates are greater than the national average; (1) Native Hawaiian and other Pacific Islander; (2) excludes Taiwanese; (3) includes Chamorro; (4) county does not meet population threshold but is shown in order to allow inclusion of city

Place	Total foreign-born population	Total Asian population	Asians who are foreign born	Total NHPI[1] population	NHPIs[1] who are foreign born	Asian Indian	Bangladeshi	Cambodian	Chinese[2]	Fijian	Filipino	Guamanian[3]	Hawaiian, Native	Hmong	Indonesian	Japanese	Korean	Laotian	Malaysian	Pakistani	Samoan	Sri Lankan	Taiwanese	Thai	Tongan	Vietnamese
Lawrence County	1,261 1.33	293	198 67.58 67.58 15.70	-	-	-	-	-	-	-	-	-	-	-	-	-	-	-	-	-	-	-	-	-	-	-
Lebanon County	2,907 2.42	1,108	831 75.00 75.00 28.59	-	-	-	-	-	-	-	-	-	-	-	-	-	-	-	-	-	-	-	-	-	-	-
Lehigh County	19,331 6.19	6,841	5,137 75.09 75.09 26.57	-	-	1,710 79.24 33.29 25.00 8.85	-	-	1,192 72.82 23.20 17.42 6.17	-	-	-	-	-	-	-	509 71.29 9.91 7.44 2.63	-	-	-	-	-	-	-	-	1,049 72.15 20.42 15.33 5.43
Fullerton (cdp)	1,644 11.57	687	564 82.10 82.10 34.31	-	-	-	-	-	-	-	-	-	-	-	-	-	-	-	-	-	-	-	-	-	-	-
Lower Macungie (township)	1,273 6.62	874	593 67.85 67.85 46.58	-	-	-	-	-	264 64.55 44.52 30.21 20.74	-	-	-	-	-	-	-	-	-	-	-	-	-	-	-	-	-
Upper Macungie (township)	987 7.10	627	451 71.93 71.93 45.69	-	-	-	-	-	-	-	-	-	-	-	-	-	-	-	-	-	-	-	-	-	-	-
Luzerne County	6,171 1.93	1,534	1,118 72.88 72.88 18.12	-	-	283 68.86 25.31 18.45 4.59	-	-	-	-	-	-	-	-	-	-	-	-	-	-	-	-	-	-	-	-
Lycoming County	1,407 1.17	490	378 77.14 77.14 26.87	-	-	-	-	-	-	-	-	-	-	-	-	-	-	-	-	-	-	-	-	-	-	-
Mercer County	1,956 1.63	671	556 82.86 82.86 28.43	-	-	-	-	-	-	-	-	-	-	-	-	-	-	-	-	-	-	-	-	-	-	-
Monroe County	8,066 5.82	1,395	947 67.89 67.89 11.74	-	-	291 69.29 30.73 20.86 3.61	-	-	-	-	-	-	-	-	-	-	-	-	-	-	-	-	-	-	-	-

Notes: Please refer to the User's Guide for an explanation of data; data is arranged alphabetically by state, then county, then city within each county; table includes counties with populations greater than 49,999 unless noted and cities with populations greater than 9,999 whose Asian and/or NHPI population rates are greater than the national average; (1) Native Hawaiian and other Pacific Islander; (2) excludes Taiwanese; (3) includes Chamorro; (4) county does not meet population threshold but is shown in order to allow inclusion of city

Place	Total foreign-born population	Total Asian population	Asians who are foreign born	Total NHPI[1] population	NHPIs[1] who are foreign born	Asian Indian	Bangladeshi	Cambodian	Chinese[2]	Fijian	Filipino	Guamanian[3]	Hawaiian, Native	Hmong	Indonesian	Japanese	Korean	Laotian	Malaysian	Pakistani	Samoan	Sri Lankan	Taiwanese	Thai	Tongan	Vietnamese
Montgomery County	52,152 6.95	29,431	21,920 74.48 74.48 42.03	-	-	5,695 76.62 25.98 19.35 10.92	-	-	4,078 74.19 18.60 13.86 7.82	-	1,424 72.65 6.50 4.84 2.73	-	-	-	-	389 54.41 1.77 1.32 0.75	7,019 76.27 32.02 23.85 13.46	-	-	-	-	-	-	-	-	1,732 71.31 7.90 5.88 3.32
Cheltenham (township)	4,020 10.90	2,391	1,920 80.30 80.30 47.76	-	-	-	-	-	-	-	-	-	-	-	-	-	989 88.38 51.51 41.36 24.60	-	-	-	-	-	-	-	-	-
East Norriton (township)	955 7.27	538	467 86.80 86.80 48.90	-	-	-	-	-	-	-	-	-	-	-	-	-	-	-	-	-	-	-	-	-	-	-
Hatfield (township)	2,100 12.62	1,819	1,425 78.34 78.34 67.86	-	-	782 80.37 54.88 42.99 37.24	-	-	-	-	-	-	-	-	-	-	-	-	-	-	-	-	-	-	-	-
Horsham (township)	1,662 6.86	1,150	871 75.74 75.74 52.41	-	-	-	-	-	-	-	-	-	-	-	-	-	371 72.46 42.59 32.26 22.32	-	-	-	-	-	-	-	-	-
King of Prussia (cdp)	2,527 13.63	1,895	1,509 79.63 79.63 59.72	-	-	665 86.59 44.07 35.09 26.32	-	-	296 72.91 19.62 15.62 11.71	-	-	-	-	-	-	-	-	-	-	-	-	-	-	-	-	-
Lansdale (borough)	1,833 11.41	1,329	1,050 79.01 79.01 57.28	-	-	435 96.67 41.43 32.73 23.73	-	-	-	-	-	-	-	-	-	-	-	-	-	-	-	-	-	-	-	-
Lower Gwynedd (township)	753 7.23	403	303 75.19 75.19 40.24	-	-	-	-	-	-	-	-	-	-	-	-	-	-	-	-	-	-	-	-	-	-	-
Lower Providence (township)	1,443 6.44	1,014	772 76.13 76.13 53.50	-	-	-	-	-	368 77.64 47.67 36.29 25.50	-	-	-	-	-	-	-	-	-	-	-	-	-	-	-	-	-
Montgomery (township)	2,155 9.78	1,827	1,310 71.70 71.70 60.79	-	-	430 74.52 32.82 23.54 19.95	-	-	-	-	-	-	-	-	-	-	524 72.48 40.00 28.68 24.32	-	-	-	-	-	-	-	-	-

Notes: Please refer to the User's Guide for an explanation of data; data is arranged alphabetically by state, then county, then city within each county; table includes counties with populations greater than 49,999 unless noted and cities with populations greater than 9,999 whose Asian and/or NHPI population rates are greater than the national average; (1) Native Hawaiian and other Pacific Islander; (2) excludes Taiwanese; (3) includes Chamorro; (4) county does not meet population threshold but is shown in order to allow inclusion of city

Place	Total foreign-born population	Total Asian population	Asians who are foreign born	Total NHPI[1] population	NHPIs[1] who are foreign born	Asian Indian	Bangladeshi	Cambodian	Chinese[2]	Fijian	Filipino	Guamanian[3]	Hawaiian, Native	Hmong	Indonesian	Japanese	Korean	Laotian	Malaysian	Pakistani	Samoan	Sri Lankan	Taiwanese	Thai	Tongan	Vietnamese
Montgomeryville (cdp)	1,129 9.44	820	635 77.44 77.44 56.24	-	-	-	-	-	-	-	-	-	-	-	-	-	-	-	-	-	-	-	-	-	-	-
Plymouth (township)	1,215 7.57	832	682 81.97 81.97 56.13	-	-	-	-	-	-	-	-	-	-	-	-	-	260 78.31 38.12 31.25 21.40	-	-	-	-	-	-	-	-	-
Towamencin (township)	1,289 7.32	1,043	789 75.65 75.65 61.21	-	-	-	-	-	-	-	-	-	-	-	-	-	-	-	-	-	-	-	-	-	-	-
Upper Dublin (township)	2,126 8.22	1,514	1,050 69.35 69.35 49.39	-	-	-	-	-	-	-	-	-	-	-	-	-	544 65.54 51.81 35.93 25.59	-	-	-	-	-	-	-	-	-
Upper Gwynedd (township)	1,365 9.58	1,144	764 66.78 66.78 55.97	-	-	-	-	-	212 66.46 27.75 18.53 15.53	-	-	-	-	-	-	-	-	-	-	-	-	-	-	-	-	-
Upper Merion (township)	3,085 11.49	2,161	1,672 77.37 77.37 54.20	-	-	741 81.43 44.32 34.29 24.02	-	-	324 72.97 19.38 14.99 10.50	-	-	-	-	-	-	-	-	-	-	-	-	-	-	-	-	-
Whitpain (township)	1,793 9.59	1,247	897 71.93 71.93 50.03	-	-	-	-	-	-	-	-	-	-	-	-	-	430 73.38 47.94 34.48 23.98	-	-	-	-	-	-	-	-	-
Northampton County	12,227 4.58	3,756	2,674 71.19 71.19 21.87	-	-	843 67.93 31.53 22.44 6.89	-	-	502 66.31 18.77 13.37 4.11	-	-	-	-	-	-	-	421 91.32 15.74 11.21 3.44	-	-	-	-	-	-	-	-	345 72.94 12.90 9.19 2.82
Northumberland County	1,056 1.12	373	258 69.17 69.17 24.43	-	-	-	-	-	-	-	-	-	-	-	-	-	-	-	-	-	-	-	-	-	-	-
Philadelphia County	137,205 9.04	65,171	46,567 71.45 71.45 33.94	790	146 18.48 18.48 0.11	8,665 69.09 18.61 13.30 6.32	-	4,181 65.26 8.98 6.42 3.05	12,888 72.38 27.68 19.78 9.39	-	2,541 66.45 5.46 3.90 1.85	-	-	-	-	792 71.67 1.70 1.22 0.58	4,948 75.78 10.63 7.59 3.61	860 70.84 1.85 1.32 0.63	-	546 86.80 1.17 0.84 0.40	-	-	-	-	-	8,937 80.70 19.19 13.71 6.51

Notes: Please refer to the User's Guide for an explanation of data; data is arranged alphabetically by state, then county, then city within each county; table includes counties with populations greater than 49,999 unless noted and cities with populations greater than 9,999 whose Asian and/or NHPI population rates are greater than the national average; (1) Native Hawaiian and other Pacific Islander; (2) excludes Taiwanese; (3) includes Chamorro; (4) county does not meet population threshold but is shown in order to allow inclusion of city

Place	Total foreign-born population	Total Asian population	Asians who are foreign born	Total NHPI[1] population	NHPIs[1] who are foreign born	Asian Indian	Bangladeshi	Cambodian	Chinese[2]	Fijian	Filipino	Guamanian[3]	Hawaiian, Native	Hmong	Indonesian	Japanese	Korean	Laotian	Malaysian	Pakistani	Samoan	Sri Lankan	Taiwanese	Thai	Tongan	Vietnamese
Philadelphia (city)	137,205 9.04	65,171	46,567 71.45 71.45 33.94	790	146 18.48 18.48 0.11	8,665 69.09 18.61 13.30 6.32	-	4,181 65.26 8.98 6.42 3.05	12,888 72.38 27.68 19.78 9.39	-	2,541 66.45 5.46 3.90 1.85	-	-	-	-	792 71.67 1.70 1.22 0.58	4,948 75.78 10.63 7.59 3.61	860 70.84 1.85 1.32 0.63	-	546 86.80 1.17 0.84 0.40	-	-	-	-	-	8,937 80.70 19.19 13.71 6.51
Schuylkill County	1,500 1.00	553	366 66.18 66.18 24.40	-	-	-	-	-	-	-	-	-	-	-	-	-	-	-	-	-	-	-	-	-	-	-
Washington County	2,404 1.18	631	432 68.46 68.46 17.97	-	-	-	-	-	-	-	-	-	-	-	-	-	-	-	-	-	-	-	-	-	-	-
Westmoreland County	5,277 1.43	1,724	1,258 72.97 72.97 23.84	-	-	264 59.06 20.99 15.31 5.00	-	-	-	-	-	-	-	-	-	-	-	-	-	-	-	-	-	-	-	-
York County	8,280 2.17	3,150	2,320 73.65 73.65 28.02	-	-	355 67.36 15.30 11.27 4.29	-	-	556 82.13 23.97 17.65 6.71	-	-	-	-	-	-	-	458 73.28 19.74 14.54 5.53	-	-	-	-	-	-	-	-	464 79.45 20.00 14.73 5.60
RHODE ISLAND	119,277 11.38	23,825	15,724 66.00 66.00 13.18	441	111 25.17 25.17 0.09	1,789 70.21 11.38 7.51 1.50	-	3,073 60.20 19.54 12.90 2.58	2,976 65.23 18.93 12.49 2.50	-	1,556 73.19 9.90 6.53 1.30	-	-	606 63.06 3.85 2.54 0.51	-	510 64.97 3.24 2.14 0.43	1,317 68.49 8.38 5.53 1.10	2,061 71.34 13.11 8.65 1.73	-	-	-	-	-	-	-	758 73.74 4.82 3.18 0.64
Bristol County	5,090 10.05	420	275 65.48 65.48 5.40	-	-	-	-	-	-	-	-	-	-	-	-	-	-	-	-	-	-	-	-	-	-	-
Kent County	8,107 4.85	2,187	1,565 71.56 71.56 19.30	-	-	-	-	-	260 70.46 16.61 11.89 3.21	-	-	-	-	-	-	-	276 66.03 17.64 12.62 3.40	-	-	-	-	-	-	-	-	-
Newport County	4,216 4.93	982	580 59.06 59.06 13.76	-	-	-	-	-	-	-	278 60.30 47.93 28.31 6.59	-	-	-	-	-	-	-	-	-	-	-	-	-	-	-
Providence County	96,676 15.55	18,319	11,950 65.23 65.23 12.36	-	-	1,269 68.12 10.62 6.93 1.31	-	2,834 58.74 23.72 15.47 2.93	2,034 63.88 17.02 11.10 2.10	-	843 76.57 7.05 4.60 0.87	-	-	531 63.90 4.44 2.90 0.55	-	-	788 66.89 6.59 4.30 0.82	1,960 71.27 16.40 10.70 2.03	-	-	-	-	-	-	-	623 77.10 5.21 3.40 0.64

Notes: Please refer to the User's Guide for an explanation of data; data is arranged alphabetically by state, then county, then city within each county; table includes counties with populations greater than 49,999 unless noted and cities with populations greater than 9,999 whose Asian and/or NHPI population rates are greater than the national average; (1) Native Hawaiian and other Pacific Islander; (2) excludes Taiwanese; (3) includes Chamorro; (4) county does not meet population threshold but is shown in order to allow inclusion of city

Place	Total foreign-born population	Total Asian population	Asians who are foreign born	Total NHPI[1] population	NHPIs[1] who are foreign born	Asian Indian	Bangladeshi	Cambodian	Chinese[2]	Fijian	Filipino	Guamanian[3]	Hawaiian, Native	Hmong	Indonesian	Japanese	Korean	Laotian	Malaysian	Pakistani	Samoan	Sri Lankan	Taiwanese	Thai	Tongan	Vietnamese
Providence (city)	43,947 25.31	10,707	6,619 61.82 61.82 15.06	-	-	554 60.75 8.37 5.17 1.26	-	2,204 61.53 33.30 20.58 5.02	873 58.24 13.19 8.15 1.99	-	400 77.37 6.04 3.74 0.91	-	-	439 65.13 6.63 4.10 1.00	-	-	409 57.28 6.18 3.82 0.93	923 69.61 13.94 8.62 2.10	-	-	-	-	-	-	-	-
Woonsocket (city)	3,239 7.49	1,646	1,193 72.48 72.48 36.83	-	-	-	-	-	-	-	-	-	-	-	-	-	-	714 78.29 59.85 43.38 22.04	-	-	-	-	-	-	-	-
Washington County	5,188 4.20	1,917	1,354 70.63 70.63 26.10	-	-	-	-	-	417 72.65 30.80 21.75 8.04	-	-	-	-	-	-	-	-	-	-	-	-	-	-	-	-	-
SOUTH CAROLINA	115,978 2.89	36,505	25,942 71.06 71.06 22.37	1,384	401 28.97 28.97 0.35	6,191 75.36 23.86 16.96 5.34	-	249 73.02 0.96 0.68 0.21	4,614 73.68 17.79 12.64 3.98	-	4,650 66.88 17.92 12.74 4.01	100 27.86 24.94 7.23 0.09	57 11.49 14.21 4.12 0.05	377 43.84 1.45 1.03 0.33	-	1,663 72.87 6.41 4.56 1.43	2,748 77.50 10.59 7.53 2.37	859 64.88 3.31 2.35 0.74	-	-	-	-	-	573 83.28 2.21 1.57 0.49	-	2,950 77.35 11.37 8.08 2.54
Aiken County	3,252 2.28	940	626 66.60 66.60 19.25	-	-	-	-	-	-	-	-	-	-	-	-	-	-	-	-	-	-	-	-	-	-	-
Anderson County	2,516 1.52	836	596 71.29 71.29 23.69	-	-	-	-	-	-	-	-	-	-	-	-	-	-	-	-	-	-	-	-	-	-	-
Beaufort County	7,596 6.28	1,014	697 68.74 68.74 9.18	-	-	-	-	-	-	-	-	-	-	-	-	-	-	-	-	-	-	-	-	-	-	-
Berkeley County	4,443 3.11	2,933	2,041 69.59 69.59 45.94	-	-	-	-	-	-	-	1,232 68.03 60.36 42.00 27.73	-	-	-	-	-	-	-	-	-	-	-	-	-	-	-
Charleston County	11,124 3.59	3,502	2,411 68.85 68.85 21.67	-	-	489 77.25 20.28 13.96 4.40	-	-	515 73.47 21.36 14.71 4.63	-	586 58.78 24.31 16.73 5.27	-	-	-	-	-	-	-	-	-	-	-	-	-	-	-
Dorchester County	2,690 2.79	1,254	829 66.11 66.11 30.82	-	-	-	-	-	-	-	421 65.99 50.78 33.57 15.65	-	-	-	-	-	-	-	-	-	-	-	-	-	-	-

Notes: Please refer to the User's Guide for an explanation of data; data is arranged alphabetically by state, then county, then city within each county; table includes counties with populations greater than 49,999 unless noted and cities with populations greater than 9,999 whose Asian and/or NHPI population rates are greater than the national average; (1) Native Hawaiian and other Pacific Islander; (2) excludes Taiwanese; (3) includes Chamorro; (4) county does not meet population threshold but is shown in order to allow inclusion of city

Place	Total foreign-born population	Total Asian population	Asians who are foreign born	Total NHPI[1] population	NHPIs[1] who are foreign born	Asian Indian	Bangladeshi	Cambodian	Chinese[2]	Fijian	Filipino	Guamanian[3]	Hawaiian, Native	Hmong	Indonesian	Japanese	Korean	Laotian	Malaysian	Pakistani	Samoan	Sri Lankan	Taiwanese	Thai	Tongan	Vietnamese
Florence County	2,240 1.78	1,026	705 68.71 68.71 31.47	-	-	-	-	-	-	-	-	-	-	-	-	-	-	-	-	-	-	-	-	-	-	-
Greenville County	18,420 4.85	4,893	3,627 74.13 74.13 19.69	-	-	1,129 78.95 31.13 23.07 6.13	-	-	466 64.99 12.85 9.52 2.53	-	336 63.04 9.26 6.87 1.82	-	-	-	-	-	-	-	-	-	-	-	-	-	-	967 84.90 26.66 19.76 5.25
Greenwood County	1,842 2.78	422	326 77.25 77.25 17.70	-	-	-	-	-	-	-	-	-	-	-	-	-	-	-	-	-	-	-	-	-	-	-
Horry County	7,806 3.97	1,548	1,125 72.67 72.67 14.41	-	-	-	-	-	-	-	-	-	-	-	-	-	-	-	-	-	-	-	-	-	-	-
Lexington County	6,283 2.91	1,945	1,359 69.87 69.87 21.63	-	-	461 76.58 33.92 23.70 7.34	-	-	367 64.84 27.01 18.87 5.84	-	-	-	-	-	-	-	-	-	-	-	-	-	-	-	-	-
Oconee County	1,596 2.41	264	193 73.11 73.11 12.09	-	-	-	-	-	-	-	-	-	-	-	-	-	-	-	-	-	-	-	-	-	-	-
Pickens County	3,168 2.86	1,316	1,055 80.17 80.17 33.30	-	-	409 78.96 38.77 31.08 12.91	-	-	339 88.51 32.13 25.76 10.70	-	-	-	-	-	-	-	-	-	-	-	-	-	-	-	-	-
Clemson (city)	1,048 8.65	598	534 89.30 89.30 50.95	-	-	-	-	-	-	-	-	-	-	-	-	-	-	-	-	-	-	-	-	-	-	-
Richland County	12,646 3.94	5,611	4,180 74.50 74.50 33.05	-	-	1,145 76.64 27.39 20.41 9.05	-	-	890 80.62 21.29 15.86 7.04	-	330 63.22 7.89 5.88 2.61	-	-	-	-	-	1,004 79.62 24.02 17.89 7.94	-	-	-	-	-	-	-	-	367 69.51 8.78 6.54 2.90
Spartanburg County	9,396 3.70	4,152	2,633 63.42 63.42 28.02	-	-	550 71.99 20.89 13.25 5.85	-	-	-	-	-	-	-	327 43.60 12.42 7.88 3.48	-	-	-	419 61.80 15.91 10.09 4.46	-	-	-	-	-	-	-	-

Notes: Please refer to the User's Guide for an explanation of data; data is arranged alphabetically by state, then county, then city within each county; table includes counties with populations greater than 49,999 unless noted and cities with populations greater than 9,999 whose Asian and/or NHPI population rates are greater than the national average; (1) Native Hawaiian and other Pacific Islander; (2) excludes Taiwanese; (3) includes Chamorro; (4) county does not meet population threshold but is shown in order to allow inclusion of city

Place	Total foreign-born population	Total Asian population	Asians who are foreign born	Total NHPI[1] population	NHPIs[1] who are foreign born	Asian Indian	Bangladeshi	Cambodian	Chinese[2]	Fijian	Filipino	Guamanian[3]	Hawaiian, Native	Hmong	Indonesian	Japanese	Korean	Laotian	Malaysian	Pakistani	Samoan	Sri Lankan	Taiwanese	Thai	Tongan	Vietnamese
Sumter County	2,149 2.05	932	684 73.39 73.39 31.83	-	-	-	-	-	-	-	-	-	-	-	-	-	-	-	-	-	-	-	-	-	-	-
York County	3,980 2.42	1,312	968 73.78 73.78 24.32	-	-	-	-	-	-	-	-	-	-	-	-	-	-	-	-	-	-	-	-	-	-	309 69.44 31.92 23.55 7.76
SOUTH DAKOTA	13,495 1.79	4,729	3,360 71.05 71.05 24.90	-	-	457 78.66 13.60 9.66 3.39	-	-	568 83.65 16.90 12.01 4.21	-	490 69.60 14.58 10.36 3.63	-	-	-	-	193 46.84 5.74 4.08 1.43	604 81.07 17.98 12.77 4.48	143 65.60 4.26 3.02 1.06	-	-	-	-	-	-	-	540 75.52 16.07 11.42 4.00
Minnehaha County	6,028 4.07	1,585	1,153 72.74 72.74 19.13	-	-	-	-	-	-	-	-	-	-	-	-	-	-	-	-	-	-	-	-	-	-	396 75.72 34.35 24.98 6.57
Pennington County	1,899 2.14	914	555 60.72 60.72 29.23	-	-	-	-	-	-	-	-	-	-	-	-	-	-	-	-	-	-	-	-	-	-	-
TENNESSEE	159,004 2.79	54,132	40,361 74.56 74.56 25.38	2,159	493 22.83 22.83 0.31	9,070 75.86 22.47 16.76 5.70	-	858 72.10 2.13 1.59 0.54	6,199 74.66 15.36 11.45 3.90	-	3,631 68.74 9.00 6.71 2.28	190 30.69 38.54 8.80 0.12	18 3.21 3.65 0.83 0.01	-	-	3,051 78.88 7.56 5.64 1.92	5,603 81.18 13.88 10.35 3.52	2,901 72.25 7.19 5.36 1.82	-	582 76.18 1.44 1.08 0.37	132 24.44 26.77 6.11 0.08	-	468 80.69 1.16 0.86 0.29	750 75.38 1.86 1.39 0.47	-	5,575 78.95 13.81 10.30 3.51
Anderson County	1,390 1.95	513	407 79.34 79.34 29.28	-	-	-	-	-	-	-	-	-	-	-	-	-	-	-	-	-	-	-	-	-	-	-
Blount County	1,634 1.54	638	544 85.27 85.27 33.29	-	-	-	-	-	-	-	-	-	-	-	-	-	-	-	-	-	-	-	-	-	-	-
Bradley County	1,956 2.22	480	410 85.42 85.42 20.96	-	-	-	-	-	-	-	-	-	-	-	-	-	-	-	-	-	-	-	-	-	-	-
Davidson County	39,596 6.95	11,691	8,951 76.56 76.56 22.61	400	56 14.00 14.00 0.14	1,897 75.04 21.19 16.23 4.79	-	-	1,278 84.19 14.28 10.93 3.23	-	568 70.91 6.35 4.86 1.43	-	-	-	-	643 74.85 7.18 5.50 1.62	1,072 82.46 11.98 9.17 2.71	999 76.20 11.16 8.55 2.52	-	-	-	-	-	-	-	1,355 80.37 15.14 11.59 3.42

Notes: Please refer to the User's Guide for an explanation of data; data is arranged alphabetically by state, then county, then city within each county; table includes counties with populations greater than 49,999 unless noted and cities with populations greater than 9,999 whose Asian and/or NHPI population rates are greater than the national average; (1) Native Hawaiian and other Pacific Islander; (2) excludes Taiwanese; (3) includes Chamorro; (4) county does not meet population threshold but is shown in order to allow inclusion of city

Place	Total foreign-born population	Total Asian population	Asians who are foreign born	Total NHPI[1] population	NHPIs[1] who are foreign born	Asian Indian	Bangladeshi	Cambodian	Chinese[2]	Fijian	Filipino	Guamanian[3]	Hawaiian, Native	Hmong	Indonesian	Japanese	Korean	Laotian	Malaysian	Pakistani	Samoan	Sri Lankan	Taiwanese	Thai	Tongan	Vietnamese
Hamilton County	9,297 3.02	3,852	2,909 75.52 75.52 31.29	-	-	881 77.28 30.29 22.87 9.48	-	-	-	-	288 69.40 9.90 7.48 3.10	-	-	-	-	-	418 79.77 14.37 10.85 4.50	-	-	-	-	-	-	-	-	367 84.17 12.62 9.53 3.95
Knox County	9,568 2.50	4,548	3,313 72.85 72.85 34.63	-	-	923 68.88 27.86 20.29 9.65	-	-	680 73.35 20.53 14.95 7.11	-	-	-	-	-	-	-	429 80.49 12.95 9.43 4.48	-	-	-	-	-	-	-	-	369 78.01 11.14 8.11 3.86
Madison County	2,074 2.26	557	424 76.12 76.12 20.44	-	-	-	-	-	-	-	-	-	-	-	-	-	-	-	-	-	-	-	-	-	-	-
Montgomery County	5,905 4.38	2,448	1,806 73.77 73.77 30.58	-	-	-	-	-	-	-	-	-	-	-	-	-	963 86.68 53.32 39.34 16.31	-	-	-	-	-	-	-	-	-
Putnam County	2,130 3.42	581	448 77.11 77.11 21.03	-	-	-	-	-	-	-	-	-	-	-	-	-	-	-	-	-	-	-	-	-	-	-
Rutherford County	6,608 3.63	3,253	2,438 74.95 74.95 36.89	-	-	-	-	-	-	-	-	-	-	-	-	-	-	1,102 70.42 45.20 33.88 16.68	-	-	-	-	-	-	-	-
Shelby County	34,373 3.83	14,925	11,043 73.99 73.99 32.13	493	192 38.95 38.95 0.56	2,810 78.45 25.45 18.83 8.18	-	404 78.29 3.66 2.71 1.18	1,947 69.54 17.63 13.05 5.66	-	950 69.75 8.60 6.37 2.76	-	-	-	-	384 74.56 3.48 2.57 1.12	874 70.88 7.91 5.86 2.54	-	-	-	-	-	-	-	-	2,661 79.62 24.10 17.83 7.74
Germantown (city)	1,971 5.29	1,380	994 72.03 72.03 50.43	-	-	364 68.55 36.62 26.38 18.47	-	-	249 59.14 25.05 18.04 12.63	-	-	-	-	-	-	-	-	-	-	-	-	-	-	-	-	-
Sullivan County	1,936 1.26	585	447 76.41 76.41 23.09	-	-	-	-	-	-	-	-	-	-	-	-	-	-	-	-	-	-	-	-	-	-	-
Sumner County	3,108 2.38	877	675 76.97 76.97 21.72	-	-	-	-	-	-	-	-	-	-	-	-	-	-	-	-	-	-	-	-	-	-	-

Notes: Please refer to the User's Guide for an explanation of data; data is arranged alphabetically by state, then county, then city within each county; table includes counties with populations greater than 49,999 unless noted and cities with populations greater than 9,999 whose Asian and/or NHPI population rates are greater than the national average; (1) Native Hawaiian and other Pacific Islander; (2) excludes Taiwanese; (3) includes Chamorro; (4) county does not meet population threshold but is shown in order to allow inclusion of city

Place	Total foreign-born population	Total Asian population	Asians who are foreign born	Total NHPI[1] population	NHPIs[1] who are foreign born	Asian Indian	Bangladeshi	Cambodian	Chinese[2]	Fijian	Filipino	Guamanian[3]	Hawaiian, Native	Hmong	Indonesian	Japanese	Korean	Laotian	Malaysian	Pakistani	Samoan	Sri Lankan	Taiwanese	Thai	Tongan	Vietnamese
Washington County	2,003	729	504	-	-	-	-	-	-	-	-	-	-	-	-	-	-	-	-	-	-	-	-	-	-	-
	1.87		69.14																							
			69.14																							
			25.16																							
Weakley County[4]	706	467	390	-	-	-	-	-	-	-	-	-	-	-	-	-	-	-	-	-	-	-	-	-	-	-
	2.02		83.51																							
			83.51																							
			55.24																							
Martin (city)	593	430	366	-	-	-	-	-	-	-	-	-	-	-	-	-	-	-	-	-	-	-	-	-	-	-
	5.62		85.12																							
			85.12																							
			61.72																							
Williamson County	4,944	1,497	1,156	-	-	-	-	-	-	-	-	-	-	-	-	-	-	-	-	-	-	-	-	-	-	-
	3.90		77.22																							
			77.22																							
			23.38																							
Wilson County	1,260	303	193	-	-	-	-	-	-	-	-	-	-	-	-	-	-	-	-	-	-	-	-	-	-	-
	1.42		63.70																							
			63.70																							
			15.32																							
TEXAS	2,899,642	555,928	408,383	12,464	2,669	95,796	2,153	5,169	72,607	-	41,554	373	260	-	1,591	10,507	34,378	6,938	599	14,288	367	781	5,902	5,263	284	99,579
	13.91		73.46		21.41	75.28	83.64	67.99	73.84		70.89	11.29	7.11		89.84	65.20	77.47	70.35	89.40	75.71	18.05	80.02	75.10	73.98	56.69	74.23
						23.46	0.53	1.27	17.78		10.18	13.98	9.74		0.39	2.57	8.42	1.70	0.15	3.50	13.75	0.19	1.45	1.29	10.64	24.38
			73.46		21.41	17.23	0.39	0.93	13.06		7.47	2.99	2.09		0.29	1.89	6.18	1.25	0.11	2.57	2.94	0.14	1.06	0.95	2.28	17.91
			14.08		0.09	3.30	0.07	0.18	2.50		1.43	0.01	0.01		0.05	0.36	1.19	0.24	0.02	0.49	0.01	0.03	0.20	0.18	0.01	3.43
Anderson County	1,782	406	279	-	-	-	-	-	-	-	-	-	-	-	-	-	-	-	-	-	-	-	-	-	-	-
	3.23		68.72																							
			68.72																							
			15.66																							
Angelina County	5,561	539	371	-	-	-	-	-	-	-	-	-	-	-	-	-	-	-	-	-	-	-	-	-	-	-
	6.94		68.83																							
			68.83																							
			6.67																							
Bell County	17,322	6,114	4,502	1,264	154	391	-	-	-	-	1,116	18	-	-	-	262	1,978	-	-	-	-	-	-	-	-	-
	7.28		73.63		12.18	67.07					68.30	3.02				68.59	83.53									
						8.69					24.79	11.69				5.82	43.94									
			73.63		12.18	6.40					18.25	1.42				4.29	32.35									
			25.99		0.89	2.26					6.44	0.10				1.51	11.42									
Killeen (city)	8,922	3,805	2,842	1,046	130	-	-	-	-	-	771	18	-	-	-	-	1,349	-	-	-	-	-	-	-	-	-
	10.28		74.69		12.43						70.09	3.60					85.92									
											27.13	13.85					47.47									
			74.69		12.43						20.26	1.72					35.45									
			31.85		1.46						8.64	0.20					15.12									

Notes: Please refer to the User's Guide for an explanation of data; data is arranged alphabetically by state, then county, then city within each county; table includes counties with populations greater than 49,999 unless noted and cities with populations greater than 9,999 whose Asian and/or NHPI population rates are greater than the national average; (1) Native Hawaiian and other Pacific Islander; (2) excludes Taiwanese; (3) includes Chamorro; (4) county does not meet population threshold but is shown in order to allow inclusion of city

Place	Total foreign-born population	Total Asian population	Asians who are foreign born	Total NHPI[1] population	NHPIs[1] who are foreign born	Asian Indian	Bangladeshi	Cambodian	Chinese[2]	Fijian	Filipino	Guamanian[3]	Hawaiian, Native	Hmong	Indonesian	Japanese	Korean	Laotian	Malaysian	Pakistani	Samoan	Sri Lankan	Taiwanese	Thai	Tongan	Vietnamese
Bexar County	151,340 10.86	22,586	15,479 68.53 68.53 10.23	1,130	169 14.96 14.96 0.11	2,653 70.97 17.14 11.75 1.75	-	-	2,533 68.37 16.36 11.21 1.67	-	3,458 66.40 22.34 15.31 2.28	-	16 3.81 9.47 1.42 0.01	-	-	958 55.86 6.19 4.24 0.63	1,955 75.83 12.63 8.66 1.29	296 76.88 1.91 1.31 0.20	-	-	-	-	-	599 73.59 3.87 2.65 0.40	-	2,229 77.42 14.40 9.87 1.47
Bowie County	1,332 1.49	448	277 61.83 61.83 20.80	-	-	-	-	-	-	-	-	-	-	-	-	-	-	-	-	-	-	-	-	-	-	-
Brazoria County	20,597 8.52	4,720	3,106 65.81 65.81 15.08	-	-	628 69.24 20.22 13.31 3.05	-	233 60.84 7.50 4.94 1.13	379 59.13 12.20 8.03 1.84	-	462 67.84 14.87 9.79 2.24	-	-	-	-	-	-	-	-	-	-	-	-	-	-	901 68.05 29.01 19.09 4.37
Brazos County	15,636 10.26	6,238	4,783 76.68 76.68 30.59	-	-	1,416 79.73 29.60 22.70 9.06	-	-	1,287 78.00 26.91 20.63 8.23	-	-	-	-	-	-	-	768 84.58 16.06 12.31 4.91	-	-	-	-	-	-	-	-	308 65.81 6.44 4.94 1.97
College Station (city)	7,568 11.15	5,160	3,843 74.48 74.48 50.78	-	-	1,005 76.60 26.15 19.48 13.28	-	-	1,110 76.45 28.88 21.51 14.67	-	-	-	-	-	-	-	638 82.01 16.60 12.36 8.43	-	-	-	-	-	-	-	-	-
Calhoun County[4]	1,756 8.50	683	512 74.96 74.96 29.16	-	-	-	-	-	-	-	-	-	-	-	-	-	-	-	-	-	-	-	-	-	-	107 64.85 20.90 15.67 6.09
Port Lavaca (city)	1,315 10.95	493	383 77.69 77.69 29.13	-	-	-	-	-	-	-	-	-	-	-	-	-	-	-	-	-	-	-	-	-	-	-
Cameron County	85,723 25.57	1,509	1,123 74.42 74.42 1.31	-	-	-	-	-	-	-	487 83.39 43.37 32.27 0.57	-	-	-	-	-	-	-	-	-	-	-	-	-	-	-
Collin County	65,279 13.28	33,606	24,914 74.14 74.14 38.17	-	-	6,735 77.01 27.03 20.04 10.32	-	-	9,270 74.01 37.21 27.58 14.20	-	1,068 73.60 4.29 3.18 1.64	-	-	-	-	694 75.93 2.79 2.07 1.06	2,103 74.02 8.44 6.26 3.22	-	-	661 69.00 2.65 1.97 1.01	-	-	543 63.88 2.18 1.62 0.83	346 76.21 1.39 1.03 0.53	-	2,512 71.92 10.08 7.47 3.85
Allen (city)	3,178 7.31	1,639	1,105 67.42 67.42 34.77	-	-	304 67.41 27.51 18.55 9.57	-	-	-	-	-	-	-	-	-	-	-	-	-	-	-	-	-	-	-	264 66.67 23.89 16.11 8.31

Notes: Please refer to the User's Guide for an explanation of data; data is arranged alphabetically by state, then county, then city within each county; table includes counties with populations greater than 49,999 unless noted and cities with populations greater than 9,999 whose Asian and/or NHPI population rates are greater than the national average; (1) Native Hawaiian and other Pacific Islander; (2) excludes Taiwanese; (3) includes Chamorro; (4) county does not meet population threshold but is shown in order to allow inclusion of city

Place	Total foreign-born population	Total Asian population	Asians who are foreign born	Total NHPI[1] population	NHPIs[1] who are foreign born	Asian Indian	Bangladeshi	Cambodian	Chinese[2]	Fijian	Filipino	Guamanian[3]	Hawaiian, Native	Hmong	Indonesian	Japanese	Korean	Laotian	Malaysian	Pakistani	Samoan	Sri Lankan	Taiwanese	Thai	Tongan	Vietnamese
	37,923	22,465	16,470	-	-	4,287	-	-	6,796	-	592	-	-	-	-	377	1,545	-	-	393	-	-	377	-	-	1,328
	17.06		73.31			75.48			73.04		75.90					75.55	72.23			65.07			66.84			73.61
Plano (city)						26.03			41.26		3.59					2.29	9.38			2.39			2.29			8.06
			73.31			19.08			30.25		2.64					1.68	6.88			1.75			1.68			5.91
			43.43			11.30			17.92		1.56					0.99	4.07			1.04			0.99			3.50
	3,721	443	231	-	-	-	-	-	-	-	-	-	-	-	-	-	-	-	-	-	-	-	-	-	-	-
	4.77		52.14																							
Comal County																										
			52.14																							
			6.21																							
	3,966	1,380	894	433	66	-	-	-	-	-	-	-	-	-	-	-	366	-	-	-	-	-	-	-	-	-
	5.29		64.78		15.24												73.94									
Coryell County																	40.94									
			64.78		15.24												26.52									
			22.54		1.66												9.23									
	463,574	87,446	66,715	987	290	18,579	560	1,493	9,026	-	4,387	-	-	-	-	1,570	7,416	1,609	-	2,679	-	-	593	819	-	15,465
	20.89		76.29		29.38	78.27	83.21	63.34	76.92		73.19					70.59	79.40	68.85		72.15			73.76	74.12		77.80
Dallas County						27.85	0.84	2.24	13.53		6.58					2.35	11.12	2.41		4.02			0.89	1.23		23.18
			76.29		29.38	21.25	0.64	1.71	10.32		5.02					1.80	8.48	1.84		3.06			0.68	0.94		17.69
			14.39		0.06	4.01	0.12	0.32	1.95		0.95					0.34	1.60	0.35		0.58			0.13	0.18		3.34
	3,747	1,104	857	-	-	524	-	-	-	-	-	-	-	-	-	-	-	-	-	-	-	-	-	-	-	-
	27.15		77.63			86.47																				
Addison (town)						61.14																				
			77.63			47.46																				
			22.87			13.98																				
	4,296	3,444	2,419	-	-	819	-	-	511	-	-	-	-	-	-	-	473	-	-	-	-	-	-	-	-	-
	11.95		70.24			71.84			65.85								69.56									
Coppell (city)						33.86			21.12								19.55									
			70.24			23.78			14.84								13.73									
			56.31			19.06			11.89								11.01									
	7,125	1,051	846	-	-	-	-	-	-	-	-	-	-	-	-	-	-	-	-	-	-	-	-	-	-	-
	25.15		80.49																							
Farmers Branch (city)																										
			80.49																							
			11.87																							
	43,588	15,646	11,621	-	-	2,342	-	-	1,232	-	794	-	-	-	-	-	933	-	-	519	-	-	-	-	-	4,927
	20.18		74.27			75.50			73.55		71.34						81.99			62.45						78.19
Garland (city)						20.15			10.60		6.83						8.03			4.47						42.40
			74.27			14.97			7.87		5.07						5.96			3.32						31.49
			26.66			5.37			2.83		1.82						2.14			1.19						11.30
	20,841	5,295	3,653	-	-	526	-	-	-	-	470	-	-	-	-	-	-	278	-	-	-	-	-	-	-	1,603
	16.40		68.99			71.76					66.76							71.10								67.27
Grand Prairie (city)						14.40					12.87							7.61								43.88
			68.99			9.93					8.88							5.25								30.27
			17.53			2.52					2.26							1.33								7.69
	50,696	15,637	12,388	-	-	4,850	-	-	1,302	-	572	-	-	-	-	527	1,939	375	-	327	-	-	-	-	-	1,199
	26.46		79.22			79.60			84.16		73.90					77.73	78.19	78.29		76.22						76.18
Irving (city)						39.15			10.51		4.62					4.25	15.65	3.03		2.64						9.68
			79.22			31.02			8.33		3.66					3.37	12.40	2.40		2.09						7.67
			24.44			9.57			2.57		1.13					1.04	3.82	0.74		0.65						2.37

Notes: Please refer to the User's Guide for an explanation of data; data is arranged alphabetically by state, then county, then city within each county; table includes counties with populations greater than 49,999 unless noted and cities with populations greater than 9,999 whose Asian and/or NHPI population rates are greater than the national average; (1) Native Hawaiian and other Pacific Islander; (2) excludes Taiwanese; (3) includes Chamorro; (4) county does not meet population threshold but is shown in order to allow inclusion of city

Place	Total foreign-born population	Total Asian population	Asians who are foreign born	Total NHPI[1] population	NHPIs[1] who are foreign born	Asian Indian	Bangladeshi	Cambodian	Chinese[2]	Fijian	Filipino	Guamanian[3]	Hawaiian, Native	Hmong	Indonesian	Japanese	Korean	Laotian	Malaysian	Pakistani	Samoan	Sri Lankan	Taiwanese	Thai	Tongan	Vietnamese
Mesquite (city)	11,409 9.16	4,557	3,254 71.41 71.41 28.52	-	-	1,694 73.88 52.06 37.17 14.85	-	-	-	-	684 74.35 21.02 15.01 6.00	-	-	-	-	-	-	-	-	-	-	-	-	-	-	-
Richardson (city)	17,274 18.85	10,196	8,005 78.51 78.51 46.34	-	-	1,963 81.05 24.52 19.25 11.36	-	-	2,407 78.79 30.07 23.61 13.93	-	302 80.53 3.77 2.96 1.75	-	-	-	-	-	866 84.00 10.82 8.49 5.01	-	-	347 82.03 4.33 3.40 2.01	-	-	-	-	-	1,220 70.07 15.24 11.97 7.06
Rowlett (city)	2,846 6.42	1,681	1,128 67.10 67.10 39.63	-	-	375 66.02 33.24 22.31 13.18	-	-	-	-	-	-	-	-	-	-	-	-	-	-	-	-	-	-	-	-
Denton County	40,591 9.37	17,110	12,283 71.79 71.79 30.26	-	-	4,308 71.43 35.07 25.18 10.61	-	502 69.15 4.09 2.93 1.24	1,585 78.78 12.90 9.26 3.90	-	585 68.66 4.76 3.42 1.44	-	-	-	-	334 69.87 2.72 1.95 0.82	1,688 74.66 13.74 9.87 4.16	-	-	534 63.57 4.35 3.12 1.32	-	-	-	-	-	1,849 70.95 15.05 10.81 4.56
Carrollton (city)	21,796 19.96	11,415	8,433 73.88 73.88 38.69	-	-	3,239 73.88 38.41 28.37 14.86	-	516 63.08 6.12 4.52 2.37	535 79.14 6.34 4.69 2.45	-	-	-	-	-	-	-	819 77.78 9.71 7.17 3.76	-	-	795 68.18 9.43 6.96 3.65	-	-	-	-	-	1,811 75.33 21.48 15.87 8.31
Lewisville (city)	9,824 12.67	3,043	2,099 68.98 68.98 21.37	-	-	868 70.92 41.35 28.52 8.84	-	-	-	-	-	-	-	-	-	-	-	-	-	-	-	-	-	-	-	314 69.47 14.96 10.32 3.20
Ector County	12,873 10.63	880	614 69.77 69.77 4.77	-	-	-	-	-	-	-	-	-	-	-	-	-	-	-	-	-	-	-	-	-	-	-
El Paso County	186,168 27.39	6,956	4,776 68.66 68.66 2.57	554	49 8.84 8.84 0.03	804 79.29 16.83 11.56 0.43	-	-	582 71.67 12.19 8.37 0.31	-	999 55.62 20.92 14.36 0.54	-	-	-	-	580 72.77 12.14 8.34 0.31	1,255 73.26 26.28 18.04 0.67	-	-	-	-	-	-	-	-	-
Ellis County	7,907 7.10	441	294 66.67 66.67 3.72	-	-	-	-	-	-	-	-	-	-	-	-	-	-	-	-	-	-	-	-	-	-	-
Fort Bend County	64,878 18.30	38,774	27,470 70.85 70.85 42.34	-	-	9,161 71.64 33.35 23.63 14.12	-	-	6,931 70.37 25.23 17.88 10.68	-	3,023 68.78 11.00 7.80 4.66	-	-	-	-	-	847 73.91 3.08 2.18 1.31	-	-	1,847 75.67 6.72 4.76 2.85	-	-	919 75.58 3.35 2.37 1.42	-	-	3,693 70.91 13.44 9.52 5.69

Notes: Please refer to the User's Guide for an explanation of data; data is arranged alphabetically by state, then county, then city within each county; table includes counties with populations greater than 49,999 unless noted and cities with populations greater than 9,999 whose Asian and/or NHPI population rates are greater than the national average; (1) Native Hawaiian and other Pacific Islander; (2) excludes Taiwanese; (3) includes Chamorro; (4) county does not meet population threshold but is shown in order to allow inclusion of city

Place	Total foreign-born population	Total Asian population	Asians who are foreign born	Total NHPI[1] population	NHPIs[1] who are foreign born	Asian Indian	Bangladeshi	Cambodian	Chinese[2]	Fijian	Filipino	Guamanian[3]	Hawaiian, Native	Hmong	Indonesian	Japanese	Korean	Laotian	Malaysian	Pakistani	Samoan	Sri Lankan	Taiwanese	Thai	Tongan	Vietnamese
Cinco Ranch (cdp)	1,546 13.76	690	462 66.96 66.96 29.88	-	-	-	-	-	-	-	-	-	-	-	-	-	-	-	-	-	-	-	-	-	-	-
Mission Bend (cdp)	9,164 29.66	5,175	3,761 72.68 72.68 41.04	-	-	1,028 78.47 27.33 19.86 11.22	-	-	437 63.61 11.62 8.44 4.77	-	719 78.07 19.12 13.89 7.85	-	-	-	-	-	-	-	-	402 83.75 10.69 7.77 4.39	-	-	-	-	-	899 71.18 23.90 17.37 9.81
Missouri City (city)	9,220 17.57	5,746	4,142 72.08 72.08 44.92	-	-	1,425 74.10 34.40 24.80 15.46	-	-	993 71.70 23.97 17.28 10.77	-	743 71.79 17.94 12.93 8.06	-	-	-	-	-	-	-	-	-	-	-	-	-	-	423 72.31 10.21 7.36 4.59
New Territory (cdp)	3,250 23.40	3,250	2,140 65.85 65.85 65.85	-	-	1,032 65.77 48.22 31.75 31.75	-	-	438 62.75 20.47 13.48 13.48	-	-	-	-	-	-	-	-	-	-	-	-	-	-	-	-	-
Stafford (city)	4,334 27.75	3,312	2,421 73.10 73.10 55.86	-	-	930 72.66 38.41 28.08 21.46	-	-	399 74.72 16.48 12.05 9.21	-	373 72.01 15.41 11.26 8.61	-	-	-	-	-	-	-	-	-	-	-	-	-	-	445 73.55 18.38 13.44 10.27
Sugar Land (city)	14,917 23.49	14,417	10,270 71.24 71.24 68.85	-	-	3,109 71.67 30.27 21.56 20.84	-	-	3,802 71.91 37.02 26.37 25.49	-	638 64.06 6.21 4.43 4.28	-	-	-	-	-	347 78.86 3.38 2.41 2.33	-	-	444 71.84 4.32 3.08 2.98	-	-	714 76.20 6.95 4.95 4.79	-	-	853 66.85 8.31 5.92 5.72
Galveston County	20,678 8.27	5,275	3,794 71.92 71.92 18.35	-	-	730 75.41 19.24 13.84 3.53	-	-	664 75.20 17.50 12.59 3.21	-	603 74.08 15.89 11.43 2.92	-	-	-	-	-	-	-	-	-	-	-	-	-	-	1,128 65.89 29.73 21.38 5.46
Grayson County	4,329 3.91	647	517 79.91 79.91 11.94	-	-	-	-	-	-	-	-	-	-	-	-	-	-	-	-	-	-	-	-	-	-	
Gregg County	6,053 5.43	644	462 71.74 71.74 7.63	-	-	-	-	-	-	-	-	-	-	-	-	-	-	-	-	-	-	-	-	-	-	-
Guadalupe County	5,801 6.52	896	660 73.66 73.66 11.38	-	-	-	-	-	-	-	-	-	-	-	-	-	-	-	-	-	-	-	-	-	-	-

Notes: Please refer to the User's Guide for an explanation of data; data is arranged alphabetically by state, then county, then city within each county; table includes counties with populations greater than 49,999 unless noted and cities with populations greater than 9,999 whose Asian and/or NHPI population rates are greater than the national average; (1) Native Hawaiian and other Pacific Islander; (2) excludes Taiwanese; (3) includes Chamorro; (4) county does not meet population threshold but is shown in order to allow inclusion of city

Place	Total foreign-born population	Total Asian population	Asians who are foreign born	Total NHPI[1] population	NHPIs[1] who are foreign born	Asian Indian	Bangladeshi	Cambodian	Chinese[2]	Fijian	Filipino	Guamanian[3]	Hawaiian, Native	Hmong	Indonesian	Japanese	Korean	Laotian	Malaysian	Pakistani	Samoan	Sri Lankan	Taiwanese	Thai	Tongan	Vietnamese
	756,548	171,977	129,827	1,514	348	27,263	578	1,472	23,660	-	11,470	76	-	-	651	2,374	6,550	872	-	5,966	-	-	1,853	1,024	-	42,202
	22.25		75.49		22.99	75.74	84.01	73.16	75.31		72.71	11.89			94.35	64.53	80.72	73.77		81.37			83.36	76.82		76.12
Harris County						21.00	0.45	1.13	18.22		8.83	21.84			0.50	1.83	5.05	0.67		4.60			1.43	0.79		32.51
			75.49		22.99	15.85	0.34	0.86	13.76		6.67	5.02			0.38	1.38	3.81	0.51		3.47			1.08	0.60		24.54
			17.16		0.05	3.60	0.08	0.19	3.13		1.52	0.01			0.09	0.31	0.87	0.12		0.79			0.24	0.14		5.58
	1,672	1,052	661	-	-	-	-	-	263	-	-	-	-	-	-	-	-	-	-	-	-	-	-	-	-	-
	10.73		62.83						57.93																	
Bellaire (city)									39.79																	
			62.83						25.00																	
			39.53						15.73																	
	516,105	102,484	80,093	876	246	15,810	-	585	17,136	-	5,793	54	-	-	503	1,745	4,200	-	-	4,081	-	-	1,262	704	-	25,244
	26.40		78.15		28.08	77.21		80.91	78.40		75.37	12.22			97.29	72.50	80.92			81.67			84.58	79.91		79.33
Houston (city)						19.74		0.73	21.40		7.23	21.95			0.63	2.18	5.24			5.10			1.58	0.88		31.52
			78.15		28.08	15.43		0.57	16.72		5.65	6.16			0.49	1.70	4.10			3.98			1.23	0.69		24.63
			15.52		0.05	3.06		0.11	3.32		1.12	0.01			0.10	0.34	0.81			0.79			0.24	0.14		4.89
	1,131	745	426	-	-	-	-	-	-	-	-	-	-	-	-	-	-	-	-	-	-	-	-	-	-	-
	7.96		57.18																							
West University Place (city)																										
			57.18																							
			37.67																							
	5,438	851	540	-	-	-	-	-	-	-	-	-	-	-	-	-	-	-	-	-	-	-	-	-	-	-
	5.57		63.45																							
Hays County																										
			63.45																							
			9.93																							
	168,215	3,156	2,313	-	-	441	-	-	-	-	1,248	-	-	-	-	-	-	-	-	-	-	-	-	-	-	-
	29.54		73.29			70.00					82.76															
Hidalgo County						19.07					53.96															
			73.29			13.97					39.54															
			1.38			0.26					0.74															
	3,601	557	365	-	-	-	-	-	-	-	-	-	-	-	-	-	-	-	-	-	-	-	-	-	-	-
	4.70		65.53																							
Hunt County																										
			65.53																							
			10.14																							
	15,608	7,033	4,302	-	-	647	-	-	358	-	700	-	-	-	-	-	-	-	-	-	-	-	-	-	-	2,243
	6.19		61.17			71.81			73.66		73.38															54.77
Jefferson County						15.04			8.32		16.27															52.14
			61.17			9.20			5.09		9.95															31.89
			27.56			4.15			2.29		4.48															14.37
	7,168	3,388	2,004	-	-	-	-	-	-	-	-	-	-	-	-	-	-	-	-	-	-	-	-	-	-	1,551
	12.41		59.15																							54.83
Port Arthur (city)																										77.40
			59.15																							45.78
			27.96																							21.64
	6,570	650	435	-	-	-	-	-	-	-	-	-	-	-	-	-	-	-	-	-	-	-	-	-	-	-
	5.18		66.92																							
Johnson County																										
			66.92																							
			6.62																							

Notes: Please refer to the User's Guide for an explanation of data; data is arranged alphabetically by state, then county, then city within each county; table includes counties with populations greater than 49,999 unless noted and cities with populations greater than 9,999 whose Asian and/or NHPI population rates are greater than the national average; (1) Native Hawaiian and other Pacific Islander; (2) excludes Taiwanese; (3) includes Chamorro; (4) county does not meet population threshold but is shown in order to allow inclusion of city

Place	Total foreign-born population	Total Asian population	Asians who are foreign born	Total NHPI[1] population	NHPIs[1] who are foreign born	Asian Indian	Bangladeshi	Cambodian	Chinese[2]	Fijian	Filipino	Guamanian[3]	Hawaiian, Native	Hmong	Indonesian	Japanese	Korean	Laotian	Malaysian	Pakistani	Samoan	Sri Lankan	Taiwanese	Thai	Tongan	Vietnamese
Kaufman County	4,039	487	359	-	-	-	-	-	-	-	-	-	-	-	-	-	-	-	-	-	-	-	-	-	-	-
	5.66		73.72																							
			73.72																							
			8.89																							
Lubbock County	8,115	2,971	2,352	-	-	545	-	-	506	-	-	-	-	-	-	-	-	-	-	-	-	-	-	-	-	313
	3.34		79.17			71.43			84.76																	85.05
						23.17			21.51																	13.31
			79.17			18.34			17.03																	10.54
			28.98			6.72			6.24																	3.86
McLennan County	13,119	2,134	1,501	-	-	240	-	-	-	-	-	-	-	-	-	-	-	-	-	-	-	-	-	-	-	-
	6.14		70.34			60.91																				
						15.99																				
			70.34			11.25																				
			11.44			1.83																				
Midland County	8,787	1,065	788	-	-	259	-	-	-	-	-	-	-	-	-	-	-	-	-	-	-	-	-	-	-	-
	7.57		73.99			65.08																				
						32.87																				
			73.99			24.32																				
			8.97			2.95																				
Montgomery County	25,276	3,133	2,360	-	-	797	-	-	505	-	355	-	-	-	-	-	-	-	-	-	-	-	-	-	-	-
	8.60		75.33			81.83			73.08		76.18															
						33.77			21.40		15.04															
			75.33			25.44			16.12		11.33															
			9.34			3.15			2.00		1.40															
Nacogdoches County	3,680	383	265	-	-	-	-	-	-	-	-	-	-	-	-	-	-	-	-	-	-	-	-	-	-	-
	6.22		69.19																							
			69.19																							
			7.20																							
Nueces County	20,506	3,507	2,622	-	-	463	-	-	-	-	1,212	-	-	-	-	-	-	-	-	-	-	-	-	-	-	-
	6.54		74.76			74.08					75.09															
						17.66					46.22															
			74.76			13.20					34.56															
			12.79			2.26					5.91															
Orange County	1,763	697	522	-	-	-	-	-	-	-	-	-	-	-	-	-	-	-	-	-	-	-	-	-	-	250
	2.07		74.89																							66.31
																										47.89
			74.89																							35.87
			29.61																							14.18
Potter County	10,693	2,990	2,102	-	-	-	-	-	-	-	-	-	-	-	-	-	-	717	-	-	-	-	-	-	-	807
	9.42		70.30															67.71								75.92
																		34.11								38.39
			70.30															23.98								26.99
			19.66															6.71								7.55
Randall County	2,748	1,131	840	-	-	-	-	-	-	-	-	-	-	-	-	-	-	-	-	-	-	-	-	-	-	-
	2.63		74.27																							
			74.27																							
			30.57																							

Notes: Please refer to the User's Guide for an explanation of data; data is arranged alphabetically by state, then county, then city within each county; table includes counties with populations greater than 49,999 unless noted and cities with populations greater than 9,999 whose Asian and/or NHPI population rates are greater than the national average; (1) Native Hawaiian and other Pacific Islander; (2) excludes Taiwanese; (3) includes Chamorro; (4) county does not meet population threshold but is shown in order to allow inclusion of city

Place	Total foreign-born population	Total Asian population	Asians who are foreign born	Total NHPI[1] population	NHPIs[1] who are foreign born	Asian Indian	Bangladeshi	Cambodian	Chinese[2]	Fijian	Filipino	Guamanian[3]	Hawaiian, Native	Hmong	Indonesian	Japanese	Korean	Laotian	Malaysian	Pakistani	Samoan	Sri Lankan	Taiwanese	Thai	Tongan	Vietnamese
San Patricio County	2,205 3.28	451	259 57.43 57.43 11.75	-	-	-	-	-	-	-	-	-	-	-	-	-	-	-	-	-	-	-	-	-	-	-
Smith County	11,603 6.64	1,105	715 64.71 64.71 6.16	-	-	-	-	-	-	-	-	-	-	-	-	-	-	-	-	-	-	-	-	-	-	-
Tarrant County	183,223 12.67	51,202	37,666 73.56 73.56 20.56	1,646	553 33.60 33.60 0.30	7,288 76.93 19.35 14.23 3.98	-	517 66.45 1.37 1.01 0.28	4,119 74.22 10.94 8.04 2.25	-	2,472 71.03 6.56 4.83 1.35	-	-	-	-	697 67.47 1.85 1.36 0.38	2,492 78.12 6.62 4.87 1.36	2,174 68.09 5.77 4.25 1.19	-	743 75.35 1.97 1.45 0.41	-	-	513 76.34 1.36 1.00 0.28	568 73.29 1.51 1.11 0.31	199 54.52 35.99 12.09 0.11	14,302 74.60 37.97 27.93 7.81
Arlington (city)	50,911 15.30	19,271	14,810 76.85 76.85 29.09	-	-	2,399 79.78 16.20 12.45 4.71	-	-	2,103 76.11 14.20 10.91 4.13	-	879 73.74 5.94 4.56 1.73	-	-	-	-	-	759 83.77 5.12 3.94 1.49	-	-	-	-	-	326 78.55 2.20 1.69 0.64	-	-	6,946 76.98 46.90 36.04 13.64
Euless (city)	6,484 14.07	3,232	2,392 74.01 74.01 36.89	-	-	970 77.97 40.55 30.01 14.96	-	-	-	-	-	-	-	-	-	-	-	-	-	-	-	-	-	-	-	-
Haltom City (city)	5,539 14.12	3,106	2,210 71.15 71.15 39.90	-	-	-	-	-	-	-	-	-	-	-	-	-	-	531 65.39 24.03 17.10 9.59	-	-	-	-	-	-	-	1,161 73.67 52.53 37.38 20.96
Taylor County	5,022 3.97	1,678	1,110 66.15 66.15 22.10	-	-	-	-	-	-	-	393 65.83 35.41 23.42 7.83	-	-	-	-	-	-	-	-	-	-	-	-	-	-	-
Tom Green County	6,161 5.92	724	516 71.27 71.27 8.38	-	-	-	-	-	-	-	-	-	-	-	-	-	-	-	-	-	-	-	-	-	-	-
Travis County	122,621 15.10	36,119	25,622 70.94 70.94 20.90	676	179 26.48 26.48 0.15	6,196 73.49 24.18 17.15 5.05	-	-	6,314 71.77 24.64 17.48 5.15	-	1,363 61.45 5.32 3.77 1.11	-	-	-	-	850 69.96 3.32 2.35 0.69	2,940 70.78 11.47 8.14 2.40	-	-	547 75.55 2.13 1.51 0.45	-	-	576 68.57 2.25 1.59 0.47	251 62.44 0.98 0.69 0.20	-	5,349 72.42 20.88 14.81 4.36
Austin (city)	109,006 16.61	30,866	21,947 71.10 71.10 20.13	445	33 7.42 7.42 0.03	5,458 74.40 24.87 17.68 5.01	-	-	5,778 72.03 26.33 18.72 5.30	-	1,001 57.79 4.56 3.24 0.92	-	-	-	-	797 70.22 3.63 2.58 0.73	2,567 70.68 11.70 8.32 2.35	-	-	434 82.51 1.98 1.41 0.40	-	-	508 67.91 2.31 1.65 0.47	-	-	4,159 71.84 18.95 13.47 3.82

Notes: Please refer to the User's Guide for an explanation of data; data is arranged alphabetically by state, then county, then city within each county; table includes counties with populations greater than 49,999 unless noted and cities with populations greater than 9,999 whose Asian and/or NHPI population rates are greater than the national average; (1) Native Hawaiian and other Pacific Islander; (2) excludes Taiwanese; (3) includes Chamorro; (4) county does not meet population threshold but is shown in order to allow inclusion of city

Place	Total foreign-born population	Total Asian population	Asians who are foreign born	Total NHPI[1] population	NHPIs[1] who are foreign born	Asian Indian	Bangladeshi	Cambodian	Chinese[2]	Fijian	Filipino	Guamanian[3]	Hawaiian, Native	Hmong	Indonesian	Japanese	Korean	Laotian	Malaysian	Pakistani	Samoan	Sri Lankan	Taiwanese	Thai	Tongan	Vietnamese
Pflugerville (city)	1,052 6.43	728	528 72.53 72.53 50.19	-	-	-	-	-	-	-	-	-	-	-	-	-	-	-	-	-	-	-	-	-	-	-
Wells Branch (cdp)	1,458 12.96	1,077	771 71.59 71.59 52.88	-	-	-	-	-	-	-	-	-	-	-	-	-	-	-	-	-	-	-	-	-	-	-
Victoria County	3,585 4.26	492	361 73.37 73.37 10.07	-	-	-	-	-	-	-	-	-	-	-	-	-	-	-	-	-	-	-	-	-	-	-
Webb County	56,029 29.01	801	592 73.91 73.91 1.06	-	-	-	-	-	-	-	-	-	-	-	-	-	-	-	-	-	-	-	-	-	-	-
Wichita County	6,731 5.11	2,538	1,730 68.16 68.16 25.70	-	-	-	-	-	-	-	343 59.04 19.83 13.51 5.10	-	-	-	-	-	-	-	-	-	-	-	-	-	-	593 74.31 34.28 23.36 8.81
Williamson County	18,449 7.38	6,457	4,624 71.61 71.61 25.06	-	-	1,226 73.33 26.51 18.99 6.65	-	-	1,000 69.54 21.63 15.49 5.42	-	-	-	-	-	-	-	571 81.46 12.35 8.84 3.10	-	-	-	-	-	-	-	-	771 70.22 16.67 11.94 4.18
Brushy Creek (cdp)	1,391 8.75	933	607 65.06 65.06 43.64	-	-	-	-	-	-	-	-	-	-	-	-	-	-	-	-	-	-	-	-	-	-	-
Jollyville (cdp)	1,694 10.95	1,181	822 69.60 69.60 48.52	-	-	-	-	-	-	-	-	-	-	-	-	-	-	-	-	-	-	-	-	-	-	-
UTAH	158,664 7.10	36,878	23,509 63.75 63.75 14.82	14,366	5,118 35.63 35.63 3.23	2,473 78.33 10.52 6.71 1.56	-	992 68.09 4.22 2.69 0.63	5,332 73.60 22.68 14.46 3.36	-	2,278 61.48 9.69 6.18 1.44	-	30 2.24 0.59 0.21 0.02	-	-	1,840 30.77 7.83 4.99 1.16	2,832 79.06 12.05 7.68 1.78	1,469 66.65 6.25 3.98 0.93	-	261 65.09 1.11 0.71 0.16	1,080 28.72 21.10 7.52 0.68	-	243 65.68 1.03 0.66 0.15	548 77.51 2.33 1.49 0.35	3,099 45.61 60.55 21.57 1.95	4,121 74.21 17.53 11.17 2.60
Cache County	6,082 6.65	1,733	1,289 74.38 74.38 21.19	-	-	-	-	-	512 89.82 39.72 29.54 8.42	-	-	-	-	-	-	-	-	-	-	-	-	-	-	-	-	-

Notes: Please refer to the User's Guide for an explanation of data; data is arranged alphabetically by state, then county, then city within each county; table includes counties with populations greater than 49,999 unless noted and cities with populations greater than 9,999 whose Asian and/or NHPI population rates are greater than the national average; (1) Native Hawaiian and other Pacific Islander; (2) excludes Taiwanese; (3) includes Chamorro; (4) county does not meet population threshold but is shown in order to allow inclusion of city

Place	Total foreign-born population	Total Asian population	Asians who are foreign born	Total NHPI[1] population	NHPIs[1] who are foreign born	Asian Indian	Bangladeshi	Cambodian	Chinese[2]	Fijian	Filipino	Guamanian[3]	Hawaiian, Native	Hmong	Indonesian	Japanese	Korean	Laotian	Malaysian	Pakistani	Samoan	Sri Lankan	Taiwanese	Thai	Tongan	Vietnamese
Davis County	8,694 3.64	3,497	1,902 54.39 54.39 21.88	928	186 20.04 20.04 2.14	-	-	-	-	-	534 64.57 28.08 15.27 6.14	-	-	-	-	155 19.50 8.15 4.43 1.78	290 76.92 15.25 8.29 3.34	-	-	-	-	-	-	-	-	-
Salt Lake County	93,276 10.38	23,211	15,086 65.00 65.00 16.17	10,334	4,201 40.65 40.65 4.50	1,758 79.95 11.65 7.57 1.88	-	752 67.81 4.98 3.24 0.81	3,228 71.05 21.40 13.91 3.46	-	1,086 61.43 7.20 4.68 1.16	-	20 4.17 0.48 0.19 0.02	-	-	816 26.10 5.41 3.52 0.87	1,428 78.98 9.47 6.15 1.53	1,203 67.24 7.97 5.18 1.29	-	-	838 32.41 19.95 8.11 0.90	-	-	-	2,812 47.36 66.94 27.21 3.01	3,578 76.65 23.72 15.42 3.84
Kearns (cdp)	4,493 13.36	862	590 68.45 68.45 13.13	406	128 31.53 31.53 2.85	-	-	-	-	-	-	-	-	-	-	-	-	-	-	-	-	-	-	-	-	-
Salt Lake City (city)	33,252 18.33	6,484	4,436 68.41 68.41 13.34	3,315	1,475 44.49 44.49 4.44	511 76.38 11.52 7.88 1.54	-	-	1,140 72.38 25.70 17.58 3.43	-	296 56.70 6.67 4.57 0.89	-	-	-	-	266 27.65 6.00 4.10 0.80	468 91.94 10.55 7.22 1.41	-	-	-	142 31.28 9.63 4.28 0.43	-	-	-	1,201 49.08 81.42 36.23 3.61	1,117 82.68 25.18 17.23 3.36
Sandy (city)	4,590 5.20	1,544	789 51.10 51.10 17.19	383	109 28.46 28.46 2.37	-	-	-	241 59.07 30.54 15.61 5.25	-	-	-	-	-	-	-	-	-	-	-	-	-	-	-	-	-
Taylorsville (city)	5,673 9.80	1,736	1,140 65.67 65.67 20.10	713	247 34.64 34.64 4.35	-	-	-	-	-	-	-	-	-	-	-	-	-	-	-	-	-	-	-	-	402 67.79 35.26 23.16 7.09
West Jordan (city)	3,731 5.47	1,198	735 61.35 61.35 19.70	699	242 34.62 34.62 6.49	-	-	-	-	-	-	-	-	-	-	-	-	-	-	-	-	-	-	-	188 40.00 77.69 26.90 5.04	-
West Valley City (city)	15,683 14.41	4,764	3,538 74.27 74.27 22.56	3,126	1,286 41.14 41.14 8.20	-	-	443 67.12 12.52 9.30 2.82	612 89.21 17.30 12.85 3.90	-	-	-	-	-	-	-	-	308 66.81 8.71 6.47 1.96	-	-	317 36.82 24.65 10.14 2.02	-	-	-	846 46.84 65.79 27.06 5.39	1,275 84.89 36.04 26.76 8.13
Utah County	23,187 6.29	3,959	2,667 67.37 67.37 11.50	1,805	457 25.32 25.32 1.97	-	-	-	925 75.70 34.68 23.36 3.99	-	204 49.88 7.65 5.15 0.88	-	10 2.58 2.19 0.55 0.04	-	-	411 54.01 15.41 10.38 1.77	428 81.99 16.05 10.81 1.85	-	-	-	116 21.13 25.38 6.43 0.50	-	-	-	169 36.58 36.98 9.36 0.73	-
Orem (city)	6,941 8.23	1,233	837 67.88 67.88 12.06	700	166 23.71 23.71 2.39	-	-	-	-	-	-	-	-	-	-	-	-	-	-	-	-	-	-	-	-	-

Notes: Please refer to the User's Guide for an explanation of data; data is arranged alphabetically by state, then county, then city within each county; table includes counties with populations greater than 49,999 unless noted and cities with populations greater than 9,999 whose Asian and/or NHPI population rates are greater than the national average; (1) Native Hawaiian and other Pacific Islander; (2) excludes Taiwanese; (3) includes Chamorro; (4) county does not meet population threshold but is shown in order to allow inclusion of city

Place	Total foreign-born population	Total Asian population	Asians who are foreign born	Total NHPI[1] population	NHPIs[1] who are foreign born	Asian Indian	Bangladeshi	Cambodian	Chinese[2]	Fijian	Filipino	Guamanian[3]	Hawaiian, Native	Hmong	Indonesian	Japanese	Korean	Laotian	Malaysian	Pakistani	Samoan	Sri Lankan	Taiwanese	Thai	Tongan	Vietnamese
Provo (city)	10,084	1,972	1,422	668	145	-	-	-	621	-	-	-	-	-	-	253	-	-	-	-	-	-	-	-	-	-
	9.58		72.11		21.71				81.18							58.43										
									43.67							17.79										
			72.11		21.71				31.49							12.83										
			14.10		1.44				6.16							2.51										
Washington County	3,714	459	313	462	59	-	-	-	-	-	-	-	-	-	-	-	-	-	-	-	-	-	-	-	-	-
	4.11		68.19		12.77																					
			68.19		12.77																					
			8.43		1.59																					
St. George (city)	2,713	388	275	418	47	-	-	-	-	-	-	-	-	-	-	-	-	-	-	-	-	-	-	-	-	-
	5.47		70.88		11.24																					
			70.88		11.24																					
			10.14		1.73																					
Weber County	12,538	2,352	1,280	-	-	-	-	-	-	-	-	-	-	-	-	120	-	-	-	-	-	-	-	-	-	-
	6.38		54.42													18.90										
																9.38										
			54.42													5.10										
			10.21													0.96										
VERMONT	23,245	4,851	3,785	-	-	592	-	-	783	-	197	-	-	-	-	286	601	-	-	-	-	-	-	-	-	895
	3.82		78.03			84.94			68.93		62.74					76.06	88.38									83.49
						15.64			20.69		5.20					7.56	15.88									23.65
			78.03			12.20			16.14		4.06					5.90	12.39									18.45
			16.28			2.55			3.37		0.85					1.23	2.59									3.85
Chittenden County	8,669	2,732	2,074	-	-	330	-	-	461	-	-	-	-	-	-	-	-	-	-	-	-	-	-	-	-	687
	5.91		75.92			89.19			68.91																	82.08
						15.91			22.23																	33.12
			75.92			12.08			16.87																	25.15
			23.92			3.81			5.32																	7.92
Rutland County	1,247	213	162	-	-	-	-	-	-	-	-	-	-	-	-	-	-	-	-	-	-	-	-	-	-	-
	1.97		76.06																							
			76.06																							
			12.99																							
Washington County	2,115	262	221	-	-	-	-	-	-	-	-	-	-	-	-	-	-	-	-	-	-	-	-	-	-	-
	3.64		84.35																							
			84.35																							
			10.45																							
Windsor County	1,708	446	375	-	-	-	-	-	-	-	-	-	-	-	-	-	-	-	-	-	-	-	-	-	-	-
	2.97		84.08																							
			84.08																							
			21.96																							
VIRGINIA	570,279	256,355	191,051	3,617	821	36,114	1,492	3,703	25,378	-	33,142	132	23	-	962	5,956	36,120	2,135	-	7,884	188	527	978	2,894	-	28,155
	8.06		74.53		22.70	75.90	82.52	74.54	74.09		69.02	13.00	2.49		87.85	67.27	80.16	71.14		75.38	36.15	82.86	74.37	80.82		79.44
						18.90	0.78	1.94	13.28		17.35	16.08	2.80		0.50	3.12	18.91	1.12		4.13	22.90	0.28	0.51	1.51		14.74
			74.53		22.70	14.09	0.58	1.44	9.90		12.93	3.65	0.64		0.38	2.32	14.09	0.83		3.08	5.20	0.21	0.38	1.13		10.98
			33.50		0.14	6.33	0.26	0.65	4.45		5.81	0.02	<0.01		0.17	1.04	6.33	0.37		1.38	0.03	0.09	0.17	0.51		4.94

Notes: Please refer to the User's Guide for an explanation of data; data is arranged alphabetically by state, then county, then city within each county; table includes counties with populations greater than 49,999 unless noted and cities with populations greater than 9,999 whose Asian and/or NHPI population rates are greater than the national average; (1) Native Hawaiian and other Pacific Islander; (2) excludes Taiwanese; (3) includes Chamorro; (4) county does not meet population threshold but is shown in order to allow inclusion of city

Place	Total foreign-born population	Total Asian population	Asians who are foreign born	Total NHPI[1] population	NHPIs[1] who are foreign born	Asian Indian	Bangladeshi	Cambodian	Chinese[2]	Fijian	Filipino	Guamanian[3]	Hawaiian, Native	Hmong	Indonesian	Japanese	Korean	Laotian	Malaysian	Pakistani	Samoan	Sri Lankan	Taiwanese	Thai	Tongan	Vietnamese
Albemarle County	5,753 7.26	2,458	1,983 80.68 80.68 34.47	-	-	580 80.56 29.25 23.60 10.08	-	-	794 88.32 40.04 32.30 13.80	-	-	-	-	-	-	-	-	-	-	-	-	-	-	-	-	-
Alexandria Independent City	32,600 25.41	6,985	5,768 82.58 82.58 17.69	-	-	1,289 81.53 22.35 18.45 3.95	-	-	615 76.59 10.66 8.80 1.89	-	838 77.38 14.53 12.00 2.57	-	-	-	-	-	1,130 90.76 19.59 16.18 3.47	-	-	518 90.24 8.98 7.42 1.59	-	-	-	-	-	432 89.26 7.49 6.18 1.33
Arlington County	52,693 27.81	15,761	12,485 79.21 79.21 23.69	-	-	2,852 81.93 22.84 18.10 5.41	-	282 79.89 2.26 1.79 0.54	1,788 76.18 14.32 11.34 3.39	-	1,543 75.31 12.36 9.79 2.93	-	-	-	-	830 73.06 6.65 5.27 1.58	1,090 78.30 8.73 6.92 2.07	-	-	662 82.65 5.30 4.20 1.26	-	-	-	-	-	1,747 79.81 13.99 11.08 3.32
Arlington (cdp)	52,693 27.81	15,761	12,485 79.21 79.21 23.69	-	-	2,852 81.93 22.84 18.10 5.41	-	282 79.89 2.26 1.79 0.54	1,788 76.18 14.32 11.34 3.39	-	1,543 75.31 12.36 9.79 2.93	-	-	-	-	830 73.06 6.65 5.27 1.58	1,090 78.30 8.73 6.92 2.07	-	-	662 82.65 5.30 4.20 1.26	-	-	-	-	-	1,747 79.81 13.99 11.08 3.32
Bedford County	1,098 1.82	581	411 70.74 70.74 37.43	-	-	-	-	-	-	-	-	-	-	-	-	-	-	-	-	-	-	-	-	-	-	-
Charlottesville Independent City	3,107 6.90	2,172	1,216 55.99 55.99 39.14	-	-	205 41.50 16.86 9.44 6.60	-	-	437 62.34 35.94 20.12 14.07	-	-	-	-	-	-	-	-	-	-	-	-	-	-	-	-	-
Chesapeake Independent City	5,971 3.00	3,440	2,401 69.80 69.80 40.21	-	-	-	-	-	-	-	1,256 69.74 52.31 36.51 21.04	-	-	-	-	-	-	-	-	-	-	-	-	-	-	-
Chesterfield County	13,523 5.20	6,363	4,406 69.24 69.24 32.58	-	-	824 79.15 18.70 12.95 6.09	-	452 67.87 10.26 7.10 3.34	651 68.89 14.78 10.23 4.81	-	498 71.04 11.30 7.83 3.68	-	-	-	-	-	1,034 68.21 23.47 16.25 7.65	-	-	-	-	-	-	-	-	512 68.82 11.62 8.05 3.79
Fairfax Independent City	5,451 25.36	2,530	2,085 82.41 82.41 38.25	-	-	437 86.36 20.96 17.27 8.02	-	-	443 86.19 21.25 17.51 8.13	-	-	-	-	-	-	-	488 88.89 23.41 19.29 8.95	-	-	-	-	-	-	-	-	334 77.31 16.02 13.20 6.13
Fairfax County	237,677 24.51	123,612	94,805 76.70 76.70 39.89	884	226 25.57 25.57 0.10	19,087 76.49 20.13 15.44 8.03	690 76.50 0.73 0.56 0.29	1,361 73.77 1.44 1.10 0.57	12,006 74.18 12.66 9.71 5.05	-	9,089 71.42 9.59 7.35 3.82	-	-	-	506 85.04 0.53 0.41 0.21	2,025 69.66 2.14 1.64 0.85	22,492 81.25 23.72 18.20 9.46	1,044 68.87 1.10 0.84 0.44	-	4,676 74.35 4.93 3.78 1.97	-	-	560 75.88 0.59 0.45 0.24	1,182 79.22 1.25 0.96 0.50	-	17,312 81.31 18.26 14.01 7.28

Notes: Please refer to the User's Guide for an explanation of data; data is arranged alphabetically by state, then county, then city within each county; table includes counties with populations greater than 49,999 unless noted and cities with populations greater than 9,999 whose Asian and/or NHPI population rates are greater than the national average; (1) Native Hawaiian and other Pacific Islander; (2) excludes Taiwanese; (3) includes Chamorro; (4) county does not meet population threshold but is shown in order to allow inclusion of city

Place	Total foreign-born population	Total Asian population	Asians who are foreign born	Total NHPI[1] population	NHPIs[1] who are foreign born	Asian Indian	Bangladeshi	Cambodian	Chinese[2]	Fijian	Filipino	Guamanian[3]	Hawaiian, Native	Hmong	Indonesian	Japanese	Korean	Laotian	Malaysian	Pakistani	Samoan	Sri Lankan	Taiwanese	Thai	Tongan	Vietnamese
Annandale (cdp)	18,961 34.45	10,446	8,530 81.66 81.66 44.99	-	-	930 81.15 10.90 8.90 4.90	-	-	732 75.31 8.58 7.01 3.86	-	460 71.88 5.39 4.40 2.43	-	-	-	-	-	2,869 85.49 33.63 27.47 15.13	-	-	-	-	-	-	-	-	2,821 84.23 33.07 27.01 14.88
Bailey's Crossroads (cdp)	12,502 54.69	2,502	2,119 84.69 84.69 16.95	-	-	-	-	-	-	-	-	-	-	-	-	-	-	-	-	296 82.45 13.97 11.83 2.37	-	-	-	-	-	485 84.35 22.89 19.38 3.88
Burke (cdp)	11,690 20.28	8,266	6,142 74.30 74.30 52.54	-	-	1,038 72.94 16.90 12.56 8.88	-	-	544 72.05 8.86 6.58 4.65	-	717 66.76 11.67 8.67 6.13	-	-	-	-	-	2,460 79.00 40.05 29.76 21.04	-	-	-	-	-	-	-	-	896 78.87 14.59 10.84 7.66
Centreville (cdp)	9,892 20.38	6,337	4,659 73.52 73.52 47.10	-	-	1,240 75.11 26.62 19.57 12.54	-	-	744 78.40 15.97 11.74 7.52	-	606 66.30 13.01 9.56 6.13	-	-	-	-	-	1,318 81.31 28.29 20.80 13.32	-	-	-	-	-	-	-	-	297 70.71 6.37 4.69 3.00
Chantilly (cdp)	9,095 22.13	6,492	4,993 76.91 76.91 54.90	-	-	1,661 79.47 33.27 25.59 18.26	-	-	663 68.78 13.28 10.21 7.29	-	-	-	-	-	-	-	973 83.30 19.49 14.99 10.70	-	-	-	-	-	-	-	-	776 78.38 15.54 11.95 8.53
Franconia (cdp)	5,890 18.42	3,142	2,347 74.70 74.70 39.85	-	-	326 78.74 13.89 10.38 5.53	-	-	-	-	434 73.94 18.49 13.81 7.37	-	-	-	-	-	467 78.62 19.90 14.86 7.93	-	-	-	-	-	-	-	-	382 72.76 16.28 12.16 6.49
Groveton (cdp)	5,152 24.23	1,628	1,240 76.17 76.17 24.07	-	-	-	-	-	-	-	-	-	-	-	-	-	-	-	-	-	-	-	-	-	-	-
Herndon (town)	7,907 36.50	3,199	2,326 72.71 72.71 29.42	-	-	821 77.75 35.30 25.66 10.38	-	-	-	-	-	-	-	-	-	-	-	-	-	-	-	-	-	-	-	350 82.55 15.05 10.94 4.43
Hybla Valley (cdp)	4,419 26.28	1,281	933 72.83 72.83 21.11	-	-	-	-	-	-	-	-	-	-	-	-	-	-	-	-	-	-	-	-	-	-	-
Idylwood (cdp)	6,024 37.52	3,183	2,642 83.00 83.00 43.86	-	-	830 83.25 31.42 26.08 13.78	-	-	454 79.37 17.18 14.26 7.54	-	-	-	-	-	-	-	-	-	-	-	-	-	-	-	-	540 83.08 20.44 16.97 8.96

Notes: Please refer to the User's Guide for an explanation of data; data is arranged alphabetically by state, then county, then city within each county; table includes counties with populations greater than 49,999 unless noted and cities with populations greater than 9,999 whose Asian and/or NHPI population rates are greater than the national average; (1) Native Hawaiian and other Pacific Islander; (2) excludes Taiwanese; (3) includes Chamorro; (4) county does not meet population threshold but is shown in order to allow inclusion of city

Place	Total foreign-born population	Total Asian population	Asians who are foreign born	Total NHPI[1] population	NHPIs[1] who are foreign born	Asian Indian	Bangladeshi	Cambodian	Chinese[2]	Fijian	Filipino	Guamanian[3]	Hawaiian, Native	Hmong	Indonesian	Japanese	Korean	Laotian	Malaysian	Pakistani	Samoan	Sri Lankan	Taiwanese	Thai	Tongan	Vietnamese
Jefferson (cdp)	10,378	5,249	4,266	-	-	740	-	-	414	-	374	-	-	-	-	-	-	-	-	-	-	-	-	-	-	1,904
	37.96		81.27			87.68			75.69		74.21															83.18
						17.35			9.70		8.77															44.63
			81.27			14.10			7.89		7.13															36.27
			41.11			7.13			3.99		3.60															18.35
Lincolnia (cdp)	7,526	2,337	1,778	-	-	-	-	-	-	-	-	-	-	-	-	-	-	-	-	395	-	-	-	-	-	391
	47.43		76.08																	76.40						77.89
																				22.22						21.99
			76.08																	16.90						16.73
			23.62																	5.25						5.20
Lorton (cdp)	2,730	1,425	1,050	-	-	-	-	-	-	-	-	-	-	-	-	-	-	-	-	-	-	-	-	-	-	-
	15.37		73.68																							
			73.68																							
			38.46																							
McLean (cdp)	8,320	4,229	3,337	-	-	710	-	-	604	-	359	-	-	-	-	492	713	-	-	-	-	-	-	-	-	-
	21.33		78.91			74.50			78.34		70.81					89.29	86.42									
						21.28			18.10		10.76					14.74	21.37									
			78.91			16.79			14.28		8.49					11.63	16.86									
			40.11			8.53			7.26		4.31					5.91	8.57									
Merrifield (cdp)	4,635	3,156	2,624	-	-	683	-	-	-	-	-	-	-	-	-	-	763	-	-	-	-	-	-	-	-	559
	41.83		83.14			80.35											89.87									79.52
						26.03											29.08									21.30
			83.14			21.64											24.18									17.71
			56.61			14.74											16.46									12.06
Mount Vernon (cdp)	5,986	1,856	1,381	-	-	-	-	-	-	-	-	-	-	-	-	-	366	-	-	-	-	-	-	-	-	-
	20.94		74.41														79.22									
																	26.50									
			74.41														19.72									
			23.07														6.11									
Newington (cdp)	3,825	2,141	1,488	-	-	262	-	-	-	-	321	-	-	-	-	-	336	-	-	-	-	-	-	-	-	-
	19.41		69.50			70.05					67.01						69.85									
						17.61					21.57						22.58									
			69.50			12.24					14.99						15.69									
			38.90			6.85					8.39						8.78									
Oakton (cdp)	7,663	4,123	3,208	-	-	791	-	-	770	-	-	-	-	-	-	-	986	-	-	-	-	-	-	-	-	362
	26.08		77.81			83.79			76.85								87.57									79.04
						24.66			24.00								30.74									11.28
			77.81			19.19			18.68								23.91									8.78
			41.86			10.32			10.05								12.87									4.72
Reston (cdp)	12,413	5,237	4,170	-	-	1,616	-	-	503	-	426	-	-	-	-	-	527	-	-	-	-	-	-	-	-	-
	21.99		79.63			84.78			70.45		73.32						77.50									
						38.75			12.06		10.22						12.64									
			79.63			30.86			9.60		8.13						10.06									
			33.59			13.02			4.05		3.43						4.25									
Rose Hill (cdp)	2,926	1,223	985	-	-	-	-	-	-	-	-	-	-	-	-	-	-	-	-	-	-	-	-	-	-	-
	19.57		80.54																							
			80.54																							
			33.66																							

Notes: Please refer to the User's Guide for an explanation of data; data is arranged alphabetically by state, then county, then city within each county; table includes counties with populations greater than 49,999 unless noted and cities with populations greater than 9,999 whose Asian and/or NHPI population rates are greater than the national average; (1) Native Hawaiian and other Pacific Islander; (2) excludes Taiwanese; (3) includes Chamorro; (4) county does not meet population threshold but is shown in order to allow inclusion of city

Place	Total foreign-born population	Total Asian population	Asians who are foreign born	Total NHPI[1] population	NHPIs[1] who are foreign born	Asian Indian	Bangladeshi	Cambodian	Chinese[2]	Fijian	Filipino	Guamanian[3]	Hawaiian, Native	Hmong	Indonesian	Japanese	Korean	Laotian	Malaysian	Pakistani	Samoan	Sri Lankan	Taiwanese	Thai	Tongan	Vietnamese
Springfield (cdp)	11,229 37.11	6,589	5,050 76.64 76.64 44.97	-	-	741 76.95 14.67 11.25 6.60	-	-	260 61.03 5.15 3.95 2.32	-	792 77.04 15.68 12.02 7.05	-	-	-	-	-	622 77.85 12.32 9.44 5.54	246 61.81 4.87 3.73 2.19	-	-	-	-	-	-	-	1,608 87.01 31.84 24.40 14.32
Tysons Corner (cdp)	6,398 34.58	3,155	2,519 79.84 79.84 39.37	-	-	585 79.48 23.22 18.54 9.14	-	-	519 79.36 20.60 16.45 8.11	-	-	-	-	-	-	-	672 85.50 26.68 21.30 10.50	-	-	-	-	-	-	-	-	-
Vienna (town)	2,671 18.36	1,207	900 74.57 74.57 33.70	-	-	-	-	-	-	-	-	-	-	-	-	-	-	-	-	-	-	-	-	-	-	-
West Springfield (cdp)	5,702 19.93	3,917	2,912 74.34 74.34 51.07	-	-	332 74.61 11.40 8.48 5.82	-	-	187 55.65 6.42 4.77 3.28	-	-	-	-	-	-	-	1,164 85.34 39.97 29.72 20.41	-	-	-	-	-	-	-	-	592 65.63 20.33 15.11 10.38
Wolf Trap (cdp)	2,271 16.36	1,254	887 70.73 70.73 39.06	-	-	205 56.79 23.11 16.35 9.03	-	-	200 73.80 22.55 15.95 8.81	-	-	-	-	-	-	-	-	-	-	-	-	-	-	-	-	-
Falls Church Independent City	1,667 16.06	674	555 82.34 82.34 33.29	-	-	-	-	-	-	-	-	-	-	-	-	-	-	-	-	-	-	-	-	-	-	-
Fauquier County	1,982 3.59	471	401 85.14 85.14 20.23	-	-	-	-	-	-	-	-	-	-	-	-	-	-	-	-	-	-	-	-	-	-	-
Frederick County	1,406 2.37	515	330 64.08 64.08 23.47	-	-	-	-	-	-	-	-	-	-	-	-	-	-	-	-	-	-	-	-	-	-	-
Hampton Independent City	5,778 3.95	2,570	1,905 74.12 74.12 32.97	-	-	-	-	-	-	-	501 74.66 26.30 19.49 8.67	-	-	-	-	-	-	-	-	-	-	-	-	-	-	456 86.53 23.94 17.74 7.89
Hanover County	1,527 1.77	539	334 61.97 61.97 21.87	-	-	-	-	-	-	-	-	-	-	-	-	-	-	-	-	-	-	-	-	-	-	-

Notes: Please refer to the User's Guide for an explanation of data; data is arranged alphabetically by state, then county, then city within each county; table includes counties with populations greater than 49,999 unless noted and cities with populations greater than 9,999 whose Asian and/or NHPI population rates are greater than the national average; (1) Native Hawaiian and other Pacific Islander; (2) excludes Taiwanese; (3) includes Chamorro; (4) county does not meet population threshold but is shown in order to allow inclusion of city

Place	Total foreign-born population	Total Asian population	Asians who are foreign born	Total NHPI[1] population	NHPIs[1] who are foreign born	Asian Indian	Bangladeshi	Cambodian	Chinese[2]	Fijian	Filipino	Guamanian[3]	Hawaiian, Native	Hmong	Indonesian	Japanese	Korean	Laotian	Malaysian	Pakistani	Samoan	Sri Lankan	Taiwanese	Thai	Tongan	Vietnamese
Henrico County	17,465 6.66	9,273	6,964 75.10 75.10 39.87	-	-	2,144 79.61 30.79 23.12 12.28	-	658 80.84 9.45 7.10 3.77	1,121 68.27 16.10 12.09 6.42	-	397 57.12 5.70 4.28 2.27	-	-	-	-	-	771 83.71 11.07 8.31 4.41	-	-	-	-	-	-	-	-	1,190 80.30 17.09 12.83 6.81
Glen Allen (cdp)	521 4.08	467	313 67.02 67.02 60.08	-	-	-	-	-	-	-	-	-	-	-	-	-	-	-	-	-	-	-	-	-	-	-
Laurel (cdp)	1,554 10.64	775	600 77.42 77.42 38.61	-	-	-	-	-	-	-	-	-	-	-	-	-	-	-	-	-	-	-	-	-	-	-
Loudoun County	19,116 11.27	8,927	6,405 71.75 71.75 33.51	-	-	1,456 76.59 22.73 16.31 7.62	-	-	857 74.65 13.38 9.60 4.48	-	825 70.51 12.88 9.24 4.32	-	-	-	-	-	766 70.08 11.96 8.58 4.01	-	-	452 72.09 7.06 5.06 2.36	-	-	-	-	-	1,291 73.98 20.16 14.46 6.75
Lynchburg Independent City	2,073 3.18	960	823 85.73 85.73 39.70	-	-	-	-	-	-	-	-	-	-	-	-	-	-	-	-	-	-	-	-	-	-	-
Manassas Park Indep. City	1,543 15.00	385	305 79.22 79.22 19.77	-	-	-	-	-	-	-	-	-	-	-	-	-	-	-	-	-	-	-	-	-	-	-
Montgomery County	4,813 5.76	3,132	2,229 71.17 71.17 46.31	-	-	490 76.44 21.98 15.64 10.18	-	-	705 80.57 31.63 22.51 14.65	-	-	-	-	-	-	-	538 69.78 24.14 17.18 11.18	-	-	-	-	-	-	-	-	-
Blacksburg (town)	4,253 10.80	2,885	2,016 69.88 69.88 47.40	-	-	446 75.21 22.12 15.46 10.49	-	-	667 79.69 33.09 23.12 15.68	-	-	-	-	-	-	-	468 66.76 23.21 16.22 11.00	-	-	-	-	-	-	-	-	-
Newport News Independent City	8,610 4.78	4,212	3,109 73.81 73.81 36.11	-	-	-	-	-	334 75.74 10.74 7.93 3.88	-	431 57.01 13.86 10.23 5.01	-	-	-	-	-	944 84.21 30.36 22.41 10.96	-	-	-	-	-	-	-	-	549 77.54 17.66 13.03 6.38
Norfolk Independent City	11,634 4.96	7,007	4,971 70.94 70.94 42.73	-	-	233 57.39 4.69 3.33 2.00	-	-	622 82.93 12.51 8.88 5.35	-	3,125 73.12 62.86 44.60 26.86	-	-	-	-	-	-	-	-	-	-	-	-	-	-	261 72.70 5.25 3.72 2.24

Notes: Please refer to the User's Guide for an explanation of data; data is arranged alphabetically by state, then county, then city within each county; table includes counties with populations greater than 49,999 unless noted and cities with populations greater than 9,999 whose Asian and/or NHPI population rates are greater than the national average; (1) Native Hawaiian and other Pacific Islander; (2) excludes Taiwanese; (3) includes Chamorro; (4) county does not meet population threshold but is shown in order to allow inclusion of city

Place	Total foreign-born population	Total Asian population	Asians who are foreign born	Total NHPI[1] population	NHPIs[1] who are foreign born	Asian Indian	Bangladeshi	Cambodian	Chinese[2]	Fijian	Filipino	Guamanian[3]	Hawaiian, Native	Hmong	Indonesian	Japanese	Korean	Laotian	Malaysian	Pakistani	Samoan	Sri Lankan	Taiwanese	Thai	Tongan	Vietnamese
Portsmouth Independent City	1,595 1.59	815	498 61.10 61.10 31.22	-	-	-	-	-	-	-	277 58.56 55.62 33.99 17.37	-	-	-	-	-	-	-	-	-	-	-	-	-	-	-
Prince William County	32,186 11.46	10,436	7,633 73.14 73.14 23.72	-	-	1,387 68.33 18.17 13.29 4.31	-	-	755 80.23 9.89 7.23 2.35	-	1,583 72.15 20.74 15.17 4.92	-	-	-	-	272 59.65 3.56 2.61 0.85	1,346 79.98 17.63 12.90 4.18	-	-	625 76.88 8.19 5.99 1.94	-	-	-	-	-	724 75.50 9.49 6.94 2.25
Bull Run (cdp)	2,218 19.46	598	467 78.09 78.09 21.06	-	-	-	-	-	-	-	-	-	-	-	-	-	-	-	-	-	-	-	-	-	-	-
Dale City (cdp)	7,298 13.02	2,864	2,154 75.21 75.21 29.51	-	-	439 69.79 20.38 15.33 6.02	-	-	-	-	529 77.45 24.56 18.47 7.25	-	-	-	-	-	-	-	-	255 78.70 11.84 8.90 3.49	-	-	-	-	-	-
Lake Ridge (cdp)	3,012 9.85	1,116	771 69.09 69.09 25.60	-	-	-	-	-	-	-	-	-	-	-	-	-	-	-	-	-	-	-	-	-	-	-
Woodbridge (cdp)	6,045 18.97	1,512	1,168 77.25 77.25 19.32	-	-	-	-	-	-	-	-	-	-	-	-	-	-	-	-	-	-	-	-	-	-	-
Richmond Independent City	7,643 3.86	2,438	1,559 63.95 63.95 20.40	-	-	303 58.83 19.44 12.43 3.96	-	-	-	-	220 52.01 14.11 9.02 2.88	-	-	-	-	-	-	-	-	-	-	-	-	-	-	-
Roanoke Independent City	2,904 3.06	1,004	755 75.20 75.20 26.00	-	-	-	-	-	-	-	-	-	-	-	-	-	-	-	-	-	-	-	-	-	-	-
Roanoke County	2,631 3.07	999	802 80.28 80.28 30.48	-	-	-	-	-	-	-	-	-	-	-	-	-	-	-	-	-	-	-	-	-	-	-
Spotsylvania County	2,917 3.23	1,281	843 65.81 65.81 28.90	-	-	-	-	-	-	-	-	-	-	-	-	-	-	-	-	-	-	-	-	-	-	-

Notes: Please refer to the User's Guide for an explanation of data; data is arranged alphabetically by state, then county, then city within each county; table includes counties with populations greater than 49,999 unless noted and cities with populations greater than 9,999 whose Asian and/or NHPI population rates are greater than the national average; (1) Native Hawaiian and other Pacific Islander; (2) excludes Taiwanese; (3) includes Chamorro; (4) county does not meet population threshold but is shown in order to allow inclusion of city

Place	Total foreign-born population	Total Asian population	Asians who are foreign born	Total NHPI[1] population	NHPIs[1] who are foreign born	Asian Indian	Bangladeshi	Cambodian	Chinese[2]	Fijian	Filipino	Guamanian[3]	Hawaiian, Native	Hmong	Indonesian	Japanese	Korean	Laotian	Malaysian	Pakistani	Samoan	Sri Lankan	Taiwanese	Thai	Tongan	Vietnamese
Stafford County	3,713	1,497	1,179	-	-	-	-	-	-	-	300	-	-	-	-	-	-	-	-	-	-	-	-	-	-	-
	4.02		78.76								79.37															
											25.45															
			78.76								20.04															
			31.75								8.08															
Suffolk Independent City	1,180	533	384	-	-	-	-	-	-	-	-	-	-	-	-	-	-	-	-	-	-	-	-	-	-	-
	1.85		72.05																							
			72.05																							
			32.54																							
Virginia Beach Independent City	28,276	20,207	13,661	-	-	930	-	-	1,107	-	9,010	-	-	-	-	504	618	-	-	-	-	-	-	-	-	932
	6.65		67.61			75.98			68.17		66.58					67.56	78.93									78.39
						6.81			8.10		65.95					3.69	4.52									6.82
			67.61			4.60			5.48		44.59					2.49	3.06									4.61
			48.31			3.29			3.91		31.86					1.78	2.19									3.30
Williamsburg Independent City	622	521	247	-	-	-	-	-	-	-	-	-	-	-	-	-	-	-	-	-	-	-	-	-	-	-
	5.18		47.41																							
			47.41																							
			39.71																							
York County	2,931	1,836	1,231	-	-	202	-	-	-	-	-	-	-	-	-	-	396	-	-	-	-	-	-	-	-	-
	5.21		67.05			77.39											71.74									
						16.41											32.17									
			67.05			11.00											21.57									
			42.00			6.89											13.51									
WASHINGTON	614,457	320,979	215,582	21,738	3,743	17,257	-	9,709	39,376	535	42,578	181	106	915	1,113	15,363	36,214	5,457	-	903	1,430	345	2,895	3,207	460	34,853
	10.42		67.16		17.22	76.74		65.75	68.75	75.46	65.45	3.36	2.35	61.24	89.61	41.19	77.89	67.40		71.72	20.22	81.75	76.43	82.40	54.50	78.04
						8.00		4.50	18.26	14.29	19.75	4.84	2.83	0.42	0.52	7.13	16.80	2.53		0.42	38.20	0.16	1.34	1.49	12.29	16.17
			67.16		17.22	5.38		3.02	12.27	2.46	13.27	0.83	0.49	0.29	0.35	4.79	11.28	1.70		0.28	6.58	0.11	0.90	1.00	2.12	10.86
			35.08		0.61	2.81		1.58	6.41	0.09	6.93	0.03	0.02	0.15	0.18	2.50	5.89	0.89		0.15	0.23	0.06	0.47	0.52	0.07	5.67
Benton County	12,051	2,934	2,028	-	-	353	-	-	384	-	-	-	-	-	-	-	285	-	-	-	-	-	-	-	-	351
	8.46		69.12			87.38			72.05								69.68									69.78
						17.41			18.93								14.05									17.31
			69.12			12.03			13.09								9.71									11.96
			16.83			2.93			3.19								2.36									2.91
Richland (city)	2,782	1,566	1,104	-	-	-	-	-	281	-	-	-	-	-	-	-	-	-	-	-	-	-	-	-	-	-
	7.20		70.50						68.54																	
									25.45																	
			70.50						17.94																	
			39.68						10.10																	
Chelan County	8,608	417	261	-	-	-	-	-	-	-	-	-	-	-	-	-	-	-	-	-	-	-	-	-	-	-
	12.92		62.59																							
			62.59																							
			3.03																							
Clallam County	2,877	870	509	-	-	-	-	-	-	-	-	-	-	-	-	-	-	-	-	-	-	-	-	-	-	-
	4.46		58.51																							
			58.51																							
			17.69																							

Notes: Please refer to the User's Guide for an explanation of data; data is arranged alphabetically by state, then county, then city within each county; table includes counties with populations greater than 49,999 unless noted and cities with populations greater than 9,999 whose Asian and/or NHPI population rates are greater than the national average; (1) Native Hawaiian and other Pacific Islander; (2) excludes Taiwanese; (3) includes Chamorro; (4) county does not meet population threshold but is shown in order to allow inclusion of city

Place	Total foreign-born population	Total Asian population	Asians who are foreign born	Total NHPI[1] population	NHPIs[1] who are foreign born	Asian Indian	Bangladeshi	Cambodian	Chinese[2]	Fijian	Filipino	Guamanian[3]	Hawaiian, Native	Hmong	Indonesian	Japanese	Korean	Laotian	Malaysian	Pakistani	Samoan	Sri Lankan	Taiwanese	Thai	Tongan	Vietnamese
Clark County	29,357 8.50	10,622	7,336 69.06 69.06 24.99	1,329	158 11.89 11.89 0.54	553 74.23 7.54 5.21 1.88	-	324 75.88 4.42 3.05 1.10	1,165 70.61 15.88 10.97 3.97	-	1,101 63.02 15.01 10.37 3.75	-	-	-	-	643 50.16 8.76 6.05 2.19	992 76.19 13.52 9.34 3.38	300 72.64 4.09 2.82 1.02	-	-	-	-	-	-	-	1,860 79.05 25.35 17.51 6.34
Five Corners (cdp)	928 7.66	585	414 70.77 70.77 44.61	-	-	-	-	-	-	-	-	-	-	-	-	-	-	-	-	-	-	-	-	-	-	-
Orchards (cdp)	1,517 8.46	768	460 59.90 59.90 30.32	-	-	-	-	-	-	-	-	-	-	-	-	-	-	-	-	-	-	-	-	-	-	-
Vancouver (city)	17,506 12.22	6,155	4,313 70.07 70.07 24.64	943	132 14.00 14.00 0.75	-	-	-	762 74.93 17.67 12.38 4.35	-	635 70.40 14.72 10.32 3.63	-	-	-	-	381 47.57 8.83 6.19 2.18	512 74.53 11.87 8.32 2.92	-	-	-	-	-	-	-	-	1,149 76.45 26.64 18.67 6.56
Cowlitz County	3,452 3.71	1,259	781 62.03 62.03 22.62	-	-	-	-	221 62.43 28.30 17.55 6.40	-	-	-	-	-	-	-	-	-	-	-	-	-	-	-	-	-	285 71.97 36.49 22.64 8.26
Grant County	12,803 17.14	569	290 50.97 50.97 2.27	-	-	-	-	-	-	-	-	-	-	-	-	-	-	-	-	-	-	-	-	-	-	-
Grays Harbor County	2,798 4.16	640	451 70.47 70.47 16.12	-	-	-	-	-	-	-	-	-	-	-	-	-	-	-	-	-	-	-	-	-	-	-
Island County	4,613 6.45	2,847	1,987 69.79 69.79 43.07	-	-	-	-	-	-	-	1,402 74.02 70.56 49.24 30.39	-	-	-	-	194 50.00 9.76 6.81 4.21	-	-	-	-	-	-	-	-	-	-
Oak Harbor (city)	1,952 9.81	1,739	1,216 69.93 69.93 62.30	-	-	-	-	-	-	-	970 71.32 79.77 55.78 49.69	-	-	-	-	-	-	-	-	-	-	-	-	-	-	-
King County	268,285 15.45	187,788	125,632 66.90 66.90 46.83	8,270	2,309 27.92 27.92 0.86	11,100 79.10 8.84 5.91 4.14	-	4,442 67.07 3.54 2.37 1.66	30,141 68.84 23.99 16.05 11.23	427 78.64 18.49 5.16 0.16	22,395 66.30 17.83 11.93 8.35	102 12.23 4.42 1.23 0.04	44 3.20 1.91 0.53 0.02	504 56.69 0.40 0.27 0.19	732 88.19 0.58 0.39 0.27	8,253 36.82 6.57 4.39 3.08	15,671 77.64 12.47 8.35 5.84	3,379 67.04 2.69 1.80 1.26	-	351 66.73 0.28 0.19 0.13	963 24.56 41.71 11.64 0.36	-	2,283 75.50 1.82 1.22 0.85	1,760 90.26 1.40 0.94 0.66	321 63.94 13.90 3.88 0.12	21,227 78.50 16.90 11.30 7.91

Notes: Please refer to the User's Guide for an explanation of data; data is arranged alphabetically by state, then county, then city within each county; table includes counties with populations greater than 49,999 unless noted and cities with populations greater than 9,999 whose Asian and/or NHPI population rates are greater than the national average; (1) Native Hawaiian and other Pacific Islander; (2) excludes Taiwanese; (3) includes Chamorro; (4) county does not meet population threshold but is shown in order to allow inclusion of city

Place	Total foreign-born population	Total Asian population	Asians who are foreign born	Total NHPI[1] population	NHPIs[1] who are foreign born	Asian Indian	Bangladeshi	Cambodian	Chinese[2]	Fijian	Filipino	Guamanian[3]	Hawaiian, Native	Hmong	Indonesian	Japanese	Korean	Laotian	Malaysian	Pakistani	Samoan	Sri Lankan	Taiwanese	Thai	Tongan	Vietnamese
Auburn (city)	4,504 11.18	1,565	970 61.98 61.98 21.54	-	-	-	-	-	-	-	-	-	-	-	-	-	-	-	-	-	-	-	-	-	-	-
Bellevue (city)	26,782 24.53	18,828	13,292 70.60 70.60 49.63	-	-	2,129 87.94 16.02 11.31 7.95	-	-	4,101 70.48 30.85 21.78 15.31	-	776 72.66 5.84 4.12 2.90	-	-	-	-	1,511 50.60 11.37 8.03 5.64	1,813 74.58 13.64 9.63 6.77	367 79.09 2.76 1.95 1.37	-	-	-	-	645 69.43 4.85 3.43 2.41	-	-	1,145 85.45 8.61 6.08 4.28
Bothell (city)	3,346 11.20	2,317	1,407 60.73 60.73 42.05	-	-	-	-	-	387 66.38 27.51 16.70 11.57	-	-	-	-	-	-	-	-	-	-	-	-	-	-	-	-	-
Bryn Mawr-Skyway (cdp)	2,536 18.05	3,055	1,838 60.16 60.16 72.48	-	-	-	-	-	-	-	611 69.91 33.24 20.00 24.09	-	-	-	-	62 10.11 3.37 2.03 2.44	-	-	-	-	-	-	-	-	-	362 85.18 19.70 11.85 14.27
Burien (city)	4,840 15.25	2,138	1,389 64.97 64.97 28.70	-	-	-	-	-	-	-	318 62.11 22.89 14.87 6.57	-	-	-	-	-	-	-	-	-	-	-	-	-	-	303 75.19 21.81 14.17 6.26
Cascade-Fairwood (cdp)	4,652 13.51	4,647	2,791 60.06 60.06 60.00	-	-	-	-	-	603 66.78 21.61 12.98 12.96	-	754 61.25 27.02 16.23 16.21	-	-	-	-	39 7.40 1.40 0.84 0.84	-	-	-	-	-	-	-	-	-	566 75.67 20.28 12.18 12.17
Cottage Lake (cdp)	1,676 6.90	1,051	582 55.38 55.38 34.73	-	-	-	-	-	-	-	-	-	-	-	-	-	-	-	-	-	-	-	-	-	-	-
Des Moines (city)	3,612 12.28	2,465	1,583 64.22 64.22 43.83	390	211 54.10 54.10 5.84	-	-	-	-	-	256 55.05 16.17 10.39 7.09	-	-	-	-	-	-	-	-	-	-	-	-	-	-	396 73.33 25.02 16.06 10.96
East Hill-Meridian (cdp)	4,606 15.55	3,905	2,555 65.43 65.43 55.47	-	-	568 75.03 22.23 14.55 12.33	-	-	506 63.57 19.80 12.96 10.99	-	416 60.47 16.28 10.65 9.03	-	-	-	-	-	-	-	-	-	-	-	-	-	-	398 70.82 15.58 10.19 8.64
Federal Way (city)	14,525 17.45	10,162	6,983 68.72 68.72 48.08	895	315 35.20 35.20 2.17	-	-	-	546 63.86 7.82 5.37 3.76	-	1,091 57.45 15.62 10.74 7.51	-	-	-	-	289 46.61 4.14 2.84 1.99	3,435 77.45 49.19 33.80 23.65	-	-	-	204 41.55 64.76 22.79 1.40	-	-	-	-	843 74.27 12.07 8.30 5.80

Notes: Please refer to the User's Guide for an explanation of data; data is arranged alphabetically by state, then county, then city within each county; table includes counties with populations greater than 49,999 unless noted and cities with populations greater than 9,999 whose Asian and/or NHPI population rates are greater than the national average; (1) Native Hawaiian and other Pacific Islander; (2) excludes Taiwanese; (3) includes Chamorro; (4) county does not meet population threshold but is shown in order to allow inclusion of city

Place	Total foreign-born population	Total Asian population	Asians who are foreign born	Total NHPI[1] population	NHPIs[1] who are foreign born	Asian Indian	Bangladeshi	Cambodian	Chinese[2]	Fijian	Filipino	Guamanian[3]	Hawaiian, Native	Hmong	Indonesian	Japanese	Korean	Laotian	Malaysian	Pakistani	Samoan	Sri Lankan	Taiwanese	Thai	Tongan	Vietnamese
Inglewood-Finn Hill (cdp)	2,632 11.62	1,679	1,055 62.84 62.84 40.08	-	-	-	-	-	286 69.59 27.11 17.03 10.87	-	-	-	-	-	-	-	-	-	-	-	-	-	-	-	-	-
Issaquah (city)	1,372 12.24	704	499 70.88 70.88 36.37	-	-	-	-	-	-	-	-	-	-	-	-	-	-	-	-	-	-	-	-	-	-	-
Kenmore (city)	1,928 10.40	1,226	713 58.16 58.16 36.98	-	-	-	-	-	-	-	-	-	-	-	-	-	-	-	-	-	-	-	-	-	-	-
Kent (city)	13,426 16.93	7,720	5,074 65.73 65.73 37.79	-	-	1,127 76.10 22.21 14.60 8.39	-	-	661 66.03 13.03 8.56 4.92	-	960 59.26 18.92 12.44 7.15	-	-	-	-	116 20.94 2.29 1.50 0.86	611 73.53 12.04 7.91 4.55	-	-	-	-	-	-	-	-	1,168 80.77 23.02 15.13 8.70
Kingsgate (cdp)	2,089 17.37	1,503	1,077 71.66 71.66 51.56	-	-	-	-	-	256 70.72 23.77 17.03 12.25	-	-	-	-	-	-	-	-	-	-	-	-	-	-	-	-	-
Kirkland (city)	6,466 14.37	3,476	2,480 71.35 71.35 38.35	-	-	-	-	-	591 73.78 23.83 17.00 9.14	-	-	-	-	-	-	273 52.30 11.01 7.85 4.22	-	-	-	-	-	-	-	-	-	416 77.90 16.77 11.97 6.43
Lake Forest Park (city)	1,586 11.80	1,157	797 68.89 68.89 50.25	-	-	-	-	-	-	-	-	-	-	-	-	-	-	-	-	-	-	-	-	-	-	-
Lakeland North (cdp)	1,744 11.51	941	616 65.46 65.46 35.32	-	-	-	-	-	-	-	-	-	-	-	-	-	-	-	-	-	-	-	-	-	-	-
Lakeland South (cdp)	913 7.94	665	413 62.11 62.11 45.24	-	-	-	-	-	-	-	-	-	-	-	-	-	-	-	-	-	-	-	-	-	-	-
Lea Hill (cdp)	1,011 9.48	519	373 71.87 71.87 36.89	-	-	-	-	-	-	-	-	-	-	-	-	-	-	-	-	-	-	-	-	-	-	-

Notes: Please refer to the User's Guide for an explanation of data; data is arranged alphabetically by state, then county, then city within each county; table includes counties with populations greater than 49,999 unless noted and cities with populations greater than 9,999 whose Asian and/or NHPI population rates are greater than the national average; (1) Native Hawaiian and other Pacific Islander; (2) excludes Taiwanese; (3) includes Chamorro; (4) county does not meet population threshold but is shown in order to allow inclusion of city

Place	Total foreign-born population	Total Asian population	Asians who are foreign born	Total NHPI[1] population	NHPIs[1] who are foreign born	Asian Indian	Bangladeshi	Cambodian	Chinese[2]	Fijian	Filipino	Guamanian[3]	Hawaiian, Native	Hmong	Indonesian	Japanese	Korean	Laotian	Malaysian	Pakistani	Samoan	Sri Lankan	Taiwanese	Thai	Tongan	Vietnamese
Mercer Island (city)	3,046 13.82	2,436	1,316 54.02 54.02 43.20	-	-	-	-	-	546 52.50 41.49 22.41 17.93	-	-	-	-	-	-	179 31.51 13.60 7.35 5.88	-	-	-	-	-	-	-	-	-	-
Redmond (city)	9,368 20.64	6,028	4,389 72.81 72.81 46.85	-	-	1,112 88.89 25.34 18.45 11.87	-	-	1,468 75.98 33.45 24.35 15.67	-	-	-	-	-	-	423 54.65 9.64 7.02 4.52	437 89.92 9.96 7.25 4.66	-	-	-	-	-	-	-	-	-
Renton (city)	9,590 19.22	6,648	4,387 65.99 65.99 45.75	-	-	-	-	-	807 66.42 18.40 12.14 8.42	-	994 63.64 22.66 14.95 10.36	-	-	-	-	165 26.19 3.76 2.48 1.72	-	-	-	-	-	-	-	-	-	1,428 80.36 32.55 21.48 14.89
Riverton-Boulevard Park (cdp)	2,522 22.14	1,524	998 65.49 65.49 39.57	-	-	-	-	-	-	-	-	-	-	-	-	-	-	-	-	-	-	-	-	-	-	-
Sammamish (city)	3,370 9.88	2,530	1,593 62.96 62.96 47.27	-	-	-	-	-	822 73.99 51.60 32.49 24.39	-	-	-	-	-	-	-	-	-	-	-	-	-	-	-	-	-
SeaTac (city)	5,763 22.58	2,945	2,030 68.93 68.93 35.22	614	168 27.36 27.36 2.92	479 83.16 23.60 16.26 8.31	-	-	-	-	505 69.66 24.88 17.15 8.76	-	-	-	-	-	-	-	-	-	-	-	-	-	-	380 69.60 18.72 12.90 6.59
Seattle (city)	94,952 16.85	73,849	49,573 67.13 67.13 52.21	2,514	458 18.22 18.22 0.48	2,062 75.53 4.16 2.79 2.17	-	1,653 65.49 3.33 2.24 1.74	13,204 69.97 26.64 17.88 13.91	-	11,308 69.69 22.81 15.31 11.91	-	-	-	343 90.74 0.69 0.46 0.36	3,182 34.14 6.42 4.31 3.35	3,957 79.78 7.98 5.36 4.17	1,754 66.26 3.54 2.38 1.85	-	-	243 18.08 53.06 9.67 0.26	-	804 82.29 1.62 1.09 0.85	804 91.57 1.62 1.09 0.85	-	9,139 79.87 18.44 12.38 9.62
Shoreline (city)	8,942 16.89	6,613	4,871 73.66 73.66 54.47	-	-	300 78.13 6.16 4.54 3.35	-	-	1,267 72.19 26.01 19.16 14.17	-	743 63.29 15.25 11.24 8.31	-	-	-	-	234 57.78 4.80 3.54 2.62	1,104 81.12 22.66 16.69 12.35	-	-	-	-	-	-	-	-	701 78.94 14.39 10.60 7.84
Tukwila (city)	4,512 26.23	1,788	1,252 70.02 70.02 27.75	332	152 45.78 45.78 3.37	-	-	-	-	-	461 76.07 36.82 25.78 10.22	-	-	-	-	-	-	-	-	-	-	-	-	-	-	-
Union Hill-Novelty Hill (cdp)	1,158 10.36	528	326 61.74 61.74 28.15	-	-	-	-	-	-	-	-	-	-	-	-	-	-	-	-	-	-	-	-	-	-	-

Notes: Please refer to the User's Guide for an explanation of data; data is arranged alphabetically by state, then county, then city within each county; table includes counties with populations greater than 49,999 unless noted and cities with populations greater than 9,999 whose Asian and/or NHPI population rates are greater than the national average; (1) Native Hawaiian and other Pacific Islander; (2) excludes Taiwanese; (3) includes Chamorro; (4) county does not meet population threshold but is shown in order to allow inclusion of city

Place	Total foreign-born population	Total Asian population	Asians who are foreign born	Total NHPI[1] population	NHPIs[1] who are foreign born	Asian Indian	Bangladeshi	Cambodian	Chinese[2]	Fijian	Filipino	Guamanian[3]	Hawaiian, Native	Hmong	Indonesian	Japanese	Korean	Laotian	Malaysian	Pakistani	Samoan	Sri Lankan	Taiwanese	Thai	Tongan	Vietnamese
White Center (cdp)	5,652 27.11	4,478	3,209 71.66 71.66 56.78	-	-	-	-	747 62.98 23.28 16.68 13.22	-	-	346 73.00 10.78 7.73 6.12	-	-	-	-	-	-	-	-	-	-	-	-	-	-	1,614 79.08 50.30 36.04 28.56
Kitsap County	13,180 5.68	10,465	6,845 65.41 65.41 51.93	1,698	111 6.54 6.54 0.84	-	-	-	295 62.63 4.31 2.82 2.24	-	4,636 66.49 67.73 44.30 35.17	0 0.00 0.00 0.00 0.00	-	-	-	645 53.97 9.42 6.16 4.89	526 86.37 7.68 5.03 3.99	-	-	-	-	-	-	-	-	295 67.05 4.31 2.82 2.24
Bremerton (city)	2,681 7.24	2,074	1,451 69.96 69.96 54.12	-	-	-	-	-	-	-	1,030 70.16 70.99 49.66 38.42	-	-	-	-	-	-	-	-	-	-	-	-	-	-	-
Silverdale (cdp)	1,590 10.08	1,751	1,075 61.39 61.39 67.61	-	-	-	-	-	-	-	866 58.63 80.56 49.46 54.47	-	-	-	-	-	-	-	-	-	-	-	-	-	-	-
Lewis County	2,799 4.08	380	217 57.11 57.11 7.75	-	-	-	-	-	-	-	-	-	-	-	-	-	-	-	-	-	-	-	-	-	-	-
Pierce County	56,525 8.07	34,671	23,593 68.05 68.05 41.74	5,075	547 10.78 10.78 0.97	516 65.48 2.19 1.49 0.91	-	2,569 63.31 10.89 7.41 4.54	1,077 61.37 4.56 3.11 1.91	-	4,007 59.15 16.98 11.56 7.09	17 0.93 3.11 0.33 0.03	0 0.00 0.00 0.00 0.00	-	-	1,851 52.57 7.85 5.34 3.27	8,736 78.55 37.03 25.20 15.46	332 77.75 1.41 0.96 0.59	-	-	348 20.13 63.62 6.86 0.62	-	-	310 78.28 1.31 0.89 0.55	-	3,487 81.36 14.78 10.06 6.17
Elk Plain (cdp)	909 5.79	627	353 56.30 56.30 38.83	-	-	-	-	-	-	-	-	-	-	-	-	-	-	-	-	-	-	-	-	-	-	-
Fort Lewis (cdp)	1,192 6.27	659	404 61.31 61.31 33.89	317	63 19.87 19.87 5.29	-	-	-	-	-	209 53.59 51.73 31.71 17.53	-	-	-	-	-	-	-	-	-	-	-	-	-	-	-
Lakewood (city)	7,397 12.68	5,181	3,614 69.75 69.75 48.86	746	106 14.21 14.21 1.43	-	-	-	-	-	783 64.08 21.67 15.11 10.59	-	-	-	-	419 65.37 11.59 8.09 5.66	1,875 80.23 51.88 36.19 25.35	-	-	-	62 21.16 58.49 8.31 0.84	-	-	-	-	-
Parkland (cdp)	2,270 9.49	1,589	1,150 72.37 72.37 50.66	415	16 3.86 3.86 0.70	-	-	-	-	-	-	-	-	-	-	-	615 76.78 53.48 38.70 27.09	-	-	-	-	-	-	-	-	-

Notes: Please refer to the User's Guide for an explanation of data; data is arranged alphabetically by state, then county, then city within each county; table includes counties with populations greater than 49,999 unless noted and cities with populations greater than 9,999 whose Asian and/or NHPI population rates are greater than the national average; (1) Native Hawaiian and other Pacific Islander; (2) excludes Taiwanese; (3) includes Chamorro; (4) county does not meet population threshold but is shown in order to allow inclusion of city

Place	Total foreign-born population	Total Asian population	Asians who are foreign born	Total NHPI[1] population	NHPIs[1] who are foreign born	Asian Indian	Bangladeshi	Cambodian	Chinese[2]	Fijian	Filipino	Guamanian[3]	Hawaiian, Native	Hmong	Indonesian	Japanese	Korean	Laotian	Malaysian	Pakistani	Samoan	Sri Lankan	Taiwanese	Thai	Tongan	Vietnamese
Spanaway (cdp)	1,788 8.34	1,275	914 71.69 71.69 51.12	578	20 3.46 3.46 1.12	-	-	-	-	-	307 58.37 33.59 24.08 17.17	-	-	-	-	-	481 82.50 52.63 37.73 26.90	-	-	-	-	-	-	-	-	-
Tacoma (city)	23,047 11.93	14,336	9,978 69.60 69.60 43.29	1,347	193 14.33 14.33 0.84	-	-	1,979 62.69 19.83 13.80 8.59	445 59.81 4.46 3.10 1.93	-	1,179 59.34 11.82 8.22 5.12	0 0.00 0.00 0.00 0.00	-	-	-	464 48.84 4.65 3.24 2.01	2,424 78.83 24.29 16.91 10.52	254 81.94 2.55 1.77 1.10	-	-	154 24.56 79.79 11.43 0.67	-	-	-	-	2,619 83.94 26.25 18.27 11.36
University Place (city)	3,021 10.03	2,311	1,713 74.12 74.12 56.70	-	-	-	-	-	-	-	-	-	-	-	-	-	1,014 81.97 59.19 43.88 33.57	-	-	-	-	-	-	-	-	-
Skagit County	9,093 8.83	1,459	1,005 68.88 68.88 11.05	-	-	-	-	-	-	-	328 67.77 32.64 22.48 3.61	-	-	-	-	-	-	-	-	-	-	-	-	-	-	-
Snohomish County	59,014 9.74	35,534	24,593 69.21 69.21 41.67	1,250	238 19.04 19.04 0.40	1,968 73.38 8.00 5.54 3.33	-	1,374 68.77 5.59 3.87 2.33	3,124 70.57 12.70 8.79 5.29	-	4,973 65.15 20.22 14.00 8.43	-	12 2.36 5.04 0.96 0.02	-	-	1,093 44.54 4.44 3.08 1.85	5,862 78.92 23.84 16.50 9.93	435 56.94 1.77 1.22 0.74	-	321 74.31 1.31 0.90 0.54	-	-	-	-	-	3,965 75.52 16.12 11.16 6.72
Alderwood Manor (cdp)	1,638 10.74	1,245	920 73.90 73.90 56.17	-	-	-	-	-	-	-	-	-	-	-	-	-	-	-	-	-	-	-	-	-	-	-
Edmonds (city)	4,351 10.98	2,187	1,481 67.72 67.72 34.04	-	-	-	-	-	-	-	239 65.66 16.14 10.93 5.49	-	-	-	-	-	469 81.57 31.67 21.44 10.78	-	-	-	-	-	-	-	-	-
Everett (city)	11,327 12.41	6,057	4,393 72.53 72.53 38.78	-	-	432 73.34 9.83 7.13 3.81	-	450 70.53 10.24 7.43 3.97	-	-	1,262 69.61 28.73 20.84 11.14	-	-	-	-	-	-	-	-	-	-	-	-	-	-	976 82.09 22.22 16.11 8.62
Lynnwood (city)	7,213 21.38	4,706	3,519 74.78 74.78 48.79	-	-	-	-	-	451 72.28 12.82 9.58 6.25	-	655 71.58 18.61 13.92 9.08	-	-	-	-	-	845 81.49 24.01 17.96 11.71	-	-	-	-	-	-	-	-	805 82.23 22.88 17.11 11.16
Martha Lake (cdp)	1,323 10.47	1,171	744 63.54 63.54 56.24	-	-	-	-	-	-	-	-	-	-	-	-	-	-	-	-	-	-	-	-	-	-	-

Notes: Please refer to the User's Guide for an explanation of data; data is arranged alphabetically by state, then county, then city within each county; table includes counties with populations greater than 49,999 unless noted and cities with populations greater than 9,999 whose Asian and/or NHPI population rates are greater than the national average; (1) Native Hawaiian and other Pacific Islander; (2) excludes Taiwanese; (3) includes Chamorro; (4) county does not meet population threshold but is shown in order to allow inclusion of city

Place	Total foreign-born population	Total Asian population	Asians who are foreign born	Total NHPI[1] population	NHPIs[1] who are foreign born	Asian Indian	Bangladeshi	Cambodian	Chinese[2]	Fijian	Filipino	Guamanian[3]	Hawaiian, Native	Hmong	Indonesian	Japanese	Korean	Laotian	Malaysian	Pakistani	Samoan	Sri Lankan	Taiwanese	Thai	Tongan	Vietnamese
Marysville (city)	1,860 7.37	953	600 62.96 62.96 32.26	-	-	-	-	-	-	-	-	-	-	-	-	-	-	-	-	-	-	-	-	-	-	-
Mill Creek (city)	1,794 15.68	1,187	814 68.58 68.58 45.37	-	-	-	-	-	-	-	-	-	-	-	-	-	335 75.45 41.15 28.22 18.67	-	-	-	-	-	-	-	-	-
Mountlake Terrace (city)	3,436 16.93	2,347	1,730 73.71 73.71 50.35	-	-	-	-	-	-	-	406 73.29 23.47 17.30 11.82	-	-	-	-	-	494 82.33 28.55 21.05 14.38	-	-	-	-	-	-	-	-	-
Mukilteo (city)	2,477 13.73	2,092	1,411 67.45 67.45 56.96	-	-	-	-	-	-	-	-	-	-	-	-	-	699 69.48 49.54 33.41 28.22	-	-	-	-	-	-	-	-	-
North Creek (cdp)	2,147 8.26	1,537	967 62.91 62.91 45.04	-	-	-	-	-	-	-	-	-	-	-	-	-	-	-	-	-	-	-	-	-	-	-
Paine Field-Lk. Stickney (cdp)	3,247 13.39	1,572	1,086 69.08 69.08 33.45	-	-	-	-	-	-	-	-	-	-	-	-	-	-	-	-	-	-	-	-	-	-	-
Picnic Pt.-N. Lynnwood (cdp)	3,780 16.56	2,482	1,889 76.11 76.11 49.97	-	-	-	-	-	-	-	291 72.03 15.40 11.72 7.70	-	-	-	-	-	728 83.58 38.54 29.33 19.26	-	-	-	-	-	-	-	-	-
Seattle Hill-Silver Firs (cdp)	3,257 9.16	2,755	1,718 62.36 62.36 52.75	-	-	-	-	-	-	-	290 48.90 16.88 10.53 8.90	-	-	-	-	-	454 73.46 26.43 16.48 13.94	-	-	-	-	-	-	-	-	349 76.37 20.31 12.67 10.72
Spokane County	18,711 4.48	7,444	4,729 63.53 63.53 25.27	695	107 15.40 15.40 0.57	466 74.44 9.85 6.26 2.49	-	-	617 67.58 13.05 8.29 3.30	-	618 63.38 13.07 8.30 3.30	-	-	356 66.79 7.53 4.78 1.90	-	562 33.69 11.88 7.55 3.00	544 80.95 11.50 7.31 2.91	-	-	-	-	-	-	-	-	1,081 86.90 22.86 14.52 5.78
Spokane (city)	11,096 5.66	4,379	2,687 61.36 61.36 24.22	422	68 16.11 16.11 0.61	-	-	-	374 68.50 13.92 8.54 3.37	-	296 62.32 11.02 6.76 2.67	-	-	265 64.48 9.86 6.05 2.39	-	260 25.54 9.68 5.94 2.34	302 80.75 11.24 6.90 2.72	-	-	-	-	-	-	-	-	684 86.69 25.46 15.62 6.16

Notes: Please refer to the User's Guide for an explanation of data; data is arranged alphabetically by state, then county, then city within each county; table includes counties with populations greater than 49,999 unless noted and cities with populations greater than 9,999 whose Asian and/or NHPI population rates are greater than the national average; (1) Native Hawaiian and other Pacific Islander; (2) excludes Taiwanese; (3) includes Chamorro; (4) county does not meet population threshold but is shown in order to allow inclusion of city

Place	Total foreign-born population	Total Asian population	Asians who are foreign born	Total NHPI[1] population	NHPIs[1] who are foreign born	Asian Indian	Bangladeshi	Cambodian	Chinese[2]	Fijian	Filipino	Guamanian[3]	Hawaiian, Native	Hmong	Indonesian	Japanese	Korean	Laotian	Malaysian	Pakistani	Samoan	Sri Lankan	Taiwanese	Thai	Tongan	Vietnamese
Thurston County	12,738	9,424	6,334	1,205	39	358	-	511	559	-	1,037	11	-	-	-	383	1,609	-	-	-	-	-	-	-	-	1,349
	6.14		67.21		3.24	73.97		61.05	63.16		63.97	1.51				48.67	74.70									76.56
						5.65		8.07	8.83		16.37	28.21				6.05	25.40									21.30
			67.21		3.24	3.80		5.42	5.93		11.00	0.91				4.06	17.07									14.31
			49.73		0.31	2.81		4.01	4.39		8.14	0.09				3.01	12.63									10.59
Lacey (city)	2,919	2,517	1,778	-	-	-	-	-	-	-	282	-	-	-	-	-	477	-	-	-	-	-	-	-	-	444
	9.38		70.64								60.00						77.94									75.64
											15.86						26.83									24.97
			70.64								11.20						18.95									17.64
			60.91								9.66						16.34									15.21
Olympia (city)	2,787	2,326	1,559	-	-	-	-	-	-	-	-	-	-	-	-	-	-	-	-	-	-	-	-	-	-	525
	6.58		67.02																							74.15
																										33.68
			67.02																							22.57
			55.94																							18.84
Tumwater (city)	782	479	332	-	-	-	-	-	-	-	-	-	-	-	-	-	-	-	-	-	-	-	-	-	-	-
	6.18		69.31																							
			69.31																							
			42.46																							
Walla Walla County	5,206	772	352	-	-	-	-	-	-	-	-	-	-	-	-	-	-	-	-	-	-	-	-	-	-	-
	9.43		45.60																							
			45.60																							
			6.76																							
Whatcom County	16,342	4,416	3,064	-	-	979	-	-	358	-	326	-	-	-	-	278	326	-	-	-	-	-	-	-	-	464
	9.80		69.38			78.95			68.06		63.67					55.71	71.96									74.48
						31.95			11.68		10.64					9.07	10.64									15.14
			69.38			22.17			8.11		7.38					6.30	7.38									10.51
			18.75			5.99			2.19		1.99					1.70	1.99									2.84
Bellingham (city)	6,088	2,680	1,796	-	-	479	-	-	-	-	-	-	-	-	-	-	-	-	-	-	-	-	-	-	-	360
	9.11		67.01			78.52																				76.27
						26.67																				20.04
			67.01			17.87																				13.43
			29.50			7.87																				5.91
Whitman County[4]	3,121	2,230	1,608	-	-	-	-	-	546	-	-	-	-	-	-	399	-	-	-	-	-	-	-	-	-	-
	7.66		72.11						79.71							65.41										
									33.96							24.81										
			72.11						24.48							17.89										
			51.52						17.49							12.78										
Pullman (city)	2,863	1,992	1,497	-	-	-	-	-	491	-	-	-	-	-	-	395	-	-	-	-	-	-	-	-	-	-
	11.57		75.15						84.36							70.28										
									32.80							26.39										
			75.15						24.65							19.83										
			52.29						17.15							13.80										
Yakima County	37,575	2,180	1,295	-	-	-	-	-	-	-	571	-	-	-	-	-	-	-	-	-	-	-	-	-	-	-
	16.88		59.40								61.40															
											44.09															
			59.40								26.19															
			3.45								1.52															

Notes: Please refer to the User's Guide for an explanation of data; data is arranged alphabetically by state, then county, then city within each county; table includes counties with populations greater than 49,999 unless noted and cities with populations greater than 9,999 whose Asian and/or NHPI population rates are greater than the national average; (1) Native Hawaiian and other Pacific Islander; (2) excludes Taiwanese; (3) includes Chamorro; (4) county does not meet population threshold but is shown in order to allow inclusion of city

Place	Total foreign-born population	Total Asian population	Asians who are foreign born	Total NHPI[1] population	NHPIs[1] who are foreign born	Asian Indian	Bangladeshi	Cambodian	Chinese[2]	Fijian	Filipino	Guamanian[3]	Hawaiian, Native	Hmong	Indonesian	Japanese	Korean	Laotian	Malaysian	Pakistani	Samoan	Sri Lankan	Taiwanese	Thai	Tongan	Vietnamese
WEST VIRGINIA	19,390	9,445	6,843	405	83	1,932	-	-	1,320	-	1,101	-	-	-	-	734	730	-	-	224	-	-	-	-	-	287
	1.07		72.45		20.49	76.39			79.95		66.41					83.50	81.66			69.14						64.93
						28.23			19.29		16.09					10.73	10.67			3.27						4.19
			72.45		20.49	20.46			13.98		11.66					7.77	7.73			2.37						3.04
			35.29		0.43	9.96			6.81		5.68					3.79	3.76			1.16						1.48
Cabell County	1,216	748	524	-	-	-	-	-	-	-	-	-	-	-	-	-	-	-	-	-	-	-	-	-	-	-
	1.26		70.05																							
			70.05																							
			43.09																							
Harrison County	947	398	336	-	-	-	-	-	-	-	-	-	-	-	-	-	-	-	-	-	-	-	-	-	-	-
	1.38		84.42																							
			84.42																							
			35.48																							
Kanawha County	2,864	1,670	1,217	-	-	463	-	-	-	-	-	-	-	-	-	-	-	-	-	-	-	-	-	-	-	-
	1.43		72.87			81.09																				
						38.04																				
			72.87			27.72																				
			42.49			16.17																				
Monongalia County	3,140	1,910	1,435	-	-	460	-	-	484	-	-	-	-	-	-	-	-	-	-	-	-	-	-	-	-	-
	3.84		75.13			83.03			78.83																	
						32.06			33.73																	
			75.13			24.08			25.34																	
			45.70			14.65			15.41																	
Putnam County	530	300	186	-	-	-	-	-	-	-	-	-	-	-	-	-	-	-	-	-	-	-	-	-	-	-
	1.03		62.00																							
			62.00																							
			35.09																							
Raleigh County	945	663	477	-	-	-	-	-	-	-	-	-	-	-	-	-	-	-	-	-	-	-	-	-	-	-
	1.19		71.95																							
			71.95																							
			50.48																							
Wood County	926	395	283	-	-	-	-	-	-	-	-	-	-	-	-	-	-	-	-	-	-	-	-	-	-	-
	1.05		71.65																							
			71.65																							
			30.56																							
WISCONSIN	193,751	83,077	55,567	1,577	202	8,630	-	365	7,393	-	3,674	6	14	17,783	366	1,869	5,802	2,586	-	718	-	-	529	729	-	2,762
	3.61		66.89		12.81	76.51		58.21	76.93		67.30	1.41	3.23	57.35	90.15	62.59	84.75	62.54		77.45			78.60	83.79		71.35
						15.53		0.66	13.30		6.61	2.97	6.93	32.00	0.66	3.36	10.44	4.65		1.29			0.95	1.31		4.97
			66.89		12.81	10.39		0.44	8.90		4.42	0.38	0.89	21.41	0.44	2.25	6.98	3.11		0.86			0.64	0.88		3.32
			28.68		0.10	4.45		0.19	3.82		1.90	<0.01	0.01	9.18	0.19	0.96	2.99	1.33		0.37			0.27	0.38		1.43
Brown County	8,914	4,596	2,797	-	-	235	-	-	-	-	-	-	-	1,445	-	-	-	280	-	-	-	-	-	-	-	-
	3.93		60.86			76.80								59.78				63.64								
						8.40								51.66				10.01								
			60.86			5.11								31.44				6.09								
			31.38			2.64								16.21				3.14								

Notes: Please refer to the User's Guide for an explanation of data; data is arranged alphabetically by state, then county, then city within each county; table includes counties with populations greater than 49,999 unless noted and cities with populations greater than 9,999 whose Asian and/or NHPI population rates are greater than the national average; (1) Native Hawaiian and other Pacific Islander; (2) excludes Taiwanese; (3) includes Chamorro; (4) county does not meet population threshold but is shown in order to allow inclusion of city

Place	Total foreign-born population	Total Asian population	Asians who are foreign born	Total NHPI[1] population	NHPIs[1] who are foreign born	Asian Indian	Bangladeshi	Cambodian	Chinese[2]	Fijian	Filipino	Guamanian[3]	Hawaiian, Native	Hmong	Indonesian	Japanese	Korean	Laotian	Malaysian	Pakistani	Samoan	Sri Lankan	Taiwanese	Thai	Tongan	Vietnamese
Chippewa County	520 0.94	469	189 40.30 40.30 36.35	-	-	-	-	-	-	-	-	-	-	116 32.31 61.38 24.73 22.31	-	-	-	-	-	-	-	-	-	-	-	-
Columbia County	693 1.32	177	118 66.67 66.67 17.03	-	-	-	-	-	-	-	-	-	-	-	-	-	-	-	-	-	-	-	-	-	-	-
Dane County	26,786 6.28	14,296	10,705 74.88 74.88 39.96	-	-	1,685 77.65 15.74 11.79 6.29	-	-	2,582 81.48 24.12 18.06 9.64	-	456 68.26 4.26 3.19 1.70	-	-	1,309 56.99 12.23 9.16 4.89	-	603 75.47 5.63 4.22 2.25	1,658 86.99 15.49 11.60 6.19	246 71.51 2.30 1.72 0.92	-	-	-	-	360 84.51 3.36 2.52 1.34	-	-	523 71.16 4.89 3.66 1.95
Madison (city)	18,792 9.06	11,641	8,945 76.84 76.84 47.60	-	-	1,119 78.20 12.51 9.61 5.95	-	-	2,311 83.01 25.84 19.85 12.30	-	305 68.23 3.41 2.62 1.62	-	-	1,047 57.56 11.70 8.99 5.57	-	554 80.41 6.19 4.76 2.95	1,460 86.19 16.32 12.54 7.77	-	-	-	-	-	360 85.11 4.02 3.09 1.92	-	-	454 71.50 5.08 3.90 2.42
Dodge County	1,380 1.61	268	205 76.49 76.49 14.86	-	-	-	-	-	-	-	-	-	-	-	-	-	-	-	-	-	-	-	-	-	-	-
Eau Claire County	2,092 2.25	2,323	1,236 53.21 53.21 59.08	-	-	-	-	-	-	-	-	-	-	685 49.49 55.42 29.49 32.74	-	-	-	-	-	-	-	-	-	-	-	-
Fond du Lac County	1,957 2.01	588	446 75.85 75.85 22.79	-	-	-	-	-	-	-	-	-	-	206 77.74 46.19 35.03 10.53	-	-	-	-	-	-	-	-	-	-	-	-
Jefferson County	2,064 2.79	215	155 72.09 72.09 7.51	-	-	-	-	-	-	-	-	-	-	-	-	-	-	-	-	-	-	-	-	-	-	-
Kenosha County	7,144 4.78	1,381	1,017 73.64 73.64 14.24	-	-	-	-	-	-	-	-	-	-	-	-	-	-	-	-	-	-	-	-	-	-	-
La Crosse County	2,706 2.53	2,855	1,712 59.96 59.96 63.27	-	-	-	-	-	-	-	-	-	-	1,046 53.89 61.10 36.64 38.65	-	-	-	-	-	-	-	-	-	-	-	-

Notes: Please refer to the User's Guide for an explanation of data; data is arranged alphabetically by state, then county, then city within each county; table includes counties with populations greater than 49,999 unless noted and cities with populations greater than 9,999 whose Asian and/or NHPI population rates are greater than the national average; (1) Native Hawaiian and other Pacific Islander; (2) excludes Taiwanese; (3) includes Chamorro; (4) county does not meet population threshold but is shown in order to allow inclusion of city

Place	Total foreign-born population	Total Asian population	Asians who are foreign born	Total NHPI[1] population	NHPIs[1] who are foreign born	Asian Indian	Bangladeshi	Cambodian	Chinese[2]	Fijian	Filipino	Guamanian[3]	Hawaiian, Native	Hmong	Indonesian	Japanese	Korean	Laotian	Malaysian	Pakistani	Samoan	Sri Lankan	Taiwanese	Thai	Tongan	Vietnamese
La Crosse (city)	1,683 3.26	1,943	1,160 59.70 59.70 68.92	-	-	-	-	-	-	-	-	-	-	733 54.62 63.19 37.73 43.55	-	-	-	-	-	-	-	-	-	-	-	-
Manitowoc County	1,939 2.34	1,471	874 59.42 59.42 45.07	-	-	-	-	-	-	-	-	-	-	572 60.92 65.45 38.89 29.50	-	-	-	-	-	-	-	-	-	-	-	-
Marathon County	4,390 3.49	5,156	3,132 60.74 60.74 71.34	-	-	-	-	-	-	-	-	-	-	2,435 59.29 77.75 47.23 55.47	-	-	-	-	-	-	-	-	-	-	-	-
Wausau (city)	3,209 8.36	4,168	2,615 62.74 62.74 81.49	-	-	-	-	-	-	-	-	-	-	2,112 61.50 80.76 50.67 65.81	-	-	-	-	-	-	-	-	-	-	-	-
Milwaukee County	63,648 6.77	22,356	15,047 67.31 67.31 23.64	520	98 18.85 18.85 0.15	2,981 78.45 19.81 13.33 4.68	-	-	1,695 75.40 11.26 7.58 2.66	-	1,032 63.59 6.86 4.62 1.62	-	-	4,374 58.44 29.07 19.57 6.87	-	385 51.82 2.56 1.72 0.60	1,064 83.06 7.07 4.76 1.67	1,219 70.95 8.10 5.45 1.92	-	339 95.49 2.25 1.52 0.53	-	-	-	-	-	991 75.82 6.59 4.43 1.56
Outagamie County	5,057 3.14	3,635	2,221 61.10 61.10 43.92	-	-	267 60.14 12.02 7.35 5.28	-	-	-	-	-	-	-	1,398 60.05 62.94 38.46 27.64	-	-	-	-	-	-	-	-	-	-	-	-
Appleton (city)	3,559 5.08	3,192	1,963 61.50 61.50 55.16	-	-	-	-	-	-	-	-	-	-	1,426 61.18 72.64 44.67 40.07	-	-	-	-	-	-	-	-	-	-	-	-
Ozaukee County	2,719 3.30	670	481 71.79 71.79 17.69	-	-	-	-	-	-	-	-	-	-	-	-	-	-	-	-	-	-	-	-	-	-	-
Portage County	1,458 2.17	1,295	748 57.76 57.76 51.30	-	-	-	-	-	-	-	-	-	-	446 51.32 59.63 34.44 30.59	-	-	-	-	-	-	-	-	-	-	-	-
Stevens Point (city)	926 3.78	1,035	581 56.14 56.14 62.74	-	-	-	-	-	-	-	-	-	-	379 50.07 65.23 36.62 40.93	-	-	-	-	-	-	-	-	-	-	-	-

Notes: Please refer to the User's Guide for an explanation of data; data is arranged alphabetically by state, then county, then city within each county; table includes counties with populations greater than 49,999 unless noted and cities with populations greater than 9,999 whose Asian and/or NHPI population rates are greater than the national average; (1) Native Hawaiian and other Pacific Islander; (2) excludes Taiwanese; (3) includes Chamorro; (4) county does not meet population threshold but is shown in order to allow inclusion of city

Place	Total foreign-born population	Total Asian population	Asians who are foreign born	Total NHPI[1] population	NHPIs[1] who are foreign born	Asian Indian	Bangladeshi	Cambodian	Chinese[2]	Fijian	Filipino	Guamanian[3]	Hawaiian, Native	Hmong	Indonesian	Japanese	Korean	Laotian	Malaysian	Pakistani	Samoan	Sri Lankan	Taiwanese	Thai	Tongan	Vietnamese
Racine County	7,710 4.08	1,277	1,013 79.33 79.33 13.14	-	-	-	-	-	-	-	-	-	-	-	-	-	-	-	-	-	-	-	-	-	-	-
Rock County	5,048 3.31	1,338	984 73.54 73.54 19.49	-	-	-	-	-	-	-	-	-	-	-	-	-	-	-	-	-	-	-	-	-	-	-
St. Croix County	692 1.10	263	169 64.26 64.26 24.42	-	-	-	-	-	-	-	-	-	-	-	-	-	-	-	-	-	-	-	-	-	-	-
Sauk County	1,068 1.93	209	110 52.63 52.63 10.30	-	-	-	-	-	-	-	-	-	-	-	-	-	-	-	-	-	-	-	-	-	-	-
Sheboygan County	4,817 4.28	3,575	2,140 59.86 59.86 44.43	-	-	-	-	-	-	-	-	-	-	1,406 56.42 65.70 39.33 29.19	-	-	-	-	-	-	-	-	-	-	-	-
Sheboygan (city)	3,895 7.67	3,289	1,958 59.53 59.53 50.27	-	-	-	-	-	-	-	-	-	-	1,372 57.48 70.07 41.71 35.22	-	-	-	-	-	-	-	-	-	-	-	-
Walworth County	5,036 5.37	567	431 76.01 76.01 8.56	-	-	-	-	-	-	-	-	-	-	-	-	-	-	-	-	-	-	-	-	-	-	-
Washington County	2,190 1.86	513	299 58.28 58.28 13.65	-	-	-	-	-	-	-	-	-	-	-	-	-	-	-	-	-	-	-	-	-	-	-
Waukesha County	13,017 3.61	5,005	3,664 73.21 73.21 28.15	-	-	1,234 74.70 33.68 24.66 9.48	-	-	818 71.44 22.33 16.34 6.28	-	304 75.43 8.30 6.07 2.34	-	-	-	-	-	517 87.33 14.11 10.33 3.97	-	-	-	-	-	-	-	-	-
Winnebago County	4,351 2.78	2,456	1,599 65.11 65.11 36.75	-	-	-	-	-	-	-	-	-	-	807 54.05 50.47 32.86 18.55	-	-	-	-	-	-	-	-	-	-	-	-

Notes: Please refer to the User's Guide for an explanation of data; data is arranged alphabetically by state, then county, then city within each county; table includes counties with populations greater than 49,999 unless noted and cities with populations greater than 9,999 whose Asian and/or NHPI population rates are greater than the national average; (1) Native Hawaiian and other Pacific Islander; (2) excludes Taiwanese; (3) includes Chamorro; (4) county does not meet population threshold but is shown in order to allow inclusion of city

Place	Total foreign-born population	Total Asian population	Asians who are foreign born	Total NHPI[1] population	NHPIs[1] who are foreign born	Asian Indian	Bangladeshi	Cambodian	Chinese[2]	Fijian	Filipino	Guamanian[3]	Hawaiian, Native	Hmong	Indonesian	Japanese	Korean	Laotian	Malaysian	Pakistani	Samoan	Sri Lankan	Taiwanese	Thai	Tongan	Vietnamese
Wood County	1,555 2.06	1,160	740 63.79 63.79 47.59	-	-	-	-	-	-	-	-	-	-	341 57.70 46.08 29.40 21.93	-	-	-	-	-	-	-	-	-	-	-	-
WYOMING	11,205 2.27	2,972	1,926 64.80 64.80 17.19	-	-	307 72.58 15.94 10.33 2.74	-	-	418 67.97 21.70 14.06 3.73	-	303 57.93 15.73 10.20 2.70	-	-	-	-	250 47.80 12.98 8.41 2.23	396 84.26 20.56 13.32 3.53	-	-	-	-	-	-	-	-	-
Laramie County	2,399 2.94	817	539 65.97 65.97 22.47	-	-	-	-	-	-	-	-	-	-	-	-	-	-	-	-	-	-	-	-	-	-	-
Natrona County	1,197 1.80	409	221 54.03 54.03 18.46	-	-	-	-	-	-	-	-	-	-	-	-	-	-	-	-	-	-	-	-	-	-	-

Notes: Please refer to the User's Guide for an explanation of data; data is arranged alphabetically by state, then county, then city within each county; table includes counties with populations greater than 49,999 unless noted and cities with populations greater than 9,999 whose Asian and/or NHPI population rates are greater than the national average; (1) Native Hawaiian and other Pacific Islander; (2) excludes Taiwanese; (3) includes Chamorro; (4) county does not meet population threshold but is shown in order to allow inclusion of city

Foreign-Born Naturalized Citizens

(Universe: Total Population)

Place	Total foreign-born naturalized citizens	Total Asian population	Asians who are foreign-born naturalized citizens	Total NHPI¹ population	NHPIs¹ who are foreign-born naturalized citizens	Asian Indian	Bangladeshi	Cambodian	Chinese²
UNITED STATES	12,542,626 4.46	10,171,820	3,502,021 34.43 34.43 27.92	378,782	30,284 8.00 8.00 0.24	487,795 29.64 13.93 4.80 3.89	10,515 25.38 0.30 0.10 0.08	53,496 30.05 1.53 0.53 0.43	857,071 37.26 24.47 8.43 6.83
ALABAMA	32,200 0.72	29,908	10,033 33.55 33.55 31.16	1,187	39 3.29 3.29 0.12	2,157 32.26 21.50 7.21 6.70	-	147 26.02 1.47 0.49 0.46	1,449 25.38 14.44 4.84 4.50
Baldwin County	1,143 0.81	535	157 29.35 29.35 13.74	-	-	-	-	-	-
Calhoun County	946 0.84	671	251 37.41 37.41 26.53	-	-	-	-	-	-
Etowah County	446 0.43	361	111 30.75 30.75 24.89	-	-	-	-	-	-
Houston County	571 0.64	500	196 39.20 39.20 34.33	-	-	-	-	-	-
Jefferson County	4,946 0.75	5,793	1,676 28.93 28.93 33.89	-	-	514 36.69 30.67 8.87 10.39	-	-	338 17.86 20.17 5.83 6.83
Lee County	1,063 0.92	1,834	462 25.19 25.19 43.46	-	-	-	-	-	193 30.68 41.77 10.52 18.16
Madison County	4,820 1.74	4,706	1,554 33.02 33.02 32.24	-	-	453 30.61 29.15 9.63 9.40	-	-	160 23.19 10.30 3.40 3.32

Place	Fijian	Filipino	Guamanian³	Hawaiian, Native	Hmong	Indonesian	Japanese	Korean	Laotian	Malaysian	Pakistani	Samoan	Sri Lankan	Taiwanese	Thai	Tongan	Vietnamese
UNITED STATES	2,901 28.26 9.58 0.77 0.02	775,400 41.60 22.14 7.62 6.18	2,308 4.19 7.62 0.61 0.02	1,459 1.05 4.82 0.39 0.01	29,664 17.44 0.85 0.29 0.24	7,646 20.57 0.22 0.08 0.06	80,119 10.08 2.29 0.79 0.64	423,393 39.47 12.09 4.16 3.38	55,076 32.82 1.57 0.54 0.44	1,391 12.99 0.04 0.01 0.01	47,923 30.74 1.37 0.47 0.38	10,283 12.06 33.96 2.71 0.08	5,950 31.19 0.17 0.06 0.05	52,483 42.76 1.50 0.52 0.42	36,227 32.68 1.03 0.36 0.29	5,434 19.63 17.94 1.43 0.04	488,874 44.03 13.96 4.81 3.90
ALABAMA	-	1,058 43.34 10.55 3.54 3.29	22 5.19 56.41 1.85 0.07	-	-	-	445 23.52 4.44 1.49 1.38	1,842 45.78 18.36 6.16 5.72	352 42.46 3.51 1.18 1.09	-	138 35.84 1.38 0.46 0.43	-	-	-	217 34.94 2.16 0.73 0.67	-	1,769 38.20 17.63 5.91 5.49
Baldwin County	-	-	-	-	-	-	-	-	-	-	-	-	-	-	-	-	-
Calhoun County	-	-	-	-	-	-	-	-	-	-	-	-	-	-	-	-	-
Etowah County	-	-	-	-	-	-	-	-	-	-	-	-	-	-	-	-	-
Houston County	-	-	-	-	-	-	-	-	-	-	-	-	-	-	-	-	-
Jefferson County	-	-	-	-	-	-	-	217 46.77 12.95 3.75 4.39	-	-	-	-	-	-	-	-	314 36.18 18.74 5.42 6.35
Lee County	-	-	-	-	-	-	-	-	-	-	-	-	-	-	-	-	-
Madison County	-	-	-	-	-	-	-	476 49.17 30.63 10.11 9.88	-	-	-	-	-	-	-	-	183 48.54 11.78 3.89 3.80

Notes: Please refer to the User's Guide for an explanation of data; data is arranged alphabetically by state, then county, then city within each county; table includes counties with populations greater than 49,999 unless noted and cities with populations greater than 9,999 whose Asian and/or NHPI population rates are greater than the national average; (1) Native Hawaiian and other Pacific Islander; (2) excludes Taiwanese; (3) includes Chamorro; (4) county does not meet population threshold but is shown in order to allow inclusion of city

Place	Total foreign-born naturalized citizens	Total Asian population	Asians who are foreign-born naturalized citizens	Total NHPI[1] population	NHPIs[1] who are foreign-born naturalized citizens	Asian Indian	Bangladeshi	Cambodian	Chinese[2]	Fijian	Filipino	Guamanian[3]	Hawaiian, Native	Hmong	Indonesian	Japanese	Korean	Laotian	Malaysian	Pakistani	Samoan	Sri Lankan	Taiwanese	Thai	Tongan	Vietnamese
Mobile County	3,792	5,256	1,617	-	-	170	-	75	188	-	136	-	-	-	-	-	-	107	-	-	-	-	-	-	-	675
	0.95		30.76			29.31		19.28	28.10		36.86							34.08								32.88
						10.51		4.64	11.63		8.41							6.62								41.74
			30.76			3.23		1.43	3.58		2.59							2.04								12.84
			42.64			4.48		1.98	4.96		3.59							2.82								17.80
Montgomery County	2,205	1,779	811	-	-	-	-	-	-	-	-	-	-	-	-	-	-	-	-	-	-	-	-	-	-	-
	0.99		45.59																							
			45.59																							
			36.78																							
Morgan County	1,156	571	235	-	-	-	-	-	-	-	-	-	-	-	-	-	-	-	-	-	-	-	-	-	-	-
	1.04		41.16																							
			41.16																							
			20.33																							
Shelby County	1,300	1,006	446	-	-	192	-	-	-	-	-	-	-	-	-	-	-	-	-	-	-	-	-	-	-	-
	0.91		44.33			49.61																				
						43.05																				
			44.33			19.09																				
			34.31			14.77																				
Tuscaloosa County	1,098	1,533	422	-	-	-	-	-	-	-	-	-	-	-	-	-	-	-	-	-	-	-	-	-	-	-
	0.67		27.53																							
			27.53																							
			38.43																							
ALASKA	20,011	25,496	9,849	3,122	430	233	-	-	688	-	5,112	-	7	113	-	241	2,303	192	-	-	248	-	-	318	82	306
	3.19		38.63		13.77	42.67			43.99		40.94		1.40	21.65		16.91	50.57	14.04			16.17			40.66	19.57	31.58
						2.37			6.99		51.90		1.63	1.15		2.45	23.38	1.95			57.67			3.23	19.07	3.11
			38.63		13.77	0.91			2.70		20.05		0.22	0.44		0.95	9.03	0.75			7.94			1.25	2.63	1.20
			49.22		2.15	1.16			3.44		25.55		0.03	0.56		1.20	11.51	0.96			1.24			1.59	0.41	1.53
Anchorage Borough	11,631	14,266	5,626	2,027	330	144	-	-	429	-	2,226	-	-	113	-	180	1,744	187	-	-	194	-	-	213	-	153
	4.47		39.44		16.28	45.57			49.65		44.20			21.65		20.34	50.58	14.78			16.06			36.92		31.61
						2.56			7.63		39.57			2.01		3.20	31.00	3.32			58.79			3.79		2.72
			39.44		16.28	1.01			3.01		15.60			0.79		1.26	12.22	1.31			9.57			1.49		1.07
			48.37		2.84	1.24			3.69		19.14			0.97		1.55	14.99	1.61			1.67			1.83		1.32
Fairbanks North Star Borough	1,735	2,001	818	-	-	-	-	-	122	-	304	-	-	-	-	-	243	-	-	-	-	-	-	-	-	-
	2.09		40.88						34.46		53.33						44.34									
									14.91		37.16						29.71									
			40.88						6.10		15.19						12.14									
			47.15						7.03		17.52						14.01									
Juneau City and Borough	1,042	1,396	592	-	-	-	-	-	-	-	471	-	-	-	-	-	-	-	-	-	-	-	-	-	-	-
	3.39		42.41								45.20															
											79.56															
			42.41								33.74															
			56.81								45.20															
Matanuska-Susitna Borough	813	385	195	-	-	-	-	-	-	-	-	-	-	-	-	-	-	-	-	-	-	-	-	-	-	-
	1.37		50.65																							
			50.65																							
			23.99																							

Notes: Please refer to the User's Guide for an explanation of data; data is arranged alphabetically by state, then county, then city within each county; table includes counties with populations greater than 49,999 unless noted and cities with populations greater than 9,999 whose Asian and/or NHPI population rates are greater than the national average; (1) Native Hawaiian and other Pacific Islander; (2) excludes Taiwanese; (3) includes Chamorro; (4) county does not meet population threshold but is shown in order to allow inclusion of city

Place	Total foreign-born naturalized citizens	Total Asian population	Asians who are foreign-born naturalized citizens	Total NHPI[1] population	NHPIs[1] who are foreign-born naturalized citizens	Asian Indian	Bangladeshi	Cambodian	Chinese[2]	Fijian	Filipino	Guamanian[3]	Hawaiian, Native	Hmong	Indonesian	Japanese	Korean	Laotian	Malaysian	Pakistani	Samoan	Sri Lankan	Taiwanese	Thai	Tongan	Vietnamese
ARIZONA	193,944	91,223	28,524	6,166	487	3,806	-	380	6,621	-	5,409	60	35	-	138	1,431	4,198	349	-	212	49	-	267	516	121	4,173
	3.78		31.27		7.90	26.23		30.65	31.43		33.38	4.74	1.76		24.08	19.22	42.25	39.17		31.55	5.76		33.63	31.64	19.09	35.65
						13.34		1.33	23.21		18.96	12.32	7.19		0.48	5.02	14.72	1.22		0.74	10.06		0.94	1.81	24.85	14.63
			31.27		7.90	4.17		0.42	7.26		5.93	0.97	0.57		0.15	1.57	4.60	0.38		0.23	0.79		0.29	0.57	1.96	4.57
			14.71		0.25	1.96		0.20	3.41		2.79	0.03	0.02		0.07	0.74	2.16	0.18		0.11	0.03		0.14	0.27	0.06	2.15
Cochise County	7,083	1,960	983	-	-	-	-	-	-	-	157	-	-	-	-	-	463	-	-	-	-	-	-	-	-	-
	6.02		50.15								36.60						60.37									
											15.97						47.10									
			50.15								8.01						23.62									
			13.88								2.22						6.54									
Coconino County	1,609	894	218	-	-	-	-	-	-	-	-	-	-	-	-	-	-	-	-	-	-	-	-	-	-	-
	1.38		24.38																							
			24.38																							
			13.55																							
Maricopa County	114,048	66,294	20,181	3,811	318	2,916	-	335	5,077	-	3,871	9	0	-	114	790	2,428	240	-	159	30	-	221	332	119	3,029
	3.71		30.44		8.34	25.83		28.25	32.74		32.53	1.39	0.00		27.67	16.21	40.15	39.93		30.58	5.42		34.42	28.97	22.58	33.98
						14.45		1.66	25.16		19.18	2.83	0.00		0.56	3.91	12.03	1.19		0.79	9.43		1.10	1.65	37.42	15.01
			30.44		8.34	4.40		0.51	7.66		5.84	0.24	0.00		0.17	1.19	3.66	0.36		0.24	0.79		0.33	0.50	3.12	4.57
			17.70		0.28	2.56		0.29	4.45		3.39	0.01	0.00		0.10	0.69	2.13	0.21		0.14	0.03		0.19	0.29	0.10	2.66
Chandler (city)	7,224	7,460	2,469	-	-	454	-	-	705	-	437	-	-	-	-	-	-	-	-	-	-	-	-	-	-	457
	4.10		33.10			29.25			34.76		37.58															47.90
						18.39			28.55		17.70															18.51
			33.10			6.09			9.45		5.86															6.13
			34.18			6.28			9.76		6.05															6.33
Gilbert (town)	3,211	4,016	1,244	-	-	285	-	-	338	-	154	-	-	-	-	-	-	-	-	-	-	-	-	-	-	-
	2.92		30.98			38.20			28.55		20.92															
						22.91			27.17		12.38															
			30.98			7.10			8.42		3.83															
			38.74			8.88			10.53		4.80															
Mesa (city)	11,573	6,022	2,028	647	54	193	-	-	352	-	557	-	-	-	-	104	323	-	-	-	-	-	-	-	-	317
	2.91		33.68		8.35	32.66			34.68		37.84					17.75	44.99									42.04
						9.52			17.36		27.47					5.13	15.93									15.63
			33.68		8.35	3.20			5.85		9.25					1.73	5.36									5.26
			17.52		0.47	1.67			3.04		4.81					0.90	2.79									2.74
Phoenix (city)	52,874	25,613	7,205	1,745	174	1,106	-	193	1,853	-	1,470	-	0	-	-	303	716	-	-	-	-	-	-	-	-	1,031
	4.00		28.13		9.97	24.95		34.90	33.28		29.21		0.00			19.15	36.22									23.26
						15.35		2.68	25.72		20.40		0.00			4.21	9.94									14.31
			28.13		9.97	4.32		0.75	7.23		5.74		0.00			1.18	2.80									4.03
			13.63		0.33	2.09		0.37	3.50		2.78		0.00			0.57	1.35									1.95
Tempe (city)	5,478	7,920	1,725	-	-	213	-	-	456	-	138	-	-	-	-	58	247	-	-	-	-	-	-	-	-	257
	3.46		21.78			11.28			23.51		23.35					9.08	35.80									32.13
						12.35			26.43		8.00					3.36	14.32									14.90
			21.78			2.69			5.76		1.74					0.73	3.12									3.24
			31.49			3.89			8.32		2.52					1.06	4.51									4.69
Mohave County	3,666	921	300	-	-	-	-	-	-	-	-	-	-	-	-	-	-	-	-	-	-	-	-	-	-	-
	2.36		32.57																							
			32.57																							
			8.18																							

Notes: Please refer to the User's Guide for an explanation of data; data is arranged alphabetically by state, then county, then city within each county; table includes counties with populations greater than 49,999 unless noted and cities with populations greater than 9,999 whose Asian and/or NHPI population rates are greater than the national average; (1) Native Hawaiian and other Pacific Islander; (2) excludes Taiwanese; (3) includes Chamorro; (4) county does not meet population threshold but is shown in order to allow inclusion of city

Place	Total foreign-born naturalized citizens	Total Asian population	Asians who are foreign-born naturalized citizens	Total NHPI[1] population	NHPIs[1] who are foreign-born naturalized citizens	Asian Indian	Bangladeshi	Cambodian	Chinese[2]	Fijian	Filipino	Guamanian[3]	Hawaiian, Native	Hmong	Indonesian	Japanese	Korean	Laotian	Malaysian	Pakistani	Samoan	Sri Lankan	Taiwanese	Thai	Tongan	Vietnamese
Pima County	39,665 4.70	16,907	5,481 32.42 32.42 13.82	1,084	110 10.15 10.15 0.28	593 29.75 10.82 3.51 1.50	-	-	1,190 25.36 21.71 7.04 3.00	-	885 36.86 16.15 5.23 2.23	-	35 7.51 31.82 3.23 0.09	-	-	325 21.75 5.93 1.92 0.82	922 41.27 16.82 5.45 2.32	-	-	-	-	-	-	-	-	905 39.92 16.51 5.35 2.28
Tucson (city)	24,548 5.04	11,641	3,192 27.42 27.42 13.00	734	80 10.90 10.90 0.33	301 22.41 9.43 2.59 1.23	-	-	566 17.82 17.73 4.86 2.31	-	541 30.90 16.95 4.65 2.20	-	-	-	-	241 24.20 7.55 2.07 0.98	434 34.01 13.60 3.73 1.77	-	-	-	-	-	-	-	-	686 36.92 21.49 5.89 2.79
Pinal County	4,326 2.41	993	254 25.58 25.58 5.87	-	-	-	-	-	-	-	-	-	-	-	-	-	-	-	-	-	-	-	-	-	-	-
Yavapai County	3,868 2.31	847	280 33.06 33.06 7.24	-	-	-	-	-	-	-	-	-	-	-	-	-	-	-	-	-	-	-	-	-	-	-
Yuma County	10,225 6.39	1,345	512 38.07 38.07 5.01	-	-	-	-	-	-	-	154 34.53 30.08 11.45 1.51	-	-	-	-	-	-	-	-	-	-	-	-	-	-	-
ARKANSAS	22,055 0.82	19,081	5,729 30.02 30.02 25.98	1,534	225 14.67 14.67 1.02	608 22.57 10.61 3.19 2.76	-	-	832 28.15 14.52 4.36 3.77	-	833 36.17 14.54 4.37 3.78	-	0 0.00 0.00 0.00 0.00	-	-	324 29.62 5.66 1.70 1.47	566 37.83 9.88 2.97 2.57	722 26.62 12.60 3.78 3.27	-	-	-	-	-	90 30.82 1.57 0.47 0.41	-	1,443 37.34 25.19 7.56 6.54
Benton County	2,393 1.56	1,495	405 27.09 27.09 16.92	-	-	36 8.59 8.89 2.41 1.50	-	-	-	-	-	-	-	-	-	-	-	-	-	-	-	-	-	-	-	158 41.15 39.01 10.57 6.60
Craighead County	316 0.38	517	83 16.05 16.05 26.27	-	-	-	-	-	-	-	-	-	-	-	-	-	-	-	-	-	-	-	-	-	-	-
Crawford County	506 0.95	631	172 27.26 27.26 33.99	-	-	-	-	-	-	-	-	-	-	-	-	-	-	-	-	-	-	-	-	-	-	-
Faulkner County	523 0.61	526	108 20.53 20.53 20.65	-	-	-	-	-	-	-	-	-	-	-	-	-	-	-	-	-	-	-	-	-	-	-

Notes: Please refer to the User's Guide for an explanation of data; data is arranged alphabetically by state, then county, then city within each county; table includes counties with populations greater than 49,999 unless noted and cities with populations greater than 9,999 whose Asian and/or NHPI population rates are greater than the national average; (1) Native Hawaiian and other Pacific Islander; (2) excludes Taiwanese; (3) includes Chamorro; (4) county does not meet population threshold but is shown in order to allow inclusion of city

Place	Total foreign-born naturalized citizens	Total Asian population	Asians who are foreign-born naturalized citizens	Total NHPI[1] population	NHPIs[1] who are foreign-born naturalized citizens	Asian Indian	Bangladeshi	Cambodian	Chinese[2]	Fijian	Filipino	Guamanian[3]	Hawaiian, Native	Hmong	Indonesian	Japanese	Korean	Laotian	Malaysian	Pakistani	Samoan	Sri Lankan	Taiwanese	Thai	Tongan	Vietnamese
Jefferson County	299	443	103	-	-	-	-	-	-	-	-	-	-	-	-	-	-	-	-	-	-	-	-	-	-	-
	0.35		23.25																							
			23.25																							
			34.45																							
Pulaski County	4,457	4,335	1,407	-	-	216	-	-	267	-	299	-	-	-	-	-	-	-	-	-	-	-	-	-	-	-
	1.23		32.46			22.34			30.69		44.76															
						15.35			18.98		21.25															
			32.46			4.98			6.16		6.90															
			31.57			4.85			5.99		6.71															
Saline County	475	454	143	-	-	-	-	-	-	-	-	-	-	-	-	-	-	-	-	-	-	-	-	-	-	-
	0.57		31.50																							
			31.50																							
			30.11																							
Sebastian County	2,208	3,581	1,303	-	-	-	-	-	-	-	-	-	-	-	-	-	-	416	-	-	-	-	-	-	-	687
	1.92		36.39															36.05								38.29
																		31.93								52.72
			36.39															11.62								19.18
			59.01															18.84								31.11
Fort Smith (city)	1,924	3,277	1,178	-	-	-	-	-	-	-	-	-	-	-	-	-	-	404	-	-	-	-	-	-	-	638
	2.39		35.95															35.98								37.24
																		34.30								54.16
			35.95															12.33								19.47
			61.23															21.00								33.16
Washington County	2,305	2,607	481	756	134	-	-	-	70	-	-	-	-	-	-	-	-	134	-	-	-	-	-	-	-	-
	1.46		18.45		17.72				8.92									24.32								
									14.55									27.86								
			18.45		17.72				2.69									5.14								
			20.87		5.81				3.04									5.81								
Springdale (city)	1,355	739	178	694	134	-	-	-	-	-	-	-	-	-	-	-	-	87	-	-	-	-	-	-	-	-
	2.94		24.09		19.31													20.67								
																		48.88								
			24.09		19.31													11.77								
			13.14		9.89													6.42								
CALIFORNIA	3,473,266	3,682,975	1,368,752	113,858	13,049	89,028	693	20,801	380,526	2,291	392,117	552	507	12,094	3,787	29,825	125,636	16,663	350	6,615	5,324	1,932	27,328	12,432	2,175	213,824
	10.25		37.16		11.46	28.99	25.22	29.19	41.63	27.24	42.62	2.70	2.58	17.60	23.11	10.31	36.55	29.29	19.88	33.35	13.68	35.67	42.98	34.39	17.88	47.89
						6.50	0.05	1.52	27.80	17.56	28.65	4.23	3.89	0.88	0.28	2.18	9.18	1.22	0.03	0.48	40.80	0.14	2.00	0.91	16.67	15.62
			37.16		11.46	2.42	0.02	0.56	10.33	2.01	10.65	0.48	0.45	0.33	0.10	0.81	3.41	0.45	0.01	0.18	4.68	0.05	0.74	0.34	1.91	5.81
			39.41		0.38	2.56	0.02	0.60	10.96	0.07	11.29	0.02	0.01	0.35	0.11	0.86	3.62	0.48	0.01	0.19	0.15	0.06	0.79	0.36	0.06	6.16
Alameda County	169,708	293,807	104,462	9,188	967	10,236	-	1,205	40,041	280	29,904	13	24	-	169	1,018	5,459	955	-	545	160	-	1,475	346	324	10,289
	11.75		35.55		10.52	24.47		30.87	37.44	19.14	42.92	0.99	1.87		26.28	8.19	37.57	30.20		27.54	6.65		37.48	23.81	17.69	43.73
						9.80		1.15	38.33	28.96	28.63	1.34	2.48		0.16	0.97	5.23	0.91		0.52	16.55		1.41	0.33	33.51	9.85
			35.55		10.52	3.48		0.41	13.63	3.05	10.18	0.14	0.26		0.06	0.35	1.86	0.33		0.19	1.74		0.50	0.12	3.53	3.50
			61.55		0.57	6.03		0.71	23.59	0.16	17.62	0.01	0.01		0.10	0.60	3.22	0.56		0.32	0.09		0.87	0.20	0.19	6.06
Alameda (city)	10,439	18,698	7,423	796	87	200	-	-	2,916	-	2,732	-	-	-	-	101	538	-	-	-	-	-	-	-	-	665
	14.45		39.70		10.93	18.66			39.23		45.18					14.39	43.70									51.04
						2.69			39.28		36.80					1.36	7.25									8.96
			39.70		10.93	1.07			15.60		14.61					0.54	2.88									3.56
			71.11		0.83	1.92			27.93		26.17					0.97	5.15									6.37

Notes: Please refer to the User's Guide for an explanation of data; data is arranged alphabetically by state, then county, then city within each county; table includes counties with populations greater than 49,999 unless noted and cities with populations greater than 9,999 whose Asian and/or NHPI population rates are greater than the national average; (1) Native Hawaiian and other Pacific Islander; (2) excludes Taiwanese; (3) includes Chamorro; (4) county does not meet population threshold but is shown in order to allow inclusion of city

Place	Total foreign-born naturalized citizens	Total Asian population	Asians who are foreign-born naturalized citizens	Total NHPI[1] population	NHPIs[1] who are foreign-born naturalized citizens	Asian Indian	Bangladeshi	Cambodian	Chinese[2]	Fijian	Filipino	Guamanian[3]	Hawaiian, Native	Hmong	Indonesian	Japanese	Korean	Laotian	Malaysian	Pakistani	Samoan	Sri Lankan	Taiwanese	Thai	Tongan	Vietnamese
Albany (city)	1,814	4,246	1,001	-	-	32	-	-	570	-	-	-	-	-	-	35	82	-	-	-	-	-	-	-	-	-
	11.03		23.58			9.67			27.70							5.44	15.77									
						3.20			56.94							3.50	8.19									
			23.58			0.75			13.42							0.82	1.93									
			55.18			1.76			31.42							1.93	4.52									
Ashland (cdp)	2,320	3,127	1,403	-	-	-	-	-	540	-	608	-	-	-	-	-	-	-	-	-	-	-	-	-	-	-
	11.17		44.87						55.96		45.85															
									38.49		43.34															
			44.87						17.27		19.44															
			60.47						23.28		26.21															
Berkeley (city)	8,916	16,660	4,311	-	-	355	-	-	1,954	-	384	-	-	-	-	115	524	-	-	-	-	-	157	-	-	427
	8.68		25.88			20.07			27.04		32.96					5.31	32.33						38.48			45.82
						8.23			45.33		8.91					2.67	12.15						3.64			9.90
			25.88			2.13			11.73		2.30					0.69	3.15						0.94			2.56
			48.35			3.98			21.92		4.31					1.29	5.88						1.76			4.79
Castro Valley (cdp)	5,712	7,317	2,826	-	-	336	-	-	1,260	-	615	-	-	-	-	62	344	-	-	-	-	-	-	-	-	-
	9.95		38.62			40.24			36.51		51.90					9.97	45.99									
						11.89			44.59		21.76					2.19	12.17									
			38.62			4.59			17.22		8.41					0.85	4.70									
			49.47			5.88			22.06		10.77					1.09	6.02									
Cherryland (cdp)	1,036	1,182	326	-	-	-	-	-	-	-	192	-	-	-	-	-	-	-	-	-	-	-	-	-	-	-
	7.52		27.58								30.72															
											58.90															
			27.58								16.24															
			31.47								18.53															
Dublin (city)	1,956	2,965	1,042	-	-	182	-	-	323	-	408	-	-	-	-	-	-	-	-	-	-	-	-	-	-	-
	6.51		35.14			31.82			35.53		51.78															
						17.47			31.00		39.16															
			35.14			6.14			10.89		13.76															
			53.27			9.30			16.51		20.86															
Fremont (city)	33,755	74,753	23,950	670	36	4,322	-	-	9,207	-	4,826	-	-	-	-	130	1,290	-	-	249	-	-	851	-	-	2,142
	16.59		32.04		5.37	20.89			35.02		42.33					8.37	32.40			22.60			34.71			49.30
						18.05			38.44		20.15					0.54	5.39			1.04			3.55			8.94
			32.04		5.37	5.78			12.32		6.46					0.17	1.73			0.33			1.14			2.87
			70.95		0.11	12.80			27.28		14.30					0.39	3.82			0.74			2.52			6.35
Hayward (city)	19,046	26,106	10,260	2,357	227	1,160	-	-	1,648	140	5,289	-	-	-	-	110	334	-	-	-	30	-	-	-	-	1,124
	13.61		39.30		9.63	32.53			44.86	16.61	42.11					8.65	40.83				5.15					43.11
						11.31			16.06	61.67	51.55					1.07	3.26				13.22					10.96
			39.30		9.63	4.44			6.31	5.94	20.26					0.42	1.28				1.27					4.31
			53.87		1.19	6.09			8.65	0.74	27.77					0.58	1.75				0.16					5.90
Livermore (city)	3,762	4,261	1,388	-	-	181	-	-	242	-	574	-	-	-	-	-	-	-	-	-	-	-	-	-	-	206
	5.12		32.57			29.92			31.80		35.34															43.83
						13.04			17.44		41.35															14.84
			32.57			4.25			5.68		13.47															4.83
			36.90			4.81			6.43		15.26															5.48
Newark (city)	5,922	9,249	3,402	-	-	495	-	-	609	-	1,282	-	-	-	-	-	193	-	-	-	-	-	-	-	-	385
	13.94		36.78			30.76			35.95		36.89						35.41									52.31
						14.55			17.90		37.68						5.67									11.32
			36.78			5.35			6.58		13.86						2.09									4.16
			57.45			8.36			10.28		21.65						3.26									6.50

Notes: Please refer to the User's Guide for an explanation of data; data is arranged alphabetically by state, then county, then city within each county; table includes counties with populations greater than 49,999 unless noted and cities with populations greater than 9,999 whose Asian and/or NHPI population rates are greater than the national average; (1) Native Hawaiian and other Pacific Islander; (2) excludes Taiwanese; (3) includes Chamorro; (4) county does not meet population threshold but is shown in order to allow inclusion of city

Place	Total foreign-born naturalized citizens	Total Asian population	Asians who are foreign-born naturalized citizens	Total NHPI[1] population	NHPIs[1] who are foreign-born naturalized citizens	Asian Indian	Bangladeshi	Cambodian	Chinese[2]	Fijian	Filipino	Guamanian[3]	Hawaiian, Native	Hmong	Indonesian	Japanese	Korean	Laotian	Malaysian	Pakistani	Samoan	Sri Lankan	Taiwanese	Thai	Tongan	Vietnamese
	37,783	60,110	22,333	2,581	275	539	-	756	12,900	-	2,918	-	-	-	-	158	781	604	-	-	-	-	-	-	183	2,940
	9.46		37.15		10.65	31.34		25.76	40.92		43.70					7.52	44.22	25.28							13.95	35.78
Oakland (city)						2.41		3.39	57.76		13.07					0.71	3.50	2.70							66.55	13.16
			37.15		10.65	0.90		1.26	21.46		4.85					0.26	1.30	1.00							7.09	4.89
			59.11		0.73	1.43		2.00	34.14		7.72					0.42	2.07	1.60							0.48	7.78
	936	1,805	615	-	-	-	-	-	497	-	-	-	-	-	-	-	-	-	-	-	-	-	-	-	-	-
	8.55		34.07						36.54																	
Piedmont (city)									80.81																	
			34.07						27.53																	
			65.71						53.10																	
	4,098	7,392	1,896	-	-	349	-	-	665	-	325	-	-	-	-	23	282	-	-	-	-	-	-	-	-	-
	6.45		25.65			22.07			25.42		38.88					3.33	43.79									
Pleasanton (city)						18.41			35.07		17.14					1.21	14.87									
			25.65			4.72			9.00		4.40					0.31	3.81									
			46.27			8.52			16.23		7.93					0.56	6.88									
	11,338	18,317	7,326	608	20	172	-	-	3,318	-	2,550	-	-	-	-	43	181	-	-	-	-	-	-	-	-	752
	14.30		40.00		3.29	24.50			40.36		41.05					8.13	39.52									58.29
San Leandro (city)						2.35			45.29		34.81					0.59	2.47									10.26
			40.00		3.29	0.94			18.11		13.92					0.23	0.99									4.11
			64.61		0.18	1.52			29.26		22.49					0.38	1.60									6.63
	2,571	3,479	1,513	-	-	-	-	-	376	-	726	-	-	-	-	-	-	-	-	-	-	-	-	-	-	92
	11.71		43.49						38.56		52.61															30.56
San Lorenzo (cdp)									24.85		47.98															6.08
			43.49						10.81		20.87															2.64
			58.85						14.62		28.24															3.58
	15,600	29,442	12,005	634	120	1,552	-	-	2,520	-	5,954	-	-	-	-	79	391	-	-	-	-	-	-	-	-	936
	23.33		40.78		18.93	28.86			42.29		45.35					16.22	41.46									45.73
Union City (city)						12.93			20.99		49.60					0.66	3.26									7.80
			40.78		18.93	5.27			8.56		20.22					0.27	1.33									3.18
			76.96		0.77	9.95			16.15		38.17					0.51	2.51									6.00
	5,920	6,553	1,435	-	-	114	-	-	294	-	90	-	-	436	-	87	-	128	-	-	-	-	-	-	-	-
	2.91		21.90			26.39			41.23		24.93			15.44		13.90		23.23								
Butte County						7.94			20.49		6.27			30.38		6.06		8.92								
			21.90			1.74			4.49		1.37			6.65		1.33		1.95								
			24.24			1.93			4.97		1.52			7.36		1.47		2.16								
	1,801	2,278	504	-	-	-	-	-	155	-	-	-	-	146	-	-	-	-	-	-	-	-	-	-	-	-
	3.03		22.12						37.90					20.03												
Chico (city)									30.75					28.97												
			22.12						6.80					6.41												
			27.98						8.61					8.11												
	395	729	128	-	-	-	-	-	-	-	-	-	-	100	-	-	-	-	-	-	-	-	-	-	-	-
	3.05		17.56											20.70												
Oroville (city)														78.13												
			17.56											13.72												
			32.41											25.32												
	82,317	103,198	38,076	3,391	487	3,772	-	-	10,854	121	14,339	11	25	-	144	697	1,738	1,714	-	234	121	-	792	224	90	2,471
	8.68		36.90		14.36	33.68			39.20	22.49	41.64	2.02	4.20		30.44	8.40	38.69	40.09		33.05	15.94		62.81	35.28	19.96	45.49
Contra Costa County						9.91			28.51	24.85	37.66	2.26	5.13		0.38	1.83	4.56	4.50		0.61	24.85		2.08	0.59	18.48	6.49
			36.90		14.36	3.66			10.52	3.57	13.89	0.32	0.74		0.14	0.68	1.68	1.66		0.23	3.57		0.77	0.22	2.65	2.39
			46.26		0.59	4.58			13.19	0.15	17.42	0.01	0.03		0.17	0.85	2.11	2.08		0.28	0.15		0.96	0.27	0.11	3.00

Notes: Please refer to the User's Guide for an explanation of data; data is arranged alphabetically by state, then county, then city within each county; table includes counties with populations greater than 49,999 unless noted and cities with populations greater than 9,999 whose Asian and/or NHPI population rates are greater than the national average; (1) Native Hawaiian and other Pacific Islander; (2) excludes Taiwanese; (3) includes Chamorro; (4) county does not meet population threshold but is shown in order to allow inclusion of city

Place	Total foreign-born naturalized citizens	Total Asian population	Asians who are foreign-born naturalized citizens	Total NHPI[1] population	NHPIs[1] who are foreign-born naturalized citizens	Asian Indian	Bangladeshi	Cambodian	Chinese[2]	Fijian	Filipino	Guamanian[3]	Hawaiian, Native	Hmong	Indonesian	Japanese	Korean	Laotian	Malaysian	Pakistani	Samoan	Sri Lankan	Taiwanese	Thai	Tongan	Vietnamese
Alamo (cdp)	1,057 6.98	863	292 33.84 33.84 27.63	-	-	-	-	-	-	-	-	-	-	-	-	-	-	-	-	-	-	-	-	-	-	-
Antioch (city)	5,724 6.30	6,674	2,422 36.29 36.29 42.31	408	53 12.99 12.99 0.93	82 23.23 3.39 1.23 1.43	-	-	392 35.00 16.18 5.87 6.85	-	1,279 36.37 52.81 19.16 22.34	-	-	-	-	-	-	-	-	-	-	-	-	-	-	268 56.42 11.07 4.02 4.68
Bay Point (cdp)	2,453 11.45	2,471	1,050 42.49 42.49 42.80	-	-	-	-	-	-	-	498 40.89 47.43 20.15 20.30	-	-	-	-	-	-	-	-	-	-	-	-	-	-	-
Blackhawk-Camino-Tass. (cdp)	1,217 12.21	1,682	694 41.26 41.26 57.03	-	-	-	-	-	381 39.56 54.90 22.65 31.31	-	-	-	-	-	-	-	-	-	-	-	-	-	-	-	-	-
Clayton (city)	584 5.41	596	170 28.52 28.52 29.11	-	-	-	-	-	-	-	-	-	-	-	-	-	-	-	-	-	-	-	-	-	-	-
Concord (city)	10,410 8.55	11,117	4,036 36.30 36.30 38.77	468	149 31.84 31.84 1.43	631 41.03 15.63 5.68 6.06	-	-	1,025 39.30 25.40 9.22 9.85	-	1,496 36.14 37.07 13.46 14.37	-	-	-	-	104 12.18 2.58 0.94 1.00	194 42.36 4.81 1.75 1.86	-	-	-	-	-	-	-	-	277 42.03 6.86 2.49 2.66
Danville (town)	2,909 6.91	3,588	1,200 33.44 33.44 41.25	-	-	163 35.51 13.58 4.54 5.60	-	-	514 33.05 42.83 14.33 17.67	-	201 43.70 16.75 5.60 6.91	-	-	-	-	-	-	-	-	-	-	-	-	-	-	-
El Cerrito (city)	3,061 13.21	5,634	1,919 34.06 34.06 62.69	-	-	96 25.60 5.00 1.70 3.14	-	-	1,179 47.79 61.44 20.93 38.52	-	179 37.45 9.33 3.18 5.85	-	-	-	-	75 6.09 3.91 1.33 2.45	-	-	-	-	-	-	-	-	-	-
El Sobrante (cdp)	871 7.51	1,349	393 29.13 29.13 45.12	-	-	52 14.40 13.23 3.85 5.97	-	-	-	-	-	-	-	-	-	-	-	-	-	-	-	-	-	-	-	-
Hercules (city)	4,442 23.02	8,291	3,776 45.54 45.54 85.01	-	-	261 38.61 6.91 3.15 5.88	-	-	797 49.72 21.11 9.61 17.94	-	2,296 46.52 60.81 27.69 51.69	-	-	-	-	-	-	-	-	-	-	-	-	-	-	-

Notes: Please refer to the User's Guide for an explanation of data; data is arranged alphabetically by state, then county, then city within each county; table includes counties with populations greater than 49,999 unless noted and cities with populations greater than 9,999 whose Asian and/or NHPI population rates are greater than the national average; (1) Native Hawaiian and other Pacific Islander; (2) excludes Taiwanese; (3) includes Chamorro; (4) county does not meet population threshold but is shown in order to allow inclusion of city

Place	Total foreign-born naturalized citizens	Total Asian population	Asians who are foreign-born naturalized citizens	Total NHPI[1] population	NHPIs[1] who are foreign-born naturalized citizens	Asian Indian	Bangladeshi	Cambodian	Chinese[2]	Fijian	Filipino	Guamanian[3]	Hawaiian, Native	Hmong	Indonesian	Japanese	Korean	Laotian	Malaysian	Pakistani	Samoan	Sri Lankan	Taiwanese	Thai	Tongan	Vietnamese
Lafayette (city)	1,447 6.17	1,660	583 35.12 35.12 40.29	-	-	-	-	-	361 44.35 61.92 21.75 24.95	-	-	-	-	-	-	-	-	-	-	-	-	-	-	-	-	-
Martinez (city)	1,950 5.39	2,319	865 37.30 37.30 44.36	-	-	-	-	-	205 42.44 23.70 8.84 10.51	-	373 38.30 43.12 16.08 19.13	-	-	-	-	-	-	-	-	-	-	-	-	-	-	-
Moraga (town)	1,602 9.63	2,163	804 37.17 37.17 50.19	-	-	-	-	-	456 37.07 56.72 21.08 28.46	-	-	-	-	-	-	-	-	-	-	-	-	-	-	-	-	-
Orinda (city)	1,283 7.35	1,524	436 28.61 28.61 33.98	-	-	-	-	-	273 30.57 62.61 17.91 21.28	-	-	-	-	-	-	-	-	-	-	-	-	-	-	-	-	-
Pinole (city)	2,725 14.05	4,095	1,752 42.78 42.78 64.29	-	-	-	-	-	414 47.05 23.63 10.11 15.19	-	974 48.39 55.59 23.79 35.74	-	-	-	-	-	-	-	-	-	-	-	-	-	-	-
Pittsburg (city)	5,723 10.07	7,248	2,760 38.08 38.08 48.23	554	109 19.68 19.68 1.90	254 26.60 9.20 3.50 4.44	-	-	182 40.44 6.59 2.51 3.18	-	2,001 41.91 72.50 27.61 34.96	-	-	-	-	-	-	-	-	-	-	-	-	-	-	-
Pleasant Hill (city)	2,123 6.46	3,286	759 23.10 23.10 35.75	-	-	-	-	-	184 20.04 24.24 5.60 8.67	-	234 27.89 30.83 7.12 11.02	-	-	-	-	-	148 28.35 19.50 4.50 6.97	-	-	-	-	-	-	-	-	-
Richmond (city)	9,452 9.48	12,088	4,530 37.48 37.48 47.93	401	44 10.97 10.97 0.47	418 37.59 9.23 3.46 4.42	-	-	1,230 39.51 27.15 10.18 13.01	-	1,271 45.79 28.06 10.51 13.45	-	-	-	-	65 7.36 1.43 0.54 0.69	102 22.08 2.25 0.84 1.08	1,023 43.00 22.58 8.46 10.82	-	-	-	-	-	-	-	121 26.13 2.67 1.00 1.28
San Pablo (city)	4,033 13.39	4,912	1,964 39.98 39.98 48.70	-	-	200 33.06 10.18 4.07 4.96	-	-	-	-	803 46.18 40.89 16.35 19.91	-	-	-	-	-	-	391 35.04 19.91 7.96 9.70	-	-	-	-	-	-	-	267 37.61 13.59 5.44 6.62
San Ramon (city)	4,039 9.08	6,804	2,328 34.22 34.22 57.64	-	-	323 23.19 13.87 4.75 8.00	-	-	1,024 38.05 43.99 15.05 25.35	-	442 47.07 18.99 6.50 10.94	-	-	-	-	20 4.43 0.86 0.29 0.50	-	-	-	-	-	-	-	-	-	-

Notes: Please refer to the User's Guide for an explanation of data; data is arranged alphabetically by state, then county, then city within each county; table includes counties with populations greater than 49,999 unless noted and cities with populations greater than 9,999 whose Asian and/or NHPI population rates are greater than the national average; (1) Native Hawaiian and other Pacific Islander; (2) excludes Taiwanese; (3) includes Chamorro; (4) county does not meet population threshold but is shown in order to allow inclusion of city

Place	Total foreign-born naturalized citizens	Total Asian population	Asians who are foreign-born naturalized citizens	Total NHPI[1] population	NHPIs[1] who are foreign-born naturalized citizens	Asian Indian	Bangladeshi	Cambodian	Chinese[2]	Fijian	Filipino	Guamanian[3]	Hawaiian, Native	Hmong	Indonesian	Japanese	Korean	Laotian	Malaysian	Pakistani	Samoan	Sri Lankan	Taiwanese	Thai	Tongan	Vietnamese
Walnut Creek (city)	6,266 9.70	6,201	2,205 35.56 35.56 35.19	-	-	258 46.15 11.70 4.16 4.12	-	-	982 37.11 44.54 15.84 15.67	-	481 39.56 21.81 7.76 7.68	-	-	-	-	49 5.88 2.22 0.79 0.78	226 46.03 10.25 3.64 3.61	-	-	-	-	-	-	-	-	-
El Dorado County	4,548 2.91	3,055	835 27.33 27.33 18.36	-	-	-	-	-	-	-	376 27.67 45.03 12.31 8.27	-	-	-	-	18 3.56 2.16 0.59 0.40	-	-	-	-	-	-	-	-	-	-
El Dorado Hills (cdp)	564 3.12	658	162 24.62 24.62 28.72	-	-	-	-	-	-	-	-	-	-	-	-	-	-	-	-	-	-	-	-	-	-	-
South Lake Tahoe (city)	1,251 5.27	1,415	395 27.92 27.92 31.57	-	-	-	-	-	-	-	263 26.75 66.58 18.59 21.02	-	-	-	-	-	-	-	-	-	-	-	-	-	-	-
Fresno County	49,397 6.18	63,895	14,662 22.95 22.95 29.68	652	21 3.22 3.22 0.04	2,056 29.52 14.02 3.22 4.16	-	697 17.72 4.75 1.09 1.41	1,587 32.75 10.82 2.48 3.21	-	2,513 40.47 17.14 3.93 5.09	-	-	4,418 18.37 30.13 6.91 8.94	-	418 7.31 2.85 0.65 0.85	478 35.83 3.26 0.75 0.97	1,167 18.61 7.96 1.83 2.36	-	-	-	-	-	-	-	863 40.61 5.89 1.35 1.75
Clovis (city)	2,580 3.78	4,429	1,171 26.44 26.44 45.39	-	-	-	-	-	-	-	217 31.91 18.53 4.90 8.41	-	-	424 23.57 36.21 9.57 16.43	-	45 8.21 3.84 1.02 1.74	-	-	-	-	-	-	-	-	-	-
Fresno (city)	26,304 6.16	48,485	10,739 22.15 22.15 40.83	-	-	995 26.75 9.27 2.05 3.78	-	648 17.95 6.03 1.34 2.46	1,327 35.65 12.36 2.74 5.04	-	1,776 40.14 16.54 3.66 6.75	-	-	3,518 17.29 32.76 7.26 13.37	-	211 7.93 1.96 0.44 0.80	315 33.58 2.93 0.65 1.20	1,002 18.28 9.33 2.07 3.81	-	-	-	-	-	-	-	658 38.08 6.13 1.36 2.50
Reedley (city)	1,657 7.98	782	220 28.13 28.13 13.28	-	-	-	-	-	-	-	-	-	-	-	-	-	-	-	-	-	-	-	-	-	-	-
Humboldt County	2,739 2.16	1,859	436 23.45 23.45 15.92	-	-	-	-	-	-	-	-	-	-	-	-	15 5.24 3.44 0.81 0.55	-	-	-	-	-	-	-	-	-	-
Imperial County	17,942 12.60	2,819	640 22.70 22.70 3.57	-	-	-	-	-	139 23.44 21.72 4.93 0.77	-	275 31.21 42.97 9.76 1.53	-	-	-	-	-	109 22.11 17.03 3.87 0.61	-	-	-	-	-	-	-	-	-

Notes: Please refer to the User's Guide for an explanation of data; data is arranged alphabetically by state, then county, then city within each county; table includes counties with populations greater than 49,999 unless noted and cities with populations greater than 9,999 whose Asian and/or NHPI population rates are greater than the national average; (1) Native Hawaiian and other Pacific Islander; (2) excludes Taiwanese; (3) includes Chamorro; (4) county does not meet population threshold but is shown in order to allow inclusion of city

Place	Total foreign-born naturalized citizens	Total Asian population	Asians who are foreign-born naturalized citizens	Total NHPI[1] population	NHPIs[1] who are foreign-born naturalized citizens	Asian Indian	Bangladeshi	Cambodian	Chinese[2]	Fijian	Filipino	Guamanian[3]	Hawaiian, Native	Hmong	Indonesian	Japanese	Korean	Laotian	Malaysian	Pakistani	Samoan	Sri Lankan	Taiwanese	Thai	Tongan	Vietnamese
Kern County	33,590	21,562	7,151	778	21	1,386	-	92	679	-	3,651	-	-	-	-	121	485	-	-	-	-	-	-	-	-	364
	5.08		33.16		2.70	33.37		21.35	32.69		34.60					11.60	38.40									56.09
						19.38		1.29	9.50		51.06					1.69	6.78									5.09
			33.16		2.70	6.43		0.43	3.15		16.93					0.56	2.25									1.69
			21.29		0.06	4.13		0.27	2.02		10.87					0.36	1.44									1.08
Bakersfield (city)	11,229	10,499	3,284	468	21	986	-	-	449	-	939	-	-	-	-	51	280	-	-	-	-	-	-	-	-	268
	4.54		31.28		4.49	31.31			29.81		34.28					7.86	28.99									61.05
						30.02			13.67		28.59					1.55	8.53									8.16
			31.28		4.49	9.39			4.28		8.94					0.49	2.67									2.55
			29.25		0.19	8.78			4.00		8.36					0.45	2.49									2.39
Delano (city)	5,097	6,027	1,997	-	-	-	-	-	-	-	1,868	-	-	-	-	-	-	-	-	-	-	-	-	-	-	-
	13.08		33.13								33.24															
											93.54															
			33.13								30.99															
			39.18								36.65															
Ridgecrest (city)	721	1,036	395	-	-	-	-	-	-	-	220	-	-	-	-	-	-	-	-	-	-	-	-	-	-	-
	2.86		38.13								44.99															
											55.70															
			38.13								21.24															
			54.79								30.51															
Kings County	6,206	3,771	1,488	-	-	-	-	-	-	-	1,158	-	-	-	-	-	-	-	-	-	-	-	-	-	-	-
	4.79		39.46								47.05															
											77.82															
			39.46								30.71															
			23.98								18.66															
Lemoore (city)	1,322	1,434	688	-	-	-	-	-	-	-	563	-	-	-	-	-	-	-	-	-	-	-	-	-	-	-
	6.77		47.98								52.52															
											81.83															
			47.98								39.26															
			52.04								42.59															
Lake County	1,706	529	132	-	-	-	-	-	-	-	-	-	-	-	-	-	-	-	-	-	-	-	-	-	-	-
	2.93		24.95																							
			24.95																							
			7.74																							
Los Angeles County	1,311,755	1,134,263	428,680	27,221	3,474	21,396	309	9,733	123,835	179	115,150	187	102	58	1,322	10,510	65,641	1,364	115	1,711	2,212	812	15,073	7,115	322	40,661
	13.78		37.79		12.76	36.27	23.32	32.39	42.50	36.31	43.95	5.96	2.32	13.18	23.50	9.34	35.40	43.27	21.54	36.18	16.32	33.27	43.38	36.37	14.15	51.96
						4.99	0.07	2.27	28.89	5.15	26.86	5.38	2.94	0.01	0.31	2.45	15.31	0.32	0.03	0.40	63.67	0.19	3.52	1.66	9.27	9.49
			37.79		12.76	1.89	0.03	0.86	10.92	0.66	10.15	0.69	0.37	0.01	0.12	0.93	5.79	0.12	0.01	0.15	8.13	0.07	1.33	0.63	1.18	3.58
			32.68		0.26	1.63	0.02	0.74	9.44	0.01	8.78	0.01	0.01	<0.01	0.10	0.80	5.00	0.10	0.01	0.13	0.17	0.06	1.15	0.54	0.02	3.10
Agoura Hills (city)	1,653	1,242	521	-	-	-	-	-	-	-	-	-	-	-	-	-	-	-	-	-	-	-	-	-	-	-
	8.13		41.95																							
			41.95																							
			31.52																							
Alhambra (city)	22,888	40,563	17,714	-	-	177	-	-	11,593	-	849	-	-	-	-	184	369	-	-	-	-	-	749	-	-	2,407
	26.63		43.67			34.44			44.00		44.47					12.25	41.84						48.07			54.77
						1.00			65.45		4.79					1.04	2.08						4.23			13.59
			43.67			0.44			28.58		2.09					0.45	0.91						1.85			5.93
			77.39			0.77			50.65		3.71					0.80	1.61						3.27			10.52

Notes: Please refer to the User's Guide for an explanation of data; data is arranged alphabetically by state, then county, then city within each county; table includes counties with populations greater than 49,999 unless noted and cities with populations greater than 9,999 whose Asian and/or NHPI population rates are greater than the national average; (1) Native Hawaiian and other Pacific Islander; (2) excludes Taiwanese; (3) includes Chamorro; (4) county does not meet population threshold but is shown in order to allow inclusion of city

Place	Total foreign-born naturalized citizens	Total Asian population	Asians who are foreign-born naturalized citizens	Total NHPI[1] population	NHPIs[1] who are foreign-born naturalized citizens	Asian Indian	Bangladeshi	Cambodian	Chinese[2]	Fijian	Filipino	Guamanian[3]	Hawaiian, Native	Hmong	Indonesian	Japanese	Korean	Laotian	Malaysian	Pakistani	Samoan	Sri Lankan	Taiwanese	Thai	Tongan	Vietnamese
Altadena (cdp)	4,070 9.57	1,758	505 28.73 28.73 12.41	-	-	-	-	-	-	-	134 42.68 26.53 7.62 3.29	-	-	-	-	20 3.19 3.96 1.14 0.49	-	-	-	-	-	-	-	-	-	-
Arcadia (city)	11,540 21.79	23,996	8,867 36.95 36.95 76.84	-	-	279 42.47 3.15 1.16 2.42	-	-	5,383 38.47 60.71 22.43 46.65	-	403 50.12 4.54 1.68 3.49	-	-	-	-	63 5.49 0.71 0.26 0.55	622 32.18 7.01 2.59 5.39	-	-	-	-	-	1,518 40.45 17.12 6.33 13.15	-	-	-
Artesia (city)	3,377 20.62	4,524	1,480 32.71 32.71 43.83	-	-	93 19.42 6.28 2.06 2.75	-	-	264 41.44 17.84 5.84 7.82	-	638 35.66 43.11 14.10 18.89	-	-	-	-	-	182 20.80 12.30 4.02 5.39	-	-	-	-	-	-	-	-	-
Avocado Heights (cdp)	2,468 16.30	1,362	578 42.44 42.44 23.42	-	-	-	-	-	-	-	-	-	-	-	-	-	-	-	-	-	-	-	-	-	-	-
Azusa (city)	4,467 10.07	2,430	946 38.93 38.93 21.18	-	-	-	-	-	-	-	487 40.82 51.48 20.04 10.90	-	-	-	-	-	-	-	-	-	-	-	-	-	-	-
Baldwin Park (city)	13,228 17.46	9,017	3,955 43.86 43.86 29.90	-	-	-	-	-	1,282 45.87 32.41 14.22 9.69	-	1,661 40.84 42.00 18.42 12.56	-	-	-	-	-	-	-	-	-	-	-	-	-	-	515 54.21 13.02 5.71 3.89
Bellflower (city)	8,188 11.24	7,181	2,800 38.99 38.99 34.20	-	-	-	-	288 53.93 10.29 4.01 3.52	-	-	1,310 35.86 46.79 18.24 16.00	-	-	-	-	-	298 32.08 10.64 4.15 3.64	-	-	-	-	-	-	140 35.99 5.00 1.95 1.71	-	-
Beverly Hills (city)	7,979 23.59	2,570	864 33.62 33.62 10.83	-	-	-	-	-	232 45.22 26.85 9.03 2.91	-	-	-	-	-	-	-	245 26.86 28.36 9.53 3.07	-	-	-	-	-	-	-	-	-
Burbank (city)	16,180 16.13	9,089	3,463 38.10 38.10 21.40	-	-	346 36.31 9.99 3.81 2.14	-	-	401 44.56 11.58 4.41 2.48	-	1,326 40.17 38.29 14.59 8.20	-	-	-	-	65 10.38 1.88 0.72 0.40	708 35.76 20.44 7.79 4.38	-	-	-	-	-	-	-	-	261 49.81 7.54 2.87 1.61
Calabasas (city)	2,350 11.69	1,652	650 39.35 39.35 27.66	-	-	-	-	-	204 40.16 31.38 12.35 8.68	-	-	-	-	-	-	-	-	-	-	-	-	-	-	-	-	-

Notes: Please refer to the User's Guide for an explanation of data; data is arranged alphabetically by state, then county, then city within each county; table includes counties with populations greater than 49,999 unless noted and cities with populations greater than 9,999 whose Asian and/or NHPI population rates are greater than the national average; (1) Native Hawaiian and other Pacific Islander; (2) excludes Taiwanese; (3) includes Chamorro; (4) county does not meet population threshold but is shown in order to allow inclusion of city

Place	Total foreign-born naturalized citizens	Total Asian population	Asians who are foreign-born naturalized citizens	Total NHPI[1] population	NHPIs[1] who are foreign-born naturalized citizens	Asian Indian	Bangladeshi	Cambodian	Chinese[2]	Fijian	Filipino	Guamanian[3]	Hawaiian, Native	Hmong	Indonesian	Japanese	Korean	Laotian	Malaysian	Pakistani	Samoan	Sri Lankan	Taiwanese	Thai	Tongan	Vietnamese
Carson (city)	15,728	20,156	8,748	1,929	127	-	-	-	181	-	7,727	-	-	-	-	35	-	-	-	-	121	-	-	-	-	267
	17.56		43.40		6.58				36.13		44.58					5.55					8.41					83.18
									2.07		88.33					0.40					95.28					3.05
			43.40		6.58				0.90		38.34					0.17					6.27					1.32
			55.62		0.81				1.15		49.13					0.22					0.77					1.70
Cerritos (city)	14,909	30,185	12,578	-	-	1,184	-	-	2,647	-	3,071	-	-	-	-	187	3,089	-	-	-	-	-	798	185	-	823
	28.95		41.67			40.19			45.71		53.64					9.32	34.99						44.56	39.70		65.32
						9.41			21.04		24.42					1.49	24.56						6.34	1.47		6.54
			41.67			3.92			8.77		10.17					0.62	10.23						2.64	0.61		2.73
			84.37			7.94			17.75		20.60					1.25	20.72						5.35	1.24		5.52
Citrus (cdp)	1,467	784	318	-	-	-	-	-	-	-	-	-	-	-	-	-	-	-	-	-	-	-	-	-	-	-
	13.78		40.56																							
			40.56																							
			21.68																							
Claremont (city)	2,989	3,983	1,246	-	-	147	-	-	317	-	-	-	-	-	-	-	206	-	-	-	-	-	-	-	-	-
	8.80		31.28			27.43			29.68								33.72									
						11.80			25.44								16.53									
			31.28			3.69			7.96								5.17									
			41.69			4.92			10.61								6.89									
Compton (city)	7,041	420	155	1,028	240	-	-	-	-	-	-	-	-	-	-	-	-	-	-	-	211	-	-	-	-	-
	7.55		36.90		23.35																21.51					
																					87.92					
			36.90		23.35																20.53					
			2.20		3.41																3.00					
Covina (city)	4,776	4,565	1,866	-	-	-	-	-	537	-	495	-	-	-	-	50	-	-	-	-	-	-	-	-	-	256
	10.13		40.88						46.02		36.59					12.53										57.92
									28.78		26.53					2.68										13.72
			40.88						11.76		10.84					1.10										5.61
			39.07						11.24		10.36					1.05										5.36
Culver City (city)	5,341	4,738	1,693	-	-	215	-	-	364	-	516	-	-	-	-	178	-	-	-	-	-	-	-	-	-	-
	13.76		35.73			34.62			47.09		51.70					12.95										
						12.70			21.50		30.48					10.51										
			35.73			4.54			7.68		10.89					3.76										
			31.70			4.03			6.82		9.66					3.33										
Diamond Bar (city)	12,799	23,831	9,358	-	-	974	-	-	2,857	-	1,491	-	-	-	-	70	2,097	-	-	-	-	-	908	-	-	418
	22.71		39.27			39.24			37.25		47.51					10.16	37.47						43.26			60.06
						10.41			30.53		15.93					0.75	22.41						9.70			4.47
			39.27			4.09			11.99		6.26					0.29	8.80						3.81			1.75
			73.12			7.61			22.32		11.65					0.55	16.38						7.09			3.27
Downey (city)	17,241	7,814	2,995	-	-	173	-	-	245	-	756	-	-	-	-	47	1,125	-	-	-	-	-	-	-	-	265
	16.06		38.33			38.36			47.76		39.27					12.47	35.39									64.32
						5.78			8.18		25.24					1.57	37.56									8.85
			38.33			2.21			3.14		9.67					0.60	14.40									3.39
			17.37			1.00			1.42		4.38					0.27	6.53									1.54
Duarte (city)	3,445	2,730	1,113	-	-	-	-	-	210	-	533	-	-	-	-	-	-	-	-	-	-	-	-	-	-	-
	16.03		40.77						47.84		37.77															
									18.87		47.89															
			40.77						7.69		19.52															
			32.31						6.10		15.47															

Notes: Please refer to the User's Guide for an explanation of data; data is arranged alphabetically by state, then county, then city within each county; table includes counties with populations greater than 49,999 unless noted and cities with populations greater than 9,999 whose Asian and/or NHPI population rates are greater than the national average; (1) Native Hawaiian and other Pacific Islander; (2) excludes Taiwanese; (3) includes Chamorro; (4) county does not meet population threshold but is shown in order to allow inclusion of city

Place	Total foreign-born naturalized citizens	Total Asian population	Asians who are foreign-born naturalized citizens	Total NHPI[1] population	NHPIs[1] who are foreign-born naturalized citizens	Asian Indian	Bangladeshi	Cambodian	Chinese[2]	Fijian	Filipino	Guamanian[3]	Hawaiian, Native	Hmong	Indonesian	Japanese	Korean	Laotian	Malaysian	Pakistani	Samoan	Sri Lankan	Taiwanese	Thai	Tongan	Vietnamese
East San Gabriel (cdp)	3,363	6,104	2,452	-	-	-	-	-	1,527	-	-	-	-	-	-	91	-	-	-	-	-	-	241	-	-	-
	23.05		40.17						43.58							16.28							37.60			
									62.28							3.71							9.83			
			40.17						25.02							1.49							3.95			
			72.91						45.41							2.71							7.17			
El Monte (city)	19,300	21,529	9,791	-	-	-	-	-	5,518	-	515	-	-	-	-	-	-	-	-	-	-	-	206	-	-	2,832
	16.60		45.48						47.16		53.15												51.37			44.47
									56.36		5.26												2.10			28.92
			45.48						25.63		2.39												0.96			13.15
			50.73						28.59		2.67												1.07			14.67
El Segundo (city)	1,020	1,063	417	-	-	-	-	-	-	-	-	-	-	-	-	-	-	-	-	-	-	-	-	-	-	-
	6.39		39.23																							
			39.23																							
			40.88																							
Gardena (city)	8,106	15,458	4,280	-	-	-	-	-	446	-	781	-	-	-	-	660	1,454	-	-	-	-	-	-	-	-	646
	14.02		27.69						50.62		44.20					9.87	38.83									50.04
									10.42		18.25					15.42	33.97									15.09
			27.69						2.89		5.05					4.27	9.41									4.18
			52.80						5.50		9.63					8.14	17.94									7.97
Glendale (city)	52,023	31,944	12,017	-	-	321	-	-	1,260	-	5,099	-	-	-	-	149	4,005	-	-	-	-	-	-	152	-	675
	26.67		37.62			33.09			46.46		44.11					8.86	32.10							36.19		70.90
						2.67			10.49		42.43					1.24	33.33							1.26		5.62
			37.62			1.00			3.94		15.96					0.47	12.54							0.48		2.11
			23.10			0.62			2.42		9.80					0.29	7.70							0.29		1.30
Glendora (city)	4,368	3,254	1,422	-	-	187	-	-	406	-	408	-	-	-	-	-	-	-	-	-	-	-	-	-	-	-
	8.79		43.70			35.08			46.77		49.33															
						13.15			28.55		28.69															
			43.70			5.75			12.48		12.54															
			32.55			4.28			9.29		9.34															
Hacienda Heights (cdp)	11,520	19,225	7,693	-	-	-	-	-	3,993	-	534	-	-	-	-	132	1,024	-	-	-	-	-	1,215	-	-	197
	21.69		40.02						43.77		39.79					9.92	39.83						42.26			40.87
									51.90		6.94					1.72	13.31						15.79			2.56
			40.02						20.77		2.78					0.69	5.33						6.32			1.02
			66.78						34.66		4.64					1.15	8.89						10.55			1.71
Hawaiian Gardens (city)	1,914	1,292	492	-	-	-	-	-	-	-	-	-	-	-	-	-	333	-	-	-	-	-	-	-	-	-
	12.83		38.08														44.11									
																	67.68									
			38.08														25.77									
			25.71														17.40									
Hawthorne (city)	10,183	5,948	2,632	546	8	198	-	-	295	-	1,006	-	-	-	-	13	-	-	-	-	-	-	-	-	-	790
	12.13		44.25		1.47	41.16			54.23		45.19					2.90										53.49
						7.52			11.21		38.22					0.49										30.02
			44.25		1.47	3.33			4.96		16.91					0.22										13.28
			25.85		0.08	1.94			2.90		9.88					0.13										7.76
Hermosa Beach (city)	638	864	135	-	-	-	-	-	-	-	-	-	-	-	-	-	-	-	-	-	-	-	-	-	-	-
	3.46		15.63																							
			15.63																							
			21.16																							

Notes: Please refer to the User's Guide for an explanation of data; data is arranged alphabetically by state, then county, then city within each county; table includes counties with populations greater than 49,999 unless noted and cities with populations greater than 9,999 whose Asian and/or NHPI population rates are greater than the national average; (1) Native Hawaiian and other Pacific Islander; (2) excludes Taiwanese; (3) includes Chamorro; (4) county does not meet population threshold but is shown in order to allow inclusion of city

Place	Total foreign-born naturalized citizens	Total Asian population	Asians who are foreign-born naturalized citizens	Total NHPI[1] population	NHPIs[1] who are foreign-born naturalized citizens	Asian Indian	Bangladeshi	Cambodian	Chinese[2]	Fijian	Filipino	Guamanian[3]	Hawaiian, Native	Hmong	Indonesian	Japanese	Korean	Laotian	Malaysian	Pakistani	Samoan	Sri Lankan	Taiwanese	Thai	Tongan	Vietnamese
La Canada Flintridge (city)	2,497	3,981	1,323	-	-	-	-	-	331	-	-	-	-	-	-	19	766	-	-	-	-	-	-	-	-	-
	12.25		33.23						43.04							4.99	34.35									
									25.02							1.44	57.90									
			33.23						8.31							0.48	19.24									
			52.98						13.26							0.76	30.68									
La Crescenta-Montrose (cdp)	2,939	3,524	1,259	-	-	-	-	-	-	-	136	-	-	-	-	-	871	-	-	-	-	-	-	-	-	-
	15.97		35.73								39.08						34.83									
											10.80						69.18									
			35.73								3.86						24.72									
			42.84								4.63						29.64									
La Mirada (city)	6,132	6,968	2,969	-	-	219	-	-	362	-	1,049	-	-	-	-	33	845	-	-	-	-	-	-	-	-	-
	13.11		42.61			42.20			51.27		47.68					8.46	36.52									
						7.38			12.19		35.33					1.11	28.46									
			42.61			3.14			5.20		15.05					0.47	12.13									
			48.42			3.57			5.90		17.11					0.54	13.78									
La Puente (city)	6,046	2,883	1,369	-	-	-	-	-	361	-	548	-	-	-	-	-	-	-	-	-	-	-	-	-	-	-
	14.74		47.49						40.93		54.69															
									26.37		40.03															
			47.49						12.52		19.01															
			22.64						5.97		9.06															
La Verne (city)	2,693	2,372	989	-	-	-	-	-	-	-	336	-	-	-	-	-	-	-	-	-	-	-	-	-	-	-
	8.46		41.69								38.40															
											33.97															
			41.69								14.17															
			36.72								12.48															
Lakewood (city)	8,110	10,432	4,014	762	255	205	-	293	437	-	2,030	-	-	-	-	75	433	-	-	-	241	-	-	-	-	282
	10.21		38.48		33.46	47.56		40.03	43.10		42.50					10.36	29.99				40.30					63.80
						5.11		7.30	10.89		50.57					1.87	10.79				94.51					7.03
			38.48		33.46	1.97		2.81	4.19		19.46					0.72	4.15				31.63					2.70
			49.49		3.14	2.53		3.61	5.39		25.03					0.92	5.34				2.97					3.48
Lancaster (city)	6,844	4,596	1,877	-	-	278	-	-	189	-	884	-	-	-	-	-	-	-	-	-	-	-	-	-	-	-
	5.76		40.84			43.57			37.95		42.50															
						14.81			10.07		47.10															
			40.84			6.05			4.11		19.23															
			27.43			4.06			2.76		12.92															
Lawndale (city)	4,737	2,928	1,374	463	18	-	-	-	-	-	305	-	-	-	-	-	-	-	-	-	-	-	-	-	-	712
	14.93		46.93		3.89						46.49															54.06
											22.20															51.82
			46.93		3.89						10.42															24.32
			29.01		0.38						6.44															15.03
Lomita (city)	1,915	2,265	648	-	-	-	-	-	-	-	197	-	-	-	-	46	165	-	-	-	-	-	-	-	-	-
	9.58		28.61								43.01					7.41	30.84									
											30.40					7.10	25.46									
			28.61								8.70					2.03	7.28									
			33.84								10.29					2.40	8.62									
Long Beach (city)	45,713	55,040	19,452	5,145	886	403	-	4,978	1,209	-	7,857	-	-	-	-	391	798	181	-	-	710	-	-	197	-	2,455
	9.91		35.34		17.22	33.81		28.11	38.55		43.74					10.90	45.97	24.39			19.02			32.62		48.39
						2.07		25.59	6.22		40.39					2.01	4.10	0.93			80.14			1.01		12.62
			35.34		17.22	0.73		9.04	2.20		14.28					0.71	1.45	0.33			13.80			0.36		4.46
			42.55		1.94	0.88		10.89	2.64		17.19					0.86	1.75	0.40			1.55			0.43		5.37

Notes: Please refer to the User's Guide for an explanation of data; data is arranged alphabetically by state, then county, then city within each county; table includes counties with populations greater than 49,999 unless noted and cities with populations greater than 9,999 whose Asian and/or NHPI population rates are greater than the national average; (1) Native Hawaiian and other Pacific Islander; (2) excludes Taiwanese; (3) includes Chamorro; (4) county does not meet population threshold but is shown in order to allow inclusion of city

Place	Total foreign-born naturalized citizens	Total Asian population	Asians who are foreign-born naturalized citizens	Total NHPI[1] population	NHPIs[1] who are foreign-born naturalized citizens	Asian Indian	Bangladeshi	Cambodian	Chinese[2]	Fijian	Filipino	Guamanian[3]	Hawaiian, Native	Hmong	Indonesian	Japanese	Korean	Laotian	Malaysian	Pakistani	Samoan	Sri Lankan	Taiwanese	Thai	Tongan	Vietnamese
Los Angeles (city)	509,841	368,644	132,527	6,445	740	7,948	171	1,359	24,725	-	43,826	118	33	-	419	3,657	31,191	372	-	416	300	261	1,583	2,946	64	10,072
	13.80		35.95		11.48	32.94	20.58	32.30	41.16		42.97	10.27	2.05		23.41	9.95	34.17	53.99		24.82	14.60	21.61	47.59	32.43	18.71	51.63
						6.00	0.13	1.03	18.66		33.07	15.95	4.46		0.32	2.76	23.54	0.28		0.31	40.54	0.20	1.19	2.22	8.65	7.60
			35.95		11.48	2.16	0.05	0.37	6.71		11.89	1.83	0.51		0.11	0.99	8.46	0.10		0.11	4.65	0.07	0.43	0.80	0.99	2.73
			25.99		0.15	1.56	0.03	0.27	4.85		8.60	0.02	0.01		0.08	0.72	6.12	0.07		0.08	0.06	0.05	0.31	0.58	0.01	1.98
Manhattan Beach (city)	1,853	2,023	624	-	-	-	-	-	216	-	-	-	-	-	-	44	-	-	-	-	-	-	-	-	-	-
	5.44		30.85						38.71							7.21										
									34.62							7.05										
			30.85						10.68							2.17										
			33.68						11.66							2.37										
Monrovia (city)	3,469	2,480	994	-	-	-	-	-	266	-	389	-	-	-	-	-	-	-	-	-	-	-	-	-	-	-
	9.42		40.08						37.89		42.24															
									26.76		39.13															
			40.08						10.73		15.69															
			28.65						7.67		11.21															
Montebello (city)	11,101	7,022	2,424	-	-	-	-	-	1,201	-	398	-	-	-	-	161	248	-	-	-	-	-	-	-	-	-
	17.92		34.52						47.56		45.75					8.99	39.49									
									49.55		16.42					6.64	10.23									
			34.52						17.10		5.67					2.29	3.53									
			21.84						10.82		3.59					1.45	2.23									
Monterey Park (city)	18,086	36,674	14,952	-	-	-	-	142	10,432	-	360	-	-	-	-	480	479	-	-	-	-	-	496	-	-	1,540
	30.18		40.77					34.38	45.91		42.65					9.97	55.76						47.19			47.55
								0.95	69.77		2.41					3.21	3.20						3.32			10.30
			40.77					0.39	28.45		0.98					1.31	1.31						1.35			4.20
			82.67					0.79	57.68		1.99					2.65	2.65						2.74			8.51
Norwalk (city)	14,845	12,174	5,101	-	-	474	-	261	380	-	1,959	-	-	-	-	66	875	-	-	-	-	-	-	-	-	535
	14.38		41.90			35.35		51.89	40.86		43.75					13.81	34.76									62.35
						9.29		5.12	7.45		38.40					1.29	17.15									10.49
			41.90			3.89		2.14	3.12		16.09					0.54	7.19									4.39
			34.36			3.19		1.76	2.56		13.20					0.44	5.89									3.60
Palmdale (city)	10,113	4,308	2,125	-	-	196	-	-	-	-	1,109	-	-	-	-	-	-	-	-	-	-	-	-	-	-	-
	8.68		49.33			46.12					50.57															
						9.22					52.19															
			49.33			4.55					25.74															
			21.01			1.94					10.97															
Palos Verdes Estates (city)	1,467	2,317	730	-	-	-	-	-	249	-	-	-	-	-	-	50	121	-	-	-	-	-	-	-	-	-
	11.00		31.51						45.36							7.50	41.87									
									34.11							6.85	16.58									
			31.51						10.75							2.16	5.22									
			49.76						16.97							3.41	8.25									
Pasadena (city)	16,378	13,378	4,020	-	-	270	-	-	1,374	-	962	-	-	-	-	80	429	-	-	-	-	-	-	-	-	547
	12.23		30.05			31.65			32.88		37.03					3.56	30.80									71.13
						6.72			34.18		23.93					1.99	10.67									13.61
			30.05			2.02			10.27		7.19					0.60	3.21									4.09
			24.55			1.65			8.39		5.87					0.49	2.62									3.34
Pomona (city)	16,417	10,733	3,841	-	-	216	-	179	622	-	1,211	-	-	-	-	71	-	211	-	-	-	-	-	-	-	765
	10.97		35.79			34.02		23.65	31.10		42.48					13.76		39.59								43.79
						5.62		4.66	16.19		31.53					1.85		5.49								19.92
			35.79			2.01		1.67	5.80		11.28					0.66		1.97								7.13
			23.40			1.32		1.09	3.79		7.38					0.43		1.29								4.66

Notes: Please refer to the User's Guide for an explanation of data; data is arranged alphabetically by state, then county, then city within each county; table includes counties with populations greater than 49,999 unless noted and cities with populations greater than 9,999 whose Asian and/or NHPI population rates are greater than the national average; (1) Native Hawaiian and other Pacific Islander; (2) excludes Taiwanese; (3) includes Chamorro; (4) county does not meet population threshold but is shown in order to allow inclusion of city

Place	Total foreign-born naturalized citizens	Total Asian population	Asians who are foreign-born naturalized citizens	Total NHPI[1] population	NHPIs[1] who are foreign-born naturalized citizens	Asian Indian	Bangladeshi	Cambodian	Chinese[2]	Fijian	Filipino	Guamanian[3]	Hawaiian, Native	Hmong	Indonesian	Japanese	Korean	Laotian	Malaysian	Pakistani	Samoan	Sri Lankan	Taiwanese	Thai	Tongan	Vietnamese
Rancho Palos Verdes (city)	6,450	10,372	3,555	-	-	247	-	-	1,312	-	344	-	-	-	-	289	918	-	-	-	-	-	303	-	-	-
	15.62		34.27			43.64			49.60		58.70					9.46	37.78						56.11			
						6.95			36.91		9.68					8.13	25.82						8.52			
			34.27			2.38			12.65		3.32					2.79	8.85						2.92			
			55.12			3.83			20.34		5.33					4.48	14.23						4.70			
Redondo Beach (city)	5,555	5,896	1,718	-	-	173	-	-	417	-	387	-	-	-	-	118	306	-	-	-	-	-	-	-	-	-
	8.78		29.14			34.39			34.52		48.68					5.91	45.74									
						10.07			24.27		22.53					6.87	17.81									
			29.14			2.93			7.07		6.56					2.00	5.19									
			30.93			3.11			7.51		6.97					2.12	5.51									
Rosemead (city)	14,755	25,917	11,380	-	-	-	-	318	6,788	-	321	-	-	-	-	82	-	-	-	-	-	-	-	-	-	2,653
	27.69		43.91					41.03	45.34		44.71					10.50										44.68
								2.79	59.65		2.82					0.72										23.31
			43.91					1.23	26.19		1.24					0.32										10.24
			77.13					2.16	46.00		2.18					0.56										17.98
Rowland Heights (cdp)	12,306	24,773	9,616	-	-	454	-	-	4,393	-	1,579	-	-	-	-	52	1,295	-	-	-	-	-	962	-	-	366
	25.46		38.82			43.49			38.46		48.20					7.90	34.77						37.10			58.65
						4.72			45.68		16.42					0.54	13.47						10.00			3.81
			38.82			1.83			17.73		6.37					0.21	5.23						3.88			1.48
			78.14			3.69			35.70		12.83					0.42	10.52						7.82			2.97
San Dimas (city)	3,756	3,172	1,442	-	-	-	-	-	581	-	340	-	-	-	-	-	-	-	-	-	-	-	-	-	-	-
	10.71		45.46						48.58		44.16															
									40.29		23.58															
			45.46						18.32		10.72															
			38.39						15.47		9.05															
San Gabriel (city)	10,371	19,190	8,082	-	-	-	-	-	5,036	-	681	-	-	-	-	39	-	-	-	-	-	-	291	-	-	1,214
	26.39		42.12						42.98		58.61					6.22							38.14			45.52
									62.31		8.43					0.48							3.60			15.02
			42.12						26.24		3.55					0.20							1.52			6.33
			77.93						48.56		6.57					0.38							2.81			11.71
San Marino (city)	3,225	6,071	2,739	-	-	-	-	-	1,679	-	-	-	-	-	-	-	-	-	-	-	-	-	838	-	-	-
	24.86		45.12						42.89														54.91			
									61.30														30.60			
			45.12						27.66														13.80			
			84.93						52.06														25.98			
Santa Clarita (city)	10,700	7,586	3,000	-	-	391	-	-	412	-	1,181	-	-	-	-	84	329	-	-	-	-	-	-	-	-	295
	7.07		39.55			51.45			47.91		47.45					7.51	40.72									58.30
						13.03			13.73		39.37					2.80	10.97									9.83
			39.55			5.15			5.43		15.57					1.11	4.34									3.89
			28.04			3.65			3.85		11.04					0.79	3.07									2.76
Santa Monica (city)	10,594	5,986	1,819	-	-	242	-	-	550	-	254	-	-	-	-	183	341	-	-	-	-	-	-	-	-	-
	12.60		30.39			38.47			34.59		52.05					9.98	45.90									
						13.30			30.24		13.96					10.06	18.75									
			30.39			4.04			9.19		4.24					3.06	5.70									
			17.17			2.28			5.19		2.40					1.73	3.22									
Sierra Madre (city)	707	566	165	-	-	-	-	-	-	-	-	-	-	-	-	-	-	-	-	-	-	-	-	-	-	-
	6.68		29.15																							
			29.15																							
			23.34																							

Notes: Please refer to the User's Guide for an explanation of data; data is arranged alphabetically by state, then county, then city within each county; table includes counties with populations greater than 49,999 unless noted and cities with populations greater than 9,999 whose Asian and/or NHPI population rates are greater than the national average; (1) Native Hawaiian and other Pacific Islander; (2) excludes Taiwanese; (3) includes Chamorro; (4) county does not meet population threshold but is shown in order to allow inclusion of city

Place	Total foreign-born naturalized citizens	Total Asian population	Asians who are foreign-born naturalized citizens	Total NHPI[1] population	NHPIs[1] who are foreign-born naturalized citizens	Asian Indian	Bangladeshi	Cambodian	Chinese[2]	Fijian	Filipino	Guamanian[3]	Hawaiian, Native	Hmong	Indonesian	Japanese	Korean	Laotian	Malaysian	Pakistani	Samoan	Sri Lankan	Taiwanese	Thai	Tongan	Vietnamese
South El Monte (city)	3,002	1,597	712	-	-	-	-	-	346	-	-	-	-	-	-	-	-	-	-	-	-	-	-	-	-	246
	14.34		44.58						50.07																	38.92
									48.60																	34.55
			44.58						21.67																	15.40
			23.72						11.53																	8.19
South Pasadena (city)	3,070	6,249	2,000	-	-	-	-	-	1,386	-	-	-	-	-	-	50	113	-	-	-	-	-	-	-	-	-
	12.63		32.01						41.50							5.02	16.64									
									69.30							2.50	5.65									
			32.01						22.18							0.80	1.81									
			65.15						45.15							1.63	3.68									
South San Jose Hills (cdp)	3,018	1,241	458	-	-	-	-	-	-	-	300	-	-	-	-	-	-	-	-	-	-	-	-	-	-	-
	14.95		36.91								41.15															
											65.50															
			36.91								24.17															
			15.18								9.94															
Temple City (city)	7,410	12,936	5,487	-	-	-	-	-	3,252	-	338	-	-	-	-	48	203	-	-	-	-	-	670	-	-	525
	22.25		42.42						41.10		52.08					8.33	40.44						43.73			61.98
									59.27		6.16					0.87	3.70						12.21			9.57
			42.42						25.14		2.61					0.37	1.57						5.18			4.06
			74.05						43.89		4.56					0.65	2.74						9.04			7.09
Torrance (city)	18,711	39,445	10,840	-	-	773	-	-	2,291	-	1,643	-	-	-	-	1,002	2,985	-	-	246	-	-	533	-	-	888
	13.57		27.48			35.07			38.80		46.29					7.42	34.99			37.50			41.32			48.34
						7.13			21.13		15.16					9.24	27.54			2.27			4.92			8.19
			27.48			1.96			5.81		4.17					2.54	7.57			0.62			1.35			2.25
			57.93			4.13			12.24		8.78					5.36	15.95			1.31			2.85			4.75
Valinda (cdp)	3,606	1,936	849	-	-	-	-	-	-	-	420	-	-	-	-	-	-	-	-	-	-	-	-	-	-	274
	16.55		43.85								41.63															57.81
											49.47															32.27
			43.85								21.69															14.15
			23.54								11.65															7.60
Vincent (cdp)	2,064	1,093	497	-	-	-	-	-	-	-	288	-	-	-	-	-	-	-	-	-	-	-	-	-	-	-
	13.67		45.47								46.45															
											57.95															
			45.47								26.35															
			24.08								13.95															
Walnut (city)	8,215	16,880	6,853	-	-	358	-	-	2,426	-	1,770	-	-	-	-	32	770	-	-	-	-	-	677	-	-	324
	27.38		40.60			44.75			38.43		51.27					7.34	40.70						35.15			56.35
						5.22			35.40		25.83					0.47	11.24						9.88			4.73
			40.60			2.12			14.37		10.49					0.19	4.56						4.01			1.92
			83.42			4.36			29.53		21.55					0.39	9.37						8.24			3.94
West Carson (cdp)	3,689	5,067	1,735	-	-	-	-	-	-	-	883	-	-	-	-	85	449	-	-	-	-	-	-	-	-	-
	17.45		34.24								41.63					7.60	52.21									
											50.89					4.90	25.88									
			34.24								17.43					1.68	8.86									
			47.03								23.94					2.30	12.17									
West Covina (city)	19,213	23,749	10,294	449	30	185	-	-	3,044	-	4,485	-	-	-	-	27	339	-	-	-	-	-	402	-	-	1,205
	18.32		43.34		6.68	36.93			46.04		44.66					3.73	36.97						42.41			55.79
						1.80			29.57		43.57					0.26	3.29						3.91			11.71
			43.34		6.68	0.78			12.82		18.89					0.11	1.43						1.69			5.07
			53.58		0.16	0.96			15.84		23.34					0.14	1.76						2.09			6.27

Notes: Please refer to the User's Guide for an explanation of data; data is arranged alphabetically by state, then county, then city within each county; table includes counties with populations greater than 49,999 unless noted and cities with populations greater than 9,999 whose Asian and/or NHPI population rates are greater than the national average; (1) Native Hawaiian and other Pacific Islander; (2) excludes Taiwanese; (3) includes Chamorro; (4) county does not meet population threshold but is shown in order to allow inclusion of city

Place	Total foreign-born naturalized citizens	Total Asian population	Asians who are foreign-born naturalized citizens	Total NHPI[1] population	NHPIs[1] who are foreign-born naturalized citizens	Asian Indian	Bangladeshi	Cambodian	Chinese[2]	Fijian	Filipino	Guamanian[3]	Hawaiian, Native	Hmong	Indonesian	Japanese	Korean	Laotian	Malaysian	Pakistani	Samoan	Sri Lankan	Taiwanese	Thai	Tongan	Vietnamese
West Hollywood (city)	7,200 20.16	1,412	455 32.22 32.22 6.32	-	-	-	-	-	-	-	-	-	-	-	-	-	-	-	-	-	-	-	-	-	-	-
West Puente Valley (cdp)	4,143 18.06	1,733	837 48.30 48.30 20.20	-	-	-	-	-	-	-	343 46.99 40.98 19.79 8.28	-	-	-	-	-	-	-	-	-	-	-	-	-	-	240 51.95 28.67 13.85 5.79
Whittier (city)	6,532 7.79	3,270	1,127 34.46 34.46 17.25	-	-	-	-	-	425 35.48 37.71 13.00 6.51	-	286 43.47 25.38 8.75 4.38	-	-	-	-	28 6.47 2.48 0.86 0.43	131 37.32 11.62 4.01 2.01	-	-	-	-	-	-	-	-	-
Madera County	6,089 4.95	1,544	548 35.49 35.49 9.00	-	-	251 43.58 45.80 16.26 4.12	-	-	-	-	173 39.41 31.57 11.20 2.84	-	-	-	-	-	-	-	-	-	-	-	-	-	-	-
Marin County	17,086 6.91	10,961	3,685 33.62 33.62 21.57	-	-	472 32.71 12.81 4.31 2.76	-	-	1,158 36.40 31.42 10.56 6.78	-	408 32.80 11.07 3.72 2.39	-	-	-	-	236 14.63 6.40 2.15 1.38	442 37.62 11.99 4.03 2.59	-	-	-	-	-	-	-	-	631 49.61 17.12 5.76 3.69
Larkspur (city)	865 7.21	440	124 28.18 28.18 14.34	-	-	-	-	-	-	-	-	-	-	-	-	-	-	-	-	-	-	-	-	-	-	-
Novato (city)	3,568 7.47	2,515	963 38.29 38.29 26.99	-	-	-	-	-	281 43.36 29.18 11.17 7.88	-	173 36.89 17.96 6.88 4.85	-	-	-	-	-	-	-	-	-	-	-	-	-	-	-
San Rafael (city)	4,633 8.25	3,163	1,090 34.46 34.46 23.53	-	-	119 22.93 10.92 3.76 2.57	-	-	334 33.27 30.64 10.56 7.21	-	-	-	-	-	-	-	-	-	-	-	-	-	-	-	-	334 49.63 30.64 10.56 7.21
Tamalpais-Homestead (cdp)	720 6.80	508	143 28.15 28.15 19.86	-	-	-	-	-	-	-	-	-	-	-	-	-	-	-	-	-	-	-	-	-	-	-
Mendocino County	2,485 2.88	826	261 31.60 31.60 10.50	-	-	-	-	-	-	-	-	-	-	-	-	-	-	-	-	-	-	-	-	-	-	-

Notes: Please refer to the User's Guide for an explanation of data; data is arranged alphabetically by state, then county, then city within each county; table includes counties with populations greater than 49,999 unless noted and cities with populations greater than 9,999 whose Asian and/or NHPI population rates are greater than the national average; (1) Native Hawaiian and other Pacific Islander; (2) excludes Taiwanese; (3) includes Chamorro; (4) county does not meet population threshold but is shown in order to allow inclusion of city

Place	Total foreign-born naturalized citizens	Total Asian population	Asians who are foreign-born naturalized citizens	Total NHPI[1] population	NHPIs[1] who are foreign-born naturalized citizens	Asian Indian	Bangladeshi	Cambodian	Chinese[2]	Fijian	Filipino	Guamanian[3]	Hawaiian, Native	Hmong	Indonesian	Japanese	Korean	Laotian	Malaysian	Pakistani	Samoan	Sri Lankan	Taiwanese	Thai	Tongan	Vietnamese
Merced County	16,809 7.98	14,464	3,811 26.35 26.35 22.67	-	-	739 34.57 19.39 5.11 4.40	-	-	206 45.68 5.41 1.42 1.23	-	562 37.10 14.75 3.89 3.34	-	-	1,207 18.33 31.67 8.34 7.18	-	68 12.57 1.78 0.47 0.40	-	528 30.64 13.85 3.65 3.14	-	-	-	-	-	-	-	-
Atwater (city)	1,651 7.21	1,238	469 37.88 37.88 28.41	-	-	-	-	-	-	-	-	-	-	96 24.43 20.47 7.75 5.81	-	-	-	-	-	-	-	-	-	-	-	-
Livingston (city)	1,463 14.14	1,553	470 30.26 30.26 32.13	-	-	390 31.33 82.98 25.11 26.66	-	-	-	-	-	-	-	-	-	-	-	-	-	-	-	-	-	-	-	-
Merced (city)	4,663 7.29	7,099	1,629 22.95 22.95 34.93	-	-	-	-	-	-	-	-	-	-	782 18.50 48.00 11.02 16.77	-	-	-	441 31.64 27.07 6.21 9.46	-	-	-	-	-	-	-	-
Monterey County	33,530 8.35	24,221	8,311 34.31 34.31 24.79	1,823	125 6.86 6.86 0.37	306 23.72 3.68 1.26 0.91	-	-	647 30.16 7.78 2.67 1.93	-	4,201 36.48 50.55 17.34 12.53	9 1.34 7.20 0.49 0.03	-	-	-	821 24.64 9.88 3.39 2.45	1,336 46.88 16.08 5.52 3.98	-	-	-	-	-	-	-	-	705 36.12 8.48 2.91 2.10
Marina (city)	2,614 10.43	4,223	1,619 38.34 38.34 61.94	504	52 10.32 10.32 1.99	-	-	-	-	-	576 45.50 35.58 13.64 22.04	-	-	-	-	129 34.49 7.97 3.05 4.93	557 44.49 34.40 13.19 21.31	-	-	-	-	-	-	-	-	228 31.02 14.08 5.40 8.72
Monterey (city)	2,312 7.77	2,342	593 25.32 25.32 25.65	-	-	-	-	-	97 22.15 16.36 4.14 4.20	-	149 33.79 25.13 6.36 6.44	-	-	-	-	85 11.61 14.33 3.63 3.68	-	-	-	-	-	-	-	-	-	-
Pacific Grove (city)	1,104 7.14	660	279 42.27 42.27 25.27	-	-	-	-	-	-	-	-	-	-	-	-	-	-	-	-	-	-	-	-	-	-	-
Salinas (city)	12,814 8.50	9,091	2,742 30.16 30.16 21.40	547	46 8.41 8.41 0.36	139 24.05 5.07 1.53 1.08	-	-	124 21.57 4.52 1.36 0.97	-	1,921 32.33 70.06 21.13 14.99	-	-	-	-	133 16.92 4.85 1.46 1.04	174 37.02 6.35 1.91 1.36	-	-	-	-	-	-	-	-	211 44.23 7.70 2.32 1.65
Seaside (city)	2,992 9.41	3,347	1,219 36.42 36.42 40.74	-	-	-	-	-	-	-	767 38.76 62.92 22.92 25.64	-	-	-	-	160 38.28 13.13 4.78 5.35	-	-	-	-	-	-	-	-	-	110 23.45 9.02 3.29 3.68

Notes: Please refer to the User's Guide for an explanation of data; data is arranged alphabetically by state, then county, then city within each county; table includes counties with populations greater than 49,999 unless noted and cities with populations greater than 9,999 whose Asian and/or NHPI population rates are greater than the national average; (1) Native Hawaiian and other Pacific Islander; (2) excludes Taiwanese; (3) includes Chamorro; (4) county does not meet population threshold but is shown in order to allow inclusion of city

Place	Total foreign-born naturalized citizens	Total Asian population	Asians who are foreign-born naturalized citizens	Total NHPI[1] population	NHPIs[1] who are foreign-born naturalized citizens	Asian Indian	Bangladeshi	Cambodian	Chinese[2]	Fijian	Filipino	Guamanian[3]	Hawaiian, Native	Hmong	Indonesian	Japanese	Korean	Laotian	Malaysian	Pakistani	Samoan	Sri Lankan	Taiwanese	Thai	Tongan	Vietnamese
Napa County	7,241 5.83	3,936	1,498 38.06 38.06 20.69	-	-	-	-	-	153 27.57 10.21 3.89 2.11	-	880 44.09 58.74 22.36 12.15	-	-	-	-	19 4.58 1.27 0.48 0.26	-	-	-	-	-	-	-	-	-	-
Nevada County	2,061 2.24	593	94 15.85 15.85 4.56	-	-	-	-	-	-	-	-	-	-	-	-	-	-	-	-	-	-	-	-	-	-	-
Orange County	322,592 11.33	386,344	155,731 40.31 40.31 48.27	8,530	933 10.94 10.94 0.29	9,372 34.83 6.02 2.43 2.91	-	2,066 46.24 1.33 0.53 0.64	22,062 44.28 14.17 5.71 6.84	-	19,697 40.26 12.65 5.10 6.11	20 1.81 2.14 0.23 0.01	28 1.65 3.00 0.33 0.01	415 39.34 0.27 0.11 0.13	506 26.52 0.32 0.13 0.16	3,007 10.03 1.93 0.78 0.93	20,621 35.87 13.24 5.34 6.39	1,041 35.72 0.67 0.27 0.32	-	985 37.42 0.63 0.25 0.31	628 16.88 67.31 7.36 0.19	238 35.16 0.15 0.06 0.07	4,114 44.51 2.64 1.06 1.28	1,074 34.00 0.69 0.28 0.33	71 12.22 7.61 0.83 0.02	67,030 49.22 43.04 17.35 20.78
Aliso Viejo (cdp)	3,902 9.70	4,377	1,557 35.57 35.57 39.90	-	-	134 24.68 8.61 3.06 3.43	-	-	290 41.43 18.63 6.63 7.43	-	311 35.95 19.97 7.11 7.97	-	-	-	-	61 10.45 3.92 1.39 1.56	187 38.80 12.01 4.27 4.79	-	-	-	-	-	-	-	-	344 67.06 22.09 7.86 8.82
Anaheim (city)	38,125 11.65	39,590	15,633 39.49 39.49 41.00	1,094	73 6.67 6.67 0.19	1,598 38.74 10.22 4.04 4.19	-	-	1,684 43.31 10.77 4.25 4.42	-	2,979 38.48 19.06 7.52 7.81	-	-	-	-	292 13.25 1.87 0.74 0.77	2,449 36.88 15.67 6.19 6.42	259 32.54 1.66 0.65 0.68	-	135 31.84 0.86 0.34 0.35	51 9.19 69.86 4.66 0.13	-	263 39.31 1.68 0.66 0.69	153 33.55 0.98 0.39 0.40	-	5,175 48.97 33.10 13.07 13.57
Brea (city)	2,936 8.36	3,155	1,201 38.07 38.07 40.91	-	-	212 46.39 17.65 6.72 7.22	-	-	275 56.35 22.90 8.72 9.37	-	206 40.95 17.15 6.53 7.02	-	-	-	-	-	235 28.62 19.57 7.45 8.00	-	-	-	-	-	-	-	-	-
Buena Park (city)	10,678 13.63	16,914	6,021 35.60 35.60 56.39	-	-	801 46.01 13.30 4.74 7.50	-	-	613 44.65 10.18 3.62 5.74	-	1,968 38.65 32.69 11.64 18.43	-	-	-	-	78 10.46 1.30 0.46 0.73	1,471 27.63 24.43 8.70 13.78	-	-	-	-	-	-	-	-	487 48.99 8.09 2.88 4.56
Costa Mesa (city)	8,665 7.97	7,878	3,107 39.44 39.44 35.86	652	65 9.97 9.97 0.75	66 15.38 2.12 0.84 0.76	-	-	405 42.32 13.04 5.14 4.67	-	555 41.64 17.86 7.04 6.41	-	-	-	-	110 7.29 3.54 1.40 1.27	297 50.34 9.56 3.77 3.43	-	-	-	-	-	-	-	-	1,289 57.52 41.49 16.36 14.88
Cypress (city)	5,752 12.36	9,470	3,594 37.95 37.95 62.48	-	-	285 41.07 7.93 3.01 4.95	-	-	699 47.45 19.45 7.38 12.15	-	782 44.89 21.76 8.26 13.60	-	-	-	-	106 11.25 2.95 1.12 1.84	844 32.80 23.48 8.91 14.67	-	-	-	-	-	324 43.55 9.02 3.42 5.63	-	-	380 49.61 10.57 4.01 6.61
Foothill Ranch (cdp)	970 8.89	1,713	590 34.44 34.44 60.82	-	-	-	-	-	-	-	-	-	-	-	-	-	-	-	-	-	-	-	-	-	-	-

Notes: Please refer to the User's Guide for an explanation of data; data is arranged alphabetically by state, then county, then city within each county; table includes counties with populations greater than 49,999 unless noted and cities with populations greater than 9,999 whose Asian and/or NHPI population rates are greater than the national average; (1) Native Hawaiian and other Pacific Islander; (2) excludes Taiwanese; (3) includes Chamorro; (4) county does not meet population threshold but is shown in order to allow inclusion of city

Place	Total foreign-born naturalized citizens	Total Asian population	Asians who are foreign-born naturalized citizens	Total NHPI[1] population	NHPIs[1] who are foreign-born naturalized citizens	Asian Indian	Bangladeshi	Cambodian	Chinese[2]	Fijian	Filipino	Guamanian[3]	Hawaiian, Native	Hmong	Indonesian	Japanese	Korean	Laotian	Malaysian	Pakistani	Samoan	Sri Lankan	Taiwanese	Thai	Tongan	Vietnamese
Fountain Valley (city)	9,764	14,421	6,784	-	-	201	-	-	1,282	-	241	-	-	-	-	168	464	-	-	-	-	-	184	-	-	3,952
	17.75		47.04			27.20			52.65		40.64					11.86	43.57						46.35			55.53
						2.96			18.90		3.55					2.48	6.84						2.71			58.25
			47.04			1.39			8.89		1.67					1.16	3.22						1.28			27.40
			69.48			2.06			13.13		2.47					1.72	4.75						1.88			40.48
Fullerton (city)	13,582	20,248	7,010	-	-	675	-	-	1,169	-	787	-	-	-	-	130	2,936	-	-	-	-	-	-	-	-	795
	10.76		34.62			36.78			41.91		35.76					11.48	32.67									50.32
						9.63			16.68		11.23					1.85	41.88									11.34
			34.62			3.33			5.77		3.89					0.64	14.50									3.93
			51.61			4.97			8.61		5.79					0.96	21.62									5.85
Garden Grove (city)	29,909	51,029	21,200	1,266	211	260	-	260	1,259	-	1,175	-	-	-	-	130	1,817	-	-	-	153	-	-	-	-	15,575
	18.05		41.55		16.67	35.91		52.00	48.93		39.94					12.45	29.97				19.79					44.47
						1.23		1.23	5.94		5.54					0.61	8.57				72.51					73.47
			41.55		16.67	0.51		0.51	2.47		2.30					0.25	3.56				12.09					30.52
			70.88		0.71	0.87		0.87	4.21		3.93					0.43	6.08				0.51					52.07
Huntington Beach (city)	16,744	17,636	7,573	359	24	449	-	-	1,417	-	654	-	-	-	-	269	867	-	-	-	-	-	354	-	-	3,238
	8.82		42.94		6.69	44.41			47.92		39.16					9.42	51.85						61.35			55.11
						5.93			18.71		8.64					3.55	11.45						4.67			42.76
			42.94		6.69	2.55			8.03		3.71					1.53	4.92						2.01			18.36
			45.23		0.14	2.68			8.46		3.91					1.61	5.18						2.11			19.34
Irvine (city)	22,294	42,386	13,670	-	-	1,220	-	-	4,176	-	1,073	-	-	-	-	331	2,397	-	-	-	-	-	1,093	-	-	2,796
	15.59		32.25			26.23			36.55		32.20					6.45	30.02						41.69			57.63
						8.92			30.55		7.85					2.42	17.53						8.00			20.45
			32.25			2.88			9.85		2.53					0.78	5.66						2.58			6.60
			61.32			5.47			18.73		4.81					1.48	10.75						4.90			12.54
La Habra (city)	5,395	3,397	1,193	-	-	-	-	-	200	-	251	-	-	-	-	-	447	-	-	-	-	-	-	-	-	-
	9.11		35.12						41.93		42.40						36.70									
									16.76		21.04						37.47									
			35.12						5.89		7.39						13.16									
			22.11						3.71		4.65						8.29									
La Palma (city)	3,167	6,574	2,508	-	-	248	-	-	412	-	598	-	-	-	-	58	844	-	-	-	-	-	-	-	-	-
	20.93		38.15			41.33			44.21		48.54					8.07	35.15									
						9.89			16.43		23.84					2.31	33.65									
			38.15			3.77			6.27		9.10					0.88	12.84									
			79.19			7.83			13.01		18.88					1.83	26.65									
Laguna Hills (city)	3,584	3,259	1,373	-	-	-	-	-	241	-	328	-	-	-	-	-	-	-	-	-	-	-	-	-	-	325
	11.46		42.13						42.28		52.48															57.02
									17.55		23.89															23.67
			42.13						7.39		10.06															9.97
			38.31						6.72		9.15															9.07
Laguna Niguel (city)	5,763	4,689	2,089	-	-	-	-	-	543	-	371	-	-	-	-	141	344	-	-	-	-	-	-	-	-	304
	9.30		44.55						54.14		43.85					16.51	50.89									65.52
									25.99		17.76					6.75	16.47									14.55
			44.55						11.58		7.91					3.01	7.34									6.48
			36.25						9.42		6.44					2.45	5.97									5.28
Lake Forest (city)	5,372	5,447	2,219	-	-	225	-	-	382	-	337	-	-	-	-	73	310	-	-	-	-	-	-	-	-	723
	9.14		40.74			30.49			56.43		32.31					12.72	53.73									52.01
						10.14			17.21		15.19					3.29	13.97									32.58
			40.74			4.13			7.01		6.19					1.34	5.69									13.27
			41.31			4.19			7.11		6.27					1.36	5.77									13.46

Notes: Please refer to the User's Guide for an explanation of data; data is arranged alphabetically by state, then county, then city within each county; table includes counties with populations greater than 49,999 unless noted and cities with populations greater than 9,999 whose Asian and/or NHPI population rates are greater than the national average; (1) Native Hawaiian and other Pacific Islander; (2) excludes Taiwanese; (3) includes Chamorro; (4) county does not meet population threshold but is shown in order to allow inclusion of city

Place	Total foreign-born naturalized citizens	Total Asian population	Asians who are foreign-born naturalized citizens	Total NHPI[1] population	NHPIs[1] who are foreign-born naturalized citizens	Asian Indian	Bangladeshi	Cambodian	Chinese[2]	Fijian	Filipino	Guamanian[3]	Hawaiian, Native	Hmong	Indonesian	Japanese	Korean	Laotian	Malaysian	Pakistani	Samoan	Sri Lankan	Taiwanese	Thai	Tongan	Vietnamese
Los Alamitos (city)	684 6.07	1,050	227 21.62 21.62 33.19	-	-	-	-	-	-	-	-	-	-	-	-	-	-	-	-	-	-	-	-	-	-	-
Mission Viejo (city)	8,677 9.35	7,380	2,782 37.70 37.70 32.06	-	-	220 35.48 7.91 2.98 2.54	-	-	537 41.79 19.30 7.28 6.19	-	634 42.35 22.79 8.59 7.31	-	-	-	-	103 9.54 3.70 1.40 1.19	407 50.81 14.63 5.51 4.69	-	-	-	-	-	-	-	-	701 53.11 25.20 9.50 8.08
Newport Beach (city)	4,144 5.92	2,762	1,014 36.71 36.71 24.47	-	-	-	-	-	295 41.61 29.09 10.68 7.12	-	-	-	-	-	-	18 3.67 1.78 0.65 0.43	-	-	-	-	-	-	-	-	-	-
Orange (city)	11,715 9.12	11,711	5,447 46.51 46.51 46.50	-	-	319 37.27 5.86 2.72 2.72	-	-	696 53.33 12.78 5.94 5.94	-	909 44.80 16.69 7.76 7.76	-	-	-	-	86 11.07 1.58 0.73 0.73	842 52.17 15.46 7.19 7.19	-	-	-	-	-	239 51.73 4.39 2.04 2.04	-	-	1,961 51.17 36.00 16.74 16.74
Placentia (city)	4,599 9.76	5,254	2,321 44.18 44.18 50.47	-	-	199 37.98 8.57 3.79 4.33	-	-	472 41.33 20.34 8.98 10.26	-	461 60.10 19.86 8.77 10.02	-	-	-	-	23 4.87 0.99 0.44 0.50	318 45.69 13.70 6.05 6.91	-	-	-	-	-	-	-	-	518 55.40 22.32 9.86 11.26
Rancho Santa Margarita (city)	3,388 7.10	3,836	1,564 40.77 40.77 46.16	-	-	-	-	-	253 42.10 16.18 6.60 7.47	-	493 45.06 31.52 12.85 14.55	-	-	-	-	-	-	-	-	-	-	-	-	-	-	314 59.47 20.08 8.19 9.27
Rossmoor (cdp)	529 5.16	514	142 27.63 27.63 26.84	-	-	-	-	-	-	-	-	-	-	-	-	-	-	-	-	-	-	-	-	-	-	-
Santa Ana (city)	42,269 12.52	29,802	13,986 46.93 46.93 33.09	1,276	152 11.91 11.91 0.36	71 12.18 0.51 0.24 0.17	-	638 36.75 4.56 2.14 1.51	1,139 56.08 8.14 3.82 2.69	-	1,004 44.74 7.18 3.37 2.38	-	-	215 40.72 1.54 0.72 0.51	-	125 15.01 0.89 0.42 0.30	292 42.57 2.09 0.98 0.69	354 36.61 2.53 1.19 0.84	-	-	134 19.14 88.16 10.50 0.32	-	-	-	-	9,728 50.64 69.56 32.64 23.01
Seal Beach (city)	1,957 8.06	1,255	399 31.79 31.79 20.39	-	-	-	-	-	-	-	-	-	-	-	-	45 12.26 11.28 3.59 2.30	-	-	-	-	-	-	-	-	-	-
Stanton (city)	4,339 11.75	5,727	2,284 39.88 39.88 52.64	-	-	-	-	-	-	-	427 35.73 18.70 7.46 9.84	-	-	-	-	-	222 28.21 9.72 3.88 5.12	-	-	-	-	-	-	-	-	1,260 46.07 55.17 22.00 29.04

Notes: Please refer to the User's Guide for an explanation of data; data is arranged alphabetically by state, then county, then city within each county; table includes counties with populations greater than 49,999 unless noted and cities with populations greater than 9,999 whose Asian and/or NHPI population rates are greater than the national average; (1) Native Hawaiian and other Pacific Islander; (2) excludes Taiwanese; (3) includes Chamorro; (4) county does not meet population threshold but is shown in order to allow inclusion of city

Place	Total foreign-born naturalized citizens	Total Asian population	Asians who are foreign-born naturalized citizens	Total NHPI[1] population	NHPIs[1] who are foreign-born naturalized citizens	Asian Indian	Bangladeshi	Cambodian	Chinese[2]	Fijian	Filipino	Guamanian[3]	Hawaiian, Native	Hmong	Indonesian	Japanese	Korean	Laotian	Malaysian	Pakistani	Samoan	Sri Lankan	Taiwanese	Thai	Tongan	Vietnamese
Tustin (city)	7,825 11.58	9,359	3,750 40.07 40.07 47.92	-	-	364 28.17 9.71 3.89 4.65	-	-	575 43.66 15.33 6.14 7.35	-	623 36.16 16.61 6.66 7.96	-	-	-	-	71 10.29 1.89 0.76 0.91	579 49.49 15.44 6.19 7.40	-	-	-	-	-	192 41.11 5.12 2.05 2.45	-	-	954 55.37 25.44 10.19 12.19
Tustin Foothills (cdp)	2,059 8.57	1,707	873 51.14 51.14 42.40	-	-	-	-	-	274 56.26 31.39 16.05 13.31	-	-	-	-	-	-	-	-	-	-	-	-	-	-	-	-	-
Westminster (city)	19,200 21.85	33,351	15,152 45.43 45.43 78.92	435	123 28.28 28.28 0.64	139 33.10 0.92 0.42 0.72	-	-	761 49.00 5.02 2.28 3.96	-	597 42.52 3.94 1.79 3.11	-	-	-	-	151 14.73 1.00 0.45 0.79	320 45.52 2.11 0.96 1.67	-	-	-	123 32.71 100.00 28.28 0.64	-	-	-	-	12,604 46.47 83.18 37.79 65.65
Yorba Linda (city)	5,086 8.68	6,403	2,530 39.51 39.51 49.74	-	-	277 39.86 10.95 4.33 5.45	-	-	798 49.41 31.54 12.46 15.69	-	354 38.35 13.99 5.53 6.96	-	-	-	-	28 3.34 1.11 0.44 0.55	346 39.18 13.68 5.40 6.80	-	-	-	-	-	-	-	-	358 55.68 14.15 5.59 7.04
Placer County	8,402 3.38	7,256	2,096 28.89 28.89 24.95	-	-	271 31.55 12.93 3.73 3.23	-	-	493 37.04 23.52 6.79 5.87	-	573 29.22 27.34 7.90 6.82	-	-	-	-	168 9.26 8.02 2.32 2.00	257 51.71 12.26 3.54 3.06	-	-	-	-	-	-	-	-	221 49.66 10.54 3.05 2.63
Rocklin (city)	1,155 3.16	1,314	369 28.08 28.08 31.95	-	-	-	-	-	-	-	-	-	-	-	-	21 4.76 5.69 1.60 1.82	-	-	-	-	-	-	-	-	-	-
Roseville (city)	3,427 4.28	3,358	1,011 30.11 30.11 29.50	-	-	186 29.15 18.40 5.54 5.43	-	-	225 32.70 22.26 6.70 6.57	-	321 32.49 31.75 9.56 9.37	-	-	-	-	72 14.26 7.12 2.14 2.10	-	-	-	-	-	-	-	-	-	-
Riverside County	106,834 6.91	54,648	20,545 37.60 37.60 19.23	3,719	213 5.73 5.73 0.20	1,947 34.58 9.48 3.56 1.82	-	222 37.00 1.08 0.41 0.21	2,272 37.91 11.06 4.16 2.13	-	7,965 40.58 38.77 14.58 7.46	10 1.06 4.69 0.27 0.01	15 1.85 7.04 0.40 0.01	127 26.08 0.62 0.23 0.12	-	840 18.89 4.09 1.54 0.79	2,126 37.06 10.35 3.89 1.99	525 35.28 2.56 0.96 0.49	-	151 34.01 0.73 0.28 0.14	98 10.39 46.01 2.64 0.09	-	257 51.61 1.25 0.47 0.24	356 40.64 1.73 0.65 0.33	-	3,069 49.85 14.94 5.62 2.87
Banning (city)	1,357 5.79	1,057	296 28.00 28.00 21.81	-	-	-	-	-	-	-	-	-	-	-	-	-	-	89 26.10 30.07 8.42 6.56	-	-	-	-	-	-	-	-
Corona (city)	10,833 8.67	9,285	3,689 39.73 39.73 34.05	-	-	592 39.31 16.05 6.38 5.46	-	-	337 37.99 9.14 3.63 3.11	-	1,316 43.20 35.67 14.17 12.15	-	-	-	-	69 11.54 1.87 0.74 0.64	403 32.82 10.92 4.34 3.72	-	-	-	-	-	-	-	-	777 54.45 21.06 8.37 7.17

Notes: Please refer to the User's Guide for an explanation of data; data is arranged alphabetically by state, then county, then city within each county; table includes counties with populations greater than 49,999 unless noted and cities with populations greater than 9,999 whose Asian and/or NHPI population rates are greater than the national average; (1) Native Hawaiian and other Pacific Islander; (2) excludes Taiwanese; (3) includes Chamorro; (4) county does not meet population threshold but is shown in order to allow inclusion of city

Place	Total foreign-born naturalized citizens	Total Asian population	Asians who are foreign-born naturalized citizens	Total NHPI[1] population	NHPIs[1] who are foreign-born naturalized citizens	Asian Indian	Bangladeshi	Cambodian	Chinese[2]	Fijian	Filipino	Guamanian[3]	Hawaiian, Native	Hmong	Indonesian	Japanese	Korean	Laotian	Malaysian	Pakistani	Samoan	Sri Lankan	Taiwanese	Thai	Tongan	Vietnamese
Moreno Valley (city)	12,241 8.59	7,995	3,355 41.96 41.96 27.41	-	-	-	-	-	194 41.36 5.78 2.43 1.58	-	1,739 43.76 51.83 21.75 14.21	-	-	-	-	160 32.06 4.77 2.00 1.31	312 46.15 9.30 3.90 2.55	119 24.39 3.55 1.49 0.97	-	-	-	-	-	-	-	342 56.81 10.19 4.28 2.79
Palm Springs (city)	3,457 8.07	1,756	600 34.17 34.17 17.36	-	-	-	-	-	-	-	408 35.51 68.00 23.23 11.80	-	-	-	-	-	-	-	-	-	-	-	-	-	-	-
Pedley (cdp)	1,069 9.65	459	230 50.11 50.11 21.52	-	-	-	-	-	-	-	-	-	-	-	-	-	-	-	-	-	-	-	-	-	-	-
Riverside (city)	18,788 7.37	14,185	4,931 34.76 34.76 26.25	1,061	77 7.26 7.26 0.41	430 29.17 8.72 3.03 2.29	-	-	794 33.86 16.10 5.60 4.23	-	1,154 36.34 23.40 8.14 6.14	-	-	-	-	121 10.72 2.45 0.85 0.64	544 29.36 11.03 3.84 2.90	169 49.13 3.43 1.19 0.90	-	-	-	-	-	-	-	1,174 51.27 23.81 8.28 6.25
Temecula (city)	3,019 5.26	2,668	1,033 38.72 38.72 34.22	-	-	-	-	-	121 31.59 11.71 4.54 4.01	-	597 43.36 57.79 22.38 19.77	-	-	-	-	-	-	-	-	-	-	-	-	-	-	-
Sacramento County	83,982 6.86	134,881	41,775 30.97 30.97 49.74	6,269	1,066 17.00 17.00 1.27	3,765 29.55 9.01 2.79 4.48	-	403 36.08 0.96 0.30 0.48	10,663 37.12 25.52 7.91 12.70	458 26.16 42.96 7.31 0.55	9,220 38.34 22.07 6.84 10.98	32 3.66 3.00 0.51 0.04	8 1.22 0.75 0.13 0.01	2,710 15.65 6.49 2.01 3.23	-	1,317 10.70 3.15 0.98 1.57	2,134 45.66 5.11 1.58 2.54	2,210 22.91 5.29 1.64 2.63	-	521 36.28 1.25 0.39 0.62	118 9.52 11.07 1.88 0.14	-	220 54.19 0.53 0.16 0.26	227 30.72 0.54 0.17 0.27	210 28.34 19.70 3.35 0.25	7,191 43.43 17.21 5.33 8.56
Arden-Arcade (cdp)	5,026 5.24	4,766	1,661 34.85 34.85 33.05	-	-	257 35.79 15.47 5.39 5.11	-	-	303 33.85 18.24 6.36 6.03	-	402 36.68 24.20 8.43 8.00	-	-	44 12.54 2.65 0.92 0.88	-	77 15.19 4.64 1.62 1.53	-	-	-	-	-	-	-	-	-	206 51.63 12.40 4.32 4.10
Elk Grove (cdp)	6,162 10.23	10,532	4,292 40.75 40.75 69.65	-	-	433 29.97 10.09 4.11 7.03	-	-	768 52.03 17.89 7.29 12.46	-	1,395 41.19 32.50 13.25 22.64	-	-	-	-	26 5.71 0.61 0.25 0.42	-	-	-	-	-	-	-	-	-	1,057 48.62 24.63 10.04 17.15
Fair Oaks (cdp)	1,255 4.48	1,200	317 26.42 26.42 25.26	-	-	-	-	-	-	-	-	-	-	-	-	-	-	-	-	-	-	-	-	-	-	-
Florin (cdp)	2,537 9.20	5,500	1,616 29.38 29.38 63.70	-	-	117 38.36 7.24 2.13 4.61	-	-	236 35.17 14.60 4.29 9.30	-	426 45.17 26.36 7.75 16.79	-	-	107 10.08 6.62 1.95 4.22	-	-	-	-	-	-	-	-	-	-	-	431 33.10 26.67 7.84 16.99

Notes: Please refer to the User's Guide for an explanation of data; data is arranged alphabetically by state, then county, then city within each county; table includes counties with populations greater than 49,999 unless noted and cities with populations greater than 9,999 whose Asian and/or NHPI population rates are greater than the national average; (1) Native Hawaiian and other Pacific Islander; (2) excludes Taiwanese; (3) includes Chamorro; (4) county does not meet population threshold but is shown in order to allow inclusion of city

Place	Total foreign-born naturalized citizens	Total Asian population	Asians who are foreign-born naturalized citizens	Total NHPI[1] population	NHPIs[1] who are foreign-born naturalized citizens	Asian Indian	Bangladeshi	Cambodian	Chinese[2]	Fijian	Filipino	Guamanian[3]	Hawaiian, Native	Hmong	Indonesian	Japanese	Korean	Laotian	Malaysian	Pakistani	Samoan	Sri Lankan	Taiwanese	Thai	Tongan	Vietnamese
Folsom (city)	1,997 3.85	3,626	990 27.30 27.30 49.57	-	-	311 22.45 31.41 8.58 15.57	-	-	167 27.79 16.87 4.61 8.36	-	172 27.13 17.37 4.74 8.61	-	-	-	-	-	-	-	-	-	-	-	-	-	-	-
Foothill Farms (cdp)	833 4.79	798	310 38.85 38.85 37.21	-	-	-	-	-	-	-	-	-	-	-	-	-	-	-	-	-	-	-	-	-	-	-
La Riviera (cdp)	710 6.91	883	358 40.54 40.54 50.42	-	-	-	-	-	-	-	-	-	-	-	-	-	-	-	-	-	-	-	-	-	-	-
Laguna (cdp)	3,571 10.38	6,259	2,501 39.96 39.96 70.04	-	-	262 36.90 10.48 4.19 7.34	-	-	824 42.28 32.95 13.17 23.07	-	804 44.13 32.15 12.85 22.51	-	-	-	-	26 4.65 1.04 0.42 0.73	-	-	-	-	-	-	-	-	-	329 65.15 13.15 5.26 9.21
North Highlands (cdp)	2,394 5.43	2,463	974 39.55 39.55 40.69	-	-	-	-	-	-	-	329 39.93 33.78 13.36 13.74	-	-	-	-	-	-	-	-	-	-	-	-	-	-	354 55.23 36.34 14.37 14.79
Parkway-S. Sacramento (cdp)	2,698 7.39	6,735	1,336 19.84 19.84 49.52	-	-	-	-	-	226 42.97 16.92 3.36 8.38	-	-	-	-	314 11.42 23.50 4.66 11.64	-	-	-	201 14.44 15.04 2.98 7.45	-	-	-	-	-	-	-	401 36.13 30.01 5.95 14.86
Rancho Cordova (cdp)	3,133 5.74	4,375	1,330 30.40 30.40 42.45	-	-	52 8.70 3.91 1.19 1.66	-	-	123 25.36 9.25 2.81 3.93	-	404 39.88 30.38 9.23 12.89	-	-	-	-	-	172 40.19 12.93 3.93 5.49	-	-	-	-	-	-	-	-	283 33.69 21.28 6.47 9.03
Rosemont (cdp)	1,961 8.59	2,698	1,037 38.44 38.44 52.88	-	-	-	-	-	-	-	85 19.54 8.20 3.15 4.33	-	-	-	-	-	224 46.86 21.60 8.30 11.42	-	-	-	-	-	-	-	-	322 59.63 31.05 11.93 16.42
Sacramento (city)	34,257 8.42	67,400	18,545 27.51 27.51 54.13	3,692	712 19.28 19.28 2.08	1,188 29.31 6.41 1.76 3.47	-	195 40.37 1.05 0.29 0.57	6,872 36.20 37.06 10.20 20.06	338 27.26 47.47 9.15 0.99	2,960 36.16 15.96 4.39 8.64	-	-	1,913 15.85 10.32 2.84 5.58	-	371 5.52 2.00 0.55 1.08	333 47.71 1.80 0.49 0.97	1,440 22.84 7.76 2.14 4.20	-	282 36.20 1.52 0.42 0.82	46 6.28 6.46 1.25 0.13	-	-	-	156 27.18 21.91 4.23 0.46	2,408 37.06 12.98 3.57 7.03
Vineyard (cdp)	994 9.93	1,629	704 43.22 43.22 70.82	-	-	-	-	-	-	-	300 42.31 42.61 18.42 30.18	-	-	-	-	-	-	-	-	-	-	-	-	-	-	-

Notes: Please refer to the User's Guide for an explanation of data; data is arranged alphabetically by state, then county, then city within each county; table includes counties with populations greater than 49,999 unless noted and cities with populations greater than 9,999 whose Asian and/or NHPI population rates are greater than the national average; (1) Native Hawaiian and other Pacific Islander; (2) excludes Taiwanese; (3) includes Chamorro; (4) county does not meet population threshold but is shown in order to allow inclusion of city

Place	Total foreign-born naturalized citizens	Total Asian population	Asians who are foreign-born naturalized citizens	Total NHPI[1] population	NHPIs[1] who are foreign-born naturalized citizens	Asian Indian	Bangladeshi	Cambodian	Chinese[2]	Fijian	Filipino	Guamanian[3]	Hawaiian, Native	Hmong	Indonesian	Japanese	Korean	Laotian	Malaysian	Pakistani	Samoan	Sri Lankan	Taiwanese	Thai	Tongan	Vietnamese
San Benito County	3,282	1,033	332	-	-	-	-	-	-	-	225	-	-	-	-	-	-	-	-	-	-	-	-	-	-	-
	6.17		32.14								41.98															
											67.77															
			32.14								21.78															
			10.12								6.86															
San Bernardino County	120,983	79,103	30,535	5,019	652	3,010	-	546	4,310	-	11,138	15	24	-	635	644	2,912	188	-	300	445	-	800	643	75	4,530
	7.08		38.60		12.99	37.79		31.34	40.40		43.47	1.44	3.93		19.24	14.93	40.61	39.58		43.92	21.86		39.23	37.71	9.26	43.95
						9.86		1.79	14.11		36.48	2.30	3.68		2.08	2.11	9.54	0.62		0.98	68.25		2.62	2.11	11.50	14.84
			38.60		12.99	3.81		0.69	5.45		14.08	0.30	0.48		0.80	0.81	3.68	0.24		0.38	8.87		1.01	0.81	1.49	5.73
			25.24		0.54	2.49		0.45	3.56		9.21	0.01	0.02		0.52	0.53	2.41	0.16		0.25	0.37		0.66	0.53	0.06	3.74
Chino (city)	5,978	3,351	1,280	-	-	-	-	-	-	-	610	-	-	-	-	-	-	-	-	-	-	-	-	-	-	195
	8.84		38.20								38.80															41.67
											47.66															15.23
			38.20								18.20															5.82
			21.41								10.20															3.26
Chino Hills (city)	9,817	14,256	6,332	-	-	545	-	-	1,468	-	2,556	-	-	-	-	5	509	-	-	-	-	-	269	-	-	493
	14.71		44.42			46.26			42.10		45.92					0.91	48.62						42.43			62.09
						8.61			23.18		40.37					0.08	8.04						4.25			7.79
			44.42			3.82			10.30		17.93					0.04	3.57						1.89			3.46
			64.50			5.55			14.95		26.04					0.05	5.18						2.74			5.02
Colton (city)	3,965	2,440	809	-	-	-	-	-	-	-	206	-	-	-	-	-	-	-	-	-	-	-	-	-	-	-
	8.26		33.16								34.97															
											25.46															
			33.16								8.44															
			20.40								5.20															
Fontana (city)	12,337	5,898	2,152	604	48	235	-	-	-	-	1,154	-	-	-	-	-	-	-	-	-	-	-	-	-	-	-
	9.63		36.49		7.95	35.71					38.78															
						10.92					53.62															
			36.49		7.95	3.98					19.57															
			17.44		0.39	1.90					9.35															
Grand Terrace (city)	760	602	175	-	-	-	-	-	-	-	-	-	-	-	-	-	-	-	-	-	-	-	-	-	-	-
	6.44		29.07																							
			29.07																							
			23.03																							
Highland (city)	2,848	2,832	1,073	-	-	-	-	-	-	-	308	-	-	-	-	-	-	-	-	-	-	-	-	-	-	324
	6.38		37.89								32.08															53.55
											28.70															30.20
			37.89								10.88															11.44
			37.68								10.81															11.38
Loma Linda (city)	2,649	4,351	1,584	-	-	173	-	-	252	-	444	-	-	-	75	-	346	-	-	-	-	-	-	-	-	-
	14.26		36.41			42.82			35.00		42.61				14.37		42.72									
						10.92			15.91		28.03				4.73		21.84									
			36.41			3.98			5.79		10.20				1.72		7.95									
			59.80			6.53			9.51		16.76				2.83		13.06									
Montclair (city)	3,675	2,645	936	-	-	-	-	-	-	-	-	-	-	-	-	-	-	-	-	-	-	-	-	-	-	430
	11.10		35.39																							35.16
																										45.94
			35.39																							16.26
			25.47																							11.70

Notes: Please refer to the User's Guide for an explanation of data; data is arranged alphabetically by state, then county, then city within each county; table includes counties with populations greater than 49,999 unless noted and cities with populations greater than 9,999 whose Asian and/or NHPI population rates are greater than the national average; (1) Native Hawaiian and other Pacific Islander; (2) excludes Taiwanese; (3) includes Chamorro; (4) county does not meet population threshold but is shown in order to allow inclusion of city

Place	Total foreign-born naturalized citizens	Total Asian population	Asians who are foreign-born naturalized citizens	Total NHPI[1] population	NHPIs[1] who are foreign-born naturalized citizens	Asian Indian	Bangladeshi	Cambodian	Chinese[2]	Fijian	Filipino	Guamanian[3]	Hawaiian, Native	Hmong	Indonesian	Japanese	Korean	Laotian	Malaysian	Pakistani	Samoan	Sri Lankan	Taiwanese	Thai	Tongan	Vietnamese
Ontario (city)	14,603 9.28	6,130	2,716 44.31 44.31 18.60	544	64 11.76 11.76 0.44	214 42.04 7.88 3.49 1.47	-	-	212 45.20 7.81 3.46 1.45	-	1,068 46.15 39.32 17.42 7.31	-	-	-	-	-	-	-	-	-	-	-	-	-	-	815 50.68 30.01 13.30 5.58
Rancho Cucamonga (city)	9,449 7.37	7,360	2,944 40.00 40.00 31.16	-	-	362 36.83 12.30 4.92 3.83	-	-	517 38.64 17.56 7.02 5.47	-	968 44.53 32.88 13.15 10.24	-	-	-	-	76 14.42 2.58 1.03 0.80	319 42.03 10.84 4.33 3.38	-	-	-	-	-	-	-	-	285 54.08 9.68 3.87 3.02
Redlands (city)	3,716 5.84	3,292	1,191 36.18 36.18 32.05	-	-	185 46.48 15.53 5.62 4.98	-	-	190 38.85 15.95 5.77 5.11	-	296 46.03 24.85 8.99 7.97	-	-	-	-	-	188 34.06 15.79 5.71 5.06	-	-	-	-	-	-	-	-	-
Rialto (city)	6,971 7.60	1,748	657 37.59 37.59 9.42	532	107 20.11 20.11 1.53	-	-	-	-	-	212 42.66 32.27 12.13 3.04	-	-	-	-	-	-	-	-	-	-	-	-	-	-	-
San Bernardino (city)	11,881 6.41	7,501	2,407 32.09 32.09 20.26	748	84 11.23 11.23 0.71	258 28.99 10.72 3.44 2.17	-	99 22.20 4.11 1.32 0.83	233 38.77 9.68 3.11 1.96	-	861 48.13 35.77 11.48 7.25	-	-	-	71 15.81 2.95 0.95 0.60	-	150 38.07 6.23 2.00 1.26	-	-	-	53 11.09 63.10 7.09 0.45	-	-	-	-	423 27.94 17.57 5.64 3.56
Upland (city)	4,767 6.97	4,996	1,606 32.15 32.15 33.69	-	-	153 26.29 9.53 3.06 3.21	-	-	184 26.21 11.46 3.68 3.86	-	315 55.56 19.61 6.31 6.61	-	-	-	-	-	240 24.87 14.94 4.80 5.03	-	-	-	-	-	174 37.18 10.83 3.48 3.65	-	-	362 42.64 22.54 7.25 7.59
Victorville (city)	3,454 5.35	2,398	892 37.20 37.20 25.83	-	-	-	-	-	-	-	440 36.04 49.33 18.35 12.74	-	-	-	-	-	-	-	-	-	-	-	-	-	-	-
San Diego County	250,125 8.89	248,653	95,664 38.47 38.47 38.25	13,482	756 5.61 5.61 0.30	2,859 29.70 2.99 1.15 1.14	-	822 18.81 0.86 0.33 0.33	10,739 37.11 11.23 4.32 4.29	-	52,849 43.80 55.24 21.25 21.13	84 1.81 11.11 0.62 0.03	12 0.54 1.59 0.09 <0.01	280 20.36 0.29 0.11 0.11	102 20.82 0.11 0.04 0.04	2,978 15.87 3.11 1.20 1.19	3,958 34.79 4.14 1.59 1.58	2,610 36.67 2.73 1.05 1.04	-	144 26.67 0.15 0.06 0.06	318 6.42 42.06 2.36 0.13	-	1,025 43.40 1.07 0.41 0.41	407 31.09 0.43 0.16 0.16	84 19.31 11.11 0.62 0.03	15,169 43.97 15.86 6.10 6.06
Bonita (cdp)	1,400 11.65	994	484 48.69 48.69 34.57	-	-	-	-	-	-	-	333 61.67 68.80 33.50 23.79	-	-	-	-	-	-	-	-	-	-	-	-	-	-	-
Carlsbad (city)	4,559 5.85	3,177	1,186 37.33 37.33 26.01	-	-	-	-	-	215 30.15 18.13 6.77 4.72	-	231 37.32 19.48 7.27 5.07	-	-	-	-	99 20.75 8.35 3.12 2.17	-	-	-	-	-	-	-	-	-	-

Notes: Please refer to the User's Guide for an explanation of data; data is arranged alphabetically by state, then county, then city within each county; table includes counties with populations greater than 49,999 unless noted and cities with populations greater than 9,999 whose Asian and/or NHPI population rates are greater than the national average; (1) Native Hawaiian and other Pacific Islander; (2) excludes Taiwanese; (3) includes Chamorro; (4) county does not meet population threshold but is shown in order to allow inclusion of city

Place	Total foreign-born naturalized citizens	Total Asian population	Asians who are foreign-born naturalized citizens	Total NHPI[1] population	NHPIs[1] who are foreign-born naturalized citizens	Asian Indian	Bangladeshi	Cambodian	Chinese[2]	Fijian	Filipino	Guamanian[3]	Hawaiian, Native	Hmong	Indonesian	Japanese	Korean	Laotian	Malaysian	Pakistani	Samoan	Sri Lankan	Taiwanese	Thai	Tongan	Vietnamese
Chula Vista (city)	24,203	18,851	7,380	752	47	-	-	-	369	-	5,912	21	-	-	-	326	353	-	-	-	-	-	-	-	-	-
	13.92		39.15		6.25				34.62		45.21	4.94				16.12	25.07									
									5.00		80.11	44.68				4.42	4.78									
			39.15		6.25				1.96		31.36	2.79				1.73	1.87									
			30.49		0.19				1.52		24.43	0.09				1.35	1.46									
Coronado (city)	960	907	320	-	-	-	-	-	-	-	177	-	-	-	-	-	-	-	-	-	-	-	-	-	-	-
	3.96		35.28								38.06															
											55.31															
			35.28								19.51															
			33.33								18.44															
Escondido (city)	8,855	5,552	2,387	-	-	-	-	-	224	-	944	-	-	-	-	-	-	201	-	-	-	-	-	-	-	586
	6.63		42.99						51.73		46.30							41.96								45.67
									9.38		39.55							8.42								24.55
			42.99						4.03		17.00							3.62								10.55
			26.96						2.53		10.66							2.27								6.62
Imperial Beach (city)	2,238	1,826	715	-	-	-	-	-	-	-	605	-	-	-	-	-	-	-	-	-	-	-	-	-	-	-
	8.30		39.16								40.04															
											84.62															
			39.16								33.13															
			31.95								27.03															
La Mesa (city)	3,017	2,255	660	-	-	-	-	-	-	-	215	-	-	-	-	-	-	-	-	-	-	-	-	-	-	-
	5.51		29.27								37.52															
											32.58															
			29.27								9.53															
			21.88								7.13															
La Presa (cdp)	3,493	3,397	1,475	-	-	-	-	-	-	-	1,322	-	-	-	-	-	-	-	-	-	-	-	-	-	-	-
	10.63		43.42								43.09															
											89.63															
			43.42								38.92															
			42.23								37.85															
Lemon Grove (city)	1,631	1,447	600	-	-	-	-	-	-	-	290	-	-	-	-	-	-	-	-	-	-	-	-	-	-	181
	6.54		41.47								40.56															49.59
											48.33															30.17
			41.47								20.04															12.51
			36.79								17.78															11.10
National City (city)	9,192	9,966	4,394	-	-	-	-	-	-	-	4,063	-	-	-	-	-	-	-	-	-	-	-	-	-	-	-
	16.90		44.09								44.84															
											92.47															
			44.09								40.77															
			47.80								44.20															
Oceanside (city)	11,548	8,991	3,233	2,274	135	-	-	-	172	-	1,987	-	-	-	-	237	-	-	-	-	86	-	-	-	-	397
	7.18		35.96		5.94				34.40		37.81					19.93					5.61					45.68
									5.32		61.46					7.33					63.70					12.28
			35.96		5.94				1.91		22.10					2.64					3.78					4.42
			28.00		1.17				1.49		17.21					2.05					0.74					3.44
Poway (city)	2,627	3,458	1,261	-	-	-	-	-	285	-	447	-	-	-	-	-	-	-	-	-	-	-	-	-	-	-
	5.44		36.47						41.13		32.60															
									22.60		35.45															
			36.47						8.24		12.93															
			48.00						10.85		17.02															

Notes: Please refer to the User's Guide for an explanation of data; data is arranged alphabetically by state, then county, then city within each county; table includes counties with populations greater than 49,999 unless noted and cities with populations greater than 9,999 whose Asian and/or NHPI population rates are greater than the national average; (1) Native Hawaiian and other Pacific Islander; (2) excludes Taiwanese; (3) includes Chamorro; (4) county does not meet population threshold but is shown in order to allow inclusion of city

Place	Total foreign-born naturalized citizens	Total Asian population	Asians who are foreign-born naturalized citizens	Total NHPI[1] population	NHPIs[1] who are foreign-born naturalized citizens	Asian Indian	Bangladeshi	Cambodian	Chinese[2]	Fijian	Filipino	Guamanian[3]	Hawaiian, Native	Hmong	Indonesian	Japanese	Korean	Laotian	Malaysian	Pakistani	Samoan	Sri Lankan	Taiwanese	Thai	Tongan	Vietnamese
Rancho San Diego (cdp)	1,720 8.58	1,010	430 42.57 42.57 25.00	-	-	-	-	-	-	-	252 46.15 58.60 24.95 14.65	-	-	-	-	-	-	-	-	-	-	-	-	-	-	-
San Diego (city)	134,456 10.99	166,326	63,508 38.18 38.18 47.23	6,216	413 6.64 6.64 0.31	1,641 25.17 2.58 0.99 1.22	-	658 16.80 1.04 0.40 0.49	8,035 36.59 12.65 4.83 5.98	-	32,765 44.41 51.59 19.70 24.37	27 1.30 6.54 0.43 0.02	0 0.00 0.00 0.00 0.00	227 20.79 0.36 0.14 0.17	-	1,339 13.13 2.11 0.81 1.00	2,293 33.70 3.61 1.38 1.71	2,105 34.87 3.31 1.27 1.57	-	-	167 7.69 40.44 2.69 0.12	-	658 41.46 1.04 0.40 0.49	268 32.56 0.42 0.16 0.20	-	12,321 43.16 19.40 7.41 9.16
San Marcos (city)	4,145 7.51	2,463	919 37.31 37.31 22.17	-	-	-	-	-	196 46.23 21.33 7.96 4.73	-	485 38.74 52.77 19.69 11.70	-	-	-	-	-	-	-	-	-	-	-	-	-	-	-
Solana Beach (city)	769 5.97	529	209 39.51 39.51 27.18	-	-	-	-	-	-	-	-	-	-	-	-	-	-	-	-	-	-	-	-	-	-	-
Spring Valley (cdp)	1,939 7.28	1,361	579 42.54 42.54 29.86	-	-	-	-	-	-	-	310 49.28 53.54 22.78 15.99	-	-	-	-	-	-	-	-	-	-	-	-	-	-	-
Vista (city)	5,701 6.33	3,160	1,106 35.00 35.00 19.40	582	21 3.61 3.61 0.37	-	-	-	-	-	463 39.07 41.86 14.65 8.12	-	-	-	-	102 17.32 9.22 3.23 1.79	-	-	-	-	-	-	-	-	-	-
San Francisco County	163,426 21.04	239,938	111,416 46.44 46.44 68.18	3,581	547 15.28 15.28 0.33	1,697 35.11 1.52 0.71 1.04	-	281 43.50 0.25 0.12 0.17	75,337 48.76 67.62 31.40 46.10	-	19,939 49.76 17.90 8.31 12.20	-	-	-	141 16.15 0.13 0.06 0.09	1,225 11.32 1.10 0.51 0.75	3,075 43.10 2.76 1.28 1.88	-	-	204 36.69 0.18 0.09 0.12	400 17.55 73.13 11.17 0.24	-	275 35.67 0.25 0.11 0.17	366 25.05 0.33 0.15 0.22	-	5,704 54.69 5.12 2.38 3.49
San Francisco (city)	163,426 21.04	239,938	111,416 46.44 46.44 68.18	3,581	547 15.28 15.28 0.33	1,697 35.11 1.52 0.71 1.04	-	281 43.50 0.25 0.12 0.17	75,337 48.76 67.62 31.40 46.10	-	19,939 49.76 17.90 8.31 12.20	-	-	-	141 16.15 0.13 0.06 0.09	1,225 11.32 1.10 0.51 0.75	3,075 43.10 2.76 1.28 1.88	-	-	204 36.69 0.18 0.09 0.12	400 17.55 73.13 11.17 0.24	-	275 35.67 0.25 0.11 0.17	366 25.05 0.33 0.15 0.22	-	5,704 54.69 5.12 2.38 3.49
San Joaquin County	39,437 7.00	65,065	17,968 27.62 27.62 45.56	1,785	167 9.36 9.36 0.42	1,782 34.24 9.92 2.74 4.52	-	1,530 16.16 8.52 2.35 3.88	2,384 42.21 13.27 3.66 6.05	-	7,473 35.30 41.59 11.49 18.95	-	17 4.10 10.18 0.95 0.04	772 12.98 4.30 1.19 1.96	-	278 7.80 1.55 0.43 0.70	371 44.48 2.06 0.57 0.94	503 16.33 2.80 0.77 1.28	-	322 24.08 1.79 0.49 0.82	38 10.56 22.75 2.13 0.10	-	-	-	-	2,064 32.66 11.49 3.17 5.23
Lathrop (city)	1,288 12.46	1,463	710 48.53 48.53 55.12	-	-	-	-	-	-	-	599 56.35 84.37 40.94 46.51	-	-	-	-	-	-	-	-	-	-	-	-	-	-	-

Notes: Please refer to the User's Guide for an explanation of data; data is arranged alphabetically by state, then county, then city within each county; table includes counties with populations greater than 49,999 unless noted and cities with populations greater than 9,999 whose Asian and/or NHPI population rates are greater than the national average; (1) Native Hawaiian and other Pacific Islander; (2) excludes Taiwanese; (3) includes Chamorro; (4) county does not meet population threshold but is shown in order to allow inclusion of city

Place	Total foreign-born naturalized citizens	Total Asian population	Asians who are foreign-born naturalized citizens	Total NHPI[1] population	NHPIs[1] who are foreign-born naturalized citizens	Asian Indian	Bangladeshi	Cambodian	Chinese[2]	Fijian	Filipino	Guamanian[3]	Hawaiian, Native	Hmong	Indonesian	Japanese	Korean	Laotian	Malaysian	Pakistani	Samoan	Sri Lankan	Taiwanese	Thai	Tongan	Vietnamese
Lodi (city)	3,244	3,114	884	-	-	294	-	-	-	-	177	-	-	-	-	48	-	-	-	-	-	-	-	-	-	-
	5.69		28.39			38.28					27.74					7.25										
						33.26					20.02					5.43										
			28.39			9.44					5.68					1.54										
			27.25			9.06					5.46					1.48										
Stockton (city)	21,734	48,681	13,177	1,036	49	739	-	1,492	1,832	-	5,351	-	-	616	-	122	-	471	-	198	-	-	-	-	-	1,785
	8.95		27.07		4.73	34.57		16.39	42.75		35.60			12.44		7.54		15.87		28.21						31.04
						5.61		11.32	13.90		40.61			4.67		0.93		3.57		1.50						13.55
			27.07		4.73	1.52		3.06	3.76		10.99			1.27		0.25		0.97		0.41						3.67
			60.63		0.23	3.40		6.86	8.43		24.62			2.83		0.56		2.17		0.91						8.21
Tracy (city)	3,753	4,763	1,475	-	-	372	-	-	129	-	636	-	-	-	-	-	-	-	-	-	-	-	-	-	-	-
	6.60		30.97			32.72			34.96		31.61															
						25.22			8.75		43.12															
			30.97			7.81			2.71		13.35															
			39.30			9.91			3.44		16.95															
San Luis Obispo County	8,924	6,850	2,208	-	-	258	-	-	472	-	865	-	-	-	-	79	361	-	-	-	-	-	-	-	-	-
	3.62		32.23			41.48			42.29		35.23					7.79	48.85									
						11.68			21.38		39.18					3.58	16.35									
			32.23			3.77			6.89		12.63					1.15	5.27									
			24.74			2.89			5.29		9.69					0.89	4.05									
Baywood-Los Osos (cdp)	662	845	352	-	-	-	-	-	-	-	267	-	-	-	-	-	-	-	-	-	-	-	-	-	-	-
	4.68		41.66								45.64															
											75.85															
			41.66								31.60															
			53.17								40.33															
Grover Beach (city)	539	501	170	-	-	-	-	-	-	-	-	-	-	-	-	-	-	-	-	-	-	-	-	-	-	-
	4.14		33.93																							
			33.93																							
			31.54																							
San Luis Obispo (city)	1,902	2,273	719	-	-	-	-	-	225	-	153	-	-	-	-	-	-	-	-	-	-	-	-	-	-	-
	4.31		31.63						40.32		28.54															
									31.29		21.28															
			31.63						9.90		6.73															
			37.80						11.83		8.04															
San Mateo County	111,735	142,162	57,371	8,533	1,677	2,961	-	-	20,610	442	26,856	15	29	-	199	887	1,991	-	-	-	164	-	386	236	812	1,751
	15.80		40.36		19.65	26.69			43.47	38.20	44.68	3.73	3.60		26.32	9.37	45.69				11.30		49.55	33.67	22.22	62.54
						5.16			35.92	26.36	46.81	0.89	1.73		0.35	1.55	3.47				9.78		0.67	0.41	48.42	3.05
			40.36		19.65	2.08			14.50	5.18	18.89	0.18	0.34		0.14	0.62	1.40				1.92		0.27	0.17	9.52	1.23
			51.35		1.50	2.65			18.45	0.40	24.04	0.01	0.03		0.18	0.79	1.78				0.15		0.35	0.21	0.73	1.57
Belmont (city)	2,996	3,923	1,144	-	-	114	-	-	575	-	209	-	-	-	-	54	-	-	-	-	-	-	-	-	-	-
	11.92		29.16			15.77			33.98		32.55					12.19										
						9.97			50.26		18.27					4.72										
			29.16			2.91			14.66		5.33					1.38										
			38.18			3.81			19.19		6.98					1.80										
Burlingame (city)	3,651	3,739	1,446	-	-	-	-	-	765	-	252	-	-	-	-	30	-	-	-	-	-	-	-	-	-	-
	13.05		38.67						41.71		44.13					7.75										
									52.90		17.43					2.07										
			38.67						20.46		6.74					0.80										
			39.61						20.95		6.90					0.82										

Notes: Please refer to the User's Guide for an explanation of data; data is arranged alphabetically by state, then county, then city within each county; table includes counties with populations greater than 49,999 unless noted and cities with populations greater than 9,999 whose Asian and/or NHPI population rates are greater than the national average; (1) Native Hawaiian and other Pacific Islander; (2) excludes Taiwanese; (3) includes Chamorro; (4) county does not meet population threshold but is shown in order to allow inclusion of city

Place	Total foreign-born naturalized citizens	Total Asian population	Asians who are foreign-born naturalized citizens	Total NHPI[1] population	NHPIs[1] who are foreign-born naturalized citizens	Asian Indian	Bangladeshi	Cambodian	Chinese[2]	Fijian	Filipino	Guamanian[3]	Hawaiian, Native	Hmong	Indonesian	Japanese	Korean	Laotian	Malaysian	Pakistani	Samoan	Sri Lankan	Taiwanese	Thai	Tongan	Vietnamese
Daly City (city)	32,278 31.17	52,289	23,708 45.34 45.34 73.45	866	159 18.36 18.36 0.49	332 31.38 1.40 0.63 1.03	-	-	6,634 48.23 27.98 12.69 20.55	-	15,067 45.76 63.55 28.81 46.68	-	-	-	-	130 15.83 0.55 0.25 0.40	278 34.88 1.17 0.53 0.86	-	-	-	-	-	-	-	-	564 60.97 2.38 1.08 1.75
East Palo Alto (city)	2,856 9.70	563	207 36.77 36.77 7.25	2,211	509 23.02 23.02 17.82	-	-	-	-	-	-	-	-	-	-	-	-	-	-	-	-	-	-	-	404 27.04 79.37 18.27 14.15	-
Foster City (city)	4,928 17.11	9,377	2,929 31.24 31.24 59.44	-	-	259 14.57 8.84 2.76 5.26	-	-	1,779 42.05 60.74 18.97 36.10	-	333 41.63 11.37 3.55 6.76	-	-	-	-	43 2.87 1.47 0.46 0.87	254 65.13 8.67 2.71 5.15	-	-	-	-	-	-	-	-	-
Hillsborough (town)	1,894 17.50	2,702	1,229 45.48 45.48 64.89	-	-	-	-	-	967 48.47 78.68 35.79 51.06	-	-	-	-	-	-	-	-	-	-	-	-	-	-	-	-	-
Menlo Park (city)	2,453 7.97	2,154	687 31.89 31.89 28.01	-	-	-	-	-	341 39.65 49.64 15.83 13.90	-	-	-	-	-	-	30 6.62 4.37 1.39 1.22	-	-	-	-	-	-	-	-	-	-
Millbrae (city)	4,514 21.78	5,898	2,385 40.44 40.44 52.84	-	-	152 40.75 6.37 2.58 3.37	-	-	1,760 46.00 73.79 29.84 38.99	-	213 31.51 8.93 3.61 4.72	-	-	-	-	19 4.68 0.80 0.32 0.42	113 35.31 4.74 1.92 2.50	-	-	-	-	-	-	-	-	-
Pacifica (city)	4,404 11.46	5,897	2,356 39.95 39.95 53.50	-	-	-	-	-	614 40.32 26.06 10.41 13.94	-	1,338 41.06 56.79 22.69 30.38	-	-	-	-	80 22.10 3.40 1.36 1.82	-	-	-	-	-	-	-	-	-	-
Redwood City (city)	7,730 10.25	6,932	2,275 32.82 32.82 29.43	566	108 19.08 19.08 1.40	204 16.13 8.97 2.94 2.64	-	-	1,038 40.87 45.63 14.97 13.43	-	590 40.83 25.93 8.51 7.63	-	-	-	-	39 6.55 1.71 0.56 0.50	-	-	-	-	-	-	-	-	-	-
San Bruno (city)	6,791 16.91	7,496	2,901 38.70 38.70 42.72	1,017	175 17.21 17.21 2.58	266 25.29 9.17 3.55 3.92	-	-	840 38.82 28.96 11.21 12.37	-	1,385 45.26 47.74 18.48 20.39	-	-	-	-	60 12.42 2.07 0.80 0.88	-	-	-	-	-	-	-	-	47 8.82 26.86 4.62 0.69	-
San Carlos (city)	2,439 8.81	1,841	678 36.83 36.83 27.80	-	-	-	-	-	311 44.30 45.87 16.89 12.75	-	-	-	-	-	-	-	-	-	-	-	-	-	-	-	-	-

Notes: Please refer to the User's Guide for an explanation of data; data is arranged alphabetically by state, then county, then city within each county; table includes counties with populations greater than 49,999 unless noted and cities with populations greater than 9,999 whose Asian and/or NHPI population rates are greater than the national average; (1) Native Hawaiian and other Pacific Islander; (2) excludes Taiwanese; (3) includes Chamorro; (4) county does not meet population threshold but is shown in order to allow inclusion of city

Place	Total foreign-born naturalized citizens	Total Asian population	Asians who are foreign-born naturalized citizens	Total NHPI[1] population	NHPIs[1] who are foreign-born naturalized citizens	Asian Indian	Bangladeshi	Cambodian	Chinese[2]	Fijian	Filipino	Guamanian[3]	Hawaiian, Native	Hmong	Indonesian	Japanese	Korean	Laotian	Malaysian	Pakistani	Samoan	Sri Lankan	Taiwanese	Thai	Tongan	Vietnamese
San Mateo (city)	12,379	14,221	4,884	1,369	330	624	-	-	2,134	-	1,238	-	-	-	-	171	224	-	-	-	-	-	-	-	174	215
	13.40		34.34		24.11	28.62			40.32		42.05					8.49	38.96								27.27	53.35
						12.78			43.69		25.35					3.50	4.59								52.73	4.40
			34.34		24.11	4.39			15.01		8.71					1.20	1.58								12.71	1.51
			39.45		2.67	5.04			17.24		10.00					1.38	1.81								1.41	1.74
South San Francisco (city)	13,264	17,618	7,528	874	174	310	-	-	1,804	-	4,681	-	-	-	-	87	-	-	-	-	-	-	-	-	-	-
	21.84		42.73		19.91	42.29			39.04		45.19					16.57										
						4.12			23.96		62.18					1.16										
			42.73		19.91	1.76			10.24		26.57					0.49										
			56.76		1.31	2.34			13.60		35.29					0.66										
Santa Barbara County	27,490	15,630	5,275	905	107	279	-	-	759	-	1,929	-	-	45	-	345	628	-	-	-	-	-	-	-	-	671
	6.88		33.75		11.82	31.89			29.16		39.53			12.68		14.99	38.86									54.82
						5.29			14.39		36.57			0.85		6.54	11.91									12.72
			33.75		11.82	1.79			4.86		12.34			0.29		2.21	4.02									4.29
			19.19		0.39	1.01			2.76		7.02			0.16		1.26	2.28									2.44
Goleta (cdp)	4,477	3,247	1,180	-	-	-	-	-	263	-	236	-	-	-	-	19	-	-	-	-	-	-	-	-	-	279
	8.09		36.34						33.89		44.53					4.18										56.59
									22.29		20.00					1.61										23.64
			36.34						8.10		7.27					0.59										8.59
			26.36						5.87		5.27					0.42										6.23
Isla Vista (cdp)	787	1,973	385	-	-	-	-	-	115	-	-	-	-	-	-	-	98	-	-	-	-	-	-	-	-	-
	4.28		19.51						17.06								23.00									
									29.87								25.45									
			19.51						5.83								4.97									
			48.92						14.61								12.45									
Lompoc (city)	2,538	1,539	616	-	-	-	-	-	-	-	154	-	-	-	-	-	-	-	-	-	-	-	-	-	-	-
	6.18		40.03								43.14															
											25.00															
			40.03								10.01															
			24.27								6.07															
Orcutt (cdp)	1,364	1,056	393	-	-	-	-	-	-	-	-	-	-	-	-	-	-	-	-	-	-	-	-	-	-	-
	4.73		37.22																							
			37.22																							
			28.81																							
Santa Maria (city)	5,854	3,639	1,373	-	-	-	-	-	-	-	978	-	-	-	-	102	-	-	-	-	-	-	-	-	-	-
	7.59		37.73								40.70					22.97										
											71.23					7.43										
			37.73								26.88					2.80										
			23.45								16.71					1.74										
Santa Clara County	235,952	430,201	149,168	5,793	596	11,950	168	1,482	42,232	185	31,256	53	34	-	139	1,715	7,240	731	-	853	247	-	2,039	273	-	45,526
	14.02		34.67		10.29	18.36	34.71	33.69	37.51	36.20	40.17	3.81	2.97		20.23	6.36	33.41	35.45		31.01	14.37		38.49	20.46		46.73
						8.01	0.11	0.99	28.31	31.04	20.95	8.89	5.70		0.09	1.15	4.85	0.49		0.57	41.44		1.37	0.18		30.52
			34.67		10.29	2.78	0.04	0.34	9.82	3.19	7.27	0.91	0.59		0.03	0.40	1.68	0.17		0.20	4.26		0.47	0.06		10.58
			63.22		0.25	5.06	0.07	0.63	17.90	0.08	13.25	0.02	0.01		0.06	0.73	3.07	0.31		0.36	0.10		0.86	0.12		19.29
Alum Rock (cdp)	1,763	1,258	611	-	-	-	-	-	-	-	-	-	-	-	-	-	-	-	-	-	-	-	-	-	-	315
	12.79		48.57																							56.55
																										51.55
			48.57																							25.04
			34.66																							17.87

Notes: Please refer to the User's Guide for an explanation of data; data is arranged alphabetically by state, then county, then city within each county; table includes counties with populations greater than 49,999 unless noted and cities with populations greater than 9,999 whose Asian and/or NHPI population rates are greater than the national average; (1) Native Hawaiian and other Pacific Islander; (2) excludes Taiwanese; (3) includes Chamorro; (4) county does not meet population threshold but is shown in order to allow inclusion of city

Place	Total foreign-born naturalized citizens	Total Asian population	Asians who are foreign-born naturalized citizens	Total NHPI[1] population	NHPIs[1] who are foreign-born naturalized citizens	Asian Indian	Bangladeshi	Cambodian	Chinese[2]	Fijian	Filipino	Guamanian[3]	Hawaiian, Native	Hmong	Indonesian	Japanese	Korean	Laotian	Malaysian	Pakistani	Samoan	Sri Lankan	Taiwanese	Thai	Tongan	Vietnamese
Campbell (city)	3,377	5,641	1,623	-	-	110	-	-	406	-	176	-	-	-	-	83	273	-	-	-	-	-	-	-	-	516
	8.84		28.77			14.30			27.58		28.12					10.48	31.97									56.70
						6.78			25.02		10.84					5.11	16.82									31.79
			28.77			1.95			7.20		3.12					1.47	4.84									9.15
			48.06			3.26			12.02		5.21					2.46	8.08									15.28
Cupertino (city)	8,153	22,599	6,072	-	-	738	-	-	3,821	-	170	-	-	-	-	59	462	-	-	-	-	-	268	-	-	406
	16.09		26.87			15.47			36.32		41.56					2.44	20.67						33.84			55.31
						12.15			62.93		2.80					0.97	7.61						4.41			6.69
			26.87			3.27			16.91		0.75					0.26	2.04						1.19			1.80
			74.48			9.05			46.87		2.09					0.72	5.67						3.29			4.98
Gilroy (city)	2,575	1,912	681	-	-	-	-	-	142	-	284	-	-	-	-	-	-	-	-	-	-	-	-	-	-	-
	6.19		35.62						36.98		43.23															
									20.85		41.70															
			35.62						7.43		14.85															
			26.45						5.51		11.03															
Los Altos (city)	2,967	4,177	1,625	-	-	189	-	-	965	-	-	-	-	-	-	70	-	-	-	-	-	-	-	-	-	-
	10.76		38.90			36.21			47.14							10.22										
						11.63			59.38							4.31										
			38.90			4.52			23.10							1.68										
			54.77			6.37			32.52							2.36										
Los Gatos (town)	2,144	2,338	798	-	-	-	-	-	497	-	-	-	-	-	-	24	-	-	-	-	-	-	-	-	-	-
	7.47		34.13						55.10							4.90										
									62.28							3.01										
			34.13						21.26							1.03										
			37.22						23.18							1.12										
Milpitas (city)	14,982	32,766	13,088	631	66	912	-	-	3,331	-	3,694	-	-	-	-	74	440	-	-	-	-	-	-	-	-	4,121
	23.89		39.94		10.46	19.29			41.10		40.96					12.59	51.76									52.02
						6.97			25.45		28.22					0.57	3.36									31.49
			39.94		10.46	2.78			10.17		11.27					0.23	1.34									12.58
			87.36		0.44	6.09			22.23		24.66					0.49	2.94									27.51
Morgan Hill (city)	2,055	2,113	700	-	-	-	-	-	182	-	-	-	-	-	-	5	-	-	-	-	-	-	-	-	-	-
	6.11		33.13						43.44							1.07										
									26.00							0.71										
			33.13						8.61							0.24										
			34.06						8.86							0.24										
Mountain View (city)	7,252	14,561	3,708	-	-	277	-	-	1,641	-	775	-	-	-	-	80	276	-	-	-	-	-	-	-	-	464
	10.29		25.47			9.53			29.90		36.90					4.80	39.66									53.77
						7.47			44.26		20.90					2.16	7.44									12.51
			25.47			1.90			11.27		5.32					0.55	1.90									3.19
			51.13			3.82			22.63		10.69					1.10	3.81									6.40
Palo Alto (city)	6,768	10,307	3,171	-	-	391	-	-	1,933	-	195	-	-	-	-	56	243	-	-	-	-	-	-	-	-	-
	11.51		30.77			26.91			35.42		46.76					4.69	24.72									
						12.33			60.96		6.15					1.77	7.66									
			30.77			3.79			18.75		1.89					0.54	2.36									
			46.85			5.78			28.56		2.88					0.83	3.59									
San Jose (city)	140,542	239,465	90,797	3,234	387	6,266	-	1,297	20,063	-	19,826	26	20	-	-	886	3,334	637	-	469	165	-	782	137	-	34,500
	15.72		37.92		11.97	24.99		32.51	39.41		39.97	3.55	3.74			7.91	35.55	33.65		35.56	13.55		38.09	21.71		45.42
						6.90		1.43	22.10		21.84	6.72	5.17			0.98	3.67	0.70		0.52	42.64		0.86	0.15		38.00
			37.92		11.97	2.62		0.54	8.38		8.28	0.80	0.62			0.37	1.39	0.27		0.20	5.10		0.33	0.06		14.41
			64.60		0.28	4.46		0.92	14.28		14.11	0.02	0.01			0.63	2.37	0.45		0.33	0.12		0.56	0.10		24.55

Notes: Please refer to the User's Guide for an explanation of data; data is arranged alphabetically by state, then county, then city within each county; table includes counties with populations greater than 49,999 unless noted and cities with populations greater than 9,999 whose Asian and/or NHPI population rates are greater than the national average; (1) Native Hawaiian and other Pacific Islander; (2) excludes Taiwanese; (3) includes Chamorro; (4) county does not meet population threshold but is shown in order to allow inclusion of city

Place	Total foreign-born naturalized citizens	Total Asian population	Asians who are foreign-born naturalized citizens	Total NHPI[1] population	NHPIs[1] who are foreign-born naturalized citizens	Asian Indian	Bangladeshi	Cambodian	Chinese[2]	Fijian	Filipino	Guamanian[3]	Hawaiian, Native	Hmong	Indonesian	Japanese	Korean	Laotian	Malaysian	Pakistani	Samoan	Sri Lankan	Taiwanese	Thai	Tongan	Vietnamese
Santa Clara (city)	13,057	29,195	8,125	382	24	860	-	-	1,501	-	2,473	-	-	-	-	64	664	-	-	96	-	-	-	-	-	2,183
	12.79		27.83		6.28	9.70			31.98		41.68					4.42	32.15			20.47						47.07
						10.58			18.47		30.44					0.79	8.17			1.18						26.87
			27.83		6.28	2.95			5.14		8.47					0.22	2.27			0.33						7.48
			62.23		0.18	6.59			11.50		18.94					0.49	5.09			0.74						16.72
Saratoga (city)	4,680	8,531	3,358	-	-	413	-	-	2,175	-	-	-	-	-	-	25	201	-	-	-	-	-	183	-	-	-
	15.68		39.36			33.36			43.58							4.66	36.41						55.12			
						12.30			64.77							0.74	5.99						5.45			
			39.36			4.84			25.50							0.29	2.36						2.15			
			71.75			8.82			46.47							0.53	4.29						3.91			
Stanford (cdp)	699	3,460	366	-	-	84	-	-	168	-	-	-	-	-	-	-	39	-	-	-	-	-	-	-	-	-
	5.25		10.58			12.80			10.57								10.60									
						22.95			45.90								10.66									
			10.58			2.43			4.86								1.13									
			52.36			12.02			24.03								5.58									
Sunnyvale (city)	17,067	42,604	11,072	536	83	1,100	-	-	3,893	-	2,756	-	-	-	-	188	862	-	-	-	-	-	217	-	-	1,673
	12.94		25.99		15.49	9.01			31.63		41.97					5.46	31.96						32.34			52.68
						9.93			35.16		24.89					1.70	7.79						1.96			15.11
			25.99		15.49	2.58			9.14		6.47					0.44	2.02						0.51			3.93
			64.87		0.49	6.45			22.81		16.15					1.10	5.05						1.27			9.80
Santa Cruz County	14,643	8,390	2,075	-	-	294	-	-	564	-	619	-	-	-	-	98	193	-	-	-	-	-	-	-	-	155
	5.73		24.73			30.06			27.84		30.28					5.60	39.96									36.21
						14.17			27.18		29.83					4.72	9.30									7.47
			24.73			3.50			6.72		7.38					1.17	2.30									1.85
			14.17			2.01			3.85		4.23					0.67	1.32									1.06
Capitola (city)	519	484	179	-	-	-	-	-	-	-	-	-	-	-	-	-	-	-	-	-	-	-	-	-	-	-
	5.09		36.98																							
			36.98																							
			34.49																							
Santa Cruz (city)	2,518	2,795	584	-	-	99	-	-	207	-	152	-	-	-	-	18	-	-	-	-	-	-	-	-	-	-
	4.63		20.89			23.24			22.67		28.79					4.20										
						16.95			35.45		26.03					3.08										
			20.89			3.54			7.41		5.44					0.64										
			23.19			3.93			8.22		6.04					0.71										
Scotts Valley (city)	610	655	197	-	-	-	-	-	-	-	-	-	-	-	-	-	-	-	-	-	-	-	-	-	-	-
	5.30		30.08																							
			30.08																							
			32.30																							
Shasta County	3,012	3,219	910	-	-	-	-	-	-	-	205	-	-	-	-	-	-	408	-	-	-	-	-	-	-	-
	1.84		28.27								45.66							23.38								
											22.53							44.84								
			28.27								6.37							12.67								
			30.21								6.81							13.55								
Solano County	35,301	49,899	21,021	3,189	189	1,021	-	-	1,325	-	16,033	16	7	111	-	622	502	138	-	-	31	-	-	-	-	547
	8.95		42.13		5.93	36.04			42.20		44.71	1.18	1.07	27.01		31.21	51.86	18.30			4.96					38.96
						4.86			6.30		76.27	8.47	3.70	0.53		2.96	2.39	0.66			16.40					2.60
			42.13		5.93	2.05			2.66		32.13	0.50	0.22	0.22		1.25	1.01	0.28			0.97					1.10
			59.55		0.54	2.89			3.75		45.42	0.05	0.02	0.31		1.76	1.42	0.39			0.09					1.55

Notes: Please refer to the User's Guide for an explanation of data; data is arranged alphabetically by state, then county, then city within each county; table includes counties with populations greater than 49,999 unless noted and cities with populations greater than 9,999 whose Asian and/or NHPI population rates are greater than the national average; (1) Native Hawaiian and other Pacific Islander; (2) excludes Taiwanese; (3) includes Chamorro; (4) county does not meet population threshold but is shown in order to allow inclusion of city

Place	Total foreign-born naturalized citizens	Total Asian population	Asians who are foreign-born naturalized citizens	Total NHPI[1] population	NHPIs[1] who are foreign-born naturalized citizens	Asian Indian	Bangladeshi	Cambodian	Chinese[2]	Fijian	Filipino	Guamanian[3]	Hawaiian, Native	Hmong	Indonesian	Japanese	Korean	Laotian	Malaysian	Pakistani	Samoan	Sri Lankan	Taiwanese	Thai	Tongan	Vietnamese
Benicia (city)	1,529 5.67	1,941	744 38.33 38.33 48.66	-	-	-	-	-	174 37.74 23.39 8.96 11.38	-	446 42.44 59.95 22.98 29.17	-	-	-	-	-	-	-	-	-	-	-	-	-	-	-
Fairfield (city)	7,848 8.16	10,596	4,186 39.51 39.51 53.34	1,037	58 5.59 5.59 0.74	405 42.95 9.68 3.82 5.16	-	-	399 42.77 9.53 3.77 5.08	-	2,475 40.86 59.13 23.36 31.54	0 0.00 0.00 0.00 0.00	-	-	-	263 37.57 6.28 2.48 3.35	187 47.95 4.47 1.76 2.38	79 20.31 1.89 0.75 1.01	-	-	-	-	-	-	-	-
Suisun City (city)	3,134 12.03	4,803	2,210 46.01 46.01 70.52	-	-	171 40.62 7.74 3.56 5.46	-	-	-	-	1,515 48.89 68.55 31.54 48.34	-	-	-	-	-	-	-	-	-	-	-	-	-	-	-
Vacaville (city)	3,996 4.51	3,700	1,433 38.73 38.73 35.86	-	-	-	-	-	-	-	821 42.92 57.29 22.19 20.55	-	-	-	-	-	-	-	-	-	-	-	-	-	-	-
Vallejo (city)	16,443 14.13	27,632	12,075 43.70 43.70 73.44	1,396	109 7.81 7.81 0.66	288 31.27 2.39 1.04 1.75	-	-	399 44.28 3.30 1.44 2.43	-	10,605 45.57 87.83 38.38 64.50	16 2.80 14.68 1.15 0.10	-	-	-	93 25.34 0.77 0.34 0.57	-	-	-	-	-	-	-	-	-	220 34.70 1.82 0.80 1.34
Sonoma County	22,335 4.87	14,070	4,453 31.65 31.65 19.94	750	37 4.93 4.93 0.17	448 25.76 10.06 3.18 2.01	-	179 21.06 4.02 1.27 0.80	913 32.97 20.50 6.49 4.09	-	938 37.58 21.06 6.67 4.20	-	-	-	-	274 17.58 6.15 1.95 1.23	418 46.91 9.39 2.97 1.87	360 33.27 8.08 2.56 1.61	-	-	-	-	-	-	-	706 52.18 15.85 5.02 3.16
Petaluma (city)	3,087 5.66	2,232	825 36.96 36.96 26.72	-	-	-	-	-	280 40.82 33.94 12.54 9.07	-	-	-	-	-	-	-	-	-	-	-	-	-	-	-	-	-
Rohnert Park (city)	2,088 4.93	2,473	728 29.44 29.44 34.87	-	-	-	-	-	105 23.18 14.42 4.25 5.03	-	315 43.99 43.27 12.74 15.09	-	-	-	-	-	-	-	-	-	-	-	-	-	-	-
Santa Rosa (city)	7,472 5.06	5,607	1,675 29.87 29.87 22.42	-	-	231 32.72 13.79 4.12 3.09	-	145 22.45 8.66 2.59 1.94	230 28.40 13.73 4.10 3.08	-	214 29.12 12.78 3.82 2.86	-	-	-	-	37 9.09 2.21 0.66 0.50	-	199 31.44 11.88 3.55 2.66	-	-	-	-	-	-	-	385 49.61 22.99 6.87 5.15
Stanislaus County	30,603 6.85	18,392	5,655 30.75 30.75 18.48	1,804	322 17.85 17.85 1.05	1,441 33.13 25.48 7.83 4.71	-	751 23.25 13.28 4.08 2.45	662 35.73 11.71 3.60 2.16	232 33.24 72.05 12.86 0.76	903 32.66 15.97 4.91 2.95	-	-	181 18.68 3.20 0.98 0.59	-	99 12.16 1.75 0.54 0.32	-	531 33.42 9.39 2.89 1.74	-	-	-	-	-	-	-	624 44.80 11.03 3.39 2.04

Notes: Please refer to the User's Guide for an explanation of data; data is arranged alphabetically by state, then county, then city within each county; table includes counties with populations greater than 49,999 unless noted and cities with populations greater than 9,999 whose Asian and/or NHPI population rates are greater than the national average; (1) Native Hawaiian and other Pacific Islander; (2) excludes Taiwanese; (3) includes Chamorro; (4) county does not meet population threshold but is shown in order to allow inclusion of city

Place	Total foreign-born naturalized citizens	Total Asian population	Asians who are foreign-born naturalized citizens	Total NHPI[1] population	NHPIs[1] who are foreign-born naturalized citizens	Asian Indian	Bangladeshi	Cambodian	Chinese[2]	Fijian	Filipino	Guamanian[3]	Hawaiian, Native	Hmong	Indonesian	Japanese	Korean	Laotian	Malaysian	Pakistani	Samoan	Sri Lankan	Taiwanese	Thai	Tongan	Vietnamese
Ceres (city)	2,582 7.48	1,759	519 29.51 29.51 20.10	-	-	250 29.38 48.17 14.21 9.68	-	-	-	-	-	-	-	-	-	-	-	-	-	-	-	-	-	-	-	-
Modesto (city)	12,744 6.73	11,219	3,562 31.75 31.75 27.95	1,217	231 18.98 18.98 1.81	683 34.88 19.17 6.09 5.36	-	656 25.85 18.42 5.85 5.15	451 39.53 12.66 4.02 3.54	152 30.77 65.80 12.49 1.19	535 34.67 15.02 4.77 4.20	-	-	68 16.75 1.91 0.61 0.53	-	67 17.27 1.88 0.60 0.53	-	375 32.87 10.53 3.34 2.94	-	-	-	-	-	-	-	486 42.59 13.64 4.33 3.81
Salida (cdp)	768 6.11	487	174 35.73 35.73 22.66	-	-	-	-	-	-	-	-	-	-	-	-	-	-	-	-	-	-	-	-	-	-	-
Turlock (city)	4,991 8.99	2,410	675 28.01 28.01 13.52	-	-	373 34.93 55.26 15.48 7.47	-	-	-	-	-	-	-	-	-	-	-	-	-	-	-	-	-	-	-	-
Sutter County	5,333 6.76	8,869	2,476 27.92 27.92 46.43	-	-	2,022 27.77 81.66 22.80 37.91	-	-	-	-	134 32.60 5.41 1.51 2.51	-	-	-	-	50 13.74 2.02 0.56 0.94	-	-	-	-	-	-	-	-	-	-
South Yuba City (cdp)	1,355 10.52	2,922	979 33.50 33.50 72.25	-	-	870 32.56 88.87 29.77 64.21	-	-	-	-	-	-	-	-	-	-	-	-	-	-	-	-	-	-	-	-
Yuba City (city)	2,214 6.05	3,087	722 23.39 23.39 32.61	-	-	485 21.83 67.17 15.71 21.91	-	-	-	-	-	-	-	-	-	-	-	-	-	-	-	-	-	-	-	-
Tehama County	1,378 2.46	415	79 19.04 19.04 5.73	-	-	-	-	-	-	-	-	-	-	-	-	-	-	-	-	-	-	-	-	-	-	-
Tulare County	21,567 5.86	12,336	3,485 28.25 28.25 16.16	-	-	210 20.33 6.03 1.70 0.97	-	-	249 34.49 7.14 2.02 1.15	-	1,597 34.93 45.82 12.95 7.40	-	-	245 22.54 7.03 1.99 1.14	-	81 13.66 2.32 0.66 0.38	161 43.51 4.62 1.31 0.75	726 23.11 20.83 5.89 3.37	-	-	-	-	-	-	-	-
Porterville (city)	2,433 6.08	2,100	640 30.48 30.48 26.30	-	-	-	-	-	-	-	332 33.40 51.88 15.81 13.65	-	-	-	-	-	-	-	-	-	-	-	-	-	-	-

Notes: Please refer to the User's Guide for an explanation of data; data is arranged alphabetically by state, then county, then city within each county; table includes counties with populations greater than 49,999 unless noted and cities with populations greater than 9,999 whose Asian and/or NHPI population rates are greater than the national average; (1) Native Hawaiian and other Pacific Islander; (2) excludes Taiwanese; (3) includes Chamorro; (4) county does not meet population threshold but is shown in order to allow inclusion of city

Place	Total foreign-born naturalized citizens	Total Asian population	Asians who are foreign-born naturalized citizens	Total NHPI[1] population	NHPIs[1] who are foreign-born naturalized citizens	Asian Indian	Bangladeshi	Cambodian	Chinese[2]	Fijian	Filipino	Guamanian[3]	Hawaiian, Native	Hmong	Indonesian	Japanese	Korean	Laotian	Malaysian	Pakistani	Samoan	Sri Lankan	Taiwanese	Thai	Tongan	Vietnamese
Visalia (city)	4,004	5,077	1,278	-	-	-	-	-	-	-	271	-	-	125	-	-	-	523	-	-	-	-	-	-	-	-
	4.38		25.17								33.83			23.11				24.28								
											21.21			9.78				40.92								
			25.17								5.34			2.46				10.30								
			31.92								6.77			3.12				13.06								
Tuolumne County	1,075	451	91	-	-	-	-	-	-	-	-	-	-	-	-	-	-	-	-	-	-	-	-	-	-	-
	1.97		20.18																							
			20.18																							
			8.47																							
Ventura County	61,540	39,182	16,214	1,669	269	1,515	-	-	2,348	-	7,049	-	78	-	-	690	1,430	-	-	-	134	-	436	-	-	1,678
	8.17		41.38		16.12	35.68			46.08		46.21		13.57			13.23	55.23				21.90		54.71			51.90
						9.34			14.48		43.47		29.00			4.26	8.82				49.81		2.69			10.35
			41.38		16.12	3.87			5.99		17.99		4.67			1.76	3.65				8.03		1.11			4.28
			26.35		0.44	2.46			3.82		11.45		0.13			1.12	2.32				0.22		0.71			2.73
Camarillo (city)	4,256	4,014	1,469	-	-	-	-	-	186	-	556	-	-	-	-	87	215	-	-	-	-	-	-	-	-	205
	7.45		36.60						38.67		40.70					12.38	48.53									47.24
									12.66		37.85					5.92	14.64									13.96
			36.60						4.63		13.85					2.17	5.36									5.11
			34.52						4.37		13.06					2.04	5.05									4.82
Moorpark (city)	2,336	1,353	604	-	-	-	-	-	-	-	-	-	-	-	-	-	-	-	-	-	-	-	-	-	-	-
	7.47		44.64																							
			44.64																							
			25.86																							
Oxnard (city)	20,862	12,641	5,904	869	196	250	-	-	177	-	4,363	-	-	-	-	297	277	-	-	-	129	-	-	-	-	343
	12.23		46.71		22.55	53.42			48.36		48.45					24.83	65.48				23.84					44.03
						4.23			3.00		73.90					5.03	4.69				65.82					5.81
			46.71		22.55	1.98			1.40		34.51					2.35	2.19				14.84					2.71
			28.30		0.94	1.20			0.85		20.91					1.42	1.33				0.62					1.64
Port Hueneme (city)	1,824	1,314	541	-	-	-	-	-	-	-	401	-	-	-	-	-	-	-	-	-	-	-	-	-	-	-
	8.35		41.17								40.63															
											74.12															
			41.17								30.52															
			29.66								21.98															
Simi Valley (city)	8,454	6,710	2,775	-	-	505	-	-	551	-	586	-	-	-	-	53	294	-	-	-	-	-	-	-	-	486
	7.58		41.36			36.70			53.34		45.89					6.73	50.09									50.31
						18.20			19.86		21.12					1.91	10.59									17.51
			41.36			7.53			8.21		8.73					0.79	4.38									7.24
			32.82			5.97			6.52		6.93					0.63	3.48									5.75
Thousand Oaks (city)	8,928	6,378	2,472	-	-	346	-	-	857	-	259	-	-	-	-	26	236	-	-	-	-	-	-	-	-	236
	7.65		38.76			30.40			46.45		46.25					3.03	48.96									49.58
						14.00			34.67		10.48					1.05	9.55									9.55
			38.76			5.42			13.44		4.06					0.41	3.70									3.70
			27.69			3.88			9.60		2.90					0.29	2.64									2.64
Yolo County	11,911	15,792	4,116	715	64	404	-	-	1,629	44	419	-	-	128	-	107	341	74	-	-	-	-	-	-	-	595
	7.06		26.06		8.95	22.54			28.93	8.37	24.81			19.25		7.21	30.83	14.12								42.65
						9.82			39.58	68.75	10.18			3.11		2.60	8.28	1.80								14.46
			26.06		8.95	2.56			10.32	6.15	2.65			0.81		0.68	2.16	0.47								3.77
			34.56		0.54	3.39			13.68	0.37	3.52			1.07		0.90	2.86	0.62								5.00

Notes: Please refer to the User's Guide for an explanation of data; data is arranged alphabetically by state, then county, then city within each county; table includes counties with populations greater than 49,999 unless noted and cities with populations greater than 9,999 whose Asian and/or NHPI population rates are greater than the national average; (1) Native Hawaiian and other Pacific Islander; (2) excludes Taiwanese; (3) includes Chamorro; (4) county does not meet population threshold but is shown in order to allow inclusion of city

Place	Total foreign-born naturalized citizens	Total Asian population	Asians who are foreign-born naturalized citizens	Total NHPI[1] population	NHPIs[1] who are foreign-born naturalized citizens	Asian Indian	Bangladeshi	Cambodian	Chinese[2]	Fijian	Filipino	Guamanian[3]	Hawaiian, Native	Hmong	Indonesian	Japanese	Korean	Laotian	Malaysian	Pakistani	Samoan	Sri Lankan	Taiwanese	Thai	Tongan	Vietnamese
Davis (city)	4,740	9,963	2,930	-	-	160	-	-	1,441	-	238	-	-	-	-	41	281	-	-	-	-	-	-	-	-	527
	7.86		29.41			20.57			32.43		21.52					4.77	34.69									50.87
						5.46			49.18		8.12					1.40	9.59									17.99
			29.41			1.61			14.46		2.39					0.41	2.82									5.29
			61.81			3.38			30.40		5.02					0.86	5.93									11.12
West Sacramento (city)	2,371	2,251	468	-	-	109	-	-	-	-	-	-	-	102	-	-	-	-	-	-	-	-	-	-	-	-
	7.50		20.79			23.34								17.62												
						23.29								21.79												
			20.79			4.84								4.53												
			19.74			4.60								4.30												
Woodland (city)	2,907	1,781	474	-	-	124	-	-	-	-	-	-	-	-	-	-	-	-	-	-	-	-	-	-	-	-
	5.92		26.61			29.45																				
						26.16																				
			26.61			6.96																				
			16.31			4.27																				
Yuba County	2,595	4,551	1,042	-	-	-	-	-	-	-	168	-	-	508	-	-	-	-	-	-	-	-	-	-	-	-
	4.31		22.90								31.58			18.81												
											16.12			48.75												
			22.90								3.69			11.16												
			40.15								6.47			19.58												
Linda (cdp)	887	2,539	466	-	-	-	-	-	-	-	-	-	-	370	-	-	-	-	-	-	-	-	-	-	-	-
	6.61		18.35											18.22												
														79.40												
			18.35											14.57												
			52.54											41.71												
Marysville (city)	515	767	252	-	-	-	-	-	-	-	-	-	-	-	-	-	-	-	-	-	-	-	-	-	-	-
	4.19		32.86																							
			32.86																							
			48.93																							
Olivehurst (cdp)	463	547	147	-	-	-	-	-	-	-	-	-	-	-	-	-	-	-	-	-	-	-	-	-	-	-
	4.17		26.87																							
			26.87																							
			31.75																							
COLORADO	116,875	93,306	29,575	4,298	199	2,268	-	493	5,204	-	3,698	24	17	689	184	1,615	6,877	708	-	307	59	-	239	586	-	5,487
	2.72		31.70		4.63	19.18		33.36	35.10		39.68	2.37	1.17	22.86	23.90	13.58	44.97	30.58		37.76	6.44		35.15	30.10		40.15
						7.67		1.67	17.60		12.50	12.06	8.54	2.33	0.62	5.46	23.25	2.39		1.04	29.65		0.81	1.98		18.55
			31.70		4.63	2.43		0.53	5.58		3.96	0.56	0.40	0.74	0.20	1.73	7.37	0.76		0.33	1.37		0.26	0.63		5.88
			25.30		0.17	1.94		0.42	4.45		3.16	0.02	0.01	0.59	0.16	1.38	5.88	0.61		0.26	0.05		0.20	0.50		4.69
Adams County	12,266	11,508	3,556	-	-	94	-	-	478	-	298	-	-	468	-	134	465	291	-	-	-	-	-	-	-	924
	3.37		30.90			14.60			42.45		35.22			21.83		14.00	50.49	27.27								41.27
						2.64			13.44		8.38			13.16		3.77	13.08	8.18								25.98
			30.90			0.82			4.15		2.59			4.07		1.16	4.04	2.53								8.03
			28.99			0.77			3.90		2.43			3.82		1.09	3.79	2.37								7.53
Berkley (cdp)	439	419	143	-	-	-	-	-	-	-	-	-	-	-	-	-	-	-	-	-	-	-	-	-	-	-
	4.14		34.13																							
			34.13																							
			32.57																							

Notes: Please refer to the User's Guide for an explanation of data; data is arranged alphabetically by state, then county, then city within each county; table includes counties with populations greater than 49,999 unless noted and cities with populations greater than 9,999 whose Asian and/or NHPI population rates are greater than the national average; (1) Native Hawaiian and other Pacific Islander; (2) excludes Taiwanese; (3) includes Chamorro; (4) county does not meet population threshold but is shown in order to allow inclusion of city

Place	Total foreign-born naturalized citizens	Total Asian population	Asians who are foreign-born naturalized citizens	Total NHPI[1] population	NHPIs[1] who are foreign-born naturalized citizens	Asian Indian	Bangladeshi	Cambodian	Chinese[2]	Fijian	Filipino	Guamanian[3]	Hawaiian, Native	Hmong	Indonesian	Japanese	Korean	Laotian	Malaysian	Pakistani	Samoan	Sri Lankan	Taiwanese	Thai	Tongan	Vietnamese
Federal Heights (city)	364	748	202	-	-	-	-	-	-	-	-	-	-	-	-	-	-	-	-	-	-	-	-	-	-	-
	3.02		27.01																							
			27.01																							
			55.49																							
Westminster (city)	3,680	5,460	1,787	-	-	164	-	-	274	-	-	-	-	248	-	-	265	255	-	-	-	-	-	-	-	281
	3.64		32.73			34.97			42.75					24.43			47.92	37.72								34.14
						9.18			15.33					13.88			14.83	14.27								15.72
			32.73			3.00			5.02					4.54			4.85	4.67								5.15
			48.56			4.46			7.45					6.74			7.20	6.93								7.64
Arapahoe County	19,668	18,693	6,916	554	20	523	-	-	1,115	-	958	-	-	-	-	212	1,840	-	-	-	-	-	-	-	-	1,391
	4.03		37.00		3.61	22.03			36.44		43.94					12.26	41.02									50.80
						7.56			16.12		13.85					3.07	26.60									20.11
			37.00		3.61	2.80			5.96		5.12					1.13	9.84									7.44
			35.16		0.10	2.66			5.67		4.87					1.08	9.36									7.07
Aurora (city)	13,456	11,335	4,463	387	48	289	-	155	658	-	702	-	-	-	-	178	1,046	-	-	-	-	-	-	-	-	906
	4.88		39.37		12.40	27.76		35.15	40.57		47.69					17.42	41.69									47.31
						6.48		3.47	14.74		15.73					3.99	23.44									20.30
			39.37		12.40	2.55		1.37	5.81		6.19					1.57	9.23									7.99
			33.17		0.36	2.15		1.15	4.89		5.22					1.32	7.77									6.73
Boulder County	7,923	9,175	2,277	-	-	217	-	-	723	-	89	-	-	-	-	61	403	-	-	-	-	-	-	-	-	322
	2.72		24.82			18.53			29.06		21.98					4.60	32.76									44.17
						9.53			31.75		3.91					2.68	17.70									14.14
			24.82			2.37			7.88		0.97					0.66	4.39									3.51
			28.74			2.74			9.13		1.12					0.77	5.09									4.06
Boulder (city)	2,648	3,604	723	-	-	67	-	-	258	-	-	-	-	-	-	25	187	-	-	-	-	-	-	-	-	-
	2.80		20.06			16.14			27.36							4.81	24.22									
						9.27			35.68							3.46	25.86									
			20.06			1.86			7.16							0.69	5.19									
			27.30			2.53			9.74							0.94	7.06									
Broomfield (city)	1,006	1,648	588	-	-	-	-	-	108	-	-	-	-	-	-	-	-	-	-	-	-	-	-	-	-	-
	2.63		35.68						32.05																	
									18.37																	
			35.68						6.55																	
			58.45						10.74																	
Lafayette (city)	696	892	254	-	-	-	-	-	-	-	-	-	-	-	-	-	-	-	-	-	-	-	-	-	-	-
	2.98		28.48																							
			28.48																							
			36.49																							
Denver County	22,144	15,172	3,801	447	29	243	-	103	661	-	402	-	-	-	-	192	498	-	-	-	-	-	-	83	-	1,366
	3.99		25.05		6.49	11.89		25.88	30.87		41.74					9.73	39.03							20.44		30.70
						6.39		2.71	17.39		10.58					5.05	13.10							2.18		35.94
			25.05		6.49	1.60		0.68	4.36		2.65					1.27	3.28							0.55		9.00
			17.16		0.13	1.10		0.47	2.99		1.82					0.87	2.25							0.37		6.17
Douglas County	4,244	4,303	1,489	-	-	146	-	-	557	-	-	-	-	-	-	-	366	-	-	-	-	-	-	-	-	-
	2.41		34.60			17.12			43.35								60.20									
						9.81			37.41								24.58									
			34.60			3.39			12.94								8.51									
			35.08			3.44			13.12								8.62									

Notes: Please refer to the User's Guide for an explanation of data; data is arranged alphabetically by state, then county, then city within each county; table includes counties with populations greater than 49,999 unless noted and cities with populations greater than 9,999 whose Asian and/or NHPI population rates are greater than the national average; (1) Native Hawaiian and other Pacific Islander; (2) excludes Taiwanese; (3) includes Chamorro; (4) county does not meet population threshold but is shown in order to allow inclusion of city

Place	Total foreign-born naturalized citizens	Total Asian population	Asians who are foreign-born naturalized citizens	Total NHPI[1] population	NHPIs[1] who are foreign-born naturalized citizens	Asian Indian	Bangladeshi	Cambodian	Chinese[2]	Fijian	Filipino	Guamanian[3]	Hawaiian, Native	Hmong	Indonesian	Japanese	Korean	Laotian	Malaysian	Pakistani	Samoan	Sri Lankan	Taiwanese	Thai	Tongan	Vietnamese
Highlands Ranch (cdp)	2,043 2.88	2,913	947 32.51 32.51 46.35	-	-	104 16.00 10.98 3.57 5.09	-	-	384 41.33 40.55 13.18 18.80	-	-	-	-	-	-	-	-	-	-	-	-	-	-	-	-	-
El Paso County	16,122 3.12	13,154	4,794 36.45 36.45 29.74	1,291	63 4.88 4.88 0.39	261 13.44 5.44 1.98 1.62	-	-	351 34.31 7.32 2.67 2.18	-	1,006 39.48 20.98 7.65 6.24	11 2.24 17.46 0.85 0.07	-	-	-	532 36.26 11.10 4.04 3.30	1,847 46.93 38.53 14.04 11.46	-	-	-	-	-	-	-	-	372 40.92 7.76 2.83 2.31
Colorado Springs (city)	11,331 3.14	10,295	3,389 32.92 32.92 29.91	798	56 7.02 7.02 0.49	233 12.38 6.88 2.26 2.06	-	-	283 33.53 8.35 2.75 2.50	-	582 33.51 17.17 5.65 5.14	-	-	-	-	310 30.13 9.15 3.01 2.74	1,373 45.69 40.51 13.34 12.12	-	-	-	-	-	-	-	-	279 36.86 8.23 2.71 2.46
Jefferson County	12,367 2.35	11,752	3,875 32.97 32.97 31.33	437	13 2.97 2.97 0.11	457 31.60 11.79 3.89 3.70	-	-	670 34.99 17.29 5.70 5.42	-	414 43.81 10.68 3.52 3.35	-	-	100 24.27 2.58 0.85 0.81	-	220 11.60 5.68 1.87 1.78	832 56.06 21.47 7.08 6.73	271 29.46 6.99 2.31 2.19	-	-	-	-	-	-	-	647 37.49 16.70 5.51 5.23
Larimer County	4,229 1.68	3,616	1,084 29.98 29.98 25.63	-	-	139 22.20 12.82 3.84 3.29	-	-	242 27.94 22.32 6.69 5.72	-	-	-	-	-	-	40 6.94 3.69 1.11 0.95	215 35.95 19.83 5.95 5.08	-	-	-	-	-	-	-	-	-
Mesa County	1,360 1.17	424	183 43.16 43.16 13.46	-	-	-	-	-	-	-	-	-	-	-	-	-	-	-	-	-	-	-	-	-	-	-
Pueblo County	1,803 1.27	761	323 42.44 42.44 17.91	-	-	-	-	-	-	-	-	-	-	-	-	-	-	-	-	-	-	-	-	-	-	-
Weld County	4,411 2.44	1,533	427 27.85 27.85 9.68	-	-	-	-	-	-	-	-	-	-	-	-	45 9.09 10.54 2.94 1.02	-	-	-	-	-	-	-	-	-	-
CONNECTICUT	180,267 5.29	82,277	27,408 33.31 33.31 15.20	1,357	67 4.94 4.94 0.04	7,409 30.99 27.03 9.00 4.11	69 19.83 0.25 0.08 0.04	942 43.59 3.44 1.14 0.52	6,334 33.73 23.11 7.70 3.51	-	2,864 38.13 10.45 3.48 1.59	12 2.86 17.91 0.88 0.01	-	-	-	357 7.84 1.30 0.43 0.20	2,936 43.65 10.71 3.57 1.63	1,102 35.47 4.02 1.34 0.61	-	575 27.23 2.10 0.70 0.32	-	-	257 31.38 0.94 0.31 0.14	239 30.48 0.87 0.29 0.13	-	3,251 43.94 11.86 3.95 1.80
Fairfield County	62,953 7.13	28,452	9,292 32.66 32.66 14.76	-	-	2,605 31.22 28.03 9.16 4.14	-	624 43.27 6.72 2.19 0.99	2,166 37.34 23.31 7.61 3.44	-	927 38.07 9.98 3.26 1.47	-	-	-	-	98 3.71 1.05 0.34 0.16	822 42.55 8.85 2.89 1.31	396 38.41 4.26 1.39 0.63	-	189 34.81 2.03 0.66 0.30	-	-	-	-	-	911 38.02 9.80 3.20 1.45

Notes: Please refer to the User's Guide for an explanation of data; data is arranged alphabetically by state, then county, then city within each county; table includes counties with populations greater than 49,999 unless noted and cities with populations greater than 9,999 whose Asian and/or NHPI population rates are greater than the national average; (1) Native Hawaiian and other Pacific Islander; (2) excludes Taiwanese; (3) includes Chamorro; (4) county does not meet population threshold but is shown in order to allow inclusion of city

Place	Total foreign-born naturalized citizens	Total Asian population	Asians who are foreign-born naturalized citizens	Total NHPI[1] population	NHPIs[1] who are foreign-born naturalized citizens	Asian Indian	Bangladeshi	Cambodian	Chinese[2]	Fijian	Filipino	Guamanian[3]	Hawaiian, Native	Hmong	Indonesian	Japanese	Korean	Laotian	Malaysian	Pakistani	Samoan	Sri Lankan	Taiwanese	Thai	Tongan	Vietnamese
Danbury (city)	6,193 8.27	3,671	1,334 36.34 36.34 21.54	-	-	345 28.80 25.86 9.40 5.57	-	195 34.09 14.62 5.31 3.15	179 37.45 13.42 4.88 2.89	-	-	-	-	-	-	-	-	-	-	-	-	-	-	-	-	-
Greenwich (town)	4,850 7.94	3,259	769 23.60 23.60 15.86	-	-	166 41.71 21.59 5.09 3.42	-	-	343 53.68 44.60 10.52 7.07	-	-	-	-	-	-	26 1.88 3.38 0.80 0.54	-	-	-	-	-	-	-	-	-	-
Stamford (city)	12,880 11.00	5,735	1,773 30.92 30.92 13.77	-	-	654 22.78 36.89 11.40 5.08	-	-	496 43.13 27.98 8.65 3.85	-	240 29.81 13.54 4.18 1.86	-	-	-	-	-	-	-	-	-	-	-	-	-	-	-
Hartford County	54,803 6.39	21,058	7,483 35.54 35.54 13.65	-	-	2,146 31.91 28.68 10.19 3.92	-	-	1,427 37.01 19.07 6.78 2.60	-	642 36.46 8.58 3.05 1.17	-	-	-	-	91 16.82 1.22 0.43 0.17	698 48.30 9.33 3.31 1.27	396 32.59 5.29 1.88 0.72	-	152 22.75 2.03 0.72 0.28	-	-	-	-	-	1,509 47.14 20.17 7.17 2.75
East Hartford (town)	3,882 7.83	2,091	863 41.27 41.27 22.23	-	-	289 46.46 33.49 13.82 7.44	-	-	-	-	-	-	-	-	-	-	-	-	-	-	-	-	-	-	-	254 45.93 29.43 12.15 6.54
Farmington (town)	1,848 7.82	972	368 37.86 37.86 19.91	-	-	-	-	-	-	-	-	-	-	-	-	-	-	-	-	-	-	-	-	-	-	-
Glastonbury (town)	1,434 4.50	1,212	491 40.51 40.51 34.24	-	-	205 40.92 41.75 16.91 14.30	-	-	-	-	-	-	-	-	-	-	-	-	-	-	-	-	-	-	-	-
Rocky Hill (town)	1,381 7.70	711	239 33.61 33.61 17.31	-	-	-	-	-	-	-	-	-	-	-	-	-	-	-	-	-	-	-	-	-	-	-
South Windsor (town)	1,547 6.32	965	385 39.90 39.90 24.89	-	-	-	-	-	-	-	-	-	-	-	-	-	-	-	-	-	-	-	-	-	-	-
West Hartford (town)	5,758 9.06	3,063	1,282 41.85 41.85 22.26	-	-	265 34.33 20.67 8.65 4.60	-	-	357 43.33 27.85 11.66 6.20	-	-	-	-	-	-	-	-	-	-	-	-	-	-	-	-	337 50.30 26.29 11.00 5.85

Notes: Please refer to the User's Guide for an explanation of data; data is arranged alphabetically by state, then county, then city within each county; table includes counties with populations greater than 49,999 unless noted and cities with populations greater than 9,999 whose Asian and/or NHPI population rates are greater than the national average; (1) Native Hawaiian and other Pacific Islander; (2) excludes Taiwanese; (3) includes Chamorro; (4) county does not meet population threshold but is shown in order to allow inclusion of city

Place	Total foreign-born naturalized citizens	Total Asian population	Asians who are foreign-born naturalized citizens	Total NHPI[1] population	NHPIs[1] who are foreign-born naturalized citizens	Asian Indian	Bangladeshi	Cambodian	Chinese[2]	Fijian	Filipino	Guamanian[3]	Hawaiian, Native	Hmong	Indonesian	Japanese	Korean	Laotian	Malaysian	Pakistani	Samoan	Sri Lankan	Taiwanese	Thai	Tongan	Vietnamese
Litchfield County	5,928	2,278	914	-	-	224	-	-	100	-	-	-	-	-	-	-	189	-	-	-	-	-	-	-	-	81
	3.25		40.12			48.70			24.39								51.36									30.57
						24.51			10.94								20.68									8.86
			40.12			9.83			4.39								8.30									3.56
			15.42			3.78			1.69								3.19									1.37
Middlesex County	5,208	2,272	856	-	-	170	-	-	178	-	-	-	-	-	-	-	-	-	-	-	-	-	-	-	-	-
	3.36		37.68			26.11			32.66																	
						19.86			20.79																	
			37.68			7.48			7.83																	
			16.44			3.26			3.42																	
New Haven County	36,699	19,615	5,784	-	-	1,636	-	-	1,580	-	594	-	-	-	-	48	642	183	-	156	-	-	-	-	-	454
	4.45		29.49			27.65			29.47		36.76					5.39	31.26	36.31		23.89						51.01
						28.28			27.32		10.27					0.83	11.10	3.16		2.70						7.85
			29.49			8.34			8.06		3.03					0.24	3.27	0.93		0.80						2.31
			15.76			4.46			4.31		1.62					0.13	1.75	0.50		0.43						1.24
New Haven (city)	4,727	4,623	931	-	-	191	-	-	344	-	-	-	-	-	-	-	93	-	-	-	-	-	-	-	-	-
	3.82		20.14			23.67			19.36								17.22									
						20.52			36.95								9.99									
			20.14			4.13			7.44								2.01									
			19.70			4.04			7.28								1.97									
New London County	7,955	4,806	1,855	-	-	286	-	-	597	-	407	-	-	-	-	-	-	-	-	-	-	-	-	-	-	-
	3.07		38.60			31.12			38.42		39.44															
						15.42			32.18		21.94															
			38.60			5.95			12.42		8.47															
			23.32			3.60			7.50		5.12															
Tolland County	4,203	3,123	982	-	-	315	-	-	198	-	-	-	-	-	-	-	-	-	-	-	-	-	-	-	-	-
	3.08		31.44			36.84			18.45																	
						32.08			20.16																	
			31.44			10.09			6.34																	
			23.36			7.49			4.71																	
Mansfield (town)	883	1,487	309	-	-	154	-	-	52	-	-	-	-	-	-	-	-	-	-	-	-	-	-	-	-	-
	4.26		20.78			34.84			8.58																	
						49.84			16.83																	
			20.78			10.36			3.50																	
			34.99			17.44			5.89																	
Storrs (cdp)	402	1,064	148	-	-	-	-	-	52	-	-	-	-	-	-	-	-	-	-	-	-	-	-	-	-	-
	3.60		13.91						9.54																	
									35.14																	
			13.91						4.89																	
			36.82						12.94																	
Windham County	2,518	673	242	-	-	-	-	-	-	-	-	-	-	-	-	-	-	-	-	-	-	-	-	-	-	-
	2.31		35.96																							
			35.96																							
			9.61																							
DELAWARE	19,052	16,053	5,742	335	17	1,456	-	-	1,327	-	917	-	-	-	-	191	827	-	-	160	-	-	-	-	-	345
	2.43		35.77		5.07	27.83			32.35		50.25					31.57	44.70			42.22						50.29
						25.36			23.11		15.97					3.33	14.40			2.79						6.01
			35.77		5.07	9.07			8.27		5.71					1.19	5.15			1.00						2.15
			30.14		0.09	7.64			6.97		4.81					1.00	4.34			0.84						1.81

Notes: Please refer to the User's Guide for an explanation of data; data is arranged alphabetically by state, then county, then city within each county; table includes counties with populations greater than 49,999 unless noted and cities with populations greater than 9,999 whose Asian and/or NHPI population rates are greater than the national average; (1) Native Hawaiian and other Pacific Islander; (2) excludes Taiwanese; (3) includes Chamorro; (4) county does not meet population threshold but is shown in order to allow inclusion of city

Place	Total foreign-born naturalized citizens	Total Asian population	Asians who are foreign-born naturalized citizens	Total NHPI[1] population	NHPIs[1] who are foreign-born naturalized citizens	Asian Indian	Bangladeshi	Cambodian	Chinese[2]	Fijian	Filipino	Guamanian[3]	Hawaiian, Native	Hmong	Indonesian	Japanese	Korean	Laotian	Malaysian	Pakistani	Samoan	Sri Lankan	Taiwanese	Thai	Tongan	Vietnamese
Kent County	2,605 2.06	2,083	865 41.53 41.53 33.21	-	-	123 29.36 14.22 5.90 4.72	-	-	-	-	244 48.90 28.21 11.71 9.37	-	-	-	-	-	-	-	-	-	-	-	-	-	-	-
New Castle County	14,272 2.85	13,182	4,647 35.25 35.25 32.56	-	-	1,314 28.27 28.28 9.97 9.21	-	-	1,191 31.74 25.63 9.04 8.35	-	564 50.67 12.14 4.28 3.95	-	-	-	-	102 26.42 2.19 0.77 0.71	671 47.76 14.44 5.09 4.70	-	-	-	-	-	-	-	-	302 56.34 6.50 2.29 2.12
Hockessin (cdp)	781 6.06	837	338 40.38 40.38 43.28	-	-	-	-	-	-	-	-	-	-	-	-	-	-	-	-	-	-	-	-	-	-	-
Newark (city)	596 2.09	1,219	217 17.80 17.80 36.41	-	-	-	-	-	54 9.98 24.88 4.43 9.06	-	-	-	-	-	-	-	-	-	-	-	-	-	-	-	-	-
Pike Creek (cdp)	981 4.97	1,085	487 44.88 44.88 49.64	-	-	-	-	-	-	-	-	-	-	-	-	-	-	-	-	-	-	-	-	-	-	-
Sussex County	2,175 1.39	788	230 29.19 29.19 10.57	-	-	-	-	-	-	-	-	-	-	-	-	-	-	-	-	-	-	-	-	-	-	-
DISTRICT OF COLUMBIA	22,050 3.85	14,762	3,599 24.38 24.38 16.32	-	-	647 26.79 17.98 4.38 2.93	-	-	1,173 30.52 32.59 7.95 5.32	-	447 21.09 12.42 3.03 2.03	-	-	-	-	36 3.47 1.00 0.24 0.16	456 39.04 12.67 3.09 2.07	-	-	-	-	-	-	-	-	455 25.43 12.64 3.08 2.06
FLORIDA	1,207,502 7.56	264,377	99,107 37.49 37.49 8.21	6,812	700 10.28 10.28 0.06	21,913 32.32 22.11 8.29 1.81	328 26.03 0.33 0.12 0.03	1,171 42.40 1.18 0.44 0.10	17,580 39.18 17.74 6.65 1.46	-	23,541 43.33 23.75 8.90 1.95	66 3.27 9.43 0.97 0.01	41 2.08 5.86 0.60 <0.01	-	346 38.70 0.35 0.13 0.03	2,972 26.19 3.00 1.12 0.25	8,158 42.76 8.23 3.09 0.68	1,438 35.67 1.45 0.54 0.12	-	1,810 33.24 1.83 0.68 0.15	190 22.38 27.14 2.79 0.02	155 38.56 0.16 0.06 0.01	988 48.74 1.00 0.37 0.08	2,470 37.58 2.49 0.93 0.20	-	13,645 40.86 13.77 5.16 1.13
Alachua County	5,956 2.73	7,858	2,010 25.58 25.58 33.75	-	-	562 28.84 27.96 7.15 9.44	-	-	367 17.19 18.26 4.67 6.16	-	386 36.90 19.20 4.91 6.48	-	-	-	-	91 21.02 4.53 1.16 1.53	132 13.13 6.57 1.68 2.22	-	-	-	-	-	-	-	-	294 47.65 14.63 3.74 4.94
Gainesville (city)	2,832 2.96	4,399	897 20.39 20.39 31.67	-	-	201 19.03 22.41 4.57 7.10	-	-	215 14.77 23.97 4.89 7.59	-	-	-	-	-	-	-	53 10.58 5.91 1.20 1.87	-	-	-	-	-	-	-	-	-

Notes: Please refer to the User's Guide for an explanation of data; data is arranged alphabetically by state, then county, then city within each county; table includes counties with populations greater than 49,999 unless noted and cities with populations greater than 9,999 whose Asian and/or NHPI population rates are greater than the national average; (1) Native Hawaiian and other Pacific Islander; (2) excludes Taiwanese; (3) includes Chamorro; (4) county does not meet population threshold but is shown in order to allow inclusion of city

Place	Total foreign-born naturalized citizens	Total Asian population	Asians who are foreign-born naturalized citizens	Total NHPI population	NHPIs[1] who are foreign-born naturalized citizens	Asian Indian	Bangladeshi	Cambodian	Chinese[2]	Fijian	Filipino	Guamanian[3]	Hawaiian, Native	Hmong	Indonesian	Japanese	Korean	Laotian	Malaysian	Pakistani	Samoan	Sri Lankan	Taiwanese	Thai	Tongan	Vietnamese
Bay County	2,885 1.95	2,369	944 39.85 39.85 32.72	-	-	-	-	-	-	-	201 41.53 21.29 8.48 6.97	-	-	-	-	-	-	-	-	-	-	-	-	-	-	252 37.84 26.69 10.64 8.73
Callaway (city)	500 3.51	530	217 40.94 40.94 43.40	-	-	-	-	-	-	-	-	-	-	-	-	-	-	-	-	-	-	-	-	-	-	-
Brevard County	18,374 3.86	7,122	2,983 41.88 41.88 16.23	-	-	683 34.65 22.90 9.59 3.72	-	-	344 38.57 11.53 4.83 1.87	-	769 50.03 25.78 10.80 4.19	-	-	-	-	131 24.95 4.39 1.84 0.71	312 50.24 10.46 4.38 1.70	-	-	-	-	-	-	-	-	406 53.21 13.61 5.70 2.21
Broward County	183,641 11.31	36,505	13,921 38.13 38.13 7.58	645	176 27.29 27.29 0.10	4,500 34.59 32.33 12.33 2.45	-	-	3,658 42.75 26.28 10.02 1.99	-	2,112 43.37 15.17 5.79 1.15	-	-	-	-	205 19.62 1.47 0.56 0.11	916 40.53 6.58 2.51 0.50	-	-	287 26.16 2.06 0.79 0.16	-	-	-	154 25.71 1.11 0.42 0.08	-	1,353 47.19 9.72 3.71 0.74
Cooper City (city)	3,037 10.97	1,241	587 47.30 47.30 19.33	-	-	303 51.10 51.62 24.42 9.98	-	-	-	-	-	-	-	-	-	-	-	-	-	-	-	-	-	-	-	-
Pembroke Pines (city)	22,597 16.48	5,004	2,069 41.35 41.35 9.16	-	-	683 38.98 33.01 13.65 3.02	-	-	497 43.10 24.02 9.93 2.20	-	460 49.62 22.23 9.19 2.04	-	-	-	-	-	-	-	-	-	-	-	-	-	-	-
Charlotte County	6,815 4.81	872	382 43.81 43.81 5.61	-	-	-	-	-	-	-	-	-	-	-	-	-	-	-	-	-	-	-	-	-	-	-
Citrus County	3,861 3.27	1,145	508 44.37 44.37 13.16	-	-	-	-	-	-	-	-	-	-	-	-	-	-	-	-	-	-	-	-	-	-	-
Clay County	3,472 2.47	2,901	1,206 41.57 41.57 34.74	-	-	-	-	-	-	-	867 50.29 71.89 29.89 24.97	-	-	-	-	-	-	-	-	-	-	-	-	-	-	-
Bellair-Meadowbrook Ter. (cdp)	526 3.18	635	277 43.62 43.62 52.66	-	-	-	-	-	-	-	-	-	-	-	-	-	-	-	-	-	-	-	-	-	-	-

Notes: Please refer to the User's Guide for an explanation of data; data is arranged alphabetically by state, then county, then city within each county; table includes counties with populations greater than 49,999 unless noted and cities with populations greater than 9,999 whose Asian and/or NHPI population rates are greater than the national average; (1) Native Hawaiian and other Pacific Islander; (2) excludes Taiwanese; (3) includes Chamorro; (4) county does not meet population threshold but is shown in order to allow inclusion of city

Place	Total foreign-born naturalized citizens	Total Asian population	Asians who are foreign-born naturalized citizens	Total NHPI[1] population	NHPIs[1] who are foreign-born naturalized citizens	Asian Indian	Bangladeshi	Cambodian	Chinese[2]	Fijian	Filipino	Guamanian[3]	Hawaiian, Native	Hmong	Indonesian	Japanese	Korean	Laotian	Malaysian	Pakistani	Samoan	Sri Lankan	Taiwanese	Thai	Tongan	Vietnamese
	14,194	1,200	526	-	-	-	-	-	-	-	-	-	-	-	-	-	-	-	-	-	-	-	-	-	-	-
	5.65		43.83																							
Collier County																										
			43.83																							
			3.71																							
	779	386	177	-	-	-	-	-	-	-	-	-	-	-	-	-	-	-	-	-	-	-	-	-	-	-
	1.38		45.85																							
Columbia County																										
			45.85																							
			22.72																							
	21,813	20,554	7,933	507	15	674	-	349	645	-	4,580	-	-	-	-	163	416	-	-	-	-	-	-	-	-	714
	2.80		38.60		2.96	24.36		34.87	39.28		44.88					29.64	43.02									33.81
Duval County						8.50		4.40	8.13		57.73					2.05	5.24									9.00
			38.60		2.96	3.28		1.70	3.14		22.28					0.79	2.02									3.47
			36.37		0.07	3.09		1.60	2.96		21.00					0.75	1.91									3.27
	6,088	6,565	2,693	-	-	199	-	-	202	-	1,258	-	-	-	-	-	-	-	-	-	-	-	-	-	-	578
	2.07		41.02			38.57			34.41		46.30															36.19
Escambia County						7.39			7.50		46.71															21.46
			41.02			3.03			3.08		19.16															8.80
			44.23			3.27			3.32		20.66															9.49
	590	787	323	-	-	-	-	-	-	-	205	-	-	-	-	-	-	-	-	-	-	-	-	-	-	-
	2.80		41.04								49.76															
Bellview (cdp)											63.47															
			41.04								26.05															
			54.75								34.75															
	565	812	332	-	-	-	-	-	-	-	239	-	-	-	-	-	-	-	-	-	-	-	-	-	-	-
	3.26		40.89								50.74															
Myrtle Grove (cdp)											71.99															
			40.89								29.43															
			58.76								42.30															
	4,701	773	298	-	-	-	-	-	-	-	-	-	-	-	-	-	-	-	-	-	-	-	-	-	-	-
	3.59		38.55																							
Hernando County																										
			38.55																							
			6.34																							
	2,795	964	320	-	-	-	-	-	-	-	156	-	-	-	-	-	-	-	-	-	-	-	-	-	-	-
	3.20		33.20								34.90															
Highlands County											48.75															
			33.20								16.18															
			11.45								5.58															
	47,127	21,571	7,068	540	34	1,558	-	-	749	-	1,172	-	-	-	-	285	951	-	-	-	-	-	-	264	-	1,556
	4.72		32.77		6.30	26.40			27.96		36.59					33.02	34.99							39.05		38.97
Hillsborough County						22.04			10.60		16.58					4.03	13.46							3.74		22.01
			32.77		6.30	7.22			3.47		5.43					1.32	4.41							1.22		7.21
			15.00		0.07	3.31			1.59		2.49					0.60	2.02							0.56		3.30
	577	508	176	-	-	-	-	-	-	-	-	-	-	-	-	-	-	-	-	-	-	-	-	-	-	-
	5.19		34.65																							
Westchase (cdp)																										
			34.65																							
			30.50																							

Notes: Please refer to the User's Guide for an explanation of data; data is arranged alphabetically by state, then county, then city within each county; table includes counties with populations greater than 49,999 unless noted and cities with populations greater than 9,999 whose Asian and/or NHPI population rates are greater than the national average; (1) Native Hawaiian and other Pacific Islander; (2) excludes Taiwanese; (3) includes Chamorro; (4) county does not meet population threshold but is shown in order to allow inclusion of city

Place	Total foreign-born naturalized citizens	Total Asian population	Asians who are foreign-born naturalized citizens	Total NHPI[1] population	NHPIs[1] who are foreign-born naturalized citizens	Asian Indian	Bangladeshi	Cambodian	Chinese[2]	Fijian	Filipino	Guamanian[3]	Hawaiian, Native	Hmong	Indonesian	Japanese	Korean	Laotian	Malaysian	Pakistani	Samoan	Sri Lankan	Taiwanese	Thai	Tongan	Vietnamese
Indian River County	4,120 3.65	864	358 41.44 41.44 8.69	-	-	-	-	-	-	-	-	-	-	-	-	-	-	-	-	-	-	-	-	-	-	-
Lake County	5,084 2.41	1,422	566 39.80 39.80 11.13	-	-	-	-	-	-	-	-	-	-	-	-	-	-	-	-	-	-	-	-	-	-	-
Lee County	15,380 3.49	3,159	1,359 43.02 43.02 8.84	-	-	257 38.42 18.91 8.14 1.67	-	-	297 49.83 21.85 9.40 1.93	-	456 41.30 33.55 14.43 2.96	-	-	-	-	-	-	-	-	-	-	-	-	-	-	-
Leon County	4,776 1.99	4,858	1,560 32.11 32.11 32.66	-	-	516 34.22 33.08 10.62 10.80	-	-	274 25.25 17.56 5.64 5.74	-	169 32.13 10.83 3.48 3.54	-	-	-	-	-	165 37.00 10.58 3.40 3.45	-	-	-	-	-	-	-	-	-
Manatee County	8,466 3.21	2,237	1,050 46.94 46.94 12.40	-	-	-	-	-	-	-	227 42.19 21.62 10.15 2.68	-	-	-	-	-	-	-	-	-	-	-	-	-	-	-
Marion County	7,516 2.90	2,221	840 37.82 37.82 11.18	-	-	305 32.14 36.31 13.73 4.06	-	-	-	-	-	-	-	-	-	-	-	-	-	-	-	-	-	-	-	-
Martin County	4,482 3.54	701	364 51.93 51.93 8.12	-	-	-	-	-	-	-	-	-	-	-	-	-	-	-	-	-	-	-	-	-	-	-
Miami-Dade County	535,080 23.75	30,692	11,851 38.61 38.61 2.21	605	220 36.36 36.36 0.04	2,962 33.14 24.99 9.65 0.55	-	-	4,020 45.22 33.92 13.10 0.75	-	1,874 41.45 15.81 6.11 0.35	-	-	-	-	218 15.53 1.84 0.71 0.04	600 44.91 5.06 1.95 0.11	-	-	357 44.96 3.01 1.16 0.07	-	-	-	256 29.02 2.16 0.83 0.05	-	702 44.01 5.92 2.29 0.13
Doral (cdp)	3,753 18.30	1,186	186 15.68 15.68 4.96	-	-	-	-	-	-	-	-	-	-	-	-	-	-	-	-	-	-	-	-	-	-	-
Ives Estates (cdp)	3,439 19.75	831	381 45.85 45.85 11.08	-	-	-	-	-	-	-	-	-	-	-	-	-	-	-	-	-	-	-	-	-	-	-

Notes: Please refer to the User's Guide for an explanation of data; data is arranged alphabetically by state, then county, then city within each county; table includes counties with populations greater than 49,999 unless noted and cities with populations greater than 9,999 whose Asian and/or NHPI population rates are greater than the national average; (1) Native Hawaiian and other Pacific Islander; (2) excludes Taiwanese; (3) includes Chamorro; (4) county does not meet population threshold but is shown in order to allow inclusion of city

Place	Total foreign-born naturalized citizens	Total Asian population	Asians who are foreign-born naturalized citizens	Total NHPI[1] population	NHPIs[1] who are foreign-born naturalized citizens	Asian Indian	Bangladeshi	Cambodian	Chinese[2]	Fijian	Filipino	Guamanian[3]	Hawaiian, Native	Hmong	Indonesian	Japanese	Korean	Laotian	Malaysian	Pakistani	Samoan	Sri Lankan	Taiwanese	Thai	Tongan	Vietnamese
North Miami Beach (city)	8,469	1,706	607	-	-	103	-	-	360	-	-	-	-	-	-	-	-	-	-	-	-	-	-	-	-	-
	20.82		35.58			26.01			48.58																	
						16.97			59.31																	
			35.58			6.04			21.10																	
			7.17			1.22			4.25																	
Pinecrest (village)	2,830	884	364	-	-	-	-	-	-	-	-	-	-	-	-	-	-	-	-	-	-	-	-	-	-	-
	14.75		41.18																							
			41.18																							
			12.86																							
Monroe County	5,004	566	185	-	-	-	-	-	-	-	-	-	-	-	-	-	-	-	-	-	-	-	-	-	-	-
	6.29		32.69																							
			32.69																							
			3.70																							
Nassau County	666	422	177	-	-	-	-	-	-	-	-	-	-	-	-	-	-	-	-	-	-	-	-	-	-	-
	1.15		41.94																							
			41.94																							
			26.58																							
Okaloosa County	5,715	4,432	2,115	-	-	-	-	-	-	-	748	-	-	-	-	-	392	-	-	-	-	-	-	389	-	181
	3.35		47.72								42.94						54.44							62.34		45.25
											35.37						18.53							18.39		8.56
			47.72								16.88						8.84							8.78		4.08
			37.01								13.09						6.86							6.81		3.17
Wright (cdp)	964	825	385	-	-	-	-	-	-	-	-	-	-	-	-	-	-	-	-	-	-	-	-	-	-	-
	4.47		46.67																							
			46.67																							
			39.94																							
Orange County	53,651	28,748	10,922	853	53	2,510	-	-	1,479	-	1,835	-	-	-	-	271	872	-	-	285	-	-	-	-	-	2,892
	5.99		37.99		6.21	32.81			37.05		40.56					22.58	40.65			31.63						45.49
						22.98			13.54		16.80					2.48	7.98			2.61						26.48
			37.99		6.21	8.73			5.14		6.38					0.94	3.03			0.99						10.06
			20.36		0.10	4.68			2.76		3.42					0.51	1.63			0.53						5.39
Oak Ridge (cdp)	2,133	1,306	465	-	-	-	-	-	-	-	-	-	-	-	-	-	-	-	-	-	-	-	-	-	-	226
	9.52		35.60																							42.88
																										48.60
			35.60																							17.30
			21.80																							10.60
Osceola County	9,514	3,642	1,480	-	-	241	-	-	286	-	440	-	-	-	-	-	-	-	-	-	-	-	-	-	-	-
	5.52		40.64			24.95			48.97		49.83															
						16.28			19.32		29.73															
			40.64			6.62			7.85		12.08															
			15.56			2.53			3.01		4.62															
Palm Beach County	83,681	16,895	6,076	423	17	1,577	-	-	1,380	-	889	-	-	-	-	179	403	-	-	-	-	-	-	257	-	841
	7.40		35.96		4.02	30.93			37.90		39.72					31.18	43.24							33.82		42.18
						25.95			22.71		14.63					2.95	6.63							4.23		13.84
			35.96		4.02	9.33			8.17		5.26					1.06	2.39							1.52		4.98
			7.26		0.02	1.88			1.65		1.06					0.21	0.48							0.31		1.01

Notes: Please refer to the User's Guide for an explanation of data; data is arranged alphabetically by state, then county, then city within each county; table includes counties with populations greater than 49,999 unless noted and cities with populations greater than 9,999 whose Asian and/or NHPI population rates are greater than the national average; (1) Native Hawaiian and other Pacific Islander; (2) excludes Taiwanese; (3) includes Chamorro; (4) county does not meet population threshold but is shown in order to allow inclusion of city

Place	Total foreign-born naturalized citizens	Total Asian population	Asians who are foreign-born naturalized citizens	Total NHPI[1] population	NHPIs[1] who are foreign-born naturalized citizens	Asian Indian	Bangladeshi	Cambodian	Chinese[2]	Fijian	Filipino	Guamanian[3]	Hawaiian, Native	Hmong	Indonesian	Japanese	Korean	Laotian	Malaysian	Pakistani	Samoan	Sri Lankan	Taiwanese	Thai	Tongan	Vietnamese
Pasco County	13,303 3.86	3,489	1,432 41.04 41.04 10.76	-	-	247 24.87 17.25 7.08 1.86	-	-	226 44.84 15.78 6.48 1.70	-	481 48.39 33.59 13.79 3.62	-	-	-	-	-	-	-	-	-	-	-	-	-	-	-
Pinellas County	40,786 4.43	18,783	6,215 33.09 33.09 15.24	-	-	1,211 33.20 19.49 6.45 2.97	-	203 28.27 3.27 1.08 0.50	793 38.03 12.76 4.22 1.94	-	1,026 33.82 16.51 5.46 2.52	-	-	-	-	125 22.01 2.01 0.67 0.31	419 49.06 6.74 2.23 1.03	624 33.64 10.04 3.32 1.53	-	-	-	-	-	97 19.88 1.56 0.52 0.24	-	1,356 32.03 21.82 7.22 3.32
Pinellas Park (city)	1,901 4.19	1,811	595 32.85 32.85 31.30	-	-	-	-	-	-	-	-	-	-	-	-	-	-	-	-	-	-	-	-	-	-	159 30.23 26.72 8.78 8.36
Polk County	11,908 2.46	5,805	1,942 33.45 33.45 16.31	-	-	507 29.53 26.11 8.73 4.26	-	-	180 30.25 9.27 3.10 1.51	-	427 47.34 21.99 7.36 3.59	-	-	-	-	-	-	84 20.95 4.33 1.45 0.71	-	-	-	-	-	-	-	330 37.84 16.99 5.68 2.77
Putnam County	986 1.40	291	142 48.80 48.80 14.40	-	-	-	-	-	-	-	-	-	-	-	-	-	-	-	-	-	-	-	-	-	-	-
St. Johns County	3,604 2.93	1,244	563 45.26 45.26 15.62	-	-	-	-	-	-	-	-	-	-	-	-	-	-	-	-	-	-	-	-	-	-	-
St. Lucie County	8,746 4.54	1,885	693 36.76 36.76 7.92	-	-	-	-	-	-	-	-	-	-	-	-	-	-	-	-	-	-	-	-	-	-	-
Santa Rosa County	2,065 1.75	1,608	853 53.05 53.05 41.31	-	-	-	-	-	-	-	410 57.99 48.07 25.50 19.85	-	-	-	-	-	-	-	-	-	-	-	-	-	-	-
Sarasota County	14,642 4.49	2,624	918 34.98 34.98 6.27	-	-	-	-	-	127 29.81 13.83 4.84 0.87	-	264 48.89 28.76 10.06 1.80	-	-	-	-	-	-	-	-	-	-	-	-	-	-	200 29.28 21.79 7.62 1.37
Seminole County	16,507 4.52	8,682	3,298 37.99 37.99 19.98	-	-	1,038 37.32 31.47 11.96 6.29	-	-	502 36.25 15.22 5.78 3.04	-	521 39.68 15.80 6.00 3.16	-	-	-	-	-	365 37.40 11.07 4.20 2.21	-	-	-	-	-	-	-	-	523 49.15 15.86 6.02 3.17

Notes: Please refer to the User's Guide for an explanation of data; data is arranged alphabetically by state, then county, then city within each county; table includes counties with populations greater than 49,999 unless noted and cities with populations greater than 9,999 whose Asian and/or NHPI population rates are greater than the national average; (1) Native Hawaiian and other Pacific Islander; (2) excludes Taiwanese; (3) includes Chamorro; (4) county does not meet population threshold but is shown in order to allow inclusion of city

Place	Total foreign-born naturalized citizens	Total Asian population	Asians who are foreign-born naturalized citizens	Total NHPI[1] population	NHPIs[1] who are foreign-born naturalized citizens	Asian Indian	Bangladeshi	Cambodian	Chinese[2]	Fijian	Filipino	Guamanian[3]	Hawaiian, Native	Hmong	Indonesian	Japanese	Korean	Laotian	Malaysian	Pakistani	Samoan	Sri Lankan	Taiwanese	Thai	Tongan	Vietnamese
Volusia County	14,955 3.37	4,812	1,962 40.77 40.77 13.12	-	-	593 37.30 30.22 12.32 3.97	-	-	299 45.44 15.24 6.21 2.00	-	460 52.21 23.45 9.56 3.08	-	-	-	-	-	204 44.16 10.40 4.24 1.36	-	-	-	-	-	-	-	-	-
GEORGIA	169,232 2.07	171,463	52,201 30.44 30.44 30.85	3,866	234 6.05 6.05 0.14	12,863 28.76 24.64 7.50 7.60	413 32.86 0.79 0.24 0.24	1,234 35.47 2.36 0.72 0.73	8,318 32.70 15.93 4.85 4.92	-	4,175 40.01 8.00 2.43 2.47	104 7.21 44.44 2.69 0.06	25 3.07 10.68 0.65 0.01	229 19.08 0.44 0.13 0.14	91 16.55 0.17 0.05 0.05	1,120 14.91 2.15 0.65 0.66	9,472 34.19 18.15 5.52 5.60	1,582 33.45 3.03 0.92 0.93	-	1,176 30.11 2.25 0.69 0.69	77 10.10 32.91 1.99 0.05	-	830 45.01 1.59 0.48 0.49	627 27.87 1.20 0.37 0.37	-	8,497 28.81 16.28 4.96 5.02
Bartow County	552 0.73	616	148 24.03 24.03 26.81	-	-	-	-	-	-	-	-	-	-	-	-	-	-	-	-	-	-	-	-	-	-	-
Bibb County	1,234 0.80	1,593	458 28.75 28.75 37.12	-	-	-	-	-	-	-	-	-	-	-	-	-	-	-	-	-	-	-	-	-	-	-
Bulloch County	700 1.25	591	148 25.04 25.04 21.14	-	-	-	-	-	-	-	-	-	-	-	-	-	-	-	-	-	-	-	-	-	-	-
Carroll County	687 0.79	471	224 47.56 47.56 32.61	-	-	-	-	-	-	-	-	-	-	-	-	-	-	-	-	-	-	-	-	-	-	-
Catoosa County	301 0.56	419	75 17.90 17.90 24.92	-	-	-	-	-	-	-	-	-	-	-	-	-	-	-	-	-	-	-	-	-	-	-
Chatham County	3,851 1.66	4,048	1,277 31.55 31.55 33.16	-	-	186 24.54 14.57 4.59 4.83	-	-	220 28.68 17.23 5.43 5.71	-	-	-	-	-	-	-	160 34.86 12.53 3.95 4.15	-	-	-	-	-	-	-	-	314 30.97 24.59 7.76 8.15
Cherokee County	2,247 1.58	1,428	458 32.07 32.07 20.38	-	-	74 21.83 16.16 5.18 3.29	-	-	-	-	-	-	-	-	-	-	-	-	-	-	-	-	-	-	-	-
Clarke County	1,795 1.77	3,250	609 18.74 18.74 33.93	-	-	152 20.60 24.96 4.68 8.47	-	-	150 15.67 24.63 4.62 8.36	-	-	-	-	-	-	-	74 13.50 12.15 2.28 4.12	-	-	-	-	-	-	-	-	-

Notes: Please refer to the User's Guide for an explanation of data; data is arranged alphabetically by state, then county, then city within each county; table includes counties with populations greater than 49,999 unless noted and cities with populations greater than 9,999 whose Asian and/or NHPI population rates are greater than the national average; (1) Native Hawaiian and other Pacific Islander; (2) excludes Taiwanese; (3) includes Chamorro; (4) county does not meet population threshold but is shown in order to allow inclusion of city

Place	Total foreign-born naturalized citizens	Total Asian population	Asians who are foreign-born naturalized citizens	Total NHPI[1] population	NHPIs[1] who are foreign-born naturalized citizens	Asian Indian	Bangladeshi	Cambodian	Chinese[2]	Fijian	Filipino	Guamanian[3]	Hawaiian, Native	Hmong	Indonesian	Japanese	Korean	Laotian	Malaysian	Pakistani	Samoan	Sri Lankan	Taiwanese	Thai	Tongan	Vietnamese
Clayton County	7,841 3.32	10,344	2,767 26.75 26.75 35.29	-	-	516 39.66 18.65 4.99 6.58	-	294 28.05 10.63 2.84 3.75	220 40.07 7.95 2.13 2.81	-	-	-	-	-	-	-	-	421 33.47 15.22 4.07 5.37	-	111 26.49 4.01 1.07 1.42	-	-	-	-	-	872 19.86 31.51 8.43 11.12
Forest Park (city)	947 4.45	1,297	333 25.67 25.67 35.16	-	-	-	-	-	-	-	-	-	-	-	-	-	-	-	-	-	-	-	-	-	-	232 24.22 69.67 17.89 24.50
Riverdale (city)	575 4.62	1,030	259 25.15 25.15 45.04	-	-	-	-	-	-	-	-	-	-	-	-	-	-	-	-	-	-	-	-	-	-	95 20.21 36.68 9.22 16.52
Cobb County	20,701 3.41	18,486	5,832 31.55 31.55 28.17	-	-	1,447 26.85 24.81 7.83 6.99	-	-	1,389 40.33 23.82 7.51 6.71	-	425 35.83 7.29 2.30 2.05	-	-	-	-	73 7.34 1.25 0.39 0.35	975 32.53 16.72 5.27 4.71	-	-	190 29.37 3.26 1.03 0.92	-	-	-	-	-	571 34.17 9.79 3.09 2.76
Smyrna (city)	1,627 3.99	1,619	387 23.90 23.90 23.79	-	-	78 13.68 20.16 4.82 4.79	-	-	-	-	-	-	-	-	-	-	-	-	-	-	-	-	-	-	-	-
Columbia County	2,632 2.95	2,878	1,385 48.12 48.12 52.62	-	-	428 46.88 30.90 14.87 16.26	-	-	272 49.64 19.64 9.45 10.33	-	-	-	-	-	-	-	213 48.85 15.38 7.40 8.09	-	-	-	-	-	-	-	-	-
Martinez (cdp)	1,171 4.25	1,409	702 49.82 49.82 59.95	-	-	235 48.55 33.48 16.68 20.07	-	-	-	-	-	-	-	-	-	-	-	-	-	-	-	-	-	-	-	-
Coweta County	982 1.10	584	232 39.73 39.73 23.63	-	-	-	-	-	-	-	-	-	-	-	-	-	-	-	-	-	-	-	-	-	-	-
DeKalb County	26,531 3.98	26,537	7,321 27.59 27.59 27.59	-	-	2,012 27.41 27.48 7.58 7.58	155 28.18 2.12 0.58 0.58	170 27.87 2.32 0.64 0.64	1,103 28.23 15.07 4.16 4.16	-	287 43.82 3.92 1.08 1.08	-	-	-	-	52 5.83 0.71 0.20 0.20	1,117 33.85 15.26 4.21 4.21	-	-	-	-	-	-	-	-	1,662 25.51 22.70 6.26 6.26
Druid Hills (cdp)	449 3.54	867	164 18.92 18.92 36.53	-	-	-	-	-	-	-	-	-	-	-	-	-	-	-	-	-	-	-	-	-	-	-

Notes: Please refer to the User's Guide for an explanation of data; data is arranged alphabetically by state, then county, then city within each county; table includes counties with populations greater than 49,999 unless noted and cities with populations greater than 9,999 whose Asian and/or NHPI population rates are greater than the national average; (1) Native Hawaiian and other Pacific Islander; (2) excludes Taiwanese; (3) includes Chamorro; (4) county does not meet population threshold but is shown in order to allow inclusion of city

Place	Total foreign-born naturalized citizens	Total Asian population	Asians who are foreign-born naturalized citizens	Total NHPI[1] population	NHPIs[1] who are foreign-born naturalized citizens	Asian Indian	Bangladeshi	Cambodian	Chinese[2]	Fijian	Filipino	Guamanian[3]	Hawaiian, Native	Hmong	Indonesian	Japanese	Korean	Laotian	Malaysian	Pakistani	Samoan	Sri Lankan	Taiwanese	Thai	Tongan	Vietnamese
Dunwoody (cdp)	1,586 4.83	2,480	632 25.48 25.48 39.85	-	-	206 19.06 32.59 8.31 12.99	-	-	-	-	-	-	-	-	-	-	160 35.79 25.32 6.45 10.09	-	-	-	-	-	-	-	-	-
North Atlanta (cdp)	1,830 4.77	1,710	401 23.45 23.45 21.91	-	-	-	-	-	-	-	-	-	-	-	-	-	-	-	-	-	-	-	-	-	-	-
North Decatur (cdp)	663 4.37	847	223 26.33 26.33 33.63	-	-	-	-	-	-	-	-	-	-	-	-	-	-	-	-	-	-	-	-	-	-	-
North Druid Hills (cdp)	1,015 5.38	1,268	201 15.85 15.85 19.80	-	-	52 9.04 25.87 4.10 5.12	-	-	-	-	-	-	-	-	-	-	-	-	-	-	-	-	-	-	-	-
Tucker (cdp)	1,369 5.14	1,987	701 35.28 35.28 51.21	-	-	-	-	-	-	-	-	-	-	-	-	-	-	-	-	-	-	-	-	-	-	139 42.64 19.83 7.00 10.15
Dougherty County	620 0.65	696	201 28.88 28.88 32.42	-	-	-	-	-	-	-	-	-	-	-	-	-	-	-	-	-	-	-	-	-	-	-
Douglas County	1,348 1.46	897	270 30.10 30.10 20.03	-	-	-	-	-	-	-	-	-	-	-	-	-	-	-	-	-	-	-	-	-	-	-
Fayette County	2,146 2.35	2,071	654 31.58 31.58 30.48	-	-	-	-	-	-	-	-	-	-	-	-	48 7.61 7.34 2.32 2.24	-	-	-	-	-	-	-	-	-	-
Peachtree City (city)	898 2.82	1,263	284 22.49 22.49 31.63	-	-	-	-	-	-	-	-	-	-	-	-	34 5.63 11.97 2.69 3.79	-	-	-	-	-	-	-	-	-	-
Floyd County	1,349 1.49	1,212	471 38.86 38.86 34.91	-	-	239 50.64 50.74 19.72 17.72	-	-	-	-	-	-	-	-	-	-	-	-	-	-	-	-	-	-	-	-

Notes: Please refer to the User's Guide for an explanation of data; data is arranged alphabetically by state, then county, then city within each county; table includes counties with populations greater than 49,999 unless noted and cities with populations greater than 9,999 whose Asian and/or NHPI population rates are greater than the national average; (1) Native Hawaiian and other Pacific Islander; (2) excludes Taiwanese; (3) includes Chamorro; (4) county does not meet population threshold but is shown in order to allow inclusion of city

Place	Total foreign-born naturalized citizens	Total Asian population	Asians who are foreign-born naturalized citizens	Total NHPI[1] population	NHPIs[1] who are foreign-born naturalized citizens	Asian Indian	Bangladeshi	Cambodian	Chinese[2]	Fijian	Filipino	Guamanian[3]	Hawaiian, Native	Hmong	Indonesian	Japanese	Korean	Laotian	Malaysian	Pakistani	Samoan	Sri Lankan	Taiwanese	Thai	Tongan	Vietnamese
Forsyth County	1,576 1.60	756	247 32.67 32.67 15.67	-	-	-	-	-	-	-	-	-	-	-	-	-	-	-	-	-	-	-	-	-	-	-
Fulton County	21,268 2.61	23,763	5,971 25.13 25.13 28.08	-	-	1,538 21.29 25.76 6.47 7.23	-	-	1,353 25.06 22.66 5.69 6.36	-	293 33.83 4.91 1.23 1.38	-	-	-	-	60 6.41 1.00 0.25 0.28	1,238 30.37 20.73 5.21 5.82	-	-	-	-	-	-	-	-	887 29.74 14.86 3.73 4.17
Alpharetta (city)	1,275 3.68	1,709	557 32.59 32.59 43.69	-	-	123 19.49 22.08 7.20 9.65	-	-	209 44.66 37.52 12.23 16.39	-	-	-	-	-	-	-	-	-	-	-	-	-	-	-	-	-
Roswell (city)	3,128 3.92	2,963	1,020 34.42 34.42 32.61	-	-	263 31.72 25.78 8.88 8.41	-	-	236 40.27 23.14 7.96 7.54	-	-	-	-	-	-	-	313 36.52 30.69 10.56 10.01	-	-	-	-	-	-	-	-	-
Glynn County	916 1.36	553	203 36.71 36.71 22.16	-	-	-	-	-	-	-	-	-	-	-	-	-	-	-	-	-	-	-	-	-	-	-
Gwinnett County	29,838 5.07	41,021	13,179 32.13 32.13 44.17	506	20 3.95 3.95 0.07	3,362 30.56 25.51 8.20 11.27	-	316 35.03 2.40 0.77 1.06	2,075 40.89 15.74 5.06 6.95	-	545 44.53 4.14 1.33 1.83	-	-	-	-	118 13.63 0.90 0.29 0.40	2,673 28.87 20.28 6.52 8.96	466 42.63 3.54 1.14 1.56	-	381 33.36 2.89 0.93 1.28	-	-	243 51.27 1.84 0.59 0.81	-	-	2,330 31.20 17.68 5.68 7.81
Duluth (city)	1,367 6.11	2,725	718 26.35 26.35 52.52	-	-	185 20.29 25.77 6.79 13.53	-	-	195 37.14 27.16 7.16 14.26	-	-	-	-	-	-	-	153 22.24 21.31 5.61 11.19	-	-	-	-	-	-	-	-	-
Lilburn (city)	857 7.55	1,466	532 36.29 36.29 62.08	-	-	164 42.27 30.83 11.19 19.14	-	-	-	-	-	-	-	-	-	-	-	-	-	-	-	-	-	-	-	180 38.96 33.83 12.28 21.00
Mountain Park (cdp)	625 5.44	1,055	373 35.36 35.36 59.68	-	-	227 32.90 60.86 21.52 36.32	-	-	-	-	-	-	-	-	-	-	-	-	-	-	-	-	-	-	-	-
Hall County	3,356 2.41	1,817	444 24.44 24.44 13.23	-	-	-	-	-	-	-	-	-	-	-	-	-	-	-	-	-	-	-	-	-	-	256 21.26 57.66 14.09 7.63

Notes: Please refer to the User's Guide for an explanation of data; data is arranged alphabetically by state, then county, then city within each county; table includes counties with populations greater than 49,999 unless noted and cities with populations greater than 9,999 whose Asian and/or NHPI population rates are greater than the national average; (1) Native Hawaiian and other Pacific Islander; (2) excludes Taiwanese; (3) includes Chamorro; (4) county does not meet population threshold but is shown in order to allow inclusion of city

Place	Total foreign-born naturalized citizens	Total Asian population	Asians who are foreign-born naturalized citizens	Total NHPI[1] population	NHPIs[1] who are foreign-born naturalized citizens	Asian Indian	Bangladeshi	Cambodian	Chinese[2]	Fijian	Filipino	Guamanian[3]	Hawaiian, Native	Hmong	Indonesian	Japanese	Korean	Laotian	Malaysian	Pakistani	Samoan	Sri Lankan	Taiwanese	Thai	Tongan	Vietnamese
Henry County	2,206	2,134	815	-	-	323	-	-	-	-	-	-	-	-	-	-	-	-	-	-	-	-	-	-	-	-
	1.85		38.19			39.39																				
						39.63																				
			38.19			15.14																				
			36.94			14.64																				
Houston County	1,737	1,777	733	-	-	-	-	-	-	-	182	-	-	-	-	-	-	-	-	-	-	-	-	-	-	-
	1.57		41.25								33.09															
											24.83															
			41.25								10.24															
			42.20								10.48															
Liberty County	1,404	957	467	-	-	-	-	-	-	-	-	-	-	-	-	-	210	-	-	-	-	-	-	-	-	-
	2.28		48.80														55.70									
																	44.97									
			48.80														21.94									
			33.26														14.96									
Lowndes County	1,069	852	339	-	-	-	-	-	-	-	-	-	-	-	-	-	-	-	-	-	-	-	-	-	-	-
	1.16		39.79																							
			39.79																							
			31.71																							
Muscogee County	4,197	2,983	1,034	385	22	122	-	-	104	-	224	-	-	-	-	-	320	-	-	-	-	-	-	-	-	-
	2.25		34.66		5.71	21.94			28.42		49.67						41.03									
						11.80			10.06		21.66						30.95									
			34.66		5.71	4.09			3.49		7.51						10.73									
			24.64		0.52	2.91			2.48		5.34						7.62									
Columbus (sp. city)	4,195	2,983	1,034	385	22	122	-	-	104	-	224	-	-	-	-	-	320	-	-	-	-	-	-	-	-	-
	2.26		34.66		5.71	21.94			28.42		49.67						41.03									
						11.80			10.06		21.66						30.95									
			34.66		5.71	4.09			3.49		7.51						10.73									
			24.65		0.52	2.91			2.48		5.34						7.63									
Newton County	706	442	112	-	-	-	-	-	-	-	-	-	-	-	-	-	-	-	-	-	-	-	-	-	-	-
	1.14		25.34																							
			25.34																							
			15.86																							
Richmond County	4,024	3,023	1,324	-	-	218	-	-	188	-	-	-	-	-	-	-	526	-	-	-	-	-	-	-	-	-
	2.01		43.80			32.20			35.54								60.46									
						16.47			14.20								39.73									
			43.80			7.21			6.22								17.40									
			32.90			5.42			4.67								13.07									
Rockdale County	1,361	1,140	295	-	-	-	-	-	-	-	-	-	-	-	-	-	-	-	-	-	-	-	-	-	-	-
	1.94		25.88																							
			25.88																							
			21.68																							
Spalding County	325	418	122	-	-	-	-	-	-	-	-	-	-	-	-	-	-	-	-	-	-	-	-	-	-	-
	0.56		29.19																							
			29.19																							
			37.54																							

Notes: Please refer to the User's Guide for an explanation of data; data is arranged alphabetically by state, then county, then city within each county; table includes counties with populations greater than 49,999 unless noted and cities with populations greater than 9,999 whose Asian and/or NHPI population rates are greater than the national average; (1) Native Hawaiian and other Pacific Islander; (2) excludes Taiwanese; (3) includes Chamorro; (4) county does not meet population threshold but is shown in order to allow inclusion of city

Place	Total foreign-born naturalized citizens	Total Asian population	Asians who are foreign-born naturalized citizens	Total NHPI[1] population	NHPIs[1] who are foreign-born naturalized citizens	Asian Indian	Bangladeshi	Cambodian	Chinese[2]	Fijian	Filipino	Guamanian[3]	Hawaiian, Native	Hmong	Indonesian	Japanese	Korean	Laotian	Malaysian	Pakistani	Samoan	Sri Lankan	Taiwanese	Thai	Tongan	Vietnamese
	367	415	112	-	-	-	-	-	-	-	-	-	-	-	-	-	-	-	-	-	-	-	-	-	-	-
	0.62		26.99																							
Troup County																										
			26.99																							
			30.52																							
	490	478	171	-	-	-	-	-	-	-	-	-	-	-	-	-	-	-	-	-	-	-	-	-	-	-
	0.81		35.77																							
Walton County																										
			35.77																							
			34.90																							
	2,103	864	305	-	-	-	-	-	-	-	-	-	-	-	-	-	-	-	-	-	-	-	-	-	-	-
	2.52		35.30																							
Whitfield County																										
			35.30																							
			14.50																							
	127,532	503,950	107,282	112,561	3,874	437	-	105	15,982	-	63,468	20	383	-	-	8,300	10,197	771	-	-	1,616	-	413	442	1,006	4,573
	10.53		21.29		3.44	35.13		49.76	28.68		36.97	1.34	0.47			4.14	43.01	45.73			11.25		50.30	31.62	24.06	54.80
HAWAII						0.41		0.10	14.90		59.16	0.52	9.89			7.74	9.50	0.72			41.71		0.38	0.41	25.97	4.26
			21.29		3.44	0.09		0.02	3.17		12.59	0.02	0.34			1.65	2.02	0.15			1.44		0.08	0.09	0.89	0.91
			84.12		3.04	0.34		0.08	12.53		49.77	0.02	0.30			6.51	8.00	0.60			1.27		0.32	0.35	0.79	3.59
	7,839	39,708	5,724	16,227	267	-	-	-	256	-	4,184	-	71	-	-	599	306	-	-	-	44	-	-	-	-	-
	5.27		14.42		1.65				19.05		31.94		0.51			2.90	35.01				14.86					
Hawaii County									4.47		73.10		26.59			10.46	5.35				16.48					
			14.42		1.65				0.64		10.54		0.44			1.51	0.77				0.27					
			73.02		3.41				3.27		53.37		0.91			7.64	3.90				0.56					
	1,460	15,349	1,099	4,969	90	-	-	-	97	-	534	-	17	-	-	243	131	-	-	-	-	-	-	-	-	-
	3.58		7.16		1.81				19.52		26.01		0.41			2.19	33.08									
Hilo (cdp)									8.83		48.59		18.89			22.11	11.92									
			7.16		1.81				0.63		3.48		0.34			1.58	0.85									
			75.27		6.16				6.64		36.58		1.16			16.64	8.97									
	102,311	404,493	87,775	77,175	3,217	352	-	-	15,414	-	47,418	20	293	-	-	7,185	9,333	751	-	-	1,512	-	405	382	728	4,267
	11.68		21.70		4.17	35.06			29.15		37.67	1.51	0.58			4.50	42.99	45.65			10.92		51.20	33.25	23.62	54.88
Honolulu County						0.40			17.56		54.02	0.62	9.11			8.19	10.63	0.86			47.00		0.46	0.44	22.63	4.86
			21.70		4.17	0.09			3.81		11.72	0.03	0.38			1.78	2.31	0.19			1.96		0.10	0.09	0.94	1.05
			85.79		3.14	0.34			15.07		46.35	0.02	0.29			7.02	9.12	0.73			1.48		0.40	0.37	0.71	4.17
	2,592	7,204	2,394	1,456	50	-	-	-	-	-	2,229	-	0	-	-	34	-	-	-	-	41	-	-	-	-	-
	17.69		33.23		3.43						39.68		0.00			4.15					9.74					
Ewa Beach (cdp)											93.11		0.00			1.42					82.00					
			33.23		3.43						30.94		0.00			0.47					2.82					
			92.36		1.93						86.00		0.00			1.31					1.58					
	1,969	7,231	1,695	1,512	65	-	-	-	163	-	1,134	-	0	-	-	143	-	-	-	-	30	-	-	-	-	-
	14.11		23.44		4.30				22.27		39.71		0.00			5.72					4.54					
Halawa (cdp)									9.62		66.90		0.00			8.44					46.15					
			23.44		4.30				2.25		15.68		0.00			1.98					1.98					
			86.08		3.30				8.28		57.59		0.00			7.26					1.52					
	53,278	208,028	46,284	25,856	1,383	200	-	-	12,129	-	17,054	0	107	-	-	4,316	6,546	453	-	-	561	-	405	199	367	3,488
	14.34		22.25		5.35	32.57			31.17		39.07	0.00	0.74			5.04	42.37	46.04			12.60		57.69	37.20	23.56	53.13
Honolulu (cdp)						0.43			26.21		36.85	0.00	7.74			9.33	14.14	0.98			40.56		0.88	0.43	26.54	7.54
			22.25		5.35	0.10			5.83		8.20	0.00	0.41			2.07	3.15	0.22			2.17		0.19	0.10	1.42	1.68
			86.87		2.60	0.38			22.77		32.01	0.00	0.20			8.10	12.29	0.85			1.05		0.76	0.37	0.69	6.55

Notes: Please refer to the User's Guide for an explanation of data; data is arranged alphabetically by state, then county, then city within each county; table includes counties with populations greater than 49,999 unless noted and cities with populations greater than 9,999 whose Asian and/or NHPI population rates are greater than the national average; (1) Native Hawaiian and other Pacific Islander; (2) excludes Taiwanese; (3) includes Chamorro; (4) county does not meet population threshold but is shown in order to allow inclusion of city

Place	Total foreign-born naturalized citizens	Total Asian population	Asians who are foreign-born naturalized citizens	Total NHPI[1] population	NHPIs[1] who are foreign-born naturalized citizens	Asian Indian	Bangladeshi	Cambodian	Chinese[2]	Fijian	Filipino	Guamanian[3]	Hawaiian, Native	Hmong	Indonesian	Japanese	Korean	Laotian	Malaysian	Pakistani	Samoan	Sri Lankan	Taiwanese	Thai	Tongan	Vietnamese
Kailua (cdp)	1,660 4.54	7,872	1,027 13.05 13.05 61.87	2,743	26 0.95 0.95 1.57	-	-	-	225 18.69 21.91 2.86 13.55	-	386 39.47 37.59 4.90 23.25	-	0 0.00 0.00 0.00 0.00	-	-	115 2.66 11.20 1.46 6.93	148 39.36 14.41 1.88 8.92	-	-	-	-	-	-	-	-	-
Kaneohe (cdp)	1,445 4.13	13,801	1,158 8.39 8.39 80.14	4,046	49 1.21 1.21 3.39	-	-	-	139 9.69 12.00 1.01 9.62	-	498 29.73 43.01 3.61 34.46	-	8 0.24 16.33 0.20 0.55	-	-	214 2.54 18.48 1.55 14.81	208 46.33 17.96 1.51 14.39	-	-	-	-	-	-	-	-	-
Kaneohe Station (cdp)	431 3.64	629	236 37.52 37.52 54.76	-	-	-	-	-	-	-	-	-	-	-	-	-	-	-	-	-	-	-	-	-	-	-
Makakilo City (cdp)	1,396 10.61	4,415	1,224 27.72 27.72 87.68	1,355	21 1.55 1.55 1.50	-	-	-	-	-	891 37.69 72.79 20.18 63.83	-	0 0.00 0.00 0.00 0.00	-	-	100 10.30 8.17 2.27 7.16	-	-	-	-	-	-	-	-	-	-
Mililani Town (cdp)	2,256 7.90	13,195	1,846 13.99 13.99 81.83	1,173	80 6.82 6.82 3.55	-	-	-	308 31.65 16.68 2.33 13.65	-	970 30.83 52.55 7.35 43.00	-	4 0.46 5.00 0.34 0.18	-	-	237 3.37 12.84 1.80 10.51	212 42.66 11.48 1.61 9.40	-	-	-	-	-	-	-	-	-
Nanakuli (cdp)	219 2.05	1,059	120 11.33 11.33 54.79	4,104	49 1.19 1.19 22.37	-	-	-	-	-	112 17.34 93.33 10.58 51.14	-	6 0.19 12.24 0.15 2.74	-	-	-	-	-	-	-	37 4.91 75.51 0.90 16.89	-	-	-	-	-
Pearl City (cdp)	2,904 9.42	16,882	2,592 15.35 15.35 89.26	1,791	38 2.12 2.12 1.31	-	-	-	333 26.34 12.85 1.97 11.47	-	1,600 37.49 61.73 9.48 55.10	-	7 0.52 18.42 0.39 0.24	-	-	359 3.80 13.85 2.13 12.36	145 38.36 5.59 0.86 4.99	-	-	-	-	-	-	-	-	-
Schofield Barracks (cdp)	356 2.47	525	128 24.38 24.38 35.96	-	-	-	-	-	-	-	-	-	-	-	-	-	-	-	-	-	-	-	-	-	-	-
Wahiawa (cdp)	1,414 8.75	7,193	1,247 17.34 17.34 88.19	1,734	18 1.04 1.04 1.27	-	-	-	-	-	988 33.82 79.23 13.74 69.87	-	6 0.64 33.33 0.35 0.42	-	-	132 4.07 10.59 1.84 9.34	-	-	-	-	-	-	-	-	-	-
Waianae (cdp)	442 4.15	1,928	351 18.21 18.21 79.41	2,793	62 2.22 2.22 14.03	-	-	-	-	-	231 22.74 65.81 11.98 52.26	-	10 0.42 16.13 0.36 2.26	-	-	15 2.72 4.27 0.78 3.39	-	-	-	-	-	-	-	-	-	-

Notes: Please refer to the User's Guide for an explanation of data; data is arranged alphabetically by state, then county, then city within each county; table includes counties with populations greater than 49,999 unless noted and cities with populations greater than 9,999 whose Asian and/or NHPI population rates are greater than the national average; (1) Native Hawaiian and other Pacific Islander; (2) excludes Taiwanese; (3) includes Chamorro; (4) county does not meet population threshold but is shown in order to allow inclusion of city

Place	Total foreign-born naturalized citizens	Total Asian population	Asians who are foreign-born naturalized citizens	Total NHPI[1] population	NHPIs[1] who are foreign-born naturalized citizens	Asian Indian	Bangladeshi	Cambodian	Chinese[2]	Fijian	Filipino	Guamanian[3]	Hawaiian, Native	Hmong	Indonesian	Japanese	Korean	Laotian	Malaysian	Pakistani	Samoan	Sri Lankan	Taiwanese	Thai	Tongan	Vietnamese
Waimalu (cdp)	2,995	15,849	2,658	1,564	123	-	-	-	339	-	1,127	-	0	-	-	363	630	-	-	-	-	-	-	-	-	-
	10.15		16.77		7.86				26.57		33.79		0.00			4.58	50.36									
									12.75		42.40		0.00			13.66	23.70									
			16.77		7.86				2.14		7.11		0.00			2.29	3.98									
			88.75		4.11				11.32		37.63		0.00			12.12	21.04									
Waipahu (cdp)	7,861	21,657	7,230	4,026	225	-	-	-	89	-	6,740	-	0	-	-	141	-	-	-	-	161	-	-	-	-	-
	23.74		33.38		5.59				15.29		40.75		0.00			4.22					7.59					
									1.23		93.22		0.00			1.95					71.56					
			33.38		5.59				0.41		31.12		0.00			0.65					4.00					
			91.97		2.86				1.13		85.74		0.00			1.79					2.05					
Waipio (cdp)	1,449	6,544	1,296	627	35	-	-	-	-	-	946	-	22	-	-	115	-	-	-	-	-	-	-	-	-	-
	12.45		19.80		5.58						38.90		5.05			4.00										
											72.99		62.86			8.87										
			19.80		5.58						14.46		3.51			1.76										
			89.44		2.42						65.29		1.52			7.94										
Kauai County	4,806	20,929	4,106	5,314	27	-	-	-	77	-	3,643	-	5	-	-	183	-	-	-	-	-	-	-	-	-	-
	8.22		19.62		0.51				18.29		32.77		0.10			2.41										
									1.88		88.72		18.52			4.46										
			19.62		0.51				0.37		17.41		0.09			0.87										
			85.43		0.56				1.60		75.80		0.10			3.81										
Maui County	12,546	38,790	9,662	13,757	363	-	-	-	235	-	8,208	-	14	-	-	333	458	-	-	-	-	-	-	-	215	-
	9.79		24.91		2.64				21.56		38.08		0.12			2.66	48.57								27.08	
									2.43		84.95		3.86			3.45	4.74								59.23	
			24.91		2.64				0.61		21.16		0.10			0.86	1.18								1.56	
			77.01		2.89				1.87		65.42		0.11			2.65	3.65								1.71	
Kahului (cdp)	3,036	10,796	2,785	1,834	0	-	-	-	-	-	2,493	-	0	-	-	104	-	-	-	-	-	-	-	-	-	-
	15.16		25.80		<0.01						38.85		<0.01			3.02										
											89.52		***.**			3.73										
			25.80		<0.01						23.09		<0.01			0.96										
			91.73		<0.01						82.11		<0.01			3.43										
Kihei (cdp)	1,959	4,134	1,284	1,137	94	-	-	-	-	-	1,134	-	0	-	-	15	-	-	-	-	-	-	-	-	-	-
	11.64		31.06		8.27						35.73		0.00			3.23										
											88.32		0.00			1.17										
			31.06		8.27						27.43		0.00			0.36										
			65.54		4.80						57.89		0.00			0.77										
Wailuku (cdp)	824	5,045	692	1,378	0	-	-	-	-	-	508	-	0	-	-	57	-	-	-	-	-	-	-	-	-	-
	6.63		13.72		<0.01						32.07		<0.01			2.15										
											73.41		***.**			8.24										
			13.72		<0.01						10.07		<0.01			1.13										
			83.98		<0.01						61.65		<0.01			6.92										
IDAHO	21,203	11,321	3,272	1,232	54	280	-	-	577	-	629	-	0	-	-	293	615	176	-	-	-	-	-	-	-	534
	1.64		28.90		4.38	24.52			31.98		38.35		0.00			11.05	48.31	34.65								39.26
						8.56			17.63		19.22		0.00			8.95	18.80	5.38								16.32
			28.90		4.38	2.47			5.10		5.56		0.00			2.59	5.43	1.55								4.72
			15.43		0.25	1.32			2.72		2.97		0.00			1.38	2.90	0.83								2.52
Ada County	5,116	4,738	1,474	413	11	122	-	-	222	-	210	-	-	-	-	91	288	-	-	-	-	-	-	-	-	387
	1.70		31.11		2.66	19.71			31.71		41.92					12.69	57.37									40.02
						8.28			15.06		14.25					6.17	19.54									26.26
			31.11		2.66	2.57			4.69		4.43					1.92	6.08									8.17
			28.81		0.22	2.38			4.34		4.10					1.78	5.63									7.56

Notes: Please refer to the User's Guide for an explanation of data; data is arranged alphabetically by state, then county, then city within each county; table includes counties with populations greater than 49,999 unless noted and cities with populations greater than 9,999 whose Asian and/or NHPI population rates are greater than the national average; (1) Native Hawaiian and other Pacific Islander; (2) excludes Taiwanese; (3) includes Chamorro; (4) county does not meet population threshold but is shown in order to allow inclusion of city

Place	Total foreign-born naturalized citizens	Total Asian population	Asians who are foreign-born naturalized citizens	Total NHPI[1] population	NHPIs[1] who are foreign-born naturalized citizens	Asian Indian	Bangladeshi	Cambodian	Chinese[2]	Fijian	Filipino	Guamanian[3]	Hawaiian, Native	Hmong	Indonesian	Japanese	Korean	Laotian	Malaysian	Pakistani	Samoan	Sri Lankan	Taiwanese	Thai	Tongan	Vietnamese
Bannock County	815 1.08	785	213 27.13 27.13 26.13	-	-	-	-	-	-	-	-	-	-	-	-	-	-	-	-	-	-	-	-	-	-	-
Bonneville County	1,170 1.42	486	199 40.95 40.95 17.01	-	-	-	-	-	-	-	-	-	-	-	-	-	-	-	-	-	-	-	-	-	-	-
Canyon County	3,322 2.53	1,090	312 28.62 28.62 9.39	-	-	-	-	-	-	-	-	-	-	-	-	38 12.38 12.18 3.49 1.14	-	-	-	-	-	-	-	-	-	-
Kootenai County	1,464 1.35	581	204 35.11 35.11 13.93	-	-	-	-	-	-	-	-	-	-	-	-	-	-	-	-	-	-	-	-	-	-	-
Twin Falls County	1,353 2.10	384	130 33.85 33.85 9.61	-	-	-	-	-	-	-	-	-	-	-	-	-	-	-	-	-	-	-	-	-	-	-
ILLINOIS	603,521 4.86	423,440	147,868 34.92 34.92 24.50	3,811	443 11.62 11.62 0.07	36,868 29.91 24.93 8.71 6.11	242 30.06 0.16 0.06 0.04	1,402 40.02 0.95 0.33 0.23	25,552 34.72 17.28 6.03 4.23	-	37,691 43.70 25.49 8.90 6.25	86 10.55 19.41 2.26 0.01	6 0.66 1.35 0.16 <0.01	-	75 7.85 0.05 0.02 0.01	1,769 8.49 1.20 0.42 0.29	22,062 42.36 14.92 5.21 3.66	2,171 44.17 1.47 0.51 0.36	13 2.29 0.01 <0.01 <0.01	5,358 34.37 3.62 1.27 0.89	71 8.12 16.03 1.86 0.01	155 27.98 0.10 0.04 0.03	1,609 45.07 1.09 0.38 0.27	1,730 29.58 1.17 0.41 0.29	-	7,808 42.39 5.28 1.84 1.29
Champaign County	3,936 2.19	11,602	1,902 16.39 16.39 48.32	-	-	329 13.62 17.30 2.84 8.36	-	-	406 12.39 21.35 3.50 10.32	-	196 27.15 10.30 1.69 4.98	-	-	-	-	22 3.71 1.16 0.19 0.56	457 17.95 24.03 3.94 11.61	-	-	-	-	-	-	-	-	214 32.04 11.25 1.84 5.44
Champaign (city)	1,726 2.54	4,602	836 18.17 18.17 48.44	-	-	183 16.37 21.89 3.98 10.60	-	-	159 14.96 19.02 3.46 9.21	-	-	-	-	-	-	-	167 18.96 19.98 3.63 9.68	-	-	-	-	-	-	-	-	131 30.47 15.67 2.85 7.59
Urbana (city)	1,243 3.43	5,283	615 11.64 11.64 49.48	-	-	98 9.99 15.93 1.86 7.88	-	-	181 10.04 29.43 3.43 14.56	-	-	-	-	-	-	-	140 12.10 22.76 2.65 11.26	-	-	-	-	-	-	-	-	-
Coles County	410 0.77	364	138 37.91 37.91 33.66	-	-	-	-	-	-	-	-	-	-	-	-	-	-	-	-	-	-	-	-	-	-	-

Notes: Please refer to the User's Guide for an explanation of data; data is arranged alphabetically by state, then county, then city within each county; table includes counties with populations greater than 49,999 unless noted and cities with populations greater than 9,999 whose Asian and/or NHPI population rates are greater than the national average; (1) Native Hawaiian and other Pacific Islander; (2) excludes Taiwanese; (3) includes Chamorro; (4) county does not meet population threshold but is shown in order to allow inclusion of city

Place	Total foreign-born naturalized citizens	Total Asian population	Asians who are foreign-born naturalized citizens	Total NHPI[1] population	NHPIs[1] who are foreign-born naturalized citizens	Asian Indian	Bangladeshi	Cambodian	Chinese[2]	Fijian	Filipino	Guamanian[3]	Hawaiian, Native	Hmong	Indonesian	Japanese	Korean	Laotian	Malaysian	Pakistani	Samoan	Sri Lankan	Taiwanese	Thai	Tongan	Vietnamese
Cook County	420,739	260,996	92,410	1,596	259	20,229	-	838	17,436	-	25,052	-	-	-	26	920	15,086	720	-	3,373	-	-	692	1,176	-	4,813
	7.83		35.41		16.23	29.11		37.63	36.95		45.89				5.26	6.45	42.39	57.46		31.78			39.50	29.39		43.71
						21.89		0.91	18.87		27.11				0.03	1.00	16.33	0.78		3.65			0.75	1.27		5.21
			35.41		16.23	7.75		0.32	6.68		9.60				0.01	0.35	5.78	0.28		1.29			0.27	0.45		1.84
			21.96		0.06	4.81		0.20	4.14		5.95				0.01	0.22	3.59	0.17		0.80			0.16	0.28		1.14
Arlington Heights (village)	4,863	4,671	1,330	-	-	141	-	-	174	-	395	-	-	-	-	35	341	-	-	-	-	-	-	-	-	-
	6.39		28.47			11.47			31.87		57.33					3.52	42.84									
						10.60			13.08		29.70					2.63	25.64									
			28.47			3.02			3.73		8.46					0.75	7.30									
			27.35			2.90			3.58		8.12					0.72	7.01									
Chicago (city)	223,984	127,052	44,502	1,065	221	6,121	-	692	11,704	-	12,744	-	-	-	-	463	5,533	-	-	1,802	-	-	239	468	-	3,316
	7.73		35.03		20.75	25.29		36.21	37.25		45.72					7.66	44.00			27.99			30.80	21.83		40.54
						13.75		1.55	26.30		28.64					1.04	12.43			4.05			0.54	1.05		7.45
			35.03		20.75	4.82		0.54	9.21		10.03					0.36	4.35			1.42			0.19	0.37		2.61
			19.87		0.10	2.73		0.31	5.23		5.69					0.21	2.47			0.80			0.11	0.21		1.48
Des Plaines (city)	6,827	4,382	1,776	-	-	776	-	-	183	-	417	-	-	-	-	-	-	-	-	-	-	-	-	-	-	-
	11.63		40.53			39.73			36.09		44.03															
						43.69			10.30		23.48															
			40.53			17.71			4.18		9.52															
			26.01			11.37			2.68		6.11															
Elk Grove Village (village)	2,387	3,311	1,050	-	-	365	-	-	212	-	249	-	-	-	-	0	-	-	-	-	-	-	-	-	-	-
	6.87		31.71			34.18			50.60		42.13					0.00										
						34.76			20.19		23.71					0.00										
			31.71			11.02			6.40		7.52					0.00										
			43.99			15.29			8.88		10.43					0.00										
Evanston (city)	4,396	4,493	822	-	-	213	-	-	192	-	216	-	-	-	-	39	82	-	-	-	-	-	-	-	-	-
	5.92		18.30			17.69			16.05		41.30					10.37	12.39									
						25.91			23.36		26.28					4.74	9.98									
			18.30			4.74			4.27		4.81					0.87	1.83									
			18.70			4.85			4.37		4.91					0.89	1.87									
Forest Park (village)	923	1,048	421	-	-	-	-	-	-	-	-	-	-	-	-	-	-	-	-	-	-	-	-	-	-	-
	5.88		40.17																							
			40.17																							
			45.61																							
Glenview (village)	5,026	4,212	1,798	-	-	250	-	-	370	-	277	-	-	-	-	22	750	-	-	-	-	-	-	-	-	-
	12.06		42.69			40.19			52.86		47.76					7.01	46.96									
						13.90			20.58		15.41					1.22	41.71									
			42.69			5.94			8.78		6.58					0.52	17.81									
			35.77			4.97			7.36		5.51					0.44	14.92									
Hanover Park (village)	3,882	4,249	1,827	-	-	772	-	-	-	-	479	-	-	-	-	-	-	-	-	-	-	-	-	-	-	-
	10.12		43.00			40.74					41.19															
						42.26					26.22															
			43.00			18.17					11.27															
			47.06			19.89					12.34															
Hoffman Estates (village)	5,088	7,480	2,489	-	-	904	-	-	299	-	441	-	-	-	-	8	595	-	-	-	-	-	-	-	-	-
	10.10		33.28			32.99			36.42		50.98					0.96	41.73									
						36.32			12.01		17.72					0.32	23.91									
			33.28			12.09			4.00		5.90					0.11	7.95									
			48.92			17.77			5.88		8.67					0.16	11.69									

Notes: Please refer to the User's Guide for an explanation of data; data is arranged alphabetically by state, then county, then city within each county; table includes counties with populations greater than 49,999 unless noted and cities with populations greater than 9,999 whose Asian and/or NHPI population rates are greater than the national average; (1) Native Hawaiian and other Pacific Islander; (2) excludes Taiwanese; (3) includes Chamorro; (4) county does not meet population threshold but is shown in order to allow inclusion of city

Place	Total foreign-born naturalized citizens	Total Asian population	Asians who are foreign-born naturalized citizens	Total NHPI[1] population	NHPIs[1] who are foreign-born naturalized citizens	Asian Indian	Bangladeshi	Cambodian	Chinese[2]	Fijian	Filipino	Guamanian[3]	Hawaiian, Native	Hmong	Indonesian	Japanese	Korean	Laotian	Malaysian	Pakistani	Samoan	Sri Lankan	Taiwanese	Thai	Tongan	Vietnamese
Lincolnwood (village)	3,232	2,641	1,159	-	-	312	-	-	-	-	267	-	-	-	-	-	337	-	-	-	-	-	-	-	-	-
	26.15		43.88			39.39					54.16						51.85									
						26.92					23.04						29.08									
			43.88			11.81					10.11						12.76									
			35.86			9.65					8.26						10.43									
Morton Grove (village)	5,235	4,931	2,134	-	-	494	-	-	-	-	879	-	-	-	-	-	431	-	-	-	-	-	-	-	-	-
	23.32		43.28			32.25					49.22						49.54									
						23.15					41.19						20.20									
			43.28			10.02					17.83						8.74									
			40.76			9.44					16.79						8.23									
Mount Prospect (village)	5,875	6,482	1,831	-	-	735	-	-	120	-	234	-	-	-	-	0	604	-	-	-	-	-	-	-	-	-
	10.36		28.25			23.30			20.44		48.65					0.00	41.77									
						40.14			6.55		12.78					0.00	32.99									
			28.25			11.34			1.85		3.61					0.00	9.32									
			31.17			12.51			2.04		3.98					0.00	10.28									
Niles (village)	6,401	3,381	1,346	-	-	452	-	-	-	-	266	-	-	-	-	-	450	-	-	-	-	-	-	-	-	-
	21.23		39.81			33.09					42.36						44.78									
						33.58					19.76						33.43									
			39.81			13.37					7.87						13.31									
			21.03			7.06					4.16						7.03									
Northbrook (village)	3,484	2,920	1,345	-	-	-	-	-	295	-	-	-	-	-	-	-	730	-	-	-	-	-	-	-	-	-
	10.42		46.06						58.88								47.16									
									21.93								54.28									
			46.06						10.10								25.00									
			38.61						8.47								20.95									
Oak Park (village)	2,229	2,267	653	-	-	247	-	-	124	-	-	-	-	-	-	-	-	-	-	-	-	-	-	-	-	-
	4.24		28.80			31.99			25.36																	
						37.83			18.99																	
			28.80			10.90			5.47																	
			29.30			11.08			5.56																	
Orland Park (village)	3,731	2,132	1,000	-	-	307	-	-	-	-	314	-	-	-	-	-	-	-	-	-	-	-	-	-	-	-
	7.30		46.90			47.45					46.31															
						30.70					31.40															
			46.90			14.40					14.73															
			26.80			8.23					8.42															
Palatine (village)	4,818	5,225	1,601	-	-	506	-	-	246	-	361	-	-	-	-	-	255	-	-	-	-	-	-	-	-	-
	7.39		30.64			22.90			35.81		50.85						42.43									
						31.61			15.37		22.55						15.93									
			30.64			9.68			4.71		6.91						4.88									
			33.23			10.50			5.11		7.49						5.29									
Prospect Heights (city)	1,757	630	186	-	-	-	-	-	-	-	-	-	-	-	-	-	-	-	-	-	-	-	-	-	-	-
	10.02		29.52																							
			29.52																							
			10.59																							
Rolling Meadows (city)	1,368	1,478	409	-	-	116	-	-	-	-	-	-	-	-	-	-	-	-	-	-	-	-	-	-	-	-
	5.56		27.67			25.38																				
						28.36																				
			27.67			7.85																				
			29.90			8.48																				

Notes: Please refer to the User's Guide for an explanation of data; data is arranged alphabetically by state, then county, then city within each county; table includes counties with populations greater than 49,999 unless noted and cities with populations greater than 9,999 whose Asian and/or NHPI population rates are greater than the national average; (1) Native Hawaiian and other Pacific Islander; (2) excludes Taiwanese; (3) includes Chamorro; (4) county does not meet population threshold but is shown in order to allow inclusion of city

Place	Total foreign-born naturalized citizens	Total Asian population	Asians who are foreign-born naturalized citizens	Total NHPI[1] population	NHPIs[1] who are foreign-born naturalized citizens	Asian Indian	Bangladeshi	Cambodian	Chinese[2]	Fijian	Filipino	Guamanian[3]	Hawaiian, Native	Hmong	Indonesian	Japanese	Korean	Laotian	Malaysian	Pakistani	Samoan	Sri Lankan	Taiwanese	Thai	Tongan	Vietnamese
Schaumburg (village)	6,120 8.21	10,285	2,972 28.90 28.90 48.56	-	-	1,075 23.74 36.17 10.45 17.57	-	-	509 38.10 17.13 4.95 8.32	-	448 48.38 15.07 4.36 7.32	-	-	-	-	35 3.72 1.18 0.34 0.57	637 35.89 21.43 6.19 10.41	-	-	-	-	-	-	-	-	-
Schiller Park (village)	1,751 14.86	715	292 40.84 40.84 16.68	-	-	-	-	-	-	-	-	-	-	-	-	-	-	-	-	-	-	-	-	-	-	-
Skokie (village)	13,753 21.72	13,321	5,748 43.15 43.15 41.79	-	-	1,693 44.03 29.45 12.71 12.31	-	-	532 32.11 9.26 3.99 3.87	-	1,408 45.57 24.50 10.57 10.24	-	-	-	-	-	1,241 49.17 21.59 9.32 9.02	-	-	232 46.87 4.04 1.74 1.69	-	-	-	-	-	-
Streamwood (village)	3,095 8.43	3,314	1,217 36.72 36.72 39.32	-	-	374 30.26 30.73 11.29 12.08	-	-	-	-	505 42.69 41.50 15.24 16.32	-	-	-	-	-	-	-	-	-	-	-	-	-	-	-
Wheeling (village)	3,924 11.40	2,968	857 28.87 28.87 21.84	-	-	345 24.68 40.26 11.62 8.79	-	-	-	-	190 32.48 22.17 6.40 4.84	-	-	-	-	-	-	-	-	-	-	-	-	-	-	-
Wilmette (village)	2,220 8.02	2,214	765 34.55 34.55 34.46	-	-	-	-	-	185 44.90 24.18 8.36 8.33	-	-	-	-	-	-	3 0.87 0.39 0.14 0.14	326 42.01 42.61 14.72 14.68	-	-	-	-	-	-	-	-	-
DeKalb County	1,849 2.08	2,089	486 23.26 23.26 26.28	-	-	149 23.24 30.66 7.13 8.06	-	-	-	-	-	-	-	-	-	-	-	-	-	-	-	-	-	-	-	-
DeKalb (city)	1,183 3.05	1,778	371 20.87 20.87 31.36	-	-	143 25.27 38.54 8.04 12.09	-	-	-	-	-	-	-	-	-	-	-	-	-	-	-	-	-	-	-	-
DuPage County	61,601 6.81	71,389	25,806 36.15 36.15 41.89	-	-	10,374 32.55 40.20 14.53 16.84	-	-	3,579 35.43 13.87 5.01 5.81	-	5,887 41.72 22.81 8.25 9.56	-	-	-	-	168 11.49 0.65 0.24 0.27	1,979 46.92 7.67 2.77 3.21	-	-	1,050 37.30 4.07 1.47 1.70	-	-	504 60.00 1.95 0.71 0.82	94 22.49 0.36 0.13 0.15	-	1,150 40.68 4.46 1.61 1.87
Addison (village)	4,362 12.22	2,954	984 33.31 33.31 22.56	-	-	502 30.39 51.02 16.99 11.51	-	-	-	-	227 45.22 23.07 7.68 5.20	-	-	-	-	-	-	-	-	-	-	-	-	-	-	-

Notes: Please refer to the User's Guide for an explanation of data; data is arranged alphabetically by state, then county, then city within each county; table includes counties with populations greater than 49,999 unless noted and cities with populations greater than 9,999 whose Asian and/or NHPI population rates are greater than the national average; (1) Native Hawaiian and other Pacific Islander; (2) excludes Taiwanese; (3) includes Chamorro; (4) county does not meet population threshold but is shown in order to allow inclusion of city

Place	Total foreign-born naturalized citizens	Total Asian population	Asians who are foreign-born naturalized citizens	Total NHPI[1] population	NHPIs[1] who are foreign-born naturalized citizens	Asian Indian	Bangladeshi	Cambodian	Chinese[2]	Fijian	Filipino	Guamanian[3]	Hawaiian, Native	Hmong	Indonesian	Japanese	Korean	Laotian	Malaysian	Pakistani	Samoan	Sri Lankan	Taiwanese	Thai	Tongan	Vietnamese
Bartlett (village)	2,357 6.40	2,934	1,138 38.79 38.79 48.28	-	-	545 36.45 47.89 18.58 23.12	-	-	-	-	286 43.40 25.13 9.75 12.13	-	-	-	-	-	-	-	-	-	-	-	-	-	-	-
Bensenville (village)	1,717 8.37	1,242	403 32.45 32.45 23.47	-	-	197 26.09 48.88 15.86 11.47	-	-	-	-	-	-	-	-	-	-	-	-	-	-	-	-	-	-	-	-
Bloomingdale (village)	1,738 8.05	1,932	790 40.89 40.89 45.45	-	-	393 42.90 49.75 20.34 22.61	-	-	-	-	-	-	-	-	-	-	-	-	-	-	-	-	-	-	-	-
Burr Ridge (village)	1,139 11.03	1,032	588 56.98 56.98 51.62	-	-	340 53.38 57.82 32.95 29.85	-	-	-	-	-	-	-	-	-	-	-	-	-	-	-	-	-	-	-	-
Carol Stream (village)	3,014 7.57	4,071	1,613 39.62 39.62 53.52	-	-	647 35.49 40.11 15.89 21.47	-	-	-	-	468 43.58 29.01 11.50 15.53	-	-	-	-	-	-	-	-	-	-	-	-	-	-	188 39.83 11.66 4.62 6.24
Darien (city)	2,401 10.45	2,909	1,405 48.30 48.30 58.52	-	-	640 42.84 45.55 22.00 26.66	-	-	-	-	444 56.42 31.60 15.26 18.49	-	-	-	-	-	-	-	-	-	-	-	-	-	-	-
Downers Grove (village)	2,391 4.92	2,976	1,076 36.16 36.16 45.00	-	-	496 36.99 46.10 16.67 20.74	-	-	190 32.65 17.66 6.38 7.95	-	258 47.87 23.98 8.67 10.79	-	-	-	-	-	-	-	-	-	-	-	-	-	-	-
Glen Ellyn (village)	989 3.66	1,318	355 26.93 26.93 35.89	-	-	112 21.96 31.55 8.50 11.32	-	-	-	-	-	-	-	-	-	-	-	-	-	-	-	-	-	-	-	-
Glendale Heights (village)	3,813 12.04	6,298	2,075 32.95 32.95 54.42	-	-	786 28.27 37.88 12.48 20.61	-	-	-	-	523 29.99 25.20 8.30 13.72	-	-	-	-	-	-	-	-	-	-	-	-	-	-	338 42.30 16.29 5.37 8.86
Hinsdale (village)	864 4.94	866	345 39.84 39.84 39.93	-	-	-	-	-	-	-	-	-	-	-	-	-	-	-	-	-	-	-	-	-	-	-

Notes: Please refer to the User's Guide for an explanation of data; data is arranged alphabetically by state, then county, then city within each county; table includes counties with populations greater than 49,999 unless noted and cities with populations greater than 9,999 whose Asian and/or NHPI population rates are greater than the national average; (1) Native Hawaiian and other Pacific Islander; (2) excludes Taiwanese; (3) includes Chamorro; (4) county does not meet population threshold but is shown in order to allow inclusion of city

Place	Total foreign-born naturalized citizens	Total Asian population	Asians who are foreign-born naturalized citizens	Total NHPI[1] population	NHPIs[1] who are foreign-born naturalized citizens	Asian Indian	Bangladeshi	Cambodian	Chinese[2]	Fijian	Filipino	Guamanian[3]	Hawaiian, Native	Hmong	Indonesian	Japanese	Korean	Laotian	Malaysian	Pakistani	Samoan	Sri Lankan	Taiwanese	Thai	Tongan	Vietnamese
Lisle (village)	1,068 5.06	2,175	540 24.83 24.83 50.56	-	-	140 18.18 25.93 6.44 13.11	-	-	180 27.03 33.33 8.28 16.85	-	-	-	-	-	-	-	-	-	-	-	-	-	-	-	-	-
Lombard (village)	2,450 5.85	2,912	1,090 37.43 37.43 44.49	-	-	365 27.99 33.49 12.53 14.90	-	-	-	-	375 56.22 34.40 12.88 15.31	-	-	-	-	-	-	-	-	-	-	-	-	-	-	-
Naperville (city)	6,400 4.99	11,700	3,709 31.70 31.70 57.95	-	-	1,297 27.75 34.97 11.09 20.27	-	-	1,280 31.65 34.51 10.94 20.00	-	253 36.67 6.82 2.16 3.95	-	-	-	-	-	319 36.67 8.60 2.73 4.98	-	-	-	-	-	203 47.10 5.47 1.74 3.17	-	-	-
Roselle (village)	1,878 8.07	1,816	730 40.20 40.20 38.87	-	-	301 35.20 41.23 16.57 16.03	-	-	-	-	-	-	-	-	-	-	-	-	-	-	-	-	-	-	-	-
Villa Park (village)	963 4.32	896	275 30.69 30.69 28.56	-	-	-	-	-	-	-	-	-	-	-	-	-	-	-	-	-	-	-	-	-	-	-
Warrenville (city)	602 4.56	521	232 44.53 44.53 38.54	-	-	-	-	-	-	-	-	-	-	-	-	-	-	-	-	-	-	-	-	-	-	-
Westmont (village)	1,886 7.75	2,900	771 26.59 26.59 40.88	-	-	210 15.53 27.24 7.24 11.13	-	-	171 35.70 22.18 5.90 9.07	-	145 28.83 18.81 5.00 7.69	-	-	-	-	-	-	-	-	-	-	-	-	-	-	-
Wheaton (city)	2,327 4.20	2,711	995 36.70 36.70 42.76	-	-	345 36.32 34.67 12.73 14.83	-	-	-	-	-	-	-	-	-	-	-	-	-	-	-	-	-	-	-	89 23.30 8.94 3.28 3.82
Woodridge (village)	2,264 7.29	3,503	1,255 35.83 35.83 55.43	-	-	479 29.14 38.17 13.67 21.16	-	-	-	-	510 43.89 40.64 14.56 22.53	-	-	-	-	-	-	-	-	-	-	-	-	-	-	-
Jackson County	630 1.06	1,931	267 13.83 13.83 42.38	-	-	-	-	-	38 9.13 14.23 1.97 6.03	-	-	-	-	-	-	-	-	-	-	-	-	-	-	-	-	-

Notes: Please refer to the User's Guide for an explanation of data; data is arranged alphabetically by state, then county, then city within each county; table includes counties with populations greater than 49,999 unless noted and cities with populations greater than 9,999 whose Asian and/or NHPI population rates are greater than the national average; (1) Native Hawaiian and other Pacific Islander; (2) excludes Taiwanese; (3) includes Chamorro; (4) county does not meet population threshold but is shown in order to allow inclusion of city

Place	Total foreign-born naturalized citizens	Total Asian population	Asians who are foreign-born naturalized citizens	Total NHPI[1] population	NHPIs[1] who are foreign-born naturalized citizens	Asian Indian	Bangladeshi	Cambodian	Chinese[2]	Fijian	Filipino	Guamanian[3]	Hawaiian, Native	Hmong	Indonesian	Japanese	Korean	Laotian	Malaysian	Pakistani	Samoan	Sri Lankan	Taiwanese	Thai	Tongan	Vietnamese
Carbondale (city)	395 1.91	1,429	144 10.08 10.08 36.46	-	-	-	-	-	-	-	-	-	-	-	-	-	-	-	-	-	-	-	-	-	-	-
Kane County	18,252 4.52	7,056	2,818 39.94 39.94 15.44	-	-	582 36.08 20.65 8.25 3.19	-	-	414 48.42 14.69 5.87 2.27	-	454 34.24 16.11 6.43 2.49	-	-	-	-	-	252 52.61 8.94 3.57 1.38	428 40.92 15.19 6.07 2.34	-	-	-	-	-	-	-	233 48.74 8.27 3.30 1.28
South Elgin (village)	785 5.01	842	351 41.69 41.69 44.71	-	-	-	-	-	-	-	-	-	-	-	-	-	-	-	-	-	-	-	-	-	-	-
Kankakee County	1,532 1.48	730	405 55.48 55.48 26.44	-	-	-	-	-	-	-	-	-	-	-	-	-	-	-	-	-	-	-	-	-	-	-
Kendall County	1,451 2.66	671	212 31.59 31.59 14.61	-	-	-	-	-	-	-	-	-	-	-	-	-	-	-	-	-	-	-	-	-	-	-
Knox County	453 0.81	448	101 22.54 22.54 22.30	-	-	-	-	-	-	-	-	-	-	-	-	-	-	-	-	-	-	-	-	-	-	-
La Salle County	1,460 1.31	506	226 44.66 44.66 15.48	-	-	-	-	-	-	-	-	-	-	-	-	-	-	-	-	-	-	-	-	-	-	-
Lake County	35,300 5.48	25,305	8,739 34.53 34.53 24.76	-	-	1,688 29.78 19.32 6.67 4.78	-	-	1,449 29.87 16.58 5.73 4.10	-	2,809 40.20 32.14 11.10 7.96	-	-	-	-	154 10.35 1.76 0.61 0.44	1,651 42.23 18.89 6.52 4.68	-	-	195 37.57 2.23 0.77 0.55	-	-	-	-	-	305 52.14 3.49 1.21 0.86
Buffalo Grove (village)	4,479 10.52	3,687	1,040 28.21 28.21 23.22	-	-	195 25.73 18.75 5.29 4.35	-	-	242 39.87 23.27 6.56 5.40	-	195 44.93 18.75 5.29 4.35	-	-	-	-	36 5.89 3.46 0.98 0.80	352 32.15 33.85 9.55 7.86	-	-	-	-	-	-	-	-	-
Gages Lake (cdp)	484 4.63	411	183 44.53 44.53 37.81	-	-	-	-	-	-	-	-	-	-	-	-	-	-	-	-	-	-	-	-	-	-	-

Notes: Please refer to the User's Guide for an explanation of data; data is arranged alphabetically by state, then county, then city within each county; table includes counties with populations greater than 49,999 unless noted and cities with populations greater than 9,999 whose Asian and/or NHPI population rates are greater than the national average; (1) Native Hawaiian and other Pacific Islander; (2) excludes Taiwanese; (3) includes Chamorro; (4) county does not meet population threshold but is shown in order to allow inclusion of city

Place	Total foreign-born naturalized citizens	Total Asian population	Asians who are foreign-born naturalized citizens	Total NHPI[1] population	NHPIs[1] who are foreign-born naturalized citizens	Asian Indian	Bangladeshi	Cambodian	Chinese[2]	Fijian	Filipino	Guamanian[3]	Hawaiian, Native	Hmong	Indonesian	Japanese	Korean	Laotian	Malaysian	Pakistani	Samoan	Sri Lankan	Taiwanese	Thai	Tongan	Vietnamese
Grayslake (village)	928 5.02	905	356 39.34 39.34 38.36	-	-	-	-	-	-	-	-	-	-	-	-	-	-	-	-	-	-	-	-	-	-	-
Gurnee (village)	1,648 5.76	2,361	750 31.77 31.77 45.51	-	-	203 27.69 27.07 8.60 12.32	-	-	107 29.16 14.27 4.53 6.49	-	303 39.50 40.40 12.83 18.39	-	-	-	-	-	-	-	-	-	-	-	-	-	-	-
Lake Zurich (village)	802 4.42	691	236 34.15 34.15 29.43	-	-	-	-	-	-	-	-	-	-	-	-	-	-	-	-	-	-	-	-	-	-	-
Libertyville (village)	1,071 5.17	986	368 37.32 37.32 34.36	-	-	-	-	-	-	-	-	-	-	-	-	-	-	-	-	-	-	-	-	-	-	-
Mundelein (village)	2,067 6.76	2,054	695 33.84 33.84 33.62	-	-	-	-	-	186 34.32 26.76 9.06 9.00	-	279 45.22 40.14 13.58 13.50	-	-	-	-	-	-	-	-	-	-	-	-	-	-	-
Vernon Hills (village)	1,992 9.67	2,316	813 35.10 35.10 40.81	-	-	186 34.57 22.88 8.03 9.34	-	-	204 30.04 25.09 8.81 10.24	-	-	-	-	-	-	-	233 36.24 28.66 10.06 11.70	-	-	-	-	-	-	-	-	-
Macon County	753 0.66	745	266 35.70 35.70 35.33	-	-	-	-	-	-	-	-	-	-	-	-	-	-	-	-	-	-	-	-	-	-	-
Madison County	1,811 0.70	1,264	513 40.59 40.59 28.33	-	-	140 39.33 27.29 11.08 7.73	-	-	-	-	-	-	-	-	-	-	-	-	-	-	-	-	-	-	-	-
McHenry County	7,253 2.79	3,408	1,280 37.56 37.56 17.65	-	-	357 37.42 27.89 10.48 4.92	-	-	187 34.19 14.61 5.49 2.58	-	392 40.08 30.63 11.50 5.40	-	-	-	-	-	-	-	-	-	-	-	-	-	-	-
McLean County	1,729 1.15	3,117	702 22.52 22.52 40.60	-	-	245 19.71 34.90 7.86 14.17	-	-	104 15.25 14.81 3.34 6.02	-	-	-	-	-	-	-	-	-	-	-	-	-	-	-	-	-

Notes: Please refer to the User's Guide for an explanation of data; data is arranged alphabetically by state, then county, then city within each county; table includes counties with populations greater than 49,999 unless noted and cities with populations greater than 9,999 whose Asian and/or NHPI population rates are greater than the national average; (1) Native Hawaiian and other Pacific Islander; (2) excludes Taiwanese; (3) includes Chamorro; (4) county does not meet population threshold but is shown in order to allow inclusion of city

Place	Total foreign-born naturalized citizens	Total Asian population	Asians who are foreign-born naturalized citizens	Total NHPI[1] population	NHPIs[1] who are foreign-born naturalized citizens	Asian Indian	Bangladeshi	Cambodian	Chinese[2]	Fijian	Filipino	Guamanian[3]	Hawaiian, Native	Hmong	Indonesian	Japanese	Korean	Laotian	Malaysian	Pakistani	Samoan	Sri Lankan	Taiwanese	Thai	Tongan	Vietnamese
Peoria County	2,768 1.51	3,159	977 30.93 30.93 35.30	-	-	231 21.79 23.64 7.31 8.35	-	-	268 29.88 27.43 8.48 9.68	-	-	-	-	-	-	-	-	-	-	-	-	-	-	-	-	119 38.39 12.18 3.77 4.30
Rock Island County	2,873 1.92	1,469	463 31.52 31.52 16.12	-	-	136 22.78 29.37 9.26 4.73	-	-	-	-	-	-	-	-	-	-	-	-	-	-	-	-	-	-	-	-
St. Clair County	2,743 1.07	2,269	971 42.79 42.79 35.40	-	-	-	-	-	-	-	292 45.77 30.07 12.87 10.65	-	-	-	-	-	248 61.39 25.54 10.93 9.04	-	-	-	-	-	-	-	-	-
Sangamon County	1,928 1.02	1,988	809 40.69 40.69 41.96	-	-	206 30.07 25.46 10.36 10.68	-	-	206 56.91 25.46 10.36 10.68	-	-	-	-	-	-	-	-	-	-	-	-	-	-	-	-	-
Tazewell County	789 0.61	572	237 41.43 41.43 30.04	-	-	-	-	-	-	-	-	-	-	-	-	-	-	-	-	-	-	-	-	-	-	-
Vermilion County	646 0.77	512	218 42.58 42.58 33.75	-	-	-	-	-	-	-	-	-	-	-	-	-	-	-	-	-	-	-	-	-	-	-
Will County	15,449 3.08	11,282	4,304 38.15 38.15 27.86	-	-	965 33.10 22.42 8.55 6.25	-	-	621 40.12 14.43 5.50 4.02	-	1,178 38.80 27.37 10.44 7.63	-	-	-	-	-	514 54.80 11.94 4.56 3.33	-	-	194 44.39 4.51 1.72 1.26	-	-	-	-	-	248 40.06 5.76 2.20 1.61
Bolingbrook (village)	3,174 5.62	3,786	1,519 40.12 40.12 47.86	-	-	347 31.81 22.84 9.17 10.93	-	-	-	-	527 45.20 34.69 13.92 16.60	-	-	-	-	-	-	-	-	-	-	-	-	-	-	-
Winnebago County	6,160 2.21	4,448	1,413 31.77 31.77 22.94	-	-	147 22.69 10.40 3.30 2.39	-	-	-	-	187 34.38 13.23 4.20 3.04	-	-	-	-	-	248 54.15 17.55 5.58 4.03	483 37.18 34.18 10.86 7.84	-	-	-	-	-	-	-	150 25.91 10.62 3.37 2.44
INDIANA	70,983 1.17	57,193	17,253 30.17 30.17 24.31	1,762	102 5.79 5.79 0.14	3,871 27.34 22.44 6.77 5.45	-	185 31.73 1.07 0.32 0.26	2,695 23.36 15.62 4.71 3.80	-	2,926 42.46 16.96 5.12 4.12	22 4.18 21.57 1.25 0.03	0 0.00 0.00 0.00 0.00	-	-	646 13.42 3.74 1.13 0.91	3,016 42.48 17.48 5.27 4.25	419 42.62 2.43 0.73 0.59	-	259 36.33 1.50 0.45 0.36	-	-	266 36.29 1.54 0.47 0.37	306 33.85 1.77 0.54 0.43	-	1,930 40.94 11.19 3.37 2.72

Notes: Please refer to the User's Guide for an explanation of data; data is arranged alphabetically by state, then county, then city within each county; table includes counties with populations greater than 49,999 unless noted and cities with populations greater than 9,999 whose Asian and/or NHPI population rates are greater than the national average; (1) Native Hawaiian and other Pacific Islander; (2) excludes Taiwanese; (3) includes Chamorro; (4) county does not meet population threshold but is shown in order to allow inclusion of city

Place	Total foreign-born naturalized citizens	Total Asian population	Asians who are foreign-born naturalized citizens	Total NHPI[1] population	NHPIs[1] who are foreign-born naturalized citizens	Asian Indian	Bangladeshi	Cambodian	Chinese[2]	Fijian	Filipino	Guamanian[3]	Hawaiian, Native	Hmong	Indonesian	Japanese	Korean	Laotian	Malaysian	Pakistani	Samoan	Sri Lankan	Taiwanese	Thai	Tongan	Vietnamese
	5,235	4,452	1,473	-	-	358	-	-	195	-	200	-	-	-	-	-	-	-	-	-	-	-	-	-	-	216
	1.58		33.09			35.10			37.21		41.32															26.70
Allen County						24.30			13.24		13.58															14.66
			33.09			8.04			4.38		4.49															4.85
			28.14			6.84			3.72		3.82															4.13
	720	1,182	266	-	-	20	-	-	-	-	-	-	-	-	-	-	-	-	-	-	-	-	-	-	-	-
	1.01		22.50			4.69																				
Bartholomew County						7.52																				
			22.50			1.69																				
			36.94			2.78																				
	695	428	120	-	-	-	-	-	-	-	-	-	-	-	-	-	-	-	-	-	-	-	-	-	-	-
	0.72		28.04																							
Clark County																										
			28.04																							
			17.27																							
	551	752	147	-	-	-	-	-	-	-	-	-	-	-	-	-	-	-	-	-	-	-	-	-	-	-
	0.46		19.55																							
Delaware County																										
			19.55																							
			26.68																							
	3,072	1,606	477	-	-	-	-	-	-	-	-	-	-	-	-	-	-	-	-	-	-	-	-	-	-	-
	1.68		29.70																							
Elkhart County																										
			29.70																							
			15.53																							
	495	469	203	-	-	-	-	-	-	-	-	-	-	-	-	-	-	-	-	-	-	-	-	-	-	-
	0.67		43.28																							
Grant County																										
			43.28																							
			41.01																							
	3,550	4,119	1,619	-	-	369	-	-	209	-	-	-	-	-	-	-	-	-	-	-	-	-	-	-	-	-
	1.94		39.31			34.07			24.59																	
Hamilton County						22.79			12.91																	
			39.31			8.96			5.07																	
			45.61			10.39			5.89																	
	1,251	1,636	657	-	-	-	-	-	-	-	-	-	-	-	-	-	-	-	-	-	-	-	-	-	-	-
	3.31		40.16																							
Carmel (city)																										
			40.16																							
			52.52																							
	856	673	257	-	-	-	-	-	-	-	-	-	-	-	-	-	-	-	-	-	-	-	-	-	-	-
	0.82		38.19																							
Hendricks County																										
			38.19																							
			30.02																							
	708	682	163	-	-	-	-	-	-	-	-	-	-	-	-	-	-	-	-	-	-	-	-	-	-	-
	0.83		23.90																							
Howard County																										
			23.90																							
			23.02																							

Notes: Please refer to the User's Guide for an explanation of data; data is arranged alphabetically by state, then county, then city within each county; table includes counties with populations greater than 49,999 unless noted and cities with populations greater than 9,999 whose Asian and/or NHPI population rates are greater than the national average; (1) Native Hawaiian and other Pacific Islander; (2) excludes Taiwanese; (3) includes Chamorro; (4) county does not meet population threshold but is shown in order to allow inclusion of city

Place	Total foreign-born naturalized citizens	Total Asian population	Asians who are foreign-born naturalized citizens	Total NHPI[1] population	NHPIs[1] who are foreign-born naturalized citizens	Asian Indian	Bangladeshi	Cambodian	Chinese[2]	Fijian	Filipino	Guamanian[3]	Hawaiian, Native	Hmong	Indonesian	Japanese	Korean	Laotian	Malaysian	Pakistani	Samoan	Sri Lankan	Taiwanese	Thai	Tongan	Vietnamese
Johnson County	807 0.70	955	348 36.44 36.44 43.12	-	-	-	-	-	-	-	-	-	-	-	-	-	-	-	-	-	-	-	-	-	-	-
Kosciusko County	672 0.91	378	130 34.39 34.39 19.35	-	-	-	-	-	-	-	-	-	-	-	-	-	-	-	-	-	-	-	-	-	-	-
Lake County	14,319 2.96	3,940	1,559 39.57 39.57 10.89	-	-	490 34.12 31.43 12.44 3.42	-	-	211 33.55 13.53 5.36 1.47	-	366 46.56 23.48 9.29 2.56	-	-	-	-	-	350 64.58 22.45 8.88 2.44	-	-	-	-	-	-	-	-	-
Munster (town)	1,028 4.78	952	432 45.38 45.38 42.02	-	-	155 36.99 35.88 16.28 15.08	-	-	-	-	-	-	-	-	-	-	-	-	-	-	-	-	-	-	-	-
LaPorte County	1,464 1.33	361	132 36.57 36.57 9.02	-	-	-	-	-	-	-	-	-	-	-	-	-	-	-	-	-	-	-	-	-	-	-
Madison County	540 0.40	502	159 31.67 31.67 29.44	-	-	-	-	-	-	-	-	-	-	-	-	-	-	-	-	-	-	-	-	-	-	-
Marion County	13,380 1.55	11,505	3,873 33.66 33.66 28.95	-	-	934 27.72 24.12 8.12 6.98	-	-	514 22.69 13.27 4.47 3.84	-	632 43.41 16.32 5.49 4.72	-	-	-	-	109 21.46 2.81 0.95 0.81	629 52.24 16.24 5.47 4.70	-	-	-	-	-	-	-	-	542 42.48 13.99 4.71 4.05
Monroe County	1,785 1.48	3,912	679 17.36 17.36 38.04	-	-	107 15.31 15.76 2.74 5.99	-	-	162 19.98 23.86 4.14 9.08	-	-	-	-	-	-	-	209 19.53 30.78 5.34 11.71	-	-	-	-	-	-	-	-	-
Bloomington (city)	1,328 1.92	3,458	477 13.79 13.79 35.92	-	-	59 10.31 12.37 1.71 4.44	-	-	130 17.15 27.25 3.76 9.79	-	-	-	-	-	-	-	146 15.04 30.61 4.22 10.99	-	-	-	-	-	-	-	-	-
Porter County	2,349 1.60	1,053	457 43.40 43.40 19.46	-	-	-	-	-	-	-	-	-	-	-	-	-	-	-	-	-	-	-	-	-	-	-

Notes: Please refer to the User's Guide for an explanation of data; data is arranged alphabetically by state, then county, then city within each county; table includes counties with populations greater than 49,999 unless noted and cities with populations greater than 9,999 whose Asian and/or NHPI population rates are greater than the national average; (1) Native Hawaiian and other Pacific Islander; (2) excludes Taiwanese; (3) includes Chamorro; (4) county does not meet population threshold but is shown in order to allow inclusion of city

Place	Total foreign-born naturalized citizens	Total Asian population	Asians who are foreign-born naturalized citizens	Total NHPI[1] population	NHPIs[1] who are foreign-born naturalized citizens	Asian Indian	Bangladeshi	Cambodian	Chinese[2]	Fijian	Filipino	Guamanian[3]	Hawaiian, Native	Hmong	Indonesian	Japanese	Korean	Laotian	Malaysian	Pakistani	Samoan	Sri Lankan	Taiwanese	Thai	Tongan	Vietnamese
St. Joseph County	4,629 1.74	3,464	939 27.11 27.11 20.29	-	-	167 24.63 17.78 4.82 3.61	-	-	235 27.74 25.03 6.78 5.08	-	-	-	-	-	-	-	194 42.27 20.66 5.60 4.19	-	-	-	-	-	-	-	-	-
Tippecanoe County	2,430 1.63	6,760	971 14.36 14.36 39.96	-	-	187 11.29 19.26 2.77 7.70	-	-	320 14.84 32.96 4.73 13.17	-	-	-	-	-	-	19 4.87 1.96 0.28 0.78	83 8.03 8.55 1.23 3.42	-	-	-	-	-	-	-	-	-
West Lafayette (city)	724 2.50	3,159	361 11.43 11.43 49.86	-	-	95 9.71 26.32 3.01 13.12	-	-	118 12.36 32.69 3.74 16.30	-	-	-	-	-	-	-	-	-	-	-	-	-	-	-	-	-
Vanderburgh County	1,235 0.72	1,589	586 36.88 36.88 47.45	-	-	-	-	-	-	-	-	-	-	-	-	-	-	-	-	-	-	-	-	-	-	-
Vigo County	759 0.72	1,096	205 18.70 18.70 27.01	-	-	-	-	-	-	-	-	-	-	-	-	-	-	-	-	-	-	-	-	-	-	-
Wayne County	424 0.60	476	190 39.92 39.92 44.81	-	-	-	-	-	-	-	-	-	-	-	-	-	-	-	-	-	-	-	-	-	-	-
IOWA	29,951 1.02	35,023	11,527 32.91 32.91 38.49	955	35 3.66 3.66 0.12	1,358 25.12 11.78 3.88 4.53	-	271 32.89 2.35 0.77 0.90	1,152 20.56 9.99 3.29 3.85	-	990 44.02 8.59 2.83 3.31	-	-	-	-	148 11.52 1.28 0.42 0.49	2,524 51.70 21.90 7.21 8.43	1,513 38.13 13.13 4.32 5.05	-	80 20.51 0.69 0.23 0.27	-	-	157 35.20 1.36 0.45 0.52	464 49.89 4.03 1.32 1.55	-	2,305 34.04 20.00 6.58 7.70
Black Hawk County	1,499 1.17	1,316	441 33.51 33.51 29.42	-	-	-	-	-	-	-	-	-	-	-	-	-	-	-	-	-	-	-	-	-	-	-
Buena Vista County[4]	587 2.88	885	246 27.80 27.80 41.91	-	-	-	-	-	-	-	-	-	-	-	-	-	-	171 29.58 69.51 19.32 29.13	-	-	-	-	-	-	-	-
Storm Lake (city)	448 4.41	769	217 28.22 28.22 48.44	-	-	-	-	-	-	-	-	-	-	-	-	-	-	164 31.12 75.58 21.33 36.61	-	-	-	-	-	-	-	-

Notes: Please refer to the User's Guide for an explanation of data; data is arranged alphabetically by state, then county, then city within each county; table includes counties with populations greater than 49,999 unless noted and cities with populations greater than 9,999 whose Asian and/or NHPI population rates are greater than the national average; (1) Native Hawaiian and other Pacific Islander; (2) excludes Taiwanese; (3) includes Chamorro; (4) county does not meet population threshold but is shown in order to allow inclusion of city

Place	Total foreign-born naturalized citizens	Total Asian population	Asians who are foreign-born naturalized citizens	Total NHPI[1] population	NHPIs[1] who are foreign-born naturalized citizens	Asian Indian	Bangladeshi	Cambodian	Chinese[2]	Fijian	Filipino	Guamanian[3]	Hawaiian, Native	Hmong	Indonesian	Japanese	Korean	Laotian	Malaysian	Pakistani	Samoan	Sri Lankan	Taiwanese	Thai	Tongan	Vietnamese
	1,946	4,406	1,073	-	-	192	-	-	240	-	-	-	-	-	-	-	173	-	-	-	-	-	-	-	-	-
	1.75		24.35			23.82			16.10								23.04									
Johnson County						17.89			22.37								16.12									
			24.35			4.36			5.45								3.93									
			55.14			9.87			12.33								8.89									
	265	647	148	-	-	-	-	-	-	-	-	-	-	-	-	-	-	-	-	-	-	-	-	-	-	-
	1.75		22.87																							
Coralville (city)																										
			22.87																							
			55.85																							
	1,287	3,495	774	-	-	123	-	-	202	-	-	-	-	-	-	-	150	-	-	-	-	-	-	-	-	-
	2.06		22.15			20.67			15.30								28.68									
Iowa City (city)						15.89			26.10								19.38									
			22.15			3.52			5.78								4.29									
			60.14			9.56			15.70								11.66									
	2,002	2,647	833	-	-	109	-	-	-	-	-	-	-	-	-	-	207	-	-	-	-	-	-	-	-	-
	1.04		31.47			13.10											62.54									
Linn County						13.09											24.85									
			31.47			4.12											7.82									
			41.61			5.44											10.34									
	7,072	9,173	3,547	-	-	384	-	176	258	-	-	-	-	-	-	-	420	738	-	-	-	-	-	198	-	920
	1.89		38.67			29.58		42.00	24.43								57.07	44.62						55.31		36.68
Polk County						10.83		4.96	7.27								11.84	20.81						5.58		25.94
			38.67			4.19		1.92	2.81								4.58	8.05						2.16		10.03
			50.16			5.43		2.49	3.65								5.94	10.44						2.80		13.01
	776	548	300	-	-	-	-	-	-	-	-	-	-	-	-	-	-	-	-	-	-	-	-	-	-	-
	0.88		54.74																							
Pottawattamie County																										
			54.74																							
			38.66																							
	2,064	2,274	794	-	-	-	-	-	-	-	-	-	-	-	-	-	-	-	-	-	-	-	-	-	-	305
	1.30		34.92																							30.56
Scott County																										38.41
			34.92																							13.41
			38.47																							14.78
	935	3,620	507	-	-	151	-	-	52	-	-	-	-	-	-	-	130	-	-	-	-	-	-	-	-	-
	1.17		14.01			21.57			4.46								17.08									
Story County						29.78			10.26								25.64									
			14.01			4.17			1.44								3.59									
			54.22			16.15			5.56								13.90									
	785	3,471	433	-	-	130	-	-	50	-	-	-	-	-	-	-	104	-	-	-	-	-	-	-	-	-
	1.55		12.47			19.70			4.40								14.21									
Ames (city)						30.02			11.55								24.02									
			12.47			3.75			1.44								3.00									
			55.16			16.56			6.37								13.25									
	1,921	2,386	616	-	-	-	-	-	-	-	-	-	-	-	-	-	-	-	-	-	-	-	-	-	-	293
	1.85		25.82																							20.43
Woodbury County																										47.56
			25.82																							12.28
			32.07																							15.25

Notes: Please refer to the User's Guide for an explanation of data; data is arranged alphabetically by state, then county, then city within each county; table includes counties with populations greater than 49,999 unless noted and cities with populations greater than 9,999 whose Asian and/or NHPI population rates are greater than the national average; (1) Native Hawaiian and other Pacific Islander; (2) excludes Taiwanese; (3) includes Chamorro; (4) county does not meet population threshold but is shown in order to allow inclusion of city

Place	Total foreign-born naturalized citizens	Total Asian population	Asians who are foreign-born naturalized citizens	Total NHPI[1] population	NHPIs[1] who are foreign-born naturalized citizens	Asian Indian	Bangladeshi	Cambodian	Chinese[2]	Fijian	Filipino	Guamanian[3]	Hawaiian, Native	Hmong	Indonesian	Japanese	Korean	Laotian	Malaysian	Pakistani	Samoan	Sri Lankan	Taiwanese	Thai	Tongan	Vietnamese
	44,763	44,772	15,233	1,208	65	2,197	-	185	2,255	-	1,363	-	0	218	-	370	1,843	1,083	-	207	-	-	174	210	-	4,560
	1.67		34.02		5.38	28.60		26.17	31.96		40.31		0.00	23.42		20.19	42.26	38.11		26.57			33.59	32.31		40.38
KANSAS						14.42		1.21	14.80		8.95		0.00	1.43		2.43	12.10	7.11		1.36			1.14	1.38		29.94
			34.02		5.38	4.91		0.41	5.04		3.04		0.00	0.49		0.83	4.12	2.42		0.46			0.39	0.47		10.18
			34.03		0.15	4.91		0.41	5.04		3.04		0.00	0.49		0.83	4.12	2.42		0.46			0.39	0.47		10.19
	279	552	200	-	-	-	-	-	-	-	-	-	-	-	-	-	-	124	-	-	-	-	-	-	-	-
	0.77		36.23															35.63								
Cowley County[4]																		62.00								
			36.23															22.46								
			71.68															44.44								
	216	485	177	-	-	-	-	-	-	-	-	-	-	-	-	-	-	124	-	-	-	-	-	-	-	-
	1.77		36.49															36.05								
Winfield (city)																		70.06								
			36.49															25.57								
			81.94															57.41								
	1,452	3,335	622	-	-	77	-	-	176	-	-	-	-	-	-	-	96	-	-	-	-	-	-	-	-	-
	1.45		18.65			15.68			18.20								18.25									
Douglas County						12.38			28.30								15.43									
			18.65			2.31			5.28								2.88									
			42.84			5.30			12.12								6.61									
	1,351	3,296	603	-	-	69	-	-	176	-	-	-	-	-	-	-	92	-	-	-	-	-	-	-	-	-
	1.69		18.29			14.53			18.20								17.62									
Lawrence (city)						11.44			29.19								15.26									
			18.29			2.09			5.34								2.79									
			44.63			5.11			13.03								6.81									
	10,528	12,582	4,355	-	-	1,164	-	-	988	-	403	-	-	-	-	70	596	318	-	-	-	-	-	-	-	540
	2.33		34.61			28.71			38.13		42.69					15.73	44.78	49.69								40.45
Johnson County						26.73			22.69		9.25					1.61	13.69	7.30								12.40
			34.61			9.25			7.85		3.20					0.56	4.74	2.53								4.29
			41.37			11.06			9.38		3.83					0.66	5.66	3.02								5.13
	4,526	5,672	1,853	-	-	430	-	-	533	-	-	-	-	-	-	-	258	-	-	-	-	-	-	-	-	281
	3.04		32.67			21.71			41.22								42.93									47.71
Overland Park (city)						23.21			28.76								13.92									15.16
			32.67			7.58			9.40								4.55									4.95
			40.94			9.50			11.78								5.70									6.21
	1,020	747	357	-	-	-	-	-	-	-	-	-	-	-	-	-	-	-	-	-	-	-	-	-	-	-
	1.48		47.79																							
Leavenworth County																										
			47.79																							
			35.00																							
	1,152	1,992	453	-	-	-	-	-	76	-	-	-	-	-	-	-	115	-	-	-	-	-	-	-	-	-
	1.83		22.74						11.28								27.12									
Riley County									16.78								25.39									
			22.74						3.82								5.77									
			39.32						6.60								9.98									
	794	1,712	341	-	-	-	-	-	62	-	-	-	-	-	-	-	-	-	-	-	-	-	-	-	-	-
	1.77		19.92						9.61																	
Manhattan (city)									18.18																	
			19.92						3.62																	
			42.95						7.81																	

Notes: Please refer to the User's Guide for an explanation of data; data is arranged alphabetically by state, then county, then city within each county; table includes counties with populations greater than 49,999 unless noted and cities with populations greater than 9,999 whose Asian and/or NHPI population rates are greater than the national average; (1) Native Hawaiian and other Pacific Islander; (2) excludes Taiwanese; (3) includes Chamorro; (4) county does not meet population threshold but is shown in order to allow inclusion of city

Place	Total foreign-born naturalized citizens	Total Asian population	Asians who are foreign-born naturalized citizens	Total NHPI[1] population	NHPIs[1] who are foreign-born naturalized citizens	Asian Indian	Bangladeshi	Cambodian	Chinese[2]	Fijian	Filipino	Guamanian[3]	Hawaiian, Native	Hmong	Indonesian	Japanese	Korean	Laotian	Malaysian	Pakistani	Samoan	Sri Lankan	Taiwanese	Thai	Tongan	Vietnamese
Saline County	900 1.68	861	423 49.13 49.13 47.00	-	-	-	-	-	-	-	-	-	-	-	-	-	-	-	-	-	-	-	-	-	-	177 47.58 41.84 20.56 19.67
Sedgwick County	11,250 2.48	14,175	5,394 38.05 38.05 47.95	431	25 5.80 5.80 0.22	410 31.51 7.60 2.89 3.64	-	115 24.95 2.13 0.81 1.02	559 38.39 10.36 3.94 4.97	-	326 47.25 6.04 2.30 2.90	-	-	-	-	-	219 39.25 4.06 1.54 1.95	314 29.82 5.82 2.22 2.79	-	-	-	-	-	-	-	2,862 42.51 53.06 20.19 25.44
Wichita (city)	10,068 2.93	12,682	4,865 38.36 38.36 48.32	-	-	392 31.39 8.06 3.09 3.89	-	-	530 39.06 10.89 4.18 5.26	-	268 49.91 5.51 2.11 2.66	-	-	-	-	-	151 31.46 3.10 1.19 1.50	219 31.56 4.50 1.73 2.18	-	-	-	-	-	-	-	2,704 42.17 55.58 21.32 26.86
Shawnee County	1,711 1.01	1,478	516 34.91 34.91 30.16	-	-	-	-	-	-	-	-	-	-	-	-	-	-	-	-	-	-	-	-	-	-	-
Wyandotte County	3,199 2.03	2,225	588 26.43 26.43 18.38	-	-	-	-	-	-	-	-	-	-	147 18.87 25.00 6.61 4.60	-	-	-	-	-	-	-	-	-	-	-	-
KENTUCKY	27,569 0.68	28,994	8,732 30.12 30.12 31.67	1,155	79 6.84 6.84 0.29	1,694 25.16 19.40 5.84 6.14	-	-	1,531 29.25 17.53 5.28 5.55	-	1,394 44.55 15.96 4.81 5.06	12 3.26 15.19 1.04 0.04	-	-	-	444 13.98 5.08 1.53 1.61	1,910 47.27 21.87 6.59 6.93	-	-	139 24.69 1.59 0.48 0.50	-	-	-	74 17.54 0.85 0.26 0.27	-	1,000 31.19 11.45 3.45 3.63
Boone County	780 0.91	1,014	231 22.78 22.78 29.62	-	-	-	-	-	-	-	-	-	-	-	-	38 8.28 16.45 3.75 4.87	-	-	-	-	-	-	-	-	-	-
Campbell County	507 0.57	580	189 32.59 32.59 37.28	-	-	-	-	-	-	-	-	-	-	-	-	-	-	-	-	-	-	-	-	-	-	-
Christian County	856 1.18	617	203 32.90 32.90 23.71	-	-	-	-	-	-	-	-	-	-	-	-	-	-	-	-	-	-	-	-	-	-	-
Fayette County	3,913 1.50	5,824	1,128 19.37 19.37 28.83	-	-	262 19.07 23.23 4.50 6.70	-	-	329 18.92 29.17 5.65 8.41	-	-	-	-	-	-	53 5.84 4.70 0.91 1.35	-	-	-	-	-	-	-	-	-	-

Notes: Please refer to the User's Guide for an explanation of data; data is arranged alphabetically by state, then county, then city within each county; table includes counties with populations greater than 49,999 unless noted and cities with populations greater than 9,999 whose Asian and/or NHPI population rates are greater than the national average; (1) Native Hawaiian and other Pacific Islander; (2) excludes Taiwanese; (3) includes Chamorro; (4) county does not meet population threshold but is shown in order to allow inclusion of city

Place	Total foreign-born naturalized citizens	Total Asian population	Asians who are foreign-born naturalized citizens	Total NHPI[1] population	NHPIs[1] who are foreign-born naturalized citizens	Asian Indian	Bangladeshi	Cambodian	Chinese[2]	Fijian	Filipino	Guamanian[3]	Hawaiian, Native	Hmong	Indonesian	Japanese	Korean	Laotian	Malaysian	Pakistani	Samoan	Sri Lankan	Taiwanese	Thai	Tongan	Vietnamese
Hardin County	2,405 2.55	1,892	806 42.60 42.60 33.51	-	-	-	-	-	-	-	-	-	-	-	-	-	420 56.00 52.11 22.20 17.46	-	-	-	-	-	-	-	-	-
Radcliff (city)	1,191 5.45	939	486 51.76 51.76 40.81	-	-	-	-	-	-	-	-	-	-	-	-	-	-	-	-	-	-	-	-	-	-	-
Jefferson County	8,317 1.20	9,043	2,932 32.42 32.42 35.25	-	-	624 25.21 21.28 6.90 7.50	-	-	437 30.69 14.90 4.83 5.25	-	471 50.92 16.06 5.21 5.66	-	-	-	-	96 27.04 3.27 1.06 1.15	504 47.86 17.19 5.57 6.06	-	-	-	-	-	-	-	-	497 27.86 16.95 5.50 5.98
Kenton County	1,122 0.74	866	287 33.14 33.14 25.58	-	-	-	-	-	-	-	-	-	-	-	-	-	-	-	-	-	-	-	-	-	-	-
Madison County	367 0.52	567	145 25.57 25.57 39.51	-	-	-	-	-	-	-	-	-	-	-	-	-	-	-	-	-	-	-	-	-	-	-
Warren County	874 0.94	1,102	368 33.39 33.39 42.11	-	-	-	-	-	-	-	-	-	-	-	-	-	-	-	-	-	-	-	-	-	-	-
LOUISIANA	56,102 1.26	55,492	18,233 32.86 32.86 32.50	1,379	66 4.79 4.79 0.12	2,412 27.91 13.23 4.35 4.30	-	-	1,918 28.24 10.52 3.46 3.42	-	1,949 41.23 10.69 3.51 3.47	7 1.50 10.61 0.51 0.01	0 0.00 0.00 0.00 0.00	-	-	360 25.26 1.97 0.65 0.64	1,066 38.98 5.85 1.92 1.90	357 27.59 1.96 0.64 0.64	-	271 27.79 1.49 0.49 0.48	-	-	219 44.33 1.20 0.39 0.39	273 42.33 1.50 0.49 0.49	-	8,832 35.26 48.44 15.92 15.74
Ascension Parish	477 0.62	320	63 19.69 19.69 13.21	-	-	-	-	-	-	-	-	-	-	-	-	-	-	-	-	-	-	-	-	-	-	-
Bossier Parish	1,182 1.20	1,151	451 39.18 39.18 38.16	-	-	-	-	-	-	-	-	-	-	-	-	-	-	-	-	-	-	-	-	-	-	-
Caddo Parish	1,894 0.75	1,914	586 30.62 30.62 30.94	-	-	145 29.35 24.74 7.58 7.66	-	-	-	-	-	-	-	-	-	-	-	-	-	-	-	-	-	-	-	-

Notes: Please refer to the User's Guide for an explanation of data; data is arranged alphabetically by state, then county, then city within each county; table includes counties with populations greater than 49,999 unless noted and cities with populations greater than 9,999 whose Asian and/or NHPI population rates are greater than the national average; (1) Native Hawaiian and other Pacific Islander; (2) excludes Taiwanese; (3) includes Chamorro; (4) county does not meet population threshold but is shown in order to allow inclusion of city

Place	Total foreign-born naturalized citizens	Total Asian population	Asians who are foreign-born naturalized citizens	Total NHPI population	NHPIs[1] who are foreign-born naturalized citizens	Asian Indian	Bangladeshi	Cambodian	Chinese[2]	Fijian	Filipino	Guamanian[3]	Hawaiian, Native	Hmong	Indonesian	Japanese	Korean	Laotian	Malaysian	Pakistani	Samoan	Sri Lankan	Taiwanese	Thai	Tongan	Vietnamese
Calcasieu Parish	1,081 0.59	1,096	399 36.41 36.41 36.91	-	-	-	-	-	-	-	-	-	-	-	-	-	-	-	-	-	-	-	-	-	-	-
East Baton Rouge Parish	6,273 1.52	8,729	2,485 28.47 28.47 39.61	-	-	478 25.28 19.24 5.48 7.62	-	-	364 21.41 14.65 4.17 5.80	-	196 42.33 7.89 2.25 3.12	-	-	-	-	-	-	-	-	-	-	-	-	-	-	1,091 31.04 43.90 12.50 17.39
Iberia Parish	644 0.88	1,474	378 25.64 25.64 58.70	-	-	-	-	-	-	-	-	-	-	-	-	-	-	263 29.22 69.58 17.84 40.84	-	-	-	-	-	-	-	87 22.25 23.02 5.90 13.51
Jefferson Parish	17,850 3.92	13,790	5,206 37.75 37.75 29.17	-	-	582 33.47 11.18 4.22 3.26	-	-	672 34.71 12.91 4.87 3.76	-	376 38.41 7.22 2.73 2.11	-	-	-	-	-	227 37.46 4.36 1.65 1.27	-	-	156 35.06 3.00 1.13 0.87	-	-	-	-	-	2,796 40.47 53.71 20.28 15.66
Gretna (city)	432 2.49	642	215 33.49 33.49 49.77	-	-	-	-	-	-	-	-	-	-	-	-	-	-	-	-	-	-	-	-	-	-	122 32.88 56.74 19.00 28.24
Harvey (cdp)	1,048 4.71	1,147	575 50.13 50.13 54.87	-	-	-	-	-	-	-	-	-	-	-	-	-	-	-	-	-	-	-	-	-	-	393 46.02 68.35 34.26 37.50
Timberlane (cdp)	708 6.18	638	363 56.90 56.90 51.27	-	-	-	-	-	-	-	-	-	-	-	-	-	-	-	-	-	-	-	-	-	-	303 53.35 83.47 47.49 42.80
Woodmere (cdp)	558 4.26	711	300 42.19 42.19 53.76	-	-	-	-	-	-	-	-	-	-	-	-	-	-	-	-	-	-	-	-	-	-	198 39.36 66.00 27.85 35.48
Lafayette Parish	1,823 0.96	2,142	683 31.89 31.89 37.47	-	-	162 25.92 23.72 7.56 8.89	-	-	-	-	-	-	-	-	-	-	-	-	-	-	-	-	-	-	-	326 44.11 47.73 15.22 17.88
Lafourche Parish	614 0.68	525	212 40.38 40.38 34.53	-	-	-	-	-	-	-	-	-	-	-	-	-	-	-	-	-	-	-	-	-	-	-

Notes: Please refer to the User's Guide for an explanation of data; data is arranged alphabetically by state, then county, then city within each county; table includes counties with populations greater than 49,999 unless noted and cities with populations greater than 9,999 whose Asian and/or NHPI population rates are greater than the national average; (1) Native Hawaiian and other Pacific Islander; (2) excludes Taiwanese; (3) includes Chamorro; (4) county does not meet population threshold but is shown in order to allow inclusion of city

Place	Total foreign-born naturalized citizens	Total Asian population	Asians who are foreign-born naturalized citizens	Total NHPI[1] population	NHPIs[1] who are foreign-born naturalized citizens	Asian Indian	Bangladeshi	Cambodian	Chinese[2]	Fijian	Filipino	Guamanian[3]	Hawaiian, Native	Hmong	Indonesian	Japanese	Korean	Laotian	Malaysian	Pakistani	Samoan	Sri Lankan	Taiwanese	Thai	Tongan	Vietnamese
Orleans Parish	10,227 2.11	10,503	3,466 33.00 33.00 33.89	-	-	276 22.12 7.96 2.63 2.70	-	-	183 22.70 5.28 1.74 1.79	-	235 50.21 6.78 2.24 2.30	-	-	-	-	-	-	-	-	-	-	-	-	-	-	2,541 36.50 73.31 24.19 24.85
Ouachita Parish	816 0.55	784	306 39.03 39.03 37.50	-	-	-	-	-	-	-	-	-	-	-	-	-	-	-	-	-	-	-	-	-	-	-
Rapides Parish	801 0.63	1,090	302 27.71 27.71 37.70	-	-	-	-	-	-	-	-	-	-	-	-	-	-	-	-	-	-	-	-	-	-	-
St. Bernard Parish	1,260 1.87	1,079	444 41.15 41.15 35.24	-	-	-	-	-	-	-	-	-	-	-	-	-	-	-	-	-	-	-	-	-	-	190 38.31 42.79 17.61 15.08
St. Mary Parish	407 0.76	979	175 17.88 17.88 43.00	-	-	-	-	-	-	-	-	-	-	-	-	-	-	-	-	-	-	-	-	-	-	159 18.01 90.86 16.24 39.07
St. Tammany Parish	2,735 1.43	1,456	535 36.74 36.74 19.56	-	-	-	-	-	-	-	-	-	-	-	-	-	-	-	-	-	-	-	-	-	-	148 47.90 27.66 10.16 5.41
Terrebonne Parish	710 0.68	868	228 26.27 26.27 32.11	-	-	-	-	-	-	-	-	-	-	-	-	-	-	-	-	-	-	-	-	-	-	84 21.59 36.84 9.68 11.83
Vermilion Parish	423 0.79	1,045	273 26.12 26.12 64.54	-	-	-	-	-	-	-	-	-	-	-	-	-	-	-	-	-	-	-	-	-	-	246 26.34 90.11 23.54 58.16
Abbeville (city)	219 1.84	684	189 27.63 27.63 86.30	-	-	-	-	-	-	-	-	-	-	-	-	-	-	-	-	-	-	-	-	-	-	189 28.90 100.00 27.63 86.30
Vernon Parish	1,168 2.22	1,125	432 38.40 38.40 36.99	-	-	-	-	-	-	-	-	-	-	-	-	-	190 54.76 43.98 16.89 16.27	-	-	-	-	-	-	-	-	-

Notes: Please refer to the User's Guide for an explanation of data; data is arranged alphabetically by state, then county, then city within each county; table includes counties with populations greater than 49,999 unless noted and cities with populations greater than 9,999 whose Asian and/or NHPI population rates are greater than the national average; (1) Native Hawaiian and other Pacific Islander; (2) excludes Taiwanese; (3) includes Chamorro; (4) county does not meet population threshold but is shown in order to allow inclusion of city

Place	Total foreign-born naturalized citizens	Total Asian population	Asians who are foreign-born naturalized citizens	Total NHPI[1] population	NHPIs[1] who are foreign-born naturalized citizens	Asian Indian	Bangladeshi	Cambodian	Chinese[2]	Fijian	Filipino	Guamanian[3]	Hawaiian, Native	Hmong	Indonesian	Japanese	Korean	Laotian	Malaysian	Pakistani	Samoan	Sri Lankan	Taiwanese	Thai	Tongan	Vietnamese
	20,252	8,259	3,153	301	33	372	-	235	575	-	553	-	-	-	-	195	390	-	-	-	-	-	-	-	-	515
	1.59		38.18		10.96	38.04		23.27	35.23		47.26					32.94	53.06									46.19
MAINE						11.80		7.45	18.24		17.54					6.18	12.37									16.33
			38.18		10.96	4.50		2.85	6.96		6.70					2.36	4.72									6.24
			15.57		0.16	1.84		1.16	2.84		2.73					0.96	1.93									2.54
	1,601	533	214	-	-	-	-	-	-	-	-	-	-	-	-	-	-	-	-	-	-	-	-	-	-	-
	1.54		40.15																							
Androscoggin County																										
			40.15																							
			13.37																							
	2,558	404	125	-	-	-	-	-	-	-	-	-	-	-	-	-	-	-	-	-	-	-	-	-	-	-
	3.46		30.94																							
Aroostook County																										
			30.94																							
			4.89																							
	4,923	3,325	1,197	-	-	-	-	119	112	-	127	-	-	-	-	-	-	-	-	-	-	-	-	-	-	311
	1.85		36.00					18.00	25.40		39.08															47.70
Cumberland County								9.94	9.36		10.61															25.98
			36.00					3.58	3.37		3.82															9.35
			24.31					2.42	2.28		2.58															6.32
	598	194	63	-	-	-	-	-	-	-	-	-	-	-	-	-	-	-	-	-	-	-	-	-	-	-
	1.15		32.47																							
Hancock County																										
			32.47																							
			10.54																							
	1,577	654	240	-	-	-	-	-	-	-	-	-	-	-	-	-	-	-	-	-	-	-	-	-	-	-
	1.35		36.70																							
Kennebec County																										
			36.70																							
			15.22																							
	631	253	118	-	-	-	-	-	-	-	-	-	-	-	-	-	-	-	-	-	-	-	-	-	-	-
	1.15		46.64																							
Oxford County																										
			46.64																							
			18.70																							
	1,869	998	404	-	-	-	-	-	125	-	-	-	-	-	-	-	-	-	-	-	-	-	-	-	-	-
	1.29		40.48						42.52																	
Penobscot County									30.94																	
			40.48						12.53																	
			21.62						6.69																	
	3,090	946	317	-	-	-	-	-	-	-	-	-	-	-	-	-	-	-	-	-	-	-	-	-	-	-
	1.65		33.51																							
York County																										
			33.51																							
			10.26																							
	234,711	209,713	82,219	2,030	187	17,794	423	836	17,854	-	11,527	44	13	-	143	1,253	17,203	409	-	1,681	-	388	1,066	988	-	8,490
	4.43		39.21		9.21	35.76	35.13	48.95	37.82		43.22	6.28	2.52		12.91	18.10	43.98	55.57		33.00		34.58	44.85	34.62		50.89
MARYLAND						21.64	0.51	1.02	21.72		14.02	23.53	6.95		0.17	1.52	20.92	0.50		2.04		0.47	1.30	1.20		10.33
			39.21		9.21	8.48	0.20	0.40	8.51		5.50	2.17	0.64		0.07	0.60	8.20	0.20		0.80		0.19	0.51	0.47		4.05
			35.03		0.08	7.58	0.18	0.36	7.61		4.91	0.02	0.01		0.06	0.53	7.33	0.17		0.72		0.17	0.45	0.42		3.62

Notes: Please refer to the User's Guide for an explanation of data; data is arranged alphabetically by state, then county, then city within each county; table includes counties with populations greater than 49,999 unless noted and cities with populations greater than 9,999 whose Asian and/or NHPI population rates are greater than the national average; (1) Native Hawaiian and other Pacific Islander; (2) excludes Taiwanese; (3) includes Chamorro; (4) county does not meet population threshold but is shown in order to allow inclusion of city

Place	Total foreign-born naturalized citizens	Total Asian population	Asians who are foreign-born naturalized citizens	Total NHPI[1] population	NHPIs[1] who are foreign-born naturalized citizens	Asian Indian	Bangladeshi	Cambodian	Chinese[2]	Fijian	Filipino	Guamanian[3]	Hawaiian, Native	Hmong	Indonesian	Japanese	Korean	Laotian	Malaysian	Pakistani	Samoan	Sri Lankan	Taiwanese	Thai	Tongan	Vietnamese
Allegany County	464 0.62	454	182 40.09 40.09 39.22	-	-	-	-	-	-	-	-	-	-	-	-	-	-	-	-	-	-	-	-	-	-	-
Anne Arundel County	12,441 2.54	11,380	4,721 41.49 41.49 37.95	-	-	654 38.63 13.85 5.75 5.26	-	-	670 44.88 14.19 5.89 5.39	-	1,035 41.75 21.92 9.09 8.32	-	-	-	-	229 33.53 4.85 2.01 1.84	1,680 45.58 35.59 14.76 13.50	-	-	-	-	-	-	-	-	-
Severn (cdp)	1,480 4.21	1,624	685 42.18 42.18 46.28	-	-	-	-	-	-	-	-	-	-	-	-	-	324 42.08 47.30 19.95 21.89	-	-	-	-	-	-	-	-	-
South Gate (cdp)	936 3.26	1,436	510 35.52 35.52 54.49	-	-	-	-	-	-	-	-	-	-	-	-	-	261 30.56 51.18 18.18 27.88	-	-	-	-	-	-	-	-	-
Baltimore Independent City	13,521 2.08	10,256	2,787 27.17 27.17 20.61	-	-	530 25.06 19.02 5.17 3.92	-	-	494 21.73 17.73 4.82 3.65	-	433 30.97 15.54 4.22 3.20	-	-	-	-	-	660 37.29 23.68 6.44 4.88	-	-	-	-	-	-	-	-	265 32.72 9.51 2.58 1.96
Baltimore County	28,791 3.82	23,723	9,390 39.58 39.58 32.61	-	-	2,355 38.06 25.08 9.93 8.18	-	-	1,454 32.20 15.48 6.13 5.05	-	1,711 52.32 18.22 7.21 5.94	-	-	-	-	80 11.83 0.85 0.34 0.28	2,335 45.66 24.87 9.84 8.11	-	-	250 24.93 2.66 1.05 0.87	-	-	-	-	-	561 45.13 5.97 2.36 1.95
Arbutus (cdp)	657 3.27	970	388 40.00 40.00 59.06	-	-	-	-	-	-	-	-	-	-	-	-	-	-	-	-	-	-	-	-	-	-	-
Carney (cdp)	1,175 4.14	1,589	551 34.68 34.68 46.89	-	-	-	-	-	45 12.82 8.17 2.83 3.83	-	-	-	-	-	-	-	309 40.23 56.08 19.45 26.30	-	-	-	-	-	-	-	-	-
Cockeysville (cdp)	976 4.99	1,741	483 27.74 27.74 49.49	-	-	-	-	-	-	-	-	-	-	-	-	-	172 25.75 35.61 9.88 17.62	-	-	-	-	-	-	-	-	-
Lutherville-Timonium (cdp)	895 5.74	662	338 51.06 51.06 37.77	-	-	-	-	-	-	-	-	-	-	-	-	-	-	-	-	-	-	-	-	-	-	-

Notes: Please refer to the User's Guide for an explanation of data; data is arranged alphabetically by state, then county, then city within each county; table includes counties with populations greater than 49,999 unless noted and cities with populations greater than 9,999 whose Asian and/or NHPI population rates are greater than the national average; (1) Native Hawaiian and other Pacific Islander; (2) excludes Taiwanese; (3) includes Chamorro; (4) county does not meet population threshold but is shown in order to allow inclusion of city

Place	Total foreign-born naturalized citizens	Total Asian population	Asians who are foreign-born naturalized citizens	Total NHPI[1] population	NHPIs[1] who are foreign-born naturalized citizens	Asian Indian	Bangladeshi	Cambodian	Chinese[2]	Fijian	Filipino	Guamanian[3]	Hawaiian, Native	Hmong	Indonesian	Japanese	Korean	Laotian	Malaysian	Pakistani	Samoan	Sri Lankan	Taiwanese	Thai	Tongan	Vietnamese
Mays Chapel (cdp)	613 5.37	821	370 45.07 45.07 60.36	-	-	-	-	-	-	-	-	-	-	-	-	-	-	-	-	-	-	-	-	-	-	-
Owings Mills (cdp)	882 4.36	775	267 34.45 34.45 30.27	-	-	-	-	-	-	-	-	-	-	-	-	-	-	-	-	-	-	-	-	-	-	-
Perry Hall (cdp)	1,258 4.40	1,497	816 54.51 54.51 64.86	-	-	-	-	-	-	-	-	-	-	-	-	-	245 46.67 30.02 16.37 19.48	-	-	-	-	-	-	-	-	-
Reisterstown (cdp)	1,894 8.42	1,030	292 28.35 28.35 15.42	-	-	180 31.91 61.64 17.48 9.50	-	-	-	-	-	-	-	-	-	-	-	-	-	-	-	-	-	-	-	-
Rossville (cdp)	509 4.37	556	204 36.69 36.69 40.08	-	-	-	-	-	-	-	-	-	-	-	-	-	-	-	-	-	-	-	-	-	-	-
Towson (cdp)	1,661 3.20	1,938	513 26.47 26.47 30.89	-	-	-	-	-	192 22.70 37.43 9.91 11.56	-	-	-	-	-	-	-	-	-	-	-	-	-	-	-	-	-
Woodlawn (cdp)	1,726 4.78	2,170	842 38.80 38.80 48.78	-	-	358 40.54 42.52 16.50 20.74	-	-	-	-	-	-	-	-	-	-	-	-	-	-	-	-	-	-	-	-
Calvert County	902 1.21	655	265 40.46 40.46 29.38	-	-	-	-	-	-	-	-	-	-	-	-	-	-	-	-	-	-	-	-	-	-	-
Carroll County	1,826 1.21	1,299	540 41.57 41.57 29.57	-	-	-	-	-	-	-	-	-	-	-	-	-	-	-	-	-	-	-	-	-	-	-
Cecil County	849 0.99	564	172 30.50 30.50 20.26	-	-	-	-	-	-	-	-	-	-	-	-	-	-	-	-	-	-	-	-	-	-	-

Notes: Please refer to the User's Guide for an explanation of data; data is arranged alphabetically by state, then county, then city within each county; table includes counties with populations greater than 49,999 unless noted and cities with populations greater than 9,999 whose Asian and/or NHPI population rates are greater than the national average; (1) Native Hawaiian and other Pacific Islander; (2) excludes Taiwanese; (3) includes Chamorro; (4) county does not meet population threshold but is shown in order to allow inclusion of city

Place	Total foreign-born naturalized citizens	Total Asian population	Asians who are foreign-born naturalized citizens	Total NHPI[1] population	NHPIs[1] who are foreign-born naturalized citizens	Asian Indian	Bangladeshi	Cambodian	Chinese[2]	Fijian	Filipino	Guamanian[3]	Hawaiian, Native	Hmong	Indonesian	Japanese	Korean	Laotian	Malaysian	Pakistani	Samoan	Sri Lankan	Taiwanese	Thai	Tongan	Vietnamese
Charles County	2,021 1.68	1,884	799 42.41 42.41 39.53	-	-	-	-	-	-	-	116 24.58 14.52 6.16 5.74	-	-	-	-	-	-	-	-	-	-	-	-	-	-	-
Frederick County	3,886 1.99	3,327	1,173 35.26 35.26 30.19	-	-	244 39.17 20.80 7.33 6.28	-	-	154 19.57 13.13 4.63 3.96	-	-	-	-	-	-	-	250 47.44 21.31 7.51 6.43	-	-	-	-	-	-	-	-	-
Harford County	4,787 2.19	3,169	1,508 47.59 47.59 31.50	-	-	282 44.06 18.70 8.90 5.89	-	-	-	-	170 30.30 11.27 5.36 3.55	-	-	-	-	-	462 60.71 30.64 14.58 9.65	-	-	-	-	-	-	-	-	-
Howard County	14,714 5.94	18,712	7,507 40.12 40.12 51.02	-	-	1,830 38.46 24.38 9.78 12.44	-	-	1,545 41.75 20.58 8.26 10.50	-	642 46.52 8.55 3.43 4.36	-	-	-	-	-	2,360 39.25 31.44 12.61 16.04	-	-	265 40.64 3.53 1.42 1.80	-	-	-	-	-	413 56.81 5.50 2.21 2.81
Columbia (cdp)	5,745 6.50	6,274	2,627 41.87 41.87 45.73	-	-	631 35.04 24.02 10.06 10.98	-	-	630 40.13 23.98 10.04 10.97	-	268 52.65 10.20 4.27 4.66	-	-	-	-	-	660 45.64 25.12 10.52 11.49	-	-	-	-	-	-	-	-	-
Elkridge (cdp)	1,117 5.07	1,406	587 41.75 41.75 52.55	-	-	-	-	-	-	-	-	-	-	-	-	-	116 31.02 19.76 8.25 10.38	-	-	-	-	-	-	-	-	-
Ellicott City (cdp)	3,848 6.83	6,661	2,332 35.01 35.01 60.60	-	-	419 37.08 17.97 6.29 10.89	-	-	441 34.92 18.91 6.62 11.46	-	171 42.22 7.33 2.57 4.44	-	-	-	-	-	976 34.03 41.85 14.65 25.36	-	-	141 35.70 6.05 2.12 3.66	-	-	-	-	-	-
North Laurel (cdp)	1,368 6.63	1,390	644 46.33 46.33 47.08	-	-	265 63.70 41.15 19.06 19.37	-	-	-	-	-	-	-	-	-	-	148 35.07 22.98 10.65 10.82	-	-	-	-	-	-	-	-	-
Savage-Guilford (cdp)	569 4.51	730	273 37.40 37.40 47.98	-	-	-	-	-	-	-	-	-	-	-	-	-	-	-	-	-	-	-	-	-	-	-
Montgomery County	100,658 11.53	97,994	39,168 39.97 39.97 38.91	489	97 19.84 19.84 0.10	8,686 35.58 22.18 8.86 8.63	314 38.01 0.80 0.32 0.31	524 45.13 1.34 0.53 0.52	11,092 40.51 28.32 11.32 11.02	-	2,790 40.45 7.12 2.85 2.77	-	-	-	114 12.28 0.29 0.12 0.11	408 12.92 1.04 0.42 0.41	6,953 44.98 17.75 7.10 6.91	-	-	689 37.65 1.76 0.70 0.68	-	226 30.21 0.58 0.23 0.22	561 49.04 1.43 0.57 0.56	404 30.44 1.03 0.41 0.40	-	5,180 55.20 13.23 5.29 5.15

Notes: Please refer to the User's Guide for an explanation of data; data is arranged alphabetically by state, then county, then city within each county; table includes counties with populations greater than 49,999 unless noted and cities with populations greater than 9,999 whose Asian and/or NHPI population rates are greater than the national average; (1) Native Hawaiian and other Pacific Islander; (2) excludes Taiwanese; (3) includes Chamorro; (4) county does not meet population threshold but is shown in order to allow inclusion of city

Place	Total foreign-born naturalized citizens	Total Asian population	Asians who are foreign-born naturalized citizens	Total NHPI[1] population	NHPIs[1] who are foreign-born naturalized citizens	Asian Indian	Bangladeshi	Cambodian	Chinese[2]	Fijian	Filipino	Guamanian[3]	Hawaiian, Native	Hmong	Indonesian	Japanese	Korean	Laotian	Malaysian	Pakistani	Samoan	Sri Lankan	Taiwanese	Thai	Tongan	Vietnamese
Aspen Hill (cdp)	6,710	5,557	2,419	-	-	275	-	-	817	-	345	-	-	-	-	-	459	-	-	-	-	-	-	-	-	243
	13.36		43.53			39.63			45.44		50.81						45.90									56.38
						11.37			33.77		14.26						18.97									10.05
			43.53			4.95			14.70		6.21						8.26									4.37
			36.05			4.10			12.18		5.14						6.84									3.62
Bethesda (cdp)	5,005	4,261	1,482	-	-	220	-	-	511	-	174	-	-	-	-	57	323	-	-	-	-	-	-	-	-	-
	9.05		34.78			21.80			40.81		44.27					12.90	53.13									
						14.84			34.48		11.74					3.85	21.79									
			34.78			5.16			11.99		4.08					1.34	7.58									
			29.61			4.40			10.21		3.48					1.14	6.45									
Calverton (cdp)	1,634	2,095	828	-	-	262	-	-	-	-	-	-	-	-	-	-	223	-	-	-	-	-	-	-	-	-
	12.96		39.52			37.32											39.26									
						31.64											26.93									
			39.52			12.51											10.64									
			50.67			16.03											13.65									
Colesville (cdp)	3,052	3,390	1,768	-	-	398	-	-	358	-	-	-	-	-	-	-	589	-	-	-	-	-	-	-	-	238
	15.37		52.15			54.30			49.45								50.95									71.90
						22.51			20.25								33.31									13.46
			52.15			11.74			10.56								17.37									7.02
			57.93			13.04			11.73								19.30									7.80
Fairland (cdp)	2,672	3,328	1,266	-	-	220	-	-	333	-	-	-	-	-	-	-	461	-	-	-	-	-	-	-	-	-
	12.38		38.04			26.96			54.41								36.53									
						17.38			26.30								36.41									
			38.04			6.61			10.01								13.85									
			47.38			8.23			12.46								17.25									
Gaithersburg (city)	6,297	6,935	2,510	-	-	456	-	-	789	-	161	-	-	-	-	-	510	-	-	-	-	-	-	-	-	296
	11.93		36.19			26.98			32.31		36.76						55.74									51.30
						18.17			31.43		6.41						20.32									11.79
			36.19			6.58			11.38		2.32						7.35									4.27
			39.86			7.24			12.53		2.56						8.10									4.70
Germantown (cdp)	5,154	5,283	1,952	-	-	700	-	-	381	-	-	-	-	-	-	-	178	-	-	-	-	-	-	-	-	264
	9.35		36.95			33.33			37.65								45.41									51.87
						35.86			19.52								9.12									13.52
			36.95			13.25			7.21								3.37									5.00
			37.87			13.58			7.39								3.45									5.12
Montgomery Village (cdp)	4,588	4,276	1,640	-	-	383	-	-	386	-	209	-	-	-	-	-	-	-	-	-	-	-	-	-	-	244
	12.11		38.35			21.79			55.06		36.60															60.55
						23.35			23.54		12.74															14.88
			38.35			8.96			9.03		4.89															5.71
			35.75			8.35			8.41		4.56															5.32
North Bethesda (cdp)	4,499	4,536	1,435	-	-	258	-	-	480	-	152	-	-	-	-	31	279	-	-	-	-	-	-	-	-	-
	11.64		31.64			24.69			33.22		40.43					5.94	41.15									
						17.98			33.45		10.59					2.16	19.44									
			31.64			5.69			10.58		3.35					0.68	6.15									
			31.90			5.73			10.67		3.38					0.69	6.20									
North Potomac (cdp)	3,843	6,183	2,529	-	-	572	-	-	1,193	-	-	-	-	-	-	-	381	-	-	-	-	-	-	-	-	-
	16.75		40.90			49.10			36.78								36.29									
						22.62			47.17								15.07									
			40.90			9.25			19.29								6.16									
			65.81			14.88			31.04								9.91									

Notes: Please refer to the User's Guide for an explanation of data; data is arranged alphabetically by state, then county, then city within each county; table includes counties with populations greater than 49,999 unless noted and cities with populations greater than 9,999 whose Asian and/or NHPI population rates are greater than the national average; (1) Native Hawaiian and other Pacific Islander; (2) excludes Taiwanese; (3) includes Chamorro; (4) county does not meet population threshold but is shown in order to allow inclusion of city

Place	Total foreign-born naturalized citizens	Total Asian population	Asians who are foreign-born naturalized citizens	Total NHPI[1] population	NHPIs[1] who are foreign-born naturalized citizens	Asian Indian	Bangladeshi	Cambodian	Chinese[2]	Fijian	Filipino	Guamanian[3]	Hawaiian, Native	Hmong	Indonesian	Japanese	Korean	Laotian	Malaysian	Pakistani	Samoan	Sri Lankan	Taiwanese	Thai	Tongan	Vietnamese
Olney (cdp)	2,803 8.86	2,585	1,117 43.21 43.21 39.85	-	-	323 46.34 28.92 12.50 11.52	-	-	238 37.48 21.31 9.21 8.49	-	-	-	-	-	-	-	280 43.01 25.07 10.83 9.99	-	-	-	-	-	-	-	-	-
Potomac (cdp)	5,778 12.89	5,819	2,731 46.93 46.93 47.27	-	-	716 48.25 26.22 12.30 12.39	-	-	928 47.69 33.98 15.95 16.06	-	99 26.61 3.63 1.70 1.71	-	-	-	-	-	571 51.16 20.91 9.81 9.88	-	-	-	-	-	-	-	-	-
Redland (cdp)	2,393 13.87	2,930	1,160 39.59 39.59 48.47	-	-	320 42.78 27.59 10.92 13.37	-	-	265 33.21 22.84 9.04 11.07	-	93 30.10 8.02 3.17 3.89	-	-	-	-	-	149 36.25 12.84 5.09 6.23	-	-	-	-	-	-	-	-	-
Rockville (city)	5,266 11.14	6,677	2,015 30.18 30.18 38.26	-	-	319 32.00 15.83 4.78 6.06	-	-	820 30.61 40.69 12.28 15.57	-	122 28.44 6.05 1.83 2.32	-	-	-	-	17 3.83 0.84 0.25 0.32	254 27.94 12.61 3.80 4.82	-	-	-	-	-	-	-	-	213 47.87 10.57 3.19 4.04
Silver Spring (cdp)	7,727 10.07	6,302	2,015 31.97 31.97 26.08	-	-	385 27.09 19.11 6.11 4.98	-	141 43.25 7.00 2.24 1.82	232 31.10 11.51 3.68 3.00	-	53 11.30 2.63 0.84 0.69	-	-	-	-	-	226 50.22 11.22 3.59 2.92	-	-	-	-	-	-	-	-	711 40.15 35.29 11.28 9.20
Takoma Park (city)	1,919 11.17	714	241 33.75 33.75 12.56	-	-	-	-	-	-	-	-	-	-	-	-	-	-	-	-	-	-	-	-	-	-	-
Wheaton-Glenmont (cdp)	9,708 16.82	7,096	3,214 45.29 45.29 33.11	-	-	503 42.02 15.65 7.09 5.18	-	-	944 50.56 29.37 13.30 9.72	-	240 35.19 7.47 3.38 2.47	-	-	-	-	-	389 46.59 12.10 5.48 4.01	-	-	-	-	-	-	-	-	777 66.58 24.18 10.95 8.00
White Oak (cdp)	2,812 13.46	2,508	1,019 40.63 40.63 36.24	-	-	201 37.08 19.73 8.01 7.15	-	-	214 47.87 21.00 8.53 7.61	-	-	-	-	-	-	-	186 29.11 18.25 7.42 6.61	-	-	-	-	-	-	-	-	364 55.49 35.72 14.51 12.94
Prince George's County	42,817 5.34	30,390	11,775 38.75 38.75 27.50	-	-	2,285 32.05 19.41 7.52 5.34	-	-	1,692 34.40 14.37 5.57 3.95	-	3,793 46.04 32.21 12.48 8.86	-	-	-	-	168 26.42 1.43 0.55 0.39	1,524 41.29 12.94 5.01 3.56	-	-	180 26.47 1.53 0.59 0.42	-	-	-	86 25.75 0.73 0.28 0.20	-	1,234 47.01 10.48 4.06 2.88
Adelphi (cdp)	1,879 12.51	1,400	405 28.93 28.93 21.55	-	-	-	-	-	-	-	-	-	-	-	-	-	-	-	-	-	-	-	-	-	-	-

Notes: Please refer to the User's Guide for an explanation of data; data is arranged alphabetically by state, then county, then city within each county; table includes counties with populations greater than 49,999 unless noted and cities with populations greater than 9,999 whose Asian and/or NHPI population rates are greater than the national average; (1) Native Hawaiian and other Pacific Islander; (2) excludes Taiwanese; (3) includes Chamorro; (4) county does not meet population threshold but is shown in order to allow inclusion of city

Place	Total foreign-born naturalized citizens	Total Asian population	Asians who are foreign-born naturalized citizens	Total NHPI[1] population	NHPIs[1] who are foreign-born naturalized citizens	Asian Indian	Bangladeshi	Cambodian	Chinese[2]	Fijian	Filipino	Guamanian[3]	Hawaiian, Native	Hmong	Indonesian	Japanese	Korean	Laotian	Malaysian	Pakistani	Samoan	Sri Lankan	Taiwanese	Thai	Tongan	Vietnamese
Beltsville (cdp)	1,696 10.79	1,706	584 34.23 34.23 34.43	-	-	150 29.01 25.68 8.79 8.84	-	-	-	-	-	-	-	-	-	-	83 29.23 14.21 4.87 4.89	-	-	-	-	-	-	-	-	-
College Park (city)	1,334 5.42	2,236	577 25.81 25.81 43.25	-	-	124 19.44 21.49 5.55 9.30	-	-	223 31.72 38.65 9.97 16.72	-	-	-	-	-	-	-	-	-	-	-	-	-	-	-	-	-
Fort Washington (cdp)	1,897 7.84	2,413	1,081 44.80 44.80 56.98	-	-	-	-	-	-	-	879 45.50 81.31 36.43 46.34	-	-	-	-	-	-	-	-	-	-	-	-	-	-	-
Friendly (cdp)	632 5.76	657	355 54.03 54.03 56.17	-	-	-	-	-	-	-	274 52.39 77.18 41.70 43.35	-	-	-	-	-	-	-	-	-	-	-	-	-	-	-
Glenn Dale (cdp)	1,052 8.21	1,008	477 47.32 47.32 45.34	-	-	-	-	-	-	-	-	-	-	-	-	-	-	-	-	-	-	-	-	-	-	-
Greenbelt (city)	1,558 7.28	2,577	669 25.96 25.96 42.94	-	-	128 17.63 19.13 4.97 8.22	-	-	122 20.54 18.24 4.73 7.83	-	-	-	-	-	-	-	234 38.81 34.98 9.08 15.02	-	-	-	-	-	-	-	-	-
Hyattsville (city)	1,239 8.35	695	255 36.69 36.69 20.58	-	-	-	-	-	-	-	-	-	-	-	-	-	-	-	-	-	-	-	-	-	-	-
Lanham-Seabrook (cdp)	1,452 8.03	916	396 43.23 43.23 27.27	-	-	-	-	-	-	-	-	-	-	-	-	-	-	-	-	-	-	-	-	-	-	-
Laurel (city)	1,197 5.97	1,215	378 31.11 31.11 31.58	-	-	-	-	-	-	-	-	-	-	-	-	-	-	-	-	-	-	-	-	-	-	-
New Carrollton (city)	1,025 7.98	517	191 36.94 36.94 18.63	-	-	-	-	-	-	-	-	-	-	-	-	-	-	-	-	-	-	-	-	-	-	-

Notes: Please refer to the User's Guide for an explanation of data; data is arranged alphabetically by state, then county, then city within each county; table includes counties with populations greater than 49,999 unless noted and cities with populations greater than 9,999 whose Asian and/or NHPI population rates are greater than the national average; (1) Native Hawaiian and other Pacific Islander; (2) excludes Taiwanese; (3) includes Chamorro; (4) county does not meet population threshold but is shown in order to allow inclusion of city

Place	Total foreign-born naturalized citizens	Total Asian population	Asians who are foreign-born naturalized citizens	Total NHPI[1] population	NHPIs[1] who are foreign-born naturalized citizens	Asian Indian	Bangladeshi	Cambodian	Chinese[2]	Fijian	Filipino	Guamanian[3]	Hawaiian, Native	Hmong	Indonesian	Japanese	Korean	Laotian	Malaysian	Pakistani	Samoan	Sri Lankan	Taiwanese	Thai	Tongan	Vietnamese
South Laurel (cdp)	1,454 6.99	1,164	441 37.89 37.89 30.33	-	-	-	-	-	-	-	-	-	-	-	-	-	-	-	-	-	-	-	-	-	-	-
St. Mary's County	1,420 1.65	1,623	694 42.76 42.76 48.87	-	-	106 37.99 15.27 6.53 7.46	-	-	-	-	304 46.48 43.80 18.73 21.41	-	-	-	-	-	-	-	-	-	-	-	-	-	-	-
Lexington Park (cdp)	337 3.11	436	183 41.97 41.97 54.30	-	-	-	-	-	-	-	-	-	-	-	-	-	-	-	-	-	-	-	-	-	-	-
Washington County	1,360 1.03	1,000	358 35.80 35.80 26.32	-	-	-	-	-	-	-	-	-	-	-	-	-	-	-	-	-	-	-	-	-	-	-
Wicomico County	1,467 1.73	1,746	657 37.63 37.63 44.79	-	-	212 48.18 32.27 12.14 14.45	-	-	-	-	-	-	-	-	-	-	180 30.51 27.40 10.31 12.27	-	-	-	-	-	-	-	-	-
Salisbury (city)	539 2.23	997	298 29.89 29.89 55.29	-	-	-	-	-	-	-	-	-	-	-	-	-	-	-	-	-	-	-	-	-	-	-
MASSACHUSETTS	337,617 5.32	238,246	72,105 30.26 30.26 21.36	1,835	122 6.65 6.65 0.04	10,161 24.23 14.09 4.26 3.01	157 27.99 0.22 0.07 0.05	4,346 21.34 6.03 1.82 1.29	28,392 34.60 39.38 11.92 8.41	-	3,657 39.38 5.07 1.53 1.08	37 8.31 30.33 2.02 0.01	0 0.00 0.00 0.00 0.00	160 16.11 0.22 0.07 0.05	155 21.83 0.21 0.07 0.05	961 8.77 1.33 0.40 0.28	6,345 36.47 8.80 2.66 1.88	892 24.46 1.24 0.37 0.26	-	536 22.75 0.74 0.22 0.16	-	194 41.36 0.27 0.08 0.06	887 34.98 1.23 0.37 0.26	487 21.60 0.68 0.20 0.14	-	12,790 37.21 17.74 5.37 3.79
Barnstable County	5,784 2.60	1,372	466 33.97 33.97 8.06	-	-	-	-	-	156 36.11 33.48 11.37 2.70	-	-	-	-	-	-	-	-	-	-	-	-	-	-	-	-	-
Berkshire County	2,740 2.03	1,259	379 30.10 30.10 13.83	-	-	59 17.10 15.57 4.69 2.15	-	-	-	-	-	-	-	-	-	-	-	-	-	-	-	-	-	-	-	-
Bristol County	36,225 6.78	7,292	2,295 31.47 31.47 6.34	-	-	450 29.62 19.61 6.17 1.24	-	384 17.67 16.73 5.27 1.06	474 33.88 20.65 6.50 1.31	-	197 47.58 8.58 2.70 0.54	-	-	-	-	-	363 64.59 15.82 4.98 1.00	-	-	-	-	-	-	-	-	215 47.57 9.37 2.95 0.59

Notes: Please refer to the User's Guide for an explanation of data; data is arranged alphabetically by state, then county, then city within each county; table includes counties with populations greater than 49,999 unless noted and cities with populations greater than 9,999 whose Asian and/or NHPI population rates are greater than the national average; (1) Native Hawaiian and other Pacific Islander; (2) excludes Taiwanese; (3) includes Chamorro; (4) county does not meet population threshold but is shown in order to allow inclusion of city

Place	Total foreign-born naturalized citizens	Total Asian population	Asians who are foreign-born naturalized citizens	Total NHPI[1] population	NHPIs[1] who are foreign-born naturalized citizens	Asian Indian	Bangladeshi	Cambodian	Chinese[2]	Fijian	Filipino	Guamanian[3]	Hawaiian, Native	Hmong	Indonesian	Japanese	Korean	Laotian	Malaysian	Pakistani	Samoan	Sri Lankan	Taiwanese	Thai	Tongan	Vietnamese
Essex County	33,707	17,261	5,374	-	-	781	-	898	1,103	-	273	-	-	-	-	81	686	85	-	-	-	-	-	-	-	1,133
	4.66		31.13			31.67		23.92	33.55		40.44					7.94	44.37	21.96								37.31
						14.53		16.71	20.52		5.08					1.51	12.77	1.58								21.08
			31.13			4.52		5.20	6.39		1.58					0.47	3.97	0.49								6.56
			15.94			2.32		2.66	3.27		0.81					0.24	2.04	0.25								3.36
Andover (town)	1,569	2,078	664	-	-	177	-	-	198	-	-	-	-	-	-	-	-	-	-	-	-	-	-	-	-	-
	5.02		31.95			35.19			24.18																	
						26.66			29.82																	
			31.95			8.52			9.53																	
			42.32			11.28			12.62																	
Lynn (city)	6,764	5,899	1,372	-	-	82	-	688	-	-	-	-	-	-	-	-	-	-	-	-	-	-	-	-	-	269
	7.59		23.26			19.95		22.94																		22.82
						5.98		50.15																		19.61
			23.26			1.39		11.66																		4.56
			20.28			1.21		10.17																		3.98
North Andover (town)	1,132	1,084	388	-	-	-	-	-	143	-	-	-	-	-	-	-	-	-	-	-	-	-	-	-	-	-
	4.16		35.79						41.57																	
									36.86																	
			35.79						13.19																	
			34.28						12.63																	
Franklin County	1,162	641	189	-	-	-	-	-	-	-	-	-	-	-	-	-	-	-	-	-	-	-	-	-	-	-
	1.62		29.49																							
			29.49																							
			16.27																							
Hampden County	16,458	6,054	2,043	-	-	260	-	105	374	-	-	-	-	-	-	-	270	-	-	-	-	-	-	-	-	618
	3.61		33.75			36.26		23.08	31.30								59.47									31.87
						12.73		5.14	18.31								13.22									30.25
			33.75			4.29		1.73	6.18								4.46									10.21
			12.41			1.58		0.64	2.27								1.64									3.76
Hampshire County	4,380	4,811	1,270	-	-	207	-	-	418	-	-	-	-	-	-	-	248	-	-	-	-	-	-	-	-	-
	2.88		26.40			24.47			26.14								32.63									
						16.30			32.91								19.53									
			26.40			4.30			8.69								5.15									
			29.00			4.73			9.54								5.66									
Amherst Center (cdp)	660	1,356	337	-	-	-	-	-	-	-	-	-	-	-	-	-	-	-	-	-	-	-	-	-	-	-
	3.85		24.85																							
			24.85																							
			51.06																							
Amherst (town)	1,415	2,992	621	-	-	-	-	-	225	-	-	-	-	-	-	-	-	-	-	-	-	-	-	-	-	-
	4.06		20.76						21.05																	
									36.23																	
			20.76						7.52																	
			43.89						15.90																	
Middlesex County	91,978	91,645	25,037	-	-	4,987	-	1,973	9,630	-	1,005	-	-	-	-	358	2,248	442	-	82	-	-	519	177	-	2,769
	6.28		27.32			22.74		17.98	32.14		39.41					9.24	31.66	24.46		13.83			40.80	19.64		41.11
						19.92		7.88	38.46		4.01					1.43	8.98	1.77		0.33			2.07	0.71		11.06
			27.32			5.44		2.15	10.51		1.10					0.39	2.45	0.48		0.09			0.57	0.19		3.02
			27.22			5.42		2.15	10.47		1.09					0.39	2.44	0.48		0.09			0.56	0.19		3.01

Notes: Please refer to the User's Guide for an explanation of data; data is arranged alphabetically by state, then county, then city within each county; table includes counties with populations greater than 49,999 unless noted and cities with populations greater than 9,999 whose Asian and/or NHPI population rates are greater than the national average; (1) Native Hawaiian and other Pacific Islander; (2) excludes Taiwanese; (3) includes Chamorro; (4) county does not meet population threshold but is shown in order to allow inclusion of city

Place	Total foreign-born naturalized citizens	Total Asian population	Asians who are foreign-born naturalized citizens	Total NHPI[1] population	NHPIs[1] who are foreign-born naturalized citizens	Asian Indian	Bangladeshi	Cambodian	Chinese[2]	Fijian	Filipino	Guamanian[3]	Hawaiian, Native	Hmong	Indonesian	Japanese	Korean	Laotian	Malaysian	Pakistani	Samoan	Sri Lankan	Taiwanese	Thai	Tongan	Vietnamese
Acton (town)	1,070 5.26	1,813	530 29.23 29.23 49.53	-	-	126 19.33 23.77 6.95 11.78	-	-	264 32.55 49.81 14.56 24.67	-	-	-	-	-	-	-	-	-	-	-	-	-	-	-	-	-
Arlington (town)	2,823 6.66	2,006	601 29.96 29.96 21.29	-	-	-	-	-	237 32.51 39.43 11.81 8.40	-	-	-	-	-	-	-	-	-	-	-	-	-	-	-	-	-
Bedford (town)	693 5.50	789	260 32.95 32.95 37.52	-	-	-	-	-	-	-	-	-	-	-	-	-	-	-	-	-	-	-	-	-	-	-
Belmont (cdp)	1,912 7.90	1,297	376 28.99 28.99 19.67	-	-	-	-	-	184 32.80 48.94 14.19 9.62	-	-	-	-	-	-	-	-	-	-	-	-	-	-	-	-	-
Belmont (town)	1,912 7.90	1,297	376 28.99 28.99 19.67	-	-	-	-	-	184 32.80 48.94 14.19 9.62	-	-	-	-	-	-	-	-	-	-	-	-	-	-	-	-	-
Burlington (town)	1,606 7.02	2,314	582 25.15 25.15 36.24	-	-	346 22.88 59.45 14.95 21.54	-	-	-	-	-	-	-	-	-	-	-	-	-	-	-	-	-	-	-	-
Cambridge (city)	8,283 8.17	12,112	2,377 19.63 19.63 28.70	-	-	444 16.04 18.68 3.67 5.36	-	-	1,041 23.99 43.79 8.59 12.57	-	-	-	-	-	-	57 5.36 2.40 0.47 0.69	408 21.13 17.16 3.37 4.93	-	-	-	-	-	-	-	-	-
Chelmsford (town)	1,429 4.22	1,550	567 36.58 36.58 39.68	-	-	78 21.14 13.76 5.03 5.46	-	-	215 37.52 37.92 13.87 15.05	-	-	-	-	-	-	-	-	-	-	-	-	-	-	-	-	-
Framingham (town)	4,325 6.46	3,446	1,185 34.39 34.39 27.40	-	-	458 33.26 38.65 13.29 10.59	-	-	387 36.86 32.66 11.23 8.95	-	-	-	-	-	-	-	-	-	-	-	-	-	-	-	-	-
Lexington (town)	2,704 8.91	3,251	1,173 36.08 36.08 43.38	-	-	304 36.19 25.92 9.35 11.24	-	-	600 44.81 51.15 18.46 22.19	-	-	-	-	-	-	-	121 26.77 10.32 3.72 4.47	-	-	-	-	-	-	-	-	-

Notes: Please refer to the User's Guide for an explanation of data; data is arranged alphabetically by state, then county, then city within each county; table includes counties with populations greater than 49,999 unless noted and cities with populations greater than 9,999 whose Asian and/or NHPI population rates are greater than the national average; (1) Native Hawaiian and other Pacific Islander; (2) excludes Taiwanese; (3) includes Chamorro; (4) county does not meet population threshold but is shown in order to allow inclusion of city

Place	Total foreign-born naturalized citizens	Total Asian population	Asians who are foreign-born naturalized citizens	Total NHPI[1] population	NHPIs[1] who are foreign-born naturalized citizens	Asian Indian	Bangladeshi	Cambodian	Chinese[2]	Fijian	Filipino	Guamanian[3]	Hawaiian, Native	Hmong	Indonesian	Japanese	Korean	Laotian	Malaysian	Pakistani	Samoan	Sri Lankan	Taiwanese	Thai	Tongan	Vietnamese
Lowell (city)	7,022	17,161	3,015	-	-	333	-	1,483	189	-	-	-	-	-	-	-	-	337	-	-	-	-	-	-	-	470
	6.68		17.57			12.84		15.58	24.90									22.97								31.54
						11.04		49.19	6.27									11.18								15.59
			17.57			1.94		8.64	1.10									1.96								2.74
			42.94			4.74		21.12	2.69									4.80								6.69
Malden (city)	5,658	7,879	2,666	-	-	202	-	-	1,471	-	-	-	-	-	-	-	-	-	-	-	-	-	-	-	-	587
	10.04		33.84			19.31			35.82																	43.84
						7.58			55.18																	22.02
			33.84			2.56			18.67																	7.45
			47.12			3.57			26.00																	10.37
Marlborough (city)	1,682	1,601	386	-	-	80	-	-	-	-	-	-	-	-	-	-	-	-	-	-	-	-	-	-	-	-
	4.64		24.11			11.49																				
						20.73																				
			24.11			5.00																				
			22.95			4.76																				
Medford (city)	4,364	2,338	645	-	-	87	-	-	191	-	-	-	-	-	-	-	-	-	-	-	-	-	-	-	-	159
	7.83		27.59			21.59			21.95																	43.80
						13.49			29.61																	24.65
			27.59			3.72			8.17																	6.80
			14.78			1.99			4.38																	3.64
Natick (town)	1,513	1,294	432	-	-	-	-	-	253	-	-	-	-	-	-	-	-	-	-	-	-	-	-	-	-	-
	4.70		33.38						38.63																	
									58.56																	
			33.38						19.55																	
			28.55						16.72																	
Newton (city)	8,615	6,323	2,140	-	-	238	-	-	1,365	-	-	-	-	-	-	-	148	-	-	-	-	-	-	-	-	-
	10.28		33.84			41.18			34.57								22.12									
						11.12			63.79								6.92									
			33.84			3.76			21.59								2.34									
			24.84			2.76			15.84								1.72									
Somerville (city)	7,077	5,013	1,234	-	-	327	-	-	532	-	-	-	-	-	-	-	69	-	-	-	-	-	-	-	-	-
	9.13		24.62			25.33			26.05								15.23									
						26.50			43.11								5.59									
			24.62			6.52			10.61								1.38									
			17.44			4.62			7.52								0.97									
Sudbury (town)	683	615	263	-	-	-	-	-	-	-	-	-	-	-	-	-	-	-	-	-	-	-	-	-	-	-
	4.06		42.76																							
			42.76																							
			38.51																							
Waltham (city)	4,561	4,638	1,059	-	-	237	-	-	432	-	-	-	-	-	-	-	-	-	-	-	-	-	-	-	-	-
	7.70		22.83			12.07			29.03																	
						22.38			40.79																	
			22.83			5.11			9.31																	
			23.22			5.20			9.47																	
Wayland (town)	740	682	279	-	-	-	-	-	-	-	-	-	-	-	-	-	-	-	-	-	-	-	-	-	-	-
	5.65		40.91																							
			40.91																							
			37.70																							

Notes: Please refer to the User's Guide for an explanation of data; data is arranged alphabetically by state, then county, then city within each county; table includes counties with populations greater than 49,999 unless noted and cities with populations greater than 9,999 whose Asian and/or NHPI population rates are greater than the national average; (1) Native Hawaiian and other Pacific Islander; (2) excludes Taiwanese; (3) includes Chamorro; (4) county does not meet population threshold but is shown in order to allow inclusion of city

Place	Total foreign-born naturalized citizens	Total Asian population	Asians who are foreign-born naturalized citizens	Total NHPI[1] population	NHPIs[1] who are foreign-born naturalized citizens	Asian Indian	Bangladeshi	Cambodian	Chinese[2]	Fijian	Filipino	Guamanian[3]	Hawaiian, Native	Hmong	Indonesian	Japanese	Korean	Laotian	Malaysian	Pakistani	Samoan	Sri Lankan	Taiwanese	Thai	Tongan	Vietnamese
Westford (town)	712 3.43	951	339 35.65 35.65 47.61	-	-	-	-	-	126 34.05 37.17 13.25 17.70	-	-	-	-	-	-	-	-	-	-	-	-	-	-	-	-	-
Weston (town)	797 6.95	910	378 41.54 41.54 47.43	-	-	-	-	-	180 46.75 47.62 19.78 22.58	-	-	-	-	-	-	-	-	-	-	-	-	-	-	-	-	-
Winchester (town)	1,017 4.89	794	242 30.48 30.48 23.80	-	-	-	-	-	-	-	-	-	-	-	-	-	-	-	-	-	-	-	-	-	-	-
Woburn (city)	1,561 4.19	1,827	573 31.36 31.36 36.71	-	-	214 21.36 37.35 11.71 13.71	-	-	-	-	-	-	-	-	-	-	-	-	-	-	-	-	-	-	-	-
Norfolk County	42,260 6.50	36,121	13,222 36.60 36.60 31.29	-	-	1,268 25.03 9.59 3.51 3.00	-	-	7,814 40.73 59.10 21.63 18.49	-	851 45.07 6.44 2.36 2.01	-	-	-	-	93 4.47 0.70 0.26 0.22	823 36.59 6.22 2.28 1.95	-	-	-	-	-	113 26.71 0.85 0.31 0.27	-	-	1,337 47.44 10.11 3.70 3.16
Brookline (town)	6,599 11.56	7,787	2,042 26.22 26.22 30.94	-	-	287 26.48 14.05 3.69 4.35	-	-	1,267 35.34 62.05 16.27 19.20	-	-	-	-	-	-	10 0.75 0.49 0.13 0.15	191 19.25 9.35 2.45 2.89	-	-	-	-	-	-	-	-	-
Needham (town)	1,802 6.23	1,062	331 31.17 31.17 18.37	-	-	-	-	-	173 28.55 52.27 16.29 9.60	-	-	-	-	-	-	-	-	-	-	-	-	-	-	-	-	-
Norwood (town)	1,574 5.51	1,384	258 18.64 18.64 16.39	-	-	54 7.12 20.93 3.90 3.43	-	-	-	-	-	-	-	-	-	-	-	-	-	-	-	-	-	-	-	-
Quincy (city)	9,271 10.53	14,007	5,798 41.39 41.39 62.54	-	-	156 16.10 2.69 1.11 1.68	-	-	4,065 43.05 70.11 29.02 43.85	-	410 47.73 7.07 2.93 4.42	-	-	-	-	-	-	-	-	-	-	-	-	-	-	657 44.91 11.33 4.69 7.09
Randolph (town)	4,022 12.98	3,152	1,492 47.34 47.34 37.10	-	-	-	-	-	752 49.28 50.40 23.86 18.70	-	-	-	-	-	-	-	-	-	-	-	-	-	-	-	-	318 48.25 21.31 10.09 7.91

Notes: Please refer to the User's Guide for an explanation of data; data is arranged alphabetically by state, then county, then city within each county; table includes counties with populations greater than 49,999 unless noted and cities with populations greater than 9,999 whose Asian and/or NHPI population rates are greater than the national average; (1) Native Hawaiian and other Pacific Islander; (2) excludes Taiwanese; (3) includes Chamorro; (4) county does not meet population threshold but is shown in order to allow inclusion of city

Place	Total foreign-born naturalized citizens	Total Asian population	Asians who are foreign-born naturalized citizens	Total NHPI[1] population	NHPIs[1] who are foreign-born naturalized citizens	Asian Indian	Bangladeshi	Cambodian	Chinese[2]	Fijian	Filipino	Guamanian[3]	Hawaiian, Native	Hmong	Indonesian	Japanese	Korean	Laotian	Malaysian	Pakistani	Samoan	Sri Lankan	Taiwanese	Thai	Tongan	Vietnamese
Sharon (town)	1,424 8.18	694	285 41.07 41.07 20.01	-	-	-	-	-	-	-	-	-	-	-	-	-	-	-	-	-	-	-	-	-	-	-
Wellesley (town)	1,310 4.92	1,784	487 27.30 27.30 37.18	-	-	-	-	-	316 34.92 64.89 17.71 24.12	-	-	-	-	-	-	-	-	-	-	-	-	-	-	-	-	-
Plymouth County	13,636 2.88	4,491	1,626 36.21 36.21 11.92	-	-	203 32.43 12.48 4.52 1.49	-	-	354 33.62 21.77 7.88 2.60	-	254 47.30 15.62 5.66 1.86	-	-	-	-	-	-	-	-	-	-	-	-	-	-	285 40.14 17.53 6.35 2.09
Suffolk County	63,450 9.20	48,115	14,763 30.68 30.68 23.27	-	-	994 22.83 6.73 2.07 1.57	-	502 29.22 3.40 1.04 0.79	6,869 34.47 46.53 14.28 10.83	-	504 27.16 3.41 1.05 0.79	-	-	-	-	69 3.04 0.47 0.14 0.11	704 27.18 4.77 1.46 1.11	-	-	-	-	-	67 14.41 0.45 0.14 0.11	-	-	4,515 36.24 30.58 9.38 7.12
Boston (city)	56,681 9.62	44,345	13,531 30.51 30.51 23.87	-	-	977 24.12 7.22 2.20 1.72	-	225 35.94 1.66 0.51 0.40	6,543 33.69 48.36 14.75 11.54	-	470 27.00 3.47 1.06 0.83	-	-	-	-	69 3.09 0.51 0.16 0.12	672 27.73 4.97 1.52 1.19	-	-	-	-	-	67 14.41 0.50 0.15 0.12	-	-	4,044 36.35 29.89 9.12 7.13
Chelsea (city)	2,548 7.26	1,455	412 28.32 28.32 16.17	-	-	-	-	-	-	-	-	-	-	-	-	-	-	-	-	-	-	-	-	-	-	251 33.96 60.92 17.25 9.85
Revere (city)	3,596 7.61	2,161	755 34.94 34.94 21.00	-	-	-	-	242 29.88 32.05 11.20 6.73	-	-	-	-	-	-	-	-	-	-	-	-	-	-	-	-	-	211 36.70 27.95 9.76 5.87
Worcester County	25,327 3.37	18,965	5,368 28.30 28.30 21.19	-	-	910 23.36 16.95 4.80 3.59	-	74 18.73 1.38 0.39 0.29	990 28.63 18.44 5.22 3.91	-	166 34.73 3.09 0.88 0.66	-	-	88 13.27 1.64 0.46 0.35	-	71 18.16 1.32 0.37 0.28	588 49.04 10.95 3.10 2.32	242 23.89 4.51 1.28 0.96	-	107 26.95 1.99 0.56 0.42	-	-	-	-	-	1,729 30.63 32.21 9.12 6.83
Fitchburg (city)	1,498 3.83	1,748	345 19.74 19.74 23.03	-	-	-	-	-	-	-	-	-	-	88 14.47 25.51 5.03 5.87	-	-	-	73 18.72 21.16 4.18 4.87	-	-	-	-	-	-	-	-
Northborough (town)	559 3.99	762	269 35.30 35.30 48.12	-	-	-	-	-	-	-	-	-	-	-	-	-	-	-	-	-	-	-	-	-	-	-

Notes: Please refer to the User's Guide for an explanation of data; data is arranged alphabetically by state, then county, then city within each county; table includes counties with populations greater than 49,999 unless noted and cities with populations greater than 9,999 whose Asian and/or NHPI population rates are greater than the national average; (1) Native Hawaiian and other Pacific Islander; (2) excludes Taiwanese; (3) includes Chamorro; (4) county does not meet population threshold but is shown in order to allow inclusion of city

Place	Total foreign-born naturalized citizens	Total Asian population	Asians who are foreign-born naturalized citizens	Total NHPI[1] population	NHPIs[1] who are foreign-born naturalized citizens	Asian Indian	Bangladeshi	Cambodian	Chinese[2]	Fijian	Filipino	Guamanian[3]	Hawaiian, Native	Hmong	Indonesian	Japanese	Korean	Laotian	Malaysian	Pakistani	Samoan	Sri Lankan	Taiwanese	Thai	Tongan	Vietnamese
Shrewsbury (town)	1,365 4.31	2,574	673 26.15 26.15 49.30	-	-	221 19.40 32.84 8.59 16.19	-	-	145 22.17 21.55 5.63 10.62	-	-	-	-	-	-	-	-	-	-	-	-	-	-	-	-	237 45.93 35.22 9.21 17.36
Westborough (town)	790 4.39	1,429	347 24.28 24.28 43.92	-	-	88 14.64 25.36 6.16 11.14	-	-	146 30.29 42.07 10.22 18.48	-	-	-	-	-	-	-	-	-	-	-	-	-	-	-	-	-
Worcester (city)	8,988 5.21	7,893	2,102 26.63 26.63 23.39	-	-	240 22.68 11.42 3.04 2.67	-	-	290 30.21 13.80 3.67 3.23	-	-	-	-	-	-	-	-	-	-	-	-	-	-	-	-	1,115 26.01 53.04 14.13 12.41
MICHIGAN	239,955 2.41	174,824	53,383 30.54 30.54 22.25	2,669	175 6.56 6.56 0.07	13,965 25.64 26.16 7.99 5.82	431 25.61 0.81 0.25 0.18	576 36.14 1.08 0.33 0.24	8,285 28.14 15.52 4.74 3.45	-	7,578 43.08 14.20 4.33 3.16	85 12.41 48.57 3.18 0.04	7 0.88 4.00 0.26 <0.01	1,274 22.52 2.39 0.73 0.53	105 16.10 0.20 0.06 0.04	929 8.73 1.74 0.53 0.39	9,583 45.60 17.95 5.48 3.99	1,001 35.92 1.88 0.57 0.42	32 7.00 0.06 0.02 0.01	1,412 28.36 2.65 0.81 0.59	25 5.27 14.29 0.94 0.01	122 34.27 0.23 0.07 0.05	983 43.04 1.84 0.56 0.41	436 27.18 0.82 0.25 0.18	-	4,766 36.74 8.93 2.73 1.99
Allegan County	1,269 1.20	592	264 44.59 44.59 20.80	-	-	-	-	-	-	-	-	-	-	-	-	-	-	-	-	-	-	-	-	-	-	-
Bay County	859 0.78	617	226 36.63 36.63 26.31	-	-	-	-	-	-	-	-	-	-	-	-	-	-	-	-	-	-	-	-	-	-	-
Berrien County	3,029 1.86	1,671	455 27.23 27.23 15.02	-	-	151 31.92 33.19 9.04 4.99	-	-	-	-	142 44.65 31.21 8.50 4.69	-	-	-	-	-	87 22.25 19.12 5.21 2.87	-	-	-	-	-	-	-	-	-
Calhoun County	1,320 0.96	1,473	377 25.59 25.59 28.56	-	-	-	-	-	-	-	-	-	-	-	-	30 6.73 7.96 2.04 2.27	-	-	-	-	-	-	-	-	-	-
Cass County	470 0.92	324	131 40.43 40.43 27.87	-	-	-	-	-	-	-	-	-	-	-	-	-	-	44 30.77 33.59 13.58 9.36	-	-	-	-	-	-	-	-
Clinton County	418 0.65	358	129 36.03 36.03 30.86	-	-	-	-	-	-	-	-	-	-	-	-	-	-	-	-	-	-	-	-	-	-	-

Notes: Please refer to the User's Guide for an explanation of data; data is arranged alphabetically by state, then county, then city within each county; table includes counties with populations greater than 49,999 unless noted and cities with populations greater than 9,999 whose Asian and/or NHPI population rates are greater than the national average; (1) Native Hawaiian and other Pacific Islander; (2) excludes Taiwanese; (3) includes Chamorro; (4) county does not meet population threshold but is shown in order to allow inclusion of city

Place	Total foreign-born naturalized citizens	Total Asian population	Asians who are foreign-born naturalized citizens	Total NHPI[1] population	NHPIs[1] who are foreign-born naturalized citizens	Asian Indian	Bangladeshi	Cambodian	Chinese[2]	Fijian	Filipino	Guamanian[3]	Hawaiian, Native	Hmong	Indonesian	Japanese	Korean	Laotian	Malaysian	Pakistani	Samoan	Sri Lankan	Taiwanese	Thai	Tongan	Vietnamese
Eaton County	1,110 1.07	1,222	433 35.43 35.43 39.01	-	-	80 22.16 18.48 6.55 7.21	-	-	-	-	-	-	-	-	-	-	-	-	-	-	-	-	-	-	-	124 42.18 28.64 10.15 11.17
Genesee County	5,867 1.35	3,161	1,144 36.19 36.19 19.50	-	-	382 32.71 33.39 12.08 6.51	-	-	145 36.43 12.67 4.59 2.47	-	188 44.44 16.43 5.95 3.20	-	-	-	-	-	244 53.74 21.33 7.72 4.16	-	-	-	-	-	-	-	-	-
Ingham County	5,577 2.00	9,991	2,132 21.34 21.34 38.23	-	-	405 20.05 19.00 4.05 7.26	-	-	423 23.76 19.84 4.23 7.58	-	194 31.24 9.10 1.94 3.48	-	-	59 9.92 2.77 0.59 1.06	-	53 10.15 2.49 0.53 0.95	354 20.26 16.60 3.54 6.35	-	-	-	-	-	-	-	-	401 30.01 18.81 4.01 7.19
East Lansing (city)	934 2.00	3,836	307 8.00 8.00 32.87	-	-	69 9.10 22.48 1.80 7.39	-	-	79 9.18 25.73 2.06 8.46	-	-	-	-	-	-	-	98 9.90 31.92 2.55 10.49	-	-	-	-	-	-	-	-	-
Meridian charter (township)	1,458 3.74	2,453	790 32.21 32.21 54.18	-	-	257 28.46 32.53 10.48 17.63	-	-	172 32.33 21.77 7.01 11.80	-	-	-	-	-	-	-	120 31.58 15.19 4.89 8.23	-	-	-	-	-	-	-	-	-
Okemos (cdp)	1,064 4.69	1,916	597 31.16 31.16 56.11	-	-	209 27.72 35.01 10.91 19.64	-	-	98 26.34 16.42 5.11 9.21	-	-	-	-	-	-	-	-	-	-	-	-	-	-	-	-	-
Ionia County	241 0.39	219	64 29.22 29.22 26.56	-	-	-	-	-	-	-	-	-	-	-	-	-	-	-	-	-	-	-	-	-	-	-
Isabella County	487 0.77	799	157 19.65 19.65 32.24	-	-	-	-	-	-	-	-	-	-	-	-	-	-	-	-	-	-	-	-	-	-	-
Jackson County	1,334 0.84	732	314 42.90 42.90 23.54	-	-	-	-	-	-	-	-	-	-	-	-	-	-	-	-	-	-	-	-	-	-	-
Kalamazoo County	3,849 1.61	4,315	1,167 27.05 27.05 30.32	-	-	330 25.76 28.28 7.65 8.57	-	-	155 18.04 13.28 3.59 4.03	-	-	-	-	-	-	-	309 43.58 26.48 7.16 8.03	-	-	-	-	-	-	-	-	-

Notes: Please refer to the User's Guide for an explanation of data; data is arranged alphabetically by state, then county, then city within each county; table includes counties with populations greater than 49,999 unless noted and cities with populations greater than 9,999 whose Asian and/or NHPI population rates are greater than the national average; (1) Native Hawaiian and other Pacific Islander; (2) excludes Taiwanese; (3) includes Chamorro; (4) county does not meet population threshold but is shown in order to allow inclusion of city

Place	Total foreign-born naturalized citizens	Total Asian population	Asians who are foreign-born naturalized citizens	Total NHPI[1] population	NHPIs[1] who are foreign-born naturalized citizens	Asian Indian	Bangladeshi	Cambodian	Chinese[2]	Fijian	Filipino	Guamanian[3]	Hawaiian, Native	Hmong	Indonesian	Japanese	Korean	Laotian	Malaysian	Pakistani	Samoan	Sri Lankan	Taiwanese	Thai	Tongan	Vietnamese
Kent County	12,040 2.10	10,515	3,772 35.87 35.87 31.33	-	-	303 21.88 8.03 2.88 2.52	-	-	308 29.33 8.17 2.93 2.56	-	216 34.18 5.73 2.05 1.79	-	-	-	-	-	1,015 53.56 26.91 9.65 8.43	-	-	-	-	-	-	-	-	1,531 35.48 40.59 14.56 12.72
Kentwood (city)	1,574 3.48	2,504	833 33.27 33.27 52.92	-	-	-	-	-	-	-	-	-	-	-	-	-	193 43.37 23.17 7.71 12.26	-	-	-	-	-	-	-	-	439 35.90 52.70 17.53 27.89
Lenawee County	788 0.80	533	190 35.65 35.65 24.11	-	-	-	-	-	-	-	-	-	-	-	-	-	-	-	-	-	-	-	-	-	-	-
Livingston County	2,397 1.53	1,059	485 45.80 45.80 20.23	-	-	-	-	-	-	-	-	-	-	-	-	-	-	-	-	-	-	-	-	-	-	-
Macomb County	36,883 4.68	17,378	5,948 34.23 34.23 16.13	-	-	1,482 26.73 24.92 8.53 4.02	-	-	804 33.60 13.52 4.63 2.18	-	1,424 41.76 23.94 8.19 3.86	-	-	292 26.99 4.91 1.68 0.79	-	-	789 52.08 13.26 4.54 2.14	-	-	241 45.47 4.05 1.39 0.65	-	-	-	-	-	536 37.64 9.01 3.08 1.45
Sterling Heights (city)	11,165 8.97	6,510	2,366 36.34 36.34 21.19	-	-	831 34.34 35.12 12.76 7.44	-	-	324 33.03 13.69 4.98 2.90	-	564 42.34 23.84 8.66 5.05	-	-	-	-	-	195 30.90 8.24 3.00 1.75	-	-	-	-	-	-	-	-	206 45.98 8.71 3.16 1.85
Marquette County	544 0.84	306	129 42.16 42.16 23.71	-	-	-	-	-	-	-	-	-	-	-	-	-	-	-	-	-	-	-	-	-	-	-
Midland County	918 1.11	1,165	347 29.79 29.79 37.80	-	-	109 28.68 31.41 9.36 11.87	-	-	130 33.42 37.46 11.16 14.16	-	-	-	-	-	-	-	-	-	-	-	-	-	-	-	-	-
Monroe County	1,527 1.05	944	294 31.14 31.14 19.25	-	-	-	-	-	-	-	-	-	-	-	-	-	-	-	-	-	-	-	-	-	-	-
Muskegon County	1,602 0.94	745	358 48.05 48.05 22.35	-	-	-	-	-	-	-	-	-	-	-	-	-	-	-	-	-	-	-	-	-	-	-

Notes: Please refer to the User's Guide for an explanation of data; data is arranged alphabetically by state, then county, then city within each county; table includes counties with populations greater than 49,999 unless noted and cities with populations greater than 9,999 whose Asian and/or NHPI population rates are greater than the national average; (1) Native Hawaiian and other Pacific Islander; (2) excludes Taiwanese; (3) includes Chamorro; (4) county does not meet population threshold but is shown in order to allow inclusion of city

Place	Total foreign-born naturalized citizens	Total Asian population	Asians who are foreign-born naturalized citizens	Total NHPI[1] population	NHPIs[1] who are foreign-born naturalized citizens	Asian Indian	Bangladeshi	Cambodian	Chinese[2]	Fijian	Filipino	Guamanian[3]	Hawaiian, Native	Hmong	Indonesian	Japanese	Korean	Laotian	Malaysian	Pakistani	Samoan	Sri Lankan	Taiwanese	Thai	Tongan	Vietnamese
Oakland County	58,944 4.94	48,378	14,720 30.43 30.43 24.97	-	-	4,834 25.24 32.84 9.99 8.20	-	-	2,926 33.64 19.88 6.05 4.96	-	1,839 45.95 12.49 3.80 3.12	-	-	290 26.83 1.97 0.60 0.49	-	188 4.39 1.28 0.39 0.32	2,219 45.98 15.07 4.59 3.76	-	-	334 34.33 2.27 0.69 0.57	-	-	547 43.45 3.72 1.13 0.93	-	-	661 40.13 4.49 1.37 1.12
Auburn Hills (city)	425 2.15	1,229	159 12.94 12.94 37.41	-	-	33 4.88 20.75 2.69 7.76	-	-	-	-	-	-	-	-	-	-	-	-	-	-	-	-	-	-	-	-
Bloomfield (township)	3,782 8.79	2,717	1,355 49.87 49.87 35.83	-	-	552 46.94 40.74 20.32 14.60	-	-	-	-	-	-	-	-	-	-	277 48.01 20.44 10.20 7.32	-	-	-	-	-	-	-	-	-
Farmington (city)	369 3.54	1,065	56 5.26 5.26 15.18	-	-	26 3.16 46.43 2.44 7.05	-	-	-	-	-	-	-	-	-	-	-	-	-	-	-	-	-	-	-	-
Farmington Hills (city)	6,380 7.77	5,722	1,348 23.56 23.56 21.13	-	-	506 14.79 37.54 8.84 7.93	-	-	404 45.91 29.97 7.06 6.33	-	183 48.80 13.58 3.20 2.87	-	-	-	-	-	-	-	-	-	-	-	-	-	-	-
Madison Heights (city)	1,800 5.79	1,595	399 25.02 25.02 22.17	-	-	-	-	-	143 26.14 35.84 8.97 7.94	-	-	-	-	-	-	-	-	-	-	-	-	-	-	-	-	-
Novi (city)	2,286 4.82	3,991	883 22.12 22.12 38.63	-	-	248 22.20 28.09 6.21 10.85	-	-	255 31.37 28.88 6.39 11.15	-	-	-	-	-	-	68 5.92 7.70 1.70 2.97	-	-	-	-	-	-	-	-	-	-
Rochester (city)	456 4.36	549	175 31.88 31.88 38.38	-	-	-	-	-	-	-	-	-	-	-	-	-	-	-	-	-	-	-	-	-	-	-
Rochester Hills (city)	3,955 5.75	4,596	1,610 35.03 35.03 40.71	-	-	618 31.68 38.39 13.45 15.63	-	-	292 28.74 18.14 6.35 7.38	-	-	-	-	-	-	-	218 58.60 13.54 4.74 5.51	-	-	-	-	-	-	-	-	-
Troy (city)	7,683 9.49	10,378	3,179 30.63 30.63 41.38	-	-	1,348 28.95 42.40 12.99 17.55	-	-	588 25.74 18.50 5.67 7.65	-	391 52.06 12.30 3.77 5.09	-	-	-	-	-	376 30.52 11.83 3.62 4.89	-	-	-	-	-	272 48.75 8.56 2.62 3.54	-	-	-

Notes: Please refer to the User's Guide for an explanation of data; data is arranged alphabetically by state, then county, then city within each county; table includes counties with populations greater than 49,999 unless noted and cities with populations greater than 9,999 whose Asian and/or NHPI population rates are greater than the national average; (1) Native Hawaiian and other Pacific Islander; (2) excludes Taiwanese; (3) includes Chamorro; (4) county does not meet population threshold but is shown in order to allow inclusion of city

Place	Total foreign-born naturalized citizens	Total Asian population	Asians who are foreign-born naturalized citizens	Total NHPI[1] population	NHPIs[1] who are foreign-born naturalized citizens	Asian Indian	Bangladeshi	Cambodian	Chinese[2]	Fijian	Filipino	Guamanian[3]	Hawaiian, Native	Hmong	Indonesian	Japanese	Korean	Laotian	Malaysian	Pakistani	Samoan	Sri Lankan	Taiwanese	Thai	Tongan	Vietnamese
West Bloomfield (township)	7,501 11.57	4,994	1,442 28.87 28.87 19.22	-	-	620 36.66 43.00 12.41 8.27	-	-	251 42.11 17.41 5.03 3.35	-	198 46.26 13.73 3.96 2.64	-	-	-	-	5 0.39 0.35 0.10 0.07	232 46.49 16.09 4.65 3.09	-	-	-	-	-	-	-	-	-
Ottawa County	5,584 2.34	5,180	2,127 41.06 41.06 38.09	-	-	233 49.68 10.95 4.50 4.17	-	371 34.26 17.44 7.16 6.64	155 36.56 7.29 2.99 2.78	-	-	-	-	-	-	-	444 82.99 20.87 8.57 7.95	447 38.97 21.02 8.63 8.01	-	-	-	-	-	-	-	245 33.24 11.52 4.73 4.39
Holland (city)	1,437 4.08	1,271	532 41.86 41.86 37.02	-	-	-	-	-	-	-	-	-	-	-	-	-	-	-	-	-	-	-	-	-	-	-
Saginaw County	2,252 1.07	1,747	614 35.15 35.15 27.26	-	-	139 41.00 22.64 7.96 6.17	-	-	-	-	151 40.27 24.59 8.64 6.71	-	-	-	-	-	158 46.75 25.73 9.04 7.02	-	-	-	-	-	-	-	-	-
St. Clair County	2,548 1.55	424	191 45.05 45.05 7.50	-	-	-	-	-	-	-	-	-	-	-	-	-	-	-	-	-	-	-	-	-	-	-
St. Joseph County	682 1.09	297	145 48.82 48.82 21.26	-	-	-	-	-	-	-	-	-	-	-	-	-	-	-	-	-	-	-	-	-	-	-
Washtenaw County	10,713 3.32	20,021	4,227 21.11 21.11 39.46	-	-	1,044 22.03 24.70 5.21 9.75	-	-	1,125 18.56 26.61 5.62 10.50	-	351 37.10 8.30 1.75 3.28	-	-	-	-	57 3.34 1.35 0.28 0.53	934 25.31 22.10 4.67 8.72	-	-	95 20.43 2.25 0.47 0.89	-	-	193 37.12 4.57 0.96 1.80	-	-	165 36.03 3.90 0.82 1.54
Ann Arbor (city)	5,355 4.69	13,389	2,424 18.10 18.10 45.27	-	-	623 19.20 25.70 4.65 11.63	-	-	730 17.35 30.12 5.45 13.63	-	173 32.70 7.14 1.29 3.23	-	-	-	-	34 2.67 1.40 0.25 0.63	463 18.34 19.10 3.46 8.65	-	-	-	-	-	183 41.50 7.55 1.37 3.42	-	-	-
Pittsfield charter (township)	1,708 5.67	2,769	699 25.24 25.24 40.93	-	-	195 29.55 27.90 7.04 11.42	-	-	125 15.94 17.88 4.51 7.32	-	-	-	-	-	-	-	200 35.34 28.61 7.22 11.71	-	-	-	-	-	-	-	-	-
Scio (township)	460 2.93	611	213 34.86 34.86 46.30	-	-	-	-	-	-	-	-	-	-	-	-	-	-	-	-	-	-	-	-	-	-	-

Notes: Please refer to the User's Guide for an explanation of data; data is arranged alphabetically by state, then county, then city within each county; table includes counties with populations greater than 49,999 unless noted and cities with populations greater than 9,999 whose Asian and/or NHPI population rates are greater than the national average; (1) Native Hawaiian and other Pacific Islander; (2) excludes Taiwanese; (3) includes Chamorro; (4) county does not meet population threshold but is shown in order to allow inclusion of city

Place	Total foreign-born naturalized citizens	Total Asian population	Asians who are foreign-born naturalized citizens	Total NHPI[1] population	NHPIs[1] who are foreign-born naturalized citizens	Asian Indian	Bangladeshi	Cambodian	Chinese[2]	Fijian	Filipino	Guamanian[3]	Hawaiian, Native	Hmong	Indonesian	Japanese	Korean	Laotian	Malaysian	Pakistani	Samoan	Sri Lankan	Taiwanese	Thai	Tongan	Vietnamese
Wayne County	62,926	35,273	10,832	495	17	3,612	282	-	1,388	-	2,104	-	-	410	-	136	1,046	-	-	596	-	-	-	-	-	554
	3.05		30.71		3.43	24.91	24.25		27.84		48.95			22.37		12.99	58.01			27.36						45.67
						33.35	2.60		12.81		19.42			3.79		1.26	9.66			5.50						5.11
			30.71		3.43	10.24	0.80		3.94		5.96			1.16		0.39	2.97			1.69						1.57
			17.21		0.03	5.74	0.45		2.21		3.34			0.65		0.22	1.66			0.95						0.88
Brownstown (township)	592	925	275	-	-	-	-	-	-	-	-	-	-	-	-	-	-	-	-	-	-	-	-	-	-	-
	2.58		29.73																							
			29.73																							
			46.45																							
Canton (township)	3,736	6,569	1,993	-	-	997	-	-	258	-	310	-	-	-	-	-	159	-	-	-	-	-	-	-	-	-
	4.90		30.34			28.04			20.74		50.57						53.18									
						50.03			12.95		15.55						7.98									
			30.34			15.18			3.93		4.72						2.42									
			53.35			26.69			6.91		8.30						4.26									
Hamtramck (city)	2,539	2,358	611	-	-	238	221	-	-	-	-	-	-	-	-	-	-	-	-	-	-	-	-	-	-	-
	11.05		25.91			21.06	29.86																			
						38.95	36.17																			
			25.91			10.09	9.37																			
			24.06			9.37	8.70																			
Inkster (city)	383	1,140	96	-	-	39	-	-	-	-	-	-	-	-	-	-	-	-	-	-	-	-	-	-	-	-
	1.27		8.42			5.26																				
						40.63																				
			8.42			3.42																				
			25.07			10.18																				
Northville (township)	961	922	261	-	-	126	-	-	-	-	-	-	-	-	-	-	-	-	-	-	-	-	-	-	-	-
	4.57		28.31			29.37																				
						48.28																				
			28.31			13.67																				
			27.16			13.11																				
MINNESOTA	97,308	139,245	42,403	1,724	143	4,180	-	1,697	4,597	-	2,363	46	23	7,541	-	524	8,932	2,419	-	254	-	-	191	337	-	7,739
	1.98		30.45		8.29	25.68		33.09	30.82		40.05	10.77	3.97	17.47		12.53	69.49	26.89		23.13			41.25	36.63		42.10
						9.86		4.00	10.84		5.57	32.17	16.08	17.78		1.24	21.06	5.70		0.60			0.45	0.79		18.25
			30.45		8.29	3.00		1.22	3.30		1.70	2.67	1.33	5.42		0.38	6.41	1.74		0.18			0.14	0.24		5.56
			43.58		0.15	4.30		1.74	4.72		2.43	0.05	0.02	7.75		0.54	9.18	2.49		0.26			0.20	0.35		7.95
Anoka County	5,232	4,992	2,050	-	-	334	-	-	137	-	166	-	-	174	-	-	574	-	-	-	-	-	-	-	-	371
	1.76		41.07			36.74			31.14		43.68			30.47			81.07									39.14
						16.29			6.68		8.10			8.49			28.00									18.10
			41.07			6.69			2.74		3.33			3.49			11.50									7.43
			39.18			6.38			2.62		3.17			3.33			10.97									7.09
Columbia Heights (city)	763	672	266	-	-	-	-	-	-	-	-	-	-	-	-	-	-	-	-	-	-	-	-	-	-	-
	4.12		39.58																							
			39.58																							
			34.86																							
Blue Earth County	645	883	303	-	-	-	-	-	-	-	-	-	-	-	-	-	-	-	-	-	-	-	-	-	-	-
	1.15		34.31																							
			34.31																							
			46.98																							

Notes: Please refer to the User's Guide for an explanation of data; data is arranged alphabetically by state, then county, then city within each county; table includes counties with populations greater than 49,999 unless noted and cities with populations greater than 9,999 whose Asian and/or NHPI population rates are greater than the national average; (1) Native Hawaiian and other Pacific Islander; (2) excludes Taiwanese; (3) includes Chamorro; (4) county does not meet population threshold but is shown in order to allow inclusion of city

Place	Total foreign-born naturalized citizens	Total Asian population	Asians who are foreign-born naturalized citizens	Total NHPI[1] population	NHPIs[1] who are foreign-born naturalized citizens	Asian Indian	Bangladeshi	Cambodian	Chinese[2]	Fijian	Filipino	Guamanian[3]	Hawaiian, Native	Hmong	Indonesian	Japanese	Korean	Laotian	Malaysian	Pakistani	Samoan	Sri Lankan	Taiwanese	Thai	Tongan	Vietnamese
Carver County	900	1,039	450	-	-	-	-	-	-	-	-	-	-	-	-	-	-	-	-	-	-	-	-	-	-	-
	1.28		43.31																							
			43.31																							
			50.00																							
Clay County	530	394	161	-	-	-	-	-	-	-	-	-	-	-	-	-	-	-	-	-	-	-	-	-	-	-
	1.03		40.86																							
			40.86																							
			30.38																							
Crow Wing County	400	218	111	-	-	-	-	-	-	-	-	-	-	-	-	-	-	-	-	-	-	-	-	-	-	-
	0.73		50.92																							
			50.92																							
			27.75																							
Dakota County	8,456	9,152	3,691	-	-	275	-	202	581	-	274	-	-	-	-	-	818	295	-	-	-	-	-	-	-	846
	2.38		40.33			16.22		44.79	42.07		33.54						73.50	40.47								48.21
						7.45		5.47	15.74		7.42						22.16	7.99								22.92
			40.33			3.00		2.21	6.35		2.99						8.94	3.22								9.24
			43.65			3.25		2.39	6.87		3.24						9.67	3.49								10.00
Eagan (city)	2,198	3,087	1,080	-	-	64	-	-	178	-	-	-	-	-	-	-	-	-	-	-	-	-	-	-	-	231
	3.45		34.99			9.58			35.60																	40.53
						5.93			16.48																	21.39
			34.99			2.07			5.77																	7.48
			49.14			2.91			8.10																	10.51
Hennepin County	36,519	53,136	15,909	583	94	1,860	-	541	1,790	-	757	-	-	2,052	-	154	3,192	1,445	-	86	-	-	-	-	-	3,346
	3.27		29.94		16.12	23.83		30.26	29.63		40.37			15.40		9.15	67.50	32.77		21.08						41.06
						11.69		3.40	11.25		4.76			12.90		0.97	20.06	9.08		0.54						21.03
			29.94		16.12	3.50		1.02	3.37		1.42			3.86		0.29	6.01	2.72		0.16						6.30
			43.56		0.26	5.09		1.48	4.90		2.07			5.62		0.42	8.74	3.96		0.24						9.16
Bloomington (city)	3,014	4,254	1,643	-	-	178	-	144	319	-	-	-	-	-	-	-	361	-	-	-	-	-	-	-	-	478
	3.54		38.62			32.90		29.45	40.08								71.63									40.82
						10.83		8.76	19.42								21.97									29.09
			38.62			4.18		3.39	7.50								8.49									11.24
			54.51			5.91		4.78	10.58								11.98									15.86
Brooklyn Center (city)	1,398	2,606	866	-	-	-	-	-	-	-	-	-	-	387	-	-	-	106	-	-	-	-	-	-	-	-
	4.81		33.23											26.65				33.13								
														44.69				12.24								
			33.23											14.85				4.07								
			61.95											27.68				7.58								
Brooklyn Park (city)	3,370	6,200	2,159	-	-	304	-	-	-	-	-	-	-	162	-	-	-	573	-	-	-	-	-	-	-	510
	5.00		34.82			33.26								14.73				39.65								34.32
						14.08								7.50				26.54								23.62
			34.82			4.90								2.61				9.24								8.23
			64.07			9.02								4.81				17.00								15.13
Eden Prairie (city)	1,779	2,793	890	-	-	92	-	-	216	-	-	-	-	-	-	-	-	-	-	-	-	-	-	-	-	175
	3.24		31.87			15.70			32.10																	33.02
						10.34			24.27																	19.66
			31.87			3.29			7.73																	6.27
			50.03			5.17			12.14																	9.84

Notes: Please refer to the User's Guide for an explanation of data; data is arranged alphabetically by state, then county, then city within each county; table includes counties with populations greater than 49,999 unless noted and cities with populations greater than 9,999 whose Asian and/or NHPI population rates are greater than the national average; (1) Native Hawaiian and other Pacific Islander; (2) excludes Taiwanese; (3) includes Chamorro; (4) county does not meet population threshold but is shown in order to allow inclusion of city

Place	Total foreign-born naturalized citizens	Total Asian population	Asians who are foreign-born naturalized citizens	Total NHPI[1] population	NHPIs[1] who are foreign-born naturalized citizens	Asian Indian	Bangladeshi	Cambodian	Chinese[2]	Fijian	Filipino	Guamanian[3]	Hawaiian, Native	Hmong	Indonesian	Japanese	Korean	Laotian	Malaysian	Pakistani	Samoan	Sri Lankan	Taiwanese	Thai	Tongan	Vietnamese
Hopkins (city)	499 2.92	964	136 14.11 14.11 27.25	-	-	8 1.74 5.88 0.83 1.60	-	-	-	-	-	-	-	-	-	-	-	-	-	-	-	-	-	-	-	-
Minneapolis (city)	13,508 3.53	23,912	5,384 22.52 22.52 39.86	-	-	465 22.21 8.64 1.94 3.44	-	83 16.67 1.54 0.35 0.61	477 23.11 8.86 1.99 3.53	-	246 33.84 4.57 1.03 1.82	-	-	1,326 12.92 24.63 5.55 9.82	-	70 9.19 1.30 0.29 0.52	924 56.93 17.16 3.86 6.84	369 22.68 6.85 1.54 2.73	-	-	-	-	-	-	-	1,096 39.09 20.36 4.58 8.11
Plymouth (city)	2,089 3.17	2,463	727 29.52 29.52 34.80	-	-	191 20.78 26.27 7.75 9.14	-	-	116 27.17 15.96 4.71 5.55	-	-	-	-	-	-	-	183 50.69 25.17 7.43 8.76	-	-	-	-	-	-	-	-	-
Richfield (city)	1,301 3.78	1,760	645 36.65 36.65 49.58	-	-	-	-	-	-	-	-	-	-	-	-	-	-	-	-	-	-	-	-	-	-	183 43.47 28.37 10.40 14.07
Nobles County[4]	379 1.82	774	110 14.21 14.21 29.02	-	-	-	-	-	-	-	-	-	-	-	-	-	-	33 8.17 30.00 4.26 8.71	-	-	-	-	-	-	-	-
Worthington (city)	324 2.87	706	93 13.17 13.17 28.70	-	-	-	-	-	-	-	-	-	-	-	-	-	-	31 8.36 33.33 4.39 9.57	-	-	-	-	-	-	-	-
Olmsted County	3,224 2.59	5,329	1,542 28.94 28.94 47.83	-	-	135 13.31 8.75 2.53 4.19	-	255 35.32 16.54 4.79 7.91	171 29.03 11.09 3.21 5.30	-	-	-	-	108 27.00 7.00 2.03 3.35	-	30 6.99 1.95 0.56 0.93	331 67.28 21.47 6.21 10.27	99 22.50 6.42 1.86 3.07	-	-	-	-	-	-	-	296 40.77 19.20 5.55 9.18
Rochester (city)	2,580 3.02	4,806	1,280 26.63 26.63 49.61	-	-	107 11.17 8.36 2.23 4.15	-	188 33.63 14.69 3.91 7.29	146 26.50 11.41 3.04 5.66	-	-	-	-	108 27.00 8.44 2.25 4.19	-	-	232 61.21 18.13 4.83 8.99	97 22.15 7.58 2.02 3.76	-	-	-	-	-	-	-	274 39.42 21.41 5.70 10.62
Otter Tail County	455 0.80	171	57 33.33 33.33 12.53	-	-	-	-	-	-	-	-	-	-	-	-	-	-	-	-	-	-	-	-	-	-	-
Ramsey County	18,812 3.68	44,030	10,641 24.17 24.17 56.56	-	-	736 31.74 6.92 1.67 3.91	-	395 35.59 3.71 0.90 2.10	905 26.16 8.50 2.06 4.81	-	352 39.29 3.31 0.80 1.87	-	-	4,626 17.38 43.47 10.51 24.59	-	51 9.41 0.48 0.12 0.27	1,303 65.51 12.25 2.96 6.93	149 15.97 1.40 0.34 0.79	-	-	-	-	-	-	-	1,452 40.32 13.65 3.30 7.72

Notes: Please refer to the User's Guide for an explanation of data; data is arranged alphabetically by state, then county, then city within each county; table includes counties with populations greater than 49,999 unless noted and cities with populations greater than 9,999 whose Asian and/or NHPI population rates are greater than the national average; (1) Native Hawaiian and other Pacific Islander; (2) excludes Taiwanese; (3) includes Chamorro; (4) county does not meet population threshold but is shown in order to allow inclusion of city

Place	Total foreign-born naturalized citizens	Total Asian population	Asians who are foreign-born naturalized citizens	Total NHPI[1] population	NHPIs[1] who are foreign-born naturalized citizens	Asian Indian	Bangladeshi	Cambodian	Chinese[2]	Fijian	Filipino	Guamanian[3]	Hawaiian, Native	Hmong	Indonesian	Japanese	Korean	Laotian	Malaysian	Pakistani	Samoan	Sri Lankan	Taiwanese	Thai	Tongan	Vietnamese
Maplewood (city)	966 2.76	1,358	551 40.57 40.57 57.04	-	-	-	-	-	67 21.82 12.16 4.93 6.94	-	-	-	-	139 35.10 25.23 10.24 14.39	-	-	-	-	-	-	-	-	-	-	-	-
New Brighton (city)	803 3.61	916	468 51.09 51.09 58.28	-	-	-	-	-	-	-	-	-	-	-	-	-	-	-	-	-	-	-	-	-	-	-
Roseville (city)	1,080 3.20	1,624	687 42.30 42.30 63.61	-	-	-	-	-	237 34.90 34.50 14.59 21.94	-	-	-	-	-	-	-	-	-	-	-	-	-	-	-	-	-
St. Paul (city)	12,402 4.32	35,316	7,282 20.62 20.62 58.72	-	-	202 23.79 2.77 0.57 1.63	-	285 30.71 3.91 0.81 2.30	228 23.17 3.13 0.65 1.84	-	193 35.87 2.65 0.55 1.56	-	-	4,319 16.95 59.31 12.23 34.83	-	-	588 64.40 8.07 1.66 4.74	111 12.89 1.52 0.31 0.90	-	-	-	-	-	-	-	887 34.74 12.18 2.51 7.15
Vadnais Heights (city)	422 3.23	567	236 41.62 41.62 55.92	-	-	-	-	-	-	-	-	-	-	-	-	-	-	-	-	-	-	-	-	-	-	-
Rice County	688 1.21	885	282 31.86 31.86 40.99	-	-	-	-	-	-	-	-	-	-	-	-	-	-	-	-	-	-	-	-	-	-	-
St. Louis County	2,624 1.31	1,504	785 52.19 52.19 29.92	-	-	-	-	-	-	-	-	-	-	-	-	-	273 75.62 34.78 18.15 10.40	-	-	-	-	-	-	-	-	-
Scott County	1,496 1.67	1,867	717 38.40 38.40 47.93	-	-	-	-	87 24.03 12.13 4.66 5.82	-	-	-	-	-	-	-	-	-	-	-	-	-	-	-	-	-	207 52.54 28.87 11.09 13.84
Savage (city)	679 3.21	1,101	410 37.24 37.24 60.38	-	-	-	-	-	-	-	-	-	-	-	-	-	-	-	-	-	-	-	-	-	-	-
Sherburne County	647 1.00	374	148 39.57 39.57 22.87	-	-	-	-	-	-	-	-	-	-	-	-	-	-	-	-	-	-	-	-	-	-	-

Notes: Please refer to the User's Guide for an explanation of data; data is arranged alphabetically by state, then county, then city within each county; table includes counties with populations greater than 49,999 unless noted and cities with populations greater than 9,999 whose Asian and/or NHPI population rates are greater than the national average; (1) Native Hawaiian and other Pacific Islander; (2) excludes Taiwanese; (3) includes Chamorro; (4) county does not meet population threshold but is shown in order to allow inclusion of city

Place	Total foreign-born naturalized citizens	Total Asian population	Asians who are foreign-born naturalized citizens	Total NHPI[1] population	NHPIs[1] who are foreign-born naturalized citizens	Asian Indian	Bangladeshi	Cambodian	Chinese[2]	Fijian	Filipino	Guamanian[3]	Hawaiian, Native	Hmong	Indonesian	Japanese	Korean	Laotian	Malaysian	Pakistani	Samoan	Sri Lankan	Taiwanese	Thai	Tongan	Vietnamese
Stearns County	1,147 0.86	1,796	547 30.46 30.46 47.69	-	-	-	-	-	-	-	-	-	-	-	-	-	-	-	-	-	-	-	-	-	-	273 44.75 49.91 15.20 23.80
Washington County	3,709 1.84	4,362	1,758 40.30 40.30 47.40	-	-	175 30.76 9.95 4.01 4.72	-	-	300 42.49 17.06 6.88 8.09	-	-	-	-	219 28.40 12.46 5.02 5.90	-	-	405 59.56 23.04 9.28 10.92	-	-	-	-	-	-	-	-	247 46.69 14.05 5.66 6.66
Woodbury (city)	1,545 3.33	2,382	872 36.61 36.61 56.44	-	-	100 23.42 11.47 4.20 6.47	-	-	145 38.46 16.63 6.09 9.39	-	-	-	-	83 23.51 9.52 3.48 5.37	-	-	-	-	-	-	-	-	-	-	-	-
Wright County	470 0.52	196	115 58.67 58.67 24.47	-	-	-	-	-	-	-	-	-	-	-	-	-	-	-	-	-	-	-	-	-	-	-
MISSISSIPPI	16,098 0.57	17,709	6,151 34.73 34.73 38.21	677	7 1.03 1.03 0.04	1,099 33.05 17.87 6.21 6.83	-	-	940 35.26 15.28 5.31 5.84	-	982 37.50 15.96 5.55 6.10	-	-	-	-	171 31.78 2.78 0.97 1.06	715 51.89 11.62 4.04 4.44	-	-	-	-	-	-	-	-	1,666 31.22 27.09 9.41 10.35
DeSoto County	703 0.66	676	276 40.83 40.83 39.26	-	-	-	-	-	-	-	-	-	-	-	-	-	-	-	-	-	-	-	-	-	-	-
Forrest County	353 0.49	626	100 15.97 15.97 28.33	-	-	-	-	-	-	-	-	-	-	-	-	-	-	-	-	-	-	-	-	-	-	-
Harrison County	3,501 1.85	4,976	1,739 34.95 34.95 49.67	-	-	-	-	-	-	-	266 32.68 15.30 5.35 7.60	-	-	-	-	-	-	-	-	-	-	-	-	-	-	834 29.82 47.96 16.76 23.82
Biloxi (city)	1,276 2.52	2,451	719 29.33 29.33 56.35	-	-	-	-	-	-	-	131 30.47 18.22 5.34 10.27	-	-	-	-	-	-	-	-	-	-	-	-	-	-	394 26.57 54.80 16.08 30.88
Hinds County	1,189 0.47	1,315	398 30.27 30.27 33.47	-	-	183 31.55 45.98 13.92 15.39	-	-	-	-	-	-	-	-	-	-	-	-	-	-	-	-	-	-	-	-

Notes: Please refer to the User's Guide for an explanation of data; data is arranged alphabetically by state, then county, then city within each county; table includes counties with populations greater than 49,999 unless noted and cities with populations greater than 9,999 whose Asian and/or NHPI population rates are greater than the national average; (1) Native Hawaiian and other Pacific Islander; (2) excludes Taiwanese; (3) includes Chamorro; (4) county does not meet population threshold but is shown in order to allow inclusion of city

Place	Total foreign-born naturalized citizens	Total Asian population	Asians who are foreign-born naturalized citizens	Total NHPI[1] population	NHPIs[1] who are foreign-born naturalized citizens	Asian Indian	Bangladeshi	Cambodian	Chinese[2]	Fijian	Filipino	Guamanian[3]	Hawaiian, Native	Hmong	Indonesian	Japanese	Korean	Laotian	Malaysian	Pakistani	Samoan	Sri Lankan	Taiwanese	Thai	Tongan	Vietnamese
Jackson County	1,749 1.33	1,945	749 38.51 38.51 42.82	-	-	-	-	-	-	-	-	-	-	-	-	-	-	-	-	-	-	-	-	-	-	316 29.81 42.19 16.25 18.07
Madison County	743 0.99	585	367 62.74 62.74 49.39	-	-	-	-	-	-	-	-	-	-	-	-	-	-	-	-	-	-	-	-	-	-	-
Oktibbeha County[4]	232 0.54	1,077	130 12.07 12.07 56.03	-	-	-	-	-	-	-	-	-	-	-	-	-	-	-	-	-	-	-	-	-	-	-
Starkville (city)	151 0.69	798	103 12.91 12.91 68.21	-	-	-	-	-	-	-	-	-	-	-	-	-	-	-	-	-	-	-	-	-	-	-
Rankin County	706 0.61	554	280 50.54 50.54 39.66	-	-	-	-	-	-	-	-	-	-	-	-	-	-	-	-	-	-	-	-	-	-	-
MISSOURI	61,786 1.10	60,429	20,840 34.49 34.49 33.73	3,071	314 10.22 10.22 0.51	3,399 28.70 16.31 5.62 5.50	-	189 21.50 0.91 0.31 0.31	3,996 31.30 19.17 6.61 6.47	-	3,346 46.13 16.06 5.54 5.42	13 2.12 4.14 0.42 0.02	0 0.00 0.00 0.00 0.00	-	-	744 21.72 3.57 1.23 1.20	3,160 48.56 15.16 5.23 5.11	298 41.62 1.43 0.49 0.48	-	456 43.30 2.19 0.75 0.74	132 13.15 42.04 4.30 0.21	-	394 40.53 1.89 0.65 0.64	448 32.65 2.15 0.74 0.73	-	3,759 35.78 18.04 6.22 6.08
Boone County	1,829 1.35	3,865	905 23.42 23.42 49.48	-	-	256 31.68 28.29 6.62 14.00	-	-	264 21.96 29.17 6.83 14.43	-	-	-	-	-	-	-	116 22.61 12.82 3.00 6.34	-	-	-	-	-	-	-	-	-
Columbia (city)	1,503 1.77	3,574	820 22.94 22.94 54.56	-	-	249 31.88 30.37 6.97 16.57	-	-	258 22.40 31.46 7.22 17.17	-	-	-	-	-	-	-	83 19.53 10.12 2.32 5.52	-	-	-	-	-	-	-	-	-
Cape Girardeau County	363 0.53	446	123 27.58 27.58 33.88	-	-	-	-	-	-	-	-	-	-	-	-	-	-	-	-	-	-	-	-	-	-	-
Cass County	620 0.76	346	128 36.99 36.99 20.65	-	-	-	-	-	-	-	-	-	-	-	-	-	-	-	-	-	-	-	-	-	-	-

Notes: Please refer to the User's Guide for an explanation of data; data is arranged alphabetically by state, then county, then city within each county; table includes counties with populations greater than 49,999 unless noted and cities with populations greater than 9,999 whose Asian and/or NHPI population rates are greater than the national average; (1) Native Hawaiian and other Pacific Islander; (2) excludes Taiwanese; (3) includes Chamorro; (4) county does not meet population threshold but is shown in order to allow inclusion of city

Place	Total foreign-born naturalized citizens	Total Asian population	Asians who are foreign-born naturalized citizens	Total NHPI[1] population	NHPIs[1] who are foreign-born naturalized citizens	Asian Indian	Bangladeshi	Cambodian	Chinese[2]	Fijian	Filipino	Guamanian[3]	Hawaiian, Native	Hmong	Indonesian	Japanese	Korean	Laotian	Malaysian	Pakistani	Samoan	Sri Lankan	Taiwanese	Thai	Tongan	Vietnamese
Clay County	2,163 1.18	2,165	694 32.06 32.06 32.09	-	-	99 24.44 14.27 4.57 4.58	-	-	-	-	-	-	-	-	-	-	-	-	-	-	-	-	-	-	-	228 36.95 32.85 10.53 10.54
Cole County	550 0.77	661	171 25.87 25.87 31.09	-	-	-	-	-	-	-	-	-	-	-	-	-	-	-	-	-	-	-	-	-	-	-
Franklin County	511 0.54	326	165 50.61 50.61 32.29	-	-	-	-	-	-	-	-	-	-	-	-	-	-	-	-	-	-	-	-	-	-	-
Greene County	2,118 0.88	2,207	819 37.11 37.11 38.67	-	-	-	-	-	67 18.41 8.18 3.04 3.16	-	-	-	-	-	-	-	134 37.33 16.36 6.07 6.33	-	-	-	-	-	-	-	-	244 58.51 29.79 11.06 11.52
Jackson County	10,043 1.53	8,646	2,809 32.49 32.49 27.97	926	138 14.90 14.90 1.37	238 22.24 8.47 2.75 2.37	-	-	414 32.42 14.74 4.79 4.12	-	689 53.95 24.53 7.97 6.86	-	-	-	-	101 24.75 3.60 1.17 1.01	253 44.54 9.01 2.93 2.52	-	-	-	97 20.64 70.29 10.48 0.97	-	-	-	-	815 28.30 29.01 9.43 8.12
Independence (city)	1,509 1.33	1,022	373 36.50 36.50 24.72	405	39 9.63 9.63 2.58	-	-	-	-	-	-	-	-	-	-	-	-	-	-	-	-	-	-	-	-	-
Jasper County	843 0.81	598	266 44.48 44.48 31.55	-	-	-	-	-	-	-	-	-	-	-	-	-	-	-	-	-	-	-	-	-	-	-
Jefferson County	1,107 0.56	745	296 39.73 39.73 26.74	-	-	-	-	-	-	-	-	-	-	-	-	-	-	-	-	-	-	-	-	-	-	-
Newton County	275 0.52	177	61 34.46 34.46 22.18	-	-	-	-	-	-	-	-	-	-	-	-	-	-	-	-	-	-	-	-	-	-	-
Phelps County[4]	486 1.22	836	223 26.67 26.67 45.88	-	-	119 36.62 53.36 14.23 24.49	-	-	-	-	-	-	-	-	-	-	-	-	-	-	-	-	-	-	-	-

Notes: Please refer to the User's Guide for an explanation of data; data is arranged alphabetically by state, then county, then city within each county; table includes counties with populations greater than 49,999 unless noted and cities with populations greater than 9,999 whose Asian and/or NHPI population rates are greater than the national average; (1) Native Hawaiian and other Pacific Islander; (2) excludes Taiwanese; (3) includes Chamorro; (4) county does not meet population threshold but is shown in order to allow inclusion of city

Place	Total foreign-born naturalized citizens	Total Asian population	Asians who are foreign-born naturalized citizens	Total NHPI[1] population	NHPIs[1] who are foreign-born naturalized citizens	Asian Indian	Bangladeshi	Cambodian	Chinese[2]	Fijian	Filipino	Guamanian[3]	Hawaiian, Native	Hmong	Indonesian	Japanese	Korean	Laotian	Malaysian	Pakistani	Samoan	Sri Lankan	Taiwanese	Thai	Tongan	Vietnamese
Rolla (city)	321 1.94	684	174 25.44 25.44 54.21	-	-	-	-	-	-	-	-	-	-	-	-	-	-	-	-	-	-	-	-	-	-	-
Platte County	1,175 1.59	1,115	435 39.01 39.01 37.02	-	-	-	-	-	-	-	-	-	-	-	-	-	-	-	-	-	-	-	-	-	-	-
St. Charles County	2,921 1.03	2,392	944 39.46 39.46 32.32	-	-	231 40.03 24.47 9.66 7.91	-	-	129 31.08 13.67 5.39 4.42	-	190 47.15 20.13 7.94 6.50	-	-	-	-	-	-	-	-	-	-	-	-	-	-	-
Saint Louis Independent City	5,348 1.54	7,075	1,996 28.21 28.21 37.32	-	-	133 18.05 6.66 1.88 2.49	-	-	242 21.45 12.12 3.42 4.53	-	199 36.31 9.97 2.81 3.72	-	-	-	-	-	-	-	-	-	-	-	-	-	-	1,043 32.40 52.25 14.74 19.50
St. Louis County	20,781 2.04	21,534	7,786 36.16 36.16 37.47	437	29 6.64 6.64 0.14	1,659 29.11 21.31 7.70 7.98	-	-	1,987 33.10 25.52 9.23 9.56	-	944 46.92 12.12 4.38 4.54	-	-	-	-	199 16.43 2.56 0.92 0.96	1,351 53.06 17.35 6.27 6.50	-	-	258 45.34 3.31 1.20 1.24	-	-	279 43.06 3.58 1.30 1.34	154 40.74 1.98 0.72 0.74	-	635 43.26 8.16 2.95 3.06
Chesterfield (city)	2,065 4.40	2,442	1,064 43.57 43.57 51.53	-	-	210 31.67 19.74 8.60 10.17	-	-	362 45.65 34.02 14.82 17.53	-	-	-	-	-	-	-	-	-	-	-	-	-	-	-	-	-
Clayton (city)	360 2.81	788	162 20.56 20.56 45.00	-	-	-	-	-	-	-	-	-	-	-	-	-	-	-	-	-	-	-	-	-	-	-
Creve Coeur (city)	792 4.86	872	352 40.37 40.37 44.44	-	-	-	-	-	-	-	-	-	-	-	-	-	-	-	-	-	-	-	-	-	-	-
Manchester (city)	625 3.28	935	266 28.45 28.45 42.56	-	-	-	-	-	-	-	-	-	-	-	-	-	-	-	-	-	-	-	-	-	-	-
Maryland Heights (city)	777 3.00	1,788	450 25.17 25.17 57.92	-	-	60 8.62 13.33 3.36 7.72	-	-	119 23.24 26.44 6.66 15.32	-	-	-	-	-	-	-	-	-	-	-	-	-	-	-	-	-

Notes: Please refer to the User's Guide for an explanation of data; data is arranged alphabetically by state, then county, then city within each county; table includes counties with populations greater than 49,999 unless noted and cities with populations greater than 9,999 whose Asian and/or NHPI population rates are greater than the national average; (1) Native Hawaiian and other Pacific Islander; (2) excludes Taiwanese; (3) includes Chamorro; (4) county does not meet population threshold but is shown in order to allow inclusion of city

Place	Total foreign-born naturalized citizens	Total Asian population	Asians who are foreign-born naturalized citizens	Total NHPI[1] population	NHPIs[1] who are foreign-born naturalized citizens	Asian Indian	Bangladeshi	Cambodian	Chinese[2]	Fijian	Filipino	Guamanian[3]	Hawaiian, Native	Hmong	Indonesian	Japanese	Korean	Laotian	Malaysian	Pakistani	Samoan	Sri Lankan	Taiwanese	Thai	Tongan	Vietnamese
Town and Country (city)	850	829	540	-	-	241	-	-	-	-	-	-	-	-	-	-	-	-	-	-	-	-	-	-	-	-
	7.81		65.14			63.25																				
						44.63																				
			65.14			29.07																				
			63.53			28.35																				
MONTANA	9,482	4,363	1,545	447	28	108	-	-	212	-	317	-	0	-	-	136	548	-	-	-	-	-	-	-	-	-
	1.05		35.41		6.26	24.00			32.62		40.38		0.00			16.00	65.32									
						6.99			13.72		20.52		0.00			8.80	35.47									
			35.41		6.26	2.48			4.86		7.27		0.00			3.12	12.56									
			16.29		0.30	1.14			2.24		3.34		0.00			1.43	5.78									
Cascade County	1,208	498	223	-	-	-	-	-	-	-	-	-	-	-	-	-	-	-	-	-	-	-	-	-	-	-
	1.50		44.78																							
			44.78																							
			18.46																							
Flathead County	875	251	151	-	-	-	-	-	-	-	-	-	-	-	-	-	-	-	-	-	-	-	-	-	-	-
	1.17		60.16																							
			60.16																							
			17.26																							
Gallatin County	815	693	151	-	-	-	-	-	-	-	-	-	-	-	-	-	-	-	-	-	-	-	-	-	-	-
	1.20		21.79																							
			21.79																							
			18.53																							
Missoula County	1,207	919	227	-	-	-	-	-	-	-	-	-	-	-	-	-	-	-	-	-	-	-	-	-	-	-
	1.26		24.70																							
			24.70																							
			18.81																							
Yellowstone County	1,134	666	307	-	-	-	-	-	-	-	-	-	-	-	-	-	-	-	-	-	-	-	-	-	-	-
	0.88		46.10																							
			46.10																							
			27.07																							
NEBRASKA	23,918	21,126	6,801	673	19	747	-	-	635	-	970	-	-	-	-	198	1,296	271	-	-	-	-	-	139	-	2,289
	1.40		32.19		2.82	23.35			22.30		46.97					14.32	58.14	33.21						30.15		34.27
						10.98			9.34		14.26					2.91	19.06	3.98						2.04		33.66
			32.19		2.82	3.54			3.01		4.59					0.94	6.13	1.28						0.66		10.83
			28.43		0.08	3.12			2.65		4.06					0.83	5.42	1.13						0.58		9.57
Douglas County	8,445	7,912	2,338	-	-	409	-	-	356	-	438	-	-	-	-	44	452	-	-	-	-	-	-	-	-	499
	1.82		29.55			20.06			25.63		49.49					6.33	55.26									38.92
						17.49			15.23		18.73					1.88	19.33									21.34
			29.55			5.17			4.50		5.54					0.56	5.71									6.31
			27.69			4.84			4.22		5.19					0.52	5.35									5.91
Hall County	927	544	178	-	-	-	-	-	-	-	-	-	-	-	-	-	-	-	-	-	-	-	-	-	-	-
	1.73		32.72																							
			32.72																							
			19.20																							

Notes: Please refer to the User's Guide for an explanation of data; data is arranged alphabetically by state, then county, then city within each county; table includes counties with populations greater than 49,999 unless noted and cities with populations greater than 9,999 whose Asian and/or NHPI population rates are greater than the national average; (1) Native Hawaiian and other Pacific Islander; (2) excludes Taiwanese; (3) includes Chamorro; (4) county does not meet population threshold but is shown in order to allow inclusion of city

Place	Total foreign-born naturalized citizens	Total Asian population	Asians who are foreign-born naturalized citizens	Total NHPI[1] population	NHPIs[1] who are foreign-born naturalized citizens	Asian Indian	Bangladeshi	Cambodian	Chinese[2]	Fijian	Filipino	Guamanian[3]	Hawaiian, Native	Hmong	Indonesian	Japanese	Korean	Laotian	Malaysian	Pakistani	Samoan	Sri Lankan	Taiwanese	Thai	Tongan	Vietnamese
Lancaster County	4,363	6,700	2,038	-	-	199	-	-	112	-	-	-	-	-	-	-	200	-	-	-	-	-	-	-	-	1,333
	1.74		30.42			30.62			11.58								55.10									35.30
						9.76			5.50								9.81									65.41
			30.42			2.97			1.67								2.99									19.90
			46.71			4.56			2.57								4.58									30.55
Sarpy County	2,434	2,230	945	-	-	-	-	-	-	-	285	-	-	-	-	-	231	-	-	-	-	-	-	-	-	147
	1.99		42.38								57.81						50.44									34.83
											30.16						24.44									15.56
			42.38								12.78						10.36									6.59
			38.82								11.71						9.49									6.04
NEVADA	116,786	89,121	34,206	7,806	512	1,852	-	317	5,275	-	16,410	96	56	-	-	1,424	3,422	479	-	260	139	-	262	1,097	115	2,128
	5.84		38.38		6.56	38.11		42.95	38.96		40.49	8.43	1.64			16.96	45.13	40.29		48.87	8.87		43.89	36.85	14.56	51.97
						5.41		0.93	15.42		47.97	18.75	10.94			4.16	10.00	1.40		0.76	27.15		0.77	3.21	22.46	6.22
			38.38		6.56	2.08		0.36	5.92		18.41	1.23	0.72			1.60	3.84	0.54		0.29	1.78		0.29	1.23	1.47	2.39
			29.29		0.44	1.59		0.27	4.52		14.05	0.08	0.05			1.22	2.93	0.41		0.22	0.12		0.22	0.94	0.10	1.82
Carson City Independent City	1,655	1,070	338	-	-	-	-	-	-	-	95	-	-	-	-	-	-	-	-	-	-	-	-	-	-	-
	3.15		31.59								34.42															
											28.11															
			31.59								8.88															
			20.42								5.74															
Clark County	90,437	71,495	27,736	5,918	327	1,137	-	303	4,197	-	13,283	96	48	-	-	1,192	2,889	479	-	-	93	-	186	1,006	-	1,783
	6.57		38.79		5.53	38.94		42.20	39.11		40.71	10.02	1.56			17.81	44.26	40.70			8.33		43.36	38.40		54.16
						4.10		1.09	15.13		47.89	29.36	14.68			4.30	10.42	1.73			28.44		0.67	3.63		6.43
			38.79		5.53	1.59		0.42	5.87		18.58	1.62	0.81			1.67	4.04	0.67			1.57		0.26	1.41		2.49
			30.67		0.36	1.26		0.34	4.64		14.69	0.11	0.05			1.32	3.19	0.53			0.10		0.21	1.11		1.97
Enterprise (cdp)	755	701	240	-	-	-	-	-	-	-	-	-	-	-	-	-	-	-	-	-	-	-	-	-	-	-
	5.23		34.24																							
			34.24																							
			31.79																							
Henderson (city)	8,171	6,683	2,706	758	23	215	-	-	269	-	1,272	-	0	-	-	109	310	-	-	-	-	-	-	-	-	-
	4.64		40.49		3.03	46.14			33.50		46.54		0.00			14.03	37.76									
						7.95			9.94		47.01		0.00			4.03	11.46									
			40.49		3.03	3.22			4.03		19.03		0.00			1.63	4.64									
			33.12		0.28	2.63			3.29		15.57		0.00			1.33	3.79									
Las Vegas (city)	30,945	21,634	8,304	1,673	98	435	-	-	1,042	-	4,392	-	29	-	-	457	675	-	-	-	-	-	-	197	-	418
	6.46		38.38		5.86	43.20			38.31		40.70		3.71			18.63	47.04							28.14		68.52
						5.24			12.55		52.89		29.59			5.50	8.13							2.37		5.03
			38.38		5.86	2.01			4.82		20.30		1.73			2.11	3.12							0.91		1.93
			26.83		0.32	1.41			3.37		14.19		0.09			1.48	2.18							0.64		1.35
North Las Vegas (city)	7,034	3,845	1,435	747	68	-	-	-	-	-	784	-	-	-	-	-	-	-	-	-	-	-	-	-	-	-
	6.09		37.32		9.10						35.72															
											54.63															
			37.32		9.10						20.39															
			20.40		0.97						11.15															
Paradise (cdp)	14,647	12,628	4,404	841	64	191	-	-	648	-	1,970	-	19	-	-	150	601	-	-	-	-	-	-	-	-	332
	7.88		34.87		7.61	29.75			35.31		34.61		3.17			10.65	44.13									56.85
						4.34			14.71		44.73		29.69			3.41	13.65									7.54
			34.87		7.61	1.51			5.13		15.60		2.26			1.19	4.76									2.63
			30.07		0.44	1.30			4.42		13.45		0.13			1.02	4.10									2.27

Notes: Please refer to the User's Guide for an explanation of data; data is arranged alphabetically by state, then county, then city within each county; table includes counties with populations greater than 49,999 unless noted and cities with populations greater than 9,999 whose Asian and/or NHPI population rates are greater than the national average; (1) Native Hawaiian and other Pacific Islander; (2) excludes Taiwanese; (3) includes Chamorro; (4) county does not meet population threshold but is shown in order to allow inclusion of city

Place	Total foreign-born naturalized citizens	Total Asian population	Asians who are foreign-born naturalized citizens	Total NHPI[1] population	NHPIs[1] who are foreign-born naturalized citizens	Asian Indian	Bangladeshi	Cambodian	Chinese[2]	Fijian	Filipino	Guamanian[3]	Hawaiian, Native	Hmong	Indonesian	Japanese	Korean	Laotian	Malaysian	Pakistani	Samoan	Sri Lankan	Taiwanese	Thai	Tongan	Vietnamese
Spring Valley (cdp)	11,002 9.35	12,944	5,208 40.23 40.23 47.34	657	19 2.89 2.89 0.17	-	-	-	1,673 39.63 32.12 12.92 15.21	-	1,678 42.92 32.22 12.96 15.25	-	-	-	-	144 20.00 2.76 1.11 1.31	509 37.62 9.77 3.93 4.63	-	-	-	-	-	-	165 33.20 3.17 1.27 1.50	-	491 50.36 9.43 3.79 4.46
Sunrise Manor (cdp)	10,423 6.70	8,644	3,661 42.35 42.35 35.12	429	15 3.50 3.50 0.14	-	-	-	223 46.27 6.09 2.58 2.14	-	2,133 44.16 58.26 24.68 20.46	-	-	-	-	185 30.78 5.05 2.14 1.77	428 58.55 11.69 4.95 4.11	-	-	-	-	-	-	-	-	-
Winchester (cdp)	2,703 10.09	1,480	637 43.04 43.04 23.57	-	-	-	-	-	-	-	227 50.56 35.64 15.34 8.40	-	-	-	-	-	-	-	-	-	-	-	-	-	-	-
Washoe County	18,007 5.30	14,327	5,279 36.85 36.85 29.32	1,502	167 11.12 11.12 0.93	584 36.43 11.06 4.08 3.24	-	-	918 38.69 17.39 6.41 5.10	-	2,540 39.55 48.12 17.73 14.11	-	-	-	-	162 12.62 3.07 1.13 0.90	377 50.07 7.14 2.63 2.09	-	-	-	-	-	-	-	89 15.42 53.29 5.93 0.49	299 41.99 5.66 2.09 1.66
Reno (city)	10,830 5.99	9,438	3,265 34.59 34.59 30.15	952	86 9.03 9.03 0.79	363 38.21 11.12 3.85 3.35	-	-	522 35.10 15.99 5.53 4.82	-	1,587 37.15 48.61 16.82 14.65	-	-	-	-	87 9.31 2.66 0.92 0.80	212 47.01 6.49 2.25 1.96	-	-	-	-	-	-	-	-	184 40.09 5.64 1.95 1.70
Sparks (city)	4,080 6.13	3,133	1,233 39.36 39.36 30.22	-	-	-	-	-	265 40.46 21.49 8.46 6.50	-	645 44.36 52.31 20.59 15.81	-	-	-	-	-	-	-	-	-	-	-	-	-	-	-
NEW HAMPSHIRE	25,761 2.08	15,422	4,642 30.10 30.10 18.02	-	-	776 21.68 16.72 5.03 3.01	-	-	1,311 33.85 28.24 8.50 5.09	-	504 39.62 10.86 3.27 1.96	-	-	-	-	164 17.52 3.53 1.06 0.64	942 48.31 20.29 6.11 3.66	112 30.19 2.41 0.73 0.43	-	-	-	-	-	-	-	447 26.58 9.63 2.90 1.74
Belknap County	778 1.38	347	120 34.58 34.58 15.42	-	-	-	-	-	-	-	-	-	-	-	-	-	-	-	-	-	-	-	-	-	-	-
Cheshire County	949 1.29	486	144 29.63 29.63 15.17	-	-	-	-	-	-	-	-	-	-	-	-	-	-	-	-	-	-	-	-	-	-	-
Grafton County	1,527 1.87	1,251	373 29.82 29.82 24.43	-	-	-	-	-	118 27.96 31.64 9.43 7.73	-	-	-	-	-	-	-	-	-	-	-	-	-	-	-	-	-

Notes: Please refer to the User's Guide for an explanation of data; data is arranged alphabetically by state, then county, then city within each county; table includes counties with populations greater than 49,999 unless noted and cities with populations greater than 9,999 whose Asian and/or NHPI population rates are greater than the national average; (1) Native Hawaiian and other Pacific Islander; (2) excludes Taiwanese; (3) includes Chamorro; (4) county does not meet population threshold but is shown in order to allow inclusion of city

Place	Total foreign-born naturalized citizens	Total Asian population	Asians who are foreign-born naturalized citizens	Total NHPI[1] population	NHPIs[1] who are foreign-born naturalized citizens	Asian Indian	Bangladeshi	Cambodian	Chinese[2]	Fijian	Filipino	Guamanian[3]	Hawaiian, Native	Hmong	Indonesian	Japanese	Korean	Laotian	Malaysian	Pakistani	Samoan	Sri Lankan	Taiwanese	Thai	Tongan	Vietnamese
Hanover (town)	447 4.12	653	161 24.66 24.66 36.02	-	-	-	-	-	-	-	-	-	-	-	-	-	-	-	-	-	-	-	-	-	-	-
Hillsborough County	10,465 2.75	7,366	1,946 26.42 26.42 18.60	-	-	371 17.10 19.06 5.04 3.55	-	-	594 31.56 30.52 8.06 5.68	-	189 47.61 9.71 2.57 1.81	-	-	-	-	-	283 46.62 14.54 3.84 2.70	-	-	-	-	-	-	-	-	219 20.11 11.25 2.97 2.09
Nashua (city)	3,013 3.48	3,387	789 23.29 23.29 26.19	-	-	187 12.91 23.70 5.52 6.21	-	-	233 29.42 29.53 6.88 7.73	-	-	-	-	-	-	-	-	-	-	-	-	-	-	-	-	-
Merrimack County	2,258 1.66	1,134	413 36.42 36.42 18.29	-	-	-	-	-	-	-	-	-	-	-	-	-	-	-	-	-	-	-	-	-	-	-
Rockingham County	5,849 2.11	2,946	1,051 35.68 35.68 17.97	-	-	124 25.94 11.80 4.21 2.12	-	-	347 41.26 33.02 11.78 5.93	-	116 28.02 11.04 3.94 1.98	-	-	-	-	-	225 53.19 21.41 7.64 3.85	-	-	-	-	-	-	-	-	-
Strafford County	1,831 1.63	1,477	467 31.62 31.62 25.51	-	-	-	-	-	142 41.16 30.41 9.61 7.76	-	-	-	-	-	-	-	-	-	-	-	-	-	-	-	-	-
NEW JERSEY	682,304 8.11	481,794	167,391 34.74 34.74 24.53	2,709	373 13.77 13.77 0.05	52,534 31.05 31.38 10.90 7.70	771 34.18 0.46 0.16 0.11	304 46.20 0.18 0.06 0.04	35,954 38.07 21.48 7.46 5.27	-	37,071 41.93 22.15 7.69 5.43	95 15.78 25.47 3.51 0.01	20 3.07 5.36 0.74 <0.01	-	176 17.25 0.11 0.04 0.03	1,576 11.44 0.94 0.33 0.23	21,611 33.60 12.91 4.49 3.17	154 32.08 0.09 0.03 0.02	-	4,313 34.64 2.58 0.90 0.63	65 10.17 17.43 2.40 0.01	417 31.24 0.25 0.09 0.06	2,599 44.42 1.55 0.54 0.38	542 29.38 0.32 0.11 0.08	-	6,281 41.93 3.75 1.30 0.92
Atlantic County	12,826 5.08	12,952	5,181 40.00 40.00 40.39	-	-	1,556 38.58 30.03 12.01 12.13	157 38.57 3.03 1.21 1.22	-	913 44.30 17.62 7.05 7.12	-	883 40.65 17.04 6.82 6.88	-	-	-	-	-	245 39.07 4.73 1.89 1.91	-	-	201 39.96 3.88 1.55 1.57	-	-	-	-	-	814 39.51 15.71 6.28 6.35
Atlantic City (city)	3,462 8.54	4,131	1,554 37.62 37.62 44.89	-	-	269 29.72 17.31 6.51 7.77	-	-	284 39.44 18.28 6.87 8.20	-	242 47.36 15.57 5.86 6.99	-	-	-	-	-	-	-	-	-	-	-	-	-	-	486 40.94 31.27 11.76 14.04
Brigantine (city)	813 6.46	780	350 44.87 44.87 43.05	-	-	-	-	-	-	-	-	-	-	-	-	-	-	-	-	-	-	-	-	-	-	-

Notes: Please refer to the User's Guide for an explanation of data; data is arranged alphabetically by state, then county, then city within each county; table includes counties with populations greater than 49,999 unless noted and cities with populations greater than 9,999 whose Asian and/or NHPI population rates are greater than the national average; (1) Native Hawaiian and other Pacific Islander; (2) excludes Taiwanese; (3) includes Chamorro; (4) county does not meet population threshold but is shown in order to allow inclusion of city

Place	Total foreign-born naturalized citizens	Total Asian population	Asians who are foreign-born naturalized citizens	Total NHPI[1] population	NHPIs[1] who are foreign-born naturalized citizens	Asian Indian	Bangladeshi	Cambodian	Chinese[2]	Fijian	Filipino	Guamanian[3]	Hawaiian, Native	Hmong	Indonesian	Japanese	Korean	Laotian	Malaysian	Pakistani	Samoan	Sri Lankan	Taiwanese	Thai	Tongan	Vietnamese
Egg Harbor (township)	1,365 4.46	1,704	653 38.32 38.32 47.84	-	-	-	-	-	-	-	-	-	-	-	-	-	-	-	-	-	-	-	-	-	-	-
Galloway (township)	1,827 5.86	2,657	1,053 39.63 39.63 57.64	-	-	495 38.31 47.01 18.63 27.09	-	-	-	-	-	-	-	-	-	-	-	-	-	-	-	-	-	-	-	-
Ventnor City (city)	1,302 10.09	1,048	478 45.61 45.61 36.71	-	-	-	-	-	-	-	-	-	-	-	-	-	-	-	-	-	-	-	-	-	-	-
Bergen County	112,882 12.77	94,124	29,180 31.00 31.00 25.85	-	-	5,607 32.23 19.22 5.96 4.97	-	-	5,038 38.58 17.27 5.35 4.46	-	6,196 41.59 21.23 6.58 5.49	-	-	-	-	480 6.86 1.64 0.51 0.43	9,992 27.68 34.24 10.62 8.85	-	-	546 36.38 1.87 0.58 0.48	-	-	403 48.61 1.38 0.43 0.36	109 21.67 0.37 0.12 0.10	-	223 42.40 0.76 0.24 0.20
Bergenfield (borough)	4,657 17.74	5,347	1,888 35.31 35.31 40.54	-	-	489 32.38 25.90 9.15 10.50	-	-	-	-	1,212 37.55 64.19 22.67 26.03	-	-	-	-	-	-	-	-	-	-	-	-	-	-	-
Cliffside Park (borough)	4,783 20.79	2,650	805 30.38 30.38 16.83	-	-	-	-	-	-	-	-	-	-	-	-	68 15.25 8.45 2.57 1.42	452 30.50 56.15 17.06 9.45	-	-	-	-	-	-	-	-	-
Dumont (borough)	1,937 11.07	1,927	821 42.61 42.61 42.39	-	-	195 36.04 23.75 10.12 10.07	-	-	-	-	300 49.59 36.54 15.57 15.49	-	-	-	-	-	-	-	-	-	-	-	-	-	-	-
Elmwood Park (borough)	2,919 15.42	1,638	462 28.21 28.21 15.83	-	-	259 25.49 56.06 15.81 8.87	-	-	-	-	-	-	-	-	-	-	-	-	-	-	-	-	-	-	-	-
Englewood (city)	3,585 13.68	1,388	379 27.31 27.31 10.57	-	-	-	-	-	-	-	182 43.44 48.02 13.11 5.08	-	-	-	-	-	-	-	-	-	-	-	-	-	-	-
Fair Lawn (borough)	5,440 17.20	1,829	729 39.86 39.86 13.40	-	-	223 34.15 30.59 12.19 4.10	-	-	-	-	241 44.96 33.06 13.18 4.43	-	-	-	-	-	-	-	-	-	-	-	-	-	-	-

Notes: Please refer to the User's Guide for an explanation of data; data is arranged alphabetically by state, then county, then city within each county; table includes counties with populations greater than 49,999 unless noted and cities with populations greater than 9,999 whose Asian and/or NHPI population rates are greater than the national average; (1) Native Hawaiian and other Pacific Islander; (2) excludes Taiwanese; (3) includes Chamorro; (4) county does not meet population threshold but is shown in order to allow inclusion of city

Place	Total foreign-born naturalized citizens	Total Asian population	Asians who are foreign-born naturalized citizens	Total NHPI[1] population	NHPIs[1] who are foreign-born naturalized citizens	Asian Indian	Bangladeshi	Cambodian	Chinese[2]	Fijian	Filipino	Guamanian[3]	Hawaiian, Native	Hmong	Indonesian	Japanese	Korean	Laotian	Malaysian	Pakistani	Samoan	Sri Lankan	Taiwanese	Thai	Tongan	Vietnamese
Fairview (borough)	2,806 21.17	679	137 20.18 20.18 4.88	-	-	-	-	-	-	-	-	-	-	-	-	-	-	-	-	-	-	-	-	-	-	-
Fort Lee (borough)	7,469 21.06	11,004	2,699 24.53 24.53 36.14	-	-	220 36.30 8.15 2.00 2.95	-	-	552 32.02 20.45 5.02 7.39	-	-	-	-	-	-	90 4.48 3.33 0.82 1.20	1,555 26.31 57.61 14.13 20.82	-	-	-	-	-	-	-	-	-
Franklin Lakes (borough)	939 9.01	713	285 39.97 39.97 30.35	-	-	-	-	-	-	-	-	-	-	-	-	-	-	-	-	-	-	-	-	-	-	-
Glen Rock (borough)	792 6.86	722	221 30.61 30.61 27.90	-	-	-	-	-	-	-	-	-	-	-	-	-	-	-	-	-	-	-	-	-	-	-
Hackensack (city)	5,348 12.53	3,192	856 26.82 26.82 16.01	-	-	136 14.05 15.89 4.26 2.54	-	-	-	-	254 35.62 29.67 7.96 4.75	-	-	-	-	-	203 31.77 23.71 6.36 3.80	-	-	-	-	-	-	-	-	-
Hasbrouck Heights (borough)	1,204 10.32	626	159 25.40 25.40 13.21	-	-	-	-	-	-	-	-	-	-	-	-	-	-	-	-	-	-	-	-	-	-	-
Hillsdale (borough)	936 9.28	515	307 59.61 59.61 32.80	-	-	-	-	-	-	-	-	-	-	-	-	-	-	-	-	-	-	-	-	-	-	-
Little Ferry (borough)	1,539 14.25	1,845	461 24.99 24.99 29.95	-	-	113 26.16 24.51 6.12 7.34	-	-	-	-	185 48.18 40.13 10.03 12.02	-	-	-	-	-	124 16.80 26.90 6.72 8.06	-	-	-	-	-	-	-	-	-
Lodi (borough)	3,298 13.76	2,036	526 25.83 25.83 15.95	-	-	264 24.44 50.19 12.97 8.00	-	-	-	-	154 27.26 29.28 7.56 4.67	-	-	-	-	-	-	-	-	-	-	-	-	-	-	-
Lyndhurst (township)	1,850 9.54	1,160	353 30.43 30.43 19.08	-	-	-	-	-	-	-	-	-	-	-	-	-	-	-	-	-	-	-	-	-	-	-

Notes: Please refer to the User's Guide for an explanation of data; data is arranged alphabetically by state, then county, then city within each county; table includes counties with populations greater than 49,999 unless noted and cities with populations greater than 9,999 whose Asian and/or NHPI population rates are greater than the national average; (1) Native Hawaiian and other Pacific Islander; (2) excludes Taiwanese; (3) includes Chamorro; (4) county does not meet population threshold but is shown in order to allow inclusion of city

Place	Total foreign-born naturalized citizens	Total Asian population	Asians who are foreign-born naturalized citizens	Total NHPI[1] population	NHPIs[1] who are foreign-born naturalized citizens	Asian Indian	Bangladeshi	Cambodian	Chinese[2]	Fijian	Filipino	Guamanian[3]	Hawaiian, Native	Hmong	Indonesian	Japanese	Korean	Laotian	Malaysian	Pakistani	Samoan	Sri Lankan	Taiwanese	Thai	Tongan	Vietnamese
Mahwah (township)	1,724 7.16	1,551	508 32.75 32.75 29.47	-	-	216 42.11 42.52 13.93 12.53	-	-	-	-	-	-	-	-	-	-	-	-	-	-	-	-	-	-	-	-
New Milford (borough)	2,335 14.24	2,311	977 42.28 42.28 41.84	-	-	252 40.58 25.79 10.90 10.79	-	-	-	-	400 41.97 40.94 17.31 17.13	-	-	-	-	-	-	-	-	-	-	-	-	-	-	-
North Arlington (borough)	1,921 12.65	828	177 21.38 21.38 9.21	-	-	-	-	-	-	-	-	-	-	-	-	-	-	-	-	-	-	-	-	-	-	-
Palisades Park (borough)	3,580 20.97	7,002	1,606 22.94 22.94 44.86	-	-	-	-	-	-	-	-	-	-	-	-	-	1,291 21.87 80.39 18.44 36.06	-	-	-	-	-	-	-	-	-
Paramus (borough)	4,052 15.74	4,413	1,548 35.08 35.08 38.20	-	-	543 41.55 35.08 12.30 13.40	-	-	164 35.73 10.59 3.72 4.05	-	375 45.40 24.22 8.50 9.25	-	-	-	-	-	349 25.11 22.55 7.91 8.61	-	-	-	-	-	-	-	-	-
Ramsey (borough)	824 5.74	825	206 24.97 24.97 25.00	-	-	-	-	-	-	-	-	-	-	-	-	-	-	-	-	-	-	-	-	-	-	-
Ridgefield (borough)	1,988 18.36	1,776	399 22.47 22.47 20.07	-	-	-	-	-	-	-	-	-	-	-	-	-	311 23.19 77.94 17.51 15.64	-	-	-	-	-	-	-	-	-
Ridgefield Park (village)	1,548 12.03	1,104	299 27.08 27.08 19.32	-	-	-	-	-	-	-	-	-	-	-	-	-	118 26.16 39.46 10.69 7.62	-	-	-	-	-	-	-	-	-
Ridgewood (village)	1,733 6.95	2,111	568 26.91 26.91 32.78	-	-	-	-	-	-	-	-	-	-	-	-	25 5.59 4.40 1.18 1.44	152 26.67 26.76 7.20 8.77	-	-	-	-	-	-	-	-	-
River Edge (borough)	1,186 10.84	1,350	392 29.04 29.04 33.05	-	-	-	-	-	-	-	-	-	-	-	-	-	98 20.72 25.00 7.26 8.26	-	-	-	-	-	-	-	-	-

Notes: Please refer to the User's Guide for an explanation of data; data is arranged alphabetically by state, then county, then city within each county; table includes counties with populations greater than 49,999 unless noted and cities with populations greater than 9,999 whose Asian and/or NHPI population rates are greater than the national average; (1) Native Hawaiian and other Pacific Islander; (2) excludes Taiwanese; (3) includes Chamorro; (4) county does not meet population threshold but is shown in order to allow inclusion of city

Place	Total foreign-born naturalized citizens	Total Asian population	Asians who are foreign-born naturalized citizens	Total NHPI[1] population	NHPIs[1] who are foreign-born naturalized citizens	Asian Indian	Bangladeshi	Cambodian	Chinese[2]	Fijian	Filipino	Guamanian[3]	Hawaiian, Native	Hmong	Indonesian	Japanese	Korean	Laotian	Malaysian	Pakistani	Samoan	Sri Lankan	Taiwanese	Thai	Tongan	Vietnamese
Rutherford (borough)	2,130 11.76	2,079	783 37.66 37.66 36.76	-	-	182 52.30 23.24 8.75 8.54	-	-	-	-	-	-	-	-	-	-	303 33.52 38.70 14.57 14.23	-	-	-	-	-	-	-	-	-
Saddle Brook (township)	1,228 9.33	728	330 45.33 45.33 26.87	-	-	-	-	-	-	-	-	-	-	-	-	-	-	-	-	-	-	-	-	-	-	-
Teaneck (township)	5,879 14.97	2,829	1,118 39.52 39.52 19.02	-	-	329 40.67 29.43 11.63 5.60	-	-	-	-	436 50.23 39.00 15.41 7.42	-	-	-	-	-	-	-	-	-	-	-	-	-	-	-
Tenafly (borough)	1,881 13.62	2,587	790 30.54 30.54 42.00	-	-	-	-	-	315 42.28 39.87 12.18 16.75	-	-	-	-	-	-	-	355 30.11 44.94 13.72 18.87	-	-	-	-	-	-	-	-	-
Wallington (borough)	1,658 14.31	546	108 19.78 19.78 6.51	-	-	-	-	-	-	-	-	-	-	-	-	-	-	-	-	-	-	-	-	-	-	-
Westwood (borough)	910 8.27	527	192 36.43 36.43 21.10	-	-	-	-	-	-	-	-	-	-	-	-	-	-	-	-	-	-	-	-	-	-	-
Wyckoff (township)	1,071 6.49	641	229 35.73 35.73 21.38	-	-	-	-	-	-	-	-	-	-	-	-	-	-	-	-	-	-	-	-	-	-	-
Burlington County	15,591 3.68	11,170	4,380 39.21 39.21 28.09	-	-	1,182 31.60 26.99 10.58 7.58	-	-	550 35.05 12.56 4.92 3.53	-	851 41.74 19.43 7.62 5.46	-	-	-	-	219 44.79 5.00 1.96 1.40	1,017 51.60 23.22 9.10 6.52	-	-	-	-	-	-	-	-	244 45.19 5.57 2.18 1.57
Browns Mills (cdp)	586 5.16	478	232 48.54 48.54 39.59	-	-	-	-	-	-	-	-	-	-	-	-	-	168 48.00 72.41 35.15 28.67	-	-	-	-	-	-	-	-	-
Evesham (township)	1,572 3.71	1,597	528 33.06 33.06 33.59	-	-	134 37.33 25.38 8.39 8.52	-	-	147 32.81 27.84 9.20 9.35	-	-	-	-	-	-	-	-	-	-	-	-	-	-	-	-	-

Notes: Please refer to the User's Guide for an explanation of data; data is arranged alphabetically by state, then county, then city within each county; table includes counties with populations greater than 49,999 unless noted and cities with populations greater than 9,999 whose Asian and/or NHPI population rates are greater than the national average; (1) Native Hawaiian and other Pacific Islander; (2) excludes Taiwanese; (3) includes Chamorro; (4) county does not meet population threshold but is shown in order to allow inclusion of city

Place	Total foreign-born naturalized citizens	Total Asian population	Asians who are foreign-born naturalized citizens	Total NHPI[1] population	NHPIs[1] who are foreign-born naturalized citizens	Asian Indian	Bangladeshi	Cambodian	Chinese[2]	Fijian	Filipino	Guamanian[3]	Hawaiian, Native	Hmong	Indonesian	Japanese	Korean	Laotian	Malaysian	Pakistani	Samoan	Sri Lankan	Taiwanese	Thai	Tongan	Vietnamese
Maple Shade (township)	520 2.73	1,083	227 20.96 20.96 43.65	-	-	55 8.45 24.23 5.08 10.58	-	-	-	-	-	-	-	-	-	-	-	-	-	-	-	-	-	-	-	-
Marlton (cdp)	356 3.47	392	123 31.38 31.38 34.55	-	-	-	-	-	-	-	-	-	-	-	-	-	-	-	-	-	-	-	-	-	-	-
Mount Laurel (township)	1,806 4.49	1,722	721 41.87 41.87 39.92	-	-	203 35.61 28.16 11.79 11.24	-	-	192 39.02 26.63 11.15 10.63	-	-	-	-	-	-	-	-	-	-	-	-	-	-	-	-	-
Camden County	18,694 3.67	19,842	8,055 40.60 40.60 43.09	-	-	2,095 41.58 26.01 10.56 11.21	-	110 35.14 1.37 0.55 0.59	1,580 40.33 19.62 7.96 8.45	-	1,971 52.10 24.47 9.93 10.54	-	-	-	-	-	648 37.37 8.04 3.27 3.47	-	-	117 31.12 1.45 0.59 0.63	-	-	-	-	-	1,070 33.81 13.28 5.39 5.72
Barclay-Kingston (cdp)	793 7.36	883	500 56.63 56.63 63.05	-	-	-	-	-	-	-	-	-	-	-	-	-	-	-	-	-	-	-	-	-	-	-
Bellmawr (borough)	382 3.39	450	124 27.56 27.56 32.46	-	-	-	-	-	-	-	-	-	-	-	-	-	-	-	-	-	-	-	-	-	-	-
Cherry Hill Mall (cdp)	1,168 8.67	1,291	532 41.21 41.21 45.55	-	-	-	-	-	-	-	-	-	-	-	-	-	-	-	-	-	-	-	-	-	-	-
Cherry Hill (township)	5,725 8.18	6,595	2,832 42.94 42.94 49.47	-	-	639 46.27 22.56 9.69 11.16	-	-	755 41.19 26.66 11.45 13.19	-	802 54.23 28.32 12.16 14.01	-	-	-	-	-	295 29.01 10.42 4.47 5.15	-	-	-	-	-	-	-	-	-
Echelon (cdp)	833 8.02	1,347	496 36.82 36.82 59.54	-	-	296 36.59 59.68 21.97 35.53	-	-	-	-	-	-	-	-	-	-	-	-	-	-	-	-	-	-	-	-
Greentree (cdp)	1,380 12.00	1,925	892 46.34 46.34 64.64	-	-	287 48.81 32.17 14.91 20.80	-	-	341 44.23 38.23 17.71 24.71	-	-	-	-	-	-	-	-	-	-	-	-	-	-	-	-	-

Notes: Please refer to the User's Guide for an explanation of data; data is arranged alphabetically by state, then county, then city within each county; table includes counties with populations greater than 49,999 unless noted and cities with populations greater than 9,999 whose Asian and/or NHPI population rates are greater than the national average; (1) Native Hawaiian and other Pacific Islander; (2) excludes Taiwanese; (3) includes Chamorro; (4) county does not meet population threshold but is shown in order to allow inclusion of city

Place	Total foreign-born naturalized citizens	Total Asian population	Asians who are foreign-born naturalized citizens	Total NHPI[1] population	NHPIs[1] who are foreign-born naturalized citizens	Asian Indian	Bangladeshi	Cambodian	Chinese[2]	Fijian	Filipino	Guamanian[3]	Hawaiian, Native	Hmong	Indonesian	Japanese	Korean	Laotian	Malaysian	Pakistani	Samoan	Sri Lankan	Taiwanese	Thai	Tongan	Vietnamese
Pennsauken (township)	1,484	1,556	610	-	-	-	-	-	-	-	-	-	-	-	-	-	-	-	-	-	-	-	-	-	-	263
	4.16		39.20																							38.01
																										43.11
			39.20																							16.90
			41.11																							17.72
Springdale (cdp)	1,093	1,196	442	-	-	-	-	-	144	-	-	-	-	-	-	-	-	-	-	-	-	-	-	-	-	-
	7.58		36.96						30.84																	
									32.58																	
			36.96						12.04																	
			40.44						13.17																	
Voorhees (township)	2,409	3,077	1,368	-	-	728	-	-	314	-	202	-	-	-	-	-	-	-	-	-	-	-	-	-	-	-
	8.57		44.46			41.15			50.81		49.39															
						53.22			22.95		14.77															
			44.46			23.66			10.20		6.56															
			56.79			30.22			13.03		8.39															
Cape May County	2,020	615	382	-	-	-	-	-	-	-	-	-	-	-	-	-	-	-	-	-	-	-	-	-	-	-
	1.97		62.11																							
			62.11																							
			18.91																							
Cumberland County	3,514	1,171	406	-	-	89	-	-	-	-	-	-	-	-	-	-	-	-	-	-	-	-	-	-	-	-
	2.40		34.67			21.50																				
						21.92																				
			34.67			7.60																				
			11.55			2.53																				
Essex County	73,983	29,468	10,998	458	62	2,960	-	-	2,401	-	3,275	-	-	-	-	78	1,200	-	-	231	-	-	183	-	-	328
	9.32		37.32		13.54	34.04			39.24		41.24					13.00	43.00			37.93			38.36			31.15
						26.91			21.83		29.78					0.71	10.91			2.10			1.66			2.98
			37.32		13.54	10.04			8.15		11.11					0.26	4.07			0.78			0.62			1.11
			14.87		0.08	4.00			3.25		4.43					0.11	1.62			0.31			0.25			0.44
Belleville (township)	4,850	4,228	1,513	-	-	260	-	-	-	-	801	-	-	-	-	-	-	-	-	-	-	-	-	-	-	160
	13.50		35.79			29.21					37.62															37.74
						17.18					52.94															10.58
			35.79			6.15					18.95															3.78
			31.20			5.36					16.52															3.30
Bloomfield (township)	5,565	4,056	1,547	-	-	507	-	-	149	-	743	-	-	-	-	-	-	-	-	-	-	-	-	-	-	-
	11.67		38.14			33.71			30.10		46.76															
						32.77			9.63		48.03															
			38.14			12.50			3.67		18.32															
			27.80			9.11			2.68		13.35															
Cedar Grove (township)	965	605	246	-	-	-	-	-	-	-	-	-	-	-	-	-	-	-	-	-	-	-	-	-	-	-
	7.85		40.66																							
			40.66																							
			25.49																							
Livingston (township)	3,325	3,990	1,581	-	-	335	-	-	626	-	218	-	-	-	-	-	310	-	-	-	-	-	-	-	-	-
	12.14		39.62			44.97			39.77		37.85						38.99									
						21.19			39.60		13.79						19.61									
			39.62			8.40			15.69		5.46						7.77									
			47.55			10.08			18.83		6.56						9.32									

Notes: Please refer to the User's Guide for an explanation of data; data is arranged alphabetically by state, then county, then city within each county; table includes counties with populations greater than 49,999 unless noted and cities with populations greater than 9,999 whose Asian and/or NHPI population rates are greater than the national average; (1) Native Hawaiian and other Pacific Islander; (2) excludes Taiwanese; (3) includes Chamorro; (4) county does not meet population threshold but is shown in order to allow inclusion of city

Place	Total foreign-born naturalized citizens	Total Asian population	Asians who are foreign-born naturalized citizens	Total NHPI[1] population	NHPIs[1] who are foreign-born naturalized citizens	Asian Indian	Bangladeshi	Cambodian	Chinese[2]	Fijian	Filipino	Guamanian[3]	Hawaiian, Native	Hmong	Indonesian	Japanese	Korean	Laotian	Malaysian	Pakistani	Samoan	Sri Lankan	Taiwanese	Thai	Tongan	Vietnamese
Millburn (township)	1,783	1,508	626	-	-	-	-	-	254	-	-	-	-	-	-	-	-	-	-	-	-	-	-	-	-	-
	9.02		41.51						38.90																	
									40.58																	
			41.51						16.84																	
			35.11						14.25																	
Nutley (township)	2,427	1,995	786	-	-	262	-	-	-	-	186	-	-	-	-	-	-	-	-	-	-	-	-	-	-	-
	8.87		39.40			35.65					38.19															
						33.33					23.66															
			39.40			13.13					9.32															
			32.39			10.80					7.66															
Verona (township)	816	612	247	-	-	-	-	-	-	-	-	-	-	-	-	-	-	-	-	-	-	-	-	-	-	-
	6.03		40.36																							
			40.36																							
			30.27																							
West Caldwell (township)	674	413	218	-	-	-	-	-	-	-	-	-	-	-	-	-	-	-	-	-	-	-	-	-	-	-
	6.00		52.78																							
			52.78																							
			32.34																							
West Orange (township)	6,553	3,756	1,728	-	-	391	-	-	408	-	525	-	-	-	-	-	269	-	-	-	-	-	-	-	-	-
	14.61		46.01			37.89			51.78		54.57						42.63									
						22.63			23.61		30.38						15.57									
			46.01			10.41			10.86		13.98						7.16									
			26.37			5.97			6.23		8.01						4.10									
Gloucester County	5,321	4,162	1,870	-	-	378	-	-	320	-	672	-	-	-	-	-	228	-	-	-	-	-	-	-	-	-
	2.09		44.93			38.07			42.67		49.19						52.53									
						20.21			17.11		35.94						12.19									
			44.93			9.08			7.69		16.15						5.48									
			35.14			7.10			6.01		12.63						4.28									
Hudson County	97,376	57,191	19,289	-	-	6,547	-	-	1,659	-	8,283	-	-	-	-	77	888	-	-	713	-	-	-	-	-	613
	15.99		33.73			31.78			24.64		41.67					8.23	27.70			30.73						37.38
						33.94			8.60		42.94					0.40	4.60			3.70						3.18
			33.73			11.45			2.90		14.48					0.13	1.55			1.25						1.07
			19.81			6.72			1.70		8.51					0.08	0.91			0.73						0.63
Bayonne (city)	5,912	2,599	962	-	-	220	-	-	-	-	507	-	-	-	-	-	123	-	-	-	-	-	-	-	-	-
	9.56		37.01			41.20					38.15						41.69									
						22.87					52.70						12.79									
			37.01			8.46					19.51						4.73									
			16.27			3.72					8.58						2.08									
Guttenberg (town)	2,192	743	223	-	-	-	-	-	-	-	-	-	-	-	-	-	-	-	-	-	-	-	-	-	-	-
	20.50		30.01																							
			30.01																							
			10.17																							
Harrison (town)	2,467	1,759	279	-	-	-	-	-	185	-	-	-	-	-	-	-	-	-	-	-	-	-	-	-	-	-
	17.10		15.86						14.08																	
									66.31																	
			15.86						10.52																	
			11.31						7.50																	

Notes: Please refer to the User's Guide for an explanation of data; data is arranged alphabetically by state, then county, then city within each county; table includes counties with populations greater than 49,999 unless noted and cities with populations greater than 9,999 whose Asian and/or NHPI population rates are greater than the national average; (1) Native Hawaiian and other Pacific Islander; (2) excludes Taiwanese; (3) includes Chamorro; (4) county does not meet population threshold but is shown in order to allow inclusion of city

Place	Total foreign-born naturalized citizens	Total Asian population	Asians who are foreign-born naturalized citizens	Total NHPI[1] population	NHPIs[1] who are foreign-born naturalized citizens	Asian Indian	Bangladeshi	Cambodian	Chinese[2]	Fijian	Filipino	Guamanian[3]	Hawaiian, Native	Hmong	Indonesian	Japanese	Korean	Laotian	Malaysian	Pakistani	Samoan	Sri Lankan	Taiwanese	Thai	Tongan	Vietnamese
Hoboken (city)	2,658	1,694	507	-	-	235	-	-	101	-	-	-	-	-	-	-	-	-	-	-	-	-	-	-	-	-
	6.87		29.93			36.04			20.57																	
						46.35			19.92																	
			29.93			13.87			5.96																	
			19.07			8.84			3.80																	
Jersey City (city)	33,609	39,070	13,927	-	-	4,300	-	-	809	-	6,932	-	-	-	-	-	390	-	-	620	-	-	-	-	-	530
	14.00		35.65			32.13			27.83		42.12						26.33			33.01						38.02
						30.88			5.81		49.77						2.80			4.45						3.81
			35.65			11.01			2.07		17.74						1.00			1.59						1.36
			41.44			12.79			2.41		20.63						1.16			1.84						1.58
Kearny (town)	5,895	2,280	551	-	-	159	-	-	198	-	-	-	-	-	-	-	-	-	-	-	-	-	-	-	-	-
	14.55		24.17			19.51			21.59																	
						28.86			35.93																	
			24.17			6.97			8.68																	
			9.35			2.70			3.36																	
North Bergen (township)	14,485	3,516	1,424	-	-	993	-	-	141	-	-	-	-	-	-	-	-	-	-	-	-	-	-	-	-	-
	24.89		40.50			42.01			44.20																	
						69.73			9.90																	
			40.50			28.24			4.01																	
			9.83			6.86			0.97																	
Secaucus (town)	1,745	1,853	523	-	-	111	-	-	-	-	235	-	-	-	-	-	-	-	-	-	-	-	-	-	-	-
	11.02		28.22			20.83					37.01															
						21.22					44.93															
			28.22			5.99					12.68															
			29.97			6.36					13.47															
Weehawken (township)	2,620	608	132	-	-	-	-	-	-	-	-	-	-	-	-	-	-	-	-	-	-	-	-	-	-	-
	19.41		21.71																							
			21.71																							
			5.04																							
Hunterdon County	4,374	2,595	1,123	-	-	464	-	-	235	-	-	-	-	-	-	-	-	-	-	-	-	-	-	-	-	-
	3.59		43.28			43.77			33.24																	
						41.32			20.93																	
			43.28			17.88			9.06																	
			25.67			10.61			5.37																	
Mercer County	20,225	17,429	5,835	-	-	2,081	-	-	1,503	-	541	-	-	-	-	64	798	-	-	196	-	-	205	-	-	-
	5.77		33.48			30.44			32.56		46.88					10.32	40.28			29.70			42.01			
						35.66			25.76		9.27					1.10	13.68			3.36			3.51			
			33.48			11.94			8.62		3.10					0.37	4.58			1.12			1.18			
			28.85			10.29			7.43		2.67					0.32	3.95			0.97			1.01			
East Windsor (township)	2,273	2,363	765	-	-	537	-	-	-	-	-	-	-	-	-	-	-	-	-	-	-	-	-	-	-	-
	9.12		32.37			35.99																				
						70.20																				
			32.37			22.73																				
			33.66			23.63																				
Hopewell (township)	682	668	278	-	-	-	-	-	-	-	-	-	-	-	-	-	-	-	-	-	-	-	-	-	-	-
	4.23		41.62																							
			41.62																							
			40.76																							

Notes: Please refer to the User's Guide for an explanation of data; data is arranged alphabetically by state, then county, then city within each county; table includes counties with populations greater than 49,999 unless noted and cities with populations greater than 9,999 whose Asian and/or NHPI population rates are greater than the national average; (1) Native Hawaiian and other Pacific Islander; (2) excludes Taiwanese; (3) includes Chamorro; (4) county does not meet population threshold but is shown in order to allow inclusion of city

Place	Total foreign-born naturalized citizens	Total Asian population	Asians who are foreign-born naturalized citizens	Total NHPI[1] population	NHPIs[1] who are foreign-born naturalized citizens	Asian Indian	Bangladeshi	Cambodian	Chinese[2]	Fijian	Filipino	Guamanian[3]	Hawaiian, Native	Hmong	Indonesian	Japanese	Korean	Laotian	Malaysian	Pakistani	Samoan	Sri Lankan	Taiwanese	Thai	Tongan	Vietnamese
Lawrence (township)	2,225 7.63	2,291	699 30.51 30.51 31.42	-	-	282 24.12 40.34 12.31 12.67	-	-	211 32.31 30.19 9.21 9.48	-	-	-	-	-	-	-	-	-	-	-	-	-	-	-	-	-
Princeton (borough)	457 3.22	931	71 7.63 7.63 15.54	-	-	-	-	-	-	-	-	-	-	-	-	-	-	-	-	-	-	-	-	-	-	-
Princeton (township)	1,618 10.10	1,684	572 33.97 33.97 35.35	-	-	141 33.49 24.65 8.37 8.71	-	-	212 29.36 37.06 12.59 13.10	-	-	-	-	-	-	-	-	-	-	-	-	-	-	-	-	-
West Windsor (township)	2,583 11.79	4,798	1,831 38.16 38.16 70.89	-	-	600 37.20 32.77 12.51 23.23	-	-	719 39.59 39.27 14.99 27.84	-	-	-	-	-	-	-	135 31.47 7.37 2.81 5.23	-	-	-	-	-	-	-	-	-
Middlesex County	77,921 10.39	104,114	32,067 30.80 30.80 41.15	-	-	14,056 25.95 43.83 13.50 18.04	106 27.39 0.33 0.10 0.14	-	7,574 35.60 23.62 7.27 9.72	-	4,740 37.92 14.78 4.55 6.08	-	-	-	37 7.58 0.12 0.04 0.05	58 8.76 0.18 0.06 0.07	1,858 34.72 5.79 1.78 2.38	-	-	1,218 38.37 3.80 1.17 1.56	-	168 33.80 0.52 0.16 0.22	563 41.40 1.76 0.54 0.72	-	-	1,181 52.49 3.68 1.13 1.52
Avenel (cdp)	1,433 8.16	3,296	621 18.84 18.84 43.34	-	-	345 15.80 55.56 10.47 24.08	-	-	-	-	-	-	-	-	-	-	-	-	-	-	-	-	-	-	-	-
Carteret (borough)	2,226 10.75	1,656	686 41.43 41.43 30.82	-	-	377 34.21 54.96 22.77 16.94	-	-	-	-	-	-	-	-	-	-	-	-	-	-	-	-	-	-	-	-
Colonia (cdp)	1,873 10.55	1,263	548 43.39 43.39 29.26	-	-	252 40.32 45.99 19.95 13.45	-	-	-	-	205 62.12 37.41 16.23 10.95	-	-	-	-	-	-	-	-	-	-	-	-	-	-	-
East Brunswick (township)	6,510 13.92	7,634	3,017 39.52 39.52 46.34	-	-	1,009 38.53 33.44 13.22 15.50	-	-	1,285 41.45 42.59 16.83 19.74	-	194 34.34 6.43 2.54 2.98	-	-	-	-	-	141 32.12 4.67 1.85 2.17	-	-	-	-	-	-	-	-	-
Edison (township)	14,460 14.80	28,438	8,567 30.13 30.13 59.25	-	-	4,185 25.60 48.85 14.72 28.94	-	-	2,151 36.92 25.11 7.56 14.88	-	997 38.76 11.64 3.51 6.89	-	-	-	-	-	476 37.75 5.56 1.67 3.29	-	-	220 32.64 2.57 0.77 1.52	-	-	227 34.24 2.65 0.80 1.57	-	-	-

Notes: Please refer to the User's Guide for an explanation of data; data is arranged alphabetically by state, then county, then city within each county; table includes counties with populations greater than 49,999 unless noted and cities with populations greater than 9,999 whose Asian and/or NHPI population rates are greater than the national average; (1) Native Hawaiian and other Pacific Islander; (2) excludes Taiwanese; (3) includes Chamorro; (4) county does not meet population threshold but is shown in order to allow inclusion of city

Place	Total foreign-born naturalized citizens	Total Asian population	Asians who are foreign-born naturalized citizens	Total NHPI[1] population	NHPIs[1] who are foreign-born naturalized citizens	Asian Indian	Bangladeshi	Cambodian	Chinese[2]	Fijian	Filipino	Guamanian[3]	Hawaiian, Native	Hmong	Indonesian	Japanese	Korean	Laotian	Malaysian	Pakistani	Samoan	Sri Lankan	Taiwanese	Thai	Tongan	Vietnamese
Fords (cdp)	1,692 11.18	2,383	771 32.35 32.35 45.57	-	-	315 27.44 40.86 13.22 18.62	-	-	-	-	235 35.66 30.48 9.86 13.89	-	-	-	-	-	-	-	-	-	-	-	-	-	-	-
Highland Park (borough)	1,398 9.99	1,926	210 10.90 10.90 15.02	-	-	28 4.47 13.33 1.45 2.00	-	-	92 10.67 43.81 4.78 6.58	-	-	-	-	-	-	-	-	-	-	-	-	-	-	-	-	-
Iselin (cdp)	2,083 12.55	3,982	1,131 28.40 28.40 54.30	-	-	769 27.30 67.99 19.31 36.92	-	-	147 28.77 13.00 3.69 7.06	-	-	-	-	-	-	-	-	-	-	-	-	-	-	-	-	-
Metuchen (borough)	1,034 8.05	941	416 44.21 44.21 40.23	-	-	-	-	-	-	-	-	-	-	-	-	-	-	-	-	-	-	-	-	-	-	-
Middlesex (borough)	932 6.79	609	196 32.18 32.18 21.03	-	-	-	-	-	-	-	-	-	-	-	-	-	-	-	-	-	-	-	-	-	-	-
New Brunswick (city)	3,002 6.18	2,719	596 21.92 21.92 19.85	-	-	230 20.50 38.59 8.46 7.66	-	-	134 30.18 22.48 4.93 4.46	-	-	-	-	-	-	-	-	-	-	-	-	-	-	-	-	-
North Brunswick (township)	4,258 11.73	5,148	1,895 36.81 36.81 44.50	-	-	915 30.40 48.28 17.77 21.49	-	-	401 48.14 21.16 7.79 9.42	-	235 53.41 12.40 4.56 5.52	-	-	-	-	-	168 36.13 8.87 3.26 3.95	-	-	-	-	-	-	-	-	-
Old Bridge (township)	6,068 10.04	6,489	2,255 34.75 34.75 37.16	-	-	917 32.44 40.67 14.13 15.11	-	-	389 32.31 17.25 5.99 6.41	-	428 33.57 18.98 6.60 7.05	-	-	-	-	-	-	-	-	262 49.81 11.62 4.04 4.32	-	-	-	-	-	-
Piscataway (township)	6,724 13.32	12,562	4,092 32.57 32.57 60.86	-	-	1,722 28.99 42.08 13.71 25.61	-	-	830 33.27 20.28 6.61 12.34	-	878 40.78 21.46 6.99 13.06	-	-	-	-	-	215 27.15 5.25 1.71 3.20	-	-	-	-	-	-	-	-	-
Plainsboro (township)	2,101 10.39	6,164	1,256 20.38 20.38 59.78	-	-	525 16.07 41.80 8.52 24.99	-	-	414 24.73 32.96 6.72 19.70	-	-	-	-	-	-	-	-	-	-	-	-	-	-	-	-	-

Notes: Please refer to the User's Guide for an explanation of data; data is arranged alphabetically by state, then county, then city within each county; table includes counties with populations greater than 49,999 unless noted and cities with populations greater than 9,999 whose Asian and/or NHPI population rates are greater than the national average; (1) Native Hawaiian and other Pacific Islander; (2) excludes Taiwanese; (3) includes Chamorro; (4) county does not meet population threshold but is shown in order to allow inclusion of city

Place	Total foreign-born naturalized citizens	Total Asian population	Asians who are foreign-born naturalized citizens	Total NHPI[1] population	NHPIs[1] who are foreign-born naturalized citizens	Asian Indian	Bangladeshi	Cambodian	Chinese[2]	Fijian	Filipino	Guamanian[3]	Hawaiian, Native	Hmong	Indonesian	Japanese	Korean	Laotian	Malaysian	Pakistani	Samoan	Sri Lankan	Taiwanese	Thai	Tongan	Vietnamese
Princeton Meadows (cdp)	1,236 9.33	3,875	747 19.28 19.28 60.44	-	-	293 13.45 39.22 7.56 23.71	-	-	225 25.28 30.12 5.81 18.20	-	-	-	-	-	-	-	-	-	-	-	-	-	-	-	-	-
Sayreville (borough)	3,291 8.15	4,184	888 21.22 21.22 26.98	-	-	466 18.63 52.48 11.14 14.16	-	-	157 23.64 17.68 3.75 4.77	-	139 21.09 15.65 3.32 4.22	-	-	-	-	-	-	-	-	-	-	-	-	-	-	-
South Brunswick (township)	4,048 10.73	6,888	2,223 32.27 32.27 54.92	-	-	1,001 25.93 45.03 14.53 24.73	-	-	640 45.26 28.79 9.29 15.81	-	209 38.70 9.40 3.03 5.16	-	-	-	-	-	-	-	-	-	-	-	-	-	-	-
South Plainfield (borough)	2,003 9.18	1,761	725 41.17 41.17 36.20	-	-	269 37.05 37.10 15.28 13.43	-	-	-	-	162 41.75 22.34 9.20 8.09	-	-	-	-	-	-	-	-	-	-	-	-	-	-	188 51.37 25.93 10.68 9.39
Woodbridge (township)	9,502 9.78	13,949	3,699 26.52 26.52 38.93	-	-	1,930 21.92 52.18 13.84 20.31	-	-	446 33.16 12.06 3.20 4.69	-	719 37.08 19.44 5.15 7.57	-	-	-	-	-	255 39.72 6.89 1.83 2.68	-	-	166 35.55 4.49 1.19 1.75	-	-	-	-	-	-
Monmouth County	34,090 5.54	24,047	9,630 40.05 40.05 28.25	-	-	2,246 32.87 23.32 9.34 6.59	-	-	3,913 42.11 40.63 16.27 11.48	-	1,527 45.72 15.86 6.35 4.48	-	-	-	-	101 27.98 1.05 0.42 0.30	1,025 51.64 10.64 4.26 3.01	-	-	97 23.60 1.01 0.40 0.28	-	-	-	-	-	411 56.77 4.27 1.71 1.21
Aberdeen (township)	1,175 6.76	943	358 37.96 37.96 30.47	-	-	121 30.71 33.80 12.83 10.30	-	-	169 43.33 47.21 17.92 14.38	-	-	-	-	-	-	-	-	-	-	-	-	-	-	-	-	-
Colts Neck (township)	734 5.95	519	230 44.32 44.32 31.34	-	-	-	-	-	-	-	-	-	-	-	-	-	-	-	-	-	-	-	-	-	-	-
Eatontown (borough)	901 6.44	1,262	309 24.48 24.48 34.30	-	-	-	-	-		-	-	-	-	-	-	-	-	-	-	-	-	-	-	-	-	-
Freehold (township)	2,158 6.84	1,711	763 44.59 44.59 35.36	-	-	234 48.55 30.67 13.68 10.84	-	-	239 43.85 31.32 13.97 11.08	-	177 45.27 23.20 10.34 8.20	-	-	-	-	-	-	-	-	-	-	-	-	-	-	-

Notes: Please refer to the User's Guide for an explanation of data; data is arranged alphabetically by state, then county, then city within each county; table includes counties with populations greater than 49,999 unless noted and cities with populations greater than 9,999 whose Asian and/or NHPI population rates are greater than the national average; (1) Native Hawaiian and other Pacific Islander; (2) excludes Taiwanese; (3) includes Chamorro; (4) county does not meet population threshold but is shown in order to allow inclusion of city

Place	Total foreign-born naturalized citizens	Total Asian population	Asians who are foreign-born naturalized citizens	Total NHPI[1] population	NHPIs[1] who are foreign-born naturalized citizens	Asian Indian	Bangladeshi	Cambodian	Chinese[2]	Fijian	Filipino	Guamanian[3]	Hawaiian, Native	Hmong	Indonesian	Japanese	Korean	Laotian	Malaysian	Pakistani	Samoan	Sri Lankan	Taiwanese	Thai	Tongan	Vietnamese
Holmdel (township)	2,060 13.05	2,610	1,072 41.07 41.07 52.04	-	-	126 27.69 11.75 4.83 6.12	-	-	685 42.36 63.90 26.25 33.25	-	-	-	-	-	-	-	-	-	-	-	-	-	-	-	-	-
Howell (township)	2,851 5.83	1,849	793 42.89 42.89 27.81	-	-	169 26.00 21.31 9.14 5.93	-	-	-	-	188 39.00 23.71 10.17 6.59	-	-	-	-	-	-	-	-	-	-	-	-	-	-	-
Manalapan (township)	2,609 7.81	1,528	618 40.45 40.45 23.69	-	-	281 45.99 45.47 18.39 10.77	-	-	191 37.16 30.91 12.50 7.32	-	-	-	-	-	-	-	-	-	-	-	-	-	-	-	-	-
Marlboro (township)	3,866 10.62	4,550	1,911 42.00 42.00 49.43	-	-	412 39.69 21.56 9.05 10.66	-	-	1,105 42.06 57.82 24.29 28.58	-	-	-	-	-	-	-	-	-	-	-	-	-	-	-	-	-
Morganville (cdp)	1,175 10.55	1,058	460 43.48 43.48 39.15	-	-	-	-	-	326 50.39 70.87 30.81 27.74	-	-	-	-	-	-	-	-	-	-	-	-	-	-	-	-	-
Ocean (township)	2,043 7.58	1,525	563 36.92 36.92 27.56	-	-	189 32.81 33.57 12.39 9.25	-	-	-	-	-	-	-	-	-	-	-	-	-	-	-	-	-	-	-	-
Tinton Falls (borough)	903 6.00	797	335 42.03 42.03 37.10	-	-	-	-	-	-	-	-	-	-	-	-	-	-	-	-	-	-	-	-	-	-	-
West Freehold (cdp)	844 6.73	581	259 44.58 44.58 30.69	-	-	-	-	-	-	-	-	-	-	-	-	-	-	-	-	-	-	-	-	-	-	-
Morris County	36,134 7.68	30,070	11,903 39.58 39.58 32.94	-	-	3,690 34.88 31.00 12.27 10.21	-	-	3,998 42.96 33.59 13.30 11.06	-	1,484 46.07 12.47 4.94 4.11	-	-	-	-	104 13.77 0.87 0.35 0.29	1,129 42.10 9.49 3.75 3.12	-	-	307 40.50 2.58 1.02 0.85	-	-	315 44.87 2.65 1.05 0.87	-	-	396 52.45 3.33 1.32 1.10
Chatham (township)	592 5.87	565	170 30.09 30.09 28.72	-	-	-	-	-	-	-	-	-	-	-	-	-	-	-	-	-	-	-	-	-	-	-

Notes: Please refer to the User's Guide for an explanation of data; data is arranged alphabetically by state, then county, then city within each county; table includes counties with populations greater than 49,999 unless noted and cities with populations greater than 9,999 whose Asian and/or NHPI population rates are greater than the national average; (1) Native Hawaiian and other Pacific Islander; (2) excludes Taiwanese; (3) includes Chamorro; (4) county does not meet population threshold but is shown in order to allow inclusion of city

Place	Total foreign-born naturalized citizens	Total Asian population	Asians who are foreign-born naturalized citizens	Total NHPI[1] population	NHPIs[1] who are foreign-born naturalized citizens	Asian Indian	Bangladeshi	Cambodian	Chinese[2]	Fijian	Filipino	Guamanian[3]	Hawaiian, Native	Hmong	Indonesian	Japanese	Korean	Laotian	Malaysian	Pakistani	Samoan	Sri Lankan	Taiwanese	Thai	Tongan	Vietnamese
Denville (township)	1,148 7.25	810	382 47.16 47.16 33.28	-	-	-	-	-	-	-	-	-	-	-	-	-	-	-	-	-	-	-	-	-	-	-
East Hanover (township)	1,580 13.87	1,245	601 48.27 48.27 38.04	-	-	-	-	-	304 49.35 50.58 24.42 19.24	-	-	-	-	-	-	-	-	-	-	-	-	-	-	-	-	-
Hanover (township)	1,336 10.36	1,237	579 46.81 46.81 43.34	-	-	158 40.31 27.29 12.77 11.83	-	-	276 49.02 47.67 22.31 20.66	-	-	-	-	-	-	-	-	-	-	-	-	-	-	-	-	-
Lincoln Park (borough)	888 8.12	617	255 41.33 41.33 28.72	-	-	-	-	-	-	-	-	-	-	-	-	-	-	-	-	-	-	-	-	-	-	-
Montville (township)	2,359 11.32	2,652	1,172 44.19 44.19 49.68	-	-	420 42.08 35.84 15.84 17.80	-	-	461 48.58 39.33 17.38 19.54	-	-	-	-	-	-	-	-	-	-	-	-	-	-	-	-	-
Morris (township)	1,237 5.68	911	411 45.12 45.12 33.23	-	-	-	-	-	-	-	-	-	-	-	-	-	-	-	-	-	-	-	-	-	-	-
Mount Olive (township)	1,212 5.01	1,639	436 26.60 26.60 35.97	-	-	150 22.06 34.40 9.15 12.38	-	-	-	-	-	-	-	-	-	-	-	-	-	-	-	-	-	-	-	-
Parsippany-Troy Hills (twp)	7,119 14.06	9,048	3,309 36.57 36.57 46.48	-	-	1,306 31.70 39.47 14.43 18.35	-	-	1,022 39.07 30.89 11.30 14.36	-	397 52.10 12.00 4.39 5.58	-	-	-	-	-	208 44.16 6.29 2.30 2.92	-	-	-	-	-	-	-	-	-
Randolph (township)	1,936 7.79	2,495	778 31.18 31.18 40.19	-	-	213 23.33 27.38 8.54 11.00	-	-	289 37.39 37.15 11.58 14.93	-	-	-	-	-	-	-	-	-	-	-	-	-	-	-	-	-
Rockaway (township)	1,683 7.34	1,317	562 42.67 42.67 33.39	-	-	286 45.32 50.89 21.72 16.99	-	-	-	-	-	-	-	-	-	-	-	-	-	-	-	-	-	-	-	-

Notes: Please refer to the User's Guide for an explanation of data; data is arranged alphabetically by state, then county, then city within each county; table includes counties with populations greater than 49,999 unless noted and cities with populations greater than 9,999 whose Asian and/or NHPI population rates are greater than the national average; (1) Native Hawaiian and other Pacific Islander; (2) excludes Taiwanese; (3) includes Chamorro; (4) county does not meet population threshold but is shown in order to allow inclusion of city

Place	Total foreign-born naturalized citizens	Total Asian population	Asians who are foreign-born naturalized citizens	Total NHPI[1] population	NHPIs[1] who are foreign-born naturalized citizens	Asian Indian	Bangladeshi	Cambodian	Chinese[2]	Fijian	Filipino	Guamanian[3]	Hawaiian, Native	Hmong	Indonesian	Japanese	Korean	Laotian	Malaysian	Pakistani	Samoan	Sri Lankan	Taiwanese	Thai	Tongan	Vietnamese
Roxbury (township)	1,479 6.19	874	398 45.54 45.54 26.91	-	-	-	-	-	-	-	-	-	-	-	-	-	-	-	-	-	-	-	-	-	-	-
Succasunna-Kenvil (cdp)	768 6.13	521	242 46.45 46.45 31.51	-	-	-	-	-	-	-	-	-	-	-	-	-	-	-	-	-	-	-	-	-	-	-
Ocean County	20,293 3.97	6,657	2,748 41.28 41.28 13.54	-	-	572 35.44 20.82 8.59 2.82	-	-	499 43.32 18.16 7.50 2.46	-	914 37.17 33.26 13.73 4.50	-	-	-	-	-	427 79.37 15.54 6.41 2.10	-	-	-	-	-	-	-	-	-
Passaic County	53,888 11.02	18,458	6,864 37.19 37.19 12.74	-	-	3,210 35.61 46.77 17.39 5.96	197 36.15 2.87 1.07 0.37	-	730 37.67 10.64 3.95 1.35	-	1,642 47.18 23.92 8.90 3.05	-	-	-	-	-	531 32.52 7.74 2.88 0.99	-	-	-	-	-	-	-	-	-
Clifton (city)	11,677 14.84	5,425	2,132 39.30 39.30 18.26	-	-	1,134 38.77 53.19 20.90 9.71	-	-	186 45.59 8.72 3.43 1.59	-	594 47.71 27.86 10.95 5.09	-	-	-	-	-	105 32.61 4.92 1.94 0.90	-	-	-	-	-	-	-	-	-
Little Falls (township)	841 7.75	459	142 30.94 30.94 16.88	-	-	-	-	-	-	-	-	-	-	-	-	-	-	-	-	-	-	-	-	-	-	-
Passaic (city)	8,094 11.93	3,830	1,408 36.76 36.76 17.40	-	-	885 35.09 62.86 23.11 10.93	-	-	-	-	394 52.12 27.98 10.29 4.87	-	-	-	-	-	-	-	-	-	-	-	-	-	-	-
Wayne (township)	5,484 10.13	3,245	1,104 34.02 34.02 20.13	-	-	412 37.97 37.32 12.70 7.51	-	-	191 27.80 17.30 5.89 3.48	-	130 36.52 11.78 4.01 2.37	-	-	-	-	-	263 30.16 23.82 8.10 4.80	-	-	-	-	-	-	-	-	-
Salem County	890 1.38	370	148 40.00 40.00 16.63	-	-	-	-	-	-	-	-	-	-	-	-	-	-	-	-	-	-	-	-	-	-	-
Somerset County	25,253 8.49	25,117	8,872 35.32 35.32 35.13	-	-	3,086 30.23 34.78 12.29 12.22	-	-	3,005 40.80 33.87 11.96 11.90	-	1,093 35.50 12.32 4.35 4.33	-	-	-	-	48 8.07 0.54 0.19 0.19	597 42.70 6.73 2.38 2.36	-	-	268 32.92 3.02 1.07 1.06	-	-	328 59.74 3.70 1.31 1.30	-	-	237 48.07 2.67 0.94 0.94

Notes: Please refer to the User's Guide for an explanation of data; data is arranged alphabetically by state, then county, then city within each county; table includes counties with populations greater than 49,999 unless noted and cities with populations greater than 9,999 whose Asian and/or NHPI population rates are greater than the national average; (1) Native Hawaiian and other Pacific Islander; (2) excludes Taiwanese; (3) includes Chamorro; (4) county does not meet population threshold but is shown in order to allow inclusion of city

Place	Total foreign-born naturalized citizens	Total Asian population	Asians who are foreign-born naturalized citizens	Total NHPI[1] population	NHPIs[1] who are foreign-born naturalized citizens	Asian Indian	Bangladeshi	Cambodian	Chinese[2]	Fijian	Filipino	Guamanian[3]	Hawaiian, Native	Hmong	Indonesian	Japanese	Korean	Laotian	Malaysian	Pakistani	Samoan	Sri Lankan	Taiwanese	Thai	Tongan	Vietnamese
Bernards (township)	1,733 7.05	1,926	719 37.33 37.33 41.49	-	-	159 29.07 22.11 8.26 9.17	-	-	426 45.37 59.25 22.12 24.58	-	-	-	-	-	-	-	-	-	-	-	-	-	-	-	-	-
Branchburg (township)	892 6.13	1,065	413 38.78 38.78 46.30	-	-	236 40.00 57.14 22.16 26.46	-	-	-	-	-	-	-	-	-	-	-	-	-	-	-	-	-	-	-	-
Bridgewater (township)	3,591 8.37	4,723	1,679 35.55 35.55 46.76	-	-	586 29.94 34.90 12.41 16.32	-	-	689 42.82 41.04 14.59 19.19	-	-	-	-	-	-	-	-	-	-	-	-	-	-	-	-	-
Franklin (township)	5,806 11.41	6,404	2,053 32.06 32.06 35.36	-	-	829 25.04 40.38 12.95 14.28	-	-	498 37.81 24.26 7.78 8.58	-	368 44.23 17.92 5.75 6.34	-	-	-	-	-	-	-	-	-	-	-	-	-	-	-
Hillsborough (township)	2,283 6.23	2,548	976 38.30 38.30 42.75	-	-	347 36.22 35.55 13.62 15.20	-	-	279 38.75 28.59 10.95 12.22	-	-	-	-	-	-	-	-	-	-	-	-	-	-	-	-	-
Montgomery (township)	1,510 8.65	1,971	751 38.10 38.10 49.74	-	-	187 31.48 24.90 9.49 12.38	-	-	342 37.17 45.54 17.35 22.65	-	-	-	-	-	-	-	-	-	-	-	-	-	-	-	-	-
North Plainfield (borough)	2,328 11.03	1,059	286 27.01 27.01 12.29	-	-	-	-	-	-	-	-	-	-	-	-	-	-	-	-	-	-	-	-	-	-	-
Somerset (cdp)	2,478 10.75	1,831	586 32.00 32.00 23.65	-	-	198 27.69 33.79 10.81 7.99	-	-	148 35.84 25.26 8.08 5.97	-	202 36.40 34.47 11.03 8.15	-	-	-	-	-	-	-	-	-	-	-	-	-	-	-
Somerville (borough)	770 6.17	868	197 22.70 22.70 25.58	-	-	-	-	-	-	-	-	-	-	-	-	-	-	-	-	-	-	-	-	-	-	-
Warren (township)	1,666 11.68	1,602	749 46.75 46.75 44.96	-	-	234 45.00 31.24 14.61 14.05	-	-	274 43.84 36.58 17.10 16.45	-	-	-	-	-	-	-	-	-	-	-	-	-	-	-	-	-

Notes: Please refer to the User's Guide for an explanation of data; data is arranged alphabetically by state, then county, then city within each county; table includes counties with populations greater than 49,999 unless noted and cities with populations greater than 9,999 whose Asian and/or NHPI population rates are greater than the national average; (1) Native Hawaiian and other Pacific Islander; (2) excludes Taiwanese; (3) includes Chamorro; (4) county does not meet population threshold but is shown in order to allow inclusion of city

Place	Total foreign-born naturalized citizens	Total Asian population	Asians who are foreign-born naturalized citizens	Total NHPI[1] population	NHPIs[1] who are foreign-born naturalized citizens	Asian Indian	Bangladeshi	Cambodian	Chinese[2]	Fijian	Filipino	Guamanian[3]	Hawaiian, Native	Hmong	Indonesian	Japanese	Korean	Laotian	Malaysian	Pakistani	Samoan	Sri Lankan	Taiwanese	Thai	Tongan	Vietnamese
Sussex County	5,191 3.60	1,628	689 42.32 42.32 13.27	-	-	195 47.68 28.30 11.98 3.76	-	-	-	-	159 31.86 23.08 9.77 3.06	-	-	-	-	-	-	-	-	-	-	-	-	-	-	-
Union County	58,826 11.26	19,393	7,355 37.93 37.93 12.50	-	-	2,254 33.02 30.65 11.62 3.83	-	-	1,724 45.50 23.44 8.89 2.93	-	2,380 41.53 32.36 12.27 4.05	-	-	-	-	-	502 44.86 6.83 2.59 0.85	-	-	105 29.17 1.43 0.54 0.18	-	-	-	-	-	182 41.18 2.47 0.94 0.31
Berkeley Heights (township)	1,014 7.56	1,050	474 45.14 45.14 46.75	-	-	-	-	-	185 44.26 39.03 17.62 18.24	-	-	-	-	-	-	-	-	-	-	-	-	-	-	-	-	-
New Providence (borough)	979 8.22	896	320 35.71 35.71 32.69	-	-	-	-	-	184 49.33 57.50 20.54 18.79	-	-	-	-	-	-	-	-	-	-	-	-	-	-	-	-	-
Rahway (city)	2,211 8.34	1,149	473 41.17 41.17 21.39	-	-	-	-	-	-	-	241 46.71 50.95 20.97 10.90	-	-	-	-	-	-	-	-	-	-	-	-	-	-	-
Roselle Park (borough)	1,499 11.29	1,243	360 28.96 28.96 24.02	-	-	233 26.54 64.72 18.74 15.54	-	-	-	-	-	-	-	-	-	-	-	-	-	-	-	-	-	-	-	-
Scotch Plains (township)	2,083 9.16	1,593	680 42.69 42.69 32.65	-	-	154 24.33 22.65 9.67 7.39	-	-	304 66.09 44.71 19.08 14.59	-	-	-	-	-	-	-	-	-	-	-	-	-	-	-	-	-
Springfield (township)	1,832 12.70	559	167 29.87 29.87 9.12	-	-	-	-	-	-	-	-	-	-	-	-	-	-	-	-	-	-	-	-	-	-	-
Summit (city)	1,647 7.79	812	259 31.90 31.90 15.73	-	-	95 24.36 36.68 11.70 5.77	-	-	-	-	-	-	-	-	-	-	-	-	-	-	-	-	-	-	-	-
Union (township)	8,054 14.80	4,258	1,528 35.89 35.89 18.97	-	-	349 33.82 22.84 8.20 4.33	-	-	191 37.23 12.50 4.49 2.37	-	792 37.17 51.83 18.60 9.83	-	-	-	-	-	-	-	-	-	-	-	-	-	-	-

Notes: Please refer to the User's Guide for an explanation of data; data is arranged alphabetically by state, then county, then city within each county; table includes counties with populations greater than 49,999 unless noted and cities with populations greater than 9,999 whose Asian and/or NHPI population rates are greater than the national average; (1) Native Hawaiian and other Pacific Islander; (2) excludes Taiwanese; (3) includes Chamorro; (4) county does not meet population threshold but is shown in order to allow inclusion of city

Place	Total foreign-born naturalized citizens	Total Asian population	Asians who are foreign-born naturalized citizens	Total NHPI[1] population	NHPIs[1] who are foreign-born naturalized citizens	Asian Indian	Bangladeshi	Cambodian	Chinese[2]	Fijian	Filipino	Guamanian[3]	Hawaiian, Native	Hmong	Indonesian	Japanese	Korean	Laotian	Malaysian	Pakistani	Samoan	Sri Lankan	Taiwanese	Thai	Tongan	Vietnamese
Westfield (town)	1,501 5.06	1,109	405 36.52 36.52 26.98	-	-	-	-	-	-	-	-	-	-	-	-	-	-	-	-	-	-	-	-	-	-	-
Warren County	3,012 2.94	1,221	416 34.07 34.07 13.81	-	-	143 26.34 34.38 11.71 4.75	-	-	-	-	-	-	-	-	-	-	-	-	-	-	-	-	-	-	-	-
NEW MEXICO	52,103 2.86	18,286	6,274 34.31 34.31 12.04	1,248	12 0.96 0.96 0.02	792 32.67 12.62 4.33 1.52	-	-	1,134 28.41 18.07 6.20 2.18	-	1,164 39.56 18.55 6.37 2.23	6 1.64 50.00 0.48 0.01	0 0.00 0.00 0.00 0.00	-	-	465 22.52 7.41 2.54 0.89	934 53.77 14.89 5.11 1.79	-	-	-	-	-	-	200 49.88 3.19 1.09 0.38	-	1,165 41.65 18.57 6.37 2.24
Bernalillo County	17,332 3.11	9,864	3,484 35.32 35.32 20.10	532	10 1.88 1.88 0.06	397 34.37 11.39 4.02 2.29	-	-	577 28.27 16.56 5.85 3.33	-	406 38.59 11.65 4.12 2.34	-	-	-	-	231 20.64 6.63 2.34 1.33	527 61.00 15.13 5.34 3.04	-	-	-	-	-	-	-	-	1,012 40.82 29.05 10.26 5.84
Chaves County	2,350 3.83	387	159 41.09 41.09 6.77	-	-	-	-	-	-	-	-	-	-	-	-	-	-	-	-	-	-	-	-	-	-	-
Dona Ana County	11,233 6.43	1,386	426 30.74 30.74 3.79	-	-	-	-	-	113 28.46 26.53 8.15 1.01	-	-	-	-	-	-	-	-	-	-	-	-	-	-	-	-	-
Los Alamos County[4]	567 3.09	798	233 29.20 29.20 41.09	-	-	-	-	-	-	-	-	-	-	-	-	-	-	-	-	-	-	-	-	-	-	-
Los Alamos (cdp)	398 3.34	609	193 31.69 31.69 48.49	-	-	-	-	-	-	-	-	-	-	-	-	-	-	-	-	-	-	-	-	-	-	-
Otero County	2,105 3.38	714	313 43.84 43.84 14.87	-	-	-	-	-	-	-	-	-	-	-	-	-	-	-	-	-	-	-	-	-	-	-
Sandoval County	1,985 2.21	748	359 47.99 47.99 18.09	-	-	-	-	-	-	-	201 60.54 55.99 26.87 10.13	-	-	-	-	-	-	-	-	-	-	-	-	-	-	-

Notes: Please refer to the User's Guide for an explanation of data; data is arranged alphabetically by state, then county, then city within each county; table includes counties with populations greater than 49,999 unless noted and cities with populations greater than 9,999 whose Asian and/or NHPI population rates are greater than the national average; (1) Native Hawaiian and other Pacific Islander; (2) excludes Taiwanese; (3) includes Chamorro; (4) county does not meet population threshold but is shown in order to allow inclusion of city

Place	Total foreign-born naturalized citizens	Total Asian population	Asians who are foreign-born naturalized citizens	Total NHPI[1] population	NHPIs[1] who are foreign-born naturalized citizens	Asian Indian	Bangladeshi	Cambodian	Chinese[2]	Fijian	Filipino	Guamanian[3]	Hawaiian, Native	Hmong	Indonesian	Japanese	Korean	Laotian	Malaysian	Pakistani	Samoan	Sri Lankan	Taiwanese	Thai	Tongan	Vietnamese
Santa Fe County	3,587 2.77	944	271 28.71 28.71 7.56	-	-	-	-	-	-	-	-	-	-	-	-	-	-	-	-	-	-	-	-	-	-	-
NEW YORK	1,783,744 9.40	1,044,423	353,021 33.80 33.80 19.79	7,903	1,096 13.87 13.87 0.06	81,517 32.60 23.09 7.80 4.57	4,791 23.85 1.36 0.46 0.27	987 33.92 0.28 0.09 0.06	151,848 36.42 43.01 14.54 8.51	-	34,693 40.00 9.83 3.32 1.94	222 12.62 20.26 2.81 0.01	116 8.04 10.58 1.47 0.01	-	440 18.08 0.12 0.04 0.02	3,251 8.65 0.92 0.31 0.18	39,957 33.08 11.32 3.83 2.24	1,438 44.71 0.41 0.14 0.08	246 17.55 0.07 0.02 0.01	9,393 29.24 2.66 0.90 0.53	46 3.20 4.20 0.58 <0.01	680 25.29 0.19 0.07 0.04	3,478 44.65 0.99 0.33 0.19	1,787 27.09 0.51 0.17 0.10	-	10,404 44.89 2.95 1.00 0.58
Albany County	11,141 3.78	7,887	2,837 35.97 35.97 25.46	-	-	909 37.07 32.04 11.53 8.16	-	-	493 25.09 17.38 6.25 4.43	-	362 51.64 12.76 4.59 3.25	-	-	-	-	-	391 40.06 13.78 4.96 3.51	-	-	-	-	-	-	-	-	291 54.60 10.26 3.69 2.61
Colonie (town)	3,596 4.54	2,919	1,457 49.91 49.91 40.52	-	-	571 46.84 39.19 19.56 15.88	-	-	269 43.95 18.46 9.22 7.48	-	-	-	-	-	-	-	-	-	-	-	-	-	-	-	-	-
Guilderland (town)	1,073 3.28	1,238	261 21.08 21.08 24.32	-	-	86 20.77 32.95 6.95 8.01	-	-	-	-	-	-	-	-	-	-	-	-	-	-	-	-	-	-	-	-
Bronx County (Bronx)	152,521 11.44	39,076	12,434 31.82 31.82 8.15	1,099	193 17.56 17.56 0.13	5,092 34.54 40.95 13.03 3.34	451 22.64 3.63 1.15 0.30	179 22.10 1.44 0.46 0.12	2,214 34.89 17.81 5.67 1.45	-	1,419 28.76 11.41 3.63 0.93	-	-	-	-	30 5.78 0.24 0.08 0.02	1,227 35.44 9.87 3.14 0.80	-	-	317 28.20 2.55 0.81 0.21	-	-	-	-	-	1,015 33.89 8.16 2.60 0.67
Broome County	5,834 2.91	5,321	1,855 34.86 34.86 31.80	-	-	387 41.26 20.86 7.27 6.63	-	-	394 25.31 21.24 7.40 6.75	-	-	-	-	-	-	-	260 33.21 14.02 4.89 4.46	161 31.14 8.68 3.03 2.76	-	-	-	-	-	-	-	258 50.29 13.91 4.85 4.42
Johnson City (village)	525 3.38	826	254 30.75 30.75 48.38	-	-	-	-	-	-	-	-	-	-	-	-	-	-	-	-	-	-	-	-	-	-	-
Vestal (town)	1,469 5.54	2,105	713 33.87 33.87 48.54	-	-	-	-	-	163 19.18 22.86 7.74 11.10	-	-	-	-	-	-	-	-	-	-	-	-	-	-	-	-	-
Cattaraugus County	678 0.81	441	153 34.69 34.69 22.57	-	-	-	-	-	-	-	-	-	-	-	-	-	-	-	-	-	-	-	-	-	-	-

Notes: Please refer to the User's Guide for an explanation of data; data is arranged alphabetically by state, then county, then city within each county; table includes counties with populations greater than 49,999 unless noted and cities with populations greater than 9,999 whose Asian and/or NHPI population rates are greater than the national average; (1) Native Hawaiian and other Pacific Islander; (2) excludes Taiwanese; (3) includes Chamorro; (4) county does not meet population threshold but is shown in order to allow inclusion of city

Place	Total foreign-born naturalized citizens	Total Asian population	Asians who are foreign-born naturalized citizens	Total NHPI[1] population	NHPIs[1] who are foreign-born naturalized citizens	Asian Indian	Bangladeshi	Cambodian	Chinese[2]	Fijian	Filipino	Guamanian[3]	Hawaiian, Native	Hmong	Indonesian	Japanese	Korean	Laotian	Malaysian	Pakistani	Samoan	Sri Lankan	Taiwanese	Thai	Tongan	Vietnamese
Cayuga County	1,039 1.27	343	149 43.44 43.44 14.34	-	-	-	-	-	-	-	-	-	-	-	-	-	-	-	-	-	-	-	-	-	-	-
Chautauqua County	1,665 1.19	462	251 54.33 54.33 15.08	-	-	-	-	-	-	-	-	-	-	-	-	-	-	-	-	-	-	-	-	-	-	-
Chemung County	938 1.03	796	253 31.78 31.78 26.97	-	-	-	-	-	-	-	-	-	-	-	-	-	-	-	-	-	-	-	-	-	-	-
Chenango County	591 1.15	171	88 51.46 51.46 14.89	-	-	-	-	-	-	-	-	-	-	-	-	-	-	-	-	-	-	-	-	-	-	-
Clinton County	1,578 1.98	714	303 42.44 42.44 19.20	-	-	-	-	-	-	-	-	-	-	-	-	-	-	-	-	-	-	-	-	-	-	-
Columbia County	1,615 2.56	461	162 35.14 35.14 10.03	-	-	-	-	-	-	-	-	-	-	-	-	-	-	-	-	-	-	-	-	-	-	-
Dutchess County	11,282 4.03	7,091	2,223 31.35 31.35 19.70	-	-	763 26.66 34.32 10.76 6.76	-	-	730 35.37 32.84 10.29 6.47	-	-	-	-	-	-	-	301 39.87 13.54 4.24 2.67	-	-	-	-	-	-	-	-	-
Arlington (cdp)	715 5.75	766	197 25.72 25.72 27.55	-	-	-	-	-	-	-	-	-	-	-	-	-	-	-	-	-	-	-	-	-	-	-
Poughkeepsie (town)	2,152 5.03	1,835	609 33.19 33.19 28.30	-	-	224 23.16 36.78 12.21 10.41	-	-	176 43.35 28.90 9.59 8.18	-	-	-	-	-	-	-	-	-	-	-	-	-	-	-	-	-
Wappinger (town)	1,373 5.22	1,180	334 28.31 28.31 24.33	-	-	87 19.25 26.05 7.37 6.34	-	-	-	-	-	-	-	-	-	-	-	-	-	-	-	-	-	-	-	-

Notes: Please refer to the User's Guide for an explanation of data; data is arranged alphabetically by state, then county, then city within each county; table includes counties with populations greater than 49,999 unless noted and cities with populations greater than 9,999 whose Asian and/or NHPI population rates are greater than the national average; (1) Native Hawaiian and other Pacific Islander; (2) excludes Taiwanese; (3) includes Chamorro; (4) county does not meet population threshold but is shown in order to allow inclusion of city

Place	Total foreign-born naturalized citizens	Total Asian population	Asians who are foreign-born naturalized citizens	Total NHPI[1] population	NHPIs[1] who are foreign-born naturalized citizens	Asian Indian	Bangladeshi	Cambodian	Chinese[2]	Fijian	Filipino	Guamanian[3]	Hawaiian, Native	Hmong	Indonesian	Japanese	Korean	Laotian	Malaysian	Pakistani	Samoan	Sri Lankan	Taiwanese	Thai	Tongan	Vietnamese
Erie County	25,043 2.64	12,893	4,580 35.52 35.52 18.29	-	-	1,219 35.64 26.62 9.45 4.87	-	-	864 28.26 18.86 6.70 3.45	-	316 46.81 6.90 2.45 1.26	-	-	-	-	61 12.30 1.33 0.47 0.24	854 42.96 18.65 6.62 3.41	-	-	-	-	-	-	-	-	624 41.08 13.62 4.84 2.49
Amherst (town)	5,724 4.91	5,559	1,730 31.12 31.12 30.22	-	-	678 37.56 39.19 12.20 11.84	-	-	462 27.45 26.71 8.31 8.07	-	-	-	-	-	-	-	247 26.30 14.28 4.44 4.32	-	-	-	-	-	-	-	-	-
Herkimer County	938 1.46	255	106 41.57 41.57 11.30	-	-	-	-	-	-	-	-	-	-	-	-	-	-	-	-	-	-	-	-	-	-	-
Jefferson County	1,872 1.68	1,171	465 39.71 39.71 24.84	-	-	-	-	-	-	-	120 38.71 25.81 10.25 6.41	-	-	-	-	-	180 50.28 38.71 15.37 9.62	-	-	-	-	-	-	-	-	-
Kings County (Brooklyn)	439,973 17.85	185,814	64,153 34.53 34.53 14.58	1,549	271 17.50 17.50 0.06	7,869 31.74 12.27 4.23 1.79	949 24.16 1.48 0.51 0.22	216 43.11 0.34 0.12 0.05	44,109 36.51 68.76 23.74 10.03	-	2,805 39.24 4.37 1.51 0.64	42 8.59 15.50 2.71 0.01	-	-	-	187 8.59 0.29 0.10 0.04	1,975 29.21 3.08 1.06 0.45	-	-	2,157 22.42 3.36 1.16 0.49	-	-	-	-	-	1,930 50.39 3.01 1.04 0.44
Livingston County	967 1.50	685	336 49.05 49.05 34.75	-	-	-	-	-	-	-	-	-	-	-	-	-	-	-	-	-	-	-	-	-	-	-
Madison County	880 1.27	478	181 37.87 37.87 20.57	-	-	-	-	-	-	-	-	-	-	-	-	-	-	-	-	-	-	-	-	-	-	-
Monroe County	29,655 4.03	17,744	6,983 39.35 39.35 23.55	-	-	1,421 31.61 20.35 8.01 4.79	-	74 19.42 1.06 0.42 0.25	1,309 32.92 18.75 7.38 4.41	-	324 52.94 4.64 1.83 1.09	-	-	-	-	95 16.30 1.36 0.54 0.32	1,557 62.16 22.30 8.77 5.25	619 45.68 8.86 3.49 2.09	-	146 31.60 2.09 0.82 0.49	-	-	-	-	-	1,106 48.79 15.84 6.23 3.73
Brighton (town)	2,425 6.81	2,811	830 29.53 29.53 34.23	-	-	259 25.77 31.20 9.21 10.68	-	-	235 36.72 28.31 8.36 9.69	-	-	-	-	-	-	-	-	-	-	-	-	-	-	-	-	-
Henrietta (town)	1,557 3.99	2,028	549 27.07 27.07 35.26	-	-	104 22.03 18.94 5.13 6.68	-	-	76 15.08 13.84 3.75 4.88	-	-	-	-	-	-	-	-	-	-	-	-	-	-	-	-	-

Notes: Please refer to the User's Guide for an explanation of data; data is arranged alphabetically by state, then county, then city within each county; table includes counties with populations greater than 49,999 unless noted and cities with populations greater than 9,999 whose Asian and/or NHPI population rates are greater than the national average; (1) Native Hawaiian and other Pacific Islander; (2) excludes Taiwanese; (3) includes Chamorro; (4) county does not meet population threshold but is shown in order to allow inclusion of city

Place	Total foreign-born naturalized citizens	Total Asian population	Asians who are foreign-born naturalized citizens	Total NHPI[1] population	NHPIs[1] who are foreign-born naturalized citizens	Asian Indian	Bangladeshi	Cambodian	Chinese[2]	Fijian	Filipino	Guamanian[3]	Hawaiian, Native	Hmong	Indonesian	Japanese	Korean	Laotian	Malaysian	Pakistani	Samoan	Sri Lankan	Taiwanese	Thai	Tongan	Vietnamese
Pittsford (town)	1,266 4.65	1,274	564 44.27 44.27 44.55	-	-	278 48.18 49.29 21.82 21.96	-	-	-	-	-	-	-	-	-	-	-	-	-	-	-	-	-	-	-	-
Nassau County	132,767 9.95	62,536	24,149 38.62 38.62 18.19	410	55 13.41 13.41 0.04	8,834 37.63 36.58 14.13 6.65	-	-	6,387 42.77 26.45 10.21 4.81	-	2,881 40.19 11.93 4.61 2.17	-	-	-	-	149 8.34 0.62 0.24 0.11	3,648 40.15 15.11 5.83 2.75	-	-	720 30.66 2.98 1.15 0.54	-	-	314 51.99 1.30 0.50 0.24	114 30.32 0.47 0.18 0.09	-	260 57.78 1.08 0.42 0.20
East Meadow (cdp)	3,438 9.17	2,418	897 37.10 37.10 26.09	-	-	417 36.94 46.49 17.25 12.13	-	-	-	-	128 36.78 14.27 5.29 3.72	-	-	-	-	-	-	-	-	-	-	-	-	-	-	-
Elmont (cdp)	6,799 20.82	3,178	1,159 36.47 36.47 17.05	-	-	730 38.22 62.99 22.97 10.74	-	-	-	-	165 30.00 14.24 5.19 2.43	-	-	-	-	-	-	-	-	-	-	-	-	-	-	-
Franklin Square (cdp)	3,386 11.54	1,173	559 47.66 47.66 16.51	-	-	200 44.05 35.78 17.05 5.91	-	-	-	-	-	-	-	-	-	-	-	-	-	-	-	-	-	-	-	-
Glen Cove (city)	3,109 11.68	1,053	362 34.38 34.38 11.64	-	-	93 28.62 25.69 8.83 2.99	-	-	-	-	-	-	-	-	-	-	140 35.18 38.67 13.30 4.50	-	-	-	-	-	-	-	-	-
Hicksville (cdp)	4,306 10.44	3,689	1,619 43.89 43.89 37.60	-	-	661 35.65 40.83 17.92 15.35	-	-	413 55.36 25.51 11.20 9.59	-	288 55.71 17.79 7.81 6.69	-	-	-	-	-	-	-	-	-	-	-	-	-	-	-
Jericho (cdp)	1,143 8.80	1,483	556 37.49 37.49 48.64	-	-	-	-	-	-	-	-	-	-	-	-	-	242 33.75 43.53 16.32 21.17	-	-	-	-	-	-	-	-	-
Mineola (village)	2,526 13.13	903	285 31.56 31.56 11.28	-	-	79 22.90 27.72 8.75 3.13	-	-	-	-	-	-	-	-	-	-	-	-	-	-	-	-	-	-	-	-
North Hempstead (town)	30,865 13.86	20,579	7,690 37.37 37.37 24.91	-	-	2,720 35.59 35.37 13.22 8.81	-	-	2,305 41.18 29.97 11.20 7.47	-	649 47.83 8.44 3.15 2.10	-	-	-	-	55 5.76 0.72 0.27 0.18	1,259 38.76 16.37 6.12 4.08	-	-	231 37.38 3.00 1.12 0.75	-	-	139 49.12 1.81 0.68 0.45	-	-	-

Notes: Please refer to the User's Guide for an explanation of data; data is arranged alphabetically by state, then county, then city within each county; table includes counties with populations greater than 49,999 unless noted and cities with populations greater than 9,999 whose Asian and/or NHPI population rates are greater than the national average; (1) Native Hawaiian and other Pacific Islander; (2) excludes Taiwanese; (3) includes Chamorro; (4) county does not meet population threshold but is shown in order to allow inclusion of city

Place	Total foreign-born naturalized citizens	Total Asian population	Asians who are foreign-born naturalized citizens	Total NHPI[1] population	NHPIs[1] who are foreign-born naturalized citizens	Asian Indian	Bangladeshi	Cambodian	Chinese[2]	Fijian	Filipino	Guamanian[3]	Hawaiian, Native	Hmong	Indonesian	Japanese	Korean	Laotian	Malaysian	Pakistani	Samoan	Sri Lankan	Taiwanese	Thai	Tongan	Vietnamese
North Merrick (cdp)	643 5.43	479	172 35.91 35.91 26.75	-	-	-	-	-	-	-	-	-	-	-	-	-	-	-	-	-	-	-	-	-	-	-
North New Hyde Park (cdp)	2,086 14.34	2,141	782 36.52 36.52 37.49	-	-	358 29.91 45.78 16.72 17.16	-	-	308 42.78 39.39 14.39 14.77	-	-	-	-	-	-	-	-	-	-	-	-	-	-	-	-	-
North Valley Stream (cdp)	3,360 21.28	1,469	522 35.53 35.53 15.54	-	-	283 44.71 54.21 19.26 8.42	-	-	-	-	-	-	-	-	-	-	-	-	-	-	-	-	-	-	-	-
Oyster Bay (town)	22,589 7.69	13,857	5,746 41.47 41.47 25.44	-	-	1,991 38.73 34.65 14.37 8.81	-	-	1,670 45.45 29.06 12.05 7.39	-	663 51.68 11.54 4.78 2.94	-	-	-	-	30 8.02 0.52 0.22 0.13	994 40.21 17.30 7.17 4.40	-	-	-	-	-	-	-	-	-
Plainview (cdp)	2,206 8.60	1,250	422 33.76 33.76 19.13	-	-	101 29.53 23.93 8.08 4.58	-	-	133 37.89 31.52 10.64 6.03	-	-	-	-	-	-	-	97 25.06 22.99 7.76 4.40	-	-	-	-	-	-	-	-	-
Port Washington (cdp)	1,559 10.26	962	330 34.30 34.30 21.17	-	-	90 35.16 27.27 9.36 5.77	-	-	-	-	-	-	-	-	-	-	-	-	-	-	-	-	-	-	-	-
Salisbury (cdp)	1,350 10.97	1,089	422 38.75 38.75 31.26	-	-	181 47.88 42.89 16.62 13.41	-	-	-	-	-	-	-	-	-	-	-	-	-	-	-	-	-	-	-	-
Syosset (cdp)	2,166 11.68	2,327	947 40.70 40.70 43.72	-	-	329 45.13 34.74 14.14 15.19	-	-	284 36.46 29.99 12.20 13.11	-	-	-	-	-	-	-	254 45.36 26.82 10.92 11.73	-	-	-	-	-	-	-	-	-
Valley Stream (village)	4,420 12.14	2,553	1,018 39.87 39.87 23.03	-	-	-	-	-	352 44.22 34.58 13.79 7.96	-	171 27.94 16.80 6.70 3.87	-	-	-	-	-	-	-	-	-	-	-	-	-	-	-
West Hempstead (cdp)	2,078 11.11	994	367 36.92 36.92 17.66	-	-	129 37.28 35.15 12.98 6.21	-	-	-	-	-	-	-	-	-	-	-	-	-	-	-	-	-	-	-	-

Notes: Please refer to the User's Guide for an explanation of data; data is arranged alphabetically by state, then county, then city within each county; table includes counties with populations greater than 49,999 unless noted and cities with populations greater than 9,999 whose Asian and/or NHPI population rates are greater than the national average; (1) Native Hawaiian and other Pacific Islander; (2) excludes Taiwanese; (3) includes Chamorro; (4) county does not meet population threshold but is shown in order to allow inclusion of city

Place	Total foreign-born naturalized citizens	Total Asian population	Asians who are foreign-born naturalized citizens	Total NHPI[1] population	NHPIs[1] who are foreign-born naturalized citizens	Asian Indian	Bangladeshi	Cambodian	Chinese[2]	Fijian	Filipino	Guamanian[3]	Hawaiian, Native	Hmong	Indonesian	Japanese	Korean	Laotian	Malaysian	Pakistani	Samoan	Sri Lankan	Taiwanese	Thai	Tongan	Vietnamese
Westbury (village)	1,928 13.52	694	294 42.36 42.36 15.25	-	-	-	-	-	-	-	-	-	-	-	-	-	-	-	-	-	-	-	-	-	-	-
Woodmere (cdp)	1,746 10.62	607	121 19.93 19.93 6.93	-	-	-	-	-	-	-	-	-	-	-	-	-	-	-	-	-	-	-	-	-	-	-
New York City	1,278,687 15.97	788,110	263,102 33.38 33.38 20.58	4,870	819 16.82 16.82 0.06	54,421 31.98 20.68 6.91 4.26	4,495 23.47 1.71 0.57 0.35	524 32.37 0.20 0.07 0.04	131,495 36.78 49.98 16.68 10.28	-	23,421 39.73 8.90 2.97 1.83	156 13.27 19.05 3.20 0.01	116 14.95 14.16 2.38 0.01	-	305 16.80 0.12 0.04 0.02	1,707 7.65 0.65 0.22 0.13	24,991 28.68 9.50 3.17 1.95	-	179 14.95 0.07 0.02 0.01	6,614 27.73 2.51 0.84 0.52	20 2.74 2.44 0.41 <0.01	431 21.51 0.16 0.05 0.03	2,281 46.48 0.87 0.29 0.18	958 25.06 0.36 0.12 0.07	-	5,654 45.93 2.15 0.72 0.44
New York County (Manhattan)	179,785 11.70	144,368	43,667 30.25 30.25 24.29	612	79 12.91 12.91 0.04	3,630 25.43 8.31 2.51 2.02	217 27.71 0.50 0.15 0.12	-	29,121 34.13 66.69 20.17 16.20	-	3,621 41.00 8.29 2.51 2.01	-	-	-	-	882 6.24 2.02 0.61 0.49	3,615 31.66 8.28 2.50 2.01	-	-	269 24.77 0.62 0.19 0.15	-	-	316 30.07 0.72 0.22 0.18	234 28.02 0.54 0.16 0.13	-	849 54.11 1.94 0.59 0.47
Niagara County	5,212 2.37	1,148	431 37.54 37.54 8.27	-	-	155 35.96 35.96 13.50 2.97	-	-	-	-	-	-	-	-	-	-	-	-	-	-	-	-	-	-	-	-
Oneida County	4,861 2.06	2,740	1,068 38.98 38.98 21.97	-	-	210 36.52 19.66 7.66 4.32	-	-	132 44.90 12.36 4.82 2.72	-	-	-	-	-	-	-	-	-	-	-	-	-	-	-	-	338 30.98 31.65 12.34 6.95
Onondaga County	13,498 2.95	9,593	3,161 32.95 32.95 23.42	-	-	579 29.20 18.32 6.04 4.29	-	-	496 29.25 15.69 5.17 3.67	-	362 47.69 11.45 3.77 2.68	-	-	-	-	42 11.97 1.33 0.44 0.31	611 46.82 19.33 6.37 4.53	-	-	-	-	-	-	-	-	607 35.23 19.20 6.33 4.50
Ontario County	1,575 1.57	696	347 49.86 49.86 22.03	-	-	-	-	-	-	-	-	-	-	-	-	-	-	-	-	-	-	-	-	-	-	-
Orange County	13,889 4.07	5,476	2,110 38.53 38.53 15.19	-	-	564 32.77 26.73 10.30 4.06	-	-	459 35.61 21.75 8.38 3.30	-	227 29.29 10.76 4.15 1.63	-	-	-	-	-	468 57.49 22.18 8.55 3.37	-	-	-	-	-	-	-	-	-
Oswego County	1,181 0.97	540	200 37.04 37.04 16.93	-	-	-	-	-	-	-	-	-	-	-	-	-	-	-	-	-	-	-	-	-	-	-

Notes: Please refer to the User's Guide for an explanation of data; data is arranged alphabetically by state, then county, then city within each county; table includes counties with populations greater than 49,999 unless noted and cities with populations greater than 9,999 whose Asian and/or NHPI population rates are greater than the national average; (1) Native Hawaiian and other Pacific Islander; (2) excludes Taiwanese; (3) includes Chamorro; (4) county does not meet population threshold but is shown in order to allow inclusion of city

Place	Total foreign-born naturalized citizens	Total Asian population	Asians who are foreign-born naturalized citizens	Total NHPI[1] population	NHPIs[1] who are foreign-born naturalized citizens	Asian Indian	Bangladeshi	Cambodian	Chinese[2]	Fijian	Filipino	Guamanian[3]	Hawaiian, Native	Hmong	Indonesian	Japanese	Korean	Laotian	Malaysian	Pakistani	Samoan	Sri Lankan	Taiwanese	Thai	Tongan	Vietnamese
Otsego County	993 1.61	304	82 26.97 26.97 8.26	-	-	-	-	-	-	-	-	-	-	-	-	-	-	-	-	-	-	-	-	-	-	-
Putnam County	4,356 4.55	1,213	389 32.07 32.07 8.93	-	-	149 35.90 38.30 12.28 3.42	-	-	95 22.41 24.42 7.83 2.18	-	-	-	-	-	-	-	-	-	-	-	-	-	-	-	-	-
Queens County (Queens)	466,608 20.93	394,314	132,674 33.65 33.65 28.43	1,394	276 19.80 19.80 0.06	35,512 32.30 26.77 9.01 7.61	2,862 23.08 2.16 0.73 0.61	-	52,997 38.48 39.95 13.44 11.36	-	13,073 39.80 9.85 3.32 2.80	-	-	-	200 16.09 0.15 0.05 0.04	537 10.16 0.40 0.14 0.12	16,736 26.88 12.61 4.24 3.59	-	83 14.64 0.06 0.02 0.02	3,573 31.75 2.69 0.91 0.77	-	231 24.65 0.17 0.06 0.05	1,758 50.77 1.33 0.45 0.38	557 23.56 0.42 0.14 0.12	-	1,779 47.58 1.34 0.45 0.38
Rensselaer County	2,963 1.94	2,430	439 18.07 18.07 14.82	-	-	51 11.70 11.62 2.10 1.72	-	-	167 15.41 38.04 6.87 5.64	-	-	-	-	-	-	-	124 33.24 28.25 5.10 4.18	-	-	-	-	-	-	-	-	-
Richmond Co. (Staten Island)	39,800 8.97	24,538	10,174 41.46 41.46 25.56	-	-	2,318 36.00 22.78 9.45 5.82	-	-	3,054 41.71 30.02 12.45 7.67	-	2,503 48.24 24.60 10.20 6.29	-	-	-	-	-	1,438 44.36 14.13 5.86 3.61	-	-	298 38.60 2.93 1.21 0.75	-	134 25.43 1.32 0.55 0.34	-	-	-	-
Rockland County	27,846 9.71	16,130	6,076 37.67 37.67 21.82	-	-	1,975 35.38 32.50 12.24 7.09	-	-	831 41.55 13.68 5.15 2.98	-	1,838 40.80 30.25 11.39 6.60	-	-	-	-	-	693 36.26 11.41 4.30 2.49	-	-	-	-	-	-	-	-	-
Clarkstown (town)	8,128 9.90	6,705	2,437 36.35 36.35 29.98	-	-	820 34.25 33.65 12.23 10.09	-	-	271 34.13 11.12 4.04 3.33	-	873 40.01 35.82 13.02 10.74	-	-	-	-	-	247 34.26 10.14 3.68 3.04	-	-	-	-	-	-	-	-	-
Nanuet (cdp)	2,038 12.20	1,559	518 33.23 33.23 25.42	-	-	183 31.61 35.33 11.74 8.98	-	-	-	-	-	-	-	-	-	-	-	-	-	-	-	-	-	-	-	-
New City (cdp)	3,301 9.67	2,583	939 36.35 36.35 28.45	-	-	319 29.90 33.97 12.35 9.66	-	-	-	-	238 40.34 25.35 9.21 7.21	-	-	-	-	-	-	-	-	-	-	-	-	-	-	-
Orangetown (town)	4,141 8.66	3,001	1,148 38.25 38.25 27.72	-	-	261 38.33 22.74 8.70 6.30	-	-	246 42.34 21.43 8.20 5.94	-	322 45.22 28.05 10.73 7.78	-	-	-	-	-	192 33.80 16.72 6.40 4.64	-	-	-	-	-	-	-	-	-

Notes: Please refer to the User's Guide for an explanation of data; data is arranged alphabetically by state, then county, then city within each county; table includes counties with populations greater than 49,999 unless noted and cities with populations greater than 9,999 whose Asian and/or NHPI population rates are greater than the national average; (1) Native Hawaiian and other Pacific Islander; (2) excludes Taiwanese; (3) includes Chamorro; (4) county does not meet population threshold but is shown in order to allow inclusion of city

Place	Total foreign-born naturalized citizens	Total Asian population	Asians who are foreign-born naturalized citizens	Total NHPI[1] population	NHPIs[1] who are foreign-born naturalized citizens	Asian Indian	Bangladeshi	Cambodian	Chinese[2]	Fijian	Filipino	Guamanian[3]	Hawaiian, Native	Hmong	Indonesian	Japanese	Korean	Laotian	Malaysian	Pakistani	Samoan	Sri Lankan	Taiwanese	Thai	Tongan	Vietnamese
Ramapo (town)	11,707 10.75	5,131	1,969 38.37 38.37 16.82	-	-	722 35.83 36.67 14.07 6.17	-	-	253 53.49 12.85 4.93 2.16	-	530 39.09 26.92 10.33 4.53	-	-	-	-	-	209 38.78 10.61 4.07 1.79	-	-	-	-	-	-	-	-	-
Spring Valley (village)	3,393 13.37	1,479	447 30.22 30.22 13.17	-	-	185 23.90 41.39 12.51 5.45	-	-	-	-	-	-	-	-	-	-	-	-	-	-	-	-	-	-	-	-
St. Lawrence County	1,908 1.70	657	184 28.01 28.01 9.64	-	-	-	-	-	-	-	-	-	-	-	-	-	-	-	-	-	-	-	-	-	-	-
Saratoga County	3,881 1.93	2,179	1,023 46.95 46.95 26.36	-	-	292 42.07 28.54 13.40 7.52	-	-	156 39.59 15.25 7.16 4.02	-	-	-	-	-	-	-	322 72.20 31.48 14.78 8.30	-	-	-	-	-	-	-	-	-
Schenectady County	4,932 3.37	2,850	907 31.82 31.82 18.39	-	-	292 25.46 32.19 10.25 5.92	-	-	279 33.14 30.76 9.79 5.66	-	-	-	-	-	-	-	-	-	-	-	-	-	-	-	-	-
Niskayuna (town)	1,269 6.26	1,175	402 34.21 34.21 31.68	-	-	130 25.05 32.34 11.06 10.24	-	-	-	-	-	-	-	-	-	-	-	-	-	-	-	-	-	-	-	-
Steuben County	1,084 1.10	799	302 37.80 37.80 27.86	-	-	-	-	-	-	-	-	-	-	-	-	-	-	-	-	-	-	-	-	-	-	-
Suffolk County	77,416 5.45	34,143	12,799 37.49 37.49 16.53	427	55 12.88 12.88 0.07	3,682 35.89 28.77 10.78 4.76	-	-	3,273 33.59 25.57 9.59 4.23	-	1,791 44.17 13.99 5.25 2.31	-	-	-	-	244 23.37 1.91 0.71 0.32	1,898 48.55 14.83 5.56 2.45	-	-	695 34.63 5.43 2.04 0.90	-	-	248 57.94 1.94 0.73 0.32	121 31.27 0.95 0.35 0.16	-	334 47.44 2.61 0.98 0.43
Coram (cdp)	1,992 5.69	1,284	364 28.35 28.35 18.27	-	-	-	-	-	117 27.34 32.14 9.11 5.87	-	-	-	-	-	-	-	-	-	-	-	-	-	-	-	-	-
Dix Hills (cdp)	2,736 10.48	1,955	881 45.06 45.06 32.20	-	-	330 39.71 37.46 16.88 12.06	-	-	224 50.22 25.43 11.46 8.19	-	-	-	-	-	-	-	-	-	-	-	-	-	-	-	-	-

Notes: Please refer to the User's Guide for an explanation of data; data is arranged alphabetically by state, then county, then city within each county; table includes counties with populations greater than 49,999 unless noted and cities with populations greater than 9,999 whose Asian and/or NHPI population rates are greater than the national average; (1) Native Hawaiian and other Pacific Islander; (2) excludes Taiwanese; (3) includes Chamorro; (4) county does not meet population threshold but is shown in order to allow inclusion of city

Place	Total foreign-born naturalized citizens	Total Asian population	Asians who are foreign-born naturalized citizens	Total NHPI[1] population	NHPIs[1] who are foreign-born naturalized citizens	Asian Indian	Bangladeshi	Cambodian	Chinese[2]	Fijian	Filipino	Guamanian[3]	Hawaiian, Native	Hmong	Indonesian	Japanese	Korean	Laotian	Malaysian	Pakistani	Samoan	Sri Lankan	Taiwanese	Thai	Tongan	Vietnamese
Elwood (cdp)	835 7.70	712	309 43.40 43.40 37.01	-	-	-	-	-	-	-	-	-	-	-	-	-	-	-	-	-	-	-	-	-	-	-
Lake Grove (village)	467 4.49	554	99 17.87 17.87 21.20	-	-	-	-	-	-	-	-	-	-	-	-	-	-	-	-	-	-	-	-	-	-	-
Melville (cdp)	1,052 7.24	637	297 46.62 46.62 28.23	-	-	-	-	-	-	-	-	-	-	-	-	-	-	-	-	-	-	-	-	-	-	-
Setauket-East Setauket (cdp)	905 5.67	1,477	372 25.19 25.19 41.10	-	-	-	-	-	124 18.34 33.33 8.40 13.70	-	-	-	-	-	-	-	-	-	-	-	-	-	-	-	-	-
Stony Brook (cdp)	891 6.51	802	348 43.39 43.39 39.06	-	-	-	-	-	189 44.89 54.31 23.57 21.21	-	-	-	-	-	-	-	-	-	-	-	-	-	-	-	-	-
Sullivan County	3,038 4.11	855	257 30.06 30.06 8.46	-	-	-	-	-	-	-	-	-	-	-	-	-	-	-	-	-	-	-	-	-	-	-
Tioga County	558 1.08	349	155 44.41 44.41 27.78	-	-	-	-	-	-	-	-	-	-	-	-	-	-	-	-	-	-	-	-	-	-	-
Tompkins County	2,874 2.98	7,146	988 13.83 13.83 34.38	-	-	183 17.43 18.52 2.56 6.37	-	-	424 13.63 42.91 5.93 14.75	-	-	-	-	-	-	18 3.09 1.82 0.25 0.63	141 11.72 14.27 1.97 4.91	-	-	-	-	-	-	-	-	-
Ithaca (city)	1,203 4.15	4,039	510 12.63 12.63 42.39	-	-	47 8.92 9.22 1.16 3.91	-	-	262 13.14 51.37 6.49 21.78	-	-	-	-	-	-	-	59 12.42 11.57 1.46 4.90	-	-	-	-	-	-	-	-	-
Lansing (town)	409 3.97	1,071	210 19.61 19.61 51.34	-	-	-	-	-	-	-	-	-	-	-	-	-	-	-	-	-	-	-	-	-	-	-

Notes: Please refer to the User's Guide for an explanation of data; data is arranged alphabetically by state, then county, then city within each county; table includes counties with populations greater than 49,999 unless noted and cities with populations greater than 9,999 whose Asian and/or NHPI population rates are greater than the national average; (1) Native Hawaiian and other Pacific Islander; (2) excludes Taiwanese; (3) includes Chamorro; (4) county does not meet population threshold but is shown in order to allow inclusion of city

Place	Total foreign-born naturalized citizens	Total Asian population	Asians who are foreign-born naturalized citizens	Total NHPI[1] population	NHPIs[1] who are foreign-born naturalized citizens	Asian Indian	Bangladeshi	Cambodian	Chinese[2]	Fijian	Filipino	Guamanian[3]	Hawaiian, Native	Hmong	Indonesian	Japanese	Korean	Laotian	Malaysian	Pakistani	Samoan	Sri Lankan	Taiwanese	Thai	Tongan	Vietnamese
Ulster County	5,482 3.08	1,815	532 29.31 29.31 9.70	-	-	-	-	-	190 35.32 35.71 10.47 3.47	-	-	-	-	-	-	-	-	-	-	-	-	-	-	-	-	-
New Paltz (town)	605 4.72	576	111 19.27 19.27 18.35	-	-	-	-	-	-	-	-	-	-	-	-	-	-	-	-	-	-	-	-	-	-	-
Warren County	996 1.57	504	209 41.47 41.47 20.98	-	-	-	-	-	-	-	-	-	-	-	-	-	-	-	-	-	-	-	-	-	-	-
Wayne County	1,388 1.48	394	209 53.05 53.05 15.06	-	-	-	-	-	-	-	-	-	-	-	-	-	-	-	-	-	-	-	-	-	-	-
Westchester County	85,546 9.26	41,751	11,746 28.13 28.13 13.73	-	-	4,078 28.13 34.72 9.77 4.77	-	-	2,749 38.79 23.40 6.58 3.21	-	1,737 35.05 14.79 4.16 2.03	-	-	-	-	425 5.67 3.62 1.02 0.50	1,723 40.75 14.67 4.13 2.01	-	-	244 28.98 2.08 0.58 0.29	-	-	132 39.05 1.12 0.32 0.15	165 27.78 1.40 0.40 0.19	-	-
Dobbs Ferry (village)	962 9.06	750	216 28.80 28.80 22.45	-	-	-	-	-	-	-	-	-	-	-	-	-	-	-	-	-	-	-	-	-	-	-
Eastchester (cdp)	1,483 7.99	1,293	238 18.41 18.41 16.05	-	-	-	-	-	-	-	-	-	-	-	-	4 0.73 1.68 0.31 0.27	-	-	-	-	-	-	-	-	-	-
Eastchester (town)	2,278 7.27	2,265	338 14.92 14.92 14.84	-	-	-	-	-	-	-	-	-	-	-	-	11 0.91 3.25 0.49 0.48	-	-	-	-	-	-	-	-	-	-
Greenburgh (town)	8,370 9.65	7,818	2,207 28.23 28.23 26.37	-	-	778 30.09 35.25 9.95 9.30	-	-	490 38.43 22.20 6.27 5.85	-	268 46.29 12.14 3.43 3.20	-	-	-	-	117 5.98 5.30 1.50 1.40	421 42.10 19.08 5.39 5.03	-	-	-	-	-	-	-	-	-
Harrison (village)	1,988 8.23	1,336	186 13.92 13.92 9.36	-	-	-	-	-	-	-	-	-	-	-	-	20 2.89 10.75 1.50 1.01	-	-	-	-	-	-	-	-	-	-

Notes: Please refer to the User's Guide for an explanation of data; data is arranged alphabetically by state, then county, then city within each county; table includes counties with populations greater than 49,999 unless noted and cities with populations greater than 9,999 whose Asian and/or NHPI population rates are greater than the national average; (1) Native Hawaiian and other Pacific Islander; (2) excludes Taiwanese; (3) includes Chamorro; (4) county does not meet population threshold but is shown in order to allow inclusion of city

Place	Total foreign-born naturalized citizens	Total Asian population	Asians who are foreign-born naturalized citizens	Total NHPI[1] population	NHPIs[1] who are foreign-born naturalized citizens	Asian Indian	Bangladeshi	Cambodian	Chinese[2]	Fijian	Filipino	Guamanian[3]	Hawaiian, Native	Hmong	Indonesian	Japanese	Korean	Laotian	Malaysian	Pakistani	Samoan	Sri Lankan	Taiwanese	Thai	Tongan	Vietnamese
New Castle (town)	1,228 7.02	1,014	391 38.56 38.56 31.84	-	-	119 29.46 30.43 11.74 9.69	-	-	162 52.60 41.43 15.98 13.19	-	-	-	-	-	-	-	-	-	-	-	-	-	-	-	-	-
New Rochelle (city)	7,268 10.07	2,686	862 32.09 32.09 11.86	-	-	402 34.21 46.64 14.97 5.53	-	-	199 36.78 23.09 7.41 2.74	-	-	-	-	-	-	-	-	-	-	-	-	-	-	-	-	-
North Castle (town)	805 7.42	471	189 40.13 40.13 23.48	-	-	-	-	-	-	-	-	-	-	-	-	-	-	-	-	-	-	-	-	-	-	-
Ossining (town)	2,862 7.83	1,510	481 31.85 31.85 16.81	-	-	247 35.49 51.35 16.36 8.63	-	-	-	-	-	-	-	-	-	-	-	-	-	-	-	-	-	-	-	-
Ossining (village)	2,030 8.45	937	244 26.04 26.04 12.02	-	-	84 27.54 34.43 8.96 4.14	-	-	-	-	-	-	-	-	-	-	-	-	-	-	-	-	-	-	-	-
Pelham (town)	833 7.02	454	187 41.19 41.19 22.45	-	-	-	-	-	-	-	-	-	-	-	-	-	-	-	-	-	-	-	-	-	-	-
Rye (city)	1,050 7.02	1,075	164 15.26 15.26 15.62	-	-	-	-	-	-	-	-	-	-	-	-	23 3.57 14.02 2.14 2.19	-	-	-	-	-	-	-	-	-	-
Scarsdale (village)	1,318 7.39	2,225	480 21.57 21.57 36.42	-	-	99 23.86 20.63 4.45 7.51	-	-	158 42.02 32.92 7.10 11.99	-	-	-	-	-	-	32 4.08 6.67 1.44 2.43	113 29.50 23.54 5.08 8.57	-	-	-	-	-	-	-	-	-
Tarrytown (village)	980 8.84	638	122 19.12 19.12 12.45	-	-	-	-	-	-	-	-	-	-	-	-	-	-	-	-	-	-	-	-	-	-	-
White Plains (city)	5,579 10.51	2,199	468 21.28 21.28 8.39	-	-	117 14.87 25.00 5.32 2.10	-	-	199 35.41 42.52 9.05 3.57	-	-	-	-	-	-	-	-	-	-	-	-	-	-	-	-	-

Notes: Please refer to the User's Guide for an explanation of data; data is arranged alphabetically by state, then county, then city within each county; table includes counties with populations greater than 49,999 unless noted and cities with populations greater than 9,999 whose Asian and/or NHPI population rates are greater than the national average; (1) Native Hawaiian and other Pacific Islander; (2) excludes Taiwanese; (3) includes Chamorro; (4) county does not meet population threshold but is shown in order to allow inclusion of city

Place	Total foreign-born naturalized citizens	Total Asian population	Asians who are foreign-born naturalized citizens	Total NHPI[1] population	NHPIs[1] who are foreign-born naturalized citizens	Asian Indian	Bangladeshi	Cambodian	Chinese[2]	Fijian	Filipino	Guamanian[3]	Hawaiian, Native	Hmong	Indonesian	Japanese	Korean	Laotian	Malaysian	Pakistani	Samoan	Sri Lankan	Taiwanese	Thai	Tongan	Vietnamese
Yonkers (city)	22,521 11.49	9,564	2,828 29.57 29.57 12.56	-	-	1,070 22.82 37.84 11.19 4.75	-	-	455 52.06 16.09 4.76 2.02	-	570 31.37 20.16 5.96 2.53	-	-	-	-	-	410 38.57 14.50 4.29 1.82	-	-	-	-	-	-	-	-	-
NORTH CAROLINA	112,822 1.40	111,292	32,092 28.84 28.84 28.44	3,699	257 6.95 6.95 0.23	6,553 25.85 20.42 5.89 5.81	-	697 29.41 2.17 0.63 0.62	4,804 27.45 14.97 4.32 4.26	-	3,933 38.58 12.26 3.53 3.49	81 6.77 31.52 2.19 0.07	0 0.00 0.00 0.00 0.00	936 13.73 2.92 0.84 0.83	-	1,139 18.87 3.55 1.02 1.01	5,068 40.86 15.79 4.55 4.49	1,256 25.29 3.91 1.13 1.11	-	516 27.53 1.61 0.46 0.46	82 16.57 31.91 2.22 0.07	-	465 47.89 1.45 0.42 0.41	471 28.98 1.47 0.42 0.42	-	5,284 33.86 16.47 4.75 4.68
Alamance County	1,530 1.17	1,155	343 29.70 29.70 22.42	-	-	-	-	-	-	-	-	-	-	-	-	-	-	-	-	-	-	-	-	-	-	-
Buncombe County	2,672 1.30	1,849	482 26.07 26.07 18.04	-	-	123 22.28 25.52 6.65 4.60	-	-	-	-	-	-	-	-	-	-	-	-	-	-	-	-	-	-	-	-
Burke County	1,131 1.27	3,023	683 22.59 22.59 60.39	-	-	-	-	-	-	-	-	-	-	319 15.91 46.71 10.55 28.21	-	-	-	191 38.51 27.96 6.32 16.89	-	-	-	-	-	-	-	-
Cabarrus County	1,304 0.99	1,072	308 28.73 28.73 23.62	-	-	-	-	-	-	-	-	-	-	-	-	-	-	-	-	-	-	-	-	-	-	-
Catawba County	1,910 1.35	3,792	699 18.43 18.43 36.60	-	-	-	-	-	-	-	-	-	-	180 10.03 25.75 4.75 9.42	-	-	-	60 9.23 8.58 1.58 3.14	-	-	-	-	-	-	-	91 18.09 13.02 2.40 4.76
Hickory (city)	832 2.22	1,616	300 18.56 18.56 36.06	-	-	-	-	-	-	-	-	-	-	7 1.29 2.33 0.43 0.84	-	-	-	-	-	-	-	-	-	-	-	-
Cleveland County	507 0.53	785	225 28.66 28.66 44.38	-	-	-	-	-	-	-	-	-	-	-	-	-	-	-	-	-	-	-	-	-	-	-
Craven County	1,226 1.34	1,148	409 35.63 35.63 33.36	-	-	-	-	-	-	-	202 42.35 49.39 17.60 16.48	-	-	-	-	-	-	-	-	-	-	-	-	-	-	-

Notes: Please refer to the User's Guide for an explanation of data; data is arranged alphabetically by state, then county, then city within each county; table includes counties with populations greater than 49,999 unless noted and cities with populations greater than 9,999 whose Asian and/or NHPI population rates are greater than the national average; (1) Native Hawaiian and other Pacific Islander; (2) excludes Taiwanese; (3) includes Chamorro; (4) county does not meet population threshold but is shown in order to allow inclusion of city

Place	Total foreign-born naturalized citizens	Total Asian population	Asians who are foreign-born naturalized citizens	Total NHPI[1] population	NHPIs[1] who are foreign-born naturalized citizens	Asian Indian	Bangladeshi	Cambodian	Chinese[2]	Fijian	Filipino	Guamanian[3]	Hawaiian, Native	Hmong	Indonesian	Japanese	Korean	Laotian	Malaysian	Pakistani	Samoan	Sri Lankan	Taiwanese	Thai	Tongan	Vietnamese
Cumberland County	8,185	6,126	2,786	503	9	184	-	-	-	-	453	-	-	-	-	227	1,151	-	-	-	-	-	-	-	-	431
	2.70		45.48		1.79	27.71					46.13					50.33	54.81									59.78
						6.60					16.26					8.15	41.31									15.47
			45.48		1.79	3.00					7.39					3.71	18.79									7.04
			34.04		0.11	2.25					5.53					2.77	14.06									5.27
Davidson County	1,061	1,267	289	-	-	-	-	88	-	-	-	-	-	-	-	-	-	-	-	-	-	-	-	-	-	-
	0.72		22.81					17.02																		
								30.45																		
			22.81					6.95																		
			27.24					8.29																		
Durham County	4,592	7,052	1,608	-	-	498	-	-	372	-	161	-	-	-	-	22	224	-	-	-	-	-	-	-	-	-
	2.06		22.80			18.38			22.99		27.57					5.70	37.21									
						30.97			23.13		10.01					1.37	13.93									
			22.80			7.06			5.28		2.28					0.31	3.18									
			35.02			10.84			8.10		3.51					0.48	4.88									
Forsyth County	3,942	3,227	1,058	-	-	147	-	-	200	-	104	-	-	-	-	-	-	-	-	-	-	-	-	-	-	243
	1.29		32.79			24.22			21.76		36.75															46.73
						13.89			18.90		9.83															22.97
			32.79			4.56			6.20		3.22															7.53
			26.84			3.73			5.07		2.64															6.16
Gaston County	1,455	1,508	516	-	-	-	-	-	-	-	-	-	-	-	-	-	-	-	-	-	-	-	-	-	-	190
	0.76		34.22																							37.62
																										36.82
			34.22																							12.60
			35.46																							13.06
Guilford County	6,901	9,341	2,129	-	-	492	-	-	330	-	147	-	-	-	-	-	309	141	-	57	-	-	-	-	-	424
	1.64		22.79			28.16			32.45		27.17						32.05	28.89		13.94						14.30
						23.11			15.50		6.90						14.51	6.62		2.68						19.92
			22.79			5.27			3.53		1.57						3.31	1.51		0.61						4.54
			30.85			7.13			4.78		2.13						4.48	2.04		0.83						6.14
Halifax County	198	375	54	-	-	-	-	-	-	-	-	-	-	-	-	-	-	-	-	-	-	-	-	-	-	-
	0.35		14.40																							
			14.40																							
			27.27																							
Harnett County	1,155	639	217	-	-	-	-	-	-	-	-	-	-	-	-	-	-	-	-	-	-	-	-	-	-	-
	1.27		33.96																							
			33.96																							
			18.79																							
Henderson County	1,801	440	219	-	-	-	-	-	-	-	-	-	-	-	-	-	-	-	-	-	-	-	-	-	-	-
	2.02		49.77																							
			49.77																							
			12.16																							
Iredell County	1,031	1,110	284	-	-	-	-	-	-	-	-	-	-	-	-	-	-	-	-	-	-	-	-	-	-	-
	0.84		25.59																							
			25.59																							
			27.55																							

Notes: Please refer to the User's Guide for an explanation of data; data is arranged alphabetically by state, then county, then city within each county; table includes counties with populations greater than 49,999 unless noted and cities with populations greater than 9,999 whose Asian and/or NHPI population rates are greater than the national average; (1) Native Hawaiian and other Pacific Islander; (2) excludes Taiwanese; (3) includes Chamorro; (4) county does not meet population threshold but is shown in order to allow inclusion of city

Place	Total foreign-born naturalized citizens	Total Asian population	Asians who are foreign-born naturalized citizens	Total NHPI[1] population	NHPIs[1] who are foreign-born naturalized citizens	Asian Indian	Bangladeshi	Cambodian	Chinese[2]	Fijian	Filipino	Guamanian[3]	Hawaiian, Native	Hmong	Indonesian	Japanese	Korean	Laotian	Malaysian	Pakistani	Samoan	Sri Lankan	Taiwanese	Thai	Tongan	Vietnamese
Johnston County	1,312 1.08	579	160 27.63 27.63 12.20	-	-	-	-	-	-	-	-	-	-	-	-	-	-	-	-	-	-	-	-	-	-	-
Lenoir County	494 0.83	392	128 32.65 32.65 25.91	-	-	-	-	-	-	-	-	-	-	-	-	-	-	-	-	-	-	-	-	-	-	-
Mecklenburg County	19,810 2.85	20,819	6,305 30.28 30.28 31.83	-	-	1,497 28.98 23.74 7.19 7.56	-	221 28.81 3.51 1.06 1.12	846 28.91 13.42 4.06 4.27	-	516 44.68 8.18 2.48 2.60	-	-	23 4.04 0.36 0.11 0.12	-	78 9.35 1.24 0.37 0.39	937 38.35 14.86 4.50 4.73	303 34.59 4.81 1.46 1.53	-	-	-	-	-	-	-	1,695 36.44 26.88 8.14 8.56
Nash County	726 0.83	413	122 29.54 29.54 16.80	-	-	-	-	-	-	-	-	-	-	-	-	-	-	-	-	-	-	-	-	-	-	-
New Hanover County	2,099 1.31	1,381	465 33.67 33.67 22.15	-	-	-	-	-	-	-	-	-	-	-	-	-	-	-	-	-	-	-	-	-	-	-
Onslow County	2,686 1.79	2,566	947 36.91 36.91 35.26	400	44 11.00 11.00 1.64	-	-	-	-	-	444 38.81 46.88 17.30 16.53	-	-	-	-	150 30.80 15.84 5.85 5.58	-	-	-	-	-	-	-	-	-	-
Orange County	2,683 2.27	4,646	911 19.61 19.61 33.95	-	-	179 25.28 19.65 3.85 6.67	-	-	288 17.12 31.61 6.20 10.73	-	-	-	-	-	-	27 5.18 2.96 0.58 1.01	152 19.39 16.68 3.27 5.67	-	-	-	-	-	-	-	-	-
Carrboro (town)	348 2.08	802	65 8.10 8.10 18.68	-	-	-	-	-	-	-	-	-	-	-	-	-	-	-	-	-	-	-	-	-	-	-
Chapel Hill (town)	1,394 2.86	3,327	568 17.07 17.07 40.75	-	-	147 25.65 25.88 4.42 10.55	-	-	161 13.27 28.35 4.84 11.55	-	-	-	-	-	-	-	96 17.20 16.90 2.89 6.89	-	-	-	-	-	-	-	-	-
Pitt County	1,174 0.88	1,245	348 27.95 27.95 29.64	-	-	-	-	-	-	-	-	-	-	-	-	-	-	-	-	-	-	-	-	-	-	-

Notes: Please refer to the User's Guide for an explanation of data; data is arranged alphabetically by state, then county, then city within each county; table includes counties with populations greater than 49,999 unless noted and cities with populations greater than 9,999 whose Asian and/or NHPI population rates are greater than the national average; (1) Native Hawaiian and other Pacific Islander; (2) excludes Taiwanese; (3) includes Chamorro; (4) county does not meet population threshold but is shown in order to allow inclusion of city

Place	Total foreign-born naturalized citizens	Total Asian population	Asians who are foreign-born naturalized citizens	Total NHPI[1] population	NHPIs[1] who are foreign-born naturalized citizens	Asian Indian	Bangladeshi	Cambodian	Chinese[2]	Fijian	Filipino	Guamanian[3]	Hawaiian, Native	Hmong	Indonesian	Japanese	Korean	Laotian	Malaysian	Pakistani	Samoan	Sri Lankan	Taiwanese	Thai	Tongan	Vietnamese
Randolph County	1,138 0.87	785	200 25.48 25.48 17.57	-	-	-	-	-	-	-	-	-	-	-	-	-	-	-	-	-	-	-	-	-	-	-
Robeson County	770 0.62	936	308 32.91 32.91 40.00	-	-	-	-	-	-	-	-	-	-	-	-	-	-	-	-	-	-	-	-	-	-	-
Rowan County	821 0.63	808	172 21.29 21.29 20.95	-	-	-	-	-	-	-	-	-	-	-	-	-	-	-	-	-	-	-	-	-	-	-
Stanly County	401 0.69	752	157 20.88 20.88 39.15	-	-	-	-	-	-	-	-	-	-	25 7.86 15.92 3.32 6.23	-	-	-	-	-	-	-	-	-	-	-	-
Surry County	636 0.89	478	77 16.11 16.11 12.11	-	-	-	-	-	-	-	-	-	-	-	-	-	-	-	-	-	-	-	-	-	-	-
Union County	1,533 1.24	586	240 40.96 40.96 15.66	-	-	-	-	-	-	-	-	-	-	-	-	-	-	-	-	-	-	-	-	-	-	-
Wake County	16,362 2.61	20,722	6,092 29.40 29.40 37.23	-	-	1,687 24.30 27.69 8.14 10.31	-	-	1,421 28.83 23.33 6.86 8.68	-	472 38.94 7.75 2.28 2.88	-	-	-	-	80 9.63 1.31 0.39 0.49	611 27.81 10.03 2.95 3.73	-	-	202 45.39 3.32 0.97 1.23	-	-	-	-	-	1,054 45.18 17.30 5.09 6.44
Apex (town)	443 2.21	761	183 24.05 24.05 41.31	-	-	-	-	-	-	-	-	-	-	-	-	-	-	-	-	-	-	-	-	-	-	-
Cary (town)	4,145 4.38	7,521	2,184 29.04 29.04 52.69	-	-	861 25.47 39.42 11.45 20.77	-	-	542 28.41 24.82 7.21 13.08	-	-	-	-	-	-	28 7.82 1.28 0.37 0.68	178 34.63 8.15 2.37 4.29	-	-	-	-	-	-	-	-	248 54.63 11.36 3.30 5.98
Wayne County	1,515 1.34	1,078	506 46.94 46.94 33.40	-	-	-	-	-	-	-	-	-	-	-	-	-	-	-	-	-	-	-	-	-	-	-

Notes: Please refer to the User's Guide for an explanation of data; data is arranged alphabetically by state, then county, then city within each county; table includes counties with populations greater than 49,999 unless noted and cities with populations greater than 9,999 whose Asian and/or NHPI population rates are greater than the national average; (1) Native Hawaiian and other Pacific Islander; (2) excludes Taiwanese; (3) includes Chamorro; (4) county does not meet population threshold but is shown in order to allow inclusion of city

Place	Total foreign-born naturalized citizens	Total Asian population	Asians who are foreign-born naturalized citizens	Total NHPI[1] population	NHPIs[1] who are foreign-born naturalized citizens	Asian Indian	Bangladeshi	Cambodian	Chinese[2]	Fijian	Filipino	Guamanian[3]	Hawaiian, Native	Hmong	Indonesian	Japanese	Korean	Laotian	Malaysian	Pakistani	Samoan	Sri Lankan	Taiwanese	Thai	Tongan	Vietnamese
Wilkes County	360 0.55	332	51 15.36 15.36 14.17	-	-	-	-	-	-	-	-	-	-	-	-	-	-	-	-	-	-	-	-	-	-	-
NORTH DAKOTA	5,156 0.80	3,342	1,038 31.06 31.06 20.13	-	-	280 26.87 26.97 8.38 5.43	-	-	103 24.01 9.92 3.08 2.00	-	168 29.12 16.18 5.03 3.26	-	-	-	-	-	190 52.05 18.30 5.69 3.69	-	-	-	-	-	-	-	-	-
Cass County	1,006 0.82	1,422	359 25.25 25.25 35.69	-	-	85 20.53 23.68 5.98 8.45	-	-	-	-	-	-	-	-	-	-	-	-	-	-	-	-	-	-	-	-
Grand Forks County	704 1.06	632	159 25.16 25.16 22.59	-	-	-	-	-	-	-	-	-	-	-	-	-	-	-	-	-	-	-	-	-	-	-
Ward County	639 1.09	307	130 42.35 42.35 20.34	-	-	-	-	-	-	-	-	-	-	-	-	-	-	-	-	-	-	-	-	-	-	-
OHIO	169,295 1.49	132,131	41,939 31.74 31.74 24.77	2,641	115 4.35 4.35 0.07	10,665 28.35 25.43 8.07 6.30	153 23.61 0.36 0.12 0.09	762 29.14 1.82 0.58 0.45	7,995 28.89 19.06 6.05 4.72	-	5,811 44.09 13.86 4.40 3.43	22 3.30 19.13 0.83 0.01	0 0.00 0.00 0.00 0.00	-	120 11.31 0.29 0.09 0.07	1,117 10.85 2.66 0.85 0.66	6,083 43.81 14.50 4.60 3.59	1,162 38.76 2.77 0.88 0.69	55 15.80 0.13 0.04 0.03	463 28.21 1.10 0.35 0.27	37 7.54 32.17 1.40 0.02	114 22.18 0.27 0.09 0.07	863 39.00 2.06 0.65 0.51	568 29.89 1.35 0.43 0.34	-	4,763 45.99 11.36 3.60 2.81
Allen County	652 0.60	534	234 43.82 43.82 35.89	-	-	-	-	-	-	-	-	-	-	-	-	-	-	-	-	-	-	-	-	-	-	-
Ashtabula County	974 0.95	287	136 47.39 47.39 13.96	-	-	-	-	-	-	-	-	-	-	-	-	-	-	-	-	-	-	-	-	-	-	-
Athens County	399 0.64	1,116	99 8.87 8.87 24.81	-	-	-	-	-	-	-	-	-	-	-	-	-	-	-	-	-	-	-	-	-	-	-
Athens (city)	177 0.84	876	51 5.82 5.82 28.81	-	-	-	-	-	-	-	-	-	-	-	-	-	-	-	-	-	-	-	-	-	-	-

Notes: Please refer to the User's Guide for an explanation of data; data is arranged alphabetically by state, then county, then city within each county; table includes counties with populations greater than 49,999 unless noted and cities with populations greater than 9,999 whose Asian and/or NHPI population rates are greater than the national average; (1) Native Hawaiian and other Pacific Islander; (2) excludes Taiwanese; (3) includes Chamorro; (4) county does not meet population threshold but is shown in order to allow inclusion of city

Place	Total foreign-born naturalized citizens	Total Asian population	Asians who are foreign-born naturalized citizens	Total NHPI[1] population	NHPIs[1] who are foreign-born naturalized citizens	Asian Indian	Bangladeshi	Cambodian	Chinese[2]	Fijian	Filipino	Guamanian[3]	Hawaiian, Native	Hmong	Indonesian	Japanese	Korean	Laotian	Malaysian	Pakistani	Samoan	Sri Lankan	Taiwanese	Thai	Tongan	Vietnamese
Butler County	4,374 1.31	5,077	1,983 39.06 39.06 45.34	-	-	554 30.97 27.94 10.91 12.67	-	-	448 44.49 22.59 8.82 10.24	-	176 39.11 8.88 3.47 4.02	-	-	-	-	-	237 50.32 11.95 4.67 5.42	-	-	-	-	-	-	-	-	321 49.38 16.19 6.32 7.34
Clark County	1,115 0.77	671	318 47.39 47.39 28.52	-	-	-	-	-	-	-	-	-	-	-	-	-	-	-	-	-	-	-	-	-	-	-
Clermont County	1,469 0.83	1,078	448 41.56 41.56 30.50	-	-	120 31.41 26.79 11.13 8.17	-	-	-	-	-	-	-	-	-	-	-	-	-	-	-	-	-	-	-	-
Columbiana County	630 0.56	325	134 41.23 41.23 21.27	-	-	-	-	-	-	-	-	-	-	-	-	-	-	-	-	-	-	-	-	-	-	-
Cuyahoga County	50,362 3.61	25,831	8,802 34.08 34.08 17.48	-	-	3,013 33.27 34.23 11.66 5.98	-	143 29.55 1.62 0.55 0.28	1,787 29.43 20.30 6.92 3.55	-	1,306 46.83 14.84 5.06 2.59	-	-	-	-	85 6.71 0.97 0.33 0.17	846 46.10 9.61 3.28 1.68	-	-	-	-	-	-	-	-	916 43.93 10.41 3.55 1.82
Mayfield Heights (city)	1,700 8.77	798	146 18.30 18.30 8.59	-	-	62 15.98 42.47 7.77 3.65	-	-	-	-	-	-	-	-	-	-	-	-	-	-	-	-	-	-	-	-
Richmond Heights (city)	1,050 9.59	515	104 20.19 20.19 9.90	-	-	-	-	-	-	-	-	-	-	-	-	-	-	-	-	-	-	-	-	-	-	-
Solon (city)	1,186 5.44	1,070	465 43.46 43.46 39.21	-	-	229 48.72 49.25 21.40 19.31	-	-	130 37.57 27.96 12.15 10.96	-	-	-	-	-	-	-	-	-	-	-	-	-	-	-	-	-
Westlake (city)	1,905 5.98	1,354	665 49.11 49.11 34.91	-	-	258 47.69 38.80 19.05 13.54	-	-	-	-	-	-	-	-	-	-	-	-	-	-	-	-	-	-	-	-
Delaware County	1,418 1.29	1,755	588 33.50 33.50 41.47	-	-	121 27.82 20.58 6.89 8.53	-	-	169 30.51 28.74 9.63 11.92	-	-	-	-	-	-	-	-	-	-	-	-	-	-	-	-	-

Notes: Please refer to the User's Guide for an explanation of data; data is arranged alphabetically by state, then county, then city within each county; table includes counties with populations greater than 49,999 unless noted and cities with populations greater than 9,999 whose Asian and/or NHPI population rates are greater than the national average; (1) Native Hawaiian and other Pacific Islander; (2) excludes Taiwanese; (3) includes Chamorro; (4) county does not meet population threshold but is shown in order to allow inclusion of city

Place	Total foreign-born naturalized citizens	Total Asian population	Asians who are foreign-born naturalized citizens	Total NHPI[1] population	NHPIs[1] who are foreign-born naturalized citizens	Asian Indian	Bangladeshi	Cambodian	Chinese[2]	Fijian	Filipino	Guamanian[3]	Hawaiian, Native	Hmong	Indonesian	Japanese	Korean	Laotian	Malaysian	Pakistani	Samoan	Sri Lankan	Taiwanese	Thai	Tongan	Vietnamese
Fairfield County	1,015 0.83	874	307 35.13 35.13 30.25	-	-	-	-	-	-	-	-	-	-	-	-	-	-	-	-	-	-	-	-	-	-	-
Franklin County	20,851 1.95	32,912	7,770 23.61 23.61 37.26	362	5 1.38 1.38 0.02	1,439 17.46 18.52 4.37 6.90	-	351 26.81 4.52 1.07 1.68	1,727 23.78 22.23 5.25 8.28	-	726 40.47 9.34 2.21 3.48	-	-	-	16 3.02 0.21 0.05 0.08	142 4.40 1.83 0.43 0.68	974 29.21 12.54 2.96 4.67	511 44.98 6.58 1.55 2.45	-	125 24.37 1.61 0.38 0.60	-	-	269 35.58 3.46 0.82 1.29	87 20.33 1.12 0.26 0.42	-	1,001 40.97 12.88 3.04 4.80
Dublin (city)	1,035 3.29	2,497	528 21.15 21.15 51.01	-	-	154 23.12 29.17 6.17 14.88	-	-	171 33.53 32.39 6.85 16.52	-	-	-	-	-	-	10 1.22 1.89 0.40 0.97	-	-	-	-	-	-	-	-	-	-
Hilliard (city)	426 1.76	1,006	251 24.95 24.95 58.92	-	-	-	-	-	-	-	-	-	-	-	-	-	-	-	-	-	-	-	-	-	-	-
Geauga County	1,723 1.90	370	221 59.73 59.73 12.83	-	-	-	-	-	-	-	-	-	-	-	-	-	-	-	-	-	-	-	-	-	-	-
Greene County	2,593 1.75	2,883	1,138 39.47 39.47 43.89	-	-	349 39.89 30.67 12.11 13.46	-	-	147 34.35 12.92 5.10 5.67	-	-	-	-	-	-	-	236 41.40 20.74 8.19 9.10	-	-	-	-	-	-	-	-	-
Hamilton County	12,251 1.45	12,652	3,789 29.95 29.95 30.93	-	-	897 22.60 23.67 7.09 7.32	-	82 23.36 2.16 0.65 0.67	963 32.11 25.42 7.61 7.86	-	401 30.49 10.58 3.17 3.27	-	-	-	-	92 15.11 2.43 0.73 0.75	462 40.38 12.19 3.65 3.77	-	-	-	-	-	-	-	-	500 47.35 13.20 3.95 4.08
Blue Ash (city)	493 3.87	898	217 24.16 24.16 44.02	-	-	68 16.79 31.34 7.57 13.79	-	-	-	-	-	-	-	-	-	-	-	-	-	-	-	-	-	-	-	-
Sharonville (city)	264 1.93	556	94 16.91 16.91 35.61	-	-	45 11.45 47.87 8.09 17.05	-	-	-	-	-	-	-	-	-	-	-	-	-	-	-	-	-	-	-	-
Hancock County	559 0.78	764	211 27.62 27.62 37.75	-	-	-	-	-	-	-	-	-	-	-	-	-	-	-	-	-	-	-	-	-	-	-

Notes: Please refer to the User's Guide for an explanation of data; data is arranged alphabetically by state, then county, then city within each county; table includes counties with populations greater than 49,999 unless noted and cities with populations greater than 9,999 whose Asian and/or NHPI population rates are greater than the national average; (1) Native Hawaiian and other Pacific Islander; (2) excludes Taiwanese; (3) includes Chamorro; (4) county does not meet population threshold but is shown in order to allow inclusion of city

Place	Total foreign-born naturalized citizens	Total Asian population	Asians who are foreign-born naturalized citizens	Total NHPI[1] population	NHPIs[1] who are foreign-born naturalized citizens	Asian Indian	Bangladeshi	Cambodian	Chinese[2]	Fijian	Filipino	Guamanian[3]	Hawaiian, Native	Hmong	Indonesian	Japanese	Korean	Laotian	Malaysian	Pakistani	Samoan	Sri Lankan	Taiwanese	Thai	Tongan	Vietnamese
Lake County	5,365 2.36	2,234	752 33.66 33.66 14.02	-	-	181 26.66 24.07 8.10 3.37	-	-	172 32.27 22.87 7.70 3.21	-	-	-	-	-	-	-	-	-	-	-	-	-	-	-	-	-
Licking County	808 0.56	687	271 39.45 39.45 33.54	-	-	-	-	-	-	-	-	-	-	-	-	-	-	-	-	-	-	-	-	-	-	-
Lorain County	4,567 1.60	1,715	704 41.05 41.05 15.41	-	-	116 29.44 16.48 6.76 2.54	-	-	-	-	241 55.66 34.23 14.05 5.28	-	-	-	-	-	-	-	-	-	-	-	-	-	-	-
Lucas County	7,621 1.67	5,326	1,788 33.57 33.57 23.46	-	-	446 27.56 24.94 8.37 5.85	-	-	395 27.78 22.09 7.42 5.18	-	295 49.33 16.50 5.54 3.87	-	-	-	-	-	279 54.17 15.60 5.24 3.66	-	-	-	-	-	-	-	-	-
Mahoning County	4,382 1.70	1,018	323 31.73 31.73 7.37	-	-	-	-	-	-	-	-	-	-	-	-	-	-	-	-	-	-	-	-	-	-	-
Marion County	388 0.59	364	132 36.26 36.26 34.02	-	-	-	-	-	-	-	-	-	-	-	-	-	-	-	-	-	-	-	-	-	-	-
Medina County	2,997 1.98	1,153	467 40.50 40.50 15.58	-	-	180 40.72 38.54 15.61 6.01	-	-	-	-	-	-	-	-	-	-	-	-	-	-	-	-	-	-	-	-
Miami County	715 0.72	845	246 29.11 29.11 34.41	-	-	-	-	-	-	-	-	-	-	-	-	-	-	-	-	-	-	-	-	-	-	-
Montgomery County	7,277 1.30	7,190	2,587 35.98 35.98 35.55	-	-	693 32.72 26.79 9.64 9.52	-	-	390 34.54 15.08 5.42 5.36	-	336 46.93 12.99 4.67 4.62	-	-	-	-	63 9.84 2.44 0.88 0.87	305 38.51 11.79 4.24 4.19	-	-	-	-	-	-	-	-	606 58.44 23.42 8.43 8.33
Portage County	1,430 0.94	1,156	348 30.10 30.10 24.34	-	-	-	-	-	-	-	-	-	-	-	-	-	-	-	-	-	-	-	-	-	-	-

Notes: Please refer to the User's Guide for an explanation of data; data is arranged alphabetically by state, then county, then city within each county; table includes counties with populations greater than 49,999 unless noted and cities with populations greater than 9,999 whose Asian and/or NHPI population rates are greater than the national average; (1) Native Hawaiian and other Pacific Islander; (2) excludes Taiwanese; (3) includes Chamorro; (4) county does not meet population threshold but is shown in order to allow inclusion of city

Place	Total foreign-born naturalized citizens	Total Asian population	Asians who are foreign-born naturalized citizens	Total NHPI[1] population	NHPIs[1] who are foreign-born naturalized citizens	Asian Indian	Bangladeshi	Cambodian	Chinese[2]	Fijian	Filipino	Guamanian[3]	Hawaiian, Native	Hmong	Indonesian	Japanese	Korean	Laotian	Malaysian	Pakistani	Samoan	Sri Lankan	Taiwanese	Thai	Tongan	Vietnamese
Richland County	1,502	709	332	-	-	-	-	-	-	-	-	-	-	-	-	-	-	-	-	-	-	-	-	-	-	-
	1.17		46.83																							
			46.83																							
			22.10																							
Stark County	4,148	1,811	864	-	-	196	-	-	152	-	-	-	-	-	-	-	-	-	-	-	-	-	-	-	-	-
	1.10		47.71			43.85			39.18																	
						22.69			17.59																	
			47.71			10.82			8.39																	
			20.83			4.73			3.66																	
Summit County	9,514	7,735	2,217	-	-	583	-	-	422	-	209	-	-	-	-	61	323	216	-	-	-	-	-	-	-	250
	1.75		28.66			28.55			24.49		42.22					14.15	34.96	28.31								36.93
						26.30			19.03		9.43					2.75	14.57	9.74								11.28
			28.66			7.54			5.46		2.70					0.79	4.18	2.79								3.23
			23.30			6.13			4.44		2.20					0.64	3.39	2.27								2.63
Trumbull County	2,852	1,009	458	-	-	-	-	-	-	-	-	-	-	-	-	-	-	-	-	-	-	-	-	-	-	-
	1.27		45.39																							
			45.39																							
			16.06																							
Warren County	1,714	2,167	703	-	-	160	-	-	116	-	-	-	-	-	-	-	-	-	-	-	-	-	-	-	-	-
	1.08		32.44			23.85			22.39																	
						22.76			16.50																	
			32.44			7.38			5.35																	
			41.02			9.33			6.77																	
Wayne County	756	767	198	-	-	-	-	-	-	-	-	-	-	-	-	-	-	-	-	-	-	-	-	-	-	-
	0.68		25.81																							
			25.81																							
			26.19																							
Wood County	1,186	1,170	303	-	-	-	-	-	-	-	-	-	-	-	-	-	-	-	-	-	-	-	-	-	-	-
	0.98		25.90																							
			25.90																							
			25.55																							
OKLAHOMA	45,766	45,546	15,804	1,840	166	2,519	-	149	1,472	-	1,634	12	15	96	-	600	2,498	379	18	217	-	-	67	315	-	5,438
	1.33		34.70		9.02	30.34		45.29	22.16		39.05	3.00	2.22	28.66		21.51	54.00	43.02	3.50	19.34			18.93	38.27		44.50
						15.94		0.94	9.31		10.34	7.23	9.04	0.61		3.80	15.81	2.40	0.11	1.37			0.42	1.99		34.41
			34.70		9.02	5.53		0.33	3.23		3.59	0.65	0.82	0.21		1.32	5.48	0.83	0.04	0.48			0.15	0.69		11.94
			34.53		0.36	5.50		0.33	3.22		3.57	0.03	0.03	0.21		1.31	5.46	0.83	0.04	0.47			0.15	0.69		11.88
Canadian County	1,474	2,180	904	-	-	360	-	-	-	-	-	-	-	-	-	-	-	-	-	-	-	-	-	-	-	361
	1.68		41.47			29.78																				61.08
						39.82																				39.93
			41.47			16.51																				16.56
			61.33			24.42																				24.49
Cleveland County	4,255	5,879	2,025	-	-	260	-	-	194	-	182	-	-	-	-	-	361	-	-	-	-	-	-	-	-	849
	2.05		34.44			29.05			17.88		32.50						50.99									49.94
						12.84			9.58		8.99						17.83									41.93
			34.44			4.42			3.30		3.10						6.14									14.44
			47.59			6.11			4.56		4.28						8.48									19.95

Notes: Please refer to the User's Guide for an explanation of data; data is arranged alphabetically by state, then county, then city within each county; table includes counties with populations greater than 49,999 unless noted and cities with populations greater than 9,999 whose Asian and/or NHPI population rates are greater than the national average; (1) Native Hawaiian and other Pacific Islander; (2) excludes Taiwanese; (3) includes Chamorro; (4) county does not meet population threshold but is shown in order to allow inclusion of city

Place	Total foreign-born naturalized citizens	Total Asian population	Asians who are foreign-born naturalized citizens	Total NHPI[1] population	NHPIs[1] who are foreign-born naturalized citizens	Asian Indian	Bangladeshi	Cambodian	Chinese[2]	Fijian	Filipino	Guamanian[3]	Hawaiian, Native	Hmong	Indonesian	Japanese	Korean	Laotian	Malaysian	Pakistani	Samoan	Sri Lankan	Taiwanese	Thai	Tongan	Vietnamese
Comanche County	3,586 3.12	2,430	1,164 47.90 47.90 32.46	-	-	-	-	-	-	-	212 38.69 18.21 8.72 5.91	-	-	-	-	-	474 56.70 40.72 19.51 13.22	-	-	-	-	-	-	-	-	-
Garfield County	640 1.11	499	197 39.48 39.48 30.78	-	-	-	-	-	-	-	-	-	-	-	-	-	-	-	-	-	-	-	-	-	-	-
Muskogee County	409 0.59	351	170 48.43 48.43 41.56	-	-	-	-	-	-	-	-	-	-	-	-	-	-	-	-	-	-	-	-	-	-	-
Oklahoma County	15,175 2.30	18,171	6,199 34.11 34.11 40.85	-	-	916 32.06 14.78 5.04 6.04	-	-	490 22.28 7.90 2.70 3.23	-	528 42.00 8.52 2.91 3.48	-	-	-	-	173 17.21 2.79 0.95 1.14	643 52.97 10.37 3.54 4.24	209 42.39 3.37 1.15 1.38	-	-	-	-	-	153 38.54 2.47 0.84 1.01	-	2,795 40.85 45.09 15.38 18.42
Payne County	527 0.77	1,906	191 10.02 10.02 36.24	-	-	-	-	-	54 8.10 28.27 2.83 10.25	-	-	-	-	-	-	-	-	-	-	-	-	-	-	-	-	-
Stillwater (city)	430 1.10	1,869	174 9.31 9.31 40.47	-	-	-	-	-	54 8.14 31.03 2.89 12.56	-	-	-	-	-	-	-	-	-	-	-	-	-	-	-	-	-
Pottawatomie County	275 0.42	372	63 16.94 16.94 22.91	-	-	-	-	-	-	-	-	-	-	-	-	-	-	-	-	-	-	-	-	-	-	-
Tulsa County	9,454 1.68	8,601	3,114 36.21 36.21 32.94	-	-	567 29.12 18.21 6.59 6.00	-	-	411 26.58 13.20 4.78 4.35	-	173 36.97 5.56 2.01 1.83	-	-	-	-	-	531 59.46 17.05 6.17 5.62	-	-	113 20.77 3.63 1.31 1.20	-	-	-	-	-	933 45.56 29.96 10.85 9.87
Wagoner County	523 0.91	489	197 40.29 40.29 37.67	-	-	-	-	-	-	-	-	-	-	-	-	-	-	-	-	-	-	-	-	-	-	-
OREGON	97,381 2.85	99,136	32,409 32.69 32.69 33.28	7,583	777 10.25 10.25 0.80	2,627 25.79 8.11 2.65 2.70	-	1,088 39.58 3.36 1.10 1.12	6,375 34.43 19.67 6.43 6.55	134 35.92 17.25 1.77 0.14	3,738 35.02 11.53 3.77 3.84	35 3.15 4.50 0.46 0.04	6 0.30 0.77 0.08 0.01	148 10.83 0.46 0.15 0.15	123 19.19 0.38 0.12 0.13	1,240 10.64 3.83 1.25 1.27	5,738 44.78 17.70 5.79 5.89	1,373 37.10 4.24 1.38 1.41	-	113 28.97 0.35 0.11 0.12	51 6.60 6.56 0.67 0.05	-	200 25.00 0.62 0.20 0.21	470 31.42 1.45 0.47 0.48	100 22.47 12.87 1.32 0.10	7,949 41.75 24.53 8.02 8.16

Notes: Please refer to the User's Guide for an explanation of data; data is arranged alphabetically by state, then county, then city within each county; table includes counties with populations greater than 49,999 unless noted and cities with populations greater than 9,999 whose Asian and/or NHPI population rates are greater than the national average; (1) Native Hawaiian and other Pacific Islander; (2) excludes Taiwanese; (3) includes Chamorro; (4) county does not meet population threshold but is shown in order to allow inclusion of city

Place	Total foreign-born naturalized citizens	Total Asian population	Asians who are foreign-born naturalized citizens	Total NHPI[1] population	NHPIs[1] who are foreign-born naturalized citizens	Asian Indian	Bangladeshi	Cambodian	Chinese[2]	Fijian	Filipino	Guamanian[3]	Hawaiian, Native	Hmong	Indonesian	Japanese	Korean	Laotian	Malaysian	Pakistani	Samoan	Sri Lankan	Taiwanese	Thai	Tongan	Vietnamese
Benton County	2,111 2.70	3,331	820 24.62 24.62 38.84	-	-	-	-	-	305 32.34 37.20 9.16 14.45	-	-	-	-	-	-	23 5.32 2.80 0.69 1.09	254 34.75 30.98 7.63 12.03	-	-	-	-	-	-	-	-	-
Corvallis (city)	1,463 2.97	3,031	674 22.24 22.24 46.07	-	-	-	-	-	289 31.90 42.88 9.53 19.75	-	-	-	-	-	-	-	186 29.43 27.60 6.14 12.71	-	-	-	-	-	-	-	-	-
Clackamas County	9,300 2.75	8,114	3,061 37.72 37.72 32.91	616	27 4.38 4.38 0.29	319 45.51 10.42 3.93 3.43	-	-	791 42.83 25.84 9.75 8.51	-	261 26.91 8.53 3.22 2.81	-	-	-	-	137 13.66 4.48 1.69 1.47	751 44.44 24.53 9.26 8.08	-	-	-	-	-	-	-	-	458 48.26 14.96 5.64 4.92
Lake Oswego (city)	1,576 4.47	1,494	481 32.20 32.20 30.52	-	-	-	-	-	217 51.42 45.11 14.52 13.77	-	-	-	-	-	-	-	-	-	-	-	-	-	-	-	-	-
Coos County	791 1.26	345	130 37.68 37.68 16.43	-	-	-	-	-	-	-	-	-	-	-	-	-	-	-	-	-	-	-	-	-	-	-
Deschutes County	1,440 1.25	615	259 42.11 42.11 17.99	-	-	-	-	-	-	-	-	-	-	-	-	-	-	-	-	-	-	-	-	-	-	-
Douglas County	1,320 1.31	593	225 37.94 37.94 17.05	-	-	-	-	-	-	-	-	-	-	-	-	-	-	-	-	-	-	-	-	-	-	-
Jackson County	3,431 1.89	1,398	508 36.34 36.34 14.81	-	-	-	-	-	-	-	-	-	-	-	-	-	-	-	-	-	-	-	-	-	-	-
Josephine County	1,356 1.79	396	184 46.46 46.46 13.57	-	-	-	-	-	-	-	-	-	-	-	-	-	-	-	-	-	-	-	-	-	-	-
Klamath County	1,260 1.98	474	215 45.36 45.36 17.06	-	-	-	-	-	-	-	-	-	-	-	-	-	-	-	-	-	-	-	-	-	-	-

Notes: Please refer to the User's Guide for an explanation of data; data is arranged alphabetically by state, then county, then city within each county; table includes counties with populations greater than 49,999 unless noted and cities with populations greater than 9,999 whose Asian and/or NHPI population rates are greater than the national average; (1) Native Hawaiian and other Pacific Islander; (2) excludes Taiwanese; (3) includes Chamorro; (4) county does not meet population threshold but is shown in order to allow inclusion of city

Place	Total foreign-born naturalized citizens	Total Asian population	Asians who are foreign-born naturalized citizens	Total NHPI[1] population	NHPIs[1] who are foreign-born naturalized citizens	Asian Indian	Bangladeshi	Cambodian	Chinese[2]	Fijian	Filipino	Guamanian[3]	Hawaiian, Native	Hmong	Indonesian	Japanese	Korean	Laotian	Malaysian	Pakistani	Samoan	Sri Lankan	Taiwanese	Thai	Tongan	Vietnamese
Lane County	6,074	6,103	1,454	588	39	166	-	-	289	-	206	-	-	-	-	153	339	-	-	-	-	-	-	-	-	-
	1.88		23.82		6.63	27.53			24.39		36.08					11.94	27.67									
						11.42			19.88		14.17					10.52	23.31									
			23.82		6.63	2.72			4.74		3.38					2.51	5.55									
			23.94		0.64	2.73			4.76		3.39					2.52	5.58									
Linn County	1,569	780	368	-	-	-	-	-	-	-	-	-	-	-	-	-	-	-	-	-	-	-	-	-	-	-
	1.52		47.18																							
			47.18																							
			23.45																							
Marion County	9,186	4,801	1,682	761	117	136	-	-	248	-	251	-	-	-	-	74	350	-	-	-	-	-	-	-	-	393
	3.23		35.03		15.37	37.78			31.59		38.20					12.17	56.45									47.35
						8.09			14.74		14.92					4.40	20.81									23.37
			35.03		15.37	2.83			5.17		5.23					1.54	7.29									8.19
			18.31		1.27	1.48			2.70		2.73					0.81	3.81									4.28
Salem (city)	4,213	3,310	1,079	382	115	-	-	-	205	-	138	-	-	-	-	59	-	-	-	-	-	-	-	-	-	237
	3.08		32.60		30.10				31.25		36.22					15.21										48.17
									19.00		12.79					5.47										21.96
			32.60		30.10				6.19		4.17					1.78										7.16
			25.61		2.73				4.87		3.28					1.40										5.63
Multnomah County	28,946	37,280	12,585	2,511	382	689	-	382	2,455	-	1,305	-	6	133	-	280	1,287	956	-	-	-	-	-	107	69	4,465
	4.38		33.76		15.21	37.75		35.80	35.00		39.26		1.28	12.58		7.89	49.85	36.74						21.75	19.22	38.96
						5.47		3.04	19.51		10.37		1.57	1.06		2.22	10.23	7.60						0.85	18.06	35.48
			33.76		15.21	1.85		1.02	6.59		3.50		0.24	0.36		0.75	3.45	2.56						0.29	2.75	11.98
			43.48		1.32	2.38		1.32	8.48		4.51		0.02	0.46		0.97	4.45	3.30						0.37	0.24	15.43
Portland (city)	24,617	33,683	11,452	2,010	351	610	-	363	2,241	-	1,058	-	6	120	-	247	1,144	870	-	-	-	-	-	89	69	4,216
	4.65		34.00		17.46	40.13		34.94	34.63		38.57		1.72	12.89		8.09	52.14	37.79						19.78	19.60	38.77
						5.33		3.17	19.57		9.24		1.71	1.05		2.16	9.99	7.60						0.78	19.66	36.81
			34.00		17.46	1.81		1.08	6.65		3.14		0.30	0.36		0.73	3.40	2.58						0.26	3.43	12.52
			46.52		1.43	2.48		1.47	9.10		4.30		0.02	0.49		1.00	4.65	3.53						0.36	0.28	17.13
Polk County	1,226	773	291	-	-	-	-	-	-	-	-	-	-	-	-	-	-	-	-	-	-	-	-	-	-	-
	1.97		37.65																							
			37.65																							
			23.74																							
Umatilla County	1,594	492	96	-	-	-	-	-	-	-	-	-	-	-	-	-	-	-	-	-	-	-	-	-	-	-
	2.26		19.51																							
			19.51																							
			6.02																							
Washington County	20,343	29,946	9,456	1,399	116	958	-	499	1,631	-	1,058	-	0	-	-	224	1,726	254	-	-	-	-	-	-	-	2,313
	4.57		31.58		8.29	17.21		45.20	33.25		33.80		0.00			8.31	40.16	40.84								46.08
						10.13		5.28	17.25		11.19		0.00			2.37	18.25	2.69								24.46
			31.58		8.29	3.20		1.67	5.45		3.53		0.00			0.75	5.76	0.85								7.72
			46.48		0.57	4.71		2.45	8.02		5.20		0.00			1.10	8.48	1.25								11.37
Aloha (cdp)	1,889	3,122	1,067	-	-	-	-	-	-	-	163	-	-	-	-	-	-	-	-	-	-	-	-	-	-	415
	4.49		34.18								39.18															37.12
											15.28															38.89
			34.18								5.22															13.29
			56.48								8.63															21.97

Notes: Please refer to the User's Guide for an explanation of data; data is arranged alphabetically by state, then county, then city within each county; table includes counties with populations greater than 49,999 unless noted and cities with populations greater than 9,999 whose Asian and/or NHPI population rates are greater than the national average; (1) Native Hawaiian and other Pacific Islander; (2) excludes Taiwanese; (3) includes Chamorro; (4) county does not meet population threshold but is shown in order to allow inclusion of city

Place	Total foreign-born naturalized citizens	Total Asian population	Asians who are foreign-born naturalized citizens	Total NHPI[1] population	NHPIs[1] who are foreign-born naturalized citizens	Asian Indian	Bangladeshi	Cambodian	Chinese[2]	Fijian	Filipino	Guamanian[3]	Hawaiian, Native	Hmong	Indonesian	Japanese	Korean	Laotian	Malaysian	Pakistani	Samoan	Sri Lankan	Taiwanese	Thai	Tongan	Vietnamese
Beaverton (city)	4,405	7,449	2,212	-	-	244	-	174	313	-	233	-	-	-	-	43	496	-	-	-	-	-	-	-	-	506
	5.80		29.70			14.01		48.74	30.51		32.09					6.34	40.16									55.24
						11.03		7.87	14.15		10.53					1.94	22.42									22.88
			29.70			3.28		2.34	4.20		3.13					0.58	6.66									6.79
			50.22			5.54		3.95	7.11		5.29					0.98	11.26									11.49
Cedar Mill (cdp)	745	982	433	-	-	-	-	-	-	-	-	-	-	-	-	-	-	-	-	-	-	-	-	-	-	-
	5.83		44.09																							
			44.09																							
			58.12																							
Hillsboro (city)	2,718	4,366	1,248	-	-	242	-	-	149	-	-	-	-	-	-	-	232	-	-	-	-	-	-	-	-	346
	3.89		28.58			18.38			24.96								44.02									46.44
						19.39			11.94								18.59									27.72
			28.58			5.54			3.41								5.31									7.92
			45.92			8.90			5.48								8.54									12.73
Tigard (city)	1,992	2,458	852	-	-	-	-	-	191	-	-	-	-	-	-	-	-	-	-	-	-	-	-	-	-	188
	4.83		34.66						30.71																	42.34
									22.42																	22.07
			34.66						7.77																	7.65
			42.77						9.59																	9.44
Tualatin (city)	917	1,007	388	-	-	-	-	-	-	-	-	-	-	-	-	-	-	-	-	-	-	-	-	-	-	-
	4.06		38.53																							
			38.53																							
			42.31																							
Yamhill County	1,685	872	246	-	-	-	-	-	-	-	-	-	-	-	-	-	-	-	-	-	-	-	-	-	-	-
	1.98		28.21																							
			28.21																							
			14.60																							
PENNSYLVANIA	257,339	216,631	72,517	3,721	259	16,255	232	2,462	14,784	-	6,124	40	25	71	54	1,045	14,572	679	-	932	92	112	873	528	-	12,032
	2.10		33.47		6.96	28.91	32.86	28.31	30.77		41.62	4.97	2.49	9.01	10.07	14.54	44.32	29.94		30.80	10.90	33.94	38.34	29.37		42.03
						22.42	0.32	3.40	20.39		8.44	15.44	9.65	0.10	0.07	1.44	20.09	0.94		1.29	35.52	0.15	1.20	0.73		16.59
			33.47		6.96	7.50	0.11	1.14	6.82		2.83	1.07	0.67	0.03	0.02	0.48	6.73	0.31		0.43	2.47	0.05	0.40	0.24		5.55
			28.18		0.10	6.32	0.09	0.96	5.74		2.38	0.02	0.01	0.03	0.02	0.41	5.66	0.26		0.36	0.04	0.04	0.34	0.21		4.68
Adams County	1,113	639	291	-	-	-	-	-	-	-	-	-	-	-	-	-	-	-	-	-	-	-	-	-	-	-
	1.22		45.54																							
			45.54																							
			26.15																							
Allegheny County	23,771	20,851	5,411	650	69	1,927	-	-	1,368	-	331	-	-	-	-	75	845	-	-	-	-	-	108	-	-	420
	1.85		25.95		10.62	25.58			27.60		29.61					6.16	37.44						23.95			32.63
						35.61			25.28		6.12					1.39	15.62						2.00			7.76
			25.95		10.62	9.24			6.56		1.59					0.36	4.05						0.52			2.01
			22.76		0.29	8.11			5.75		1.39					0.32	3.55						0.45			1.77
Muni. of Monroeville (borough)	909	1,165	301	-	-	130	-	-	-	-	-	-	-	-	-	-	-	-	-	-	-	-	-	-	-	-
	3.10		25.84			19.03																				
						43.19																				
			25.84			11.16																				
			33.11			14.30																				

Notes: Please refer to the User's Guide for an explanation of data; data is arranged alphabetically by state, then county, then city within each county; table includes counties with populations greater than 49,999 unless noted and cities with populations greater than 9,999 whose Asian and/or NHPI population rates are greater than the national average; (1) Native Hawaiian and other Pacific Islander; (2) excludes Taiwanese; (3) includes Chamorro; (4) county does not meet population threshold but is shown in order to allow inclusion of city

Place	Total foreign-born naturalized citizens	Total Asian population	Asians who are foreign-born naturalized citizens	Total NHPI[1] population	NHPIs[1] who are foreign-born naturalized citizens	Asian Indian	Bangladeshi	Cambodian	Chinese[2]	Fijian	Filipino	Guamanian[3]	Hawaiian, Native	Hmong	Indonesian	Japanese	Korean	Laotian	Malaysian	Pakistani	Samoan	Sri Lankan	Taiwanese	Thai	Tongan	Vietnamese
Scott (township)	437 2.53	1,000	107 10.70 10.70 24.49	-	-	46 5.53 42.99 4.60 10.53	-	-	-	-	-	-	-	-	-	-	-	-	-	-	-	-	-	-	-	-
Scott Township (cdp)	437 2.53	1,000	107 10.70 10.70 24.49	-	-	46 5.53 42.99 4.60 10.53	-	-	-	-	-	-	-	-	-	-	-	-	-	-	-	-	-	-	-	-
Upper St. Clair (township)	787 3.92	779	353 45.31 45.31 44.85	-	-	207 39.81 58.64 26.57 26.30	-	-	-	-	-	-	-	-	-	-	-	-	-	-	-	-	-	-	-	-
Beaver County	2,205 1.22	451	196 43.46 43.46 8.89	-	-	-	-	-	-	-	-	-	-	-	-	-	-	-	-	-	-	-	-	-	-	-
Berks County	7,116 1.90	3,621	1,594 44.02 44.02 22.40	-	-	282 36.11 17.69 7.79 3.96	-	-	258 41.28 16.19 7.13 3.63	-	-	-	-	-	-	-	246 78.34 15.43 6.79 3.46	-	-	-	-	-	-	-	-	483 41.53 30.30 13.34 6.79
Blair County	918 0.71	562	297 52.85 52.85 32.35	-	-	-	-	-	-	-	-	-	-	-	-	-	-	-	-	-	-	-	-	-	-	-
Bradford County	433 0.69	198	90 45.45 45.45 20.79	-	-	-	-	-	-	-	-	-	-	-	-	-	-	-	-	-	-	-	-	-	-	-
Bucks County	20,395 3.41	14,171	5,390 38.04 38.04 26.43	-	-	2,120 36.01 39.33 14.96 10.39	-	-	702 32.87 13.02 4.95 3.44	-	729 46.70 13.53 5.14 3.57	-	-	-	-	-	1,034 46.83 19.18 7.30 5.07	-	-	-	-	-	-	-	-	329 58.86 6.10 2.32 1.61
Bensalem (township)	3,362 5.75	3,807	1,092 28.68 28.68 32.48	-	-	500 26.54 45.79 13.13 14.87	-	-	-	-	-	-	-	-	-	-	197 28.72 18.04 5.17 5.86	-	-	-	-	-	-	-	-	-
Lower Makefield (township)	1,534 4.69	1,351	649 48.04 48.04 42.31	-	-	297 52.85 45.76 21.98 19.36	-	-	-	-	-	-	-	-	-	-	-	-	-	-	-	-	-	-	-	-

Notes: Please refer to the User's Guide for an explanation of data; data is arranged alphabetically by state, then county, then city within each county; table includes counties with populations greater than 49,999 unless noted and cities with populations greater than 9,999 whose Asian and/or NHPI population rates are greater than the national average; (1) Native Hawaiian and other Pacific Islander; (2) excludes Taiwanese; (3) includes Chamorro; (4) county does not meet population threshold but is shown in order to allow inclusion of city

Place	Total foreign-born naturalized citizens	Total Asian population	Asians who are foreign-born naturalized citizens	Total NHPI[1] population	NHPIs[1] who are foreign-born naturalized citizens	Asian Indian	Bangladeshi	Cambodian	Chinese[2]	Fijian	Filipino	Guamanian[3]	Hawaiian, Native	Hmong	Indonesian	Japanese	Korean	Laotian	Malaysian	Pakistani	Samoan	Sri Lankan	Taiwanese	Thai	Tongan	Vietnamese
Newtown (township)	855 4.69	899	354 39.38 39.38 41.40	-	-	-	-	-	-	-	-	-	-	-	-	-	-	-	-	-	-	-	-	-	-	-
Butler County	1,212 0.70	942	343 36.41 36.41 28.30	-	-	114 25.45 33.24 12.10 9.41	-	-	-	-	-	-	-	-	-	-	-	-	-	-	-	-	-	-	-	-
Cambria County	948 0.62	560	180 32.14 32.14 18.99	-	-	-	-	-	-	-	-	-	-	-	-	-	-	-	-	-	-	-	-	-	-	-
Centre County	1,963 1.45	5,369	879 16.37 16.37 44.78	-	-	235 18.67 26.73 4.38 11.97	-	-	187 10.71 21.27 3.48 9.53	-	-	-	-	-	-	-	256 24.81 29.12 4.77 13.04	-	-	-	-	-	-	-	-	-
Ferguson (township)	321 2.28	1,012	196 19.37 19.37 61.06	-	-	-	-	-	-	-	-	-	-	-	-	-	-	-	-	-	-	-	-	-	-	-
Patton (township)	169 1.48	516	77 14.92 14.92 45.56	-	-	-	-	-	-	-	-	-	-	-	-	-	-	-	-	-	-	-	-	-	-	-
State College (borough)	971 2.53	3,462	474 13.69 13.69 48.82	-	-	107 13.93 22.57 3.09 11.02	-	-	124 10.64 26.16 3.58 12.77	-	-	-	-	-	-	-	132 22.37 27.85 3.81 13.59	-	-	-	-	-	-	-	-	-
Chester County	10,513 2.43	8,755	3,124 35.68 35.68 29.72	-	-	746 26.79 23.88 8.52 7.10	-	-	753 32.15 24.10 8.60 7.16	-	203 35.80 6.50 2.32 1.93	-	-	-	-	53 13.25 1.70 0.61 0.50	692 63.96 22.15 7.90 6.58	-	-	-	-	-	-	-	-	423 50.72 13.54 4.83 4.02
Tredyffrin (township)	1,200 4.13	1,694	518 30.58 30.58 43.17	-	-	84 12.94 16.22 4.96 7.00	-	-	231 37.68 44.59 13.64 19.25	-	-	-	-	-	-	-	-	-	-	-	-	-	-	-	-	-
West Goshen (township)	504 2.46	777	214 27.54 27.54 42.46	-	-	-	-	-	-	-	-	-	-	-	-	-	-	-	-	-	-	-	-	-	-	-

Notes: Please refer to the User's Guide for an explanation of data; data is arranged alphabetically by state, then county, then city within each county; table includes counties with populations greater than 49,999 unless noted and cities with populations greater than 9,999 whose Asian and/or NHPI population rates are greater than the national average; (1) Native Hawaiian and other Pacific Islander; (2) excludes Taiwanese; (3) includes Chamorro; (4) county does not meet population threshold but is shown in order to allow inclusion of city

Place	Total foreign-born naturalized citizens	Total Asian population	Asians who are foreign-born naturalized citizens	Total NHPI[1] population	NHPIs[1] who are foreign-born naturalized citizens	Asian Indian	Bangladeshi	Cambodian	Chinese[2]	Fijian	Filipino	Guamanian[3]	Hawaiian, Native	Hmong	Indonesian	Japanese	Korean	Laotian	Malaysian	Pakistani	Samoan	Sri Lankan	Taiwanese	Thai	Tongan	Vietnamese
West Whiteland (township)	413 2.50	608	167 27.47 27.47 40.44	-	-	-	-	-	-	-	-	-	-	-	-	-	-	-	-	-	-	-	-	-	-	-
Clearfield County	349 0.42	268	131 48.88 48.88 37.54	-	-	-	-	-	-	-	-	-	-	-	-	-	-	-	-	-	-	-	-	-	-	-
Columbia County	518 0.81	295	146 49.49 49.49 28.19	-	-	-	-	-	-	-	-	-	-	-	-	-	-	-	-	-	-	-	-	-	-	-
Crawford County	645 0.71	288	142 49.31 49.31 22.02	-	-	-	-	-	-	-	-	-	-	-	-	-	-	-	-	-	-	-	-	-	-	-
Cumberland County	3,619 1.69	3,444	1,587 46.08 46.08 43.85	-	-	414 39.81 26.09 12.02 11.44	-	-	242 47.27 15.25 7.03 6.69	-	-	-	-	-	-	-	395 57.16 24.89 11.47 10.91	-	-	-	-	-	-	-	-	315 51.98 19.85 9.15 8.70
Hampden (township)	536 2.22	889	341 38.36 38.36 63.62	-	-	-	-	-	-	-	-	-	-	-	-	-	-	-	-	-	-	-	-	-	-	-
Dauphin County	4,819 1.91	5,028	1,775 35.30 35.30 36.83	-	-	388 36.40 21.86 7.72 8.05	-	-	201 24.16 11.32 4.00 4.17	-	-	-	-	-	-	-	260 60.89 14.65 5.17 5.40	-	-	-	-	-	-	-	-	652 37.17 36.73 12.97 13.53
Derry (township)	568 2.67	886	302 34.09 34.09 53.17	-	-	-	-	-	-	-	-	-	-	-	-	-	-	-	-	-	-	-	-	-	-	-
Hershey (cdp)	401 3.14	547	181 33.09 33.09 45.14	-	-	-	-	-	-	-	-	-	-	-	-	-	-	-	-	-	-	-	-	-	-	-
Delaware County	19,609 3.56	18,290	6,341 34.67 34.67 32.34	-	-	1,455 28.05 22.95 7.96 7.42	-	-	1,183 33.48 18.66 6.47 6.03	-	381 31.78 6.01 2.08 1.94	-	-	-	-	66 9.32 1.04 0.36 0.34	1,449 41.94 22.85 7.92 7.39	-	-	251 38.91 3.96 1.37 1.28	-	-	-	-	-	943 48.53 14.87 5.16 4.81

Notes: Please refer to the User's Guide for an explanation of data; data is arranged alphabetically by state, then county, then city within each county; table includes counties with populations greater than 49,999 unless noted and cities with populations greater than 9,999 whose Asian and/or NHPI population rates are greater than the national average; (1) Native Hawaiian and other Pacific Islander; (2) excludes Taiwanese; (3) includes Chamorro; (4) county does not meet population threshold but is shown in order to allow inclusion of city

Place	Total foreign-born naturalized citizens	Total Asian population	Asians who are foreign-born naturalized citizens	Total NHPI[1] population	NHPIs[1] who are foreign-born naturalized citizens	Asian Indian	Bangladeshi	Cambodian	Chinese[2]	Fijian	Filipino	Guamanian[3]	Hawaiian, Native	Hmong	Indonesian	Japanese	Korean	Laotian	Malaysian	Pakistani	Samoan	Sri Lankan	Taiwanese	Thai	Tongan	Vietnamese
Broomall (cdp)	954 8.54	777	302 38.87 38.87 31.66	-	-	-	-	-	-	-	-	-	-	-	-	-	180 38.63 59.60 23.17 18.87	-	-	-	-	-	-	-	-	-
Drexel Hill (cdp)	1,050 3.58	1,138	300 26.36 26.36 28.57	-	-	-	-	-	21 5.92 7.00 1.85 2.00	-	-	-	-	-	-	-	-	-	-	-	-	-	-	-	-	-
Marple (township)	1,791 7.55	1,265	541 42.77 42.77 30.21	-	-	-	-	-	-	-	-	-	-	-	-	-	281 42.26 51.94 22.21 15.69	-	-	-	-	-	-	-	-	-
Radnor (township)	1,269 4.11	1,600	497 31.06 31.06 39.16	-	-	-	-	-	201 51.02 40.44 12.56 15.84	-	-	-	-	-	-	-	-	-	-	-	-	-	-	-	-	-
Upper Darby (township)	5,068 6.19	7,107	2,254 31.72 31.72 44.48	-	-	407 20.07 18.06 5.73 8.03	-	-	486 31.91 21.56 6.84 9.59	-	-	-	-	-	-	-	333 33.47 14.77 4.69 6.57	-	-	-	-	-	-	-	-	595 50.47 26.40 8.37 11.74
Erie County	3,632 1.29	1,811	629 34.73 34.73 17.32	-	-	136 26.00 21.62 7.51 3.74	-	-	-	-	-	-	-	-	-	-	-	-	-	-	-	-	-	-	-	-
Franklin County	1,020 0.79	909	244 26.84 26.84 23.92	-	-	-	-	-	-	-	-	-	-	-	-	-	-	-	-	-	-	-	-	-	-	-
Indiana County	541 0.60	663	215 32.43 32.43 39.74	-	-	-	-	-	-	-	-	-	-	-	-	-	-	-	-	-	-	-	-	-	-	-
Lackawanna County	2,907 1.36	1,806	691 38.26 38.26 23.77	-	-	210 31.34 30.39 11.63 7.22	-	-	-	-	-	-	-	-	-	-	-	-	-	-	-	-	-	-	-	-
Lancaster County	7,207 1.53	6,563	2,663 40.58 40.58 36.95	-	-	271 34.79 10.18 4.13 3.76	-	-	559 43.17 20.99 8.52 7.76	-	-	-	-	44 9.61 1.65 0.67 0.61	-	-	396 69.72 14.87 6.03 5.49	-	-	-	-	-	-	-	-	961 46.58 36.09 14.64 13.33

Notes: Please refer to the User's Guide for an explanation of data; data is arranged alphabetically by state, then county, then city within each county; table includes counties with populations greater than 49,999 unless noted and cities with populations greater than 9,999 whose Asian and/or NHPI population rates are greater than the national average; (1) Native Hawaiian and other Pacific Islander; (2) excludes Taiwanese; (3) includes Chamorro; (4) county does not meet population threshold but is shown in order to allow inclusion of city

Place	Total foreign-born naturalized citizens	Total Asian population	Asians who are foreign-born naturalized citizens	Total NHPI[1] population	NHPIs[1] who are foreign-born naturalized citizens	Asian Indian	Bangladeshi	Cambodian	Chinese[2]	Fijian	Filipino	Guamanian[3]	Hawaiian, Native	Hmong	Indonesian	Japanese	Korean	Laotian	Malaysian	Pakistani	Samoan	Sri Lankan	Taiwanese	Thai	Tongan	Vietnamese
Lawrence County	889 0.94	293	108 36.86 36.86 12.15	-	-	-	-	-	-	-	-	-	-	-	-	-	-	-	-	-	-	-	-	-	-	-
Lebanon County	1,544 1.28	1,108	536 48.38 48.38 34.72	-	-	-	-	-	-	-	-	-	-	-	-	-	-	-	-	-	-	-	-	-	-	-
Lehigh County	9,487 3.04	6,841	2,269 33.17 33.17 23.92	-	-	566 26.23 24.94 8.27 5.97	-	-	537 32.80 23.67 7.85 5.66	-	-	-	-	-	-	-	296 41.46 13.05 4.33 3.12	-	-	-	-	-	-	-	-	561 38.58 24.72 8.20 5.91
Fullerton (cdp)	787 5.54	687	185 26.93 26.93 23.51	-	-	-	-	-	-	-	-	-	-	-	-	-	-	-	-	-	-	-	-	-	-	-
Lower Macungie (township)	791 4.12	874	465 53.20 53.20 58.79	-	-	-	-	-	193 47.19 41.51 22.08 24.40	-	-	-	-	-	-	-	-	-	-	-	-	-	-	-	-	-
Upper Macungie (township)	466 3.35	627	151 24.08 24.08 32.40	-	-	-	-	-	-	-	-	-	-	-	-	-	-	-	-	-	-	-	-	-	-	-
Luzerne County	3,731 1.17	1,534	690 44.98 44.98 18.49	-	-	164 39.90 23.77 10.69 4.40	-	-	-	-	-	-	-	-	-	-	-	-	-	-	-	-	-	-	-	-
Lycoming County	829 0.69	490	216 44.08 44.08 26.06	-	-	-	-	-	-	-	-	-	-	-	-	-	-	-	-	-	-	-	-	-	-	-
Mercer County	1,331 1.11	671	295 43.96 43.96 22.16	-	-	-	-	-	-	-	-	-	-	-	-	-	-	-	-	-	-	-	-	-	-	-
Monroe County	5,052 3.64	1,395	518 37.13 37.13 10.25	-	-	144 34.29 27.80 10.32 2.85	-	-	-	-	-	-	-	-	-	-	-	-	-	-	-	-	-	-	-	-

Notes: Please refer to the User's Guide for an explanation of data; data is arranged alphabetically by state, then county, then city within each county; table includes counties with populations greater than 49,999 unless noted and cities with populations greater than 9,999 whose Asian and/or NHPI population rates are greater than the national average; (1) Native Hawaiian and other Pacific Islander; (2) excludes Taiwanese; (3) includes Chamorro; (4) county does not meet population threshold but is shown in order to allow inclusion of city

Place	Total foreign-born naturalized citizens	Total Asian population	Asians who are foreign-born naturalized citizens	Total NHPI[1] population	NHPIs[1] who are foreign-born naturalized citizens	Asian Indian	Bangladeshi	Cambodian	Chinese[2]	Fijian	Filipino	Guamanian[3]	Hawaiian, Native	Hmong	Indonesian	Japanese	Korean	Laotian	Malaysian	Pakistani	Samoan	Sri Lankan	Taiwanese	Thai	Tongan	Vietnamese
Montgomery County	27,822 3.71	29,431	10,508 35.70 35.70 37.77	-	-	2,222 29.89 21.15 7.55 7.99	-	-	1,877 34.15 17.86 6.38 6.75	-	849 43.32 8.08 2.88 3.05	-	-	-	-	83 11.61 0.79 0.28 0.30	3,700 40.20 35.21 12.57 13.30	-	-	-	-	-	-	-	-	1,130 46.52 10.75 3.84 4.06
Cheltenham (township)	2,177 5.90	2,391	919 38.44 38.44 42.21	-	-	-	-	-	-	-	-	-	-	-	-	-	414 37.00 45.05 17.31 19.02	-	-	-	-	-	-	-	-	-
East Norriton (township)	528 4.02	538	201 37.36 37.36 38.07	-	-	-	-	-	-	-	-	-	-	-	-	-	-	-	-	-	-	-	-	-	-	-
Hatfield (township)	1,030 6.19	1,819	572 31.45 31.45 55.53	-	-	266 27.34 46.50 14.62 25.83	-	-	-	-	-	-	-	-	-	-	-	-	-	-	-	-	-	-	-	-
Horsham (township)	882 3.64	1,150	410 35.65 35.65 46.49	-	-	-	-	-	-	-	-	-	-	-	-	-	244 47.66 59.51 21.22 27.66	-	-	-	-	-	-	-	-	-
King of Prussia (cdp)	1,041 5.62	1,895	468 24.70 24.70 44.96	-	-	168 21.88 35.90 8.87 16.14	-	-	73 17.98 15.60 3.85 7.01	-	-	-	-	-	-	-	-	-	-	-	-	-	-	-	-	-
Lansdale (borough)	767 4.77	1,329	373 28.07 28.07 48.63	-	-	158 35.11 42.36 11.89 20.60	-	-	-	-	-	-	-	-	-	-	-	-	-	-	-	-	-	-	-	-
Lower Gwynedd (township)	515 4.94	403	201 49.88 49.88 39.03	-	-	-	-	-	-	-	-	-	-	-	-	-	-	-	-	-	-	-	-	-	-	-
Lower Providence (township)	628 2.80	1,014	285 28.11 28.11 45.38	-	-	-	-	-	126 26.58 44.21 12.43 20.06	-	-	-	-	-	-	-	-	-	-	-	-	-	-	-	-	-
Montgomery (township)	1,307 5.93	1,827	747 40.89 40.89 57.15	-	-	198 34.32 26.51 10.84 15.15	-	-	-	-	-	-	-	-	-	-	347 47.99 46.45 18.99 26.55	-	-	-	-	-	-	-	-	-

Notes: Please refer to the User's Guide for an explanation of data; data is arranged alphabetically by state, then county, then city within each county; table includes counties with populations greater than 49,999 unless noted and cities with populations greater than 9,999 whose Asian and/or NHPI population rates are greater than the national average; (1) Native Hawaiian and other Pacific Islander; (2) excludes Taiwanese; (3) includes Chamorro; (4) county does not meet population threshold but is shown in order to allow inclusion of city

Place	Total foreign-born naturalized citizens	Total Asian population	Asians who are foreign-born naturalized citizens	Total NHPI[1] population	NHPIs[1] who are foreign-born naturalized citizens	Asian Indian	Bangladeshi	Cambodian	Chinese[2]	Fijian	Filipino	Guamanian[3]	Hawaiian, Native	Hmong	Indonesian	Japanese	Korean	Laotian	Malaysian	Pakistani	Samoan	Sri Lankan	Taiwanese	Thai	Tongan	Vietnamese
Montgomeryville (cdp)	576 4.82	820	308 37.56 37.56 53.47	-	-	-	-	-	-	-	-	-	-	-	-	-	-	-	-	-	-	-	-	-	-	-
Plymouth (township)	722 4.50	832	373 44.83 44.83 51.66	-	-	-	-	-	-	-	-	-	-	-	-	-	157 47.29 42.09 18.87 21.75	-	-	-	-	-	-	-	-	-
Towamencin (township)	612 3.48	1,043	343 32.89 32.89 56.05	-	-	-	-	-	-	-	-	-	-	-	-	-	-	-	-	-	-	-	-	-	-	-
Upper Dublin (township)	1,422 5.50	1,514	578 38.18 38.18 40.65	-	-	-	-	-	-	-	-	-	-	-	-	-	246 29.64 42.56 16.25 17.30	-	-	-	-	-	-	-	-	-
Upper Gwynedd (township)	817 5.74	1,144	485 42.40 42.40 59.36	-	-	-	-	-	102 31.97 21.03 8.92 12.48	-	-	-	-	-	-	-	-	-	-	-	-	-	-	-	-	-
Upper Merion (township)	1,285 4.79	2,161	568 26.28 26.28 44.20	-	-	192 21.10 33.80 8.88 14.94	-	-	101 22.75 17.78 4.67 7.86	-	-	-	-	-	-	-	-	-	-	-	-	-	-	-	-	-
Whitpain (township)	915 4.89	1,247	467 37.45 37.45 51.04	-	-	-	-	-	-	-	-	-	-	-	-	-	260 44.37 55.67 20.85 28.42	-	-	-	-	-	-	-	-	-
Northampton County	6,515 2.44	3,756	1,450 38.60 38.60 22.26	-	-	438 35.29 30.21 11.66 6.72	-	-	206 27.21 14.21 5.48 3.16	-	-	-	-	-	-	-	253 54.88 17.45 6.74 3.88	-	-	-	-	-	-	-	-	177 37.42 12.21 4.71 2.72
Northumberland County	686 0.73	373	201 53.89 53.89 29.30	-	-	-	-	-	-	-	-	-	-	-	-	-	-	-	-	-	-	-	-	-	-	-
Philadelphia County	64,786 4.27	65,171	19,477 29.89 29.89 30.06	790	110 13.92 13.92 0.17	3,033 24.18 15.57 4.65 4.68	-	1,571 24.52 8.07 2.41 2.42	5,123 28.77 26.30 7.86 7.91	-	1,712 44.77 8.79 2.63 2.64	-	-	-	-	122 11.04 0.63 0.19 0.19	2,342 35.87 12.02 3.59 3.61	308 25.37 1.58 0.47 0.48	-	203 32.27 1.04 0.31 0.31	-	-	-	-	-	4,417 39.89 22.68 6.78 6.82

Notes: Please refer to the User's Guide for an explanation of data; data is arranged alphabetically by state, then county, then city within each county; table includes counties with populations greater than 49,999 unless noted and cities with populations greater than 9,999 whose Asian and/or NHPI population rates are greater than the national average; (1) Native Hawaiian and other Pacific Islander; (2) excludes Taiwanese; (3) includes Chamorro; (4) county does not meet population threshold but is shown in order to allow inclusion of city

Place	Total foreign-born naturalized citizens	Total Asian population	Asians who are foreign-born naturalized citizens	Total NHPI[1] population	NHPIs[1] who are foreign-born naturalized citizens	Asian Indian	Bangladeshi	Cambodian	Chinese[2]	Fijian	Filipino	Guamanian[3]	Hawaiian, Native	Hmong	Indonesian	Japanese	Korean	Laotian	Malaysian	Pakistani	Samoan	Sri Lankan	Taiwanese	Thai	Tongan	Vietnamese
Philadelphia (city)	64,786	65,171	19,477	790	110	3,033	-	1,571	5,123	-	1,712	-	-	-	-	122	2,342	308	-	203	-	-	-	-	-	4,417
	4.27		29.89		13.92	24.18		24.52	28.77		44.77					11.04	35.87	25.37		32.27						39.89
						15.57		8.07	26.30		8.79					0.63	12.02	1.58		1.04						22.68
			29.89		13.92	4.65		2.41	7.86		2.63					0.19	3.59	0.47		0.31						6.78
			30.06		0.17	4.68		2.42	7.91		2.64					0.19	3.61	0.48		0.31						6.82
Schuylkill County	970	553	223	-	-	-	-	-	-	-	-	-	-	-	-	-	-	-	-	-	-	-	-	-	-	-
	0.65		40.33																							
			40.33																							
			22.99																							
Washington County	1,630	631	193	-	-	-	-	-	-	-	-	-	-	-	-	-	-	-	-	-	-	-	-	-	-	-
	0.80		30.59																							
			30.59																							
			11.84																							
Westmoreland County	3,311	1,724	619	-	-	179	-	-	-	-	-	-	-	-	-	-	-	-	-	-	-	-	-	-	-	-
	0.89		35.90			40.04																				
						28.92																				
			35.90			10.38																				
			18.70			5.41																				
York County	4,267	3,150	1,360	-	-	171	-	-	271	-	-	-	-	-	-	-	349	-	-	-	-	-	-	-	-	215
	1.12		43.17			32.45			40.03								55.84									36.82
						12.57			19.93								25.66									15.81
			43.17			5.43			8.60								11.08									6.83
			31.87			4.01			6.35								8.18									5.04
RHODE ISLAND	56,184	23,825	7,420	441	25	681	-	1,299	1,598	-	1,049	-	-	155	-	150	671	914	-	-	-	-	-	-	-	417
	5.36		31.14		5.67	26.73		25.45	35.03		49.34			16.13		19.11	34.89	31.64								40.56
						9.18		17.51	21.54		14.14			2.09		2.02	9.04	12.32								5.62
			31.14		5.67	2.86		5.45	6.71		4.40			0.65		0.63	2.82	3.84								1.75
			13.21		0.04	1.21		2.31	2.84		1.87			0.28		0.27	1.19	1.63								0.74
Bristol County	3,329	420	184	-	-	-	-	-	-	-	-	-	-	-	-	-	-	-	-	-	-	-	-	-	-	-
	6.57		43.81																							
			43.81																							
			5.53																							
Kent County	5,260	2,187	970	-	-	-	-	-	203	-	-	-	-	-	-	-	165	-	-	-	-	-	-	-	-	-
	3.15		44.35						55.01								39.47									
									20.93								17.01									
			44.35						9.28								7.54									
			18.44						3.86								3.14									
Newport County	2,272	982	344	-	-	-	-	-	-	-	187	-	-	-	-	-	-	-	-	-	-	-	-	-	-	-
	2.66		35.03								40.56															
											54.36															
			35.03								19.04															
			15.14								8.23															
Providence County	42,285	18,319	5,260	-	-	485	-	1,137	1,059	-	537	-	-	121	-	-	374	868	-	-	-	-	-	-	-	294
	6.80		28.71			26.03		23.56	33.26		48.77			14.56			31.75	31.56								36.39
						9.22		21.62	20.13		10.21			2.30			7.11	16.50								5.59
			28.71			2.65		6.21	5.78		2.93			0.66			2.04	4.74								1.60
			12.44			1.15		2.69	2.50		1.27			0.29			0.88	2.05								0.70

Notes: Please refer to the User's Guide for an explanation of data; data is arranged alphabetically by state, then county, then city within each county; table includes counties with populations greater than 49,999 unless noted and cities with populations greater than 9,999 whose Asian and/or NHPI population rates are greater than the national average; (1) Native Hawaiian and other Pacific Islander; (2) excludes Taiwanese; (3) includes Chamorro; (4) county does not meet population threshold but is shown in order to allow inclusion of city

Place	Total foreign-born naturalized citizens	Total Asian population	Asians who are foreign-born naturalized citizens	Total NHPI[1] population	NHPIs[1] who are foreign-born naturalized citizens	Asian Indian	Bangladeshi	Cambodian	Chinese[2]	Fijian	Filipino	Guamanian[3]	Hawaiian, Native	Hmong	Indonesian	Japanese	Korean	Laotian	Malaysian	Pakistani	Samoan	Sri Lankan	Taiwanese	Thai	Tongan	Vietnamese
Providence (city)	15,117 8.71	10,707	2,403 22.44 22.44 15.90	-	-	186 20.39 7.74 1.74 1.23	-	764 21.33 31.79 7.14 5.05	383 25.55 15.94 3.58 2.53	-	215 41.59 8.95 2.01 1.42	-	-	72 10.68 3.00 0.67 0.48	-	-	116 16.25 4.83 1.08 0.77	380 28.66 15.81 3.55 2.51	-	-	-	-	-	-	-	-
Woonsocket (city)	1,453 3.36	1,646	441 26.79 26.79 30.35	-	-	-	-	-	-	-	-	-	-	-	-	-	-	269 29.50 61.00 16.34 18.51	-	-	-	-	-	-	-	-
Washington County	3,038 2.46	1,917	662 34.53 34.53 21.79	-	-	-	-	-	154 26.83 23.26 8.03 5.07	-	-	-	-	-	-	-	-	-	-	-	-	-	-	-	-	-
SOUTH CAROLINA	42,983 1.07	36,505	12,657 34.67 34.67 29.45	1,384	85 6.14 6.14 0.20	2,559 31.15 20.22 7.01 5.95	-	102 29.91 0.81 0.28 0.24	2,004 32.00 15.83 5.49 4.66	-	3,080 44.30 24.33 8.44 7.17	2 0.56 2.35 0.14 <0.01	13 2.62 15.29 0.94 0.03	167 19.42 1.32 0.46 0.39	-	524 22.96 4.14 1.44 1.22	1,460 41.17 11.54 4.00 3.40	340 25.68 2.69 0.93 0.79	-	-	-	-	-	306 44.48 2.42 0.84 0.71	-	1,689 44.28 13.34 4.63 3.93
Aiken County	1,411 0.99	940	446 47.45 47.45 31.61	-	-	-	-	-	-	-	-	-	-	-	-	-	-	-	-	-	-	-	-	-	-	-
Anderson County	1,100 0.66	836	278 33.25 33.25 25.27	-	-	-	-	-	-	-	-	-	-	-	-	-	-	-	-	-	-	-	-	-	-	-
Beaufort County	2,332 1.93	1,014	406 40.04 40.04 17.41	-	-	-	-	-	-	-	-	-	-	-	-	-	-	-	-	-	-	-	-	-	-	-
Berkeley County	2,387 1.67	2,933	1,339 45.65 45.65 56.10	-	-	-	-	-	-	-	916 50.58 68.41 31.23 38.37	-	-	-	-	-	-	-	-	-	-	-	-	-	-	-
Charleston County	4,193 1.35	3,502	1,191 34.01 34.01 28.40	-	-	175 27.65 14.69 5.00 4.17	-	-	221 31.53 18.56 6.31 5.27	-	391 39.22 32.83 11.17 9.33	-	-	-	-	-	-	-	-	-	-	-	-	-	-	-
Dorchester County	1,379 1.43	1,254	530 42.26 42.26 38.43	-	-	-	-	-	-	-	297 46.55 56.04 23.68 21.54	-	-	-	-	-	-	-	-	-	-	-	-	-	-	-

Notes: Please refer to the User's Guide for an explanation of data; data is arranged alphabetically by state, then county, then city within each county; table includes counties with populations greater than 49,999 unless noted and cities with populations greater than 9,999 whose Asian and/or NHPI population rates are greater than the national average; (1) Native Hawaiian and other Pacific Islander; (2) excludes Taiwanese; (3) includes Chamorro; (4) county does not meet population threshold but is shown in order to allow inclusion of city

Place	Total foreign-born naturalized citizens	Total Asian population	Asians who are foreign-born naturalized citizens	Total NHPI[1] population	NHPIs[1] who are foreign-born naturalized citizens	Asian Indian	Bangladeshi	Cambodian	Chinese[2]	Fijian	Filipino	Guamanian[3]	Hawaiian, Native	Hmong	Indonesian	Japanese	Korean	Laotian	Malaysian	Pakistani	Samoan	Sri Lankan	Taiwanese	Thai	Tongan	Vietnamese
Florence County	986 0.78	1,026	313 30.51 30.51 31.74	-	-	-	-	-	-	-	-	-	-	-	-	-	-	-	-	-	-	-	-	-	-	-
Greenville County	5,451 1.44	4,893	1,572 32.13 32.13 28.84	-	-	423 29.58 26.91 8.65 7.76	-	-	231 32.22 14.69 4.72 4.24	-	176 33.02 11.20 3.60 3.23	-	-	-	-	-	-	-	-	-	-	-	-	-	-	484 42.49 30.79 9.89 8.88
Greenwood County	455 0.69	422	67 15.88 15.88 14.73	-	-	-	-	-	-	-	-	-	-	-	-	-	-	-	-	-	-	-	-	-	-	-
Horry County	3,250 1.65	1,548	638 41.21 41.21 19.63	-	-	-	-	-	-	-	-	-	-	-	-	-	-	-	-	-	-	-	-	-	-	-
Lexington County	2,177 1.01	1,945	602 30.95 30.95 27.65	-	-	162 26.91 26.91 8.33 7.44	-	-	111 19.61 18.44 5.71 5.10	-	-	-	-	-	-	-	-	-	-	-	-	-	-	-	-	-
Oconee County	649 0.98	264	104 39.39 39.39 16.02	-	-	-	-	-	-	-	-	-	-	-	-	-	-	-	-	-	-	-	-	-	-	-
Pickens County	852 0.77	1,316	224 17.02 17.02 26.29	-	-	56 10.81 25.00 4.26 6.57	-	-	81 21.15 36.16 6.16 9.51	-	-	-	-	-	-	-	-	-	-	-	-	-	-	-	-	-
Clemson (city)	188 1.55	598	40 6.69 6.69 21.28	-	-	-	-	-	-	-	-	-	-	-	-	-	-	-	-	-	-	-	-	-	-	-
Richland County	5,444 1.70	5,611	1,735 30.92 30.92 31.87	-	-	350 23.43 20.17 6.24 6.43	-	-	272 24.64 15.68 4.85 5.00	-	238 45.59 13.72 4.24 4.37	-	-	-	-	-	484 38.38 27.90 8.63 8.89	-	-	-	-	-	-	-	-	188 35.61 10.84 3.35 3.45
Spartanburg County	3,599 1.42	4,152	1,407 33.89 33.89 39.09	-	-	341 44.63 24.24 8.21 9.47	-	-	-	-	-	-	-	140 18.67 9.95 3.37 3.89	-	-	-	176 25.96 12.51 4.24 4.89	-	-	-	-	-	-	-	-

Notes: Please refer to the User's Guide for an explanation of data; data is arranged alphabetically by state, then county, then city within each county; table includes counties with populations greater than 49,999 unless noted and cities with populations greater than 9,999 whose Asian and/or NHPI population rates are greater than the national average; (1) Native Hawaiian and other Pacific Islander; (2) excludes Taiwanese; (3) includes Chamorro; (4) county does not meet population threshold but is shown in order to allow inclusion of city

Place	Total foreign-born naturalized citizens	Total Asian population	Asians who are foreign-born naturalized citizens	Total NHPI[1] population	NHPIs[1] who are foreign-born naturalized citizens	Asian Indian	Bangladeshi	Cambodian	Chinese[2]	Fijian	Filipino	Guamanian[3]	Hawaiian, Native	Hmong	Indonesian	Japanese	Korean	Laotian	Malaysian	Pakistani	Samoan	Sri Lankan	Taiwanese	Thai	Tongan	Vietnamese
Sumter County	990 0.95	932	373 40.02 40.02 37.68	-	-	-	-	-	-	-	-	-	-	-	-	-	-	-	-	-	-	-	-	-	-	-
York County	1,478 0.90	1,312	480 36.59 36.59 32.48	-	-	-	-	-	-	-	-	-	-	-	-	-	-	-	-	-	-	-	-	-	-	194 43.60 40.42 14.79 13.13
SOUTH DAKOTA	5,452 0.72	4,729	1,611 34.07 34.07 29.55	-	-	100 17.21 6.21 2.11 1.83	-	-	206 30.34 12.79 4.36 3.78	-	284 40.34 17.63 6.01 5.21	-	-	-	-	73 17.72 4.53 1.54 1.34	488 65.50 30.29 10.32 8.95	44 20.18 2.73 0.93 0.81	-	-	-	-	-	-	-	252 35.24 15.64 5.33 4.62
Minnehaha County	1,749 1.18	1,585	582 36.72 36.72 33.28	-	-	-	-	-	-	-	-	-	-	-	-	-	-	-	-	-	-	-	-	-	-	157 30.02 26.98 9.91 8.98
Pennington County	1,044 1.18	914	326 35.67 35.67 31.23	-	-	-	-	-	-	-	-	-	-	-	-	-	-	-	-	-	-	-	-	-	-	-
TENNESSEE	53,185 0.93	54,132	16,916 31.25 31.25 31.81	2,159	233 10.79 10.79 0.44	3,536 29.58 20.90 6.53 6.65	-	328 27.56 1.94 0.61 0.62	2,344 28.23 13.86 4.33 4.41	-	2,000 37.86 11.82 3.69 3.76	145 23.42 62.23 6.72 0.27	9 1.61 3.86 0.42 0.02	-	-	486 12.56 2.87 0.90 0.91	2,831 41.02 16.74 5.23 5.32	1,681 41.87 9.94 3.11 3.16	-	256 33.51 1.51 0.47 0.48	55 10.19 23.61 2.55 0.10	-	301 51.90 1.78 0.56 0.57	262 26.33 1.55 0.48 0.49	-	2,233 31.62 13.20 4.13 4.20
Anderson County	552 0.77	513	146 28.46 28.46 26.45	-	-	-	-	-	-	-	-	-	-	-	-	-	-	-	-	-	-	-	-	-	-	-
Blount County	721 0.68	638	182 28.53 28.53 25.24	-	-	-	-	-	-	-	-	-	-	-	-	-	-	-	-	-	-	-	-	-	-	-
Bradley County	649 0.74	480	149 31.04 31.04 22.96	-	-	-	-	-	-	-	-	-	-	-	-	-	-	-	-	-	-	-	-	-	-	-
Davidson County	9,891 1.74	11,691	3,020 25.83 25.83 30.53	400	21 5.25 5.25 0.21	780 30.85 25.83 6.67 7.89	-	-	301 19.83 9.97 2.57 3.04	-	324 40.45 10.73 2.77 3.28	-	-	-	-	57 6.64 1.89 0.49 0.58	368 28.31 12.19 3.15 3.72	499 38.06 16.52 4.27 5.04	-	-	-	-	-	-	-	363 21.53 12.02 3.10 3.67

Notes: Please refer to the User's Guide for an explanation of data; data is arranged alphabetically by state, then county, then city within each county; table includes counties with populations greater than 49,999 unless noted and cities with populations greater than 9,999 whose Asian and/or NHPI population rates are greater than the national average; (1) Native Hawaiian and other Pacific Islander; (2) excludes Taiwanese; (3) includes Chamorro; (4) county does not meet population threshold but is shown in order to allow inclusion of city

Place	Total foreign-born naturalized citizens	Total Asian population	Asians who are foreign-born naturalized citizens	Total NHPI[1] population	NHPIs[1] who are foreign-born naturalized citizens	Asian Indian	Bangladeshi	Cambodian	Chinese[2]	Fijian	Filipino	Guamanian[3]	Hawaiian, Native	Hmong	Indonesian	Japanese	Korean	Laotian	Malaysian	Pakistani	Samoan	Sri Lankan	Taiwanese	Thai	Tongan	Vietnamese
Hamilton County	4,038 1.31	3,852	1,637 42.50 42.50 40.54	-	-	427 37.46 26.08 11.09 10.57	-	-	-	-	233 56.14 14.23 6.05 5.77	-	-	-	-	-	247 47.14 15.09 6.41 6.12	-	-	-	-	-	-	-	-	149 34.17 9.10 3.87 3.69
Knox County	4,004 1.05	4,548	1,295 28.47 28.47 32.34	-	-	362 27.01 27.95 7.96 9.04	-	-	293 31.61 22.63 6.44 7.32	-	-	-	-	-	-	-	170 31.89 13.13 3.74 4.25	-	-	-	-	-	-	-	-	172 36.36 13.28 3.78 4.30
Madison County	474 0.52	557	125 22.44 22.44 26.37	-	-	-	-	-	-	-	-	-	-	-	-	-	-	-	-	-	-	-	-	-	-	-
Montgomery County	3,117 2.31	2,448	992 40.52 40.52 31.83	-	-	-	-	-	-	-	-	-	-	-	-	-	577 51.94 58.17 23.57 18.51	-	-	-	-	-	-	-	-	-
Putnam County	583 0.94	581	171 29.43 29.43 29.33	-	-	-	-	-	-	-	-	-	-	-	-	-	-	-	-	-	-	-	-	-	-	-
Rutherford County	2,590 1.42	3,253	1,293 39.75 39.75 49.92	-	-	-	-	-	-	-	-	-	-	-	-	-	-	722 46.13 55.84 22.19 27.88	-	-	-	-	-	-	-	-
Shelby County	11,314 1.26	14,925	4,148 27.79 27.79 36.66	493	113 22.92 22.92 1.00	778 21.72 18.76 5.21 6.88	-	186 36.05 4.48 1.25 1.64	718 25.64 17.31 4.81 6.35	-	503 36.93 12.13 3.37 4.45	-	-	-	-	51 9.90 1.23 0.34 0.45	434 35.20 10.46 2.91 3.84	-	-	-	-	-	-	-	-	1,046 31.30 25.22 7.01 9.25
Germantown (city)	1,104 2.96	1,380	537 38.91 38.91 48.64	-	-	200 37.66 37.24 14.49 18.12	-	-	179 42.52 33.33 12.97 16.21	-	-	-	-	-	-	-	-	-	-	-	-	-	-	-	-	-
Sullivan County	942 0.62	585	282 48.21 48.21 29.94	-	-	-	-	-	-	-	-	-	-	-	-	-	-	-	-	-	-	-	-	-	-	-
Sumner County	1,177 0.90	877	429 48.92 48.92 36.45	-	-	-	-	-	-	-	-	-	-	-	-	-	-	-	-	-	-	-	-	-	-	-

Notes: Please refer to the User's Guide for an explanation of data; data is arranged alphabetically by state, then county, then city within each county; table includes counties with populations greater than 49,999 unless noted and cities with populations greater than 9,999 whose Asian and/or NHPI population rates are greater than the national average; (1) Native Hawaiian and other Pacific Islander; (2) excludes Taiwanese; (3) includes Chamorro; (4) county does not meet population threshold but is shown in order to allow inclusion of city

Place	Total foreign-born naturalized citizens	Total Asian population	Asians who are foreign-born naturalized citizens	Total NHPI[1] population	NHPIs[1] who are foreign-born naturalized citizens	Asian Indian	Bangladeshi	Cambodian	Chinese[2]	Fijian	Filipino	Guamanian[3]	Hawaiian, Native	Hmong	Indonesian	Japanese	Korean	Laotian	Malaysian	Pakistani	Samoan	Sri Lankan	Taiwanese	Thai	Tongan	Vietnamese
	734	729	313	-	-	-	-	-	-	-	-	-	-	-	-	-	-	-	-	-	-	-	-	-	-	-
	0.68		42.94																							
Washington County																										
			42.94																							
			42.64																							
	238	467	94	-	-	-	-	-	-	-	-	-	-	-	-	-	-	-	-	-	-	-	-	-	-	-
	0.68		20.13																							
Weakley County[4]																										
			20.13																							
			39.50																							
	156	430	76	-	-	-	-	-	-	-	-	-	-	-	-	-	-	-	-	-	-	-	-	-	-	-
	1.48		17.67																							
Martin (city)																										
			17.67																							
			48.72																							
	1,804	1,497	470	-	-	-	-	-	-	-	-	-	-	-	-	-	-	-	-	-	-	-	-	-	-	-
	1.42		31.40																							
Williamson County																										
			31.40																							
			26.05																							
	525	303	100	-	-	-	-	-	-	-	-	-	-	-	-	-	-	-	-	-	-	-	-	-	-	-
	0.59		33.00																							
Wilson County																										
			33.00																							
			19.05																							
	914,326	555,928	191,788	12,464	771	35,431	717	2,588	32,313	-	22,366	97	61	-	224	3,247	16,692	4,006	95	5,225	155	243	3,502	2,129	111	57,884
	4.38		34.50		6.19	27.84	27.86	34.04	32.86		38.16	2.94	1.67		12.65	20.15	37.62	40.62	14.18	27.69	7.62	24.90	44.56	29.93	22.16	43.15
TEXAS						18.47	0.37	1.35	16.85		11.66	12.58	7.91		0.12	1.69	8.70	2.09	0.05	2.72	20.10	0.13	1.83	1.11	14.40	30.18
			34.50		6.19	6.37	0.13	0.47	5.81		4.02	0.78	0.49		0.04	0.58	3.00	0.72	0.02	0.94	1.24	0.04	0.63	0.38	0.89	10.41
			20.98		0.08	3.88	0.08	0.28	3.53		2.45	0.01	0.01		0.02	0.36	1.83	0.44	0.01	0.57	0.02	0.03	0.38	0.23	0.01	6.33
	596	406	34	-	-	-	-	-	-	-	-	-	-	-	-	-	-	-	-	-	-	-	-	-	-	-
	1.08		8.37																							
Anderson County																										
			8.37																							
			5.70																							
	1,810	539	137	-	-	-	-	-	-	-	-	-	-	-	-	-	-	-	-	-	-	-	-	-	-	-
	2.26		25.42																							
Angelina County																										
			25.42																							
			7.57																							
	8,278	6,114	2,557	1,264	43	212	-	-	-	-	652	0	-	-	-	198	1,021	-	-	-	-	-	-	-	-	-
	3.48		41.82		3.40	36.36					39.90	0.00				51.83	43.12									
Bell County						8.29					25.50	0.00				7.74	39.93									
			41.82		3.40	3.47					10.66	0.00				3.24	16.70									
			30.89		0.52	2.56					7.88	0.00				2.39	12.33									
	4,708	3,805	1,618	1,046	43	-	-	-	-	-	455	0	-	-	-	-	654	-	-	-	-	-	-	-	-	-
	5.42		42.52		4.11						41.36	0.00					41.66									
Killeen (city)											28.12	0.00					40.42									
			42.52		4.11						11.96	0.00					17.19									
			34.37		0.91						9.66	0.00					13.89									

Notes: Please refer to the User's Guide for an explanation of data; data is arranged alphabetically by state, then county, then city within each county; table includes counties with populations greater than 49,999 unless noted and cities with populations greater than 9,999 whose Asian and/or NHPI population rates are greater than the national average; (1) Native Hawaiian and other Pacific Islander; (2) excludes Taiwanese; (3) includes Chamorro; (4) county does not meet population threshold but is shown in order to allow inclusion of city

Place	Total foreign-born naturalized citizens	Total Asian population	Asians who are foreign-born naturalized citizens	Total NHPI[1] population	NHPIs[1] who are foreign-born naturalized citizens	Asian Indian	Bangladeshi	Cambodian	Chinese[2]	Fijian	Filipino	Guamanian[3]	Hawaiian, Native	Hmong	Indonesian	Japanese	Korean	Laotian	Malaysian	Pakistani	Samoan	Sri Lankan	Taiwanese	Thai	Tongan	Vietnamese
Bexar County	63,432	22,586	9,130	1,130	61	1,393	-	-	1,216	-	2,179	-	8	-	-	570	1,286	162	-	-	-	-	-	375	-	1,571
	4.55		40.42		5.40	37.27			32.82		41.84		1.90			33.24	49.88	42.08						46.07		54.57
						15.26			13.32		23.87		13.11			6.24	14.09	1.77						4.11		17.21
			40.42		5.40	6.17			5.38		9.65		0.71			2.52	5.69	0.72						1.66		6.96
			14.39		0.10	2.20			1.92		3.44		0.01			0.90	2.03	0.26						0.59		2.48
Bowie County	528	448	181	-	-	-	-	-	-	-	-	-	-	-	-	-	-	-	-	-	-	-	-	-	-	-
	0.59		40.40																							
			40.40																							
			34.28																							
Brazoria County	7,511	4,720	1,775	-	-	332	-	60	160	-	292	-	-	-	-	-	-	-	-	-	-	-	-	-	-	720
	3.11		37.61			36.60		15.67	24.96		42.88															54.38
						18.70		3.38	9.01		16.45															40.56
			37.61			7.03		1.27	3.39		6.19															15.25
			23.63			4.42		0.80	2.13		3.89															9.59
Brazos County	3,325	6,238	1,047	-	-	386	-	-	185	-	-	-	-	-	-	-	63	-	-	-	-	-	-	-	-	158
	2.18		16.78			21.73			11.21								6.94									33.76
						36.87			17.67								6.02									15.09
			16.78			6.19			2.97								1.01									2.53
			31.49			11.61			5.56								1.89									4.75
College Station (city)	1,653	5,160	864	-	-	313	-	-	185	-	-	-	-	-	-	-	28	-	-	-	-	-	-	-	-	-
	2.43		16.74			23.86			12.74								3.60									
						36.23			21.41								3.24									
			16.74			6.07			3.59								0.54									
			52.27			18.94			11.19								1.69									
Calhoun County[4]	554	683	241	-	-	-	-	-	-	-	-	-	-	-	-	-	-	-	-	-	-	-	-	-	-	51
	2.68		35.29																							30.91
																										21.16
			35.29																							7.47
			43.50																							9.21
Port Lavaca (city)	416	493	194	-	-	-	-	-	-	-	-	-	-	-	-	-	-	-	-	-	-	-	-	-	-	-
	3.46		39.35																							
			39.35																							
			46.63																							
Cameron County	29,571	1,509	403	-	-	-	-	-	-	-	146	-	-	-	-	-	-	-	-	-	-	-	-	-	-	-
	8.82		26.71								25.00															
											36.23															
			26.71								9.68															
			1.36								0.49															
Collin County	22,237	33,606	10,507	-	-	2,020	-	-	3,849	-	415	-	-	-	-	46	1,067	-	-	218	-	-	431	127	-	1,877
	4.52		31.27			23.10			30.73		28.60					5.03	37.56			22.76			50.71	27.97		53.74
						19.23			36.63		3.95					0.44	10.16			2.07			4.10	1.21		17.86
			31.27			6.01			11.45		1.23					0.14	3.18			0.65			1.28	0.38		5.59
			47.25			9.08			17.31		1.87					0.21	4.80			0.98			1.94	0.57		8.44
Allen (city)	1,375	1,639	541	-	-	125	-	-	-	-	-	-	-	-	-	-	-	-	-	-	-	-	-	-	-	183
	3.16		33.01			27.72																				46.21
						23.11																				33.83
			33.01			7.63																				11.17
			39.35			9.09																				13.31

Notes: Please refer to the User's Guide for an explanation of data; data is arranged alphabetically by state, then county, then city within each county; table includes counties with populations greater than 49,999 unless noted and cities with populations greater than 9,999 whose Asian and/or NHPI population rates are greater than the national average; (1) Native Hawaiian and other Pacific Islander; (2) excludes Taiwanese; (3) includes Chamorro; (4) county does not meet population threshold but is shown in order to allow inclusion of city

Place	Total foreign-born naturalized citizens	Total Asian population	Asians who are foreign-born naturalized citizens	Total NHPI[1] population	NHPIs[1] who are foreign-born naturalized citizens	Asian Indian	Bangladeshi	Cambodian	Chinese[2]	Fijian	Filipino	Guamanian[3]	Hawaiian, Native	Hmong	Indonesian	Japanese	Korean	Laotian	Malaysian	Pakistani	Samoan	Sri Lankan	Taiwanese	Thai	Tongan	Vietnamese
Plano (city)	13,559 6.10	22,465	7,003 31.17 31.17 51.65	-	-	1,280 22.54 18.28 5.70 9.44	-	-	2,882 30.97 41.15 12.83 21.26	-	244 31.28 3.48 1.09 1.80	-	-	-	-	18 3.61 0.26 0.08 0.13	811 37.91 11.58 3.61 5.98	-	-	141 23.34 2.01 0.63 1.04	-	-	300 53.19 4.28 1.34 2.21	-	-	941 52.16 13.44 4.19 6.94
Comal County	1,540 1.97	443	156 35.21 35.21 10.13	-	-	-	-	-	-	-	-	-	-	-	-	-	-	-	-	-	-	-	-	-	-	-
Coryell County	2,069 2.76	1,380	594 43.04 43.04 28.71	433	15 3.46 3.46 0.72	-	-	-	-	-	-	-	-	-	-	-	257 51.92 43.27 18.62 12.42	-	-	-	-	-	-	-	-	-
Dallas County	102,201 4.61	87,446	25,655 29.34 29.34 25.10	987	87 8.81 8.81 0.09	5,206 21.93 20.29 5.95 5.09	119 17.68 0.46 0.14 0.12	791 33.56 3.08 0.90 0.77	3,852 32.83 15.01 4.41 3.77	-	2,482 41.41 9.67 2.84 2.43	-	-	-	-	265 11.92 1.03 0.30 0.26	3,098 33.17 12.08 3.54 3.03	686 29.35 2.67 0.78 0.67	-	910 24.51 3.55 1.04 0.89	-	-	309 38.43 1.20 0.35 0.30	262 23.71 1.02 0.30 0.26	-	6,970 35.06 27.17 7.97 6.82
Addison (town)	866 6.28	1,104	309 27.99 27.99 35.68	-	-	100 16.50 32.36 9.06 11.55	-	-	-	-	-	-	-	-	-	-	-	-	-	-	-	-	-	-	-	-
Coppell (city)	1,443 4.01	3,444	958 27.82 27.82 66.39	-	-	193 16.93 20.15 5.60 13.37	-	-	270 34.79 28.18 7.84 18.71	-	-	-	-	-	-	-	232 34.12 24.22 6.74 16.08	-	-	-	-	-	-	-	-	-
Farmers Branch (city)	1,620 5.72	1,051	342 32.54 32.54 21.11	-	-	-	-	-	-	-	-	-	-	-	-	-	-	-	-	-	-	-	-	-	-	-
Garland (city)	12,339 5.71	15,646	5,176 33.08 33.08 41.95	-	-	811 26.14 15.67 5.18 6.57	-	-	702 41.91 13.56 4.49 5.69	-	474 42.59 9.16 3.03 3.84	-	-	-	-	-	309 27.15 5.97 1.97 2.50	-	-	207 24.91 4.00 1.32 1.68	-	-	-	-	-	2,274 36.09 43.93 14.53 18.43
Grand Prairie (city)	6,584 5.18	5,295	2,013 38.02 38.02 30.57	-	-	272 37.11 13.51 5.14 4.13	-	-	-	-	276 39.20 13.71 5.21 4.19	-	-	-	-	-	-	128 32.74 6.36 2.42 1.94	-	-	-	-	-	-	-	944 39.61 46.90 17.83 14.34
Irving (city)	10,262 5.36	15,637	3,474 22.22 22.22 33.85	-	-	849 13.93 24.44 5.43 8.27	-	-	332 21.46 9.56 2.12 3.24	-	341 44.06 9.82 2.18 3.32	-	-	-	-	21 3.10 0.60 0.13 0.20	705 28.43 20.29 4.51 6.87	102 21.29 2.94 0.65 0.99	-	96 22.38 2.76 0.61 0.94	-	-	-	-	-	667 42.38 19.20 4.27 6.50

Notes: Please refer to the User's Guide for an explanation of data; data is arranged alphabetically by state, then county, then city within each county; table includes counties with populations greater than 49,999 unless noted and cities with populations greater than 9,999 whose Asian and/or NHPI population rates are greater than the national average; (1) Native Hawaiian and other Pacific Islander; (2) excludes Taiwanese; (3) includes Chamorro; (4) county does not meet population threshold but is shown in order to allow inclusion of city

Place	Total foreign-born naturalized citizens	Total Asian population	Asians who are foreign-born naturalized citizens	Total NHPI[1] population	NHPIs[1] who are foreign-born naturalized citizens	Asian Indian	Bangladeshi	Cambodian	Chinese[2]	Fijian	Filipino	Guamanian[3]	Hawaiian, Native	Hmong	Indonesian	Japanese	Korean	Laotian	Malaysian	Pakistani	Samoan	Sri Lankan	Taiwanese	Thai	Tongan	Vietnamese
Mesquite (city)	4,168	4,557	1,509	-	-	655	-	-	-	-	372	-	-	-	-	-	-	-	-	-	-	-	-	-	-	-
	3.35		33.11			28.57					40.43															
						43.41					24.65															
			33.11			14.37					8.16															
			36.20			15.71					8.93															
Richardson (city)	6,156	10,196	3,485	-	-	562	-	-	1,153	-	150	-	-	-	-	-	351	-	-	125	-	-	-	-	-	817
	6.72		34.18			23.20			37.74		40.00						34.04			29.55						46.93
						16.13			33.08		4.30						10.07			3.59						23.44
			34.18			5.51			11.31		1.47						3.44			1.23						8.01
			56.61			9.13			18.73		2.44						5.70			2.03						13.27
Rowlett (city)	1,549	1,681	739	-	-	183	-	-	-	-	-	-	-	-	-	-	-	-	-	-	-	-	-	-	-	-
	3.49		43.96			32.22																				
						24.76																				
			43.96			10.89																				
			47.71			11.81																				
Denton County	14,061	17,110	5,439	-	-	1,580	-	264	513	-	371	-	-	-	-	68	733	-	-	212	-	-	-	-	-	1,334
	3.25		31.79			26.20		36.36	25.50		43.54					14.23	32.42			25.24						51.19
						29.05		4.85	9.43		6.82					1.25	13.48			3.90						24.53
			31.79			9.23		1.54	3.00		2.17					0.40	4.28			1.24						7.80
			38.68			11.24		1.88	3.65		2.64					0.48	5.21			1.51						9.49
Carrollton (city)	7,095	11,415	3,755	-	-	1,193	-	244	256	-	-	-	-	-	-	-	367	-	-	290	-	-	-	-	-	1,136
	6.50		32.90			27.21		29.83	37.87								34.85			24.87						47.25
						31.77		6.50	6.82								9.77			7.72						30.25
			32.90			10.45		2.14	2.24								3.22			2.54						9.95
			52.92			16.81		3.44	3.61								5.17			4.09						16.01
Lewisville (city)	2,999	3,043	1,040	-	-	287	-	-	-	-	-	-	-	-	-	-	-	-	-	-	-	-	-	-	-	265
	3.87		34.18			23.45																				58.63
						27.60																				25.48
			34.18			9.43																				8.71
			34.68			9.57																				8.84
Ector County	5,156	880	297	-	-	-	-	-	-	-	-	-	-	-	-	-	-	-	-	-	-	-	-	-	-	-
	4.26		33.75																							
			33.75																							
			5.76																							
El Paso County	77,821	6,956	2,490	554	21	334	-	-	201	-	571	-	-	-	-	364	715	-	-	-	-	-	-	-	-	-
	11.45		35.80		3.79	32.94			24.75		31.79					45.67	41.74									
						13.41			8.07		22.93					14.62	28.71									
			35.80		3.79	4.80			2.89		8.21					5.23	10.28									
			3.20		0.03	0.43			0.26		0.73					0.47	0.92									
Ellis County	2,031	441	188	-	-	-	-	-	-	-	-	-	-	-	-	-	-	-	-	-	-	-	-	-	-	-
	1.82		42.63																							
			42.63																							
			9.26																							
Fort Bend County	30,828	38,774	16,090	-	-	4,778	-	-	3,947	-	1,892	-	-	-	-	-	550	-	-	875	-	-	459	-	-	2,919
	8.70		41.50			37.36			40.08		43.05						47.99			35.85			37.75			56.05
						29.70			24.53		11.76						3.42			5.44			2.85			18.14
			41.50			12.32			10.18		4.88						1.42			2.26			1.18			7.53
			52.19			15.50			12.80		6.14						1.78			2.84			1.49			9.47

Notes: Please refer to the User's Guide for an explanation of data; data is arranged alphabetically by state, then county, then city within each county; table includes counties with populations greater than 49,999 unless noted and cities with populations greater than 9,999 whose Asian and/or NHPI population rates are greater than the national average; (1) Native Hawaiian and other Pacific Islander; (2) excludes Taiwanese; (3) includes Chamorro; (4) county does not meet population threshold but is shown in order to allow inclusion of city

Place	Total foreign-born naturalized citizens	Total Asian population	Asians who are foreign-born naturalized citizens	Total NHPI[1] population	NHPIs[1] who are foreign-born naturalized citizens	Asian Indian	Bangladeshi	Cambodian	Chinese[2]	Fijian	Filipino	Guamanian[3]	Hawaiian, Native	Hmong	Indonesian	Japanese	Korean	Laotian	Malaysian	Pakistani	Samoan	Sri Lankan	Taiwanese	Thai	Tongan	Vietnamese
Cinco Ranch (cdp)	474	690	233	-	-	-	-	-	-	-	-	-	-	-	-	-	-	-	-	-	-	-	-	-	-	-
	4.22		33.77																							
			33.77																							
			49.16																							
Mission Bend (cdp)	4,993	5,175	2,422	-	-	700	-	-	308	-	542	-	-	-	-	-	-	-	-	133	-	-	-	-	-	607
	16.16		46.80			53.44			44.83		58.85									27.71						48.06
						28.90			12.72		22.38									5.49						25.06
			46.80			13.53			5.95		10.47									2.57						11.73
			48.51			14.02			6.17		10.86									2.66						12.16
Missouri City (city)	5,110	5,746	2,503	-	-	845	-	-	591	-	429	-	-	-	-	-	-	-	-	-	-	-	-	-	-	354
	9.74		43.56			43.94			42.67		41.45															60.51
						33.76			23.61		17.14															14.14
			43.56			14.71			10.29		7.47															6.16
			48.98			16.54			11.57		8.40															6.93
New Territory (cdp)	1,907	3,250	1,377	-	-	616	-	-	217	-	-	-	-	-	-	-	-	-	-	-	-	-	-	-	-	-
	13.73		42.37			39.26			31.09																	
						44.73			15.76																	
			42.37			18.95			6.68																	
			72.21			32.30			11.38																	
Stafford (city)	1,643	3,312	1,118	-	-	205	-	-	221	-	193	-	-	-	-	-	-	-	-	-	-	-	-	-	-	371
	10.52		33.76			16.02			41.39		37.26															61.32
						18.34			19.77		17.26															33.18
			33.76			6.19			6.67		5.83															11.20
			68.05			12.48			13.45		11.75															22.58
Sugar Land (city)	8,766	14,417	6,257	-	-	1,684	-	-	2,270	-	409	-	-	-	-	-	234	-	-	263	-	-	400	-	-	720
	13.80		43.40			38.82			42.94		41.06						53.18			42.56			42.69			56.43
						26.91			36.28		6.54						3.74			4.20			6.39			11.51
			43.40			11.68			15.75		2.84						1.62			1.82			2.77			4.99
			71.38			19.21			25.90		4.67						2.67			3.00			4.56			8.21
Galveston County	7,233	5,275	1,861	-	-	265	-	-	220	-	380	-	-	-	-	-	-	-	-	-	-	-	-	-	-	684
	2.89		35.28			27.38			24.92		46.68															39.95
						14.24			11.82		20.42															36.75
			35.28			5.02			4.17		7.20															12.97
			25.73			3.66			3.04		5.25															9.46
Grayson County	1,096	647	257	-	-	-	-	-	-	-	-	-	-	-	-	-	-	-	-	-	-	-	-	-	-	-
	0.99		39.72																							
			39.72																							
			23.45																							
Gregg County	1,691	644	238	-	-	-	-	-	-	-	-	-	-	-	-	-	-	-	-	-	-	-	-	-	-	-
	1.52		36.96																							
			36.96																							
			14.07																							
Guadalupe County	2,505	896	479	-	-	-	-	-	-	-	-	-	-	-	-	-	-	-	-	-	-	-	-	-	-	-
	2.81		53.46																							
			53.46																							
			19.12																							

Notes: Please refer to the User's Guide for an explanation of data; data is arranged alphabetically by state, then county, then city within each county; table includes counties with populations greater than 49,999 unless noted and cities with populations greater than 9,999 whose Asian and/or NHPI population rates are greater than the national average; (1) Native Hawaiian and other Pacific Islander; (2) excludes Taiwanese; (3) includes Chamorro; (4) county does not meet population threshold but is shown in order to allow inclusion of city

Place	Total foreign-born naturalized citizens	Total Asian population	Asians who are foreign-born naturalized citizens	Total NHPI[1] population	NHPIs[1] who are foreign-born naturalized citizens	Asian Indian	Bangladeshi	Cambodian	Chinese[2]	Fijian	Filipino	Guamanian[3]	Hawaiian, Native	Hmong	Indonesian	Japanese	Korean	Laotian	Malaysian	Pakistani	Samoan	Sri Lankan	Taiwanese	Thai	Tongan	Vietnamese
Harris County	223,609 6.58	171,977	63,865 37.14 37.14 28.56	1,514	107 7.07 7.07 0.05	10,332 28.70 16.18 6.01 4.62	285 41.42 0.45 0.17 0.13	803 39.91 1.26 0.47 0.36	10,804 34.39 16.92 6.28 4.83	-	5,999 38.03 9.39 3.49 2.68	10 1.56 9.35 0.66 <0.01	-	-	57 8.26 0.09 0.03 0.03	438 11.91 0.69 0.25 0.20	3,377 41.62 5.29 1.96 1.51	581 49.15 0.91 0.34 0.26	-	2,088 28.48 3.27 1.21 0.93	-	-	1,161 52.23 1.82 0.68 0.52	331 24.83 0.52 0.19 0.15	-	25,833 46.59 40.45 15.02 11.55
Bellaire (city)	1,114 7.15	1,052	485 46.10 46.10 43.54	-	-	-	-	-	191 42.07 39.38 18.16 17.15	-	-	-	-	-	-	-	-	-	-	-	-	-	-	-	-	-
Houston (city)	136,472 6.98	102,484	35,425 34.57 34.57 25.96	876	79 9.02 9.02 0.06	5,190 25.35 14.65 5.06 3.80	-	254 35.13 0.72 0.25 0.19	7,033 32.18 19.85 6.86 5.15	-	2,941 38.26 8.30 2.87 2.16	10 2.26 12.66 1.14 0.01	-	-	14 2.71 0.04 0.01 0.01	225 9.35 0.64 0.22 0.16	1,999 38.52 5.64 1.95 1.46	-	-	1,249 24.99 3.53 1.22 0.92	-	-	762 51.07 2.15 0.74 0.56	233 26.45 0.66 0.23 0.17	-	14,200 44.63 40.08 13.86 10.41
West University Place (city)	675 4.75	745	350 46.98 46.98 51.85	-	-	-	-	-	-	-	-	-	-	-	-	-	-	-	-	-	-	-	-	-	-	-
Hays County	1,831 1.88	851	270 31.73 31.73 14.75	-	-	-	-	-	-	-	-	-	-	-	-	-	-	-	-	-	-	-	-	-	-	-
Hidalgo County	48,474 8.51	3,156	694 21.99 21.99 1.43	-	-	197 31.27 28.39 6.24 0.41	-	-	-	-	232 15.38 33.43 7.35 0.48	-	-	-	-	-	-	-	-	-	-	-	-	-	-	-
Hunt County	967 1.26	557	106 19.03 19.03 10.96	-	-	-	-	-	-	-	-	-	-	-	-	-	-	-	-	-	-	-	-	-	-	-
Jefferson County	5,727 2.27	7,033	2,213 31.47 31.47 38.64	-	-	314 34.85 14.19 4.46 5.48	-	-	192 39.51 8.68 2.73 3.35	-	251 26.31 11.34 3.57 4.38	-	-	-	-	-	-	-	-	-	-	-	-	-	-	1,300 31.75 58.74 18.48 22.70
Port Arthur (city)	2,319 4.02	3,388	1,025 30.25 30.25 44.20	-	-	-	-	-	-	-	-	-	-	-	-	-	-	-	-	-	-	-	-	-	-	918 32.45 89.56 27.10 39.59
Johnson County	2,312 1.82	650	211 32.46 32.46 9.13	-	-	-	-	-	-	-	-	-	-	-	-	-	-	-	-	-	-	-	-	-	-	-

Notes: Please refer to the User's Guide for an explanation of data; data is arranged alphabetically by state, then county, then city within each county; table includes counties with populations greater than 49,999 unless noted and cities with populations greater than 9,999 whose Asian and/or NHPI population rates are greater than the national average; (1) Native Hawaiian and other Pacific Islander; (2) excludes Taiwanese; (3) includes Chamorro; (4) county does not meet population threshold but is shown in order to allow inclusion of city

Place	Total foreign-born naturalized citizens	Total Asian population	Asians who are foreign-born naturalized citizens	Total NHPI[1] population	NHPIs[1] who are foreign-born naturalized citizens	Asian Indian	Bangladeshi	Cambodian	Chinese[2]	Fijian	Filipino	Guamanian[3]	Hawaiian, Native	Hmong	Indonesian	Japanese	Korean	Laotian	Malaysian	Pakistani	Samoan	Sri Lankan	Taiwanese	Thai	Tongan	Vietnamese
Kaufman County	1,303	487	313	-	-	-	-	-	-	-	-	-	-	-	-	-	-	-	-	-	-	-	-	-	-	-
	1.83		64.27																							
			64.27																							
			24.02																							
Lubbock County	3,617	2,971	931	-	-	231	-	-	127	-	-	-	-	-	-	-	-	-	-	-	-	-	-	-	-	135
	1.49		31.34			30.28			21.27																	36.68
						24.81			13.64																	14.50
			31.34			7.78			4.27																	4.54
			25.74			6.39			3.51																	3.73
McLennan County	3,707	2,134	687	-	-	141	-	-	-	-	-	-	-	-	-	-	-	-	-	-	-	-	-	-	-	-
	1.74		32.19			35.79																				
						20.52																				
			32.19			6.61																				
			18.53			3.80																				
Midland County	3,514	1,065	415	-	-	143	-	-	-	-	-	-	-	-	-	-	-	-	-	-	-	-	-	-	-	-
	3.03		38.97			35.93																				
						34.46																				
			38.97			13.43																				
			11.81			4.07																				
Montgomery County	7,715	3,133	1,374	-	-	483	-	-	285	-	223	-	-	-	-	-	-	-	-	-	-	-	-	-	-	-
	2.63		43.86			49.59			41.24		47.85															
						35.15			20.74		16.23															
			43.86			15.42			9.10		7.12															
			17.81			6.26			3.69		2.89															
Nacogdoches County	871	383	149	-	-	-	-	-	-	-	-	-	-	-	-	-	-	-	-	-	-	-	-	-	-	-
	1.47		38.90																							
			38.90																							
			17.11																							
Nueces County	9,113	3,507	1,640	-	-	296	-	-	-	-	788	-	-	-	-	-	-	-	-	-	-	-	-	-	-	-
	2.91		46.76			47.36					48.82															
						18.05					48.05															
			46.76			8.44					22.47															
			18.00			3.25					8.65															
Orange County	874	697	344	-	-	-	-	-	-	-	-	-	-	-	-	-	-	-	-	-	-	-	-	-	-	179
	1.03		49.35																							47.48
																										52.03
			49.35																							25.68
			39.36																							20.48
Potter County	3,859	2,990	1,085	-	-	-	-	-	-	-	-	-	-	-	-	-	-	464	-	-	-	-	-	-	-	350
	3.40		36.29															43.81								32.93
																		42.76								32.26
			36.29															15.52								11.71
			28.12															12.02								9.07
Randall County	1,183	1,131	346	-	-	-	-	-	-	-	-	-	-	-	-	-	-	-	-	-	-	-	-	-	-	-
	1.13		30.59																							
			30.59																							
			29.25																							

Notes: Please refer to the User's Guide for an explanation of data; data is arranged alphabetically by state, then county, then city within each county; table includes counties with populations greater than 49,999 unless noted and cities with populations greater than 9,999 whose Asian and/or NHPI population rates are greater than the national average; (1) Native Hawaiian and other Pacific Islander; (2) excludes Taiwanese; (3) includes Chamorro; (4) county does not meet population threshold but is shown in order to allow inclusion of city

Place	Total foreign-born naturalized citizens	Total Asian population	Asians who are foreign-born naturalized citizens	Total NHPI[1] population	NHPIs[1] who are foreign-born naturalized citizens	Asian Indian	Bangladeshi	Cambodian	Chinese[2]	Fijian	Filipino	Guamanian[3]	Hawaiian, Native	Hmong	Indonesian	Japanese	Korean	Laotian	Malaysian	Pakistani	Samoan	Sri Lankan	Taiwanese	Thai	Tongan	Vietnamese
San Patricio County	990	451	137	-	-	-	-	-	-	-	-	-	-	-	-	-	-	-	-	-	-	-	-	-	-	-
	1.47		30.38																							
			30.38																							
			13.84																							
Smith County	3,344	1,105	377	-	-	-	-	-	-	-	-	-	-	-	-	-	-	-	-	-	-	-	-	-	-	-
	1.91		34.12																							
			34.12																							
			11.27																							
Tarrant County	56,074	51,202	17,224	1,646	174	2,417	-	144	1,953	-	1,479	-	-	-	-	342	1,154	1,331	-	277	-	-	282	225	92	7,011
	3.88		33.64		10.57	25.51		18.51	35.19		42.50					33.11	36.18	41.68		28.09			41.96	29.03	25.21	36.57
						14.03		0.84	11.34		8.59					1.99	6.70	7.73		1.61			1.64	1.31	52.87	40.70
			33.64		10.57	4.72		0.28	3.81		2.89					0.67	2.25	2.60		0.54			0.55	0.44	5.59	13.69
			30.72		0.31	4.31		0.26	3.48		2.64					0.61	2.06	2.37		0.49			0.50	0.40	0.16	12.50
Arlington (city)	15,569	19,271	6,207	-	-	740	-	-	913	-	547	-	-	-	-	-	289	-	-	-	-	-	177	-	-	3,143
	4.68		32.21			24.61			33.04		45.89						31.90						42.65			34.83
						11.92			14.71		8.81						4.66						2.85			50.64
			32.21			3.84			4.74		2.84						1.50						0.92			16.31
			39.87			4.75			5.86		3.51						1.86						1.14			20.19
Euless (city)	2,199	3,232	863	-	-	284	-	-	-	-	-	-	-	-	-	-	-	-	-	-	-	-	-	-	-	-
	4.77		26.70			22.83																				
						32.91																				
			26.70			8.79																				
			39.25			12.91																				
Haltom City (city)	1,714	3,106	952	-	-	-	-	-	-	-	-	-	-	-	-	-	-	344	-	-	-	-	-	-	-	392
	4.37		30.65															42.36								24.87
																		36.13								41.18
			30.65															11.08								12.62
			55.54															20.07								22.87
Taylor County	2,008	1,678	465	-	-	-	-	-	-	-	146	-	-	-	-	-	-	-	-	-	-	-	-	-	-	-
	1.59		27.71								24.46															
											31.40															
			27.71								8.70															
			23.16								7.27															
Tom Green County	2,825	724	316	-	-	-	-	-	-	-	-	-	-	-	-	-	-	-	-	-	-	-	-	-	-	-
	2.72		43.65																							
			43.65																							
			11.19																							
Travis County	32,375	36,119	10,477	676	21	1,714	-	-	2,484	-	842	-	-	-	-	173	994	-	-	110	-	-	331	92	-	3,252
	3.99		29.01		3.11	20.33			28.23		37.96					14.24	23.93			15.19			39.40	22.89		44.03
						16.36			23.71		8.04					1.65	9.49			1.05			3.16	0.88		31.04
			29.01		3.11	4.75			6.88		2.33					0.48	2.75			0.30			0.92	0.25		9.00
			32.36		0.06	5.29			7.67		2.60					0.53	3.07			0.34			1.02	0.28		10.04
Austin (city)	26,747	30,866	8,452	445	5	1,385	-	-	2,165	-	551	-	-	-	-	151	764	-	-	86	-	-	270	-	-	2,614
	4.08		27.38		1.12	18.88			26.99		31.81					13.30	21.04			16.35			36.10			45.15
						16.39			25.62		6.52					1.79	9.04			1.02			3.19			30.93
			27.38		1.12	4.49			7.01		1.79					0.49	2.48			0.28			0.87			8.47
			31.60		0.02	5.18			8.09		2.06					0.56	2.86			0.32			1.01			9.77

Notes: Please refer to the User's Guide for an explanation of data; data is arranged alphabetically by state, then county, then city within each county; table includes counties with populations greater than 49,999 unless noted and cities with populations greater than 9,999 whose Asian and/or NHPI population rates are greater than the national average; (1) Native Hawaiian and other Pacific Islander; (2) excludes Taiwanese; (3) includes Chamorro; (4) county does not meet population threshold but is shown in order to allow inclusion of city

Place	Total foreign-born naturalized citizens	Total Asian population	Asians who are foreign-born naturalized citizens	Total NHPI[1] population	NHPIs[1] who are foreign-born naturalized citizens	Asian Indian	Bangladeshi	Cambodian	Chinese[2]	Fijian	Filipino	Guamanian[3]	Hawaiian, Native	Hmong	Indonesian	Japanese	Korean	Laotian	Malaysian	Pakistani	Samoan	Sri Lankan	Taiwanese	Thai	Tongan	Vietnamese
Pflugerville (city)	651 3.98	728	371 50.96 50.96 56.99	-	-	-	-	-	-	-	-	-	-	-	-	-	-	-	-	-	-	-	-	-	-	-
Wells Branch (cdp)	679 6.04	1,077	413 38.35 38.35 60.82	-	-	-	-	-	-	-	-	-	-	-	-	-	-	-	-	-	-	-	-	-	-	-
Victoria County	1,407 1.67	492	205 41.67 41.67 14.57	-	-	-	-	-	-	-	-	-	-	-	-	-	-	-	-	-	-	-	-	-	-	-
Webb County	18,867 9.77	801	200 24.97 24.97 1.06	-	-	-	-	-	-	-	-	-	-	-	-	-	-	-	-	-	-	-	-	-	-	-
Wichita County	2,924 2.22	2,538	991 39.05 39.05 33.89	-	-	-	-	-	-	-	233 40.10 23.51 9.18 7.97	-	-	-	-	-	-	-	-	-	-	-	-	-	-	292 36.59 29.47 11.51 9.99
Williamson County	7,485 2.99	6,457	2,462 38.13 38.13 32.89	-	-	576 34.45 23.40 8.92 7.70	-	-	501 34.84 20.35 7.76 6.69	-	-	-	-	-	-	-	335 47.79 13.61 5.19 4.48	-	-	-	-	-	-	-	-	508 46.27 20.63 7.87 6.79
Brushy Creek (cdp)	675 4.25	933	296 31.73 31.73 43.85	-	-	-	-	-	-	-	-	-	-	-	-	-	-	-	-	-	-	-	-	-	-	-
Jollyville (cdp)	771 4.99	1,181	485 41.07 41.07 62.91	-	-	-	-	-	-	-	-	-	-	-	-	-	-	-	-	-	-	-	-	-	-	-
UTAH	48,178 2.16	36,878	10,311 27.96 27.96 21.40	14,366	2,300 16.01 16.01 4.77	952 30.16 9.23 2.58 1.98	-	472 32.40 4.58 1.28 0.98	2,041 28.17 19.79 5.53 4.24	-	1,162 31.36 11.27 3.15 2.41	-	10 0.75 0.43 0.07 0.02	-	-	363 6.07 3.52 0.98 0.75	1,276 35.62 12.38 3.46 2.65	789 35.80 7.65 2.14 1.64	-	119 29.68 1.15 0.32 0.25	595 15.82 25.87 4.14 1.24	-	108 29.19 1.05 0.29 0.22	230 32.53 2.23 0.62 0.48	1,377 20.26 59.87 9.59 2.86	2,361 42.52 22.90 6.40 4.90
Cache County	1,338 1.46	1,733	274 15.81 15.81 20.48	-	-	-	-	-	82 14.39 29.93 4.73 6.13	-	-	-	-	-	-	-	-	-	-	-	-	-	-	-	-	-

Notes: Please refer to the User's Guide for an explanation of data; data is arranged alphabetically by state, then county, then city within each county; table includes counties with populations greater than 49,999 unless noted and cities with populations greater than 9,999 whose Asian and/or NHPI population rates are greater than the national average; (1) Native Hawaiian and other Pacific Islander; (2) excludes Taiwanese; (3) includes Chamorro; (4) county does not meet population threshold but is shown in order to allow inclusion of city

Place	Total foreign-born naturalized citizens	Total Asian population	Asians who are foreign-born naturalized citizens	Total NHPI[1] population	NHPIs[1] who are foreign-born naturalized citizens	Asian Indian	Bangladeshi	Cambodian	Chinese[2]	Fijian	Filipino	Guamanian[3]	Hawaiian, Native	Hmong	Indonesian	Japanese	Korean	Laotian	Malaysian	Pakistani	Samoan	Sri Lankan	Taiwanese	Thai	Tongan	Vietnamese
Davis County	4,262 1.78	3,497	1,065 30.45 30.45 24.99	928	99 10.67 10.67 2.32	-	-	-	-	-	229 27.69 21.50 6.55 5.37	-	-	-	-	57 7.17 5.35 1.63 1.34	184 48.81 17.28 5.26 4.32	-	-	-	-	-	-	-	-	-
Salt Lake County	28,519 3.17	23,211	7,080 30.50 30.50 24.83	10,334	1,931 18.69 18.69 6.77	688 31.29 9.72 2.96 2.41	-	388 34.99 5.48 1.67 1.36	1,383 30.44 19.53 5.96 4.85	-	629 35.58 8.88 2.71 2.21	-	0 0.00 0.00 0.00 0.00	-	-	197 6.30 2.78 0.85 0.69	626 34.62 8.84 2.70 2.20	594 33.20 8.39 2.56 2.08	-	-	479 18.52 24.81 4.64 1.68	-	-	-	1,263 21.27 65.41 12.22 4.43	2,076 44.47 29.32 8.94 7.28
Kearns (cdp)	1,204 3.58	862	202 23.43 23.43 16.78	406	41 10.10 10.10 3.41	-	-	-	-	-	-	-	-	-	-	-	-	-	-	-	-	-	-	-	-	-
Salt Lake City (city)	7,711 4.25	6,484	1,796 27.70 27.70 23.29	3,315	673 20.30 20.30 8.73	172 25.71 9.58 2.65 2.23	-	-	365 23.17 20.32 5.63 4.73	-	225 43.10 12.53 3.47 2.92	-	-	-	-	52 5.41 2.90 0.80 0.67	84 16.50 4.68 1.30 1.09	-	-	-	107 23.57 15.90 3.23 1.39	-	-	-	526 21.50 78.16 15.87 6.82	546 40.41 30.40 8.42 7.08
Sandy (city)	2,392 2.71	1,544	522 33.81 33.81 21.82	383	78 20.37 20.37 3.26	-	-	-	127 31.13 24.33 8.23 5.31	-	-	-	-	-	-	-	-	-	-	-	-	-	-	-	-	-
Taylorsville (city)	1,948 3.37	1,736	690 39.75 39.75 35.42	713	168 23.56 23.56 8.62	-	-	-	-	-	-	-	-	-	-	-	-	-	-	-	-	-	-	-	-	294 49.58 42.61 16.94 15.09
West Jordan (city)	1,474 2.16	1,198	379 31.64 31.64 25.71	699	130 18.60 18.60 8.82	-	-	-	-	-	-	-	-	-	-	-	-	-	-	-	-	-	-	-	115 24.47 88.46 16.45 7.80	-
West Valley City (city)	4,774 4.39	4,764	1,605 33.69 33.69 33.62	3,126	531 16.99 16.99 11.12	-	-	242 36.67 15.08 5.08 5.07	210 30.61 13.08 4.41 4.40	-	-	-	-	-	-	-	-	126 27.33 7.85 2.64 2.64	-	-	160 18.58 30.13 5.12 3.35	-	-	-	319 17.66 60.08 10.20 6.68	710 47.27 44.24 14.90 14.87
Utah County	6,049 1.64	3,959	876 22.13 22.13 14.48	1,805	183 10.14 10.14 3.03	-	-	-	260 21.28 29.68 6.57 4.30	-	130 31.78 14.84 3.28 2.15	-	10 2.58 5.46 0.55 0.17	-	-	50 6.57 5.71 1.26 0.83	165 31.61 18.84 4.17 2.73	-	-	-	38 6.92 20.77 2.11 0.63	-	-	-	76 16.45 41.53 4.21 1.26	-
Orem (city)	1,853 2.20	1,233	302 24.49 24.49 16.30	700	50 7.14 7.14 2.70	-	-	-	-	-	-	-	-	-	-	-	-	-	-	-	-	-	-	-	-	-

Notes: Please refer to the User's Guide for an explanation of data; data is arranged alphabetically by state, then county, then city within each county; table includes counties with populations greater than 49,999 unless noted and cities with populations greater than 9,999 whose Asian and/or NHPI population rates are greater than the national average; (1) Native Hawaiian and other Pacific Islander; (2) excludes Taiwanese; (3) includes Chamorro; (4) county does not meet population threshold but is shown in order to allow inclusion of city

Place	Total foreign-born naturalized citizens	Total Asian population	Asians who are foreign-born naturalized citizens	Total NHPI[1] population	NHPIs[1] who are foreign-born naturalized citizens	Asian Indian	Bangladeshi	Cambodian	Chinese[2]	Fijian	Filipino	Guamanian[3]	Hawaiian, Native	Hmong	Indonesian	Japanese	Korean	Laotian	Malaysian	Pakistani	Samoan	Sri Lankan	Taiwanese	Thai	Tongan	Vietnamese
Provo (city)	2,094 1.99	1,972	347 17.60 17.60 16.57	668	73 10.93 10.93 3.49	-	-	-	186 24.31 53.60 9.43 8.88	-	-	-	-	-	-	6 1.39 1.73 0.30 0.29	-	-	-	-	-	-	-	-	-	-
Washington County	1,398 1.55	459	59 12.85 12.85 4.22	462	25 5.41 5.41 1.79	-	-	-	-	-	-	-	-	-	-	-	-	-	-	-	-	-	-	-	-	-
St. George (city)	931 1.88	388	46 11.86 11.86 4.94	418	25 5.98 5.98 2.69	-	-	-	-	-	-	-	-	-	-	-	-	-	-	-	-	-	-	-	-	-
Weber County	3,248 1.65	2,352	603 25.64 25.64 18.57	-	-	-	-	-	-	-	-	-	-	-	-	21 3.31 3.48 0.89 0.65	-	-	-	-	-	-	-	-	-	-
VERMONT	12,451 2.05	4,851	2,006 41.35 41.35 16.11	-	-	316 45.34 15.75 6.51 2.54	-	-	373 32.83 18.59 7.69 3.00	-	164 52.23 8.18 3.38 1.32	-	-	-	-	40 10.64 1.99 0.82 0.32	417 61.32 20.79 8.60 3.35	-	-	-	-	-	-	-	-	520 48.51 25.92 10.72 4.18
Chittenden County	3,939 2.69	2,732	1,003 36.71 36.71 25.46	-	-	111 30.00 11.07 4.06 2.82	-	-	189 28.25 18.84 6.92 4.80	-	-	-	-	-	-	-	-	-	-	-	-	-	-	-	-	369 44.09 36.79 13.51 9.37
Rutland County	797 1.26	213	94 44.13 44.13 11.79	-	-	-	-	-	-	-	-	-	-	-	-	-	-	-	-	-	-	-	-	-	-	-
Washington County	1,117 1.92	262	150 57.25 57.25 13.43	-	-	-	-	-	-	-	-	-	-	-	-	-	-	-	-	-	-	-	-	-	-	-
Windsor County	1,026 1.79	446	266 59.64 59.64 25.93	-	-	-	-	-	-	-	-	-	-	-	-	-	-	-	-	-	-	-	-	-	-	-
VIRGINIA	232,767 3.29	256,355	97,291 37.95 37.95 41.80	3,617	323 8.93 8.93 0.14	13,777 28.96 14.16 5.37 5.92	452 25.00 0.46 0.18 0.19	1,828 36.80 1.88 0.71 0.79	12,674 37.00 13.03 4.94 5.44	-	20,620 42.94 21.19 8.04 8.86	40 3.94 12.38 1.11 0.02	17 1.84 5.26 0.47 0.01	-	262 23.93 0.27 0.10 0.11	1,862 21.03 1.91 0.73 0.80	18,627 41.34 19.15 7.27 8.00	1,287 42.89 1.32 0.50 0.55	-	3,138 30.00 3.23 1.22 1.35	88 16.92 27.24 2.43 0.04	243 38.21 0.25 0.09 0.10	618 47.00 0.64 0.24 0.27	1,176 32.84 1.21 0.46 0.51	-	18,278 51.57 18.79 7.13 7.85

Notes: Please refer to the User's Guide for an explanation of data; data is arranged alphabetically by state, then county, then city within each county; table includes counties with populations greater than 49,999 unless noted and cities with populations greater than 9,999 whose Asian and/or NHPI population rates are greater than the national average; (1) Native Hawaiian and other Pacific Islander; (2) excludes Taiwanese; (3) includes Chamorro; (4) county does not meet population threshold but is shown in order to allow inclusion of city

Place	Total foreign-born naturalized citizens	Total Asian population	Asians who are foreign-born naturalized citizens	Total NHPI[1] population	NHPIs[1] who are foreign-born naturalized citizens	Asian Indian	Bangladeshi	Cambodian	Chinese[2]	Fijian	Filipino	Guamanian[3]	Hawaiian, Native	Hmong	Indonesian	Japanese	Korean	Laotian	Malaysian	Pakistani	Samoan	Sri Lankan	Taiwanese	Thai	Tongan	Vietnamese
Albemarle County	1,791	2,458	584	-	-	142	-	-	195	-	-	-	-	-	-	-	-	-	-	-	-	-	-	-	-	-
	2.26		23.76			19.72			21.69																	
						24.32			33.39																	
			23.76			5.78			7.93																	
			32.61			7.93			10.89																	
Alexandria Independent City	9,248	6,985	2,387	-	-	278	-	-	432	-	309	-	-	-	-	-	584	-	-	152	-	-	-	-	-	318
	7.21		34.17			17.58			53.80		28.53						46.91			26.48						65.70
						11.65			18.10		12.95						24.47			6.37						13.32
			34.17			3.98			6.18		4.42						8.36			2.18						4.55
			25.81			3.01			4.67		3.34						6.31			1.64						3.44
Arlington County	14,393	15,761	4,689	-	-	825	-	95	669	-	759	-	-	-	-	79	618	-	-	165	-	-	-	-	-	1,125
	7.60		29.75			23.70		26.91	28.50		37.04					6.95	44.40			20.60						51.39
						17.59		2.03	14.27		16.19					1.68	13.18			3.52						23.99
			29.75			5.23		0.60	4.24		4.82					0.50	3.92			1.05						7.14
			32.58			5.73		0.66	4.65		5.27					0.55	4.29			1.15						7.82
Arlington (cdp)	14,393	15,761	4,689	-	-	825	-	95	669	-	759	-	-	-	-	79	618	-	-	165	-	-	-	-	-	1,125
	7.60		29.75			23.70		26.91	28.50		37.04					6.95	44.40			20.60						51.39
						17.59		2.03	14.27		16.19					1.68	13.18			3.52						23.99
			29.75			5.23		0.60	4.24		4.82					0.50	3.92			1.05						7.14
			32.58			5.73		0.66	4.65		5.27					0.55	4.29			1.15						7.82
Bedford County	635	581	248	-	-	-	-	-	-	-	-	-	-	-	-	-	-	-	-	-	-	-	-	-	-	-
	1.05		42.69																							
			42.69																							
			39.06																							
Charlottesville Independent City	1,017	2,172	450	-	-	61	-	-	94	-	-	-	-	-	-	-	-	-	-	-	-	-	-	-	-	-
	2.26		20.72			12.35			13.41																	
						13.56			20.89																	
			20.72			2.81			4.33																	
			44.25			6.00			9.24																	
Chesapeake Independent City	3,627	3,440	1,704	-	-	-	-	-	-	-	988	-	-	-	-	-	-	-	-	-	-	-	-	-	-	-
	1.82		49.53								54.86															
											57.98															
			49.53								28.72															
			46.98								27.24															
Chesterfield County	6,444	6,363	2,363	-	-	435	-	95	381	-	325	-	-	-	-	-	602	-	-	-	-	-	-	-	-	305
	2.48		37.14			41.79		14.26	40.32		46.36						39.71									40.99
						18.41		4.02	16.12		13.75						25.48									12.91
			37.14			6.84		1.49	5.99		5.11						9.46									4.79
			36.67			6.75		1.47	5.91		5.04						9.34									4.73
Fairfax Independent City	1,906	2,530	906	-	-	82	-	-	215	-	-	-	-	-	-	-	128	-	-	-	-	-	-	-	-	252
	8.87		35.81			16.21			41.83								23.32									58.33
						9.05			23.73								14.13									27.81
			35.81			3.24			8.50								5.06									9.96
			47.53			4.30			11.28								6.72									13.22
Fairfax County	98,601	123,612	47,287	884	118	7,156	237	833	6,592	-	4,722	-	-	-	112	558	10,933	716	-	1,836	-	-	408	483	-	11,431
	10.17		38.25		13.35	28.68	26.27	45.15	40.73		37.10				18.82	19.20	39.49	47.23		29.19			55.28	32.37		53.69
						15.13	0.50	1.76	13.94		9.99				0.24	1.18	23.12	1.51		3.88			0.86	1.02		24.17
			38.25		13.35	5.79	0.19	0.67	5.33		3.82				0.09	0.45	8.84	0.58		1.49			0.33	0.39		9.25
			47.96		0.12	7.26	0.24	0.84	6.69		4.79				0.11	0.57	11.09	0.73		1.86			0.41	0.49		11.59

Notes: Please refer to the User's Guide for an explanation of data; data is arranged alphabetically by state, then county, then city within each county; table includes counties with populations greater than 49,999 unless noted and cities with populations greater than 9,999 whose Asian and/or NHPI population rates are greater than the national average; (1) Native Hawaiian and other Pacific Islander; (2) excludes Taiwanese; (3) includes Chamorro; (4) county does not meet population threshold but is shown in order to allow inclusion of city

Place	Total foreign-born naturalized citizens	Total Asian population	Asians who are foreign-born naturalized citizens	Total NHPI[1] population	NHPIs[1] who are foreign-born naturalized citizens	Asian Indian	Bangladeshi	Cambodian	Chinese[2]	Fijian	Filipino	Guamanian[3]	Hawaiian, Native	Hmong	Indonesian	Japanese	Korean	Laotian	Malaysian	Pakistani	Samoan	Sri Lankan	Taiwanese	Thai	Tongan	Vietnamese
Annandale (cdp)	7,303	10,446	4,070	-	-	270	-	-	335	-	282	-	-	-	-	-	1,072	-	-	-	-	-	-	-	-	1,748
	13.27		38.96			23.56			34.47		44.06						31.94									52.19
						6.63			8.23		6.93						26.34									42.95
			38.96			2.58			3.21		2.70						10.26									16.73
			55.73			3.70			4.59		3.86						14.68									23.94
Bailey's Crossroads (cdp)	2,902	2,502	838	-	-	-	-	-	-	-	-	-	-	-	-	-	-	-	-	58	-	-	-	-	-	275
	12.69		33.49																	16.16						47.83
																				6.92						32.82
			33.49																	2.32						10.99
			28.88																	2.00						9.48
Burke (cdp)	6,230	8,266	3,660	-	-	634	-	-	337	-	454	-	-	-	-	-	1,279	-	-	-	-	-	-	-	-	680
	10.81		44.28			44.55			44.64		42.27						41.07									59.86
						17.32			9.21		12.40						34.95									18.58
			44.28			7.67			4.08		5.49						15.47									8.23
			58.75			10.18			5.41		7.29						20.53									10.91
Centreville (cdp)	4,364	6,337	2,070	-	-	339	-	-	342	-	349	-	-	-	-	-	625	-	-	-	-	-	-	-	-	214
	8.99		32.67			20.53			36.04		38.18						38.56									50.95
						16.38			16.52		16.86						30.19									10.34
			32.67			5.35			5.40		5.51						9.86									3.38
			47.43			7.77			7.84		8.00						14.32									4.90
Chantilly (cdp)	4,518	6,492	2,509	-	-	505	-	-	414	-	-	-	-	-	-	-	458	-	-	-	-	-	-	-	-	567
	11.00		38.65			24.16			42.95								39.21									57.27
						20.13			16.50								18.25									22.60
			38.65			7.78			6.38								7.05									8.73
			55.53			11.18			9.16								10.14									12.55
Franconia (cdp)	3,235	3,142	1,371	-	-	179	-	-	-	-	228	-	-	-	-	-	260	-	-	-	-	-	-	-	-	349
	10.12		43.63			43.24					38.84						43.77									66.48
						13.06					16.63						18.96									25.46
			43.63			5.70					7.26						8.27									11.11
			42.38			5.53					7.05						8.04									10.79
Groveton (cdp)	1,787	1,628	661	-	-	-	-	-	-	-	-	-	-	-	-	-	-	-	-	-	-	-	-	-	-	-
	8.40		40.60																							
			40.60																							
			36.99																							
Herndon (town)	1,843	3,199	1,019	-	-	318	-	-	-	-	-	-	-	-	-	-	-	-	-	-	-	-	-	-	-	280
	8.51		31.85			30.11																				66.04
						31.21																				27.48
			31.85			9.94																				8.75
			55.29			17.25																				15.19
Hybla Valley (cdp)	1,107	1,281	344	-	-	-	-	-	-	-	-	-	-	-	-	-	-	-	-	-	-	-	-	-	-	-
	6.58		26.85																							
			26.85																							
			31.07																							
Idylwood (cdp)	1,994	3,183	900	-	-	132	-	-	142	-	-	-	-	-	-	-	-	-	-	-	-	-	-	-	-	318
	12.42		28.28			13.24			24.83																	48.92
						14.67			15.78																	35.33
			28.28			4.15			4.46																	9.99
			45.14			6.62			7.12																	15.95

Notes: Please refer to the User's Guide for an explanation of data; data is arranged alphabetically by state, then county, then city within each county; table includes counties with populations greater than 49,999 unless noted and cities with populations greater than 9,999 whose Asian and/or NHPI population rates are greater than the national average; (1) Native Hawaiian and other Pacific Islander; (2) excludes Taiwanese; (3) includes Chamorro; (4) county does not meet population threshold but is shown in order to allow inclusion of city

Place	Total foreign-born naturalized citizens	Total Asian population	Asians who are foreign-born naturalized citizens	Total NHPI[1] population	NHPIs[1] who are foreign-born naturalized citizens	Asian Indian	Bangladeshi	Cambodian	Chinese[2]	Fijian	Filipino	Guamanian[3]	Hawaiian, Native	Hmong	Indonesian	Japanese	Korean	Laotian	Malaysian	Pakistani	Samoan	Sri Lankan	Taiwanese	Thai	Tongan	Vietnamese
Jefferson (cdp)	4,040 14.78	5,249	2,327 44.33 44.33 57.60	-	-	145 17.18 6.23 2.76 3.59	-	-	246 44.97 10.57 4.69 6.09	-	208 41.27 8.94 3.96 5.15	-	-	-	-	-	-	-	-	-	-	-	-	-	-	1,248 54.52 53.63 23.78 30.89
Lincolnia (cdp)	2,489 15.69	2,337	1,036 44.33 44.33 41.62	-	-	-	-	-	-	-	-	-	-	-	-	-	-	-	-	114 22.05 11.00 4.88 4.58	-	-	-	-	-	317 63.15 30.60 13.56 12.74
Lorton (cdp)	1,330 7.49	1,425	641 44.98 44.98 48.20	-	-	-	-	-	-	-	-	-	-	-	-	-	-	-	-	-	-	-	-	-	-	-
McLean (cdp)	3,469 8.89	4,229	1,436 33.96 33.96 41.40	-	-	314 32.95 21.87 7.42 9.05	-	-	352 45.65 24.51 8.32 10.15	-	119 23.47 8.29 2.81 3.43	-	-	-	-	22 3.99 1.53 0.52 0.63	303 36.73 21.10 7.16 8.73	-	-	-	-	-	-	-	-	-
Merrifield (cdp)	1,782 16.08	3,156	977 30.96 30.96 54.83	-	-	267 31.41 27.33 8.46 14.98	-	-	-	-	-	-	-	-	-	-	156 18.37 15.97 4.94 8.75	-	-	-	-	-	-	-	-	332 47.23 33.98 10.52 18.63
Mount Vernon (cdp)	2,271 7.95	1,856	812 43.75 43.75 35.76	-	-	-	-	-	-	-	-	-	-	-	-	-	264 57.14 32.51 14.22 11.62	-	-	-	-	-	-	-	-	-
Newington (cdp)	2,108 10.70	2,141	909 42.46 42.46 43.12	-	-	196 52.41 21.56 9.15 9.30	-	-	-	-	195 40.71 21.45 9.11 9.25	-	-	-	-	-	153 31.81 16.83 7.15 7.26	-	-	-	-	-	-	-	-	-
Oakton (cdp)	2,554 8.69	4,123	1,204 29.20 29.20 47.14	-	-	125 13.24 10.38 3.03 4.89	-	-	466 46.51 38.70 11.30 18.25	-	-	-	-	-	-	-	300 26.64 24.92 7.28 11.75	-	-	-	-	-	-	-	-	205 44.76 17.03 4.97 8.03
Reston (cdp)	4,693 8.31	5,237	1,549 29.58 29.58 33.01	-	-	373 19.57 24.08 7.12 7.95	-	-	258 36.13 16.66 4.93 5.50	-	148 25.47 9.55 2.83 3.15	-	-	-	-	-	350 51.47 22.60 6.68 7.46	-	-	-	-	-	-	-	-	-
Rose Hill (cdp)	1,323 8.85	1,223	573 46.85 46.85 43.31	-	-	-	-	-	-	-	-	-	-	-	-	-	-	-	-	-	-	-	-	-	-	-

Notes: Please refer to the User's Guide for an explanation of data; data is arranged alphabetically by state, then county, then city within each county; table includes counties with populations greater than 49,999 unless noted and cities with populations greater than 9,999 whose Asian and/or NHPI population rates are greater than the national average; (1) Native Hawaiian and other Pacific Islander; (2) excludes Taiwanese; (3) includes Chamorro; (4) county does not meet population threshold but is shown in order to allow inclusion of city

Place	Total foreign-born naturalized citizens	Total Asian population	Asians who are foreign-born naturalized citizens	Total NHPI[1] population	NHPIs[1] who are foreign-born naturalized citizens	Asian Indian	Bangladeshi	Cambodian	Chinese[2]	Fijian	Filipino	Guamanian[3]	Hawaiian, Native	Hmong	Indonesian	Japanese	Korean	Laotian	Malaysian	Pakistani	Samoan	Sri Lankan	Taiwanese	Thai	Tongan	Vietnamese
Springfield (cdp)	4,888 16.15	6,589	2,668 40.49 40.49 54.58	-	-	338 35.10 12.67 5.13 6.91	-	-	154 36.15 5.77 2.34 3.15	-	292 28.40 10.94 4.43 5.97	-	-	-	-	-	355 44.43 13.31 5.39 7.26	182 45.73 6.82 2.76 3.72	-	-	-	-	-	-	-	1,043 56.44 39.09 15.83 21.34
Tysons Corner (cdp)	2,230 12.05	3,155	850 26.94 26.94 38.12	-	-	114 15.49 13.41 3.61 5.11	-	-	225 34.40 26.47 7.13 10.09	-	-	-	-	-	-	-	251 31.93 29.53 7.96 11.26	-	-	-	-	-	-	-	-	-
Vienna (town)	1,276 8.77	1,207	467 38.69 38.69 36.60	-	-	-	-	-	-	-	-	-	-	-	-	-	-	-	-	-	-	-	-	-	-	-
West Springfield (cdp)	3,226 11.28	3,917	1,626 41.51 41.51 50.40	-	-	183 41.12 11.25 4.67 5.67	-	-	134 39.88 8.24 3.42 4.15	-	-	-	-	-	-	-	527 38.64 32.41 13.45 16.34	-	-	-	-	-	-	-	-	399 44.24 24.54 10.19 12.37
Wolf Trap (cdp)	1,383 9.96	1,254	644 51.36 51.36 46.57	-	-	151 41.83 23.45 12.04 10.92	-	-	141 52.03 21.89 11.24 10.20	-	-	-	-	-	-	-	-	-	-	-	-	-	-	-	-	-
Falls Church Independent City	706 6.80	674	277 41.10 41.10 39.24	-	-	-	-	-	-	-	-	-	-	-	-	-	-	-	-	-	-	-	-	-	-	-
Fauquier County	927 1.68	471	211 44.80 44.80 22.76	-	-	-	-	-	-	-	-	-	-	-	-	-	-	-	-	-	-	-	-	-	-	-
Frederick County	594 1.00	515	190 36.89 36.89 31.99	-	-	-	-	-	-	-	-	-	-	-	-	-	-	-	-	-	-	-	-	-	-	-
Hampton Independent City	3,335 2.28	2,570	1,140 44.36 44.36 34.18	-	-	-	-	-	-	-	288 42.92 25.26 11.21 8.64	-	-	-	-	-	-	-	-	-	-	-	-	-	-	288 54.65 25.26 11.21 8.64
Hanover County	792 0.92	539	234 43.41 43.41 29.55	-	-	-	-	-	-	-	-	-	-	-	-	-	-	-	-	-	-	-	-	-	-	-

Notes: Please refer to the User's Guide for an explanation of data; data is arranged alphabetically by state, then county, then city within each county; table includes counties with populations greater than 49,999 unless noted and cities with populations greater than 9,999 whose Asian and/or NHPI population rates are greater than the national average; (1) Native Hawaiian and other Pacific Islander; (2) excludes Taiwanese; (3) includes Chamorro; (4) county does not meet population threshold but is shown in order to allow inclusion of city

Place	Total foreign-born naturalized citizens	Total Asian population	Asians who are foreign-born naturalized citizens	Total NHPI[1] population	NHPIs[1] who are foreign-born naturalized citizens	Asian Indian	Bangladeshi	Cambodian	Chinese[2]	Fijian	Filipino	Guamanian[3]	Hawaiian, Native	Hmong	Indonesian	Japanese	Korean	Laotian	Malaysian	Pakistani	Samoan	Sri Lankan	Taiwanese	Thai	Tongan	Vietnamese
Henrico County	7,215	9,273	3,250	-	-	737	-	303	554	-	235	-	-	-	-	-	461	-	-	-	-	-	-	-	-	632
	2.75		35.05			27.37		37.22	33.74		33.81						50.05									42.65
						22.68		9.32	17.05		7.23						14.18									19.45
			35.05			7.95		3.27	5.97		2.53						4.97									6.82
			45.05			10.21		4.20	7.68		3.26						6.39									8.76
Glen Allen (cdp)	353	467	210	-	-	-	-	-	-	-	-	-	-	-	-	-	-	-	-	-	-	-	-	-	-	-
	2.76		44.97																							
			44.97																							
			59.49																							
Laurel (cdp)	555	775	223	-	-	-	-	-	-	-	-	-	-	-	-	-	-	-	-	-	-	-	-	-	-	-
	3.80		28.77																							
			28.77																							
			40.18																							
Loudoun County	7,998	8,927	3,311	-	-	513	-	-	377	-	440	-	-	-	-	-	539	-	-	218	-	-	-	-	-	916
	4.72		37.09			26.99			32.84		37.61						49.31			34.77						52.49
						15.49			11.39		13.29						16.28			6.58						27.67
			37.09			5.75			4.22		4.93						6.04			2.44						10.26
			41.40			6.41			4.71		5.50						6.74			2.73						11.45
Lynchburg Independent City	754	960	347	-	-	-	-	-	-	-	-	-	-	-	-	-	-	-	-	-	-	-	-	-	-	-
	1.16		36.15																							
			36.15																							
			46.02																							
Manassas Park Indep. City	422	385	140	-	-	-	-	-	-	-	-	-	-	-	-	-	-	-	-	-	-	-	-	-	-	-
	4.10		36.36																							
			36.36																							
			33.18																							
Montgomery County	1,192	3,132	503	-	-	89	-	-	114	-	-	-	-	-	-	-	163	-	-	-	-	-	-	-	-	-
	1.43		16.06			13.88			13.03								21.14									
						17.69			22.66								32.41									
			16.06			2.84			3.64								5.20									
			42.20			7.47			9.56								13.67									
Blacksburg (town)	1,006	2,885	402	-	-	59	-	-	93	-	-	-	-	-	-	-	125	-	-	-	-	-	-	-	-	-
	2.55		13.93			9.95			11.11								17.83									
						14.68			23.13								31.09									
			13.93			2.05			3.22								4.33									
			39.96			5.86			9.24								12.43									
Newport News Independent City	4,540	4,212	1,728	-	-	-	-	-	133	-	279	-	-	-	-	-	542	-	-	-	-	-	-	-	-	309
	2.52		41.03						30.16		36.90						48.35									43.64
									7.70		16.15						31.37									17.88
			41.03						3.16		6.62						12.87									7.34
			38.06						2.93		6.15						11.94									6.81
Norfolk Independent City	5,675	7,007	2,834	-	-	124	-	-	216	-	1,992	-	-	-	-	-	-	-	-	-	-	-	-	-	-	214
	2.42		40.45			30.54			28.80		46.61															59.61
						4.38			7.62		70.29															7.55
			40.45			1.77			3.08		28.43															3.05
			49.94			2.19			3.81		35.10															3.77

Notes: Please refer to the User's Guide for an explanation of data; data is arranged alphabetically by state, then county, then city within each county; table includes counties with populations greater than 49,999 unless noted and cities with populations greater than 9,999 whose Asian and/or NHPI population rates are greater than the national average; (1) Native Hawaiian and other Pacific Islander; (2) excludes Taiwanese; (3) includes Chamorro; (4) county does not meet population threshold but is shown in order to allow inclusion of city

Place	Total foreign-born naturalized citizens	Total Asian population	Asians who are foreign-born naturalized citizens	Total NHPI[1] population	NHPIs[1] who are foreign-born naturalized citizens	Asian Indian	Bangladeshi	Cambodian	Chinese[2]	Fijian	Filipino	Guamanian[3]	Hawaiian, Native	Hmong	Indonesian	Japanese	Korean	Laotian	Malaysian	Pakistani	Samoan	Sri Lankan	Taiwanese	Thai	Tongan	Vietnamese
Portsmouth Independent City	879 0.87	815	336 41.23 41.23 38.23	-	-	-	-	-	-	-	218 46.09 64.88 26.75 24.80	-	-	-	-	-	-	-	-	-	-	-	-	-	-	-
Prince William County	13,391 4.77	10,436	4,241 40.64 40.64 31.67	-	-	675 33.25 15.92 6.47 5.04	-	-	363 38.58 8.56 3.48 2.71	-	998 45.49 23.53 9.56 7.45	-	-	-	-	104 22.81 2.45 1.00 0.78	829 49.26 19.55 7.94 6.19	-	-	306 37.64 7.22 2.93 2.29	-	-	-	-	-	441 45.99 10.40 4.23 3.29
Bull Run (cdp)	606 5.32	598	187 31.27 31.27 30.86	-	-	-	-	-	-	-	-	-	-	-	-	-	-	-	-	-	-	-	-	-	-	-
Dale City (cdp)	3,670 6.55	2,864	1,284 44.83 44.83 34.99	-	-	148 23.53 11.53 5.17 4.03	-	-	-	-	343 50.22 26.71 11.98 9.35	-	-	-	-	-	-	-	-	205 63.27 15.97 7.16 5.59	-	-	-	-	-	-
Lake Ridge (cdp)	1,448 4.74	1,116	504 45.16 45.16 34.81	-	-	-	-	-	-	-	-	-	-	-	-	-	-	-	-	-	-	-	-	-	-	-
Woodbridge (cdp)	1,802 5.66	1,512	548 36.24 36.24 30.41	-	-	-	-	-	-	-	-	-	-	-	-	-	-	-	-	-	-	-	-	-	-	-
Richmond Independent City	2,715 1.37	2,438	759 31.13 31.13 27.96	-	-	151 29.32 19.89 6.19 5.56	-	-	-	-	154 36.41 20.29 6.32 5.67	-	-	-	-	-	-	-	-	-	-	-	-	-	-	-
Roanoke Independent City	835 0.88	1,004	256 25.50 25.50 30.66	-	-	-	-	-	-	-	-	-	-	-	-	-	-	-	-	-	-	-	-	-	-	-
Roanoke County	1,231 1.44	999	418 41.84 41.84 33.96	-	-	-	-	-	-	-	-	-	-	-	-	-	-	-	-	-	-	-	-	-	-	-
Spotsylvania County	1,736 1.92	1,281	588 45.90 45.90 33.87	-	-	-	-	-	-	-	-	-	-	-	-	-	-	-	-	-	-	-	-	-	-	-

Notes: Please refer to the User's Guide for an explanation of data; data is arranged alphabetically by state, then county, then city within each county; table includes counties with populations greater than 49,999 unless noted and cities with populations greater than 9,999 whose Asian and/or NHPI population rates are greater than the national average; (1) Native Hawaiian and other Pacific Islander; (2) excludes Taiwanese; (3) includes Chamorro; (4) county does not meet population threshold but is shown in order to allow inclusion of city

Place	Total foreign-born naturalized citizens	Total Asian population	Asians who are foreign-born naturalized citizens	Total NHPI[1] population	NHPIs[1] who are foreign-born naturalized citizens	Asian Indian	Bangladeshi	Cambodian	Chinese[2]	Fijian	Filipino	Guamanian[3]	Hawaiian, Native	Hmong	Indonesian	Japanese	Korean	Laotian	Malaysian	Pakistani	Samoan	Sri Lankan	Taiwanese	Thai	Tongan	Vietnamese
Stafford County	2,404 2.60	1,497	816 54.51 54.51 33.94	-	-	-	-	-	-	-	232 61.38 28.43 15.50 9.65	-	-	-	-	-	-	-	-	-	-	-	-	-	-	-
Suffolk Independent City	683 1.07	533	250 46.90 46.90 36.60	-	-	-	-	-	-	-	-	-	-	-	-	-	-	-	-	-	-	-	-	-	-	-
Virginia Beach Independent City	16,696 3.93	20,207	9,500 47.01 47.01 56.90	-	-	474 38.73 4.99 2.35 2.84	-	-	771 47.48 8.12 3.82 4.62	-	6,585 48.66 69.32 32.59 39.44	-	-	-	-	265 35.52 2.79 1.31 1.59	448 57.22 4.72 2.22 2.68	-	-	-	-	-	-	-	-	536 45.08 5.64 2.65 3.21
Williamsburg Independent City	253 2.11	521	90 17.27 17.27 35.57	-	-	-	-	-	-	-	-	-	-	-	-	-	-	-	-	-	-	-	-	-	-	-
York County	1,787 3.17	1,836	853 46.46 46.46 47.73	-	-	154 59.00 18.05 8.39 8.62	-	-	-	-	-	-	-	-	-	-	251 45.47 29.43 13.67 14.05	-	-	-	-	-	-	-	-	-
WASHINGTON	257,648 4.37	320,979	117,072 36.47 36.47 45.44	21,738	1,605 7.38 7.38 0.62	6,613 29.41 5.65 2.06 2.57	-	4,286 29.03 3.66 1.34 1.66	22,315 38.96 19.06 6.95 8.66	200 28.21 12.46 0.92 0.08	28,194 43.34 24.08 8.78 10.94	46 0.86 2.87 0.21 0.02	31 0.69 1.93 0.14 0.01	355 23.76 0.30 0.11 0.14	269 21.66 0.23 0.08 0.10	4,541 12.18 3.88 1.41 1.76	20,965 45.09 17.91 6.53 8.14	2,755 34.02 2.35 0.86 1.07	-	442 35.11 0.38 0.14 0.17	808 11.43 50.34 3.72 0.31	104 24.64 0.09 0.03 0.04	1,657 43.74 1.42 0.52 0.64	1,261 32.40 1.08 0.39 0.49	170 20.14 10.59 0.78 0.07	20,345 45.56 17.38 6.34 7.90
Benton County	4,230 2.97	2,934	1,348 45.94 45.94 31.87	-	-	181 44.80 13.43 6.17 4.28	-	-	247 46.34 18.32 8.42 5.84	-	-	-	-	-	-	-	209 51.10 15.50 7.12 4.94	-	-	-	-	-	-	-	-	300 59.64 22.26 10.22 7.09
Richland (city)	1,261 3.26	1,566	715 45.66 45.66 56.70	-	-	-	-	-	185 45.12 25.87 11.81 14.67	-	-	-	-	-	-	-	-	-	-	-	-	-	-	-	-	-
Chelan County	2,434 3.65	417	195 46.76 46.76 8.01	-	-	-	-	-	-	-	-	-	-	-	-	-	-	-	-	-	-	-	-	-	-	-
Clallam County	1,675 2.60	870	340 39.08 39.08 20.30	-	-	-	-	-	-	-	-	-	-	-	-	-	-	-	-	-	-	-	-	-	-	-

Notes: Please refer to the User's Guide for an explanation of data; data is arranged alphabetically by state, then county, then city within each county; table includes counties with populations greater than 49,999 unless noted and cities with populations greater than 9,999 whose Asian and/or NHPI population rates are greater than the national average; (1) Native Hawaiian and other Pacific Islander; (2) excludes Taiwanese; (3) includes Chamorro; (4) county does not meet population threshold but is shown in order to allow inclusion of city

Place	Total foreign-born naturalized citizens	Total Asian population	Asians who are foreign-born naturalized citizens	Total NHPI[1] population	NHPIs[1] who are foreign-born naturalized citizens	Asian Indian	Bangladeshi	Cambodian	Chinese[2]	Fijian	Filipino	Guamanian[3]	Hawaiian, Native	Hmong	Indonesian	Japanese	Korean	Laotian	Malaysian	Pakistani	Samoan	Sri Lankan	Taiwanese	Thai	Tongan	Vietnamese
	10,146	10,622	3,847	1,329	48	272	-	75	554	-	731	-	-	-	-	170	679	164	-	-	-	-	-	-	-	973
	2.94		36.22		3.61	36.51		17.56	33.58		41.84					13.26	52.15	39.71								41.35
Clark County						7.07		1.95	14.40		19.00					4.42	17.65	4.26								25.29
			36.22		3.61	2.56		0.71	5.22		6.88					1.60	6.39	1.54								9.16
			37.92		0.47	2.68		0.74	5.46		7.20					1.68	6.69	1.62								9.59
	443	585	236	-	-	-	-	-	-	-	-	-	-	-	-	-	-	-	-	-	-	-	-	-	-	-
	3.66		40.34																							
Five Corners (cdp)																										
			40.34																							
			53.27																							
	512	768	215	-	-	-	-	-	-	-	-	-	-	-	-	-	-	-	-	-	-	-	-	-	-	-
	2.86		27.99																							
Orchards (cdp)																										
			27.99																							
			41.99																							
	5,295	6,155	2,184	943	22	-	-	-	333	-	429	-	-	-	-	81	324	-	-	-	-	-	-	-	-	623
	3.70		35.48		2.33				32.74		47.56					10.11	47.16									41.45
Vancouver (city)									15.25		19.64					3.71	14.84									28.53
			35.48		2.33				5.41		6.97					1.32	5.26									10.12
			41.25		0.42				6.29		8.10					1.53	6.12									11.77
	1,478	1,259	432	-	-	-	-	65	-	-	-	-	-	-	-	-	-	-	-	-	-	-	-	-	-	177
	1.59		34.31					18.36																		44.70
Cowlitz County								15.05																		40.97
			34.31					5.16																		14.06
			29.23					4.40																		11.98
	2,574	569	139	-	-	-	-	-	-	-	-	-	-	-	-	-	-	-	-	-	-	-	-	-	-	-
	3.45		24.43																							
Grant County																										
			24.43																							
			5.40																							
	1,037	640	213	-	-	-	-	-	-	-	-	-	-	-	-	-	-	-	-	-	-	-	-	-	-	-
	1.54		33.28																							
Grays Harbor County																										
			33.28																							
			20.54																							
	2,784	2,847	1,143	-	-	-	-	-	-	-	839	-	-	-	-	60	-	-	-	-	-	-	-	-	-	-
	3.89		40.15								44.30					15.46										
Island County											73.40					5.25										
			40.15								29.47					2.11										
			41.06								30.14					2.16										
	1,122	1,739	698	-	-	-	-	-	-	-	578	-	-	-	-	-	-	-	-	-	-	-	-	-	-	-
	5.64		40.14								42.50															
Oak Harbor (city)											82.81															
			40.14								33.24															
			62.21								51.52															
	118,436	187,788	65,954	8,270	961	3,631	-	2,067	17,092	168	14,355	27	13	166	158	1,818	8,503	1,762	-	154	488	-	1,300	591	126	12,499
	6.82		35.12		11.62	25.87		31.21	39.04	30.94	42.50	3.24	0.94	18.67	19.04	8.11	42.13	34.96		29.28	12.45		42.99	30.31	25.10	46.22
King County						5.51		3.13	25.92	17.48	21.77	2.81	1.35	0.25	0.24	2.76	12.89	2.67		0.23	50.78		1.97	0.90	13.11	18.95
			35.12		11.62	1.93		1.10	9.10	2.03	7.64	0.33	0.16	0.09	0.08	0.97	4.53	0.94		0.08	5.90		0.69	0.31	1.52	6.66
			55.69		0.81	3.07		1.75	14.43	0.14	12.12	0.02	0.01	0.14	0.13	1.54	7.18	1.49		0.13	0.41		1.10	0.50	0.11	10.55

Notes: Please refer to the User's Guide for an explanation of data; data is arranged alphabetically by state, then county, then city within each county; table includes counties with populations greater than 49,999 unless noted and cities with populations greater than 9,999 whose Asian and/or NHPI population rates are greater than the national average; (1) Native Hawaiian and other Pacific Islander; (2) excludes Taiwanese; (3) includes Chamorro; (4) county does not meet population threshold but is shown in order to allow inclusion of city

Place	Total foreign-born naturalized citizens	Total Asian population	Asians who are foreign-born naturalized citizens	Total NHPI[1] population	NHPIs[1] who are foreign-born naturalized citizens	Asian Indian	Bangladeshi	Cambodian	Chinese[2]	Fijian	Filipino	Guamanian[3]	Hawaiian, Native	Hmong	Indonesian	Japanese	Korean	Laotian	Malaysian	Pakistani	Samoan	Sri Lankan	Taiwanese	Thai	Tongan	Vietnamese
Auburn (city)	1,519 3.77	1,565	592 37.83 37.83 38.97	-	-	-	-	-	-	-	-	-	-	-	-	-	-	-	-	-	-	-	-	-	-	-
Bellevue (city)	11,034 10.11	18,828	5,885 31.26 31.26 53.34	-	-	296 12.23 5.03 1.57 2.68	-	-	2,197 37.76 37.33 11.67 19.91	-	540 50.56 9.18 2.87 4.89	-	-	-	-	192 6.43 3.26 1.02 1.74	1,008 41.46 17.13 5.35 9.14	236 50.86 4.01 1.25 2.14	-	-	-	-	381 41.01 6.47 2.02 3.45	-	-	668 49.85 11.35 3.55 6.05
Bothell (city)	1,494 5.00	2,317	774 33.41 33.41 51.81	-	-	-	-	-	157 26.93 20.28 6.78 10.51	-	-	-	-	-	-	-	-	-	-	-	-	-	-	-	-	-
Bryn Mawr-Skyway (cdp)	1,387 9.87	3,055	1,124 36.79 36.79 81.04	-	-	-	-	-	-	-	365 41.76 32.47 11.95 26.32	-	-	-	-	36 5.87 3.20 1.18 2.60	-	-	-	-	-	-	-	-	-	149 35.06 13.26 4.88 10.74
Burien (city)	1,916 6.04	2,138	763 35.69 35.69 39.82	-	-	-	-	-	-	-	185 36.13 24.25 8.65 9.66	-	-	-	-	-	-	-	-	-	-	-	-	-	-	218 54.09 28.57 10.20 11.38
Cascade-Fairwood (cdp)	2,405 6.98	4,647	1,654 35.59 35.59 68.77	-	-	-	-	-	338 37.43 20.44 7.27 14.05	-	545 44.27 32.95 11.73 22.66	-	-	-	-	23 4.36 1.39 0.49 0.96	-	-	-	-	-	-	-	-	-	379 50.67 22.91 8.16 15.76
Cottage Lake (cdp)	911 3.75	1,051	370 35.20 35.20 40.61	-	-	-	-	-	-	-	-	-	-	-	-	-	-	-	-	-	-	-	-	-	-	-
Des Moines (city)	1,562 5.31	2,465	802 32.54 32.54 51.34	390	44 11.28 11.28 2.82	-	-	-	-	-	172 36.99 21.45 6.98 11.01	-	-	-	-	-	-	-	-	-	-	-	-	-	-	193 35.74 24.06 7.83 12.36
East Hill-Meridian (cdp)	2,403 8.11	3,905	1,620 41.49 41.49 67.42	-	-	243 32.10 15.00 6.22 10.11	-	-	396 49.75 24.44 10.14 16.48	-	306 44.48 18.89 7.84 12.73	-	-	-	-	-	-	-	-	-	-	-	-	-	-	266 47.33 16.42 6.81 11.07
Federal Way (city)	5,920 7.11	10,162	3,697 36.38 36.38 62.45	895	194 21.68 21.68 3.28	-	-	-	343 40.12 9.28 3.38 5.79	-	763 40.18 20.64 7.51 12.89	-	-	-	-	104 16.77 2.81 1.02 1.76	1,506 33.96 40.74 14.82 25.44	-	-	-	158 32.18 81.44 17.65 2.67	-	-	-	-	595 52.42 16.09 5.86 10.05

Notes: Please refer to the User's Guide for an explanation of data; data is arranged alphabetically by state, then county, then city within each county; table includes counties with populations greater than 49,999 unless noted and cities with populations greater than 9,999 whose Asian and/or NHPI population rates are greater than the national average; (1) Native Hawaiian and other Pacific Islander; (2) excludes Taiwanese; (3) includes Chamorro; (4) county does not meet population threshold but is shown in order to allow inclusion of city

Place	Total foreign-born naturalized citizens	Total Asian population	Asians who are foreign-born naturalized citizens	Total NHPI[1] population	NHPIs[1] who are foreign-born naturalized citizens	Asian Indian	Bangladeshi	Cambodian	Chinese[2]	Fijian	Filipino	Guamanian[3]	Hawaiian, Native	Hmong	Indonesian	Japanese	Korean	Laotian	Malaysian	Pakistani	Samoan	Sri Lankan	Taiwanese	Thai	Tongan	Vietnamese
Inglewood-Finn Hill (cdp)	1,332 5.88	1,679	653 38.89 38.89 49.02	-	-	-	-	-	166 40.39 25.42 9.89 12.46	-	-	-	-	-	-	-	-	-	-	-	-	-	-	-	-	-
Issaquah (city)	645 5.76	704	265 37.64 37.64 41.09	-	-	-	-	-	-	-	-	-	-	-	-	-	-	-	-	-	-	-	-	-	-	-
Kenmore (city)	1,128 6.08	1,226	430 35.07 35.07 38.12	-	-	-	-	-	-	-	-	-	-	-	-	-	-	-	-	-	-	-	-	-	-	-
Kent (city)	4,983 6.28	7,720	2,781 36.02 36.02 55.81	-	-	511 34.50 18.37 6.62 10.25	-	-	406 40.56 14.60 5.26 8.15	-	614 37.90 22.08 7.95 12.32	-	-	-	-	9 1.62 0.32 0.12 0.18	245 29.48 8.81 3.17 4.92	-	-	-	-	-	-	-	-	788 54.50 28.34 10.21 15.81
Kingsgate (cdp)	801 6.66	1,503	481 32.00 32.00 60.05	-	-	-	-	-	138 38.12 28.69 9.18 17.23	-	-	-	-	-	-	-	-	-	-	-	-	-	-	-	-	-
Kirkland (city)	2,747 6.11	3,476	1,200 34.52 34.52 43.68	-	-	-	-	-	217 27.09 18.08 6.24 7.90	-	-	-	-	-	-	26 4.98 2.17 0.75 0.95	-	-	-	-	-	-	-	-	-	269 50.37 22.42 7.74 9.79
Lake Forest Park (city)	969 7.21	1,157	598 51.69 51.69 61.71	-	-	-	-	-	-	-	-	-	-	-	-	-	-	-	-	-	-	-	-	-	-	-
Lakeland North (cdp)	732 4.83	941	294 31.24 31.24 40.16	-	-	-	-	-	-	-	-	-	-	-	-	-	-	-	-	-	-	-	-	-	-	-
Lakeland South (cdp)	511 4.44	665	213 32.03 32.03 41.68	-	-	-	-	-	-	-	-	-	-	-	-	-	-	-	-	-	-	-	-	-	-	-
Lea Hill (cdp)	401 3.76	519	110 21.19 21.19 27.43	-	-	-	-	-	-	-	-	-	-	-	-	-	-	-	-	-	-	-	-	-	-	-

Notes: Please refer to the User's Guide for an explanation of data; data is arranged alphabetically by state, then county, then city within each county; table includes counties with populations greater than 49,999 unless noted and cities with populations greater than 9,999 whose Asian and/or NHPI population rates are greater than the national average; (1) Native Hawaiian and other Pacific Islander; (2) excludes Taiwanese; (3) includes Chamorro; (4) county does not meet population threshold but is shown in order to allow inclusion of city

Place	Total foreign-born naturalized citizens	Total Asian population	Asians who are foreign-born naturalized citizens	Total NHPI[1] population	NHPIs[1] who are foreign-born naturalized citizens	Asian Indian	Bangladeshi	Cambodian	Chinese[2]	Fijian	Filipino	Guamanian[3]	Hawaiian, Native	Hmong	Indonesian	Japanese	Korean	Laotian	Malaysian	Pakistani	Samoan	Sri Lankan	Taiwanese	Thai	Tongan	Vietnamese
Mercer Island (city)	1,943	2,436	832	-	-	-	-	-	392	-	-	-	-	-	-	94	-	-	-	-	-	-	-	-	-	-
	8.82		34.15						37.69							16.55										
									47.12							11.30										
			34.15						16.09							3.86										
			42.82						20.17							4.84										
Redmond (city)	2,900	6,028	1,475	-	-	86	-	-	612	-	-	-	-	-	-	52	228	-	-	-	-	-	-	-	-	-
	6.39		24.47			6.87			31.68							6.72	46.91									
						5.83			41.49							3.53	15.46									
			24.47			1.43			10.15							0.86	3.78									
			50.86			2.97			21.10							1.79	7.86									
Renton (city)	4,207	6,648	2,804	-	-	-	-	-	577	-	734	-	-	-	-	35	-	-	-	-	-	-	-	-	-	903
	8.43		42.18						47.49		46.99					5.56										50.82
									20.58		26.18					1.25										32.20
			42.18						8.68		11.04					0.53										13.58
			66.65						13.72		17.45					0.83										21.46
Riverton-Boulevard Park (cdp)	924	1,524	485	-	-	-	-	-	-	-	-	-	-	-	-	-	-	-	-	-	-	-	-	-	-	-
	8.11		31.82																							
			31.82																							
			52.49																							
Sammamish (city)	1,511	2,530	699	-	-	-	-	-	306	-	-	-	-	-	-	-	-	-	-	-	-	-	-	-	-	-
	4.43		27.63						27.54																	
									43.78																	
			27.63						12.09																	
			46.26						20.25																	
SeaTac (city)	1,707	2,945	1,017	614	56	115	-	-	-	-	228	-	-	-	-	-	-	-	-	-	-	-	-	-	-	227
	6.69		34.53		9.12	19.97					31.45															41.58
						11.31					22.42															22.32
			34.53		9.12	3.90					7.74															7.71
			59.58		3.28	6.74					13.36															13.30
Seattle (city)	44,334	73,849	26,324	2,514	252	776	-	764	7,566	-	7,045	-	-	-	42	621	2,263	849	-	-	168	-	375	220	-	5,060
	7.87		35.65		10.02	28.42		30.27	40.09		43.42				11.11	6.66	45.63	32.07			12.50		38.38	25.06		44.22
						2.95		2.90	28.74		26.76				0.16	2.36	8.60	3.23			66.67		1.42	0.84		19.22
			35.65		10.02	1.05		1.03	10.25		9.54				0.06	0.84	3.06	1.15			6.68		0.51	0.30		6.85
			59.38		0.57	1.75		1.72	17.07		15.89				0.09	1.40	5.10	1.92			0.38		0.85	0.50		11.41
Shoreline (city)	4,723	6,613	2,857	-	-	159	-	-	802	-	545	-	-	-	-	74	519	-	-	-	-	-	-	-	-	469
	8.92		43.20			41.41			45.70		46.42					18.27	38.13									52.82
						5.57			28.07		19.08					2.59	18.17									16.42
			43.20			2.40			12.13		8.24					1.12	7.85									7.09
			60.49			3.37			16.98		11.54					1.57	10.99									9.93
Tukwila (city)	1,422	1,788	600	332	45	-	-	-	-	-	225	-	-	-	-	-	-	-	-	-	-	-	-	-	-	-
	8.27		33.56		13.55						37.13															
											37.50															
			33.56		13.55						12.58															
			42.19		3.16						15.82															
Union Hill-Novelty Hill (cdp)	529	528	257	-	-	-	-	-	-	-	-	-	-	-	-	-	-	-	-	-	-	-	-	-	-	-
	4.73		48.67																							
			48.67																							
			48.58																							

Notes: Please refer to the User's Guide for an explanation of data; data is arranged alphabetically by state, then county, then city within each county; table includes counties with populations greater than 49,999 unless noted and cities with populations greater than 9,999 whose Asian and/or NHPI population rates are greater than the national average; (1) Native Hawaiian and other Pacific Islander; (2) excludes Taiwanese; (3) includes Chamorro; (4) county does not meet population threshold but is shown in order to allow inclusion of city

Place	Total foreign-born naturalized citizens	Total Asian population	Asians who are foreign-born naturalized citizens	Total NHPI[1] population	NHPIs[1] who are foreign-born naturalized citizens	Asian Indian	Bangladeshi	Cambodian	Chinese[2]	Fijian	Filipino	Guamanian[3]	Hawaiian, Native	Hmong	Indonesian	Japanese	Korean	Laotian	Malaysian	Pakistani	Samoan	Sri Lankan	Taiwanese	Thai	Tongan	Vietnamese
White Center (cdp)	1,909	4,478	1,301	-	-	-	-	219	-	-	228	-	-	-	-	-	-	-	-	-	-	-	-	-	-	671
	9.16		29.05					18.47			48.10															32.88
								16.83			17.52															51.58
			29.05					4.89			5.09															14.98
			68.15					11.47			11.94															35.15
Kitsap County	8,094	10,465	4,794	1,698	62	-	-	-	209	-	3,593	0	-	-	-	248	342	-	-	-	-	-	-	-	-	129
	3.49		45.81		3.65				44.37		51.53	0.00				20.75	56.16									29.32
									4.36		74.95	0.00				5.17	7.13									2.69
			45.81		3.65				2.00		34.33	0.00				2.37	3.27									1.23
			59.23		0.77				2.58		44.39	0.00				3.06	4.23									1.59
Bremerton (city)	1,357	2,074	810	-	-	-	-	-	-	-	597	-	-	-	-	-	-	-	-	-	-	-	-	-	-	-
	3.66		39.05								40.67															
											73.70															
			39.05								28.78															
			59.69								43.99															
Silverdale (cdp)	1,260	1,751	911	-	-	-	-	-	-	-	761	-	-	-	-	-	-	-	-	-	-	-	-	-	-	-
	7.99		52.03								51.52															
											83.53															
			52.03								43.46															
			72.30								60.40															
Lewis County	972	380	157	-	-	-	-	-	-	-	-	-	-	-	-	-	-	-	-	-	-	-	-	-	-	-
	1.42		41.32																							
			41.32																							
			16.15																							
Pierce County	28,370	34,671	13,372	5,075	304	272	-	935	692	-	2,843	6	0	-	-	1,116	5,091	121	-	-	219	-	-	132	-	1,755
	4.05		38.57		5.99	34.52		23.04	39.43		41.97	0.33	0.00			31.70	45.77	28.34			12.67			33.33		40.95
						2.03		6.99	5.17		21.26	1.97	0.00			8.35	38.07	0.90			72.04			0.99		13.12
			38.57		5.99	0.78		2.70	2.00		8.20	0.12	0.00			3.22	14.68	0.35			4.32			0.38		5.06
			47.13		1.07	0.96		3.30	2.44		10.02	0.02	0.00			3.93	17.95	0.43			0.77			0.47		6.19
Elk Plain (cdp)	510	627	219	-	-	-	-	-	-	-	-	-	-	-	-	-	-	-	-	-	-	-	-	-	-	-
	3.25		34.93																							
			34.93																							
			42.94																							
Fort Lewis (cdp)	457	659	186	317	40	-	-	-	-	-	123	-	-	-	-	-	-	-	-	-	-	-	-	-	-	-
	2.40		28.22		12.62						31.54															
											66.13															
			28.22		12.62						18.66															
			40.70		8.75						26.91															
Lakewood (city)	4,119	5,181	2,197	746	86	-	-	-	-	-	604	-	-	-	-	294	1,033	-	-	-	59	-	-	-	-	-
	7.06		42.40		11.53						49.43					45.87	44.20				20.14					
											27.49					13.38	47.02				68.60					
			42.40		11.53						11.66					5.67	19.94				7.91					
			53.34		2.09						14.66					7.14	25.08				1.43					
Parkland (cdp)	1,242	1,589	727	415	8	-	-	-	-	-	-	-	-	-	-	-	332	-	-	-	-	-	-	-	-	-
	5.19		45.75		1.93												41.45									
																	45.67									
			45.75		1.93												20.89									
			58.53		0.64												26.73									

Notes: Please refer to the User's Guide for an explanation of data; data is arranged alphabetically by state, then county, then city within each county; table includes counties with populations greater than 49,999 unless noted and cities with populations greater than 9,999 whose Asian and/or NHPI population rates are greater than the national average; (1) Native Hawaiian and other Pacific Islander; (2) excludes Taiwanese; (3) includes Chamorro; (4) county does not meet population threshold but is shown in order to allow inclusion of city

Place	Total foreign-born naturalized citizens	Total Asian population	Asians who are foreign-born naturalized citizens	Total NHPI[1] population	NHPIs[1] who are foreign-born naturalized citizens	Asian Indian	Bangladeshi	Cambodian	Chinese[2]	Fijian	Filipino	Guamanian[3]	Hawaiian, Native	Hmong	Indonesian	Japanese	Korean	Laotian	Malaysian	Pakistani	Samoan	Sri Lankan	Taiwanese	Thai	Tongan	Vietnamese
Spanaway (cdp)	1,103	1,275	671	578	6	-	-	-	-	-	221	-	-	-	-	-	345	-	-	-	-	-	-	-	-	-
	5.14		52.63		1.04						42.02						59.18									
											32.94						51.42									
			52.63		1.04						17.33						27.06									
			60.83		0.54						20.04						31.28									
Tacoma (city)	9,657	14,336	4,780	1,347	88	-	-	677	271	-	753	0	-	-	-	214	1,365	76	-	-	65	-	-	-	-	1,125
	5.00		33.34		6.53			21.44	36.42		37.90	0.00				22.53	44.39	24.52			10.37					36.06
								14.16	5.67		15.75	0.00				4.48	28.56	1.59			73.86					23.54
			33.34		6.53			4.72	1.89		5.25	0.00				1.49	9.52	0.53			4.83					7.85
			49.50		0.91			7.01	2.81		7.80	0.00				2.22	14.13	0.79			0.67					11.65
University Place (city)	1,781	2,311	1,044	-	-	-	-	-	-	-	-	-	-	-	-	-	490	-	-	-	-	-	-	-	-	-
	5.91		45.18														39.61									
																	46.93									
			45.18														21.20									
			58.62														27.51									
Skagit County	2,985	1,459	487	-	-	-	-	-	-	-	215	-	-	-	-	-	-	-	-	-	-	-	-	-	-	-
	2.90		33.38								44.42															
											44.15															
			33.38								14.74															
			16.31								7.20															
Snohomish County	27,587	35,534	14,242	1,250	27	892	-	796	1,886	-	3,311	-	0	-	-	397	3,403	245	-	163	-	-	-	-	-	2,526
	4.55		40.08		2.16	33.26		39.84	42.60		43.38		0.00			16.18	45.81	32.07		37.73						48.11
						6.26		5.59	13.24		23.25		0.00			2.79	23.89	1.72		1.14						17.74
			40.08		2.16	2.51		2.24	5.31		9.32		0.00			1.12	9.58	0.69		0.46						7.11
			51.63		0.10	3.23		2.89	6.84		12.00		0.00			1.44	12.34	0.89		0.59						9.16
Alderwood Manor (cdp)	957	1,245	642	-	-	-	-	-	-	-	-	-	-	-	-	-	-	-	-	-	-	-	-	-	-	-
	6.27		51.57																							
			51.57																							
			67.08																							
Edmonds (city)	2,211	2,187	893	-	-	-	-	-	-	-	175	-	-	-	-	-	279	-	-	-	-	-	-	-	-	-
	5.58		40.83								48.08						48.52									
											19.60						31.24									
			40.83								8.00						12.76									
			40.39								7.91						12.62									
Everett (city)	4,026	6,057	2,217	-	-	165	-	208	-	-	829	-	-	-	-	-	-	-	-	-	-	-	-	-	-	500
	4.41		36.60			28.01		32.60			45.73															42.05
						7.44		9.38			37.39															22.55
			36.60			2.72		3.43			13.69															8.25
			55.07			4.10		5.17			20.59															12.42
Lynnwood (city)	3,159	4,706	1,976	-	-	-	-	-	273	-	401	-	-	-	-	-	433	-	-	-	-	-	-	-	-	489
	9.37		41.99						43.75		43.83						41.76									49.95
									13.82		20.29						21.91									24.75
			41.99						5.80		8.52						9.20									10.39
			62.55						8.64		12.69						13.71									15.48
Martha Lake (cdp)	803	1,171	433	-	-	-	-	-	-	-	-	-	-	-	-	-	-	-	-	-	-	-	-	-	-	-
	6.35		36.98																							
			36.98																							
			53.92																							

Notes: Please refer to the User's Guide for an explanation of data; data is arranged alphabetically by state, then county, then city within each county; table includes counties with populations greater than 49,999 unless noted and cities with populations greater than 9,999 whose Asian and/or NHPI population rates are greater than the national average; (1) Native Hawaiian and other Pacific Islander; (2) excludes Taiwanese; (3) includes Chamorro; (4) county does not meet population threshold but is shown in order to allow inclusion of city

Place	Total foreign-born naturalized citizens	Total Asian population	Asians who are foreign-born naturalized citizens	Total NHPI[1] population	NHPIs[1] who are foreign-born naturalized citizens	Asian Indian	Bangladeshi	Cambodian	Chinese[2]	Fijian	Filipino	Guamanian[3]	Hawaiian, Native	Hmong	Indonesian	Japanese	Korean	Laotian	Malaysian	Pakistani	Samoan	Sri Lankan	Taiwanese	Thai	Tongan	Vietnamese
Marysville (city)	1,029 4.08	953	405 42.50 42.50 39.36	-	-	-	-	-	-	-	-	-	-	-	-	-	-	-	-	-	-	-	-	-	-	-
Mill Creek (city)	990 8.65	1,187	548 46.17 46.17 55.35	-	-	-	-	-	-	-	-	-	-	-	-	-	184 41.44 33.58 15.50 18.59	-	-	-	-	-	-	-	-	-
Mountlake Terrace (city)	1,655 8.15	2,347	829 35.32 35.32 50.09	-	-	-	-	-	-	-	253 45.67 30.52 10.78 15.29	-	-	-	-	-	251 41.83 30.28 10.69 15.17	-	-	-	-	-	-	-	-	-
Mukilteo (city)	1,403 7.78	2,092	880 42.07 42.07 62.72	-	-	-	-	-	-	-	-	-	-	-	-	-	346 34.39 39.32 16.54 24.66	-	-	-	-	-	-	-	-	-
North Creek (cdp)	1,055 4.06	1,537	650 42.29 42.29 61.61	-	-	-	-	-	-	-	-	-	-	-	-	-	-	-	-	-	-	-	-	-	-	-
Paine Field-Lk. Stickney (cdp)	977 4.03	1,572	503 32.00 32.00 51.48	-	-	-	-	-	-	-	-	-	-	-	-	-	-	-	-	-	-	-	-	-	-	-
Picnic Pt.-N. Lynnwood (cdp)	1,495 6.55	2,482	864 34.81 34.81 57.79	-	-	-	-	-	-	-	168 41.58 19.44 6.77 11.24	-	-	-	-	-	361 41.45 41.78 14.54 24.15	-	-	-	-	-	-	-	-	-
Seattle Hill-Silver Firs (cdp)	1,890 5.32	2,755	1,172 42.54 42.54 62.01	-	-	-	-	-	-	-	182 30.69 15.53 6.61 9.63	-	-	-	-	-	377 61.00 32.17 13.68 19.95	-	-	-	-	-	-	-	-	257 56.24 21.93 9.33 13.60
Spokane County	8,051 1.93	7,444	2,493 33.49 33.49 30.97	695	79 11.37 11.37 0.98	311 49.68 12.47 4.18 3.86	-	-	302 33.08 12.11 4.06 3.75	-	373 38.26 14.96 5.01 4.63	-	-	154 28.89 6.18 2.07 1.91	-	145 8.69 5.82 1.95 1.80	342 50.89 13.72 4.59 4.25	-	-	-	-	-	-	-	-	602 48.39 24.15 8.09 7.48
Spokane (city)	4,486 2.29	4,379	1,509 34.46 34.46 33.64	422	40 9.48 9.48 0.89	-	-	-	211 38.64 13.98 4.82 4.70	-	177 37.26 11.73 4.04 3.95	-	-	77 18.73 5.10 1.76 1.72	-	88 8.64 5.83 2.01 1.96	201 53.74 13.32 4.59 4.48	-	-	-	-	-	-	-	-	372 47.15 24.65 8.50 8.29

Notes: Please refer to the User's Guide for an explanation of data; data is arranged alphabetically by state, then county, then city within each county; table includes counties with populations greater than 49,999 unless noted and cities with populations greater than 9,999 whose Asian and/or NHPI population rates are greater than the national average; (1) Native Hawaiian and other Pacific Islander; (2) excludes Taiwanese; (3) includes Chamorro; (4) county does not meet population threshold but is shown in order to allow inclusion of city

Place	Total foreign-born naturalized citizens	Total Asian population	Asians who are foreign-born naturalized citizens	Total NHPI[1] population	NHPIs[1] who are foreign-born naturalized citizens	Asian Indian	Bangladeshi	Cambodian	Chinese[2]	Fijian	Filipino	Guamanian[3]	Hawaiian, Native	Hmong	Indonesian	Japanese	Korean	Laotian	Malaysian	Pakistani	Samoan	Sri Lankan	Taiwanese	Thai	Tongan	Vietnamese
Thurston County	7,094 3.42	9,424	3,769 39.99 39.99 53.13	1,205	25 2.07 2.07 0.35	121 25.00 3.21 1.28 1.71	-	250 29.87 6.63 2.65 3.52	370 41.81 9.82 3.93 5.22	-	701 43.24 18.60 7.44 9.88	5 0.68 20.00 0.41 0.07	-	-	-	140 17.79 3.71 1.49 1.97	1,041 48.33 27.62 11.05 14.67	-	-	-	-	-	-	-	-	862 48.92 22.87 9.15 12.15
Lacey (city)	1,632 5.25	2,517	1,043 41.44 41.44 63.91	-	-	-	-	-	-	-	188 40.00 18.02 7.47 11.52	-	-	-	-	-	345 56.37 33.08 13.71 21.14	-	-	-	-	-	-	-	-	289 49.23 27.71 11.48 17.71
Olympia (city)	1,602 3.78	2,326	966 41.53 41.53 60.30	-	-	-	-	-	-	-	-	-	-	-	-	-	-	-	-	-	-	-	-	-	-	351 49.58 36.34 15.09 21.91
Tumwater (city)	277 2.19	479	91 19.00 19.00 32.85	-	-	-	-	-	-	-	-	-	-	-	-	-	-	-	-	-	-	-	-	-	-	-
Walla Walla County	1,680 3.04	772	206 26.68 26.68 12.26	-	-	-	-	-	-	-	-	-	-	-	-	-	-	-	-	-	-	-	-	-	-	-
Whatcom County	6,583 3.95	4,416	1,399 31.68 31.68 21.25	-	-	405 32.66 28.95 9.17 6.15	-	-	202 38.40 14.44 4.57 3.07	-	113 22.07 8.08 2.56 1.72	-	-	-	-	59 11.82 4.22 1.34 0.90	235 51.88 16.80 5.32 3.57	-	-	-	-	-	-	-	-	238 38.20 17.01 5.39 3.62
Bellingham (city)	2,694 4.03	2,680	805 30.04 30.04 29.88	-	-	165 27.05 20.50 6.16 6.12	-	-	-	-	-	-	-	-	-	-	-	-	-	-	-	-	-	-	-	160 33.90 19.88 5.97 5.94
Whitman County[4]	851 2.09	2,230	421 18.88 18.88 49.47	-	-	-	-	-	159 23.21 37.77 7.13 18.68	-	-	-	-	-	-	12 1.97 2.85 0.54 1.41	-	-	-	-	-	-	-	-	-	-
Pullman (city)	730 2.95	1,992	368 18.47 18.47 50.41	-	-	-	-	-	145 24.91 39.40 7.28 19.86	-	-	-	-	-	-	10 1.78 2.72 0.50 1.37	-	-	-	-	-	-	-	-	-	-
Yakima County	9,925 4.46	2,180	785 36.01 36.01 7.91	-	-	-	-	-	-	-	398 42.80 50.70 18.26 4.01	-	-	-	-	-	-	-	-	-	-	-	-	-	-	-

Notes: Please refer to the User's Guide for an explanation of data; data is arranged alphabetically by state, then county, then city within each county; table includes counties with populations greater than 49,999 unless noted and cities with populations greater than 9,999 whose Asian and/or NHPI population rates are greater than the national average; (1) Native Hawaiian and other Pacific Islander; (2) excludes Taiwanese; (3) includes Chamorro; (4) county does not meet population threshold but is shown in order to allow inclusion of city

Place	Total foreign-born naturalized citizens	Total Asian population	Asians who are foreign-born naturalized citizens	Total NHPI[1] population	NHPIs[1] who are foreign-born naturalized citizens	Asian Indian	Bangladeshi	Cambodian	Chinese[2]	Fijian	Filipino	Guamanian[3]	Hawaiian, Native	Hmong	Indonesian	Japanese	Korean	Laotian	Malaysian	Pakistani	Samoan	Sri Lankan	Taiwanese	Thai	Tongan	Vietnamese
WEST VIRGINIA	10,446 0.58	9,445	3,516 37.23 37.23 33.66	405	27 6.67 6.67 0.26	1,030 40.73 29.29 10.91 9.86	-	-	401 24.29 11.41 4.25 3.84	-	827 49.88 23.52 8.76 7.92	-	-	-	-	210 23.89 5.97 2.22 2.01	535 59.84 15.22 5.66 5.12	-	-	57 17.59 1.62 0.60 0.55	-	-	-	-	-	231 52.26 6.57 2.45 2.21
Cabell County	705 0.73	748	313 41.84 41.84 44.40	-	-	-	-	-	-	-	-	-	-	-	-	-	-	-	-	-	-	-	-	-	-	-
Harrison County	503 0.73	398	98 24.62 24.62 19.48	-	-	-	-	-	-	-	-	-	-	-	-	-	-	-	-	-	-	-	-	-	-	-
Kanawha County	1,801 0.90	1,670	787 47.13 47.13 43.70	-	-	270 47.29 34.31 16.17 14.99	-	-	-	-	-	-	-	-	-	-	-	-	-	-	-	-	-	-	-	-
Monongalia County	1,033 1.26	1,910	484 25.34 25.34 46.85	-	-	146 26.35 30.17 7.64 14.13	-	-	115 18.73 23.76 6.02 11.13	-	-	-	-	-	-	-	-	-	-	-	-	-	-	-	-	-
Putnam County	316 0.61	300	118 39.33 39.33 37.34	-	-	-	-	-	-	-	-	-	-	-	-	-	-	-	-	-	-	-	-	-	-	-
Raleigh County	442 0.56	663	249 37.56 37.56 56.33	-	-	-	-	-	-	-	-	-	-	-	-	-	-	-	-	-	-	-	-	-	-	-
Wood County	520 0.59	395	209 52.91 52.91 40.19	-	-	-	-	-	-	-	-	-	-	-	-	-	-	-	-	-	-	-	-	-	-	-
WISCONSIN	76,223 1.42	83,077	20,437 24.60 24.60 26.81	1,577	104 6.59 6.59 0.14	2,931 25.98 14.34 3.53 3.85	-	165 26.32 0.81 0.20 0.22	2,355 24.51 11.52 2.83 3.09	-	2,269 41.56 11.10 2.73 2.98	6 1.41 5.77 0.38 0.01	4 0.92 3.85 0.25 0.01	4,813 15.52 23.55 5.79 6.31	27 6.65 0.13 0.03 0.04	475 15.91 2.32 0.57 0.62	3,451 50.41 16.89 4.15 4.53	902 21.81 4.41 1.09 1.18	-	250 26.97 1.22 0.30 0.33	-	-	176 26.15 0.86 0.21 0.23	166 19.08 0.81 0.20 0.22	-	1,815 46.89 8.88 2.18 2.38
Brown County	2,192 0.97	4,596	756 16.45 16.45 34.49	-	-	36 11.76 4.76 0.78 1.64	-	-	-	-	-	-	-	258 10.67 34.13 5.61 11.77	-	-	-	83 18.86 10.98 1.81 3.79	-	-	-	-	-	-	-	-

Notes: Please refer to the User's Guide for an explanation of data; data is arranged alphabetically by state, then county, then city within each county; table includes counties with populations greater than 49,999 unless noted and cities with populations greater than 9,999 whose Asian and/or NHPI population rates are greater than the national average; (1) Native Hawaiian and other Pacific Islander; (2) excludes Taiwanese; (3) includes Chamorro; (4) county does not meet population threshold but is shown in order to allow inclusion of city

Place	Total foreign-born naturalized citizens	Total Asian population	Asians who are foreign-born naturalized citizens	Total NHPI population	NHPIs[1] who are foreign-born naturalized citizens	Asian Indian	Bangladeshi	Cambodian	Chinese[2]	Fijian	Filipino	Guamanian[3]	Hawaiian, Native	Hmong	Indonesian	Japanese	Korean	Laotian	Malaysian	Pakistani	Samoan	Sri Lankan	Taiwanese	Thai	Tongan	Vietnamese
Chippewa County	270 0.49	469	73 15.57 15.57 27.04	-	-	-	-	-	-	-	-	-	-	38 10.58 52.05 8.10 14.07	-	-	-	-	-	-	-	-	-	-	-	-
Columbia County	293 0.56	177	24 13.56 13.56 8.19	-	-	-	-	-	-	-	-	-	-	-	-	-	-	-	-	-	-	-	-	-	-	-
Dane County	7,822 1.83	14,296	3,110 21.75 21.75 39.76	-	-	462 21.29 14.86 3.23 5.91	-	-	553 17.45 17.78 3.87 7.07	-	263 39.37 8.46 1.84 3.36	-	-	430 18.72 13.83 3.01 5.50	-	63 7.88 2.03 0.44 0.81	478 25.08 15.37 3.34 6.11	97 28.20 3.12 0.68 1.24	-	-	-	-	68 15.96 2.19 0.48 0.87	-	-	368 50.07 11.83 2.57 4.70
Madison (city)	5,119 2.47	11,641	2,378 20.43 20.43 46.45	-	-	278 19.43 11.69 2.39 5.43	-	-	454 16.31 19.09 3.90 8.87	-	194 43.40 8.16 1.67 3.79	-	-	372 20.45 15.64 3.20 7.27	-	50 7.26 2.10 0.43 0.98	324 19.13 13.62 2.78 6.33	-	-	-	-	-	68 16.08 2.86 0.58 1.33	-	-	315 49.61 13.25 2.71 6.15
Dodge County	685 0.80	268	104 38.81 38.81 15.18	-	-	-	-	-	-	-	-	-	-	-	-	-	-	-	-	-	-	-	-	-	-	-
Eau Claire County	908 0.97	2,323	548 23.59 23.59 60.35	-	-	-	-	-	-	-	-	-	-	291 21.03 53.10 12.53 32.05	-	-	-	-	-	-	-	-	-	-	-	-
Fond du Lac County	759 0.78	588	139 23.64 23.64 18.31	-	-	-	-	-	-	-	-	-	-	47 17.74 33.81 7.99 6.19	-	-	-	-	-	-	-	-	-	-	-	-
Jefferson County	664 0.90	215	78 36.28 36.28 11.75	-	-	-	-	-	-	-	-	-	-	-	-	-	-	-	-	-	-	-	-	-	-	-
Kenosha County	3,486 2.33	1,381	488 35.34 35.34 14.00	-	-	-	-	-	-	-	-	-	-	-	-	-	-	-	-	-	-	-	-	-	-	-
La Crosse County	1,370 1.28	2,855	852 29.84 29.84 62.19	-	-	-	-	-	-	-	-	-	-	417 21.48 48.94 14.61 30.44	-	-	-	-	-	-	-	-	-	-	-	-

Notes: Please refer to the User's Guide for an explanation of data; data is arranged alphabetically by state, then county, then city within each county; table includes counties with populations greater than 49,999 unless noted and cities with populations greater than 9,999 whose Asian and/or NHPI population rates are greater than the national average; (1) Native Hawaiian and other Pacific Islander; (2) excludes Taiwanese; (3) includes Chamorro; (4) county does not meet population threshold but is shown in order to allow inclusion of city

Place	Total foreign-born naturalized citizens	Total Asian population	Asians who are foreign-born naturalized citizens	Total NHPI[1] population	NHPIs[1] who are foreign-born naturalized citizens	Asian Indian	Bangladeshi	Cambodian	Chinese[2]	Fijian	Filipino	Guamanian[3]	Hawaiian, Native	Hmong	Indonesian	Japanese	Korean	Laotian	Malaysian	Pakistani	Samoan	Sri Lankan	Taiwanese	Thai	Tongan	Vietnamese
La Crosse (city)	772 1.50	1,943	463 23.83 23.83 59.97	-	-	-	-	-	-	-	-	-	-	226 16.84 48.81 11.63 29.27	-	-	-	-	-	-	-	-	-	-	-	-
Manitowoc County	565 0.68	1,471	236 16.04 16.04 41.77	-	-	-	-	-	-	-	-	-	-	80 8.52 33.90 5.44 14.16	-	-	-	-	-	-	-	-	-	-	-	-
Marathon County	1,539 1.22	5,156	824 15.98 15.98 53.54	-	-	-	-	-	-	-	-	-	-	569 13.85 69.05 11.04 36.97	-	-	-	-	-	-	-	-	-	-	-	-
Wausau (city)	943 2.46	4,168	615 14.76 14.76 65.22	-	-	-	-	-	-	-	-	-	-	453 13.19 73.66 10.87 48.04	-	-	-	-	-	-	-	-	-	-	-	-
Milwaukee County	23,894 2.54	22,356	5,899 26.39 26.39 24.69	520	54 10.38 10.38 0.23	945 24.87 16.02 4.23 3.95	-	-	604 26.87 10.24 2.70 2.53	-	620 38.20 10.51 2.77 2.59	-	-	1,467 19.60 24.87 6.56 6.14	-	145 19.52 2.46 0.65 0.61	732 57.14 12.41 3.27 3.06	341 19.85 5.78 1.53 1.43	-	94 26.48 1.59 0.42 0.39	-	-	-	-	-	642 49.12 10.88 2.87 2.69
Outagamie County	1,623 1.01	3,635	558 15.35 15.35 34.38	-	-	43 9.68 7.71 1.18 2.65	-	-	-	-	-	-	-	301 12.93 53.94 8.28 18.55	-	-	-	-	-	-	-	-	-	-	-	-
Appleton (city)	1,029 1.47	3,192	429 13.44 13.44 41.69	-	-	-	-	-	-	-	-	-	-	267 11.45 62.24 8.36 25.95	-	-	-	-	-	-	-	-	-	-	-	-
Ozaukee County	1,397 1.70	670	223 33.28 33.28 15.96	-	-	-	-	-	-	-	-	-	-	-	-	-	-	-	-	-	-	-	-	-	-	-
Portage County	624 0.93	1,295	254 19.61 19.61 40.71	-	-	-	-	-	-	-	-	-	-	135 15.54 53.15 10.42 21.63	-	-	-	-	-	-	-	-	-	-	-	-
Stevens Point (city)	325 1.33	1,035	174 16.81 16.81 53.54	-	-	-	-	-	-	-	-	-	-	129 17.04 74.14 12.46 39.69	-	-	-	-	-	-	-	-	-	-	-	-

Notes: Please refer to the User's Guide for an explanation of data; data is arranged alphabetically by state, then county, then city within each county; table includes counties with populations greater than 49,999 unless noted and cities with populations greater than 9,999 whose Asian and/or NHPI population rates are greater than the national average; (1) Native Hawaiian and other Pacific Islander; (2) excludes Taiwanese; (3) includes Chamorro; (4) county does not meet population threshold but is shown in order to allow inclusion of city

Place	Total foreign-born naturalized citizens	Total Asian population	Asians who are foreign-born naturalized citizens	Total NHPI[1] population	NHPIs[1] who are foreign-born naturalized citizens	Asian Indian	Bangladeshi	Cambodian	Chinese[2]	Fijian	Filipino	Guamanian[3]	Hawaiian, Native	Hmong	Indonesian	Japanese	Korean	Laotian	Malaysian	Pakistani	Samoan	Sri Lankan	Taiwanese	Thai	Tongan	Vietnamese
Racine County	3,487 1.85	1,277	524 41.03 41.03 15.03	-	-	-	-	-	-	-	-	-	-	-	-	-	-	-	-	-	-	-	-	-	-	-
Rock County	1,660 1.09	1,338	508 37.97 37.97 30.60	-	-	-	-	-	-	-	-	-	-	-	-	-	-	-	-	-	-	-	-	-	-	-
St. Croix County	346 0.55	263	76 28.90 28.90 21.97	-	-	-	-	-	-	-	-	-	-	-	-	-	-	-	-	-	-	-	-	-	-	-
Sauk County	496 0.90	209	60 28.71 28.71 12.10	-	-	-	-	-	-	-	-	-	-	-	-	-	-	-	-	-	-	-	-	-	-	-
Sheboygan County	1,541 1.37	3,575	475 13.29 13.29 30.82	-	-	-	-	-	-	-	-	-	-	303 12.16 63.79 8.48 19.66	-	-	-	-	-	-	-	-	-	-	-	-
Sheboygan (city)	1,109 2.18	3,289	424 12.89 12.89 38.23	-	-	-	-	-	-	-	-	-	-	290 12.15 68.40 8.82 26.15	-	-	-	-	-	-	-	-	-	-	-	-
Walworth County	2,046 2.18	567	244 43.03 43.03 11.93	-	-	-	-	-	-	-	-	-	-	-	-	-	-	-	-	-	-	-	-	-	-	-
Washington County	1,167 0.99	513	159 30.99 30.99 13.62	-	-	-	-	-	-	-	-	-	-	-	-	-	-	-	-	-	-	-	-	-	-	-
Waukesha County	7,241 2.01	5,005	1,814 36.24 36.24 25.05	-	-	488 29.54 26.90 9.75 6.74	-	-	344 30.04 18.96 6.87 4.75	-	205 50.87 11.30 4.10 2.83	-	-	-	-	-	427 72.13 23.54 8.53 5.90	-	-	-	-	-	-	-	-	-
Winnebago County	1,696 1.08	2,456	612 24.92 24.92 36.08	-	-	-	-	-	-	-	-	-	-	240 16.08 39.22 9.77 14.15	-	-	-	-	-	-	-	-	-	-	-	-

Notes: Please refer to the User's Guide for an explanation of data; data is arranged alphabetically by state, then county, then city within each county; table includes counties with populations greater than 49,999 unless noted and cities with populations greater than 9,999 whose Asian and/or NHPI population rates are greater than the national average; (1) Native Hawaiian and other Pacific Islander; (2) excludes Taiwanese; (3) includes Chamorro; (4) county does not meet population threshold but is shown in order to allow inclusion of city

Place	Total foreign-born naturalized citizens	Total Asian population	Asians who are foreign-born naturalized citizens	Total NHPI[1] population	NHPIs[1] who are foreign-born naturalized citizens	Asian Indian	Bangladeshi	Cambodian	Chinese[2]	Fijian	Filipino	Guamanian[3]	Hawaiian, Native	Hmong	Indonesian	Japanese	Korean	Laotian	Malaysian	Pakistani	Samoan	Sri Lankan	Taiwanese	Thai	Tongan	Vietnamese
Wood County	679 0.90	1,160	240 20.69 20.69 35.35	-	-	-	-	-	-	-	-	-	-	42 7.11 17.50 3.62 6.19	-	-	-	-	-	-	-	-	-	-	-	-
WYOMING	5,121 1.04	2,972	1,144 38.49 38.49 22.34	-	-	169 39.95 14.77 5.69 3.30	-	-	192 31.22 16.78 6.46 3.75	-	261 49.90 22.81 8.78 5.10	-	-	-	-	88 16.83 7.69 2.96 1.72	289 61.49 25.26 9.72 5.64	-	-	-	-	-	-	-	-	-
Laramie County	1,533 1.88	817	407 49.82 49.82 26.55	-	-	-	-	-	-	-	-	-	-	-	-	-	-	-	-	-	-	-	-	-	-	-
Natrona County	574 0.86	409	156 38.14 38.14 27.18	-	-	-	-	-	-	-	-	-	-	-	-	-	-	-	-	-	-	-	-	-	-	-

Notes: Please refer to the User's Guide for an explanation of data; data is arranged alphabetically by state, then county, then city within each county; table includes counties with populations greater than 49,999 unless noted and cities with populations greater than 9,999 whose Asian and/or NHPI population rates are greater than the national average; (1) Native Hawaiian and other Pacific Islander; (2) excludes Taiwanese; (3) includes Chamorro; (4) county does not meet population threshold but is shown in order to allow inclusion of city

Educational Attainment: High School Graduates

(Universe: Population 25 Years and Over)

Place	Total population 25 years and over who are high school graduates	Asian population 25 years and over	Asians 25 years and over who are high school graduates	NHPI[1] population 25 years and over	NHPIs[1] 25 years and over who are high school graduates	Asian Indian	Bangladeshi	Cambodian	Chinese[2]	Fijian	Filipino	Guamanian[3]	Hawaiian, Native	Hmong	Indonesian	Japanese	Korean	Laotian	Malaysian	Pakistani	Samoan	Sri Lankan	Taiwanese	Thai	Tongan	Vietnamese
UNITED STATES	146,496,014 80.40	6,640,671	5,340,921 80.43 80.43 3.65	206,675	161,732 78.25 78.25 0.11	906,483 86.69 16.97 13.65 0.62	19,556 78.22 0.37 0.29 0.01	40,287 46.66 0.75 0.61 0.03	1,205,190 76.20 22.57 18.15 0.82	3,914 66.84 2.42 1.89 <0.01	1,097,808 87.34 20.55 16.53 0.75	25,286 77.85 15.63 12.23 0.02	70,074 83.17 43.33 33.91 0.05	21,922 40.40 0.41 0.33 0.01	21,566 92.60 0.40 0.32 0.01	577,286 91.12 10.81 8.69 0.39	599,278 86.31 11.22 9.02 0.41	43,977 50.40 0.82 0.66 0.03	6,004 89.05 0.11 0.09 <0.01	71,715 82.03 1.34 1.08 0.05	31,625 75.81 19.55 15.30 0.02	11,612 86.55 0.22 0.17 0.01	75,069 93.01 1.41 1.13 0.05	62,006 79.12 1.16 0.93 0.04	8,559 65.27 5.29 4.14 0.01	429,134 61.88 8.03 6.46 0.29
ALABAMA	2,173,319 75.27	18,999	15,404 81.08 81.08 0.71	639	451 70.58 70.58 0.02	3,793 91.71 24.62 19.96 0.17	-	59 22.61 0.38 0.31 <0.01	3,426 90.42 22.24 18.03 0.16	-	1,571 87.86 10.20 8.27 0.07	147 76.96 32.59 23.00 0.01	-	-	-	1,203 88.46 7.81 6.33 0.06	2,024 75.41 13.14 10.65 0.09	390 76.47 2.53 2.05 0.02	-	192 94.12 1.25 1.01 0.01	-	-	-	273 62.19 1.77 1.44 0.01	-	1,328 51.67 8.62 6.99 0.06
Baldwin County	78,752 82.02	336	297 88.39 88.39 0.38	-	-	-	-	-	-	-	-	-	-	-	-	-	-	-	-	-	-	-	-	-	-	-
Calhoun County	54,697 73.90	433	309 71.36 71.36 0.56	-	-	-	-	-	-	-	-	-	-	-	-	-	-	-	-	-	-	-	-	-	-	-
Etowah County	51,714 74.06	229	191 83.41 83.41 0.37	-	-	-	-	-	-	-	-	-	-	-	-	-	-	-	-	-	-	-	-	-	-	-
Houston County	44,900 76.53	355	279 78.59 78.59 0.62	-	-	-	-	-	-	-	-	-	-	-	-	-	-	-	-	-	-	-	-	-	-	-
Jefferson County	351,208 80.89	3,682	3,227 87.64 87.64 0.92	-	-	781 92.32 24.20 21.21 0.22	-	-	1,261 94.81 39.08 34.25 0.36	-	-	-	-	-	-	-	231 82.50 7.16 6.27 0.07	-	-	-	-	-	-	-	-	222 53.62 6.88 6.03 0.06
Lee County	50,613 81.41	1,193	1,111 93.13 93.13 2.20	-	-	-	-	-	491 100.00 44.19 41.16 0.97	-	-	-	-	-	-	-	-	-	-	-	-	-	-	-	-	-
Madison County	154,081 85.42	3,074	2,633 85.65 85.65 1.71	-	-	898 94.03 34.11 29.21 0.58	-	-	446 95.50 16.94 14.51 0.29	-	-	-	-	-	-	-	505 75.60 19.18 16.43 0.33	-	-	-	-	-	-	-	-	178 61.38 6.76 5.79 0.12

Notes: Please refer to the User's Guide for an explanation of data; data is arranged alphabetically by state, then county, then city within each county; table includes counties with populations greater than 49,999 unless noted and cities with populations greater than 9,999 whose Asian and/or NHPI population rates are greater than the national average; (1) Native Hawaiian and other Pacific Islander; (2) excludes Taiwanese; (3) includes Chamorro; (4) county does not meet population threshold but is shown in order to allow inclusion of city

Place	Total population 25 years and over who are high school graduates	Asian population 25 years and over	Asians 25 years and over who are high school graduates	NHPI[1] population 25 years and over	NHPIs[1] 25 years and over who are high school graduates	Asian Indian	Bangladeshi	Cambodian	Chinese[2]	Fijian	Filipino	Guamanian[3]	Hawaiian, Native	Hmong	Indonesian	Japanese	Korean	Laotian	Malaysian	Pakistani	Samoan	Sri Lankan	Taiwanese	Thai	Tongan	Vietnamese
Mobile County	191,899 76.72	2,856	1,787 62.57 62.57 0.93	-	-	271 93.77 15.17 9.49 0.14	-	30 19.48 1.68 1.05 0.02	276 75.62 15.44 9.66 0.14	-	270 90.30 15.11 9.45 0.14	-	-	-	-	-	-	108 64.67 6.04 3.78 0.06	-	-	-	-	-	-	-	377 35.73 21.10 13.20 0.20
Montgomery County	113,437 80.26	1,341	1,052 78.45 78.45 0.93	-	-	-	-	-	-	-	-	-	-	-	-	-	-	-	-	-	-	-	-	-	-	-
Morgan County	55,984 76.34	311	284 91.32 91.32 0.51	-	-	-	-	-	-	-	-	-	-	-	-	-	-	-	-	-	-	-	-	-	-	-
Shelby County	81,799 86.85	715	639 89.37 89.37 0.78	-	-	289 91.17 45.23 40.42 0.35	-	-	-	-	-	-	-	-	-	-	-	-	-	-	-	-	-	-	-	-
Tuscaloosa County	78,058 78.82	904	813 89.93 89.93 1.04	-	-	-	-	-	-	-	-	-	-	-	-	-	-	-	-	-	-	-	-	-	-	-
ALASKA	335,274 88.33	16,576	12,108 73.05 73.05 3.61	1,322	1,002 75.79 75.79 0.30	263 84.29 2.17 1.59 0.08	-	-	801 79.15 6.62 4.83 0.24	-	6,195 75.78 51.16 37.37 1.85	-	244 86.52 24.35 18.46 0.07	42 21.76 0.35 0.25 0.01	-	1,118 94.59 9.23 6.74 0.33	2,179 68.57 18.00 13.15 0.65	172 29.05 1.42 1.04 0.05	-	-	397 70.89 39.62 30.03 0.12	-	-	273 51.22 2.25 1.65 0.08	82 53.95 8.18 6.20 0.02	442 67.48 3.65 2.67 0.13
Anchorage Borough	144,409 90.29	9,043	6,620 73.21 73.21 4.58	825	626 75.88 75.88 0.43	188 89.95 2.84 2.08 0.13	-	-	477 78.45 7.21 5.27 0.33	-	2,620 81.72 39.58 28.97 1.81	-	-	42 21.76 0.63 0.46 0.03	-	742 95.87 11.21 8.21 0.51	1,734 71.48 26.19 19.18 1.20	142 25.91 2.15 1.57 0.10	-	-	289 71.71 46.17 35.03 0.20	-	-	170 44.62 2.57 1.88 0.12	-	139 53.88 2.10 1.54 0.10
Fairbanks North Star Borough	44,056 91.83	1,293	933 72.16 72.16 2.12	-	-	-	-	-	181 86.60 19.40 14.00 0.41	-	259 72.75 27.76 20.03 0.59	-	-	-	-	-	176 47.44 18.86 13.61 0.40	-	-	-	-	-	-	-	-	-
Juneau City and Borough	18,540 93.17	882	749 84.92 84.92 4.04	-	-	-	-	-	-	-	557 85.43 74.37 63.15 3.00	-	-	-	-	-	-	-	-	-	-	-	-	-	-	-
Matanuska-Susitna Borough	31,488 88.15	266	187 70.30 70.30 0.59	-	-	-	-	-	-	-	-	-	-	-	-	-	-	-	-	-	-	-	-	-	-	-

Notes: Please refer to the User's Guide for an explanation of data; data is arranged alphabetically by state, then county, then city within each county; table includes counties with populations greater than 49,999 unless noted and cities with populations greater than 9,999 whose Asian and/or NHPI population rates are greater than the national average; (1) Native Hawaiian and other Pacific Islander; (2) excludes Taiwanese; (3) includes Chamorro; (4) county does not meet population threshold but is shown in order to allow inclusion of city

Place	Total population 25 years and over who are high school graduates	Asian population 25 years and over	Asians 25 years and over who are high school graduates	NHPI[1] population 25 years and over	NHPIs[1] 25 years and over who are high school graduates	Asian Indian	Bangladeshi	Cambodian	Chinese[2]	Fijian	Filipino	Guamanian[3]	Hawaiian, Native	Hmong	Indonesian	Japanese	Korean	Laotian	Malaysian	Pakistani	Samoan	Sri Lankan	Taiwanese	Thai	Tongan	Vietnamese
ARIZONA	2,636,637 80.97	60,212	50,210 83.39 83.39 1.90	3,068	2,571 83.80 83.80 0.10	8,268 90.69 16.47 13.73 0.31	-	416 67.97 0.83 0.69 0.02	12,211 85.53 24.32 20.28 0.46	-	9,327 86.51 18.58 15.49 0.35	579 84.53 22.52 18.87 0.02	894 88.69 34.77 29.14 0.03	-	349 88.58 0.70 0.58 0.01	5,503 91.08 10.96 9.14 0.21	5,450 84.56 10.85 9.05 0.21	376 71.48 0.75 0.62 0.01	-	392 98.74 0.78 0.65 0.01	393 79.55 15.29 12.81 0.01	-	441 90.74 0.88 0.73 0.02	873 76.85 1.74 1.45 0.03	188 73.44 7.31 6.13 0.01	4,616 61.12 9.19 7.67 0.18
Cochise County	60,211 79.46	1,452	1,075 74.04 74.04 1.79	-	-	-	-	-	-	-	236 82.52 21.95 16.25 0.39	-	-	-	-	-	381 64.80 35.44 26.24 0.63	-	-	-	-	-	-	-	-	-
Coconino County	55,272 83.78	475	378 79.58 79.58 0.68	-	-	-	-	-	-	-	-	-	-	-	-	-	-	-	-	-	-	-	-	-	-	-
Maricopa County	1,596,366 82.50	44,020	37,479 85.14 85.14 2.35	1,933	1,635 84.58 84.58 0.10	6,712 92.22 17.91 15.25 0.42	-	378 65.85 1.01 0.86 0.02	9,152 85.48 24.42 20.79 0.57	-	7,018 88.66 18.73 15.94 0.44	323 84.33 19.76 16.71 0.02	486 89.83 29.72 25.14 0.03	-	283 94.33 0.76 0.64 0.02	3,781 93.87 10.09 8.59 0.24	3,533 87.86 9.43 8.03 0.22	278 81.05 0.74 0.63 0.02	-	288 98.29 0.77 0.65 0.02	258 80.63 15.78 13.35 0.02	-	404 92.45 1.08 0.92 0.03	602 80.05 1.61 1.37 0.04	182 73.39 11.13 9.42 0.01	3,606 64.10 9.62 8.19 0.23
Chandler (city)	95,521 87.80	4,957	4,510 90.98 90.98 4.72	-	-	999 98.52 22.15 20.15 1.05	-	-	1,242 90.79 27.54 25.06 1.30	-	723 90.72 16.03 14.59 0.76	-	-	-	-	-	-	-	-	-	-	-	-	-	-	516 79.14 11.44 10.41 0.54
Gilbert (town)	60,771 94.27	2,561	2,387 93.21 93.21 3.93	-	-	443 96.30 18.56 17.30 0.73	-	-	764 94.79 32.01 29.83 1.26	-	439 96.06 18.39 17.14 0.72	-	-	-	-	-	-	-	-	-	-	-	-	-	-	-
Mesa (city)	207,509 84.66	4,120	3,476 84.37 84.37 1.68	230	210 91.30 91.30 0.10	373 86.74 10.73 9.05 0.18	-	-	594 79.52 17.09 14.42 0.29	-	870 91.19 25.03 21.12 0.42	-	-	-	-	439 93.40 12.63 10.66 0.21	425 82.05 12.23 10.32 0.20	-	-	-	-	-	-	-	-	376 74.31 10.82 9.13 0.18
Phoenix (city)	609,329 76.62	16,997	13,615 80.10 80.10 2.23	921	787 85.45 85.45 0.13	2,512 88.11 18.45 14.78 0.41	-	208 72.98 1.53 1.22 0.03	3,185 80.41 23.39 18.74 0.52	-	2,870 85.98 21.08 16.89 0.47	-	231 87.83 29.35 25.08 0.04	-	-	1,201 91.05 8.82 7.07 0.20	1,112 89.03 8.17 6.54 0.18	-	-	-	-	-	-	-	-	1,427 53.81 10.48 8.40 0.23
Tempe (city)	84,006 90.06	4,878	4,375 89.69 89.69 5.21	-	-	1,082 96.35 24.73 22.18 1.29	-	-	1,123 91.30 25.67 23.02 1.34	-	322 87.50 7.36 6.60 0.38	-	-	-	-	472 98.13 10.79 9.68 0.56	507 100.00 11.59 10.39 0.60	-	-	-	-	-	-	-	-	328 67.63 7.50 6.72 0.39
Mohave County	84,751 77.51	702	505 71.94 71.94 0.60	-	-	-	-	-	-	-	-	-	-	-	-	-	-	-	-	-	-	-	-	-	-	-

Notes: Please refer to the User's Guide for an explanation of data; data is arranged alphabetically by state, then county, then city within each county; table includes counties with populations greater than 49,999 unless noted and cities with populations greater than 9,999 whose Asian and/or NHPI population rates are greater than the national average; (1) Native Hawaiian and other Pacific Islander; (2) excludes Taiwanese; (3) includes Chamorro; (4) county does not meet population threshold but is shown in order to allow inclusion of city

Place	Total population 25 years and over who are high school graduates	Asian population 25 years and over	Asians 25 years and over who are high school graduates	NHPI[1] population 25 years and over	NHPIs[1] 25 years and over who are high school graduates	Asian Indian	Bangladeshi	Cambodian	Chinese[2]	Fijian	Filipino	Guamanian[3]	Hawaiian, Native	Hmong	Indonesian	Japanese	Korean	Laotian	Malaysian	Pakistani	Samoan	Sri Lankan	Taiwanese	Thai	Tongan	Vietnamese
Pima County	455,717 83.43	10,638	8,560 80.47 80.47 1.88	569	452 79.44 79.44 0.10	988 90.89 11.54 9.29 0.22	-	-	2,556 86.67 29.86 24.03 0.56	-	1,227 80.20 14.33 11.53 0.27	-	206 83.40 45.58 36.20 0.05	-	-	1,025 89.99 11.97 9.64 0.22	1,083 81.55 12.65 10.18 0.24	-	-	-	-	-	-	-	-	833 54.87 9.73 7.83 0.18
Tucson (city)	242,013 80.39	7,114	5,476 76.97 76.97 2.26	354	274 77.40 77.40 0.11	608 89.54 11.10 8.55 0.25	-	-	1,678 86.05 30.64 23.59 0.69	-	785 74.34 14.34 11.03 0.32	-	-	-	-	632 87.29 11.54 8.88 0.26	586 77.11 10.70 8.24 0.24	-	-	-	-	-	-	-	-	652 53.18 11.91 9.17 0.27
Pinal County	86,589 72.70	648	457 70.52 70.52 0.53	-	-	-	-	-	-	-	-	-	-	-	-	-	-	-	-	-	-	-	-	-	-	-
Yavapai County	101,847 84.72	572	449 78.50 78.50 0.44	-	-	-	-	-	-	-	-	-	-	-	-	-	-	-	-	-	-	-	-	-	-	-
Yuma County	64,283 65.81	957	734 76.70 76.70 1.14	-	-	-	-	-	-	-	240 81.91 32.70 25.08 0.37	-	-	-	-	-	-	-	-	-	-	-	-	-	-	-
ARKANSAS	1,303,751 75.31	12,097	8,819 72.90 72.90 0.68	561	388 69.16 69.16 0.03	1,558 87.97 17.67 12.88 0.12	-	-	1,607 83.70 18.22 13.28 0.12	-	1,306 80.82 14.81 10.80 0.10	-	107 67.30 27.58 19.07 0.01	-	-	732 84.53 8.30 6.05 0.06	706 73.93 8.01 5.84 0.05	631 45.36 7.16 5.22 0.05	-	-	-	-	-	105 55.26 1.19 0.87 0.01	-	1,351 56.65 15.32 11.17 0.10
Benton County	79,971 80.42	985	719 72.99 72.99 0.90	-	-	273 93.49 37.97 27.72 0.34	-	-	-	-	-	-	-	-	-	-	-	-	-	-	-	-	-	-	-	100 39.22 13.91 10.15 0.13
Craighead County	39,210 77.30	232	115 49.57 49.57 0.29	-	-	-	-	-	-	-	-	-	-	-	-	-	-	-	-	-	-	-	-	-	-	-
Crawford County	24,137 71.49	374	212 56.68 56.68 0.88	-	-	-	-	-	-	-	-	-	-	-	-	-	-	-	-	-	-	-	-	-	-	-
Faulkner County	42,381 83.35	261	227 86.97 86.97 0.54	-	-	-	-	-	-	-	-	-	-	-	-	-	-	-	-	-	-	-	-	-	-	-

Notes: Please refer to the User's Guide for an explanation of data; data is arranged alphabetically by state, then county, then city within each county; table includes counties with populations greater than 49,999 unless noted and cities with populations greater than 9,999 whose Asian and/or NHPI population rates are greater than the national average; (1) Native Hawaiian and other Pacific Islander; (2) excludes Taiwanese; (3) includes Chamorro; (4) county does not meet population threshold but is shown in order to allow inclusion of city

Place	Total population 25 years and over who are high school graduates	Asian population 25 years and over	Asians 25 years and over who are high school graduates	NHPI[1] population 25 years and over	NHPIs[1] 25 years and over who are high school graduates	Asian Indian	Bangladeshi	Cambodian	Chinese[2]	Fijian	Filipino	Guamanian[3]	Hawaiian, Native	Hmong	Indonesian	Japanese	Korean	Laotian	Malaysian	Pakistani	Samoan	Sri Lankan	Taiwanese	Thai	Tongan	Vietnamese
Jefferson County	39,755	315	276	-	-	-	-	-	-	-	-	-	-	-	-	-	-	-	-	-	-	-	-	-	-	-
	74.82		87.62																							
			87.62																							
			0.69																							
Pulaski County	199,048	2,966	2,441	-	-	588	-	-	532	-	369	-	-	-	-	-	-	-	-	-	-	-	-	-	-	-
	84.37		82.30			93.78			90.78		80.92															
						24.09			21.79		15.12															
			82.30			19.82			17.94		12.44															
			1.23			0.30			0.27		0.19															
Saline County	45,938	275	206	-	-	-	-	-	-	-	-	-	-	-	-	-	-	-	-	-	-	-	-	-	-	-
	82.33		74.91																							
			74.91																							
			0.45																							
Sebastian County	57,126	2,205	1,209	-	-	-	-	-	-	-	-	-	-	-	-	-	-	268	-	-	-	-	-	-	-	629
	76.58		54.83															42.95								55.08
																		22.17								52.03
			54.83															12.15								28.53
			2.12															0.47								1.10
Fort Smith (city)	39,430	2,011	1,027	-	-	-	-	-	-	-	-	-	-	-	-	-	-	256	-	-	-	-	-	-	-	570
	75.72		51.07															41.83								52.83
																		24.93								55.50
			51.07															12.73								28.34
			2.60															0.65								1.45
Washington County	74,757	1,521	1,286	190	150	-	-	-	486	-	-	-	-	-	-	-	-	136	-	-	-	-	-	-	-	-
	79.51		84.55		78.95				96.24									50.56								
									37.79									10.58								
			84.55		78.95				31.95									8.94								
			1.72		0.20				0.65									0.18								
Springdale (city)	20,333	422	266	168	137	-	-	-	-	-	-	-	-	-	-	-	-	106	-	-	-	-	-	-	-	-
	73.56		63.03		81.55													48.85								
																		39.85								
			63.03		81.55													25.12								
			1.31		0.67													0.52								
CALIFORNIA	16,356,157	2,434,151	1,960,603	63,077	47,954	169,100	1,482	14,622	486,125	3,046	537,348	10,299	11,022	7,347	9,483	216,928	204,612	11,233	1,070	9,177	14,243	3,228	38,659	20,228	3,686	181,849
	76.79		80.55		76.02	85.48	85.52	43.84	76.30	65.11	87.78	79.90	83.34	34.37	91.39	92.94	88.12	41.60	87.63	83.31	76.07	85.35	92.57	81.39	60.73	64.47
						8.62	0.08	0.75	24.79	6.35	27.41	21.48	22.98	0.37	0.48	11.06	10.44	0.57	0.05	0.47	29.70	0.16	1.97	1.03	7.69	9.28
			80.55		76.02	6.95	0.06	0.60	19.97	4.83	22.08	16.33	17.47	0.30	0.39	8.91	8.41	0.46	0.04	0.38	22.58	0.13	1.59	0.83	5.84	7.47
			11.99		0.29	1.03	0.01	0.09	2.97	0.02	3.29	0.06	0.07	0.04	0.06	1.33	1.25	0.07	0.01	0.06	0.09	0.02	0.24	0.12	0.02	1.11
Alameda County	785,435	193,930	157,804	4,871	3,667	24,110	-	813	54,704	562	41,572	822	777	-	320	9,429	8,557	642	-	1,081	664	-	2,476	727	522	9,232
	82.36		81.37		75.28	88.21		47.91	75.13	75.13	89.29	87.45	83.37		84.66	93.98	89.25	43.38		87.60	67.76		96.38	79.45	61.63	64.93
						15.28		0.52	34.67	15.33	26.34	22.42	21.19		0.20	5.98	5.42	0.41		0.69	18.11		1.57	0.46	14.24	5.85
			81.37		75.28	12.43		0.42	28.21	11.54	21.44	16.88	15.95		0.17	4.86	4.41	0.33		0.56	13.63		1.28	0.37	10.72	4.76
			20.09		0.47	3.07		0.10	6.96	0.07	5.29	0.10	0.10		0.04	1.20	1.09	0.08		0.14	0.08		0.32	0.09	0.07	1.18
Alameda (city)	45,946	12,761	10,480	458	364	615	-	-	3,900	-	3,674	-	-	-	-	615	769	-	-	-	-	-	-	-	-	521
	88.44		82.13		79.48	88.87			76.89		87.10					96.09	86.21									68.64
						5.87			37.21		35.06					5.87	7.34									4.97
			82.13		79.48	4.82			30.56		28.79					4.82	6.03									4.08
			22.81		0.79	1.34			8.49		8.00					1.34	1.67									1.13

Notes: Please refer to the User's Guide for an explanation of data; data is arranged alphabetically by state, then county, then city within each county; table includes counties with populations greater than 49,999 unless noted and cities with populations greater than 9,999 whose Asian and/or NHPI population rates are greater than the national average; (1) Native Hawaiian and other Pacific Islander; (2) excludes Taiwanese; (3) includes Chamorro; (4) county does not meet population threshold but is shown in order to allow inclusion of city

Place	Total population 25 years and over who are high school graduates	Asian population 25 years and over	Asians 25 years and over who are high school graduates	NHPI[1] population 25 years and over	NHPIs[1] 25 years and over who are high school graduates	Asian Indian	Bangladeshi	Cambodian	Chinese[2]	Fijian	Filipino	Guamanian[3]	Hawaiian, Native	Hmong	Indonesian	Japanese	Korean	Laotian	Malaysian	Pakistani	Samoan	Sri Lankan	Taiwanese	Thai	Tongan	Vietnamese
Albany (city)	10,854	2,855	2,635	-	-	223	-	-	1,214	-	-	-	-	-	-	446	324	-	-	-	-	-	-	-	-	-
	93.78		92.29			96.96			90.60							93.31	93.91									
						8.46			46.07							16.93	12.30									
			92.29			7.81			42.52							15.62	11.35									
			24.28			2.05			11.18							4.11	2.99									
Ashland (cdp)	9,346	2,146	1,704	-	-	-	-	-	523	-	788	-	-	-	-	-	-	-	-	-	-	-	-	-	-	-
	72.80		79.40						72.44		88.24															
									30.69		46.24															
			79.40						24.37		36.72															
			18.23						5.60		8.43															
Berkeley (city)	60,999	7,757	7,083	-	-	660	-	-	2,681	-	664	-	-	-	-	1,526	630	-	-	-	-	-	129	-	-	304
	92.24		91.31			92.31			89.10		93.79					96.64	98.75						100.00			80.21
						9.32			37.85		9.37					21.54	8.89						1.82			4.29
			91.31			8.51			34.56		8.56					19.67	8.12						1.66			3.92
			11.61			1.08			4.40		1.09					2.50	1.03						0.21			0.50
Castro Valley (cdp)	35,494	5,086	4,545	-	-	515	-	-	2,097	-	808	-	-	-	-	432	485	-	-	-	-	-	-	-	-	-
	88.99		89.36			90.83			88.48		94.39					94.32	88.99									
						11.33			46.14		17.78					9.50	10.67									
			89.36			10.13			41.23		15.89					8.49	9.54									
			12.80			1.45			5.91		2.28					1.22	1.37									
Cherryland (cdp)	5,778	813	637	-	-	-	-	-	-	-	339	-	-	-	-	-	-	-	-	-	-	-	-	-	-	-
	66.71		78.35								85.82															
											53.22															
			78.35								41.70															
			11.02								5.87															
Dublin (city)	18,120	2,192	1,952	-	-	347	-	-	642	-	547	-	-	-	-	-	-	-	-	-	-	-	-	-	-	-
	86.31		89.05			87.85			93.59		88.51															
						17.78			32.89		28.02															
			89.05			15.83			29.29		24.95															
			10.77			1.92			3.54		3.02															
Fremont (city)	120,443	50,516	45,807	446	424	12,909	-	-	16,273	-	6,969	-	-	-	-	1,279	2,206	-	-	616	-	-	1,649	-	-	2,410
	88.40		90.68		95.07	92.19			89.74		91.48					96.38	87.92			87.01			96.55			85.01
						28.18			35.53		15.21					2.79	4.82			1.34			3.60			5.26
			90.68		95.07	25.55			32.21		13.80					2.53	4.37			1.22			3.26			4.77
			38.03		0.35	10.72			13.51		5.79					1.06	1.83			0.51			1.37			2.00
Hayward (city)	65,940	16,992	14,229	1,334	945	1,765	-	-	2,166	283	7,246	-	-	-	-	824	568	-	-	-	202	-	-	-	-	1,045
	75.11		83.74		70.84	79.61			80.46	68.19	88.60					91.05	89.73				64.74					69.11
						12.40			15.22	29.95	50.92					5.79	3.99				21.38					7.34
			83.74		70.84	10.39			12.75	21.21	42.64					4.85	3.34				15.14					6.15
			21.58		1.43	2.68			3.28	0.43	10.99					1.25	0.86				0.31					1.58
Livermore (city)	42,516	2,902	2,505	-	-	327	-	-	525	-	1,003	-	-	-	-	-	-	-	-	-	-	-	-	-	-	166
	89.60		86.32			77.86			93.75		88.76															57.44
						13.05			20.96		40.04															6.63
			86.32			11.27			18.09		34.56															5.72
			5.89			0.77			1.23		2.36															0.39
Newark (city)	21,060	6,160	5,248	-	-	955	-	-	1,040	-	1,954	-	-	-	-	-	348	-	-	-	-	-	-	-	-	297
	79.23		85.19			88.34			83.94		88.14						93.30									69.56
						18.20			19.82		37.23						6.63									5.66
			85.19			15.50			16.88		31.72						5.65									4.82
			24.92			4.53			4.94		9.28						1.65									1.41

Notes: Please refer to the User's Guide for an explanation of data; data is arranged alphabetically by state, then county, then city within each county; table includes counties with populations greater than 49,999 unless noted and cities with populations greater than 9,999 whose Asian and/or NHPI population rates are greater than the national average; (1) Native Hawaiian and other Pacific Islander; (2) excludes Taiwanese; (3) includes Chamorro; (4) county does not meet population threshold but is shown in order to allow inclusion of city

Place	Total population 25 years and over who are high school graduates	Asian population 25 years and over	Asians 25 years and over who are high school graduates	NHPI[1] population 25 years and over	NHPIs[1] 25 years and over who are high school graduates	Asian Indian	Bangladeshi	Cambodian	Chinese[2]	Fijian	Filipino	Guamanian[3]	Hawaiian, Native	Hmong	Indonesian	Japanese	Korean	Laotian	Malaysian	Pakistani	Samoan	Sri Lankan	Taiwanese	Thai	Tongan	Vietnamese
Oakland (city)	193,305	40,634	24,448	1,102	699	1,007	-	430	12,161	-	4,044	-	-	-	-	1,704	1,144	345	-	-	-	-	-	-	333	2,520
	73.95		60.17		63.43	83.29		36.23	54.08		83.61					91.37	80.91	33.66							61.21	50.00
						4.12		1.76	49.74		16.54					6.97	4.68	1.41							47.64	10.31
			60.17		63.43	2.48		1.06	29.93		9.95					4.19	2.82	0.85							30.22	6.20
			12.65		0.36	0.52		0.22	6.29		2.09					0.88	0.59	0.18							0.17	1.30
Piedmont (city)	7,122	1,228	1,175	-	-	-	-	-	848	-	-	-	-	-	-	-	-	-	-	-	-	-	-	-	-	-
	98.13		95.68						94.85																	
									72.17																	
			95.68						69.06																	
			16.50						11.91																	
Pleasanton (city)	39,925	4,818	4,649	-	-	1,030	-	-	1,627	-	571	-	-	-	-	513	400	-	-	-	-	-	-	-	-	-
	94.23		96.49			96.71			95.76		94.54					98.84	100.00									
						22.16			35.00		12.28					11.03	8.60									
			96.49			21.38			33.77		11.85					10.65	8.30									
			11.64			2.58			4.08		1.43					1.28	1.00									
San Leandro (city)	45,155	12,667	9,870	264	195	422	-	-	3,831	-	3,790	-	-	-	-	459	268	-	-	-	-	-	-	-	-	539
	80.86		77.92		73.86	87.01			66.36		91.24					95.82	89.63									65.73
						4.28			38.81		38.40					4.65	2.72									5.46
			77.92		73.86	3.33			30.24		29.92					3.62	2.12									4.26
			21.86		0.43	0.93			8.48		8.39					1.02	0.59									1.19
San Lorenzo (cdp)	11,986	2,340	1,845	-	-	-	-	-	451	-	850	-	-	-	-	-	-	-	-	-	-	-	-	-	-	80
	81.23		78.85						66.62		91.20															45.45
									24.44		46.07															4.34
			78.85						19.27		36.32															3.42
			15.39						3.76		7.09															0.67
Union City (city)	33,824	18,906	16,154	370	312	2,669	-	-	3,561	-	7,487	-	-	-	-	349	626	-	-	-	-	-	-	-	-	770
	80.46		85.44		84.32	79.58			85.62		89.69					84.10	91.12									65.87
						16.52			22.04		46.35					2.16	3.88									4.77
			85.44		84.32	14.12			18.84		39.60					1.85	3.31									4.07
			47.76		0.92	7.89			10.53		22.14					1.03	1.85									2.28
Butte County	104,259	2,718	1,698	-	-	201	-	-	337	-	220	-	-	292	-	278	-	42	-	-	-	-	-	-	-	-
	82.26		62.47			77.31			74.39		97.35			38.47		82.74		19.72								
						11.84			19.85		12.96			17.20		16.37		2.47								
			62.47			7.40			12.40		8.09			10.74		10.23		1.55								
			1.63			0.19			0.32		0.21			0.28		0.27		0.04								
Chico (city)	27,130	898	657	-	-	-	-	-	175	-	-	-	-	86	-	-	-	-	-	-	-	-	-	-	-	-
	87.31		73.16						76.09					39.63												
									26.64					13.09												
			73.16						19.49					9.58												
			2.42						0.65					0.32												
Oroville (city)	5,717	198	89	-	-	-	-	-	-	-	-	-	-	41	-	-	-	-	-	-	-	-	-	-	-	-
	73.64		44.95											42.27												
														46.07												
			44.95											20.71												
			1.56											0.72												
Contra Costa County	543,774	69,241	60,536	1,792	1,455	6,247	-	-	18,073	193	20,433	292	328	-	363	6,363	2,660	829	-	378	266	-	946	333	139	2,272
	86.91		87.43		81.19	84.98			90.78	73.38	89.82	88.48	82.41		97.84	95.08	91.13	39.36		91.30	75.57		93.48	78.17	78.98	69.23
						10.32			29.85	13.26	33.75	20.07	22.54		0.60	10.51	4.39	1.37		0.62	18.28		1.56	0.55	9.55	3.75
			87.43		81.19	9.02			26.10	10.77	29.51	16.29	18.30		0.52	9.19	3.84	1.20		0.55	14.84		1.37	0.48	7.76	3.28
			11.13		0.27	1.15			3.32	0.04	3.76	0.05	0.06		0.07	1.17	0.49	0.15		0.07	0.05		0.17	0.06	0.03	0.42

Notes: Please refer to the User's Guide for an explanation of data; data is arranged alphabetically by state, then county, then city within each county; table includes counties with populations greater than 49,999 unless noted and cities with populations greater than 9,999 whose Asian and/or NHPI population rates are greater than the national average; (1) Native Hawaiian and other Pacific Islander; (2) excludes Taiwanese; (3) includes Chamorro; (4) county does not meet population threshold but is shown in order to allow inclusion of city

Place	Total population 25 years and over who are high school graduates	Asian population 25 years and over	Asians 25 years and over who are high school graduates	NHPI[1] population 25 years and over	NHPIs[1] 25 years and over who are high school graduates	Asian Indian	Bangladeshi	Cambodian	Chinese[2]	Fijian	Filipino	Guamanian[3]	Hawaiian, Native	Hmong	Indonesian	Japanese	Korean	Laotian	Malaysian	Pakistani	Samoan	Sri Lankan	Taiwanese	Thai	Tongan	Vietnamese
Alamo (cdp)	10,113	577	566	-	-	-	-	-	-	-	-	-	-	-	-	-	-	-	-	-	-	-	-	-	-	-
	98.37		98.09																							
			98.09																							
			5.60																							
Antioch (city)	46,306	4,221	3,611	183	136	173	-	-	699	-	1,909	-	-	-	-	-	-	-	-	-	-	-	-	-	-	201
	85.69		85.55		74.32	82.78			84.42		91.87															62.23
						4.79			19.36		52.87															5.57
			85.55		74.32	4.10			16.56		45.23															4.76
			7.80		0.29	0.37			1.51		4.12															0.43
Bay Point (cdp)	8,860	1,480	1,275	-	-	-	-	-	-	-	699	-	-	-	-	-	-	-	-	-	-	-	-	-	-	-
	71.80		86.15								92.71															
											54.82															
			86.15								47.23															
			14.39								7.89															
Blackhawk-Camino-Tass. (cdp)	6,535	1,079	1,058	-	-	-	-	-	561	-	-	-	-	-	-	-	-	-	-	-	-	-	-	-	-	-
	97.03		98.05						97.57																	
									53.02																	
			98.05						51.99																	
			16.19						8.58																	
Clayton (city)	7,255	451	445	-	-	-	-	-	-	-	-	-	-	-	-	-	-	-	-	-	-	-	-	-	-	-
	97.51		98.67																							
			98.67																							
			6.13																							
Concord (city)	67,886	7,719	6,647	187	145	952	-	-	1,740	-	2,341	-	-	-	-	688	248	-	-	-	-	-	-	-	-	276
	84.72		86.11		77.54	84.32			91.05		86.19					99.14	84.07									62.30
						14.32			26.18		35.22					10.35	3.73									4.15
			86.11		77.54	12.33			22.54		30.33					8.91	3.21									3.58
			9.79		0.21	1.40			2.56		3.45					1.01	0.37									0.41
Danville (town)	27,463	2,355	2,229	-	-	282	-	-	912	-	355	-	-	-	-	-	-	-	-	-	-	-	-	-	-	-
	96.55		94.65			97.58			93.44		98.34															
						12.65			40.92		15.93															
			94.65			11.97			38.73		15.07															
			8.12			1.03			3.32		1.29															
El Cerrito (city)	16,671	4,203	3,764	-	-	241	-	-	1,698	-	318	-	-	-	-	932	-	-	-	-	-	-	-	-	-	-
	92.62		89.56			94.88			87.80		90.34					93.01										
						6.40			45.11		8.45					24.76										
			89.56			5.73			40.40		7.57					22.17										
			22.58			1.45			10.19		1.91					5.59										
El Sobrante (cdp)	6,833	939	715	-	-	124	-	-	-	-	-	-	-	-	-	-	-	-	-	-	-	-	-	-	-	-
	86.44		76.14			63.59																				
						17.34																				
			76.14			13.21																				
			10.46			1.81																				
Hercules (city)	11,211	5,219	4,628	-	-	312	-	-	1,011	-	2,728	-	-	-	-	-	-	-	-	-	-	-	-	-	-	-
	90.54		88.68			81.89			84.46		92.19															
						6.74			21.85		58.95															
			88.68			5.98			19.37		52.27															
			41.28			2.78			9.02		24.33															

Notes: Please refer to the User's Guide for an explanation of data; data is arranged alphabetically by state, then county, then city within each county; table includes counties with populations greater than 49,999 unless noted and cities with populations greater than 9,999 whose Asian and/or NHPI population rates are greater than the national average; (1) Native Hawaiian and other Pacific Islander; (2) excludes Taiwanese; (3) includes Chamorro; (4) county does not meet population threshold but is shown in order to allow inclusion of city

Place	Total population 25 years and over who are high school graduates	Asian population 25 years and over	Asians 25 years and over who are high school graduates	NHPI[1] population 25 years and over	NHPIs[1] 25 years and over who are high school graduates	Asian Indian	Bangladeshi	Cambodian	Chinese[2]	Fijian	Filipino	Guamanian[3]	Hawaiian, Native	Hmong	Indonesian	Japanese	Korean	Laotian	Malaysian	Pakistani	Samoan	Sri Lankan	Taiwanese	Thai	Tongan	Vietnamese
Lafayette (city)	16,242	1,228	1,195	-	-	-	-	-	577	-	-	-	-	-	-	-	-	-	-	-	-	-	-	-	-	-
	97.68		97.31						98.63																	
									48.28																	
			97.31						46.99																	
			7.36						3.55																	
Martinez (city)	22,950	1,684	1,549	-	-	-	-	-	344	-	675	-	-	-	-	-	-	-	-	-	-	-	-	-	-	-
	91.07		91.98						92.97		94.80															
									22.21		43.58															
			91.98						20.43		40.08															
			6.75						1.50		2.94															
Moraga (town)	10,290	1,422	1,367	-	-	-	-	-	832	-	-	-	-	-	-	-	-	-	-	-	-	-	-	-	-	-
	97.07		96.13						97.08																	
									60.86																	
			96.13						58.51																	
			13.28						8.09																	
Orinda (city)	12,084	1,003	933	-	-	-	-	-	544	-	-	-	-	-	-	-	-	-	-	-	-	-	-	-	-	-
	97.77		93.02						91.12																	
									58.31																	
			93.02						54.24																	
			7.72						4.50																	
Pinole (city)	11,514	2,688	2,336	-	-	-	-	-	556	-	1,204	-	-	-	-	-	-	-	-	-	-	-	-	-	-	-
	88.26		86.90						88.39		89.52															
									23.80		51.54															
			86.90						20.68		44.79															
			20.29						4.83		10.46															
Pittsburg (city)	25,262	4,589	3,759	262	226	306	-	-	290	-	2,667	-	-	-	-	-	-	-	-	-	-	-	-	-	-	-
	75.66		81.91		86.26	59.42			82.86		85.84															
						8.14			7.71		70.95															
			81.91		86.26	6.67			6.32		58.12															
			14.88		0.89	1.21			1.15		10.56															
Pleasant Hill (city)	21,927	2,114	2,006	-	-	-	-	-	647	-	526	-	-	-	-	-	260	-	-	-	-	-	-	-	-	-
	93.09		94.89						98.93		93.76						91.55									
									32.25		26.22						12.96									
			94.89						30.61		24.88						12.30									
			9.15						2.95		2.40						1.19									
Richmond (city)	47,216	8,016	6,256	248	164	541	-	-	1,963	-	1,689	-	-	-	-	696	285	475	-	-	-	-	-	-	-	199
	75.35		78.04		66.13	71.18			84.61		86.26					93.55	95.32	40.98								78.66
						8.65			31.38		27.00					11.13	4.56	7.59								3.18
			78.04		66.13	6.75			24.49		21.07					8.68	3.56	5.93								2.48
			13.25		0.35	1.15			4.16		3.58					1.47	0.60	1.01								0.42
San Pablo (city)	10,825	2,912	2,037	-	-	252	-	-	-	-	947	-	-	-	-	-	-	234	-	-	-	-	-	-	-	223
	62.40		69.95			75.22					84.40							39.86								57.62
						12.37					46.49							11.49								10.95
			69.95			8.65					32.52							8.04								7.66
			18.82			2.33					8.75							2.16								2.06
San Ramon (city)	29,247	4,565	4,396	-	-	912	-	-	1,732	-	681	-	-	-	-	346	-	-	-	-	-	-	-	-	-	-
	96.53		96.30			97.75			95.53		96.19					100.00										
						20.75			39.40		15.49					7.87										
			96.30			19.98			37.94		14.92					7.58										
			15.03			3.12			5.92		2.33					1.18										

Notes: Please refer to the User's Guide for an explanation of data; data is arranged alphabetically by state, then county, then city within each county; table includes counties with populations greater than 49,999 unless noted and cities with populations greater than 9,999 whose Asian and/or NHPI population rates are greater than the national average; (1) Native Hawaiian and other Pacific Islander; (2) excludes Taiwanese; (3) includes Chamorro; (4) county does not meet population threshold but is shown in order to allow inclusion of city

Place	Total population 25 years and over who are high school graduates	Asian population 25 years and over	Asians 25 years and over who are high school graduates	NHPI[1] population 25 years and over	NHPIs[1] 25 years and over who are high school graduates	Asian Indian	Bangladeshi	Cambodian	Chinese[2]	Fijian	Filipino	Guamanian[3]	Hawaiian, Native	Hmong	Indonesian	Japanese	Korean	Laotian	Malaysian	Pakistani	Samoan	Sri Lankan	Taiwanese	Thai	Tongan	Vietnamese
Walnut Creek (city)	47,465 94.96	4,635	4,464 96.31 96.31 9.40	-	-	409 95.78 9.16 8.82 0.86	-	-	1,837 96.48 41.15 39.63 3.87	-	930 97.38 20.83 20.06 1.96	-	-	-	-	700 98.59 15.68 15.10 1.47	324 93.91 7.26 6.99 0.68	-	-	-	-	-	-	-	-	-
El Dorado County	93,554 89.07	2,105	1,758 83.52 83.52 1.88	-	-	-	-	-	-	-	666 76.73 37.88 31.64 0.71	-	-	-	-	404 92.87 22.98 19.19 0.43	-	-	-	-	-	-	-	-	-	-
El Dorado Hills (cdp)	11,040 97.31	428	413 96.50 96.50 3.74	-	-	-	-	-	-	-	-	-	-	-	-	-	-	-	-	-	-	-	-	-	-	-
South Lake Tahoe (city)	12,128 80.79	945	688 72.80 72.80 5.67	-	-	-	-	-	-	-	446 71.13 64.83 47.20 3.68	-	-	-	-	-	-	-	-	-	-	-	-	-	-	-
Fresno County	307,603 67.52	31,409	18,562 59.10 59.10 6.03	306	189 61.76 61.76 0.06	2,349 58.49 12.65 7.48 0.76	-	483 30.43 2.60 1.54 0.16	2,596 76.56 13.99 8.27 0.84	-	3,611 86.74 19.45 11.50 1.17	-	-	2,259 30.32 12.17 7.19 0.73	-	4,338 91.58 23.37 13.81 1.41	768 89.10 4.14 2.45 0.25	671 25.14 3.61 2.14 0.22	-	-	-	-	-	-	-	522 45.12 2.81 1.66 0.17
Clovis (city)	34,961 84.99	2,266	1,687 74.45 74.45 4.83	-	-	-	-	-	-	-	338 94.68 20.04 14.92 0.97	-	-	302 48.24 17.90 13.33 0.86	-	422 91.74 25.01 18.62 1.21	-	-	-	-	-	-	-	-	-	-
Fresno (city)	163,456 69.06	22,295	12,066 54.12 54.12 7.38	-	-	1,284 61.61 10.64 5.76 0.79	-	430 29.68 3.56 1.93 0.26	1,917 74.22 15.89 8.60 1.17	-	2,575 88.12 21.34 11.55 1.58	-	-	1,754 27.99 14.54 7.87 1.07	-	1,986 93.90 16.46 8.91 1.22	540 87.38 4.48 2.42 0.33	561 23.85 4.65 2.52 0.34	-	-	-	-	-	-	-	329 36.43 2.73 1.48 0.20
Reedley (city)	6,888 59.19	606	517 85.31 85.31 7.51	-	-	-	-	-	-	-	-	-	-	-	-	-	-	-	-	-	-	-	-	-	-	-
Humboldt County	69,203 84.91	982	729 74.24 74.24 1.05	-	-	-	-	-	-	-	-	-	-	-	-	222 100.00 30.45 22.61 0.32	-	-	-	-	-	-	-	-	-	-
Imperial County	49,374 59.04	1,836	1,474 80.28 80.28 2.99	-	-	-	-	-	217 49.89 14.72 11.82 0.44	-	498 87.37 33.79 27.12 1.01	-	-	-	-	-	268 97.81 18.18 14.60 0.54	-	-	-	-	-	-	-	-	-

Notes: Please refer to the User's Guide for an explanation of data; data is arranged alphabetically by state, then county, then city within each county; table includes counties with populations greater than 49,999 unless noted and cities with populations greater than 9,999 whose Asian and/or NHPI population rates are greater than the national average; (1) Native Hawaiian and other Pacific Islander; (2) excludes Taiwanese; (3) includes Chamorro; (4) county does not meet population threshold but is shown in order to allow inclusion of city

Place	Total population 25 years and over who are high school graduates	Asian population 25 years and over	Asians 25 years and over who are high school graduates	NHPI[1] population 25 years and over	NHPIs[1] 25 years and over who are high school graduates	Asian Indian	Bangladeshi	Cambodian	Chinese[2]	Fijian	Filipino	Guamanian[3]	Hawaiian, Native	Hmong	Indonesian	Japanese	Korean	Laotian	Malaysian	Pakistani	Samoan	Sri Lankan	Taiwanese	Thai	Tongan	Vietnamese
Kern County	262,686 68.47	13,549	9,603 70.88 70.88 3.66	395	315 79.75 79.75 0.12	1,463 58.26 15.23 10.80 0.56	-	84 42.00 0.87 0.62 0.03	1,247 83.19 12.99 9.20 0.47	-	4,581 68.26 47.70 33.81 1.74	-	-	-	-	679 95.63 7.07 5.01 0.26	723 92.34 7.53 5.34 0.28	-	-	-	-	-	-	-	-	266 69.09 2.77 1.96 0.10
Bakersfield (city)	107,797 75.88	6,464	4,867 75.29 75.29 4.51	222	186 83.78 83.78 0.17	1,017 55.18 20.90 15.73 0.94	-	-	859 83.56 17.65 13.29 0.80	-	1,439 81.76 29.57 22.26 1.33	-	-	-	-	395 94.27 8.12 6.11 0.37	543 94.76 11.16 8.40 0.50	-	-	-	-	-	-	-	-	221 80.66 4.54 3.42 0.21
Delano (city)	10,604 48.67	3,739	2,243 59.99 59.99 21.15	-	-	-	-	-	-	-	2,075 59.12 92.51 55.50 19.57	-	-	-	-	-	-	-	-	-	-	-	-	-	-	-
Ridgecrest (city)	13,722 87.39	660	543 82.27 82.27 3.96	-	-	-	-	-	-	-	254 78.64 46.78 38.48 1.85	-	-	-	-	-	-	-	-	-	-	-	-	-	-	-
Kings County	53,062 68.83	2,449	1,844 75.30 75.30 3.48	-	-	-	-	-	-	-	1,252 78.54 67.90 51.12 2.36	-	-	-	-	-	-	-	-	-	-	-	-	-	-	-
Lemoore (city)	8,302 79.00	982	769 78.31 78.31 9.26	-	-	-	-	-	-	-	605 83.68 78.67 61.61 7.29	-	-	-	-	-	-	-	-	-	-	-	-	-	-	-
Lake County	31,461 77.27	402	344 85.57 85.57 1.09	-	-	-	-	-	-	-	-	-	-	-	-	-	-	-	-	-	-	-	-	-	-	-
Los Angeles County	4,112,424 69.90	773,327	637,192 82.40 82.40 15.49	14,489	10,732 74.07 74.07 0.26	33,497 87.62 5.26 4.33 0.81	677 81.57 0.11 0.09 0.02	6,385 43.54 1.00 0.83 0.16	150,074 74.52 23.55 19.41 3.65	245 70.20 2.28 1.69 0.01	159,702 90.01 25.06 20.65 3.88	1,330 70.07 12.39 9.18 0.03	2,318 82.08 21.60 16.00 0.06	57 55.34 0.01 0.01 <0.01	3,169 89.52 0.50 0.41 0.08	84,489 92.72 13.26 10.93 2.05	112,155 87.64 17.60 14.50 2.73	1,139 65.69 0.18 0.15 0.03	303 86.08 0.05 0.04 0.01	2,284 83.72 0.36 0.30 0.06	4,893 74.90 45.59 33.77 0.12	1,368 80.23 0.21 0.18 0.03	20,831 91.94 3.27 2.69 0.51	11,042 81.36 1.73 1.43 0.27	656 61.25 6.11 4.53 0.02	31,702 62.28 4.98 4.10 0.77
Agoura Hills (city)	12,187 94.77	912	894 98.03 98.03 7.34	-	-	-	-	-	-	-	-	-	-	-	-	-	-	-	-	-	-	-	-	-	-	-
Alhambra (city)	42,762 73.00	28,975	20,489 70.71 70.71 47.91	-	-	294 83.05 1.43 1.01 0.69	-	-	13,090 68.38 63.89 45.18 30.61	-	1,161 85.37 5.67 4.01 2.72	-	-	-	-	1,106 91.25 5.40 3.82 2.59	590 92.19 2.88 2.04 1.38	-	-	-	-	-	979 84.11 4.78 3.38 2.29	-	-	1,801 62.25 8.79 6.22 4.21

Notes: Please refer to the User's Guide for an explanation of data; data is arranged alphabetically by state, then county, then city within each county; table includes counties with populations greater than 49,999 unless noted and cities with populations greater than 9,999 whose Asian and/or NHPI population rates are greater than the national average; (1) Native Hawaiian and other Pacific Islander; (2) excludes Taiwanese; (3) includes Chamorro; (4) county does not meet population threshold but is shown in order to allow inclusion of city

Place	Total population 25 years and over who are high school graduates	Asian population 25 years and over	Asians 25 years and over who are high school graduates	NHPI[1] population 25 years and over	NHPIs[1] 25 years and over who are high school graduates	Asian Indian	Bangladeshi	Cambodian	Chinese[2]	Fijian	Filipino	Guamanian[3]	Hawaiian, Native	Hmong	Indonesian	Japanese	Korean	Laotian	Malaysian	Pakistani	Samoan	Sri Lankan	Taiwanese	Thai	Tongan	Vietnamese
Altadena (cdp)	24,123 84.67	1,421	1,327 93.38 93.38 5.50	-	-	-	-	-	-	-	207 95.39 15.60 14.57 0.86	-	-	-	-	531 92.99 40.02 37.37 2.20	-	-	-	-	-	-	-	-	-	-
Arcadia (city)	32,992 89.65	15,136	13,582 89.73 89.73 41.17	-	-	321 77.72 2.36 2.12 0.97	-	-	7,898 88.00 58.15 52.18 23.94	-	544 95.61 4.01 3.59 1.65	-	-	-	-	792 99.12 5.83 5.23 2.40	1,066 93.51 7.85 7.04 3.23	-	-	-	-	-	2,108 92.66 15.52 13.93 6.39	-	-	-
Artesia (city)	6,795 65.96	2,997	2,490 83.08 83.08 36.64	-	-	247 73.08 9.92 8.24 3.64	-	-	412 88.98 16.55 13.75 6.06	-	949 84.13 38.11 31.66 13.97	-	-	-	-	-	476 83.07 19.12 15.88 7.01	-	-	-	-	-	-	-	-	-
Avocado Heights (cdp)	5,112 57.67	981	783 79.82 79.82 15.32	-	-	-	-	-	-	-	-	-	-	-	-	-	-	-	-	-	-	-	-	-	-	-
Azusa (city)	14,408 60.73	1,531	1,354 88.44 88.44 9.40	-	-	-	-	-	-	-	725 92.36 53.55 47.35 5.03	-	-	-	-	-	-	-	-	-	-	-	-	-	-	-
Baldwin Park (city)	19,211 47.53	6,040	4,639 76.80 76.80 24.15	-	-	-	-	-	1,379 71.56 29.73 22.83 7.18	-	2,217 88.36 47.79 36.71 11.54	-	-	-	-	-	-	-	-	-	-	-	-	-	-	349 51.55 7.52 5.78 1.82
Bellflower (city)	29,947 70.85	4,615	3,808 82.51 82.51 12.72	-	-	-	-	155 51.16 4.07 3.36 0.52	-	-	1,993 91.38 52.34 43.19 6.66	-	-	-	-	-	554 86.43 14.55 12.00 1.85	-	-	-	-	-	-	227 86.31 5.96 4.92 0.76	-	-
Beverly Hills (city)	22,762 90.76	1,804	1,706 94.57 94.57 7.49	-	-	-	-	-	374 95.41 21.92 20.73 1.64	-	-	-	-	-	-	-	561 95.90 32.88 31.10 2.46	-	-	-	-	-	-	-	-	-
Burbank (city)	58,603 83.10	6,186	5,474 88.49 88.49 9.34	-	-	521 85.27 9.52 8.42 0.89	-	-	632 84.95 11.55 10.22 1.08	-	2,000 92.08 36.54 32.33 3.41	-	-	-	-	499 93.97 9.12 8.07 0.85	1,210 93.44 22.10 19.56 2.06	-	-	-	-	-	-	-	-	234 74.05 4.27 3.78 0.40
Calabasas (city)	12,891 97.20	1,100	1,069 97.18 97.18 8.29	-	-	-	-	-	350 100.00 32.74 31.82 2.72	-	-	-	-	-	-	-	-	-	-	-	-	-	-	-	-	-

Notes: Please refer to the User's Guide for an explanation of data; data is arranged alphabetically by state, then county, then city within each county; table includes counties with populations greater than 49,999 unless noted and cities with populations greater than 9,999 whose Asian and/or NHPI population rates are greater than the national average; (1) Native Hawaiian and other Pacific Islander; (2) excludes Taiwanese; (3) includes Chamorro; (4) county does not meet population threshold but is shown in order to allow inclusion of city

Place	Total population 25 years and over who are high school graduates	Asian population 25 years and over	Asians 25 years and over who are high school graduates	NHPI[1] population 25 years and over	NHPIs[1] 25 years and over who are high school graduates	Asian Indian	Bangladeshi	Cambodian	Chinese[2]	Fijian	Filipino	Guamanian[3]	Hawaiian, Native	Hmong	Indonesian	Japanese	Korean	Laotian	Malaysian	Pakistani	Samoan	Sri Lankan	Taiwanese	Thai	Tongan	Vietnamese
	39,024	13,465	11,263	953	696	-	-	-	239	-	9,654	-	-	-	-	513	-	-	-	-	507	-	-	-	-	191
	70.64		83.65		73.03				77.60		84.95					83.69					72.02					69.45
Carson (city)									2.12		85.71					4.55					72.84					1.70
			83.65		73.03				1.77		71.70					3.81					53.20					1.42
			28.86		1.78				0.61		24.74					1.31					1.30					0.49
	31,144	19,456	17,944	-	-	1,732	-	-	3,450	-	3,582	-	-	-	-	1,394	4,940	-	-	-	-	-	1,150	304	-	709
	90.66		92.23			93.62			88.69		93.26					95.35	92.63						100.00	92.12		86.46
Cerritos (city)						9.65			19.23		19.96					7.77	27.53						6.41	1.69		3.95
			92.23			8.90			17.73		18.41					7.16	25.39						5.91	1.56		3.64
			57.62			5.56			11.08		11.50					4.48	15.86						3.69	0.98		2.28
	3,729	542	471	-	-	-	-	-	-	-	-	-	-	-	-	-	-	-	-	-	-	-	-	-	-	-
	62.21		86.90																							
Citrus (cdp)																										
			86.90																							
			12.63																							
	19,250	2,147	1,941	-	-	296	-	-	568	-	-	-	-	-	-	-	270	-	-	-	-	-	-	-	-	-
	92.42		90.41			100.00			93.57								90.60									
Claremont (city)						15.25			29.26								13.91									
			90.41			13.79			26.46								12.58									
			10.08			1.54			2.95								1.40									
	22,379	306	219	372	251	-	-	-	-	-	-	-	-	-	-	-	-	-	-	-	227	-	-	-	-	-
	48.02		71.57		67.47																67.76					
Compton (city)																					90.44					
			71.57		67.47																61.02					
			0.98		1.12																1.01					
	24,087	2,959	2,559	-	-	-	-	-	643	-	850	-	-	-	-	262	-	-	-	-	-	-	-	-	-	137
	81.87		86.48						81.19		98.27					94.24										56.38
Covina (city)									25.13		33.22					10.24										5.35
			86.48						21.73		28.73					8.85										4.63
			10.62						2.67		3.53					1.09										0.57
	24,711	3,608	3,272	-	-	380	-	-	544	-	635	-	-	-	-	1,095	-	-	-	-	-	-	-	-	-	-
	87.19		90.69			83.70			90.22		89.44					94.23										
Culver City (city)						11.61			16.63		19.41					33.47										
			90.69			10.53			15.08		17.60					30.35										
			13.24			1.54			2.20		2.57					4.43										
	32,951	14,972	13,873	-	-	1,331	-	-	4,469	-	1,899	-	-	-	-	557	3,303	-	-	-	-	-	1,179	-	-	388
	90.72		92.66			87.85			90.67		94.86					97.72	95.43						92.04			88.99
Diamond Bar (city)						9.59			32.21		13.69					4.01	23.81						8.50			2.80
			92.66			8.89			29.85		12.68					3.72	22.06						7.87			2.59
			42.10			4.04			13.56		5.76					1.69	10.02						3.58			1.18
	47,563	5,437	4,883	-	-	293	-	-	379	-	1,184	-	-	-	-	287	1,963	-	-	-	-	-	-	-	-	283
	72.31		89.81			91.85			83.85		90.80					91.40	91.99									92.18
Downey (city)						6.00			7.76		24.25					5.88	40.20									5.80
			89.81			5.39			6.97		21.78					5.28	36.10									5.21
			10.27			0.62			0.80		2.49					0.60	4.13									0.60
	10,134	1,844	1,617	-	-	-	-	-	289	-	790	-	-	-	-	-	-	-	-	-	-	-	-	-	-	-
	74.42		87.69						90.03		90.39															
Duarte (city)									17.87		48.86															
			87.69						15.67		42.84															
			15.96						2.85		7.80															

Notes: Please refer to the User's Guide for an explanation of data; data is arranged alphabetically by state, then county, then city within each county; table includes counties with populations greater than 49,999 unless noted and cities with populations greater than 9,999 whose Asian and/or NHPI population rates are greater than the national average; (1) Native Hawaiian and other Pacific Islander; (2) excludes Taiwanese; (3) includes Chamorro; (4) county does not meet population threshold but is shown in order to allow inclusion of city

Place	Total population 25 years and over who are high school graduates	Asian population 25 years and over	Asians 25 years and over who are high school graduates	NHPI[1] population 25 years and over	NHPIs[1] 25 years and over who are high school graduates	Asian Indian	Bangladeshi	Cambodian	Chinese[2]	Fijian	Filipino	Guamanian[3]	Hawaiian, Native	Hmong	Indonesian	Japanese	Korean	Laotian	Malaysian	Pakistani	Samoan	Sri Lankan	Taiwanese	Thai	Tongan	Vietnamese
East San Gabriel (cdp)	8,429 84.75	4,113	3,535 85.95 85.95 41.94	-	-	-	-	-	2,038 84.49 57.65 49.55 24.18	-	-	-	-	-	-	382 93.63 10.81 9.29 4.53	-	-	-	-	-	-	342 94.21 9.67 8.32 4.06	-	-	-
El Monte (city)	27,609 44.23	14,064	8,005 56.92 56.92 28.99	-	-	-	-	-	4,307 55.02 53.80 30.62 15.60	-	509 83.86 6.36 3.62 1.84	-	-	-	-	-	-	-	-	-	-	-	267 85.58 3.34 1.90 0.97	-	-	1,942 49.57 24.26 13.81 7.03
El Segundo (city)	10,601 92.83	801	792 98.88 98.88 7.47	-	-	-	-	-	-	-	-	-	-	-	-	-	-	-	-	-	-	-	-	-	-	-
Gardena (city)	28,259 73.98	12,341	10,447 84.65 84.65 36.97	-	-	-	-	-	550 80.17 5.26 4.46 1.95	-	1,175 91.23 11.25 9.52 4.16	-	-	-	-	5,336 89.04 51.08 43.24 18.88	2,316 83.10 22.17 18.77 8.20	-	-	-	-	-	-	-	-	505 59.13 4.83 4.09 1.79
Glendale (city)	106,665 78.98	21,923	20,118 91.77 91.77 18.86	-	-	638 94.94 3.17 2.91 0.60	-	-	1,727 84.66 8.58 7.88 1.62	-	7,475 93.71 37.16 34.10 7.01	-	-	-	-	1,209 96.18 6.01 5.51 1.13	7,695 93.05 38.25 35.10 7.21	-	-	-	-	-	-	285 85.07 1.42 1.30 0.27	-	491 73.50 2.44 2.24 0.46
Glendora (city)	28,094 87.11	2,190	1,944 88.77 88.77 6.92	-	-	298 88.69 15.33 13.61 1.06	-	-	488 83.85 25.10 22.28 1.74	-	508 91.86 26.13 23.20 1.81	-	-	-	-	-	-	-	-	-	-	-	-	-	-	-
Hacienda Heights (cdp)	28,269 81.59	12,958	11,489 88.66 88.66 40.64	-	-	-	-	-	5,298 84.84 46.11 40.89 18.74	-	832 94.98 7.24 6.42 2.94	-	-	-	-	1,005 92.29 8.75 7.76 3.56	1,529 93.98 13.31 11.80 5.41	-	-	-	-	-	1,667 91.59 14.51 12.86 5.90	-	-	254 77.20 2.21 1.96 0.90
Hawaiian Gardens (city)	3,482 45.63	831	697 83.87 83.87 20.02	-	-	-	-	-	-	-	-	-	-	-	-	-	446 86.27 63.99 53.67 12.81	-	-	-	-	-	-	-	-	-
Hawthorne (city)	32,300 66.82	4,076	3,121 76.57 76.57 9.66	322	254 78.88 78.88 0.79	259 66.93 8.30 6.35 0.80	-	-	250 58.00 8.01 6.13 0.77	-	1,375 85.83 44.06 33.73 4.26	-	-	-	-	256 88.89 8.20 6.28 0.79	-	-	-	-	-	-	-	-	-	577 63.83 18.49 14.16 1.79
Hermosa Beach (city)	14,825 97.49	733	722 98.50 98.50 4.87	-	-	-	-	-	-	-	-	-	-	-	-	-	-	-	-	-	-	-	-	-	-	-

Notes: Please refer to the User's Guide for an explanation of data; data is arranged alphabetically by state, then county, then city within each county; table includes counties with populations greater than 49,999 unless noted and cities with populations greater than 9,999 whose Asian and/or NHPI population rates are greater than the national average; (1) Native Hawaiian and other Pacific Islander; (2) excludes Taiwanese; (3) includes Chamorro; (4) county does not meet population threshold but is shown in order to allow inclusion of city

Place	Total population 25 years and over who are high school graduates	Asian population 25 years and over	Asians 25 years and over who are high school graduates	NHPI[1] population 25 years and over	NHPIs[1] 25 years and over who are high school graduates	Asian Indian	Bangladeshi	Cambodian	Chinese[2]	Fijian	Filipino	Guamanian[3]	Hawaiian, Native	Hmong	Indonesian	Japanese	Korean	Laotian	Malaysian	Pakistani	Samoan	Sri Lankan	Taiwanese	Thai	Tongan	Vietnamese
La Canada Flintridge (city)	12,754	2,334	2,204	-	-	-	-	-	451	-	-	-	-	-	-	300	1,138	-	-	-	-	-	-	-	-	-
	95.87		94.43						98.69							97.09	93.74									
									20.46							13.61	51.63									
			94.43						19.32							12.85	48.76									
			17.28						3.54							2.35	8.92									
La Crescenta-Montrose (cdp)	11,413	2,199	1,983	-	-	-	-	-	-	-	240	-	-	-	-	-	1,284	-	-	-	-	-	-	-	-	-
	91.71		90.18								93.39						88.25									
											12.10						64.75									
			90.18								10.91						58.39									
			17.37								2.10						11.25									
La Mirada (city)	24,913	4,682	4,309	-	-	300	-	-	466	-	1,360	-	-	-	-	348	1,412	-	-	-	-	-	-	-	-	-
	84.48		92.03			92.59			98.52		94.44					98.31	88.97									
						6.96			10.81		31.56					8.08	32.77									
			92.03			6.41			9.95		29.05					7.43	30.16									
			17.30			1.20			1.87		5.46					1.40	5.67									
La Puente (city)	11,134	2,032	1,546	-	-	-	-	-	469	-	600	-	-	-	-	-	-	-	-	-	-	-	-	-	-	-
	49.65		76.08						79.49		80.54															
									30.34		38.81															
			76.08						23.08		29.53															
			13.89						4.21		5.39															
La Verne (city)	18,131	1,587	1,508	-	-	-	-	-	-	-	525	-	-	-	-	-	-	-	-	-	-	-	-	-	-	-
	88.67		95.02								96.33															
											34.81															
			95.02								33.08															
			8.32								2.90															
Lakewood (city)	43,510	6,780	5,910	403	357	268	-	245	597	-	2,726	-	-	-	-	531	861	-	-	-	295	-	-	-	-	258
	85.08		87.17		88.59	91.78		64.64	80.46		90.35					94.48	87.32				92.77					81.90
						4.53		4.15	10.10		46.13					8.98	14.57				82.63					4.37
			87.17		88.59	3.95		3.61	8.81		40.21					7.83	12.70				73.20					3.81
			13.58		0.82	0.62		0.56	1.37		6.27					1.22	1.98				0.68					0.59
Lancaster (city)	54,265	3,095	2,665	-	-	313	-	-	269	-	1,387	-	-	-	-	-	-	-	-	-	-	-	-	-	-	-
	78.32		86.11			84.14			87.91		96.72															
						11.74			10.09		52.05															
			86.11			10.11			8.69		44.81															
			4.91			0.58			0.50		2.56															
Lawndale (city)	11,633	1,954	1,495	226	157	-	-	-	-	-	399	-	-	-	-	-	-	-	-	-	-	-	-	-	-	577
	63.38		76.51		69.47						94.77															63.83
											26.69															38.60
			76.51		69.47						20.42															29.53
			12.85		1.35						3.43															4.96
Lomita (city)	10,767	1,694	1,497	-	-	-	-	-	-	-	334	-	-	-	-	489	283	-	-	-	-	-	-	-	-	-
	80.21		88.37								88.83					91.23	79.94									
											22.31					32.67	18.90									
			88.37								19.72					28.87	16.71									
			13.90								3.10					4.54	2.63									
Long Beach (city)	201,578	32,626	22,732	2,423	1,708	586	-	3,174	1,723	-	10,059	-	-	-	-	2,593	1,040	136	-	-	1,229	-	-	360	-	1,849
	72.66		69.67		70.49	82.54		39.41	76.21		85.35					89.63	78.91	40.00			71.87			90.91		57.60
						2.58		13.96	7.58		44.25					11.41	4.58	0.60			71.96			1.58		8.13
			69.67		70.49	1.80		9.73	5.28		30.83					7.95	3.19	0.42			50.72			1.10		5.67
			11.28		0.85	0.29		1.57	0.85		4.99					1.29	0.52	0.07			0.61			0.18		0.92

Notes: Please refer to the User's Guide for an explanation of data; data is arranged alphabetically by state, then county, then city within each county; table includes counties with populations greater than 49,999 unless noted and cities with populations greater than 9,999 whose Asian and/or NHPI population rates are greater than the national average; (1) Native Hawaiian and other Pacific Islander; (2) excludes Taiwanese; (3) includes Chamorro; (4) county does not meet population threshold but is shown in order to allow inclusion of city

Place	Total population 25 years and over who are high school graduates	Asian population 25 years and over	Asians 25 years and over who are high school graduates	NHPI[1] population 25 years and over	NHPIs[1] 25 years and over who are high school graduates	Asian Indian	Bangladeshi	Cambodian	Chinese[2]	Fijian	Filipino	Guamanian[3]	Hawaiian, Native	Hmong	Indonesian	Japanese	Korean	Laotian	Malaysian	Pakistani	Samoan	Sri Lankan	Taiwanese	Thai	Tongan	Vietnamese
	1,538,715	258,082	211,832	3,969	2,963	13,137	433	833	27,634	-	63,567	496	891	-	1,116	27,754	55,698	339	-	717	952	647	2,106	4,777	92	7,924
	66.64		82.08		74.65	85.95	80.19	37.37	66.34		90.18	66.58	80.85		94.50	90.78	84.54	81.29		78.02	82.07	78.71	95.12	74.68	58.23	63.16
Los Angeles (city)						6.20	0.20	0.39	13.05		30.01	16.74	30.07		0.53	13.10	26.29	0.16		0.34	32.13	0.31	0.99	2.26	3.10	3.74
			82.08		74.65	5.09	0.17	0.32	10.71		24.63	12.50	22.45		0.43	10.75	21.58	0.13		0.28	23.99	0.25	0.82	1.85	2.32	3.07
			13.77		0.19	0.85	0.03	0.05	1.80		4.13	0.03	0.06		0.07	1.80	3.62	0.02		0.05	0.06	0.04	0.14	0.31	0.01	0.51
	24,270	1,582	1,522	-	-	-	-	-	429	-	-	-	-	-	-	504	-	-	-	-	-	-	-	-	-	-
	96.82		96.21						98.39							95.09										
Manhattan Beach (city)									28.19							33.11										
			96.21						27.12							31.86										
			6.27						1.77							2.08										
	18,444	1,783	1,613	-	-	-	-	-	407	-	628	-	-	-	-	-	-	-	-	-	-	-	-	-	-	-
	78.04		90.47						82.89		98.90															
Monrovia (city)									25.23		38.93															
			90.47						22.83		35.22															
			8.75						2.21		3.40															
	23,511	5,330	4,426	-	-	-	-	-	1,421	-	595	-	-	-	-	1,384	426	-	-	-	-	-	-	-	-	-
	62.10		83.04						74.20		90.84					91.59	86.76									
Montebello (city)									32.11		13.44					31.27	9.62									
			83.04						26.66		11.16					25.97	7.99									
			18.83						6.04		2.53					5.89	1.81									
	30,253	26,901	19,276	-	-	-	-	82	11,287	-	604	-	-	-	-	3,766	618	-	-	-	-	-	702	-	-	1,023
	71.57		71.66					39.05	67.64		92.35					92.15	93.21						86.88			50.34
Monterey Park (city)								0.43	58.55		3.13					19.54	3.21						3.64			5.31
			71.66					0.30	41.96		2.25					14.00	2.30						2.61			3.80
			63.72					0.27	37.31		2.00					12.45	2.04						2.32			3.38
	37,339	8,040	6,766	-	-	645	-	201	543	-	2,426	-	-	-	-	351	1,562	-	-	-	-	-	-	-	-	457
	63.01		84.15			84.09		64.42	80.44		85.69					92.86	88.75									75.29
Norwalk (city)						9.53		2.97	8.03		35.86					5.19	23.09									6.75
			84.15			8.02		2.50	6.75		30.17					4.37	19.43									5.68
			18.12			1.73		0.54	1.45		6.50					0.94	4.18									1.22
	46,651	2,975	2,649	-	-	217	-	-	-	-	1,339	-	-	-	-	-	-	-	-	-	-	-	-	-	-	-
	74.04		89.04			90.79					90.05															
Palmdale (city)						8.19					50.55															
			89.04			7.29					45.01															
			5.68			0.47					2.87															
	9,556	1,537	1,509	-	-	-	-	-	385	-	-	-	-	-	-	433	183	-	-	-	-	-	-	-	-	-
	98.35		98.18						98.72							100.00	95.31									
Palos Verdes Estates (city)									25.51							28.69	12.13									
			98.18						25.05							28.17	11.91									
			15.79						4.03							4.53	1.92									
	72,281	10,006	9,328	-	-	630	-	-	2,861	-	1,836	-	-	-	-	1,830	1,003	-	-	-	-	-	-	-	-	455
	79.49		93.22			95.74			91.88		93.29					95.66	99.50									78.18
Pasadena (city)						6.75			30.67		19.68					19.62	10.75									4.88
			93.22			6.30			28.59		18.35					18.29	10.02									4.55
			12.91			0.87			3.96		2.54					2.53	1.39									0.63
	43,280	5,876	4,468	-	-	307	-	124	847	-	1,533	-	-	-	-	284	-	109	-	-	-	-	-	-	-	631
	54.92		76.04			82.53		47.15	73.27		91.36					89.59		43.60								58.75
Pomona (city)						6.87		2.78	18.96		34.31					6.36		2.44								14.12
			76.04			5.22		2.11	14.41		26.09					4.83		1.86								10.74
			10.32			0.71		0.29	1.96		3.54					0.66		0.25								1.46

Notes: Please refer to the User's Guide for an explanation of data; data is arranged alphabetically by state, then county, then city within each county; table includes counties with populations greater than 49,999 unless noted and cities with populations greater than 9,999 whose Asian and/or NHPI population rates are greater than the national average; (1) Native Hawaiian and other Pacific Islander; (2) excludes Taiwanese; (3) includes Chamorro; (4) county does not meet population threshold but is shown in order to allow inclusion of city

Place	Total population 25 years and over who are high school graduates	Asian population 25 years and over	Asians 25 years and over who are high school graduates	NHPI[1] population 25 years and over	NHPIs[1] 25 years and over who are high school graduates	Asian Indian	Bangladeshi	Cambodian	Chinese[2]	Fijian	Filipino	Guamanian[3]	Hawaiian, Native	Hmong	Indonesian	Japanese	Korean	Laotian	Malaysian	Pakistani	Samoan	Sri Lankan	Taiwanese	Thai	Tongan	Vietnamese
Rancho Palos Verdes (city)	28,753	7,013	6,813	-	-	375	-	-	1,818	-	408	-	-	-	-	2,085	1,481	-	-	-	-	-	382	-	-	-
	95.77		97.15			98.43			96.75		94.66					97.98	97.05						98.96			
						5.50			26.68		5.99					30.60	21.74						5.61			
			97.15			5.35			25.92		5.82					29.73	21.12						5.45			
			23.69			1.30			6.32		1.42					7.25	5.15						1.33			
Redondo Beach (city)	44,284	4,644	4,528	-	-	337	-	-	900	-	651	-	-	-	-	1,626	474	-	-	-	-	-	-	-	-	-
	92.55		97.50			96.29			96.88		97.02					98.91	95.56									
						7.44			19.88		14.38					35.91	10.47									
			97.50			7.26			19.38		14.02					35.01	10.21									
			10.22			0.76			2.03		1.47					3.67	1.07									
Rosemead (city)	17,489	16,782	8,635	-	-	-	-	211	4,310	-	447	-	-	-	-	576	-	-	-	-	-	-	-	-	-	1,842
	53.19		51.45					46.27	45.30		85.96					86.75										48.44
								2.44	49.91		5.18					6.67										21.33
			51.45					1.26	25.68		2.66					3.43										10.98
			49.37					1.21	24.64		2.56					3.29										10.53
Rowland Heights (cdp)	25,178	16,523	14,575	-	-	558	-	-	6,804	-	1,961	-	-	-	-	473	2,150	-	-	-	-	-	1,501	-	-	314
	82.08		88.21			85.71			88.56		90.75					90.79	88.30						89.72			70.09
						3.83			46.68		13.45					3.25	14.75						10.30			2.15
			88.21			3.38			41.18		11.87					2.86	13.01						9.08			1.90
			57.89			2.22			27.02		7.79					1.88	8.54						5.96			1.25
San Dimas (city)	20,123	2,165	2,015	-	-	-	-	-	762	-	458	-	-	-	-	-	-	-	-	-	-	-	-	-	-	-
	87.28		93.07						91.04		98.07															
									37.82		22.73															
			93.07						35.20		21.15															
			10.01						3.79		2.28															
San Gabriel (city)	18,651	13,439	8,901	-	-	-	-	-	5,624	-	710	-	-	-	-	445	-	-	-	-	-	-	486	-	-	792
	69.18		66.23						67.24		85.44					92.52							85.26			45.75
									63.18		7.98					5.00							5.46			8.90
			66.23						41.85		5.28					3.31							3.62			5.89
			47.72						30.15		3.81					2.39							2.61			4.25
San Marino (city)	8,338	3,644	3,485	-	-	-	-	-	2,193	-	-	-	-	-	-	-	-	-	-	-	-	-	899	-	-	-
	95.43		95.64						95.68														95.33			
									62.93														25.80			
			95.64						60.18														24.67			
			41.80						26.30														10.78			
Santa Clarita (city)	82,066	5,151	4,848	-	-	514	-	-	561	-	1,674	-	-	-	-	827	470	-	-	-	-	-	-	-	-	263
	87.63		94.12			100.00			85.52		94.42					99.28	98.33									87.96
						10.60			11.57		34.53					17.06	9.69									5.42
			94.12			9.98			10.89		32.50					16.06	9.12									5.11
			5.91			0.63			0.68		2.04					1.01	0.57									0.32
Santa Monica (city)	61,114	4,653	4,456	-	-	467	-	-	1,121	-	403	-	-	-	-	1,400	553	-	-	-	-	-	-	-	-	-
	90.98		95.77			92.29			95.73		97.82					97.56	96.85									
						10.48			25.16		9.04					31.42	12.41									
			95.77			10.04			24.09		8.66					30.09	11.88									
			7.29			0.76			1.83		0.66					2.29	0.90									
Sierra Madre (city)	7,645	472	450	-	-	-	-	-	-	-	-	-	-	-	-	-	-	-	-	-	-	-	-	-	-	-
	94.45		95.34																							
			95.34																							
			5.89																							

Notes: Please refer to the User's Guide for an explanation of data; data is arranged alphabetically by state, then county, then city within each county; table includes counties with populations greater than 49,999 unless noted and cities with populations greater than 9,999 whose Asian and/or NHPI population rates are greater than the national average; (1) Native Hawaiian and other Pacific Islander; (2) excludes Taiwanese; (3) includes Chamorro; (4) county does not meet population threshold but is shown in order to allow inclusion of city

Place	Total population 25 years and over who are high school graduates	Asian population 25 years and over	Asians 25 years and over who are high school graduates	NHPI¹ population 25 years and over	NHPIs¹ 25 years and over who are high school graduates	Asian Indian	Bangladeshi	Cambodian	Chinese²	Fijian	Filipino	Guamanian³	Hawaiian, Native	Hmong	Indonesian	Japanese	Korean	Laotian	Malaysian	Pakistani	Samoan	Sri Lankan	Taiwanese	Thai	Tongan	Vietnamese
South El Monte (city)	3,966	1,061	404	-	-	-	-	-	103	-	-	-	-	-	-	-	-	-	-	-	-	-	-	-	-	189
	35.61		38.08						24.47																	43.45
									25.50																	46.78
			38.08						9.71																	17.81
			10.19						2.60																	4.77
South Pasadena (city)	15,974	4,270	4,030	-	-	-	-	-	2,173	-	-	-	-	-	-	776	372	-	-	-	-	-	-	-	-	-
	93.61		94.38						92.08							100.00	97.13									
									53.92							19.26	9.23									
			94.38						50.89							18.17	8.71									
			25.23						13.60							4.86	2.33									
South San Jose Hills (cdp)	4,666	787	675	-	-	-	-	-	-	-	468	-	-	-	-	-	-	-	-	-	-	-	-	-	-	-
	43.78		85.77								91.59															
											69.33															
			85.77								59.47															
			14.47								10.03															
Temple City (city)	18,656	8,496	6,917	-	-	-	-	-	4,120	-	372	-	-	-	-	423	260	-	-	-	-	-	822	-	-	417
	83.55		81.41						79.60		87.74					89.43	81.50						87.63			69.73
									59.56		5.38					6.12	3.76						11.88			6.03
			81.41						48.49		4.38					4.98	3.06						9.68			4.91
			37.08						22.08		1.99					2.27	1.39						4.41			2.24
Torrance (city)	87,897	27,233	25,227	-	-	1,417	-	-	3,825	-	2,357	-	-	-	-	9,768	5,112	-	-	336	-	-	805	-	-	713
	90.60		92.63			95.16			89.75		94.51					95.76	92.73			87.05			91.89			68.69
						5.62			15.16		9.34					38.72	20.26			1.33			3.19			2.83
			92.63			5.20			14.05		8.65					35.87	18.77			1.23			2.96			2.62
			28.70			1.61			4.35		2.68					11.11	5.82			0.38			0.92			0.81
Valinda (cdp)	6,870	1,288	1,005	-	-	-	-	-	-	-	623	-	-	-	-	-	-	-	-	-	-	-	-	-	-	186
	57.91		78.03								86.41															65.96
											61.99															18.51
			78.03								48.37															14.44
			14.63								9.07															2.71
Vincent (cdp)	5,775	741	603	-	-	-	-	-	-	-	369	-	-	-	-	-	-	-	-	-	-	-	-	-	-	-
	68.29		81.38								85.81															
											61.19															
			81.38								49.80															
			10.44								6.39															
Walnut (city)	16,596	10,456	9,481	-	-	447	-	-	3,561	-	2,088	-	-	-	-	304	1,083	-	-	-	-	-	1,077	-	-	233
	88.75		90.68			90.67			88.56		95.87					100.00	91.70						91.04			69.97
						4.71			37.56		22.02					3.21	11.42						11.36			2.46
			90.68			4.28			34.06		19.97					2.91	10.36						10.30			2.23
			57.13			2.69			21.46		12.58					1.83	6.53						6.49			1.40
West Carson (cdp)	10,975	3,733	3,303	-	-	-	-	-	-	-	1,258	-	-	-	-	893	598	-	-	-	-	-	-	-	-	-
	74.66		88.48								86.05					94.10	93.88									
											38.09					27.04	18.10									
			88.48								33.70					23.92	16.02									
			30.10								11.46					8.14	5.45									
West Covina (city)	50,804	15,582	12,785	217	163	329	-	-	3,233	-	5,780	-	-	-	-	488	582	-	-	-	-	-	584	-	-	942
	78.15		82.05		75.12	90.38			73.81		88.81					94.21	90.80						95.74			65.83
						2.57			25.29		45.21					3.82	4.55						4.57			7.37
			82.05		75.12	2.11			20.75		37.09					3.13	3.74						3.75			6.05
			25.17		0.32	0.65			6.36		11.38					0.96	1.15						1.15			1.85

Notes: Please refer to the User's Guide for an explanation of data; data is arranged alphabetically by state, then county, then city within each county; table includes counties with populations greater than 49,999 unless noted and cities with populations greater than 9,999 whose Asian and/or NHPI population rates are greater than the national average; (1) Native Hawaiian and other Pacific Islander; (2) excludes Taiwanese; (3) includes Chamorro; (4) county does not meet population threshold but is shown in order to allow inclusion of city

Place	Total population 25 years and over who are high school graduates	Asian population 25 years and over	Asians 25 years and over who are high school graduates	NHPI[1] population 25 years and over	NHPIs[1] 25 years and over who are high school graduates	Asian Indian	Bangladeshi	Cambodian	Chinese[2]	Fijian	Filipino	Guamanian[3]	Hawaiian, Native	Hmong	Indonesian	Japanese	Korean	Laotian	Malaysian	Pakistani	Samoan	Sri Lankan	Taiwanese	Thai	Tongan	Vietnamese
West Hollywood (city)	28,915 91.14	1,261	1,201 95.24 95.24 4.15	-	-	-	-	-	-	-	-	-	-	-	-	-	-	-	-	-	-	-	-	-	-	-
West Puente Valley (cdp)	6,501 50.35	1,156	833 72.06 72.06 12.81	-	-	-	-	-	-	-	402 77.76 48.26 34.78 6.18	-	-	-	-	-	-	-	-	-	-	-	-	-	-	128 46.21 15.37 11.07 1.97
Whittier (city)	40,688 78.78	2,218	1,980 89.27 89.27 4.87	-	-	-	-	-	701 85.70 35.40 31.61 1.72	-	377 91.73 19.04 17.00 0.93	-	-	-	-	378 96.92 19.09 17.04 0.93	214 91.06 10.81 9.65 0.53	-	-	-	-	-	-	-	-	-
Madera County	48,929 65.39	1,057	729 68.97 68.97 1.49	-	-	192 52.60 26.34 18.16 0.39	-	-	-	-	255 82.52 34.98 24.12 0.52	-	-	-	-	-	-	-	-	-	-	-	-	-	-	-
Marin County	167,614 91.25	8,269	7,462 90.24 90.24 4.45	-	-	956 90.44 12.81 11.56 0.57	-	-	2,270 92.54 30.42 27.45 1.35	-	898 93.25 12.03 10.86 0.54	-	-	-	-	1,422 98.00 19.06 17.20 0.85	789 92.39 10.57 9.54 0.47	-	-	-	-	-	-	-	-	516 63.70 6.92 6.24 0.31
Larkspur (city)	9,473 97.23	377	377 100.00 100.00 3.98	-	-	-	-	-	-	-	-	-	-	-	-	-	-	-	-	-	-	-	-	-	-	-
Novato (city)	30,422 90.53	1,735	1,521 87.67 87.67 5.00	-	-	-	-	-	359 80.67 23.60 20.69 1.18	-	272 100.00 17.88 15.68 0.89	-	-	-	-	-	-	-	-	-	-	-	-	-	-	-
San Rafael (city)	34,479 84.75	2,294	1,965 85.66 85.66 5.70	-	-	297 86.84 15.11 12.95 0.86	-	-	708 92.07 36.03 30.86 2.05	-	-	-	-	-	-	-	-	-	-	-	-	-	-	-	-	228 55.34 11.60 9.94 0.66
Tamalpais-Homestead (cdp)	7,993 99.03	399	389 97.49 97.49 4.87	-	-	-	-	-	-	-	-	-	-	-	-	-	-	-	-	-	-	-	-	-	-	-
Mendocino County	45,980 80.83	656	492 75.00 75.00 1.07	-	-	-	-	-	-	-	-	-	-	-	-	-	-	-	-	-	-	-	-	-	-	-

Notes: Please refer to the User's Guide for an explanation of data; data is arranged alphabetically by state, then county, then city within each county; table includes counties with populations greater than 49,999 unless noted and cities with populations greater than 9,999 whose Asian and/or NHPI population rates are greater than the national average; (1) Native Hawaiian and other Pacific Islander; (2) excludes Taiwanese; (3) includes Chamorro; (4) county does not meet population threshold but is shown in order to allow inclusion of city

Place	Total population 25 years and over who are high school graduates	Asian population 25 years and over	Asians 25 years and over who are high school graduates	NHPI[1] population 25 years and over	NHPIs[1] 25 years and over who are high school graduates	Asian Indian	Bangladeshi	Cambodian	Chinese[2]	Fijian	Filipino	Guamanian[3]	Hawaiian, Native	Hmong	Indonesian	Japanese	Korean	Laotian	Malaysian	Pakistani	Samoan	Sri Lankan	Taiwanese	Thai	Tongan	Vietnamese
Merced County	74,478	6,570	3,287	-	-	570	-	-	251	-	864	-	-	617	-	431		252	-	-	-	-	-	-	-	-
	63.81		50.03			45.24			80.97		82.36			30.87		88.32		33.11								
						17.34			7.64		26.29			18.77		13.11		7.67								
			50.03			8.68			3.82		13.15			9.39		6.56		3.84								
			4.41			0.77			0.34		1.16			0.83		0.58		0.34								
Atwater (city)	8,747	702	413	-	-	-	-	-	-	-	-	-	-	62	-	-	-	-	-	-	-	-	-	-	-	-
	70.31		58.83											43.66												
														15.01												
			58.83											8.83												
			4.72											0.71												
Livingston (city)	1,936	912	419	-	-	294	-	-	-	-	-	-	-	-	-	-	-	-	-	-	-	-	-	-	-	-
	37.07		45.94			40.27																				
						70.17																				
			45.94			32.24																				
			21.64			15.19																				
Merced (city)	23,571	2,688	1,041	-	-	-	-	-	-	-	-	-	-	361	-	-	-	168	-	-	-	-	-	-	-	-
	68.48		38.73											28.79				26.62								
														34.68				16.14								
			38.73											13.43				6.25								
			4.42											1.53				0.71								
Monterey County	167,067	16,816	13,055	1,040	829	615	-	-	1,409	-	5,984	308	-	-	-	2,427	1,506	-	-	-	-	-	-	-	-	569
	68.43		77.63		79.71	76.68			84.88		77.43	89.80				87.24	75.53									48.47
						4.71			10.79		45.84	37.15				18.59	11.54									4.36
			77.63		79.71	3.66			8.38		35.59	29.62				14.43	8.96									3.38
			7.81		0.50	0.37			0.84		3.58	0.18				1.45	0.90									0.34
Marina (city)	11,711	2,828	1,923	336	241	-	-	-		-	622	-	-	-	-	287	579	-	-	-	-	-	-	-	-	175
	71.82		68.00		71.73						75.49					83.43	66.40									41.87
											32.35					14.92	30.11									9.10
			68.00		71.73						21.99					10.15	20.47									6.19
			16.42		2.06						5.31					2.45	4.94									1.49
Monterey (city)	19,058	1,649	1,494	-	-	-	-	-	324	-	259	-	-	-	-	476	-	-	-	-	-	-	-	-	-	-
	91.59		90.60						100.00		89.62					90.15										
									21.69		17.34					31.86										
			90.60						19.65		15.71					28.87										
			7.84						1.70		1.36					2.50										
Pacific Grove (city)	10,955	537	464	-	-	-	-	-	-	-	-	-	-	-	-	-	-	-	-	-	-	-	-	-	-	-
	92.18		86.41																							
			86.41																							
			4.24																							
Salinas (city)	47,329	6,151	4,951	218	160	320	-	-	348	-	3,184	-	-	-	-	550	237	-	-	-	-	-	-	-	-	177
	56.00		80.49		73.39	82.05			76.99		80.49					90.31	76.95									61.67
						6.46			7.03		64.31					11.11	4.79									3.58
			80.49		73.39	5.20			5.66		51.76					8.94	3.85									2.88
			10.46		0.34	0.68			0.74		6.73					1.16	0.50									0.37
Seaside (city)	13,206	2,293	1,549	-	-	-	-	-	-	-	960	-	-	-	-	308	-	-	-	-	-	-	-	-	-	75
	70.13		67.55								72.56					80.21										28.52
											61.98					19.88										4.84
			67.55								41.87					13.43										3.27
			11.73								7.27					2.33										0.57

Notes: Please refer to the User's Guide for an explanation of data; data is arranged alphabetically by state, then county, then city within each county; table includes counties with populations greater than 49,999 unless noted and cities with populations greater than 9,999 whose Asian and/or NHPI population rates are greater than the national average; (1) Native Hawaiian and other Pacific Islander; (2) excludes Taiwanese; (3) includes Chamorro; (4) county does not meet population threshold but is shown in order to allow inclusion of city

Place	Total population 25 years and over who are high school graduates	Asian population 25 years and over	Asians 25 years and over who are high school graduates	NHPI[1] population 25 years and over	NHPIs[1] 25 years and over who are high school graduates	Asian Indian	Bangladeshi	Cambodian	Chinese[2]	Fijian	Filipino	Guamanian[3]	Hawaiian, Native	Hmong	Indonesian	Japanese	Korean	Laotian	Malaysian	Pakistani	Samoan	Sri Lankan	Taiwanese	Thai	Tongan	Vietnamese
Napa County	67,483	2,587	2,206	-	-	-	-	-	324	-	1,195	-	-	-	-	271	-	-	-	-	-	-	-	-	-	-
	80.40		85.27						81.00		89.65					86.58										
									14.69		54.17					12.28										
			85.27						12.52		46.19					10.48										
			3.27						0.48		1.77					0.40										
Nevada County	58,839	470	431	-	-	-	-	-	-	-	-	-	-	-	-	-	-	-	-	-	-	-	-	-	-	-
	90.32		91.70																							
			91.70																							
			0.73																							
Orange County	1,441,037	253,320	205,628	4,737	3,790	14,733	-	1,672	29,719	-	29,895	638	1,046	237	1,110	22,106	33,879	949	-	1,264	1,492	412	5,551	1,810	115	57,593
	79.46		81.17		80.01	87.22		62.30	87.34		92.05	80.25	89.71	51.41	90.76	95.03	90.21	55.53		86.93	80.00	87.66	94.01	87.57	45.10	65.92
						7.16		0.81	14.45		14.54	16.83	27.60	0.12	0.54	10.75	16.48	0.46		0.61	39.37	0.20	2.70	0.88	3.03	28.01
			81.17		80.01	5.82		0.66	11.73		11.80	13.47	22.08	0.09	0.44	8.73	13.37	0.37		0.50	31.50	0.16	2.19	0.71	2.43	22.74
			14.27		0.26	1.02		0.12	2.06		2.07	0.04	0.07	0.02	0.08	1.53	2.35	0.07		0.09	0.10	0.03	0.39	0.13	0.01	4.00
Aliso Viejo (cdp)	26,809	3,181	3,078	-	-	330	-	-	510	-	599	-	-	-	-	483	357	-	-	-	-	-	-	-	-	364
	96.11		96.76			94.29			93.24		99.17					100.00	98.35									93.09
						10.72			16.57		19.46					15.69	11.60									11.83
			96.76			10.37			16.03		18.83					15.18	11.22									11.44
			11.48			1.23			1.90		2.23					1.80	1.33									1.36
Anaheim (city)	134,633	26,483	21,941	567	449	2,132	-	-	2,389	-	4,760	-	-	-	-	1,659	4,170	332	-	181	233	-	379	252	-	4,739
	69.26		82.85		79.19	79.40			84.45		91.54					90.11	90.30	67.48		84.58	80.90		100.00	81.55		70.72
						9.72			10.89		21.69					7.56	19.01	1.51		0.82	51.89		1.73	1.15		21.60
			82.85		79.19	8.05			9.02		17.97					6.26	15.75	1.25		0.68	41.09		1.43	0.95		17.89
			16.30		0.33	1.58			1.77		3.54					1.23	3.10	0.25		0.13	0.17		0.28	0.19		3.52
Brea (city)	20,427	2,106	1,942	-	-	255	-	-	327	-	320	-	-	-	-	-	511	-	-	-	-	-	-	-	-	-
	88.44		92.21			86.73			89.34		96.39						95.87									
						13.13			16.84		16.48						26.31									
			92.21			12.11			15.53		15.19						24.26									
			9.51			1.25			1.60		1.57						2.50									
Buena Park (city)	36,426	10,955	9,632	-	-	922	-	-	674	-	3,026	-	-	-	-	546	3,272	-	-	-	-	-	-	-	-	454
	75.78		87.92			81.38			73.50		93.54					92.07	91.88									72.99
						9.57			7.00		31.42					5.67	33.97									4.71
			87.92			8.42			6.15		27.62					4.98	29.87									4.14
			26.44			2.53			1.85		8.31					1.50	8.98									1.25
Costa Mesa (city)	56,642	5,366	4,700	334	242	247	-	-	622	-	953	-	-	-	-	914	405	-	-	-	-	-	-	-	-	1,096
	79.08		87.59		72.46	92.86			87.98		97.84					94.72	93.10									73.31
						5.26			13.23		20.28					19.45	8.62									23.32
			87.59		72.46	4.60			11.59		17.76					17.03	7.55									20.42
			8.30		0.43	0.44			1.10		1.68					1.61	0.72									1.93
Cypress (city)	27,049	6,185	5,594	-	-	408	-	-	887	-	1,058	-	-	-	-	773	1,361	-	-	-	-	-	415	-	-	405
	89.66		90.44			86.44			90.97		90.43					93.58	91.28						94.97			80.68
						7.29			15.86		18.91					13.82	24.33						7.42			7.24
			90.44			6.60			14.34		17.11					12.50	22.00						6.71			6.55
			20.68			1.51			3.28		3.91					2.86	5.03						1.53			1.50
Foothill Ranch (cdp)	6,765	1,175	1,144	-	-	-	-	-	-	-	-	-	-	-	-	-	-	-	-	-	-	-	-	-	-	-
	96.85		97.36																							
			97.36																							
			16.91																							

Notes: Please refer to the User's Guide for an explanation of data; data is arranged alphabetically by state, then county, then city within each county; table includes counties with populations greater than 49,999 unless noted and cities with populations greater than 9,999 whose Asian and/or NHPI population rates are greater than the national average; (1) Native Hawaiian and other Pacific Islander; (2) excludes Taiwanese; (3) includes Chamorro; (4) county does not meet population threshold but is shown in order to allow inclusion of city

Place	Total population 25 years and over who are high school graduates	Asian population 25 years and over	Asians 25 years and over who are high school graduates	NHPI[1] population 25 years and over	NHPIs[1] 25 years and over who are high school graduates	Asian Indian	Bangladeshi	Cambodian	Chinese[2]	Fijian	Filipino	Guamanian[3]	Hawaiian, Native	Hmong	Indonesian	Japanese	Korean	Laotian	Malaysian	Pakistani	Samoan	Sri Lankan	Taiwanese	Thai	Tongan	Vietnamese
Fountain Valley (city)	33,280	9,527	7,881	-	-	365	-	-	1,463	-	417	-	-	-	-	951	645	-	-	-	-	-	235	-	-	3,433
	88.62		82.72			78.83			85.41		92.67					92.78	88.24						93.63			76.37
						4.63			18.56		5.29					12.07	8.18						2.98			43.56
			82.72			3.83			15.36		4.38					9.98	6.77						2.47			36.03
			23.68			1.10			4.40		1.25					2.86	1.94						0.71			10.32
Fullerton (city)	65,435	13,004	11,658	-	-	1,024	-	-	1,752	-	1,284	-	-	-	-	893	5,271	-	-	-	-	-	-	-	-	570
	81.78		89.65			84.77			92.31		91.65					97.92	94.31									57.75
						8.78			15.03		11.01					7.66	45.21									4.89
			89.65			7.87			13.47		9.87					6.87	40.53									4.38
			17.82			1.56			2.68		1.96					1.36	8.06									0.87
Garden Grove (city)	70,136	33,577	21,984	605	419	301	-	198	1,185	-	1,595	-	-	-	-	828	3,268	-	-	-	290	-	-	-	-	13,797
	67.79		65.47		69.26	70.66		58.41	66.61		83.60					90.59	77.42				80.33					60.62
						1.37		0.90	5.39		7.26					3.77	14.87				69.21					62.76
			65.47		69.26	0.90		0.59	3.53		4.75					2.47	9.73				47.93					41.09
			31.34		0.60	0.43		0.28	1.69		2.27					1.18	4.66				0.41					19.67
Huntington Beach (city)	118,233	12,456	10,859	236	204	662	-	-	2,069	-	1,165	-	-	-	-	2,238	1,077	-	-	-	-	-	392	-	-	2,719
	89.58		87.18		86.44	93.37			90.63		95.81					96.84	90.96						85.96			74.49
						6.10			19.05		10.73					20.61	9.92						3.61			25.04
			87.18		86.44	5.31			16.61		9.35					17.97	8.65						3.15			21.83
			9.18		0.17	0.56			1.75		0.99					1.89	0.91						0.33			2.30
Irvine (city)	84,756	23,640	22,338	-	-	2,421	-	-	6,130	-	1,515	-	-	-	-	3,211	4,195	-	-	-	-	-	1,498	-	-	2,435
	95.27		94.49			95.50			94.63		95.70					97.69	96.24						95.05			88.19
						10.84			27.44		6.78					14.37	18.78						6.71			10.90
			94.49			10.24			25.93		6.41					13.58	17.75						6.34			10.30
			26.36			2.86			7.23		1.79					3.79	4.95						1.77			2.87
La Habra (city)	26,514	2,305	2,105	-	-	-	-	-	336	-	425	-	-	-	-	-	735	-	-	-	-	-	-	-	-	-
	73.44		91.32						98.82		90.43						94.35									
									15.96		20.19						34.92									
			91.32						14.58		18.44						31.89									
			7.94						1.27		1.60						2.77									
La Palma (city)	9,341	4,396	4,009	-	-	291	-	-	599	-	764	-	-	-	-	564	1,415	-	-	-	-	-	-	-	-	-
	90.38		91.20			85.84			92.72		92.16					98.95	91.00									
						7.26			14.94		19.06					14.07	35.30									
			91.20			6.62			13.63		17.38					12.83	32.19									
			42.92			3.12			6.41		8.18					6.04	15.15									
Laguna Hills (city)	19,127	2,266	2,141	-	-	-	-	-	407	-	448	-	-	-	-	-	-	-	-	-	-	-	-	-	-	316
	90.97		94.48						95.32		95.73															94.61
									19.01		20.92															14.76
			94.48						17.96		19.77															13.95
			11.19						2.13		2.34															1.65
Laguna Niguel (city)	39,876	3,307	3,136	-	-	-	-	-	664	-	589	-	-	-	-	663	413	-	-	-	-	-	-	-	-	317
	95.17		94.83						95.95		93.34					94.99	94.51									95.48
									21.17		18.78					21.14	13.17									10.11
			94.83						20.08		17.81					20.05	12.49									9.59
			7.86						1.67		1.48					1.66	1.04									0.79
Lake Forest (city)	33,777	3,766	3,270	-	-	434	-	-	396	-	627	-	-	-	-	469	396	-	-	-	-	-	-	-	-	677
	88.75		86.83			98.41			81.31		85.31					92.69	92.74									75.98
						13.27			12.11		19.17					14.34	12.11									20.70
			86.83			11.52			10.52		16.65					12.45	10.52									17.98
			9.68			1.28			1.17		1.86					1.39	1.17									2.00

Notes: Please refer to the User's Guide for an explanation of data; data is arranged alphabetically by state, then county, then city within each county; table includes counties with populations greater than 49,999 unless noted and cities with populations greater than 9,999 whose Asian and/or NHPI population rates are greater than the national average; (1) Native Hawaiian and other Pacific Islander; (2) excludes Taiwanese; (3) includes Chamorro; (4) county does not meet population threshold but is shown in order to allow inclusion of city

Place	Total population 25 years and over who are high school graduates	Asian population 25 years and over	Asians 25 years and over who are high school graduates	NHPI[1] population 25 years and over	NHPIs[1] 25 years and over who are high school graduates	Asian Indian	Bangladeshi	Cambodian	Chinese[2]	Fijian	Filipino	Guamanian[3]	Hawaiian, Native	Hmong	Indonesian	Japanese	Korean	Laotian	Malaysian	Pakistani	Samoan	Sri Lankan	Taiwanese	Thai	Tongan	Vietnamese
Los Alamitos (city)	6,699 87.29	718	641 89.28 89.28 9.57	-	-	-	-	-	-	-	-	-	-	-	-	-	-	-	-	-	-	-	-	-	-	-
Mission Viejo (city)	57,651 93.77	5,045	4,703 93.22 93.22 8.16	-	-	350 93.58 7.44 6.94 0.61	-	-	858 89.56 18.24 17.01 1.49	-	957 92.91 20.35 18.97 1.66	-	-	-	-	801 97.56 17.03 15.88 1.39	577 98.97 12.27 11.44 1.00	-	-	-	-	-	-	-	-	727 86.75 15.46 14.41 1.26
Newport Beach (city)	52,970 96.74	2,061	1,968 95.49 95.49 3.72	-	-	-	-	-	441 93.04 22.41 21.40 0.83	-	-	-	-	-	-	386 100.00 19.61 18.73 0.73	-	-	-	-	-	-	-	-	-	-
Orange (city)	66,034 80.39	7,952	6,679 83.99 83.99 10.11	-	-	478 86.91 7.16 6.01 0.72	-	-	859 87.39 12.86 10.80 1.30	-	1,289 93.14 19.30 16.21 1.95	-	-	-	-	562 94.14 8.41 7.07 0.85	996 83.56 14.91 12.53 1.51	-	-	-	-	-	334 97.95 5.00 4.20 0.51	-	-	1,705 72.12 25.53 21.44 2.58
Placentia (city)	24,422 81.49	3,524	3,071 87.15 87.15 12.57	-	-	246 82.55 8.01 6.98 1.01	-	-	729 94.92 23.74 20.69 2.99	-	483 88.79 15.73 13.71 1.98	-	-	-	-	350 88.61 11.40 9.93 1.43	410 91.52 13.35 11.63 1.68	-	-	-	-	-	-	-	-	509 82.23 16.57 14.44 2.08
Rancho Santa Margarita (city)	27,543 95.14	2,615	2,499 95.56 95.56 9.07	-	-	-	-	-	434 100.00 17.37 16.60 1.58	-	726 97.45 29.05 27.76 2.64	-	-	-	-	-	-	-	-	-	-	-	-	-	-	306 90.27 12.24 11.70 1.11
Rossmoor (cdp)	6,719 95.01	374	374 100.00 100.00 5.57	-	-	-	-	-	-	-	-	-	-	-	-	-	-	-	-	-	-	-	-	-	-	-
Santa Ana (city)	77,270 43.23	19,479	12,075 61.99 61.99 15.63	700	517 73.86 73.86 0.67	284 79.78 2.35 1.46 0.37	-	437 44.32 3.62 2.24 0.57	972 65.90 8.05 4.99 1.26	-	1,269 84.77 10.51 6.51 1.64	-	-	71 29.96 0.59 0.36 0.09	-	662 92.72 5.48 3.40 0.86	332 67.48 2.75 1.70 0.43	213 43.20 1.76 1.09 0.28	-	-	310 84.01 59.96 44.29 0.40	-	-	-	-	7,450 58.91 61.70 38.25 9.64
Seal Beach (city)	18,107 90.55	968	945 97.62 97.62 5.22	-	-	-	-	-	-	-	-	-	-	-	-	288 100.00 30.48 29.75 1.59	-	-	-	-	-	-	-	-	-	-
Stanton (city)	13,792 62.69	3,902	2,724 69.81 69.81 19.75	-	-	-	-	-	-	-	632 83.27 23.20 16.20 4.58	-	-	-	-	-	436 81.04 16.01 11.17 3.16	-	-	-	-	-	-	-	-	1,098 58.44 40.31 28.14 7.96

Notes: Please refer to the User's Guide for an explanation of data; data is arranged alphabetically by state, then county, then city within each county; table includes counties with populations greater than 49,999 unless noted and cities with populations greater than 9,999 whose Asian and/or NHPI population rates are greater than the national average; (1) Native Hawaiian and other Pacific Islander; (2) excludes Taiwanese; (3) includes Chamorro; (4) county does not meet population threshold but is shown in order to allow inclusion of city

Place	Total population 25 years and over who are high school graduates	Asian population 25 years and over	Asians 25 years and over who are high school graduates	NHPI[1] population 25 years and over	NHPIs'[1] 25 years and over who are high school graduates	Asian Indian	Bangladeshi	Cambodian	Chinese[2]	Fijian	Filipino	Guamanian[3]	Hawaiian, Native	Hmong	Indonesian	Japanese	Korean	Laotian	Malaysian	Pakistani	Samoan	Sri Lankan	Taiwanese	Thai	Tongan	Vietnamese
Tustin (city)	34,343 79.93	6,170	5,508 89.27 89.27 16.04	-	-	691 83.86 12.55 11.20 2.01	-	-	867 92.83 15.74 14.05 2.52	-	1,046 95.09 18.99 16.95 3.05	-	-	-	-	481 95.63 8.73 7.80 1.40	747 92.68 13.56 12.11 2.18	-	-	-	-	-	307 90.83 5.57 4.98 0.89	-	-	905 82.95 16.43 14.67 2.64
Tustin Foothills (cdp)	15,988 95.95	1,255	1,151 91.71 91.71 7.20	-	-	-	-	-	316 90.80 27.45 25.18 1.98	-	-	-	-	-	-	-	-	-	-	-	-	-	-	-	-	-
Westminster (city)	40,995 71.53	21,648	13,864 64.04 64.04 33.82	202	168 83.17 83.17 0.41	200 82.64 1.44 0.92 0.49	-	-	745 69.82 5.37 3.44 1.82	-	908 89.11 6.55 4.19 2.21	-	-	-	-	755 88.30 5.45 3.49 1.84	399 81.60 2.88 1.84 0.97	-	-	-	145 81.01 86.31 71.78 0.35	-	-	-	-	10,336 59.96 74.55 47.75 25.21
Yorba Linda (city)	35,000 93.44	4,158	3,984 95.82 95.82 11.38	-	-	428 98.62 10.74 10.29 1.22	-	-	1,044 93.05 26.20 25.11 2.98	-	558 96.37 14.01 13.42 1.59	-	-	-	-	645 100.00 16.19 15.51 1.84	506 96.02 12.70 12.17 1.45	-	-	-	-	-	-	-	-	368 95.09 9.24 8.85 1.05
Placer County	150,059 90.45	5,070	4,637 91.46 91.46 3.09	-	-	442 88.05 9.53 8.72 0.29	-	-	906 91.70 19.54 17.87 0.60	-	1,204 89.92 25.97 23.75 0.80	-	-	-	-	1,388 95.53 29.93 27.38 0.92	260 93.19 5.61 5.13 0.17	-	-	-	-	-	-	-	-	227 81.07 4.90 4.48 0.15
Rocklin (city)	21,746 94.43	895	828 92.51 92.51 3.81	-	-	-	-	-	-	-	-	-	-	-	-	283 88.16 34.18 31.62 1.30	-	-	-	-	-	-	-	-	-	-
Roseville (city)	48,179 90.89	2,220	2,053 92.48 92.48 4.26	-	-	317 87.81 15.44 14.28 0.66	-	-	466 96.28 22.70 20.99 0.97	-	638 92.20 31.08 28.74 1.32	-	-	-	-	360 100.00 17.54 16.22 0.75	-	-	-	-	-	-	-	-	-	-
Riverside County	701,551 74.95	33,180	27,541 83.00 83.00 3.93	2,206	1,651 74.84 74.84 0.24	2,793 83.17 10.14 8.42 0.40	-	186 60.59 0.68 0.56 0.03	2,818 82.45 10.23 8.49 0.40	-	10,947 88.46 39.75 32.99 1.56	443 69.22 26.83 20.08 0.06	474 80.20 28.71 21.49 0.07	94 61.84 0.34 0.28 0.01	-	3,013 88.72 10.94 9.08 0.43	3,017 85.08 10.95 9.09 0.43	450 54.74 1.63 1.36 0.06	-	218 92.37 0.79 0.66 0.03	399 87.31 24.17 18.09 0.06	-	228 92.31 0.83 0.69 0.03	426 68.60 1.55 1.28 0.06	-	2,408 67.53 8.74 7.26 0.34
Banning (city)	11,695 76.01	490	350 71.43 71.43 2.99	-	-	-	-	-	-	-	-	-	-	-	-	-	-	97 52.72 27.71 19.80 0.83	-	-	-	-	-	-	-	-
Corona (city)	58,305 80.56	5,865	5,218 88.97 88.97 8.95	-	-	810 85.53 15.52 13.81 1.39	-	-	450 84.59 8.62 7.67 0.77	-	1,821 92.86 34.90 31.05 3.12	-	-	-	-	416 93.27 7.97 7.09 0.71	742 90.27 14.22 12.65 1.27	-	-	-	-	-	-	-	-	773 87.44 14.81 13.18 1.33

Notes: Please refer to the User's Guide for an explanation of data; data is arranged alphabetically by state, then county, then city within each county; table includes counties with populations greater than 49,999 unless noted and cities with populations greater than 9,999 whose Asian and/or NHPI population rates are greater than the national average; (1) Native Hawaiian and other Pacific Islander; (2) excludes Taiwanese; (3) includes Chamorro; (4) county does not meet population threshold but is shown in order to allow inclusion of city

Place	Total population 25 years and over who are high school graduates	Asian population 25 years and over	Asians 25 years and over who are high school graduates	NHPI[1] population 25 years and over	NHPIs[1] 25 years and over who are high school graduates	Asian Indian	Bangladeshi	Cambodian	Chinese[2]	Fijian	Filipino	Guamanian[3]	Hawaiian, Native	Hmong	Indonesian	Japanese	Korean	Laotian	Malaysian	Pakistani	Samoan	Sri Lankan	Taiwanese	Thai	Tongan	Vietnamese
Moreno Valley (city)	55,864	4,890	4,017	-	-	-	-	-	246	-	2,260	-	-	-	-	316	379	129	-	-	-	-	-	-	-	202
	74.51		82.15						87.54		90.87					84.72	89.60	49.81								54.16
									6.12		56.26					7.87	9.43	3.21								5.03
			82.15						5.03		46.22					6.46	7.75	2.64								4.13
			7.19						0.44		4.05					0.57	0.68	0.23								0.36
Palm Springs (city)	26,780	1,205	895	-	-	-	-	-	-	-	524	-	-	-	-	-	-	-	-	-	-	-	-	-	-	-
	81.70		74.27								68.59															
											58.55															
			74.27								43.49															
			3.34								1.96															
Pedley (cdp)	4,744	282	180	-	-	-	-	-	-	-	-	-	-	-	-	-	-	-	-	-	-	-	-	-	-	-
	73.14		63.83																							
			63.83																							
			3.79																							
Riverside (city)	109,490	7,348	6,087	666	487	665	-	-	895	-	1,706	-	-	-	-	664	764	120	-	-	-	-	-	-	-	725
	74.90		82.84		73.12	82.10			91.89		95.15					94.86	81.62	62.83								56.77
						10.92			14.70		28.03					10.91	12.55	1.97								11.91
			82.84		73.12	9.05			12.18		23.22					9.04	10.40	1.63								9.87
			5.56		0.44	0.61			0.82		1.56					0.61	0.70	0.11								0.66
Temecula (city)	29,602	1,693	1,408	-	-	-	-	-	203	-	760	-	-	-	-	-	-	-	-	-	-	-	-	-	-	-
	90.13		83.17						81.53		85.01															
									14.42		53.98															
			83.17						11.99		44.89															
			4.76						0.69		2.57															
Sacramento County	643,218	80,510	58,349	3,435	2,351	5,963	-	253	13,832	632	13,953	429	340	1,957	-	9,729	2,430	1,291	-	504	377	-	267	341	229	5,850
	83.27		72.47		68.44	77.35		46.85	69.67	60.77	87.72	81.40	78.89	37.38		92.83	78.54	32.51		69.33	76.01		87.83	74.78	59.17	60.92
						10.22		0.43	23.71	26.88	23.91	18.25	14.46	3.35		16.67	4.16	2.21		0.86	16.04		0.46	0.58	9.74	10.03
			72.47		68.44	7.41		0.31	17.18	18.40	17.33	12.49	9.90	2.43		12.08	3.02	1.60		0.63	10.98		0.33	0.42	6.67	7.27
			9.07		0.37	0.93		0.04	2.15	0.10	2.17	0.07	0.05	0.30		1.51	0.38	0.20		0.08	0.06		0.04	0.05	0.04	0.91
Arden-Arcade (cdp)	58,071	3,189	2,750	-	-	398	-	-	515	-	636	-	-	73	-	392	-	-	-	-	-	-	-	-	-	236
	89.05		86.23			88.84			77.33		86.06			64.04		94.69										86.76
						14.47			18.73		23.13			2.65		14.25										8.58
			86.23			12.48			16.15		19.94			2.29		12.29										7.40
			4.74			0.69			0.89		1.10			0.13		0.68										0.41
Elk Grove (cdp)	30,850	6,340	4,923	-	-	567	-	-	738	-	1,912	-	-	-	-	375	-	-	-	-	-	-	-	-	-	736
	86.73		77.65			68.56			79.96		90.49					91.69										58.37
						11.52			14.99		38.84					7.62										14.95
			77.65			8.94			11.64		30.16					5.91										11.61
			15.96			1.84			2.39		6.20					1.22										2.39
Fair Oaks (cdp)	18,446	794	772	-	-	-	-	-	-	-	-	-	-	-	-	-	-	-	-	-	-	-	-	-	-	-
	93.87		97.23																							
			97.23																							
			4.19																							
Florin (cdp)	11,712	2,840	1,615	-	-	120	-	-	199	-	605	-	-	74	-	-	-	-	-	-	-	-	-	-	-	310
	72.04		56.87			57.97			50.38		85.09			32.60												44.03
						7.43			12.32		37.46			4.58												19.20
			56.87			4.23			7.01		21.30			2.61												10.92
			13.79			1.02			1.70		5.17			0.63												2.65

Notes: Please refer to the User's Guide for an explanation of data; data is arranged alphabetically by state, then county, then city within each county; table includes counties with populations greater than 49,999 unless noted and cities with populations greater than 9,999 whose Asian and/or NHPI population rates are greater than the national average; (1) Native Hawaiian and other Pacific Islander; (2) excludes Taiwanese; (3) includes Chamorro; (4) county does not meet population threshold but is shown in order to allow inclusion of city

Place	Total population 25 years and over who are high school graduates	Asian population 25 years and over	Asians 25 years and over who are high school graduates	NHPI[1] population 25 years and over	NHPIs[1] 25 years and over who are high school graduates	Asian Indian	Bangladeshi	Cambodian	Chinese[2]	Fijian	Filipino	Guamanian[3]	Hawaiian, Native	Hmong	Indonesian	Japanese	Korean	Laotian	Malaysian	Pakistani	Samoan	Sri Lankan	Taiwanese	Thai	Tongan	Vietnamese
Folsom (city)	32,002 88.87	2,525	2,403 95.17 95.17 7.51	-	-	854 91.04 35.54 33.82 2.67	-	-	438 100.00 18.23 17.35 1.37	-	410 97.62 17.06 16.24 1.28	-	-	-	-	-	-	-	-	-	-	-	-	-	-	-
Foothill Farms (cdp)	8,599 84.02	571	453 79.33 79.33 5.27	-	-	-	-	-	-	-	-	-	-	-	-	-	-	-	-	-	-	-	-	-	-	-
La Riviera (cdp)	6,234 90.57	655	572 87.33 87.33 9.18	-	-	-	-	-	-	-	-	-	-	-	-	-	-	-	-	-	-	-	-	-	-	-
Laguna (cdp)	19,633 94.05	4,033	3,621 89.78 89.78 18.44	-	-	343 78.31 9.47 8.50 1.75	-	-	1,149 88.86 31.73 28.49 5.85	-	1,123 96.07 31.01 27.85 5.72	-	-	-	-	442 95.88 12.21 10.96 2.25	-	-	-	-	-	-	-	-	-	279 85.85 7.71 6.92 1.42
North Highlands (cdp)	19,476 75.53	1,559	975 62.54 62.54 5.01	-	-	-	-	-	-	-	343 65.58 35.18 22.00 1.76	-	-	-	-	-	-	-	-	-	-	-	-	-	-	283 66.12 29.03 18.15 1.45
Parkway-S. Sacramento (cdp)	12,346 63.84	2,915	1,327 45.52 45.52 10.75	-	-	-	-	-	138 50.36 10.40 4.73 1.12	-	-	-	-	349 42.56 26.30 11.97 2.83	-	-	-	136 22.52 10.25 4.67 1.10	-	-	-	-	-	-	-	298 46.27 22.46 10.22 2.41
Rancho Cordova (cdp)	28,230 83.89	2,743	2,114 77.07 77.07 7.49	-	-	330 83.12 15.61 12.03 1.17	-	-	211 76.17 9.98 7.69 0.75	-	641 95.96 30.32 23.37 2.27	-	-	-	-	-	243 77.14 11.49 8.86 0.86	-	-	-	-	-	-	-	-	293 58.84 13.86 10.68 1.04
Rosemont (cdp)	12,520 88.06	1,834	1,383 75.41 75.41 11.05	-	-	-	-	-	-	-	249 96.89 18.00 13.58 1.99	-	-	-	-	-	221 60.71 15.98 12.05 1.77	-	-	-	-	-	-	-	-	265 68.65 19.16 14.45 2.12
Sacramento (city)	197,067 77.31	38,901	25,513 65.58 65.58 12.95	1,942	1,280 65.91 65.91 0.65	1,608 68.34 6.30 4.13 0.82	-	133 53.85 0.52 0.34 0.07	8,476 63.76 33.22 21.79 4.30	454 62.53 35.47 23.38 0.23	4,541 83.88 17.80 11.67 2.30	-	-	1,247 34.21 4.89 3.21 0.63	-	5,353 93.49 20.98 13.76 2.72	392 77.62 1.54 1.01 0.20	777 30.89 3.05 2.00 0.39	-	279 72.47 1.09 0.72 0.14	163 66.26 12.73 8.39 0.08	-	-	-	158 60.08 12.34 8.14 0.08	1,805 52.36 7.07 4.64 0.92
Vineyard (cdp)	5,609 89.82	1,045	832 79.62 79.62 14.83	-	-	-	-	-	-	-	359 82.53 43.15 34.35 6.40	-	-	-	-	-	-	-	-	-	-	-	-	-	-	-

Notes: Please refer to the User's Guide for an explanation of data; data is arranged alphabetically by state, then county, then city within each county; table includes counties with populations greater than 49,999 unless noted and cities with populations greater than 9,999 whose Asian and/or NHPI population rates are greater than the national average; (1) Native Hawaiian and other Pacific Islander; (2) excludes Taiwanese; (3) includes Chamorro; (4) county does not meet population threshold but is shown in order to allow inclusion of city

Place	Total population 25 years and over who are high school graduates	Asian population 25 years and over	Asians 25 years and over who are high school graduates	NHPI[1] population 25 years and over	NHPIs[1] 25 years and over who are high school graduates	Asian Indian	Bangladeshi	Cambodian	Chinese[2]	Fijian	Filipino	Guamanian[3]	Hawaiian, Native	Hmong	Indonesian	Japanese	Korean	Laotian	Malaysian	Pakistani	Samoan	Sri Lankan	Taiwanese	Thai	Tongan	Vietnamese
San Benito County	23,525 74.92	730	665 91.10 91.10 2.83	-	-	-	-	-	-	-	359 91.58 53.98 49.18 1.53	-	-	-	-	-	-	-	-	-	-	-	-	-	-	-
San Bernardino County	729,679 74.21	50,706	42,943 84.69 84.69 5.89	2,606	2,048 78.59 78.59 0.28	4,161 86.60 9.69 8.21 0.57	-	411 50.12 0.96 0.81 0.06	6,300 88.88 14.67 12.42 0.86	-	14,970 90.48 34.86 29.52 2.05	565 86.00 27.59 21.68 0.08	364 80.00 17.77 13.97 0.05	-	1,885 93.69 4.39 3.72 0.26	3,239 92.41 7.54 6.39 0.44	4,345 89.85 10.12 8.57 0.60	110 44.90 0.26 0.22 0.02	-	387 95.56 0.90 0.76 0.05	607 72.35 29.64 23.29 0.08	-	1,125 85.36 2.62 2.22 0.15	971 79.46 2.26 1.91 0.13	272 70.28 13.28 10.44 0.04	3,740 60.15 8.71 7.38 0.51
Chino (city)	28,301 70.68	2,166	1,899 87.67 87.67 6.71	-	-	-	-	-	-	-	884 91.99 46.55 40.81 3.12	-	-	-	-	-	-	-	-	-	-	-	-	-	-	204 62.96 10.74 9.42 0.72
Chino Hills (city)	35,982 89.88	9,051	8,509 94.01 94.01 23.65	-	-	703 94.62 8.26 7.77 1.95	-	-	2,163 95.75 25.42 23.90 6.01	-	3,213 96.14 37.76 35.50 8.93	-	-	-	-	432 100.00 5.08 4.77 1.20	702 93.23 8.25 7.76 1.95	-	-	-	-	-	348 88.10 4.09 3.84 0.97	-	-	392 74.95 4.61 4.33 1.09
Colton (city)	17,705 68.79	1,580	1,415 89.56 89.56 7.99	-	-	-	-	-	-	-	350 92.11 24.73 22.15 1.98	-	-	-	-	-	-	-	-	-	-	-	-	-	-	-
Fontana (city)	43,645 65.43	3,558	3,004 84.43 84.43 6.88	302	241 79.80 79.80 0.55	321 83.16 10.69 9.02 0.74	-	-	-	-	1,683 91.27 56.03 47.30 3.86	-	-	-	-	-	-	-	-	-	-	-	-	-	-	-
Grand Terrace (city)	6,677 87.89	373	285 76.41 76.41 4.27	-	-	-	-	-	-	-	-	-	-	-	-	-	-	-	-	-	-	-	-	-	-	-
Highland (city)	17,759 72.02	1,688	1,270 75.24 75.24 7.15	-	-	-	-	-	-	-	507 87.56 39.92 30.04 2.85	-	-	-	-	-	-	-	-	-	-	-	-	-	-	157 49.06 12.36 9.30 0.88
Loma Linda (city)	11,054 88.12	2,919	2,636 90.30 90.30 23.85	-	-	242 85.82 9.18 8.29 2.19	-	-	381 90.93 14.45 13.05 3.45	-	627 88.68 23.79 21.48 5.67	-	-	-	279 100.00 10.58 9.56 2.52	-	537 91.95 20.37 18.40 4.86	-	-	-	-	-	-	-	-	-
Montclair (city)	11,338 60.42	1,734	1,229 70.88 70.88 10.84	-	-	-	-	-	-	-	-	-	-	-	-	-	-	-	-	-	-	-	-	-	-	433 55.02 35.23 24.97 3.82

Notes: Please refer to the User's Guide for an explanation of data; data is arranged alphabetically by state, then county, then city within each county; table includes counties with populations greater than 49,999 unless noted and cities with populations greater than 9,999 whose Asian and/or NHPI population rates are greater than the national average; (1) Native Hawaiian and other Pacific Islander; (2) excludes Taiwanese; (3) includes Chamorro; (4) county does not meet population threshold but is shown in order to allow inclusion of city

Place	Total population 25 years and over who are high school graduates	Asian population 25 years and over	Asians 25 years and over who are high school graduates	NHPI[1] population 25 years and over	NHPIs[1] 25 years and over who are high school graduates	Asian Indian	Bangladeshi	Cambodian	Chinese[2]	Fijian	Filipino	Guamanian[3]	Hawaiian, Native	Hmong	Indonesian	Japanese	Korean	Laotian	Malaysian	Pakistani	Samoan	Sri Lankan	Taiwanese	Thai	Tongan	Vietnamese
Ontario (city)	53,532 62.49	4,050	3,224 79.60 79.60 6.02	253	138 54.55 54.55 0.26	261 90.31 8.10 6.44 0.49	-	-	298 85.14 9.24 7.36 0.56	-	1,437 89.76 44.57 35.48 2.68	-	-	-	-	-	-	-	-	-	-	-	-	-	-	535 54.26 16.59 13.21 1.00
Rancho Cucamonga (city)	66,474 86.00	4,799	4,318 89.98 89.98 6.50	-	-	481 84.98 11.14 10.02 0.72	-	-	870 91.19 20.15 18.13 1.31	-	1,307 93.02 30.27 27.23 1.97	-	-	-	-	434 96.23 10.05 9.04 0.65	423 91.96 9.80 8.81 0.64	-	-	-	-	-	-	-	-	236 76.13 5.47 4.92 0.36
Redlands (city)	34,891 86.63	2,238	2,035 90.93 90.93 5.83	-	-	234 91.76 11.50 10.46 0.67	-	-	305 87.64 14.99 13.63 0.87	-	467 90.50 22.95 20.87 1.34	-	-	-	-	-	330 96.77 16.22 14.75 0.95	-	-	-	-	-	-	-	-	-
Rialto (city)	31,752 66.47	1,066	867 81.33 81.33 2.73	289	226 78.20 78.20 0.71	-	-	-	-	-	275 90.76 31.72 25.80 0.87	-	-	-	-	-	-	-	-	-	-	-	-	-	-	-
San Bernardino (city)	64,473 64.91	4,350	2,976 68.41 68.41 4.62	355	264 74.37 74.37 0.41	353 76.08 11.86 8.11 0.55	-	71 38.59 2.39 1.63 0.11	269 67.76 9.04 6.18 0.42	-	877 76.26 29.47 20.16 1.36	-	-	-	158 87.29 5.31 3.63 0.25	-	232 84.98 7.80 5.33 0.36	-	-	-	93 53.45 35.23 26.20 0.14	-	-	-	-	398 49.75 13.37 9.15 0.62
Upland (city)	36,296 83.80	3,264	2,853 87.41 87.41 7.86	-	-	360 96.51 12.62 11.03 0.99	-	-	427 88.59 14.97 13.08 1.18	-	438 89.39 15.35 13.42 1.21	-	-	-	-	-	491 89.76 17.21 15.04 1.35	-	-	-	-	-	266 88.96 9.32 8.15 0.73	-	-	356 66.67 12.48 10.91 0.98
Victorville (city)	28,214 76.72	1,540	1,231 79.94 79.94 4.36	-	-	-	-	-	-	-	617 86.54 50.12 40.06 2.19	-	-	-	-	-	-	-	-	-	-	-	-	-	-	-
San Diego County	1,464,478 82.58	160,925	130,772 81.26 81.26 8.93	7,805	6,585 84.37 84.37 0.45	5,756 92.20 4.40 3.58 0.39	-	726 37.73 0.56 0.45 0.05	15,830 83.29 12.11 9.84 1.08	-	67,912 85.68 51.93 42.20 4.64	2,343 80.54 35.58 30.02 0.16	1,343 89.06 20.39 17.21 0.09	255 45.86 0.19 0.16 0.02	327 97.61 0.25 0.20 0.02	13,331 90.53 10.19 8.28 0.91	6,349 89.80 4.86 3.95 0.43	2,048 52.99 1.57 1.27 0.14	-	260 94.55 0.20 0.16 0.02	2,164 85.84 32.86 27.73 0.15	-	1,404 93.66 1.07 0.87 0.10	782 86.70 0.60 0.49 0.05	176 84.21 2.67 2.25 0.01	12,907 59.80 9.87 8.02 0.88
Bonita (cdp)	7,527 90.36	760	697 91.71 91.71 9.26	-	-	-	-	-	-	-	435 92.36 62.41 57.24 5.78	-	-	-	-	-	-	-	-	-	-	-	-	-	-	-
Carlsbad (city)	50,866 93.07	2,327	2,080 89.39 89.39 4.09	-	-	-	-	-	476 100.00 22.88 20.46 0.94	-	432 89.07 20.77 18.56 0.85	-	-	-	-	364 87.29 17.50 15.64 0.72	-	-	-	-	-	-	-	-	-	-

Notes: Please refer to the User's Guide for an explanation of data; data is arranged alphabetically by state, then county, then city within each county; table includes counties with populations greater than 49,999 unless noted and cities with populations greater than 9,999 whose Asian and/or NHPI population rates are greater than the national average; (1) Native Hawaiian and other Pacific Islander; (2) excludes Taiwanese; (3) includes Chamorro; (4) county does not meet population threshold but is shown in order to allow inclusion of city

Place	Total population 25 years and over who are high school graduates	Asian population 25 years and over	Asians 25 years and over who are high school graduates	NHPI[1] population 25 years and over	NHPIs[1] 25 years and over who are high school graduates	Asian Indian	Bangladeshi	Cambodian	Chinese[2]	Fijian	Filipino	Guamanian[3]	Hawaiian, Native	Hmong	Indonesian	Japanese	Korean	Laotian	Malaysian	Pakistani	Samoan	Sri Lankan	Taiwanese	Thai	Tongan	Vietnamese
Chula Vista (city)	84,401	12,722	11,264	513	420	-	-	-	613	-	7,834	207	-	-	-	1,445	786	-	-	-	-	-	-	-	-	-
	78.52		88.54		81.87				79.61		90.12	72.38				89.75	85.34									
									5.44		69.55	49.29				12.83	6.98									
			88.54		81.87				4.82		61.58	40.35				11.36	6.18									
			13.35		0.50				0.73		9.28	0.25				1.71	0.93									
Coronado (city)	14,666	508	441	-	-	-	-	-	-	-	189	-	-	-	-	-	-	-	-	-	-	-	-	-	-	-
	96.13		86.81								78.10															
											42.86															
			86.81								37.20															
			3.01								1.29															
Escondido (city)	57,843	3,525	2,716	-	-	-	-	-	310	-	1,068	-	-	-	-	-	-	134	-	-	-	-	-	-	-	520
	72.58		77.05						86.83		87.25							58.01								63.73
									11.41		39.32							4.93								19.15
			77.05						8.79		30.30							3.80								14.75
			4.70						0.54		1.85							0.23								0.90
Imperial Beach (city)	11,792	1,297	1,084	-	-	-	-	-	-	-	888	-	-	-	-	-	-	-	-	-	-	-	-	-	-	-
	76.97		83.58								82.22															
											81.92															
			83.58								68.47															
			9.19								7.53															
La Mesa (city)	34,401	1,525	1,301	-	-	-	-	-	-	-	335	-	-	-	-	-	-	-	-	-	-	-	-	-	-	-
	89.56		85.31								87.93															
											25.75															
			85.31								21.97															
			3.78								0.97															
La Presa (cdp)	15,402	2,305	1,883	-	-	-	-	-	-	-	1,684	-	-	-	-	-	-	-	-	-	-	-	-	-	-	-
	79.15		81.69								83.00															
											89.43															
			81.69								73.06															
			12.23								10.93															
Lemon Grove (city)	12,553	890	664	-	-	-	-	-	-	-	371	-	-	-	-	-	-	-	-	-	-	-	-	-	-	108
	79.99		74.61								85.88															54.55
											55.87															16.27
			74.61								41.69															12.13
			5.29								2.96															0.86
National City (city)	17,358	6,771	4,860	-	-	-	-	-	-	-	4,534	-	-	-	-	-	-	-	-	-	-	-	-	-	-	-
	57.24		71.78								72.94															
											93.29															
			71.78								66.96															
			28.00								26.12															
Oceanside (city)	81,384	6,170	5,064	1,203	1,041	-	-	-	350	-	2,748	-	-	-	-	920	-	-	-	-	679	-	-	-	-	385
	80.83		82.07		86.53				86.42		80.63					89.67					86.83					72.37
									6.91		54.27					18.17					65.23					7.60
			82.07		86.53				5.67		44.54					14.91					56.44					6.24
			6.22		1.28				0.43		3.38					1.13					0.83					0.47
Poway (city)	27,743	2,107	1,876	-	-	-	-	-	434	-	731	-	-	-	-	-	-	-	-	-	-	-	-	-	-	-
	93.13		89.04						92.74		90.69															
									23.13		38.97															
			89.04						20.60		34.69															
			6.76						1.56		2.63															

Notes: Please refer to the User's Guide for an explanation of data; data is arranged alphabetically by state, then county, then city within each county; table includes counties with populations greater than 49,999 unless noted and cities with populations greater than 9,999 whose Asian and/or NHPI population rates are greater than the national average; (1) Native Hawaiian and other Pacific Islander; (2) excludes Taiwanese; (3) includes Chamorro; (4) county does not meet population threshold but is shown in order to allow inclusion of city

Place	Total population 25 years and over who are high school graduates	Asian population 25 years and over	Asians 25 years and over who are high school graduates	NHPI[1] population 25 years and over	NHPIs[1] 25 years and over who are high school graduates	Asian Indian	Bangladeshi	Cambodian	Chinese[2]	Fijian	Filipino	Guamanian[3]	Hawaiian, Native	Hmong	Indonesian	Japanese	Korean	Laotian	Malaysian	Pakistani	Samoan	Sri Lankan	Taiwanese	Thai	Tongan	Vietnamese
Rancho San Diego (cdp)	11,740 92.11	646	607 93.96 93.96 5.17	-	-	-	-	-	-	-	329 91.90 54.20 50.93 2.80	-	-	-	-	-	-	-	-	-	-	-	-	-	-	-
San Diego (city)	645,200 82.80	105,087	84,066 80.00 80.00 13.03	3,519	3,011 85.56 85.56 0.47	3,893 94.19 4.63 3.70 0.60	-	583 34.38 0.69 0.55 0.09	11,545 82.46 13.73 10.99 1.79	-	41,658 86.82 49.55 39.64 6.46	1,074 83.45 35.67 30.52 0.17	682 91.54 22.65 19.38 0.11	190 45.35 0.23 0.18 0.03	-	7,027 91.84 8.36 6.69 1.09	3,676 90.99 4.37 3.50 0.57	1,684 50.91 2.00 1.60 0.26	-	-	868 85.77 28.83 24.67 0.13	-	953 97.15 1.13 0.91 0.15	492 92.13 0.59 0.47 0.08	-	10,334 58.13 12.29 9.83 1.60
San Marcos (city)	25,544 75.06	1,715	1,438 83.85 83.85 5.63	-	-	-	-	-	253 81.35 17.59 14.75 0.99	-	668 83.71 46.45 38.95 2.62	-	-	-	-	-	-	-	-	-	-	-	-	-	-	-
Solana Beach (city)	9,004 92.14	418	398 95.22 95.22 4.42	-	-	-	-	-	-	-	-	-	-	-	-	-	-	-	-	-	-	-	-	-	-	-
Spring Valley (cdp)	14,135 84.38	960	811 84.48 84.48 5.74	-	-	-	-	-	-	-	378 79.75 46.61 39.38 2.67	-	-	-	-	-	-	-	-	-	-	-	-	-	-	-
Vista (city)	40,209 75.86	2,160	1,915 88.66 88.66 4.76	274	237 86.50 86.50 0.59	-	-	-	-	-	780 94.89 40.73 36.11 1.94	-	-	-	-	321 84.25 16.76 14.86 0.80	-	-	-	-	-	-	-	-	-	-
San Francisco County	483,740 81.19	176,086	118,501 67.30 67.30 24.50	2,004	1,291 64.42 64.42 0.27	2,993 85.25 2.53 1.70 0.62	-	175 50.14 0.15 0.10 0.04	68,731 60.14 58.00 39.03 14.21	-	23,842 82.62 20.12 13.54 4.93	-	-	-	473 95.75 0.40 0.27 0.10	8,584 93.26 7.24 4.87 1.77	4,841 85.53 4.09 2.75 1.00	-	-	199 77.13 0.17 0.11 0.04	639 58.95 49.50 31.89 0.13	-	524 93.40 0.44 0.30 0.11	969 89.81 0.82 0.55 0.20	-	3,774 54.03 3.18 2.14 0.78
San Francisco (city)	483,740 81.19	176,086	118,501 67.30 67.30 24.50	2,004	1,291 64.42 64.42 0.27	2,993 85.25 2.53 1.70 0.62	-	175 50.14 0.15 0.10 0.04	68,731 60.14 58.00 39.03 14.21	-	23,842 82.62 20.12 13.54 4.93	-	-	-	473 95.75 0.40 0.27 0.10	8,584 93.26 7.24 4.87 1.77	4,841 85.53 4.09 2.75 1.00	-	-	199 77.13 0.17 0.11 0.04	639 58.95 49.50 31.89 0.13	-	524 93.40 0.44 0.30 0.11	969 89.81 0.82 0.55 0.20	-	3,774 54.03 3.18 2.14 0.78
San Joaquin County	237,619 71.23	35,054	21,948 62.61 62.61 9.24	942	724 76.86 76.86 0.30	1,977 67.34 9.01 5.64 0.83	-	1,023 28.00 4.66 2.92 0.43	2,438 62.61 11.11 6.95 1.03	-	10,366 77.57 47.23 29.57 4.36	-	228 88.03 31.49 24.20 0.10	555 29.35 2.53 1.58 0.23	-	2,521 87.44 11.49 7.19 1.06	435 74.74 1.98 1.24 0.18	462 33.48 2.10 1.32 0.19	-	256 47.32 1.17 0.73 0.11	133 64.25 18.37 14.12 0.06	-	-	-	-	1,362 46.09 6.21 3.89 0.57
Lathrop (city)	4,310 74.03	855	679 79.42 79.42 15.75	-	-	-	-	-	-	-	536 82.33 78.94 62.69 12.44	-	-	-	-	-	-	-	-	-	-	-	-	-	-	-

Notes: Please refer to the User's Guide for an explanation of data; data is arranged alphabetically by state, then county, then city within each county; table includes counties with populations greater than 49,999 unless noted and cities with populations greater than 9,999 whose Asian and/or NHPI population rates are greater than the national average; (1) Native Hawaiian and other Pacific Islander; (2) excludes Taiwanese; (3) includes Chamorro; (4) county does not meet population threshold but is shown in order to allow inclusion of city

Place	Total population 25 years and over who are high school graduates	Asian population 25 years and over	Asians 25 years and over who are high school graduates	NHPI[1] population 25 years and over	NHPIs[1] 25 years and over who are high school graduates	Asian Indian	Bangladeshi	Cambodian	Chinese[2]	Fijian	Filipino	Guamanian[3]	Hawaiian, Native	Hmong	Indonesian	Japanese	Korean	Laotian	Malaysian	Pakistani	Samoan	Sri Lankan	Taiwanese	Thai	Tongan	Vietnamese
	25,536	1,918	1,362	-	-	233	-	-	-	-	321	-	-	-	-	447	-	-	-	-	-	-	-	-	-	-
	72.86		71.01			51.21					85.60					86.13										
Lodi (city)						17.11					23.57					32.82										
			71.01			12.15					16.74					23.31										
			5.33			0.91					1.26					1.75										
	94,299	25,316	14,462	539	396	707	-	962	1,698	-	7,290	-	-	464	-	1,112	-	418	-	159	-	-	-	-	-	1,096
	68.16		57.13		73.47	62.07		27.37	57.66		75.48			30.51		86.27		31.55		52.65						41.74
Stockton (city)						4.89		6.65	11.74		50.41			3.21		7.69		2.89		1.10						7.58
			57.13		73.47	2.79		3.80	6.71		28.80			1.83		4.39		1.65		0.63						4.33
			15.34		0.42	0.75		1.02	1.80		7.73			0.49		1.18		0.44		0.17						1.16
	26,938	2,795	2,333	-	-	533	-	-	207	-	1,001	-	-	-	-	-	-	-	-	-	-	-	-	-	-	-
	81.49		83.47			80.88			84.49		86.07															
Tracy (city)						22.85			8.87		42.91															
			83.47			19.07			7.41		35.81															
			8.66			1.98			0.77		3.72															
	136,232	3,844	3,342	-	-	274	-	-	447	-	1,262	-	-	-	-	689	387	-	-	-	-	-	-	-	-	-
	85.58		86.94			83.79			92.55		85.56					96.23	86.97									
San Luis Obispo County						8.20			13.38		37.76					20.62	11.58									
			86.94			7.13			11.63		32.83					17.92	10.07									
			2.45			0.20			0.33		0.93					0.51	0.28									
	9,326	553	428	-	-	-	-	-	-	-	307	-	-	-	-	-	-	-	-	-	-	-	-	-	-	-
	92.03		77.40								79.53															
Baywood-Los Osos (cdp)											71.73															
			77.40								55.52															
			4.59								3.29															
	7,053	348	316	-	-	-	-	-	-	-	-	-	-	-	-	-	-	-	-	-	-	-	-	-	-	-
	82.76		90.80																							
Grover Beach (city)																										
			90.80																							
			4.48																							
	21,151	899	836	-	-	-	-	-	139	-	170	-	-	-	-	-	-	-	-	-	-	-	-	-	-	-
	91.09		92.99						100.00		87.18															
San Luis Obispo (city)									16.63		20.33															
			92.99						15.46		18.91															
			3.95						0.66		0.80															
	418,121	99,081	88,220	4,855	3,341	7,102	-	-	29,810	376	35,825	250	480	-	415	7,342	3,017	-	-	-	610	-	612	448	1,179	1,501
	85.28		89.04		68.82	90.68			86.31	54.81	90.01	87.41	88.56		96.74	94.24	94.76				79.43		100.00	94.12	60.06	77.49
San Mateo County						8.05			33.79	11.25	40.61	7.48	14.37		0.47	8.32	3.42				18.26		0.69	0.51	35.29	1.70
			89.04		68.82	7.17			30.09	7.74	36.16	5.15	9.89		0.42	7.41	3.04				12.56		0.62	0.45	24.28	1.51
			21.10		0.80	1.70			7.13	0.09	8.57	0.06	0.11		0.10	1.76	0.72				0.15		0.15	0.11	0.28	0.36
	17,703	2,878	2,644	-	-	468	-	-	1,218	-	404	-	-	-	-	341	-	-	-	-	-	-	-	-	-	-
	94.20		91.87			93.98			93.69		95.28					91.42										
Belmont (city)						17.70			46.07		15.28					12.90										
			91.87			16.26			42.32		14.04					11.85										
			14.94			2.64			6.88		2.28					1.93										
	19,611	2,786	2,580	-	-	-	-	-	1,236	-	424	-	-	-	-	320	-	-	-	-	-	-	-	-	-	-
	92.89		92.61						88.86		97.70					93.02										
Burlingame (city)									47.91		16.43					12.40										
			92.61						44.36		15.22					11.49										
			13.16						6.30		2.16					1.63										

Notes: Please refer to the User's Guide for an explanation of data; data is arranged alphabetically by state, then county, then city within each county; table includes counties with populations greater than 49,999 unless noted and cities with populations greater than 9,999 whose Asian and/or NHPI population rates are greater than the national average; (1) Native Hawaiian and other Pacific Islander; (2) excludes Taiwanese; (3) includes Chamorro; (4) county does not meet population threshold but is shown in order to allow inclusion of city

Place	Total population 25 years and over who are high school graduates	Asian population 25 years and over	Asians 25 years and over who are high school graduates	NHPI[1] population 25 years and over	NHPIs[1] 25 years and over who are high school graduates	Asian Indian	Bangladeshi	Cambodian	Chinese[2]	Fijian	Filipino	Guamanian[3]	Hawaiian, Native	Hmong	Indonesian	Japanese	Korean	Laotian	Malaysian	Pakistani	Samoan	Sri Lankan	Taiwanese	Thai	Tongan	Vietnamese
Daly City (city)	57,147 82.04	35,014	30,006 85.70 85.70 52.51	563	470 83.48 83.48 0.82	701 89.53 2.34 2.00 1.23	-	-	7,622 78.46 25.40 21.77 13.34	-	19,102 88.62 63.66 54.56 33.43	-	-	-	-	666 94.07 2.22 1.90 1.17	510 95.86 1.70 1.46 0.89	-	-	-	-	-	-	-	-	453 69.37 1.51 1.29 0.79
East Palo Alto (city)	7,315 48.22	437	372 85.13 85.13 5.09	1,134	652 57.50 57.50 8.91	-	-	-	-	-	-	-	-	-	-	-	-	-	-	-	-	-	-	-	435 57.39 66.72 38.36 5.95	-
Foster City (city)	20,296 95.59	6,823	6,442 94.42 94.42 31.74	-	-	1,288 98.17 19.99 18.88 6.35	-	-	2,953 91.91 45.84 43.28 14.55	-	536 96.75 8.32 7.86 2.64	-	-	-	-	1,027 96.34 15.94 15.05 5.06	288 98.63 4.47 4.22 1.42	-	-	-	-	-	-	-	-	-
Hillsborough (town)	7,318 96.38	1,864	1,691 90.72 90.72 23.11	-	-	-	-	-	1,218 88.26 72.03 65.34 16.64	-	-	-	-	-	-	-	-	-	-	-	-	-	-	-	-	-
Menlo Park (city)	19,994 89.04	1,688	1,616 95.73 95.73 8.08	-	-	-	-	-	603 93.06 37.31 35.72 3.02	-	-	-	-	-	-	353 98.06 21.84 20.91 1.77	-	-	-	-	-	-	-	-	-	-
Millbrae (city)	13,303 87.10	3,810	3,311 86.90 86.90 24.89	-	-	244 92.42 7.37 6.40 1.83	-	-	2,063 83.32 62.31 54.15 15.51	-	405 90.60 12.23 10.63 3.04	-	-	-	-	248 98.02 7.49 6.51 1.86	179 90.40 5.41 4.70 1.35	-	-	-	-	-	-	-	-	-
Pacifica (city)	24,189 91.49	3,987	3,591 90.07 90.07 14.85	-	-	-	-	-	947 88.34 26.37 23.75 3.92	-	1,842 89.20 51.29 46.20 7.62	-	-	-	-	306 100.00 8.52 7.67 1.27	-	-	-	-	-	-	-	-	-	-
Redwood City (city)	42,844 82.91	5,073	4,717 92.98 92.98 11.01	327	224 68.50 68.50 0.52	803 98.41 17.02 15.83 1.87	-	-	1,872 93.88 39.69 36.90 4.37	-	916 94.05 19.42 18.06 2.14	-	-	-	-	553 95.67 11.72 10.90 1.29	-	-	-	-	-	-	-	-	-	-
San Bruno (city)	23,384 84.48	5,244	4,664 88.94 88.94 19.95	551	468 84.94 84.94 2.00	489 71.91 10.48 9.32 2.09	-	-	1,401 89.07 30.04 26.72 5.99	-	1,917 90.94 41.10 36.56 8.20	-	-	-	-	384 96.97 8.23 7.32 1.64	-	-	-	-	-	-	-	-	216 90.38 46.15 39.20 0.92	-
San Carlos (city)	19,296 94.62	1,435	1,313 91.50 91.50 6.80	-	-	-	-	-	494 90.31 37.62 34.43 2.56	-	-	-	-	-	-	-	-	-	-	-	-	-	-	-	-	-

Notes: Please refer to the User's Guide for an explanation of data; data is arranged alphabetically by state, then county, then city within each county; table includes counties with populations greater than 49,999 unless noted and cities with populations greater than 9,999 whose Asian and/or NHPI population rates are greater than the national average; (1) Native Hawaiian and other Pacific Islander; (2) excludes Taiwanese; (3) includes Chamorro; (4) county does not meet population threshold but is shown in order to allow inclusion of city

Place	Total population 25 years and over who are high school graduates	Asian population 25 years and over	Asians 25 years and over who are high school graduates	NHPI[1] population 25 years and over	NHPIs[1] 25 years and over who are high school graduates	Asian Indian	Bangladeshi	Cambodian	Chinese[2]	Fijian	Filipino	Guamanian[3]	Hawaiian, Native	Hmong	Indonesian	Japanese	Korean	Laotian	Malaysian	Pakistani	Samoan	Sri Lankan	Taiwanese	Thai	Tongan	Vietnamese
San Mateo (city)	57,697	10,837	9,675	833	488	1,410	-	-	3,617	-	1,939	-	-	-	-	1,540	432	-	-	-	-	-	-	-	183	209
	85.94		89.28		58.58	89.24			85.79		93.99					90.01	98.63								46.10	85.66
						14.57			37.39		20.04					15.92	4.47								37.50	2.16
			89.28		58.58	13.01			33.38		17.89					14.21	3.99								21.97	1.93
			16.77		0.85	2.44			6.27		3.36					2.67	0.75								0.32	0.36
South San Francisco (city)	32,273	11,705	10,597	497	372	372	-	-	2,845	-	6,228	-	-	-	-	408	-	-	-	-	-	-	-	-	-	-
	79.84		90.53		74.85	72.51			89.80		92.47					90.27										
						3.51			26.85		58.77					3.85										
			90.53		74.85	3.18			24.31		53.21					3.49										
			32.84		1.15	1.15			8.82		19.30					1.26										
Santa Barbara County	195,509	9,580	7,915	516	359	484	-	-	1,301	-	2,547	-	-	69	-	1,602	803	-	-	-	-	-	-	-	-	408
	79.24		82.62		69.57	93.80			85.76		79.77			69.00		89.15	94.36									64.25
						6.11			16.44		32.18			0.87		20.24	10.15									5.15
			82.62		69.57	5.05			13.58		26.59			0.72		16.72	8.38									4.26
			4.05		0.18	0.25			0.67		1.30			0.04		0.82	0.41									0.21
Goleta (cdp)	32,893	2,040	1,749	-	-	-	-	-	466	-	302	-	-	-	-	320	-	-	-	-	-	-	-	-	-	172
	87.82		85.74						88.43		90.42					95.24										65.15
									26.64		17.27					18.30										9.83
			85.74						22.84		14.80					15.69										8.43
			5.32						1.42		0.92					0.97										0.52
Isla Vista (cdp)	2,464	478	434	-	-	-	-	-	200	-	-	-	-	-	-	-	76	-	-	-	-	-	-	-	-	-
	75.65		90.79						88.11								100.00									
									46.08								17.51									
			90.79						41.84								15.90									
			17.61						8.12								3.08									
Lompoc (city)	18,593	967	762	-	-	-	-	-	-	-	221	-	-	-	-	-	-	-	-	-	-	-	-	-	-	-
	74.45		78.80								87.35															
											29.00															
			78.80								22.85															
			4.10								1.19															
Orcutt (cdp)	17,210	757	627	-	-	-	-	-	-	-	-	-	-	-	-	-	-	-	-	-	-	-	-	-	-	-
	89.32		82.83																							
			82.83																							
			3.64																							
Santa Maria (city)	26,708	2,449	1,831	-	-	-	-	-	-	-	1,129	-	-	-	-	311	-	-	-	-	-	-	-	-	-	-
	61.02		74.77								72.56					79.95										
											61.66					16.99										
			74.77								46.10					12.70										
			6.86								4.23					1.16										
Santa Clara County	928,258	288,844	244,928	3,431	2,763	41,274	323	1,059	69,664	219	44,284	714	656	-	395	20,872	12,876	558	-	1,397	697	-	3,457	740	-	42,976
	83.40		84.80		80.53	93.22	95.00	48.91	88.94	74.24	87.80	90.27	85.31		93.60	95.08	89.75	55.03		86.77	74.07		93.99	85.06		68.17
						16.85	0.13	0.43	28.44	7.93	18.08	25.84	23.74		0.16	8.52	5.26	0.23		0.57	25.23		1.41	0.30		17.55
			84.80		80.53	14.29	0.11	0.37	24.12	6.38	15.33	20.81	19.12		0.14	7.23	4.46	0.19		0.48	20.31		1.20	0.26		14.88
			26.39		0.30	4.45	0.03	0.11	7.50	0.02	4.77	0.08	0.07		0.04	2.25	1.39	0.06		0.15	0.08		0.37	0.08		4.63
Alum Rock (cdp)	4,946	821	586	-	-	-	-	-	-	-	-	-	-	-	-	-	-	-	-	-	-	-	-	-	-	219
	60.42		71.38																							62.93
																										37.37
			71.38																							26.67
			11.85																							4.43

Notes: Please refer to the User's Guide for an explanation of data; data is arranged alphabetically by state, then county, then city within each county; table includes counties with populations greater than 49,999 unless noted and cities with populations greater than 9,999 whose Asian and/or NHPI population rates are greater than the national average; (1) Native Hawaiian and other Pacific Islander; (2) excludes Taiwanese; (3) includes Chamorro; (4) county does not meet population threshold but is shown in order to allow inclusion of city

Place	Total population 25 years and over who are high school graduates	Asian population 25 years and over	Asians 25 years and over who are high school graduates	NHPI[1] population 25 years and over	NHPIs[1] 25 years and over who are high school graduates	Asian Indian	Bangladeshi	Cambodian	Chinese[2]	Fijian	Filipino	Guamanian[3]	Hawaiian, Native	Hmong	Indonesian	Japanese	Korean	Laotian	Malaysian	Pakistani	Samoan	Sri Lankan	Taiwanese	Thai	Tongan	Vietnamese
Campbell (city)	24,420 89.74	4,110	3,589 87.32 87.32 14.70	-	-	504 91.64 14.04 12.26 2.06	-	-	991 90.67 27.61 24.11 4.06	-	408 91.48 11.37 9.93 1.67	-	-	-	-	641 91.44 17.86 15.60 2.62	472 80.14 13.15 11.48 1.93	-	-	-	-	-	-	-	-	449 73.97 12.51 10.92 1.84
Cupertino (city)	32,954 95.46	14,254	13,582 95.29 95.29 41.22	-	-	2,846 96.70 20.95 19.97 8.64	-	-	6,327 95.24 46.58 44.39 19.20	-	324 99.39 2.39 2.27 0.98	-	-	-	-	1,635 98.14 12.04 11.47 4.96	1,219 93.41 8.98 8.55 3.70	-	-	-	-	-	535 96.92 3.94 3.75 1.62	-	-	374 82.93 2.75 2.62 1.13
Gilroy (city)	16,893 70.08	1,280	1,112 86.88 86.88 6.58	-	-	-	-	-	210 75.81 18.88 16.41 1.24	-	406 95.08 36.51 31.72 2.40	-	-	-	-	-	-	-	-	-	-	-	-	-	-	-
Los Altos (city)	19,574 97.25	2,929	2,817 96.18 96.18 14.39	-	-	381 100.00 13.53 13.01 1.95	-	-	1,286 95.83 45.65 43.91 6.57	-	-	-	-	-	-	526 94.10 18.67 17.96 2.69	-	-	-	-	-	-	-	-	-	-
Los Gatos (town)	20,545 95.99	1,651	1,534 92.91 92.91 7.47	-	-	-	-	-	640 95.95 41.72 38.76 3.12	-	-	-	-	-	-	293 89.60 19.10 17.75 1.43	-	-	-	-	-	-	-	-	-	-
Milpitas (city)	34,184 83.20	22,053	18,646 84.55 84.55 54.55	295	264 89.49 89.49 0.77	2,709 88.10 14.53 12.28 7.92	-	-	4,888 83.31 26.21 22.16 14.30	-	5,156 90.00 27.65 23.38 15.08	-	-	-	-	492 95.16 2.64 2.23 1.44	578 85.13 3.10 2.62 1.69	-	-	-	-	-	-	-	-	4,012 76.68 21.52 18.19 11.74
Morgan Hill (city)	17,925 86.77	1,521	1,402 92.18 92.18 7.82	-	-	-	-	-	255 80.70 18.19 16.77 1.42	-	-	-	-	-	-	349 98.31 24.89 22.95 1.95	-	-	-	-	-	-	-	-	-	-
Mountain View (city)	46,595 89.00	11,074	10,298 92.99 92.99 22.10	-	-	2,102 96.20 20.41 18.98 4.51	-	-	3,938 92.99 38.24 35.56 8.45	-	1,363 91.72 13.24 12.31 2.93	-	-	-	-	1,447 94.64 14.05 13.07 3.11	522 98.12 5.07 4.71 1.12	-	-	-	-	-	-	-	-	471 77.59 4.57 4.25 1.01
Palo Alto (city)	41,914 96.21	7,310	6,994 95.68 95.68 16.69	-	-	1,029 96.71 14.71 14.08 2.46	-	-	3,663 96.75 52.37 50.11 8.74	-	282 90.97 4.03 3.86 0.67	-	-	-	-	955 95.40 13.65 13.06 2.28	636 98.91 9.09 8.70 1.52	-	-	-	-	-	-	-	-	-
San Jose (city)	447,071 78.33	157,466	125,491 79.69 79.69 28.07	1,884	1,463 77.65 77.65 0.33	14,880 89.75 11.86 9.45 3.33	-	970 49.67 0.77 0.62 0.22	29,873 85.00 23.80 18.97 6.68	-	27,510 86.47 21.92 17.47 6.15	427 90.85 29.19 22.66 0.10	308 84.85 21.05 16.35 0.07	-	-	8,768 94.58 6.99 5.57 1.96	5,374 86.59 4.28 3.41 1.20	479 52.75 0.38 0.30 0.11	-	631 81.84 0.50 0.40 0.14	445 70.97 30.42 23.62 0.10	-	1,321 91.04 1.05 0.84 0.30	340 85.43 0.27 0.22 0.08	-	32,125 65.87 25.60 20.40 7.19

Notes: Please refer to the User's Guide for an explanation of data; data is arranged alphabetically by state, then county, then city within each county; table includes counties with populations greater than 49,999 unless noted and cities with populations greater than 9,999 whose Asian and/or NHPI population rates are greater than the national average; (1) Native Hawaiian and other Pacific Islander; (2) excludes Taiwanese; (3) includes Chamorro; (4) county does not meet population threshold but is shown in order to allow inclusion of city

Place	Total population 25 years and over who are high school graduates	Asian population 25 years and over	Asians 25 years and over who are high school graduates	NHPI[1] population 25 years and over	NHPIs[1] 25 years and over who are high school graduates	Asian Indian	Bangladeshi	Cambodian	Chinese[2]	Fijian	Filipino	Guamanian[3]	Hawaiian, Native	Hmong	Indonesian	Japanese	Korean	Laotian	Malaysian	Pakistani	Samoan	Sri Lankan	Taiwanese	Thai	Tongan	Vietnamese
Santa Clara (city)	60,910	20,579	18,355	250	207	5,892	-	-	3,350	-	3,430	-	-	-	-	1,178	1,398	-	-	203	-	-	-	-	-	2,288
	86.89		89.19		82.80	94.73			91.76		88.93					98.66	92.77			82.52						71.50
						32.10			18.25		18.69					6.42	7.62			1.11						12.47
			89.19		82.80	28.63			16.28		16.67					5.72	6.79			0.99						11.12
			30.13		0.34	9.67			5.50		5.63					1.93	2.30			0.33						3.76
Saratoga (city)	20,217	5,339	5,158	-	-	770	-	-	2,923	-	-	-	-	-	-	423	314	-	-	-	-	-	174	-	-	-
	96.49		96.61			98.84			95.87							96.14	96.91						97.75			
						14.93			56.67							8.20	6.09						3.37			
			96.61			14.42			54.75							7.92	5.88						3.26			
			25.51			3.81			14.46							2.09	1.55						0.86			
Stanford (cdp)	4,407	1,152	1,142	-	-	162	-	-	558	-	-	-	-	-	-	-	122	-	-	-	-	-	-	-	-	-
	99.06		99.13			100.00			98.76								100.00									
						14.19			48.86								10.68									
			99.13			14.06			48.44								10.59									
			25.91			3.68			12.66								2.77									
Sunnyvale (city)	85,189	31,043	28,568	337	255	8,774	-	-	8,820	-	3,813	-	-	-	-	2,629	1,605	-	-	-	-	-	492	-	-	1,588
	89.41		92.03		75.67	96.96			93.15		90.04					94.67	90.37						94.80			73.08
						30.71			30.87		13.35					9.20	5.62						1.72			5.56
			92.03		75.67	28.26			28.41		12.28					8.47	5.17						1.58			5.12
			33.53		0.30	10.30			10.35		4.48					3.09	1.88						0.58			1.86
Santa Cruz County	137,315	5,342	4,605	-	-	557	-	-	999	-	1,117	-	-	-	-	1,272	249	-	-	-	-	-	-	-	-	126
	83.22		86.20			89.84			86.19		84.37					89.26	88.93									70.39
						12.10			21.69		24.26					27.62	5.41									2.74
			86.20			10.43			18.70		20.91					23.81	4.66									2.36
			3.35			0.41			0.73		0.81					0.93	0.18									0.09
Capitola (city)	6,818	293	224	-	-	-	-	-	-	-	-	-	-	-	-	-	-	-	-	-	-	-	-	-	-	-
	91.30		76.45																							
			76.45																							
			3.29																							
Santa Cruz (city)	30,203	1,432	1,312	-	-	256	-	-	356	-	261	-	-	-	-	277	-	-	-	-	-	-	-	-	-	-
	89.10		91.62			92.75			84.56		91.58					100.00										
						19.51			27.13		19.89					21.11										
			91.62			17.88			24.86		18.23					19.34										
			4.34			0.85			1.18		0.86					0.92										
Scotts Valley (city)	7,304	477	459	-	-	-	-	-	-	-	-	-	-	-	-	-	-	-	-	-	-	-	-	-	-	-
	94.83		96.23																							
			96.23																							
			6.28																							
Shasta County	89,320	1,726	1,003	-	-	-	-	-	-	-	307	-	-	-	-	-	-	231	-	-	-	-	-	-	-	-
	83.26		58.11								87.22							32.72								
											30.61							23.03								
			58.11								17.79							13.38								
			1.12								0.34							0.26								
Solano County	206,460	32,267	27,574	1,975	1,472	1,246	-	-	1,852	-	20,677	755	334	58	-	1,463	538	139	-	-	250	-	-	-	-	519
	83.76		85.46		74.53	77.06			80.80		88.47	78.00	73.89	38.93		86.93	77.86	36.20			79.87					64.96
						4.52			6.72		74.99	51.29	22.69	0.21		5.31	1.95	0.50			16.98					1.88
			85.46		74.53	3.86			5.74		64.08	38.23	16.91	0.18		4.53	1.67	0.43			12.66					1.61
			13.36		0.71	0.60			0.90		10.02	0.37	0.16	0.03		0.71	0.26	0.07			0.12					0.25

Notes: Please refer to the User's Guide for an explanation of data; data is arranged alphabetically by state, then county, then city within each county; table includes counties with populations greater than 49,999 unless noted and cities with populations greater than 9,999 whose Asian and/or NHPI population rates are greater than the national average; (1) Native Hawaiian and other Pacific Islander; (2) excludes Taiwanese; (3) includes Chamorro; (4) county does not meet population threshold but is shown in order to allow inclusion of city

Place	Total population 25 years and over who are high school graduates	Asian population 25 years and over	Asians 25 years and over who are high school graduates	NHPI[1] population 25 years and over	NHPIs[1] 25 years and over who are high school graduates	Asian Indian	Bangladeshi	Cambodian	Chinese[2]	Fijian	Filipino	Guamanian[3]	Hawaiian, Native	Hmong	Indonesian	Japanese	Korean	Laotian	Malaysian	Pakistani	Samoan	Sri Lankan	Taiwanese	Thai	Tongan	Vietnamese
Benicia (city)	16,441	1,336	1,229	-	-	-	-	-	276	-	683	-	-	-	-	-	-	-	-	-	-	-	-	-	-	-
	91.70		91.99						86.52		94.21															
									22.46		55.57															
			91.99						20.66		51.12															
			7.48						1.68		4.15															
Fairfield (city)	48,061	6,689	5,611	681	540	470	-	-	530	-	3,449	288	-	-	-	476	190	66	-	-	-	-	-	-	-	-
	85.05		83.88		79.30	81.46			80.79		90.83	78.26				83.51	71.16	34.02								
						8.38			9.45		61.47	53.33				8.48	3.39	1.18								
			83.88		79.30	7.03			7.92		51.56	42.29				7.12	2.84	0.99								
			11.67		1.12	0.98			1.10		7.18	0.60				0.99	0.40	0.14								
Suisun City (city)	12,995	3,032	2,526	-	-	144	-	-	-	-	1,853	-	-	-	-	-	-	-	-	-	-	-	-	-	-	-
	85.57		83.31			65.16					90.66															
						5.70					73.36															
			83.31			4.75					61.11															
			19.44			1.11					14.26															
Vacaville (city)	47,919	2,520	2,183	-	-	-	-	-	-	-	1,112	-	-	-	-	-	-	-	-	-	-	-	-	-	-	-
	83.94		86.63								88.46															
											50.94															
			86.63								44.13															
			4.56								2.32															
Vallejo (city)	60,618	17,842	15,330	854	638	397	-	-	549	-	13,229	330	-	-	-	273	-	-	-	-	-	-	-	-	-	210
	81.74		85.92		74.71	76.79			78.32		87.23	79.90				86.39										65.63
						2.59			3.58		86.29	51.72				1.78										1.37
			85.92		74.71	2.23			3.08		74.15	38.64				1.53										1.18
			25.29		1.05	0.65			0.91		21.82	0.54				0.45										0.35
Sonoma County	260,327	9,302	7,513	447	341	818	-	133	1,804	-	1,618	-	-	-	-	1,197	471	276	-	-	-	-	-	-	-	587
	84.92		80.77		76.29	77.76		36.04	90.97		92.40					90.61	81.35	47.42								66.10
						10.89		1.77	24.01		21.54					15.93	6.27	3.67								7.81
			80.77		76.29	8.79		1.43	19.39		17.39					12.87	5.06	2.97								6.31
			2.89		0.13	0.31		0.05	0.69		0.62					0.46	0.18	0.11								0.23
Petaluma (city)	31,262	1,426	1,187	-	-	-	-	-	458	-	-	-	-	-	-	-	-	-	-	-	-	-	-	-	-	-
	85.94		83.24						92.53																	
									38.58																	
			83.24						32.12																	
			3.80						1.47																	
Rohnert Park (city)	22,456	1,495	1,237	-	-	-	-	-	237	-	432	-	-	-	-	-	-	-	-	-	-	-	-	-	-	-
	88.00		82.74						90.46		97.08															
									19.16		34.92															
			82.74						15.85		28.90															
			5.51						1.06		1.92															
Santa Rosa (city)	82,112	3,564	2,657	-	-	343	-	102	531	-	440	-	-	-	-	323	-	179	-	-	-	-	-	-	-	343
	84.21		74.55			74.08		37.50	90.15		86.96					96.13		50.14								65.33
						12.91		3.84	19.98		16.56					12.16		6.74								12.91
			74.55			9.62		2.86	14.90		12.35					9.06		5.02								9.62
			3.24			0.42		0.12	0.65		0.54					0.39		0.22								0.42
Stanislaus County	186,151	10,090	6,337	944	644	1,444	-	550	845	217	1,604	-	-	81	-	549	-	309	-	-	-	-	-	-	-	388
	70.36		62.80		68.22	58.06		43.69	68.15	65.96	84.11			28.62		86.59		39.16								50.72
						22.79		8.68	13.33	33.70	25.31			1.28		8.66		4.88								6.12
			62.80		68.22	14.31		5.45	8.37	22.99	15.90			0.80		5.44		3.06								3.85
			3.40		0.35	0.78		0.30	0.45	0.12	0.86			0.04		0.29		0.17								0.21

Notes: Please refer to the User's Guide for an explanation of data; data is arranged alphabetically by state, then county, then city within each county; table includes counties with populations greater than 49,999 unless noted and cities with populations greater than 9,999 whose Asian and/or NHPI population rates are greater than the national average; (1) Native Hawaiian and other Pacific Islander; (2) excludes Taiwanese; (3) includes Chamorro; (4) county does not meet population threshold but is shown in order to allow inclusion of city

Place	Total population 25 years and over who are high school graduates	Asian population 25 years and over	Asians 25 years and over who are high school graduates	NHPI[1] population 25 years and over	NHPIs[1] 25 years and over who are high school graduates	Asian Indian	Bangladeshi	Cambodian	Chinese[2]	Fijian	Filipino	Guamanian[3]	Hawaiian, Native	Hmong	Indonesian	Japanese	Korean	Laotian	Malaysian	Pakistani	Samoan	Sri Lankan	Taiwanese	Thai	Tongan	Vietnamese
Ceres (city)	12,832 67.01	985	623 63.25 63.25 4.86	-	-	271 62.88 43.50 27.51 2.11	-	-	-	-	-	-	-	-	-	-	-	-	-	-	-	-	-	-	-	-
Modesto (city)	86,045 75.04	5,985	3,592 60.02 60.02 4.17	624	427 68.43 68.43 0.50	676 57.19 18.82 11.29 0.79	-	409 39.82 11.39 6.83 0.48	488 64.98 13.59 8.15 0.57	164 68.62 38.41 26.28 0.19	868 85.01 24.16 14.50 1.01	-	-	52 50.98 1.45 0.87 0.06	-	260 88.74 7.24 4.34 0.30	-	223 39.19 6.21 3.73 0.26	-	-	-	-	-	-	-	306 51.00 8.52 5.11 0.36
Salida (cdp)	5,427 76.75	308	253 82.14 82.14 4.66	-	-	-	-	-	-	-	-	-	-	-	-	-	-	-	-	-	-	-	-	-	-	-
Turlock (city)	22,984 70.44	1,425	946 66.39 66.39 4.12	-	-	328 51.65 34.67 23.02 1.43	-	-	-	-	-	-	-	-	-	-	-	-	-	-	-	-	-	-	-	-
Sutter County	35,811 72.98	5,426	3,174 58.50 58.50 8.86	-	-	2,251 52.68 70.92 41.49 6.29	-	-	-	-	234 84.17 7.37 4.31 0.65	-	-	-	-	295 87.28 9.29 5.44 0.82	-	-	-	-	-	-	-	-	-	-
South Yuba City (cdp)	6,617 80.29	1,663	952 57.25 57.25 14.39	-	-	797 53.92 83.72 47.93 12.04	-	-	-	-	-	-	-	-	-	-	-	-	-	-	-	-	-	-	-	-
Yuba City (city)	16,110 72.56	1,986	1,223 61.58 61.58 7.59	-	-	681 50.26 55.68 34.29 4.23	-	-	-	-	-	-	-	-	-	-	-	-	-	-	-	-	-	-	-	-
Tehama County	27,435 75.66	222	156 70.27 70.27 0.57	-	-	-	-	-	-	-	-	-	-	-	-	-	-	-	-	-	-	-	-	-	-	-
Tulare County	126,376 61.68	6,683	3,838 57.43 57.43 3.04	-	-	399 75.57 10.40 5.97 0.32	-	-	358 69.92 9.33 5.36 0.28	-	1,820 64.04 47.42 27.23 1.44	-	-	79 23.94 2.06 1.18 0.06	-	513 95.53 13.37 7.68 0.41	250 95.42 6.51 3.74 0.20	201 15.93 5.24 3.01 0.16	-	-	-	-	-	-	-	-
Porterville (city)	13,455 61.75	1,128	598 53.01 53.01 4.44	-	-	-	-	-	-	-	384 67.49 64.21 34.04 2.85	-	-	-	-	-	-	-	-	-	-	-	-	-	-	-

Notes: Please refer to the User's Guide for an explanation of data; data is arranged alphabetically by state, then county, then city within each county; table includes counties with populations greater than 49,999 unless noted and cities with populations greater than 9,999 whose Asian and/or NHPI population rates are greater than the national average; (1) Native Hawaiian and other Pacific Islander; (2) excludes Taiwanese; (3) includes Chamorro; (4) county does not meet population threshold but is shown in order to allow inclusion of city

Place	Total population 25 years and over who are high school graduates	Asian population 25 years and over	Asians 25 years and over who are high school graduates	NHPI[1] population 25 years and over	NHPIs[1] 25 years and over who are high school graduates	Asian Indian	Bangladeshi	Cambodian	Chinese[2]	Fijian	Filipino	Guamanian[3]	Hawaiian, Native	Hmong	Indonesian	Japanese	Korean	Laotian	Malaysian	Pakistani	Samoan	Sri Lankan	Taiwanese	Thai	Tongan	Vietnamese
Visalia (city)	41,184 76.39	2,481	1,374 55.38 55.38 3.34	-	-	-	-	-	-	-	434 83.30 31.59 17.49 1.05	-	-	31 20.39 2.26 1.25 0.08	-	-	-	114 13.44 8.30 4.59 0.28	-	-	-	-	-	-	-	-
Tuolumne County	32,848 84.28	282	255 90.43 90.43 0.78	-	-	-	-	-	-	-	-	-	-	-	-	-	-	-	-	-	-	-	-	-	-	-
Ventura County	377,884 80.10	27,138	23,823 87.78 87.78 6.30	1,012	899 88.83 88.83 0.24	2,516 90.18 10.56 9.27 0.67	-	-	3,296 90.97 13.84 12.15 0.87	-	9,139 86.56 38.36 33.68 2.42	-	370 93.43 41.16 36.56 0.10	-	-	3,841 93.57 16.12 14.15 1.02	1,466 86.54 6.15 5.40 0.39	-	-	-	261 84.19 29.03 25.79 0.07	-	505 96.19 2.12 1.86 0.13	-	-	1,584 73.30 6.65 5.84 0.42
Camarillo (city)	35,300 90.58	2,695	2,377 88.20 88.20 6.73	-	-	-	-	-	356 98.34 14.98 13.21 1.01	-	791 85.42 33.28 29.35 2.24	-	-	-	-	504 88.58 21.20 18.70 1.43	238 91.54 10.01 8.83 0.67	-	-	-	-	-	-	-	-	173 71.19 7.28 6.42 0.49
Moorpark (city)	15,208 84.74	949	910 95.89 95.89 5.98	-	-	-	-	-	-	-	-	-	-	-	-	-	-	-	-	-	-	-	-	-	-	-
Oxnard (city)	57,322 59.46	8,602	7,185 83.53 83.53 12.53	515	447 86.80 86.80 0.78	163 65.20 2.27 1.89 0.28	-	-	150 60.98 2.09 1.74 0.26	-	5,198 85.82 72.35 60.43 9.07	-	-	-	-	867 89.84 12.07 10.08 1.51	241 78.50 3.35 2.80 0.42	-	-	-	218 81.65 48.77 42.33 0.38	-	-	-	-	309 66.17 4.30 3.59 0.54
Port Hueneme (city)	9,735 75.44	958	762 79.54 79.54 7.83	-	-	-	-	-	-	-	562 82.65 73.75 58.66 5.77	-	-	-	-	-	-	-	-	-	-	-	-	-	-	-
Simi Valley (city)	61,823 86.92	4,699	4,097 87.19 87.19 6.63	-	-	821 88.37 20.04 17.47 1.33	-	-	633 86.24 15.45 13.47 1.02	-	858 90.13 20.94 18.26 1.39	-	-	-	-	570 95.96 13.91 12.13 0.92	304 87.86 7.42 6.47 0.49	-	-	-	-	-	-	-	-	482 71.30 11.76 10.26 0.78
Thousand Oaks (city)	71,737 91.43	4,502	4,236 94.09 94.09 5.90	-	-	715 96.36 16.88 15.88 1.00	-	-	1,239 95.45 29.25 27.52 1.73	-	432 91.72 10.20 9.60 0.60	-	-	-	-	718 100.00 16.95 15.95 1.00	286 88.27 6.75 6.35 0.40	-	-	-	-	-	-	-	-	264 85.71 6.23 5.86 0.37
Yolo County	76,124 79.78	6,355	5,525 86.94 86.94 7.26	369	257 69.65 69.65 0.34	621 76.10 11.24 9.77 0.82	-	-	2,069 96.05 37.45 32.56 2.72	148 58.96 57.59 40.11 0.19	643 87.36 11.64 10.12 0.84	-	-	95 55.56 1.72 1.49 0.12	-	898 97.50 16.25 14.13 1.18	432 98.41 7.82 6.80 0.57	44 22.22 0.80 0.69 0.06	-	-	-	-	-	-	-	238 74.38 4.31 3.75 0.31

Notes: Please refer to the User's Guide for an explanation of data; data is arranged alphabetically by state, then county, then city within each county; table includes counties with populations greater than 49,999 unless noted and cities with populations greater than 9,999 whose Asian and/or NHPI population rates are greater than the national average; (1) Native Hawaiian and other Pacific Islander; (2) excludes Taiwanese; (3) includes Chamorro; (4) county does not meet population threshold but is shown in order to allow inclusion of city

Place	Total population 25 years and over who are high school graduates	Asian population 25 years and over	Asians 25 years and over who are high school graduates	NHPI[1] population 25 years and over	NHPIs[1] 25 years and over who are high school graduates	Asian Indian	Bangladeshi	Cambodian	Chinese[2]	Fijian	Filipino	Guamanian[3]	Hawaiian, Native	Hmong	Indonesian	Japanese	Korean	Laotian	Malaysian	Pakistani	Samoan	Sri Lankan	Taiwanese	Thai	Tongan	Vietnamese
Davis (city)	29,287	3,331	3,257	-	-	297	-	-	1,372	-	332	-	-	-	-	504	282	-	-	-	-	-	-	-	-	171
	96.42		97.78			97.70			97.17		94.32					100.00	100.00									96.07
						9.12			42.12		10.19					15.47	8.66									5.25
			97.78			8.92			41.19		9.97					15.13	8.47									5.13
			11.12			1.01			4.68		1.13					1.72	0.96									0.58
West Sacramento (city)	13,428	1,123	680	-	-	156	-	-	-	-	-	-	-	90	-	-	-	-	-	-	-	-	-	-	-	-
	69.93		60.55			58.87								54.22												
						22.94								13.24												
			60.55			13.89								8.01												
			5.06			1.16								0.67												
Woodland (city)	21,844	1,028	748	-	-	152	-	-	-	-	-	-	-	-	-	-	-	-	-	-	-	-	-	-	-	-
	73.00		72.76			65.80																				
						20.32																				
			72.76			14.79																				
			3.42			0.70																				
Yuba County	25,294	1,954	924	-	-	-	-	-	-	-	268	-	-	259	-	-	-	-	-	-	-	-	-	-	-	-
	71.82		47.29								73.02			31.43												
											29.00			28.03												
			47.29								13.72			13.25												
			3.65								1.06			1.02												
Linda (cdp)	4,065	820	259	-	-	-	-	-	-	-	-	-	-	145	-	-	-	-	-	-	-	-	-	-	-	-
	58.90		31.59											25.48												
														55.98												
			31.59											17.68												
			6.37											3.57												
Marysville (city)	5,517	430	269	-	-	-	-	-	-	-	-	-	-	-	-	-	-	-	-	-	-	-	-	-	-	-
	73.78		62.56																							
			62.56																							
			4.88																							
Olivehurst (cdp)	3,741	275	123	-	-	-	-	-	-	-	-	-	-	-	-	-	-	-	-	-	-	-	-	-	-	-
	58.40		44.73																							
			44.73																							
			3.29																							
COLORADO	2,413,593	60,422	49,425	2,357	1,984	7,267	-	329	8,454	-	5,709	517	738	637	442	8,754	7,951	725	-	427	372	-	427	1,162	-	4,881
	86.93		81.80		84.17	94.16		45.95	84.27		89.99	79.42	86.93	55.49	96.72	91.75	81.42	59.43		96.83	88.36		95.31	84.26		58.15
						14.70		0.67	17.10		11.55	26.06	37.20	1.29	0.89	17.71	16.09	1.47		0.86	18.75		0.86	2.35		9.88
			81.80		84.17	12.03		0.54	13.99		9.45	21.93	31.31	1.05	0.73	14.49	13.16	1.20		0.71	15.78		0.71	1.92		8.08
			2.05		0.08	0.30		0.01	0.35		0.24	0.02	0.03	0.03	0.02	0.36	0.33	0.03		0.02	0.02		0.02	0.05		0.20
Adams County	175,854	6,899	4,784	-	-	279	-	-	537	-	581	-	-	553	-	754	530	286	-	-	-	-	-	-	-	706
	78.83		69.34			80.17			69.20		95.56			64.45		89.76	78.52	52.19								51.12
						5.83			11.22		12.14			11.56		15.76	11.08	5.98								14.76
			69.34			4.04			7.78		8.42			8.02		10.93	7.68	4.15								10.23
			2.72			0.16			0.31		0.33			0.31		0.43	0.30	0.16								0.40
Berkley (cdp)	4,410	208	100	-	-	-	-	-	-	-	-	-	-	-	-	-	-	-	-	-	-	-	-	-	-	-
	67.98		48.08																							
			48.08																							
			2.27																							

Notes: Please refer to the User's Guide for an explanation of data; data is arranged alphabetically by state, then county, then city within each county; table includes counties with populations greater than 49,999 unless noted and cities with populations greater than 9,999 whose Asian and/or NHPI population rates are greater than the national average; (1) Native Hawaiian and other Pacific Islander; (2) excludes Taiwanese; (3) includes Chamorro; (4) county does not meet population threshold but is shown in order to allow inclusion of city

Place	Total population 25 years and over who are high school graduates	Asian population 25 years and over	Asians 25 years and over who are high school graduates	NHPI[1] population 25 years and over	NHPIs[1] 25 years and over who are high school graduates	Asian Indian	Bangladeshi	Cambodian	Chinese[2]	Fijian	Filipino	Guamanian[3]	Hawaiian, Native	Hmong	Indonesian	Japanese	Korean	Laotian	Malaysian	Pakistani	Samoan	Sri Lankan	Taiwanese	Thai	Tongan	Vietnamese
Federal Heights (city)	5,615	441	277	-	-	-	-	-	-	-	-	-	-	-	-	-	-	-	-	-	-	-	-	-	-	-
	74.38		62.81																							
			62.81																							
			4.93																							
Westminster (city)	57,642	3,133	2,359	-	-	262	-	-	301	-	-	-	-	209	-	-	329	237	-	-	-	-	-	-	-	312
	89.11		75.30			84.24			70.49					58.87			83.93	60.46								64.33
						11.11			12.76					8.86			13.95	10.05								13.23
			75.30			8.36			9.61					6.67			10.50	7.56								9.96
			4.09			0.45			0.52					0.36			0.57	0.41								0.54
Arapahoe County	286,986	12,547	10,354	379	306	1,461	-	-	1,763	-	1,346	-	-	-	-	1,253	2,275	-	-	-	-	-	-	-	-	1,155
	90.66		82.52		80.74	95.87			81.92		88.55					90.60	79.38									62.37
						14.11			17.03		13.00					12.10	21.97									11.16
			82.52		80.74	11.64			14.05		10.73					9.99	18.13									9.21
			3.61		0.11	0.51			0.61		0.47					0.44	0.79									0.40
Aurora (city)	146,565	7,737	5,810	275	222	547	-	68	907	-	938	-	-	-	-	750	1,283	-	-	-	-	-	-	-	-	636
	84.99		75.09		80.73	90.41		33.33	77.59		86.29					89.61	74.29									49.11
						9.41		1.17	15.61		16.14					12.91	22.08									10.95
			75.09		80.73	7.07		0.88	11.72		12.12					9.69	16.58									8.22
			3.96		0.15	0.37		0.05	0.62		0.64					0.51	0.88									0.43
Boulder County	172,722	5,711	5,148	-	-	745	-	-	1,512	-	263	-	-	-	-	931	665	-	-	-	-	-	-	-	-	296
	92.80		90.14			98.54			94.74		94.60					98.62	97.36									74.56
						14.47			29.37		5.11					18.08	12.92									5.75
			90.14			13.05			26.48		4.61					16.30	11.64									5.18
			2.98			0.43			0.88		0.15					0.54	0.39									0.17
Boulder (city)	53,251	2,145	1,975	-	-	242	-	-	599	-	-	-	-	-	-	339	439	-	-	-	-	-	-	-	-	-
	94.70		92.07			100.00			96.93							100.00	97.56									
						12.25			30.33							17.16	22.23									
			92.07			11.28			27.93							15.80	20.47									
			3.71			0.45			1.12							0.64	0.82									
Broomfield (city)	22,628	965	736	-	-	-	-	-	181	-	-	-	-	-	-	-	-	-	-	-	-	-	-	-	-	-
	93.06		76.27						81.17																	
									24.59																	
			76.27						18.76																	
			3.25						0.80																	
Lafayette (city)	13,783	585	530	-	-	-	-	-	-	-	-	-	-	-	-	-	-	-	-	-	-	-	-	-	-	-
	91.01		90.60																							
			90.60																							
			3.85																							
Denver County	295,444	10,055	7,741	223	170	1,321	-	46	1,155	-	607	-	-	-	-	1,593	756	-	-	-	-	-	-	207	-	1,397
	78.89		76.99		76.23	94.09		22.44	77.31		88.10					92.67	85.52							79.01		53.00
						17.06		0.59	14.92		7.84					20.58	9.77							2.67		18.05
			76.99		76.23	13.14		0.46	11.49		6.04					15.84	7.52							2.06		13.89
			2.62		0.06	0.45		0.02	0.39		0.21					0.54	0.26							0.07		0.47
Douglas County	109,013	2,866	2,547	-	-	482	-	-	749	-	-	-	-	-	-	-	361	-	-	-	-	-	-	-	-	-
	96.96		88.87			92.51			85.11								91.39									
						18.92			29.41								14.17									
			88.87			16.82			26.13								12.60									
			2.34			0.44			0.69								0.33									

Notes: Please refer to the User's Guide for an explanation of data; data is arranged alphabetically by state, then county, then city within each county; table includes counties with populations greater than 49,999 unless noted and cities with populations greater than 9,999 whose Asian and/or NHPI population rates are greater than the national average; (1) Native Hawaiian and other Pacific Islander; (2) excludes Taiwanese; (3) includes Chamorro; (4) county does not meet population threshold but is shown in order to allow inclusion of city

Place	Total population 25 years and over who are high school graduates	Asian population 25 years and over	Asians 25 years and over who are high school graduates	NHPI[1] population 25 years and over	NHPIs[1] 25 years and over who are high school graduates	Asian Indian	Bangladeshi	Cambodian	Chinese[2]	Fijian	Filipino	Guamanian[3]	Hawaiian, Native	Hmong	Indonesian	Japanese	Korean	Laotian	Malaysian	Pakistani	Samoan	Sri Lankan	Taiwanese	Thai	Tongan	Vietnamese
Highlands Ranch (cdp)	43,893	1,932	1,693	-	-	385	-	-	524	-	-	-	-	-	-	-	-	-	-	-	-	-	-	-	-	-
	97.84		87.63			100.00			84.11																	
						22.74			30.95																	
			87.63			19.93			27.12																	
			3.86			0.88			1.19																	
El Paso County	292,391	9,028	7,454	670	620	1,350	-	-	650	-	1,447	284	-	-	-	1,017	1,996	-	-	-	-	-	-	-	-	368
	91.25		82.57		92.54	96.64			95.73		86.91	94.98				84.68	73.25									60.73
						18.11			8.72		19.41	45.81				13.64	26.78									4.94
			82.57		92.54	14.95			7.20		16.03	42.39				11.26	22.11									4.08
			2.55		0.21	0.46			0.22		0.49	0.10				0.35	0.68									0.13
Colorado Springs (city)	207,770	6,993	5,817	407	357	1,319	-	-	518	-	944	-	-	-	-	718	1,562	-	-	-	-	-	-	-	-	273
	90.90		83.18		87.71	96.56			94.70		85.05					85.68	76.57									56.17
						22.67			8.90		16.23					12.34	26.85									4.69
			83.18		87.71	18.86			7.41		13.50					10.27	22.34									3.90
			2.80		0.17	0.63			0.25		0.45					0.35	0.75									0.13
Jefferson County	322,832	7,358	6,255	230	214	948	-	-	1,012	-	628	-	-	29	-	1,435	817	340	-	-	-	-	-	-	-	628
	91.82		85.01		93.04	96.93			82.21		96.17			25.00		93.30	88.23	70.10								65.21
						15.16			16.18		10.04			0.46		22.94	13.06	5.44								10.04
			85.01		93.04	12.88			13.75		8.53			0.39		19.50	11.10	4.62								8.53
			1.94		0.07	0.29			0.31		0.19			0.01		0.44	0.25	0.11								0.19
Larimer County	144,413	2,165	1,947	-	-	307	-	-	549	-	-	-	-	-	-	332	246	-	-	-	-	-	-	-	-	-
	92.32		89.93			88.22			88.12							90.22	100.00									
						15.77			28.20							17.05	12.63									
			89.93			14.18			25.36							15.33	11.36									
			1.35			0.21			0.38							0.23	0.17									
Mesa County	64,905	278	236	-	-	-	-	-	-	-	-	-	-	-	-	-	-	-	-	-	-	-	-	-	-	-
	85.00		84.89																							
			84.89																							
			0.36																							
Pueblo County	74,881	538	470	-	-	-	-	-	-	-	-	-	-	-	-	-	-	-	-	-	-	-	-	-	-	-
	81.32		87.36																							
			87.36																							
			0.63																							
Weld County	84,612	821	681	-	-	-	-	-	-	-	-	-	-	-	-	302	-	-	-	-	-	-	-	-	-	-
	79.64		82.95													89.09										
																44.35										
			82.95													36.78										
			0.80													0.36										
CONNECTICUT	1,927,961	51,977	44,186	700	562	14,003	193	616	10,779	-	4,949	207	-	-	-	2,730	3,248	1,075	-	1,113	-	-	376	364	-	2,898
	83.98		85.01		80.29	88.08	88.53	52.83	86.85		93.50	88.84				93.94	90.63	59.16		94.08			98.43	78.96		63.33
						31.69	0.44	1.39	24.39		11.20	36.83				6.18	7.35	2.43		2.52			0.85	0.82		6.56
			85.01		80.29	26.94	0.37	1.19	20.74		9.52	29.57				5.25	6.25	2.07		2.14			0.72	0.70		5.58
			2.29		0.03	0.73	0.01	0.03	0.56		0.26	0.01				0.14	0.17	0.06		0.06			0.02	0.02		0.15
Fairfield County	503,136	18,576	15,826	-	-	5,255	-	383	3,636	-	1,659	-	-	-	-	1,534	1,008	304	-	275	-	-	-	-	-	865
	84.37		85.20			89.25		50.93	89.12		96.01					96.36	91.97	50.08		92.28						58.25
						33.20		2.42	22.97		10.48					9.69	6.37	1.92		1.74						5.47
			85.20			28.29		2.06	19.57		8.93					8.26	5.43	1.64		1.48						4.66
			3.15			1.04		0.08	0.72		0.33					0.30	0.20	0.06		0.05						0.17

Notes: Please refer to the User's Guide for an explanation of data; data is arranged alphabetically by state, then county, then city within each county; table includes counties with populations greater than 49,999 unless noted and cities with populations greater than 9,999 whose Asian and/or NHPI population rates are greater than the national average; (1) Native Hawaiian and other Pacific Islander; (2) excludes Taiwanese; (3) includes Chamorro; (4) county does not meet population threshold but is shown in order to allow inclusion of city

Place	Total population 25 years and over who are high school graduates	Asian population 25 years and over	Asians 25 years and over who are high school graduates	NHPI[1] population 25 years and over	NHPIs[1] 25 years and over who are high school graduates	Asian Indian	Bangladeshi	Cambodian	Chinese[2]	Fijian	Filipino	Guamanian[3]	Hawaiian, Native	Hmong	Indonesian	Japanese	Korean	Laotian	Malaysian	Pakistani	Samoan	Sri Lankan	Taiwanese	Thai	Tongan	Vietnamese
Danbury (city)	39,434 76.98	2,374	1,807 76.12 76.12 4.58	-	-	677 77.37 37.47 28.52 1.72	-	136 48.57 7.53 5.73 0.34	263 70.70 14.55 11.08 0.67	-	-	-	-	-	-	-	-	-	-	-	-	-	-	-	-	-
Greenwich (town)	39,659 92.08	2,039	1,864 91.42 91.42 4.70	-	-	262 87.04 14.06 12.85 0.66	-	-	448 93.53 24.03 21.97 1.13	-	-	-	-	-	-	731 97.73 39.22 35.85 1.84	-	-	-	-	-	-	-	-	-	-
Stamford (city)	68,145 82.22	4,159	3,784 90.98 90.98 5.55	-	-	1,969 92.97 52.03 47.34 2.89	-	-	807 94.39 21.33 19.40 1.18	-	502 94.18 13.27 12.07 0.74	-	-	-	-	-	-	-	-	-	-	-	-	-	-	-
Hartford County	477,537 82.36	13,339	10,839 81.26 81.26 2.27	-	-	3,748 85.24 34.58 28.10 0.78	-	-	2,119 82.97 19.55 15.89 0.44	-	1,138 92.07 10.50 8.53 0.24	-	-	-	-	294 83.29 2.71 2.20 0.06	729 86.37 6.73 5.47 0.15	445 60.30 4.11 3.34 0.09	-	363 98.91 3.35 2.72 0.08	-	-	-	-	-	1,307 65.74 12.06 9.80 0.27
East Hartford (town)	26,290 77.42	1,385	990 71.48 71.48 3.77	-	-	281 67.87 28.38 20.29 1.07	-	-	-	-	-	-	-	-	-	-	-	-	-	-	-	-	-	-	-	266 69.63 26.87 19.21 1.01
Farmington (town)	15,386 91.62	650	605 93.08 93.08 3.93	-	-	-	-	-	-	-	-	-	-	-	-	-	-	-	-	-	-	-	-	-	-	-
Glastonbury (town)	20,617 93.73	747	655 87.68 87.68 3.18	-	-	273 86.12 41.68 36.55 1.32	-	-	-	-	-	-	-	-	-	-	-	-	-	-	-	-	-	-	-	-
Rocky Hill (town)	11,690 88.21	477	464 97.27 97.27 3.97	-	-	-	-	-	-	-	-	-	-	-	-	-	-	-	-	-	-	-	-	-	-	-
South Windsor (town)	15,112 91.38	583	468 80.27 80.27 3.10	-	-	-	-	-	-	-	-	-	-	-	-	-	-	-	-	-	-	-	-	-	-	-
West Hartford (town)	39,235 90.29	1,960	1,619 82.60 82.60 4.13	-	-	446 89.38 27.55 22.76 1.14	-	-	429 78.28 26.50 21.89 1.09	-	-	-	-	-	-	-	-	-	-	-	-	-	-	-	-	311 75.49 19.21 15.87 0.79

Notes: Please refer to the User's Guide for an explanation of data; data is arranged alphabetically by state, then county, then city within each county; table includes counties with populations greater than 49,999 unless noted and cities with populations greater than 9,999 whose Asian and/or NHPI population rates are greater than the national average; (1) Native Hawaiian and other Pacific Islander; (2) excludes Taiwanese; (3) includes Chamorro; (4) county does not meet population threshold but is shown in order to allow inclusion of city

Place	Total population 25 years and over who are high school graduates	Asian population 25 years and over	Asians 25 years and over who are high school graduates	NHPI[1] population 25 years and over	NHPIs[1] 25 years and over who are high school graduates	Asian Indian	Bangladeshi	Cambodian	Chinese[2]	Fijian	Filipino	Guamanian[3]	Hawaiian, Native	Hmong	Indonesian	Japanese	Korean	Laotian	Malaysian	Pakistani	Samoan	Sri Lankan	Taiwanese	Thai	Tongan	Vietnamese
Litchfield County	109,342	1,321	966	-	-	285	-	-	128	-	-	-	-	-	-	-	119	-	-	-	-	-	-	-	-	72
	85.89		73.13			93.14			57.92								75.32									41.62
						29.50			13.25								12.32									7.45
			73.13			21.57			9.69								9.01									5.45
			0.88			0.26			0.12								0.11									0.07
Middlesex County	95,922	1,311	1,148	-	-	358	-	-	333	-	-	-	-	-	-	-	-	-	-	-	-	-	-	-	-	-
	88.73		87.57			84.43			89.28																	
						31.18			29.01																	
			87.57			27.31			25.40																	
			1.20			0.37			0.35																	
New Haven County	457,905	12,209	10,957	-	-	3,324	-	-	3,118	-	1,113	-	-	-	-	581	1,015	215	-	337	-	-	-	-	-	433
	83.01		89.75			88.10			90.40		95.37					96.19	94.68	73.63		88.68						72.77
						30.34			28.46		10.16					5.30	9.26	1.96		3.08						3.95
			89.75			27.23			25.54		9.12					4.76	8.31	1.76		2.76						3.55
			2.39			0.73			0.68		0.24					0.13	0.22	0.05		0.07						0.09
New Haven (city)	53,096	2,635	2,468	-	-	427	-	-	1,081	-	-	-	-	-	-	-	235	-	-	-	-	-	-	-	-	-
	73.57		93.66			91.83			97.92								92.16									
						17.30			43.80								9.52									
			93.66			16.20			41.02								8.92									
			4.65			0.80			2.04								0.44									
New London County	149,634	3,023	2,556	-	-	587	-	-	725	-	676	-	-	-	-	-	-	-	-	-	-	-	-	-	-	-
	86.04		84.55			92.30			80.82		88.14															
						22.97			28.36		26.45															
			84.55			19.42			23.98		22.36															
			1.71			0.39			0.48		0.45															
Tolland County	77,778	1,820	1,597	-	-	419	-	-	633	-	-	-	-	-	-	-	-	-	-	-	-	-	-	-	-	-
	89.19		87.75			93.74			89.28																	
						26.24			39.64																	
			87.75			23.02			34.78																	
			2.05			0.54			0.81																	
Mansfield (town)	7,927	732	732	-	-	178	-	-	369	-	-	-	-	-	-	-	-	-	-	-	-	-	-	-	-	-
	91.32		100.00			100.00			100.00																	
						24.32			50.41																	
			100.00			24.32			50.41																	
			9.23			2.25			4.65																	
Storrs (cdp)	2,082	487	487	-	-	-	-	-	317	-	-	-	-	-	-	-	-	-	-	-	-	-	-	-	-	-
	92.49		100.00						100.00																	
									65.09																	
			100.00						65.09																	
			23.39						15.23																	
Windham County	56,707	378	297	-	-	-	-	-	-	-	-	-	-	-	-	-	-	-	-	-	-	-	-	-	-	-
	79.60		78.57																							
			78.57																							
			0.52																							
DELAWARE	425,122	10,915	9,616	150	80	3,218	-	-	2,535	-	1,171	-	-	-	-	421	999	-	-	209	-	-	-	-	-	277
	82.60		88.10		53.33	92.05			88.39		87.00					84.20	86.64			96.76						61.83
						33.47			26.36		12.18					4.38	10.39			2.17						2.88
			88.10		53.33	29.48			23.22		10.73					3.86	9.15			1.91						2.54
			2.26		0.02	0.76			0.60		0.28					0.10	0.23			0.05						0.07

Notes: Please refer to the User's Guide for an explanation of data; data is arranged alphabetically by state, then county, then city within each county; table includes counties with populations greater than 49,999 unless noted and cities with populations greater than 9,999 whose Asian and/or NHPI population rates are greater than the national average; (1) Native Hawaiian and other Pacific Islander; (2) excludes Taiwanese; (3) includes Chamorro; (4) county does not meet population threshold but is shown in order to allow inclusion of city

Place	Total population 25 years and over who are high school graduates	Asian population 25 years and over	Asians 25 years and over who are high school graduates	NHPI[1] population 25 years and over	NHPIs[1] 25 years and over who are high school graduates	Asian Indian	Bangladeshi	Cambodian	Chinese[2]	Fijian	Filipino	Guamanian[3]	Hawaiian, Native	Hmong	Indonesian	Japanese	Korean	Laotian	Malaysian	Pakistani	Samoan	Sri Lankan	Taiwanese	Thai	Tongan	Vietnamese
Kent County	62,937 79.42	1,477	1,108 75.02 75.02 1.76	-	-	268 97.81 24.19 18.14 0.43	-	-	-	-	244 67.40 22.02 16.52 0.39	-	-	-	-	-	-	-	-	-	-	-	-	-	-	-
New Castle County	277,565 85.45	8,883	8,091 91.08 91.08 2.91	-	-	2,885 92.77 35.66 32.48 1.04	-	-	2,350 89.29 29.04 26.46 0.85	-	776 96.64 9.59 8.74 0.28	-	-	-	-	287 92.58 3.55 3.23 0.10	755 90.10 9.33 8.50 0.27	-	-	-	-	-	-	-	-	258 72.88 3.19 2.90 0.09
Hockessin (cdp)	8,419 96.31	544	528 97.06 97.06 6.27	-	-	-	-	-	-	-	-	-	-	-	-	-	-	-	-	-	-	-	-	-	-	-
Newark (city)	11,780 93.42	735	725 98.64 98.64 6.15	-	-	-	-	-	403 97.58 55.59 54.83 3.42	-	-	-	-	-	-	-	-	-	-	-	-	-	-	-	-	-
Pike Creek (cdp)	13,068 95.60	688	680 98.84 98.84 5.20	-	-	-	-	-	-	-	-	-	-	-	-	-	-	-	-	-	-	-	-	-	-	-
Sussex County	84,620 76.51	555	417 75.14 75.14 0.49	-	-	-	-	-	-	-	-	-	-	-	-	-	-	-	-	-	-	-	-	-	-	-
DISTRICT OF COLUMBIA	299,286 77.83	9,875	8,083 81.85 81.85 2.70	-	-	1,593 92.83 19.71 16.13 0.53	-	-	1,961 73.09 24.26 19.86 0.66	-	1,374 87.74 17.00 13.91 0.46	-	-	-	-	743 93.69 9.19 7.52 0.25	796 99.13 9.85 8.06 0.27	-	-	-	-	-	-	-	-	610 55.61 7.55 6.18 0.20
FLORIDA	8,804,697 79.86	177,289	143,001 80.66 80.66 1.62	4,096	2,930 71.53 71.53 0.03	37,097 85.72 25.94 20.92 0.42	678 80.43 0.47 0.38 0.01	823 53.55 0.58 0.46 0.01	24,216 77.01 16.93 13.66 0.28	-	33,761 88.44 23.61 19.04 0.38	745 62.87 25.43 18.19 0.01	1,010 76.05 34.47 24.66 0.01	-	647 93.63 0.45 0.36 0.01	8,143 88.12 5.69 4.59 0.09	10,830 82.56 7.57 6.11 0.12	1,443 59.36 1.01 0.81 0.02	-	2,797 84.60 1.96 1.58 0.03	376 75.35 12.83 9.18 <0.01	268 93.06 0.19 0.15 <0.01	1,289 92.80 0.90 0.73 0.01	3,625 71.27 2.53 2.04 0.04	-	13,059 61.58 9.13 7.37 0.15
Alachua County	108,766 88.05	4,231	4,096 96.81 96.81 3.77	-	-	831 96.63 20.29 19.64 0.76	-	-	1,268 98.68 30.96 29.97 1.17	-	586 98.16 14.31 13.85 0.54	-	-	-	-	288 96.64 7.03 6.81 0.26	569 98.27 13.89 13.45 0.52	-	-	-	-	-	-	-	-	271 84.42 6.62 6.41 0.25
Gainesville (city)	44,391 87.77	2,330	2,232 95.79 95.79 5.03	-	-	407 96.90 18.23 17.47 0.92	-	-	874 98.09 39.16 37.51 1.97	-	-	-	-	-	-	-	270 96.43 12.10 11.59 0.61	-	-	-	-	-	-	-	-	-

Notes: Please refer to the User's Guide for an explanation of data; data is arranged alphabetically by state, then county, then city within each county; table includes counties with populations greater than 49,999 unless noted and cities with populations greater than 9,999 whose Asian and/or NHPI population rates are greater than the national average; (1) Native Hawaiian and other Pacific Islander; (2) excludes Taiwanese; (3) includes Chamorro; (4) county does not meet population threshold but is shown in order to allow inclusion of city

Place	Total population 25 years and over who are high school graduates	Asian population 25 years and over	Asians 25 years and over who are high school graduates	NHPI[1] population 25 years and over	NHPIs[1] 25 years and over who are high school graduates	Asian Indian	Bangladeshi	Cambodian	Chinese[2]	Fijian	Filipino	Guamanian[3]	Hawaiian, Native	Hmong	Indonesian	Japanese	Korean	Laotian	Malaysian	Pakistani	Samoan	Sri Lankan	Taiwanese	Thai	Tongan	Vietnamese
Bay County	80,855 81.04	1,586	1,020 64.31 64.31 1.26	-	-	-	-	-	-	-	238 73.46 23.33 15.01 0.29	-	-	-	-	-	-	-	-	-	-	-	-	-	-	153 42.27 15.00 9.65 0.19
Callaway (city)	7,267 83.25	355	231 65.07 65.07 3.18	-	-	-	-	-	-	-	-	-	-	-	-	-	-	-	-	-	-	-	-	-	-	-
Brevard County	293,322 86.34	5,153	4,249 82.46 82.46 1.45	-	-	1,125 87.07 26.48 21.83 0.38	-	-	533 75.60 12.54 10.34 0.18	-	973 84.61 22.90 18.88 0.33	-	-	-	-	415 94.32 9.77 8.05 0.14	385 73.33 9.06 7.47 0.13	-	-	-	-	-	-	-	-	394 81.24 9.27 7.65 0.13
Broward County	923,268 81.96	24,543	19,872 80.97 80.97 2.15	439	346 78.82 78.82 0.04	7,050 83.63 35.48 28.73 0.76	-	-	4,202 70.30 21.15 17.12 0.46	-	3,117 90.03 15.69 12.70 0.34	-	-	-	-	805 93.28 4.05 3.28 0.09	1,367 91.74 6.88 5.57 0.15	-	-	580 87.75 2.92 2.36 0.06	-	-	-	384 78.85 1.93 1.56 0.04	-	1,219 65.43 6.13 4.97 0.13
Cooper City (city)	15,873 92.14	735	648 88.16 88.16 4.08	-	-	328 90.86 50.62 44.63 2.07	-	-	-	-	-	-	-	-	-	-	-	-	-	-	-	-	-	-	-	-
Pembroke Pines (city)	82,419 88.05	3,411	2,957 86.69 86.69 3.59	-	-	1,059 91.85 35.81 31.05 1.28	-	-	532 69.00 17.99 15.60 0.65	-	655 93.57 22.15 19.20 0.79	-	-	-	-	-	-	-	-	-	-	-	-	-	-	-
Charlotte County	92,886 82.15	674	573 85.01 85.01 0.62	-	-	-	-	-	-	-	-	-	-	-	-	-	-	-	-	-	-	-	-	-	-	-
Citrus County	72,516 78.32	834	684 82.01 82.01 0.94	-	-	-	-	-	-	-	-	-	-	-	-	-	-	-	-	-	-	-	-	-	-	-
Clay County	78,085 86.39	2,076	1,709 82.32 82.32 2.19	-	-	-	-	-	-	-	1,117 86.52 65.36 53.81 1.43	-	-	-	-	-	-	-	-	-	-	-	-	-	-	-
Bellair-Meadowbrook Ter. (cdp)	9,192 87.09	517	439 84.91 84.91 4.78	-	-	-	-	-	-	-	-	-	-	-	-	-	-	-	-	-	-	-	-	-	-	-

Notes: Please refer to the User's Guide for an explanation of data; data is arranged alphabetically by state, then county, then city within each county; table includes counties with populations greater than 49,999 unless noted and cities with populations greater than 9,999 whose Asian and/or NHPI population rates are greater than the national average; (1) Native Hawaiian and other Pacific Islander; (2) excludes Taiwanese; (3) includes Chamorro; (4) county does not meet population threshold but is shown in order to allow inclusion of city

Place	Total population 25 years and over who are high school graduates	Asian population 25 years and over	Asians 25 years and over who are high school graduates	NHPI[1] population 25 years and over	NHPIs[1] 25 years and over who are high school graduates	Asian Indian	Bangladeshi	Cambodian	Chinese[2]	Fijian	Filipino	Guamanian[3]	Hawaiian, Native	Hmong	Indonesian	Japanese	Korean	Laotian	Malaysian	Pakistani	Samoan	Sri Lankan	Taiwanese	Thai	Tongan	Vietnamese
Collier County	151,535 81.75	876	762 86.99 86.99 0.50	-	-	-	-	-	-	-	-	-	-	-	-	-	-	-	-	-	-	-	-	-	-	-
Columbia County	27,547 74.69	249	202 81.12 81.12 0.73	-	-	-	-	-	-	-	-	-	-	-	-	-	-	-	-	-	-	-	-	-	-	-
Duval County	413,266 82.72	13,470	10,931 81.15 81.15 2.65	286	220 76.92 76.92 0.05	1,684 91.92 15.41 12.50 0.41	-	249 46.89 2.28 1.85 0.06	877 83.05 8.02 6.51 0.21	-	6,003 87.62 54.92 44.57 1.45	-	-	-	-	382 83.22 3.49 2.84 0.09	497 75.19 4.55 3.69 0.12	-	-	-	-	-	-	-	-	611 48.11 5.59 4.54 0.15
Escambia County	155,668 82.06	4,153	3,073 73.99 73.99 1.97	-	-	300 88.24 9.76 7.22 0.19	-	-	253 67.29 8.23 6.09 0.16	-	1,546 83.79 50.31 37.23 0.99	-	-	-	-	-	-	-	-	-	-	-	-	-	-	326 41.69 10.61 7.85 0.21
Bellview (cdp)	11,439 83.36	518	391 75.48 75.48 3.42	-	-	-	-	-	-	-	245 83.33 62.66 47.30 2.14	-	-	-	-	-	-	-	-	-	-	-	-	-	-	-
Myrtle Grove (cdp)	8,947 84.09	521	373 71.59 71.59 4.17	-	-	-	-	-	-	-	275 81.12 73.73 52.78 3.07	-	-	-	-	-	-	-	-	-	-	-	-	-	-	-
Hernando County	77,747 78.47	545	423 77.61 77.61 0.54	-	-	-	-	-	-	-	-	-	-	-	-	-	-	-	-	-	-	-	-	-	-	-
Highlands County	48,500 74.52	648	522 80.56 80.56 1.08	-	-	-	-	-	-	-	268 87.30 51.34 41.36 0.55	-	-	-	-	-	-	-	-	-	-	-	-	-	-	-
Hillsborough County	528,058 80.76	14,352	11,689 81.45 81.45 2.21	325	237 72.92 72.92 0.04	3,170 88.08 27.12 22.09 0.60	-	-	1,464 80.97 12.52 10.20 0.28	-	2,031 93.98 17.38 14.15 0.38	-	-	-	-	619 82.86 5.30 4.31 0.12	1,554 82.48 13.29 10.83 0.29	-	-	-	-	-	-	426 78.74 3.64 2.97 0.08	-	1,628 61.57 13.93 11.34 0.31
Westchase (cdp)	7,377 96.62	341	289 84.75 84.75 3.92	-	-	-	-	-	-	-	-	-	-	-	-	-	-	-	-	-	-	-	-	-	-	-

Notes: Please refer to the User's Guide for an explanation of data; data is arranged alphabetically by state, then county, then city within each county; table includes counties with populations greater than 49,999 unless noted and cities with populations greater than 9,999 whose Asian and/or NHPI population rates are greater than the national average; (1) Native Hawaiian and other Pacific Islander; (2) excludes Taiwanese; (3) includes Chamorro; (4) county does not meet population threshold but is shown in order to allow inclusion of city

Place	Total population 25 years and over who are high school graduates	Asian population 25 years and over	Asians 25 years and over who are high school graduates	NHPI[1] population 25 years and over	NHPIs[1] 25 years and over who are high school graduates	Asian Indian	Bangladeshi	Cambodian	Chinese[2]	Fijian	Filipino	Guamanian[3]	Hawaiian, Native	Hmong	Indonesian	Japanese	Korean	Laotian	Malaysian	Pakistani	Samoan	Sri Lankan	Taiwanese	Thai	Tongan	Vietnamese
Indian River County	68,940 81.56	592	521 88.01 88.01 0.76	-	-	-	-	-	-	-	-	-	-	-	-	-	-	-	-	-	-	-	-	-	-	-
Lake County	124,090 79.76	1,000	798 79.80 79.80 0.64	-	-	-	-	-	-	-	-	-	-	-	-	-	-	-	-	-	-	-	-	-	-	-
Lee County	269,652 82.29	2,321	1,921 82.77 82.77 0.71	-	-	377 86.07 19.63 16.24 0.14	-	-	332 80.98 17.28 14.30 0.12	-	755 87.89 39.30 32.53 0.28	-	-	-	-	-	-	-	-	-	-	-	-	-	-	-
Leon County	122,570 89.12	3,165	2,909 91.91 91.91 2.37	-	-	894 96.13 30.73 28.25 0.73	-	-	726 96.41 24.96 22.94 0.59	-	305 95.31 10.48 9.64 0.25	-	-	-	-	-	298 91.41 10.24 9.42 0.24	-	-	-	-	-	-	-	-	-
Manatee County	157,012 81.44	1,589	1,164 73.25 73.25 0.74	-	-	-	-	-	-	-	279 76.65 23.97 17.56 0.18	-	-	-	-	-	-	-	-	-	-	-	-	-	-	-
Marion County	146,374 78.20	1,485	1,149 77.37 77.37 0.78	-	-	489 83.16 42.56 32.93 0.33	-	-	-	-	-	-	-	-	-	-	-	-	-	-	-	-	-	-	-	-
Martin County	82,284 85.30	509	453 89.00 89.00 0.55	-	-	-	-	-	-	-	-	-	-	-	-	-	-	-	-	-	-	-	-	-	-	-
Miami-Dade County	1,012,436 67.87	20,980	16,886 80.49 80.49 1.67	384	252 65.63 65.63 0.02	4,621 81.36 27.37 22.03 0.46	-	-	4,825 74.38 28.57 23.00 0.48	-	2,972 90.91 17.60 14.17 0.29	-	-	-	-	964 91.29 5.71 4.59 0.10	823 87.65 4.87 3.92 0.08	-	-	446 81.83 2.64 2.13 0.04	-	-	-	571 82.75 3.38 2.72 0.06	-	610 64.35 3.61 2.91 0.06
Doral (cdp)	12,631 91.29	789	662 83.90 83.90 5.24	-	-	-	-	-	-	-	-	-	-	-	-	-	-	-	-	-	-	-	-	-	-	-
Ives Estates (cdp)	9,869 85.07	561	465 82.89 82.89 4.71	-	-	-	-	-	-	-	-	-	-	-	-	-	-	-	-	-	-	-	-	-	-	-

Notes: Please refer to the User's Guide for an explanation of data; data is arranged alphabetically by state, then county, then city within each county; table includes counties with populations greater than 49,999 unless noted and cities with populations greater than 9,999 whose Asian and/or NHPI population rates are greater than the national average; (1) Native Hawaiian and other Pacific Islander; (2) excludes Taiwanese; (3) includes Chamorro; (4) county does not meet population threshold but is shown in order to allow inclusion of city

Place	Total population 25 years and over who are high school graduates	Asian population 25 years and over	Asians 25 years and over who are high school graduates	NHPI[1] population 25 years and over	NHPIs[1] 25 years and over who are high school graduates	Asian Indian	Bangladeshi	Cambodian	Chinese[2]	Fijian	Filipino	Guamanian[3]	Hawaiian, Native	Hmong	Indonesian	Japanese	Korean	Laotian	Malaysian	Pakistani	Samoan	Sri Lankan	Taiwanese	Thai	Tongan	Vietnamese
North Miami Beach (city)	17,683 68.34	1,087	737 67.80 67.80 4.17	-	-	188 78.66 25.51 17.30 1.06	-	-	249 50.92 33.79 22.91 1.41	-	-	-	-	-	-	-	-	-	-	-	-	-	-	-	-	-
Pinecrest (village)	11,395 94.24	587	509 86.71 86.71 4.47	-	-	-	-	-	-	-	-	-	-	-	-	-	-	-	-	-	-	-	-	-	-	-
Monroe County	51,929 84.91	432	325 75.23 75.23 0.63	-	-	-	-	-	-	-	-	-	-	-	-	-	-	-	-	-	-	-	-	-	-	-
Nassau County	31,574 81.02	278	214 76.98 76.98 0.68	-	-	-	-	-	-	-	-	-	-	-	-	-	-	-	-	-	-	-	-	-	-	-
Okaloosa County	98,958 88.02	3,161	2,139 67.67 67.67 2.16	-	-	-	-	-	-	-	877 72.48 41.00 27.74 0.89	-	-	-	-	-	349 66.48 16.32 11.04 0.35	-	-	-	-	-	-	230 43.40 10.75 7.28 0.23	-	141 62.39 6.59 4.46 0.14
Wright (cdp)	12,248 87.70	604	382 63.25 63.25 3.12	-	-	-	-	-	-	-	-	-	-	-	-	-	-	-	-	-	-	-	-	-	-	-
Orange County	469,510 81.78	19,367	15,500 80.03 80.03 3.30	411	327 79.56 79.56 0.07	4,011 82.45 25.88 20.71 0.85	-	-	2,318 82.02 14.95 11.97 0.49	-	2,796 92.00 18.04 14.44 0.60	-	-	-	-	921 93.12 5.94 4.76 0.20	1,298 88.72 8.37 6.70 0.28	-	-	480 87.43 3.10 2.48 0.10	-	-	-	-	-	2,713 62.90 17.50 14.01 0.58
Oak Ridge (cdp)	8,738 67.13	864	469 54.28 54.28 5.37	-	-	-	-	-	-	-	-	-	-	-	-	-	-	-	-	-	-	-	-	-	-	154 38.21 32.84 17.82 1.76
Osceola County	87,512 79.12	2,425	2,031 83.75 83.75 2.32	-	-	442 85.83 21.76 18.23 0.51	-	-	387 82.87 19.05 15.96 0.44	-	540 91.22 26.59 22.27 0.62	-	-	-	-	-	-	-	-	-	-	-	-	-	-	-
Palm Beach County	683,553 83.57	11,637	9,680 83.18 83.18 1.42	270	147 54.44 54.44 0.02	2,938 85.71 30.35 25.25 0.43	-	-	1,993 77.01 20.59 17.13 0.29	-	1,569 94.35 16.21 13.48 0.23	-	-	-	-	405 84.91 4.18 3.48 0.06	600 87.46 6.20 5.16 0.09	-	-	-	-	-	-	438 83.11 4.52 3.76 0.06	-	994 77.54 10.27 8.54 0.15

Notes: Please refer to the User's Guide for an explanation of data; data is arranged alphabetically by state, then county, then city within each county; table includes counties with populations greater than 49,999 unless noted and cities with populations greater than 9,999 whose Asian and/or NHPI population rates are greater than the national average; (1) Native Hawaiian and other Pacific Islander; (2) excludes Taiwanese; (3) includes Chamorro; (4) county does not meet population threshold but is shown in order to allow inclusion of city

Place	Total population 25 years and over who are high school graduates	Asian population 25 years and over	Asians 25 years and over who are high school graduates	NHPI[1] population 25 years and over	NHPIs[1] 25 years and over who are high school graduates	Asian Indian	Bangladeshi	Cambodian	Chinese[2]	Fijian	Filipino	Guamanian[3]	Hawaiian, Native	Hmong	Indonesian	Japanese	Korean	Laotian	Malaysian	Pakistani	Samoan	Sri Lankan	Taiwanese	Thai	Tongan	Vietnamese
Pasco County	198,175 77.57	2,251	1,922 85.38 85.38 0.97	-	-	525 87.35 27.32 23.32 0.26	-	-	212 73.61 11.03 9.42 0.11	-	612 87.06 31.84 27.19 0.31	-	-	-	-	-	-	-	-	-	-	-	-	-	-	-
Pinellas County	576,396 84.01	12,435	9,148 73.57 73.57 1.59	-	-	2,150 88.04 23.50 17.29 0.37	-	161 44.35 1.76 1.29 0.03	1,213 76.53 13.26 9.75 0.21	-	1,826 84.62 19.96 14.68 0.32	-	-	-	-	439 92.81 4.80 3.53 0.08	488 80.00 5.33 3.92 0.08	531 49.72 5.80 4.27 0.09	-	-	-	-	-	265 76.81 2.90 2.13 0.05	-	1,523 55.28 16.65 12.25 0.26
Pinellas Park (city)	26,327 80.19	1,175	855 72.77 72.77 3.25	-	-	-	-	-	-	-	-	-	-	-	-	-	-	-	-	-	-	-	-	-	-	278 75.75 32.51 23.66 1.06
Polk County	243,868 74.76	3,533	2,669 75.54 75.54 1.09	-	-	901 82.43 33.76 25.50 0.37	-	-	259 70.00 9.70 7.33 0.11	-	513 88.75 19.22 14.52 0.21	-	-	-	-	-	-	132 59.46 4.95 3.74 0.05	-	-	-	-	-	-	-	225 46.49 8.43 6.37 0.09
Putnam County	33,601 70.35	208	124 59.62 59.62 0.37	-	-	-	-	-	-	-	-	-	-	-	-	-	-	-	-	-	-	-	-	-	-	-
St. Johns County	75,162 87.20	862	753 87.35 87.35 1.00	-	-	-	-	-	-	-	-	-	-	-	-	-	-	-	-	-	-	-	-	-	-	-
St. Lucie County	105,985 77.67	1,269	970 76.44 76.44 0.92	-	-	-	-	-	-	-	-	-	-	-	-	-	-	-	-	-	-	-	-	-	-	-
Santa Rosa County	66,781 85.43	1,232	924 75.00 75.00 1.38	-	-	-	-	-	-	-	446 79.93 48.27 36.20 0.67	-	-	-	-	-	-	-	-	-	-	-	-	-	-	-
Sarasota County	223,638 87.09	1,694	1,270 74.97 74.97 0.57	-	-	-	-	-	146 63.48 11.50 8.62 0.07	-	316 79.40 24.88 18.65 0.14	-	-	-	-	-	-	-	-	-	-	-	-	-	-	252 60.87 19.84 14.88 0.11
Seminole County	215,693 88.68	5,863	5,225 89.12 89.12 2.42	-	-	1,661 92.07 31.79 28.33 0.77	-	-	798 80.36 15.27 13.61 0.37	-	888 94.77 17.00 15.15 0.41	-	-	-	-	-	583 94.18 11.16 9.94 0.27	-	-	-	-	-	-	-	-	603 85.29 11.54 10.28 0.28

Notes: Please refer to the User's Guide for an explanation of data; data is arranged alphabetically by state, then county, then city within each county; table includes counties with populations greater than 49,999 unless noted and cities with populations greater than 9,999 whose Asian and/or NHPI population rates are greater than the national average; (1) Native Hawaiian and other Pacific Islander; (2) excludes Taiwanese; (3) includes Chamorro; (4) county does not meet population threshold but is shown in order to allow inclusion of city

Place	Total population 25 years and over who are high school graduates	Asian population 25 years and over	Asians 25 years and over who are high school graduates	NHPI[1] population 25 years and over	NHPIs[1] 25 years and over who are high school graduates	Asian Indian	Bangladeshi	Cambodian	Chinese[2]	Fijian	Filipino	Guamanian[3]	Hawaiian, Native	Hmong	Indonesian	Japanese	Korean	Laotian	Malaysian	Pakistani	Samoan	Sri Lankan	Taiwanese	Thai	Tongan	Vietnamese
Volusia County	260,243 82.04	3,243	2,711 83.60 83.60 1.04	-	-	867 84.50 31.98 26.73 0.33	-	-	364 79.48 13.43 11.22 0.14	-	591 90.23 21.80 18.22 0.23	-	-	-	-	-	246 85.12 9.07 7.59 0.09	-	-	-	-	-	-	-	-	-
GEORGIA	4,074,616 78.57	109,098	86,749 79.51 79.51 2.13	2,101	1,499 71.35 71.35 0.04	24,647 88.75 28.41 22.59 0.60	644 83.20 0.74 0.59 0.02	908 48.30 1.05 0.83 0.02	14,585 84.86 16.81 13.37 0.36	-	6,314 87.87 7.28 5.79 0.15	463 59.28 30.89 22.04 0.01	411 69.78 27.42 19.56 0.01	206 45.78 0.24 0.19 0.01	304 81.50 0.35 0.28 0.01	5,163 93.25 5.95 4.73 0.13	15,271 84.59 17.60 14.00 0.37	1,312 50.91 1.51 1.20 0.03	-	1,955 83.01 2.25 1.79 0.05	324 82.65 21.61 15.42 0.01	-	1,216 97.51 1.40 1.11 0.03	1,205 70.10 1.39 1.10 0.03	-	10,003 54.50 11.53 9.17 0.25
Bartow County	34,987 71.83	316	225 71.20 71.20 0.64	-	-	-	-	-	-	-	-	-	-	-	-	-	-	-	-	-	-	-	-	-	-	-
Bibb County	75,251 77.21	899	747 83.09 83.09 0.99	-	-	-	-	-	-	-	-	-	-	-	-	-	-	-	-	-	-	-	-	-	-	-
Bulloch County	22,400 77.94	296	280 94.59 94.59 1.25	-	-	-	-	-	-	-	-	-	-	-	-	-	-	-	-	-	-	-	-	-	-	-
Carroll County	37,990 71.06	280	250 89.29 89.29 0.66	-	-	-	-	-	-	-	-	-	-	-	-	-	-	-	-	-	-	-	-	-	-	-
Catoosa County	26,786 76.03	232	157 67.67 67.67 0.59	-	-	-	-	-	-	-	-	-	-	-	-	-	-	-	-	-	-	-	-	-	-	-
Chatham County	118,570 80.20	2,509	1,820 72.54 72.54 1.53	-	-	347 81.07 19.07 13.83 0.29	-	-	461 83.06 25.33 18.37 0.39	-	-	-	-	-	-	-	211 85.43 11.59 8.41 0.18	-	-	-	-	-	-	-	-	266 44.19 14.62 10.60 0.22
Cherokee County	76,956 84.44	905	681 75.25 75.25 0.88	-	-	168 91.30 24.67 18.56 0.22	-	-	-	-	-	-	-	-	-	-	-	-	-	-	-	-	-	-	-	-
Clarke County	42,017 81.04	1,778	1,654 93.03 93.03 3.94	-	-	309 89.57 18.68 17.38 0.74	-	-	622 94.10 37.61 34.98 1.48	-	-	-	-	-	-	-	238 92.97 14.39 13.39 0.57	-	-	-	-	-	-	-	-	-

Notes: Please refer to the User's Guide for an explanation of data; data is arranged alphabetically by state, then county, then city within each county; table includes counties with populations greater than 49,999 unless noted and cities with populations greater than 9,999 whose Asian and/or NHPI population rates are greater than the national average; (1) Native Hawaiian and other Pacific Islander; (2) excludes Taiwanese; (3) includes Chamorro; (4) county does not meet population threshold but is shown in order to allow inclusion of city

Place	Total population 25 years and over who are high school graduates	Asian population 25 years and over	Asians 25 years and over who are high school graduates	NHPI[1] population 25 years and over	NHPIs[1] 25 years and over who are high school graduates	Asian Indian	Bangladeshi	Cambodian	Chinese[2]	Fijian	Filipino	Guamanian[3]	Hawaiian, Native	Hmong	Indonesian	Japanese	Korean	Laotian	Malaysian	Pakistani	Samoan	Sri Lankan	Taiwanese	Thai	Tongan	Vietnamese
Clayton County	113,333 80.06	6,363	3,695 58.07 58.07 3.26	-	-	775 89.60 20.97 12.18 0.68	-	150 29.53 4.06 2.36 0.13	140 42.30 3.79 2.20 0.12	-	-	-	-	-	-	-	-	336 49.70 9.09 5.28 0.30	-	203 87.88 5.49 3.19 0.18	-	-	-	-	-	1,418 49.41 38.38 22.29 1.25
Forest Park (city)	8,101 64.83	760	342 45.00 45.00 4.22	-	-	-	-	-	-	-	-	-	-	-	-	-	-	-	-	-	-	-	-	-	-	232 40.99 67.84 30.53 2.86
Riverdale (city)	5,558 76.73	637	295 46.31 46.31 5.31	-	-	-	-	-	-	-	-	-	-	-	-	-	-	-	-	-	-	-	-	-	-	108 34.73 36.61 16.95 1.94
Cobb County	351,035 88.79	12,169	10,400 85.46 85.46 2.96	-	-	3,236 91.98 31.12 26.59 0.92	-	-	2,000 84.42 19.23 16.44 0.57	-	772 90.72 7.42 6.34 0.22	-	-	-	-	697 100.00 6.70 5.73 0.20	1,749 88.20 16.82 14.37 0.50	-	-	318 81.54 3.06 2.61 0.09	-	-	-	-	-	608 61.29 5.85 5.00 0.17
Smyrna (city)	24,633 85.84	1,183	1,092 92.31 92.31 4.43	-	-	371 100.00 33.97 31.36 1.51	-	-	-	-	-	-	-	-	-	-	-	-	-	-	-	-	-	-	-	-
Columbia County	49,702 87.87	1,924	1,629 84.67 84.67 3.28	-	-	564 94.00 34.62 29.31 1.13	-	-	239 72.42 14.67 12.42 0.48	-	-	-	-	-	-	-	205 69.26 12.58 10.65 0.41	-	-	-	-	-	-	-	-	-
Martinez (cdp)	16,131 91.36	925	788 85.19 85.19 4.89	-	-	303 92.66 38.45 32.76 1.88	-	-	-	-	-	-	-	-	-	-	-	-	-	-	-	-	-	-	-	-
Coweta County	46,379 81.62	383	309 80.68 80.68 0.67	-	-	-	-	-	-	-	-	-	-	-	-	-	-	-	-	-	-	-	-	-	-	-
DeKalb County	365,721 85.06	17,436	13,309 76.33 76.33 3.64	-	-	4,107 87.03 30.86 23.55 1.12	261 75.22 1.96 1.50 0.07	189 49.22 1.42 1.08 0.05	2,285 83.85 17.17 13.11 0.62	-	417 85.80 3.13 2.39 0.11	-	-	-	-	708 97.12 5.32 4.06 0.19	2,033 83.90 15.28 11.66 0.56	-	-	-	-	-	-	-	-	2,061 51.62 15.49 11.82 0.56
Druid Hills (cdp)	7,010 98.06	319	312 97.81 97.81 4.45	-	-	-	-	-	-	-	-	-	-	-	-	-	-	-	-	-	-	-	-	-	-	-

Notes: Please refer to the User's Guide for an explanation of data; data is arranged alphabetically by state, then county, then city within each county; table includes counties with populations greater than 49,999 unless noted and cities with populations greater than 9,999 whose Asian and/or NHPI population rates are greater than the national average; (1) Native Hawaiian and other Pacific Islander; (2) excludes Taiwanese; (3) includes Chamorro; (4) county does not meet population threshold but is shown in order to allow inclusion of city

Place	Total population 25 years and over who are high school graduates	Asian population 25 years and over	Asians 25 years and over who are high school graduates	NHPI[1] population 25 years and over	NHPIs[1] 25 years and over who are high school graduates	Asian Indian	Bangladeshi	Cambodian	Chinese[2]	Fijian	Filipino	Guamanian[3]	Hawaiian, Native	Hmong	Indonesian	Japanese	Korean	Laotian	Malaysian	Pakistani	Samoan	Sri Lankan	Taiwanese	Thai	Tongan	Vietnamese
Dunwoody (cdp)	23,227 96.07	1,675	1,616 96.48 96.48 6.96	-	-	730 97.72 45.17 43.58 3.14	-	-	-	-	-	-	-	-	-	-	303 92.66 18.75 18.09 1.30	-	-	-	-	-	-	-	-	-
North Atlanta (cdp)	21,257 79.46	1,142	956 83.71 83.71 4.50	-	-	-	-	-	-	-	-	-	-	-	-	-	-	-	-	-	-	-	-	-	-	-
North Decatur (cdp)	11,293 93.98	582	500 85.91 85.91 4.43	-	-	-	-	-	-	-	-	-	-	-	-	-	-	-	-	-	-	-	-	-	-	-
North Druid Hills (cdp)	13,157 94.23	861	855 99.30 99.30 6.50	-	-	373 98.42 43.63 43.32 2.83	-	-	-	-	-	-	-	-	-	-	-	-	-	-	-	-	-	-	-	-
Tucker (cdp)	17,189 89.04	1,361	1,075 78.99 78.99 6.25	-	-	-	-	-	-	-	-	-	-	-	-	-	-	-	-	-	-	-	-	-	-	123 54.91 11.44 9.04 0.72
Dougherty County	42,738 73.66	474	307 64.77 64.77 0.72	-	-	-	-	-	-	-	-	-	-	-	-	-	-	-	-	-	-	-	-	-	-	-
Douglas County	47,621 81.14	606	536 88.45 88.45 1.13	-	-	-	-	-	-	-	-	-	-	-	-	-	-	-	-	-	-	-	-	-	-	-
Fayette County	54,514 92.37	1,326	1,227 92.53 92.53 2.25	-	-	-	-	-	-	-	-	-	-	-	-	409 98.55 33.33 30.84 0.75	-	-	-	-	-	-	-	-	-	-
Peachtree City (city)	19,458 96.22	805	780 96.89 96.89 4.01	-	-	-	-	-	-	-	-	-	-	-	-	388 98.48 49.74 48.20 1.99	-	-	-	-	-	-	-	-	-	-
Floyd County	41,915 71.47	691	564 81.62 81.62 1.35	-	-	237 84.34 42.02 34.30 0.57	-	-	-	-	-	-	-	-	-	-	-	-	-	-	-	-	-	-	-	-

Notes: Please refer to the User's Guide for an explanation of data; data is arranged alphabetically by state, then county, then city within each county; table includes counties with populations greater than 49,999 unless noted and cities with populations greater than 9,999 whose Asian and/or NHPI population rates are greater than the national average; (1) Native Hawaiian and other Pacific Islander; (2) excludes Taiwanese; (3) includes Chamorro; (4) county does not meet population threshold but is shown in order to allow inclusion of city

Place	Total population 25 years and over who are high school graduates	Asian population 25 years and over	Asians 25 years and over who are high school graduates	NHPI[1] population 25 years and over	NHPIs[1] 25 years and over who are high school graduates	Asian Indian	Bangladeshi	Cambodian	Chinese[2]	Fijian	Filipino	Guamanian[3]	Hawaiian, Native	Hmong	Indonesian	Japanese	Korean	Laotian	Malaysian	Pakistani	Samoan	Sri Lankan	Taiwanese	Thai	Tongan	Vietnamese
Forsyth County	55,741 85.72	552	512 92.75 92.75 0.92	-	-	-	-	-	-	-	-	-	-	-	-	-	-	-	-	-	-	-	-	-	-	-
Fulton County	443,368 84.01	15,006	12,965 86.40 86.40 2.92	-	-	4,037 92.98 31.14 26.90 0.91	-	-	3,077 89.06 23.73 20.51 0.69	-	581 93.41 4.48 3.87 0.13	-	-	-	-	634 93.10 4.89 4.22 0.14	2,398 93.38 18.50 15.98 0.54	-	-	-	-	-	-	-	-	815 46.49 6.29 5.43 0.18
Alpharetta (city)	21,505 95.19	1,117	1,038 92.93 92.93 4.83	-	-	406 97.13 39.11 36.35 1.89	-	-	275 82.58 26.49 24.62 1.28	-	-	-	-	-	-	-	-	-	-	-	-	-	-	-	-	-
Roswell (city)	49,850 92.83	1,960	1,753 89.44 89.44 3.52	-	-	540 93.26 30.80 27.55 1.08	-	-	330 83.76 18.82 16.84 0.66	-	-	-	-	-	-	-	437 83.88 24.93 22.30 0.88	-	-	-	-	-	-	-	-	-
Glynn County	36,841 82.22	329	281 85.41 85.41 0.76	-	-	-	-	-	-	-	-	-	-	-	-	-	-	-	-	-	-	-	-	-	-	-
Gwinnett County	325,256 87.29	26,336	21,181 80.43 80.43 6.51	276	177 64.13 64.13 0.05	6,055 87.13 28.59 22.99 1.86	-	233 54.95 1.10 0.88 0.07	3,220 88.95 15.20 12.23 0.99	-	832 92.04 3.93 3.16 0.26	-	-	-	-	631 95.17 2.98 2.40 0.19	5,064 85.95 23.91 19.23 1.56	377 57.21 1.78 1.43 0.12	-	536 81.71 2.53 2.04 0.16	-	-	353 98.88 1.67 1.34 0.11	-	-	2,745 57.61 12.96 10.42 0.84
Duluth (city)	13,957 92.79	1,719	1,594 92.73 92.73 11.42	-	-	508 93.90 31.87 29.55 3.64	-	-	304 95.30 19.07 17.68 2.18	-	-	-	-	-	-	-	436 97.32 27.35 25.36 3.12	-	-	-	-	-	-	-	-	-
Lilburn (city)	6,219 84.35	883	707 80.07 80.07 11.37	-	-	156 75.00 22.07 17.67 2.51	-	-	-	-	-	-	-	-	-	-	-	-	-	-	-	-	-	-	-	203 69.76 28.71 22.99 3.26
Mountain Park (cdp)	7,260 90.89	625	572 91.52 91.52 7.88	-	-	350 94.85 61.19 56.00 4.82	-	-	-	-	-	-	-	-	-	-	-	-	-	-	-	-	-	-	-	-
Hall County	61,217 70.51	1,041	567 54.47 54.47 0.93	-	-	-	-	-	-	-	-	-	-	-	-	-	-	-	-	-	-	-	-	-	-	289 43.39 50.97 27.76 0.47

Notes: Please refer to the User's Guide for an explanation of data; data is arranged alphabetically by state, then county, then city within each county; table includes counties with populations greater than 49,999 unless noted and cities with populations greater than 9,999 whose Asian and/or NHPI population rates are greater than the national average; (1) Native Hawaiian and other Pacific Islander; (2) excludes Taiwanese; (3) includes Chamorro; (4) county does not meet population threshold but is shown in order to allow inclusion of city

Place	Total population 25 years and over who are high school graduates	Asian population 25 years and over	Asians 25 years and over who are high school graduates	NHPI[1] population 25 years and over	NHPIs[1] 25 years and over who are high school graduates	Asian Indian	Bangladeshi	Cambodian	Chinese[2]	Fijian	Filipino	Guamanian[3]	Hawaiian, Native	Hmong	Indonesian	Japanese	Korean	Laotian	Malaysian	Pakistani	Samoan	Sri Lankan	Taiwanese	Thai	Tongan	Vietnamese
Henry County	63,594 84.23	1,363	1,136 83.35 83.35 1.79	-	-	456 94.21 40.14 33.46 0.72	-	-	-	-	-	-	-	-	-	-	-	-	-	-	-	-	-	-	-	-
Houston County	58,196 84.30	1,216	935 76.89 76.89 1.61	-	-	-	-	-	-	-	292 79.56 31.23 24.01 0.50	-	-	-	-	-	-	-	-	-	-	-	-	-	-	-
Liberty County	26,723 86.77	598	460 76.92 76.92 1.72	-	-	-	-	-	-	-	-	-	-	-	-	-	244 83.56 53.04 40.80 0.91	-	-	-	-	-	-	-	-	-
Lowndes County	42,118 77.66	553	390 70.52 70.52 0.93	-	-	-	-	-	-	-	-	-	-	-	-	-	-	-	-	-	-	-	-	-	-	-
Muscogee County	90,001 78.92	1,961	1,626 82.92 82.92 1.81	170	154 90.59 90.59 0.17	320 96.10 19.68 16.32 0.36	-	-	216 81.51 13.28 11.01 0.24	-	284 91.61 17.47 14.48 0.32	-	-	-	-	-	380 72.24 23.37 19.38 0.42	-	-	-	-	-	-	-	-	-
Columbus (sp. city)	89,852 79.01	1,961	1,626 82.92 82.92 1.81	170	154 90.59 90.59 0.17	320 96.10 19.68 16.32 0.36	-	-	216 81.51 13.28 11.01 0.24	-	284 91.61 17.47 14.48 0.32	-	-	-	-	-	380 72.24 23.37 19.38 0.42	-	-	-	-	-	-	-	-	-
Newton County	29,244 74.71	212	210 99.06 99.06 0.72	-	-	-	-	-	-	-	-	-	-	-	-	-	-	-	-	-	-	-	-	-	-	-
Richmond County	95,581 77.97	2,028	1,654 81.56 81.56 1.73	-	-	342 85.71 20.68 16.86 0.36	-	-	284 85.54 17.17 14.00 0.30	-	-	-	-	-	-	-	507 74.56 30.65 25.00 0.53	-	-	-	-	-	-	-	-	-
Rockdale County	36,914 82.41	721	625 86.69 86.69 1.69	-	-	-	-	-	-	-	-	-	-	-	-	-	-	-	-	-	-	-	-	-	-	-
Spalding County	25,145 67.76	269	224 83.27 83.27 0.89	-	-	-	-	-	-	-	-	-	-	-	-	-	-	-	-	-	-	-	-	-	-	-

Notes: Please refer to the User's Guide for an explanation of data; data is arranged alphabetically by state, then county, then city within each county; table includes counties with populations greater than 49,999 unless noted and cities with populations greater than 9,999 whose Asian and/or NHPI population rates are greater than the national average; (1) Native Hawaiian and other Pacific Islander; (2) excludes Taiwanese; (3) includes Chamorro; (4) county does not meet population threshold but is shown in order to allow inclusion of city

Place	Total population 25 years and over who are high school graduates	Asian population 25 years and over	Asians 25 years and over who are high school graduates	NHPI[1] population 25 years and over	NHPIs[1] 25 years and over who are high school graduates	Asian Indian	Bangladeshi	Cambodian	Chinese[2]	Fijian	Filipino	Guamanian[3]	Hawaiian, Native	Hmong	Indonesian	Japanese	Korean	Laotian	Malaysian	Pakistani	Samoan	Sri Lankan	Taiwanese	Thai	Tongan	Vietnamese
Troup County	26,868 72.98	295	245 83.05 83.05 0.91	-	-	-	-	-	-	-	-	-	-	-	-	-	-	-	-	-	-	-	-	-	-	-
Walton County	28,313 73.49	225	179 79.56 79.56 0.63	-	-	-	-	-	-	-	-	-	-	-	-	-	-	-	-	-	-	-	-	-	-	-
Whitfield County	33,114 62.99	563	439 77.98 77.98 1.33	-	-	-	-	-	-	-	-	-	-	-	-	-	-	-	-	-	-	-	-	-	-	-
HAWAII	678,666 84.57	378,686	302,581 79.90 79.90 44.58	61,930	50,133 80.95 80.95 7.39	886 88.96 0.29 0.23 0.13	-	42 51.85 0.01 0.01 0.01	34,541 77.75 11.42 9.12 5.09	-	82,883 71.39 27.39 21.89 12.21	780 89.66 1.56 1.26 0.11	39,279 83.51 78.35 63.42 5.79	-	-	147,066 86.26 48.60 38.84 21.67	14,333 78.40 4.74 3.78 2.11	426 44.51 0.14 0.11 0.06	-	-	5,249 74.55 10.47 8.48 0.77	-	525 83.73 0.17 0.14 0.08	729 71.26 0.24 0.19 0.11	1,421 65.12 2.83 2.29 0.21	2,850 52.65 0.94 0.75 0.42
Hawaii County	82,620 84.56	30,732	24,102 78.43 78.43 29.17	8,953	7,328 81.85 81.85 8.87	-	-	-	912 86.94 3.78 2.97 1.10	-	6,075 66.66 25.21 19.77 7.35	-	6,644 83.93 90.67 74.21 8.04	-	-	14,660 82.99 60.82 47.70 17.74	504 77.66 2.09 1.64 0.61	-	-	-	138 66.99 1.88 1.54 0.17	-	-	-	-	-
Hilo (cdp)	22,806 85.89	12,185	10,337 84.83 84.83 45.33	2,602	2,198 84.47 84.47 9.64	-	-	-	395 94.05 3.82 3.24 1.73	-	1,158 76.74 11.20 9.50 5.08	-	1,971 87.52 89.67 75.75 8.64	-	-	7,885 85.62 76.28 64.71 34.57	246 76.16 2.38 2.02 1.08	-	-	-	-	-	-	-	-	-
Honolulu County	492,110 84.85	303,546	245,141 80.76 80.76 49.81	42,410	34,509 81.37 81.37 7.01	737 88.90 0.30 0.24 0.15	-	-	32,662 77.47 13.32 10.76 6.64	-	61,702 72.76 25.17 20.33 12.54	714 91.89 2.07 1.68 0.15	25,178 84.46 72.96 59.37 5.12	-	-	118,013 87.29 48.14 38.88 23.98	13,163 78.31 5.37 4.34 2.67	401 43.30 0.16 0.13 0.08	-	-	4,986 74.60 14.45 11.76 1.01	-	498 83.42 0.20 0.16 0.10	597 72.01 0.24 0.20 0.12	1,053 65.98 3.05 2.48 0.21	2,524 50.44 1.03 0.83 0.51
Ewa Beach (cdp)	6,417 71.47	4,764	3,235 67.91 67.91 50.41	822	636 77.37 77.37 9.91	-	-	-	-	-	2,288 65.20 70.73 48.03 35.66	-	421 77.53 66.19 51.22 6.56	-	-	551 74.56 17.03 11.57 8.59	-	-	-	-	146 73.00 22.96 17.76 2.28	-	-	-	-	-
Halawa (cdp)	7,830 83.72	5,415	4,333 80.02 80.02 55.34	868	680 78.34 78.34 8.68	-	-	-	408 72.60 9.42 7.53 5.21	-	1,552 75.93 35.82 28.66 19.82	-	416 80.31 61.18 47.93 5.31	-	-	1,872 87.27 43.20 34.57 23.91	-	-	-	-	202 73.19 29.71 23.27 2.58	-	-	-	-	-
Honolulu (cdp)	223,118 83.38	159,892	127,006 79.43 79.43 56.92	14,980	11,854 79.13 79.13 5.31	468 96.49 0.37 0.29 0.21	-	-	23,224 74.81 18.29 14.52 10.41	-	20,843 70.13 16.41 13.04 9.34	313 87.43 2.64 2.09 0.14	7,988 83.47 67.39 53.32 3.58	-	-	63,255 86.28 49.80 39.56 28.35	9,375 78.40 7.38 5.86 4.20	217 37.80 0.17 0.14 0.10	-	-	1,616 72.86 13.63 10.79 0.72	-	448 82.66 0.35 0.28 0.20	301 76.59 0.24 0.19 0.13	494 59.95 4.17 3.30 0.22	1,970 47.84 1.55 1.23 0.88

Notes: Please refer to the User's Guide for an explanation of data; data is arranged alphabetically by state, then county, then city within each county; table includes counties with populations greater than 49,999 unless noted and cities with populations greater than 9,999 whose Asian and/or NHPI population rates are greater than the national average; (1) Native Hawaiian and other Pacific Islander; (2) excludes Taiwanese; (3) includes Chamorro; (4) county does not meet population threshold but is shown in order to allow inclusion of city

Place	Total population 25 years and over who are high school graduates	Asian population 25 years and over	Asians 25 years and over who are high school graduates	NHPI[1] population 25 years and over	NHPIs[1] 25 years and over who are high school graduates	Asian Indian	Bangladeshi	Cambodian	Chinese[2]	Fijian	Filipino	Guamanian[3]	Hawaiian, Native	Hmong	Indonesian	Japanese	Korean	Laotian	Malaysian	Pakistani	Samoan	Sri Lankan	Taiwanese	Thai	Tongan	Vietnamese
Kailua (cdp)	23,292 92.82	6,329	5,553 87.74 87.74 23.84	1,667	1,529 91.72 91.72 6.56	-	-	-	855 89.91 15.40 13.51 3.67	-	574 76.74 10.34 9.07 2.46	-	1,398 91.73 91.43 83.86 6.00	-	-	3,310 88.62 59.61 52.30 14.21	326 92.88 5.87 5.15 1.40	-	-	-	-	-	-	-	-	-
Kaneohe (cdp)	21,225 89.67	10,798	9,549 88.43 88.43 44.99	2,297	2,047 89.12 89.12 9.64	-	-	-	1,059 88.03 11.09 9.81 4.99	-	1,073 82.79 11.24 9.94 5.06	-	1,733 89.89 84.66 75.45 8.16	-	-	6,190 89.12 64.82 57.33 29.16	305 85.92 3.19 2.82 1.44	-	-	-	-	-	-	-	-	-
Kaneohe Station (cdp)	3,665 97.58	363	320 88.15 88.15 8.73	-	-	-	-	-	-	-	-	-	-	-	-	-	-	-	-	-	-	-	-	-	-	-
Makakilo City (cdp)	7,297 90.12	3,076	2,654 86.28 86.28 36.37	743	650 87.48 87.48 8.91	-	-	-	-	-	1,212 82.67 45.67 39.40 16.61	-	497 93.25 76.46 66.89 6.81	-	-	750 91.24 28.26 24.38 10.28	-	-	-	-	-	-	-	-	-	-
Mililani Town (cdp)	17,202 94.27	9,601	8,874 92.43 92.43 51.59	713	679 95.23 95.23 3.95	-	-	-	774 92.81 8.72 8.06 4.50	-	1,945 87.73 21.92 20.26 11.31	-	550 100.00 81.00 77.14 3.20	-	-	5,177 95.15 58.34 53.92 30.10	334 82.88 3.76 3.48 1.94	-	-	-	-	-	-	-	-	-
Nanakuli (cdp)	4,181 75.46	717	472 65.83 65.83 11.29	2,084	1,564 75.05 75.05 37.41	-	-	-	-	-	210 52.50 44.49 29.29 5.02	-	1,318 76.41 84.27 63.24 31.52	-	-	-	-	-	-	-	216 69.68 13.81 10.36 5.17	-	-	-	-	-
Pearl City (cdp)	18,036 86.74	13,505	11,468 84.92 84.92 63.58	1,054	860 81.59 81.59 4.77	-	-	-	922 80.59 8.04 6.83 5.11	-	2,415 79.89 21.06 17.88 13.39	-	650 82.59 75.58 61.67 3.60	-	-	7,175 87.28 62.57 53.13 39.78	222 78.45 1.94 1.64 1.23	-	-	-	-	-	-	-	-	-
Schofield Barracks (cdp)	5,343 96.11	273	245 89.74 89.74 4.59	-	-	-	-	-	-	-	-	-	-	-	-	-	-	-	-	-	-	-	-	-	-	-
Wahiawa (cdp)	8,218 77.96	5,713	4,274 74.81 74.81 52.01	847	647 76.39 76.39 7.87	-	-	-	-	-	1,370 68.33 32.05 23.98 16.67	-	454 83.46 70.17 53.60 5.52	-	-	2,234 77.19 52.27 39.10 27.18	-	-	-	-	-	-	-	-	-	-
Waianae (cdp)	4,751 79.71	1,466	1,134 77.35 77.35 23.87	1,473	1,213 82.35 82.35 25.53	-	-	-	-	-	549 75.41 48.41 37.45 11.56	-	1,087 83.42 89.61 73.79 22.88	-	-	428 83.76 37.74 29.20 9.01	-	-	-	-	-	-	-	-	-	-

Notes: Please refer to the User's Guide for an explanation of data; data is arranged alphabetically by state, then county, then city within each county; table includes counties with populations greater than 49,999 unless noted and cities with populations greater than 9,999 whose Asian and/or NHPI population rates are greater than the national average; (1) Native Hawaiian and other Pacific Islander; (2) excludes Taiwanese; (3) includes Chamorro; (4) county does not meet population threshold but is shown in order to allow inclusion of city

Place	Total population 25 years and over who are high school graduates	Asian population 25 years and over	Asians 25 years and over who are high school graduates	NHPI[1] population 25 years and over	NHPIs[1] 25 years and over who are high school graduates	Asian Indian	Bangladeshi	Cambodian	Chinese[2]	Fijian	Filipino	Guamanian[3]	Hawaiian, Native	Hmong	Indonesian	Japanese	Korean	Laotian	Malaysian	Pakistani	Samoan	Sri Lankan	Taiwanese	Thai	Tongan	Vietnamese
Waimalu (cdp)	18,369	11,779	10,433	894	760	-	-	-	946	-	1,858	-	499	-	-	6,134	602	-	-	-	-	-	-	-	-	-
	90.56		88.57		85.01				87.76		82.91		86.63			93.21	71.50									
									9.07		17.81		65.66			58.79	5.77									
			88.57		85.01				8.03		15.77		55.82			52.08	5.11									
			56.80		4.14				5.15		10.11		2.72			33.39	3.28									
Waipahu (cdp)	14,458	15,322	10,347	1,766	1,205	-	-	-	312	-	7,213	-	434	-	-	2,318	-	-	-	-	567	-	-	-	-	-
	68.57		67.53		68.23				70.11		65.51		76.14			73.59					64.65					
									3.02		69.71		36.02			22.40					47.05					
			67.53		68.23				2.04		47.08		24.58			15.13					32.11					
			71.57		8.33				2.16		49.89		3.00			16.03					3.92					
Waipio (cdp)	6,615	4,488	3,925	346	328	-	-	-	-	-	1,264	-	216	-	-	2,024	-	-	-	-	-	-	-	-	-	-
	89.77		87.46		94.80						80.77		95.15			93.66										
											32.20		65.85			51.57										
			87.46		94.80						28.16		62.43			45.10										
			59.33		4.96						19.11		3.27			30.60										
Kauai County	32,368	15,803	11,989	2,900	2,374	-	-	-	253	-	5,496	-	2,241	-	-	5,365	-	-	-	-	-	-	-	-	-	-
	83.27		75.87		81.86				73.98		71.08		83.18			80.27										
									2.11		45.84		94.40			44.75										
			75.87		81.86				1.60		34.78		77.28			33.95										
			37.04		7.33				0.78		16.98		6.92			16.58										
Maui County	71,510	28,575	21,334	7,579	5,893	-	-	-	714	-	9,595	-	5,187	-	-	9,028	559	-	-	-	-	-	-	-	258	-
	83.39		74.66		77.75				81.79		66.44		79.48			82.54	81.84								61.28	
									3.35		44.98		88.02			42.32	2.62								4.38	
			74.66		77.75				2.50		33.58		68.44			31.59	1.96								3.40	
			29.83		8.24				1.00		13.42		7.25			12.62	0.78								0.36	
Kahului (cdp)	9,269	8,063	5,608	990	670	-	-	-	-	-	2,789	-	567	-	-	2,298	-	-	-	-	-	-	-	-	-	-
	70.96		69.55		67.68						63.13		68.98			76.32										
											49.73		84.63			40.98										
			69.55		67.68						34.59		57.27			28.50										
			60.50		7.23						30.09		6.12			24.79										
Kihei (cdp)	9,975	2,752	2,171	712	565	-	-	-	-	-	1,452	-	384	-	-	434	-	-	-	-	-	-	-	-	-	-
	88.27		78.89		79.35						73.22		82.05			98.86										
											66.88		67.96			19.99										
			78.89		79.35						52.76		53.93			15.77										
			21.76		5.66						14.56		3.85			4.35										
Wailuku (cdp)	7,011	4,031	3,212	714	533	-	-	-	-	-	725	-	510	-	-	2,033	-	-	-	-	-	-	-	-	-	-
	82.12		79.68		74.65						68.01		74.67			84.89										
											22.57		95.68			63.29										
			79.68		74.65						17.99		71.43			50.43										
			45.81		7.60						10.34		7.27			29.00										
IDAHO	667,144	7,654	6,279	557	446	621	-	-	1,001	-	1,015	-	164	-	-	1,965	595	152	-	-	-	-	-	-	-	462
	84.72		82.04		80.07	87.96			86.82		84.72		85.42			92.73	83.10	45.37								53.78
						9.89			15.94		16.16		36.77			31.29	9.48	2.42								7.36
			82.04		80.07	8.11			13.08		13.26		29.44			25.67	7.77	1.99								6.04
			0.94		0.07	0.09			0.15		0.15		0.02			0.29	0.09	0.02								0.07
Ada County	171,285	3,286	2,669	187	165	407	-	-	448	-	352	-	-	-	-	538	213	-	-	-	-	-	-	-	-	338
	90.79		81.22		88.24	93.35			94.51		90.49					95.39	76.34									52.65
						15.25			16.79		13.19					20.16	7.98									12.66
			81.22		88.24	12.39			13.63		10.71					16.37	6.48									10.29
			1.56		0.10	0.24			0.26		0.21					0.31	0.12									0.20

Notes: Please refer to the User's Guide for an explanation of data; data is arranged alphabetically by state, then county, then city within each county; table includes counties with populations greater than 49,999 unless noted and cities with populations greater than 9,999 whose Asian and/or NHPI population rates are greater than the national average; (1) Native Hawaiian and other Pacific Islander; (2) excludes Taiwanese; (3) includes Chamorro; (4) county does not meet population threshold but is shown in order to allow inclusion of city

Place	Total population 25 years and over who are high school graduates	Asian population 25 years and over	Asians 25 years and over who are high school graduates	NHPI[1] population 25 years and over	NHPIs[1] 25 years and over who are high school graduates	Asian Indian	Bangladeshi	Cambodian	Chinese[2]	Fijian	Filipino	Guamanian[3]	Hawaiian, Native	Hmong	Indonesian	Japanese	Korean	Laotian	Malaysian	Pakistani	Samoan	Sri Lankan	Taiwanese	Thai	Tongan	Vietnamese
Bannock County	37,894 87.55	556	496 89.21 89.21 1.31	-	-	-	-	-	-	-	-	-	-	-	-	-	-	-	-	-	-	-	-	-	-	-
Bonneville County	42,583 87.80	313	268 85.62 85.62 0.63	-	-	-	-	-	-	-	-	-	-	-	-	-	-	-	-	-	-	-	-	-	-	-
Canyon County	58,248 76.02	718	558 77.72 77.72 0.96	-	-	-	-	-	-	-	-	-	-	-	-	215 91.10 38.53 29.94 0.37	-	-	-	-	-	-	-	-	-	-
Kootenai County	60,995 87.30	343	272 79.30 79.30 0.45	-	-	-	-	-	-	-	-	-	-	-	-	-	-	-	-	-	-	-	-	-	-	-
Twin Falls County	32,141 81.28	248	147 59.27 59.27 0.46	-	-	-	-	-	-	-	-	-	-	-	-	-	-	-	-	-	-	-	-	-	-	-
ILLINOIS	6,493,228 81.43	276,697	240,406 86.88 86.88 3.70	2,172	1,532 70.53 70.53 0.02	67,930 88.28 28.26 24.55 1.05	396 89.59 0.16 0.14 0.01	1,041 56.70 0.43 0.38 0.02	39,919 79.57 16.60 14.43 0.61	-	55,631 93.45 23.14 20.11 0.86	397 69.53 25.91 18.28 0.01	418 73.85 27.28 19.24 0.01	-	650 98.93 0.27 0.23 0.01	15,480 95.57 6.44 5.59 0.24	30,264 88.65 12.59 10.94 0.47	1,915 67.55 0.80 0.69 0.03	332 98.52 0.14 0.12 0.01	7,609 85.09 3.17 2.75 0.12	292 66.97 19.06 13.44 <0.01	405 92.05 0.17 0.15 0.01	2,189 95.80 0.91 0.79 0.03	3,788 93.03 1.58 1.37 0.06	-	7,475 65.75 3.11 2.70 0.12
Champaign County	91,487 90.98	5,453	5,030 92.24 92.24 5.50	-	-	941 98.64 18.71 17.26 1.03	-	-	1,620 98.00 32.21 29.71 1.77	-	252 80.77 5.01 4.62 0.28	-	-	-	-	340 96.87 6.76 6.24 0.37	1,180 97.84 23.46 21.64 1.29	-	-	-	-	-	-	-	-	194 46.30 3.86 3.56 0.21
Champaign (city)	31,461 91.58	2,132	1,857 87.10 87.10 5.90	-	-	444 100.00 23.91 20.83 1.41	-	-	526 100.00 28.33 24.67 1.67	-	-	-	-	-	-	-	401 96.16 21.59 18.81 1.27	-	-	-	-	-	-	-	-	98 36.84 5.28 4.60 0.31
Urbana (city)	16,126 90.80	2,292	2,252 98.25 98.25 13.97	-	-	317 100.00 14.08 13.83 1.97	-	-	909 97.64 40.36 39.66 5.64	-	-	-	-	-	-	-	482 100.00 21.40 21.03 2.99	-	-	-	-	-	-	-	-	-
Coles County	25,151 82.94	206	181 87.86 87.86 0.72	-	-	-	-	-	-	-	-	-	-	-	-	-	-	-	-	-	-	-	-	-	-	-

Notes: Please refer to the User's Guide for an explanation of data; data is arranged alphabetically by state, then county, then city within each county; table includes counties with populations greater than 49,999 unless noted and cities with populations greater than 9,999 whose Asian and/or NHPI population rates are greater than the national average; (1) Native Hawaiian and other Pacific Islander; (2) excludes Taiwanese; (3) includes Chamorro; (4) county does not meet population threshold but is shown in order to allow inclusion of city

Place	Total population 25 years and over who are high school graduates	Asian population 25 years and over	Asians 25 years and over who are high school graduates	NHPI[1] population 25 years and over	NHPIs[1] 25 years and over who are high school graduates	Asian Indian	Bangladeshi	Cambodian	Chinese[2]	Fijian	Filipino	Guamanian[3]	Hawaiian, Native	Hmong	Indonesian	Japanese	Korean	Laotian	Malaysian	Pakistani	Samoan	Sri Lankan	Taiwanese	Thai	Tongan	Vietnamese
Cook County	2,684,397 77.70	175,671	149,516 85.11 85.11 5.57	930	600 64.52 64.52 0.02	37,972 86.25 25.40 21.62 1.41	-	593 50.38 0.40 0.34 0.02	24,424 73.45 16.34 13.90 0.91	-	36,115 93.55 24.15 20.56 1.35	-	-	-	344 100.00 0.23 0.20 0.01	10,973 95.90 7.34 6.25 0.41	21,454 87.64 14.35 12.21 0.80	594 68.75 0.40 0.34 0.02	-	5,074 82.37 3.39 2.89 0.19	-	-	1,137 96.27 0.76 0.65 0.04	2,631 92.80 1.76 1.50 0.10	-	4,421 65.45 2.96 2.52 0.16
Arlington Heights (village)	50,106 92.75	3,310	3,146 95.05 95.05 6.28	-	-	846 94.84 26.89 25.56 1.69	-	-	350 95.63 11.13 10.57 0.70	-	494 93.56 15.70 14.92 0.99	-	-	-	-	779 99.24 24.76 23.53 1.55	458 92.90 14.56 13.84 0.91	-	-	-	-	-	-	-	-	-
Chicago (city)	1,304,122 71.82	87,469	69,751 79.74 79.74 5.35	602	348 57.81 57.81 0.03	12,640 83.24 18.12 14.45 0.97	-	482 47.25 0.69 0.55 0.04	14,871 66.21 21.32 17.00 1.14	-	18,689 92.65 26.79 21.37 1.43	-	-	-	-	4,925 94.62 7.06 5.63 0.38	7,533 79.40 10.80 8.61 0.58	-	-	3,088 79.16 4.43 3.53 0.24	-	-	437 95.83 0.63 0.50 0.03	1,424 93.62 2.04 1.63 0.11	-	3,147 62.50 4.51 3.60 0.24
Des Plaines (city)	34,033 81.91	2,836	2,441 86.07 86.07 7.17	-	-	930 76.48 38.10 32.79 2.73	-	-	304 86.12 12.45 10.72 0.89	-	586 100.00 24.01 20.66 1.72	-	-	-	-	-	-	-	-	-	-	-	-	-	-	-
Elk Grove Village (village)	21,445 90.33	2,205	2,060 93.42 93.42 9.61	-	-	586 88.52 28.45 26.58 2.73	-	-	283 88.44 13.74 12.83 1.32	-	378 96.18 18.35 17.14 1.76	-	-	-	-	420 100.00 20.39 19.05 1.96	-	-	-	-	-	-	-	-	-	-
Evanston (city)	43,244 91.37	2,358	2,313 98.09 98.09 5.35	-	-	567 98.61 24.51 24.05 1.31	-	-	542 100.00 23.43 22.99 1.25	-	316 91.33 13.66 13.40 0.73	-	-	-	-	284 97.59 12.28 12.04 0.66	360 100.00 15.56 15.27 0.83	-	-	-	-	-	-	-	-	-
Forest Park (village)	10,260 88.27	833	764 91.72 91.72 7.45	-	-	-	-	-	-	-	-	-	-	-	-	-	-	-	-	-	-	-	-	-	-	-
Glenview (village)	27,215 94.32	2,810	2,697 95.98 95.98 9.91	-	-	383 95.04 14.20 13.63 1.41	-	-	467 90.68 17.32 16.62 1.72	-	396 96.82 14.68 14.09 1.46	-	-	-	-	248 100.00 9.20 8.83 0.91	972 97.69 36.04 34.59 3.57	-	-	-	-	-	-	-	-	-
Hanover Park (village)	17,543 78.69	2,668	2,367 88.72 88.72 13.49	-	-	1,030 89.02 43.51 38.61 5.87	-	-	-	-	730 94.81 30.84 27.36 4.16	-	-	-	-	-	-	-	-	-	-	-	-	-	-	-
Hoffman Estates (village)	28,275 89.64	4,746	4,231 89.15 89.15 14.96	-	-	1,505 86.15 35.57 31.71 5.32	-	-	501 94.89 11.84 10.56 1.77	-	597 90.73 14.11 12.58 2.11	-	-	-	-	481 93.58 11.37 10.13 1.70	785 89.10 18.55 16.54 2.78	-	-	-	-	-	-	-	-	-

Notes: Please refer to the User's Guide for an explanation of data; data is arranged alphabetically by state, then county, then city within each county; table includes counties with populations greater than 49,999 unless noted and cities with populations greater than 9,999 whose Asian and/or NHPI population rates are greater than the national average; (1) Native Hawaiian and other Pacific Islander; (2) excludes Taiwanese; (3) includes Chamorro; (4) county does not meet population threshold but is shown in order to allow inclusion of city

Place	Total population 25 years and over who are high school graduates	Asian population 25 years and over	Asians 25 years and over who are high school graduates	NHPI[1] population 25 years and over	NHPIs[1] 25 years and over who are high school graduates	Asian Indian	Bangladeshi	Cambodian	Chinese[2]	Fijian	Filipino	Guamanian[3]	Hawaiian, Native	Hmong	Indonesian	Japanese	Korean	Laotian	Malaysian	Pakistani	Samoan	Sri Lankan	Taiwanese	Thai	Tongan	Vietnamese
Lincolnwood (village)	7,790 89.21	1,600	1,418 88.63 88.63 18.20	-	-	387 81.47 27.29 24.19 4.97	-	-	-	-	286 98.62 20.17 17.88 3.67	-	-	-	-	-	363 90.30 25.60 22.69 4.66	-	-	-	-	-	-	-	-	-
Morton Grove (village)	14,387 87.38	3,243	2,933 90.44 90.44 20.39	-	-	772 87.43 26.32 23.81 5.37	-	-	-	-	1,122 95.08 38.25 34.60 7.80	-	-	-	-	-	533 88.54 18.17 16.44 3.70	-	-	-	-	-	-	-	-	-
Mount Prospect (village)	33,565 85.66	4,457	3,746 84.05 84.05 11.16	-	-	1,719 78.31 45.89 38.57 5.12	-	-	323 81.16 8.62 7.25 0.96	-	303 98.06 8.09 6.80 0.90	-	-	-	-	359 100.00 9.58 8.05 1.07	812 87.03 21.68 18.22 2.42	-	-	-	-	-	-	-	-	-
Niles (village)	18,563 81.40	2,221	2,016 90.77 90.77 10.86	-	-	717 91.45 35.57 32.28 3.86	-	-	-	-	375 91.69 18.60 16.88 2.02	-	-	-	-	-	653 91.71 32.39 29.40 3.52	-	-	-	-	-	-	-	-	-
Northbrook (village)	22,529 95.57	1,978	1,881 95.10 95.10 8.35	-	-	-	-	-	315 89.24 16.75 15.93 1.40	-	-	-	-	-	-	-	974 96.06 51.78 49.24 4.32	-	-	-	-	-	-	-	-	-
Oak Park (village)	34,397 94.40	1,624	1,583 97.48 97.48 4.60	-	-	554 98.05 35.00 34.11 1.61	-	-	296 97.69 18.70 18.23 0.86	-	-	-	-	-	-	-	-	-	-	-	-	-	-	-	-	-
Orland Park (village)	31,330 89.86	1,323	1,212 91.61 91.61 3.87	-	-	370 95.85 30.53 27.97 1.18	-	-	-	-	437 98.87 36.06 33.03 1.39	-	-	-	-	-	-	-	-	-	-	-	-	-	-	-
Palatine (village)	38,852 89.13	3,479	3,155 90.69 90.69 8.12	-	-	1,240 89.08 39.30 35.64 3.19	-	-	456 86.36 14.45 13.11 1.17	-	497 92.21 15.75 14.29 1.28	-	-	-	-	-	390 98.24 12.36 11.21 1.00	-	-	-	-	-	-	-	-	-
Prospect Heights (city)	9,043 77.40	418	418 100.00 100.00 4.62	-	-	-	-	-	-	-	-	-	-	-	-	-	-	-	-	-	-	-	-	-	-	-
Rolling Meadows (city)	13,615 83.66	926	856 92.44 92.44 6.29	-	-	279 97.21 32.59 30.13 2.05	-	-	-	-	-	-	-	-	-	-	-	-	-	-	-	-	-	-	-	-

Notes: Please refer to the User's Guide for an explanation of data; data is arranged alphabetically by state, then county, then city within each county; table includes counties with populations greater than 49,999 unless noted and cities with populations greater than 9,999 whose Asian and/or NHPI population rates are greater than the national average; (1) Native Hawaiian and other Pacific Islander; (2) excludes Taiwanese; (3) includes Chamorro; (4) county does not meet population threshold but is shown in order to allow inclusion of city

Place	Total population 25 years and over who are high school graduates	Asian population 25 years and over	Asians 25 years and over who are high school graduates	NHPI[1] population 25 years and over	NHPIs[1] 25 years and over who are high school graduates	Asian Indian	Bangladeshi	Cambodian	Chinese[2]	Fijian	Filipino	Guamanian[3]	Hawaiian, Native	Hmong	Indonesian	Japanese	Korean	Laotian	Malaysian	Pakistani	Samoan	Sri Lankan	Taiwanese	Thai	Tongan	Vietnamese
Schaumburg (village)	47,877 91.82	7,048	6,663 94.54 94.54 13.92	-	-	2,987 94.95 44.83 42.38 6.24	-	-	850 91.79 12.76 12.06 1.78	-	733 98.79 11.00 10.40 1.53	-	-	-	-	671 99.11 10.07 9.52 1.40	1,042 92.62 15.64 14.78 2.18	-	-	-	-	-	-	-	-	-
Schiller Park (village)	5,566 72.55	487	402 82.55 82.55 7.22	-	-	-	-	-	-	-	-	-	-	-	-	-	-	-	-	-	-	-	-	-	-	-
Skokie (village)	38,697 87.35	8,599	7,656 89.03 89.03 19.78	-	-	1,853 83.66 24.20 21.55 4.79	-	-	1,046 88.64 13.66 12.16 2.70	-	1,848 92.45 24.14 21.49 4.78	-	-	-	-	-	1,650 92.13 21.55 19.19 4.26	-	-	197 70.61 2.57 2.29 0.51	-	-	-	-	-	-
Streamwood (village)	20,087 85.35	2,239	2,046 91.38 91.38 10.19	-	-	760 91.24 37.15 33.94 3.78	-	-	-	-	775 98.73 37.88 34.61 3.86	-	-	-	-	-	-	-	-	-	-	-	-	-	-	-
Wheeling (village)	18,914 82.57	1,967	1,833 93.19 93.19 9.69	-	-	842 93.45 45.94 42.81 4.45	-	-	-	-	355 94.41 19.37 18.05 1.88	-	-	-	-	-	-	-	-	-	-	-	-	-	-	-
Wilmette (village)	17,794 96.76	1,361	1,317 96.77 96.77 7.40	-	-	-	-	-	237 89.10 18.00 17.41 1.33	-	-	-	-	-	-	209 100.00 15.87 15.36 1.17	472 98.74 35.84 34.68 2.65	-	-	-	-	-	-	-	-	-
DeKalb County	42,802 87.51	674	629 93.32 93.32 1.47	-	-	161 87.50 25.60 23.89 0.38	-	-	-	-	-	-	-	-	-	-	-	-	-	-	-	-	-	-	-	-
DeKalb (city)	14,973 87.58	542	519 95.76 95.76 3.47	-	-	136 85.53 26.20 25.09 0.91	-	-	-	-	-	-	-	-	-	-	-	-	-	-	-	-	-	-	-	-
DuPage County	530,429 90.04	46,209	41,883 90.64 90.64 7.90	-	-	18,127 90.53 43.28 39.23 3.42	-	-	6,251 92.36 14.92 13.53 1.18	-	9,106 94.45 21.74 19.71 1.72	-	-	-	-	1,206 97.97 2.88 2.61 0.23	2,561 91.24 6.11 5.54 0.48	-	-	1,339 87.92 3.20 2.90 0.25	-	-	527 95.82 1.26 1.14 0.10	277 97.54 0.66 0.60 0.05	-	1,162 64.23 2.77 2.51 0.22
Addison (village)	16,423 73.50	1,934	1,523 78.75 78.75 9.27	-	-	841 77.58 55.22 43.49 5.12	-	-	-	-	322 84.29 21.14 16.65 1.96	-	-	-	-	-	-	-	-	-	-	-	-	-	-	-

Notes: Please refer to the User's Guide for an explanation of data; data is arranged alphabetically by state, then county, then city within each county; table includes counties with populations greater than 49,999 unless noted and cities with populations greater than 9,999 whose Asian and/or NHPI population rates are greater than the national average; (1) Native Hawaiian and other Pacific Islander; (2) excludes Taiwanese; (3) includes Chamorro; (4) county does not meet population threshold but is shown in order to allow inclusion of city

Place	Total population 25 years and over who are high school graduates	Asian population 25 years and over	Asians 25 years and over who are high school graduates	NHPI[1] population 25 years and over	NHPIs[1] 25 years and over who are high school graduates	Asian Indian	Bangladeshi	Cambodian	Chinese[2]	Fijian	Filipino	Guamanian[3]	Hawaiian, Native	Hmong	Indonesian	Japanese	Korean	Laotian	Malaysian	Pakistani	Samoan	Sri Lankan	Taiwanese	Thai	Tongan	Vietnamese
Bartlett (village)	21,342 92.33	1,863	1,687 90.55 90.55 7.90	-	-	849 90.22 50.33 45.57 3.98	-	-	-	-	411 97.86 24.36 22.06 1.93	-	-	-	-	-	-	-	-	-	-	-	-	-	-	-
Bensenville (village)	9,392 71.13	866	786 90.76 90.76 8.37	-	-	436 94.17 55.47 50.35 4.64	-	-	-	-	-	-	-	-	-	-	-	-	-	-	-	-	-	-	-	-
Bloomingdale (village)	13,526 89.23	1,301	1,167 89.70 89.70 8.63	-	-	517 88.68 44.30 39.74 3.82	-	-	-	-	-	-	-	-	-	-	-	-	-	-	-	-	-	-	-	-
Burr Ridge (village)	6,519 95.28	701	672 95.86 95.86 10.31	-	-	356 96.22 52.98 50.78 5.46	-	-	-	-	-	-	-	-	-	-	-	-	-	-	-	-	-	-	-	-
Carol Stream (village)	21,811 89.88	2,555	2,200 86.11 86.11 10.09	-	-	999 84.95 45.41 39.10 4.58	-	-	-	-	622 96.43 28.27 24.34 2.85	-	-	-	-	-	-	-	-	-	-	-	-	-	-	156 58.65 7.09 6.11 0.72
Darien (city)	15,049 93.54	1,803	1,709 94.79 94.79 11.36	-	-	801 94.12 46.87 44.43 5.32	-	-	-	-	521 93.37 30.49 28.90 3.46	-	-	-	-	-	-	-	-	-	-	-	-	-	-	-
Downers Grove (village)	31,110 93.03	1,981	1,845 93.13 93.13 5.93	-	-	856 95.64 46.40 43.21 2.75	-	-	366 83.56 19.84 18.48 1.18	-	327 95.06 17.72 16.51 1.05	-	-	-	-	-	-	-	-	-	-	-	-	-	-	-
Glen Ellyn (village)	16,716 94.50	822	775 94.28 94.28 4.64	-	-	329 97.63 42.45 40.02 1.97	-	-	-	-	-	-	-	-	-	-	-	-	-	-	-	-	-	-	-	-
Glendale Heights (village)	15,889 81.50	3,867	3,035 78.48 78.48 19.10	-	-	1,116 72.89 36.77 28.86 7.02	-	-	-	-	1,084 95.93 35.72 28.03 6.82	-	-	-	-	-	-	-	-	-	-	-	-	-	-	254 50.10 8.37 6.57 1.60
Hinsdale (village)	10,697 97.33	584	536 91.78 91.78 5.01	-	-	-	-	-	-	-	-	-	-	-	-	-	-	-	-	-	-	-	-	-	-	-

Notes: Please refer to the User's Guide for an explanation of data; data is arranged alphabetically by state, then county, then city within each county; table includes counties with populations greater than 49,999 unless noted and cities with populations greater than 9,999 whose Asian and/or NHPI population rates are greater than the national average; (1) Native Hawaiian and other Pacific Islander; (2) excludes Taiwanese; (3) includes Chamorro; (4) county does not meet population threshold but is shown in order to allow inclusion of city

Place	Total population 25 years and over who are high school graduates	Asian population 25 years and over	Asians 25 years and over who are high school graduates	NHPI[1] population 25 years and over	NHPIs[1] 25 years and over who are high school graduates	Asian Indian	Bangladeshi	Cambodian	Chinese[2]	Fijian	Filipino	Guamanian[3]	Hawaiian, Native	Hmong	Indonesian	Japanese	Korean	Laotian	Malaysian	Pakistani	Samoan	Sri Lankan	Taiwanese	Thai	Tongan	Vietnamese
Lisle (village)	13,555 95.42	1,388	1,355 97.62 97.62 10.00	-	-	483 100.00 35.65 34.80 3.56	-	-	402 92.41 29.67 28.96 2.97	-	-	-	-	-	-	-	-	-	-	-	-	-	-	-	-	-
Lombard (village)	26,353 90.42	2,041	1,894 92.80 92.80 7.19	-	-	804 92.31 42.45 39.39 3.05	-	-	-	-	477 96.36 25.18 23.37 1.81	-	-	-	-	-	-	-	-	-	-	-	-	-	-	-
Naperville (city)	75,935 96.31	7,267	6,863 94.44 94.44 9.04	-	-	2,709 91.89 39.47 37.28 3.57	-	-	2,391 95.99 34.84 32.90 3.15	-	424 100.00 6.18 5.83 0.56	-	-	-	-	-	483 94.15 7.04 6.65 0.64	-	-	-	-	-	240 91.25 3.50 3.30 0.32	-	-	-
Roselle (village)	13,946 91.02	1,262	1,207 95.64 95.64 8.65	-	-	585 93.90 48.47 46.35 4.19	-	-	-	-	-	-	-	-	-	-	-	-	-	-	-	-	-	-	-	-
Villa Park (village)	12,291 85.98	555	494 89.01 89.01 4.02	-	-	-	-	-	-	-	-	-	-	-	-	-	-	-	-	-	-	-	-	-	-	-
Warrenville (city)	7,815 92.85	356	316 88.76 88.76 4.04	-	-	-	-	-	-	-	-	-	-	-	-	-	-	-	-	-	-	-	-	-	-	-
Westmont (village)	14,827 86.59	2,078	1,940 93.36 93.36 13.08	-	-	912 96.92 47.01 43.89 6.15	-	-	343 88.40 17.68 16.51 2.31	-	317 85.91 16.34 15.26 2.14	-	-	-	-	-	-	-	-	-	-	-	-	-	-	-
Wheaton (city)	33,355 94.42	1,680	1,438 85.60 85.60 4.31	-	-	622 96.88 43.25 37.02 1.86	-	-	-	-	-	-	-	-	-	-	-	-	-	-	-	-	-	-	-	55 27.64 3.82 3.27 0.16
Woodridge (village)	17,908 90.02	2,289	2,063 90.13 90.13 11.52	-	-	978 89.72 47.41 42.73 5.46	-	-	-	-	671 91.54 32.53 29.31 3.75	-	-	-	-	-	-	-	-	-	-	-	-	-	-	-
Jackson County	27,838 85.24	1,109	1,084 97.75 97.75 3.89	-	-	-	-	-	265 100.00 24.45 23.90 0.95	-	-	-	-	-	-	-	-	-	-	-	-	-	-	-	-	-

Notes: Please refer to the User's Guide for an explanation of data; data is arranged alphabetically by state, then county, then city within each county; table includes counties with populations greater than 49,999 unless noted and cities with populations greater than 9,999 whose Asian and/or NHPI population rates are greater than the national average; (1) Native Hawaiian and other Pacific Islander; (2) excludes Taiwanese; (3) includes Chamorro; (4) county does not meet population threshold but is shown in order to allow inclusion of city

Place	Total population 25 years and over who are high school graduates	Asian population 25 years and over	Asians 25 years and over who are high school graduates	NHPI[1] population 25 years and over	NHPIs[1] 25 years and over who are high school graduates	Asian Indian	Bangladeshi	Cambodian	Chinese[2]	Fijian	Filipino	Guamanian[3]	Hawaiian, Native	Hmong	Indonesian	Japanese	Korean	Laotian	Malaysian	Pakistani	Samoan	Sri Lankan	Taiwanese	Thai	Tongan	Vietnamese
Carbondale (city)	9,222 90.68	831	820 98.68 98.68 8.89	-	-	-	-	-	-	-	-	-	-	-	-	-	-	-	-	-	-	-	-	-	-	-
Kane County	196,798 80.17	4,380	3,771 86.10 86.10 1.92	-	-	842 89.57 22.33 19.22 0.43	-	-	506 81.22 13.42 11.55 0.26	-	884 98.22 23.44 20.18 0.45	-	-	-	-	-	237 86.50 6.28 5.41 0.12	418 73.46 11.08 9.54 0.21	-	-	-	-	-	-	-	227 70.50 6.02 5.18 0.12
South Elgin (village)	9,080 90.38	507	382 75.35 75.35 4.21	-	-	-	-	-	-	-	-	-	-	-	-	-	-	-	-	-	-	-	-	-	-	-
Kankakee County	52,545 79.80	424	306 72.17 72.17 0.58	-	-	-	-	-	-	-	-	-	-	-	-	-	-	-	-	-	-	-	-	-	-	-
Kendall County	30,882 89.87	366	325 88.80 88.80 1.05	-	-	-	-	-	-	-	-	-	-	-	-	-	-	-	-	-	-	-	-	-	-	-
Knox County	31,137 81.83	175	137 78.29 78.29 0.44	-	-	-	-	-	-	-	-	-	-	-	-	-	-	-	-	-	-	-	-	-	-	-
La Salle County	60,559 81.36	354	322 90.96 90.96 0.53	-	-	-	-	-	-	-	-	-	-	-	-	-	-	-	-	-	-	-	-	-	-	-
Lake County	344,806 86.58	16,241	15,074 92.81 92.81 4.37	-	-	3,287 91.82 21.81 20.24 0.95	-	-	3,005 93.27 19.93 18.50 0.87	-	4,089 92.41 27.13 25.18 1.19	-	-	-	-	1,015 95.66 6.73 6.25 0.29	2,409 95.94 15.98 14.83 0.70	-	-	279 94.90 1.85 1.72 0.08	-	-	-	-	-	339 84.12 2.25 2.09 0.10
Buffalo Grove (village)	26,710 95.31	2,323	2,230 96.00 96.00 8.35	-	-	427 94.47 19.15 18.38 1.60	-	-	410 96.02 18.39 17.65 1.54	-	270 93.75 12.11 11.62 1.01	-	-	-	-	396 100.00 17.76 17.05 1.48	600 95.85 26.91 25.83 2.25	-	-	-	-	-	-	-	-	-
Gages Lake (cdp)	6,223 92.69	277	252 90.97 90.97 4.05	-	-	-	-	-	-	-	-	-	-	-	-	-	-	-	-	-	-	-	-	-	-	-

Notes: Please refer to the User's Guide for an explanation of data; data is arranged alphabetically by state, then county, then city within each county; table includes counties with populations greater than 49,999 unless noted and cities with populations greater than 9,999 whose Asian and/or NHPI population rates are greater than the national average; (1) Native Hawaiian and other Pacific Islander; (2) excludes Taiwanese; (3) includes Chamorro; (4) county does not meet population threshold but is shown in order to allow inclusion of city

Place	Total population 25 years and over who are high school graduates	Asian population 25 years and over	Asians 25 years and over who are high school graduates	NHPI[1] population 25 years and over	NHPIs[1] 25 years and over who are high school graduates	Asian Indian	Bangladeshi	Cambodian	Chinese[2]	Fijian	Filipino	Guamanian[3]	Hawaiian, Native	Hmong	Indonesian	Japanese	Korean	Laotian	Malaysian	Pakistani	Samoan	Sri Lankan	Taiwanese	Thai	Tongan	Vietnamese
Grayslake (village)	10,844 94.63	599	583 97.33 97.33 5.38	-	-	-	-	-	-	-	-	-	-	-	-	-	-	-	-	-	-	-	-	-	-	-
Gurnee (village)	17,280 94.12	1,482	1,435 96.83 96.83 8.30	-	-	448 94.51 31.22 30.23 2.59	-	-	240 95.24 16.72 16.19 1.39	-	445 98.02 31.01 30.03 2.58	-	-	-	-	-	-	-	-	-	-	-	-	-	-	-
Lake Zurich (village)	10,257 93.79	436	415 95.18 95.18 4.05	-	-	-	-	-	-	-	-	-	-	-	-	-	-	-	-	-	-	-	-	-	-	-
Libertyville (village)	12,877 94.15	669	611 91.33 91.33 4.74	-	-	-	-	-	-	-	-	-	-	-	-	-	-	-	-	-	-	-	-	-	-	-
Mundelein (village)	15,529 83.53	1,244	1,145 92.04 92.04 7.37	-	-	-	-	-	327 91.60 28.56 26.29 2.11	-	339 96.03 29.61 27.25 2.18	-	-	-	-	-	-	-	-	-	-	-	-	-	-	-
Vernon Hills (village)	12,341 93.97	1,509	1,453 96.29 96.29 11.77	-	-	338 100.00 23.26 22.40 2.74	-	-	418 94.14 28.77 27.70 3.39	-	-	-	-	-	-	-	420 97.67 28.91 27.83 3.40	-	-	-	-	-	-	-	-	-
Macon County	62,543 83.17	427	379 88.76 88.76 0.61	-	-	-	-	-	-	-	-	-	-	-	-	-	-	-	-	-	-	-	-	-	-	-
Madison County	143,600 84.26	831	707 85.08 85.08 0.49	-	-	231 89.88 32.67 27.80 0.16	-	-	-	-	-	-	-	-	-	-	-	-	-	-	-	-	-	-	-	-
McHenry County	146,130 89.22	2,188	1,953 89.26 89.26 1.34	-	-	458 81.49 23.45 20.93 0.31	-	-	352 95.39 18.02 16.09 0.24	-	629 98.28 32.21 28.75 0.43	-	-	-	-	-	-	-	-	-	-	-	-	-	-	-
McLean County	79,125 90.72	1,934	1,840 95.14 95.14 2.33	-	-	771 100.00 41.90 39.87 0.97	-	-	404 89.98 21.96 20.89 0.51	-	-	-	-	-	-	-	-	-	-	-	-	-	-	-	-	-

Notes: Please refer to the User's Guide for an explanation of data; data is arranged alphabetically by state, then county, then city within each county; table includes counties with populations greater than 49,999 unless noted and cities with populations greater than 9,999 whose Asian and/or NHPI population rates are greater than the national average; (1) Native Hawaiian and other Pacific Islander; (2) excludes Taiwanese; (3) includes Chamorro; (4) county does not meet population threshold but is shown in order to allow inclusion of city

Place	Total population 25 years and over who are high school graduates	Asian population 25 years and over	Asians 25 years and over who are high school graduates	NHPI[1] population 25 years and over	NHPIs[1] 25 years and over who are high school graduates	Asian Indian	Bangladeshi	Cambodian	Chinese[2]	Fijian	Filipino	Guamanian[3]	Hawaiian, Native	Hmong	Indonesian	Japanese	Korean	Laotian	Malaysian	Pakistani	Samoan	Sri Lankan	Taiwanese	Thai	Tongan	Vietnamese
Peoria County	99,342 83.83	2,123	1,911 90.01 90.01 1.92	-	-	712 100.00 37.26 33.54 0.72	-	-	584 88.35 30.56 27.51 0.59	-	-	-	-	-	-	-	-	-	-	-	-	-	-	-	-	128 60.66 6.70 6.03 0.13
Rock Island County	81,627 82.56	909	826 90.87 90.87 1.01	-	-	373 96.38 45.16 41.03 0.46	-	-	-	-	-	-	-	-	-	-	-	-	-	-	-	-	-	-	-	-
St. Clair County	131,611 80.88	1,575	1,286 81.65 81.65 0.98	-	-	-	-	-	-	-	345 80.99 26.83 21.90 0.26	-	-	-	-	-	256 77.11 19.91 16.25 0.19	-	-	-	-	-	-	-	-	-
Sangamon County	111,520 88.07	1,332	1,216 91.29 91.29 1.09	-	-	433 100.00 35.61 32.51 0.39	-	-	233 86.62 19.16 17.49 0.21	-	-	-	-	-	-	-	-	-	-	-	-	-	-	-	-	-
Tazewell County	73,653 84.98	402	273 67.91 67.91 0.37	-	-	-	-	-	-	-	-	-	-	-	-	-	-	-	-	-	-	-	-	-	-	-
Vermilion County	43,921 78.74	316	285 90.19 90.19 0.65	-	-	-	-	-	-	-	-	-	-	-	-	-	-	-	-	-	-	-	-	-	-	-
Will County	270,085 86.87	6,979	6,329 90.69 90.69 2.34	-	-	1,537 88.03 24.29 22.02 0.57	-	-	880 91.67 13.90 12.61 0.33	-	2,005 96.16 31.68 28.73 0.74	-	-	-	-	-	450 88.06 7.11 6.45 0.17	-	-	202 94.39 3.19 2.89 0.07	-	-	-	-	-	290 83.57 4.58 4.16 0.11
Bolingbrook (village)	29,351 87.18	2,417	2,123 87.84 87.84 7.23	-	-	558 85.45 26.28 23.09 1.90	-	-	-	-	790 95.53 37.21 32.69 2.69	-	-	-	-	-	-	-	-	-	-	-	-	-	-	-
Winnebago County	148,039 81.43	2,674	2,063 77.15 77.15 1.39	-	-	371 87.91 17.98 13.87 0.25	-	-	-	-	349 95.10 16.92 13.05 0.24	-	-	-	-	-	229 87.07 11.10 8.56 0.15	459 62.28 22.25 17.17 0.31	-	-	-	-	-	-	-	191 49.87 9.26 7.14 0.13
INDIANA	3,197,738 82.13	35,529	30,624 86.19 86.19 0.96	929	715 76.96 76.96 0.02	7,762 91.66 25.35 21.85 0.24	-	94 34.81 0.31 0.26 <0.01	6,469 88.11 21.12 18.21 0.20	-	4,284 90.65 13.99 12.06 0.13	147 58.57 20.56 15.82 <0.01	332 91.21 46.43 35.74 0.01	-	-	3,058 92.84 9.99 8.61 0.10	3,729 86.56 12.18 10.50 0.12	345 58.57 1.13 0.97 0.01	-	327 87.90 1.07 0.92 0.01	-	-	504 97.49 1.65 1.42 0.02	442 69.72 1.44 1.24 0.01	-	1,796 63.37 5.86 5.06 0.06

Notes: Please refer to the User's Guide for an explanation of data; data is arranged alphabetically by state, then county, then city within each county; table includes counties with populations greater than 49,999 unless noted and cities with populations greater than 9,999 whose Asian and/or NHPI population rates are greater than the national average; (1) Native Hawaiian and other Pacific Islander; (2) excludes Taiwanese; (3) includes Chamorro; (4) county does not meet population threshold but is shown in order to allow inclusion of city

Place	Total population 25 years and over who are high school graduates	Asian population 25 years and over	Asians 25 years and over who are high school graduates	NHPI[1] population 25 years and over	NHPIs[1] 25 years and over who are high school graduates	Asian Indian	Bangladeshi	Cambodian	Chinese[2]	Fijian	Filipino	Guamanian[3]	Hawaiian, Native	Hmong	Indonesian	Japanese	Korean	Laotian	Malaysian	Pakistani	Samoan	Sri Lankan	Taiwanese	Thai	Tongan	Vietnamese
Allen County	178,884 85.69	2,868	2,261 78.84 78.84 1.26	-	-	624 93.41 27.60 21.76 0.35	-	-	280 77.13 12.38 9.76 0.16	-	322 88.46 14.24 11.23 0.18	-	-	-	-	-	-	-	-	-	-	-	-	-	-	281 58.54 12.43 9.80 0.16
Bartholomew County	39,469 83.78	841	801 95.24 95.24 2.03	-	-	277 98.23 34.58 32.94 0.70	-	-	-	-	-	-	-	-	-	-	-	-	-	-	-	-	-	-	-	-
Clark County	51,415 79.85	335	294 87.76 87.76 0.57	-	-	-	-	-	-	-	-	-	-	-	-	-	-	-	-	-	-	-	-	-	-	-
Delaware County	59,114 81.60	385	357 92.73 92.73 0.60	-	-	-	-	-	-	-	-	-	-	-	-	-	-	-	-	-	-	-	-	-	-	-
Elkhart County	85,517 75.74	968	670 69.21 69.21 0.78	-	-	-	-	-	-	-	-	-	-	-	-	-	-	-	-	-	-	-	-	-	-	-
Grant County	37,537 79.18	258	208 80.62 80.62 0.55	-	-	-	-	-	-	-	-	-	-	-	-	-	-	-	-	-	-	-	-	-	-	-
Hamilton County	109,692 94.19	2,670	2,498 93.56 93.56 2.28	-	-	638 96.67 25.54 23.90 0.58	-	-	547 93.83 21.90 20.49 0.50	-	-	-	-	-	-	-	-	-	-	-	-	-	-	-	-	-
Carmel (city)	23,867 97.02	1,000	921 92.10 92.10 3.86	-	-	-	-	-	-	-	-	-	-	-	-	-	-	-	-	-	-	-	-	-	-	-
Hendricks County	59,903 88.51	476	366 76.89 76.89 0.61	-	-	-	-	-	-	-	-	-	-	-	-	-	-	-	-	-	-	-	-	-	-	-
Howard County	46,844 83.32	484	420 86.78 86.78 0.90	-	-	-	-	-	-	-	-	-	-	-	-	-	-	-	-	-	-	-	-	-	-	-

Notes: Please refer to the User's Guide for an explanation of data; data is arranged alphabetically by state, then county, then city within each county; table includes counties with populations greater than 49,999 unless noted and cities with populations greater than 9,999 whose Asian and/or NHPI population rates are greater than the national average; (1) Native Hawaiian and other Pacific Islander; (2) excludes Taiwanese; (3) includes Chamorro; (4) county does not meet population threshold but is shown in order to allow inclusion of city

Place	Total population 25 years and over who are high school graduates	Asian population 25 years and over	Asians 25 years and over who are high school graduates	NHPI[1] population 25 years and over	NHPIs[1] 25 years and over who are high school graduates	Asian Indian	Bangladeshi	Cambodian	Chinese[2]	Fijian	Filipino	Guamanian[3]	Hawaiian, Native	Hmong	Indonesian	Japanese	Korean	Laotian	Malaysian	Pakistani	Samoan	Sri Lankan	Taiwanese	Thai	Tongan	Vietnamese
Johnson County	63,391 85.70	619	550 88.85 88.85 0.87	-	-	-	-	-	-	-	-	-	-	-	-	-	-	-	-	-	-	-	-	-	-	-
Kosciusko County	38,439 81.61	257	234 91.05 91.05 0.61	-	-	-	-	-	-	-	-	-	-	-	-	-	-	-	-	-	-	-	-	-	-	-
Lake County	250,349 80.70	2,657	2,448 92.13 92.13 0.98	-	-	853 96.38 34.84 32.10 0.34	-	-	381 97.44 15.56 14.34 0.15	-	541 93.12 22.10 20.36 0.22	-	-	-	-	-	352 79.10 14.38 13.25 0.14	-	-	-	-	-	-	-	-	-
Munster (town)	14,006 92.95	649	634 97.69 97.69 4.53	-	-	241 100.00 38.01 37.13 1.72	-	-	-	-	-	-	-	-	-	-	-	-	-	-	-	-	-	-	-	-
LaPorte County	59,409 80.58	220	169 76.82 76.82 0.28	-	-	-	-	-	-	-	-	-	-	-	-	-	-	-	-	-	-	-	-	-	-	-
Madison County	71,677 80.12	326	244 74.85 74.85 0.34	-	-	-	-	-	-	-	-	-	-	-	-	-	-	-	-	-	-	-	-	-	-	-
Marion County	451,863 81.64	7,867	6,722 85.45 85.45 1.49	-	-	2,103 90.03 31.29 26.73 0.47	-	-	1,408 87.34 20.95 17.90 0.31	-	935 91.67 13.91 11.89 0.21	-	-	-	-	402 95.49 5.98 5.11 0.09	674 85.32 10.03 8.57 0.15	-	-	-	-	-	-	-	-	589 70.04 8.76 7.49 0.13
Monroe County	57,952 88.49	2,068	2,011 97.24 97.24 3.47	-	-	341 97.15 16.96 16.49 0.59	-	-	465 94.32 23.12 22.49 0.80	-	-	-	-	-	-	-	559 98.07 27.80 27.03 0.96	-	-	-	-	-	-	-	-	-
Bloomington (city)	28,564 91.17	1,786	1,734 97.09 97.09 6.07	-	-	255 98.08 14.71 14.28 0.89	-	-	432 93.91 24.91 24.19 1.51	-	-	-	-	-	-	-	520 97.93 29.99 29.12 1.82	-	-	-	-	-	-	-	-	-
Porter County	83,372 88.26	643	516 80.25 80.25 0.62	-	-	-	-	-	-	-	-	-	-	-	-	-	-	-	-	-	-	-	-	-	-	-

Notes: Please refer to the User's Guide for an explanation of data; data is arranged alphabetically by state, then county, then city within each county; table includes counties with populations greater than 49,999 unless noted and cities with populations greater than 9,999 whose Asian and/or NHPI population rates are greater than the national average; (1) Native Hawaiian and other Pacific Islander; (2) excludes Taiwanese; (3) includes Chamorro; (4) county does not meet population threshold but is shown in order to allow inclusion of city

Place	Total population 25 years and over who are high school graduates	Asian population 25 years and over	Asians 25 years and over who are high school graduates	NHPI[1] population 25 years and over	NHPIs[1] 25 years and over who are high school graduates	Asian Indian	Bangladeshi	Cambodian	Chinese[2]	Fijian	Filipino	Guamanian[3]	Hawaiian, Native	Hmong	Indonesian	Japanese	Korean	Laotian	Malaysian	Pakistani	Samoan	Sri Lankan	Taiwanese	Thai	Tongan	Vietnamese
St. Joseph County	136,825 82.39	2,210	1,887 85.38 85.38 1.38	-	-	422 97.01 22.36 19.10 0.31	-	-	514 91.62 27.24 23.26 0.38	-	-	-	-	-	-	-	211 79.32 11.18 9.55 0.15	-	-	-	-	-	-	-	-	-
Tippecanoe County	70,160 87.80	3,381	3,170 93.76 93.76 4.52	-	-	533 86.81 16.81 15.76 0.76	-	-	1,174 97.27 37.03 34.72 1.67	-	-	-	-	-	-	260 100.00 8.20 7.69 0.37	581 95.72 18.33 17.18 0.83	-	-	-	-	-	-	-	-	-
West Lafayette (city)	9,778 96.25	1,279	1,238 96.79 96.79 12.66	-	-	296 98.67 23.91 23.14 3.03	-	-	395 96.11 31.91 30.88 4.04	-	-	-	-	-	-	-	-	-	-	-	-	-	-	-	-	-
Vanderburgh County	93,243 83.12	988	878 88.87 88.87 0.94	-	-	-	-	-	-	-	-	-	-	-	-	-	-	-	-	-	-	-	-	-	-	-
Vigo County	54,059 81.03	679	572 84.24 84.24 1.06	-	-	-	-	-	-	-	-	-	-	-	-	-	-	-	-	-	-	-	-	-	-	-
Wayne County	36,969 78.12	248	188 75.81 75.81 0.51	-	-	-	-	-	-	-	-	-	-	-	-	-	-	-	-	-	-	-	-	-	-	-
IOWA	1,632,420 86.10	20,157	14,974 74.29 74.29 0.92	440	346 78.64 78.64 0.02	3,022 94.73 20.18 14.99 0.19	-	108 28.95 0.72 0.54 0.01	3,232 92.05 21.58 16.03 0.20	-	1,362 85.34 9.10 6.76 0.08	-	-	-	-	786 91.50 5.25 3.90 0.05	1,824 89.94 12.18 9.05 0.11	1,154 53.43 7.71 5.73 0.07	-	181 100.00 1.21 0.90 0.01	-	-	264 95.31 1.76 1.31 0.02	479 70.86 3.20 2.38 0.03	-	1,839 41.72 12.28 9.12 0.11
Black Hawk County	67,780 86.45	822	721 87.71 87.71 1.06	-	-	-	-	-	-	-	-	-	-	-	-	-	-	-	-	-	-	-	-	-	-	-
Buena Vista County[4]	10,358 81.33	475	228 48.00 48.00 2.20	-	-	-	-	-	-	-	-	-	-	-	-	-	-	89 30.17 39.04 18.74 0.86	-	-	-	-	-	-	-	-
Storm Lake (city)	4,287 73.31	412	192 46.60 46.60 4.48	-	-	-	-	-	-	-	-	-	-	-	-	-	-	84 30.32 43.75 20.39 1.96	-	-	-	-	-	-	-	-

Notes: Please refer to the User's Guide for an explanation of data; data is arranged alphabetically by state, then county, then city within each county; table includes counties with populations greater than 49,999 unless noted and cities with populations greater than 9,999 whose Asian and/or NHPI population rates are greater than the national average; (1) Native Hawaiian and other Pacific Islander; (2) excludes Taiwanese; (3) includes Chamorro; (4) county does not meet population threshold but is shown in order to allow inclusion of city

Place	Total population 25 years and over who are high school graduates	Asian population 25 years and over	Asians 25 years and over who are high school graduates	NHPI[1] population 25 years and over	NHPIs[1] 25 years and over who are high school graduates	Asian Indian	Bangladeshi	Cambodian	Chinese[2]	Fijian	Filipino	Guamanian[3]	Hawaiian, Native	Hmong	Indonesian	Japanese	Korean	Laotian	Malaysian	Pakistani	Samoan	Sri Lankan	Taiwanese	Thai	Tongan	Vietnamese
Johnson County	58,876 93.66	2,618	2,352 89.84 89.84 3.99	-	-	440 91.67 18.71 16.81 0.75	-	-	904 95.97 38.44 34.53 1.54	-	-	-	-	-	-	-	367 98.13 15.60 14.02 0.62	-	-	-	-	-	-	-	-	-
Coralville (city)	9,125 96.34	418	377 90.19 90.19 4.13	-	-	-	-	-	-	-	-	-	-	-	-	-	-	-	-	-	-	-	-	-	-	-
Iowa City (city)	30,260 94.76	2,030	1,824 89.85 89.85 6.03	-	-	346 95.05 18.97 17.04 1.14	-	-	781 95.36 42.82 38.47 2.58	-	-	-	-	-	-	-	247 100.00 13.54 12.17 0.82	-	-	-	-	-	-	-	-	-
Linn County	112,229 90.58	1,538	1,400 91.03 91.03 1.25	-	-	552 98.57 39.43 35.89 0.49	-	-	-	-	-	-	-	-	-	-	72 90.00 5.14 4.68 0.06	-	-	-	-	-	-	-	-	-
Polk County	215,056 88.33	5,633	3,788 67.25 67.25 1.76	-	-	806 94.05 21.28 14.31 0.37	-	49 24.02 1.29 0.87 0.02	632 88.52 16.68 11.22 0.29	-	-	-	-	-	-	-	334 85.20 8.82 5.93 0.16	627 66.21 16.55 11.13 0.29	-	-	-	-	-	147 58.10 3.88 2.61 0.07	-	709 43.26 18.72 12.59 0.33
Pottawattamie County	47,912 84.04	346	258 74.57 74.57 0.54	-	-	-	-	-	-	-	-	-	-	-	-	-	-	-	-	-	-	-	-	-	-	-
Scott County	88,170 86.32	1,402	865 61.70 61.70 0.98	-	-	-	-	-	-	-	-	-	-	-	-	-	-	-	-	-	-	-	-	-	-	179 29.88 20.69 12.77 0.20
Story County	39,423 93.53	1,969	1,920 97.51 97.51 4.87	-	-	314 95.44 16.35 15.95 0.80	-	-	767 100.00 39.95 38.95 1.95	-	-	-	-	-	-	-	373 96.88 19.43 18.94 0.95	-	-	-	-	-	-	-	-	-
Ames (city)	21,860 95.33	1,895	1,846 97.41 97.41 8.44	-	-	293 95.13 15.87 15.46 1.34	-	-	751 100.00 40.68 39.63 3.44	-	-	-	-	-	-	-	370 96.86 20.04 19.53 1.69	-	-	-	-	-	-	-	-	-
Woodbury County	52,883 81.44	1,367	544 39.80 39.80 1.03	-	-	-	-	-	-	-	-	-	-	-	-	-	-	-	-	-	-	-	-	-	-	288 31.75 52.94 21.07 0.54

Notes: Please refer to the User's Guide for an explanation of data; data is arranged alphabetically by state, then county, then city within each county; table includes counties with populations greater than 49,999 unless noted and cities with populations greater than 9,999 whose Asian and/or NHPI population rates are greater than the national average; (1) Native Hawaiian and other Pacific Islander; (2) excludes Taiwanese; (3) includes Chamorro; (4) county does not meet population threshold but is shown in order to allow inclusion of city

Place	Total population 25 years and over who are high school graduates	Asian population 25 years and over	Asians 25 years and over who are high school graduates	NHPI[1] population 25 years and over	NHPIs[1] 25 years and over who are high school graduates	Asian Indian	Bangladeshi	Cambodian	Chinese[2]	Fijian	Filipino	Guamanian[3]	Hawaiian, Native	Hmong	Indonesian	Japanese	Korean	Laotian	Malaysian	Pakistani	Samoan	Sri Lankan	Taiwanese	Thai	Tongan	Vietnamese
KANSAS	1,463,408 86.02	27,227	20,371 74.82 74.82 1.39	714	633 88.66 88.66 0.04	4,284 89.14 21.03 15.73 0.29	-	185 50.27 0.91 0.68 0.01	4,073 88.12 19.99 14.96 0.28	-	2,086 86.16 10.24 7.66 0.14	-	244 95.69 38.55 34.17 0.02	126 40.26 0.62 0.46 0.01	-	1,185 89.91 5.82 4.35 0.08	2,286 82.26 11.22 8.40 0.16	855 53.81 4.20 3.14 0.06	-	414 91.59 2.03 1.52 0.03	-	-	291 85.84 1.43 1.07 0.02	354 81.76 1.74 1.30 0.02	-	3,167 48.74 15.55 11.63 0.22
Cowley County[4]	19,635 85.44	318	169 53.14 53.14 0.86	-	-	-	-	-	-	-	-	-	-	-	-	-	-	114 52.05 67.46 35.85 0.58	-	-	-	-	-	-	-	-
Winfield (city)	6,472 86.34	280	143 51.07 51.07 2.21	-	-	-	-	-	-	-	-	-	-	-	-	-	-	114 52.53 79.72 40.71 1.76	-	-	-	-	-	-	-	-
Douglas County	49,188 92.36	1,729	1,620 93.70 93.70 3.29	-	-	209 92.89 12.90 12.09 0.42	-	-	603 100.00 37.22 34.88 1.23	-	-	-	-	-	-	-	256 93.77 15.80 14.81 0.52	-	-	-	-	-	-	-	-	-
Lawrence (city)	37,814 92.81	1,706	1,597 93.61 93.61 4.22	-	-	201 92.63 12.59 11.78 0.53	-	-	603 100.00 37.76 35.35 1.59	-	-	-	-	-	-	-	254 93.73 15.90 14.89 0.67	-	-	-	-	-	-	-	-	-
Johnson County	280,763 94.91	8,235	7,286 88.48 88.48 2.60	-	-	2,560 93.36 35.14 31.09 0.91	-	-	1,610 90.45 22.10 19.55 0.57	-	626 96.60 8.59 7.60 0.22	-	-	-	-	335 93.58 4.60 4.07 0.12	761 89.32 10.44 9.24 0.27	288 66.51 3.95 3.50 0.10	-	-	-	-	-	-	-	506 65.46 6.94 6.14 0.18
Overland Park (city)	96,275 95.82	3,756	3,419 91.03 91.03 3.55	-	-	1,282 95.53 37.50 34.13 1.33	-	-	808 89.98 23.63 21.51 0.84	-	-	-	-	-	-	-	361 90.93 10.56 9.61 0.37	-	-	-	-	-	-	-	-	214 64.46 6.26 5.70 0.22
Leavenworth County	38,751 86.51	556	458 82.37 82.37 1.18	-	-	-	-	-	-	-	-	-	-	-	-	-	-	-	-	-	-	-	-	-	-	-
Riley County	27,550 93.84	1,262	1,192 94.45 94.45 4.33	-	-	-	-	-	507 100.00 42.53 40.17 1.84	-	-	-	-	-	-	-	233 88.26 19.55 18.46 0.85	-	-	-	-	-	-	-	-	-
Manhattan (city)	19,249 94.90	1,110	1,052 94.77 94.77 5.47	-	-	-	-	-	493 100.00 46.86 44.41 2.56	-	-	-	-	-	-	-	-	-	-	-	-	-	-	-	-	-

Notes: Please refer to the User's Guide for an explanation of data; data is arranged alphabetically by state, then county, then city within each county; table includes counties with populations greater than 49,999 unless noted and cities with populations greater than 9,999 whose Asian and/or NHPI population rates are greater than the national average; (1) Native Hawaiian and other Pacific Islander; (2) excludes Taiwanese; (3) includes Chamorro; (4) county does not meet population threshold but is shown in order to allow inclusion of city

Place	Total population 25 years and over who are high school graduates	Asian population 25 years and over	Asians 25 years and over who are high school graduates	NHPI[1] population 25 years and over	NHPIs[1] 25 years and over who are high school graduates	Asian Indian	Bangladeshi	Cambodian	Chinese[2]	Fijian	Filipino	Guamanian[3]	Hawaiian, Native	Hmong	Indonesian	Japanese	Korean	Laotian	Malaysian	Pakistani	Samoan	Sri Lankan	Taiwanese	Thai	Tongan	Vietnamese
Saline County	30,172 87.00	555	343 61.80 61.80 1.14	-	-	-	-	-	-	-	-	-	-	-	-	-	-	-	-	-	-	-	-	-	-	118 50.00 34.40 21.26 0.39
Sedgwick County	240,438 85.09	8,357	5,203 62.26 62.26 2.16	230	203 88.26 88.26 0.08	613 82.06 11.78 7.34 0.25	-	143 57.89 2.75 1.71 0.06	710 77.77 13.65 8.50 0.30	-	388 70.80 7.46 4.64 0.16	-	-	-	-	-	304 83.52 5.84 3.64 0.13	234 46.34 4.50 2.80 0.10	-	-	-	-	-	-	-	1,902 49.24 36.56 22.76 0.79
Wichita (city)	181,390 83.79	7,492	4,682 62.49 62.49 2.58	-	-	572 81.48 12.22 7.63 0.32	-	-	667 78.66 14.25 8.90 0.37	-	325 73.86 6.94 4.34 0.18	-	-	-	-	-	268 85.62 5.72 3.58 0.15	162 48.94 3.46 2.16 0.09	-	-	-	-	-	-	-	1,773 48.34 37.87 23.67 0.98
Shawnee County	98,442 88.12	911	767 84.19 84.19 0.78	-	-	-	-	-	-	-	-	-	-	-	-	-	-	-	-	-	-	-	-	-	-	-
Wyandotte County	71,487 74.00	1,062	678 63.84 63.84 0.95	-	-	-	-	-	-	-	-	-	-	108 42.02 15.93 10.17 0.15	-	-	-	-	-	-	-	-	-	-	-	-
KENTUCKY	1,961,397 74.12	18,667	16,089 86.19 86.19 0.82	649	507 78.12 78.12 0.03	3,854 89.34 23.95 20.65 0.20	-	-	3,077 88.14 19.12 16.48 0.16	-	2,022 91.49 12.57 10.83 0.10	132 66.67 26.04 20.34 0.01	-	-	-	2,089 93.59 12.98 11.19 0.11	2,103 81.39 13.07 11.27 0.11	-	-	329 100.00 2.04 1.76 0.02	-	-	-	277 86.56 1.72 1.48 0.01	-	1,242 66.13 7.72 6.65 0.06
Boone County	46,094 85.10	685	651 95.04 95.04 1.41	-	-	-	-	-	-	-	-	-	-	-	-	326 97.60 50.08 47.59 0.71	-	-	-	-	-	-	-	-	-	-
Campbell County	46,228 80.84	329	293 89.06 89.06 0.63	-	-	-	-	-	-	-	-	-	-	-	-	-	-	-	-	-	-	-	-	-	-	-
Christian County	31,159 77.23	300	282 94.00 94.00 0.91	-	-	-	-	-	-	-	-	-	-	-	-	-	-	-	-	-	-	-	-	-	-	-
Fayette County	143,483 85.80	3,793	3,474 91.59 91.59 2.42	-	-	727 90.42 20.93 19.17 0.51	-	-	1,148 94.25 33.05 30.27 0.80	-	-	-	-	-	-	493 92.50 14.19 13.00 0.34	-	-	-	-	-	-	-	-	-	-

Notes: Please refer to the User's Guide for an explanation of data; data is arranged alphabetically by state, then county, then city within each county; table includes counties with populations greater than 49,999 unless noted and cities with populations greater than 9,999 whose Asian and/or NHPI population rates are greater than the national average; (1) Native Hawaiian and other Pacific Islander; (2) excludes Taiwanese; (3) includes Chamorro; (4) county does not meet population threshold but is shown in order to allow inclusion of city

Place	Total population 25 years and over who are high school graduates	Asian population 25 years and over	Asians 25 years and over who are high school graduates	NHPI[1] population 25 years and over	NHPIs[1] 25 years and over who are high school graduates	Asian Indian	Bangladeshi	Cambodian	Chinese[2]	Fijian	Filipino	Guamanian[3]	Hawaiian, Native	Hmong	Indonesian	Japanese	Korean	Laotian	Malaysian	Pakistani	Samoan	Sri Lankan	Taiwanese	Thai	Tongan	Vietnamese
Hardin County	48,035 82.31	1,290	1,001 77.60 77.60 2.08	-	-	-	-	-	-	-	-	-	-	-	-	-	377 64.44 37.66 29.22 0.78	-	-	-	-	-	-	-	-	-
Radcliff (city)	11,576 84.70	718	546 76.04 76.04 4.72	-	-	-	-	-	-	-	-	-	-	-	-	-	-	-	-	-	-	-	-	-	-	-
Jefferson County	380,016 81.85	6,046	5,125 84.77 84.77 1.35	-	-	1,510 93.67 29.46 24.98 0.40	-	-	859 83.97 16.76 14.21 0.23	-	675 90.60 13.17 11.16 0.18	-	-	-	-	266 88.08 5.19 4.40 0.07	619 88.18 12.08 10.24 0.16	-	-	-	-	-	-	-	-	638 60.94 12.45 10.55 0.17
Kenton County	80,267 82.13	519	463 89.21 89.21 0.58	-	-	-	-	-	-	-	-	-	-	-	-	-	-	-	-	-	-	-	-	-	-	-
Madison County	31,697 75.25	322	287 89.13 89.13 0.91	-	-	-	-	-	-	-	-	-	-	-	-	-	-	-	-	-	-	-	-	-	-	-
Warren County	45,019 80.29	599	476 79.47 79.47 1.06	-	-	-	-	-	-	-	-	-	-	-	-	-	-	-	-	-	-	-	-	-	-	-
LOUISIANA	2,076,416 74.81	33,366	22,500 67.43 67.43 1.08	833	664 79.71 79.71 0.03	4,608 86.42 20.48 13.81 0.22	-	-	3,848 83.42 17.10 11.53 0.19	-	2,726 80.18 12.12 8.17 0.13	225 72.58 33.89 27.01 0.01	198 83.19 29.82 23.77 0.01	-	-	917 85.38 4.08 2.75 0.04	1,400 79.32 6.22 4.20 0.07	187 27.02 0.83 0.56 0.01	-	490 84.48 2.18 1.47 0.02	-	-	328 92.13 1.46 0.98 0.02	402 76.28 1.79 1.20 0.02	-	6,599 48.49 29.33 19.78 0.32
Ascension Parish	36,819 79.59	203	107 52.71 52.71 0.29	-	-	-	-	-	-	-	-	-	-	-	-	-	-	-	-	-	-	-	-	-	-	-
Bossier Parish	50,828 83.00	749	549 73.30 73.30 1.08	-	-	-	-	-	-	-	-	-	-	-	-	-	-	-	-	-	-	-	-	-	-	-
Caddo Parish	125,087 78.67	1,247	961 77.06 77.06 0.77	-	-	267 86.69 27.78 21.41 0.21	-	-	-	-	-	-	-	-	-	-	-	-	-	-	-	-	-	-	-	-

Notes: Please refer to the User's Guide for an explanation of data; data is arranged alphabetically by state, then county, then city within each county; table includes counties with populations greater than 49,999 unless noted and cities with populations greater than 9,999 whose Asian and/or NHPI population rates are greater than the national average; (1) Native Hawaiian and other Pacific Islander; (2) excludes Taiwanese; (3) includes Chamorro; (4) county does not meet population threshold but is shown in order to allow inclusion of city

Place	Total population 25 years and over who are high school graduates	Asian population 25 years and over	Asians 25 years and over who are high school graduates	NHPI[1] population 25 years and over	NHPIs[1] 25 years and over who are high school graduates	Asian Indian	Bangladeshi	Cambodian	Chinese[2]	Fijian	Filipino	Guamanian[3]	Hawaiian, Native	Hmong	Indonesian	Japanese	Korean	Laotian	Malaysian	Pakistani	Samoan	Sri Lankan	Taiwanese	Thai	Tongan	Vietnamese
Calcasieu Parish	88,258 77.04	766	558 72.85 72.85 0.63	-	-	-	-	-	-	-	-	-	-	-	-	-	-	-	-	-	-	-	-	-	-	-
East Baton Rouge Parish	205,789 83.89	4,903	3,749 76.46 76.46 1.82	-	-	1,065 93.59 28.41 21.72 0.52	-	-	1,002 92.52 26.73 20.44 0.49	-	215 86.35 5.73 4.39 0.10	-	-	-	-	-	-	-	-	-	-	-	-	-	-	881 49.38 23.50 17.97 0.43
Iberia Parish	29,415 66.91	756	204 26.98 26.98 0.69	-	-	-	-	-	-	-	-	-	-	-	-	-	-	80 17.09 39.22 10.58 0.27	-	-	-	-	-	-	-	60 36.81 29.41 7.94 0.20
Jefferson Parish	236,816 79.27	8,819	6,112 69.30 69.30 2.58	-	-	1,019 87.24 16.67 11.55 0.43	-	-	946 72.60 15.48 10.73 0.40	-	617 82.16 10.09 7.00 0.26	-	-	-	-	-	356 78.24 5.82 4.04 0.15	-	-	230 74.92 3.76 2.61 0.10	-	-	-	-	-	2,236 55.80 36.58 25.35 0.94
Gretna (city)	8,090 70.26	426	288 67.61 67.61 3.56	-	-	-	-	-	-	-	-	-	-	-	-	-	-	-	-	-	-	-	-	-	-	120 57.97 41.67 28.17 1.48
Harvey (cdp)	9,516 71.23	684	418 61.11 61.11 4.39	-	-	-	-	-	-	-	-	-	-	-	-	-	-	-	-	-	-	-	-	-	-	308 62.99 73.68 45.03 3.24
Timberlane (cdp)	6,206 83.75	424	294 69.34 69.34 4.74	-	-	-	-	-	-	-	-	-	-	-	-	-	-	-	-	-	-	-	-	-	-	241 66.21 81.97 56.84 3.88
Woodmere (cdp)	5,687 80.64	427	301 70.49 70.49 5.29	-	-	-	-	-	-	-	-	-	-	-	-	-	-	-	-	-	-	-	-	-	-	183 60.60 60.80 42.86 3.22
Lafayette Parish	92,753 79.83	1,241	1,050 84.61 84.61 1.13	-	-	307 93.60 29.24 24.74 0.33	-	-	-	-	-	-	-	-	-	-	-	-	-	-	-	-	-	-	-	285 73.83 27.14 22.97 0.31
Lafourche Parish	37,073 66.33	346	263 76.01 76.01 0.71	-	-	-	-	-	-	-	-	-	-	-	-	-	-	-	-	-	-	-	-	-	-	-

Notes: Please refer to the User's Guide for an explanation of data; data is arranged alphabetically by state, then county, then city within each county; table includes counties with populations greater than 49,999 unless noted and cities with populations greater than 9,999 whose Asian and/or NHPI population rates are greater than the national average; (1) Native Hawaiian and other Pacific Islander; (2) excludes Taiwanese; (3) includes Chamorro; (4) county does not meet population threshold but is shown in order to allow inclusion of city

Place	Total population 25 years and over who are high school graduates	Asian population 25 years and over	Asians 25 years and over who are high school graduates	NHPI[1] population 25 years and over	NHPIs[1] 25 years and over who are high school graduates	Asian Indian	Bangladeshi	Cambodian	Chinese[2]	Fijian	Filipino	Guamanian[3]	Hawaiian, Native	Hmong	Indonesian	Japanese	Korean	Laotian	Malaysian	Pakistani	Samoan	Sri Lankan	Taiwanese	Thai	Tongan	Vietnamese
Orleans Parish	224,486 74.69	6,330	3,679 58.12 58.12 1.64	-	-	632 81.03 17.18 9.98 0.28	-	-	535 84.65 14.54 8.45 0.24	-	332 83.84 9.02 5.24 0.15	-	-	-	-	-	-	-	-	-	-	-	-	-	-	1,598 41.63 43.44 25.24 0.71
Ouachita Parish	69,518 78.61	543	443 81.58 81.58 0.64	-	-	-	-	-	-	-	-	-	-	-	-	-	-	-	-	-	-	-	-	-	-	-
Rapides Parish	59,550 74.61	659	489 74.20 74.20 0.82	-	-	-	-	-	-	-	-	-	-	-	-	-	-	-	-	-	-	-	-	-	-	-
St. Bernard Parish	32,268 73.13	601	389 64.73 64.73 1.21	-	-	-	-	-	-	-	-	-	-	-	-	-	-	-	-	-	-	-	-	-	-	137 57.56 35.22 22.80 0.42
St. Mary Parish	21,863 65.94	421	193 45.84 45.84 0.88	-	-	-	-	-	-	-	-	-	-	-	-	-	-	-	-	-	-	-	-	-	-	137 38.38 70.98 32.54 0.63
St. Tammany Parish	103,124 83.87	908	724 79.74 79.74 0.70	-	-	-	-	-	-	-	-	-	-	-	-	-	-	-	-	-	-	-	-	-	-	106 53.27 14.64 11.67 0.10
Terrebonne Parish	42,425 67.05	445	281 63.15 63.15 0.66	-	-	-	-	-	-	-	-	-	-	-	-	-	-	-	-	-	-	-	-	-	-	59 35.12 21.00 13.26 0.14
Vermilion Parish	22,064 65.64	524	200 38.17 38.17 0.91	-	-	-	-	-	-	-	-	-	-	-	-	-	-	-	-	-	-	-	-	-	-	153 33.92 76.50 29.20 0.69
Abbeville (city)	4,040 55.68	318	116 36.48 36.48 2.87	-	-	-	-	-	-	-	-	-	-	-	-	-	-	-	-	-	-	-	-	-	-	116 37.79 100.00 36.48 2.87
Vernon Parish	23,504 80.14	681	531 77.97 77.97 2.26	-	-	-	-	-	-	-	-	-	-	-	-	-	130 59.91 24.48 19.09 0.55	-	-	-	-	-	-	-	-	-

Notes: Please refer to the User's Guide for an explanation of data; data is arranged alphabetically by state, then county, then city within each county; table includes counties with populations greater than 49,999 unless noted and cities with populations greater than 9,999 whose Asian and/or NHPI population rates are greater than the national average; (1) Native Hawaiian and other Pacific Islander; (2) excludes Taiwanese; (3) includes Chamorro; (4) county does not meet population threshold but is shown in order to allow inclusion of city

Place	Total population 25 years and over who are high school graduates	Asian population 25 years and over	Asians 25 years and over who are high school graduates	NHPI[1] population 25 years and over	NHPIs[1] 25 years and over who are high school graduates	Asian Indian	Bangladeshi	Cambodian	Chinese[2]	Fijian	Filipino	Guamanian[3]	Hawaiian, Native	Hmong	Indonesian	Japanese	Korean	Laotian	Malaysian	Pakistani	Samoan	Sri Lankan	Taiwanese	Thai	Tongan	Vietnamese
MAINE	742,605 85.37	4,513	3,367 74.61 74.61 0.45	193	155 80.31 80.31 0.02	456 89.41 13.54 10.10 0.06	-	203 47.32 6.03 4.50 0.03	657 71.57 19.51 14.56 0.09	-	681 86.86 20.23 15.09 0.09	-	-	-	-	345 80.05 10.25 7.64 0.05	297 81.15 8.82 6.58 0.04	-	-	-	-	-	-	-	-	385 62.20 11.43 8.53 0.05
Androscoggin County	55,537 79.84	264	173 65.53 65.53 0.31	-	-	-	-	-	-	-	-	-	-	-	-	-	-	-	-	-	-	-	-	-	-	-
Aroostook County	39,571 76.93	212	176 83.02 83.02 0.44	-	-	-	-	-	-	-	-	-	-	-	-	-	-	-	-	-	-	-	-	-	-	-
Cumberland County	163,376 90.13	1,719	1,114 64.81 64.81 0.68	-	-	-	-	84 34.01 7.54 4.89 0.05	140 68.63 12.57 8.14 0.09	-	161 81.73 14.45 9.37 0.10	-	-	-	-	-	-	-	-	-	-	-	-	-	-	213 53.25 19.12 12.39 0.13
Hancock County	31,960 87.76	131	112 85.50 85.50 0.35	-	-	-	-	-	-	-	-	-	-	-	-	-	-	-	-	-	-	-	-	-	-	-
Kennebec County	67,651 85.24	413	284 68.77 68.77 0.42	-	-	-	-	-	-	-	-	-	-	-	-	-	-	-	-	-	-	-	-	-	-	-
Oxford County	31,236 82.35	126	107 84.92 84.92 0.34	-	-	-	-	-	-	-	-	-	-	-	-	-	-	-	-	-	-	-	-	-	-	-
Penobscot County	81,845 85.70	507	470 92.70 92.70 0.57	-	-	-	-	-	168 92.82 35.74 33.14 0.21	-	-	-	-	-	-	-	-	-	-	-	-	-	-	-	-	-
York County	110,414 86.54	557	450 80.79 80.79 0.41	-	-	-	-	-	-	-	-	-	-	-	-	-	-	-	-	-	-	-	-	-	-	-
MARYLAND	2,930,509 83.83	139,018	118,907 85.53 85.53 4.06	1,238	1,003 81.02 81.02 0.03	29,433 90.48 24.75 21.17 1.00	661 84.53 0.56 0.48 0.02	649 61.40 0.55 0.47 0.02	27,623 85.06 23.23 19.87 0.94	-	16,518 90.36 13.89 11.88 0.56	362 86.60 36.09 29.24 0.01	314 85.79 31.31 25.36 0.01	-	654 87.67 0.55 0.47 0.02	5,138 93.18 4.32 3.70 0.18	21,374 84.88 17.98 15.37 0.73	328 68.62 0.28 0.24 0.01	-	2,409 83.47 2.03 1.73 0.08	-	746 90.31 0.63 0.54 0.03	1,439 93.02 1.21 1.04 0.05	1,673 78.77 1.41 1.20 0.06	-	7,118 65.90 5.99 5.12 0.24

Notes: Please refer to the User's Guide for an explanation of data; data is arranged alphabetically by state, then county, then city within each county; table includes counties with populations greater than 49,999 unless noted and cities with populations greater than 9,999 whose Asian and/or NHPI population rates are greater than the national average; (1) Native Hawaiian and other Pacific Islander; (2) excludes Taiwanese; (3) includes Chamorro; (4) county does not meet population threshold but is shown in order to allow inclusion of city

Place	Total population 25 years and over who are high school graduates	Asian population 25 years and over	Asians 25 years and over who are high school graduates	NHPI[1] population 25 years and over	NHPIs[1] 25 years and over who are high school graduates	Asian Indian	Bangladeshi	Cambodian	Chinese[2]	Fijian	Filipino	Guamanian[3]	Hawaiian, Native	Hmong	Indonesian	Japanese	Korean	Laotian	Malaysian	Pakistani	Samoan	Sri Lankan	Taiwanese	Thai	Tongan	Vietnamese
Allegany County	40,915 79.90	259	210 81.08 81.08 0.51	-	-	-	-	-	-	-	-	-	-	-	-	-	-	-	-	-	-	-	-	-	-	-
Anne Arundel County	282,676 86.45	7,511	6,166 82.09 82.09 2.18	-	-	1,000 89.53 16.22 13.31 0.35	-	-	810 83.25 13.14 10.78 0.29	-	1,470 89.42 23.84 19.57 0.52	-	-	-	-	491 80.10 7.96 6.54 0.17	1,783 74.17 28.92 23.74 0.63	-	-	-	-	-	-	-	-	-
Severn (cdp)	19,410 88.61	1,101	845 76.75 76.75 4.35	-	-	-	-	-	-	-	-	-	-	-	-	-	419 73.77 49.59 38.06 2.16	-	-	-	-	-	-	-	-	-
South Gate (cdp)	15,930 86.57	974	702 72.07 72.07 4.41	-	-	-	-	-	-	-	-	-	-	-	-	-	347 68.31 49.43 35.63 2.18	-	-	-	-	-	-	-	-	-
Baltimore Independent City	286,882 68.37	6,067	4,722 77.83 77.83 1.65	-	-	1,095 91.17 23.19 18.05 0.38	-	-	1,068 75.32 22.62 17.60 0.37	-	653 83.72 13.83 10.76 0.23	-	-	-	-	-	805 72.33 17.05 13.27 0.28	-	-	-	-	-	-	-	-	287 54.88 6.08 4.73 0.10
Baltimore County	431,380 84.35	15,318	13,080 85.39 85.39 3.03	-	-	3,521 90.37 26.92 22.99 0.82	-	-	2,440 77.73 18.65 15.93 0.57	-	2,154 93.69 16.47 14.06 0.50	-	-	-	-	480 94.67 3.67 3.13 0.11	2,740 86.03 20.95 17.89 0.64	-	-	414 73.53 3.17 2.70 0.10	-	-	-	-	-	500 68.12 3.82 3.26 0.12
Arbutus (cdp)	11,428 82.27	667	599 89.81 89.81 5.24	-	-	-	-	-	-	-	-	-	-	-	-	-	-	-	-	-	-	-	-	-	-	-
Carney (cdp)	17,338 87.92	1,056	948 89.77 89.77 5.47	-	-	-	-	-	194 80.83 20.46 18.37 1.12	-	-	-	-	-	-	-	427 92.62 45.04 40.44 2.46	-	-	-	-	-	-	-	-	-
Cockeysville (cdp)	11,763 90.09	1,170	1,028 87.86 87.86 8.74	-	-	-	-	-	-	-	-	-	-	-	-	-	399 87.31 38.81 34.10 3.39	-	-	-	-	-	-	-	-	-
Lutherville-Timonium (cdp)	10,449 88.81	497	381 76.66 76.66 3.65	-	-	-	-	-	-	-	-	-	-	-	-	-	-	-	-	-	-	-	-	-	-	-

Notes: Please refer to the User's Guide for an explanation of data; data is arranged alphabetically by state, then county, then city within each county; table includes counties with populations greater than 49,999 unless noted and cities with populations greater than 9,999 whose Asian and/or NHPI population rates are greater than the national average; (1) Native Hawaiian and other Pacific Islander; (2) excludes Taiwanese; (3) includes Chamorro; (4) county does not meet population threshold but is shown in order to allow inclusion of city

Place	Total population 25 years and over who are high school graduates	Asian population 25 years and over	Asians 25 years and over who are high school graduates	NHPI[1] population 25 years and over	NHPIs[1] 25 years and over who are high school graduates	Asian Indian	Bangladeshi	Cambodian	Chinese[2]	Fijian	Filipino	Guamanian[3]	Hawaiian, Native	Hmong	Indonesian	Japanese	Korean	Laotian	Malaysian	Pakistani	Samoan	Sri Lankan	Taiwanese	Thai	Tongan	Vietnamese
Mays Chapel (cdp)	7,666 95.29	508	452 88.98 88.98 5.90	-	-	-	-	-	-	-	-	-	-	-	-	-	-	-	-	-	-	-	-	-	-	-
Owings Mills (cdp)	12,489 90.53	564	492 87.23 87.23 3.94	-	-	-	-	-	-	-	-	-	-	-	-	-	-	-	-	-	-	-	-	-	-	-
Perry Hall (cdp)	17,201 87.60	991	749 75.58 75.58 4.35	-	-	-	-	-	-	-	-	-	-	-	-	-	239 72.87 31.91 24.12 1.39	-	-	-	-	-	-	-	-	-
Reisterstown (cdp)	13,136 88.05	600	489 81.50 81.50 3.72	-	-	271 78.32 55.42 45.17 2.06	-	-	-	-	-	-	-	-	-	-	-	-	-	-	-	-	-	-	-	-
Rossville (cdp)	6,532 84.22	393	356 90.59 90.59 5.45	-	-	-	-	-	-	-	-	-	-	-	-	-	-	-	-	-	-	-	-	-	-	-
Towson (cdp)	30,723 90.93	1,180	1,091 92.46 92.46 3.55	-	-	-	-	-	551 90.77 50.50 46.69 1.79	-	-	-	-	-	-	-	-	-	-	-	-	-	-	-	-	-
Woodlawn (cdp)	20,139 85.12	1,317	1,046 79.42 79.42 5.19	-	-	513 90.64 49.04 38.95 2.55	-	-	-	-	-	-	-	-	-	-	-	-	-	-	-	-	-	-	-	-
Calvert County	41,527 86.93	470	423 90.00 90.00 1.02	-	-	-	-	-	-	-	-	-	-	-	-	-	-	-	-	-	-	-	-	-	-	-
Carroll County	84,182 85.30	736	595 80.84 80.84 0.71	-	-	-	-	-	-	-	-	-	-	-	-	-	-	-	-	-	-	-	-	-	-	-
Cecil County	45,302 81.17	363	299 82.37 82.37 0.66	-	-	-	-	-	-	-	-	-	-	-	-	-	-	-	-	-	-	-	-	-	-	-

Notes: Please refer to the User's Guide for an explanation of data; data is arranged alphabetically by state, then county, then city within each county; table includes counties with populations greater than 49,999 unless noted and cities with populations greater than 9,999 whose Asian and/or NHPI population rates are greater than the national average; (1) Native Hawaiian and other Pacific Islander; (2) excludes Taiwanese; (3) includes Chamorro; (4) county does not meet population threshold but is shown in order to allow inclusion of city

Place	Total population 25 years and over who are high school graduates	Asian population 25 years and over	Asians 25 years and over who are high school graduates	NHPI[1] population 25 years and over	NHPIs[1] 25 years and over who are high school graduates	Asian Indian	Bangladeshi	Cambodian	Chinese[2]	Fijian	Filipino	Guamanian[3]	Hawaiian, Native	Hmong	Indonesian	Japanese	Korean	Laotian	Malaysian	Pakistani	Samoan	Sri Lankan	Taiwanese	Thai	Tongan	Vietnamese
Charles County	66,077 85.83	1,196	901 75.33 75.33 1.36	-	-	-	-	-	-	-	293 94.52 32.52 24.50 0.44	-	-	-	-	-	-	-	-	-	-	-	-	-	-	-
Frederick County	110,832 87.09	2,098	1,864 88.85 88.85 1.68	-	-	374 92.12 20.06 17.83 0.34	-	-	500 90.09 26.82 23.83 0.45	-	-	-	-	-	-	-	255 82.26 13.68 12.15 0.23	-	-	-	-	-	-	-	-	-
Harford County	124,069 86.73	2,079	1,597 76.82 76.82 1.29	-	-	311 76.60 19.47 14.96 0.25	-	-	-	-	351 93.60 21.98 16.88 0.28	-	-	-	-	-	311 67.46 19.47 14.96 0.25	-	-	-	-	-	-	-	-	-
Howard County	152,041 93.10	12,165	10,903 89.63 89.63 7.17	-	-	2,793 90.42 25.62 22.96 1.84	-	-	2,296 91.47 21.06 18.87 1.51	-	912 94.02 8.36 7.50 0.60	-	-	-	-	-	3,374 89.76 30.95 27.74 2.22	-	-	312 92.04 2.86 2.56 0.21	-	-	-	-	-	338 67.60 3.10 2.78 0.22
Columbia (cdp)	56,180 94.33	4,219	3,797 90.00 90.00 6.76	-	-	1,056 90.64 27.81 25.03 1.88	-	-	1,004 89.72 26.44 23.80 1.79	-	357 95.45 9.40 8.46 0.64	-	-	-	-	-	851 90.63 22.41 20.17 1.51	-	-	-	-	-	-	-	-	-
Elkridge (cdp)	12,966 91.14	904	822 90.93 90.93 6.34	-	-	-	-	-	-	-	-	-	-	-	-	-	209 95.00 25.43 23.12 1.61	-	-	-	-	-	-	-	-	-
Ellicott City (cdp)	34,670 93.59	4,147	3,748 90.38 90.38 10.81	-	-	671 93.45 17.90 16.18 1.94	-	-	780 96.65 20.81 18.81 2.25	-	246 92.83 6.56 5.93 0.71	-	-	-	-	-	1,574 88.08 42.00 37.96 4.54	-	-	158 85.41 4.22 3.81 0.46	-	-	-	-	-	-
North Laurel (cdp)	11,669 89.73	972	876 90.12 90.12 7.51	-	-	276 96.84 31.51 28.40 2.37	-	-	-	-	-	-	-	-	-	-	242 88.00 27.63 24.90 2.07	-	-	-	-	-	-	-	-	-
Savage-Guilford (cdp)	7,390 91.55	499	411 82.36 82.36 5.56	-	-	-	-	-	-	-	-	-	-	-	-	-	-	-	-	-	-	-	-	-	-	-
Montgomery County	536,558 90.32	67,048	58,509 87.26 87.26 10.90	334	287 85.93 85.93 0.05	15,197 92.46 25.97 22.67 2.83	472 82.81 0.81 0.70 0.09	483 65.27 0.83 0.72 0.09	16,763 87.27 28.65 25.00 3.12	-	4,635 91.42 7.92 6.91 0.86	-	-	-	552 85.71 0.94 0.82 0.10	2,490 96.74 4.26 3.71 0.46	9,131 89.28 15.61 13.62 1.70	-	-	916 85.13 1.57 1.37 0.17	-	467 86.16 0.80 0.70 0.09	720 94.74 1.23 1.07 0.13	860 81.90 1.47 1.28 0.16	-	4,216 67.43 7.21 6.29 0.79

Notes: Please refer to the User's Guide for an explanation of data; data is arranged alphabetically by state, then county, then city within each county; table includes counties with populations greater than 49,999 unless noted and cities with populations greater than 9,999 whose Asian and/or NHPI population rates are greater than the national average; (1) Native Hawaiian and other Pacific Islander; (2) excludes Taiwanese; (3) includes Chamorro; (4) county does not meet population threshold but is shown in order to allow inclusion of city

Place	Total population 25 years and over who are high school graduates	Asian population 25 years and over	Asians 25 years and over who are high school graduates	NHPI[1] population 25 years and over	NHPIs[1] 25 years and over who are high school graduates	Asian Indian	Bangladeshi	Cambodian	Chinese[2]	Fijian	Filipino	Guamanian[3]	Hawaiian, Native	Hmong	Indonesian	Japanese	Korean	Laotian	Malaysian	Pakistani	Samoan	Sri Lankan	Taiwanese	Thai	Tongan	Vietnamese
Aspen Hill (cdp)	29,880	3,816	3,196	-	-	429	-	-	1,020	-	453	-	-	-	-	-	631	-	-	-	-	-	-	-	-	188
	87.67		83.75			97.06			82.06		94.97						89.63									58.93
						13.42			31.91		14.17						19.74									5.88
			83.75			11.24			26.73		11.87						16.54									4.93
			10.70			1.44			3.41		1.52						2.11									0.63
Bethesda (cdp)	39,528	3,127	2,878	-	-	679	-	-	858	-	246	-	-	-	-	346	361	-	-	-	-	-	-	-	-	-
	96.97		92.04			91.76			93.36		86.93					98.02	88.92									
						23.59			29.81		8.55					12.02	12.54									
			92.04			21.71			27.44		7.87					11.06	11.54									
			7.28			1.72			2.17		0.62					0.88	0.91									
Calverton (cdp)	7,792	1,394	1,142	-	-	400	-	-	-	-	-	-	-	-	-	-	317	-	-	-	-	-	-	-	-	-
	91.71		81.92			79.21											90.83									
						35.03											27.76									
			81.92			28.69											22.74									
			14.66			5.13											4.07									
Colesville (cdp)	12,676	2,226	1,950	-	-	465	-	-	416	-	-	-	-	-	-	-	632	-	-	-	-	-	-	-	-	170
	93.38		87.60			91.90			91.23								85.41									79.44
						23.85			21.33								32.41									8.72
			87.60			20.89			18.69								28.39									7.64
			15.38			3.67			3.28								4.99									1.34
Fairland (cdp)	13,569	2,198	1,883	-	-	526	-	-	324	-	-	-	-	-	-	-	759	-	-	-	-	-	-	-	-	-
	93.99		85.67			93.76			76.42								91.12									
						27.93			17.21								40.31									
			85.67			23.93			14.74								34.53									
			13.88			3.88			2.39								5.59									
Gaithersburg (city)	29,950	4,815	4,288	-	-	1,038	-	-	1,577	-	301	-	-	-	-	-	574	-	-	-	-	-	-	-	-	261
	85.60		89.06			91.05			89.15		89.32						91.11									75.43
						24.21			36.78		7.02						13.39									6.09
			89.06			21.56			32.75		6.25						11.92									5.42
			14.32			3.47			5.27		1.01						1.92									0.87
Germantown (cdp)	32,846	3,586	3,263	-	-	1,414	-	-	655	-	-	-	-	-	-	-	239	-	-	-	-	-	-	-	-	227
	93.52		90.99			96.72			86.41								90.87									76.69
						43.33			20.07								7.32									6.96
			90.99			39.43			18.27								6.66									6.33
			9.93			4.30			1.99								0.73									0.69
Montgomery Village (cdp)	23,179	2,919	2,683	-	-	1,042	-	-	471	-	374	-	-	-	-	-	-	-	-	-	-	-	-	-	-	232
	91.67		91.92			90.61			89.71		95.65															90.27
						38.84			17.55		13.94															8.65
			91.92			35.70			16.14		12.81															7.95
			11.58			4.50			2.03		1.61															1.00
North Bethesda (cdp)	27,418	3,349	3,159	-	-	771	-	-	989	-	262	-	-	-	-	426	409	-	-	-	-	-	-	-	-	-
	93.07		94.33			96.50			90.48		94.93					100.00	95.56									
						24.41			31.31		8.29					13.49	12.95									
			94.33			23.02			29.53		7.82					12.72	12.21									
			11.52			2.81			3.61		0.96					1.55	1.49									
North Potomac (cdp)	13,338	3,960	3,695	-	-	714	-	-	1,948	-	-	-	-	-	-	-	593	-	-	-	-	-	-	-	-	-
	96.08		93.31			91.30			93.83								95.34									
						19.32			52.72								16.05									
			93.31			18.03			49.19								14.97									
			27.70			5.35			14.60								4.45									

Notes: Please refer to the User's Guide for an explanation of data; data is arranged alphabetically by state, then county, then city within each county; table includes counties with populations greater than 49,999 unless noted and cities with populations greater than 9,999 whose Asian and/or NHPI population rates are greater than the national average; (1) Native Hawaiian and other Pacific Islander; (2) excludes Taiwanese; (3) includes Chamorro; (4) county does not meet population threshold but is shown in order to allow inclusion of city

Place	Total population 25 years and over who are high school graduates	Asian population 25 years and over	Asians 25 years and over who are high school graduates	NHPI[1] population 25 years and over	NHPIs[1] 25 years and over who are high school graduates	Asian Indian	Bangladeshi	Cambodian	Chinese[2]	Fijian	Filipino	Guamanian[3]	Hawaiian, Native	Hmong	Indonesian	Japanese	Korean	Laotian	Malaysian	Pakistani	Samoan	Sri Lankan	Taiwanese	Thai	Tongan	Vietnamese
Olney (cdp)	19,234 95.73	1,700	1,517 89.24 89.24 7.89	-	-	365 84.69 24.06 21.47 1.90	-	-	398 91.71 26.24 23.41 2.07	-	-	-	-	-	-	-	338 88.95 22.28 19.88 1.76	-	-	-	-	-	-	-	-	-
Potomac (cdp)	30,158 96.49	4,076	3,840 94.21 94.21 12.73	-	-	992 96.03 25.83 24.34 3.29	-	-	1,304 96.45 33.96 31.99 4.32	-	231 81.34 6.02 5.67 0.77	-	-	-	-	-	683 92.55 17.79 16.76 2.26	-	-	-	-	-	-	-	-	-
Redland (cdp)	9,558 88.05	1,932	1,731 89.60 89.60 18.11	-	-	498 93.08 28.77 25.78 5.21	-	-	411 80.12 23.74 21.27 4.30	-	197 100.00 11.38 10.20 2.06	-	-	-	-	-	271 94.10 15.66 14.03 2.84	-	-	-	-	-	-	-	-	-
Rockville (city)	29,601 89.12	4,640	4,205 90.63 90.63 14.21	-	-	678 96.17 16.12 14.61 2.29	-	-	1,791 91.52 42.59 38.60 6.05	-	279 91.18 6.63 6.01 0.94	-	-	-	-	297 100.00 7.06 6.40 1.00	540 96.60 12.84 11.64 1.82	-	-	-	-	-	-	-	-	218 69.21 5.18 4.70 0.74
Silver Spring (cdp)	42,791 81.95	4,402	3,000 68.15 68.15 7.01	-	-	754 83.31 25.13 17.13 1.76	-	106 54.64 3.53 2.41 0.25	391 68.72 13.03 8.88 0.91	-	312 84.10 10.40 7.09 0.73	-	-	-	-	-	260 71.43 8.67 5.91 0.61	-	-	-	-	-	-	-	-	468 41.38 15.60 10.63 1.09
Takoma Park (city)	9,933 85.09	539	438 81.26 81.26 4.41	-	-	-	-	-	-	-	-	-	-	-	-	-	-	-	-	-	-	-	-	-	-	-
Wheaton-Glenmont (cdp)	30,178 78.09	4,862	3,652 75.11 75.11 12.10	-	-	726 88.21 19.88 14.93 2.41	-	-	962 70.42 26.34 19.79 3.19	-	379 84.22 10.38 7.80 1.26	-	-	-	-	-	501 84.20 13.72 10.30 1.66	-	-	-	-	-	-	-	-	448 56.28 12.27 9.21 1.48
White Oak (cdp)	12,027 87.58	1,620	1,279 78.95 78.95 10.63	-	-	343 92.20 26.82 21.17 2.85	-	-	187 62.13 14.62 11.54 1.55	-	-	-	-	-	-	-	307 78.52 24.00 18.95 2.55	-	-	-	-	-	-	-	-	279 70.99 21.81 17.22 2.32
Prince George's County	427,557 84.88	19,849	16,550 83.38 83.38 3.87	-	-	3,918 86.07 23.67 19.74 0.92	-	-	2,747 82.92 16.60 13.84 0.64	-	4,803 88.47 29.02 24.20 1.12	-	-	-	-	484 95.65 2.92 2.44 0.11	1,987 80.35 12.01 10.01 0.46	-	-	376 88.47 2.27 1.89 0.09	-	-	-	185 80.43 1.12 0.93 0.04	-	1,007 59.59 6.08 5.07 0.24
Adelphi (cdp)	7,615 78.99	1,031	867 84.09 84.09 11.39	-	-	-	-	-	-	-	-	-	-	-	-	-	-	-	-	-	-	-	-	-	-	-

Notes: Please refer to the User's Guide for an explanation of data; data is arranged alphabetically by state, then county, then city within each county; table includes counties with populations greater than 49,999 unless noted and cities with populations greater than 9,999 whose Asian and/or NHPI population rates are greater than the national average; (1) Native Hawaiian and other Pacific Islander; (2) excludes Taiwanese; (3) includes Chamorro; (4) county does not meet population threshold but is shown in order to allow inclusion of city

Place	Total population 25 years and over who are high school graduates	Asian population 25 years and over	Asians 25 years and over who are high school graduates	NHPI[1] population 25 years and over	NHPIs[1] 25 years and over who are high school graduates	Asian Indian	Bangladeshi	Cambodian	Chinese[2]	Fijian	Filipino	Guamanian[3]	Hawaiian, Native	Hmong	Indonesian	Japanese	Korean	Laotian	Malaysian	Pakistani	Samoan	Sri Lankan	Taiwanese	Thai	Tongan	Vietnamese
Beltsville (cdp)	9,228 89.19	1,130	917 81.15 81.15 9.94	-	-	254 85.23 27.70 22.48 2.75	-	-	-	-	-	-	-	-	-	-	188 83.93 20.50 16.64 2.04	-	-	-	-	-	-	-	-	-
College Park (city)	8,232 87.61	970	855 88.14 88.14 10.39	-	-	251 92.96 29.36 25.88 3.05	-	-	264 90.41 30.88 27.22 3.21	-	-	-	-	-	-	-	-	-	-	-	-	-	-	-	-	-
Fort Washington (cdp)	14,821 89.87	1,674	1,428 85.30 85.30 9.63	-	-	-	-	-	-	-	1,141 86.44 79.90 68.16 7.70	-	-	-	-	-	-	-	-	-	-	-	-	-	-	-
Friendly (cdp)	6,425 91.21	394	368 93.40 93.40 5.73	-	-	-	-	-	-	-	285 96.28 77.45 72.34 4.44	-	-	-	-	-	-	-	-	-	-	-	-	-	-	-
Glenn Dale (cdp)	7,375 91.91	704	606 86.08 86.08 8.22	-	-	-	-	-	-	-	-	-	-	-	-	-	-	-	-	-	-	-	-	-	-	-
Greenbelt (city)	12,744 91.53	1,748	1,554 88.90 88.90 12.19	-	-	428 91.45 27.54 24.49 3.36	-	-	395 89.77 25.42 22.60 3.10	-	-	-	-	-	-	-	295 79.95 18.98 16.88 2.31	-	-	-	-	-	-	-	-	-
Hyattsville (city)	7,775 80.51	412	360 87.38 87.38 4.63	-	-	-	-	-	-	-	-	-	-	-	-	-	-	-	-	-	-	-	-	-	-	-
Lanham-Seabrook (cdp)	10,314 87.50	623	508 81.54 81.54 4.93	-	-	-	-	-	-	-	-	-	-	-	-	-	-	-	-	-	-	-	-	-	-	-
Laurel (city)	12,390 88.16	828	736 88.89 88.89 5.94	-	-	-	-	-	-	-	-	-	-	-	-	-	-	-	-	-	-	-	-	-	-	-
New Carrollton (city)	6,808 84.85	338	296 87.57 87.57 4.35	-	-	-	-	-	-	-	-	-	-	-	-	-	-	-	-	-	-	-	-	-	-	-

Notes: Please refer to the User's Guide for an explanation of data; data is arranged alphabetically by state, then county, then city within each county; table includes counties with populations greater than 49,999 unless noted and cities with populations greater than 9,999 whose Asian and/or NHPI population rates are greater than the national average; (1) Native Hawaiian and other Pacific Islander; (2) excludes Taiwanese; (3) includes Chamorro; (4) county does not meet population threshold but is shown in order to allow inclusion of city

Place	Total population 25 years and over who are high school graduates	Asian population 25 years and over	Asians 25 years and over who are high school graduates	NHPI[1] population 25 years and over	NHPIs[1] 25 years and over who are high school graduates	Asian Indian	Bangladeshi	Cambodian	Chinese[2]	Fijian	Filipino	Guamanian[3]	Hawaiian, Native	Hmong	Indonesian	Japanese	Korean	Laotian	Malaysian	Pakistani	Samoan	Sri Lankan	Taiwanese	Thai	Tongan	Vietnamese
South Laurel (cdp)	11,431 86.86	829	700 84.44 84.44 6.12	-	-	-	-	-	-	-	-	-	-	-	-	-	-	-	-	-	-	-	-	-	-	-
St. Mary's County	46,559 85.35	1,124	974 86.65 86.65 2.09	-	-	173 98.86 17.76 15.39 0.37	-	-	-	-	385 83.33 39.53 34.25 0.83	-	-	-	-	-	-	-	-	-	-	-	-	-	-	-
Lexington Park (cdp)	5,142 86.68	291	198 68.04 68.04 3.85	-	-	-	-	-	-	-	-	-	-	-	-	-	-	-	-	-	-	-	-	-	-	-
Washington County	70,301 77.79	712	528 74.16 74.16 0.75	-	-	-	-	-	-	-	-	-	-	-	-	-	-	-	-	-	-	-	-	-	-	-
Wicomico County	43,182 80.68	1,114	877 78.73 78.73 2.03	-	-	247 85.17 28.16 22.17 0.57	-	-	-	-	-	-	-	-	-	-	299 81.03 34.09 26.84 0.69	-	-	-	-	-	-	-	-	-
Salisbury (city)	10,327 76.43	583	414 71.01 71.01 4.01	-	-	-	-	-	-	-	-	-	-	-	-	-	-	-	-	-	-	-	-	-	-	-
MASSACHUSETTS	3,622,182 84.76	145,125	110,603 76.21 76.21 3.05	1,119	855 76.41 76.41 0.02	24,363 91.88 22.03 16.79 0.67	305 92.15 0.28 0.21 0.01	4,022 43.36 3.64 2.77 0.11	40,700 75.24 36.80 28.04 1.12	-	6,126 92.36 5.54 4.22 0.17	194 73.21 22.69 17.34 0.01	230 98.29 26.90 20.55 0.01	165 50.61 0.15 0.11 <0.01	315 87.50 0.28 0.22 0.01	6,792 94.95 6.14 4.68 0.19	8,629 90.84 7.80 5.95 0.24	926 48.33 0.84 0.64 0.03	-	984 81.19 0.89 0.68 0.03	-	322 92.00 0.29 0.22 0.01	1,433 95.41 1.30 0.99 0.04	1,299 87.53 1.17 0.90 0.04	-	11,135 55.16 10.07 7.67 0.31
Barnstable County	151,594 91.81	904	703 77.77 77.77 0.46	-	-	-	-	-	202 69.18 28.73 22.35 0.13	-	-	-	-	-	-	-	-	-	-	-	-	-	-	-	-	-
Berkshire County	79,388 85.05	626	556 88.82 88.82 0.70	-	-	193 100.00 34.71 30.83 0.24	-	-	-	-	-	-	-	-	-	-	-	-	-	-	-	-	-	-	-	-
Bristol County	261,910 73.19	4,308	2,959 68.69 68.69 1.13	-	-	867 86.61 29.30 20.13 0.33	-	434 46.07 14.67 10.07 0.17	637 65.47 21.53 14.79 0.24	-	289 89.47 9.77 6.71 0.11	-	-	-	-	-	182 73.39 6.15 4.22 0.07	-	-	-	-	-	-	-	-	159 49.69 5.37 3.69 0.06

Notes: Please refer to the User's Guide for an explanation of data; data is arranged alphabetically by state, then county, then city within each county; table includes counties with populations greater than 49,999 unless noted and cities with populations greater than 9,999 whose Asian and/or NHPI population rates are greater than the national average; (1) Native Hawaiian and other Pacific Islander; (2) excludes Taiwanese; (3) includes Chamorro; (4) county does not meet population threshold but is shown in order to allow inclusion of city

Place	Total population 25 years and over who are high school graduates	Asian population 25 years and over	Asians 25 years and over who are high school graduates	NHPI[1] population 25 years and over	NHPIs[1] 25 years and over who are high school graduates	Asian Indian	Bangladeshi	Cambodian	Chinese[2]	Fijian	Filipino	Guamanian[3]	Hawaiian, Native	Hmong	Indonesian	Japanese	Korean	Laotian	Malaysian	Pakistani	Samoan	Sri Lankan	Taiwanese	Thai	Tongan	Vietnamese
Essex County	412,136	10,137	7,304	-	-	1,420	-	713	1,817	-	492	-	-	-	-	569	828	95	-	-	-	-	-	-	-	937
	84.61		72.05			86.85		41.70	83.69		94.98					92.37	87.16	45.45								53.97
						19.44		9.76	24.88		6.74					7.79	11.34	1.30								12.83
			72.05			14.01		7.03	17.92		4.85					5.61	8.17	0.94								9.24
			1.77			0.34		0.17	0.44		0.12					0.14	0.20	0.02								0.23
Andover (town)	19,960	1,341	1,321	-	-	338	-	-	519	-	-	-	-	-	-	-	-	-	-	-	-	-	-	-	-	-
	95.52		98.51			100.00			96.29																	
						25.59			39.29																	
			98.51			25.21			38.70																	
			6.62			1.69			2.60																	
Lynn (city)	42,336	2,896	1,352	-	-	132	-	488	-	-	-	-	-	-	-	-	-	-	-	-	-	-	-	-	-	278
	74.15		46.69			56.17		36.17																		46.10
						9.76		36.09																		20.56
			46.69			4.56		16.85																		9.60
			3.19			0.31		1.15																		0.66
North Andover (town)	16,445	714	650	-	-	-	-	-	196	-	-	-	-	-	-	-	-	-	-	-	-	-	-	-	-	-
	93.06		91.04						86.34																	
									30.15																	
			91.04						27.45																	
			3.95						1.19																	
Franklin County	43,204	344	298	-	-	-	-	-	-	-	-	-	-	-	-	-	-	-	-	-	-	-	-	-	-	-
	87.95		86.63																							
			86.63																							
			0.69																							
Hampden County	234,374	3,595	2,351	-	-	332	-	119	516	-	-	-	-	-	-	-	210	-	-	-	-	-	-	-	-	544
	79.22		65.40			76.67		53.13	72.27								90.13									47.43
						14.12		5.06	21.95								8.93									23.14
			65.40			9.24		3.31	14.35								5.84									15.13
			1.00			0.14		0.05	0.22								0.09									0.23
Hampshire County	83,274	2,014	1,758	-	-	291	-	-	713	-	-	-	-	-	-	-	177	-	-	-	-	-	-	-	-	-
	89.36		87.29			93.57			89.57								97.25									
						16.55			40.56								10.07									
			87.29			14.45			35.40								8.79									
			2.11			0.35			0.86								0.21									
Amherst Center (cdp)	4,250	340	313	-	-	-	-	-		-	-	-	-	-	-	-	-	-	-	-	-	-	-	-	-	-
	95.94		92.06																							
			92.06																							
			7.36																							
Amherst (town)	12,288	1,092	951	-	-	-	-	-	466	-	-	-	-	-	-	-	-	-	-	-	-	-	-	-	-	-
	95.06		87.09						89.79																	
									49.00																	
			87.09						42.67																	
			7.74						3.79																	
Middlesex County	890,431	56,096	46,531	-	-	13,247	-	2,148	16,898	-	1,722	-	-	-	-	2,749	3,786	402	-	267	-	-	743	500	-	2,431
	88.47		82.95			92.76		42.71	86.72		94.88					98.07	93.25	44.42		91.75			96.37	87.11		60.19
						28.47		4.62	36.32		3.70					5.91	8.14	0.86		0.57			1.60	1.07		5.22
			82.95			23.61		3.83	30.12		3.07					4.90	6.75	0.72		0.48			1.32	0.89		4.33
			5.23			1.49		0.24	1.90		0.19					0.31	0.43	0.05		0.03			0.08	0.06		0.27

Notes: Please refer to the User's Guide for an explanation of data; data is arranged alphabetically by state, then county, then city within each county; table includes counties with populations greater than 49,999 unless noted and cities with populations greater than 9,999 whose Asian and/or NHPI population rates are greater than the national average; (1) Native Hawaiian and other Pacific Islander; (2) excludes Taiwanese; (3) includes Chamorro; (4) county does not meet population threshold but is shown in order to allow inclusion of city

Place	Total population 25 years and over who are high school graduates	Asian population 25 years and over	Asians 25 years and over who are high school graduates	NHPI[1] population 25 years and over	NHPIs[1] 25 years and over who are high school graduates	Asian Indian	Bangladeshi	Cambodian	Chinese[2]	Fijian	Filipino	Guamanian[3]	Hawaiian, Native	Hmong	Indonesian	Japanese	Korean	Laotian	Malaysian	Pakistani	Samoan	Sri Lankan	Taiwanese	Thai	Tongan	Vietnamese
Acton (town)	13,198 97.76	1,208	1,187 98.26 98.26 8.99	-	-	431 100.00 36.31 35.68 3.27	-	-	550 98.39 46.34 45.53 4.17	-	-	-	-	-	-	-	-	-	-	-	-	-	-	-	-	-
Arlington (town)	29,734 91.67	1,451	1,308 90.14 90.14 4.40	-	-	-	-	-	482 90.43 36.85 33.22 1.62	-	-	-	-	-	-	-	-	-	-	-	-	-	-	-	-	-
Bedford (town)	8,632 94.90	574	551 95.99 95.99 6.38	-	-	-	-	-	-	-	-	-	-	-	-	-	-	-	-	-	-	-	-	-	-	-
Belmont (cdp)	16,638 94.61	869	820 94.36 94.36 4.93	-	-	-	-	-	346 90.34 42.20 39.82 2.08	-	-	-	-	-	-	-	-	-	-	-	-	-	-	-	-	-
Belmont (town)	16,638 94.61	869	820 94.36 94.36 4.93	-	-	-	-	-	346 90.34 42.20 39.82 2.08	-	-	-	-	-	-	-	-	-	-	-	-	-	-	-	-	-
Burlington (town)	14,781 92.27	1,599	1,538 96.19 96.19 10.41	-	-	1,000 97.28 65.02 62.54 6.77	-	-	-	-	-	-	-	-	-	-	-	-	-	-	-	-	-	-	-	-
Cambridge (city)	59,375 89.53	6,739	6,282 93.22 93.22 10.58	-	-	1,395 90.35 22.21 20.70 2.35	-	-	2,138 91.92 34.03 31.73 3.60	-	-	-	-	-	-	795 99.25 12.66 11.80 1.34	1,059 97.78 16.86 15.71 1.78	-	-	-	-	-	-	-	-	-
Chelmsford (town)	22,000 93.01	1,035	971 93.82 93.82 4.41	-	-	260 96.65 26.78 25.12 1.18	-	-	390 93.98 40.16 37.68 1.77	-	-	-	-	-	-	-	-	-	-	-	-	-	-	-	-	-
Framingham (town)	40,848 87.15	2,396	2,149 89.69 89.69 5.26	-	-	949 95.19 44.16 39.61 2.32	-	-	680 87.52 31.64 28.38 1.66	-	-	-	-	-	-	-	-	-	-	-	-	-	-	-	-	-
Lexington (town)	20,510 96.31	1,984	1,915 96.52 96.52 9.34	-	-	493 97.62 25.74 24.85 2.40	-	-	839 97.11 43.81 42.29 4.09	-	-	-	-	-	-	-	221 88.76 11.54 11.14 1.08	-	-	-	-	-	-	-	-	-

Notes: Please refer to the User's Guide for an explanation of data; data is arranged alphabetically by state, then county, then city within each county; table includes counties with populations greater than 49,999 unless noted and cities with populations greater than 9,999 whose Asian and/or NHPI population rates are greater than the national average; (1) Native Hawaiian and other Pacific Islander; (2) excludes Taiwanese; (3) includes Chamorro; (4) county does not meet population threshold but is shown in order to allow inclusion of city

Place	Total population 25 years and over who are high school graduates	Asian population 25 years and over	Asians 25 years and over who are high school graduates	NHPI[1] population 25 years and over	NHPIs[1] 25 years and over who are high school graduates	Asian Indian	Bangladeshi	Cambodian	Chinese[2]	Fijian	Filipino	Guamanian[3]	Hawaiian, Native	Hmong	Indonesian	Japanese	Korean	Laotian	Malaysian	Pakistani	Samoan	Sri Lankan	Taiwanese	Thai	Tongan	Vietnamese
Lowell (city)	45,880 71.22	8,731	4,776 54.70 54.70 10.41	-	-	1,347 84.88 28.20 15.43 2.94	-	1,733 40.26 36.29 19.85 3.78	526 93.93 11.01 6.02 1.15	-	-	-	-	-	-	-	-	316 42.82 6.62 3.62 0.69	-	-	-	-	-	-	-	413 48.99 8.65 4.73 0.90
Malden (city)	33,853 83.44	5,301	3,714 70.06 70.06 10.97	-	-	738 94.49 19.87 13.92 2.18	-	-	1,747 62.66 47.04 32.96 5.16	-	-	-	-	-	-	-	-	-	-	-	-	-	-	-	-	456 54.42 12.28 8.60 1.35
Marlborough (city)	22,274 87.31	1,116	1,011 90.59 90.59 4.54	-	-	439 94.82 43.42 39.34 1.97	-	-	-	-	-	-	-	-	-	-	-	-	-	-	-	-	-	-	-	-
Medford (city)	34,020 85.56	1,407	1,214 86.28 86.28 3.57	-	-	255 94.44 21.00 18.12 0.75	-	-	497 86.74 40.94 35.32 1.46	-	-	-	-	-	-	-	-	-	-	-	-	-	-	-	-	153 76.88 12.60 10.87 0.45
Natick (town)	21,866 94.00	865	779 90.06 90.06 3.56	-	-	-	-	-	381 90.93 48.91 44.05 1.74	-	-	-	-	-	-	-	-	-	-	-	-	-	-	-	-	-
Newton (city)	54,543 94.55	4,031	3,689 91.52 91.52 6.76	-	-	415 93.68 11.25 10.30 0.76	-	-	2,303 89.54 62.43 57.13 4.22	-	-	-	-	-	-	-	328 100.00 8.89 8.14 0.60	-	-	-	-	-	-	-	-	-
Somerville (city)	43,285 80.62	2,990	2,469 82.58 82.58 5.70	-	-	607 77.72 24.58 20.30 1.40	-	-	998 80.03 40.42 33.38 2.31	-	-	-	-	-	-	-	177 96.72 7.17 5.92 0.41	-	-	-	-	-	-	-	-	-
Sudbury (town)	10,426 96.32	409	401 98.04 98.04 3.85	-	-	-	-	-	-	-	-	-	-	-	-	-	-	-	-	-	-	-	-	-	-	-
Waltham (city)	34,070 85.36	2,740	2,447 89.31 89.31 7.18	-	-	1,117 93.63 45.65 40.77 3.28	-	-	845 91.75 34.53 30.84 2.48	-	-	-	-	-	-	-	-	-	-	-	-	-	-	-	-	-
Wayland (town)	8,652 96.48	448	443 98.88 98.88 5.12	-	-	-	-	-	-	-	-	-	-	-	-	-	-	-	-	-	-	-	-	-	-	-

Notes: Please refer to the User's Guide for an explanation of data; data is arranged alphabetically by state, then county, then city within each county; table includes counties with populations greater than 49,999 unless noted and cities with populations greater than 9,999 whose Asian and/or NHPI population rates are greater than the national average; (1) Native Hawaiian and other Pacific Islander; (2) excludes Taiwanese; (3) includes Chamorro; (4) county does not meet population threshold but is shown in order to allow inclusion of city

Place	Total population 25 years and over who are high school graduates	Asian population 25 years and over	Asians 25 years and over who are high school graduates	NHPI[1] population 25 years and over	NHPIs[1] 25 years and over who are high school graduates	Asian Indian	Bangladeshi	Cambodian	Chinese[2]	Fijian	Filipino	Guamanian[3]	Hawaiian, Native	Hmong	Indonesian	Japanese	Korean	Laotian	Malaysian	Pakistani	Samoan	Sri Lankan	Taiwanese	Thai	Tongan	Vietnamese
Westford (town)	12,498 94.15	605	601 99.34 99.34 4.81	-	-	-	-	-	227 98.27 37.77 37.52 1.82	-	-	-	-	-	-	-	-	-	-	-	-	-	-	-	-	-
Weston (town)	7,082 96.05	548	493 89.96 89.96 6.96	-	-	-	-	-	225 82.12 45.64 41.06 3.18	-	-	-	-	-	-	-	-	-	-	-	-	-	-	-	-	-
Winchester (town)	13,991 94.53	545	514 94.31 94.31 3.67	-	-	-	-	-	-	-	-	-	-	-	-	-	-	-	-	-	-	-	-	-	-	-
Woburn (city)	23,625 88.06	1,301	1,203 92.47 92.47 5.09	-	-	616 95.50 51.21 47.35 2.61	-	-	-	-	-	-	-	-	-	-	-	-	-	-	-	-	-	-	-	-
Norfolk County	413,038 91.28	23,571	18,957 80.43 80.43 4.59	-	-	3,277 94.77 17.29 13.90 0.79	-	-	9,501 74.06 50.12 40.31 2.30	-	1,230 89.20 6.49 5.22 0.30	-	-	-	-	1,328 97.22 7.01 5.63 0.32	1,153 94.90 6.08 4.89 0.28	-	-	-	-	-	180 91.84 0.95 0.76 0.04	-	-	1,215 69.83 6.41 5.15 0.29
Brookline (town)	39,534 96.28	5,270	4,849 92.01 92.01 12.27	-	-	671 96.27 13.84 12.73 1.70	-	-	2,253 87.06 46.46 42.75 5.70	-	-	-	-	-	-	880 98.10 18.15 16.70 2.23	603 100.00 12.44 11.44 1.53	-	-	-	-	-	-	-	-	-
Needham (town)	19,025 96.43	630	605 96.03 96.03 3.18	-	-	-	-	-	349 93.32 57.69 55.40 1.83	-	-	-	-	-	-	-	-	-	-	-	-	-	-	-	-	-
Norwood (town)	19,088 91.82	989	957 96.76 96.76 5.01	-	-	546 100.00 57.05 55.21 2.86	-	-	-	-	-	-	-	-	-	-	-	-	-	-	-	-	-	-	-	-
Quincy (city)	55,804 85.17	9,374	6,385 68.11 68.11 11.44	-	-	723 95.51 11.32 7.71 1.30	-	-	3,922 62.97 61.43 41.84 7.03	-	530 81.54 8.30 5.65 0.95	-	-	-	-	-	-	-	-	-	-	-	-	-	-	542 62.80 8.49 5.78 0.97
Randolph (town)	18,866 87.25	2,126	1,558 73.28 73.28 8.26	-	-	-	-	-	707 65.89 45.38 33.25 3.75	-	-	-	-	-	-	-	-	-	-	-	-	-	-	-	-	337 73.42 21.63 15.85 1.79

Notes: Please refer to the User's Guide for an explanation of data; data is arranged alphabetically by state, then county, then city within each county; table includes counties with populations greater than 49,999 unless noted and cities with populations greater than 9,999 whose Asian and/or NHPI population rates are greater than the national average; (1) Native Hawaiian and other Pacific Islander; (2) excludes Taiwanese; (3) includes Chamorro; (4) county does not meet population threshold but is shown in order to allow inclusion of city

Place	Total population 25 years and over who are high school graduates	Asian population 25 years and over	Asians 25 years and over who are high school graduates	NHPI[1] population 25 years and over	NHPIs[1] 25 years and over who are high school graduates	Asian Indian	Bangladeshi	Cambodian	Chinese[2]	Fijian	Filipino	Guamanian[3]	Hawaiian, Native	Hmong	Indonesian	Japanese	Korean	Laotian	Malaysian	Pakistani	Samoan	Sri Lankan	Taiwanese	Thai	Tongan	Vietnamese
Sharon (town)	11,109 96.80	480	463 96.46 96.46 4.17	-	-	-	-	-	-	-	-	-	-	-	-	-	-	-	-	-	-	-	-	-	-	-
Wellesley (town)	15,844 97.63	629	607 96.50 96.50 3.83	-	-	-	-	-	356 96.74 58.65 56.60 2.25	-	-	-	-	-	-	-	-	-	-	-	-	-	-	-	-	-
Plymouth County	274,037 87.64	2,656	1,981 74.59 74.59 0.72	-	-	313 84.14 15.80 11.78 0.11	-	-	405 68.41 20.44 15.25 0.15	-	362 87.65 18.27 13.63 0.13	-	-	-	-	-	-	-	-	-	-	-	-	-	-	270 63.83 13.63 10.17 0.10
Suffolk County	348,894 78.14	29,562	18,876 63.85 63.85 5.41	-	-	2,082 89.39 11.03 7.04 0.60	-	310 39.79 1.64 1.05 0.09	7,844 57.28 41.56 26.53 2.25	-	1,097 94.98 5.81 3.71 0.31	-	-	-	-	1,126 95.42 5.97 3.81 0.32	1,396 94.32 7.40 4.72 0.40	-	-	-	-	-	290 100.00 1.54 0.98 0.08	-	-	3,661 50.48 19.39 12.38 1.05
Boston (city)	297,945 78.91	27,436	17,629 64.25 64.25 5.92	-	-	1,884 89.84 10.69 6.87 0.63	-	148 47.13 0.84 0.54 0.05	7,600 56.99 43.11 27.70 2.55	-	1,018 95.50 5.77 3.71 0.34	-	-	-	-	1,098 95.31 6.23 4.00 0.37	1,288 93.88 7.31 4.69 0.43	-	-	-	-	-	290 100.00 1.65 1.06 0.10	-	-	3,302 50.53 18.73 12.04 1.11
Chelsea (city)	12,844 59.47	864	438 50.69 50.69 3.41	-	-	-	-	-	-	-	-	-	-	-	-	-	-	-	-	-	-	-	-	-	-	192 45.93 43.84 22.22 1.49
Revere (city)	25,858 76.68	1,182	729 61.68 61.68 2.82	-	-	-	-	116 35.80 15.91 9.81 0.45	-	-	-	-	-	-	-	-	-	-	-	-	-	-	-	-	-	167 55.85 22.91 14.13 0.65
Worcester County	413,842 83.46	11,163	8,205 73.50 73.50 1.98	-	-	2,251 93.29 27.43 20.16 0.54	-	73 37.63 0.89 0.65 0.02	1,890 85.21 23.03 16.93 0.46	-	336 88.19 4.10 3.01 0.08	-	-	55 28.21 0.67 0.49 0.01	-	210 97.22 2.56 1.88 0.05	564 78.55 6.87 5.05 0.14	313 55.11 3.81 2.80 0.08	-	176 80.73 2.15 1.58 0.04	-	-	-	-	-	1,755 52.91 21.39 15.72 0.42
Fitchburg (city)	18,743 75.39	726	355 48.90 48.90 1.89	-	-	-	-	-	-	-	-	-	-	52 29.89 14.65 7.16 0.28	-	-	-	109 57.07 30.70 15.01 0.58	-	-	-	-	-	-	-	-
Northborough (town)	8,616 93.44	466	447 95.92 95.92 5.19	-	-	-	-	-	-	-	-	-	-	-	-	-	-	-	-	-	-	-	-	-	-	-

Notes: Please refer to the User's Guide for an explanation of data; data is arranged alphabetically by state, then county, then city within each county; table includes counties with populations greater than 49,999 unless noted and cities with populations greater than 9,999 whose Asian and/or NHPI population rates are greater than the national average; (1) Native Hawaiian and other Pacific Islander; (2) excludes Taiwanese; (3) includes Chamorro; (4) county does not meet population threshold but is shown in order to allow inclusion of city

Place	Total population 25 years and over who are high school graduates	Asian population 25 years and over	Asians 25 years and over who are high school graduates	NHPI[1] population 25 years and over	NHPIs[1] 25 years and over who are high school graduates	Asian Indian	Bangladeshi	Cambodian	Chinese[2]	Fijian	Filipino	Guamanian[3]	Hawaiian, Native	Hmong	Indonesian	Japanese	Korean	Laotian	Malaysian	Pakistani	Samoan	Sri Lankan	Taiwanese	Thai	Tongan	Vietnamese
Shrewsbury (town)	20,073 91.76	1,694	1,531 90.38 90.38 7.63	-	-	733 96.96 47.88 43.27 3.65	-	-	416 97.65 27.17 24.56 2.07	-	-	-	-	-	-	-	-	-	-	-	-	-	-	-	-	216 63.53 14.11 12.75 1.08
Westborough (town)	11,154 93.35	927	869 93.74 93.74 7.79	-	-	368 95.09 42.35 39.70 3.30	-	-	296 92.79 34.06 31.93 2.65	-	-	-	-	-	-	-	-	-	-	-	-	-	-	-	-	-
Worcester (city)	83,382 76.66	4,517	2,719 60.19 60.19 3.26	-	-	518 87.06 19.05 11.47 0.62	-	-	382 68.71 14.05 8.46 0.46	-	-	-	-	-	-	-	-	-	-	-	-	-	-	-	-	1,215 48.68 44.69 26.90 1.46
MICHIGAN	5,351,808 83.41	107,112	91,693 85.60 85.60 1.71	1,354	995 73.49 73.49 0.02	31,318 90.04 34.16 29.24 0.59	508 53.31 0.55 0.47 0.01	398 46.66 0.43 0.37 0.01	16,817 85.83 18.34 15.70 0.31	-	11,692 92.78 12.75 10.92 0.22	186 59.24 18.69 13.74 <0.01	327 77.67 32.86 24.15 0.01	796 43.10 0.87 0.74 0.01	307 88.47 0.33 0.29 0.01	7,168 95.32 7.82 6.69 0.13	9,222 89.44 10.06 8.61 0.17	758 56.57 0.83 0.71 0.01	161 95.27 0.18 0.15 <0.01	2,419 86.49 2.64 2.26 0.05	193 76.89 19.40 14.25 <0.01	248 94.30 0.27 0.23 <0.01	1,471 99.12 1.60 1.37 0.03	924 82.80 1.01 0.86 0.02	-	4,901 63.01 5.35 4.58 0.09
Allegan County	55,090 82.32	313	222 70.93 70.93 0.40	-	-	-	-	-	-	-	-	-	-	-	-	-	-	-	-	-	-	-	-	-	-	-
Bay County	61,119 82.43	376	270 71.81 71.81 0.44	-	-	-	-	-	-	-	-	-	-	-	-	-	-	-	-	-	-	-	-	-	-	-
Berrien County	87,406 81.93	996	857 86.04 86.04 0.98	-	-	242 84.32 28.24 24.30 0.28	-	-	-	-	185 85.65 21.59 18.57 0.21	-	-	-	-	-	187 100.00 21.82 18.78 0.21	-	-	-	-	-	-	-	-	-
Calhoun County	75,025 83.23	986	881 89.35 89.35 1.17	-	-	-	-	-	-	-	-	-	-	-	-	277 94.86 31.44 28.09 0.37	-	-	-	-	-	-	-	-	-	-
Cass County	27,579 80.44	196	104 53.06 53.06 0.38	-	-	-	-	-	-	-	-	-	-	-	-	-	-	23 28.05 22.12 11.73 0.08	-	-	-	-	-	-	-	-
Clinton County	37,342 89.20	158	98 62.03 62.03 0.26	-	-	-	-	-	-	-	-	-	-	-	-	-	-	-	-	-	-	-	-	-	-	-

Notes: Please refer to the User's Guide for an explanation of data; data is arranged alphabetically by state, then county, then city within each county; table includes counties with populations greater than 49,999 unless noted and cities with populations greater than 9,999 whose Asian and/or NHPI population rates are greater than the national average; (1) Native Hawaiian and other Pacific Islander; (2) excludes Taiwanese; (3) includes Chamorro; (4) county does not meet population threshold but is shown in order to allow inclusion of city

Place	Total population 25 years and over who are high school graduates	Asian population 25 years and over	Asians 25 years and over who are high school graduates	NHPI[1] population 25 years and over	NHPIs[1] 25 years and over who are high school graduates	Asian Indian	Bangladeshi	Cambodian	Chinese[2]	Fijian	Filipino	Guamanian[3]	Hawaiian, Native	Hmong	Indonesian	Japanese	Korean	Laotian	Malaysian	Pakistani	Samoan	Sri Lankan	Taiwanese	Thai	Tongan	Vietnamese
Eaton County	60,027 89.53	695	548 78.85 78.85 0.91	-	-	218 100.00 39.78 31.37 0.36	-	-	-	-	-	-	-	-	-	-	-	-	-	-	-	-	-	-	-	96 52.75 17.52 13.81 0.16
Genesee County	230,850 83.14	2,027	1,797 88.65 88.65 0.78	-	-	746 95.76 41.51 36.80 0.32	-	-	221 77.82 12.30 10.90 0.10	-	320 94.12 17.81 15.79 0.14	-	-	-	-	-	154 79.79 8.57 7.60 0.07	-	-	-	-	-	-	-	-	-
Ingham County	143,568 88.13	5,517	4,807 87.13 87.13 3.35	-	-	1,114 90.94 23.17 20.19 0.78	-	-	1,036 92.91 21.55 18.78 0.72	-	338 88.25 7.03 6.13 0.24	-	-	44 29.14 0.92 0.80 0.03	-	349 97.49 7.26 6.33 0.24	890 100.00 18.51 16.13 0.62	-	-	-	-	-	-	-	-	444 62.71 9.24 8.05 0.31
East Lansing (city)	14,824 96.94	1,967	1,948 99.03 99.03 13.14	-	-	376 95.19 19.30 19.12 2.54	-	-	535 100.00 27.46 27.20 3.61	-	-	-	-	-	-	-	511 100.00 26.23 25.98 3.45	-	-	-	-	-	-	-	-	-
Meridian charter (township)	23,624 95.60	1,526	1,413 92.60 92.60 5.98	-	-	522 90.47 36.94 34.21 2.21	-	-	294 92.16 20.81 19.27 1.24	-	-	-	-	-	-	-	194 100.00 13.73 12.71 0.82	-	-	-	-	-	-	-	-	-
Okemos (cdp)	13,645 97.02	1,157	1,083 93.60 93.60 7.94	-	-	403 87.99 37.21 34.83 2.95	-	-	220 96.49 20.31 19.01 1.61	-	-	-	-	-	-	-	-	-	-	-	-	-	-	-	-	-
Ionia County	31,554 83.40	117	91 77.78 77.78 0.29	-	-	-	-	-	-	-	-	-	-	-	-	-	-	-	-	-	-	-	-	-	-	-
Isabella County	27,263 86.07	439	413 94.08 94.08 1.51	-	-	-	-	-	-	-	-	-	-	-	-	-	-	-	-	-	-	-	-	-	-	-
Jackson County	88,335 84.22	464	439 94.61 94.61 0.50	-	-	-	-	-	-	-	-	-	-	-	-	-	-	-	-	-	-	-	-	-	-	-
Kalamazoo County	128,721 88.78	2,439	2,273 93.19 93.19 1.77	-	-	736 94.85 32.38 30.18 0.57	-	-	471 94.96 20.72 19.31 0.37	-	-	-	-	-	-	-	262 92.25 11.53 10.74 0.20	-	-	-	-	-	-	-	-	-

Notes: Please refer to the User's Guide for an explanation of data; data is arranged alphabetically by state, then county, then city within each county; table includes counties with populations greater than 49,999 unless noted and cities with populations greater than 9,999 whose Asian and/or NHPI population rates are greater than the national average; (1) Native Hawaiian and other Pacific Islander; (2) excludes Taiwanese; (3) includes Chamorro; (4) county does not meet population threshold but is shown in order to allow inclusion of city

Place	Total population 25 years and over who are high school graduates	Asian population 25 years and over	Asians 25 years and over who are high school graduates	NHPI[1] population 25 years and over	NHPIs[1] 25 years and over who are high school graduates	Asian Indian	Bangladeshi	Cambodian	Chinese[2]	Fijian	Filipino	Guamanian[3]	Hawaiian, Native	Hmong	Indonesian	Japanese	Korean	Laotian	Malaysian	Pakistani	Samoan	Sri Lankan	Taiwanese	Thai	Tongan	Vietnamese
Kent County	297,727 84.61	6,054	4,261 70.38 70.38 1.43	-	-	682 80.24 16.01 11.27 0.23	-	-	500 80.00 11.73 8.26 0.17	-	383 92.74 8.99 6.33 0.13	-	-	-	-	-	609 81.97 14.29 10.06 0.20	-	-	-	-	-	-	-	-	1,492 54.57 35.02 24.64 0.50
Kentwood (city)	25,437 89.20	1,561	1,191 76.30 76.30 4.68	-	-	-	-	-	-	-	-	-	-	-	-	-	203 87.12 17.04 13.00 0.80	-	-	-	-	-	-	-	-	458 60.50 38.46 29.34 1.80
Lenawee County	53,636 83.40	350	294 84.00 84.00 0.55	-	-	-	-	-	-	-	-	-	-	-	-	-	-	-	-	-	-	-	-	-	-	-
Livingston County	92,650 91.39	623	519 83.31 83.31 0.56	-	-	-	-	-	-	-	-	-	-	-	-	-	-	-	-	-	-	-	-	-	-	-
Macomb County	444,465 82.95	10,937	8,762 80.11 80.11 1.97	-	-	2,982 83.91 34.03 27.27 0.67	-	-	1,152 69.40 13.15 10.53 0.26	-	2,222 91.18 25.36 20.32 0.50	-	-	269 61.28 3.07 2.46 0.06	-	-	626 82.15 7.14 5.72 0.14	-	-	252 80.51 2.88 2.30 0.06	-	-	-	-	-	580 64.95 6.62 5.30 0.13
Sterling Heights (city)	70,347 83.97	4,233	3,600 85.05 85.05 5.12	-	-	1,343 86.70 37.31 31.73 1.91	-	-	495 72.16 13.75 11.69 0.70	-	940 97.11 26.11 22.21 1.34	-	-	-	-	-	259 77.54 7.19 6.12 0.37	-	-	-	-	-	-	-	-	239 77.85 6.64 5.65 0.34
Marquette County	37,101 88.47	200	138 69.00 69.00 0.37	-	-	-	-	-	-	-	-	-	-	-	-	-	-	-	-	-	-	-	-	-	-	-
Midland County	47,596 88.97	715	678 94.83 94.83 1.42	-	-	255 100.00 37.61 35.66 0.54	-	-	213 89.12 31.42 29.79 0.45	-	-	-	-	-	-	-	-	-	-	-	-	-	-	-	-	-
Monroe County	78,363 83.12	538	455 84.57 84.57 0.58	-	-	-	-	-	-	-	-	-	-	-	-	-	-	-	-	-	-	-	-	-	-	-
Muskegon County	90,258 83.06	406	319 78.57 78.57 0.35	-	-	-	-	-	-	-	-	-	-	-	-	-	-	-	-	-	-	-	-	-	-	-

Notes: Please refer to the User's Guide for an explanation of data; data is arranged alphabetically by state, then county, then city within each county; table includes counties with populations greater than 49,999 unless noted and cities with populations greater than 9,999 whose Asian and/or NHPI population rates are greater than the national average; (1) Native Hawaiian and other Pacific Islander; (2) excludes Taiwanese; (3) includes Chamorro; (4) county does not meet population threshold but is shown in order to allow inclusion of city

Place	Total population 25 years and over who are high school graduates	Asian population 25 years and over	Asians 25 years and over who are high school graduates	NHPI[1] population 25 years and over	NHPIs[1] 25 years and over who are high school graduates	Asian Indian	Bangladeshi	Cambodian	Chinese[2]	Fijian	Filipino	Guamanian[3]	Hawaiian, Native	Hmong	Indonesian	Japanese	Korean	Laotian	Malaysian	Pakistani	Samoan	Sri Lankan	Taiwanese	Thai	Tongan	Vietnamese
Oakland County	721,193 89.27	31,940	29,178 91.35 91.35 4.05	-	-	12,378 94.68 42.42 38.75 1.72	-	-	5,174 85.96 17.73 16.20 0.72	-	2,819 94.98 9.66 8.83 0.39	-	-	155 38.56 0.53 0.49 0.02	-	2,934 97.93 10.06 9.19 0.41	2,688 93.20 9.21 8.42 0.37	-	-	474 87.94 1.62 1.48 0.07	-	-	748 99.07 2.56 2.34 0.10	-	-	643 69.66 2.20 2.01 0.09
Auburn Hills (city)	11,083 87.93	799	710 88.86 88.86 6.41	-	-	388 94.17 54.65 48.56 3.50	-	-	-	-	-	-	-	-	-	-	-	-	-	-	-	-	-	-	-	-
Bloomfield (township)	29,931 96.15	1,926	1,815 94.24 94.24 6.06	-	-	732 91.16 40.33 38.01 2.45	-	-	-	-	-	-	-	-	-	-	364 95.29 20.06 18.90 1.22	-	-	-	-	-	-	-	-	-
Farmington (city)	7,201 91.58	763	725 95.02 95.02 10.07	-	-	578 97.31 79.72 75.75 8.03	-	-	-	-	-	-	-	-	-	-	-	-	-	-	-	-	-	-	-	-
Farmington Hills (city)	52,782 91.68	4,039	3,855 95.44 95.44 7.30	-	-	2,370 97.37 61.48 58.68 4.49	-	-	565 91.42 14.66 13.99 1.07	-	224 91.43 5.81 5.55 0.42	-	-	-	-	-	-	-	-	-	-	-	-	-	-	-
Madison Heights (city)	17,179 78.84	1,206	1,030 85.41 85.41 6.00	-	-	-	-	-	310 77.69 30.10 25.70 1.80	-	-	-	-	-	-	-	-	-	-	-	-	-	-	-	-	-
Novi (city)	29,329 93.96	2,587	2,424 93.70 93.70 8.26	-	-	674 92.71 27.81 26.05 2.30	-	-	509 93.57 21.00 19.68 1.74	-	-	-	-	-	-	751 97.15 30.98 29.03 2.56	-	-	-	-	-	-	-	-	-	-
Rochester (city)	6,929 94.12	352	332 94.32 94.32 4.79	-	-	-	-	-	-	-	-	-	-	-	-	-	-	-	-	-	-	-	-	-	-	-
Rochester Hills (city)	43,001 92.72	3,011	2,776 92.20 92.20 6.46	-	-	1,243 93.88 44.78 41.28 2.89	-	-	620 92.12 22.33 20.59 1.44	-	-	-	-	-	-	-	177 95.16 6.38 5.88 0.41	-	-	-	-	-	-	-	-	-
Troy (city)	50,020 92.22	6,651	6,239 93.81 93.81 12.47	-	-	2,912 96.14 46.67 43.78 5.82	-	-	1,355 90.64 21.72 20.37 2.71	-	537 95.72 8.61 8.07 1.07	-	-	-	-	-	668 90.88 10.71 10.04 1.34	-	-	-	-	-	324 100.00 5.19 4.87 0.65	-	-	-

Notes: Please refer to the User's Guide for an explanation of data; data is arranged alphabetically by state, then county, then city within each county; table includes counties with populations greater than 49,999 unless noted and cities with populations greater than 9,999 whose Asian and/or NHPI population rates are greater than the national average; (1) Native Hawaiian and other Pacific Islander; (2) excludes Taiwanese; (3) includes Chamorro; (4) county does not meet population threshold but is shown in order to allow inclusion of city

Place	Total population 25 years and over who are high school graduates	Asian population 25 years and over	Asians 25 years and over who are high school graduates	NHPI[1] population 25 years and over	NHPIs[1] 25 years and over who are high school graduates	Asian Indian	Bangladeshi	Cambodian	Chinese[2]	Fijian	Filipino	Guamanian[3]	Hawaiian, Native	Hmong	Indonesian	Japanese	Korean	Laotian	Malaysian	Pakistani	Samoan	Sri Lankan	Taiwanese	Thai	Tongan	Vietnamese
West Bloomfield (township)	41,434 93.29	3,127	2,984 95.43 95.43 7.20	-	-	1,074 95.13 35.99 34.35 2.59	-	-	388 90.23 13.00 12.41 0.94	-	271 100.00 9.08 8.67 0.65	-	-	-	-	787 100.00 26.37 25.17 1.90	273 93.81 9.15 8.73 0.66	-	-	-	-	-	-	-	-	-
Ottawa County	122,899 86.63	2,551	1,713 67.15 67.15 1.39	-	-	127 67.91 7.41 4.98 0.10	-	267 50.47 15.59 10.47 0.22	157 59.70 9.17 6.15 0.13	-	-	-	-	-	-	-	97 100.00 5.66 3.80 0.08	364 61.18 21.25 14.27 0.30	-	-	-	-	-	-	-	315 71.59 18.39 12.35 0.26
Holland (city)	15,779 78.53	749	522 69.69 69.69 3.31	-	-	-	-	-	-	-	-	-	-	-	-	-	-	-	-	-	-	-	-	-	-	-
Saginaw County	110,292 81.58	1,052	916 87.07 87.07 0.83	-	-	184 88.04 20.09 17.49 0.17	-	-	-	-	214 92.24 23.36 20.34 0.19	-	-	-	-	-	168 91.30 18.34 15.97 0.15	-	-	-	-	-	-	-	-	-
St. Clair County	89,122 82.84	271	217 80.07 80.07 0.24	-	-	-	-	-	-	-	-	-	-	-	-	-	-	-	-	-	-	-	-	-	-	-
St. Joseph County	31,283 78.59	205	160 78.05 78.05 0.51	-	-	-	-	-	-	-	-	-	-	-	-	-	-	-	-	-	-	-	-	-	-	-
Washtenaw County	180,698 91.53	11,479	10,899 94.95 94.95 6.03	-	-	2,459 96.47 22.56 21.42 1.36	-	-	3,479 95.76 31.92 30.31 1.93	-	622 98.26 5.71 5.42 0.34	-	-	-	-	1,127 99.21 10.34 9.82 0.62	1,880 94.42 17.25 16.38 1.04	-	-	217 93.13 1.99 1.89 0.12	-	-	346 98.30 3.17 3.01 0.19	-	-	178 81.65 1.63 1.55 0.10
Ann Arbor (city)	61,878 95.68	7,121	6,898 96.87 96.87 11.15	-	-	1,542 97.29 22.35 21.65 2.49	-	-	2,263 97.38 32.81 31.78 3.66	-	285 98.62 4.13 4.00 0.46	-	-	-	-	804 98.89 11.66 11.29 1.30	1,219 95.38 17.67 17.12 1.97	-	-	-	-	-	286 97.95 4.15 4.02 0.46	-	-	-
Pittsfield charter (township)	17,288 89.53	1,770	1,591 89.89 89.89 9.20	-	-	427 95.96 26.84 24.12 2.47	-	-	470 89.87 29.54 26.55 2.72	-	-	-	-	-	-	-	307 88.22 19.30 17.34 1.78	-	-	-	-	-	-	-	-	-
Scio (township)	9,899 95.09	433	433 100.00 100.00 4.37	-	-	-	-	-	-	-	-	-	-	-	-	-	-	-	-	-	-	-	-	-	-	-

Notes: Please refer to the User's Guide for an explanation of data; data is arranged alphabetically by state, then county, then city within each county; table includes counties with populations greater than 49,999 unless noted and cities with populations greater than 9,999 whose Asian and/or NHPI population rates are greater than the national average; (1) Native Hawaiian and other Pacific Islander; (2) excludes Taiwanese; (3) includes Chamorro; (4) county does not meet population threshold but is shown in order to allow inclusion of city

Place	Total population 25 years and over who are high school graduates	Asian population 25 years and over	Asians 25 years and over who are high school graduates	NHPI[1] population 25 years and over	NHPIs[1] 25 years and over who are high school graduates	Asian Indian	Bangladeshi	Cambodian	Chinese[2]	Fijian	Filipino	Guamanian[3]	Hawaiian, Native	Hmong	Indonesian	Japanese	Korean	Laotian	Malaysian	Pakistani	Samoan	Sri Lankan	Taiwanese	Thai	Tongan	Vietnamese
Wayne County	1,004,782 76.98	22,048	17,833 80.88 80.88 1.77	291	177 60.82 60.82 0.02	7,651 83.53 42.90 34.70 0.76	249 39.09 1.40 1.13 0.02	-	3,036 84.24 17.02 13.77 0.30	-	2,983 94.43 16.73 13.53 0.30	-	-	138 26.54 0.77 0.63 0.01	-	729 86.89 4.09 3.31 0.07	741 74.85 4.16 3.36 0.07	-	-	1,014 83.11 5.69 4.60 0.10	-	-	-	-	-	551 72.31 3.09 2.50 0.05
Brownstown (township)	12,144 85.09	505	462 91.49 91.49 3.80	-	-	-	-	-	-	-	-	-	-	-	-	-	-	-	-	-	-	-	-	-	-	-
Canton (township)	44,215 91.98	4,161	3,788 91.04 91.04 8.57	-	-	1,935 88.48 51.08 46.50 4.38	-	-	768 94.12 20.27 18.46 1.74	-	469 100.00 12.38 11.27 1.06	-	-	-	-	-	145 85.29 3.83 3.48 0.33	-	-	-	-	-	-	-	-	-
Hamtramck (city)	8,825 62.20	1,165	526 45.15 45.15 5.96	-	-	265 50.19 50.38 22.75 3.00	135 36.59 25.67 11.59 1.53	-	-	-	-	-	-	-	-	-	-	-	-	-	-	-	-	-	-	-
Inkster (city)	13,655 74.32	820	780 95.12 95.12 5.71	-	-	552 95.34 70.77 67.32 4.04	-	-	-	-	-	-	-	-	-	-	-	-	-	-	-	-	-	-	-	-
Northville (township)	14,038 91.70	658	612 93.01 93.01 4.36	-	-	261 91.90 42.65 39.67 1.86	-	-	-	-	-	-	-	-	-	-	-	-	-	-	-	-	-	-	-	-
MINNESOTA	2,783,000 87.95	68,939	49,024 71.11 71.11 1.76	1,060	830 78.30 78.30 0.03	9,381 90.97 19.14 13.61 0.34	-	1,324 52.60 2.70 1.92 0.05	8,222 85.26 16.77 11.93 0.30	-	3,507 87.85 7.15 5.09 0.13	196 77.47 23.61 18.49 0.01	315 79.95 37.95 29.72 0.01	6,220 44.92 12.69 9.02 0.22	-	2,873 95.07 5.86 4.17 0.10	4,276 87.39 8.72 6.20 0.15	2,371 52.57 4.84 3.44 0.09	-	566 89.27 1.15 0.82 0.02	-	-	299 96.14 0.61 0.43 0.01	423 68.01 0.86 0.61 0.02	-	7,229 63.09 14.75 10.49 0.26
Anoka County	170,332 91.03	2,735	2,124 77.66 77.66 1.25	-	-	459 80.95 21.61 16.78 0.27	-	-	255 85.86 12.01 9.32 0.15	-	247 81.79 11.63 9.03 0.15	-	-	196 82.01 9.23 7.17 0.12	-	-	190 75.10 8.95 6.95 0.11	-	-	-	-	-	-	-	-	364 66.67 17.14 13.31 0.21
Columbia Heights (city)	11,040 84.18	407	322 79.12 79.12 2.92	-	-	-	-	-	-	-	-	-	-	-	-	-	-	-	-	-	-	-	-	-	-	-
Blue Earth County	27,782 87.68	335	268 80.00 80.00 0.96	-	-	-	-	-	-	-	-	-	-	-	-	-	-	-	-	-	-	-	-	-	-	-

Notes: Please refer to the User's Guide for an explanation of data; data is arranged alphabetically by state, then county, then city within each county; table includes counties with populations greater than 49,999 unless noted and cities with populations greater than 9,999 whose Asian and/or NHPI population rates are greater than the national average; (1) Native Hawaiian and other Pacific Islander; (2) excludes Taiwanese; (3) includes Chamorro; (4) county does not meet population threshold but is shown in order to allow inclusion of city

Place	Total population 25 years and over who are high school graduates	Asian population 25 years and over	Asians 25 years and over who are high school graduates	NHPI[1] population 25 years and over	NHPIs[1] 25 years and over who are high school graduates	Asian Indian	Bangladeshi	Cambodian	Chinese[2]	Fijian	Filipino	Guamanian[3]	Hawaiian, Native	Hmong	Indonesian	Japanese	Korean	Laotian	Malaysian	Pakistani	Samoan	Sri Lankan	Taiwanese	Thai	Tongan	Vietnamese
Carver County	39,486 91.36	599	483 80.63 80.63 1.22	-	-	-	-	-	-	-	-	-	-	-	-	-	-	-	-	-	-	-	-	-	-	-
Clay County	25,648 86.71	190	155 81.58 81.58 0.60	-	-	-	-	-	-	-	-	-	-	-	-	-	-	-	-	-	-	-	-	-	-	-
Crow Wing County	32,022 86.33	97	93 95.88 95.88 0.29	-	-	-	-	-	-	-	-	-	-	-	-	-	-	-	-	-	-	-	-	-	-	-
Dakota County	209,093 93.21	5,370	4,287 79.83 79.83 2.05	-	-	1,037 95.05 24.19 19.31 0.50	-	148 64.07 3.45 2.76 0.07	775 84.61 18.08 14.43 0.37	-	436 88.26 10.17 8.12 0.21	-	-	-	-	-	285 77.24 6.65 5.31 0.14	254 67.20 5.92 4.73 0.12	-	-	-	-	-	-	-	755 67.59 17.61 14.06 0.36
Eagan (city)	38,627 95.98	1,861	1,524 81.89 81.89 3.95	-	-	457 97.23 29.99 24.56 1.18	-	-	353 95.15 23.16 18.97 0.91	-	-	-	-	-	-	-	-	-	-	-	-	-	-	-	-	194 60.82 12.73 10.42 0.50
Hennepin County	671,196 90.65	28,202	20,402 72.34 72.34 3.04	373	316 84.72 84.72 0.05	4,576 89.25 22.43 16.23 0.68	-	556 62.26 2.73 1.97 0.08	3,389 84.37 16.61 12.02 0.50	-	1,206 93.27 5.91 4.28 0.18	-	-	1,571 39.05 7.70 5.57 0.23	-	1,232 95.88 6.04 4.37 0.18	1,914 87.16 9.38 6.79 0.29	1,393 58.55 6.83 4.94 0.21	-	219 87.25 1.07 0.78 0.03	-	-	-	-	-	3,197 61.91 15.67 11.34 0.48
Bloomington (city)	56,269 92.16	2,620	2,027 77.37 77.37 3.60	-	-	320 90.91 15.79 12.21 0.57	-	156 61.18 7.70 5.95 0.28	515 86.41 25.41 19.66 0.92	-	-	-	-	-	-	-	213 98.16 10.51 8.13 0.38	-	-	-	-	-	-	-	-	472 60.36 23.29 18.02 0.84
Brooklyn Center (city)	16,577 86.87	1,119	667 59.61 59.61 4.02	-	-	-	-	-	-	-	-	-	-	215 46.84 32.23 19.21 1.30	-	-	-	107 55.15 16.04 9.56 0.65	-	-	-	-	-	-	-	-
Brooklyn Park (city)	37,398 90.54	3,354	2,238 66.73 66.73 5.98	-	-	455 77.91 20.33 13.57 1.22	-	-	-	-	-	-	-	142 48.14 6.34 4.23 0.38	-	-	-	445 58.17 19.88 13.27 1.19	-	-	-	-	-	-	-	580 61.70 25.92 17.29 1.55
Eden Prairie (city)	33,862 97.22	1,695	1,426 84.13 84.13 4.21	-	-	393 100.00 27.56 23.19 1.16	-	-	358 91.33 25.11 21.12 1.06	-	-	-	-	-	-	-	-	-	-	-	-	-	-	-	-	194 54.96 13.60 11.45 0.57

Notes: Please refer to the User's Guide for an explanation of data; data is arranged alphabetically by state, then county, then city within each county; table includes counties with populations greater than 49,999 unless noted and cities with populations greater than 9,999 whose Asian and/or NHPI population rates are greater than the national average; (1) Native Hawaiian and other Pacific Islander; (2) excludes Taiwanese; (3) includes Chamorro; (4) county does not meet population threshold but is shown in order to allow inclusion of city

Place	Total population 25 years and over who are high school graduates	Asian population 25 years and over	Asians 25 years and over who are high school graduates	NHPI[1] population 25 years and over	NHPIs[1] 25 years and over who are high school graduates	Asian Indian	Bangladeshi	Cambodian	Chinese[2]	Fijian	Filipino	Guamanian[3]	Hawaiian, Native	Hmong	Indonesian	Japanese	Korean	Laotian	Malaysian	Pakistani	Samoan	Sri Lankan	Taiwanese	Thai	Tongan	Vietnamese
Hopkins (city)	10,791 91.04	649	551 84.90 84.90 5.11	-	-	327 95.34 59.35 50.39 3.03	-	-	-	-	-	-	-	-	-	-	-	-	-	-	-	-	-	-	-	-
Minneapolis (city)	206,788 84.95	11,135	7,024 63.08 63.08 3.40	-	-	1,000 79.30 14.24 8.98 0.48	-	84 50.91 1.20 0.75 0.04	1,131 83.53 16.10 10.16 0.55	-	504 96.18 7.18 4.53 0.24	-	-	1,083 35.63 15.42 9.73 0.52	-	576 97.96 8.20 5.17 0.28	742 77.45 10.56 6.66 0.36	407 51.13 5.79 3.66 0.20	-	-	-	-	-	-	-	969 59.23 13.80 8.70 0.47
Plymouth (city)	41,835 96.19	1,512	1,425 94.25 94.25 3.41	-	-	609 99.02 42.74 40.28 1.46	-	-	247 94.64 17.33 16.34 0.59	-	-	-	-	-	-	-	200 100.00 14.04 13.23 0.48	-	-	-	-	-	-	-	-	-
Richfield (city)	21,797 89.67	1,137	770 67.72 67.72 3.53	-	-	-	-	-	-	-	-	-	-	-	-	-	-	-	-	-	-	-	-	-	-	140 50.91 18.18 12.31 0.64
Nobles County[4]	10,348 75.79	448	137 30.58 30.58 1.32	-	-	-	-	-	-	-	-	-	-	-	-	-	-	59 26.70 43.07 13.17 0.57	-	-	-	-	-	-	-	-
Worthington (city)	5,259 71.69	423	126 29.79 29.79 2.40	-	-	-	-	-	-	-	-	-	-	-	-	-	-	55 26.57 43.65 13.00 1.05	-	-	-	-	-	-	-	-
Olmsted County	73,138 91.11	2,972	2,418 81.36 81.36 3.31	-	-	646 98.93 26.72 21.74 0.88	-	117 40.21 4.84 3.94 0.16	436 100.00 18.03 14.67 0.60	-	-	-	-	109 69.87 4.51 3.67 0.15	-	295 100.00 12.20 9.93 0.40	205 100.00 8.48 6.90 0.28	55 32.74 2.27 1.85 0.08	-	-	-	-	-	-	-	296 64.07 12.24 9.96 0.40
Rochester (city)	50,564 91.05	2,684	2,186 81.45 81.45 4.32	-	-	614 98.87 28.09 22.88 1.21	-	82 36.12 3.75 3.06 0.16	401 100.00 18.34 14.94 0.79	-	-	-	-	109 69.87 4.99 4.06 0.22	-	-	168 100.00 7.69 6.26 0.33	53 31.93 2.42 1.97 0.10	-	-	-	-	-	-	-	282 65.13 12.90 10.51 0.56
Otter Tail County	31,542 81.42	101	48 47.52 47.52 0.15	-	-	-	-	-	-	-	-	-	-	-	-	-	-	-	-	-	-	-	-	-	-	-
Ramsey County	283,200 87.62	18,538	11,550 62.30 62.30 4.08	-	-	1,421 94.04 12.30 7.67 0.50	-	251 43.65 2.17 1.35 0.09	1,970 87.67 17.06 10.63 0.70	-	496 84.21 4.29 2.68 0.18	-	-	3,947 44.99 34.17 21.29 1.39	-	387 97.24 3.35 2.09 0.14	715 92.86 6.19 3.86 0.25	176 46.19 1.52 0.95 0.06	-	-	-	-	-	-	-	1,344 62.75 11.64 7.25 0.47

Notes: Please refer to the User's Guide for an explanation of data; data is arranged alphabetically by state, then county, then city within each county; table includes counties with populations greater than 49,999 unless noted and cities with populations greater than 9,999 whose Asian and/or NHPI population rates are greater than the national average; (1) Native Hawaiian and other Pacific Islander; (2) excludes Taiwanese; (3) includes Chamorro; (4) county does not meet population threshold but is shown in order to allow inclusion of city

Place	Total population 25 years and over who are high school graduates	Asian population 25 years and over	Asians 25 years and over who are high school graduates	NHPI[1] population 25 years and over	NHPIs[1] 25 years and over who are high school graduates	Asian Indian	Bangladeshi	Cambodian	Chinese[2]	Fijian	Filipino	Guamanian[3]	Hawaiian, Native	Hmong	Indonesian	Japanese	Korean	Laotian	Malaysian	Pakistani	Samoan	Sri Lankan	Taiwanese	Thai	Tongan	Vietnamese
Maplewood (city)	21,323 90.06	767	653 85.14 85.14 3.06	-	-	-	-	-	190 90.91 29.10 24.77 0.89	-	-	-	-	140 84.34 21.44 18.25 0.66	-	-	-	-	-	-	-	-	-	-	-	-
New Brighton (city)	13,757 92.89	624	590 94.55 94.55 4.29	-	-	-	-	-	-	-	-	-	-	-	-	-	-	-	-	-	-	-	-	-	-	-
Roseville (city)	21,701 91.41	958	832 86.85 86.85 3.83	-	-	-	-	-	345 85.19 41.47 36.01 1.59	-	-	-	-	-	-	-	-	-	-	-	-	-	-	-	-	-
St. Paul (city)	145,922 83.77	13,340	7,023 52.65 52.65 4.81	-	-	424 86.35 6.04 3.18 0.29	-	184 37.94 2.62 1.38 0.13	519 85.08 7.39 3.89 0.36	-	282 86.77 4.02 2.11 0.19	-	-	3,612 43.21 51.43 27.08 2.48	-	-	312 94.83 4.44 2.34 0.21	127 38.25 1.81 0.95 0.09	-	-	-	-	-	-	-	875 59.81 12.46 6.56 0.60
Vadnais Heights (city)	7,871 93.38	291	228 78.35 78.35 2.90	-	-	-	-	-	-	-	-	-	-	-	-	-	-	-	-	-	-	-	-	-	-	-
Rice County	28,464 85.22	381	246 64.57 64.57 0.86	-	-	-	-	-	-	-	-	-	-	-	-	-	-	-	-	-	-	-	-	-	-	-
St. Louis County	115,861 87.24	681	542 79.59 79.59 0.47	-	-	-	-	-	-	-	-	-	-	-	-	-	77 97.47 14.21 11.31 0.07	-	-	-	-	-	-	-	-	-
Scott County	50,587 91.04	1,121	893 79.66 79.66 1.77	-	-	-	-	116 53.70 12.99 10.35 0.23	-	-	-	-	-	-	-	-	-	-	-	-	-	-	-	-	-	221 89.84 24.75 19.71 0.44
Savage (city)	12,187 95.41	717	537 74.90 74.90 4.41	-	-	-	-	-	-	-	-	-	-	-	-	-	-	-	-	-	-	-	-	-	-	-
Sherburne County	34,480 89.91	156	122 78.21 78.21 0.35	-	-	-	-	-	-	-	-	-	-	-	-	-	-	-	-	-	-	-	-	-	-	-

Notes: Please refer to the User's Guide for an explanation of data; data is arranged alphabetically by state, then county, then city within each county; table includes counties with populations greater than 49,999 unless noted and cities with populations greater than 9,999 whose Asian and/or NHPI population rates are greater than the national average; (1) Native Hawaiian and other Pacific Islander; (2) excludes Taiwanese; (3) includes Chamorro; (4) county does not meet population threshold but is shown in order to allow inclusion of city

Place	Total population 25 years and over who are high school graduates	Asian population 25 years and over	Asians 25 years and over who are high school graduates	NHPI[1] population 25 years and over	NHPIs[1] 25 years and over who are high school graduates	Asian Indian	Bangladeshi	Cambodian	Chinese[2]	Fijian	Filipino	Guamanian[3]	Hawaiian, Native	Hmong	Indonesian	Japanese	Korean	Laotian	Malaysian	Pakistani	Samoan	Sri Lankan	Taiwanese	Thai	Tongan	Vietnamese
Stearns County	66,853 86.24	806	618 76.67 76.67 0.92	-	-	-	-	-	-	-	-	-	-	-	-	-	-	-	-	-	-	-	-	-	-	230 61.01 37.22 28.54 0.34
Washington County	120,549 94.02	2,318	1,976 85.25 85.25 1.64	-	-	348 98.03 17.61 15.01 0.29	-	-	365 84.49 18.47 15.75 0.30	-	-	-	-	228 78.35 11.54 9.84 0.19	-	-	249 97.65 12.60 10.74 0.21	-	-	-	-	-	-	-	-	234 70.27 11.84 10.09 0.19
Woodbury (city)	28,433 96.44	1,346	1,206 89.60 89.60 4.24	-	-	264 97.42 21.89 19.61 0.93	-	-	224 93.33 18.57 16.64 0.79	-	-	-	-	85 68.55 7.05 6.32 0.30	-	-	-	-	-	-	-	-	-	-	-	-
Wright County	48,652 88.08	91	73 80.22 80.22 0.15	-	-	-	-	-	-	-	-	-	-	-	-	-	-	-	-	-	-	-	-	-	-	-
MISSISSIPPI	1,280,487 72.86	10,890	7,894 72.49 72.49 0.62	385	309 80.26 80.26 0.02	1,810 85.50 22.93 16.62 0.14	-	-	1,484 79.66 18.80 13.63 0.12	-	1,555 82.45 19.70 14.28 0.12	-	-	-	-	374 85.00 4.74 3.43 0.03	671 75.90 8.50 6.16 0.05	-	-	-	-	-	-	-	-	1,219 45.90 15.44 11.19 0.10
DeSoto County	55,734 81.60	431	309 71.69 71.69 0.55	-	-	-	-	-	-	-	-	-	-	-	-	-	-	-	-	-	-	-	-	-	-	-
Forrest County	32,926 79.29	259	196 75.68 75.68 0.60	-	-	-	-	-	-	-	-	-	-	-	-	-	-	-	-	-	-	-	-	-	-	-
Harrison County	95,639 80.25	2,956	1,693 57.27 57.27 1.77	-	-	-	-	-	-	-	425 79.89 25.10 14.38 0.44	-	-	-	-	-	-	-	-	-	-	-	-	-	-	458 33.07 27.05 15.49 0.48
Biloxi (city)	25,433 81.90	1,355	677 49.96 49.96 2.66	-	-	-	-	-	-	-	209 83.27 30.87 15.42 0.82	-	-	-	-	-	-	-	-	-	-	-	-	-	-	160 22.32 23.63 11.81 0.63
Hinds County	120,803 80.38	874	724 82.84 82.84 0.60	-	-	367 87.59 50.69 41.99 0.30	-	-	-	-	-	-	-	-	-	-	-	-	-	-	-	-	-	-	-	-

Notes: Please refer to the User's Guide for an explanation of data; data is arranged alphabetically by state, then county, then city within each county; table includes counties with populations greater than 49,999 unless noted and cities with populations greater than 9,999 whose Asian and/or NHPI population rates are greater than the national average; (1) Native Hawaiian and other Pacific Islander; (2) excludes Taiwanese; (3) includes Chamorro; (4) county does not meet population threshold but is shown in order to allow inclusion of city

Place	Total population 25 years and over who are high school graduates	Asian population 25 years and over	Asians 25 years and over who are high school graduates	NHPI[1] population 25 years and over	NHPIs[1] 25 years and over who are high school graduates	Asian Indian	Bangladeshi	Cambodian	Chinese[2]	Fijian	Filipino	Guamanian[3]	Hawaiian, Native	Hmong	Indonesian	Japanese	Korean	Laotian	Malaysian	Pakistani	Samoan	Sri Lankan	Taiwanese	Thai	Tongan	Vietnamese
Jackson County	67,074 80.99	1,159	804 69.37 69.37 1.20	-	-	-	-	-	-	-	-	-	-	-	-	-	-	-	-	-	-	-	-	-	-	263 50.67 32.71 22.69 0.39
Madison County	38,827 83.01	465	382 82.15 82.15 0.98	-	-	-	-	-	-	-	-	-	-	-	-	-	-	-	-	-	-	-	-	-	-	-
Oktibbeha County[4]	16,991 79.96	577	555 96.19 96.19 3.27	-	-	-	-	-	-	-	-	-	-	-	-	-	-	-	-	-	-	-	-	-	-	-
Starkville (city)	9,428 85.06	481	461 95.84 95.84 4.89	-	-	-	-	-	-	-	-	-	-	-	-	-	-	-	-	-	-	-	-	-	-	-
Rankin County	61,263 81.81	374	282 75.40 75.40 0.46	-	-	-	-	-	-	-	-	-	-	-	-	-	-	-	-	-	-	-	-	-	-	-
MISSOURI	2,955,811 81.32	39,231	32,256 82.22 82.22 1.09	1,630	1,366 83.80 83.80 0.05	7,002 93.31 21.71 17.85 0.24	-	174 44.05 0.54 0.44 0.01	7,373 87.46 22.86 18.79 0.25	-	4,540 88.43 14.07 11.57 0.15	294 82.12 21.52 18.04 0.01	356 85.58 26.06 21.84 0.01	-	-	2,339 88.73 7.25 5.96 0.08	3,538 85.31 10.97 9.02 0.12	176 37.53 0.55 0.45 0.01	-	588 91.02 1.82 1.50 0.02	402 82.21 29.43 24.66 0.01	-	670 98.10 2.08 1.71 0.02	761 79.27 2.36 1.94 0.03	-	3,508 54.80 10.88 8.94 0.12
Boone County	69,496 89.19	2,358	2,162 91.69 91.69 3.11	-	-	488 100.00 22.57 20.70 0.70	-	-	699 91.49 32.33 29.64 1.01	-	-	-	-	-	-	-	254 92.03 11.75 10.77 0.37	-	-	-	-	-	-	-	-	-
Columbia (city)	41,583 91.09	2,194	2,024 92.25 92.25 4.87	-	-	468 100.00 23.12 21.33 1.13	-	-	662 91.06 32.71 30.17 1.59	-	-	-	-	-	-	-	236 94.02 11.66 10.76 0.57	-	-	-	-	-	-	-	-	-
Cape Girardeau County	35,228 81.10	205	189 92.20 92.20 0.54	-	-	-	-	-	-	-	-	-	-	-	-	-	-	-	-	-	-	-	-	-	-	-
Cass County	45,761 86.72	214	155 72.43 72.43 0.34	-	-	-	-	-	-	-	-	-	-	-	-	-	-	-	-	-	-	-	-	-	-	-

Notes: Please refer to the User's Guide for an explanation of data; data is arranged alphabetically by state, then county, then city within each county; table includes counties with populations greater than 49,999 unless noted and cities with populations greater than 9,999 whose Asian and/or NHPI population rates are greater than the national average; (1) Native Hawaiian and other Pacific Islander; (2) excludes Taiwanese; (3) includes Chamorro; (4) county does not meet population threshold but is shown in order to allow inclusion of city

Place	Total population 25 years and over who are high school graduates	Asian population 25 years and over	Asians 25 years and over who are high school graduates	NHPI[1] population 25 years and over	NHPIs[1] 25 years and over who are high school graduates	Asian Indian	Bangladeshi	Cambodian	Chinese[2]	Fijian	Filipino	Guamanian[3]	Hawaiian, Native	Hmong	Indonesian	Japanese	Korean	Laotian	Malaysian	Pakistani	Samoan	Sri Lankan	Taiwanese	Thai	Tongan	Vietnamese
Clay County	106,913 88.72	1,361	1,071 78.69 78.69 1.00	-	-	203 91.44 18.95 14.92 0.19	-	-	-	-	-	-	-	-	-	-	-	-	-	-	-	-	-	-	-	244 65.77 22.78 17.93 0.23
Cole County	40,395 85.33	472	409 86.65 86.65 1.01	-	-	-	-	-	-	-	-	-	-	-	-	-	-	-	-	-	-	-	-	-	-	-
Franklin County	46,953 77.65	202	150 74.26 74.26 0.32	-	-	-	-	-	-	-	-	-	-	-	-	-	-	-	-	-	-	-	-	-	-	-
Greene County	130,427 84.73	1,274	1,019 79.98 79.98 0.78	-	-	-	-	-	135 74.59 13.25 10.60 0.10	-	-	-	-	-	-	-	168 87.96 16.49 13.19 0.13	-	-	-	-	-	-	-	-	192 72.18 18.84 15.07 0.15
Jackson County	356,191 83.40	5,505	3,993 72.53 72.53 1.12	493	419 84.99 84.99 0.12	595 87.12 14.90 10.81 0.17	-	-	791 85.42 19.81 14.37 0.22	-	800 90.70 20.04 14.53 0.22	-	-	-	-	288 83.24 7.21 5.23 0.08	323 83.46 8.09 5.87 0.09	-	-	-	174 75.65 41.53 35.29 0.05	-	-	-	-	751 45.74 18.81 13.64 0.21
Independence (city)	63,482 82.92	709	554 78.14 78.14 0.87	196	157 80.10 80.10 0.25	-	-	-	-	-	-	-	-	-	-	-	-	-	-	-	-	-	-	-	-	-
Jasper County	52,645 79.52	419	367 87.59 87.59 0.70	-	-	-	-	-	-	-	-	-	-	-	-	-	-	-	-	-	-	-	-	-	-	-
Jefferson County	99,960 79.36	475	372 78.32 78.32 0.37	-	-	-	-	-	-	-	-	-	-	-	-	-	-	-	-	-	-	-	-	-	-	-
Newton County	27,284 79.75	112	82 73.21 73.21 0.30	-	-	-	-	-	-	-	-	-	-	-	-	-	-	-	-	-	-	-	-	-	-	-
Phelps County[4]	19,494 79.04	556	528 94.96 94.96 2.71	-	-	162 90.00 30.68 29.14 0.83	-	-	-	-	-	-	-	-	-	-	-	-	-	-	-	-	-	-	-	-

Notes: Please refer to the User's Guide for an explanation of data; data is arranged alphabetically by state, then county, then city within each county; table includes counties with populations greater than 49,999 unless noted and cities with populations greater than 9,999 whose Asian and/or NHPI population rates are greater than the national average; (1) Native Hawaiian and other Pacific Islander; (2) excludes Taiwanese; (3) includes Chamorro; (4) county does not meet population threshold but is shown in order to allow inclusion of city

Place	Total population 25 years and over who are high school graduates	Asian population 25 years and over	Asians 25 years and over who are high school graduates	NHPI[1] population 25 years and over	NHPIs[1] 25 years and over who are high school graduates	Asian Indian	Bangladeshi	Cambodian	Chinese[2]	Fijian	Filipino	Guamanian[3]	Hawaiian, Native	Hmong	Indonesian	Japanese	Korean	Laotian	Malaysian	Pakistani	Samoan	Sri Lankan	Taiwanese	Thai	Tongan	Vietnamese
Rolla (city)	7,540 82.47	472	459 97.25 97.25 6.09	-	-	-	-	-	-	-	-	-	-	-	-	-	-	-	-	-	-	-	-	-	-	-
Platte County	44,706 91.76	713	640 89.76 89.76 1.43	-	-	-	-	-	-	-	-	-	-	-	-	-	-	-	-	-	-	-	-	-	-	-
St. Charles County	159,107 89.14	1,543	1,408 91.25 91.25 0.88	-	-	358 97.55 25.43 23.20 0.23	-	-	244 93.13 17.33 15.81 0.15	-	244 86.22 17.33 15.81 0.15	-	-	-	-	-	-	-	-	-	-	-	-	-	-	-
Saint Louis Independent City	158,236 71.29	4,595	3,068 66.77 66.77 1.94	-	-	421 95.03 13.72 9.16 0.27	-	-	595 85.73 19.39 12.95 0.38	-	358 86.27 11.67 7.79 0.23	-	-	-	-	-	-	-	-	-	-	-	-	-	-	962 47.58 31.36 20.94 0.61
St. Louis County	595,492 87.96	14,654	13,056 89.10 89.10 2.19	215	172 80.00 80.00 0.03	3,586 94.64 27.47 24.47 0.60	-	-	3,597 88.66 27.55 24.55 0.60	-	1,428 91.83 10.94 9.74 0.24	-	-	-	-	848 89.64 6.50 5.79 0.14	1,393 88.44 10.67 9.51 0.23	-	-	326 89.56 2.50 2.22 0.05	-	-	450 98.90 3.45 3.07 0.08	199 73.98 1.52 1.36 0.03	-	654 63.74 5.01 4.46 0.11
Chesterfield (city)	31,348 95.90	1,640	1,544 94.15 94.15 4.93	-	-	377 95.69 24.42 22.99 1.20	-	-	490 91.76 31.74 29.88 1.56	-	-	-	-	-	-	-	-	-	-	-	-	-	-	-	-	-
Clayton (city)	8,542 96.47	526	518 98.48 98.48 6.06	-	-	-	-	-	-	-	-	-	-	-	-	-	-	-	-	-	-	-	-	-	-	-
Creve Coeur (city)	11,357 96.56	651	605 92.93 92.93 5.33	-	-	-	-	-	-	-	-	-	-	-	-	-	-	-	-	-	-	-	-	-	-	-
Manchester (city)	11,853 95.53	586	578 98.63 98.63 4.88	-	-	-	-	-	-	-	-	-	-	-	-	-	-	-	-	-	-	-	-	-	-	-
Maryland Heights (city)	15,734 88.19	1,290	1,083 83.95 83.95 6.88	-	-	495 98.80 45.71 38.37 3.15	-	-	256 69.75 23.64 19.84 1.63	-	-	-	-	-	-	-	-	-	-	-	-	-	-	-	-	-

Notes: Please refer to the User's Guide for an explanation of data; data is arranged alphabetically by state, then county, then city within each county; table includes counties with populations greater than 49,999 unless noted and cities with populations greater than 9,999 whose Asian and/or NHPI population rates are greater than the national average; (1) Native Hawaiian and other Pacific Islander; (2) excludes Taiwanese; (3) includes Chamorro; (4) county does not meet population threshold but is shown in order to allow inclusion of city

Place	Total population 25 years and over who are high school graduates	Asian population 25 years and over	Asians 25 years and over who are high school graduates	NHPI[1] population 25 years and over	NHPIs[1] 25 years and over who are high school graduates	Asian Indian	Bangladeshi	Cambodian	Chinese[2]	Fijian	Filipino	Guamanian[3]	Hawaiian, Native	Hmong	Indonesian	Japanese	Korean	Laotian	Malaysian	Pakistani	Samoan	Sri Lankan	Taiwanese	Thai	Tongan	Vietnamese
Town and Country (city)	7,055 92.74	626	576 92.01 92.01 8.16	-	-	264 93.62 45.83 42.17 3.74	-	-	-	-	-	-	-	-	-	-	-	-	-	-	-	-	-	-	-	-
MONTANA	511,263 87.15	2,562	2,184 85.25 85.25 0.43	250	200 80.00 80.00 0.04	246 96.47 11.26 9.60 0.05	-	-	330 92.18 15.11 12.88 0.06	-	442 76.74 20.24 17.25 0.09	-	126 90.65 63.00 50.40 0.02	-	-	552 91.24 25.27 21.55 0.11	268 79.53 12.27 10.46 0.05	-	-	-	-	-	-	-	-	-
Cascade County	45,585 87.11	400	309 77.25 77.25 0.68	-	-	-	-	-	-	-	-	-	-	-	-	-	-	-	-	-	-	-	-	-	-	-
Flathead County	43,376 87.37	166	143 86.14 86.14 0.33	-	-	-	-	-	-	-	-	-	-	-	-	-	-	-	-	-	-	-	-	-	-	-
Gallatin County	37,770 93.35	317	298 94.01 94.01 0.79	-	-	-	-	-	-	-	-	-	-	-	-	-	-	-	-	-	-	-	-	-	-	-
Missoula County	53,954 90.99	468	397 84.83 84.83 0.74	-	-	-	-	-	-	-	-	-	-	-	-	-	-	-	-	-	-	-	-	-	-	-
Yellowstone County	74,510 88.46	356	321 90.17 90.17 0.43	-	-	-	-	-	-	-	-	-	-	-	-	-	-	-	-	-	-	-	-	-	-	-
NEBRASKA	941,380 86.58	12,594	9,780 77.66 77.66 1.04	339	210 61.95 61.95 0.02	1,806 93.04 18.47 14.34 0.19	-	-	1,795 93.64 18.35 14.25 0.19	-	1,239 85.21 12.67 9.84 0.13	-	-	-	-	972 97.30 9.94 7.72 0.10	887 88.97 9.07 7.04 0.09	252 53.85 2.58 2.00 0.03	-	-	-	-	-	306 82.93 3.13 2.43 0.03	-	1,838 49.88 18.79 14.59 0.20
Douglas County	255,866 87.30	4,690	4,152 88.53 88.53 1.62	-	-	1,148 96.71 27.65 24.48 0.45	-	-	841 94.28 20.26 17.93 0.33	-	539 85.83 12.98 11.49 0.21	-	-	-	-	423 97.69 10.19 9.02 0.17	335 95.44 8.07 7.14 0.13	-	-	-	-	-	-	-	-	412 60.06 9.92 8.78 0.16
Hall County	28,256 82.21	319	211 66.14 66.14 0.75	-	-	-	-	-	-	-	-	-	-	-	-	-	-	-	-	-	-	-	-	-	-	-

Notes: Please refer to the User's Guide for an explanation of data; data is arranged alphabetically by state, then county, then city within each county; table includes counties with populations greater than 49,999 unless noted and cities with populations greater than 9,999 whose Asian and/or NHPI population rates are greater than the national average; (1) Native Hawaiian and other Pacific Islander; (2) excludes Taiwanese; (3) includes Chamorro; (4) county does not meet population threshold but is shown in order to allow inclusion of city

Place	Total population 25 years and over who are high school graduates	Asian population 25 years and over	Asians 25 years and over who are high school graduates	NHPI[1] population 25 years and over	NHPIs[1] 25 years and over who are high school graduates	Asian Indian	Bangladeshi	Cambodian	Chinese[2]	Fijian	Filipino	Guamanian[3]	Hawaiian, Native	Hmong	Indonesian	Japanese	Korean	Laotian	Malaysian	Pakistani	Samoan	Sri Lankan	Taiwanese	Thai	Tongan	Vietnamese
Lancaster County	138,233	3,896	2,642	-	-	375	-	-	692	-	-	-	-	-	-	-	163	-	-	-	-	-	-	-	-	934
	90.50		67.81			90.80			97.46								88.11									45.56
						14.19			26.19								6.17									35.35
			67.81			9.63			17.76								4.18									23.97
			1.91			0.27			0.50								0.12									0.68
Sarpy County	68,837	1,469	1,171	-	-	-	-	-	-	-	287	-	-	-	-	-	252	-	-	-	-	-	-	-	-	110
	93.27		79.71								76.94						87.20									46.03
											24.51						21.52									9.39
			79.71								19.54						17.15									7.49
			1.70								0.42						0.37									0.16
NEVADA	1,056,802	62,181	50,969	4,572	3,670	2,725	-	254	7,520	-	23,420	574	1,901	-	-	6,072	4,457	445	-	257	608	-	324	1,535	232	1,901
	80.66		81.97		80.27	82.03		53.03	77.61		86.42	81.42	84.71			89.49	80.77	58.78		81.59	77.45		71.68	68.77	59.18	64.01
						5.35		0.50	14.75		45.95	15.64	51.80			11.91	8.74	0.87		0.50	16.57		0.64	3.01	6.32	3.73
			81.97		80.27	4.38		0.41	12.09		37.66	12.55	41.58			9.77	7.17	0.72		0.41	13.30		0.52	2.47	5.07	3.06
			4.82		0.35	0.26		0.02	0.71		2.22	0.05	0.18			0.57	0.42	0.04		0.02	0.06		0.03	0.15	0.02	0.18
Carson City Independent City	29,649	711	647	-	-	-	-	-	-	-	174	-	-	-	-	-	-	-	-	-	-	-	-	-	-	-
	82.47		91.00								92.55															
											26.89															
			91.00								24.47															
			2.18								0.59															
Clark County	715,402	50,502	41,211	3,637	3,000	1,731	-	240	5,992	-	18,897	517	1,720	-	-	4,858	3,904	445	-	-	433	-	203	1,379	-	1,611
	79.45		81.60		82.49	81.54		51.61	76.92		86.00	82.85	85.87			88.60	81.79	58.78			78.73		63.04	69.40		65.28
						4.20		0.58	14.54		45.85	17.23	57.33			11.79	9.47	1.08			14.43		0.49	3.35		3.91
			81.60		82.49	3.43		0.48	11.86		37.42	14.22	47.29			9.62	7.73	0.88			11.91		0.40	2.73		3.19
			5.76		0.42	0.24		0.03	0.84		2.64	0.07	0.24			0.68	0.55	0.06			0.06		0.03	0.19		0.23
Enterprise (cdp)	8,669	501	474	-	-	-	-	-	-	-	-	-	-	-	-	-	-	-	-	-	-	-	-	-	-	-
	85.37		94.61																							
			94.61																							
			5.47																							
Henderson (city)	104,988	4,903	4,404	503	466	271	-	-	535	-	1,754	-	297	-	-	638	490	-	-	-	-	-	-	-	-	-
	88.50		89.82		92.64	78.10			88.87		93.70		95.50			92.87	90.07									
						6.15			12.15		39.83		63.73			14.49	11.13									
			89.82		92.64	5.53			10.91		35.77		59.05			13.01	9.99									
			4.19		0.44	0.26			0.51		1.67		0.28			0.61	0.47									
Las Vegas (city)	245,804	15,432	12,845	1,095	826	661	-	-	1,622	-	6,271	-	463	-	-	1,786	913	-	-	-	-	-	-	404	-	365
	78.48		83.24		75.43	85.84			78.28		86.52		81.37			89.30	83.76							76.52		67.84
						5.15			12.63		48.82		56.05			13.90	7.11							3.15		2.84
			83.24		75.43	4.28			10.51		40.64		42.28			11.57	5.92							2.62		2.37
			5.23		0.34	0.27			0.66		2.55		0.19			0.73	0.37							0.16		0.15
North Las Vegas (city)	43,607	2,672	2,055	430	345	-	-	-	-	-	1,148	-	-	-	-	-	-	-	-	-	-	-	-	-	-	-
	66.55		76.91		80.23						80.17															
											55.86															
			76.91		80.23						42.96															
			4.71		0.79						2.63															
Paradise (cdp)	101,298	8,845	7,459	462	363	386	-	-	1,233	-	3,317	-	233	-	-	904	779	-	-	-	-	-	-	-	-	304
	79.95		84.33		78.57	85.78			85.63		86.58		72.14			90.76	82.43									67.71
						5.17			16.53		44.47		64.19			12.12	10.44									4.08
			84.33		78.57	4.36			13.94		37.50		50.43			10.22	8.81									3.44
			7.36		0.36	0.38			1.22		3.27		0.23			0.89	0.77									0.30

Notes: Please refer to the User's Guide for an explanation of data; data is arranged alphabetically by state, then county, then city within each county; table includes counties with populations greater than 49,999 unless noted and cities with populations greater than 9,999 whose Asian and/or NHPI population rates are greater than the national average; (1) Native Hawaiian and other Pacific Islander; (2) excludes Taiwanese; (3) includes Chamorro; (4) county does not meet population threshold but is shown in order to allow inclusion of city

Place	Total population 25 years and over who are high school graduates	Asian population 25 years and over	Asians 25 years and over who are high school graduates	NHPI[1] population 25 years and over	NHPIs[1] 25 years and over who are high school graduates	Asian Indian	Bangladeshi	Cambodian	Chinese[2]	Fijian	Filipino	Guamanian[3]	Hawaiian, Native	Hmong	Indonesian	Japanese	Korean	Laotian	Malaysian	Pakistani	Samoan	Sri Lankan	Taiwanese	Thai	Tongan	Vietnamese
	69,413	9,008	7,033	347	315	-	-	-	1,989	-	2,364	-	-	-	-	550	834	-	-	-	-	-	-	252	-	330
	84.64		78.08		90.78				70.56		88.97					91.06	79.89							70.99		50.54
Spring Valley (cdp)									28.28		33.61					7.82	11.86							3.58		4.69
			78.08		90.78				22.08		26.24					6.11	9.26							2.80		3.66
			10.13		0.45				2.87		3.41					0.79	1.20							0.36		0.48
	69,633	6,010	4,612	275	222	-	-	-	269	-	2,722	-	-	-	-	460	416	-	-	-	-	-	-	-	-	-
	73.84		76.74		80.73				70.98		82.74					84.56	78.94									
Sunrise Manor (cdp)									5.83		59.02					9.97	9.02									
			76.74		80.73				4.48		45.29					7.65	6.92									
			6.62		0.32				0.39		3.91					0.66	0.60									
	14,523	1,095	795	-	-	-	-	-	-	-	247	-	-	-	-	-	-	-	-	-	-	-	-	-	-	-
	74.62		72.60								73.29															
Winchester (cdp)											31.07															
			72.60								22.56															
			5.47								1.70															
	186,211	9,324	7,761	675	472	776	-	-	1,308	-	3,603	-	-	-	-	869	454	-	-	-	-	-	-	-	172	241
	83.94		83.24		69.93	79.67			79.76		88.42					93.74	81.07								63.70	53.67
Washoe County						10.00			16.85		46.42					11.20	5.85								36.44	3.11
			83.24		69.93	8.32			14.03		38.64					9.32	4.87								25.48	2.58
			4.17		0.25	0.42			0.70		1.93					0.47	0.24								0.09	0.13
	96,762	6,100	5,106	455	320	512	-	-	896	-	2,383	-	-	-	-	548	271	-	-	-	-	-	-	-	-	161
	82.36		83.70		70.33	82.71			82.50		88.49					92.72	80.90									57.30
Reno (city)						10.03			17.55		46.67					10.73	5.31									3.15
			83.70		70.33	8.39			14.69		39.07					8.98	4.44									2.64
			5.28		0.33	0.53			0.93		2.46					0.57	0.28									0.17
	34,847	2,033	1,636	-	-	-	-	-	284	-	813	-	-	-	-	-	-	-	-	-	-	-	-	-	-	-
	82.18		80.47						74.54		88.95															
Sparks (city)									17.36		49.69															
			80.47						13.97		39.99															
			4.69						0.81		2.33															
	720,233	9,476	8,043	-	-	2,217	-	-	2,097	-	785	-	-	-	-	591	824	116	-	-	-	-	-	-	-	607
	87.41		84.88			97.24			84.93		92.14					92.63	84.60	55.24								54.39
NEW HAMPSHIRE						27.56			26.07		9.76					7.35	10.24	1.44								7.55
			84.88			23.40			22.13		8.28					6.24	8.70	1.22								6.41
			1.12			0.31			0.29		0.11					0.08	0.11	0.02								0.08
	33,637	217	165	-	-	-	-	-	-	-	-	-	-	-	-	-	-	-	-	-	-	-	-	-	-	-
	85.68		76.04																							
Belknap County																										
			76.04																							
			0.49																							
	41,405	260	228	-	-	-	-	-	-	-	-	-	-	-	-	-	-	-	-	-	-	-	-	-	-	-
	86.20		87.69																							
Cheshire County																										
			87.69																							
			0.55																							
	46,288	507	434	-	-	-	-	-	147	-	-	-	-	-	-	-	-	-	-	-	-	-	-	-	-	-
	87.67		85.60						88.55																	
Grafton County									33.87																	
			85.60						28.99																	
			0.94						0.32																	

Notes: Please refer to the User's Guide for an explanation of data; data is arranged alphabetically by state, then county, then city within each county; table includes counties with populations greater than 49,999 unless noted and cities with populations greater than 9,999 whose Asian and/or NHPI population rates are greater than the national average; (1) Native Hawaiian and other Pacific Islander; (2) excludes Taiwanese; (3) includes Chamorro; (4) county does not meet population threshold but is shown in order to allow inclusion of city

Place	Total population 25 years and over who are high school graduates	Asian population 25 years and over	Asians 25 years and over who are high school graduates	NHPI[1] population 25 years and over	NHPIs[1] 25 years and over who are high school graduates	Asian Indian	Bangladeshi	Cambodian	Chinese[2]	Fijian	Filipino	Guamanian[3]	Hawaiian, Native	Hmong	Indonesian	Japanese	Korean	Laotian	Malaysian	Pakistani	Samoan	Sri Lankan	Taiwanese	Thai	Tongan	Vietnamese
Hanover (town)	4,990 96.59	173	147 84.97 84.97 2.95	-	-	-	-	-	-	-	-	-	-	-	-	-	-	-	-	-	-	-	-	-	-	-
Hillsborough County	219,055 86.96	4,828	4,035 83.57 83.57 1.84	-	-	1,434 97.75 35.54 29.70 0.65	-	-	1,074 82.11 26.62 22.25 0.49	-	268 94.70 6.64 5.55 0.12	-	-	-	-	-	299 89.52 7.41 6.19 0.14	-	-	-	-	-	-	-	-	355 47.91 8.80 7.35 0.16
Nashua (city)	50,443 86.57	2,303	2,081 90.36 90.36 4.13	-	-	964 97.67 46.32 41.86 1.91	-	-	578 95.07 27.78 25.10 1.15	-	-	-	-	-	-	-	-	-	-	-	-	-	-	-	-	-
Merrimack County	80,469 88.16	681	629 92.36 92.36 0.78	-	-	-	-	-	-	-	-	-	-	-	-	-	-	-	-	-	-	-	-	-	-	-
Rockingham County	169,367 90.49	1,845	1,663 90.14 90.14 0.98	-	-	310 98.73 18.64 16.80 0.18	-	-	499 90.89 30.01 27.05 0.29	-	236 91.47 14.19 12.79 0.14	-	-	-	-	-	196 90.32 11.79 10.62 0.12	-	-	-	-	-	-	-	-	-
Strafford County	60,727 86.36	868	686 79.03 79.03 1.13	-	-	-	-	-	181 88.73 26.38 20.85 0.30	-	-	-	-	-	-	-	-	-	-	-	-	-	-	-	-	-
NEW JERSEY	4,643,322 82.07	315,460	279,179 88.50 88.50 6.01	1,686	1,159 68.74 68.74 0.02	95,797 87.17 34.31 30.37 2.06	959 73.71 0.34 0.30 0.02	216 59.18 0.08 0.07 <0.01	56,475 87.87 20.23 17.90 1.22	-	55,374 94.45 19.83 17.55 1.19	175 54.35 15.10 10.38 <0.01	321 72.13 27.70 19.04 0.01	-	686 95.81 0.25 0.22 0.01	9,945 94.99 3.56 3.15 0.21	36,886 90.79 13.21 11.69 0.79	174 67.18 0.06 0.06 <0.01	-	5,659 82.56 2.03 1.79 0.12	292 69.03 25.19 17.32 0.01	803 86.44 0.29 0.25 0.02	3,713 94.53 1.33 1.18 0.08	1,137 86.27 0.41 0.36 0.02	-	6,232 64.23 2.23 1.98 0.13
Atlantic County	131,737 78.16	8,493	5,996 70.60 70.60 4.55	-	-	1,951 75.91 32.54 22.97 1.48	148 66.67 2.47 1.74 0.11	-	877 58.58 14.63 10.33 0.67	-	1,225 87.94 20.43 14.42 0.93	-	-	-	-	-	331 84.87 5.52 3.90 0.25	-	-	223 70.79 3.72 2.63 0.17	-	-	-	-	-	833 57.09 13.89 9.81 0.63
Atlantic City (city)	16,403 61.85	2,915	1,615 55.40 55.40 9.85	-	-	295 48.68 18.27 10.12 1.80	-	-	254 45.77 15.73 8.71 1.55	-	273 73.78 16.90 9.37 1.66	-	-	-	-	-	-	-	-	-	-	-	-	-	-	476 54.03 29.47 16.33 2.90
Brigantine (city)	7,871 84.51	456	363 79.61 79.61 4.61	-	-	-	-	-	-	-	-	-	-	-	-	-	-	-	-	-	-	-	-	-	-	-

Notes: Please refer to the User's Guide for an explanation of data; data is arranged alphabetically by state, then county, then city within each county; table includes counties with populations greater than 49,999 unless noted and cities with populations greater than 9,999 whose Asian and/or NHPI population rates are greater than the national average; (1) Native Hawaiian and other Pacific Islander; (2) excludes Taiwanese; (3) includes Chamorro; (4) county does not meet population threshold but is shown in order to allow inclusion of city

Place	Total population 25 years and over who are high school graduates	Asian population 25 years and over	Asians 25 years and over who are high school graduates	NHPI[1] population 25 years and over	NHPIs[1] 25 years and over who are high school graduates	Asian Indian	Bangladeshi	Cambodian	Chinese[2]	Fijian	Filipino	Guamanian[3]	Hawaiian, Native	Hmong	Indonesian	Japanese	Korean	Laotian	Malaysian	Pakistani	Samoan	Sri Lankan	Taiwanese	Thai	Tongan	Vietnamese
Egg Harbor (township)	16,617 82.79	1,097	863 78.67 78.67 5.19	-	-	-	-	-	-	-	-	-	-	-	-	-	-	-	-	-	-	-	-	-	-	-
Galloway (township)	16,358 87.32	1,586	1,296 81.72 81.72 7.92	-	-	639 82.45 49.31 40.29 3.91	-	-	-	-	-	-	-	-	-	-	-	-	-	-	-	-	-	-	-	-
Ventnor City (city)	7,601 80.26	651	494 75.88 75.88 6.50	-	-	-	-	-	-	-	-	-	-	-	-	-	-	-	-	-	-	-	-	-	-	-
Bergen County	539,849 86.59	62,554	57,437 91.82 91.82 10.64	-	-	10,222 88.78 17.80 16.34 1.89	-	-	8,247 90.46 14.36 13.18 1.53	-	9,486 96.02 16.52 15.16 1.76	-	-	-	-	4,874 98.11 8.49 7.79 0.90	21,587 91.58 37.58 34.51 4.00	-	-	707 81.17 1.23 1.13 0.13	-	-	540 95.24 0.94 0.86 0.10	337 92.84 0.59 0.54 0.06	-	190 65.97 0.33 0.30 0.04
Bergenfield (borough)	15,440 86.59	3,299	3,011 91.27 91.27 19.50	-	-	766 87.14 25.44 23.22 4.96	-	-	-	-	1,867 93.49 62.01 56.59 12.09	-	-	-	-	-	-	-	-	-	-	-	-	-	-	-
Cliffside Park (borough)	13,673 78.66	2,024	1,844 91.11 91.11 13.49	-	-	-	-	-	-	-	-	-	-	-	-	335 96.26 18.17 16.55 2.45	985 90.12 53.42 48.67 7.20	-	-	-	-	-	-	-	-	-
Dumont (borough)	10,824 88.51	1,215	1,106 91.03 91.03 10.22	-	-	260 86.38 23.51 21.40 2.40	-	-	-	-	404 98.30 36.53 33.25 3.73	-	-	-	-	-	-	-	-	-	-	-	-	-	-	-
Elmwood Park (borough)	10,830 80.00	1,058	989 93.48 93.48 9.13	-	-	622 96.14 62.89 58.79 5.74	-	-	-	-	-	-	-	-	-	-	-	-	-	-	-	-	-	-	-	-
Englewood (city)	14,887 82.66	1,013	932 92.00 92.00 6.26	-	-	-	-	-	-	-	299 97.39 32.08 29.52 2.01	-	-	-	-	-	-	-	-	-	-	-	-	-	-	-
Fair Lawn (borough)	20,185 89.90	1,118	1,048 93.74 93.74 5.19	-	-	377 92.18 35.97 33.72 1.87	-	-	-	-	304 96.51 29.01 27.19 1.51	-	-	-	-	-	-	-	-	-	-	-	-	-	-	-

Notes: Please refer to the User's Guide for an explanation of data; data is arranged alphabetically by state, then county, then city within each county; table includes counties with populations greater than 49,999 unless noted and cities with populations greater than 9,999 whose Asian and/or NHPI population rates are greater than the national average; (1) Native Hawaiian and other Pacific Islander; (2) excludes Taiwanese; (3) includes Chamorro; (4) county does not meet population threshold but is shown in order to allow inclusion of city

Place	Total population 25 years and over who are high school graduates	Asian population 25 years and over	Asians 25 years and over who are high school graduates	NHPI[1] population 25 years and over	NHPIs[1] 25 years and over who are high school graduates	Asian Indian	Bangladeshi	Cambodian	Chinese[2]	Fijian	Filipino	Guamanian[3]	Hawaiian, Native	Hmong	Indonesian	Japanese	Korean	Laotian	Malaysian	Pakistani	Samoan	Sri Lankan	Taiwanese	Thai	Tongan	Vietnamese
Fairview (borough)	5,792 65.38	462	430 93.07 93.07 7.42	-	-	-	-	-	-	-	-	-	-	-	-	-	-	-	-	-	-	-	-	-	-	-
Fort Lee (borough)	24,598 89.48	7,622	7,194 94.38 94.38 29.25	-	-	438 97.77 6.09 5.75 1.78	-	-	1,137 94.51 15.80 14.92 4.62	-	-	-	-	-	-	1,316 98.50 18.29 17.27 5.35	3,745 92.63 52.06 49.13 15.22	-	-	-	-	-	-	-	-	-
Franklin Lakes (borough)	6,518 94.67	422	422 100.00 100.00 6.47	-	-	-	-	-	-	-	-	-	-	-	-	-	-	-	-	-	-	-	-	-	-	-
Glen Rock (borough)	7,409 96.05	479	469 97.91 97.91 6.33	-	-	-	-	-	-	-	-	-	-	-	-	-	-	-	-	-	-	-	-	-	-	-
Hackensack (city)	25,118 79.69	2,434	2,276 93.51 93.51 9.06	-	-	699 92.83 30.71 28.72 2.78	-	-	-	-	519 93.85 22.80 21.32 2.07	-	-	-	-	-	467 96.69 20.52 19.19 1.86	-	-	-	-	-	-	-	-	-
Hasbrouck Heights (borough)	7,222 86.90	378	350 92.59 92.59 4.85	-	-	-	-	-	-	-	-	-	-	-	-	-	-	-	-	-	-	-	-	-	-	-
Hillsdale (borough)	6,381 92.44	340	321 94.41 94.41 5.03	-	-	-	-	-	-	-	-	-	-	-	-	-	-	-	-	-	-	-	-	-	-	-
Little Ferry (borough)	6,323 81.46	1,234	1,121 90.84 90.84 17.73	-	-	194 77.29 17.31 15.72 3.07	-	-	-	-	242 100.00 21.59 19.61 3.83	-	-	-	-	-	488 89.71 43.53 39.55 7.72	-	-	-	-	-	-	-	-	-
Lodi (borough)	12,899 75.80	1,321	1,042 78.88 78.88 8.08	-	-	539 70.37 51.73 40.80 4.18	-	-	-	-	304 97.44 29.17 23.01 2.36	-	-	-	-	-	-	-	-	-	-	-	-	-	-	-
Lyndhurst (township)	11,612 81.41	735	639 86.94 86.94 5.50	-	-	-	-	-	-	-	-	-	-	-	-	-	-	-	-	-	-	-	-	-	-	-

Notes: Please refer to the User's Guide for an explanation of data; data is arranged alphabetically by state, then county, then city within each county; table includes counties with populations greater than 49,999 unless noted and cities with populations greater than 9,999 whose Asian and/or NHPI population rates are greater than the national average; (1) Native Hawaiian and other Pacific Islander; (2) excludes Taiwanese; (3) includes Chamorro; (4) county does not meet population threshold but is shown in order to allow inclusion of city

Place	Total population 25 years and over who are high school graduates	Asian population 25 years and over	Asians 25 years and over who are high school graduates	NHPI[1] population 25 years and over	NHPIs[1] 25 years and over who are high school graduates	Asian Indian	Bangladeshi	Cambodian	Chinese[2]	Fijian	Filipino	Guamanian[3]	Hawaiian, Native	Hmong	Indonesian	Japanese	Korean	Laotian	Malaysian	Pakistani	Samoan	Sri Lankan	Taiwanese	Thai	Tongan	Vietnamese
Mahwah (township)	15,320 93.56	1,014	976 96.25 96.25 6.37	-	-	357 97.81 36.58 35.21 2.33	-	-	-	-	-	-	-	-	-	-	-	-	-	-	-	-	-	-	-	-
New Milford (borough)	10,387 87.63	1,571	1,433 91.22 91.22 13.80	-	-	381 90.93 26.59 24.25 3.67	-	-	-	-	553 96.68 38.59 35.20 5.32	-	-	-	-	-	-	-	-	-	-	-	-	-	-	-
North Arlington (borough)	9,241 82.13	571	532 93.17 93.17 5.76	-	-	-	-	-	-	-	-	-	-	-	-	-	-	-	-	-	-	-	-	-	-	-
Palisades Park (borough)	9,659 79.35	4,841	4,344 89.73 89.73 44.97	-	-	-	-	-	-	-	-	-	-	-	-	-	3,669 89.16 84.46 75.79 37.99	-	-	-	-	-	-	-	-	-
Paramus (borough)	15,747 86.22	2,730	2,488 91.14 91.14 15.80	-	-	736 89.65 29.58 26.96 4.67	-	-	333 97.37 13.38 12.20 2.11	-	499 96.52 20.06 18.28 3.17	-	-	-	-	-	653 83.40 26.25 23.92 4.15	-	-	-	-	-	-	-	-	-
Ramsey (borough)	9,291 95.50	552	514 93.12 93.12 5.53	-	-	-	-	-	-	-	-	-	-	-	-	-	-	-	-	-	-	-	-	-	-	-
Ridgefield (borough)	6,097 78.80	1,100	925 84.09 84.09 15.17	-	-	-	-	-	-	-	-	-	-	-	-	-	641 81.14 69.30 58.27 10.51	-	-	-	-	-	-	-	-	-
Ridgefield Park (village)	7,676 85.06	758	691 91.16 91.16 9.00	-	-	-	-	-	-	-	-	-	-	-	-	-	297 93.99 42.98 39.18 3.87	-	-	-	-	-	-	-	-	-
Ridgewood (village)	15,731 95.88	1,248	1,164 93.27 93.27 7.40	-	-	-	-	-	-	-	-	-	-	-	-	288 100.00 24.74 23.08 1.83	272 95.77 23.37 21.79 1.73	-	-	-	-	-	-	-	-	-
River Edge (borough)	7,310 93.63	880	846 96.14 96.14 11.57	-	-	-	-	-	-	-	-	-	-	-	-	-	271 95.76 32.03 30.80 3.71	-	-	-	-	-	-	-	-	-

Notes: Please refer to the User's Guide for an explanation of data; data is arranged alphabetically by state, then county, then city within each county; table includes counties with populations greater than 49,999 unless noted and cities with populations greater than 9,999 whose Asian and/or NHPI population rates are greater than the national average; (1) Native Hawaiian and other Pacific Islander; (2) excludes Taiwanese; (3) includes Chamorro; (4) county does not meet population threshold but is shown in order to allow inclusion of city

Place	Total population 25 years and over who are high school graduates	Asian population 25 years and over	Asians 25 years and over who are high school graduates	NHPI[1] population 25 years and over	NHPIs[1] 25 years and over who are high school graduates	Asian Indian	Bangladeshi	Cambodian	Chinese[2]	Fijian	Filipino	Guamanian[3]	Hawaiian, Native	Hmong	Indonesian	Japanese	Korean	Laotian	Malaysian	Pakistani	Samoan	Sri Lankan	Taiwanese	Thai	Tongan	Vietnamese
Rutherford (borough)	11,478	1,358	1,219	-	-	227	-	-	-	-	-	-	-	-	-	-	489	-	-	-	-	-	-	-	-	-
	88.31		89.76			91.16											90.89									
						18.62											40.11									
			89.76			16.72											36.01									
			10.62			1.98											4.26									
Saddle Brook (township)	8,274	527	498	-	-	-	-	-	-	-	-	-	-	-	-	-	-	-	-	-	-	-	-	-	-	-
	85.27		94.50																							
			94.50																							
			6.02																							
Teaneck (township)	23,376	1,931	1,678	-	-	497	-	-	-	-	550	-	-	-	-	-	-	-	-	-	-	-	-	-	-	-
	89.72		86.90			81.74					98.39															
						29.62					32.78															
			86.90			25.74					28.48															
			7.18			2.13					2.35															
Tenafly (borough)	8,580	1,522	1,433	-	-	-	-	-	438	-	-	-	-	-	-	-	568	-	-	-	-	-	-	-	-	-
	93.54		94.15						92.99								94.51									
									30.57								39.64									
			94.15						28.78								37.32									
			16.70						5.10								6.62									
Wallington (borough)	6,106	378	319	-	-	-	-	-	-	-	-	-	-	-	-	-	-	-	-	-	-	-	-	-	-	-
	72.40		84.39																							
			84.39																							
			5.22																							
Westwood (borough)	7,095	381	343	-	-	-	-	-	-	-	-	-	-	-	-	-	-	-	-	-	-	-	-	-	-	-
	88.11		90.03																							
			90.03																							
			4.83																							
Wyckoff (township)	10,434	429	408	-	-	-	-	-	-	-	-	-	-	-	-	-	-	-	-	-	-	-	-	-	-	-
	93.81		95.10																							
			95.10																							
			3.91																							
Burlington County	248,894	7,682	6,309	-	-	2,088	-	-	784	-	1,319	-	-	-	-	337	1,040	-	-	-	-	-	-	-	-	292
	87.16		82.13			85.57			73.27		91.03					71.10	81.76									73.18
						33.10			12.43		20.91					5.34	16.48									4.63
			82.13			27.18			10.21		17.17					4.39	13.54									3.80
			2.53			0.84			0.31		0.53					0.14	0.42									0.12
Browns Mills (cdp)	5,573	337	215	-	-	-	-	-	-	-	-	-	-	-	-	-	162	-	-	-	-	-	-	-	-	-
	78.80		63.80														69.23									
																	75.35									
			63.80														48.07									
			3.86														2.91									
Evesham (township)	26,650	1,080	900	-	-	221	-	-	184	-	-	-	-	-	-	-	-	-	-	-	-	-	-	-	-	-
	93.30		83.33			90.57			65.95																	
						24.56			20.44																	
			83.33			20.46			17.04																	
			3.38			0.83			0.69																	

Notes: Please refer to the User's Guide for an explanation of data; data is arranged alphabetically by state, then county, then city within each county; table includes counties with populations greater than 49,999 unless noted and cities with populations greater than 9,999 whose Asian and/or NHPI population rates are greater than the national average; (1) Native Hawaiian and other Pacific Islander; (2) excludes Taiwanese; (3) includes Chamorro; (4) county does not meet population threshold but is shown in order to allow inclusion of city

Place	Total population 25 years and over who are high school graduates	Asian population 25 years and over	Asians 25 years and over who are high school graduates	NHPI[1] population 25 years and over	NHPIs[1] 25 years and over who are high school graduates	Asian Indian	Bangladeshi	Cambodian	Chinese[2]	Fijian	Filipino	Guamanian[3]	Hawaiian, Native	Hmong	Indonesian	Japanese	Korean	Laotian	Malaysian	Pakistani	Samoan	Sri Lankan	Taiwanese	Thai	Tongan	Vietnamese
Maple Shade (township)	11,286 82.31	752	641 85.24 85.24 5.68	-	-	385 90.16 60.06 51.20 3.41	-	-	-	-	-	-	-	-	-	-	-	-	-	-	-	-	-	-	-	-
Marlton (cdp)	6,441 89.91	271	209 77.12 77.12 3.24	-	-	-	-	-	-	-	-	-	-	-	-	-	-	-	-	-	-	-	-	-	-	-
Mount Laurel (township)	26,645 92.12	1,182	1,054 89.17 89.17 3.96	-	-	319 85.52 30.27 26.99 1.20	-	-	287 85.16 27.23 24.28 1.08	-	-	-	-	-	-	-	-	-	-	-	-	-	-	-	-	-
Camden County	266,308 80.27	12,299	9,870 80.25 80.25 3.71	-	-	2,897 90.67 29.35 23.55 1.09	-	68 40.48 0.69 0.55 0.03	2,054 80.45 20.81 16.70 0.77	-	2,256 94.04 22.86 18.34 0.85	-	-	-	-	-	840 85.89 8.51 6.83 0.32	-	-	163 83.16 1.65 1.33 0.06	-	-	-	-	-	917 47.12 9.29 7.46 0.34
Barclay-Kingston (cdp)	7,108 94.36	511	503 98.43 98.43 7.08	-	-	-	-	-	-	-	-	-	-	-	-	-	-	-	-	-	-	-	-	-	-	-
Bellmawr (borough)	5,908 74.55	251	162 64.54 64.54 2.74	-	-	-	-	-	-	-	-	-	-	-	-	-	-	-	-	-	-	-	-	-	-	-
Cherry Hill Mall (cdp)	8,291 87.49	765	615 80.39 80.39 7.42	-	-	-	-	-	-	-	-	-	-	-	-	-	-	-	-	-	-	-	-	-	-	-
Cherry Hill (township)	44,938 90.97	3,945	3,529 89.46 89.46 7.85	-	-	793 93.08 22.47 20.10 1.76	-	-	995 86.52 28.19 25.22 2.21	-	864 94.74 24.48 21.90 1.92	-	-	-	-	-	465 86.43 13.18 11.79 1.03	-	-	-	-	-	-	-	-	-
Echelon (cdp)	6,733 89.21	922	823 89.26 89.26 12.22	-	-	490 89.25 59.54 53.15 7.28	-	-	-	-	-	-	-	-	-	-	-	-	-	-	-	-	-	-	-	-
Greentree (cdp)	7,120 93.63	1,204	1,091 90.61 90.61 15.32	-	-	334 96.81 30.61 27.74 4.69	-	-	453 88.82 41.52 37.62 6.36	-	-	-	-	-	-	-	-	-	-	-	-	-	-	-	-	-

Notes: Please refer to the User's Guide for an explanation of data; data is arranged alphabetically by state, then county, then city within each county; table includes counties with populations greater than 49,999 unless noted and cities with populations greater than 9,999 whose Asian and/or NHPI population rates are greater than the national average; (1) Native Hawaiian and other Pacific Islander; (2) excludes Taiwanese; (3) includes Chamorro; (4) county does not meet population threshold but is shown in order to allow inclusion of city

Place	Total population 25 years and over who are high school graduates	Asian population 25 years and over	Asians 25 years and over who are high school graduates	NHPI[1] population 25 years and over	NHPIs[1] 25 years and over who are high school graduates	Asian Indian	Bangladeshi	Cambodian	Chinese[2]	Fijian	Filipino	Guamanian[3]	Hawaiian, Native	Hmong	Indonesian	Japanese	Korean	Laotian	Malaysian	Pakistani	Samoan	Sri Lankan	Taiwanese	Thai	Tongan	Vietnamese
Pennsauken (township)	17,746 77.21	945	580 61.38 61.38 3.27	-	-	-	-	-	-	-	-	-	-	-	-	-	-	-	-	-	-	-	-	-	-	195 47.56 33.62 20.63 1.10
Springdale (cdp)	9,597 93.67	702	653 93.02 93.02 6.80	-	-	-	-	-	241 94.14 36.91 34.33 2.51	-	-	-	-	-	-	-	-	-	-	-	-	-	-	-	-	-
Voorhees (township)	17,285 91.16	2,048	1,891 92.33 92.33 10.94	-	-	1,111 92.35 58.75 54.25 6.43	-	-	386 88.33 20.41 18.85 2.23	-	229 97.86 12.11 11.18 1.32	-	-	-	-	-	-	-	-	-	-	-	-	-	-	-
Cape May County	59,668 81.87	430	382 88.84 88.84 0.64	-	-	-	-	-	-	-	-	-	-	-	-	-	-	-	-	-	-	-	-	-	-	-
Cumberland County	66,386 68.51	823	707 85.91 85.91 1.06	-	-	233 86.94 32.96 28.31 0.35	-	-	-	-	-	-	-	-	-	-	-	-	-	-	-	-	-	-	-	-
Essex County	388,166 75.58	19,327	17,521 90.66 90.66 4.51	325	270 83.08 83.08 0.07	4,942 87.45 28.21 25.57 1.27	-	-	3,746 90.90 21.38 19.38 0.97	-	4,978 96.04 28.41 25.76 1.28	-	-	-	-	482 98.57 2.75 2.49 0.12	1,608 91.31 9.18 8.32 0.41	-	-	314 79.09 1.79 1.62 0.08	-	-	327 99.39 1.87 1.69 0.08	-	-	503 72.37 2.87 2.60 0.13
Belleville (township)	19,638 78.20	2,709	2,453 90.55 90.55 12.49	-	-	546 92.70 22.26 20.16 2.78	-	-	-	-	1,271 97.25 51.81 46.92 6.47	-	-	-	-	-	-	-	-	-	-	-	-	-	-	192 68.09 7.83 7.09 0.98
Bloomfield (township)	28,115 83.49	2,722	2,421 88.94 88.94 8.61	-	-	819 81.25 33.83 30.09 2.91	-	-	254 78.40 10.49 9.33 0.90	-	1,076 97.73 44.44 39.53 3.83	-	-	-	-	-	-	-	-	-	-	-	-	-	-	-
Cedar Grove (township)	8,185 88.35	434	418 96.31 96.31 5.11	-	-	-	-	-	-	-	-	-	-	-	-	-	-	-	-	-	-	-	-	-	-	-
Livingston (township)	17,639 93.98	2,463	2,256 91.60 91.60 12.79	-	-	346 74.73 15.34 14.05 1.96	-	-	959 96.48 42.51 38.94 5.44	-	307 98.08 13.61 12.46 1.74	-	-	-	-	-	444 90.06 19.68 18.03 2.52	-	-	-	-	-	-	-	-	-

Notes: Please refer to the User's Guide for an explanation of data; data is arranged alphabetically by state, then county, then city within each county; table includes counties with populations greater than 49,999 unless noted and cities with populations greater than 9,999 whose Asian and/or NHPI population rates are greater than the national average; (1) Native Hawaiian and other Pacific Islander; (2) excludes Taiwanese; (3) includes Chamorro; (4) county does not meet population threshold but is shown in order to allow inclusion of city

Place	Total population 25 years and over who are high school graduates	Asian population 25 years and over	Asians 25 years and over who are high school graduates	NHPI[1] population 25 years and over	NHPIs[1] 25 years and over who are high school graduates	Asian Indian	Bangladeshi	Cambodian	Chinese[2]	Fijian	Filipino	Guamanian[3]	Hawaiian, Native	Hmong	Indonesian	Japanese	Korean	Laotian	Malaysian	Pakistani	Samoan	Sri Lankan	Taiwanese	Thai	Tongan	Vietnamese
Millburn (township)	12,738 96.57	952	930 97.69 97.69 7.30	-	-	-	-	-	381 98.20 40.97 40.02 2.99	-	-	-	-	-	-	-	-	-	-	-	-	-	-	-	-	-
Nutley (township)	17,036 86.53	1,315	1,181 89.81 89.81 6.93	-	-	414 88.46 35.06 31.48 2.43	-	-	-	-	332 100.00 28.11 25.25 1.95	-	-	-	-	-	-	-	-	-	-	-	-	-	-	-
Verona (township)	9,221 92.39	417	372 89.21 89.21 4.03	-	-	-	-	-	-	-	-	-	-	-	-	-	-	-	-	-	-	-	-	-	-	-
West Caldwell (township)	7,454 93.39	304	264 86.84 86.84 3.54	-	-	-	-	-	-	-	-	-	-	-	-	-	-	-	-	-	-	-	-	-	-	-
West Orange (township)	27,366 86.34	2,478	2,265 91.40 91.40 8.28	-	-	652 96.17 28.79 26.31 2.38	-	-	507 90.37 22.38 20.46 1.85	-	585 93.15 25.83 23.61 2.14	-	-	-	-	-	320 86.72 14.13 12.91 1.17	-	-	-	-	-	-	-	-	-
Gloucester County	138,995 84.34	2,492	2,170 87.08 87.08 1.56	-	-	492 78.59 22.67 19.74 0.35	-	-	358 78.17 16.50 14.37 0.26	-	842 94.93 38.80 33.79 0.61	-	-	-	-	-	160 86.02 7.37 6.42 0.12	-	-	-	-	-	-	-	-	-
Hudson County	288,316 70.53	38,508	32,589 84.63 84.63 11.30	-	-	10,481 77.97 32.16 27.22 3.64	-	-	4,255 86.61 13.06 11.05 1.48	-	12,316 92.07 37.79 31.98 4.27	-	-	-	-	737 97.62 2.26 1.91 0.26	2,146 88.39 6.59 5.57 0.74	-	-	945 75.18 2.90 2.45 0.33	-	-	-	-	-	619 57.64 1.90 1.61 0.21
Bayonne (city)	34,152 78.77	1,632	1,357 83.15 83.15 3.97	-	-	255 76.35 18.79 15.63 0.75	-	-	-	-	767 90.88 56.52 47.00 2.25	-	-	-	-	-	162 77.51 11.94 9.93 0.47	-	-	-	-	-	-	-	-	-
Guttenberg (town)	5,676 75.02	566	543 95.94 95.94 9.57	-	-	-	-	-	-	-	-	-	-	-	-	-	-	-	-	-	-	-	-	-	-	-
Harrison (town)	6,750 69.32	1,266	1,160 91.63 91.63 17.19	-	-	-	-	-	868 91.08 74.83 68.56 12.86	-	-	-	-	-	-	-	-	-	-	-	-	-	-	-	-	-

Notes: Please refer to the User's Guide for an explanation of data; data is arranged alphabetically by state, then county, then city within each county; table includes counties with populations greater than 49,999 unless noted and cities with populations greater than 9,999 whose Asian and/or NHPI population rates are greater than the national average; (1) Native Hawaiian and other Pacific Islander; (2) excludes Taiwanese; (3) includes Chamorro; (4) county does not meet population threshold but is shown in order to allow inclusion of city

Place	Total population 25 years and over who are high school graduates	Asian population 25 years and over	Asians 25 years and over who are high school graduates	NHPI[1] population 25 years and over	NHPIs[1] 25 years and over who are high school graduates	Asian Indian	Bangladeshi	Cambodian	Chinese[2]	Fijian	Filipino	Guamanian[3]	Hawaiian, Native	Hmong	Indonesian	Japanese	Korean	Laotian	Malaysian	Pakistani	Samoan	Sri Lankan	Taiwanese	Thai	Tongan	Vietnamese
Hoboken (city)	23,842 83.26	1,073	1,010 94.13 94.13 4.24	-	-	310 89.60 30.69 28.89 1.30	-	-	292 94.19 28.91 27.21 1.22	-	-	-	-	-	-	-	-	-	-	-	-	-	-	-	-	-
Jersey City (city)	112,835 72.58	26,224	21,923 83.60 83.60 19.43	-	-	6,788 76.82 30.96 25.88 6.02	-	-	1,746 81.74 7.96 6.66 1.55	-	10,197 91.59 46.51 38.88 9.04	-	-	-	-	-	1,003 88.92 4.58 3.82 0.89	-	-	763 74.29 3.48 2.91 0.68	-	-	-	-	-	476 53.36 2.17 1.82 0.42
Kearny (town)	19,633 70.90	1,574	1,420 90.22 90.22 7.23	-	-	409 81.47 28.80 25.98 2.08	-	-	660 94.42 46.48 41.93 3.36	-	-	-	-	-	-	-	-	-	-	-	-	-	-	-	-	-
North Bergen (township)	27,301 68.74	2,394	1,929 80.58 80.58 7.07	-	-	1,207 77.67 62.57 50.42 4.42	-	-	144 68.25 7.47 6.02 0.53	-	-	-	-	-	-	-	-	-	-	-	-	-	-	-	-	-
Secaucus (town)	9,684 82.21	1,195	1,077 90.13 90.13 11.12	-	-	333 92.24 30.92 27.87 3.44	-	-	-	-	348 93.55 32.31 29.12 3.59	-	-	-	-	-	-	-	-	-	-	-	-	-	-	-
Weehawken (township)	7,610 76.02	480	443 92.29 92.29 5.82	-	-	-	-	-	-	-	-	-	-	-	-	-	-	-	-	-	-	-	-	-	-	-
Hunterdon County	76,443 91.50	1,674	1,596 95.34 95.34 2.09	-	-	647 93.90 40.54 38.65 0.85	-	-	485 97.78 30.39 28.97 0.63	-	-	-	-	-	-	-	-	-	-	-	-	-	-	-	-	-
Mercer County	189,134 81.83	11,118	10,147 91.27 91.27 5.36	-	-	3,809 89.90 37.54 34.26 2.01	-	-	2,942 92.54 28.99 26.46 1.56	-	738 96.47 7.27 6.64 0.39	-	-	-	-	418 96.54 4.12 3.76 0.22	1,067 92.46 10.52 9.60 0.56	-	-	280 82.11 2.76 2.52 0.15	-	-	304 98.06 3.00 2.73 0.16	-	-	-
East Windsor (township)	15,242 88.64	1,650	1,416 85.82 85.82 9.29	-	-	894 85.63 63.14 54.18 5.87	-	-	-	-	-	-	-	-	-	-	-	-	-	-	-	-	-	-	-	-
Hopewell (township)	10,193 93.04	458	444 96.94 96.94 4.36	-	-	-	-	-	-	-	-	-	-	-	-	-	-	-	-	-	-	-	-	-	-	-

Notes: Please refer to the User's Guide for an explanation of data; data is arranged alphabetically by state, then county, then city within each county; table includes counties with populations greater than 49,999 unless noted and cities with populations greater than 9,999 whose Asian and/or NHPI population rates are greater than the national average; (1) Native Hawaiian and other Pacific Islander; (2) excludes Taiwanese; (3) includes Chamorro; (4) county does not meet population threshold but is shown in order to allow inclusion of city

Place	Total population 25 years and over who are high school graduates	Asian population 25 years and over	Asians 25 years and over who are high school graduates	NHPI[1] population 25 years and over	NHPIs[1] 25 years and over who are high school graduates	Asian Indian	Bangladeshi	Cambodian	Chinese[2]	Fijian	Filipino	Guamanian[3]	Hawaiian, Native	Hmong	Indonesian	Japanese	Korean	Laotian	Malaysian	Pakistani	Samoan	Sri Lankan	Taiwanese	Thai	Tongan	Vietnamese
Lawrence (township)	17,088 89.23	1,512	1,273 84.19 84.19 7.45	-	-	536 76.68 42.11 35.45 3.14	-	-	431 89.42 33.86 28.51 2.52	-	-	-	-	-	-	-	-	-	-	-	-	-	-	-	-	-
Princeton (borough)	6,390 89.40	456	426 93.42 93.42 6.67	-	-	-	-	-	-	-	-	-	-	-	-	-	-	-	-	-	-	-	-	-	-	-
Princeton (township)	10,700 94.23	1,208	1,164 96.36 96.36 10.88	-	-	258 95.91 22.16 21.36 2.41	-	-	549 97.51 47.16 45.45 5.13	-	-	-	-	-	-	-	-	-	-	-	-	-	-	-	-	-
West Windsor (township)	13,593 96.91	3,051	2,923 95.80 95.80 21.50	-	-	957 97.55 32.74 31.37 7.04	-	-	1,107 94.29 37.87 36.28 8.14	-	-	-	-	-	-	-	236 93.28 8.07 7.74 1.74	-	-	-	-	-	-	-	-	-
Middlesex County	423,088 84.36	66,773	60,403 90.46 90.46 14.28	-	-	31,877 90.27 52.77 47.74 7.53	210 97.22 0.35 0.31 0.05	-	12,511 89.19 20.71 18.74 2.96	-	7,613 96.57 12.60 11.40 1.80	-	-	-	316 96.34 0.52 0.47 0.07	483 95.08 0.80 0.72 0.11	2,793 90.80 4.62 4.18 0.66	-	-	1,522 90.92 2.52 2.28 0.36	-	274 85.89 0.45 0.41 0.06	869 95.49 1.44 1.30 0.21	-	-	894 67.37 1.48 1.34 0.21
Avenel (cdp)	10,190 79.45	2,175	1,928 88.64 88.64 18.92	-	-	1,331 87.97 69.04 61.20 13.06	-	-	-	-	-	-	-	-	-	-	-	-	-	-	-	-	-	-	-	-
Carteret (borough)	10,301 74.94	1,046	780 74.57 74.57 7.57	-	-	469 67.97 60.13 44.84 4.55	-	-	-	-	-	-	-	-	-	-	-	-	-	-	-	-	-	-	-	-
Colonia (cdp)	10,759 86.52	742	678 91.37 91.37 6.30	-	-	331 88.74 48.82 44.61 3.08	-	-	-	-	209 97.66 30.83 28.17 1.94	-	-	-	-	-	-	-	-	-	-	-	-	-	-	-
East Brunswick (township)	29,164 92.14	4,801	4,394 91.52 91.52 15.07	-	-	1,530 92.62 34.82 31.87 5.25	-	-	1,812 88.65 41.24 37.74 6.21	-	290 100.00 6.60 6.04 0.99	-	-	-	-	-	227 90.44 5.17 4.73 0.78	-	-	-	-	-	-	-	-	-
Edison (township)	59,269 87.61	18,640	16,835 90.32 90.32 28.40	-	-	9,784 90.12 58.12 52.49 16.51	-	-	3,278 86.47 19.47 17.59 5.53	-	1,701 99.42 10.10 9.13 2.87	-	-	-	-	-	780 93.75 4.63 4.18 1.32	-	-	332 88.06 1.97 1.78 0.56	-	-	357 92.73 2.12 1.92 0.60	-	-	-

Notes: Please refer to the User's Guide for an explanation of data; data is arranged alphabetically by state, then county, then city within each county; table includes counties with populations greater than 49,999 unless noted and cities with populations greater than 9,999 whose Asian and/or NHPI population rates are greater than the national average; (1) Native Hawaiian and other Pacific Islander; (2) excludes Taiwanese; (3) includes Chamorro; (4) county does not meet population threshold but is shown in order to allow inclusion of city

Place	Total population 25 years and over who are high school graduates	Asian population 25 years and over	Asians 25 years and over who are high school graduates	NHPI[1] population 25 years and over	NHPIs[1] 25 years and over who are high school graduates	Asian Indian	Bangladeshi	Cambodian	Chinese[2]	Fijian	Filipino	Guamanian[3]	Hawaiian, Native	Hmong	Indonesian	Japanese	Korean	Laotian	Malaysian	Pakistani	Samoan	Sri Lankan	Taiwanese	Thai	Tongan	Vietnamese
Fords (cdp)	9,219	1,604	1,528	-	-	790	-	-	-	-	396	-	-	-	-	-	-	-	-	-	-	-	-	-	-	-
	86.26		95.26			96.58					93.18															
						51.70					25.92															
			95.26			49.25					24.69															
			16.57			8.57					4.30															
Highland Park (borough)	8,929	1,363	1,307	-	-	445	-	-	591	-	-	-	-	-	-	-	-	-	-	-	-	-	-	-	-	-
	91.10		95.89			96.11			95.79																	
						34.05			45.22																	
			95.89			32.65			43.36																	
			14.64			4.98			6.62																	
Iselin (cdp)	10,028	2,648	2,248	-	-	1,548	-	-	304	-	-	-	-	-	-	-	-	-	-	-	-	-	-	-	-	-
	85.37		84.89			83.50			81.94																	
						68.86			13.52																	
			84.89			58.46			11.48																	
			22.42			15.44			3.03																	
Metuchen (borough)	8,524	643	549	-	-	-	-	-	-	-	-	-	-	-	-	-	-	-	-	-	-	-	-	-	-	-
	92.11		85.38																							
			85.38																							
			6.44																							
Middlesex (borough)	8,145	399	376	-	-	-	-	-	-	-	-	-	-	-	-	-	-	-	-	-	-	-	-	-	-	-
	85.40		94.24																							
			94.24																							
			4.62																							
New Brunswick (city)	13,817	1,028	912	-	-	420	-	-	166	-	-	-	-	-	-	-	-	-	-	-	-	-	-	-	-	-
	62.55		88.72			86.42			91.21																	
						46.05			18.20																	
			88.72			40.86			16.15																	
			6.60			3.04			1.20																	
North Brunswick (township)	21,537	3,392	3,077	-	-	1,866	-	-	508	-	290	-	-	-	-	-	218	-	-	-	-	-	-	-	-	-
	85.84		90.71			92.10			87.29		93.85						83.85									
						60.64			16.51		9.42						7.08									
			90.71			55.01			14.98		8.55						6.43									
			14.29			8.66			2.36		1.35						1.01									
Old Bridge (township)	35,959	4,086	3,717	-	-	1,571	-	-	701	-	794	-	-	-	-	-	-	-	-	284	-	-	-	-	-	-
	88.40		90.97			89.36			88.62		98.39									91.91						
						42.27			18.86		21.36									7.64						
			90.97			38.45			17.16		19.43									6.95						
			10.34			4.37			1.95		2.21									0.79						
Piscataway (township)	28,436	7,688	6,905	-	-	3,413	-	-	1,480	-	1,181	-	-	-	-	-	324	-	-	-	-	-	-	-	-	-
	88.54		89.82			88.60			94.93		95.09						89.50									
						49.43			21.43		17.10						4.69									
			89.82			44.39			19.25		15.36						4.21									
			24.28			12.00			5.20		4.15						1.14									
Plainsboro (township)	13,569	4,039	3,915	-	-	2,101	-	-	1,046	-	-	-	-	-	-	-	-	-	-	-	-	-	-	-	-	-
	97.29		96.93			98.04			96.76																	
						53.67			26.72																	
			96.93			52.02			25.90																	
			28.85			15.48			7.71																	

Notes: Please refer to the User's Guide for an explanation of data; data is arranged alphabetically by state, then county, then city within each county; table includes counties with populations greater than 49,999 unless noted and cities with populations greater than 9,999 whose Asian and/or NHPI population rates are greater than the national average; (1) Native Hawaiian and other Pacific Islander; (2) excludes Taiwanese; (3) includes Chamorro; (4) county does not meet population threshold but is shown in order to allow inclusion of city

Place	Total population 25 years and over who are high school graduates	Asian population 25 years and over	Asians 25 years and over who are high school graduates	NHPI[1] population 25 years and over	NHPIs[1] 25 years and over who are high school graduates	Asian Indian	Bangladeshi	Cambodian	Chinese[2]	Fijian	Filipino	Guamanian[3]	Hawaiian, Native	Hmong	Indonesian	Japanese	Korean	Laotian	Malaysian	Pakistani	Samoan	Sri Lankan	Taiwanese	Thai	Tongan	Vietnamese
Princeton Meadows (cdp)	8,826	2,531	2,438	-	-	1,359	-	-	597	-	-	-	-	-	-	-	-	-	-	-	-	-	-	-	-	-
	96.85		96.33			97.42			97.23																	
						55.74			24.49																	
			96.33			53.69			23.59																	
			27.62			15.40			6.76																	
Sayreville (borough)	23,860	2,683	2,470	-	-	1,522	-	-	345	-	397	-	-	-	-	-	-	-	-	-	-	-	-	-	-	-
	85.61		92.06			93.83			80.42		96.13															
						61.62			13.97		16.07															
			92.06			56.73			12.86		14.80															
			10.35			6.38			1.45		1.66															
South Brunswick (township)	23,194	4,476	4,214	-	-	2,279	-	-	926	-	378	-	-	-	-	-	-	-	-	-	-	-	-	-	-	-
	93.25		94.15			94.72			92.32		92.87															
						54.08			21.97		8.97															
			94.15			50.92			20.69		8.45															
			18.17			9.83			3.99		1.63															
South Plainfield (borough)	12,592	1,142	851	-	-	320	-	-	-	-	212	-	-	-	-	-	-	-	-	-	-	-	-	-	-	172
	84.28		74.52			71.43					87.24															66.93
						37.60					24.91															20.21
			74.52			28.02					18.56															15.06
			6.76			2.54					1.68															1.37
Woodbridge (township)	57,841	9,355	8,417	-	-	5,419	-	-	822	-	1,195	-	-	-	-	-	387	-	-	199	-	-	-	-	-	-
	84.02		89.97			89.78			85.80		95.14						87.56			89.64						
						64.38			9.77		14.20						4.60			2.36						
			89.97			57.93			8.79		12.77						4.14			2.13						
			14.55			9.37			1.42		2.07						0.67			0.34						
Monmouth County	363,164	15,942	14,156	-	-	4,068	-	-	5,271	-	2,210	-	-	-	-	274	1,114	-	-	191	-	-	-	-	-	428
	87.92		88.80			90.97			84.78		95.34					85.36	90.20			91.39						82.79
						28.74			37.24		15.61					1.94	7.87			1.35						3.02
			88.80			25.52			33.06		13.86					1.72	6.99			1.20						2.68
			3.90			1.12			1.45		0.61					0.08	0.31			0.05						0.12
Aberdeen (township)	10,774	665	575	-	-	247	-	-	238	-	-	-	-	-	-	-	-	-	-	-	-	-	-	-	-	-
	87.86		86.47			87.59			89.14																	
						42.96			41.39																	
			86.47			37.14			35.79																	
			5.34			2.29			2.21																	
Colts Neck (township)	6,891	342	322	-	-	-	-	-	-	-	-	-	-	-	-	-	-	-	-	-	-	-	-	-	-	-
	95.00		94.15																							
			94.15																							
			4.67																							
Eatontown (borough)	8,800	914	830	-	-	-	-	-	-	-	-	-	-	-	-	-	-	-	-	-	-	-	-	-	-	-
	89.10		90.81																							
			90.81																							
			9.43																							
Freehold (township)	19,355	1,187	1,018	-	-	251	-	-	335	-	314	-	-	-	-	-	-	-	-	-	-	-	-	-	-	-
	88.75		85.76			84.51			82.51		98.13															
						24.66			32.91		30.84															
			85.76			21.15			28.22		26.45															
			5.26			1.30			1.73		1.62															

Notes: Please refer to the User's Guide for an explanation of data; data is arranged alphabetically by state, then county, then city within each county; table includes counties with populations greater than 49,999 unless noted and cities with populations greater than 9,999 whose Asian and/or NHPI population rates are greater than the national average; (1) Native Hawaiian and other Pacific Islander; (2) excludes Taiwanese; (3) includes Chamorro; (4) county does not meet population threshold but is shown in order to allow inclusion of city

Place	Total population 25 years and over who are high school graduates	Asian population 25 years and over	Asians 25 years and over who are high school graduates	NHPI[1] population 25 years and over	NHPIs[1] 25 years and over who are high school graduates	Asian Indian	Bangladeshi	Cambodian	Chinese[2]	Fijian	Filipino	Guamanian[3]	Hawaiian, Native	Hmong	Indonesian	Japanese	Korean	Laotian	Malaysian	Pakistani	Samoan	Sri Lankan	Taiwanese	Thai	Tongan	Vietnamese
Holmdel (township)	9,479 91.14	1,632	1,543 94.55 94.55 16.28	-	-	283 94.97 18.34 17.34 2.99	-	-	916 93.18 59.36 56.13 9.66	-	-	-	-	-	-	-	-	-	-	-	-	-	-	-	-	-
Howell (township)	27,241 88.22	1,283	1,093 85.19 85.19 4.01	-	-	339 88.28 31.02 26.42 1.24	-	-	-	-	307 98.40 28.09 23.93 1.13	-	-	-	-	-	-	-	-	-	-	-	-	-	-	-
Manalapan (township)	19,683 92.47	919	874 95.10 95.10 4.44	-	-	356 94.68 40.73 38.74 1.81	-	-	319 93.82 36.50 34.71 1.62	-	-	-	-	-	-	-	-	-	-	-	-	-	-	-	-	-
Marlboro (township)	22,049 94.01	2,862	2,640 92.24 92.24 11.97	-	-	593 97.05 22.46 20.72 2.69	-	-	1,479 89.69 56.02 51.68 6.71	-	-	-	-	-	-	-	-	-	-	-	-	-	-	-	-	-
Morganville (cdp)	7,050 96.43	629	619 98.41 98.41 8.78	-	-	-	-	-	381 97.44 61.55 60.57 5.40	-	-	-	-	-	-	-	-	-	-	-	-	-	-	-	-	-
Ocean (township)	16,544 90.24	1,034	909 87.91 87.91 5.49	-	-	334 85.20 36.74 32.30 2.02	-	-	-	-	-	-	-	-	-	-	-	-	-	-	-	-	-	-	-	-
Tinton Falls (borough)	9,692 92.68	488	409 83.81 83.81 4.22	-	-	-	-	-	-	-	-	-	-	-	-	-	-	-	-	-	-	-	-	-	-	-
West Freehold (cdp)	8,170 90.43	420	380 90.48 90.48 4.65	-	-	-	-	-	-	-	-	-	-	-	-	-	-	-	-	-	-	-	-	-	-	-
Morris County	293,387 90.58	19,859	18,254 91.92 91.92 6.22	-	-	6,382 90.47 34.96 32.14 2.18	-	-	6,011 94.07 32.93 30.27 2.05	-	2,116 95.27 11.59 10.66 0.72	-	-	-	-	583 93.88 3.19 2.94 0.20	1,377 92.23 7.54 6.93 0.47	-	-	351 87.31 1.92 1.77 0.12	-	-	452 97.84 2.48 2.28 0.15	-	-	360 74.69 1.97 1.81 0.12
Chatham (township)	6,777 96.63	405	377 93.09 93.09 5.56	-	-	-	-	-	-	-	-	-	-	-	-	-	-	-	-	-	-	-	-	-	-	-

Notes: Please refer to the User's Guide for an explanation of data; data is arranged alphabetically by state, then county, then city within each county; table includes counties with populations greater than 49,999 unless noted and cities with populations greater than 9,999 whose Asian and/or NHPI population rates are greater than the national average; (1) Native Hawaiian and other Pacific Islander; (2) excludes Taiwanese; (3) includes Chamorro; (4) county does not meet population threshold but is shown in order to allow inclusion of city

Place	Total population 25 years and over who are high school graduates	Asian population 25 years and over	Asians 25 years and over who are high school graduates	NHPI[1] population 25 years and over	NHPIs[1] 25 years and over who are high school graduates	Asian Indian	Bangladeshi	Cambodian	Chinese[2]	Fijian	Filipino	Guamanian[3]	Hawaiian, Native	Hmong	Indonesian	Japanese	Korean	Laotian	Malaysian	Pakistani	Samoan	Sri Lankan	Taiwanese	Thai	Tongan	Vietnamese
Denville (township)	10,443 92.26	532	468 87.97 87.97 4.48	-	-	-	-	-	-	-	-	-	-	-	-	-	-	-	-	-	-	-	-	-	-	-
East Hanover (township)	7,174 88.06	813	737 90.65 90.65 10.27	-	-	-	-	-	333 84.95 45.18 40.96 4.64	-	-	-	-	-	-	-	-	-	-	-	-	-	-	-	-	-
Hanover (township)	8,302 89.54	791	749 94.69 94.69 9.02	-	-	204 89.08 27.24 25.79 2.46	-	-	355 98.89 47.40 44.88 4.28	-	-	-	-	-	-	-	-	-	-	-	-	-	-	-	-	-
Lincoln Park (borough)	7,026 86.33	411	378 91.97 91.97 5.38	-	-	-	-	-	-	-	-	-	-	-	-	-	-	-	-	-	-	-	-	-	-	-
Montville (township)	13,506 93.50	1,761	1,696 96.31 96.31 12.56	-	-	648 92.70 38.21 36.80 4.80	-	-	681 97.99 40.15 38.67 5.04	-	-	-	-	-	-	-	-	-	-	-	-	-	-	-	-	-
Morris (township)	14,805 95.12	697	670 96.13 96.13 4.53	-	-	-	-	-	-	-	-	-	-	-	-	-	-	-	-	-	-	-	-	-	-	-
Mount Olive (township)	14,482 91.87	1,019	954 93.62 93.62 6.59	-	-	422 93.78 44.23 41.41 2.91	-	-	-	-	-	-	-	-	-	-	-	-	-	-	-	-	-	-	-	-
Parsippany-Troy Hills (twp)	32,943 89.90	5,946	5,301 89.15 89.15 16.09	-	-	2,356 86.24 44.44 39.62 7.15	-	-	1,618 91.41 30.52 27.21 4.91	-	485 97.59 9.15 8.16 1.47	-	-	-	-	-	320 100.00 6.04 5.38 0.97	-	-	-	-	-	-	-	-	-
Randolph (township)	15,551 95.68	1,587	1,565 98.61 98.61 10.06	-	-	625 100.00 39.94 39.38 4.02	-	-	436 99.09 27.86 27.47 2.80	-	-	-	-	-	-	-	-	-	-	-	-	-	-	-	-	-
Rockaway (township)	14,398 92.96	833	780 93.64 93.64 5.42	-	-	373 91.42 47.82 44.78 2.59	-	-	-	-	-	-	-	-	-	-	-	-	-	-	-	-	-	-	-	-

Notes: Please refer to the User's Guide for an explanation of data; data is arranged alphabetically by state, then county, then city within each county; table includes counties with populations greater than 49,999 unless noted and cities with populations greater than 9,999 whose Asian and/or NHPI population rates are greater than the national average; (1) Native Hawaiian and other Pacific Islander; (2) excludes Taiwanese; (3) includes Chamorro; (4) county does not meet population threshold but is shown in order to allow inclusion of city

Place	Total population 25 years and over who are high school graduates	Asian population 25 years and over	Asians 25 years and over who are high school graduates	NHPI[1] population 25 years and over	NHPIs[1] 25 years and over who are high school graduates	Asian Indian	Bangladeshi	Cambodian	Chinese[2]	Fijian	Filipino	Guamanian[3]	Hawaiian, Native	Hmong	Indonesian	Japanese	Korean	Laotian	Malaysian	Pakistani	Samoan	Sri Lankan	Taiwanese	Thai	Tongan	Vietnamese
Roxbury (township)	14,537 90.01	609	560 91.95 91.95 3.85	-	-	-	-	-	-	-	-	-	-	-	-	-	-	-	-	-	-	-	-	-	-	-
Succasunna-Kenvil (cdp)	7,599 91.68	354	313 88.42 88.42 4.12	-	-	-	-	-	-	-	-	-	-	-	-	-	-	-	-	-	-	-	-	-	-	-
Ocean County	297,455 83.01	4,313	3,613 83.77 83.77 1.21	-	-	887 85.37 24.55 20.57 0.30	-	-	551 67.94 15.25 12.78 0.19	-	1,483 92.28 41.05 34.38 0.50	-	-	-	-	-	163 75.81 4.51 3.78 0.05	-	-	-	-	-	-	-	-	-
Passaic County	231,991 73.32	11,790	9,425 79.94 79.94 4.06	-	-	4,110 73.93 43.61 34.86 1.77	162 54.73 1.72 1.37 0.07	-	1,032 81.13 10.95 8.75 0.44	-	2,270 93.53 24.08 19.25 0.98	-	-	-	-	-	954 91.03 10.12 8.09 0.41	-	-	-	-	-	-	-	-	-
Clifton (city)	43,783 78.56	3,464	2,758 79.62 79.62 6.30	-	-	1,345 74.85 48.77 38.83 3.07	-	-	175 71.43 6.35 5.05 0.40	-	772 92.34 27.99 22.29 1.76	-	-	-	-	-	215 89.21 7.80 6.21 0.49	-	-	-	-	-	-	-	-	-
Little Falls (township)	6,972 85.25	313	273 87.22 87.22 3.92	-	-	-	-	-	-	-	-	-	-	-	-	-	-	-	-	-	-	-	-	-	-	-
Passaic (city)	21,342 55.52	2,548	1,962 77.00 77.00 9.19	-	-	1,194 72.58 60.86 46.86 5.59	-	-	-	-	473 90.79 24.11 18.56 2.22	-	-	-	-	-	-	-	-	-	-	-	-	-	-	-
Wayne (township)	33,272 89.21	2,160	2,029 93.94 93.94 6.10	-	-	698 94.07 34.40 32.31 2.10	-	-	410 93.61 20.21 18.98 1.23	-	216 94.74 10.65 10.00 0.65	-	-	-	-	-	507 92.69 24.99 23.47 1.52	-	-	-	-	-	-	-	-	-
Salem County	33,995 79.45	231	205 88.74 88.74 0.60	-	-	-	-	-	-	-	-	-	-	-	-	-	-	-	-	-	-	-	-	-	-	-
Somerset County	183,031 89.57	16,364	15,402 94.12 94.12 8.41	-	-	6,192 93.11 40.20 37.84 3.38	-	-	4,617 94.07 29.98 28.21 2.52	-	1,984 99.20 12.88 12.12 1.08	-	-	-	-	453 96.18 2.94 2.77 0.25	710 90.79 4.61 4.34 0.39	-	-	408 87.55 2.65 2.49 0.22	-	-	356 95.19 2.31 2.18 0.19	-	-	280 90.03 1.82 1.71 0.15

Notes: Please refer to the User's Guide for an explanation of data; data is arranged alphabetically by state, then county, then city within each county; table includes counties with populations greater than 49,999 unless noted and cities with populations greater than 9,999 whose Asian and/or NHPI population rates are greater than the national average; (1) Native Hawaiian and other Pacific Islander; (2) excludes Taiwanese; (3) includes Chamorro; (4) county does not meet population threshold but is shown in order to allow inclusion of city

Place	Total population 25 years and over who are high school graduates	Asian population 25 years and over	Asians 25 years and over who are high school graduates	NHPI[1] population 25 years and over	NHPIs[1] 25 years and over who are high school graduates	Asian Indian	Bangladeshi	Cambodian	Chinese[2]	Fijian	Filipino	Guamanian[3]	Hawaiian, Native	Hmong	Indonesian	Japanese	Korean	Laotian	Malaysian	Pakistani	Samoan	Sri Lankan	Taiwanese	Thai	Tongan	Vietnamese
Bernards (township)	16,239 95.81	1,272	1,207 94.89 94.89 7.43	-	-	347 97.20 28.75 27.28 2.14	-	-	575 92.30 47.64 45.20 3.54	-	-	-	-	-	-	-	-	-	-	-	-	-	-	-	-	-
Branchburg (township)	9,435 94.79	695	648 93.24 93.24 6.87	-	-	345 92.00 53.24 49.64 3.66	-	-	-	-	-	-	-	-	-	-	-	-	-	-	-	-	-	-	-	-
Bridgewater (township)	27,312 92.00	2,964	2,837 95.72 95.72 10.39	-	-	1,193 96.29 42.05 40.25 4.37	-	-	974 94.84 34.33 32.86 3.57	-	-	-	-	-	-	-	-	-	-	-	-	-	-	-	-	-
Franklin (township)	31,855 88.21	4,431	4,203 94.85 94.85 13.19	-	-	2,019 92.91 48.04 45.57 6.34	-	-	927 94.59 22.06 20.92 2.91	-	613 100.00 14.58 13.83 1.92	-	-	-	-	-	-	-	-	-	-	-	-	-	-	-
Hillsborough (township)	22,004 92.68	1,559	1,423 91.28 91.28 6.47	-	-	538 89.37 37.81 34.51 2.45	-	-	432 90.76 30.36 27.71 1.96	-	-	-	-	-	-	-	-	-	-	-	-	-	-	-	-	-
Montgomery (township)	10,736 97.32	1,220	1,191 97.62 97.62 11.09	-	-	376 100.00 31.57 30.82 3.50	-	-	540 96.26 45.34 44.26 5.03	-	-	-	-	-	-	-	-	-	-	-	-	-	-	-	-	-
North Plainfield (borough)	11,181 80.65	660	600 90.91 90.91 5.37	-	-	-	-	-	-	-	-	-	-	-	-	-	-	-	-	-	-	-	-	-	-	-
Somerset (cdp)	13,347 85.00	1,290	1,266 98.14 98.14 9.49	-	-	453 94.97 35.78 35.12 3.39	-	-	311 100.00 24.57 24.11 2.33	-	393 100.00 31.04 30.47 2.94	-	-	-	-	-	-	-	-	-	-	-	-	-	-	-
Somerville (borough)	7,042 81.86	552	509 92.21 92.21 7.23	-	-	-	-	-	-	-	-	-	-	-	-	-	-	-	-	-	-	-	-	-	-	-
Warren (township)	8,779 93.43	977	914 93.55 93.55 10.41	-	-	303 94.98 33.15 31.01 3.45	-	-	372 95.14 40.70 38.08 4.24	-	-	-	-	-	-	-	-	-	-	-	-	-	-	-	-	-

Notes: Please refer to the User's Guide for an explanation of data; data is arranged alphabetically by state, then county, then city within each county; table includes counties with populations greater than 49,999 unless noted and cities with populations greater than 9,999 whose Asian and/or NHPI population rates are greater than the national average; (1) Native Hawaiian and other Pacific Islander; (2) excludes Taiwanese; (3) includes Chamorro; (4) county does not meet population threshold but is shown in order to allow inclusion of city

Place	Total population 25 years and over who are high school graduates	Asian population 25 years and over	Asians 25 years and over who are high school graduates	NHPI[1] population 25 years and over	NHPIs[1] 25 years and over who are high school graduates	Asian Indian	Bangladeshi	Cambodian	Chinese[2]	Fijian	Filipino	Guamanian[3]	Hawaiian, Native	Hmong	Indonesian	Japanese	Korean	Laotian	Malaysian	Pakistani	Samoan	Sri Lankan	Taiwanese	Thai	Tongan	Vietnamese
Sussex County	85,369 89.77	996	888 89.16 89.16 1.04	-	-	273 94.14 30.74 27.41 0.32	-	-	-	-	313 97.81 35.25 31.43 0.37	-	-	-	-	-	-	-	-	-	-	-	-	-	-	-
Union County	279,004 79.28	13,099	11,536 88.07 88.07 4.13	-	-	3,905 88.57 33.85 29.81 1.40	-	-	2,331 84.58 20.21 17.80 0.84	-	3,612 92.97 31.31 27.57 1.29	-	-	-	-	-	728 95.66 6.31 5.56 0.26	-	-	135 79.41 1.17 1.03 0.05	-	-	-	-	-	212 59.55 1.84 1.62 0.08
Berkeley Heights (township)	8,572 92.50	674	645 95.70 95.70 7.52	-	-	-	-	-	264 94.62 40.93 39.17 3.08	-	-	-	-	-	-	-	-	-	-	-	-	-	-	-	-	-
New Providence (borough)	7,910 95.08	626	608 97.12 97.12 7.69	-	-	-	-	-	238 96.36 39.14 38.02 3.01	-	-	-	-	-	-	-	-	-	-	-	-	-	-	-	-	-
Rahway (city)	14,778 81.47	743	608 81.83 81.83 4.11	-	-	-	-	-	-	-	305 89.44 50.16 41.05 2.06	-	-	-	-	-	-	-	-	-	-	-	-	-	-	-
Roselle Park (borough)	7,541 82.91	810	709 87.53 87.53 9.40	-	-	455 82.43 64.17 56.17 6.03	-	-	-	-	-	-	-	-	-	-	-	-	-	-	-	-	-	-	-	-
Scotch Plains (township)	14,646 92.05	1,114	1,022 91.74 91.74 6.98	-	-	414 94.74 40.51 37.16 2.83	-	-	266 81.10 26.03 23.88 1.82	-	-	-	-	-	-	-	-	-	-	-	-	-	-	-	-	-
Springfield (township)	9,929 90.34	399	390 97.74 97.74 3.93	-	-	-	-	-	-	-	-	-	-	-	-	-	-	-	-	-	-	-	-	-	-	-
Summit (city)	13,418 92.43	556	511 91.91 91.91 3.81	-	-	249 91.54 48.73 44.78 1.86	-	-	-	-	-	-	-	-	-	-	-	-	-	-	-	-	-	-	-	-
Union (township)	30,416 80.90	2,678	2,378 88.80 88.80 7.82	-	-	551 89.89 23.17 20.58 1.81	-	-	307 80.79 12.91 11.46 1.01	-	1,268 96.13 53.32 47.35 4.17	-	-	-	-	-	-	-	-	-	-	-	-	-	-	-

Notes: Please refer to the User's Guide for an explanation of data; data is arranged alphabetically by state, then county, then city within each county; table includes counties with populations greater than 49,999 unless noted and cities with populations greater than 9,999 whose Asian and/or NHPI population rates are greater than the national average; (1) Native Hawaiian and other Pacific Islander; (2) excludes Taiwanese; (3) includes Chamorro; (4) county does not meet population threshold but is shown in order to allow inclusion of city

Place	Total population 25 years and over who are high school graduates	Asian population 25 years and over	Asians 25 years and over who are high school graduates	NHPI[1] population 25 years and over	NHPIs[1] 25 years and over who are high school graduates	Asian Indian	Bangladeshi	Cambodian	Chinese[2]	Fijian	Filipino	Guamanian[3]	Hawaiian, Native	Hmong	Indonesian	Japanese	Korean	Laotian	Malaysian	Pakistani	Samoan	Sri Lankan	Taiwanese	Thai	Tongan	Vietnamese
Westfield (town)	19,121 95.36	769	704 91.55 91.55 3.68	-	-	-	-	-	-	-	-	-	-	-	-	-	-	-	-	-	-	-	-	-	-	-
Warren County	58,942 84.86	693	573 82.68 82.68 0.97	-	-	191 64.75 33.33 27.56 0.32	-	-	-	-	-	-	-	-	-	-	-	-	-	-	-	-	-	-	-	-
NEW MEXICO	894,820 78.85	11,987	9,959 83.08 83.08 1.11	846	661 78.13 78.13 0.07	1,468 91.52 14.74 12.25 0.16	-	-	2,333 89.22 23.43 19.46 0.26	-	1,651 86.99 16.58 13.77 0.18	176 87.56 26.63 20.80 0.02	258 85.71 39.03 30.50 0.03	-	-	1,549 90.58 15.55 12.92 0.17	863 80.20 8.67 7.20 0.10	-	-	-	-	-	-	175 57.19 1.76 1.46 0.02	-	1,205 64.23 12.10 10.05 0.13
Bernalillo County	302,822 84.43	6,522	5,284 81.02 81.02 1.74	357	298 83.47 83.47 0.10	672 94.38 12.72 10.30 0.22	-	-	1,136 88.96 21.50 17.42 0.38	-	678 91.62 12.83 10.40 0.22	-	-	-	-	831 87.20 15.73 12.74 0.27	440 82.24 8.33 6.75 0.15	-	-	-	-	-	-	-	-	1,046 62.75 19.80 16.04 0.35
Chaves County	27,433 72.55	277	238 85.92 85.92 0.87	-	-	-	-	-	-	-	-	-	-	-	-	-	-	-	-	-	-	-	-	-	-	-
Dona Ana County	69,971 70.05	943	838 88.87 88.87 1.20	-	-	-	-	-	293 94.52 34.96 31.07 0.42	-	-	-	-	-	-	-	-	-	-	-	-	-	-	-	-	-
Los Alamos County[4]	12,352 96.33	510	482 94.51 94.51 3.90	-	-	-	-	-	-	-	-	-	-	-	-	-	-	-	-	-	-	-	-	-	-	-
Los Alamos (cdp)	8,047 96.36	406	378 93.10 93.10 4.70	-	-	-	-	-	-	-	-	-	-	-	-	-	-	-	-	-	-	-	-	-	-	-
Otero County	30,839 81.03	510	403 79.02 79.02 1.31	-	-	-	-	-	-	-	-	-	-	-	-	-	-	-	-	-	-	-	-	-	-	-
Sandoval County	48,578 86.01	465	368 79.14 79.14 0.76	-	-	-	-	-	-	-	153 77.66 41.58 32.90 0.31	-	-	-	-	-	-	-	-	-	-	-	-	-	-	-

Notes: Please refer to the User's Guide for an explanation of data; data is arranged alphabetically by state, then county, then city within each county; table includes counties with populations greater than 49,999 unless noted and cities with populations greater than 9,999 whose Asian and/or NHPI population rates are greater than the national average; (1) Native Hawaiian and other Pacific Islander; (2) excludes Taiwanese; (3) includes Chamorro; (4) county does not meet population threshold but is shown in order to allow inclusion of city

Place	Total population 25 years and over who are high school graduates	Asian population 25 years and over	Asians 25 years and over who are high school graduates	NHPI[1] population 25 years and over	NHPIs[1] 25 years and over who are high school graduates	Asian Indian	Bangladeshi	Cambodian	Chinese[2]	Fijian	Filipino	Guamanian[3]	Hawaiian, Native	Hmong	Indonesian	Japanese	Korean	Laotian	Malaysian	Pakistani	Samoan	Sri Lankan	Taiwanese	Thai	Tongan	Vietnamese
Santa Fe County	74,240 84.49	659	582 88.32 88.32 0.78	-	-	-	-	-	-	-	-	-	-	-	-	-	-	-	-	-	-	-	-	-	-	-
NEW YORK	9,916,212 79.06	693,502	508,574 73.33 73.33 5.13	4,567	3,238 70.90 70.90 0.03	123,734 78.62 24.33 17.84 1.25	8,732 72.77 1.72 1.26 0.09	693 49.15 0.14 0.10 0.01	174,641 60.87 34.34 25.18 1.76	-	57,009 93.68 11.21 8.22 0.57	618 66.24 19.09 13.53 0.01	772 79.92 23.84 16.90 0.01	-	1,464 93.07 0.29 0.21 0.01	27,401 95.90 5.39 3.95 0.28	68,335 85.87 13.44 9.85 0.69	883 49.11 0.17 0.13 0.01	756 68.11 0.15 0.11 0.01	12,923 72.62 2.54 1.86 0.13	537 69.83 16.58 11.76 0.01	1,371 74.19 0.27 0.20 0.01	4,998 91.35 0.98 0.72 0.05	3,860 84.15 0.76 0.56 0.04	-	8,285 56.45 1.63 1.19 0.08
Albany County	168,664 86.33	4,627	4,065 87.85 87.85 2.41	-	-	1,414 92.12 34.78 30.56 0.84	-	-	1,004 86.70 24.70 21.70 0.60	-	448 95.52 11.02 9.68 0.27	-	-	-	-	-	309 90.35 7.60 6.68 0.18	-	-	-	-	-	-	-	-	230 61.50 5.66 4.97 0.14
Colonie (town)	48,999 88.95	1,803	1,577 87.47 87.47 3.22	-	-	740 91.70 46.92 41.04 1.51	-	-	315 80.15 19.97 17.47 0.64	-	-	-	-	-	-	-	-	-	-	-	-	-	-	-	-	-
Guilderland (town)	21,180 92.53	845	760 89.94 89.94 3.59	-	-	268 92.73 35.26 31.72 1.27	-	-	-	-	-	-	-	-	-	-	-	-	-	-	-	-	-	-	-	-
Bronx County (Bronx)	495,106 62.29	25,252	17,416 68.97 68.97 3.52	560	370 66.07 66.07 0.07	6,115 65.94 35.11 24.22 1.24	696 62.20 4.00 2.76 0.14	124 38.04 0.71 0.49 0.03	2,655 57.89 15.24 10.51 0.54	-	3,141 95.01 18.04 12.44 0.63	-	-	-	-	408 96.68 2.34 1.62 0.08	1,958 79.05 11.24 7.75 0.40	-	-	463 71.01 2.66 1.83 0.09	-	-	-	-	-	735 43.65 4.22 2.91 0.15
Broome County	111,080 83.81	2,276	1,783 78.34 78.34 1.61	-	-	443 91.53 24.85 19.46 0.40	-	-	392 85.96 21.99 17.22 0.35	-	-	-	-	-	-	-	260 89.35 14.58 11.42 0.23	97 41.63 5.44 4.26 0.09	-	-	-	-	-	-	-	125 41.53 7.01 5.49 0.11
Johnson City (village)	8,838 81.72	411	308 74.94 74.94 3.48	-	-	-	-	-	-	-	-	-	-	-	-	-	-	-	-	-	-	-	-	-	-	-
Vestal (town)	14,155 92.61	579	556 96.03 96.03 3.93	-	-	-	-	-	124 89.86 22.30 21.42 0.88	-	-	-	-	-	-	-	-	-	-	-	-	-	-	-	-	-
Cattaraugus County	43,964 81.18	259	193 74.52 74.52 0.44	-	-	-	-	-	-	-	-	-	-	-	-	-	-	-	-	-	-	-	-	-	-	-

Notes: Please refer to the User's Guide for an explanation of data; data is arranged alphabetically by state, then county, then city within each county; table includes counties with populations greater than 49,999 unless noted and cities with populations greater than 9,999 whose Asian and/or NHPI population rates are greater than the national average; (1) Native Hawaiian and other Pacific Islander; (2) excludes Taiwanese; (3) includes Chamorro; (4) county does not meet population threshold but is shown in order to allow inclusion of city

Place	Total population 25 years and over who are high school graduates	Asian population 25 years and over	Asians 25 years and over who are high school graduates	NHPI[1] population 25 years and over	NHPIs[1] 25 years and over who are high school graduates	Asian Indian	Bangladeshi	Cambodian	Chinese[2]	Fijian	Filipino	Guamanian[3]	Hawaiian, Native	Hmong	Indonesian	Japanese	Korean	Laotian	Malaysian	Pakistani	Samoan	Sri Lankan	Taiwanese	Thai	Tongan	Vietnamese
Cayuga County	43,207 79.06	234	159 67.95 67.95 0.37	-	-	-	-	-	-	-	-	-	-	-	-	-	-	-	-	-	-	-	-	-	-	-
Chautauqua County	74,095 81.19	217	182 83.87 83.87 0.25	-	-	-	-	-	-	-	-	-	-	-	-	-	-	-	-	-	-	-	-	-	-	-
Chemung County	49,889 82.06	481	375 77.96 77.96 0.75	-	-	-	-	-	-	-	-	-	-	-	-	-	-	-	-	-	-	-	-	-	-	-
Chenango County	27,687 80.57	129	112 86.82 86.82 0.40	-	-	-	-	-	-	-	-	-	-	-	-	-	-	-	-	-	-	-	-	-	-	-
Clinton County	39,427 76.41	408	305 74.75 74.75 0.77	-	-	-	-	-	-	-	-	-	-	-	-	-	-	-	-	-	-	-	-	-	-	-
Columbia County	35,618 80.97	272	195 71.69 71.69 0.55	-	-	-	-	-	-	-	-	-	-	-	-	-	-	-	-	-	-	-	-	-	-	-
Dutchess County	154,251 83.96	4,589	3,980 86.73 86.73 2.58	-	-	1,587 87.29 39.87 34.58 1.03	-	-	1,120 83.40 28.14 24.41 0.73	-	-	-	-	-	-	-	432 92.90 10.85 9.41 0.28	-	-	-	-	-	-	-	-	-
Arlington (cdp)	5,867 83.47	379	279 73.61 73.61 4.76	-	-	-	-	-	-	-	-	-	-	-	-	-	-	-	-	-	-	-	-	-	-	-
Poughkeepsie (town)	22,630 87.14	1,097	942 85.87 85.87 4.16	-	-	483 81.73 51.27 44.03 2.13	-	-	221 96.09 23.46 20.15 0.98	-	-	-	-	-	-	-	-	-	-	-	-	-	-	-	-	-
Wappinger (town)	15,743 88.71	853	789 92.50 92.50 5.01	-	-	253 88.77 32.07 29.66 1.61	-	-	-	-	-	-	-	-	-	-	-	-	-	-	-	-	-	-	-	-

Notes: Please refer to the User's Guide for an explanation of data; data is arranged alphabetically by state, then county, then city within each county; table includes counties with populations greater than 49,999 unless noted and cities with populations greater than 9,999 whose Asian and/or NHPI population rates are greater than the national average; (1) Native Hawaiian and other Pacific Islander; (2) excludes Taiwanese; (3) includes Chamorro; (4) county does not meet population threshold but is shown in order to allow inclusion of city

Place	Total population 25 years and over who are high school graduates	Asian population 25 years and over	Asians 25 years and over who are high school graduates	NHPI[1] population 25 years and over	NHPIs[1] 25 years and over who are high school graduates	Asian Indian	Bangladeshi	Cambodian	Chinese[2]	Fijian	Filipino	Guamanian[3]	Hawaiian, Native	Hmong	Indonesian	Japanese	Korean	Laotian	Malaysian	Pakistani	Samoan	Sri Lankan	Taiwanese	Thai	Tongan	Vietnamese
Erie County	528,556	7,807	6,578	-	-	2,052	-	-	1,641	-	382	-	-	-	-	295	834	-	-	-	-	-	-	-	-	494
	82.89		84.26			92.64			87.85		90.31					96.09	88.25									52.00
						31.19			24.95		5.81					4.48	12.68									7.51
			84.26			26.28			21.02		4.89					3.78	10.68									6.33
			1.24			0.39			0.31		0.07					0.06	0.16									0.09
Amherst (town)	72,062	3,239	2,950	-	-	1,102	-	-	821	-	-	-	-	-	-	-	397	-	-	-	-	-	-	-	-	-
	91.93		91.08			95.25			88.57								87.44									
						37.36			27.83								13.46									
			91.08			34.02			25.35								12.26									
			4.09			1.53			1.14								0.55									
Herkimer County	34,496	165	121	-	-	-	-	-	-	-	-	-	-	-	-	-	-	-	-	-	-	-	-	-	-	-
	79.38		73.33																							
			73.33																							
			0.35																							
Jefferson County	57,163	694	581	-	-	-	-	-	-	-	167	-	-	-	-	-	168	-	-	-	-	-	-	-	-	-
	82.89		83.72								95.43						74.01									
											28.74						28.92									
			83.72								24.06						24.21									
			1.02								0.29						0.29									
Kings County (Brooklyn)	1,068,564	121,889	69,539	767	483	11,244	1,525	137	39,646	-	4,761	121	-	-	-	1,603	3,844	-	-	2,874	-	-	-	-	-	1,236
	68.81		57.05		62.97	72.24	67.15	44.05	49.06		93.35	67.60				97.21	82.56			55.44						52.17
						16.17	2.19	0.20	57.01		6.85	25.05				2.31	5.53			4.13						1.78
			57.05		62.97	9.22	1.25	0.11	32.53		3.91	15.78				1.32	3.15			2.36						1.01
			6.51		0.05	1.05	0.14	0.01	3.71		0.45	0.01				0.15	0.36			0.27						0.12
Livingston County	33,003	286	187	-	-	-	-	-	-	-	-	-	-	-	-	-	-	-	-	-	-	-	-	-	-	-
	82.34		65.38																							
			65.38																							
			0.57																							
Madison County	36,471	182	148	-	-	-	-	-	-	-	-	-	-	-	-	-	-	-	-	-	-	-	-	-	-	-
	83.34		81.32																							
			81.32																							
			0.41																							
Monroe County	405,547	10,231	8,273	-	-	2,398	-	59	2,151	-	357	-	-	-	-	400	799	450	-	198	-	-	-	-	-	898
	84.85		80.86			88.75		35.33	85.42		92.25					94.79	87.13	58.37		70.21						63.24
						28.99		0.71	26.00		4.32					4.84	9.66	5.44		2.39						10.85
			80.86			23.44		0.58	21.02		3.49					3.91	7.81	4.40		1.94						8.78
			2.04			0.59		0.01	0.53		0.09					0.10	0.20	0.11		0.05						0.22
Brighton (town)	23,626	1,921	1,595	-	-	628	-	-	310	-	-	-	-	-	-	-	-	-	-	-	-	-	-	-	-	-
	91.47		83.03			89.08			76.17																	
						39.37			19.44																	
			83.03			32.69			16.14																	
			6.75			2.66			1.31																	
Henrietta (town)	19,625	981	868	-	-	168	-	-	241	-	-	-	-	-	-	-	-	-	-	-	-	-	-	-	-	-
	90.26		88.48			100.00			95.26																	
						19.35			27.76																	
			88.48			17.13			24.57																	
			4.42			0.86			1.23																	

Notes: Please refer to the User's Guide for an explanation of data; data is arranged alphabetically by state, then county, then city within each county; table includes counties with populations greater than 49,999 unless noted and cities with populations greater than 9,999 whose Asian and/or NHPI population rates are greater than the national average; (1) Native Hawaiian and other Pacific Islander; (2) excludes Taiwanese; (3) includes Chamorro; (4) county does not meet population threshold but is shown in order to allow inclusion of city

Place	Total population 25 years and over who are high school graduates	Asian population 25 years and over	Asians 25 years and over who are high school graduates	NHPI[1] population 25 years and over	NHPIs[1] 25 years and over who are high school graduates	Asian Indian	Bangladeshi	Cambodian	Chinese[2]	Fijian	Filipino	Guamanian[3]	Hawaiian, Native	Hmong	Indonesian	Japanese	Korean	Laotian	Malaysian	Pakistani	Samoan	Sri Lankan	Taiwanese	Thai	Tongan	Vietnamese
Pittsford (town)	17,223 96.20	755	672 89.01 89.01 3.90	-	-	340 93.41 50.60 45.03 1.97	-	-	-	-	-	-	-	-	-	-	-	-	-	-	-	-	-	-	-	-
Nassau County	787,955 86.71	39,330	34,757 88.37 88.37 4.41	232	161 69.40 69.40 0.02	12,658 88.23 36.42 32.18 1.61	-	-	8,373 84.89 24.09 21.29 1.06	-	4,444 92.87 12.79 11.30 0.56	-	-	-	-	1,330 93.73 3.83 3.38 0.17	4,981 91.80 14.33 12.66 0.63	-	-	1,009 82.50 2.90 2.57 0.13	-	-	335 88.86 0.96 0.85 0.04	211 85.77 0.61 0.54 0.03	-	264 80.73 0.76 0.67 0.03
East Meadow (cdp)	22,418 86.54	1,463	1,348 92.14 92.14 6.01	-	-	618 92.24 45.85 42.24 2.76	-	-	-	-	222 100.00 16.47 15.17 0.99	-	-	-	-	-	-	-	-	-	-	-	-	-	-	-
Elmont (cdp)	16,939 80.03	1,926	1,585 82.29 82.29 9.36	-	-	827 75.87 52.18 42.94 4.88	-	-	-	-	306 88.44 19.31 15.89 1.81	-	-	-	-	-	-	-	-	-	-	-	-	-	-	-
Franklin Square (cdp)	17,317 83.02	695	625 89.93 89.93 3.61	-	-	237 89.77 37.92 34.10 1.37	-	-	-	-	-	-	-	-	-	-	-	-	-	-	-	-	-	-	-	-
Glen Cove (city)	14,570 77.56	658	543 82.52 82.52 3.73	-	-	136 77.27 25.05 20.67 0.93	-	-	-	-	-	-	-	-	-	-	196 80.33 36.10 29.79 1.35	-	-	-	-	-	-	-	-	-
Hicksville (cdp)	25,019 86.44	2,187	1,909 87.29 87.29 7.63	-	-	915 86.73 47.93 41.84 3.66	-	-	414 83.81 21.69 18.93 1.65	-	284 95.30 14.88 12.99 1.14	-	-	-	-	-	-	-	-	-	-	-	-	-	-	-
Jericho (cdp)	8,845 95.95	892	855 95.85 95.85 9.67	-	-	-	-	-	-	-	-	-	-	-	-	-	415 96.96 48.54 46.52 4.69	-	-	-	-	-	-	-	-	-
Mineola (village)	11,505 82.01	626	615 98.24 98.24 5.35	-	-	238 100.00 38.70 38.02 2.07	-	-	-	-	-	-	-	-	-	-	-	-	-	-	-	-	-	-	-	-
North Hempstead (town)	133,811 87.15	12,953	11,451 88.40 88.40 8.56	-	-	4,083 86.67 35.66 31.52 3.05	-	-	3,015 84.41 26.33 23.28 2.25	-	905 93.88 7.90 6.99 0.68	-	-	-	-	750 99.73 6.55 5.79 0.56	1,780 92.32 15.54 13.74 1.33	-	-	285 91.94 2.49 2.20 0.21	-	-	167 95.43 1.46 1.29 0.12	-	-	-

Notes: Please refer to the User's Guide for an explanation of data; data is arranged alphabetically by state, then county, then city within each county; table includes counties with populations greater than 49,999 unless noted and cities with populations greater than 9,999 whose Asian and/or NHPI population rates are greater than the national average; (1) Native Hawaiian and other Pacific Islander; (2) excludes Taiwanese; (3) includes Chamorro; (4) county does not meet population threshold but is shown in order to allow inclusion of city

Place	Total population 25 years and over who are high school graduates	Asian population 25 years and over	Asians 25 years and over who are high school graduates	NHPI[1] population 25 years and over	NHPIs[1] 25 years and over who are high school graduates	Asian Indian	Bangladeshi	Cambodian	Chinese[2]	Fijian	Filipino	Guamanian[3]	Hawaiian, Native	Hmong	Indonesian	Japanese	Korean	Laotian	Malaysian	Pakistani	Samoan	Sri Lankan	Taiwanese	Thai	Tongan	Vietnamese
North Merrick (cdp)	7,614 92.86	291	264 90.72 90.72 3.47	-	-	-	-	-	-	-	-	-	-	-	-	-	-	-	-	-	-	-	-	-	-	-
North New Hyde Park (cdp)	9,076 87.52	1,291	1,127 87.30 87.30 12.42	-	-	590 84.53 52.35 45.70 6.50	-	-	401 87.75 35.58 31.06 4.42	-	-	-	-	-	-	-	-	-	-	-	-	-	-	-	-	-
North Valley Stream (cdp)	8,902 85.57	828	689 83.21 83.21 7.74	-	-	342 88.83 49.64 41.30 3.84	-	-	-	-	-	-	-	-	-	-	-	-	-	-	-	-	-	-	-	-
Oyster Bay (town)	184,305 89.99	8,794	7,886 89.67 89.67 4.28	-	-	2,829 89.95 35.87 32.17 1.53	-	-	2,121 86.78 26.90 24.12 1.15	-	819 94.14 10.39 9.31 0.44	-	-	-	-	271 95.76 3.44 3.08 0.15	1,377 92.42 17.46 15.66 0.75	-	-	-	-	-	-	-	-	-
Plainview (cdp)	16,461 92.20	799	715 89.49 89.49 4.34	-	-	187 96.89 26.15 23.40 1.14	-	-	199 81.56 27.83 24.91 1.21	-	-	-	-	-	-	-	201 85.90 28.11 25.16 1.22	-	-	-	-	-	-	-	-	-
Port Washington (cdp)	9,626 90.09	652	618 94.79 94.79 6.42	-	-	140 92.11 22.65 21.47 1.45	-	-	-	-	-	-	-	-	-	-	-	-	-	-	-	-	-	-	-	-
Salisbury (cdp)	7,739 90.14	779	744 95.51 95.51 9.61	-	-	259 92.83 34.81 33.25 3.35	-	-	-	-	-	-	-	-	-	-	-	-	-	-	-	-	-	-	-	-
Syosset (cdp)	12,006 94.02	1,491	1,415 94.90 94.90 11.79	-	-	407 96.67 28.76 27.30 3.39	-	-	508 94.95 35.90 34.07 4.23	-	-	-	-	-	-	-	348 92.55 24.59 23.34 2.90	-	-	-	-	-	-	-	-	-
Valley Stream (village)	21,404 86.15	1,563	1,402 89.70 89.70 6.55	-	-	-	-	-	406 84.23 28.96 25.98 1.90	-	284 88.20 20.26 18.17 1.33	-	-	-	-	-	-	-	-	-	-	-	-	-	-	-
West Hempstead (cdp)	11,030 88.08	671	602 89.72 89.72 5.46	-	-	208 95.85 34.55 31.00 1.89	-	-	-	-	-	-	-	-	-	-	-	-	-	-	-	-	-	-	-	-

Notes: Please refer to the User's Guide for an explanation of data; data is arranged alphabetically by state, then county, then city within each county; table includes counties with populations greater than 49,999 unless noted and cities with populations greater than 9,999 whose Asian and/or NHPI population rates are greater than the national average; (1) Native Hawaiian and other Pacific Islander; (2) excludes Taiwanese; (3) includes Chamorro; (4) county does not meet population threshold but is shown in order to allow inclusion of city

Place	Total population 25 years and over who are high school graduates	Asian population 25 years and over	Asians 25 years and over who are high school graduates	NHPI[1] population 25 years and over	NHPIs[1] 25 years and over who are high school graduates	Asian Indian	Bangladeshi	Cambodian	Chinese[2]	Fijian	Filipino	Guamanian[3]	Hawaiian, Native	Hmong	Indonesian	Japanese	Korean	Laotian	Malaysian	Pakistani	Samoan	Sri Lankan	Taiwanese	Thai	Tongan	Vietnamese
Westbury (village)	7,697	452	370	-	-	-	-	-	-	-	-	-	-	-	-	-	-	-	-	-	-	-	-	-	-	-
	79.42		81.86																							
			81.86																							
			4.81																							
Woodmere (cdp)	10,269	335	284	-	-	-	-	-	-	-	-	-	-	-	-	-	-	-	-	-	-	-	-	-	-	-
	93.94		84.78																							
			84.78																							
			2.77																							
New York City	3,814,256	536,408	372,377	2,682	1,791	79,753	8,232	398	143,665	-	39,562	401	388	-	1,087	17,426	51,832	-	636	9,002	169	950	3,251	2,395	-	4,482
	72.28		69.42		66.78	74.08	72.10	48.01	57.36		93.73	68.66	72.93		92.12	96.17	84.27		65.16	68.35	56.52	70.68	89.78	86.46		57.63
						21.42	2.21	0.11	38.58		10.62	22.39	21.66		0.29	4.68	13.92		0.17	2.42	9.44	0.26	0.87	0.64		1.20
			69.42		66.78	14.87	1.53	0.07	26.78		7.38	14.95	14.47		0.20	3.25	9.66		0.12	1.68	6.30	0.18	0.61	0.45		0.84
			9.76		0.05	2.09	0.22	0.01	3.77		1.04	0.01	0.01		0.03	0.46	1.36		0.02	0.24	<0.01	0.02	0.09	0.06		0.12
New York County (Manhattan)	885,633	106,507	70,174	385	227	8,351	222	-	29,595	-	7,087	-	-	-	-	11,497	7,991	-	-	638	-	-	699	608	-	1,009
	78.65		65.89		58.96	86.61	51.03		47.64		96.57					97.00	94.29			89.48			99.01	91.02		84.36
						11.90	0.32		42.17		10.10					16.38	11.39			0.91			1.00	0.87		1.44
			65.89		58.96	7.84	0.21		27.79		6.65					10.79	7.50			0.60			0.66	0.57		0.95
			7.92		0.03	0.94	0.03		3.34		0.80					1.30	0.90			0.07			0.08	0.07		0.11
Niagara County	122,519	689	546	-	-	215	-	-	-	-	-	-	-	-	-	-	-	-	-	-	-	-	-	-	-	-
	83.26		79.25			88.11																				
						39.38																				
			79.25			31.20																				
			0.45			0.18																				
Oneida County	125,565	1,615	903	-	-	238	-	-	142	-	-	-	-	-	-	-	-	-	-	-	-	-	-	-	-	177
	79.05		55.91			85.61			70.30																	27.27
						26.36			15.73																	19.60
			55.91			14.74			8.79																	10.96
			0.72			0.19			0.11																	0.14
Onondaga County	254,356	5,718	4,397	-	-	1,108	-	-	885	-	435	-	-	-	-	249	601	-	-	-	-	-	-	-	-	466
	85.67		76.90			89.86			82.17		94.98					95.40	94.20									42.87
						25.20			20.13		9.89					5.66	13.67									10.60
			76.90			19.38			15.48		7.61					4.35	10.51									8.15
			1.73			0.44			0.35		0.17					0.10	0.24									0.18
Ontario County	58,133	360	317	-	-	-	-	-	-	-	-	-	-	-	-	-	-	-	-	-	-	-	-	-	-	-
	87.37		88.06																							
			88.06																							
			0.55																							
Orange County	174,187	3,459	2,956	-	-	964	-	-	647	-	482	-	-	-	-	-	385	-	-	-	-	-	-	-	-	-
	81.85		85.46			90.35			77.86		89.42						91.23									
						32.61			21.89		16.31						13.02									
			85.46			27.87			18.70		13.93						11.13									
			1.70			0.55			0.37		0.28						0.22									
Oswego County	61,270	294	262	-	-	-	-	-	-	-	-	-	-	-	-	-	-	-	-	-	-	-	-	-	-	-
	80.44		89.12																							
			89.12																							
			0.43																							

Notes: Please refer to the User's Guide for an explanation of data; data is arranged alphabetically by state, then county, then city within each county; table includes counties with populations greater than 49,999 unless noted and cities with populations greater than 9,999 whose Asian and/or NHPI population rates are greater than the national average; (1) Native Hawaiian and other Pacific Islander; (2) excludes Taiwanese; (3) includes Chamorro; (4) county does not meet population threshold but is shown in order to allow inclusion of city

Place	Total population 25 years and over who are high school graduates	Asian population 25 years and over	Asians 25 years and over who are high school graduates	NHPI[1] population 25 years and over	NHPIs[1] 25 years and over who are high school graduates	Asian Indian	Bangladeshi	Cambodian	Chinese[2]	Fijian	Filipino	Guamanian[3]	Hawaiian, Native	Hmong	Indonesian	Japanese	Korean	Laotian	Malaysian	Pakistani	Samoan	Sri Lankan	Taiwanese	Thai	Tongan	Vietnamese
Otsego County	32,203	143	128	-	-	-	-	-	-	-	-	-	-	-	-	-	-	-	-	-	-	-	-	-	-	-
	82.98		89.51																							
			89.51																							
			0.40																							
Putnam County	58,263	813	780	-	-	261	-	-	272	-	-	-	-	-	-	-	-	-	-	-	-	-	-	-	-	-
	90.16		95.94			100.00			89.77																	
						33.46			34.87																	
			95.94			32.10			33.46																	
			1.34			0.45			0.47																	
Queens County (Queens)	1,122,321	266,430	201,479	821	584	50,401	5,773	-	68,231	-	21,176	-	-	-	720	3,783	35,930	-	349	4,710	-	448	2,313	1,307	-	1,451
	74.35		75.62		71.13	72.94	76.20		69.58		92.52				93.75	93.52	82.61		71.52	75.60		75.55	88.38	81.64		59.47
						25.02	2.87		33.87		10.51				0.36	1.88	17.83		0.17	2.34		0.22	1.15	0.65		0.72
			75.62		71.13	18.92	2.17		25.61		7.95				0.27	1.42	13.49		0.13	1.77		0.17	0.87	0.49		0.54
			17.95		0.05	4.49	0.51		6.08		1.89				0.06	0.34	3.20		0.03	0.42		0.04	0.21	0.12		0.13
Rensselaer County	85,101	1,218	1,109	-	-	239	-	-	506	-	-	-	-	-	-	-	118	-	-	-	-	-	-	-	-	-
	84.90		91.05			97.95			87.85								96.72									
						21.55			45.63								10.64									
			91.05			19.62			41.54								9.69									
			1.30			0.28			0.59								0.14									
Richmond Co. (Staten Island)	242,632	16,330	13,769	-	-	3,642	-	-	3,538	-	3,397	-	-	-	-	-	2,109	-	-	317	-	203	-	-	-	-
	82.59		84.32			89.24			72.74		94.97						87.69			80.87		62.27				
						26.45			25.70		24.67						15.32			2.30		1.47				
			84.32			22.30			21.67		20.80						12.91			1.94		1.24				
			5.67			1.50			1.46		1.40						0.87			0.13		0.08				
Rockland County	156,996	10,376	9,144	-	-	3,088	-	-	1,033	-	2,856	-	-	-	-	-	1,128	-	-	-	-	-	-	-	-	-
	85.32		88.13			88.18			79.34		95.36						92.46									
						33.77			11.30		31.23						12.34									
			88.13			29.76			9.96		27.53						10.87									
			5.82			1.97			0.66		1.82						0.72									
Clarkstown (town)	50,821	4,196	3,824	-	-	1,290	-	-	416	-	1,399	-	-	-	-	-	407	-	-	-	-	-	-	-	-	-
	89.99		91.13			88.84			83.70		98.38						91.67									
						33.73			10.88		36.58						10.64									
			91.13			30.74			9.91		33.34						9.70									
			7.52			2.54			0.82		2.75						0.80									
Nanuet (cdp)	10,127	1,043	968	-	-	349	-	-	-	-	-	-	-	-	-	-	-	-	-	-	-	-	-	-	-	-
	87.76		92.81			94.84																				
						36.05																				
			92.81			33.46																				
			9.56			3.45																				
New City (cdp)	21,306	1,540	1,358	-	-	501	-	-	-	-	340	-	-	-	-	-	-	-	-	-	-	-	-	-	-	-
	90.99		88.18			80.03					98.27															
						36.89					25.04															
			88.18			32.53					22.08															
			6.37			2.35					1.60															
Orangetown (town)	29,843	1,956	1,777	-	-	409	-	-	275	-	486	-	-	-	-	-	350	-	-	-	-	-	-	-	-	-
	90.15		90.85			93.38			75.55		96.24						96.15									
						23.02			15.48		27.35						19.70									
			90.85			20.91			14.06		24.85						17.89									
			5.95			1.37			0.92		1.63						1.17									

Notes: Please refer to the User's Guide for an explanation of data; data is arranged alphabetically by state, then county, then city within each county; table includes counties with populations greater than 49,999 unless noted and cities with populations greater than 9,999 whose Asian and/or NHPI population rates are greater than the national average; (1) Native Hawaiian and other Pacific Islander; (2) excludes Taiwanese; (3) includes Chamorro; (4) county does not meet population threshold but is shown in order to allow inclusion of city

Place	Total population 25 years and over who are high school graduates	Asian population 25 years and over	Asians 25 years and over who are high school graduates	NHPI[1] population 25 years and over	NHPIs[1] 25 years and over who are high school graduates	Asian Indian	Bangladeshi	Cambodian	Chinese[2]	Fijian	Filipino	Guamanian[3]	Hawaiian, Native	Hmong	Indonesian	Japanese	Korean	Laotian	Malaysian	Pakistani	Samoan	Sri Lankan	Taiwanese	Thai	Tongan	Vietnamese
Ramapo (town)	51,177 81.55	3,364	2,861 85.05 85.05 5.59	-	-	1,127 89.30 39.39 33.50 2.20	-	-	261 78.14 9.12 7.76 0.51	-	828 91.09 28.94 24.61 1.62	-	-	-	-	-	320 89.64 11.18 9.51 0.63	-	-	-	-	-	-	-	-	-
Spring Valley (village)	10,107 70.10	923	784 84.94 84.94 7.76	-	-	403 89.76 51.40 43.66 3.99	-	-	-	-	-	-	-	-	-	-	-	-	-	-	-	-	-	-	-	-
St. Lawrence County	55,624 79.24	326	291 89.26 89.26 0.52	-	-	-	-	-	-	-	-	-	-	-	-	-	-	-	-	-	-	-	-	-	-	-
Saratoga County	119,086 88.20	1,319	1,212 91.89 91.89 1.02	-	-	466 95.49 38.45 35.33 0.39	-	-	230 100.00 18.98 17.44 0.19	-	-	-	-	-	-	-	137 84.05 11.30 10.39 0.12	-	-	-	-	-	-	-	-	-
Schenectady County	84,433 84.80	1,688	1,497 88.68 88.68 1.77	-	-	629 92.50 42.02 37.26 0.74	-	-	492 87.23 32.87 29.15 0.58	-	-	-	-	-	-	-	-	-	-	-	-	-	-	-	-	-
Niskayuna (town)	13,084 92.57	783	763 97.45 97.45 5.83	-	-	359 100.00 47.05 45.85 2.74	-	-	-	-	-	-	-	-	-	-	-	-	-	-	-	-	-	-	-	-
Steuben County	54,437 82.78	513	474 92.40 92.40 0.87	-	-	-	-	-	-	-	-	-	-	-	-	-	-	-	-	-	-	-	-	-	-	-
Suffolk County	812,227 86.19	21,127	18,410 87.14 87.14 2.27	299	244 81.61 81.61 0.03	5,587 86.74 30.35 26.44 0.69	-	-	4,888 83.64 26.55 23.14 0.60	-	2,653 95.40 14.41 12.56 0.33	-	-	-	-	779 87.92 4.23 3.69 0.10	2,077 95.23 11.28 9.83 0.26	-	-	947 86.33 5.14 4.48 0.12	-	-	268 94.70 1.46 1.27 0.03	182 75.52 0.99 0.86 0.02	-	309 63.45 1.68 1.46 0.04
Coram (cdp)	20,700 88.33	872	736 84.40 84.40 3.56	-	-	-	-	-	214 68.37 29.08 24.54 1.03	-	-	-	-	-	-	-	-	-	-	-	-	-	-	-	-	-
Dix Hills (cdp)	16,189 93.57	1,210	1,148 94.88 94.88 7.09	-	-	522 97.39 45.47 43.14 3.22	-	-	261 96.31 22.74 21.57 1.61	-	-	-	-	-	-	-	-	-	-	-	-	-	-	-	-	-

Notes: Please refer to the User's Guide for an explanation of data; data is arranged alphabetically by state, then county, then city within each county; table includes counties with populations greater than 49,999 unless noted and cities with populations greater than 9,999 whose Asian and/or NHPI population rates are greater than the national average; (1) Native Hawaiian and other Pacific Islander; (2) excludes Taiwanese; (3) includes Chamorro; (4) county does not meet population threshold but is shown in order to allow inclusion of city

Place	Total population 25 years and over who are high school graduates	Asian population 25 years and over	Asians 25 years and over who are high school graduates	NHPI[1] population 25 years and over	NHPIs[1] 25 years and over who are high school graduates	Asian Indian	Bangladeshi	Cambodian	Chinese[2]	Fijian	Filipino	Guamanian[3]	Hawaiian, Native	Hmong	Indonesian	Japanese	Korean	Laotian	Malaysian	Pakistani	Samoan	Sri Lankan	Taiwanese	Thai	Tongan	Vietnamese
Elwood (cdp)	6,762 89.85	465	438 94.19 94.19 6.48	-	-	-	-	-	-	-	-	-	-	-	-	-	-	-	-	-	-	-	-	-	-	-
Lake Grove (village)	6,369 91.21	380	344 90.53 90.53 5.40	-	-	-	-	-	-	-	-	-	-	-	-	-	-	-	-	-	-	-	-	-	-	-
Melville (cdp)	9,252 92.44	463	447 96.54 96.54 4.83	-	-	-	-	-	-	-	-	-	-	-	-	-	-	-	-	-	-	-	-	-	-	-
Setauket-East Setauket (cdp)	9,984 95.06	990	936 94.55 94.55 9.38	-	-	-	-	-	478 97.95 51.07 48.28 4.79	-	-	-	-	-	-	-	-	-	-	-	-	-	-	-	-	-
Stony Brook (cdp)	8,857 95.01	522	474 90.80 90.80 5.35	-	-	-	-	-	230 85.50 48.52 44.06 2.60	-	-	-	-	-	-	-	-	-	-	-	-	-	-	-	-	-
Sullivan County	38,275 76.20	585	444 75.90 75.90 1.16	-	-	-	-	-	-	-	-	-	-	-	-	-	-	-	-	-	-	-	-	-	-	-
Tioga County	29,009 84.76	208	118 56.73 56.73 0.41	-	-	-	-	-	-	-	-	-	-	-	-	-	-	-	-	-	-	-	-	-	-	-
Tompkins County	48,491 91.36	2,854	2,744 96.15 96.15 5.66	-	-	454 98.48 16.55 15.91 0.94	-	-	1,052 97.14 38.34 36.86 2.17	-	-	-	-	-	-	293 100.00 10.68 10.27 0.60	547 100.00 19.93 19.17 1.13	-	-	-	-	-	-	-	-	-
Ithaca (city)	9,619 89.53	848	770 90.80 90.80 8.00	-	-	133 95.00 17.27 15.68 1.38	-	-	295 93.65 38.31 34.79 3.07	-	-	-	-	-	-	-	77 100.00 10.00 9.08 0.80	-	-	-	-	-	-	-	-	-
Lansing (town)	6,372 93.21	733	715 97.54 97.54 11.22	-	-	-	-	-	-	-	-	-	-	-	-	-	-	-	-	-	-	-	-	-	-	-

Notes: Please refer to the User's Guide for an explanation of data; data is arranged alphabetically by state, then county, then city within each county; table includes counties with populations greater than 49,999 unless noted and cities with populations greater than 9,999 whose Asian and/or NHPI population rates are greater than the national average; (1) Native Hawaiian and other Pacific Islander; (2) excludes Taiwanese; (3) includes Chamorro; (4) county does not meet population threshold but is shown in order to allow inclusion of city

Place	Total population 25 years and over who are high school graduates	Asian population 25 years and over	Asians 25 years and over who are high school graduates	NHPI[1] population 25 years and over	NHPIs[1] 25 years and over who are high school graduates	Asian Indian	Bangladeshi	Cambodian	Chinese[2]	Fijian	Filipino	Guamanian[3]	Hawaiian, Native	Hmong	Indonesian	Japanese	Korean	Laotian	Malaysian	Pakistani	Samoan	Sri Lankan	Taiwanese	Thai	Tongan	Vietnamese
Ulster County	98,558 81.68	1,050	886 84.38 84.38 0.90	-	-	-	-	-	236 83.69 26.64 22.48 0.24	-	-	-	-	-	-	-	-	-	-	-	-	-	-	-	-	-
New Paltz (town)	6,042 90.10	202	177 87.62 87.62 2.93	-	-	-	-	-	-	-	-	-	-	-	-	-	-	-	-	-	-	-	-	-	-	-
Warren County	36,692 84.61	300	247 82.33 82.33 0.67	-	-	-	-	-	-	-	-	-	-	-	-	-	-	-	-	-	-	-	-	-	-	-
Wayne County	50,777 82.26	205	146 71.22 71.22 0.29	-	-	-	-	-	-	-	-	-	-	-	-	-	-	-	-	-	-	-	-	-	-	-
Westchester County	525,485 83.55	28,190	25,752 91.35 91.35 4.90	-	-	8,384 87.60 32.56 29.74 1.60	-	-	4,554 89.05 17.68 16.15 0.87	-	3,317 95.34 12.88 11.77 0.63	-	-	-	-	4,858 98.56 18.86 17.23 0.92	2,673 93.69 10.38 9.48 0.51	-	-	411 91.74 1.60 1.46 0.08	-	-	231 100.00 0.90 0.82 0.04	366 85.71 1.42 1.30 0.07	-	-
Dobbs Ferry (village)	6,142 87.38	483	433 89.65 89.65 7.05	-	-	-	-	-	-	-	-	-	-	-	-	-	-	-	-	-	-	-	-	-	-	-
Eastchester (cdp)	12,345 90.68	866	829 95.73 95.73 6.72	-	-	-	-	-	-	-	-	-	-	-	-	350 100.00 42.22 40.42 2.84	-	-	-	-	-	-	-	-	-	-
Eastchester (town)	20,160 90.98	1,539	1,499 97.40 97.40 7.44	-	-	-	-	-	-	-	-	-	-	-	-	800 100.00 53.37 51.98 3.97	-	-	-	-	-	-	-	-	-	-
Greenburgh (town)	55,774 90.96	5,314	5,057 95.16 95.16 9.07	-	-	1,628 92.29 32.19 30.64 2.92	-	-	884 95.88 17.48 16.64 1.58	-	407 99.27 8.05 7.66 0.73	-	-	-	-	1,279 98.23 25.29 24.07 2.29	615 95.05 12.16 11.57 1.10	-	-	-	-	-	-	-	-	-
Harrison (village)	13,830 87.02	821	796 96.95 96.95 5.76	-	-	-	-	-	-	-	-	-	-	-	-	406 100.00 51.01 49.45 2.94	-	-	-	-	-	-	-	-	-	-

Notes: Please refer to the User's Guide for an explanation of data; data is arranged alphabetically by state, then county, then city within each county; table includes counties with populations greater than 49,999 unless noted and cities with populations greater than 9,999 whose Asian and/or NHPI population rates are greater than the national average; (1) Native Hawaiian and other Pacific Islander; (2) excludes Taiwanese; (3) includes Chamorro; (4) county does not meet population threshold but is shown in order to allow inclusion of city

Place	Total population 25 years and over who are high school graduates	Asian population 25 years and over	Asians 25 years and over who are high school graduates	NHPI[1] population 25 years and over	NHPIs[1] 25 years and over who are high school graduates	Asian Indian	Bangladeshi	Cambodian	Chinese[2]	Fijian	Filipino	Guamanian[3]	Hawaiian, Native	Hmong	Indonesian	Japanese	Korean	Laotian	Malaysian	Pakistani	Samoan	Sri Lankan	Taiwanese	Thai	Tongan	Vietnamese
New Castle (town)	10,994 96.54	650	629 96.77 96.77 5.72	-	-	260 96.30 41.34 40.00 2.36	-	-	188 94.47 29.89 28.92 1.71	-	-	-	-	-	-	-	-	-	-	-	-	-	-	-	-	-
New Rochelle (city)	39,106 80.02	1,862	1,682 90.33 90.33 4.30	-	-	698 92.21 41.50 37.49 1.78	-	-	353 85.89 20.99 18.96 0.90	-	-	-	-	-	-	-	-	-	-	-	-	-	-	-	-	-
North Castle (town)	6,581 92.36	289	236 81.66 81.66 3.59	-	-	-	-	-	-	-	-	-	-	-	-	-	-	-	-	-	-	-	-	-	-	-
Ossining (town)	20,143 78.12	1,070	1,001 93.55 93.55 4.97	-	-	477 93.71 47.65 44.58 2.37	-	-	-	-	-	-	-	-	-	-	-	-	-	-	-	-	-	-	-	-
Ossining (village)	12,021 70.16	638	574 89.97 89.97 4.77	-	-	183 85.12 31.88 28.68 1.52	-	-	-	-	-	-	-	-	-	-	-	-	-	-	-	-	-	-	-	-
Pelham (town)	7,228 91.67	317	257 81.07 81.07 3.56	-	-	-	-	-	-	-	-	-	-	-	-	-	-	-	-	-	-	-	-	-	-	-
Rye (city)	9,565 94.29	700	673 96.14 96.14 7.04	-	-	-	-	-	-	-	-	-	-	-	-	396 98.51 58.84 56.57 4.14	-	-	-	-	-	-	-	-	-	-
Scarsdale (village)	10,936 97.11	1,274	1,208 94.82 94.82 11.05	-	-	228 90.48 18.87 17.90 2.08	-	-	242 97.98 20.03 19.00 2.21	-	-	-	-	-	-	396 97.06 32.78 31.08 3.62	194 94.17 16.06 15.23 1.77	-	-	-	-	-	-	-	-	-
Tarrytown (village)	7,037 87.93	416	401 96.39 96.39 5.70	-	-	-	-	-	-	-	-	-	-	-	-	-	-	-	-	-	-	-	-	-	-	-
White Plains (city)	31,159 82.03	1,701	1,592 93.59 93.59 5.11	-	-	540 93.43 33.92 31.75 1.73	-	-	339 84.75 21.29 19.93 1.09	-	-	-	-	-	-	-	-	-	-	-	-	-	-	-	-	-

Notes: Please refer to the User's Guide for an explanation of data; data is arranged alphabetically by state, then county, then city within each county; table includes counties with populations greater than 49,999 unless noted and cities with populations greater than 9,999 whose Asian and/or NHPI population rates are greater than the national average; (1) Native Hawaiian and other Pacific Islander; (2) excludes Taiwanese; (3) includes Chamorro; (4) county does not meet population threshold but is shown in order to allow inclusion of city

Place	Total population 25 years and over who are high school graduates	Asian population 25 years and over	Asians 25 years and over who are high school graduates	NHPI[1] population 25 years and over	NHPIs[1] 25 years and over who are high school graduates	Asian Indian	Bangladeshi	Cambodian	Chinese[2]	Fijian	Filipino	Guamanian[3]	Hawaiian, Native	Hmong	Indonesian	Japanese	Korean	Laotian	Malaysian	Pakistani	Samoan	Sri Lankan	Taiwanese	Thai	Tongan	Vietnamese
Yonkers (city)	101,090 76.73	6,391	5,341 83.57 83.57 5.28	-	-	2,292 78.25 42.91 35.86 2.27	-	-	560 81.16 10.48 8.76 0.55	-	1,152 94.74 21.57 18.03 1.14	-	-	-	-	-	695 86.23 13.01 10.87 0.69	-	-	-	-	-	-	-	-	-
NORTH CAROLINA	4,128,270 78.14	67,753	53,737 79.31 79.31 1.30	1,939	1,601 82.57 82.57 0.04	14,254 89.63 26.53 21.04 0.35	-	468 39.46 0.87 0.69 0.01	10,017 87.58 18.64 14.78 0.24	-	6,100 87.69 11.35 9.00 0.15	567 82.89 35.42 29.24 0.01	514 84.96 32.10 26.51 0.01	929 42.93 1.73 1.37 0.02	-	4,177 91.42 7.77 6.17 0.10	6,863 84.57 12.77 10.13 0.17	1,182 47.17 2.20 1.74 0.03	-	813 76.41 1.51 1.20 0.02	218 85.83 13.62 11.24 0.01	-	609 89.69 1.13 0.90 0.01	804 70.65 1.50 1.19 0.02	-	5,400 57.49 10.05 7.97 0.13
Alamance County	66,319 76.55	658	474 72.04 72.04 0.71	-	-	-	-	-	-	-	-	-	-	-	-	-	-	-	-	-	-	-	-	-	-	-
Buncombe County	117,655 81.90	1,178	1,010 85.74 85.74 0.86	-	-	300 81.74 29.70 25.47 0.25	-	-	-	-	-	-	-	-	-	-	-	-	-	-	-	-	-	-	-	-
Burke County	40,514 67.61	1,111	430 38.70 38.70 1.06	-	-	-	-	-	-	-	-	-	-	167 29.25 38.84 15.03 0.41	-	-	-	47 23.04 10.93 4.23 0.12	-	-	-	-	-	-	-	-
Cabarrus County	67,841 78.22	583	487 83.53 83.53 0.72	-	-	-	-	-	-	-	-	-	-	-	-	-	-	-	-	-	-	-	-	-	-	-
Catawba County	70,878 74.81	1,679	941 56.05 56.05 1.33	-	-	-	-	-	-	-	-	-	-	248 39.68 26.35 14.77 0.35	-	-	-	120 50.00 12.75 7.15 0.17	-	-	-	-	-	-	-	143 53.76 15.20 8.52 0.20
Hickory (city)	19,272 79.13	715	412 57.62 57.62 2.14	-	-	-	-	-	-	-	-	-	-	88 42.11 21.36 12.31 0.46	-	-	-	-	-	-	-	-	-	-	-	-
Cleveland County	45,771 72.20	388	285 73.45 73.45 0.62	-	-	-	-	-	-	-	-	-	-	-	-	-	-	-	-	-	-	-	-	-	-	-
Craven County	46,796 82.06	738	579 78.46 78.46 1.24	-	-	-	-	-	-	-	213 71.24 36.79 28.86 0.46	-	-	-	-	-	-	-	-	-	-	-	-	-	-	-

Notes: Please refer to the User's Guide for an explanation of data; data is arranged alphabetically by state, then county, then city within each county; table includes counties with populations greater than 49,999 unless noted and cities with populations greater than 9,999 whose Asian and/or NHPI population rates are greater than the national average; (1) Native Hawaiian and other Pacific Islander; (2) excludes Taiwanese; (3) includes Chamorro; (4) county does not meet population threshold but is shown in order to allow inclusion of city

Place	Total population 25 years and over who are high school graduates	Asian population 25 years and over	Asians 25 years and over who are high school graduates	NHPI[1] population 25 years and over	NHPIs[1] 25 years and over who are high school graduates	Asian Indian	Bangladeshi	Cambodian	Chinese[2]	Fijian	Filipino	Guamanian[3]	Hawaiian, Native	Hmong	Indonesian	Japanese	Korean	Laotian	Malaysian	Pakistani	Samoan	Sri Lankan	Taiwanese	Thai	Tongan	Vietnamese
Cumberland County	150,188 84.99	4,110	3,258 79.27 79.27 2.17	268	227 84.70 84.70 0.15	356 89.45 10.93 8.66 0.24	-	-	-	-	625 94.41 19.18 15.21 0.42	-	-	-	-	273 71.47 8.38 6.64 0.18	1,225 78.73 37.60 29.81 0.82	-	-	-	-	-	-	-	-	310 67.98 9.52 7.54 0.21
Davidson County	72,136 72.04	654	362 55.35 55.35 0.50	-	-	-	-	53 22.46 14.64 8.10 0.07	-	-	-	-	-	-	-	-	-	-	-	-	-	-	-	-	-	-
Durham County	119,297 82.96	4,393	4,152 94.51 94.51 3.48	-	-	1,560 94.09 37.57 35.51 1.31	-	-	948 95.95 22.83 21.58 0.79	-	438 100.00 10.55 9.97 0.37	-	-	-	-	309 100.00 7.44 7.03 0.26	294 93.33 7.08 6.69 0.25	-	-	-	-	-	-	-	-	-
Forsyth County	167,333 81.99	2,267	1,846 81.43 81.43 1.10	-	-	394 95.86 21.34 17.38 0.24	-	-	512 75.18 27.74 22.58 0.31	-	193 96.02 10.46 8.51 0.12	-	-	-	-	-	-	-	-	-	-	-	-	-	-	217 67.60 11.76 9.57 0.13
Gaston County	91,226 71.41	969	578 59.65 59.65 0.63	-	-	-	-	-	-	-	-	-	-	-	-	-	-	-	-	-	-	-	-	-	-	114 38.91 19.72 11.76 0.12
Guilford County	228,582 82.97	5,710	3,825 66.99 66.99 1.67	-	-	990 90.25 25.88 17.34 0.43	-	-	617 90.60 16.13 10.81 0.27	-	361 94.50 9.44 6.32 0.16	-	-	-	-	-	584 91.97 15.27 10.23 0.26	137 46.60 3.58 2.40 0.06	-	129 62.62 3.37 2.26 0.06	-	-	-	-	-	623 35.24 16.29 10.91 0.27
Halifax County	24,659 65.38	208	128 61.54 61.54 0.52	-	-	-	-	-	-	-	-	-	-	-	-	-	-	-	-	-	-	-	-	-	-	-
Harnett County	42,867 75.02	395	298 75.44 75.44 0.70	-	-	-	-	-	-	-	-	-	-	-	-	-	-	-	-	-	-	-	-	-	-	-
Henderson County	54,084 83.16	308	213 69.16 69.16 0.39	-	-	-	-	-	-	-	-	-	-	-	-	-	-	-	-	-	-	-	-	-	-	-
Iredell County	64,288 78.37	675	497 73.63 73.63 0.77	-	-	-	-	-	-	-	-	-	-	-	-	-	-	-	-	-	-	-	-	-	-	-

Notes: Please refer to the User's Guide for an explanation of data; data is arranged alphabetically by state, then county, then city within each county; table includes counties with populations greater than 49,999 unless noted and cities with populations greater than 9,999 whose Asian and/or NHPI population rates are greater than the national average; (1) Native Hawaiian and other Pacific Islander; (2) excludes Taiwanese; (3) includes Chamorro; (4) county does not meet population threshold but is shown in order to allow inclusion of city

Place	Total population 25 years and over who are high school graduates	Asian population 25 years and over	Asians 25 years and over who are high school graduates	NHPI[1] population 25 years and over	NHPIs[1] 25 years and over who are high school graduates	Asian Indian	Bangladeshi	Cambodian	Chinese[2]	Fijian	Filipino	Guamanian[3]	Hawaiian, Native	Hmong	Indonesian	Japanese	Korean	Laotian	Malaysian	Pakistani	Samoan	Sri Lankan	Taiwanese	Thai	Tongan	Vietnamese
Johnston County	60,945 75.93	280	248 88.57 88.57 0.41	-	-	-	-	-	-	-	-	-	-	-	-	-	-	-	-	-	-	-	-	-	-	-
Lenoir County	28,658 71.95	229	175 76.42 76.42 0.61	-	-	-	-	-	-	-	-	-	-	-	-	-	-	-	-	-	-	-	-	-	-	-
Mecklenburg County	392,470 86.23	12,894	10,082 78.19 78.19 2.57	-	-	3,060 90.86 30.35 23.73 0.78	-	199 52.65 1.97 1.54 0.05	1,617 85.24 16.04 12.54 0.41	-	728 90.43 7.22 5.65 0.19	-	-	58 39.73 0.58 0.45 0.01	-	569 96.77 5.64 4.41 0.14	1,354 84.63 13.43 10.50 0.34	292 51.05 2.90 2.26 0.07	-	-	-	-	-	-	-	1,623 56.91 16.10 12.59 0.41
Nash County	43,506 75.63	269	244 90.71 90.71 0.56	-	-	-	-	-	-	-	-	-	-	-	-	-	-	-	-	-	-	-	-	-	-	-
New Hanover County	92,915 86.30	897	741 82.61 82.61 0.80	-	-	-	-	-	-	-	-	-	-	-	-	-	-	-	-	-	-	-	-	-	-	-
Onslow County	63,482 84.32	1,660	1,148 69.16 69.16 1.81	180	164 91.11 91.11 0.26	-	-	-	-	-	465 64.94 40.51 28.01 0.73	-	-	-	-	297 79.41 25.87 17.89 0.47	-	-	-	-	-	-	-	-	-	-
Orange County	60,915 87.61	2,708	2,628 97.05 97.05 4.31	-	-	351 98.04 13.36 12.96 0.58	-	-	1,108 98.49 42.16 40.92 1.82	-	-	-	-	-	-	361 100.00 13.74 13.33 0.59	360 100.00 13.70 13.29 0.59	-	-	-	-	-	-	-	-	-
Carrboro (town)	8,904 90.21	488	453 92.83 92.83 5.09	-	-	-	-	-	-	-	-	-	-	-	-	-	-	-	-	-	-	-	-	-	-	-
Chapel Hill (town)	22,276 94.29	1,858	1,813 97.58 97.58 8.14	-	-	253 97.31 13.95 13.62 1.14	-	-	805 97.93 44.40 43.33 3.61	-	-	-	-	-	-	-	249 100.00 13.73 13.40 1.12	-	-	-	-	-	-	-	-	-
Pitt County	63,185 79.94	770	713 92.60 92.60 1.13	-	-	-	-	-	-	-	-	-	-	-	-	-	-	-	-	-	-	-	-	-	-	-

Notes: Please refer to the User's Guide for an explanation of data; data is arranged alphabetically by state, then county, then city within each county; table includes counties with populations greater than 49,999 unless noted and cities with populations greater than 9,999 whose Asian and/or NHPI population rates are greater than the national average; (1) Native Hawaiian and other Pacific Islander; (2) excludes Taiwanese; (3) includes Chamorro; (4) county does not meet population threshold but is shown in order to allow inclusion of city

Place	Total population 25 years and over who are high school graduates	Asian population 25 years and over	Asians 25 years and over who are high school graduates	NHPI[1] population 25 years and over	NHPIs[1] 25 years and over who are high school graduates	Asian Indian	Bangladeshi	Cambodian	Chinese[2]	Fijian	Filipino	Guamanian[3]	Hawaiian, Native	Hmong	Indonesian	Japanese	Korean	Laotian	Malaysian	Pakistani	Samoan	Sri Lankan	Taiwanese	Thai	Tongan	Vietnamese
Randolph County	61,191 69.97	479	347 72.44 72.44 0.57	-	-	-	-	-	-	-	-	-	-	-	-	-	-	-	-	-	-	-	-	-	-	-
Robeson County	48,302 64.87	563	420 74.60 74.60 0.87	-	-	-	-	-	-	-	-	-	-	-	-	-	-	-	-	-	-	-	-	-	-	-
Rowan County	64,067 74.20	432	236 54.63 54.63 0.37	-	-	-	-	-	-	-	-	-	-	-	-	-	-	-	-	-	-	-	-	-	-	-
Stanly County	28,418 73.43	292	165 56.51 56.51 0.58	-	-	-	-	-	-	-	-	-	-	31 30.39 18.79 10.62 0.11	-	-	-	-	-	-	-	-	-	-	-	-
Surry County	32,857 67.03	146	55 37.67 37.67 0.17	-	-	-	-	-	-	-	-	-	-	-	-	-	-	-	-	-	-	-	-	-	-	-
Union County	63,289 80.24	338	311 92.01 92.01 0.49	-	-	-	-	-	-	-	-	-	-	-	-	-	-	-	-	-	-	-	-	-	-	-
Wake County	360,395 89.32	13,302	11,918 89.60 89.60 3.31	-	-	4,101 92.20 34.41 30.83 1.14	-	-	3,054 93.80 25.63 22.96 0.85	-	809 93.53 6.79 6.08 0.22	-	-	-	-	557 97.89 4.67 4.19 0.15	1,193 91.42 10.01 8.97 0.33	-	-	219 85.88 1.84 1.65 0.06	-	-	-	-	-	1,010 69.04 8.47 7.59 0.28
Apex (town)	12,362 95.98	504	451 89.48 89.48 3.65	-	-	-	-	-	-	-	-	-	-	-	-	-	-	-	-	-	-	-	-	-	-	-
Cary (town)	58,098 95.06	4,876	4,509 92.47 92.47 7.76	-	-	1,952 92.03 43.29 40.03 3.36	-	-	1,175 93.77 26.06 24.10 2.02	-	-	-	-	-	-	234 97.91 5.19 4.80 0.40	346 95.32 7.67 7.10 0.60	-	-	-	-	-	-	-	-	260 83.60 5.77 5.33 0.45
Wayne County	56,270 77.19	730	603 82.60 82.60 1.07	-	-	-	-	-	-	-	-	-	-	-	-	-	-	-	-	-	-	-	-	-	-	-

Notes: Please refer to the User's Guide for an explanation of data; data is arranged alphabetically by state, then county, then city within each county; table includes counties with populations greater than 49,999 unless noted and cities with populations greater than 9,999 whose Asian and/or NHPI population rates are greater than the national average; (1) Native Hawaiian and other Pacific Islander; (2) excludes Taiwanese; (3) includes Chamorro; (4) county does not meet population threshold but is shown in order to allow inclusion of city

Place	Total population 25 years and over who are high school graduates	Asian population 25 years and over	Asians 25 years and over who are high school graduates	NHPI[1] population 25 years and over	NHPIs[1] 25 years and over who are high school graduates	Asian Indian	Bangladeshi	Cambodian	Chinese[2]	Fijian	Filipino	Guamanian[3]	Hawaiian, Native	Hmong	Indonesian	Japanese	Korean	Laotian	Malaysian	Pakistani	Samoan	Sri Lankan	Taiwanese	Thai	Tongan	Vietnamese
Wilkes County	30,017 65.97	169	113 66.86 66.86 0.38	-	-	-	-	-	-	-	-	-	-	-	-	-	-	-	-	-	-	-	-	-	-	-
NORTH DAKOTA	342,629 83.86	2,046	1,726 84.36 84.36 0.50	-	-	560 99.47 32.44 27.37 0.16	-	-	268 96.06 15.53 13.10 0.08	-	339 87.82 19.64 16.57 0.10	-	-	-	-	-	191 77.64 11.07 9.34 0.06	-	-	-	-	-	-	-	-	-
Cass County	67,874 90.90	828	688 83.09 83.09 1.01	-	-	244 100.00 35.47 29.47 0.36	-	-	-	-	-	-	-	-	-	-	-	-	-	-	-	-	-	-	-	-
Grand Forks County	33,315 89.16	425	389 91.53 91.53 1.17	-	-	-	-	-	-	-	-	-	-	-	-	-	-	-	-	-	-	-	-	-	-	-
Ward County	31,411 87.36	210	165 78.57 78.57 0.53	-	-	-	-	-	-	-	-	-	-	-	-	-	-	-	-	-	-	-	-	-	-	-
OHIO	6,149,655 82.97	85,861	74,335 86.58 86.58 1.21	1,363	1,070 78.50 78.50 0.02	22,734 92.81 30.58 26.48 0.37	409 94.68 0.55 0.48 0.01	582 45.79 0.78 0.68 0.01	16,508 87.05 22.21 19.23 0.27	-	8,641 91.27 11.62 10.06 0.14	292 79.78 27.29 21.42 <0.01	368 81.96 34.39 27.00 0.01	-	446 97.38 0.60 0.52 0.01	6,659 93.13 8.96 7.76 0.11	7,429 85.39 9.99 8.65 0.12	825 53.09 1.11 0.96 0.01	187 93.97 0.25 0.22 <0.01	846 87.40 1.14 0.99 0.01	188 72.87 17.57 13.79 <0.01	349 90.18 0.47 0.41 0.01	1,310 91.74 1.76 1.53 0.02	1,000 77.64 1.35 1.16 0.02	-	4,338 66.66 5.84 5.05 0.07
Allen County	57,479 82.50	338	261 77.22 77.22 0.45	-	-	-	-	-	-	-	-	-	-	-	-	-	-	-	-	-	-	-	-	-	-	-
Ashtabula County	54,335 79.91	217	156 71.89 71.89 0.29	-	-	-	-	-	-	-	-	-	-	-	-	-	-	-	-	-	-	-	-	-	-	-
Athens County	26,179 82.94	607	588 96.87 96.87 2.25	-	-	-	-	-	-	-	-	-	-	-	-	-	-	-	-	-	-	-	-	-	-	-
Athens (city)	5,131 93.51	437	429 98.17 98.17 8.36	-	-	-	-	-	-	-	-	-	-	-	-	-	-	-	-	-	-	-	-	-	-	-

Notes: Please refer to the User's Guide for an explanation of data; data is arranged alphabetically by state, then county, then city within each county; table includes counties with populations greater than 49,999 unless noted and cities with populations greater than 9,999 whose Asian and/or NHPI population rates are greater than the national average; (1) Native Hawaiian and other Pacific Islander; (2) excludes Taiwanese; (3) includes Chamorro; (4) county does not meet population threshold but is shown in order to allow inclusion of city

Place	Total population 25 years and over who are high school graduates	Asian population 25 years and over	Asians 25 years and over who are high school graduates	NHPI[1] population 25 years and over	NHPIs[1] 25 years and over who are high school graduates	Asian Indian	Bangladeshi	Cambodian	Chinese[2]	Fijian	Filipino	Guamanian[3]	Hawaiian, Native	Hmong	Indonesian	Japanese	Korean	Laotian	Malaysian	Pakistani	Samoan	Sri Lankan	Taiwanese	Thai	Tongan	Vietnamese
	172,511	3,112	2,749	-	-	981	-	-	553	-	306	-	-	-	-	-	217	-	-	-	-	-	-	-	-	334
	83.25		88.34			93.97			87.78		97.14						87.85									74.72
Butler County						35.69			20.12		11.13						7.89									12.15
			88.34			31.52			17.77		9.83						6.97									10.73
			1.59			0.57			0.32		0.18						0.13									0.19
	77,416	398	352	-	-	-	-	-	-	-	-	-	-	-	-	-	-	-	-	-	-	-	-	-	-	-
	81.24		88.44																							
Clark County																										
			88.44																							
			0.45																							
	93,136	829	744	-	-	275	-	-	-	-	-	-	-	-	-	-	-	-	-	-	-	-	-	-	-	-
	82.05		89.75			92.91																				
Clermont County						36.96																				
			89.75			33.17																				
			0.80			0.30																				
	61,252	248	193	-	-	-	-	-	-	-	-	-	-	-	-	-	-	-	-	-	-	-	-	-	-	-
	80.57		77.82																							
Columbiana County																										
			77.82																							
			0.32																							
	764,186	17,649	15,035	-	-	5,549	-	107	3,342	-	2,046	-	-	-	-	860	1,135	-	-	-	-	-	-	-	-	787
	81.63		85.19			92.68		41.96	79.18		92.96					95.03	86.25									58.91
Cuyahoga County						36.91		0.71	22.23		13.61					5.72	7.55									5.23
			85.19			31.44		0.61	18.94		11.59					4.87	6.43									4.46
			1.97			0.73		0.01	0.44		0.27					0.11	0.15									0.10
	12,861	538	464	-	-	256	-	-	-	-	-	-	-	-	-	-	-	-	-	-	-	-	-	-	-	-
	85.77		86.25			94.81																				
Mayfield Heights (city)						55.17																				
			86.25			47.58																				
			3.61			1.99																				
	7,129	393	364	-	-	-	-	-	-	-	-	-	-	-	-	-	-	-	-	-	-	-	-	-	-	-
	89.34		92.62																							
Richmond Heights (city)																										
			92.62																							
			5.11																							
	13,375	693	660	-	-	299	-	-	220	-	-	-	-	-	-	-	-	-	-	-	-	-	-	-	-	-
	94.60		95.24			92.00			100.00																	
Solon (city)						45.30			33.33																	
			95.24			43.15			31.75																	
			4.93			2.24			1.64																	
	21,124	954	866	-	-	386	-	-	-	-	-	-	-	-	-	-	-	-	-	-	-	-	-	-	-	-
	92.14		90.78			98.22																				
Westlake (city)						44.57																				
			90.78			40.46																				
			4.10			1.83																				
	65,569	1,151	1,074	-	-	274	-	-	358	-	-	-	-	-	-	-	-	-	-	-	-	-	-	-	-	-
	92.85		93.31			90.43			98.08																	
Delaware County						25.51			33.33																	
			93.31			23.81			31.10																	
			1.64			0.42			0.55																	

Notes: Please refer to the User's Guide for an explanation of data; data is arranged alphabetically by state, then county, then city within each county; table includes counties with populations greater than 49,999 unless noted and cities with populations greater than 9,999 whose Asian and/or NHPI population rates are greater than the national average; (1) Native Hawaiian and other Pacific Islander; (2) excludes Taiwanese; (3) includes Chamorro; (4) county does not meet population threshold but is shown in order to allow inclusion of city

Place	Total population 25 years and over who are high school graduates	Asian population 25 years and over	Asians 25 years and over who are high school graduates	NHPI[1] population 25 years and over	NHPIs[1] 25 years and over who are high school graduates	Asian Indian	Bangladeshi	Cambodian	Chinese[2]	Fijian	Filipino	Guamanian[3]	Hawaiian, Native	Hmong	Indonesian	Japanese	Korean	Laotian	Malaysian	Pakistani	Samoan	Sri Lankan	Taiwanese	Thai	Tongan	Vietnamese
Fairfield County	70,037 87.60	512	450 87.89 87.89 0.64	-	-	-	-	-	-	-	-	-	-	-	-	-	-	-	-	-	-	-	-	-	-	-
Franklin County	579,896 85.74	20,437	17,546 85.85 85.85 3.03	169	156 92.31 92.31 0.03	4,880 92.21 27.81 23.88 0.84	-	297 47.29 1.69 1.45 0.05	4,244 86.63 24.19 20.77 0.73	-	1,098 88.05 6.26 5.37 0.19	-	-	-	111 100.00 0.63 0.54 0.02	1,959 97.37 11.16 9.59 0.34	1,928 90.52 10.99 9.43 0.33	369 57.84 2.10 1.81 0.06	-	231 89.53 1.32 1.13 0.04	-	-	470 95.92 2.68 2.30 0.08	239 87.23 1.36 1.17 0.04	-	944 62.81 5.38 4.62 0.16
Dublin (city)	19,179 97.27	1,546	1,464 94.70 94.70 7.63	-	-	422 100.00 28.83 27.30 2.20	-	-	268 89.04 18.31 17.34 1.40	-	-	-	-	-	-	491 96.27 33.54 31.76 2.56	-	-	-	-	-	-	-	-	-	-
Hilliard (city)	14,059 92.54	598	569 95.15 95.15 4.05	-	-	-	-	-	-	-	-	-	-	-	-	-	-	-	-	-	-	-	-	-	-	-
Geauga County	51,117 86.32	254	246 96.85 96.85 0.48	-	-	-	-	-	-	-	-	-	-	-	-	-	-	-	-	-	-	-	-	-	-	-
Greene County	81,185 87.85	1,963	1,626 82.83 82.83 2.00	-	-	530 86.60 32.60 27.00 0.65	-	-	252 91.30 15.50 12.84 0.31	-	-	-	-	-	-	-	307 76.37 18.88 15.64 0.38	-	-	-	-	-	-	-	-	-
Hamilton County	451,841 82.75	8,475	7,640 90.15 90.15 1.69	-	-	2,523 95.57 33.02 29.77 0.56	-	70 37.23 0.92 0.83 0.02	1,988 92.72 26.02 23.46 0.44	-	844 96.02 11.05 9.96 0.19	-	-	-	-	451 92.23 5.90 5.32 0.10	653 91.97 8.55 7.71 0.14	-	-	-	-	-	-	-	-	424 67.19 5.55 5.00 0.09
Blue Ash (city)	7,972 90.81	571	557 97.55 97.55 6.99	-	-	262 100.00 47.04 45.88 3.29	-	-	-	-	-	-	-	-	-	-	-	-	-	-	-	-	-	-	-	-
Sharonville (city)	8,560 87.85	378	349 92.33 92.33 4.08	-	-	240 96.39 68.77 63.49 2.80	-	-	-	-	-	-	-	-	-	-	-	-	-	-	-	-	-	-	-	-
Hancock County	40,563 88.43	443	423 95.49 95.49 1.04	-	-	-	-	-	-	-	-	-	-	-	-	-	-	-	-	-	-	-	-	-	-	-

Notes: Please refer to the User's Guide for an explanation of data; data is arranged alphabetically by state, then county, then city within each county; table includes counties with populations greater than 49,999 unless noted and cities with populations greater than 9,999 whose Asian and/or NHPI population rates are greater than the national average; (1) Native Hawaiian and other Pacific Islander; (2) excludes Taiwanese; (3) includes Chamorro; (4) county does not meet population threshold but is shown in order to allow inclusion of city

Place	Total population 25 years and over who are high school graduates	Asian population 25 years and over	Asians 25 years and over who are high school graduates	NHPI[1] population 25 years and over	NHPIs[1] 25 years and over who are high school graduates	Asian Indian	Bangladeshi	Cambodian	Chinese[2]	Fijian	Filipino	Guamanian[3]	Hawaiian, Native	Hmong	Indonesian	Japanese	Korean	Laotian	Malaysian	Pakistani	Samoan	Sri Lankan	Taiwanese	Thai	Tongan	Vietnamese
Lake County	134,958 86.41	1,557	1,361 87.41 87.41 1.01	-	-	434 93.94 31.89 27.87 0.32	-	-	333 92.24 24.47 21.39 0.25	-	-	-	-	-	-	-	-	-	-	-	-	-	-	-	-	-
Licking County	80,432 84.66	450	337 74.89 74.89 0.42	-	-	-	-	-	-	-	-	-	-	-	-	-	-	-	-	-	-	-	-	-	-	-
Lorain County	153,611 82.81	1,088	947 87.04 87.04 0.62	-	-	241 94.88 25.45 22.15 0.16	-	-	-	-	330 95.93 34.85 30.33 0.21	-	-	-	-	-	-	-	-	-	-	-	-	-	-	-
Lucas County	241,323 82.92	3,736	3,248 86.94 86.94 1.35	-	-	964 94.79 29.68 25.80 0.40	-	-	972 84.38 29.93 26.02 0.40	-	419 90.50 12.90 11.22 0.17	-	-	-	-	-	296 86.55 9.11 7.92 0.12	-	-	-	-	-	-	-	-	-
Mahoning County	144,100 82.44	683	573 83.89 83.89 0.40	-	-	-	-	-	-	-	-	-	-	-	-	-	-	-	-	-	-	-	-	-	-	-
Marion County	35,713 80.32	221	193 87.33 87.33 0.54	-	-	-	-	-	-	-	-	-	-	-	-	-	-	-	-	-	-	-	-	-	-	-
Medina County	87,918 88.80	738	652 88.35 88.35 0.74	-	-	251 88.69 38.50 34.01 0.29	-	-	-	-	-	-	-	-	-	-	-	-	-	-	-	-	-	-	-	-
Miami County	54,368 82.67	605	529 87.44 87.44 0.97	-	-	-	-	-	-	-	-	-	-	-	-	-	-	-	-	-	-	-	-	-	-	-
Montgomery County	306,504 83.49	4,771	4,183 87.68 87.68 1.36	-	-	1,319 92.76 31.53 27.65 0.43	-	-	677 89.43 16.18 14.19 0.22	-	474 89.10 11.33 9.94 0.15	-	-	-	-	424 95.07 10.14 8.89 0.14	420 80.15 10.04 8.80 0.14	-	-	-	-	-	-	-	-	478 74.69 11.43 10.02 0.16
Portage County	80,829 85.92	763	753 98.69 98.69 0.93	-	-	-	-	-	-	-	-	-	-	-	-	-	-	-	-	-	-	-	-	-	-	-

Notes: Please refer to the User's Guide for an explanation of data; data is arranged alphabetically by state, then county, then city within each county; table includes counties with populations greater than 49,999 unless noted and cities with populations greater than 9,999 whose Asian and/or NHPI population rates are greater than the national average; (1) Native Hawaiian and other Pacific Islander; (2) excludes Taiwanese; (3) includes Chamorro; (4) county does not meet population threshold but is shown in order to allow inclusion of city

Place	Total population 25 years and over who are high school graduates	Asian population 25 years and over	Asians 25 years and over who are high school graduates	NHPI[1] population 25 years and over	NHPIs[1] 25 years and over who are high school graduates	Asian Indian	Bangladeshi	Cambodian	Chinese[2]	Fijian	Filipino	Guamanian[3]	Hawaiian, Native	Hmong	Indonesian	Japanese	Korean	Laotian	Malaysian	Pakistani	Samoan	Sri Lankan	Taiwanese	Thai	Tongan	Vietnamese
Richland County	69,077 80.15	457	394 86.21 86.21 0.57	-	-	-	-	-	-	-	-	-	-	-	-	-	-	-	-	-	-	-	-	-	-	-
Stark County	211,059 83.43	1,269	1,002 78.96 78.96 0.47	-	-	253 84.33 25.25 19.94 0.12	-	-	208 85.25 20.76 16.39 0.10	-	-	-	-	-	-	-	-	-	-	-	-	-	-	-	-	-
Summit County	310,769 85.70	4,814	4,195 87.14 87.14 1.35	-	-	1,186 92.87 28.27 24.64 0.38	-	-	1,068 91.44 25.46 22.19 0.34	-	332 90.22 7.91 6.90 0.11	-	-	-	-	310 99.04 7.39 6.44 0.10	517 96.28 12.32 10.74 0.17	172 52.92 4.10 3.57 0.06	-	-	-	-	-	-	-	276 68.32 6.58 5.73 0.09
Trumbull County	126,250 82.49	682	531 77.86 77.86 0.42	-	-	-	-	-	-	-	-	-	-	-	-	-	-	-	-	-	-	-	-	-	-	-
Warren County	89,029 86.18	1,375	1,312 95.42 95.42 1.47	-	-	420 99.53 32.01 30.55 0.47	-	-	339 97.41 25.84 24.65 0.38	-	-	-	-	-	-	-	-	-	-	-	-	-	-	-	-	-
Wayne County	55,994 80.05	441	372 84.35 84.35 0.66	-	-	-	-	-	-	-	-	-	-	-	-	-	-	-	-	-	-	-	-	-	-	-
Wood County	63,401 88.61	750	634 84.53 84.53 1.00	-	-	-	-	-	-	-	-	-	-	-	-	-	-	-	-	-	-	-	-	-	-	-
OKLAHOMA	1,775,940 80.61	28,009	21,627 77.21 77.21 1.22	1,019	766 75.17 75.17 0.04	4,267 86.67 19.73 15.23 0.24	-	117 64.64 0.54 0.42 0.01	3,696 86.33 17.09 13.20 0.21	-	2,348 83.83 10.86 8.38 0.13	228 80.00 29.77 22.37 0.01	326 76.35 42.56 31.99 0.02	59 48.36 0.27 0.21 <0.01	-	1,646 87.14 7.61 5.88 0.09	2,263 75.18 10.46 8.08 0.13	258 55.97 1.19 0.92 0.01	174 95.08 0.80 0.62 0.01	537 87.18 2.48 1.92 0.03	-	-	270 96.77 1.25 0.96 0.02	395 63.81 1.83 1.41 0.02	-	4,627 61.94 21.39 16.52 0.26
Canadian County	49,060 87.28	1,258	951 75.60 75.60 1.94	-	-	536 79.17 56.36 42.61 1.09	-	-	-	-	-	-	-	-	-	-	-	-	-	-	-	-	-	-	-	233 67.15 24.50 18.52 0.47
Cleveland County	111,548 88.13	3,328	2,793 83.92 83.92 2.50	-	-	359 87.56 12.85 10.79 0.32	-	-	655 96.75 23.45 19.68 0.59	-	233 75.90 8.34 7.00 0.21	-	-	-	-	-	379 84.41 13.57 11.39 0.34	-	-	-	-	-	-	-	-	687 73.01 24.60 20.64 0.62

Notes: Please refer to the User's Guide for an explanation of data; data is arranged alphabetically by state, then county, then city within each county; table includes counties with populations greater than 49,999 unless noted and cities with populations greater than 9,999 whose Asian and/or NHPI population rates are greater than the national average; (1) Native Hawaiian and other Pacific Islander; (2) excludes Taiwanese; (3) includes Chamorro; (4) county does not meet population threshold but is shown in order to allow inclusion of city

Place	Total population 25 years and over who are high school graduates	Asian population 25 years and over	Asians 25 years and over who are high school graduates	NHPI[1] population 25 years and over	NHPIs[1] 25 years and over who are high school graduates	Asian Indian	Bangladeshi	Cambodian	Chinese[2]	Fijian	Filipino	Guamanian[3]	Hawaiian, Native	Hmong	Indonesian	Japanese	Korean	Laotian	Malaysian	Pakistani	Samoan	Sri Lankan	Taiwanese	Thai	Tongan	Vietnamese
Comanche County	57,240	1,677	1,220	-	-	-	-	-	-	-	323	-	-	-	-	-	386	-	-	-	-	-	-	-	-	-
	85.15		72.75								95.85						58.48									
											26.48						31.64									
			72.75								19.26						23.02									
			2.13								0.56						0.67									
Garfield County	31,295	350	223	-	-	-	-	-	-	-	-	-	-	-	-	-	-	-	-	-	-	-	-	-	-	-
	82.21		63.71																							
			63.71																							
			0.71																							
Muskogee County	33,693	210	174	-	-	-	-	-	-	-	-	-	-	-	-	-	-	-	-	-	-	-	-	-	-	-
	75.06		82.86																							
			82.86																							
			0.52																							
Oklahoma County	347,275	11,611	8,682	-	-	1,678	-	-	1,295	-	759	-	-	-	-	516	652	145	-	-	-	-	-	210	-	2,532
	82.52		74.77			89.97			85.88		87.54					89.12	80.10	49.83						68.40		58.33
						19.33			14.92		8.74					5.94	7.51	1.67						2.42		29.16
			74.77			14.45			11.15		6.54					4.44	5.62	1.25						1.81		21.81
			2.50			0.48			0.37		0.22					0.15	0.19	0.04						0.06		0.73
Payne County	32,296	919	877	-	-	-	-	-	298	-	-	-	-	-	-	-	-	-	-	-	-	-	-	-	-	-
	86.73		95.43						96.75																	
									33.98																	
			95.43						32.43																	
			2.72						0.92																	
Stillwater (city)	16,794	900	858	-	-	-	-	-	298	-	-	-	-	-	-	-	-	-	-	-	-	-	-	-	-	-
	91.60		95.33						96.75																	
									34.73																	
			95.33						33.11																	
			5.11						1.77																	
Pottawatomie County	32,608	207	174	-	-	-	-	-	-	-	-	-	-	-	-	-	-	-	-	-	-	-	-	-	-	-
	79.26		84.06																							
			84.06																							
			0.53																							
Tulsa County	305,677	5,234	4,091	-	-	1,057	-	-	848	-	271	-	-	-	-	-	440	-	-	202	-	-	-	-	-	788
	85.06		78.16			87.00			80.38		85.22						83.49			78.91						64.38
						25.84			20.73		6.62						10.76			4.94						19.26
			78.16			20.19			16.20		5.18						8.41			3.86						15.06
			1.34			0.35			0.28		0.09						0.14			0.07						0.26
Wagoner County	29,993	254	198	-	-	-	-	-	-	-	-	-	-	-	-	-	-	-	-	-	-	-	-	-	-	-
	81.29		77.95																							
			77.95																							
			0.66																							
OREGON	1,916,187	63,124	50,156	4,123	3,387	5,794	-	909	9,436	163	6,204	548	1,162	234	295	8,056	6,524	1,107	-	206	308	-	444	897	127	7,899
	85.13		79.46		82.15	90.66		56.49	75.43	74.09	85.27	85.89	86.91	54.93	91.61	94.32	85.52	56.71		96.26	81.05		95.28	82.90	74.27	65.43
						11.55		1.81	18.81	4.81	12.37	16.18	34.31	0.47	0.59	16.06	13.01	2.21		0.41	9.09		0.89	1.79	3.75	15.75
			79.46		82.15	9.18		1.44	14.95	3.95	9.83	13.29	28.18	0.37	0.47	12.76	10.34	1.75		0.33	7.47		0.70	1.42	3.08	12.51
			2.62		0.18	0.30		0.05	0.49	0.01	0.32	0.03	0.06	0.01	0.02	0.42	0.34	0.06		0.01	0.02		0.02	0.05	0.01	0.41

Notes: Please refer to the User's Guide for an explanation of data; data is arranged alphabetically by state, then county, then city within each county; table includes counties with populations greater than 49,999 unless noted and cities with populations greater than 9,999 whose Asian and/or NHPI population rates are greater than the national average; (1) Native Hawaiian and other Pacific Islander; (2) excludes Taiwanese; (3) includes Chamorro; (4) county does not meet population threshold but is shown in order to allow inclusion of city

Place	Total population 25 years and over who are high school graduates	Asian population 25 years and over	Asians 25 years and over who are high school graduates	NHPI[1] population 25 years and over	NHPIs[1] 25 years and over who are high school graduates	Asian Indian	Bangladeshi	Cambodian	Chinese[2]	Fijian	Filipino	Guamanian[3]	Hawaiian, Native	Hmong	Indonesian	Japanese	Korean	Laotian	Malaysian	Pakistani	Samoan	Sri Lankan	Taiwanese	Thai	Tongan	Vietnamese
Benton County	42,609	1,741	1,603	-	-	-	-	-	468	-	-	-	-	-	-	218	335	-	-	-	-	-	-	-	-	-
	93.12		92.07						89.66							95.61	97.95									
									29.20							13.60	20.90									
			92.07						26.88							12.52	19.24									
			3.76						1.10							0.51	0.79									
Corvallis (city)	24,681	1,543	1,410	-	-	-	-	-	447	-	-	-	-	-	-	-	297	-	-	-	-	-	-	-	-	-
	93.00		91.38						89.22								97.70									
									31.70								21.06									
			91.38						28.97								19.25									
			5.71						1.81								1.20									
Clackamas County	198,537	5,404	4,719	340	287	393	-	-	1,122	-	632	-	-	-	-	793	888	-	-	-	-	-	-	-	-	362
	88.95		87.32		84.41	89.52			89.26		93.91					94.29	87.06									66.18
						8.33			23.78		13.39					16.80	18.82									7.67
			87.32		84.41	7.27			20.76		11.70					14.67	16.43									6.70
			2.38		0.14	0.20			0.57		0.32					0.40	0.45									0.18
Lake Oswego (city)	24,054	1,025	1,001	-	-	-	-	-	266	-	-	-	-	-	-	-	-	-	-	-	-	-	-	-	-	-
	97.66		97.66						96.38																	
									26.57																	
			97.66						25.95																	
			4.16						1.11																	
Coos County	36,430	199	151	-	-	-	-	-	-	-	-	-	-	-	-	-	-	-	-	-	-	-	-	-	-	-
	81.56		75.88																							
			75.88																							
			0.41																							
Deschutes County	68,906	376	294	-	-	-	-	-	-	-	-	-	-	-	-	-	-	-	-	-	-	-	-	-	-	-
	88.36		78.19																							
			78.19																							
			0.43																							
Douglas County	55,698	413	345	-	-	-	-	-	-	-	-	-	-	-	-	-	-	-	-	-	-	-	-	-	-	-
	80.98		83.54																							
			83.54																							
			0.62																							
Jackson County	102,968	891	759	-	-	-	-	-	-	-	-	-	-	-	-	-	-	-	-	-	-	-	-	-	-	-
	84.99		85.19																							
			85.19																							
			0.74																							
Josephine County	43,682	273	189	-	-	-	-	-	-	-	-	-	-	-	-	-	-	-	-	-	-	-	-	-	-	-
	81.76		69.23																							
			69.23																							
			0.43																							
Klamath County	34,088	273	236	-	-	-	-	-	-	-	-	-	-	-	-	-	-	-	-	-	-	-	-	-	-	-
	81.49		86.45																							
			86.45																							
			0.69																							

Notes: Please refer to the User's Guide for an explanation of data; data is arranged alphabetically by state, then county, then city within each county; table includes counties with populations greater than 49,999 unless noted and cities with populations greater than 9,999 whose Asian and/or NHPI population rates are greater than the national average; (1) Native Hawaiian and other Pacific Islander; (2) excludes Taiwanese; (3) includes Chamorro; (4) county does not meet population threshold but is shown in order to allow inclusion of city

Place	Total population 25 years and over who are high school graduates	Asian population 25 years and over	Asians 25 years and over who are high school graduates	NHPI[1] population 25 years and over	NHPIs[1] 25 years and over who are high school graduates	Asian Indian	Bangladeshi	Cambodian	Chinese[2]	Fijian	Filipino	Guamanian[3]	Hawaiian, Native	Hmong	Indonesian	Japanese	Korean	Laotian	Malaysian	Pakistani	Samoan	Sri Lankan	Taiwanese	Thai	Tongan	Vietnamese
Lane County	184,336	3,322	2,924	299	225	276	-	-	569	-	303	-	-	-	-	750	568	-	-	-	-	-	-	-	-	-
	87.53		88.02		75.25	91.69			89.32		83.01					94.46	91.32									
						9.44			19.46		10.36					25.65	19.43									
			88.02		75.25	8.31			17.13		9.12					22.58	17.10									
			1.59		0.12	0.15			0.31		0.16					0.41	0.31									
Linn County	55,353	450	247	-	-	-	-	-	-	-	-	-	-	-	-	-	-	-	-	-	-	-	-	-	-	-
	81.88		54.89																							
			54.89																							
			0.45																							
Marion County	140,892	3,060	2,234	402	309	184	-	-	351	-	400	-	-	-	-	278	294	-	-	-	-	-	-	-	-	403
	79.29		73.01		76.87	81.42			63.24		79.37					89.10	79.25									74.77
						8.24			15.71		17.91					12.44	13.16									18.04
			73.01		76.87	6.01			11.47		13.07					9.08	9.61									13.17
			1.59		0.22	0.13			0.25		0.28					0.20	0.21									0.29
Salem (city)	70,300	2,077	1,456	207	158	-	-	-	287	-	200	-	-	-	-	156	-	-	-	-	-	-	-	-	-	242
	81.55		70.10		76.33				63.08		68.49					91.23										73.56
									19.71		13.74					10.71										16.62
			70.10		76.33				13.82		9.63					7.51										11.65
			2.07		0.22				0.41		0.28					0.22										0.34
Multnomah County	382,235	24,041	16,858	1,253	1,010	844	-	282	3,092	-	1,966	-	271	164	-	2,740	1,428	709	-	-	-	-	-	293	114	4,407
	85.64		70.12		80.61	76.87		52.22	64.20		85.22		91.86	50.93		95.44	81.18	52.48						85.42	89.76	59.43
						5.01		1.67	18.34		11.66		26.83	0.97		16.25	8.47	4.21						1.74	11.29	26.14
			70.12		80.61	3.51		1.17	12.86		8.18		21.63	0.68		11.40	5.94	2.95						1.22	9.10	18.33
			4.41		0.26	0.22		0.07	0.81		0.51		0.07	0.04		0.72	0.37	0.19						0.08	0.03	1.15
Portland (city)	311,725	21,756	14,896	994	804	696	-	267	2,779	-	1,598	-	201	137	-	2,320	1,195	638	-	-	-	-	-	260	107	4,176
	85.67		68.47		80.89	74.84		51.74	62.41		84.95		92.20	49.82		95.28	78.57	52.00						83.87	89.17	58.81
						4.67		1.79	18.66		10.73		25.00	0.92		15.57	8.02	4.28						1.75	13.31	28.03
			68.47		80.89	3.20		1.23	12.77		7.35		20.22	0.63		10.66	5.49	2.93						1.20	10.76	19.19
			4.78		0.26	0.22		0.09	0.89		0.51		0.06	0.04		0.74	0.38	0.20						0.08	0.03	1.34
Polk County	33,634	431	358	-	-	-	-	-	-	-	-	-	-	-	-	-	-	-	-	-	-	-	-	-	-	-
	85.46		83.06																							
			83.06																							
			1.06																							
Umatilla County	34,618	282	159	-	-	-	-	-	-	-	-	-	-	-	-	-	-	-	-	-	-	-	-	-	-	-
	77.77		56.38																							
			56.38																							
			0.46																							
Washington County	253,848	19,371	17,055	883	766	3,546	-	462	3,055	-	1,781	-	284	-	-	1,891	2,377	227	-	-	-	-	-	-	-	2,408
	88.91		88.04		86.75	97.71		64.98	89.15		85.91		88.20			98.70	87.07	64.12								77.48
						20.79		2.71	17.91		10.44		37.08			11.09	13.94	1.33								14.12
			88.04		86.75	18.31		2.39	15.77		9.19		32.16			9.76	12.27	1.17								12.43
			6.72		0.30	1.40		0.18	1.20		0.70		0.11			0.74	0.94	0.09								0.95
Aloha (cdp)	22,099	1,923	1,549	-	-	-	-	-	-	-	229	-	-	-	-	-	-	-	-	-	-	-	-	-	-	507
	86.14		80.55								92.34															74.01
											14.78															32.73
			80.55								11.91															26.37
			7.01								1.04															2.29

Notes: Please refer to the User's Guide for an explanation of data; data is arranged alphabetically by state, then county, then city within each county; table includes counties with populations greater than 49,999 unless noted and cities with populations greater than 9,999 whose Asian and/or NHPI population rates are greater than the national average; (1) Native Hawaiian and other Pacific Islander; (2) excludes Taiwanese; (3) includes Chamorro; (4) county does not meet population threshold but is shown in order to allow inclusion of city

Place	Total population 25 years and over who are high school graduates	Asian population 25 years and over	Asians 25 years and over who are high school graduates	NHPI[1] population 25 years and over	NHPIs[1] 25 years and over who are high school graduates	Asian Indian	Bangladeshi	Cambodian	Chinese[2]	Fijian	Filipino	Guamanian[3]	Hawaiian, Native	Hmong	Indonesian	Japanese	Korean	Laotian	Malaysian	Pakistani	Samoan	Sri Lankan	Taiwanese	Thai	Tongan	Vietnamese
Beaverton (city)	44,032	4,854	4,245	-	-	1,127	-	146	637	-	407	-	-	-	-	461	667	-	-	-	-	-	-	-	-	462
	90.03		87.45			97.16		61.34	86.31		84.27					100.00	82.45									78.84
						26.55		3.44	15.01		9.59					10.86	15.71									10.88
			87.45			23.22		3.01	13.12		8.38					9.50	13.74									9.52
			9.64			2.56		0.33	1.45		0.92					1.05	1.51									1.05
Cedar Mill (cdp)	7,690	696	641	-	-	-	-	-	-	-	-	-	-	-	-	-	-	-	-	-	-	-	-	-	-	-
	93.56		92.10																							
			92.10																							
			8.34																							
Hillsboro (city)	35,821	2,881	2,653	-	-	918	-	-	424	-	-	-	-	-	-	-	287	-	-	-	-	-	-	-	-	369
	84.23		92.09			98.39			94.43								85.93									82.37
						34.60			15.98								10.82									13.91
			92.09			31.86			14.72								9.96									12.81
			7.41			2.56			1.18								0.80									1.03
Tigard (city)	24,657	1,613	1,388	-	-	-	-	-	310	-	-	-	-	-	-	-	-	-	-	-	-	-	-	-	-	210
	90.84		86.05						82.01																	70.23
									22.33																	15.13
			86.05						19.22																	13.02
			5.63						1.26																	0.85
Tualatin (city)	13,248	626	568	-	-	-	-	-	-	-	-	-	-	-	-	-	-	-	-	-	-	-	-	-	-	-
	92.93		90.73																							
			90.73																							
			4.29																							
Yamhill County	43,581	542	389	-	-	-	-	-	-	-	-	-	-	-	-	-	-	-	-	-	-	-	-	-	-	-
	82.78		71.77																							
			71.77																							
			0.89																							
PENNSYLVANIA	6,770,179	132,374	103,777	2,029	1,557	30,570	351	1,523	23,086	-	9,285	275	464	123	320	4,534	17,001	588	-	1,507	359	232	1,365	964	-	9,578
	81.90		78.40		76.74	88.17	83.18	36.65	75.84		91.41	70.88	75.69	42.41	89.39	90.09	86.50	47.04		87.46	76.71	95.08	93.17	81.08		55.10
						29.46	0.34	1.47	22.25		8.95	17.66	29.80	0.12	0.31	4.37	16.38	0.57		1.45	23.06	0.22	1.32	0.93		9.23
			78.40		76.74	23.09	0.27	1.15	17.44		7.01	13.55	22.87	0.09	0.24	3.43	12.84	0.44		1.14	17.69	0.18	1.03	0.73		7.24
			1.53		0.02	0.45	0.01	0.02	0.34		0.14	<0.01	0.01	<0.01	<0.01	0.07	0.25	0.01		0.02	0.01	<0.01	0.02	0.01		0.14
Adams County	47,966	375	344	-	-	-	-	-	-	-	-	-	-	-	-	-	-	-	-	-	-	-	-	-	-	-
	79.71		91.73																							
			91.73																							
			0.72																							
Allegheny County	769,335	13,093	11,954	350	325	4,826	-	-	2,975	-	677	-	-	-	-	842	1,189	-	-	-	-	-	256	-	-	406
	86.33		91.30		92.86	96.71			90.23		90.75					95.90	92.82						96.24			53.35
						40.37			24.89		5.66					7.04	9.95						2.14			3.40
			91.30		92.86	36.86			22.72		5.17					6.43	9.08						1.96			3.10
			1.55		0.04	0.63			0.39		0.09					0.11	0.15						0.03			0.05
Muni. of Monroeville (borough)	19,275	779	729	-	-	432	-	-	-	-	-	-	-	-	-	-	-	-	-	-	-	-	-	-	-	-
	89.22		93.58			96.43																				
						59.26																				
			93.58			55.46																				
			3.78			2.24																				

Notes: Please refer to the User's Guide for an explanation of data; data is arranged alphabetically by state, then county, then city within each county; table includes counties with populations greater than 49,999 unless noted and cities with populations greater than 9,999 whose Asian and/or NHPI population rates are greater than the national average; (1) Native Hawaiian and other Pacific Islander; (2) excludes Taiwanese; (3) includes Chamorro; (4) county does not meet population threshold but is shown in order to allow inclusion of city

Place	Total population 25 years and over who are high school graduates	Asian population 25 years and over	Asians 25 years and over who are high school graduates	NHPI[1] population 25 years and over	NHPIs[1] 25 years and over who are high school graduates	Asian Indian	Bangladeshi	Cambodian	Chinese[2]	Fijian	Filipino	Guamanian[3]	Hawaiian, Native	Hmong	Indonesian	Japanese	Korean	Laotian	Malaysian	Pakistani	Samoan	Sri Lankan	Taiwanese	Thai	Tongan	Vietnamese
Scott (township)	11,612 87.73	740	740 100.00 100.00 6.37	-	-	647 100.00 87.43 87.43 5.57	-	-	-	-	-	-	-	-	-	-	-	-	-	-	-	-	-	-	-	-
Scott Township (cdp)	11,612 87.73	740	740 100.00 100.00 6.37	-	-	647 100.00 87.43 87.43 5.57	-	-	-	-	-	-	-	-	-	-	-	-	-	-	-	-	-	-	-	-
Upper St. Clair (township)	13,224 97.21	508	490 96.46 96.46 3.71	-	-	307 94.46 62.65 60.43 2.32	-	-	-	-	-	-	-	-	-	-	-	-	-	-	-	-	-	-	-	-
Beaver County	106,110 83.60	296	244 82.43 82.43 0.23	-	-	-	-	-	-	-	-	-	-	-	-	-	-	-	-	-	-	-	-	-	-	-
Berks County	194,213 78.04	2,252	1,562 69.36 69.36 0.80	-	-	426 79.33 27.27 18.92 0.22	-	-	292 82.25 18.69 12.97 0.15	-	-	-	-	-	-	-	168 84.00 10.76 7.46 0.09	-	-	-	-	-	-	-	-	298 44.15 19.08 13.23 0.15
Blair County	74,014 83.76	336	292 86.90 86.90 0.39	-	-	-	-	-	-	-	-	-	-	-	-	-	-	-	-	-	-	-	-	-	-	-
Bradford County	34,668 81.71	115	90 78.26 78.26 0.26	-	-	-	-	-	-	-	-	-	-	-	-	-	-	-	-	-	-	-	-	-	-	-
Bucks County	356,646 88.59	8,946	7,949 88.86 88.86 2.23	-	-	3,290 88.16 41.39 36.78 0.92	-	-	1,256 89.97 15.80 14.04 0.35	-	996 95.49 12.53 11.13 0.28	-	-	-	-	-	1,222 90.72 15.37 13.66 0.34	-	-	-	-	-	-	-	-	265 74.44 3.33 2.96 0.07
Bensalem (township)	33,495 84.31	2,481	2,154 86.82 86.82 6.43	-	-	1,081 82.96 50.19 43.57 3.23	-	-	-	-	-	-	-	-	-	-	402 88.16 18.66 16.20 1.20	-	-	-	-	-	-	-	-	-
Lower Makefield (township)	21,531 96.12	865	853 98.61 98.61 3.96	-	-	384 98.71 45.02 44.39 1.78	-	-	-	-	-	-	-	-	-	-	-	-	-	-	-	-	-	-	-	-

Notes: Please refer to the User's Guide for an explanation of data; data is arranged alphabetically by state, then county, then city within each county; table includes counties with populations greater than 49,999 unless noted and cities with populations greater than 9,999 whose Asian and/or NHPI population rates are greater than the national average; (1) Native Hawaiian and other Pacific Islander; (2) excludes Taiwanese; (3) includes Chamorro; (4) county does not meet population threshold but is shown in order to allow inclusion of city

Place	Total population 25 years and over who are high school graduates	Asian population 25 years and over	Asians 25 years and over who are high school graduates	NHPI[1] population 25 years and over	NHPIs[1] 25 years and over who are high school graduates	Asian Indian	Bangladeshi	Cambodian	Chinese[2]	Fijian	Filipino	Guamanian[3]	Hawaiian, Native	Hmong	Indonesian	Japanese	Korean	Laotian	Malaysian	Pakistani	Samoan	Sri Lankan	Taiwanese	Thai	Tongan	Vietnamese
Newtown (township)	11,652 95.82	540	510 94.44 94.44 4.38	-	-	-	-	-	-	-	-	-	-	-	-	-	-	-	-	-	-	-	-	-	-	-
Butler County	100,724 86.78	648	591 91.20 91.20 0.59	-	-	281 94.61 47.55 43.36 0.28	-	-	-	-	-	-	-	-	-	-	-	-	-	-	-	-	-	-	-	-
Cambria County	85,476 80.05	384	263 68.49 68.49 0.31	-	-	-	-	-	-	-	-	-	-	-	-	-	-	-	-	-	-	-	-	-	-	-
Centre County	65,954 88.19	2,814	2,703 96.06 96.06 4.10	-	-	582 95.25 21.53 20.68 0.88	-	-	1,014 97.41 37.51 36.03 1.54	-	-	-	-	-	-	-	512 95.70 18.94 18.19 0.78	-	-	-	-	-	-	-	-	-
Ferguson (township)	8,140 94.98	712	676 94.94 94.94 8.30	-	-	-	-	-	-	-	-	-	-	-	-	-	-	-	-	-	-	-	-	-	-	-
Patton (township)	6,062 94.48	298	285 95.64 95.64 4.70	-	-	-	-	-	-	-	-	-	-	-	-	-	-	-	-	-	-	-	-	-	-	-
State College (borough)	10,472 95.91	1,556	1,504 96.66 96.66 14.36	-	-	277 96.18 18.42 17.80 2.65	-	-	609 96.82 40.49 39.14 5.82	-	-	-	-	-	-	-	209 100.00 13.90 13.43 2.00	-	-	-	-	-	-	-	-	-
Chester County	255,240 89.30	5,656	5,253 92.87 92.87 2.06	-	-	1,836 97.66 34.95 32.46 0.72	-	-	1,469 95.95 27.96 25.97 0.58	-	385 100.00 7.33 6.81 0.15	-	-	-	-	268 95.71 5.10 4.74 0.10	517 86.89 9.84 9.14 0.20	-	-	-	-	-	-	-	-	452 75.46 8.60 7.99 0.18
Tredyffrin (township)	20,198 96.16	1,143	1,094 95.71 95.71 5.42	-	-	411 100.00 37.57 35.96 2.03	-	-	423 97.47 38.67 37.01 2.09	-	-	-	-	-	-	-	-	-	-	-	-	-	-	-	-	-
West Goshen (township)	13,009 94.22	562	509 90.57 90.57 3.91	-	-	-	-	-	-	-	-	-	-	-	-	-	-	-	-	-	-	-	-	-	-	-

Notes: Please refer to the User's Guide for an explanation of data; data is arranged alphabetically by state, then county, then city within each county; table includes counties with populations greater than 49,999 unless noted and cities with populations greater than 9,999 whose Asian and/or NHPI population rates are greater than the national average; (1) Native Hawaiian and other Pacific Islander; (2) excludes Taiwanese; (3) includes Chamorro; (4) county does not meet population threshold but is shown in order to allow inclusion of city

Place	Total population 25 years and over who are high school graduates	Asian population 25 years and over	Asians 25 years and over who are high school graduates	NHPI[1] population 25 years and over	NHPIs[1] 25 years and over who are high school graduates	Asian Indian	Bangladeshi	Cambodian	Chinese[2]	Fijian	Filipino	Guamanian[3]	Hawaiian, Native	Hmong	Indonesian	Japanese	Korean	Laotian	Malaysian	Pakistani	Samoan	Sri Lankan	Taiwanese	Thai	Tongan	Vietnamese
West Whiteland (township)	10,864 94.80	416	366 87.98 87.98 3.37	-	-	-	-	-	-	-	-	-	-	-	-	-	-	-	-	-	-	-	-	-	-	-
Clearfield County	45,986 79.10	188	170 90.43 90.43 0.37	-	-	-	-	-	-	-	-	-	-	-	-	-	-	-	-	-	-	-	-	-	-	-
Columbia County	33,583 80.62	198	169 85.35 85.35 0.50	-	-	-	-	-	-	-	-	-	-	-	-	-	-	-	-	-	-	-	-	-	-	-
Crawford County	48,675 81.55	186	152 81.72 81.72 0.31	-	-	-	-	-	-	-	-	-	-	-	-	-	-	-	-	-	-	-	-	-	-	-
Cumberland County	124,154 86.09	2,089	1,708 81.76 81.76 1.38	-	-	584 89.02 34.19 27.96 0.47	-	-	270 80.36 15.81 12.92 0.22	-	-	-	-	-	-	-	354 80.45 20.73 16.95 0.29	-	-	-	-	-	-	-	-	215 65.15 12.59 10.29 0.17
Hampden (township)	15,753 93.06	547	439 80.26 80.26 2.79	-	-	-	-	-	-	-	-	-	-	-	-	-	-	-	-	-	-	-	-	-	-	-
Dauphin County	143,236 83.38	3,245	2,404 74.08 74.08 1.68	-	-	618 88.67 25.71 19.04 0.43	-	-	470 80.90 19.55 14.48 0.33	-	-	-	-	-	-	-	212 95.07 8.82 6.53 0.15	-	-	-	-	-	-	-	-	641 56.83 26.66 19.75 0.45
Derry (township)	13,721 91.28	583	493 84.56 84.56 3.59	-	-	-	-	-	-	-	-	-	-	-	-	-	-	-	-	-	-	-	-	-	-	-
Hershey (cdp)	8,265 89.18	368	285 77.45 77.45 3.45	-	-	-	-	-	-	-	-	-	-	-	-	-	-	-	-	-	-	-	-	-	-	-
Delaware County	315,948 86.52	11,411	9,297 81.47 81.47 2.94	-	-	2,748 83.91 29.56 24.08 0.87	-	-	1,874 79.51 20.16 16.42 0.59	-	735 92.34 7.91 6.44 0.23	-	-	-	-	393 90.34 4.23 3.44 0.12	1,828 86.55 19.66 16.02 0.58	-	-	327 86.51 3.52 2.87 0.10	-	-	-	-	-	744 62.05 8.00 6.52 0.24

Notes: Please refer to the User's Guide for an explanation of data; data is arranged alphabetically by state, then county, then city within each county; table includes counties with populations greater than 49,999 unless noted and cities with populations greater than 9,999 whose Asian and/or NHPI population rates are greater than the national average; (1) Native Hawaiian and other Pacific Islander; (2) excludes Taiwanese; (3) includes Chamorro; (4) county does not meet population threshold but is shown in order to allow inclusion of city

Place	Total population 25 years and over who are high school graduates	Asian population 25 years and over	Asians 25 years and over who are high school graduates	NHPI[1] population 25 years and over	NHPIs[1] 25 years and over who are high school graduates	Asian Indian	Bangladeshi	Cambodian	Chinese[2]	Fijian	Filipino	Guamanian[3]	Hawaiian, Native	Hmong	Indonesian	Japanese	Korean	Laotian	Malaysian	Pakistani	Samoan	Sri Lankan	Taiwanese	Thai	Tongan	Vietnamese
Broomall (cdp)	6,972 86.79	495	430 86.87 86.87 6.17	-	-	-	-	-	-	-	-	-	-	-	-	-	240 82.47 55.81 48.48 3.44	-	-	-	-	-	-	-	-	-
Drexel Hill (cdp)	18,274 90.72	765	700 91.50 91.50 3.83	-	-	-	-	-	251 95.44 35.86 32.81 1.37	-	-	-	-	-	-	-	-	-	-	-	-	-	-	-	-	-
Marple (township)	15,035 88.03	836	704 84.21 84.21 4.68	-	-	-	-	-	-	-	-	-	-	-	-	-	360 84.31 51.14 43.06 2.39	-	-	-	-	-	-	-	-	-
Radnor (township)	16,546 95.05	914	890 97.37 97.37 5.38	-	-	-	-	-	232 94.31 26.07 25.38 1.40	-	-	-	-	-	-	-	-	-	-	-	-	-	-	-	-	-
Upper Darby (township)	46,341 85.44	4,525	3,304 73.02 73.02 7.13	-	-	988 79.49 29.90 21.83 2.13	-	-	698 66.54 21.13 15.43 1.51	-	-	-	-	-	-	-	540 82.07 16.34 11.93 1.17	-	-	-	-	-	-	-	-	428 57.37 12.95 9.46 0.92
Erie County	152,458 84.65	1,047	880 84.05 84.05 0.58	-	-	287 94.10 32.61 27.41 0.19	-	-	-	-	-	-	-	-	-	-	-	-	-	-	-	-	-	-	-	-
Franklin County	69,422 78.93	459	374 81.48 81.48 0.54	-	-	-	-	-	-	-	-	-	-	-	-	-	-	-	-	-	-	-	-	-	-	-
Indiana County	45,382 81.05	407	317 77.89 77.89 0.70	-	-	-	-	-	-	-	-	-	-	-	-	-	-	-	-	-	-	-	-	-	-	-
Lackawanna County	121,477 82.01	1,033	824 79.77 79.77 0.68	-	-	292 78.49 35.44 28.27 0.24	-	-	-	-	-	-	-	-	-	-	-	-	-	-	-	-	-	-	-	-
Lancaster County	234,021 77.36	3,687	2,412 65.42 65.42 1.03	-	-	400 93.02 16.58 10.85 0.17	-	-	424 54.01 17.58 11.50 0.18	-	-	-	-	63 37.28 2.61 1.71 0.03	-	-	133 62.44 5.51 3.61 0.06	-	-	-	-	-	-	-	-	845 65.15 35.03 22.92 0.36

Notes: Please refer to the User's Guide for an explanation of data; data is arranged alphabetically by state, then county, then city within each county; table includes counties with populations greater than 49,999 unless noted and cities with populations greater than 9,999 whose Asian and/or NHPI population rates are greater than the national average; (1) Native Hawaiian and other Pacific Islander; (2) excludes Taiwanese; (3) includes Chamorro; (4) county does not meet population threshold but is shown in order to allow inclusion of city

Place	Total population 25 years and over who are high school graduates	Asian population 25 years and over	Asians 25 years and over who are high school graduates	NHPI[1] population 25 years and over	NHPIs[1] 25 years and over who are high school graduates	Asian Indian	Bangladeshi	Cambodian	Chinese[2]	Fijian	Filipino	Guamanian[3]	Hawaiian, Native	Hmong	Indonesian	Japanese	Korean	Laotian	Malaysian	Pakistani	Samoan	Sri Lankan	Taiwanese	Thai	Tongan	Vietnamese
Lawrence County	52,834 81.58	184	167 90.76 90.76 0.32	-	-	-	-	-	-	-	-	-	-	-	-	-	-	-	-	-	-	-	-	-	-	-
Lebanon County	64,466 78.61	686	536 78.13 78.13 0.83	-	-	-	-	-	-	-	-	-	-	-	-	-	-	-	-	-	-	-	-	-	-	-
Lehigh County	172,561 81.14	4,472	3,622 80.99 80.99 2.10	-	-	1,328 89.79 36.66 29.70 0.77	-	-	961 88.49 26.53 21.49 0.56	-	-	-	-	-	-	-	332 76.32 9.17 7.42 0.19	-	-	-	-	-	-	-	-	488 57.62 13.47 10.91 0.28
Fullerton (cdp)	8,488 82.32	458	430 93.89 93.89 5.07	-	-	-	-	-	-	-	-	-	-	-	-	-	-	-	-	-	-	-	-	-	-	-
Lower Macungie (township)	12,205 91.23	557	517 92.82 92.82 4.24	-	-	-	-	-	247 92.86 47.78 44.34 2.02	-	-	-	-	-	-	-	-	-	-	-	-	-	-	-	-	-
Upper Macungie (township)	8,208 85.89	414	414 100.00 100.00 5.04	-	-	-	-	-	-	-	-	-	-	-	-	-	-	-	-	-	-	-	-	-	-	-
Luzerne County	183,484 81.05	927	767 82.74 82.74 0.42	-	-	265 93.64 34.55 28.59 0.14	-	-	-	-	-	-	-	-	-	-	-	-	-	-	-	-	-	-	-	-
Lycoming County	64,864 80.58	310	243 78.39 78.39 0.37	-	-	-	-	-	-	-	-	-	-	-	-	-	-	-	-	-	-	-	-	-	-	-
Mercer County	67,603 82.95	396	302 76.26 76.26 0.45	-	-	-	-	-	-	-	-	-	-	-	-	-	-	-	-	-	-	-	-	-	-	-
Monroe County	75,271 83.83	851	746 87.66 87.66 0.99	-	-	182 83.49 24.40 21.39 0.24	-	-	-	-	-	-	-	-	-	-	-	-	-	-	-	-	-	-	-	-

Notes: Please refer to the User's Guide for an explanation of data; data is arranged alphabetically by state, then county, then city within each county; table includes counties with populations greater than 49,999 unless noted and cities with populations greater than 9,999 whose Asian and/or NHPI population rates are greater than the national average; (1) Native Hawaiian and other Pacific Islander; (2) excludes Taiwanese; (3) includes Chamorro; (4) county does not meet population threshold but is shown in order to allow inclusion of city

Place	Total population 25 years and over who are high school graduates	Asian population 25 years and over	Asians 25 years and over who are high school graduates	NHPI[1] population 25 years and over	NHPIs[1] 25 years and over who are high school graduates	Asian Indian	Bangladeshi	Cambodian	Chinese[2]	Fijian	Filipino	Guamanian[3]	Hawaiian, Native	Hmong	Indonesian	Japanese	Korean	Laotian	Malaysian	Pakistani	Samoan	Sri Lankan	Taiwanese	Thai	Tongan	Vietnamese
Montgomery County	456,564 88.50	18,943	16,737 88.35 88.35 3.67	-	-	4,318 91.15 25.80 22.79 0.95	-	-	3,234 89.58 19.32 17.07 0.71	-	1,346 96.28 8.04 7.11 0.29	-	-	-	-	479 92.29 2.86 2.53 0.10	5,443 91.25 32.52 28.73 1.19	-	-	-	-	-	-	-	-	921 62.65 5.50 4.86 0.20
Cheltenham (township)	23,364 91.99	1,551	1,457 93.94 93.94 6.24	-	-	-	-	-	-	-	-	-	-	-	-	-	732 96.32 50.24 47.20 3.13	-	-	-	-	-	-	-	-	-
East Norriton (township)	8,652 87.19	424	357 84.20 84.20 4.13	-	-	-	-	-	-	-	-	-	-	-	-	-	-	-	-	-	-	-	-	-	-	-
Hatfield (township)	9,791 88.34	1,126	869 77.18 77.18 8.88	-	-	501 84.77 57.65 44.49 5.12	-	-	-	-	-	-	-	-	-	-	-	-	-	-	-	-	-	-	-	-
Horsham (township)	14,788 92.03	746	698 93.57 93.57 4.72	-	-	-	-	-	-	-	-	-	-	-	-	-	313 91.52 44.84 41.96 2.12	-	-	-	-	-	-	-	-	-
King of Prussia (cdp)	12,789 93.49	1,366	1,277 93.48 93.48 9.99	-	-	522 94.22 40.88 38.21 4.08	-	-	274 97.86 21.46 20.06 2.14	-	-	-	-	-	-	-	-	-	-	-	-	-	-	-	-	-
Lansdale (borough)	9,255 83.06	804	585 72.76 72.76 6.32	-	-	229 81.21 39.15 28.48 2.47	-	-	-	-	-	-	-	-	-	-	-	-	-	-	-	-	-	-	-	-
Lower Gwynedd (township)	6,851 92.66	266	260 97.74 97.74 3.80	-	-	-	-	-	-	-	-	-	-	-	-	-	-	-	-	-	-	-	-	-	-	-
Lower Providence (township)	13,135 87.49	672	637 94.79 94.79 4.85	-	-	-	-	-	294 94.84 46.15 43.75 2.24	-	-	-	-	-	-	-	-	-	-	-	-	-	-	-	-	-
Montgomery (township)	13,791 92.82	1,160	1,010 87.07 87.07 7.32	-	-	271 86.86 26.83 23.36 1.97	-	-	-	-	-	-	-	-	-	-	418 83.60 41.39 36.03 3.03	-	-	-	-	-	-	-	-	-

Notes: Please refer to the User's Guide for an explanation of data; data is arranged alphabetically by state, then county, then city within each county; table includes counties with populations greater than 49,999 unless noted and cities with populations greater than 9,999 whose Asian and/or NHPI population rates are greater than the national average; (1) Native Hawaiian and other Pacific Islander; (2) excludes Taiwanese; (3) includes Chamorro; (4) county does not meet population threshold but is shown in order to allow inclusion of city

Place	Total population 25 years and over who are high school graduates	Asian population 25 years and over	Asians 25 years and over who are high school graduates	NHPI[1] population 25 years and over	NHPIs[1] 25 years and over who are high school graduates	Asian Indian	Bangladeshi	Cambodian	Chinese[2]	Fijian	Filipino	Guamanian[3]	Hawaiian, Native	Hmong	Indonesian	Japanese	Korean	Laotian	Malaysian	Pakistani	Samoan	Sri Lankan	Taiwanese	Thai	Tongan	Vietnamese
Montgomeryville (cdp)	7,281 93.19	504	417 82.74 82.74 5.73	-	-	-	-	-	-	-	-	-	-	-	-	-	-	-	-	-	-	-	-	-	-	-
Plymouth (township)	10,076 86.27	632	569 90.03 90.03 5.65	-	-	-	-	-	-	-	-	-	-	-	-	-	232 92.43 40.77 36.71 2.30	-	-	-	-	-	-	-	-	-
Towamencin (township)	11,106 91.90	670	590 88.06 88.06 5.31	-	-	-	-	-	-	-	-	-	-	-	-	-	-	-	-	-	-	-	-	-	-	-
Upper Dublin (township)	16,229 92.77	967	881 91.11 91.11 5.43	-	-	-	-	-	-	-	-	-	-	-	-	-	419 87.11 47.56 43.33 2.58	-	-	-	-	-	-	-	-	-
Upper Gwynedd (township)	9,229 92.29	754	667 88.46 88.46 7.23	-	-	-	-	-	170 91.40 25.49 22.55 1.84	-	-	-	-	-	-	-	-	-	-	-	-	-	-	-	-	-
Upper Merion (township)	18,420 93.02	1,534	1,445 94.20 94.20 7.84	-	-	605 94.98 41.87 39.44 3.28	-	-	306 98.08 21.18 19.95 1.66	-	-	-	-	-	-	-	-	-	-	-	-	-	-	-	-	-
Whitpain (township)	12,220 94.04	796	744 93.47 93.47 6.09	-	-	-	-	-	-	-	-	-	-	-	-	-	340 93.92 45.70 42.71 2.78	-	-	-	-	-	-	-	-	-
Northampton County	145,288 80.71	2,111	1,857 87.97 87.97 1.28	-	-	626 92.33 33.71 29.65 0.43	-	-	396 96.12 21.32 18.76 0.27	-	-	-	-	-	-	-	186 88.57 10.02 8.81 0.13	-	-	-	-	-	-	-	-	156 65.55 8.40 7.39 0.11
Northumberland County	52,229 77.82	255	212 83.14 83.14 0.41	-	-	-	-	-	-	-	-	-	-	-	-	-	-	-	-	-	-	-	-	-	-	-
Philadelphia County	688,107 71.22	38,394	24,136 62.86 62.86 3.51	383	286 74.67 74.67 0.04	5,466 77.86 22.65 14.24 0.79	-	959 32.39 3.97 2.50 0.14	6,395 58.02 26.50 16.66 0.93	-	2,293 89.08 9.50 5.97 0.33	-	-	-	-	751 92.37 3.11 1.96 0.11	3,285 80.34 13.61 8.56 0.48	276 41.19 1.14 0.72 0.04	-	288 77.01 1.19 0.75 0.04	-	-	-	-	-	3,009 44.84 12.47 7.84 0.44

Notes: Please refer to the User's Guide for an explanation of data; data is arranged alphabetically by state, then county, then city within each county; table includes counties with populations greater than 49,999 unless noted and cities with populations greater than 9,999 whose Asian and/or NHPI population rates are greater than the national average; (1) Native Hawaiian and other Pacific Islander; (2) excludes Taiwanese; (3) includes Chamorro; (4) county does not meet population threshold but is shown in order to allow inclusion of city

Place	Total population 25 years and over who are high school graduates	Asian population 25 years and over	Asians 25 years and over who are high school graduates	NHPI[1] population 25 years and over	NHPIs[1] 25 years and over who are high school graduates	Asian Indian	Bangladeshi	Cambodian	Chinese[2]	Fijian	Filipino	Guamanian[3]	Hawaiian, Native	Hmong	Indonesian	Japanese	Korean	Laotian	Malaysian	Pakistani	Samoan	Sri Lankan	Taiwanese	Thai	Tongan	Vietnamese
Philadelphia (city)	688,107 71.22	38,394	24,136 62.86 62.86 3.51	383	286 74.67 74.67 0.04	5,466 77.86 22.65 14.24 0.79	-	959 32.39 3.97 2.50 0.14	6,395 58.02 26.50 16.66 0.93	-	2,293 89.08 9.50 5.97 0.33	-	-	-	-	751 92.37 3.11 1.96 0.11	3,285 80.34 13.61 8.56 0.48	276 41.19 1.14 0.72 0.04	-	288 77.01 1.19 0.75 0.04	-	-	-	-	-	3,009 44.84 12.47 7.84 0.44
Schuylkill County	83,343 77.16	375	288 76.80 76.80 0.35	-	-	-	-	-	-	-	-	-	-	-	-	-	-	-	-	-	-	-	-	-	-	-
Washington County	117,457 82.65	337	298 88.43 88.43 0.25	-	-	-	-	-	-	-	-	-	-	-	-	-	-	-	-	-	-	-	-	-	-	-
Westmoreland County	225,525 85.56	1,021	867 84.92 84.92 0.38	-	-	235 95.53 27.10 23.02 0.10	-	-	-	-	-	-	-	-	-	-	-	-	-	-	-	-	-	-	-	-
York County	209,046 80.70	1,890	1,421 75.19 75.19 0.68	-	-	322 91.22 22.66 17.04 0.15	-	-	271 62.59 19.07 14.34 0.13	-	-	-	-	-	-	-	224 75.68 15.76 11.85 0.11	-	-	-	-	-	-	-	-	237 69.71 16.68 12.54 0.11
RHODE ISLAND	541,487 77.96	12,863	8,901 69.20 69.20 1.64	213	123 57.75 57.75 0.02	1,269 88.00 14.26 9.87 0.23	-	1,082 45.75 12.16 8.41 0.20	1,913 75.85 21.49 14.87 0.35	-	1,303 83.42 14.64 10.13 0.24	-	-	181 62.20 2.03 1.41 0.03	-	529 92.00 5.94 4.11 0.10	862 92.00 9.68 6.70 0.16	709 42.23 7.97 5.51 0.13	-	-	-	-	-	-	-	389 64.83 4.37 3.02 0.07
Bristol County	27,616 80.71	207	196 94.69 94.69 0.71	-	-	-	-	-	-	-	-	-	-	-	-	-	-	-	-	-	-	-	-	-	-	-
Kent County	97,845 83.89	1,374	1,150 83.70 83.70 1.18	-	-	-	-	-	178 74.17 15.48 12.95 0.18	-	-	-	-	-	-	-	177 83.10 15.39 12.88 0.18	-	-	-	-	-	-	-	-	-
Newport County	51,837 87.73	643	518 80.56 80.56 1.00	-	-	-	-	-	-	-	272 83.44 52.51 42.30 0.52	-	-	-	-	-	-	-	-	-	-	-	-	-	-	-
Providence County	292,566 72.46	9,556	6,146 64.32 64.32 2.10	-	-	865 87.73 14.07 9.05 0.30	-	1,007 44.44 16.38 10.54 0.34	1,263 73.99 20.55 13.22 0.43	-	655 81.47 10.66 6.85 0.22	-	-	164 65.86 2.67 1.72 0.06	-	-	558 95.88 9.08 5.84 0.19	676 41.65 11.00 7.07 0.23	-	-	-	-	-	-	-	281 59.53 4.57 2.94 0.10

Notes: Please refer to the User's Guide for an explanation of data; data is arranged alphabetically by state, then county, then city within each county; table includes counties with populations greater than 49,999 unless noted and cities with populations greater than 9,999 whose Asian and/or NHPI population rates are greater than the national average; (1) Native Hawaiian and other Pacific Islander; (2) excludes Taiwanese; (3) includes Chamorro; (4) county does not meet population threshold but is shown in order to allow inclusion of city

Place	Total population 25 years and over who are high school graduates	Asian population 25 years and over	Asians 25 years and over who are high school graduates	NHPI[1] population 25 years and over	NHPIs[1] 25 years and over who are high school graduates	Asian Indian	Bangladeshi	Cambodian	Chinese[2]	Fijian	Filipino	Guamanian[3]	Hawaiian, Native	Hmong	Indonesian	Japanese	Korean	Laotian	Malaysian	Pakistani	Samoan	Sri Lankan	Taiwanese	Thai	Tongan	Vietnamese
Providence (city)	63,250 65.78	4,899	2,915 59.50 59.50 4.61	-	-	372 86.11 12.76 7.59 0.59	-	662 40.49 22.71 13.51 1.05	478 76.48 16.40 9.76 0.76	-	286 79.01 9.81 5.84 0.45	-	-	125 72.67 4.29 2.55 0.20	-	-	281 100.00 9.64 5.74 0.44	287 36.10 9.85 5.86 0.45	-	-	-	-	-	-	-	-
Woonsocket (city)	17,977 63.95	906	422 46.58 46.58 2.35	-	-	-	-	-	-	-	-	-	-	-	-	-	-	201 39.26 47.63 22.19 1.12	-	-	-	-	-	-	-	-
Washington County	71,623 88.57	1,083	891 82.27 82.27 1.24	-	-	-	-	-	261 82.59 29.29 24.10 0.36	-	-	-	-	-	-	-	-	-	-	-	-	-	-	-	-	-
SOUTH CAROLINA	1,981,731 76.34	23,216	18,462 79.52 79.52 0.93	875	634 72.46 72.46 0.03	4,227 87.61 22.90 18.21 0.21	-	92 49.20 0.50 0.40 <0.01	3,248 80.70 17.59 13.99 0.16	-	3,864 83.13 20.93 16.64 0.19	154 64.17 24.29 17.60 0.01	285 79.17 44.95 32.57 0.01	125 38.46 0.68 0.54 0.01	-	1,649 91.05 8.93 7.10 0.08	2,010 80.27 10.89 8.66 0.10	423 61.39 2.29 1.82 0.02	-	-	-	-	-	436 73.77 2.36 1.88 0.02	-	1,427 57.91 7.73 6.15 0.07
Aiken County	72,217 77.72	627	468 74.64 74.64 0.65	-	-	-	-	-	-	-	-	-	-	-	-	-	-	-	-	-	-	-	-	-	-	-
Anderson County	81,454 73.36	480	388 80.83 80.83 0.48	-	-	-	-	-	-	-	-	-	-	-	-	-	-	-	-	-	-	-	-	-	-	-
Beaufort County	68,957 87.84	628	538 85.67 85.67 0.78	-	-	-	-	-	-	-	-	-	-	-	-	-	-	-	-	-	-	-	-	-	-	-
Berkeley County	68,978 80.19	1,978	1,488 75.23 75.23 2.16	-	-	-	-	-	-	-	1,024 80.38 68.82 51.77 1.48	-	-	-	-	-	-	-	-	-	-	-	-	-	-	-
Charleston County	162,509 81.51	2,202	1,769 80.34 80.34 1.09	-	-	319 84.39 18.03 14.49 0.20	-	-	350 80.83 19.79 15.89 0.22	-	461 79.62 26.06 20.94 0.28	-	-	-	-	-	-	-	-	-	-	-	-	-	-	-
Dorchester County	50,405 82.18	857	739 86.23 86.23 1.47	-	-	-	-	-	-	-	340 82.73 46.01 39.67 0.67	-	-	-	-	-	-	-	-	-	-	-	-	-	-	-

Notes: Please refer to the User's Guide for an explanation of data; data is arranged alphabetically by state, then county, then city within each county; table includes counties with populations greater than 49,999 unless noted and cities with populations greater than 9,999 whose Asian and/or NHPI population rates are greater than the national average; (1) Native Hawaiian and other Pacific Islander; (2) excludes Taiwanese; (3) includes Chamorro; (4) county does not meet population threshold but is shown in order to allow inclusion of city

Place	Total population 25 years and over who are high school graduates	Asian population 25 years and over	Asians 25 years and over who are high school graduates	NHPI[1] population 25 years and over	NHPIs[1] 25 years and over who are high school graduates	Asian Indian	Bangladeshi	Cambodian	Chinese[2]	Fijian	Filipino	Guamanian[3]	Hawaiian, Native	Hmong	Indonesian	Japanese	Korean	Laotian	Malaysian	Pakistani	Samoan	Sri Lankan	Taiwanese	Thai	Tongan	Vietnamese
Florence County	59,152 73.11	715	661 92.45 92.45 1.12	-	-	-	-	-	-	-	-	-	-	-	-	-	-	-	-	-	-	-	-	-	-	-
Greenville County	198,846 79.46	3,265	2,657 81.38 81.38 1.34	-	-	792 86.65 29.81 24.26 0.40	-	-	402 91.78 15.13 12.31 0.20	-	332 93.26 12.50 10.17 0.17	-	-	-	-	-	-	-	-	-	-	-	-	-	-	513 62.56 19.31 15.71 0.26
Greenwood County	31,020 73.14	252	218 86.51 86.51 0.70	-	-	-	-	-	-	-	-	-	-	-	-	-	-	-	-	-	-	-	-	-	-	-
Horry County	110,808 81.15	1,083	785 72.48 72.48 0.71	-	-	-	-	-	-	-	-	-	-	-	-	-	-	-	-	-	-	-	-	-	-	-
Lexington County	117,936 83.01	1,248	1,073 85.98 85.98 0.91	-	-	356 93.44 33.18 28.53 0.30	-	-	259 82.48 24.14 20.75 0.22	-	-	-	-	-	-	-	-	-	-	-	-	-	-	-	-	-
Oconee County	33,901 73.86	213	182 85.45 85.45 0.54	-	-	-	-	-	-	-	-	-	-	-	-	-	-	-	-	-	-	-	-	-	-	-
Pickens County	49,189 73.65	729	679 93.14 93.14 1.38	-	-	157 100.00 23.12 21.54 0.32	-	-	282 100.00 41.53 38.68 0.57	-	-	-	-	-	-	-	-	-	-	-	-	-	-	-	-	-
Clemson (city)	5,400 91.39	253	242 95.65 95.65 4.48	-	-	-	-	-	-	-	-	-	-	-	-	-	-	-	-	-	-	-	-	-	-	-
Richland County	169,197 85.15	3,444	2,898 84.15 84.15 1.71	-	-	752 95.55 25.95 21.84 0.44	-	-	596 81.98 20.57 17.31 0.35	-	295 98.33 10.18 8.57 0.17	-	-	-	-	-	702 78.26 24.22 20.38 0.41	-	-	-	-	-	-	-	-	192 68.82 6.63 5.57 0.11
Spartanburg County	122,659 73.10	2,352	1,631 69.35 69.35 1.33	-	-	417 82.25 25.57 17.73 0.34	-	-	-	-	-	-	-	111 37.50 6.81 4.72 0.09	-	-	-	240 71.01 14.71 10.20 0.20	-	-	-	-	-	-	-	-

Notes: Please refer to the User's Guide for an explanation of data; data is arranged alphabetically by state, then county, then city within each county; table includes counties with populations greater than 49,999 unless noted and cities with populations greater than 9,999 whose Asian and/or NHPI population rates are greater than the national average; (1) Native Hawaiian and other Pacific Islander; (2) excludes Taiwanese; (3) includes Chamorro; (4) county does not meet population threshold but is shown in order to allow inclusion of city

Place	Total population 25 years and over who are high school graduates	Asian population 25 years and over	Asians 25 years and over who are high school graduates	NHPI[1] population 25 years and over	NHPIs[1] 25 years and over who are high school graduates	Asian Indian	Bangladeshi	Cambodian	Chinese[2]	Fijian	Filipino	Guamanian[3]	Hawaiian, Native	Hmong	Indonesian	Japanese	Korean	Laotian	Malaysian	Pakistani	Samoan	Sri Lankan	Taiwanese	Thai	Tongan	Vietnamese
Sumter County	47,643 74.28	654	483 73.85 73.85 1.01	-	-	-	-	-	-	-	-	-	-	-	-	-	-	-	-	-	-	-	-	-	-	-
York County	81,692 77.25	805	554 68.82 68.82 0.68	-	-	-	-	-	-	-	-	-	-	-	-	-	-	-	-	-	-	-	-	-	-	155 51.67 27.98 19.25 0.19
SOUTH DAKOTA	401,179 84.57	2,669	1,929 72.27 72.27 0.48	-	-	288 97.30 14.93 10.79 0.07	-	-	383 78.81 19.85 14.35 0.10	-	426 81.92 22.08 15.96 0.11	-	-	-	-	183 84.72 9.49 6.86 0.05	202 84.87 10.47 7.57 0.05	38 35.85 1.97 1.42 0.01	-	-	-	-	-	-	-	147 34.67 7.62 5.51 0.04
Minnehaha County	82,632 88.47	826	435 52.66 52.66 0.53	-	-	-	-	-	-	-	-	-	-	-	-	-	-	-	-	-	-	-	-	-	-	90 29.03 20.69 10.90 0.11
Pennington County	48,768 87.81	486	385 79.22 79.22 0.79	-	-	-	-	-	-	-	-	-	-	-	-	-	-	-	-	-	-	-	-	-	-	-
TENNESSEE	2,843,244 75.92	34,168	28,061 82.13 82.13 0.99	1,289	942 73.08 73.08 0.03	6,778 90.54 24.15 19.84 0.24	-	215 35.54 0.77 0.63 0.01	4,736 84.77 16.88 13.86 0.17	-	3,467 93.25 12.36 10.15 0.12	162 51.76 17.20 12.57 0.01	292 77.04 31.00 22.65 0.01	-	-	2,425 92.91 8.64 7.10 0.09	3,784 81.53 13.48 11.07 0.13	1,616 67.84 5.76 4.73 0.06	-	354 96.99 1.26 1.04 0.01	278 83.73 29.51 21.57 0.01	-	330 96.49 1.18 0.97 0.01	582 85.21 2.07 1.70 0.02	-	2,427 58.94 8.65 7.10 0.09
Anderson County	39,036 78.86	354	339 95.76 95.76 0.87	-	-	-	-	-	-	-	-	-	-	-	-	-	-	-	-	-	-	-	-	-	-	-
Blount County	57,214 78.44	385	297 77.14 77.14 0.52	-	-	-	-	-	-	-	-	-	-	-	-	-	-	-	-	-	-	-	-	-	-	-
Bradley County	41,908 73.31	349	296 84.81 84.81 0.71	-	-	-	-	-	-	-	-	-	-	-	-	-	-	-	-	-	-	-	-	-	-	-
Davidson County	307,933 81.52	7,264	5,897 81.18 81.18 1.92	172	124 72.09 72.09 0.04	1,466 89.83 24.86 20.18 0.48	-	-	860 92.37 14.58 11.84 0.28	-	563 94.15 9.55 7.75 0.18	-	-	-	-	569 98.27 9.65 7.83 0.18	728 83.68 12.35 10.02 0.24	472 63.27 8.00 6.50 0.15	-	-	-	-	-	-	-	512 53.00 8.68 7.05 0.17

Notes: Please refer to the User's Guide for an explanation of data; data is arranged alphabetically by state, then county, then city within each county; table includes counties with populations greater than 49,999 unless noted and cities with populations greater than 9,999 whose Asian and/or NHPI population rates are greater than the national average; (1) Native Hawaiian and other Pacific Islander; (2) excludes Taiwanese; (3) includes Chamorro; (4) county does not meet population threshold but is shown in order to allow inclusion of city

Place	Total population 25 years and over who are high school graduates	Asian population 25 years and over	Asians 25 years and over who are high school graduates	NHPI[1] population 25 years and over	NHPIs[1] 25 years and over who are high school graduates	Asian Indian	Bangladeshi	Cambodian	Chinese[2]	Fijian	Filipino	Guamanian[3]	Hawaiian, Native	Hmong	Indonesian	Japanese	Korean	Laotian	Malaysian	Pakistani	Samoan	Sri Lankan	Taiwanese	Thai	Tongan	Vietnamese
Hamilton County	167,216 80.71	2,440	2,122 86.97 86.97 1.27	-	-	631 89.89 29.74 25.86 0.38	-	-	-	-	321 100.00 15.13 13.16 0.19	-	-	-	-	-	301 88.01 14.18 12.34 0.18	-	-	-	-	-	-	-	-	191 70.74 9.00 7.83 0.11
Knox County	208,456 82.55	2,791	2,495 89.39 89.39 1.20	-	-	732 93.37 29.34 26.23 0.35	-	-	598 90.47 23.97 21.43 0.29	-	-	-	-	-	-	-	287 89.13 11.50 10.28 0.14	-	-	-	-	-	-	-	-	158 63.20 6.33 5.66 0.08
Madison County	45,711 78.76	300	268 89.33 89.33 0.59	-	-	-	-	-	-	-	-	-	-	-	-	-	-	-	-	-	-	-	-	-	-	-
Montgomery County	67,314 84.33	1,707	1,279 74.93 74.93 1.90	-	-	-	-	-	-	-	-	-	-	-	-	-	577 65.49 45.11 33.80 0.86	-	-	-	-	-	-	-	-	-
Putnam County	28,590 72.56	325	301 92.62 92.62 1.05	-	-	-	-	-	-	-	-	-	-	-	-	-	-	-	-	-	-	-	-	-	-	-
Rutherford County	89,871 81.77	2,069	1,613 77.96 77.96 1.79	-	-	-	-	-	-	-	-	-	-	-	-	-	-	691 70.65 42.84 33.40 0.77	-	-	-	-	-	-	-	-
Shelby County	450,794 80.78	9,556	7,572 79.24 79.24 1.68	378	222 58.73 58.73 0.05	2,135 92.79 28.20 22.34 0.47	-	80 25.72 1.06 0.84 0.02	1,598 81.12 21.10 16.72 0.35	-	894 89.13 11.81 9.36 0.20	-	-	-	-	347 92.53 4.58 3.63 0.08	758 91.55 10.01 7.93 0.17	-	-	-	-	-	-	-	-	1,029 54.24 13.59 10.77 0.23
Germantown (city)	24,282 98.05	896	836 93.30 93.30 3.44	-	-	298 88.69 35.65 33.26 1.23	-	-	262 98.87 31.34 29.24 1.08	-	-	-	-	-	-	-	-	-	-	-	-	-	-	-	-	-
Sullivan County	82,272 75.75	348	322 92.53 92.53 0.39	-	-	-	-	-	-	-	-	-	-	-	-	-	-	-	-	-	-	-	-	-	-	-
Sumner County	68,274 79.71	676	565 83.58 83.58 0.83	-	-	-	-	-	-	-	-	-	-	-	-	-	-	-	-	-	-	-	-	-	-	-

Notes: Please refer to the User's Guide for an explanation of data; data is arranged alphabetically by state, then county, then city within each county; table includes counties with populations greater than 49,999 unless noted and cities with populations greater than 9,999 whose Asian and/or NHPI population rates are greater than the national average; (1) Native Hawaiian and other Pacific Islander; (2) excludes Taiwanese; (3) includes Chamorro; (4) county does not meet population threshold but is shown in order to allow inclusion of city

Place	Total population 25 years and over who are high school graduates	Asian population 25 years and over	Asians 25 years and over who are high school graduates	NHPI[1] population 25 years and over	NHPIs[1] 25 years and over who are high school graduates	Asian Indian	Bangladeshi	Cambodian	Chinese[2]	Fijian	Filipino	Guamanian[3]	Hawaiian, Native	Hmong	Indonesian	Japanese	Korean	Laotian	Malaysian	Pakistani	Samoan	Sri Lankan	Taiwanese	Thai	Tongan	Vietnamese
Washington County	56,322	430	420	-	-	-	-	-	-	-	-	-	-	-	-	-	-	-	-	-	-	-	-	-	-	-
	77.21		97.67																							
			97.67																							
			0.75																							
Weakley County[4]	15,391	279	279	-	-	-	-	-	-	-	-	-	-	-	-	-	-	-	-	-	-	-	-	-	-	-
	70.25		100.00																							
			100.00																							
			1.81																							
Martin (city)	4,206	252	252	-	-	-	-	-	-	-	-	-	-	-	-	-	-	-	-	-	-	-	-	-	-	-
	76.65		100.00																							
			100.00																							
			5.99																							
Williamson County	73,504	931	826	-	-	-	-	-	-	-	-	-	-	-	-	-	-	-	-	-	-	-	-	-	-	-
	90.06		88.72																							
			88.72																							
			1.12																							
Wilson County	47,470	197	137	-	-	-	-	-	-	-	-	-	-	-	-	-	-	-	-	-	-	-	-	-	-	-
	80.89		69.54																							
			69.54																							
			0.29																							
TEXAS	9,676,332	356,028	287,359	6,826	5,098	70,213	1,556	2,165	58,339	-	35,950	1,542	1,557	-	1,081	11,169	24,572	3,162	453	8,755	666	563	4,792	4,084	169	52,438
	75.65		80.71		74.69	88.32	92.73	53.88	87.74		91.73	78.39	71.13		98.18	91.88	83.12	55.89	93.98	81.91	71.23	86.88	93.63	78.10	68.42	62.42
						24.43	0.54	0.75	20.30		12.51	30.25	30.54		0.38	3.89	8.55	1.10	0.16	3.05	13.06	0.20	1.67	1.42	3.32	18.25
			80.71		74.69	19.72	0.44	0.61	16.39		10.10	22.59	22.81		0.30	3.14	6.90	0.89	0.13	2.46	9.76	0.16	1.35	1.15	2.48	14.73
			2.97		0.05	0.73	0.02	0.02	0.60		0.37	0.02	0.02		0.01	0.12	0.25	0.03	<0.01	0.09	0.01	0.01	0.05	0.04	<0.01	0.54
Anderson County	24,793	257	183	-	-	-	-	-	-	-	-	-	-	-	-	-	-	-	-	-	-	-	-	-	-	-
	64.39		71.21																							
			71.21																							
			0.74																							
Angelina County	35,825	314	238	-	-	-	-	-	-	-	-	-	-	-	-	-	-	-	-	-	-	-	-	-	-	-
	71.24		75.80																							
			75.80																							
			0.66																							
Bell County	116,349	4,207	3,242	655	558	327	-	-	-	-	868	316	-	-	-	255	1,218	-	-	-	-	-	-	-	-	-
	84.66		77.06		85.19	79.95					87.50	87.05				77.98	69.09									
						10.09					26.77	56.63				7.87	37.57									
			77.06		85.19	7.77					20.63	48.24				6.06	28.95									
			2.79		0.48	0.28					0.75	0.27				0.22	1.05									
Killeen (city)	41,887	2,620	2,005	537	440	-	-	-	-	-	619	257	-	-	-	-	790	-	-	-	-	-	-	-	-	-
	89.26		76.53		81.94						90.23	84.54					66.72									
											30.87	58.41					39.40									
			76.53		81.94						23.63	47.86					30.15									
			4.79		1.05						1.48	0.61					1.89									

Notes: Please refer to the User's Guide for an explanation of data; data is arranged alphabetically by state, then county, then city within each county; table includes counties with populations greater than 49,999 unless noted and cities with populations greater than 9,999 whose Asian and/or NHPI population rates are greater than the national average; (1) Native Hawaiian and other Pacific Islander; (2) excludes Taiwanese; (3) includes Chamorro; (4) county does not meet population threshold but is shown in order to allow inclusion of city

Place	Total population 25 years and over who are high school graduates	Asian population 25 years and over	Asians 25 years and over who are high school graduates	NHPI[1] population 25 years and over	NHPIs[1] 25 years and over who are high school graduates	Asian Indian	Bangladeshi	Cambodian	Chinese[2]	Fijian	Filipino	Guamanian[3]	Hawaiian, Native	Hmong	Indonesian	Japanese	Korean	Laotian	Malaysian	Pakistani	Samoan	Sri Lankan	Taiwanese	Thai	Tongan	Vietnamese
Bexar County	653,124 76.93	15,401	12,584 81.71 81.71 1.93	662	517 78.10 78.10 0.08	2,017 86.46 16.03 13.10 0.31	-	-	2,114 85.59 16.80 13.73 0.32	-	3,169 87.11 25.18 20.58 0.49	-	226 74.59 43.71 34.14 0.03	-	-	1,164 87.39 9.25 7.56 0.18	1,295 69.33 10.29 8.41 0.20	109 47.81 0.87 0.71 0.02	-	-	-	-	-	523 76.24 4.16 3.40 0.08	-	1,441 72.56 11.45 9.36 0.22
Bowie County	45,420 77.29	308	239 77.60 77.60 0.53	-	-	-	-	-	-	-	-	-	-	-	-	-	-	-	-	-	-	-	-	-	-	-
Brazoria County	121,091 79.54	2,971	2,450 82.46 82.46 2.02	-	-	588 95.92 24.00 19.79 0.49	-	60 30.00 2.45 2.02 0.05	357 90.15 14.57 12.02 0.29	-	459 96.23 18.73 15.45 0.38	-	-	-	-	-	-	-	-	-	-	-	-	-	-	629 78.72 25.67 21.17 0.52
Brazos County	57,502 81.32	3,350	3,220 96.12 96.12 5.60	-	-	774 94.85 24.04 23.10 1.35	-	-	985 98.50 30.59 29.40 1.71	-	-	-	-	-	-	-	572 100.00 17.76 17.07 0.99	-	-	-	-	-	-	-	-	190 92.23 5.90 5.67 0.33
College Station (city)	21,863 93.83	2,731	2,618 95.86 95.86 11.97	-	-	576 93.20 22.00 21.09 2.63	-	-	835 98.24 31.89 30.57 3.82	-	-	-	-	-	-	-	442 100.00 16.88 16.18 2.02	-	-	-	-	-	-	-	-	-
Calhoun County[4]	8,983 69.04	402	335 83.33 83.33 3.73	-	-	-	-	-	-	-	-	-	-	-	-	-	-	-	-	-	-	-	-	-	-	38 41.30 11.34 9.45 0.42
Port Lavaca (city)	4,928 68.12	291	278 95.53 95.53 5.64	-	-	-	-	-	-	-	-	-	-	-	-	-	-	-	-	-	-	-	-	-	-	-
Cameron County	103,348 55.25	1,008	921 91.37 91.37 0.89	-	-	-	-	-	-	-	399 99.50 43.32 39.58 0.39	-	-	-	-	-	-	-	-	-	-	-	-	-	-	-
Collin County	289,823 91.81	22,117	20,742 93.78 93.78 7.16	-	-	5,518 95.88 26.60 24.95 1.90	-	-	7,950 94.69 38.33 35.95 2.74	-	1,000 97.28 4.82 4.52 0.35	-	-	-	-	701 99.01 3.38 3.17 0.24	1,541 91.51 7.43 6.97 0.53	-	-	489 86.40 2.36 2.21 0.17	-	-	519 95.23 2.50 2.35 0.18	291 84.84 1.40 1.32 0.10	-	1,944 86.55 9.37 8.79 0.67
Allen (city)	25,022 95.62	1,015	921 90.74 90.74 3.68	-	-	219 91.25 23.78 21.58 0.88	-	-	-	-	-	-	-	-	-	-	-	-	-	-	-	-	-	-	-	200 86.58 21.72 19.70 0.80

Notes: Please refer to the User's Guide for an explanation of data; data is arranged alphabetically by state, then county, then city within each county; table includes counties with populations greater than 49,999 unless noted and cities with populations greater than 9,999 whose Asian and/or NHPI population rates are greater than the national average; (1) Native Hawaiian and other Pacific Islander; (2) excludes Taiwanese; (3) includes Chamorro; (4) county does not meet population threshold but is shown in order to allow inclusion of city

Place	Total population 25 years and over who are high school graduates	Asian population 25 years and over	Asians 25 years and over who are high school graduates	NHPI[1] population 25 years and over	NHPIs[1] 25 years and over who are high school graduates	Asian Indian	Bangladeshi	Cambodian	Chinese[2]	Fijian	Filipino	Guamanian[3]	Hawaiian, Native	Hmong	Indonesian	Japanese	Korean	Laotian	Malaysian	Pakistani	Samoan	Sri Lankan	Taiwanese	Thai	Tongan	Vietnamese
Plano (city)	135,274	14,539	13,713	-	-	3,600	-	-	5,731	-	545	-	-	-	-	386	1,193	-	-	300	-	-	366	-	-	963
	93.91		94.32			96.23			94.82		98.73					98.72	94.31			87.72			96.57			83.74
						26.25			41.79		3.97					2.81	8.70			2.19			2.67			7.02
			94.32			24.76			39.42		3.75					2.65	8.21			2.06			2.52			6.62
			10.14			2.66			4.24		0.40					0.29	0.88			0.22			0.27			0.71
Comal County	44,066	280	263	-	-	-	-	-	-	-	-	-	-	-	-	-	-	-	-	-	-	-	-	-	-	-
	83.86		93.93																							
			93.93																							
			0.60																							
Coryell County	33,881	865	598	192	192	-	-	-	-	-	-	-	-	-	-	-	183	-	-	-	-	-	-	-	-	-
	81.12		69.13		100.00												53.35									
																	30.60									
			69.13		100.00												21.16									
			1.77		0.57												0.54									
Dallas County	1,023,752	57,080	45,172	551	356	13,377	357	607	6,828	-	4,035	-	-	-	-	1,669	5,443	731	-	1,698	-	-	489	737	-	7,504
	74.95		79.14		64.61	87.20	92.97	51.75	85.18		93.71					97.03	82.62	57.20		80.28			89.72	85.30		59.23
						29.61	0.79	1.34	15.12		8.93					3.69	12.05	1.62		3.76			1.08	1.63		16.61
			79.14		64.61	23.44	0.63	1.06	11.96		7.07					2.92	9.54	1.28		2.97			0.86	1.29		13.15
			4.41		0.03	1.31	0.03	0.06	0.67		0.39					0.16	0.53	0.07		0.17			0.05	0.07		0.73
Addison (town)	9,060	830	736	-	-	408	-	-	-	-	-	-	-	-	-	-	-	-	-	-	-	-	-	-	-	-
	90.53		88.67			86.62																				
						55.43																				
			88.67			49.16																				
			8.12			4.50																				
Coppell (city)	21,225	2,132	1,919	-	-	697	-	-	439	-	-	-	-	-	-	-	366	-	-	-	-	-	-	-	-	-
	96.64		90.01			91.47			95.85								87.56									
						36.32			22.88								19.07									
			90.01			32.69			20.59								17.17									
			9.04			3.28			2.07								1.72									
Farmers Branch (city)	13,821	679	534	-	-	-	-	-	-	-	-	-	-	-	-	-	-	-	-	-	-	-	-	-	-	-
	76.16		78.65																							
			78.65																							
			3.86																							
Garland (city)	102,825	9,660	6,849	-	-	1,479	-	-	655	-	792	-	-	-	-	-	589	-	-	333	-	-	-	-	-	2,392
	78.32		70.90			80.25			66.77		95.54						77.70			75.00						60.66
						21.59			9.56		11.56						8.60			4.86						34.92
			70.90			15.31			6.78		8.20						6.10			3.45						24.76
			6.66			1.44			0.64		0.77						0.57			0.32						2.33
Grand Prairie (city)	56,564	3,213	2,256	-	-	367	-	-	-	-	343	-	-	-	-	-	-	103	-	-	-	-	-	-	-	886
	74.88		70.21			83.60					81.86							60.23								59.86
						16.27					15.20							4.57								39.27
			70.21			11.42					10.68							3.21								27.58
			3.99			0.65					0.61							0.18								1.57
Irving (city)	94,347	10,780	9,548	-	-	3,842	-	-	1,010	-	562	-	-	-	-	497	1,383	196	-	243	-	-	-	-	-	819
	77.98		88.57			92.60			89.62		94.77					100.00	85.74	70.00		85.26						72.61
						40.24			10.58		5.89					5.21	14.48	2.05		2.55						8.58
			88.57			35.64			9.37		5.21					4.61	12.83	1.82		2.25						7.60
			10.12			4.07			1.07		0.60					0.53	1.47	0.21		0.26						0.87

Notes: Please refer to the User's Guide for an explanation of data; data is arranged alphabetically by state, then county, then city within each county; table includes counties with populations greater than 49,999 unless noted and cities with populations greater than 9,999 whose Asian and/or NHPI population rates are greater than the national average; (1) Native Hawaiian and other Pacific Islander; (2) excludes Taiwanese; (3) includes Chamorro; (4) county does not meet population threshold but is shown in order to allow inclusion of city

Place	Total population 25 years and over who are high school graduates	Asian population 25 years and over	Asians 25 years and over who are high school graduates	NHPI[1] population 25 years and over	NHPIs[1] 25 years and over who are high school graduates	Asian Indian	Bangladeshi	Cambodian	Chinese[2]	Fijian	Filipino	Guamanian[3]	Hawaiian, Native	Hmong	Indonesian	Japanese	Korean	Laotian	Malaysian	Pakistani	Samoan	Sri Lankan	Taiwanese	Thai	Tongan	Vietnamese
Mesquite (city)	62,674 83.04	2,733	2,304 84.30 84.30 3.68	-	-	1,183 85.42 51.35 43.29 1.89	-	-	-	-	554 90.82 24.05 20.27 0.88	-	-	-	-	-	-	-	-	-	-	-	-	-	-	-
Richardson (city)	55,700 91.49	6,698	5,721 85.41 85.41 10.27	-	-	1,307 91.33 22.85 19.51 2.35	-	-	1,853 86.63 32.39 27.66 3.33	-	250 97.28 4.37 3.73 0.45	-	-	-	-	-	627 82.72 10.96 9.36 1.13	-	-	199 76.54 3.48 2.97 0.36	-	-	-	-	-	833 76.85 14.56 12.44 1.50
Rowlett (city)	25,091 92.38	988	850 86.03 86.03 3.39	-	-	293 93.02 34.47 29.66 1.17	-	-	-	-	-	-	-	-	-	-	-	-	-	-	-	-	-	-	-	-
Denton County	237,025 89.37	10,564	9,044 85.61 85.61 3.82	-	-	3,263 90.99 36.08 30.89 1.38	-	289 67.52 3.20 2.74 0.12	1,193 85.52 13.19 11.29 0.50	-	551 95.00 6.09 5.22 0.23	-	-	-	-	301 100.00 3.33 2.85 0.13	1,237 88.86 13.68 11.71 0.52	-	-	347 83.82 3.84 3.28 0.15	-	-	-	-	-	1,126 71.09 12.45 10.66 0.48
Carrollton (city)	60,523 86.35	7,046	5,507 78.16 78.16 9.10	-	-	2,289 85.19 41.57 32.49 3.78	-	217 52.93 3.94 3.08 0.36	350 74.47 6.36 4.97 0.58	-	-	-	-	-	-	-	614 88.47 11.15 8.71 1.01	-	-	430 74.91 7.81 6.10 0.71	-	-	-	-	-	1,096 69.63 19.90 15.55 1.81
Lewisville (city)	41,694 87.02	2,016	1,705 84.57 84.57 4.09	-	-	715 93.83 41.94 35.47 1.71	-	-	-	-	-	-	-	-	-	-	-	-	-	-	-	-	-	-	-	167 58.19 9.79 8.28 0.40
Ector County	48,768 67.96	537	424 78.96 78.96 0.87	-	-	-	-	-	-	-	-	-	-	-	-	-	-	-	-	-	-	-	-	-	-	-
El Paso County	257,532 65.77	4,760	3,959 83.17 83.17 1.54	300	218 72.67 72.67 0.08	645 87.64 16.29 13.55 0.25	-	-	507 94.41 12.81 10.65 0.20	-	1,028 90.41 25.97 21.60 0.40	-	-	-	-	547 81.40 13.82 11.49 0.21	805 70.80 20.33 16.91 0.31	-	-	-	-	-	-	-	-	-
Ellis County	52,489 77.80	269	216 80.30 80.30 0.41	-	-	-	-	-	-	-	-	-	-	-	-	-	-	-	-	-	-	-	-	-	-	-
Fort Bend County	180,858 84.33	24,102	20,755 86.11 86.11 11.48	-	-	6,733 87.78 32.44 27.94 3.72	-	-	5,773 87.70 27.81 23.95 3.19	-	2,469 93.91 11.90 10.24 1.37	-	-	-	-	-	622 87.11 3.00 2.58 0.34	-	-	1,111 79.36 5.35 4.61 0.61	-	-	647 89.12 3.12 2.68 0.36	-	-	2,543 76.18 12.25 10.55 1.41

Notes: Please refer to the User's Guide for an explanation of data; data is arranged alphabetically by state, then county, then city within each county; table includes counties with populations greater than 49,999 unless noted and cities with populations greater than 9,999 whose Asian and/or NHPI population rates are greater than the national average; (1) Native Hawaiian and other Pacific Islander; (2) excludes Taiwanese; (3) includes Chamorro; (4) county does not meet population threshold but is shown in order to allow inclusion of city

Place	Total population 25 years and over who are high school graduates	Asian population 25 years and over	Asians 25 years and over who are high school graduates	NHPI[1] population 25 years and over	NHPIs[1] 25 years and over who are high school graduates	Asian Indian	Bangladeshi	Cambodian	Chinese[2]	Fijian	Filipino	Guamanian[3]	Hawaiian, Native	Hmong	Indonesian	Japanese	Korean	Laotian	Malaysian	Pakistani	Samoan	Sri Lankan	Taiwanese	Thai	Tongan	Vietnamese
Cinco Ranch (cdp)	6,429 98.53	402	390 97.01 97.01 6.07	-	-	-	-	-	-	-	-	-	-	-	-	-	-	-	-	-	-	-	-	-	-	-
Mission Bend (cdp)	15,423 85.30	3,162	2,556 80.83 80.83 16.57	-	-	757 88.95 29.62 23.94 4.91	-	-	362 80.44 14.16 11.45 2.35	-	544 95.94 21.28 17.20 3.53	-	-	-	-	-	-	-	-	175 68.90 6.85 5.53 1.13	-	-	-	-	-	529 66.46 20.70 16.73 3.43
Missouri City (city)	30,376 92.18	3,682	3,329 90.41 90.41 10.96	-	-	1,131 90.92 33.97 30.72 3.72	-	-	837 92.38 25.14 22.73 2.76	-	625 93.98 18.77 16.97 2.06	-	-	-	-	-	-	-	-	-	-	-	-	-	-	345 85.40 10.36 9.37 1.14
New Territory (cdp)	7,418 92.01	1,960	1,675 85.46 85.46 22.58	-	-	755 82.69 45.07 38.52 10.18	-	-	349 81.16 20.84 17.81 4.70	-	-	-	-	-	-	-	-	-	-	-	-	-	-	-	-	-
Stafford (city)	8,304 85.89	2,008	1,673 83.32 83.32 20.15	-	-	589 83.31 35.21 29.33 7.09	-	-	286 76.06 17.10 14.24 3.44	-	228 97.02 13.63 11.35 2.75	-	-	-	-	-	-	-	-	-	-	-	-	-	-	398 90.87 23.79 19.82 4.79
Sugar Land (city)	37,124 93.39	8,967	7,886 87.94 87.94 21.24	-	-	2,338 89.82 29.65 26.07 6.30	-	-	3,150 90.03 39.94 35.13 8.49	-	536 92.73 6.80 5.98 1.44	-	-	-	-	-	260 89.04 3.30 2.90 0.70	-	-	301 91.49 3.82 3.36 0.81	-	-	496 88.41 6.29 5.53 1.34	-	-	521 68.28 6.61 5.81 1.40
Galveston County	130,716 80.94	3,482	2,676 76.85 76.85 2.05	-	-	534 80.18 19.96 15.34 0.41	-	-	523 84.76 19.54 15.02 0.40	-	488 85.61 18.24 14.01 0.37	-	-	-	-	-	-	-	-	-	-	-	-	-	-	606 59.41 22.65 17.40 0.46
Grayson County	58,074 80.23	402	328 81.59 81.59 0.56	-	-	-	-	-	-	-	-	-	-	-	-	-	-	-	-	-	-	-	-	-	-	-
Gregg County	55,372 79.10	372	329 88.44 88.44 0.59	-	-	-	-	-	-	-	-	-	-	-	-	-	-	-	-	-	-	-	-	-	-	-
Guadalupe County	43,491 78.11	593	415 69.98 69.98 0.95	-	-	-	-	-	-	-	-	-	-	-	-	-	-	-	-	-	-	-	-	-	-	-

Notes: Please refer to the User's Guide for an explanation of data; data is arranged alphabetically by state, then county, then city within each county; table includes counties with populations greater than 49,999 unless noted and cities with populations greater than 9,999 whose Asian and/or NHPI population rates are greater than the national average; (1) Native Hawaiian and other Pacific Islander; (2) excludes Taiwanese; (3) includes Chamorro; (4) county does not meet population threshold but is shown in order to allow inclusion of city

Place	Total population 25 years and over who are high school graduates	Asian population 25 years and over	Asians 25 years and over who are high school graduates	NHPI[1] population 25 years and over	NHPIs[1] 25 years and over who are high school graduates	Asian Indian	Bangladeshi	Cambodian	Chinese[2]	Fijian	Filipino	Guamanian[3]	Hawaiian, Native	Hmong	Indonesian	Japanese	Korean	Laotian	Malaysian	Pakistani	Samoan	Sri Lankan	Taiwanese	Thai	Tongan	Vietnamese
Harris County	1,542,977 74.63	113,074	89,039 78.74 78.74 5.77	868	699 80.53 80.53 0.05	19,776 86.93 22.21 17.49 1.28	384 88.48 0.43 0.34 0.02	671 55.92 0.75 0.59 0.04	18,982 84.28 21.32 16.79 1.23	-	10,039 93.49 11.27 8.88 0.65	297 78.16 42.49 34.22 0.02	-	-	448 95.73 0.50 0.40 0.03	2,496 94.44 2.80 2.21 0.16	5,117 89.85 5.75 4.53 0.33	435 61.27 0.49 0.38 0.03	-	3,494 82.68 3.92 3.09 0.23	-	-	1,535 94.11 1.72 1.36 0.10	785 85.33 0.88 0.69 0.05	-	22,323 62.38 25.07 19.74 1.45
Bellaire (city)	10,094 95.41	669	583 87.14 87.14 5.78	-	-	-	-	-	260 90.91 44.60 38.86 2.58	-	-	-	-	-	-	-	-	-	-	-	-	-	-	-	-	-
Houston (city)	845,709 70.41	69,174	54,429 78.68 78.68 6.44	539	388 71.99 71.99 0.05	11,565 86.99 21.25 16.72 1.37	-	158 36.83 0.29 0.23 0.02	13,722 85.59 25.21 19.84 1.62	-	5,091 93.86 9.35 7.36 0.60	205 73.21 52.84 38.03 0.02	-	-	325 95.87 0.60 0.47 0.04	1,621 96.83 2.98 2.34 0.19	3,333 89.91 6.12 4.82 0.39	-	-	2,382 84.44 4.38 3.44 0.28	-	-	1,038 93.60 1.91 1.50 0.12	563 87.56 1.03 0.81 0.07	-	12,718 60.27 23.37 18.39 1.50
West University Place (city)	9,429 97.96	540	497 92.04 92.04 5.27	-	-	-	-	-	-	-	-	-	-	-	-	-	-	-	-	-	-	-	-	-	-	-
Hays County	45,423 84.69	426	336 78.87 78.87 0.74	-	-	-	-	-	-	-	-	-	-	-	-	-	-	-	-	-	-	-	-	-	-	-
Hidalgo County	153,709 50.45	2,015	1,828 90.72 90.72 1.19	-	-	359 89.75 19.64 17.82 0.23	-	-	-	-	951 99.17 52.02 47.20 0.62	-	-	-	-	-	-	-	-	-	-	-	-	-	-	-
Hunt County	37,314 76.86	302	267 88.41 88.41 0.72	-	-	-	-	-	-	-	-	-	-	-	-	-	-	-	-	-	-	-	-	-	-	-
Jefferson County	126,521 78.46	3,685	2,262 61.38 61.38 1.79	-	-	492 87.08 21.75 13.35 0.39	-	-	294 94.53 13.00 7.98 0.23	-	523 98.49 23.12 14.19 0.41	-	-	-	-	-	-	-	-	-	-	-	-	-	-	751 37.74 33.20 20.38 0.59
Port Arthur (city)	24,812 69.74	1,694	798 47.11 47.11 3.22	-	-	-	-	-	-	-	-	-	-	-	-	-	-	-	-	-	-	-	-	-	-	500 37.15 62.66 29.52 2.02
Johnson County	61,591 77.55	382	277 72.51 72.51 0.45	-	-	-	-	-	-	-	-	-	-	-	-	-	-	-	-	-	-	-	-	-	-	-

Notes: Please refer to the User's Guide for an explanation of data; data is arranged alphabetically by state, then county, then city within each county; table includes counties with populations greater than 49,999 unless noted and cities with populations greater than 9,999 whose Asian and/or NHPI population rates are greater than the national average; (1) Native Hawaiian and other Pacific Islander; (2) excludes Taiwanese; (3) includes Chamorro; (4) county does not meet population threshold but is shown in order to allow inclusion of city

Place	Total population 25 years and over who are high school graduates	Asian population 25 years and over	Asians 25 years and over who are high school graduates	NHPI[1] population 25 years and over	NHPIs[1] 25 years and over who are high school graduates	Asian Indian	Bangladeshi	Cambodian	Chinese[2]	Fijian	Filipino	Guamanian[3]	Hawaiian, Native	Hmong	Indonesian	Japanese	Korean	Laotian	Malaysian	Pakistani	Samoan	Sri Lankan	Taiwanese	Thai	Tongan	Vietnamese
Kaufman County	33,422 74.50	334	208 62.28 62.28 0.62	-	-	-	-	-	-	-	-	-	-	-	-	-	-	-	-	-	-	-	-	-	-	-
Lubbock County	110,818 78.39	1,817	1,657 91.19 91.19 1.50	-	-	333 93.02 20.10 18.33 0.30	-	-	425 100.00 25.65 23.39 0.38	-	-	-	-	-	-	-	-	-	-	-	-	-	-	-	-	150 72.12 9.05 8.26 0.14
McLennan County	96,519 76.63	1,129	987 87.42 87.42 1.02	-	-	160 89.89 16.21 14.17 0.17	-	-	-	-	-	-	-	-	-	-	-	-	-	-	-	-	-	-	-	-
Midland County	56,233 79.19	639	564 88.26 88.26 1.00	-	-	187 81.30 33.16 29.26 0.33	-	-	-	-	-	-	-	-	-	-	-	-	-	-	-	-	-	-	-	-
Montgomery County	149,928 81.60	2,062	1,750 84.87 84.87 1.17	-	-	634 93.51 36.23 30.75 0.42	-	-	364 83.68 20.80 17.65 0.24	-	305 93.27 17.43 14.79 0.20	-	-	-	-	-	-	-	-	-	-	-	-	-	-	-
Nacogdoches County	24,434 73.65	266	253 95.11 95.11 1.04	-	-	-	-	-	-	-	-	-	-	-	-	-	-	-	-	-	-	-	-	-	-	-
Nueces County	142,668 74.37	2,436	2,086 85.63 85.63 1.46	-	-	353 88.47 16.92 14.49 0.25	-	-	-	-	1,075 90.87 51.53 44.13 0.75	-	-	-	-	-	-	-	-	-	-	-	-	-	-	-
Orange County	42,868 79.05	429	219 51.05 51.05 0.51	-	-	-	-	-	-	-	-	-	-	-	-	-	-	-	-	-	-	-	-	-	-	61 29.61 27.85 14.22 0.14
Potter County	49,345 71.07	1,762	918 52.10 52.10 1.86	-	-	-	-	-	-	-	-	-	-	-	-	-	-	228 40.43 24.84 12.94 0.46	-	-	-	-	-	-	-	334 51.38 36.38 18.96 0.68
Randall County	58,751 89.52	824	738 89.56 89.56 1.26	-	-	-	-	-	-	-	-	-	-	-	-	-	-	-	-	-	-	-	-	-	-	-

Notes: Please refer to the User's Guide for an explanation of data; data is arranged alphabetically by state, then county, then city within each county; table includes counties with populations greater than 49,999 unless noted and cities with populations greater than 9,999 whose Asian and/or NHPI population rates are greater than the national average; (1) Native Hawaiian and other Pacific Islander; (2) excludes Taiwanese; (3) includes Chamorro; (4) county does not meet population threshold but is shown in order to allow inclusion of city

Place	Total population 25 years and over who are high school graduates	Asian population 25 years and over	Asians 25 years and over who are high school graduates	NHPI[1] population 25 years and over	NHPIs[1] 25 years and over who are high school graduates	Asian Indian	Bangladeshi	Cambodian	Chinese[2]	Fijian	Filipino	Guamanian[3]	Hawaiian, Native	Hmong	Indonesian	Japanese	Korean	Laotian	Malaysian	Pakistani	Samoan	Sri Lankan	Taiwanese	Thai	Tongan	Vietnamese
	28,251	267	181	-	-	-	-	-	-	-	-	-	-	-	-	-	-	-	-	-	-	-	-	-	-	-
	71.43		67.79																							
San Patricio County																										
			67.79																							
			0.64																							
	89,048	627	489	-	-	-	-	-	-	-	-	-	-	-	-	-	-	-	-	-	-	-	-	-	-	-
	80.21		77.99																							
Smith County																										
			77.99																							
			0.55																							
	730,928	31,748	22,951	869	678	5,366	-	69	3,016	-	2,152	-	-	-	-	673	1,782	1,068	-	468	-	-	428	388	129	6,412
	81.32		72.29		78.02	89.76		19.49	84.79		92.01					85.08	86.30	57.76		83.13			97.49	71.32	73.71	54.44
Tarrant County						23.38		0.30	13.14		9.38					2.93	7.76	4.65		2.04			1.86	1.69	19.03	27.94
			72.29		78.02	16.90		0.22	9.50		6.78					2.12	5.61	3.36		1.47			1.35	1.22	14.84	20.20
			3.14		0.09	0.73		0.01	0.41		0.29					0.09	0.24	0.15		0.06			0.06	0.05	0.02	0.88
	172,717	11,737	8,428	-	-	1,573	-	-	1,478	-	711	-	-	-	-	-	465	-	-	-	-	-	267	-	-	3,062
	84.93		71.81			90.72			84.60		87.35						81.58						100.00			55.47
Arlington (city)						18.66			17.54		8.44						5.52						3.17			36.33
			71.81			13.40			12.59		6.06						3.96						2.27			26.09
			4.88			0.91			0.86		0.41						0.27						0.15			1.77
	26,757	2,009	1,527	-	-	733	-	-	-	-	-	-	-	-	-	-	-	-	-	-	-	-	-	-	-	-
	88.49		76.01			85.83																				
Euless (city)						48.00																				
			76.01			36.49																				
			5.71			2.74																				
	18,171	1,850	983	-	-	-	-	-	-	-	-	-	-	-	-	-	-	222	-	-	-	-	-	-	-	420
	73.26		53.14															51.51								43.30
Haltom City (city)																		22.58								42.73
			53.14															12.00								22.70
			5.41															1.22								2.31
	61,329	988	752	-	-	-	-	-	-	-	292	-	-	-	-	-	-	-	-	-	-	-	-	-	-	-
	81.23		76.11								79.35															
Taylor County											38.83															
			76.11								29.55															
			1.23								0.48															
	48,365	493	400	-	-	-	-	-	-	-	-	-	-	-	-	-	-	-	-	-	-	-	-	-	-	-
	76.25		81.14																							
Tom Green County																										
			81.14																							
			0.83																							
	424,575	21,300	19,051	358	267	4,543	-	-	5,253	-	1,203	-	-	-	-	866	2,138	-	-	267	-	-	388	225	-	3,302
	84.68		89.44		74.58	94.00			96.65		89.38					95.06	93.16			72.36			96.04	80.36		75.23
Travis County						23.85			27.57		6.31					4.55	11.22			1.40			2.04	1.18		17.33
			89.44		74.58	21.33			24.66		5.65					4.07	10.04			1.25			1.82	1.06		15.50
			4.49		0.06	1.07			1.24		0.28					0.20	0.50			0.06			0.09	0.05		0.78
	334,626	17,873	16,212	248	205	3,993	-	-	4,719	-	867	-	-	-	-	795	1,810	-	-	194	-	-	327	-	-	2,613
	83.42		90.71		82.66	95.69			96.88		89.20					94.64	93.83			72.93			95.34			76.38
Austin (city)						24.63			29.11		5.35					4.90	11.16			1.20			2.02			16.12
			90.71		82.66	22.34			26.40		4.85					4.45	10.13			1.09			1.83			14.62
			4.84		0.06	1.19			1.41		0.26					0.24	0.54			0.06			0.10			0.78

Notes: Please refer to the User's Guide for an explanation of data; data is arranged alphabetically by state, then county, then city within each county; table includes counties with populations greater than 49,999 unless noted and cities with populations greater than 9,999 whose Asian and/or NHPI population rates are greater than the national average; (1) Native Hawaiian and other Pacific Islander; (2) excludes Taiwanese; (3) includes Chamorro; (4) county does not meet population threshold but is shown in order to allow inclusion of city

Place	Total population 25 years and over who are high school graduates	Asian population 25 years and over	Asians 25 years and over who are high school graduates	NHPI[1] population 25 years and over	NHPIs[1] 25 years and over who are high school graduates	Asian Indian	Bangladeshi	Cambodian	Chinese[2]	Fijian	Filipino	Guamanian[3]	Hawaiian, Native	Hmong	Indonesian	Japanese	Korean	Laotian	Malaysian	Pakistani	Samoan	Sri Lankan	Taiwanese	Thai	Tongan	Vietnamese
Pflugerville (city)	9,308 94.65	462	373 80.74 80.74 4.01	-	-	-	-	-	-	-	-	-	-	-	-	-	-	-	-	-	-	-	-	-	-	-
Wells Branch (cdp)	7,088 94.98	689	616 89.40 89.40 8.69	-	-	-	-	-	-	-	-	-	-	-	-	-	-	-	-	-	-	-	-	-	-	-
Victoria County	39,633 76.24	321	273 85.05 85.05 0.69	-	-	-	-	-	-	-	-	-	-	-	-	-	-	-	-	-	-	-	-	-	-	-
Webb County	53,616 52.99	510	422 82.75 82.75 0.79	-	-	-	-	-	-	-	-	-	-	-	-	-	-	-	-	-	-	-	-	-	-	-
Wichita County	64,500 79.89	1,506	955 63.41 63.41 1.48	-	-	-	-	-	-	-	262 85.34 27.43 17.40 0.41	-	-	-	-	-	-	-	-	-	-	-	-	-	-	197 43.49 20.63 13.08 0.31
Williamson County	138,201 88.84	4,033	3,440 85.30 85.30 2.49	-	-	921 86.32 26.77 22.84 0.67	-	-	805 88.36 23.40 19.96 0.58	-	-	-	-	-	-	-	361 83.95 10.49 8.95 0.26	-	-	-	-	-	-	-	-	510 77.27 14.83 12.65 0.37
Brushy Creek (cdp)	9,124 95.71	565	516 91.33 91.33 5.66	-	-	-	-	-	-	-	-	-	-	-	-	-	-	-	-	-	-	-	-	-	-	-
Jollyville (cdp)	9,365 95.72	779	723 92.81 92.81 7.72	-	-	-	-	-	-	-	-	-	-	-	-	-	-	-	-	-	-	-	-	-	-	-
UTAH	1,050,881 87.73	22,120	17,679 79.92 79.92 1.68	6,116	4,692 76.72 76.72 0.45	1,445 82.38 8.17 6.53 0.14	-	396 58.32 2.24 1.79 0.04	3,794 81.63 21.46 17.15 0.36	-	2,037 88.41 11.52 9.21 0.19	-	625 85.62 13.32 10.22 0.06	-	-	3,953 92.10 22.36 17.87 0.38	1,825 91.39 10.32 8.25 0.17	767 68.79 4.34 3.47 0.07	-	156 77.61 0.88 0.71 0.01	1,300 81.30 27.71 21.26 0.12	-	220 100.00 1.24 0.99 0.02	390 75.14 2.21 1.76 0.04	1,932 70.93 41.18 31.59 0.18	1,927 57.20 10.90 8.71 0.18
Cache County	38,463 90.41	853	768 90.04 90.04 2.00	-	-	-	-	-	300 95.24 39.06 35.17 0.78	-	-	-	-	-	-	-	-	-	-	-	-	-	-	-	-	-

Notes: Please refer to the User's Guide for an explanation of data; data is arranged alphabetically by state, then county, then city within each county; table includes counties with populations greater than 49,999 unless noted and cities with populations greater than 9,999 whose Asian and/or NHPI population rates are greater than the national average; (1) Native Hawaiian and other Pacific Islander; (2) excludes Taiwanese; (3) includes Chamorro; (4) county does not meet population threshold but is shown in order to allow inclusion of city

Place	Total population 25 years and over who are high school graduates	Asian population 25 years and over	Asians 25 years and over who are high school graduates	NHPI[1] population 25 years and over	NHPIs[1] 25 years and over who are high school graduates	Asian Indian	Bangladeshi	Cambodian	Chinese[2]	Fijian	Filipino	Guamanian[3]	Hawaiian, Native	Hmong	Indonesian	Japanese	Korean	Laotian	Malaysian	Pakistani	Samoan	Sri Lankan	Taiwanese	Thai	Tongan	Vietnamese
Davis County	115,797 92.25	2,282	1,817 79.62 79.62 1.57	432	388 89.81 89.81 0.34	-	-	-	-	-	462 81.63 25.43 20.25 0.40	-	-	-	-	545 89.79 29.99 23.88 0.47	195 92.42 10.73 8.55 0.17	-	-	-	-	-	-	-	-	-
Salt Lake County	442,368 86.83	14,214	11,012 77.47 77.47 2.49	4,408	3,226 73.19 73.19 0.73	1,001 78.94 9.09 7.04 0.23	-	282 56.29 2.56 1.98 0.06	2,369 80.06 21.51 16.67 0.54	-	982 89.52 8.92 6.91 0.22	-	248 86.11 7.69 5.63 0.06	-	-	2,241 92.83 20.35 15.77 0.51	964 89.84 8.75 6.78 0.22	658 73.77 5.98 4.63 0.15	-	-	867 76.79 26.88 19.67 0.20	-	-	-	1,647 69.26 51.05 37.36 0.37	1,649 57.04 14.97 11.60 0.37
Kearns (cdp)	13,149 75.44	449	378 84.19 84.19 2.87	178	119 66.85 66.85 0.91	-	-	-	-	-	-	-	-	-	-	-	-	-	-	-	-	-	-	-	-	-
Salt Lake City (city)	92,405 83.36	4,335	3,345 77.16 77.16 3.62	1,437	961 66.88 66.88 1.04	332 89.01 9.93 7.66 0.36	-	-	866 83.59 25.89 19.98 0.94	-	282 87.04 8.43 6.51 0.31	-	-	-	-	718 90.54 21.46 16.56 0.78	341 97.15 10.19 7.87 0.37	-	-	-	158 69.00 16.44 11.00 0.17	-	-	-	606 62.60 63.06 42.17 0.66	393 44.01 11.75 9.07 0.43
Sandy (city)	44,834 93.61	934	793 84.90 84.90 1.77	139	109 78.42 78.42 0.24	-	-	-	217 84.77 27.36 23.23 0.48	-	-	-	-	-	-	-	-	-	-	-	-	-	-	-	-	-
Taylorsville (city)	27,600 87.49	961	689 71.70 71.70 2.50	296	249 84.12 84.12 0.90	-	-	-	-	-	-	-	-	-	-	-	-	-	-	-	-	-	-	-	-	185 52.26 26.85 19.25 0.67
West Jordan (city)	30,430 89.30	711	598 84.11 84.11 1.97	291	240 82.47 82.47 0.79	-	-	-	-	-	-	-	-	-	-	-	-	-	-	-	-	-	-	-	153 85.00 63.75 52.58 0.50	-
West Valley City (city)	45,544 78.35	2,672	1,695 63.44 63.44 3.72	1,244	883 70.98 70.98 1.94	-	-	138 47.75 8.14 5.16 0.30	229 52.52 13.51 8.57 0.50	-	-	-	-	-	-	-	-	160 70.18 9.44 5.99 0.35	-	-	272 72.34 30.80 21.86 0.60	-	-	-	457 66.81 51.76 36.74 1.00	634 65.70 37.40 23.73 1.39
Utah County	151,063 90.87	2,018	1,846 91.48 91.48 1.22	736	615 83.56 83.56 0.41	-	-	-	623 87.38 33.75 30.87 0.41	-	194 93.27 10.51 9.61 0.13	-	114 78.08 18.54 15.49 0.08	-	-	355 94.16 19.23 17.59 0.24	252 100.00 13.65 12.49 0.17	-	-	-	190 92.23 30.89 25.82 0.13	-	-	-	171 84.24 27.80 23.23 0.11	-
Orem (city)	36,576 91.49	746	700 93.83 93.83 1.91	313	258 82.43 82.43 0.71	-	-	-	-	-	-	-	-	-	-	-	-	-	-	-	-	-	-	-	-	-

Notes: Please refer to the User's Guide for an explanation of data; data is arranged alphabetically by state, then county, then city within each county; table includes counties with populations greater than 49,999 unless noted and cities with populations greater than 9,999 whose Asian and/or NHPI population rates are greater than the national average; (1) Native Hawaiian and other Pacific Islander; (2) excludes Taiwanese; (3) includes Chamorro; (4) county does not meet population threshold but is shown in order to allow inclusion of city

Place	Total population 25 years and over who are high school graduates	Asian population 25 years and over	Asians 25 years and over who are high school graduates	NHPI[1] population 25 years and over	NHPIs[1] 25 years and over who are high school graduates	Asian Indian	Bangladeshi	Cambodian	Chinese[2]	Fijian	Filipino	Guamanian[3]	Hawaiian, Native	Hmong	Indonesian	Japanese	Korean	Laotian	Malaysian	Pakistani	Samoan	Sri Lankan	Taiwanese	Thai	Tongan	Vietnamese
Provo (city)	35,623	944	835	253	210	-	-	-	345	-	-	-	-	-	-	156	-	-	-	-	-	-	-	-	-	-
	89.42		88.45		83.00				80.05							92.86										
									41.32							18.68										
			88.45		83.00				36.55							16.53										
			2.34		0.59				0.97							0.44										
Washington County	45,400	273	218	153	140	-	-	-	-	-	-	-	-	-	-	-	-	-	-	-	-	-	-	-	-	-
	87.57		79.85		91.50																					
			79.85		91.50																					
			0.48		0.31																					
St. George (city)	25,331	232	180	131	118	-	-	-	-	-	-	-	-	-	-	-	-	-	-	-	-	-	-	-	-	-
	87.79		77.59		90.08																					
			77.59		90.08																					
			0.71		0.47																					
Weber County	94,534	1,511	1,260	-	-	-	-	-	-	-	-	-	-	-	-	443	-	-	-	-	-	-	-	-	-	-
	85.05		83.39													91.53										
																35.16										
			83.39													29.32										
			1.33													0.47										
VERMONT	349,327	2,418	1,895	-	-	318	-	-	501	-	197	-	-	-	-	218	235	-	-	-	-	-	-	-	-	227
	86.42		78.37			96.95			83.22		87.95					96.04	89.35									45.13
						16.78			26.44		10.40					11.50	12.40									11.98
			78.37			13.15			20.72		8.15					9.02	9.72									9.39
			0.54			0.09			0.14		0.06					0.06	0.07									0.06
Chittenden County	83,958	1,375	1,049	-	-	175	-	-	288	-	-	-	-	-	-	-	-	-	-	-	-	-	-	-	-	210
	90.62		76.29			100.00			83.72																	49.41
						16.68			27.45																	20.02
			76.29			12.73			20.95																	15.27
			1.25			0.21			0.34																	0.25
Rutland County	36,487	110	91	-	-	-	-	-	-	-	-	-	-	-	-	-	-	-	-	-	-	-	-	-	-	-
	84.29		82.73																							
			82.73																							
			0.25																							
Washington County	34,627	147	129	-	-	-	-	-	-	-	-	-	-	-	-	-	-	-	-	-	-	-	-	-	-	-
	88.41		87.76																							
			87.76																							
			0.37																							
Windsor County	35,790	247	183	-	-	-	-	-	-	-	-	-	-	-	-	-	-	-	-	-	-	-	-	-	-	-
	88.11		74.09																							
			74.09																							
			0.51																							
VIRGINIA	3,801,964	169,251	142,432	2,036	1,793	27,869	869	1,535	19,808	-	29,211	497	560	-	618	6,406	25,936	1,159	-	4,578	230	380	866	2,124	-	16,511
	81.47		84.15		88.06	90.43	80.24	58.57	83.71		89.62	82.70	94.28		92.10	92.40	86.37	64.32		81.42	86.79	83.89	91.06	80.09		69.05
						19.57	0.61	1.08	13.91		20.51	27.72	31.23		0.43	4.50	18.21	0.81		3.21	12.83	0.27	0.61	1.49		11.59
			84.15		88.06	16.47	0.51	0.91	11.70		17.26	24.41	27.50		0.37	3.78	15.32	0.68		2.70	11.30	0.22	0.51	1.25		9.76
			3.75		0.05	0.73	0.02	0.04	0.52		0.77	0.01	0.01		0.02	0.17	0.68	0.03		0.12	0.01	0.01	0.02	0.06		0.43

Notes: Please refer to the User's Guide for an explanation of data; data is arranged alphabetically by state, then county, then city within each county; table includes counties with populations greater than 49,999 unless noted and cities with populations greater than 9,999 whose Asian and/or NHPI population rates are greater than the national average; (1) Native Hawaiian and other Pacific Islander; (2) excludes Taiwanese; (3) includes Chamorro; (4) county does not meet population threshold but is shown in order to allow inclusion of city

Place	Total population 25 years and over who are high school graduates	Asian population 25 years and over	Asians 25 years and over who are high school graduates	NHPI[1] population 25 years and over	NHPIs[1] 25 years and over who are high school graduates	Asian Indian	Bangladeshi	Cambodian	Chinese[2]	Fijian	Filipino	Guamanian[3]	Hawaiian, Native	Hmong	Indonesian	Japanese	Korean	Laotian	Malaysian	Pakistani	Samoan	Sri Lankan	Taiwanese	Thai	Tongan	Vietnamese
Albemarle County	47,088	1,639	1,531	-	-	420	-	-	617	-	-	-	-	-	-	-	-	-	-	-	-	-	-	-	-	-
	87.45		93.41			92.11			94.92																	
						27.43			40.30																	
			93.41			25.63			37.64																	
			3.25			0.89			1.31																	
Alexandria Independent City	83,133	5,075	4,412	-	-	969	-	-	510	-	766	-	-	-	-	-	834	-	-	265	-	-	-	-	-	304
	86.84		86.94			90.99			82.93		94.22						80.66			80.30						78.76
						21.96			11.56		17.36						18.90			6.01						6.89
			86.94			19.09			10.05		15.09						16.43			5.22						5.99
			5.31			1.17			0.61		0.92						1.00			0.32						0.37
Arlington County	121,919	11,536	9,476	-	-	2,312	-	104	1,538	-	1,343	-	-	-	-	989	938	-	-	273	-	-	-	-	-	863
	87.81		82.14			90.38		60.47	84.69		87.49					98.41	88.66			61.21						54.97
						24.40		1.10	16.23		14.17					10.44	9.90			2.88						9.11
			82.14			20.04		0.90	13.33		11.64					8.57	8.13			2.37						7.48
			7.77			1.90		0.09	1.26		1.10					0.81	0.77			0.22						0.71
Arlington (cdp)	121,919	11,536	9,476	-	-	2,312	-	104	1,538	-	1,343	-	-	-	-	989	938	-	-	273	-	-	-	-	-	863
	87.81		82.14			90.38		60.47	84.69		87.49					98.41	88.66			61.21						54.97
						24.40		1.10	16.23		14.17					10.44	9.90			2.88						9.11
			82.14			20.04		0.90	13.33		11.64					8.57	8.13			2.37						7.48
			7.77			1.90		0.09	1.26		1.10					0.81	0.77			0.22						0.71
Bedford County	33,982	377	315	-	-	-	-	-	-	-	-	-	-	-	-	-	-	-	-	-	-	-	-	-	-	-
	80.12		83.55																							
			83.55																							
			0.93																							
Charlottesville Independent City	18,486	637	618	-	-	88	-	-	263	-	-	-	-	-	-	-	-	-	-	-	-	-	-	-	-	-
	80.84		97.02			100.00			97.77																	
						14.24			42.56																	
			97.02			13.81			41.29																	
			3.34			0.48			1.42																	
Chesapeake Independent City	106,851	2,430	2,142	-	-	-	-	-	-	-	1,199	-	-	-	-	-	-	-	-	-	-	-	-	-	-	-
	85.14		88.15								89.48															
											55.98															
			88.15								49.34															
			2.00								1.12															
Chesterfield County	147,209	3,892	3,089	-	-	585	-	142	462	-	415	-	-	-	-	-	776	-	-	-	-	-	-	-	-	269
	88.13		79.37			84.17		45.51	81.48		85.57						83.08									62.41
						18.94		4.60	14.96		13.43						25.12									8.71
			79.37			15.03		3.65	11.87		10.66						19.94									6.91
			2.10			0.40		0.10	0.31		0.28						0.53									0.18
Fairfax Independent City	13,486	1,750	1,518	-	-	313	-	-	288	-	-	-	-	-	-	-	331	-	-	-	-	-	-	-	-	246
	88.60		86.74			95.14			76.60								89.70									81.19
						20.62			18.97								21.81									16.21
			86.74			17.89			16.46								18.91									14.06
			11.26			2.32			2.14								2.45									1.82
Fairfax County	592,760	82,972	70,859	474	446	15,018	420	807	9,738	-	8,301	-	-	-	278	2,117	16,493	645	-	2,790	-	-	495	934	-	10,700
	90.74		85.40		94.09	90.76	79.55	75.77	84.69		92.80				85.28	96.53	88.22	70.18		81.77			89.03	83.02		72.69
						21.19	0.59	1.14	13.74		11.71				0.39	2.99	23.28	0.91		3.94			0.70	1.32		15.10
			85.40		94.09	18.10	0.51	0.97	11.74		10.00				0.34	2.55	19.88	0.78		3.36			0.60	1.13		12.90
			11.95		0.08	2.53	0.07	0.14	1.64		1.40				0.05	0.36	2.78	0.11		0.47			0.08	0.16		1.81

Notes: Please refer to the User's Guide for an explanation of data; data is arranged alphabetically by state, then county, then city within each county; table includes counties with populations greater than 49,999 unless noted and cities with populations greater than 9,999 whose Asian and/or NHPI population rates are greater than the national average; (1) Native Hawaiian and other Pacific Islander; (2) excludes Taiwanese; (3) includes Chamorro; (4) county does not meet population threshold but is shown in order to allow inclusion of city

Place	Total population 25 years and over who are high school graduates	Asian population 25 years and over	Asians 25 years and over who are high school graduates	NHPI[1] population 25 years and over	NHPIs[1] 25 years and over who are high school graduates	Asian Indian	Bangladeshi	Cambodian	Chinese[2]	Fijian	Filipino	Guamanian[3]	Hawaiian, Native	Hmong	Indonesian	Japanese	Korean	Laotian	Malaysian	Pakistani	Samoan	Sri Lankan	Taiwanese	Thai	Tongan	Vietnamese
Annandale (cdp)	34,645	7,361	6,170	-	-	820	-	-	510	-	468	-	-	-	-	-	2,097	-	-	-	-	-	-	-	-	1,724
	89.70		83.82			98.44			80.57		94.55						88.18									71.95
						13.29			8.27		7.59						33.99									27.94
			83.82			11.14			6.93		6.36						28.49									23.42
			17.81			2.37			1.47		1.35						6.05									4.98
Bailey's Crossroads (cdp)	10,957	1,675	1,238	-	-	-	-	-	-	-	-	-	-	-	-	-	-	-	-	100	-	-	-	-	-	255
	71.67		73.91																	55.25						63.59
																				8.08						20.60
			73.91																	5.97						15.22
			11.30																	0.91						2.33
Burke (cdp)	35,623	5,342	4,733	-	-	798	-	-	456	-	740	-	-	-	-	-	1,764	-	-	-	-	-	-	-	-	554
	94.88		88.60			91.72			82.31		97.63						89.54									74.16
						16.86			9.63		15.63						37.27									11.71
			88.60			14.94			8.54		13.85						33.02									10.37
			13.29			2.24			1.28		2.08						4.95									1.56
Centreville (cdp)	28,784	4,067	3,586	-	-	931	-	-	508	-	578	-	-	-	-	-	973	-	-	-	-	-	-	-	-	195
	93.54		88.17			88.41			76.74		98.97						92.31									71.96
						25.96			14.17		16.12						27.13									5.44
			88.17			22.89			12.49		14.21						23.92									4.79
			12.46			3.23			1.76		2.01						3.38									0.68
Chantilly (cdp)	25,858	4,299	3,921	-	-	1,169	-	-	626	-	-	-	-	-	-	-	751	-	-	-	-	-	-	-	-	547
	94.72		91.21			89.03			96.31								90.48									85.60
						29.81			15.97								19.15									13.95
			91.21			27.19			14.56								17.47									12.72
			15.16			4.52			2.42								2.90									2.12
Franconia (cdp)	21,937	2,255	2,027	-	-	239	-	-	-	-	425	-	-	-	-	-	416	-	-	-	-	-	-	-	-	335
	95.04		89.89			87.23					97.03						91.03									87.93
						11.79					20.97						20.52									16.53
			89.89			10.60					18.85						18.45									14.86
			9.24			1.09					1.94						1.90									1.53
Groveton (cdp)	11,755	1,068	776	-	-	-	-	-	-	-	-	-	-	-	-	-	-	-	-	-	-	-	-	-	-	-
	81.68		72.66																							
			72.66																							
			6.60																							
Herndon (town)	11,102	2,083	1,703	-	-	568	-	-	-	-	-	-	-	-	-	-	-	-	-	-	-	-	-	-	-	150
	80.91		81.76			81.73																				58.82
						33.35																				8.81
			81.76			27.27																				7.20
			15.34			5.12																				1.35
Hybla Valley (cdp)	8,298	778	515	-	-	-	-	-	-	-	-	-	-	-	-	-	-	-	-	-	-	-	-	-	-	-
	76.39		66.20																							
			66.20																							
			6.21																							
Idylwood (cdp)	9,840	2,264	1,802	-	-	690	-	-	338	-	-	-	-	-	-	-	-	-	-	-	-	-	-	-	-	259
	86.41		79.59			98.85			76.99																	52.11
						38.29			18.76																	14.37
			79.59			30.48			14.93																	11.44
			18.31			7.01			3.43																	2.63

Notes: Please refer to the User's Guide for an explanation of data; data is arranged alphabetically by state, then county, then city within each county; table includes counties with populations greater than 49,999 unless noted and cities with populations greater than 9,999 whose Asian and/or NHPI population rates are greater than the national average; (1) Native Hawaiian and other Pacific Islander; (2) excludes Taiwanese; (3) includes Chamorro; (4) county does not meet population threshold but is shown in order to allow inclusion of city

Place	Total population 25 years and over who are high school graduates	Asian population 25 years and over	Asians 25 years and over who are high school graduates	NHPI[1] population 25 years and over	NHPIs[1] 25 years and over who are high school graduates	Asian Indian	Bangladeshi	Cambodian	Chinese[2]	Fijian	Filipino	Guamanian[3]	Hawaiian, Native	Hmong	Indonesian	Japanese	Korean	Laotian	Malaysian	Pakistani	Samoan	Sri Lankan	Taiwanese	Thai	Tongan	Vietnamese
Jefferson (cdp)	15,730	3,672	2,701	-	-	515	-	-	312	-	305	-	-	-	-	-	-	-	-	-	-	-	-	-	-	1,034
	81.49		73.56			86.41			77.04		89.71															64.14
						19.07			11.55		11.29															38.28
			73.56			14.03			8.50		8.31															28.16
			17.17			3.27			1.98		1.94															6.57
Lincolnia (cdp)	8,200	1,492	1,197	-	-	-	-	-	-	-	-	-	-	-	-	-	-	-	-	195	-	-	-	-	-	239
	79.76		80.23																	74.71						78.88
																				16.29						19.97
			80.23																	13.07						16.02
			14.60																	2.38						2.91
Lorton (cdp)	9,565	979	796	-	-	-	-	-	-	-	-	-	-	-	-	-	-	-	-	-	-	-	-	-	-	-
	79.47		81.31																							
			81.31																							
			8.32																							
McLean (cdp)	26,876	2,982	2,809	-	-	654	-	-	515	-	359	-	-	-	-	338	553	-	-	-	-	-	-	-	-	-
	97.07		94.20			96.60			90.67		94.47					100.00	95.18									
						23.28			18.33		12.78					12.03	19.69									
			94.20			21.93			17.27		12.04					11.33	18.54									
			10.45			2.43			1.92		1.34					1.26	2.06									
Merrifield (cdp)	6,940	2,155	1,925	-	-	574	-	-	-	-	-	-	-	-	-	-	500	-	-	-	-	-	-	-	-	380
	90.73		89.33			90.82											93.81									80.51
						29.82											25.97									19.74
			89.33			26.64											23.20									17.63
			27.74			8.27											7.20									5.48
Mount Vernon (cdp)	16,110	1,248	960	-	-	-	-	-	-	-	-	-	-	-	-	-	262	-	-	-	-	-	-	-	-	-
	85.07		76.92														75.29									
																	27.29									
			76.92														20.99									
			5.96														1.63									
Newington (cdp)	11,672	1,379	1,081	-	-	192	-	-	-	-	310	-	-	-	-	-	220	-	-	-	-	-	-	-	-	-
	91.32		78.39			90.57					85.87						72.13									
						17.76					28.68						20.35									
			78.39			13.92					22.48						15.95									
			9.26			1.64					2.66						1.88									
Oakton (cdp)	19,155	2,779	2,457	-	-	599	-	-	660	-	-	-	-	-	-	-	629	-	-	-	-	-	-	-	-	211
	93.63		88.41			89.27			91.67								85.81									75.36
						24.38			26.86								25.60									8.59
			88.41			21.55			23.75								22.63									7.59
			12.83			3.13			3.45								3.28									1.10
Reston (cdp)	37,220	3,624	3,298	-	-	1,253	-	-	552	-	371	-	-	-	-	-	447	-	-	-	-	-	-	-	-	-
	93.23		91.00			93.86			97.01		95.87						88.69									
						37.99			16.74		11.25						13.55									
			91.00			34.58			15.23		10.24						12.33									
			8.86			3.37			1.48		1.00						1.20									
Rose Hill (cdp)	9,534	825	681	-	-	-	-	-	-	-	-	-	-	-	-	-	-	-	-	-	-	-	-	-	-	-
	90.05		82.55																							
			82.55																							
			7.14																							

Notes: Please refer to the User's Guide for an explanation of data; data is arranged alphabetically by state, then county, then city within each county; table includes counties with populations greater than 49,999 unless noted and cities with populations greater than 9,999 whose Asian and/or NHPI population rates are greater than the national average; (1) Native Hawaiian and other Pacific Islander; (2) excludes Taiwanese; (3) includes Chamorro; (4) county does not meet population threshold but is shown in order to allow inclusion of city

Place	Total population 25 years and over who are high school graduates	Asian population 25 years and over	Asians 25 years and over who are high school graduates	NHPI[1] population 25 years and over	NHPIs[1] 25 years and over who are high school graduates	Asian Indian	Bangladeshi	Cambodian	Chinese[2]	Fijian	Filipino	Guamanian[3]	Hawaiian, Native	Hmong	Indonesian	Japanese	Korean	Laotian	Malaysian	Pakistani	Samoan	Sri Lankan	Taiwanese	Thai	Tongan	Vietnamese
	17,274	4,164	3,253	-	-	424	-	-	185	-	548	-	-	-	-	-	520	158	-	-	-	-	-	-	-	896
	83.31		78.12			74.26			72.55		81.43						94.37	73.49								70.94
Springfield (cdp)						13.03			5.69		16.85						15.99	4.86								27.54
			78.12			10.18			4.44		13.16						12.49	3.79								21.52
			18.83			2.45			1.07		3.17						3.01	0.91								5.19
	13,269	2,239	2,045	-	-	556	-	-	444	-	-	-	-	-	-	-	464	-	-	-	-	-	-	-	-	-
	95.03		91.34			100.00			90.98								85.61									
Tysons Corner (cdp)						27.19			21.71								22.69									
			91.34			24.83			19.83								20.72									
			15.41			4.19			3.35								3.50									
	9,542	858	675	-	-	-	-	-	-	-	-	-	-	-	-	-	-	-	-	-	-	-	-	-	-	-
	92.05		78.67																							
Vienna (town)																										
			78.67																							
			7.07																							
	18,557	2,486	2,131	-	-	210	-	-	179	-	-	-	-	-	-	-	814	-	-	-	-	-	-	-	-	396
	95.50		85.72			87.50			89.05								89.75									73.20
West Springfield (cdp)						9.85			8.40								38.20									18.58
			85.72			8.45			7.20								32.74									15.93
			11.48			1.13			0.96								4.39									2.13
	9,088	826	787	-	-	206	-	-	169	-	-	-	-	-	-	-	-	-	-	-	-	-	-	-	-	-
	98.28		95.28			100.00			88.02																	
Wolf Trap (cdp)						26.18			21.47																	
			95.28			24.94			20.46																	
			8.66			2.27			1.86																	
	7,156	526	451	-	-	-	-	-	-	-	-	-	-	-	-	-	-	-	-	-	-	-	-	-	-	-
	95.87		85.74																							
Falls Church Independent City																										
			85.74																							
			6.30																							
	31,090	314	244	-	-	-	-	-	-	-	-	-	-	-	-	-	-	-	-	-	-	-	-	-	-	-
	84.50		77.71																							
Fauquier County																										
			77.71																							
			0.78																							
	30,858	309	241	-	-	-	-	-	-	-	-	-	-	-	-	-	-	-	-	-	-	-	-	-	-	-
	78.58		77.99																							
Frederick County																										
			77.99																							
			0.78																							
	79,075	1,735	1,301	-	-	-	-	-	-	-	360	-	-	-	-	-	-	-	-	-	-	-	-	-	-	232
	85.51		74.99								84.91															59.79
Hampton Independent City											27.67															17.83
			74.99								20.75															13.37
			1.65								0.46															0.29
	49,275	385	337	-	-	-	-	-	-	-	-	-	-	-	-	-	-	-	-	-	-	-	-	-	-	-
	86.61		87.53																							
Hanover County																										
			87.53																							
			0.68																							

Notes: Please refer to the User's Guide for an explanation of data; data is arranged alphabetically by state, then county, then city within each county; table includes counties with populations greater than 49,999 unless noted and cities with populations greater than 9,999 whose Asian and/or NHPI population rates are greater than the national average; (1) Native Hawaiian and other Pacific Islander; (2) excludes Taiwanese; (3) includes Chamorro; (4) county does not meet population threshold but is shown in order to allow inclusion of city

Place	Total population 25 years and over who are high school graduates	Asian population 25 years and over	Asians 25 years and over who are high school graduates	NHPI[1] population 25 years and over	NHPIs[1] 25 years and over who are high school graduates	Asian Indian	Bangladeshi	Cambodian	Chinese[2]	Fijian	Filipino	Guamanian[3]	Hawaiian, Native	Hmong	Indonesian	Japanese	Korean	Laotian	Malaysian	Pakistani	Samoan	Sri Lankan	Taiwanese	Thai	Tongan	Vietnamese
Henrico County	153,476	6,143	4,723	-	-	1,722	-	109	881	-	396	-	-	-	-	-	556	-	-	-	-	-	-	-	-	551
	86.62		76.88			92.58		27.46	76.28		89.19						89.97									54.13
						36.46		2.31	18.65		8.38						11.77									11.67
			76.88			28.03		1.77	14.34		6.45						9.05									8.97
			3.08			1.12		0.07	0.57		0.26						0.36									0.36
Glen Allen (cdp)	7,952	301	213	-	-	-	-	-	-	-	-	-	-	-	-	-	-	-	-	-	-	-	-	-	-	-
	92.04		70.76																							
			70.76																							
			2.68																							
Laurel (cdp)	8,452	478	396	-	-	-	-	-	-	-	-	-	-	-	-	-	-	-	-	-	-	-	-	-	-	-
	84.07		82.85																							
			82.85																							
			4.69																							
Loudoun County	101,385	5,842	5,075	-	-	1,101	-	-	745	-	722	-	-	-	-	-	652	-	-	319	-	-	-	-	-	887
	92.53		86.87			89.29			89.22		96.52						91.96			87.40						77.81
						21.69			14.68		14.23						12.85			6.29						17.48
			86.87			18.85			12.75		12.36						11.16			5.46						15.18
			5.01			1.09			0.73		0.71						0.64			0.31						0.87
Lynchburg Independent City	31,835	576	520	-	-	-	-	-	-	-	-	-	-	-	-	-	-	-	-	-	-	-	-	-	-	-
	78.02		90.28																							
			90.28																							
			1.63																							
Manassas Park Indep. City	4,757	241	216	-	-	-	-	-	-	-	-	-	-	-	-	-	-	-	-	-	-	-	-	-	-	-
	76.43		89.63																							
			89.63																							
			4.54																							
Montgomery County	35,679	1,371	1,328	-	-	275	-	-	456	-	-	-	-	-	-	-	316	-	-	-	-	-	-	-	-	-
	82.77		96.86			100.00			98.70								96.64									
						20.71			34.34								23.80									
			96.86			20.06			33.26								23.05									
			3.72			0.77			1.28								0.89									
Blacksburg (town)	11,951	1,184	1,152	-	-	227	-	-	428	-	-	-	-	-	-	-	276	-	-	-	-	-	-	-	-	-
	92.91		97.30			100.00			98.62								100.00									
						19.70			37.15								23.96									
			97.30			19.17			36.15								23.31									
			9.64			1.90			3.58								2.31									
Newport News Independent City	93,030	2,898	2,292	-	-	-	-	-	302	-	394	-	-	-	-	-	673	-	-	-	-	-	-	-	-	302
	84.51		79.09						86.78		89.75						77.98									64.12
									13.18		17.19						29.36									13.18
			79.09						10.42		13.60						23.22									10.42
			2.46						0.32		0.42						0.72									0.32
Norfolk Independent City	106,020	4,370	3,483	-	-	221	-	-	416	-	2,358	-	-	-	-	-	-	-	-	-	-	-	-	-	-	116
	78.38		79.70			94.04			85.77		82.36															54.98
						6.35			11.94		67.70															3.33
			79.70			5.06			9.52		53.96															2.65
			3.29			0.21			0.39		2.22															0.11

Notes: Please refer to the User's Guide for an explanation of data; data is arranged alphabetically by state, then county, then city within each county; table includes counties with populations greater than 49,999 unless noted and cities with populations greater than 9,999 whose Asian and/or NHPI population rates are greater than the national average; (1) Native Hawaiian and other Pacific Islander; (2) excludes Taiwanese; (3) includes Chamorro; (4) county does not meet population threshold but is shown in order to allow inclusion of city

Place	Total population 25 years and over who are high school graduates	Asian population 25 years and over	Asians 25 years and over who are high school graduates	NHPI[1] population 25 years and over	NHPIs[1] 25 years and over who are high school graduates	Asian Indian	Bangladeshi	Cambodian	Chinese[2]	Fijian	Filipino	Guamanian[3]	Hawaiian, Native	Hmong	Indonesian	Japanese	Korean	Laotian	Malaysian	Pakistani	Samoan	Sri Lankan	Taiwanese	Thai	Tongan	Vietnamese
Portsmouth Independent City	47,862 75.15	484	407 84.09 84.09 0.85	-	-	-	-	-	-	-	279 94.58 68.55 57.64 0.58	-	-	-	-	-	-	-	-	-	-	-	-	-	-	-
Prince William County	151,849 88.77	6,977	5,833 83.60 83.60 3.84	-	-	936 81.18 16.05 13.42 0.62	-	-	619 85.50 10.61 8.87 0.41	-	1,460 91.77 25.03 20.93 0.96	-	-	-	-	323 89.72 5.54 4.63 0.21	981 81.55 16.82 14.06 0.65	-	-	368 90.42 6.31 5.27 0.24	-	-	-	-	-	482 72.81 8.26 6.91 0.32
Bull Run (cdp)	5,949 84.55	432	398 92.13 92.13 6.69	-	-	-	-	-	-	-	-	-	-	-	-	-	-	-	-	-	-	-	-	-	-	-
Dale City (cdp)	29,386 89.05	1,894	1,536 81.10 81.10 5.23	-	-	272 70.65 17.71 14.36 0.93	-	-	-	-	378 81.64 24.61 19.96 1.29	-	-	-	-	-	-	-	-	147 86.47 9.57 7.76 0.50	-	-	-	-	-	-
Lake Ridge (cdp)	18,434 95.07	756	718 94.97 94.97 3.89	-	-	-	-	-	-	-	-	-	-	-	-	-	-	-	-	-	-	-	-	-	-	-
Woodbridge (cdp)	15,177 80.30	964	730 75.73 75.73 4.81	-	-	-	-	-	-	-	-	-	-	-	-	-	-	-	-	-	-	-	-	-	-	-
Richmond Independent City	96,648 75.18	1,298	1,067 82.20 82.20 1.10	-	-	204 89.08 19.12 15.72 0.21	-	-	-	-	217 93.94 20.34 16.72 0.22	-	-	-	-	-	-	-	-	-	-	-	-	-	-	-
Roanoke Independent City	49,851 76.00	620	472 76.13 76.13 0.95	-	-	-	-	-	-	-	-	-	-	-	-	-	-	-	-	-	-	-	-	-	-	-
Roanoke County	52,119 85.76	649	609 93.84 93.84 1.17	-	-	-	-	-	-	-	-	-	-	-	-	-	-	-	-	-	-	-	-	-	-	-
Spotsylvania County	47,446 83.78	840	669 79.64 79.64 1.41	-	-	-	-	-	-	-	-	-	-	-	-	-	-	-	-	-	-	-	-	-	-	-

Notes: Please refer to the User's Guide for an explanation of data; data is arranged alphabetically by state, then county, then city within each county; table includes counties with populations greater than 49,999 unless noted and cities with populations greater than 9,999 whose Asian and/or NHPI population rates are greater than the national average; (1) Native Hawaiian and other Pacific Islander; (2) excludes Taiwanese; (3) includes Chamorro; (4) county does not meet population threshold but is shown in order to allow inclusion of city

Place	Total population 25 years and over who are high school graduates	Asian population 25 years and over	Asians 25 years and over who are high school graduates	NHPI[1] population 25 years and over	NHPIs[1] 25 years and over who are high school graduates	Asian Indian	Bangladeshi	Cambodian	Chinese[2]	Fijian	Filipino	Guamanian[3]	Hawaiian, Native	Hmong	Indonesian	Japanese	Korean	Laotian	Malaysian	Pakistani	Samoan	Sri Lankan	Taiwanese	Thai	Tongan	Vietnamese
	49,650	1,106	949	-	-	-	-	-	-	-	288	-	-	-	-	-	-	-	-	-	-	-	-	-	-	-
	88.61		85.80								91.14															
Stafford County											30.35															
			85.80								26.04															
			1.91								0.58															
	32,010	406	314	-	-	-	-	-	-	-	-	-	-	-	-	-	-	-	-	-	-	-	-	-	-	-
	76.83		77.34																							
Suffolk Independent City																										
			77.34																							
			0.98																							
	241,162	13,216	11,124	-	-	704	-	-	766	-	7,842	-	-	-	-	514	461	-	-	-	-	-	-	-	-	317
	90.45		84.17			89.45			71.39		88.64					87.56	79.76									43.19
Virginia Beach Independent City						6.33			6.89		70.50					4.62	4.14									2.85
			84.17			5.33			5.80		59.34					3.89	3.49									2.40
			4.61			0.29			0.32		3.25					0.21	0.19									0.13
	4,803	193	155	-	-	-	-	-	-	-	-	-	-	-	-	-	-	-	-	-	-	-	-	-	-	-
	89.61		80.31																							
Williamsburg Independent City																										
			80.31																							
			3.23																							
	33,160	1,151	998	-	-	162	-	-	-	-	-	-	-	-	-	-	295	-	-	-	-	-	-	-	-	-
	91.68		86.71			90.50											88.32									
York County						16.23											29.56									
			86.71			14.07											25.63									
			3.01			0.49											0.89									
	3,333,171	209,271	168,561	11,598	9,621	12,358	-	3,607	32,393	288	37,981	2,520	2,566	239	730	26,520	24,900	2,123	-	654	2,542	222	2,144	2,069	366	17,493
	87.08		80.55		82.95	83.99		49.59	82.41	64.14	87.01	84.93	89.59	44.26	96.56	92.15	83.29	49.46		92.11	75.50	85.71	94.41	79.36	85.51	62.37
WASHINGTON						7.33		2.14	19.22	2.99	22.53	26.19	26.67	0.14	0.43	15.73	14.77	1.26		0.39	26.42	0.13	1.27	1.23	3.80	10.38
			80.55		82.95	5.91		1.72	15.48	2.48	18.15	21.73	22.12	0.11	0.35	12.67	11.90	1.01		0.31	21.92	0.11	1.02	0.99	3.16	8.36
			5.06		0.29	0.37		0.11	0.97	0.01	1.14	0.08	0.08	0.01	0.02	0.80	0.75	0.06		0.02	0.08	0.01	0.06	0.06	0.01	0.52
	75,076	2,003	1,723	-	-	272	-	-	387	-	-	-	-	-	-	-	153	-	-	-	-	-	-	-	-	229
	85.10		86.02			90.37			97.97								71.50									67.55
Benton County						15.79			22.46								8.88									13.29
			86.02			13.58			19.32								7.64									11.43
			2.30			0.36			0.52								0.20									0.31
	23,467	1,102	1,018	-	-	-	-	-	295	-	-	-	-	-	-	-	-	-	-	-	-	-	-	-	-	-
	92.61		92.38						97.36																	
Richland (city)									28.98																	
			92.38						26.77																	
			4.34						1.26																	
	33,546	278	208	-	-	-	-	-	-	-	-	-	-	-	-	-	-	-	-	-	-	-	-	-	-	-
	79.07		74.82																							
Chelan County																										
			74.82																							
			0.62																							
	39,079	597	459	-	-	-	-	-	-	-	-	-	-	-	-	-	-	-	-	-	-	-	-	-	-	-
	85.49		76.88																							
Clallam County																										
			76.88																							
			1.17																							

Notes: Please refer to the User's Guide for an explanation of data; data is arranged alphabetically by state, then county, then city within each county; table includes counties with populations greater than 49,999 unless noted and cities with populations greater than 9,999 whose Asian and/or NHPI population rates are greater than the national average; (1) Native Hawaiian and other Pacific Islander; (2) excludes Taiwanese; (3) includes Chamorro; (4) county does not meet population threshold but is shown in order to allow inclusion of city

Place	Total population 25 years and over who are high school graduates	Asian population 25 years and over	Asians 25 years and over who are high school graduates	NHPI[1] population 25 years and over	NHPIs[1] 25 years and over who are high school graduates	Asian Indian	Bangladeshi	Cambodian	Chinese[2]	Fijian	Filipino	Guamanian[3]	Hawaiian, Native	Hmong	Indonesian	Japanese	Korean	Laotian	Malaysian	Pakistani	Samoan	Sri Lankan	Taiwanese	Thai	Tongan	Vietnamese
	190,715	6,988	5,552	619	537	374	-	143	932	-	1,044	-	-	-	-	922	782	114	-	-	-	-	-	-	-	894
	87.77		79.45		86.75	89.47		56.52	82.84		86.00					93.41	87.08	50.00								61.83
Clark County						6.74		2.58	16.79		18.80					16.61	14.09	2.05								16.10
			79.45		86.75	5.35		2.05	13.34		14.94					13.19	11.19	1.63								12.79
			2.91		0.28	0.20		0.07	0.49		0.55					0.48	0.41	0.06								0.47
	6,402	337	239	-	-	-	-	-	-	-	-	-	-	-	-	-	-	-	-	-	-	-	-	-	-	-
	85.08		70.92																							
Five Corners (cdp)																										
			70.92																							
			3.73																							
	9,146	494	379	-	-	-	-	-	-	-	-	-	-	-	-	-	-	-	-	-	-	-	-	-	-	-
	88.79		76.72																							
Orchards (cdp)																										
			76.72																							
			4.14																							
	78,231	4,171	3,298	401	367	-	-	-	591	-	569	-	-	-	-	545	429	-	-	-	-	-	-	-	-	605
	85.96		79.07		91.52				83.24		87.54					94.13	85.12									63.95
Vancouver (city)									17.92		17.25					16.53	13.01									18.34
			79.07		91.52				14.17		13.64					13.07	10.29									14.50
			4.22		0.47				0.76		0.73					0.70	0.55									0.77
	50,195	721	412	-	-	-	-	28	-	-	-	-	-	-	-	-	-	-	-	-	-	-	-	-	-	144
	83.17		57.14					18.54																		63.44
Cowlitz County								6.80																		34.95
			57.14					3.88																		19.97
			0.82					0.06																		0.29
	31,283	417	378	-	-	-	-	-	-	-	-	-	-	-	-	-	-	-	-	-	-	-	-	-	-	-
	72.23		90.65																							
Grant County																										
			90.65																							
			1.21																							
	36,156	401	313	-	-	-	-	-	-	-	-	-	-	-	-	-	-	-	-	-	-	-	-	-	-	-
	81.09		78.05																							
Grays Harbor County																										
			78.05																							
			0.87																							
	43,388	1,843	1,486	-	-	-	-	-	-	-	1,007	-	-	-	-	231	-	-	-	-	-	-	-	-	-	-
	92.10		80.63								79.48					82.80										
Island County											67.77					15.55										
			80.63								54.64					12.53										
			3.42								2.32					0.53										
	10,169	1,110	896	-	-	-	-	-	-	-	688	-	-	-	-	-	-	-	-	-	-	-	-	-	-	-
	90.41		80.72								78.45															
Oak Harbor (city)											76.79															
			80.72								61.98															
			8.81								6.77															
	1,073,012	123,894	101,247	4,488	3,560	8,298	-	1,725	24,696	229	19,864	376	888	109	481	16,761	11,194	1,256	-	285	1,315	-	1,766	1,132	262	10,397
	90.26		81.72		79.32	86.61		52.83	81.26	65.24	87.98	88.26	92.02	37.72	97.57	94.21	87.93	47.63		94.37	69.25		95.36	84.23	86.18	62.13
King County						8.20		1.70	24.39	6.43	19.62	10.56	24.94	0.11	0.48	16.55	11.06	1.24		0.28	36.94		1.74	1.12	7.36	10.27
			81.72		79.32	6.70		1.39	19.93	5.10	16.03	8.38	19.79	0.09	0.39	13.53	9.04	1.01		0.23	29.30		1.43	0.91	5.84	8.39
			9.44		0.33	0.77		0.16	2.30	0.02	1.85	0.04	0.08	0.01	0.04	1.56	1.04	0.12		0.03	0.12		0.16	0.11	0.02	0.97

Notes: Please refer to the User's Guide for an explanation of data; data is arranged alphabetically by state, then county, then city within each county; table includes counties with populations greater than 49,999 unless noted and cities with populations greater than 9,999 whose Asian and/or NHPI population rates are greater than the national average; (1) Native Hawaiian and other Pacific Islander; (2) excludes Taiwanese; (3) includes Chamorro; (4) county does not meet population threshold but is shown in order to allow inclusion of city

Place	Total population 25 years and over who are high school graduates	Asian population 25 years and over	Asians 25 years and over who are high school graduates	NHPI[1] population 25 years and over	NHPIs[1] 25 years and over who are high school graduates	Asian Indian	Bangladeshi	Cambodian	Chinese[2]	Fijian	Filipino	Guamanian[3]	Hawaiian, Native	Hmong	Indonesian	Japanese	Korean	Laotian	Malaysian	Pakistani	Samoan	Sri Lankan	Taiwanese	Thai	Tongan	Vietnamese
Auburn (city)	21,177	1,006	787	-	-	-	-	-	-	-	-	-	-	-	-	-	-	-	-	-	-	-	-	-	-	-
	82.82		78.23																							
			78.23																							
			3.72																							
Bellevue (city)	73,619	12,766	11,847	-	-	1,754	-	-	3,686	-	778	-	-	-	-	2,227	1,473	193	-	-	-	-	518	-	-	658
	94.34		92.80			97.17			92.45		97.62					97.89	97.16	73.38					95.22			73.68
						14.81			31.11		6.57					18.80	12.43	1.63					4.37			5.55
			92.80			13.74			28.87		6.09					17.44	11.54	1.51					4.06			5.15
			16.09			2.38			5.01		1.06					3.03	2.00	0.26					0.70			0.89
Bothell (city)	18,590	1,398	1,344	-	-	-	-	-	351	-	-	-	-	-	-	-	-	-	-	-	-	-	-	-	-	-
	93.74		96.14						96.69																	
									26.12																	
			96.14						25.11																	
			7.23						1.89																	
Bryn Mawr-Skyway (cdp)	8,312	2,101	1,559	-	-	-	-	-	-	-	491	-	-	-	-	439	-	-	-	-	-	-	-	-	-	147
	84.15		74.20								82.24					88.33										49.33
											31.49					28.16										9.43
			74.20								23.37					20.89										7.00
			18.76								5.91					5.28										1.77
Burien (city)	18,964	1,374	1,129	-	-	-	-	-	-	-	297	-	-	-	-	-	-	-	-	-	-	-	-	-	-	220
	84.80		82.17								86.59															84.62
											26.31															19.49
			82.17								21.62															16.01
			5.95								1.57															1.16
Cascade-Fairwood (cdp)	20,509	3,038	2,561	-	-	-	-	-	538	-	791	-	-	-	-	378	-	-	-	-	-	-	-	-	-	328
	91.69		84.30						88.93		90.09					93.56										72.89
									21.01		30.89					14.76										12.81
			84.30						17.71		26.04					12.44										10.80
			12.49						2.62		3.86					1.84										1.60
Cottage Lake (cdp)	14,708	730	678	-	-	-	-	-	-	-	-	-	-	-	-	-	-	-	-	-	-	-	-	-	-	-
	97.13		92.88																							
			92.88																							
			4.61																							
Des Moines (city)	17,497	1,417	1,039	186	88	-	-	-	-	-	253	-	-	-	-	-	-	-	-	-	-	-	-	-	-	172
	87.52		73.32		47.31						93.36															56.77
											24.35															16.55
			73.32		47.31						17.85															12.14
			5.94		0.50						1.45															0.98
East Hill-Meridian (cdp)	16,605	2,459	1,923	-	-	343	-	-	406	-	362	-	-	-	-	-	-	-	-	-	-	-	-	-	-	235
	89.59		78.20			75.88			79.92		87.44															67.14
						17.84			21.11		18.82															12.22
			78.20			13.95			16.51		14.72															9.56
			11.58			2.07			2.45		2.18															1.42
Federal Way (city)	46,222	6,676	5,832	460	359	-	-	-	557	-	1,041	-	-	-	-	529	2,589	-	-	-	168	-	-	-	-	561
	89.26		87.36		78.04				93.30		88.00					97.42	87.85				72.10					78.46
									9.55		17.85					9.07	44.39				46.80					9.62
			87.36		78.04				8.34		15.59					7.92	38.78				36.52					8.40
			12.62		0.78				1.21		2.25					1.14	5.60				0.36					1.21

Notes: Please refer to the User's Guide for an explanation of data; data is arranged alphabetically by state, then county, then city within each county; table includes counties with populations greater than 49,999 unless noted and cities with populations greater than 9,999 whose Asian and/or NHPI population rates are greater than the national average; (1) Native Hawaiian and other Pacific Islander; (2) excludes Taiwanese; (3) includes Chamorro; (4) county does not meet population threshold but is shown in order to allow inclusion of city

Place	Total population 25 years and over who are high school graduates	Asian population 25 years and over	Asians 25 years and over who are high school graduates	NHPI[1] population 25 years and over	NHPIs[1] 25 years and over who are high school graduates	Asian Indian	Bangladeshi	Cambodian	Chinese[2]	Fijian	Filipino	Guamanian[3]	Hawaiian, Native	Hmong	Indonesian	Japanese	Korean	Laotian	Malaysian	Pakistani	Samoan	Sri Lankan	Taiwanese	Thai	Tongan	Vietnamese
Inglewood-Finn Hill (cdp)	14,422 96.05	1,141	1,049 91.94 91.94 7.27	-	-	-	-	-	255 86.73 24.31 22.35 1.77	-	-	-	-	-	-	-	-	-	-	-	-	-	-	-	-	-
Issaquah (city)	7,622 96.15	474	466 98.31 98.31 6.11	-	-	-	-	-	-	-	-	-	-	-	-	-	-	-	-	-	-	-	-	-	-	-
Kenmore (city)	11,825 92.93	792	701 88.51 88.51 5.93	-	-	-	-	-	-	-	-	-	-	-	-	-	-	-	-	-	-	-	-	-	-	-
Kent (city)	42,703 86.61	4,888	3,954 80.89 80.89 9.26	-	-	631 69.65 15.96 12.91 1.48	-	-	578 89.89 14.62 11.82 1.35	-	978 94.13 24.73 20.01 2.29	-	-	-	-	478 96.18 12.09 9.78 1.12	449 85.52 11.36 9.19 1.05	-	-	-	-	-	-	-	-	534 63.12 13.51 10.92 1.25
Kingsgate (cdp)	7,126 93.11	909	732 80.53 80.53 10.27	-	-	-	-	-	256 94.46 34.97 28.16 3.59	-	-	-	-	-	-	-	-	-	-	-	-	-	-	-	-	-
Kirkland (city)	31,240 95.36	2,537	2,353 92.75 92.75 7.53	-	-	-	-	-	553 96.68 23.50 21.80 1.77	-	-	-	-	-	-	468 100.00 19.89 18.45 1.50	-	-	-	-	-	-	-	-	-	317 81.49 13.47 12.50 1.01
Lake Forest Park (city)	9,024 93.18	834	675 80.94 80.94 7.48	-	-	-	-	-	-	-	-	-	-	-	-	-	-	-	-	-	-	-	-	-	-	-
Lakeland North (cdp)	8,691 90.38	609	496 81.44 81.44 5.71	-	-	-	-	-	-	-	-	-	-	-	-	-	-	-	-	-	-	-	-	-	-	-
Lakeland South (cdp)	6,916 91.26	446	424 95.07 95.07 6.13	-	-	-	-	-	-	-	-	-	-	-	-	-	-	-	-	-	-	-	-	-	-	-
Lea Hill (cdp)	5,882 91.76	237	184 77.64 77.64 3.13	-	-	-	-	-	-	-	-	-	-	-	-	-	-	-	-	-	-	-	-	-	-	-

Notes: Please refer to the User's Guide for an explanation of data; data is arranged alphabetically by state, then county, then city within each county; table includes counties with populations greater than 49,999 unless noted and cities with populations greater than 9,999 whose Asian and/or NHPI population rates are greater than the national average; (1) Native Hawaiian and other Pacific Islander; (2) excludes Taiwanese; (3) includes Chamorro; (4) county does not meet population threshold but is shown in order to allow inclusion of city

Place	Total population 25 years and over who are high school graduates	Asian population 25 years and over	Asians 25 years and over who are high school graduates	NHPI[1] population 25 years and over	NHPIs[1] 25 years and over who are high school graduates	Asian Indian	Bangladeshi	Cambodian	Chinese[2]	Fijian	Filipino	Guamanian[3]	Hawaiian, Native	Hmong	Indonesian	Japanese	Korean	Laotian	Malaysian	Pakistani	Samoan	Sri Lankan	Taiwanese	Thai	Tongan	Vietnamese
	15,075	1,741	1,660	-	-	-	-	-	635	-	-	-	-	-	-	512	-	-	-	-	-	-	-	-	-	-
	97.74		95.35						93.66							98.84										
Mercer Island (city)									38.25							30.84										
			95.35						36.47							29.41										
			11.01						4.21							3.40										
	29,626	4,065	3,802	-	-	860	-	-	1,309	-	-	-	-	-	-	584	286	-	-	-	-	-	-	-	-	-
	94.46		93.53			98.29			96.39							100.00	84.12									
Redmond (city)						22.62			34.43							15.36	7.52									
			93.53			21.16			32.20							14.37	7.04									
			12.83			2.90			4.42							1.97	0.97									
	29,454	4,547	3,743	-	-	-	-	-	780	-	909	-	-	-	-	539	-	-	-	-	-	-	-	-	-	730
	86.62		82.32						83.16		87.74					98.90										67.34
Renton (city)									20.84		24.29					14.40										19.50
			82.32						17.15		19.99					11.85										16.05
			12.71						2.65		3.09					1.83										2.48
	5,923	923	682	-	-	-	-	-	-	-	-	-	-	-	-	-	-	-	-	-	-	-	-	-	-	-
	79.57		73.89																							
Riverton-Boulevard Park (cdp)																										
			73.89																							
			11.51																							
	20,951	1,720	1,698	-	-	-	-	-	737	-	-	-	-	-	-	-	-	-	-	-	-	-	-	-	-	-
	98.35		98.72						100.00																	
Sammamish (city)									43.40																	
			98.72						42.85																	
			8.10						3.52																	
	13,495	1,813	1,328	335	233	261	-	-	-	-	406	-	-	-	-	-	-	-	-	-	-	-	-	-	-	173
	81.42		73.25		69.55	67.27					81.04															56.91
SeaTac (city)						19.65					30.57															13.03
			73.25		69.55	14.40					22.39															9.54
			9.84		1.73	1.93					3.01															1.28
	366,435	49,210	37,263	1,340	1,025	1,756	-	528	9,405	-	9,363	-	-	-	179	6,783	2,577	532	-	-	435	-	564	526	-	3,888
	89.47		75.72		76.49	87.71		43.89	70.16		86.57				96.76	91.03	83.00	39.76			68.50		94.16	91.96		55.27
Seattle (city)						4.71		1.42	25.24		25.13				0.48	18.20	6.92	1.43			42.44		1.51	1.41		10.43
			75.72		76.49	3.57		1.07	19.11		19.03				0.36	13.78	5.24	1.08			32.46		1.15	1.07		7.90
			10.17		0.28	0.48		0.14	2.57		2.56				0.05	1.85	0.70	0.15			0.12		0.15	0.14		1.06
	33,338	4,336	3,678	-	-	261	-	-	919	-	730	-	-	-	-	293	746	-	-	-	-	-	-	-	-	377
	90.16		84.82			95.60			76.65		90.91					97.67	88.08									74.51
Shoreline (city)						7.10			24.99		19.85					7.97	20.28									10.25
			84.82			6.02			21.19		16.84					6.76	17.20									8.69
			11.03			0.78			2.76		2.19					0.88	2.24									1.13
	9,268	1,180	993	115	72	-	-	-	-	-	363	-	-	-	-	-	-	-	-	-	-	-	-	-	-	-
	81.55		84.15		62.61						94.04															
Tukwila (city)											36.56															
			84.15		62.61						30.76															
			10.71		0.78						3.92															
	6,469	334	312	-	-	-	-	-	-	-	-	-	-	-	-	-	-	-	-	-	-	-	-	-	-	-
	94.73		93.41																							
Union Hill-Novelty Hill (cdp)																										
			93.41																							
			4.82																							

Notes: Please refer to the User's Guide for an explanation of data; data is arranged alphabetically by state, then county, then city within each county; table includes counties with populations greater than 49,999 unless noted and cities with populations greater than 9,999 whose Asian and/or NHPI population rates are greater than the national average; (1) Native Hawaiian and other Pacific Islander; (2) excludes Taiwanese; (3) includes Chamorro; (4) county does not meet population threshold but is shown in order to allow inclusion of city

Place	Total population 25 years and over who are high school graduates	Asian population 25 years and over	Asians 25 years and over who are high school graduates	NHPI[1] population 25 years and over	NHPIs[1] 25 years and over who are high school graduates	Asian Indian	Bangladeshi	Cambodian	Chinese[2]	Fijian	Filipino	Guamanian[3]	Hawaiian, Native	Hmong	Indonesian	Japanese	Korean	Laotian	Malaysian	Pakistani	Samoan	Sri Lankan	Taiwanese	Thai	Tongan	Vietnamese
White Center (cdp)	9,709	2,536	1,363	-	-	-	-	227	-	-	258	-	-	-	-	-	-	-	-	-	-	-	-	-	-	548
	73.14		53.75					43.40			77.95															45.63
								16.65			18.93															40.21
			53.75					8.95			10.17															21.61
			14.04					2.34			2.66															5.64
Kitsap County	134,973	7,097	5,874	913	830	-	-	-	301	-	3,906	472	-	-	-	862	335	-	-	-	-	-	-	-	-	167
	90.77		82.77		90.91				79.21		84.33	88.56				85.43	82.92									64.48
									5.12		66.50	56.87				14.67	5.70									2.84
			82.77		90.91				4.24		55.04	51.70				12.15	4.72									2.35
			4.35		0.61				0.22		2.89	0.35				0.64	0.25									0.12
Bremerton (city)	19,097	1,344	988	-	-	-	-	-	-	-	699	-	-	-	-	-	-	-	-	-	-	-	-	-	-	-
	86.51		73.51								73.81															
											70.75															
			73.51								52.01															
			5.17								3.66															
Silverdale (cdp)	8,985	1,055	949	-	-	-	-	-	-	-	794	-	-	-	-	-	-	-	-	-	-	-	-	-	-	-
	93.94		89.95								92.54															
											83.67															
			89.95								75.26															
			10.56								8.84															
Lewis County	36,132	243	195	-	-	-	-	-	-	-	-	-	-	-	-	-	-	-	-	-	-	-	-	-	-	-
	80.55		80.25																							
			80.25																							
			0.54																							
Pierce County	384,540	23,295	16,961	2,687	2,316	347	-	779	1,113	-	3,900	785	512	-	-	2,513	5,821	133	-	-	698	-	-	244	-	1,551
	86.87		72.81		86.19	73.21		41.55	88.19		83.83	82.72	90.62			82.77	74.16	50.96			86.60			74.85		54.61
						2.05		4.59	6.56		22.99	33.89	22.11			14.82	34.32	0.78			30.14			1.44		9.14
			72.81		86.19	1.49		3.34	4.78		16.74	29.21	19.05			10.79	24.99	0.57			25.98			1.05		6.66
			4.41		0.60	0.09		0.20	0.29		1.01	0.20	0.13			0.65	1.51	0.03			0.18			0.06		0.40
Elk Plain (cdp)	8,331	419	343	-	-	-	-	-	-	-	-	-	-	-	-	-	-	-	-	-	-	-	-	-	-	-
	88.49		81.86																							
			81.86																							
			4.12																							
Fort Lewis (cdp)	7,289	352	324	129	114	-	-	-	-	-	193	-	-	-	-	-	-	-	-	-	-	-	-	-	-	-
	96.54		92.05		88.37						91.90															
											59.57															
			92.05		88.37						54.83															
			4.45		1.56						2.65															
Lakewood (city)	32,106	3,800	2,758	385	353	-	-	-	-	-	680	-	-	-	-	464	1,292	-	-	-	129	-	-	-	-	-
	85.42		72.58		91.69						79.53					75.08	73.41				95.56					
											24.66					16.82	46.85				36.54					
			72.58		91.69						17.89					12.21	34.00				33.51					
			8.59		1.10						2.12					1.45	4.02				0.40					
Parkland (cdp)	11,736	1,117	842	203	155	-	-	-	-	-	-	-	-	-	-	-	396	-	-	-	-	-	-	-	-	-
	84.09		75.38		76.35												74.72									
																	47.03									
			75.38		76.35												35.45									
			7.17		1.32												3.37									

Notes: Please refer to the User's Guide for an explanation of data; data is arranged alphabetically by state, then county, then city within each county; table includes counties with populations greater than 49,999 unless noted and cities with populations greater than 9,999 whose Asian and/or NHPI population rates are greater than the national average; (1) Native Hawaiian and other Pacific Islander; (2) excludes Taiwanese; (3) includes Chamorro; (4) county does not meet population threshold but is shown in order to allow inclusion of city

Place	Total population 25 years and over who are high school graduates	Asian population 25 years and over	Asians 25 years and over who are high school graduates	NHPI[1] population 25 years and over	NHPIs[1] 25 years and over who are high school graduates	Asian Indian	Bangladeshi	Cambodian	Chinese[2]	Fijian	Filipino	Guamanian[3]	Hawaiian, Native	Hmong	Indonesian	Japanese	Korean	Laotian	Malaysian	Pakistani	Samoan	Sri Lankan	Taiwanese	Thai	Tongan	Vietnamese
Spanaway (cdp)	11,214 84.56	918	659 71.79 71.79 5.88	253	224 88.54 88.54 2.00	-	-	-	-	-	251 81.76 38.09 27.34 2.24	-	-	-	-	-	321 69.33 48.71 34.97 2.86	-	-	-	-	-	-	-	-	-
Tacoma (city)	103,651 83.59	9,208	5,902 64.10 64.10 5.69	734	574 78.20 78.20 0.55	-	-	574 39.70 9.73 6.23 0.55	465 87.41 7.88 5.05 0.45	-	1,185 81.61 20.08 12.87 1.14	185 74.00 32.23 25.20 0.18	-	-	-	569 80.37 9.64 6.18 0.55	1,558 69.06 26.40 16.92 1.50	88 47.57 1.49 0.96 0.08	-	-	225 82.72 39.20 30.65 0.22	-	-	-	-	1,041 51.15 17.64 11.31 1.00
University Place (city)	18,080 92.88	1,485	1,257 84.65 84.65 6.95	-	-	-	-	-	-	-	-	-	-	-	-	-	646 85.79 51.39 43.50 3.57	-	-	-	-	-	-	-	-	-
Skagit County	56,213 83.95	788	659 83.63 83.63 1.17	-	-	-	-	-	-	-	253 83.22 38.39 32.11 0.45	-	-	-	-	-	-	-	-	-	-	-	-	-	-	-
Snohomish County	346,918 89.18	22,558	19,103 84.68 84.68 5.51	733	610 83.22 83.22 0.18	1,488 83.97 7.79 6.60 0.43	-	626 57.70 3.28 2.78 0.18	2,563 88.90 13.42 11.36 0.74	-	4,449 90.91 23.29 19.72 1.28	-	270 88.82 44.26 36.83 0.08	-	-	1,736 93.79 9.09 7.70 0.50	4,236 87.63 22.17 18.78 1.22	310 74.16 1.62 1.37 0.09	-	233 95.49 1.22 1.03 0.07	-	-	-	-	-	2,396 71.29 12.54 10.62 0.69
Alderwood Manor (cdp)	9,156 91.90	856	705 82.36 82.36 7.70	-	-	-	-	-	-	-	-	-	-	-	-	-	-	-	-	-	-	-	-	-	-	-
Edmonds (city)	26,714 93.55	1,423	1,348 94.73 94.73 5.05	-	-	-	-	-	-	-	220 97.35 16.32 15.46 0.82	-	-	-	-	-	321 85.37 23.81 22.56 1.20	-	-	-	-	-	-	-	-	-
Everett (city)	48,228 84.37	3,699	2,726 73.70 73.70 5.65	-	-	327 78.23 12.00 8.84 0.68	-	119 38.39 4.37 3.22 0.25	-	-	1,005 88.94 36.87 27.17 2.08	-	-	-	-	-	-	-	-	-	-	-	-	-	-	464 61.95 17.02 12.54 0.96
Lynnwood (city)	19,206 86.87	2,957	2,459 83.16 83.16 12.80	-	-	-	-	-	316 85.64 12.85 10.69 1.65	-	556 96.03 22.61 18.80 2.89	-	-	-	-	-	578 84.38 23.51 19.55 3.01	-	-	-	-	-	-	-	-	486 75.70 19.76 16.44 2.53
Martha Lake (cdp)	7,475 91.71	739	621 84.03 84.03 8.31	-	-	-	-	-	-	-	-	-	-	-	-	-	-	-	-	-	-	-	-	-	-	-

Notes: Please refer to the User's Guide for an explanation of data; data is arranged alphabetically by state, then county, then city within each county; table includes counties with populations greater than 49,999 unless noted and cities with populations greater than 9,999 whose Asian and/or NHPI population rates are greater than the national average; (1) Native Hawaiian and other Pacific Islander; (2) excludes Taiwanese; (3) includes Chamorro; (4) county does not meet population threshold but is shown in order to allow inclusion of city

Place	Total population 25 years and over who are high school graduates	Asian population 25 years and over	Asians 25 years and over who are high school graduates	NHPI[1] population 25 years and over	NHPIs[1] 25 years and over who are high school graduates	Asian Indian	Bangladeshi	Cambodian	Chinese[2]	Fijian	Filipino	Guamanian[3]	Hawaiian, Native	Hmong	Indonesian	Japanese	Korean	Laotian	Malaysian	Pakistani	Samoan	Sri Lankan	Taiwanese	Thai	Tongan	Vietnamese
	13,660	668	504	-	-	-	-	-	-	-	-	-	-	-	-	-	-	-	-	-	-	-	-	-	-	-
	87.08		75.45																							
Marysville (city)																										
			75.45																							
			3.69																							
	7,352	771	726	-	-	-	-	-	-	-	-	-	-	-	-	-	275	-	-	-	-	-	-	-	-	-
	95.04		94.16														94.83									
Mill Creek (city)																	37.88									
			94.16														35.67									
			9.87														3.74									
	12,047	1,506	1,324	-	-	-	-	-	-	-	317	-	-	-	-	-	390	-	-	-	-	-	-	-	-	-
	90.48		87.92								91.35						91.33									
Mountlake Terrace (city)											23.94						29.46									
			87.92								21.05						25.90									
			10.99								2.63						3.24									
	11,262	1,332	1,279	-	-	-	-	-	-	-	-	-	-	-	-	-	538	-	-	-	-	-	-	-	-	-
	96.56		96.02														94.39									
Mukilteo (city)																	42.06									
			96.02														40.39									
			11.36														4.78									
	15,267	1,035	926	-	-	-	-	-	-	-	-	-	-	-	-	-	-	-	-	-	-	-	-	-	-	-
	93.74		89.47																							
North Creek (cdp)																										
			89.47																							
			6.07																							
	12,542	1,034	846	-	-	-	-	-	-	-	-	-	-	-	-	-	-	-	-	-	-	-	-	-	-	-
	83.44		81.82																							
Paine Field-Lk. Stickney (cdp)																										
			81.82																							
			6.75																							
	13,410	1,547	1,393	-	-	-	-	-	-	-	245	-	-	-	-	-	516	-	-	-	-	-	-	-	-	-
	92.13		90.05								100.00						87.16									
Picnic Pt.-N. Lynnwood (cdp)											17.59						37.04									
			90.05								15.84						33.35									
			10.39								1.83						3.85									
	20,827	1,752	1,523	-	-	-	-	-	-	-	265	-	-	-	-	-	406	-	-	-	-	-	-	-	-	259
	93.11		86.93								89.23						93.98									79.20
Seattle Hill-Silver Firs (cdp)											17.40						26.66									17.01
			86.93								15.13						23.17									14.78
			7.31								1.27						1.95									1.24
	237,740	4,488	3,472	381	330	307	-	-	523	-	584	-	-	100	-	906	287	-	-	-	-	-	-	-	-	534
	89.10		77.36		86.61	89.77			88.49		86.65			45.25		87.79	85.93									58.42
Spokane County						8.84			15.06		16.82			2.88		26.09	8.27									15.38
			77.36		86.61	6.84			11.65		13.01			2.23		20.19	6.39									11.90
			1.46		0.14	0.13			0.22		0.25			0.04		0.38	0.12									0.22
	111,054	2,571	1,828	244	231	-	-	-	259	-	274	-	-	67	-	594	124	-	-	-	-	-	-	-	-	260
	88.06		71.10		94.67				79.20		81.55			45.89		88.92	77.50									46.93
Spokane (city)									14.17		14.99			3.67		32.49	6.78									14.22
			71.10		94.67				10.07		10.66			2.61		23.10	4.82									10.11
			1.65		0.21				0.23		0.25			0.06		0.53	0.11									0.23

Notes: Please refer to the User's Guide for an explanation of data; data is arranged alphabetically by state, then county, then city within each county; table includes counties with populations greater than 49,999 unless noted and cities with populations greater than 9,999 whose Asian and/or NHPI population rates are greater than the national average; (1) Native Hawaiian and other Pacific Islander; (2) excludes Taiwanese; (3) includes Chamorro; (4) county does not meet population threshold but is shown in order to allow inclusion of city

Place	Total population 25 years and over who are high school graduates	Asian population 25 years and over	Asians 25 years and over who are high school graduates	NHPI[1] population 25 years and over	NHPIs[1] 25 years and over who are high school graduates	Asian Indian	Bangladeshi	Cambodian	Chinese[2]	Fijian	Filipino	Guamanian[3]	Hawaiian, Native	Hmong	Indonesian	Japanese	Korean	Laotian	Malaysian	Pakistani	Samoan	Sri Lankan	Taiwanese	Thai	Tongan	Vietnamese
Thurston County	121,445	6,055	4,610	709	610	279	-	189	399	-	1,007	385	-	-	-	483	1,153	-	-	-	-	-	-	-	-	766
	89.50		76.14		86.04	85.06		46.67	72.68		85.63	85.18				96.99	74.82									66.90
						6.05		4.10	8.66		21.84	63.11				10.48	25.01									16.62
			76.14		86.04	4.61		3.12	6.59		16.63	54.30				7.98	19.04									12.65
			3.80		0.50	0.23		0.16	0.33		0.83	0.32				0.40	0.95									0.63
Lacey (city)	17,739	1,690	1,265	-	-	-	-	-	-	-	271	-	-	-	-	-	362	-	-	-	-	-	-	-	-	246
	88.06		74.85								88.56						74.95									64.40
											21.42						28.62									19.45
			74.85								16.04						21.42									14.56
			7.13								1.53						2.04									1.39
Olympia (city)	25,843	1,520	1,281	-	-	-	-	-	-	-	-	-	-	-	-	-	-	-	-	-	-	-	-	-	-	325
	91.59		84.28																							70.65
																										25.37
			84.28																							21.38
			4.96																							1.26
Tumwater (city)	7,723	302	249	-	-	-	-	-	-	-	-	-	-	-	-	-	-	-	-	-	-	-	-	-	-	-
	92.38		82.45																							
			82.45																							
			3.22																							
Walla Walla County	27,889	363	255	-	-	-	-	-	-	-	-	-	-	-	-	-	-	-	-	-	-	-	-	-	-	-
	81.14		70.25																							
			70.25																							
			0.91																							
Whatcom County	89,935	2,315	1,702	-	-	419	-	-	287	-	238	-	-	-	-	288	122	-	-	-	-	-	-	-	-	187
	87.50		73.52			60.37			92.28		90.84					99.65	99.19									47.95
						24.62			16.86		13.98					16.92	7.17									10.99
			73.52			18.10			12.40		10.28					12.44	5.27									8.08
			1.89			0.47			0.32		0.26					0.32	0.14									0.21
Bellingham (city)	34,711	1,297	960	-	-	220	-	-	-	-	-	-	-	-	-	-	-	-	-	-	-	-	-	-	-	109
	88.54		74.02			70.97																				37.59
						22.92																				11.35
			74.02			16.96																				8.40
			2.77			0.63																				0.31
Whitman County[4]	18,626	1,086	1,015	-	-	-	-	-	368	-	-	-	-	-	-	248	-	-	-	-	-	-	-	-	-	-
	92.81		93.46						90.86							100.00										
									36.26							24.43										
			93.46						33.89							22.84										
			5.45						1.98							1.33										
Pullman (city)	9,033	963	916	-	-	-	-	-	313	-	-	-	-	-	-	239	-	-	-	-	-	-	-	-	-	-
	97.49		95.12						90.99							100.00										
									34.17							26.09										
			95.12						32.50							24.82										
			10.14						3.47							2.65										
Yakima County	89,774	1,474	1,251	-	-	-	-	-	-	-	614	-	-	-	-	-	-	-	-	-	-	-	-	-	-	-
	68.66		84.87								86.85															
											49.08															
			84.87								41.66															
			1.39								0.68															

Notes: Please refer to the User's Guide for an explanation of data; data is arranged alphabetically by state, then county, then city within each county; table includes counties with populations greater than 49,999 unless noted and cities with populations greater than 9,999 whose Asian and/or NHPI population rates are greater than the national average; (1) Native Hawaiian and other Pacific Islander; (2) excludes Taiwanese; (3) includes Chamorro; (4) county does not meet population threshold but is shown in order to allow inclusion of city

Place	Total population 25 years and over who are high school graduates	Asian population 25 years and over	Asians 25 years and over who are high school graduates	NHPI[1] population 25 years and over	NHPIs[1] 25 years and over who are high school graduates	Asian Indian	Bangladeshi	Cambodian	Chinese[2]	Fijian	Filipino	Guamanian[3]	Hawaiian, Native	Hmong	Indonesian	Japanese	Korean	Laotian	Malaysian	Pakistani	Samoan	Sri Lankan	Taiwanese	Thai	Tongan	Vietnamese
WEST VIRGINIA	927,767 75.21	5,937	5,364 90.35 90.35 0.58	187	161 86.10 86.10 0.02	1,528 93.34 28.49 25.74 0.16	-	-	904 89.42 16.85 15.23 0.10	-	1,117 91.86 20.82 18.81 0.12	-	-	-	-	455 95.19 8.48 7.66 0.05	386 80.58 7.20 6.50 0.04	-	-	189 92.20 3.52 3.18 0.02	-	-	-	-	-	245 76.09 4.57 4.13 0.03
Cabell County	51,527 79.96	482	404 83.82 83.82 0.78	-	-	-	-	-	-	-	-	-	-	-	-	-	-	-	-	-	-	-	-	-	-	-
Harrison County	36,769 78.45	155	134 86.45 86.45 0.36	-	-	-	-	-	-	-	-	-	-	-	-	-	-	-	-	-	-	-	-	-	-	-
Kanawha County	112,487 80.01	1,082	1,004 92.79 92.79 0.89	-	-	382 95.02 38.05 35.30 0.34	-	-	-	-	-	-	-	-	-	-	-	-	-	-	-	-	-	-	-	-
Monongalia County	40,089 83.62	1,148	1,135 98.87 98.87 2.83	-	-	288 100.00 25.37 25.09 0.72	-	-	413 100.00 36.39 35.98 1.03	-	-	-	-	-	-	-	-	-	-	-	-	-	-	-	-	-
Putnam County	29,201 83.78	172	130 75.58 75.58 0.45	-	-	-	-	-	-	-	-	-	-	-	-	-	-	-	-	-	-	-	-	-	-	-
Raleigh County	39,722 71.96	482	461 95.64 95.64 1.16	-	-	-	-	-	-	-	-	-	-	-	-	-	-	-	-	-	-	-	-	-	-	-
Wood County	49,398 81.38	261	231 88.51 88.51 0.47	-	-	-	-	-	-	-	-	-	-	-	-	-	-	-	-	-	-	-	-	-	-	-
WISCONSIN	2,957,461 85.09	39,469	28,887 73.19 73.19 0.98	795	626 78.74 78.74 0.02	6,230 90.67 21.57 15.78 0.21	-	108 40.91 0.37 0.27 <0.01	4,992 86.37 17.28 12.65 0.17	-	3,477 92.97 12.04 8.81 0.12	174 83.25 27.80 21.89 0.01	196 83.05 31.31 24.65 0.01	4,002 41.05 13.85 10.14 0.14	196 100.00 0.68 0.50 0.01	2,131 93.51 7.38 5.40 0.07	2,933 89.67 10.15 7.43 0.10	819 45.88 2.84 2.08 0.03	-	378 78.42 1.31 0.96 0.01	-	-	378 90.21 1.31 0.96 0.01	436 82.42 1.51 1.10 0.01	-	1,581 65.90 5.47 4.01 0.05
Brown County	124,429 86.31	1,816	944 51.98 51.98 0.76	-	-	141 78.33 14.94 7.76 0.11	-	-	-	-	-	-	-	243 30.99 25.74 13.38 0.20	-	-	-	48 35.82 5.08 2.64 0.04	-	-	-	-	-	-	-	-

Notes: Please refer to the User's Guide for an explanation of data; data is arranged alphabetically by state, then county, then city within each county; table includes counties with populations greater than 49,999 unless noted and cities with populations greater than 9,999 whose Asian and/or NHPI population rates are greater than the national average; (1) Native Hawaiian and other Pacific Islander; (2) excludes Taiwanese; (3) includes Chamorro; (4) county does not meet population threshold but is shown in order to allow inclusion of city

Place	Total population 25 years and over who are high school graduates	Asian population 25 years and over	Asians 25 years and over who are high school graduates	NHPI[1] population 25 years and over	NHPIs[1] 25 years and over who are high school graduates	Asian Indian	Bangladeshi	Cambodian	Chinese[2]	Fijian	Filipino	Guamanian[3]	Hawaiian, Native	Hmong	Indonesian	Japanese	Korean	Laotian	Malaysian	Pakistani	Samoan	Sri Lankan	Taiwanese	Thai	Tongan	Vietnamese
Chippewa County	30,612 84.26	189	115 60.85 60.85 0.38	-	-	-	-	-	-	-	-	-	-	35 32.11 30.43 18.52 0.11	-	-	-	-	-	-	-	-	-	-	-	-
Columbia County	30,625 86.20	105	97 92.38 92.38 0.32	-	-	-	-	-	-	-	-	-	-	-	-	-	-	-	-	-	-	-	-	-	-	-
Dane County	248,821 92.16	7,452	6,481 86.97 86.97 2.60	-	-	1,180 95.39 18.21 15.83 0.47	-	-	1,579 90.70 24.36 21.19 0.63	-	398 88.64 6.14 5.34 0.16	-	-	400 55.10 6.17 5.37 0.16	-	623 100.00 9.61 8.36 0.25	977 96.54 15.07 13.11 0.39	94 55.29 1.45 1.26 0.04	-	-	-	-	230 84.87 3.55 3.09 0.09	-	-	369 79.87 5.69 4.95 0.15
Madison (city)	117,185 92.41	5,993	5,204 86.83 86.83 4.44	-	-	751 94.11 14.43 12.53 0.64	-	-	1,338 90.47 25.71 22.33 1.14	-	273 91.61 5.25 4.56 0.23	-	-	323 56.17 6.21 5.39 0.28	-	513 100.00 9.86 8.56 0.44	918 97.56 17.64 15.32 0.78	-	-	-	-	-	227 84.70 4.36 3.79 0.19	-	-	315 78.55 6.05 5.26 0.27
Dodge County	47,300 82.33	147	104 70.75 70.75 0.22	-	-	-	-	-	-	-	-	-	-	-	-	-	-	-	-	-	-	-	-	-	-	-
Eau Claire County	49,157 88.91	845	562 66.51 66.51 1.14	-	-	-	-	-	-	-	-	-	-	248 58.91 44.13 29.35 0.50	-	-	-	-	-	-	-	-	-	-	-	-
Fond du Lac County	53,522 84.22	247	156 63.16 63.16 0.29	-	-	-	-	-	-	-	-	-	-	16 20.78 10.26 6.48 0.03	-	-	-	-	-	-	-	-	-	-	-	-
Jefferson County	41,548 84.69	118	86 72.88 72.88 0.21	-	-	-	-	-	-	-	-	-	-	-	-	-	-	-	-	-	-	-	-	-	-	-
Kenosha County	79,393 83.54	855	704 82.34 82.34 0.89	-	-	-	-	-	-	-	-	-	-	-	-	-	-	-	-	-	-	-	-	-	-	-
La Crosse County	58,514 89.66	965	618 64.04 64.04 1.06	-	-	-	-	-	-	-	-	-	-	247 44.11 39.97 25.60 0.42	-	-	-	-	-	-	-	-	-	-	-	-

Notes: Please refer to the User's Guide for an explanation of data; data is arranged alphabetically by state, then county, then city within each county; table includes counties with populations greater than 49,999 unless noted and cities with populations greater than 9,999 whose Asian and/or NHPI population rates are greater than the national average; (1) Native Hawaiian and other Pacific Islander; (2) excludes Taiwanese; (3) includes Chamorro; (4) county does not meet population threshold but is shown in order to allow inclusion of city

Place	Total population 25 years and over who are high school graduates	Asian population 25 years and over	Asians 25 years and over who are high school graduates	NHPI[1] population 25 years and over	NHPIs[1] 25 years and over who are high school graduates	Asian Indian	Bangladeshi	Cambodian	Chinese[2]	Fijian	Filipino	Guamanian[3]	Hawaiian, Native	Hmong	Indonesian	Japanese	Korean	Laotian	Malaysian	Pakistani	Samoan	Sri Lankan	Taiwanese	Thai	Tongan	Vietnamese
La Crosse (city)	25,792 87.75	642	375 58.41 58.41 1.45	-	-	-	-	-	-	-	-	-	-	135 35.90 36.00 21.03 0.52	-	-	-	-	-	-	-	-	-	-	-	-
Manitowoc County	46,890 84.56	598	318 53.18 53.18 0.68	-	-	-	-	-	-	-	-	-	-	115 34.53 36.16 19.23 0.25	-	-	-	-	-	-	-	-	-	-	-	-
Marathon County	68,643 83.79	1,645	658 40.00 40.00 0.96	-	-	-	-	-	-	-	-	-	-	376 31.31 57.14 22.86 0.55	-	-	-	-	-	-	-	-	-	-	-	-
Wausau (city)	20,296 80.77	1,304	465 35.66 35.66 2.29	-	-	-	-	-	-	-	-	-	-	284 28.43 61.08 21.78 1.40	-	-	-	-	-	-	-	-	-	-	-	-
Milwaukee County	476,973 80.25	11,781	8,598 72.98 72.98 1.80	270	163 60.37 60.37 0.03	2,169 87.18 25.23 18.41 0.45	-	-	1,340 85.46 15.59 11.37 0.28	-	1,065 97.08 12.39 9.04 0.22	-	-	1,097 42.85 12.76 9.31 0.23	-	585 93.75 6.80 4.97 0.12	643 88.32 7.48 5.46 0.13	385 46.67 4.48 3.27 0.08	-	181 80.09 2.11 1.54 0.04	-	-	-	-	-	533 59.75 6.20 4.52 0.11
Outagamie County	90,088 88.13	1,440	898 62.36 62.36 1.00	-	-	156 92.31 17.37 10.83 0.17	-	-	-	-	-	-	-	345 43.56 38.42 23.96 0.38	-	-	-	-	-	-	-	-	-	-	-	-
Appleton (city)	39,295 88.83	1,158	666 57.51 57.51 1.69	-	-	-	-	-	-	-	-	-	-	336 43.35 50.45 29.02 0.86	-	-	-	-	-	-	-	-	-	-	-	-
Ozaukee County	50,439 91.85	403	363 90.07 90.07 0.72	-	-	-	-	-	-	-	-	-	-	-	-	-	-	-	-	-	-	-	-	-	-	-
Portage County	34,704 86.45	395	253 64.05 64.05 0.73	-	-	-	-	-	-	-	-	-	-	97 45.12 38.34 24.56 0.28	-	-	-	-	-	-	-	-	-	-	-	-
Stevens Point (city)	10,623 85.11	310	194 62.58 62.58 1.83	-	-	-	-	-	-	-	-	-	-	87 47.54 44.85 28.06 0.82	-	-	-	-	-	-	-	-	-	-	-	-

Notes: Please refer to the User's Guide for an explanation of data; data is arranged alphabetically by state, then county, then city within each county; table includes counties with populations greater than 49,999 unless noted and cities with populations greater than 9,999 whose Asian and/or NHPI population rates are greater than the national average; (1) Native Hawaiian and other Pacific Islander; (2) excludes Taiwanese; (3) includes Chamorro; (4) county does not meet population threshold but is shown in order to allow inclusion of city

Place	Total population 25 years and over who are high school graduates	Asian population 25 years and over	Asians 25 years and over who are high school graduates	NHPI[1] population 25 years and over	NHPIs[1] 25 years and over who are high school graduates	Asian Indian	Bangladeshi	Cambodian	Chinese[2]	Fijian	Filipino	Guamanian[3]	Hawaiian, Native	Hmong	Indonesian	Japanese	Korean	Laotian	Malaysian	Pakistani	Samoan	Sri Lankan	Taiwanese	Thai	Tongan	Vietnamese
Racine County	101,442 82.91	755	598 79.21 79.21 0.59	-	-	-	-	-	-	-	-	-	-	-	-	-	-	-	-	-	-	-	-	-	-	-
Rock County	82,883 83.92	747	530 70.95 70.95 0.64	-	-	-	-	-	-	-	-	-	-	-	-	-	-	-	-	-	-	-	-	-	-	-
St. Croix County	36,963 91.59	153	147 96.08 96.08 0.40	-	-	-	-	-	-	-	-	-	-	-	-	-	-	-	-	-	-	-	-	-	-	-
Sauk County	30,655 83.53	113	113 100.00 100.00 0.37	-	-	-	-	-	-	-	-	-	-	-	-	-	-	-	-	-	-	-	-	-	-	-
Sheboygan County	62,956 84.44	1,347	607 45.06 45.06 0.96	-	-	-	-	-	-	-	-	-	-	269 34.22 44.32 19.97 0.43	-	-	-	-	-	-	-	-	-	-	-	-
Sheboygan (city)	27,040 81.18	1,203	512 42.56 42.56 1.89	-	-	-	-	-	-	-	-	-	-	246 32.58 48.05 20.45 0.91	-	-	-	-	-	-	-	-	-	-	-	-
Walworth County	48,949 84.17	318	251 78.93 78.93 0.51	-	-	-	-	-	-	-	-	-	-	-	-	-	-	-	-	-	-	-	-	-	-	-
Washington County	68,971 88.76	288	229 79.51 79.51 0.33	-	-	-	-	-	-	-	-	-	-	-	-	-	-	-	-	-	-	-	-	-	-	-
Waukesha County	221,889 91.96	3,100	2,835 91.45 91.45 1.28	-	-	1,010 95.73 35.63 32.58 0.46	-	-	680 96.18 23.99 21.94 0.31	-	292 97.33 10.30 9.42 0.13	-	-	-	-	-	248 90.18 8.75 8.00 0.11	-	-	-	-	-	-	-	-	-
Winnebago County	87,228 86.28	1,053	706 67.05 67.05 0.81	-	-	-	-	-	-	-	-	-	-	187 42.12 26.49 17.76 0.21	-	-	-	-	-	-	-	-	-	-	-	-

Notes: Please refer to the User's Guide for an explanation of data; data is arranged alphabetically by state, then county, then city within each county; table includes counties with populations greater than 49,999 unless noted and cities with populations greater than 9,999 whose Asian and/or NHPI population rates are greater than the national average; (1) Native Hawaiian and other Pacific Islander; (2) excludes Taiwanese; (3) includes Chamorro; (4) county does not meet population threshold but is shown in order to allow inclusion of city

Place	Total population 25 years and over who are high school graduates	Asian population 25 years and over	Asians 25 years and over who are high school graduates	NHPI[1] population 25 years and over	NHPIs[1] 25 years and over who are high school graduates	Asian Indian	Bangladeshi	Cambodian	Chinese[2]	Fijian	Filipino	Guamanian[3]	Hawaiian, Native	Hmong	Indonesian	Japanese	Korean	Laotian	Malaysian	Pakistani	Samoan	Sri Lankan	Taiwanese	Thai	Tongan	Vietnamese
Wood County	42,597 84.75	445	363 81.57 81.57 0.85	-	-	-	-	-	-	-	-	-	-	84 53.85 23.14 18.88 0.20	-	-	-	-	-	-	-	-	-	-	-	-
WYOMING	277,346 87.86	1,910	1,573 82.36 82.36 0.57	-	-	251 91.61 15.96 13.14 0.09	-	-	241 61.48 15.32 12.62 0.09	-	288 88.89 18.31 15.08 0.10	-	-	-	-	394 94.03 25.05 20.63 0.14	235 90.04 14.94 12.30 0.08	-	-	-	-	-	-	-	-	-
Laramie County	47,275 89.13	517	455 88.01 88.01 0.96	-	-	-	-	-	-	-	-	-	-	-	-	-	-	-	-	-	-	-	-	-	-	-
Natrona County	37,650 88.26	257	194 75.49 75.49 0.52	-	-	-	-	-	-	-	-	-	-	-	-	-	-	-	-	-	-	-	-	-	-	-

Notes: Please refer to the User's Guide for an explanation of data; data is arranged alphabetically by state, then county, then city within each county; table includes counties with populations greater than 49,999 unless noted and cities with populations greater than 9,999 whose Asian and/or NHPI population rates are greater than the national average; (1) Native Hawaiian and other Pacific Islander; (2) excludes Taiwanese; (3) includes Chamorro; (4) county does not meet population threshold but is shown in order to allow inclusion of city

Educational Attainment: Four-Year College Graduates

(Universe: Population 25 Years and Over)

Place	Total population 25 years and over who are 4-year college graduates	Asian population 25 years and over	Asians 25 years and over who are 4-year college graduates	NHPI[1] population 25 years and over	NHPIs[1] 25 years and over who are 4-year college graduates	Asian Indian	Bangladeshi	Cambodian	Chinese[2]	Fijian	Filipino	Guamanian[3]	Hawaiian, Native	Hmong	Indonesian	Japanese	Korean	Laotian	Malaysian	Pakistani	Samoan	Sri Lankan	Taiwanese	Thai	Tongan	Vietnamese
UNITED STATES	44,462,605	6,640,671	2,925,743	206,675	28,498	668,029	12,355	7,943	744,668	514	550,230	4,635	12,843	4,053	10,852	265,248	304,272	6,722	3,607	47,470	4,369	6,849	54,160	30,219	1,133	134,820
	24.40		44.06		13.79	63.89	49.42	9.20	47.08	8.78	43.77	14.27	15.24	7.47	46.60	41.87	43.82	7.70	53.50	54.30	10.47	51.05	67.11	38.56	8.64	19.44
						22.83	0.42	0.27	25.45	1.80	18.81	16.26	45.07	0.14	0.37	9.07	10.40	0.23	0.12	1.62	15.33	0.23	1.85	1.03	3.98	4.61
			44.06		13.79	10.06	0.19	0.12	11.21	0.25	8.29	2.24	6.21	0.06	0.16	3.99	4.58	0.10	0.05	0.71	2.11	0.10	0.82	0.46	0.55	2.03
			6.58		0.06	1.50	0.03	0.02	1.67	<0.01	1.24	0.01	0.03	0.01	0.02	0.60	0.68	0.02	0.01	0.11	0.01	0.02	0.12	0.07	<0.01	0.30
ALABAMA	549,608	18,999	9,173	639	101	2,961	-	2	2,720	-	717	38	-	-	-	510	842	69	-	158	-	-	-	106	-	404
	19.03		48.28		15.81	71.59		0.77	71.79		40.10	19.90				37.50	31.37	13.53		77.45				24.15		15.72
						32.28		0.02	29.65		7.82	37.62				5.56	9.18	0.75		1.72				1.16		4.40
			48.28		15.81	15.59		0.01	14.32		3.77	5.95				2.68	4.43	0.36		0.83				0.56		2.13
			1.67		0.02	0.54		<0.01	0.49		0.13	0.01				0.09	0.15	0.01		0.03				0.02		0.07
Baldwin County	22,146	336	97	-	-	-	-	-	-	-	-	-	-	-	-	-	-	-	-	-	-	-	-	-	-	-
	23.07		28.87																							
			28.87																							
			0.44																							
Calhoun County	11,265	433	142	-	-	-	-	-	-	-	-	-	-	-	-	-	-	-	-	-	-	-	-	-	-	-
	15.22		32.79																							
			32.79																							
			1.26																							
Etowah County	9,372	229	81	-	-	-	-	-	-	-	-	-	-	-	-	-	-	-	-	-	-	-	-	-	-	-
	13.42		35.37																							
			35.37																							
			0.86																							
Houston County	10,817	355	116	-	-	-	-	-	-	-	-	-	-	-	-	-	-	-	-	-	-	-	-	-	-	-
	18.44		32.68																							
			32.68																							
			1.07																							
Jefferson County	106,833	3,682	2,385	-	-	667	-	-	1,074	-	-	-	-	-	-	-	161	-	-	-	-	-	-	-	-	60
	24.61		64.77			78.84			80.75								57.50									14.49
						27.97			45.03								6.75									2.52
			64.77			18.12			29.17								4.37									1.63
			2.23			0.62			1.01								0.15									0.06
Lee County	17,351	1,193	777	-	-	-	-	-	393	-	-	-	-	-	-	-	-	-	-	-	-	-	-	-	-	-
	27.91		65.13						80.04																	
									50.58																	
			65.13						32.94																	
			4.48						2.26																	
Madison County	61,814	3,074	1,659	-	-	704	-	-	302	-	-	-	-	-	-	-	212	-	-	-	-	-	-	-	-	120
	34.27		53.97			73.72			64.67								31.74									41.38
						42.44			18.20								12.78									7.23
			53.97			22.90			9.82								6.90									3.90
			2.68			1.14			0.49								0.34									0.19

Notes: Please refer to the User's Guide for an explanation of data; data is arranged alphabetically by state, then county, then city within each county; table includes counties with populations greater than 49,999 unless noted and cities with populations greater than 9,999 whose Asian and/or NHPI population rates are greater than the national average; (1) Native Hawaiian and other Pacific Islander; (2) excludes Taiwanese; (3) includes Chamorro; (4) county does not meet population threshold but is shown in order to allow inclusion of city

Place	Total population 25 years and over who are 4-year college graduates	Asian population 25 years and over	Asians 25 years and over who are 4-year college graduates	NHPI[1] population 25 years and over	NHPIs[1] 25 years and over who are 4-year college graduates	Asian Indian	Bangladeshi	Cambodian	Chinese[2]	Fijian	Filipino	Guamanian[3]	Hawaiian, Native	Hmong	Indonesian	Japanese	Korean	Laotian	Malaysian	Pakistani	Samoan	Sri Lankan	Taiwanese	Thai	Tongan	Vietnamese
Mobile County	46,625 18.64	2,856	985 34.49 34.49 2.11	-	-	215 74.39 21.83 7.53 0.46	-	0 0.00 0.00 0.00 0.00	222 60.82 22.54 7.77 0.48	-	160 53.51 16.24 5.60 0.34	-	-	-	-	-	-	19 11.38 1.93 0.67 0.04	-	-	-	-	-	-	-	90 8.53 9.14 3.15 0.19
Montgomery County	40,294 28.51	1,341	441 32.89 32.89 1.09	-	-	-	-	-	-	-	-	-	-	-	-	-	-	-	-	-	-	-	-	-	-	-
Morgan County	13,490 18.40	311	169 54.34 54.34 1.25	-	-	-	-	-	-	-	-	-	-	-	-	-	-	-	-	-	-	-	-	-	-	-
Shelby County	34,649 36.79	715	517 72.31 72.31 1.49	-	-	240 75.71 46.42 33.57 0.69	-	-	-	-	-	-	-	-	-	-	-	-	-	-	-	-	-	-	-	-
Tuscaloosa County	23,804 24.03	904	607 67.15 67.15 2.55	-	-	-	-	-	-	-	-	-	-	-	-	-	-	-	-	-	-	-	-	-	-	-
ALASKA	93,807 24.71	16,576	3,519 21.23 21.23 3.75	1,322	128 9.68 9.68 0.14	154 49.36 4.38 0.93 0.16	-	-	400 39.53 11.37 2.41 0.43	-	1,541 18.85 43.79 9.30 1.64	-	28 9.93 21.88 2.12 0.03	7 3.63 0.20 0.04 0.01	-	539 45.60 15.32 3.25 0.57	553 17.40 15.71 3.34 0.59	26 4.39 0.74 0.16 0.03	-	-	41 7.32 32.03 3.10 0.04	-	-	44 8.26 1.25 0.27 0.05	20 13.16 15.63 1.51 0.02	54 8.24 1.53 0.33 0.06
Anchorage Borough	46,240 28.91	9,043	2,169 23.99 23.99 4.69	825	108 13.09 13.09 0.23	122 58.37 5.62 1.35 0.26	-	-	225 37.01 10.37 2.49 0.49	-	782 24.39 36.05 8.65 1.69	-	-	7 3.63 0.32 0.08 0.02	-	352 45.48 16.23 3.89 0.76	446 18.38 20.56 4.93 0.96	26 4.74 1.20 0.29 0.06	-	-	38 9.43 35.19 4.61 0.08	-	-	7 1.84 0.32 0.08 0.02	-	54 20.93 2.49 0.60 0.12
Fairbanks North Star Borough	12,968 27.03	1,293	337 26.06 26.06 2.60	-	-	-	-	-	120 57.42 35.61 9.28 0.93	-	53 14.89 15.73 4.10 0.41	-	-	-	-	-	48 12.94 14.24 3.71 0.37	-	-	-	-	-	-	-	-	-
Juneau City and Borough	7,167 36.02	882	304 34.47 34.47 4.24	-	-	-	-	-	-	-	220 33.74 72.37 24.94 3.07	-	-	-	-	-	-	-	-	-	-	-	-	-	-	-
Matanuska-Susitna Borough	6,524 18.26	266	50 18.80 18.80 0.77	-	-	-	-	-	-	-	-	-	-	-	-	-	-	-	-	-	-	-	-	-	-	-

Notes: Please refer to the User's Guide for an explanation of data; data is arranged alphabetically by state, then county, then city within each county; table includes counties with populations greater than 49,999 unless noted and cities with populations greater than 9,999 whose Asian and/or NHPI population rates are greater than the national average; (1) Native Hawaiian and other Pacific Islander; (2) excludes Taiwanese; (3) includes Chamorro; (4) county does not meet population threshold but is shown in order to allow inclusion of city

Place	Total population 25 years and over who are 4-year college graduates	Asian population 25 years and over	Asians 25 years and over who are 4-year college graduates	NHPI[1] population 25 years and over	NHPIs[1] 25 years and over who are 4-year college graduates	Asian Indian	Bangladeshi	Cambodian	Chinese[2]	Fijian	Filipino	Guamanian[3]	Hawaiian, Native	Hmong	Indonesian	Japanese	Korean	Laotian	Malaysian	Pakistani	Samoan	Sri Lankan	Taiwanese	Thai	Tongan	Vietnamese
	766,212	60,212	26,798	3,068	545	6,673	-	137	7,441	-	4,375	138	205	-	186	2,345	2,385	89	-	288	84	-	333	387	15	1,182
	23.53		44.51		17.76	73.19		22.39	52.12		40.58	20.15	20.34		47.21	38.81	37.01	16.92		72.54	17.00		68.52	34.07	5.86	15.65
ARIZONA						24.90		0.51	27.77		16.33	25.32	37.61		0.69	8.75	8.90	0.33		1.07	15.41		1.24	1.44	2.75	4.41
			44.51		17.76	11.08		0.23	12.36		7.27	4.50	6.68		0.31	3.89	3.96	0.15		0.48	2.74		0.55	0.64	0.49	1.96
			3.50		0.07	0.87		0.02	0.97		0.57	0.02	0.03		0.02	0.31	0.31	0.01		0.04	0.01		0.04	0.05	<0.01	0.15
	14,247	1,452	231	-	-	-	-	-	-	-	53	-	-	-	-	-	49	-	-	-	-	-	-	-	-	-
	18.80		15.91								18.53						8.33									
Cochise County											22.94						21.21									
			15.91								3.65						3.37									
			1.62								0.37						0.34									
	19,758	475	234	-	-	-	-	-	-	-	-	-	-	-	-	-	-	-	-	-	-	-	-	-	-	-
	29.95		49.26																							
Coconino County																										
			49.26																							
			1.18																							
	500,881	44,020	20,670	1,933	315	5,447	-	124	5,443	-	3,560	83	85	-	147	1,702	1,633	82	-	201	58	-	314	299	15	934
	25.89		46.96		16.30	74.84		21.60	50.84		44.97	21.67	15.71		49.00	42.25	40.61	23.91		68.60	18.13		71.85	39.76	6.05	16.60
Maricopa County						26.35		0.60	26.33		17.22	26.35	26.98		0.71	8.23	7.90	0.40		0.97	18.41		1.52	1.45	4.76	4.52
			46.96		16.30	12.37		0.28	12.36		8.09	4.29	4.40		0.33	3.87	3.71	0.19		0.46	3.00		0.71	0.68	0.78	2.12
			4.13		0.06	1.09		0.02	1.09		0.71	0.02	0.02		0.03	0.34	0.33	0.02		0.04	0.01		0.06	0.06	<0.01	0.19
	35,313	4,957	2,966	-	-	897	-	-	806	-	386	-	-	-	-	-	-	-	-	-	-	-	-	-	-	206
	32.46		59.83			88.46			58.92		48.43															31.60
Chandler (city)						30.24			27.17		13.01															6.95
			59.83			18.10			16.26		7.79															4.16
			8.40			2.54			2.28		1.09															0.58
	23,273	2,561	1,321	-	-	385	-	-	480	-	195	-	-	-	-	-	-	-	-	-	-	-	-	-	-	-
	36.10		51.58			83.70			59.55		42.67															
Gilbert (town)						29.14			36.34		14.76															
			51.58			15.03			18.74		7.61															
			5.68			1.65			2.06		0.84															
	52,929	4,120	1,635	230	28	268	-	-	388	-	466	-	-	-	-	146	146	-	-	-	-	-	-	-	-	106
	21.59		39.68		12.17	62.33			51.94		48.85					31.06	28.19									20.95
Mesa (city)						16.39			23.73		28.50					8.93	8.93									6.48
			39.68		12.17	6.50			9.42		11.31					3.54	3.54									2.57
			3.09		0.05	0.51			0.73		0.88					0.28	0.28									0.20
	180,443	16,997	7,150	921	155	1,957	-	58	1,734	-	1,462	-	29	-	-	537	483	-	-	-	-	-	-	-	-	332
	22.69		42.07		16.83	68.64		20.35	43.78		43.80		11.03			40.71	38.67									12.52
Phoenix (city)						27.37		0.81	24.25		20.45		18.71			7.51	6.76									4.64
			42.07		16.83	11.51		0.34	10.20		8.60		3.15			3.16	2.84									1.95
			3.96		0.09	1.08		0.03	0.96		0.81		0.02			0.30	0.27									0.18
	36,966	4,878	2,968	-	-	995	-	-	809	-	178	-	-	-	-	267	286	-	-	-	-	-	-	-	-	100
	39.63		60.84			88.60			65.77		48.37					55.51	56.41									20.62
Tempe (city)						33.52			27.26		6.00					9.00	9.64									3.37
			60.84			20.40			16.58		3.65					5.47	5.86									2.05
			8.03			2.69			2.19		0.48					0.72	0.77									0.27
	10,855	702	167	-	-	-	-	-	-	-	-	-	-	-	-	-	-	-	-	-	-	-	-	-	-	-
	9.93		23.79																							
Mohave County																										
			23.79																							
			1.54																							

Notes: Please refer to the User's Guide for an explanation of data; data is arranged alphabetically by state, then county, then city within each county; table includes counties with populations greater than 49,999 unless noted and cities with populations greater than 9,999 whose Asian and/or NHPI population rates are greater than the national average; (1) Native Hawaiian and other Pacific Islander; (2) excludes Taiwanese; (3) includes Chamorro; (4) county does not meet population threshold but is shown in order to allow inclusion of city

Place	Total population 25 years and over who are 4-year college graduates	Asian population 25 years and over	Asians 25 years and over who are 4-year college graduates	NHPI[1] population 25 years and over	NHPIs[1] 25 years and over who are 4-year college graduates	Asian Indian	Bangladeshi	Cambodian	Chinese[2]	Fijian	Filipino	Guamanian[3]	Hawaiian, Native	Hmong	Indonesian	Japanese	Korean	Laotian	Malaysian	Pakistani	Samoan	Sri Lankan	Taiwanese	Thai	Tongan	Vietnamese
Pima County	146,108	10,638	4,603	569	125	818	-	-	1,782	-	452	-	62	-	-	428	554	-	-	-	-	-		-	-	219
	26.75		43.27		21.97	75.25			60.43		29.54		25.10			37.58	41.72									14.43
						17.77			38.71		9.82		49.60			9.30	12.04									4.76
			43.27		21.97	7.69			16.75		4.25		10.90			4.02	5.21									2.06
			3.15		0.09	0.56			1.22		0.31		0.04			0.29	0.38									0.15
Tucson (city)	68,863	7,114	2,846	354	46	481	-	-	1,138	-	269	-	-	-	-	275	305	-	-	-	-	-	-	-	-	162
	22.88		40.01		12.99	70.84			58.36		25.47					37.98	40.13									13.21
						16.90			39.99		9.45					9.66	10.72									5.69
			40.01		12.99	6.76			16.00		3.78					3.87	4.29									2.28
			4.13		0.07	0.70			1.65		0.39					0.40	0.44									0.24
Pinal County	14,177	648	163	-	-	-	-	-	-	-	-	-	-	-	-	-	-	-	-	-	-	-	-	-	-	-
	11.90		25.15																							
			25.15																							
			1.15																							
Yavapai County	25,405	572	247	-	-	-	-	-	-	-	-	-	-	-	-	-	-	-	-	-	-	-	-	-	-	-
	21.13		43.18																							
			43.18																							
			0.97																							
Yuma County	11,569	957	243	-	-	-	-	-	-	-	59	-	-	-	-	-	-	-	-	-	-	-	-	-	-	-
	11.84		25.39								20.14															
											24.28															
			25.39								6.17															
			2.10								0.51															
ARKANSAS	288,428	12,097	3,943	561	48	1,164	-	-	1,061	-	559	-	22	-	-	201	209	38	-	-	-	-	-	17	-	254
	16.66		32.59		8.56	65.73			55.26		34.59		13.84			23.21	21.88	2.73						8.95		10.65
						29.52			26.91		14.18		45.83			5.10	5.30	0.96						0.43		6.44
			32.59		8.56	9.62			8.77		4.62		3.92			1.66	1.73	0.31						0.14		2.10
			1.37		0.02	0.40			0.37		0.19		0.01			0.07	0.07	0.01						0.01		0.09
Benton County	20,210	985	372	-	-	247	-	-	-	-	-	-	-	-	-	-	-	-	-	-	-	-	-	-	-	0
	20.32		37.77			84.59																				0.00
						66.40																				0.00
			37.77			25.08																				0.00
			1.84			1.22																				0.00
Craighead County	10,624	232	51	-	-	-	-	-	-	-	-	-	-	-	-	-	-	-	-	-	-	-	-	-	-	-
	20.94		21.98																							
			21.98																							
			0.48																							
Crawford County	3,276	374	26	-	-	-	-	-	-	-	-	-	-	-	-	-	-	-	-	-	-	-	-	-	-	-
	9.70		6.95																							
			6.95																							
			0.79																							
Faulkner County	12,820	261	107	-	-	-	-	-	-	-	-	-	-	-	-	-	-	-	-	-	-	-	-	-	-	-
	25.21		41.00																							
			41.00																							
			0.83																							

Notes: Please refer to the User's Guide for an explanation of data; data is arranged alphabetically by state, then county, then city within each county; table includes counties with populations greater than 49,999 unless noted and cities with populations greater than 9,999 whose Asian and/or NHPI population rates are greater than the national average; (1) Native Hawaiian and other Pacific Islander; (2) excludes Taiwanese; (3) includes Chamorro; (4) county does not meet population threshold but is shown in order to allow inclusion of city

Place	Total population 25 years and over who are 4-year college graduates	Asian population 25 years and over	Asians 25 years and over who are 4-year college graduates	NHPI[1] population 25 years and over	NHPIs[1] 25 years and over who are 4-year college graduates	Asian Indian	Bangladeshi	Cambodian	Chinese[2]	Fijian	Filipino	Guamanian[3]	Hawaiian, Native	Hmong	Indonesian	Japanese	Korean	Laotian	Malaysian	Pakistani	Samoan	Sri Lankan	Taiwanese	Thai	Tongan	Vietnamese
Jefferson County	8,333	315	156	-	-	-	-	-	-	-	-	-	-	-	-	-	-	-	-	-	-	-	-	-	-	-
	15.68		49.52																							
			49.52																							
			1.87																							
Pulaski County	66,324	2,966	1,421	-	-	487	-	-	367	-	163	-	-	-	-	-	-	-	-	-	-	-	-	-	-	-
	28.11		47.91			77.67			62.63		35.75															
						34.27			25.83		11.47															
			47.91			16.42			12.37		5.50															
			2.14			0.73			0.55		0.25															
Saline County	9,130	275	66	-	-	-	-	-	-	-	-	-	-	-	-	-	-	-	-	-	-	-	-	-	-	-
	16.36		24.00																							
			24.00																							
			0.72																							
Sebastian County	12,383	2,205	158	-	-	-	-	-	-	-	-	-	-	-	-	-	-	13	-	-	-	-	-	-	-	60
	16.60		7.17															2.08								5.25
																		8.23								37.97
			7.17															0.59								2.72
			1.28															0.10								0.48
Fort Smith (city)	9,686	2,011	118	-	-	-	-	-	-	-	-	-	-	-	-	-	-	13	-	-	-	-	-	-	-	52
	18.60		5.87															2.12								4.82
																		11.02								44.07
			5.87															0.65								2.59
			1.22															0.13								0.54
Washington County	23,075	1,521	848	190	17	-	-	-	399	-	-	-	-	-	-	-	-	11	-	-	-	-	-	-	-	-
	24.54		55.75		8.95				79.01									4.09								
									47.05									1.30								
			55.75		8.95				26.23									0.72								
			3.67		0.07				1.73									0.05								
Springdale (city)	4,884	422	90	168	17	-	-	-	-	-	-	-	-	-	-	-	-	12	-	-	-	-	-	-	-	-
	17.67		21.33		10.12													5.53								
																		13.33								
			21.33		10.12													2.84								
			1.84		0.35													0.25								
CALIFORNIA	5,669,966	2,434,151	1,012,851	63,077	7,925	124,573	1,062	3,004	285,136	360	258,176	1,540	2,393	1,398	4,333	101,844	105,673	1,555	597	6,230	1,713	1,506	25,927	9,574	432	59,035
	26.62		41.61		12.56	62.97	61.28	9.01	44.75	7.70	42.18	11.95	18.09	6.54	41.76	43.63	45.51	5.76	48.89	56.56	9.15	39.82	62.08	38.52	7.12	20.93
						12.30	0.10	0.30	28.15	4.54	25.49	19.43	30.20	0.14	0.43	10.06	10.43	0.15	0.06	0.62	21.62	0.15	2.56	0.95	5.45	5.83
			41.61		12.56	5.12	0.04	0.12	11.71	0.57	10.61	2.44	3.79	0.06	0.18	4.18	4.34	0.06	0.02	0.26	2.72	0.06	1.07	0.39	0.68	2.43
			17.86		0.14	2.20	0.02	0.05	5.03	0.01	4.55	0.03	0.04	0.02	0.08	1.80	1.86	0.03	0.01	0.11	0.03	0.03	0.46	0.17	0.01	1.04
Alameda County	332,954	193,930	89,420	4,871	648	18,831	-	204	31,619	86	19,509	227	155	-	192	5,171	4,790	122	-	841	62	-	1,799	448	19	3,580
	34.91		46.11		13.30	68.89		12.02	43.43	11.50	41.90	24.15	16.63		50.79	51.54	49.96	8.24		68.15	6.33		70.03	48.96	2.24	25.18
						21.06		0.23	35.36	13.27	21.82	35.03	23.92		0.21	5.78	5.36	0.14		0.94	9.57		2.01	0.50	2.93	4.00
			46.11		13.30	9.71		0.11	16.30	1.77	10.06	4.66	3.18		0.10	2.67	2.47	0.06		0.43	1.27		0.93	0.23	0.39	1.85
			26.86		0.19	5.66		0.06	9.50	0.03	5.86	0.07	0.05		0.06	1.55	1.44	0.04		0.25	0.02		0.54	0.13	0.01	1.08
Alameda (city)	21,908	12,761	5,438	458	42	470	-	-	2,077	-	1,788	-	-	-	-	257	431	-	-	-	-	-	-	-	-	162
	42.17		42.61		9.17	67.92			40.95		42.39					40.16	48.32									21.34
						8.64			38.19		32.88					4.73	7.93									2.98
			42.61		9.17	3.68			16.28		14.01					2.01	3.38									1.27
			24.82		0.19	2.15			9.48		8.16					1.17	1.97									0.74

Notes: Please refer to the User's Guide for an explanation of data; data is arranged alphabetically by state, then county, then city within each county; table includes counties with populations greater than 49,999 unless noted and cities with populations greater than 9,999 whose Asian and/or NHPI population rates are greater than the national average; (1) Native Hawaiian and other Pacific Islander; (2) excludes Taiwanese; (3) includes Chamorro; (4) county does not meet population threshold but is shown in order to allow inclusion of city

Place	Total population 25 years and over who are 4-year college graduates	Asian population 25 years and over	Asians 25 years and over who are 4-year college graduates	NHPI[1] population 25 years and over	NHPIs[1] 25 years and over who are 4-year college graduates	Asian Indian	Bangladeshi	Cambodian	Chinese[2]	Fijian	Filipino	Guamanian[3]	Hawaiian, Native	Hmong	Indonesian	Japanese	Korean	Laotian	Malaysian	Pakistani	Samoan	Sri Lankan	Taiwanese	Thai	Tongan	Vietnamese
Albany (city)	7,402	2,855	1,905	-	-	176	-	-	818	-	-	-	-	-	-	328	273	-	-	-	-	-	-	-	-	-
	63.95		66.73			76.52			61.04							68.62	79.13									
						9.24			42.94							17.22	14.33									
			66.73			6.16			28.65							11.49	9.56									
			25.74			2.38			11.05							4.43	3.69									
Ashland (cdp)	1,807	2,146	633	-	-	-	-	-	191	-	327	-	-	-	-	-	-	-	-	-	-	-	-	-	-	-
	14.08		29.50						26.45		36.62															
									30.17		51.66															
			29.50						8.90		15.24															
			35.03						10.57		18.10															
Berkeley (city)	42,491	7,757	4,984	-	-	595	-	-	1,871	-	447	-	-	-	-	922	536	-	-	-	-	-	121	-	-	159
	64.25		64.25			83.22			62.18		63.14					58.39	84.01						93.80			41.95
						11.94			37.54		8.97					18.50	10.75						2.43			3.19
			64.25			7.67			24.12		5.76					11.89	6.91						1.56			2.05
			11.73			1.40			4.40		1.05					2.17	1.26						0.28			0.37
Castro Valley (cdp)	12,202	5,086	2,653	-	-	340	-	-	1,267	-	445	-	-	-	-	246	268	-	-	-	-	-	-	-	-	-
	30.59		52.16			59.96			53.46		51.99					53.71	49.17									
						12.82			47.76		16.77					9.27	10.10									
			52.16			6.69			24.91		8.75					4.84	5.27									
			21.74			2.79			10.38		3.65					2.02	2.20									
Cherryland (cdp)	798	813	173	-	-	-	-	-	-	-	106	-	-	-	-	-	-	-	-	-	-	-	-	-	-	-
	9.21		21.28								26.84															
											61.27															
			21.28								13.04															
			21.68								13.28															
Dublin (city)	6,909	2,192	1,265	-	-	292	-	-	464	-	293	-	-	-	-	-	-	-	-	-	-	-	-	-	-	-
	32.91		57.71			73.92			67.64		47.41															
						23.08			36.68		23.16															
			57.71			13.32			21.17		13.37															
			18.31			4.23			6.72		4.24															
Fremont (city)	58,796	50,516	32,136	446	89	11,032	-	-	11,753	-	3,758	-	-	-	-	728	1,107	-	-	504	-	-	1,215	-	-	1,161
	43.16		63.62		19.96	78.78			64.81		49.33					54.86	44.12			71.19			71.14			40.95
						34.33			36.57		11.69					2.27	3.44			1.57			3.78			3.61
			63.62		19.96	21.84			23.27		7.44					1.44	2.19			1.00			2.41			2.30
			54.66		0.15	18.76			19.99		6.39					1.24	1.88			0.86			2.07			1.97
Hayward (city)	17,442	16,992	6,496	1,334	164	979	-	-	1,028	58	3,215	-	-	-	-	394	269	-	-	-	8	-	-	-	-	321
	19.87		38.23		12.29	44.16			38.19	13.98	39.31					43.54	42.50				2.56					21.23
						15.07			15.83	35.37	49.49					6.07	4.14				4.88					4.94
			38.23		12.29	5.76			6.05	4.35	18.92					2.32	1.58				0.60					1.89
			37.24		0.94	5.61			5.89	0.33	18.43					2.26	1.54				0.05					1.84
Livermore (city)	14,983	2,902	1,245	-	-	215	-	-	373	-	445	-	-	-	-	-	-	-	-	-	-	-	-	-	-	50
	31.57		42.90			51.19			66.61		39.38															17.30
						17.27			29.96		35.74															4.02
			42.90			7.41			12.85		15.33															1.72
			8.31			1.43			2.49		2.97															0.33
Newark (city)	6,431	6,160	2,649	-	-	652	-	-	584	-	833	-	-	-	-	-	183	-	-	-	-	-	-	-	-	123
	24.19		43.00			60.31			47.13		37.57						49.06									28.81
						24.61			22.05		31.45						6.91									4.64
			43.00			10.58			9.48		13.52						2.97									2.00
			41.19			10.14			9.08		12.95						2.85									1.91

Notes: Please refer to the User's Guide for an explanation of data; data is arranged alphabetically by state, then county, then city within each county; table includes counties with populations greater than 49,999 unless noted and cities with populations greater than 9,999 whose Asian and/or NHPI population rates are greater than the national average; (1) Native Hawaiian and other Pacific Islander; (2) excludes Taiwanese; (3) includes Chamorro; (4) county does not meet population threshold but is shown in order to allow inclusion of city

Place	Total population 25 years and over who are 4-year college graduates	Asian population 25 years and over	Asians 25 years and over who are 4-year college graduates	NHPI[1] population 25 years and over	NHPIs[1] 25 years and over who are 4-year college graduates	Asian Indian	Bangladeshi	Cambodian	Chinese[2]	Fijian	Filipino	Guamanian[3]	Hawaiian, Native	Hmong	Indonesian	Japanese	Korean	Laotian	Malaysian	Pakistani	Samoan	Sri Lankan	Taiwanese	Thai	Tongan	Vietnamese
Oakland (city)	80,777	40,634	10,254	1,102	134	756	-	69	4,521	-	1,771	-	-	-	-	1,135	693	34	-	-	-	-	-	-	5	747
	30.90		25.24		12.16	62.53		5.81	20.11		36.61					60.86	49.01	3.32							0.92	14.82
						7.37		0.67	44.09		17.27					11.07	6.76	0.33							3.73	7.28
			25.24		12.16	1.86		0.17	11.13		4.36					2.79	1.71	0.08							0.45	1.84
			12.69		0.17	0.94		0.09	5.60		2.19					1.41	0.86	0.04							0.01	0.92
Piedmont (city)	5,650	1,228	976	-	-	-	-	-	744	-	-	-	-	-	-	-	-	-	-	-	-	-	-	-	-	-
	77.85		79.48						83.22																	
									76.23																	
			79.48						60.59																	
			17.27						13.17																	
Pleasanton (city)	20,030	4,818	3,431	-	-	944	-	-	1,215	-	363	-	-	-	-	248	291	-	-	-	-	-	-	-	-	-
	47.27		71.21			88.64			71.51		60.10					47.78	72.75									
						27.51			35.41		10.58					7.23	8.48									
			71.21			19.59			25.22		7.53					5.15	6.04									
			17.13			4.71			6.07		1.81					1.24	1.45									
San Leandro (city)	12,992	12,667	4,320	264	22	301	-	-	1,576	-	1,600	-	-	-	-	208	131	-	-	-	-	-	-	-	-	216
	23.26		34.10		8.33	62.06			27.30		38.52					43.42	43.81									26.34
						6.97			36.48		37.04					4.81	3.03									5.00
			34.10		8.33	2.38			12.44		12.63					1.64	1.03									1.71
			33.25		0.17	2.32			12.13		12.32					1.60	1.01									1.66
San Lorenzo (cdp)	2,210	2,340	715	-	-	-	-	-	191	-	400	-	-	-	-	-	-	-	-	-	-	-	-	-	-	27
	14.98		30.56						28.21		42.92															15.34
									26.71		55.94															3.78
			30.56						8.16		17.09															1.15
			32.35						8.64		18.10															1.22
Union City (city)	12,387	18,906	8,261	370	51	1,772	-	-	2,150	-	3,236	-	-	-	-	127	215	-	-	-	-	-	-	-	-	327
	29.47		43.70		13.78	52.83			51.70		38.76					30.60	31.30									27.97
						21.45			26.03		39.17					1.54	2.60									3.96
			43.70		13.78	9.37			11.37		17.12					0.67	1.14									1.73
			66.69		0.41	14.31			17.36		26.12					1.03	1.74									2.64
Butte County	27,674	2,718	701	-	-	128	-	-	176	-	80	-	-	56	-	139	-	0	-	-	-	-	-	-	-	-
	21.84		25.79			49.23			38.85		35.40			7.38		41.37		0.00								
						18.26			25.11		11.41			7.99		19.83		0.00								
			25.79			4.71			6.48		2.94			2.06		5.11		0.00								
			2.53			0.46			0.64		0.29			0.20		0.50		0.00								
Chico (city)	10,450	898	312	-	-	-	-	-	105	-	-	-	-	7	-	-	-	-	-	-	-	-	-	-	-	-
	33.63		34.74						45.65					3.23												
									33.65					2.24												
			34.74						11.69					0.78												
			2.99						1.00					0.07												
Oroville (city)	835	198	22	-	-	-	-	-	-	-	-	-	-	6	-	-	-	-	-	-	-	-	-	-	-	-
	10.76		11.11											6.19												
														27.27												
			11.11											3.03												
			2.63											0.72												
Contra Costa County	219,048	69,241	33,822	1,792	257	4,297	-	-	11,339	19	10,283	51	102	-	176	3,505	1,463	75	-	240	29	-	674	121	24	806
	35.01		48.85		14.34	58.45			56.96	7.22	45.20	15.45	25.63		47.44	52.38	50.12	3.56		57.97	8.24		66.60	28.40	13.64	24.56
						12.70			33.53	7.39	30.40	19.84	39.69		0.52	10.36	4.33	0.22		0.71	11.28		1.99	0.36	9.34	2.38
			48.85		14.34	6.21			16.38	1.06	14.85	2.85	5.69		0.25	5.06	2.11	0.11		0.35	1.62		0.97	0.17	1.34	1.16
			15.44		0.12	1.96			5.18	0.01	4.69	0.02	0.05		0.08	1.60	0.67	0.03		0.11	0.01		0.31	0.06	0.01	0.37

Notes: Please refer to the User's Guide for an explanation of data; data is arranged alphabetically by state, then county, then city within each county; table includes counties with populations greater than 49,999 unless noted and cities with populations greater than 9,999 whose Asian and/or NHPI population rates are greater than the national average; (1) Native Hawaiian and other Pacific Islander; (2) excludes Taiwanese; (3) includes Chamorro; (4) county does not meet population threshold but is shown in order to allow inclusion of city

Place	Total population 25 years and over who are 4-year college graduates	Asian population 25 years and over	Asians 25 years and over who are 4-year college graduates	NHPI[1] population 25 years and over	NHPIs[1] 25 years and over who are 4-year college graduates	Asian Indian	Bangladeshi	Cambodian	Chinese[2]	Fijian	Filipino	Guamanian[3]	Hawaiian, Native	Hmong	Indonesian	Japanese	Korean	Laotian	Malaysian	Pakistani	Samoan	Sri Lankan	Taiwanese	Thai	Tongan	Vietnamese
Alamo (cdp)	6,546	577	402	-	-	-	-	-	-	-	-	-	-	-	-	-	-	-	-	-	-	-	-	-	-	-
	63.67		69.67																							
			69.67																							
			6.14																							
Antioch (city)	9,811	4,221	1,545	183	7	87	-	-	295	-	843	-	-	-	-	-	-	-	-	-	-	-	-	-	-	66
	18.15		36.60		3.83	41.63			35.63		40.57															20.43
						5.63			19.09		54.56															4.27
			36.60		3.83	2.06			6.99		19.97															1.56
			15.75		0.07	0.89			3.01		8.59															0.67
Bay Point (cdp)	1,497	1,480	410	-	-	-	-	-	-	-	183	-	-	-	-	-	-	-	-	-	-	-	-	-	-	-
	12.13		27.70								24.27															
											44.63															
			27.70								12.36															
			27.39								12.22															
Blackhawk-Camino-Tass. (cdp)	4,336	1,079	895	-	-	-	-	-	476	-	-	-	-	-	-	-	-	-	-	-	-	-	-	-	-	-
	64.38		82.95						82.78																	
									53.18																	
			82.95						44.11																	
			20.64						10.98																	
Clayton (city)	3,851	451	286	-	-	-	-	-	-	-	-	-	-	-	-	-	-	-	-	-	-	-	-	-	-	-
	51.76		63.41																							
			63.41																							
			7.43																							
Concord (city)	20,763	7,719	3,236	187	33	552	-	-	891	-	1,035	-	-	-	-	308	143	-	-	-	-	-	-	-	-	96
	25.91		41.92		17.65	48.89			46.62		38.11					44.38	48.47									21.67
						17.06			27.53		31.98					9.52	4.42									2.97
			41.92		17.65	7.15			11.54		13.41					3.99	1.85									1.24
			15.59		0.16	2.66			4.29		4.98					1.48	0.69									0.46
Danville (town)	16,908	2,355	1,639	-	-	235	-	-	703	-	266	-	-	-	-	-	-	-	-	-	-	-	-	-	-	-
	59.45		69.60			81.31			72.03		73.68															
						14.34			42.89		16.23															
			69.60			9.98			29.85		11.30															
			9.69			1.39			4.16		1.57															
El Cerrito (city)	10,078	4,203	2,416	-	-	199	-	-	1,137	-	209	-	-	-	-	551	-	-	-	-	-	-	-	-	-	-
	55.99		57.48			78.35			58.79		59.38					54.99										
						8.24			47.06		8.65					22.81										
			57.48			4.73			27.05		4.97					13.11										
			23.97			1.97			11.28		2.07					5.47										
El Sobrante (cdp)	1,645	939	363	-	-	67	-	-	-	-	-	-	-	-	-	-	-	-	-	-	-	-	-	-	-	-
	20.81		38.66			34.36																				
						18.46																				
			38.66			7.14																				
			22.07			4.07																				
Hercules (city)	4,447	5,219	2,292	-	-	163	-	-	449	-	1,466	-	-	-	-	-	-	-	-	-	-	-	-	-	-	-
	35.91		43.92			42.78			37.51		49.54															
						7.11			19.59		63.96															
			43.92			3.12			8.60		28.09															
			51.54			3.67			10.10		32.97															

Notes: Please refer to the User's Guide for an explanation of data; data is arranged alphabetically by state, then county, then city within each county; table includes counties with populations greater than 49,999 unless noted and cities with populations greater than 9,999 whose Asian and/or NHPI population rates are greater than the national average; (1) Native Hawaiian and other Pacific Islander; (2) excludes Taiwanese; (3) includes Chamorro; (4) county does not meet population threshold but is shown in order to allow inclusion of city

Place	Total population 25 years and over who are 4-year college graduates	Asian population 25 years and over	Asians 25 years and over who are 4-year college graduates	NHPI[1] population 25 years and over	NHPIs[1] 25 years and over who are 4-year college graduates	Asian Indian	Bangladeshi	Cambodian	Chinese[2]	Fijian	Filipino	Guamanian[3]	Hawaiian, Native	Hmong	Indonesian	Japanese	Korean	Laotian	Malaysian	Pakistani	Samoan	Sri Lankan	Taiwanese	Thai	Tongan	Vietnamese
Lafayette (city)	11,302 67.97	1,228	881 71.74 71.74 7.80	-	-	-	-	-	474 81.03 53.80 38.60 4.19	-	-	-	-	-	-	-	-	-	-	-	-	-	-	-	-	-
Martinez (city)	8,091 32.11	1,684	875 51.96 51.96 10.81	-	-	-	-	-	186 50.27 21.26 11.05 2.30	-	454 63.76 51.89 26.96 5.61	-	-	-	-	-	-	-	-	-	-	-	-	-	-	-
Moraga (town)	7,159 67.53	1,422	968 68.07 68.07 13.52	-	-	-	-	-	605 70.60 62.50 42.55 8.45	-	-	-	-	-	-	-	-	-	-	-	-	-	-	-	-	-
Orinda (city)	9,134 73.91	1,003	737 73.48 73.48 8.07	-	-	-	-	-	419 70.18 56.85 41.77 4.59	-	-	-	-	-	-	-	-	-	-	-	-	-	-	-	-	-
Pinole (city)	3,600 27.60	2,688	1,192 44.35 44.35 33.11	-	-	-	-	-	296 47.06 24.83 11.01 8.22	-	584 43.42 48.99 21.73 16.22	-	-	-	-	-	-	-	-	-	-	-	-	-	-	-
Pittsburg (city)	4,914 14.72	4,589	1,475 32.14 32.14 30.02	262	29 11.07 11.07 0.59	113 21.94 7.66 2.46 2.30	-	-	136 38.86 9.22 2.96 2.77	-	1,080 34.76 73.22 23.53 21.98	-	-	-	-	-	-	-	-	-	-	-	-	-	-	-
Pleasant Hill (city)	10,000 42.45	2,114	1,227 58.04 58.04 12.27	-	-	-	-	-	383 58.56 31.21 18.12 3.83	-	336 59.89 27.38 15.89 3.36	-	-	-	-	-	139 48.94 11.33 6.58 1.39	-	-	-	-	-	-	-	-	-
Richmond (city)	14,018 22.37	8,016	3,136 39.12 39.12 22.37	248	20 8.06 8.06 0.14	359 47.24 11.45 4.48 2.56	-	-	1,079 46.51 34.41 13.46 7.70	-	938 47.91 29.91 11.70 6.69	-	-	-	-	305 40.99 9.73 3.80 2.18	168 56.19 5.36 2.10 1.20	60 5.18 1.91 0.75 0.43	-	-	-	-	-	-	-	46 18.18 1.47 0.57 0.33
San Pablo (city)	1,807 10.42	2,912	674 23.15 23.15 37.30	-	-	69 20.60 10.24 2.37 3.82	-	-	-	-	379 33.78 56.23 13.02 20.97	-	-	-	-	-	-	4 0.68 0.59 0.14 0.22	-	-	-	-	-	-	-	33 8.53 4.90 1.13 1.83
San Ramon (city)	15,974 52.72	4,565	3,168 69.40 69.40 19.83	-	-	733 78.56 23.14 16.06 4.59	-	-	1,200 66.19 37.88 26.29 7.51	-	462 65.25 14.58 10.12 2.89	-	-	-	-	278 80.35 8.78 6.09 1.74	-	-	-	-	-	-	-	-	-	-

Notes: Please refer to the User's Guide for an explanation of data; data is arranged alphabetically by state, then county, then city within each county; table includes counties with populations greater than 49,999 unless noted and cities with populations greater than 9,999 whose Asian and/or NHPI population rates are greater than the national average; (1) Native Hawaiian and other Pacific Islander; (2) excludes Taiwanese; (3) includes Chamorro; (4) county does not meet population threshold but is shown in order to allow inclusion of city

Place	Total population 25 years and over who are 4-year college graduates	Asian population 25 years and over	Asians 25 years and over who are 4-year college graduates	NHPI[1] population 25 years and over	NHPIs[1] 25 years and over who are 4-year college graduates	Asian Indian	Bangladeshi	Cambodian	Chinese[2]	Fijian	Filipino	Guamanian[3]	Hawaiian, Native	Hmong	Indonesian	Japanese	Korean	Laotian	Malaysian	Pakistani	Samoan	Sri Lankan	Taiwanese	Thai	Tongan	Vietnamese
Walnut Creek (city)	26,971 53.96	4,635	3,218 69.43 69.43 11.93	-	-	380 88.99 11.81 8.20 1.41	-	-	1,304 68.49 40.52 28.13 4.83	-	704 73.72 21.88 15.19 2.61	-	-	-	-	441 62.11 13.70 9.51 1.64	194 56.23 6.03 4.19 0.72	-	-	-	-	-	-	-	-	-
El Dorado County	27,867 26.53	2,105	781 37.10 37.10 2.80	-	-	-	-	-	-	-	190 21.89 24.33 9.03 0.68	-	-	-	-	194 44.60 24.84 9.22 0.70	-	-	-	-	-	-	-	-	-	-
El Dorado Hills (cdp)	5,863 51.68	428	326 76.17 76.17 5.56	-	-	-	-	-	-	-	-	-	-	-	-	-	-	-	-	-	-	-	-	-	-	-
South Lake Tahoe (city)	2,798 18.64	945	200 21.16 21.16 7.15	-	-	-	-	-	-	-	121 19.30 60.50 12.80 4.32	-	-	-	-	-	-	-	-	-	-	-	-	-	-	-
Fresno County	79,927 17.55	31,409	7,708 24.54 24.54 9.64	306	56 18.30 18.30 0.07	1,111 27.66 14.41 3.54 1.39	-	91 5.73 1.18 0.29 0.11	1,395 41.14 18.10 4.44 1.75	-	1,587 38.12 20.59 5.05 1.99	-	-	502 6.74 6.51 1.60 0.63	-	1,891 39.92 24.53 6.02 2.37	406 47.10 5.27 1.29 0.51	62 2.32 0.80 0.20 0.08	-	-	-	-	-	-	-	216 18.67 2.80 0.69 0.27
Clovis (city)	9,512 23.12	2,266	760 33.54 33.54 7.99	-	-	-	-	-	-	-	161 45.10 21.18 7.11 1.69	-	-	57 9.11 7.50 2.52 0.60	-	215 46.74 28.29 9.49 2.26	-	-	-	-	-	-	-	-	-	-
Fresno (city)	44,999 19.01	22,295	5,077 22.77 22.77 11.28	-	-	652 31.29 12.84 2.92 1.45	-	91 6.28 1.79 0.41 0.20	1,013 39.22 19.95 4.54 2.25	-	1,146 39.22 22.57 5.14 2.55	-	-	385 6.14 7.58 1.73 0.86	-	987 46.67 19.44 4.43 2.19	331 53.56 6.52 1.48 0.74	45 1.91 0.89 0.20 0.10	-	-	-	-	-	-	-	131 14.51 2.58 0.59 0.29
Reedley (city)	1,678 14.42	606	249 41.09 41.09 14.84	-	-	-	-	-	-	-	-	-	-	-	-	-	-	-	-	-	-	-	-	-	-	-
Humboldt County	18,755 23.01	982	297 30.24 30.24 1.58	-	-	-	-	-	-	-	-	-	-	-	-	101 45.50 34.01 10.29 0.54	-	-	-	-	-	-	-	-	-	-
Imperial County	8,641 10.33	1,836	576 31.37 31.37 6.67	-	-	-	-	-	67 15.40 11.63 3.65 0.78	-	162 28.42 28.13 8.82 1.87	-	-	-	-	-	138 50.36 23.96 7.52 1.60	-	-	-	-	-	-	-	-	-

Notes: Please refer to the User's Guide for an explanation of data; data is arranged alphabetically by state, then county, then city within each county; table includes counties with populations greater than 49,999 unless noted and cities with populations greater than 9,999 whose Asian and/or NHPI population rates are greater than the national average; (1) Native Hawaiian and other Pacific Islander; (2) excludes Taiwanese; (3) includes Chamorro; (4) county does not meet population threshold but is shown in order to allow inclusion of city

Place	Total population 25 years and over who are 4-year college graduates	Asian population 25 years and over	Asians 25 years and over who are 4-year college graduates	NHPI[1] population 25 years and over	NHPIs[1] 25 years and over who are 4-year college graduates	Asian Indian	Bangladeshi	Cambodian	Chinese[2]	Fijian	Filipino	Guamanian[3]	Hawaiian, Native	Hmong	Indonesian	Japanese	Korean	Laotian	Malaysian	Pakistani	Samoan	Sri Lankan	Taiwanese	Thai	Tongan	Vietnamese
Kern County	51,869	13,549	3,854	395	56	674	-	5	681	-	1,518	-	-	-	-	313	305	-	-	-	-	-	-	-	-	123
	13.52		28.44		14.18	26.84		2.50	45.43		22.62					44.08	38.95									31.95
						17.49		0.13	17.67		39.39					8.12	7.91									3.19
			28.44		14.18	4.97		0.04	5.03		11.20					2.31	2.25									0.91
			7.43		0.11	1.30		0.01	1.31		2.93					0.60	0.59									0.24
Bakersfield (city)	27,487	6,464	2,382	222	34	434	-	-	519	-	739	-	-	-	-	182	230	-	-	-	-	-	-	-	-	91
	19.35		36.85		15.32	23.55			50.49		41.99					43.44	40.14									33.21
						18.22			21.79		31.02					7.64	9.66									3.82
			36.85		15.32	6.71			8.03		11.43					2.82	3.56									1.41
			8.67		0.12	1.58			1.89		2.69					0.66	0.84									0.33
Delano (city)	1,194	3,739	542	-	-	-	-	-	-	-	498	-	-	-	-	-	-	-	-	-	-	-	-	-	-	-
	5.48		14.50								14.19															
											91.88															
			14.50								13.32															
			45.39								41.71															
Ridgecrest (city)	3,830	660	200	-	-	-	-	-	-	-	62	-	-	-	-	-	-	-	-	-	-	-	-	-	-	-
	24.39		30.30								19.20															
											31.00															
			30.30								9.39															
			5.22								1.62															
Kings County	7,994	2,449	545	-	-	-	-	-	-	-	383	-	-	-	-	-	-	-	-	-	-	-	-	-	-	-
	10.37		22.25								24.03															
											70.28															
			22.25								15.64															
			6.82								4.79															
Lemoore (city)	1,736	982	186	-	-	-	-	-	-	-	146	-	-	-	-	-	-	-	-	-	-	-	-	-	-	-
	16.52		18.94								20.19															
											78.49															
			18.94								14.87															
			10.71								8.41															
Lake County	4,914	402	148	-	-	-	-	-	-	-	-	-	-	-	-	-	-	-	-	-	-	-	-	-	-	-
	12.07		36.82																							
			36.82																							
			3.01																							
Los Angeles County	1,462,389	773,327	332,020	14,489	1,845	23,544	416	1,408	83,736	26	88,860	285	481	4	1,542	37,577	55,604	195	180	1,481	582	460	12,774	4,859	69	10,564
	24.86		42.93		12.73	61.58	50.12	9.60	41.58	7.45	50.08	15.02	17.03	3.88	43.56	41.24	43.45	11.25	51.14	54.29	8.91	26.98	56.38	35.80	6.44	20.75
						7.09	0.13	0.42	25.22	1.41	26.76	15.45	26.07	<0.01	0.46	11.32	16.75	0.06	0.05	0.45	31.54	0.14	3.85	1.46	3.74	3.18
			42.93		12.73	3.04	0.05	0.18	10.83	0.18	11.49	1.97	3.32	<0.01	0.20	4.86	7.19	0.03	0.02	0.19	4.02	0.06	1.65	0.63	0.48	1.37
			22.70		0.13	1.61	0.03	0.10	5.73	<0.01	6.08	0.02	0.03	<0.01	0.11	2.57	3.80	0.01	0.01	0.10	0.04	0.03	0.87	0.33	<0.01	0.72
Agoura Hills (city)	6,230	912	550	-	-	-	-	-	-	-	-	-	-	-	-	-	-	-	-	-	-	-	-	-	-	-
	48.44		60.31																							
			60.31																							
			8.83																							
Alhambra (city)	16,089	28,975	9,553	-	-	227	-	-	6,137	-	662	-	-	-	-	524	256	-	-	-	-	-	548	-	-	548
	27.47		32.97			64.12			32.06		48.68					43.23	40.00						47.08			18.94
						2.38			64.24		6.93					5.49	2.68						5.74			5.74
			32.97			0.78			21.18		2.28					1.81	0.88						1.89			1.89
			59.38			1.41			38.14		4.11					3.26	1.59						3.41			3.41

Notes: Please refer to the User's Guide for an explanation of data; data is arranged alphabetically by state, then county, then city within each county; table includes counties with populations greater than 49,999 unless noted and cities with populations greater than 9,999 whose Asian and/or NHPI population rates are greater than the national average; (1) Native Hawaiian and other Pacific Islander; (2) excludes Taiwanese; (3) includes Chamorro; (4) county does not meet population threshold but is shown in order to allow inclusion of city

Place	Total population 25 years and over who are 4-year college graduates	Asian population 25 years and over	Asians 25 years and over who are 4-year college graduates	NHPI[1] population 25 years and over	NHPIs[1] 25 years and over who are 4-year college graduates	Asian Indian	Bangladeshi	Cambodian	Chinese[2]	Fijian	Filipino	Guamanian[3]	Hawaiian, Native	Hmong	Indonesian	Japanese	Korean	Laotian	Malaysian	Pakistani	Samoan	Sri Lankan	Taiwanese	Thai	Tongan	Vietnamese
Altadena (cdp)	11,071 38.86	1,421	750 52.78 52.78 6.77	-	-	-	-	-	-	-	116 53.46 15.47 8.16 1.05	-	-	-	-	243 42.56 32.40 17.10 2.19	-	-	-	-	-	-	-	-	-	-
Arcadia (city)	16,355 44.44	15,136	8,385 55.40 55.40 51.27	-	-	237 57.38 2.83 1.57 1.45	-	-	4,955 55.21 59.09 32.74 30.30	-	371 65.20 4.42 2.45 2.27	-	-	-	-	477 59.70 5.69 3.15 2.92	590 51.75 7.04 3.90 3.61	-	-	-	-	-	1,328 58.37 15.84 8.77 8.12	-	-	-
Artesia (city)	1,935 18.78	2,997	1,238 41.31 41.31 63.98	-	-	171 50.59 13.81 5.71 8.84	-	-	205 44.28 16.56 6.84 10.59	-	519 46.01 41.92 17.32 26.82	-	-	-	-	-	226 39.44 18.26 7.54 11.68	-	-	-	-	-	-	-	-	-
Avocado Heights (cdp)	830 9.36	981	252 25.69 25.69 30.36	-	-	-	-	-	-	-	-	-	-	-	-	-	-	-	-	-	-	-	-	-	-	-
Azusa (city)	3,380 14.25	1,531	709 46.31 46.31 20.98	-	-	-	-	-	-	-	448 57.07 63.19 29.26 13.25	-	-	-	-	-	-	-	-	-	-	-	-	-	-	-
Baldwin Park (city)	3,629 8.98	6,040	2,012 33.31 33.31 55.44	-	-	-	-	-	465 24.13 23.11 7.70 12.81	-	1,209 48.19 60.09 20.02 33.31	-	-	-	-	-	-	-	-	-	-	-	-	-	-	73 10.78 3.63 1.21 2.01
Bellflower (city)	5,443 12.88	4,615	1,739 37.68 37.68 31.95	-	-	-	-	22 7.26 1.27 0.48 0.40	-	-	1,040 47.68 59.80 22.54 19.11	-	-	-	-	-	256 39.94 14.72 5.55 4.70	-	-	-	-	-	-	85 32.32 4.89 1.84 1.56	-	-
Beverly Hills (city)	13,657 54.46	1,804	1,144 63.41 63.41 8.38	-	-	-	-	-	275 70.15 24.04 15.24 2.01	-	-	-	-	-	-	-	350 59.83 30.59 19.40 2.56	-	-	-	-	-	-	-	-	-
Burbank (city)	20,444 28.99	6,186	3,222 52.09 52.09 15.76	-	-	370 60.56 11.48 5.98 1.81	-	-	473 63.58 14.68 7.65 2.31	-	1,158 53.31 35.94 18.72 5.66	-	-	-	-	271 51.04 8.41 4.38 1.33	685 52.90 21.26 11.07 3.35	-	-	-	-	-	-	-	-	99 31.33 3.07 1.60 0.48
Calabasas (city)	7,680 57.91	1,100	805 73.18 73.18 10.48	-	-	-	-	-	279 79.71 34.66 25.36 3.63	-	-	-	-	-	-	-	-	-	-	-	-	-	-	-	-	-

Notes: Please refer to the User's Guide for an explanation of data; data is arranged alphabetically by state, then county, then city within each county; table includes counties with populations greater than 49,999 unless noted and cities with populations greater than 9,999 whose Asian and/or NHPI population rates are greater than the national average; (1) Native Hawaiian and other Pacific Islander; (2) excludes Taiwanese; (3) includes Chamorro; (4) county does not meet population threshold but is shown in order to allow inclusion of city

Place	Total population 25 years and over who are 4-year college graduates	Asian population 25 years and over	Asians 25 years and over who are 4-year college graduates	NHPI[1] population 25 years and over	NHPIs[1] 25 years and over who are 4-year college graduates	Asian Indian	Bangladeshi	Cambodian	Chinese[2]	Fijian	Filipino	Guamanian[3]	Hawaiian, Native	Hmong	Indonesian	Japanese	Korean	Laotian	Malaysian	Pakistani	Samoan	Sri Lankan	Taiwanese	Thai	Tongan	Vietnamese
Carson (city)	9,982	13,465	4,638	953	100	-	-	-	115	-	4,158	-	-	-	-	103	-	-	-	-	61	-	-	-	-	64
	18.07		34.44		10.49				37.34		36.59					16.80					8.66					23.27
									2.48		89.65					2.22					61.00					1.38
			34.44		10.49				0.85		30.88					0.76					6.40					0.48
			46.46		1.00				1.15		41.65					1.03					0.61					0.64
Cerritos (city)	14,995	19,456	10,789	-	-	1,304	-	-	2,243	-	2,255	-	-	-	-	654	2,685	-	-	-	-	-	753	149	-	373
	43.65		55.45			70.49			57.66		58.71					44.73	50.35						65.48	45.15		45.49
						12.09			20.79		20.90					6.06	24.89						6.98	1.38		3.46
			55.45			6.70			11.53		11.59					3.36	13.80						3.87	0.77		1.92
			71.95			8.70			14.96		15.04					4.36	17.91						5.02	0.99		2.49
Citrus (cdp)	555	542	185	-	-	-	-	-	-	-	-	-	-	-	-	-	-	-	-	-	-	-	-	-	-	-
	9.26		34.13																							
			34.13																							
			33.33																							
Claremont (city)	10,907	2,147	1,372	-	-	237	-	-	433	-	-	-	-	-	-	-	185	-	-	-	-	-	-	-	-	-
	52.36		63.90			80.07			71.33								62.08									
						17.27			31.56								13.48									
			63.90			11.04			20.17								8.62									
			12.58			2.17			3.97								1.70									
Compton (city)	2,747	306	74	372	59	-	-	-	-	-	-	-	-	-	-	-	-	-	-	-	46	-	-	-	-	-
	5.89		24.18		15.86																13.73					
																					77.97					
			24.18		15.86																12.37					
			2.69		2.15																1.67					
Covina (city)	5,542	2,959	1,293	-	-	-	-	-	336	-	461	-	-	-	-	71	-	-	-	-	-	-	-	-	-	38
	18.84		43.70						42.42		53.29					25.54										15.64
									25.99		35.65					5.49										2.94
			43.70						11.36		15.58					2.40										1.28
			23.33						6.06		8.32					1.28										0.69
Culver City (city)	11,684	3,608	1,941	-	-	316	-	-	340	-	424	-	-	-	-	484	-	-	-	-	-	-	-	-	-	-
	41.23		53.80			69.60			56.38		59.72					41.65										
						16.28			17.52		21.84					24.94										
			53.80			8.76			9.42		11.75					13.41										
			16.61			2.70			2.91		3.63					4.14										
Diamond Bar (city)	15,382	14,972	8,600	-	-	983	-	-	2,797	-	1,260	-	-	-	-	324	1,936	-	-	-	-	-	688	-	-	171
	42.35		57.44			64.88			56.75		62.94					56.84	55.94						53.71			39.22
						11.43			32.52		14.65					3.77	22.51						8.00			1.99
			57.44			6.57			18.68		8.42					2.16	12.93						4.60			1.14
			55.91			6.39			18.18		8.19					2.11	12.59						4.47			1.11
Downey (city)	11,363	5,437	2,390	-	-	203	-	-	182	-	779	-	-	-	-	120	792	-	-	-	-	-	-	-	-	141
	17.28		43.96			63.64			40.27		59.74					38.22	37.11									45.93
						8.49			7.62		32.59					5.02	33.14									5.90
			43.96			3.73			3.35		14.33					2.21	14.57									2.59
			21.03			1.79			1.60		6.86					1.06	6.97									1.24
Duarte (city)	3,216	1,844	1,047	-	-	-	-	-	172	-	523	-	-	-	-	-	-	-	-	-	-	-	-	-	-	-
	23.62		56.78						53.58		59.84															
									16.43		49.95															
			56.78						9.33		28.36															
			32.56						5.35		16.26															

Notes: Please refer to the User's Guide for an explanation of data; data is arranged alphabetically by state, then county, then city within each county; table includes counties with populations greater than 49,999 unless noted and cities with populations greater than 9,999 whose Asian and/or NHPI population rates are greater than the national average; (1) Native Hawaiian and other Pacific Islander; (2) excludes Taiwanese; (3) includes Chamorro; (4) county does not meet population threshold but is shown in order to allow inclusion of city

Place	Total population 25 years and over who are 4-year college graduates	Asian population 25 years and over	Asians 25 years and over who are 4-year college graduates	NHPI[1] population 25 years and over	NHPIs[1] 25 years and over who are 4-year college graduates	Asian Indian	Bangladeshi	Cambodian	Chinese[2]	Fijian	Filipino	Guamanian[3]	Hawaiian, Native	Hmong	Indonesian	Japanese	Korean	Laotian	Malaysian	Pakistani	Samoan	Sri Lankan	Taiwanese	Thai	Tongan	Vietnamese
East San Gabriel (cdp)	3,565	4,113	1,772	-	-	-	-	-	1,151	-	-	-	-	-	-	169	-	-	-	-	-	-	168	-	-	-
	35.84		43.08						47.72							41.42							46.28			
									64.95							9.54							9.48			
			43.08						27.98							4.11							4.08			
			49.71						32.29							4.74							4.71			
El Monte (city)	4,441	14,064	2,417	-	-	-	-	-	1,374	-	281	-	-	-	-	-	-	-	-	-	-	-	87	-	-	337
	7.11		17.19						17.55		46.29												27.88			8.60
									56.85		11.63												3.60			13.94
			17.19						9.77		2.00												0.62			2.40
			54.42						30.94		6.33												1.96			7.59
El Segundo (city)	4,663	801	590	-	-	-	-	-	-	-	-	-	-	-	-	-	-	-	-	-	-	-	-	-	-	-
	40.83		73.66																							
			73.66																							
			12.65																							
Gardena (city)	6,354	12,341	3,310	-	-	-	-	-	254	-	466	-	-	-	-	1,485	756	-	-	-	-	-	-	-	-	132
	16.64		26.82						37.03		36.18					24.78	27.13									15.46
									7.67		14.08					44.86	22.84									3.99
			26.82						2.06		3.78					12.03	6.13									1.07
			52.09						4.00		7.33					23.37	11.90									2.08
Glendale (city)	43,288	21,923	11,842	-	-	493	-	-	1,263	-	4,683	-	-	-	-	657	4,101	-	-	-	-	-	-	102	-	179
	32.05		54.02			73.36			61.91		58.71					52.27	49.59							30.45		26.80
						4.16			10.67		39.55					5.55	34.63							0.86		1.51
			54.02			2.25			5.76		21.36					3.00	18.71							0.47		0.82
			27.36			1.14			2.92		10.82					1.52	9.47							0.24		0.41
Glendora (city)	8,274	2,190	1,153	-	-	242	-	-	352	-	277	-	-	-	-	-	-	-	-	-	-	-	-	-	-	-
	25.65		52.65			72.02			60.48		50.09															
						20.99			30.53		24.02															
			52.65			11.05			16.07		12.65															
			13.94			2.92			4.25		3.35															
Hacienda Heights (cdp)	10,640	12,958	6,334	-	-	-	-	-	3,136	-	529	-	-	-	-	509	734	-	-	-	-	-	916	-	-	28
	30.71		48.88						50.22		60.39					46.74	45.11						50.33			8.51
									49.51		8.35					8.04	11.59						14.46			0.44
			48.88						24.20		4.08					3.93	5.66						7.07			0.22
			59.53						29.47		4.97					4.78	6.90						8.61			0.26
Hawaiian Gardens (city)	513	831	231	-	-	-	-	-	-	-	-	-	-	-	-	-	151	-	-	-	-	-	-	-	-	-
	6.72		27.80														29.21									
																	65.37									
			27.80														18.17									
			45.03														29.43									
Hawthorne (city)	6,123	4,076	1,147	322	0	69	-	-	112	-	655	-	-	-	-	62	-	-	-	-	-	-	-	-	-	114
	12.67		28.14		<0.01	17.83			25.99		40.89					21.53										12.61
						6.02			9.76		57.11					5.41										9.94
			28.14		<0.01	1.69			2.75		16.07					1.52										2.80
			18.73		<0.01	1.13			1.83		10.70					1.01										1.86
Hermosa Beach (city)	10,284	733	603	-	-	-	-	-	-	-	-	-	-	-	-	-	-	-	-	-	-	-	-	-	-	-
	67.63		82.26																							
			82.26																							
			5.86																							

Notes: Please refer to the User's Guide for an explanation of data; data is arranged alphabetically by state, then county, then city within each county; table includes counties with populations greater than 49,999 unless noted and cities with populations greater than 9,999 whose Asian and/or NHPI population rates are greater than the national average; (1) Native Hawaiian and other Pacific Islander; (2) excludes Taiwanese; (3) includes Chamorro; (4) county does not meet population threshold but is shown in order to allow inclusion of city

Place	Total population 25 years and over who are 4-year college graduates	Asian population 25 years and over	Asians 25 years and over who are 4-year college graduates	NHPI[1] population 25 years and over	NHPIs[1] 25 years and over who are 4-year college graduates	Asian Indian	Bangladeshi	Cambodian	Chinese[2]	Fijian	Filipino	Guamanian[3]	Hawaiian, Native	Hmong	Indonesian	Japanese	Korean	Laotian	Malaysian	Pakistani	Samoan	Sri Lankan	Taiwanese	Thai	Tongan	Vietnamese
La Canada Flintridge (city)	8,447	2,334	1,605	-	-	-	-	-	393	-	-	-	-	-	-	235	754	-	-	-	-	-	-	-	-	-
	63.50		68.77						86.00							76.05	62.11									
									24.49							14.64	46.98									
			68.77						16.84							10.07	32.31									
			19.00						4.65							2.78	8.93									
La Crescenta-Montrose (cdp)	4,998	2,199	1,111	-	-	-	-	-	-	-	125	-	-	-	-	-	704	-	-	-	-	-	-	-	-	-
	40.16		50.52								48.64						48.38									
											11.25						63.37									
			50.52								5.68						32.01									
			22.23								2.50						14.09									
La Mirada (city)	7,430	4,682	2,596	-	-	160	-	-	320	-	962	-	-	-	-	115	800	-	-	-	-	-	-	-	-	-
	25.20		55.45			49.38			67.65		66.81					32.49	50.41									
						6.16			12.33		37.06					4.43	30.82									
			55.45			3.42			6.83		20.55					2.46	17.09									
			34.94			2.15			4.31		12.95					1.55	10.77									
La Puente (city)	1,755	2,032	686	-	-	-	-	-	221	-	332	-	-	-	-	-	-	-	-	-	-	-	-	-	-	-
	7.83		33.76						37.46		44.56															
									32.22		48.40															
			33.76						10.88		16.34															
			39.09						12.59		18.92															
La Verne (city)	6,468	1,587	990	-	-	-	-	-	-	-	329	-	-	-	-	-	-	-	-	-	-	-	-	-	-	-
	31.63		62.38								60.37															
											33.23															
			62.38								20.73															
			15.31								5.09															
Lakewood (city)	10,566	6,780	2,803	403	100	159	-	87	378	-	1,359	-	-	-	-	222	355	-	-	-	95	-	-	-	-	71
	20.66		41.34		24.81	54.45		22.96	50.94		45.04					39.50	36.00				29.87					22.54
						5.67		3.10	13.49		48.48					7.92	12.67				95.00					2.53
			41.34		24.81	2.35		1.28	5.58		20.04					3.27	5.24				23.57					1.05
			26.53		0.95	1.50		0.82	3.58		12.86					2.10	3.36				0.90					0.67
Lancaster (city)	10,951	3,095	1,136	-	-	153	-	-	155	-	557	-	-	-	-	-	-	-	-	-	-	-	-	-	-	-
	15.81		36.70			41.13			50.65		38.84															
						13.47			13.64		49.03															
			36.70			4.94			5.01		18.00															
			10.37			1.40			1.42		5.09															
Lawndale (city)	2,298	1,954	575	226	16	-	-	-	-	-	214	-	-	-	-	-	-	-	-	-	-	-	-	-	-	112
	12.52		29.43		7.08						50.83															12.39
											37.22															19.48
			29.43		7.08						10.95															5.73
			25.02		0.70						9.31															4.87
Lomita (city)	3,068	1,694	695	-	-	-	-	-	-	-	160	-	-	-	-	186	124	-	-	-	-	-	-	-	-	-
	22.85		41.03								42.55					34.70	35.03									
											23.02					26.76	17.84									
			41.03								9.45					10.98	7.32									
			22.65								5.22					6.06	4.04									
Long Beach (city)	66,424	32,626	9,325	2,423	103	399	-	569	1,132	-	4,438	-	-	-	-	1,082	469	18	-	-	39	-	-	135	-	462
	23.94		28.58		4.25	56.20		7.07	50.07		37.65					37.40	35.58	5.29			2.28			34.09		14.39
						4.28		6.10	12.14		47.59					11.60	5.03	0.19			37.86			1.45		4.95
			28.58		4.25	1.22		1.74	3.47		13.60					3.32	1.44	0.06			1.61			0.41		1.42
			14.04		0.16	0.60		0.86	1.70		6.68					1.63	0.71	0.03			0.06			0.20		0.70

Notes: Please refer to the User's Guide for an explanation of data; data is arranged alphabetically by state, then county, then city within each county; table includes counties with populations greater than 49,999 unless noted and cities with populations greater than 9,999 whose Asian and/or NHPI population rates are greater than the national average; (1) Native Hawaiian and other Pacific Islander; (2) excludes Taiwanese; (3) includes Chamorro; (4) county does not meet population threshold but is shown in order to allow inclusion of city

Place	Total population 25 years and over who are 4-year college graduates	Asian population 25 years and over	Asians 25 years and over who are 4-year college graduates	NHPI[1] population 25 years and over	NHPIs[1] 25 years and over who are 4-year college graduates	Asian Indian	Bangladeshi	Cambodian	Chinese[2]	Fijian	Filipino	Guamanian[3]	Hawaiian, Native	Hmong	Indonesian	Japanese	Korean	Laotian	Malaysian	Pakistani	Samoan	Sri Lankan	Taiwanese	Thai	Tongan	Vietnamese
Los Angeles (city)	589,061 25.51	258,082	109,300 42.35 42.35 18.55	3,969	665 16.75 16.75 0.11	9,034 59.10 8.27 3.50 1.53	233 43.15 0.21 0.09 0.04	187 8.39 0.17 0.07 0.03	16,294 39.12 14.91 6.31 2.77	-	35,665 50.60 32.63 13.82 6.05	129 17.32 19.40 3.25 0.02	205 18.60 30.83 5.17 0.03	-	531 44.96 0.49 0.21 0.09	11,180 36.57 10.23 4.33 1.90	26,067 39.57 23.85 10.10 4.43	77 18.47 0.07 0.03 0.01	-	435 47.33 0.40 0.17 0.07	156 13.45 23.46 3.93 0.03	191 23.24 0.17 0.07 0.03	1,577 71.23 1.44 0.61 0.27	2,038 31.86 1.86 0.79 0.35	6 3.80 0.90 0.15 <0.01	3,201 25.51 2.93 1.24 0.54
Manhattan Beach (city)	16,946 67.60	1,582	1,103 69.72 69.72 6.51	-	-	-	-	-	355 81.42 32.18 22.44 2.09	-	-	-	-	-	-	342 64.53 31.01 21.62 2.02	-	-	-	-	-	-	-	-	-	-
Monrovia (city)	5,942 25.14	1,783	847 47.50 47.50 14.25	-	-	-	-	-	191 38.90 22.55 10.71 3.21	-	327 51.50 38.61 18.34 5.50	-	-	-	-	-	-	-	-	-	-	-	-	-	-	-
Montebello (city)	5,425 14.33	5,330	2,360 44.28 44.28 43.50	-	-	-	-	-	801 41.83 33.94 15.03 14.76	-	439 67.02 18.60 8.24 8.09	-	-	-	-	623 41.23 26.40 11.69 11.48	195 39.71 8.26 3.66 3.59	-	-	-	-	-	-	-	-	-
Monterey Park (city)	10,603 25.08	26,901	8,352 31.05 31.05 78.77	-	-	-	-	49 23.33 0.59 0.18 0.46	5,233 31.36 62.66 19.45 49.35	-	364 55.66 4.36 1.35 3.43	-	-	-	-	1,281 31.34 15.34 4.76 12.08	332 50.08 3.98 1.23 3.13	-	-	-	-	-	411 50.87 4.92 1.53 3.88	-	-	209 10.29 2.50 0.78 1.97
Norwalk (city)	6,301 10.63	8,040	3,066 38.13 38.13 48.66	-	-	374 48.76 12.20 4.65 5.94	-	54 17.31 1.76 0.67 0.86	231 34.22 7.53 2.87 3.67	-	1,283 45.32 41.85 15.96 20.36	-	-	-	-	82 21.69 2.67 1.02 1.30	671 38.13 21.89 8.35 10.65	-	-	-	-	-	-	-	-	155 25.54 5.06 1.93 2.46
Palmdale (city)	8,390 13.32	2,975	1,252 42.08 42.08 14.92	-	-	177 74.06 14.14 5.95 2.11	-	-	-	-	601 40.42 48.00 20.20 7.16	-	-	-	-	-	-	-	-	-	-	-	-	-	-	-
Palos Verdes Estates (city)	6,884 70.85	1,537	1,193 77.62 77.62 17.33	-	-	-	-	-	292 74.87 24.48 19.00 4.24	-	-	-	-	-	-	363 83.83 30.43 23.62 5.27	153 79.69 12.82 9.95 2.22	-	-	-	-	-	-	-	-	-
Pasadena (city)	37,590 41.34	10,006	6,309 63.05 63.05 16.78	-	-	508 77.20 8.05 5.08 1.35	-	-	2,073 66.57 32.86 20.72 5.51	-	1,081 54.93 17.13 10.80 2.88	-	-	-	-	1,074 56.14 17.02 10.73 2.86	839 83.23 13.30 8.38 2.23	-	-	-	-	-	-	-	-	245 42.10 3.88 2.45 0.65
Pomona (city)	10,081 12.79	5,876	2,244 38.19 38.19 22.26	-	-	227 61.02 10.12 3.86 2.25	-	8 3.04 0.36 0.14 0.08	387 33.48 17.25 6.59 3.84	-	992 59.12 44.21 16.88 9.84	-	-	-	-	104 32.81 4.63 1.77 1.03	-	7 2.80 0.31 0.12 0.07	-	-	-	-	-	-	-	205 19.09 9.14 3.49 2.03

Notes: Please refer to the User's Guide for an explanation of data; data is arranged alphabetically by state, then county, then city within each county; table includes counties with populations greater than 49,999 unless noted and cities with populations greater than 9,999 whose Asian and/or NHPI population rates are greater than the national average; (1) Native Hawaiian and other Pacific Islander; (2) excludes Taiwanese; (3) includes Chamorro; (4) county does not meet population threshold but is shown in order to allow inclusion of city

Place	Total population 25 years and over who are 4-year college graduates	Asian population 25 years and over	Asians 25 years and over who are 4-year college graduates	NHPI[1] population 25 years and over	NHPIs[1] 25 years and over who are 4-year college graduates	Asian Indian	Bangladeshi	Cambodian	Chinese[2]	Fijian	Filipino	Guamanian[3]	Hawaiian, Native	Hmong	Indonesian	Japanese	Korean	Laotian	Malaysian	Pakistani	Samoan	Sri Lankan	Taiwanese	Thai	Tongan	Vietnamese
Rancho Palos Verdes (city)	17,410	7,013	4,992	-	-	338	-	-	1,513	-	301	-	-	-	-	1,435	950	-	-	-	-	-	266	-	-	-
	57.99		71.18			88.71			80.52		69.84					67.43	62.25						68.91			
						6.77			30.31		6.03					28.75	19.03						5.33			
			71.18			4.82			21.57		4.29					20.46	13.55						3.79			
			28.67			1.94			8.69		1.73					8.24	5.46						1.53			
Redondo Beach (city)	22,963	4,644	2,931	-	-	282	-	-	694	-	358	-	-	-	-	972	327	-	-	-	-	-	-	-	-	-
	47.99		63.11			80.57			74.70		53.35					59.12	65.93									
						9.62			23.68		12.21					33.16	11.16									
			63.11			6.07			14.94		7.71					20.93	7.04									
			12.76			1.23			3.02		1.56					4.23	1.42									
Rosemead (city)	4,240	16,782	2,805	-	-	-	-	39	1,353	-	296	-	-	-	-	271	-	-	-	-	-	-	-	-	-	426
	12.90		16.71					8.55	14.22		56.92					40.81										11.20
								1.39	48.24		10.55					9.66										15.19
			16.71					0.23	8.06		1.76					1.61										2.54
			66.16					0.92	31.91		6.98					6.39										10.05
Rowland Heights (cdp)	10,218	16,523	7,726	-	-	391	-	-	3,701	-	1,117	-	-	-	-	234	977	-	-	-	-	-	823	-	-	132
	33.31		46.76			60.06			48.17		51.69					44.91	40.12						49.19			29.46
						5.06			47.90		14.46					3.03	12.65						10.65			1.71
			46.76			2.37			22.40		6.76					1.42	5.91						4.98			0.80
			75.61			3.83			36.22		10.93					2.29	9.56						8.05			1.29
San Dimas (city)	6,554	2,165	1,249	-	-	-	-	-	465	-	310	-	-	-	-	-	-	-	-	-	-	-	-	-	-	-
	28.43		57.69						55.56		66.38															
									37.23		24.82															
			57.69						21.48		14.32															
			19.06						7.09		4.73															
San Gabriel (city)	6,630	13,439	3,908	-	-	-	-	-	2,393	-	455	-	-	-	-	200	-	-	-	-	-	-	305	-	-	211
	24.59		29.08						28.61		54.75					41.58							53.51			12.19
									61.23		11.64					5.12							7.80			5.40
			29.08						17.81		3.39					1.49							2.27			1.57
			58.94						36.09		6.86					3.02							4.60			3.18
San Marino (city)	6,087	3,644	2,618	-	-	-	-	-	1,602	-	-	-	-	-	-	-	-	-	-	-	-	-	687	-	-	-
	69.67		71.84						69.90														72.85			
									61.19														26.24			
			71.84						43.96														18.85			
			43.01						26.32														11.29			
Santa Clarita (city)	27,209	5,151	2,935	-	-	389	-	-	375	-	1,069	-	-	-	-	423	304	-	-	-	-	-	-	-	-	140
	29.05		56.98			75.68			57.16		60.29					50.78	63.60									46.82
						13.25			12.78		36.42					14.41	10.36									4.77
			56.98			7.55			7.28		20.75					8.21	5.90									2.72
			10.79			1.43			1.38		3.93					1.55	1.12									0.51
Santa Monica (city)	36,815	4,653	2,941	-	-	332	-	-	769	-	262	-	-	-	-	802	347	-	-	-	-	-	-	-	-	-
	54.80		63.21			65.61			65.67		63.59					55.89	60.77									
						11.29			26.15		8.91					27.27	11.80									
			63.21			7.14			16.53		5.63					17.24	7.46									
			7.99			0.90			2.09		0.71					2.18	0.94									
Sierra Madre (city)	4,024	472	300	-	-	-	-	-	-	-	-	-	-	-	-	-	-	-	-	-	-	-	-	-	-	-
	49.72		63.56																							
			63.56																							
			7.46																							

Notes: Please refer to the User's Guide for an explanation of data; data is arranged alphabetically by state, then county, then city within each county; table includes counties with populations greater than 49,999 unless noted and cities with populations greater than 9,999 whose Asian and/or NHPI population rates are greater than the national average; (1) Native Hawaiian and other Pacific Islander; (2) excludes Taiwanese; (3) includes Chamorro; (4) county does not meet population threshold but is shown in order to allow inclusion of city

Place	Total population 25 years and over who are 4-year college graduates	Asian population 25 years and over	Asians 25 years and over who are 4-year college graduates	NHPI[1] population 25 years and over	NHPIs[1] 25 years and over who are 4-year college graduates	Asian Indian	Bangladeshi	Cambodian	Chinese[2]	Fijian	Filipino	Guamanian[3]	Hawaiian, Native	Hmong	Indonesian	Japanese	Korean	Laotian	Malaysian	Pakistani	Samoan	Sri Lankan	Taiwanese	Thai	Tongan	Vietnamese
South El Monte (city)	345	1,061	56	-	-	-	-	-	24	-	-	-	-	-	-	-	-	-	-	-	-	-	-	-	-	13
	3.10		5.28						5.70																	2.99
									42.86																	23.21
			5.28						2.26																	1.23
			16.23						6.96																	3.77
South Pasadena (city)	9,577	4,270	2,734	-	-	-	-	-	1,491	-	-	-	-	-	-	522	281	-	-	-	-	-	-	-	-	-
	56.12		64.03						63.18							67.27	73.37									
									54.54							19.09	10.28									
			64.03						34.92							12.22	6.58									
			28.55						15.57							5.45	2.93									
South San Jose Hills (cdp)	853	787	313	-	-	-	-	-	-	-	227	-	-	-	-	-	-	-	-	-	-	-	-	-	-	-
	8.00		39.77								44.42															
											72.52															
			39.77								28.84															
			36.69								26.61															
Temple City (city)	6,375	8,496	3,599	-	-	-	-	-	2,139	-	248	-	-	-	-	207	105	-	-	-	-	-	500	-	-	107
	28.55		42.36						41.33		58.49					43.76	32.92						53.30			17.89
									59.43		6.89					5.75	2.92						13.89			2.97
			42.36						25.18		2.92					2.44	1.24						5.89			1.26
			56.45						33.55		3.89					3.25	1.65						7.84			1.68
Torrance (city)	35,334	27,233	13,804	-	-	1,124	-	-	2,576	-	1,475	-	-	-	-	4,718	2,400	-	-	200	-	-	516	-	-	303
	36.42		50.69			75.49			60.44		59.14					46.25	43.53			51.81			58.90			29.19
						8.14			18.66		10.69					34.18	17.39			1.45			3.74			2.20
			50.69			4.13			9.46		5.42					17.32	8.81			0.73			1.89			1.11
			39.07			3.18			7.29		4.17					13.35	6.79			0.57			1.46			0.86
Valinda (cdp)	995	1,288	429	-	-	-	-	-	-	-	344	-	-	-	-	-	-	-	-	-	-	-	-	-	-	28
	8.39		33.31								47.71															9.93
											80.19															6.53
			33.31								26.71															2.17
			43.12								34.57															2.81
Vincent (cdp)	942	741	302	-	-	-	-	-	-	-	246	-	-	-	-	-	-	-	-	-	-	-	-	-	-	-
	11.14		40.76								57.21															
											81.46															
			40.76								33.20															
			32.06								26.11															
Walnut (city)	7,834	10,456	5,735	-	-	308	-	-	2,058	-	1,472	-	-	-	-	168	620	-	-	-	-	-	615	-	-	90
	41.90		54.85			62.47			51.18		67.58					55.26	52.50						51.99			27.03
						5.37			35.88		25.67					2.93	10.81						10.72			1.57
			54.85			2.95			19.68		14.08					1.61	5.93						5.88			0.86
			73.21			3.93			26.27		18.79					2.14	7.91						7.85			1.15
West Carson (cdp)	3,495	3,733	1,596	-	-	-	-	-	-	-	704	-	-	-	-	346	310	-	-	-	-	-	-	-	-	-
	23.78		42.75								48.15					36.46	48.67									
											44.11					21.68	19.42									
			42.75								18.86					9.27	8.30									
			45.67								20.14					9.90	8.87									
West Covina (city)	14,262	15,582	6,717	217	23	246	-	-	1,572	-	3,262	-	-	-	-	204	336	-	-	-	-	-	294	-	-	304
	21.94		43.11		10.60	67.58			35.89		50.12					39.38	52.42						48.20			21.24
						3.66			23.40		48.56					3.04	5.00						4.38			4.53
			43.11		10.60	1.58			10.09		20.93					1.31	2.16						1.89			1.95
			47.10		0.16	1.72			11.02		22.87					1.43	2.36						2.06			2.13

Notes: Please refer to the User's Guide for an explanation of data; data is arranged alphabetically by state, then county, then city within each county; table includes counties with populations greater than 49,999 unless noted and cities with populations greater than 9,999 whose Asian and/or NHPI population rates are greater than the national average; (1) Native Hawaiian and other Pacific Islander; (2) excludes Taiwanese; (3) includes Chamorro; (4) county does not meet population threshold but is shown in order to allow inclusion of city

Place	Total population 25 years and over who are 4-year college graduates	Asian population 25 years and over	Asians 25 years and over who are 4-year college graduates	NHPI[1] population 25 years and over	NHPIs[1] 25 years and over who are 4-year college graduates	Asian Indian	Bangladeshi	Cambodian	Chinese[2]	Fijian	Filipino	Guamanian[3]	Hawaiian, Native	Hmong	Indonesian	Japanese	Korean	Laotian	Malaysian	Pakistani	Samoan	Sri Lankan	Taiwanese	Thai	Tongan	Vietnamese
	14,853	1,261	856	-	-	-	-	-	-	-	-	-	-	-	-	-	-	-	-	-	-	-	-	-	-	-
	46.82		67.88																							
West Hollywood (city)																										
			67.88																							
			5.76																							
	1,014	1,156	357	-	-	-	-	-	-	-	227	-	-	-	-	-	-	-	-	-	-	-	-	-	-	31
	7.85		30.88								43.91															11.19
West Puente Valley (cdp)											63.59															8.68
			30.88								19.64															2.68
			35.21								22.39															3.06
	11,298	2,218	1,144	-	-	-	-	-	425	-	213	-	-	-	-	189	162	-	-	-	-	-	-	-	-	-
	21.88		51.58						51.96		51.82					48.46	68.94									
Whittier (city)									37.15		18.62					16.52	14.16									
			51.58						19.16		9.60					8.52	7.30									
			10.13						3.76		1.89					1.67	1.43									
	8,982	1,057	325	-	-	82	-	-	-	-	125	-	-	-	-	-	-	-	-	-	-	-	-	-	-	-
	12.00		30.75			22.47					40.45															
Madera County						25.23					38.46															
			30.75			7.76					11.83															
			3.62			0.91					1.39															
	94,248	8,269	4,558	-	-	723	-	-	1,499	-	507	-	-	-	-	928	463	-	-	-	-	-	-	-	-	94
	51.31		55.12			68.40			61.11		52.65					63.96	54.22									11.60
Marin County						15.86			32.89		11.12					20.36	10.16									2.06
			55.12			8.74			18.13		6.13					11.22	5.60									1.14
			4.84			0.77			1.59		0.54					0.98	0.49									0.10
	6,098	377	290	-	-	-	-	-	-	-	-	-	-	-	-	-	-	-	-	-	-	-	-	-	-	-
	62.59		76.92																							
Larkspur (city)																										
			76.92																							
			4.76																							
	12,444	1,735	770	-	-	-	-	-	129	-	125	-	-	-	-	-	-	-	-	-	-	-	-	-	-	-
	37.03		44.38						28.99		45.96															
Novato (city)									16.75		16.23															
			44.38						7.44		7.20															
			6.19						1.04		1.00															
	17,740	2,294	1,153	-	-	243	-	-	476	-	-	-	-	-	-	-	-	-	-	-	-	-	-	-	-	15
	43.60		50.26			71.05			61.90																	3.64
San Rafael (city)						21.08			41.28																	1.30
			50.26			10.59			20.75																	0.65
			6.50			1.37			2.68																	0.08
	6,115	399	252	-	-	-	-	-	-	-	-	-	-	-	-	-	-	-	-	-	-	-	-	-	-	-
	75.77		63.16																							
Tamalpais-Homestead (cdp)																										
			63.16																							
			4.12																							
	11,505	656	233	-	-	-	-	-	-	-	-	-	-	-	-	-	-	-	-	-	-	-	-	-	-	-
	20.22		35.52																							
Mendocino County																										
			35.52																							
			2.03																							

Notes: Please refer to the User's Guide for an explanation of data; data is arranged alphabetically by state, then county, then city within each county; table includes counties with populations greater than 49,999 unless noted and cities with populations greater than 9,999 whose Asian and/or NHPI population rates are greater than the national average; (1) Native Hawaiian and other Pacific Islander; (2) excludes Taiwanese; (3) includes Chamorro; (4) county does not meet population threshold but is shown in order to allow inclusion of city

Place	Total population 25 years and over who are 4-year college graduates	Asian population 25 years and over	Asians 25 years and over who are 4-year college graduates	NHPI[1] population 25 years and over	NHPIs[1] 25 years and over who are 4-year college graduates	Asian Indian	Bangladeshi	Cambodian	Chinese[2]	Fijian	Filipino	Guamanian[3]	Hawaiian, Native	Hmong	Indonesian	Japanese	Korean	Laotian	Malaysian	Pakistani	Samoan	Sri Lankan	Taiwanese	Thai	Tongan	Vietnamese
	12,896	6,570	881	-	-	253	-	-	89	-	271	-	-	86	-	120	-	13	-	-	-	-	-	-	-	-
	11.05		13.41			20.08			28.71		25.83			4.30		24.59		1.71								
Merced County						28.72			10.10		30.76			9.76		13.62		1.48								
			13.41			3.85			1.35		4.12			1.31		1.83		0.20								
			6.83			1.96			0.69		2.10			0.67		0.93		0.10								
	1,525	702	110	-	-	-	-	-	-	-	-	-	-	15	-	-	-	-	-	-	-	-	-	-	-	-
	12.26		15.67											10.56												
Atwater (city)														13.64												
			15.67											2.14												
			7.21											0.98												
	326	912	143	-	-	106	-	-	-	-	-	-	-	-	-	-	-	-	-	-	-	-	-	-	-	-
	6.24		15.68			14.52																				
Livingston (city)						74.13																				
			15.68			11.62																				
			43.87			32.52																				
	4,676	2,688	245	-	-	-	-	-	-	-	-	-	-	63	-	-	-	13	-	-	-	-	-	-	-	-
	13.58		9.11											5.02				2.06								
Merced (city)														25.71				5.31								
			9.11											2.34				0.48								
			5.24											1.35				0.28								
	54,939	16,816	4,591	1,040	148	326	-	-	790	-	1,818	7	-	-	-	791	540	-	-	-	-	-	-	-	-	156
	22.50		27.30		14.23	40.65			47.59		23.52	2.04				28.43	27.08									13.29
Monterey County						7.10			17.21		39.60	4.73				17.23	11.76									3.40
			27.30		14.23	1.94			4.70		10.81	0.67				4.70	3.21									0.93
			8.36		0.27	0.59			1.44		3.31	0.01				1.44	0.98									0.28
	2,329	2,828	491	336	17	-	-	-	-	-	139	-	-	-	-	46	132	-	-	-	-	-	-	-	-	41
	14.28		17.36		5.06						16.87					13.37	15.14									9.81
Marina (city)											28.31					9.37	26.88									8.35
			17.36		5.06						4.92					1.63	4.67									1.45
			21.08		0.73						5.97					1.98	5.67									1.76
	9,620	1,649	818	-	-	-	-	-	264	-	62	-	-	-	-	210	-	-	-	-	-	-	-	-	-	-
	46.23		49.61						81.48		21.45					39.77										
Monterey (city)									32.27		7.58					25.67										
			49.61						16.01		3.76					12.73										
			8.50						2.74		0.64					2.18										
	5,238	537	215	-	-	-	-	-	-	-	-	-	-	-	-	-	-	-	-	-	-	-	-	-	-	-
	44.08		40.04																							
Pacific Grove (city)																										
			40.04																							
			4.10																							
	10,395	6,151	1,738	218	31	158	-	-	113	-	1,113	-	-	-	-	225	70	-	-	-	-	-	-	-	-	37
	12.30		28.26		14.22	40.51			25.00		28.13					36.95	22.73									12.89
Salinas (city)						9.09			6.50		64.04					12.95	4.03									2.13
			28.26		14.22	2.57			1.84		18.09					3.66	1.14									0.60
			16.72		0.30	1.52			1.09		10.71					2.16	0.67									0.36
	3,300	2,293	326	-	-	-	-	-	-	-	177	-	-	-	-	66	-	-	-	-	-	-	-	-	-	7
	17.52		14.22								13.38					17.19										2.66
Seaside (city)											54.29					20.25										2.15
			14.22								7.72					2.88										0.31
			9.88								5.36					2.00										0.21

Notes: Please refer to the User's Guide for an explanation of data; data is arranged alphabetically by state, then county, then city within each county; table includes counties with populations greater than 49,999 unless noted and cities with populations greater than 9,999 whose Asian and/or NHPI population rates are greater than the national average; (1) Native Hawaiian and other Pacific Islander; (2) excludes Taiwanese; (3) includes Chamorro; (4) county does not meet population threshold but is shown in order to allow inclusion of city

Place	Total population 25 years and over who are 4-year college graduates	Asian population 25 years and over	Asians 25 years and over who are 4-year college graduates	NHPI[1] population 25 years and over	NHPIs[1] 25 years and over who are 4-year college graduates	Asian Indian	Bangladeshi	Cambodian	Chinese[2]	Fijian	Filipino	Guamanian[3]	Hawaiian, Native	Hmong	Indonesian	Japanese	Korean	Laotian	Malaysian	Pakistani	Samoan	Sri Lankan	Taiwanese	Thai	Tongan	Vietnamese
Napa County	22,150	2,587	1,107	-	-	-	-	-	158	-	507	-	-	-	-	211	-	-	-	-	-	-	-	-	-	-
	26.39		42.79						39.50		38.03					67.41										
									14.27		45.80					19.06										
			42.79						6.11		19.60					8.16										
			5.00						0.71		2.29					0.95										
Nevada County	17,003	470	123	-	-	-	-	-	-	-	-	-	-	-	-	-	-	-	-	-	-	-	-	-	-	-
	26.10		26.17																							
			26.17																							
			0.72																							
Orange County	558,743	253,320	104,810	4,737	659	11,008	-	459	20,358	-	16,713	119	215	57	394	11,145	18,112	120	-	890	182	200	3,792	939	26	18,296
	30.81		41.37		13.91	65.17		17.10	59.83		51.46	14.97	18.44	12.36	32.22	47.91	48.23	7.02		61.21	9.76	42.55	64.22	45.43	10.20	20.94
						10.50		0.44	19.42		15.95	18.06	32.63	0.05	0.38	10.63	17.28	0.11		0.85	27.62	0.19	3.62	0.90	3.95	17.46
			41.37		13.91	4.35		0.18	8.04		6.60	2.51	4.54	0.02	0.16	4.40	7.15	0.05		0.35	3.84	0.08	1.50	0.37	0.55	7.22
			18.76		0.12	1.97		0.08	3.64		2.99	0.02	0.04	0.01	0.07	1.99	3.24	0.02		0.16	0.03	0.04	0.68	0.17	<0.01	3.27
Aliso Viejo (cdp)	13,561	3,181	1,963	-	-	277	-	-	344	-	398	-	-	-	-	289	232	-	-	-	-	-	-	-	-	225
	48.62		61.71			79.14			62.89		65.89					59.83	63.91									57.54
						14.11			17.52		20.28					14.72	11.82									11.46
			61.71			8.71			10.81		12.51					9.09	7.29									7.07
			14.48			2.04			2.54		2.93					2.13	1.71									1.66
Anaheim (city)	38,164	26,483	10,775	567	133	1,516	-	-	1,427	-	2,660	-	-	-	-	681	1,991	42	-	135	68	-	296	107	-	1,619
	19.63		40.69		23.46	56.46			50.44		51.15					36.99	43.11	8.54		63.08	23.61		78.10	34.63		24.16
						14.07			13.24		24.69					6.32	18.48	0.39		1.25	51.13		2.75	0.99		15.03
			40.69		23.46	5.72			5.39		10.04					2.57	7.52	0.16		0.51	11.99		1.12	0.40		6.11
			28.23		0.35	3.97			3.74		6.97					1.78	5.22	0.11		0.35	0.18		0.78	0.28		4.24
Brea (city)	7,728	2,106	1,318	-	-	204	-	-	254	-	200	-	-	-	-	-	412	-	-	-	-	-	-	-	-	-
	33.46		62.58			69.39			69.40		60.24						77.30									
						15.48			19.27		15.17						31.26									
			62.58			9.69			12.06		9.50						19.56									
			17.05			2.64			3.29		2.59						5.33									
Buena Park (city)	9,454	10,955	4,772	-	-	614	-	-	370	-	1,624	-	-	-	-	190	1,494	-	-	-	-	-	-	-	-	161
	19.67		43.56			54.19			40.35		50.20					32.04	41.95									25.88
						12.87			7.75		34.03					3.98	31.31									3.37
			43.56			5.60			3.38		14.82					1.73	13.64									1.47
			50.48			6.49			3.91		17.18					2.01	15.80									1.70
Costa Mesa (city)	20,837	5,366	2,413	334	30	213	-	-	415	-	462	-	-	-	-	471	236	-	-	-	-	-	-	-	-	361
	29.09		44.97		8.98	80.08			58.70		47.43					48.81	54.25									24.15
						8.83			17.20		19.15					19.52	9.78									14.96
			44.97		8.98	3.97			7.73		8.61					8.78	4.40									6.73
			11.58		0.14	1.02			1.99		2.22					2.26	1.13									1.73
Cypress (city)	9,413	6,185	3,113	-	-	284	-	-	572	-	632	-	-	-	-	361	687	-	-	-	-	-	254	-	-	193
	31.20		50.33			60.17			58.67		54.02					43.70	46.08						58.12			38.45
						9.12			18.37		20.30					11.60	22.07						8.16			6.20
			50.33			4.59			9.25		10.22					5.84	11.11						4.11			3.12
			33.07			3.02			6.08		6.71					3.84	7.30						2.70			2.05
Foothill Ranch (cdp)	3,477	1,175	737	-	-	-	-	-	-	-	-	-	-	-	-	-	-	-	-	-	-	-	-	-	-	-
	49.78		62.72																							
			62.72																							
			21.20																							

Notes: Please refer to the User's Guide for an explanation of data; data is arranged alphabetically by state, then county, then city within each county; table includes counties with populations greater than 49,999 unless noted and cities with populations greater than 9,999 whose Asian and/or NHPI population rates are greater than the national average; (1) Native Hawaiian and other Pacific Islander; (2) excludes Taiwanese; (3) includes Chamorro; (4) county does not meet population threshold but is shown in order to allow inclusion of city

Place	Total population 25 years and over who are 4-year college graduates	Asian population 25 years and over	Asians 25 years and over who are 4-year college graduates	NHPI[1] population 25 years and over	NHPIs[1] 25 years and over who are 4-year college graduates	Asian Indian	Bangladeshi	Cambodian	Chinese[2]	Fijian	Filipino	Guamanian[3]	Hawaiian, Native	Hmong	Indonesian	Japanese	Korean	Laotian	Malaysian	Pakistani	Samoan	Sri Lankan	Taiwanese	Thai	Tongan	Vietnamese
Fountain Valley (city)	12,903	9,527	4,051	-	-	298	-	-	969	-	234	-	-	-	-	421	329	-	-	-	-	-	131	-	-	1,458
	34.36		42.52			64.36			56.57		52.00					41.07	45.01						52.19			32.44
						7.36			23.92		5.78					10.39	8.12						3.23			35.99
			42.52			3.13			10.17		2.46					4.42	3.45						1.38			15.30
			31.40			2.31			7.51		1.81					3.26	2.55						1.02			11.30
Fullerton (city)	25,036	13,004	6,942	-	-	699	-	-	1,378	-	751	-	-	-	-	438	3,023	-	-	-	-	-	-	-	-	240
	31.29		53.38			57.86			72.60		53.60					48.03	54.09									24.32
						10.07			19.85		10.82					6.31	43.55									3.46
			53.38			5.38			10.60		5.78					3.37	23.25									1.85
			27.73			2.79			5.50		3.00					1.75	12.07									0.96
Garden Grove (city)	15,522	33,577	6,050	605	32	162	-	70	465	-	699	-	-	-	-	286	1,135	-	-	-	28	-	-	-	-	2,979
	15.00		18.02		5.29	38.03		20.65	26.14		36.64					31.29	26.89				7.76					13.09
						2.68		1.16	7.69		11.55					4.73	18.76				87.50					49.24
			18.02		5.29	0.48		0.21	1.38		2.08					0.85	3.38				4.63					8.87
			38.98		0.21	1.04		0.45	3.00		4.50					1.84	7.31				0.18					19.19
Huntington Beach (city)	47,476	12,456	6,130	236	50	526	-	-	1,393	-	597	-	-	-	-	1,218	607	-	-	-	-	-	300	-	-	1,169
	35.97		49.21		21.19	74.19			61.02		49.10					52.70	51.27						65.79			32.03
						8.58			22.72		9.74					19.87	9.90						4.89			19.07
			49.21		21.19	4.22			11.18		4.79					9.78	4.87						2.41			9.39
			12.91		0.11	1.11			2.93		1.26					2.57	1.28						0.63			2.46
Irvine (city)	51,932	23,640	15,883	-	-	2,096	-	-	4,834	-	893	-	-	-	-	2,044	2,948	-	-	-	-	-	1,062	-	-	1,348
	58.38		67.19			82.68			74.62		56.41					62.18	67.63						67.39			48.82
						13.20			30.44		5.62					12.87	18.56						6.69			8.49
			67.19			8.87			20.45		3.78					8.65	12.47						4.49			5.70
			30.58			4.04			9.31		1.72					3.94	5.68						2.04			2.60
La Habra (city)	6,581	2,305	1,230	-	-	-	-	-	240	-	243	-	-	-	-	-	439	-	-	-	-	-	-	-	-	-
	18.23		53.36						70.59		51.70						56.35									
									19.51		19.76						35.69									
			53.36						10.41		10.54						19.05									
			18.69						3.65		3.69						6.67									
La Palma (city)	3,937	4,396	2,316	-	-	197	-	-	432	-	552	-	-	-	-	282	677	-	-	-	-	-	-	-	-	-
	38.09		52.68			58.11			66.87		66.59					49.47	43.54									
						8.51			18.65		23.83					12.18	29.23									
			52.68			4.48			9.83		12.56					6.41	15.40									
			58.83			5.00			10.97		14.02					7.16	17.20									
Laguna Hills (city)	8,268	2,266	1,250	-	-	-	-	-	320	-	229	-	-	-	-	-	-	-	-	-	-	-	-	-	-	189
	39.32		55.16						74.94		48.93															56.59
									25.60		18.32															15.12
			55.16						14.12		10.11															8.34
			15.12						3.87		2.77															2.29
Laguna Niguel (city)	20,046	3,307	1,930	-	-	-	-	-	516	-	266	-	-	-	-	412	209	-	-	-	-	-	-	-	-	211
	47.84		58.36						74.57		42.16					59.03	47.83									63.55
									26.74		13.78					21.35	10.83									10.93
			58.36						15.60		8.04					12.46	6.32									6.38
			9.63						2.57		1.33					2.06	1.04									1.05
Lake Forest (city)	12,900	3,766	1,720	-	-	322	-	-	196	-	345	-	-	-	-	223	197	-	-	-	-	-	-	-	-	306
	33.89		45.67			73.02			40.25		46.94					44.07	46.14									34.34
						18.72			11.40		20.06					12.97	11.45									17.79
			45.67			8.55			5.20		9.16					5.92	5.23									8.13
			13.33			2.50			1.52		2.67					1.73	1.53									2.37

Notes: Please refer to the User's Guide for an explanation of data; data is arranged alphabetically by state, then county, then city within each county; table includes counties with populations greater than 49,999 unless noted and cities with populations greater than 9,999 whose Asian and/or NHPI population rates are greater than the national average; (1) Native Hawaiian and other Pacific Islander; (2) excludes Taiwanese; (3) includes Chamorro; (4) county does not meet population threshold but is shown in order to allow inclusion of city

Place	Total population 25 years and over who are 4-year college graduates	Asian population 25 years and over	Asians 25 years and over who are 4-year college graduates	NHPI[1] population 25 years and over	NHPIs[1] 25 years and over who are 4-year college graduates	Asian Indian	Bangladeshi	Cambodian	Chinese[2]	Fijian	Filipino	Guamanian[3]	Hawaiian, Native	Hmong	Indonesian	Japanese	Korean	Laotian	Malaysian	Pakistani	Samoan	Sri Lankan	Taiwanese	Thai	Tongan	Vietnamese
Los Alamitos (city)	2,290 29.84	718	279 38.86 38.86 12.18	-	-	-	-	-	-	-	-	-	-	-	-	-	-	-	-	-	-	-	-	-	-	-
Mission Viejo (city)	25,328 41.20	5,045	2,827 56.04 56.04 11.16	-	-	266 71.12 9.41 5.27 1.05	-	-	648 67.64 22.92 12.84 2.56	-	571 55.44 20.20 11.32 2.25	-	-	-	-	448 54.57 15.85 8.88 1.77	360 61.75 12.73 7.14 1.42	-	-	-	-	-	-	-	-	333 39.74 11.78 6.60 1.31
Newport Beach (city)	32,020 58.48	2,061	1,374 66.67 66.67 4.29	-	-	-	-	-	331 69.83 24.09 16.06 1.03	-	-	-	-	-	-	225 58.29 16.38 10.92 0.70	-	-	-	-	-	-	-	-	-	-
Orange (city)	22,967 27.96	7,952	3,806 47.86 47.86 16.57	-	-	381 69.27 10.01 4.79 1.66	-	-	615 62.56 16.16 7.73 2.68	-	757 54.70 19.89 9.52 3.30	-	-	-	-	340 56.95 8.93 4.28 1.48	506 42.45 13.29 6.36 2.20	-	-	-	-	-	215 63.05 5.65 2.70 0.94	-	-	743 31.43 19.52 9.34 3.24
Placentia (city)	9,376 31.28	3,524	1,856 52.67 52.67 19.80	-	-	198 66.44 10.67 5.62 2.11	-	-	478 62.24 25.75 13.56 5.10	-	262 48.16 14.12 7.43 2.79	-	-	-	-	161 40.76 8.67 4.57 1.72	286 63.84 15.41 8.12 3.05	-	-	-	-	-	-	-	-	279 45.07 15.03 7.92 2.98
Rancho Santa Margarita (city)	12,669 43.76	2,615	1,643 62.83 62.83 12.97	-	-	-	-	-	271 62.44 16.49 10.36 2.14	-	516 69.26 31.41 19.73 4.07	-	-	-	-	-	-	-	-	-	-	-	-	-	-	147 43.36 8.95 5.62 1.16
Rossmoor (cdp)	3,458 48.90	374	213 56.95 56.95 6.16	-	-	-	-	-	-	-	-	-	-	-	-	-	-	-	-	-	-	-	-	-	-	-
Santa Ana (city)	16,416 9.18	19,479	3,609 18.53 18.53 21.98	700	43 6.14 6.14 0.26	182 51.12 5.04 0.93 1.11	-	63 6.39 1.75 0.32 0.38	337 22.85 9.34 1.73 2.05	-	583 38.94 16.15 2.99 3.55	-	-	15 6.33 0.42 0.08 0.09	-	221 30.95 6.12 1.13 1.35	116 23.58 3.21 0.60 0.71	22 4.46 0.61 0.11 0.13	-	-	14 3.79 32.56 2.00 0.09	-	-	-	-	1,934 15.29 53.59 9.93 11.78
Seal Beach (city)	7,569 37.85	968	654 67.56 67.56 8.64	-	-	-	-	-	-	-	-	-	-	-	-	178 61.81 27.22 18.39 2.35	-	-	-	-	-	-	-	-	-	-
Stanton (city)	2,625 11.93	3,902	801 20.53 20.53 30.51	-	-	-	-	-	-	-	354 46.64 44.19 9.07 13.49	-	-	-	-	-	117 21.75 14.61 3.00 4.46	-	-	-	-	-	-	-	-	204 10.86 25.47 5.23 7.77

Notes: Please refer to the User's Guide for an explanation of data; data is arranged alphabetically by state, then county, then city within each county; table includes counties with populations greater than 49,999 unless noted and cities with populations greater than 9,999 whose Asian and/or NHPI population rates are greater than the national average; (1) Native Hawaiian and other Pacific Islander; (2) excludes Taiwanese; (3) includes Chamorro; (4) county does not meet population threshold but is shown in order to allow inclusion of city

Place	Total population 25 years and over who are 4-year college graduates	Asian population 25 years and over	Asians 25 years and over who are 4-year college graduates	NHPI[1] population 25 years and over	NHPIs[1] 25 years and over who are 4-year college graduates	Asian Indian	Bangladeshi	Cambodian	Chinese[2]	Fijian	Filipino	Guamanian[3]	Hawaiian, Native	Hmong	Indonesian	Japanese	Korean	Laotian	Malaysian	Pakistani	Samoan	Sri Lankan	Taiwanese	Thai	Tongan	Vietnamese
Tustin (city)	14,350 33.40	6,170	3,174 51.44 51.44 22.12	-	-	422 51.21 13.30 6.84 2.94	-	-	592 63.38 18.65 9.59 4.13	-	558 50.73 17.58 9.04 3.89	-	-	-	-	203 40.36 6.40 3.29 1.41	436 54.09 13.74 7.07 3.04	-	-	-	-	-	231 68.34 7.28 3.74 1.61	-	-	458 41.98 14.43 7.42 3.19
Tustin Foothills (cdp)	8,965 53.80	1,255	835 66.53 66.53 9.31	-	-	-	-	-	279 80.17 33.41 22.23 3.11	-	-	-	-	-	-	-	-	-	-	-	-	-	-	-	-	-
Westminster (city)	10,382 18.11	21,648	4,141 19.13 19.13 39.89	202	17 8.42 8.42 0.16	93 38.43 2.25 0.43 0.90	-	-	393 36.83 9.49 1.82 3.79	-	526 51.62 12.70 2.43 5.07	-	-	-	-	276 32.28 6.67 1.27 2.66	168 34.36 4.06 0.78 1.62	-	-	-	17 9.50 100.00 8.42 0.16	-	-	-	-	2,534 14.70 61.19 11.71 24.41
Yorba Linda (city)	15,534 41.47	4,158	2,657 63.90 63.90 17.10	-	-	342 78.80 12.87 8.23 2.20	-	-	826 73.62 31.09 19.87 5.32	-	323 55.79 12.16 7.77 2.08	-	-	-	-	304 47.13 11.44 7.31 1.96	308 58.44 11.59 7.41 1.98	-	-	-	-	-	-	-	-	209 54.01 7.87 5.03 1.35
Placer County	50,226 30.28	5,070	2,347 46.29 46.29 4.67	-	-	328 65.34 13.98 6.47 0.65	-	-	522 52.83 22.24 10.30 1.04	-	580 43.32 24.71 11.44 1.15	-	-	-	-	584 40.19 24.88 11.52 1.16	115 41.22 4.90 2.27 0.23	-	-	-	-	-	-	-	-	111 39.64 4.73 2.19 0.22
Rocklin (city)	8,303 36.05	895	515 57.54 57.54 6.20	-	-	-	-	-	-	-	-	-	-	-	-	139 43.30 26.99 15.53 1.67	-	-	-	-	-	-	-	-	-	-
Roseville (city)	16,622 31.36	2,220	1,034 46.58 46.58 6.22	-	-	230 63.71 22.24 10.36 1.38	-	-	272 56.20 26.31 12.25 1.64	-	238 34.39 23.02 10.72 1.43	-	-	-	-	195 54.17 18.86 8.78 1.17	-	-	-	-	-	-	-	-	-	-
Riverside County	155,676 16.63	33,180	12,795 38.56 38.56 8.22	2,206	176 7.98 7.98 0.11	1,716 51.10 13.41 5.17 1.10	-	62 20.20 0.48 0.19 0.04	1,542 45.11 12.05 4.65 0.99	-	5,370 43.39 41.97 16.18 3.45	20 3.13 11.36 0.91 0.01	88 14.89 50.00 3.99 0.06	0 0.00 0.00 0.00 0.00	-	1,181 34.78 9.23 3.56 0.76	1,309 36.91 10.23 3.95 0.84	47 5.72 0.37 0.14 0.03	-	135 57.20 1.06 0.41 0.09	31 6.78 17.61 1.41 0.02	-	161 65.18 1.26 0.49 0.10	179 28.82 1.40 0.54 0.11	-	829 23.25 6.48 2.50 0.53
Banning (city)	1,932 12.56	490	85 17.35 17.35 4.40	-	-	-	-	-	-	-	-	-	-	-	-	-	-	4 2.17 4.71 0.82 0.21	-	-	-	-	-	-	-	-
Corona (city)	15,918 21.99	5,865	2,574 43.89 43.89 16.17	-	-	550 58.08 21.37 9.38 3.46	-	-	237 44.55 9.21 4.04 1.49	-	987 50.33 38.34 16.83 6.20	-	-	-	-	168 37.67 6.53 2.86 1.06	307 37.35 11.93 5.23 1.93	-	-	-	-	-	-	-	-	262 29.64 10.18 4.47 1.65

Notes: Please refer to the User's Guide for an explanation of data; data is arranged alphabetically by state, then county, then city within each county; table includes counties with populations greater than 49,999 unless noted and cities with populations greater than 9,999 whose Asian and/or NHPI population rates are greater than the national average; (1) Native Hawaiian and other Pacific Islander; (2) excludes Taiwanese; (3) includes Chamorro; (4) county does not meet population threshold but is shown in order to allow inclusion of city

Place	Total population 25 years and over who are 4-year college graduates	Asian population 25 years and over	Asians 25 years and over who are 4-year college graduates	NHPI[1] population 25 years and over	NHPIs[1] 25 years and over who are 4-year college graduates	Asian Indian	Bangladeshi	Cambodian	Chinese[2]	Fijian	Filipino	Guamanian[3]	Hawaiian, Native	Hmong	Indonesian	Japanese	Korean	Laotian	Malaysian	Pakistani	Samoan	Sri Lankan	Taiwanese	Thai	Tongan	Vietnamese
Moreno Valley (city)	10,496 14.00	4,890	1,809 36.99 36.99 17.24	-	-	-	-	-	93 33.10 5.14 1.90 0.89	-	1,180 47.45 65.23 24.13 11.24	-	-	-	-	100 26.81 5.53 2.04 0.95	135 31.91 7.46 2.76 1.29	12 4.63 0.66 0.25 0.11	-	-	-	-	-	-	-	50 13.40 2.76 1.02 0.48
Palm Springs (city)	8,710 26.57	1,205	388 32.20 32.20 4.45	-	-	-	-	-	-	-	242 31.68 62.37 20.08 2.78	-	-	-	-	-	-	-	-	-	-	-	-	-	-	-
Pedley (cdp)	626 9.65	282	59 20.92 20.92 9.42	-	-	-	-	-	-	-	-	-	-	-	-	-	-	-	-	-	-	-	-	-	-	-
Riverside (city)	27,896 19.08	7,348	3,242 44.12 44.12 11.62	666	39 5.86 5.86 0.14	489 60.37 15.08 6.65 1.75	-	-	631 64.78 19.46 8.59 2.26	-	924 51.53 28.50 12.57 3.31	-	-	-	-	297 42.43 9.16 4.04 1.06	363 38.78 11.20 4.94 1.30	31 16.23 0.96 0.42 0.11	-	-	-	-	-	-	-	256 20.05 7.90 3.48 0.92
Temecula (city)	8,211 25.00	1,693	670 39.57 39.57 8.16	-	-	-	-	-	113 45.38 16.87 6.67 1.38	-	325 36.35 48.51 19.20 3.96	-	-	-	-	-	-	-	-	-	-	-	-	-	-	-
Sacramento County	191,641 24.81	80,510	24,583 30.53 30.53 12.83	3,435	314 9.14 9.14 0.16	3,259 42.28 13.26 4.05 1.70	-	58 10.74 0.24 0.07 0.03	6,839 34.44 27.82 8.49 3.57	35 3.37 11.15 1.02 0.02	6,129 38.53 24.93 7.61 3.20	64 12.14 20.38 1.86 0.03	58 13.46 18.47 1.69 0.03	284 5.43 1.16 0.35 0.15	-	4,155 39.64 16.90 5.16 2.17	1,000 32.32 4.07 1.24 0.52	155 3.90 0.63 0.19 0.08	-	200 27.51 0.81 0.25 0.10	32 6.45 10.19 0.93 0.02	-	155 50.99 0.63 0.19 0.08	114 25.00 0.46 0.14 0.06	33 8.53 10.51 0.96 0.02	1,519 15.82 6.18 1.89 0.79
Arden-Arcade (cdp)	22,418 34.38	3,189	1,615 50.64 50.64 7.20	-	-	261 58.26 16.16 8.18 1.16	-	-	384 57.66 23.78 12.04 1.71	-	305 41.27 18.89 9.56 1.36	-	-	46 40.35 2.85 1.44 0.21	-	246 59.42 15.23 7.71 1.10	-	-	-	-	-	-	-	-	-	66 24.26 4.09 2.07 0.29
Elk Grove (cdp)	8,584 24.13	6,340	2,099 33.11 33.11 24.45	-	-	164 19.83 7.81 2.59 1.91	-	-	239 25.89 11.39 3.77 2.78	-	1,004 47.52 47.83 15.84 11.70	-	-	-	-	251 61.37 11.96 3.96 2.92	-	-	-	-	-	-	-	-	-	275 21.81 13.10 4.34 3.20
Fair Oaks (cdp)	8,327 42.38	794	497 62.59 62.59 5.97	-	-	-	-	-	-	-	-	-	-	-	-	-	-	-	-	-	-	-	-	-	-	-
Florin (cdp)	1,642 10.10	2,840	441 15.53 15.53 26.86	-	-	46 22.22 10.43 1.62 2.80	-	-	46 11.65 10.43 1.62 2.80	-	247 34.74 56.01 8.70 15.04	-	-	4 1.76 0.91 0.14 0.24	-	-	-	-	-	-	-	-	-	-	-	29 4.12 6.58 1.02 1.77

Notes: Please refer to the User's Guide for an explanation of data; data is arranged alphabetically by state, then county, then city within each county; table includes counties with populations greater than 49,999 unless noted and cities with populations greater than 9,999 whose Asian and/or NHPI population rates are greater than the national average; (1) Native Hawaiian and other Pacific Islander; (2) excludes Taiwanese; (3) includes Chamorro; (4) county does not meet population threshold but is shown in order to allow inclusion of city

Place	Total population 25 years and over who are 4-year college graduates	Asian population 25 years and over	Asians 25 years and over who are 4-year college graduates	NHPI[1] population 25 years and over	NHPIs[1] 25 years and over who are 4-year college graduates	Asian Indian	Bangladeshi	Cambodian	Chinese[2]	Fijian	Filipino	Guamanian[3]	Hawaiian, Native	Hmong	Indonesian	Japanese	Korean	Laotian	Malaysian	Pakistani	Samoan	Sri Lankan	Taiwanese	Thai	Tongan	Vietnamese
Folsom (city)	13,538	2,525	1,690	-	-	712	-	-	323	-	247	-	-	-	-	-	-	-	-	-	-	-	-	-	-	-
	37.60		66.93			75.91			73.74		58.81															
						42.13			19.11		14.62															
			66.93			28.20			12.79		9.78															
			12.48			5.26			2.39		1.82															
Foothill Farms (cdp)	1,300	571	103	-	-	-	-	-	-	-	-	-	-	-	-	-	-	-	-	-	-	-	-	-	-	-
	12.70		18.04																							
			18.04																							
			7.92																							
La Riviera (cdp)	2,485	655	298	-	-	-	-	-	-	-	-	-	-	-	-	-	-	-	-	-	-	-	-	-	-	-
	36.10		45.50																							
			45.50																							
			11.99																							
Laguna (cdp)	8,191	4,033	1,891	-	-	158	-	-	700	-	608	-	-	-	-	231	-	-	-	-	-	-	-	-	-	102
	39.24		46.89			36.07			54.14		52.01					50.11										31.38
						8.36			37.02		32.15					12.22										5.39
			46.89			3.92			17.36		15.08					5.73										2.53
			23.09			1.93			8.55		7.42					2.82										1.25
North Highlands (cdp)	2,307	1,559	78	-	-	-	-	-	-	-	47	-	-	-	-	-	-	-	-	-	-	-	-	-	-	13
	8.95		5.00								8.99															3.04
											60.26															16.67
			5.00								3.01															0.83
			3.38								2.04															0.56
Parkway-S. Sacramento (cdp)	1,571	2,915	163	-	-	-	-	-	50	-	-	-	-	8	-	-	-	15	-	-	-	-	-	-	-	20
	8.12		5.59						18.25					0.98				2.48								3.11
									30.67					4.91				9.20								12.27
			5.59						1.72					0.27				0.51								0.69
			10.38						3.18					0.51				0.95								1.27
Rancho Cordova (cdp)	6,091	2,743	864	-	-	275	-	-	127	-	233	-	-	-	-	-	50	-	-	-	-	-	-	-	-	88
	18.10		31.50			69.27			45.85		34.88						15.87									17.67
						31.83			14.70		26.97						5.79									10.19
			31.50			10.03			4.63		8.49						1.82									3.21
			14.18			4.51			2.09		3.83						0.82									1.44
Rosemont (cdp)	3,624	1,834	518	-	-	-	-	-	-	-	99	-	-	-	-	-	78	-	-	-	-	-	-	-	-	43
	25.49		28.24								38.52						21.43									11.14
											19.11						15.06									8.30
			28.24								5.40						4.25									2.34
			14.29								2.73						2.15									1.19
Sacramento (city)	61,042	38,901	9,960	1,942	157	686	-	18	3,886	32	1,850	-	-	175	-	2,230	185	81	-	113	6	-	-	-	33	416
	23.95		25.60		8.08	29.15		7.29	29.23	4.41	34.17			4.80		38.95	36.63	3.22		29.35	2.44				12.55	12.07
						6.89		0.18	39.02	20.38	18.57			1.76		22.39	1.86	0.81		1.13	3.82				21.02	4.18
			25.60		8.08	1.76		0.05	9.99	1.65	4.76			0.45		5.73	0.48	0.21		0.29	0.31				1.70	1.07
			16.32		0.26	1.12		0.03	6.37	0.05	3.03			0.29		3.65	0.30	0.13		0.19	0.01				0.05	0.68
Vineyard (cdp)	1,714	1,045	350	-	-	-	-	-	-	-	153	-	-	-	-	-	-	-	-	-	-	-	-	-	-	-
	27.45		33.49								35.17															
											43.71															
			33.49								14.64															
			20.42								8.93															

Notes: Please refer to the User's Guide for an explanation of data; data is arranged alphabetically by state, then county, then city within each county; table includes counties with populations greater than 49,999 unless noted and cities with populations greater than 9,999 whose Asian and/or NHPI population rates are greater than the national average; (1) Native Hawaiian and other Pacific Islander; (2) excludes Taiwanese; (3) includes Chamorro; (4) county does not meet population threshold but is shown in order to allow inclusion of city

Place	Total population 25 years and over who are 4-year college graduates	Asian population 25 years and over	Asians 25 years and over who are 4-year college graduates	NHPI[1] population 25 years and over	NHPIs[1] 25 years and over who are 4-year college graduates	Asian Indian	Bangladeshi	Cambodian	Chinese[2]	Fijian	Filipino	Guamanian[3]	Hawaiian, Native	Hmong	Indonesian	Japanese	Korean	Laotian	Malaysian	Pakistani	Samoan	Sri Lankan	Taiwanese	Thai	Tongan	Vietnamese
San Benito County	5,371 17.10	730	212 29.04 29.04 3.95	-	-	-	-	-	-	-	88 22.45 41.51 12.05 1.64	-	-	-	-	-	-	-	-	-	-	-	-	-	-	-
San Bernardino County	156,581 15.92	50,706	22,170 43.72 43.72 14.16	2,606	202 7.75 7.75 0.13	2,704 56.27 12.20 5.33 1.73	-	95 11.59 0.43 0.19 0.06	3,519 49.65 15.87 6.94 2.25	-	8,333 50.37 37.59 16.43 5.32	48 7.31 23.76 1.84 0.03	67 14.73 33.17 2.57 0.04	-	834 41.45 3.76 1.64 0.53	1,262 36.01 5.69 2.49 0.81	2,244 46.40 10.12 4.43 1.43	20 8.16 0.09 0.04 0.01	-	268 66.17 1.21 0.53 0.17	24 2.86 11.88 0.92 0.02	-	751 56.98 3.39 1.48 0.48	432 35.35 1.95 0.85 0.28	25 6.46 12.38 0.96 0.02	1,085 17.45 4.89 2.14 0.69
Chino (city)	5,213 13.02	2,166	896 41.37 41.37 17.19	-	-	-	-	-	-	-	421 43.81 46.99 19.44 8.08	-	-	-	-	-	-	-	-	-	-	-	-	-	-	59 18.21 6.58 2.72 1.13
Chino Hills (city)	15,037 37.56	9,051	5,553 61.35 61.35 36.93	-	-	582 78.33 10.48 6.43 3.87	-	-	1,231 54.49 22.17 13.60 8.19	-	2,234 66.85 40.23 24.68 14.86	-	-	-	-	249 57.64 4.48 2.75 1.66	419 55.64 7.55 4.63 2.79	-	-	-	-	-	283 71.65 5.10 3.13 1.88	-	-	220 42.07 3.96 2.43 1.46
Colton (city)	3,143 12.21	1,580	736 46.58 46.58 23.42	-	-	-	-	-	-	-	239 62.89 32.47 15.13 7.60	-	-	-	-	-	-	-	-	-	-	-	-	-	-	-
Fontana (city)	6,842 10.26	3,558	1,381 38.81 38.81 20.18	302	35 11.59 11.59 0.51	124 32.12 8.98 3.49 1.81	-	-	-	-	899 48.75 65.10 25.27 13.14	-	-	-	-	-	-	-	-	-	-	-	-	-	-	-
Grand Terrace (city)	1,849 24.34	373	175 46.92 46.92 9.46	-	-	-	-	-	-	-	-	-	-	-	-	-	-	-	-	-	-	-	-	-	-	-
Highland (city)	3,959 16.06	1,688	597 35.37 35.37 15.08	-	-	-	-	-	-	-	290 50.09 48.58 17.18 7.33	-	-	-	-	-	-	-	-	-	-	-	-	-	-	49 15.31 8.21 2.90 1.24
Loma Linda (city)	5,605 44.68	2,919	1,735 59.44 59.44 30.95	-	-	162 57.45 9.34 5.55 2.89	-	-	283 67.54 16.31 9.70 5.05	-	431 60.96 24.84 14.77 7.69	-	-	-	129 46.24 7.44 4.42 2.30	-	386 66.10 22.25 13.22 6.89	-	-	-	-	-	-	-	-	-
Montclair (city)	1,793 9.56	1,734	386 22.26 22.26 21.53	-	-	-	-	-	-	-	-	-	-	-	-	-	-	-	-	-	-	-	-	-	-	81 10.29 20.98 4.67 4.52

Notes: Please refer to the User's Guide for an explanation of data; data is arranged alphabetically by state, then county, then city within each county; table includes counties with populations greater than 49,999 unless noted and cities with populations greater than 9,999 whose Asian and/or NHPI population rates are greater than the national average; (1) Native Hawaiian and other Pacific Islander; (2) excludes Taiwanese; (3) includes Chamorro; (4) county does not meet population threshold but is shown in order to allow inclusion of city

Place	Total population 25 years and over who are 4-year college graduates	Asian population 25 years and over	Asians 25 years and over who are 4-year college graduates	NHPI[1] population 25 years and over	NHPIs[1] 25 years and over who are 4-year college graduates	Asian Indian	Bangladeshi	Cambodian	Chinese[2]	Fijian	Filipino	Guamanian[3]	Hawaiian, Native	Hmong	Indonesian	Japanese	Korean	Laotian	Malaysian	Pakistani	Samoan	Sri Lankan	Taiwanese	Thai	Tongan	Vietnamese
Ontario (city)	8,983	4,050	1,395	253	9	95	-	-	131	-	751	-	-	-	-	-	-	-	-	-	-	-	-	-	-	127
	10.49		34.44		3.56	32.87			37.43		46.91															12.88
						6.81			9.39		53.84															9.10
			34.44		3.56	2.35			3.23		18.54															3.14
			15.53		0.10	1.06			1.46		8.36															1.41
Rancho Cucamonga (city)	18,008	4,799	2,331	-	-	332	-	-	434	-	873	-	-	-	-	166	192	-	-	-	-	-	-	-	-	75
	23.30		48.57			58.66			45.49		62.14					36.81	41.74									24.19
						14.24			18.62		37.45					7.12	8.24									3.22
			48.57			6.92			9.04		18.19					3.46	4.00									1.56
			12.94			1.84			2.41		4.85					0.92	1.07									0.42
Redlands (city)	14,184	2,238	1,198	-	-	161	-	-	198	-	280	-	-	-	-	-	217	-	-	-	-	-	-	-	-	-
	35.22		53.53			63.14			56.90		54.26						63.64									
						13.44			16.53		23.37						18.11									
			53.53			7.19			8.85		12.51						9.70									
			8.45			1.14			1.40		1.97						1.53									
Rialto (city)	4,146	1,066	392	289	0	-	-	-	-	-	163	-	-	-	-	-	-	-	-	-	-	-	-	-	-	-
	8.68		36.77		<0.01						53.80															
											41.58															
			36.77		<0.01						15.29															
			9.45		<0.01						3.93															
San Bernardino (city)	11,558	4,350	1,360	355	30	216	-	34	136	-	372	-	-	-	49	-	121	-	-	-	14	-	-	-	-	87
	11.64		31.26		8.45	46.55		18.48	34.26		32.35				27.07		44.32				8.05					10.88
						15.88		2.50	10.00		27.35				3.60		8.90				46.67					6.40
			31.26		8.45	4.97		0.78	3.13		8.55				1.13		2.78				3.94					2.00
			11.77		0.26	1.87		0.29	1.18		3.22				0.42		1.05				0.12					0.75
Upland (city)	11,545	3,264	1,601	-	-	272	-	-	304	-	266	-	-	-	-	-	324	-	-	-	-	-	156	-	-	79
	26.66		49.05			72.92			63.07		54.29						59.23						52.17			14.79
						16.99			18.99		16.61						20.24						9.74			4.93
			49.05			8.33			9.31		8.15						9.93						4.78			2.42
			13.87			2.36			2.63		2.30						2.81						1.35			0.68
Victorville (city)	3,906	1,540	369	-	-	-	-	-	-	-	218	-	-	-	-	-	-	-	-	-	-	-	-	-	-	-
	10.62		23.96								30.58															
											59.08															
			23.96								14.16															
			9.45								5.58															
San Diego County	523,511	160,925	59,820	7,805	990	4,440	-	76	11,195	-	26,898	274	250	71	163	5,797	3,582	332	-	224	276	-	1,062	476	54	4,159
	29.52		37.17		12.68	71.12		3.95	58.90		33.93	9.42	16.58	12.77	48.66	39.37	50.66	8.59		81.45	10.95		70.85	52.77	25.84	19.27
						7.42		0.13	18.71		44.96	27.68	25.25	0.12	0.27	9.69	5.99	0.55		0.37	27.88		1.78	0.80	5.45	6.95
			37.17		12.68	2.76		0.05	6.96		16.71	3.51	3.20	0.04	0.10	3.60	2.23	0.21		0.14	3.54		0.66	0.30	0.69	2.58
			11.43		0.19	0.85		0.01	2.14		5.14	0.05	0.05	0.01	0.03	1.11	0.68	0.06		0.04	0.05		0.20	0.09	0.01	0.79
Bonita (cdp)	3,203	760	357	-	-	-	-	-	-	-	221	-	-	-	-	-	-	-	-	-	-	-	-	-	-	-
	38.45		46.97								46.92															
											61.90															
			46.97								29.08															
			11.15								6.90															
Carlsbad (city)	24,956	2,327	1,285	-	-	-	-	-	410	-	221	-	-	-	-	169	-	-	-	-	-	-	-	-	-	-
	45.66		55.22						86.13		45.57					40.53										
									31.91		17.20					13.15										
			55.22						17.62		9.50					7.26										
			5.15						1.64		0.89					0.68										

Notes: Please refer to the User's Guide for an explanation of data; data is arranged alphabetically by state, then county, then city within each county; table includes counties with populations greater than 49,999 unless noted and cities with populations greater than 9,999 whose Asian and/or NHPI population rates are greater than the national average; (1) Native Hawaiian and other Pacific Islander; (2) excludes Taiwanese; (3) includes Chamorro; (4) county does not meet population threshold but is shown in order to allow inclusion of city

Place	Total population 25 years and over who are 4-year college graduates	Asian population 25 years and over	Asians 25 years and over who are 4-year college graduates	NHPI[1] population 25 years and over	NHPIs[1] 25 years and over who are 4-year college graduates	Asian Indian	Bangladeshi	Cambodian	Chinese[2]	Fijian	Filipino	Guamanian[3]	Hawaiian, Native	Hmong	Indonesian	Japanese	Korean	Laotian	Malaysian	Pakistani	Samoan	Sri Lankan	Taiwanese	Thai	Tongan	Vietnamese
Chula Vista (city)	23,889 22.22	12,722	5,137 40.38 40.38 21.50	513	56 10.92 10.92 0.23	-	-	-	381 49.48 7.42 2.99 1.59	-	3,569 41.06 69.48 28.05 14.94	12 4.20 21.43 2.34 0.05	-	-	-	532 33.04 10.36 4.18 2.23	418 45.39 8.14 3.29 1.75	-	-	-	-	-	-	-	-	-
Coronado (city)	7,353 48.20	508	230 45.28 45.28 3.13	-	-	-	-	-	-	-	78 32.23 33.91 15.35 1.06	-	-	-	-	-	-	-	-	-	-	-	-	-	-	-
Escondido (city)	16,025 20.11	3,525	1,269 36.00 36.00 7.92	-	-	-	-	-	223 62.46 17.57 6.33 1.39	-	522 42.65 41.13 14.81 3.26	-	-	-	-	-	-	6 2.60 0.47 0.17 0.04	-	-	-	-	-	-	-	189 23.16 14.89 5.36 1.18
Imperial Beach (city)	1,785 11.65	1,297	288 22.21 22.21 16.13	-	-	-	-	-	-	-	202 18.70 70.14 15.57 11.32	-	-	-	-	-	-	-	-	-	-	-	-	-	-	-
La Mesa (city)	10,615 27.63	1,525	592 38.82 38.82 5.58	-	-	-	-	-	-	-	191 50.13 32.26 12.52 1.80	-	-	-	-	-	-	-	-	-	-	-	-	-	-	-
La Presa (cdp)	2,563 13.17	2,305	515 22.34 22.34 20.09	-	-	-	-	-	-	-	466 22.97 90.49 20.22 18.18	-	-	-	-	-	-	-	-	-	-	-	-	-	-	-
Lemon Grove (city)	2,397 15.27	890	146 16.40 16.40 6.09	-	-	-	-	-	-	-	96 22.22 65.75 10.79 4.01	-	-	-	-	-	-	-	-	-	-	-	-	-	-	18 9.09 12.33 2.02 0.75
National City (city)	2,732 9.01	6,771	1,288 19.02 19.02 47.14	-	-	-	-	-	-	-	1,249 20.09 96.97 18.45 45.72	-	-	-	-	-	-	-	-	-	-	-	-	-	-	-
Oceanside (city)	22,310 22.16	6,170	1,632 26.45 26.45 7.32	1,203	65 5.40 5.40 0.29	-	-	-	199 49.14 12.19 3.23 0.89	-	871 25.56 53.37 14.12 3.90	-	-	-	-	231 22.51 14.15 3.74 1.04	-	-	-	-	49 6.27 75.38 4.07 0.22	-	-	-	-	91 17.11 5.58 1.47 0.41
Poway (city)	11,713 39.32	2,107	1,051 49.88 49.88 8.97	-	-	-	-	-	296 63.25 28.16 14.05 2.53	-	287 35.61 27.31 13.62 2.45	-	-	-	-	-	-	-	-	-	-	-	-	-	-	-

Notes: Please refer to the User's Guide for an explanation of data; data is arranged alphabetically by state, then county, then city within each county; table includes counties with populations greater than 49,999 unless noted and cities with populations greater than 9,999 whose Asian and/or NHPI population rates are greater than the national average; (1) Native Hawaiian and other Pacific Islander; (2) excludes Taiwanese; (3) includes Chamorro; (4) county does not meet population threshold but is shown in order to allow inclusion of city

Place	Total population 25 years and over who are 4-year college graduates	Asian population 25 years and over	Asians 25 years and over who are 4-year college graduates	NHPI[1] population 25 years and over	NHPIs[1] 25 years and over who are 4-year college graduates	Asian Indian	Bangladeshi	Cambodian	Chinese[2]	Fijian	Filipino	Guamanian[3]	Hawaiian, Native	Hmong	Indonesian	Japanese	Korean	Laotian	Malaysian	Pakistani	Samoan	Sri Lankan	Taiwanese	Thai	Tongan	Vietnamese
Rancho San Diego (cdp)	4,646 36.45	646	173 26.78 26.78 3.72	-	-	-	-	-	-	-	95 26.54 54.91 14.71 2.04	-	-	-	-	-	-	-	-	-	-	-	-	-	-	-
San Diego (city)	272,785 35.01	105,087	40,376 38.42 38.42 14.80	3,519	552 15.69 15.69 0.20	3,138 75.93 7.77 2.99 1.15	-	61 3.60 0.15 0.06 0.02	8,322 59.44 20.61 7.92 3.05	-	17,093 35.62 42.33 16.27 6.27	173 13.44 31.34 4.92 0.06	166 22.28 30.07 4.72 0.06	64 15.27 0.16 0.06 0.02	-	3,579 46.78 8.86 3.41 1.31	2,341 57.95 5.80 2.23 0.86	301 9.10 0.75 0.29 0.11	-	-	84 8.30 15.22 2.39 0.03	-	745 75.94 1.85 0.71 0.27	343 64.23 0.85 0.33 0.13	-	3,316 18.65 8.21 3.16 1.22
San Marcos (city)	6,822 20.05	1,715	608 35.45 35.45 8.91	-	-	-	-	-	156 50.16 25.66 9.10 2.29	-	272 34.09 44.74 15.86 3.99	-	-	-	-	-	-	-	-	-	-	-	-	-	-	-
Solana Beach (city)	5,685 58.18	418	283 67.70 67.70 4.98	-	-	-	-	-	-	-	-	-	-	-	-	-	-	-	-	-	-	-	-	-	-	-
Spring Valley (cdp)	3,312 19.77	960	205 21.35 21.35 6.19	-	-	-	-	-	-	-	111 23.42 54.15 11.56 3.35	-	-	-	-	-	-	-	-	-	-	-	-	-	-	-
Vista (city)	10,399 19.62	2,160	890 41.20 41.20 8.56	274	24 8.76 8.76 0.23	-	-	-	-	-	234 28.47 26.29 10.83 2.25	-	-	-	-	143 37.53 16.07 6.62 1.38	-	-	-	-	-	-	-	-	-	-
San Francisco County	267,992 44.98	176,086	56,004 31.80 31.80 20.90	2,004	352 17.56 17.56 0.13	2,326 66.25 4.15 1.32 0.87	-	46 13.18 0.08 0.03 0.02	30,586 26.76 54.61 17.37 11.41	-	11,136 38.59 19.88 6.32 4.16	-	-	-	305 61.74 0.54 0.17 0.11	4,445 48.29 7.94 2.52 1.66	2,985 52.74 5.33 1.70 1.11	-	-	121 46.90 0.22 0.07 0.05	114 10.52 32.39 5.69 0.04	-	378 67.38 0.67 0.21 0.14	565 52.36 1.01 0.32 0.21	-	1,239 17.74 2.21 0.70 0.46
San Francisco (city)	267,992 44.98	176,086	56,004 31.80 31.80 20.90	2,004	352 17.56 17.56 0.13	2,326 66.25 4.15 1.32 0.87	-	46 13.18 0.08 0.03 0.02	30,586 26.76 54.61 17.37 11.41	-	11,136 38.59 19.88 6.32 4.16	-	-	-	305 61.74 0.54 0.17 0.11	4,445 48.29 7.94 2.52 1.66	2,985 52.74 5.33 1.70 1.11	-	-	121 46.90 0.22 0.07 0.05	114 10.52 32.39 5.69 0.04	-	378 67.38 0.67 0.21 0.14	565 52.36 1.01 0.32 0.21	-	1,239 17.74 2.21 0.70 0.46
San Joaquin County	48,468 14.53	35,054	7,359 20.99 20.99 15.18	942	98 10.40 10.40 0.20	964 32.83 13.10 2.75 1.99	-	117 3.20 1.59 0.33 0.24	945 24.27 12.84 2.70 1.95	-	3,410 25.52 46.34 9.73 7.04	-	70 27.03 71.43 7.43 0.14	85 4.49 1.16 0.24 0.18	-	834 28.93 11.33 2.38 1.72	201 34.54 2.73 0.57 0.41	61 4.42 0.83 0.17 0.13	-	95 17.56 1.29 0.27 0.20	4 1.93 4.08 0.42 0.01	-	-	-	-	383 12.96 5.20 1.09 0.79
Lathrop (city)	635 10.91	855	242 28.30 28.30 38.11	-	-	-	-	-	-	-	169 25.96 69.83 19.77 26.61	-	-	-	-	-	-	-	-	-	-	-	-	-	-	-

Notes: Please refer to the User's Guide for an explanation of data; data is arranged alphabetically by state, then county, then city within each county; table includes counties with populations greater than 49,999 unless noted and cities with populations greater than 9,999 whose Asian and/or NHPI population rates are greater than the national average; (1) Native Hawaiian and other Pacific Islander; (2) excludes Taiwanese; (3) includes Chamorro; (4) county does not meet population threshold but is shown in order to allow inclusion of city

Place	Total population 25 years and over who are 4-year college graduates	Asian population 25 years and over	Asians 25 years and over who are 4-year college graduates	NHPI[1] population 25 years and over	NHPIs[1] 25 years and over who are 4-year college graduates	Asian Indian	Bangladeshi	Cambodian	Chinese[2]	Fijian	Filipino	Guamanian[3]	Hawaiian, Native	Hmong	Indonesian	Japanese	Korean	Laotian	Malaysian	Pakistani	Samoan	Sri Lankan	Taiwanese	Thai	Tongan	Vietnamese
Lodi (city)	5,482 15.64	1,918	413 21.53 21.53 7.53	-	-	96 21.10 23.24 5.01 1.75	-	-	-	-	71 18.93 17.19 3.70 1.30	-	-	-	-	128 24.66 30.99 6.67 2.33	-	-	-	-	-	-	-	-	-	-
Stockton (city)	21,239 15.35	25,316	4,580 18.09 18.09 21.56	539	72 13.36 13.36 0.34	259 22.74 5.66 1.02 1.22	-	104 2.96 2.27 0.41 0.49	661 22.44 14.43 2.61 3.11	-	2,442 25.28 53.32 9.65 11.50	-	-	60 3.94 1.31 0.24 0.28	-	391 30.33 8.54 1.54 1.84	-	57 4.30 1.24 0.23 0.27	-	45 14.90 0.98 0.18 0.21	-	-	-	-	-	285 10.85 6.22 1.13 1.34
Tracy (city)	5,957 18.02	2,795	1,018 36.42 36.42 17.09	-	-	289 43.85 28.39 10.34 4.85	-	-	105 42.86 10.31 3.76 1.76	-	395 33.96 38.80 14.13 6.63	-	-	-	-	-	-	-	-	-	-	-	-	-	-	-
San Luis Obispo County	42,507 26.70	3,844	1,314 34.18 34.18 3.09	-	-	196 59.94 14.92 5.10 0.46	-	-	258 53.42 19.63 6.71 0.61	-	447 30.31 34.02 11.63 1.05	-	-	-	-	193 26.96 14.69 5.02 0.45	151 33.93 11.49 3.93 0.36	-	-	-	-	-	-	-	-	-
Baywood-Los Osos (cdp)	3,743 36.94	553	142 25.68 25.68 3.79	-	-	-	-	-	-	-	120 31.09 84.51 21.70 3.21	-	-	-	-	-	-	-	-	-	-	-	-	-	-	-
Grover Beach (city)	1,661 19.49	348	124 35.63 35.63 7.47	-	-	-	-	-	-	-	-	-	-	-	-	-	-	-	-	-	-	-	-	-	-	-
San Luis Obispo (city)	9,497 40.90	899	388 43.16 43.16 4.09	-	-	-	-	-	82 58.99 21.13 9.12 0.86	-	30 15.38 7.73 3.34 0.32	-	-	-	-	-	-	-	-	-	-	-	-	-	-	-
San Mateo County	191,277 39.01	99,081	49,684 50.14 50.14 25.97	4,855	526 10.83 10.83 0.27	5,588 71.35 11.25 5.64 2.92	-	-	17,558 50.84 35.34 17.72 9.18	51 7.43 9.70 1.05 0.03	17,642 44.32 35.51 17.81 9.22	56 19.58 10.65 1.15 0.03	105 19.37 19.96 2.16 0.05	-	203 47.32 0.41 0.20 0.11	4,101 52.64 8.25 4.14 2.14	1,850 58.10 3.72 1.87 0.97	-	-	-	103 13.41 19.58 2.12 0.05	-	552 90.20 1.11 0.56 0.29	222 46.64 0.45 0.22 0.12	151 7.69 28.71 3.11 0.08	729 37.64 1.47 0.74 0.38
Belmont (city)	9,719 51.72	2,878	1,981 68.83 68.83 20.38	-	-	436 87.55 22.01 15.15 4.49	-	-	902 69.38 45.53 31.34 9.28	-	233 54.95 11.76 8.10 2.40	-	-	-	-	232 62.20 11.71 8.06 2.39	-	-	-	-	-	-	-	-	-	-
Burlingame (city)	10,121 47.94	2,786	1,750 62.81 62.81 17.29	-	-	-	-	-	861 61.90 49.20 30.90 8.51	-	258 59.45 14.74 9.26 2.55	-	-	-	-	190 55.23 10.86 6.82 1.88	-	-	-	-	-	-	-	-	-	-

Notes: Please refer to the User's Guide for an explanation of data; data is arranged alphabetically by state, then county, then city within each county; table includes counties with populations greater than 49,999 unless noted and cities with populations greater than 9,999 whose Asian and/or NHPI population rates are greater than the national average; (1) Native Hawaiian and other Pacific Islander; (2) excludes Taiwanese; (3) includes Chamorro; (4) county does not meet population threshold but is shown in order to allow inclusion of city

Place	Total population 25 years and over who are 4-year college graduates	Asian population 25 years and over	Asians 25 years and over who are 4-year college graduates	NHPI[1] population 25 years and over	NHPIs[1] 25 years and over who are 4-year college graduates	Asian Indian	Bangladeshi	Cambodian	Chinese[2]	Fijian	Filipino	Guamanian[3]	Hawaiian, Native	Hmong	Indonesian	Japanese	Korean	Laotian	Malaysian	Pakistani	Samoan	Sri Lankan	Taiwanese	Thai	Tongan	Vietnamese
Daly City (city)	20,244 29.06	35,014	13,262 37.88 37.88 65.51	563	103 18.29 18.29 0.51	448 57.22 3.38 1.28 2.21	-	-	3,248 33.43 24.49 9.28 16.04	-	8,423 39.08 63.51 24.06 41.61	-	-	-	-	275 38.84 2.07 0.79 1.36	322 60.53 2.43 0.92 1.59	-	-	-	-	-	-	-	-	191 29.25 1.44 0.55 0.94
East Palo Alto (city)	1,614 10.64	437	197 45.08 45.08 12.21	1,134	56 4.94 4.94 3.47	-	-	-	-	-	-	-	-	-	-	-	-	-	-	-	-	-	-	-	56 7.39 100.00 4.94 3.47	-
Foster City (city)	12,705 59.84	6,823	4,787 70.16 70.16 37.68	-	-	1,177 89.71 24.59 17.25 9.26	-	-	2,067 64.33 43.18 30.29 16.27	-	373 67.33 7.79 5.47 2.94	-	-	-	-	709 66.51 14.81 10.39 5.58	186 63.70 3.89 2.73 1.46	-	-	-	-	-	-	-	-	-
Hillsborough (town)	5,318 70.04	1,864	1,309 70.23 70.23 24.61	-	-	-	-	-	921 66.74 70.36 49.41 17.32	-	-	-	-	-	-	-	-	-	-	-	-	-	-	-	-	-
Menlo Park (city)	13,845 61.66	1,688	1,231 72.93 72.93 8.89	-	-	-	-	-	459 70.83 37.29 27.19 3.32	-	-	-	-	-	-	234 65.00 19.01 13.86 1.69	-	-	-	-	-	-	-	-	-	-
Millbrae (city)	5,160 33.79	3,810	1,936 50.81 50.81 37.52	-	-	161 60.98 8.32 4.23 3.12	-	-	1,158 46.77 59.81 30.39 22.44	-	252 56.38 13.02 6.61 4.88	-	-	-	-	164 64.82 8.47 4.30 3.18	84 42.42 4.34 2.20 1.63	-	-	-	-	-	-	-	-	-
Pacifica (city)	8,941 33.82	3,987	1,776 44.54 44.54 19.86	-	-	-	-	-	429 40.02 24.16 10.76 4.80	-	883 42.76 49.72 22.15 9.88	-	-	-	-	136 44.44 7.66 3.41 1.52	-	-	-	-	-	-	-	-	-	-
Redwood City (city)	18,437 35.68	5,073	3,430 67.61 67.61 18.60	327	42 12.84 12.84 0.23	723 88.60 21.08 14.25 3.92	-	-	1,466 73.52 42.74 28.90 7.95	-	554 56.88 16.15 10.92 3.00	-	-	-	-	317 54.84 9.24 6.25 1.72	-	-	-	-	-	-	-	-	-	-
San Bruno (city)	7,239 26.15	5,244	2,514 47.94 47.94 34.73	551	42 7.62 7.62 0.58	296 43.53 11.77 5.64 4.09	-	-	740 47.04 29.44 14.11 10.22	-	1,062 50.38 42.24 20.25 14.67	-	-	-	-	199 50.25 7.92 3.79 2.75	-	-	-	-	-	-	-	-	14 5.86 33.33 2.54 0.19	-
San Carlos (city)	10,152 49.78	1,435	1,033 71.99 71.99 10.18	-	-	-	-	-	438 80.07 42.40 30.52 4.31	-	-	-	-	-	-	-	-	-	-	-	-	-	-	-	-	-

Notes: Please refer to the User's Guide for an explanation of data; data is arranged alphabetically by state, then county, then city within each county; table includes counties with populations greater than 49,999 unless noted and cities with populations greater than 9,999 whose Asian and/or NHPI population rates are greater than the national average; (1) Native Hawaiian and other Pacific Islander; (2) excludes Taiwanese; (3) includes Chamorro; (4) county does not meet population threshold but is shown in order to allow inclusion of city

Place	Total population 25 years and over who are 4-year college graduates	Asian population 25 years and over	Asians 25 years and over who are 4-year college graduates	NHPI[1] population 25 years and over	NHPIs[1] 25 years and over who are 4-year college graduates	Asian Indian	Bangladeshi	Cambodian	Chinese[2]	Fijian	Filipino	Guamanian[3]	Hawaiian, Native	Hmong	Indonesian	Japanese	Korean	Laotian	Malaysian	Pakistani	Samoan	Sri Lankan	Taiwanese	Thai	Tongan	Vietnamese
San Mateo (city)	25,900 38.58	10,837	5,789 53.42 53.42 22.35	833	83 9.96 9.96 0.32	1,023 64.75 17.67 9.44 3.95	-	-	2,283 54.15 39.44 21.07 8.81	-	1,105 53.56 19.09 10.20 4.27	-	-	-	-	713 41.67 12.32 6.58 2.75	269 61.42 4.65 2.48 1.04	-	-	-	-	-	-	-	29 7.30 34.94 3.48 0.11	60 24.59 1.04 0.55 0.23
South San Francisco (city)	10,191 25.21	11,705	5,644 48.22 48.22 55.38	497	80 16.10 16.10 0.79	216 42.11 3.83 1.85 2.12	-	-	1,447 45.68 25.64 12.36 14.20	-	3,399 50.47 60.22 29.04 33.35	-	-	-	-	186 41.15 3.30 1.59 1.83	-	-	-	-	-	-	-	-	-	-
Santa Barbara County	72,596 29.42	9,580	3,649 38.09 38.09 5.03	516	101 19.57 19.57 0.14	436 84.50 11.95 4.55 0.60	-	-	877 57.81 24.03 9.15 1.21	-	887 27.78 24.31 9.26 1.22	-	-	12 12.00 0.33 0.13 0.02	-	641 35.67 17.57 6.69 0.88	410 48.18 11.24 4.28 0.56	-	-	-	-	-	-	-	-	87 13.70 2.38 0.91 0.12
Goleta (cdp)	14,616 39.02	2,040	963 47.21 47.21 6.59	-	-	-	-	-	335 63.57 34.79 16.42 2.29	-	166 49.70 17.24 8.14 1.14	-	-	-	-	172 51.19 17.86 8.43 1.18	-	-	-	-	-	-	-	-	-	30 11.36 3.12 1.47 0.21
Isla Vista (cdp)	1,285 39.45	478	314 65.69 65.69 24.44	-	-	-	-	-	161 70.93 51.27 33.68 12.53	-	-	-	-	-	-	-	35 46.05 11.15 7.32 2.72	-	-	-	-	-	-	-	-	-
Lompoc (city)	3,455 13.83	967	254 26.27 26.27 7.35	-	-	-	-	-	-	-	85 33.60 33.46 8.79 2.46	-	-	-	-	-	-	-	-	-	-	-	-	-	-	-
Orcutt (cdp)	4,807 24.95	757	304 40.16 40.16 6.32	-	-	-	-	-	-	-	-	-	-	-	-	-	-	-	-	-	-	-	-	-	-	-
Santa Maria (city)	4,821 11.01	2,449	504 20.58 20.58 10.45	-	-	-	-	-	-	-	310 19.92 61.51 12.66 6.43	-	-	-	-	52 13.37 10.32 2.12 1.08	-	-	-	-	-	-	-	-	-	-
Santa Clara County	450,539 40.48	288,844	148,060 51.26 51.26 32.86	3,431	581 16.93 16.93 0.13	35,658 80.53 24.08 12.35 7.91	286 84.12 0.19 0.10 0.06	196 9.05 0.13 0.07 0.04	51,593 65.87 34.85 17.86 11.45	44 14.92 7.57 1.28 0.01	19,610 38.88 13.24 6.79 4.35	122 15.42 21.00 3.56 0.03	202 26.27 34.77 5.89 0.04	-	218 51.66 0.15 0.08 0.05	11,636 53.00 7.86 4.03 2.58	7,895 55.03 5.33 2.73 1.75	110 10.85 0.07 0.04 0.02	-	1,110 68.94 0.75 0.38 0.25	71 7.55 12.22 2.07 0.02	-	2,927 79.58 1.98 1.01 0.65	487 55.98 0.33 0.17 0.11	-	13,744 21.80 9.28 4.76 3.05
Alum Rock (cdp)	647 7.90	821	113 13.76 13.76 17.47	-	-	-	-	-	-	-	-	-	-	-	-	-	-	-	-	-	-	-	-	-	-	14 4.02 12.39 1.71 2.16

Notes: Please refer to the User's Guide for an explanation of data; data is arranged alphabetically by state, then county, then city within each county; table includes counties with populations greater than 49,999 unless noted and cities with populations greater than 9,999 whose Asian and/or NHPI population rates are greater than the national average; (1) Native Hawaiian and other Pacific Islander; (2) excludes Taiwanese; (3) includes Chamorro; (4) county does not meet population threshold but is shown in order to allow inclusion of city

Place	Total population 25 years and over who are 4-year college graduates	Asian population 25 years and over	Asians 25 years and over who are 4-year college graduates	NHPI[1] population 25 years and over	NHPIs[1] 25 years and over who are 4-year college graduates	Asian Indian	Bangladeshi	Cambodian	Chinese[2]	Fijian	Filipino	Guamanian[3]	Hawaiian, Native	Hmong	Indonesian	Japanese	Korean	Laotian	Malaysian	Pakistani	Samoan	Sri Lankan	Taiwanese	Thai	Tongan	Vietnamese
Campbell (city)	10,791	4,110	2,185	-	-	406	-	-	791	-	221	-	-	-	-	367	157	-	-	-	-	-	-	-	-	190
	39.66		53.16			73.82			72.37		49.55					52.35	26.66									31.30
						18.58			36.20		10.11					16.80	7.19									8.70
			53.16			9.88			19.25		5.38					8.93	3.82									4.62
			20.25			3.76			7.33		2.05					3.40	1.45									1.76
Cupertino (city)	22,563	14,254	10,847	-	-	2,645	-	-	5,203	-	234	-	-	-	-	1,044	794	-	-	-	-	-	459	-	-	224
	65.36		76.10			89.87			78.32		71.78					62.67	60.84						83.15			49.67
						24.38			47.97		2.16					9.62	7.32						4.23			2.07
			76.10			18.56			36.50		1.64					7.32	5.57						3.22			1.57
			48.07			11.72			23.06		1.04					4.63	3.52						2.03			0.99
Gilroy (city)	4,597	1,280	404	-	-	-	-	-	99	-	136	-	-	-	-	-	-	-	-	-	-	-	-	-	-	-
	19.07		31.56						35.74		31.85															
									24.50		33.66															
			31.56						7.73		10.63															
			8.79						2.15		2.96															
Los Altos (city)	14,351	2,929	2,304	-	-	358	-	-	1,170	-	-	-	-	-	-	265	-	-	-	-	-	-	-	-	-	-
	71.30		78.66			93.96			87.18							47.41										
						15.54			50.78							11.50										
			78.66			12.22			39.95							9.05										
			16.05			2.49			8.15							1.85										
Los Gatos (town)	12,606	1,651	1,133	-	-	-	-	-	466	-	-	-	-	-	-	182	-	-	-	-	-	-	-	-	-	-
	58.90		68.63						69.87							55.66										
									41.13							16.06										
			68.63						28.23							11.02										
			8.99						3.70							1.44										
Milpitas (city)	15,005	22,053	10,742	295	20	2,250	-	-	3,444	-	2,486	-	-	-	-	246	289	-	-	-	-	-	-	-	-	1,615
	36.52		48.71		6.78	73.17			58.70		43.39					47.58	42.56									30.87
						20.95			32.06		23.14					2.29	2.69									15.03
			48.71		6.78	10.20			15.62		11.27					1.12	1.31									7.32
			71.59		0.13	15.00			22.95		16.57					1.64	1.93									10.76
Morgan Hill (city)	6,913	1,521	747	-	-	-	-	-	131	-	-	-	-	-	-	152	-	-	-	-	-	-	-	-	-	-
	33.46		49.11						41.46							42.82										
									17.54							20.35										
			49.11						8.61							9.99										
			10.81						1.89							2.20										
Mountain View (city)	28,977	11,074	7,561	-	-	1,887	-	-	3,091	-	734	-	-	-	-	882	389	-	-	-	-	-	-	-	-	238
	55.35		68.28			86.36			72.99		49.39					57.68	73.12									39.21
						24.96			40.88		9.71					11.67	5.14									3.15
			68.28			17.04			27.91		6.63					7.96	3.51									2.15
			26.09			6.51			10.67		2.53					3.04	1.34									0.82
Palo Alto (city)	32,406	7,310	5,791	-	-	901	-	-	3,148	-	189	-	-	-	-	628	608	-	-	-	-	-	-	-	-	-
	74.38		79.22			84.68			83.15		60.97					62.74	94.56									
						15.56			54.36		3.26					10.84	10.50									
			79.22			12.33			43.06		2.59					8.59	8.32									
			17.87			2.78			9.71		0.58					1.94	1.88									
San Jose (city)	180,122	157,466	64,058	1,884	291	11,794	-	178	20,233	-	11,692	82	72	-	-	4,540	3,059	110	-	465	59	-	1,112	202	-	9,263
	31.56		40.68		15.45	71.13		9.11	57.57		36.75	17.45	19.83			48.98	49.29	12.11		60.31	9.41		76.64	50.75		18.99
						18.41		0.28	31.59		18.25	28.18	24.74			7.09	4.78	0.17		0.73	20.27		1.74	0.32		14.46
			40.68		15.45	7.49		0.11	12.85		7.43	4.35	3.82			2.88	1.94	0.07		0.30	3.13		0.71	0.13		5.88
			35.56		0.16	6.55		0.10	11.23		6.49	0.05	0.04			2.52	1.70	0.06		0.26	0.03		0.62	0.11		5.14

Notes: Please refer to the User's Guide for an explanation of data; data is arranged alphabetically by state, then county, then city within each county; table includes counties with populations greater than 49,999 unless noted and cities with populations greater than 9,999 whose Asian and/or NHPI population rates are greater than the national average; (1) Native Hawaiian and other Pacific Islander; (2) excludes Taiwanese; (3) includes Chamorro; (4) county does not meet population threshold but is shown in order to allow inclusion of city

Place	Total population 25 years and over who are 4-year college graduates	Asian population 25 years and over	Asians 25 years and over who are 4-year college graduates	NHPI[1] population 25 years and over	NHPIs[1] 25 years and over who are 4-year college graduates	Asian Indian	Bangladeshi	Cambodian	Chinese[2]	Fijian	Filipino	Guamanian[3]	Hawaiian, Native	Hmong	Indonesian	Japanese	Korean	Laotian	Malaysian	Pakistani	Samoan	Sri Lankan	Taiwanese	Thai	Tongan	Vietnamese
Santa Clara (city)	29,688 42.35	20,579	12,209 59.33 59.33 41.12	250	74 29.60 29.60 0.25	5,214 83.83 42.71 25.34 17.56	-	-	2,676 73.29 21.92 13.00 9.01	-	1,408 36.51 11.53 6.84 4.74	-	-	-	-	646 54.10 5.29 3.14 2.18	800 53.09 6.55 3.89 2.69	-	-	175 71.14 1.43 0.85 0.59	-	-	-	-	-	823 25.72 6.74 4.00 2.77
Saratoga (city)	14,283 68.17	5,339	4,259 79.77 79.77 29.82	-	-	726 93.20 17.05 13.60 5.08	-	-	2,478 81.27 58.18 46.41 17.35	-	-	-	-	-	-	308 70.00 7.23 5.77 2.16	184 56.79 4.32 3.45 1.29	-	-	-	-	-	154 86.52 3.62 2.88 1.08	-	-	-
Stanford (cdp)	4,207 94.56	1,152	1,107 96.09 96.09 26.31	-	-	157 96.91 14.18 13.63 3.73	-	-	558 98.76 50.41 48.44 13.26	-	-	-	-	-	-	-	122 100.00 11.02 10.59 2.90	-	-	-	-	-	-	-	-	-
Sunnyvale (city)	48,379 50.78	31,043	21,021 67.72 67.72 43.45	337	58 17.21 17.21 0.12	8,271 91.40 39.35 26.64 17.10	-	-	6,703 70.79 31.89 21.59 13.86	-	1,766 41.70 8.40 5.69 3.65	-	-	-	-	1,595 57.44 7.59 5.14 3.30	1,032 58.11 4.91 3.32 2.13	-	-	-	-	-	413 79.58 1.96 1.33 0.85	-	-	610 28.07 2.90 1.97 1.26
Santa Cruz County	56,400 34.18	5,342	2,245 42.03 42.03 3.98	-	-	424 68.39 18.89 7.94 0.75	-	-	641 55.31 28.55 12.00 1.14	-	333 25.15 14.83 6.23 0.59	-	-	-	-	519 36.42 23.12 9.72 0.92	133 47.50 5.92 2.49 0.24	-	-	-	-	-	-	-	-	63 35.20 2.81 1.18 0.11
Capitola (city)	2,586 34.63	293	102 34.81 34.81 3.94	-	-	-	-	-	-	-	-	-	-	-	-	-	-	-	-	-	-	-	-	-	-	-
Santa Cruz (city)	15,046 44.39	1,432	766 53.49 53.49 5.09	-	-	196 71.01 25.59 13.69 1.30	-	-	263 62.47 34.33 18.37 1.75	-	63 22.11 8.22 4.40 0.42	-	-	-	-	146 52.71 19.06 10.20 0.97	-	-	-	-	-	-	-	-	-	-
Scotts Valley (city)	3,150 40.90	477	311 65.20 65.20 9.87	-	-	-	-	-	-	-	-	-	-	-	-	-	-	-	-	-	-	-	-	-	-	-
Shasta County	17,808 16.60	1,726	317 18.37 18.37 1.78	-	-	-	-	-	-	-	78 22.16 24.61 4.52 0.44	-	-	-	-	-	-	25 3.54 7.89 1.45 0.14	-	-	-	-	-	-	-	-
Solano County	52,715 21.39	32,267	10,482 32.49 32.49 19.88	1,975	167 8.46 8.46 0.32	676 41.81 6.45 2.10 1.28	-	-	816 35.60 7.78 2.53 1.55	-	7,948 34.01 75.83 24.63 15.08	74 7.64 44.31 3.75 0.14	26 5.75 15.57 1.32 0.05	9 6.04 0.09 0.03 0.02	-	322 19.13 3.07 1.00 0.61	176 25.47 1.68 0.55 0.33	12 3.13 0.11 0.04 0.02	-	-	45 14.38 26.95 2.28 0.09	-	-	-	-	132 16.52 1.26 0.41 0.25

Notes: Please refer to the User's Guide for an explanation of data; data is arranged alphabetically by state, then county, then city within each county; table includes counties with populations greater than 49,999 unless noted and cities with populations greater than 9,999 whose Asian and/or NHPI population rates are greater than the national average; (1) Native Hawaiian and other Pacific Islander; (2) excludes Taiwanese; (3) includes Chamorro; (4) county does not meet population threshold but is shown in order to allow inclusion of city

Place	Total population 25 years and over who are 4-year college graduates	Asian population 25 years and over	Asians 25 years and over who are 4-year college graduates	NHPI[1] population 25 years and over	NHPIs[1] 25 years and over who are 4-year college graduates	Asian Indian	Bangladeshi	Cambodian	Chinese[2]	Fijian	Filipino	Guamanian[3]	Hawaiian, Native	Hmong	Indonesian	Japanese	Korean	Laotian	Malaysian	Pakistani	Samoan	Sri Lankan	Taiwanese	Thai	Tongan	Vietnamese
Benicia (city)	6,689 37.31	1,336	650 48.65 48.65 9.72	-	-	-	-	-	152 47.65 23.38 11.38 2.27	-	322 44.41 49.54 24.10 4.81	-	-	-	-	-	-	-	-	-	-	-	-	-	-	-
Fairfield (city)	11,524 20.39	6,689	1,869 27.94 27.94 16.22	681	35 5.14 5.14 0.30	300 51.99 16.05 4.48 2.60	-	-	236 35.98 12.63 3.53 2.05	-	1,096 28.86 58.64 16.39 9.51	30 8.15 85.71 4.41 0.26	-	-	-	95 16.67 5.08 1.42 0.82	16 5.99 0.86 0.24 0.14	5 2.58 0.27 0.07 0.04	-	-	-	-	-	-	-	-
Suisun City (city)	2,624 17.28	3,032	754 24.87 24.87 28.73	-	-	66 29.86 8.75 2.18 2.52	-	-	-	-	571 27.94 75.73 18.83 21.76	-	-	-	-	-	-	-	-	-	-	-	-	-	-	-
Vacaville (city)	11,083 19.41	2,520	833 33.06 33.06 7.52	-	-	-	-	-	-	-	488 38.82 58.58 19.37 4.40	-	-	-	-	-	-	-	-	-	-	-	-	-	-	-
Vallejo (city)	15,619 21.06	17,842	6,140 34.41 34.41 39.31	854	88 10.30 10.30 0.56	192 37.14 3.13 1.08 1.23	-	-	261 37.23 4.25 1.46 1.67	-	5,326 35.12 86.74 29.85 34.10	28 6.78 31.82 3.28 0.18	-	-	-	64 20.25 1.04 0.36 0.41	-	-	-	-	-	-	-	-	-	67 20.94 1.09 0.38 0.43
Sonoma County	87,493 28.54	9,302	3,327 35.77 35.77 3.80	447	113 25.28 25.28 0.13	453 43.06 13.62 4.87 0.52	-	12 3.25 0.36 0.13 0.01	1,022 51.54 30.72 10.99 1.17	-	694 39.63 20.86 7.46 0.79	-	-	-	-	497 37.62 14.94 5.34 0.57	148 25.56 4.45 1.59 0.17	23 3.95 0.69 0.25 0.03	-	-	-	-	-	-	-	151 17.00 4.54 1.62 0.17
Petaluma (city)	10,954 30.11	1,426	679 47.62 47.62 6.20	-	-	-	-	-	290 58.59 42.71 20.34 2.65	-	-	-	-	-	-	-	-	-	-	-	-	-	-	-	-	-
Rohnert Park (city)	6,310 24.73	1,495	663 44.35 44.35 10.51	-	-	-	-	-	161 61.45 24.28 10.77 2.55	-	186 41.80 28.05 12.44 2.95	-	-	-	-	-	-	-	-	-	-	-	-	-	-	-
Santa Rosa (city)	26,928 27.62	3,564	925 25.95 25.95 3.44	-	-	169 36.50 18.27 4.74 0.63	-	0 0.00 0.00 0.00 0.00	251 42.61 27.14 7.04 0.93	-	187 36.96 20.22 5.25 0.69	-	-	-	-	113 33.63 12.22 3.17 0.42	-	18 5.04 1.95 0.51 0.07	-	-	-	-	-	-	-	67 12.76 7.24 1.88 0.25
Stanislaus County	37,179 14.05	10,090	2,260 22.40 22.40 6.08	944	62 6.57 6.57 0.17	485 19.50 21.46 4.81 1.30	-	39 3.10 1.73 0.39 0.10	447 36.05 19.78 4.43 1.20	29 8.81 46.77 3.07 0.08	708 37.13 31.33 7.02 1.90	-	-	2 0.71 0.09 0.02 0.01	-	243 38.33 10.75 2.41 0.65	-	47 5.96 2.08 0.47 0.13	-	-	-	-	-	-	-	85 11.11 3.76 0.84 0.23

Notes: Please refer to the User's Guide for an explanation of data; data is arranged alphabetically by state, then county, then city within each county; table includes counties with populations greater than 49,999 unless noted and cities with populations greater than 9,999 whose Asian and/or NHPI population rates are greater than the national average; (1) Native Hawaiian and other Pacific Islander; (2) excludes Taiwanese; (3) includes Chamorro; (4) county does not meet population threshold but is shown in order to allow inclusion of city

Place	Total population 25 years and over who are 4-year college graduates	Asian population 25 years and over	Asians 25 years and over who are 4-year college graduates	NHPI[1] population 25 years and over	NHPIs[1] 25 years and over who are 4-year college graduates	Asian Indian	Bangladeshi	Cambodian	Chinese[2]	Fijian	Filipino	Guamanian[3]	Hawaiian, Native	Hmong	Indonesian	Japanese	Korean	Laotian	Malaysian	Pakistani	Samoan	Sri Lankan	Taiwanese	Thai	Tongan	Vietnamese
Ceres (city)	1,584 8.27	985	130 13.20 13.20 8.21	-	-	39 9.05 30.00 3.96 2.46	-	-	-	-	-	-	-	-	-	-	-	-	-	-	-	-	-	-	-	-
Modesto (city)	18,895 16.48	5,985	1,217 20.33 20.33 6.44	624	54 8.65 8.65 0.29	241 20.39 19.80 4.03 1.28	-	21 2.04 1.73 0.35 0.11	224 29.83 18.41 3.74 1.19	29 12.13 53.70 4.65 0.15	415 40.65 34.10 6.93 2.20	-	-	0 0.00 0.00 0.00 0.00	-	127 43.34 10.44 2.12 0.67	-	25 4.39 2.05 0.42 0.13	-	-	-	-	-	-	-	55 9.17 4.52 0.92 0.29
Salida (cdp)	953 13.48	308	121 39.29 39.29 12.70	-	-	-	-	-	-	-	-	-	-	-	-	-	-	-	-	-	-	-	-	-	-	-
Turlock (city)	6,227 19.08	1,425	422 29.61 29.61 6.78	-	-	118 18.58 27.96 8.28 1.89	-	-	-	-	-	-	-	-	-	-	-	-	-	-	-	-	-	-	-	-
Sutter County	7,502 15.29	5,426	1,038 19.13 19.13 13.84	-	-	740 17.32 71.29 13.64 9.86	-	-	-	-	58 20.86 5.59 1.07 0.77	-	-	-	-	108 31.95 10.40 1.99 1.44	-	-	-	-	-	-	-	-	-	-
South Yuba City (cdp)	1,581 19.18	1,663	258 15.51 15.51 16.32	-	-	205 13.87 79.46 12.33 12.97	-	-	-	-	-	-	-	-	-	-	-	-	-	-	-	-	-	-	-	-
Yuba City (city)	3,189 14.36	1,986	442 22.26 22.26 13.86	-	-	277 20.44 62.67 13.95 8.69	-	-	-	-	-	-	-	-	-	-	-	-	-	-	-	-	-	-	-	-
Tehama County	4,093 11.29	222	92 41.44 41.44 2.25	-	-	-	-	-	-	-	-	-	-	-	-	-	-	-	-	-	-	-	-	-	-	-
Tulare County	23,560 11.50	6,683	1,244 18.61 18.61 5.28	-	-	254 48.11 20.42 3.80 1.08	-	-	163 31.84 13.10 2.44 0.69	-	408 14.36 32.80 6.11 1.73	-	-	17 5.15 1.37 0.25 0.07	-	133 24.77 10.69 1.99 0.56	142 54.20 11.41 2.12 0.60	31 2.46 2.49 0.46 0.13	-	-	-	-	-	-	-	-
Porterville (city)	2,404 11.03	1,128	207 18.35 18.35 8.61	-	-	-	-	-	-	-	100 17.57 48.31 8.87 4.16	-	-	-	-	-	-	-	-	-	-	-	-	-	-	-

Notes: Please refer to the User's Guide for an explanation of data; data is arranged alphabetically by state, then county, then city within each county; table includes counties with populations greater than 49,999 unless noted and cities with populations greater than 9,999 whose Asian and/or NHPI population rates are greater than the national average; (1) Native Hawaiian and other Pacific Islander; (2) excludes Taiwanese; (3) includes Chamorro; (4) county does not meet population threshold but is shown in order to allow inclusion of city

Place	Total population 25 years and over who are 4-year college graduates	Asian population 25 years and over	Asians 25 years and over who are 4-year college graduates	NHPI[1] population 25 years and over	NHPIs[1] 25 years and over who are 4-year college graduates	Asian Indian	Bangladeshi	Cambodian	Chinese[2]	Fijian	Filipino	Guamanian[3]	Hawaiian, Native	Hmong	Indonesian	Japanese	Korean	Laotian	Malaysian	Pakistani	Samoan	Sri Lankan	Taiwanese	Thai	Tongan	Vietnamese
Visalia (city)	10,184 18.89	2,481	572 23.06 23.06 5.62	-	-	-	-	-	-	-	156 29.94 27.27 6.29 1.53	-	-	6 3.95 1.05 0.24 0.06	-	-	-	31 3.66 5.42 1.25 0.30	-	-	-	-	-	-	-	-
Tuolumne County	6,284 16.12	282	147 52.13 52.13 2.34	-	-	-	-	-	-	-	-	-	-	-	-	-	-	-	-	-	-	-	-	-	-	-
Ventura County	127,136 26.95	27,138	12,841 47.32 47.32 10.10	1,012	198 19.57 19.57 0.16	2,002 71.76 15.59 7.38 1.57	-	-	2,339 64.56 18.22 8.62 1.84	-	4,025 38.12 31.34 14.83 3.17	-	95 23.99 47.98 9.39 0.07	-	-	1,894 46.14 14.75 6.98 1.49	805 47.52 6.27 2.97 0.63	-	-	-	38 12.26 19.19 3.75 0.03	-	415 79.05 3.23 1.53 0.33	-	-	636 29.43 4.95 2.34 0.50
Camarillo (city)	12,827 32.91	2,695	1,356 50.32 50.32 10.57	-	-	-	-	-	262 72.38 19.32 9.72 2.04	-	382 41.25 28.17 14.17 2.98	-	-	-	-	270 47.45 19.91 10.02 2.10	75 28.85 5.53 2.78 0.58	-	-	-	-	-	-	-	-	98 40.33 7.23 3.64 0.76
Moorpark (city)	6,140 34.21	949	621 65.44 65.44 10.11	-	-	-	-	-	-	-	-	-	-	-	-	-	-	-	-	-	-	-	-	-	-	-
Oxnard (city)	13,207 13.70	8,602	2,667 31.00 31.00 20.19	515	48 9.32 9.32 0.36	67 26.80 2.51 0.78 0.51	-	-	60 24.39 2.25 0.70 0.45	-	2,018 33.32 75.67 23.46 15.28	-	-	-	-	216 22.38 8.10 2.51 1.64	127 41.37 4.76 1.48 0.96	-	-	-	23 8.61 47.92 4.47 0.17	-	-	-	-	68 14.56 2.55 0.79 0.51
Port Hueneme (city)	1,987 15.40	958	306 31.94 31.94 15.40	-	-	-	-	-	-	-	251 36.91 82.03 26.20 12.63	-	-	-	-	-	-	-	-	-	-	-	-	-	-	-
Simi Valley (city)	17,732 24.93	4,699	2,233 47.52 47.52 12.59	-	-	645 69.43 28.88 13.73 3.64	-	-	359 48.91 16.08 7.64 2.02	-	466 48.95 20.87 9.92 2.63	-	-	-	-	331 55.72 14.82 7.04 1.87	126 36.42 5.64 2.68 0.71	-	-	-	-	-	-	-	-	153 22.63 6.85 3.26 0.86
Thousand Oaks (city)	33,126 42.22	4,502	3,263 72.48 72.48 9.85	-	-	649 87.47 19.89 14.42 1.96	-	-	1,059 81.59 32.45 23.52 3.20	-	253 53.72 7.75 5.62 0.76	-	-	-	-	478 66.57 14.65 10.62 1.44	221 68.21 6.77 4.91 0.67	-	-	-	-	-	-	-	-	149 48.38 4.57 3.31 0.45
Yolo County	32,576 34.14	6,355	3,682 57.94 57.94 11.30	369	39 10.57 10.57 0.12	348 42.65 9.45 5.48 1.07	-	-	1,655 76.83 44.95 26.04 5.08	13 5.18 33.33 3.52 0.04	411 55.84 11.16 6.47 1.26	-	-	32 18.71 0.87 0.50 0.10	-	528 57.33 14.34 8.31 1.62	309 70.39 8.39 4.86 0.95	0 0.00 0.00 0.00 0.00	-	-	-	-	-	-	-	111 34.69 3.01 1.75 0.34

Notes: Please refer to the User's Guide for an explanation of data; data is arranged alphabetically by state, then county, then city within each county; table includes counties with populations greater than 49,999 unless noted and cities with populations greater than 9,999 whose Asian and/or NHPI population rates are greater than the national average; (1) Native Hawaiian and other Pacific Islander; (2) excludes Taiwanese; (3) includes Chamorro; (4) county does not meet population threshold but is shown in order to allow inclusion of city

Place	Total population 25 years and over who are 4-year college graduates	Asian population 25 years and over	Asians 25 years and over who are 4-year college graduates	NHPI[1] population 25 years and over	NHPIs[1] 25 years and over who are 4-year college graduates	Asian Indian	Bangladeshi	Cambodian	Chinese[2]	Fijian	Filipino	Guamanian[3]	Hawaiian, Native	Hmong	Indonesian	Japanese	Korean	Laotian	Malaysian	Pakistani	Samoan	Sri Lankan	Taiwanese	Thai	Tongan	Vietnamese
Davis (city)	20,848 68.64	3,331	2,605 78.20 78.20 12.50	-	-	263 86.51 10.10 7.90 1.26	-	-	1,162 82.29 44.61 34.88 5.57	-	263 74.72 10.10 7.90 1.26	-	-	-	-	391 77.58 15.01 11.74 1.88	224 79.43 8.60 6.72 1.07	-	-	-	-	-	-	-	-	70 39.33 2.69 2.10 0.34
West Sacramento (city)	1,885 9.82	1,123	168 14.96 14.96 8.91	-	-	44 16.60 26.19 3.92 2.33	-	-	-	-	-	-	-	27 16.27 16.07 2.40 1.43	-	-	-	-	-	-	-	-	-	-	-	-
Woodland (city)	5,393 18.02	1,028	234 22.76 22.76 4.34	-	-	25 10.82 10.68 2.43 0.46	-	-	-	-	-	-	-	-	-	-	-	-	-	-	-	-	-	-	-	-
Yuba County	3,637 10.33	1,954	204 10.44 10.44 5.61	-	-	-	-	-	-	-	85 23.16 41.67 4.35 2.34	-	-	52 6.31 25.49 2.66 1.43	-	-	-	-	-	-	-	-	-	-	-	-
Linda (cdp)	251 3.64	820	49 5.98 5.98 19.52	-	-	-	-	-	-	-	-	-	-	34 5.98 69.39 4.15 13.55	-	-	-	-	-	-	-	-	-	-	-	-
Marysville (city)	817 10.93	430	43 10.00 10.00 5.26	-	-	-	-	-	-	-	-	-	-	-	-	-	-	-	-	-	-	-	-	-	-	-
Olivehurst (cdp)	319 4.98	275	20 7.27 7.27 6.27	-	-	-	-	-	-	-	-	-	-	-	-	-	-	-	-	-	-	-	-	-	-	-
COLORADO	907,755 32.69	60,422	25,860 42.80 42.80 2.85	2,357	466 19.77 19.77 0.05	5,955 77.16 23.03 9.86 0.66	-	46 6.42 0.18 0.08 0.01	5,595 55.77 21.64 9.26 0.62	-	2,747 43.30 10.62 4.55 0.30	107 16.44 22.96 4.54 0.01	190 22.38 40.77 8.06 0.02	140 12.20 0.54 0.23 0.02	240 52.52 0.93 0.40 0.03	4,121 43.19 15.94 6.82 0.45	3,199 32.76 12.37 5.29 0.35	110 9.02 0.43 0.18 0.01	-	349 79.14 1.35 0.58 0.04	62 14.73 13.30 2.63 0.01	-	341 76.12 1.32 0.56 0.04	601 43.58 2.32 0.99 0.07	-	1,408 16.77 5.44 2.33 0.16
Adams County	38,776 17.38	6,899	1,677 24.31 24.31 4.32	-	-	162 46.55 9.66 2.35 0.42	-	-	286 36.86 17.05 4.15 0.74	-	293 48.19 17.47 4.25 0.76	-	-	117 13.64 6.98 1.70 0.30	-	239 28.45 14.25 3.46 0.62	180 26.67 10.73 2.61 0.46	16 2.92 0.95 0.23 0.04	-	-	-	-	-	-	-	150 10.86 8.94 2.17 0.39
Berkley (cdp)	577 8.89	208	24 11.54 11.54 4.16	-	-	-	-	-	-	-	-	-	-	-	-	-	-	-	-	-	-	-	-	-	-	-

Notes: Please refer to the User's Guide for an explanation of data; data is arranged alphabetically by state, then county, then city within each county; table includes counties with populations greater than 49,999 unless noted and cities with populations greater than 9,999 whose Asian and/or NHPI population rates are greater than the national average; (1) Native Hawaiian and other Pacific Islander; (2) excludes Taiwanese; (3) includes Chamorro; (4) county does not meet population threshold but is shown in order to allow inclusion of city

Place	Total population 25 years and over who are 4-year college graduates	Asian population 25 years and over	Asians 25 years and over who are 4-year college graduates	NHPI[1] population 25 years and over	NHPIs[1] 25 years and over who are 4-year college graduates	Asian Indian	Bangladeshi	Cambodian	Chinese[2]	Fijian	Filipino	Guamanian[3]	Hawaiian, Native	Hmong	Indonesian	Japanese	Korean	Laotian	Malaysian	Pakistani	Samoan	Sri Lankan	Taiwanese	Thai	Tongan	Vietnamese
Federal Heights (city)	691 9.15	441	75 17.01 17.01 10.85	-	-	-	-	-	-	-	-	-	-	-	-	-	-	-	-	-	-	-	-	-	-	-
Westminster (city)	20,242 31.29	3,133	1,111 35.46 35.46 5.49	-	-	205 65.92 18.45 6.54 1.01	-	-	182 42.62 16.38 5.81 0.90	-	-	-	-	48 13.52 4.32 1.53 0.24	-	-	162 41.33 14.58 5.17 0.80	16 4.08 1.44 0.51 0.08	-	-	-	-	-	-	-	79 16.29 7.11 2.52 0.39
Arapahoe County	117,232 37.03	12,547	5,131 40.89 40.89 4.38	379	49 12.93 12.93 0.04	1,038 68.11 20.23 8.27 0.89	-	-	973 45.21 18.96 7.75 0.83	-	601 39.54 11.71 4.79 0.51	-	-	-	-	620 44.83 12.08 4.94 0.53	852 29.73 16.60 6.79 0.73	-	-	-	-	-	-	-	-	457 24.68 8.91 3.64 0.39
Aurora (city)	42,351 24.56	7,737	2,121 27.41 27.41 5.01	275	27 9.82 9.82 0.06	298 49.26 14.05 3.85 0.70	-	9 4.41 0.42 0.12 0.02	363 31.05 17.11 4.69 0.86	-	376 34.59 17.73 4.86 0.89	-	-	-	-	283 33.81 13.34 3.66 0.67	335 19.40 15.79 4.33 0.79	-	-	-	-	-	-	-	-	186 14.36 8.77 2.40 0.44
Boulder County	97,499 52.38	5,711	3,722 65.17 65.17 3.82	-	-	693 91.67 18.62 12.13 0.71	-	-	1,187 74.37 31.89 20.78 1.22	-	155 55.76 4.16 2.71 0.16	-	-	-	-	659 69.81 17.71 11.54 0.68	518 75.84 13.92 9.07 0.53	-	-	-	-	-	-	-	-	88 22.17 2.36 1.54 0.09
Boulder (city)	37,598 66.86	2,145	1,687 78.65 78.65 4.49	-	-	237 97.93 14.05 11.05 0.63	-	-	540 87.38 32.01 25.17 1.44	-	-	-	-	-	-	281 82.89 16.66 13.10 0.75	385 85.56 22.82 17.95 1.02	-	-	-	-	-	-	-	-	-
Broomfield (city)	9,217 37.91	965	458 47.46 47.46 4.97	-	-	-	-	-	137 61.43 29.91 14.20 1.49	-	-	-	-	-	-	-	-	-	-	-	-	-	-	-	-	-
Lafayette (city)	6,913 45.65	585	369 63.08 63.08 5.34	-	-	-	-	-	-	-	-	-	-	-	-	-	-	-	-	-	-	-	-	-	-	-
Denver County	129,065 34.47	10,055	4,089 40.67 40.67 3.17	223	54 24.22 24.22 0.04	1,134 80.77 27.73 11.28 0.88	-	0 0.00 0.00 0.00 0.00	782 52.34 19.12 7.78 0.61	-	345 50.07 8.44 3.43 0.27	-	-	-	-	730 42.47 17.85 7.26 0.57	303 34.28 7.41 3.01 0.23	-	-	-	-	-	-	135 51.53 3.30 1.34 0.10	-	284 10.77 6.95 2.82 0.22
Douglas County	58,303 51.85	2,866	1,704 59.46 59.46 2.92	-	-	450 86.37 26.41 15.70 0.77	-	-	542 61.59 31.81 18.91 0.93	-	-	-	-	-	-	-	157 39.75 9.21 5.48 0.27	-	-	-	-	-	-	-	-	-

Notes: Please refer to the User's Guide for an explanation of data; data is arranged alphabetically by state, then county, then city within each county; table includes counties with populations greater than 49,999 unless noted and cities with populations greater than 9,999 whose Asian and/or NHPI population rates are greater than the national average; (1) Native Hawaiian and other Pacific Islander; (2) excludes Taiwanese; (3) includes Chamorro; (4) county does not meet population threshold but is shown in order to allow inclusion of city

Place	Total population 25 years and over who are 4-year college graduates	Asian population 25 years and over	Asians 25 years and over who are 4-year college graduates	NHPI[1] population 25 years and over	NHPIs[1] 25 years and over who are 4-year college graduates	Asian Indian	Bangladeshi	Cambodian	Chinese[2]	Fijian	Filipino	Guamanian[3]	Hawaiian, Native	Hmong	Indonesian	Japanese	Korean	Laotian	Malaysian	Pakistani	Samoan	Sri Lankan	Taiwanese	Thai	Tongan	Vietnamese
	26,461	1,932	1,178	-	-	367	-	-	401	-	-	-	-	-	-	-	-	-	-	-	-	-	-	-	-	-
	58.98		60.97			95.32			64.37																	
Highlands Ranch (cdp)						31.15			34.04																	
			60.97			19.00			20.76																	
			4.45			1.39			1.52																	
	101,762	9,028	3,193	670	80	1,122	-	-	434	-	520	49	-	-	-	341	499	-	-	-	-	-	-	-	-	74
	31.76		35.37		11.94	80.31			63.92		31.23	16.39				28.39	18.31									12.21
El Paso County						35.14			13.59		16.29	61.25				10.68	15.63									2.32
			35.37		11.94	12.43			4.81		5.76	7.31				3.78	5.53									0.82
			3.14		0.08	1.10			0.43		0.51	0.05				0.34	0.49									0.07
	76,702	6,993	2,704	407	39	1,112	-	-	361	-	315	-	-	-	-	285	403	-	-	-	-	-	-	-	-	57
	33.56		38.67		9.58	81.41			66.00		28.38					34.01	19.75									11.73
Colorado Springs (city)						41.12			13.35		11.65					10.54	14.90									2.11
			38.67		9.58	15.90			5.16		4.50					4.08	5.76									0.82
			3.53		0.05	1.45			0.47		0.41					0.37	0.53									0.07
	128,496	7,358	3,541	230	85	807	-	-	666	-	364	-	-	14	-	743	415	59	-	-	-	-	-	-	-	238
	36.55		48.12		36.96	82.52			54.10		55.74			12.07		48.31	44.82	12.16								24.71
Jefferson County						22.79			18.81		10.28			0.40		20.98	11.72	1.67								6.72
			48.12		36.96	10.97			9.05		4.95			0.19		10.10	5.64	0.80								3.23
			2.76		0.07	0.63			0.52		0.28			0.01		0.58	0.32	0.05								0.19
	61,828	2,165	1,343	-	-	281	-	-	420	-	-	-	-	-	-	177	148	-	-	-	-	-	-	-	-	-
	39.53		62.03			80.75			67.42							48.10	60.16									
Larimer County						20.92			31.27							13.18	11.02									
			62.03			12.98			19.40							8.18	6.84									
			2.17			0.45			0.68							0.29	0.24									
	16,764	278	72	-	-	-	-	-	-	-	-	-	-	-	-	-	-	-	-	-	-	-	-	-	-	-
	21.95		25.90																							
Mesa County																										
			25.90																							
			0.43																							
	16,887	538	247	-	-	-	-	-	-	-	-	-	-	-	-	-	-	-	-	-	-	-	-	-	-	-
	18.34		45.91																							
Pueblo County																										
			45.91																							
			1.46																							
	22,997	821	412	-	-	-	-	-	-	-	-	-	-	-	-	151	-	-	-	-	-	-	-	-	-	-
	21.65		50.18													44.54										
Weld County																36.65										
			50.18													18.39										
			1.79													0.66										
	720,994	51,977	29,977	700	156	10,874	163	118	8,084	-	3,204	69	-	-	-	1,813	2,044	170	-	837	-	-	306	243	-	985
	31.41		57.67		22.29	68.40	74.77	10.12	65.14		60.53	29.61				62.39	57.03	9.36		70.75			80.10	52.71		21.53
CONNECTICUT						36.27	0.54	0.39	26.97		10.69	44.23				6.05	6.82	0.57		2.79			1.02	0.81		3.29
			57.67		22.29	20.92	0.31	0.23	15.55		6.16	9.86				3.49	3.93	0.33		1.61			0.59	0.47		1.90
			4.16		0.02	1.51	0.02	0.02	1.12		0.44	0.01				0.25	0.28	0.02		0.12			0.04	0.03		0.14
	237,674	18,576	11,073	-	-	4,261	-	96	2,696	-	1,214	-	-	-	-	1,050	645	27	-	204	-	-	-	-	-	266
	39.85		59.61			72.37		12.77	66.08		70.25					65.95	58.85	4.45		68.46						17.91
Fairfield County						38.48		0.87	24.35		10.96					9.48	5.82	0.24		1.84						2.40
			59.61			22.94		0.52	14.51		6.54					5.65	3.47	0.15		1.10						1.43
			4.66			1.79		0.04	1.13		0.51					0.44	0.27	0.01		0.09						0.11

Notes: Please refer to the User's Guide for an explanation of data; data is arranged alphabetically by state, then county, then city within each county; table includes counties with populations greater than 49,999 unless noted and cities with populations greater than 9,999 whose Asian and/or NHPI population rates are greater than the national average; (1) Native Hawaiian and other Pacific Islander; (2) excludes Taiwanese; (3) includes Chamorro; (4) county does not meet population threshold but is shown in order to allow inclusion of city

Place	Total population 25 years and over who are 4-year college graduates	Asian population 25 years and over	Asians 25 years and over who are 4-year college graduates	NHPI[1] population 25 years and over	NHPIs[1] 25 years and over who are 4-year college graduates	Asian Indian	Bangladeshi	Cambodian	Chinese[2]	Fijian	Filipino	Guamanian[3]	Hawaiian, Native	Hmong	Indonesian	Japanese	Korean	Laotian	Malaysian	Pakistani	Samoan	Sri Lankan	Taiwanese	Thai	Tongan	Vietnamese
Danbury (city)	13,884 27.11	2,374	1,142 48.10 48.10 8.23	-	-	481 54.97 42.12 20.26 3.46	-	24 8.57 2.10 1.01 0.17	192 51.61 16.81 8.09 1.38	-	-	-	-	-	-	-	-	-	-	-	-	-	-	-	-	-
Greenwich (town)	25,323 58.79	2,039	1,381 67.73 67.73 5.45	-	-	203 67.44 14.70 9.96 0.80	-	-	340 70.98 24.62 16.67 1.34	-	-	-	-	-	-	522 69.79 37.80 25.60 2.06	-	-	-	-	-	-	-	-	-	-
Stamford (city)	32,785 39.55	4,159	2,912 70.02 70.02 8.88	-	-	1,720 81.21 59.07 41.36 5.25	-	-	557 65.15 19.13 13.39 1.70	-	335 62.85 11.50 8.05 1.02	-	-	-	-	-	-	-	-	-	-	-	-	-	-	-
Hartford County	171,651 29.60	13,339	6,798 50.96 50.96 3.96	-	-	2,727 62.02 40.11 20.44 1.59	-	-	1,540 60.30 22.65 11.55 0.90	-	802 64.89 11.80 6.01 0.47	-	-	-	-	135 38.24 1.99 1.01 0.08	461 54.62 6.78 3.46 0.27	37 5.01 0.54 0.28 0.02	-	284 77.38 4.18 2.13 0.17	-	-	-	-	-	446 22.43 6.56 3.34 0.26
East Hartford (town)	4,536 13.36	1,385	328 23.68 23.68 7.23	-	-	97 23.43 29.57 7.00 2.14	-	-	-	-	-	-	-	-	-	-	-	-	-	-	-	-	-	-	-	78 20.42 23.78 5.63 1.72
Farmington (town)	8,269 49.24	650	481 74.00 74.00 5.82	-	-	-	-	-	-	-	-	-	-	-	-	-	-	-	-	-	-	-	-	-	-	-
Glastonbury (town)	12,089 54.96	747	538 72.02 72.02 4.45	-	-	230 72.56 42.75 30.79 1.90	-	-	-	-	-	-	-	-	-	-	-	-	-	-	-	-	-	-	-	-
Rocky Hill (town)	4,913 37.07	477	410 85.95 85.95 8.35	-	-	-	-	-	-	-	-	-	-	-	-	-	-	-	-	-	-	-	-	-	-	-
South Windsor (town)	6,876 41.58	583	327 56.09 56.09 4.76	-	-	-	-	-	-	-	-	-	-	-	-	-	-	-	-	-	-	-	-	-	-	-
West Hartford (town)	23,022 52.98	1,960	975 49.74 49.74 4.24	-	-	319 63.93 32.72 16.28 1.39	-	-	308 56.20 31.59 15.71 1.34	-	-	-	-	-	-	-	-	-	-	-	-	-	-	-	-	126 30.58 12.92 6.43 0.55

Notes: Please refer to the User's Guide for an explanation of data; data is arranged alphabetically by state, then county, then city within each county; table includes counties with populations greater than 49,999 unless noted and cities with populations greater than 9,999 whose Asian and/or NHPI population rates are greater than the national average; (1) Native Hawaiian and other Pacific Islander; (2) excludes Taiwanese; (3) includes Chamorro; (4) county does not meet population threshold but is shown in order to allow inclusion of city

Place	Total population 25 years and over who are 4-year college graduates	Asian population 25 years and over	Asians 25 years and over who are 4-year college graduates	NHPI[1] population 25 years and over	NHPIs[1] 25 years and over who are 4-year college graduates	Asian Indian	Bangladeshi	Cambodian	Chinese[2]	Fijian	Filipino	Guamanian[3]	Hawaiian, Native	Hmong	Indonesian	Japanese	Korean	Laotian	Malaysian	Pakistani	Samoan	Sri Lankan	Taiwanese	Thai	Tongan	Vietnamese
	34,965	1,321	580	-	-	229	-	-	82	-	-	-	-	-	-	-	60	-	-	-	-	-	-	-	-	27
	27.47		43.91			74.84			37.10								37.97									15.61
Litchfield County						39.48			14.14								10.34									4.66
			43.91			17.34			6.21								4.54									2.04
			1.66			0.65			0.23								0.17									0.08
	36,545	1,311	699	-	-	265	-	-	247	-	-	-	-	-	-	-	-	-	-	-	-	-	-	-	-	-
	33.80		53.32			62.50			66.22																	
Middlesex County						37.91			35.34																	
			53.32			20.21			18.84																	
			1.91			0.73			0.68																	
	152,433	12,209	8,040	-	-	2,587	-	-	2,505	-	759	-	-	-	-	451	665	89	-	241	-	-	-	-	-	164
	27.63		65.85			68.57			72.63		65.04					74.67	62.03	30.48		63.42						27.56
New Haven County						32.18			31.16		9.44					5.61	8.27	1.11		3.00						2.04
			65.85			21.19			20.52		6.22					3.69	5.45	0.73		1.97						1.34
			5.27			1.70			1.64		0.50					0.30	0.44	0.06		0.16						0.11
	19,570	2,635	2,038	-	-	355	-	-	970	-	-	-	-	-	-	-	210	-	-	-	-	-	-	-	-	-
	27.12		77.34			76.34			87.86								82.35									
New Haven (city)						17.42			47.60								10.30									
			77.34			13.47			36.81								7.97									
			10.41			1.81			4.96								1.07									
	45,616	3,023	1,339	-	-	460	-	-	399	-	220	-	-	-	-	-	-	-	-	-	-	-	-	-	-	-
	26.23		44.29			72.33			44.48		28.68															
New London County						34.35			29.80		16.43															
			44.29			15.22			13.20		7.28															
			2.94			1.01			0.87		0.48															
	28,598	1,820	1,310	-	-	338	-	-	578	-	-	-	-	-	-	-	-	-	-	-	-	-	-	-	-	-
	32.80		71.98			75.62			81.52																	
Tolland County						25.80			44.12																	
			71.98			18.57			31.76																	
			4.58			1.18			2.02																	
	4,698	732	689	-	-	168	-	-	350	-	-	-	-	-	-	-	-	-	-	-	-	-	-	-	-	-
	54.12		94.13			94.38			94.85																	
Mansfield (town)						24.38			50.80																	
			94.13			22.95			47.81																	
			14.67			3.58			7.45																	
	1,534	487	454	-	-	-	-	-	298	-	-	-	-	-	-	-	-	-	-	-	-	-	-	-	-	-
	68.15		93.22						94.01																	
Storrs (cdp)									65.64																	
			93.22						61.19																	
			29.60						19.43																	
	13,512	378	138	-	-	-	-	-	-	-	-	-	-	-	-	-	-	-	-	-	-	-	-	-	-	-
	18.97		36.51																							
Windham County																										
			36.51																							
			1.02																							
	128,917	10,915	6,741	150	11	2,704	-	-	1,908	-	710	-	-	-	-	126	468	-	-	158	-	-	-	-	-	192
	25.05		61.76		7.33	77.35			66.53		52.75					25.20	40.59			73.15						42.86
DELAWARE						40.11			28.30		10.53					1.87	6.94			2.34						2.85
			61.76		7.33	24.77			17.48		6.50					1.15	4.29			1.45						1.76
			5.23		0.01	2.10			1.48		0.55					0.10	0.36			0.12						0.15

Notes: Please refer to the User's Guide for an explanation of data; data is arranged alphabetically by state, then county, then city within each county; table includes counties with populations greater than 49,999 unless noted and cities with populations greater than 9,999 whose Asian and/or NHPI population rates are greater than the national average; (1) Native Hawaiian and other Pacific Islander; (2) excludes Taiwanese; (3) includes Chamorro; (4) county does not meet population threshold but is shown in order to allow inclusion of city

Place	Total population 25 years and over who are 4-year college graduates	Asian population 25 years and over	Asians 25 years and over who are 4-year college graduates	NHPI[1] population 25 years and over	NHPIs[1] 25 years and over who are 4-year college graduates	Asian Indian	Bangladeshi	Cambodian	Chinese[2]	Fijian	Filipino	Guamanian[3]	Hawaiian, Native	Hmong	Indonesian	Japanese	Korean	Laotian	Malaysian	Pakistani	Samoan	Sri Lankan	Taiwanese	Thai	Tongan	Vietnamese
Kent County	14,769	1,477	506	-	-	207	-	-	-	-	98	-	-	-	-	-	-	-	-	-	-	-	-	-	-	-
	18.64		34.26			75.55					27.07															
						40.91					19.37															
			34.26			14.01					6.64															
			3.43			1.40					0.66															
New Castle County	95,774	8,883	6,022	-	-	2,456	-	-	1,848	-	534	-	-	-	-	90	373	-	-	-	-	-	-	-	-	184
	29.49		67.79			78.97			70.21		66.50					29.03	44.51									51.98
						40.78			30.69		8.87					1.49	6.19									3.06
			67.79			27.65			20.80		6.01					1.01	4.20									2.07
			6.29			2.56			1.93		0.56					0.09	0.39									0.19
Hockessin (cdp)	5,072	544	438	-	-	-	-	-	-	-	-	-	-	-	-	-	-	-	-	-	-	-	-	-	-	-
	58.02		80.51																							
			80.51																							
			8.64																							
Newark (city)	6,475	735	597	-	-	-	-	-	361	-	-	-	-	-	-	-	-	-	-	-	-	-	-	-	-	-
	51.35		81.22						87.41																	
									60.47																	
			81.22						49.12																	
			9.22						5.58																	
Pike Creek (cdp)	6,833	688	537	-	-	-	-	-	-	-	-	-	-	-	-	-	-	-	-	-	-	-	-	-	-	-
	49.99		78.05																							
			78.05																							
			7.86																							
Sussex County	18,374	555	213	-	-	-	-	-	-	-	-	-	-	-	-	-	-	-	-	-	-	-	-	-	-	-
	16.61		38.38																							
			38.38																							
			1.16																							
DISTRICT OF COLUMBIA	150,237	9,875	5,749	-	-	1,353	-	-	1,471	-	835	-	-	-	-	599	664	-	-	-	-	-	-	-	-	237
	39.07		58.22			78.85			54.83		53.32					75.54	82.69									21.60
						23.53			25.59		14.52					10.42	11.55									4.12
			58.22			13.70			14.90		8.46					6.07	6.72									2.40
			3.83			0.90			0.98		0.56					0.40	0.44									0.16
FLORIDA	2,462,328	177,289	72,564	4,096	615	22,389	364	111	13,959	-	17,128	172	158	-	269	2,928	4,715	262	-	1,784	72	194	821	1,336	-	4,165
	22.33		40.93		15.01	51.73	43.18	7.22	44.39		44.87	14.51	11.90		38.93	31.68	35.94	10.78		53.96	14.43	67.36	59.11	26.27		19.64
						30.85	0.50	0.15	19.24		23.60	27.97	25.69		0.37	4.04	6.50	0.36		2.46	11.71	0.27	1.13	1.84		5.74
			40.93		15.01	12.63	0.21	0.06	7.87		9.66	4.20	3.86		0.15	1.65	2.66	0.15		1.01	1.76	0.11	0.46	0.75		2.35
			2.95		0.02	0.91	0.01	<0.01	0.57		0.70	0.01	0.01		0.01	0.12	0.19	0.01		0.07	<0.01	0.01	0.03	0.05		0.17
Alachua County	47,803	4,231	3,333	-	-	717	-	-	1,177	-	441	-	-	-	-	149	425	-	-	-	-	-	-	-	-	211
	38.70		78.78			83.37			91.60		73.87					50.00	73.40									65.73
						21.51			35.31		13.23					4.47	12.75									6.33
			78.78			16.95			27.82		10.42					3.52	10.04									4.99
			6.97			1.50			2.46		0.92					0.31	0.89									0.44
Gainesville (city)	21,653	2,330	1,874	-	-	361	-	-	825	-	-	-	-	-	-	-	215	-	-	-	-	-	-	-	-	-
	42.81		80.43			85.95			92.59								76.79									
						19.26			44.02								11.47									
			80.43			15.49			35.41								9.23									
			8.65			1.67			3.81								0.99									

Notes: Please refer to the User's Guide for an explanation of data; data is arranged alphabetically by state, then county, then city within each county; table includes counties with populations greater than 49,999 unless noted and cities with populations greater than 9,999 whose Asian and/or NHPI population rates are greater than the national average; (1) Native Hawaiian and other Pacific Islander; (2) excludes Taiwanese; (3) includes Chamorro; (4) county does not meet population threshold but is shown in order to allow inclusion of city

Place	Total population 25 years and over who are 4-year college graduates	Asian population 25 years and over	Asians 25 years and over who are 4-year college graduates	NHPI[1] population 25 years and over	NHPIs[1] 25 years and over who are 4-year college graduates	Asian Indian	Bangladeshi	Cambodian	Chinese[2]	Fijian	Filipino	Guamanian[3]	Hawaiian, Native	Hmong	Indonesian	Japanese	Korean	Laotian	Malaysian	Pakistani	Samoan	Sri Lankan	Taiwanese	Thai	Tongan	Vietnamese
Bay County	17,636 17.68	1,586	364 22.95 22.95 2.06	-	-	-	-	-	-	-	81 25.00 22.25 5.11 0.46	-	-	-	-	-	-	-	-	-	-	-	-	-	-	19 5.25 5.22 1.20 0.11
Callaway (city)	1,226 14.05	355	28 7.89 7.89 2.28	-	-	-	-	-	-	-	-	-	-	-	-	-	-	-	-	-	-	-	-	-	-	-
Brevard County	80,020 23.55	5,153	1,946 37.76 37.76 2.43	-	-	700 54.18 35.97 13.58 0.87	-	-	319 45.25 16.39 6.19 0.40	-	398 34.61 20.45 7.72 0.50	-	-	-	-	117 26.59 6.01 2.27 0.15	122 23.24 6.27 2.37 0.15	-	-	-	-	-	-	-	-	128 26.39 6.58 2.48 0.16
Broward County	276,527 24.55	24,543	9,524 38.81 38.81 3.44	439	60 13.67 13.67 0.02	3,340 39.62 35.07 13.61 1.21	-	-	1,960 32.79 20.58 7.99 0.71	-	1,835 53.00 19.27 7.48 0.66	-	-	-	-	300 34.76 3.15 1.22 0.11	612 41.07 6.43 2.49 0.22	-	-	355 53.71 3.73 1.45 0.13	-	-	-	168 34.50 1.76 0.68 0.06	-	440 23.62 4.62 1.79 0.16
Cooper City (city)	6,575 38.17	735	392 53.33 53.33 5.96	-	-	210 58.17 53.57 28.57 3.19	-	-	-	-	-	-	-	-	-	-	-	-	-	-	-	-	-	-	-	-
Pembroke Pines (city)	26,847 28.68	3,411	1,762 51.66 51.66 6.56	-	-	653 56.63 37.06 19.14 2.43	-	-	262 33.98 14.87 7.68 0.98	-	411 58.71 23.33 12.05 1.53	-	-	-	-	-	-	-	-	-	-	-	-	-	-	-
Charlotte County	19,875 17.58	674	289 42.88 42.88 1.45	-	-	-	-	-	-	-	-	-	-	-	-	-	-	-	-	-	-	-	-	-	-	-
Citrus County	12,177 13.15	834	351 42.09 42.09 2.88	-	-	-	-	-	-	-	-	-	-	-	-	-	-	-	-	-	-	-	-	-	-	-
Clay County	18,159 20.09	2,076	654 31.50 31.50 3.60	-	-	-	-	-	-	-	437 33.85 66.82 21.05 2.41	-	-	-	-	-	-	-	-	-	-	-	-	-	-	-
Bellair-Meadowbrook Ter. (cdp)	1,887 17.88	517	180 34.82 34.82 9.54	-	-	-	-	-	-	-	-	-	-	-	-	-	-	-	-	-	-	-	-	-	-	-

Notes: Please refer to the User's Guide for an explanation of data; data is arranged alphabetically by state, then county, then city within each county; table includes counties with populations greater than 49,999 unless noted and cities with populations greater than 9,999 whose Asian and/or NHPI population rates are greater than the national average; (1) Native Hawaiian and other Pacific Islander; (2) excludes Taiwanese; (3) includes Chamorro; (4) county does not meet population threshold but is shown in order to allow inclusion of city

Place	Total population 25 years and over who are 4-year college graduates	Asian population 25 years and over	Asians 25 years and over who are 4-year college graduates	NHPI[1] population 25 years and over	NHPIs[1] 25 years and over who are 4-year college graduates	Asian Indian	Bangladeshi	Cambodian	Chinese[2]	Fijian	Filipino	Guamanian[3]	Hawaiian, Native	Hmong	Indonesian	Japanese	Korean	Laotian	Malaysian	Pakistani	Samoan	Sri Lankan	Taiwanese	Thai	Tongan	Vietnamese
Collier County	51,757	876	432	-	-	-	-	-	-	-	-	-	-	-	-	-	-	-	-	-	-	-	-	-	-	-
	27.92		49.32																							
			49.32																							
			0.83																							
Columbia County	4,028	249	131	-	-	-	-	-	-	-	-	-	-	-	-	-	-	-	-	-	-	-	-	-	-	-
	10.92		52.61																							
			52.61																							
			3.25																							
Duval County	109,473	13,470	4,638	286	42	1,267	-	32	458	-	2,178	-	-	-	-	47	107	-	-	-	-	-	-	-	-	218
	21.91		34.43		14.69	69.16		6.03	43.37		31.79					10.24	16.19									17.17
						27.32		0.69	9.87		46.96					1.01	2.31									4.70
			34.43		14.69	9.41		0.24	3.40		16.17					0.35	0.79									1.62
			4.24		0.04	1.16		0.03	0.42		1.99					0.04	0.10									0.20
Escambia County	39,789	4,153	970	-	-	125	-	-	97	-	438	-	-	-	-	-	-	-	-	-	-	-	-	-	-	50
	20.97		23.36			36.76			25.80		23.74															6.39
						12.89			10.00		45.15															5.15
			23.36			3.01			2.34		10.55															1.20
			2.44			0.31			0.24		1.10															0.13
Bellview (cdp)	1,866	518	89	-	-	-	-	-	-	-	51	-	-	-	-	-	-	-	-	-	-	-	-	-	-	-
	13.60		17.18								17.35															
											57.30															
			17.18								9.85															
			4.77								2.73															
Myrtle Grove (cdp)	1,928	521	70	-	-	-	-	-	-	-	47	-	-	-	-	-	-	-	-	-	-	-	-	-	-	-
	18.12		13.44								13.86															
											67.14															
			13.44								9.02															
			3.63								2.44															
Hernando County	12,615	545	155	-	-	-	-	-	-	-	-	-	-	-	-	-	-	-	-	-	-	-	-	-	-	-
	12.73		28.44																							
			28.44																							
			1.23																							
Highlands County	8,837	648	314	-	-	-	-	-	-	-	191	-	-	-	-	-	-	-	-	-	-	-	-	-	-	-
	13.58		48.46								62.21															
											60.83															
			48.46								29.48															
			3.55								2.16															
Hillsborough County	164,109	14,352	6,188	325	77	2,119	-	-	980	-	1,114	-	-	-	-	249	768	-	-	-	-	-	-	221	-	341
	25.10		43.12		23.69	58.88			54.20		51.55					33.33	40.76							40.85		12.90
						34.24			15.84		18.00					4.02	12.41							3.57		5.51
			43.12		23.69	14.76			6.83		7.76					1.73	5.35							1.54		2.38
			3.77		0.05	1.29			0.60		0.68					0.15	0.47							0.13		0.21
Westchase (cdp)	3,744	341	135	-	-	-	-	-	-	-	-	-	-	-	-	-	-	-	-	-	-	-	-	-	-	-
	49.04		39.59																							
			39.59																							
			3.61																							

Notes: Please refer to the User's Guide for an explanation of data; data is arranged alphabetically by state, then county, then city within each county; table includes counties with populations greater than 49,999 unless noted and cities with populations greater than 9,999 whose Asian and/or NHPI population rates are greater than the national average; (1) Native Hawaiian and other Pacific Islander; (2) excludes Taiwanese; (3) includes Chamorro; (4) county does not meet population threshold but is shown in order to allow inclusion of city

Place	Total population 25 years and over who are 4-year college graduates	Asian population 25 years and over	Asians 25 years and over who are 4-year college graduates	NHPI[1] population 25 years and over	NHPIs[1] 25 years and over who are 4-year college graduates	Asian Indian	Bangladeshi	Cambodian	Chinese[2]	Fijian	Filipino	Guamanian[3]	Hawaiian, Native	Hmong	Indonesian	Japanese	Korean	Laotian	Malaysian	Pakistani	Samoan	Sri Lankan	Taiwanese	Thai	Tongan	Vietnamese
Indian River County	19,533 23.11	592	279 47.13 47.13 1.43	-	-	-	-	-	-	-	-	-	-	-	-	-	-	-	-	-	-	-	-	-	-	-
Lake County	25,811 16.59	1,000	338 33.80 33.80 1.31	-	-	-	-	-	-	-	-	-	-	-	-	-	-	-	-	-	-	-	-	-	-	-
Lee County	69,153 21.10	2,321	982 42.31 42.31 1.42	-	-	257 58.68 26.17 11.07 0.37	-	-	196 47.80 19.96 8.44 0.28	-	390 45.40 39.71 16.80 0.56	-	-	-	-	-	-	-	-	-	-	-	-	-	-	-
Leon County	57,396 41.73	3,165	2,092 66.10 66.10 3.64	-	-	710 76.34 33.94 22.43 1.24	-	-	582 77.29 27.82 18.39 1.01	-	203 63.44 9.70 6.41 0.35	-	-	-	-	-	185 56.75 8.84 5.85 0.32	-	-	-	-	-	-	-	-	-
Manatee County	40,059 20.78	1,589	530 33.35 33.35 1.32	-	-	-	-	-	-	-	169 46.43 31.89 10.64 0.42	-	-	-	-	-	-	-	-	-	-	-	-	-	-	-
Marion County	25,626 13.69	1,485	513 34.55 34.55 2.00	-	-	302 51.36 58.87 20.34 1.18	-	-	-	-	-	-	-	-	-	-	-	-	-	-	-	-	-	-	-	-
Martin County	25,413 26.34	509	231 45.38 45.38 0.91	-	-	-	-	-	-	-	-	-	-	-	-	-	-	-	-	-	-	-	-	-	-	-
Miami-Dade County	323,399 21.68	20,980	9,467 45.12 45.12 2.93	384	88 22.92 22.92 0.03	2,676 47.11 28.27 12.76 0.83	-	-	2,581 39.79 27.26 12.30 0.80	-	1,904 58.24 20.11 9.08 0.59	-	-	-	-	511 48.39 5.40 2.44 0.16	441 46.96 4.66 2.10 0.14	-	-	308 56.51 3.25 1.47 0.10	-	-	-	280 40.58 2.96 1.33 0.09	-	232 24.47 2.45 1.11 0.07
Doral (cdp)	6,587 47.61	789	465 58.94 58.94 7.06	-	-	-	-	-	-	-	-	-	-	-	-	-	-	-	-	-	-	-	-	-	-	-
Ives Estates (cdp)	3,062 26.39	561	305 54.37 54.37 9.96	-	-	-	-	-	-	-	-	-	-	-	-	-	-	-	-	-	-	-	-	-	-	-

Notes: Please refer to the User's Guide for an explanation of data; data is arranged alphabetically by state, then county, then city within each county; table includes counties with populations greater than 49,999 unless noted and cities with populations greater than 9,999 whose Asian and/or NHPI population rates are greater than the national average; (1) Native Hawaiian and other Pacific Islander; (2) excludes Taiwanese; (3) includes Chamorro; (4) county does not meet population threshold but is shown in order to allow inclusion of city

Place	Total population 25 years and over who are 4-year college graduates	Asian population 25 years and over	Asians 25 years and over who are 4-year college graduates	NHPI[1] population 25 years and over	NHPIs[1] 25 years and over who are 4-year college graduates	Asian Indian	Bangladeshi	Cambodian	Chinese[2]	Fijian	Filipino	Guamanian[3]	Hawaiian, Native	Hmong	Indonesian	Japanese	Korean	Laotian	Malaysian	Pakistani	Samoan	Sri Lankan	Taiwanese	Thai	Tongan	Vietnamese
North Miami Beach (city)	3,671 14.19	1,087	266 24.47 24.47 7.25	-	-	62 25.94 23.31 5.70 1.69	-	-	61 12.47 22.93 5.61 1.66	-	-	-	-	-	-	-	-	-	-	-	-	-	-	-	-	-
Pinecrest (village)	7,444 61.56	587	347 59.11 59.11 4.66	-	-	-	-	-	-	-	-	-	-	-	-	-	-	-	-	-	-	-	-	-	-	-
Monroe County	15,583 25.48	432	221 51.16 51.16 1.42	-	-	-	-	-	-	-	-	-	-	-	-	-	-	-	-	-	-	-	-	-	-	-
Nassau County	7,364 18.90	278	74 26.62 26.62 1.00	-	-	-	-	-	-	-	-	-	-	-	-	-	-	-	-	-	-	-	-	-	-	-
Okaloosa County	27,250 24.24	3,161	460 14.55 14.55 1.69	-	-	-	-	-	-	-	188 15.54 40.87 5.95 0.69	-	-	-	-	-	101 19.24 21.96 3.20 0.37	-	-	-	-	-	-	10 1.89 2.17 0.32 0.04	-	66 29.20 14.35 2.09 0.24
Wright (cdp)	2,960 21.20	604	58 9.60 9.60 1.96	-	-	-	-	-	-	-	-	-	-	-	-	-	-	-	-	-	-	-	-	-	-	-
Orange County	150,009 26.13	19,367	7,945 41.02 41.02 5.30	411	76 18.49 18.49 0.05	2,243 46.10 28.23 11.58 1.50	-	-	1,489 52.69 18.74 7.69 0.99	-	1,546 50.87 19.46 7.98 1.03	-	-	-	-	337 34.07 4.24 1.74 0.22	543 37.12 6.83 2.80 0.36	-	-	326 59.38 4.10 1.68 0.22	-	-	-	-	-	998 23.14 12.56 5.15 0.67
Oak Ridge (cdp)	1,364 10.48	864	100 11.57 11.57 7.33	-	-	-	-	-	-	-	-	-	-	-	-	-	-	-	-	-	-	-	-	-	-	9 2.23 9.00 1.04 0.66
Osceola County	17,416 15.75	2,425	997 41.11 41.11 5.72	-	-	216 41.94 21.66 8.91 1.24	-	-	156 33.40 15.65 6.43 0.90	-	319 53.89 32.00 13.15 1.83	-	-	-	-	-	-	-	-	-	-	-	-	-	-	-
Palm Beach County	226,615 27.71	11,637	5,612 48.23 48.23 2.48	270	16 5.93 5.93 0.01	1,902 55.48 33.89 16.34 0.84	-	-	1,293 49.96 23.04 11.11 0.57	-	1,076 64.70 19.17 9.25 0.47	-	-	-	-	154 32.29 2.74 1.32 0.07	231 33.67 4.12 1.99 0.10	-	-	-	-	-	-	140 26.57 2.49 1.20 0.06	-	404 31.51 7.20 3.47 0.18

Notes: Please refer to the User's Guide for an explanation of data; data is arranged alphabetically by state, then county, then city within each county; table includes counties with populations greater than 49,999 unless noted and cities with populations greater than 9,999 whose Asian and/or NHPI population rates are greater than the national average; (1) Native Hawaiian and other Pacific Islander; (2) excludes Taiwanese; (3) includes Chamorro; (4) county does not meet population threshold but is shown in order to allow inclusion of city

Place	Total population 25 years and over who are 4-year college graduates	Asian population 25 years and over	Asians 25 years and over who are 4-year college graduates	NHPI[1] population 25 years and over	NHPIs[1] 25 years and over who are 4-year college graduates	Asian Indian	Bangladeshi	Cambodian	Chinese[2]	Fijian	Filipino	Guamanian[3]	Hawaiian, Native	Hmong	Indonesian	Japanese	Korean	Laotian	Malaysian	Pakistani	Samoan	Sri Lankan	Taiwanese	Thai	Tongan	Vietnamese
Pasco County	33,548 13.13	2,251	1,041 46.25 46.25 3.10	-	-	283 47.09 27.19 12.57 0.84	-	-	85 29.51 8.17 3.78 0.25	-	392 55.76 37.66 17.41 1.17	-	-	-	-	-	-	-	-	-	-	-	-	-	-	-
Pinellas County	157,235 22.92	12,435	4,198 33.76 33.76 2.67	-	-	1,519 62.20 36.18 12.22 0.97	-	6 1.65 0.14 0.05 <0.01	599 37.79 14.27 4.82 0.38	-	893 41.38 21.27 7.18 0.57	-	-	-	-	160 33.83 3.81 1.29 0.10	240 39.34 5.72 1.93 0.15	47 4.40 1.12 0.38 0.03	-	-	-	-	-	85 24.64 2.02 0.68 0.05	-	311 11.29 7.41 2.50 0.20
Pinellas Park (city)	3,897 11.87	1,175	262 22.30 22.30 6.72	-	-	-	-	-	-	-	-	-	-	-	-	-	-	-	-	-	-	-	-	-	-	29 7.90 11.07 2.47 0.74
Polk County	48,669 14.92	3,533	1,446 40.93 40.93 2.97	-	-	527 48.22 36.45 14.92 1.08	-	-	169 45.68 11.69 4.78 0.35	-	372 64.36 25.73 10.53 0.76	-	-	-	-	-	-	23 10.36 1.59 0.65 0.05	-	-	-	-	-	-	-	94 19.42 6.50 2.66 0.19
Putnam County	4,507 9.44	208	51 24.52 24.52 1.13	-	-	-	-	-	-	-	-	-	-	-	-	-	-	-	-	-	-	-	-	-	-	-
St. Johns County	28,560 33.13	862	510 59.16 59.16 1.79	-	-	-	-	-	-	-	-	-	-	-	-	-	-	-	-	-	-	-	-	-	-	-
St. Lucie County	20,562 15.07	1,269	389 30.65 30.65 1.89	-	-	-	-	-	-	-	-	-	-	-	-	-	-	-	-	-	-	-	-	-	-	-
Santa Rosa County	17,881 22.88	1,232	360 29.22 29.22 2.01	-	-	-	-	-	-	-	152 27.24 42.22 12.34 0.85	-	-	-	-	-	-	-	-	-	-	-	-	-	-	-
Sarasota County	70,446 27.43	1,694	584 34.47 34.47 0.83	-	-	-	-	-	61 26.52 10.45 3.60 0.09	-	209 52.51 35.79 12.34 0.30	-	-	-	-	-	-	-	-	-	-	-	-	-	-	79 19.08 13.53 4.66 0.11
Seminole County	75,491 31.04	5,863	2,838 48.41 48.41 3.76	-	-	1,192 66.08 42.00 20.33 1.58	-	-	490 49.35 17.27 8.36 0.65	-	423 45.14 14.90 7.21 0.56	-	-	-	-	-	208 33.60 7.33 3.55 0.28	-	-	-	-	-	-	-	-	198 28.01 6.98 3.38 0.26

Notes: Please refer to the User's Guide for an explanation of data; data is arranged alphabetically by state, then county, then city within each county; table includes counties with populations greater than 49,999 unless noted and cities with populations greater than 9,999 whose Asian and/or NHPI population rates are greater than the national average; (1) Native Hawaiian and other Pacific Islander; (2) excludes Taiwanese; (3) includes Chamorro; (4) county does not meet population threshold but is shown in order to allow inclusion of city

Place	Total population 25 years and over who are 4-year college graduates	Asian population 25 years and over	Asians 25 years and over who are 4-year college graduates	NHPI[1] population 25 years and over	NHPIs[1] 25 years and over who are 4-year college graduates	Asian Indian	Bangladeshi	Cambodian	Chinese[2]	Fijian	Filipino	Guamanian[3]	Hawaiian, Native	Hmong	Indonesian	Japanese	Korean	Laotian	Malaysian	Pakistani	Samoan	Sri Lankan	Taiwanese	Thai	Tongan	Vietnamese
Volusia County	55,961 17.64	3,243	1,190 36.69 36.69 2.13	-	-	414 40.35 34.79 12.77 0.74	-	-	171 37.34 14.37 5.27 0.31	-	351 53.59 29.50 10.82 0.63	-	-	-	-	-	46 15.92 3.87 1.42 0.08	-	-	-	-	-	-	-	-	-
GEORGIA	1,260,178 24.30	109,098	48,368 44.33 44.33 3.84	2,101	308 14.66 14.66 0.02	18,216 65.60 37.66 16.70 1.45	432 55.81 0.89 0.40 0.03	240 12.77 0.50 0.22 0.02	10,126 58.91 20.94 9.28 0.80	-	3,418 47.56 7.07 3.13 0.27	78 9.99 25.32 3.71 0.01	92 15.62 29.87 4.38 0.01	51 11.33 0.11 0.05 <0.01	147 39.41 0.30 0.13 0.01	2,672 48.26 5.52 2.45 0.21	6,388 35.38 13.21 5.86 0.51	157 6.09 0.32 0.14 0.01	-	1,116 47.39 2.31 1.02 0.09	68 17.35 22.08 3.24 0.01	-	868 69.61 1.79 0.80 0.07	660 38.39 1.36 0.60 0.05	-	2,289 12.47 4.73 2.10 0.18
Bartow County	6,881 14.13	316	93 29.43 29.43 1.35	-	-	-	-	-	-	-	-	-	-	-	-	-	-	-	-	-	-	-	-	-	-	-
Bibb County	20,799 21.34	899	425 47.27 47.27 2.04	-	-	-	-	-	-	-	-	-	-	-	-	-	-	-	-	-	-	-	-	-	-	-
Bulloch County	7,303 25.41	296	212 71.62 71.62 2.90	-	-	-	-	-	-	-	-	-	-	-	-	-	-	-	-	-	-	-	-	-	-	-
Carroll County	8,828 16.51	280	138 49.29 49.29 1.56	-	-	-	-	-	-	-	-	-	-	-	-	-	-	-	-	-	-	-	-	-	-	-
Catoosa County	4,857 13.79	232	57 24.57 24.57 1.17	-	-	-	-	-	-	-	-	-	-	-	-	-	-	-	-	-	-	-	-	-	-	-
Chatham County	36,984 25.01	2,509	916 36.51 36.51 2.48	-	-	240 56.07 26.20 9.57 0.65	-	-	234 42.16 25.55 9.33 0.63	-	-	-	-	-	-	-	125 50.61 13.65 4.98 0.34	-	-	-	-	-	-	-	-	65 10.80 7.10 2.59 0.18
Cherokee County	24,590 26.98	905	356 39.34 39.34 1.45	-	-	133 72.28 37.36 14.70 0.54	-	-	-	-	-	-	-	-	-	-	-	-	-	-	-	-	-	-	-	-
Clarke County	20,646 39.82	1,778	1,359 76.43 76.43 6.58	-	-	283 82.03 20.82 15.92 1.37	-	-	540 81.69 39.74 30.37 2.62	-	-	-	-	-	-	-	184 71.88 13.54 10.35 0.89	-	-	-	-	-	-	-	-	-

Notes: Please refer to the User's Guide for an explanation of data; data is arranged alphabetically by state, then county, then city within each county; table includes counties with populations greater than 49,999 unless noted and cities with populations greater than 9,999 whose Asian and/or NHPI population rates are greater than the national average; (1) Native Hawaiian and other Pacific Islander; (2) excludes Taiwanese; (3) includes Chamorro; (4) county does not meet population threshold but is shown in order to allow inclusion of city

Place	Total population 25 years and over who are 4-year college graduates	Asian population 25 years and over	Asians 25 years and over who are 4-year college graduates	NHPI[1] population 25 years and over	NHPIs[1] 25 years and over who are 4-year college graduates	Asian Indian	Bangladeshi	Cambodian	Chinese[2]	Fijian	Filipino	Guamanian[3]	Hawaiian, Native	Hmong	Indonesian	Japanese	Korean	Laotian	Malaysian	Pakistani	Samoan	Sri Lankan	Taiwanese	Thai	Tongan	Vietnamese
Clayton County	23,544 16.63	6,363	1,008 15.84 15.84 4.28	-	-	528 61.04 52.38 8.30 2.24	-	8 1.57 0.79 0.13 0.03	39 11.78 3.87 0.61 0.17	-	-	-	-	-	-	-	-	43 6.36 4.27 0.68 0.18	-	94 40.69 9.33 1.48 0.40	-	-	-	-	-	171 5.96 16.96 2.69 0.73
Forest Park (city)	829 6.63	760	25 3.29 3.29 3.02	-	-	-	-	-	-	-	-	-	-	-	-	-	-	-	-	-	-	-	-	-	-	4 0.71 16.00 0.53 0.48
Riverdale (city)	1,094 15.10	637	87 13.66 13.66 7.95	-	-	-	-	-	-	-	-	-	-	-	-	-	-	-	-	-	-	-	-	-	-	9 2.89 10.34 1.41 0.82
Cobb County	157,178 39.76	12,169	6,666 54.78 54.78 4.24	-	-	2,734 77.71 41.01 22.47 1.74	-	-	1,443 60.91 21.65 11.86 0.92	-	419 49.24 6.29 3.44 0.27	-	-	-	-	408 58.54 6.12 3.35 0.26	753 37.97 11.30 6.19 0.48	-	-	133 34.10 2.00 1.09 0.08	-	-	-	-	-	216 21.77 3.24 1.78 0.14
Smyrna (city)	11,572 40.33	1,183	782 66.10 66.10 6.76	-	-	343 92.45 43.86 28.99 2.96	-	-	-	-	-	-	-	-	-	-	-	-	-	-	-	-	-	-	-	-
Columbia County	18,072 31.95	1,924	1,033 53.69 53.69 5.72	-	-	388 64.67 37.56 20.17 2.15	-	-	208 63.03 20.14 10.81 1.15	-	-	-	-	-	-	-	50 16.89 4.84 2.60 0.28	-	-	-	-	-	-	-	-	-
Martinez (cdp)	6,476 36.68	925	531 57.41 57.41 8.20	-	-	210 64.22 39.55 22.70 3.24	-	-	-	-	-	-	-	-	-	-	-	-	-	-	-	-	-	-	-	-
Coweta County	11,709 20.61	383	170 44.39 44.39 1.45	-	-	-	-	-	-	-	-	-	-	-	-	-	-	-	-	-	-	-	-	-	-	-
DeKalb County	156,089 36.30	17,436	8,157 46.78 46.78 5.23	-	-	3,012 63.83 36.93 17.27 1.93	159 45.82 1.95 0.91 0.10	16 4.17 0.20 0.09 0.01	1,874 68.77 22.97 10.75 1.20	-	281 57.82 3.44 1.61 0.18	-	-	-	-	544 74.62 6.67 3.12 0.35	1,107 45.69 13.57 6.35 0.71	-	-	-	-	-	-	-	-	453 11.34 5.55 2.60 0.29
Druid Hills (cdp)	5,632 78.78	319	271 84.95 84.95 4.81	-	-	-	-	-	-	-	-	-	-	-	-	-	-	-	-	-	-	-	-	-	-	-

Notes: Please refer to the User's Guide for an explanation of data; data is arranged alphabetically by state, then county, then city within each county; table includes counties with populations greater than 49,999 unless noted and cities with populations greater than 9,999 whose Asian and/or NHPI population rates are greater than the national average; (1) Native Hawaiian and other Pacific Islander; (2) excludes Taiwanese; (3) includes Chamorro; (4) county does not meet population threshold but is shown in order to allow inclusion of city

Place	Total population 25 years and over who are 4-year college graduates	Asian population 25 years and over	Asians 25 years and over who are 4-year college graduates	NHPI[1] population 25 years and over	NHPIs[1] 25 years and over who are 4-year college graduates	Asian Indian	Bangladeshi	Cambodian	Chinese[2]	Fijian	Filipino	Guamanian[3]	Hawaiian, Native	Hmong	Indonesian	Japanese	Korean	Laotian	Malaysian	Pakistani	Samoan	Sri Lankan	Taiwanese	Thai	Tongan	Vietnamese
Dunwoody (cdp)	15,828 65.47	1,675	1,275 76.12 76.12 8.06	-	-	655 87.68 51.37 39.10 4.14	-	-	-	-	-	-	-	-	-	-	205 62.69 16.08 12.24 1.30	-	-	-	-	-	-	-	-	-
North Atlanta (cdp)	11,843 44.27	1,142	668 58.49 58.49 5.64	-	-	-	-	-	-	-	-	-	-	-	-	-	-	-	-	-	-	-	-	-	-	-
North Decatur (cdp)	6,943 57.78	582	423 72.68 72.68 6.09	-	-	-	-	-	-	-	-	-	-	-	-	-	-	-	-	-	-	-	-	-	-	-
North Druid Hills (cdp)	9,083 65.06	861	750 87.11 87.11 8.26	-	-	321 84.70 42.80 37.28 3.53	-	-	-	-	-	-	-	-	-	-	-	-	-	-	-	-	-	-	-	-
Tucker (cdp)	8,009 41.49	1,361	637 46.80 46.80 7.95	-	-	-	-	-	-	-	-	-	-	-	-	-	-	-	-	-	-	-	-	-	-	35 15.63 5.49 2.57 0.44
Dougherty County	10,347 17.83	474	73 15.40 15.40 0.71	-	-	-	-	-	-	-	-	-	-	-	-	-	-	-	-	-	-	-	-	-	-	-
Douglas County	11,285 19.23	606	300 49.50 49.50 2.66	-	-	-	-	-	-	-	-	-	-	-	-	-	-	-	-	-	-	-	-	-	-	-
Fayette County	21,347 36.17	1,326	610 46.00 46.00 2.86	-	-	-	-	-	-	-	-	-	-	-	-	184 44.34 30.16 13.88 0.86	-	-	-	-	-	-	-	-	-	-
Peachtree City (city)	9,345 46.21	805	367 45.59 45.59 3.93	-	-	-	-	-	-	-	-	-	-	-	-	163 41.37 44.41 20.25 1.74	-	-	-	-	-	-	-	-	-	-
Floyd County	9,267 15.80	691	200 28.94 28.94 2.16	-	-	85 30.25 42.50 12.30 0.92	-	-	-	-	-	-	-	-	-	-	-	-	-	-	-	-	-	-	-	-

Notes: Please refer to the User's Guide for an explanation of data; data is arranged alphabetically by state, then county, then city within each county; table includes counties with populations greater than 49,999 unless noted and cities with populations greater than 9,999 whose Asian and/or NHPI population rates are greater than the national average; (1) Native Hawaiian and other Pacific Islander; (2) excludes Taiwanese; (3) includes Chamorro; (4) county does not meet population threshold but is shown in order to allow inclusion of city

Place	Total population 25 years and over who are 4-year college graduates	Asian population 25 years and over	Asians 25 years and over who are 4-year college graduates	NHPI[1] population 25 years and over	NHPIs[1] 25 years and over who are 4-year college graduates	Asian Indian	Bangladeshi	Cambodian	Chinese[2]	Fijian	Filipino	Guamanian[3]	Hawaiian, Native	Hmong	Indonesian	Japanese	Korean	Laotian	Malaysian	Pakistani	Samoan	Sri Lankan	Taiwanese	Thai	Tongan	Vietnamese
Forsyth County	22,490 34.59	552	346 62.68 62.68 1.54	-	-	-	-	-	-	-	-	-	-	-	-	-	-	-	-	-	-	-	-	-	-	-
Fulton County	218,405 41.39	15,006	9,156 61.02 61.02 4.19	-	-	3,395 78.19 37.08 22.62 1.55	-	-	2,518 72.88 27.50 16.78 1.15	-	386 62.06 4.22 2.57 0.18	-	-	-	-	446 65.49 4.87 2.97 0.20	1,182 46.03 12.91 7.88 0.54	-	-	-	-	-	-	-	-	284 16.20 3.10 1.89 0.13
Alpharetta (city)	12,903 57.12	1,117	887 79.41 79.41 6.87	-	-	383 91.63 43.18 34.29 2.97	-	-	239 71.77 26.94 21.40 1.85	-	-	-	-	-	-	-	-	-	-	-	-	-	-	-	-	-
Roswell (city)	28,247 52.60	1,960	1,180 60.20 60.20 4.18	-	-	479 82.73 40.59 24.44 1.70	-	-	227 57.61 19.24 11.58 0.80	-	-	-	-	-	-	-	236 45.30 20.00 12.04 0.84	-	-	-	-	-	-	-	-	-
Glynn County	10,654 23.78	329	71 21.58 21.58 0.67	-	-	-	-	-	-	-	-	-	-	-	-	-	-	-	-	-	-	-	-	-	-	-
Gwinnett County	126,907 34.06	26,336	11,197 42.52 42.52 8.82	276	35 12.68 12.68 0.03	4,205 60.51 37.55 15.97 3.31	-	131 30.90 1.17 0.50 0.10	1,975 54.56 17.64 7.50 1.56	-	556 61.50 4.97 2.11 0.44	-	-	-	-	342 51.58 3.05 1.30 0.27	2,029 34.44 18.12 7.70 1.60	46 6.98 0.41 0.17 0.04	-	358 54.57 3.20 1.36 0.28	-	-	249 69.75 2.22 0.95 0.20	-	-	641 13.45 5.72 2.43 0.51
Duluth (city)	6,867 45.66	1,719	939 54.62 54.62 13.67	-	-	386 71.35 41.11 22.45 5.62	-	-	189 59.25 20.13 10.99 2.75	-	-	-	-	-	-	-	172 38.39 18.32 10.01 2.50	-	-	-	-	-	-	-	-	-
Lilburn (city)	2,345 31.81	883	371 42.02 42.02 15.82	-	-	106 50.96 28.57 12.00 4.52	-	-	-	-	-	-	-	-	-	-	-	-	-	-	-	-	-	-	-	36 12.37 9.70 4.08 1.54
Mountain Park (cdp)	2,870 35.93	625	397 63.52 63.52 13.83	-	-	230 62.33 57.93 36.80 8.01	-	-	-	-	-	-	-	-	-	-	-	-	-	-	-	-	-	-	-	-
Hall County	16,261 18.73	1,041	150 14.41 14.41 0.92	-	-	-	-	-	-	-	-	-	-	-	-	-	-	-	-	-	-	-	-	-	-	10 1.50 6.67 0.96 0.06

Notes: Please refer to the User's Guide for an explanation of data; data is arranged alphabetically by state, then county, then city within each county; table includes counties with populations greater than 49,999 unless noted and cities with populations greater than 9,999 whose Asian and/or NHPI population rates are greater than the national average; (1) Native Hawaiian and other Pacific Islander; (2) excludes Taiwanese; (3) includes Chamorro; (4) county does not meet population threshold but is shown in order to allow inclusion of city

Place	Total population 25 years and over who are 4-year college graduates	Asian population 25 years and over	Asians 25 years and over who are 4-year college graduates	NHPI[1] population 25 years and over	NHPIs[1] 25 years and over who are 4-year college graduates	Asian Indian	Bangladeshi	Cambodian	Chinese[2]	Fijian	Filipino	Guamanian[3]	Hawaiian, Native	Hmong	Indonesian	Japanese	Korean	Laotian	Malaysian	Pakistani	Samoan	Sri Lankan	Taiwanese	Thai	Tongan	Vietnamese
Henry County	14,760 19.55	1,363	601 44.09 44.09 4.07	-	-	361 74.59 60.07 26.49 2.45	-	-	-	-	-	-	-	-	-	-	-	-	-	-	-	-	-	-	-	-
Houston County	13,637 19.75	1,216	396 32.57 32.57 2.90	-	-	-	-	-	-	-	104 28.34 26.26 8.55 0.76	-	-	-	-	-	-	-	-	-	-	-	-	-	-	-
Liberty County	4,469 14.51	598	145 24.25 24.25 3.24	-	-	-	-	-	-	-	-	-	-	-	-	-	60 20.55 41.38 10.03 1.34	-	-	-	-	-	-	-	-	-
Lowndes County	10,665 19.66	553	96 17.36 17.36 0.90	-	-	-	-	-	-	-	-	-	-	-	-	-	-	-	-	-	-	-	-	-	-	-
Muscogee County	23,180 20.33	1,961	701 35.75 35.75 3.02	170	18 10.59 10.59 0.08	280 84.08 39.94 14.28 1.21	-	-	135 50.94 19.26 6.88 0.58	-	98 31.61 13.98 5.00 0.42	-	-	-	-	-	58 11.03 8.27 2.96 0.25	-	-	-	-	-	-	-	-	-
Columbus (sp. city)	23,166 20.37	1,961	701 35.75 35.75 3.03	170	18 10.59 10.59 0.08	280 84.08 39.94 14.28 1.21	-	-	135 50.94 19.26 6.88 0.58	-	98 31.61 13.98 5.00 0.42	-	-	-	-	-	58 11.03 8.27 2.96 0.25	-	-	-	-	-	-	-	-	-
Newton County	5,692 14.54	212	96 45.28 45.28 1.69	-	-	-	-	-	-	-	-	-	-	-	-	-	-	-	-	-	-	-	-	-	-	-
Richmond County	22,909 18.69	2,028	585 28.85 28.85 2.55	-	-	280 70.18 47.86 13.81 1.22	-	-	60 18.07 10.26 2.96 0.26	-	-	-	-	-	-	-	75 11.03 12.82 3.70 0.33	-	-	-	-	-	-	-	-	-
Rockdale County	10,461 23.35	721	297 41.19 41.19 2.84	-	-	-	-	-	-	-	-	-	-	-	-	-	-	-	-	-	-	-	-	-	-	-
Spalding County	4,628 12.47	269	121 44.98 44.98 2.61	-	-	-	-	-	-	-	-	-	-	-	-	-	-	-	-	-	-	-	-	-	-	-

Notes: Please refer to the User's Guide for an explanation of data; data is arranged alphabetically by state, then county, then city within each county; table includes counties with populations greater than 49,999 unless noted and cities with populations greater than 9,999 whose Asian and/or NHPI population rates are greater than the national average; (1) Native Hawaiian and other Pacific Islander; (2) excludes Taiwanese; (3) includes Chamorro; (4) county does not meet population threshold but is shown in order to allow inclusion of city

Place	Total population 25 years and over who are 4-year college graduates	Asian population 25 years and over	Asians 25 years and over who are 4-year college graduates	NHPI[1] population 25 years and over	NHPIs[1] 25 years and over who are 4-year college graduates	Asian Indian	Bangladeshi	Cambodian	Chinese[2]	Fijian	Filipino	Guamanian[3]	Hawaiian, Native	Hmong	Indonesian	Japanese	Korean	Laotian	Malaysian	Pakistani	Samoan	Sri Lankan	Taiwanese	Thai	Tongan	Vietnamese
	6,614	295	115	-	-	-	-	-	-	-	-	-	-	-	-	-	-	-	-	-	-	-	-	-	-	-
	17.97		38.98																							
Troup County																										
			38.98																							
			1.74																							
	5,024	225	82	-	-	-	-	-	-	-	-	-	-	-	-	-	-	-	-	-	-	-	-	-	-	-
	13.04		36.44																							
Walton County																										
			36.44																							
			1.63																							
	6,748	563	168	-	-	-	-	-	-	-	-	-	-	-	-	-	-	-	-	-	-	-	-	-	-	-
	12.84		29.84																							
Whitfield County																										
			29.84																							
			2.49																							
	210,041	378,686	100,682	61,930	7,301	554	-	28	15,922	-	18,838	187	5,948	-	-	53,422	4,445	73	-	-	480	-	300	256	212	573
	26.17		26.59		11.79	55.62		34.57	35.84		16.23	21.49	12.65			31.33	24.31	7.63			6.82		47.85	25.02	9.72	10.59
HAWAII						0.55		0.03	15.81		18.71	2.56	81.47			53.06	4.41	0.07			6.57		0.30	0.25	2.90	0.57
			26.59		11.79	0.15		0.01	4.20		4.97	0.30	9.60			14.11	1.17	0.02			0.78		0.08	0.07	0.34	0.15
			47.93		3.48	0.26		0.01	7.58		8.97	0.09	2.83			25.43	2.12	0.03			0.23		0.14	0.12	0.10	0.27
	21,595	30,732	6,720	8,953	975	-	-	-	296	-	912	-	915	-	-	4,727	197	-	-	-	2	-	-	-	-	-
	22.10		21.87		10.89				28.22		10.01		11.56			26.76	30.35				0.97					
Hawaii County									4.40		13.57		93.85			70.34	2.93				0.21					
			21.87		10.89				0.96		2.97		10.22			15.38	0.64				0.02					
			31.12		4.51				1.37		4.22		4.24			21.89	0.91				0.01					
	6,444	12,185	3,661	2,602	307	-	-	-	151	-	211	-	286	-	-	2,952	79	-	-	-	-	-	-	-	-	-
	24.27		30.05		11.80				35.95		13.98		12.70			32.06	24.46									
Hilo (cdp)									4.12		5.76		93.16			80.63	2.16									
			30.05		11.80				1.24		1.73		10.99			24.23	0.65									
			56.81		4.76				2.34		3.27		4.44			45.81	1.23									
	161,646	303,546	85,664	42,410	5,396	460	-	-	15,209	-	15,142	178	4,200	-	-	44,309	4,090	73	-	-	459	-	284	214	172	497
	27.87		28.22		12.72	55.49			36.07		17.86	22.91	14.09			32.77	24.33	7.88			6.87		47.57	25.81	10.78	9.93
Honolulu County						0.54			17.75		17.68	3.30	77.84			51.72	4.77	0.09			8.51		0.33	0.25	3.19	0.58
			28.22		12.72	0.15			5.01		4.99	0.42	9.90			14.60	1.35	0.02			1.08		0.09	0.07	0.41	0.16
			52.99		3.34	0.28			9.41		9.37	0.11	2.60			27.41	2.53	0.05			0.28		0.18	0.13	0.11	0.31
	954	4,764	588	822	54	-	-	-	-	-	397	-	32	-	-	128	-	-	-	-	13	-	-	-	-	-
	10.63		12.34		6.57						11.31		5.89			17.32					6.50					
Ewa Beach (cdp)											67.52		59.26			21.77					24.07					
			12.34		6.57						8.33		3.89			2.69					1.58					
			61.64		5.66						41.61		3.35			13.42					1.36					
	2,059	5,415	1,244	868	56	-	-	-	152	-	426	-	15	-	-	529	-	-	-	-	20	-	-	-	-	-
	22.01		22.97		6.45				27.05		20.84		2.90			24.66					7.25					
Halawa (cdp)									12.22		34.24		26.79			42.52					35.71					
			22.97		6.45				2.81		7.87		1.73			9.77					2.30					
			60.42		2.72				7.38		20.69		0.73			25.69					0.97					
	83,207	159,892	47,388	14,980	2,275	320	-	-	11,100	-	5,411	59	1,862	-	-	24,030	3,029	28	-	-	151	-	284	136	36	334
	31.10		29.64		15.19	65.98			35.76		18.21	16.48	19.46			32.78	25.33	4.88			6.81		52.40	34.61	4.37	8.11
Honolulu (cdp)						0.68			23.42		11.42	2.59	81.85			50.71	6.39	0.06			6.64		0.60	0.29	1.58	0.70
			29.64		15.19	0.20			6.94		3.38	0.39	12.43			15.03	1.89	0.02			1.01		0.18	0.09	0.24	0.21
			56.95		2.73	0.38			13.34		6.50	0.07	2.24			28.88	3.64	0.03			0.18		0.34	0.16	0.04	0.40

Notes: Please refer to the User's Guide for an explanation of data; data is arranged alphabetically by state, then county, then city within each county; table includes counties with populations greater than 49,999 unless noted and cities with populations greater than 9,999 whose Asian and/or NHPI population rates are greater than the national average; (1) Native Hawaiian and other Pacific Islander; (2) excludes Taiwanese; (3) includes Chamorro; (4) county does not meet population threshold but is shown in order to allow inclusion of city

Place	Total population 25 years and over who are 4-year college graduates	Asian population 25 years and over	Asians 25 years and over who are 4-year college graduates	NHPI[1] population 25 years and over	NHPIs[1] 25 years and over who are 4-year college graduates	Asian Indian	Bangladeshi	Cambodian	Chinese[2]	Fijian	Filipino	Guamanian[3]	Hawaiian, Native	Hmong	Indonesian	Japanese	Korean	Laotian	Malaysian	Pakistani	Samoan	Sri Lankan	Taiwanese	Thai	Tongan	Vietnamese
Kailua (cdp)	9,896	6,329	2,409	1,667	282	-	-	-	376	-	187	-	223	-	-	1,474	143	-	-	-	-	-	-	-	-	-
	39.44		38.06		16.92				39.54		25.00		14.63			39.46	40.74									
									15.61		7.76		79.08			61.19	5.94									
			38.06		16.92				5.94		2.95		13.38			23.29	2.26									
			24.34		2.85				3.80		1.89		2.25			14.89	1.45									
Kaneohe (cdp)	6,981	10,798	3,365	2,297	315	-	-	-	366	-	229	-	270	-	-	2,281	132	-	-	-	-	-	-	-	-	-
	29.49		31.16		13.71				30.42		17.67		14.00			32.84	37.18									
									10.88		6.81		85.71			67.79	3.92									
			31.16		13.71				3.39		2.12		11.75			21.12	1.22									
			48.20		4.51				5.24		3.28		3.87			32.67	1.89									
Kaneohe Station (cdp)	905	363	77	-	-	-	-	-	-	-	-	-	-	-	-	-	-	-	-	-	-	-	-	-	-	-
	24.09		21.21																							
			21.21																							
			8.51																							
Makakilo City (cdp)	2,126	3,076	862	743	136	-	-	-	-	-	362	-	106	-	-	303	-	-	-	-	-	-	-	-	-	-
	26.26		28.02		18.30						24.69		19.89			36.86										
											42.00		77.94			35.15										
			28.02		18.30						11.77		14.27			9.85										
			40.55		6.40						17.03		4.99			14.25										
Mililani Town (cdp)	5,805	9,601	3,439	713	144	-	-	-	404	-	451	-	136	-	-	2,270	102	-	-	-	-	-	-	-	-	-
	31.81		35.82		20.20				48.44		20.34		24.73			41.72	25.31									
									11.75		13.11		94.44			66.01	2.97									
			35.82		20.20				4.21		4.70		19.07			23.64	1.06									
			59.24		2.48				6.96		7.77		2.34			39.10	1.76									
Nanakuli (cdp)	367	717	46	2,084	64	-	-	-	-	-	38	-	64	-	-	-	-	-	-	-	0	-	-	-	-	-
	6.62		6.42		3.07						9.50		3.71								0.00					
											82.61		100.00								0.00					
			6.42		3.07						5.30		3.07								0.00					
			12.53		17.44						10.35		17.44								0.00					
Pearl City (cdp)	4,186	13,505	3,095	1,054	147	-	-	-	286	-	638	-	119	-	-	1,952	40	-	-	-	-	-	-	-	-	-
	20.13		22.92		13.95				25.00		21.10		15.12			23.74	14.13									
									9.24		20.61		80.95			63.07	1.29									
			22.92		13.95				2.12		4.72		11.29			14.45	0.30									
			73.94		3.51				6.83		15.24		2.84			46.63	0.96									
Schofield Barracks (cdp)	932	273	39	-	-	-	-	-	-	-	-	-	-	-	-	-	-	-	-	-	-	-	-	-	-	-
	16.77		14.29																							
			14.29																							
			4.18																							
Wahiawa (cdp)	1,768	5,713	1,033	847	102	-	-	-	-	-	290	-	79	-	-	604	-	-	-	-	-	-	-	-	-	-
	16.77		18.08		12.04						14.46		14.52			20.87										
											28.07		77.45			58.47										
			18.08		12.04						5.08		9.33			10.57										
			58.43		5.77						16.40		4.47			34.16										
Waianae (cdp)	446	1,466	150	1,473	78	-	-	-	-	-	61	-	78	-	-	56	-	-	-	-	-	-	-	-	-	-
	7.48		10.23		5.30						8.38		5.99			10.96										
											40.67		100.00			37.33										
			10.23		5.30						4.16		5.30			3.82										
			33.63		17.49						13.68		17.49			12.56										

Notes: Please refer to the User's Guide for an explanation of data; data is arranged alphabetically by state, then county, then city within each county; table includes counties with populations greater than 49,999 unless noted and cities with populations greater than 9,999 whose Asian and/or NHPI population rates are greater than the national average; (1) Native Hawaiian and other Pacific Islander; (2) excludes Taiwanese; (3) includes Chamorro; (4) county does not meet population threshold but is shown in order to allow inclusion of city

Place	Total population 25 years and over who are 4-year college graduates	Asian population 25 years and over	Asians 25 years and over who are 4-year college graduates	NHPI[1] population 25 years and over	NHPIs[1] 25 years and over who are 4-year college graduates	Asian Indian	Bangladeshi	Cambodian	Chinese[2]	Fijian	Filipino	Guamanian[3]	Hawaiian, Native	Hmong	Indonesian	Japanese	Korean	Laotian	Malaysian	Pakistani	Samoan	Sri Lankan	Taiwanese	Thai	Tongan	Vietnamese
Waimalu (cdp)	6,581 32.44	11,779	4,164 35.35 35.35 63.27	894	135 15.10 15.10 2.05	-	-	-	478 44.34 11.48 4.06 7.26	-	566 25.26 13.59 4.81 8.60	-	103 17.88 76.30 11.52 1.57	-	-	2,548 38.72 61.19 21.63 38.72	191 22.68 4.59 1.62 2.90	-	-	-	-	-	-	-	-	-
Waipahu (cdp)	2,349 11.14	15,322	1,985 12.96 12.96 84.50	1,766	78 4.42 4.42 3.32	-	-	-	38 8.54 1.91 0.25 1.62	-	1,522 13.82 76.68 9.93 64.79	-	31 5.44 39.74 1.76 1.32	-	-	367 11.65 18.49 2.40 15.62	-	-	-	-	27 3.08 34.62 1.53 1.15	-	-	-	-	-
Waipio (cdp)	2,070 28.09	4,488	1,439 32.06 32.06 69.52	346	28 8.09 8.09 1.35	-	-	-	-	-	264 16.87 18.35 5.88 12.75	-	28 12.33 100.00 8.09 1.35	-	-	911 42.16 63.31 20.30 44.01	-	-	-	-	-	-	-	-	-	-
Kauai County	7,551 19.43	15,803	2,515 15.91 15.91 33.31	2,900	276 9.52 9.52 3.66	-	-	-	105 30.70 4.17 0.66 1.39	-	691 8.94 27.48 4.37 9.15	-	267 9.91 96.74 9.21 3.54	-	-	1,508 22.56 59.96 9.54 19.97	-	-	-	-	-	-	-	-	-	-
Maui County	19,234 22.43	28,575	5,768 20.19 20.19 29.99	7,579	654 8.63 8.63 3.40	-	-	-	312 35.74 5.41 1.09 1.62	-	2,078 14.39 36.03 7.27 10.80	-	566 8.67 86.54 7.47 2.94	-	-	2,878 26.31 49.90 10.07 14.96	135 19.77 2.34 0.47 0.70	-	-	-	-	-	-	-	17 4.04 2.60 0.22 0.09	-
Kahului (cdp)	1,757 13.45	8,063	1,260 15.63 15.63 71.71	990	79 7.98 7.98 4.50	-	-	-	-	-	614 13.90 48.73 7.62 34.95	-	79 9.61 100.00 7.98 4.50	-	-	562 18.66 44.60 6.97 31.99	-	-	-	-	-	-	-	-	-	-
Kihei (cdp)	2,462 21.79	2,752	554 20.13 20.13 22.50	712	60 8.43 8.43 2.44	-	-	-	-	-	338 17.04 61.01 12.28 13.73	-	56 11.97 93.33 7.87 2.27	-	-	134 30.52 24.19 4.87 5.44	-	-	-	-	-	-	-	-	-	-
Wailuku (cdp)	1,845 21.61	4,031	1,005 24.93 24.93 54.47	714	106 14.85 14.85 5.75	-	-	-	-	-	163 15.29 16.22 4.04 8.83	-	91 13.32 85.85 12.75 4.93	-	-	669 27.93 66.57 16.60 36.26	-	-	-	-	-	-	-	-	-	-
IDAHO	170,615 21.67	7,654	2,932 38.31 38.31 1.72	557	89 15.98 15.98 0.05	475 67.28 16.20 6.21 0.28	-	-	575 49.87 19.61 7.51 0.34	-	451 37.65 15.38 5.89 0.26	-	37 19.27 41.57 6.64 0.02	-	-	712 33.60 24.28 9.30 0.42	297 41.48 10.13 3.88 0.17	13 3.88 0.44 0.17 0.01	-	-	-	-	-	-	-	121 14.09 4.13 1.58 0.07
Ada County	58,820 31.18	3,286	1,382 42.06 42.06 2.35	187	41 21.93 21.93 0.07	324 74.31 23.44 9.86 0.55	-	-	282 59.49 20.41 8.58 0.48	-	193 49.61 13.97 5.87 0.33	-	-	-	-	249 44.15 18.02 7.58 0.42	76 27.24 5.50 2.31 0.13	-	-	-	-	-	-	-	-	64 9.97 4.63 1.95 0.11

Notes: Please refer to the User's Guide for an explanation of data; data is arranged alphabetically by state, then county, then city within each county; table includes counties with populations greater than 49,999 unless noted and cities with populations greater than 9,999 whose Asian and/or NHPI population rates are greater than the national average; (1) Native Hawaiian and other Pacific Islander; (2) excludes Taiwanese; (3) includes Chamorro; (4) county does not meet population threshold but is shown in order to allow inclusion of city

Place	Total population 25 years and over who are 4-year college graduates	Asian population 25 years and over	Asians 25 years and over who are 4-year college graduates	NHPI[1] population 25 years and over	NHPIs[1] 25 years and over who are 4-year college graduates	Asian Indian	Bangladeshi	Cambodian	Chinese[2]	Fijian	Filipino	Guamanian[3]	Hawaiian, Native	Hmong	Indonesian	Japanese	Korean	Laotian	Malaysian	Pakistani	Samoan	Sri Lankan	Taiwanese	Thai	Tongan	Vietnamese
Bannock County	10,799 24.95	556	240 43.17 43.17 2.22	-	-	-	-	-	-	-	-	-	-	-	-	-	-	-	-	-	-	-	-	-	-	-
Bonneville County	12,674 26.13	313	120 38.34 38.34 0.95	-	-	-	-	-	-	-	-	-	-	-	-	-	-	-	-	-	-	-	-	-	-	-
Canyon County	11,415 14.90	718	166 23.12 23.12 1.45	-	-	-	-	-	-	-	-	-	-	-	-	71 30.08 42.77 9.89 0.62	-	-	-	-	-	-	-	-	-	-
Kootenai County	13,331 19.08	343	119 34.69 34.69 0.89	-	-	-	-	-	-	-	-	-	-	-	-	-	-	-	-	-	-	-	-	-	-	-
Twin Falls County	6,337 16.03	248	27 10.89 10.89 0.43	-	-	-	-	-	-	-	-	-	-	-	-	-	-	-	-	-	-	-	-	-	-	-
ILLINOIS	2,078,049 26.06	276,697	159,582 57.67 57.67 7.68	2,172	454 20.90 20.90 0.02	50,789 66.00 31.83 18.36 2.44	331 74.89 0.21 0.12 0.02	332 18.08 0.21 0.12 0.02	28,294 56.40 17.73 10.23 1.36	-	37,120 62.36 23.26 13.42 1.79	123 21.54 27.09 5.66 0.01	115 20.32 25.33 5.29 0.01	-	408 62.10 0.26 0.15 0.02	8,161 50.39 5.11 2.95 0.39	17,948 52.57 11.25 6.49 0.86	331 11.68 0.21 0.12 0.02	269 79.82 0.17 0.10 0.01	5,082 56.83 3.18 1.84 0.24	84 19.27 18.50 3.87 <0.01	291 66.14 0.18 0.11 0.01	1,841 80.57 1.15 0.67 0.09	2,389 58.67 1.50 0.86 0.11	-	2,688 23.64 1.68 0.97 0.13
Champaign County	38,202 37.99	5,453	4,327 79.35 79.35 11.33	-	-	853 89.41 19.71 15.64 2.23	-	-	1,461 88.38 33.76 26.79 3.82	-	195 62.50 4.51 3.58 0.51	-	-	-	-	286 81.48 6.61 5.24 0.75	1,070 88.72 24.73 19.62 2.80	-	-	-	-	-	-	-	-	87 20.76 2.01 1.60 0.23
Champaign (city)	15,217 44.29	2,132	1,590 74.58 74.58 10.45	-	-	396 89.19 24.91 18.57 2.60	-	-	488 92.78 30.69 22.89 3.21	-	-	-	-	-	-	-	348 83.45 21.89 16.32 2.29	-	-	-	-	-	-	-	-	41 15.41 2.58 1.92 0.27
Urbana (city)	9,508 53.54	2,292	2,006 87.52 87.52 21.10	-	-	301 94.95 15.00 13.13 3.17	-	-	795 85.39 39.63 34.69 8.36	-	-	-	-	-	-	-	474 98.34 23.63 20.68 4.99	-	-	-	-	-	-	-	-	-
Coles County	6,305 20.79	206	144 69.90 69.90 2.28	-	-	-	-	-	-	-	-	-	-	-	-	-	-	-	-	-	-	-	-	-	-	-

Notes: Please refer to the User's Guide for an explanation of data; data is arranged alphabetically by state, then county, then city within each county; table includes counties with populations greater than 49,999 unless noted and cities with populations greater than 9,999 whose Asian and/or NHPI population rates are greater than the national average; (1) Native Hawaiian and other Pacific Islander; (2) excludes Taiwanese; (3) includes Chamorro; (4) county does not meet population threshold but is shown in order to allow inclusion of city

Place	Total population 25 years and over who are 4-year college graduates	Asian population 25 years and over	Asians 25 years and over who are 4-year college graduates	NHPI[1] population 25 years and over	NHPIs[1] 25 years and over who are 4-year college graduates	Asian Indian	Bangladeshi	Cambodian	Chinese[2]	Fijian	Filipino	Guamanian[3]	Hawaiian, Native	Hmong	Indonesian	Japanese	Korean	Laotian	Malaysian	Pakistani	Samoan	Sri Lankan	Taiwanese	Thai	Tongan	Vietnamese
Cook County	968,642 28.04	175,671	96,013 54.66 54.66 9.91	930	201 21.61 21.61 0.02	27,104 61.56 28.23 15.43 2.80	-	215 18.27 0.22 0.12 0.02	15,815 47.56 16.47 9.00 1.63	-	24,393 63.18 25.41 13.89 2.52	-	-	-	240 69.77 0.25 0.14 0.02	5,627 49.18 5.86 3.20 0.58	12,552 51.27 13.07 7.15 1.30	183 21.18 0.19 0.10 0.02	-	3,283 53.30 3.42 1.87 0.34	-	-	957 81.03 1.00 0.54 0.10	1,684 59.40 1.75 0.96 0.17	-	1,585 23.46 1.65 0.90 0.16
Arlington Heights (village)	25,101 46.46	3,310	2,437 73.63 73.63 9.71	-	-	781 87.56 32.05 23.60 3.11	-	-	290 79.23 11.90 8.76 1.16	-	405 76.70 16.62 12.24 1.61	-	-	-	-	499 63.57 20.48 15.08 1.99	264 53.55 10.83 7.98 1.05	-	-	-	-	-	-	-	-	-
Chicago (city)	462,783 25.49	87,469	42,187 48.23 48.23 9.12	602	86 14.29 14.29 0.02	8,885 58.51 21.06 10.16 1.92	-	183 17.94 0.43 0.21 0.04	8,744 38.93 20.73 10.00 1.89	-	12,106 60.01 28.70 13.84 2.62	-	-	-	-	2,470 47.45 5.85 2.82 0.53	4,396 46.34 10.42 5.03 0.95	-	-	1,852 47.48 4.39 2.12 0.40	-	-	380 83.33 0.90 0.43 0.08	829 54.50 1.97 0.95 0.18	-	992 19.70 2.35 1.13 0.21
Des Plaines (city)	10,274 24.73	2,836	1,471 51.87 51.87 14.32	-	-	532 43.75 36.17 18.76 5.18	-	-	206 58.36 14.00 7.26 2.01	-	394 67.24 26.78 13.89 3.83	-	-	-	-	-	-	-	-	-	-	-	-	-	-	-
Elk Grove Village (village)	7,501 31.59	2,205	1,330 60.32 60.32 17.73	-	-	431 65.11 32.41 19.55 5.75	-	-	191 59.69 14.36 8.66 2.55	-	285 72.52 21.43 12.93 3.80	-	-	-	-	249 59.29 18.72 11.29 3.32	-	-	-	-	-	-	-	-	-	-
Evanston (city)	29,511 62.36	2,358	2,028 86.01 86.01 6.87	-	-	540 93.91 26.63 22.90 1.83	-	-	509 93.91 25.10 21.59 1.72	-	244 70.52 12.03 10.35 0.83	-	-	-	-	210 72.16 10.36 8.91 0.71	296 82.22 14.60 12.55 1.00	-	-	-	-	-	-	-	-	-
Forest Park (village)	4,217 36.28	833	614 73.71 73.71 14.56	-	-	-	-	-	-	-	-	-	-	-	-	-	-	-	-	-	-	-	-	-	-	-
Glenview (village)	16,140 55.93	2,810	1,994 70.96 70.96 12.35	-	-	342 84.86 17.15 12.17 2.12	-	-	396 76.89 19.86 14.09 2.45	-	326 79.71 16.35 11.60 2.02	-	-	-	-	126 50.81 6.32 4.48 0.78	620 62.31 31.09 22.06 3.84	-	-	-	-	-	-	-	-	-
Hanover Park (village)	4,506 20.21	2,668	1,280 47.98 47.98 28.41	-	-	599 51.77 46.80 22.45 13.29	-	-	-	-	452 58.70 35.31 16.94 10.03	-	-	-	-	-	-	-	-	-	-	-	-	-	-	-
Hoffman Estates (village)	11,327 35.91	4,746	2,647 55.77 55.77 23.37	-	-	907 51.92 34.27 19.11 8.01	-	-	397 75.19 15.00 8.36 3.50	-	423 64.29 15.98 8.91 3.73	-	-	-	-	268 52.14 10.12 5.65 2.37	415 47.11 15.68 8.74 3.66	-	-	-	-	-	-	-	-	-

Notes: Please refer to the User's Guide for an explanation of data; data is arranged alphabetically by state, then county, then city within each county; table includes counties with populations greater than 49,999 unless noted and cities with populations greater than 9,999 whose Asian and/or NHPI population rates are greater than the national average; (1) Native Hawaiian and other Pacific Islander; (2) excludes Taiwanese; (3) includes Chamorro; (4) county does not meet population threshold but is shown in order to allow inclusion of city

Place	Total population 25 years and over who are 4-year college graduates	Asian population 25 years and over	Asians 25 years and over who are 4-year college graduates	NHPI[1] population 25 years and over	NHPIs[1] 25 years and over who are 4-year college graduates	Asian Indian	Bangladeshi	Cambodian	Chinese[2]	Fijian	Filipino	Guamanian[3]	Hawaiian, Native	Hmong	Indonesian	Japanese	Korean	Laotian	Malaysian	Pakistani	Samoan	Sri Lankan	Taiwanese	Thai	Tongan	Vietnamese
Lincolnwood (village)	4,211 48.22	1,600	933 58.31 58.31 22.16	-	-	273 57.47 29.26 17.06 6.48	-	-	-	-	225 77.59 24.12 14.06 5.34	-	-	-	-	-	192 47.76 20.58 12.00 4.56	-	-	-	-	-	-	-	-	-
Morton Grove (village)	5,670 34.44	3,243	1,867 57.57 57.57 32.93	-	-	490 55.49 26.25 15.11 8.64	-	-	-	-	794 67.29 42.53 24.48 14.00	-	-	-	-	-	308 51.16 16.50 9.50 5.43	-	-	-	-	-	-	-	-	-
Mount Prospect (village)	13,852 35.35	4,457	2,466 55.33 55.33 17.80	-	-	1,165 53.08 47.24 26.14 8.41	-	-	311 78.14 12.61 6.98 2.25	-	212 68.61 8.60 4.76 1.53	-	-	-	-	207 57.66 8.39 4.64 1.49	434 46.52 17.60 9.74 3.13	-	-	-	-	-	-	-	-	-
Niles (village)	5,667 24.85	2,221	1,219 54.89 54.89 21.51	-	-	456 58.16 37.41 20.53 8.05	-	-	-	-	276 67.48 22.64 12.43 4.87	-	-	-	-	-	378 53.09 31.01 17.02 6.67	-	-	-	-	-	-	-	-	-
Northbrook (village)	14,663 62.20	1,978	1,438 72.70 72.70 9.81	-	-	-	-	-	279 79.04 19.40 14.11 1.90	-	-	-	-	-	-	-	693 68.34 48.19 35.04 4.73	-	-	-	-	-	-	-	-	-
Oak Park (village)	22,637 62.12	1,624	1,316 81.03 81.03 5.81	-	-	495 87.61 37.61 30.48 2.19	-	-	220 72.61 16.72 13.55 0.97	-	-	-	-	-	-	-	-	-	-	-	-	-	-	-	-	-
Orland Park (village)	11,035 31.65	1,323	934 70.60 70.60 8.46	-	-	293 75.91 31.37 22.15 2.66	-	-	-	-	342 77.38 36.62 25.85 3.10	-	-	-	-	-	-	-	-	-	-	-	-	-	-	-
Palatine (village)	18,062 41.43	3,479	2,293 65.91 65.91 12.70	-	-	986 70.83 43.00 28.34 5.46	-	-	397 75.19 17.31 11.41 2.20	-	330 61.22 14.39 9.49 1.83	-	-	-	-	-	265 66.75 11.56 7.62 1.47	-	-	-	-	-	-	-	-	-
Prospect Heights (city)	3,332 28.52	418	318 76.08 76.08 9.54	-	-	-	-	-	-	-	-	-	-	-	-	-	-	-	-	-	-	-	-	-	-	-
Rolling Meadows (city)	5,042 30.98	926	588 63.50 63.50 11.66	-	-	249 86.76 42.35 26.89 4.94	-	-	-	-	-	-	-	-	-	-	-	-	-	-	-	-	-	-	-	-

Notes: Please refer to the User's Guide for an explanation of data; data is arranged alphabetically by state, then county, then city within each county; table includes counties with populations greater than 49,999 unless noted and cities with populations greater than 9,999 whose Asian and/or NHPI population rates are greater than the national average; (1) Native Hawaiian and other Pacific Islander; (2) excludes Taiwanese; (3) includes Chamorro; (4) county does not meet population threshold but is shown in order to allow inclusion of city

Place	Total population 25 years and over who are 4-year college graduates	Asian population 25 years and over	Asians 25 years and over who are 4-year college graduates	NHPI[1] population 25 years and over	NHPIs[1] 25 years and over who are 4-year college graduates	Asian Indian	Bangladeshi	Cambodian	Chinese[2]	Fijian	Filipino	Guamanian[3]	Hawaiian, Native	Hmong	Indonesian	Japanese	Korean	Laotian	Malaysian	Pakistani	Samoan	Sri Lankan	Taiwanese	Thai	Tongan	Vietnamese
Schaumburg (village)	20,273 38.88	7,048	4,675 66.33 66.33 23.06	-	-	2,407 76.51 51.49 34.15 11.87	-	-	613 66.20 13.11 8.70 3.02	-	538 72.51 11.51 7.63 2.65	-	-	-	-	286 42.25 6.12 4.06 1.41	562 49.96 12.02 7.97 2.77	-	-	-	-	-	-	-	-	-
Schiller Park (village)	1,104 14.39	487	267 54.83 54.83 24.18	-	-	-	-	-	-	-	-	-	-	-	-	-	-	-	-	-	-	-	-	-	-	-
Skokie (village)	18,851 42.55	8,599	4,839 56.27 56.27 25.67	-	-	1,154 52.10 23.85 13.42 6.12	-	-	713 60.42 14.73 8.29 3.78	-	1,269 63.48 26.22 14.76 6.73	-	-	-	-	-	923 51.54 19.07 10.73 4.90	-	-	111 39.78 2.29 1.29 0.59	-	-	-	-	-	-
Streamwood (village)	6,235 26.49	2,239	1,308 58.42 58.42 20.98	-	-	502 60.26 38.38 22.42 8.05	-	-	-	-	476 60.64 36.39 21.26 7.63	-	-	-	-	-	-	-	-	-	-	-	-	-	-	-
Wheeling (village)	7,364 32.15	1,967	1,202 61.11 61.11 16.32	-	-	586 65.04 48.75 29.79 7.96	-	-	-	-	262 69.68 21.80 13.32 3.56	-	-	-	-	-	-	-	-	-	-	-	-	-	-	-
Wilmette (village)	13,347 72.58	1,361	1,022 75.09 75.09 7.66	-	-	-	-	-	225 84.59 22.02 16.53 1.69	-	-	-	-	-	-	142 67.94 13.89 10.43 1.06	348 72.80 34.05 25.57 2.61	-	-	-	-	-	-	-	-	-
DeKalb County	13,102 26.79	674	421 62.46 62.46 3.21	-	-	103 55.98 24.47 15.28 0.79	-	-	-	-	-	-	-	-	-	-	-	-	-	-	-	-	-	-	-	-
DeKalb (city)	6,490 37.96	542	356 65.68 65.68 5.49	-	-	97 61.01 27.25 17.90 1.49	-	-	-	-	-	-	-	-	-	-	-	-	-	-	-	-	-	-	-	-
DuPage County	245,452 41.66	46,209	30,733 66.51 66.51 12.52	-	-	14,096 70.40 45.87 30.50 5.74	-	-	5,237 77.38 17.04 11.33 2.13	-	6,386 66.24 20.78 13.82 2.60	-	-	-	-	777 63.12 2.53 1.68 0.32	1,500 53.44 4.88 3.25 0.61	-	-	903 59.29 2.94 1.95 0.37	-	-	466 84.73 1.52 1.01 0.19	232 81.69 0.75 0.50 0.09	-	343 18.96 1.12 0.74 0.14
Addison (village)	4,350 19.47	1,934	985 50.93 50.93 22.64	-	-	537 49.54 54.52 27.77 12.34	-	-	-	-	198 51.83 20.10 10.24 4.55	-	-	-	-	-	-	-	-	-	-	-	-	-	-	-

Notes: Please refer to the User's Guide for an explanation of data; data is arranged alphabetically by state, then county, then city within each county; table includes counties with populations greater than 49,999 unless noted and cities with populations greater than 9,999 whose Asian and/or NHPI population rates are greater than the national average; (1) Native Hawaiian and other Pacific Islander; (2) excludes Taiwanese; (3) includes Chamorro; (4) county does not meet population threshold but is shown in order to allow inclusion of city

Place	Total population 25 years and over who are 4-year college graduates	Asian population 25 years and over	Asians 25 years and over who are 4-year college graduates	NHPI[1] population 25 years and over	NHPIs[1] 25 years and over who are 4-year college graduates	Asian Indian	Bangladeshi	Cambodian	Chinese[2]	Fijian	Filipino	Guamanian[3]	Hawaiian, Native	Hmong	Indonesian	Japanese	Korean	Laotian	Malaysian	Pakistani	Samoan	Sri Lankan	Taiwanese	Thai	Tongan	Vietnamese
Bartlett (village)	8,858 38.32	1,863	1,103 59.21 59.21 12.45	-	-	598 63.55 54.22 32.10 6.75	-	-	-	-	287 68.33 26.02 15.41 3.24	-	-	-	-	-	-	-	-	-	-	-	-	-	-	-
Bensenville (village)	2,524 19.12	866	569 65.70 65.70 22.54	-	-	342 73.87 60.11 39.49 13.55	-	-	-	-	-	-	-	-	-	-	-	-	-	-	-	-	-	-	-	-
Bloomingdale (village)	5,212 34.38	1,301	831 63.87 63.87 15.94	-	-	427 73.24 51.38 32.82 8.19	-	-	-	-	-	-	-	-	-	-	-	-	-	-	-	-	-	-	-	-
Burr Ridge (village)	3,983 58.21	701	577 82.31 82.31 14.49	-	-	323 87.30 55.98 46.08 8.11	-	-	-	-	-	-	-	-	-	-	-	-	-	-	-	-	-	-	-	-
Carol Stream (village)	7,760 31.98	2,555	1,391 54.44 54.44 17.93	-	-	703 59.78 50.54 27.51 9.06	-	-	-	-	396 61.40 28.47 15.50 5.10	-	-	-	-	-	-	-	-	-	-	-	-	-	-	15 5.64 1.08 0.59 0.19
Darien (city)	7,003 43.53	1,803	1,331 73.82 73.82 19.01	-	-	651 76.50 48.91 36.11 9.30	-	-	-	-	416 74.55 31.25 23.07 5.94	-	-	-	-	-	-	-	-	-	-	-	-	-	-	-
Downers Grove (village)	15,501 46.35	1,981	1,417 71.53 71.53 9.14	-	-	680 75.98 47.99 34.33 4.39	-	-	288 65.75 20.32 14.54 1.86	-	244 70.93 17.22 12.32 1.57	-	-	-	-	-	-	-	-	-	-	-	-	-	-	-
Glen Ellyn (village)	10,409 58.84	822	535 65.09 65.09 5.14	-	-	218 64.69 40.75 26.52 2.09	-	-	-	-	-	-	-	-	-	-	-	-	-	-	-	-	-	-	-	-
Glendale Heights (village)	5,196 26.65	3,867	1,687 43.63 43.63 32.47	-	-	678 44.28 40.19 17.53 13.05	-	-	-	-	660 58.41 39.12 17.07 12.70	-	-	-	-	-	-	-	-	-	-	-	-	-	-	50 9.86 2.96 1.29 0.96
Hinsdale (village)	7,541 68.61	584 -	421 72.09 72.09 5.58	-	-	-	-	-	-	-	-	-	-	-	-	-	-	-	-	-	-	-	-	-	-	-

Notes: Please refer to the User's Guide for an explanation of data; data is arranged alphabetically by state, then county, then city within each county; table includes counties with populations greater than 49,999 unless noted and cities with populations greater than 9,999 whose Asian and/or NHPI population rates are greater than the national average; (1) Native Hawaiian and other Pacific Islander; (2) excludes Taiwanese; (3) includes Chamorro; (4) county does not meet population threshold but is shown in order to allow inclusion of city

Place	Total population 25 years and over who are 4-year college graduates	Asian population 25 years and over	Asians 25 years and over who are 4-year college graduates	NHPI[1] population 25 years and over	NHPIs[1] 25 years and over who are 4-year college graduates	Asian Indian	Bangladeshi	Cambodian	Chinese[2]	Fijian	Filipino	Guamanian[3]	Hawaiian, Native	Hmong	Indonesian	Japanese	Korean	Laotian	Malaysian	Pakistani	Samoan	Sri Lankan	Taiwanese	Thai	Tongan	Vietnamese
Lisle (village)	7,107 50.03	1,388	1,098 79.11 79.11 15.45	-	-	440 91.10 40.07 31.70 6.19	-	-	349 80.23 31.79 25.14 4.91	-	-	-	-	-	-	-	-	-	-	-	-	-	-	-	-	-
Lombard (village)	10,494 36.01	2,041	1,467 71.88 71.88 13.98	-	-	636 73.02 43.35 31.16 6.06	-	-	-	-	378 76.36 25.77 18.52 3.60	-	-	-	-	-	-	-	-	-	-	-	-	-	-	-
Naperville (city)	47,805 60.63	7,267	5,670 78.02 78.02 11.86	-	-	2,367 80.29 41.75 32.57 4.95	-	-	2,002 80.37 35.31 27.55 4.19	-	312 73.58 5.50 4.29 0.65	-	-	-	-	-	332 64.72 5.86 4.57 0.69	-	-	-	-	-	213 80.99 3.76 2.93 0.45	-	-	-
Roselle (village)	5,203 33.96	1,262	846 67.04 67.04 16.26	-	-	484 77.69 57.21 38.35 9.30	-	-	-	-	-	-	-	-	-	-	-	-	-	-	-	-	-	-	-	-
Villa Park (village)	3,391 23.72	555	242 43.60 43.60 7.14	-	-	-	-	-	-	-	-	-	-	-	-	-	-	-	-	-	-	-	-	-	-	-
Warrenville (city)	3,346 39.75	356	278 78.09 78.09 8.31	-	-	-	-	-	-	-	-	-	-	-	-	-	-	-	-	-	-	-	-	-	-	-
Westmont (village)	5,991 34.99	2,078	1,533 73.77 73.77 25.59	-	-	807 85.76 52.64 38.84 13.47	-	-	278 71.65 18.13 13.38 4.64	-	231 62.60 15.07 11.12 3.86	-	-	-	-	-	-	-	-	-	-	-	-	-	-	-
Wheaton (city)	20,247 57.31	1,680	1,126 67.02 67.02 5.56	-	-	545 84.89 48.40 32.44 2.69	-	-	-	-	-	-	-	-	-	-	-	-	-	-	-	-	-	-	-	7 3.52 0.62 0.42 0.03
Woodridge (village)	7,766 39.04	2,289	1,487 64.96 64.96 19.15	-	-	737 67.61 49.56 32.20 9.49	-	-	-	-	473 64.53 31.81 20.66 6.09	-	-	-	-	-	-	-	-	-	-	-	-	-	-	-
Jackson County	10,447 31.99	1,109	864 77.91 77.91 8.27	-	-	-	-	-	206 77.74 23.84 18.58 1.97	-	-	-	-	-	-	-	-	-	-	-	-	-	-	-	-	-

Notes: Please refer to the User's Guide for an explanation of data; data is arranged alphabetically by state, then county, then city within each county; table includes counties with populations greater than 49,999 unless noted and cities with populations greater than 9,999 whose Asian and/or NHPI population rates are greater than the national average; (1) Native Hawaiian and other Pacific Islander; (2) excludes Taiwanese; (3) includes Chamorro; (4) county does not meet population threshold but is shown in order to allow inclusion of city

Place	Total population 25 years and over who are 4-year college graduates	Asian population 25 years and over	Asians 25 years and over who are 4-year college graduates	NHPI[1] population 25 years and over	NHPIs[1] 25 years and over who are 4-year college graduates	Asian Indian	Bangladeshi	Cambodian	Chinese[2]	Fijian	Filipino	Guamanian[3]	Hawaiian, Native	Hmong	Indonesian	Japanese	Korean	Laotian	Malaysian	Pakistani	Samoan	Sri Lankan	Taiwanese	Thai	Tongan	Vietnamese
Carbondale (city)	4,863 47.82	831	636 76.53 76.53 13.08	-	-	-	-	-	-	-	-	-	-	-	-	-	-	-	-	-	-	-	-	-	-	-
Kane County	68,050 27.72	4,380	2,082 47.53 47.53 3.06	-	-	625 66.49 30.02 14.27 0.92	-	-	321 51.52 15.42 7.33 0.47	-	552 61.33 26.51 12.60 0.81	-	-	-	-	-	88 32.12 4.23 2.01 0.13	29 5.10 1.39 0.66 0.04	-	-	-	-	-	-	-	63 19.57 3.03 1.44 0.09
South Elgin (village)	2,546 25.34	507	183 36.09 36.09 7.19	-	-	-	-	-	-	-	-	-	-	-	-	-	-	-	-	-	-	-	-	-	-	-
Kankakee County	9,850 14.96	424	171 40.33 40.33 1.74	-	-	-	-	-	-	-	-	-	-	-	-	-	-	-	-	-	-	-	-	-	-	-
Kendall County	8,678 25.25	366	157 42.90 42.90 1.81	-	-	-	-	-	-	-	-	-	-	-	-	-	-	-	-	-	-	-	-	-	-	-
Knox County	5,545 14.57	175	86 49.14 49.14 1.55	-	-	-	-	-	-	-	-	-	-	-	-	-	-	-	-	-	-	-	-	-	-	-
La Salle County	9,889 13.29	354	231 65.25 65.25 2.34	-	-	-	-	-	-	-	-	-	-	-	-	-	-	-	-	-	-	-	-	-	-	-
Lake County	153,726 38.60	16,241	10,516 64.75 64.75 6.84	-	-	2,676 74.75 25.45 16.48 1.74	-	-	2,558 79.39 24.32 15.75 1.66	-	2,412 54.51 22.94 14.85 1.57	-	-	-	-	535 50.42 5.09 3.29 0.35	1,570 62.52 14.93 9.67 1.02	-	-	154 52.38 1.46 0.95 0.10	-	-	-	-	-	181 44.91 1.72 1.11 0.12
Buffalo Grove (village)	15,665 55.90	2,323	1,545 66.51 66.51 9.86	-	-	360 79.65 23.30 15.50 2.30	-	-	289 67.68 18.71 12.44 1.84	-	154 53.47 9.97 6.63 0.98	-	-	-	-	234 59.09 15.15 10.07 1.49	409 65.34 26.47 17.61 2.61	-	-	-	-	-	-	-	-	-
Gages Lake (cdp)	2,521 37.55	277	201 72.56 72.56 7.97	-	-	-	-	-	-	-	-	-	-	-	-	-	-	-	-	-	-	-	-	-	-	-

Notes: Please refer to the User's Guide for an explanation of data; data is arranged alphabetically by state, then county, then city within each county; table includes counties with populations greater than 49,999 unless noted and cities with populations greater than 9,999 whose Asian and/or NHPI population rates are greater than the national average; (1) Native Hawaiian and other Pacific Islander; (2) excludes Taiwanese; (3) includes Chamorro; (4) county does not meet population threshold but is shown in order to allow inclusion of city

Place	Total population 25 years and over who are 4-year college graduates	Asian population 25 years and over	Asians 25 years and over who are 4-year college graduates	NHPI[1] population 25 years and over	NHPIs[1] 25 years and over who are 4-year college graduates	Asian Indian	Bangladeshi	Cambodian	Chinese[2]	Fijian	Filipino	Guamanian[3]	Hawaiian, Native	Hmong	Indonesian	Japanese	Korean	Laotian	Malaysian	Pakistani	Samoan	Sri Lankan	Taiwanese	Thai	Tongan	Vietnamese
Grayslake (village)	5,822 50.81	599	469 78.30 78.30 8.06	-	-	-	-	-	-	-	-	-	-	-	-	-	-	-	-	-	-	-	-	-	-	-
Gurnee (village)	8,771 47.77	1,482	1,047 70.65 70.65 11.94	-	-	363 76.58 34.67 24.49 4.14	-	-	191 75.79 18.24 12.89 2.18	-	338 74.45 32.28 22.81 3.85	-	-	-	-	-	-	-	-	-	-	-	-	-	-	-
Lake Zurich (village)	4,793 43.83	436	298 68.35 68.35 6.22	-	-	-	-	-	-	-	-	-	-	-	-	-	-	-	-	-	-	-	-	-	-	-
Libertyville (village)	7,679 56.15	669	505 75.49 75.49 6.58	-	-	-	-	-	-	-	-	-	-	-	-	-	-	-	-	-	-	-	-	-	-	-
Mundelein (village)	7,412 39.87	1,244	903 72.59 72.59 12.18	-	-	-	-	-	287 80.39 31.78 23.07 3.87	-	272 77.05 30.12 21.86 3.67	-	-	-	-	-	-	-	-	-	-	-	-	-	-	-
Vernon Hills (village)	7,130 54.29	1,509	1,066 70.64 70.64 14.95	-	-	318 94.08 29.83 21.07 4.46	-	-	361 81.31 33.86 23.92 5.06	-	-	-	-	-	-	-	212 49.30 19.89 14.05 2.97	-	-	-	-	-	-	-	-	-
Macon County	12,722 16.92	427	237 55.50 55.50 1.86	-	-	-	-	-	-	-	-	-	-	-	-	-	-	-	-	-	-	-	-	-	-	-
Madison County	32,759 19.22	831	419 50.42 50.42 1.28	-	-	195 75.88 46.54 23.47 0.60	-	-	-	-	-	-	-	-	-	-	-	-	-	-	-	-	-	-	-	-
McHenry County	45,436 27.74	2,188	1,220 55.76 55.76 2.69	-	-	327 58.19 26.80 14.95 0.72	-	-	240 65.04 19.67 10.97 0.53	-	417 65.16 34.18 19.06 0.92	-	-	-	-	-	-	-	-	-	-	-	-	-	-	-
McLean County	31,546 36.17	1,934	1,417 73.27 73.27 4.49	-	-	679 88.07 47.92 35.11 2.15	-	-	324 72.16 22.87 16.75 1.03	-	-	-	-	-	-	-	-	-	-	-	-	-	-	-	-	-

Notes: Please refer to the User's Guide for an explanation of data; data is arranged alphabetically by state, then county, then city within each county; table includes counties with populations greater than 49,999 unless noted and cities with populations greater than 9,999 whose Asian and/or NHPI population rates are greater than the national average; (1) Native Hawaiian and other Pacific Islander; (2) excludes Taiwanese; (3) includes Chamorro; (4) county does not meet population threshold but is shown in order to allow inclusion of city

Place	Total population 25 years and over who are 4-year college graduates	Asian population 25 years and over	Asians 25 years and over who are 4-year college graduates	NHPI[1] population 25 years and over	NHPIs[1] 25 years and over who are 4-year college graduates	Asian Indian	Bangladeshi	Cambodian	Chinese[2]	Fijian	Filipino	Guamanian[3]	Hawaiian, Native	Hmong	Indonesian	Japanese	Korean	Laotian	Malaysian	Pakistani	Samoan	Sri Lankan	Taiwanese	Thai	Tongan	Vietnamese
Peoria County	27,661	2,123	1,461	-	-	640	-	-	485	-	-	-	-	-	-	-	-	-	-	-	-	-	-	-	-	46
	23.34		68.82			89.89			73.37																	21.80
						43.81			33.20																	3.15
			68.82			30.15			22.85																	2.17
			5.28			2.31			1.75																	0.17
Rock Island County	16,889	909	519	-	-	343	-	-	-	-	-	-	-	-	-	-	-	-	-	-	-	-	-	-	-	-
	17.08		57.10			88.63																				
						66.09																				
			57.10			37.73																				
			3.07			2.03																				
St. Clair County	31,362	1,575	534	-	-	-	-	-	-	-	146	-	-	-	-	-	86	-	-	-	-	-	-	-	-	-
	19.27		33.90								34.27						25.90									
											27.34						16.10									
			33.90								9.27						5.46									
			1.70								0.47						0.27									
Sangamon County	36,152	1,332	848	-	-	370	-	-	171	-	-	-	-	-	-	-	-	-	-	-	-	-	-	-	-	-
	28.55		63.66			85.45			63.57																	
						43.63			20.17																	
			63.66			27.78			12.84																	
			2.35			1.02			0.47																	
Tazewell County	15,722	402	123	-	-	-	-	-	-	-	-	-	-	-	-	-	-	-	-	-	-	-	-	-	-	-
	18.14		30.60																							
			30.60																							
			0.78																							
Vermilion County	6,945	316	196	-	-	-	-	-	-	-	-	-	-	-	-	-	-	-	-	-	-	-	-	-	-	-
	12.45		62.03																							
			62.03																							
			2.82																							
Will County	79,270	6,979	4,106	-	-	1,131	-	-	590	-	1,352	-	-	-	-	-	246	-	-	164	-	-	-	-	-	98
	25.50		58.83			64.78			61.46		64.84						48.14			76.64						28.24
						27.55			14.37		32.93						5.99			3.99						2.39
			58.83			16.21			8.45		19.37						3.52			2.35						1.40
			5.18			1.43			0.74		1.71						0.31			0.21						0.12
Bolingbrook (village)	9,839	2,417	1,271	-	-	384	-	-	-	-	507	-	-	-	-	-	-	-	-	-	-	-	-	-	-	-
	29.22		52.59			58.81					61.31															
						30.21					39.89															
			52.59			15.89					20.98															
			12.92			3.90					5.15															
Winnebago County	35,226	2,674	992	-	-	310	-	-	-	-	226	-	-	-	-	-	59	52	-	-	-	-	-	-	-	55
	19.38		37.10			73.46					61.58						22.43	7.06								14.36
						31.25					22.78						5.95	5.24								5.54
			37.10			11.59					8.45						2.21	1.94								2.06
			2.82			0.88					0.64						0.17	0.15								0.16
INDIANA	755,613	35,529	20,602	929	162	6,276	-	30	4,934	-	2,713	65	29	-	-	1,624	2,349	93	-	268	-	-	449	214	-	586
	19.41		57.99		17.44	74.11		11.11	67.20		57.41	25.90	7.97			49.30	54.53	15.79		72.04			86.85	33.75		20.68
						30.46		0.15	23.95		13.17	40.12	17.90			7.88	11.40	0.45		1.30			2.18	1.04		2.84
			57.99		17.44	17.66		0.08	13.89		7.64	7.00	3.12			4.57	6.61	0.26		0.75			1.26	0.60		1.65
			2.73		0.02	0.83		<0.01	0.65		0.36	0.01	<0.01			0.21	0.31	0.01		0.04			0.06	0.03		0.08

Notes: Please refer to the User's Guide for an explanation of data; data is arranged alphabetically by state, then county, then city within each county; table includes counties with populations greater than 49,999 unless noted and cities with populations greater than 9,999 whose Asian and/or NHPI population rates are greater than the national average; (1) Native Hawaiian and other Pacific Islander; (2) excludes Taiwanese; (3) includes Chamorro; (4) county does not meet population threshold but is shown in order to allow inclusion of city

Place	Total population 25 years and over who are 4-year college graduates	Asian population 25 years and over	Asians 25 years and over who are 4-year college graduates	NHPI[1] population 25 years and over	NHPIs[1] 25 years and over who are 4-year college graduates	Asian Indian	Bangladeshi	Cambodian	Chinese[2]	Fijian	Filipino	Guamanian[3]	Hawaiian, Native	Hmong	Indonesian	Japanese	Korean	Laotian	Malaysian	Pakistani	Samoan	Sri Lankan	Taiwanese	Thai	Tongan	Vietnamese
Allen County	47,392 22.70	2,868	1,141 39.78 39.78 2.41	-	-	469 70.21 41.10 16.35 0.99	-	-	176 48.48 15.43 6.14 0.37	-	130 35.71 11.39 4.53 0.27	-	-	-	-	-	-	-	-	-	-	-	-	-	-	53 11.04 4.65 1.85 0.11
Bartholomew County	10,379 22.03	841	614 73.01 73.01 5.92	-	-	270 95.74 43.97 32.10 2.60	-	-	-	-	-	-	-	-	-	-	-	-	-	-	-	-	-	-	-	-
Clark County	9,239 14.35	335	154 45.97 45.97 1.67	-	-	-	-	-	-	-	-	-	-	-	-	-	-	-	-	-	-	-	-	-	-	-
Delaware County	14,763 20.38	385	271 70.39 70.39 1.84	-	-	-	-	-	-	-	-	-	-	-	-	-	-	-	-	-	-	-	-	-	-	-
Elkhart County	17,509 15.51	968	352 36.36 36.36 2.01	-	-	-	-	-	-	-	-	-	-	-	-	-	-	-	-	-	-	-	-	-	-	-
Grant County	6,671 14.07	258	142 55.04 55.04 2.13	-	-	-	-	-	-	-	-	-	-	-	-	-	-	-	-	-	-	-	-	-	-	-
Hamilton County	56,909 48.87	2,670	1,865 69.85 69.85 3.28	-	-	538 81.52 28.85 20.15 0.95	-	-	441 75.64 23.65 16.52 0.77	-	-	-	-	-	-	-	-	-	-	-	-	-	-	-	-	-
Carmel (city)	14,369 58.41	1,000	676 67.60 67.60 4.70	-	-	-	-	-	-	-	-	-	-	-	-	-	-	-	-	-	-	-	-	-	-	-
Hendricks County	15,644 23.11	476	253 53.15 53.15 1.62	-	-	-	-	-	-	-	-	-	-	-	-	-	-	-	-	-	-	-	-	-	-	-
Howard County	10,163 18.08	484	280 57.85 57.85 2.76	-	-	-	-	-	-	-	-	-	-	-	-	-	-	-	-	-	-	-	-	-	-	-

Notes: Please refer to the User's Guide for an explanation of data; data is arranged alphabetically by state, then county, then city within each county; table includes counties with populations greater than 49,999 unless noted and cities with populations greater than 9,999 whose Asian and/or NHPI population rates are greater than the national average; (1) Native Hawaiian and other Pacific Islander; (2) excludes Taiwanese; (3) includes Chamorro; (4) county does not meet population threshold but is shown in order to allow inclusion of city

Place	Total population 25 years and over who are 4-year college graduates	Asian population 25 years and over	Asians 25 years and over who are 4-year college graduates	NHPI[1] population 25 years and over	NHPIs[1] 25 years and over who are 4-year college graduates	Asian Indian	Bangladeshi	Cambodian	Chinese[2]	Fijian	Filipino	Guamanian[3]	Hawaiian, Native	Hmong	Indonesian	Japanese	Korean	Laotian	Malaysian	Pakistani	Samoan	Sri Lankan	Taiwanese	Thai	Tongan	Vietnamese
Johnson County	17,076 23.09	619	355 57.35 57.35 2.08	-	-	-	-	-	-	-	-	-	-	-	-	-	-	-	-	-	-	-	-	-	-	-
Kosciusko County	6,998 14.86	257	50 19.46 19.46 0.71	-	-	-	-	-	-	-	-	-	-	-	-	-	-	-	-	-	-	-	-	-	-	-
Lake County	50,307 16.22	2,657	1,620 60.97 60.97 3.22	-	-	669 75.59 41.30 25.18 1.33	-	-	210 53.71 12.96 7.90 0.42	-	403 69.36 24.88 15.17 0.80	-	-	-	-	-	193 43.37 11.91 7.26 0.38	-	-	-	-	-	-	-	-	-
Munster (town)	5,900 39.16	649	457 70.42 70.42 7.75	-	-	198 82.16 43.33 30.51 3.36	-	-	-	-	-	-	-	-	-	-	-	-	-	-	-	-	-	-	-	-
LaPorte County	10,312 13.99	220	72 32.73 32.73 0.70	-	-	-	-	-	-	-	-	-	-	-	-	-	-	-	-	-	-	-	-	-	-	-
Madison County	12,870 14.39	326	48 14.72 14.72 0.37	-	-	-	-	-	-	-	-	-	-	-	-	-	-	-	-	-	-	-	-	-	-	-
Marion County	140,550 25.39	7,867	4,452 56.59 56.59 3.17	-	-	1,643 70.33 36.90 20.88 1.17	-	-	1,063 65.94 23.88 13.51 0.76	-	615 60.29 13.81 7.82 0.44	-	-	-	-	187 44.42 4.20 2.38 0.13	402 50.89 9.03 5.11 0.29	-	-	-	-	-	-	-	-	236 28.06 5.30 3.00 0.17
Monroe County	25,952 39.63	2,068	1,696 82.01 82.01 6.54	-	-	294 83.76 17.33 14.22 1.13	-	-	418 84.79 24.65 20.21 1.61	-	-	-	-	-	-	-	459 80.53 27.06 22.20 1.77	-	-	-	-	-	-	-	-	-
Bloomington (city)	17,174 54.82	1,786	1,496 83.76 83.76 8.71	-	-	223 85.77 14.91 12.49 1.30	-	-	385 83.70 25.74 21.56 2.24	-	-	-	-	-	-	-	441 83.05 29.48 24.69 2.57	-	-	-	-	-	-	-	-	-
Porter County	21,341 22.59	643	301 46.81 46.81 1.41	-	-	-	-	-	-	-	-	-	-	-	-	-	-	-	-	-	-	-	-	-	-	-

Notes: Please refer to the User's Guide for an explanation of data; data is arranged alphabetically by state, then county, then city within each county; table includes counties with populations greater than 49,999 unless noted and cities with populations greater than 9,999 whose Asian and/or NHPI population rates are greater than the national average; (1) Native Hawaiian and other Pacific Islander; (2) excludes Taiwanese; (3) includes Chamorro; (4) county does not meet population threshold but is shown in order to allow inclusion of city

Place	Total population 25 years and over who are 4-year college graduates	Asian population 25 years and over	Asians 25 years and over who are 4-year college graduates	NHPI[1] population 25 years and over	NHPIs[1] 25 years and over who are 4-year college graduates	Asian Indian	Bangladeshi	Cambodian	Chinese[2]	Fijian	Filipino	Guamanian[3]	Hawaiian, Native	Hmong	Indonesian	Japanese	Korean	Laotian	Malaysian	Pakistani	Samoan	Sri Lankan	Taiwanese	Thai	Tongan	Vietnamese
St. Joseph County	39,238 23.63	2,210	1,311 59.32 59.32 3.34	-	-	333 76.55 25.40 15.07 0.85	-	-	406 72.37 30.97 18.37 1.03	-	-	-	-	-	-	-	119 44.74 9.08 5.38 0.30	-	-	-	-	-	-	-	-	-
Tippecanoe County	26,496 33.16	3,381	2,780 82.22 82.22 10.49	-	-	521 84.85 18.74 15.41 1.97	-	-	1,058 87.66 38.06 31.29 3.99	-	-	-	-	-	-	218 83.85 7.84 6.45 0.82	522 86.00 18.78 15.44 1.97	-	-	-	-	-	-	-	-	-
West Lafayette (city)	7,080 69.69	1,279	1,163 90.93 90.93 16.43	-	-	292 97.33 25.11 22.83 4.12	-	-	384 93.43 33.02 30.02 5.42	-	-	-	-	-	-	-	-	-	-	-	-	-	-	-	-	-
Vanderburgh County	21,674 19.32	988	547 55.36 55.36 2.52	-	-	-	-	-	-	-	-	-	-	-	-	-	-	-	-	-	-	-	-	-	-	-
Vigo County	14,267 21.39	679	448 65.98 65.98 3.14	-	-	-	-	-	-	-	-	-	-	-	-	-	-	-	-	-	-	-	-	-	-	-
Wayne County	6,501 13.74	248	83 33.47 33.47 1.28	-	-	-	-	-	-	-	-	-	-	-	-	-	-	-	-	-	-	-	-	-	-	-
IOWA	402,090 21.21	20,157	8,642 42.87 42.87 2.15	440	94 21.36 21.36 0.02	2,507 78.59 29.01 12.44 0.62	-	3 0.80 0.03 0.01 <0.01	2,550 72.63 29.51 12.65 0.63	-	646 40.48 7.48 3.20 0.16	-	-	-	-	465 54.13 5.38 2.31 0.12	1,038 51.18 12.01 5.15 0.26	224 10.37 2.59 1.11 0.06	-	159 87.85 1.84 0.79 0.04	-	-	216 77.98 2.50 1.07 0.05	176 26.04 2.04 0.87 0.04	-	332 7.53 3.84 1.65 0.08
Black Hawk County	18,018 22.98	822	496 60.34 60.34 2.75	-	-	-	-	-	-	-	-	-	-	-	-	-	-	-	-	-	-	-	-	-	-	-
Buena Vista County[4]	2,382 18.70	475	68 14.32 14.32 2.85	-	-	-	-	-	-	-	-	-	-	-	-	-	-	35 11.86 51.47 7.37 1.47	-	-	-	-	-	-	-	-
Storm Lake (city)	1,141 19.51	412	67 16.26 16.26 5.87	-	-	-	-	-	-	-	-	-	-	-	-	-	-	35 12.64 52.24 8.50 3.07	-	-	-	-	-	-	-	-

Notes: Please refer to the User's Guide for an explanation of data; data is arranged alphabetically by state, then county, then city within each county; table includes counties with populations greater than 49,999 unless noted and cities with populations greater than 9,999 whose Asian and/or NHPI population rates are greater than the national average; (1) Native Hawaiian and other Pacific Islander; (2) excludes Taiwanese; (3) includes Chamorro; (4) county does not meet population threshold but is shown in order to allow inclusion of city

Place	Total population 25 years and over who are 4-year college graduates	Asian population 25 years and over	Asians 25 years and over who are 4-year college graduates	NHPI[1] population 25 years and over	NHPIs[1] 25 years and over who are 4-year college graduates	Asian Indian	Bangladeshi	Cambodian	Chinese[2]	Fijian	Filipino	Guamanian[3]	Hawaiian, Native	Hmong	Indonesian	Japanese	Korean	Laotian	Malaysian	Pakistani	Samoan	Sri Lankan	Taiwanese	Thai	Tongan	Vietnamese
Johnson County	29,920 47.60	2,618	2,000 76.39 76.39 6.68	-	-	381 79.38 19.05 14.55 1.27	-	-	850 90.23 42.50 32.47 2.84	-	-	-	-	-	-	-	320 85.56 16.00 12.22 1.07	-	-	-	-	-	-	-	-	-
Coralville (city)	4,906 51.79	418	315 75.36 75.36 6.42	-	-	-	-	-	-	-	-	-	-	-	-	-	-	-	-	-	-	-	-	-	-	-
Iowa City (city)	17,848 55.89	2,030	1,576 77.64 77.64 8.83	-	-	307 84.34 19.48 15.12 1.72	-	-	739 90.23 46.89 36.40 4.14	-	-	-	-	-	-	-	211 85.43 13.39 10.39 1.18	-	-	-	-	-	-	-	-	-
Linn County	34,357 27.73	1,538	848 55.14 55.14 2.47	-	-	526 93.93 62.03 34.20 1.53	-	-	-	-	-	-	-	-	-	-	11 13.75 1.30 0.72 0.03	-	-	-	-	-	-	-	-	-
Polk County	72,357 29.72	5,633	1,593 28.28 28.28 2.20	-	-	575 67.09 36.10 10.21 0.79	-	0 0.00 0.00 0.00 0.00	468 65.55 29.38 8.31 0.65	-	-	-	-	-	-	-	122 31.12 7.66 2.17 0.17	87 9.19 5.46 1.54 0.12	-	-	-	-	-	30 11.86 1.88 0.53 0.04	-	135 8.24 8.47 2.40 0.19
Pottawattamie County	8,571 15.03	346	126 36.42 36.42 1.47	-	-	-	-	-	-	-	-	-	-	-	-	-	-	-	-	-	-	-	-	-	-	-
Scott County	25,408 24.87	1,402	504 35.95 35.95 1.98	-	-	-	-	-	-	-	-	-	-	-	-	-	-	-	-	-	-	-	-	-	-	33 5.51 6.55 2.35 0.13
Story County	18,756 44.50	1,969	1,583 80.40 80.40 8.44	-	-	282 85.71 17.81 14.32 1.50	-	-	648 84.49 40.93 32.91 3.45	-	-	-	-	-	-	-	312 81.04 19.71 15.85 1.66	-	-	-	-	-	-	-	-	-
Ames (city)	13,438 58.60	1,895	1,532 80.84 80.84 11.40	-	-	261 84.74 17.04 13.77 1.94	-	-	632 84.15 41.25 33.35 4.70	-	-	-	-	-	-	-	312 81.68 20.37 16.46 2.32	-	-	-	-	-	-	-	-	-
Woodbury County	12,274 18.90	1,367	163 11.92 11.92 1.33	-	-	-	-	-	-	-	-	-	-	-	-	-	-	-	-	-	-	-	-	-	-	36 3.97 22.09 2.63 0.29

Notes: Please refer to the User's Guide for an explanation of data; data is arranged alphabetically by state, then county, then city within each county; table includes counties with populations greater than 49,999 unless noted and cities with populations greater than 9,999 whose Asian and/or NHPI population rates are greater than the national average; (1) Native Hawaiian and other Pacific Islander; (2) excludes Taiwanese; (3) includes Chamorro; (4) county does not meet population threshold but is shown in order to allow inclusion of city

Place	Total population 25 years and over who are 4-year college graduates	Asian population 25 years and over	Asians 25 years and over who are 4-year college graduates	NHPI[1] population 25 years and over	NHPIs[1] 25 years and over who are 4-year college graduates	Asian Indian	Bangladeshi	Cambodian	Chinese[2]	Fijian	Filipino	Guamanian[3]	Hawaiian, Native	Hmong	Indonesian	Japanese	Korean	Laotian	Malaysian	Pakistani	Samoan	Sri Lankan	Taiwanese	Thai	Tongan	Vietnamese
KANSAS	438,978	27,227	11,020	714	151	3,458	-	17	2,896	-	1,071	-	66	17	-	601	974	70	-	304	-	-	231	208	-	677
	25.80		40.47		21.15	71.95		4.62	62.66		44.24		25.88	5.43		45.60	35.05	4.41		67.26			68.14	48.04		10.42
						31.38		0.15	26.28		9.72		43.71	0.15		5.45	8.84	0.64		2.76			2.10	1.89		6.14
			40.47		21.15	12.70		0.06	10.64		3.93		9.24	0.06		2.21	3.58	0.26		1.12			0.85	0.76		2.49
			2.51		0.03	0.79		<0.01	0.66		0.24		0.02	<0.01		0.14	0.22	0.02		0.07			0.05	0.05		0.15
Cowley County[4]	4,198	318	10	-	-	-	-	-	-	-	-	-	-	-	-	-	-	0	-	-	-	-	-	-	-	-
	18.27		3.14															0.00								
																		0.00								
			3.14															0.00								
			0.24															0.00								
Winfield (city)	1,868	280	5	-	-	-	-	-	-	-	-	-	-	-	-	-	-	0	-	-	-	-	-	-	-	-
	24.92		1.79															0.00								
																		0.00								
			1.79															0.00								
			0.27															0.00								
Douglas County	22,732	1,729	1,233	-	-	187	-	-	510	-	-	-	-	-	-	-	199	-	-	-	-	-	-	-	-	-
	42.68		71.31			83.11			84.58								72.89									
						15.17			41.36								16.14									
			71.31			10.82			29.50								11.51									
			5.42			0.82			2.24								0.88									
Lawrence (city)	19,417	1,706	1,218	-	-	179	-	-	510	-	-	-	-	-	-	-	199	-	-	-	-	-	-	-	-	-
	47.66		71.40			82.49			84.58								73.43									
						14.70			41.87								16.34									
			71.40			10.49			29.89								11.66									
			6.27			0.92			2.63								1.02									
Johnson County	141,219	8,235	4,945	-	-	2,199	-	-	1,101	-	432	-	-	-	-	184	371	44	-	-	-	-	-	-	-	162
	47.74		60.05			80.20			61.85		66.67					51.40	43.54	10.16								20.96
						44.47			22.26		8.74					3.72	7.50	0.89								3.28
			60.05			26.70			13.37		5.25					2.23	4.51	0.53								1.97
			3.50			1.56			0.78		0.31					0.13	0.26	0.03								0.11
Overland Park (city)	52,397	3,756	2,549	-	-	1,198	-	-	581	-	-	-	-	-	-	-	184	-	-	-	-	-	-	-	-	85
	52.15		67.86			89.27			64.70								46.35									25.60
						47.00			22.79								7.22									3.33
			67.86			31.90			15.47								4.90									2.26
			4.86			2.29			1.11								0.35									0.16
Leavenworth County	10,338	556	131	-	-	-	-	-	-	-	-	-	-	-	-	-	-	-	-	-	-	-	-	-	-	-
	23.08		23.56																							
			23.56																							
			1.27																							
Riley County	11,896	1,262	885	-	-	-	-	-	448	-	-	-	-	-	-	-	145	-	-	-	-	-	-	-	-	-
	40.52		70.13						88.36								54.92									
									50.62								16.38									
			70.13						35.50								11.49									
			7.44						3.77								1.22									
Manhattan (city)	9,777	1,110	841	-	-	-	-	-	448	-	-	-	-	-	-	-	-	-	-	-	-	-	-	-	-	-
	48.20		75.77						90.87																	
									53.27																	
			75.77						40.36																	
			8.60						4.58																	

Notes: Please refer to the User's Guide for an explanation of data; data is arranged alphabetically by state, then county, then city within each county; table includes counties with populations greater than 49,999 unless noted and cities with populations greater than 9,999 whose Asian and/or NHPI population rates are greater than the national average; (1) Native Hawaiian and other Pacific Islander; (2) excludes Taiwanese; (3) includes Chamorro; (4) county does not meet population threshold but is shown in order to allow inclusion of city

Place	Total population 25 years and over who are 4-year college graduates	Asian population 25 years and over	Asians 25 years and over who are 4-year college graduates	NHPI[1] population 25 years and over	NHPIs[1] 25 years and over who are 4-year college graduates	Asian Indian	Bangladeshi	Cambodian	Chinese[2]	Fijian	Filipino	Guamanian[3]	Hawaiian, Native	Hmong	Indonesian	Japanese	Korean	Laotian	Malaysian	Pakistani	Samoan	Sri Lankan	Taiwanese	Thai	Tongan	Vietnamese
Saline County	7,058	555	67	-	-	-	-	-	-	-	-	-	-	-	-	-	-	-	-	-	-	-	-	-	-	36
	20.35		12.07																							15.25
																										53.73
			12.07																							6.49
			0.95																							0.51
Sedgwick County	71,818	8,357	1,983	230	60	473	-	12	415	-	186	-	-	-	-	-	115	0	-	-	-	-	-	-	-	370
	25.41		23.73		26.09	63.32		4.86	45.45		33.94						31.59	0.00								9.58
						23.85		0.61	20.93		9.38						5.80	0.00								18.66
			23.73		26.09	5.66		0.14	4.97		2.23						1.38	0.00								4.43
			2.76		0.08	0.66		0.02	0.58		0.26						0.16	0.00								0.52
Wichita (city)	54,692	7,492	1,835	-	-	432	-	-	394	-	170	-	-	-	-	-	107	0	-	-	-	-	-	-	-	352
	25.26		24.49			61.54			46.46		38.64						34.19	0.00								9.60
						23.54			21.47		9.26						5.83	0.00								19.18
			24.49			5.77			5.26		2.27						1.43	0.00								4.70
			3.36			0.79			0.72		0.31						0.20	0.00								0.64
Shawnee County	29,094	911	460	-	-	-	-	-	-	-	-	-	-	-	-	-	-	-	-	-	-	-	-	-	-	-
	26.04		50.49																							
			50.49																							
			1.58																							
Wyandotte County	11,636	1,062	232	-	-	-	-	-	-	-	-	-	-	6	-	-	-	-	-	-	-	-	-	-	-	-
	12.04		21.85											2.33												
														2.59												
			21.85											0.56												
			1.99											0.05												
KENTUCKY	453,469	18,667	9,940	649	96	3,169	-	-	2,273	-	1,022	17	-	-	-	1,047	982	-	-	284	-	-	-	218	-	300
	17.14		53.25		14.79	73.46			65.11		46.24	8.59				46.91	38.00			86.32				68.13		15.97
						31.88			22.87		10.28	17.71				10.53	9.88			2.86				2.19		3.02
			53.25		14.79	16.98			12.18		5.47	2.62				5.61	5.26			1.52				1.17		1.61
			2.19		0.02	0.70			0.50		0.23	<0.01				0.23	0.22			0.06				0.05		0.07
Boone County	12,364	685	442	-	-	-	-	-	-	-	-	-	-	-	-	216	-	-	-	-	-	-	-	-	-	-
	22.83		64.53													64.67										
																48.87										
			64.53													31.53										
			3.57													1.75										
Campbell County	11,748	329	181	-	-	-	-	-	-	-	-	-	-	-	-	-	-	-	-	-	-	-	-	-	-	-
	20.54		55.02																							
			55.02																							
			1.54																							
Christian County	5,028	300	125	-	-	-	-	-	-	-	-	-	-	-	-	-	-	-	-	-	-	-	-	-	-	-
	12.46		41.67																							
			41.67																							
			2.49																							
Fayette County	59,615	3,793	2,580	-	-	649	-	-	993	-	-	-	-	-	-	241	-	-	-	-	-	-	-	-	-	-
	35.65		68.02			80.72			81.53							45.22										
						25.16			38.49							9.34										
			68.02			17.11			26.18							6.35										
			4.33			1.09			1.67							0.40										

Notes: Please refer to the User's Guide for an explanation of data; data is arranged alphabetically by state, then county, then city within each county; table includes counties with populations greater than 49,999 unless noted and cities with populations greater than 9,999 whose Asian and/or NHPI population rates are greater than the national average; (1) Native Hawaiian and other Pacific Islander; (2) excludes Taiwanese; (3) includes Chamorro; (4) county does not meet population threshold but is shown in order to allow inclusion of city

Place	Total population 25 years and over who are 4-year college graduates	Asian population 25 years and over	Asians 25 years and over who are 4-year college graduates	NHPI[1] population 25 years and over	NHPIs[1] 25 years and over who are 4-year college graduates	Asian Indian	Bangladeshi	Cambodian	Chinese[2]	Fijian	Filipino	Guamanian[3]	Hawaiian, Native	Hmong	Indonesian	Japanese	Korean	Laotian	Malaysian	Pakistani	Samoan	Sri Lankan	Taiwanese	Thai	Tongan	Vietnamese
Hardin County	8,967 15.37	1,290	411 31.86 31.86 4.58	-	-	-	-	-	-	-	-	-	-	-	-	-	102 17.44 24.82 7.91 1.14	-	-	-	-	-	-	-	-	-
Radcliff (city)	1,835 13.43	718	222 30.92 30.92 12.10	-	-	-	-	-	-	-	-	-	-	-	-	-	-	-	-	-	-	-	-	-	-	-
Jefferson County	115,317 24.84	6,046	3,113 51.49 51.49 2.70	-	-	1,253 77.73 40.25 20.72 1.09	-	-	581 56.79 18.66 9.61 0.50	-	377 50.60 12.11 6.24 0.33	-	-	-	-	81 26.82 2.60 1.34 0.07	298 42.45 9.57 4.93 0.26	-	-	-	-	-	-	-	-	187 17.86 6.01 3.09 0.16
Kenton County	22,375 22.90	519	226 43.55 43.55 1.01	-	-	-	-	-	-	-	-	-	-	-	-	-	-	-	-	-	-	-	-	-	-	-
Madison County	9,196 21.83	322	217 67.39 67.39 2.36	-	-	-	-	-	-	-	-	-	-	-	-	-	-	-	-	-	-	-	-	-	-	-
Warren County	13,846 24.69	599	302 50.42 50.42 2.18	-	-	-	-	-	-	-	-	-	-	-	-	-	-	-	-	-	-	-	-	-	-	-
LOUISIANA	519,778 18.73	33,366	11,889 35.63 35.63 2.29	833	155 18.61 18.61 0.03	3,591 67.35 30.20 10.76 0.69	-	-	2,711 58.77 22.80 8.13 0.52	-	1,372 40.35 11.54 4.11 0.26	30 9.68 19.35 3.60 0.01	40 16.81 25.81 4.80 0.01	-	-	397 36.96 3.34 1.19 0.08	610 34.56 5.13 1.83 0.12	34 4.91 0.29 0.10 0.01	-	399 68.79 3.36 1.20 0.08	-	-	236 66.29 1.99 0.71 0.05	138 26.19 1.16 0.41 0.03	-	1,862 13.68 15.66 5.58 0.36
Ascension Parish	6,709 14.50	203	53 26.11 26.11 0.79	-	-	-	-	-	-	-	-	-	-	-	-	-	-	-	-	-	-	-	-	-	-	-
Bossier Parish	11,097 18.12	749	187 24.97 24.97 1.69	-	-	-	-	-	-	-	-	-	-	-	-	-	-	-	-	-	-	-	-	-	-	-
Caddo Parish	32,683 20.55	1,247	557 44.67 44.67 1.70	-	-	215 69.81 38.60 17.24 0.66	-	-	-	-	-	-	-	-	-	-	-	-	-	-	-	-	-	-	-	-

Notes: Please refer to the User's Guide for an explanation of data; data is arranged alphabetically by state, then county, then city within each county; table includes counties with populations greater than 49,999 unless noted and cities with populations greater than 9,999 whose Asian and/or NHPI population rates are greater than the national average; (1) Native Hawaiian and other Pacific Islander; (2) excludes Taiwanese; (3) includes Chamorro; (4) county does not meet population threshold but is shown in order to allow inclusion of city

Place	Total population 25 years and over who are 4-year college graduates	Asian population 25 years and over	Asians 25 years and over who are 4-year college graduates	NHPI[1] population 25 years and over	NHPIs[1] 25 years and over who are 4-year college graduates	Asian Indian	Bangladeshi	Cambodian	Chinese[2]	Fijian	Filipino	Guamanian[3]	Hawaiian, Native	Hmong	Indonesian	Japanese	Korean	Laotian	Malaysian	Pakistani	Samoan	Sri Lankan	Taiwanese	Thai	Tongan	Vietnamese
Calcasieu Parish	19,317	766	286	-	-	-	-	-	-	-	-	-	-	-	-	-	-	-	-	-	-	-	-	-	-	-
	16.86		37.34																							
			37.34																							
			1.48																							
East Baton Rouge Parish	75,487	4,903	2,540	-	-	913	-	-	798	-	148	-	-	-	-	-	-	-	-	-	-	-	-	-	-	271
	30.77		51.81			80.23			73.68		59.44															15.19
						35.94			31.42		5.83															10.67
			51.81			18.62			16.28		3.02															5.53
			3.36			1.21			1.06		0.20															0.36
Iberia Parish	4,913	756	52	-	-	-	-	-	-	-	-	-	-	-	-	-	-	9	-	-	-	-	-	-	-	11
	11.17		6.88															1.92								6.75
																		17.31								21.15
			6.88															1.19								1.46
			1.06															0.18								0.22
Jefferson Parish	64,216	8,819	3,151	-	-	897	-	-	589	-	251	-	-	-	-	-	125	-	-	209	-	-	-	-	-	719
	21.49		35.73			76.80			45.20		33.42						27.47			68.08						17.94
						28.47			18.69		7.97						3.97			6.63						22.82
			35.73			10.17			6.68		2.85						1.42			2.37						8.15
			4.91			1.40			0.92		0.39						0.19			0.33						1.12
Gretna (city)	1,269	426	98	-	-	-	-	-	-	-	-	-	-	-	-	-	-	-	-	-	-	-	-	-	-	15
	11.02		23.00																							7.25
																										15.31
			23.00																							3.52
			7.72																							1.18
Harvey (cdp)	1,876	684	154	-	-	-	-	-	-	-	-	-	-	-	-	-	-	-	-	-	-	-	-	-	-	91
	14.04		22.51																							18.61
																										59.09
			22.51																							13.30
			8.21																							4.85
Timberlane (cdp)	1,412	424	84	-	-	-	-	-	-	-	-	-	-	-	-	-	-	-	-	-	-	-	-	-	-	57
	19.06		19.81																							15.66
																										67.86
			19.81																							13.44
			5.95																							4.04
Woodmere (cdp)	1,190	427	125	-	-	-	-	-	-	-	-	-	-	-	-	-	-	-	-	-	-	-	-	-	-	68
	16.87		29.27																							22.52
																										54.40
			29.27																							15.93
			10.50																							5.71
Lafayette Parish	29,590	1,241	575	-	-	161	-	-	-	-	-	-	-	-	-	-	-	-	-	-	-	-	-	-	-	88
	25.47		46.33			49.09																				22.80
						28.00																				15.30
			46.33			12.97																				7.09
			1.94			0.54																				0.30
Lafourche Parish	6,908	346	156	-	-	-	-	-	-	-	-	-	-	-	-	-	-	-	-	-	-	-	-	-	-	-
	12.36		45.09																							
			45.09																							
			2.26																							

Notes: Please refer to the User's Guide for an explanation of data; data is arranged alphabetically by state, then county, then city within each county; table includes counties with populations greater than 49,999 unless noted and cities with populations greater than 9,999 whose Asian and/or NHPI population rates are greater than the national average; (1) Native Hawaiian and other Pacific Islander; (2) excludes Taiwanese; (3) includes Chamorro; (4) county does not meet population threshold but is shown in order to allow inclusion of city

Place	Total population 25 years and over who are 4-year college graduates	Asian population 25 years and over	Asians 25 years and over who are 4-year college graduates	NHPI[1] population 25 years and over	NHPIs[1] 25 years and over who are 4-year college graduates	Asian Indian	Bangladeshi	Cambodian	Chinese[2]	Fijian	Filipino	Guamanian[3]	Hawaiian, Native	Hmong	Indonesian	Japanese	Korean	Laotian	Malaysian	Pakistani	Samoan	Sri Lankan	Taiwanese	Thai	Tongan	Vietnamese
Orleans Parish	77,407	6,330	2,009	-	-	479	-	-	440	-	195	-	-	-	-	-	-	-	-	-	-	-	-	-	-	472
	25.75		31.74			61.41			69.62		49.24															12.29
						23.84			21.90		9.71															23.49
			31.74			7.57			6.95		3.08															7.46
			2.60			0.62			0.57		0.25															0.61
Ouachita Parish	20,104	543	268	-	-	-	-	-	-	-	-	-	-	-	-	-	-	-	-	-	-	-	-	-	-	-
	22.73		49.36																							
			49.36																							
			1.33																							
Rapides Parish	13,205	659	256	-	-	-	-	-	-	-	-	-	-	-	-	-	-	-	-	-	-	-	-	-	-	-
	16.55		38.85																							
			38.85																							
			1.94																							
St. Bernard Parish	3,942	601	122	-	-	-	-	-	-	-	-	-	-	-	-	-	-	-	-	-	-	-	-	-	-	19
	8.93		20.30																							7.98
																										15.57
			20.30																							3.16
			3.09																							0.48
St. Mary Parish	3,122	421	39	-	-	-	-	-	-	-	-	-	-	-	-	-	-	-	-	-	-	-	-	-	-	10
	9.42		9.26																							2.80
																										25.64
			9.26																							2.38
			1.25																							0.32
St. Tammany Parish	34,822	908	358	-	-	-	-	-	-	-	-	-	-	-	-	-	-	-	-	-	-	-	-	-	-	22
	28.32		39.43																							11.06
																										6.15
			39.43																							2.42
			1.03																							0.06
Terrebonne Parish	7,752	445	140	-	-	-	-	-	-	-	-	-	-	-	-	-	-	-	-	-	-	-	-	-	-	18
	12.25		31.46																							10.71
																										12.86
			31.46																							4.04
			1.81																							0.23
Vermilion Parish	3,609	524	21	-	-	-	-	-	-	-	-	-	-	-	-	-	-	-	-	-	-	-	-	-	-	5
	10.74		4.01																							1.11
																										23.81
			4.01																							0.95
			0.58																							0.14
Abbeville (city)	647	318	5	-	-	-	-	-	-	-	-	-	-	-	-	-	-	-	-	-	-	-	-	-	-	5
	8.92		1.57																							1.63
																										100.00
			1.57																							1.57
			0.77																							0.77
Vernon Parish	3,965	681	163	-	-	-	-	-	-	-	-	-	-	-	-	-	12	-	-	-	-	-	-	-	-	-
	13.52		23.94														5.53									
																	7.36									
			23.94														1.76									
			4.11														0.30									

Notes: Please refer to the User's Guide for an explanation of data; data is arranged alphabetically by state, then county, then city within each county; table includes counties with populations greater than 49,999 unless noted and cities with populations greater than 9,999 whose Asian and/or NHPI population rates are greater than the national average; (1) Native Hawaiian and other Pacific Islander; (2) excludes Taiwanese; (3) includes Chamorro; (4) county does not meet population threshold but is shown in order to allow inclusion of city

Place	Total population 25 years and over who are 4-year college graduates	Asian population 25 years and over	Asians 25 years and over who are 4-year college graduates	NHPI[1] population 25 years and over	NHPIs[1] 25 years and over who are 4-year college graduates	Asian Indian	Bangladeshi	Cambodian	Chinese[2]	Fijian	Filipino	Guamanian[3]	Hawaiian, Native	Hmong	Indonesian	Japanese	Korean	Laotian	Malaysian	Pakistani	Samoan	Sri Lankan	Taiwanese	Thai	Tongan	Vietnamese
MAINE	198,960 22.87	4,513	1,470 32.57 32.57 0.74	193	24 12.44 12.44 0.01	359 70.39 24.42 7.95 0.18	-	35 8.16 2.38 0.78 0.02	314 34.20 21.36 6.96 0.16	-	277 35.33 18.84 6.14 0.14	-	-	-	-	170 39.44 11.56 3.77 0.09	98 26.78 6.67 2.17 0.05	-	-	-	-	-	-	-	-	58 9.37 3.95 1.29 0.03
Androscoggin County	9,993 14.37	264	84 31.82 31.82 0.84	-	-	-	-	-	-	-	-	-	-	-	-	-	-	-	-	-	-	-	-	-	-	-
Aroostook County	7,534 14.65	212	88 41.51 41.51 1.17	-	-	-	-	-	-	-	-	-	-	-	-	-	-	-	-	-	-	-	-	-	-	-
Cumberland County	62,068 34.24	1,719	484 28.16 28.16 0.78	-	-	-	-	12 4.86 2.48 0.70 0.02	89 43.63 18.39 5.18 0.14	-	56 28.43 11.57 3.26 0.09	-	-	-	-	-	-	-	-	-	-	-	-	-	-	23 5.75 4.75 1.34 0.04
Hancock County	9,878 27.13	131	58 44.27 44.27 0.59	-	-	-	-	-	-	-	-	-	-	-	-	-	-	-	-	-	-	-	-	-	-	-
Kennebec County	16,402 20.67	413	120 29.06 29.06 0.73	-	-	-	-	-	-	-	-	-	-	-	-	-	-	-	-	-	-	-	-	-	-	-
Oxford County	5,959 15.71	126	37 29.37 29.37 0.62	-	-	-	-	-	-	-	-	-	-	-	-	-	-	-	-	-	-	-	-	-	-	-
Penobscot County	19,406 20.32	507	258 50.89 50.89 1.33	-	-	-	-	-	87 48.07 33.72 17.16 0.45	-	-	-	-	-	-	-	-	-	-	-	-	-	-	-	-	-
York County	29,189 22.88	557	141 25.31 25.31 0.48	-	-	-	-	-	-	-	-	-	-	-	-	-	-	-	-	-	-	-	-	-	-	-
MARYLAND	1,099,360 31.45	139,018	76,464 55.00 55.00 6.96	1,238	325 26.25 26.25 0.03	22,624 69.55 29.59 16.27 2.06	462 59.08 0.60 0.33 0.04	219 20.72 0.29 0.16 0.02	20,485 63.08 26.79 14.74 1.86	-	9,328 51.03 12.20 6.71 0.85	76 18.18 23.38 6.14 0.01	124 33.88 38.15 10.02 0.01	-	321 43.03 0.42 0.23 0.03	3,381 61.32 4.42 2.43 0.31	10,822 42.98 14.15 7.78 0.98	71 14.85 0.09 0.05 0.01	-	1,626 56.34 2.13 1.17 0.15	-	458 55.45 0.60 0.33 0.04	1,189 76.86 1.55 0.86 0.11	904 42.56 1.18 0.65 0.08	-	2,788 25.81 3.65 2.01 0.25

Notes: Please refer to the User's Guide for an explanation of data; data is arranged alphabetically by state, then county, then city within each county; table includes counties with populations greater than 49,999 unless noted and cities with populations greater than 9,999 whose Asian and/or NHPI population rates are greater than the national average; (1) Native Hawaiian and other Pacific Islander; (2) excludes Taiwanese; (3) includes Chamorro; (4) county does not meet population threshold but is shown in order to allow inclusion of city

Place	Total population 25 years and over who are 4-year college graduates	Asian population 25 years and over	Asians 25 years and over who are 4-year college graduates	NHPI[1] population 25 years and over	NHPIs[1] 25 years and over who are 4-year college graduates	Asian Indian	Bangladeshi	Cambodian	Chinese[2]	Fijian	Filipino	Guamanian[3]	Hawaiian, Native	Hmong	Indonesian	Japanese	Korean	Laotian	Malaysian	Pakistani	Samoan	Sri Lankan	Taiwanese	Thai	Tongan	Vietnamese
Allegany County	7,208 14.08	259	152 58.69 58.69 2.11	-	-	-	-	-	-	-	-	-	-	-	-	-	-	-	-	-	-	-	-	-	-	-
Anne Arundel County	100,078 30.60	7,511	3,056 40.69 40.69 3.05	-	-	761 68.13 24.90 10.13 0.76	-	-	482 49.54 15.77 6.42 0.48	-	692 42.09 22.64 9.21 0.69	-	-	-	-	213 34.75 6.97 2.84 0.21	570 23.71 18.65 7.59 0.57	-	-	-	-	-	-	-	-	-
Severn (cdp)	5,834 26.63	1,101	312 28.34 28.34 5.35	-	-	-	-	-	-	-	-	-	-	-	-	-	113 19.89 36.22 10.26 1.94	-	-	-	-	-	-	-	-	-
South Gate (cdp)	3,950 21.47	974	194 19.92 19.92 4.91	-	-	-	-	-	-	-	-	-	-	-	-	-	71 13.98 36.60 7.29 1.80	-	-	-	-	-	-	-	-	-
Baltimore Independent City	80,324 19.14	6,067	3,171 52.27 52.27 3.95	-	-	815 67.86 25.70 13.43 1.01	-	-	838 59.10 26.43 13.81 1.04	-	314 40.26 9.90 5.18 0.39	-	-	-	-	-	556 49.96 17.53 9.16 0.69	-	-	-	-	-	-	-	-	88 16.83 2.78 1.45 0.11
Baltimore County	156,341 30.57	15,318	8,478 55.35 55.35 5.42	-	-	2,593 66.56 30.59 16.93 1.66	-	-	1,905 60.69 22.47 12.44 1.22	-	1,479 64.33 17.45 9.66 0.95	-	-	-	-	324 63.91 3.82 2.12 0.21	1,301 40.85 15.35 8.49 0.83	-	-	246 43.69 2.90 1.61 0.16	-	-	-	-	-	142 19.35 1.67 0.93 0.09
Arbutus (cdp)	3,194 22.99	667	437 65.52 65.52 13.68	-	-	-	-	-	-	-	-	-	-	-	-	-	-	-	-	-	-	-	-	-	-	-
Carney (cdp)	5,887 29.85	1,056	534 50.57 50.57 9.07	-	-	-	-	-	168 70.00 31.46 15.91 2.85	-	-	-	-	-	-	-	150 32.54 28.09 14.20 2.55	-	-	-	-	-	-	-	-	-
Cockeysville (cdp)	6,120 46.87	1,170	739 63.16 63.16 12.08	-	-	-	-	-	-	-	-	-	-	-	-	-	242 52.95 32.75 20.68 3.95	-	-	-	-	-	-	-	-	-
Lutherville-Timonium (cdp)	5,412 46.00	497	288 57.95 57.95 5.32	-	-	-	-	-	-	-	-	-	-	-	-	-	-	-	-	-	-	-	-	-	-	-

Notes: Please refer to the User's Guide for an explanation of data; data is arranged alphabetically by state, then county, then city within each county; table includes counties with populations greater than 49,999 unless noted and cities with populations greater than 9,999 whose Asian and/or NHPI population rates are greater than the national average; (1) Native Hawaiian and other Pacific Islander; (2) excludes Taiwanese; (3) includes Chamorro; (4) county does not meet population threshold but is shown in order to allow inclusion of city

Place	Total population 25 years and over who are 4-year college graduates	Asian population 25 years and over	Asians 25 years and over who are 4-year college graduates	NHPI[1] population 25 years and over	NHPIs[1] 25 years and over who are 4-year college graduates	Asian Indian	Bangladeshi	Cambodian	Chinese[2]	Fijian	Filipino	Guamanian[3]	Hawaiian, Native	Hmong	Indonesian	Japanese	Korean	Laotian	Malaysian	Pakistani	Samoan	Sri Lankan	Taiwanese	Thai	Tongan	Vietnamese
Mays Chapel (cdp)	4,899 60.89	508	303 59.65 59.65 6.18	-	-	-	-	-	-	-	-	-	-	-	-	-	-	-	-	-	-	-	-	-	-	-
Owings Mills (cdp)	5,910 42.84	564	242 42.91 42.91 4.09	-	-	-	-	-	-	-	-	-	-	-	-	-	-	-	-	-	-	-	-	-	-	-
Perry Hall (cdp)	5,928 30.19	991	338 34.11 34.11 5.70	-	-	-	-	-	-	-	-	-	-	-	-	-	56 17.07 16.57 5.65 0.94	-	-	-	-	-	-	-	-	-
Reisterstown (cdp)	5,209 34.92	600	349 58.17 58.17 6.70	-	-	252 72.83 72.21 42.00 4.84	-	-	-	-	-	-	-	-	-	-	-	-	-	-	-	-	-	-	-	-
Rossville (cdp)	1,822 23.49	393	181 46.06 46.06 9.93	-	-	-	-	-	-	-	-	-	-	-	-	-	-	-	-	-	-	-	-	-	-	-
Towson (cdp)	17,988 53.24	1,180	902 76.44 76.44 5.01	-	-	-	-	-	503 82.87 55.76 42.63 2.80	-	-	-	-	-	-	-	-	-	-	-	-	-	-	-	-	-
Woodlawn (cdp)	6,405 27.07	1,317	712 54.06 54.06 11.12	-	-	381 67.31 53.51 28.93 5.95	-	-	-	-	-	-	-	-	-	-	-	-	-	-	-	-	-	-	-	-
Calvert County	10,740 22.48	470	273 58.09 58.09 2.54	-	-	-	-	-	-	-	-	-	-	-	-	-	-	-	-	-	-	-	-	-	-	-
Carroll County	24,483 24.81	736	297 40.35 40.35 1.21	-	-	-	-	-	-	-	-	-	-	-	-	-	-	-	-	-	-	-	-	-	-	-
Cecil County	9,168 16.43	363	185 50.96 50.96 2.02	-	-	-	-	-	-	-	-	-	-	-	-	-	-	-	-	-	-	-	-	-	-	-

Notes: Please refer to the User's Guide for an explanation of data; data is arranged alphabetically by state, then county, then city within each county; table includes counties with populations greater than 49,999 unless noted and cities with populations greater than 9,999 whose Asian and/or NHPI population rates are greater than the national average; (1) Native Hawaiian and other Pacific Islander; (2) excludes Taiwanese; (3) includes Chamorro; (4) county does not meet population threshold but is shown in order to allow inclusion of city

Place	Total population 25 years and over who are 4-year college graduates	Asian population 25 years and over	Asians 25 years and over who are 4-year college graduates	NHPI[1] population 25 years and over	NHPIs[1] 25 years and over who are 4-year college graduates	Asian Indian	Bangladeshi	Cambodian	Chinese[2]	Fijian	Filipino	Guamanian[3]	Hawaiian, Native	Hmong	Indonesian	Japanese	Korean	Laotian	Malaysian	Pakistani	Samoan	Sri Lankan	Taiwanese	Thai	Tongan	Vietnamese
Charles County	15,406 20.01	1,196	379 31.69 31.69 2.46	-	-	-	-	-	-	-	83 26.77 21.90 6.94 0.54	-	-	-	-	-	-	-	-	-	-	-	-	-	-	-
Frederick County	38,176 30.00	2,098	1,142 54.43 54.43 2.99	-	-	265 65.27 23.20 12.63 0.69	-	-	318 57.30 27.85 15.16 0.83	-	-	-	-	-	-	-	117 37.74 10.25 5.58 0.31	-	-	-	-	-	-	-	-	-
Harford County	39,056 27.30	2,079	772 37.13 37.13 1.98	-	-	208 51.23 26.94 10.00 0.53	-	-	-	-	234 62.40 30.31 11.26 0.60	-	-	-	-	-	88 19.09 11.40 4.23 0.23	-	-	-	-	-	-	-	-	-
Howard County	86,437 52.93	12,165	7,579 62.30 62.30 8.77	-	-	2,248 72.77 29.66 18.48 2.60	-	-	1,936 77.13 25.54 15.91 2.24	-	646 66.60 8.52 5.31 0.75	-	-	-	-	-	1,694 45.07 22.35 13.93 1.96	-	-	237 69.91 3.13 1.95 0.27	-	-	-	-	-	199 39.80 2.63 1.64 0.23
Columbia (cdp)	35,159 59.03	4,219	2,905 68.86 68.86 8.26	-	-	908 77.94 31.26 21.52 2.58	-	-	866 77.39 29.81 20.53 2.46	-	239 63.90 8.23 5.66 0.68	-	-	-	-	-	531 56.55 18.28 12.59 1.51	-	-	-	-	-	-	-	-	-
Elkridge (cdp)	6,229 43.79	904	540 59.73 59.73 8.67	-	-	-	-	-	-	-	-	-	-	-	-	-	116 52.73 21.48 12.83 1.86	-	-	-	-	-	-	-	-	-
Ellicott City (cdp)	20,900 56.42	4,147	2,465 59.44 59.44 11.79	-	-	586 81.62 23.77 14.13 2.80	-	-	673 83.40 27.30 16.23 3.22	-	207 78.11 8.40 4.99 0.99	-	-	-	-	-	663 37.10 26.90 15.99 3.17	-	-	117 63.24 4.75 2.82 0.56	-	-	-	-	-	-
North Laurel (cdp)	5,145 39.56	972	546 56.17 56.17 10.61	-	-	186 65.26 34.07 19.14 3.62	-	-	-	-	-	-	-	-	-	-	93 33.82 17.03 9.57 1.81	-	-	-	-	-	-	-	-	-
Savage-Guilford (cdp)	3,243 40.18	499	164 32.87 32.87 5.06	-	-	-	-	-	-	-	-	-	-	-	-	-	-	-	-	-	-	-	-	-	-	-
Montgomery County	324,080 54.56	67,048	40,113 59.83 59.83 12.38	334	131 39.22 39.22 0.04	12,164 74.01 30.32 18.14 3.75	357 62.63 0.89 0.53 0.11	191 25.81 0.48 0.28 0.06	12,572 65.45 31.34 18.75 3.88	-	2,855 56.31 7.12 4.26 0.88	-	-	-	243 37.73 0.61 0.36 0.07	1,899 73.78 4.73 2.83 0.59	5,224 51.08 13.02 7.79 1.61	-	-	631 58.64 1.57 0.94 0.19	-	243 44.83 0.61 0.36 0.07	605 79.61 1.51 0.90 0.19	518 49.33 1.29 0.77 0.16	-	1,710 27.35 4.26 2.55 0.53

Notes: Please refer to the User's Guide for an explanation of data; data is arranged alphabetically by state, then county, then city within each county; table includes counties with populations greater than 49,999 unless noted and cities with populations greater than 9,999 whose Asian and/or NHPI population rates are greater than the national average; (1) Native Hawaiian and other Pacific Islander; (2) excludes Taiwanese; (3) includes Chamorro; (4) county does not meet population threshold but is shown in order to allow inclusion of city

Place	Total population 25 years and over who are 4-year college graduates	Asian population 25 years and over	Asians 25 years and over who are 4-year college graduates	NHPI¹ population 25 years and over	NHPIs¹ 25 years and over who are 4-year college graduates	Asian Indian	Bangladeshi	Cambodian	Chinese²	Fijian	Filipino	Guamanian³	Hawaiian, Native	Hmong	Indonesian	Japanese	Korean	Laotian	Malaysian	Pakistani	Samoan	Sri Lankan	Taiwanese	Thai	Tongan	Vietnamese
Aspen Hill (cdp)	14,737 43.24	3,816	1,653 43.32 43.32 11.22	-	-	357 80.77 21.60 9.36 2.42	-	-	455 36.60 27.53 11.92 3.09	-	225 47.17 13.61 5.90 1.53	-	-	-	-	-	339 48.15 20.51 8.88 2.30	-	-	-	-	-	-	-	-	60 18.81 3.63 1.57 0.41
Bethesda (cdp)	32,155 78.88	3,127	2,399 76.72 76.72 7.46	-	-	626 84.59 26.09 20.02 1.95	-	-	797 86.72 33.22 25.49 2.48	-	150 53.00 6.25 4.80 0.47	-	-	-	-	279 79.04 11.63 8.92 0.87	289 71.18 12.05 9.24 0.90	-	-	-	-	-	-	-	-	-
Calverton (cdp)	4,005 47.14	1,394	758 54.38 54.38 18.93	-	-	305 60.40 40.24 21.88 7.62	-	-	-	-	-	-	-	-	-	-	206 59.03 27.18 14.78 5.14	-	-	-	-	-	-	-	-	-
Colesville (cdp)	8,047 59.28	2,226	1,167 52.43 52.43 14.50	-	-	348 68.77 29.82 15.63 4.32	-	-	302 66.23 25.88 13.57 3.75	-	-	-	-	-	-	-	300 40.54 25.71 13.48 3.73	-	-	-	-	-	-	-	-	76 35.51 6.51 3.41 0.94
Fairland (cdp)	7,434 51.50	2,198	1,047 47.63 47.63 14.08	-	-	392 69.88 37.44 17.83 5.27	-	-	263 62.03 25.12 11.97 3.54	-	-	-	-	-	-	-	240 28.81 22.92 10.92 3.23	-	-	-	-	-	-	-	-	-
Gaithersburg (city)	16,259 46.47	4,815	2,938 61.02 61.02 18.07	-	-	877 76.93 29.85 18.21 5.39	-	-	1,179 66.65 40.13 24.49 7.25	-	158 46.88 5.38 3.28 0.97	-	-	-	-	-	246 39.05 8.37 5.11 1.51	-	-	-	-	-	-	-	-	133 38.44 4.53 2.76 0.82
Germantown (cdp)	15,171 43.20	3,586	2,132 59.45 59.45 14.05	-	-	1,032 70.59 48.41 28.78 6.80	-	-	462 60.95 21.67 12.88 3.05	-	-	-	-	-	-	-	152 57.79 7.13 4.24 1.00	-	-	-	-	-	-	-	-	99 33.45 4.64 2.76 0.65
Montgomery Village (cdp)	12,566 49.70	2,919	1,870 64.06 64.06 14.88	-	-	903 78.52 48.29 30.94 7.19	-	-	335 63.81 17.91 11.48 2.67	-	272 69.57 14.55 9.32 2.16	-	-	-	-	-	-	-	-	-	-	-	-	-	-	103 40.08 5.51 3.53 0.82
North Bethesda (cdp)	18,771 63.72	3,349	2,348 70.11 70.11 12.51	-	-	664 83.10 28.28 19.83 3.54	-	-	746 68.25 31.77 22.28 3.97	-	173 62.68 7.37 5.17 0.92	-	-	-	-	383 89.91 16.31 11.44 2.04	223 52.10 9.50 6.66 1.19	-	-	-	-	-	-	-	-	-
North Potomac (cdp)	10,469 75.41	3,960	3,084 77.88 77.88 29.46	-	-	632 80.82 20.49 15.96 6.04	-	-	1,649 79.43 53.47 41.64 15.75	-	-	-	-	-	-	-	447 71.86 14.49 11.29 4.27	-	-	-	-	-	-	-	-	-

Notes: Please refer to the User's Guide for an explanation of data; data is arranged alphabetically by state, then county, then city within each county; table includes counties with populations greater than 49,999 unless noted and cities with populations greater than 9,999 whose Asian and/or NHPI population rates are greater than the national average; (1) Native Hawaiian and other Pacific Islander; (2) excludes Taiwanese; (3) includes Chamorro; (4) county does not meet population threshold but is shown in order to allow inclusion of city

Place	Total population 25 years and over who are 4-year college graduates	Asian population 25 years and over	Asians 25 years and over who are 4-year college graduates	NHPI[1] population 25 years and over	NHPIs[1] 25 years and over who are 4-year college graduates	Asian Indian	Bangladeshi	Cambodian	Chinese[2]	Fijian	Filipino	Guamanian[3]	Hawaiian, Native	Hmong	Indonesian	Japanese	Korean	Laotian	Malaysian	Pakistani	Samoan	Sri Lankan	Taiwanese	Thai	Tongan	Vietnamese
Olney (cdp)	11,299	1,700	1,014	-	-	235	-	-	311	-	-	-	-	-	-	-	203	-	-	-	-	-	-	-	-	-
	56.24		59.65			54.52			71.66								53.42									
						23.18			30.67								20.02									
			59.65			13.82			18.29								11.94									
			8.97			2.08			2.75								1.80									
Potomac (cdp)	23,879	4,076	3,193	-	-	917	-	-	1,144	-	166	-	-	-	-	-	493	-	-	-	-	-	-	-	-	-
	76.40		78.34			88.77			84.62		58.45						66.80									
						28.72			35.83		5.20						15.44									
			78.34			22.50			28.07		4.07						12.10									
			13.37			3.84			4.79		0.70						2.06									
Redland (cdp)	5,197	1,932	1,015	-	-	325	-	-	276	-	117	-	-	-	-	-	130	-	-	-	-	-	-	-	-	-
	47.88		52.54			60.75			53.80		59.39						45.14									
						32.02			27.19		11.53						12.81									
			52.54			16.82			14.29		6.06						6.73									
			19.53			6.25			5.31		2.25						2.50									
Rockville (city)	17,581	4,640	3,132	-	-	571	-	-	1,357	-	167	-	-	-	-	242	416	-	-	-	-	-	-	-	-	89
	52.93		67.50			80.99			69.34		54.58					81.48	74.42									28.25
						18.23			43.33		5.33					7.73	13.28									2.84
			67.50			12.31			29.25		3.60					5.22	8.97									1.92
			17.81			3.25			7.72		0.95					1.38	2.37									0.51
Silver Spring (cdp)	25,313	4,402	1,742	-	-	474	-	41	256	-	134	-	-	-	-	-	213	-	-	-	-	-	-	-	-	179
	48.48		39.57			52.38		21.13	44.99		36.12						58.52									15.83
						27.21		2.35	14.70		7.69						12.23									10.28
			39.57			10.77		0.93	5.82		3.04						4.84									4.07
			6.88			1.87		0.16	1.01		0.53						0.84									0.71
Takoma Park (city)	5,793	539	291	-	-	-	-	-	-	-	-	-	-	-	-	-	-	-	-	-	-	-	-	-	-	-
	49.63		53.99																							
			53.99																							
			5.02																							
Wheaton-Glenmont (cdp)	13,209	4,862	1,838	-	-	427	-	-	513	-	207	-	-	-	-	-	261	-	-	-	-	-	-	-	-	97
	34.18		37.80			51.88			37.55		46.00						43.87									12.19
						23.23			27.91		11.26						14.20									5.28
			37.80			8.78			10.55		4.26						5.37									2.00
			13.91			3.23			3.88		1.57						1.98									0.73
White Oak (cdp)	6,417	1,620	715	-	-	248	-	-	127	-	-	-	-	-	-	-	127	-	-	-	-	-	-	-	-	77
	46.73		44.14			66.67			42.19								32.48									19.59
						34.69			17.76								17.76									10.77
			44.14			15.31			7.84								7.84									4.75
			11.14			3.86			1.98								1.98									1.20
Prince George's County	136,788	19,849	9,301	-	-	2,677	-	-	1,838	-	2,441	-	-	-	-	210	905	-	-	227	-	-	-	70	-	348
	27.16		46.86			58.81			55.48		44.96					41.50	36.60			53.41				30.43		20.59
						28.78			19.76		26.24					2.26	9.73			2.44				0.75		3.74
			46.86			13.49			9.26		12.30					1.06	4.56			1.14				0.35		1.75
			6.80			1.96			1.34		1.78					0.15	0.66			0.17				0.05		0.25
Adelphi (cdp)	3,567	1,031	546	-	-	-	-	-	-	-	-	-	-	-	-	-	-	-	-	-	-	-	-	-	-	-
	37.00		52.96																							
			52.96																							
			15.31																							

Notes: Please refer to the User's Guide for an explanation of data; data is arranged alphabetically by state, then county, then city within each county; table includes counties with populations greater than 49,999 unless noted and cities with populations greater than 9,999 whose Asian and/or NHPI population rates are greater than the national average; (1) Native Hawaiian and other Pacific Islander; (2) excludes Taiwanese; (3) includes Chamorro; (4) county does not meet population threshold but is shown in order to allow inclusion of city

Place	Total population 25 years and over who are 4-year college graduates	Asian population 25 years and over	Asians 25 years and over who are 4-year college graduates	NHPI[1] population 25 years and over	NHPIs[1] 25 years and over who are 4-year college graduates	Asian Indian	Bangladeshi	Cambodian	Chinese[2]	Fijian	Filipino	Guamanian[3]	Hawaiian, Native	Hmong	Indonesian	Japanese	Korean	Laotian	Malaysian	Pakistani	Samoan	Sri Lankan	Taiwanese	Thai	Tongan	Vietnamese
Beltsville (cdp)	3,438	1,130	552	-	-	201	-	-	-	-	-	-	-	-	-	-	84	-	-	-	-	-	-	-	-	-
	33.23		48.85			67.45											37.50									
						36.41											15.22									
			48.85			17.79											7.43									
			16.06			5.85											2.44									
College Park (city)	3,826	970	678	-	-	188	-	-	241	-	-	-	-	-	-	-	-	-	-	-	-	-	-	-	-	-
	40.72		69.90			69.63			82.53																	
						27.73			35.55																	
			69.90			19.38			24.85																	
			17.72			4.91			6.30																	
Fort Washington (cdp)	5,962	1,674	793	-	-	-	-	-	-	-	588	-	-	-	-	-	-	-	-	-	-	-	-	-	-	-
	36.15		47.37								44.55															
											74.15															
			47.37								35.13															
			13.30								9.86															
Friendly (cdp)	2,038	394	167	-	-	-	-	-	-	-	136	-	-	-	-	-	-	-	-	-	-	-	-	-	-	-
	28.93		42.39								45.95															
											81.44															
			42.39								34.52															
			8.19								6.67															
Glenn Dale (cdp)	3,410	704	421	-	-	-	-	-	-	-	-	-	-	-	-	-	-	-	-	-	-	-	-	-	-	-
	42.50		59.80																							
			59.80																							
			12.35																							
Greenbelt (city)	6,257	1,748	1,051	-	-	367	-	-	336	-	-	-	-	-	-	-	101	-	-	-	-	-	-	-	-	-
	44.94		60.13			78.42			76.36								27.37									
						34.92			31.97								9.61									
			60.13			21.00			19.22								5.78									
			16.80			5.87			5.37								1.61									
Hyattsville (city)	2,564	412	152	-	-	-	-	-	-	-	-	-	-	-	-	-	-	-	-	-	-	-	-	-	-	-
	26.55		36.89																							
			36.89																							
			5.93																							
Lanham-Seabrook (cdp)	3,796	623	274	-	-	-	-	-	-	-	-	-	-	-	-	-	-	-	-	-	-	-	-	-	-	-
	32.20		43.98																							
			43.98																							
			7.22																							
Laurel (city)	5,085	828	430	-	-	-	-	-	-	-	-	-	-	-	-	-	-	-	-	-	-	-	-	-	-	-
	36.18		51.93																							
			51.93																							
			8.46																							
New Carrollton (city)	2,014	338	166	-	-	-	-	-	-	-	-	-	-	-	-	-	-	-	-	-	-	-	-	-	-	-
	25.10		49.11																							
			49.11																							
			8.24																							

Notes: Please refer to the User's Guide for an explanation of data; data is arranged alphabetically by state, then county, then city within each county; table includes counties with populations greater than 49,999 unless noted and cities with populations greater than 9,999 whose Asian and/or NHPI population rates are greater than the national average; (1) Native Hawaiian and other Pacific Islander; (2) excludes Taiwanese; (3) includes Chamorro; (4) county does not meet population threshold but is shown in order to allow inclusion of city

Place	Total population 25 years and over who are 4-year college graduates	Asian population 25 years and over	Asians 25 years and over who are 4-year college graduates	NHPI¹ population 25 years and over	NHPIs¹ 25 years and over who are 4-year college graduates	Asian Indian	Bangladeshi	Cambodian	Chinese²	Fijian	Filipino	Guamanian³	Hawaiian, Native	Hmong	Indonesian	Japanese	Korean	Laotian	Malaysian	Pakistani	Samoan	Sri Lankan	Taiwanese	Thai	Tongan	Vietnamese
South Laurel (cdp)	4,312	829	364	-	-	-	-	-	-	-	-	-	-	-	-	-	-	-	-	-	-	-	-	-	-	-
	32.76		43.91																							
			43.91																							
			8.44																							
St. Mary's County	12,302	1,124	588	-	-	154	-	-	-	-	150	-	-	-	-	-	-	-	-	-	-	-	-	-	-	-
	22.55		52.31			88.00					32.47															
						26.19					25.51															
			52.31			13.70					13.35															
			4.78			1.25					1.22															
Lexington Park (cdp)	1,235	291	96	-	-	-	-	-	-	-	-	-	-	-	-	-	-	-	-	-	-	-	-	-	-	-
	20.82		32.99																							
			32.99																							
			7.77																							
Washington County	13,224	712	234	-	-	-	-	-	-	-	-	-	-	-	-	-	-	-	-	-	-	-	-	-	-	-
	14.63		32.87																							
			32.87																							
			1.77																							
Wicomico County	11,718	1,114	364	-	-	143	-	-	-	-	-	-	-	-	-	-	109	-	-	-	-	-	-	-	-	-
	21.89		32.68			49.31											29.54									
						39.29											29.95									
			32.68			12.84											9.78									
			3.11			1.22											0.93									
Salisbury (city)	2,856	583	149	-	-	-	-	-	-	-	-	-	-	-	-	-	-	-	-	-	-	-	-	-	-	-
	21.14		25.56																							
			25.56																							
			5.22																							
MASSACHUSETTS	1,418,295	145,125	72,334	1,119	266	20,871	267	711	27,165	-	3,936	49	99	9	172	4,851	6,366	129	-	698	-	187	1,219	779	-	3,111
	33.19		49.84		23.77	78.71	80.66	7.66	50.22		59.34	18.49	42.31	2.76	47.78	67.82	67.02	6.73		57.59		53.43	81.16	52.49		15.41
						28.85	0.37	0.98	37.55		5.44	18.42	37.22	0.01	0.24	6.71	8.80	0.18		0.96		0.26	1.69	1.08		4.30
			49.84		23.77	14.38	0.18	0.49	18.72		2.71	4.38	8.85	0.01	0.12	3.34	4.39	0.09		0.48		0.13	0.84	0.54		2.14
			5.10		0.02	1.47	0.02	0.05	1.92		0.28	<0.01	0.01	<0.01	0.01	0.34	0.45	0.01		0.05		0.01	0.09	0.05		0.22
Barnstable County	55,463	904	385	-	-	-	-	-	80	-	-	-	-	-	-	-	-	-	-	-	-	-	-	-	-	-
	33.59		42.59						27.40																	
									20.78																	
			42.59						8.85																	
			0.69						0.14																	
Berkshire County	24,226	626	332	-	-	150	-	-	-	-	-	-	-	-	-	-	-	-	-	-	-	-	-	-	-	-
	25.95		53.04			77.72																				
						45.18																				
			53.04			23.96																				
			1.37			0.62																				
Bristol County	71,117	4,308	1,725	-	-	774	-	43	419	-	141	-	-	-	-	-	121	-	-	-	-	-	-	-	-	47
	19.87		40.04			77.32		4.56	43.06		43.65						48.79									14.69
						44.87		2.49	24.29		8.17						7.01									2.72
			40.04			17.97		1.00	9.73		3.27						2.81									1.09
			2.43			1.09		0.06	0.59		0.20						0.17									0.07

Notes: Please refer to the User's Guide for an explanation of data; data is arranged alphabetically by state, then county, then city within each county; table includes counties with populations greater than 49,999 unless noted and cities with populations greater than 9,999 whose Asian and/or NHPI population rates are greater than the national average; (1) Native Hawaiian and other Pacific Islander; (2) excludes Taiwanese; (3) includes Chamorro; (4) county does not meet population threshold but is shown in order to allow inclusion of city

Place	Total population 25 years and over who are 4-year college graduates	Asian population 25 years and over	Asians 25 years and over who are 4-year college graduates	NHPI[1] population 25 years and over	NHPIs[1] 25 years and over who are 4-year college graduates	Asian Indian	Bangladeshi	Cambodian	Chinese[2]	Fijian	Filipino	Guamanian[3]	Hawaiian, Native	Hmong	Indonesian	Japanese	Korean	Laotian	Malaysian	Pakistani	Samoan	Sri Lankan	Taiwanese	Thai	Tongan	Vietnamese
Essex County	152,225	10,137	4,120	-	-	1,088	-	95	1,246	-	299	-	-	-	-	286	525	8	-	-	-	-	-	-	-	306
	31.25		40.64			66.54		5.56	57.39		57.72					46.43	55.26	3.83								17.63
						26.41		2.31	30.24		7.26					6.94	12.74	0.19								7.43
			40.64			10.73		0.94	12.29		2.95					2.82	5.18	0.08								3.02
			2.71			0.71		0.06	0.82		0.20					0.19	0.34	0.01								0.20
Andover (town)	13,062	1,341	1,089	-	-	293	-	-	451	-	-	-	-	-	-	-	-	-	-	-	-	-	-	-	-	-
	62.51		81.21			86.69			83.67																	
						26.91			41.41																	
			81.21			21.85			33.63																	
			8.34			2.24			3.45																	
Lynn (city)	9,337	2,896	435	-	-	23	-	88	-	-	-	-	-	-	-	-	-	-	-	-	-	-	-	-	-	70
	16.35		15.02			9.79		6.52																		11.61
						5.29		20.23																		16.09
			15.02			0.79		3.04																		2.42
			4.66			0.25		0.94																		0.75
North Andover (town)	8,892	714	552	-	-	-	-	-	167	-	-	-	-	-	-	-	-	-	-	-	-	-	-	-	-	-
	50.32		77.31						73.57																	
									30.25																	
			77.31						23.39																	
			6.21						1.88																	
Franklin County	14,285	344	149	-	-	-	-	-	-	-	-	-	-	-	-	-	-	-	-	-	-	-	-	-	-	-
	29.08		43.31																							
			43.31																							
			1.04																							
Hampden County	60,554	3,595	1,148	-	-	284	-	19	310	-	-	-	-	-	-	-	80	-	-	-	-	-	-	-	-	106
	20.47		31.93			65.59		8.48	43.42								34.33									9.24
						24.74		1.66	27.00								6.97									9.23
			31.93			7.90		0.53	8.62								2.23									2.95
			1.90			0.47		0.03	0.51								0.13									0.18
Hampshire County	35,365	2,014	1,374	-	-	269	-	-	615	-	-	-	-	-	-	-	157	-	-	-	-	-	-	-	-	-
	37.95		68.22			86.50			77.26								86.26									
						19.58			44.76								11.43									
			68.22			13.36			30.54								7.80									
			3.89			0.76			1.74								0.44									
Amherst Center (cdp)	3,203	340	235	-	-	-	-	-	-	-	-	-	-	-	-	-	-	-	-	-	-	-	-	-	-	-
	72.30		69.12																							
			69.12																							
			7.34																							
Amherst (town)	8,876	1,092	765	-	-	-	-	-	410	-	-	-	-	-	-	-	-	-	-	-	-	-	-	-	-	-
	68.67		70.05						79.00																	
									53.59																	
			70.05						37.55																	
			8.62						4.62																	
Middlesex County	438,733	56,096	34,418	-	-	11,316	-	424	13,016	-	1,270	-	-	-	-	2,055	2,946	34	-	180	-	-	629	393	-	1,004
	43.59		61.36			79.24		8.43	66.80		69.97					73.31	72.56	3.76		61.86			81.58	68.47		24.86
						32.88		1.23	37.82		3.69					5.97	8.56	0.10		0.52			1.83	1.14		2.92
			61.36			20.17		0.76	23.20		2.26					3.66	5.25	0.06		0.32			1.12	0.70		1.79
			7.84			2.58		0.10	2.97		0.29					0.47	0.67	0.01		0.04			0.14	0.09		0.23

Notes: Please refer to the User's Guide for an explanation of data; data is arranged alphabetically by state, then county, then city within each county; table includes counties with populations greater than 49,999 unless noted and cities with populations greater than 9,999 whose Asian and/or NHPI population rates are greater than the national average; (1) Native Hawaiian and other Pacific Islander; (2) excludes Taiwanese; (3) includes Chamorro; (4) county does not meet population threshold but is shown in order to allow inclusion of city

Place	Total population 25 years and over who are 4-year college graduates	Asian population 25 years and over	Asians 25 years and over who are 4-year college graduates	NHPI[1] population 25 years and over	NHPIs[1] 25 years and over who are 4-year college graduates	Asian Indian	Bangladeshi	Cambodian	Chinese[2]	Fijian	Filipino	Guamanian[3]	Hawaiian, Native	Hmong	Indonesian	Japanese	Korean	Laotian	Malaysian	Pakistani	Samoan	Sri Lankan	Taiwanese	Thai	Tongan	Vietnamese
Acton (town)	9,354 69.29	1,208	1,062 87.91 87.91 11.35	-	-	422 97.91 39.74 34.93 4.51	-	-	492 88.01 46.33 40.73 5.26	-	-	-	-	-	-	-	-	-	-	-	-	-	-	-	-	-
Arlington (town)	17,121 52.78	1,451	1,074 74.02 74.02 6.27	-	-	-	-	-	422 79.17 39.29 29.08 2.46	-	-	-	-	-	-	-	-	-	-	-	-	-	-	-	-	-
Bedford (town)	5,221 57.40	574	458 79.79 79.79 8.77	-	-	-	-	-	-	-	-	-	-	-	-	-	-	-	-	-	-	-	-	-	-	-
Belmont (cdp)	11,099 63.11	869	690 79.40 79.40 6.22	-	-	-	-	-	310 80.94 44.93 35.67 2.79	-	-	-	-	-	-	-	-	-	-	-	-	-	-	-	-	-
Belmont (town)	11,099 63.11	869	690 79.40 79.40 6.22	-	-	-	-	-	310 80.94 44.93 35.67 2.79	-	-	-	-	-	-	-	-	-	-	-	-	-	-	-	-	-
Burlington (town)	6,827 42.62	1,599	1,272 79.55 79.55 18.63	-	-	894 86.96 70.28 55.91 13.10	-	-		-	-	-	-	-	-	-	-	-	-	-	-	-	-	-	-	-
Cambridge (city)	43,191 65.13	6,739	5,444 80.78 80.78 12.60	-	-	1,169 75.71 21.47 17.35 2.71	-	-	1,770 76.10 32.51 26.27 4.10	-	-	-	-	-	-	708 88.39 13.01 10.51 1.64	995 91.87 18.28 14.76 2.30	-	-	-	-	-	-	-	-	-
Chelmsford (town)	10,403 43.98	1,035	772 74.59 74.59 7.42	-	-	247 91.82 31.99 23.86 2.37	-	-	318 76.63 41.19 30.72 3.06	-	-	-	-	-	-	-		-	-	-	-	-	-	-	-	-
Framingham (town)	19,839 42.33	2,396	1,713 71.49 71.49 8.63	-	-	830 83.25 48.45 34.64 4.18	-	-	518 66.67 30.24 21.62 2.61	-	-	-	-	-	-	-	-	-	-	-	-	-	-	-	-	-
Lexington (town)	14,709 69.07	1,984	1,605 80.90 80.90 10.91	-	-	464 91.88 28.91 23.39 3.15	-	-	728 84.26 45.36 36.69 4.95	-	-	-	-	-	-	-	118 47.39 7.35 5.95 0.80	-	-	-	-	-	-	-	-	-

Notes: Please refer to the User's Guide for an explanation of data; data is arranged alphabetically by state, then county, then city within each county; table includes counties with populations greater than 49,999 unless noted and cities with populations greater than 9,999 whose Asian and/or NHPI population rates are greater than the national average; (1) Native Hawaiian and other Pacific Islander; (2) excludes Taiwanese; (3) includes Chamorro; (4) county does not meet population threshold but is shown in order to allow inclusion of city

Place	Total population 25 years and over who are 4-year college graduates	Asian population 25 years and over	Asians 25 years and over who are 4-year college graduates	NHPI[1] population 25 years and over	NHPIs[1] 25 years and over who are 4-year college graduates	Asian Indian	Bangladeshi	Cambodian	Chinese[2]	Fijian	Filipino	Guamanian[3]	Hawaiian, Native	Hmong	Indonesian	Japanese	Korean	Laotian	Malaysian	Pakistani	Samoan	Sri Lankan	Taiwanese	Thai	Tongan	Vietnamese
	11,675	8,731	2,108	-	-	1,028	-	264	407	-	-	-	-	-	-	-	-	22	-	-	-	-	-	-	-	95
	18.12		24.14			64.78		6.13	72.68									2.98								11.27
Lowell (city)						48.77		12.52	19.31									1.04								4.51
			24.14			11.77		3.02	4.66									0.25								1.09
			18.06			8.81		2.26	3.49									0.19								0.81
	10,611	5,301	2,258	-	-	631	-	-	949	-	-	-	-	-	-	-	-	-	-	-	-	-	-	-	-	136
	26.15		42.60			80.79			34.04																	16.23
Malden (city)						27.95			42.03																	6.02
			42.60			11.90			17.90																	2.57
			21.28			5.95			8.94																	1.28
	9,084	1,116	792	-	-	399	-	-	-	-	-	-	-	-	-	-	-	-	-	-	-	-	-	-	-	-
	35.61		70.97			86.18																				
Marlborough (city)						50.38																				
			70.97			35.75																				
			8.72			4.39																				
	12,607	1,407	844	-	-	205	-	-	379	-	-	-	-	-	-	-	-	-	-	-	-	-	-	-	-	61
	31.71		59.99			75.93			66.14																	30.65
Medford (city)						24.29			44.91																	7.23
			59.99			14.57			26.94																	4.34
			6.69			1.63			3.01																	0.48
	12,219	865	600	-	-	-	-	-	289	-	-	-	-	-	-	-	-	-	-	-	-	-	-	-	-	-
	52.53		69.36						68.97																	
Natick (town)									48.17																	
			69.36						33.41																	
			4.91						2.37																	
	39,248	4,031	2,765	-	-	373	-	-	1,668	-	-	-	-	-	-	-	269	-	-	-	-	-	-	-	-	-
	68.04		68.59			84.20			64.85								82.01									
Newton (city)						13.49			60.33								9.73									
			68.59			9.25			41.38								6.67									
			7.04			0.95			4.25								0.69									
	21,791	2,990	1,795	-	-	396	-	-	761	-	-	-	-	-	-	-	134	-	-	-	-	-	-	-	-	-
	40.58		60.03			50.70			61.03								73.22									
Somerville (city)						22.06			42.40								7.47									
			60.03			13.24			25.45								4.48									
			8.24			1.82			3.49								0.61									
	7,781	409	354	-	-	-	-	-	-	-	-	-	-	-	-	-	-	-	-	-	-	-	-	-	-	-
	71.89		86.55																							
Sudbury (town)																										
			86.55																							
			4.55																							
	15,345	2,740	1,847	-	-	906	-	-	632	-	-	-	-	-	-	-	-	-	-	-	-	-	-	-	-	-
	38.45		67.41			75.94			68.62																	
Waltham (city)						49.05			34.22																	
			67.41			33.07			23.07																	
			12.04			5.90			4.12																	
	6,128	448	346	-	-	-	-	-	-	-	-	-	-	-	-	-	-	-	-	-	-	-	-	-	-	-
	68.33		77.23																							
Wayland (town)																										
			77.23																							
			5.65																							

Notes: Please refer to the User's Guide for an explanation of data; data is arranged alphabetically by state, then county, then city within each county; table includes counties with populations greater than 49,999 unless noted and cities with populations greater than 9,999 whose Asian and/or NHPI population rates are greater than the national average; (1) Native Hawaiian and other Pacific Islander; (2) excludes Taiwanese; (3) includes Chamorro; (4) county does not meet population threshold but is shown in order to allow inclusion of city

Place	Total population 25 years and over who are 4-year college graduates	Asian population 25 years and over	Asians 25 years and over who are 4-year college graduates	NHPI[1] population 25 years and over	NHPIs[1] 25 years and over who are 4-year college graduates	Asian Indian	Bangladeshi	Cambodian	Chinese[2]	Fijian	Filipino	Guamanian[3]	Hawaiian, Native	Hmong	Indonesian	Japanese	Korean	Laotian	Malaysian	Pakistani	Samoan	Sri Lankan	Taiwanese	Thai	Tongan	Vietnamese
Westford (town)	7,542 56.81	605	520 85.95 85.95 6.89	-	-	-	-	-	201 87.01 38.65 33.22 2.67	-	-	-	-	-	-	-	-	-	-	-	-	-	-	-	-	-
Weston (town)	5,537 75.10	548	400 72.99 72.99 7.22	-	-	-	-	-	165 60.22 41.25 30.11 2.98	-	-	-	-	-	-	-	-	-	-	-	-	-	-	-	-	-
Winchester (town)	9,606 64.91	545	412 75.60 75.60 4.29	-	-	-	-	-	-	-	-	-	-	-	-	-	-	-	-	-	-	-	-	-	-	-
Woburn (city)	7,904 29.46	1,301	964 74.10 74.10 12.20	-	-	535 82.95 55.50 41.12 6.77	-	-	-	-	-	-	-	-	-	-	-	-	-	-	-	-	-	-	-	-
Norfolk County	194,349 42.95	23,571	12,260 52.01 52.01 6.31	-	-	2,980 86.18 24.31 12.64 1.53	-	-	5,372 41.88 43.82 22.79 2.76	-	799 57.94 6.52 3.39 0.41	-	-	-	-	1,038 75.99 8.47 4.40 0.53	943 77.61 7.69 4.00 0.49	-	-	-	-	-	159 81.12 1.30 0.67 0.08	-	-	391 22.47 3.19 1.66 0.20
Brookline (town)	31,595 76.95	5,270	3,907 74.14 74.14 12.37	-	-	639 91.68 16.36 12.13 2.02	-	-	1,632 63.06 41.77 30.97 5.17	-	-	-	-	-	-	765 85.28 19.58 14.52 2.42	546 90.55 13.97 10.36 1.73	-	-	-	-	-	-	-	-	-
Needham (town)	12,801 64.88	630	536 85.08 85.08 4.19	-	-	-	-	-	334 89.30 62.31 53.02 2.61	-	-	-	-	-	-	-	-	-	-	-	-	-	-	-	-	-
Norwood (town)	8,152 39.21	989	844 85.34 85.34 10.35	-	-	512 93.77 60.66 51.77 6.28	-	-	-	-	-	-	-	-	-	-	-	-	-	-	-	-	-	-	-	-
Quincy (city)	20,804 31.75	9,374	2,917 31.12 31.12 14.02	-	-	635 83.88 21.77 6.77 3.05	-	-	1,472 23.64 50.46 15.70 7.08	-	333 51.23 11.42 3.55 1.60	-	-	-	-	-	-	-	-	-	-	-	-	-	-	101 11.70 3.46 1.08 0.49
Randolph (town)	5,760 26.64	2,126	761 35.79 35.79 13.21	-	-	-	-	-	277 25.82 36.40 13.03 4.81	-	-	-	-	-	-	-	-	-	-	-	-	-	-	-	-	115 25.05 15.11 5.41 2.00

Notes: Please refer to the User's Guide for an explanation of data; data is arranged alphabetically by state, then county, then city within each county; table includes counties with populations greater than 49,999 unless noted and cities with populations greater than 9,999 whose Asian and/or NHPI population rates are greater than the national average; (1) Native Hawaiian and other Pacific Islander; (2) excludes Taiwanese; (3) includes Chamorro; (4) county does not meet population threshold but is shown in order to allow inclusion of city

Place	Total population 25 years and over who are 4-year college graduates	Asian population 25 years and over	Asians 25 years and over who are 4-year college graduates	NHPI[1] population 25 years and over	NHPIs[1] 25 years and over who are 4-year college graduates	Asian Indian	Bangladeshi	Cambodian	Chinese[2]	Fijian	Filipino	Guamanian[3]	Hawaiian, Native	Hmong	Indonesian	Japanese	Korean	Laotian	Malaysian	Pakistani	Samoan	Sri Lankan	Taiwanese	Thai	Tongan	Vietnamese
Sharon (town)	7,238 63.07	480	352 73.33 73.33 4.86	-	-	-	-	-	-	-	-	-	-	-	-	-	-	-	-	-	-	-	-	-	-	-
Wellesley (town)	12,315 75.89	629	469 74.56 74.56 3.81	-	-	-	-	-	281 76.36 59.91 44.67 2.28	-	-	-	-	-	-	-	-	-	-	-	-	-	-	-	-	-
Plymouth County	86,780 27.75	2,656	986 37.12 37.12 1.14	-	-	229 61.56 23.23 8.62 0.26	-	-	226 38.18 22.92 8.51 0.26	-	151 36.56 15.31 5.69 0.17	-	-	-	-	-	-	-	-	-	-	-	-	-	-	76 17.97 7.71 2.86 0.09
Suffolk County	144,910 32.45	29,562	10,561 35.72 35.72 7.29	-	-	1,767 75.87 16.73 5.98 1.22	-	44 5.65 0.42 0.15 0.03	4,254 31.06 40.28 14.39 2.94	-	749 64.85 7.09 2.53 0.52	-	-	-	-	895 75.85 8.47 3.03 0.62	1,175 79.39 11.13 3.97 0.81	-	-	-	-	-	254 87.59 2.41 0.86 0.18	-	-	766 10.56 7.25 2.59 0.53
Boston (city)	134,252 35.56	27,436	10,150 37.00 37.00 7.56	-	-	1,618 77.16 15.94 5.90 1.21	-	44 14.01 0.43 0.16 0.03	4,133 30.99 40.72 15.06 3.08	-	731 68.57 7.20 2.66 0.54	-	-	-	-	878 76.22 8.65 3.20 0.65	1,136 82.80 11.19 4.14 0.85	-	-	-	-	-	254 87.59 2.50 0.93 0.19	-	-	736 11.26 7.25 2.68 0.55
Chelsea (city)	2,164 10.02	864	54 6.25 6.25 2.50	-	-	-	-	-	-	-	-	-	-	-	-	-	-	-	-	-	-	-	-	-	-	11 2.63 20.37 1.27 0.51
Revere (city)	4,548 13.49	1,182	303 25.63 25.63 6.66	-	-	-	-	0 0.00 0.00 0.00 0.00	-	-	-	-	-	-	-	-	-	-	-	-	-	-	-	-	-	19 6.35 6.27 1.61 0.42
Worcester County	133,505 26.92	11,163	4,809 43.08 43.08 3.60	-	-	1,940 80.40 40.34 17.38 1.45	-	35 18.04 0.73 0.31 0.03	1,446 65.19 30.07 12.95 1.08	-	189 49.61 3.93 1.69 0.14	-	-	0 0.00 0.00 0.00 0.00	-	101 46.76 2.10 0.90 0.08	253 35.24 5.26 2.27 0.19	53 9.33 1.10 0.47 0.04	-	104 47.71 2.16 0.93 0.08	-	-	-	-	-	375 11.31 7.80 3.36 0.28
Fitchburg (city)	3,831 15.41	726	81 11.16 11.16 2.11	-	-	-	-	-	-	-	-	-	-	0 0.00 0.00 0.00 0.00	-	-	-	19 9.95 23.46 2.62 0.50	-	-	-	-	-	-	-	-
Northborough (town)	4,707 51.05	466	374 80.26 80.26 7.95	-	-	-	-	-	-	-	-	-	-	-	-	-	-	-	-	-	-	-	-	-	-	-

Notes: Please refer to the User's Guide for an explanation of data; data is arranged alphabetically by state, then county, then city within each county; table includes counties with populations greater than 49,999 unless noted and cities with populations greater than 9,999 whose Asian and/or NHPI population rates are greater than the national average; (1) Native Hawaiian and other Pacific Islander; (2) excludes Taiwanese; (3) includes Chamorro; (4) county does not meet population threshold but is shown in order to allow inclusion of city

Place	Total population 25 years and over who are 4-year college graduates	Asian population 25 years and over	Asians 25 years and over who are 4-year college graduates	NHPI[1] population 25 years and over	NHPIs[1] 25 years and over who are 4-year college graduates	Asian Indian	Bangladeshi	Cambodian	Chinese[2]	Fijian	Filipino	Guamanian[3]	Hawaiian, Native	Hmong	Indonesian	Japanese	Korean	Laotian	Malaysian	Pakistani	Samoan	Sri Lankan	Taiwanese	Thai	Tongan	Vietnamese
Shrewsbury (town)	10,085 46.10	1,694	1,181 69.72 69.72 11.71	-	-	670 88.62 56.73 39.55 6.64	-	-	335 78.64 28.37 19.78 3.32	-	-	-	-	-	-	-	-	-	-	-	-	-	-	-	-	64 18.82 5.42 3.78 0.63
Westborough (town)	6,351 53.16	927	731 78.86 78.86 11.51	-	-	346 89.41 47.33 37.32 5.45	-	-	229 71.79 31.33 24.70 3.61	-	-	-	-	-	-	-	-	-	-	-	-	-	-	-	-	-
Worcester (city)	25,362 23.32	4,517	1,150 25.46 25.46 4.53	-	-	406 68.24 35.30 8.99 1.60	-	-	249 44.78 21.65 5.51 0.98	-	-	-	-	-	-	-	-	-	-	-	-	-	-	-	-	179 7.17 15.57 3.96 0.71
MICHIGAN	1,396,259 21.76	107,112	65,379 61.04 61.04 4.68	1,354	293 21.64 21.64 0.02	26,261 75.50 40.17 24.52 1.88	280 29.38 0.43 0.26 0.02	65 7.62 0.10 0.06 <0.01	12,929 65.99 19.78 12.07 0.93	-	8,220 65.23 12.57 7.67 0.59	72 22.93 24.57 5.32 0.01	112 26.60 38.23 8.27 0.01	138 7.47 0.21 0.13 0.01	246 70.89 0.38 0.23 0.02	4,421 58.79 6.76 4.13 0.32	5,777 56.03 8.84 5.39 0.41	177 13.21 0.27 0.17 0.01	132 78.11 0.20 0.12 0.01	1,888 67.50 2.89 1.76 0.14	34 13.55 11.60 2.51 <0.01	197 74.90 0.30 0.18 0.01	1,276 85.98 1.95 1.19 0.09	533 47.76 0.82 0.50 0.04	-	1,535 19.74 2.35 1.43 0.11
Allegan County	10,595 15.83	313	100 31.95 31.95 0.94	-	-	-	-	-	-	-	-	-	-	-	-	-	-	-	-	-	-	-	-	-	-	-
Bay County	10,515 14.18	376	158 42.02 42.02 1.50	-	-	-	-	-	-	-	-	-	-	-	-	-	-	-	-	-	-	-	-	-	-	-
Berrien County	20,930 19.62	996	614 61.65 61.65 2.93	-	-	200 69.69 32.57 20.08 0.96	-	-	-	-	135 62.50 21.99 13.55 0.65	-	-	-	-	-	139 74.33 22.64 13.96 0.66	-	-	-	-	-	-	-	-	-
Calhoun County	14,439 16.02	986	411 41.68 41.68 2.85	-	-	-	-	-	-	-	-	-	-	-	-	102 34.93 24.82 10.34 0.71	-	-	-	-	-	-	-	-	-	-
Cass County	4,138 12.07	196	48 24.49 24.49 1.16	-	-	-	-	-	-	-	-	-	-	-	-	-	-	5 6.10 10.42 2.55 0.12	-	-	-	-	-	-	-	-
Clinton County	8,887 21.23	158	67 42.41 42.41 0.75	-	-	-	-	-	-	-	-	-	-	-	-	-	-	-	-	-	-	-	-	-	-	-

Notes: Please refer to the User's Guide for an explanation of data; data is arranged alphabetically by state, then county, then city within each county; table includes counties with populations greater than 49,999 unless noted and cities with populations greater than 9,999 whose Asian and/or NHPI population rates are greater than the national average; (1) Native Hawaiian and other Pacific Islander; (2) excludes Taiwanese; (3) includes Chamorro; (4) county does not meet population threshold but is shown in order to allow inclusion of city

Place	Total population 25 years and over who are 4-year college graduates	Asian population 25 years and over	Asians 25 years and over who are 4-year college graduates	NHPI[1] population 25 years and over	NHPIs[1] 25 years and over who are 4-year college graduates	Asian Indian	Bangladeshi	Cambodian	Chinese[2]	Fijian	Filipino	Guamanian[3]	Hawaiian, Native	Hmong	Indonesian	Japanese	Korean	Laotian	Malaysian	Pakistani	Samoan	Sri Lankan	Taiwanese	Thai	Tongan	Vietnamese
Eaton County	14,560	695	340	-	-	197	-	-	-	-	-	-	-	-	-	-	-	-	-	-	-	-	-	-	-	19
	21.72		48.92			90.37																				10.44
						57.94																				5.59
			48.92			28.35																				2.73
			2.34			1.35																				0.13
Genesee County	45,059	2,027	1,209	-	-	608	-	-	180	-	201	-	-	-	-	-	43	-	-	-	-	-	-	-	-	-
	16.23		59.64			78.05			63.38		59.12						22.28									
						50.29			14.89		16.63						3.56									
			59.64			30.00			8.88		9.92						2.12									
			2.68			1.35			0.40		0.45						0.10									
Ingham County	53,690	5,517	3,502	-	-	936	-	-	719	-	287	-	-	20	-	261	750	-	-	-	-	-	-	-	-	100
	32.96		63.48			76.41			64.48		74.93			13.25		72.91	84.27									14.12
						26.73			20.53		8.20			0.57		7.45	21.42									2.86
			63.48			16.97			13.03		5.20			0.36		4.73	13.59									1.81
			6.52			1.74			1.34		0.53			0.04		0.49	1.40									0.19
East Lansing (city)	10,764	1,967	1,734	-	-	366	-	-	464	-	-	-	-	-	-	-	445	-	-	-	-	-	-	-	-	-
	70.39		88.15			92.66			86.73								87.08									
						21.11			26.76								25.66									
			88.15			18.61			23.59								22.62									
			16.11			3.40			4.31								4.13									
Meridian charter (township)	14,802	1,526	1,018	-	-	409	-	-	140	-	-	-	-	-	-	-	144	-	-	-	-	-	-	-	-	-
	59.90		66.71			70.88			43.89								74.23									
						40.18			13.75								14.15									
			66.71			26.80			9.17								9.44									
			6.88			2.76			0.95								0.97									
Okemos (cdp)	9,389	1,157	811	-	-	315	-	-	115	-	-	-	-	-	-	-	-	-	-	-	-	-	-	-	-	-
	66.76		70.10			68.78			50.44																	
						38.84			14.18																	
			70.10			27.23			9.94																	
			8.64			3.35			1.22																	
Ionia County	4,075	117	30	-	-	-	-	-	-	-	-	-	-	-	-	-	-	-	-	-	-	-	-	-	-	-
	10.77		25.64																							
			25.64																							
			0.74																							
Isabella County	7,577	439	319	-	-	-	-	-	-	-	-	-	-	-	-	-	-	-	-	-	-	-	-	-	-	-
	23.92		72.67																							
			72.67																							
			4.21																							
Jackson County	17,052	464	260	-	-	-	-	-	-	-	-	-	-	-	-	-	-	-	-	-	-	-	-	-	-	-
	16.26		56.03																							
			56.03																							
			1.52																							
Kalamazoo County	45,189	2,439	1,729	-	-	609	-	-	383	-	-	-	-	-	-	-	189	-	-	-	-	-	-	-	-	-
	31.17		70.89			78.48			77.22								66.55									
						35.22			22.15								10.93									
			70.89			24.97			15.70								7.75									
			3.83			1.35			0.85								0.42									

Notes: Please refer to the User's Guide for an explanation of data; data is arranged alphabetically by state, then county, then city within each county; table includes counties with populations greater than 49,999 unless noted and cities with populations greater than 9,999 whose Asian and/or NHPI population rates are greater than the national average; (1) Native Hawaiian and other Pacific Islander; (2) excludes Taiwanese; (3) includes Chamorro; (4) county does not meet population threshold but is shown in order to allow inclusion of city

Place	Total population 25 years and over who are 4-year college graduates	Asian population 25 years and over	Asians 25 years and over who are 4-year college graduates	NHPI[1] population 25 years and over	NHPIs[1] 25 years and over who are 4-year college graduates	Asian Indian	Bangladeshi	Cambodian	Chinese[2]	Fijian	Filipino	Guamanian[3]	Hawaiian, Native	Hmong	Indonesian	Japanese	Korean	Laotian	Malaysian	Pakistani	Samoan	Sri Lankan	Taiwanese	Thai	Tongan	Vietnamese
Kent County	90,838 25.82	6,054	2,026 33.47 33.47 2.23	-	-	582 68.47 28.73 9.61 0.64	-	-	294 47.04 14.51 4.86 0.32	-	246 59.56 12.14 4.06 0.27	-	-	-	-	-	301 40.51 14.86 4.97 0.33	-	-	-	-	-	-	-	-	326 11.92 16.09 5.38 0.36
Kentwood (city)	8,972 31.46	1,561	572 36.64 36.64 6.38	-	-	-	-	-	-	-	-	-	-	-	-	-	60 25.75 10.49 3.84 0.67	-	-	-	-	-	-	-	-	107 14.13 18.71 6.85 1.19
Lenawee County	10,462 16.27	350	210 60.00 60.00 2.01	-	-	-	-	-	-	-	-	-	-	-	-	-	-	-	-	-	-	-	-	-	-	-
Livingston County	28,540 28.15	623	338 54.25 54.25 1.18	-	-	-	-	-	-	-	-	-	-	-	-	-	-	-	-	-	-	-	-	-	-	-
Macomb County	94,145 17.57	10,937	4,843 44.28 44.28 5.14	-	-	2,015 56.70 41.61 18.42 2.14	-	-	566 34.10 11.69 5.18 0.60	-	1,423 58.39 29.38 13.01 1.51	-	-	43 9.79 0.89 0.39 0.05	-	-	214 28.08 4.42 1.96 0.23	-	-	145 46.33 2.99 1.33 0.15	-	-	-	-	-	193 21.61 3.99 1.76 0.21
Sterling Heights (city)	19,236 22.96	4,233	2,221 52.47 52.47 11.55	-	-	930 60.04 41.87 21.97 4.83	-	-	251 36.59 11.30 5.93 1.30	-	654 67.56 29.45 15.45 3.40	-	-	-	-	-	116 34.73 5.22 2.74 0.60	-	-	-	-	-	-	-	-	115 37.46 5.18 2.72 0.60
Marquette County	9,943 23.71	200	43 21.50 21.50 0.43	-	-	-	-	-	-	-	-	-	-	-	-	-	-	-	-	-	-	-	-	-	-	-
Midland County	15,653 29.26	715	541 75.66 75.66 3.46	-	-	235 92.16 43.44 32.87 1.50	-	-	164 68.62 30.31 22.94 1.05	-	-	-	-	-	-	-	-	-	-	-	-	-	-	-	-	-
Monroe County	13,523 14.34	538	209 38.85 38.85 1.55	-	-	-	-	-	-	-	-	-	-	-	-	-	-	-	-	-	-	-	-	-	-	-
Muskegon County	15,090 13.89	406	118 29.06 29.06 0.78	-	-	-	-	-	-	-	-	-	-	-	-	-	-	-	-	-	-	-	-	-	-	-

Notes: Please refer to the User's Guide for an explanation of data; data is arranged alphabetically by state, then county, then city within each county; table includes counties with populations greater than 49,999 unless noted and cities with populations greater than 9,999 whose Asian and/or NHPI population rates are greater than the national average; (1) Native Hawaiian and other Pacific Islander; (2) excludes Taiwanese; (3) includes Chamorro; (4) county does not meet population threshold but is shown in order to allow inclusion of city

Place	Total population 25 years and over who are 4-year college graduates	Asian population 25 years and over	Asians 25 years and over who are 4-year college graduates	NHPI[1] population 25 years and over	NHPIs[1] 25 years and over who are 4-year college graduates	Asian Indian	Bangladeshi	Cambodian	Chinese[2]	Fijian	Filipino	Guamanian[3]	Hawaiian, Native	Hmong	Indonesian	Japanese	Korean	Laotian	Malaysian	Pakistani	Samoan	Sri Lankan	Taiwanese	Thai	Tongan	Vietnamese
Oakland County	308,723	31,940	23,242	-	-	11,318	-	-	4,077	-	2,148	-	-	34	-	1,914	1,694	-	-	382	-	-	666	-	-	235
	38.21		72.77			86.57			67.74		72.37			8.46		63.89	58.74			70.87			88.21			25.46
						48.70			17.54		9.24			0.15		8.24	7.29			1.64			2.87			1.01
			72.77			35.44			12.76		6.73			0.11		5.99	5.30			1.20			2.09			0.74
			7.53			3.67			1.32		0.70			0.01		0.62	0.55			0.12			0.22			0.08
Auburn Hills (city)	4,134	799	594	-	-	365	-	-	-	-	-	-	-	-	-	-	-	-	-	-	-	-	-	-	-	-
	32.80		74.34			88.59																				
						61.45																				
			74.34			45.68																				
			14.37			8.83																				
Bloomfield (township)	20,481	1,926	1,587	-	-	692	-	-	-	-	-	-	-	-	-	-	298	-	-	-	-	-	-	-	-	-
	65.80		82.40			86.18											78.01									
						43.60											18.78									
			82.40			35.93											15.47									
			7.75			3.38											1.46									
Farmington (city)	3,770	763	655	-	-	543	-	-	-	-	-	-	-	-	-	-	-	-	-	-	-	-	-	-	-	-
	47.95		85.85			91.41																				
						82.90																				
			85.85			71.17																				
			17.37			14.40																				
Farmington Hills (city)	27,570	4,039	3,289	-	-	2,223	-	-	452	-	156	-	-	-	-	-	-	-	-	-	-	-	-	-	-	-
	47.89		81.43			91.33			73.14		63.67															
						67.59			13.74		4.74															
			81.43			55.04			11.19		3.86															
			11.93			8.06			1.64		0.57															
Madison Heights (city)	4,042	1,206	741	-	-	-	-	-	180	-	-	-	-	-	-	-	-	-	-	-	-	-	-	-	-	-
	18.55		61.44						45.11																	
									24.29																	
			61.44						14.93																	
			18.33						4.45																	
Novi (city)	15,330	2,587	1,917	-	-	631	-	-	395	-	-	-	-	-	-	521	-	-	-	-	-	-	-	-	-	-
	49.11		74.10			86.80			72.61							67.40										
						32.92			20.61							27.18										
			74.10			24.39			15.27							20.14										
			12.50			4.12			2.58							3.40										
Rochester (city)	3,834	352	274	-	-	-	-	-	-	-	-	-	-	-	-	-	-	-	-	-	-	-	-	-	-	-
	52.08		77.84																							
			77.84																							
			7.15																							
Rochester Hills (city)	21,931	3,011	2,350	-	-	1,147	-	-	524	-	-	-	-	-	-	-	114	-	-	-	-	-	-	-	-	-
	47.29		78.05			86.63			77.86								61.29									
						48.81			22.30								4.85									
			78.05			38.09			17.40								3.79									
			10.72			5.23			2.39								0.52									
Troy (city)	27,104	6,651	5,138	-	-	2,587	-	-	1,136	-	427	-	-	-	-	-	384	-	-	-	-	-	293	-	-	-
	49.97		77.25			85.41			75.99		76.11						52.24						90.43			
						50.35			22.11		8.31						7.47						5.70			
			77.25			38.90			17.08		6.42						5.77						4.41			
			18.96			9.54			4.19		1.58						1.42						1.08			

Notes: Please refer to the User's Guide for an explanation of data; data is arranged alphabetically by state, then county, then city within each county; table includes counties with populations greater than 49,999 unless noted and cities with populations greater than 9,999 whose Asian and/or NHPI population rates are greater than the national average; (1) Native Hawaiian and other Pacific Islander; (2) excludes Taiwanese; (3) includes Chamorro; (4) county does not meet population threshold but is shown in order to allow inclusion of city

Place	Total population 25 years and over who are 4-year college graduates	Asian population 25 years and over	Asians 25 years and over who are 4-year college graduates	NHPI[1] population 25 years and over	NHPIs[1] 25 years and over who are 4-year college graduates	Asian Indian	Bangladeshi	Cambodian	Chinese[2]	Fijian	Filipino	Guamanian[3]	Hawaiian, Native	Hmong	Indonesian	Japanese	Korean	Laotian	Malaysian	Pakistani	Samoan	Sri Lankan	Taiwanese	Thai	Tongan	Vietnamese
West Bloomfield (township)	24,540 55.25	3,127	2,499 79.92 79.92 10.18	-	-	1,031 91.32 41.26 32.97 4.20	-	-	330 76.74 13.21 10.55 1.34	-	223 82.29 8.92 7.13 0.91	-	-	-	-	516 65.57 20.65 16.50 2.10	224 76.98 8.96 7.16 0.91	-	-	-	-	-	-	-	-	-
Ottawa County	36,834 25.96	2,551	665 26.07 26.07 1.81	-	-	102 54.55 15.34 4.00 0.28	-	45 8.51 6.77 1.76 0.12	103 39.16 15.49 4.04 0.28	-	-	-	-	-	-	-	57 58.76 8.57 2.23 0.15	58 9.75 8.72 2.27 0.16	-	-	-	-	-	-	-	87 19.77 13.08 3.41 0.24
Holland (city)	5,400 26.87	749	207 27.64 27.64 3.83	-	-	-	-	-	-	-	-	-	-	-	-	-	-	-	-	-	-	-	-	-	-	-
Saginaw County	21,498 15.90	1,052	612 58.17 58.17 2.85	-	-	159 76.08 25.98 15.11 0.74	-	-	-	-	140 60.34 22.88 13.31 0.65	-	-	-	-	-	96 52.17 15.69 9.13 0.45	-	-	-	-	-	-	-	-	-
St. Clair County	13,524 12.57	271	108 39.85 39.85 0.80	-	-	-	-	-	-	-	-	-	-	-	-	-	-	-	-	-	-	-	-	-	-	-
St. Joseph County	5,074 12.75	205	66 32.20 32.20 1.30	-	-	-	-	-	-	-	-	-	-	-	-	-	-	-	-	-	-	-	-	-	-	-
Washtenaw County	95,026 48.14	11,479	9,474 82.53 82.53 9.97	-	-	2,276 89.29 24.02 19.83 2.40	-	-	3,153 86.79 33.28 27.47 3.32	-	456 72.04 4.81 3.97 0.48	-	-	-	-	969 85.30 10.23 8.44 1.02	1,562 78.45 16.49 13.61 1.64	-	-	168 72.10 1.77 1.46 0.18	-	-	301 85.51 3.18 2.62 0.32	-	-	144 66.06 1.52 1.25 0.15
Ann Arbor (city)	44,810 69.29	7,121	6,222 87.38 87.38 13.89	-	-	1,436 90.60 23.08 20.17 3.20	-	-	2,083 89.63 33.48 29.25 4.65	-	218 75.43 3.50 3.06 0.49	-	-	-	-	707 86.96 11.36 9.93 1.58	1,082 84.66 17.39 15.19 2.41	-	-	-	-	-	249 85.27 4.00 3.50 0.56	-	-	-
Pittsfield charter (township)	10,099 52.30	1,770	1,374 77.63 77.63 13.61	-	-	397 89.21 28.89 22.43 3.93	-	-	443 84.70 32.24 25.03 4.39	-	-	-	-	-	-	-	240 68.97 17.47 13.56 2.38	-	-	-	-	-	-	-	-	-
Scio (township)	5,780 55.52	433	394 90.99 90.99 6.82	-	-	-	-	-	-	-	-	-	-	-	-	-	-	-	-	-	-	-	-	-	-	-

Notes: Please refer to the User's Guide for an explanation of data; data is arranged alphabetically by state, then county, then city within each county; table includes counties with populations greater than 49,999 unless noted and cities with populations greater than 9,999 whose Asian and/or NHPI population rates are greater than the national average; (1) Native Hawaiian and other Pacific Islander; (2) excludes Taiwanese; (3) includes Chamorro; (4) county does not meet population threshold but is shown in order to allow inclusion of city

Place	Total population 25 years and over who are 4-year college graduates	Asian population 25 years and over	Asians 25 years and over who are 4-year college graduates	NHPI[1] population 25 years and over	NHPIs[1] 25 years and over who are 4-year college graduates	Asian Indian	Bangladeshi	Cambodian	Chinese[2]	Fijian	Filipino	Guamanian[3]	Hawaiian, Native	Hmong	Indonesian	Japanese	Korean	Laotian	Malaysian	Pakistani	Samoan	Sri Lankan	Taiwanese	Thai	Tongan	Vietnamese
Wayne County	224,792	22,048	12,768	291	23	5,896	115	-	2,414	-	2,125	-	-	18	-	434	369	-	-	814	-	-	-	-	-	217
	17.22		57.91		7.90	64.37	18.05		66.98		67.27			3.46		51.73	37.27			66.72						28.48
						46.18	0.90		18.91		16.64			0.14		3.40	2.89			6.38						1.70
			57.91		7.90	26.74	0.52		10.95		9.64			0.08		1.97	1.67			3.69						0.98
			5.68		0.01	2.62	0.05		1.07		0.95			0.01		0.19	0.16			0.36						0.10
Brownstown (township)	2,247	505	293	-	-	-	-	-	-	-	-	-	-	-	-	-	-	-	-	-	-	-	-	-	-	-
	15.74		58.02																							
			58.02																							
			13.04																							
Canton (township)	18,943	4,161	3,024	-	-	1,562	-	-	664	-	335	-	-	-	-	-	91	-	-	-	-	-	-	-	-	-
	39.41		72.67			71.42			81.37		71.43						53.53									
						51.65			21.96		11.08						3.01									
			72.67			37.54			15.96		8.05						2.19									
			15.96			8.25			3.51		1.77						0.48									
Hamtramck (city)	1,628	1,165	172	-	-	71	35	-	-	-	-	-	-	-	-	-	-	-	-	-	-	-	-	-	-	-
	11.47		14.76			13.45	9.49																			
						41.28	20.35																			
			14.76			6.09	3.00																			
			10.57			4.36	2.15																			
Inkster (city)	2,221	820	699	-	-	532	-	-	-	-	-	-	-	-	-	-	-	-	-	-	-	-	-	-	-	-
	12.09		85.24			91.88																				
						76.11																				
			85.24			64.88																				
			31.47			23.95																				
Northville (township)	7,364	658	552	-	-	244	-	-	-	-	-	-	-	-	-	-	-	-	-	-	-	-	-	-	-	-
	48.11		83.89			85.92																				
						44.20																				
			83.89			37.08																				
			7.50			3.31																				
MINNESOTA	868,082	68,939	25,023	1,060	230	7,720	-	223	6,065	-	1,685	83	73	1,176	-	1,593	2,112	417	-	425	-	-	257	237	-	1,931
	27.43		36.30		21.70	74.86		8.86	62.89		42.21	32.81	18.53	8.49		52.71	43.16	9.25		67.03			82.64	38.10		16.85
						30.85		0.89	24.24		6.73	36.09	31.74	4.70		6.37	8.44	1.67		1.70			1.03	0.95		7.72
			36.30		21.70	11.20		0.32	8.80		2.44	7.83	6.89	1.71		2.31	3.06	0.60		0.62			0.37	0.34		2.80
			2.88		0.03	0.89		0.03	0.70		0.19	0.01	0.01	0.14		0.18	0.24	0.05		0.05			0.03	0.03		0.22
Anoka County	39,827	2,735	859	-	-	263	-	-	204	-	71	-	-	24	-	-	71	-	-	-	-	-	-	-	-	79
	21.28		31.41			46.38			68.69		23.51			10.04			28.06									14.47
						30.62			23.75		8.27			2.79			8.27									9.20
			31.41			9.62			7.46		2.60			0.88			2.60									2.89
			2.16			0.66			0.51		0.18			0.06			0.18									0.20
Columbia Heights (city)	2,309	407	123	-	-	-	-	-	-	-	-	-	-	-	-	-	-	-	-	-	-	-	-	-	-	-
	17.61		30.22																							
			30.22																							
			5.33																							
Blue Earth County	8,441	335	145	-	-	-	-	-	-	-	-	-	-	-	-	-	-	-	-	-	-	-	-	-	-	-
	26.64		43.28																							
			43.28																							
			1.72																							

Notes: Please refer to the User's Guide for an explanation of data; data is arranged alphabetically by state, then county, then city within each county; table includes counties with populations greater than 49,999 unless noted and cities with populations greater than 9,999 whose Asian and/or NHPI population rates are greater than the national average; (1) Native Hawaiian and other Pacific Islander; (2) excludes Taiwanese; (3) includes Chamorro; (4) county does not meet population threshold but is shown in order to allow inclusion of city

Place	Total population 25 years and over who are 4-year college graduates	Asian population 25 years and over	Asians 25 years and over who are 4-year college graduates	NHPI[1] population 25 years and over	NHPIs[1] 25 years and over who are 4-year college graduates	Asian Indian	Bangladeshi	Cambodian	Chinese[2]	Fijian	Filipino	Guamanian[3]	Hawaiian, Native	Hmong	Indonesian	Japanese	Korean	Laotian	Malaysian	Pakistani	Samoan	Sri Lankan	Taiwanese	Thai	Tongan	Vietnamese
Carver County	14,820	599	240	-	-	-	-	-	-	-	-	-	-	-	-	-	-	-	-	-	-	-	-	-	-	-
	34.29		40.07																							
			40.07																							
			1.62																							
Clay County	7,313	190	45	-	-	-	-	-	-	-	-	-	-	-	-	-	-	-	-	-	-	-	-	-	-	-
	24.72		23.68																							
			23.68																							
			0.62																							
Crow Wing County	6,839	97	54	-	-	-	-	-	-	-	-	-	-	-	-	-	-	-	-	-	-	-	-	-	-	-
	18.44		55.67																							
			55.67																							
			0.79																							
Dakota County	78,265	5,370	2,253	-	-	860	-	31	497	-	188	-	-	-	-	-	96	61	-	-	-	-	-	-	-	241
	34.89		41.96			78.83		13.42	54.26		38.06						26.02	16.14								21.58
						38.17		1.38	22.06		8.34						4.26	2.71								10.70
			41.96			16.01		0.58	9.26		3.50						1.79	1.14								4.49
			2.88			1.10		0.04	0.64		0.24						0.12	0.08								0.31
Eagan (city)	19,210	1,861	915	-	-	367	-	-	296	-	-	-	-	-	-	-	-	-	-	-	-	-	-	-	-	76
	47.73		49.17			78.09			79.78																	23.82
						40.11			32.35																	8.31
			49.17			19.72			15.91																	4.08
			4.76			1.91			1.54																	0.40
Hennepin County	289,405	28,202	10,956	373	83	3,856	-	132	2,372	-	658	-	-	301	-	712	999	219	-	165	-	-	-	-	-	774
	39.09		38.85		22.25	75.21		14.78	59.05		50.89			7.48		55.41	45.49	9.21		65.74						14.99
						35.20		1.20	21.65		6.01			2.75		6.50	9.12	2.00		1.51						7.06
			38.85		22.25	13.67		0.47	8.41		2.33			1.07		2.52	3.54	0.78		0.59						2.74
			3.79		0.03	1.33		0.05	0.82		0.23			0.10		0.25	0.35	0.08		0.06						0.27
Bloomington (city)	21,606	2,620	789	-	-	256	-	37	236	-	-	-	-	-	-	-	39	-	-	-	-	-	-	-	-	98
	35.39		30.11			72.73		14.51	39.60								17.97									12.53
						32.45		4.69	29.91								4.94									12.42
			30.11			9.77		1.41	9.01								1.49									3.74
			3.65			1.18		0.17	1.09								0.18									0.45
Brooklyn Center (city)	3,181	1,119	155	-	-	-	-	-	-	-	-	-	-	98	-	-	-	4	-	-	-	-	-	-	-	-
	16.67		13.85											21.35				2.06								
														63.23				2.58								
			13.85											8.76				0.36								
			4.87											3.08				0.13								
Brooklyn Park (city)	11,277	3,354	868	-	-	312	-	-	-	-	-	-	-	5	-	-	-	70	-	-	-	-	-	-	-	137
	27.30		25.88			53.42								1.69				9.15								14.57
						35.94								0.58				8.06								15.78
			25.88			9.30								0.15				2.09								4.08
			7.70			2.77								0.04				0.62								1.21
Eden Prairie (city)	19,896	1,695	982	-	-	380	-	-	245	-	-	-	-	-	-	-	-	-	-	-	-	-	-	-	-	42
	57.12		57.94			96.69			62.50																	11.90
						38.70			24.95																	4.28
			57.94			22.42			14.45																	2.48
			4.94			1.91			1.23																	0.21

Notes: Please refer to the User's Guide for an explanation of data; data is arranged alphabetically by state, then county, then city within each county; table includes counties with populations greater than 49,999 unless noted and cities with populations greater than 9,999 whose Asian and/or NHPI population rates are greater than the national average; (1) Native Hawaiian and other Pacific Islander; (2) excludes Taiwanese; (3) includes Chamorro; (4) county does not meet population threshold but is shown in order to allow inclusion of city

Place	Total population 25 years and over who are 4-year college graduates	Asian population 25 years and over	Asians 25 years and over who are 4-year college graduates	NHPI[1] population 25 years and over	NHPIs[1] 25 years and over who are 4-year college graduates	Asian Indian	Bangladeshi	Cambodian	Chinese[2]	Fijian	Filipino	Guamanian[3]	Hawaiian, Native	Hmong	Indonesian	Japanese	Korean	Laotian	Malaysian	Pakistani	Samoan	Sri Lankan	Taiwanese	Thai	Tongan	Vietnamese
Hopkins (city)	4,153 35.04	649	438 67.49 67.49 10.55	-	-	321 93.59 73.29 49.46 7.73	-	-	-	-	-	-	-	-	-	-	-	-	-	-	-	-	-	-	-	-
Minneapolis (city)	91,027 37.40	11,135	3,586 32.20 32.20 3.94	-	-	774 61.38 21.58 6.95 0.85	-	14 8.48 0.39 0.13 0.02	907 66.99 25.29 8.15 1.00	-	286 54.58 7.98 2.57 0.31	-	-	165 5.43 4.60 1.48 0.18	-	347 59.01 9.68 3.12 0.38	466 48.64 12.99 4.19 0.51	20 2.51 0.56 0.18 0.02	-	-	-	-	-	-	-	275 16.81 7.67 2.47 0.30
Plymouth (city)	22,159 50.95	1,512	1,030 68.12 68.12 4.65	-	-	565 91.87 54.85 37.37 2.55	-	-	196 75.10 19.03 12.96 0.88	-	-	-	-	-	-	-	95 47.50 9.22 6.28 0.43	-	-	-	-	-	-	-	-	-
Richfield (city)	6,625 27.25	1,137	381 33.51 33.51 5.75	-	-	-	-	-	-	-	-	-	-	-	-	-	-	-	-	-	-	-	-	-	-	36 13.09 9.45 3.17 0.54
Nobles County[4]	1,843 13.50	448	60 13.39 13.39 3.26	-	-	-	-	-	-	-	-	-	-	-	-	-	-	13 5.88 21.67 2.90 0.71	-	-	-	-	-	-	-	-
Worthington (city)	1,205 16.43	423	60 14.18 14.18 4.98	-	-	-	-	-	-	-	-	-	-	-	-	-	-	13 6.28 21.67 3.07 1.08	-	-	-	-	-	-	-	-
Olmsted County	27,865 34.71	2,972	1,610 54.17 54.17 5.78	-	-	584 89.43 36.27 19.65 2.10	-	3 1.03 0.19 0.10 0.01	392 89.91 24.35 13.19 1.41	-	-	-	-	16 10.26 0.99 0.54 0.06	-	224 75.93 13.91 7.54 0.80	141 68.78 8.76 4.74 0.51	18 10.71 1.12 0.61 0.06	-	-	-	-	-	-	-	82 17.75 5.09 2.76 0.29
Rochester (city)	21,171 38.12	2,684	1,491 55.55 55.55 7.04	-	-	560 90.18 37.56 20.86 2.65	-	0 0.00 0.00 0.00 0.00	357 89.03 23.94 13.30 1.69	-	-	-	-	16 10.26 1.07 0.60 0.08	-	-	130 77.38 8.72 4.84 0.61	16 9.64 1.07 0.60 0.08	-	-	-	-	-	-	-	70 16.17 4.69 2.61 0.33
Otter Tail County	6,662 17.20	101	24 23.76 23.76 0.36	-	-	-	-	-	-	-	-	-	-	-	-	-	-	-	-	-	-	-	-	-	-	-
Ramsey County	110,972 34.33	18,538	5,508 29.71 29.71 4.96	-	-	1,194 79.02 21.68 6.44 1.08	-	29 5.04 0.53 0.16 0.03	1,717 76.41 31.17 9.26 1.55	-	268 45.50 4.87 1.45 0.24	-	-	701 7.99 12.73 3.78 0.63	-	239 60.05 4.34 1.29 0.22	452 58.70 8.21 2.44 0.41	55 14.44 1.00 0.30 0.05	-	-	-	-	-	-	-	428 19.98 7.77 2.31 0.39

Notes: Please refer to the User's Guide for an explanation of data; data is arranged alphabetically by state, then county, then city within each county; table includes counties with populations greater than 49,999 unless noted and cities with populations greater than 9,999 whose Asian and/or NHPI population rates are greater than the national average; (1) Native Hawaiian and other Pacific Islander; (2) excludes Taiwanese; (3) includes Chamorro; (4) county does not meet population threshold but is shown in order to allow inclusion of city

Place	Total population 25 years and over who are 4-year college graduates	Asian population 25 years and over	Asians 25 years and over who are 4-year college graduates	NHPI[1] population 25 years and over	NHPIs[1] 25 years and over who are 4-year college graduates	Asian Indian	Bangladeshi	Cambodian	Chinese[2]	Fijian	Filipino	Guamanian[3]	Hawaiian, Native	Hmong	Indonesian	Japanese	Korean	Laotian	Malaysian	Pakistani	Samoan	Sri Lankan	Taiwanese	Thai	Tongan	Vietnamese
Maplewood (city)	6,050 25.55	767	385 50.20 50.20 6.36	-	-	-	-	-	163 77.99 42.34 21.25 2.69	-	-	-	-	55 33.13 14.29 7.17 0.91	-	-	-	-	-	-	-	-	-	-	-	-
New Brighton (city)	6,017 40.63	624	417 66.83 66.83 6.93	-	-	-	-	-	-	-	-	-	-	-	-	-	-	-	-	-	-	-	-	-	-	-
Roseville (city)	10,031 42.25	958	609 63.57 63.57 6.07	-	-	-	-	-	287 70.86 47.13 29.96 2.86	-	-	-	-	-	-	-	-	-	-	-	-	-	-	-	-	-
St. Paul (city)	55,788 32.02	13,340	2,301 17.25 17.25 4.12	-	-	336 68.43 14.60 2.52 0.60	-	14 2.89 0.61 0.10 0.03	449 73.61 19.51 3.37 0.80	-	167 51.38 7.26 1.25 0.30	-	-	592 7.08 25.73 4.44 1.06	-	-	198 60.18 8.60 1.48 0.35	35 10.54 1.52 0.26 0.06	-	-	-	-	-	-	-	215 14.70 9.34 1.61 0.39
Vadnais Heights (city)	3,119 37.00	291	128 43.99 43.99 4.10	-	-	-	-	-	-	-	-	-	-	-	-	-	-	-	-	-	-	-	-	-	-	-
Rice County	7,475 22.38	381	106 27.82 27.82 1.42	-	-	-	-	-	-	-	-	-	-	-	-	-	-	-	-	-	-	-	-	-	-	-
St. Louis County	29,040 21.87	681	204 29.96 29.96 0.70	-	-	-	-	-	-	-	-	-	-	-	-	-	7 8.86 3.43 1.03 0.02	-	-	-	-	-	-	-	-	-
Scott County	16,334 29.40	1,121	346 30.87 30.87 2.12	-	-	-	-	13 6.02 3.76 1.16 0.08	-	-	-	-	-	-	-	-	-	-	-	-	-	-	-	-	-	82 33.33 23.70 7.31 0.50
Savage (city)	5,283 41.36	717	211 29.43 29.43 3.99	-	-	-	-	-	-	-	-	-	-	-	-	-	-	-	-	-	-	-	-	-	-	-
Sherburne County	7,442 19.41	156	51 32.69 32.69 0.69	-	-	-	-	-	-	-	-	-	-	-	-	-	-	-	-	-	-	-	-	-	-	-

Notes: Please refer to the User's Guide for an explanation of data; data is arranged alphabetically by state, then county, then city within each county; table includes counties with populations greater than 49,999 unless noted and cities with populations greater than 9,999 whose Asian and/or NHPI population rates are greater than the national average; (1) Native Hawaiian and other Pacific Islander; (2) excludes Taiwanese; (3) includes Chamorro; (4) county does not meet population threshold but is shown in order to allow inclusion of city

Place	Total population 25 years and over who are 4-year college graduates	Asian population 25 years and over	Asians 25 years and over who are 4-year college graduates	NHPI[1] population 25 years and over	NHPIs[1] 25 years and over who are 4-year college graduates	Asian Indian	Bangladeshi	Cambodian	Chinese[2]	Fijian	Filipino	Guamanian[3]	Hawaiian, Native	Hmong	Indonesian	Japanese	Korean	Laotian	Malaysian	Pakistani	Samoan	Sri Lankan	Taiwanese	Thai	Tongan	Vietnamese
Stearns County	17,036 21.98	806	251 31.14 31.14 1.47	-	-	-	-	-	-	-	-	-	-	-	-	-	-	-	-	-	-	-	-	-	-	63 16.71 25.10 7.82 0.37
Washington County	43,428 33.87	2,318	1,220 52.63 52.63 2.81	-	-	329 92.68 26.97 14.19 0.76	-	-	262 60.65 21.48 11.30 0.60	-	-	-	-	83 28.52 6.80 3.58 0.19	-	-	118 46.27 9.67 5.09 0.27	-	-	-	-	-	-	-	-	96 28.83 7.87 4.14 0.22
Woodbury (city)	14,531 49.29	1,346	836 62.11 62.11 5.75	-	-	252 92.99 30.14 18.72 1.73	-	-	192 80.00 22.97 14.26 1.32	-	-	-	-	19 15.32 2.27 1.41 0.13	-	-	-	-	-	-	-	-	-	-	-	-
Wright County	9,864 17.86	91	30 32.97 32.97 0.30	-	-	-	-	-	-	-	-	-	-	-	-	-	-	-	-	-	-	-	-	-	-	-
MISSISSIPPI	297,091 16.90	10,890	3,906 35.87 35.87 1.31	385	65 16.88 16.88 0.02	1,209 57.11 30.95 11.10 0.41	-	-	991 53.19 25.37 9.10 0.33	-	558 29.59 14.29 5.12 0.19	-	-	-	-	127 28.86 3.25 1.17 0.04	261 29.52 6.68 2.40 0.09	-	-	-	-	-	-	-	-	345 12.99 8.83 3.17 0.12
DeSoto County	9,790 14.33	431	112 25.99 25.99 1.14	-	-	-	-	-	-	-	-	-	-	-	-	-	-	-	-	-	-	-	-	-	-	-
Forrest County	9,482 22.83	259	101 39.00 39.00 1.07	-	-	-	-	-	-	-	-	-	-	-	-	-	-	-	-	-	-	-	-	-	-	-
Harrison County	21,913 18.39	2,956	504 17.05 17.05 2.30	-	-	-	-	-	-	-	105 19.74 20.83 3.55 0.48	-	-	-	-	-	-	-	-	-	-	-	-	-	-	92 6.64 18.25 3.11 0.42
Biloxi (city)	5,952 19.17	1,355	223 16.46 16.46 3.75	-	-	-	-	-	-	-	48 19.12 21.52 3.54 0.81	-	-	-	-	-	-	-	-	-	-	-	-	-	-	21 2.93 9.42 1.55 0.35
Hinds County	40,868 27.19	874	519 59.38 59.38 1.27	-	-	320 76.37 61.66 36.61 0.78	-	-	-	-	-	-	-	-	-	-	-	-	-	-	-	-	-	-	-	-

Notes: Please refer to the User's Guide for an explanation of data; data is arranged alphabetically by state, then county, then city within each county; table includes counties with populations greater than 49,999 unless noted and cities with populations greater than 9,999 whose Asian and/or NHPI population rates are greater than the national average; (1) Native Hawaiian and other Pacific Islander; (2) excludes Taiwanese; (3) includes Chamorro; (4) county does not meet population threshold but is shown in order to allow inclusion of city

Place	Total population 25 years and over who are 4-year college graduates	Asian population 25 years and over	Asians 25 years and over who are 4-year college graduates	NHPI[1] population 25 years and over	NHPIs[1] 25 years and over who are 4-year college graduates	Asian Indian	Bangladeshi	Cambodian	Chinese[2]	Fijian	Filipino	Guamanian[3]	Hawaiian, Native	Hmong	Indonesian	Japanese	Korean	Laotian	Malaysian	Pakistani	Samoan	Sri Lankan	Taiwanese	Thai	Tongan	Vietnamese
Jackson County	13,627 16.45	1,159	249 21.48 21.48 1.83	-	-	-	-	-	-	-	-	-	-	-	-	-	-	-	-	-	-	-	-	-	-	83 15.99 33.33 7.16 0.61
Madison County	17,744 37.94	465	233 50.11 50.11 1.31	-	-	-	-	-	-	-	-	-	-	-	-	-	-	-	-	-	-	-	-	-	-	-
Oktibbeha County[4]	7,402 34.83	577	472 81.80 81.80 6.38	-	-	-	-	-	-	-	-	-	-	-	-	-	-	-	-	-	-	-	-	-	-	-
Starkville (city)	5,073 45.77	481	415 86.28 86.28 8.18	-	-	-	-	-	-	-	-	-	-	-	-	-	-	-	-	-	-	-	-	-	-	-
Rankin County	17,804 23.78	374	156 41.71 41.71 0.88	-	-	-	-	-	-	-	-	-	-	-	-	-	-	-	-	-	-	-	-	-	-	-
MISSOURI	784,476 21.58	39,231	20,190 51.46 51.46 2.57	1,630	300 18.40 18.40 0.04	5,545 73.89 27.46 14.13 0.71	-	25 6.33 0.12 0.06 <0.01	5,515 65.42 27.32 14.06 0.70	-	2,668 51.97 13.21 6.80 0.34	70 19.55 23.33 4.29 0.01	81 19.47 27.00 4.97 0.01	-	-	1,120 42.49 5.55 2.85 0.14	1,950 47.02 9.66 4.97 0.25	32 6.82 0.16 0.08 <0.01	-	423 65.48 2.10 1.08 0.05	93 19.02 31.00 5.71 0.01	-	565 82.72 2.80 1.44 0.07	434 45.21 2.15 1.11 0.06	-	886 13.84 4.39 2.26 0.11
Boone County	32,517 41.73	2,358	1,686 71.50 71.50 5.18	-	-	405 82.99 24.02 17.18 1.25	-	-	607 79.45 36.00 25.74 1.87	-	-	-	-	-	-	-	196 71.01 11.63 8.31 0.60	-	-	-	-	-	-	-	-	-
Columbia (city)	23,031 50.45	2,194	1,599 72.88 72.88 6.94	-	-	385 82.26 24.08 17.55 1.67	-	-	570 78.40 35.65 25.98 2.47	-	-	-	-	-	-	-	187 74.50 11.69 8.52 0.81	-	-	-	-	-	-	-	-	-
Cape Girardeau County	10,515 24.21	205	125 60.98 60.98 1.19	-	-	-	-	-	-	-	-	-	-	-	-	-	-	-	-	-	-	-	-	-	-	-
Cass County	9,334 17.69	214	44 20.56 20.56 0.47	-	-	-	-	-	-	-	-	-	-	-	-	-	-	-	-	-	-	-	-	-	-	-

Notes: Please refer to the User's Guide for an explanation of data; data is arranged alphabetically by state, then county, then city within each county; table includes counties with populations greater than 49,999 unless noted and cities with populations greater than 9,999 whose Asian and/or NHPI population rates are greater than the national average; (1) Native Hawaiian and other Pacific Islander; (2) excludes Taiwanese; (3) includes Chamorro; (4) county does not meet population threshold but is shown in order to allow inclusion of city

Place	Total population 25 years and over who are 4-year college graduates	Asian population 25 years and over	Asians 25 years and over who are 4-year college graduates	NHPI[1] population 25 years and over	NHPIs[1] 25 years and over who are 4-year college graduates	Asian Indian	Bangladeshi	Cambodian	Chinese[2]	Fijian	Filipino	Guamanian[3]	Hawaiian, Native	Hmong	Indonesian	Japanese	Korean	Laotian	Malaysian	Pakistani	Samoan	Sri Lankan	Taiwanese	Thai	Tongan	Vietnamese
Clay County	30,047 24.94	1,361	554 40.71 40.71 1.84	-	-	130 58.56 23.47 9.55 0.43	-	-	-	-	-	-	-	-	-	-	-	-	-	-	-	-	-	-	-	79 21.29 14.26 5.80 0.26
Cole County	12,980 27.42	472	303 64.19 64.19 2.33	-	-	-	-	-	-	-	-	-	-	-	-	-	-	-	-	-	-	-	-	-	-	-
Franklin County	7,721 12.77	202	39 19.31 19.31 0.51	-	-	-	-	-	-	-	-	-	-	-	-	-	-	-	-	-	-	-	-	-	-	-
Greene County	37,232 24.19	1,274	545 42.78 42.78 1.46	-	-	-	-	-	69 38.12 12.66 5.42 0.19	-	-	-	-	-	-	-	75 39.27 13.76 5.89 0.20	-	-	-	-	-	-	-	-	93 34.96 17.06 7.30 0.25
Jackson County	100,132 23.45	5,505	2,013 36.57 36.57 2.01	493	80 16.23 16.23 0.08	354 51.83 17.59 6.43 0.35	-	-	589 63.61 29.26 10.70 0.59	-	419 47.51 20.81 7.61 0.42	-	-	-	-	138 39.88 6.86 2.51 0.14	181 46.77 8.99 3.29 0.18	-	-	-	30 13.04 37.50 6.09 0.03	-	-	-	-	121 7.37 6.01 2.20 0.12
Independence (city)	11,663 15.23	709	249 35.12 35.12 2.13	196	42 21.43 21.43 0.36	-	-	-	-	-	-	-	-	-	-	-	-	-	-	-	-	-	-	-	-	-
Jasper County	10,912 16.48	419	158 37.71 37.71 1.45	-	-	-	-	-	-	-	-	-	-	-	-	-	-	-	-	-	-	-	-	-	-	-
Jefferson County	15,290 12.14	475	164 34.53 34.53 1.07	-	-	-	-	-	-	-	-	-	-	-	-	-	-	-	-	-	-	-	-	-	-	-
Newton County	5,524 16.15	112	40 35.71 35.71 0.72	-	-	-	-	-	-	-	-	-	-	-	-	-	-	-	-	-	-	-	-	-	-	-
Phelps County[4]	5,192 21.05	556	435 78.24 78.24 8.38	-	-	151 83.89 34.71 27.16 2.91	-	-	-	-	-	-	-	-	-	-	-	-	-	-	-	-	-	-	-	-

Notes: Please refer to the User's Guide for an explanation of data; data is arranged alphabetically by state, then county, then city within each county; table includes counties with populations greater than 49,999 unless noted and cities with populations greater than 9,999 whose Asian and/or NHPI population rates are greater than the national average; (1) Native Hawaiian and other Pacific Islander; (2) excludes Taiwanese; (3) includes Chamorro; (4) county does not meet population threshold but is shown in order to allow inclusion of city

Place	Total population 25 years and over who are 4-year college graduates	Asian population 25 years and over	Asians 25 years and over who are 4-year college graduates	NHPI[1] population 25 years and over	NHPIs[1] 25 years and over who are 4-year college graduates	Asian Indian	Bangladeshi	Cambodian	Chinese[2]	Fijian	Filipino	Guamanian[3]	Hawaiian, Native	Hmong	Indonesian	Japanese	Korean	Laotian	Malaysian	Pakistani	Samoan	Sri Lankan	Taiwanese	Thai	Tongan	Vietnamese
Rolla (city)	2,547 27.86	472	392 83.05 83.05 15.39	-	-	-	-	-	-	-	-	-	-	-	-	-	-	-	-	-	-	-	-	-	-	-
Platte County	16,230 33.31	713	331 46.42 46.42 2.04	-	-	-	-	-	-	-	-	-	-	-	-	-	-	-	-	-	-	-	-	-	-	-
St. Charles County	47,006 26.33	1,543	840 54.44 54.44 1.79	-	-	264 71.93 31.43 17.11 0.56	-	-	199 75.95 23.69 12.90 0.42	-	152 53.71 18.10 9.85 0.32	-	-	-	-	-	-	-	-	-	-	-	-	-	-	-
Saint Louis Independent City	42,338 19.08	4,595	1,524 33.17 33.17 3.60	-	-	309 69.75 20.28 6.72 0.73	-	-	384 55.33 25.20 8.36 0.91	-	203 48.92 13.32 4.42 0.48	-	-	-	-	-	-	-	-	-	-	-	-	-	-	131 6.48 8.60 2.85 0.31
St. Louis County	239,729 35.41	14,654	9,709 66.25 66.25 4.05	215	55 25.58 25.58 0.02	3,037 80.15 31.28 20.72 1.27	-	-	2,810 69.26 28.94 19.18 1.17	-	968 62.25 9.97 6.61 0.40	-	-	-	-	535 56.55 5.51 3.65 0.22	923 58.60 9.51 6.30 0.39	-	-	265 72.80 2.73 1.81 0.11	-	-	370 81.32 3.81 2.52 0.15	130 48.33 1.34 0.89 0.05	-	230 22.42 2.37 1.57 0.10
Chesterfield (city)	19,803 60.58	1,640	1,279 77.99 77.99 6.46	-	-	346 87.82 27.05 21.10 1.75	-	-	411 76.97 32.13 25.06 2.08	-	-	-	-	-	-	-	-	-	-	-	-	-	-	-	-	-
Clayton (city)	6,169 69.67	526	422 80.23 80.23 6.84	-	-	-	-	-	-	-	-	-	-	-	-	-	-	-	-	-	-	-	-	-	-	-
Creve Coeur (city)	7,394 62.86	651	497 76.34 76.34 6.72	-	-	-	-	-	-	-	-	-	-	-	-	-	-	-	-	-	-	-	-	-	-	-
Manchester (city)	6,565 52.91	586	436 74.40 74.40 6.64	-	-	-	-	-	-	-	-	-	-	-	-	-	-	-	-	-	-	-	-	-	-	-
Maryland Heights (city)	6,901 38.68	1,290	918 71.16 71.16 13.30	-	-	463 92.42 50.44 35.89 6.71	-	-	190 51.77 20.70 14.73 2.75	-	-	-	-	-	-	-	-	-	-	-	-	-	-	-	-	-

Notes: Please refer to the User's Guide for an explanation of data; data is arranged alphabetically by state, then county, then city within each county; table includes counties with populations greater than 49,999 unless noted and cities with populations greater than 9,999 whose Asian and/or NHPI population rates are greater than the national average; (1) Native Hawaiian and other Pacific Islander; (2) excludes Taiwanese; (3) includes Chamorro; (4) county does not meet population threshold but is shown in order to allow inclusion of city

Place	Total population 25 years and over who are 4-year college graduates	Asian population 25 years and over	Asians 25 years and over who are 4-year college graduates	NHPI[1] population 25 years and over	NHPIs[1] 25 years and over who are 4-year college graduates	Asian Indian	Bangladeshi	Cambodian	Chinese[2]	Fijian	Filipino	Guamanian[3]	Hawaiian, Native	Hmong	Indonesian	Japanese	Korean	Laotian	Malaysian	Pakistani	Samoan	Sri Lankan	Taiwanese	Thai	Tongan	Vietnamese
Town and Country (city)	5,034	626	483	-	-	221	-	-	-	-	-	-	-	-	-	-	-	-	-	-	-	-	-	-	-	-
	66.18		77.16			78.37																				
						45.76																				
			77.16			35.30																				
			9.59			4.39																				
MONTANA	142,961	2,562	1,050	250	45	195	-	-	194	-	171	-	30	-	-	212	135	-	-	-	-	-	-	-	-	-
	24.37		40.98		18.00	76.47			54.19		29.69		21.58			35.04	40.06									
						18.57			18.48		16.29		66.67			20.19	12.86									
			40.98		18.00	7.61			7.57		6.67		12.00			8.27	5.27									
			0.73		0.03	0.14			0.14		0.12		0.02			0.15	0.09									
Cascade County	11,239	400	105	-	-	-	-	-	-	-	-	-	-	-	-	-	-	-	-	-	-	-	-	-	-	-
	21.48		26.25																							
			26.25																							
			0.93																							
Flathead County	11,137	166	61	-	-	-	-	-	-	-	-	-	-	-	-	-	-	-	-	-	-	-	-	-	-	-
	22.43		36.75																							
			36.75																							
			0.55																							
Gallatin County	16,593	317	215	-	-	-	-	-	-	-	-	-	-	-	-	-	-	-	-	-	-	-	-	-	-	-
	41.01		67.82																							
			67.82																							
			1.30																							
Missoula County	19,450	468	203	-	-	-	-	-	-	-	-	-	-	-	-	-	-	-	-	-	-	-	-	-	-	-
	32.80		43.38																							
			43.38																							
			1.04																							
Yellowstone County	22,222	356	178	-	-	-	-	-	-	-	-	-	-	-	-	-	-	-	-	-	-	-	-	-	-	-
	26.38		50.00																							
			50.00																							
			0.80																							
NEBRASKA	258,140	12,594	5,327	339	49	1,630	-	-	1,396	-	552	-	-	-	-	325	370	13	-	-	-	-	-	188	-	457
	23.74		42.30		14.45	83.98			72.82		37.96					32.53	37.11	2.78						50.95		12.40
						30.60			26.21		10.36					6.10	6.95	0.24						3.53		8.58
			42.30		14.45	12.94			11.08		4.38					2.58	2.94	0.10						1.49		3.63
			2.06		0.02	0.63			0.54		0.21					0.13	0.14	0.01						0.07		0.18
Douglas County	89,712	4,690	2,723	-	-	1,038	-	-	677	-	217	-	-	-	-	159	178	-	-	-	-	-	-	-	-	148
	30.61		58.06			87.45			75.90		34.55					36.72	50.71									21.57
						38.12			24.86		7.97					5.84	6.54									5.44
			58.06			22.13			14.43		4.63					3.39	3.80									3.16
			3.04			1.16			0.75		0.24					0.18	0.20									0.16
Hall County	5,481	319	89	-	-	-	-	-	-	-	-	-	-	-	-	-	-	-	-	-	-	-	-	-	-	-
	15.95		27.90																							
			27.90																							
			1.62																							

Notes: Please refer to the User's Guide for an explanation of data; data is arranged alphabetically by state, then county, then city within each county; table includes counties with populations greater than 49,999 unless noted and cities with populations greater than 9,999 whose Asian and/or NHPI population rates are greater than the national average; (1) Native Hawaiian and other Pacific Islander; (2) excludes Taiwanese; (3) includes Chamorro; (4) county does not meet population threshold but is shown in order to allow inclusion of city

Place	Total population 25 years and over who are 4-year college graduates	Asian population 25 years and over	Asians 25 years and over who are 4-year college graduates	NHPI[1] population 25 years and over	NHPIs[1] 25 years and over who are 4-year college graduates	Asian Indian	Bangladeshi	Cambodian	Chinese[2]	Fijian	Filipino	Guamanian[3]	Hawaiian, Native	Hmong	Indonesian	Japanese	Korean	Laotian	Malaysian	Pakistani	Samoan	Sri Lankan	Taiwanese	Thai	Tongan	Vietnamese
	49,743	3,896	1,401	-	-	370	-	-	540	-	-	-	-	-	-	-	87	-	-	-	-	-	-	-	-	176
	32.57		35.96			89.59			76.06								47.03									8.59
Lancaster County						26.41			38.54								6.21									12.56
			35.96			9.50			13.86								2.23									4.52
			2.82			0.74			1.09								0.17									0.35
	22,325	1,469	498	-	-	-	-	-	-	-	145	-	-	-	-	-	73	-	-	-	-	-	-	-	-	28
	30.25		33.90								38.87						25.26									11.72
Sarpy County											29.12						14.66									5.62
			33.90								9.87						4.97									1.91
			2.23								0.65						0.33									0.13
	237,875	62,181	17,608	4,572	485	1,481	-	23	3,102	-	8,335	112	261	-	-	1,583	1,317	85	-	150	34	-	128	410	13	446
	18.16		28.32		10.61	44.58		4.80	32.02		30.76	15.89	11.63			23.33	23.87	11.23		47.62	4.33		28.32	18.37	3.32	15.02
NEVADA						8.41		0.13	17.62		47.34	23.09	53.81			8.99	7.48	0.48		0.85	7.01		0.73	2.33	2.68	2.53
			28.32		10.61	2.38		0.04	4.99		13.40	2.45	5.71			2.55	2.12	0.14		0.24	0.74		0.21	0.66	0.28	0.72
			7.40		0.20	0.62		0.01	1.30		3.50	0.05	0.11			0.67	0.55	0.04		0.06	0.01		0.05	0.17	0.01	0.19
	6,639	711	292	-	-	-	-	-	-	-	58	-	-	-	-	-	-	-	-	-	-	-	-	-	-	-
	18.47		41.07								30.85															
Carson City Independent City											19.86															
			41.07								8.16															
			4.40								0.87															
	156,083	50,502	13,773	3,637	402	873	-	23	2,409	-	6,680	91	244	-	-	1,187	1,182	85	-	-	14	-	47	361	-	352
	17.33		27.27		11.05	41.12		4.95	30.92		30.40	14.58	12.18			21.65	24.76	11.23			2.55		14.60	18.17		14.26
Clark County						6.34		0.17	17.49		48.50	22.64	60.70			8.62	8.58	0.62			3.48		0.34	2.62		2.56
			27.27		11.05	1.73		0.05	4.77		13.23	2.50	6.71			2.35	2.34	0.17			0.38		0.09	0.71		0.70
			8.82		0.26	0.56		0.01	1.54		4.28	0.06	0.16			0.76	0.76	0.05			0.01		0.03	0.23		0.23
	1,700	501	87	-	-	-	-	-	-	-	-	-	-	-	-	-	-	-	-	-	-	-	-	-	-	-
	16.74		17.37																							
Enterprise (cdp)																										
			17.37																							
			5.12																							
	28,121	4,903	1,777	503	69	223	-	-	258	-	684	-	55	-	-	191	213	-	-	-	-	-	-	-	-	-
	23.70		36.24		13.72	64.27			42.86		36.54		17.68			27.80	39.15									
Henderson (city)						12.55			14.52		38.49		79.71			10.75	11.99									
			36.24		13.72	4.55			5.26		13.95		10.93			3.90	4.34									
			6.32		0.25	0.79			0.92		2.43		0.20			0.68	0.76									
	56,989	15,432	4,661	1,095	90	242	-	-	713	-	2,442	-	79	-	-	469	358	-	-	-	-	-	-	106	-	88
	18.20		30.20		8.22	31.43			34.41		33.69		13.88			23.45	32.84							20.08		16.36
Las Vegas (city)						5.19			15.30		52.39		87.78			10.06	7.68							2.27		1.89
			30.20		8.22	1.57			4.62		15.82		7.21			3.04	2.32							0.69		0.57
			8.18		0.16	0.42			1.25		4.29		0.14			0.82	0.63							0.19		0.15
	6,704	2,672	595	430	52	-	-	-	-	-	377	-	-	-	-	-	-	-	-	-	-	-	-	-	-	-
	10.23		22.27		12.09						26.33															
North Las Vegas (city)											63.36															
			22.27		12.09						14.11															
			8.88		0.78						5.62															
	22,469	8,845	2,547	462	57	215	-	-	538	-	1,138	-	38	-	-	197	262	-	-	-	-	-	-	-	-	57
	17.73		28.80		12.34	47.78			37.36		29.71		11.76			19.78	27.72									12.69
Paradise (cdp)						8.44			21.12		44.68		66.67			7.73	10.29									2.24
			28.80		12.34	2.43			6.08		12.87		8.23			2.23	2.96									0.64
			11.34		0.25	0.96			2.39		5.06		0.17			0.88	1.17									0.25

Notes: Please refer to the User's Guide for an explanation of data; data is arranged alphabetically by state, then county, then city within each county; table includes counties with populations greater than 49,999 unless noted and cities with populations greater than 9,999 whose Asian and/or NHPI population rates are greater than the national average; (1) Native Hawaiian and other Pacific Islander; (2) excludes Taiwanese; (3) includes Chamorro; (4) county does not meet population threshold but is shown in order to allow inclusion of city

Place	Total population 25 years and over who are 4-year college graduates	Asian population 25 years and over	Asians 25 years and over who are 4-year college graduates	NHPI[1] population 25 years and over	NHPIs[1] 25 years and over who are 4-year college graduates	Asian Indian	Bangladeshi	Cambodian	Chinese[2]	Fijian	Filipino	Guamanian[3]	Hawaiian, Native	Hmong	Indonesian	Japanese	Korean	Laotian	Malaysian	Pakistani	Samoan	Sri Lankan	Taiwanese	Thai	Tongan	Vietnamese
	16,931	9,008	2,352	347	23	-	-	-	680	-	887	-	-	-	-	212	153	-	-	-	-	-	-	81	-	79
	20.65		26.11		6.63				24.12		33.38					35.10	14.66							22.82		12.10
Spring Valley (cdp)									28.91		37.71					9.01	6.51							3.44		3.36
			26.11		6.63				7.55		9.85					2.35	1.70							0.90		0.88
			13.89		0.14				4.02		5.24					1.25	0.90							0.48		0.47
	9,214	6,010	1,103	275	45	-	-	-	63	-	778	-	-	-	-	14	86	-	-	-	-	-	-	-	-	-
	9.77		18.35		16.36				16.62		23.65					2.57	16.32									
Sunrise Manor (cdp)									5.71		70.53					1.27	7.80									
			18.35		16.36				1.05		12.95					0.23	1.43									
			11.97		0.49				0.68		8.44					0.15	0.93									
	3,102	1,095	273	-	-	-	-	-	-	-	93	-	-	-	-	-	-	-	-	-	-	-	-	-	-	-
	15.94		24.93								27.60															
Winchester (cdp)											34.07															
			24.93								8.49															
			8.80								3.00															
	52,618	9,324	3,190	675	53	477	-	-	575	-	1,421	-	-	-	-	327	115	-	-	-	-	-	-	-	10	76
	23.72		34.21		7.85	48.97			35.06		34.87					35.28	20.54								3.70	16.93
Washoe County						14.95			18.03		44.55					10.25	3.61								18.87	2.38
			34.21		7.85	5.12			6.17		15.24					3.51	1.23								1.48	0.82
			6.06		0.10	0.91			1.09		2.70					0.62	0.22								0.02	0.14
	29,353	6,100	2,111	455	31	287	-	-	422	-	968	-	-	-	-	181	66	-	-	-	-	-	-	-	-	40
	24.98		34.61		6.81	46.37			38.86		35.95					30.63	19.70									14.23
Reno (city)						13.60			19.99		45.86					8.57	3.13									1.89
			34.61		6.81	4.70			6.92		15.87					2.97	1.08									0.66
			7.19		0.11	0.98			1.44		3.30					0.62	0.22									0.14
	7,542	2,033	560	-	-	-	-	-	72	-	284	-	-	-	-	-	-	-	-	-	-	-	-	-	-	-
	17.79		27.55						18.90		31.07															
Sparks (city)									12.86		50.71															
			27.55						3.54		13.97															
			7.43						0.95		3.77															
	236,104	9,476	5,174	-	-	1,898	-	-	1,517	-	472	-	-	-	-	321	416	24	-	-	-	-	-	-	-	124
	28.65		54.60			83.25			61.44		55.40					50.31	42.71	11.43								11.11
NEW HAMPSHIRE						36.68			29.32		9.12					6.20	8.04	0.46								2.40
			54.60			20.03			16.01		4.98					3.39	4.39	0.25								1.31
			2.19			0.80			0.64		0.20					0.14	0.18	0.01								0.05
	9,140	217	54	-	-	-	-	-	-	-	-	-	-	-	-	-	-	-	-	-	-	-	-	-	-	-
	23.28		24.88																							
Belknap County																										
			24.88																							
			0.59																							
	12,783	260	120	-	-	-	-	-	-	-	-	-	-	-	-	-	-	-	-	-	-	-	-	-	-	-
	26.61		46.15																							
Cheshire County																										
			46.15																							
			0.94																							
	17,247	507	349	-	-	-	-	-	121	-	-	-	-	-	-	-	-	-	-	-	-	-	-	-	-	-
	32.67		68.84						72.89																	
Grafton County									34.67																	
			68.84						23.87																	
			2.02						0.70																	

Notes: Please refer to the User's Guide for an explanation of data; data is arranged alphabetically by state, then county, then city within each county; table includes counties with populations greater than 49,999 unless noted and cities with populations greater than 9,999 whose Asian and/or NHPI population rates are greater than the national average; (1) Native Hawaiian and other Pacific Islander; (2) excludes Taiwanese; (3) includes Chamorro; (4) county does not meet population threshold but is shown in order to allow inclusion of city

Place	Total population 25 years and over who are 4-year college graduates	Asian population 25 years and over	Asians 25 years and over who are 4-year college graduates	NHPI[1] population 25 years and over	NHPIs[1] 25 years and over who are 4-year college graduates	Asian Indian	Bangladeshi	Cambodian	Chinese[2]	Fijian	Filipino	Guamanian[3]	Hawaiian, Native	Hmong	Indonesian	Japanese	Korean	Laotian	Malaysian	Pakistani	Samoan	Sri Lankan	Taiwanese	Thai	Tongan	Vietnamese
Hanover (town)	4,012 77.66	173	139 80.35 80.35 3.46	-	-	-	-	-	-	-	-	-	-	-	-	-	-	-	-	-	-	-	-	-	-	-
Hillsborough County	75,803 30.09	4,828	2,810 58.20 58.20 3.71	-	-	1,260 85.89 44.84 26.10 1.66	-	-	821 62.77 29.22 17.00 1.08	-	170 60.07 6.05 3.52 0.22	-	-	-	-	-	169 50.60 6.01 3.50 0.22	-	-	-	-	-	-	-	-	39 5.26 1.39 0.81 0.05
Nashua (city)	18,329 31.46	2,303	1,603 69.60 69.60 8.75	-	-	874 88.55 54.52 37.95 4.77	-	-	486 79.93 30.32 21.10 2.65	-	-	-	-	-	-	-	-	-	-	-	-	-	-	-	-	-
Merrimack County	26,573 29.11	681	396 58.15 58.15 1.49	-	-	-	-	-	-	-	-	-	-	-	-	-	-	-	-	-	-	-	-	-	-	-
Rockingham County	59,261 31.66	1,845	979 53.06 53.06 1.65	-	-	260 82.80 26.56 14.09 0.44	-	-	338 61.57 34.53 18.32 0.57	-	173 67.05 17.67 9.38 0.29	-	-	-	-	-	65 29.95 6.64 3.52 0.11	-	-	-	-	-	-	-	-	-
Strafford County	18,592 26.44	868	398 45.85 45.85 2.14	-	-	-	-	-	129 63.24 32.41 14.86 0.69	-	-	-	-	-	-	-	-	-	-	-	-	-	-	-	-	-
NEW JERSEY	1,684,861 29.78	315,460	195,903 62.10 62.10 11.63	1,686	366 21.71 21.71 0.02	74,099 67.43 37.82 23.49 4.40	518 39.82 0.26 0.16 0.03	57 15.62 0.03 0.02 <0.01	41,185 64.08 21.02 13.06 2.44	-	38,639 65.91 19.72 12.25 2.29	35 10.87 9.56 2.08 <0.01	104 23.37 28.42 6.17 0.01	-	373 52.09 0.19 0.12 0.02	5,999 57.30 3.06 1.90 0.36	21,558 53.06 11.00 6.83 1.28	31 11.97 0.02 0.01 <0.01	-	3,837 55.98 1.96 1.22 0.23	130 30.73 35.52 7.71 0.01	552 59.42 0.28 0.17 0.03	3,042 77.44 1.55 0.96 0.18	624 47.34 0.32 0.20 0.04	-	2,372 24.45 1.21 0.75 0.14
Atlantic County	31,509 18.69	8,493	2,613 30.77 30.77 8.29	-	-	1,048 40.78 40.11 12.34 3.33	75 33.78 2.87 0.88 0.24	-	255 17.03 9.76 3.00 0.81	-	773 55.49 29.58 9.10 2.45	-	-	-	-	-	93 23.85 3.56 1.10 0.30	-	-	95 30.16 3.64 1.12 0.30	-	-	-	-	-	101 6.92 3.87 1.19 0.32
Atlantic City (city)	2,751 10.37	2,915	608 20.86 20.86 22.10	-	-	181 29.87 29.77 6.21 6.58	-	-	66 11.89 10.86 2.26 2.40	-	174 47.03 28.62 5.97 6.32	-	-	-	-	-	-	-	-	-	-	-	-	-	-	59 6.70 9.70 2.02 2.14
Brigantine (city)	2,218 23.81	456	195 42.76 42.76 8.79	-	-	-	-	-	-	-	-	-	-	-	-	-	-	-	-	-	-	-	-	-	-	-

Notes: Please refer to the User's Guide for an explanation of data; data is arranged alphabetically by state, then county, then city within each county; table includes counties with populations greater than 49,999 unless noted and cities with populations greater than 9,999 whose Asian and/or NHPI population rates are greater than the national average; (1) Native Hawaiian and other Pacific Islander; (2) excludes Taiwanese; (3) includes Chamorro; (4) county does not meet population threshold but is shown in order to allow inclusion of city

Place	Total population 25 years and over who are 4-year college graduates	Asian population 25 years and over	Asians 25 years and over who are 4-year college graduates	NHPI[1] population 25 years and over	NHPIs[1] 25 years and over who are 4-year college graduates	Asian Indian	Bangladeshi	Cambodian	Chinese[2]	Fijian	Filipino	Guamanian[3]	Hawaiian, Native	Hmong	Indonesian	Japanese	Korean	Laotian	Malaysian	Pakistani	Samoan	Sri Lankan	Taiwanese	Thai	Tongan	Vietnamese
Egg Harbor (township)	3,820	1,097	378	-	-	-	-	-	-	-	-	-	-	-	-	-	-	-	-	-	-	-	-	-	-	-
	19.03		34.46																							
			34.46																							
			9.90																							
Galloway (township)	4,274	1,586	618	-	-	303	-	-	-	-	-	-	-	-	-	-	-	-	-	-	-	-	-	-	-	-
	22.82		38.97			39.10																				
						49.03																				
			38.97			19.10																				
			14.46			7.09																				
Ventnor City (city)	2,023	651	154	-	-	-	-	-	-	-	-	-	-	-	-	-	-	-	-	-	-	-	-	-	-	-
	21.36		23.66																							
			23.66																							
			7.61																							
Bergen County	238,381	62,554	38,045	-	-	7,878	-	-	5,794	-	6,708	-	-	-	-	3,078	12,600	-	-	508	-	-	439	195	-	97
	38.23		60.82			68.42			63.55		67.90					61.96	53.45			58.32			77.43	53.72		33.68
						20.71			15.23		17.63					8.09	33.12			1.34			1.15	0.51		0.25
			60.82			12.59			9.26		10.72					4.92	20.14			0.81			0.70	0.31		0.16
			15.96			3.30			2.43		2.81					1.29	5.29			0.21			0.18	0.08		0.04
Bergenfield (borough)	5,757	3,299	1,964	-	-	546	-	-	-	-	1,186	-	-	-	-	-	-	-	-	-	-	-	-	-	-	-
	32.29		59.53			62.12					59.39															
						27.80					60.39															
			59.53			16.55					35.95															
			34.11			9.48					20.60															
Cliffside Park (borough)	5,681	2,024	1,154	-	-	-	-	-	-	-	-	-	-	-	-	208	610	-	-	-	-	-	-	-	-	-
	32.68		57.02													59.77	55.81									
																18.02	52.86									
			57.02													10.28	30.14									
			20.31													3.66	10.74									
Dumont (borough)	3,346	1,215	770	-	-	220	-	-	-	-	277	-	-	-	-	-	-	-	-	-	-	-	-	-	-	-
	27.36		63.37			73.09					67.40															
						28.57					35.97															
			63.37			18.11					22.80															
			23.01			6.58					8.28															
Elmwood Park (borough)	2,785	1,058	671	-	-	458	-	-	-	-	-	-	-	-	-	-	-	-	-	-	-	-	-	-	-	-
	20.57		63.42			70.79																				
						68.26																				
			63.42			43.29																				
			24.09			16.45																				
Englewood (city)	6,611	1,013	613	-	-	-	-	-	-	-	230	-	-	-	-	-	-	-	-	-	-	-	-	-	-	-
	36.71		60.51								74.92															
											37.52															
			60.51								22.70															
			9.27								3.48															
Fair Lawn (borough)	10,062	1,118	722	-	-	284	-	-	-	-	225	-	-	-	-	-	-	-	-	-	-	-	-	-	-	-
	44.82		64.58			69.44					71.43															
						39.34					31.16															
			64.58			25.40					20.13															
			7.18			2.82					2.24															

Notes: Please refer to the User's Guide for an explanation of data; data is arranged alphabetically by state, then county, then city within each county; table includes counties with populations greater than 49,999 unless noted and cities with populations greater than 9,999 whose Asian and/or NHPI population rates are greater than the national average; (1) Native Hawaiian and other Pacific Islander; (2) excludes Taiwanese; (3) includes Chamorro; (4) county does not meet population threshold but is shown in order to allow inclusion of city

Place	Total population 25 years and over who are 4-year college graduates	Asian population 25 years and over	Asians 25 years and over who are 4-year college graduates	NHPI[1] population 25 years and over	NHPIs[1] 25 years and over who are 4-year college graduates	Asian Indian	Bangladeshi	Cambodian	Chinese[2]	Fijian	Filipino	Guamanian[3]	Hawaiian, Native	Hmong	Indonesian	Japanese	Korean	Laotian	Malaysian	Pakistani	Samoan	Sri Lankan	Taiwanese	Thai	Tongan	Vietnamese
Fairview (borough)	1,466 16.55	462	262 56.71 56.71 17.87	-	-	-	-	-	-	-	-	-	-	-	-	-	-	-	-	-	-	-	-	-	-	-
Fort Lee (borough)	13,262 48.24	7,622	4,714 61.85 61.85 35.55	-	-	339 75.67 7.19 4.45 2.56	-	-	713 59.27 15.13 9.35 5.38	-	-	-	-	-	-	907 67.89 19.24 11.90 6.84	2,357 58.30 50.00 30.92 17.77	-	-	-	-	-	-	-	-	-
Franklin Lakes (borough)	3,645 52.94	422	302 71.56 71.56 8.29	-	-	-	-	-	-	-	-	-	-	-	-	-	-	-	-	-	-	-	-	-	-	-
Glen Rock (borough)	4,712 61.08	479	307 64.09 64.09 6.52	-	-	-	-	-	-	-	-	-	-	-	-	-	-	-	-	-	-	-	-	-	-	-
Hackensack (city)	9,173 29.10	2,434	1,643 67.50 67.50 17.91	-	-	636 84.46 38.71 26.13 6.93	-	-	-	-	278 50.27 16.92 11.42 3.03	-	-	-	-	-	348 72.05 21.18 14.30 3.79	-	-	-	-	-	-	-	-	-
Hasbrouck Heights (borough)	2,486 29.91	378	212 56.08 56.08 8.53	-	-	-	-	-	-	-	-	-	-	-	-	-	-	-	-	-	-	-	-	-	-	-
Hillsdale (borough)	3,165 45.85	340	268 78.82 78.82 8.47	-	-	-	-	-	-	-	-	-	-	-	-	-	-	-	-	-	-	-	-	-	-	-
Little Ferry (borough)	1,872 24.12	1,234	620 50.24 50.24 33.12	-	-	135 53.78 21.77 10.94 7.21	-	-	-	-	152 62.81 24.52 12.32 8.12	-	-	-	-	-	213 39.15 34.35 17.26 11.38	-	-	-	-	-	-	-	-	-
Lodi (borough)	3,181 18.69	1,321	660 49.96 49.96 20.75	-	-	361 47.13 54.70 27.33 11.35	-	-	-	-	230 73.72 34.85 17.41 7.23	-	-	-	-	-	-	-	-	-	-	-	-	-	-	-
Lyndhurst (township)	3,117 21.85	735	438 59.59 59.59 14.05	-	-	-	-	-	-	-	-	-	-	-	-	-	-	-	-	-	-	-	-	-	-	-

Notes: Please refer to the User's Guide for an explanation of data; data is arranged alphabetically by state, then county, then city within each county; table includes counties with populations greater than 49,999 unless noted and cities with populations greater than 9,999 whose Asian and/or NHPI population rates are greater than the national average; (1) Native Hawaiian and other Pacific Islander; (2) excludes Taiwanese; (3) includes Chamorro; (4) county does not meet population threshold but is shown in order to allow inclusion of city

Place	Total population 25 years and over who are 4-year college graduates	Asian population 25 years and over	Asians 25 years and over who are 4-year college graduates	NHPI[1] population 25 years and over	NHPIs[1] 25 years and over who are 4-year college graduates	Asian Indian	Bangladeshi	Cambodian	Chinese[2]	Fijian	Filipino	Guamanian[3]	Hawaiian, Native	Hmong	Indonesian	Japanese	Korean	Laotian	Malaysian	Pakistani	Samoan	Sri Lankan	Taiwanese	Thai	Tongan	Vietnamese
Mahwah (township)	8,098 49.46	1,014	722 71.20 71.20 8.92	-	-	287 78.63 39.75 28.30 3.54	-	-	-	-	-	-	-	-	-	-	-	-	-	-	-	-	-	-	-	-
New Milford (borough)	3,843 32.42	1,571	963 61.30 61.30 25.06	-	-	249 59.43 25.86 15.85 6.48	-	-	-	-	406 70.98 42.16 25.84 10.56	-	-	-	-	-	-	-	-	-	-	-	-	-	-	-
North Arlington (borough)	2,198 19.53	571	314 54.99 54.99 14.29	-	-	-	-	-	-	-	-	-	-	-	-	-	-	-	-	-	-	-	-	-	-	-
Palisades Park (borough)	3,727 30.62	4,841	2,046 42.26 42.26 54.90	-	-	-	-	-	-	-	-	-	-	-	-	-	1,682 40.87 82.21 34.74 45.13	-	-	-	-	-	-	-	-	-
Paramus (borough)	7,063 38.67	2,730	1,787 65.46 65.46 25.30	-	-	592 72.11 33.13 21.68 8.38	-	-	246 71.93 13.77 9.01 3.48	-	389 75.24 21.77 14.25 5.51	-	-	-	-	-	375 47.89 20.98 13.74 5.31	-	-	-	-	-	-	-	-	-
Ramsey (borough)	5,301 54.49	552	376 68.12 68.12 7.09	-	-	-	-	-	-	-	-	-	-	-	-	-	-	-	-	-	-	-	-	-	-	-
Ridgefield (borough)	2,010 25.98	1,100	451 41.00 41.00 22.44	-	-	-	-	-	-	-	-	-	-	-	-	-	239 30.25 52.99 21.73 11.89	-	-	-	-	-	-	-	-	-
Ridgefield Park (village)	2,358 26.13	758	428 56.46 56.46 18.15	-	-	-	-	-	-	-	-	-	-	-	-	-	126 39.87 29.44 16.62 5.34	-	-	-	-	-	-	-	-	-
Ridgewood (village)	10,951 66.75	1,248	990 79.33 79.33 9.04	-	-	-	-	-	-	-	-	-	-	-	-	249 86.46 25.15 19.95 2.27	208 73.24 21.01 16.67 1.90	-	-	-	-	-	-	-	-	-
River Edge (borough)	3,543 45.38	880	517 58.75 58.75 14.59	-	-	-	-	-	-	-	-	-	-	-	-	-	125 44.17 24.18 14.20 3.53	-	-	-	-	-	-	-	-	-

Notes: Please refer to the User's Guide for an explanation of data; data is arranged alphabetically by state, then county, then city within each county; table includes counties with populations greater than 49,999 unless noted and cities with populations greater than 9,999 whose Asian and/or NHPI population rates are greater than the national average; (1) Native Hawaiian and other Pacific Islander; (2) excludes Taiwanese; (3) includes Chamorro; (4) county does not meet population threshold but is shown in order to allow inclusion of city

Place	Total population 25 years and over who are 4-year college graduates	Asian population 25 years and over	Asians 25 years and over who are 4-year college graduates	NHPI[1] population 25 years and over	NHPIs[1] 25 years and over who are 4-year college graduates	Asian Indian	Bangladeshi	Cambodian	Chinese[2]	Fijian	Filipino	Guamanian[3]	Hawaiian, Native	Hmong	Indonesian	Japanese	Korean	Laotian	Malaysian	Pakistani	Samoan	Sri Lankan	Taiwanese	Thai	Tongan	Vietnamese
Rutherford (borough)	5,240 40.32	1,358	742 54.64 54.64 14.16	-	-	173 69.48 23.32 12.74 3.30	-	-	-	-	-	-	-	-	-	-	198 36.80 26.68 14.58 3.78	-	-	-	-	-	-	-	-	-
Saddle Brook (township)	2,446 25.21	527	373 70.78 70.78 15.25	-	-	-	-	-	-	-	-	-	-	-	-	-	-	-	-	-	-	-	-	-	-	-
Teaneck (township)	12,471 47.87	1,931	1,144 59.24 59.24 9.17	-	-	303 49.84 26.49 15.69 2.43	-	-	-	-	412 73.70 36.01 21.34 3.30	-	-	-	-	-	-	-	-	-	-	-	-	-	-	-
Tenafly (borough)	5,701 62.15	1,522	978 64.26 64.26 17.15	-	-	-	-	-	350 74.31 35.79 23.00 6.14	-	-	-	-	-	-	-	361 60.07 36.91 23.72 6.33	-	-	-	-	-	-	-	-	-
Wallington (borough)	1,435 17.01	378	252 66.67 66.67 17.56	-	-	-	-	-	-	-	-	-	-	-	-	-	-	-	-	-	-	-	-	-	-	-
Westwood (borough)	3,015 37.44	381	247 64.83 64.83 8.19	-	-	-	-	-	-	-	-	-	-	-	-	-	-	-	-	-	-	-	-	-	-	-
Wyckoff (township)	6,298 56.63	429	298 69.46 69.46 4.73	-	-	-	-	-	-	-	-	-	-	-	-	-	-	-	-	-	-	-	-	-	-	-
Burlington County	81,068 28.39	7,682	3,711 48.31 48.31 4.58	-	-	1,547 63.40 41.69 20.14 1.91	-	-	505 47.20 13.61 6.57 0.62	-	832 57.42 22.42 10.83 1.03	-	-	-	-	108 22.78 2.91 1.41 0.13	367 28.85 9.89 4.78 0.45	-	-	-	-	-	-	-	-	100 25.06 2.69 1.30 0.12
Browns Mills (cdp)	516 7.30	337	69 20.47 20.47 13.37	-	-	-	-	-	-	-	-	-	-	-	-	-	33 14.10 47.83 9.79 6.40	-	-	-	-	-	-	-	-	-
Evesham (township)	11,348 39.73	1,080	625 57.87 57.87 5.51	-	-	179 73.36 28.64 16.57 1.58	-	-	114 40.86 18.24 10.56 1.00	-	-	-	-	-	-	-	-	-	-	-	-	-	-	-	-	-

Notes: Please refer to the User's Guide for an explanation of data; data is arranged alphabetically by state, then county, then city within each county; table includes counties with populations greater than 49,999 unless noted and cities with populations greater than 9,999 whose Asian and/or NHPI population rates are greater than the national average; (1) Native Hawaiian and other Pacific Islander; (2) excludes Taiwanese; (3) includes Chamorro; (4) county does not meet population threshold but is shown in order to allow inclusion of city

Place	Total population 25 years and over who are 4-year college graduates	Asian population 25 years and over	Asians 25 years and over who are 4-year college graduates	NHPI[1] population 25 years and over	NHPIs[1] 25 years and over who are 4-year college graduates	Asian Indian	Bangladeshi	Cambodian	Chinese[2]	Fijian	Filipino	Guamanian[3]	Hawaiian, Native	Hmong	Indonesian	Japanese	Korean	Laotian	Malaysian	Pakistani	Samoan	Sri Lankan	Taiwanese	Thai	Tongan	Vietnamese
Maple Shade (township)	2,939 21.44	752	464 61.70 61.70 15.79	-	-	337 78.92 72.63 44.81 11.47	-	-	-	-	-	-	-	-	-	-	-	-	-	-	-	-	-	-	-	-
Marlton (cdp)	2,241 31.28	271	123 45.39 45.39 5.49	-	-	-	-	-	-	-	-	-	-	-	-	-	-	-	-	-	-	-	-	-	-	-
Mount Laurel (township)	12,178 42.10	1,182	754 63.79 63.79 6.19	-	-	254 68.10 33.69 21.49 2.09	-	-	197 58.46 26.13 16.67 1.62	-	-	-	-	-	-	-	-	-	-	-	-	-	-	-	-	-
Camden County	79,702 24.02	12,299	5,870 47.73 47.73 7.36	-	-	2,136 66.85 36.39 17.37 2.68	-	33 19.64 0.56 0.27 0.04	1,264 49.51 21.53 10.28 1.59	-	1,389 57.90 23.66 11.29 1.74	-	-	-	-	-	368 37.63 6.27 2.99 0.46	-	-	114 58.16 1.94 0.93 0.14	-	-	-	-	-	232 11.92 3.95 1.89 0.29
Barclay-Kingston (cdp)	3,311 43.95	511	287 56.16 56.16 8.67	-	-	-	-	-	-	-	-	-	-	-	-	-	-	-	-	-	-	-	-	-	-	-
Bellmawr (borough)	821 10.36	251	89 35.46 35.46 10.84	-	-	-	-	-	-	-	-	-	-	-	-	-	-	-	-	-	-	-	-	-	-	-
Cherry Hill Mall (cdp)	3,682 38.85	765	295 38.56 38.56 8.01	-	-	-	-	-	-	-	-	-	-	-	-	-	-	-	-	-	-	-	-	-	-	-
Cherry Hill (township)	22,831 46.22	3,945	2,273 57.62 57.62 9.96	-	-	613 71.95 26.97 15.54 2.68	-	-	601 52.26 26.44 15.23 2.63	-	618 67.76 27.19 15.67 2.71	-	-	-	-	-	208 38.66 9.15 5.27 0.91	-	-	-	-	-	-	-	-	-
Echelon (cdp)	3,041 40.29	922	681 73.86 73.86 22.39	-	-	421 76.68 61.82 45.66 13.84	-	-	-	-	-	-	-	-	-	-	-	-	-	-	-	-	-	-	-	-
Greentree (cdp)	4,272 56.18	1,204	742 61.63 61.63 17.37	-	-	272 78.84 36.66 22.59 6.37	-	-	273 53.53 36.79 22.67 6.39	-	-	-	-	-	-	-	-	-	-	-	-	-	-	-	-	-

Notes: Please refer to the User's Guide for an explanation of data; data is arranged alphabetically by state, then county, then city within each county; table includes counties with populations greater than 49,999 unless noted and cities with populations greater than 9,999 whose Asian and/or NHPI population rates are greater than the national average; (1) Native Hawaiian and other Pacific Islander; (2) excludes Taiwanese; (3) includes Chamorro; (4) county does not meet population threshold but is shown in order to allow inclusion of city

Place	Total population 25 years and over who are 4-year college graduates	Asian population 25 years and over	Asians 25 years and over who are 4-year college graduates	NHPI[1] population 25 years and over	NHPIs[1] 25 years and over who are 4-year college graduates	Asian Indian	Bangladeshi	Cambodian	Chinese[2]	Fijian	Filipino	Guamanian[3]	Hawaiian, Native	Hmong	Indonesian	Japanese	Korean	Laotian	Malaysian	Pakistani	Samoan	Sri Lankan	Taiwanese	Thai	Tongan	Vietnamese
Pennsauken (township)	3,536 15.39	945	227 24.02 24.02 6.42	-	-	-	-	-	-	-	-	-	-	-	-	-	-	-	-	-	-	-	-	-	-	70 17.07 30.84 7.41 1.98
Springdale (cdp)	6,418 62.65	702	510 72.65 72.65 7.95	-	-	-	-	-	204 79.69 40.00 29.06 3.18	-	-	-	-	-	-	-	-	-	-	-	-	-	-	-	-	-
Voorhees (township)	8,755 46.17	2,048	1,522 74.32 74.32 17.38	-	-	899 74.73 59.07 43.90 10.27	-	-	320 73.23 21.02 15.63 3.66	-	177 75.64 11.63 8.64 2.02	-	-	-	-	-	-	-	-	-	-	-	-	-	-	-
Cape May County	16,048 22.02	430	238 55.35 55.35 1.48	-	-	-	-	-	-	-	-	-	-	-	-	-	-	-	-	-	-	-	-	-	-	-
Cumberland County	11,385 11.75	823	386 46.90 46.90 3.39	-	-	139 51.87 36.01 16.89 1.22	-	-	-	-	-	-	-	-	-	-	-	-	-	-	-	-	-	-	-	-
Essex County	141,167 27.49	19,327	12,239 63.33 63.33 8.67	325	117 36.00 36.00 0.08	3,523 62.34 28.79 18.23 2.50	-	-	2,682 65.08 21.91 13.88 1.90	-	3,716 71.70 30.36 19.23 2.63	-	-	-	-	239 48.88 1.95 1.24 0.17	1,084 61.56 8.86 5.61 0.77	-	-	195 49.12 1.59 1.01 0.14	-	-	232 70.52 1.90 1.20 0.16	-	-	215 30.94 1.76 1.11 0.15
Belleville (township)	5,461 21.74	2,709	1,617 59.69 59.69 29.61	-	-	336 57.05 20.78 12.40 6.15	-	-	-	-	906 69.32 56.03 33.44 16.59	-	-	-	-	-	-	-	-	-	-	-	-	-	-	83 29.43 5.13 3.06 1.52
Bloomfield (township)	10,717 31.83	2,722	1,784 65.54 65.54 16.65	-	-	600 59.52 33.63 22.04 5.60	-	-	198 61.11 11.10 7.27 1.85	-	869 78.93 48.71 31.93 8.11	-	-	-	-	-	-	-	-	-	-	-	-	-	-	-
Cedar Grove (township)	3,828 41.32	434	320 73.73 73.73 8.36	-	-	-	-	-	-	-	-	-	-	-	-	-	-	-	-	-	-	-	-	-	-	-
Livingston (township)	10,825 57.67	2,463	1,622 65.85 65.85 14.98	-	-	267 57.67 16.46 10.84 2.47	-	-	721 72.54 44.45 29.27 6.66	-	234 74.76 14.43 9.50 2.16	-	-	-	-	-	249 50.51 15.35 10.11 2.30	-	-	-	-	-	-	-	-	-

Notes: Please refer to the User's Guide for an explanation of data; data is arranged alphabetically by state, then county, then city within each county; table includes counties with populations greater than 49,999 unless noted and cities with populations greater than 9,999 whose Asian and/or NHPI population rates are greater than the national average; (1) Native Hawaiian and other Pacific Islander; (2) excludes Taiwanese; (3) includes Chamorro; (4) county does not meet population threshold but is shown in order to allow inclusion of city

Place	Total population 25 years and over who are 4-year college graduates	Asian population 25 years and over	Asians 25 years and over who are 4-year college graduates	NHPI[1] population 25 years and over	NHPIs[1] 25 years and over who are 4-year college graduates	Asian Indian	Bangladeshi	Cambodian	Chinese[2]	Fijian	Filipino	Guamanian[3]	Hawaiian, Native	Hmong	Indonesian	Japanese	Korean	Laotian	Malaysian	Pakistani	Samoan	Sri Lankan	Taiwanese	Thai	Tongan	Vietnamese
Millburn (township)	9,764 74.03	952	781 82.04 82.04 8.00	-	-	-	-	-	325 83.76 41.61 34.14 3.33	-	-	-	-	-	-	-	-	-	-	-	-	-	-	-	-	-
Nutley (township)	6,482 32.92	1,315	742 56.43 56.43 11.45	-	-	296 63.25 39.89 22.51 4.57	-	-	-	-	227 68.37 30.59 17.26 3.50	-	-	-	-	-	-	-	-	-	-	-	-	-	-	-
Verona (township)	4,944 49.54	417	281 67.39 67.39 5.68	-	-	-	-	-	-	-	-	-	-	-	-	-	-	-	-	-	-	-	-	-	-	-
West Caldwell (township)	3,843 48.15	304	231 75.99 75.99 6.01	-	-	-	-	-	-	-	-	-	-	-	-	-	-	-	-	-	-	-	-	-	-	-
West Orange (township)	13,675 43.15	2,478	1,781 71.87 71.87 13.02	-	-	546 80.53 30.66 22.03 3.99	-	-	374 66.67 21.00 15.09 2.73	-	458 72.93 25.72 18.48 3.35	-	-	-	-	-	246 66.67 13.81 9.93 1.80	-	-	-	-	-	-	-	-	-
Gloucester County	36,178 21.95	2,492	1,356 54.41 54.41 3.75	-	-	333 53.19 24.56 13.36 0.92	-	-	190 41.48 14.01 7.62 0.53	-	554 62.46 40.86 22.23 1.53	-	-	-	-	-	101 54.30 7.45 4.05 0.28	-	-	-	-	-	-	-	-	-
Hudson County	103,356 25.28	38,508	21,832 56.69 56.69 21.12	-	-	7,192 53.50 32.94 18.68 6.96	-	-	3,149 64.10 14.42 8.18 3.05	-	8,134 60.81 37.26 21.12 7.87	-	-	-	-	593 78.54 2.72 1.54 0.57	1,330 54.78 6.09 3.45 1.29	-	-	575 45.74 2.63 1.49 0.56	-	-	-	-	-	258 24.02 1.18 0.67 0.25
Bayonne (city)	9,074 20.93	1,632	704 43.14 43.14 7.76	-	-	182 54.49 25.85 11.15 2.01	-	-	-	-	425 50.36 60.37 26.04 4.68	-	-	-	-	-	18 8.61 2.56 1.10 0.20	-	-	-	-	-	-	-	-	-
Guttenberg (town)	2,257 29.83	566	431 76.15 76.15 19.10	-	-	-	-	-	-	-	-	-	-	-	-	-	-	-	-	-	-	-	-	-	-	-
Harrison (town)	2,032 20.87	1,266	864 68.25 68.25 42.52	-	-	-	-	-	616 64.64 71.30 48.66 30.31	-	-	-	-	-	-	-	-	-	-	-	-	-	-	-	-	-

Notes: Please refer to the User's Guide for an explanation of data; data is arranged alphabetically by state, then county, then city within each county; table includes counties with populations greater than 49,999 unless noted and cities with populations greater than 9,999 whose Asian and/or NHPI population rates are greater than the national average; (1) Native Hawaiian and other Pacific Islander; (2) excludes Taiwanese; (3) includes Chamorro; (4) county does not meet population threshold but is shown in order to allow inclusion of city

Place	Total population 25 years and over who are 4-year college graduates	Asian population 25 years and over	Asians 25 years and over who are 4-year college graduates	NHPI[1] population 25 years and over	NHPIs[1] 25 years and over who are 4-year college graduates	Asian Indian	Bangladeshi	Cambodian	Chinese[2]	Fijian	Filipino	Guamanian[3]	Hawaiian, Native	Hmong	Indonesian	Japanese	Korean	Laotian	Malaysian	Pakistani	Samoan	Sri Lankan	Taiwanese	Thai	Tongan	Vietnamese
Hoboken (city)	17,007 59.39	1,073	860 80.15 80.15 5.06	-	-	244 70.52 28.37 22.74 1.43	-	-	249 80.32 28.95 23.21 1.46	-	-	-	-	-	-	-	-	-	-	-	-	-	-	-	-	-
Jersey City (city)	42,676 27.45	26,224	14,554 55.50 55.50 34.10	-	-	4,574 51.77 31.43 17.44 10.72	-	-	1,356 63.48 9.32 5.17 3.18	-	6,842 61.46 47.01 26.09 16.03	-	-	-	-	-	598 53.01 4.11 2.28 1.40	-	-	433 42.16 2.98 1.65 1.01	-	-	-	-	-	186 20.85 1.28 0.71 0.44
Kearny (town)	4,810 17.37	1,574	1,019 64.74 64.74 21.19	-	-	318 63.35 31.21 20.20 6.61	-	-	483 69.10 47.40 30.69 10.04	-	-	-	-	-	-	-	-	-	-	-	-	-	-	-	-	-
North Bergen (township)	7,786 19.60	2,394	1,182 49.37 49.37 15.18	-	-	739 47.55 62.52 30.87 9.49	-	-	34 16.11 2.88 1.42 0.44	-	-	-	-	-	-	-	-	-	-	-	-	-	-	-	-	-
Secaucus (town)	3,423 29.06	1,195	715 59.83 59.83 20.89	-	-	272 75.35 38.04 22.76 7.95	-	-	-	-	210 56.45 29.37 17.57 6.13	-	-	-	-	-	-	-	-	-	-	-	-	-	-	-
Weehawken (township)	3,752 37.48	480	383 79.79 79.79 10.21	-	-	-	-	-	-	-	-	-	-	-	-	-	-	-	-	-	-	-	-	-	-	-
Hunterdon County	34,898 41.77	1,674	1,193 71.27 71.27 3.42	-	-	535 77.65 44.84 31.96 1.53	-	-	340 68.55 28.50 20.31 0.97	-	-	-	-	-	-	-	-	-	-	-	-	-	-	-	-	-
Mercer County	78,506 33.96	11,118	8,026 72.19 72.19 10.22	-	-	3,133 73.94 39.04 28.18 3.99	-	-	2,528 79.52 31.50 22.74 3.22	-	556 72.68 6.93 5.00 0.71	-	-	-	-	311 71.82 3.87 2.80 0.40	666 57.71 8.30 5.99 0.85	-	-	207 60.70 2.58 1.86 0.26	-	-	265 85.48 3.30 2.38 0.34	-	-	-
East Windsor (township)	7,224 42.01	1,650	1,083 65.64 65.64 14.99	-	-	704 67.43 65.00 42.67 9.75	-	-	-	-	-	-	-	-	-	-	-	-	-	-	-	-	-	-	-	-
Hopewell (township)	6,118 55.84	458	409 89.30 89.30 6.69	-	-	-	-	-	-	-	-	-	-	-	-	-	-	-	-	-	-	-	-	-	-	-

Notes: Please refer to the User's Guide for an explanation of data; data is arranged alphabetically by state, then county, then city within each county; table includes counties with populations greater than 49,999 unless noted and cities with populations greater than 9,999 whose Asian and/or NHPI population rates are greater than the national average; (1) Native Hawaiian and other Pacific Islander; (2) excludes Taiwanese; (3) includes Chamorro; (4) county does not meet population threshold but is shown in order to allow inclusion of city

Place	Total population 25 years and over who are 4-year college graduates	Asian population 25 years and over	Asians 25 years and over who are 4-year college graduates	NHPI[1] population 25 years and over	NHPIs[1] 25 years and over who are 4-year college graduates	Asian Indian	Bangladeshi	Cambodian	Chinese[2]	Fijian	Filipino	Guamanian[3]	Hawaiian, Native	Hmong	Indonesian	Japanese	Korean	Laotian	Malaysian	Pakistani	Samoan	Sri Lankan	Taiwanese	Thai	Tongan	Vietnamese
Lawrence (township)	9,671	1,512	1,109	-	-	465	-	-	405	-	-	-	-	-	-	-	-	-	-	-	-	-	-	-	-	-
	50.50		73.35			66.52			84.02																	
						41.93			36.52																	
			73.35			30.75			26.79																	
			11.47			4.81			4.19																	
Princeton (borough)	4,298	456	302	-	-	-	-	-	-	-	-	-	-	-	-	-	-	-	-	-	-	-	-	-	-	-
	60.13		66.23																							
			66.23																							
			7.03																							
Princeton (township)	8,618	1,208	1,002	-	-	207	-	-	516	-	-	-	-	-	-	-	-	-	-	-	-	-	-	-	-	-
	75.90		82.95			76.95			91.65																	
						20.66			51.50																	
			82.95			17.14			42.72																	
			11.63			2.40			5.99																	
West Windsor (township)	10,368	3,051	2,433	-	-	840	-	-	892	-	-	-	-	-	-	-	202	-	-	-	-	-	-	-	-	-
	73.92		79.74			85.63			75.98								79.84									
						34.53			36.66								8.30									
			79.74			27.53			29.24								6.62									
			23.47			8.10			8.60								1.95									
Middlesex County	165,533	66,773	47,058	-	-	26,441	149	-	9,285	-	5,774	-	-	-	148	337	1,727	-	-	1,124	-	202	761	-	-	348
	33.00		70.47			74.87	68.98		66.19		73.25				45.12	66.34	56.14			67.14		63.32	83.63			26.22
						56.19	0.32		19.73		12.27				0.31	0.72	3.67			2.39		0.43	1.62			0.74
			70.47			39.60	0.22		13.91		8.65				0.22	0.50	2.59			1.68		0.30	1.14			0.52
			28.43			15.97	0.09		5.61		3.49				0.09	0.20	1.04			0.68		0.12	0.46			0.21
Avenel (cdp)	3,241	2,175	1,536	-	-	1,149	-	-	-	-	-	-	-	-	-	-	-	-	-	-	-	-	-	-	-	-
	25.27		70.62			75.94																				
						74.80																				
			70.62			52.83																				
			47.39			35.45																				
Carteret (borough)	1,761	1,046	462	-	-	272	-	-	-	-	-	-	-	-	-	-	-	-	-	-	-	-	-	-	-	-
	12.81		44.17			39.42																				
						58.87																				
			44.17			26.00																				
			26.24			15.45																				
Colonia (cdp)	3,054	742	458	-	-	250	-	-	-	-	128	-	-	-	-	-	-	-	-	-	-	-	-	-	-	-
	24.56		61.73			67.02					59.81															
						54.59					27.95															
			61.73			33.69					17.25															
			15.00			8.19					4.19															
East Brunswick (township)	14,910	4,801	3,338	-	-	1,204	-	-	1,311	-	253	-	-	-	-	-	150	-	-	-	-	-	-	-	-	-
	47.11		69.53			72.88			64.14		87.24						59.76									
						36.07			39.28		7.58						4.49									
			69.53			25.08			27.31		5.27						3.12									
			22.39			8.08			8.79		1.70						1.01									
Edison (township)	28,642	18,640	13,256	-	-	8,037	-	-	2,463	-	1,242	-	-	-	-	-	505	-	-	269	-	-	317	-	-	-
	42.34		71.12			74.03			64.97		72.59						60.70			71.35			82.34			
						60.63			18.58		9.37						3.81			2.03			2.39			
			71.12			43.12			13.21		6.66						2.71			1.44			1.70			
			46.28			28.06			8.60		4.34						1.76			0.94			1.11			

Notes: Please refer to the User's Guide for an explanation of data; data is arranged alphabetically by state, then county, then city within each county; table includes counties with populations greater than 49,999 unless noted and cities with populations greater than 9,999 whose Asian and/or NHPI population rates are greater than the national average; (1) Native Hawaiian and other Pacific Islander; (2) excludes Taiwanese; (3) includes Chamorro; (4) county does not meet population threshold but is shown in order to allow inclusion of city

Place	Total population 25 years and over who are 4-year college graduates	Asian population 25 years and over	Asians 25 years and over who are 4-year college graduates	NHPI[1] population 25 years and over	NHPIs[1] 25 years and over who are 4-year college graduates	Asian Indian	Bangladeshi	Cambodian	Chinese[2]	Fijian	Filipino	Guamanian[3]	Hawaiian, Native	Hmong	Indonesian	Japanese	Korean	Laotian	Malaysian	Pakistani	Samoan	Sri Lankan	Taiwanese	Thai	Tongan	Vietnamese
Fords (cdp)	3,014	1,604	1,231	-	-	729	-	-	-	-	273	-	-	-	-	-	-	-	-	-	-	-	-	-	-	-
	28.20		76.75			89.12					64.24															
						59.22					22.18															
			76.75			45.45					17.02															
			40.84			24.19					9.06															
Highland Park (borough)	5,827	1,363	1,136	-	-	433	-	-	474	-	-	-	-	-	-	-	-	-	-	-	-	-	-	-	-	-
	59.45		83.35			93.52			76.82																	
						38.12			41.73																	
			83.35			31.77			34.78																	
			19.50			7.43			8.13																	
Iselin (cdp)	3,809	2,648	1,746	-	-	1,245	-	-	205	-	-	-	-	-	-	-	-	-	-	-	-	-	-	-	-	-
	32.43		65.94			67.15			55.26																	
						71.31			11.74																	
			65.94			47.02			7.74																	
			45.84			32.69			5.38																	
Metuchen (borough)	4,550	643	410	-	-	-	-	-	-	-	-	-	-	-	-	-	-	-	-	-	-	-	-	-	-	-
	49.17		63.76																							
			63.76																							
			9.01																							
Middlesex (borough)	2,234	399	270	-	-	-	-	-	-	-	-	-	-	-	-	-	-	-	-	-	-	-	-	-	-	-
	23.42		67.67																							
			67.67																							
			12.09																							
New Brunswick (city)	4,250	1,028	676	-	-	328	-	-	126	-	-	-	-	-	-	-	-	-	-	-	-	-	-	-	-	-
	19.24		65.76			67.49			69.23																	
						48.52			18.64																	
			65.76			31.91			12.26																	
			15.91			7.72			2.96																	
North Brunswick (township)	9,283	3,392	2,365	-	-	1,480	-	-	346	-	271	-	-	-	-	-	119	-	-	-	-	-	-	-	-	-
	37.00		69.72			73.05			59.45		87.70						45.77									
						62.58			14.63		11.46						5.03									
			69.72			43.63			10.20		7.99						3.51									
			25.48			15.94			3.73		2.92						1.28									
Old Bridge (township)	11,996	4,086	2,554	-	-	1,172	-	-	393	-	620	-	-	-	-	-	-	-	-	207	-	-	-	-	-	-
	29.49		62.51			66.67			49.68		76.83									66.99						
						45.89			15.39		24.28									8.10						
			62.51			28.68			9.62		15.17									5.07						
			21.29			9.77			3.28		5.17									1.73						
Piscataway (township)	13,012	7,688	5,338	-	-	2,753	-	-	1,179	-	852	-	-	-	-	-	187	-	-	-	-	-	-	-	-	-
	40.51		69.43			71.47			75.63		68.60						51.66									
						51.57			22.09		15.96						3.50									
			69.43			35.81			15.34		11.08						2.43									
			41.02			21.16			9.06		6.55						1.44									
Plainsboro (township)	9,800	4,039	3,435	-	-	1,913	-	-	935	-	-	-	-	-	-	-	-	-	-	-	-	-	-	-	-	-
	70.27		85.05			89.27			86.49																	
						55.69			27.22																	
			85.05			47.36			23.15																	
			35.05			19.52			9.54																	

Notes: Please refer to the User's Guide for an explanation of data; data is arranged alphabetically by state, then county, then city within each county; table includes counties with populations greater than 49,999 unless noted and cities with populations greater than 9,999 whose Asian and/or NHPI population rates are greater than the national average; (1) Native Hawaiian and other Pacific Islander; (2) excludes Taiwanese; (3) includes Chamorro; (4) county does not meet population threshold but is shown in order to allow inclusion of city

Place	Total population 25 years and over who are 4-year college graduates	Asian population 25 years and over	Asians 25 years and over who are 4-year college graduates	NHPI[1] population 25 years and over	NHPIs[1] 25 years and over who are 4-year college graduates	Asian Indian	Bangladeshi	Cambodian	Chinese[2]	Fijian	Filipino	Guamanian[3]	Hawaiian, Native	Hmong	Indonesian	Japanese	Korean	Laotian	Malaysian	Pakistani	Samoan	Sri Lankan	Taiwanese	Thai	Tongan	Vietnamese
Princeton Meadows (cdp)	6,212 68.17	2,531	2,133 84.27 84.27 34.34	-	-	1,232 88.32 57.76 48.68 19.83	-	-	539 87.79 25.27 21.30 8.68	-	-	-	-	-	-	-	-	-	-	-	-	-	-	-	-	-
Sayreville (borough)	6,954 24.95	2,683	1,968 73.35 73.35 28.30	-	-	1,299 80.09 66.01 48.42 18.68	-	-	225 52.45 11.43 8.39 3.24	-	326 78.93 16.57 12.15 4.69	-	-	-	-	-	-	-	-	-	-	-	-	-	-	-
South Brunswick (township)	12,198 49.04	4,476	3,515 78.53 78.53 28.82	-	-	2,047 85.08 58.24 45.73 16.78	-	-	705 70.29 20.06 15.75 5.78	-	326 80.10 9.27 7.28 2.67	-	-	-	-	-	-	-	-	-	-	-	-	-	-	-
South Plainfield (borough)	3,590 24.03	1,142	477 41.77 41.77 13.29	-	-	198 44.20 41.51 17.34 5.52	-	-	-	-	141 58.02 29.56 12.35 3.93	-	-	-	-	-	-	-	-	-	-	-	-	-	-	37 14.40 7.76 3.24 1.03
Woodbridge (township)	18,463 26.82	9,355	6,685 71.46 71.46 36.21	-	-	4,673 77.42 69.90 49.95 25.31	-	-	592 61.80 8.86 6.33 3.21	-	895 71.26 13.39 9.57 4.85	-	-	-	-	-	217 49.10 3.25 2.32 1.18	-	-	99 44.59 1.48 1.06 0.54	-	-	-	-	-	-
Monmouth County	142,842 34.58	15,942	10,144 63.63 63.63 7.10	-	-	3,343 74.75 32.96 20.97 2.34	-	-	3,754 60.38 37.01 23.55 2.63	-	1,565 67.52 15.43 9.82 1.10	-	-	-	-	108 33.64 1.06 0.68 0.08	611 49.47 6.02 3.83 0.43	-	-	118 56.46 1.16 0.74 0.08	-	-	-	-	-	267 51.64 2.63 1.67 0.19
Aberdeen (township)	4,221 34.42	665	381 57.29 57.29 9.03	-	-	199 70.57 52.23 29.92 4.71	-	-	133 49.81 34.91 20.00 3.15	-	-	-	-	-	-	-	-	-	-	-	-	-	-	-	-	-
Colts Neck (township)	3,448 47.53	342	225 65.79 65.79 6.53	-	-	-	-	-	-	-	-	-	-	-	-	-	-	-	-	-	-	-	-	-	-	-
Eatontown (borough)	3,304 33.45	914	595 65.10 65.10 18.01	-	-	-	-	-	-	-	-	-	-	-	-	-	-	-	-	-	-	-	-	-	-	-
Freehold (township)	8,177 37.50	1,187	784 66.05 66.05 9.59	-	-	212 71.38 27.04 17.86 2.59	-	-	229 56.40 29.21 19.29 2.80	-	252 78.75 32.14 21.23 3.08	-	-	-	-	-	-	-	-	-	-	-	-	-	-	-

Notes: Please refer to the User's Guide for an explanation of data; data is arranged alphabetically by state, then county, then city within each county; table includes counties with populations greater than 49,999 unless noted and cities with populations greater than 9,999 whose Asian and/or NHPI population rates are greater than the national average; (1) Native Hawaiian and other Pacific Islander; (2) excludes Taiwanese; (3) includes Chamorro; (4) county does not meet population threshold but is shown in order to allow inclusion of city

Place	Total population 25 years and over who are 4-year college graduates	Asian population 25 years and over	Asians 25 years and over who are 4-year college graduates	NHPI[1] population 25 years and over	NHPIs[1] 25 years and over who are 4-year college graduates	Asian Indian	Bangladeshi	Cambodian	Chinese[2]	Fijian	Filipino	Guamanian[3]	Hawaiian, Native	Hmong	Indonesian	Japanese	Korean	Laotian	Malaysian	Pakistani	Samoan	Sri Lankan	Taiwanese	Thai	Tongan	Vietnamese
Holmdel (township)	5,701	1,632	1,308	-	-	265	-	-	782	-	-	-	-	-	-	-	-	-	-	-	-	-	-	-	-	-
	54.82		80.15			88.93			79.55																	
						20.26			59.79																	
			80.15			16.24			47.92																	
			22.94			4.65			13.72																	
Howell (township)	8,940	1,283	621	-	-	239	-	-	-	-	176	-	-	-	-	-	-	-	-	-	-	-	-	-	-	-
	28.95		48.40			62.24					56.41															
						38.49					28.34															
			48.40			18.63					13.72															
			6.95			2.67					1.97															
Manalapan (township)	8,368	919	599	-	-	287	-	-	166	-	-	-	-	-	-	-	-	-	-	-	-	-	-	-	-	-
	39.31		65.18			76.33			48.82																	
						47.91			27.71																	
			65.18			31.23			18.06																	
			7.16			3.43			1.98																	
Marlboro (township)	12,266	2,862	2,178	-	-	543	-	-	1,185	-	-	-	-	-	-	-	-	-	-	-	-	-	-	-	-	-
	52.30		76.10			88.87			71.86																	
						24.93			54.41																	
			76.10			18.97			41.40																	
			17.76			4.43			9.66																	
Morganville (cdp)	3,980	629	525	-	-	-	-	-	325	-	-	-	-	-	-	-	-	-	-	-	-	-	-	-	-	-
	54.44		83.47						83.12																	
									61.90																	
			83.47						51.67																	
			13.19						8.17																	
Ocean (township)	7,167	1,034	683	-	-	273	-	-	-	-	-	-	-	-	-	-	-	-	-	-	-	-	-	-	-	-
	39.09		66.05			69.64																				
						39.97																				
			66.05			26.40																				
			9.53			3.81																				
Tinton Falls (borough)	4,428	488	266	-	-	-	-	-	-	-	-	-	-	-	-	-	-	-	-	-	-	-	-	-	-	-
	42.34		54.51																							
			54.51																							
			6.01																							
West Freehold (cdp)	3,550	420	296	-	-	-	-	-	-	-	-	-	-	-	-	-	-	-	-	-	-	-	-	-	-	-
	39.29		70.48																							
			70.48																							
			8.34																							
Morris County	142,770	19,859	13,914	-	-	5,188	-	-	4,751	-	1,562	-	-	-	-	401	865	-	-	267	-	-	335	-	-	161
	44.08		70.06			73.55			74.35		70.33					64.57	57.94			66.42			72.51			33.40
						37.29			34.15		11.23					2.88	6.22			1.92			2.41			1.16
			70.06			26.12			23.92		7.87					2.02	4.36			1.34			1.69			0.81
			9.75			3.63			3.33		1.09					0.28	0.61			0.19			0.23			0.11
Chatham (township)	4,610	405	326	-	-	-	-	-	-	-	-	-	-	-	-	-	-	-	-	-	-	-	-	-	-	-
	65.74		80.49																							
			80.49																							
			7.07																							

Notes: Please refer to the User's Guide for an explanation of data; data is arranged alphabetically by state, then county, then city within each county; table includes counties with populations greater than 49,999 unless noted and cities with populations greater than 9,999 whose Asian and/or NHPI population rates are greater than the national average; (1) Native Hawaiian and other Pacific Islander; (2) excludes Taiwanese; (3) includes Chamorro; (4) county does not meet population threshold but is shown in order to allow inclusion of city

Place	Total population 25 years and over who are 4-year college graduates	Asian population 25 years and over	Asians 25 years and over who are 4-year college graduates	NHPI[1] population 25 years and over	NHPIs[1] 25 years and over who are 4-year college graduates	Asian Indian	Bangladeshi	Cambodian	Chinese[2]	Fijian	Filipino	Guamanian[3]	Hawaiian, Native	Hmong	Indonesian	Japanese	Korean	Laotian	Malaysian	Pakistani	Samoan	Sri Lankan	Taiwanese	Thai	Tongan	Vietnamese
Denville (township)	4,981 44.01	532	326 61.28 61.28 6.54	-	-	-	-	-	-	-	-	-	-	-	-	-	-	-	-	-	-	-	-	-	-	-
East Hanover (township)	2,718 33.36	813	553 68.02 68.02 20.35	-	-	-	-	-	277 70.66 50.09 34.07 10.19	-	-	-	-	-	-	-	-	-	-	-	-	-	-	-	-	-
Hanover (township)	3,845 41.47	791	587 74.21 74.21 15.27	-	-	164 71.62 27.94 20.73 4.27	-	-	302 84.12 51.45 38.18 7.85	-	-	-	-	-	-	-	-	-	-	-	-	-	-	-	-	-
Lincoln Park (borough)	2,680 32.93	411	266 64.72 64.72 9.93	-	-	-	-	-	-	-	-	-	-	-	-	-	-	-	-	-	-	-	-	-	-	-
Montville (township)	7,402 51.24	1,761	1,424 80.86 80.86 19.24	-	-	578 82.69 40.59 32.82 7.81	-	-	563 81.01 39.54 31.97 7.61	-	-	-	-	-	-	-	-	-	-	-	-	-	-	-	-	-
Morris (township)	9,896 63.58	697	578 82.93 82.93 5.84	-	-	-	-	-	-	-	-	-	-	-	-	-	-	-	-	-	-	-	-	-	-	-
Mount Olive (township)	5,750 36.48	1,019	705 69.19 69.19 12.26	-	-	292 64.89 41.42 28.66 5.08	-	-	-	-	-	-	-	-	-	-	-	-	-	-	-	-	-	-	-	-
Parsippany-Troy Hills (twp)	15,748 42.98	5,946	3,998 67.24 67.24 25.39	-	-	1,837 67.24 45.95 30.89 11.66	-	-	1,244 70.28 31.12 20.92 7.90	-	387 77.87 9.68 6.51 2.46	-	-	-	-	-	208 65.00 5.20 3.50 1.32	-	-	-	-	-	-	-	-	-
Randolph (township)	9,660 59.44	1,587	1,293 81.47 81.47 13.39	-	-	612 97.92 47.33 38.56 6.34	-	-	352 80.00 27.22 22.18 3.64	-	-	-	-	-	-	-	-	-	-	-	-	-	-	-	-	-
Rockaway (township)	6,408 41.37	833	605 72.63 72.63 9.44	-	-	325 79.66 53.72 39.02 5.07	-	-	-	-	-	-	-	-	-	-	-	-	-	-	-	-	-	-	-	-

Notes: Please refer to the User's Guide for an explanation of data; data is arranged alphabetically by state, then county, then city within each county; table includes counties with populations greater than 49,999 unless noted and cities with populations greater than 9,999 whose Asian and/or NHPI population rates are greater than the national average; (1) Native Hawaiian and other Pacific Islander; (2) excludes Taiwanese; (3) includes Chamorro; (4) county does not meet population threshold but is shown in order to allow inclusion of city

Place	Total population 25 years and over who are 4-year college graduates	Asian population 25 years and over	Asians 25 years and over who are 4-year college graduates	NHPI[1] population 25 years and over	NHPIs[1] 25 years and over who are 4-year college graduates	Asian Indian	Bangladeshi	Cambodian	Chinese[2]	Fijian	Filipino	Guamanian[3]	Hawaiian, Native	Hmong	Indonesian	Japanese	Korean	Laotian	Malaysian	Pakistani	Samoan	Sri Lankan	Taiwanese	Thai	Tongan	Vietnamese
Roxbury (township)	5,481	609	339	-	-	-	-	-	-	-	-	-	-	-	-	-	-	-	-	-	-	-	-	-	-	-
	33.94		55.67																							
			55.67																							
			6.19																							
Succasunna-Kenvil (cdp)	3,248	354	190	-	-	-	-	-	-	-	-	-	-	-	-	-	-	-	-	-	-	-	-	-	-	-
	39.18		53.67																							
			53.67																							
			5.85																							
Ocean County	69,835	4,313	2,066	-	-	507	-	-	264	-	1,014	-	-	-	-	-	41	-	-	-	-	-	-	-	-	-
	19.49		47.90			48.80			32.55		63.10						19.07									
						24.54			12.78		49.08						1.98									
			47.90			11.76			6.12		23.51						0.95									
			2.96			0.73			0.38		1.45						0.06									
Passaic County	67,077	11,790	5,715	-	-	2,513	39	-	652	-	1,490	-	-	-	-	-	601	-	-	-	-	-	-	-	-	-
	21.20		48.47			45.21	13.18		51.26		61.39						57.35									
						43.97	0.68		11.41		26.07						10.52									
			48.47			21.31	0.33		5.53		12.64						5.10									
			8.52			3.75	0.06		0.97		2.22						0.90									
Clifton (city)	13,170	3,464	1,646	-	-	834	-	-	68	-	538	-	-	-	-	-	90	-	-	-	-	-	-	-	-	-
	23.63		47.52			46.41			27.76		64.35						37.34									
						50.67			4.13		32.69						5.47									
			47.52			24.08			1.96		15.53						2.60									
			12.50			6.33			0.52		4.09						0.68									
Little Falls (township)	2,840	313	190	-	-	-	-	-	-	-	-	-	-	-	-	-	-	-	-	-	-	-	-	-	-	-
	34.73		60.70																							
			60.70																							
			6.69																							
Passaic (city)	5,281	2,548	1,098	-	-	677	-	-	-	-	316	-	-	-	-	-	-	-	-	-	-	-	-	-	-	-
	13.74		43.09			41.16					60.65															
						61.66					28.78															
			43.09			26.57					12.40															
			20.79			12.82					5.98															
Wayne (township)	15,497	2,160	1,551	-	-	584	-	-	361	-	142	-	-	-	-	-	373	-	-	-	-	-	-	-	-	-
	41.55		71.81			78.71			82.42		62.28						68.19									
						37.65			23.28		9.16						24.05									
			71.81			27.04			16.71		6.57						17.27									
			10.01			3.77			2.33		0.92						2.41									
Salem County	6,512	231	120	-	-	-	-	-	-	-	-	-	-	-	-	-	-	-	-	-	-	-	-	-	-	-
	15.22		51.95																							
			51.95																							
			1.84																							
Somerset County	95,044	16,364	12,431	-	-	5,318	-	-	3,861	-	1,436	-	-	-	-	304	510	-	-	272	-	-	317	-	-	171
	46.51		75.97			79.97			78.67		71.80					64.54	65.22			58.37			84.76			54.98
						42.78			31.06		11.55					2.45	4.10			2.19			2.55			1.38
			75.97			32.50			23.59		8.78					1.86	3.12			1.66			1.94			1.04
			13.08			5.60			4.06		1.51					0.32	0.54			0.29			0.33			0.18

Notes: Please refer to the User's Guide for an explanation of data; data is arranged alphabetically by state, then county, then city within each county; table includes counties with populations greater than 49,999 unless noted and cities with populations greater than 9,999 whose Asian and/or NHPI population rates are greater than the national average; (1) Native Hawaiian and other Pacific Islander; (2) excludes Taiwanese; (3) includes Chamorro; (4) county does not meet population threshold but is shown in order to allow inclusion of city

Place	Total population 25 years and over who are 4-year college graduates	Asian population 25 years and over	Asians 25 years and over who are 4-year college graduates	NHPI[1] population 25 years and over	NHPIs[1] 25 years and over who are 4-year college graduates	Asian Indian	Bangladeshi	Cambodian	Chinese[2]	Fijian	Filipino	Guamanian[3]	Hawaiian, Native	Hmong	Indonesian	Japanese	Korean	Laotian	Malaysian	Pakistani	Samoan	Sri Lankan	Taiwanese	Thai	Tongan	Vietnamese
Bernards (township)	11,431 67.44	1,272	1,138 89.47 89.47 9.96	-	-	340 95.24 29.88 26.73 2.97	-	-	561 90.05 49.30 44.10 4.91	-	-	-	-	-	-	-	-	-	-	-	-	-	-	-	-	-
Branchburg (township)	5,346 53.71	695	495 71.22 71.22 9.26	-	-	293 78.13 59.19 42.16 5.48	-	-	-	-	-	-	-	-	-	-	-	-	-	-	-	-	-	-	-	-
Bridgewater (township)	14,809 49.89	2,964	2,364 79.76 79.76 15.96	-	-	1,112 89.75 47.04 37.52 7.51	-	-	815 79.36 34.48 27.50 5.50	-	-	-	-	-	-	-	-	-	-	-	-	-	-	-	-	-
Franklin (township)	15,620 43.26	4,431	3,310 74.70 74.70 21.19	-	-	1,581 72.76 47.76 35.68 10.12	-	-	761 77.65 22.99 17.17 4.87	-	524 85.48 15.83 11.83 3.35	-	-	-	-	-	-	-	-	-	-	-	-	-	-	-
Hillsborough (township)	11,064 46.60	1,559	1,126 72.23 72.23 10.18	-	-	466 77.41 41.39 29.89 4.21	-	-	327 68.70 29.04 20.97 2.96	-	-	-	-	-	-	-	-	-	-	-	-	-	-	-	-	-
Montgomery (township)	7,740 70.16	1,220	1,067 87.46 87.46 13.79	-	-	344 91.49 32.24 28.20 4.44	-	-	489 87.17 45.83 40.08 6.32	-	-	-	-	-	-	-	-	-	-	-	-	-	-	-	-	-
North Plainfield (borough)	3,677 26.52	660	442 66.97 66.97 12.02	-	-	-	-	-	-	-	-	-	-	-	-	-	-	-	-	-	-	-	-	-	-	-
Somerset (cdp)	5,752 36.63	1,290	1,026 79.53 79.53 17.84	-	-	381 79.87 37.13 29.53 6.62	-	-	240 77.17 23.39 18.60 4.17	-	317 80.66 30.90 24.57 5.51	-	-	-	-	-	-	-	-	-	-	-	-	-	-	-
Somerville (borough)	2,712 31.52	552	340 61.59 61.59 12.54	-	-	-	-	-	-	-	-	-	-	-	-	-	-	-	-	-	-	-	-	-	-	-
Warren (township)	5,467 58.18	977	761 77.89 77.89 13.92	-	-	283 88.71 37.19 28.97 5.18	-	-	316 80.82 41.52 32.34 5.78	-	-	-	-	-	-	-	-	-	-	-	-	-	-	-	-	-

Notes: Please refer to the User's Guide for an explanation of data; data is arranged alphabetically by state, then county, then city within each county; table includes counties with populations greater than 49,999 unless noted and cities with populations greater than 9,999 whose Asian and/or NHPI population rates are greater than the national average; (1) Native Hawaiian and other Pacific Islander; (2) excludes Taiwanese; (3) includes Chamorro; (4) county does not meet population threshold but is shown in order to allow inclusion of city

Place	Total population 25 years and over who are 4-year college graduates	Asian population 25 years and over	Asians 25 years and over who are 4-year college graduates	NHPI[1] population 25 years and over	NHPIs[1] 25 years and over who are 4-year college graduates	Asian Indian	Bangladeshi	Cambodian	Chinese[2]	Fijian	Filipino	Guamanian[3]	Hawaiian, Native	Hmong	Indonesian	Japanese	Korean	Laotian	Malaysian	Pakistani	Samoan	Sri Lankan	Taiwanese	Thai	Tongan	Vietnamese
Sussex County	25,881 27.22	996	561 56.33 56.33 2.17	-	-	201 69.31 35.83 20.18 0.78	-	-	-	-	201 62.81 35.83 20.18 0.78	-	-	-	-	-	-	-	-	-	-	-	-	-	-	-
Union County	100,224 28.48	13,099	8,025 61.26 61.26 8.01	-	-	2,869 65.07 35.75 21.90 2.86	-	-	1,669 60.56 20.80 12.74 1.67	-	2,555 65.77 31.84 19.51 2.55	-	-	-	-	-	400 52.56 4.98 3.05 0.40	-	-	78 45.88 0.97 0.60 0.08	-	-	-	-	-	99 27.81 1.23 0.76 0.10
Berkeley Heights (township)	4,845 52.28	674	451 66.91 66.91 9.31	-	-	-	-	-	170 60.93 37.69 25.22 3.51	-	-	-	-	-	-	-	-	-	-	-	-	-	-	-	-	-
New Providence (borough)	4,831 58.07	626	549 87.70 87.70 11.36	-	-	-	-	-	209 84.62 38.07 33.39 4.33	-	-	-	-	-	-	-	-	-	-	-	-	-	-	-	-	-
Rahway (city)	3,375 18.61	743	396 53.30 53.30 11.73	-	-	-	-	-	-	-	200 58.65 50.51 26.92 5.93	-	-	-	-	-	-	-	-	-	-	-	-	-	-	-
Roselle Park (borough)	2,330 25.62	810	423 52.22 52.22 18.15	-	-	262 47.46 61.94 32.35 11.24	-	-	-	-	-	-	-	-	-	-	-	-	-	-	-	-	-	-	-	-
Scotch Plains (township)	7,903 49.67	1,114	803 72.08 72.08 10.16	-	-	395 90.39 49.19 35.46 5.00	-	-	133 40.55 16.56 11.94 1.68	-	-	-	-	-	-	-	-	-	-	-	-	-	-	-	-	-
Springfield (township)	5,137 46.74	399	269 67.42 67.42 5.24	-	-	-	-	-	-	-	-	-	-	-	-	-	-	-	-	-	-	-	-	-	-	-
Summit (city)	8,943 61.60	556	425 76.44 76.44 4.75	-	-	202 74.26 47.53 36.33 2.26	-	-	-	-	-	-	-	-	-	-	-	-	-	-	-	-	-	-	-	-
Union (township)	9,955 26.48	2,678	1,679 62.70 62.70 16.87	-	-	354 57.75 21.08 13.22 3.56	-	-	237 62.37 14.12 8.85 2.38	-	980 74.30 58.37 36.59 9.84	-	-	-	-	-	-	-	-	-	-	-	-	-	-	-

Notes: Please refer to the User's Guide for an explanation of data; data is arranged alphabetically by state, then county, then city within each county; table includes counties with populations greater than 49,999 unless noted and cities with populations greater than 9,999 whose Asian and/or NHPI population rates are greater than the national average; (1) Native Hawaiian and other Pacific Islander; (2) excludes Taiwanese; (3) includes Chamorro; (4) county does not meet population threshold but is shown in order to allow inclusion of city

Place	Total population 25 years and over who are 4-year college graduates	Asian population 25 years and over	Asians 25 years and over who are 4-year college graduates	NHPI[1] population 25 years and over	NHPIs[1] 25 years and over who are 4-year college graduates	Asian Indian	Bangladeshi	Cambodian	Chinese[2]	Fijian	Filipino	Guamanian[3]	Hawaiian, Native	Hmong	Indonesian	Japanese	Korean	Laotian	Malaysian	Pakistani	Samoan	Sri Lankan	Taiwanese	Thai	Tongan	Vietnamese
Westfield (town)	12,541	769	603	-	-	-	-	-	-	-	-	-	-	-	-	-	-	-	-	-	-	-	-	-	-	-
	62.54		78.41																							
			78.41																							
			4.81																							
Warren County	16,945	693	360	-	-	130	-	-	-	-	-	-	-	-	-	-	-	-	-	-	-	-	-	-	-	-
	24.40		51.95			44.07																				
						36.11																				
			51.95			18.76																				
			2.12			0.77																				
NEW MEXICO	266,149	11,987	5,362	846	160	1,121	-	-	1,641	-	754	40	62	-	-	735	379	-	-	-	-	-	-	44	-	366
	23.45		44.73		18.91	69.89			62.75		39.73	19.90	20.60			42.98	35.22							14.38		19.51
						20.91			30.60		14.06	25.00	38.75			13.71	7.07							0.82		6.83
			44.73		18.91	9.35			13.69		6.29	4.73	7.33			6.13	3.16							0.37		3.05
			2.01		0.06	0.42			0.62		0.28	0.02	0.02			0.28	0.14							0.02		0.14
Bernalillo County	109,436	6,522	2,619	357	48	504	-	-	827	-	268	-	-	-	-	425	168	-	-	-	-	-	-	-	-	265
	30.51		40.16		13.45	70.79			64.76		36.22					44.60	31.40									15.90
						19.24			31.58		10.23					16.23	6.41									10.12
			40.16		13.45	7.73			12.68		4.11					6.52	2.58									4.06
			2.39		0.04	0.46			0.76		0.24					0.39	0.15									0.24
Chaves County	6,132	277	153	-	-	-	-	-	-	-	-	-	-	-	-	-	-	-	-	-	-	-	-	-	-	-
	16.22		55.23																							
			55.23																							
			2.50																							
Dona Ana County	22,269	943	634	-	-	-	-	-	246	-	-	-	-	-	-	-	-	-	-	-	-	-	-	-	-	-
	22.29		67.23						79.35																	
									38.80																	
			67.23						26.09																	
			2.85						1.10																	
Los Alamos County[4]	7,755	510	388	-	-	-	-	-	-	-	-	-	-	-	-	-	-	-	-	-	-	-	-	-	-	-
	60.48		76.08																							
			76.08																							
			5.00																							
Los Alamos (cdp)	5,183	406	333	-	-	-	-	-	-	-	-	-	-	-	-	-	-	-	-	-	-	-	-	-	-	-
	62.06		82.02																							
			82.02																							
			6.42																							
Otero County	5,880	510	131	-	-	-	-	-	-	-	-	-	-	-	-	-	-	-	-	-	-	-	-	-	-	-
	15.45		25.69																							
			25.69																							
			2.23																							
Sandoval County	14,029	465	164	-	-	-	-	-	-	-	61	-	-	-	-	-	-	-	-	-	-	-	-	-	-	-
	24.84		35.27								30.96															
											37.20															
			35.27								13.12															
			1.17								0.43															

Notes: Please refer to the User's Guide for an explanation of data; data is arranged alphabetically by state, then county, then city within each county; table includes counties with populations greater than 49,999 unless noted and cities with populations greater than 9,999 whose Asian and/or NHPI population rates are greater than the national average; (1) Native Hawaiian and other Pacific Islander; (2) excludes Taiwanese; (3) includes Chamorro; (4) county does not meet population threshold but is shown in order to allow inclusion of city

Place	Total population 25 years and over who are 4-year college graduates	Asian population 25 years and over	Asians 25 years and over who are 4-year college graduates	NHPI[1] population 25 years and over	NHPIs[1] 25 years and over who are 4-year college graduates	Asian Indian	Bangladeshi	Cambodian	Chinese[2]	Fijian	Filipino	Guamanian[3]	Hawaiian, Native	Hmong	Indonesian	Japanese	Korean	Laotian	Malaysian	Pakistani	Samoan	Sri Lankan	Taiwanese	Thai	Tongan	Vietnamese
Santa Fe County	32,443	659	378	-	-	-	-	-	-	-	-	-	-	-	-	-	-	-	-	-	-	-	-	-	-	-
	36.92		57.36																							
			57.36																							
			1.17																							
NEW YORK	3,433,212	693,502	286,761	4,567	913	73,651	4,729	176	89,028	-	39,836	112	215	-	698	17,358	36,570	190	279	7,580	179	733	3,712	1,871	-	3,207
	27.37		41.35		19.99	46.80	39.41	12.48	31.03		65.46	12.00	22.26		44.37	60.75	45.96	10.57	25.14	42.59	23.28	39.66	67.85	40.79		21.85
						25.68	1.65	0.06	31.05		13.89	12.27	23.55		0.24	6.05	12.75	0.07	0.10	2.64	19.61	0.26	1.29	0.65		1.12
			41.35		19.99	10.62	0.68	0.03	12.84		5.74	2.45	4.71		0.10	2.50	5.27	0.03	0.04	1.09	3.92	0.11	0.54	0.27		0.46
			8.35		0.03	2.15	0.14	0.01	2.59		1.16	<0.01	0.01		0.02	0.51	1.07	0.01	0.01	0.22	0.01	0.02	0.11	0.05		0.09
Albany County	65,086	4,627	3,071	-	-	1,152	-	-	877	-	327	-	-	-	-	-	214	-	-	-	-	-	-	-	-	100
	33.31		66.37			75.05			75.73		69.72						62.57									26.74
						37.51			28.56		10.65						6.97									3.26
			66.37			24.90			18.95		7.07						4.63									2.16
			4.72			1.77			1.35		0.50						0.33									0.15
Colonie (town)	17,852	1,803	1,210	-	-	634	-	-	277	-	-	-	-	-	-	-	-	-	-	-	-	-	-	-	-	-
	32.41		67.11			78.56			70.48																	
						52.40			22.89																	
			67.11			35.16			15.36																	
			6.78			3.55			1.55																	
Guilderland (town)	10,301	845	623	-	-	218	-	-	-	-	-	-	-	-	-	-	-	-	-	-	-	-	-	-	-	-
	45.00		73.73			75.43																				
						34.99																				
			73.73			25.80																				
			6.05			2.12																				
Bronx County (Bronx)	116,404	25,252	9,104	560	34	2,480	397	9	1,647	-	2,350	-	-	-	-	235	995	-	-	243	-	-	-	-	-	237
	14.65		36.05		6.07	26.74	35.48	2.76	35.91		71.08					55.69	40.17			37.27						14.07
						27.24	4.36	0.10	18.09		25.81					2.58	10.93			2.67						2.60
			36.05		6.07	9.82	1.57	0.04	6.52		9.31					0.93	3.94			0.96						0.94
			7.82		0.03	2.13	0.34	0.01	1.41		2.02					0.20	0.85			0.21						0.20
Broome County	30,021	2,276	1,147	-	-	352	-	-	306	-	-	-	-	-	-	-	158	30	-	-	-	-	-	-	-	34
	22.65		50.40			72.73			67.11								54.30	12.88								11.30
						30.69			26.68								13.78	2.62								2.96
			50.40			15.47			13.44								6.94	1.32								1.49
			3.82			1.17			1.02								0.53	0.10								0.11
Johnson City (village)	2,175	411	208	-	-	-	-	-	-	-	-	-	-	-	-	-	-	-	-	-	-	-	-	-	-	-
	20.11		50.61																							
			50.61																							
			9.56																							
Vestal (town)	5,896	579	493	-	-	-	-	-	114	-	-	-	-	-	-	-	-	-	-	-	-	-	-	-	-	-
	38.57		85.15						82.61																	
									23.12																	
			85.15						19.69																	
			8.36						1.93																	
Cattaraugus County	8,054	259	127	-	-	-	-	-	-	-	-	-	-	-	-	-	-	-	-	-	-	-	-	-	-	-
	14.87		49.03																							
			49.03																							
			1.58																							

Notes: Please refer to the User's Guide for an explanation of data; data is arranged alphabetically by state, then county, then city within each county; table includes counties with populations greater than 49,999 unless noted and cities with populations greater than 9,999 whose Asian and/or NHPI population rates are greater than the national average; (1) Native Hawaiian and other Pacific Islander; (2) excludes Taiwanese; (3) includes Chamorro; (4) county does not meet population threshold but is shown in order to allow inclusion of city

Place	Total population 25 years and over who are 4-year college graduates	Asian population 25 years and over	Asians 25 years and over who are 4-year college graduates	NHPI[1] population 25 years and over	NHPIs[1] 25 years and over who are 4-year college graduates	Asian Indian	Bangladeshi	Cambodian	Chinese[2]	Fijian	Filipino	Guamanian[3]	Hawaiian, Native	Hmong	Indonesian	Japanese	Korean	Laotian	Malaysian	Pakistani	Samoan	Sri Lankan	Taiwanese	Thai	Tongan	Vietnamese
Cayuga County	8,491 15.54	234	42 17.95 17.95 0.49	-	-	-	-	-	-	-	-	-	-	-	-	-	-	-	-	-	-	-	-	-	-	-
Chautauqua County	15,461 16.94	217	107 49.31 49.31 0.69	-	-	-	-	-	-	-	-	-	-	-	-	-	-	-	-	-	-	-	-	-	-	-
Chemung County	11,297 18.58	481	259 53.85 53.85 2.29	-	-	-	-	-	-	-	-	-	-	-	-	-	-	-	-	-	-	-	-	-	-	-
Chenango County	4,965 14.45	129	67 51.94 51.94 1.35	-	-	-	-	-	-	-	-	-	-	-	-	-	-	-	-	-	-	-	-	-	-	-
Clinton County	9,186 17.80	408	151 37.01 37.01 1.64	-	-	-	-	-	-	-	-	-	-	-	-	-	-	-	-	-	-	-	-	-	-	-
Columbia County	9,939 22.59	272	91 33.46 33.46 0.92	-	-	-	-	-	-	-	-	-	-	-	-	-	-	-	-	-	-	-	-	-	-	-
Dutchess County	50,757 27.63	4,589	2,874 62.63 62.63 5.66	-	-	1,241 68.26 43.18 27.04 2.44	-	-	823 61.28 28.64 17.93 1.62	-	-	-	-	-	-	-	341 73.33 11.86 7.43 0.67	-	-	-	-	-	-	-	-	-
Arlington (cdp)	2,002 28.48	379	238 62.80 62.80 11.89	-	-	-	-	-	-	-	-	-	-	-	-	-	-	-	-	-	-	-	-	-	-	-
Poughkeepsie (town)	7,975 30.71	1,097	766 69.83 69.83 9.61	-	-	394 66.67 51.44 35.92 4.94	-	-	210 91.30 27.42 19.14 2.63	-	-	-	-	-	-	-	-	-	-	-	-	-	-	-	-	-
Wappinger (town)	5,220 29.42	853	439 51.47 51.47 8.41	-	-	208 72.98 47.38 24.38 3.98	-	-	-	-	-	-	-	-	-	-	-	-	-	-	-	-	-	-	-	-

Notes: Please refer to the User's Guide for an explanation of data; data is arranged alphabetically by state, then county, then city within each county; table includes counties with populations greater than 49,999 unless noted and cities with populations greater than 9,999 whose Asian and/or NHPI population rates are greater than the national average; (1) Native Hawaiian and other Pacific Islander; (2) excludes Taiwanese; (3) includes Chamorro; (4) county does not meet population threshold but is shown in order to allow inclusion of city

Place	Total population 25 years and over who are 4-year college graduates	Asian population 25 years and over	Asians 25 years and over who are 4-year college graduates	NHPI[1] population 25 years and over	NHPIs[1] 25 years and over who are 4-year college graduates	Asian Indian	Bangladeshi	Cambodian	Chinese[2]	Fijian	Filipino	Guamanian[3]	Hawaiian, Native	Hmong	Indonesian	Japanese	Korean	Laotian	Malaysian	Pakistani	Samoan	Sri Lankan	Taiwanese	Thai	Tongan	Vietnamese
Erie County	156,512 24.54	7,807	5,063 64.85 64.85 3.23	-	-	1,880 84.88 37.13 24.08 1.20	-	-	1,377 73.72 27.20 17.64 0.88	-	256 60.52 5.06 3.28 0.16	-	-	-	-	155 50.49 3.06 1.99 0.10	714 75.56 14.10 9.15 0.46	-	-	-	-	-	-	-	-	156 16.42 3.08 2.00 0.10
Amherst (town)	37,147 47.39	3,239	2,595 80.12 80.12 6.99	-	-	1,022 88.33 39.38 31.55 2.75	-	-	709 76.48 27.32 21.89 1.91	-	-	-	-	-	-	-	387 85.24 14.91 11.95 1.04	-	-	-	-	-	-	-	-	-
Herkimer County	6,813 15.68	165	85 51.52 51.52 1.25	-	-	-	-	-	-	-	-	-	-	-	-	-	-	-	-	-	-	-	-	-	-	-
Jefferson County	11,059 16.04	694	173 24.93 24.93 1.56	-	-	-	-	-	-	-	58 33.14 33.53 8.36 0.52	-	-	-	-	-	3 1.32 1.73 0.43 0.03	-	-	-	-	-	-	-	-	-
Kings County (Brooklyn)	339,250 21.85	121,889	28,681 23.53 23.53 8.45	767	111 14.47 14.47 0.03	5,346 34.35 18.64 4.39 1.58	682 30.03 2.38 0.56 0.20	10 3.22 0.03 0.01 <0.01	13,628 16.86 47.52 11.18 4.02	-	3,327 65.24 11.60 2.73 0.98	6 3.35 5.41 0.78 <0.01	-	-	-	968 58.70 3.38 0.79 0.29	2,013 43.23 7.02 1.65 0.59	-	-	1,125 21.70 3.92 0.92 0.33	-	-	-	-	-	419 17.69 1.46 0.34 0.12
Livingston County	7,715 19.25	286	103 36.01 36.01 1.34	-	-	-	-	-	-	-	-	-	-	-	-	-	-	-	-	-	-	-	-	-	-	-
Madison County	9,455 21.61	182	87 47.80 47.80 0.92	-	-	-	-	-	-	-	-	-	-	-	-	-	-	-	-	-	-	-	-	-	-	-
Monroe County	148,953 31.16	10,231	5,536 54.11 54.11 3.72	-	-	1,989 73.61 35.93 19.44 1.34	-	30 17.96 0.54 0.29 0.02	1,708 67.83 30.85 16.69 1.15	-	225 58.14 4.06 2.20 0.15	-	-	-	-	235 55.69 4.24 2.30 0.16	472 51.47 8.53 4.61 0.32	91 11.80 1.64 0.89 0.06	-	130 46.10 2.35 1.27 0.09	-	-	-	-	-	253 17.82 4.57 2.47 0.17
Brighton (town)	14,821 57.38	1,921	1,305 67.93 67.93 8.81	-	-	521 73.90 39.92 27.12 3.52	-	-	265 65.11 20.31 13.79 1.79	-	-	-	-	-	-	-	-	-	-	-	-	-	-	-	-	-
Henrietta (town)	6,558 30.16	981	566 57.70 57.70 8.63	-	-	141 83.93 24.91 14.37 2.15	-	-	186 73.52 32.86 18.96 2.84	-	-	-	-	-	-	-	-	-	-	-	-	-	-	-	-	-

Notes: Please refer to the User's Guide for an explanation of data; data is arranged alphabetically by state, then county, then city within each county; table includes counties with populations greater than 49,999 unless noted and cities with populations greater than 9,999 whose Asian and/or NHPI population rates are greater than the national average; (1) Native Hawaiian and other Pacific Islander; (2) excludes Taiwanese; (3) includes Chamorro; (4) county does not meet population threshold but is shown in order to allow inclusion of city

Place	Total population 25 years and over who are 4-year college graduates	Asian population 25 years and over	Asians 25 years and over who are 4-year college graduates	NHPI[1] population 25 years and over	NHPIs[1] 25 years and over who are 4-year college graduates	Asian Indian	Bangladeshi	Cambodian	Chinese[2]	Fijian	Filipino	Guamanian[3]	Hawaiian, Native	Hmong	Indonesian	Japanese	Korean	Laotian	Malaysian	Pakistani	Samoan	Sri Lankan	Taiwanese	Thai	Tongan	Vietnamese
Pittsford (town)	11,703 65.37	755	510 67.55 67.55 4.36	-	-	295 81.04 57.84 39.07 2.52	-	-	-	-	-	-	-	-	-	-	-	-	-	-	-	-	-	-	-	-
Nassau County	321,321 35.36	39,330	22,638 57.56 57.56 7.05	232	71 30.60 30.60 0.02	8,287 57.76 36.61 21.07 2.58	-	-	5,191 52.63 22.93 13.20 1.62	-	3,216 67.21 14.21 8.18 1.00	-	-	-	-	798 56.24 3.53 2.03 0.25	3,216 59.27 14.21 8.18 1.00	-	-	696 56.91 3.07 1.77 0.22	-	-	296 78.51 1.31 0.75 0.09	120 48.78 0.53 0.31 0.04	-	111 33.94 0.49 0.28 0.03
East Meadow (cdp)	7,515 29.01	1,463	804 54.96 54.96 10.70	-	-	365 54.48 45.40 24.95 4.86	-	-	-	-	189 85.14 23.51 12.92 2.51	-	-	-	-	-	-	-	-	-	-	-	-	-	-	-
Elmont (cdp)	4,516 21.34	1,926	902 46.83 46.83 19.97	-	-	382 35.05 42.35 19.83 8.46	-	-	-	-	266 76.88 29.49 13.81 5.89	-	-	-	-	-	-	-	-	-	-	-	-	-	-	-
Franklin Square (cdp)	4,654 22.31	695	283 40.72 40.72 6.08	-	-	117 44.32 41.34 16.83 2.51	-	-	-	-	-	-	-	-	-	-	-	-	-	-	-	-	-	-	-	-
Glen Cove (city)	5,247 27.93	658	339 51.52 51.52 6.46	-	-	99 56.25 29.20 15.05 1.89	-	-	-	-	-	-	-	-	-	-	110 45.08 32.45 16.72 2.10	-	-	-	-	-	-	-	-	-
Hicksville (cdp)	7,447 25.73	2,187	1,204 55.05 55.05 16.17	-	-	554 52.51 46.01 25.33 7.44	-	-	270 54.66 22.43 12.35 3.63	-	189 63.42 15.70 8.64 2.54	-	-	-	-	-	-	-	-	-	-	-	-	-	-	-
Jericho (cdp)	5,519 59.87	892	650 72.87 72.87 11.78	-	-	-	-	-	-	-	-	-	-	-	-	-	292 68.22 44.92 32.74 5.29	-	-	-	-	-	-	-	-	-
Mineola (village)	4,192 29.88	626	447 71.41 71.41 10.66	-	-	212 89.08 47.43 33.87 5.06	-	-	-	-	-	-	-	-	-	-	-	-	-	-	-	-	-	-	-	-
North Hempstead (town)	70,290 45.78	12,953	7,894 60.94 60.94 11.23	-	-	2,863 60.77 36.27 22.10 4.07	-	-	1,958 54.82 24.80 15.12 2.79	-	691 71.68 8.75 5.33 0.98	-	-	-	-	460 61.17 5.83 3.55 0.65	1,251 64.89 15.85 9.66 1.78	-	-	223 71.94 2.82 1.72 0.32	-	-	138 78.86 1.75 1.07 0.20	-	-	-

Notes: Please refer to the User's Guide for an explanation of data; data is arranged alphabetically by state, then county, then city within each county; table includes counties with populations greater than 49,999 unless noted and cities with populations greater than 9,999 whose Asian and/or NHPI population rates are greater than the national average; (1) Native Hawaiian and other Pacific Islander; (2) excludes Taiwanese; (3) includes Chamorro; (4) county does not meet population threshold but is shown in order to allow inclusion of city

Place	Total population 25 years and over who are 4-year college graduates	Asian population 25 years and over	Asians 25 years and over who are 4-year college graduates	NHPI[1] population 25 years and over	NHPIs[1] 25 years and over who are 4-year college graduates	Asian Indian	Bangladeshi	Cambodian	Chinese[2]	Fijian	Filipino	Guamanian[3]	Hawaiian, Native	Hmong	Indonesian	Japanese	Korean	Laotian	Malaysian	Pakistani	Samoan	Sri Lankan	Taiwanese	Thai	Tongan	Vietnamese
North Merrick (cdp)	2,762 33.69	291	172 59.11 59.11 6.23	-	-	-	-	-	-	-	-	-	-	-	-	-	-	-	-	-	-	-	-	-	-	-
North New Hyde Park (cdp)	3,494 33.69	1,291	635 49.19 49.19 18.17	-	-	304 43.55 47.87 23.55 8.70	-	-	233 50.98 36.69 18.05 6.67	-	-	-	-	-	-	-	-	-	-	-	-	-	-	-	-	-
North Valley Stream (cdp)	2,926 28.13	828	354 42.75 42.75 12.10	-	-	166 43.12 46.89 20.05 5.67	-	-	-	-	-	-	-	-	-	-	-	-	-	-	-	-	-	-	-	-
Oyster Bay (town)	77,489 37.84	8,794	5,462 62.11 62.11 7.05	-	-	2,055 65.34 37.62 23.37 2.65	-	-	1,474 60.31 26.99 16.76 1.90	-	552 63.45 10.11 6.28 0.71	-	-	-	-	170 60.07 3.11 1.93 0.22	921 61.81 16.86 10.47 1.19	-	-	-	-	-	-	-	-	-
Plainview (cdp)	8,627 48.32	799	512 64.08 64.08 5.93	-	-	151 78.24 29.49 18.90 1.75	-	-	141 57.79 27.54 17.65 1.63	-	-	-	-	-	-	-	119 50.85 23.24 14.89 1.38	-	-	-	-	-	-	-	-	-
Port Washington (cdp)	5,755 53.86	652	488 74.85 74.85 8.48	-	-	108 71.05 22.13 16.56 1.88	-	-	-	-	-	-	-	-	-	-	-	-	-	-	-	-	-	-	-	-
Salisbury (cdp)	3,023 35.21	779	550 70.60 70.60 18.19	-	-	221 79.21 40.18 28.37 7.31	-	-	-	-	-	-	-	-	-	-	-	-	-	-	-	-	-	-	-	-
Syosset (cdp)	6,862 53.74	1,491	1,006 67.47 67.47 14.66	-	-	303 71.97 30.12 20.32 4.42	-	-	393 73.46 39.07 26.36 5.73	-	-	-	-	-	-	-	218 57.98 21.67 14.62 3.18	-	-	-	-	-	-	-	-	-
Valley Stream (village)	6,188 24.91	1,563	726 46.45 46.45 11.73	-	-	-	-	-	150 31.12 20.66 9.60 2.42	-	212 65.84 29.20 13.56 3.43	-	-	-	-	-	-	-	-	-	-	-	-	-	-	-
West Hempstead (cdp)	4,335 34.62	671	351 52.31 52.31 8.10	-	-	110 50.69 31.34 16.39 2.54	-	-	-	-	-	-	-	-	-	-	-	-	-	-	-	-	-	-	-	-

Notes: Please refer to the User's Guide for an explanation of data; data is arranged alphabetically by state, then county, then city within each county; table includes counties with populations greater than 49,999 unless noted and cities with populations greater than 9,999 whose Asian and/or NHPI population rates are greater than the national average; (1) Native Hawaiian and other Pacific Islander; (2) excludes Taiwanese; (3) includes Chamorro; (4) county does not meet population threshold but is shown in order to allow inclusion of city

Place	Total population 25 years and over who are 4-year college graduates	Asian population 25 years and over	Asians 25 years and over who are 4-year college graduates	NHPI[1] population 25 years and over	NHPIs[1] 25 years and over who are 4-year college graduates	Asian Indian	Bangladeshi	Cambodian	Chinese[2]	Fijian	Filipino	Guamanian[3]	Hawaiian, Native	Hmong	Indonesian	Japanese	Korean	Laotian	Malaysian	Pakistani	Samoan	Sri Lankan	Taiwanese	Thai	Tongan	Vietnamese
Westbury (village)	3,021 31.17	452	249 55.09 55.09 8.24	-	-	-	-	-	-	-	-	-	-	-	-	-	-	-	-	-	-	-	-	-	-	-
Woodmere (cdp)	6,147 56.23	335	164 48.96 48.96 2.67	-	-	-	-	-	-	-	-	-	-	-	-	-	-	-	-	-	-	-	-	-	-	-
New York City	1,446,833 27.42	536,408	193,967 36.16 36.16 13.41	2,682	447 16.67 16.67 0.03	41,883 38.90 21.59 7.81 2.89	4,366 38.24 2.25 0.81 0.30	99 11.94 0.05 0.02 0.01	66,766 26.66 34.42 12.45 4.61	-	27,520 65.20 14.19 5.13 1.90	41 7.02 9.17 1.53 <0.01	125 23.50 27.96 4.66 0.01	-	461 39.07 0.24 0.09 0.03	11,154 61.56 5.75 2.08 0.77	25,875 42.07 13.34 4.82 1.79	-	202 20.70 0.10 0.04 0.01	4,826 36.64 2.49 0.90 0.33	35 11.71 7.83 1.30 <0.01	447 33.26 0.23 0.08 0.03	2,288 63.19 1.18 0.43 0.16	1,189 42.92 0.61 0.22 0.08	-	1,980 25.46 1.02 0.37 0.14
New York County (Manhattan)	556,193 49.40	106,507	48,244 45.30 45.30 8.67	385	142 36.88 36.88 0.03	7,138 74.03 14.80 6.70 1.28	136 31.26 0.28 0.13 0.02	-	16,933 27.26 35.10 15.90 3.04	-	5,515 75.15 11.43 5.18 0.99	-	-	-	-	7,848 66.21 16.27 7.37 1.41	6,727 79.37 13.94 6.32 1.21	-	-	473 66.34 0.98 0.44 0.09	-	-	639 90.51 1.32 0.60 0.11	355 53.14 0.74 0.33 0.06	-	775 64.80 1.61 0.73 0.14
Niagara County	25,632 17.42	689	320 46.44 46.44 1.25	-	-	165 67.62 51.56 23.95 0.64	-	-	-	-	-	-	-	-	-	-	-	-	-	-	-	-	-	-	-	-
Oneida County	29,072 18.30	1,615	461 28.54 28.54 1.59	-	-	211 75.90 45.77 13.07 0.73	-	-	63 31.19 13.67 3.90 0.22	-	-	-	-	-	-	-	-	-	-	-	-	-	-	-	-	22 3.39 4.77 1.36 0.08
Onondaga County	84,601 28.49	5,718	3,202 56.00 56.00 3.78	-	-	950 77.05 29.67 16.61 1.12	-	-	711 66.02 22.20 12.43 0.84	-	301 65.72 9.40 5.26 0.36	-	-	-	-	180 68.97 5.62 3.15 0.21	466 73.04 14.55 8.15 0.55	-	-	-	-	-	-	-	-	150 13.80 4.68 2.62 0.18
Ontario County	16,430 24.69	360	187 51.94 51.94 1.14	-	-	-	-	-	-	-	-	-	-	-	-	-	-	-	-	-	-	-	-	-	-	-
Orange County	47,953 22.53	3,459	1,766 51.06 51.06 3.68	-	-	642 60.17 36.35 18.56 1.34	-	-	328 39.47 18.57 9.48 0.68	-	359 66.60 20.33 10.38 0.75	-	-	-	-	-	202 47.87 11.44 5.84 0.42	-	-	-	-	-	-	-	-	-
Oswego County	10,983 14.42	294	140 47.62 47.62 1.27	-	-	-	-	-	-	-	-	-	-	-	-	-	-	-	-	-	-	-	-	-	-	-

Notes: Please refer to the User's Guide for an explanation of data; data is arranged alphabetically by state, then county, then city within each county; table includes counties with populations greater than 49,999 unless noted and cities with populations greater than 9,999 whose Asian and/or NHPI population rates are greater than the national average; (1) Native Hawaiian and other Pacific Islander; (2) excludes Taiwanese; (3) includes Chamorro; (4) county does not meet population threshold but is shown in order to allow inclusion of city

Place	Total population 25 years and over who are 4-year college graduates	Asian population 25 years and over	Asians 25 years and over who are 4-year college graduates	NHPI[1] population 25 years and over	NHPIs[1] 25 years and over who are 4-year college graduates	Asian Indian	Bangladeshi	Cambodian	Chinese[2]	Fijian	Filipino	Guamanian[3]	Hawaiian, Native	Hmong	Indonesian	Japanese	Korean	Laotian	Malaysian	Pakistani	Samoan	Sri Lankan	Taiwanese	Thai	Tongan	Vietnamese
	8,548	143	83	-	-	-	-	-	-	-	-	-	-	-	-	-	-	-	-	-	-	-	-	-	-	-
	22.03		58.04																							
Otsego County																										
			58.04																							
			0.97																							
	21,891	813	526	-	-	168	-	-	196	-	-	-	-	-	-	-	-	-	-	-	-	-	-	-	-	-
	33.87		64.70			64.37			64.69																	
Putnam County						31.94			37.26																	
			64.70			20.66			24.11																	
			2.40			0.77			0.90																	
	366,872	266,430	100,262	821	131	24,849	3,135	-	32,937	-	14,039	-	-	-	332	2,033	15,069	-	121	2,793	-	136	1,499	540	-	527
	24.30		37.63		15.96	35.96	41.38		33.59		61.34				43.23	50.26	34.65		24.80	44.83		22.93	57.28	33.73		21.60
Queens County (Queens)						24.78	3.13		32.85		14.00				0.33	2.03	15.03		0.12	2.79		0.14	1.50	0.54		0.53
			37.63		15.96	9.33	1.18		12.36		5.27				0.12	0.76	5.66		0.05	1.05		0.05	0.56	0.20		0.20
			27.33		0.04	6.77	0.85		8.98		3.83				0.09	0.55	4.11		0.03	0.76		0.04	0.41	0.15		0.14
	23,793	1,218	873	-	-	224	-	-	393	-	-	-	-	-	-	-	93	-	-	-	-	-	-	-	-	-
	23.74		71.67			91.80			68.23								76.23									
Rensselaer County						25.66			45.02								10.65									
			71.67			18.39			32.27								7.64									
			3.67			0.94			1.65								0.39									
	68,114	16,330	7,676	-	-	2,070	-	-	1,621	-	2,289	-	-	-	-	-	1,071	-	-	192	-	103	-	-	-	-
	23.18		47.01			50.72			33.33		63.99						44.53			48.98		31.60				
Richmond Co. (Staten Island)						26.97			21.12		29.82						13.95			2.50		1.34				
			47.01			12.68			9.93		14.02						6.56			1.18		0.63				
			11.27			3.04			2.38		3.36						1.57			0.28		0.15				
	69,000	10,376	6,098	-	-	1,880	-	-	700	-	2,187	-	-	-	-	-	712	-	-	-	-	-	-	-	-	-
	37.50		58.77			53.68			53.76		73.02						58.36									
Rockland County						30.83			11.48		35.86						11.68									
			58.77			18.12			6.75		21.08						6.86									
			8.84			2.72			1.01		3.17						1.03									
	25,534	4,196	2,764	-	-	803	-	-	338	-	1,112	-	-	-	-	-	321	-	-	-	-	-	-	-	-	-
	45.22		65.87			55.30			68.01		78.20						72.30									
Clarkstown (town)						29.05			12.23		40.23						11.61									
			65.87			19.14			8.06		26.50						7.65									
			10.82			3.14			1.32		4.35						1.26									
	4,433	1,043	638	-	-	161	-	-	-	-	-	-	-	-	-	-	-	-	-	-	-	-	-	-	-	-
	38.42		61.17			43.75																				
Nanuet (cdp)						25.24																				
			61.17			15.44																				
			14.39			3.63																				
	12,251	1,540	1,025	-	-	362	-	-	-	-	277	-	-	-	-	-	-	-	-	-	-	-	-	-	-	-
	52.32		66.56			57.83					80.06															
New City (cdp)						35.32					27.02															
			66.56			23.51					17.99															
			8.37			2.95					2.26															
	14,273	1,956	1,220	-	-	246	-	-	188	-	383	-	-	-	-	-	202	-	-	-	-	-	-	-	-	-
	43.11		62.37			56.16			51.65		75.84						55.49									
Orangetown (town)						20.16			15.41		31.39						16.56									
			62.37			12.58			9.61		19.58						10.33									
			8.55			1.72			1.32		2.68						1.42									

Notes: Please refer to the User's Guide for an explanation of data; data is arranged alphabetically by state, then county, then city within each county; table includes counties with populations greater than 49,999 unless noted and cities with populations greater than 9,999 whose Asian and/or NHPI population rates are greater than the national average; (1) Native Hawaiian and other Pacific Islander; (2) excludes Taiwanese; (3) includes Chamorro; (4) county does not meet population threshold but is shown in order to allow inclusion of city

Place	Total population 25 years and over who are 4-year college graduates	Asian population 25 years and over	Asians 25 years and over who are 4-year college graduates	NHPI[1] population 25 years and over	NHPIs[1] 25 years and over who are 4-year college graduates	Asian Indian	Bangladeshi	Cambodian	Chinese[2]	Fijian	Filipino	Guamanian[3]	Hawaiian, Native	Hmong	Indonesian	Japanese	Korean	Laotian	Malaysian	Pakistani	Samoan	Sri Lankan	Taiwanese	Thai	Tongan	Vietnamese
Ramapo (town)	21,683 34.55	3,364	1,687 50.15 50.15 7.78	-	-	698 55.31 41.38 20.75 3.22	-	-	117 35.03 6.94 3.48 0.54	-	570 62.71 33.79 16.94 2.63	-	-	-	-	-	161 45.10 9.54 4.79 0.74	-	-	-	-	-	-	-	-	-
Spring Valley (village)	2,875 19.94	923	409 44.31 44.31 14.23	-	-	170 37.86 41.56 18.42 5.91	-	-	-	-	-	-	-	-	-	-	-	-	-	-	-	-	-	-	-	-
St. Lawrence County	11,526 16.42	326	208 63.80 63.80 1.80	-	-	-	-	-	-	-	-	-	-	-	-	-	-	-	-	-	-	-	-	-	-	-
Saratoga County	41,678 30.87	1,319	838 63.53 63.53 2.01	-	-	391 80.12 46.66 29.64 0.94	-	-	149 64.78 17.78 11.30 0.36	-	-	-	-	-	-	-	97 59.51 11.58 7.35 0.23	-	-	-	-	-	-	-	-	-
Schenectady County	26,218 26.33	1,688	1,049 62.14 62.14 4.00	-	-	450 66.18 42.90 26.66 1.72	-	-	387 68.62 36.89 22.93 1.48	-	-	-	-	-	-	-	-	-	-	-	-	-	-	-	-	-
Niskayuna (town)	7,750 54.83	783	643 82.12 82.12 8.30	-	-	316 88.02 49.14 40.36 4.08	-	-	-	-	-	-	-	-	-	-	-	-	-	-	-	-	-	-	-	-
Steuben County	11,775 17.90	513	356 69.40 69.40 3.02	-	-	-	-	-	-	-	-	-	-	-	-	-	-	-	-	-	-	-	-	-	-	-
Suffolk County	258,864 27.47	21,127	12,098 57.26 57.26 4.67	299	51 17.06 17.06 0.02	3,959 61.47 32.72 18.74 1.53	-	-	3,448 59.00 28.50 16.32 1.33	-	1,790 64.37 14.80 8.47 0.69	-	-	-	-	347 39.16 2.87 1.64 0.13	1,231 56.44 10.18 5.83 0.48	-	-	566 51.60 4.68 2.68 0.22	-	-	161 56.89 1.33 0.76 0.06	73 30.29 0.60 0.35 0.03	-	124 25.46 1.02 0.59 0.05
Coram (cdp)	6,163 26.30	872	544 62.39 62.39 8.83	-	-	-	-	-	150 47.92 27.57 17.20 2.43	-	-	-	-	-	-	-	-	-	-	-	-	-	-	-	-	-
Dix Hills (cdp)	9,149 52.88	1,210	911 75.29 75.29 9.96	-	-	470 87.69 51.59 38.84 5.14	-	-	194 71.59 21.30 16.03 2.12	-	-	-	-	-	-	-	-	-	-	-	-	-	-	-	-	-

Notes: Please refer to the User's Guide for an explanation of data; data is arranged alphabetically by state, then county, then city within each county; table includes counties with populations greater than 49,999 unless noted and cities with populations greater than 9,999 whose Asian and/or NHPI population rates are greater than the national average; (1) Native Hawaiian and other Pacific Islander; (2) excludes Taiwanese; (3) includes Chamorro; (4) county does not meet population threshold but is shown in order to allow inclusion of city

Place	Total population 25 years and over who are 4-year college graduates	Asian population 25 years and over	Asians 25 years and over who are 4-year college graduates	NHPI[1] population 25 years and over	NHPIs[1] 25 years and over who are 4-year college graduates	Asian Indian	Bangladeshi	Cambodian	Chinese[2]	Fijian	Filipino	Guamanian[3]	Hawaiian, Native	Hmong	Indonesian	Japanese	Korean	Laotian	Malaysian	Pakistani	Samoan	Sri Lankan	Taiwanese	Thai	Tongan	Vietnamese
Elwood (cdp)	2,992 39.76	465	274 58.92 58.92 9.16	-	-	-	-	-	-	-	-	-	-	-	-	-	-	-	-	-	-	-	-	-	-	-
Lake Grove (village)	1,977 28.31	380	230 60.53 60.53 11.63	-	-	-	-	-	-	-	-	-	-	-	-	-	-	-	-	-	-	-	-	-	-	-
Melville (cdp)	4,887 48.83	463	366 79.05 79.05 7.49	-	-	-	-	-	-	-	-	-	-	-	-	-	-	-	-	-	-	-	-	-	-	-
Setauket-East Setauket (cdp)	5,842 55.62	990	815 82.32 82.32 13.95	-	-	-	-	-	426 87.30 52.27 43.03 7.29	-	-	-	-	-	-	-	-	-	-	-	-	-	-	-	-	-
Stony Brook (cdp)	5,083 54.53	522	390 74.71 74.71 7.67	-	-	-	-	-	207 76.95 53.08 39.66 4.07	-	-	-	-	-	-	-	-	-	-	-	-	-	-	-	-	-
Sullivan County	8,367 16.66	585	227 38.80 38.80 2.71	-	-	-	-	-	-	-	-	-	-	-	-	-	-	-	-	-	-	-	-	-	-	-
Tioga County	6,733 19.67	208	87 41.83 41.83 1.29	-	-	-	-	-	-	-	-	-	-	-	-	-	-	-	-	-	-	-	-	-	-	-
Tompkins County	25,187 47.46	2,854	2,528 88.58 88.58 10.04	-	-	434 94.14 17.17 15.21 1.72	-	-	993 91.69 39.28 34.79 3.94	-	-	-	-	-	-	250 85.32 9.89 8.76 0.99	537 98.17 21.24 18.82 2.13	-	-	-	-	-	-	-	-	-
Ithaca (city)	6,222 57.91	848	644 75.94 75.94 10.35	-	-	118 84.29 18.32 13.92 1.90	-	-	260 82.54 40.37 30.66 4.18	-	-	-	-	-	-	-	74 96.10 11.49 8.73 1.19	-	-	-	-	-	-	-	-	-
Lansing (town)	3,583 52.41	733	676 92.22 92.22 18.87	-	-	-	-	-	-	-	-	-	-	-	-	-	-	-	-	-	-	-	-	-	-	-

Notes: Please refer to the User's Guide for an explanation of data; data is arranged alphabetically by state, then county, then city within each county; table includes counties with populations greater than 49,999 unless noted and cities with populations greater than 9,999 whose Asian and/or NHPI population rates are greater than the national average; (1) Native Hawaiian and other Pacific Islander; (2) excludes Taiwanese; (3) includes Chamorro; (4) county does not meet population threshold but is shown in order to allow inclusion of city

Place	Total population 25 years and over who are 4-year college graduates	Asian population 25 years and over	Asians 25 years and over who are 4-year college graduates	NHPI[1] population 25 years and over	NHPIs[1] 25 years and over who are 4-year college graduates	Asian Indian	Bangladeshi	Cambodian	Chinese[2]	Fijian	Filipino	Guamanian[3]	Hawaiian, Native	Hmong	Indonesian	Japanese	Korean	Laotian	Malaysian	Pakistani	Samoan	Sri Lankan	Taiwanese	Thai	Tongan	Vietnamese
Ulster County	30,137 24.97	1,050	549 52.29 52.29 1.82	-	-	-	-	-	140 49.65 25.50 13.33 0.46	-	-	-	-	-	-	-	-	-	-	-	-	-	-	-	-	-
New Paltz (town)	3,207 47.82	202	111 54.95 54.95 3.46	-	-	-	-	-	-	-	-	-	-	-	-	-	-	-	-	-	-	-	-	-	-	-
Warren County	10,081 23.25	300	149 49.67 49.67 1.48	-	-	-	-	-	-	-	-	-	-	-	-	-	-	-	-	-	-	-	-	-	-	-
Wayne County	10,513 17.03	205	41 20.00 20.00 0.39	-	-	-	-	-	-	-	-	-	-	-	-	-	-	-	-	-	-	-	-	-	-	-
Westchester County	256,924 40.85	28,190	18,579 65.91 65.91 7.23	-	-	6,076 63.48 32.70 21.55 2.36	-	-	3,600 70.39 19.38 12.77 1.40	-	2,475 71.14 13.32 8.78 0.96	-	-	-	-	3,380 68.57 18.19 11.99 1.32	1,746 61.20 9.40 6.19 0.68	-	-	319 71.21 1.72 1.13 0.12	-	-	191 82.68 1.03 0.68 0.07	160 37.47 0.86 0.57 0.06	-	-
Dobbs Ferry (village)	3,558 50.62	483	206 42.65 42.65 5.79	-	-	-	-	-	-	-	-	-	-	-	-	-	-	-	-	-	-	-	-	-	-	-
Eastchester (cdp)	6,919 50.82	866	585 67.55 67.55 8.45	-	-	-	-	-	-	-	-	-	-	-	-	279 79.71 47.69 32.22 4.03	-	-	-	-	-	-	-	-	-	-
Eastchester (town)	11,580 52.26	1,539	972 63.16 63.16 8.39	-	-	-	-	-	-	-	-	-	-	-	-	533 66.63 54.84 34.63 4.60	-	-	-	-	-	-	-	-	-	-
Greenburgh (town)	32,946 53.73	5,314	3,913 73.64 73.64 11.88	-	-	1,322 74.94 33.78 24.88 4.01	-	-	713 77.33 18.22 13.42 2.16	-	323 78.78 8.25 6.08 0.98	-	-	-	-	926 71.12 23.66 17.43 2.81	456 70.48 11.65 8.58 1.38	-	-	-	-	-	-	-	-	-
Harrison (village)	7,209 45.36	821	580 70.65 70.65 8.05	-	-	-	-	-	-	-	-	-	-	-	-	278 68.47 47.93 33.86 3.86	-	-	-	-	-	-	-	-	-	-

Notes: Please refer to the User's Guide for an explanation of data; data is arranged alphabetically by state, then county, then city within each county; table includes counties with populations greater than 49,999 unless noted and cities with populations greater than 9,999 whose Asian and/or NHPI population rates are greater than the national average; (1) Native Hawaiian and other Pacific Islander; (2) excludes Taiwanese; (3) includes Chamorro; (4) county does not meet population threshold but is shown in order to allow inclusion of city

Place	Total population 25 years and over who are 4-year college graduates	Asian population 25 years and over	Asians 25 years and over who are 4-year college graduates	NHPI[1] population 25 years and over	NHPIs[1] 25 years and over who are 4-year college graduates	Asian Indian	Bangladeshi	Cambodian	Chinese[2]	Fijian	Filipino	Guamanian[3]	Hawaiian, Native	Hmong	Indonesian	Japanese	Korean	Laotian	Malaysian	Pakistani	Samoan	Sri Lankan	Taiwanese	Thai	Tongan	Vietnamese
New Castle (town)	8,651 75.97	650	585 90.00 90.00 6.76	-	-	256 94.81 43.76 39.38 2.96	-	-	148 74.37 25.30 22.77 1.71	-	-	-	-	-	-	-	-	-	-	-	-	-	-	-	-	-
New Rochelle (city)	18,724 38.31	1,862	1,191 63.96 63.96 6.36	-	-	440 58.12 36.94 23.63 2.35	-	-	262 63.75 22.00 14.07 1.40	-	-	-	-	-	-	-	-	-	-	-	-	-	-	-	-	-
North Castle (town)	4,048 56.81	289	201 69.55 69.55 4.97	-	-	-	-	-	-	-	-	-	-	-	-	-	-	-	-	-	-	-	-	-	-	-
Ossining (town)	10,652 41.31	1,070	758 70.84 70.84 7.12	-	-	409 80.35 53.96 38.22 3.84	-	-	-	-	-	-	-	-	-	-	-	-	-	-	-	-	-	-	-	-
Ossining (village)	4,963 28.97	638	384 60.19 60.19 7.74	-	-	152 70.70 39.58 23.82 3.06	-	-	-	-	-	-	-	-	-	-	-	-	-	-	-	-	-	-	-	-
Pelham (town)	4,621 58.60	317	123 38.80 38.80 2.66	-	-	-	-	-	-	-	-	-	-	-	-	-	-	-	-	-	-	-	-	-	-	-
Rye (city)	6,931 68.33	700	527 75.29 75.29 7.60	-	-	-	-	-	-	-	-	-	-	-	-	296 73.63 56.17 42.29 4.27	-	-	-	-	-	-	-	-	-	-
Scarsdale (village)	8,991 79.83	1,274	957 75.12 75.12 10.64	-	-	224 88.89 23.41 17.58 2.49	-	-	217 87.85 22.68 17.03 2.41	-	-	-	-	-	-	286 70.10 29.89 22.45 3.18	118 57.28 12.33 9.26 1.31	-	-	-	-	-	-	-	-	-
Tarrytown (village)	4,024 50.28	416	333 80.05 80.05 8.28	-	-	-	-	-	-	-	-	-	-	-	-	-	-	-	-	-	-	-	-	-	-	-
White Plains (city)	15,622 41.13	1,701	1,235 72.60 72.60 7.91	-	-	426 73.70 34.49 25.04 2.73	-	-	276 69.00 22.35 16.23 1.77	-	-	-	-	-	-	-	-	-	-	-	-	-	-	-	-	-

Notes: Please refer to the User's Guide for an explanation of data; data is arranged alphabetically by state, then county, then city within each county; table includes counties with populations greater than 49,999 unless noted and cities with populations greater than 9,999 whose Asian and/or NHPI population rates are greater than the national average; (1) Native Hawaiian and other Pacific Islander; (2) excludes Taiwanese; (3) includes Chamorro; (4) county does not meet population threshold but is shown in order to allow inclusion of city

Place	Total population 25 years and over who are 4-year college graduates	Asian population 25 years and over	Asians 25 years and over who are 4-year college graduates	NHPI[1] population 25 years and over	NHPIs[1] 25 years and over who are 4-year college graduates	Asian Indian	Bangladeshi	Cambodian	Chinese[2]	Fijian	Filipino	Guamanian[3]	Hawaiian, Native	Hmong	Indonesian	Japanese	Korean	Laotian	Malaysian	Pakistani	Samoan	Sri Lankan	Taiwanese	Thai	Tongan	Vietnamese
Yonkers (city)	32,711 24.83	6,391	3,401 53.22 53.22 10.40	-	-	1,343 45.85 39.49 21.01 4.11	-	-	402 58.26 11.82 6.29 1.23	-	894 73.52 26.29 13.99 2.73	-	-	-	-	-	386 47.89 11.35 6.04 1.18	-	-	-	-	-	-	-	-	-
NORTH CAROLINA	1,186,713 22.46	67,753	29,733 43.88 43.88 2.51	1,939	258 13.31 13.31 0.02	10,849 68.22 36.49 16.01 0.91	-	87 7.34 0.29 0.13 0.01	6,991 61.12 23.51 10.32 0.59	-	3,012 43.30 10.13 4.45 0.25	68 9.94 26.36 3.51 0.01	93 15.37 36.05 4.80 0.01	77 3.56 0.26 0.11 0.01	-	1,894 41.45 6.37 2.80 0.16	2,784 34.31 9.36 4.11 0.23	57 2.27 0.19 0.08 <0.01	-	532 50.00 1.79 0.79 0.04	40 15.75 15.50 2.06 <0.01	-	478 70.40 1.61 0.71 0.04	331 29.09 1.11 0.49 0.03	-	1,505 16.02 5.06 2.22 0.13
Alamance County	16,629 19.19	658	255 38.75 38.75 1.53	-	-	-	-	-	-	-	-	-	-	-	-	-	-	-	-	-	-	-	-	-	-	-
Buncombe County	36,287 25.26	1,178	492 41.77 41.77 1.36	-	-	176 47.96 35.77 14.94 0.49	-	-	-	-	-	-	-	-	-	-	-	-	-	-	-	-	-	-	-	-
Burke County	7,653 12.77	1,111	88 7.92 7.92 1.15	-	-	-	-	-	-	-	-	-	-	10 1.75 11.36 0.90 0.13	-	-	-	0 0.00 0.00 0.00 0.00	-	-	-	-	-	-	-	-
Cabarrus County	16,574 19.11	583	200 34.31 34.31 1.21	-	-	-	-	-	-	-	-	-	-	-	-	-	-	-	-	-	-	-	-	-	-	-
Catawba County	16,126 17.02	1,679	226 13.46 13.46 1.40	-	-	-	-	-	-	-	-	-	-	18 2.88 7.96 1.07 0.11	-	-	-	8 3.33 3.54 0.48 0.05	-	-	-	-	-	-	-	20 7.52 8.85 1.19 0.12
Hickory (city)	6,824 28.02	715	138 19.30 19.30 2.02	-	-	-	-	-	-	-	-	-	-	0 0.00 0.00 0.00 0.00	-	-	-	-	-	-	-	-	-	-	-	-
Cleveland County	8,403 13.25	388	118 30.41 30.41 1.40	-	-	-	-	-	-	-	-	-	-	-	-	-	-	-	-	-	-	-	-	-	-	-
Craven County	10,987 19.27	738	177 23.98 23.98 1.61	-	-	-	-	-	-	-	74 24.75 41.81 10.03 0.67	-	-	-	-	-	-	-	-	-	-	-	-	-	-	-

Notes: Please refer to the User's Guide for an explanation of data; data is arranged alphabetically by state, then county, then city within each county; table includes counties with populations greater than 49,999 unless noted and cities with populations greater than 9,999 whose Asian and/or NHPI population rates are greater than the national average; (1) Native Hawaiian and other Pacific Islander; (2) excludes Taiwanese; (3) includes Chamorro; (4) county does not meet population threshold but is shown in order to allow inclusion of city

Place	Total population 25 years and over who are 4-year college graduates	Asian population 25 years and over	Asians 25 years and over who are 4-year college graduates	NHPI[1] population 25 years and over	NHPIs[1] 25 years and over who are 4-year college graduates	Asian Indian	Bangladeshi	Cambodian	Chinese[2]	Fijian	Filipino	Guamanian[3]	Hawaiian, Native	Hmong	Indonesian	Japanese	Korean	Laotian	Malaysian	Pakistani	Samoan	Sri Lankan	Taiwanese	Thai	Tongan	Vietnamese
Cumberland County	33,769 19.11	4,110	849 20.66 20.66 2.51	268	10 3.73 3.73 0.03	201 50.50 23.67 4.89 0.60	-	-	-	-	188 28.40 22.14 4.57 0.56	-	-	-	-	35 9.16 4.12 0.85 0.10	192 12.34 22.61 4.67 0.57	-	-	-	-	-	-	-	-	80 17.54 9.42 1.95 0.24
Davidson County	12,774 12.76	654	125 19.11 19.11 0.98	-	-	-	-	6 2.54 4.80 0.92 0.05	-	-	-	-	-	-	-	-	-	-	-	-	-	-	-	-	-	-
Durham County	57,728 40.14	4,393	3,444 78.40 78.40 5.97	-	-	1,399 84.38 40.62 31.85 2.42	-	-	804 81.38 23.34 18.30 1.39	-	322 73.52 9.35 7.33 0.56	-	-	-	-	219 70.87 6.36 4.99 0.38	244 77.46 7.08 5.55 0.42	-	-	-	-	-	-	-	-	-
Forsyth County	58,524 28.68	2,267	1,208 53.29 53.29 2.06	-	-	342 83.21 28.31 15.09 0.58	-	-	372 54.63 30.79 16.41 0.64	-	111 55.22 9.19 4.90 0.19	-	-	-	-	-	-	-	-	-	-	-	-	-	-	84 26.17 6.95 3.71 0.14
Gaston County	18,094 14.16	969	223 23.01 23.01 1.23	-	-	-	-	-	-	-	-	-	-	-	-	-	-	-	-	-	-	-	-	-	-	12 4.10 5.38 1.24 0.07
Guilford County	83,444 30.29	5,710	1,779 31.16 31.16 2.13	-	-	662 60.35 37.21 11.59 0.79	-	-	301 44.20 16.92 5.27 0.36	-	227 59.42 12.76 3.98 0.27	-	-	-	-	-	203 31.97 11.41 3.56 0.24	8 2.72 0.45 0.14 0.01	-	71 34.47 3.99 1.24 0.09	-	-	-	-	-	88 4.98 4.95 1.54 0.11
Halifax County	4,185 11.10	208	67 32.21 32.21 1.60	-	-	-	-	-	-	-	-	-	-	-	-	-	-	-	-	-	-	-	-	-	-	-
Harnett County	7,298 12.77	395	89 22.53 22.53 1.22	-	-	-	-	-	-	-	-	-	-	-	-	-	-	-	-	-	-	-	-	-	-	-
Henderson County	15,696 24.13	308	84 27.27 27.27 0.54	-	-	-	-	-	-	-	-	-	-	-	-	-	-	-	-	-	-	-	-	-	-	-
Iredell County	14,296 17.43	675	197 29.19 29.19 1.38	-	-	-	-	-	-	-	-	-	-	-	-	-	-	-	-	-	-	-	-	-	-	-

Notes: Please refer to the User's Guide for an explanation of data; data is arranged alphabetically by state, then county, then city within each county; table includes counties with populations greater than 49,999 unless noted and cities with populations greater than 9,999 whose Asian and/or NHPI population rates are greater than the national average; (1) Native Hawaiian and other Pacific Islander; (2) excludes Taiwanese; (3) includes Chamorro; (4) county does not meet population threshold but is shown in order to allow inclusion of city

Place	Total population 25 years and over who are 4-year college graduates	Asian population 25 years and over	Asians 25 years and over who are 4-year college graduates	NHPI[1] population 25 years and over	NHPIs[1] 25 years and over who are 4-year college graduates	Asian Indian	Bangladeshi	Cambodian	Chinese[2]	Fijian	Filipino	Guamanian[3]	Hawaiian, Native	Hmong	Indonesian	Japanese	Korean	Laotian	Malaysian	Pakistani	Samoan	Sri Lankan	Taiwanese	Thai	Tongan	Vietnamese
Johnston County	12,751 15.89	280	70 25.00 25.00 0.55	-	-	-	-	-	-	-	-	-	-	-	-	-	-	-	-	-	-	-	-	-	-	-
Lenoir County	5,304 13.32	229	91 39.74 39.74 1.72	-	-	-	-	-	-	-	-	-	-	-	-	-	-	-	-	-	-	-	-	-	-	-
Mecklenburg County	168,957 37.12	12,894	5,187 40.23 40.23 3.07	-	-	2,308 68.53 44.50 17.90 1.37	-	22 5.82 0.42 0.17 0.01	998 52.61 19.24 7.74 0.59	-	435 54.04 8.39 3.37 0.26	-	-	8 5.48 0.15 0.06 <0.01	-	309 52.55 5.96 2.40 0.18	446 27.88 8.60 3.46 0.26	16 2.80 0.31 0.12 0.01	-	-	-	-	-	-	-	429 15.04 8.27 3.33 0.25
Nash County	9,913 17.23	269	113 42.01 42.01 1.14	-	-	-	-	-	-	-	-	-	-	-	-	-	-	-	-	-	-	-	-	-	-	-
New Hanover County	33,340 30.96	897	434 48.38 48.38 1.30	-	-	-	-	-	-	-	-	-	-	-	-	-	-	-	-	-	-	-	-	-	-	-
Onslow County	11,121 14.77	1,660	203 12.23 12.23 1.83	180	11 6.11 6.11 0.10	-	-	-	-	-	94 13.13 46.31 5.66 0.85	-	-	-	-	5 1.34 2.46 0.30 0.04	-	-	-	-	-	-	-	-	-	-
Orange County	35,799 51.49	2,708	2,191 80.91 80.91 6.12	-	-	304 84.92 13.87 11.23 0.85	-	-	934 83.02 42.63 34.49 2.61	-	-	-	-	-	-	294 81.44 13.42 10.86 0.82	333 92.50 15.20 12.30 0.93	-	-	-	-	-	-	-	-	-
Carrboro (town)	6,006 60.85	488	362 74.18 74.18 6.03	-	-	-	-	-	-	-	-	-	-	-	-	-	-	-	-	-	-	-	-	-	-	-
Chapel Hill (town)	17,409 73.69	1,858	1,557 83.80 83.80 8.94	-	-	213 81.92 13.68 11.46 1.22	-	-	698 84.91 44.83 37.57 4.01	-	-	-	-	-	-	-	236 94.78 15.16 12.70 1.36	-	-	-	-	-	-	-	-	-
Pitt County	20,866 26.40	770	440 57.14 57.14 2.11	-	-	-	-	-	-	-	-	-	-	-	-	-	-	-	-	-	-	-	-	-	-	-

Notes: Please refer to the User's Guide for an explanation of data; data is arranged alphabetically by state, then county, then city within each county; table includes counties with populations greater than 49,999 unless noted and cities with populations greater than 9,999 whose Asian and/or NHPI population rates are greater than the national average; (1) Native Hawaiian and other Pacific Islander; (2) excludes Taiwanese; (3) includes Chamorro; (4) county does not meet population threshold but is shown in order to allow inclusion of city

Place	Total population 25 years and over who are 4-year college graduates	Asian population 25 years and over	Asians 25 years and over who are 4-year college graduates	NHPI[1] population 25 years and over	NHPIs[1] 25 years and over who are 4-year college graduates	Asian Indian	Bangladeshi	Cambodian	Chinese[2]	Fijian	Filipino	Guamanian[3]	Hawaiian, Native	Hmong	Indonesian	Japanese	Korean	Laotian	Malaysian	Pakistani	Samoan	Sri Lankan	Taiwanese	Thai	Tongan	Vietnamese
Randolph County	9,681 11.07	479	126 26.30 26.30 1.30	-	-	-	-	-	-	-	-	-	-	-	-	-	-	-	-	-	-	-	-	-	-	-
Robeson County	8,524 11.45	563	163 28.95 28.95 1.91	-	-	-	-	-	-	-	-	-	-	-	-	-	-	-	-	-	-	-	-	-	-	-
Rowan County	12,242 14.18	432	69 15.97 15.97 0.56	-	-	-	-	-	-	-	-	-	-	-	-	-	-	-	-	-	-	-	-	-	-	-
Stanly County	4,934 12.75	292	90 30.82 30.82 1.82	-	-	-	-	-	-	-	-	-	-	11 10.78 12.22 3.77 0.22	-	-	-	-	-	-	-	-	-	-	-	-
Surry County	5,904 12.04	146	22 15.07 15.07 0.37	-	-	-	-	-	-	-	-	-	-	-	-	-	-	-	-	-	-	-	-	-	-	-
Union County	16,819 21.32	338	145 42.90 42.90 0.86	-	-	-	-	-	-	-	-	-	-	-	-	-	-	-	-	-	-	-	-	-	-	-
Wake County	177,029 43.88	13,302	8,807 66.21 66.21 4.97	-	-	3,545 79.70 40.25 26.65 2.00	-	-	2,406 73.89 27.32 18.09 1.36	-	507 58.61 5.76 3.81 0.29	-	-	-	-	365 64.15 4.14 2.74 0.21	694 53.18 7.88 5.22 0.39	-	-	174 68.24 1.98 1.31 0.10	-	-	-	-	-	433 29.60 4.92 3.26 0.24
Apex (town)	7,567 58.75	504	376 74.60 74.60 4.97	-	-	-	-	-	-	-	-	-	-	-	-	-	-	-	-	-	-	-	-	-	-	-
Cary (town)	37,094 60.70	4,876	3,608 74.00 74.00 9.73	-	-	1,743 82.18 48.31 35.75 4.70	-	-	925 73.82 25.64 18.97 2.49	-	-	-	-	-	-	178 74.48 4.93 3.65 0.48	210 57.85 5.82 4.31 0.57	-	-	-	-	-	-	-	-	169 54.34 4.68 3.47 0.46
Wayne County	10,925 14.99	730	239 32.74 32.74 2.19	-	-	-	-	-	-	-	-	-	-	-	-	-	-	-	-	-	-	-	-	-	-	-

Notes: Please refer to the User's Guide for an explanation of data; data is arranged alphabetically by state, then county, then city within each county; table includes counties with populations greater than 49,999 unless noted and cities with populations greater than 9,999 whose Asian and/or NHPI population rates are greater than the national average; (1) Native Hawaiian and other Pacific Islander; (2) excludes Taiwanese; (3) includes Chamorro; (4) county does not meet population threshold but is shown in order to allow inclusion of city

Place	Total population 25 years and over who are 4-year college graduates	Asian population 25 years and over	Asians 25 years and over who are 4-year college graduates	NHPI[1] population 25 years and over	NHPIs[1] 25 years and over who are 4-year college graduates	Asian Indian	Bangladeshi	Cambodian	Chinese[2]	Fijian	Filipino	Guamanian[3]	Hawaiian, Native	Hmong	Indonesian	Japanese	Korean	Laotian	Malaysian	Pakistani	Samoan	Sri Lankan	Taiwanese	Thai	Tongan	Vietnamese
Wilkes County	5,135 11.29	169	37 21.89 21.89 0.72	-	-	-	-	-	-	-	-	-	-	-	-	-	-	-	-	-	-	-	-	-	-	-
NORTH DAKOTA	89,843 21.99	2,046	1,000 48.88 48.88 1.11	-	-	437 77.62 43.70 21.36 0.49	-	-	213 76.34 21.30 10.41 0.24	-	108 27.98 10.80 5.28 0.12	-	-	-	-	-	65 26.42 6.50 3.18 0.07	-	-	-	-	-	-	-	-	-
Cass County	23,337 31.25	828	495 59.78 59.78 2.12	-	-	201 82.38 40.61 24.28 0.86	-	-	-	-	-	-	-	-	-	-	-	-	-	-	-	-	-	-	-	-
Grand Forks County	10,405 27.85	425	179 42.12 42.12 1.72	-	-	-	-	-	-	-	-	-	-	-	-	-	-	-	-	-	-	-	-	-	-	-
Ward County	7,956 22.13	210	45 21.43 21.43 0.57	-	-	-	-	-	-	-	-	-	-	-	-	-	-	-	-	-	-	-	-	-	-	-
OHIO	1,563,532 21.10	85,861	50,338 58.63 58.63 3.22	1,363	252 18.49 18.49 0.02	18,973 77.46 37.69 22.10 1.21	333 77.08 0.66 0.39 0.02	99 7.79 0.20 0.12 0.01	12,561 66.24 24.95 14.63 0.80	-	5,140 54.29 10.21 5.99 0.33	97 26.50 38.49 7.12 0.01	92 20.49 36.51 6.75 0.01	-	297 64.85 0.59 0.35 0.02	3,257 45.55 6.47 3.79 0.21	4,394 50.51 8.73 5.12 0.28	91 5.86 0.18 0.11 0.01	142 71.36 0.28 0.17 0.01	672 69.42 1.33 0.78 0.04	42 16.28 16.67 3.08 <0.01	247 63.82 0.49 0.29 0.02	974 68.21 1.93 1.13 0.06	550 42.70 1.09 0.64 0.04	-	1,408 21.63 2.80 1.64 0.09
Allen County	9,360 13.43	338	161 47.63 47.63 1.72	-	-	-	-	-	-	-	-	-	-	-	-	-	-	-	-	-	-	-	-	-	-	-
Ashtabula County	7,517 11.06	217	60 27.65 27.65 0.80	-	-	-	-	-	-	-	-	-	-	-	-	-	-	-	-	-	-	-	-	-	-	-
Athens County	8,113 25.70	607	465 76.61 76.61 5.73	-	-	-	-	-	-	-	-	-	-	-	-	-	-	-	-	-	-	-	-	-	-	-
Athens (city)	3,501 63.81	437	378 86.50 86.50 10.80	-	-	-	-	-	-	-	-	-	-	-	-	-	-	-	-	-	-	-	-	-	-	-

Notes: Please refer to the User's Guide for an explanation of data; data is arranged alphabetically by state, then county, then city within each county; table includes counties with populations greater than 49,999 unless noted and cities with populations greater than 9,999 whose Asian and/or NHPI population rates are greater than the national average; (1) Native Hawaiian and other Pacific Islander; (2) excludes Taiwanese; (3) includes Chamorro; (4) county does not meet population threshold but is shown in order to allow inclusion of city

Place	Total population 25 years and over who are 4-year college graduates	Asian population 25 years and over	Asians 25 years and over who are 4-year college graduates	NHPI[1] population 25 years and over	NHPIs[1] 25 years and over who are 4-year college graduates	Asian Indian	Bangladeshi	Cambodian	Chinese[2]	Fijian	Filipino	Guamanian[3]	Hawaiian, Native	Hmong	Indonesian	Japanese	Korean	Laotian	Malaysian	Pakistani	Samoan	Sri Lankan	Taiwanese	Thai	Tongan	Vietnamese
Butler County	48,659 23.48	3,112	1,760 56.56 56.56 3.62	-	-	806 77.20 45.80 25.90 1.66	-	-	446 70.79 25.34 14.33 0.92	-	141 44.76 8.01 4.53 0.29	-	-	-	-	-	76 30.77 4.32 2.44 0.16	-	-	-	-	-	-	-	-	133 29.75 7.56 4.27 0.27
Clark County	14,178 14.88	398	213 53.52 53.52 1.50	-	-	-	-	-	-	-	-	-	-	-	-	-	-	-	-	-	-	-	-	-	-	-
Clermont County	23,557 20.75	829	457 55.13 55.13 1.94	-	-	227 76.69 49.67 27.38 0.96	-	-	-	-	-	-	-	-	-	-	-	-	-	-	-	-	-	-	-	-
Columbiana County	8,198 10.78	248	101 40.73 40.73 1.23	-	-	-	-	-	-	-	-	-	-	-	-	-	-	-	-	-	-	-	-	-	-	-
Cuyahoga County	235,413 25.15	17,649	10,701 60.63 60.63 4.55	-	-	4,446 74.26 41.55 25.19 1.89	-	14 5.49 0.13 0.08 0.01	2,356 55.82 22.02 13.35 1.00	-	1,383 62.84 12.92 7.84 0.59	-	-	-	-	513 56.69 4.79 2.91 0.22	778 59.12 7.27 4.41 0.33	-	-	-	-	-	-	-	-	298 22.31 2.78 1.69 0.13
Mayfield Heights (city)	4,105 27.38	538	373 69.33 69.33 9.09	-	-	221 81.85 59.25 41.08 5.38	-	-	-	-	-	-	-	-	-	-	-	-	-	-	-	-	-	-	-	-
Richmond Heights (city)	2,849 35.70	393	308 78.37 78.37 10.81	-	-	-	-	-	-	-	-	-	-	-	-	-	-	-	-	-	-	-	-	-	-	-
Solon (city)	7,131 50.44	693	522 75.32 75.32 7.32	-	-	279 85.85 53.45 40.26 3.91	-	-	165 75.00 31.61 23.81 2.31	-	-	-	-	-	-	-	-	-	-	-	-	-	-	-	-	-
Westlake (city)	10,388 45.31	954	731 76.62 76.62 7.04	-	-	358 91.09 48.97 37.53 3.45	-	-	-	-	-	-	-	-	-	-	-	-	-	-	-	-	-	-	-	-
Delaware County	28,978 41.04	1,151	816 70.89 70.89 2.82	-	-	248 81.85 30.39 21.55 0.86	-	-	273 74.79 33.46 23.72 0.94	-	-	-	-	-	-	-	-	-	-	-	-	-	-	-	-	-

Notes: Please refer to the User's Guide for an explanation of data; data is arranged alphabetically by state, then county, then city within each county; table includes counties with populations greater than 49,999 unless noted and cities with populations greater than 9,999 whose Asian and/or NHPI population rates are greater than the national average; (1) Native Hawaiian and other Pacific Islander; (2) excludes Taiwanese; (3) includes Chamorro; (4) county does not meet population threshold but is shown in order to allow inclusion of city

Place	Total population 25 years and over who are 4-year college graduates	Asian population 25 years and over	Asians 25 years and over who are 4-year college graduates	NHPI[1] population 25 years and over	NHPIs[1] 25 years and over who are 4-year college graduates	Asian Indian	Bangladeshi	Cambodian	Chinese[2]	Fijian	Filipino	Guamanian[3]	Hawaiian, Native	Hmong	Indonesian	Japanese	Korean	Laotian	Malaysian	Pakistani	Samoan	Sri Lankan	Taiwanese	Thai	Tongan	Vietnamese
Fairfield County	16,660 20.84	512	242 47.27 47.27 1.45	-	-	-	-	-	-	-	-	-	-	-	-	-	-	-	-	-	-	-	-	-	-	-
Franklin County	215,180 31.82	20,437	12,264 60.01 60.01 5.70	169	53 31.36 31.36 0.02	4,276 80.80 34.87 20.92 1.99	-	54 8.60 0.44 0.26 0.03	3,325 67.87 27.11 16.27 1.55	-	610 48.92 4.97 2.98 0.28	-	-	-	66 59.46 0.54 0.32 0.03	1,003 49.85 8.18 4.91 0.47	1,383 64.93 11.28 6.77 0.64	49 7.68 0.40 0.24 0.02	-	187 72.48 1.52 0.92 0.09	-	-	351 71.63 2.86 1.72 0.16	161 58.76 1.31 0.79 0.07	-	319 21.22 2.60 1.56 0.15
Dublin (city)	12,749 64.66	1,546	1,027 66.43 66.43 8.06	-	-	380 90.05 37.00 24.58 2.98	-	-	262 87.04 25.51 16.95 2.06	-	-	-	-	-	-	202 39.61 19.67 13.07 1.58	-	-	-	-	-	-	-	-	-	-
Hilliard (city)	7,000 46.08	598	408 68.23 68.23 5.83	-	-	-	-	-	-	-	-	-	-	-	-	-	-	-	-	-	-	-	-	-	-	-
Geauga County	18,795 31.74	254	150 59.06 59.06 0.80	-	-	-	-	-	-	-	-	-	-	-	-	-	-	-	-	-	-	-	-	-	-	-
Greene County	28,737 31.10	1,963	1,109 56.50 56.50 3.86	-	-	484 79.08 43.64 24.66 1.68	-	-	210 76.09 18.94 10.70 0.73	-	-	-	-	-	-	-	126 31.34 11.36 6.42 0.44	-	-	-	-	-	-	-	-	-
Hamilton County	159,212 29.16	8,475	5,714 67.42 67.42 3.59	-	-	2,189 82.92 38.31 25.83 1.37	-	13 6.91 0.23 0.15 0.01	1,633 76.17 28.58 19.27 1.03	-	570 64.85 9.98 6.73 0.36	-	-	-	-	278 56.85 4.87 3.28 0.17	442 62.25 7.74 5.22 0.28	-	-	-	-	-	-	-	-	130 20.60 2.28 1.53 0.08
Blue Ash (city)	4,278 48.73	571	438 76.71 76.71 10.24	-	-	227 86.64 51.83 39.75 5.31	-	-	-	-	-	-	-	-	-	-	-	-	-	-	-	-	-	-	-	-
Sharonville (city)	3,293 33.80	378	287 75.93 75.93 8.72	-	-	223 89.56 77.70 58.99 6.77	-	-	-	-	-	-	-	-	-	-	-	-	-	-	-	-	-	-	-	-
Hancock County	9,932 21.65	443	288 65.01 65.01 2.90	-	-	-	-	-	-	-	-	-	-	-	-	-	-	-	-	-	-	-	-	-	-	-

Notes: Please refer to the User's Guide for an explanation of data; data is arranged alphabetically by state, then county, then city within each county; table includes counties with populations greater than 49,999 unless noted and cities with populations greater than 9,999 whose Asian and/or NHPI population rates are greater than the national average; (1) Native Hawaiian and other Pacific Islander; (2) excludes Taiwanese; (3) includes Chamorro; (4) county does not meet population threshold but is shown in order to allow inclusion of city

Place	Total population 25 years and over who are 4-year college graduates	Asian population 25 years and over	Asians 25 years and over who are 4-year college graduates	NHPI[1] population 25 years and over	NHPIs[1] 25 years and over who are 4-year college graduates	Asian Indian	Bangladeshi	Cambodian	Chinese[2]	Fijian	Filipino	Guamanian[3]	Hawaiian, Native	Hmong	Indonesian	Japanese	Korean	Laotian	Malaysian	Pakistani	Samoan	Sri Lankan	Taiwanese	Thai	Tongan	Vietnamese
Lake County	33,645 21.54	1,557	855 54.91 54.91 2.54	-	-	331 71.65 38.71 21.26 0.98	-	-	265 73.41 30.99 17.02 0.79	-	-	-	-	-	-	-	-	-	-	-	-	-	-	-	-	-
Licking County	17,504 18.42	450	176 39.11 39.11 1.01	-	-	-	-	-	-	-	-	-	-	-	-	-	-	-	-	-	-	-	-	-	-	-
Lorain County	30,741 16.57	1,088	540 49.63 49.63 1.76	-	-	161 63.39 29.81 14.80 0.52	-	-	-	-	179 52.03 33.15 16.45 0.58	-	-	-	-	-	-	-	-	-	-	-	-	-	-	-
Lucas County	61,870 21.26	3,736	2,286 61.19 61.19 3.69	-	-	737 72.47 32.24 19.73 1.19	-	-	775 67.27 33.90 20.74 1.25	-	280 60.48 12.25 7.49 0.45	-	-	-	-	-	171 50.00 7.48 4.58 0.28	-	-	-	-	-	-	-	-	-
Mahoning County	30,557 17.48	683	313 45.83 45.83 1.02	-	-	-	-	-	-	-	-	-	-	-	-	-	-	-	-	-	-	-	-	-	-	-
Marion County	4,927 11.08	221	71 32.13 32.13 1.44	-	-	-	-	-	-	-	-	-	-	-	-	-	-	-	-	-	-	-	-	-	-	-
Medina County	24,509 24.76	738	407 55.15 55.15 1.66	-	-	216 76.33 53.07 29.27 0.88	-	-	-	-	-	-	-	-	-	-	-	-	-	-	-	-	-	-	-	-
Miami County	10,715 16.29	605	267 44.13 44.13 2.49	-	-	-	-	-	-	-	-	-	-	-	-	-	-	-	-	-	-	-	-	-	-	-
Montgomery County	83,818 22.83	4,771	2,583 54.14 54.14 3.08	-	-	1,135 79.82 43.94 23.79 1.35	-	-	496 65.52 19.20 10.40 0.59	-	232 43.61 8.98 4.86 0.28	-	-	-	-	178 39.91 6.89 3.73 0.21	212 40.46 8.21 4.44 0.25	-	-	-	-	-	-	-	-	120 18.75 4.65 2.52 0.14
Portage County	19,779 21.03	763	585 76.67 76.67 2.96	-	-	-	-	-	-	-	-	-	-	-	-	-	-	-	-	-	-	-	-	-	-	-

Notes: Please refer to the User's Guide for an explanation of data; data is arranged alphabetically by state, then county, then city within each county; table includes counties with populations greater than 49,999 unless noted and cities with populations greater than 9,999 whose Asian and/or NHPI population rates are greater than the national average; (1) Native Hawaiian and other Pacific Islander; (2) excludes Taiwanese; (3) includes Chamorro; (4) county does not meet population threshold but is shown in order to allow inclusion of city

Place	Total population 25 years and over who are 4-year college graduates	Asian population 25 years and over	Asians 25 years and over who are 4-year college graduates	NHPI[1] population 25 years and over	NHPIs[1] 25 years and over who are 4-year college graduates	Asian Indian	Bangladeshi	Cambodian	Chinese[2]	Fijian	Filipino	Guamanian[3]	Hawaiian, Native	Hmong	Indonesian	Japanese	Korean	Laotian	Malaysian	Pakistani	Samoan	Sri Lankan	Taiwanese	Thai	Tongan	Vietnamese
Richland County	10,865 12.61	457	143 31.29 31.29 1.32	-	-	-	-	-	-	-	-	-	-	-	-	-	-	-	-	-	-	-	-	-	-	-
Stark County	45,397 17.95	1,269	628 49.49 49.49 1.38	-	-	207 69.00 32.96 16.31 0.46	-	-	148 60.66 23.57 11.66 0.33	-	-	-	-	-	-	-	-	-	-	-	-	-	-	-	-	-
Summit County	91,096 25.12	4,814	2,984 61.99 61.99 3.28	-	-	979 76.66 32.81 20.34 1.07	-	-	896 76.71 30.03 18.61 0.98	-	192 52.17 6.43 3.99 0.21	-	-	-	-	175 55.91 5.86 3.64 0.19	380 70.76 12.73 7.89 0.42	15 4.62 0.50 0.31 0.02	-	-	-	-	-	-	-	108 26.73 3.62 2.24 0.12
Trumbull County	22,132 14.46	682	340 49.85 49.85 1.54	-	-	-	-	-	-	-	-	-	-	-	-	-	-	-	-	-	-	-	-	-	-	-
Warren County	29,301 28.36	1,375	932 67.78 67.78 3.18	-	-	352 83.41 37.77 25.60 1.20	-	-	276 79.31 29.61 20.07 0.94	-	-	-	-	-	-	-	-	-	-	-	-	-	-	-	-	-
Wayne County	12,013 17.17	441	239 54.20 54.20 1.99	-	-	-	-	-	-	-	-	-	-	-	-	-	-	-	-	-	-	-	-	-	-	-
Wood County	18,735 26.18	750	445 59.33 59.33 2.38	-	-	-	-	-	-	-	-	-	-	-	-	-	-	-	-	-	-	-	-	-	-	-
OKLAHOMA	446,771 20.28	28,009	10,504 37.50 37.50 2.35	1,019	154 15.11 15.11 0.03	2,940 59.72 27.99 10.50 0.66	-	26 14.36 0.25 0.09 0.01	2,642 61.71 25.15 9.43 0.59	-	931 33.24 8.86 3.32 0.21	53 18.60 34.42 5.20 0.01	78 18.27 50.65 7.65 0.02	6 4.92 0.06 0.02 <0.01	-	552 29.22 5.26 1.97 0.12	887 29.47 8.44 3.17 0.20	28 6.07 0.27 0.10 0.01	150 81.97 1.43 0.54 0.03	305 49.51 2.90 1.09 0.07	-	-	184 65.95 1.75 0.66 0.04	177 28.59 1.69 0.63 0.04	-	1,147 15.35 10.92 4.10 0.26
Canadian County	11,738 20.88	1,258	408 32.43 32.43 3.48	-	-	258 38.11 63.24 20.51 2.20	-	-	-	-	-	-	-	-	-	-	-	-	-	-	-	-	-	-	-	105 30.26 25.74 8.35 0.89
Cleveland County	35,464 28.02	3,328	1,634 49.10 49.10 4.61	-	-	261 63.66 15.97 7.84 0.74	-	-	485 71.64 29.68 14.57 1.37	-	91 29.64 5.57 2.73 0.26	-	-	-	-	-	213 47.44 13.04 6.40 0.60	-	-	-	-	-	-	-	-	281 29.86 17.20 8.44 0.79

Notes: Please refer to the User's Guide for an explanation of data; data is arranged alphabetically by state, then county, then city within each county; table includes counties with populations greater than 49,999 unless noted and cities with populations greater than 9,999 whose Asian and/or NHPI population rates are greater than the national average; (1) Native Hawaiian and other Pacific Islander; (2) excludes Taiwanese; (3) includes Chamorro; (4) county does not meet population threshold but is shown in order to allow inclusion of city

Place	Total population 25 years and over who are 4-year college graduates	Asian population 25 years and over	Asians 25 years and over who are 4-year college graduates	NHPI[1] population 25 years and over	NHPIs[1] 25 years and over who are 4-year college graduates	Asian Indian	Bangladeshi	Cambodian	Chinese[2]	Fijian	Filipino	Guamanian[3]	Hawaiian, Native	Hmong	Indonesian	Japanese	Korean	Laotian	Malaysian	Pakistani	Samoan	Sri Lankan	Taiwanese	Thai	Tongan	Vietnamese
Comanche County	12,846 19.11	1,677	387 23.08 23.08 3.01	-	-	-	-	-	-	-	150 44.51 38.76 8.94 1.17	-	-	-	-	-	50 7.58 12.92 2.98 0.39	-	-	-	-	-	-	-	-	-
Garfield County	7,443 19.55	350	98 28.00 28.00 1.32	-	-	-	-	-	-	-	-	-	-	-	-	-	-	-	-	-	-	-	-	-	-	-
Muskogee County	6,895 15.36	210	83 39.52 39.52 1.20	-	-	-	-	-	-	-	-	-	-	-	-	-	-	-	-	-	-	-	-	-	-	-
Oklahoma County	106,778 25.37	11,611	4,011 34.54 34.54 3.76	-	-	1,213 65.04 30.24 10.45 1.14	-	-	959 63.59 23.91 8.26 0.90	-	288 33.22 7.18 2.48 0.27	-	-	-	-	175 30.22 4.36 1.51 0.16	285 35.01 7.11 2.45 0.27	13 4.47 0.32 0.11 0.01	-	-	-	-	-	91 29.64 2.27 0.78 0.09	-	515 11.86 12.84 4.44 0.48
Payne County	12,733 34.19	919	741 80.63 80.63 5.82	-	-	-	-	-	292 94.81 39.41 31.77 2.29	-	-	-	-	-	-	-	-	-	-	-	-	-	-	-	-	-
Stillwater (city)	8,795 47.97	900	725 80.56 80.56 8.24	-	-	-	-	-	292 94.81 40.28 32.44 3.32	-	-	-	-	-	-	-	-	-	-	-	-	-	-	-	-	-
Pottawatomie County	6,367 15.48	207	64 30.92 30.92 1.01	-	-	-	-	-	-	-	-	-	-	-	-	-	-	-	-	-	-	-	-	-	-	-
Tulsa County	96,696 26.91	5,234	2,036 38.90 38.90 2.11	-	-	771 63.46 37.87 14.73 0.80	-	-	508 48.15 24.95 9.71 0.53	-	121 38.05 5.94 2.31 0.13	-	-	-	-	-	179 33.97 8.79 3.42 0.19	-	-	87 33.98 4.27 1.66 0.09	-	-	-	-	-	183 14.95 8.99 3.50 0.19
Wagoner County	5,690 15.42	254	35 13.78 13.78 0.62	-	-	-	-	-	-	-	-	-	-	-	-	-	-	-	-	-	-	-	-	-	-	-
OREGON	564,566 25.08	63,124	24,438 38.71 38.71 4.33	4,123	589 14.29 14.29 0.10	4,835 75.65 19.78 7.66 0.86	-	143 8.89 0.59 0.23 0.03	5,621 44.93 23.00 8.90 1.00	33 15.00 5.60 0.80 0.01	2,741 37.67 11.22 4.34 0.49	72 11.29 12.22 1.75 0.01	297 22.21 50.42 7.20 0.05	36 8.45 0.15 0.06 0.01	169 52.48 0.69 0.27 0.03	3,924 45.94 16.06 6.22 0.70	2,853 37.40 11.67 4.52 0.51	172 8.81 0.70 0.27 0.03	-	147 68.69 0.60 0.23 0.03	19 5.00 3.23 0.46 <0.01	-	307 65.88 1.26 0.49 0.05	436 40.30 1.78 0.69 0.08	9 5.26 1.53 0.22 <0.01	2,010 16.65 8.22 3.18 0.36

Notes: Please refer to the User's Guide for an explanation of data; data is arranged alphabetically by state, then county, then city within each county; table includes counties with populations greater than 49,999 unless noted and cities with populations greater than 9,999 whose Asian and/or NHPI population rates are greater than the national average; (1) Native Hawaiian and other Pacific Islander; (2) excludes Taiwanese; (3) includes Chamorro; (4) county does not meet population threshold but is shown in order to allow inclusion of city

Place	Total population 25 years and over who are 4-year college graduates	Asian population 25 years and over	Asians 25 years and over who are 4-year college graduates	NHPI[1] population 25 years and over	NHPIs[1] 25 years and over who are 4-year college graduates	Asian Indian	Bangladeshi	Cambodian	Chinese[2]	Fijian	Filipino	Guamanian[3]	Hawaiian, Native	Hmong	Indonesian	Japanese	Korean	Laotian	Malaysian	Pakistani	Samoan	Sri Lankan	Taiwanese	Thai	Tongan	Vietnamese
Benton County	21,684 47.39	1,741	1,180 67.78 67.78 5.44	-	-	-	-	-	337 64.56 28.56 19.36 1.55	-	-	-	-	-	-	146 64.04 12.37 8.39 0.67	269 78.65 22.80 15.45 1.24	-	-	-	-	-	-	-	-	-
Corvallis (city)	14,101 53.13	1,543	1,057 68.50 68.50 7.50	-	-	-	-	-	316 63.07 29.90 20.48 2.24	-	-	-	-	-	-	-	257 84.54 24.31 16.66 1.82	-	-	-	-	-	-	-	-	-
Clackamas County	63,331 28.37	5,404	2,504 46.34 46.34 3.95	340	34 10.00 10.00 0.05	358 81.55 14.30 6.62 0.57	-	-	675 53.70 26.96 12.49 1.07	-	361 53.64 14.42 6.68 0.57	-	-	-	-	338 40.19 13.50 6.25 0.53	339 33.24 13.54 6.27 0.54	-	-	-	-	-	-	-	-	193 35.28 7.71 3.57 0.30
Lake Oswego (city)	15,274 62.01	1,025	747 72.88 72.88 4.89	-	-	-	-	-	226 81.88 30.25 22.05 1.48	-	-	-	-	-	-	-	-	-	-	-	-	-	-	-	-	-
Coos County	6,712 15.03	199	50 25.13 25.13 0.74	-	-	-	-	-	-	-	-	-	-	-	-	-	-	-	-	-	-	-	-	-	-	-
Deschutes County	19,470 24.97	376	129 34.31 34.31 0.66	-	-	-	-	-	-	-	-	-	-	-	-	-	-	-	-	-	-	-	-	-	-	-
Douglas County	9,145 13.30	413	98 23.73 23.73 1.07	-	-	-	-	-	-	-	-	-	-	-	-	-	-	-	-	-	-	-	-	-	-	-
Jackson County	26,992 22.28	891	258 28.96 28.96 0.96	-	-	-	-	-	-	-	-	-	-	-	-	-	-	-	-	-	-	-	-	-	-	-
Josephine County	7,528 14.09	273	57 20.88 20.88 0.76	-	-	-	-	-	-	-	-	-	-	-	-	-	-	-	-	-	-	-	-	-	-	-
Klamath County	6,653 15.90	273	76 27.84 27.84 1.14	-	-	-	-	-	-	-	-	-	-	-	-	-	-	-	-	-	-	-	-	-	-	-

Notes: Please refer to the User's Guide for an explanation of data; data is arranged alphabetically by state, then county, then city within each county; table includes counties with populations greater than 49,999 unless noted and cities with populations greater than 9,999 whose Asian and/or NHPI population rates are greater than the national average; (1) Native Hawaiian and other Pacific Islander; (2) excludes Taiwanese; (3) includes Chamorro; (4) county does not meet population threshold but is shown in order to allow inclusion of city

Place	Total population 25 years and over who are 4-year college graduates	Asian population 25 years and over	Asians 25 years and over who are 4-year college graduates	NHPI[1] population 25 years and over	NHPIs[1] 25 years and over who are 4-year college graduates	Asian Indian	Bangladeshi	Cambodian	Chinese[2]	Fijian	Filipino	Guamanian[3]	Hawaiian, Native	Hmong	Indonesian	Japanese	Korean	Laotian	Malaysian	Pakistani	Samoan	Sri Lankan	Taiwanese	Thai	Tongan	Vietnamese
Lane County	53,723 25.51	3,322	1,642 49.43 49.43 3.06	299	59 19.73 19.73 0.11	184 61.13 11.21 5.54 0.34	-	-	379 59.50 23.08 11.41 0.71	-	144 39.45 8.77 4.33 0.27	-	-	-	-	423 53.27 25.76 12.73 0.79	337 54.18 20.52 10.14 0.63	-	-	-	-	-	-	-	-	-
Linn County	9,039 13.37	450	76 16.89 16.89 0.84	-	-	-	-	-	-	-	-	-	-	-	-	-	-	-	-	-	-	-	-	-	-	-
Marion County	35,169 19.79	3,060	822 26.86 26.86 2.34	402	37 9.20 9.20 0.11	123 54.42 14.96 4.02 0.35	-	-	199 35.86 24.21 6.50 0.57	-	104 20.63 12.65 3.40 0.30	-	-	-	-	144 46.15 17.52 4.71 0.41	110 29.65 13.38 3.59 0.31	-	-	-	-	-	-	-	-	79 14.66 9.61 2.58 0.22
Salem (city)	20,783 24.11	2,077	573 27.59 27.59 2.76	207	6 2.90 2.90 0.03	-	-	-	188 41.32 32.81 9.05 0.90	-	34 11.64 5.93 1.64 0.16	-	-	-	-	69 40.35 12.04 3.32 0.33	-	-	-	-	-	-	-	-	-	66 20.06 11.52 3.18 0.32
Multnomah County	136,828 30.66	24,041	6,686 27.81 27.81 4.89	1,253	202 16.12 16.12 0.15	563 51.28 8.42 2.34 0.41	-	41 7.59 0.61 0.17 0.03	1,508 31.31 22.55 6.27 1.10	-	908 39.36 13.58 3.78 0.66	-	89 30.17 44.06 7.10 0.07	13 4.04 0.19 0.05 0.01	-	1,409 49.08 21.07 5.86 1.03	682 38.77 10.20 2.84 0.50	92 6.81 1.38 0.38 0.07	-	-	-	-	-	116 33.82 1.73 0.48 0.08	9 7.09 4.46 0.72 0.01	828 11.17 12.38 3.44 0.61
Portland (city)	118,698 32.62	21,756	5,813 26.72 26.72 4.90	994	165 16.60 16.60 0.14	494 53.12 8.50 2.27 0.42	-	36 6.98 0.62 0.17 0.03	1,346 30.23 23.15 6.19 1.13	-	732 38.92 12.59 3.36 0.62	-	67 30.73 40.61 6.74 0.06	0 0.00 0.00 0.00 0.00	-	1,230 50.51 21.16 5.65 1.04	597 39.25 10.27 2.74 0.50	92 7.50 1.58 0.42 0.08	-	-	-	-	-	83 26.77 1.43 0.38 0.07	9 7.50 5.45 0.91 0.01	752 10.59 12.94 3.46 0.63
Polk County	9,974 25.34	431	119 27.61 27.61 1.19	-	-	-	-	-	-	-	-	-	-	-	-	-	-	-	-	-	-	-	-	-	-	-
Umatilla County	7,110 15.97	282	51 18.09 18.09 0.72	-	-	-	-	-	-	-	-	-	-	-	-	-	-	-	-	-	-	-	-	-	-	-
Washington County	98,549 34.52	19,371	10,006 51.65 51.65 10.15	883	152 17.21 17.21 0.15	3,248 89.50 32.46 16.77 3.30	-	100 14.06 1.00 0.52 0.10	2,185 63.76 21.84 11.28 2.22	-	825 39.80 8.25 4.26 0.84	-	69 21.43 45.39 7.81 0.07	-	-	1,083 56.52 10.82 5.59 1.10	997 36.52 9.96 5.15 1.01	65 18.36 0.65 0.34 0.07	-	-	-	-	-	-	-	793 25.51 7.93 4.09 0.80
Aloha (cdp)	5,632 21.95	1,923	499 25.95 25.95 8.86	-	-	-	-	-	-	-	87 35.08 17.43 4.52 1.54	-	-	-	-	-	-	-	-	-	-	-	-	-	-	140 20.44 28.06 7.28 2.49

Notes: Please refer to the User's Guide for an explanation of data; data is arranged alphabetically by state, then county, then city within each county; table includes counties with populations greater than 49,999 unless noted and cities with populations greater than 9,999 whose Asian and/or NHPI population rates are greater than the national average; (1) Native Hawaiian and other Pacific Islander; (2) excludes Taiwanese; (3) includes Chamorro; (4) county does not meet population threshold but is shown in order to allow inclusion of city

Place	Total population 25 years and over who are 4-year college graduates	Asian population 25 years and over	Asians 25 years and over who are 4-year college graduates	NHPI[1] population 25 years and over	NHPIs[1] 25 years and over who are 4-year college graduates	Asian Indian	Bangladeshi	Cambodian	Chinese[2]	Fijian	Filipino	Guamanian[3]	Hawaiian, Native	Hmong	Indonesian	Japanese	Korean	Laotian	Malaysian	Pakistani	Samoan	Sri Lankan	Taiwanese	Thai	Tongan	Vietnamese
	19,109	4,854	2,504	-	-	1,018	-	13	390	-	217	-	-	-	-	329	224	-	-	-	-	-	-	-	-	130
	39.07		51.59			87.76		5.46	52.85		44.93					71.37	27.69									22.18
Beaverton (city)						40.65		0.52	15.58		8.67					13.14	8.95									5.19
			51.59			20.97		0.27	8.03		4.47					6.78	4.61									2.68
			13.10			5.33		0.07	2.04		1.14					1.72	1.17									0.68
	4,043	696	421	-	-	-	-	-	-	-	-	-	-	-	-	-	-	-	-	-	-	-	-	-	-	-
	49.19		60.49																							
Cedar Mill (cdp)																										
			60.49																							
			10.41																							
	12,556	2,881	1,778	-	-	887	-	-	344	-	-	-	-	-	-	-	126	-	-	-	-	-	-	-	-	119
	29.52		61.71			95.07			76.61								37.72									26.56
Hillsboro (city)						49.89			19.35								7.09									6.69
			61.71			30.79			11.94								4.37									4.13
			14.16			7.06			2.74								1.00									0.95
	9,904	1,613	739	-	-	-	-	-	237	-	-	-	-	-	-	-	-	-	-	-	-	-	-	-	-	52
	36.49		45.82						62.70																	17.39
Tigard (city)									32.07																	7.04
			45.82						14.69																	3.22
			7.46						2.39																	0.53
	5,347	626	285	-	-	-	-	-	-	-	-	-	-	-	-	-	-	-	-	-	-	-	-	-	-	-
	37.51		45.53																							
Tualatin (city)																										
			45.53																							
			5.33																							
	10,857	542	132	-	-	-	-	-	-	-	-	-	-	-	-	-	-	-	-	-	-	-	-	-	-	-
	20.62		24.35																							
Yamhill County																										
			24.35																							
			1.22																							
	1,847,631	132,374	65,179	2,029	431	23,442	271	290	16,138	-	5,599	76	181	5	160	2,605	9,130	115	-	945	63	165	1,163	659	-	3,085
	22.35		49.24		21.24	67.61	64.22	6.98	53.02		55.12	19.59	29.53	1.72	44.69	51.76	46.45	9.20		54.85	13.46	67.62	79.39	55.42		17.75
PENNSYLVANIA						35.97	0.42	0.44	24.76		8.59	17.63	42.00	0.01	0.25	4.00	14.01	0.18		1.45	14.62	0.25	1.78	1.01		4.73
			49.24		21.24	17.71	0.20	0.22	12.19		4.23	3.75	8.92	<0.01	0.12	1.97	6.90	0.09		0.71	3.10	0.12	0.88	0.50		2.33
			3.53		0.02	1.27	0.01	0.02	0.87		0.30	<0.01	0.01	<0.01	0.01	0.14	0.49	0.01		0.05	<0.01	0.01	0.06	0.04		0.17
	10,025	375	208	-	-	-	-	-	-	-	-	-	-	-	-	-	-	-	-	-	-	-	-	-	-	-
	16.66		55.47																							
Adams County																										
			55.47																							
			2.07																							
	252,583	13,093	9,602	350	147	4,319	-	-	2,351	-	482	-	-	-	-	583	895	-	-	-	-	-	208	-	-	165
	28.34		73.34		42.00	86.55			71.31		64.61					66.40	69.87						78.20			21.68
Allegheny County						44.98			24.48		5.02					6.07	9.32						2.17			1.72
			73.34		42.00	32.99			17.96		3.68					4.45	6.84						1.59			1.26
			3.80		0.06	1.71			0.93		0.19					0.23	0.35						0.08			0.07
	7,681	779	591	-	-	401	-	-	-	-	-	-	-	-	-	-	-	-	-	-	-	-	-	-	-	-
	35.55		75.87			89.51																				
Muni. of Monroeville (borough)						67.85																				
			75.87			51.48																				
			7.69			5.22																				

Notes: Please refer to the User's Guide for an explanation of data; data is arranged alphabetically by state, then county, then city within each county; table includes counties with populations greater than 49,999 unless noted and cities with populations greater than 9,999 whose Asian and/or NHPI population rates are greater than the national average; (1) Native Hawaiian and other Pacific Islander; (2) excludes Taiwanese; (3) includes Chamorro; (4) county does not meet population threshold but is shown in order to allow inclusion of city

Place	Total population 25 years and over who are 4-year college graduates	Asian population 25 years and over	Asians 25 years and over who are 4-year college graduates	NHPI[1] population 25 years and over	NHPIs[1] 25 years and over who are 4-year college graduates	Asian Indian	Bangladeshi	Cambodian	Chinese[2]	Fijian	Filipino	Guamanian[3]	Hawaiian, Native	Hmong	Indonesian	Japanese	Korean	Laotian	Malaysian	Pakistani	Samoan	Sri Lankan	Taiwanese	Thai	Tongan	Vietnamese
Scott (township)	4,647 35.11	740	706 95.41 95.41 15.19	-	-	617 95.36 87.39 83.38 13.28	-	-	-	-	-	-	-	-	-	-	-	-	-	-	-	-	-	-	-	-
Scott Township (cdp)	4,647 35.11	740	706 95.41 95.41 15.19	-	-	617 95.36 87.39 83.38 13.28	-	-	-	-	-	-	-	-	-	-	-	-	-	-	-	-	-	-	-	-
Upper St. Clair (township)	8,889 65.35	508	453 89.17 89.17 5.10	-	-	281 86.46 62.03 55.31 3.16	-	-	-	-	-	-	-	-	-	-	-	-	-	-	-	-	-	-	-	-
Beaver County	20,051 15.80	296	148 50.00 50.00 0.74	-	-	-	-	-	-	-	-	-	-	-	-	-	-	-	-	-	-	-	-	-	-	-
Berks County	46,011 18.49	2,252	908 40.32 40.32 1.97	-	-	307 57.17 33.81 13.63 0.67	-	-	226 63.66 24.89 10.04 0.49	-	-	-	-	-	-	-	92 46.00 10.13 4.09 0.20	-	-	-	-	-	-	-	-	96 14.22 10.57 4.26 0.21
Blair County	12,268 13.88	336	191 56.85 56.85 1.56	-	-	-	-	-	-	-	-	-	-	-	-	-	-	-	-	-	-	-	-	-	-	-
Bradford County	6,292 14.83	115	78 67.83 67.83 1.24	-	-	-	-	-	-	-	-	-	-	-	-	-	-	-	-	-	-	-	-	-	-	-
Bucks County	125,588 31.20	8,946	5,120 57.23 57.23 4.08	-	-	2,446 65.54 47.77 27.34 1.95	-	-	991 70.99 19.36 11.08 0.79	-	601 57.62 11.74 6.72 0.48	-	-	-	-	-	551 40.91 10.76 6.16 0.44	-	-	-	-	-	-	-	-	70 19.66 1.37 0.78 0.06
Bensalem (township)	9,379 23.61	2,481	1,296 52.24 52.24 13.82	-	-	818 62.78 63.12 32.97 8.72	-	-	-	-	-	-	-	-	-	-	161 35.31 12.42 6.49 1.72	-	-	-	-	-	-	-	-	-
Lower Makefield (township)	13,705 61.18	865	692 80.00 80.00 5.05	-	-	315 80.98 45.52 36.42 2.30	-	-	-	-	-	-	-	-	-	-	-	-	-	-	-	-	-	-	-	-

Notes: Please refer to the User's Guide for an explanation of data; data is arranged alphabetically by state, then county, then city within each county; table includes counties with populations greater than 49,999 unless noted and cities with populations greater than 9,999 whose Asian and/or NHPI population rates are greater than the national average; (1) Native Hawaiian and other Pacific Islander; (2) excludes Taiwanese; (3) includes Chamorro; (4) county does not meet population threshold but is shown in order to allow inclusion of city

Place	Total population 25 years and over who are 4-year college graduates	Asian population 25 years and over	Asians 25 years and over who are 4-year college graduates	NHPI[1] population 25 years and over	NHPIs[1] 25 years and over who are 4-year college graduates	Asian Indian	Bangladeshi	Cambodian	Chinese[2]	Fijian	Filipino	Guamanian[3]	Hawaiian, Native	Hmong	Indonesian	Japanese	Korean	Laotian	Malaysian	Pakistani	Samoan	Sri Lankan	Taiwanese	Thai	Tongan	Vietnamese
Newtown (township)	6,651 54.70	540	366 67.78 67.78 5.50	-	-	-	-	-	-	-	-	-	-	-	-	-	-	-	-	-	-	-	-	-	-	-
Butler County	27,263 23.49	648	436 67.28 67.28 1.60	-	-	233 78.45 53.44 35.96 0.85	-	-	-	-	-	-	-	-	-	-	-	-	-	-	-	-	-	-	-	-
Cambria County	14,634 13.70	384	171 44.53 44.53 1.17	-	-	-	-	-	-	-	-	-	-	-	-	-	-	-	-	-	-	-	-	-	-	-
Centre County	27,131 36.28	2,814	2,385 84.75 84.75 8.79	-	-	540 88.38 22.64 19.19 1.99	-	-	945 90.78 39.62 33.58 3.48	-	-	-	-	-	-	-	426 79.63 17.86 15.14 1.57	-	-	-	-	-	-	-	-	-
Ferguson (township)	4,802 56.03	712	596 83.71 83.71 12.41	-	-	-	-	-	-	-	-	-	-	-	-	-	-	-	-	-	-	-	-	-	-	-
Patton (township)	3,824 59.60	298	231 77.52 77.52 6.04	-	-	-	-	-	-	-	-	-	-	-	-	-	-	-	-	-	-	-	-	-	-	-
State College (borough)	7,555 69.19	1,556	1,380 88.69 88.69 18.27	-	-	255 88.54 18.48 16.39 3.38	-	-	587 93.32 42.54 37.72 7.77	-	-	-	-	-	-	-	184 88.04 13.33 11.83 2.44	-	-	-	-	-	-	-	-	-
Chester County	121,352 42.46	5,656	3,982 70.40 70.40 3.28	-	-	1,657 88.14 41.61 29.30 1.37	-	-	1,198 78.25 30.09 21.18 0.99	-	243 63.12 6.10 4.30 0.20	-	-	-	-	136 48.57 3.42 2.40 0.11	315 52.94 7.91 5.57 0.26	-	-	-	-	-	-	-	-	180 30.05 4.52 3.18 0.15
Tredyffrin (township)	14,467 68.87	1,143	1,006 88.01 88.01 6.95	-	-	411 100.00 40.85 35.96 2.84	-	-	398 91.71 39.56 34.82 2.75	-	-	-	-	-	-	-	-	-	-	-	-	-	-	-	-	-
West Goshen (township)	6,572 47.60	562	440 78.29 78.29 6.70	-	-	-	-	-	-	-	-	-	-	-	-	-	-	-	-	-	-	-	-	-	-	-

Notes: Please refer to the User's Guide for an explanation of data; data is arranged alphabetically by state, then county, then city within each county; table includes counties with populations greater than 49,999 unless noted and cities with populations greater than 9,999 whose Asian and/or NHPI population rates are greater than the national average; (1) Native Hawaiian and other Pacific Islander; (2) excludes Taiwanese; (3) includes Chamorro; (4) county does not meet population threshold but is shown in order to allow inclusion of city

Place	Total population 25 years and over who are 4-year college graduates	Asian population 25 years and over	Asians 25 years and over who are 4-year college graduates	NHPI[1] population 25 years and over	NHPIs[1] 25 years and over who are 4-year college graduates	Asian Indian	Bangladeshi	Cambodian	Chinese[2]	Fijian	Filipino	Guamanian[3]	Hawaiian, Native	Hmong	Indonesian	Japanese	Korean	Laotian	Malaysian	Pakistani	Samoan	Sri Lankan	Taiwanese	Thai	Tongan	Vietnamese
West Whiteland (township)	5,691 49.66	416	251 60.34 60.34 4.41	-	-	-	-	-	-	-	-	-	-	-	-	-	-	-	-	-	-	-	-	-	-	-
Clearfield County	6,470 11.13	188	116 61.70 61.70 1.79	-	-	-	-	-	-	-	-	-	-	-	-	-	-	-	-	-	-	-	-	-	-	-
Columbia County	6,568 15.77	198	101 51.01 51.01 1.54	-	-	-	-	-	-	-	-	-	-	-	-	-	-	-	-	-	-	-	-	-	-	-
Crawford County	8,773 14.70	186	75 40.32 40.32 0.85	-	-	-	-	-	-	-	-	-	-	-	-	-	-	-	-	-	-	-	-	-	-	-
Cumberland County	40,264 27.92	2,089	976 46.72 46.72 2.42	-	-	495 75.46 50.72 23.70 1.23	-	-	154 45.83 15.78 7.37 0.38	-	-	-	-	-	-	-	137 31.14 14.04 6.56 0.34	-	-	-	-	-	-	-	-	76 23.03 7.79 3.64 0.19
Hampden (township)	7,062 41.72	547	276 50.46 50.46 3.91	-	-	-	-	-	-	-	-	-	-	-	-	-	-	-	-	-	-	-	-	-	-	-
Dauphin County	40,380 23.51	3,245	1,285 39.60 39.60 3.18	-	-	452 64.85 35.18 13.93 1.12	-	-	362 62.31 28.17 11.16 0.90	-	-	-	-	-	-	-	51 22.87 3.97 1.57 0.13	-	-	-	-	-	-	-	-	181 16.05 14.09 5.58 0.45
Derry (township)	6,895 45.87	583	413 70.84 70.84 5.99	-	-	-	-	-	-	-	-	-	-	-	-	-	-	-	-	-	-	-	-	-	-	-
Hershey (cdp)	3,879 41.85	368	230 62.50 62.50 5.93	-	-	-	-	-	-	-	-	-	-	-	-	-	-	-	-	-	-	-	-	-	-	-
Delaware County	109,670 30.03	11,411	5,834 51.13 51.13 5.32	-	-	1,806 55.15 30.96 15.83 1.65	-	-	1,464 62.11 25.09 12.83 1.33	-	543 68.22 9.31 4.76 0.50	-	-	-	-	257 59.08 4.41 2.25 0.23	853 40.39 14.62 7.48 0.78	-	-	207 54.76 3.55 1.81 0.19	-	-	-	-	-	322 26.86 5.52 2.82 0.29

Notes: Please refer to the User's Guide for an explanation of data; data is arranged alphabetically by state, then county, then city within each county; table includes counties with populations greater than 49,999 unless noted and cities with populations greater than 9,999 whose Asian and/or NHPI population rates are greater than the national average; (1) Native Hawaiian and other Pacific Islander; (2) excludes Taiwanese; (3) includes Chamorro; (4) county does not meet population threshold but is shown in order to allow inclusion of city

Place	Total population 25 years and over who are 4-year college graduates	Asian population 25 years and over	Asians 25 years and over who are 4-year college graduates	NHPI[1] population 25 years and over	NHPIs[1] 25 years and over who are 4-year college graduates	Asian Indian	Bangladeshi	Cambodian	Chinese[2]	Fijian	Filipino	Guamanian[3]	Hawaiian, Native	Hmong	Indonesian	Japanese	Korean	Laotian	Malaysian	Pakistani	Samoan	Sri Lankan	Taiwanese	Thai	Tongan	Vietnamese
Broomall (cdp)	2,143 26.68	495	151 30.51 30.51 7.05	-	-	-	-	-	-	-	-	-	-	-	-	-	72 24.74 47.68 14.55 3.36	-	-	-	-	-	-	-	-	-
Drexel Hill (cdp)	7,082 35.16	765	559 73.07 73.07 7.89	-	-	-	-	-	234 88.97 41.86 30.59 3.30	-	-	-	-	-	-	-	-	-	-	-	-	-	-	-	-	-
Marple (township)	5,775 33.81	836	269 32.18 32.18 4.66	-	-	-	-	-	-	-	-	-	-	-	-	-	106 24.82 39.41 12.68 1.84	-	-	-	-	-	-	-	-	-
Radnor (township)	11,545 66.32	914	716 78.34 78.34 6.20	-	-	-	-	-	170 69.11 23.74 18.60 1.47	-	-	-	-	-	-	-	-	-	-	-	-	-	-	-	-	-
Upper Darby (township)	14,380 26.51	4,525	2,002 44.24 44.24 13.92	-	-	621 49.96 31.02 13.72 4.32	-	-	512 48.81 25.57 11.31 3.56	-	-	-	-	-	-	-	308 46.81 15.38 6.81 2.14	-	-	-	-	-	-	-	-	189 25.34 9.44 4.18 1.31
Erie County	37,590 20.87	1,047	547 52.24 52.24 1.46	-	-	246 80.66 44.97 23.50 0.65	-	-	-	-	-	-	-	-	-	-	-	-	-	-	-	-	-	-	-	-
Franklin County	12,995 14.77	459	261 56.86 56.86 2.01	-	-	-	-	-	-	-	-	-	-	-	-	-	-	-	-	-	-	-	-	-	-	-
Indiana County	9,506 16.98	407	248 60.93 60.93 2.61	-	-	-	-	-	-	-	-	-	-	-	-	-	-	-	-	-	-	-	-	-	-	-
Lackawanna County	29,028 19.60	1,033	485 46.95 46.95 1.67	-	-	235 63.17 48.45 22.75 0.81	-	-	-	-	-	-	-	-	-	-	-	-	-	-	-	-	-	-	-	-
Lancaster County	62,039 20.51	3,687	921 24.98 24.98 1.48	-	-	281 65.35 30.51 7.62 0.45	-	-	131 16.69 14.22 3.55 0.21	-	-	-	-	5 2.96 0.54 0.14 0.01	-	-	59 27.70 6.41 1.60 0.10	-	-	-	-	-	-	-	-	218 16.81 23.67 5.91 0.35

Notes: Please refer to the User's Guide for an explanation of data; data is arranged alphabetically by state, then county, then city within each county; table includes counties with populations greater than 49,999 unless noted and cities with populations greater than 9,999 whose Asian and/or NHPI population rates are greater than the national average; (1) Native Hawaiian and other Pacific Islander; (2) excludes Taiwanese; (3) includes Chamorro; (4) county does not meet population threshold but is shown in order to allow inclusion of city

Place	Total population 25 years and over who are 4-year college graduates	Asian population 25 years and over	Asians 25 years and over who are 4-year college graduates	NHPI[1] population 25 years and over	NHPIs[1] 25 years and over who are 4-year college graduates	Asian Indian	Bangladeshi	Cambodian	Chinese[2]	Fijian	Filipino	Guamanian[3]	Hawaiian, Native	Hmong	Indonesian	Japanese	Korean	Laotian	Malaysian	Pakistani	Samoan	Sri Lankan	Taiwanese	Thai	Tongan	Vietnamese
Lawrence County	9,778 15.10	184	102 55.43 55.43 1.04	-	-	-	-	-	-	-	-	-	-	-	-	-	-	-	-	-	-	-	-	-	-	-
Lebanon County	12,622 15.39	686	241 35.13 35.13 1.91	-	-	-	-	-	-	-	-	-	-	-	-	-	-	-	-	-	-	-	-	-	-	-
Lehigh County	49,612 23.33	4,472	2,385 53.33 53.33 4.81	-	-	1,074 72.62 45.03 24.02 2.16	-	-	747 68.78 31.32 16.70 1.51	-	-	-	-	-	-	-	175 40.23 7.34 3.91 0.35	-	-	-	-	-	-	-	-	139 16.41 5.83 3.11 0.28
Fullerton (cdp)	2,247 21.79	458	353 77.07 77.07 15.71	-	-	-	-	-	-	-	-	-	-	-	-	-	-	-	-	-	-	-	-	-	-	-
Lower Macungie (township)	5,717 42.73	557	441 79.17 79.17 7.71	-	-	-	-	-	221 83.08 50.11 39.68 3.87	-	-	-	-	-	-	-	-	-	-	-	-	-	-	-	-	-
Upper Macungie (township)	3,599 37.66	414	318 76.81 76.81 8.84	-	-	-	-	-	-	-	-	-	-	-	-	-	-	-	-	-	-	-	-	-	-	-
Luzerne County	37,036 16.36	927	464 50.05 50.05 1.25	-	-	193 68.20 41.59 20.82 0.52	-	-	-	-	-	-	-	-	-	-	-	-	-	-	-	-	-	-	-	-
Lycoming County	12,123 15.06	310	129 41.61 41.61 1.06	-	-	-	-	-	-	-	-	-	-	-	-	-	-	-	-	-	-	-	-	-	-	-
Mercer County	14,093 17.29	396	181 45.71 45.71 1.28	-	-	-	-	-	-	-	-	-	-	-	-	-	-	-	-	-	-	-	-	-	-	-
Monroe County	18,422 20.52	851	402 47.24 47.24 2.18	-	-	115 52.75 28.61 13.51 0.62	-	-	-	-	-	-	-	-	-	-	-	-	-	-	-	-	-	-	-	-

Notes: Please refer to the User's Guide for an explanation of data; data is arranged alphabetically by state, then county, then city within each county; table includes counties with populations greater than 49,999 unless noted and cities with populations greater than 9,999 whose Asian and/or NHPI population rates are greater than the national average; (1) Native Hawaiian and other Pacific Islander; (2) excludes Taiwanese; (3) includes Chamorro; (4) county does not meet population threshold but is shown in order to allow inclusion of city

Place	Total population 25 years and over who are 4-year college graduates	Asian population 25 years and over	Asians 25 years and over who are 4-year college graduates	NHPI[1] population 25 years and over	NHPIs[1] 25 years and over who are 4-year college graduates	Asian Indian	Bangladeshi	Cambodian	Chinese[2]	Fijian	Filipino	Guamanian[3]	Hawaiian, Native	Hmong	Indonesian	Japanese	Korean	Laotian	Malaysian	Pakistani	Samoan	Sri Lankan	Taiwanese	Thai	Tongan	Vietnamese
Montgomery County	199,787 38.73	18,943	10,940 57.75 57.75 5.48	-	-	3,446 72.75 31.50 18.19 1.72	-	-	2,498 69.20 22.83 13.19 1.25	-	957 68.45 8.75 5.05 0.48	-	-	-	-	308 59.34 2.82 1.63 0.15	2,802 46.97 25.61 14.79 1.40	-	-	-	-	-	-	-	-	342 23.27 3.13 1.81 0.17
Cheltenham (township)	12,494 49.19	1,551	836 53.90 53.90 6.69	-	-	-	-	-	-	-	-	-	-	-	-	-	341 44.87 40.79 21.99 2.73	-	-	-	-	-	-	-	-	-
East Norriton (township)	3,201 32.26	424	229 54.01 54.01 7.15	-	-	-	-	-	-	-	-	-	-	-	-	-	-	-	-	-	-	-	-	-	-	-
Hatfield (township)	3,541 31.95	1,126	554 49.20 49.20 15.65	-	-	337 57.02 60.83 29.93 9.52	-	-	-	-	-	-	-	-	-	-	-	-	-	-	-	-	-	-	-	-
Horsham (township)	5,972 37.16	746	396 53.08 53.08 6.63	-	-	-	-	-	-	-	-	-	-	-	-	-	136 39.77 34.34 18.23 2.28	-	-	-	-	-	-	-	-	-
King of Prussia (cdp)	6,763 49.44	1,366	1,091 79.87 79.87 16.13	-	-	463 83.57 42.44 33.89 6.85	-	-	233 83.21 21.36 17.06 3.45	-	-	-	-	-	-	-	-	-	-	-	-	-	-	-	-	-
Lansdale (borough)	2,742 24.61	804	314 39.05 39.05 11.45	-	-	152 53.90 48.41 18.91 5.54	-	-	-	-	-	-	-	-	-	-	-	-	-	-	-	-	-	-	-	-
Lower Gwynedd (township)	4,045 54.71	266	222 83.46 83.46 5.49	-	-	-	-	-	-	-	-	-	-	-	-	-	-	-	-	-	-	-	-	-	-	-
Lower Providence (township)	5,226 34.81	672	539 80.21 80.21 10.31	-	-	-	-	-	278 89.68 51.58 41.37 5.32	-	-	-	-	-	-	-	-	-	-	-	-	-	-	-	-	-
Montgomery (township)	6,894 46.40	1,160	603 51.98 51.98 8.75	-	-	209 66.99 34.66 18.02 3.03	-	-	-	-	-	-	-	-	-	-	186 37.20 30.85 16.03 2.70	-	-	-	-	-	-	-	-	-

Notes: Please refer to the User's Guide for an explanation of data; data is arranged alphabetically by state, then county, then city within each county; table includes counties with populations greater than 49,999 unless noted and cities with populations greater than 9,999 whose Asian and/or NHPI population rates are greater than the national average; (1) Native Hawaiian and other Pacific Islander; (2) excludes Taiwanese; (3) includes Chamorro; (4) county does not meet population threshold but is shown in order to allow inclusion of city

Place	Total population 25 years and over who are 4-year college graduates	Asian population 25 years and over	Asians 25 years and over who are 4-year college graduates	NHPI[1] population 25 years and over	NHPIs[1] 25 years and over who are 4-year college graduates	Asian Indian	Bangladeshi	Cambodian	Chinese[2]	Fijian	Filipino	Guamanian[3]	Hawaiian, Native	Hmong	Indonesian	Japanese	Korean	Laotian	Malaysian	Pakistani	Samoan	Sri Lankan	Taiwanese	Thai	Tongan	Vietnamese
Montgomeryville (cdp)	3,303 42.28	504	231 45.83 45.83 6.99	-	-	-	-	-	-	-	-	-	-	-	-	-	-	-	-	-	-	-	-	-	-	-
Plymouth (township)	3,793 32.48	632	395 62.50 62.50 10.41	-	-	-	-	-	-	-	-	-	-	-	-	-	150 59.76 37.97 23.73 3.95	-	-	-	-	-	-	-	-	-
Towamencin (township)	5,203 43.05	670	280 41.79 41.79 5.38	-	-	-	-	-	-	-	-	-	-	-	-	-	-	-	-	-	-	-	-	-	-	-
Upper Dublin (township)	10,083 57.64	967	585 60.50 60.50 5.80	-	-	-	-	-	-	-	-	-	-	-	-	-	186 38.67 31.79 19.23 1.84	-	-	-	-	-	-	-	-	-
Upper Gwynedd (township)	4,649 46.49	754	442 58.62 58.62 9.51	-	-	-	-	-	116 62.37 26.24 15.38 2.50	-	-	-	-	-	-	-	-	-	-	-	-	-	-	-	-	-
Upper Merion (township)	9,858 49.78	1,534	1,227 79.99 79.99 12.45	-	-	541 84.93 44.09 35.27 5.49	-	-	257 82.37 20.95 16.75 2.61	-	-	-	-	-	-	-	-	-	-	-	-	-	-	-	-	-
Whitpain (township)	7,383 56.82	796	467 58.67 58.67 6.33	-	-	-	-	-	-	-	-	-	-	-	-	-	143 39.50 30.62 17.96 1.94	-	-	-	-	-	-	-	-	-
Northampton County	38,098 21.16	2,111	1,176 55.71 55.71 3.09	-	-	439 64.75 37.33 20.80 1.15	-	-	277 67.23 23.55 13.12 0.73	-	-	-	-	-	-	-	147 70.00 12.50 6.96 0.39	-	-	-	-	-	-	-	-	19 7.98 1.62 0.90 0.05
Northumberland County	7,426 11.07	255	91 35.69 35.69 1.23	-	-	-	-	-	-	-	-	-	-	-	-	-	-	-	-	-	-	-	-	-	-	-
Philadelphia County	172,641 17.87	38,394	12,559 32.71 32.71 7.27	383	65 16.97 16.97 0.04	3,470 49.43 27.63 9.04 2.01	-	168 5.67 1.34 0.44 0.10	3,508 31.82 27.93 9.14 2.03	-	1,175 45.65 9.36 3.06 0.68	-	-	-	-	480 59.04 3.82 1.25 0.28	1,823 44.58 14.52 4.75 1.06	73 10.90 0.58 0.19 0.04	-	133 35.56 1.06 0.35 0.08	-	-	-	-	-	956 14.25 7.61 2.49 0.55

Notes: Please refer to the User's Guide for an explanation of data; data is arranged alphabetically by state, then county, then city within each county; table includes counties with populations greater than 49,999 unless noted and cities with populations greater than 9,999 whose Asian and/or NHPI population rates are greater than the national average; (1) Native Hawaiian and other Pacific Islander; (2) excludes Taiwanese; (3) includes Chamorro; (4) county does not meet population threshold but is shown in order to allow inclusion of city

Place	Total population 25 years and over who are 4-year college graduates	Asian population 25 years and over	Asians 25 years and over who are 4-year college graduates	NHPI[1] population 25 years and over	NHPIs[1] 25 years and over who are 4-year college graduates	Asian Indian	Bangladeshi	Cambodian	Chinese[2]	Fijian	Filipino	Guamanian[3]	Hawaiian, Native	Hmong	Indonesian	Japanese	Korean	Laotian	Malaysian	Pakistani	Samoan	Sri Lankan	Taiwanese	Thai	Tongan	Vietnamese
Philadelphia (city)	172,641 17.87	38,394	12,559 32.71 32.71 7.27	383	65 16.97 16.97 0.04	3,470 49.43 27.63 9.04 2.01	-	168 5.67 1.34 0.44 0.10	3,508 31.82 27.93 9.14 2.03	-	1,175 45.65 9.36 3.06 0.68	-	-	-	-	480 59.04 3.82 1.25 0.28	1,823 44.58 14.52 4.75 1.06	73 10.90 0.58 0.19 0.04	-	133 35.56 1.06 0.35 0.08	-	-	-	-	-	956 14.25 7.61 2.49 0.55
Schuylkill County	11,589 10.73	375	154 41.07 41.07 1.33	-	-	-	-	-	-	-	-	-	-	-	-	-	-	-	-	-	-	-	-	-	-	-
Washington County	26,726 18.81	337	161 47.77 47.77 0.60	-	-	-	-	-	-	-	-	-	-	-	-	-	-	-	-	-	-	-	-	-	-	-
Westmoreland County	53,240 20.20	1,021	622 60.92 60.92 1.17	-	-	201 81.71 32.32 19.69 0.38	-	-	-	-	-	-	-	-	-	-	-	-	-	-	-	-	-	-	-	-
York County	47,604 18.38	1,890	701 37.09 37.09 1.47	-	-	187 52.97 26.68 9.89 0.39	-	-	146 33.72 20.83 7.72 0.31	-	-	-	-	-	-	-	133 44.93 18.97 7.04 0.28	-	-	-	-	-	-	-	-	80 23.53 11.41 4.23 0.17
RHODE ISLAND	177,817 25.60	12,863	4,676 36.35 36.35 2.63	213	20 9.39 9.39 0.01	952 66.02 20.36 7.40 0.54	-	235 9.94 5.03 1.83 0.13	1,253 49.68 26.80 9.74 0.70	-	621 39.76 13.28 4.83 0.35	-	-	38 13.06 0.81 0.30 0.02	-	279 48.52 5.97 2.17 0.16	656 70.01 14.03 5.10 0.37	159 9.47 3.40 1.24 0.09	-	-	-	-	-	-	-	156 26.00 3.34 1.21 0.09
Bristol County	11,728 34.27	207	157 75.85 75.85 1.34	-	-	-	-	-	-	-	-	-	-	-	-	-	-	-	-	-	-	-	-	-	-	-
Kent County	28,898 24.78	1,374	651 47.38 47.38 2.25	-	-	-	-	-	116 48.33 17.82 8.44 0.40	-	-	-	-	-	-	-	138 64.79 21.20 10.04 0.48	-	-	-	-	-	-	-	-	-
Newport County	22,641 38.32	643	320 49.77 49.77 1.41	-	-	-	-	-	-	-	148 45.40 46.25 23.02 0.65	-	-	-	-	-	-	-	-	-	-	-	-	-	-	-
Providence County	85,858 21.26	9,556	3,016 31.56 31.56 3.51	-	-	630 63.89 20.89 6.59 0.73	-	234 10.33 7.76 2.45 0.27	798 46.75 26.46 8.35 0.93	-	295 36.69 9.78 3.09 0.34	-	-	38 15.26 1.26 0.40 0.04	-	-	404 69.42 13.40 4.23 0.47	146 9.00 4.84 1.53 0.17	-	-	-	-	-	-	-	106 22.46 3.51 1.11 0.12

Notes: Please refer to the User's Guide for an explanation of data; data is arranged alphabetically by state, then county, then city within each county; table includes counties with populations greater than 49,999 unless noted and cities with populations greater than 9,999 whose Asian and/or NHPI population rates are greater than the national average; (1) Native Hawaiian and other Pacific Islander; (2) excludes Taiwanese; (3) includes Chamorro; (4) county does not meet population threshold but is shown in order to allow inclusion of city

Place	Total population 25 years and over who are 4-year college graduates	Asian population 25 years and over	Asians 25 years and over who are 4-year college graduates	NHPI[1] population 25 years and over	NHPIs[1] 25 years and over who are 4-year college graduates	Asian Indian	Bangladeshi	Cambodian	Chinese[2]	Fijian	Filipino	Guamanian[3]	Hawaiian, Native	Hmong	Indonesian	Japanese	Korean	Laotian	Malaysian	Pakistani	Samoan	Sri Lankan	Taiwanese	Thai	Tongan	Vietnamese
Providence (city)	23,450 24.39	4,899	1,421 29.01 29.01 6.06	-	-	254 58.80 17.87 5.18 1.08	-	165 10.09 11.61 3.37 0.70	302 48.32 21.25 6.16 1.29	-	104 28.73 7.32 2.12 0.44	-	-	38 22.09 2.67 0.78 0.16	-	-	249 88.61 17.52 5.08 1.06	67 8.43 4.71 1.37 0.29	-	-	-	-	-	-	-	-
Woonsocket (city)	2,850 10.14	906	135 14.90 14.90 4.74	-	-	-	-	-	-	-	-	-	-	-	-	-	-	27 5.27 20.00 2.98 0.95	-	-	-	-	-	-	-	-
Washington County	28,692 35.48	1,083	532 49.12 49.12 1.85	-	-	-	-	-	163 51.58 30.64 15.05 0.57	-	-	-	-	-	-	-	-	-	-	-	-	-	-	-	-	-
SOUTH CAROLINA	530,055 20.42	23,216	9,475 40.81 40.81 1.79	875	104 11.89 11.89 0.02	2,965 61.45 31.29 12.77 0.56	-	30 16.04 0.32 0.13 0.01	2,250 55.90 23.75 9.69 0.42	-	1,640 35.28 17.31 7.06 0.31	25 10.42 24.04 2.86 <0.01	43 11.94 41.35 4.91 0.01	13 4.00 0.14 0.06 <0.01	-	575 31.75 6.07 2.48 0.11	911 36.38 9.61 3.92 0.17	53 7.69 0.56 0.23 0.01	-	-	-	-	-	184 31.13 1.94 0.79 0.03	-	403 16.36 4.25 1.74 0.08
Aiken County	18,536 19.95	627	255 40.67 40.67 1.38	-	-	-	-	-	-	-	-	-	-	-	-	-	-	-	-	-	-	-	-	-	-	-
Anderson County	17,709 15.95	480	214 44.58 44.58 1.21	-	-	-	-	-	-	-	-	-	-	-	-	-	-	-	-	-	-	-	-	-	-	-
Beaufort County	26,083 33.23	628	203 32.32 32.32 0.78	-	-	-	-	-	-	-	-	-	-	-	-	-	-	-	-	-	-	-	-	-	-	-
Berkeley County	12,392 14.41	1,978	587 29.68 29.68 4.74	-	-	-	-	-	-	-	372 29.20 63.37 18.81 3.00	-	-	-	-	-	-	-	-	-	-	-	-	-	-	-
Charleston County	61,253 30.72	2,202	926 42.05 42.05 1.51	-	-	234 61.90 25.27 10.63 0.38	-	-	272 62.82 29.37 12.35 0.44	-	127 21.93 13.71 5.77 0.21	-	-	-	-	-	-	-	-	-	-	-	-	-	-	-
Dorchester County	13,133 21.41	857	402 46.91 46.91 3.06	-	-	-	-	-	-	-	198 48.18 49.25 23.10 1.51	-	-	-	-	-	-	-	-	-	-	-	-	-	-	-

Notes: Please refer to the User's Guide for an explanation of data; data is arranged alphabetically by state, then county, then city within each county; table includes counties with populations greater than 49,999 unless noted and cities with populations greater than 9,999 whose Asian and/or NHPI population rates are greater than the national average; (1) Native Hawaiian and other Pacific Islander; (2) excludes Taiwanese; (3) includes Chamorro; (4) county does not meet population threshold but is shown in order to allow inclusion of city

Place	Total population 25 years and over who are 4-year college graduates	Asian population 25 years and over	Asians 25 years and over who are 4-year college graduates	NHPI[1] population 25 years and over	NHPIs[1] 25 years and over who are 4-year college graduates	Asian Indian	Bangladeshi	Cambodian	Chinese[2]	Fijian	Filipino	Guamanian[3]	Hawaiian, Native	Hmong	Indonesian	Japanese	Korean	Laotian	Malaysian	Pakistani	Samoan	Sri Lankan	Taiwanese	Thai	Tongan	Vietnamese
Florence County	15,115 18.68	715	419 58.60 58.60 2.77	-	-	-	-	-	-	-	-	-	-	-	-	-	-	-	-	-	-	-	-	-	-	-
Greenville County	65,651 26.23	3,265	1,430 43.80 43.80 2.18	-	-	553 60.50 38.67 16.94 0.84	-	-	236 53.88 16.50 7.23 0.36	-	147 41.29 10.28 4.50 0.22	-	-	-	-	-	-	-	-	-	-	-	-	-	-	157 19.15 10.98 4.81 0.24
Greenwood County	8,020 18.91	252	109 43.25 43.25 1.36	-	-	-	-	-	-	-	-	-	-	-	-	-	-	-	-	-	-	-	-	-	-	-
Horry County	25,564 18.72	1,083	332 30.66 30.66 1.30	-	-	-	-	-	-	-	-	-	-	-	-	-	-	-	-	-	-	-	-	-	-	-
Lexington County	34,965 24.61	1,248	629 50.40 50.40 1.80	-	-	272 71.39 43.24 21.79 0.78	-	-	189 60.19 30.05 15.14 0.54	-	-	-	-	-	-	-	-	-	-	-	-	-	-	-	-	-
Oconee County	8,331 18.15	213	141 66.20 66.20 1.69	-	-	-	-	-	-	-	-	-	-	-	-	-	-	-	-	-	-	-	-	-	-	-
Pickens County	12,732 19.06	729	502 68.86 68.86 3.94	-	-	107 68.15 21.31 14.68 0.84	-	-	244 86.52 48.61 33.47 1.92	-	-	-	-	-	-	-	-	-	-	-	-	-	-	-	-	-
Clemson (city)	3,437 58.17	253	190 75.10 75.10 5.53	-	-	-	-	-	-	-	-	-	-	-	-	-	-	-	-	-	-	-	-	-	-	-
Richland County	64,552 32.49	3,444	1,748 50.75 50.75 2.71	-	-	534 67.85 30.55 15.51 0.83	-	-	486 66.85 27.80 14.11 0.75	-	174 58.00 9.95 5.05 0.27	-	-	-	-	-	332 37.01 18.99 9.64 0.51	-	-	-	-	-	-	-	-	65 23.30 3.72 1.89 0.10
Spartanburg County	30,486 18.17	2,352	624 26.53 26.53 2.05	-	-	283 55.82 45.35 12.03 0.93	-	-	-	-	-	-	-	6 2.03 0.96 0.26 0.02	-	-	-	42 12.43 6.73 1.79 0.14	-	-	-	-	-	-	-	-

Notes: Please refer to the User's Guide for an explanation of data; data is arranged alphabetically by state, then county, then city within each county; table includes counties with populations greater than 49,999 unless noted and cities with populations greater than 9,999 whose Asian and/or NHPI population rates are greater than the national average; (1) Native Hawaiian and other Pacific Islander; (2) excludes Taiwanese; (3) includes Chamorro; (4) county does not meet population threshold but is shown in order to allow inclusion of city

Place	Total population 25 years and over who are 4-year college graduates	Asian population 25 years and over	Asians 25 years and over who are 4-year college graduates	NHPI[1] population 25 years and over	NHPIs[1] 25 years and over who are 4-year college graduates	Asian Indian	Bangladeshi	Cambodian	Chinese[2]	Fijian	Filipino	Guamanian[3]	Hawaiian, Native	Hmong	Indonesian	Japanese	Korean	Laotian	Malaysian	Pakistani	Samoan	Sri Lankan	Taiwanese	Thai	Tongan	Vietnamese
Sumter County	10,147 15.82	654	138 21.10 21.10 1.36	-	-	-	-	-	-	-	-	-	-	-	-	-	-	-	-	-	-	-	-	-	-	-
York County	22,113 20.91	805	234 29.07 29.07 1.06	-	-	-	-	-	-	-	-	-	-	-	-	-	-	-	-	-	-	-	-	-	-	42 14.00 17.95 5.22 0.19
SOUTH DAKOTA	102,012 21.51	2,669	1,056 39.57 39.57 1.04	-	-	252 85.14 23.86 9.44 0.25	-	-	315 64.81 29.83 11.80 0.31	-	156 30.00 14.77 5.84 0.15	-	-	-	-	78 36.11 7.39 2.92 0.08	92 38.66 8.71 3.45 0.09	21 19.81 1.99 0.79 0.02	-	-	-	-	-	-	-	19 4.48 1.80 0.71 0.02
Minnehaha County	24,260 25.97	826	239 28.93 28.93 0.99	-	-	-	-	-	-	-	-	-	-	-	-	-	-	-	-	-	-	-	-	-	-	13 4.19 5.44 1.57 0.05
Pennington County	13,873 24.98	486	149 30.66 30.66 1.07	-	-	-	-	-	-	-	-	-	-	-	-	-	-	-	-	-	-	-	-	-	-	-
TENNESSEE	732,688 19.56	34,168	16,316 47.75 47.75 2.23	1,289	250 19.39 19.39 0.03	5,380 71.87 32.97 15.75 0.73	-	42 6.94 0.26 0.12 0.01	3,422 61.25 20.97 10.02 0.47	-	1,889 50.81 11.58 5.53 0.26	26 8.31 10.40 2.02 <0.01	92 24.27 36.80 7.14 0.01	-	-	1,321 50.61 8.10 3.87 0.18	1,679 36.18 10.29 4.91 0.23	323 13.56 1.98 0.95 0.04	-	240 65.75 1.47 0.70 0.03	71 21.39 28.40 5.51 0.01	-	268 78.36 1.64 0.78 0.04	381 55.78 2.34 1.12 0.05	-	650 15.78 3.98 1.90 0.09
Anderson County	10,283 20.77	354	242 68.36 68.36 2.35	-	-	-	-	-	-	-	-	-	-	-	-	-	-	-	-	-	-	-	-	-	-	-
Blount County	13,092 17.95	385	187 48.57 48.57 1.43	-	-	-	-	-	-	-	-	-	-	-	-	-	-	-	-	-	-	-	-	-	-	-
Bradley County	9,097 15.91	349	136 38.97 38.97 1.49	-	-	-	-	-	-	-	-	-	-	-	-	-	-	-	-	-	-	-	-	-	-	-
Davidson County	115,145 30.48	7,264	3,671 50.54 50.54 3.19	172	44 25.58 25.58 0.04	1,192 73.04 32.47 16.41 1.04	-	-	677 72.72 18.44 9.32 0.59	-	393 65.72 10.71 5.41 0.34	-	-	-	-	365 63.04 9.94 5.02 0.32	363 41.72 9.89 5.00 0.32	101 13.54 2.75 1.39 0.09	-	-	-	-	-	-	-	141 14.60 3.84 1.94 0.12

Notes: Please refer to the User's Guide for an explanation of data; data is arranged alphabetically by state, then county, then city within each county; table includes counties with populations greater than 49,999 unless noted and cities with populations greater than 9,999 whose Asian and/or NHPI population rates are greater than the national average; (1) Native Hawaiian and other Pacific Islander; (2) excludes Taiwanese; (3) includes Chamorro; (4) county does not meet population threshold but is shown in order to allow inclusion of city

Place	Total population 25 years and over who are 4-year college graduates	Asian population 25 years and over	Asians 25 years and over who are 4-year college graduates	NHPI[1] population 25 years and over	NHPIs[1] 25 years and over who are 4-year college graduates	Asian Indian	Bangladeshi	Cambodian	Chinese[2]	Fijian	Filipino	Guamanian[3]	Hawaiian, Native	Hmong	Indonesian	Japanese	Korean	Laotian	Malaysian	Pakistani	Samoan	Sri Lankan	Taiwanese	Thai	Tongan	Vietnamese
Hamilton County	49,488	2,440	1,193	-	-	507	-	-	-	-	142	-	-	-	-	-	162	-	-	-	-	-	-	-	-	58
	23.89		48.89			72.22					44.24						47.37									21.48
						42.50					11.90						13.58									4.86
			48.89			20.78					5.82						6.64									2.38
			2.41			1.02					0.29						0.33									0.12
Knox County	73,348	2,791	1,783	-	-	620	-	-	501	-	-	-	-	-	-	-	208	-	-	-	-	-	-	-	-	31
	29.05		63.88			79.08			75.79								64.60									12.40
						34.77			28.10								11.67									1.74
			63.88			22.21			17.95								7.45									1.11
			2.43			0.85			0.68								0.28									0.04
Madison County	12,489	300	162	-	-	-	-	-	-	-	-	-	-	-	-	-	-	-	-	-	-	-	-	-	-	-
	21.52		54.00																							
			54.00																							
			1.30																							
Montgomery County	15,382	1,707	300	-	-	-	-	-	-	-	-	-	-	-	-	-	78	-	-	-	-	-	-	-	-	-
	19.27		17.57														8.85									
																	26.00									
			17.57														4.57									
			1.95														0.51									
Putnam County	7,979	325	212	-	-	-	-	-	-	-	-	-	-	-	-	-	-	-	-	-	-	-	-	-	-	-
	20.25		65.23																							
			65.23																							
			2.66																							
Rutherford County	25,206	2,069	644	-	-	-	-	-	-	-	-	-	-	-	-	-	-	118	-	-	-	-	-	-	-	-
	22.93		31.13															12.07								
																		18.32								
			31.13															5.70								
			2.55															0.47								
Shelby County	141,001	9,556	4,794	378	38	1,716	-	20	1,223	-	461	-	-	-	-	185	395	-	-	-	-	-	-	-	-	300
	25.27		50.17		10.05	74.58		6.43	62.08		45.96					49.33	47.71									15.81
						35.79		0.42	25.51		9.62					3.86	8.24									6.26
			50.17		10.05	17.96		0.21	12.80		4.82					1.94	4.13									3.14
			3.40		0.03	1.22		0.01	0.87		0.33					0.13	0.28									0.21
Germantown (city)	14,863	896	600	-	-	220	-	-	226	-	-	-	-	-	-	-	-	-	-	-	-	-	-	-	-	-
	60.02		66.96			65.48			85.28																	
						36.67			37.67																	
			66.96			24.55			25.22																	
			4.04			1.48			1.52																	
Sullivan County	19,675	348	149	-	-	-	-	-	-	-	-	-	-	-	-	-	-	-	-	-	-	-	-	-	-	-
	18.12		42.82																							
			42.82																							
			0.76																							
Sumner County	15,947	676	259	-	-	-	-	-	-	-	-	-	-	-	-	-	-	-	-	-	-	-	-	-	-	-
	18.62		38.31																							
			38.31																							
			1.62																							

Notes: Please refer to the User's Guide for an explanation of data; data is arranged alphabetically by state, then county, then city within each county; table includes counties with populations greater than 49,999 unless noted and cities with populations greater than 9,999 whose Asian and/or NHPI population rates are greater than the national average; (1) Native Hawaiian and other Pacific Islander; (2) excludes Taiwanese; (3) includes Chamorro; (4) county does not meet population threshold but is shown in order to allow inclusion of city

Place	Total population 25 years and over who are 4-year college graduates	Asian population 25 years and over	Asians 25 years and over who are 4-year college graduates	NHPI[1] population 25 years and over	NHPIs[1] 25 years and over who are 4-year college graduates	Asian Indian	Bangladeshi	Cambodian	Chinese[2]	Fijian	Filipino	Guamanian[3]	Hawaiian, Native	Hmong	Indonesian	Japanese	Korean	Laotian	Malaysian	Pakistani	Samoan	Sri Lankan	Taiwanese	Thai	Tongan	Vietnamese
Washington County	16,686	430	313	-	-	-	-	-	-	-	-	-	-	-	-	-	-	-	-	-	-	-	-	-	-	-
	22.87		72.79																							
			72.79																							
			1.88																							
Weakley County[4]	3,361	279	164	-	-	-	-	-	-	-	-	-	-	-	-	-	-	-	-	-	-	-	-	-	-	-
	15.34		58.78																							
			58.78																							
			4.88																							
Martin (city)	1,460	252	160	-	-	-	-	-	-	-	-	-	-	-	-	-	-	-	-	-	-	-	-	-	-	-
	26.61		63.49																							
			63.49																							
			10.96																							
Williamson County	36,203	931	526	-	-	-	-	-	-	-	-	-	-	-	-	-	-	-	-	-	-	-	-	-	-	-
	44.36		56.50																							
			56.50																							
			1.45																							
Wilson County	11,501	197	81	-	-	-	-	-	-	-	-	-	-	-	-	-	-	-	-	-	-	-	-	-	-	-
	19.60		41.12																							
			41.12																							
			0.70																							
TEXAS	2,972,293	356,028	170,121	6,826	1,045	51,642	1,101	346	42,278	-	21,996	262	339	-	722	5,350	11,444	493	325	6,066	164	390	3,643	2,081	13	17,783
	23.24		47.78		15.31	64.96	65.61	8.61	63.58		56.12	13.32	15.49		65.58	44.01	38.71	8.71	67.43	56.75	17.54	60.19	71.18	39.80	5.26	21.17
						30.36	0.65	0.20	24.85		12.93	25.07	32.44		0.42	3.14	6.73	0.29	0.19	3.57	15.69	0.23	2.14	1.22	1.24	10.45
			47.78		15.31	14.51	0.31	0.10	11.87		6.18	3.84	4.97		0.20	1.50	3.21	0.14	0.09	1.70	2.40	0.11	1.02	0.58	0.19	4.99
			5.72		0.04	1.74	0.04	0.01	1.42		0.74	0.01	0.01		0.02	0.18	0.39	0.02	0.01	0.20	0.01	0.01	0.12	0.07	<0.01	0.60
Anderson County	4,273	257	75	-	-	-	-	-	-	-	-	-	-	-	-	-	-	-	-	-	-	-	-	-	-	-
	11.10		29.18																							
			29.18																							
			1.76																							
Angelina County	7,377	314	84	-	-	-	-	-	-	-	-	-	-	-	-	-	-	-	-	-	-	-	-	-	-	-
	14.67		26.75																							
			26.75																							
			1.14																							
Bell County	27,208	4,207	1,045	655	38	187	-	-	-	-	367	19	-	-	-	41	228	-	-	-	-	-	-	-	-	-
	19.80		24.84		5.80	45.72					37.00	5.23				12.54	12.93									
						17.89					35.12	50.00				3.92	21.82									
			24.84		5.80	4.44					8.72	2.90				0.97	5.42									
			3.84		0.14	0.69					1.35	0.07				0.15	0.84									
Killeen (city)	7,389	2,620	530	537	19	-	-	-	-	-	259	10	-	-	-	-	107	-	-	-	-	-	-	-	-	-
	15.75		20.23		3.54						37.76	3.29					9.04									
											48.87	52.63					20.19									
			20.23		3.54						9.89	1.86					4.08									
			7.17		0.26						3.51	0.14					1.45									

Notes: Please refer to the User's Guide for an explanation of data; data is arranged alphabetically by state, then county, then city within each county; table includes counties with populations greater than 49,999 unless noted and cities with populations greater than 9,999 whose Asian and/or NHPI population rates are greater than the national average; (1) Native Hawaiian and other Pacific Islander; (2) excludes Taiwanese; (3) includes Chamorro; (4) county does not meet population threshold but is shown in order to allow inclusion of city

Place	Total population 25 years and over who are 4-year college graduates	Asian population 25 years and over	Asians 25 years and over who are 4-year college graduates	NHPI[1] population 25 years and over	NHPIs[1] 25 years and over who are 4-year college graduates	Asian Indian	Bangladeshi	Cambodian	Chinese[2]	Fijian	Filipino	Guamanian[3]	Hawaiian, Native	Hmong	Indonesian	Japanese	Korean	Laotian	Malaysian	Pakistani	Samoan	Sri Lankan	Taiwanese	Thai	Tongan	Vietnamese
Bexar County	192,454 22.67	15,401	6,025 39.12 39.12 3.13	662	71 10.73 10.73 0.04	1,336 57.27 22.17 8.67 0.69	-	-	1,333 53.97 22.12 8.66 0.69	-	1,554 42.72 25.79 10.09 0.81	-	38 12.54 53.52 5.74 0.02	-	-	405 30.41 6.72 2.63 0.21	388 20.77 6.44 2.52 0.20	29 12.72 0.48 0.19 0.02	-	-	-	-	-	233 33.97 3.87 1.51 0.12	-	338 17.02 5.61 2.19 0.18
Bowie County	9,480 16.13	308	154 50.00 50.00 1.62	-	-	-	-	-	-	-	-	-	-	-	-	-	-	-	-	-	-	-	-	-	-	-
Brazoria County	29,858 19.61	2,971	1,533 51.60 51.60 5.13	-	-	415 67.70 27.07 13.97 1.39	-	0 0.00 0.00 0.00 0.00	301 76.01 19.63 10.13 1.01	-	344 72.12 22.44 11.58 1.15	-	-	-	-	-	-	-	-	-	-	-	-	-	-	317 39.67 20.68 10.67 1.06
Brazos County	26,152 36.99	3,350	2,723 81.28 81.28 10.41	-	-	681 83.46 25.01 20.33 2.60	-	-	870 87.00 31.95 25.97 3.33	-	-	-	-	-	-	-	533 93.18 19.57 15.91 2.04	-	-	-	-	-	-	-	-	68 33.01 2.50 2.03 0.26
College Station (city)	13,539 58.10	2,731	2,253 82.50 82.50 16.64	-	-	526 85.11 23.35 19.26 3.89	-	-	720 84.71 31.96 26.36 5.32	-	-	-	-	-	-	-	427 96.61 18.95 15.64 3.15	-	-	-	-	-	-	-	-	-
Calhoun County[4]	1,570 12.07	402	271 67.41 67.41 17.26	-	-	-	-	-	-	-	-	-	-	-	-	-	-	-	-	-	-	-	-	-	-	12 13.04 4.43 2.99 0.76
Port Lavaca (city)	920 12.72	291	233 80.07 80.07 25.33	-	-	-	-	-	-	-	-	-	-	-	-	-	-	-	-	-	-	-	-	-	-	-
Cameron County	24,985 13.36	1,008	589 58.43 58.43 2.36	-	-	-	-	-	-	-	298 74.31 50.59 29.56 1.19	-	-	-	-	-	-	-	-	-	-	-	-	-	-	-
Collin County	149,417 47.33	22,117	15,979 72.25 72.25 10.69	-	-	4,792 83.27 29.99 21.67 3.21	-	-	6,294 74.96 39.39 28.46 4.21	-	713 69.36 4.46 3.22 0.48	-	-	-	-	429 60.59 2.68 1.94 0.29	935 55.52 5.85 4.23 0.63	-	-	373 65.90 2.33 1.69 0.25	-	-	467 85.69 2.92 2.11 0.31	190 55.39 1.19 0.86 0.13	-	1,178 52.45 7.37 5.33 0.79
Allen (city)	12,428 47.49	1,015	607 59.80 59.80 4.88	-	-	139 57.92 22.90 13.69 1.12	-	-	-	-	-	-	-	-	-	-	-	-	-	-	-	-	-	-	-	140 60.61 23.06 13.79 1.13

Notes: Please refer to the User's Guide for an explanation of data; data is arranged alphabetically by state, then county, then city within each county; table includes counties with populations greater than 49,999 unless noted and cities with populations greater than 9,999 whose Asian and/or NHPI population rates are greater than the national average; (1) Native Hawaiian and other Pacific Islander; (2) excludes Taiwanese; (3) includes Chamorro; (4) county does not meet population threshold but is shown in order to allow inclusion of city

Place	Total population 25 years and over who are 4-year college graduates	Asian population 25 years and over	Asians 25 years and over who are 4-year college graduates	NHPI[1] population 25 years and over	NHPIs[1] 25 years and over who are 4-year college graduates	Asian Indian	Bangladeshi	Cambodian	Chinese[2]	Fijian	Filipino	Guamanian[3]	Hawaiian, Native	Hmong	Indonesian	Japanese	Korean	Laotian	Malaysian	Pakistani	Samoan	Sri Lankan	Taiwanese	Thai	Tongan	Vietnamese
Plano (city)	76,706 53.25	14,539	10,562 72.65 72.65 13.77	-	-	3,164 84.58 29.96 21.76 4.12	-	-	4,563 75.50 43.20 31.38 5.95	-	379 68.66 3.59 2.61 0.49	-	-	-	-	239 61.13 2.26 1.64 0.31	752 59.45 7.12 5.17 0.98	-	-	211 61.70 2.00 1.45 0.28	-	-	314 82.85 2.97 2.16 0.41	-	-	513 44.61 4.86 3.53 0.67
Comal County	13,752 26.17	280	140 50.00 50.00 1.02	-	-	-	-	-	-	-	-	-	-	-	-	-	-	-	-	-	-	-	-	-	-	-
Coryell County	5,172 12.38	865	142 16.42 16.42 2.75	192	46 23.96 23.96 0.89	-	-	-	-	-	-	-	-	-	-	-	25 7.29 17.61 2.89 0.48	-	-	-	-	-	-	-	-	-
Dallas County	368,149 26.95	57,080	25,966 45.49 45.49 7.05	551	109 19.78 19.78 0.03	9,327 60.80 35.92 16.34 2.53	275 71.61 1.06 0.48 0.07	64 5.46 0.25 0.11 0.02	4,886 60.95 18.82 8.56 1.33	-	2,494 57.92 9.60 4.37 0.68	-	-	-	-	944 54.88 3.64 1.65 0.26	2,277 34.56 8.77 3.99 0.62	101 7.90 0.39 0.18 0.03	-	1,232 58.25 4.74 2.16 0.33	-	-	360 66.06 1.39 0.63 0.10	534 61.81 2.06 0.94 0.15	-	2,485 19.61 9.57 4.35 0.67
Addison (town)	4,467 44.63	830	493 59.40 59.40 11.04	-	-	327 69.43 66.33 39.40 7.32	-	-	-	-	-	-	-	-	-	-	-	-	-	-	-	-	-	-	-	-
Coppell (city)	13,748 62.59	2,132	1,345 63.09 63.09 9.78	-	-	534 70.08 39.70 25.05 3.88	-	-	342 74.67 25.43 16.04 2.49	-	-	-	-	-	-	-	173 41.39 12.86 8.11 1.26	-	-	-	-	-	-	-	-	-
Farmers Branch (city)	4,928 27.15	679	269 39.62 39.62 5.46	-	-	-	-	-	-	-	-	-	-	-	-	-	-	-	-	-	-	-	-	-	-	-
Garland (city)	28,589 21.78	9,660	2,907 30.09 30.09 10.17	-	-	804 43.62 27.66 8.32 2.81	-	-	269 27.42 9.25 2.78 0.94	-	423 51.03 14.55 4.38 1.48	-	-	-	-	-	223 29.42 7.67 2.31 0.78	-	-	205 46.17 7.05 2.12 0.72	-	-	-	-	-	697 17.68 23.98 7.22 2.44
Grand Prairie (city)	14,608 19.34	3,213	958 29.82 29.82 6.56	-	-	208 47.38 21.71 6.47 1.42	-	-	-	-	232 55.37 24.22 7.22 1.59	-	-	-	-	-	-	13 7.60 1.36 0.40 0.09	-	-	-	-	-	-	-	264 17.84 27.56 8.22 1.81
Irving (city)	36,273 29.98	10,780	6,263 58.10 58.10 17.27	-	-	3,128 75.39 49.94 29.02 8.62	-	-	816 72.40 13.03 7.57 2.25	-	350 59.02 5.59 3.25 0.96	-	-	-	-	340 68.41 5.43 3.15 0.94	490 30.38 7.82 4.55 1.35	27 9.64 0.43 0.25 0.07	-	187 65.61 2.99 1.73 0.52	-	-	-	-	-	336 29.79 5.36 3.12 0.93

Notes: Please refer to the User's Guide for an explanation of data; data is arranged alphabetically by state, then county, then city within each county; table includes counties with populations greater than 49,999 unless noted and cities with populations greater than 9,999 whose Asian and/or NHPI population rates are greater than the national average; (1) Native Hawaiian and other Pacific Islander; (2) excludes Taiwanese; (3) includes Chamorro; (4) county does not meet population threshold but is shown in order to allow inclusion of city

Place	Total population 25 years and over who are 4-year college graduates	Asian population 25 years and over	Asians 25 years and over who are 4-year college graduates	NHPI[1] population 25 years and over	NHPIs[1] 25 years and over who are 4-year college graduates	Asian Indian	Bangladeshi	Cambodian	Chinese[2]	Fijian	Filipino	Guamanian[3]	Hawaiian, Native	Hmong	Indonesian	Japanese	Korean	Laotian	Malaysian	Pakistani	Samoan	Sri Lankan	Taiwanese	Thai	Tongan	Vietnamese
Mesquite (city)	13,957 18.49	2,733	1,185 43.36 43.36 8.49	-	-	594 42.89 50.13 21.73 4.26	-	-	-	-	350 57.38 29.54 12.81 2.51	-	-	-	-	-	-	-	-	-	-	-	-	-	-	-
Richardson (city)	29,060 47.73	6,698	3,776 56.38 56.38 12.99	-	-	1,044 72.96 27.65 15.59 3.59	-	-	1,287 60.17 34.08 19.21 4.43	-	166 64.59 4.40 2.48 0.57	-	-	-	-	-	281 37.07 7.44 4.20 0.97	-	-	152 58.46 4.03 2.27 0.52	-	-	-	-	-	423 39.02 11.20 6.32 1.46
Rowlett (city)	8,840 32.55	988	495 50.10 50.10 5.60	-	-	175 55.56 35.35 17.71 1.98	-	-	-	-	-	-	-	-	-	-	-	-	-	-	-	-	-	-	-	-
Denton County	97,185 36.64	10,564	4,986 47.20 47.20 5.13	-	-	2,072 57.78 41.56 19.61 2.13	-	48 11.21 0.96 0.45 0.05	866 62.08 17.37 8.20 0.89	-	311 53.62 6.24 2.94 0.32	-	-	-	-	146 48.50 2.93 1.38 0.15	534 38.36 10.71 5.05 0.55	-	-	222 53.62 4.45 2.10 0.23	-	-	-	-	-	367 23.17 7.36 3.47 0.38
Carrollton (city)	25,922 36.98	7,046	2,440 34.63 34.63 9.41	-	-	1,264 47.04 51.80 17.94 4.88	-	13 3.17 0.53 0.18 0.05	219 46.60 8.98 3.11 0.84	-	-	-	-	-	-	-	276 39.77 11.31 3.92 1.06	-	-	231 40.24 9.47 3.28 0.89	-	-	-	-	-	253 16.07 10.37 3.59 0.98
Lewisville (city)	15,540 32.43	2,016	974 48.31 48.31 6.27	-	-	485 63.65 49.79 24.06 3.12	-	-	-	-	-	-	-	-	-	-	-	-	-	-	-	-	-	-	-	56 19.51 5.75 2.78 0.36
Ector County	8,611 12.00	537	303 56.42 56.42 3.52	-	-	-	-	-	-	-	-	-	-	-	-	-	-	-	-	-	-	-	-	-	-	-
El Paso County	65,026 16.61	4,760	2,034 42.73 42.73 3.13	300	33 11.00 11.00 0.05	494 67.12 24.29 10.38 0.76	-	-	328 61.08 16.13 6.89 0.50	-	620 54.53 30.48 13.03 0.95	-	-	-	-	182 27.08 8.95 3.82 0.28	267 23.48 13.13 5.61 0.41	-	-	-	-	-	-	-	-	-
Ellis County	11,546 17.11	269	173 64.31 64.31 1.50	-	-	-	-	-	-	-	-	-	-	-	-	-	-	-	-	-	-	-	-	-	-	-
Fort Bend County	79,181 36.92	24,102	13,615 56.49 56.49 17.19	-	-	4,761 62.07 34.97 19.75 6.01	-	-	4,012 60.94 29.47 16.65 5.07	-	1,810 68.85 13.29 7.51 2.29	-	-	-	-	-	251 35.15 1.84 1.04 0.32	-	-	699 49.93 5.13 2.90 0.88	-	-	414 57.02 3.04 1.72 0.52	-	-	1,076 32.23 7.90 4.46 1.36

Notes: Please refer to the User's Guide for an explanation of data; data is arranged alphabetically by state, then county, then city within each county; table includes counties with populations greater than 49,999 unless noted and cities with populations greater than 9,999 whose Asian and/or NHPI population rates are greater than the national average; (1) Native Hawaiian and other Pacific Islander; (2) excludes Taiwanese; (3) includes Chamorro; (4) county does not meet population threshold but is shown in order to allow inclusion of city

Place	Total population 25 years and over who are 4-year college graduates	Asian population 25 years and over	Asians 25 years and over who are 4-year college graduates	NHPI[1] population 25 years and over	NHPIs[1] 25 years and over who are 4-year college graduates	Asian Indian	Bangladeshi	Cambodian	Chinese[2]	Fijian	Filipino	Guamanian[3]	Hawaiian, Native	Hmong	Indonesian	Japanese	Korean	Laotian	Malaysian	Pakistani	Samoan	Sri Lankan	Taiwanese	Thai	Tongan	Vietnamese
Cinco Ranch (cdp)	4,301 65.92	402	294 73.13 73.13 6.84	-	-	-	-	-	-	-	-	-	-	-	-	-	-	-	-	-	-	-	-	-	-	-
Mission Bend (cdp)	5,735 31.72	3,162	1,461 46.20 46.20 25.48	-	-	582 68.39 39.84 18.41 10.15	-	-	144 32.00 9.86 4.55 2.51	-	417 73.54 28.54 13.19 7.27	-	-	-	-	-	-	-	-	92 36.22 6.30 2.91 1.60	-	-	-	-	-	163 20.48 11.16 5.15 2.84
Missouri City (city)	14,671 44.52	3,682	2,304 62.57 62.57 15.70	-	-	770 61.90 33.42 20.91 5.25	-	-	640 70.64 27.78 17.38 4.36	-	467 70.23 20.27 12.68 3.18	-	-	-	-	-	-	-	-	-	-	-	-	-	-	170 42.08 7.38 4.62 1.16
New Territory (cdp)	4,525 56.13	1,960	1,235 63.01 63.01 27.29	-	-	531 58.16 43.00 27.09 11.73	-	-	269 62.56 21.78 13.72 5.94	-	-	-	-	-	-	-	-	-	-	-	-	-	-	-	-	-
Stafford (city)	3,473 35.92	2,008	1,000 49.80 49.80 28.79	-	-	351 49.65 35.10 17.48 10.11	-	-	172 45.74 17.20 8.57 4.95	-	182 77.45 18.20 9.06 5.24	-	-	-	-	-	-	-	-	-	-	-	-	-	-	169 38.58 16.90 8.42 4.87
Sugar Land (city)	21,335 53.67	8,967	5,442 60.69 60.69 25.51	-	-	1,739 66.81 31.96 19.39 8.15	-	-	2,228 63.68 40.94 24.85 10.44	-	415 71.80 7.63 4.63 1.95	-	-	-	-	-	73 25.00 1.34 0.81 0.34	-	-	203 61.70 3.73 2.26 0.95	-	-	308 54.90 5.66 3.43 1.44	-	-	248 32.50 4.56 2.77 1.16
Galveston County	36,682 22.71	3,482	1,675 48.10 48.10 4.57	-	-	449 67.42 26.81 12.89 1.22	-	-	393 63.70 23.46 11.29 1.07	-	317 55.61 18.93 9.10 0.86	-	-	-	-	-	-	-	-	-	-	-	-	-	-	223 21.86 13.31 6.40 0.61
Grayson County	12,480 17.24	402	194 48.26 48.26 1.55	-	-	-	-	-	-	-	-	-	-	-	-	-	-	-	-	-	-	-	-	-	-	-
Gregg County	13,659 19.51	372	139 37.37 37.37 1.02	-	-	-	-	-	-	-	-	-	-	-	-	-	-	-	-	-	-	-	-	-	-	-
Guadalupe County	10,637 19.10	593	102 17.20 17.20 0.96	-	-	-	-	-	-	-	-	-	-	-	-	-	-	-	-	-	-	-	-	-	-	-

Notes: Please refer to the User's Guide for an explanation of data; data is arranged alphabetically by state, then county, then city within each county; table includes counties with populations greater than 49,999 unless noted and cities with populations greater than 9,999 whose Asian and/or NHPI population rates are greater than the national average; (1) Native Hawaiian and other Pacific Islander; (2) excludes Taiwanese; (3) includes Chamorro; (4) county does not meet population threshold but is shown in order to allow inclusion of city

Place	Total population 25 years and over who are 4-year college graduates	Asian population 25 years and over	Asians 25 years and over who are 4-year college graduates	NHPI[1] population 25 years and over	NHPIs[1] 25 years and over who are 4-year college graduates	Asian Indian	Bangladeshi	Cambodian	Chinese[2]	Fijian	Filipino	Guamanian[3]	Hawaiian, Native	Hmong	Indonesian	Japanese	Korean	Laotian	Malaysian	Pakistani	Samoan	Sri Lankan	Taiwanese	Thai	Tongan	Vietnamese
	556,887	113,074	51,744	868	180	14,581	197	101	13,145	-	6,441	82	-	-	263	1,430	2,494	53	-	2,458	-	-	1,141	423	-	7,408
	26.94		45.76		20.74	64.10	45.39	8.42	58.36		59.98	21.58			56.20	54.11	43.79	7.46		58.16			69.96	45.98		20.70
Harris County						28.18	0.38	0.20	25.40		12.45	45.56			0.51	2.76	4.82	0.10		4.75			2.21	0.82		14.32
			45.76		20.74	12.90	0.17	0.09	11.63		5.70	9.45			0.23	1.26	2.21	0.05		2.17			1.01	0.37		6.55
			9.29		0.03	2.62	0.04	0.02	2.36		1.16	0.01			0.05	0.26	0.45	0.01		0.44			0.20	0.08		1.33
	7,046	669	494	-	-	-	-	-	239	-	-	-	-	-	-	-	-	-	-	-	-	-	-	-	-	-
	66.60		73.84						83.57																	
Bellaire (city)									48.38																	
			73.84						35.72																	
			7.01						3.39																	
	324,039	69,174	32,817	539	71	8,850	-	32	9,532	-	3,234	47	-	-	234	1,038	1,654	-	-	1,770	-	-	795	350	-	4,233
	26.98		47.44		13.17	66.57		7.46	59.45		59.62	16.79			69.03	62.01	44.62			62.74			71.69	54.43		20.06
Houston (city)						26.97		0.10	29.05		9.85	66.20			0.71	3.16	5.04			5.39			2.42	1.07		12.90
			47.44		13.17	12.79		0.05	13.78		4.68	8.72			0.34	1.50	2.39			2.56			1.15	0.51		6.12
			10.13		0.02	2.73		0.01	2.94		1.00	0.01			0.07	0.32	0.51			0.55			0.25	0.11		1.31
	7,642	540	440	-	-	-	-	-	-	-	-	-	-	-	-	-	-	-	-	-	-	-	-	-	-	-
	79.40		81.48																							
West University Place (city)																										
			81.48																							
			5.76																							
	16,803	426	220	-	-	-	-	-	-	-	-	-	-	-	-	-	-	-	-	-	-	-	-	-	-	-
	31.33		51.64																							
Hays County																										
			51.64																							
			1.31																							
	39,333	2,015	1,357	-	-	252	-	-	-	-	805	-	-	-	-	-	-	-	-	-	-	-	-	-	-	-
	12.91		67.34			63.00					83.94															
Hidalgo County						18.57					59.32															
			67.34			12.51					39.95															
			3.45			0.64					2.05															
	8,138	302	171	-	-	-	-	-	-	-	-	-	-	-	-	-	-	-	-	-	-	-	-	-	-	-
	16.76		56.62																							
Hunt County																										
			56.62																							
			2.10																							
	26,263	3,685	1,204	-	-	339	-	-	192	-	461	-	-	-	-	-	-	-	-	-	-	-	-	-	-	141
	16.29		32.67			60.00			61.74		86.82															7.09
Jefferson County						28.16			15.95		38.29															11.71
			32.67			9.20			5.21		12.51															3.83
			4.58			1.29			0.73		1.76															0.54
	3,315	1,694	237	-	-	-	-	-	-	-	-	-	-	-	-	-	-	-	-	-	-	-	-	-	-	81
	9.32		13.99																							6.02
Port Arthur (city)																										34.18
			13.99																							4.78
			7.15																							2.44
	10,941	382	121	-	-	-	-	-	-	-	-	-	-	-	-	-	-	-	-	-	-	-	-	-	-	-
	13.78		31.68																							
Johnson County																										
			31.68																							
			1.11																							

Notes: Please refer to the User's Guide for an explanation of data; data is arranged alphabetically by state, then county, then city within each county; table includes counties with populations greater than 49,999 unless noted and cities with populations greater than 9,999 whose Asian and/or NHPI population rates are greater than the national average; (1) Native Hawaiian and other Pacific Islander; (2) excludes Taiwanese; (3) includes Chamorro; (4) county does not meet population threshold but is shown in order to allow inclusion of city

Place	Total population 25 years and over who are 4-year college graduates	Asian population 25 years and over	Asians 25 years and over who are 4-year college graduates	NHPI[1] population 25 years and over	NHPIs[1] 25 years and over who are 4-year college graduates	Asian Indian	Bangladeshi	Cambodian	Chinese[2]	Fijian	Filipino	Guamanian[3]	Hawaiian, Native	Hmong	Indonesian	Japanese	Korean	Laotian	Malaysian	Pakistani	Samoan	Sri Lankan	Taiwanese	Thai	Tongan	Vietnamese
Kaufman County	5,521 12.31	334	124 37.13 37.13 2.25	-	-	-	-	-	-	-	-	-	-	-	-	-	-	-	-	-	-	-	-	-	-	-
Lubbock County	34,451 24.37	1,817	1,179 64.89 64.89 3.42	-	-	261 72.91 22.14 14.36 0.76	-	-	396 93.18 33.59 21.79 1.15	-	-	-	-	-	-	-	-	-	-	-	-	-	-	-	-	49 23.56 4.16 2.70 0.14
McLennan County	24,059 19.10	1,129	560 49.60 49.60 2.33	-	-	81 45.51 14.46 7.17 0.34	-	-	-	-	-	-	-	-	-	-	-	-	-	-	-	-	-	-	-	-
Midland County	17,626 24.82	639	323 50.55 50.55 1.83	-	-	132 57.39 40.87 20.66 0.75	-	-	-	-	-	-	-	-	-	-	-	-	-	-	-	-	-	-	-	-
Montgomery County	46,482 25.30	2,062	1,078 52.28 52.28 2.32	-	-	493 72.71 45.73 23.91 1.06	-	-	263 60.46 24.40 12.75 0.57	-	126 38.53 11.69 6.11 0.27	-	-	-	-	-	-	-	-	-	-	-	-	-	-	-
Nacogdoches County	7,558 22.78	266	174 65.41 65.41 2.30	-	-	-	-	-	-	-	-	-	-	-	-	-	-	-	-	-	-	-	-	-	-	-
Nueces County	36,031 18.78	2,436	1,067 43.80 43.80 2.96	-	-	231 57.89 21.65 9.48 0.64	-	-	-	-	544 45.98 50.98 22.33 1.51	-	-	-	-	-	-	-	-	-	-	-	-	-	-	-
Orange County	5,956 10.98	429	84 19.58 19.58 1.41	-	-	-	-	-	-	-	-	-	-	-	-	-	-	-	-	-	-	-	-	-	-	15 7.28 17.86 3.50 0.25
Potter County	9,385 13.52	1,762	294 16.69 16.69 3.13	-	-	-	-	-	-	-	-	-	-	-	-	-	-	23 4.08 7.82 1.31 0.25	-	-	-	-	-	-	-	63 9.69 21.43 3.58 0.67
Randall County	18,971 28.91	824	385 46.72 46.72 2.03	-	-	-	-	-	-	-	-	-	-	-	-	-	-	-	-	-	-	-	-	-	-	-

Notes: Please refer to the User's Guide for an explanation of data; data is arranged alphabetically by state, then county, then city within each county; table includes counties with populations greater than 49,999 unless noted and cities with populations greater than 9,999 whose Asian and/or NHPI population rates are greater than the national average; (1) Native Hawaiian and other Pacific Islander; (2) excludes Taiwanese; (3) includes Chamorro; (4) county does not meet population threshold but is shown in order to allow inclusion of city

Place	Total population 25 years and over who are 4-year college graduates	Asian population 25 years and over	Asians 25 years and over who are 4-year college graduates	NHPI[1] population 25 years and over	NHPIs[1] 25 years and over who are 4-year college graduates	Asian Indian	Bangladeshi	Cambodian	Chinese[2]	Fijian	Filipino	Guamanian[3]	Hawaiian, Native	Hmong	Indonesian	Japanese	Korean	Laotian	Malaysian	Pakistani	Samoan	Sri Lankan	Taiwanese	Thai	Tongan	Vietnamese
San Patricio County	5,152 13.03	267	61 22.85 22.85 1.18	-	-	-	-	-	-	-	-	-	-	-	-	-	-	-	-	-	-	-	-	-	-	-
Smith County	25,033 22.55	627	307 48.96 48.96 1.23	-	-	-	-	-	-	-	-	-	-	-	-	-	-	-	-	-	-	-	-	-	-	-
Tarrant County	239,285 26.62	31,748	11,553 36.39 36.39 4.83	869	165 18.99 18.99 0.07	3,896 65.17 33.72 12.27 1.63	-	27 7.63 0.23 0.09 0.01	2,139 60.13 18.51 6.74 0.89	-	1,046 44.72 9.05 3.29 0.44	-	-	-	-	250 31.61 2.16 0.79 0.10	867 41.99 7.50 2.73 0.36	174 9.41 1.51 0.55 0.07	-	292 51.87 2.53 0.92 0.12	-	-	324 73.80 2.80 1.02 0.14	176 32.35 1.52 0.55 0.07	0 0.00 0.00 0.00 0.00	1,887 16.02 16.33 5.94 0.79
Arlington (city)	61,837 30.41	11,737	4,320 36.81 36.81 6.99	-	-	1,089 62.80 25.21 9.28 1.76	-	-	1,111 63.59 25.72 9.47 1.80	-	272 33.42 6.30 2.32 0.44	-	-	-	-	-	293 51.40 6.78 2.50 0.47	-	-	-	-	-	206 77.15 4.77 1.76 0.33	-	-	886 16.05 20.51 7.55 1.43
Euless (city)	8,933 29.54	2,009	780 38.83 38.83 8.73	-	-	402 47.07 51.54 20.01 4.50	-	-	-	-	-	-	-	-	-	-	-	-	-	-	-	-	-	-	-	-
Haltom City (city)	3,080 12.42	1,850	283 15.30 15.30 9.19	-	-	-	-	-	-	-	-	-	-	-	-	-	-	21 4.87 7.42 1.14 0.68	-	-	-	-	-	-	-	62 6.39 21.91 3.35 2.01
Taylor County	16,951 22.45	988	270 27.33 27.33 1.59	-	-	-	-	-	-	-	140 38.04 51.85 14.17 0.83	-	-	-	-	-	-	-	-	-	-	-	-	-	-	-
Tom Green County	12,371 19.50	493	146 29.61 29.61 1.18	-	-	-	-	-	-	-	-	-	-	-	-	-	-	-	-	-	-	-	-	-	-	-
Travis County	203,666 40.62	21,300	13,649 64.08 64.08 6.70	358	52 14.53 14.53 0.03	4,022 83.22 29.47 18.88 1.97	-	-	4,474 82.32 32.78 21.00 2.20	-	691 51.34 5.06 3.24 0.34	-	-	-	-	513 56.31 3.76 2.41 0.25	1,482 64.58 10.86 6.96 0.73	-	-	188 50.95 1.38 0.88 0.09	-	-	307 75.99 2.25 1.44 0.15	121 43.21 0.89 0.57 0.06	-	1,320 30.08 9.67 6.20 0.65
Austin (city)	161,937 40.37	17,873	11,966 66.95 66.95 7.39	248	52 20.97 20.97 0.03	3,575 85.67 29.88 20.00 2.21	-	-	4,004 82.20 33.46 22.40 2.47	-	534 54.94 4.46 2.99 0.33	-	-	-	-	475 56.55 3.97 2.66 0.29	1,286 66.67 10.75 7.20 0.79	-	-	144 54.14 1.20 0.81 0.09	-	-	275 80.17 2.30 1.54 0.17	-	-	1,091 31.89 9.12 6.10 0.67

Notes: Please refer to the User's Guide for an explanation of data; data is arranged alphabetically by state, then county, then city within each county; table includes counties with populations greater than 49,999 unless noted and cities with populations greater than 9,999 whose Asian and/or NHPI population rates are greater than the national average; (1) Native Hawaiian and other Pacific Islander; (2) excludes Taiwanese; (3) includes Chamorro; (4) county does not meet population threshold but is shown in order to allow inclusion of city

Place	Total population 25 years and over who are 4-year college graduates	Asian population 25 years and over	Asians 25 years and over who are 4-year college graduates	NHPI[1] population 25 years and over	NHPIs[1] 25 years and over who are 4-year college graduates	Asian Indian	Bangladeshi	Cambodian	Chinese[2]	Fijian	Filipino	Guamanian[3]	Hawaiian, Native	Hmong	Indonesian	Japanese	Korean	Laotian	Malaysian	Pakistani	Samoan	Sri Lankan	Taiwanese	Thai	Tongan	Vietnamese
Pflugerville (city)	3,762 38.26	462	167 36.15 36.15 4.44	-	-	-	-	-	-	-	-	-	-	-	-	-	-	-	-	-	-	-	-	-	-	-
Wells Branch (cdp)	3,635 48.71	689	381 55.30 55.30 10.48	-	-	-	-	-	-	-	-	-	-	-	-	-	-	-	-	-	-	-	-	-	-	-
Victoria County	8,446 16.25	321	167 52.02 52.02 1.98	-	-	-	-	-	-	-	-	-	-	-	-	-	-	-	-	-	-	-	-	-	-	-
Webb County	14,092 13.93	510	224 43.92 43.92 1.59	-	-	-	-	-	-	-	-	-	-	-	-	-	-	-	-	-	-	-	-	-	-	-
Wichita County	16,122 19.97	1,506	317 21.05 21.05 1.97	-	-	-	-	-	-	-	79 25.73 24.92 5.25 0.49	-	-	-	-	-	-	-	-	-	-	-	-	-	-	24 5.30 7.57 1.59 0.15
Williamson County	52,309 33.63	4,033	2,258 55.99 55.99 4.32	-	-	722 67.67 31.98 17.90 1.38	-	-	603 66.19 26.71 14.95 1.15	-	-	-	-	-	-	-	235 54.65 10.41 5.83 0.45	-	-	-	-	-	-	-	-	174 26.36 7.71 4.31 0.33
Brushy Creek (cdp)	5,066 53.14	565	383 67.79 67.79 7.56	-	-	-	-	-	-	-	-	-	-	-	-	-	-	-	-	-	-	-	-	-	-	-
Jollyville (cdp)	4,459 45.57	779	435 55.84 55.84 9.76	-	-	-	-	-	-	-	-	-	-	-	-	-	-	-	-	-	-	-	-	-	-	-
UTAH	312,963 26.13	22,120	8,062 36.45 36.45 2.58	6,116	729 11.92 11.92 0.23	976 55.64 12.11 4.41 0.31	-	23 3.39 0.29 0.10 0.01	2,510 54.00 31.13 11.35 0.80	-	912 39.58 11.31 4.12 0.29	-	150 20.55 20.58 2.45 0.05	-	-	1,540 35.88 19.10 6.96 0.49	916 45.87 11.36 4.14 0.29	76 6.82 0.94 0.34 0.02	-	66 32.84 0.82 0.30 0.02	168 10.51 23.05 2.75 0.05	-	154 70.00 1.91 0.70 0.05	150 28.90 1.86 0.68 0.05	304 11.16 41.70 4.97 0.10	386 11.46 4.79 1.75 0.12
Cache County	13,562 31.88	853	466 54.63 54.63 3.44	-	-	-	-	-	238 75.56 51.07 27.90 1.75	-	-	-	-	-	-	-	-	-	-	-	-	-	-	-	-	-

Notes: Please refer to the User's Guide for an explanation of data; data is arranged alphabetically by state, then county, then city within each county; table includes counties with populations greater than 49,999 unless noted and cities with populations greater than 9,999 whose Asian and/or NHPI population rates are greater than the national average; (1) Native Hawaiian and other Pacific Islander; (2) excludes Taiwanese; (3) includes Chamorro; (4) county does not meet population threshold but is shown in order to allow inclusion of city

Place	Total population 25 years and over who are 4-year college graduates	Asian population 25 years and over	Asians 25 years and over who are 4-year college graduates	NHPI[1] population 25 years and over	NHPIs[1] 25 years and over who are 4-year college graduates	Asian Indian	Bangladeshi	Cambodian	Chinese[2]	Fijian	Filipino	Guamanian[3]	Hawaiian, Native	Hmong	Indonesian	Japanese	Korean	Laotian	Malaysian	Pakistani	Samoan	Sri Lankan	Taiwanese	Thai	Tongan	Vietnamese
Davis County	36,132 28.78	2,282	613 26.86 26.86 1.70	432	64 14.81 14.81 0.18	-	-	-	-	-	142 25.09 23.16 6.22 0.39	-	-	-	-	145 23.89 23.65 6.35 0.40	51 24.17 8.32 2.23 0.14	-	-	-	-	-	-	-	-	-
Salt Lake County	139,631 27.41	14,214	5,189 36.51 36.51 3.72	4,408	397 9.01 9.01 0.28	705 55.60 13.59 4.96 0.50	-	14 2.79 0.27 0.10 0.01	1,637 55.32 31.55 11.52 1.17	-	492 44.85 9.48 3.46 0.35	-	71 24.65 17.88 1.61 0.05	-	-	936 38.77 18.04 6.59 0.67	575 53.59 11.08 4.05 0.41	67 7.51 1.29 0.47 0.05	-	-	74 6.55 18.64 1.68 0.05	-	-	-	216 9.08 54.41 4.90 0.15	311 10.76 5.99 2.19 0.22
Kearns (cdp)	1,752 10.05	449	89 19.82 19.82 5.08	178	16 8.99 8.99 0.91	-	-	-	-	-	-	-	-	-	-	-	-	-	-	-	-	-	-	-	-	-
Salt Lake City (city)	38,686 34.90	4,335	1,973 45.51 45.51 5.10	1,437	155 10.79 10.79 0.40	234 62.73 11.86 5.40 0.60	-	-	712 68.73 36.09 16.42 1.84	-	182 56.17 9.22 4.20 0.47	-	-	-	-	319 40.23 16.17 7.36 0.82	262 74.64 13.28 6.04 0.68	-	-	-	15 6.55 9.68 1.04 0.04	-	-	-	118 12.19 76.13 8.21 0.31	38 4.26 1.93 0.88 0.10
Sandy (city)	16,641 34.75	934	457 48.93 48.93 2.75	139	16 11.51 11.51 0.10	-	-	-	144 56.25 31.51 15.42 0.87	-	-	-	-	-	-	-	-	-	-	-	-	-	-	-	-	-
Taylorsville (city)	5,607 17.77	961	232 24.14 24.14 4.14	296	48 16.22 16.22 0.86	-	-	-	-	-	-	-	-	-	-	-	-	-	-	-	-	-	-	-	-	62 17.51 26.72 6.45 1.11
West Jordan (city)	6,876 20.18	711	155 21.80 21.80 2.25	291	43 14.78 14.78 0.63	-	-	-	-	-	-	-	-	-	-	-	-	-	-	-	-	-	-	-	36 20.00 83.72 12.37 0.52	-
West Valley City (city)	6,599 11.35	2,672	335 12.54 12.54 5.08	1,244	41 3.30 3.30 0.62	-	-	0 0.00 0.00 0.00 0.00	102 23.39 30.45 3.82 1.55	-	-	-	-	-	-	-	-	6 2.63 1.79 0.22 0.09	-	-	9 2.39 21.95 0.72 0.14	-	-	-	29 4.24 70.73 2.33 0.44	82 8.50 24.48 3.07 1.24
Utah County	52,293 31.46	2,018	982 48.66 48.66 1.88	736	165 22.42 22.42 0.32	-	-	-	415 58.20 42.26 20.56 0.79	-	102 49.04 10.39 5.05 0.20	-	26 17.81 15.76 3.53 0.05	-	-	161 42.71 16.40 7.98 0.31	106 42.06 10.79 5.25 0.20	-	-	-	57 27.67 34.55 7.74 0.11	-	-	-	67 33.00 40.61 9.10 0.13	-
Orem (city)	14,111 35.30	746	369 49.46 49.46 2.61	313	47 15.02 15.02 0.33	-	-	-	-	-	-	-	-	-	-	-	-	-	-	-	-	-	-	-	-	-

Notes: Please refer to the User's Guide for an explanation of data; data is arranged alphabetically by state, then county, then city within each county; table includes counties with populations greater than 49,999 unless noted and cities with populations greater than 9,999 whose Asian and/or NHPI population rates are greater than the national average; (1) Native Hawaiian and other Pacific Islander; (2) excludes Taiwanese; (3) includes Chamorro; (4) county does not meet population threshold but is shown in order to allow inclusion of city

Place	Total population 25 years and over who are 4-year college graduates	Asian population 25 years and over	Asians 25 years and over who are 4-year college graduates	NHPI[1] population 25 years and over	NHPIs[1] 25 years and over who are 4-year college graduates	Asian Indian	Bangladeshi	Cambodian	Chinese[2]	Fijian	Filipino	Guamanian[3]	Hawaiian, Native	Hmong	Indonesian	Japanese	Korean	Laotian	Malaysian	Pakistani	Samoan	Sri Lankan	Taiwanese	Thai	Tongan	Vietnamese
	14,209	944	488	253	79	-	-	-	272	-	-	-	-	-	-	45	-	-	-	-	-	-	-	-	-	-
	35.67		51.69		31.23				63.11							26.79										
Provo (city)									55.74							9.22										
			51.69		31.23				28.81							4.77										
			3.43		0.56				1.91							0.32										
	10,868	273	49	153	32	-	-	-	-	-	-	-	-	-	-	-	-	-	-	-	-	-	-	-	-	-
	20.96		17.95		20.92																					
Washington County																										
			17.95		20.92																					
			0.45		0.29																					
	6,343	232	33	131	30	-	-	-	-	-	-	-	-	-	-	-	-	-	-	-	-	-	-	-	-	-
	21.98		14.22		22.90																					
St. George (city)																										
			14.22		22.90																					
			0.52		0.47																					
	22,165	1,511	466	-	-	-	-	-	-	-	-	-	-	-	-	167	-	-	-	-	-	-	-	-	-	-
	19.94		30.84													34.50										
Weber County																35.84										
			30.84													11.05										
			2.10													0.75										
	119,025	2,418	1,128	-	-	256	-	-	360	-	109	-	-	-	-	115	107	-	-	-	-	-	-	-	-	87
	29.45		46.65			78.05			59.80		48.66					50.66	40.68									17.30
VERMONT						22.70			31.91		9.66					10.20	9.49									7.71
			46.65			10.59			14.89		4.51					4.76	4.43									3.60
			0.95			0.22			0.30		0.09					0.10	0.09									0.07
	38,138	1,375	640	-	-	152	-	-	206	-	-	-	-	-	-	-	-	-	-	-	-	-	-	-	-	81
	41.16		46.55			86.86			59.88																	19.06
Chittenden County						23.75			32.19																	12.66
			46.55			11.05			14.98																	5.89
			1.68			0.40			0.54																	0.21
	10,044	110	53	-	-	-	-	-	-	-	-	-	-	-	-	-	-	-	-	-	-	-	-	-	-	-
	23.20		48.18																							
Rutland County																										
			48.18																							
			0.53																							
	12,614	147	60	-	-	-	-	-	-	-	-	-	-	-	-	-	-	-	-	-	-	-	-	-	-	-
	32.21		40.82																							
Washington County																										
			40.82																							
			0.48																							
	12,266	247	132	-	-	-	-	-	-	-	-	-	-	-	-	-	-	-	-	-	-	-	-	-	-	-
	30.20		53.44																							
Windsor County																										
			53.44																							
			1.08																							
	1,374,988	169,251	82,539	2,036	582	22,420	684	392	14,347	-	14,917	138	199	-	318	3,549	12,394	205	-	2,663	59	195	713	911	-	6,262
	29.46		48.77		28.59	72.75	63.16	14.96	60.63		45.76	22.96	33.50		47.39	51.19	41.27	11.38		47.36	22.26	43.05	74.97	34.35		26.19
VIRGINIA						27.16	0.83	0.47	17.38		18.07	23.71	34.19		0.39	4.30	15.02	0.25		3.23	10.14	0.24	0.86	1.10		7.59
			48.77		28.59	13.25	0.40	0.23	8.48		8.81	6.78	9.77		0.19	2.10	7.32	0.12		1.57	2.90	0.12	0.42	0.54		3.70
			6.00		0.04	1.63	0.05	0.03	1.04		1.08	0.01	0.01		0.02	0.26	0.90	0.01		0.19	<0.01	0.01	0.05	0.07		0.46

Notes: Please refer to the User's Guide for an explanation of data; data is arranged alphabetically by state, then county, then city within each county; table includes counties with populations greater than 49,999 unless noted and cities with populations greater than 9,999 whose Asian and/or NHPI population rates are greater than the national average; (1) Native Hawaiian and other Pacific Islander; (2) excludes Taiwanese; (3) includes Chamorro; (4) county does not meet population threshold but is shown in order to allow inclusion of city

Place	Total population 25 years and over who are 4-year college graduates	Asian population 25 years and over	Asians 25 years and over who are 4-year college graduates	NHPI[1] population 25 years and over	NHPIs[1] 25 years and over who are 4-year college graduates	Asian Indian	Bangladeshi	Cambodian	Chinese[2]	Fijian	Filipino	Guamanian[3]	Hawaiian, Native	Hmong	Indonesian	Japanese	Korean	Laotian	Malaysian	Pakistani	Samoan	Sri Lankan	Taiwanese	Thai	Tongan	Vietnamese
Albemarle County	25,675	1,639	1,269	-	-	307	-	-	545	-	-	-	-	-	-	-	-	-	-	-	-	-	-	-	-	-
	47.68		77.43			67.32			83.85																	
						24.19			42.95																	
			77.43			18.73			33.25																	
			4.94			1.20			2.12																	
Alexandria Independent City	51,982	5,075	2,838	-	-	850	-	-	358	-	485	-	-	-	-	-	438	-	-	158	-	-	-	-	-	165
	54.30		55.92			79.81			58.21		59.66						42.36			47.88						42.75
						29.95			12.61		17.09						15.43			5.57						5.81
			55.92			16.75			7.05		9.56						8.63			3.11						3.25
			5.46			1.64			0.69		0.93						0.84			0.30						0.32
Arlington County	83,613	11,536	6,878	-	-	1,852	-	29	1,281	-	810	-	-	-	-	730	757	-	-	136	-	-	-	-	-	423
	60.22		59.62			72.40		16.86	70.54		52.77					72.64	71.55			30.49						26.94
						26.93		0.42	18.62		11.78					10.61	11.01			1.98						6.15
			59.62			16.05		0.25	11.10		7.02					6.33	6.56			1.18						3.67
			8.23			2.21		0.03	1.53		0.97					0.87	0.91			0.16						0.51
Arlington (cdp)	83,613	11,536	6,878	-	-	1,852	-	29	1,281	-	810	-	-	-	-	730	757	-	-	136	-	-	-	-	-	423
	60.22		59.62			72.40		16.86	70.54		52.77					72.64	71.55			30.49						26.94
						26.93		0.42	18.62		11.78					10.61	11.01			1.98						6.15
			59.62			16.05		0.25	11.10		7.02					6.33	6.56			1.18						3.67
			8.23			2.21		0.03	1.53		0.97					0.87	0.91			0.16						0.51
Bedford County	8,869	377	165	-	-	-	-	-	-	-	-	-	-	-	-	-	-	-	-	-	-	-	-	-	-	-
	20.91		43.77																							
			43.77																							
			1.86																							
Charlottesville Independent City	9,323	637	482	-	-	88	-	-	257	-	-	-	-	-	-	-	-	-	-	-	-	-	-	-	-	-
	40.77		75.67			100.00			95.54																	
						18.26			53.32																	
			75.67			13.81			40.35																	
			5.17			0.94			2.76																	
Chesapeake Independent City	30,943	2,430	1,239	-	-	-	-	-	-	-	518	-	-	-	-	-	-	-	-	-	-	-	-	-	-	-
	24.66		50.99								38.66															
											41.81															
			50.99								21.32															
			4.00								1.67															
Chesterfield County	54,514	3,892	1,759	-	-	482	-	14	250	-	322	-	-	-	-	-	328	-	-	-	-	-	-	-	-	116
	32.64		45.20			69.35		4.49	44.09		66.39						35.12									26.91
						27.40		0.80	14.21		18.31						18.65									6.59
			45.20			12.38		0.36	6.42		8.27						8.43									2.98
			3.23			0.88		0.03	0.46		0.59						0.60									0.21
Fairfax Independent City	6,949	1,750	920	-	-	270	-	-	192	-	-	-	-	-	-	-	145	-	-	-	-	-	-	-	-	136
	45.65		52.57			82.07			51.06								39.30									44.88
						29.35			20.87								15.76									14.78
			52.57			15.43			10.97								8.29									7.77
			13.24			3.89			2.76								2.09									1.96
Fairfax County	357,861	82,972	42,878	474	205	12,434	344	277	7,086	-	5,280	-	-	-	105	1,417	8,054	126	-	1,573	-	-	416	346	-	4,127
	54.78		51.68		43.25	75.14	65.15	26.01	61.63		59.03				32.21	64.61	43.08	13.71		46.10			74.82	30.76		28.04
						29.00	0.80	0.65	16.53		12.31				0.24	3.30	18.78	0.29		3.67			0.97	0.81		9.62
			51.68		43.25	14.99	0.41	0.33	8.54		6.36				0.13	1.71	9.71	0.15		1.90			0.50	0.42		4.97
			11.98		0.06	3.47	0.10	0.08	1.98		1.48				0.03	0.40	2.25	0.04		0.44			0.12	0.10		1.15

Notes: Please refer to the User's Guide for an explanation of data; data is arranged alphabetically by state, then county, then city within each county; table includes counties with populations greater than 49,999 unless noted and cities with populations greater than 9,999 whose Asian and/or NHPI population rates are greater than the national average; (1) Native Hawaiian and other Pacific Islander; (2) excludes Taiwanese; (3) includes Chamorro; (4) county does not meet population threshold but is shown in order to allow inclusion of city

Place	Total population 25 years and over who are 4-year college graduates	Asian population 25 years and over	Asians 25 years and over who are 4-year college graduates	NHPI[1] population 25 years and over	NHPIs[1] 25 years and over who are 4-year college graduates	Asian Indian	Bangladeshi	Cambodian	Chinese[2]	Fijian	Filipino	Guamanian[3]	Hawaiian, Native	Hmong	Indonesian	Japanese	Korean	Laotian	Malaysian	Pakistani	Samoan	Sri Lankan	Taiwanese	Thai	Tongan	Vietnamese
Annandale (cdp)	19,002 49.20	7,361	3,039 41.29 41.29 15.99	-	-	661 79.35 21.75 8.98 3.48	-	-	286 45.18 9.41 3.89 1.51	-	301 60.81 9.90 4.09 1.58	-	-	-	-	-	777 32.67 25.57 10.56 4.09	-	-	-	-	-	-	-	-	668 27.88 21.98 9.07 3.52
Bailey's Crossroads (cdp)	5,747 37.59	1,675	488 29.13 29.13 8.49	-	-	-	-	-	-	-	-	-	-	-	-	-	-	-	-	49 27.07 10.04 2.93 0.85	-	-	-	-	-	78 19.45 15.98 4.66 1.36
Burke (cdp)	22,166 59.04	5,342	2,714 50.80 50.80 12.24	-	-	524 60.23 19.31 9.81 2.36	-	-	338 61.01 12.45 6.33 1.52	-	483 63.72 17.80 9.04 2.18	-	-	-	-	-	852 43.25 31.39 15.95 3.84	-	-	-	-	-	-	-	-	239 31.99 8.81 4.47 1.08
Centreville (cdp)	15,045 48.89	4,067	2,238 55.03 55.03 14.88	-	-	763 72.46 34.09 18.76 5.07	-	-	260 39.27 11.62 6.39 1.73	-	385 65.92 17.20 9.47 2.56	-	-	-	-	-	502 47.63 22.43 12.34 3.34	-	-	-	-	-	-	-	-	56 20.66 2.50 1.38 0.37
Chantilly (cdp)	16,564 60.68	4,299	2,811 65.39 65.39 16.97	-	-	982 74.79 34.93 22.84 5.93	-	-	504 77.54 17.93 11.72 3.04	-	-	-	-	-	-	-	433 52.17 15.40 10.07 2.61	-	-	-	-	-	-	-	-	300 46.95 10.67 6.98 1.81
Franconia (cdp)	13,553 58.72	2,255	1,172 51.97 51.97 8.65	-	-	197 71.90 16.81 8.74 1.45	-	-	-	-	324 73.97 27.65 14.37 2.39	-	-	-	-	-	158 34.57 13.48 7.01 1.17	-	-	-	-	-	-	-	-	157 41.21 13.40 6.96 1.16
Groveton (cdp)	5,542 38.51	1,068	402 37.64 37.64 7.25	-	-	-	-	-	-	-	-	-	-	-	-	-	-	-	-	-	-	-	-	-	-	-
Herndon (town)	5,604 40.84	2,083	1,039 49.88 49.88 18.54	-	-	424 61.01 40.81 20.36 7.57	-	-	-	-	-	-	-	-	-	-	-	-	-	-	-	-	-	-	-	84 32.94 8.08 4.03 1.50
Hybla Valley (cdp)	3,458 31.83	778	187 24.04 24.04 5.41	-	-	-	-	-	-	-	-	-	-	-	-	-	-	-	-	-	-	-	-	-	-	-
Idylwood (cdp)	6,205 54.49	2,264	1,276 56.36 56.36 20.56	-	-	629 90.11 49.29 27.78 10.14	-	-	270 61.50 21.16 11.93 4.35	-	-	-	-	-	-	-	-	-	-	-	-	-	-	-	-	103 20.72 8.07 4.55 1.66

Notes: Please refer to the User's Guide for an explanation of data; data is arranged alphabetically by state, then county, then city within each county; table includes counties with populations greater than 49,999 unless noted and cities with populations greater than 9,999 whose Asian and/or NHPI population rates are greater than the national average; (1) Native Hawaiian and other Pacific Islander; (2) excludes Taiwanese; (3) includes Chamorro; (4) county does not meet population threshold but is shown in order to allow inclusion of city

Place	Total population 25 years and over who are 4-year college graduates	Asian population 25 years and over	Asians 25 years and over who are 4-year college graduates	NHPI[1] population 25 years and over	NHPIs[1] 25 years and over who are 4-year college graduates	Asian Indian	Bangladeshi	Cambodian	Chinese[2]	Fijian	Filipino	Guamanian[3]	Hawaiian, Native	Hmong	Indonesian	Japanese	Korean	Laotian	Malaysian	Pakistani	Samoan	Sri Lankan	Taiwanese	Thai	Tongan	Vietnamese
Jefferson (cdp)	7,790 40.36	3,672	1,360 37.04 37.04 17.46	-	-	420 70.47 30.88 11.44 5.39	-	-	184 45.43 13.53 5.01 2.36	-	188 55.29 13.82 5.12 2.41	-	-	-	-	-	-	-	-	-	-	-	-	-	-	366 22.70 26.91 9.97 4.70
Lincolnia (cdp)	4,055 39.44	1,492	585 39.21 39.21 14.43	-	-	-	-	-	-	-	-	-	-	-	-	-	-	-	-	81 31.03 13.85 5.43 2.00	-	-	-	-	-	69 22.77 11.79 4.62 1.70
Lorton (cdp)	3,490 29.00	979	363 37.08 37.08 10.40	-	-	-	-	-	-	-	-	-	-	-	-	-	-	-	-	-	-	-	-	-	-	-
McLean (cdp)	20,865 75.36	2,982	2,193 73.54 73.54 10.51	-	-	614 90.69 28.00 20.59 2.94	-	-	391 68.84 17.83 13.11 1.87	-	218 57.37 9.94 7.31 1.04	-	-	-	-	275 81.36 12.54 9.22 1.32	385 66.27 17.56 12.91 1.85	-	-	-	-	-	-	-	-	-
Merrifield (cdp)	4,394 57.45	2,155	1,143 53.04 53.04 26.01	-	-	432 68.35 37.80 20.05 9.83	-	-	-	-	-	-	-	-	-	-	251 47.09 21.96 11.65 5.71	-	-	-	-	-	-	-	-	120 25.42 10.50 5.57 2.73
Mount Vernon (cdp)	6,962 36.76	1,248	466 37.34 37.34 6.69	-	-	-	-	-	-	-	-	-	-	-	-	-	127 36.49 27.25 10.18 1.82	-	-	-	-	-	-	-	-	-
Newington (cdp)	6,576 51.45	1,379	582 42.20 42.20 8.85	-	-	120 56.60 20.62 8.70 1.82	-	-	-	-	174 48.20 29.90 12.62 2.65	-	-	-	-	-	96 31.48 16.49 6.96 1.46	-	-	-	-	-	-	-	-	-
Oakton (cdp)	12,889 63.00	2,779	1,842 66.28 66.28 14.29	-	-	531 79.14 28.83 19.11 4.12	-	-	551 76.53 29.91 19.83 4.27	-	-	-	-	-	-	-	430 58.66 23.34 15.47 3.34	-	-	-	-	-	-	-	-	97 34.64 5.27 3.49 0.75
Reston (cdp)	25,085 62.84	3,624	2,476 68.32 68.32 9.87	-	-	1,121 83.97 45.27 30.93 4.47	-	-	474 83.30 19.14 13.08 1.89	-	236 60.98 9.53 6.51 0.94	-	-	-	-	-	314 62.30 12.68 8.66 1.25	-	-	-	-	-	-	-	-	-
Rose Hill (cdp)	5,056 47.75	825	355 43.03 43.03 7.02	-	-	-	-	-	-	-	-	-	-	-	-	-	-	-	-	-	-	-	-	-	-	-

Notes: Please refer to the User's Guide for an explanation of data; data is arranged alphabetically by state, then county, then city within each county; table includes counties with populations greater than 49,999 unless noted and cities with populations greater than 9,999 whose Asian and/or NHPI population rates are greater than the national average; (1) Native Hawaiian and other Pacific Islander; (2) excludes Taiwanese; (3) includes Chamorro; (4) county does not meet population threshold but is shown in order to allow inclusion of city

Place	Total population 25 years and over who are 4-year college graduates	Asian population 25 years and over	Asians 25 years and over who are 4-year college graduates	NHPI[1] population 25 years and over	NHPIs[1] 25 years and over who are 4-year college graduates	Asian Indian	Bangladeshi	Cambodian	Chinese[2]	Fijian	Filipino	Guamanian[3]	Hawaiian, Native	Hmong	Indonesian	Japanese	Korean	Laotian	Malaysian	Pakistani	Samoan	Sri Lankan	Taiwanese	Thai	Tongan	Vietnamese
Springfield (cdp)	7,863 37.92	4,164	1,358 32.61 32.61 17.27	-	-	287 50.26 21.13 6.89 3.65	-	-	113 44.31 8.32 2.71 1.44	-	277 41.16 20.40 6.65 3.52	-	-	-	-	-	159 28.86 11.71 3.82 2.02	39 18.14 2.87 0.94 0.50	-	-	-	-	-	-	-	252 19.95 18.56 6.05 3.20
Tysons Corner (cdp)	9,746 69.80	2,239	1,613 72.04 72.04 16.55	-	-	505 90.83 31.31 22.55 5.18	-	-	412 84.43 25.54 18.40 4.23	-	-	-	-	-	-	-	331 61.07 20.52 14.78 3.40	-	-	-	-	-	-	-	-	-
Vienna (town)	5,847 56.41	858	436 50.82 50.82 7.46	-	-	-	-	-	-	-	-	-	-	-	-	-	-	-	-	-	-	-	-	-	-	-
West Springfield (cdp)	11,218 57.73	2,486	1,091 43.89 43.89 9.73	-	-	180 75.00 16.50 7.24 1.60	-	-	134 66.67 12.28 5.39 1.19	-	-	-	-	-	-	-	327 36.05 29.97 13.15 2.91	-	-	-	-	-	-	-	-	158 29.21 14.48 6.36 1.41
Wolf Trap (cdp)	7,113 76.92	826	630 76.27 76.27 8.86	-	-	176 85.44 27.94 21.31 2.47	-	-	147 76.56 23.33 17.80 2.07	-	-	-	-	-	-	-	-	-	-	-	-	-	-	-	-	-
Falls Church Independent City	4,758 63.75	526	292 55.51 55.51 6.14	-	-	-	-	-	-	-	-	-	-	-	-	-	-	-	-	-	-	-	-	-	-	-
Fauquier County	9,956 27.06	314	110 35.03 35.03 1.10	-	-	-	-	-	-	-	-	-	-	-	-	-	-	-	-	-	-	-	-	-	-	-
Frederick County	7,291 18.57	309	121 39.16 39.16 1.66	-	-	-	-	-	-	-	-	-	-	-	-	-	-	-	-	-	-	-	-	-	-	-
Hampton Independent City	20,138 21.78	1,735	437 25.19 25.19 2.17	-	-	-	-	-	-	-	91 21.46 20.82 5.24 0.45	-	-	-	-	-	-	-	-	-	-	-	-	-	-	19 4.90 4.35 1.10 0.09
Hanover County	16,324 28.69	385	159 41.30 41.30 0.97	-	-	-	-	-	-	-	-	-	-	-	-	-	-	-	-	-	-	-	-	-	-	-

Notes: Please refer to the User's Guide for an explanation of data; data is arranged alphabetically by state, then county, then city within each county; table includes counties with populations greater than 49,999 unless noted and cities with populations greater than 9,999 whose Asian and/or NHPI population rates are greater than the national average; (1) Native Hawaiian and other Pacific Islander; (2) excludes Taiwanese; (3) includes Chamorro; (4) county does not meet population threshold but is shown in order to allow inclusion of city

Place	Total population 25 years and over who are 4-year college graduates	Asian population 25 years and over	Asians 25 years and over who are 4-year college graduates	NHPI[1] population 25 years and over	NHPIs[1] 25 years and over who are 4-year college graduates	Asian Indian	Bangladeshi	Cambodian	Chinese[2]	Fijian	Filipino	Guamanian[3]	Hawaiian, Native	Hmong	Indonesian	Japanese	Korean	Laotian	Malaysian	Pakistani	Samoan	Sri Lankan	Taiwanese	Thai	Tongan	Vietnamese
Henrico County	61,887	6,143	3,100	-	-	1,492	-	11	601	-	248	-	-	-	-	-	255	-	-	-	-	-	-	-	-	198
	34.93		50.46			80.22		2.77	52.03		55.86						41.26									19.45
						48.13		0.35	19.39		8.00						8.23									6.39
			50.46			24.29		0.18	9.78		4.04						4.15									3.22
			5.01			2.41		0.02	0.97		0.40						0.41									0.32
Glen Allen (cdp)	3,139	301	129	-	-	-	-	-	-	-	-	-	-	-	-	-	-	-	-	-	-	-	-	-	-	-
	36.33		42.86																							
			42.86																							
			4.11																							
Laurel (cdp)	2,637	478	259	-	-	-	-	-	-	-	-	-	-	-	-	-	-	-	-	-	-	-	-	-	-	-
	26.23		54.18																							
			54.18																							
			9.82																							
Loudoun County	51,709	5,842	3,094	-	-	808	-	-	547	-	537	-	-	-	-	-	305	-	-	225	-	-	-	-	-	302
	47.19		52.96			65.53			65.51		71.79						43.02			61.64						26.49
						26.12			17.68		17.36						9.86			7.27						9.76
			52.96			13.83			9.36		9.19						5.22			3.85						5.17
			5.98			1.56			1.06		1.04						0.59			0.44						0.58
Lynchburg Independent City	10,301	576	342	-	-	-	-	-	-	-	-	-	-	-	-	-	-	-	-	-	-	-	-	-	-	-
	25.24		59.38																							
			59.38																							
			3.32																							
Manassas Park Indep. City	1,265	241	164	-	-	-	-	-	-	-	-	-	-	-	-	-	-	-	-	-	-	-	-	-	-	-
	20.32		68.05																							
			68.05																							
			12.96																							
Montgomery County	15,468	1,371	1,173	-	-	264	-	-	441	-	-	-	-	-	-	-	250	-	-	-	-	-	-	-	-	-
	35.88		85.56			96.00			95.45								76.45									
						22.51			37.60								21.31									
			85.56			19.26			32.17								18.23									
			7.58			1.71			2.85								1.62									
Blacksburg (town)	8,255	1,184	1,031	-	-	221	-	-	413	-	-	-	-	-	-	-	234	-	-	-	-	-	-	-	-	-
	64.18		87.08			97.36			95.16								84.78									
						21.44			40.06								22.70									
			87.08			18.67			34.88								19.76									
			12.49			2.68			5.00								2.83									
Newport News Independent City	21,890	2,898	753	-	-	-	-	-	206	-	136	-	-	-	-	-	83	-	-	-	-	-	-	-	-	58
	19.88		25.98						59.20		30.98						9.62									12.31
									27.36		18.06						11.02									7.70
			25.98						7.11		4.69						2.86									2.00
			3.44						0.94		0.62						0.38									0.26
Norfolk Independent City	26,505	4,370	1,524	-	-	146	-	-	340	-	780	-	-	-	-	-	-	-	-	-	-	-	-	-	-	22
	19.60		34.87			62.13			70.10		27.24															10.43
						9.58			22.31		51.18															1.44
			34.87			3.34			7.78		17.85															0.50
			5.75			0.55			1.28		2.94															0.08

Notes: Please refer to the User's Guide for an explanation of data; data is arranged alphabetically by state, then county, then city within each county; table includes counties with populations greater than 49,999 unless noted and cities with populations greater than 9,999 whose Asian and/or NHPI population rates are greater than the national average; (1) Native Hawaiian and other Pacific Islander; (2) excludes Taiwanese; (3) includes Chamorro; (4) county does not meet population threshold but is shown in order to allow inclusion of city

Place	Total population 25 years and over who are 4-year college graduates	Asian population 25 years and over	Asians 25 years and over who are 4-year college graduates	NHPI[1] population 25 years and over	NHPIs[1] 25 years and over who are 4-year college graduates	Asian Indian	Bangladeshi	Cambodian	Chinese[2]	Fijian	Filipino	Guamanian[3]	Hawaiian, Native	Hmong	Indonesian	Japanese	Korean	Laotian	Malaysian	Pakistani	Samoan	Sri Lankan	Taiwanese	Thai	Tongan	Vietnamese
Portsmouth Independent City	8,795 13.81	484	111 22.93 22.93 1.26	-	-	-	-	-	-	-	86 29.15 77.48 17.77 0.98	-	-	-	-	-	-	-	-	-	-	-	-	-	-	-
Prince William County	53,819 31.46	6,977	2,852 40.88 40.88 5.30	-	-	568 49.26 19.92 8.14 1.06	-	-	394 54.42 13.81 5.65 0.73	-	799 50.22 28.02 11.45 1.48	-	-	-	-	146 40.56 5.12 2.09 0.27	321 26.68 11.26 4.60 0.60	-	-	183 44.96 6.42 2.62 0.34	-	-	-	-	-	187 28.25 6.56 2.68 0.35
Bull Run (cdp)	2,230 31.69	432	290 67.13 67.13 13.00	-	-	-	-	-	-	-	-	-	-	-	-	-	-	-	-	-	-	-	-	-	-	-
Dale City (cdp)	7,485 22.68	1,894	548 28.93 28.93 7.32	-	-	148 38.44 27.01 7.81 1.98	-	-	-	-	119 25.70 21.72 6.28 1.59	-	-	-	-	-	-	-	-	46 27.06 8.39 2.43 0.61	-	-	-	-	-	-
Lake Ridge (cdp)	8,597 44.34	756	335 44.31 44.31 3.90	-	-	-	-	-	-	-	-	-	-	-	-	-	-	-	-	-	-	-	-	-	-	-
Woodbridge (cdp)	2,983 15.78	964	264 27.39 27.39 8.85	-	-	-	-	-	-	-	-	-	-	-	-	-	-	-	-	-	-	-	-	-	-	-
Richmond Independent City	37,861 29.45	1,298	646 49.77 49.77 1.71	-	-	165 72.05 25.54 12.71 0.44	-	-	-	-	117 50.65 18.11 9.01 0.31	-	-	-	-	-	-	-	-	-	-	-	-	-	-	-
Roanoke Independent City	12,289 18.74	620	234 37.74 37.74 1.90	-	-	-	-	-	-	-	-	-	-	-	-	-	-	-	-	-	-	-	-	-	-	-
Roanoke County	17,151 28.22	649	334 51.46 51.46 1.95	-	-	-	-	-	-	-	-	-	-	-	-	-	-	-	-	-	-	-	-	-	-	-
Spotsylvania County	12,928 22.83	840	230 27.38 27.38 1.78	-	-	-	-	-	-	-	-	-	-	-	-	-	-	-	-	-	-	-	-	-	-	-

Notes: Please refer to the User's Guide for an explanation of data; data is arranged alphabetically by state, then county, then city within each county; table includes counties with populations greater than 49,999 unless noted and cities with populations greater than 9,999 whose Asian and/or NHPI population rates are greater than the national average; (1) Native Hawaiian and other Pacific Islander; (2) excludes Taiwanese; (3) includes Chamorro; (4) county does not meet population threshold but is shown in order to allow inclusion of city

Place	Total population 25 years and over who are 4-year college graduates	Asian population 25 years and over	Asians 25 years and over who are 4-year college graduates	NHPI[1] population 25 years and over	NHPIs[1] 25 years and over who are 4-year college graduates	Asian Indian	Bangladeshi	Cambodian	Chinese[2]	Fijian	Filipino	Guamanian[3]	Hawaiian, Native	Hmong	Indonesian	Japanese	Korean	Laotian	Malaysian	Pakistani	Samoan	Sri Lankan	Taiwanese	Thai	Tongan	Vietnamese
Stafford County	16,606 29.64	1,106	369 33.36 33.36 2.22	-	-	-	-	-	-	-	88 27.85 23.85 7.96 0.53	-	-	-	-	-	-	-	-	-	-	-	-	-	-	-
Suffolk Independent City	7,210 17.31	406	173 42.61 42.61 2.40	-	-	-	-	-	-	-	-	-	-	-	-	-	-	-	-	-	-	-	-	-	-	-
Virginia Beach Independent City	74,949 28.11	13,216	4,416 33.41 33.41 5.89	-	-	414 52.60 9.38 3.13 0.55	-	-	422 39.33 9.56 3.19 0.56	-	3,036 34.32 68.75 22.97 4.05	-	-	-	-	146 24.87 3.31 1.10 0.19	170 29.41 3.85 1.29 0.23	-	-	-	-	-	-	-	-	58 7.90 1.31 0.44 0.08
Williamsburg Independent City	2,413 45.02	193	75 38.86 38.86 3.11	-	-	-	-	-	-	-	-	-	-	-	-	-	-	-	-	-	-	-	-	-	-	-
York County	13,512 37.36	1,151	532 46.22 46.22 3.94	-	-	114 63.69 21.43 9.90 0.84	-	-	-	-	-	-	-	-	-	-	92 27.54 17.29 7.99 0.68	-	-	-	-	-	-	-	-	-
WASHINGTON	1,061,425 27.73	209,271	76,936 36.76 36.76 7.25	11,598	1,406 12.12 12.12 0.13	8,590 58.38 11.17 4.10 0.81	-	478 6.57 0.62 0.23 0.05	19,501 49.61 25.35 9.32 1.84	19 4.23 1.35 0.16 <0.01	15,369 35.21 19.98 7.34 1.45	382 12.87 27.17 3.29 0.04	471 16.45 33.50 4.06 0.04	58 10.74 0.08 0.03 0.01	379 50.13 0.49 0.18 0.04	12,423 43.17 16.15 5.94 1.17	9,917 33.17 12.89 4.74 0.93	215 5.01 0.28 0.10 0.02	-	466 65.63 0.61 0.22 0.04	231 6.86 16.43 1.99 0.02	136 52.51 0.18 0.06 0.01	1,516 66.75 1.97 0.72 0.14	974 37.36 1.27 0.47 0.09	55 12.85 3.91 0.47 0.01	4,414 15.74 5.74 2.11 0.42
Benton County	23,188 26.29	2,003	1,027 51.27 51.27 4.43	-	-	237 78.74 23.08 11.83 1.02	-	-	338 85.57 32.91 16.87 1.46	-	-	-	-	-	-	-	47 21.96 4.58 2.35 0.20	-	-	-	-	-	-	-	-	43 12.68 4.19 2.15 0.19
Richland (city)	9,867 38.94	1,102	692 62.79 62.79 7.01	-	-	-	-	-	253 83.50 36.56 22.96 2.56	-	-	-	-	-	-	-	-	-	-	-	-	-	-	-	-	-
Chelan County	9,294 21.91	278	55 19.78 19.78 0.59	-	-	-	-	-	-	-	-	-	-	-	-	-	-	-	-	-	-	-	-	-	-	-
Clallam County	9,490 20.76	597	151 25.29 25.29 1.59	-	-	-	-	-	-	-	-	-	-	-	-	-	-	-	-	-	-	-	-	-	-	-

Notes: Please refer to the User's Guide for an explanation of data; data is arranged alphabetically by state, then county, then city within each county; table includes counties with populations greater than 49,999 unless noted and cities with populations greater than 9,999 whose Asian and/or NHPI population rates are greater than the national average; (1) Native Hawaiian and other Pacific Islander; (2) excludes Taiwanese; (3) includes Chamorro; (4) county does not meet population threshold but is shown in order to allow inclusion of city

Place	Total population 25 years and over who are 4-year college graduates	Asian population 25 years and over	Asians 25 years and over who are 4-year college graduates	NHPI[1] population 25 years and over	NHPIs[1] 25 years and over who are 4-year college graduates	Asian Indian	Bangladeshi	Cambodian	Chinese[2]	Fijian	Filipino	Guamanian[3]	Hawaiian, Native	Hmong	Indonesian	Japanese	Korean	Laotian	Malaysian	Pakistani	Samoan	Sri Lankan	Taiwanese	Thai	Tongan	Vietnamese
Clark County	47,997 22.09	6,988	2,228 31.88 31.88 4.64	619	47 7.59 7.59 0.10	203 48.56 9.11 2.90 0.42	-	22 8.70 0.99 0.31 0.05	553 49.16 24.82 7.91 1.15	-	435 35.83 19.52 6.22 0.91	-	-	-	-	397 40.22 17.82 5.68 0.83	252 28.06 11.31 3.61 0.53	4 1.75 0.18 0.06 0.01	-	-	-	-	-	-	-	176 12.17 7.90 2.52 0.37
Five Corners (cdp)	1,185 15.75	337	104 30.86 30.86 8.78	-	-	-	-	-	-	-	-	-	-	-	-	-	-	-	-	-	-	-	-	-	-	-
Orchards (cdp)	1,452 14.10	494	76 15.38 15.38 5.23	-	-	-	-	-	-	-	-	-	-	-	-	-	-	-	-	-	-	-	-	-	-	-
Vancouver (city)	19,747 21.70	4,171	1,397 33.49 33.49 7.07	401	23 5.74 5.74 0.12	-	-	-	407 57.32 29.13 9.76 2.06	-	253 38.92 18.11 6.07 1.28	-	-	-	-	244 42.14 17.47 5.85 1.24	146 28.97 10.45 3.50 0.74	-	-	-	-	-	-	-	-	116 12.26 8.30 2.78 0.59
Cowlitz County	8,016 13.28	721	91 12.62 12.62 1.14	-	-	-	-	0 0.00 0.00 0.00 0.00	-	-	-	-	-	-	-	-	-	-	-	-	-	-	-	-	-	8 3.52 8.79 1.11 0.10
Grant County	5,946 13.73	417	120 28.78 28.78 2.02	-	-	-	-	-	-	-	-	-	-	-	-	-	-	-	-	-	-	-	-	-	-	-
Grays Harbor County	5,646 12.66	401	113 28.18 28.18 2.00	-	-	-	-	-	-	-	-	-	-	-	-	-	-	-	-	-	-	-	-	-	-	-
Island County	12,736 27.03	1,843	408 22.14 22.14 3.20	-	-	-	-	-	-	-	257 20.28 62.99 13.94 2.02	-	-	-	-	51 18.28 12.50 2.77 0.40	-	-	-	-	-	-	-	-	-	-
Oak Harbor (city)	2,513 22.34	1,110	221 19.91 19.91 8.79	-	-	-	-	-	-	-	178 20.30 80.54 16.04 7.08	-	-	-	-	-	-	-	-	-	-	-	-	-	-	-
King County	474,948 39.95	123,894	51,821 41.83 41.83 10.91	4,488	642 14.30 14.30 0.14	6,042 63.06 11.66 4.88 1.27	-	206 6.31 0.40 0.17 0.04	15,081 49.62 29.10 12.17 3.18	6 1.71 0.93 0.13 <0.01	9,145 40.51 17.65 7.38 1.93	126 29.58 19.63 2.81 0.03	221 22.90 34.42 4.92 0.05	38 13.15 0.07 0.03 0.01	263 53.35 0.51 0.21 0.06	8,749 49.17 16.88 7.06 1.84	5,541 43.53 10.69 4.47 1.17	115 4.36 0.22 0.09 0.02	-	225 74.50 0.43 0.18 0.05	137 7.21 21.34 3.05 0.03	-	1,305 70.46 2.52 1.05 0.27	602 44.79 1.16 0.49 0.13	55 18.09 8.57 1.23 0.01	2,705 16.16 5.22 2.18 0.57

Notes: Please refer to the User's Guide for an explanation of data; data is arranged alphabetically by state, then county, then city within each county; table includes counties with populations greater than 49,999 unless noted and cities with populations greater than 9,999 whose Asian and/or NHPI population rates are greater than the national average; (1) Native Hawaiian and other Pacific Islander; (2) excludes Taiwanese; (3) includes Chamorro; (4) county does not meet population threshold but is shown in order to allow inclusion of city

Place	Total population 25 years and over who are 4-year college graduates	Asian population 25 years and over	Asians 25 years and over who are 4-year college graduates	NHPI[1] population 25 years and over	NHPIs[1] 25 years and over who are 4-year college graduates	Asian Indian	Bangladeshi	Cambodian	Chinese[2]	Fijian	Filipino	Guamanian[3]	Hawaiian, Native	Hmong	Indonesian	Japanese	Korean	Laotian	Malaysian	Pakistani	Samoan	Sri Lankan	Taiwanese	Thai	Tongan	Vietnamese
Auburn (city)	3,997	1,006	266	-	-	-	-	-	-	-	-	-	-	-	-	-	-	-	-	-	-	-	-	-	-	-
	15.63		26.44																							
			26.44																							
			6.65																							
Bellevue (city)	42,221	12,766	8,039	-	-	1,619	-	-	2,724	-	468	-	-	-	-	1,330	803	44	-	-	-	-	383	-	-	273
	54.11		62.97			89.70			68.32		58.72					58.46	52.97	16.73					70.40			30.57
						20.14			33.88		5.82					16.54	9.99	0.55					4.76			3.40
			62.97			12.68			21.34		3.67					10.42	6.29	0.34					3.00			2.14
			19.04			3.83			6.45		1.11					3.15	1.90	0.10					0.91			0.65
Bothell (city)	7,658	1,398	898	-	-	-	-	-	284	-	-	-	-	-	-	-	-	-	-	-	-	-	-	-	-	-
	38.62		64.23						78.24																	
									31.63																	
			64.23						20.31																	
			11.73						3.71																	
Bryn Mawr-Skyway (cdp)	2,343	2,101	515	-	-	-	-	-	-	-	244	-	-	-	-	154	-	-	-	-	-	-	-	-	-	15
	23.72		24.51								40.87					30.99										5.03
											47.38					29.90										2.91
			24.51								11.61					7.33										0.71
			21.98								10.41					6.57										0.64
Burien (city)	4,749	1,374	326	-	-	-	-	-	-	-	99	-	-	-	-	-	-	-	-	-	-	-	-	-	-	43
	21.24		23.73								28.86															16.54
											30.37															13.19
			23.73								7.21															3.13
			6.86								2.08															0.91
Cascade-Fairwood (cdp)	7,004	3,038	1,149	-	-	-	-	-	219	-	369	-	-	-	-	201	-	-	-	-	-	-	-	-	-	99
	31.31		37.82						36.20		42.03					49.75										22.00
									19.06		32.11					17.49										8.62
			37.82						7.21		12.15					6.62										3.26
			16.40						3.13		5.27					2.87										1.41
Cottage Lake (cdp)	8,050	730	482	-	-	-	-	-	-	-	-	-	-	-	-	-	-	-	-	-	-	-	-	-	-	-
	53.16		66.03																							
			66.03																							
			5.99																							
Des Moines (city)	4,568	1,417	381	186	11	-	-	-	-	-	147	-	-	-	-	-	-	-	-	-	-	-	-	-	-	44
	22.85		26.89		5.91						54.24															14.52
											38.58															11.55
			26.89		5.91						10.37															3.11
			8.34		0.24						3.22															0.96
East Hill-Meridian (cdp)	5,200	2,459	944	-	-	195	-	-	260	-	172	-	-	-	-	-	-	-	-	-	-	-	-	-	-	89
	28.06		38.39			43.14			51.18		41.55															25.43
						20.66			27.54		18.22															9.43
			38.39			7.93			10.57		6.99															3.62
			18.15			3.75			5.00		3.31															1.71
Federal Way (city)	13,563	6,676	2,212	460	46	-	-	-	301	-	471	-	-	-	-	210	929	-	-	-	23	-	-	-	-	86
	26.19		33.13		10.00				50.42		39.81					38.67	31.52				9.87					12.03
									13.61		21.29					9.49	42.00				50.00					3.89
			33.13		10.00				4.51		7.06					3.15	13.92				5.00					1.29
			16.31		0.34				2.22		3.47					1.55	6.85				0.17					0.63

Notes: Please refer to the User's Guide for an explanation of data; data is arranged alphabetically by state, then county, then city within each county; table includes counties with populations greater than 49,999 unless noted and cities with populations greater than 9,999 whose Asian and/or NHPI population rates are greater than the national average; (1) Native Hawaiian and other Pacific Islander; (2) excludes Taiwanese; (3) includes Chamorro; (4) county does not meet population threshold but is shown in order to allow inclusion of city

Place	Total population 25 years and over who are 4-year college graduates	Asian population 25 years and over	Asians 25 years and over who are 4-year college graduates	NHPI[1] population 25 years and over	NHPIs[1] 25 years and over who are 4-year college graduates	Asian Indian	Bangladeshi	Cambodian	Chinese[2]	Fijian	Filipino	Guamanian[3]	Hawaiian, Native	Hmong	Indonesian	Japanese	Korean	Laotian	Malaysian	Pakistani	Samoan	Sri Lankan	Taiwanese	Thai	Tongan	Vietnamese
Inglewood-Finn Hill (cdp)	6,472 43.10	1,141	572 50.13 50.13 8.84	-	-	-	-	-	204 69.39 35.66 17.88 3.15	-	-	-	-	-	-	-	-	-	-	-	-	-	-	-	-	-
Issaquah (city)	3,826 48.27	474	297 62.66 62.66 7.76	-	-	-	-	-	-	-	-	-	-	-	-	-	-	-	-	-	-	-	-	-	-	-
Kenmore (city)	5,282 41.51	792	359 45.33 45.33 6.80	-	-	-	-	-	-	-	-	-	-	-	-	-	-	-	-	-	-	-	-	-	-	-
Kent (city)	11,821 23.97	4,888	1,457 29.81 29.81 12.33	-	-	279 30.79 19.15 5.71 2.36	-	-	280 43.55 19.22 5.73 2.37	-	318 30.61 21.83 6.51 2.69	-	-	-	-	218 43.86 14.96 4.46 1.84	113 21.52 7.76 2.31 0.96	-	-	-	-	-	-	-	-	143 16.90 9.81 2.93 1.21
Kingsgate (cdp)	3,081 40.26	909	374 41.14 41.14 12.14	-	-	-	-	-	192 70.85 51.34 21.12 6.23	-	-	-	-	-	-	-	-	-	-	-	-	-	-	-	-	-
Kirkland (city)	15,528 47.40	2,537	1,380 54.39 54.39 8.89	-	-	-	-	-	409 71.50 29.64 16.12 2.63	-	-	-	-	-	-	205 43.80 14.86 8.08 1.32	-	-	-	-	-	-	-	-	-	81 20.82 5.87 3.19 0.52
Lake Forest Park (city)	4,951 51.13	834	377 45.20 45.20 7.61	-	-	-	-	-	-	-	-	-	-	-	-	-	-	-	-	-	-	-	-	-	-	-
Lakeland North (cdp)	2,281 23.72	609	176 28.90 28.90 7.72	-	-	-	-	-	-	-	-	-	-	-	-	-	-	-	-	-	-	-	-	-	-	-
Lakeland South (cdp)	1,908 25.18	446	187 41.93 41.93 9.80	-	-	-	-	-	-	-	-	-	-	-	-	-	-	-	-	-	-	-	-	-	-	-
Lea Hill (cdp)	1,806 28.17	237	68 28.69 28.69 3.77	-	-	-	-	-	-	-	-	-	-	-	-	-	-	-	-	-	-	-	-	-	-	-

Notes: Please refer to the User's Guide for an explanation of data; data is arranged alphabetically by state, then county, then city within each county; table includes counties with populations greater than 49,999 unless noted and cities with populations greater than 9,999 whose Asian and/or NHPI population rates are greater than the national average; (1) Native Hawaiian and other Pacific Islander; (2) excludes Taiwanese; (3) includes Chamorro; (4) county does not meet population threshold but is shown in order to allow inclusion of city

Place	Total population 25 years and over who are 4-year college graduates	Asian population 25 years and over	Asians 25 years and over who are 4-year college graduates	NHPI[1] population 25 years and over	NHPIs[1] 25 years and over who are 4-year college graduates	Asian Indian	Bangladeshi	Cambodian	Chinese[2]	Fijian	Filipino	Guamanian[3]	Hawaiian, Native	Hmong	Indonesian	Japanese	Korean	Laotian	Malaysian	Pakistani	Samoan	Sri Lankan	Taiwanese	Thai	Tongan	Vietnamese
Mercer Island (city)	10,658 69.10	1,741	1,143 65.65 65.65 10.72	-	-	-	-	-	471 69.47 41.21 27.05 4.42	-	-	-	-	-	-	312 60.23 27.30 17.92 2.93	-	-	-	-	-	-	-	-	-	-
Redmond (city)	16,581 52.87	4,065	2,720 66.91 66.91 16.40	-	-	837 95.66 30.77 20.59 5.05	-	-	991 72.97 36.43 24.38 5.98	-	-	-	-	-	-	342 58.56 12.57 8.41 2.06	138 40.59 5.07 3.39 0.83	-	-	-	-	-	-	-	-	-
Renton (city)	9,465 27.84	4,547	1,818 39.98 39.98 19.21	-	-	-	-	-	454 48.40 24.97 9.98 4.80	-	464 44.79 25.52 10.20 4.90	-	-	-	-	258 47.34 14.19 5.67 2.73	-	-	-	-	-	-	-	-	-	266 24.54 14.63 5.85 2.81
Riverton-Boulevard Park (cdp)	1,190 15.99	923	122 13.22 13.22 10.25	-	-	-	-	-	-	-	-	-	-	-	-	-	-	-	-	-	-	-	-	-	-	-
Sammamish (city)	13,095 61.47	1,720	1,346 78.26 78.26 10.28	-	-	-	-	-	549 74.49 40.79 31.92 4.19	-	-	-	-	-	-	-	-	-	-	-	-	-	-	-	-	-
SeaTac (city)	2,537 15.31	1,813	385 21.24 21.24 15.18	335	0 <0.01 <0.01 <0.01	75 19.33 19.48 4.14 2.96	-	-	-	-	112 22.36 29.09 6.18 4.41	-	-	-	-	-	-	-	-	-	-	-	-	-	-	4 1.32 1.04 0.22 0.16
Seattle (city)	193,322 47.20	49,210	18,212 37.01 37.01 9.42	1,340	256 19.10 19.10 0.13	1,140 56.94 6.26 2.32 0.59	-	100 8.31 0.55 0.20 0.05	5,150 38.42 28.28 10.47 2.66	-	4,314 39.89 23.69 8.77 2.23	-	-	-	133 71.89 0.73 0.27 0.07	3,563 47.82 19.56 7.24 1.84	1,548 49.86 8.50 3.15 0.80	34 2.54 0.19 0.07 0.02	-	-	66 10.39 25.78 4.93 0.03	-	418 69.78 2.30 0.85 0.22	302 52.80 1.66 0.61 0.16	-	877 12.47 4.82 1.78 0.45
Shoreline (city)	13,807 37.34	4,336	2,003 46.19 46.19 14.51	-	-	204 74.73 10.18 4.70 1.48	-	-	513 42.79 25.61 11.83 3.72	-	425 52.93 21.22 9.80 3.08	-	-	-	-	153 51.00 7.64 3.53 1.11	435 51.36 21.72 10.03 3.15	-	-	-	-	-	-	-	-	112 22.13 5.59 2.58 0.81
Tukwila (city)	1,991 17.52	1,180	277 23.47 23.47 13.91	115	6 5.22 5.22 0.30	-	-	-	-	-	87 22.54 31.41 7.37 4.37	-	-	-	-	-	-	-	-	-	-	-	-	-	-	-
Union Hill-Novelty Hill (cdp)	3,645 53.38	334	235 70.36 70.36 6.45	-	-	-	-	-	-	-	-	-	-	-	-	-	-	-	-	-	-	-	-	-	-	-

Notes: Please refer to the User's Guide for an explanation of data; data is arranged alphabetically by state, then county, then city within each county; table includes counties with populations greater than 49,999 unless noted and cities with populations greater than 9,999 whose Asian and/or NHPI population rates are greater than the national average; (1) Native Hawaiian and other Pacific Islander; (2) excludes Taiwanese; (3) includes Chamorro; (4) county does not meet population threshold but is shown in order to allow inclusion of city

Place	Total population 25 years and over who are 4-year college graduates	Asian population 25 years and over	Asians 25 years and over who are 4-year college graduates	NHPI[1] population 25 years and over	NHPIs[1] 25 years and over who are 4-year college graduates	Asian Indian	Bangladeshi	Cambodian	Chinese[2]	Fijian	Filipino	Guamanian[3]	Hawaiian, Native	Hmong	Indonesian	Japanese	Korean	Laotian	Malaysian	Pakistani	Samoan	Sri Lankan	Taiwanese	Thai	Tongan	Vietnamese
White Center (cdp)	1,772	2,536	197	-	-	-	-	0	-	-	54	-	-	-	-	-	-	-	-	-	-	-	-	-	-	36
	13.35		7.77					0.00			16.31															3.00
								0.00			27.41															18.27
			7.77					0.00			2.13															1.42
			11.12					0.00			3.05															2.03
Kitsap County	37,667	7,097	1,870	913	50	-	-	-	135	-	1,130	29	-	-	-	273	128	-	-	-	-	-	-	-	-	28
	25.33		26.35		5.48				35.53		24.40	5.44				27.06	31.68									10.81
									7.22		60.43	58.00				14.60	6.84									1.50
			26.35		5.48				1.90		15.92	3.18				3.85	1.80									0.39
			4.96		0.13				0.36		3.00	0.08				0.72	0.34									0.07
Bremerton (city)	3,260	1,344	272	-	-	-	-	-	-	-	189	-	-	-	-	-	-	-	-	-	-	-	-	-	-	-
	14.77		20.24								19.96															
											69.49															
			20.24								14.06															
			8.34								5.80															
Silverdale (cdp)	2,913	1,055	315	-	-	-	-	-	-	-	290	-	-	-	-	-	-	-	-	-	-	-	-	-	-	-
	30.45		29.86								33.80															
											92.06															
			29.86								27.49															
			10.81								9.96															
Lewis County	5,777	243	54	-	-	-	-	-	-	-	-	-	-	-	-	-	-	-	-	-	-	-	-	-	-	-
	12.88		22.22																							
			22.22																							
			0.93																							
Pierce County	91,161	23,295	4,844	2,687	219	163	-	98	627	-	1,191	89	63	-	-	741	1,464	33	-	-	37	-	-	73	-	273
	20.59		20.79		8.15	34.39		5.23	49.68		25.60	9.38	11.15			24.41	18.65	12.64			4.59			22.39		9.61
						3.36		2.02	12.94		24.59	40.64	28.77			15.30	30.22	0.68			16.89			1.51		5.64
			20.79		8.15	0.70		0.42	2.69		5.11	3.31	2.34			3.18	6.28	0.14			1.38			0.31		1.17
			5.31		0.24	0.18		0.11	0.69		1.31	0.10	0.07			0.81	1.61	0.04			0.04			0.08		0.30
Elk Plain (cdp)	1,349	419	108	-	-	-	-	-	-	-	-	-	-	-	-	-	-	-	-	-	-	-	-	-	-	-
	14.33		25.78																							
			25.78																							
			8.01																							
Fort Lewis (cdp)	1,286	352	75	129	0	-	-	-	-	-	58	-	-	-	-	-	-	-	-	-	-	-	-	-	-	-
	17.03		21.31		<0.01						27.62															
											77.33															
			21.31		<0.01						16.48															
			5.83		<0.01						4.51															
Lakewood (city)	8,210	3,800	626	385	27	-	-	-	-	-	176	-	-	-	-	74	246	-	-	-	9	-	-	-	-	-
	21.84		16.47		7.01						20.58					11.97	13.98				6.67					
											28.12					11.82	39.30				33.33					
			16.47		7.01						4.63					1.95	6.47				2.34					
			7.62		0.33						2.14					0.90	3.00				0.11					
Parkland (cdp)	2,075	1,117	195	203	20	-	-	-	-	-	-	-	-	-	-	-	98	-	-	-	-	-	-	-	-	-
	14.87		17.46		9.85												18.49									
																	50.26									
			17.46		9.85												8.77									
			9.40		0.96												4.72									

Notes: Please refer to the User's Guide for an explanation of data; data is arranged alphabetically by state, then county, then city within each county; table includes counties with populations greater than 49,999 unless noted and cities with populations greater than 9,999 whose Asian and/or NHPI population rates are greater than the national average; (1) Native Hawaiian and other Pacific Islander; (2) excludes Taiwanese; (3) includes Chamorro; (4) county does not meet population threshold but is shown in order to allow inclusion of city

Place	Total population 25 years and over who are 4-year college graduates	Asian population 25 years and over	Asians 25 years and over who are 4-year college graduates	NHPI[1] population 25 years and over	NHPIs[1] 25 years and over who are 4-year college graduates	Asian Indian	Bangladeshi	Cambodian	Chinese[2]	Fijian	Filipino	Guamanian[3]	Hawaiian, Native	Hmong	Indonesian	Japanese	Korean	Laotian	Malaysian	Pakistani	Samoan	Sri Lankan	Taiwanese	Thai	Tongan	Vietnamese
Spanaway (cdp)	1,488 11.22	918	112 12.20 12.20 7.53	253	5 1.98 1.98 0.34	-	-	-	-	-	67 21.82 59.82 7.30 4.50	-	-	-	-	-	33 7.13 29.46 3.59 2.22	-	-	-	-	-	-	-	-	-
Tacoma (city)	24,748 19.96	9,208	1,607 17.45 17.45 6.49	734	71 9.67 9.67 0.29	-	-	63 4.36 3.92 0.68 0.25	255 47.93 15.87 2.77 1.03	-	323 22.25 20.10 3.51 1.31	18 7.20 25.35 2.45 0.07	-	-	-	223 31.50 13.88 2.42 0.90	393 17.42 24.46 4.27 1.59	30 16.22 1.87 0.33 0.12	-	-	13 4.78 18.31 1.77 0.05	-	-	-	-	151 7.42 9.40 1.64 0.61
University Place (city)	6,591 33.86	1,485	502 33.80 33.80 7.62	-	-	-	-	-	-	-	-	-	-	-	-	-	239 31.74 47.61 16.09 3.63	-	-	-	-	-	-	-	-	-
Skagit County	13,904 20.76	788	278 35.28 35.28 2.00	-	-	-	-	-	-	-	110 36.18 39.57 13.96 0.79	-	-	-	-	-	-	-	-	-	-	-	-	-	-	-
Snohomish County	95,107 24.45	22,558	8,359 37.06 37.06 8.79	733	159 21.69 21.69 0.17	965 54.46 11.54 4.28 1.01	-	106 9.77 1.27 0.47 0.11	1,400 48.56 16.75 6.21 1.47	-	1,809 36.96 21.64 8.02 1.90	-	65 21.38 40.88 8.87 0.07	-	-	888 47.97 10.62 3.94 0.93	1,746 36.12 20.89 7.74 1.84	34 8.13 0.41 0.15 0.04	-	143 58.61 1.71 0.63 0.15	-	-	-	-	-	747 22.23 8.94 3.31 0.79
Alderwood Manor (cdp)	2,787 27.97	856	379 44.28 44.28 13.60	-	-	-	-	-	-	-	-	-	-	-	-	-	-	-	-	-	-	-	-	-	-	-
Edmonds (city)	10,401 36.42	1,423	725 50.95 50.95 6.97	-	-	-	-	-	-	-	111 49.12 15.31 7.80 1.07	-	-	-	-	-	167 44.41 23.03 11.74 1.61	-	-	-	-	-	-	-	-	-
Everett (city)	10,553 18.46	3,699	922 24.93 24.93 8.74	-	-	205 49.04 22.23 5.54 1.94	-	3 0.97 0.33 0.08 0.03	-	-	354 31.33 38.39 9.57 3.35	-	-	-	-	-	-	-	-	-	-	-	-	-	-	121 16.15 13.12 3.27 1.15
Lynnwood (city)	4,944 22.36	2,957	977 33.04 33.04 19.76	-	-	-	-	-	135 36.59 13.82 4.57 2.73	-	279 48.19 28.56 9.44 5.64	-	-	-	-	-	181 26.42 18.53 6.12 3.66	-	-	-	-	-	-	-	-	94 14.64 9.62 3.18 1.90
Martha Lake (cdp)	2,247 27.57	739	249 33.69 33.69 11.08	-	-	-	-	-	-	-	-	-	-	-	-	-	-	-	-	-	-	-	-	-	-	-

Notes: Please refer to the User's Guide for an explanation of data; data is arranged alphabetically by state, then county, then city within each county; table includes counties with populations greater than 49,999 unless noted and cities with populations greater than 9,999 whose Asian and/or NHPI population rates are greater than the national average; (1) Native Hawaiian and other Pacific Islander; (2) excludes Taiwanese; (3) includes Chamorro; (4) county does not meet population threshold but is shown in order to allow inclusion of city

Place	Total population 25 years and over who are 4-year college graduates	Asian population 25 years and over	Asians 25 years and over who are 4-year college graduates	NHPI[1] population 25 years and over	NHPIs[1] 25 years and over who are 4-year college graduates	Asian Indian	Bangladeshi	Cambodian	Chinese[2]	Fijian	Filipino	Guamanian[3]	Hawaiian, Native	Hmong	Indonesian	Japanese	Korean	Laotian	Malaysian	Pakistani	Samoan	Sri Lankan	Taiwanese	Thai	Tongan	Vietnamese
Marysville (city)	2,987 19.04	668	270 40.42 40.42 9.04	-	-	-	-	-	-	-	-	-	-	-	-	-	-	-	-	-	-	-	-	-	-	-
Mill Creek (city)	3,688 47.67	771	407 52.79 52.79 11.04	-	-	-	-	-	-	-	-	-	-	-	-	-	160 55.17 39.31 20.75 4.34	-	-	-	-	-	-	-	-	-
Mountlake Terrace (city)	3,246 24.38	1,506	536 35.59 35.59 16.51	-	-	-	-	-	-	-	85 24.50 15.86 5.64 2.62	-	-	-	-	-	197 46.14 36.75 13.08 6.07	-	-	-	-	-	-	-	-	-
Mukilteo (city)	4,979 42.69	1,332	663 49.77 49.77 13.32	-	-	-	-	-	-	-	-	-	-	-	-	-	237 41.58 35.75 17.79 4.76	-	-	-	-	-	-	-	-	-
North Creek (cdp)	5,722 35.13	1,035	515 49.76 49.76 9.00	-	-	-	-	-	-	-	-	-	-	-	-	-	-	-	-	-	-	-	-	-	-	-
Paine Field-Lk. Stickney (cdp)	2,045 13.61	1,034	218 21.08 21.08 10.66	-	-	-	-	-	-	-	-	-	-	-	-	-	-	-	-	-	-	-	-	-	-	-
Picnic Pt.-N. Lynnwood (cdp)	4,663 32.04	1,547	672 43.44 43.44 14.41	-	-	-	-	-	-	-	114 46.53 16.96 7.37 2.44	-	-	-	-	-	236 39.86 35.12 15.26 5.06	-	-	-	-	-	-	-	-	-
Seattle Hill-Silver Firs (cdp)	7,141 31.93	1,752	754 43.04 43.04 10.56	-	-	-	-	-	-	-	91 30.64 12.07 5.19 1.27	-	-	-	-	-	183 42.36 24.27 10.45 2.56	-	-	-	-	-	-	-	-	141 43.12 18.70 8.05 1.97
Spokane County	66,764 25.02	4,488	1,275 28.41 28.41 1.91	381	41 10.76 10.76 0.06	214 62.57 16.78 4.77 0.32	-	-	303 51.27 23.76 6.75 0.45	-	198 29.38 15.53 4.41 0.30	-	-	12 5.43 0.94 0.27 0.02	-	328 31.78 25.73 7.31 0.49	65 19.46 5.10 1.45 0.10	-	-	-	-	-	-	-	-	113 12.36 8.86 2.52 0.17
Spokane (city)	31,992 25.37	2,571	537 20.89 20.89 1.68	244	36 14.75 14.75 0.11	-	-	-	110 33.64 20.48 4.28 0.34	-	87 25.89 16.20 3.38 0.27	-	-	6 4.11 1.12 0.23 0.02	-	205 30.69 38.18 7.97 0.64	31 19.38 5.77 1.21 0.10	-	-	-	-	-	-	-	-	46 8.30 8.57 1.79 0.14

Notes: Please refer to the User's Guide for an explanation of data; data is arranged alphabetically by state, then county, then city within each county; table includes counties with populations greater than 49,999 unless noted and cities with populations greater than 9,999 whose Asian and/or NHPI population rates are greater than the national average; (1) Native Hawaiian and other Pacific Islander; (2) excludes Taiwanese; (3) includes Chamorro; (4) county does not meet population threshold but is shown in order to allow inclusion of city

Place	Total population 25 years and over who are 4-year college graduates	Asian population 25 years and over	Asians 25 years and over who are 4-year college graduates	NHPI[1] population 25 years and over	NHPIs[1] 25 years and over who are 4-year college graduates	Asian Indian	Bangladeshi	Cambodian	Chinese[2]	Fijian	Filipino	Guamanian[3]	Hawaiian, Native	Hmong	Indonesian	Japanese	Korean	Laotian	Malaysian	Pakistani	Samoan	Sri Lankan	Taiwanese	Thai	Tongan	Vietnamese
Thurston County	40,491 29.84	6,055	1,608 26.56 26.56 3.97	709	78 11.00 11.00 0.19	189 57.62 11.75 3.12 0.47	-	20 4.94 1.24 0.33 0.05	239 43.53 14.86 3.95 0.59	-	355 30.19 22.08 5.86 0.88	69 15.27 88.46 9.73 0.17	-	-	-	191 38.35 11.88 3.15 0.47	323 20.96 20.09 5.33 0.80	-	-	-	-	-	-	-	-	231 20.17 14.37 3.82 0.57
Lacey (city)	5,418 26.90	1,690	355 21.01 21.01 6.55	-	-	-	-	-	-	-	72 23.53 20.28 4.26 1.33	-	-	-	-	-	85 17.60 23.94 5.03 1.57	-	-	-	-	-	-	-	-	69 18.06 19.44 4.08 1.27
Olympia (city)	11,377 40.32	1,520	536 35.26 35.26 4.71	-	-	-	-	-	-	-	-	-	-	-	-	-	-	-	-	-	-	-	-	-	-	68 14.78 12.69 4.47 0.60
Tumwater (city)	2,777 33.22	302	126 41.72 41.72 4.54	-	-	-	-	-	-	-	-	-	-	-	-	-	-	-	-	-	-	-	-	-	-	-
Walla Walla County	8,010 23.30	363	112 30.85 30.85 1.40	-	-	-	-	-	-	-	-	-	-	-	-	-	-	-	-	-	-	-	-	-	-	-
Whatcom County	27,988 27.23	2,315	716 30.93 30.93 2.56	-	-	214 30.84 29.89 9.24 0.76	-	-	119 38.26 16.62 5.14 0.43	-	102 38.93 14.25 4.41 0.36	-	-	-	-	107 37.02 14.94 4.62 0.38	62 50.41 8.66 2.68 0.22	-	-	-	-	-	-	-	-	33 8.46 4.61 1.43 0.12
Bellingham (city)	12,947 33.03	1,297	438 33.77 33.77 3.38	-	-	131 42.26 29.91 10.10 1.01	-	-	-	-	-	-	-	-	-	-	-	-	-	-	-	-	-	-	-	18 6.21 4.11 1.39 0.14
Whitman County[4]	8,839 44.04	1,086	803 73.94 73.94 9.08	-	-	-	-	-	320 79.01 39.85 29.47 3.62	-	-	-	-	-	-	172 69.35 21.42 15.84 1.95	-	-	-	-	-	-	-	-	-	-
Pullman (city)	6,051 65.30	963	738 76.64 76.64 12.20	-	-	-	-	-	285 82.85 38.62 29.60 4.71	-	-	-	-	-	-	165 69.04 22.36 17.13 2.73	-	-	-	-	-	-	-	-	-	-
Yakima County	20,005 15.30	1,474	382 25.92 25.92 1.91	-	-	-	-	-	-	-	142 20.08 37.17 9.63 0.71	-	-	-	-	-	-	-	-	-	-	-	-	-	-	-

Notes: Please refer to the User's Guide for an explanation of data; data is arranged alphabetically by state, then county, then city within each county; table includes counties with populations greater than 49,999 unless noted and cities with populations greater than 9,999 whose Asian and/or NHPI population rates are greater than the national average; (1) Native Hawaiian and other Pacific Islander; (2) excludes Taiwanese; (3) includes Chamorro; (4) county does not meet population threshold but is shown in order to allow inclusion of city

Place	Total population 25 years and over who are 4-year college graduates	Asian population 25 years and over	Asians 25 years and over who are 4-year college graduates	NHPI[1] population 25 years and over	NHPIs[1] 25 years and over who are 4-year college graduates	Asian Indian	Bangladeshi	Cambodian	Chinese[2]	Fijian	Filipino	Guamanian[3]	Hawaiian, Native	Hmong	Indonesian	Japanese	Korean	Laotian	Malaysian	Pakistani	Samoan	Sri Lankan	Taiwanese	Thai	Tongan	Vietnamese
WEST VIRGINIA	182,960	5,937	3,792	187	8	1,361	-	-	675	-	841	-	-	-	-	193	230	-	-	163	-	-	-	-	-	49
	14.83		63.87		4.28	83.14			66.77		69.16					40.38	48.02			79.51						15.22
						35.89			17.80		22.18					5.09	6.07			4.30						1.29
			63.87		4.28	22.92			11.37		14.17					3.25	3.87			2.75						0.83
			2.07		<0.01	0.74			0.37		0.46					0.11	0.13			0.09						0.03
Cabell County	13,501	482	259	-	-	-	-	-	-	-	-	-	-	-	-	-	-	-	-	-	-	-	-	-	-	-
	20.95		53.73																							
			53.73																							
			1.92																							
Harrison County	7,630	155	86	-	-	-	-	-	-	-	-	-	-	-	-	-	-	-	-	-	-	-	-	-	-	-
	16.28		55.48																							
			55.48																							
			1.13																							
Kanawha County	28,937	1,082	767	-	-	354	-	-	-	-	-	-	-	-	-	-	-	-	-	-	-	-	-	-	-	-
	20.58		70.89			88.06																				
						46.15																				
			70.89			32.72																				
			2.65			1.22																				
Monongalia County	15,551	1,148	939	-	-	276	-	-	377	-	-	-	-	-	-	-	-	-	-	-	-	-	-	-	-	-
	32.44		81.79			95.83			91.28																	
						29.39			40.15																	
			81.79			24.04			32.84																	
			6.04			1.77			2.42																	
Putnam County	6,859	172	87	-	-	-	-	-	-	-	-	-	-	-	-	-	-	-	-	-	-	-	-	-	-	-
	19.68		50.58																							
			50.58																							
			1.27																							
Raleigh County	6,991	482	323	-	-	-	-	-	-	-	-	-	-	-	-	-	-	-	-	-	-	-	-	-	-	-
	12.66		67.01																							
			67.01																							
			4.62																							
Wood County	9,250	261	151	-	-	-	-	-	-	-	-	-	-	-	-	-	-	-	-	-	-	-	-	-	-	-
	15.24		57.85																							
			57.85																							
			1.63																							
WISCONSIN	779,273	39,469	16,973	795	141	5,090	-	28	3,841	-	2,063	39	48	698	137	1,133	1,830	191	-	248	-	-	306	317	-	442
	22.42		43.00		17.74	74.08		10.61	66.45		55.16	18.66	20.34	7.16	69.90	49.71	55.95	10.70		51.45			73.03	59.92		18.42
						29.99		0.16	22.63		12.15	27.66	34.04	4.11	0.81	6.68	10.78	1.13		1.46			1.80	1.87		2.60
			43.00		17.74	12.90		0.07	9.73		5.23	4.91	6.04	1.77	0.35	2.87	4.64	0.48		0.63			0.78	0.80		1.12
			2.18		0.02	0.65		<0.01	0.49		0.26	0.01	0.01	0.09	0.02	0.15	0.23	0.02		0.03			0.04	0.04		0.06
Brown County	32,389	1,816	387	-	-	118	-	-	-	-	-	-	-	22	-	-	-	0	-	-	-	-	-	-	-	-
	22.47		21.31			65.56								2.81				0.00								
						30.49								5.68				0.00								
			21.31			6.50								1.21				0.00								
			1.19			0.36								0.07				0.00								

Notes: Please refer to the User's Guide for an explanation of data; data is arranged alphabetically by state, then county, then city within each county; table includes counties with populations greater than 49,999 unless noted and cities with populations greater than 9,999 whose Asian and/or NHPI population rates are greater than the national average; (1) Native Hawaiian and other Pacific Islander; (2) excludes Taiwanese; (3) includes Chamorro; (4) county does not meet population threshold but is shown in order to allow inclusion of city

Place	Total population 25 years and over who are 4-year college graduates	Asian population 25 years and over	Asians 25 years and over who are 4-year college graduates	NHPI[1] population 25 years and over	NHPIs[1] 25 years and over who are 4-year college graduates	Asian Indian	Bangladeshi	Cambodian	Chinese[2]	Fijian	Filipino	Guamanian[3]	Hawaiian, Native	Hmong	Indonesian	Japanese	Korean	Laotian	Malaysian	Pakistani	Samoan	Sri Lankan	Taiwanese	Thai	Tongan	Vietnamese
Chippewa County	5,328 14.67	189	55 29.10 29.10 1.03	-	-	-	-	-	-	-	-	-	-	15 13.76 27.27 7.94 0.28	-	-	-	-	-	-	-	-	-	-	-	-
Columbia County	5,941 16.72	105	44 41.90 41.90 0.74	-	-	-	-	-	-	-	-	-	-	-	-	-	-	-	-	-	-	-	-	-	-	-
Dane County	109,723 40.64	7,452	4,881 65.50 65.50 4.45	-	-	975 78.82 19.98 13.08 0.89	-	-	1,371 78.75 28.09 18.40 1.25	-	280 62.36 5.74 3.76 0.26	-	-	65 8.95 1.33 0.87 0.06	-	439 70.47 8.99 5.89 0.40	881 87.06 18.05 11.82 0.80	18 10.59 0.37 0.24 0.02	-	-	-	-	205 75.65 4.20 2.75 0.19	-	-	152 32.90 3.11 2.04 0.14
Madison (city)	61,057 48.15	5,993	4,022 67.11 67.11 6.59	-	-	648 81.20 16.11 10.81 1.06	-	-	1,152 77.89 28.64 19.22 1.89	-	191 64.09 4.75 3.19 0.31	-	-	56 9.74 1.39 0.93 0.09	-	375 73.10 9.32 6.26 0.61	844 89.69 20.98 14.08 1.38	-	-	-	-	-	202 75.37 5.02 3.37 0.33	-	-	130 32.42 3.23 2.17 0.21
Dodge County	7,602 13.23	147	68 46.26 46.26 0.89	-	-	-	-	-	-	-	-	-	-	-	-	-	-	-	-	-	-	-	-	-	-	-
Eau Claire County	14,936 27.01	845	224 26.51 26.51 1.50	-	-	-	-	-	-	-	-	-	-	55 13.06 24.55 6.51 0.37	-	-	-	-	-	-	-	-	-	-	-	-
Fond du Lac County	10,715 16.86	247	93 37.65 37.65 0.87	-	-	-	-	-	-	-	-	-	-	0 0.00 0.00 0.00 0.00	-	-	-	-	-	-	-	-	-	-	-	-
Jefferson County	8,521 17.37	118	47 39.83 39.83 0.55	-	-	-	-	-	-	-	-	-	-	-	-	-	-	-	-	-	-	-	-	-	-	-
Kenosha County	18,246 19.20	855	456 53.33 53.33 2.50	-	-	-	-	-	-	-	-	-	-	-	-	-	-	-	-	-	-	-	-	-	-	-
La Crosse County	16,570 25.39	965	270 27.98 27.98 1.63	-	-	-	-	-	-	-	-	-	-	36 6.43 13.33 3.73 0.22	-	-	-	-	-	-	-	-	-	-	-	-

Notes: Please refer to the User's Guide for an explanation of data; data is arranged alphabetically by state, then county, then city within each county; table includes counties with populations greater than 49,999 unless noted and cities with populations greater than 9,999 whose Asian and/or NHPI population rates are greater than the national average; (1) Native Hawaiian and other Pacific Islander; (2) excludes Taiwanese; (3) includes Chamorro; (4) county does not meet population threshold but is shown in order to allow inclusion of city

Place	Total population 25 years and over who are 4-year college graduates	Asian population 25 years and over	Asians 25 years and over who are 4-year college graduates	NHPI[1] population 25 years and over	NHPIs[1] 25 years and over who are 4-year college graduates	Asian Indian	Bangladeshi	Cambodian	Chinese[2]	Fijian	Filipino	Guamanian[3]	Hawaiian, Native	Hmong	Indonesian	Japanese	Korean	Laotian	Malaysian	Pakistani	Samoan	Sri Lankan	Taiwanese	Thai	Tongan	Vietnamese
La Crosse (city)	7,081 24.09	642	166 25.86 25.86 2.34	-	-	-	-	-	-	-	-	-	-	8 2.13 4.82 1.25 0.11	-	-	-	-	-	-	-	-	-	-	-	-
Manitowoc County	8,579 15.47	598	128 21.40 21.40 1.49	-	-	-	-	-	-	-	-	-	-	20 6.01 15.63 3.34 0.23	-	-	-	-	-	-	-	-	-	-	-	-
Marathon County	14,994 18.30	1,645	184 11.19 11.19 1.23	-	-	-	-	-	-	-	-	-	-	53 4.41 28.80 3.22 0.35	-	-	-	-	-	-	-	-	-	-	-	-
Wausau (city)	5,409 21.53	1,304	128 9.82 9.82 2.37	-	-	-	-	-	-	-	-	-	-	36 3.60 28.13 2.76 0.67	-	-	-	-	-	-	-	-	-	-	-	-
Milwaukee County	140,460 23.63	11,781	4,757 40.38 40.38 3.39	270	50 18.52 18.52 0.04	1,676 67.36 35.23 14.23 1.19	-	-	938 59.82 19.72 7.96 0.67	-	678 61.80 14.25 5.76 0.48	-	-	210 8.20 4.41 1.78 0.15	-	225 36.06 4.73 1.91 0.16	350 48.08 7.36 2.97 0.25	92 11.15 1.93 0.78 0.07	-	114 50.44 2.40 0.97 0.08	-	-	-	-	-	136 15.25 2.86 1.15 0.10
Outagamie County	23,016 22.52	1,440	413 28.68 28.68 1.79	-	-	104 61.54 25.18 7.22 0.45	-	-	-	-	-	-	-	49 6.19 11.86 3.40 0.21	-	-	-	-	-	-	-	-	-	-	-	-
Appleton (city)	13,137 29.70	1,158	258 22.28 22.28 1.96	-	-	-	-	-	-	-	-	-	-	56 7.23 21.71 4.84 0.43	-	-	-	-	-	-	-	-	-	-	-	-
Ozaukee County	21,201 38.61	403	290 71.96 71.96 1.37	-	-	-	-	-	-	-	-	-	-	-	-	-	-	-	-	-	-	-	-	-	-	-
Portage County	9,378 23.36	395	60 15.19 15.19 0.64	-	-	-	-	-	-	-	-	-	-	3 1.40 5.00 0.76 0.03	-	-	-	-	-	-	-	-	-	-	-	-
Stevens Point (city)	3,259 26.11	310	29 9.35 9.35 0.89	-	-	-	-	-	-	-	-	-	-	3 1.64 10.34 0.97 0.09	-	-	-	-	-	-	-	-	-	-	-	-

Notes: Please refer to the User's Guide for an explanation of data; data is arranged alphabetically by state, then county, then city within each county; table includes counties with populations greater than 49,999 unless noted and cities with populations greater than 9,999 whose Asian and/or NHPI population rates are greater than the national average; (1) Native Hawaiian and other Pacific Islander; (2) excludes Taiwanese; (3) includes Chamorro; (4) county does not meet population threshold but is shown in order to allow inclusion of city

Place	Total population 25 years and over who are 4-year college graduates	Asian population 25 years and over	Asians 25 years and over who are 4-year college graduates	NHPI[1] population 25 years and over	NHPIs[1] 25 years and over who are 4-year college graduates	Asian Indian	Bangladeshi	Cambodian	Chinese[2]	Fijian	Filipino	Guamanian[3]	Hawaiian, Native	Hmong	Indonesian	Japanese	Korean	Laotian	Malaysian	Pakistani	Samoan	Sri Lankan	Taiwanese	Thai	Tongan	Vietnamese
Racine County	24,799 20.27	755	345 45.70 45.70 1.39	-	-	-	-	-	-	-	-	-	-	-	-	-	-	-	-	-	-	-	-	-	-	-
Rock County	16,479 16.68	747	290 38.82 38.82 1.76	-	-	-	-	-	-	-	-	-	-	-	-	-	-	-	-	-	-	-	-	-	-	-
St. Croix County	10,606 26.28	153	75 49.02 49.02 0.71	-	-	-	-	-	-	-	-	-	-	-	-	-	-	-	-	-	-	-	-	-	-	-
Sauk County	6,460 17.60	113	55 48.67 48.67 0.85	-	-	-	-	-	-	-	-	-	-	-	-	-	-	-	-	-	-	-	-	-	-	-
Sheboygan County	13,356 17.91	1,347	206 15.29 15.29 1.54	-	-	-	-	-	-	-	-	-	-	61 7.76 29.61 4.53 0.46	-	-	-	-	-	-	-	-	-	-	-	-
Sheboygan (city)	5,281 15.85	1,203	176 14.63 14.63 3.33	-	-	-	-	-	-	-	-	-	-	61 8.08 34.66 5.07 1.16	-	-	-	-	-	-	-	-	-	-	-	-
Walworth County	12,672 21.79	318	139 43.71 43.71 1.10	-	-	-	-	-	-	-	-	-	-	-	-	-	-	-	-	-	-	-	-	-	-	-
Washington County	17,057 21.95	288	91 31.60 31.60 0.53	-	-	-	-	-	-	-	-	-	-	-	-	-	-	-	-	-	-	-	-	-	-	-
Waukesha County	82,263 34.09	3,100	2,114 68.19 68.19 2.57	-	-	927 87.87 43.85 29.90 1.13	-	-	568 80.34 26.87 18.32 0.69	-	208 69.33 9.84 6.71 0.25	-	-	-	-	-	98 35.64 4.64 3.16 0.12	-	-	-	-	-	-	-	-	-
Winnebago County	23,028 22.78	1,053	405 38.46 38.46 1.76	-	-	-	-	-	-	-	-	-	-	50 11.26 12.35 4.75 0.22	-	-	-	-	-	-	-	-	-	-	-	-

Notes: Please refer to the User's Guide for an explanation of data; data is arranged alphabetically by state, then county, then city within each county; table includes counties with populations greater than 49,999 unless noted and cities with populations greater than 9,999 whose Asian and/or NHPI population rates are greater than the national average; (1) Native Hawaiian and other Pacific Islander; (2) excludes Taiwanese; (3) includes Chamorro; (4) county does not meet population threshold but is shown in order to allow inclusion of city

Place	Total population 25 years and over who are 4-year college graduates	Asian population 25 years and over	Asians 25 years and over who are 4-year college graduates	NHPI[1] population 25 years and over	NHPIs[1] 25 years and over who are 4-year college graduates	Asian Indian	Bangladeshi	Cambodian	Chinese[2]	Fijian	Filipino	Guamanian[3]	Hawaiian, Native	Hmong	Indonesian	Japanese	Korean	Laotian	Malaysian	Pakistani	Samoan	Sri Lankan	Taiwanese	Thai	Tongan	Vietnamese
Wood County	8,486 16.88	445	177 39.78 39.78 2.09	-	-	-	-	-	-	-	-	-	-	4 2.56 2.26 0.90 0.05	-	-	-	-	-	-	-	-	-	-	-	-
WYOMING	69,162 21.91	1,910	694 36.34 36.34 1.00	-	-	170 62.04 24.50 8.90 0.25	-	-	167 42.60 24.06 8.74 0.24	-	112 34.57 16.14 5.86 0.16	-	-	-	-	112 26.73 16.14 5.86 0.16	69 26.44 9.94 3.61 0.10	-	-	-	-	-	-	-	-	-
Laramie County	12,438 23.45	517	137 26.50 26.50 1.10	-	-	-	-	-	-	-	-	-	-	-	-	-	-	-	-	-	-	-	-	-	-	-
Natrona County	8,538 20.02	257	94 36.58 36.58 1.10	-	-	-	-	-	-	-	-	-	-	-	-	-	-	-	-	-	-	-	-	-	-	-

Notes: Please refer to the User's Guide for an explanation of data; data is arranged alphabetically by state, then county, then city within each county; table includes counties with populations greater than 49,999 unless noted and cities with populations greater than 9,999 whose Asian and/or NHPI population rates are greater than the national average; (1) Native Hawaiian and other Pacific Islander; (2) excludes Taiwanese; (3) includes Chamorro; (4) county does not meet population threshold but is shown in order to allow inclusion of city

Median Household Income

(Universe: Households)

Place	All households	Asian households	NHPI[1] households	Asian Indian	Bangladeshi	Cambodian	Chinese[2]	Fijian	Filipino	Guamanian[3]	Hawaiian, Native	Hmong	Indonesian	Japanese	Korean	Laotian	Malaysian	Pakistani	Samoan	Sri Lankan	Taiwanese	Thai	Tongan	Vietnamese
UNITED STATES	41,994	51,908	42,717	63,669	39,321	36,155	51,321	45,420	60,570	46,306	44,554	32,076	38,175	52,060	40,037	42,978	35,767	47,241	40,620	52,661	54,928	40,329	45,700	45,085
ALABAMA	34,135	42,007	37,583	54,113	-	28,661	33,281	-	46,429	37,625	-	-	-	44,524	31,445	37,500	-	51,875	-	-	-	26,406	-	38,750
Baldwin County	40,250	53,864	-	-	-	-	-	-	-	-	-	-	-	-	-	-	-	-	-	-	-	-	-	-
Calhoun County	31,768	35,179	-	-	-	-	-	-	-	-	-	-	-	-	-	-	-	-	-	-	-	-	-	-
Etowah County	31,170	55,500	-	-	-	-	-	-	-	-	-	-	-	-	-	-	-	-	-	-	-	-	-	-
Houston County	34,431	32,083	-	-	-	-	-	-	-	-	-	-	-	-	-	-	-	-	-	-	-	-	-	-
Jefferson County	36,868	44,224	-	51,964	-	-	41,042	-	-	-	-	-	-	-	17,153	-	-	-	-	-	-	-	-	31,250
Lee County	30,952	30,602	-	-	-	-	33,958	-	-	-	-	-	-	-	-	-	-	-	-	-	-	-	-	-
Madison County	44,704	50,884	-	61,759	-	-	47,167	-	-	-	-	-	-	-	34,107	-	-	-	-	-	-	-	-	63,750
Mobile County	33,710	37,762	-	50,048	-	22,679	38,833	-	47,321	-	-	-	-	-	-	32,344	-	-	-	-	-	-	-	36,250
Montgomery County	35,962	49,423	-	-	-	-	-	-	-	-	-	-	-	-	-	-	-	-	-	-	-	-	-	-
Morgan County	37,803	52,065	-	-	-	-	-	-	-	-	-	-	-	-	-	-	-	-	-	-	-	-	-	-
Shelby County	55,440	67,763	-	69,408	-	-	-	-	-	-	-	-	-	-	-	-	-	-	-	-	-	-	-	-
Tuscaloosa County	34,436	17,941	-	-	-	-	-	-	-	-	-	-	-	-	-	-	-	-	-	-	-	-	-	-
ALASKA	51,571	47,121	38,258	45,417	-	-	58,375	-	53,507	-	51,625	25,179	-	51,898	30,442	31,563	-	-	40,750	-	-	52,125	48,167	55,455
Anchorage Borough	55,546	44,575	41,875	47,417	-	-	58,125	-	49,367	-	-	25,179	-	50,625	30,505	30,625	-	-	39,934	-	-	49,286	-	50,000
Fairbanks North Star Borough	49,076	39,514	-	-	-	-	56,250	-	58,750	-	-	-	-	-	18,750	-	-	-	-	-	-	-	-	-
Juneau City and Borough	62,034	69,118	-	-	-	-	-	-	71,094	-	-	-	-	-	-	-	-	-	-	-	-	-	-	-
Matanuska-Susitna Borough	51,221	75,942	-	-	-	-	-	-	-	-	-	-	-	-	-	-	-	-	-	-	-	-	-	-
ARIZONA	40,558	45,802	39,688	64,122	-	53,958	46,576	-	47,237	47,663	36,033	-	28,125	44,227	34,528	49,375	-	63,214	43,152	-	54,911	29,336	46,964	42,308
Cochise County	32,105	37,531	-	-	-	-	-	-	39,485	-	-	-	-	-	26,838	-	-	-	-	-	-	-	-	-
Coconino County	38,256	49,716	-	-	-	-	-	-	-	-	-	-	-	-	-	-	-	-	-	-	-	-	-	-
Maricopa County	45,358	50,991	41,295	68,345	-	53,449	51,705	-	52,170	40,833	39,395	-	28,125	48,787	39,252	63,281	-	62,679	50,268	-	61,250	29,583	46,964	45,527
Chandler (city)	58,416	71,621	-	93,709	-	-	61,250	-	65,104	-	-	-	-	-	-	-	-	-	-	-	-	-	-	59,911
Gilbert (town)	68,032	74,750	-	92,947	-	-	77,400	-	77,379	-	-	-	-	-	-	-	-	-	-	-	-	-	-	-
Mesa (city)	42,817	49,813	66,875	48,472	-	-	53,333	-	63,869	-	-	-	-	47,218	39,565	-	-	-	-	-	-	-	-	48,125
Phoenix (city)	41,207	48,519	38,654	63,036	-	53,438	49,713	-	48,042	-	35,417	-	-	49,323	41,625	-	-	-	-	-	-	-	-	38,352
Tempe (city)	42,361	34,558	-	46,667	-	-	35,795	-	30,972	-	-	-	-	40,476	15,250	-	-	-	-	-	-	-	-	43,750
Mohave County	31,521	43,906	-	-	-	-	-	-	-	-	-	-	-	-	-	-	-	-	-	-	-	-	-	-
Pima County	36,758	31,673	30,125	40,658	-	-	30,889	-	31,581	-	24,155	-	-	23,229	23,629	-	-	-	-	-	-	-	-	38,000
Tucson (city)	30,981	25,282	23,547	28,750	-	-	22,241	-	31,121	-	-	-	-	16,406	16,470	-	-	-	-	-	-	-	-	33,571
Pinal County	35,856	36,304	-	-	-	-	-	-	-	-	-	-	-	-	-	-	-	-	-	-	-	-	-	-
Yavapai County	34,901	36,957	-	-	-	-	-	-	-	-	-	-	-	-	-	-	-	-	-	-	-	-	-	-
Yuma County	32,182	36,250	-	-	-	-	-	-	37,583	-	-	-	-	-	-	-	-	-	-	-	-	-	-	-
ARKANSAS	32,182	37,841	28,322	56,833	-	-	40,275	-	35,765	-	22,143	-	-	31,310	26,625	36,906	-	-	-	-	-	26,250	-	38,102
Benton County	40,281	51,131	-	58,869	-	-	-	-	-	-	-	-	-	-	-	-	-	-	-	-	-	-	-	46,250
Craighead County	32,425	23,147	-	-	-	-	-	-	-	-	-	-	-	-	-	-	-	-	-	-	-	-	-	-
Crawford County	32,871	38,382	-	-	-	-	-	-	-	-	-	-	-	-	-	-	-	-	-	-	-	-	-	-

Notes: Please refer to the User's Guide for an explanation of data; data is arranged alphabetically by state, then county, then city within each county; table includes counties with populations greater than 49,999 unless noted and cities with populations greater than 9,999 whose Asian and/or NHPI population rates are greater than the national average; (1) Native Hawaiian and other Pacific Islander; (2) excludes Taiwanese; (3) includes Chamorro; (4) county does not meet population threshold but is shown in order to allow inclusion of city

Place	All households	Asian households	NHPI[1] households	Asian Indian	Bangladeshi	Cambodian	Chinese[2]	Fijian	Filipino	Guamanian[3]	Hawaiian, Native	Hmong	Indonesian	Japanese	Korean	Laotian	Malaysian	Pakistani	Samoan	Sri Lankan	Taiwanese	Thai	Tongan	Vietnamese
Faulkner County	38,204	38,333	-	-	-	-	-	-	-	-	-	-	-	-	-	-	-	-	-	-	-	-	-	-
Jefferson County	31,327	36,875	-	-	-	-	-	-	-	-	-	-	-	-	-	-	-	-	-	-	-	-	-	-
Pulaski County	38,120	41,397	-	52,500	-	-	45,156	-	41,875	-	-	-	-	-	-	-	-	-	-	-	-	-	-	-
Saline County	42,569	62,500	-	-	-	-	-	-	-	-	-	-	-	-	-	-	-	-	-	-	-	-	-	-
Sebastian County	33,889	34,873	-	-	-	-	-	-	-	-	-	-	-	-	-	31,779	-	-	-	-	-	-	-	38,750
Fort Smith (city)	32,157	34,492	-	-	-	-	-	-	-	-	-	-	-	-	-	32,163	-	-	-	-	-	-	-	37,813
Washington County	34,691	27,039	30,391	-	-	-	16,250	-	-	-	-	-	-	-	-	41,339	-	-	-	-	-	-	-	-
Springdale (city)	36,729	40,592	30,625	-	-	-	-	-	-	-	-	-	-	-	-	42,396	-	-	-	-	-	-	-	-
CALIFORNIA	47,493	55,366	48,650	72,130	46,488	27,579	57,457	45,656	62,143	52,475	50,395	24,542	44,538	55,577	40,758	31,353	62,404	52,393	45,169	61,731	56,986	45,533	49,470	48,443
Alameda County	55,946	62,450	54,231	80,674	-	29,483	58,158	52,054	70,645	61,654	51,667	-	85,155	56,333	46,356	35,603	-	68,594	58,000	-	70,595	41,450	47,596	42,397
Alameda (city)	56,285	57,922	50,982	87,408	-	-	65,988	-	54,203	-	-	-	-	49,097	51,218	-	-	-	-	-	-	-	-	28,625
Albany (city)	54,919	48,354	-	52,917	-	-	46,653	-	-	-	-	-	-	54,773	30,759	-	-	-	-	-	-	-	-	-
Ashland (cdp)	40,811	45,139	-	-	-	-	72,857	-	44,688	-	-	-	-	-	-	-	-	-	-	-	-	-	-	-
Berkeley (city)	44,485	22,533	-	22,083	-	-	19,622	-	37,768	-	-	-	-	35,200	6,833	-	-	-	-	-	8,864	-	-	17,019
Castro Valley (cdp)	64,874	82,549	-	87,571	-	-	92,843	-	79,284	-	-	-	-	50,865	61,563	-	-	-	-	-	-	-	-	-
Cherryland (cdp)	42,880	47,120	-	-	-	-	-	-	55,417	-	-	-	-	-	-	-	-	-	-	-	-	-	-	-
Dublin (city)	77,283	90,117	-	92,153	-	-	95,717	-	90,784	-	-	-	-	-	-	-	-	-	-	-	-	-	-	-
Fremont (city)	76,579	85,194	71,705	90,894	-	-	87,634	-	79,104	-	-	-	-	89,474	71,711	-	-	83,398	-	-	87,735	-	-	93,544
Hayward (city)	51,177	61,220	55,250	58,125	-	-	52,470	52,083	69,438	-	-	-	-	37,361	35,179	-	-	-	45,938	-	-	-	-	44,432
Livermore (city)	75,322	71,840	-	75,778	-	-	77,500	-	66,346	-	-	-	-	-	-	-	-	-	-	-	-	-	-	31,313
Newark (city)	69,350	77,442	-	82,066	-	-	70,455	-	85,080	-	-	-	-	-	59,934	-	-	-	-	-	-	-	-	60,648
Oakland (city)	40,055	33,614	42,378	51,324	-	24,453	32,395	-	50,497	-	-	-	-	56,118	22,500	26,364	-	-	-	-	-	-	51,000	24,657
Piedmont (city)	134,270	132,304	-	-	-	-	151,126	-	-	-	-	-	-	-	-	-	-	-	-	-	-	-	-	-
Pleasanton (city)	90,859	97,360	-	101,765	-	-	105,441	-	93,593	-	-	-	-	82,439	87,461	-	-	-	-	-	-	-	-	-
San Leandro (city)	51,081	62,417	49,500	60,536	-	-	62,155	-	66,250	-	-	-	-	43,846	60,294	-	-	-	-	-	-	-	-	60,769
San Lorenzo (cdp)	56,170	68,897	-	-	-	-	62,292	-	73,654	-	-	-	-	-	-	-	-	-	-	-	-	-	-	55,469
Union City (city)	71,926	82,557	67,188	82,063	-	-	86,495	-	83,161	-	-	-	-	52,292	62,321	-	-	-	-	-	-	-	-	72,639
Butte County	31,924	21,777	-	31,058	-	-	37,250	-	38,889	-	-	17,778	-	18,981	-	14,297	-	-	-	-	-	-	-	-
Chico (city)	29,359	19,962	-	-	-	-	39,226	-	-	-	-	13,917	-	-	-	-	-	-	-	-	-	-	-	-
Oroville (city)	21,911	13,929	-	-	-	-	-	-	-	-	-	13,846	-	-	-	-	-	-	-	-	-	-	-	-
Contra Costa County	63,675	69,600	63,589	73,301	-	-	75,113	85,000	71,906	67,614	66,174	-	57,344	66,064	56,897	38,095	-	37,578	56,705	-	65,859	83,433	70,500	48,187
Alamo (cdp)	137,105	134,432	-	-	-	-	-	-	-	-	-	-	-	-	-	-	-	-	-	-	-	-	-	-
Antioch (city)	60,359	65,767	51,607	68,214	-	-	68,603	-	75,000	-	-	-	-	-	-	-	-	-	-	-	-	-	-	48,750
Bay Point (cdp)	44,951	60,694	-	-	-	-	-	-	65,250	-	-	-	-	-	-	-	-	-	-	-	-	-	-	-
Blackhawk-Camino-Tass. (cdp)	154,598	130,793	-	-	-	-	118,693	-	-	-	-	-	-	-	-	-	-	-	-	-	-	-	-	-
Clayton (city)	101,651	89,718	-	-	-	-	-	-	-	-	-	-	-	-	-	-	-	-	-	-	-	-	-	-
Concord (city)	55,597	56,250	34,500	66,250	-	-	57,083	-	54,694	-	-	-	-	61,823	32,981	-	-	-	-	-	-	-	-	46,333
Danville (town)	114,064	115,054	-	163,809	-	-	123,183	-	108,866	-	-	-	-	-	-	-	-	-	-	-	-	-	-	-
El Cerrito (city)	57,253	55,231	-	68,958	-	-	55,000	-	74,000	-	-	-	-	58,000	-	-	-	-	-	-	-	-	-	-
El Sobrante (cdp)	48,272	57,150	-	55,859	-	-	-	-	-	-	-	-	-	-	-	-	-	-	-	-	-	-	-	-
Hercules (city)	75,196	79,883	-	65,375	-	-	73,958	-	88,089	-	-	-	-	-	-	-	-	-	-	-	-	-	-	-

Notes: Please refer to the User's Guide for an explanation of data; data is arranged alphabetically by state, then county, then city within each county; table includes counties with populations greater than 49,999 unless noted and cities with populations greater than 9,999 whose Asian and/or NHPI population rates are greater than the national average; (1) Native Hawaiian and other Pacific Islander; (2) excludes Taiwanese; (3) includes Chamorro; (4) county does not meet population threshold but is shown in order to allow inclusion of city

Place	All households	Asian households	NHPI[1] households	Asian Indian	Bangladeshi	Cambodian	Chinese[2]	Fijian	Filipino	Guamanian[3]	Hawaiian, Native	Hmong	Indonesian	Japanese	Korean	Laotian	Malaysian	Pakistani	Samoan	Sri Lankan	Taiwanese	Thai	Tongan	Vietnamese
Lafayette (city)	102,107	102,254	-	-	-	-	101,223	-	-	-	-	-	-	-	-	-	-	-	-	-	-	-	-	-
Martinez (city)	63,010	70,962	-	-	-	-	71,719	-	75,318	-	-	-	-	-	-	-	-	-	-	-	-	-	-	-
Moraga (town)	98,080	93,686	-	-	-	-	94,693	-	-	-	-	-	-	-	-	-	-	-	-	-	-	-	-	-
Orinda (city)	117,637	126,283	-	-	-	-	109,341	-	-	-	-	-	-	-	-	-	-	-	-	-	-	-	-	-
Pinole (city)	62,256	72,297	-	-	-	-	71,587	-	81,001	-	-	-	-	-	-	-	-	-	-	-	-	-	-	-
Pittsburg (city)	50,557	69,173	78,677	54,844	-	-	76,412	-	71,528	-	-	-	-	-	-	-	-	-	-	-	-	-	-	-
Pleasant Hill (city)	67,489	61,705	-	-	-	-	72,885	-	60,500	-	-	-	-	-	60,625	-	-	-	-	-	-	-	-	-
Richmond (city)	44,210	56,558	29,063	66,895	-	-	58,023	-	71,042	-	-	-	-	59,205	50,781	39,444	-	-	-	-	-	-	-	31,379
San Pablo (city)	37,184	47,736	-	48,750	-	-	-	-	71,442	-	-	-	-	-	-	33,750	-	-	-	-	-	-	-	27,813
San Ramon (city)	95,856	102,115	-	84,140	-	-	107,900	-	104,190	-	-	-	-	103,014	-	-	-	-	-	-	-	-	-	-
Walnut Creek (city)	63,238	68,639	-	68,889	-	-	71,528	-	55,260	-	-	-	-	60,152	70,156	-	-	-	-	-	-	-	-	-
El Dorado County	51,484	53,667	-	-	-	-	-	-	44,740	-	-	-	-	65,806	-	-	-	-	-	-	-	-	-	-
El Dorado Hills (cdp)	93,483	113,984	-	-	-	-	-	-	-	-	-	-	-	-	-	-	-	-	-	-	-	-	-	-
South Lake Tahoe (city)	34,707	43,750	-	-	-	-	-	-	42,222	-	-	-	-	-	-	-	-	-	-	-	-	-	-	-
Fresno County	34,725	31,542	31,250	41,557	-	20,682	47,614	-	43,872	-	-	23,168	-	45,000	49,211	16,821	-	-	-	-	-	-	-	19,130
Clovis (city)	42,283	41,635	-	-	-	-	-	-	67,188	-	-	24,203	-	45,893	-	-	-	-	-	-	-	-	-	-
Fresno (city)	32,236	27,610	-	35,833	-	22,768	45,000	-	42,348	-	-	22,663	-	48,047	51,250	16,497	-	-	-	-	-	-	-	16,346
Reedley (city)	34,682	42,409	-	-	-	-	-	-	-	-	-	-	-	-	-	-	-	-	-	-	-	-	-	-
Humboldt County	31,226	30,145	-	-	-	-	-	-	-	-	-	-	-	27,321	-	-	-	-	-	-	-	-	-	-
Imperial County	31,870	44,706	-	-	-	-	33,917	-	50,000	-	-	-	-	-	53,250	-	-	-	-	-	-	-	-	-
Kern County	35,446	44,113	43,846	52,654	-	41,250	53,011	-	37,973	-	-	-	-	50,982	46,212	-	-	-	-	-	-	-	-	43,750
Bakersfield (city)	39,982	48,438	44,327	53,298	-	-	57,560	-	39,583	-	-	-	-	58,011	45,795	-	-	-	-	-	-	-	-	43,250
Delano (city)	28,143	39,013	-	-	-	-	-	-	37,993	-	-	-	-	-	-	-	-	-	-	-	-	-	-	-
Ridgecrest (city)	44,971	51,250	-	-	-	-	-	-	40,547	-	-	-	-	-	-	-	-	-	-	-	-	-	-	-
Kings County	35,749	37,986	-	-	-	-	-	-	37,938	-	-	-	-	-	-	-	-	-	-	-	-	-	-	-
Lemoore (city)	40,314	40,729	-	-	-	-	-	-	38,750	-	-	-	-	-	-	-	-	-	-	-	-	-	-	-
Lake County	29,627	36,786	-	-	-	-	-	-	-	-	-	-	-	-	-	-	-	-	-	-	-	-	-	-
Los Angeles County	42,189	47,631	42,363	59,085	35,769	26,779	46,503	38,487	58,499	52,321	44,148	26,094	37,304	51,736	35,292	38,007	50,694	41,563	40,885	60,116	50,925	45,325	39,861	40,505
Agoura Hills (city)	87,008	80,399	-	-	-	-	-	-	-	-	-	-	-	-	-	-	-	-	-	-	-	-	-	-
Alhambra (city)	39,213	36,960	-	30,875	-	-	35,754	-	60,144	-	-	-	-	48,839	39,250	-	-	-	-	-	37,426	-	-	29,046
Altadena (cdp)	60,549	59,479	-	-	-	-	-	-	60,156	-	-	-	-	58,333	-	-	-	-	-	-	-	-	-	-
Arcadia (city)	56,100	59,673	-	82,362	-	-	58,319	-	58,438	-	-	-	-	80,381	57,250	-	-	-	-	-	58,319	-	-	-
Artesia (city)	44,500	48,438	-	35,962	-	-	60,625	-	55,000	-	-	-	-	-	50,179	-	-	-	-	-	-	-	-	-
Avocado Heights (cdp)	48,712	62,109	-	-	-	-	-	-	-	-	-	-	-	-	-	-	-	-	-	-	-	-	-	-
Azusa (city)	39,191	50,368	-	-	-	-	-	-	51,912	-	-	-	-	-	-	-	-	-	-	-	-	-	-	-
Baldwin Park (city)	41,629	52,561	-	-	-	-	49,125	-	70,455	-	-	-	-	-	-	-	-	-	-	-	-	-	-	47,981
Bellflower (city)	39,362	47,796	-	-	-	39,821	-	-	51,357	-	-	-	-	-	41,094	-	-	-	-	-	-	51,058	-	-
Beverly Hills (city)	70,945	61,985	-	-	-	-	85,531	-	-	-	-	-	-	-	60,795	-	-	-	-	-	-	-	-	-
Burbank (city)	47,467	56,204	-	51,250	-	-	59,000	-	57,391	-	-	-	-	57,813	43,025	-	-	-	-	-	-	-	-	60,917
Calabasas (city)	93,860	87,760	-	-	-	-	155,292	-	-	-	-	-	-	-	-	-	-	-	-	-	-	-	-	-
Carson (city)	52,284	60,516	53,487	-	-	-	48,958	-	62,694	-	-	-	-	51,131	-	-	-	-	55,139	-	-	-	-	43,542

Notes: Please refer to the User's Guide for an explanation of data; data is arranged alphabetically by state, then county, then city within each county; table includes counties with populations greater than 49,999 unless noted and cities with populations greater than 9,999 whose Asian and/or NHPI population rates are greater than the national average; (1) Native Hawaiian and other Pacific Islander; (2) excludes Taiwanese; (3) includes Chamorro; (4) county does not meet population threshold but is shown in order to allow inclusion of city

Place	All households	Asian households	NHPI[1] households	Asian Indian	Bangladeshi	Cambodian	Chinese[2]	Fijian	Filipino	Guamanian[3]	Hawaiian, Native	Hmong	Indonesian	Japanese	Korean	Laotian	Malaysian	Pakistani	Samoan	Sri Lankan	Taiwanese	Thai	Tongan	Vietnamese
Cerritos (city)	73,030	75,253	-	90,601	-	-	73,929	-	90,525	-	-	-	-	85,066	60,480	-	-	-	-	-	66,518	69,464	-	87,732
Citrus (cdp)	55,110	58,036	-	-	-	-	-	-	-	-	-	-	-	-	-	-	-	-	-	-	-	-	-	-
Claremont (city)	65,910	65,417	-	88,867	-	-	71,648	-	-	-	-	-	-	-	31,528	-	-	-	-	-	-	-	-	-
Compton (city)	31,819	21,750	28,450	-	-	-	-	-	-	-	-	-	-	-	-	-	-	-	27,900	-	-	-	-	-
Covina (city)	48,474	58,618	-	-	-	-	51,000	-	68,359	-	-	-	-	59,063	-	-	-	-	-	-	-	-	-	34,904
Culver City (city)	51,792	53,479	-	68,333	-	-	61,250	-	67,841	-	-	-	-	49,211	-	-	-	-	-	-	-	-	-	-
Diamond Bar (city)	68,871	66,961	-	77,893	-	-	65,278	-	84,957	-	-	-	-	80,810	57,165	-	-	-	-	-	56,691	-	-	86,058
Downey (city)	45,667	55,717	-	65,592	-	-	56,250	-	60,625	-	-	-	-	62,857	51,406	-	-	-	-	-	-	-	-	67,813
Duarte (city)	50,744	71,688	-	-	-	-	61,250	-	85,127	-	-	-	-	-	-	-	-	-	-	-	-	-	-	-
East San Gabriel (cdp)	51,301	58,125	-	-	-	-	58,523	-	-	-	-	-	-	77,177	-	-	-	-	-	-	42,188	-	-	-
El Monte (city)	32,439	38,316	-	-	-	-	39,549	-	57,697	-	-	-	-	-	-	-	-	-	-	-	20,833	-	-	32,424
El Segundo (city)	61,341	56,806	-	-	-	-	-	-	-	-	-	-	-	-	-	-	-	-	-	-	-	-	-	-
Gardena (city)	38,988	42,668	-	-	-	-	61,875	-	53,221	-	-	-	-	43,171	32,835	-	-	-	-	-	-	-	-	40,655
Glendale (city)	41,805	52,068	-	51,992	-	-	68,542	-	57,507	-	-	-	-	51,711	44,622	-	-	-	-	-	-	50,357	-	44,792
Glendora (city)	60,013	78,024	-	79,785	-	-	82,976	-	78,173	-	-	-	-	-	-	-	-	-	-	-	-	-	-	-
Hacienda Heights (cdp)	59,485	54,375	-	-	-	-	51,181	-	66,118	-	-	-	-	67,262	41,301	-	-	-	-	-	56,875	-	-	93,496
Hawaiian Gardens (city)	34,500	21,607	-	-	-	-	-	-	-	-	-	-	-	-	18,438	-	-	-	-	-	-	-	-	-
Hawthorne (city)	31,887	41,409	29,792	49,063	-	-	45,833	-	56,328	-	-	-	-	23,750	-	-	-	-	-	-	-	-	-	30,417
Hermosa Beach (city)	81,153	61,964	-	-	-	-	-	-	-	-	-	-	-	-	-	-	-	-	-	-	-	-	-	-
La Canada Flintridge (city)	109,989	106,816	-	-	-	-	133,375	-	-	-	-	-	-	161,585	90,942	-	-	-	-	-	-	-	-	-
La Crescenta-Montrose (cdp)	60,089	57,762	-	-	-	-	-	-	60,341	-	-	-	-	-	53,696	-	-	-	-	-	-	-	-	-
La Mirada (city)	61,632	67,481	-	76,997	-	-	87,391	-	87,987	-	-	-	-	55,000	40,852	-	-	-	-	-	-	-	-	-
La Puente (city)	41,222	42,930	-	-	-	-	41,705	-	46,429	-	-	-	-	-	-	-	-	-	-	-	-	-	-	-
La Verne (city)	61,326	69,018	-	-	-	-	-	-	80,717	-	-	-	-	-	-	-	-	-	-	-	-	-	-	-
Lakewood (city)	58,214	58,115	56,250	49,875	-	53,958	59,130	-	69,760	-	-	-	-	65,938	27,050	-	-	-	51,750	-	-	-	-	39,792
Lancaster (city)	41,127	51,797	-	58,917	-	-	57,273	-	52,422	-	-	-	-	-	-	-	-	-	-	-	-	-	-	-
Lawndale (city)	39,012	50,017	37,813	-	-	-	-	-	50,052	-	-	-	-	-	-	-	-	-	-	-	-	-	-	56,382
Lomita (city)	43,303	42,005	-	-	-	-	-	-	51,111	-	-	-	-	45,156	27,083	-	-	-	-	-	-	-	-	-
Long Beach (city)	37,270	36,449	31,438	46,528	-	22,673	40,650	-	52,138	-	-	-	-	35,568	22,188	23,819	-	-	30,400	-	-	31,215	-	31,867
Los Angeles (city)	36,687	37,186	40,156	47,665	33,036	26,406	33,691	-	51,090	42,083	41,976	-	27,759	40,554	26,506	34,313	-	37,201	38,438	42,733	35,029	37,769	37,083	35,146
Manhattan Beach (city)	100,750	107,770	-	-	-	-	119,220	-	-	-	-	-	-	112,207	-	-	-	-	-	-	-	-	-	-
Monrovia (city)	45,375	54,875	-	-	-	-	52,212	-	67,857	-	-	-	-	-	-	-	-	-	-	-	-	-	-	-
Montebello (city)	38,805	61,791	-	-	-	-	60,344	-	90,263	-	-	-	-	66,518	31,705	-	-	-	-	-	-	-	-	-
Monterey Park (city)	40,724	40,150	-	-	-	19,279	35,829	-	56,406	-	-	-	-	58,125	46,696	-	-	-	-	-	39,948	-	-	30,424
Norwalk (city)	46,047	52,475	-	60,114	-	79,229	51,458	-	60,000	-	-	-	-	51,563	35,583	-	-	-	-	-	-	-	-	48,333
Palmdale (city)	46,941	63,375	-	126,216	-	-	-	-	66,964	-	-	-	-	-	-	-	-	-	-	-	-	-	-	-
Palos Verdes Estates (city)	123,534	114,521	-	-	-	-	110,260	-	-	-	-	-	-	130,014	109,957	-	-	-	-	-	-	-	-	-
Pasadena (city)	46,012	49,010	-	50,069	-	-	48,079	-	56,200	-	-	-	-	55,147	36,653	-	-	-	-	-	-	-	-	46,897
Pomona (city)	40,021	46,721	-	83,353	-	21,657	38,190	-	69,063	-	-	-	-	32,228	-	42,875	-	-	-	-	-	-	-	31,131
Rancho Palos Verdes (city)	95,503	103,493	-	125,973	-	-	98,471	-	91,156	-	-	-	-	126,440	77,798	-	-	-	-	-	50,625	-	-	-
Redondo Beach (city)	69,173	80,821	-	85,860	-	-	97,293	-	73,571	-	-	-	-	85,818	62,917	-	-	-	-	-	-	-	-	-

Notes: Please refer to the User's Guide for an explanation of data; data is arranged alphabetically by state, then county, then city within each county; table includes counties with populations greater than 49,999 unless noted and cities with populations greater than 9,999 whose Asian and/or NHPI population rates are greater than the national average; (1) Native Hawaiian and other Pacific Islander; (2) excludes Taiwanese; (3) includes Chamorro; (4) county does not meet population threshold but is shown in order to allow inclusion of city

Place	All households	Asian households	NHPI[1] households	Asian Indian	Bangladeshi	Cambodian	Chinese[2]	Fijian	Filipino	Guamanian[3]	Hawaiian, Native	Hmong	Indonesian	Japanese	Korean	Laotian	Malaysian	Pakistani	Samoan	Sri Lankan	Taiwanese	Thai	Tongan	Vietnamese
Rosemead (city)	36,181	36,919	-	-	-	21,250	35,953	-	52,083	-	-	-	-	46,394	-	-	-	-	-	-	-	-	-	33,352
Rowland Heights (cdp)	52,270	50,863	-	99,704	-	-	45,993	-	64,402	-	-	-	-	63,214	45,000	-	-	-	-	-	50,893	-	-	60,625
San Dimas (city)	62,885	75,828	-	-	-	-	85,957	-	66,591	-	-	-	-	-	-	-	-	-	-	-	-	-	-	-
San Gabriel (city)	41,791	38,669	-	-	-	-	36,857	-	62,550	-	-	-	-	52,361	-	-	-	-	-	-	40,395	-	-	31,327
San Marino (city)	117,267	108,078	-	-	-	-	104,762	-	-	-	-	-	-	-	-	-	-	-	-	-	100,334	-	-	-
Santa Clarita (city)	66,717	68,375	-	61,394	-	-	82,388	-	66,447	-	-	-	-	72,390	52,361	-	-	-	-	-	-	-	-	70,625
Santa Monica (city)	50,714	47,409	-	75,296	-	-	50,965	-	44,808	-	-	-	-	42,237	40,000	-	-	-	-	-	-	-	-	-
Sierra Madre (city)	65,900	78,055	-	-	-	-	-	-	-	-	-	-	-	-	-	-	-	-	-	-	-	-	-	-
South El Monte (city)	34,656	37,500	-	-	-	-	38,229	-	-	-	-	-	-	-	-	-	-	-	-	-	-	-	-	35,703
South Pasadena (city)	55,728	57,077	-	-	-	-	64,545	-	-	-	-	-	-	60,125	43,500	-	-	-	-	-	-	-	-	-
South San Jose Hills (cdp)	48,655	61,500	-	-	-	-	-	-	77,061	-	-	-	-	-	-	-	-	-	-	-	-	-	-	-
Temple City (city)	48,722	50,653	-	-	-	-	49,223	-	76,235	-	-	-	-	69,500	55,833	-	-	-	-	-	44,688	-	-	42,000
Torrance (city)	56,489	60,912	-	66,944	-	-	70,773	-	65,900	-	-	-	-	66,324	42,394	-	-	41,094	-	-	55,962	-	-	56,161
Valinda (cdp)	49,578	55,357	-	-	-	-	-	-	82,110	-	-	-	-	-	-	-	-	-	-	-	-	-	-	47,969
Vincent (cdp)	52,349	60,486	-	-	-	-	-	-	72,321	-	-	-	-	-	-	-	-	-	-	-	-	-	-	-
Walnut (city)	81,015	79,258	-	102,813	-	-	68,313	-	94,984	-	-	-	-	63,558	72,829	-	-	-	-	-	71,458	-	-	97,790
West Carson (cdp)	49,118	60,682	-	-	-	-	-	-	63,403	-	-	-	-	62,679	43,036	-	-	-	-	-	-	-	-	-
West Covina (city)	53,002	58,185	44,107	71,786	-	-	47,933	-	71,022	-	-	-	-	57,955	34,861	-	-	-	-	-	53,646	-	-	52,569
West Hollywood (city)	38,914	47,018	-	-	-	-	-	-	-	-	-	-	-	-	-	-	-	-	-	-	-	-	-	-
West Puente Valley (cdp)	49,923	57,344	-	-	-	-	-	-	66,667	-	-	-	-	-	-	-	-	-	-	-	-	-	-	36,375
Whittier (city)	49,256	66,289	-	-	-	-	65,721	-	76,669	-	-	-	-	57,679	69,083	-	-	-	-	-	-	-	-	-
Madera County	36,286	51,964	-	51,406	-	-	-	-	49,470	-	-	-	-	-	-	-	-	-	-	-	-	-	-	-
Marin County	71,306	70,815	-	64,792	-	-	86,034	-	85,530	-	-	-	-	62,670	57,981	-	-	-	-	-	-	-	-	22,404
Larkspur (city)	66,710	70,536	-	-	-	-	-	-	-	-	-	-	-	-	-	-	-	-	-	-	-	-	-	-
Novato (city)	63,453	57,708	-	-	-	-	76,497	-	59,688	-	-	-	-	-	-	-	-	-	-	-	-	-	-	-
San Rafael (city)	60,994	75,425	-	73,571	-	-	85,980	-	-	-	-	-	-	-	-	-	-	-	-	-	-	-	-	26,458
Tamalpais-Homestead (cdp)	102,094	97,636	-	-	-	-	-	-	-	-	-	-	-	-	-	-	-	-	-	-	-	-	-	-
Mendocino County	35,996	47,083	-	-	-	-	-	-	-	-	-	-	-	-	-	-	-	-	-	-	-	-	-	-
Merced County	35,532	30,500	-	40,500	-	-	45,583	-	53,958	-	-	21,031	-	48,750	-	24,615	-	-	-	-	-	-	-	-
Atwater (city)	37,344	39,013	-	-	-	-	-	-	-	-	-	29,286	-	-	-	-	-	-	-	-	-	-	-	-
Livingston (city)	32,500	36,190	-	32,368	-	-	-	-	-	-	-	-	-	-	-	-	-	-	-	-	-	-	-	-
Merced (city)	30,429	21,934	-	-	-	-	-	-	-	-	-	20,226	-	-	-	23,795	-	-	-	-	-	-	-	-
Monterey County	48,305	48,243	43,839	51,250	-	-	50,700	-	50,284	41,667	-	-	-	47,615	45,556	-	-	-	-	-	-	-	-	37,632
Marina (city)	43,000	40,433	44,844	-	-	-	-	-	41,012	-	-	-	-	40,750	39,583	-	-	-	-	-	-	-	-	36,750
Monterey (city)	49,109	39,427	-	-	-	-	44,643	-	38,500	-	-	-	-	30,735	-	-	-	-	-	-	-	-	-	-
Pacific Grove (city)	50,254	38,589	-	-	-	-	-	-	-	-	-	-	-	-	-	-	-	-	-	-	-	-	-	-
Salinas (city)	43,720	51,930	42,109	52,333	-	-	45,987	-	54,232	-	-	-	-	49,940	51,111	-	-	-	-	-	-	-	-	46,071
Seaside (city)	41,393	47,106	-	-	-	-	-	-	50,667	-	-	-	-	35,750	-	-	-	-	-	-	-	-	-	35,391
Napa County	51,738	69,555	-	-	-	-	76,944	-	74,229	-	-	-	-	69,444	-	-	-	-	-	-	-	-	-	-
Nevada County	45,864	45,395	-	-	-	-	-	-	-	-	-	-	-	-	-	-	-	-	-	-	-	-	-	-
Orange County	58,820	58,501	53,929	76,211	-	51,188	67,965	-	67,818	57,188	56,406	71,397	50,122	65,477	47,374	66,161	-	58,938	57,206	54,509	58,553	52,599	24,375	51,311

Notes: Please refer to the User's Guide for an explanation of data; data is arranged alphabetically by state, then county, then city within each county; table includes counties with populations greater than 49,999 unless noted and cities with populations greater than 9,999 whose Asian and/or NHPI population rates are greater than the national average; (1) Native Hawaiian and other Pacific Islander; (2) excludes Taiwanese; (3) includes Chamorro; (4) county does not meet population threshold but is shown in order to allow inclusion of city

Place	All households	Asian households	NHPI[1] households	Asian Indian	Bangladeshi	Cambodian	Chinese[2]	Fijian	Filipino	Guamanian[3]	Hawaiian, Native	Hmong	Indonesian	Japanese	Korean	Laotian	Malaysian	Pakistani	Samoan	Sri Lankan	Taiwanese	Thai	Tongan	Vietnamese
Aliso Viejo (cdp)	76,409	76,610	-	96,141	-	-	60,893	-	78,944	-	-	-	-	80,325	50,074	-	-	-	-	-	-	-	-	83,636
Anaheim (city)	47,122	52,343	53,750	70,085	-	-	53,438	-	59,297	-	-	-	-	53,580	45,085	82,492	-	42,308	68,839	-	45,781	43,214	-	50,316
Brea (city)	59,759	62,760	-	85,000	-	-	101,292	-	77,570	-	-	-	-	-	36,076	-	-	-	-	-	-	-	-	-
Buena Park (city)	50,336	56,171	-	65,850	-	-	48,611	-	72,049	-	-	-	-	50,357	45,456	-	-	-	-	-	-	-	-	62,583
Costa Mesa (city)	50,732	51,993	50,476	48,250	-	-	50,724	-	64,732	-	-	-	-	43,077	31,042	-	-	-	-	-	-	-	-	55,333
Cypress (city)	64,377	66,635	-	79,236	-	-	76,472	-	68,851	-	-	-	-	69,423	54,292	-	-	-	-	-	41,023	-	-	53,854
Foothill Ranch (cdp)	89,038	96,558	-	-	-	-	-	-	-	-	-	-	-	-	-	-	-	-	-	-	-	-	-	-
Fountain Valley (city)	69,734	66,066	-	61,705	-	-	71,439	-	71,500	-	-	-	-	56,875	60,000	-	-	-	-	-	42,813	-	-	69,120
Fullerton (city)	50,269	50,817	-	52,115	-	-	60,227	-	60,375	-	-	-	-	43,194	50,045	-	-	-	-	-	-	-	-	40,764
Garden Grove (city)	47,754	44,111	41,111	38,203	-	47,679	46,447	-	77,267	-	-	-	-	46,964	35,587	-	-	-	67,500	-	-	-	-	43,444
Huntington Beach (city)	64,824	66,077	43,594	82,932	-	-	70,256	-	80,540	-	-	-	-	71,453	54,286	-	-	-	-	-	76,158	-	-	56,204
Irvine (city)	72,057	67,246	-	90,766	-	-	70,219	-	56,250	-	-	-	-	76,149	49,067	-	-	-	-	-	64,900	-	-	95,768
La Habra (city)	47,652	67,171	-	-	-	-	82,377	-	70,341	-	-	-	-	-	50,789	-	-	-	-	-	-	-	-	-
La Palma (city)	68,438	68,750	-	67,292	-	-	88,188	-	94,288	-	-	-	-	81,990	50,982	-	-	-	-	-	-	-	-	-
Laguna Hills (city)	70,234	86,682	-	-	-	-	127,021	-	88,665	-	-	-	-	-	-	-	-	-	-	-	-	-	-	100,401
Laguna Niguel (city)	80,733	79,232	-	-	-	-	100,078	-	70,227	-	-	-	-	87,979	50,980	-	-	-	-	-	-	-	-	98,474
Lake Forest (city)	67,967	71,094	-	72,039	-	-	70,694	-	78,006	-	-	-	-	76,089	44,185	-	-	-	-	-	-	-	-	74,643
Los Alamitos (city)	55,286	47,440	-	-	-	-	-	-	-	-	-	-	-	-	-	-	-	-	-	-	-	-	-	-
Mission Viejo (city)	78,248	87,584	-	91,029	-	-	96,734	-	96,489	-	-	-	-	90,533	80,513	-	-	-	-	-	-	-	-	93,461
Newport Beach (city)	83,455	72,578	-	-	-	-	67,656	-	-	-	-	-	-	84,280	-	-	-	-	-	-	-	-	-	-
Orange (city)	58,994	65,678	-	66,136	-	-	81,339	-	75,655	-	-	-	-	73,889	40,833	-	-	-	-	-	53,269	-	-	66,196
Placentia (city)	62,803	72,375	-	81,586	-	-	68,056	-	61,750	-	-	-	-	78,664	72,688	-	-	-	-	-	-	-	-	89,868
Rancho Santa Margarita (city)	78,475	85,935	-	-	-	-	76,473	-	86,454	-	-	-	-	-	-	-	-	-	-	-	-	-	-	91,238
Rossmoor (cdp)	86,457	95,155	-	-	-	-	-	-	-	-	-	-	-	-	-	-	-	-	-	-	-	-	-	-
Santa Ana (city)	43,412	47,993	44,708	80,546	-	43,125	39,879	-	48,654	-	-	74,000	-	50,128	15,208	60,938	-	-	53,750	-	-	-	-	49,745
Seal Beach (city)	42,079	95,556	-	-	-	-	-	-	-	-	-	-	-	93,796	-	-	-	-	-	-	-	-	-	-
Stanton (city)	39,127	45,052	-	-	-	-	-	-	54,773	-	-	-	-	-	25,930	-	-	-	-	-	-	-	-	46,458
Tustin (city)	55,985	63,073	-	59,833	-	-	77,734	-	63,241	-	-	-	-	55,192	74,205	-	-	-	-	-	56,827	-	-	71,094
Tustin Foothills (cdp)	96,230	81,691	-	-	-	-	104,925	-	-	-	-	-	-	-	-	-	-	-	-	-	-	-	-	-
Westminster (city)	49,450	44,395	47,750	55,882	-	-	60,078	-	63,191	-	-	-	-	63,598	41,250	-	-	-	49,625	-	-	-	-	40,805
Yorba Linda (city)	89,593	88,532	-	100,650	-	-	85,076	-	95,894	-	-	-	-	96,088	70,677	-	-	-	-	-	-	-	-	89,310
Placer County	57,535	64,167	-	75,781	-	-	66,118	-	62,981	-	-	-	-	54,358	41,563	-	-	-	-	-	-	-	-	90,470
Rocklin (city)	64,737	63,929	-	-	-	-	-	-	-	-	-	-	-	63,214	-	-	-	-	-	-	-	-	-	-
Roseville (city)	57,367	73,077	-	72,375	-	-	77,278	-	82,024	-	-	-	-	60,313	-	-	-	-	-	-	-	-	-	-
Riverside County	42,887	50,923	41,815	64,125	-	56,750	42,546	-	62,179	51,250	55,865	16,750	-	52,167	40,947	39,706	-	48,750	37,350	-	35,987	30,667	-	45,000
Banning (city)	32,076	32,188	-	-	-	-	-	-	-	-	-	-	-	-	-	48,750	-	-	-	-	-	-	-	-
Corona (city)	59,615	73,198	-	82,541	-	-	52,039	-	78,245	-	-	-	-	63,929	71,544	-	-	-	-	-	-	-	-	74,338
Moreno Valley (city)	47,387	52,829	-	-	-	-	43,750	-	60,684	-	-	-	-	50,909	48,333	30,682	-	-	-	-	-	-	-	40,833
Palm Springs (city)	35,973	47,955	-	-	-	-	-	-	55,217	-	-	-	-	-	-	-	-	-	-	-	-	-	-	-
Pedley (cdp)	60,567	67,721	-	-	-	-	-	-	-	-	-	-	-	-	-	-	-	-	-	-	-	-	-	-
Riverside (city)	41,646	35,670	41,450	45,625	-	-	20,833	-	47,049	-	-	-	-	31,691	35,380	36,146	-	-	-	-	-	-	-	36,190

Notes: Please refer to the User's Guide for an explanation of data; data is arranged alphabetically by state, then county, then city within each county; table includes counties with populations greater than 49,999 unless noted and cities with populations greater than 9,999 whose Asian and/or NHPI population rates are greater than the national average; (1) Native Hawaiian and other Pacific Islander; (2) excludes Taiwanese; (3) includes Chamorro; (4) county does not meet population threshold but is shown in order to allow inclusion of city

Place	All households	Asian households	NHPI[1] households	Asian Indian	Bangladeshi	Cambodian	Chinese[2]	Fijian	Filipino	Guamanian[3]	Hawaiian, Native	Hmong	Indonesian	Japanese	Korean	Laotian	Malaysian	Pakistani	Samoan	Sri Lankan	Taiwanese	Thai	Tongan	Vietnamese
Temecula (city)	59,516	71,053	-	-	-	-	61,364	-	77,242	-	-	-	-	-	-	-	-	-	-	-	-	-	-	-
Sacramento County	43,816	44,501	41,047	54,918	-	30,795	46,008	35,179	50,428	52,813	39,167	27,474	-	56,352	43,519	29,797	-	50,962	34,044	-	31,818	32,679	66,094	29,250
Arden-Arcade (cdp)	40,335	33,966	-	29,279	-	-	49,432	-	34,500	-	-	36,652	-	44,286	-	-	-	-	-	-	-	-	-	21,394
Elk Grove (cdp)	60,661	60,757	-	68,333	-	-	55,673	-	70,433	-	-	-	-	79,336	-	-	-	-	-	-	-	-	-	46,339
Fair Oaks (cdp)	63,252	76,180	-	-	-	-	-	-	-	-	-	-	-	-	-	-	-	-	-	-	-	-	-	-
Florin (cdp)	33,793	35,063	-	50,500	-	-	35,263	-	41,053	-	-	25,268	-	-	-	-	-	-	-	-	-	-	-	19,028
Folsom (city)	73,175	89,531	-	100,568	-	-	93,874	-	84,702	-	-	-	-	-	-	-	-	-	-	-	-	-	-	-
Foothill Farms (cdp)	38,049	40,357	-	-	-	-	-	-	-	-	-	-	-	-	-	-	-	-	-	-	-	-	-	-
La Riviera (cdp)	49,110	41,484	-	-	-	-	-	-	-	-	-	-	-	-	-	-	-	-	-	-	-	-	-	-
Laguna (cdp)	67,447	65,717	-	70,125	-	-	61,821	-	71,029	-	-	-	-	82,569	-	-	-	-	-	-	-	-	-	41,591
North Highlands (cdp)	32,278	31,295	-	-	-	-	-	-	40,987	-	-	-	-	-	-	-	-	-	-	-	-	-	-	23,393
Parkway-S. Sacramento (cdp)	31,194	23,561	-	-	-	-	16,319	-	-	-	-	20,915	-	-	-	30,208	-	-	-	-	-	-	-	26,964
Rancho Cordova (cdp)	40,095	44,263	-	56,587	-	-	46,786	-	50,987	-	-	-	-	-	31,188	-	-	-	-	-	-	-	-	35,739
Rosemont (cdp)	45,044	37,759	-	-	-	-	-	-	36,513	-	-	-	-	-	32,656	-	-	-	-	-	-	-	-	25,938
Sacramento (city)	37,049	38,398	36,033	43,421	-	31,250	40,318	33,365	43,089	-	-	28,405	-	55,357	41,786	26,929	-	37,656	29,250	-	-	-	65,781	22,977
Vineyard (cdp)	65,192	65,050	-	-	-	-	-	-	62,176	-	-	-	-	-	-	-	-	-	-	-	-	-	-	-
San Benito County	57,469	59,250	-	-	-	-	-	-	70,625	-	-	-	-	-	-	-	-	-	-	-	-	-	-	-
San Bernardino County	42,066	54,704	45,134	62,917	-	35,216	56,567	-	66,944	62,024	48,906	-	46,898	52,355	43,567	31,806	-	44,500	34,853	-	43,750	44,942	30,625	35,659
Chino (city)	55,401	60,962	-	-	-	-	-	-	71,464	-	-	-	-	-	-	-	-	-	-	-	-	-	-	64,028
Chino Hills (city)	78,374	80,216	-	95,115	-	-	63,368	-	94,700	-	-	-	-	74,318	70,511	-	-	-	-	-	53,750	-	-	91,714
Colton (city)	35,777	50,427	-	-	-	-	-	-	51,111	-	-	-	-	-	-	-	-	-	-	-	-	-	-	-
Fontana (city)	45,782	66,250	60,833	64,750	-	-	-	-	73,750	-	-	-	-	-	-	-	-	-	-	-	-	-	-	-
Grand Terrace (city)	53,649	51,991	-	-	-	-	-	-	-	-	-	-	-	-	-	-	-	-	-	-	-	-	-	-
Highland (city)	41,230	46,979	-	-	-	-	-	-	63,864	-	-	-	-	-	-	-	-	-	-	-	-	-	-	28,750
Loma Linda (city)	38,204	45,417	-	55,536	-	-	52,813	-	51,645	-	-	-	42,237	-	30,938	-	-	-	-	-	-	-	-	-
Montclair (city)	40,797	37,500	-	-	-	-	-	-	-	-	-	-	-	-	-	-	-	-	-	-	-	-	-	27,000
Ontario (city)	42,452	46,917	28,382	48,636	-	-	49,500	-	66,607	-	-	-	-	-	-	-	-	-	-	-	-	-	-	46,058
Rancho Cucamonga (city)	60,931	66,056	-	82,542	-	-	57,628	-	72,083	-	-	-	-	87,500	39,250	-	-	-	-	-	-	-	-	63,333
Redlands (city)	48,155	44,375	-	57,109	-	-	64,063	-	43,000	-	-	-	-	-	36,847	-	-	-	-	-	-	-	-	-
Rialto (city)	41,254	58,750	54,500	-	-	-	-	-	69,306	-	-	-	-	-	-	-	-	-	-	-	-	-	-	-
San Bernardino (city)	31,140	32,195	40,441	41,759	-	20,865	20,000	-	45,469	-	-	-	27,321	-	26,429	-	-	-	33,882	-	-	-	-	22,049
Upland (city)	48,734	40,978	-	69,250	-	-	48,558	-	38,125	-	-	-	-	-	41,875	-	-	-	-	-	50,000	-	-	20,260
Victorville (city)	36,187	38,924	-	-	-	-	-	-	41,607	-	-	-	-	-	-	-	-	-	-	-	-	-	-	-
San Diego County	47,067	51,981	47,097	70,244	-	26,436	60,884	-	56,264	46,875	49,667	38,947	50,000	45,659	40,274	39,527	-	61,500	48,906	-	61,544	31,354	46,250	41,203
Bonita (cdp)	70,109	64,545	-	-	-	-	-	-	65,536	-	-	-	-	-	-	-	-	-	-	-	-	-	-	-
Carlsbad (city)	65,145	77,815	-	-	-	-	104,230	-	73,125	-	-	-	-	63,056	-	-	-	-	-	-	-	-	-	-
Chula Vista (city)	44,861	62,861	51,630	-	-	-	60,507	-	66,850	52,500	-	-	-	57,667	51,086	-	-	-	-	-	-	-	-	-
Coronado (city)	66,544	58,036	-	-	-	-	-	-	44,000	-	-	-	-	-	-	-	-	-	-	-	-	-	-	-
Escondido (city)	42,567	51,653	-	-	-	-	58,750	-	56,125	-	-	-	-	-	-	79,544	-	-	-	-	-	-	-	57,813
Imperial Beach (city)	35,882	47,917	-	-	-	-	-	-	45,114	-	-	-	-	-	-	-	-	-	-	-	-	-	-	-
La Mesa (city)	41,693	37,335	-	-	-	-	-	-	59,250	-	-	-	-	-	-	-	-	-	-	-	-	-	-	-

Notes: Please refer to the User's Guide for an explanation of data; data is arranged alphabetically by state, then county, then city within each county; table includes counties with populations greater than 49,999 unless noted and cities with populations greater than 9,999 whose Asian and/or NHPI population rates are greater than the national average; (1) Native Hawaiian and other Pacific Islander; (2) excludes Taiwanese; (3) includes Chamorro; (4) county does not meet population threshold but is shown in order to allow inclusion of city

Place	All households	Asian households	NHPI[1] households	Asian Indian	Bangladeshi	Cambodian	Chinese[2]	Fijian	Filipino	Guamanian[3]	Hawaiian, Native	Hmong	Indonesian	Japanese	Korean	Laotian	Malaysian	Pakistani	Samoan	Sri Lankan	Taiwanese	Thai	Tongan	Vietnamese
La Presa (cdp)	45,939	53,173	-	-	-	-	-	-	55,250	-	-	-	-	-	-	-	-	-	-	-	-	-	-	-
Lemon Grove (city)	39,823	43,355	-	-	-	-	-	-	52,237	-	-	-	-	-	-	-	-	-	-	-	-	-	-	-
National City (city)	29,826	34,235	-	-	-	-	-	-	35,189	-	-	-	-	-	-	-	-	-	-	-	-	-	-	37,083
Oceanside (city)	46,301	51,720	51,759	-	-	-	44,444	-	52,572	-	-	-	-	49,063	-	-	-	-	51,759	-	-	-	-	65,288
Poway (city)	71,708	80,793	-	-	-	-	79,816	-	61,250	-	-	-	-	-	-	-	-	-	-	-	-	-	-	-
Rancho San Diego (cdp)	68,185	66,731	-	-	-	-	-	-	81,594	-	-	-	-	-	-	-	-	-	-	-	-	-	-	-
San Diego (city)	45,733	51,436	47,165	67,500	-	25,441	59,946	-	58,431	45,769	48,889	39,474	-	42,750	38,327	37,419	-	-	46,635	-	61,507	25,500	-	38,110
San Marcos (city)	45,908	57,902	-	-	-	-	63,750	-	67,895	-	-	-	-	-	-	-	-	-	-	-	-	-	-	-
Solana Beach (city)	71,774	86,578	-	-	-	-	-	-	-	-	-	-	-	-	-	-	-	-	-	-	-	-	-	-
Spring Valley (cdp)	48,271	59,219	-	-	-	-	-	-	62,727	-	-	-	-	-	-	-	-	-	-	-	-	-	-	-
Vista (city)	42,594	45,225	38,162	-	-	-	-	-	52,273	-	-	-	-	23,261	-	-	-	-	-	-	-	-	-	-
San Francisco County	55,221	49,596	33,750	72,018	-	31,458	47,545	-	60,395	-	-	-	40,801	48,531	42,323	-	-	70,461	25,469	-	63,203	40,363	-	38,778
San Francisco (city)	55,221	49,596	33,750	72,018	-	31,458	47,545	-	60,395	-	-	-	40,801	48,531	42,323	-	-	70,461	25,469	-	63,203	40,363	-	38,778
San Joaquin County	41,282	36,952	44,356	50,875	-	17,377	35,508	-	47,618	-	58,942	25,979	-	46,657	25,515	23,364	-	31,406	48,750	-	-	-	-	21,324
Lathrop (city)	55,037	49,583	-	-	-	-	-	-	55,278	-	-	-	-	-	-	-	-	-	-	-	-	-	-	-
Lodi (city)	39,570	36,352	-	36,875	-	-	-	-	52,917	-	-	-	-	44,792	-	-	-	-	-	-	-	-	-	-
Stockton (city)	35,453	31,743	39,286	40,163	-	17,264	35,148	-	45,039	-	-	25,448	-	45,872	-	22,932	-	36,776	-	-	-	-	-	20,625
Tracy (city)	62,794	75,863	-	80,000	-	-	64,167	-	82,375	-	-	-	-	-	-	-	-	-	-	-	-	-	-	-
San Luis Obispo County	42,428	39,688	-	61,250	-	-	23,281	-	42,578	-	-	-	-	40,903	31,000	-	-	-	-	-	-	-	-	-
Baywood-Los Osos (cdp)	46,558	42,228	-	-	-	-	-	-	53,882	-	-	-	-	-	-	-	-	-	-	-	-	-	-	-
Grover Beach (city)	38,087	50,833	-	-	-	-	-	-	-	-	-	-	-	-	-	-	-	-	-	-	-	-	-	-
San Luis Obispo (city)	31,926	20,144	-	-	-	-	12,436	-	14,615	-	-	-	-	-	-	-	-	-	-	-	-	-	-	-
San Mateo County	70,819	78,263	65,510	83,621	-	-	79,671	60,313	77,763	58,750	56,125	-	62,891	70,694	62,443	-	-	-	86,781	-	71,071	69,773	75,074	79,314
Belmont (city)	80,905	79,343	-	78,262	-	-	94,841	-	62,500	-	-	-	-	63,264	-	-	-	-	-	-	-	-	-	-
Burlingame (city)	68,526	62,052	-	-	-	-	65,625	-	55,625	-	-	-	-	81,813	-	-	-	-	-	-	-	-	-	-
Daly City (city)	62,310	73,941	49,911	56,875	-	-	71,469	-	77,702	-	-	-	-	59,271	40,819	-	-	-	-	-	-	-	-	-
East Palo Alto (city)	45,006	46,442	68,333	-	-	-	-	-	-	-	-	-	-	-	-	-	-	-	-	-	-	-	-	69,167
Foster City (city)	95,279	94,316	-	94,225	-	-	89,615	-	81,323	-	-	-	-	108,026	106,881	-	-	-	-	-	-	-	70,625	-
Hillsborough (town)	193,157	161,576	-	-	-	-	154,640	-	-	-	-	-	-	-	-	-	-	-	-	-	-	-	-	-
Menlo Park (city)	84,609	99,598	-	-	-	-	91,921	-	-	-	-	-	-	57,500	-	-	-	-	-	-	-	-	-	-
Millbrae (city)	68,404	82,508	-	81,159	-	-	83,012	-	59,583	-	-	-	-	104,727	66,719	-	-	-	-	-	-	-	-	-
Pacifica (city)	71,737	81,803	-	-	-	-	94,144	-	78,995	-	-	-	-	58,929	-	-	-	-	-	-	-	-	-	-
Redwood City (city)	66,748	82,545	47,212	85,000	-	-	90,085	-	71,583	-	-	-	-	70,833	-	-	-	-	-	-	-	-	-	-
San Bruno (city)	62,081	73,542	77,561	65,069	-	-	68,750	-	83,954	-	-	-	-	72,232	-	-	-	-	-	-	-	-	78,135	-
San Carlos (city)	88,460	122,401	-	-	-	-	148,885	-	-	-	-	-	-	-	-	-	-	-	-	-	-	-	-	-
San Mateo (city)	64,757	70,724	65,859	81,322	-	-	69,970	-	81,420	-	-	-	-	56,484	65,789	-	-	-	-	-	-	-	-	-
South San Francisco (city)	61,764	75,918	59,107	67,813	-	-	74,448	-	80,467	-	-	-	-	47,356	-	-	-	-	-	-	-	-	100,718	65,893
Santa Barbara County	46,677	42,800	66,467	53,690	-	-	38,318	-	49,290	-	-	33,750	-	43,304	26,985	-	-	-	-	-	-	-	-	-
Goleta (cdp)	60,314	51,576	-	-	-	-	57,679	-	52,000	-	-	-	-	62,083	-	-	-	-	-	-	-	-	-	39,471
Isla Vista (cdp)	16,151	9,643	-	-	-	-	10,677	-	-	-	-	-	-	-	6,184	-	-	-	-	-	-	-	-	34,167
Lompoc (city)	37,587	44,135	-	-	-	-	-	-	53,750	-	-	-	-	-	-	-	-	-	-	-	-	-	-	-

Notes: Please refer to the User's Guide for an explanation of data; data is arranged alphabetically by state, then county, then city within each county; table includes counties with populations greater than 49,999 unless noted and cities with populations greater than 9,999 whose Asian and/or NHPI population rates are greater than the national average; (1) Native Hawaiian and other Pacific Islander; (2) excludes Taiwanese; (3) includes Chamorro; (4) county does not meet population threshold but is shown in order to allow inclusion of city

Place	All households	Asian households	NHPI[1] households	Asian Indian	Bangladeshi	Cambodian	Chinese[2]	Fijian	Filipino	Guamanian[3]	Hawaiian, Native	Hmong	Indonesian	Japanese	Korean	Laotian	Malaysian	Pakistani	Samoan	Sri Lankan	Taiwanese	Thai	Tongan	Vietnamese
Orcutt (cdp)	53,251	57,283	-	-	-	-	-	-	-	-	-	-	-	-	-	-	-	-	-	-	-	-	-	-
Santa Maria (city)	36,541	48,438	-	-	-	-	-	-	53,631	-	-	-	-	42,000	-	-	-	-	-	-	-	-	-	-
Santa Clara County	74,335	82,804	65,275	93,374	92,942	53,482	92,516	61,339	81,884	68,750	65,260	-	62,019	80,162	65,417	72,941	-	92,530	63,125	-	90,763	60,441	-	68,797
Alum Rock (cdp)	54,567	57,143	-	-	-	-	-	-	-	-	-	-	-	-	-	-	-	-	-	-	-	-	-	43,523
Campbell (city)	67,214	74,737	-	70,278	-	-	95,364	-	75,988	-	-	-	-	63,125	62,353	-	-	-	-	-	-	-	-	45,774
Cupertino (city)	100,411	105,737	-	122,832	-	-	109,207	-	93,911	-	-	-	-	104,074	81,424	-	-	-	-	-	78,945	-	-	76,996
Gilroy (city)	62,135	74,438	-	-	-	-	68,333	-	87,801	-	-	-	-	-	-	-	-	-	-	-	-	-	-	-
Los Altos (city)	126,740	155,651	-	200,001	-	-	165,961	-	-	-	-	-	-	105,461	-	-	-	-	-	-	-	-	-	-
Los Gatos (town)	94,319	107,609	-	-	-	-	104,469	-	-	-	-	-	-	77,064	-	-	-	-	-	-	-	-	-	-
Milpitas (city)	84,429	92,450	70,417	95,821	-	-	101,370	-	89,964	-	-	-	-	88,074	64,500	-	-	-	-	-	-	-	-	90,700
Morgan Hill (city)	81,958	95,677	-	-	-	-	98,786	-	-	-	-	-	-	84,257	-	-	-	-	-	-	-	-	-	-
Mountain View (city)	69,362	76,960	-	85,901	-	-	79,097	-	71,184	-	-	-	-	74,063	50,938	-	-	-	-	-	-	-	-	73,092
Palo Alto (city)	90,377	88,310	-	93,126	-	-	99,196	-	46,786	-	-	-	-	80,061	59,766	-	-	-	-	-	-	-	-	-
San Jose (city)	70,243	78,537	58,173	96,408	-	52,319	86,482	-	82,210	69,706	65,000	-	-	76,327	66,379	73,897	-	77,046	54,643	-	83,806	85,192	-	66,711
Santa Clara (city)	69,466	79,792	68,438	85,125	-	-	78,020	-	82,156	-	-	-	-	72,188	51,477	-	-	97,831	-	-	-	-	-	75,104
Saratoga (city)	139,895	155,207	-	176,313	-	-	158,514	-	-	-	-	-	-	177,278	83,434	-	-	-	-	-	153,050	-	-	-
Stanford (cdp)	41,106	26,806	-	22,778	-	-	27,578	-	-	-	-	-	-	-	13,472	-	-	-	-	-	-	-	-	-
Sunnyvale (city)	74,409	81,371	70,179	86,817	-	-	86,292	-	67,250	-	-	-	-	81,931	61,384	-	-	-	-	-	89,777	-	-	66,926
Santa Cruz County	53,998	56,176	-	66,509	-	-	60,750	-	55,750	-	-	-	-	55,727	45,625	-	-	-	-	-	-	-	-	46,985
Capitola (city)	46,048	48,750	-	-	-	-	-	-	-	-	-	-	-	-	-	-	-	-	-	-	-	-	-	-
Santa Cruz (city)	50,605	51,736	-	67,026	-	-	50,357	-	33,500	-	-	-	-	57,917	-	-	-	-	-	-	-	-	-	-
Scotts Valley (city)	72,449	91,323	-	-	-	-	-	-	-	-	-	-	-	-	-	-	-	-	-	-	-	-	-	-
Shasta County	34,335	32,039	-	-	-	-	-	-	33,981	-	-	-	-	-	-	23,883	-	-	-	-	-	-	-	-
Solano County	54,099	64,569	57,125	56,713	-	-	61,683	-	68,615	72,813	60,952	32,778	-	40,815	49,750	40,938	-	-	51,250	-	-	-	-	53,553
Benicia (city)	67,617	72,708	-	-	-	-	86,130	-	61,920	-	-	-	-	-	-	-	-	-	-	-	-	-	-	-
Fairfield (city)	51,151	54,955	56,875	70,833	-	-	70,446	-	60,793	77,912	-	-	-	24,143	46,250	41,719	-	-	-	-	-	-	-	-
Suisun City (city)	60,848	62,356	-	70,313	-	-	-	-	74,688	-	-	-	-	-	-	-	-	-	-	-	-	-	-	-
Vacaville (city)	57,667	61,942	-	-	-	-	-	-	60,081	-	-	-	-	-	-	-	-	-	-	-	-	-	-	-
Vallejo (city)	50,030	68,392	54,167	38,667	-	-	57,875	-	70,770	73,417	-	-	-	48,250	-	-	-	-	-	-	-	-	-	41,071
Sonoma County	53,076	58,333	59,188	60,962	-	25,357	75,199	-	59,650	-	-	-	-	46,653	55,833	33,750	-	-	-	-	-	-	-	55,000
Petaluma (city)	61,679	75,583	-	-	-	-	89,487	-	-	-	-	-	-	-	-	-	-	-	-	-	-	-	-	-
Rohnert Park (city)	51,942	61,324	-	-	-	-	61,786	-	81,066	-	-	-	-	-	-	-	-	-	-	-	-	-	-	-
Santa Rosa (city)	50,931	45,288	-	61,920	-	33,393	65,521	-	44,015	-	-	-	-	26,000	-	28,333	-	-	-	-	-	-	-	46,500
Stanislaus County	40,101	41,641	37,167	50,208	-	25,781	50,542	39,167	52,399	-	-	20,938	-	75,308	-	20,357	-	-	-	-	-	-	-	39,000
Ceres (city)	40,736	50,429	-	39,569	-	-	-	-	-	-	-	-	-	-	-	-	-	-	-	-	-	-	-	-
Modesto (city)	40,394	39,283	34,063	53,173	-	20,938	49,773	38,000	55,144	-	-	24,583	-	94,218	-	17,750	-	-	-	-	-	-	-	37,833
Salida (cdp)	57,874	72,500	-	-	-	-	-	-	-	-	-	-	-	-	-	-	-	-	-	-	-	-	-	-
Turlock (city)	39,050	40,192	-	44,500	-	-	-	-	-	-	-	-	-	-	-	-	-	-	-	-	-	-	-	-
Sutter County	38,375	41,274	-	39,193	-	-	-	-	38,750	-	-	-	-	49,511	-	-	-	-	-	-	-	-	-	-
South Yuba City (cdp)	54,518	48,438	-	48,292	-	-	-	-	-	-	-	-	-	-	-	-	-	-	-	-	-	-	-	-
Yuba City (city)	32,858	35,331	-	31,761	-	-	-	-	-	-	-	-	-	-	-	-	-	-	-	-	-	-	-	-

Notes: Please refer to the User's Guide for an explanation of data; data is arranged alphabetically by state, then county, then city within each county; table includes counties with populations greater than 49,999 unless noted and cities with populations greater than 9,999 whose Asian and/or NHPI population rates are greater than the national average; (1) Native Hawaiian and other Pacific Islander; (2) excludes Taiwanese; (3) includes Chamorro; (4) county does not meet population threshold but is shown in order to allow inclusion of city

Place	All households	Asian households	NHPI[1] households	Asian Indian	Bangladeshi	Cambodian	Chinese[2]	Fijian	Filipino	Guamanian[3]	Hawaiian, Native	Hmong	Indonesian	Japanese	Korean	Laotian	Malaysian	Pakistani	Samoan	Sri Lankan	Taiwanese	Thai	Tongan	Vietnamese
Tehama County	31,206	39,107	-	-	-	-	-	-	-	-	-	-	-	-	-	-	-	-	-	-	-	-	-	-
Tulare County	33,983	36,637	-	54,000	-	-	46,793	-	40,110	-	-	25,521	-	39,118	28,333	24,392	-	-	-	-	-	-	-	-
Porterville (city)	32,046	40,463	-	-	-	-	-	-	51,397	-	-	-	-	-	-	-	-	-	-	-	-	-	-	-
Visalia (city)	41,349	35,741	-	-	-	-	-	-	41,250	-	-	17,031	-	-	-	22,792	-	-	-	-	-	-	-	-
Tuolumne County	38,725	40,341	-	-	-	-	-	-	-	-	-	-	-	-	-	-	-	-	-	-	-	-	-	-
Ventura County	59,666	71,851	62,054	86,227	-	-	86,639	-	66,461	-	68,563	-	-	64,439	51,875	-	-	-	46,528	-	100,000	-	-	68,750
Camarillo (city)	62,457	79,860	-	-	-	-	90,766	-	75,195	-	-	-	-	73,625	48,173	-	-	-	-	-	-	-	-	121,279
Moorpark (city)	76,642	88,482	-	-	-	-	-	-	-	-	-	-	-	-	-	-	-	-	-	-	-	-	-	-
Oxnard (city)	48,603	61,150	50,208	51,111	-	-	44,464	-	67,872	-	-	-	-	41,250	43,542	-	-	-	42,708	-	-	-	-	59,643
Port Hueneme (city)	42,246	47,643	-	-	-	-	-	-	48,375	-	-	-	-	-	-	-	-	-	-	-	-	-	-	-
Simi Valley (city)	70,370	78,752	-	81,113	-	-	72,917	-	85,359	-	-	-	-	81,843	66,250	-	-	-	-	-	-	-	-	73,224
Thousand Oaks (city)	76,815	93,479	-	106,869	-	-	101,135	-	56,818	-	-	-	-	97,419	49,643	-	-	-	-	-	-	-	-	55,250
Yolo County	40,769	24,200	31,406	26,979	-	-	24,777	28,676	32,037	-	-	18,750	-	49,712	21,507	13,942	-	-	-	-	-	-	-	16,007
Davis (city)	42,454	20,621	-	20,278	-	-	21,462	-	22,260	-	-	-	-	52,411	20,905	-	-	-	-	-	-	-	-	13,042
West Sacramento (city)	31,718	24,125	-	23,125	-	-	-	-	-	-	-	18,403	-	-	-	-	-	-	-	-	-	-	-	-
Woodland (city)	44,449	42,112	-	32,237	-	-	-	-	-	-	-	-	-	-	-	-	-	-	-	-	-	-	-	-
Yuba County	30,460	31,284	-	-	-	-	-	-	35,341	-	-	30,668	-	-	-	-	-	-	-	-	-	-	-	-
Linda (cdp)	22,753	30,208	-	-	-	-	-	-	-	-	-	30,060	-	-	-	-	-	-	-	-	-	-	-	-
Marysville (city)	28,494	30,809	-	-	-	-	-	-	-	-	-	-	-	-	-	-	-	-	-	-	-	-	-	-
Olivehurst (cdp)	29,854	53,625	-	-	-	-	-	-	-	-	-	-	-	-	-	-	-	-	-	-	-	-	-	-
COLORADO	47,203	48,619	39,729	63,891	-	55,481	51,481	-	49,500	40,054	37,838	50,058	26,125	44,842	40,206	55,245	-	40,769	58,882	-	30,921	40,171	-	44,719
Adams County	47,323	51,007	-	64,013	-	-	49,375	-	57,083	-	-	52,180	-	45,972	49,375	52,031	-	-	-	-	-	-	-	46,250
Berkley (cdp)	36,945	54,500	-	-	-	-	-	-	-	-	-	-	-	-	-	-	-	-	-	-	-	-	-	-
Federal Heights (city)	33,750	53,750	-	-	-	-	-	-	-	-	-	-	-	-	-	-	-	-	-	-	-	-	-	-
Westminster (city)	56,323	55,262	-	71,333	-	-	45,882	-	-	-	-	52,407	-	-	55,313	46,765	-	-	-	-	-	-	-	53,098
Arapahoe County	53,570	48,849	58,438	57,303	-	-	48,000	-	51,985	-	-	-	-	49,167	42,259	-	-	-	-	-	-	-	-	57,228
Aurora (city)	46,507	41,917	22,813	41,563	-	59,375	41,400	-	45,357	-	-	-	-	36,910	36,284	-	-	-	-	-	-	-	-	47,375
Boulder County	55,861	52,724	-	73,281	-	-	61,622	-	52,734	-	-	-	-	60,972	30,893	-	-	-	-	-	-	-	-	32,930
Boulder (city)	44,748	34,138	-	64,318	-	-	44,643	-	-	-	-	-	-	24,597	18,000	-	-	-	-	-	-	-	-	-
Broomfield (city)	63,903	62,841	-	-	-	-	71,250	-	-	-	-	-	-	-	-	-	-	-	-	-	-	-	-	-
Lafayette (city)	56,376	55,000	-	-	-	-	-	-	-	-	-	-	-	-	-	-	-	-	-	-	-	-	-	-
Denver County	39,500	36,184	29,458	56,229	-	52,639	38,696	-	45,903	-	-	-	-	31,050	29,048	-	-	-	-	-	-	28,125	-	34,200
Douglas County	82,929	85,037	-	101,958	-	-	81,441	-	-	-	-	-	-	-	67,292	-	-	-	-	-	-	-	-	-
Highlands Ranch (cdp)	86,792	86,902	-	100,925	-	-	80,543	-	-	-	-	-	-	-	-	-	-	-	-	-	-	-	-	-
El Paso County	46,844	46,138	44,423	62,264	-	-	64,625	-	38,090	50,132	-	-	-	42,206	30,481	-	-	-	-	-	-	-	-	51,696
Colorado Springs (city)	45,081	46,966	31,481	62,264	-	-	62,986	-	34,871	-	-	-	-	43,409	31,346	-	-	-	-	-	-	-	-	50,268
Jefferson County	57,339	58,514	59,688	73,869	-	-	49,211	-	56,724	-	-	41,607	-	65,924	54,167	56,912	-	-	-	-	-	-	-	50,950
Larimer County	48,655	47,563	-	64,464	-	-	52,227	-	-	-	-	-	-	48,958	15,795	-	-	-	-	-	-	-	-	-
Mesa County	35,864	50,938	-	-	-	-	-	-	-	-	-	-	-	-	-	-	-	-	-	-	-	-	-	-
Pueblo County	32,775	31,667	-	-	-	-	-	-	-	-	-	-	-	-	-	-	-	-	-	-	-	-	-	-
Weld County	42,321	40,333	-	-	-	-	-	-	-	-	-	-	-	25,500	-	-	-	-	-	-	-	-	-	-

Notes: Please refer to the User's Guide for an explanation of data; data is arranged alphabetically by state, then county, then city within each county; table includes counties with populations greater than 49,999 unless noted and cities with populations greater than 9,999 whose Asian and/or NHPI population rates are greater than the national average; (1) Native Hawaiian and other Pacific Islander; (2) excludes Taiwanese; (3) includes Chamorro; (4) county does not meet population threshold but is shown in order to allow inclusion of city

Place	All households	Asian households	NHPI[1] households	Asian Indian	Bangladeshi	Cambodian	Chinese[2]	Fijian	Filipino	Guamanian[3]	Hawaiian, Native	Hmong	Indonesian	Japanese	Korean	Laotian	Malaysian	Pakistani	Samoan	Sri Lankan	Taiwanese	Thai	Tongan	Vietnamese
CONNECTICUT	53,935	61,587	60,536	66,903	48,750	69,688	63,762	-	62,614	65,625	-	-	-	70,871	43,194	60,112	-	52,868	-	-	55,625	40,227	-	53,378
Fairfield County	65,249	79,191	-	78,837	-	75,961	85,952	-	75,754	-	-	-	-	121,599	52,076	63,403	-	61,406	-	-	-	-	-	68,050
Danbury (city)	53,664	71,534	-	72,163	-	70,750	65,521	-	-	-	-	-	-	-	-	-	-	-	-	-	-	-	-	-
Greenwich (town)	99,086	107,718	-	84,509	-	-	117,714	-	-	-	-	-	-	109,944	-	-	-	-	-	-	-	-	-	-
Stamford (city)	60,556	75,835	-	75,838	-	-	83,726	-	68,750	-	-	-	-	-	-	-	-	-	-	-	-	-	-	-
Hartford County	50,756	56,071	-	60,526	-	-	56,537	-	61,688	-	-	-	-	41,667	39,643	61,029	-	48,750	-	-	-	-	-	46,000
East Hartford (town)	41,424	47,868	-	48,529	-	-	-	-	-	-	-	-	-	-	-	-	-	-	-	-	-	-	-	31,731
Farmington (town)	67,073	65,515	-	-	-	-	-	-	-	-	-	-	-	-	-	-	-	-	-	-	-	-	-	-
Glastonbury (town)	80,660	94,807	-	109,563	-	-	-	-	-	-	-	-	-	-	-	-	-	-	-	-	-	-	-	-
Rocky Hill (town)	60,247	63,750	-	-	-	-	-	-	-	-	-	-	-	-	-	-	-	-	-	-	-	-	-	-
South Windsor (town)	73,990	72,159	-	-	-	-	-	-	-	-	-	-	-	-	-	-	-	-	-	-	-	-	-	-
West Hartford (town)	61,665	61,510	-	60,833	-	-	55,655	-	-	-	-	-	-	-	-	-	-	-	-	-	-	-	-	65,000
Litchfield County	56,273	61,375	-	60,089	-	-	65,682	-	-	-	-	-	-	-	43,750	-	-	-	-	-	-	-	-	60,938
Middlesex County	59,175	56,827	-	71,250	-	-	40,156	-	-	-	-	-	-	-	-	-	-	-	-	-	-	-	-	-
New Haven County	48,834	52,474	-	59,351	-	-	54,323	-	63,017	-	-	-	-	31,929	33,333	57,917	-	48,553	-	-	-	-	-	47,125
New Haven (city)	29,604	26,297	-	33,409	-	-	28,362	-	-	-	-	-	-	-	8,929	-	-	-	-	-	-	-	-	-
New London County	50,646	58,182	-	65,000	-	-	70,677	-	46,964	-	-	-	-	-	-	-	-	-	-	-	-	-	-	-
Tolland County	59,044	44,464	-	75,302	-	-	30,946	-	-	-	-	-	-	-	-	-	-	-	-	-	-	-	-	-
Mansfield (town)	48,888	18,889	-	31,563	-	-	16,250	-	-	-	-	-	-	-	-	-	-	-	-	-	-	-	-	-
Storrs (cdp)	26,371	14,750	-	-	-	-	14,600	-	-	-	-	-	-	-	-	-	-	-	-	-	-	-	-	-
Windham County	45,115	28,571	-	-	-	-	-	-	-	-	-	-	-	-	-	-	-	-	-	-	-	-	-	-
DELAWARE	47,381	65,190	66,250	76,392	-	-	60,694	-	61,250	-	-	-	-	49,167	31,216	-	-	98,964	-	-	-	-	-	92,565
Kent County	40,950	35,288	-	80,412	-	-	-	-	40,208	-	-	-	-	-	-	-	-	-	-	-	-	-	-	-
New Castle County	52,419	71,025	-	76,883	-	-	65,417	-	74,286	-	-	-	-	51,750	42,656	-	-	-	-	-	-	-	-	95,127
Hockessin (cdp)	100,844	132,562	-	-	-	-	-	-	-	-	-	-	-	-	-	-	-	-	-	-	-	-	-	-
Newark (city)	48,758	36,477	-	-	-	-	39,219	-	-	-	-	-	-	-	-	-	-	-	-	-	-	-	-	-
Pike Creek (cdp)	71,655	79,504	-	-	-	-	-	-	-	-	-	-	-	-	-	-	-	-	-	-	-	-	-	-
Sussex County	39,208	47,031	-	-	-	-	-	-	-	-	-	-	-	-	-	-	-	-	-	-	-	-	-	-
DISTRICT OF COLUMBIA	40,127	36,031	-	47,011	-	-	31,611	-	35,887	-	-	-	-	39,224	35,500	-	-	-	-	-	-	-	-	35,660
FLORIDA	38,819	44,780	39,050	50,390	36,570	40,345	40,680	-	52,039	39,929	34,479	-	38,167	34,663	36,368	42,808	-	50,150	40,956	23,750	45,583	37,139	-	38,877
Alachua County	31,426	18,082	-	26,250	-	-	18,549	-	41,250	-	-	-	-	8,750	12,330	-	-	-	-	-	-	-	-	17,917
Gainesville (city)	28,164	15,551	-	14,550	-	-	17,708	-	-	-	-	-	-	-	11,506	-	-	-	-	-	-	-	-	-
Bay County	36,092	32,420	-	-	-	-	-	-	40,682	-	-	-	-	-	-	-	-	-	-	-	-	-	-	30,435
Callaway (city)	36,064	31,016	-	-	-	-	-	-	-	-	-	-	-	-	-	-	-	-	-	-	-	-	-	-
Brevard County	40,099	42,278	-	59,107	-	-	38,015	-	41,821	-	-	-	-	28,958	30,455	-	-	-	-	-	-	-	-	46,103
Broward County	41,691	47,731	40,819	49,518	-	-	41,049	-	69,201	-	-	-	-	52,917	36,121	-	-	41,875	-	-	-	46,058	-	41,333
Cooper City (city)	75,166	61,806	-	57,750	-	-	-	-	-	-	-	-	-	-	-	-	-	-	-	-	-	-	-	-
Pembroke Pines (city)	52,629	60,089	-	60,294	-	-	50,469	-	68,906	-	-	-	-	-	-	-	-	-	-	-	-	-	-	-
Charlotte County	36,379	61,000	-	-	-	-	-	-	-	-	-	-	-	-	-	-	-	-	-	-	-	-	-	-
Citrus County	31,001	44,375	-	-	-	-	-	-	-	-	-	-	-	-	-	-	-	-	-	-	-	-	-	-
Clay County	48,854	55,822	-	-	-	-	-	-	62,888	-	-	-	-	-	-	-	-	-	-	-	-	-	-	-

Notes: Please refer to the User's Guide for an explanation of data; data is arranged alphabetically by state, then county, then city within each county; table includes counties with populations greater than 49,999 unless noted and cities with populations greater than 9,999 whose Asian and/or NHPI population rates are greater than the national average; (1) Native Hawaiian and other Pacific Islander; (2) excludes Taiwanese; (3) includes Chamorro; (4) county does not meet population threshold but is shown in order to allow inclusion of city

Place	All households	Asian households	NHPI[1] households	Asian Indian	Bangladeshi	Cambodian	Chinese[2]	Fijian	Filipino	Guamanian[3]	Hawaiian, Native	Hmong	Indonesian	Japanese	Korean	Laotian	Malaysian	Pakistani	Samoan	Sri Lankan	Taiwanese	Thai	Tongan	Vietnamese
Bellair-Meadowbrook Ter. (cdp)	42,426	52,875	-	-	-	-	-	-	-	-	-	-	-	-	-	-	-	-	-	-	-	-	-	-
Collier County	48,289	62,742	-	-	-	-	-	-	-	-	-	-	-	-	-	-	-	-	-	-	-	-	-	-
Columbia County	30,881	40,139	-	-	-	-	-	-	-	-	-	-	-	-	-	-	-	-	-	-	-	-	-	-
Duval County	40,703	51,603	40,294	58,892	-	42,292	48,472	-	54,076	-	-	-	-	35,063	39,688	-	-	-	-	-	-	-	-	31,842
Escambia County	35,234	36,726	-	48,750	-	-	46,071	-	37,835	-	-	-	-	-	-	-	-	-	-	-	-	-	-	27,118
Bellview (cdp)	38,725	43,750	-	-	-	-	-	-	47,083	-	-	-	-	-	-	-	-	-	-	-	-	-	-	-
Myrtle Grove (cdp)	33,601	27,750	-	-	-	-	-	-	29,167	-	-	-	-	-	-	-	-	-	-	-	-	-	-	-
Hernando County	32,572	51,583	-	-	-	-	-	-	-	-	-	-	-	-	-	-	-	-	-	-	-	-	-	-
Highlands County	30,160	56,354	-	-	-	-	-	-	91,662	-	-	-	-	-	-	-	-	-	-	-	-	-	-	-
Hillsborough County	40,663	46,081	44,531	52,464	-	-	42,656	-	45,919	-	-	-	-	32,188	49,722	-	-	-	-	-	-	30,972	-	38,750
Westchase (cdp)	79,561	54,375	-	-	-	-	-	-	-	-	-	-	-	-	-	-	-	-	-	-	-	-	-	-
Indian River County	39,635	51,111	-	-	-	-	-	-	-	-	-	-	-	-	-	-	-	-	-	-	-	-	-	-
Lake County	36,903	45,083	-	-	-	-	-	-	-	-	-	-	-	-	-	-	-	-	-	-	-	-	-	-
Lee County	40,319	40,382	-	37,750	-	-	46,406	-	46,029	-	-	-	-	-	-	-	-	-	-	-	-	-	-	-
Leon County	37,517	40,531	-	56,574	-	-	41,779	-	33,047	-	-	-	-	-	30,952	-	-	-	-	-	-	-	-	-
Manatee County	38,673	52,539	-	-	-	-	-	-	56,484	-	-	-	-	-	-	-	-	-	-	-	-	-	-	-
Marion County	31,944	38,589	-	41,579	-	-	-	-	-	-	-	-	-	-	-	-	-	-	-	-	-	-	-	-
Martin County	43,083	36,250	-	-	-	-	-	-	-	-	-	-	-	-	-	-	-	-	-	-	-	-	-	-
Miami-Dade County	35,966	42,961	56,719	43,600	-	-	36,386	-	59,049	-	-	-	-	41,630	47,130	-	-	42,917	-	-	-	41,699	-	32,447
Doral (cdp)	53,060	55,909	-	-	-	-	-	-	-	-	-	-	-	-	-	-	-	-	-	-	-	-	-	-
Ives Estates (cdp)	40,717	40,556	-	-	-	-	-	-	-	-	-	-	-	-	-	-	-	-	-	-	-	-	-	-
North Miami Beach (city)	31,377	21,696	-	17,500	-	-	26,389	-	-	-	-	-	-	-	-	-	-	-	-	-	-	-	-	-
Pinecrest (village)	107,507	68,913	-	-	-	-	-	-	-	-	-	-	-	-	-	-	-	-	-	-	-	-	-	-
Monroe County	42,283	47,188	-	-	-	-	-	-	-	-	-	-	-	-	-	-	-	-	-	-	-	-	-	-
Nassau County	46,022	55,268	-	-	-	-	-	-	-	-	-	-	-	-	-	-	-	-	-	-	-	-	-	-
Okaloosa County	41,474	36,458	-	-	-	-	-	-	35,221	-	-	-	-	-	32,396	-	-	-	-	-	-	34,464	-	55,795
Wright (cdp)	36,940	38,889	-	-	-	-	-	-	-	-	-	-	-	-	-	-	-	-	-	-	-	-	-	-
Orange County	41,311	45,409	42,609	45,961	-	-	50,000	-	55,833	-	-	-	-	32,308	32,875	-	-	65,515	-	-	-	-	-	40,761
Oak Ridge (cdp)	30,290	34,500	-	-	-	-	-	-	-	-	-	-	-	-	-	-	-	-	-	-	-	-	-	39,293
Osceola County	38,214	41,840	-	32,143	-	-	52,120	-	53,864	-	-	-	-	-	-	-	-	-	-	-	-	-	-	-
Palm Beach County	45,062	47,829	48,750	55,041	-	-	45,927	-	56,354	-	-	-	-	41,071	40,042	-	-	-	-	-	-	33,750	-	43,533
Pasco County	32,969	51,761	-	65,163	-	-	34,464	-	57,976	-	-	-	-	-	-	-	-	-	-	-	-	-	-	-
Pinellas County	37,111	43,313	-	60,488	-	34,602	39,569	-	40,375	-	-	-	-	18,281	42,548	43,561	-	-	-	-	-	41,250	-	39,527
Pinellas Park (city)	35,048	34,856	-	-	-	-	-	-	-	-	-	-	-	-	-	-	-	-	-	-	-	-	-	34,196
Polk County	36,036	51,344	-	57,823	-	-	35,900	-	56,563	-	-	-	-	-	-	61,150	-	-	-	-	-	-	-	50,662
Putnam County	28,180	63,542	-	-	-	-	-	-	-	-	-	-	-	-	-	-	-	-	-	-	-	-	-	-
St. Johns County	50,099	53,500	-	-	-	-	-	-	-	-	-	-	-	-	-	-	-	-	-	-	-	-	-	-
St. Lucie County	36,363	39,728	-	-	-	-	-	-	-	-	-	-	-	-	-	-	-	-	-	-	-	-	-	-
Santa Rosa County	41,881	40,030	-	-	-	-	-	-	34,224	-	-	-	-	-	-	-	-	-	-	-	-	-	-	-
Sarasota County	41,957	42,813	-	-	-	-	37,656	-	36,579	-	-	-	-	-	-	-	-	-	-	-	-	-	-	50,313
Seminole County	49,326	56,111	-	65,292	-	-	46,528	-	64,792	-	-	-	-	-	45,625	-	-	-	-	-	-	-	-	70,521

Notes: Please refer to the User's Guide for an explanation of data; data is arranged alphabetically by state, then county, then city within each county; table includes counties with populations greater than 49,999 unless noted and cities with populations greater than 9,999 whose Asian and/or NHPI population rates are greater than the national average; (1) Native Hawaiian and other Pacific Islander; (2) excludes Taiwanese; (3) includes Chamorro; (4) county does not meet population threshold but is shown in order to allow inclusion of city

Place	All households	Asian households	NHPI[1] households	Asian Indian	Bangladeshi	Cambodian	Chinese[2]	Fijian	Filipino	Guamanian[3]	Hawaiian, Native	Hmong	Indonesian	Japanese	Korean	Laotian	Malaysian	Pakistani	Samoan	Sri Lankan	Taiwanese	Thai	Tongan	Vietnamese
Volusia County	35,219	31,528	-	37,206	-	-	31,842	-	39,083	-	-	-	-	-	29,375	-	-	-	-	-	-	-	-	-
GEORGIA	42,433	50,496	46,303	59,378	41,947	54,241	51,814	-	50,064	47,235	54,773	54,000	35,500	44,757	39,085	50,992	-	50,260	37,727	-	74,583	39,457	-	47,849
Bartow County	43,660	42,188	-	-	-	-	-	-	-	-	-	-	-	-	-	-	-	-	-	-	-	-	-	-
Bibb County	34,532	47,426	-	-	-	-	-	-	-	-	-	-	-	-	-	-	-	-	-	-	-	-	-	-
Bulloch County	29,499	38,882	-	-	-	-	-	-	-	-	-	-	-	-	-	-	-	-	-	-	-	-	-	-
Carroll County	38,799	39,500	-	-	-	-	-	-	-	-	-	-	-	-	-	-	-	-	-	-	-	-	-	-
Catoosa County	39,998	35,750	-	-	-	-	-	-	-	-	-	-	-	-	-	-	-	-	-	-	-	-	-	-
Chatham County	37,752	40,318	-	41,912	-	-	35,850	-	-	-	-	-	-	-	20,938	-	-	-	-	-	-	-	-	41,548
Cherokee County	60,896	69,653	-	90,000	-	-	-	-	-	-	-	-	-	-	-	-	-	-	-	-	-	-	-	-
Clarke County	28,403	22,926	-	29,444	-	-	25,577	-	-	-	-	-	-	-	7,917	-	-	-	-	-	-	-	-	-
Clayton County	42,697	47,015	-	35,139	-	57,440	41,250	-	-	-	-	-	-	-	-	59,688	-	43,438	-	-	-	-	-	48,601
Forest Park (city)	33,556	40,774	-	-	-	-	-	-	-	-	-	-	-	-	-	-	-	-	-	-	-	-	-	40,595
Riverdale (city)	39,530	46,471	-	-	-	-	-	-	-	-	-	-	-	-	-	-	-	-	-	-	-	-	-	60,341
Cobb County	58,289	57,690	-	63,145	-	-	57,072	-	61,806	-	-	-	-	66,719	47,200	-	-	57,868	-	-	-	-	-	53,491
Smyrna (city)	47,572	48,482	-	49,911	-	-	-	-	-	-	-	-	-	-	-	-	-	-	-	-	-	-	-	-
Columbia County	55,682	58,897	-	63,558	-	-	62,212	-	-	-	-	-	-	-	51,500	-	-	-	-	-	-	-	-	-
Martinez (cdp)	58,069	56,719	-	62,885	-	-	-	-	-	-	-	-	-	-	-	-	-	-	-	-	-	-	-	-
Coweta County	52,706	49,722	-	-	-	-	-	-	-	-	-	-	-	-	-	-	-	-	-	-	-	-	-	-
DeKalb County	49,117	44,173	-	52,281	37,115	66,648	42,500	-	36,458	-	-	-	-	51,250	26,587	-	-	-	-	-	-	-	-	42,215
Druid Hills (cdp)	62,953	28,750	-	-	-	-	-	-	-	-	-	-	-	-	-	-	-	-	-	-	-	-	-	-
Dunwoody (cdp)	82,838	70,988	-	71,680	-	-	-	-	-	-	-	-	-	-	45,139	-	-	-	-	-	-	-	-	-
North Atlanta (cdp)	52,333	40,750	-	-	-	-	-	-	-	-	-	-	-	-	-	-	-	-	-	-	-	-	-	-
North Decatur (cdp)	50,047	36,154	-	-	-	-	-	-	-	-	-	-	-	-	-	-	-	-	-	-	-	-	-	-
North Druid Hills (cdp)	48,530	38,150	-	22,393	-	-	-	-	-	-	-	-	-	-	-	-	-	-	-	-	-	-	-	-
Tucker (cdp)	59,953	60,074	-	-	-	-	-	-	-	-	-	-	-	-	-	-	-	-	-	-	-	-	-	29,500
Dougherty County	30,934	36,607	-	-	-	-	-	-	-	-	-	-	-	-	-	-	-	-	-	-	-	-	-	-
Douglas County	50,108	52,813	-	-	-	-	-	-	-	-	-	-	-	-	-	-	-	-	-	-	-	-	-	-
Fayette County	71,227	81,210	-	-	-	-	-	-	-	-	-	-	-	100,386	-	-	-	-	-	-	-	-	-	-
Peachtree City (city)	76,458	83,143	-	-	-	-	-	-	-	-	-	-	-	100,386	-	-	-	-	-	-	-	-	-	-
Floyd County	35,615	53,000	-	53,750	-	-	-	-	-	-	-	-	-	-	-	-	-	-	-	-	-	-	-	-
Forsyth County	68,890	89,554	-	-	-	-	-	-	-	-	-	-	-	-	-	-	-	-	-	-	-	-	-	-
Fulton County	47,321	61,068	-	73,472	-	-	60,571	-	54,607	-	-	-	-	70,329	48,208	-	-	-	-	-	-	-	-	50,250
Alpharetta (city)	71,207	82,963	-	71,181	-	-	81,759	-	-	-	-	-	-	-	-	-	-	-	-	-	-	-	-	-
Roswell (city)	71,726	56,688	-	71,932	-	-	50,795	-	-	-	-	-	-	-	45,625	-	-	-	-	-	-	-	-	-
Glynn County	38,765	46,538	-	-	-	-	-	-	-	-	-	-	-	-	-	-	-	-	-	-	-	-	-	-
Gwinnett County	60,537	53,519	59,655	60,602	-	45,909	60,403	-	46,618	-	-	-	-	36,779	47,569	58,382	-	48,472	-	-	82,072	-	-	56,958
Duluth (city)	60,088	67,917	-	101,265	-	-	68,750	-	-	-	-	-	-	-	67,159	-	-	-	-	-	-	-	-	-
Lilburn (city)	53,707	51,641	-	76,074	-	-	-	-	-	-	-	-	-	-	-	-	-	-	-	-	-	-	-	43,333
Mountain Park (cdp)	62,892	75,540	-	79,593	-	-	-	-	-	-	-	-	-	-	-	-	-	-	-	-	-	-	-	-
Hall County	44,908	43,015	-	-	-	-	-	-	-	-	-	-	-	-	-	-	-	-	-	-	-	-	-	39,519
Henry County	57,309	62,113	-	63,333	-	-	-	-	-	-	-	-	-	-	-	-	-	-	-	-	-	-	-	-

Notes: Please refer to the User's Guide for an explanation of data; data is arranged alphabetically by state, then county, then city within each county; table includes counties with populations greater than 49,999 unless noted and cities with populations greater than 9,999 whose Asian and/or NHPI population rates are greater than the national average; (1) Native Hawaiian and other Pacific Islander; (2) excludes Taiwanese; (3) includes Chamorro; (4) county does not meet population threshold but is shown in order to allow inclusion of city

Place	All households	Asian households	NHPI[1] households	Asian Indian	Bangladeshi	Cambodian	Chinese[2]	Fijian	Filipino	Guamanian[3]	Hawaiian, Native	Hmong	Indonesian	Japanese	Korean	Laotian	Malaysian	Pakistani	Samoan	Sri Lankan	Taiwanese	Thai	Tongan	Vietnamese
Houston County	43,638	46,905	-	-	-	-	-	-	43,229	-	-	-	-	-	-	-	-	-	-	-	-	-	-	-
Liberty County	33,477	23,482	-	-	-	-	-	-	-	-	-	-	-	-	13,875	-	-	-	-	-	-	-	-	-
Lowndes County	32,132	34,934	-	-	-	-	-	-	-	-	-	-	-	-	-	-	-	-	-	-	-	-	-	-
Muscogee County	34,798	43,967	28,631	69,583	-	-	31,630	-	51,250	-	-	-	-	-	23,438	-	-	-	-	-	-	-	-	-
Columbus (sp. city)	34,853	43,967	28,631	69,583	-	-	31,630	-	51,250	-	-	-	-	-	23,438	-	-	-	-	-	-	-	-	-
Newton County	44,875	42,500	-	-	-	-	-	-	-	-	-	-	-	-	-	-	-	-	-	-	-	-	-	-
Richmond County	33,086	29,817	-	44,926	-	-	41,719	-	-	-	-	-	-	-	20,931	-	-	-	-	-	-	-	-	-
Rockdale County	53,599	55,417	-	-	-	-	-	-	-	-	-	-	-	-	-	-	-	-	-	-	-	-	-	-
Spalding County	36,221	43,889	-	-	-	-	-	-	-	-	-	-	-	-	-	-	-	-	-	-	-	-	-	-
Troup County	35,469	65,250	-	-	-	-	-	-	-	-	-	-	-	-	-	-	-	-	-	-	-	-	-	-
Walton County	46,479	60,893	-	-	-	-	-	-	-	-	-	-	-	-	-	-	-	-	-	-	-	-	-	-
Whitfield County	39,377	30,645	-	-	-	-	-	-	-	-	-	-	-	-	-	-	-	-	-	-	-	-	-	-
HAWAII	49,820	54,232	41,779	61,523	-	12,917	53,405	-	55,305	36,767	45,486	-	-	57,134	33,365	24,792	-	-	31,477	-	47,500	34,531	38,365	26,389
Hawaii County	39,805	43,454	35,596	-	-	-	52,563	-	40,354	-	37,068	-	-	44,709	43,239	-	-	-	34,167	-	-	-	-	-
Hilo (cdp)	39,139	47,725	30,168	-	-	-	49,583	-	31,129	-	32,625	-	-	49,302	49,545	-	-	-	-	-	-	-	-	-
Honolulu County	51,914	56,030	43,442	61,172	-	-	53,354	-	56,994	41,875	50,019	-	-	60,748	32,298	24,083	-	-	31,250	-	50,446	32,045	34,375	25,694
Ewa Beach (cdp)	57,073	64,315	47,639	-	-	-	-	-	64,293	-	54,583	-	-	66,050	-	-	-	-	42,188	-	-	-	-	-
Halawa (cdp)	63,176	66,701	53,409	-	-	-	68,625	-	76,741	-	56,827	-	-	62,443	-	-	-	-	21,447	-	-	-	-	-
Honolulu (cdp)	45,112	47,273	35,673	57,292	-	-	47,204	-	49,349	35,278	43,418	-	-	51,857	29,393	22,188	-	-	25,302	-	51,339	25,694	23,750	24,037
Kailua (cdp)	72,784	79,318	64,505	-	-	-	72,857	-	71,953	-	64,565	-	-	82,773	64,583	-	-	-	-	-	-	-	-	-
Kaneohe (cdp)	66,006	71,289	56,917	-	-	-	68,209	-	68,409	-	53,750	-	-	74,424	58,750	-	-	-	-	-	-	-	-	-
Kaneohe Station (cdp)	34,757	28,393	-	-	-	-	-	-	-	-	-	-	-	-	-	-	-	-	-	-	-	-	-	-
Makakilo City (cdp)	66,515	68,509	75,435	-	-	-	-	-	67,700	-	77,007	-	-	73,103	-	-	-	-	-	-	-	-	-	-
Mililani Town (cdp)	73,067	79,464	87,188	-	-	-	75,818	-	73,016	-	90,776	-	-	84,567	61,563	-	-	-	-	-	-	-	-	-
Nanakuli (cdp)	45,352	42,969	42,132	-	-	-	-	-	40,000	-	41,625	-	-	-	-	-	-	-	47,321	-	-	-	-	-
Pearl City (cdp)	62,036	67,083	72,543	-	-	-	64,342	-	66,964	-	72,563	-	-	68,639	53,750	-	-	-	-	-	-	-	-	-
Schofield Barracks (cdp)	33,788	24,444	-	-	-	-	-	-	-	-	-	-	-	-	-	-	-	-	-	-	-	-	-	-
Wahiawa (cdp)	41,257	46,964	33,750	-	-	-	-	-	38,542	-	37,589	-	-	52,031	-	-	-	-	-	-	-	-	-	-
Waianae (cdp)	46,717	50,764	38,438	-	-	-	-	-	47,417	-	40,167	-	-	70,074	-	-	-	-	-	-	-	-	-	-
Waimalu (cdp)	61,210	67,103	43,942	-	-	-	68,571	-	63,088	-	46,250	-	-	73,140	35,000	-	-	-	-	-	-	-	-	-
Waipahu (cdp)	49,444	57,484	24,909	-	-	-	46,250	-	59,443	-	47,031	-	-	53,869	-	-	-	-	23,536	-	-	-	-	-
Waipio (cdp)	61,276	70,509	44,688	-	-	-	-	-	67,308	-	51,184	-	-	76,393	-	-	-	-	-	-	-	-	-	-
Kauai County	45,020	48,750	41,217	-	-	-	53,542	-	50,816	-	41,118	-	-	45,232	-	-	-	-	-	-	-	-	-	-
Maui County	49,489	54,307	43,813	-	-	-	56,875	-	59,289	-	44,053	-	-	49,729	46,167	-	-	-	-	-	-	-	49,153	-
Kahului (cdp)	46,656	53,963	35,188	-	-	-	-	-	59,787	-	37,000	-	-	48,654	-	-	-	-	-	-	-	-	-	-
Kihei (cdp)	46,215	53,500	44,038	-	-	-	-	-	65,000	-	39,150	-	-	42,118	-	-	-	-	-	-	-	-	-	-
Wailuku (cdp)	45,587	48,438	43,008	-	-	-	-	-	50,714	-	43,073	-	-	48,750	-	-	-	-	-	-	-	-	-	-
IDAHO	37,572	45,746	36,429	53,600	-	-	50,500	-	41,071	-	35,688	-	-	44,856	35,577	50,865	-	-	-	-	-	-	-	39,007
Ada County	46,140	51,925	37,279	53,850	-	-	62,391	-	52,083	-	-	-	-	55,417	61,563	-	-	-	-	-	-	-	-	39,669
Bannock County	36,683	31,705	-	-	-	-	-	-	-	-	-	-	-	-	-	-	-	-	-	-	-	-	-	-
Bonneville County	41,805	51,458	-	-	-	-	-	-	-	-	-	-	-	-	-	-	-	-	-	-	-	-	-	-

Notes: Please refer to the User's Guide for an explanation of data; data is arranged alphabetically by state, then county, then city within each county; table includes counties with populations greater than 49,999 unless noted and cities with populations greater than 9,999 whose Asian and/or NHPI population rates are greater than the national average; (1) Native Hawaiian and other Pacific Islander; (2) excludes Taiwanese; (3) includes Chamorro; (4) county does not meet population threshold but is shown in order to allow inclusion of city

Place	All households	Asian households	NHPI[1] households	Asian Indian	Bangladeshi	Cambodian	Chinese[2]	Fijian	Filipino	Guamanian[3]	Hawaiian, Native	Hmong	Indonesian	Japanese	Korean	Laotian	Malaysian	Pakistani	Samoan	Sri Lankan	Taiwanese	Thai	Tongan	Vietnamese
Canyon County	35,884	37,273	-	-	-	-	-	-	-	-	-	-	-	31,667	-	-	-	-	-	-	-	-	-	-
Kootenai County	37,754	33,482	-	-	-	-	-	-	-	-	-	-	-	-	-	-	-	-	-	-	-	-	-	-
Twin Falls County	34,506	37,750	-	-	-	-	-	-	-	-	-	-	-	-	-	-	-	-	-	-	-	-	-	-
ILLINOIS	46,590	57,333	41,276	64,969	50,625	55,817	50,519	-	67,293	31,607	40,667	-	21,667	53,750	42,258	58,098	37,000	46,179	50,682	57,000	51,486	46,735	-	44,177
Champaign County	37,780	20,170	-	24,554	-	-	19,621	-	30,714	-	-	-	-	25,313	13,000	-	-	-	-	-	-	-	-	35,250
Champaign (city)	32,795	17,773	-	21,679	-	-	13,125	-	-	-	-	-	-	-	8,452	-	-	-	-	-	-	-	-	29,063
Urbana (city)	27,819	17,319	-	16,512	-	-	19,269	-	-	-	-	-	-	-	13,250	-	-	-	-	-	-	-	-	-
Coles County	32,286	12,250	-	-	-	-	-	-	-	-	-	-	-	-	-	-	-	-	-	-	-	-	-	-
Cook County	45,922	52,283	37,153	60,428	-	55,233	44,240	-	63,925	-	-	-	19,375	53,886	40,955	60,347	-	39,464	-	-	38,125	46,490	-	41,064
Arlington Heights (village)	67,807	71,471	-	67,974	-	-	89,667	-	82,563	-	-	-	-	70,625	68,036	-	-	-	-	-	-	-	-	-
Chicago (city)	38,625	40,519	29,375	42,979	-	52,500	37,145	-	55,164	-	-	-	-	45,750	20,401	-	-	28,981	-	-	30,938	39,479	-	35,774
Des Plaines (city)	53,638	76,999	-	72,875	-	-	74,444	-	89,828	-	-	-	-	-	-	-	-	-	-	-	-	-	-	-
Elk Grove Village (village)	62,132	73,875	-	83,376	-	-	62,250	-	80,520	-	-	-	-	79,246	-	-	-	-	-	-	-	-	-	-
Evanston (city)	56,335	37,604	-	71,667	-	-	35,000	-	56,250	-	-	-	-	36,250	21,213	-	-	-	-	-	-	-	-	-
Forest Park (village)	44,103	39,153	-	-	-	-	-	-	-	-	-	-	-	-	-	-	-	-	-	-	-	-	-	-
Glenview (village)	80,730	85,821	-	150,000	-	-	71,667	-	91,021	-	-	-	-	91,985	70,987	-	-	-	-	-	-	-	-	-
Hanover Park (village)	61,358	64,176	-	60,625	-	-	-	-	77,832	-	-	-	-	-	-	-	-	-	-	-	-	-	-	-
Hoffman Estates (village)	65,937	67,621	-	66,250	-	-	80,921	-	76,605	-	-	-	-	100,146	67,500	-	-	-	-	-	-	-	-	-
Lincolnwood (village)	71,234	82,019	-	72,188	-	-	-	-	89,341	-	-	-	-	-	72,604	-	-	-	-	-	-	-	-	-
Morton Grove (village)	63,511	76,982	-	72,171	-	-	-	-	92,310	-	-	-	-	-	61,875	-	-	-	-	-	-	-	-	-
Mount Prospect (village)	57,165	59,258	-	57,955	-	-	60,897	-	66,979	-	-	-	-	41,458	50,729	-	-	-	-	-	-	-	-	-
Niles (village)	48,627	56,815	-	68,646	-	-	-	-	67,596	-	-	-	-	-	44,028	-	-	-	-	-	-	-	-	-
Northbrook (village)	95,665	105,894	-	-	-	-	95,318	-	-	-	-	-	-	-	72,500	-	-	-	-	-	-	-	-	-
Oak Park (village)	59,183	55,929	-	60,375	-	-	60,234	-	-	-	-	-	-	-	-	-	-	-	-	-	-	-	-	-
Orland Park (village)	67,574	92,001	-	115,985	-	-	-	-	97,711	-	-	-	-	-	-	-	-	-	-	-	-	-	-	-
Palatine (village)	63,321	63,750	-	66,818	-	-	63,221	-	90,255	-	-	-	-	-	62,198	-	-	-	-	-	-	-	-	-
Prospect Heights (city)	55,641	67,604	-	-	-	-	-	-	-	-	-	-	-	-	-	-	-	-	-	-	-	-	-	-
Rolling Meadows (city)	59,535	69,844	-	69,688	-	-	-	-	-	-	-	-	-	-	-	-	-	-	-	-	-	-	-	-
Schaumburg (village)	60,941	63,068	-	72,073	-	-	60,029	-	62,841	-	-	-	-	59,345	52,131	-	-	-	-	-	-	-	-	-
Schiller Park (village)	41,583	50,865	-	-	-	-	-	-	-	-	-	-	-	-	-	-	-	-	-	-	-	-	-	-
Skokie (village)	57,375	68,372	-	66,071	-	-	63,068	-	90,930	-	-	-	-	-	60,049	-	-	78,844	-	-	-	-	-	-
Streamwood (village)	65,076	76,272	-	72,292	-	-	-	-	80,539	-	-	-	-	-	-	-	-	-	-	-	-	-	-	-
Wheeling (village)	55,491	62,500	-	68,514	-	-	-	-	80,402	-	-	-	-	-	-	-	-	-	-	-	-	-	-	-
Wilmette (village)	106,773	75,000	-	-	-	-	77,620	-	-	-	-	-	-	106,933	61,012	-	-	-	-	-	-	-	-	-
DeKalb County	45,828	17,684	-	18,750	-	-	-	-	-	-	-	-	-	-	-	-	-	-	-	-	-	-	-	-
DeKalb (city)	35,153	12,022	-	15,000	-	-	-	-	-	-	-	-	-	-	-	-	-	-	-	-	-	-	-	-
DuPage County	67,887	75,334	-	76,555	-	-	87,952	-	77,082	-	-	-	-	62,986	61,522	-	-	60,833	-	-	131,110	70,750	-	62,222
Addison (village)	54,090	56,016	-	61,304	-	-	-	-	74,432	-	-	-	-	-	-	-	-	-	-	-	-	-	-	-
Bartlett (village)	79,718	82,229	-	87,227	-	-	-	-	85,657	-	-	-	-	-	-	-	-	-	-	-	-	-	-	-
Bensenville (village)	54,662	49,688	-	60,764	-	-	-	-	-	-	-	-	-	-	-	-	-	-	-	-	-	-	-	-
Bloomingdale (village)	67,365	78,120	-	67,391	-	-	-	-	-	-	-	-	-	-	-	-	-	-	-	-	-	-	-	-

Notes: Please refer to the User's Guide for an explanation of data; data is arranged alphabetically by state, then county, then city within each county; table includes counties with populations greater than 49,999 unless noted and cities with populations greater than 9,999 whose Asian and/or NHPI population rates are greater than the national average; (1) Native Hawaiian and other Pacific Islander; (2) excludes Taiwanese; (3) includes Chamorro; (4) county does not meet population threshold but is shown in order to allow inclusion of city

Place	All households	Asian households	NHPI[1] households	Asian Indian	Bangladeshi	Cambodian	Chinese[2]	Fijian	Filipino	Guamanian[3]	Hawaiian, Native	Hmong	Indonesian	Japanese	Korean	Laotian	Malaysian	Pakistani	Samoan	Sri Lankan	Taiwanese	Thai	Tongan	Vietnamese
Burr Ridge (village)	129,507	184,734	-	161,233	-	-	-	-	-	-	-	-	-	-	-	-	-	-	-	-	-	-	-	-
Carol Stream (village)	64,893	65,000	-	62,885	-	-	-	-	72,632	-	-	-	-	-	-	-	-	-	-	-	-	-	-	61,250
Darien (city)	74,836	94,990	-	98,984	-	-	-	-	90,728	-	-	-	-	-	-	-	-	-	-	-	-	-	-	-
Downers Grove (village)	65,539	80,374	-	82,809	-	-	75,515	-	90,442	-	-	-	-	-	-	-	-	-	-	-	-	-	-	-
Glen Ellyn (village)	74,846	54,750	-	58,750	-	-	-	-	-	-	-	-	-	-	-	-	-	-	-	-	-	-	-	-
Glendale Heights (village)	56,285	62,451	-	57,063	-	-	-	-	71,538	-	-	-	-	-	-	-	-	-	-	-	-	-	-	68,026
Hinsdale (village)	104,551	75,120	-	-	-	-	-	-	-	-	-	-	-	-	-	-	-	-	-	-	-	-	-	-
Lisle (village)	65,821	82,694	-	82,705	-	-	127,681	-	-	-	-	-	-	-	-	-	-	-	-	-	-	-	-	-
Lombard (village)	60,015	65,947	-	65,353	-	-	-	-	73,250	-	-	-	-	-	-	-	-	-	-	-	-	-	-	-
Naperville (city)	88,771	95,001	-	92,686	-	-	102,958	-	109,761	-	-	-	-	-	59,868	-	-	-	-	-	97,763	-	-	-
Roselle (village)	65,254	69,750	-	71,250	-	-	-	-	-	-	-	-	-	-	-	-	-	-	-	-	-	-	-	-
Villa Park (village)	55,706	81,953	-	-	-	-	-	-	-	-	-	-	-	-	-	-	-	-	-	-	-	-	-	-
Warrenville (city)	62,430	88,687	-	-	-	-	-	-	-	-	-	-	-	-	-	-	-	-	-	-	-	-	-	-
Westmont (village)	51,422	67,188	-	66,875	-	-	76,890	-	62,222	-	-	-	-	-	-	-	-	-	-	-	-	-	-	-
Wheaton (city)	73,385	75,610	-	97,918	-	-	-	-	-	-	-	-	-	-	-	-	-	-	-	-	-	-	-	36,458
Woodridge (village)	61,944	69,042	-	60,817	-	-	-	-	75,433	-	-	-	-	-	-	-	-	-	-	-	-	-	-	-
Jackson County	24,946	6,667	-	-	-	-	3,162	-	-	-	-	-	-	-	-	-	-	-	-	-	-	-	-	-
Carbondale (city)	15,882	4,118	-	-	-	-	-	-	-	-	-	-	-	-	-	-	-	-	-	-	-	-	-	-
Kane County	59,351	69,491	-	70,104	-	-	87,019	-	75,707	-	-	-	-	-	68,750	64,706	-	-	-	-	-	-	-	45,114
South Elgin (village)	67,323	71,964	-	-	-	-	-	-	-	-	-	-	-	-	-	-	-	-	-	-	-	-	-	-
Kankakee County	41,532	51,429	-	-	-	-	-	-	-	-	-	-	-	-	-	-	-	-	-	-	-	-	-	-
Kendall County	64,625	63,068	-	-	-	-	-	-	-	-	-	-	-	-	-	-	-	-	-	-	-	-	-	-
Knox County	35,407	71,000	-	-	-	-	-	-	-	-	-	-	-	-	-	-	-	-	-	-	-	-	-	-
La Salle County	40,308	61,058	-	-	-	-	-	-	-	-	-	-	-	-	-	-	-	-	-	-	-	-	-	-
Lake County	66,973	81,889	-	81,090	-	-	94,146	-	77,418	-	-	-	-	82,053	77,190	-	-	82,759	-	-	-	-	-	40,536
Buffalo Grove (village)	80,525	81,908	-	85,355	-	-	90,859	-	72,917	-	-	-	-	85,598	83,219	-	-	-	-	-	-	-	-	-
Gages Lake (cdp)	71,750	92,209	-	-	-	-	-	-	-	-	-	-	-	-	-	-	-	-	-	-	-	-	-	-
Grayslake (village)	73,143	95,444	-	-	-	-	-	-	-	-	-	-	-	-	-	-	-	-	-	-	-	-	-	-
Gurnee (village)	75,742	86,693	-	80,000	-	-	86,331	-	95,181	-	-	-	-	-	-	-	-	-	-	-	-	-	-	-
Lake Zurich (village)	84,125	109,994	-	-	-	-	-	-	-	-	-	-	-	-	-	-	-	-	-	-	-	-	-	-
Libertyville (village)	88,828	89,557	-	-	-	-	-	-	-	-	-	-	-	-	-	-	-	-	-	-	-	-	-	-
Mundelein (village)	69,651	93,512	-	-	-	-	104,592	-	98,932	-	-	-	-	-	-	-	-	-	-	-	-	-	-	-
Vernon Hills (village)	71,297	90,655	-	100,883	-	-	113,180	-	-	-	-	-	-	-	66,875	-	-	-	-	-	-	-	-	-
Macon County	37,859	61,923	-	-	-	-	-	-	-	-	-	-	-	-	-	-	-	-	-	-	-	-	-	-
Madison County	41,541	32,344	-	50,694	-	-	-	-	-	-	-	-	-	-	-	-	-	-	-	-	-	-	-	-
McHenry County	64,826	72,763	-	76,783	-	-	58,000	-	85,355	-	-	-	-	-	-	-	-	-	-	-	-	-	-	-
McLean County	47,021	55,363	-	56,048	-	-	56,250	-	-	-	-	-	-	-	-	-	-	-	-	-	-	-	-	-
Peoria County	39,978	60,768	-	71,563	-	-	66,250	-	-	-	-	-	-	-	-	-	-	-	-	-	-	-	-	35,096
Rock Island County	38,608	65,200	-	65,703	-	-	-	-	-	-	-	-	-	-	-	-	-	-	-	-	-	-	-	-
St. Clair County	39,148	44,861	-	-	-	-	-	-	55,208	-	-	-	-	-	18,375	-	-	-	-	-	-	-	-	-
Sangamon County	42,957	42,417	-	45,417	-	-	41,250	-	-	-	-	-	-	-	-	-	-	-	-	-	-	-	-	-

Notes: Please refer to the User's Guide for an explanation of data; data is arranged alphabetically by state, then county, then city within each county; table includes counties with populations greater than 49,999 unless noted and cities with populations greater than 9,999 whose Asian and/or NHPI population rates are greater than the national average; (1) Native Hawaiian and other Pacific Islander; (2) excludes Taiwanese; (3) includes Chamorro; (4) county does not meet population threshold but is shown in order to allow inclusion of city

Place	All households	Asian households	NHPI[1] households	Asian Indian	Bangladeshi	Cambodian	Chinese[2]	Fijian	Filipino	Guamanian[3]	Hawaiian, Native	Hmong	Indonesian	Japanese	Korean	Laotian	Malaysian	Pakistani	Samoan	Sri Lankan	Taiwanese	Thai	Tongan	Vietnamese
Tazewell County	45,250	45,288	-	-	-	-	-	-	-	-	-	-	-	-	-	-	-	-	-	-	-	-	-	-
Vermilion County	34,071	101,808	-	-	-	-	-	-	-	-	-	-	-	-	-	-	-	-	-	-	-	-	-	-
Will County	62,238	76,517	-	81,721	-	-	84,350	-	72,614	-	-	-	-	-	81,131	-	-	98,099	-	-	-	-	-	74,583
Bolingbrook (village)	67,852	75,555	-	83,264	-	-	-	-	67,361	-	-	-	-	-	-	-	-	-	-	-	-	-	-	-
Winnebago County	43,886	57,500	-	59,632	-	-	-	-	67,361	-	-	-	-	-	42,250	58,375	-	-	-	-	-	-	-	43,304
INDIANA	41,567	42,933	35,625	56,630	-	42,344	37,120	-	54,324	38,365	41,250	-	-	45,341	21,824	50,455	-	67,941	-	-	26,382	32,756	-	41,099
Allen County	42,671	44,196	-	61,250	-	-	57,250	-	46,167	-	-	-	-	-	-	-	-	-	-	-	-	-	-	45,645
Bartholomew County	44,184	56,417	-	51,607	-	-	-	-	-	-	-	-	-	-	-	-	-	-	-	-	-	-	-	-
Clark County	40,111	31,250	-	-	-	-	-	-	-	-	-	-	-	-	-	-	-	-	-	-	-	-	-	-
Delaware County	34,659	8,484	-	-	-	-	-	-	-	-	-	-	-	-	-	-	-	-	-	-	-	-	-	-
Elkhart County	44,478	50,435	-	-	-	-	-	-	-	-	-	-	-	-	-	-	-	-	-	-	-	-	-	-
Grant County	36,162	43,083	-	-	-	-	-	-	-	-	-	-	-	-	-	-	-	-	-	-	-	-	-	-
Hamilton County	71,026	80,076	-	94,784	-	-	89,788	-	-	-	-	-	-	-	-	-	-	-	-	-	-	-	-	-
Carmel (city)	81,583	83,915	-	-	-	-	-	-	-	-	-	-	-	-	-	-	-	-	-	-	-	-	-	-
Hendricks County	55,208	60,096	-	-	-	-	-	-	-	-	-	-	-	-	-	-	-	-	-	-	-	-	-	-
Howard County	43,487	67,500	-	-	-	-	-	-	-	-	-	-	-	-	-	-	-	-	-	-	-	-	-	-
Johnson County	52,693	54,583	-	-	-	-	-	-	-	-	-	-	-	-	-	-	-	-	-	-	-	-	-	-
Kosciusko County	43,939	70,446	-	-	-	-	-	-	-	-	-	-	-	-	-	-	-	-	-	-	-	-	-	-
Lake County	41,829	62,862	-	76,755	-	-	65,139	-	62,500	-	-	-	-	-	51,250	-	-	-	-	-	-	-	-	-
Munster (town)	63,243	95,399	-	119,134	-	-	-	-	-	-	-	-	-	-	-	-	-	-	-	-	-	-	-	-
LaPorte County	41,430	40,139	-	-	-	-	-	-	-	-	-	-	-	-	-	-	-	-	-	-	-	-	-	-
Madison County	38,925	35,313	-	-	-	-	-	-	-	-	-	-	-	-	-	-	-	-	-	-	-	-	-	-
Marion County	40,421	44,507	-	51,464	-	-	37,885	-	55,000	-	-	-	-	49,712	36,688	-	-	-	-	-	-	-	-	36,250
Monroe County	33,311	9,171	-	17,625	-	-	18,750	-	-	-	-	-	-	-	6,712	-	-	-	-	-	-	-	-	-
Bloomington (city)	25,377	7,624	-	8,854	-	-	17,292	-	-	-	-	-	-	-	6,495	-	-	-	-	-	-	-	-	-
Porter County	53,100	76,601	-	-	-	-	-	-	-	-	-	-	-	-	-	-	-	-	-	-	-	-	-	-
St. Joseph County	40,420	46,574	-	55,781	-	-	42,262	-	-	-	-	-	-	-	23,214	-	-	-	-	-	-	-	-	-
Tippecanoe County	38,652	17,671	-	26,875	-	-	15,337	-	-	-	-	-	-	51,719	11,319	-	-	-	-	-	-	-	-	-
West Lafayette (city)	24,869	15,769	-	26,200	-	-	11,528	-	-	-	-	-	-	-	-	-	-	-	-	-	-	-	-	-
Vanderburgh County	36,823	51,350	-	-	-	-	-	-	-	-	-	-	-	-	-	-	-	-	-	-	-	-	-	-
Vigo County	33,184	10,972	-	-	-	-	-	-	-	-	-	-	-	-	-	-	-	-	-	-	-	-	-	-
Wayne County	34,885	37,159	-	-	-	-	-	-	-	-	-	-	-	-	-	-	-	-	-	-	-	-	-	-
IOWA	39,469	40,348	35,568	60,145	-	39,286	35,363	-	39,279	-	-	-	-	22,500	19,477	45,469	-	93,358	-	-	32,353	45,781	-	44,237
Black Hawk County	37,266	47,500	-	-	-	-	-	-	-	-	-	-	-	-	-	-	-	-	-	-	-	-	-	-
Buena Vista County[4]	35,300	51,154	-	-	-	-	-	-	-	-	-	-	-	-	-	53,375	-	-	-	-	-	-	-	-
Storm Lake (city)	35,270	51,923	-	-	-	-	-	-	-	-	-	-	-	-	-	53,938	-	-	-	-	-	-	-	-
Johnson County	40,060	26,235	-	37,446	-	-	30,515	-	-	-	-	-	-	-	4,467	-	-	-	-	-	-	-	-	-
Coralville (city)	38,080	25,833	-	-	-	-	-	-	-	-	-	-	-	-	-	-	-	-	-	-	-	-	-	-
Iowa City (city)	34,977	24,847	-	39,821	-	-	26,367	-	-	-	-	-	-	-	4,428	-	-	-	-	-	-	-	-	-
Linn County	46,206	60,154	-	69,000	-	-	-	-	-	-	-	-	-	-	19,444	-	-	-	-	-	-	-	-	-
Polk County	46,116	45,029	-	51,719	-	39,107	60,625	-	-	-	-	-	-	-	45,139	48,984	-	-	-	-	-	45,781	-	40,521

Notes: Please refer to the User's Guide for an explanation of data; data is arranged alphabetically by state, then county, then city within each county; table includes counties with populations greater than 49,999 unless noted and cities with populations greater than 9,999 whose Asian and/or NHPI population rates are greater than the national average; (1) Native Hawaiian and other Pacific Islander; (2) excludes Taiwanese; (3) includes Chamorro; (4) county does not meet population threshold but is shown in order to allow inclusion of city

Place	All households	Asian households	NHPI[1] households	Asian Indian	Bangladeshi	Cambodian	Chinese[2]	Fijian	Filipino	Guamanian[3]	Hawaiian, Native	Hmong	Indonesian	Japanese	Korean	Laotian	Malaysian	Pakistani	Samoan	Sri Lankan	Taiwanese	Thai	Tongan	Vietnamese
Pottawattamie County	40,089	39,375	-	-	-	-	-	-	-	-	-	-	-	-	-	-	-	-	-	-	-	-	-	-
Scott County	42,701	48,083	-	-	-	-	-	-	-	-	-	-	-	-	-	-	-	-	-	-	-	-	-	49,306
Story County	40,442	20,899	-	50,833	-	-	21,372	-	-	-	-	-	-	-	15,938	-	-	-	-	-	-	-	-	-
Ames (city)	36,042	20,927	-	50,347	-	-	21,220	-	-	-	-	-	-	-	16,146	-	-	-	-	-	-	-	-	-
Woodbury County	38,509	44,650	-	-	-	-	-	-	-	-	-	-	-	-	-	-	-	-	-	-	-	-	-	48,750
KANSAS	40,624	42,767	37,788	55,306	-	45,833	41,497	-	47,847	-	40,000	43,750	-	29,250	33,107	46,138	-	46,797	-	-	31,429	37,054	-	45,000
Cowley County[4]	34,406	41,500	-	-	-	-	-	-	-	-	-	-	-	-	-	46,250	-	-	-	-	-	-	-	-
Winfield (city)	34,443	40,682	-	-	-	-	-	-	-	-	-	-	-	-	-	47,917	-	-	-	-	-	-	-	-
Douglas County	37,547	24,125	-	33,897	-	-	29,625	-	-	-	-	-	-	-	25,852	-	-	-	-	-	-	-	-	-
Lawrence (city)	34,669	24,075	-	33,897	-	-	29,625	-	-	-	-	-	-	-	25,739	-	-	-	-	-	-	-	-	-
Johnson County	61,455	57,684	-	65,915	-	-	58,500	-	66,518	-	-	-	-	47,024	54,875	47,955	-	-	-	-	-	-	-	51,696
Overland Park (city)	62,116	60,739	-	67,875	-	-	58,839	-	-	-	-	-	-	-	55,714	-	-	-	-	-	-	-	-	56,023
Leavenworth County	48,114	43,250	-	-	-	-	-	-	-	-	-	-	-	-	-	-	-	-	-	-	-	-	-	-
Riley County	32,042	21,813	-	-	-	-	22,500	-	-	-	-	-	-	-	13,750	-	-	-	-	-	-	-	-	-
Manhattan (city)	30,463	21,281	-	-	-	-	21,979	-	-	-	-	-	-	-	-	-	-	-	-	-	-	-	-	-
Saline County	37,308	55,938	-	-	-	-	-	-	-	-	-	-	-	-	-	-	-	-	-	-	-	-	-	61,750
Sedgwick County	42,485	39,220	35,694	30,804	-	47,202	32,350	-	45,972	-	-	-	-	-	37,049	46,042	-	-	-	-	-	-	-	41,938
Wichita (city)	39,939	37,512	-	26,731	-	-	31,500	-	42,031	-	-	-	-	-	40,673	45,550	-	-	-	-	-	-	-	41,995
Shawnee County	40,988	45,250	-	-	-	-	-	-	-	-	-	-	-	-	-	-	-	-	-	-	-	-	-	-
Wyandotte County	33,784	35,938	-	-	-	-	-	-	-	-	-	45,917	-	-	-	-	-	-	-	-	-	-	-	-
KENTUCKY	33,672	46,225	29,135	59,817	-	-	41,092	-	47,569	33,594	-	-	-	51,488	33,702	-	-	66,250	-	-	-	24,167	-	40,030
Boone County	53,593	72,794	-	-	-	-	-	-	-	-	-	-	-	84,616	-	-	-	-	-	-	-	-	-	-
Campbell County	41,903	66,042	-	-	-	-	-	-	-	-	-	-	-	-	-	-	-	-	-	-	-	-	-	-
Christian County	31,177	35,357	-	-	-	-	-	-	-	-	-	-	-	-	-	-	-	-	-	-	-	-	-	-
Fayette County	39,813	35,651	-	38,661	-	-	31,758	-	-	-	-	-	-	42,500	-	-	-	-	-	-	-	-	-	-
Hardin County	37,744	41,302	-	-	-	-	-	-	-	-	-	-	-	-	33,438	-	-	-	-	-	-	-	-	-
Radcliff (city)	35,763	28,365	-	-	-	-	-	-	-	-	-	-	-	-	-	-	-	-	-	-	-	-	-	-
Jefferson County	39,457	47,192	-	54,855	-	-	47,266	-	47,411	-	-	-	-	52,019	27,463	-	-	-	-	-	-	-	-	38,508
Kenton County	43,906	60,750	-	-	-	-	-	-	-	-	-	-	-	-	-	-	-	-	-	-	-	-	-	-
Madison County	32,861	65,298	-	-	-	-	-	-	-	-	-	-	-	-	-	-	-	-	-	-	-	-	-	-
Warren County	36,151	43,060	-	-	-	-	-	-	-	-	-	-	-	-	-	-	-	-	-	-	-	-	-	-
LOUISIANA	32,566	36,115	42,875	54,461	-	-	36,090	-	42,571	45,833	29,643	-	-	32,734	24,028	42,237	-	37,955	-	-	39,107	39,750	-	30,807
Ascension Parish	44,288	61,538	-	-	-	-	-	-	-	-	-	-	-	-	-	-	-	-	-	-	-	-	-	-
Bossier Parish	39,203	36,991	-	-	-	-	-	-	-	-	-	-	-	-	-	-	-	-	-	-	-	-	-	-
Caddo Parish	31,467	37,639	-	53,214	-	-	-	-	-	-	-	-	-	-	-	-	-	-	-	-	-	-	-	-
Calcasieu Parish	35,372	47,604	-	-	-	-	-	-	-	-	-	-	-	-	-	-	-	-	-	-	-	-	-	-
East Baton Rouge Parish	37,224	30,931	-	50,275	-	-	35,962	-	29,500	-	-	-	-	-	-	-	-	-	-	-	-	-	-	24,028
Iberia Parish	31,204	41,053	-	-	-	-	-	-	-	-	-	-	-	-	-	48,500	-	-	-	-	-	-	-	32,083
Jefferson Parish	38,435	41,127	-	67,283	-	-	38,839	-	55,789	-	-	-	-	-	40,813	-	-	37,321	-	-	-	-	-	35,511
Gretna (city)	28,065	30,272	-	-	-	-	-	-	-	-	-	-	-	-	-	-	-	-	-	-	-	-	-	20,625
Harvey (cdp)	30,010	32,917	-	-	-	-	-	-	-	-	-	-	-	-	-	-	-	-	-	-	-	-	-	35,781

Notes: Please refer to the User's Guide for an explanation of data; data is arranged alphabetically by state, then county, then city within each county; table includes counties with populations greater than 49,999 unless noted and cities with populations greater than 9,999 whose Asian and/or NHPI population rates are greater than the national average; (1) Native Hawaiian and other Pacific Islander; (2) excludes Taiwanese; (3) includes Chamorro; (4) county does not meet population threshold but is shown in order to allow inclusion of city

Place	All households	Asian households	NHPI[1] households	Asian Indian	Bangladeshi	Cambodian	Chinese[2]	Fijian	Filipino	Guamanian[3]	Hawaiian, Native	Hmong	Indonesian	Japanese	Korean	Laotian	Malaysian	Pakistani	Samoan	Sri Lankan	Taiwanese	Thai	Tongan	Vietnamese
Timberlane (cdp)	49,278	44,554	-	-	-	-	-	-	-	-	-	-	-	-	-	-	-	-	-	-	-	-	-	44,583
Woodmere (cdp)	44,892	26,719	-	-	-	-	-	-	-	-	-	-	-	-	-	-	-	-	-	-	-	-	-	28,750
Lafayette Parish	36,518	36,250	-	49,219	-	-	-	-	-	-	-	-	-	-	-	-	-	-	-	-	-	-	-	29,792
Lafourche Parish	34,910	35,441	-	-	-	-	-	-	-	-	-	-	-	-	-	-	-	-	-	-	-	-	-	-
Orleans Parish	27,133	30,269	-	45,500	-	-	36,354	-	24,737	-	-	-	-	-	-	-	-	-	-	-	-	-	-	28,073
Ouachita Parish	32,047	39,038	-	-	-	-	-	-	-	-	-	-	-	-	-	-	-	-	-	-	-	-	-	-
Rapides Parish	29,856	44,375	-	-	-	-	-	-	-	-	-	-	-	-	-	-	-	-	-	-	-	-	-	-
St. Bernard Parish	35,939	45,083	-	-	-	-	-	-	-	-	-	-	-	-	-	-	-	-	-	-	-	-	-	47,727
St. Mary Parish	28,072	36,500	-	-	-	-	-	-	-	-	-	-	-	-	-	-	-	-	-	-	-	-	-	32,105
St. Tammany Parish	47,883	54,375	-	-	-	-	-	-	-	-	-	-	-	-	-	-	-	-	-	-	-	-	-	34,844
Terrebonne Parish	35,235	41,806	-	-	-	-	-	-	-	-	-	-	-	-	-	-	-	-	-	-	-	-	-	26,875
Vermilion Parish	29,500	32,143	-	-	-	-	-	-	-	-	-	-	-	-	-	-	-	-	-	-	-	-	-	31,310
Abbeville (city)	19,714	29,141	-	-	-	-	-	-	-	-	-	-	-	-	-	-	-	-	-	-	-	-	-	29,688
Vernon Parish	31,216	30,769	-	-	-	-	-	-	-	-	-	-	-	-	21,429	-	-	-	-	-	-	-	-	-
MAINE	37,240	37,873	48,000	49,943	-	26,378	38,977	-	52,813	-	-	-	-	29,141	31,161	-	-	-	-	-	-	-	-	28,611
Androscoggin County	35,793	48,750	-	-	-	-	-	-	-	-	-	-	-	-	-	-	-	-	-	-	-	-	-	-
Aroostook County	28,837	36,719	-	-	-	-	-	-	-	-	-	-	-	-	-	-	-	-	-	-	-	-	-	-
Cumberland County	44,048	37,368	-	-	-	25,000	63,056	-	40,000	-	-	-	-	-	-	-	-	-	-	-	-	-	-	37,083
Hancock County	35,811	32,031	-	-	-	-	-	-	-	-	-	-	-	-	-	-	-	-	-	-	-	-	-	-
Kennebec County	36,498	28,611	-	-	-	-	-	-	-	-	-	-	-	-	-	-	-	-	-	-	-	-	-	-
Oxford County	33,435	45,250	-	-	-	-	-	-	-	-	-	-	-	-	-	-	-	-	-	-	-	-	-	-
Penobscot County	34,274	40,536	-	-	-	-	37,386	-	-	-	-	-	-	-	-	-	-	-	-	-	-	-	-	-
York County	43,630	44,643	-	-	-	-	-	-	-	-	-	-	-	-	-	-	-	-	-	-	-	-	-	-
MARYLAND	52,868	59,589	55,288	71,336	51,534	53,056	61,042	-	65,512	64,167	53,906	-	48,750	53,185	47,085	54,119	-	47,389	-	63,906	65,417	51,974	-	54,557
Allegany County	30,821	83,100	-	-	-	-	-	-	-	-	-	-	-	-	-	-	-	-	-	-	-	-	-	-
Anne Arundel County	61,768	50,845	-	61,326	-	-	51,607	-	64,716	-	-	-	-	70,938	44,250	-	-	-	-	-	-	-	-	-
Severn (cdp)	66,204	56,042	-	-	-	-	-	-	-	-	-	-	-	-	52,153	-	-	-	-	-	-	-	-	-
South Gate (cdp)	48,867	37,431	-	-	-	-	-	-	-	-	-	-	-	-	36,989	-	-	-	-	-	-	-	-	-
Baltimore Independent City	30,078	24,065	-	28,472	-	-	20,694	-	41,019	-	-	-	-	-	13,125	-	-	-	-	-	-	-	-	33,083
Baltimore County	50,667	50,957	-	57,106	-	-	47,966	-	75,879	-	-	-	-	41,458	43,533	-	-	29,135	-	-	-	-	-	50,100
Arbutus (cdp)	47,792	30,179	-	-	-	-	-	-	-	-	-	-	-	-	-	-	-	-	-	-	-	-	-	-
Carney (cdp)	49,365	50,441	-	-	-	-	37,143	-	-	-	-	-	-	-	49,583	-	-	-	-	-	-	-	-	-
Cockeysville (cdp)	43,681	38,661	-	-	-	-	-	-	-	-	-	-	-	-	28,125	-	-	-	-	-	-	-	-	-
Lutherville-Timonium (cdp)	61,573	51,333	-	-	-	-	-	-	-	-	-	-	-	-	-	-	-	-	-	-	-	-	-	-
Mays Chapel (cdp)	71,786	79,204	-	-	-	-	-	-	-	-	-	-	-	-	-	-	-	-	-	-	-	-	-	-
Owings Mills (cdp)	53,424	47,222	-	-	-	-	-	-	-	-	-	-	-	-	-	-	-	-	-	-	-	-	-	-
Perry Hall (cdp)	57,033	58,889	-	-	-	-	-	-	-	-	-	-	-	-	42,543	-	-	-	-	-	-	-	-	-
Reisterstown (cdp)	47,587	46,250	-	44,000	-	-	-	-	-	-	-	-	-	-	-	-	-	-	-	-	-	-	-	-
Rossville (cdp)	47,545	45,060	-	-	-	-	-	-	-	-	-	-	-	-	-	-	-	-	-	-	-	-	-	-
Towson (cdp)	53,775	49,389	-	-	-	-	51,161	-	-	-	-	-	-	-	-	-	-	-	-	-	-	-	-	-
Woodlawn (cdp)	48,878	44,194	-	45,417	-	-	-	-	-	-	-	-	-	-	-	-	-	-	-	-	-	-	-	-

Notes: Please refer to the User's Guide for an explanation of data; data is arranged alphabetically by state, then county, then city within each county; table includes counties with populations greater than 49,999 unless noted and cities with populations greater than 9,999 whose Asian and/or NHPI population rates are greater than the national average; (1) Native Hawaiian and other Pacific Islander; (2) excludes Taiwanese; (3) includes Chamorro; (4) county does not meet population threshold but is shown in order to allow inclusion of city

Place	All households	Asian households	NHPI[1] households	Asian Indian	Bangladeshi	Cambodian	Chinese[2]	Fijian	Filipino	Guamanian[3]	Hawaiian, Native	Hmong	Indonesian	Japanese	Korean	Laotian	Malaysian	Pakistani	Samoan	Sri Lankan	Taiwanese	Thai	Tongan	Vietnamese
Calvert County	65,945	93,352	-	-	-	-	-	-	-	-	-	-	-	-	-	-	-	-	-	-	-	-	-	-
Carroll County	60,021	71,094	-	-	-	-	-	-	-	-	-	-	-	-	-	-	-	-	-	-	-	-	-	-
Cecil County	50,510	60,500	-	-	-	-	-	-	-	-	-	-	-	-	-	-	-	-	-	-	-	-	-	-
Charles County	62,199	65,250	-	-	-	-	-	-	51,458	-	-	-	-	-	-	-	-	-	-	-	-	-	-	-
Frederick County	60,276	50,577	-	46,544	-	-	38,846	-	-	-	-	-	-	-	32,875	-	-	-	-	-	-	-	-	-
Harford County	57,234	50,000	-	46,563	-	-	-	-	61,518	-	-	-	-	-	30,486	-	-	-	-	-	-	-	-	-
Howard County	74,167	67,450	-	82,457	-	-	71,964	-	70,817	-	-	-	-	-	51,631	-	-	60,000	-	-	-	-	-	61,346
Columbia (cdp)	71,524	68,293	-	77,790	-	-	69,138	-	55,417	-	-	-	-	-	55,000	-	-	-	-	-	-	-	-	-
Elkridge (cdp)	65,835	64,219	-	-	-	-	-	-	-	-	-	-	-	-	59,063	-	-	-	-	-	-	-	-	-
Ellicott City (cdp)	79,031	67,208	-	89,898	-	-	78,856	-	94,877	-	-	-	-	-	49,208	-	-	82,894	-	-	-	-	-	-
North Laurel (cdp)	66,836	61,397	-	67,917	-	-	-	-	-	-	-	-	-	-	31,875	-	-	-	-	-	-	-	-	-
Savage-Guilford (cdp)	64,983	62,105	-	-	-	-	-	-	-	-	-	-	-	-	-	-	-	-	-	-	-	-	-	-
Montgomery County	71,551	69,738	56,731	82,753	60,417	58,162	70,418	-	67,875	-	-	-	49,833	68,405	56,685	-	-	67,292	-	63,047	100,119	54,531	-	58,884
Aspen Hill (cdp)	63,340	61,603	-	73,636	-	-	51,500	-	82,847	-	-	-	-	-	61,852	-	-	-	-	-	-	-	-	67,167
Bethesda (cdp)	99,102	73,333	-	110,306	-	-	51,932	-	57,500	-	-	-	-	96,786	63,304	-	-	-	-	-	-	-	-	-
Calverton (cdp)	63,990	54,625	-	62,708	-	-	-	-	-	-	-	-	-	-	46,696	-	-	-	-	-	-	-	-	-
Colesville (cdp)	91,696	88,687	-	104,364	-	-	127,961	-	-	-	-	-	-	-	64,688	-	-	-	-	-	-	-	-	59,250
Fairland (cdp)	56,624	56,786	-	71,250	-	-	82,489	-	-	-	-	-	-	-	44,750	-	-	-	-	-	-	-	-	-
Gaithersburg (city)	59,879	63,441	-	67,212	-	-	66,518	-	45,536	-	-	-	-	-	53,281	-	-	-	-	-	-	-	-	71,071
Germantown (cdp)	62,431	67,284	-	72,241	-	-	63,203	-	-	-	-	-	-	-	76,628	-	-	-	-	-	-	-	-	56,042
Montgomery Village (cdp)	66,828	70,405	-	63,194	-	-	64,318	-	77,319	-	-	-	-	-	-	-	-	-	-	-	-	-	-	76,363
North Bethesda (cdp)	72,614	59,205	-	80,744	-	-	58,980	-	49,438	-	-	-	-	54,028	56,750	-	-	-	-	-	-	-	-	-
North Potomac (cdp)	109,173	99,376	-	108,893	-	-	104,728	-	-	-	-	-	-	-	81,086	-	-	-	-	-	-	-	-	-
Olney (cdp)	94,818	94,294	-	96,654	-	-	101,127	-	-	-	-	-	-	-	77,167	-	-	-	-	-	-	-	-	-
Potomac (cdp)	128,936	129,295	-	155,091	-	-	138,500	-	66,875	-	-	-	-	-	86,907	-	-	-	-	-	-	-	-	-
Redland (cdp)	80,821	75,377	-	83,476	-	-	69,219	-	98,246	-	-	-	-	-	81,071	-	-	-	-	-	-	-	-	-
Rockville (city)	68,074	52,850	-	69,688	-	-	51,583	-	48,864	-	-	-	-	32,273	56,250	-	-	-	-	-	-	-	-	40,179
Silver Spring (cdp)	51,653	43,327	-	38,194	-	60,114	51,207	-	42,375	-	-	-	-	-	15,000	-	-	-	-	-	-	-	-	37,102
Takoma Park (city)	48,490	42,708	-	-	-	-	-	-	-	-	-	-	-	-	-	-	-	-	-	-	-	-	-	-
Wheaton-Glenmont (cdp)	59,211	56,591	-	69,773	-	-	54,766	-	80,000	-	-	-	-	-	46,875	-	-	-	-	-	-	-	-	50,170
White Oak (cdp)	54,276	56,818	-	73,056	-	-	47,574	-	-	-	-	-	-	-	45,139	-	-	-	-	-	-	-	-	53,750
Prince George's County	55,256	54,201	-	58,809	-	-	49,923	-	67,034	-	-	-	-	27,344	34,178	-	-	55,833	-	-	-	41,750	-	60,508
Adelphi (cdp)	45,827	37,643	-	-	-	-	-	-	-	-	-	-	-	-	-	-	-	-	-	-	-	-	-	-
Beltsville (cdp)	57,722	53,438	-	80,285	-	-	-	-	-	-	-	-	-	-	20,750	-	-	-	-	-	-	-	-	-
College Park (city)	50,168	46,350	-	49,500	-	-	55,000	-	-	-	-	-	-	-	-	-	-	-	-	-	-	-	-	-
Fort Washington (cdp)	81,177	81,803	-	-	-	-	-	-	84,524	-	-	-	-	-	-	-	-	-	-	-	-	-	-	-
Friendly (cdp)	80,214	76,707	-	-	-	-	-	-	82,536	-	-	-	-	-	-	-	-	-	-	-	-	-	-	-
Glenn Dale (cdp)	80,851	102,868	-	-	-	-	-	-	-	-	-	-	-	-	-	-	-	-	-	-	-	-	-	-
Greenbelt (city)	46,328	47,350	-	54,737	-	-	46,838	-	-	-	-	-	-	-	29,643	-	-	-	-	-	-	-	-	-
Hyattsville (city)	45,355	46,528	-	-	-	-	-	-	-	-	-	-	-	-	-	-	-	-	-	-	-	-	-	-
Lanham-Seabrook (cdp)	63,450	92,500	-	-	-	-	-	-	-	-	-	-	-	-	-	-	-	-	-	-	-	-	-	-

Notes: Please refer to the User's Guide for an explanation of data; data is arranged alphabetically by state, then county, then city within each county; table includes counties with populations greater than 49,999 unless noted and cities with populations greater than 9,999 whose Asian and/or NHPI population rates are greater than the national average; (1) Native Hawaiian and other Pacific Islander; (2) excludes Taiwanese; (3) includes Chamorro; (4) county does not meet population threshold but is shown in order to allow inclusion of city

Place	All households	Asian households	NHPI[1] households	Asian Indian	Bangladeshi	Cambodian	Chinese[2]	Fijian	Filipino	Guamanian[3]	Hawaiian, Native	Hmong	Indonesian	Japanese	Korean	Laotian	Malaysian	Pakistani	Samoan	Sri Lankan	Taiwanese	Thai	Tongan	Vietnamese
Laurel (city)	49,415	47,614	-	-	-	-	-	-	-	-	-	-	-	-	-	-	-	-	-	-	-	-	-	-
New Carrollton (city)	51,930	56,705	-	-	-	-	-	-	-	-	-	-	-	-	-	-	-	-	-	-	-	-	-	-
South Laurel (cdp)	51,043	59,063	-	-	-	-	-	-	-	-	-	-	-	-	-	-	-	-	-	-	-	-	-	-
St. Mary's County	54,706	66,302	-	95,981	-	-	-	-	65,333	-	-	-	-	-	-	-	-	-	-	-	-	-	-	-
Lexington Park (cdp)	39,214	40,536	-	-	-	-	-	-	-	-	-	-	-	-	-	-	-	-	-	-	-	-	-	-
Washington County	40,617	35,104	-	-	-	-	-	-	-	-	-	-	-	-	-	-	-	-	-	-	-	-	-	-
Wicomico County	39,035	41,848	-	55,729	-	-	-	-	-	-	-	-	-	-	14,519	-	-	-	-	-	-	-	-	-
Salisbury (city)	29,191	35,500	-	-	-	-	-	-	-	-	-	-	-	-	-	-	-	-	-	-	-	-	-	-
MASSACHUSETTS	50,502	51,273	34,891	71,265	43,214	37,058	51,669	-	57,400	35,481	35,509	47,153	16,500	38,033	40,056	50,030	-	45,087	-	50,714	58,281	43,631	-	42,570
Barnstable County	45,933	35,329	-	-	-	-	33,571	-	-	-	-	-	-	-	-	-	-	-	-	-	-	-	-	-
Berkshire County	39,047	46,000	-	52,589	-	-	-	-	-	-	-	-	-	-	-	-	-	-	-	-	-	-	-	-
Bristol County	43,496	48,651	-	79,775	-	21,439	50,089	-	52,679	-	-	-	-	-	30,833	-	-	-	-	-	-	-	-	58,750
Essex County	51,576	56,831	-	89,301	-	36,779	63,472	-	61,771	-	-	-	-	39,688	46,905	55,000	-	-	-	-	-	-	-	53,480
Andover (town)	87,683	100,684	-	109,819	-	-	106,024	-	-	-	-	-	-	-	-	-	-	-	-	-	-	-	-	-
Lynn (city)	37,364	40,098	-	14,688	-	36,667	-	-	-	-	-	-	-	-	-	-	-	-	-	-	-	-	-	41,111
North Andover (town)	72,728	117,750	-	-	-	-	118,985	-	-	-	-	-	-	-	-	-	-	-	-	-	-	-	-	-
Franklin County	40,768	38,224	-	-	-	-	-	-	-	-	-	-	-	-	-	-	-	-	-	-	-	-	-	-
Hampden County	39,718	44,038	-	80,402	-	36,429	52,841	-	-	-	-	-	-	-	45,714	-	-	-	-	-	-	-	-	43,707
Hampshire County	46,098	39,978	-	56,458	-	-	33,456	-	-	-	-	-	-	-	21,681	-	-	-	-	-	-	-	-	-
Amherst Center (cdp)	35,754	38,977	-	-	-	-	-	-	-	-	-	-	-	-	-	-	-	-	-	-	-	-	-	-
Amherst (town)	40,017	27,750	-	-	-	-	28,125	-	-	-	-	-	-	-	-	-	-	-	-	-	-	-	-	-
Middlesex County	60,821	62,250	-	75,871	-	41,701	67,038	-	59,391	-	-	-	-	51,696	41,646	51,583	-	33,125	-	-	88,971	45,833	-	56,000
Acton (town)	91,624	98,090	-	99,202	-	-	108,801	-	-	-	-	-	-	-	-	-	-	-	-	-	-	-	-	-
Arlington (town)	64,344	71,556	-	-	-	-	65,481	-	-	-	-	-	-	-	-	-	-	-	-	-	-	-	-	-
Bedford (town)	87,962	119,795	-	-	-	-	-	-	-	-	-	-	-	-	-	-	-	-	-	-	-	-	-	-
Belmont (cdp)	80,295	69,792	-	-	-	-	70,781	-	-	-	-	-	-	-	-	-	-	-	-	-	-	-	-	-
Belmont (town)	80,295	69,792	-	-	-	-	70,781	-	-	-	-	-	-	-	-	-	-	-	-	-	-	-	-	-
Burlington (town)	75,240	80,251	-	86,959	-	-	-	-	-	-	-	-	-	-	-	-	-	-	-	-	-	-	-	-
Cambridge (city)	47,979	40,582	-	59,438	-	-	35,625	-	-	-	-	-	-	43,934	36,583	-	-	-	-	-	-	-	-	-
Chelmsford (town)	70,207	89,028	-	78,856	-	-	101,697	-	-	-	-	-	-	-	-	-	-	-	-	-	-	-	-	-
Framingham (town)	54,288	69,107	-	71,389	-	-	63,295	-	-	-	-	-	-	-	-	-	-	-	-	-	-	-	-	-
Lexington (town)	96,825	115,114	-	140,393	-	-	110,008	-	-	-	-	-	-	-	60,139	-	-	-	-	-	-	-	-	-
Lowell (city)	39,192	45,814	-	60,833	-	39,929	45,909	-	-	-	-	-	-	-	-	49,734	-	-	-	-	-	-	-	51,058
Malden (city)	45,654	51,250	-	71,528	-	-	49,835	-	-	-	-	-	-	-	-	-	-	-	-	-	-	-	-	49,375
Marlborough (city)	56,879	70,543	-	75,396	-	-	-	-	-	-	-	-	-	-	-	-	-	-	-	-	-	-	-	-
Medford (city)	52,476	54,940	-	52,305	-	-	73,125	-	-	-	-	-	-	-	-	-	-	-	-	-	-	-	-	44,583
Natick (town)	69,755	86,833	-	-	-	-	90,897	-	-	-	-	-	-	-	-	-	-	-	-	-	-	-	-	-
Newton (city)	86,052	86,122	-	131,348	-	-	76,733	-	-	-	-	-	-	-	94,770	-	-	-	-	-	-	-	-	-
Somerville (city)	46,315	50,130	-	52,143	-	-	52,060	-	-	-	-	-	-	-	30,294	-	-	-	-	-	-	-	-	-
Sudbury (town)	118,579	131,455	-	-	-	-	-	-	-	-	-	-	-	-	-	-	-	-	-	-	-	-	-	-
Waltham (city)	54,010	59,984	-	64,866	-	-	71,131	-	-	-	-	-	-	-	-	-	-	-	-	-	-	-	-	-

Notes: Please refer to the User's Guide for an explanation of data; data is arranged alphabetically by state, then county, then city within each county; table includes counties with populations greater than 49,999 unless noted and cities with populations greater than 9,999 whose Asian and/or NHPI population rates are greater than the national average; (1) Native Hawaiian and other Pacific Islander; (2) excludes Taiwanese; (3) includes Chamorro; (4) county does not meet population threshold but is shown in order to allow inclusion of city

Place	All households	Asian households	NHPI[1] households	Asian Indian	Bangladeshi	Cambodian	Chinese[2]	Fijian	Filipino	Guamanian[3]	Hawaiian, Native	Hmong	Indonesian	Japanese	Korean	Laotian	Malaysian	Pakistani	Samoan	Sri Lankan	Taiwanese	Thai	Tongan	Vietnamese
Wayland (town)	101,036	100,360	-	-	-	-	-	-	-	-	-	-	-	-	-	-	-	-	-	-	-	-	-	-
Westford (town)	98,272	118,027	-	-	-	-	145,096	-	-	-	-	-	-	-	-	-	-	-	-	-	-	-	-	-
Weston (town)	153,918	151,010	-	-	-	-	130,239	-	-	-	-	-	-	-	-	-	-	-	-	-	-	-	-	-
Winchester (town)	94,049	99,672	-	-	-	-	-	-	-	-	-	-	-	-	-	-	-	-	-	-	-	-	-	-
Woburn (city)	54,897	53,250	-	50,417	-	-	-	-	-	-	-	-	-	-	-	-	-	-	-	-	-	-	-	-
Norfolk County	63,432	61,063	-	78,066	-	-	57,341	-	74,180	-	-	-	-	42,500	60,221	-	-	-	-	-	33,750	-	-	51,513
Brookline (town)	66,711	56,968	-	77,709	-	-	63,229	-	-	-	-	-	-	32,159	50,550	-	-	-	-	-	-	-	-	-
Needham (town)	88,079	105,607	-	-	-	-	117,657	-	-	-	-	-	-	-	-	-	-	-	-	-	-	-	-	-
Norwood (town)	58,421	74,297	-	72,344	-	-	-	-	-	-	-	-	-	-	-	-	-	-	-	-	-	-	-	-
Quincy (city)	47,121	49,808	-	64,545	-	-	46,798	-	63,696	-	-	-	-	-	-	-	-	-	-	-	-	-	-	40,517
Randolph (town)	55,255	60,673	-	-	-	-	43,375	-	-	-	-	-	-	-	-	-	-	-	-	-	-	-	-	47,188
Sharon (town)	89,256	145,183	-	-	-	-	-	-	-	-	-	-	-	-	-	-	-	-	-	-	-	-	-	-
Wellesley (town)	113,686	105,979	-	-	-	-	103,013	-	-	-	-	-	-	-	-	-	-	-	-	-	-	-	-	-
Plymouth County	55,615	63,359	-	59,250	-	-	66,042	-	66,250	-	-	-	-	-	-	-	-	-	-	-	-	-	-	42,045
Suffolk County	39,355	28,208	-	39,816	-	26,286	26,201	-	46,719	-	-	-	-	11,278	18,750	-	-	-	-	-	21,591	-	-	31,982
Boston (city)	39,629	27,963	-	38,787	-	24,886	25,957	-	47,500	-	-	-	-	11,108	18,698	-	-	-	-	-	21,591	-	-	32,904
Chelsea (city)	30,161	26,159	-	-	-	-	-	-	-	-	-	-	-	-	-	-	-	-	-	-	-	-	-	27,277
Revere (city)	37,067	35,000	-	-	-	26,250	-	-	-	-	-	-	-	-	-	-	-	-	-	-	-	-	-	19,375
Worcester County	47,874	53,258	-	67,386	-	65,682	64,063	-	56,944	-	-	45,750	-	36,417	47,135	51,354	-	40,313	-	-	-	-	-	37,946
Fitchburg (city)	37,004	41,563	-	-	-	-	-	-	-	-	-	53,500	-	-	-	41,094	-	-	-	-	-	-	-	-
Northborough (town)	79,781	116,221	-	-	-	-	-	-	-	-	-	-	-	-	-	-	-	-	-	-	-	-	-	-
Shrewsbury (town)	64,237	68,833	-	73,594	-	-	65,625	-	-	-	-	-	-	-	-	-	-	-	-	-	-	-	-	80,850
Westborough (town)	73,418	80,122	-	82,474	-	-	75,580	-	-	-	-	-	-	-	-	-	-	-	-	-	-	-	-	-
Worcester (city)	35,623	38,722	-	43,971	-	-	31,800	-	-	-	-	-	-	-	-	-	-	-	-	-	-	-	-	34,773
MICHIGAN	44,667	57,966	35,903	70,011	40,179	58,972	52,888	-	70,486	68,750	37,250	37,868	27,092	60,317	35,326	51,042	22,031	58,987	22,056	49,583	70,260	25,766	-	51,276
Allegan County	45,813	45,139	-	-	-	-	-	-	-	-	-	-	-	-	-	-	-	-	-	-	-	-	-	-
Bay County	38,646	44,107	-	-	-	-	-	-	-	-	-	-	-	-	-	-	-	-	-	-	-	-	-	-
Berrien County	38,567	52,357	-	52,708	-	-	-	-	68,942	-	-	-	-	-	16,042	-	-	-	-	-	-	-	-	-
Calhoun County	38,918	54,758	-	-	-	-	-	-	-	-	-	-	-	60,991	-	-	-	-	-	-	-	-	-	-
Cass County	41,264	65,417	-	-	-	-	-	-	-	-	-	-	-	-	-	59,375	-	-	-	-	-	-	-	-
Clinton County	52,806	40,000	-	-	-	-	-	-	-	-	-	-	-	-	-	-	-	-	-	-	-	-	-	-
Eaton County	49,588	48,281	-	58,125	-	-	-	-	-	-	-	-	-	-	-	-	-	-	-	-	-	-	-	64,097
Genesee County	41,951	69,694	-	81,489	-	-	64,643	-	74,464	-	-	-	-	-	45,536	-	-	-	-	-	-	-	-	-
Ingham County	40,774	25,213	-	60,694	-	-	27,396	-	43,854	-	-	15,625	-	24,219	11,857	-	-	-	-	-	-	-	-	29,886
East Lansing (city)	28,217	17,196	-	35,313	-	-	17,328	-	-	-	-	-	-	-	12,500	-	-	-	-	-	-	-	-	-
Meridian charter (township)	55,203	50,370	-	70,776	-	-	42,917	-	-	-	-	-	-	-	2,499	-	-	-	-	-	-	-	-	-
Okemos (cdp)	62,810	50,956	-	68,438	-	-	57,083	-	-	-	-	-	-	-	-	-	-	-	-	-	-	-	-	-
Ionia County	43,074	38,281	-	-	-	-	-	-	-	-	-	-	-	-	-	-	-	-	-	-	-	-	-	-
Isabella County	34,262	18,125	-	-	-	-	-	-	-	-	-	-	-	-	-	-	-	-	-	-	-	-	-	-
Jackson County	43,171	60,000	-	-	-	-	-	-	-	-	-	-	-	-	-	-	-	-	-	-	-	-	-	-
Kalamazoo County	42,022	40,721	-	51,336	-	-	37,717	-	-	-	-	-	-	-	20,125	-	-	-	-	-	-	-	-	-

Notes: Please refer to the User's Guide for an explanation of data; data is arranged alphabetically by state, then county, then city within each county; table includes counties with populations greater than 49,999 unless noted and cities with populations greater than 9,999 whose Asian and/or NHPI population rates are greater than the national average; (1) Native Hawaiian and other Pacific Islander; (2) excludes Taiwanese; (3) includes Chamorro; (4) county does not meet population threshold but is shown in order to allow inclusion of city

Place	All households	Asian households	NHPI[1] households	Asian Indian	Bangladeshi	Cambodian	Chinese[2]	Fijian	Filipino	Guamanian[3]	Hawaiian, Native	Hmong	Indonesian	Japanese	Korean	Laotian	Malaysian	Pakistani	Samoan	Sri Lankan	Taiwanese	Thai	Tongan	Vietnamese
Kent County	45,980	50,845	-	66,442	-	-	39,783	-	42,232	-	-	-	-	-	40,759	-	-	-	-	-	-	-	-	51,442
Kentwood (city)	45,812	55,500	-	-	-	-	-	-	-	-	-	-	-	-	69,464	-	-	-	-	-	-	-	-	49,676
Lenawee County	45,739	46,953	-	-	-	-	-	-	-	-	-	-	-	-	-	-	-	-	-	-	-	-	-	-
Livingston County	67,400	88,177	-	-	-	-	-	-	-	-	-	-	-	-	-	-	-	-	-	-	-	-	-	-
Macomb County	52,102	57,516	-	61,313	-	-	44,417	-	72,453	-	-	52,065	-	-	44,904	-	-	47,450	-	-	-	-	-	49,625
Sterling Heights (city)	60,494	67,200	-	70,966	-	-	58,920	-	88,249	-	-	-	-	-	43,558	-	-	-	-	-	-	-	-	61,964
Marquette County	35,548	33,854	-	-	-	-	-	-	-	-	-	-	-	-	-	-	-	-	-	-	-	-	-	-
Midland County	45,674	87,855	-	86,203	-	-	94,755	-	-	-	-	-	-	-	-	-	-	-	-	-	-	-	-	-
Monroe County	51,743	60,125	-	-	-	-	-	-	-	-	-	-	-	-	-	-	-	-	-	-	-	-	-	-
Muskegon County	38,008	36,328	-	-	-	-	-	-	-	-	-	-	-	-	-	-	-	-	-	-	-	-	-	-
Oakland County	61,907	76,579	-	85,233	-	-	72,009	-	73,500	-	-	47,708	-	77,268	65,515	-	-	69,038	-	-	80,000	-	-	61,528
Auburn Hills (city)	51,376	61,944	-	64,583	-	-	-	-	-	-	-	-	-	-	-	-	-	-	-	-	-	-	-	-
Bloomfield (township)	103,897	154,306	-	167,536	-	-	-	-	-	-	-	-	-	-	132,124	-	-	-	-	-	-	-	-	-
Farmington (city)	56,442	57,400	-	61,316	-	-	-	-	-	-	-	-	-	-	-	-	-	-	-	-	-	-	-	-
Farmington Hills (city)	67,493	75,322	-	76,204	-	-	92,952	-	84,743	-	-	-	-	-	-	-	-	-	-	-	-	-	-	-
Madison Heights (city)	42,326	44,826	-	-	-	-	42,386	-	-	-	-	-	-	-	-	-	-	-	-	-	-	-	-	-
Novi (city)	71,918	96,801	-	122,776	-	-	111,146	-	-	-	-	-	-	71,420	-	-	-	-	-	-	-	-	-	-
Rochester (city)	65,179	94,188	-	-	-	-	-	-	-	-	-	-	-	-	-	-	-	-	-	-	-	-	-	-
Rochester Hills (city)	74,912	88,404	-	98,985	-	-	72,938	-	-	-	-	-	-	-	90,383	-	-	-	-	-	-	-	-	-
Troy (city)	77,538	80,290	-	89,395	-	-	75,599	-	83,764	-	-	-	-	-	62,273	-	-	-	-	-	84,507	-	-	-
West Bloomfield (township)	91,661	110,736	-	116,703	-	-	151,123	-	101,739	-	-	-	-	123,905	66,719	-	-	-	-	-	-	-	-	-
Ottawa County	52,347	58,450	-	51,250	-	59,335	71,375	-	-	-	-	-	-	-	17,404	56,667	-	-	-	-	-	-	-	62,083
Holland (city)	42,291	57,292	-	-	-	-	-	-	-	-	-	-	-	-	-	-	-	-	-	-	-	-	-	-
Saginaw County	38,637	54,028	-	97,325	-	-	-	-	61,563	-	-	-	-	-	41,250	-	-	-	-	-	-	-	-	-
St. Clair County	46,313	73,750	-	-	-	-	-	-	-	-	-	-	-	-	-	-	-	-	-	-	-	-	-	-
St. Joseph County	40,355	47,917	-	-	-	-	-	-	-	-	-	-	-	-	-	-	-	-	-	-	-	-	-	-
Washtenaw County	51,990	42,129	-	50,250	-	-	43,817	-	75,645	-	-	-	-	46,563	24,696	-	-	87,136	-	-	46,250	-	-	52,813
Ann Arbor (city)	46,299	35,829	-	45,346	-	-	35,066	-	58,750	-	-	-	-	50,050	21,027	-	-	-	-	-	37,045	-	-	-
Pittsfield charter (township)	61,262	64,375	-	63,947	-	-	73,750	-	-	-	-	-	-	-	37,083	-	-	-	-	-	-	-	-	-
Scio (township)	73,705	104,155	-	-	-	-	-	-	-	-	-	-	-	-	-	-	-	-	-	-	-	-	-	-
Wayne County	40,776	55,978	32,054	61,081	33,750	-	57,794	-	75,193	-	-	33,382	-	51,500	25,938	-	-	51,875	-	-	-	-	-	60,179
Brownstown (township)	55,239	74,531	-	-	-	-	-	-	-	-	-	-	-	-	-	-	-	-	-	-	-	-	-	-
Canton (township)	72,495	84,934	-	86,469	-	-	87,402	-	101,457	-	-	-	-	-	63,929	-	-	-	-	-	-	-	-	-
Hamtramck (city)	26,616	29,145	-	28,182	30,625	-	-	-	-	-	-	-	-	-	-	-	-	-	-	-	-	-	-	-
Inkster (city)	35,950	55,347	-	61,731	-	-	-	-	-	-	-	-	-	-	-	-	-	-	-	-	-	-	-	-
Northville (township)	81,541	94,106	-	125,000	-	-	-	-	-	-	-	-	-	-	-	-	-	-	-	-	-	-	-	-
MINNESOTA	47,111	45,520	48,214	62,146	-	39,858	51,542	-	56,750	76,050	43,500	35,864	-	41,364	34,457	42,454	-	62,159	-	-	74,414	35,125	-	45,884
Anoka County	57,754	63,661	-	62,969	-	-	88,676	-	63,636	-	-	79,545	-	-	43,611	-	-	-	-	-	-	-	-	64,844
Columbia Heights (city)	40,562	45,667	-	-	-	-	-	-	-	-	-	-	-	-	-	-	-	-	-	-	-	-	-	-
Blue Earth County	38,940	26,827	-	-	-	-	-	-	-	-	-	-	-	-	-	-	-	-	-	-	-	-	-	-
Carver County	65,540	76,638	-	-	-	-	-	-	-	-	-	-	-	-	-	-	-	-	-	-	-	-	-	-

Notes: Please refer to the User's Guide for an explanation of data; data is arranged alphabetically by state, then county, then city within each county; table includes counties with populations greater than 49,999 unless noted and cities with populations greater than 9,999 whose Asian and/or NHPI population rates are greater than the national average; (1) Native Hawaiian and other Pacific Islander; (2) excludes Taiwanese; (3) includes Chamorro; (4) county does not meet population threshold but is shown in order to allow inclusion of city

Place	All households	Asian households	NHPI[1] households	Asian Indian	Bangladeshi	Cambodian	Chinese[2]	Fijian	Filipino	Guamanian[3]	Hawaiian, Native	Hmong	Indonesian	Japanese	Korean	Laotian	Malaysian	Pakistani	Samoan	Sri Lankan	Taiwanese	Thai	Tongan	Vietnamese
Clay County	37,889	14,375	-	-	-	-	-	-	-	-	-	-	-	-	-	-	-	-	-	-	-	-	-	-
Crow Wing County	37,589	18,000	-	-	-	-	-	-	-	-	-	-	-	-	-	-	-	-	-	-	-	-	-	-
Dakota County	61,863	60,708	-	70,240	-	45,750	61,071	-	76,593	-	-	-	-	-	46,150	44,167	-	-	-	-	-	-	-	55,938
Eagan (city)	67,388	60,133	-	62,436	-	-	60,179	-	-	-	-	-	-	-	-	-	-	-	-	-	-	-	-	70,250
Hennepin County	51,711	47,385	42,500	61,284	-	42,452	45,903	-	56,607	-	-	35,041	-	45,357	32,255	54,063	-	61,339	-	-	-	-	-	47,520
Bloomington (city)	54,628	54,800	-	65,741	-	41,250	55,536	-	-	-	-	-	-	-	34,286	-	-	-	-	-	-	-	-	61,705
Brooklyn Center (city)	44,570	57,269	-	-	-	-	-	-	-	-	-	54,545	-	-	-	63,542	-	-	-	-	-	-	-	-
Brooklyn Park (city)	56,572	60,642	-	62,228	-	-	-	-	-	-	-	42,083	-	-	-	64,250	-	-	-	-	-	-	-	59,167
Eden Prairie (city)	78,328	70,156	-	61,447	-	-	71,250	-	-	-	-	-	-	-	-	-	-	-	-	-	-	-	-	57,768
Hopkins (city)	39,203	41,029	-	48,333	-	-	-	-	-	-	-	-	-	-	-	-	-	-	-	-	-	-	-	-
Minneapolis (city)	37,974	30,890	-	36,774	-	26,477	33,487	-	43,750	-	-	28,772	-	35,000	20,977	31,767	-	-	-	-	-	-	-	25,951
Plymouth (city)	77,008	75,524	-	86,528	-	-	56,500	-	-	-	-	-	-	-	67,639	-	-	-	-	-	-	-	-	-
Richfield (city)	45,519	48,611	-	-	-	-	-	-	-	-	-	-	-	-	-	-	-	-	-	-	-	-	-	45,156
Nobles County[4]	35,684	30,938	-	-	-	-	-	-	-	-	-	-	-	-	-	24,338	-	-	-	-	-	-	-	-
Worthington (city)	36,250	30,938	-	-	-	-	-	-	-	-	-	-	-	-	-	24,250	-	-	-	-	-	-	-	-
Olmsted County	51,316	44,071	-	60,042	-	27,315	62,625	-	-	-	-	50,774	-	35,179	52,321	25,625	-	-	-	-	-	-	-	40,268
Rochester (city)	49,090	43,333	-	58,542	-	26,111	56,500	-	-	-	-	50,774	-	-	52,321	25,625	-	-	-	-	-	-	-	31,944
Otter Tail County	35,395	40,000	-	-	-	-	-	-	-	-	-	-	-	-	-	-	-	-	-	-	-	-	-	-
Ramsey County	45,722	37,828	-	65,474	-	31,250	52,292	-	40,982	-	-	34,801	-	50,167	31,250	25,875	-	-	-	-	-	-	-	33,750
Maplewood (city)	51,596	51,585	-	-	-	-	85,931	-	-	-	-	50,143	-	-	-	-	-	-	-	-	-	-	-	-
New Brighton (city)	52,856	57,059	-	-	-	-	-	-	-	-	-	-	-	-	-	-	-	-	-	-	-	-	-	-
Roseville (city)	51,056	56,509	-	-	-	-	60,625	-	-	-	-	-	-	-	-	-	-	-	-	-	-	-	-	-
St. Paul (city)	38,774	32,149	-	42,583	-	26,964	35,179	-	32,083	-	-	34,046	-	-	27,159	24,931	-	-	-	-	-	-	-	26,343
Vadnais Heights (city)	60,804	76,370	-	-	-	-	-	-	-	-	-	-	-	-	-	-	-	-	-	-	-	-	-	-
Rice County	48,651	60,185	-	-	-	-	-	-	-	-	-	-	-	-	-	-	-	-	-	-	-	-	-	-
St. Louis County	36,306	33,000	-	-	-	-	-	-	-	-	-	-	-	-	26,111	-	-	-	-	-	-	-	-	-
Scott County	66,612	65,870	-	-	-	57,552	-	-	-	-	-	-	-	-	-	-	-	-	-	-	-	-	-	78,364
Savage (city)	75,097	65,326	-	-	-	-	-	-	-	-	-	-	-	-	-	-	-	-	-	-	-	-	-	-
Sherburne County	57,014	30,938	-	-	-	-	-	-	-	-	-	-	-	-	-	-	-	-	-	-	-	-	-	-
Stearns County	42,426	26,795	-	-	-	-	-	-	-	-	-	-	-	-	-	-	-	-	-	-	-	-	-	40,278
Washington County	66,305	84,223	-	112,435	-	-	102,679	-	-	-	-	59,750	-	-	60,536	-	-	-	-	-	-	-	-	68,500
Woodbury (city)	76,109	92,855	-	111,815	-	-	109,671	-	-	-	-	78,730	-	-	-	-	-	-	-	-	-	-	-	-
Wright County	53,945	27,321	-	-	-	-	-	-	-	-	-	-	-	-	-	-	-	-	-	-	-	-	-	-
MISSISSIPPI	31,330	40,427	50,446	48,846	-	-	37,420	-	47,045	-	-	-	-	22,083	32,143	-	-	-	-	-	-	-	-	31,694
DeSoto County	48,206	56,771	-	-	-	-	-	-	-	-	-	-	-	-	-	-	-	-	-	-	-	-	-	-
Forrest County	27,420	6,875	-	-	-	-	-	-	-	-	-	-	-	-	-	-	-	-	-	-	-	-	-	-
Harrison County	35,624	36,336	-	-	-	-	-	-	42,717	-	-	-	-	-	-	-	-	-	-	-	-	-	-	30,726
Biloxi (city)	34,106	29,708	-	-	-	-	-	-	41,397	-	-	-	-	-	-	-	-	-	-	-	-	-	-	26,319
Hinds County	33,991	48,036	-	60,375	-	-	-	-	-	-	-	-	-	-	-	-	-	-	-	-	-	-	-	-
Jackson County	39,118	42,986	-	-	-	-	-	-	-	-	-	-	-	-	-	-	-	-	-	-	-	-	-	43,229
Madison County	46,970	53,250	-	-	-	-	-	-	-	-	-	-	-	-	-	-	-	-	-	-	-	-	-	-

Notes: Please refer to the User's Guide for an explanation of data; data is arranged alphabetically by state, then county, then city within each county; table includes counties with populations greater than 49,999 unless noted and cities with populations greater than 9,999 whose Asian and/or NHPI population rates are greater than the national average; (1) Native Hawaiian and other Pacific Islander; (2) excludes Taiwanese; (3) includes Chamorro; (4) county does not meet population threshold but is shown in order to allow inclusion of city

Place	All households	Asian households	NHPI[1] households	Asian Indian	Bangladeshi	Cambodian	Chinese[2]	Fijian	Filipino	Guamanian[3]	Hawaiian, Native	Hmong	Indonesian	Japanese	Korean	Laotian	Malaysian	Pakistani	Samoan	Sri Lankan	Taiwanese	Thai	Tongan	Vietnamese
Oktibbeha County[4]	24,899	19,526	-	-	-	-	-	-	-	-	-	-	-	-	-	-	-	-	-	-	-	-	-	-
Starkville (city)	22,590	17,976	-	-	-	-	-	-	-	-	-	-	-	-	-	-	-	-	-	-	-	-	-	-
Rankin County	44,946	46,553	-	-	-	-	-	-	-	-	-	-	-	-	-	-	-	-	-	-	-	-	-	-
MISSOURI	37,934	41,075	32,773	55,833	-	38,207	39,473	-	50,908	43,750	35,208	-	-	34,423	33,983	31,944	-	39,838	35,000	-	52,266	33,917	-	33,784
Boone County	37,485	29,917	-	45,268	-	-	22,118	-	-	-	-	-	-	-	10,583	-	-	-	-	-	-	-	-	-
Columbia (city)	33,729	27,917	-	43,625	-	-	21,319	-	-	-	-	-	-	-	10,250	-	-	-	-	-	-	-	-	-
Cape Girardeau County	36,458	12,083	-	-	-	-	-	-	-	-	-	-	-	-	-	-	-	-	-	-	-	-	-	-
Cass County	49,562	65,417	-	-	-	-	-	-	-	-	-	-	-	-	-	-	-	-	-	-	-	-	-	-
Clay County	48,347	47,148	-	59,875	-	-	-	-	-	-	-	-	-	-	-	-	-	-	-	-	-	-	-	40,536
Cole County	42,924	63,684	-	-	-	-	-	-	-	-	-	-	-	-	-	-	-	-	-	-	-	-	-	-
Franklin County	43,474	59,167	-	-	-	-	-	-	-	-	-	-	-	-	-	-	-	-	-	-	-	-	-	-
Greene County	34,157	30,081	-	-	-	-	23,452	-	-	-	-	-	-	-	21,750	-	-	-	-	-	-	-	-	44,000
Jackson County	39,277	34,821	42,955	43,417	-	-	32,244	-	51,875	-	-	-	-	37,614	24,444	-	-	-	43,594	-	-	-	-	31,743
Independence (city)	38,012	43,884	58,690	-	-	-	-	-	-	-	-	-	-	-	-	-	-	-	-	-	-	-	-	-
Jasper County	31,323	32,604	-	-	-	-	-	-	-	-	-	-	-	-	-	-	-	-	-	-	-	-	-	-
Jefferson County	46,338	41,923	-	-	-	-	-	-	-	-	-	-	-	-	-	-	-	-	-	-	-	-	-	-
Newton County	35,041	23,438	-	-	-	-	-	-	-	-	-	-	-	-	-	-	-	-	-	-	-	-	-	-
Phelps County[4]	29,378	17,216	-	60,500	-	-	-	-	-	-	-	-	-	-	-	-	-	-	-	-	-	-	-	-
Rolla (city)	26,479	15,625	-	-	-	-	-	-	-	-	-	-	-	-	-	-	-	-	-	-	-	-	-	-
Platte County	55,849	51,250	-	-	-	-	-	-	-	-	-	-	-	-	-	-	-	-	-	-	-	-	-	-
St. Charles County	57,258	63,803	-	69,688	-	-	55,375	-	61,576	-	-	-	-	-	-	-	-	-	-	-	-	-	-	-
Saint Louis Independent City	27,156	28,093	-	35,150	-	-	20,948	-	39,219	-	-	-	-	-	-	-	-	-	-	-	-	-	-	27,860
St. Louis County	50,532	55,534	19,219	68,385	-	-	52,163	-	61,591	-	-	-	-	46,094	40,455	-	-	39,410	-	-	66,932	50,000	-	54,300
Chesterfield (city)	83,802	89,072	-	82,600	-	-	103,903	-	-	-	-	-	-	-	-	-	-	-	-	-	-	-	-	-
Clayton (city)	64,184	49,122	-	-	-	-	-	-	-	-	-	-	-	-	-	-	-	-	-	-	-	-	-	-
Creve Coeur (city)	75,032	86,676	-	-	-	-	-	-	-	-	-	-	-	-	-	-	-	-	-	-	-	-	-	-
Manchester (city)	64,381	66,250	-	-	-	-	-	-	-	-	-	-	-	-	-	-	-	-	-	-	-	-	-	-
Maryland Heights (city)	48,689	47,905	-	55,833	-	-	38,125	-	-	-	-	-	-	-	-	-	-	-	-	-	-	-	-	-
Town and Country (city)	139,967	200,001	-	200,001	-	-	-	-	-	-	-	-	-	-	-	-	-	-	-	-	-	-	-	-
MONTANA	33,024	24,419	39,063	33,438	-	-	30,720	-	35,556	-	36,250	-	-	16,680	22,583	-	-	-	-	-	-	-	-	-
Cascade County	32,971	22,614	-	-	-	-	-	-	-	-	-	-	-	-	-	-	-	-	-	-	-	-	-	-
Flathead County	34,466	31,607	-	-	-	-	-	-	-	-	-	-	-	-	-	-	-	-	-	-	-	-	-	-
Gallatin County	38,120	16,400	-	-	-	-	-	-	-	-	-	-	-	-	-	-	-	-	-	-	-	-	-	-
Missoula County	34,454	19,211	-	-	-	-	-	-	-	-	-	-	-	-	-	-	-	-	-	-	-	-	-	-
Yellowstone County	36,727	39,286	-	-	-	-	-	-	-	-	-	-	-	-	-	-	-	-	-	-	-	-	-	-
NEBRASKA	39,250	41,945	34,120	55,530	-	-	30,115	-	46,307	-	-	-	-	25,592	30,208	45,078	-	-	-	-	-	34,018	-	48,594
Douglas County	43,209	38,966	-	51,811	-	-	34,917	-	42,763	-	-	-	-	18,879	40,536	-	-	-	-	-	-	-	-	44,583
Hall County	36,972	54,063	-	-	-	-	-	-	-	-	-	-	-	-	-	-	-	-	-	-	-	-	-	-
Lancaster County	41,850	40,333	-	64,167	-	-	22,931	-	-	-	-	-	-	-	25,250	-	-	-	-	-	-	-	-	48,214
Sarpy County	53,804	46,375	-	-	-	-	-	-	51,339	-	-	-	-	-	53,281	-	-	-	-	-	-	-	-	61,953
NEVADA	44,581	46,328	43,086	42,326	-	39,327	50,568	-	48,692	50,598	42,436	-	-	40,757	40,016	49,149	-	50,781	40,048	-	43,712	40,313	44,904	43,929

Notes: Please refer to the User's Guide for an explanation of data; data is arranged alphabetically by state, then county, then city within each county; table includes counties with populations greater than 49,999 unless noted and cities with populations greater than 9,999 whose Asian and/or NHPI population rates are greater than the national average; (1) Native Hawaiian and other Pacific Islander; (2) excludes Taiwanese; (3) includes Chamorro; (4) county does not meet population threshold but is shown in order to allow inclusion of city

Place	All households	Asian households	NHPI[1] households	Asian Indian	Bangladeshi	Cambodian	Chinese[2]	Fijian	Filipino	Guamanian[3]	Hawaiian, Native	Hmong	Indonesian	Japanese	Korean	Laotian	Malaysian	Pakistani	Samoan	Sri Lankan	Taiwanese	Thai	Tongan	Vietnamese
Carson City Independent City	41,809	63,542	-	-	-	-	-	-	72,750	-	-	-	-	-	-	-	-	-	-	-	-	-	-	-
Clark County	44,616	46,475	43,250	40,727	-	39,856	51,409	-	48,219	52,063	42,013	-	-	42,455	40,875	49,149	-	-	37,361	-	43,144	36,604	-	43,272
Enterprise (cdp)	50,667	44,167	-	-	-	-	-	-	-	-	-	-	-	-	-	-	-	-	-	-	-	-	-	-
Henderson (city)	55,949	60,340	45,446	71,111	-	-	60,224	-	52,056	-	41,198	-	-	51,691	70,982	-	-	-	-	-	-	-	-	-
Las Vegas (city)	44,069	47,069	41,833	41,875	-	-	66,141	-	49,007	-	38,229	-	-	42,039	38,098	-	-	-	-	-	-	35,350	-	35,331
North Las Vegas (city)	46,057	54,556	51,023	-	-	-	-	-	59,583	-	-	-	-	-	-	-	-	-	-	-	-	-	-	-
Paradise (cdp)	39,376	37,158	36,890	38,846	-	-	34,659	-	39,583	-	43,309	-	-	41,944	30,865	-	-	-	-	-	-	-	-	37,083
Spring Valley (cdp)	48,563	51,087	39,389	-	-	-	57,153	-	50,708	-	-	-	-	43,750	43,462	-	-	-	-	-	-	41,146	-	56,667
Sunrise Manor (cdp)	41,066	47,296	49,464	-	-	-	43,594	-	48,081	-	-	-	-	47,188	39,650	-	-	-	-	-	-	-	-	-
Winchester (cdp)	32,251	32,692	-	-	-	-	-	-	32,054	-	-	-	-	-	-	-	-	-	-	-	-	-	-	-
Washoe County	45,815	44,571	42,981	45,000	-	-	48,448	-	50,399	-	-	-	-	30,833	30,950	-	-	-	-	-	-	-	44,327	46,208
Reno (city)	40,530	39,595	41,146	39,650	-	-	39,013	-	45,284	-	-	-	-	17,399	29,659	-	-	-	-	-	-	-	-	43,594
Sparks (city)	45,745	51,676	-	-	-	-	50,655	-	52,917	-	-	-	-	-	-	-	-	-	-	-	-	-	-	-
NEW HAMPSHIRE	49,467	56,344	-	71,415	-	-	60,750	-	51,667	-	-	-	-	40,815	46,422	46,190	-	-	-	-	-	-	-	52,269
Belknap County	43,605	41,806	-	-	-	-	-	-	-	-	-	-	-	-	-	-	-	-	-	-	-	-	-	-
Cheshire County	42,382	41,000	-	-	-	-	-	-	-	-	-	-	-	-	-	-	-	-	-	-	-	-	-	-
Grafton County	41,962	45,781	-	-	-	-	50,714	-	-	-	-	-	-	-	-	-	-	-	-	-	-	-	-	-
Hanover (town)	72,470	42,031	-	-	-	-	-	-	-	-	-	-	-	-	-	-	-	-	-	-	-	-	-	-
Hillsborough County	53,384	62,300	-	76,711	-	-	68,393	-	60,764	-	-	-	-	-	34,028	-	-	-	-	-	-	-	-	60,875
Nashua (city)	51,969	73,527	-	85,238	-	-	78,222	-	-	-	-	-	-	-	-	-	-	-	-	-	-	-	-	-
Merrimack County	48,522	44,018	-	-	-	-	-	-	-	-	-	-	-	-	-	-	-	-	-	-	-	-	-	-
Rockingham County	58,150	66,524	-	65,515	-	-	89,251	-	52,292	-	-	-	-	-	58,929	-	-	-	-	-	-	-	-	-
Strafford County	44,803	57,708	-	-	-	-	34,722	-	-	-	-	-	-	-	-	-	-	-	-	-	-	-	-	-
NEW JERSEY	55,146	72,224	56,080	75,677	45,324	59,773	80,310	-	80,946	50,313	68,611	-	54,000	70,292	53,502	63,594	-	56,566	56,042	76,930	84,297	58,021	-	54,745
Atlantic County	43,933	52,731	-	46,406	45,563	-	54,883	-	76,552	-	-	-	-	-	50,625	-	-	26,205	-	-	-	-	-	51,875
Atlantic City (city)	26,969	44,688	-	31,150	-	-	52,891	-	63,438	-	-	-	-	-	-	-	-	-	-	-	-	-	-	54,250
Brigantine (city)	44,639	42,568	-	-	-	-	-	-	-	-	-	-	-	-	-	-	-	-	-	-	-	-	-	-
Egg Harbor (township)	52,550	66,090	-	-	-	-	-	-	-	-	-	-	-	-	-	-	-	-	-	-	-	-	-	-
Galloway (township)	51,592	66,905	-	64,205	-	-	-	-	-	-	-	-	-	-	-	-	-	-	-	-	-	-	-	-
Ventnor City (city)	42,478	51,208	-	-	-	-	-	-	-	-	-	-	-	-	-	-	-	-	-	-	-	-	-	-
Bergen County	65,241	69,609	-	79,161	-	-	75,583	-	87,226	-	-	-	-	78,049	51,724	-	-	75,947	-	-	79,249	56,250	-	127,674
Bergenfield (borough)	62,172	84,780	-	82,928	-	-	-	-	91,125	-	-	-	-	-	-	-	-	-	-	-	-	-	-	-
Cliffside Park (borough)	46,288	50,887	-	-	-	-	-	-	-	-	-	-	-	65,750	43,500	-	-	-	-	-	-	-	-	-
Dumont (borough)	65,490	95,373	-	102,499	-	-	-	-	102,526	-	-	-	-	-	-	-	-	-	-	-	-	-	-	-
Elmwood Park (borough)	52,319	53,221	-	54,605	-	-	-	-	-	-	-	-	-	-	-	-	-	-	-	-	-	-	-	-
Englewood (city)	58,379	67,750	-	-	-	-	-	-	80,000	-	-	-	-	-	-	-	-	-	-	-	-	-	-	-
Fair Lawn (borough)	72,127	73,906	-	86,702	-	-	-	-	78,115	-	-	-	-	-	-	-	-	-	-	-	-	-	-	-
Fairview (borough)	40,393	39,150	-	-	-	-	-	-	-	-	-	-	-	-	-	-	-	-	-	-	-	-	-	-
Fort Lee (borough)	58,161	61,037	-	81,592	-	-	65,417	-	-	-	-	-	-	75,865	56,354	-	-	-	-	-	-	-	-	-
Franklin Lakes (borough)	132,373	107,010	-	-	-	-	-	-	-	-	-	-	-	-	-	-	-	-	-	-	-	-	-	-
Glen Rock (borough)	104,192	84,744	-	-	-	-	-	-	-	-	-	-	-	-	-	-	-	-	-	-	-	-	-	-

Notes: Please refer to the User's Guide for an explanation of data; data is arranged alphabetically by state, then county, then city within each county; table includes counties with populations greater than 49,999 unless noted and cities with populations greater than 9,999 whose Asian and/or NHPI population rates are greater than the national average; (1) Native Hawaiian and other Pacific Islander; (2) excludes Taiwanese; (3) includes Chamorro; (4) county does not meet population threshold but is shown in order to allow inclusion of city

Place	All households	Asian households	NHPI[1] households	Asian Indian	Bangladeshi	Cambodian	Chinese[2]	Fijian	Filipino	Guamanian[3]	Hawaiian, Native	Hmong	Indonesian	Japanese	Korean	Laotian	Malaysian	Pakistani	Samoan	Sri Lankan	Taiwanese	Thai	Tongan	Vietnamese
Hackensack (city)	49,316	56,413	-	64,688	-	-	-	-	71,146	-	-	-	-	-	48,600	-	-	-	-	-	-	-	-	-
Hasbrouck Heights (borough)	64,529	47,344	-	-	-	-	-	-	-	-	-	-	-	-	-	-	-	-	-	-	-	-	-	-
Hillsdale (borough)	82,904	89,555	-	-	-	-	-	-	-	-	-	-	-	-	-	-	-	-	-	-	-	-	-	-
Little Ferry (borough)	49,958	46,563	-	67,969	-	-	-	-	97,804	-	-	-	-	-	34,205	-	-	-	-	-	-	-	-	-
Lodi (borough)	43,421	52,072	-	50,066	-	-	-	-	54,750	-	-	-	-	-	-	-	-	-	-	-	-	-	-	-
Lyndhurst (township)	53,375	62,708	-	-	-	-	-	-	-	-	-	-	-	-	-	-	-	-	-	-	-	-	-	-
Mahwah (township)	79,500	87,953	-	129,690	-	-	-	-	-	-	-	-	-	-	-	-	-	-	-	-	-	-	-	-
New Milford (borough)	59,118	78,600	-	79,359	-	-	-	-	93,337	-	-	-	-	-	-	-	-	-	-	-	-	-	-	-
North Arlington (borough)	51,787	60,667	-	-	-	-	-	-	-	-	-	-	-	-	-	-	-	-	-	-	-	-	-	-
Palisades Park (borough)	48,015	48,438	-	-	-	-	-	-	-	-	-	-	-	-	45,383	-	-	-	-	-	-	-	-	-
Paramus (borough)	76,918	90,343	-	104,111	-	-	102,747	-	108,116	-	-	-	-	-	71,151	-	-	-	-	-	-	-	-	-
Ramsey (borough)	88,187	102,001	-	-	-	-	-	-	-	-	-	-	-	-	-	-	-	-	-	-	-	-	-	-
Ridgefield (borough)	54,081	40,236	-	-	-	-	-	-	-	-	-	-	-	-	40,845	-	-	-	-	-	-	-	-	-
Ridgefield Park (village)	51,825	54,750	-	-	-	-	-	-	-	-	-	-	-	-	44,583	-	-	-	-	-	-	-	-	-
Ridgewood (village)	104,286	100,668	-	-	-	-	-	-	-	-	-	-	-	123,293	56,000	-	-	-	-	-	-	-	-	-
River Edge (borough)	71,792	68,250	-	-	-	-	-	-	-	-	-	-	-	-	36,705	-	-	-	-	-	-	-	-	-
Rutherford (borough)	63,820	47,056	-	63,750	-	-	-	-	-	-	-	-	-	-	33,750	-	-	-	-	-	-	-	-	-
Saddle Brook (township)	63,545	79,440	-	-	-	-	-	-	-	-	-	-	-	-	-	-	-	-	-	-	-	-	-	-
Teaneck (township)	74,903	80,399	-	82,486	-	-	-	-	82,509	-	-	-	-	-	-	-	-	-	-	-	-	-	-	-
Tenafly (borough)	90,931	67,109	-	-	-	-	80,468	-	-	-	-	-	-	-	50,217	-	-	-	-	-	-	-	-	-
Wallington (borough)	45,656	55,179	-	-	-	-	-	-	-	-	-	-	-	-	-	-	-	-	-	-	-	-	-	-
Westwood (borough)	59,868	64,196	-	-	-	-	-	-	-	-	-	-	-	-	-	-	-	-	-	-	-	-	-	-
Wyckoff (township)	103,614	132,300	-	-	-	-	-	-	-	-	-	-	-	-	-	-	-	-	-	-	-	-	-	-
Burlington County	58,608	61,463	-	66,351	-	-	75,275	-	67,386	-	-	-	-	31,282	40,417	-	-	-	-	-	-	-	-	58,929
Browns Mills (cdp)	45,008	24,333	-	-	-	-	-	-	-	-	-	-	-	-	22,750	-	-	-	-	-	-	-	-	-
Evesham (township)	67,010	66,053	-	74,609	-	-	56,964	-	-	-	-	-	-	-	-	-	-	-	-	-	-	-	-	-
Maple Shade (township)	45,426	50,865	-	59,181	-	-	-	-	-	-	-	-	-	-	-	-	-	-	-	-	-	-	-	-
Marlton (cdp)	52,271	57,159	-	-	-	-	-	-	-	-	-	-	-	-	-	-	-	-	-	-	-	-	-	-
Mount Laurel (township)	63,750	81,009	-	82,570	-	-	80,691	-	-	-	-	-	-	-	-	-	-	-	-	-	-	-	-	-
Camden County	48,097	57,643	-	73,553	-	39,063	57,104	-	70,568	-	-	-	-	-	46,484	-	-	57,574	-	-	-	-	-	37,202
Barclay-Kingston (cdp)	68,561	85,000	-	-	-	-	-	-	-	-	-	-	-	-	-	-	-	-	-	-	-	-	-	-
Bellmawr (borough)	44,653	31,607	-	-	-	-	-	-	-	-	-	-	-	-	-	-	-	-	-	-	-	-	-	-
Cherry Hill Mall (cdp)	61,620	55,625	-	-	-	-	-	-	-	-	-	-	-	-	-	-	-	-	-	-	-	-	-	-
Cherry Hill (township)	69,421	71,883	-	92,853	-	-	70,833	-	82,861	-	-	-	-	-	54,079	-	-	-	-	-	-	-	-	-
Echelon (cdp)	49,410	65,909	-	80,705	-	-	-	-	-	-	-	-	-	-	-	-	-	-	-	-	-	-	-	-
Greentree (cdp)	85,816	72,377	-	96,938	-	-	72,361	-	-	-	-	-	-	-	-	-	-	-	-	-	-	-	-	-
Pennsauken (township)	47,538	40,809	-	-	-	-	-	-	-	-	-	-	-	-	-	-	-	-	-	-	-	-	-	38,750
Springdale (cdp)	96,412	91,198	-	-	-	-	85,000	-	-	-	-	-	-	-	-	-	-	-	-	-	-	-	-	-
Voorhees (township)	68,402	82,187	-	91,812	-	-	79,643	-	80,664	-	-	-	-	-	-	-	-	-	-	-	-	-	-	-
Cape May County	41,591	71,548	-	-	-	-	-	-	-	-	-	-	-	-	-	-	-	-	-	-	-	-	-	-
Cumberland County	39,150	49,479	-	51,544	-	-	-	-	-	-	-	-	-	-	-	-	-	-	-	-	-	-	-	-

Notes: Please refer to the User's Guide for an explanation of data; data is arranged alphabetically by state, then county, then city within each county; table includes counties with populations greater than 49,999 unless noted and cities with populations greater than 9,999 whose Asian and/or NHPI population rates are greater than the national average; (1) Native Hawaiian and other Pacific Islander; (2) excludes Taiwanese; (3) includes Chamorro; (4) county does not meet population threshold but is shown in order to allow inclusion of city

Place	All households	Asian households	NHPI[1] households	Asian Indian	Bangladeshi	Cambodian	Chinese[2]	Fijian	Filipino	Guamanian[3]	Hawaiian, Native	Hmong	Indonesian	Japanese	Korean	Laotian	Malaysian	Pakistani	Samoan	Sri Lankan	Taiwanese	Thai	Tongan	Vietnamese
Essex County	44,944	77,066	34,712	69,811	-	-	94,282	-	86,197	-	-	-	-	56,250	59,250	-	-	46,875	-	-	86,299	-	-	47,292
Belleville (township)	48,576	63,438	-	55,781	-	-	-	-	86,115	-	-	-	-	-	-	-	-	-	-	-	-	-	-	52,917
Bloomfield (township)	53,289	74,618	-	65,568	-	-	75,550	-	89,547	-	-	-	-	-	-	-	-	-	-	-	-	-	-	-
Cedar Grove (township)	78,863	111,281	-	-	-	-	-	-	-	-	-	-	-	-	-	-	-	-	-	-	-	-	-	-
Livingston (township)	98,869	105,950	-	119,226	-	-	113,944	-	117,601	-	-	-	-	-	69,250	-	-	-	-	-	-	-	-	-
Millburn (township)	130,848	106,808	-	-	-	-	102,752	-	-	-	-	-	-	-	-	-	-	-	-	-	-	-	-	-
Nutley (township)	59,634	83,837	-	102,021	-	-	-	-	89,529	-	-	-	-	-	-	-	-	-	-	-	-	-	-	-
Verona (township)	74,619	89,333	-	-	-	-	-	-	-	-	-	-	-	-	-	-	-	-	-	-	-	-	-	-
West Caldwell (township)	83,396	100,000	-	-	-	-	-	-	-	-	-	-	-	-	-	-	-	-	-	-	-	-	-	-
West Orange (township)	69,254	99,324	-	93,814	-	-	111,683	-	100,991	-	-	-	-	-	92,491	-	-	-	-	-	-	-	-	-
Gloucester County	54,273	72,083	-	62,120	-	-	72,625	-	86,246	-	-	-	-	-	65,000	-	-	-	-	-	-	-	-	-
Hudson County	40,293	54,504	-	51,185	-	-	51,024	-	65,707	-	-	-	-	56,250	42,269	-	-	39,625	-	-	-	-	-	38,542
Bayonne (city)	41,566	52,955	-	40,000	-	-	-	-	68,750	-	-	-	-	-	30,938	-	-	-	-	-	-	-	-	-
Guttenberg (town)	44,515	58,831	-	-	-	-	-	-	-	-	-	-	-	-	-	-	-	-	-	-	-	-	-	-
Harrison (town)	41,350	54,063	-	-	-	-	60,739	-	-	-	-	-	-	-	-	-	-	-	-	-	-	-	-	-
Hoboken (city)	62,550	67,000	-	78,696	-	-	51,518	-	-	-	-	-	-	-	-	-	-	-	-	-	-	-	-	-
Jersey City (city)	37,862	54,338	-	50,824	-	-	47,973	-	65,696	-	-	-	-	-	40,229	-	-	37,171	-	-	-	-	-	36,071
Kearny (town)	47,757	50,504	-	51,696	-	-	50,664	-	-	-	-	-	-	-	-	-	-	-	-	-	-	-	-	-
North Bergen (township)	40,844	51,354	-	51,563	-	-	47,614	-	-	-	-	-	-	-	-	-	-	-	-	-	-	-	-	-
Secaucus (town)	59,800	81,470	-	81,168	-	-	-	-	90,444	-	-	-	-	-	-	-	-	-	-	-	-	-	-	-
Weehawken (township)	50,196	90,834	-	-	-	-	-	-	-	-	-	-	-	-	-	-	-	-	-	-	-	-	-	-
Hunterdon County	79,888	95,454	-	106,398	-	-	97,948	-	-	-	-	-	-	-	-	-	-	-	-	-	-	-	-	-
Mercer County	56,613	83,288	-	84,779	-	-	91,269	-	73,438	-	-	-	-	84,544	68,810	-	-	69,583	-	-	107,803	-	-	-
East Windsor (township)	63,616	65,469	-	81,439	-	-	-	-	-	-	-	-	-	-	-	-	-	-	-	-	-	-	-	-
Hopewell (township)	93,640	129,801	-	-	-	-	-	-	-	-	-	-	-	-	-	-	-	-	-	-	-	-	-	-
Lawrence (township)	67,959	78,688	-	67,045	-	-	79,032	-	-	-	-	-	-	-	-	-	-	-	-	-	-	-	-	-
Princeton (borough)	67,346	38,438	-	-	-	-	-	-	-	-	-	-	-	-	-	-	-	-	-	-	-	-	-	-
Princeton (township)	94,580	75,487	-	62,054	-	-	71,979	-	-	-	-	-	-	-	-	-	-	-	-	-	-	-	-	-
West Windsor (township)	116,335	128,100	-	146,885	-	-	132,330	-	-	-	-	-	-	-	96,481	-	-	-	-	-	-	-	-	-
Middlesex County	61,446	77,613	-	78,504	46,125	-	80,575	-	92,326	-	-	-	51,705	47,143	52,125	-	-	59,635	-	81,586	76,100	-	-	67,500
Avenel (cdp)	54,929	69,500	-	70,417	-	-	-	-	-	-	-	-	-	-	-	-	-	-	-	-	-	-	-	-
Carteret (borough)	47,148	49,485	-	48,235	-	-	-	-	-	-	-	-	-	-	-	-	-	-	-	-	-	-	-	-
Colonia (cdp)	67,372	90,892	-	101,303	-	-	-	-	84,228	-	-	-	-	-	-	-	-	-	-	-	-	-	-	-
East Brunswick (township)	75,956	85,327	-	90,000	-	-	85,937	-	100,863	-	-	-	-	-	36,944	-	-	-	-	-	-	-	-	-
Edison (township)	69,746	83,087	-	81,845	-	-	93,376	-	98,827	-	-	-	-	-	52,174	-	-	68,295	-	-	95,163	-	-	-
Fords (cdp)	61,015	76,464	-	72,381	-	-	-	-	91,118	-	-	-	-	-	-	-	-	-	-	-	-	-	-	-
Highland Park (borough)	53,250	49,669	-	58,646	-	-	45,885	-	-	-	-	-	-	-	-	-	-	-	-	-	-	-	-	-
Iselin (cdp)	65,424	80,875	-	80,453	-	-	92,301	-	-	-	-	-	-	-	-	-	-	-	-	-	-	-	-	-
Metuchen (borough)	75,546	82,720	-	-	-	-	-	-	-	-	-	-	-	-	-	-	-	-	-	-	-	-	-	-
Middlesex (borough)	60,723	85,187	-	-	-	-	-	-	-	-	-	-	-	-	-	-	-	-	-	-	-	-	-	-
New Brunswick (city)	36,080	39,583	-	41,985	-	-	47,813	-	-	-	-	-	-	-	-	-	-	-	-	-	-	-	-	-

Notes: Please refer to the User's Guide for an explanation of data; data is arranged alphabetically by state, then county, then city within each county; table includes counties with populations greater than 49,999 unless noted and cities with populations greater than 9,999 whose Asian and/or NHPI population rates are greater than the national average; (1) Native Hawaiian and other Pacific Islander; (2) excludes Taiwanese; (3) includes Chamorro; (4) county does not meet population threshold but is shown in order to allow inclusion of city

Place	All households	Asian households	NHPI[1] households	Asian Indian	Bangladeshi	Cambodian	Chinese[2]	Fijian	Filipino	Guamanian[3]	Hawaiian, Native	Hmong	Indonesian	Japanese	Korean	Laotian	Malaysian	Pakistani	Samoan	Sri Lankan	Taiwanese	Thai	Tongan	Vietnamese
North Brunswick (township)	61,325	73,375	-	76,925	-	-	65,192	-	109,672	-	-	-	-	-	59,250	-	-	-	-	-	-	-	-	-
Old Bridge (township)	64,707	75,543	-	77,068	-	-	81,826	-	93,469	-	-	-	-	-	-	-	-	66,750	-	-	-	-	-	-
Piscataway (township)	68,721	76,871	-	77,259	-	-	63,854	-	100,000	-	-	-	-	-	69,659	-	-	-	-	-	-	-	-	-
Plainsboro (township)	72,097	78,540	-	82,548	-	-	85,106	-	-	-	-	-	-	-	-	-	-	-	-	-	-	-	-	-
Princeton Meadows (cdp)	66,415	75,399	-	82,099	-	-	76,527	-	-	-	-	-	-	-	-	-	-	-	-	-	-	-	-	-
Sayreville (borough)	58,919	67,466	-	66,356	-	-	71,607	-	80,688	-	-	-	-	-	-	-	-	-	-	-	-	-	-	-
South Brunswick (township)	78,737	92,944	-	106,753	-	-	87,106	-	79,729	-	-	-	-	-	-	-	-	-	-	-	-	-	-	-
South Plainfield (borough)	67,466	75,099	-	75,510	-	-	-	-	89,459	-	-	-	-	-	-	-	-	-	-	-	-	-	-	65,288
Woodbridge (township)	60,683	78,980	-	78,350	-	-	93,107	-	89,427	-	-	-	-	-	47,115	-	-	51,944	-	-	-	-	-	-
Monmouth County	64,271	92,164	-	99,955	-	-	96,560	-	94,607	-	-	-	-	44,375	58,250	-	-	60,750	-	-	-	-	-	88,372
Aberdeen (township)	68,125	74,615	-	84,240	-	-	73,558	-	-	-	-	-	-	-	-	-	-	-	-	-	-	-	-	-
Colts Neck (township)	109,190	127,581	-	-	-	-	-	-	-	-	-	-	-	-	-	-	-	-	-	-	-	-	-	-
Eatontown (borough)	53,833	65,673	-	-	-	-	-	-	-	-	-	-	-	-	-	-	-	-	-	-	-	-	-	-
Freehold (township)	77,185	95,349	-	114,070	-	-	77,925	-	99,090	-	-	-	-	-	-	-	-	-	-	-	-	-	-	-
Holmdel (township)	112,879	129,322	-	123,283	-	-	139,211	-	-	-	-	-	-	-	-	-	-	-	-	-	-	-	-	-
Howell (township)	68,069	96,301	-	115,175	-	-	-	-	109,992	-	-	-	-	-	-	-	-	-	-	-	-	-	-	-
Manalapan (township)	83,575	103,862	-	114,288	-	-	82,500	-	-	-	-	-	-	-	-	-	-	-	-	-	-	-	-	-
Marlboro (township)	101,322	119,784	-	125,271	-	-	117,303	-	-	-	-	-	-	-	-	-	-	-	-	-	-	-	-	-
Morganville (cdp)	99,035	107,555	-	-	-	-	107,148	-	-	-	-	-	-	-	-	-	-	-	-	-	-	-	-	-
Ocean (township)	62,058	76,184	-	85,093	-	-	-	-	-	-	-	-	-	-	-	-	-	-	-	-	-	-	-	-
Tinton Falls (borough)	68,697	64,063	-	-	-	-	-	-	-	-	-	-	-	-	-	-	-	-	-	-	-	-	-	-
West Freehold (cdp)	72,577	68,393	-	-	-	-	-	-	-	-	-	-	-	-	-	-	-	-	-	-	-	-	-	-
Morris County	77,340	90,386	-	91,882	-	-	95,268	-	94,969	-	-	-	-	99,531	74,083	-	-	65,481	-	-	96,657	-	-	65,625
Chatham (township)	106,208	94,069	-	-	-	-	-	-	-	-	-	-	-	-	-	-	-	-	-	-	-	-	-	-
Denville (township)	76,778	115,954	-	-	-	-	-	-	-	-	-	-	-	-	-	-	-	-	-	-	-	-	-	-
East Hanover (township)	82,133	104,745	-	-	-	-	112,671	-	-	-	-	-	-	-	-	-	-	-	-	-	-	-	-	-
Hanover (township)	84,115	103,543	-	69,667	-	-	130,918	-	-	-	-	-	-	-	-	-	-	-	-	-	-	-	-	-
Lincoln Park (borough)	69,050	101,397	-	-	-	-	-	-	-	-	-	-	-	-	-	-	-	-	-	-	-	-	-	-
Montville (township)	94,557	117,761	-	123,454	-	-	120,500	-	-	-	-	-	-	-	-	-	-	-	-	-	-	-	-	-
Morris (township)	101,902	110,045	-	-	-	-	-	-	-	-	-	-	-	-	-	-	-	-	-	-	-	-	-	-
Mount Olive (township)	64,515	65,089	-	62,794	-	-	-	-	-	-	-	-	-	-	-	-	-	-	-	-	-	-	-	-
Parsippany-Troy Hills (twp)	68,133	79,914	-	81,968	-	-	87,867	-	85,850	-	-	-	-	-	82,046	-	-	-	-	-	-	-	-	-
Randolph (township)	97,589	92,537	-	90,984	-	-	94,714	-	-	-	-	-	-	-	-	-	-	-	-	-	-	-	-	-
Rockaway (township)	80,939	98,177	-	105,412	-	-	-	-	-	-	-	-	-	-	-	-	-	-	-	-	-	-	-	-
Roxbury (township)	72,982	96,325	-	-	-	-	-	-	-	-	-	-	-	-	-	-	-	-	-	-	-	-	-	-
Succasunna-Kenvil (cdp)	83,614	95,944	-	-	-	-	-	-	-	-	-	-	-	-	-	-	-	-	-	-	-	-	-	-
Ocean County	46,443	68,094	-	64,773	-	-	80,935	-	80,365	-	-	-	-	-	38,417	-	-	-	-	-	-	-	-	-
Passaic County	49,210	63,194	-	57,609	31,413	-	68,214	-	90,530	-	-	-	-	-	56,042	-	-	-	-	-	-	-	-	-
Clifton (city)	50,619	70,526	-	69,132	-	-	63,750	-	102,672	-	-	-	-	-	41,328	-	-	-	-	-	-	-	-	-
Little Falls (township)	58,857	52,019	-	-	-	-	-	-	-	-	-	-	-	-	-	-	-	-	-	-	-	-	-	-
Passaic (city)	33,594	51,505	-	50,093	-	-	-	-	61,429	-	-	-	-	-	-	-	-	-	-	-	-	-	-	-

Notes: Please refer to the User's Guide for an explanation of data; data is arranged alphabetically by state, then county, then city within each county; table includes counties with populations greater than 49,999 unless noted and cities with populations greater than 9,999 whose Asian and/or NHPI population rates are greater than the national average; (1) Native Hawaiian and other Pacific Islander; (2) excludes Taiwanese; (3) includes Chamorro; (4) county does not meet population threshold but is shown in order to allow inclusion of city

Place	All households	Asian households	NHPI[1] households	Asian Indian	Bangladeshi	Cambodian	Chinese[2]	Fijian	Filipino	Guamanian[3]	Hawaiian, Native	Hmong	Indonesian	Japanese	Korean	Laotian	Malaysian	Pakistani	Samoan	Sri Lankan	Taiwanese	Thai	Tongan	Vietnamese
Wayne (township)	83,651	95,013	-	126,503	-	-	102,565	-	101,949	-	-	-	-	-	60,481	-	-	-	-	-	-	-	-	-
Salem County	45,573	61,250	-	-	-	-	-	-	-	-	-	-	-	-	-	-	-	-	-	-	-	-	-	-
Somerset County	76,933	101,349	-	103,249	-	-	109,693	-	81,424	-	-	-	-	91,883	82,775	-	-	52,037	-	-	117,355	-	-	103,511
Bernards (township)	107,204	132,683	-	156,915	-	-	130,561	-	-	-	-	-	-	-	-	-	-	-	-	-	-	-	-	-
Branchburg (township)	96,864	125,000	-	117,786	-	-	-	-	-	-	-	-	-	-	-	-	-	-	-	-	-	-	-	-
Bridgewater (township)	88,308	123,362	-	145,490	-	-	125,597	-	-	-	-	-	-	-	-	-	-	-	-	-	-	-	-	-
Franklin (township)	67,923	80,402	-	72,672	-	-	85,902	-	85,469	-	-	-	-	-	-	-	-	-	-	-	-	-	-	-
Hillsborough (township)	83,290	88,223	-	88,831	-	-	84,886	-	-	-	-	-	-	-	-	-	-	-	-	-	-	-	-	-
Montgomery (township)	118,850	136,301	-	153,791	-	-	134,367	-	-	-	-	-	-	-	-	-	-	-	-	-	-	-	-	-
North Plainfield (borough)	55,322	67,692	-	-	-	-	-	-	-	-	-	-	-	-	-	-	-	-	-	-	-	-	-	-
Somerset (cdp)	65,831	75,252	-	72,841	-	-	73,750	-	78,830	-	-	-	-	-	-	-	-	-	-	-	-	-	-	-
Somerville (borough)	51,237	60,901	-	-	-	-	-	-	-	-	-	-	-	-	-	-	-	-	-	-	-	-	-	-
Warren (township)	103,677	158,816	-	176,569	-	-	142,984	-	-	-	-	-	-	-	-	-	-	-	-	-	-	-	-	-
Sussex County	65,266	75,104	-	94,500	-	-	-	-	66,875	-	-	-	-	-	-	-	-	-	-	-	-	-	-	-
Union County	55,339	75,082	-	75,230	-	-	76,818	-	84,567	-	-	-	-	-	59,423	-	-	45,208	-	-	-	-	-	46,528
Berkeley Heights (township)	107,716	128,361	-	-	-	-	115,068	-	-	-	-	-	-	-	-	-	-	-	-	-	-	-	-	-
New Providence (borough)	90,964	121,393	-	-	-	-	111,618	-	-	-	-	-	-	-	-	-	-	-	-	-	-	-	-	-
Rahway (city)	50,729	64,306	-	-	-	-	-	-	64,583	-	-	-	-	-	-	-	-	-	-	-	-	-	-	-
Roselle Park (borough)	53,717	56,500	-	51,193	-	-	-	-	-	-	-	-	-	-	-	-	-	-	-	-	-	-	-	-
Scotch Plains (township)	81,599	104,925	-	126,618	-	-	66,779	-	-	-	-	-	-	-	-	-	-	-	-	-	-	-	-	-
Springfield (township)	73,790	95,609	-	-	-	-	-	-	-	-	-	-	-	-	-	-	-	-	-	-	-	-	-	-
Summit (city)	92,964	83,701	-	104,733	-	-	-	-	-	-	-	-	-	-	-	-	-	-	-	-	-	-	-	-
Union (township)	59,173	92,725	-	73,036	-	-	101,443	-	101,179	-	-	-	-	-	-	-	-	-	-	-	-	-	-	-
Westfield (town)	98,390	96,633	-	-	-	-	-	-	-	-	-	-	-	-	-	-	-	-	-	-	-	-	-	-
Warren County	56,100	60,208	-	60,714	-	-	-	-	-	-	-	-	-	-	-	-	-	-	-	-	-	-	-	-
NEW MEXICO	34,133	42,010	42,716	57,759	-	-	48,103	-	41,875	52,500	43,125	-	-	40,000	31,136	-	-	-	-	-	-	38,750	-	35,938
Bernalillo County	38,788	41,607	46,250	71,108	-	-	49,267	-	38,958	-	-	-	-	50,345	31,172	-	-	-	-	-	-	-	-	33,776
Chaves County	28,513	46,250	-	-	-	-	-	-	-	-	-	-	-	-	-	-	-	-	-	-	-	-	-	-
Dona Ana County	29,808	48,036	-	-	-	-	34,083	-	-	-	-	-	-	-	-	-	-	-	-	-	-	-	-	-
Los Alamos County[4]	78,993	61,953	-	-	-	-	-	-	-	-	-	-	-	-	-	-	-	-	-	-	-	-	-	-
Los Alamos (cdp)	71,536	80,094	-	-	-	-	-	-	-	-	-	-	-	-	-	-	-	-	-	-	-	-	-	-
Otero County	30,861	31,364	-	-	-	-	-	-	-	-	-	-	-	-	-	-	-	-	-	-	-	-	-	-
Sandoval County	44,949	55,000	-	-	-	-	-	-	57,083	-	-	-	-	-	-	-	-	-	-	-	-	-	-	-
Santa Fe County	42,207	45,625	-	-	-	-	-	-	-	-	-	-	-	-	-	-	-	-	-	-	-	-	-	-
NEW YORK	43,393	45,402	28,713	54,150	34,136	39,205	39,243	-	72,850	25,163	32,614	-	40,566	44,927	39,267	41,744	34,005	41,675	46,071	48,587	52,088	47,677	-	37,194
Albany County	42,935	49,896	-	60,938	-	-	55,682	-	71,563	-	-	-	-	-	23,281	-	-	-	-	-	-	-	-	48,250
Colonie (town)	51,817	73,447	-	70,682	-	-	91,601	-	-	-	-	-	-	-	-	-	-	-	-	-	-	-	-	-
Guilderland (town)	58,669	53,750	-	65,541	-	-	-	-	-	-	-	-	-	-	-	-	-	-	-	-	-	-	-	-
Bronx County (Bronx)	27,611	40,105	15,000	39,547	25,430	30,789	37,456	-	72,013	-	-	-	-	8,906	34,527	-	-	34,712	-	-	-	-	-	27,560
Broome County	35,347	24,191	-	69,946	-	-	12,465	-	-	-	-	-	-	-	2,499	32,344	-	-	-	-	-	-	-	27,000
Johnson City (village)	27,438	26,328	-	-	-	-	-	-	-	-	-	-	-	-	-	-	-	-	-	-	-	-	-	-

Notes: Please refer to the User's Guide for an explanation of data; data is arranged alphabetically by state, then county, then city within each county; table includes counties with populations greater than 49,999 unless noted and cities with populations greater than 9,999 whose Asian and/or NHPI population rates are greater than the national average; (1) Native Hawaiian and other Pacific Islander; (2) excludes Taiwanese; (3) includes Chamorro; (4) county does not meet population threshold but is shown in order to allow inclusion of city

Place	All households	Asian households	NHPI[1] households	Asian Indian	Bangladeshi	Cambodian	Chinese[2]	Fijian	Filipino	Guamanian[3]	Hawaiian, Native	Hmong	Indonesian	Japanese	Korean	Laotian	Malaysian	Pakistani	Samoan	Sri Lankan	Taiwanese	Thai	Tongan	Vietnamese
Vestal (town)	51,098	68,636	-	-	-	-	14,615	-	-	-	-	-	-	-	-	-	-	-	-	-	-	-	-	-
Cattaraugus County	33,404	58,214	-	-	-	-	-	-	-	-	-	-	-	-	-	-	-	-	-	-	-	-	-	-
Cayuga County	37,487	31,667	-	-	-	-	-	-	-	-	-	-	-	-	-	-	-	-	-	-	-	-	-	-
Chautauqua County	33,458	51,250	-	-	-	-	-	-	-	-	-	-	-	-	-	-	-	-	-	-	-	-	-	-
Chemung County	36,415	129,226	-	-	-	-	-	-	-	-	-	-	-	-	-	-	-	-	-	-	-	-	-	-
Chenango County	33,679	51,875	-	-	-	-	-	-	-	-	-	-	-	-	-	-	-	-	-	-	-	-	-	-
Clinton County	37,028	18,750	-	-	-	-	-	-	-	-	-	-	-	-	-	-	-	-	-	-	-	-	-	-
Columbia County	41,915	31,875	-	-	-	-	-	-	-	-	-	-	-	-	-	-	-	-	-	-	-	-	-	-
Dutchess County	53,086	68,078	-	61,964	-	-	70,903	-	-	-	-	-	-	-	72,083	-	-	-	-	-	-	-	-	-
Arlington (cdp)	43,141	31,042	-	-	-	-	-	-	-	-	-	-	-	-	-	-	-	-	-	-	-	-	-	-
Poughkeepsie (town)	55,327	66,375	-	56,250	-	-	71,875	-	-	-	-	-	-	-	-	-	-	-	-	-	-	-	-	-
Wappinger (town)	58,079	61,500	-	51,985	-	-	-	-	-	-	-	-	-	-	-	-	-	-	-	-	-	-	-	-
Erie County	38,567	32,292	-	54,120	-	-	28,810	-	61,875	-	-	-	-	15,750	18,405	-	-	-	-	-	-	-	-	26,474
Amherst (town)	55,427	50,901	-	79,773	-	-	30,938	-	-	-	-	-	-	-	22,083	-	-	-	-	-	-	-	-	-
Herkimer County	32,924	50,625	-	-	-	-	-	-	-	-	-	-	-	-	-	-	-	-	-	-	-	-	-	-
Jefferson County	34,006	37,125	-	-	-	-	-	-	36,750	-	-	-	-	-	28,500	-	-	-	-	-	-	-	-	-
Kings County (Brooklyn)	32,135	35,275	30,000	36,662	25,741	35,078	33,564	-	70,316	37,697	-	-	-	25,486	36,377	-	-	29,375	-	-	-	-	-	35,194
Livingston County	42,066	70,000	-	-	-	-	-	-	-	-	-	-	-	-	-	-	-	-	-	-	-	-	-	-
Madison County	40,184	46,484	-	-	-	-	-	-	-	-	-	-	-	-	-	-	-	-	-	-	-	-	-	-
Monroe County	44,891	50,510	-	72,500	-	35,938	44,784	-	43,000	-	-	-	-	46,250	40,993	45,313	-	27,614	-	-	-	-	-	50,500
Brighton (town)	52,066	45,080	-	56,719	-	-	39,792	-	-	-	-	-	-	-	-	-	-	-	-	-	-	-	-	-
Henrietta (town)	51,081	50,221	-	31,618	-	-	46,641	-	-	-	-	-	-	-	-	-	-	-	-	-	-	-	-	-
Pittsford (town)	88,232	112,915	-	129,814	-	-	-	-	-	-	-	-	-	-	-	-	-	-	-	-	-	-	-	-
Nassau County	72,030	83,948	20,625	89,657	-	-	81,338	-	93,280	-	-	-	-	72,120	71,474	-	-	73,750	-	-	73,611	86,648	-	77,428
East Meadow (cdp)	67,185	84,809	-	93,429	-	-	-	-	91,195	-	-	-	-	-	-	-	-	-	-	-	-	-	-	-
Elmont (cdp)	62,511	78,063	-	75,000	-	-	-	-	94,779	-	-	-	-	-	-	-	-	-	-	-	-	-	-	-
Franklin Square (cdp)	60,998	62,500	-	96,147	-	-	-	-	-	-	-	-	-	-	-	-	-	-	-	-	-	-	-	-
Glen Cove (city)	55,503	50,000	-	60,909	-	-	-	-	-	-	-	-	-	-	28,661	-	-	-	-	-	-	-	-	-
Hicksville (cdp)	67,703	81,810	-	87,860	-	-	54,609	-	117,280	-	-	-	-	-	-	-	-	-	-	-	-	-	-	-
Jericho (cdp)	101,477	80,957	-	-	-	-	-	-	-	-	-	-	-	-	67,692	-	-	-	-	-	-	-	-	-
Mineola (village)	60,706	68,036	-	86,569	-	-	-	-	-	-	-	-	-	-	-	-	-	-	-	-	-	-	-	-
North Hempstead (town)	81,039	93,494	-	100,606	-	-	92,438	-	102,601	-	-	-	-	83,201	86,969	-	-	76,005	-	-	73,333	-	-	-
North Merrick (cdp)	80,786	78,834	-	-	-	-	-	-	-	-	-	-	-	-	-	-	-	-	-	-	-	-	-	-
North New Hyde Park (cdp)	69,792	95,246	-	88,864	-	-	103,622	-	-	-	-	-	-	-	-	-	-	-	-	-	-	-	-	-
North Valley Stream (cdp)	73,621	77,871	-	66,125	-	-	-	-	-	-	-	-	-	-	-	-	-	-	-	-	-	-	-	-
Oyster Bay (town)	78,839	92,577	-	104,560	-	-	90,899	-	100,529	-	-	-	-	78,685	73,194	-	-	-	-	-	-	-	-	-
Plainview (cdp)	90,529	88,953	-	126,123	-	-	65,000	-	-	-	-	-	-	-	78,077	-	-	-	-	-	-	-	-	-
Port Washington (cdp)	85,837	103,481	-	142,846	-	-	-	-	-	-	-	-	-	-	-	-	-	-	-	-	-	-	-	-
Salisbury (cdp)	73,641	91,606	-	69,063	-	-	-	-	-	-	-	-	-	-	-	-	-	-	-	-	-	-	-	-
Syosset (cdp)	90,929	90,594	-	117,909	-	-	102,288	-	-	-	-	-	-	-	72,250	-	-	-	-	-	-	-	-	-
Valley Stream (village)	63,243	73,438	-	-	-	-	60,063	-	92,281	-	-	-	-	-	-	-	-	-	-	-	-	-	-	-

Notes: Please refer to the User's Guide for an explanation of data; data is arranged alphabetically by state, then county, then city within each county; table includes counties with populations greater than 49,999 unless noted and cities with populations greater than 9,999 whose Asian and/or NHPI population rates are greater than the national average; (1) Native Hawaiian and other Pacific Islander; (2) excludes Taiwanese; (3) includes Chamorro; (4) county does not meet population threshold but is shown in order to allow inclusion of city

Place	All households	Asian households	NHPI[1] households	Asian Indian	Bangladeshi	Cambodian	Chinese[2]	Fijian	Filipino	Guamanian[3]	Hawaiian, Native	Hmong	Indonesian	Japanese	Korean	Laotian	Malaysian	Pakistani	Samoan	Sri Lankan	Taiwanese	Thai	Tongan	Vietnamese
West Hempstead (cdp)	71,260	81,609	-	106,749	-	-	-	-	-	-	-	-	-	-	-	-	-	-	-	-	-	-	-	-
Westbury (village)	74,032	89,335	-	-	-	-	-	-	-	-	-	-	-	-	-	-	-	-	-	-	-	-	-	-
Woodmere (cdp)	93,212	100,000	-	-	-	-	-	-	-	-	-	-	-	-	-	-	-	-	-	-	-	-	-	-
New York City	38,293	41,119	27,143	46,090	33,071	37,422	36,964	-	70,217	22,708	34,432	-	39,338	39,568	36,986	-	33,929	37,093	35,313	42,069	52,123	46,897	-	37,393
New York County (Manhattan)	47,030	39,656	26,389	70,457	33,523	-	28,473	-	63,562	-	-	-	-	47,646	47,231	-	-	51,473	-	-	61,458	38,672	-	62,292
Niagara County	38,136	35,667	-	55,250	-	-	-	-	-	-	-	-	-	-	-	-	-	-	-	-	-	-	-	-
Oneida County	35,909	34,219	-	82,699	-	-	36,071	-	-	-	-	-	-	-	-	-	-	-	-	-	-	-	-	27,813
Onondaga County	40,847	33,976	-	49,408	-	-	21,167	-	62,788	-	-	-	-	31,250	2,499	-	-	-	-	-	-	-	-	33,345
Ontario County	44,579	49,750	-	-	-	-	-	-	-	-	-	-	-	-	-	-	-	-	-	-	-	-	-	-
Orange County	52,058	61,377	-	63,696	-	-	52,656	-	71,563	-	-	-	-	-	46,111	-	-	-	-	-	-	-	-	-
Oswego County	36,598	36,750	-	-	-	-	-	-	-	-	-	-	-	-	-	-	-	-	-	-	-	-	-	-
Otsego County	33,444	30,781	-	-	-	-	-	-	-	-	-	-	-	-	-	-	-	-	-	-	-	-	-	-
Putnam County	72,279	90,169	-	107,596	-	-	88,065	-	-	-	-	-	-	-	-	-	-	-	-	-	-	-	-	-
Queens County (Queens)	42,439	43,620	38,854	46,368	35,890	-	44,903	-	71,291	-	-	-	40,726	28,986	35,185	-	29,214	40,102	-	34,896	52,695	47,817	-	42,257
Rensselaer County	42,905	28,548	-	35,833	-	-	23,565	-	-	-	-	-	-	-	27,083	-	-	-	-	-	-	-	-	-
Richmond Co. (Staten Island)	55,039	62,391	-	74,688	-	-	59,968	-	80,661	-	-	-	-	-	47,188	-	-	51,406	-	42,639	-	-	-	-
Rockland County	67,971	79,562	-	80,070	-	-	86,311	-	96,988	-	-	-	-	-	60,347	-	-	-	-	-	-	-	-	-
Clarkstown (town)	82,107	91,687	-	86,502	-	-	92,970	-	101,218	-	-	-	-	-	63,375	-	-	-	-	-	-	-	-	-
Nanuet (cdp)	71,178	99,882	-	105,611	-	-	-	-	-	-	-	-	-	-	-	-	-	-	-	-	-	-	-	-
New City (cdp)	92,261	86,244	-	76,685	-	-	-	-	102,806	-	-	-	-	-	-	-	-	-	-	-	-	-	-	-
Orangetown (town)	70,477	79,780	-	93,774	-	-	50,673	-	124,458	-	-	-	-	-	62,632	-	-	-	-	-	-	-	-	-
Ramapo (town)	60,352	67,015	-	74,265	-	-	62,386	-	75,214	-	-	-	-	-	58,750	-	-	-	-	-	-	-	-	-
Spring Valley (village)	41,311	47,371	-	53,988	-	-	-	-	-	-	-	-	-	-	-	-	-	-	-	-	-	-	-	-
St. Lawrence County	32,356	20,938	-	-	-	-	-	-	-	-	-	-	-	-	-	-	-	-	-	-	-	-	-	-
Saratoga County	49,460	63,977	-	95,342	-	-	89,554	-	-	-	-	-	-	-	63,239	-	-	-	-	-	-	-	-	-
Schenectady County	41,739	52,554	-	51,307	-	-	69,464	-	-	-	-	-	-	-	-	-	-	-	-	-	-	-	-	-
Niskayuna (town)	70,800	88,331	-	72,250	-	-	-	-	-	-	-	-	-	-	-	-	-	-	-	-	-	-	-	-
Steuben County	35,479	73,125	-	-	-	-	-	-	-	-	-	-	-	-	-	-	-	-	-	-	-	-	-	-
Suffolk County	65,288	71,059	49,792	75,893	-	-	65,053	-	90,391	-	-	-	-	63,400	55,848	-	-	55,380	-	-	95,997	74,531	-	66,477
Coram (cdp)	61,309	50,909	-	-	-	-	49,464	-	-	-	-	-	-	-	-	-	-	-	-	-	-	-	-	-
Dix Hills (cdp)	104,160	119,464	-	119,053	-	-	103,986	-	-	-	-	-	-	-	-	-	-	-	-	-	-	-	-	-
Elwood (cdp)	89,424	69,333	-	-	-	-	-	-	-	-	-	-	-	-	-	-	-	-	-	-	-	-	-	-
Lake Grove (village)	67,174	65,750	-	-	-	-	-	-	-	-	-	-	-	-	-	-	-	-	-	-	-	-	-	-
Melville (cdp)	92,527	104,862	-	-	-	-	-	-	-	-	-	-	-	-	-	-	-	-	-	-	-	-	-	-
Setauket-East Setauket (cdp)	86,986	31,450	-	-	-	-	17,071	-	-	-	-	-	-	-	-	-	-	-	-	-	-	-	-	-
Stony Brook (cdp)	90,009	86,214	-	-	-	-	91,483	-	-	-	-	-	-	-	-	-	-	-	-	-	-	-	-	-
Sullivan County	36,998	45,536	-	-	-	-	-	-	-	-	-	-	-	-	-	-	-	-	-	-	-	-	-	-
Tioga County	40,266	62,059	-	-	-	-	-	-	-	-	-	-	-	-	-	-	-	-	-	-	-	-	-	-
Tompkins County	37,272	19,741	-	52,143	-	-	19,504	-	-	-	-	-	-	17,857	17,586	-	-	-	-	-	-	-	-	-
Ithaca (city)	21,441	10,997	-	12,361	-	-	10,539	-	-	-	-	-	-	-	10,625	-	-	-	-	-	-	-	-	-
Lansing (town)	48,250	34,853	-	-	-	-	-	-	-	-	-	-	-	-	-	-	-	-	-	-	-	-	-	-

Notes: Please refer to the User's Guide for an explanation of data; data is arranged alphabetically by state, then county, then city within each county; table includes counties with populations greater than 49,999 unless noted and cities with populations greater than 9,999 whose Asian and/or NHPI population rates are greater than the national average; (1) Native Hawaiian and other Pacific Islander; (2) excludes Taiwanese; (3) includes Chamorro; (4) county does not meet population threshold but is shown in order to allow inclusion of city

Place	All households	Asian households	NHPI[1] households	Asian Indian	Bangladeshi	Cambodian	Chinese[2]	Fijian	Filipino	Guamanian[3]	Hawaiian, Native	Hmong	Indonesian	Japanese	Korean	Laotian	Malaysian	Pakistani	Samoan	Sri Lankan	Taiwanese	Thai	Tongan	Vietnamese
Ulster County	42,551	26,563	-	-	-	-	22,054	-	-	-	-	-	-	-	-	-	-	-	-	-	-	-	-	-
New Paltz (town)	40,542	9,125	-	-	-	-	-	-	-	-	-	-	-	-	-	-	-	-	-	-	-	-	-	-
Warren County	39,198	65,750	-	-	-	-	-	-	-	-	-	-	-	-	-	-	-	-	-	-	-	-	-	-
Wayne County	44,157	69,583	-	-	-	-	-	-	-	-	-	-	-	-	-	-	-	-	-	-	-	-	-	-
Westchester County	63,582	86,892	-	84,791	-	-	90,665	-	85,623	-	-	-	-	104,489	74,904	-	-	71,719	-	-	83,050	72,000	-	-
Dobbs Ferry (village)	70,333	61,750	-	-	-	-	-	-	-	-	-	-	-	-	-	-	-	-	-	-	-	-	-	-
Eastchester (cdp)	75,117	76,609	-	-	-	-	-	-	-	-	-	-	-	108,728	-	-	-	-	-	-	-	-	-	-
Eastchester (town)	78,224	85,476	-	-	-	-	-	-	-	-	-	-	-	110,772	-	-	-	-	-	-	-	-	-	-
Greenburgh (town)	80,379	98,380	-	102,225	-	-	113,220	-	78,132	-	-	-	-	91,717	105,965	-	-	-	-	-	-	-	-	-
Harrison (village)	80,738	121,587	-	-	-	-	-	-	-	-	-	-	-	152,015	-	-	-	-	-	-	-	-	-	-
New Castle (town)	159,691	162,255	-	200,001	-	-	124,081	-	-	-	-	-	-	-	-	-	-	-	-	-	-	-	-	-
New Rochelle (city)	55,513	66,902	-	58,750	-	-	60,833	-	-	-	-	-	-	-	-	-	-	-	-	-	-	-	-	-
North Castle (town)	117,815	153,354	-	-	-	-	-	-	-	-	-	-	-	-	-	-	-	-	-	-	-	-	-	-
Ossining (town)	65,485	88,819	-	88,735	-	-	-	-	-	-	-	-	-	-	-	-	-	-	-	-	-	-	-	-
Ossining (village)	52,185	77,021	-	71,250	-	-	-	-	-	-	-	-	-	-	-	-	-	-	-	-	-	-	-	-
Pelham (town)	91,810	106,294	-	-	-	-	-	-	-	-	-	-	-	-	-	-	-	-	-	-	-	-	-	-
Rye (city)	110,894	165,155	-	-	-	-	-	-	-	-	-	-	-	172,971	-	-	-	-	-	-	-	-	-	-
Scarsdale (village)	182,792	143,001	-	200,001	-	-	127,232	-	-	-	-	-	-	121,839	170,098	-	-	-	-	-	-	-	-	-
Tarrytown (village)	68,762	82,917	-	-	-	-	-	-	-	-	-	-	-	-	-	-	-	-	-	-	-	-	-	-
White Plains (city)	58,545	66,534	-	69,180	-	-	59,773	-	-	-	-	-	-	-	-	-	-	-	-	-	-	-	-	-
Yonkers (city)	44,663	64,552	-	65,066	-	-	61,250	-	96,335	-	-	-	-	-	43,333	-	-	-	-	-	-	-	-	-
NORTH CAROLINA	39,184	49,497	37,778	60,188	-	39,643	55,710	-	46,372	38,500	35,583	42,544	-	43,272	38,662	44,354	-	45,089	47,292	-	60,000	37,222	-	41,875
Alamance County	39,168	53,750	-	-	-	-	-	-	-	-	-	-	-	-	-	-	-	-	-	-	-	-	-	-
Buncombe County	36,666	42,583	-	46,875	-	-	-	-	-	-	-	-	-	-	-	-	-	-	-	-	-	-	-	-
Burke County	35,629	42,117	-	-	-	-	-	-	-	-	-	43,056	-	-	-	41,563	-	-	-	-	-	-	-	-
Cabarrus County	46,140	53,207	-	-	-	-	-	-	-	-	-	-	-	-	-	-	-	-	-	-	-	-	-	-
Catawba County	40,536	46,046	-	-	-	-	-	-	-	-	-	37,019	-	-	-	45,234	-	-	-	-	-	-	-	46,667
Hickory (city)	37,236	40,583	-	-	-	-	-	-	-	-	-	30,417	-	-	-	-	-	-	-	-	-	-	-	-
Cleveland County	35,283	49,663	-	-	-	-	-	-	-	-	-	-	-	-	-	-	-	-	-	-	-	-	-	-
Craven County	35,966	33,462	-	-	-	-	-	-	36,875	-	-	-	-	-	-	-	-	-	-	-	-	-	-	-
Cumberland County	37,466	34,869	29,650	45,375	-	-	-	-	38,348	-	-	-	-	31,250	27,702	-	-	-	-	-	-	-	-	34,196
Davidson County	38,640	40,147	-	-	-	31,000	-	-	-	-	-	-	-	-	-	-	-	-	-	-	-	-	-	-
Durham County	43,337	50,783	-	60,188	-	-	41,413	-	59,205	-	-	-	-	23,750	27,250	-	-	-	-	-	-	-	-	-
Forsyth County	42,097	47,125	-	57,537	-	-	46,447	-	34,423	-	-	-	-	-	-	-	-	-	-	-	-	-	-	50,625
Gaston County	39,482	48,611	-	-	-	-	-	-	-	-	-	-	-	-	-	-	-	-	-	-	-	-	-	53,125
Guilford County	42,618	46,719	-	61,133	-	-	61,964	-	61,083	-	-	-	-	-	41,150	43,077	-	26,250	-	-	-	-	-	35,170
Halifax County	26,459	36,250	-	-	-	-	-	-	-	-	-	-	-	-	-	-	-	-	-	-	-	-	-	-
Harnett County	35,105	16,667	-	-	-	-	-	-	-	-	-	-	-	-	-	-	-	-	-	-	-	-	-	-
Henderson County	38,109	52,917	-	-	-	-	-	-	-	-	-	-	-	-	-	-	-	-	-	-	-	-	-	-
Iredell County	41,920	42,230	-	-	-	-	-	-	-	-	-	-	-	-	-	-	-	-	-	-	-	-	-	-
Johnston County	40,872	63,603	-	-	-	-	-	-	-	-	-	-	-	-	-	-	-	-	-	-	-	-	-	-

Notes: Please refer to the User's Guide for an explanation of data; data is arranged alphabetically by state, then county, then city within each county; table includes counties with populations greater than 49,999 unless noted and cities with populations greater than 9,999 whose Asian and/or NHPI population rates are greater than the national average; (1) Native Hawaiian and other Pacific Islander; (2) excludes Taiwanese; (3) includes Chamorro; (4) county does not meet population threshold but is shown in order to allow inclusion of city

Place	All households	Asian households	NHPI[1] households	Asian Indian	Bangladeshi	Cambodian	Chinese[2]	Fijian	Filipino	Guamanian[3]	Hawaiian, Native	Hmong	Indonesian	Japanese	Korean	Laotian	Malaysian	Pakistani	Samoan	Sri Lankan	Taiwanese	Thai	Tongan	Vietnamese
Lenoir County	31,191	36,250	-	-	-	-	-	-	-	-	-	-	-	-	-	-	-	-	-	-	-	-	-	-
Mecklenburg County	50,579	55,171	-	60,690	-	37,500	63,839	-	68,289	-	-	65,313	-	63,348	51,833	49,118	-	-	-	-	-	-	-	43,681
Nash County	37,147	44,934	-	-	-	-	-	-	-	-	-	-	-	-	-	-	-	-	-	-	-	-	-	-
New Hanover County	40,172	39,107	-	-	-	-	-	-	-	-	-	-	-	-	-	-	-	-	-	-	-	-	-	-
Onslow County	33,756	24,936	40,625	-	-	-	-	-	27,731	-	-	-	-	16,912	-	-	-	-	-	-	-	-	-	-
Orange County	42,372	34,489	-	37,578	-	-	48,365	-	-	-	-	-	-	47,667	16,767	-	-	-	-	-	-	-	-	-
Carrboro (town)	33,527	26,429	-	-	-	-	-	-	-	-	-	-	-	-	-	-	-	-	-	-	-	-	-	-
Chapel Hill (town)	39,140	35,579	-	31,667	-	-	48,813	-	-	-	-	-	-	-	16,705	-	-	-	-	-	-	-	-	-
Pitt County	32,868	50,938	-	-	-	-	-	-	-	-	-	-	-	-	-	-	-	-	-	-	-	-	-	-
Randolph County	38,348	51,875	-	-	-	-	-	-	-	-	-	-	-	-	-	-	-	-	-	-	-	-	-	-
Robeson County	28,202	42,917	-	-	-	-	-	-	-	-	-	-	-	-	-	-	-	-	-	-	-	-	-	-
Rowan County	37,494	53,393	-	-	-	-	-	-	-	-	-	-	-	-	-	-	-	-	-	-	-	-	-	-
Stanly County	36,898	41,875	-	-	-	-	-	-	-	-	-	40,625	-	-	-	-	-	-	-	-	-	-	-	-
Surry County	33,046	32,250	-	-	-	-	-	-	-	-	-	-	-	-	-	-	-	-	-	-	-	-	-	-
Union County	50,638	48,438	-	-	-	-	-	-	-	-	-	-	-	-	-	-	-	-	-	-	-	-	-	-
Wake County	54,988	64,329	-	66,892	-	-	70,822	-	59,250	-	-	-	-	74,345	41,830	-	-	62,279	-	-	-	-	-	60,302
Apex (town)	71,052	65,875	-	-	-	-	-	-	-	-	-	-	-	-	-	-	-	-	-	-	-	-	-	-
Cary (town)	75,122	83,373	-	87,008	-	-	88,051	-	-	-	-	-	-	92,562	70,250	-	-	-	-	-	-	-	-	78,230
Wayne County	33,942	43,906	-	-	-	-	-	-	-	-	-	-	-	-	-	-	-	-	-	-	-	-	-	-
Wilkes County	34,258	42,625	-	-	-	-	-	-	-	-	-	-	-	-	-	-	-	-	-	-	-	-	-	-
NORTH DAKOTA	34,604	35,441	-	54,286	-	-	34,167	-	43,625	-	-	-	-	-	20,625	-	-	-	-	-	-	-	-	-
Cass County	38,147	24,130	-	46,250	-	-	-	-	-	-	-	-	-	-	-	-	-	-	-	-	-	-	-	-
Grand Forks County	35,785	39,107	-	-	-	-	-	-	-	-	-	-	-	-	-	-	-	-	-	-	-	-	-	-
Ward County	33,670	50,833	-	-	-	-	-	-	-	-	-	-	-	-	-	-	-	-	-	-	-	-	-	-
OHIO	40,956	49,266	40,718	62,119	53,000	36,750	44,380	-	53,909	43,155	50,313	-	12,159	51,854	34,067	51,339	33,393	41,595	40,673	47,857	46,635	26,833	-	41,433
Allen County	37,048	54,219	-	-	-	-	-	-	-	-	-	-	-	-	-	-	-	-	-	-	-	-	-	-
Ashtabula County	35,607	54,464	-	-	-	-	-	-	-	-	-	-	-	-	-	-	-	-	-	-	-	-	-	-
Athens County	27,322	11,797	-	-	-	-	-	-	-	-	-	-	-	-	-	-	-	-	-	-	-	-	-	-
Athens (city)	17,122	10,742	-	-	-	-	-	-	-	-	-	-	-	-	-	-	-	-	-	-	-	-	-	-
Butler County	47,885	63,000	-	80,065	-	-	73,750	-	54,792	-	-	-	-	-	73,750	-	-	-	-	-	-	-	-	42,083
Clark County	40,340	66,731	-	-	-	-	-	-	-	-	-	-	-	-	-	-	-	-	-	-	-	-	-	-
Clermont County	49,386	69,583	-	94,304	-	-	-	-	-	-	-	-	-	-	-	-	-	-	-	-	-	-	-	-
Columbiana County	34,226	44,464	-	-	-	-	-	-	-	-	-	-	-	-	-	-	-	-	-	-	-	-	-	-
Cuyahoga County	39,168	48,930	-	68,220	-	45,625	39,000	-	50,225	-	-	-	-	49,861	36,786	-	-	-	-	-	-	-	-	40,208
Mayfield Heights (city)	37,236	61,875	-	67,250	-	-	-	-	-	-	-	-	-	-	-	-	-	-	-	-	-	-	-	-
Richmond Heights (city)	43,625	55,833	-	-	-	-	-	-	-	-	-	-	-	-	-	-	-	-	-	-	-	-	-	-
Solon (city)	78,903	99,394	-	134,386	-	-	81,203	-	-	-	-	-	-	-	-	-	-	-	-	-	-	-	-	-
Westlake (city)	64,963	105,940	-	104,242	-	-	-	-	-	-	-	-	-	-	-	-	-	-	-	-	-	-	-	-
Delaware County	67,258	84,131	-	103,983	-	-	95,489	-	-	-	-	-	-	-	-	-	-	-	-	-	-	-	-	-
Fairfield County	47,962	70,391	-	-	-	-	-	-	-	-	-	-	-	-	-	-	-	-	-	-	-	-	-	-
Franklin County	42,734	44,470	40,048	56,510	-	31,346	41,193	-	46,118	-	-	-	3,125	54,956	21,760	45,294	-	63,365	-	-	41,484	21,250	-	37,091

Notes: Please refer to the User's Guide for an explanation of data; data is arranged alphabetically by state, then county, then city within each county; table includes counties with populations greater than 49,999 unless noted and cities with populations greater than 9,999 whose Asian and/or NHPI population rates are greater than the national average; (1) Native Hawaiian and other Pacific Islander; (2) excludes Taiwanese; (3) includes Chamorro; (4) county does not meet population threshold but is shown in order to allow inclusion of city

Place	All households	Asian households	NHPI[1] households	Asian Indian	Bangladeshi	Cambodian	Chinese[2]	Fijian	Filipino	Guamanian[3]	Hawaiian, Native	Hmong	Indonesian	Japanese	Korean	Laotian	Malaysian	Pakistani	Samoan	Sri Lankan	Taiwanese	Thai	Tongan	Vietnamese
Dublin (city)	91,162	86,889	-	102,288	-	-	118,591	-	-	-	-	-	-	80,830	-	-	-	-	-	-	-	-	-	-
Hilliard (city)	69,015	76,512	-	-	-	-	-	-	-	-	-	-	-	-	-	-	-	-	-	-	-	-	-	-
Geauga County	60,200	94,327	-	-	-	-	-	-	-	-	-	-	-	-	-	-	-	-	-	-	-	-	-	-
Greene County	48,656	47,852	-	81,283	-	-	28,194	-	-	-	-	-	-	-	26,094	-	-	-	-	-	-	-	-	-
Hamilton County	40,964	46,661	-	55,352	-	33,571	46,210	-	65,750	-	-	-	-	45,109	30,987	-	-	-	-	-	-	-	-	50,893
Blue Ash (city)	61,591	61,985	-	75,506	-	-	-	-	-	-	-	-	-	-	-	-	-	-	-	-	-	-	-	-
Sharonville (city)	47,055	46,618	-	44,250	-	-	-	-	-	-	-	-	-	-	-	-	-	-	-	-	-	-	-	-
Hancock County	43,856	63,281	-	-	-	-	-	-	-	-	-	-	-	-	-	-	-	-	-	-	-	-	-	-
Lake County	48,763	64,135	-	70,179	-	-	73,333	-	-	-	-	-	-	-	-	-	-	-	-	-	-	-	-	-
Licking County	44,124	47,500	-	-	-	-	-	-	-	-	-	-	-	-	-	-	-	-	-	-	-	-	-	-
Lorain County	45,042	53,125	-	57,212	-	-	-	-	54,688	-	-	-	-	-	-	-	-	-	-	-	-	-	-	-
Lucas County	38,004	41,554	-	49,403	-	-	33,618	-	50,781	-	-	-	-	-	46,346	-	-	-	-	-	-	-	-	-
Mahoning County	35,248	40,568	-	-	-	-	-	-	-	-	-	-	-	-	-	-	-	-	-	-	-	-	-	-
Marion County	38,709	60,938	-	-	-	-	-	-	-	-	-	-	-	-	-	-	-	-	-	-	-	-	-	-
Medina County	55,811	69,917	-	72,500	-	-	-	-	-	-	-	-	-	-	-	-	-	-	-	-	-	-	-	-
Miami County	44,109	57,804	-	-	-	-	-	-	-	-	-	-	-	-	-	-	-	-	-	-	-	-	-	-
Montgomery County	40,156	51,176	-	65,526	-	-	50,625	-	57,500	-	-	-	-	31,382	42,885	-	-	-	-	-	-	-	-	38,482
Portage County	44,347	16,094	-	-	-	-	-	-	-	-	-	-	-	-	-	-	-	-	-	-	-	-	-	-
Richland County	37,397	52,895	-	-	-	-	-	-	-	-	-	-	-	-	-	-	-	-	-	-	-	-	-	-
Stark County	39,824	50,089	-	92,318	-	-	51,518	-	-	-	-	-	-	-	-	-	-	-	-	-	-	-	-	-
Summit County	42,304	55,188	-	58,594	-	-	51,833	-	79,238	-	-	-	-	60,515	47,321	56,184	-	-	-	-	-	-	-	41,364
Trumbull County	38,298	43,456	-	-	-	-	-	-	-	-	-	-	-	-	-	-	-	-	-	-	-	-	-	-
Warren County	57,952	83,432	-	80,766	-	-	96,272	-	-	-	-	-	-	-	-	-	-	-	-	-	-	-	-	-
Wayne County	41,538	50,893	-	-	-	-	-	-	-	-	-	-	-	-	-	-	-	-	-	-	-	-	-	-
Wood County	44,442	36,182	-	-	-	-	-	-	-	-	-	-	-	-	-	-	-	-	-	-	-	-	-	-
OKLAHOMA	33,400	34,547	37,957	48,333	-	42,969	25,127	-	35,295	39,853	38,250	39,844	-	20,714	25,250	45,778	5,583	31,875	-	-	7,604	25,066	-	39,850
Canadian County	45,439	59,167	-	57,273	-	-	-	-	-	-	-	-	-	-	-	-	-	-	-	-	-	-	-	65,417
Cleveland County	41,846	34,455	-	57,000	-	-	23,611	-	29,583	-	-	-	-	-	26,406	-	-	-	-	-	-	-	-	53,669
Comanche County	33,867	36,034	-	-	-	-	-	-	38,333	-	-	-	-	-	32,841	-	-	-	-	-	-	-	-	-
Garfield County	33,006	26,563	-	-	-	-	-	-	-	-	-	-	-	-	-	-	-	-	-	-	-	-	-	-
Muskogee County	28,438	50,250	-	-	-	-	-	-	-	-	-	-	-	-	-	-	-	-	-	-	-	-	-	-
Oklahoma County	35,063	30,317	-	42,727	-	-	17,500	-	35,833	-	-	-	-	13,417	11,979	44,688	-	-	-	-	-	33,750	-	35,331
Payne County	28,733	12,981	-	-	-	-	17,000	-	-	-	-	-	-	-	-	-	-	-	-	-	-	-	-	-
Stillwater (city)	25,432	12,644	-	-	-	-	17,000	-	-	-	-	-	-	-	-	-	-	-	-	-	-	-	-	-
Pottawatomie County	31,573	23,375	-	-	-	-	-	-	-	-	-	-	-	-	-	-	-	-	-	-	-	-	-	-
Tulsa County	38,213	42,610	-	52,031	-	-	36,667	-	40,875	-	-	-	-	-	45,795	-	-	32,031	-	-	-	-	-	43,700
Wagoner County	41,744	46,250	-	-	-	-	-	-	-	-	-	-	-	-	-	-	-	-	-	-	-	-	-	-
OREGON	40,916	46,955	39,218	67,191	-	40,417	47,213	45,694	45,000	42,043	44,896	36,836	19,531	40,199	36,934	52,102	-	72,778	32,083	-	25,250	29,688	35,000	51,349
Benton County	41,897	17,574	-	-	-	-	22,679	-	-	-	-	-	-	31,500	11,184	-	-	-	-	-	-	-	-	-
Corvallis (city)	35,236	15,400	-	-	-	-	17,188	-	-	-	-	-	-	-	10,526	-	-	-	-	-	-	-	-	-
Clackamas County	52,080	60,774	44,479	103,321	-	-	66,172	-	57,206	-	-	-	-	55,781	46,667	-	-	-	-	-	-	-	-	65,000

Notes: Please refer to the User's Guide for an explanation of data; data is arranged alphabetically by state, then county, then city within each county; table includes counties with populations greater than 49,999 unless noted and cities with populations greater than 9,999 whose Asian and/or NHPI population rates are greater than the national average; (1) Native Hawaiian and other Pacific Islander; (2) excludes Taiwanese; (3) includes Chamorro; (4) county does not meet population threshold but is shown in order to allow inclusion of city

Place	All households	Asian households	NHPI[1] households	Asian Indian	Bangladeshi	Cambodian	Chinese[2]	Fijian	Filipino	Guamanian[3]	Hawaiian, Native	Hmong	Indonesian	Japanese	Korean	Laotian	Malaysian	Pakistani	Samoan	Sri Lankan	Taiwanese	Thai	Tongan	Vietnamese
Lake Oswego (city)	71,597	70,833	-	-	-	-	92,449	-	-	-	-	-	-	-	-	-	-	-	-	-	-	-	-	-
Coos County	31,542	21,875	-	-	-	-	-	-	-	-	-	-	-	-	-	-	-	-	-	-	-	-	-	-
Deschutes County	41,847	39,250	-	-	-	-	-	-	-	-	-	-	-	-	-	-	-	-	-	-	-	-	-	-
Douglas County	33,223	37,813	-	-	-	-	-	-	-	-	-	-	-	-	-	-	-	-	-	-	-	-	-	-
Jackson County	36,461	32,917	-	-	-	-	-	-	-	-	-	-	-	-	-	-	-	-	-	-	-	-	-	-
Josephine County	31,229	37,240	-	-	-	-	-	-	-	-	-	-	-	-	-	-	-	-	-	-	-	-	-	-
Klamath County	31,537	32,188	-	-	-	-	-	-	-	-	-	-	-	-	-	-	-	-	-	-	-	-	-	-
Lane County	36,942	18,004	31,190	31,389	-	-	23,558	-	39,125	-	-	-	-	13,793	15,909	-	-	-	-	-	-	-	-	-
Linn County	37,518	38,047	-	-	-	-	-	-	-	-	-	-	-	-	-	-	-	-	-	-	-	-	-	-
Marion County	40,314	38,558	33,750	60,511	-	-	36,635	-	37,232	-	-	-	-	47,917	19,297	-	-	-	-	-	-	-	-	59,000
Salem (city)	38,881	40,833	26,042	-	-	-	38,313	-	36,042	-	-	-	-	33,750	-	-	-	-	-	-	-	-	-	66,875
Multnomah County	41,278	43,117	39,861	54,219	-	38,885	42,417	-	43,722	-	60,893	45,938	-	38,580	38,426	51,307	-	-	-	-	-	22,061	45,667	47,552
Portland (city)	40,146	42,576	39,115	52,813	-	38,378	42,271	-	42,111	-	50,625	43,000	-	36,505	33,194	52,250	-	-	-	-	-	21,892	45,667	45,755
Polk County	42,311	52,361	-	-	-	-	-	-	-	-	-	-	-	-	-	-	-	-	-	-	-	-	-	-
Umatilla County	36,249	31,458	-	-	-	-	-	-	-	-	-	-	-	-	-	-	-	-	-	-	-	-	-	-
Washington County	52,122	60,809	41,196	72,788	-	44,250	66,831	-	53,819	-	50,417	-	-	56,641	43,229	47,368	-	-	-	-	-	-	-	60,526
Aloha (cdp)	52,299	57,647	-	-	-	-	-	-	60,357	-	-	-	-	-	-	-	-	-	-	-	-	-	-	72,738
Beaverton (city)	47,863	56,950	-	65,063	-	29,688	56,413	-	42,885	-	-	-	-	78,889	42,614	-	-	-	-	-	-	-	-	58,839
Cedar Mill (cdp)	65,730	95,717	-	-	-	-	-	-	-	-	-	-	-	-	-	-	-	-	-	-	-	-	-	-
Hillsboro (city)	51,737	64,028	-	70,074	-	-	68,571	-	-	-	-	-	-	-	60,694	-	-	-	-	-	-	-	-	56,875
Tigard (city)	51,581	64,342	-	-	-	-	76,836	-	-	-	-	-	-	-	-	-	-	-	-	-	-	-	-	56,250
Tualatin (city)	55,762	54,342	-	-	-	-	-	-	-	-	-	-	-	-	-	-	-	-	-	-	-	-	-	-
Yamhill County	44,111	31,705	-	-	-	-	-	-	-	-	-	-	-	-	-	-	-	-	-	-	-	-	-	-
PENNSYLVANIA	40,106	44,205	42,656	59,643	35,179	26,536	40,072	-	53,083	46,202	52,941	43,889	43,462	29,397	36,585	48,163	-	50,707	30,625	70,729	26,250	18,510	-	38,549
Adams County	42,704	42,708	-	-	-	-	-	-	-	-	-	-	-	-	-	-	-	-	-	-	-	-	-	-
Allegheny County	38,329	42,254	25,000	61,743	-	-	36,184	-	40,909	-	-	-	-	10,000	25,174	-	-	-	-	-	13,750	-	-	35,000
Muni. of Monroeville (borough)	44,653	62,216	-	66,094	-	-	-	-	-	-	-	-	-	-	-	-	-	-	-	-	-	-	-	-
Scott (township)	44,434	57,206	-	59,750	-	-	-	-	-	-	-	-	-	-	-	-	-	-	-	-	-	-	-	-
Scott Township (cdp)	44,434	57,206	-	59,750	-	-	-	-	-	-	-	-	-	-	-	-	-	-	-	-	-	-	-	-
Upper St. Clair (township)	87,581	151,569	-	186,873	-	-	-	-	-	-	-	-	-	-	-	-	-	-	-	-	-	-	-	-
Beaver County	36,995	48,068	-	-	-	-	-	-	-	-	-	-	-	-	-	-	-	-	-	-	-	-	-	-
Berks County	44,714	56,172	-	68,750	-	-	91,715	-	-	-	-	-	-	-	94,714	-	-	-	-	-	-	-	-	46,563
Blair County	32,861	59,107	-	-	-	-	-	-	-	-	-	-	-	-	-	-	-	-	-	-	-	-	-	-
Bradford County	35,038	39,453	-	-	-	-	-	-	-	-	-	-	-	-	-	-	-	-	-	-	-	-	-	-
Bucks County	59,727	61,972	-	64,803	-	-	75,955	-	55,962	-	-	-	-	-	46,116	-	-	-	-	-	-	-	-	50,833
Bensalem (township)	49,737	54,878	-	54,848	-	-	-	-	-	-	-	-	-	-	45,625	-	-	-	-	-	-	-	-	-
Lower Makefield (township)	98,090	84,059	-	81,704	-	-	-	-	-	-	-	-	-	-	-	-	-	-	-	-	-	-	-	-
Newtown (township)	80,532	83,149	-	-	-	-	-	-	-	-	-	-	-	-	-	-	-	-	-	-	-	-	-	-
Butler County	42,308	69,205	-	91,583	-	-	-	-	-	-	-	-	-	-	-	-	-	-	-	-	-	-	-	-
Cambria County	30,179	36,346	-	-	-	-	-	-	-	-	-	-	-	-	-	-	-	-	-	-	-	-	-	-
Centre County	36,165	19,205	-	31,131	-	-	20,859	-	-	-	-	-	-	-	13,889	-	-	-	-	-	-	-	-	-

Notes: Please refer to the User's Guide for an explanation of data; data is arranged alphabetically by state, then county, then city within each county; table includes counties with populations greater than 49,999 unless noted and cities with populations greater than 9,999 whose Asian and/or NHPI population rates are greater than the national average; (1) Native Hawaiian and other Pacific Islander; (2) excludes Taiwanese; (3) includes Chamorro; (4) county does not meet population threshold but is shown in order to allow inclusion of city

Place	All households	Asian households	NHPI[1] households	Asian Indian	Bangladeshi	Cambodian	Chinese[2]	Fijian	Filipino	Guamanian[3]	Hawaiian, Native	Hmong	Indonesian	Japanese	Korean	Laotian	Malaysian	Pakistani	Samoan	Sri Lankan	Taiwanese	Thai	Tongan	Vietnamese
Ferguson (township)	46,703	30,673	-	-	-	-	-	-	-	-	-	-	-	-	-	-	-	-	-	-	-	-	-	-
Patton (township)	41,993	42,361	-	-	-	-	-	-	-	-	-	-	-	-	-	-	-	-	-	-	-	-	-	-
State College (borough)	21,186	15,827	-	18,594	-	-	16,189	-	-	-	-	-	-	-	6,597	-	-	-	-	-	-	-	-	-
Chester County	65,295	75,576	-	90,087	-	-	90,629	-	51,500	-	-	-	-	52,679	57,721	-	-	-	-	-	-	-	-	65,694
Tredyffrin (township)	82,258	77,883	-	77,228	-	-	100,451	-	-	-	-	-	-	-	-	-	-	-	-	-	-	-	-	-
West Goshen (township)	71,055	55,750	-	-	-	-	-	-	-	-	-	-	-	-	-	-	-	-	-	-	-	-	-	-
West Whiteland (township)	71,545	80,634	-	-	-	-	-	-	-	-	-	-	-	-	-	-	-	-	-	-	-	-	-	-
Clearfield County	31,357	83,193	-	-	-	-	-	-	-	-	-	-	-	-	-	-	-	-	-	-	-	-	-	-
Columbia County	34,094	30,714	-	-	-	-	-	-	-	-	-	-	-	-	-	-	-	-	-	-	-	-	-	-
Crawford County	33,560	40,781	-	-	-	-	-	-	-	-	-	-	-	-	-	-	-	-	-	-	-	-	-	-
Cumberland County	46,707	56,417	-	62,206	-	-	69,861	-	-	-	-	-	-	-	54,833	-	-	-	-	-	-	-	-	71,063
Hampden (township)	60,011	58,500	-	-	-	-	-	-	-	-	-	-	-	-	-	-	-	-	-	-	-	-	-	-
Dauphin County	41,507	43,662	-	52,115	-	-	42,083	-	-	-	-	-	-	-	22,813	-	-	-	-	-	-	-	-	42,654
Derry (township)	52,290	49,063	-	-	-	-	-	-	-	-	-	-	-	-	-	-	-	-	-	-	-	-	-	-
Hershey (cdp)	45,098	50,357	-	-	-	-	-	-	-	-	-	-	-	-	-	-	-	-	-	-	-	-	-	-
Delaware County	50,092	50,722	-	60,025	-	-	47,074	-	61,940	-	-	-	-	41,641	48,636	-	-	46,875	-	-	-	-	-	46,944
Broomall (cdp)	52,354	52,167	-	-	-	-	-	-	-	-	-	-	-	-	46,250	-	-	-	-	-	-	-	-	-
Drexel Hill (cdp)	48,765	35,125	-	-	-	-	33,750	-	-	-	-	-	-	-	-	-	-	-	-	-	-	-	-	-
Marple (township)	59,577	63,542	-	-	-	-	-	-	-	-	-	-	-	-	55,625	-	-	-	-	-	-	-	-	-
Radnor (township)	74,272	52,969	-	-	-	-	50,114	-	-	-	-	-	-	-	-	-	-	-	-	-	-	-	-	-
Upper Darby (township)	41,489	40,775	-	48,036	-	-	32,800	-	-	-	-	-	-	-	37,679	-	-	-	-	-	-	-	-	49,250
Erie County	36,627	37,188	-	43,125	-	-	-	-	-	-	-	-	-	-	-	-	-	-	-	-	-	-	-	-
Franklin County	40,476	75,000	-	-	-	-	-	-	-	-	-	-	-	-	-	-	-	-	-	-	-	-	-	-
Indiana County	30,233	18,824	-	-	-	-	-	-	-	-	-	-	-	-	-	-	-	-	-	-	-	-	-	-
Lackawanna County	34,438	56,188	-	73,214	-	-	-	-	-	-	-	-	-	-	-	-	-	-	-	-	-	-	-	-
Lancaster County	45,507	49,972	-	51,477	-	-	40,529	-	-	-	-	48,214	-	-	35,938	-	-	-	-	-	-	-	-	55,607
Lawrence County	33,152	41,786	-	-	-	-	-	-	-	-	-	-	-	-	-	-	-	-	-	-	-	-	-	-
Lebanon County	40,838	46,250	-	-	-	-	-	-	-	-	-	-	-	-	-	-	-	-	-	-	-	-	-	-
Lehigh County	43,449	60,701	-	63,438	-	-	72,198	-	-	-	-	-	-	-	49,318	-	-	-	-	-	-	-	-	47,411
Fullerton (cdp)	43,048	61,250	-	-	-	-	-	-	-	-	-	-	-	-	-	-	-	-	-	-	-	-	-	-
Lower Macungie (township)	69,592	102,207	-	-	-	-	105,976	-	-	-	-	-	-	-	-	-	-	-	-	-	-	-	-	-
Upper Macungie (township)	65,062	95,045	-	-	-	-	-	-	-	-	-	-	-	-	-	-	-	-	-	-	-	-	-	-
Luzerne County	33,771	61,429	-	81,194	-	-	-	-	-	-	-	-	-	-	-	-	-	-	-	-	-	-	-	-
Lycoming County	34,016	41,157	-	-	-	-	-	-	-	-	-	-	-	-	-	-	-	-	-	-	-	-	-	-
Mercer County	34,666	61,563	-	-	-	-	-	-	-	-	-	-	-	-	-	-	-	-	-	-	-	-	-	-
Monroe County	46,257	72,609	-	52,344	-	-	-	-	-	-	-	-	-	-	-	-	-	-	-	-	-	-	-	-
Montgomery County	60,829	60,667	-	71,422	-	-	70,240	-	71,719	-	-	-	-	54,000	46,469	-	-	-	-	-	-	-	-	60,950
Cheltenham (township)	61,713	41,450	-	-	-	-	-	-	-	-	-	-	-	-	35,223	-	-	-	-	-	-	-	-	-
East Norriton (township)	60,536	61,250	-	-	-	-	-	-	-	-	-	-	-	-	-	-	-	-	-	-	-	-	-	-
Hatfield (township)	57,247	55,987	-	61,875	-	-	-	-	-	-	-	-	-	-	-	-	-	-	-	-	-	-	-	-
Horsham (township)	61,998	52,772	-	-	-	-	-	-	-	-	-	-	-	-	42,778	-	-	-	-	-	-	-	-	-

Notes: Please refer to the User's Guide for an explanation of data; data is arranged alphabetically by state, then county, then city within each county; table includes counties with populations greater than 49,999 unless noted and cities with populations greater than 9,999 whose Asian and/or NHPI population rates are greater than the national average; (1) Native Hawaiian and other Pacific Islander; (2) excludes Taiwanese; (3) includes Chamorro; (4) county does not meet population threshold but is shown in order to allow inclusion of city

Place	All households	Asian households	NHPI[1] households	Asian Indian	Bangladeshi	Cambodian	Chinese[2]	Fijian	Filipino	Guamanian[3]	Hawaiian, Native	Hmong	Indonesian	Japanese	Korean	Laotian	Malaysian	Pakistani	Samoan	Sri Lankan	Taiwanese	Thai	Tongan	Vietnamese
King of Prussia (cdp)	62,012	63,688	-	69,375	-	-	68,958	-	-	-	-	-	-	-	-	-	-	-	-	-	-	-	-	-
Lansdale (borough)	46,232	45,583	-	60,370	-	-	-	-	-	-	-	-	-	-	-	-	-	-	-	-	-	-	-	-
Lower Gwynedd (township)	74,351	107,014	-	-	-	-	-	-	-	-	-	-	-	-	-	-	-	-	-	-	-	-	-	-
Lower Providence (township)	66,250	63,194	-	-	-	-	104,905	-	-	-	-	-	-	-	-	-	-	-	-	-	-	-	-	-
Montgomery (township)	78,953	78,723	-	77,597	-	-	-	-	-	-	-	-	-	-	66,111	-	-	-	-	-	-	-	-	-
Montgomeryville (cdp)	77,097	59,911	-	-	-	-	-	-	-	-	-	-	-	-	-	-	-	-	-	-	-	-	-	-
Plymouth (township)	54,069	65,972	-	-	-	-	-	-	-	-	-	-	-	-	53,125	-	-	-	-	-	-	-	-	-
Towamencin (township)	66,736	69,886	-	-	-	-	-	-	-	-	-	-	-	-	-	-	-	-	-	-	-	-	-	-
Upper Dublin (township)	80,093	70,250	-	-	-	-	-	-	-	-	-	-	-	-	58,375	-	-	-	-	-	-	-	-	-
Upper Gwynedd (township)	71,078	82,697	-	-	-	-	81,776	-	-	-	-	-	-	-	-	-	-	-	-	-	-	-	-	-
Upper Merion (township)	65,636	66,250	-	74,500	-	-	72,500	-	-	-	-	-	-	-	-	-	-	-	-	-	-	-	-	-
Whitpain (township)	88,933	81,685	-	-	-	-	-	-	-	-	-	-	-	-	67,813	-	-	-	-	-	-	-	-	-
Northampton County	45,234	49,861	-	90,432	-	-	43,824	-	-	-	-	-	-	-	16,154	-	-	-	-	-	-	-	-	39,038
Northumberland County	31,314	41,319	-	-	-	-	-	-	-	-	-	-	-	-	-	-	-	-	-	-	-	-	-	-
Philadelphia County	30,746	27,794	19,500	40,995	-	20,746	25,569	-	42,202	-	-	-	-	15,083	19,510	45,741	-	30,417	-	-	-	-	-	25,658
Philadelphia (city)	30,746	27,794	19,500	40,995	-	20,746	25,569	-	42,202	-	-	-	-	15,083	19,510	45,741	-	30,417	-	-	-	-	-	25,658
Schuylkill County	32,699	43,125	-	-	-	-	-	-	-	-	-	-	-	-	-	-	-	-	-	-	-	-	-	-
Washington County	37,607	51,667	-	-	-	-	-	-	-	-	-	-	-	-	-	-	-	-	-	-	-	-	-	-
Westmoreland County	37,106	127,242	-	134,883	-	-	-	-	-	-	-	-	-	-	-	-	-	-	-	-	-	-	-	-
York County	45,268	52,250	-	58,438	-	-	35,781	-	-	-	-	-	-	-	61,000	-	-	-	-	-	-	-	-	56,806
RHODE ISLAND	42,090	36,473	29,423	47,227	-	27,212	37,262	-	45,648	-	-	45,156	-	61,417	17,344	41,667	-	-	-	-	-	-	-	43,409
Bristol County	50,737	89,451	-	-	-	-	-	-	-	-	-	-	-	-	-	-	-	-	-	-	-	-	-	-
Kent County	47,617	58,750	-	-	-	-	40,455	-	-	-	-	-	-	-	47,031	-	-	-	-	-	-	-	-	-
Newport County	50,448	41,667	-	-	-	-	-	-	41,964	-	-	-	-	-	-	-	-	-	-	-	-	-	-	-
Providence County	36,950	32,387	-	42,639	-	25,288	35,365	-	37,188	-	-	40,938	-	-	10,625	41,500	-	-	-	-	-	-	-	38,438
Providence (city)	26,867	24,094	-	29,643	-	23,297	25,435	-	31,667	-	-	37,361	-	-	2,499	27,688	-	-	-	-	-	-	-	-
Woonsocket (city)	30,819	41,042	-	-	-	-	-	-	-	-	-	-	-	-	-	41,447	-	-	-	-	-	-	-	-
Washington County	53,103	45,341	-	-	-	-	43,875	-	-	-	-	-	-	-	-	-	-	-	-	-	-	-	-	-
SOUTH CAROLINA	37,082	43,915	56,833	51,250	-	26,667	44,178	-	44,793	87,720	55,000	45,268	-	35,991	31,616	44,100	-	-	-	-	-	38,958	-	39,444
Aiken County	37,889	54,773	-	-	-	-	-	-	-	-	-	-	-	-	-	-	-	-	-	-	-	-	-	-
Anderson County	36,807	34,338	-	-	-	-	-	-	-	-	-	-	-	-	-	-	-	-	-	-	-	-	-	-
Beaufort County	46,992	72,905	-	-	-	-	-	-	-	-	-	-	-	-	-	-	-	-	-	-	-	-	-	-
Berkeley County	39,908	44,652	-	-	-	-	-	-	44,740	-	-	-	-	-	-	-	-	-	-	-	-	-	-	-
Charleston County	37,810	34,833	-	41,700	-	-	38,320	-	36,364	-	-	-	-	-	-	-	-	-	-	-	-	-	-	-
Dorchester County	43,316	51,318	-	-	-	-	-	-	72,727	-	-	-	-	-	-	-	-	-	-	-	-	-	-	-
Florence County	35,144	52,589	-	-	-	-	-	-	-	-	-	-	-	-	-	-	-	-	-	-	-	-	-	-
Greenville County	41,149	52,421	-	54,063	-	-	57,045	-	46,974	-	-	-	-	-	-	-	-	-	-	-	-	-	-	45,208
Greenwood County	34,702	62,250	-	-	-	-	-	-	-	-	-	-	-	-	-	-	-	-	-	-	-	-	-	-
Horry County	36,470	45,179	-	-	-	-	-	-	-	-	-	-	-	-	-	-	-	-	-	-	-	-	-	-
Lexington County	44,659	37,083	-	72,841	-	-	25,865	-	-	-	-	-	-	-	-	-	-	-	-	-	-	-	-	-
Oconee County	36,666	61,625	-	-	-	-	-	-	-	-	-	-	-	-	-	-	-	-	-	-	-	-	-	-

Notes: Please refer to the User's Guide for an explanation of data; data is arranged alphabetically by state, then county, then city within each county; table includes counties with populations greater than 49,999 unless noted and cities with populations greater than 9,999 whose Asian and/or NHPI population rates are greater than the national average; (1) Native Hawaiian and other Pacific Islander; (2) excludes Taiwanese; (3) includes Chamorro; (4) county does not meet population threshold but is shown in order to allow inclusion of city

Place	All households	Asian households	NHPI[1] households	Asian Indian	Bangladeshi	Cambodian	Chinese[2]	Fijian	Filipino	Guamanian[3]	Hawaiian, Native	Hmong	Indonesian	Japanese	Korean	Laotian	Malaysian	Pakistani	Samoan	Sri Lankan	Taiwanese	Thai	Tongan	Vietnamese
Pickens County	36,214	21,652	-	14,219	-	-	21,618	-	-	-	-	-	-	-	-	-	-	-	-	-	-	-	-	-
Clemson (city)	26,892	13,981	-	-	-	-	-	-	-	-	-	-	-	-	-	-	-	-	-	-	-	-	-	-
Richland County	39,961	35,833	-	48,189	-	-	31,438	-	31,500	-	-	-	-	-	22,243	-	-	-	-	-	-	-	-	61,607
Spartanburg County	37,579	44,321	-	51,667	-	-	-	-	-	-	-	46,607	-	-	-	42,102	-	-	-	-	-	-	-	-
Sumter County	33,278	40,682	-	-	-	-	-	-	-	-	-	-	-	-	-	-	-	-	-	-	-	-	-	-
York County	44,539	52,375	-	-	-	-	-	-	-	-	-	-	-	-	-	-	-	-	-	-	-	-	-	46,055
SOUTH DAKOTA	35,282	38,346	-	51,042	-	-	41,369	-	47,778	-	-	-	-	27,750	35,568	43,333	-	-	-	-	-	-	-	42,500
Minnehaha County	42,566	43,333	-	-	-	-	-	-	-	-	-	-	-	-	-	-	-	-	-	-	-	-	-	44,167
Pennington County	37,485	33,846	-	-	-	-	-	-	-	-	-	-	-	-	-	-	-	-	-	-	-	-	-	-
TENNESSEE	36,360	45,497	34,441	53,508	-	41,944	46,238	-	52,396	27,083	42,083	-	-	40,645	28,793	51,684	-	62,679	35,833	-	61,103	39,375	-	39,268
Anderson County	35,483	51,023	-	-	-	-	-	-	-	-	-	-	-	-	-	-	-	-	-	-	-	-	-	-
Blount County	37,862	57,167	-	-	-	-	-	-	-	-	-	-	-	-	-	-	-	-	-	-	-	-	-	-
Bradley County	35,034	41,875	-	-	-	-	-	-	-	-	-	-	-	-	-	-	-	-	-	-	-	-	-	-
Davidson County	39,797	38,851	28,875	40,417	-	-	36,089	-	50,673	-	-	-	-	32,875	30,856	45,469	-	-	-	-	-	-	-	40,898
Hamilton County	38,930	46,967	-	65,391	-	-	-	-	31,944	-	-	-	-	-	38,625	-	-	-	-	-	-	-	-	32,500
Knox County	37,454	38,864	-	44,539	-	-	47,019	-	-	-	-	-	-	-	15,583	-	-	-	-	-	-	-	-	38,917
Madison County	36,982	62,067	-	-	-	-	-	-	-	-	-	-	-	-	-	-	-	-	-	-	-	-	-	-
Montgomery County	38,981	31,442	-	-	-	-	-	-	-	-	-	-	-	-	22,000	-	-	-	-	-	-	-	-	-
Putnam County	30,914	31,250	-	-	-	-	-	-	-	-	-	-	-	-	-	-	-	-	-	-	-	-	-	-
Rutherford County	46,312	56,750	-	-	-	-	-	-	-	-	-	-	-	-	-	61,364	-	-	-	-	-	-	-	-
Shelby County	39,593	48,947	38,977	54,878	-	40,000	51,285	-	61,637	-	-	-	-	31,438	35,298	-	-	-	-	-	-	-	-	39,537
Germantown (city)	94,609	92,071	-	126,177	-	-	78,986	-	-	-	-	-	-	-	-	-	-	-	-	-	-	-	-	-
Sullivan County	33,529	54,583	-	-	-	-	-	-	-	-	-	-	-	-	-	-	-	-	-	-	-	-	-	-
Sumner County	46,030	62,500	-	-	-	-	-	-	-	-	-	-	-	-	-	-	-	-	-	-	-	-	-	-
Washington County	33,116	82,566	-	-	-	-	-	-	-	-	-	-	-	-	-	-	-	-	-	-	-	-	-	-
Weakley County[4]	30,008	3,125	-	-	-	-	-	-	-	-	-	-	-	-	-	-	-	-	-	-	-	-	-	-
Martin (city)	26,493	2,917	-	-	-	-	-	-	-	-	-	-	-	-	-	-	-	-	-	-	-	-	-	-
Williamson County	69,104	83,452	-	-	-	-	-	-	-	-	-	-	-	-	-	-	-	-	-	-	-	-	-	-
Wilson County	50,140	54,464	-	-	-	-	-	-	-	-	-	-	-	-	-	-	-	-	-	-	-	-	-	-
TEXAS	39,927	50,049	41,072	60,173	43,897	50,036	50,812	-	54,970	40,795	35,788	-	46,094	46,312	34,870	45,787	42,292	41,148	45,347	46,346	52,065	34,500	38,125	45,947
Anderson County	31,957	57,708	-	-	-	-	-	-	-	-	-	-	-	-	-	-	-	-	-	-	-	-	-	-
Angelina County	33,806	48,920	-	-	-	-	-	-	-	-	-	-	-	-	-	-	-	-	-	-	-	-	-	-
Bell County	36,872	32,981	50,224	51,696	-	-	-	-	35,278	49,712	-	-	-	14,107	32,019	-	-	-	-	-	-	-	-	-
Killeen (city)	34,461	30,701	51,763	-	-	-	-	-	40,924	51,382	-	-	-	-	26,190	-	-	-	-	-	-	-	-	-
Bexar County	38,328	39,823	37,222	55,950	-	-	39,659	-	37,560	-	47,768	-	-	39,861	29,792	32,500	-	-	-	-	-	37,098	-	38,125
Bowie County	33,001	60,750	-	-	-	-	-	-	-	-	-	-	-	-	-	-	-	-	-	-	-	-	-	-
Brazoria County	48,632	68,938	-	100,243	-	35,536	86,856	-	87,940	-	-	-	-	-	-	-	-	-	-	-	-	-	-	54,722
Brazos County	29,104	18,181	-	31,750	-	-	18,969	-	-	-	-	-	-	-	11,635	-	-	-	-	-	-	-	-	6,250
College Station (city)	21,180	17,679	-	37,898	-	-	19,632	-	-	-	-	-	-	-	9,417	-	-	-	-	-	-	-	-	-
Calhoun County[4]	35,849	53,438	-	-	-	-	-	-	-	-	-	-	-	-	-	-	-	-	-	-	-	-	-	38,068
Port Lavaca (city)	33,626	58,929	-	-	-	-	-	-	-	-	-	-	-	-	-	-	-	-	-	-	-	-	-	-

Notes: Please refer to the User's Guide for an explanation of data; data is arranged alphabetically by state, then county, then city within each county; table includes counties with populations greater than 49,999 unless noted and cities with populations greater than 9,999 whose Asian and/or NHPI population rates are greater than the national average; (1) Native Hawaiian and other Pacific Islander; (2) excludes Taiwanese; (3) includes Chamorro; (4) county does not meet population threshold but is shown in order to allow inclusion of city

Place	All households	Asian households	NHPI[1] households	Asian Indian	Bangladeshi	Cambodian	Chinese[2]	Fijian	Filipino	Guamanian[3]	Hawaiian, Native	Hmong	Indonesian	Japanese	Korean	Laotian	Malaysian	Pakistani	Samoan	Sri Lankan	Taiwanese	Thai	Tongan	Vietnamese
Cameron County	26,155	56,023	-	-	-	-	-	-	49,097	-	-	-	-	-	-	-	-	-	-	-	-	-	-	-
Collin County	70,835	78,545	-	80,446	-	-	80,992	-	70,139	-	-	-	-	89,728	62,472	-	-	59,375	-	-	101,912	70,294	-	85,269
Allen (city)	78,924	69,188	-	67,692	-	-	-	-	-	-	-	-	-	-	-	-	-	-	-	-	-	-	-	85,248
Plano (city)	78,722	85,819	-	97,786	-	-	87,840	-	63,533	-	-	-	-	82,610	71,129	-	-	66,518	-	-	103,208	-	-	84,195
Comal County	46,147	56,250	-	-	-	-	-	-	-	-	-	-	-	-	-	-	-	-	-	-	-	-	-	-
Coryell County	35,999	21,923	44,583	-	-	-	-	-	-	-	-	-	-	-	16,979	-	-	-	-	-	-	-	-	-
Dallas County	43,324	49,382	39,438	56,759	45,833	52,426	47,125	-	54,960	-	-	-	-	53,357	36,522	41,471	-	38,425	-	-	49,076	42,125	-	46,061
Addison (town)	48,566	49,550	-	48,400	-	-	-	-	-	-	-	-	-	-	-	-	-	-	-	-	-	-	-	-
Coppell (city)	96,935	81,503	-	91,374	-	-	98,517	-	-	-	-	-	-	-	64,453	-	-	-	-	-	-	-	-	-
Farmers Branch (city)	54,734	50,789	-	-	-	-	-	-	-	-	-	-	-	-	-	-	-	-	-	-	-	-	-	-
Garland (city)	49,156	47,530	-	60,035	-	-	43,750	-	53,917	-	-	-	-	-	28,958	-	-	35,903	-	-	-	-	-	47,422
Grand Prairie (city)	46,816	56,080	-	65,227	-	-	-	-	68,929	-	-	-	-	-	-	44,531	-	-	-	-	-	-	-	55,365
Irving (city)	44,956	52,459	-	61,592	-	-	51,331	-	51,071	-	-	-	-	49,063	32,012	39,821	-	37,500	-	-	-	-	-	51,579
Mesquite (city)	50,424	59,167	-	57,917	-	-	-	-	85,848	-	-	-	-	-	-	-	-	-	-	-	-	-	-	-
Richardson (city)	62,392	57,069	-	61,905	-	-	47,037	-	55,804	-	-	-	-	-	44,000	-	-	50,461	-	-	-	-	-	67,569
Rowlett (city)	70,947	82,269	-	84,725	-	-	-	-	-	-	-	-	-	-	-	-	-	-	-	-	-	-	-	-
Denton County	58,216	55,342	-	67,679	-	65,817	56,205	-	46,250	-	-	-	-	16,635	24,583	-	-	64,000	-	-	-	-	-	55,433
Carrollton (city)	62,406	58,136	-	61,397	-	56,667	58,571	-	-	-	-	-	-	-	55,156	-	-	45,368	-	-	-	-	-	60,909
Lewisville (city)	54,771	61,354	-	69,643	-	-	-	-	-	-	-	-	-	-	-	-	-	-	-	-	-	-	-	58,438
Ector County	31,152	58,583	-	-	-	-	-	-	-	-	-	-	-	-	-	-	-	-	-	-	-	-	-	-
El Paso County	31,051	37,636	31,818	34,821	-	-	48,095	-	53,333	-	-	-	-	30,833	33,026	-	-	-	-	-	-	-	-	-
Ellis County	50,350	52,143	-	-	-	-	-	-	-	-	-	-	-	-	-	-	-	-	-	-	-	-	-	-
Fort Bend County	63,831	76,627	-	83,834	-	-	76,238	-	84,297	-	-	-	-	-	71,179	-	-	61,563	-	-	54,919	-	-	66,731
Cinco Ranch (cdp)	111,517	126,858	-	-	-	-	-	-	-	-	-	-	-	-	-	-	-	-	-	-	-	-	-	-
Mission Bend (cdp)	60,222	65,329	-	76,025	-	-	60,054	-	82,023	-	-	-	-	-	-	-	-	36,979	-	-	-	-	-	61,146
Missouri City (city)	72,434	86,116	-	91,862	-	-	85,080	-	90,276	-	-	-	-	-	-	-	-	-	-	-	-	-	-	69,219
New Territory (cdp)	93,972	99,113	-	96,924	-	-	97,586	-	-	-	-	-	-	-	-	-	-	-	-	-	-	-	-	-
Stafford (city)	50,323	52,500	-	42,875	-	-	50,139	-	65,313	-	-	-	-	-	-	-	-	-	-	-	-	-	-	72,250
Sugar Land (city)	81,767	83,475	-	97,045	-	-	83,033	-	91,286	-	-	-	-	-	74,375	-	-	81,006	-	-	54,597	-	-	67,778
Galveston County	42,419	40,298	-	41,786	-	-	31,027	-	58,021	-	-	-	-	-	-	-	-	-	-	-	-	-	-	45,443
Grayson County	37,178	59,375	-	-	-	-	-	-	-	-	-	-	-	-	-	-	-	-	-	-	-	-	-	-
Gregg County	35,006	36,607	-	-	-	-	-	-	-	-	-	-	-	-	-	-	-	-	-	-	-	-	-	-
Guadalupe County	43,949	56,417	-	-	-	-	-	-	-	-	-	-	-	-	-	-	-	-	-	-	-	-	-	-
Harris County	42,598	46,487	45,688	53,786	40,938	40,655	44,599	-	60,582	44,861	-	-	48,875	52,979	36,159	50,341	-	35,833	-	-	50,184	31,336	-	42,622
Bellaire (city)	89,775	101,159	-	-	-	-	79,178	-	-	-	-	-	-	-	-	-	-	-	-	-	-	-	-	-
Houston (city)	36,616	40,514	43,712	47,570	-	33,618	39,270	-	55,469	46,389	-	-	50,000	53,194	31,257	-	-	33,281	-	-	40,486	30,388	-	35,751
West University Place (city)	130,721	112,773	-	-	-	-	-	-	-	-	-	-	-	-	-	-	-	-	-	-	-	-	-	-
Hays County	45,006	44,750	-	-	-	-	-	-	-	-	-	-	-	-	-	-	-	-	-	-	-	-	-	-
Hidalgo County	24,863	56,344	-	87,131	-	-	-	-	57,061	-	-	-	-	-	-	-	-	-	-	-	-	-	-	-
Hunt County	36,752	34,559	-	-	-	-	-	-	-	-	-	-	-	-	-	-	-	-	-	-	-	-	-	-
Jefferson County	34,706	38,408	-	57,540	-	-	56,667	-	62,121	-	-	-	-	-	-	-	-	-	-	-	-	-	-	27,803

Notes: Please refer to the User's Guide for an explanation of data; data is arranged alphabetically by state, then county, then city within each county; table includes counties with populations greater than 49,999 unless noted and cities with populations greater than 9,999 whose Asian and/or NHPI population rates are greater than the national average; (1) Native Hawaiian and other Pacific Islander; (2) excludes Taiwanese; (3) includes Chamorro; (4) county does not meet population threshold but is shown in order to allow inclusion of city

Place	All households	Asian households	NHPI[1] households	Asian Indian	Bangladeshi	Cambodian	Chinese[2]	Fijian	Filipino	Guamanian[3]	Hawaiian, Native	Hmong	Indonesian	Japanese	Korean	Laotian	Malaysian	Pakistani	Samoan	Sri Lankan	Taiwanese	Thai	Tongan	Vietnamese
Port Arthur (city)	26,455	30,394	-	-	-	-	-	-	-	-	-	-	-	-	-	-	-	-	-	-	-	-	-	26,983
Johnson County	44,621	44,306	-	-	-	-	-	-	-	-	-	-	-	-	-	-	-	-	-	-	-	-	-	-
Kaufman County	44,783	61,765	-	-	-	-	-	-	-	-	-	-	-	-	-	-	-	-	-	-	-	-	-	-
Lubbock County	32,198	26,130	-	25,848	-	-	21,111	-	-	-	-	-	-	-	-	-	-	-	-	-	-	-	-	34,464
McLennan County	33,560	24,444	-	76,637	-	-	-	-	-	-	-	-	-	-	-	-	-	-	-	-	-	-	-	-
Midland County	39,082	49,327	-	55,313	-	-	-	-	-	-	-	-	-	-	-	-	-	-	-	-	-	-	-	-
Montgomery County	50,864	75,673	-	87,805	-	-	79,796	-	49,375	-	-	-	-	-	-	-	-	-	-	-	-	-	-	-
Nacogdoches County	28,301	52,679	-	-	-	-	-	-	-	-	-	-	-	-	-	-	-	-	-	-	-	-	-	-
Nueces County	35,959	51,447	-	56,250	-	-	-	-	53,802	-	-	-	-	-	-	-	-	-	-	-	-	-	-	-
Orange County	37,586	49,423	-	-	-	-	-	-	-	-	-	-	-	-	-	-	-	-	-	-	-	-	-	39,167
Potter County	29,492	43,409	-	-	-	-	-	-	-	-	-	-	-	-	-	46,429	-	-	-	-	-	-	-	46,500
Randall County	42,712	29,526	-	-	-	-	-	-	-	-	-	-	-	-	-	-	-	-	-	-	-	-	-	-
San Patricio County	34,836	24,934	-	-	-	-	-	-	-	-	-	-	-	-	-	-	-	-	-	-	-	-	-	-
Smith County	37,148	51,964	-	-	-	-	-	-	-	-	-	-	-	-	-	-	-	-	-	-	-	-	-	-
Tarrant County	46,179	48,642	36,146	59,167	-	41,518	48,883	-	48,311	-	-	-	-	46,875	28,889	49,732	-	35,500	-	-	56,333	34,375	49,750	49,337
Arlington (city)	47,622	44,035	-	53,214	-	-	46,361	-	34,007	-	-	-	-	-	23,750	-	-	-	-	-	50,875	-	-	48,594
Euless (city)	49,582	49,643	-	60,592	-	-	-	-	-	-	-	-	-	-	-	-	-	-	-	-	-	-	-	-
Haltom City (city)	38,818	41,875	-	-	-	-	-	-	-	-	-	-	-	-	-	39,464	-	-	-	-	-	-	-	38,512
Taylor County	34,035	28,646	-	-	-	-	-	-	38,482	-	-	-	-	-	-	-	-	-	-	-	-	-	-	-
Tom Green County	33,148	26,897	-	-	-	-	-	-	-	-	-	-	-	-	-	-	-	-	-	-	-	-	-	-
Travis County	46,761	46,478	35,357	53,860	-	-	42,899	-	48,750	-	-	-	-	51,992	20,953	-	-	26,384	-	-	36,458	38,194	-	51,817
Austin (city)	42,689	41,904	32,222	51,816	-	-	40,479	-	41,477	-	-	-	-	51,211	19,144	-	-	25,263	-	-	34,464	-	-	50,029
Pflugerville (city)	71,985	78,250	-	-	-	-	-	-	-	-	-	-	-	-	-	-	-	-	-	-	-	-	-	-
Wells Branch (cdp)	46,934	53,000	-	-	-	-	-	-	-	-	-	-	-	-	-	-	-	-	-	-	-	-	-	-
Victoria County	38,732	51,898	-	-	-	-	-	-	-	-	-	-	-	-	-	-	-	-	-	-	-	-	-	-
Webb County	28,100	50,278	-	-	-	-	-	-	-	-	-	-	-	-	-	-	-	-	-	-	-	-	-	-
Wichita County	33,780	36,218	-	-	-	-	-	-	35,478	-	-	-	-	-	-	-	-	-	-	-	-	-	-	38,426
Williamson County	60,642	71,295	-	76,403	-	-	74,000	-	-	-	-	-	-	-	49,500	-	-	-	-	-	-	-	-	71,083
Brushy Creek (cdp)	84,472	86,844	-	-	-	-	-	-	-	-	-	-	-	-	-	-	-	-	-	-	-	-	-	-
Jollyville (cdp)	66,999	65,292	-	-	-	-	-	-	-	-	-	-	-	-	-	-	-	-	-	-	-	-	-	-
UTAH	45,726	42,219	43,575	48,431	-	51,458	38,822	-	49,327	-	44,271	-	-	42,989	28,000	43,191	-	72,788	47,542	-	28,229	41,346	46,648	46,420
Cache County	39,730	24,479	-	-	-	-	20,417	-	-	-	-	-	-	-	-	-	-	-	-	-	-	-	-	-
Davis County	53,726	51,611	49,545	-	-	-	-	-	58,750	-	-	-	-	46,250	66,250	-	-	-	-	-	-	-	-	-
Salt Lake County	48,373	44,660	43,219	48,799	-	52,596	43,924	-	49,773	-	38,333	-	-	44,417	25,031	48,750	-	-	46,406	-	-	-	50,526	46,269
Kearns (cdp)	45,711	57,760	60,417	-	-	-	-	-	-	-	-	-	-	-	-	-	-	-	-	-	-	-	-	-
Salt Lake City (city)	36,944	31,358	38,649	47,625	-	-	30,443	-	46,827	-	-	-	-	36,250	14,091	-	-	-	39,286	-	-	-	43,382	23,784
Sandy (city)	66,458	81,821	57,019	-	-	-	74,444	-	-	-	-	-	-	-	-	-	-	-	-	-	-	-	-	-
Taylorsville (city)	47,236	45,664	36,000	-	-	-	-	-	-	-	-	-	-	-	-	-	-	-	-	-	-	-	-	61,250
West Jordan (city)	55,794	50,000	61,563	-	-	-	-	-	-	-	-	-	-	-	-	-	-	-	-	-	-	-	64,018	-
West Valley City (city)	45,773	50,000	44,732	-	-	52,500	41,250	-	-	-	-	-	-	-	-	49,444	-	-	40,938	-	-	-	51,875	55,602
Utah County	45,833	37,036	45,000	-	-	-	30,882	-	42,277	-	45,417	-	-	36,125	42,153	-	-	-	63,125	-	-	-	42,625	-

Notes: Please refer to the User's Guide for an explanation of data; data is arranged alphabetically by state, then county, then city within each county; table includes counties with populations greater than 49,999 unless noted and cities with populations greater than 9,999 whose Asian and/or NHPI population rates are greater than the national average; (1) Native Hawaiian and other Pacific Islander; (2) excludes Taiwanese; (3) includes Chamorro; (4) county does not meet population threshold but is shown in order to allow inclusion of city

Place	All households	Asian households	NHPI[1] households	Asian Indian	Bangladeshi	Cambodian	Chinese[2]	Fijian	Filipino	Guamanian[3]	Hawaiian, Native	Hmong	Indonesian	Japanese	Korean	Laotian	Malaysian	Pakistani	Samoan	Sri Lankan	Taiwanese	Thai	Tongan	Vietnamese
Orem (city)	47,529	38,056	49,000	-	-	-	-	-	-	-	-	-	-	-	-	-	-	-	-	-	-	-	-	-
Provo (city)	34,313	33,889	38,750	-	-	-	28,125	-	-	-	-	-	-	14,821	-	-	-	-	-	-	-	-	-	-
Washington County	37,212	21,406	38,611	-	-	-	-	-	-	-	-	-	-	-	-	-	-	-	-	-	-	-	-	-
St. George (city)	36,505	21,198	35,000	-	-	-	-	-	-	-	-	-	-	-	-	-	-	-	-	-	-	-	-	-
Weber County	44,014	39,848	-	-	-	-	-	-	-	-	-	-	-	50,893	-	-	-	-	-	-	-	-	-	-
VERMONT	40,856	39,630	-	51,932	-	-	48,125	-	46,042	-	-	-	-	50,125	20,625	-	-	-	-	-	-	-	-	30,000
Chittenden County	47,673	36,576	-	44,286	-	-	31,957	-	-	-	-	-	-	-	-	-	-	-	-	-	-	-	-	32,500
Rutland County	36,743	40,417	-	-	-	-	-	-	-	-	-	-	-	-	-	-	-	-	-	-	-	-	-	-
Washington County	40,972	29,327	-	-	-	-	-	-	-	-	-	-	-	-	-	-	-	-	-	-	-	-	-	-
Windsor County	40,688	41,618	-	-	-	-	-	-	-	-	-	-	-	-	-	-	-	-	-	-	-	-	-	-
VIRGINIA	46,677	57,420	51,553	70,392	45,893	57,179	59,524	-	59,873	44,524	57,206	-	57,344	52,475	47,871	58,092	-	44,063	52,000	47,670	64,539	39,063	-	56,972
Albemarle County	50,749	43,125	-	55,556	-	-	42,679	-	-	-	-	-	-	-	-	-	-	-	-	-	-	-	-	-
Alexandria Independent City	56,054	44,644	-	51,953	-	-	66,500	-	45,938	-	-	-	-	-	25,475	-	-	43,828	-	-	-	-	-	52,083
Arlington County	63,001	47,102	-	58,177	-	38,971	55,601	-	53,609	-	-	-	-	52,361	37,984	-	-	39,414	-	-	-	-	-	36,047
Arlington (cdp)	63,001	47,102	-	58,177	-	38,971	55,601	-	53,609	-	-	-	-	52,361	37,984	-	-	39,414	-	-	-	-	-	36,047
Bedford County	43,136	68,807	-	-	-	-	-	-	-	-	-	-	-	-	-	-	-	-	-	-	-	-	-	-
Charlottesville Independent City	31,007	21,563	-	18,214	-	-	22,344	-	-	-	-	-	-	-	-	-	-	-	-	-	-	-	-	-
Chesapeake Independent City	50,743	67,759	-	-	-	-	-	-	73,587	-	-	-	-	-	-	-	-	-	-	-	-	-	-	-
Chesterfield County	58,537	57,778	-	60,750	-	53,900	54,766	-	71,434	-	-	-	-	-	45,795	-	-	-	-	-	-	-	-	54,773
Fairfax Independent City	67,642	60,208	-	69,904	-	-	51,063	-	-	-	-	-	-	-	42,361	-	-	-	-	-	-	-	-	75,426
Fairfax County	81,050	70,634	90,000	84,084	51,691	73,750	77,408	-	78,943	-	-	-	56,406	84,127	55,336	61,250	-	46,574	-	-	97,621	56,413	-	66,696
Annandale (cdp)	72,561	57,104	-	68,650	-	-	60,000	-	69,375	-	-	-	-	-	42,357	-	-	-	-	-	-	-	-	65,054
Bailey's Crossroads (cdp)	51,650	41,429	-	-	-	-	-	-	-	-	-	-	-	-	-	-	-	24,565	-	-	-	-	-	37,917
Burke (cdp)	93,561	75,502	-	89,659	-	-	82,557	-	92,638	-	-	-	-	-	57,438	-	-	-	-	-	-	-	-	86,179
Centreville (cdp)	71,232	61,439	-	77,829	-	-	51,484	-	63,194	-	-	-	-	-	53,641	-	-	-	-	-	-	-	-	65,500
Chantilly (cdp)	87,991	82,610	-	92,663	-	-	88,189	-	-	-	-	-	-	-	58,684	-	-	-	-	-	-	-	-	81,156
Franconia (cdp)	78,946	71,932	-	77,366	-	-	-	-	65,559	-	-	-	-	-	80,730	-	-	-	-	-	-	-	-	93,787
Groveton (cdp)	60,150	53,824	-	-	-	-	-	-	-	-	-	-	-	-	-	-	-	-	-	-	-	-	-	-
Herndon (town)	72,912	66,417	-	69,219	-	-	-	-	-	-	-	-	-	-	-	-	-	-	-	-	-	-	-	81,634
Hybla Valley (cdp)	49,087	26,844	-	-	-	-	-	-	-	-	-	-	-	-	-	-	-	-	-	-	-	-	-	-
Idylwood (cdp)	66,895	59,028	-	77,434	-	-	59,219	-	-	-	-	-	-	-	-	-	-	-	-	-	-	-	-	55,227
Jefferson (cdp)	66,445	59,079	-	77,982	-	-	68,864	-	48,409	-	-	-	-	-	-	-	-	-	-	-	-	-	-	56,349
Lincolnia (cdp)	64,148	59,583	-	-	-	-	-	-	-	-	-	-	-	-	-	-	-	22,198	-	-	-	-	-	90,927
Lorton (cdp)	60,150	52,734	-	-	-	-	-	-	-	-	-	-	-	-	-	-	-	-	-	-	-	-	-	-
McLean (cdp)	121,138	106,417	-	134,952	-	-	99,522	-	118,814	-	-	-	-	108,684	87,826	-	-	-	-	-	-	-	-	-
Merrifield (cdp)	70,363	65,066	-	75,286	-	-	-	-	-	-	-	-	-	-	43,472	-	-	-	-	-	-	-	-	66,800
Mount Vernon (cdp)	61,119	48,021	-	-	-	-	-	-	-	-	-	-	-	-	50,156	-	-	-	-	-	-	-	-	-
Newington (cdp)	82,291	76,210	-	108,302	-	-	-	-	104,805	-	-	-	-	-	48,333	-	-	-	-	-	-	-	-	-
Oakton (cdp)	87,898	66,339	-	78,417	-	-	73,472	-	-	-	-	-	-	-	41,833	-	-	-	-	-	-	-	-	79,430
Reston (cdp)	80,018	67,440	-	80,260	-	-	81,301	-	77,858	-	-	-	-	-	51,771	-	-	-	-	-	-	-	-	-
Rose Hill (cdp)	80,815	68,125	-	-	-	-	-	-	-	-	-	-	-	-	-	-	-	-	-	-	-	-	-	-

Notes: Please refer to the User's Guide for an explanation of data; data is arranged alphabetically by state, then county, then city within each county; table includes counties with populations greater than 49,999 unless noted and cities with populations greater than 9,999 whose Asian and/or NHPI population rates are greater than the national average; (1) Native Hawaiian and other Pacific Islander; (2) excludes Taiwanese; (3) includes Chamorro; (4) county does not meet population threshold but is shown in order to allow inclusion of city

Place	All households	Asian households	NHPI[1] households	Asian Indian	Bangladeshi	Cambodian	Chinese[2]	Fijian	Filipino	Guamanian[3]	Hawaiian, Native	Hmong	Indonesian	Japanese	Korean	Laotian	Malaysian	Pakistani	Samoan	Sri Lankan	Taiwanese	Thai	Tongan	Vietnamese
Springfield (cdp)	69,640	68,726	-	74,107	-	-	69,306	-	93,599	-	-	-	-	-	62,368	68,077	-	-	-	-	-	-	-	73,958
Tysons Corner (cdp)	74,151	69,844	-	84,618	-	-	55,893	-	-	-	-	-	-	-	55,357	-	-	-	-	-	-	-	-	-
Vienna (town)	85,519	71,250	-	-	-	-	-	-	-	-	-	-	-	-	-	-	-	-	-	-	-	-	-	-
West Springfield (cdp)	84,250	70,542	-	59,821	-	-	81,337	-	-	-	-	-	-	-	54,286	-	-	-	-	-	-	-	-	79,702
Wolf Trap (cdp)	135,782	124,510	-	133,711	-	-	115,590	-	-	-	-	-	-	-	-	-	-	-	-	-	-	-	-	-
Falls Church Independent City	74,924	54,432	-	-	-	-	-	-	-	-	-	-	-	-	-	-	-	-	-	-	-	-	-	-
Fauquier County	61,999	58,214	-	-	-	-	-	-	-	-	-	-	-	-	-	-	-	-	-	-	-	-	-	-
Frederick County	46,941	61,667	-	-	-	-	-	-	-	-	-	-	-	-	-	-	-	-	-	-	-	-	-	-
Hampton Independent City	39,532	32,461	-	-	-	-	-	-	44,688	-	-	-	-	-	-	-	-	-	-	-	-	-	-	31,875
Hanover County	59,223	51,750	-	-	-	-	-	-	-	-	-	-	-	-	-	-	-	-	-	-	-	-	-	-
Henrico County	49,185	51,311	-	58,958	-	52,283	52,773	-	46,818	-	-	-	-	-	50,781	-	-	-	-	-	-	-	-	44,375
Glen Allen (cdp)	55,205	57,656	-	-	-	-	-	-	-	-	-	-	-	-	-	-	-	-	-	-	-	-	-	-
Laurel (cdp)	42,128	40,938	-	-	-	-	-	-	-	-	-	-	-	-	-	-	-	-	-	-	-	-	-	-
Loudoun County	80,648	79,032	-	77,933	-	-	91,681	-	98,407	-	-	-	-	-	68,472	-	-	75,208	-	-	-	-	-	79,866
Lynchburg Independent City	32,234	34,342	-	-	-	-	-	-	-	-	-	-	-	-	-	-	-	-	-	-	-	-	-	-
Manassas Park Indep. City	60,794	58,958	-	-	-	-	-	-	-	-	-	-	-	-	-	-	-	-	-	-	-	-	-	-
Montgomery County	32,330	16,298	-	22,500	-	-	21,283	-	-	-	-	-	-	-	9,943	-	-	-	-	-	-	-	-	-
Blacksburg (town)	22,513	15,024	-	20,278	-	-	20,658	-	-	-	-	-	-	-	8,693	-	-	-	-	-	-	-	-	-
Newport News Independent City	36,597	37,303	-	-	-	-	36,250	-	36,471	-	-	-	-	-	32,031	-	-	-	-	-	-	-	-	38,542
Norfolk Independent City	31,815	34,986	-	36,458	-	-	36,413	-	38,701	-	-	-	-	-	-	-	-	-	-	-	-	-	-	30,694
Portsmouth Independent City	33,742	38,611	-	-	-	-	-	-	49,375	-	-	-	-	-	-	-	-	-	-	-	-	-	-	-
Prince William County	65,960	57,134	-	58,250	-	-	56,250	-	61,484	-	-	-	-	51,667	53,750	-	-	50,946	-	-	-	-	-	71,563
Bull Run (cdp)	49,519	55,278	-	-	-	-	-	-	-	-	-	-	-	-	-	-	-	-	-	-	-	-	-	-
Dale City (cdp)	65,355	51,629	-	41,103	-	-	-	-	62,625	-	-	-	-	-	-	-	-	50,568	-	-	-	-	-	-
Lake Ridge (cdp)	71,458	65,655	-	-	-	-	-	-	-	-	-	-	-	-	-	-	-	-	-	-	-	-	-	-
Woodbridge (cdp)	50,525	44,926	-	-	-	-	-	-	-	-	-	-	-	-	-	-	-	-	-	-	-	-	-	-
Richmond Independent City	31,121	20,341	-	22,857	-	-	-	-	30,000	-	-	-	-	-	-	-	-	-	-	-	-	-	-	-
Roanoke Independent City	30,719	23,472	-	-	-	-	-	-	-	-	-	-	-	-	-	-	-	-	-	-	-	-	-	-
Roanoke County	47,689	51,406	-	-	-	-	-	-	-	-	-	-	-	-	-	-	-	-	-	-	-	-	-	-
Spotsylvania County	57,525	40,078	-	-	-	-	-	-	-	-	-	-	-	-	-	-	-	-	-	-	-	-	-	-
Stafford County	66,809	54,609	-	-	-	-	-	-	40,536	-	-	-	-	-	-	-	-	-	-	-	-	-	-	-
Suffolk Independent City	41,115	61,023	-	-	-	-	-	-	-	-	-	-	-	-	-	-	-	-	-	-	-	-	-	-
Virginia Beach Independent City	48,705	52,526	-	50,880	-	-	50,263	-	56,841	-	-	-	-	50,000	41,667	-	-	-	-	-	-	-	-	29,917
Williamsburg Independent City	37,093	53,594	-	-	-	-	-	-	-	-	-	-	-	-	-	-	-	-	-	-	-	-	-	-
York County	57,956	57,500	-	115,437	-	-	-	-	-	-	-	-	-	-	32,885	-	-	-	-	-	-	-	-	-
WASHINGTON	45,776	47,517	41,656	60,846	-	36,127	52,555	40,625	52,393	47,287	40,870	29,375	31,776	47,438	36,670	42,887	-	55,139	39,614	47,063	50,691	40,435	65,388	40,113
Benton County	47,044	64,464	-	84,605	-	-	73,750	-	-	-	-	-	-	-	24,038	-	-	-	-	-	-	-	-	56,917
Richland (city)	53,092	71,739	-	-	-	-	78,120	-	-	-	-	-	-	-	-	-	-	-	-	-	-	-	-	-
Chelan County	37,316	41,053	-	-	-	-	-	-	-	-	-	-	-	-	-	-	-	-	-	-	-	-	-	-
Clallam County	36,449	44,583	-	-	-	-	-	-	-	-	-	-	-	-	-	-	-	-	-	-	-	-	-	-
Clark County	48,376	50,625	40,357	66,389	-	47,125	57,361	-	50,679	-	-	-	-	51,284	48,917	50,938	-	-	-	-	-	-	-	43,550

Notes: Please refer to the User's Guide for an explanation of data; data is arranged alphabetically by state, then county, then city within each county; table includes counties with populations greater than 49,999 unless noted and cities with populations greater than 9,999 whose Asian and/or NHPI population rates are greater than the national average; (1) Native Hawaiian and other Pacific Islander; (2) excludes Taiwanese; (3) includes Chamorro; (4) county does not meet population threshold but is shown in order to allow inclusion of city

Place	All households	Asian households	NHPI[1] households	Asian Indian	Bangladeshi	Cambodian	Chinese[2]	Fijian	Filipino	Guamanian[3]	Hawaiian, Native	Hmong	Indonesian	Japanese	Korean	Laotian	Malaysian	Pakistani	Samoan	Sri Lankan	Taiwanese	Thai	Tongan	Vietnamese
Five Corners (cdp)	51,688	61,442	-	-	-	-	-	-	-	-	-	-	-	-	-	-	-	-	-	-	-	-	-	-
Orchards (cdp)	49,216	50,764	-	-	-	-	-	-	-	-	-	-	-	-	-	-	-	-	-	-	-	-	-	-
Vancouver (city)	41,618	47,524	42,171	-	-	-	60,972	-	47,554	-	-	-	-	49,375	43,056	-	-	-	-	-	-	-	-	41,389
Cowlitz County	39,797	24,861	-	-	-	20,417	-	-	-	-	-	-	-	-	-	-	-	-	-	-	-	-	-	37,917
Grant County	35,276	35,114	-	-	-	-	-	-	-	-	-	-	-	-	-	-	-	-	-	-	-	-	-	-
Grays Harbor County	34,160	31,563	-	-	-	-	-	-	-	-	-	-	-	-	-	-	-	-	-	-	-	-	-	-
Island County	45,513	35,441	-	-	-	-	-	-	35,662	-	-	-	-	40,125	-	-	-	-	-	-	-	-	-	-
Oak Harbor (city)	36,641	35,588	-	-	-	-	-	-	34,955	-	-	-	-	-	-	-	-	-	-	-	-	-	-	-
King County	53,157	50,864	45,104	62,500	-	34,344	55,040	41,953	55,809	37,257	52,557	36,250	28,984	52,156	37,945	43,750	-	48,438	39,844	-	55,446	39,167	67,069	40,510
Auburn (city)	39,208	51,613	-	-	-	-	-	-	-	-	-	-	-	-	-	-	-	-	-	-	-	-	-	-
Bellevue (city)	62,338	62,418	-	66,635	-	-	70,103	-	56,544	-	-	-	-	68,875	55,048	61,125	-	-	-	-	59,048	-	-	53,333
Bothell (city)	59,264	67,500	-	-	-	-	60,900	-	-	-	-	-	-	-	-	-	-	-	-	-	-	-	-	-
Bryn Mawr-Skyway (cdp)	47,385	59,653	-	-	-	-	-	-	60,945	-	-	-	-	76,666	-	-	-	-	-	-	-	-	-	65,792
Burien (city)	41,577	56,250	-	-	-	-	-	-	56,765	-	-	-	-	-	-	-	-	-	-	-	-	-	-	60,625
Cascade-Fairwood (cdp)	57,996	57,946	-	-	-	-	48,315	-	61,223	-	-	-	-	73,958	-	-	-	-	-	-	-	-	-	70,643
Cottage Lake (cdp)	92,388	102,386	-	-	-	-	-	-	-	-	-	-	-	-	-	-	-	-	-	-	-	-	-	-
Des Moines (city)	48,971	38,661	43,250	-	-	-	-	-	48,125	-	-	-	-	-	-	-	-	-	-	-	-	-	-	36,591
East Hill-Meridian (cdp)	65,721	65,554	-	56,094	-	-	67,833	-	86,919	-	-	-	-	-	-	-	-	-	-	-	-	-	-	41,957
Federal Way (city)	49,278	43,210	38,274	-	-	-	50,750	-	52,679	-	-	-	-	64,097	36,398	-	-	-	50,938	-	-	-	-	50,139
Inglewood-Finn Hill (cdp)	72,130	69,375	-	-	-	-	86,944	-	-	-	-	-	-	-	-	-	-	-	-	-	-	-	-	-
Issaquah (city)	57,892	56,458	-	-	-	-	-	-	-	-	-	-	-	-	-	-	-	-	-	-	-	-	-	-
Kenmore (city)	61,756	66,806	-	-	-	-	-	-	-	-	-	-	-	-	-	-	-	-	-	-	-	-	-	-
Kent (city)	46,046	48,965	-	34,440	-	-	53,654	-	60,481	-	-	-	-	48,185	36,833	-	-	-	-	-	-	-	-	47,667
Kingsgate (cdp)	65,046	54,107	-	-	-	-	76,021	-	-	-	-	-	-	-	-	-	-	-	-	-	-	-	-	-
Kirkland (city)	60,332	57,647	-	-	-	-	64,958	-	-	-	-	-	-	68,036	-	-	-	-	-	-	-	-	-	56,250
Lake Forest Park (city)	74,149	82,435	-	-	-	-	-	-	-	-	-	-	-	-	-	-	-	-	-	-	-	-	-	-
Lakeland North (cdp)	62,292	63,239	-	-	-	-	-	-	-	-	-	-	-	-	-	-	-	-	-	-	-	-	-	-
Lakeland South (cdp)	62,529	66,875	-	-	-	-	-	-	-	-	-	-	-	-	-	-	-	-	-	-	-	-	-	-
Lea Hill (cdp)	65,706	36,250	-	-	-	-	-	-	-	-	-	-	-	-	-	-	-	-	-	-	-	-	-	-
Mercer Island (city)	91,904	86,830	-	-	-	-	83,031	-	-	-	-	-	-	104,686	-	-	-	-	-	-	-	-	-	-
Redmond (city)	66,735	74,475	-	78,011	-	-	71,771	-	-	-	-	-	-	90,706	60,357	-	-	-	-	-	-	-	-	-
Renton (city)	45,820	54,505	-	-	-	-	60,469	-	60,250	-	-	-	-	56,786	-	-	-	-	-	-	-	-	-	48,250
Riverton-Boulevard Park (cdp)	39,034	38,698	-	-	-	-	-	-	-	-	-	-	-	-	-	-	-	-	-	-	-	-	-	-
Sammamish (city)	101,592	104,981	-	-	-	-	97,806	-	-	-	-	-	-	-	-	-	-	-	-	-	-	-	-	-
SeaTac (city)	41,202	48,108	50,865	37,708	-	-	-	-	54,297	-	-	-	-	-	-	-	-	-	-	-	-	-	-	63,056
Seattle (city)	45,736	39,124	35,300	47,368	-	20,069	40,725	-	50,088	-	-	-	27,578	39,465	25,990	44,917	-	-	30,000	-	25,313	27,100	-	31,237
Shoreline (city)	51,658	51,701	-	66,719	-	-	62,292	-	54,722	-	-	-	-	52,708	35,893	-	-	-	-	-	-	-	-	43,173
Tukwila (city)	40,718	37,125	60,250	-	-	-	-	-	52,031	-	-	-	-	-	-	-	-	-	-	-	-	-	-	-
Union Hill-Novelty Hill (cdp)	98,061	155,737	-	-	-	-	-	-	-	-	-	-	-	-	-	-	-	-	-	-	-	-	-	-
White Center (cdp)	40,480	37,600	-	-	-	29,844	-	-	65,625	-	-	-	-	-	-	-	-	-	-	-	-	-	-	25,833
Kitsap County	46,840	46,204	33,152	-	-	-	40,625	-	46,804	40,250	-	-	-	48,864	48,750	-	-	-	-	-	-	-	-	18,958

Notes: Please refer to the User's Guide for an explanation of data; data is arranged alphabetically by state, then county, then city within each county; table includes counties with populations greater than 49,999 unless noted and cities with populations greater than 9,999 whose Asian and/or NHPI population rates are greater than the national average; (1) Native Hawaiian and other Pacific Islander; (2) excludes Taiwanese; (3) includes Chamorro; (4) county does not meet population threshold but is shown in order to allow inclusion of city

Place	All households	Asian households	NHPI[1] households	Asian Indian	Bangladeshi	Cambodian	Chinese[2]	Fijian	Filipino	Guamanian[3]	Hawaiian, Native	Hmong	Indonesian	Japanese	Korean	Laotian	Malaysian	Pakistani	Samoan	Sri Lankan	Taiwanese	Thai	Tongan	Vietnamese
Bremerton (city)	30,950	28,378	-	-	-	-	-	-	29,848	-	-	-	-	-	-	-	-	-	-	-	-	-	-	-
Silverdale (cdp)	48,164	53,676	-	-	-	-	-	-	56,786	-	-	-	-	-	-	-	-	-	-	-	-	-	-	-
Lewis County	35,511	38,846	-	-	-	-	-	-	-	-	-	-	-	-	-	-	-	-	-	-	-	-	-	-
Pierce County	45,204	36,921	40,647	52,404	-	31,712	44,605	-	47,772	47,235	26,761	-	-	33,011	28,824	23,563	-	-	38,984	-	-	46,161	-	32,371
Elk Plain (cdp)	54,400	47,396	-	-	-	-	-	-	-	-	-	-	-	-	-	-	-	-	-	-	-	-	-	-
Fort Lewis (cdp)	32,384	33,816	42,212	-	-	-	-	-	40,179	-	-	-	-	-	-	-	-	-	-	-	-	-	-	-
Lakewood (city)	36,422	28,480	48,125	-	-	-	-	-	38,828	-	-	-	-	26,450	23,320	-	-	-	49,531	-	-	-	-	-
Parkland (cdp)	39,653	27,708	40,469	-	-	-	-	-	-	-	-	-	-	-	25,125	-	-	-	-	-	-	-	-	-
Spanaway (cdp)	46,210	43,676	50,893	-	-	-	-	-	61,458	-	-	-	-	-	31,667	-	-	-	-	-	-	-	-	-
Tacoma (city)	37,879	32,312	36,000	-	-	31,250	43,947	-	52,941	41,719	-	-	-	25,536	25,172	21,250	-	-	35,250	-	-	-	-	25,278
University Place (city)	50,287	51,136	-	-	-	-	-	-	-	-	-	-	-	-	38,073	-	-	-	-	-	-	-	-	-
Skagit County	42,381	28,906	-	-	-	-	-	-	41,591	-	-	-	-	-	-	-	-	-	-	-	-	-	-	-
Snohomish County	53,060	53,790	47,092	57,841	-	51,652	52,941	-	58,500	-	46,549	-	-	60,227	46,351	65,625	-	58,281	-	-	-	-	-	53,834
Alderwood Manor (cdp)	61,199	66,250	-	-	-	-	-	-	-	-	-	-	-	-	-	-	-	-	-	-	-	-	-	-
Edmonds (city)	53,522	41,083	-	-	-	-	-	-	59,792	-	-	-	-	-	24,076	-	-	-	-	-	-	-	-	-
Everett (city)	40,100	40,000	-	39,444	-	31,250	-	-	48,229	-	-	-	-	-	-	-	-	-	-	-	-	-	-	39,702
Lynnwood (city)	42,814	54,051	-	-	-	-	51,932	-	75,000	-	-	-	-	-	42,391	-	-	-	-	-	-	-	-	45,625
Martha Lake (cdp)	57,568	63,958	-	-	-	-	-	-	-	-	-	-	-	-	-	-	-	-	-	-	-	-	-	-
Marysville (city)	47,088	47,560	-	-	-	-	-	-	-	-	-	-	-	-	-	-	-	-	-	-	-	-	-	-
Mill Creek (city)	69,702	64,034	-	-	-	-	-	-	-	-	-	-	-	-	80,761	-	-	-	-	-	-	-	-	-
Mountlake Terrace (city)	47,238	45,625	-	-	-	-	-	-	72,632	-	-	-	-	-	25,000	-	-	-	-	-	-	-	-	-
Mukilteo (city)	67,323	73,375	-	-	-	-	-	-	-	-	-	-	-	-	60,924	-	-	-	-	-	-	-	-	-
North Creek (cdp)	67,289	71,215	-	-	-	-	-	-	-	-	-	-	-	-	-	-	-	-	-	-	-	-	-	-
Paine Field-Lk. Stickney (cdp)	40,831	47,759	-	-	-	-	-	-	-	-	-	-	-	-	-	-	-	-	-	-	-	-	-	-
Picnic Pt.-N. Lynnwood (cdp)	54,913	48,958	-	-	-	-	-	-	53,125	-	-	-	-	-	26,296	-	-	-	-	-	-	-	-	-
Seattle Hill-Silver Firs (cdp)	72,554	68,750	-	-	-	-	-	-	69,167	-	-	-	-	-	70,197	-	-	-	-	-	-	-	-	70,721
Spokane County	37,308	32,427	34,219	53,295	-	-	33,594	-	44,000	-	-	14,904	-	23,565	21,607	-	-	-	-	-	-	-	-	37,627
Spokane (city)	32,273	28,500	38,387	-	-	-	33,929	-	45,694	-	-	13,580	-	24,792	20,179	-	-	-	-	-	-	-	-	32,500
Thurston County	46,975	44,816	56,926	53,750	-	30,000	56,250	-	50,388	60,000	-	-	-	45,385	38,026	-	-	-	-	-	-	-	-	34,792
Lacey (city)	43,848	52,321	-	-	-	-	-	-	54,145	-	-	-	-	-	37,763	-	-	-	-	-	-	-	-	34,375
Olympia (city)	40,846	36,563	-	-	-	-	-	-	-	-	-	-	-	-	-	-	-	-	-	-	-	-	-	23,846
Tumwater (city)	43,329	46,042	-	-	-	-	-	-	-	-	-	-	-	-	-	-	-	-	-	-	-	-	-	-
Walla Walla County	35,900	52,917	-	-	-	-	-	-	-	-	-	-	-	-	-	-	-	-	-	-	-	-	-	-
Whatcom County	40,005	31,116	-	34,671	-	-	39,063	-	46,250	-	-	-	-	11,442	20,962	-	-	-	-	-	-	-	-	28,221
Bellingham (city)	32,530	24,276	-	31,875	-	-	-	-	-	-	-	-	-	-	-	-	-	-	-	-	-	-	-	28,750
Whitman County[4]	28,584	12,210	-	-	-	-	14,306	-	-	-	-	-	-	2,499	-	-	-	-	-	-	-	-	-	-
Pullman (city)	20,652	11,897	-	-	-	-	13,843	-	-	-	-	-	-	2,499	-	-	-	-	-	-	-	-	-	-
Yakima County	34,828	34,667	-	-	-	-	-	-	32,212	-	-	-	-	-	-	-	-	-	-	-	-	-	-	-
WEST VIRGINIA	29,696	50,658	29,375	72,813	-	-	36,875	-	76,919	-	-	-	-	7,813	30,455	-	-	64,722	-	-	-	-	-	51,023
Cabell County	28,479	35,000	-	-	-	-	-	-	-	-	-	-	-	-	-	-	-	-	-	-	-	-	-	-
Harrison County	30,562	2,499	-	-	-	-	-	-	-	-	-	-	-	-	-	-	-	-	-	-	-	-	-	-

Notes: Please refer to the User's Guide for an explanation of data; data is arranged alphabetically by state, then county, then city within each county; table includes counties with populations greater than 49,999 unless noted and cities with populations greater than 9,999 whose Asian and/or NHPI population rates are greater than the national average; (1) Native Hawaiian and other Pacific Islander; (2) excludes Taiwanese; (3) includes Chamorro; (4) county does not meet population threshold but is shown in order to allow inclusion of city

Place	All households	Asian households	NHPI[1] households	Asian Indian	Bangladeshi	Cambodian	Chinese[2]	Fijian	Filipino	Guamanian[3]	Hawaiian, Native	Hmong	Indonesian	Japanese	Korean	Laotian	Malaysian	Pakistani	Samoan	Sri Lankan	Taiwanese	Thai	Tongan	Vietnamese
Kanawha County	33,766	70,441	-	99,647	-	-	-	-	-	-	-	-	-	-	-	-	-	-	-	-	-	-	-	-
Monongalia County	28,625	18,000	-	32,550	-	-	26,731	-	-	-	-	-	-	-	-	-	-	-	-	-	-	-	-	-
Putnam County	41,892	71,250	-	-	-	-	-	-	-	-	-	-	-	-	-	-	-	-	-	-	-	-	-	-
Raleigh County	28,181	131,870	-	-	-	-	-	-	-	-	-	-	-	-	-	-	-	-	-	-	-	-	-	-
Wood County	33,285	70,208	-	-	-	-	-	-	-	-	-	-	-	-	-	-	-	-	-	-	-	-	-	-
WISCONSIN	43,791	39,847	47,670	52,344	-	21,985	43,151	-	58,851	65,313	46,875	35,898	33,281	32,446	23,167	40,985	-	34,274	-	-	8,661	21,122	-	38,510
Brown County	46,447	42,500	-	61,484	-	-	-	-	-	-	-	33,750	-	-	-	38,250	-	-	-	-	-	-	-	-
Chippewa County	39,596	31,518	-	-	-	-	-	-	-	-	-	29,453	-	-	-	-	-	-	-	-	-	-	-	-
Columbia County	45,064	48,542	-	-	-	-	-	-	-	-	-	-	-	-	-	-	-	-	-	-	-	-	-	-
Dane County	49,223	27,697	-	45,532	-	-	23,203	-	59,500	-	-	35,000	-	27,023	10,255	39,297	-	-	-	-	4,360	-	-	28,616
Madison (city)	41,941	22,604	-	39,211	-	-	20,685	-	57,950	-	-	36,429	-	26,273	10,313	-	-	-	-	-	4,360	-	-	27,589
Dodge County	45,190	30,000	-	-	-	-	-	-	-	-	-	-	-	-	-	-	-	-	-	-	-	-	-	-
Eau Claire County	39,219	39,125	-	-	-	-	-	-	-	-	-	36,786	-	-	-	-	-	-	-	-	-	-	-	-
Fond du Lac County	45,578	28,958	-	-	-	-	-	-	-	-	-	11,750	-	-	-	-	-	-	-	-	-	-	-	-
Jefferson County	46,901	43,333	-	-	-	-	-	-	-	-	-	-	-	-	-	-	-	-	-	-	-	-	-	-
Kenosha County	46,970	48,370	-	-	-	-	-	-	-	-	-	-	-	-	-	-	-	-	-	-	-	-	-	-
La Crosse County	39,472	44,286	-	-	-	-	-	-	-	-	-	36,250	-	-	-	-	-	-	-	-	-	-	-	-
La Crosse (city)	31,103	38,359	-	-	-	-	-	-	-	-	-	30,565	-	-	-	-	-	-	-	-	-	-	-	-
Manitowoc County	43,286	36,406	-	-	-	-	-	-	-	-	-	35,870	-	-	-	-	-	-	-	-	-	-	-	-
Marathon County	45,165	33,902	-	-	-	-	-	-	-	-	-	29,611	-	-	-	-	-	-	-	-	-	-	-	-
Wausau (city)	36,831	30,595	-	-	-	-	-	-	-	-	-	27,237	-	-	-	-	-	-	-	-	-	-	-	-
Milwaukee County	38,100	39,338	47,891	43,333	-	-	40,833	-	56,852	-	-	40,272	-	31,875	22,104	36,500	-	33,813	-	-	-	-	-	40,417
Outagamie County	49,613	40,669	-	29,013	-	-	-	-	-	-	-	38,958	-	-	-	-	-	-	-	-	-	-	-	-
Appleton (city)	47,285	36,964	-	-	-	-	-	-	-	-	-	41,765	-	-	-	-	-	-	-	-	-	-	-	-
Ozaukee County	62,745	76,919	-	-	-	-	-	-	-	-	-	-	-	-	-	-	-	-	-	-	-	-	-	-
Portage County	43,487	34,861	-	-	-	-	-	-	-	-	-	36,875	-	-	-	-	-	-	-	-	-	-	-	-
Stevens Point (city)	33,178	29,773	-	-	-	-	-	-	-	-	-	37,596	-	-	-	-	-	-	-	-	-	-	-	-
Racine County	48,059	47,778	-	-	-	-	-	-	-	-	-	-	-	-	-	-	-	-	-	-	-	-	-	-
Rock County	45,517	34,519	-	-	-	-	-	-	-	-	-	-	-	-	-	-	-	-	-	-	-	-	-	-
St. Croix County	54,930	51,875	-	-	-	-	-	-	-	-	-	-	-	-	-	-	-	-	-	-	-	-	-	-
Sauk County	41,941	46,250	-	-	-	-	-	-	-	-	-	-	-	-	-	-	-	-	-	-	-	-	-	-
Sheboygan County	46,237	43,378	-	-	-	-	-	-	-	-	-	42,656	-	-	-	-	-	-	-	-	-	-	-	-
Sheboygan (city)	40,066	42,872	-	-	-	-	-	-	-	-	-	41,992	-	-	-	-	-	-	-	-	-	-	-	-
Walworth County	46,274	37,875	-	-	-	-	-	-	-	-	-	-	-	-	-	-	-	-	-	-	-	-	-	-
Washington County	57,033	61,964	-	-	-	-	-	-	-	-	-	-	-	-	-	-	-	-	-	-	-	-	-	-
Waukesha County	62,839	79,762	-	104,699	-	-	83,440	-	106,001	-	-	-	-	-	57,639	-	-	-	-	-	-	-	-	-
Winnebago County	44,445	44,741	-	-	-	-	-	-	-	-	-	34,565	-	-	-	-	-	-	-	-	-	-	-	-
Wood County	41,595	40,865	-	-	-	-	-	-	-	-	-	29,483	-	-	-	-	-	-	-	-	-	-	-	-
WYOMING	37,892	40,293	-	25,313	-	-	40,227	-	63,393	-	-	-	-	35,417	42,024	-	-	-	-	-	-	-	-	-
Laramie County	39,607	35,313	-	-	-	-	-	-	-	-	-	-	-	-	-	-	-	-	-	-	-	-	-	-
Natrona County	36,619	51,250	-	-	-	-	-	-	-	-	-	-	-	-	-	-	-	-	-	-	-	-	-	-

Notes: Please refer to the User's Guide for an explanation of data; data is arranged alphabetically by state, then county, then city within each county; table includes counties with populations greater than 49,999 unless noted and cities with populations greater than 9,999 whose Asian and/or NHPI population rates are greater than the national average; (1) Native Hawaiian and other Pacific Islander; (2) excludes Taiwanese; (3) includes Chamorro; (4) county does not meet population threshold but is shown in order to allow inclusion of city

Per Capita Income

(Universe: Total Population)

Place	Total population	Total Asian population	Total NHPI[1] population	Asian Indian	Bangladeshi	Cambodian	Chinese[2]	Fijian	Filipino	Guamanian[3]	Hawaiian, Native	Hmong	Indonesian	Japanese	Korean	Laotian	Malaysian	Pakistani	Samoan	Sri Lankan	Taiwanese	Thai	Tongan	Vietnamese
UNITED STATES	21,587	21,823	15,054	27,514	13,971	10,366	23,642	14,745	21,267	17,583	17,697	6,600	18,932	30,075	18,805	11,830	19,895	18,096	12,160	27,478	25,890	19,066	10,680	15,655
ALABAMA	18,189	20,488	14,089	28,786	-	10,633	20,768	-	24,946	14,678	-	-	-	22,150	15,228	11,932	-	31,172	-	-	-	13,700	-	13,468
Baldwin County	20,826	23,301	-	-	-	-	-	-	-	-	-	-	-	-	-	-	-	-	-	-	-	-	-	-
Calhoun County	17,367	18,576	-	-	-	-	-	-	-	-	-	-	-	-	-	-	-	-	-	-	-	-	-	-
Etowah County	16,783	29,333	-	-	-	-	-	-	-	-	-	-	-	-	-	-	-	-	-	-	-	-	-	-
Houston County	18,759	20,652	-	-	-	-	-	-	-	-	-	-	-	-	-	-	-	-	-	-	-	-	-	-
Jefferson County	20,892	20,308	-	29,224	-	-	19,048	-	-	-	-	-	-	-	12,901	-	-	-	-	-	-	-	-	11,220
Lee County	17,158	22,198	-	-	-	-	35,014	-	-	-	-	-	-	-	-	-	-	-	-	-	-	-	-	-
Madison County	23,091	22,347	-	28,135	-	-	23,021	-	-	-	-	-	-	-	20,265	-	-	-	-	-	-	-	-	24,351
Mobile County	17,178	13,221	-	15,441	-	5,926	13,100	-	24,293	-	-	-	-	-	-	11,894	-	-	-	-	-	-	-	10,449
Montgomery County	19,358	23,624	-	-	-	-	-	-	-	-	-	-	-	-	-	-	-	-	-	-	-	-	-	-
Morgan County	19,223	14,462	-	-	-	-	-	-	-	-	-	-	-	-	-	-	-	-	-	-	-	-	-	-
Shelby County	27,176	40,140	-	62,543	-	-	-	-	-	-	-	-	-	-	-	-	-	-	-	-	-	-	-	-
Tuscaloosa County	18,998	18,119	-	-	-	-	-	-	-	-	-	-	-	-	-	-	-	-	-	-	-	-	-	-
ALASKA	22,660	16,694	13,557	18,295	-	-	22,128	-	16,084	-	25,817	4,572	-	25,421	16,689	8,522	-	-	11,614	-	-	18,371	7,725	20,204
Anchorage Borough	25,287	16,605	13,251	24,088	-	-	24,649	-	17,010	-	-	4,572	-	26,407	16,623	8,244	-	-	9,323	-	-	14,151	-	18,489
Fairbanks North Star Borough	21,553	16,604	-	-	-	-	19,952	-	13,782	-	-	-	-	-	12,989	-	-	-	-	-	-	-	-	-
Juneau City and Borough	26,719	19,465	-	-	-	-	-	-	19,279	-	-	-	-	-	-	-	-	-	-	-	-	-	-	-
Matanuska-Susitna Borough	21,105	14,482	-	-	-	-	-	-	-	-	-	-	-	-	-	-	-	-	-	-	-	-	-	-
ARIZONA	20,275	21,876	15,224	31,036	-	15,637	23,789	-	18,758	17,047	13,851	-	15,306	25,787	17,120	15,583	-	25,063	25,291	-	23,225	16,476	8,683	16,729
Cochise County	15,988	13,992	-	-	-	-	-	-	16,042	-	-	-	-	-	8,495	-	-	-	-	-	-	-	-	-
Coconino County	17,139	28,149	-	-	-	-	-	-	-	-	-	-	-	-	-	-	-	-	-	-	-	-	-	-
Maricopa County	22,251	23,325	16,360	33,277	-	15,003	25,247	-	20,519	19,186	13,023	-	18,569	27,691	16,417	17,853	-	20,581	30,842	-	25,412	16,733	10,446	17,820
Chandler (city)	23,904	28,905	-	32,818	-	-	33,191	-	21,567	-	-	-	-	-	-	-	-	-	-	-	-	-	-	23,574
Gilbert (town)	24,795	28,167	-	48,228	-	-	29,979	-	21,794	-	-	-	-	-	-	-	-	-	-	-	-	-	-	-
Mesa (city)	19,601	19,994	13,575	28,747	-	-	22,362	-	20,533	-	-	-	-	23,897	14,195	-	-	-	-	-	-	-	-	17,854
Phoenix (city)	19,833	23,628	16,855	36,057	-	13,910	24,776	-	20,852	-	12,797	-	-	27,678	17,916	-	-	-	-	-	-	-	-	16,427
Tempe (city)	22,406	18,730	-	25,222	-	-	19,788	-	13,625	-	-	-	-	20,323	15,294	-	-	-	-	-	-	-	-	16,150
Mohave County	16,788	21,305	-	-	-	-	-	-	-	-	-	-	-	-	-	-	-	-	-	-	-	-	-	-
Pima County	19,785	17,708	12,678	23,500	-	-	17,857	-	12,593	-	10,811	-	-	20,421	22,172	-	-	-	-	-	-	-	-	13,119
Tucson (city)	16,322	14,216	9,888	16,517	-	-	13,339	-	12,095	-	-	-	-	14,617	20,223	-	-	-	-	-	-	-	-	12,690
Pinal County	16,025	15,626	-	-	-	-	-	-	-	-	-	-	-	-	-	-	-	-	-	-	-	-	-	-
Yavapai County	19,727	19,013	-	-	-	-	-	-	-	-	-	-	-	-	-	-	-	-	-	-	-	-	-	-
Yuma County	14,802	19,116	-	-	-	-	-	-	12,221	-	-	-	-	-	-	-	-	-	-	-	-	-	-	-
ARKANSAS	16,904	16,494	8,267	26,458	-	-	17,303	-	17,458	-	12,391	-	-	20,286	12,637	10,590	-	-	-	-	-	10,283	-	14,447
Benton County	19,377	17,941	-	26,798	-	-	-	-	-	-	-	-	-	-	-	-	-	-	-	-	-	-	-	16,385
Craighead County	17,091	7,636	-	-	-	-	-	-	-	-	-	-	-	-	-	-	-	-	-	-	-	-	-	-
Crawford County	15,015	9,654	-	-	-	-	-	-	-	-	-	-	-	-	-	-	-	-	-	-	-	-	-	-

Notes: Please refer to the User's Guide for an explanation of data; data is arranged alphabetically by state, then county, then city within each county; table includes counties with populations greater than 49,999 unless noted and cities with populations greater than 9,999 whose Asian and/or NHPI population rates are greater than the national average; (1) Native Hawaiian and other Pacific Islander; (2) excludes Taiwanese; (3) includes Chamorro; (4) county does not meet population threshold but is shown in order to allow inclusion of city

Place	Total population	Total Asian population	Total NHPI[1] population	Asian Indian	Bangladeshi	Cambodian	Chinese[2]	Fijian	Filipino	Guamanian[3]	Hawaiian, Native	Hmong	Indonesian	Japanese	Korean	Laotian	Malaysian	Pakistani	Samoan	Sri Lankan	Taiwanese	Thai	Tongan	Vietnamese
Faulkner County	17,988	14,519	-	-	-	-	-	-	-	-	-	-	-	-	-	-	-	-	-	-	-	-	-	-
Jefferson County	15,417	20,793	-	-	-	-	-	-	-	-	-	-	-	-	-	-	-	-	-	-	-	-	-	-
Pulaski County	21,466	21,516	-	27,205	-	-	24,537	-	21,513	-	-	-	-	-	-	-	-	-	-	-	-	-	-	-
Saline County	19,214	20,103	-	-	-	-	-	-	-	-	-	-	-	-	-	-	-	-	-	-	-	-	-	-
Sebastian County	18,424	14,737	-	-	-	-	-	-	-	-	-	-	-	-	-	9,468	-	-	-	-	-	-	-	15,890
Fort Smith (city)	18,994	13,950	-	-	-	-	-	-	-	-	-	-	-	-	-	9,673	-	-	-	-	-	-	-	15,441
Washington County	17,347	13,412	6,382	-	-	-	12,512	-	-	-	-	-	-	-	-	13,319	-	-	-	-	-	-	-	-
Springdale (city)	16,855	13,887	6,578	-	-	-	-	-	-	-	-	-	-	-	-	13,381	-	-	-	-	-	-	-	-
CALIFORNIA	22,711	22,050	15,610	29,232	18,496	8,534	25,485	13,586	20,543	19,930	22,404	5,263	19,544	32,745	19,643	8,745	24,535	19,254	11,558	28,482	24,408	18,477	11,198	16,000
Alameda County	26,680	24,335	16,584	31,899	-	8,503	25,200	14,584	22,323	25,970	28,556	-	24,372	33,645	21,022	10,543	-	21,978	11,759	-	27,995	17,880	9,543	16,654
Alameda (city)	30,982	23,153	28,163	33,201	-	-	26,103	-	20,180	-	-	-	-	35,264	20,126	-	-	-	-	-	-	-	-	13,103
Albany (city)	28,494	21,673	-	25,886	-	-	21,216	-	-	-	-	-	-	27,226	13,949	-	-	-	-	-	-	-	-	-
Ashland (cdp)	18,134	17,280	-	-	-	-	23,602	-	15,917	-	-	-	-	-	-	-	-	-	-	-	-	-	-	-
Berkeley (city)	30,477	17,069	-	20,705	-	-	16,121	-	23,369	-	-	-	-	24,234	12,214	-	-	-	-	-	8,985	-	-	10,809
Castro Valley (cdp)	30,454	29,866	-	31,144	-	-	29,363	-	37,374	-	-	-	-	27,426	25,225	-	-	-	-	-	-	-	-	-
Cherryland (cdp)	16,929	17,439	-	-	-	-	-	-	16,547	-	-	-	-	-	-	-	-	-	-	-	-	-	-	-
Dublin (city)	29,451	31,880	-	31,990	-	-	40,273	-	27,270	-	-	-	-	-	-	-	-	-	-	-	-	-	-	-
Fremont (city)	31,411	32,640	27,061	36,900	-	-	34,159	-	27,852	-	-	-	-	45,120	21,810	-	-	26,966	-	-	31,906	-	-	27,259
Hayward (city)	19,695	20,347	15,138	21,247	-	-	27,063	14,616	19,925	-	-	-	-	21,613	18,205	-	-	-	10,882	-	-	-	-	15,562
Livermore (city)	31,062	25,436	-	26,656	-	-	35,157	-	22,510	-	-	-	-	-	-	-	-	-	-	-	-	-	-	13,197
Newark (city)	23,641	24,664	-	29,286	-	-	26,884	-	21,107	-	-	-	-	-	19,388	-	-	-	-	-	-	-	-	16,656
Oakland (city)	21,936	16,590	9,507	28,189	-	6,246	16,793	-	20,641	-	-	-	-	37,488	21,401	7,522	-	-	-	-	-	-	8,674	10,812
Piedmont (city)	70,539	47,136	-	-	-	-	48,684	-	-	-	-	-	-	-	-	-	-	-	-	-	-	-	-	-
Pleasanton (city)	41,623	37,315	-	43,736	-	-	37,819	-	34,196	-	-	-	-	43,345	31,431	-	-	-	-	-	-	-	-	-
San Leandro (city)	23,895	20,937	10,668	24,802	-	-	20,260	-	20,196	-	-	-	-	30,497	23,631	-	-	-	-	-	-	-	-	21,056
San Lorenzo (cdp)	21,922	21,232	-	-	-	-	23,131	-	22,396	-	-	-	-	-	-	-	-	-	-	-	-	-	-	9,444
Union City (city)	22,890	23,384	20,783	26,312	-	-	28,223	-	20,947	-	-	-	-	25,802	22,240	-	-	-	-	-	-	-	-	20,154
Butte County	17,517	8,422	-	14,049	-	-	14,043	-	21,431	-	-	3,433	-	14,252	-	3,542	-	-	-	-	-	-	-	-
Chico (city)	16,970	9,111	-	-	-	-	14,850	-	-	-	-	2,880	-	-	-	-	-	-	-	-	-	-	-	-
Oroville (city)	12,345	3,778	-	-	-	-	-	-	-	-	-	2,598	-	-	-	-	-	-	-	-	-	-	-	-
Contra Costa County	30,615	26,674	19,330	28,610	-	-	32,985	13,739	23,909	28,706	31,594	-	23,976	36,171	23,280	9,082	-	15,173	15,601	-	32,328	21,825	10,882	16,265
Alamo (cdp)	65,705	51,021	-	-	-	-	-	-	-	-	-	-	-	-	-	-	-	-	-	-	-	-	-	-
Antioch (city)	22,152	22,216	14,677	22,687	-	-	25,295	-	20,508	-	-	-	-	-	-	-	-	-	-	-	-	-	-	15,615
Bay Point (cdp)	16,743	16,233	-	-	-	-	-	-	16,365	-	-	-	-	-	-	-	-	-	-	-	-	-	-	-
Blackhawk-Camino-Tass. (cdp)	66,972	49,068	-	-	-	-	48,096	-	-	-	-	-	-	-	-	-	-	-	-	-	-	-	-	-
Clayton (city)	42,048	34,718	-	-	-	-	-	-	-	-	-	-	-	-	-	-	-	-	-	-	-	-	-	-
Concord (city)	24,727	24,450	13,116	25,617	-	-	31,394	-	22,343	-	-	-	-	27,415	17,148	-	-	-	-	-	-	-	-	18,750
Danville (town)	50,773	38,103	-	48,080	-	-	37,082	-	43,211	-	-	-	-	-	-	-	-	-	-	-	-	-	-	-
El Cerrito (city)	32,593	26,132	-	24,689	-	-	26,791	-	31,561	-	-	-	-	31,985	-	-	-	-	-	-	-	-	-	-
El Sobrante (cdp)	24,525	19,564	-	14,161	-	-	-	-	-	-	-	-	-	-	-	-	-	-	-	-	-	-	-	-
Hercules (city)	27,699	25,062	-	17,956	-	-	29,648	-	25,664	-	-	-	-	-	-	-	-	-	-	-	-	-	-	-

Notes: Please refer to the User's Guide for an explanation of data; data is arranged alphabetically by state, then county, then city within each county; table includes counties with populations greater than 49,999 unless noted and cities with populations greater than 9,999 whose Asian and/or NHPI population rates are greater than the national average; (1) Native Hawaiian and other Pacific Islander; (2) excludes Taiwanese; (3) includes Chamorro; (4) county does not meet population threshold but is shown in order to allow inclusion of city

Place	Total population	Total Asian population	Total NHPI[1] population	Asian Indian	Bangladeshi	Cambodian	Chinese[2]	Fijian	Filipino	Guamanian[3]	Hawaiian, Native	Hmong	Indonesian	Japanese	Korean	Laotian	Malaysian	Pakistani	Samoan	Sri Lankan	Taiwanese	Thai	Tongan	Vietnamese
Lafayette (city)	54,319	47,532	-	-	-	-	46,178	-	-	-	-	-	-	-	-	-	-	-	-	-	-	-	-	-
Martinez (city)	29,701	29,717	-	-	-	-	38,973	-	31,329	-	-	-	-	-	-	-	-	-	-	-	-	-	-	-
Moraga (town)	45,437	35,197	-	-	-	-	34,358	-	-	-	-	-	-	-	-	-	-	-	-	-	-	-	-	-
Orinda (city)	65,428	41,246	-	-	-	-	42,138	-	-	-	-	-	-	-	-	-	-	-	-	-	-	-	-	-
Pinole (city)	25,170	23,303	-	-	-	-	29,740	-	23,374	-	-	-	-	-	-	-	-	-	-	-	-	-	-	-
Pittsburg (city)	18,241	21,063	21,716	23,293	-	-	25,828	-	22,140	-	-	-	-	-	-	-	-	-	-	-	-	-	-	-
Pleasant Hill (city)	33,076	27,115	-	-	-	-	31,436	-	24,511	-	-	-	-	-	20,052	-	-	-	-	-	-	-	-	-
Richmond (city)	19,788	20,543	14,709	21,739	-	-	25,035	-	22,631	-	-	-	-	31,771	17,642	8,062	-	-	-	-	-	-	-	10,147
San Pablo (city)	14,303	13,817	-	15,742	-	-	-	-	18,577	-	-	-	-	-	-	8,646	-	-	-	-	-	-	-	7,708
San Ramon (city)	42,336	33,486	-	33,024	-	-	33,598	-	33,883	-	-	-	-	48,400	-	-	-	-	-	-	-	-	-	-
Walnut Creek (city)	39,875	37,145	-	43,568	-	-	39,871	-	31,400	-	-	-	-	38,783	28,443	-	-	-	-	-	-	-	-	-
El Dorado County	25,560	30,460	-	-	-	-	-	-	25,980	-	-	-	-	32,573	-	-	-	-	-	-	-	-	-	-
El Dorado Hills (cdp)	40,239	36,322	-	-	-	-	-	-	-	-	-	-	-	-	-	-	-	-	-	-	-	-	-	-
South Lake Tahoe (city)	18,452	24,322	-	-	-	-	-	-	22,219	-	-	-	-	-	-	-	-	-	-	-	-	-	-	-
Fresno County	15,495	11,524	19,634	15,699	-	4,558	23,323	-	17,984	-	-	4,445	-	28,726	21,767	4,399	-	-	-	-	-	-	-	11,033
Clovis (city)	18,690	14,096	-	-	-	-	-	-	18,106	-	-	5,317	-	26,191	-	-	-	-	-	-	-	-	-	-
Fresno (city)	15,010	10,250	-	16,040	-	4,573	22,402	-	17,935	-	-	4,328	-	31,586	24,421	4,223	-	-	-	-	-	-	-	9,662
Reedley (city)	12,096	21,081	-	-	-	-	-	-	-	-	-	-	-	-	-	-	-	-	-	-	-	-	-	-
Humboldt County	17,203	12,074	-	-	-	-	-	-	-	-	-	-	-	19,420	-	-	-	-	-	-	-	-	-	-
Imperial County	13,239	24,655	-	-	-	-	18,440	-	17,821	-	-	-	-	-	32,890	-	-	-	-	-	-	-	-	-
Kern County	15,760	16,608	14,320	15,382	-	8,698	26,959	-	14,255	-	-	-	-	25,322	18,929	-	-	-	-	-	-	-	-	14,416
Bakersfield (city)	17,678	18,700	11,759	15,905	-	-	24,313	-	20,007	-	-	-	-	23,399	19,143	-	-	-	-	-	-	-	-	16,835
Delano (city)	11,068	11,656	-	-	-	-	-	-	11,635	-	-	-	-	-	-	-	-	-	-	-	-	-	-	-
Ridgecrest (city)	21,312	18,195	-	-	-	-	-	-	13,975	-	-	-	-	-	-	-	-	-	-	-	-	-	-	-
Kings County	15,848	14,477	-	-	-	-	-	-	15,682	-	-	-	-	-	-	-	-	-	-	-	-	-	-	-
Lemoore (city)	15,876	14,908	-	-	-	-	-	-	16,321	-	-	-	-	-	-	-	-	-	-	-	-	-	-	-
Lake County	16,825	17,779	-	-	-	-	-	-	-	-	-	-	-	-	-	-	-	-	-	-	-	-	-	-
Los Angeles County	20,683	20,595	13,344	26,461	13,324	8,373	21,011	14,291	20,304	16,790	19,095	6,956	16,839	31,213	18,254	10,738	22,298	14,608	11,106	24,099	22,113	18,034	9,711	14,237
Agoura Hills (city)	39,700	37,047	-	-	-	-	-	-	-	-	-	-	-	-	-	-	-	-	-	-	-	-	-	-
Alhambra (city)	17,350	15,542	-	16,349	-	-	15,547	-	20,604	-	-	-	-	24,483	14,342	-	-	-	-	-	15,548	-	-	12,578
Altadena (cdp)	27,604	30,770	-	-	-	-	-	-	22,657	-	-	-	-	32,086	-	-	-	-	-	-	-	-	-	-
Arcadia (city)	28,400	23,076	-	27,051	-	-	23,686	-	22,113	-	-	-	-	33,034	19,889	-	-	-	-	-	19,917	-	-	-
Artesia (city)	15,763	14,337	-	10,932	-	-	15,959	-	13,886	-	-	-	-	-	14,090	-	-	-	-	-	-	-	-	-
Avocado Heights (cdp)	14,570	21,149	-	-	-	-	-	-	-	-	-	-	-	-	-	-	-	-	-	-	-	-	-	-
Azusa (city)	13,412	17,386	-	-	-	-	-	-	19,399	-	-	-	-	-	-	-	-	-	-	-	-	-	-	-
Baldwin Park (city)	11,562	15,763	-	-	-	-	15,043	-	17,076	-	-	-	-	-	-	-	-	-	-	-	-	-	-	10,824
Bellflower (city)	15,982	16,522	-	-	-	12,966	-	-	16,316	-	-	-	-	-	17,412	-	-	-	-	-	-	19,081	-	-
Beverly Hills (city)	65,507	40,111	-	-	-	-	48,299	-	-	-	-	-	-	-	41,264	-	-	-	-	-	-	-	-	-
Burbank (city)	25,713	22,562	-	19,009	-	-	29,431	-	21,333	-	-	-	-	36,036	21,303	-	-	-	-	-	-	-	-	20,210
Calabasas (city)	48,189	46,438	-	-	-	-	59,680	-	-	-	-	-	-	-	-	-	-	-	-	-	-	-	-	-
Carson (city)	17,107	16,657	11,745	-	-	-	18,757	-	16,409	-	-	-	-	25,011	-	-	-	-	11,053	-	-	-	-	19,249

Notes: Please refer to the User's Guide for an explanation of data; data is arranged alphabetically by state, then county, then city within each county; table includes counties with populations greater than 49,999 unless noted and cities with populations greater than 9,999 whose Asian and/or NHPI population rates are greater than the national average; (1) Native Hawaiian and other Pacific Islander; (2) excludes Taiwanese; (3) includes Chamorro; (4) county does not meet population threshold but is shown in order to allow inclusion of city

Place	Total population	Total Asian population	Total NHPI[1] population	Asian Indian	Bangladeshi	Cambodian	Chinese[2]	Fijian	Filipino	Guamanian[3]	Hawaiian, Native	Hmong	Indonesian	Japanese	Korean	Laotian	Malaysian	Pakistani	Samoan	Sri Lankan	Taiwanese	Thai	Tongan	Vietnamese
Cerritos (city)	25,249	23,665	-	26,725	-	-	24,402	-	26,175	-	-	-	-	31,196	17,898	-	-	-	-	-	29,492	24,844	-	24,359
Citrus (cdp)	15,848	20,080	-	-	-	-	-	-	-	-	-	-	-	-	-	-	-	-	-	-	-	-	-	-
Claremont (city)	28,843	26,368	-	52,618	-	-	27,761	-	-	-	-	-	-	-	15,171	-	-	-	-	-	-	-	-	-
Compton (city)	10,389	12,943	5,305	-	-	-	-	-	-	-	-	-	-	-	-	-	-	-	4,983	-	-	-	-	-
Covina (city)	20,231	19,534	-	-	-	-	20,473	-	21,484	-	-	-	-	23,796	-	-	-	-	-	-	-	-	-	8,976
Culver City (city)	29,025	24,094	-	23,228	-	-	25,270	-	21,513	-	-	-	-	27,157	-	-	-	-	-	-	-	-	-	-
Diamond Bar (city)	25,472	23,223	-	30,457	-	-	23,241	-	22,832	-	-	-	-	37,754	19,745	-	-	-	-	-	23,538	-	-	25,492
Downey (city)	18,197	20,416	-	23,974	-	-	23,716	-	23,185	-	-	-	-	31,545	17,783	-	-	-	-	-	-	-	-	17,921
Duarte (city)	19,648	22,515	-	-	-	-	25,968	-	20,821	-	-	-	-	-	-	-	-	-	-	-	-	-	-	-
East San Gabriel (cdp)	23,571	20,012	-	-	-	-	21,409	-	-	-	-	-	-	22,625	-	-	-	-	-	-	15,370	-	-	-
El Monte (city)	10,316	13,420	-	-	-	-	15,143	-	16,173	-	-	-	-	-	-	-	-	-	-	-	14,463	-	-	9,587
El Segundo (city)	33,996	37,115	-	-	-	-	-	-	-	-	-	-	-	-	-	-	-	-	-	-	-	-	-	-
Gardena (city)	17,263	20,877	-	-	-	-	27,273	-	18,805	-	-	-	-	26,212	14,818	-	-	-	-	-	-	-	-	11,365
Glendale (city)	22,227	22,108	-	26,604	-	-	34,821	-	21,445	-	-	-	-	37,818	17,639	-	-	-	-	-	-	24,885	-	21,212
Glendora (city)	25,993	26,426	-	24,024	-	-	32,899	-	23,116	-	-	-	-	-	-	-	-	-	-	-	-	-	-	-
Hacienda Heights (cdp)	21,893	19,753	-	-	-	-	18,954	-	20,294	-	-	-	-	36,031	19,090	-	-	-	-	-	16,425	-	-	11,414
Hawaiian Gardens (city)	10,728	10,807	-	-	-	-	-	-	-	-	-	-	-	-	10,270	-	-	-	-	-	-	-	-	-
Hawthorne (city)	15,022	16,587	11,227	12,819	-	-	21,562	-	19,122	-	-	-	-	17,811	-	-	-	-	-	-	-	-	-	12,492
Hermosa Beach (city)	54,244	54,068	-	-	-	-	-	-	-	-	-	-	-	-	-	-	-	-	-	-	-	-	-	-
La Canada Flintridge (city)	52,838	37,337	-	-	-	-	52,100	-	-	-	-	-	-	73,265	27,373	-	-	-	-	-	-	-	-	-
La Crescenta-Montrose (cdp)	30,196	23,605	-	-	-	-	-	-	31,737	-	-	-	-	-	19,267	-	-	-	-	-	-	-	-	-
La Mirada (city)	22,404	22,537	-	23,365	-	-	31,611	-	25,017	-	-	-	-	28,165	18,241	-	-	-	-	-	-	-	-	-
La Puente (city)	11,336	16,863	-	-	-	-	13,600	-	22,881	-	-	-	-	-	-	-	-	-	-	-	-	-	-	-
La Verne (city)	26,689	27,912	-	-	-	-	-	-	30,465	-	-	-	-	-	-	-	-	-	-	-	-	-	-	-
Lakewood (city)	22,095	17,889	14,757	18,747	-	11,695	20,653	-	18,213	-	-	-	-	31,309	13,077	-	-	-	13,875	-	-	-	-	19,172
Lancaster (city)	16,935	19,204	-	22,997	-	-	20,451	-	19,713	-	-	-	-	-	-	-	-	-	-	-	-	-	-	-
Lawndale (city)	13,702	15,818	8,247	-	-	-	-	-	19,113	-	-	-	-	-	-	-	-	-	-	-	-	-	-	14,139
Lomita (city)	22,127	21,507	-	-	-	-	-	-	26,694	-	-	-	-	29,500	10,736	-	-	-	-	-	-	-	-	-
Long Beach (city)	19,040	14,367	8,364	27,361	-	6,670	22,881	-	17,628	-	-	-	-	26,528	17,768	6,921	-	-	7,416	-	-	19,930	-	12,961
Los Angeles (city)	20,671	19,553	16,038	23,502	12,064	8,718	19,969	-	19,999	16,317	18,260	-	16,385	28,142	16,686	10,066	-	11,898	15,065	22,726	22,757	16,742	7,663	14,847
Manhattan Beach (city)	61,136	48,773	-	-	-	-	63,372	-	-	-	-	-	-	53,314	-	-	-	-	-	-	-	-	-	-
Monrovia (city)	21,686	22,427	-	-	-	-	23,690	-	18,727	-	-	-	-	-	-	-	-	-	-	-	-	-	-	-
Montebello (city)	15,125	24,651	-	-	-	-	23,896	-	29,019	-	-	-	-	32,732	14,402	-	-	-	-	-	-	-	-	-
Monterey Park (city)	17,661	17,654	-	-	-	8,568	16,817	-	18,325	-	-	-	-	28,743	20,867	-	-	-	-	-	17,186	-	-	10,518
Norwalk (city)	14,022	16,194	-	17,859	-	17,043	18,082	-	15,650	-	-	-	-	18,007	14,506	-	-	-	-	-	-	-	-	16,204
Palmdale (city)	16,384	23,574	-	29,495	-	-	-	-	18,607	-	-	-	-	-	-	-	-	-	-	-	-	-	-	-
Palos Verdes Estates (city)	69,040	52,830	-	-	-	-	51,508	-	-	-	-	-	-	58,912	56,187	-	-	-	-	-	-	-	-	-
Pasadena (city)	28,186	27,657	-	29,171	-	-	31,615	-	21,962	-	-	-	-	37,836	23,684	-	-	-	-	-	-	-	-	18,006
Pomona (city)	13,336	14,983	-	27,034	-	8,861	13,049	-	18,510	-	-	-	-	21,055	-	8,687	-	-	-	-	-	-	-	9,880
Rancho Palos Verdes (city)	46,250	42,306	-	53,260	-	-	43,677	-	37,245	-	-	-	-	49,798	35,417	-	-	-	-	-	27,161	-	-	-
Redondo Beach (city)	38,305	36,305	-	33,603	-	-	40,408	-	37,976	-	-	-	-	40,627	25,521	-	-	-	-	-	-	-	-	-

Notes: Please refer to the User's Guide for an explanation of data; data is arranged alphabetically by state, then county, then city within each county; table includes counties with populations greater than 49,999 unless noted and cities with populations greater than 9,999 whose Asian and/or NHPI population rates are greater than the national average; (1) Native Hawaiian and other Pacific Islander; (2) excludes Taiwanese; (3) includes Chamorro; (4) county does not meet population threshold but is shown in order to allow inclusion of city

Place	Total population	Total Asian population	Total NHPI[1] population	Asian Indian	Bangladeshi	Cambodian	Chinese[2]	Fijian	Filipino	Guamanian[3]	Hawaiian, Native	Hmong	Indonesian	Japanese	Korean	Laotian	Malaysian	Pakistani	Samoan	Sri Lankan	Taiwanese	Thai	Tongan	Vietnamese
Rosemead (city)	12,146	11,651	-	-	-	9,626	11,030	-	19,545	-	-	-	-	27,592	-	-	-	-	-	-	-	-	-	9,898
Rowland Heights (cdp)	19,315	18,988	-	29,433	-	-	18,386	-	18,892	-	-	-	-	30,460	15,563	-	-	-	-	-	18,959	-	-	21,074
San Dimas (city)	28,321	33,911	-	-	-	-	29,358	-	23,824	-	-	-	-	-	-	-	-	-	-	-	-	-	-	-
San Gabriel (city)	16,807	14,244	-	-	-	-	14,161	-	19,140	-	-	-	-	25,845	-	-	-	-	-	-	16,546	-	-	10,629
San Marino (city)	59,150	40,487	-	-	-	-	41,316	-	-	-	-	-	-	-	-	-	-	-	-	-	36,291	-	-	-
Santa Clarita (city)	26,841	23,690	-	23,006	-	-	26,783	-	25,592	-	-	-	-	28,099	17,495	-	-	-	-	-	-	-	-	22,800
Santa Monica (city)	42,874	35,693	-	42,244	-	-	38,182	-	40,566	-	-	-	-	33,154	34,760	-	-	-	-	-	-	-	-	-
Sierra Madre (city)	41,104	44,268	-	-	-	-	-	-	-	-	-	-	-	-	-	-	-	-	-	-	-	-	-	-
South El Monte (city)	10,130	10,128	-	-	-	-	10,628	-	-	-	-	-	-	-	-	-	-	-	-	-	-	-	-	9,489
South Pasadena (city)	32,620	31,144	-	-	-	-	34,019	-	-	-	-	-	-	40,661	18,899	-	-	-	-	-	-	-	-	-
South San Jose Hills (cdp)	11,324	21,856	-	-	-	-	-	-	19,373	-	-	-	-	-	-	-	-	-	-	-	-	-	-	-
Temple City (city)	20,267	17,640	-	-	-	-	16,589	-	20,736	-	-	-	-	28,507	16,551	-	-	-	-	-	16,747	-	-	15,332
Torrance (city)	28,144	26,065	-	28,578	-	-	27,688	-	25,259	-	-	-	-	32,708	19,119	-	-	12,070	-	-	32,702	-	-	16,771
Valinda (cdp)	12,949	16,048	-	-	-	-	-	-	19,095	-	-	-	-	-	-	-	-	-	-	-	-	-	-	12,143
Vincent (cdp)	15,522	17,336	-	-	-	-	-	-	19,870	-	-	-	-	-	-	-	-	-	-	-	-	-	-	-
Walnut (city)	25,196	22,982	-	30,119	-	-	23,182	-	25,247	-	-	-	-	41,452	18,489	-	-	-	-	-	19,709	-	-	16,615
West Carson (cdp)	21,023	25,186	-	-	-	-	-	-	22,161	-	-	-	-	35,037	25,001	-	-	-	-	-	-	-	-	-
West Covina (city)	19,342	19,116	12,840	24,655	-	-	17,936	-	20,442	-	-	-	-	24,853	19,352	-	-	-	-	-	18,667	-	-	15,715
West Hollywood (city)	38,302	35,372	-	-	-	-	-	-	-	-	-	-	-	-	-	-	-	-	-	-	-	-	-	-
West Puente Valley (cdp)	12,806	14,489	-	-	-	-	-	-	17,431	-	-	-	-	-	-	-	-	-	-	-	-	-	-	10,450
Whittier (city)	21,409	28,126	-	-	-	-	27,753	-	27,257	-	-	-	-	30,194	26,167	-	-	-	-	-	-	-	-	-
Madera County	14,682	24,435	-	24,368	-	-	-	-	17,017	-	-	-	-	-	-	-	-	-	-	-	-	-	-	-
Marin County	44,962	37,371	-	38,155	-	-	48,210	-	34,157	-	-	-	-	43,768	25,501	-	-	-	-	-	-	-	-	13,158
Larkspur (city)	56,983	43,575	-	-	-	-	-	-	-	-	-	-	-	-	-	-	-	-	-	-	-	-	-	-
Novato (city)	32,402	27,280	-	-	-	-	28,946	-	20,137	-	-	-	-	-	-	-	-	-	-	-	-	-	-	-
San Rafael (city)	35,762	31,209	-	30,320	-	-	37,054	-	-	-	-	-	-	-	-	-	-	-	-	-	-	-	-	12,910
Tamalpais-Homestead (cdp)	56,913	54,189	-	-	-	-	-	-	-	-	-	-	-	-	-	-	-	-	-	-	-	-	-	-
Mendocino County	19,443	21,621	-	-	-	-	-	-	-	-	-	-	-	-	-	-	-	-	-	-	-	-	-	-
Merced County	14,257	9,899	-	18,032	-	-	24,921	-	20,994	-	-	4,178	-	23,692	-	5,404	-	-	-	-	-	-	-	-
Atwater (city)	15,162	10,407	-	-	-	-	-	-	-	-	-	5,142	-	-	-	-	-	-	-	-	-	-	-	-
Livingston (city)	9,231	9,367	-	9,038	-	-	-	-	-	-	-	-	-	-	-	-	-	-	-	-	-	-	-	-
Merced (city)	13,115	6,350	-	-	-	-	-	-	-	-	-	3,917	-	-	-	5,134	-	-	-	-	-	-	-	-
Monterey County	20,165	19,634	15,253	24,738	-	-	25,606	-	16,786	15,216	-	-	-	27,926	21,607	-	-	-	-	-	-	-	-	12,239
Marina (city)	18,860	16,974	16,644	-	-	-	-	-	15,681	-	-	-	-	23,324	20,913	-	-	-	-	-	-	-	-	9,547
Monterey (city)	27,133	23,763	-	-	-	-	25,556	-	16,138	-	-	-	-	25,899	-	-	-	-	-	-	-	-	-	-
Pacific Grove (city)	31,277	22,577	-	-	-	-	-	-	-	-	-	-	-	-	-	-	-	-	-	-	-	-	-	-
Salinas (city)	14,495	18,310	9,977	19,446	-	-	20,178	-	16,605	-	-	-	-	32,161	17,643	-	-	-	-	-	-	-	-	15,210
Seaside (city)	15,183	15,169	-	-	-	-	-	-	14,739	-	-	-	-	24,605	-	-	-	-	-	-	-	-	-	9,383
Napa County	26,395	27,414	-	-	-	-	60,000	-	20,085	-	-	-	-	40,802	-	-	-	-	-	-	-	-	-	-
Nevada County	24,007	28,721	-	-	-	-	-	-	-	-	-	-	-	-	-	-	-	-	-	-	-	-	-	-
Orange County	25,826	21,137	16,373	27,911	-	13,710	28,732	-	22,489	24,232	26,073	11,417	17,904	34,027	18,732	14,297	-	21,482	12,701	22,609	22,009	20,811	5,883	15,434

Notes: Please refer to the User's Guide for an explanation of data; data is arranged alphabetically by state, then county, then city within each county; table includes counties with populations greater than 49,999 unless noted and cities with populations greater than 9,999 whose Asian and/or NHPI population rates are greater than the national average; (1) Native Hawaiian and other Pacific Islander; (2) excludes Taiwanese; (3) includes Chamorro; (4) county does not meet population threshold but is shown in order to allow inclusion of city

Place	Total population	Total Asian population	Total NHPI[1] population	Asian Indian	Bangladeshi	Cambodian	Chinese[2]	Fijian	Filipino	Guamanian[3]	Hawaiian, Native	Hmong	Indonesian	Japanese	Korean	Laotian	Malaysian	Pakistani	Samoan	Sri Lankan	Taiwanese	Thai	Tongan	Vietnamese
Aliso Viejo (cdp)	35,244	29,360	-	36,799	-	-	26,697	-	31,078	-	-	-	-	35,559	23,069	-	-	-	-	-	-	-	-	37,489
Anaheim (city)	18,266	20,385	13,998	29,962	-	-	28,727	-	20,426	-	-	-	-	32,135	17,156	16,010	-	18,457	14,152	-	15,732	18,314	-	15,300
Brea (city)	26,307	26,114	-	24,551	-	-	37,092	-	24,690	-	-	-	-	-	16,463	-	-	-	-	-	-	-	-	-
Buena Park (city)	18,031	17,698	-	18,385	-	-	18,002	-	19,328	-	-	-	-	23,856	15,985	-	-	-	-	-	-	-	-	17,526
Costa Mesa (city)	23,342	22,815	12,933	30,153	-	-	25,231	-	25,200	-	-	-	-	24,276	17,556	-	-	-	-	-	-	-	-	18,886
Cypress (city)	25,798	22,424	-	23,734	-	-	24,493	-	23,838	-	-	-	-	39,509	16,072	-	-	-	-	-	15,647	-	-	19,401
Foothill Ranch (cdp)	36,013	33,926	-	-	-	-	-	-	-	-	-	-	-	-	-	-	-	-	-	-	-	-	-	-
Fountain Valley (city)	26,521	20,970	-	19,128	-	-	24,697	-	25,689	-	-	-	-	27,768	20,638	-	-	-	-	-	16,187	-	-	18,505
Fullerton (city)	23,370	20,548	-	24,320	-	-	26,106	-	21,004	-	-	-	-	31,155	18,670	-	-	-	-	-	-	-	-	13,238
Garden Grove (city)	16,209	13,263	12,001	13,610	-	11,917	15,018	-	18,533	-	-	-	-	26,888	15,274	-	-	-	12,798	-	-	-	-	11,927
Huntington Beach (city)	31,964	28,311	20,270	35,275	-	-	34,894	-	30,304	-	-	-	-	34,431	24,857	-	-	-	-	-	28,092	-	-	21,697
Irvine (city)	32,196	24,273	-	29,942	-	-	26,136	-	17,882	-	-	-	-	32,009	17,177	-	-	-	-	-	22,703	-	-	26,518
La Habra (city)	18,923	24,125	-	-	-	-	35,500	-	24,718	-	-	-	-	-	19,518	-	-	-	-	-	-	-	-	-
La Palma (city)	26,598	22,322	-	21,194	-	-	29,390	-	24,208	-	-	-	-	33,155	16,115	-	-	-	-	-	-	-	-	-
Laguna Hills (city)	36,133	30,317	-	-	-	-	42,198	-	21,760	-	-	-	-	-	-	-	-	-	-	-	-	-	-	30,799
Laguna Niguel (city)	39,167	35,029	-	-	-	-	52,135	-	25,135	-	-	-	-	48,256	25,222	-	-	-	-	-	-	-	-	31,448
Lake Forest (city)	28,583	26,443	-	24,128	-	-	24,585	-	27,292	-	-	-	-	40,875	21,304	-	-	-	-	-	-	-	-	25,800
Los Alamitos (city)	26,014	21,932	-	-	-	-	-	-	-	-	-	-	-	-	-	-	-	-	-	-	-	-	-	-
Mission Viejo (city)	33,302	28,806	-	24,477	-	-	36,255	-	25,344	-	-	-	-	36,032	26,954	-	-	-	-	-	-	-	-	23,705
Newport Beach (city)	63,015	42,619	-	-	-	-	38,887	-	-	-	-	-	-	57,139	-	-	-	-	-	-	-	-	-	-
Orange (city)	24,294	24,353	-	28,418	-	-	33,388	-	21,804	-	-	-	-	38,559	22,233	-	-	-	-	-	36,324	-	-	18,330
Placentia (city)	23,843	24,263	-	25,431	-	-	22,984	-	21,739	-	-	-	-	30,361	27,625	-	-	-	-	-	-	-	-	24,804
Rancho Santa Margarita (city)	31,531	29,455	-	-	-	-	34,418	-	27,802	-	-	-	-	-	-	-	-	-	-	-	-	-	-	26,696
Rossmoor (cdp)	38,642	41,496	-	-	-	-	-	-	-	-	-	-	-	-	-	-	-	-	-	-	-	-	-	-
Santa Ana (city)	12,152	14,740	13,404	25,998	-	10,875	19,611	-	19,406	-	-	9,958	-	29,376	12,012	12,295	-	-	11,319	-	-	-	-	13,456
Seal Beach (city)	34,589	37,776	-	-	-	-	-	-	-	-	-	-	-	42,179	-	-	-	-	-	-	-	-	-	-
Stanton (city)	14,197	14,480	-	-	-	-	-	-	15,224	-	-	-	-	-	12,295	-	-	-	-	-	-	-	-	14,023
Tustin (city)	25,932	26,458	-	23,863	-	-	33,844	-	22,580	-	-	-	-	30,781	31,420	-	-	-	-	-	29,218	-	-	26,912
Tustin Foothills (cdp)	42,656	33,225	-	-	-	-	50,133	-	-	-	-	-	-	-	-	-	-	-	-	-	-	-	-	-
Westminster (city)	18,218	14,271	9,002	16,499	-	-	20,784	-	19,268	-	-	-	-	31,086	18,653	-	-	-	8,125	-	-	-	-	12,737
Yorba Linda (city)	36,173	29,137	-	34,073	-	-	33,347	-	27,370	-	-	-	-	30,581	21,290	-	-	-	-	-	-	-	-	27,200
Placer County	27,963	26,402	-	31,520	-	-	32,575	-	20,189	-	-	-	-	31,738	12,276	-	-	-	-	-	-	-	-	22,747
Rocklin (city)	26,910	26,078	-	-	-	-	-	-	-	-	-	-	-	28,122	-	-	-	-	-	-	-	-	-	-
Roseville (city)	27,021	24,349	-	32,763	-	-	27,950	-	18,881	-	-	-	-	30,487	-	-	-	-	-	-	-	-	-	-
Riverside County	18,689	18,589	17,415	23,329	-	11,989	18,106	-	19,459	17,590	25,722	4,483	-	26,026	16,259	9,803	-	17,881	10,557	-	11,811	11,277	-	15,944
Banning (city)	16,231	7,449	-	-	-	-	-	-	-	-	-	-	-	-	-	9,090	-	-	-	-	-	-	-	-
Corona (city)	21,001	22,515	-	22,943	-	-	23,374	-	24,529	-	-	-	-	25,381	21,060	-	-	-	-	-	-	-	-	20,980
Moreno Valley (city)	14,983	15,861	-	-	-	-	19,632	-	17,683	-	-	-	-	21,837	12,858	7,267	-	-	-	-	-	-	-	10,847
Palm Springs (city)	25,957	16,682	-	-	-	-	-	-	15,292	-	-	-	-	-	-	-	-	-	-	-	-	-	-	-
Pedley (cdp)	20,623	21,497	-	-	-	-	-	-	-	-	-	-	-	-	-	-	-	-	-	-	-	-	-	-
Riverside (city)	17,882	16,766	13,441	21,109	-	-	12,878	-	19,203	-	-	-	-	28,736	14,332	10,160	-	-	-	-	-	-	-	15,830

Notes: Please refer to the User's Guide for an explanation of data; data is arranged alphabetically by state, then county, then city within each county; table includes counties with populations greater than 49,999 unless noted and cities with populations greater than 9,999 whose Asian and/or NHPI population rates are greater than the national average; (1) Native Hawaiian and other Pacific Islander; (2) excludes Taiwanese; (3) includes Chamorro; (4) county does not meet population threshold but is shown in order to allow inclusion of city

Place	Total population	Total Asian population	Total NHPI[1] population	Asian Indian	Bangladeshi	Cambodian	Chinese[2]	Fijian	Filipino	Guamanian[3]	Hawaiian, Native	Hmong	Indonesian	Japanese	Korean	Laotian	Malaysian	Pakistani	Samoan	Sri Lankan	Taiwanese	Thai	Tongan	Vietnamese
Temecula (city)	21,557	24,905	-	-	-	-	30,520	-	19,576	-	-	-	-	-	-	-	-	-	-	-	-	-	-	-
Sacramento County	21,142	17,333	13,768	21,399	-	8,219	21,781	11,112	19,288	19,964	23,429	5,937	-	32,700	17,034	7,103	-	10,211	9,608	-	23,841	14,432	11,942	12,042
Arden-Arcade (cdp)	26,530	23,614	-	31,552	-	-	29,931	-	19,628	-	-	11,530	-	29,366	-	-	-	-	-	-	-	-	-	13,929
Elk Grove (cdp)	20,916	17,763	-	15,175	-	-	17,945	-	18,929	-	-	-	-	46,432	-	-	-	-	-	-	-	-	-	14,690
Fair Oaks (cdp)	31,874	28,322	-	-	-	-	-	-	-	-	-	-	-	-	-	-	-	-	-	-	-	-	-	-
Florin (cdp)	14,606	11,760	-	15,059	-	-	10,850	-	16,982	-	-	9,741	-	-	-	-	-	-	-	-	-	-	-	6,802
Folsom (city)	30,210	38,850	-	43,883	-	-	36,153	-	35,141	-	-	-	-	-	-	-	-	-	-	-	-	-	-	-
Foothill Farms (cdp)	16,358	15,335	-	-	-	-	-	-	-	-	-	-	-	-	-	-	-	-	-	-	-	-	-	-
La Riviera (cdp)	24,034	22,653	-	-	-	-	-	-	-	-	-	-	-	-	-	-	-	-	-	-	-	-	-	-
Laguna (cdp)	25,280	22,537	-	18,390	-	-	23,045	-	23,129	-	-	-	-	37,940	-	-	-	-	-	-	-	-	-	17,766
North Highlands (cdp)	14,109	11,249	-	-	-	-	-	-	13,897	-	-	-	-	-	-	-	-	-	-	-	-	-	-	9,388
Parkway-S. Sacramento (cdp)	12,702	9,727	-	-	-	-	9,268	-	-	-	-	6,449	-	-	-	7,082	-	-	-	-	-	-	-	19,838
Rancho Cordova (cdp)	18,121	18,867	-	34,706	-	-	19,315	-	21,061	-	-	-	-	-	11,383	-	-	-	-	-	-	-	-	14,160
Rosemont (cdp)	19,467	15,846	-	-	-	-	-	-	15,329	-	-	-	-	-	15,443	-	-	-	-	-	-	-	-	10,059
Sacramento (city)	18,721	15,207	11,196	15,355	-	8,045	20,292	10,153	17,788	-	-	4,885	-	33,238	21,672	6,265	-	8,564	7,161	-	-	-	9,665	8,030
Vineyard (cdp)	24,178	21,138	-	-	-	-	-	-	18,833	-	-	-	-	-	-	-	-	-	-	-	-	-	-	-
San Benito County	20,932	27,272	-	-	-	-	-	-	30,473	-	-	-	-	-	-	-	-	-	-	-	-	-	-	-
San Bernardino County	16,856	19,557	12,580	22,291	-	12,555	21,300	-	21,383	18,350	22,071	-	15,762	27,045	19,694	9,269	-	19,806	7,924	-	18,562	15,847	8,750	12,484
Chino (city)	17,574	18,007	-	-	-	-	-	-	17,750	-	-	-	-	-	-	-	-	-	-	-	-	-	-	16,394
Chino Hills (city)	26,182	24,884	-	33,937	-	-	21,117	-	26,082	-	-	-	-	31,786	26,305	-	-	-	-	-	22,912	-	-	21,059
Colton (city)	13,460	17,117	-	-	-	-	-	-	14,229	-	-	-	-	-	-	-	-	-	-	-	-	-	-	-
Fontana (city)	14,208	18,092	15,326	15,124	-	-	-	-	19,903	-	-	-	-	-	-	-	-	-	-	-	-	-	-	-
Grand Terrace (city)	21,787	18,374	-	-	-	-	-	-	-	-	-	-	-	-	-	-	-	-	-	-	-	-	-	-
Highland (city)	16,039	15,797	-	-	-	-	-	-	17,027	-	-	-	-	-	-	-	-	-	-	-	-	-	-	8,833
Loma Linda (city)	20,189	20,720	-	25,549	-	-	20,396	-	18,969	-	-	-	13,205	-	21,268	-	-	-	-	-	-	-	-	-
Montclair (city)	13,556	12,673	-	-	-	-	-	-	-	-	-	-	-	-	-	-	-	-	-	-	-	-	-	10,741
Ontario (city)	14,244	17,259	9,161	15,451	-	-	24,340	-	21,418	-	-	-	-	-	-	-	-	-	-	-	-	-	-	11,267
Rancho Cucamonga (city)	23,702	24,467	-	24,293	-	-	24,339	-	25,391	-	-	-	-	34,171	20,241	-	-	-	-	-	-	-	-	19,695
Redlands (city)	24,237	22,666	-	23,770	-	-	26,457	-	28,842	-	-	-	-	-	20,319	-	-	-	-	-	-	-	-	-
Rialto (city)	13,375	19,360	11,535	-	-	-	-	-	21,706	-	-	-	-	-	-	-	-	-	-	-	-	-	-	-
San Bernardino (city)	12,925	10,925	12,017	10,439	-	5,584	10,348	-	16,019	-	-	-	7,845	-	16,060	-	-	-	8,430	-	-	-	-	7,796
Upland (city)	23,343	20,780	-	25,346	-	-	23,541	-	39,987	-	-	-	-	-	18,112	-	-	-	-	-	21,595	-	-	8,110
Victorville (city)	14,454	13,167	-	-	-	-	-	-	13,721	-	-	-	-	-	-	-	-	-	-	-	-	-	-	-
San Diego County	22,926	19,039	17,080	29,254	-	7,721	25,228	-	17,835	18,508	23,391	7,141	21,078	26,543	19,442	11,448	-	21,960	12,711	-	26,687	18,667	9,661	14,751
Bonita (cdp)	31,131	26,223	-	-	-	-	-	-	23,349	-	-	-	-	-	-	-	-	-	-	-	-	-	-	-
Carlsbad (city)	34,863	29,689	-	-	-	-	35,540	-	30,731	-	-	-	-	30,084	-	-	-	-	-	-	-	-	-	-
Chula Vista (city)	18,556	20,580	28,340	-	-	-	23,846	-	19,553	29,771	-	-	-	28,279	18,273	-	-	-	-	-	-	-	-	-
Coronado (city)	34,656	19,659	-	-	-	-	-	-	15,128	-	-	-	-	-	-	-	-	-	-	-	-	-	-	-
Escondido (city)	18,241	18,187	-	-	-	-	28,493	-	18,545	-	-	-	-	-	-	13,271	-	-	-	-	-	-	-	16,918
Imperial Beach (city)	16,003	23,588	-	-	-	-	-	-	22,183	-	-	-	-	-	-	-	-	-	-	-	-	-	-	-
La Mesa (city)	22,372	18,182	-	-	-	-	-	-	22,603	-	-	-	-	-	-	-	-	-	-	-	-	-	-	-

Notes: Please refer to the User's Guide for an explanation of data; data is arranged alphabetically by state, then county, then city within each county; table includes counties with populations greater than 49,999 unless noted and cities with populations greater than 9,999 whose Asian and/or NHPI population rates are greater than the national average; (1) Native Hawaiian and other Pacific Islander; (2) excludes Taiwanese; (3) includes Chamorro; (4) county does not meet population threshold but is shown in order to allow inclusion of city

Place	Total population	Total Asian population	Total NHPI[1] population	Asian Indian	Bangladeshi	Cambodian	Chinese[2]	Fijian	Filipino	Guamanian[3]	Hawaiian, Native	Hmong	Indonesian	Japanese	Korean	Laotian	Malaysian	Pakistani	Samoan	Sri Lankan	Taiwanese	Thai	Tongan	Vietnamese
La Presa (cdp)	15,998	15,714	-	-	-	-	-	-	15,948	-	-	-	-	-	-	-	-	-	-	-	-	-	-	-
Lemon Grove (city)	17,002	15,398	-	-	-	-	-	-	18,556	-	-	-	-	-	-	-	-	-	-	-	-	-	-	10,108
National City (city)	11,582	13,951	-	-	-	-	-	-	14,326	-	-	-	-	-	-	-	-	-	-	-	-	-	-	-
Oceanside (city)	20,329	18,376	14,486	-	-	-	21,359	-	16,771	-	-	-	-	24,549	-	-	-	-	14,011	-	-	-	-	15,793
Poway (city)	29,788	27,632	-	-	-	-	45,230	-	20,888	-	-	-	-	-	-	-	-	-	-	-	-	-	-	-
Rancho San Diego (cdp)	29,834	22,314	-	-	-	-	-	-	24,398	-	-	-	-	-	-	-	-	-	-	-	-	-	-	-
San Diego (city)	23,609	18,364	15,854	28,336	-	7,251	24,158	-	17,660	16,127	23,322	7,327	-	26,121	18,646	11,036	-	-	10,467	-	28,668	20,688	-	14,165
San Marcos (city)	18,657	19,146	-	-	-	-	20,344	-	16,451	-	-	-	-	-	-	-	-	-	-	-	-	-	-	-
Solana Beach (city)	48,547	40,493	-	-	-	-	-	-	-	-	-	-	-	-	-	-	-	-	-	-	-	-	-	-
Spring Valley (cdp)	19,504	19,272	-	-	-	-	-	-	21,738	-	-	-	-	-	-	-	-	-	-	-	-	-	-	-
Vista (city)	18,027	20,188	16,883	-	-	-	-	-	17,028	-	-	-	-	17,880	-	-	-	-	-	-	-	-	-	-
San Francisco County	34,556	22,357	12,476	40,986	-	15,481	21,272	-	21,125	-	-	-	17,975	36,223	30,471	-	-	27,818	7,359	-	28,898	24,511	-	15,160
San Francisco (city)	34,556	22,357	12,476	40,986	-	15,481	21,272	-	21,125	-	-	-	17,975	36,223	30,471	-	-	27,818	7,359	-	28,898	24,511	-	15,160
San Joaquin County	17,365	13,506	20,236	17,816	-	5,107	19,542	-	17,380	-	21,687	4,984	-	26,317	22,633	7,405	-	7,495	13,376	-	-	-	-	8,493
Lathrop (city)	16,032	16,428	-	-	-	-	-	-	16,296	-	-	-	-	-	-	-	-	-	-	-	-	-	-	-
Lodi (city)	18,719	18,844	-	13,432	-	-	-	-	33,539	-	-	-	-	23,681	-	-	-	-	-	-	-	-	-	-
Stockton (city)	15,405	11,578	15,730	15,516	-	4,945	18,254	-	15,820	-	-	4,932	-	27,830	-	7,318	-	8,920	-	-	-	-	-	7,406
Tracy (city)	21,397	22,072	-	24,634	-	-	22,850	-	21,735	-	-	-	-	-	-	-	-	-	-	-	-	-	-	-
San Luis Obispo County	21,864	16,552	-	26,960	-	-	14,068	-	14,425	-	-	-	-	25,596	12,722	-	-	-	-	-	-	-	-	-
Baywood-Los Osos (cdp)	24,838	12,004	-	-	-	-	-	-	12,538	-	-	-	-	-	-	-	-	-	-	-	-	-	-	-
Grover Beach (city)	18,812	17,370	-	-	-	-	-	-	-	-	-	-	-	-	-	-	-	-	-	-	-	-	-	-
San Luis Obispo (city)	20,386	14,689	-	-	-	-	11,101	-	9,171	-	-	-	-	-	-	-	-	-	-	-	-	-	-	-
San Mateo County	36,045	30,119	16,470	39,943	-	-	35,969	16,743	22,426	22,367	23,455	-	27,521	39,382	32,099	-	-	-	16,179	-	49,502	25,038	14,039	27,197
Belmont (city)	42,812	38,369	-	37,106	-	-	44,447	-	23,559	-	-	-	-	43,318	-	-	-	-	-	-	-	-	-	-
Burlingame (city)	43,565	35,849	-	-	-	-	35,260	-	37,572	-	-	-	-	47,107	-	-	-	-	-	-	-	-	-	-
Daly City (city)	21,900	21,626	16,635	27,158	-	-	24,907	-	19,743	-	-	-	-	30,952	22,181	-	-	-	-	-	-	-	-	20,902
East Palo Alto (city)	13,774	24,025	12,379	-	-	-	-	-	-	-	-	-	-	-	-	-	-	-	-	-	-	-	11,806	-
Foster City (city)	45,754	40,598	-	54,315	-	-	38,135	-	29,149	-	-	-	-	41,221	41,613	-	-	-	-	-	-	-	-	-
Hillsborough (town)	98,643	66,556	-	-	-	-	63,717	-	-	-	-	-	-	-	-	-	-	-	-	-	-	-	-	-
Menlo Park (city)	53,341	50,785	-	-	-	-	58,014	-	-	-	-	-	-	35,464	-	-	-	-	-	-	-	-	-	-
Millbrae (city)	33,193	27,296	-	35,907	-	-	26,556	-	23,594	-	-	-	-	35,181	26,333	-	-	-	-	-	-	-	-	-
Pacifica (city)	30,183	26,206	-	-	-	-	31,898	-	22,091	-	-	-	-	31,284	-	-	-	-	-	-	-	-	-	-
Redwood City (city)	34,042	39,621	20,505	39,746	-	-	45,592	-	33,439	-	-	-	-	44,011	-	-	-	-	-	-	-	-	-	-
San Bruno (city)	26,360	27,377	16,384	21,222	-	-	29,028	-	27,166	-	-	-	-	35,842	-	-	-	-	-	-	-	-	-	-
San Carlos (city)	46,628	55,839	-	-	-	-	56,493	-	-	-	-	-	-	-	-	-	-	-	-	-	-	-	10,657	-
San Mateo (city)	36,176	34,915	14,443	32,723	-	-	40,312	-	29,123	-	-	-	-	36,297	33,425	-	-	-	-	-	-	-	-	-
South San Francisco (city)	23,562	24,864	18,598	25,191	-	-	29,657	-	22,843	-	-	-	-	37,434	-	-	-	-	-	-	-	-	13,738	20,614
Santa Barbara County	23,059	18,441	19,145	29,236	-	-	18,921	-	17,841	-	-	6,722	-	25,713	15,146	-	-	-	-	-	-	-	-	13,876
Goleta (cdp)	28,890	20,545	-	-	-	-	25,836	-	20,014	-	-	-	-	29,871	-	-	-	-	-	-	-	-	-	13,400
Isla Vista (cdp)	7,644	7,010	-	-	-	-	6,987	-	-	-	-	-	-	-	6,518	-	-	-	-	-	-	-	-	-
Lompoc (city)	15,509	14,280	-	-	-	-	-	-	18,755	-	-	-	-	-	-	-	-	-	-	-	-	-	-	-

Notes: Please refer to the User's Guide for an explanation of data; data is arranged alphabetically by state, then county, then city within each county; table includes counties with populations greater than 49,999 unless noted and cities with populations greater than 9,999 whose Asian and/or NHPI population rates are greater than the national average; (1) Native Hawaiian and other Pacific Islander; (2) excludes Taiwanese; (3) includes Chamorro; (4) county does not meet population threshold but is shown in order to allow inclusion of city

Place	Total population	Total Asian population	Total NHPI[1] population	Asian Indian	Bangladeshi	Cambodian	Chinese[2]	Fijian	Filipino	Guamanian[3]	Hawaiian, Native	Hmong	Indonesian	Japanese	Korean	Laotian	Malaysian	Pakistani	Samoan	Sri Lankan	Taiwanese	Thai	Tongan	Vietnamese
Orcutt (cdp)	23,373	23,572	-	-	-	-	-	-	-	-	-	-	-	-	-	-	-	-	-	-	-	-	-	-
Santa Maria (city)	13,780	16,108	-	-	-	-	-	-	16,868	-	-	-	-	19,607	-	-	-	-	-	-	-	-	-	-
Santa Clara County	32,795	29,926	21,014	38,619	34,979	12,334	37,128	19,301	23,032	23,186	23,784	-	30,430	43,273	27,255	17,129	-	32,141	14,744	-	35,291	22,578	-	19,908
Alum Rock (cdp)	15,359	18,484	-	-	-	-	-	-	-	-	-	-	-	-	-	-	-	-	-	-	-	-	-	13,440
Campbell (city)	34,441	28,700	-	24,900	-	-	36,997	-	26,342	-	-	-	-	35,245	22,674	-	-	-	-	-	-	-	-	19,565
Cupertino (city)	44,749	37,784	-	41,625	-	-	41,012	-	36,393	-	-	-	-	40,885	22,386	-	-	-	-	-	28,848	-	-	26,094
Gilroy (city)	22,071	30,920	-	-	-	-	25,768	-	29,288	-	-	-	-	-	-	-	-	-	-	-	-	-	-	-
Los Altos (city)	66,776	60,680	-	83,270	-	-	55,655	-	-	-	-	-	-	55,318	-	-	-	-	-	-	-	-	-	-
Los Gatos (town)	56,094	44,325	-	-	-	-	49,034	-	-	-	-	-	-	35,402	-	-	-	-	-	-	-	-	-	-
Milpitas (city)	27,823	28,144	19,092	31,508	-	-	35,268	-	23,182	-	-	-	-	61,066	26,072	-	-	-	-	-	-	-	-	23,581
Morgan Hill (city)	33,047	46,219	-	-	-	-	53,129	-	-	-	-	-	-	37,184	-	-	-	-	-	-	-	-	-	-
Mountain View (city)	39,693	37,401	-	45,209	-	-	38,419	-	27,229	-	-	-	-	47,222	37,352	-	-	-	-	-	-	-	-	23,835
Palo Alto (city)	56,257	48,381	-	48,456	-	-	50,977	-	29,960	-	-	-	-	49,163	52,382	-	-	-	-	-	-	-	-	-
San Jose (city)	26,697	25,051	19,130	34,759	-	12,034	31,758	-	21,788	26,048	22,027	-	-	39,489	24,535	16,772	-	23,206	11,597	-	33,215	21,393	-	18,569
Santa Clara (city)	31,755	30,752	19,571	36,483	-	-	37,410	-	23,305	-	-	-	-	42,265	20,921	-	-	41,617	-	-	-	-	-	23,642
Saratoga (city)	65,400	50,043	-	56,009	-	-	48,623	-	-	-	-	-	-	65,996	44,579	-	-	-	-	-	37,878	-	-	-
Stanford (cdp)	22,443	13,802	-	10,680	-	-	17,084	-	-	-	-	-	-	-	5,489	-	-	-	-	-	-	-	-	-
Sunnyvale (city)	36,524	35,274	22,385	40,736	-	-	40,002	-	23,433	-	-	-	-	40,917	24,754	-	-	-	-	-	37,861	-	-	24,879
Santa Cruz County	26,396	26,472	-	43,616	-	-	26,059	-	19,800	-	-	-	-	32,364	17,074	-	-	-	-	-	-	-	-	20,569
Capitola (city)	27,609	18,491	-	-	-	-	-	-	-	-	-	-	-	-	-	-	-	-	-	-	-	-	-	-
Santa Cruz (city)	25,758	22,096	-	45,553	-	-	16,203	-	15,504	-	-	-	-	31,163	-	-	-	-	-	-	-	-	-	-
Scotts Valley (city)	35,684	36,363	-	-	-	-	-	-	-	-	-	-	-	-	-	-	-	-	-	-	-	-	-	-
Shasta County	17,738	13,487	-	-	-	-	-	-	17,242	-	-	-	-	-	-	4,876	-	-	-	-	-	-	-	-
Solano County	21,731	20,543	17,089	17,291	-	-	26,228	-	20,651	20,049	21,597	4,815	-	30,132	15,722	8,357	-	-	12,546	-	-	-	-	16,559
Benicia (city)	31,226	30,630	-	-	-	-	25,304	-	30,518	-	-	-	-	-	-	-	-	-	-	-	-	-	-	-
Fairfield (city)	20,617	19,578	19,132	18,997	-	-	29,524	-	20,465	22,266	-	-	-	18,769	12,406	9,638	-	-	-	-	-	-	-	-
Suisun City (city)	20,386	17,729	-	19,025	-	-	-	-	19,443	-	-	-	-	-	-	-	-	-	-	-	-	-	-	-
Vacaville (city)	21,557	23,046	-	-	-	-	-	-	19,290	-	-	-	-	-	-	-	-	-	-	-	-	-	-	-
Vallejo (city)	20,415	20,343	15,821	14,075	-	-	24,742	-	20,517	20,313	-	-	-	28,382	-	-	-	-	-	-	-	-	-	12,795
Sonoma County	25,724	21,533	19,283	19,656	-	7,250	30,998	-	23,011	-	-	-	-	26,576	21,963	11,746	-	-	-	-	-	-	-	16,541
Petaluma (city)	27,087	24,205	-	-	-	-	29,858	-	-	-	-	-	-	-	-	-	-	-	-	-	-	-	-	-
Rohnert Park (city)	23,035	19,991	-	-	-	-	22,094	-	20,023	-	-	-	-	-	-	-	-	-	-	-	-	-	-	-
Santa Rosa (city)	24,495	18,135	-	16,742	-	6,515	31,801	-	18,859	-	-	-	-	23,891	-	12,306	-	-	-	-	-	-	-	15,156
Stanislaus County	16,913	15,658	9,656	14,430	-	6,225	23,544	9,538	21,528	-	-	4,376	-	34,017	-	6,950	-	-	-	-	-	-	-	23,558
Ceres (city)	14,420	16,675	-	15,286	-	-	-	-	-	-	-	-	-	-	-	-	-	-	-	-	-	-	-	-
Modesto (city)	17,797	14,824	9,534	15,592	-	5,986	21,942	9,358	22,110	-	-	4,094	-	35,774	-	6,687	-	-	-	-	-	-	-	22,147
Salida (cdp)	18,173	21,291	-	-	-	-	-	-	-	-	-	-	-	-	-	-	-	-	-	-	-	-	-	-
Turlock (city)	16,844	16,333	-	11,606	-	-	-	-	-	-	-	-	-	-	-	-	-	-	-	-	-	-	-	-
Sutter County	17,428	14,013	-	11,844	-	-	-	-	18,355	-	-	-	-	27,487	-	-	-	-	-	-	-	-	-	-
South Yuba City (cdp)	21,423	12,711	-	11,850	-	-	-	-	-	-	-	-	-	-	-	-	-	-	-	-	-	-	-	-
Yuba City (city)	15,928	16,037	-	10,931	-	-	-	-	-	-	-	-	-	-	-	-	-	-	-	-	-	-	-	-

Notes: Please refer to the User's Guide for an explanation of data; data is arranged alphabetically by state, then county, then city within each county; table includes counties with populations greater than 49,999 unless noted and cities with populations greater than 9,999 whose Asian and/or NHPI population rates are greater than the national average; (1) Native Hawaiian and other Pacific Islander; (2) excludes Taiwanese; (3) includes Chamorro; (4) county does not meet population threshold but is shown in order to allow inclusion of city

Place	Total population	Total Asian population	Total NHPI[1] population	Asian Indian	Bangladeshi	Cambodian	Chinese[2]	Fijian	Filipino	Guamanian[3]	Hawaiian, Native	Hmong	Indonesian	Japanese	Korean	Laotian	Malaysian	Pakistani	Samoan	Sri Lankan	Taiwanese	Thai	Tongan	Vietnamese
Tehama County	15,793	21,792	-	-	-	-	-	-	-	-	-	-	-	-	-	-	-	-	-	-	-	-	-	-
Tulare County	14,006	11,418	-	15,956	-	-	17,732	-	12,537	-	-	3,833	-	26,818	15,293	5,261	-	-	-	-	-	-	-	-
Porterville (city)	12,745	12,032	-	-	-	-	-	-	13,608	-	-	-	-	-	-	-	-	-	-	-	-	-	-	-
Visalia (city)	18,422	10,591	-	-	-	-	-	-	17,182	-	-	3,308	-	-	-	5,151	-	-	-	-	-	-	-	-
Tuolumne County	21,015	27,335	-	-	-	-	-	-	-	-	-	-	-	-	-	-	-	-	-	-	-	-	-	-
Ventura County	24,600	26,188	18,766	32,052	-	-	35,070	-	19,767	-	24,314	-	-	35,749	25,763	-	-	-	13,158	-	29,587	-	-	19,638
Camarillo (city)	28,635	27,183	-	-	-	-	34,399	-	25,417	-	-	-	-	30,677	18,320	-	-	-	-	-	-	-	-	21,965
Moorpark (city)	25,383	39,480	-	-	-	-	-	-	-	-	-	-	-	-	-	-	-	-	-	-	-	-	-	-
Oxnard (city)	15,288	18,235	16,649	12,543	-	-	21,719	-	17,303	-	-	-	-	22,497	21,525	-	-	-	11,872	-	-	-	-	16,153
Port Hueneme (city)	17,311	17,557	-	-	-	-	-	-	17,075	-	-	-	-	-	-	-	-	-	-	-	-	-	-	-
Simi Valley (city)	26,586	27,252	-	30,888	-	-	26,758	-	24,951	-	-	-	-	37,398	30,442	-	-	-	-	-	-	-	-	17,359
Thousand Oaks (city)	34,314	37,446	-	34,603	-	-	41,835	-	25,915	-	-	-	-	54,147	34,510	-	-	-	-	-	-	-	-	22,727
Yolo County	19,365	13,837	11,064	12,198	-	-	14,509	6,557	19,979	-	-	3,251	-	23,848	11,742	5,254	-	-	-	-	-	-	-	7,625
Davis (city)	22,937	14,535	-	17,039	-	-	14,306	-	15,804	-	-	-	-	25,474	12,881	-	-	-	-	-	-	-	-	5,641
West Sacramento (city)	15,245	9,073	-	8,304	-	-	-	-	-	-	-	3,085	-	-	-	-	-	-	-	-	-	-	-	-
Woodland (city)	18,042	14,672	-	9,374	-	-	-	-	-	-	-	-	-	-	-	-	-	-	-	-	-	-	-	-
Yuba County	14,124	8,485	-	-	-	-	-	-	16,278	-	-	6,358	-	-	-	-	-	-	-	-	-	-	-	-
Linda (cdp)	9,826	6,897	-	-	-	-	-	-	-	-	-	6,701	-	-	-	-	-	-	-	-	-	-	-	-
Marysville (city)	15,315	9,657	-	-	-	-	-	-	-	-	-	-	-	-	-	-	-	-	-	-	-	-	-	-
Olivehurst (cdp)	12,020	7,981	-	-	-	-	-	-	-	-	-	-	-	-	-	-	-	-	-	-	-	-	-	-
COLORADO	24,049	20,958	16,314	30,580	-	12,241	23,898	-	20,037	16,276	18,272	10,400	14,208	27,528	18,076	14,002	-	19,396	14,292	-	21,721	16,202	-	15,395
Adams County	19,944	17,044	-	25,485	-	-	21,953	-	24,392	-	-	10,841	-	25,644	17,381	13,642	-	-	-	-	-	-	-	13,227
Berkley (cdp)	17,295	11,381	-	-	-	-	-	-	-	-	-	-	-	-	-	-	-	-	-	-	-	-	-	-
Federal Heights (city)	16,801	15,584	-	-	-	-	-	-	-	-	-	-	-	-	-	-	-	-	-	-	-	-	-	-
Westminster (city)	25,482	19,076	-	23,304	-	-	22,580	-	-	-	-	10,945	-	-	22,104	13,396	-	-	-	-	-	-	-	13,678
Arapahoe County	28,147	21,775	22,295	23,131	-	-	22,905	-	19,046	-	-	-	-	30,989	20,357	-	-	-	-	-	-	-	-	21,141
Aurora (city)	21,095	17,520	16,872	17,083	-	15,516	16,890	-	18,630	-	-	-	-	26,201	15,633	-	-	-	-	-	-	-	-	17,808
Boulder County	28,976	23,816	-	41,322	-	-	26,023	-	19,660	-	-	-	-	29,381	14,272	-	-	-	-	-	-	-	-	16,859
Boulder (city)	27,262	18,565	-	32,358	-	-	22,748	-	-	-	-	-	-	21,743	12,014	-	-	-	-	-	-	-	-	-
Broomfield (city)	26,488	21,755	-	-	-	-	29,765	-	-	-	-	-	-	-	-	-	-	-	-	-	-	-	-	-
Lafayette (city)	27,780	22,666	-	-	-	-	-	-	-	-	-	-	-	-	-	-	-	-	-	-	-	-	-	-
Denver County	24,101	18,769	12,867	26,455	-	9,316	24,338	-	21,992	-	-	-	-	25,171	23,103	-	-	-	-	-	-	14,595	-	11,955
Douglas County	34,848	29,418	-	36,835	-	-	29,127	-	-	-	-	-	-	-	27,189	-	-	-	-	-	-	-	-	-
Highlands Ranch (cdp)	34,707	29,604	-	37,051	-	-	29,238	-	-	-	-	-	-	-	-	-	-	-	-	-	-	-	-	-
El Paso County	22,005	19,921	15,113	31,961	-	-	26,216	-	16,794	18,682	-	-	-	20,644	15,816	-	-	-	-	-	-	-	-	15,500
Colorado Springs (city)	22,496	20,402	13,704	32,707	-	-	24,813	-	16,478	-	-	-	-	21,869	16,905	-	-	-	-	-	-	-	-	14,487
Jefferson County	28,066	22,457	21,412	38,761	-	-	19,108	-	22,514	-	-	11,037	-	33,972	19,701	14,096	-	-	-	-	-	-	-	15,120
Larimer County	23,689	22,111	-	31,463	-	-	24,602	-	-	-	-	-	-	23,203	8,156	-	-	-	-	-	-	-	-	-
Mesa County	18,715	14,939	-	-	-	-	-	-	-	-	-	-	-	-	-	-	-	-	-	-	-	-	-	-
Pueblo County	17,163	22,055	-	-	-	-	-	-	-	-	-	-	-	-	-	-	-	-	-	-	-	-	-	-
Weld County	18,957	16,823	-	-	-	-	-	-	-	-	-	-	-	23,302	-	-	-	-	-	-	-	-	-	-

Notes: Please refer to the User's Guide for an explanation of data; data is arranged alphabetically by state, then county, then city within each county; table includes counties with populations greater than 49,999 unless noted and cities with populations greater than 9,999 whose Asian and/or NHPI population rates are greater than the national average; (1) Native Hawaiian and other Pacific Islander; (2) excludes Taiwanese; (3) includes Chamorro; (4) county does not meet population threshold but is shown in order to allow inclusion of city

Place	Total population	Total Asian population	Total NHPI[1] population	Asian Indian	Bangladeshi	Cambodian	Chinese[2]	Fijian	Filipino	Guamanian[3]	Hawaiian, Native	Hmong	Indonesian	Japanese	Korean	Laotian	Malaysian	Pakistani	Samoan	Sri Lankan	Taiwanese	Thai	Tongan	Vietnamese
CONNECTICUT	28,766	27,948	18,345	33,234	20,172	17,016	30,673	-	26,690	19,263	-	-	-	35,833	23,528	16,180	-	22,521	-	-	19,531	20,725	-	17,396
Fairfield County	38,350	37,087	-	45,228	-	16,893	45,523	-	27,866	-	-	-	-	38,952	38,901	17,244	-	21,761	-	-	-	-	-	18,419
Danbury (city)	24,500	24,940	-	27,079	-	13,770	34,205	-	-	-	-	-	-	-	-	-	-	-	-	-	-	-	-	-
Greenwich (town)	74,346	55,416	-	93,678	-	-	55,836	-	-	-	-	-	-	32,399	-	-	-	-	-	-	-	-	-	-
Stamford (city)	34,987	36,026	-	36,160	-	-	47,953	-	23,508	-	-	-	-	-	-	-	-	-	-	-	-	-	-	-
Hartford County	26,047	23,475	-	25,644	-	-	28,168	-	29,295	-	-	-	-	37,285	19,522	15,406	-	20,195	-	-	-	-	-	16,065
East Hartford (town)	21,763	16,022	-	15,216	-	-	-	-	-	-	-	-	-	-	-	-	-	-	-	-	-	-	-	15,701
Farmington (town)	39,102	31,207	-	-	-	-	-	-	-	-	-	-	-	-	-	-	-	-	-	-	-	-	-	-
Glastonbury (town)	40,820	33,284	-	31,840	-	-	-	-	-	-	-	-	-	-	-	-	-	-	-	-	-	-	-	-
Rocky Hill (town)	29,701	29,466	-	-	-	-	-	-	-	-	-	-	-	-	-	-	-	-	-	-	-	-	-	-
South Windsor (town)	30,966	23,848	-	-	-	-	-	-	-	-	-	-	-	-	-	-	-	-	-	-	-	-	-	-
West Hartford (town)	33,468	22,070	-	20,065	-	-	30,095	-	-	-	-	-	-	-	-	-	-	-	-	-	-	-	-	17,103
Litchfield County	28,408	19,731	-	28,780	-	-	17,847	-	-	-	-	-	-	-	10,889	-	-	-	-	-	-	-	-	14,619
Middlesex County	28,251	23,310	-	26,227	-	-	20,219	-	-	-	-	-	-	-	-	-	-	-	-	-	-	-	-	-
New Haven County	24,439	23,585	-	27,153	-	-	23,655	-	24,965	-	-	-	-	31,402	18,638	15,626	-	16,992	-	-	-	-	-	20,634
New Haven (city)	16,393	17,917	-	22,190	-	-	15,488	-	-	-	-	-	-	-	11,458	-	-	-	-	-	-	-	-	-
New London County	24,678	24,952	-	33,833	-	-	25,221	-	23,146	-	-	-	-	-	-	-	-	-	-	-	-	-	-	-
Tolland County	25,474	19,239	-	24,426	-	-	15,026	-	-	-	-	-	-	-	-	-	-	-	-	-	-	-	-	-
Mansfield (town)	18,094	12,461	-	18,224	-	-	8,598	-	-	-	-	-	-	-	-	-	-	-	-	-	-	-	-	-
Storrs (cdp)	9,947	6,831	-	-	-	-	7,058	-	-	-	-	-	-	-	-	-	-	-	-	-	-	-	-	-
Windham County	20,443	13,962	-	-	-	-	-	-	-	-	-	-	-	-	-	-	-	-	-	-	-	-	-	-
DELAWARE	23,305	28,411	16,281	33,056	-	-	28,813	-	32,429	-	-	-	-	21,235	22,575	-	-	30,615	-	-	-	-	-	21,857
Kent County	18,662	20,995	-	46,421	-	-	-	-	20,077	-	-	-	-	-	-	-	-	-	-	-	-	-	-	-
New Castle County	25,413	30,134	-	32,692	-	-	30,219	-	37,700	-	-	-	-	24,178	26,179	-	-	-	-	-	-	-	-	25,206
Hockessin (cdp)	40,516	67,211	-	-	-	-	-	-	-	-	-	-	-	-	-	-	-	-	-	-	-	-	-	-
Newark (city)	20,376	17,367	-	-	-	-	17,519	-	-	-	-	-	-	-	-	-	-	-	-	-	-	-	-	-
Pike Creek (cdp)	32,939	30,874	-	-	-	-	-	-	-	-	-	-	-	-	-	-	-	-	-	-	-	-	-	-
Sussex County	20,328	19,190	-	-	-	-	-	-	-	-	-	-	-	-	-	-	-	-	-	-	-	-	-	-
DISTRICT OF COLUMBIA	28,659	27,162	-	41,209	-	-	27,447	-	23,532	-	-	-	-	32,873	27,307	-	-	-	-	-	-	-	-	20,618
FLORIDA	21,557	20,429	15,251	24,363	11,343	12,325	21,313	-	20,901	14,108	16,057	-	20,935	22,113	16,577	13,014	-	20,603	15,628	43,144	40,339	17,104	-	14,962
Alachua County	18,465	16,659	-	19,398	-	-	14,240	-	19,853	-	-	-	-	18,282	8,958	-	-	-	-	-	-	-	-	15,805
Gainesville (city)	16,779	12,149	-	14,123	-	-	10,383	-	-	-	-	-	-	-	7,384	-	-	-	-	-	-	-	-	-
Bay County	18,700	13,995	-	-	-	-	-	-	11,480	-	-	-	-	-	-	-	-	-	-	-	-	-	-	8,841
Callaway (city)	16,102	9,226	-	-	-	-	-	-	-	-	-	-	-	-	-	-	-	-	-	-	-	-	-	-
Brevard County	21,484	19,087	-	23,246	-	-	17,910	-	16,420	-	-	-	-	17,682	18,074	-	-	-	-	-	-	-	-	17,474
Broward County	23,170	20,147	19,375	20,230	-	-	21,094	-	24,606	-	-	-	-	24,222	15,533	-	-	13,943	-	-	-	16,263	-	18,109
Cooper City (city)	27,474	22,066	-	22,102	-	-	-	-	-	-	-	-	-	-	-	-	-	-	-	-	-	-	-	-
Pembroke Pines (city)	23,843	21,611	-	22,365	-	-	18,843	-	25,764	-	-	-	-	-	-	-	-	-	-	-	-	-	-	-
Charlotte County	21,806	20,973	-	-	-	-	-	-	-	-	-	-	-	-	-	-	-	-	-	-	-	-	-	-
Citrus County	18,585	34,576	-	-	-	-	-	-	-	-	-	-	-	-	-	-	-	-	-	-	-	-	-	-
Clay County	20,868	18,699	-	-	-	-	-	-	20,396	-	-	-	-	-	-	-	-	-	-	-	-	-	-	-

Notes: Please refer to the User's Guide for an explanation of data; data is arranged alphabetically by state, then county, then city within each county; table includes counties with populations greater than 49,999 unless noted and cities with populations greater than 9,999 whose Asian and/or NHPI population rates are greater than the national average; (1) Native Hawaiian and other Pacific Islander; (2) excludes Taiwanese; (3) includes Chamorro; (4) county does not meet population threshold but is shown in order to allow inclusion of city

Place	Total population	Total Asian population	Total NHPI[1] population	Asian Indian	Bangladeshi	Cambodian	Chinese[2]	Fijian	Filipino	Guamanian[3]	Hawaiian, Native	Hmong	Indonesian	Japanese	Korean	Laotian	Malaysian	Pakistani	Samoan	Sri Lankan	Taiwanese	Thai	Tongan	Vietnamese
Bellair-Meadowbrook Ter. (cdp)	21,095	23,173	-	-	-	-	-	-	-	-	-	-	-	-	-	-	-	-	-	-	-	-	-	-
Collier County	31,195	33,926	-	-	-	-	-	-	-	-	-	-	-	-	-	-	-	-	-	-	-	-	-	-
Columbia County	14,598	19,896	-	-	-	-	-	-	-	-	-	-	-	-	-	-	-	-	-	-	-	-	-	-
Duval County	20,753	19,721	15,447	29,720	-	11,706	22,730	-	19,817	-	-	-	-	14,698	14,941	-	-	-	-	-	-	-	-	13,540
Escambia County	18,641	15,540	-	19,732	-	-	23,954	-	15,163	-	-	-	-	-	-	-	-	-	-	-	-	-	-	9,134
Bellview (cdp)	18,173	12,806	-	-	-	-	-	-	15,612	-	-	-	-	-	-	-	-	-	-	-	-	-	-	-
Myrtle Grove (cdp)	18,268	11,260	-	-	-	-	-	-	13,996	-	-	-	-	-	-	-	-	-	-	-	-	-	-	-
Hernando County	18,321	23,110	-	-	-	-	-	-	-	-	-	-	-	-	-	-	-	-	-	-	-	-	-	-
Highlands County	17,222	25,879	-	-	-	-	-	-	31,556	-	-	-	-	-	-	-	-	-	-	-	-	-	-	-
Hillsborough County	21,812	20,690	17,270	28,174	-	-	21,060	-	20,375	-	-	-	-	19,906	18,563	-	-	-	-	-	-	17,085	-	12,130
Westchase (cdp)	37,630	19,745	-	-	-	-	-	-	-	-	-	-	-	-	-	-	-	-	-	-	-	-	-	-
Indian River County	27,227	28,557	-	-	-	-	-	-	-	-	-	-	-	-	-	-	-	-	-	-	-	-	-	-
Lake County	20,199	21,089	-	-	-	-	-	-	-	-	-	-	-	-	-	-	-	-	-	-	-	-	-	-
Lee County	24,542	17,908	-	22,339	-	-	19,205	-	18,579	-	-	-	-	-	-	-	-	-	-	-	-	-	-	-
Leon County	21,024	22,009	-	30,481	-	-	24,031	-	13,619	-	-	-	-	-	16,709	-	-	-	-	-	-	-	-	-
Manatee County	22,388	18,041	-	-	-	-	-	-	21,237	-	-	-	-	-	-	-	-	-	-	-	-	-	-	-
Marion County	17,848	19,852	-	25,928	-	-	-	-	-	-	-	-	-	-	-	-	-	-	-	-	-	-	-	-
Martin County	29,584	18,328	-	-	-	-	-	-	-	-	-	-	-	-	-	-	-	-	-	-	-	-	-	-
Miami-Dade County	18,497	21,336	16,570	20,039	-	-	20,553	-	23,913	-	-	-	-	47,220	19,982	-	-	19,747	-	-	-	19,015	-	16,236
Doral (cdp)	27,705	23,653	-	-	-	-	-	-	-	-	-	-	-	-	-	-	-	-	-	-	-	-	-	-
Ives Estates (cdp)	19,118	18,795	-	-	-	-	-	-	-	-	-	-	-	-	-	-	-	-	-	-	-	-	-	-
North Miami Beach (city)	14,699	14,597	-	8,817	-	-	19,120	-	-	-	-	-	-	-	-	-	-	-	-	-	-	-	-	-
Pinecrest (village)	51,181	58,647	-	-	-	-	-	-	-	-	-	-	-	-	-	-	-	-	-	-	-	-	-	-
Monroe County	26,102	21,969	-	-	-	-	-	-	-	-	-	-	-	-	-	-	-	-	-	-	-	-	-	-
Nassau County	22,836	13,991	-	-	-	-	-	-	-	-	-	-	-	-	-	-	-	-	-	-	-	-	-	-
Okaloosa County	20,918	15,213	-	-	-	-	-	-	14,849	-	-	-	-	-	13,818	-	-	-	-	-	-	11,397	-	17,425
Wright (cdp)	18,746	15,114	-	-	-	-	-	-	-	-	-	-	-	-	-	-	-	-	-	-	-	-	-	-
Orange County	20,916	20,259	13,933	23,770	-	-	20,860	-	19,048	-	-	-	-	18,295	18,071	-	-	23,458	-	-	-	-	-	17,443
Oak Ridge (cdp)	12,347	11,530	-	-	-	-	-	-	-	-	-	-	-	-	-	-	-	-	-	-	-	-	-	11,864
Osceola County	17,022	19,318	-	9,148	-	-	33,080	-	23,791	-	-	-	-	-	-	-	-	-	-	-	-	-	-	-
Palm Beach County	28,801	23,964	17,329	26,198	-	-	22,400	-	26,303	-	-	-	-	20,400	22,165	-	-	-	-	-	-	14,587	-	16,834
Pasco County	18,439	21,713	-	25,124	-	-	16,405	-	21,928	-	-	-	-	-	-	-	-	-	-	-	-	-	-	-
Pinellas County	23,497	19,028	-	31,591	-	10,582	19,729	-	19,797	-	-	-	-	17,260	16,234	11,534	-	-	-	-	-	16,847	-	14,143
Pinellas Park (city)	18,701	14,175	-	-	-	-	-	-	-	-	-	-	-	-	-	-	-	-	-	-	-	-	-	15,915
Polk County	18,302	18,106	-	18,923	-	-	17,818	-	25,142	-	-	-	-	-	-	16,796	-	-	-	-	-	-	-	12,065
Putnam County	15,603	32,782	-	-	-	-	-	-	-	-	-	-	-	-	-	-	-	-	-	-	-	-	-	-
St. Johns County	28,674	40,366	-	-	-	-	-	-	-	-	-	-	-	-	-	-	-	-	-	-	-	-	-	-
St. Lucie County	18,790	19,054	-	-	-	-	-	-	-	-	-	-	-	-	-	-	-	-	-	-	-	-	-	-
Santa Rosa County	20,089	22,558	-	-	-	-	-	-	11,037	-	-	-	-	-	-	-	-	-	-	-	-	-	-	-
Sarasota County	28,326	19,140	-	-	-	-	22,142	-	18,028	-	-	-	-	-	-	-	-	-	-	-	-	-	-	12,661
Seminole County	24,591	24,961	-	31,121	-	-	23,797	-	25,876	-	-	-	-	-	16,430	-	-	-	-	-	-	-	-	21,038

Notes: Please refer to the User's Guide for an explanation of data; data is arranged alphabetically by state, then county, then city within each county; table includes counties with populations greater than 49,999 unless noted and cities with populations greater than 9,999 whose Asian and/or NHPI population rates are greater than the national average; (1) Native Hawaiian and other Pacific Islander; (2) excludes Taiwanese; (3) includes Chamorro; (4) county does not meet population threshold but is shown in order to allow inclusion of city

Place	Total population	Total Asian population	Total NHPI[1] population	Asian Indian	Bangladeshi	Cambodian	Chinese[2]	Fijian	Filipino	Guamanian[3]	Hawaiian, Native	Hmong	Indonesian	Japanese	Korean	Laotian	Malaysian	Pakistani	Samoan	Sri Lankan	Taiwanese	Thai	Tongan	Vietnamese
Volusia County	19,664	20,853	-	25,792	-	-	18,972	-	22,985	-	-	-	-	-	13,006	-	-	-	-	-	-	-	-	-
GEORGIA	21,154	20,155	15,333	24,917	15,316	13,843	22,718	-	20,910	16,385	17,974	10,712	13,792	25,799	17,180	14,323	-	20,927	13,243	-	35,996	23,004	-	14,029
Bartow County	18,989	20,359	-	-	-	-	-	-	-	-	-	-	-	-	-	-	-	-	-	-	-	-	-	-
Bibb County	19,058	22,249	-	-	-	-	-	-	-	-	-	-	-	-	-	-	-	-	-	-	-	-	-	-
Bulloch County	16,080	23,158	-	-	-	-	-	-	-	-	-	-	-	-	-	-	-	-	-	-	-	-	-	-
Carroll County	17,656	11,528	-	-	-	-	-	-	-	-	-	-	-	-	-	-	-	-	-	-	-	-	-	-
Catoosa County	18,009	16,326	-	-	-	-	-	-	-	-	-	-	-	-	-	-	-	-	-	-	-	-	-	-
Chatham County	21,152	16,407	-	16,257	-	-	21,271	-	-	-	-	-	-	-	9,174	-	-	-	-	-	-	-	-	13,761
Cherokee County	24,871	21,573	-	23,393	-	-	-	-	-	-	-	-	-	-	-	-	-	-	-	-	-	-	-	-
Clarke County	17,123	13,068	-	17,854	-	-	12,610	-	-	-	-	-	-	-	5,222	-	-	-	-	-	-	-	-	-
Clayton County	18,079	14,237	-	21,183	-	13,505	10,896	-	-	-	-	-	-	-	-	13,695	-	14,256	-	-	-	-	-	13,554
Forest Park (city)	14,932	13,172	-	-	-	-	-	-	-	-	-	-	-	-	-	-	-	-	-	-	-	-	-	13,732
Riverdale (city)	15,377	12,441	-	-	-	-	-	-	-	-	-	-	-	-	-	-	-	-	-	-	-	-	-	11,913
Cobb County	27,863	24,247	-	27,948	-	-	24,313	-	24,190	-	-	-	-	40,265	22,056	-	-	19,416	-	-	-	-	-	16,280
Smyrna (city)	27,637	23,575	-	25,250	-	-	-	-	-	-	-	-	-	-	-	-	-	-	-	-	-	-	-	-
Columbia County	23,496	19,510	-	21,045	-	-	22,454	-	-	-	-	-	-	-	13,400	-	-	-	-	-	-	-	-	-
Martinez (cdp)	26,734	17,705	-	19,658	-	-	-	-	-	-	-	-	-	-	-	-	-	-	-	-	-	-	-	-
Coweta County	21,949	17,530	-	-	-	-	-	-	-	-	-	-	-	-	-	-	-	-	-	-	-	-	-	-
DeKalb County	23,968	19,422	-	23,367	15,366	15,339	21,405	-	22,571	-	-	-	-	30,896	17,201	-	-	-	-	-	-	-	-	12,881
Druid Hills (cdp)	34,829	12,651	-	-	-	-	-	-	-	-	-	-	-	-	-	-	-	-	-	-	-	-	-	-
Dunwoody (cdp)	43,523	31,373	-	33,991	-	-	-	-	-	-	-	-	-	-	23,649	-	-	-	-	-	-	-	-	-
North Atlanta (cdp)	32,087	27,713	-	-	-	-	-	-	-	-	-	-	-	-	-	-	-	-	-	-	-	-	-	-
North Decatur (cdp)	33,739	17,206	-	-	-	-	-	-	-	-	-	-	-	-	-	-	-	-	-	-	-	-	-	-
North Druid Hills (cdp)	33,288	22,329	-	21,767	-	-	-	-	-	-	-	-	-	-	-	-	-	-	-	-	-	-	-	-
Tucker (cdp)	28,318	20,472	-	-	-	-	-	-	-	-	-	-	-	-	-	-	-	-	-	-	-	-	-	15,562
Dougherty County	16,645	16,484	-	-	-	-	-	-	-	-	-	-	-	-	-	-	-	-	-	-	-	-	-	-
Douglas County	21,172	21,670	-	-	-	-	-	-	-	-	-	-	-	-	-	-	-	-	-	-	-	-	-	-
Fayette County	29,464	22,924	-	-	-	-	-	-	-	-	-	-	-	30,814	-	-	-	-	-	-	-	-	-	-
Peachtree City (city)	31,667	26,365	-	-	-	-	-	-	-	-	-	-	-	31,305	-	-	-	-	-	-	-	-	-	-
Floyd County	17,808	16,306	-	19,683	-	-	-	-	-	-	-	-	-	-	-	-	-	-	-	-	-	-	-	-
Forsyth County	29,114	38,507	-	-	-	-	-	-	-	-	-	-	-	-	-	-	-	-	-	-	-	-	-	-
Fulton County	30,003	24,950	-	29,449	-	-	25,949	-	26,468	-	-	-	-	31,348	21,569	-	-	-	-	-	-	-	-	15,240
Alpharetta (city)	39,432	32,842	-	37,055	-	-	31,518	-	-	-	-	-	-	-	-	-	-	-	-	-	-	-	-	-
Roswell (city)	36,012	24,379	-	33,163	-	-	25,563	-	-	-	-	-	-	-	16,324	-	-	-	-	-	-	-	-	-
Glynn County	21,707	20,972	-	-	-	-	-	-	-	-	-	-	-	-	-	-	-	-	-	-	-	-	-	-
Gwinnett County	25,006	20,536	17,184	24,390	-	11,536	26,622	-	25,170	-	-	-	-	20,961	17,653	18,913	-	17,195	-	-	57,843	-	-	14,665
Duluth (city)	29,185	21,517	-	27,488	-	-	21,331	-	-	-	-	-	-	-	21,171	-	-	-	-	-	-	-	-	-
Lilburn (city)	22,503	17,223	-	18,352	-	-	-	-	-	-	-	-	-	-	-	-	-	-	-	-	-	-	-	11,016
Mountain Park (cdp)	28,454	48,064	-	41,964	-	-	-	-	-	-	-	-	-	-	-	-	-	-	-	-	-	-	-	-
Hall County	19,690	12,115	-	-	-	-	-	-	-	-	-	-	-	-	-	-	-	-	-	-	-	-	-	8,660
Henry County	22,945	22,376	-	31,390	-	-	-	-	-	-	-	-	-	-	-	-	-	-	-	-	-	-	-	-

Notes: Please refer to the User's Guide for an explanation of data; data is arranged alphabetically by state, then county, then city within each county; table includes counties with populations greater than 49,999 unless noted and cities with populations greater than 9,999 whose Asian and/or NHPI population rates are greater than the national average; (1) Native Hawaiian and other Pacific Islander; (2) excludes Taiwanese; (3) includes Chamorro; (4) county does not meet population threshold but is shown in order to allow inclusion of city

Place	Total population	Total Asian population	Total NHPI[1] population	Asian Indian	Bangladeshi	Cambodian	Chinese[2]	Fijian	Filipino	Guamanian[3]	Hawaiian, Native	Hmong	Indonesian	Japanese	Korean	Laotian	Malaysian	Pakistani	Samoan	Sri Lankan	Taiwanese	Thai	Tongan	Vietnamese
Houston County	19,515	15,087	-	-	-	-	-	-	12,025	-	-	-	-	-	-	-	-	-	-	-	-	-	-	-
Liberty County	13,855	9,824	-	-	-	-	-	-	-	-	-	-	-	-	6,968	-	-	-	-	-	-	-	-	-
Lowndes County	16,683	12,390	-	-	-	-	-	-	-	-	-	-	-	-	-	-	-	-	-	-	-	-	-	-
Muscogee County	18,262	18,786	11,761	27,486	-	-	18,320	-	17,447	-	-	-	-	-	8,211	-	-	-	-	-	-	-	-	-
Columbus (sp. city)	18,276	18,786	11,761	27,486	-	-	18,320	-	17,447	-	-	-	-	-	8,211	-	-	-	-	-	-	-	-	-
Newton County	19,317	14,588	-	-	-	-	-	-	-	-	-	-	-	-	-	-	-	-	-	-	-	-	-	-
Richmond County	17,088	17,343	-	27,397	-	-	13,108	-	-	-	-	-	-	-	14,437	-	-	-	-	-	-	-	-	-
Rockdale County	22,300	22,882	-	-	-	-	-	-	-	-	-	-	-	-	-	-	-	-	-	-	-	-	-	-
Spalding County	16,791	13,105	-	-	-	-	-	-	-	-	-	-	-	-	-	-	-	-	-	-	-	-	-	-
Troup County	17,626	21,448	-	-	-	-	-	-	-	-	-	-	-	-	-	-	-	-	-	-	-	-	-	-
Walton County	19,470	21,808	-	-	-	-	-	-	-	-	-	-	-	-	-	-	-	-	-	-	-	-	-	-
Whitfield County	18,515	15,726	-	-	-	-	-	-	-	-	-	-	-	-	-	-	-	-	-	-	-	-	-	-
HAWAII	21,525	22,884	14,375	29,742	-	6,649	27,259	-	16,426	16,745	16,071	-	-	29,257	18,447	8,669	-	-	10,537	-	26,021	13,263	11,953	12,124
Hawaii County	18,791	20,915	12,619	-	-	-	21,393	-	14,746	-	13,516	-	-	25,449	19,697	-	-	-	12,741	-	-	-	-	-
Hilo (cdp)	18,220	23,740	10,653	-	-	-	25,135	-	16,547	-	11,688	-	-	25,589	23,121	-	-	-	-	-	-	-	-	-
Honolulu County	21,998	23,317	14,748	28,832	-	-	27,288	-	16,420	17,120	17,279	-	-	29,928	18,389	8,242	-	-	10,373	-	25,706	12,782	11,428	12,060
Ewa Beach (cdp)	14,807	15,690	10,429	-	-	-	-	-	14,884	-	10,764	-	-	22,740	-	-	-	-	9,163	-	-	-	-	-
Halawa (cdp)	21,868	22,750	13,009	-	-	-	26,502	-	20,440	-	17,239	-	-	27,962	-	-	-	-	8,686	-	-	-	-	-
Honolulu (cdp)	24,191	23,609	16,382	31,828	-	-	26,547	-	15,591	13,227	22,392	-	-	29,488	17,836	6,125	-	-	9,698	-	27,409	14,792	8,358	11,258
Kailua (cdp)	29,299	31,978	18,908	-	-	-	33,761	-	23,343	-	18,612	-	-	35,717	28,733	-	-	-	-	-	-	-	-	-
Kaneohe (cdp)	23,476	27,485	16,670	-	-	-	30,808	-	20,953	-	16,080	-	-	30,210	24,475	-	-	-	-	-	-	-	-	-
Kaneohe Station (cdp)	12,983	10,357	-	-	-	-	-	-	-	-	-	-	-	-	-	-	-	-	-	-	-	-	-	-
Makakilo City (cdp)	20,945	21,741	17,141	-	-	-	-	-	17,551	-	18,649	-	-	30,975	-	-	-	-	-	-	-	-	-	-
Mililani Town (cdp)	24,427	27,503	24,563	-	-	-	35,871	-	22,409	-	27,001	-	-	31,457	21,163	-	-	-	-	-	-	-	-	-
Nanakuli (cdp)	11,690	12,109	10,632	-	-	-	-	-	10,224	-	11,595	-	-	-	-	-	-	-	8,883	-	-	-	-	-
Pearl City (cdp)	21,683	24,668	16,538	-	-	-	28,082	-	17,974	-	17,521	-	-	28,962	17,535	-	-	-	-	-	-	-	-	-
Schofield Barracks (cdp)	12,316	13,212	-	-	-	-	-	-	-	-	-	-	-	-	-	-	-	-	-	-	-	-	-	-
Wahiawa (cdp)	16,366	19,241	11,057	-	-	-	-	-	13,154	-	15,538	-	-	24,250	-	-	-	-	-	-	-	-	-	-
Waianae (cdp)	13,348	19,656	10,455	-	-	-	-	-	15,621	-	10,830	-	-	26,680	-	-	-	-	-	-	-	-	-	-
Waimalu (cdp)	25,913	28,084	19,163	-	-	-	31,479	-	19,700	-	21,039	-	-	35,550	16,279	-	-	-	-	-	-	-	-	-
Waipahu (cdp)	14,484	16,227	7,238	-	-	-	17,064	-	14,877	-	10,227	-	-	23,144	-	-	-	-	6,664	-	-	-	-	-
Waipio (cdp)	24,451	26,133	18,607	-	-	-	-	-	19,356	-	19,725	-	-	33,444	-	-	-	-	-	-	-	-	-	-
Kauai County	20,301	20,727	13,939	-	-	-	28,145	-	17,225	-	14,269	-	-	26,325	-	-	-	-	-	-	-	-	-	-
Maui County	22,033	21,555	14,547	-	-	-	32,721	-	17,070	-	14,721	-	-	28,791	19,327	-	-	-	-	-	-	-	15,322	-
Kahului (cdp)	18,049	20,098	14,816	-	-	-	-	-	16,408	-	16,254	-	-	26,932	-	-	-	-	-	-	-	-	-	-
Kihei (cdp)	21,591	19,466	15,172	-	-	-	-	-	17,083	-	13,750	-	-	33,808	-	-	-	-	-	-	-	-	-	-
Wailuku (cdp)	20,503	25,746	14,952	-	-	-	-	-	20,478	-	15,058	-	-	29,319	-	-	-	-	-	-	-	-	-	-
IDAHO	17,841	20,143	12,666	25,191	-	-	22,853	-	20,278	-	15,524	-	-	26,461	10,875	16,303	-	-	-	-	-	-	-	12,857
Ada County	22,519	24,415	13,398	30,519	-	-	32,547	-	33,309	-	-	-	-	31,670	13,663	-	-	-	-	-	-	-	-	12,598
Bannock County	17,148	18,907	-	-	-	-	-	-	-	-	-	-	-	-	-	-	-	-	-	-	-	-	-	-
Bonneville County	18,326	26,131	-	-	-	-	-	-	-	-	-	-	-	-	-	-	-	-	-	-	-	-	-	-

Notes: Please refer to the User's Guide for an explanation of data; data is arranged alphabetically by state, then county, then city within each county; table includes counties with populations greater than 49,999 unless noted and cities with populations greater than 9,999 whose Asian and/or NHPI population rates are greater than the national average; (1) Native Hawaiian and other Pacific Islander; (2) excludes Taiwanese; (3) includes Chamorro; (4) county does not meet population threshold but is shown in order to allow inclusion of city

Place	Total population	Total Asian population	Total NHPI[1] population	Asian Indian	Bangladeshi	Cambodian	Chinese[2]	Fijian	Filipino	Guamanian[3]	Hawaiian, Native	Hmong	Indonesian	Japanese	Korean	Laotian	Malaysian	Pakistani	Samoan	Sri Lankan	Taiwanese	Thai	Tongan	Vietnamese
Canyon County	15,155	15,615	-	-	-	-	-	-	-	-	-	-	-	20,326	-	-	-	-	-	-	-	-	-	-
Kootenai County	18,430	17,851	-	-	-	-	-	-	-	-	-	-	-	-	-	-	-	-	-	-	-	-	-	-
Twin Falls County	16,678	12,516	-	-	-	-	-	-	-	-	-	-	-	-	-	-	-	-	-	-	-	-	-	-
ILLINOIS	23,104	24,137	15,523	26,094	18,007	13,431	24,016	-	25,616	17,353	17,849	-	12,594	33,059	21,179	16,398	21,426	17,792	12,728	30,961	32,430	22,438	-	16,764
Champaign County	19,708	13,208	-	16,464	-	-	12,312	-	11,279	-	-	-	-	18,718	12,165	-	-	-	-	-	-	-	-	13,801
Champaign (city)	18,664	13,063	-	18,401	-	-	12,656	-	-	-	-	-	-	-	10,037	-	-	-	-	-	-	-	-	11,643
Urbana (city)	15,969	9,199	-	9,513	-	-	10,400	-	-	-	-	-	-	-	6,407	-	-	-	-	-	-	-	-	-
Coles County	17,370	14,883	-	-	-	-	-	-	-	-	-	-	-	-	-	-	-	-	-	-	-	-	-	-
Cook County	23,227	22,874	15,820	24,114	-	12,331	21,578	-	25,249	-	-	-	14,824	34,130	21,140	20,582	-	14,513	-	-	26,272	22,807	-	15,359
Arlington Heights (village)	33,544	31,177	-	34,648	-	-	27,530	-	30,558	-	-	-	-	39,086	21,723	-	-	-	-	-	-	-	-	-
Chicago (city)	20,175	19,822	13,017	21,262	-	11,594	18,731	-	23,304	-	-	-	-	30,684	17,983	-	-	11,816	-	-	20,133	20,073	-	13,354
Des Plaines (city)	24,146	23,115	-	19,098	-	-	28,994	-	25,659	-	-	-	-	-	-	-	-	-	-	-	-	-	-	-
Elk Grove Village (village)	28,515	28,344	-	33,183	-	-	30,299	-	26,721	-	-	-	-	26,878	-	-	-	-	-	-	-	-	-	-
Evanston (city)	33,645	21,165	-	28,157	-	-	16,201	-	22,556	-	-	-	-	34,676	11,700	-	-	-	-	-	-	-	-	-
Forest Park (village)	26,045	20,027	-	-	-	-	-	-	-	-	-	-	-	-	-	-	-	-	-	-	-	-	-	-
Glenview (village)	43,384	36,457	-	47,032	-	-	38,217	-	35,960	-	-	-	-	70,887	27,676	-	-	-	-	-	-	-	-	-
Hanover Park (village)	19,960	20,790	-	17,340	-	-	-	-	25,804	-	-	-	-	-	-	-	-	-	-	-	-	-	-	-
Hoffman Estates (village)	26,669	22,918	-	20,262	-	-	27,911	-	27,182	-	-	-	-	34,573	19,956	-	-	-	-	-	-	-	-	-
Lincolnwood (village)	35,911	26,253	-	19,020	-	-	-	-	31,924	-	-	-	-	-	26,025	-	-	-	-	-	-	-	-	-
Morton Grove (village)	26,973	23,690	-	18,983	-	-	-	-	27,613	-	-	-	-	-	22,730	-	-	-	-	-	-	-	-	-
Mount Prospect (village)	26,464	21,610	-	19,337	-	-	25,630	-	27,552	-	-	-	-	28,904	20,028	-	-	-	-	-	-	-	-	-
Niles (village)	23,543	19,634	-	17,120	-	-	-	-	21,531	-	-	-	-	-	18,392	-	-	-	-	-	-	-	-	-
Northbrook (village)	50,765	41,764	-	-	-	-	46,018	-	-	-	-	-	-	-	32,694	-	-	-	-	-	-	-	-	-
Oak Park (village)	36,340	28,628	-	27,842	-	-	27,665	-	-	-	-	-	-	-	-	-	-	-	-	-	-	-	-	-
Orland Park (village)	30,467	35,951	-	58,181	-	-	-	-	30,372	-	-	-	-	-	-	-	-	-	-	-	-	-	-	-
Palatine (village)	30,661	27,053	-	25,663	-	-	30,817	-	34,352	-	-	-	-	-	23,000	-	-	-	-	-	-	-	-	-
Prospect Heights (city)	28,200	27,182	-	-	-	-	-	-	-	-	-	-	-	-	-	-	-	-	-	-	-	-	-	-
Rolling Meadows (city)	26,178	26,861	-	29,311	-	-	-	-	-	-	-	-	-	-	-	-	-	-	-	-	-	-	-	-
Schaumburg (village)	30,587	29,201	-	33,111	-	-	24,698	-	37,440	-	-	-	-	30,714	18,798	-	-	-	-	-	-	-	-	-
Schiller Park (village)	17,781	19,156	-	-	-	-	-	-	-	-	-	-	-	-	-	-	-	-	-	-	-	-	-	-
Skokie (village)	27,136	23,001	-	20,697	-	-	24,525	-	25,632	-	-	-	-	-	23,504	-	-	22,213	-	-	-	-	-	-
Streamwood (village)	23,961	26,228	-	25,977	-	-	-	-	25,681	-	-	-	-	-	-	-	-	-	-	-	-	-	-	-
Wheeling (village)	24,989	25,260	-	24,691	-	-	-	-	23,602	-	-	-	-	-	-	-	-	-	-	-	-	-	-	-
Wilmette (village)	55,611	31,200	-	-	-	-	32,381	-	-	-	-	-	-	42,897	24,224	-	-	-	-	-	-	-	-	-
DeKalb County	19,462	9,042	-	11,231	-	-	-	-	-	-	-	-	-	-	-	-	-	-	-	-	-	-	-	-
DeKalb (city)	16,261	7,925	-	10,563	-	-	-	-	-	-	-	-	-	-	-	-	-	-	-	-	-	-	-	-
DuPage County	31,315	28,568	-	28,240	-	-	34,020	-	27,709	-	-	-	-	44,250	26,421	-	-	23,227	-	-	45,231	22,729	-	19,820
Addison (village)	21,201	20,477	-	21,910	-	-	-	-	20,482	-	-	-	-	-	-	-	-	-	-	-	-	-	-	-
Bartlett (village)	29,652	24,511	-	23,854	-	-	-	-	24,686	-	-	-	-	-	-	-	-	-	-	-	-	-	-	-
Bensenville (village)	20,040	20,558	-	19,031	-	-	-	-	-	-	-	-	-	-	-	-	-	-	-	-	-	-	-	-
Bloomingdale (village)	30,941	26,205	-	20,879	-	-	-	-	-	-	-	-	-	-	-	-	-	-	-	-	-	-	-	-

Notes: Please refer to the User's Guide for an explanation of data; data is arranged alphabetically by state, then county, then city within each county; table includes counties with populations greater than 49,999 unless noted and cities with populations greater than 9,999 whose Asian and/or NHPI population rates are greater than the national average; (1) Native Hawaiian and other Pacific Islander; (2) excludes Taiwanese; (3) includes Chamorro; (4) county does not meet population threshold but is shown in order to allow inclusion of city

Place	Total population	Total Asian population	Total NHPI[1] population	Asian Indian	Bangladeshi	Cambodian	Chinese[2]	Fijian	Filipino	Guamanian[3]	Hawaiian, Native	Hmong	Indonesian	Japanese	Korean	Laotian	Malaysian	Pakistani	Samoan	Sri Lankan	Taiwanese	Thai	Tongan	Vietnamese
Burr Ridge (village)	58,518	56,585	-	40,125	-	-	-	-	-	-	-	-	-	-	-	-	-	-	-	-	-	-	-	-
Carol Stream (village)	25,152	21,835	-	21,193	-	-	-	-	21,891	-	-	-	-	-	-	-	-	-	-	-	-	-	-	18,204
Darien (city)	34,795	31,253	-	32,664	-	-	-	-	30,665	-	-	-	-	-	-	-	-	-	-	-	-	-	-	-
Downers Grove (village)	31,580	27,048	-	27,728	-	-	26,609	-	29,359	-	-	-	-	-	-	-	-	-	-	-	-	-	-	-
Glen Ellyn (village)	39,783	21,565	-	16,748	-	-	-	-	-	-	-	-	-	-	-	-	-	-	-	-	-	-	-	-
Glendale Heights (village)	21,911	18,815	-	14,857	-	-	-	-	22,630	-	-	-	-	-	-	-	-	-	-	-	-	-	-	-
Hinsdale (village)	63,765	34,031	-	-	-	-	-	-	-	-	-	-	-	-	-	-	-	-	-	-	-	-	-	20,530
Lisle (village)	35,693	34,079	-	35,708	-	-	45,114	-	-	-	-	-	-	-	-	-	-	-	-	-	-	-	-	-
Lombard (village)	27,667	26,917	-	24,596	-	-	-	-	33,356	-	-	-	-	-	-	-	-	-	-	-	-	-	-	-
Naperville (city)	35,551	30,560	-	31,557	-	-	31,004	-	31,584	-	-	-	-	-	21,560	-	-	-	-	-	35,047	-	-	-
Roselle (village)	28,501	29,668	-	28,171	-	-	-	-	-	-	-	-	-	-	-	-	-	-	-	-	-	-	-	-
Villa Park (village)	22,354	19,349	-	-	-	-	-	-	-	-	-	-	-	-	-	-	-	-	-	-	-	-	-	-
Warrenville (city)	28,922	35,662	-	-	-	-	-	-	-	-	-	-	-	-	-	-	-	-	-	-	-	-	-	-
Westmont (village)	26,394	27,932	-	23,883	-	-	35,526	-	22,511	-	-	-	-	-	-	-	-	-	-	-	-	-	-	-
Wheaton (city)	34,147	31,055	-	49,501	-	-	-	-	-	-	-	-	-	-	-	-	-	-	-	-	-	-	-	10,257
Woodridge (village)	27,851	25,130	-	27,879	-	-	-	-	23,591	-	-	-	-	-	-	-	-	-	-	-	-	-	-	-
Jackson County	15,755	12,485	-	-	-	-	6,854	-	-	-	-	-	-	-	-	-	-	-	-	-	-	-	-	-
Carbondale (city)	13,346	9,253	-	-	-	-	-	-	-	-	-	-	-	-	-	-	-	-	-	-	-	-	-	-
Kane County	24,315	23,666	-	22,647	-	-	36,229	-	27,590	-	-	-	-	-	18,949	16,242	-	-	-	-	-	-	-	15,513
South Elgin (village)	25,676	18,015	-	-	-	-	-	-	-	-	-	-	-	-	-	-	-	-	-	-	-	-	-	-
Kankakee County	19,055	26,546	-	-	-	-	-	-	-	-	-	-	-	-	-	-	-	-	-	-	-	-	-	-
Kendall County	25,188	17,750	-	-	-	-	-	-	-	-	-	-	-	-	-	-	-	-	-	-	-	-	-	-
Knox County	17,985	39,912	-	-	-	-	-	-	-	-	-	-	-	-	-	-	-	-	-	-	-	-	-	-
La Salle County	19,185	39,317	-	-	-	-	-	-	-	-	-	-	-	-	-	-	-	-	-	-	-	-	-	-
Lake County	32,102	29,561	-	32,105	-	-	34,374	-	24,207	-	-	-	-	33,796	29,801	-	-	31,170	-	-	-	-	-	17,924
Buffalo Grove (village)	36,696	32,055	-	29,094	-	-	31,647	-	27,877	-	-	-	-	51,519	28,119	-	-	-	-	-	-	-	-	-
Gages Lake (cdp)	28,391	24,691	-	-	-	-	-	-	-	-	-	-	-	-	-	-	-	-	-	-	-	-	-	-
Grayslake (village)	28,898	29,039	-	-	-	-	-	-	-	-	-	-	-	-	-	-	-	-	-	-	-	-	-	-
Gurnee (village)	31,517	25,152	-	26,282	-	-	28,715	-	25,016	-	-	-	-	-	-	-	-	-	-	-	-	-	-	-
Lake Zurich (village)	30,287	36,924	-	-	-	-	-	-	-	-	-	-	-	-	-	-	-	-	-	-	-	-	-	-
Libertyville (village)	40,426	35,493	-	-	-	-	-	-	-	-	-	-	-	-	-	-	-	-	-	-	-	-	-	-
Mundelein (village)	26,280	26,747	-	-	-	-	33,137	-	25,764	-	-	-	-	-	-	-	-	-	-	-	-	-	-	-
Vernon Hills (village)	32,246	30,587	-	33,786	-	-	38,354	-	-	-	-	-	-	-	22,381	-	-	-	-	-	-	-	-	-
Macon County	20,067	25,714	-	-	-	-	-	-	-	-	-	-	-	-	-	-	-	-	-	-	-	-	-	-
Madison County	20,509	23,214	-	39,699	-	-	-	-	-	-	-	-	-	-	-	-	-	-	-	-	-	-	-	-
McHenry County	26,476	27,280	-	33,904	-	-	25,808	-	25,500	-	-	-	-	-	-	-	-	-	-	-	-	-	-	-
McLean County	22,227	24,677	-	26,552	-	-	27,068	-	-	-	-	-	-	-	-	-	-	-	-	-	-	-	-	-
Peoria County	21,219	29,611	-	37,932	-	-	28,389	-	-	-	-	-	-	-	-	-	-	-	-	-	-	-	-	-
Rock Island County	20,164	30,268	-	39,398	-	-	-	-	-	-	-	-	-	-	-	-	-	-	-	-	-	-	-	25,105
St. Clair County	18,932	21,174	-	-	-	-	-	-	20,048	-	-	-	-	-	10,613	-	-	-	-	-	-	-	-	-
Sangamon County	23,173	25,726	-	30,711	-	-	25,659	-	-	-	-	-	-	-	-	-	-	-	-	-	-	-	-	-

Notes: Please refer to the User's Guide for an explanation of data; data is arranged alphabetically by state, then county, then city within each county; table includes counties with populations greater than 49,999 unless noted and cities with populations greater than 9,999 whose Asian and/or NHPI population rates are greater than the national average; (1) Native Hawaiian and other Pacific Islander; (2) excludes Taiwanese; (3) includes Chamorro; (4) county does not meet population threshold but is shown in order to allow inclusion of city

Place	Total population	Total Asian population	Total NHPI[1] population	Asian Indian	Bangladeshi	Cambodian	Chinese[2]	Fijian	Filipino	Guamanian[3]	Hawaiian, Native	Hmong	Indonesian	Japanese	Korean	Laotian	Malaysian	Pakistani	Samoan	Sri Lankan	Taiwanese	Thai	Tongan	Vietnamese
Tazewell County	21,511	19,547	-	-	-	-	-	-	-	-	-	-	-	-	-	-	-	-	-	-	-	-	-	-
Vermilion County	16,787	37,289	-	-	-	-	-	-	-	-	-	-	-	-	-	-	-	-	-	-	-	-	-	-
Will County	24,613	26,456	-	27,942	-	-	26,714	-	27,029	-	-	-	-	-	23,188	-	-	22,340	-	-	-	-	-	34,182
Bolingbrook (village)	23,468	23,891	-	25,388	-	-	-	-	24,841	-	-	-	-	-	-	-	-	-	-	-	-	-	-	-
Winnebago County	21,194	19,774	-	30,706	-	-	-	-	26,909	-	-	-	-	-	15,472	15,245	-	-	-	-	-	-	-	13,354
INDIANA	20,397	22,421	15,504	29,602	-	14,662	19,791	-	24,631	12,699	17,121	-	-	23,767	16,802	19,344	-	28,822	-	-	27,881	32,579	-	15,726
Allen County	21,544	21,008	-	36,276	-	-	23,975	-	19,738	-	-	-	-	-	-	-	-	-	-	-	-	-	-	13,447
Bartholomew County	21,536	28,832	-	26,204	-	-	-	-	-	-	-	-	-	-	-	-	-	-	-	-	-	-	-	-
Clark County	19,936	26,140	-	-	-	-	-	-	-	-	-	-	-	-	-	-	-	-	-	-	-	-	-	-
Delaware County	19,233	10,509	-	-	-	-	-	-	-	-	-	-	-	-	-	-	-	-	-	-	-	-	-	-
Elkhart County	20,250	24,121	-	-	-	-	-	-	-	-	-	-	-	-	-	-	-	-	-	-	-	-	-	-
Grant County	18,003	27,430	-	-	-	-	-	-	-	-	-	-	-	-	-	-	-	-	-	-	-	-	-	-
Hamilton County	33,109	32,978	-	45,525	-	-	33,726	-	-	-	-	-	-	-	-	-	-	-	-	-	-	-	-	-
Carmel (city)	38,906	30,560	-	-	-	-	-	-	-	-	-	-	-	-	-	-	-	-	-	-	-	-	-	-
Hendricks County	23,129	21,725	-	-	-	-	-	-	-	-	-	-	-	-	-	-	-	-	-	-	-	-	-	-
Howard County	22,049	24,037	-	-	-	-	-	-	-	-	-	-	-	-	-	-	-	-	-	-	-	-	-	-
Johnson County	22,976	30,853	-	-	-	-	-	-	-	-	-	-	-	-	-	-	-	-	-	-	-	-	-	-
Kosciusko County	19,806	22,149	-	-	-	-	-	-	-	-	-	-	-	-	-	-	-	-	-	-	-	-	-	-
Lake County	19,639	32,442	-	40,903	-	-	24,790	-	30,840	-	-	-	-	-	34,497	-	-	-	-	-	-	-	-	-
Munster (town)	30,952	48,676	-	61,671	-	-	-	-	-	-	-	-	-	-	-	-	-	-	-	-	-	-	-	-
LaPorte County	18,913	15,312	-	-	-	-	-	-	-	-	-	-	-	-	-	-	-	-	-	-	-	-	-	-
Madison County	20,090	16,169	-	-	-	-	-	-	-	-	-	-	-	-	-	-	-	-	-	-	-	-	-	-
Marion County	21,789	22,153	-	24,635	-	-	19,690	-	27,932	-	-	-	-	32,144	19,276	-	-	-	-	-	-	-	-	17,748
Monroe County	18,534	11,236	-	18,019	-	-	13,395	-	-	-	-	-	-	-	7,162	-	-	-	-	-	-	-	-	-
Bloomington (city)	16,481	9,993	-	14,280	-	-	12,894	-	-	-	-	-	-	-	6,585	-	-	-	-	-	-	-	-	-
Porter County	23,957	49,691	-	-	-	-	-	-	-	-	-	-	-	-	-	-	-	-	-	-	-	-	-	-
St. Joseph County	19,756	23,274	-	24,342	-	-	23,281	-	-	-	-	-	-	-	16,764	-	-	-	-	-	-	-	-	-
Tippecanoe County	19,375	13,486	-	14,240	-	-	12,847	-	-	-	-	-	-	35,963	7,044	-	-	-	-	-	-	-	-	-
West Lafayette (city)	18,337	14,400	-	16,132	-	-	13,138	-	-	-	-	-	-	-	-	-	-	-	-	-	-	-	-	-
Vanderburgh County	20,655	22,068	-	-	-	-	-	-	-	-	-	-	-	-	-	-	-	-	-	-	-	-	-	-
Vigo County	17,620	16,362	-	-	-	-	-	-	-	-	-	-	-	-	-	-	-	-	-	-	-	-	-	-
Wayne County	17,727	11,749	-	-	-	-	-	-	-	-	-	-	-	-	-	-	-	-	-	-	-	-	-	-
IOWA	19,674	18,279	21,436	34,605	-	11,204	19,273	-	19,451	-	-	-	-	15,325	11,389	12,775	-	48,604	-	-	22,219	20,238	-	13,480
Black Hawk County	18,885	37,428	-	-	-	-	-	-	-	-	-	-	-	-	-	-	-	-	-	-	-	-	-	-
Buena Vista County[4]	16,042	11,709	-	-	-	-	-	-	-	-	-	-	-	-	-	11,213	-	-	-	-	-	-	-	-
Storm Lake (city)	15,150	11,650	-	-	-	-	-	-	-	-	-	-	-	-	-	11,258	-	-	-	-	-	-	-	-
Johnson County	22,220	16,355	-	25,200	-	-	18,724	-	-	-	-	-	-	-	5,161	-	-	-	-	-	-	-	-	-
Coralville (city)	23,283	12,824	-	-	-	-	-	-	-	-	-	-	-	-	-	-	-	-	-	-	-	-	-	-
Iowa City (city)	20,269	15,885	-	26,427	-	-	18,148	-	-	-	-	-	-	-	5,978	-	-	-	-	-	-	-	-	-
Linn County	22,977	25,203	-	38,929	-	-	-	-	-	-	-	-	-	-	10,137	-	-	-	-	-	-	-	-	-
Polk County	23,654	17,121	-	28,706	-	10,609	25,279	-	-	-	-	-	-	-	14,101	13,254	-	-	-	-	-	15,344	-	14,204

Notes: Please refer to the User's Guide for an explanation of data; data is arranged alphabetically by state, then county, then city within each county; table includes counties with populations greater than 49,999 unless noted and cities with populations greater than 9,999 whose Asian and/or NHPI population rates are greater than the national average; (1) Native Hawaiian and other Pacific Islander; (2) excludes Taiwanese; (3) includes Chamorro; (4) county does not meet population threshold but is shown in order to allow inclusion of city

Place	Total population	Total Asian population	Total NHPI[1] population	Asian Indian	Bangladeshi	Cambodian	Chinese[2]	Fijian	Filipino	Guamanian[3]	Hawaiian, Native	Hmong	Indonesian	Japanese	Korean	Laotian	Malaysian	Pakistani	Samoan	Sri Lankan	Taiwanese	Thai	Tongan	Vietnamese
Pottawattamie County	19,275	26,106	-	-	-	-	-	-	-	-	-	-	-	-	-	-	-	-	-	-	-	-	-	-
Scott County	21,310	23,382	-	-	-	-	-	-	-	-	-	-	-	-	-	-	-	-	-	-	-	-	-	11,625
Story County	19,949	13,387	-	26,289	-	-	11,514	-	-	-	-	-	-	-	7,339	-	-	-	-	-	-	-	-	-
Ames (city)	18,881	13,410	-	26,087	-	-	11,542	-	-	-	-	-	-	-	7,544	-	-	-	-	-	-	-	-	-
Woodbury County	18,771	14,897	-	-	-	-	-	-	-	-	-	-	-	-	-	-	-	-	-	-	-	-	-	12,538
KANSAS	20,506	18,182	17,272	26,686	-	11,174	19,708	-	22,824	-	20,457	7,769	-	20,556	14,539	13,877	-	29,412	-	-	25,962	19,173	-	13,896
Cowley County[4]	17,509	10,868	-	-	-	-	-	-	-	-	-	-	-	-	-	13,709	-	-	-	-	-	-	-	-
Winfield (city)	19,162	11,170	-	-	-	-	-	-	-	-	-	-	-	-	-	13,741	-	-	-	-	-	-	-	-
Douglas County	19,952	14,423	-	18,067	-	-	16,331	-	-	-	-	-	-	-	10,025	-	-	-	-	-	-	-	-	-
Lawrence (city)	19,378	14,424	-	18,052	-	-	16,331	-	-	-	-	-	-	-	9,979	-	-	-	-	-	-	-	-	-
Johnson County	30,919	25,410	-	32,109	-	-	24,762	-	30,038	-	-	-	-	31,222	20,093	15,405	-	-	-	-	-	-	-	18,520
Overland Park (city)	32,069	26,722	-	32,274	-	-	26,760	-	-	-	-	-	-	-	24,675	-	-	-	-	-	-	-	-	21,682
Leavenworth County	20,292	16,082	-	-	-	-	-	-	-	-	-	-	-	-	-	-	-	-	-	-	-	-	-	-
Riley County	16,349	13,762	-	-	-	-	14,061	-	-	-	-	-	-	-	7,707	-	-	-	-	-	-	-	-	-
Manhattan (city)	16,566	13,281	-	-	-	-	14,070	-	-	-	-	-	-	-	-	-	-	-	-	-	-	-	-	-
Saline County	19,073	15,757	-	-	-	-	-	-	-	-	-	-	-	-	-	-	-	-	-	-	-	-	-	14,677
Sedgwick County	20,907	15,767	16,739	19,652	-	12,544	18,666	-	18,743	-	-	-	-	-	16,466	12,402	-	-	-	-	-	-	-	14,013
Wichita (city)	20,647	15,601	-	18,347	-	-	18,654	-	19,979	-	-	-	-	-	16,213	12,224	-	-	-	-	-	-	-	13,845
Shawnee County	20,904	21,751	-	-	-	-	-	-	-	-	-	-	-	-	-	-	-	-	-	-	-	-	-	-
Wyandotte County	16,005	11,402	-	-	-	-	-	-	-	-	-	6,946	-	-	-	-	-	-	-	-	-	-	-	-
KENTUCKY	18,093	24,349	12,710	35,162	-	-	20,882	-	24,954	15,390	-	-	-	28,544	16,352	-	-	50,931	-	-	-	18,459	-	13,349
Boone County	23,535	34,855	-	-	-	-	-	-	-	-	-	-	-	29,936	-	-	-	-	-	-	-	-	-	-
Campbell County	20,637	28,592	-	-	-	-	-	-	-	-	-	-	-	-	-	-	-	-	-	-	-	-	-	-
Christian County	14,611	17,854	-	-	-	-	-	-	-	-	-	-	-	-	-	-	-	-	-	-	-	-	-	-
Fayette County	23,109	23,176	-	32,805	-	-	17,563	-	-	-	-	-	-	22,660	-	-	-	-	-	-	-	-	-	-
Hardin County	17,487	30,292	-	-	-	-	-	-	-	-	-	-	-	-	18,826	-	-	-	-	-	-	-	-	-
Radcliff (city)	16,436	16,441	-	-	-	-	-	-	-	-	-	-	-	-	-	-	-	-	-	-	-	-	-	-
Jefferson County	22,352	21,523	-	30,078	-	-	19,618	-	26,806	-	-	-	-	32,764	14,572	-	-	-	-	-	-	-	-	12,388
Kenton County	22,085	20,943	-	-	-	-	-	-	-	-	-	-	-	-	-	-	-	-	-	-	-	-	-	-
Madison County	16,790	26,804	-	-	-	-	-	-	-	-	-	-	-	-	-	-	-	-	-	-	-	-	-	-
Warren County	18,847	24,931	-	-	-	-	-	-	-	-	-	-	-	-	-	-	-	-	-	-	-	-	-	-
LOUISIANA	16,912	16,304	14,975	27,624	-	-	20,664	-	18,460	15,597	11,370	-	-	17,392	15,814	10,847	-	14,767	-	-	23,830	16,331	-	11,162
Ascension Parish	17,858	17,956	-	-	-	-	-	-	-	-	-	-	-	-	-	-	-	-	-	-	-	-	-	-
Bossier Parish	18,119	15,712	-	-	-	-	-	-	-	-	-	-	-	-	-	-	-	-	-	-	-	-	-	-
Caddo Parish	17,839	26,913	-	61,737	-	-	-	-	-	-	-	-	-	-	-	-	-	-	-	-	-	-	-	-
Calcasieu Parish	17,710	16,533	-	-	-	-	-	-	-	-	-	-	-	-	-	-	-	-	-	-	-	-	-	-
East Baton Rouge Parish	19,790	16,079	-	25,818	-	-	19,679	-	13,394	-	-	-	-	-	-	-	-	-	-	-	-	-	-	10,030
Iberia Parish	14,145	9,647	-	-	-	-	-	-	-	-	-	-	-	-	-	9,488	-	-	-	-	-	-	-	9,810
Jefferson Parish	19,953	17,948	-	33,272	-	-	18,303	-	19,842	-	-	-	-	-	19,306	-	-	15,756	-	-	-	-	-	13,472
Gretna (city)	15,735	14,279	-	-	-	-	-	-	-	-	-	-	-	-	-	-	-	-	-	-	-	-	-	7,061
Harvey (cdp)	14,885	13,569	-	-	-	-	-	-	-	-	-	-	-	-	-	-	-	-	-	-	-	-	-	14,236

Notes: Please refer to the User's Guide for an explanation of data; data is arranged alphabetically by state, then county, then city within each county; table includes counties with populations greater than 49,999 unless noted and cities with populations greater than 9,999 whose Asian and/or NHPI population rates are greater than the national average; (1) Native Hawaiian and other Pacific Islander; (2) excludes Taiwanese; (3) includes Chamorro; (4) county does not meet population threshold but is shown in order to allow inclusion of city

Place	Total population	Total Asian population	Total NHPI[1] population	Asian Indian	Bangladeshi	Cambodian	Chinese[2]	Fijian	Filipino	Guamanian[3]	Hawaiian, Native	Hmong	Indonesian	Japanese	Korean	Laotian	Malaysian	Pakistani	Samoan	Sri Lankan	Taiwanese	Thai	Tongan	Vietnamese
Timberlane (cdp)	20,674	11,323	-	-	-	-	-	-	-	-	-	-	-	-	-	-	-	-	-	-	-	-	-	11,367
Woodmere (cdp)	14,494	11,865	-	-	-	-	-	-	-	-	-	-	-	-	-	-	-	-	-	-	-	-	-	11,324
Lafayette Parish	19,371	15,921	-	19,584	-	-	-	-	-	-	-	-	-	-	-	-	-	-	-	-	-	-	-	9,152
Lafourche Parish	15,809	11,995	-	-	-	-	-	-	-	-	-	-	-	-	-	-	-	-	-	-	-	-	-	-
Orleans Parish	17,258	13,826	-	16,210	-	-	32,780	-	21,907	-	-	-	-	-	-	-	-	-	-	-	-	-	-	10,659
Ouachita Parish	17,084	28,597	-	-	-	-	-	-	-	-	-	-	-	-	-	-	-	-	-	-	-	-	-	-
Rapides Parish	16,088	17,515	-	-	-	-	-	-	-	-	-	-	-	-	-	-	-	-	-	-	-	-	-	-
St. Bernard Parish	16,718	13,093	-	-	-	-	-	-	-	-	-	-	-	-	-	-	-	-	-	-	-	-	-	9,672
St. Mary Parish	13,399	8,914	-	-	-	-	-	-	-	-	-	-	-	-	-	-	-	-	-	-	-	-	-	7,097
St. Tammany Parish	22,514	23,122	-	-	-	-	-	-	-	-	-	-	-	-	-	-	-	-	-	-	-	-	-	13,773
Terrebonne Parish	16,051	15,758	-	-	-	-	-	-	-	-	-	-	-	-	-	-	-	-	-	-	-	-	-	9,232
Vermilion Parish	14,201	9,212	-	-	-	-	-	-	-	-	-	-	-	-	-	-	-	-	-	-	-	-	-	9,089
Abbeville (city)	11,680	7,326	-	-	-	-	-	-	-	-	-	-	-	-	-	-	-	-	-	-	-	-	-	7,598
Vernon Parish	14,036	15,662	-	-	-	-	-	-	-	-	-	-	-	-	7,190	-	-	-	-	-	-	-	-	-
MAINE	19,533	14,592	16,353	21,863	-	8,362	14,666	-	20,578	-	-	-	-	14,154	10,952	-	-	-	-	-	-	-	-	12,425
Androscoggin County	18,734	19,038	-	-	-	-	-	-	-	-	-	-	-	-	-	-	-	-	-	-	-	-	-	-
Aroostook County	15,033	11,368	-	-	-	-	-	-	-	-	-	-	-	-	-	-	-	-	-	-	-	-	-	-
Cumberland County	23,949	13,610	-	-	-	6,147	19,826	-	21,106	-	-	-	-	-	-	-	-	-	-	-	-	-	-	12,061
Hancock County	19,809	14,433	-	-	-	-	-	-	-	-	-	-	-	-	-	-	-	-	-	-	-	-	-	-
Kennebec County	18,520	13,713	-	-	-	-	-	-	-	-	-	-	-	-	-	-	-	-	-	-	-	-	-	-
Oxford County	16,945	19,530	-	-	-	-	-	-	-	-	-	-	-	-	-	-	-	-	-	-	-	-	-	-
Penobscot County	17,801	15,267	-	-	-	-	16,764	-	-	-	-	-	-	-	-	-	-	-	-	-	-	-	-	-
York County	21,225	15,008	-	-	-	-	-	-	-	-	-	-	-	-	-	-	-	-	-	-	-	-	-	-
MARYLAND	25,614	24,025	19,600	28,509	23,182	15,594	26,431	-	23,754	20,891	23,647	-	16,208	32,588	19,623	16,308	-	16,518	-	27,876	25,611	22,898	-	17,981
Allegany County	16,780	32,378	-	-	-	-	-	-	-	-	-	-	-	-	-	-	-	-	-	-	-	-	-	-
Anne Arundel County	27,578	22,355	-	29,710	-	-	25,425	-	22,727	-	-	-	-	39,047	16,757	-	-	-	-	-	-	-	-	-
Severn (cdp)	24,640	19,301	-	-	-	-	-	-	-	-	-	-	-	-	19,161	-	-	-	-	-	-	-	-	-
South Gate (cdp)	22,061	19,054	-	-	-	-	-	-	-	-	-	-	-	-	17,343	-	-	-	-	-	-	-	-	-
Baltimore Independent City	16,978	15,737	-	21,457	-	-	14,691	-	16,456	-	-	-	-	-	13,416	-	-	-	-	-	-	-	-	10,028
Baltimore County	26,167	22,584	-	25,931	-	-	21,052	-	30,226	-	-	-	-	23,479	20,142	-	-	12,315	-	-	-	-	-	14,271
Arbutus (cdp)	22,456	17,207	-	-	-	-	-	-	-	-	-	-	-	-	-	-	-	-	-	-	-	-	-	-
Carney (cdp)	24,428	18,768	-	-	-	-	16,935	-	-	-	-	-	-	-	14,956	-	-	-	-	-	-	-	-	-
Cockeysville (cdp)	29,080	21,303	-	-	-	-	-	-	-	-	-	-	-	-	12,583	-	-	-	-	-	-	-	-	-
Lutherville-Timonium (cdp)	32,369	26,252	-	-	-	-	-	-	-	-	-	-	-	-	-	-	-	-	-	-	-	-	-	-
Mays Chapel (cdp)	41,086	28,857	-	-	-	-	-	-	-	-	-	-	-	-	-	-	-	-	-	-	-	-	-	-
Owings Mills (cdp)	27,107	17,940	-	-	-	-	-	-	-	-	-	-	-	-	-	-	-	-	-	-	-	-	-	-
Perry Hall (cdp)	26,361	18,607	-	-	-	-	-	-	-	-	-	-	-	-	10,254	-	-	-	-	-	-	-	-	-
Reisterstown (cdp)	22,206	14,586	-	14,079	-	-	-	-	-	-	-	-	-	-	-	-	-	-	-	-	-	-	-	-
Rossville (cdp)	22,608	22,135	-	-	-	-	-	-	-	-	-	-	-	-	-	-	-	-	-	-	-	-	-	-
Towson (cdp)	32,502	23,261	-	-	-	-	22,541	-	-	-	-	-	-	-	-	-	-	-	-	-	-	-	-	-
Woodlawn (cdp)	21,710	21,056	-	15,048	-	-	-	-	-	-	-	-	-	-	-	-	-	-	-	-	-	-	-	-

Notes: Please refer to the User's Guide for an explanation of data; data is arranged alphabetically by state, then county, then city within each county; table includes counties with populations greater than 49,999 unless noted and cities with populations greater than 9,999 whose Asian and/or NHPI population rates are greater than the national average; (1) Native Hawaiian and other Pacific Islander; (2) excludes Taiwanese; (3) includes Chamorro; (4) county does not meet population threshold but is shown in order to allow inclusion of city

Place	Total population	Total Asian population	Total NHPI[1] population	Asian Indian	Bangladeshi	Cambodian	Chinese[2]	Fijian	Filipino	Guamanian[3]	Hawaiian, Native	Hmong	Indonesian	Japanese	Korean	Laotian	Malaysian	Pakistani	Samoan	Sri Lankan	Taiwanese	Thai	Tongan	Vietnamese
Calvert County	25,410	46,295	-	-	-	-	-	-	-	-	-	-	-	-	-	-	-	-	-	-	-	-	-	-
Carroll County	23,829	19,175	-	-	-	-	-	-	-	-	-	-	-	-	-	-	-	-	-	-	-	-	-	-
Cecil County	21,384	20,399	-	-	-	-	-	-	-	-	-	-	-	-	-	-	-	-	-	-	-	-	-	-
Charles County	24,285	19,429	-	-	-	-	-	-	17,887	-	-	-	-	-	-	-	-	-	-	-	-	-	-	-
Frederick County	25,404	18,248	-	19,887	-	-	21,160	-	-	-	-	-	-	-	12,531	-	-	-	-	-	-	-	-	-
Harford County	24,232	20,321	-	19,030	-	-	-	-	28,706	-	-	-	-	-	11,071	-	-	-	-	-	-	-	-	-
Howard County	32,402	25,968	-	31,494	-	-	28,187	-	31,104	-	-	-	-	-	19,971	-	-	17,234	-	-	-	-	-	20,784
Columbia (cdp)	32,833	27,082	-	31,445	-	-	27,277	-	28,208	-	-	-	-	-	21,526	-	-	-	-	-	-	-	-	-
Elkridge (cdp)	27,629	23,444	-	-	-	-	-	-	-	-	-	-	-	-	23,369	-	-	-	-	-	-	-	-	-
Ellicott City (cdp)	33,316	25,803	-	35,160	-	-	27,423	-	38,141	-	-	-	-	-	20,227	-	-	19,633	-	-	-	-	-	-
North Laurel (cdp)	27,991	24,117	-	28,199	-	-	-	-	-	-	-	-	-	-	13,146	-	-	-	-	-	-	-	-	-
Savage-Guilford (cdp)	25,798	17,786	-	-	-	-	-	-	-	-	-	-	-	-	-	-	-	-	-	-	-	-	-	-
Montgomery County	35,684	27,015	21,258	31,436	27,231	16,721	29,778	-	25,009	-	-	-	15,695	38,480	22,812	-	-	19,589	-	26,199	33,599	21,235	-	18,990
Aspen Hill (cdp)	27,905	22,219	-	23,604	-	-	23,477	-	24,283	-	-	-	-	-	24,822	-	-	-	-	-	-	-	-	18,257
Bethesda (cdp)	58,479	34,802	-	47,375	-	-	30,331	-	21,907	-	-	-	-	46,233	27,745	-	-	-	-	-	-	-	-	-
Calverton (cdp)	28,107	20,098	-	29,266	-	-	-	-	-	-	-	-	-	-	14,108	-	-	-	-	-	-	-	-	-
Colesville (cdp)	34,942	26,407	-	32,340	-	-	31,629	-	-	-	-	-	-	-	21,273	-	-	-	-	-	-	-	-	20,750
Fairland (cdp)	28,603	20,589	-	21,851	-	-	31,064	-	-	-	-	-	-	-	15,156	-	-	-	-	-	-	-	-	-
Gaithersburg (city)	27,323	25,326	-	28,996	-	-	25,509	-	23,643	-	-	-	-	-	22,859	-	-	-	-	-	-	-	-	22,704
Germantown (cdp)	26,709	24,112	-	28,022	-	-	25,956	-	-	-	-	-	-	-	23,202	-	-	-	-	-	-	-	-	18,188
Montgomery Village (cdp)	29,620	24,106	-	24,150	-	-	30,621	-	22,743	-	-	-	-	-	-	-	-	-	-	-	-	-	-	19,446
North Bethesda (cdp)	44,316	30,602	-	38,273	-	-	29,222	-	24,644	-	-	-	-	34,486	30,241	-	-	-	-	-	-	-	-	-
North Potomac (cdp)	37,573	33,281	-	43,906	-	-	33,189	-	-	-	-	-	-	-	23,814	-	-	-	-	-	-	-	-	-
Olney (cdp)	35,267	29,917	-	29,711	-	-	33,653	-	-	-	-	-	-	-	23,093	-	-	-	-	-	-	-	-	-
Potomac (cdp)	64,875	49,146	-	59,404	-	-	50,969	-	26,999	-	-	-	-	-	38,849	-	-	-	-	-	-	-	-	-
Redland (cdp)	27,542	22,725	-	26,878	-	-	20,958	-	29,462	-	-	-	-	-	22,832	-	-	-	-	-	-	-	-	-
Rockville (city)	30,518	22,348	-	27,786	-	-	22,945	-	22,592	-	-	-	-	18,788	20,103	-	-	-	-	-	-	-	-	17,878
Silver Spring (cdp)	26,357	17,096	-	17,900	-	14,909	24,531	-	18,954	-	-	-	-	-	16,825	-	-	-	-	-	-	-	-	11,925
Takoma Park (city)	26,437	21,686	-	-	-	-	-	-	-	-	-	-	-	-	-	-	-	-	-	-	-	-	-	-
Wheaton-Glenmont (cdp)	23,927	20,540	-	25,065	-	-	22,515	-	22,665	-	-	-	-	-	14,483	-	-	-	-	-	-	-	-	18,647
White Oak (cdp)	25,893	20,333	-	25,938	-	-	21,716	-	-	-	-	-	-	-	15,504	-	-	-	-	-	-	-	-	16,014
Prince George's County	23,360	19,782	-	21,558	-	-	20,118	-	21,126	-	-	-	-	18,758	17,028	-	-	15,996	-	-	-	17,912	-	18,395
Adelphi (cdp)	20,952	17,463	-	-	-	-	-	-	-	-	-	-	-	-	-	-	-	-	-	-	-	-	-	-
Beltsville (cdp)	24,679	18,848	-	20,693	-	-	-	-	-	-	-	-	-	-	15,429	-	-	-	-	-	-	-	-	-
College Park (city)	16,026	12,363	-	15,018	-	-	11,575	-	-	-	-	-	-	-	-	-	-	-	-	-	-	-	-	-
Fort Washington (cdp)	30,871	22,322	-	-	-	-	-	-	23,470	-	-	-	-	-	-	-	-	-	-	-	-	-	-	-
Friendly (cdp)	28,545	18,977	-	-	-	-	-	-	19,522	-	-	-	-	-	-	-	-	-	-	-	-	-	-	-
Glenn Dale (cdp)	27,920	29,595	-	-	-	-	-	-	-	-	-	-	-	-	-	-	-	-	-	-	-	-	-	-
Greenbelt (city)	25,236	20,890	-	21,983	-	-	19,776	-	-	-	-	-	-	-	22,921	-	-	-	-	-	-	-	-	-
Hyattsville (city)	20,152	14,634	-	-	-	-	-	-	-	-	-	-	-	-	-	-	-	-	-	-	-	-	-	-
Lanham-Seabrook (cdp)	25,066	31,270	-	-	-	-	-	-	-	-	-	-	-	-	-	-	-	-	-	-	-	-	-	-

Notes: Please refer to the User's Guide for an explanation of data; data is arranged alphabetically by state, then county, then city within each county; table includes counties with populations greater than 49,999 unless noted and cities with populations greater than 9,999 whose Asian and/or NHPI population rates are greater than the national average; (1) Native Hawaiian and other Pacific Islander; (2) excludes Taiwanese; (3) includes Chamorro; (4) county does not meet population threshold but is shown in order to allow inclusion of city

Place	Total population	Total Asian population	Total NHPI[1] population	Asian Indian	Bangladeshi	Cambodian	Chinese[2]	Fijian	Filipino	Guamanian[3]	Hawaiian, Native	Hmong	Indonesian	Japanese	Korean	Laotian	Malaysian	Pakistani	Samoan	Sri Lankan	Taiwanese	Thai	Tongan	Vietnamese
Laurel (city)	26,717	19,702	-	-	-	-	-	-	-	-	-	-	-	-	-	-	-	-	-	-	-	-	-	-
New Carrollton (city)	21,654	26,313	-	-	-	-	-	-	-	-	-	-	-	-	-	-	-	-	-	-	-	-	-	-
South Laurel (cdp)	24,564	22,426	-	-	-	-	-	-	-	-	-	-	-	-	-	-	-	-	-	-	-	-	-	-
St. Mary's County	22,662	23,393	-	42,322	-	-	-	-	18,898	-	-	-	-	-	-	-	-	-	-	-	-	-	-	-
Lexington Park (cdp)	17,605	14,502	-	-	-	-	-	-	-	-	-	-	-	-	-	-	-	-	-	-	-	-	-	-
Washington County	20,062	17,468	-	-	-	-	-	-	-	-	-	-	-	-	-	-	-	-	-	-	-	-	-	-
Wicomico County	19,171	15,358	-	24,079	-	-	-	-	-	-	-	-	-	-	10,180	-	-	-	-	-	-	-	-	-
Salisbury (city)	15,228	12,451	-	-	-	-	-	-	-	-	-	-	-	-	-	-	-	-	-	-	-	-	-	-
MASSACHUSETTS	25,952	21,452	16,948	31,702	18,694	10,306	23,101	-	26,109	15,809	16,939	8,472	15,264	23,302	19,827	14,299	-	14,809	-	23,204	26,526	19,885	-	13,522
Barnstable County	25,318	22,341	-	-	-	-	18,325	-	-	-	-	-	-	-	-	-	-	-	-	-	-	-	-	-
Berkshire County	21,807	15,190	-	15,208	-	-	-	-	-	-	-	-	-	-	-	-	-	-	-	-	-	-	-	-
Bristol County	20,978	20,098	-	39,881	-	7,781	20,272	-	27,109	-	-	-	-	-	9,698	-	-	-	-	-	-	-	-	22,373
Essex County	26,358	21,085	-	36,905	-	10,347	28,082	-	26,729	-	-	-	-	20,616	20,799	13,354	-	-	-	-	-	-	-	15,166
Andover (town)	41,133	38,603	-	48,406	-	-	35,276	-	-	-	-	-	-	-	-	-	-	-	-	-	-	-	-	-
Lynn (city)	17,492	10,764	-	6,026	-	10,275	-	-	-	-	-	-	-	-	-	-	-	-	-	-	-	-	-	10,549
North Andover (town)	34,335	38,044	-	-	-	-	47,069	-	-	-	-	-	-	-	-	-	-	-	-	-	-	-	-	-
Franklin County	20,672	12,788	-	-	-	-	-	-	-	-	-	-	-	-	-	-	-	-	-	-	-	-	-	-
Hampden County	19,541	19,409	-	41,072	-	9,831	24,340	-	-	-	-	-	-	-	17,354	-	-	-	-	-	-	-	-	12,344
Hampshire County	21,685	14,592	-	21,741	-	-	12,746	-	-	-	-	-	-	-	9,769	-	-	-	-	-	-	-	-	-
Amherst Center (cdp)	13,791	7,679	-	-	-	-	-	-	-	-	-	-	-	-	-	-	-	-	-	-	-	-	-	-
Amherst (town)	17,427	10,956	-	-	-	-	10,075	-	-	-	-	-	-	-	-	-	-	-	-	-	-	-	-	-
Middlesex County	31,199	24,582	-	31,656	-	10,583	28,322	-	26,282	-	-	-	-	29,225	20,341	15,515	-	13,983	-	-	29,949	19,501	-	17,048
Acton (town)	41,901	40,746	-	49,138	-	-	40,437	-	-	-	-	-	-	-	-	-	-	-	-	-	-	-	-	-
Arlington (town)	34,399	30,696	-	-	-	-	24,552	-	-	-	-	-	-	-	-	-	-	-	-	-	-	-	-	-
Bedford (town)	39,212	44,515	-	-	-	-	-	-	-	-	-	-	-	-	-	-	-	-	-	-	-	-	-	-
Belmont (cdp)	42,485	31,802	-	-	-	-	36,606	-	-	-	-	-	-	-	-	-	-	-	-	-	-	-	-	-
Belmont (town)	42,485	31,802	-	-	-	-	36,606	-	-	-	-	-	-	-	-	-	-	-	-	-	-	-	-	-
Burlington (town)	30,732	31,268	-	33,078	-	-	-	-	-	-	-	-	-	-	-	-	-	-	-	-	-	-	-	-
Cambridge (city)	31,156	21,066	-	24,682	-	-	20,684	-	-	-	-	-	-	24,948	19,621	-	-	-	-	-	-	-	-	-
Chelmsford (town)	30,465	32,496	-	46,651	-	-	35,371	-	-	-	-	-	-	-	-	-	-	-	-	-	-	-	-	-
Framingham (town)	27,758	28,806	-	34,141	-	-	30,444	-	-	-	-	-	-	-	-	-	-	-	-	-	-	-	-	-
Lexington (town)	46,119	36,177	-	46,360	-	-	35,504	-	-	-	-	-	-	-	18,215	-	-	-	-	-	-	-	-	-
Lowell (city)	17,557	12,729	-	20,327	-	9,727	19,938	-	-	-	-	-	-	-	-	15,844	-	-	-	-	-	-	-	13,983
Malden (city)	22,004	18,894	-	29,964	-	-	18,173	-	-	-	-	-	-	-	-	-	-	-	-	-	-	-	-	14,690
Marlborough (city)	28,723	28,657	-	33,368	-	-	-	-	-	-	-	-	-	-	-	-	-	-	-	-	-	-	-	-
Medford (city)	24,707	18,645	-	26,280	-	-	20,102	-	-	-	-	-	-	-	-	-	-	-	-	-	-	-	-	14,841
Natick (town)	36,358	29,058	-	-	-	-	31,487	-	-	-	-	-	-	-	-	-	-	-	-	-	-	-	-	-
Newton (city)	45,708	32,796	-	52,375	-	-	32,185	-	-	-	-	-	-	-	29,795	-	-	-	-	-	-	-	-	-
Somerville (city)	23,628	19,311	-	20,366	-	-	17,070	-	-	-	-	-	-	-	18,789	-	-	-	-	-	-	-	-	-
Sudbury (town)	53,285	48,446	-	-	-	-	-	-	-	-	-	-	-	-	-	-	-	-	-	-	-	-	-	-
Waltham (city)	26,364	24,248	-	24,643	-	-	29,198	-	-	-	-	-	-	-	-	-	-	-	-	-	-	-	-	-

Notes: Please refer to the User's Guide for an explanation of data; data is arranged alphabetically by state, then county, then city within each county; table includes counties with populations greater than 49,999 unless noted and cities with populations greater than 9,999 whose Asian and/or NHPI population rates are greater than the national average; (1) Native Hawaiian and other Pacific Islander; (2) excludes Taiwanese; (3) includes Chamorro; (4) county does not meet population threshold but is shown in order to allow inclusion of city

Place	Total population	Total Asian population	Total NHPI[1] population	Asian Indian	Bangladeshi	Cambodian	Chinese[2]	Fijian	Filipino	Guamanian[3]	Hawaiian, Native	Hmong	Indonesian	Japanese	Korean	Laotian	Malaysian	Pakistani	Samoan	Sri Lankan	Taiwanese	Thai	Tongan	Vietnamese
Wayland (town)	52,717	40,943	-	-	-	-	-	-	-	-	-	-	-	-	-	-	-	-	-	-	-	-	-	-
Westford (town)	37,979	41,456	-	-	-	-	54,309	-	-	-	-	-	-	-	-	-	-	-	-	-	-	-	-	-
Weston (town)	79,640	38,718	-	-	-	-	39,268	-	-	-	-	-	-	-	-	-	-	-	-	-	-	-	-	-
Winchester (town)	50,414	36,340	-	-	-	-	-	-	-	-	-	-	-	-	-	-	-	-	-	-	-	-	-	-
Woburn (city)	26,207	26,110	-	25,875	-	-	-	-	-	-	-	-	-	-	-	-	-	-	-	-	-	-	-	-
Norfolk County	32,484	24,578	-	37,442	-	-	22,943	-	30,648	-	-	-	-	21,306	25,252	-	-	-	-	-	15,070	-	-	16,907
Brookline (town)	44,327	28,730	-	42,496	-	-	28,172	-	-	-	-	-	-	21,238	31,325	-	-	-	-	-	-	-	-	-
Needham (town)	44,549	39,176	-	-	-	-	46,730	-	-	-	-	-	-	-	-	-	-	-	-	-	-	-	-	-
Norwood (town)	27,720	33,544	-	31,794	-	-	-	-	-	-	-	-	-	-	-	-	-	-	-	-	-	-	-	-
Quincy (city)	26,001	17,287	-	33,991	-	-	15,548	-	25,144	-	-	-	-	-	-	-	-	-	-	-	-	-	-	13,290
Randolph (town)	23,413	20,952	-	-	-	-	16,642	-	-	-	-	-	-	-	-	-	-	-	-	-	-	-	-	18,353
Sharon (town)	41,323	60,619	-	-	-	-	-	-	-	-	-	-	-	-	-	-	-	-	-	-	-	-	-	-
Wellesley (town)	52,866	22,957	-	-	-	-	28,116	-	-	-	-	-	-	-	-	-	-	-	-	-	-	-	-	-
Plymouth County	24,789	20,837	-	29,086	-	-	18,121	-	24,102	-	-	-	-	-	-	-	-	-	-	-	-	-	-	16,383
Suffolk County	22,766	15,218	-	22,857	-	8,699	15,864	-	21,985	-	-	-	-	15,753	19,900	-	-	-	-	-	18,845	-	-	10,221
Boston (city)	23,353	15,513	-	22,713	-	11,274	15,777	-	21,955	-	-	-	-	15,681	20,520	-	-	-	-	-	18,845	-	-	10,434
Chelsea (city)	14,628	9,204	-	-	-	-	-	-	-	-	-	-	-	-	-	-	-	-	-	-	-	-	-	9,302
Revere (city)	19,698	12,417	-	-	-	6,330	-	-	-	-	-	-	-	-	-	-	-	-	-	-	-	-	-	7,622
Worcester County	22,983	20,261	-	30,755	-	13,107	24,527	-	29,488	-	-	6,916	-	18,261	20,018	14,035	-	16,063	-	-	-	-	-	13,637
Fitchburg (city)	17,256	9,867	-	-	-	-	-	-	-	-	-	6,828	-	-	-	11,417	-	-	-	-	-	-	-	-
Northborough (town)	32,889	33,696	-	-	-	-	-	-	-	-	-	-	-	-	-	-	-	-	-	-	-	-	-	-
Shrewsbury (town)	31,570	29,799	-	37,033	-	-	27,776	-	-	-	-	-	-	-	-	-	-	-	-	-	-	-	-	16,092
Westborough (town)	35,063	31,207	-	29,413	-	-	31,202	-	-	-	-	-	-	-	-	-	-	-	-	-	-	-	-	-
Worcester (city)	18,614	13,814	-	18,612	-	-	13,794	-	-	-	-	-	-	-	-	-	-	-	-	-	-	-	-	12,073
MICHIGAN	22,168	24,581	16,378	31,216	12,217	14,121	24,906	-	28,788	15,127	19,340	7,696	14,904	29,197	16,109	16,755	14,191	22,883	11,358	24,031	29,836	19,980	-	17,020
Allegan County	19,918	17,976	-	-	-	-	-	-	-	-	-	-	-	-	-	-	-	-	-	-	-	-	-	-
Bay County	19,698	19,073	-	-	-	-	-	-	-	-	-	-	-	-	-	-	-	-	-	-	-	-	-	-
Berrien County	19,952	20,385	-	27,198	-	-	-	-	26,328	-	-	-	-	-	8,449	-	-	-	-	-	-	-	-	-
Calhoun County	19,230	29,004	-	-	-	-	-	-	-	-	-	-	-	26,076	-	-	-	-	-	-	-	-	-	-
Cass County	19,474	15,319	-	-	-	-	-	-	-	-	-	-	-	-	-	12,224	-	-	-	-	-	-	-	-
Clinton County	22,913	13,812	-	-	-	-	-	-	-	-	-	-	-	-	-	-	-	-	-	-	-	-	-	-
Eaton County	22,411	16,879	-	22,262	-	-	-	-	-	-	-	-	-	-	-	-	-	-	-	-	-	-	-	13,970
Genesee County	20,883	36,055	-	53,544	-	-	27,673	-	31,221	-	-	-	-	-	15,515	-	-	-	-	-	-	-	-	-
Ingham County	21,079	15,558	-	30,445	-	-	16,017	-	16,651	-	-	2,213	-	20,011	7,484	-	-	-	-	-	-	-	-	9,945
East Lansing (city)	16,333	12,998	-	29,665	-	-	13,139	-	-	-	-	-	-	-	7,054	-	-	-	-	-	-	-	-	-
Meridian charter (township)	32,190	22,502	-	30,498	-	-	18,323	-	-	-	-	-	-	-	9,935	-	-	-	-	-	-	-	-	-
Okemos (cdp)	33,401	21,126	-	23,678	-	-	22,246	-	-	-	-	-	-	-	-	-	-	-	-	-	-	-	-	-
Ionia County	17,451	11,655	-	-	-	-	-	-	-	-	-	-	-	-	-	-	-	-	-	-	-	-	-	-
Isabella County	16,242	15,106	-	-	-	-	-	-	-	-	-	-	-	-	-	-	-	-	-	-	-	-	-	-
Jackson County	20,171	30,483	-	-	-	-	-	-	-	-	-	-	-	-	-	-	-	-	-	-	-	-	-	-
Kalamazoo County	21,739	19,261	-	21,266	-	-	21,518	-	-	-	-	-	-	-	9,485	-	-	-	-	-	-	-	-	-

Notes: Please refer to the User's Guide for an explanation of data; data is arranged alphabetically by state, then county, then city within each county; table includes counties with populations greater than 49,999 unless noted and cities with populations greater than 9,999 whose Asian and/or NHPI population rates are greater than the national average; (1) Native Hawaiian and other Pacific Islander; (2) excludes Taiwanese; (3) includes Chamorro; (4) county does not meet population threshold but is shown in order to allow inclusion of city

Place	Total population	Total Asian population	Total NHPI[1] population	Asian Indian	Bangladeshi	Cambodian	Chinese[2]	Fijian	Filipino	Guamanian[3]	Hawaiian, Native	Hmong	Indonesian	Japanese	Korean	Laotian	Malaysian	Pakistani	Samoan	Sri Lankan	Taiwanese	Thai	Tongan	Vietnamese
Kent County	21,629	17,766	-	29,170	-	-	19,419	-	19,220	-	-	-	-	-	11,859	-	-	-	-	-	-	-	-	16,008
Kentwood (city)	22,463	17,816	-	-	-	-	-	-	-	-	-	-	-	-	14,761	-	-	-	-	-	-	-	-	14,071
Lenawee County	20,186	26,058	-	-	-	-	-	-	-	-	-	-	-	-	-	-	-	-	-	-	-	-	-	-
Livingston County	28,069	32,592	-	-	-	-	-	-	-	-	-	-	-	-	-	-	-	-	-	-	-	-	-	-
Macomb County	24,446	19,850	-	20,938	-	-	17,825	-	26,885	-	-	11,946	-	-	15,356	-	-	14,589	-	-	-	-	-	17,431
Sterling Heights (city)	24,958	22,610	-	22,328	-	-	21,479	-	30,633	-	-	-	-	-	14,232	-	-	-	-	-	-	-	-	24,701
Marquette County	18,070	13,586	-	-	-	-	-	-	-	-	-	-	-	-	-	-	-	-	-	-	-	-	-	-
Midland County	23,383	34,555	-	40,152	-	-	33,872	-	-	-	-	-	-	-	-	-	-	-	-	-	-	-	-	-
Monroe County	22,458	25,188	-	-	-	-	-	-	-	-	-	-	-	-	-	-	-	-	-	-	-	-	-	-
Muskegon County	17,967	13,750	-	-	-	-	-	-	-	-	-	-	-	-	-	-	-	-	-	-	-	-	-	-
Oakland County	32,534	32,992	-	38,716	-	-	30,346	-	32,748	-	-	10,256	-	35,824	27,171	-	-	30,793	-	-	32,874	-	-	18,511
Auburn Hills (city)	25,529	22,205	-	25,638	-	-	-	-	-	-	-	-	-	-	-	-	-	-	-	-	-	-	-	-
Bloomfield (township)	62,716	62,343	-	71,576	-	-	-	-	-	-	-	-	-	-	54,346	-	-	-	-	-	-	-	-	-
Farmington (city)	32,452	26,369	-	28,447	-	-	-	-	-	-	-	-	-	-	-	-	-	-	-	-	-	-	-	-
Farmington Hills (city)	36,134	34,705	-	37,368	-	-	32,798	-	28,042	-	-	-	-	-	-	-	-	-	-	-	-	-	-	-
Madison Heights (city)	21,429	25,394	-	-	-	-	23,129	-	-	-	-	-	-	-	-	-	-	-	-	-	-	-	-	-
Novi (city)	35,992	35,422	-	41,201	-	-	38,433	-	-	-	-	-	-	33,251	-	-	-	-	-	-	-	-	-	-
Rochester (city)	36,989	32,901	-	-	-	-	-	-	-	-	-	-	-	-	-	-	-	-	-	-	-	-	-	-
Rochester Hills (city)	35,070	32,191	-	37,373	-	-	27,549	-	-	-	-	-	-	-	19,401	-	-	-	-	-	-	-	-	-
Troy (city)	35,936	31,938	-	35,652	-	-	29,436	-	34,817	-	-	-	-	-	22,828	-	-	-	-	-	34,534	-	-	-
West Bloomfield (township)	44,885	38,866	-	47,579	-	-	48,152	-	30,533	-	-	-	-	36,297	28,268	-	-	-	-	-	-	-	-	-
Ottawa County	21,676	16,239	-	16,216	-	13,892	17,410	-	-	-	-	-	-	-	4,888	18,180	-	-	-	-	-	-	-	18,188
Holland (city)	18,823	20,162	-	-	-	-	-	-	-	-	-	-	-	-	-	-	-	-	-	-	-	-	-	-
Saginaw County	19,438	27,443	-	47,365	-	-	-	-	22,569	-	-	-	-	-	19,837	-	-	-	-	-	-	-	-	-
St. Clair County	21,582	33,931	-	-	-	-	-	-	-	-	-	-	-	-	-	-	-	-	-	-	-	-	-	-
St. Joseph County	18,247	28,460	-	-	-	-	-	-	-	-	-	-	-	-	-	-	-	-	-	-	-	-	-	-
Washtenaw County	27,173	23,088	-	29,749	-	-	22,284	-	34,948	-	-	-	-	24,423	15,225	-	-	22,061	-	-	26,708	-	-	15,692
Ann Arbor (city)	26,419	19,979	-	23,444	-	-	18,834	-	32,120	-	-	-	-	25,201	13,158	-	-	-	-	-	27,877	-	-	-
Pittsfield charter (township)	29,645	29,230	-	45,845	-	-	32,682	-	-	-	-	-	-	-	18,003	-	-	-	-	-	-	-	-	-
Scio (township)	36,837	44,728	-	-	-	-	-	-	-	-	-	-	-	-	-	-	-	-	-	-	-	-	-	-
Wayne County	20,058	22,743	19,981	24,105	8,771	-	28,251	-	29,087	-	-	5,691	-	29,990	16,584	-	-	18,064	-	-	-	-	-	28,621
Brownstown (township)	22,523	22,262	-	-	-	-	-	-	-	-	-	-	-	-	-	-	-	-	-	-	-	-	-	-
Canton (township)	28,609	27,620	-	26,905	-	-	30,017	-	33,159	-	-	-	-	-	19,996	-	-	-	-	-	-	-	-	-
Hamtramck (city)	12,691	8,326	-	7,659	6,694	-	-	-	-	-	-	-	-	-	-	-	-	-	-	-	-	-	-	-
Inkster (city)	16,711	26,008	-	28,559	-	-	-	-	-	-	-	-	-	-	-	-	-	-	-	-	-	-	-	-
Northville (township)	40,258	38,755	-	45,454	-	-	-	-	-	-	-	-	-	-	-	-	-	-	-	-	-	-	-	-
MINNESOTA	23,198	15,389	16,948	27,156	-	11,432	23,935	-	21,393	19,113	16,050	7,210	-	23,586	13,081	12,640	-	27,195	-	-	31,856	25,672	-	16,509
Anoka County	23,297	18,563	-	19,978	-	-	27,497	-	20,470	-	-	13,137	-	-	14,068	-	-	-	-	-	-	-	-	18,927
Columbia Heights (city)	21,368	13,434	-	-	-	-	-	-	-	-	-	-	-	-	-	-	-	-	-	-	-	-	-	-
Blue Earth County	18,712	11,260	-	-	-	-	-	-	-	-	-	-	-	-	-	-	-	-	-	-	-	-	-	-
Carver County	28,486	24,147	-	-	-	-	-	-	-	-	-	-	-	-	-	-	-	-	-	-	-	-	-	-

Notes: Please refer to the User's Guide for an explanation of data; data is arranged alphabetically by state, then county, then city within each county; table includes counties with populations greater than 49,999 unless noted and cities with populations greater than 9,999 whose Asian and/or NHPI population rates are greater than the national average; (1) Native Hawaiian and other Pacific Islander; (2) excludes Taiwanese; (3) includes Chamorro; (4) county does not meet population threshold but is shown in order to allow inclusion of city

Place	Total population	Total Asian population	Total NHPI[1] population	Asian Indian	Bangladeshi	Cambodian	Chinese[2]	Fijian	Filipino	Guamanian[3]	Hawaiian, Native	Hmong	Indonesian	Japanese	Korean	Laotian	Malaysian	Pakistani	Samoan	Sri Lankan	Taiwanese	Thai	Tongan	Vietnamese
Clay County	17,557	13,836	-	-	-	-	-	-	-	-	-	-	-	-	-	-	-	-	-	-	-	-	-	-
Crow Wing County	19,174	13,537	-	-	-	-	-	-	-	-	-	-	-	-	-	-	-	-	-	-	-	-	-	-
Dakota County	27,008	20,395	-	29,637	-	12,735	25,931	-	20,105	-	-	-	-	-	11,505	13,960	-	-	-	-	-	-	-	16,764
Eagan (city)	30,167	21,946	-	29,023	-	-	33,093	-	-	-	-	-	-	-	-	-	-	-	-	-	-	-	-	13,262
Hennepin County	28,789	16,734	19,761	27,856	-	12,711	23,689	-	23,805	-	-	6,365	-	27,247	15,973	14,584	-	23,567	-	-	-	-	-	16,441
Bloomington (city)	29,782	20,198	-	23,307	-	11,991	22,432	-	-	-	-	-	-	-	20,092	-	-	-	-	-	-	-	-	21,822
Brooklyn Center (city)	19,695	11,925	-	-	-	-	-	-	-	-	-	9,347	-	-	-	15,005	-	-	-	-	-	-	-	-
Brooklyn Park (city)	23,199	15,702	-	23,990	-	-	-	-	-	-	-	7,047	-	-	-	15,326	-	-	-	-	-	-	-	16,985
Eden Prairie (city)	38,854	24,649	-	31,834	-	-	27,833	-	-	-	-	-	-	-	-	-	-	-	-	-	-	-	-	19,433
Hopkins (city)	26,759	17,105	-	20,933	-	-	-	-	-	-	-	-	-	-	-	-	-	-	-	-	-	-	-	-
Minneapolis (city)	22,685	11,460	-	19,405	-	9,176	18,438	-	21,800	-	-	5,500	-	29,814	15,002	10,817	-	-	-	-	-	-	-	11,987
Plymouth (city)	36,309	28,360	-	36,398	-	-	32,721	-	-	-	-	-	-	-	21,196	-	-	-	-	-	-	-	-	-
Richfield (city)	24,709	20,752	-	-	-	-	-	-	-	-	-	-	-	-	-	-	-	-	-	-	-	-	-	16,304
Nobles County[4]	16,987	10,272	-	-	-	-	-	-	-	-	-	-	-	-	-	7,918	-	-	-	-	-	-	-	-
Worthington (city)	18,078	10,560	-	-	-	-	-	-	-	-	-	-	-	-	-	7,667	-	-	-	-	-	-	-	-
Olmsted County	24,939	19,573	-	27,162	-	11,003	36,833	-	-	-	-	7,772	-	18,856	14,388	9,940	-	-	-	-	-	-	-	15,938
Rochester (city)	24,811	18,500	-	25,398	-	7,192	35,846	-	-	-	-	7,772	-	-	14,845	9,839	-	-	-	-	-	-	-	13,572
Otter Tail County	18,014	15,664	-	-	-	-	-	-	-	-	-	-	-	-	-	-	-	-	-	-	-	-	-	-
Ramsey County	23,536	11,501	-	29,446	-	8,859	21,327	-	18,177	-	-	7,222	-	26,790	12,279	7,182	-	-	-	-	-	-	-	15,936
Maplewood (city)	24,387	17,081	-	-	-	-	24,536	-	-	-	-	9,096	-	-	-	-	-	-	-	-	-	-	-	-
New Brighton (city)	27,574	26,614	-	-	-	-	-	-	-	-	-	-	-	-	-	-	-	-	-	-	-	-	-	-
Roseville (city)	27,755	19,880	-	-	-	-	17,810	-	-	-	-	-	-	-	-	-	-	-	-	-	-	-	-	-
St. Paul (city)	20,216	8,581	-	17,883	-	8,255	19,000	-	16,113	-	-	6,996	-	-	10,267	6,328	-	-	-	-	-	-	-	12,705
Vadnais Heights (city)	30,891	29,365	-	-	-	-	-	-	-	-	-	-	-	-	-	-	-	-	-	-	-	-	-	-
Rice County	19,695	15,772	-	-	-	-	-	-	-	-	-	-	-	-	-	-	-	-	-	-	-	-	-	-
St. Louis County	18,982	13,655	-	-	-	-	-	-	-	-	-	-	-	-	7,852	-	-	-	-	-	-	-	-	-
Scott County	26,418	20,017	-	-	-	14,085	-	-	-	-	-	-	-	-	-	-	-	-	-	-	-	-	-	21,538
Savage (city)	26,858	21,134	-	-	-	-	-	-	-	-	-	-	-	-	-	-	-	-	-	-	-	-	-	-
Sherburne County	21,322	13,973	-	-	-	-	-	-	-	-	-	-	-	-	-	-	-	-	-	-	-	-	-	-
Stearns County	19,211	10,955	-	-	-	-	-	-	-	-	-	-	-	-	-	-	-	-	-	-	-	-	-	13,125
Washington County	28,148	25,280	-	38,363	-	-	34,567	-	-	-	-	15,276	-	-	20,894	-	-	-	-	-	-	-	-	20,035
Woodbury (city)	32,606	29,606	-	37,909	-	-	42,889	-	-	-	-	20,353	-	-	-	-	-	-	-	-	-	-	-	-
Wright County	21,844	11,861	-	-	-	-	-	-	-	-	-	-	-	-	-	-	-	-	-	-	-	-	-	-
MISSISSIPPI	15,853	17,504	19,794	25,253	-	-	19,600	-	19,272	-	-	-	-	15,612	13,374	-	-	-	-	-	-	-	-	11,715
DeSoto County	20,468	17,027	-	-	-	-	-	-	-	-	-	-	-	-	-	-	-	-	-	-	-	-	-	-
Forrest County	15,160	6,426	-	-	-	-	-	-	-	-	-	-	-	-	-	-	-	-	-	-	-	-	-	-
Harrison County	18,024	14,111	-	-	-	-	-	-	13,864	-	-	-	-	-	-	-	-	-	-	-	-	-	-	10,834
Biloxi (city)	17,809	13,073	-	-	-	-	-	-	12,096	-	-	-	-	-	-	-	-	-	-	-	-	-	-	11,232
Hinds County	17,785	28,392	-	40,563	-	-	-	-	-	-	-	-	-	-	-	-	-	-	-	-	-	-	-	-
Jackson County	17,768	16,203	-	-	-	-	-	-	-	-	-	-	-	-	-	-	-	-	-	-	-	-	-	14,108
Madison County	23,469	27,106	-	-	-	-	-	-	-	-	-	-	-	-	-	-	-	-	-	-	-	-	-	-

Notes: Please refer to the User's Guide for an explanation of data; data is arranged alphabetically by state, then county, then city within each county; table includes counties with populations greater than 49,999 unless noted and cities with populations greater than 9,999 whose Asian and/or NHPI population rates are greater than the national average; (1) Native Hawaiian and other Pacific Islander; (2) excludes Taiwanese; (3) includes Chamorro; (4) county does not meet population threshold but is shown in order to allow inclusion of city

Place	Total population	Total Asian population	Total NHPI[1] population	Asian Indian	Bangladeshi	Cambodian	Chinese[2]	Fijian	Filipino	Guamanian[3]	Hawaiian, Native	Hmong	Indonesian	Japanese	Korean	Laotian	Malaysian	Pakistani	Samoan	Sri Lankan	Taiwanese	Thai	Tongan	Vietnamese
Oktibbeha County[4]	14,998	12,519	-	-	-	-	-	-	-	-	-	-	-	-	-	-	-	-	-	-	-	-	-	-
Starkville (city)	16,272	13,269	-	-	-	-	-	-	-	-	-	-	-	-	-	-	-	-	-	-	-	-	-	-
Rankin County	20,412	20,413	-	-	-	-	-	-	-	-	-	-	-	-	-	-	-	-	-	-	-	-	-	-
MISSOURI	19,936	21,297	14,012	32,027	-	10,068	19,597	-	23,686	16,965	15,832	-	-	19,581	17,552	16,214	-	17,647	12,563	-	35,060	19,771	-	14,208
Boone County	19,844	18,240	-	33,971	-	-	15,140	-	-	-	-	-	-	-	11,085	-	-	-	-	-	-	-	-	-
Columbia (city)	19,507	17,811	-	33,846	-	-	13,371	-	-	-	-	-	-	-	11,696	-	-	-	-	-	-	-	-	-
Cape Girardeau County	18,593	18,037	-	-	-	-	-	-	-	-	-	-	-	-	-	-	-	-	-	-	-	-	-	-
Cass County	21,073	17,820	-	-	-	-	-	-	-	-	-	-	-	-	-	-	-	-	-	-	-	-	-	-
Clay County	23,144	19,674	-	28,433	-	-	-	-	-	-	-	-	-	-	-	-	-	-	-	-	-	-	-	15,365
Cole County	20,739	25,242	-	-	-	-	-	-	-	-	-	-	-	-	-	-	-	-	-	-	-	-	-	-
Franklin County	19,705	12,447	-	-	-	-	-	-	-	-	-	-	-	-	-	-	-	-	-	-	-	-	-	-
Greene County	19,185	17,419	-	-	-	-	6,949	-	-	-	-	-	-	-	12,577	-	-	-	-	-	-	-	-	20,809
Jackson County	20,788	15,264	13,013	20,815	-	-	16,883	-	20,336	-	-	-	-	19,357	14,537	-	-	-	13,235	-	-	-	-	11,235
Independence (city)	19,384	18,175	12,077	-	-	-	-	-	-	-	-	-	-	-	-	-	-	-	-	-	-	-	-	-
Jasper County	16,227	13,272	-	-	-	-	-	-	-	-	-	-	-	-	-	-	-	-	-	-	-	-	-	-
Jefferson County	19,435	15,597	-	-	-	-	-	-	-	-	-	-	-	-	-	-	-	-	-	-	-	-	-	-
Newton County	17,502	23,607	-	-	-	-	-	-	-	-	-	-	-	-	-	-	-	-	-	-	-	-	-	-
Phelps County[4]	16,084	16,681	-	25,099	-	-	-	-	-	-	-	-	-	-	-	-	-	-	-	-	-	-	-	-
Rolla (city)	15,916	16,527	-	-	-	-	-	-	-	-	-	-	-	-	-	-	-	-	-	-	-	-	-	-
Platte County	26,356	22,647	-	-	-	-	-	-	-	-	-	-	-	-	-	-	-	-	-	-	-	-	-	-
St. Charles County	23,592	25,780	-	39,300	-	-	24,250	-	19,176	-	-	-	-	-	-	-	-	-	-	-	-	-	-	-
Saint Louis Independent City	16,108	15,403	-	21,079	-	-	13,940	-	25,241	-	-	-	-	-	-	-	-	-	-	-	-	-	-	12,663
St. Louis County	27,595	28,425	11,793	37,875	-	-	23,710	-	33,176	-	-	-	-	23,722	21,159	-	-	16,187	-	-	41,750	23,860	-	22,016
Chesterfield (city)	43,288	36,305	-	33,944	-	-	33,970	-	-	-	-	-	-	-	-	-	-	-	-	-	-	-	-	-
Clayton (city)	48,055	30,256	-	-	-	-	-	-	-	-	-	-	-	-	-	-	-	-	-	-	-	-	-	-
Creve Coeur (city)	47,905	53,566	-	-	-	-	-	-	-	-	-	-	-	-	-	-	-	-	-	-	-	-	-	-
Manchester (city)	27,663	21,867	-	-	-	-	-	-	-	-	-	-	-	-	-	-	-	-	-	-	-	-	-	-
Maryland Heights (city)	24,918	22,542	-	26,865	-	-	18,283	-	-	-	-	-	-	-	-	-	-	-	-	-	-	-	-	-
Town and Country (city)	69,347	78,526	-	114,911	-	-	-	-	-	-	-	-	-	-	-	-	-	-	-	-	-	-	-	-
MONTANA	17,151	14,464	11,373	13,398	-	-	15,506	-	22,382	-	10,578	-	-	14,220	7,704	-	-	-	-	-	-	-	-	-
Cascade County	17,566	22,148	-	-	-	-	-	-	-	-	-	-	-	-	-	-	-	-	-	-	-	-	-	-
Flathead County	18,112	10,902	-	-	-	-	-	-	-	-	-	-	-	-	-	-	-	-	-	-	-	-	-	-
Gallatin County	19,074	10,980	-	-	-	-	-	-	-	-	-	-	-	-	-	-	-	-	-	-	-	-	-	-
Missoula County	17,808	13,565	-	-	-	-	-	-	-	-	-	-	-	-	-	-	-	-	-	-	-	-	-	-
Yellowstone County	19,303	17,198	-	-	-	-	-	-	-	-	-	-	-	-	-	-	-	-	-	-	-	-	-	-
NEBRASKA	19,613	16,739	13,670	27,837	-	-	18,160	-	17,915	-	-	-	-	18,593	10,162	12,523	-	-	-	-	-	20,796	-	13,242
Douglas County	22,879	19,061	-	27,705	-	-	20,595	-	19,646	-	-	-	-	13,911	10,707	-	-	-	-	-	-	-	-	14,232
Hall County	17,386	13,758	-	-	-	-	-	-	-	-	-	-	-	-	-	-	-	-	-	-	-	-	-	-
Lancaster County	21,265	15,251	-	31,448	-	-	14,302	-	-	-	-	-	-	-	10,814	-	-	-	-	-	-	-	-	12,975
Sarpy County	21,985	17,049	-	-	-	-	-	-	15,314	-	-	-	-	-	14,241	-	-	-	-	-	-	-	-	15,060
NEVADA	21,989	20,018	18,652	20,849	-	12,874	25,777	-	18,029	17,541	24,912	-	-	22,756	21,187	14,026	-	16,824	11,245	-	17,802	19,255	12,155	18,879

Notes: Please refer to the User's Guide for an explanation of data; data is arranged alphabetically by state, then county, then city within each county; table includes counties with populations greater than 49,999 unless noted and cities with populations greater than 9,999 whose Asian and/or NHPI population rates are greater than the national average; (1) Native Hawaiian and other Pacific Islander; (2) excludes Taiwanese; (3) includes Chamorro; (4) county does not meet population threshold but is shown in order to allow inclusion of city

Place	Total population	Total Asian population	Total NHPI[1] population	Asian Indian	Bangladeshi	Cambodian	Chinese[2]	Fijian	Filipino	Guamanian[3]	Hawaiian, Native	Hmong	Indonesian	Japanese	Korean	Laotian	Malaysian	Pakistani	Samoan	Sri Lankan	Taiwanese	Thai	Tongan	Vietnamese
Carson City Independent City	20,943	20,096	-	-	-	-	-	-	15,869	-	-	-	-	-	-	-	-	-	-	-	-	-	-	-
Clark County	21,785	20,493	18,425	23,631	-	12,902	27,286	-	18,108	18,397	21,412	-	-	22,764	21,463	14,160	-	-	11,440	-	19,970	19,629	-	20,105
Enterprise (cdp)	25,063	14,297	-	-	-	-	-	-	-	-	-	-	-	-	-	-	-	-	-	-	-	-	-	-
Henderson (city)	26,815	23,581	16,424	27,303	-	-	26,723	-	21,581	-	16,029	-	-	22,857	27,733	-	-	-	-	-	-	-	-	-
Las Vegas (city)	22,060	23,963	26,250	26,738	-	-	41,789	-	19,727	-	37,112	-	-	24,324	25,847	-	-	-	-	-	-	25,999	-	22,843
North Las Vegas (city)	16,023	18,468	13,761	-	-	-	-	-	19,102	-	-	-	-	-	-	-	-	-	-	-	-	-	-	-
Paradise (cdp)	21,258	17,999	14,830	19,883	-	-	19,593	-	16,787	-	15,474	-	-	22,127	16,518	-	-	-	-	-	-	-	-	18,328
Spring Valley (cdp)	26,321	20,510	16,166	-	-	-	22,984	-	17,891	-	-	-	-	23,261	23,142	-	-	-	-	-	-	16,895	-	18,965
Sunrise Manor (cdp)	16,659	15,736	16,146	-	-	-	20,995	-	15,599	-	-	-	-	16,185	17,187	-	-	-	-	-	-	-	-	-
Winchester (cdp)	20,615	19,668	-	-	-	-	-	-	14,264	-	-	-	-	-	-	-	-	-	-	-	-	-	-	-
Washoe County	24,277	18,011	12,222	15,228	-	-	20,631	-	17,604	-	-	-	-	23,047	22,120	-	-	-	-	-	-	-	10,787	13,760
Reno (city)	22,520	17,184	11,071	14,852	-	-	19,494	-	17,274	-	-	-	-	20,612	21,629	-	-	-	-	-	-	-	-	13,438
Sparks (city)	21,122	18,539	-	-	-	-	19,706	-	17,619	-	-	-	-	-	-	-	-	-	-	-	-	-	-	-
NEW HAMPSHIRE	23,844	21,538	-	27,991	-	-	24,960	-	18,245	-	-	-	-	17,712	14,026	16,022	-	-	-	-	-	-	-	17,582
Belknap County	22,758	13,667	-	-	-	-	-	-	-	-	-	-	-	-	-	-	-	-	-	-	-	-	-	-
Cheshire County	20,685	14,814	-	-	-	-	-	-	-	-	-	-	-	-	-	-	-	-	-	-	-	-	-	-
Grafton County	22,227	17,283	-	-	-	-	22,123	-	-	-	-	-	-	-	-	-	-	-	-	-	-	-	-	-
Hanover (town)	30,393	15,211	-	-	-	-	-	-	-	-	-	-	-	-	-	-	-	-	-	-	-	-	-	-
Hillsborough County	25,198	24,561	-	32,059	-	-	28,169	-	21,038	-	-	-	-	-	14,271	-	-	-	-	-	-	-	-	17,652
Nashua (city)	25,209	29,263	-	33,188	-	-	33,818	-	-	-	-	-	-	-	-	-	-	-	-	-	-	-	-	-
Merrimack County	23,208	15,952	-	-	-	-	-	-	-	-	-	-	-	-	-	-	-	-	-	-	-	-	-	-
Rockingham County	26,656	22,280	-	23,205	-	-	27,675	-	19,299	-	-	-	-	-	17,080	-	-	-	-	-	-	-	-	-
Strafford County	20,479	18,541	-	-	-	-	16,717	-	-	-	-	-	-	-	-	-	-	-	-	-	-	-	-	-
NEW JERSEY	27,006	27,581	23,745	28,828	14,400	14,827	32,113	-	26,970	18,139	35,864	-	26,385	37,964	21,384	14,294	-	20,291	26,074	30,753	31,184	23,932	-	18,492
Atlantic County	21,034	17,827	-	16,457	10,319	-	20,339	-	22,455	-	-	-	-	-	15,275	-	-	11,289	-	-	-	-	-	17,129
Atlantic City (city)	15,402	16,440	-	13,801	-	-	20,161	-	19,037	-	-	-	-	-	-	-	-	-	-	-	-	-	-	17,139
Brigantine (city)	23,950	15,158	-	-	-	-	-	-	-	-	-	-	-	-	-	-	-	-	-	-	-	-	-	-
Egg Harbor (township)	22,328	20,067	-	-	-	-	-	-	-	-	-	-	-	-	-	-	-	-	-	-	-	-	-	-
Galloway (township)	21,048	18,282	-	17,888	-	-	-	-	-	-	-	-	-	-	-	-	-	-	-	-	-	-	-	-
Ventnor City (city)	22,631	17,147	-	-	-	-	-	-	-	-	-	-	-	-	-	-	-	-	-	-	-	-	-	-
Bergen County	33,638	27,750	-	30,498	-	-	33,835	-	28,654	-	-	-	-	41,917	21,012	-	-	21,657	-	-	35,756	26,346	-	40,802
Bergenfield (borough)	24,706	21,812	-	20,949	-	-	-	-	22,299	-	-	-	-	-	-	-	-	-	-	-	-	-	-	-
Cliffside Park (borough)	28,516	30,967	-	-	-	-	-	-	-	-	-	-	-	51,674	19,979	-	-	-	-	-	-	-	-	-
Dumont (borough)	26,489	25,715	-	21,095	-	-	-	-	29,493	-	-	-	-	-	-	-	-	-	-	-	-	-	-	-
Elmwood Park (borough)	22,588	18,616	-	18,148	-	-	-	-	-	-	-	-	-	-	-	-	-	-	-	-	-	-	-	-
Englewood (city)	35,275	34,171	-	-	-	-	-	-	24,887	-	-	-	-	-	-	-	-	-	-	-	-	-	-	-
Fair Lawn (borough)	32,273	22,311	-	24,599	-	-	-	-	17,986	-	-	-	-	-	-	-	-	-	-	-	-	-	-	-
Fairview (borough)	18,835	15,282	-	-	-	-	-	-	-	-	-	-	-	-	-	-	-	-	-	-	-	-	-	-
Fort Lee (borough)	37,899	28,899	-	31,387	-	-	30,035	-	-	-	-	-	-	42,503	23,989	-	-	-	-	-	-	-	-	-
Franklin Lakes (borough)	59,763	41,712	-	-	-	-	-	-	-	-	-	-	-	-	-	-	-	-	-	-	-	-	-	-
Glen Rock (borough)	45,091	38,656	-	-	-	-	-	-	-	-	-	-	-	-	-	-	-	-	-	-	-	-	-	-

Notes: Please refer to the User's Guide for an explanation of data; data is arranged alphabetically by state, then county, then city within each county; table includes counties with populations greater than 49,999 unless noted and cities with populations greater than 9,999 whose Asian and/or NHPI population rates are greater than the national average; (1) Native Hawaiian and other Pacific Islander; (2) excludes Taiwanese; (3) includes Chamorro; (4) county does not meet population threshold but is shown in order to allow inclusion of city

Place	Total population	Total Asian population	Total NHPI[1] population	Asian Indian	Bangladeshi	Cambodian	Chinese[2]	Fijian	Filipino	Guamanian[3]	Hawaiian, Native	Hmong	Indonesian	Japanese	Korean	Laotian	Malaysian	Pakistani	Samoan	Sri Lankan	Taiwanese	Thai	Tongan	Vietnamese
Hackensack (city)	26,856	27,657	-	32,397	-	-	-	-	27,626	-	-	-	-	-	20,092	-	-	-	-	-	-	-	-	-
Hasbrouck Heights (borough)	29,626	24,014	-	-	-	-	-	-	-	-	-	-	-	-	-	-	-	-	-	-	-	-	-	-
Hillsdale (borough)	34,651	27,643	-	-	-	-	-	-	-	-	-	-	-	-	-	-	-	-	-	-	-	-	-	-
Little Ferry (borough)	24,210	20,525	-	22,246	-	-	-	-	28,826	-	-	-	-	-	14,717	-	-	-	-	-	-	-	-	-
Lodi (borough)	21,667	18,917	-	17,948	-	-	-	-	19,410	-	-	-	-	-	-	-	-	-	-	-	-	-	-	-
Lyndhurst (township)	25,940	22,454	-	-	-	-	-	-	-	-	-	-	-	-	-	-	-	-	-	-	-	-	-	-
Mahwah (township)	44,709	34,873	-	44,158	-	-	-	-	-	-	-	-	-	-	-	-	-	-	-	-	-	-	-	-
New Milford (borough)	29,064	27,282	-	26,559	-	-	-	-	28,009	-	-	-	-	-	-	-	-	-	-	-	-	-	-	-
North Arlington (borough)	24,441	21,025	-	-	-	-	-	-	-	-	-	-	-	-	-	-	-	-	-	-	-	-	-	-
Palisades Park (borough)	22,607	19,252	-	-	-	-	-	-	-	-	-	-	-	-	18,160	-	-	-	-	-	-	-	-	-
Paramus (borough)	29,295	26,283	-	28,205	-	-	30,453	-	30,621	-	-	-	-	-	19,378	-	-	-	-	-	-	-	-	-
Ramsey (borough)	41,964	34,333	-	-	-	-	-	-	-	-	-	-	-	-	-	-	-	-	-	-	-	-	-	-
Ridgefield (borough)	25,558	15,112	-	-	-	-	-	-	-	-	-	-	-	-	13,137	-	-	-	-	-	-	-	-	-
Ridgefield Park (village)	24,290	21,934	-	-	-	-	-	-	-	-	-	-	-	-	16,747	-	-	-	-	-	-	-	-	-
Ridgewood (village)	51,658	31,257	-	-	-	-	-	-	-	-	-	-	-	48,407	16,802	-	-	-	-	-	-	-	-	-
River Edge (borough)	33,188	29,047	-	-	-	-	-	-	-	-	-	-	-	-	10,871	-	-	-	-	-	-	-	-	-
Rutherford (borough)	30,495	22,724	-	25,509	-	-	-	-	-	-	-	-	-	-	13,380	-	-	-	-	-	-	-	-	-
Saddle Brook (township)	27,561	28,662	-	-	-	-	-	-	-	-	-	-	-	-	-	-	-	-	-	-	-	-	-	-
Teaneck (township)	32,212	26,283	-	25,993	-	-	-	-	29,950	-	-	-	-	-	-	-	-	-	-	-	-	-	-	-
Tenafly (borough)	53,170	24,412	-	-	-	-	29,216	-	-	-	-	-	-	-	14,634	-	-	-	-	-	-	-	-	-
Wallington (borough)	24,431	19,398	-	-	-	-	-	-	-	-	-	-	-	-	-	-	-	-	-	-	-	-	-	-
Westwood (borough)	32,083	24,776	-	-	-	-	-	-	-	-	-	-	-	-	-	-	-	-	-	-	-	-	-	-
Wyckoff (township)	49,375	47,763	-	-	-	-	-	-	-	-	-	-	-	-	-	-	-	-	-	-	-	-	-	-
Burlington County	26,339	25,621	-	27,272	-	-	25,446	-	31,062	-	-	-	-	31,851	17,477	-	-	-	-	-	-	-	-	20,292
Browns Mills (cdp)	17,678	11,775	-	-	-	-	-	-	-	-	-	-	-	-	12,284	-	-	-	-	-	-	-	-	-
Evesham (township)	29,494	25,712	-	27,569	-	-	17,452	-	-	-	-	-	-	-	-	-	-	-	-	-	-	-	-	-
Maple Shade (township)	23,812	21,472	-	22,722	-	-	-	-	-	-	-	-	-	-	-	-	-	-	-	-	-	-	-	-
Marlton (cdp)	25,145	17,919	-	-	-	-	-	-	-	-	-	-	-	-	-	-	-	-	-	-	-	-	-	-
Mount Laurel (township)	32,245	35,400	-	43,265	-	-	26,292	-	-	-	-	-	-	-	-	-	-	-	-	-	-	-	-	-
Camden County	22,354	19,276	-	24,961	-	10,977	20,026	-	22,390	-	-	-	-	-	15,460	-	-	16,002	-	-	-	-	-	11,212
Barclay-Kingston (cdp)	32,259	21,848	-	-	-	-	-	-	-	-	-	-	-	-	-	-	-	-	-	-	-	-	-	-
Bellmawr (borough)	19,863	13,696	-	-	-	-	-	-	-	-	-	-	-	-	-	-	-	-	-	-	-	-	-	-
Cherry Hill Mall (cdp)	28,892	15,585	-	-	-	-	-	-	-	-	-	-	-	-	-	-	-	-	-	-	-	-	-	-
Cherry Hill (township)	32,658	21,647	-	27,133	-	-	20,610	-	23,728	-	-	-	-	-	17,012	-	-	-	-	-	-	-	-	-
Echelon (cdp)	26,850	24,463	-	25,747	-	-	-	-	-	-	-	-	-	-	-	-	-	-	-	-	-	-	-	-
Greentree (cdp)	34,371	23,382	-	29,262	-	-	21,748	-	-	-	-	-	-	-	-	-	-	-	-	-	-	-	-	-
Pennsauken (township)	19,004	12,281	-	-	-	-	-	-	-	-	-	-	-	-	-	-	-	-	-	-	-	-	-	9,783
Springdale (cdp)	43,752	25,193	-	-	-	-	23,015	-	-	-	-	-	-	-	-	-	-	-	-	-	-	-	-	-
Voorhees (township)	33,635	28,243	-	29,804	-	-	30,971	-	23,285	-	-	-	-	-	-	-	-	-	-	-	-	-	-	-
Cape May County	24,172	30,638	-	-	-	-	-	-	-	-	-	-	-	-	-	-	-	-	-	-	-	-	-	-
Cumberland County	17,376	28,100	-	18,992	-	-	-	-	-	-	-	-	-	-	-	-	-	-	-	-	-	-	-	-

Notes: Please refer to the User's Guide for an explanation of data; data is arranged alphabetically by state, then county, then city within each county; table includes counties with populations greater than 49,999 unless noted and cities with populations greater than 9,999 whose Asian and/or NHPI population rates are greater than the national average; (1) Native Hawaiian and other Pacific Islander; (2) excludes Taiwanese; (3) includes Chamorro; (4) county does not meet population threshold but is shown in order to allow inclusion of city

Place	Total population	Total Asian population	Total NHPI[1] population	Asian Indian	Bangladeshi	Cambodian	Chinese[2]	Fijian	Filipino	Guamanian[3]	Hawaiian, Native	Hmong	Indonesian	Japanese	Korean	Laotian	Malaysian	Pakistani	Samoan	Sri Lankan	Taiwanese	Thai	Tongan	Vietnamese
Essex County	24,943	29,138	21,839	31,562	-	-	33,097	-	27,823	-	-	-	-	28,900	26,276	-	-	28,261	-	-	32,249	-	-	15,819
Belleville (township)	22,093	21,523	-	20,786	-	-	-	-	23,832	-	-	-	-	-	-	-	-	-	-	-	-	-	-	14,185
Bloomfield (township)	26,049	24,856	-	24,102	-	-	24,545	-	27,330	-	-	-	-	-	-	-	-	-	-	-	-	-	-	-
Cedar Grove (township)	36,558	47,386	-	-	-	-	-	-	-	-	-	-	-	-	-	-	-	-	-	-	-	-	-	-
Livingston (township)	47,218	33,609	-	50,008	-	-	33,590	-	27,757	-	-	-	-	-	23,860	-	-	-	-	-	-	-	-	-
Millburn (township)	76,796	46,240	-	-	-	-	39,629	-	-	-	-	-	-	-	-	-	-	-	-	-	-	-	-	-
Nutley (township)	28,039	27,337	-	30,016	-	-	-	-	29,248	-	-	-	-	-	-	-	-	-	-	-	-	-	-	-
Verona (township)	41,202	36,246	-	-	-	-	-	-	-	-	-	-	-	-	-	-	-	-	-	-	-	-	-	-
West Caldwell (township)	38,345	40,800	-	-	-	-	-	-	-	-	-	-	-	-	-	-	-	-	-	-	-	-	-	-
West Orange (township)	34,412	32,331	-	41,266	-	-	31,309	-	29,902	-	-	-	-	-	25,116	-	-	-	-	-	-	-	-	-
Gloucester County	22,708	22,919	-	24,123	-	-	21,077	-	28,388	-	-	-	-	-	12,466	-	-	-	-	-	-	-	-	-
Hudson County	21,154	23,135	-	20,866	-	-	28,796	-	23,730	-	-	-	-	37,369	27,456	-	-	13,912	-	-	-	-	-	18,326
Bayonne (city)	21,553	18,792	-	16,472	-	-	-	-	22,511	-	-	-	-	-	15,052	-	-	-	-	-	-	-	-	-
Guttenberg (town)	27,931	51,251	-	-	-	-	-	-	-	-	-	-	-	-	-	-	-	-	-	-	-	-	-	-
Harrison (town)	18,490	22,285	-	-	-	-	20,805	-	-	-	-	-	-	-	-	-	-	-	-	-	-	-	-	-
Hoboken (city)	43,195	35,272	-	31,540	-	-	32,662	-	-	-	-	-	-	-	-	-	-	-	-	-	-	-	-	-
Jersey City (city)	19,410	22,078	-	20,710	-	-	29,117	-	22,874	-	-	-	-	-	25,957	-	-	12,578	-	-	-	-	-	17,294
Kearny (town)	20,886	24,923	-	27,002	-	-	21,136	-	-	-	-	-	-	-	-	-	-	-	-	-	-	-	-	-
North Bergen (township)	20,058	19,496	-	16,372	-	-	16,534	-	-	-	-	-	-	-	-	-	-	-	-	-	-	-	-	-
Secaucus (town)	31,684	29,839	-	24,185	-	-	-	-	38,309	-	-	-	-	-	-	-	-	-	-	-	-	-	-	-
Weehawken (township)	29,269	44,587	-	-	-	-	-	-	-	-	-	-	-	-	-	-	-	-	-	-	-	-	-	-
Hunterdon County	36,370	32,445	-	37,069	-	-	34,648	-	-	-	-	-	-	-	-	-	-	-	-	-	-	-	-	-
Mercer County	27,914	32,224	-	32,133	-	-	36,218	-	27,411	-	-	-	-	36,899	30,040	-	-	30,655	-	-	29,092	-	-	-
East Windsor (township)	28,695	26,200	-	29,218	-	-	-	-	-	-	-	-	-	-	-	-	-	-	-	-	-	-	-	-
Hopewell (township)	43,947	57,581	-	-	-	-	-	-	-	-	-	-	-	-	-	-	-	-	-	-	-	-	-	-
Lawrence (township)	33,120	34,578	-	25,518	-	-	51,123	-	-	-	-	-	-	-	-	-	-	-	-	-	-	-	-	-
Princeton (borough)	27,292	13,643	-	-	-	-	-	-	-	-	-	-	-	-	-	-	-	-	-	-	-	-	-	-
Princeton (township)	56,360	44,173	-	45,741	-	-	35,773	-	-	-	-	-	-	-	-	-	-	-	-	-	-	-	-	-
West Windsor (township)	48,511	40,216	-	43,969	-	-	38,445	-	-	-	-	-	-	-	40,483	-	-	-	-	-	-	-	-	-
Middlesex County	26,535	27,439	-	28,658	17,069	-	29,295	-	27,717	-	-	-	23,436	28,021	19,201	-	-	19,699	-	28,666	28,526	-	-	16,564
Avenel (cdp)	19,794	24,042	-	25,916	-	-	-	-	-	-	-	-	-	-	-	-	-	-	-	-	-	-	-	-
Carteret (borough)	18,967	15,656	-	15,309	-	-	-	-	-	-	-	-	-	-	-	-	-	-	-	-	-	-	-	-
Colonia (cdp)	27,732	27,022	-	28,754	-	-	-	-	28,845	-	-	-	-	-	-	-	-	-	-	-	-	-	-	-
East Brunswick (township)	33,286	29,772	-	33,518	-	-	29,375	-	28,430	-	-	-	-	-	22,456	-	-	-	-	-	-	-	-	-
Edison (township)	30,148	29,219	-	29,866	-	-	30,554	-	29,463	-	-	-	-	-	21,023	-	-	24,735	-	-	25,150	-	-	-
Fords (cdp)	25,917	27,547	-	30,491	-	-	-	-	25,537	-	-	-	-	-	-	-	-	-	-	-	-	-	-	-
Highland Park (borough)	28,767	22,392	-	29,204	-	-	21,041	-	-	-	-	-	-	-	-	-	-	-	-	-	-	-	-	-
Iselin (cdp)	26,793	28,242	-	28,196	-	-	30,344	-	-	-	-	-	-	-	-	-	-	-	-	-	-	-	-	-
Metuchen (borough)	36,749	25,892	-	-	-	-	-	-	-	-	-	-	-	-	-	-	-	-	-	-	-	-	-	-
Middlesex (borough)	27,834	21,128	-	-	-	-	-	-	-	-	-	-	-	-	-	-	-	-	-	-	-	-	-	-
New Brunswick (city)	14,308	14,655	-	17,201	-	-	9,270	-	-	-	-	-	-	-	-	-	-	-	-	-	-	-	-	-

Notes: Please refer to the User's Guide for an explanation of data; data is arranged alphabetically by state, then county, then city within each county; table includes counties with populations greater than 49,999 unless noted and cities with populations greater than 9,999 whose Asian and/or NHPI population rates are greater than the national average; (1) Native Hawaiian and other Pacific Islander; (2) excludes Taiwanese; (3) includes Chamorro; (4) county does not meet population threshold but is shown in order to allow inclusion of city

Place	Total population	Total Asian population	Total NHPI[1] population	Asian Indian	Bangladeshi	Cambodian	Chinese[2]	Fijian	Filipino	Guamanian[3]	Hawaiian, Native	Hmong	Indonesian	Japanese	Korean	Laotian	Malaysian	Pakistani	Samoan	Sri Lankan	Taiwanese	Thai	Tongan	Vietnamese
North Brunswick (township)	28,431	27,779	-	28,252	-	-	28,589	-	36,775	-	-	-	-	-	17,449	-	-	-	-	-	-	-	-	-
Old Bridge (township)	26,814	24,097	-	23,244	-	-	28,261	-	28,025	-	-	-	-	-	-	-	-	18,890	-	-	-	-	-	-
Piscataway (township)	26,321	25,716	-	26,746	-	-	30,350	-	24,502	-	-	-	-	-	12,867	-	-	-	-	-	-	-	-	-
Plainsboro (township)	38,982	33,237	-	34,075	-	-	32,902	-	-	-	-	-	-	-	-	-	-	-	-	-	-	-	-	-
Princeton Meadows (cdp)	36,654	32,306	-	32,590	-	-	34,470	-	-	-	-	-	-	-	-	-	-	-	-	-	-	-	-	-
Sayreville (borough)	24,736	23,915	-	24,724	-	-	23,018	-	24,296	-	-	-	-	-	-	-	-	-	-	-	-	-	-	-
South Brunswick (township)	32,104	31,060	-	32,910	-	-	32,099	-	30,093	-	-	-	-	-	-	-	-	-	-	-	-	-	-	-
South Plainfield (borough)	25,270	19,035	-	18,179	-	-	-	-	23,780	-	-	-	-	-	-	-	-	-	-	-	-	-	-	14,796
Woodbridge (township)	25,087	28,278	-	30,193	-	-	32,018	-	27,947	-	-	-	-	-	19,699	-	-	11,505	-	-	-	-	-	-
Monmouth County	31,149	32,951	-	37,363	-	-	34,139	-	31,924	-	-	-	-	36,514	19,576	-	-	26,356	-	-	-	-	-	31,510
Aberdeen (township)	28,984	35,677	-	38,942	-	-	35,335	-	-	-	-	-	-	-	-	-	-	-	-	-	-	-	-	-
Colts Neck (township)	46,795	57,788	-	-	-	-	-	-	-	-	-	-	-	-	-	-	-	-	-	-	-	-	-	-
Eatontown (borough)	26,965	30,568	-	-	-	-	-	-	-	-	-	-	-	-	-	-	-	-	-	-	-	-	-	-
Freehold (township)	31,505	31,168	-	30,112	-	-	30,861	-	41,349	-	-	-	-	-	-	-	-	-	-	-	-	-	-	-
Holmdel (township)	47,898	40,925	-	47,531	-	-	41,902	-	-	-	-	-	-	-	-	-	-	-	-	-	-	-	-	-
Howell (township)	26,143	29,992	-	34,161	-	-	-	-	28,344	-	-	-	-	-	-	-	-	-	-	-	-	-	-	-
Manalapan (township)	32,142	32,020	-	36,113	-	-	25,889	-	-	-	-	-	-	-	-	-	-	-	-	-	-	-	-	-
Marlboro (township)	38,635	34,097	-	38,347	-	-	33,808	-	-	-	-	-	-	-	-	-	-	-	-	-	-	-	-	-
Morganville (cdp)	39,802	29,307	-	-	-	-	31,398	-	-	-	-	-	-	-	-	-	-	-	-	-	-	-	-	-
Ocean (township)	30,581	31,081	-	30,424	-	-	-	-	-	-	-	-	-	-	-	-	-	-	-	-	-	-	-	-
Tinton Falls (borough)	31,520	24,349	-	-	-	-	-	-	-	-	-	-	-	-	-	-	-	-	-	-	-	-	-	-
West Freehold (cdp)	33,218	33,162	-	-	-	-	-	-	-	-	-	-	-	-	-	-	-	-	-	-	-	-	-	-
Morris County	36,964	33,772	-	35,825	-	-	38,953	-	29,723	-	-	-	-	41,511	24,069	-	-	18,792	-	-	32,378	-	-	22,368
Chatham (township)	65,497	52,506	-	-	-	-	-	-	-	-	-	-	-	-	-	-	-	-	-	-	-	-	-	-
Denville (township)	38,607	38,118	-	-	-	-	-	-	-	-	-	-	-	-	-	-	-	-	-	-	-	-	-	-
East Hanover (township)	32,129	33,657	-	-	-	-	38,036	-	-	-	-	-	-	-	-	-	-	-	-	-	-	-	-	-
Hanover (township)	37,661	30,364	-	20,561	-	-	37,456	-	-	-	-	-	-	-	-	-	-	-	-	-	-	-	-	-
Lincoln Park (borough)	30,389	31,576	-	-	-	-	-	-	-	-	-	-	-	-	-	-	-	-	-	-	-	-	-	-
Montville (township)	43,341	44,973	-	58,050	-	-	44,624	-	-	-	-	-	-	-	-	-	-	-	-	-	-	-	-	-
Morris (township)	54,782	47,668	-	-	-	-	-	-	-	-	-	-	-	-	-	-	-	-	-	-	-	-	-	-
Mount Olive (township)	28,691	24,710	-	26,348	-	-	-	-	-	-	-	-	-	-	-	-	-	-	-	-	-	-	-	-
Parsippany-Troy Hills (twp)	32,220	28,283	-	27,666	-	-	32,250	-	29,830	-	-	-	-	-	36,333	-	-	-	-	-	-	-	-	-
Randolph (township)	43,072	37,362	-	46,150	-	-	37,436	-	-	-	-	-	-	-	-	-	-	-	-	-	-	-	-	-
Rockaway (township)	33,184	31,085	-	31,203	-	-	-	-	-	-	-	-	-	-	-	-	-	-	-	-	-	-	-	-
Roxbury (township)	30,174	29,199	-	-	-	-	-	-	-	-	-	-	-	-	-	-	-	-	-	-	-	-	-	-
Succasunna-Kenvil (cdp)	31,923	28,514	-	-	-	-	-	-	-	-	-	-	-	-	-	-	-	-	-	-	-	-	-	-
Ocean County	23,054	26,680	-	33,608	-	-	29,107	-	26,571	-	-	-	-	-	6,509	-	-	-	-	-	-	-	-	-
Passaic County	21,370	20,617	-	18,491	8,834	-	25,188	-	26,140	-	-	-	-	-	20,478	-	-	-	-	-	-	-	-	-
Clifton (city)	23,638	20,001	-	16,595	-	-	23,680	-	28,620	-	-	-	-	-	18,608	-	-	-	-	-	-	-	-	-
Little Falls (township)	33,242	18,072	-	-	-	-	-	-	-	-	-	-	-	-	-	-	-	-	-	-	-	-	-	-
Passaic (city)	12,874	15,972	-	14,060	-	-	-	-	22,418	-	-	-	-	-	-	-	-	-	-	-	-	-	-	-

Notes: Please refer to the User's Guide for an explanation of data; data is arranged alphabetically by state, then county, then city within each county; table includes counties with populations greater than 49,999 unless noted and cities with populations greater than 9,999 whose Asian and/or NHPI population rates are greater than the national average; (1) Native Hawaiian and other Pacific Islander; (2) excludes Taiwanese; (3) includes Chamorro; (4) county does not meet population threshold but is shown in order to allow inclusion of city

Place	Total population	Total Asian population	Total NHPI[1] population	Asian Indian	Bangladeshi	Cambodian	Chinese[2]	Fijian	Filipino	Guamanian[3]	Hawaiian, Native	Hmong	Indonesian	Japanese	Korean	Laotian	Malaysian	Pakistani	Samoan	Sri Lankan	Taiwanese	Thai	Tongan	Vietnamese
Wayne (township)	35,349	33,692	-	42,725	-	-	34,022	-	29,275	-	-	-	-	-	21,960	-	-	-	-	-	-	-	-	-
Salem County	20,874	21,026	-	-	-	-	-	-	-	-	-	-	-	-	-	-	-	-	-	-	-	-	-	-
Somerset County	37,970	37,092	-	39,465	-	-	39,393	-	30,222	-	-	-	-	43,008	29,458	-	-	25,715	-	-	42,561	-	-	28,933
Bernards (township)	56,521	50,892	-	67,934	-	-	47,784	-	-	-	-	-	-	-	-	-	-	-	-	-	-	-	-	-
Branchburg (township)	41,241	41,046	-	37,310	-	-	-	-	-	-	-	-	-	-	-	-	-	-	-	-	-	-	-	-
Bridgewater (township)	39,555	41,832	-	45,291	-	-	47,897	-	-	-	-	-	-	-	-	-	-	-	-	-	-	-	-	-
Franklin (township)	31,209	30,758	-	29,719	-	-	32,463	-	32,064	-	-	-	-	-	-	-	-	-	-	-	-	-	-	-
Hillsborough (township)	33,091	27,604	-	28,967	-	-	30,267	-	-	-	-	-	-	-	-	-	-	-	-	-	-	-	-	-
Montgomery (township)	48,699	42,835	-	54,172	-	-	38,064	-	-	-	-	-	-	-	-	-	-	-	-	-	-	-	-	-
North Plainfield (borough)	22,791	23,993	-	-	-	-	-	-	-	-	-	-	-	-	-	-	-	-	-	-	-	-	-	-
Somerset (cdp)	26,798	29,375	-	30,867	-	-	30,692	-	27,309	-	-	-	-	-	-	-	-	-	-	-	-	-	-	-
Somerville (borough)	23,310	24,534	-	-	-	-	-	-	-	-	-	-	-	-	-	-	-	-	-	-	-	-	-	-
Warren (township)	49,475	48,260	-	55,959	-	-	39,258	-	-	-	-	-	-	-	-	-	-	-	-	-	-	-	-	-
Sussex County	26,992	25,959	-	40,361	-	-	-	-	26,337	-	-	-	-	-	-	-	-	-	-	-	-	-	-	-
Union County	26,992	29,438	-	31,044	-	-	35,360	-	26,890	-	-	-	-	-	21,759	-	-	11,608	-	-	-	-	-	23,633
Berkeley Heights (township)	43,981	39,440	-	-	-	-	37,552	-	-	-	-	-	-	-	-	-	-	-	-	-	-	-	-	-
New Providence (borough)	42,995	48,041	-	-	-	-	48,735	-	-	-	-	-	-	-	-	-	-	-	-	-	-	-	-	-
Rahway (city)	22,481	23,304	-	-	-	-	-	-	22,655	-	-	-	-	-	-	-	-	-	-	-	-	-	-	-
Roselle Park (borough)	24,101	20,602	-	17,612	-	-	-	-	-	-	-	-	-	-	-	-	-	-	-	-	-	-	-	-
Scotch Plains (township)	39,913	40,662	-	53,428	-	-	27,897	-	-	-	-	-	-	-	-	-	-	-	-	-	-	-	-	-
Springfield (township)	36,754	33,204	-	-	-	-	-	-	-	-	-	-	-	-	-	-	-	-	-	-	-	-	-	-
Summit (city)	62,598	38,394	-	41,598	-	-	-	-	-	-	-	-	-	-	-	-	-	-	-	-	-	-	-	-
Union (township)	24,768	26,095	-	24,949	-	-	29,112	-	27,753	-	-	-	-	-	-	-	-	-	-	-	-	-	-	-
Westfield (town)	47,187	44,293	-	-	-	-	-	-	-	-	-	-	-	-	-	-	-	-	-	-	-	-	-	-
Warren County	25,728	22,116	-	26,753	-	-	-	-	-	-	-	-	-	-	-	-	-	-	-	-	-	-	-	-
NEW MEXICO	17,261	21,435	16,738	31,264	-	-	25,135	-	17,825	13,814	21,473	-	-	28,344	16,296	-	-	-	-	-	-	14,374	-	13,405
Bernalillo County	20,790	20,774	17,343	31,932	-	-	24,170	-	18,163	-	-	-	-	33,520	16,572	-	-	-	-	-	-	-	-	12,209
Chaves County	14,990	21,710	-	-	-	-	-	-	-	-	-	-	-	-	-	-	-	-	-	-	-	-	-	-
Dona Ana County	13,999	26,173	-	-	-	-	22,496	-	-	-	-	-	-	-	-	-	-	-	-	-	-	-	-	-
Los Alamos County[4]	34,646	34,231	-	-	-	-	-	-	-	-	-	-	-	-	-	-	-	-	-	-	-	-	-	-
Los Alamos (cdp)	34,240	38,278	-	-	-	-	-	-	-	-	-	-	-	-	-	-	-	-	-	-	-	-	-	-
Otero County	14,345	12,314	-	-	-	-	-	-	-	-	-	-	-	-	-	-	-	-	-	-	-	-	-	-
Sandoval County	19,174	20,691	-	-	-	-	-	-	18,720	-	-	-	-	-	-	-	-	-	-	-	-	-	-	-
Santa Fe County	23,594	21,606	-	-	-	-	-	-	-	-	-	-	-	-	-	-	-	-	-	-	-	-	-	-
NEW YORK	23,389	20,618	13,485	23,028	10,899	12,096	17,784	-	28,130	11,480	15,882	-	18,044	37,011	19,160	13,761	17,889	14,535	15,292	24,983	28,698	21,540	-	15,805
Albany County	23,345	21,745	-	30,061	-	-	20,679	-	24,350	-	-	-	-	-	10,659	-	-	-	-	-	-	-	-	14,482
Colonie (town)	25,231	27,266	-	32,726	-	-	28,342	-	-	-	-	-	-	-	-	-	-	-	-	-	-	-	-	-
Guilderland (town)	29,508	20,100	-	27,817	-	-	-	-	-	-	-	-	-	-	-	-	-	-	-	-	-	-	-	-
Bronx County (Bronx)	13,959	16,454	8,474	16,555	6,466	8,645	16,061	-	26,925	-	-	-	-	21,095	16,692	-	-	11,160	-	-	-	-	-	9,504
Broome County	19,168	16,128	-	29,359	-	-	8,394	-	-	-	-	-	-	-	10,803	8,946	-	-	-	-	-	-	-	25,561
Johnson City (village)	17,511	17,532	-	-	-	-	-	-	-	-	-	-	-	-	-	-	-	-	-	-	-	-	-	-

Notes: Please refer to the User's Guide for an explanation of data; data is arranged alphabetically by state, then county, then city within each county; table includes counties with populations greater than 49,999 unless noted and cities with populations greater than 9,999 whose Asian and/or NHPI population rates are greater than the national average; (1) Native Hawaiian and other Pacific Islander; (2) excludes Taiwanese; (3) includes Chamorro; (4) county does not meet population threshold but is shown in order to allow inclusion of city

Place	Total population	Total Asian population	Total NHPI[1] population	Asian Indian	Bangladeshi	Cambodian	Chinese[2]	Fijian	Filipino	Guamanian[3]	Hawaiian, Native	Hmong	Indonesian	Japanese	Korean	Laotian	Malaysian	Pakistani	Samoan	Sri Lankan	Taiwanese	Thai	Tongan	Vietnamese
Vestal (town)	22,363	16,845	-	-	-	-	7,372	-	-	-	-	-	-	-	-	-	-	-	-	-	-	-	-	-
Cattaraugus County	15,959	24,500	-	-	-	-	-	-	-	-	-	-	-	-	-	-	-	-	-	-	-	-	-	-
Cayuga County	18,003	16,274	-	-	-	-	-	-	-	-	-	-	-	-	-	-	-	-	-	-	-	-	-	-
Chautauqua County	16,840	18,658	-	-	-	-	-	-	-	-	-	-	-	-	-	-	-	-	-	-	-	-	-	-
Chemung County	18,264	36,102	-	-	-	-	-	-	-	-	-	-	-	-	-	-	-	-	-	-	-	-	-	-
Chenango County	16,427	24,698	-	-	-	-	-	-	-	-	-	-	-	-	-	-	-	-	-	-	-	-	-	-
Clinton County	17,946	12,918	-	-	-	-	-	-	-	-	-	-	-	-	-	-	-	-	-	-	-	-	-	-
Columbia County	22,265	12,752	-	-	-	-	-	-	-	-	-	-	-	-	-	-	-	-	-	-	-	-	-	-
Dutchess County	23,940	28,565	-	23,595	-	-	35,647	-	-	-	-	-	-	-	31,783	-	-	-	-	-	-	-	-	-
Arlington (cdp)	19,563	16,583	-	-	-	-	-	-	-	-	-	-	-	-	-	-	-	-	-	-	-	-	-	-
Poughkeepsie (town)	23,589	32,977	-	20,958	-	-	60,914	-	-	-	-	-	-	-	-	-	-	-	-	-	-	-	-	-
Wappinger (town)	25,817	29,517	-	32,443	-	-	-	-	-	-	-	-	-	-	-	-	-	-	-	-	-	-	-	-
Erie County	20,357	21,218	-	33,649	-	-	18,867	-	23,475	-	-	-	-	15,351	13,954	-	-	-	-	-	-	-	-	12,273
Amherst (town)	27,647	26,308	-	42,602	-	-	18,291	-	-	-	-	-	-	-	14,618	-	-	-	-	-	-	-	-	-
Herkimer County	16,141	42,294	-	-	-	-	-	-	-	-	-	-	-	-	-	-	-	-	-	-	-	-	-	-
Jefferson County	16,202	17,231	-	-	-	-	-	-	22,514	-	-	-	-	-	10,123	-	-	-	-	-	-	-	-	-
Kings County (Brooklyn)	16,775	13,818	12,972	14,055	9,001	14,446	12,705	-	29,716	11,490	-	-	-	21,189	18,289	-	-	9,685	-	-	-	-	-	14,837
Livingston County	18,062	17,675	-	-	-	-	-	-	-	-	-	-	-	-	-	-	-	-	-	-	-	-	-	-
Madison County	19,105	15,334	-	-	-	-	-	-	-	-	-	-	-	-	-	-	-	-	-	-	-	-	-	-
Monroe County	22,821	20,938	-	33,785	-	9,025	19,856	-	24,293	-	-	-	-	18,857	11,586	12,801	-	11,914	-	-	-	-	-	15,341
Brighton (town)	32,642	25,245	-	35,658	-	-	19,028	-	-	-	-	-	-	-	-	-	-	-	-	-	-	-	-	-
Henrietta (town)	19,821	13,649	-	16,181	-	-	12,142	-	-	-	-	-	-	-	-	-	-	-	-	-	-	-	-	-
Pittsford (town)	42,723	36,174	-	52,366	-	-	-	-	-	-	-	-	-	-	-	-	-	-	-	-	-	-	-	-
Nassau County	32,151	30,416	11,576	32,777	-	-	32,115	-	27,506	-	-	-	-	45,071	22,844	-	-	21,860	-	-	28,651	25,711	-	32,126
East Meadow (cdp)	27,076	23,496	-	22,666	-	-	-	-	28,873	-	-	-	-	-	-	-	-	-	-	-	-	-	-	-
Elmont (cdp)	22,111	26,689	-	19,873	-	-	-	-	22,463	-	-	-	-	-	-	-	-	-	-	-	-	-	-	-
Franklin Square (cdp)	24,149	18,173	-	24,185	-	-	-	-	-	-	-	-	-	-	-	-	-	-	-	-	-	-	-	-
Glen Cove (city)	26,627	16,806	-	17,646	-	-	-	-	-	-	-	-	-	-	11,185	-	-	-	-	-	-	-	-	-
Hicksville (cdp)	26,741	26,132	-	30,263	-	-	24,450	-	24,793	-	-	-	-	-	-	-	-	-	-	-	-	-	-	-
Jericho (cdp)	45,312	29,643	-	-	-	-	-	-	-	-	-	-	-	-	19,015	-	-	-	-	-	-	-	-	-
Mineola (village)	28,890	27,274	-	33,586	-	-	-	-	-	-	-	-	-	-	-	-	-	-	-	-	-	-	-	-
North Hempstead (town)	41,621	35,372	-	39,149	-	-	33,651	-	38,800	-	-	-	-	44,889	27,269	-	-	24,302	-	-	27,918	-	-	-
North Merrick (cdp)	30,791	21,359	-	-	-	-	-	-	-	-	-	-	-	-	-	-	-	-	-	-	-	-	-	-
North New Hyde Park (cdp)	31,998	29,052	-	25,655	-	-	28,033	-	-	-	-	-	-	-	-	-	-	-	-	-	-	-	-	-
North Valley Stream (cdp)	24,727	19,685	-	21,037	-	-	-	-	-	-	-	-	-	-	-	-	-	-	-	-	-	-	-	-
Oyster Bay (town)	35,895	35,663	-	42,469	-	-	34,004	-	27,656	-	-	-	-	66,261	23,257	-	-	-	-	-	-	-	-	-
Plainview (cdp)	36,634	38,021	-	41,303	-	-	47,866	-	-	-	-	-	-	-	18,054	-	-	-	-	-	-	-	-	-
Port Washington (cdp)	43,815	39,524	-	58,821	-	-	-	-	-	-	-	-	-	-	-	-	-	-	-	-	-	-	-	-
Salisbury (cdp)	27,579	27,547	-	27,387	-	-	-	-	-	-	-	-	-	-	-	-	-	-	-	-	-	-	-	-
Syosset (cdp)	38,537	34,396	-	34,390	-	-	36,392	-	-	-	-	-	-	-	22,256	-	-	-	-	-	-	-	-	-
Valley Stream (village)	25,636	23,164	-	-	-	-	33,168	-	20,344	-	-	-	-	-	-	-	-	-	-	-	-	-	-	-

Notes: Please refer to the User's Guide for an explanation of data; data is arranged alphabetically by state, then county, then city within each county; table includes counties with populations greater than 49,999 unless noted and cities with populations greater than 9,999 whose Asian and/or NHPI population rates are greater than the national average; (1) Native Hawaiian and other Pacific Islander; (2) excludes Taiwanese; (3) includes Chamorro; (4) county does not meet population threshold but is shown in order to allow inclusion of city

Place	Total population	Total Asian population	Total NHPI[1] population	Asian Indian	Bangladeshi	Cambodian	Chinese[2]	Fijian	Filipino	Guamanian[3]	Hawaiian, Native	Hmong	Indonesian	Japanese	Korean	Laotian	Malaysian	Pakistani	Samoan	Sri Lankan	Taiwanese	Thai	Tongan	Vietnamese
West Hempstead (cdp)	26,732	24,557	-	26,294	-	-	-	-	-	-	-	-	-	-	-	-	-	-	-	-	-	-	-	-
Westbury (village)	28,018	26,636	-	-	-	-	-	-	-	-	-	-	-	-	-	-	-	-	-	-	-	-	-	-
Woodmere (cdp)	41,699	25,748	-	-	-	-	-	-	-	-	-	-	-	-	-	-	-	-	-	-	-	-	-	-
New York City	22,402	18,739	13,118	19,111	10,364	13,582	16,527	-	27,982	11,529	17,095	-	17,028	38,572	19,049	-	16,545	12,108	13,721	21,876	30,329	22,566	-	16,043
New York County (Manhattan)	42,922	29,878	21,147	53,013	12,293	-	19,546	-	40,799	-	-	-	-	48,981	43,744	-	-	27,661	-	-	61,900	26,820	-	35,376
Niagara County	19,219	21,824	-	31,594	-	-	-	-	-	-	-	-	-	-	-	-	-	-	-	-	-	-	-	-
Oneida County	18,516	18,044	-	23,582	-	-	15,941	-	-	-	-	-	-	-	-	-	-	-	-	-	-	-	-	10,461
Onondaga County	21,336	18,122	-	29,407	-	-	15,972	-	32,559	-	-	-	-	22,839	10,078	-	-	-	-	-	-	-	-	12,539
Ontario County	21,533	24,319	-	-	-	-	-	-	-	-	-	-	-	-	-	-	-	-	-	-	-	-	-	-
Orange County	21,597	25,167	-	26,989	-	-	19,472	-	29,365	-	-	-	-	-	18,303	-	-	-	-	-	-	-	-	-
Oswego County	16,853	23,694	-	-	-	-	-	-	-	-	-	-	-	-	-	-	-	-	-	-	-	-	-	-
Otsego County	16,806	14,138	-	-	-	-	-	-	-	-	-	-	-	-	-	-	-	-	-	-	-	-	-	-
Putnam County	30,127	30,350	-	33,182	-	-	31,843	-	-	-	-	-	-	-	-	-	-	-	-	-	-	-	-	-
Queens County (Queens)	19,222	16,902	12,957	15,728	11,291	-	17,822	-	24,489	-	-	-	16,291	20,387	14,664	-	15,569	12,559	-	14,907	21,933	18,175	-	14,617
Rensselaer County	21,095	11,923	-	20,023	-	-	9,812	-	-	-	-	-	-	-	7,385	-	-	-	-	-	-	-	-	-
Richmond Co. (Staten Island)	23,905	23,611	-	27,060	-	-	20,420	-	26,890	-	-	-	-	-	20,390	-	-	15,235	-	30,431	-	-	-	-
Rockland County	28,082	25,228	-	24,956	-	-	24,317	-	31,171	-	-	-	-	-	21,025	-	-	-	-	-	-	-	-	-
Clarkstown (town)	34,430	27,267	-	24,498	-	-	30,539	-	32,491	-	-	-	-	-	20,716	-	-	-	-	-	-	-	-	-
Nanuet (cdp)	30,338	28,677	-	26,360	-	-	-	-	-	-	-	-	-	-	-	-	-	-	-	-	-	-	-	-
New City (cdp)	37,519	26,965	-	19,181	-	-	-	-	42,877	-	-	-	-	-	-	-	-	-	-	-	-	-	-	-
Orangetown (town)	33,170	26,014	-	30,212	-	-	18,604	-	37,602	-	-	-	-	-	20,085	-	-	-	-	-	-	-	-	-
Ramapo (town)	22,868	22,854	-	23,895	-	-	21,562	-	27,205	-	-	-	-	-	23,049	-	-	-	-	-	-	-	-	-
Spring Valley (village)	14,861	15,035	-	16,805	-	-	-	-	-	-	-	-	-	-	-	-	-	-	-	-	-	-	-	-
St. Lawrence County	15,728	14,042	-	-	-	-	-	-	-	-	-	-	-	-	-	-	-	-	-	-	-	-	-	-
Saratoga County	23,945	27,807	-	40,371	-	-	41,904	-	-	-	-	-	-	-	14,146	-	-	-	-	-	-	-	-	-
Schenectady County	21,992	20,771	-	20,718	-	-	23,121	-	-	-	-	-	-	-	-	-	-	-	-	-	-	-	-	-
Niskayuna (town)	33,257	30,386	-	28,389	-	-	-	-	-	-	-	-	-	-	-	-	-	-	-	-	-	-	-	-
Steuben County	18,197	37,357	-	-	-	-	-	-	-	-	-	-	-	-	-	-	-	-	-	-	-	-	-	-
Suffolk County	26,577	23,940	13,948	26,829	-	-	21,989	-	31,203	-	-	-	-	30,012	18,219	-	-	15,863	-	-	24,805	21,922	-	20,409
Coram (cdp)	24,597	23,624	-	-	-	-	22,496	-	-	-	-	-	-	-	-	-	-	-	-	-	-	-	-	-
Dix Hills (cdp)	41,426	42,633	-	45,282	-	-	28,511	-	-	-	-	-	-	-	-	-	-	-	-	-	-	-	-	-
Elwood (cdp)	32,655	22,191	-	-	-	-	-	-	-	-	-	-	-	-	-	-	-	-	-	-	-	-	-	-
Lake Grove (village)	26,321	18,208	-	-	-	-	-	-	-	-	-	-	-	-	-	-	-	-	-	-	-	-	-	-
Melville (cdp)	41,053	48,605	-	-	-	-	-	-	-	-	-	-	-	-	-	-	-	-	-	-	-	-	-	-
Setauket-East Setauket (cdp)	37,736	24,187	-	-	-	-	18,826	-	-	-	-	-	-	-	-	-	-	-	-	-	-	-	-	-
Stony Brook (cdp)	35,247	23,804	-	-	-	-	26,586	-	-	-	-	-	-	-	-	-	-	-	-	-	-	-	-	-
Sullivan County	18,892	21,293	-	-	-	-	-	-	-	-	-	-	-	-	-	-	-	-	-	-	-	-	-	-
Tioga County	18,673	18,231	-	-	-	-	-	-	-	-	-	-	-	-	-	-	-	-	-	-	-	-	-	-
Tompkins County	19,659	12,107	-	24,142	-	-	10,611	-	-	-	-	-	-	12,211	8,286	-	-	-	-	-	-	-	-	-
Ithaca (city)	13,408	6,778	-	9,310	-	-	6,128	-	-	-	-	-	-	-	3,510	-	-	-	-	-	-	-	-	-
Lansing (town)	25,634	24,990	-	-	-	-	-	-	-	-	-	-	-	-	-	-	-	-	-	-	-	-	-	-

Notes: Please refer to the User's Guide for an explanation of data; data is arranged alphabetically by state, then county, then city within each county; table includes counties with populations greater than 49,999 unless noted and cities with populations greater than 9,999 whose Asian and/or NHPI population rates are greater than the national average; (1) Native Hawaiian and other Pacific Islander; (2) excludes Taiwanese; (3) includes Chamorro; (4) county does not meet population threshold but is shown in order to allow inclusion of city

Place	Total population	Total Asian population	Total NHPI[1] population	Asian Indian	Bangladeshi	Cambodian	Chinese[2]	Fijian	Filipino	Guamanian[3]	Hawaiian, Native	Hmong	Indonesian	Japanese	Korean	Laotian	Malaysian	Pakistani	Samoan	Sri Lankan	Taiwanese	Thai	Tongan	Vietnamese
Ulster County	20,846	15,892	-	-	-	-	11,720	-	-	-	-	-	-	-	-	-	-	-	-	-	-	-	-	-
New Paltz (town)	18,436	8,274	-	-	-	-	-	-	-	-	-	-	-	-	-	-	-	-	-	-	-	-	-	-
Warren County	20,727	29,751	-	-	-	-	-	-	-	-	-	-	-	-	-	-	-	-	-	-	-	-	-	-
Wayne County	19,258	14,786	-	-	-	-	-	-	-	-	-	-	-	-	-	-	-	-	-	-	-	-	-	-
Westchester County	36,726	36,944	-	37,127	-	-	39,793	-	31,022	-	-	-	-	43,036	33,966	-	-	24,481	-	-	57,896	23,705	-	-
Dobbs Ferry (village)	35,090	25,576	-	-	-	-	-	-	-	-	-	-	-	-	-	-	-	-	-	-	-	-	-	-
Eastchester (cdp)	42,067	39,045	-	-	-	-	-	-	-	-	-	-	-	44,199	-	-	-	-	-	-	-	-	-	-
Eastchester (town)	49,941	38,290	-	-	-	-	-	-	-	-	-	-	-	40,102	-	-	-	-	-	-	-	-	-	-
Greenburgh (town)	43,778	42,871	-	43,432	-	-	40,941	-	35,692	-	-	-	-	50,784	39,625	-	-	-	-	-	-	-	-	-
Harrison (village)	49,652	46,737	-	-	-	-	-	-	-	-	-	-	-	37,554	-	-	-	-	-	-	-	-	-	-
New Castle (town)	73,888	53,580	-	71,684	-	-	39,683	-	-	-	-	-	-	-	-	-	-	-	-	-	-	-	-	-
New Rochelle (city)	31,956	31,484	-	27,353	-	-	27,182	-	-	-	-	-	-	-	-	-	-	-	-	-	-	-	-	-
North Castle (town)	60,628	38,427	-	-	-	-	-	-	-	-	-	-	-	-	-	-	-	-	-	-	-	-	-	-
Ossining (town)	34,195	39,326	-	46,263	-	-	-	-	-	-	-	-	-	-	-	-	-	-	-	-	-	-	-	-
Ossining (village)	25,036	27,023	-	29,459	-	-	-	-	-	-	-	-	-	-	-	-	-	-	-	-	-	-	-	-
Pelham (town)	51,548	29,724	-	-	-	-	-	-	-	-	-	-	-	-	-	-	-	-	-	-	-	-	-	-
Rye (city)	76,566	69,806	-	-	-	-	-	-	-	-	-	-	-	57,629	-	-	-	-	-	-	-	-	-	-
Scarsdale (village)	89,907	53,178	-	89,444	-	-	55,691	-	-	-	-	-	-	36,925	48,602	-	-	-	-	-	-	-	-	-
Tarrytown (village)	39,472	36,154	-	-	-	-	-	-	-	-	-	-	-	-	-	-	-	-	-	-	-	-	-	-
White Plains (city)	33,825	37,084	-	40,851	-	-	30,986	-	-	-	-	-	-	-	-	-	-	-	-	-	-	-	-	-
Yonkers (city)	22,793	23,112	-	21,524	-	-	26,811	-	27,767	-	-	-	-	-	18,833	-	-	-	-	-	-	-	-	-
NORTH CAROLINA	20,307	19,815	14,703	27,265	-	11,109	23,914	-	19,636	15,410	17,923	9,358	-	23,879	17,560	11,179	-	17,839	11,365	-	28,053	16,170	-	14,235
Alamance County	19,391	16,839	-	-	-	-	-	-	-	-	-	-	-	-	-	-	-	-	-	-	-	-	-	-
Buncombe County	20,384	15,219	-	18,327	-	-	-	-	-	-	-	-	-	-	-	-	-	-	-	-	-	-	-	-
Burke County	17,397	8,871	-	-	-	-	-	-	-	-	-	6,899	-	-	-	8,552	-	-	-	-	-	-	-	-
Cabarrus County	21,121	18,564	-	-	-	-	-	-	-	-	-	-	-	-	-	-	-	-	-	-	-	-	-	-
Catawba County	20,358	11,933	-	-	-	-	-	-	-	-	-	8,151	-	-	-	8,346	-	-	-	-	-	-	-	15,811
Hickory (city)	23,263	13,114	-	-	-	-	-	-	-	-	-	6,640	-	-	-	-	-	-	-	-	-	-	-	-
Cleveland County	17,395	13,807	-	-	-	-	-	-	-	-	-	-	-	-	-	-	-	-	-	-	-	-	-	-
Craven County	18,423	12,538	-	-	-	-	-	-	10,879	-	-	-	-	-	-	-	-	-	-	-	-	-	-	-
Cumberland County	17,376	16,924	11,631	31,224	-	-	-	-	17,507	-	-	-	-	15,600	12,572	-	-	-	-	-	-	-	-	11,258
Davidson County	18,703	13,427	-	-	-	8,890	-	-	-	-	-	-	-	-	-	-	-	-	-	-	-	-	-	-
Durham County	23,156	21,949	-	24,995	-	-	22,186	-	26,393	-	-	-	-	20,313	17,165	-	-	-	-	-	-	-	-	-
Forsyth County	23,023	22,426	-	24,863	-	-	24,518	-	24,973	-	-	-	-	-	-	-	-	-	-	-	-	-	-	19,850
Gaston County	19,225	16,451	-	-	-	-	-	-	-	-	-	-	-	-	-	-	-	-	-	-	-	-	-	14,087
Guilford County	23,340	16,981	-	24,884	-	-	26,179	-	26,383	-	-	-	-	-	16,811	13,260	-	8,399	-	-	-	-	-	10,571
Halifax County	13,810	13,310	-	-	-	-	-	-	-	-	-	-	-	-	-	-	-	-	-	-	-	-	-	-
Harnett County	16,775	11,804	-	-	-	-	-	-	-	-	-	-	-	-	-	-	-	-	-	-	-	-	-	-
Henderson County	21,110	27,455	-	-	-	-	-	-	-	-	-	-	-	-	-	-	-	-	-	-	-	-	-	-
Iredell County	21,148	15,210	-	-	-	-	-	-	-	-	-	-	-	-	-	-	-	-	-	-	-	-	-	-
Johnston County	18,788	16,439	-	-	-	-	-	-	-	-	-	-	-	-	-	-	-	-	-	-	-	-	-	-

Notes: Please refer to the User's Guide for an explanation of data; data is arranged alphabetically by state, then county, then city within each county; table includes counties with populations greater than 49,999 unless noted and cities with populations greater than 9,999 whose Asian and/or NHPI population rates are greater than the national average; (1) Native Hawaiian and other Pacific Islander; (2) excludes Taiwanese; (3) includes Chamorro; (4) county does not meet population threshold but is shown in order to allow inclusion of city

Place	Total population	Total Asian population	Total NHPI[1] population	Asian Indian	Bangladeshi	Cambodian	Chinese[2]	Fijian	Filipino	Guamanian[3]	Hawaiian, Native	Hmong	Indonesian	Japanese	Korean	Laotian	Malaysian	Pakistani	Samoan	Sri Lankan	Taiwanese	Thai	Tongan	Vietnamese
Lenoir County	16,744	14,574	-	-	-	-	-	-	-	-	-	-	-	-	-	-	-	-	-	-	-	-	-	-
Mecklenburg County	27,352	23,006	-	29,762	-	11,251	26,364	-	26,652	-	-	31,970	-	36,489	22,097	14,922	-	-	-	-	-	-	-	14,789
Nash County	18,863	24,714	-	-	-	-	-	-	-	-	-	-	-	-	-	-	-	-	-	-	-	-	-	-
New Hanover County	23,123	19,187	-	-	-	-	-	-	-	-	-	-	-	-	-	-	-	-	-	-	-	-	-	-
Onslow County	14,853	11,835	10,170	-	-	-	-	-	11,199	-	-	-	-	8,727	-	-	-	-	-	-	-	-	-	-
Orange County	24,873	18,340	-	21,403	-	-	20,668	-	-	-	-	-	-	25,060	11,531	-	-	-	-	-	-	-	-	-
Carrboro (town)	21,429	12,999	-	-	-	-	-	-	-	-	-	-	-	-	-	-	-	-	-	-	-	-	-	-
Chapel Hill (town)	24,133	18,086	-	15,545	-	-	21,336	-	-	-	-	-	-	-	13,568	-	-	-	-	-	-	-	-	-
Pitt County	18,243	24,226	-	-	-	-	-	-	-	-	-	-	-	-	-	-	-	-	-	-	-	-	-	-
Randolph County	18,236	18,791	-	-	-	-	-	-	-	-	-	-	-	-	-	-	-	-	-	-	-	-	-	-
Robeson County	13,224	18,827	-	-	-	-	-	-	-	-	-	-	-	-	-	-	-	-	-	-	-	-	-	-
Rowan County	18,071	14,723	-	-	-	-	-	-	-	-	-	-	-	-	-	-	-	-	-	-	-	-	-	-
Stanly County	17,825	8,494	-	-	-	-	-	-	-	-	-	5,999	-	-	-	-	-	-	-	-	-	-	-	-
Surry County	17,722	5,420	-	-	-	-	-	-	-	-	-	-	-	-	-	-	-	-	-	-	-	-	-	-
Union County	21,978	19,916	-	-	-	-	-	-	-	-	-	-	-	-	-	-	-	-	-	-	-	-	-	-
Wake County	27,004	26,472	-	31,607	-	-	27,413	-	25,792	-	-	-	-	30,623	16,727	-	-	31,332	-	-	-	-	-	19,838
Apex (town)	28,727	33,099	-	-	-	-	-	-	-	-	-	-	-	-	-	-	-	-	-	-	-	-	-	-
Cary (town)	32,974	31,613	-	33,948	-	-	29,585	-	-	-	-	-	-	36,930	22,391	-	-	-	-	-	-	-	-	30,099
Wayne County	17,010	31,860	-	-	-	-	-	-	-	-	-	-	-	-	-	-	-	-	-	-	-	-	-	-
Wilkes County	17,516	13,297	-	-	-	-	-	-	-	-	-	-	-	-	-	-	-	-	-	-	-	-	-	-
NORTH DAKOTA	17,769	21,265	-	30,528	-	-	22,751	-	19,543	-	-	-	-	-	11,826	-	-	-	-	-	-	-	-	-
Cass County	20,889	21,010	-	37,466	-	-	-	-	-	-	-	-	-	-	-	-	-	-	-	-	-	-	-	-
Grand Forks County	17,868	16,594	-	-	-	-	-	-	-	-	-	-	-	-	-	-	-	-	-	-	-	-	-	-
Ward County	16,926	24,283	-	-	-	-	-	-	-	-	-	-	-	-	-	-	-	-	-	-	-	-	-	-
OHIO	21,003	24,912	12,919	31,900	20,613	14,136	23,961	-	26,272	15,310	15,678	-	15,888	27,470	20,209	14,405	17,259	24,819	9,826	24,167	30,126	13,662	-	17,099
Allen County	17,511	27,597	-	-	-	-	-	-	-	-	-	-	-	-	-	-	-	-	-	-	-	-	-	-
Ashtabula County	16,814	22,705	-	-	-	-	-	-	-	-	-	-	-	-	-	-	-	-	-	-	-	-	-	-
Athens County	14,171	12,066	-	-	-	-	-	-	-	-	-	-	-	-	-	-	-	-	-	-	-	-	-	-
Athens (city)	11,061	10,491	-	-	-	-	-	-	-	-	-	-	-	-	-	-	-	-	-	-	-	-	-	-
Butler County	22,076	23,472	-	27,377	-	-	29,354	-	18,264	-	-	-	-	-	19,311	-	-	-	-	-	-	-	-	16,642
Clark County	19,501	27,738	-	-	-	-	-	-	-	-	-	-	-	-	-	-	-	-	-	-	-	-	-	-
Clermont County	22,370	33,175	-	38,095	-	-	-	-	-	-	-	-	-	-	-	-	-	-	-	-	-	-	-	-
Columbiana County	16,655	19,161	-	-	-	-	-	-	-	-	-	-	-	-	-	-	-	-	-	-	-	-	-	-
Cuyahoga County	22,272	25,604	-	31,354	-	11,647	22,433	-	26,745	-	-	-	-	27,075	24,117	-	-	-	-	-	-	-	-	17,773
Mayfield Heights (city)	24,392	22,435	-	26,494	-	-	-	-	-	-	-	-	-	-	-	-	-	-	-	-	-	-	-	-
Richmond Heights (city)	25,738	26,733	-	-	-	-	-	-	-	-	-	-	-	-	-	-	-	-	-	-	-	-	-	-
Solon (city)	35,394	41,367	-	47,197	-	-	37,218	-	-	-	-	-	-	-	-	-	-	-	-	-	-	-	-	-
Westlake (city)	37,142	46,367	-	55,467	-	-	-	-	-	-	-	-	-	-	-	-	-	-	-	-	-	-	-	-
Delaware County	31,600	34,378	-	36,477	-	-	34,242	-	-	-	-	-	-	-	-	-	-	-	-	-	-	-	-	-
Fairfield County	21,671	27,549	-	-	-	-	-	-	-	-	-	-	-	-	-	-	-	-	-	-	-	-	-	-
Franklin County	23,059	22,714	15,327	27,641	-	17,145	23,346	-	28,017	-	-	-	9,726	26,810	18,807	13,426	-	17,769	-	-	35,973	11,804	-	15,685

Notes: Please refer to the User's Guide for an explanation of data; data is arranged alphabetically by state, then county, then city within each county; table includes counties with populations greater than 49,999 unless noted and cities with populations greater than 9,999 whose Asian and/or NHPI population rates are greater than the national average; (1) Native Hawaiian and other Pacific Islander; (2) excludes Taiwanese; (3) includes Chamorro; (4) county does not meet population threshold but is shown in order to allow inclusion of city

Place	Total population	Total Asian population	Total NHPI[1] population	Asian Indian	Bangladeshi	Cambodian	Chinese[2]	Fijian	Filipino	Guamanian[3]	Hawaiian, Native	Hmong	Indonesian	Japanese	Korean	Laotian	Malaysian	Pakistani	Samoan	Sri Lankan	Taiwanese	Thai	Tongan	Vietnamese
Dublin (city)	41,122	33,203	-	38,436	-	-	35,393	-	-	-	-	-	-	31,854	-	-	-	-	-	-	-	-	-	-
Hilliard (city)	28,496	25,875	-	-	-	-	-	-	-	-	-	-	-	-	-	-	-	-	-	-	-	-	-	-
Geauga County	27,944	32,547	-	-	-	-	-	-	-	-	-	-	-	-	-	-	-	-	-	-	-	-	-	-
Greene County	23,057	24,322	-	40,267	-	-	17,713	-	-	-	-	-	-	-	13,369	-	-	-	-	-	-	-	-	-
Hamilton County	24,053	25,584	-	30,553	-	9,644	27,033	-	26,251	-	-	-	-	31,019	18,614	-	-	-	-	-	-	-	-	15,621
Blue Ash (city)	33,801	21,880	-	25,038	-	-	-	-	-	-	-	-	-	-	-	-	-	-	-	-	-	-	-	-
Sharonville (city)	27,483	24,858	-	24,412	-	-	-	-	-	-	-	-	-	-	-	-	-	-	-	-	-	-	-	-
Hancock County	20,991	25,236	-	-	-	-	-	-	-	-	-	-	-	-	-	-	-	-	-	-	-	-	-	-
Lake County	23,160	24,636	-	27,184	-	-	23,322	-	-	-	-	-	-	-	-	-	-	-	-	-	-	-	-	-
Licking County	20,581	21,162	-	-	-	-	-	-	-	-	-	-	-	-	-	-	-	-	-	-	-	-	-	-
Lorain County	21,054	26,770	-	30,739	-	-	-	-	35,018	-	-	-	-	-	-	-	-	-	-	-	-	-	-	-
Lucas County	20,518	24,387	-	32,002	-	-	21,177	-	21,396	-	-	-	-	-	22,878	-	-	-	-	-	-	-	-	-
Mahoning County	18,818	33,705	-	-	-	-	-	-	-	-	-	-	-	-	-	-	-	-	-	-	-	-	-	-
Marion County	18,255	36,776	-	-	-	-	-	-	-	-	-	-	-	-	-	-	-	-	-	-	-	-	-	-
Medina County	24,251	32,289	-	47,997	-	-	-	-	-	-	-	-	-	-	-	-	-	-	-	-	-	-	-	-
Miami County	21,669	42,809	-	-	-	-	-	-	-	-	-	-	-	-	-	-	-	-	-	-	-	-	-	-
Montgomery County	21,743	24,581	-	32,320	-	-	22,794	-	23,092	-	-	-	-	31,211	14,471	-	-	-	-	-	-	-	-	14,311
Portage County	20,428	16,631	-	-	-	-	-	-	-	-	-	-	-	-	-	-	-	-	-	-	-	-	-	-
Richland County	18,582	22,586	-	-	-	-	-	-	-	-	-	-	-	-	-	-	-	-	-	-	-	-	-	-
Stark County	20,417	30,524	-	40,249	-	-	20,469	-	-	-	-	-	-	-	-	-	-	-	-	-	-	-	-	-
Summit County	22,842	24,402	-	26,715	-	-	23,510	-	38,788	-	-	-	-	36,608	15,730	16,422	-	-	-	-	-	-	-	28,770
Trumbull County	19,188	23,436	-	-	-	-	-	-	-	-	-	-	-	-	-	-	-	-	-	-	-	-	-	-
Warren County	25,517	31,611	-	28,504	-	-	38,059	-	-	-	-	-	-	-	-	-	-	-	-	-	-	-	-	-
Wayne County	18,330	24,650	-	-	-	-	-	-	-	-	-	-	-	-	-	-	-	-	-	-	-	-	-	-
Wood County	21,284	21,280	-	-	-	-	-	-	-	-	-	-	-	-	-	-	-	-	-	-	-	-	-	-
OKLAHOMA	17,646	15,691	11,963	23,169	-	11,062	15,900	-	17,480	17,228	13,559	6,644	-	15,250	12,410	11,433	6,229	12,274	-	-	11,139	13,687	-	14,018
Canadian County	19,691	16,246	-	16,067	-	-	-	-	-	-	-	-	-	-	-	-	-	-	-	-	-	-	-	17,138
Cleveland County	20,114	16,628	-	24,063	-	-	16,025	-	18,959	-	-	-	-	-	15,171	-	-	-	-	-	-	-	-	16,789
Comanche County	15,728	15,991	-	-	-	-	-	-	15,098	-	-	-	-	-	14,371	-	-	-	-	-	-	-	-	-
Garfield County	17,457	19,187	-	-	-	-	-	-	-	-	-	-	-	-	-	-	-	-	-	-	-	-	-	-
Muskogee County	14,828	22,130	-	-	-	-	-	-	-	-	-	-	-	-	-	-	-	-	-	-	-	-	-	-
Oklahoma County	19,551	14,913	-	25,867	-	-	14,076	-	18,840	-	-	-	-	10,341	10,533	11,054	-	-	-	-	-	14,624	-	13,115
Payne County	15,983	9,231	-	-	-	-	9,445	-	-	-	-	-	-	-	-	-	-	-	-	-	-	-	-	-
Stillwater (city)	15,789	9,159	-	-	-	-	9,502	-	-	-	-	-	-	-	-	-	-	-	-	-	-	-	-	-
Pottawatomie County	15,972	9,109	-	-	-	-	-	-	-	-	-	-	-	-	-	-	-	-	-	-	-	-	-	-
Tulsa County	21,115	17,407	-	24,855	-	-	18,274	-	18,015	-	-	-	-	-	13,998	-	-	9,838	-	-	-	-	-	14,274
Wagoner County	18,272	13,058	-	-	-	-	-	-	-	-	-	-	-	-	-	-	-	-	-	-	-	-	-	-
OREGON	20,940	19,790	15,516	30,723	-	12,079	20,884	18,604	17,697	15,924	21,517	8,802	13,912	26,217	16,657	13,299	-	26,386	11,526	-	20,251	15,819	8,321	16,132
Benton County	21,868	14,995	-	-	-	-	16,586	-	-	-	-	-	-	14,242	9,707	-	-	-	-	-	-	-	-	-
Corvallis (city)	19,317	13,253	-	-	-	-	16,458	-	-	-	-	-	-	-	6,965	-	-	-	-	-	-	-	-	-
Clackamas County	25,973	25,096	18,912	33,118	-	-	26,593	-	22,346	-	-	-	-	35,776	20,149	-	-	-	-	-	-	-	-	17,874

Notes: Please refer to the User's Guide for an explanation of data; data is arranged alphabetically by state, then county, then city within each county; table includes counties with populations greater than 49,999 unless noted and cities with populations greater than 9,999 whose Asian and/or NHPI population rates are greater than the national average; (1) Native Hawaiian and other Pacific Islander; (2) excludes Taiwanese; (3) includes Chamorro; (4) county does not meet population threshold but is shown in order to allow inclusion of city

Place	Total population	Total Asian population	Total NHPI[1] population	Asian Indian	Bangladeshi	Cambodian	Chinese[2]	Fijian	Filipino	Guamanian[3]	Hawaiian, Native	Hmong	Indonesian	Japanese	Korean	Laotian	Malaysian	Pakistani	Samoan	Sri Lankan	Taiwanese	Thai	Tongan	Vietnamese
Lake Oswego (city)	42,166	30,435	-	-	-	-	26,388	-	-	-	-	-	-	-	-	-	-	-	-	-	-	-	-	-
Coos County	17,547	11,147	-	-	-	-	-	-	-	-	-	-	-	-	-	-	-	-	-	-	-	-	-	-
Deschutes County	21,767	19,868	-	-	-	-	-	-	-	-	-	-	-	-	-	-	-	-	-	-	-	-	-	-
Douglas County	16,581	16,574	-	-	-	-	-	-	-	-	-	-	-	-	-	-	-	-	-	-	-	-	-	-
Jackson County	19,498	17,597	-	-	-	-	-	-	-	-	-	-	-	-	-	-	-	-	-	-	-	-	-	-
Josephine County	17,234	20,610	-	-	-	-	-	-	-	-	-	-	-	-	-	-	-	-	-	-	-	-	-	-
Klamath County	16,719	39,437	-	-	-	-	-	-	-	-	-	-	-	-	-	-	-	-	-	-	-	-	-	-
Lane County	19,681	12,691	12,407	15,663	-	-	14,634	-	11,925	-	-	-	-	15,064	9,367	-	-	-	-	-	-	-	-	-
Linn County	17,633	14,883	-	-	-	-	-	-	-	-	-	-	-	-	-	-	-	-	-	-	-	-	-	-
Marion County	18,408	14,910	10,990	19,412	-	-	16,031	-	17,782	-	-	-	-	14,063	11,549	-	-	-	-	-	-	-	-	17,143
Salem (city)	19,141	13,863	9,570	-	-	-	17,188	-	15,891	-	-	-	-	10,820	-	-	-	-	-	-	-	-	-	19,628
Multnomah County	22,606	17,559	16,024	25,380	-	10,666	17,833	-	17,846	-	23,193	9,485	-	29,619	24,005	12,596	-	-	-	-	-	11,644	8,537	14,468
Portland (city)	22,643	17,165	15,905	25,822	-	10,104	17,831	-	17,661	-	23,391	9,303	-	29,496	21,626	12,755	-	-	-	-	-	10,911	7,961	14,275
Polk County	19,282	15,052	-	-	-	-	-	-	-	-	-	-	-	-	-	-	-	-	-	-	-	-	-	-
Umatilla County	16,410	11,339	-	-	-	-	-	-	-	-	-	-	-	-	-	-	-	-	-	-	-	-	-	-
Washington County	24,969	24,156	16,716	36,158	-	14,452	27,547	-	18,954	-	20,728	-	-	28,637	16,637	15,383	-	-	-	-	-	-	-	19,766
Aloha (cdp)	19,685	16,511	-	-	-	-	-	-	15,271	-	-	-	-	-	-	-	-	-	-	-	-	-	-	18,699
Beaverton (city)	25,419	23,254	-	33,362	-	16,788	22,476	-	20,680	-	-	-	-	30,407	16,081	-	-	-	-	-	-	-	-	20,795
Cedar Mill (cdp)	33,555	50,850	-	-	-	-	-	-	-	-	-	-	-	-	-	-	-	-	-	-	-	-	-	-
Hillsboro (city)	21,680	25,440	-	30,587	-	-	32,029	-	-	-	-	-	-	-	22,256	-	-	-	-	-	-	-	-	18,162
Tigard (city)	25,110	23,258	-	-	-	-	23,242	-	-	-	-	-	-	-	-	-	-	-	-	-	-	-	-	15,759
Tualatin (city)	26,694	26,885	-	-	-	-	-	-	-	-	-	-	-	-	-	-	-	-	-	-	-	-	-	-
Yamhill County	18,951	14,760	-	-	-	-	-	-	-	-	-	-	-	-	-	-	-	-	-	-	-	-	-	-
PENNSYLVANIA	20,880	20,096	15,003	26,600	18,415	8,025	19,938	-	25,848	13,512	17,552	8,432	17,168	20,241	17,434	13,555	-	19,794	15,630	37,754	25,031	16,940	-	14,052
Adams County	18,577	18,371	-	-	-	-	-	-	-	-	-	-	-	-	-	-	-	-	-	-	-	-	-	-
Allegheny County	22,491	26,250	15,186	35,919	-	-	22,537	-	24,524	-	-	-	-	17,075	24,932	-	-	-	-	-	19,668	-	-	13,719
Muni. of Monroeville (borough)	24,031	31,106	-	25,921	-	-	-	-	-	-	-	-	-	-	-	-	-	-	-	-	-	-	-	-
Scott (township)	24,439	28,806	-	29,106	-	-	-	-	-	-	-	-	-	-	-	-	-	-	-	-	-	-	-	-
Scott Township (cdp)	24,439	28,806	-	29,106	-	-	-	-	-	-	-	-	-	-	-	-	-	-	-	-	-	-	-	-
Upper St. Clair (township)	42,413	60,605	-	56,045	-	-	-	-	-	-	-	-	-	-	-	-	-	-	-	-	-	-	-	-
Beaver County	18,402	25,183	-	-	-	-	-	-	-	-	-	-	-	-	-	-	-	-	-	-	-	-	-	-
Berks County	21,232	22,427	-	27,330	-	-	25,339	-	-	-	-	-	-	-	42,579	-	-	-	-	-	-	-	-	13,179
Blair County	16,743	37,964	-	-	-	-	-	-	-	-	-	-	-	-	-	-	-	-	-	-	-	-	-	-
Bradford County	17,148	17,609	-	-	-	-	-	-	-	-	-	-	-	-	-	-	-	-	-	-	-	-	-	-
Bucks County	27,430	25,197	-	26,832	-	-	29,867	-	25,613	-	-	-	-	-	20,040	-	-	-	-	-	-	-	-	20,993
Bensalem (township)	22,517	19,931	-	21,867	-	-	-	-	-	-	-	-	-	-	12,289	-	-	-	-	-	-	-	-	-
Lower Makefield (township)	43,983	37,896	-	42,294	-	-	-	-	-	-	-	-	-	-	-	-	-	-	-	-	-	-	-	-
Newtown (township)	34,335	26,776	-	-	-	-	-	-	-	-	-	-	-	-	-	-	-	-	-	-	-	-	-	-
Butler County	20,794	37,632	-	45,619	-	-	-	-	-	-	-	-	-	-	-	-	-	-	-	-	-	-	-	-
Cambria County	16,058	24,030	-	-	-	-	-	-	-	-	-	-	-	-	-	-	-	-	-	-	-	-	-	-
Centre County	18,020	13,016	-	18,969	-	-	13,140	-	-	-	-	-	-	-	7,685	-	-	-	-	-	-	-	-	-

Notes: Please refer to the User's Guide for an explanation of data; data is arranged alphabetically by state, then county, then city within each county; table includes counties with populations greater than 49,999 unless noted and cities with populations greater than 9,999 whose Asian and/or NHPI population rates are greater than the national average; (1) Native Hawaiian and other Pacific Islander; (2) excludes Taiwanese; (3) includes Chamorro; (4) county does not meet population threshold but is shown in order to allow inclusion of city

Place	Total population	Total Asian population	Total NHPI[1] population	Asian Indian	Bangladeshi	Cambodian	Chinese[2]	Fijian	Filipino	Guamanian[3]	Hawaiian, Native	Hmong	Indonesian	Japanese	Korean	Laotian	Malaysian	Pakistani	Samoan	Sri Lankan	Taiwanese	Thai	Tongan	Vietnamese
Ferguson (township)	22,724	19,717	-	-	-	-	-	-	-	-	-	-	-	-	-	-	-	-	-	-	-	-	-	-
Patton (township)	22,860	20,573	-	-	-	-	-	-	-	-	-	-	-	-	-	-	-	-	-	-	-	-	-	-
State College (borough)	12,155	8,912	-	10,956	-	-	9,139	-	-	-	-	-	-	-	4,678	-	-	-	-	-	-	-	-	-
Chester County	31,627	30,197	-	34,893	-	-	33,400	-	30,403	-	-	-	-	28,272	22,390	-	-	-	-	-	-	-	-	21,169
Tredyffrin (township)	47,584	34,714	-	32,443	-	-	46,713	-	-	-	-	-	-	-	-	-	-	-	-	-	-	-	-	-
West Goshen (township)	32,487	27,286	-	-	-	-	-	-	-	-	-	-	-	-	-	-	-	-	-	-	-	-	-	-
West Whiteland (township)	35,031	38,400	-	-	-	-	-	-	-	-	-	-	-	-	-	-	-	-	-	-	-	-	-	-
Clearfield County	16,010	41,419	-	-	-	-	-	-	-	-	-	-	-	-	-	-	-	-	-	-	-	-	-	-
Columbia County	16,973	21,876	-	-	-	-	-	-	-	-	-	-	-	-	-	-	-	-	-	-	-	-	-	-
Crawford County	16,870	17,907	-	-	-	-	-	-	-	-	-	-	-	-	-	-	-	-	-	-	-	-	-	-
Cumberland County	23,610	24,401	-	30,079	-	-	23,646	-	-	-	-	-	-	-	26,552	-	-	-	-	-	-	-	-	21,066
Hampden (township)	28,977	22,828	-	-	-	-	-	-	-	-	-	-	-	-	-	-	-	-	-	-	-	-	-	-
Dauphin County	22,134	18,463	-	22,359	-	-	18,874	-	-	-	-	-	-	-	8,191	-	-	-	-	-	-	-	-	16,051
Derry (township)	31,365	22,538	-	-	-	-	-	-	-	-	-	-	-	-	-	-	-	-	-	-	-	-	-	-
Hershey (cdp)	28,487	18,607	-	-	-	-	-	-	-	-	-	-	-	-	-	-	-	-	-	-	-	-	-	-
Delaware County	25,040	20,532	-	23,548	-	-	23,612	-	31,442	-	-	-	-	17,562	16,237	-	-	14,450	-	-	-	-	-	14,512
Broomall (cdp)	24,940	18,319	-	-	-	-	-	-	-	-	-	-	-	-	15,385	-	-	-	-	-	-	-	-	-
Drexel Hill (cdp)	25,471	22,523	-	-	-	-	30,271	-	-	-	-	-	-	-	-	-	-	-	-	-	-	-	-	-
Marple (township)	28,494	20,127	-	-	-	-	-	-	-	-	-	-	-	-	17,107	-	-	-	-	-	-	-	-	-
Radnor (township)	39,813	29,966	-	-	-	-	39,069	-	-	-	-	-	-	-	-	-	-	-	-	-	-	-	-	-
Upper Darby (township)	20,770	15,494	-	16,395	-	-	15,627	-	-	-	-	-	-	-	15,324	-	-	-	-	-	-	-	-	13,575
Erie County	17,932	21,884	-	28,858	-	-	-	-	-	-	-	-	-	-	-	-	-	-	-	-	-	-	-	-
Franklin County	19,339	21,718	-	-	-	-	-	-	-	-	-	-	-	-	-	-	-	-	-	-	-	-	-	-
Indiana County	15,312	23,794	-	-	-	-	-	-	-	-	-	-	-	-	-	-	-	-	-	-	-	-	-	-
Lackawanna County	18,710	25,035	-	29,832	-	-	-	-	-	-	-	-	-	-	-	-	-	-	-	-	-	-	-	-
Lancaster County	20,398	15,247	-	18,050	-	-	14,558	-	-	-	-	8,771	-	-	10,860	-	-	-	-	-	-	-	-	16,748
Lawrence County	16,835	28,722	-	-	-	-	-	-	-	-	-	-	-	-	-	-	-	-	-	-	-	-	-	-
Lebanon County	19,773	19,672	-	-	-	-	-	-	-	-	-	-	-	-	-	-	-	-	-	-	-	-	-	-
Lehigh County	21,897	23,542	-	27,649	-	-	27,951	-	-	-	-	-	-	-	19,403	-	-	-	-	-	-	-	-	17,357
Fullerton (cdp)	22,164	26,083	-	-	-	-	-	-	-	-	-	-	-	-	-	-	-	-	-	-	-	-	-	-
Lower Macungie (township)	30,202	29,688	-	-	-	-	33,584	-	-	-	-	-	-	-	-	-	-	-	-	-	-	-	-	-
Upper Macungie (township)	28,801	35,143	-	-	-	-	-	-	-	-	-	-	-	-	-	-	-	-	-	-	-	-	-	-
Luzerne County	18,228	23,283	-	34,394	-	-	-	-	-	-	-	-	-	-	-	-	-	-	-	-	-	-	-	-
Lycoming County	17,224	23,565	-	-	-	-	-	-	-	-	-	-	-	-	-	-	-	-	-	-	-	-	-	-
Mercer County	17,636	30,630	-	-	-	-	-	-	-	-	-	-	-	-	-	-	-	-	-	-	-	-	-	-
Monroe County	20,011	28,539	-	28,709	-	-	-	-	-	-	-	-	-	-	-	-	-	-	-	-	-	-	-	-
Montgomery County	30,898	24,422	-	29,263	-	-	27,591	-	32,370	-	-	-	-	28,432	18,243	-	-	-	-	-	-	-	-	20,316
Cheltenham (township)	31,424	20,718	-	-	-	-	-	-	-	-	-	-	-	-	16,292	-	-	-	-	-	-	-	-	-
East Norriton (township)	28,749	28,099	-	-	-	-	-	-	-	-	-	-	-	-	-	-	-	-	-	-	-	-	-	-
Hatfield (township)	25,051	16,529	-	18,395	-	-	-	-	-	-	-	-	-	-	-	-	-	-	-	-	-	-	-	-
Horsham (township)	28,542	25,166	-	-	-	-	-	-	-	-	-	-	-	-	17,939	-	-	-	-	-	-	-	-	-

Notes: Please refer to the User's Guide for an explanation of data; data is arranged alphabetically by state, then county, then city within each county; table includes counties with populations greater than 49,999 unless noted and cities with populations greater than 9,999 whose Asian and/or NHPI population rates are greater than the national average; (1) Native Hawaiian and other Pacific Islander; (2) excludes Taiwanese; (3) includes Chamorro; (4) county does not meet population threshold but is shown in order to allow inclusion of city

Place	Total population	Total Asian population	Total NHPI[1] population	Asian Indian	Bangladeshi	Cambodian	Chinese[2]	Fijian	Filipino	Guamanian[3]	Hawaiian, Native	Hmong	Indonesian	Japanese	Korean	Laotian	Malaysian	Pakistani	Samoan	Sri Lankan	Taiwanese	Thai	Tongan	Vietnamese
King of Prussia (cdp)	32,070	30,745	-	31,715	-	-	32,952	-	-	-	-	-	-	-	-	-	-	-	-	-	-	-	-	-
Lansdale (borough)	22,096	16,815	-	21,504	-	-	-	-	-	-	-	-	-	-	-	-	-	-	-	-	-	-	-	-
Lower Gwynedd (township)	41,868	37,370	-	-	-	-	-	-	-	-	-	-	-	-	-	-	-	-	-	-	-	-	-	-
Lower Providence (township)	26,186	26,921	-	-	-	-	31,998	-	-	-	-	-	-	-	-	-	-	-	-	-	-	-	-	-
Montgomery (township)	32,349	23,568	-	19,911	-	-	-	-	-	-	-	-	-	-	20,441	-	-	-	-	-	-	-	-	-
Montgomeryville (cdp)	28,967	18,662	-	-	-	-	-	-	-	-	-	-	-	-	-	-	-	-	-	-	-	-	-	-
Plymouth (township)	28,862	31,550	-	-	-	-	-	-	-	-	-	-	-	-	27,488	-	-	-	-	-	-	-	-	-
Towamencin (township)	30,559	20,555	-	-	-	-	-	-	-	-	-	-	-	-	-	-	-	-	-	-	-	-	-	-
Upper Dublin (township)	37,994	23,144	-	-	-	-	-	-	-	-	-	-	-	-	16,273	-	-	-	-	-	-	-	-	-
Upper Gwynedd (township)	32,806	29,658	-	-	-	-	21,122	-	-	-	-	-	-	-	-	-	-	-	-	-	-	-	-	-
Upper Merion (township)	34,961	32,021	-	34,329	-	-	33,067	-	-	-	-	-	-	-	-	-	-	-	-	-	-	-	-	-
Whitpain (township)	41,739	28,327	-	-	-	-	-	-	-	-	-	-	-	-	21,414	-	-	-	-	-	-	-	-	-
Northampton County	21,399	24,772	-	35,512	-	-	19,890	-	-	-	-	-	-	-	16,735	-	-	-	-	-	-	-	-	11,473
Northumberland County	16,489	21,193	-	-	-	-	-	-	-	-	-	-	-	-	-	-	-	-	-	-	-	-	-	-
Philadelphia County	16,509	12,367	8,418	16,575	-	6,675	12,298	-	18,831	-	-	-	-	16,250	12,176	12,947	-	12,004	-	-	-	-	-	9,597
Philadelphia (city)	16,509	12,367	8,418	16,575	-	6,675	12,298	-	18,831	-	-	-	-	16,250	12,176	12,947	-	12,004	-	-	-	-	-	9,597
Schuylkill County	17,230	19,022	-	-	-	-	-	-	-	-	-	-	-	-	-	-	-	-	-	-	-	-	-	-
Washington County	19,935	17,072	-	-	-	-	-	-	-	-	-	-	-	-	-	-	-	-	-	-	-	-	-	-
Westmoreland County	19,674	34,887	-	50,327	-	-	-	-	-	-	-	-	-	-	-	-	-	-	-	-	-	-	-	-
York County	21,086	18,753	-	23,939	-	-	14,467	-	-	-	-	-	-	-	17,466	-	-	-	-	-	-	-	-	18,113
RHODE ISLAND	21,688	15,010	10,327	23,030	-	8,252	17,150	-	20,428	-	-	6,664	-	26,409	16,737	13,278	-	-	-	-	-	-	-	13,505
Bristol County	26,503	30,989	-	-	-	-	-	-	-	-	-	-	-	-	-	-	-	-	-	-	-	-	-	-
Kent County	23,833	23,752	-	-	-	-	17,344	-	-	-	-	-	-	-	14,473	-	-	-	-	-	-	-	-	-
Newport County	26,779	19,616	-	-	-	-	-	-	19,064	-	-	-	-	-	-	-	-	-	-	-	-	-	-	-
Providence County	19,255	13,244	-	18,846	-	8,247	15,533	-	20,787	-	-	6,123	-	-	17,565	13,311	-	-	-	-	-	-	-	13,640
Providence (city)	15,525	10,035	-	14,463	-	7,237	13,229	-	13,347	-	-	5,496	-	-	10,424	10,469	-	-	-	-	-	-	-	-
Woonsocket (city)	16,223	12,825	-	-	-	-	-	-	-	-	-	-	-	-	-	13,413	-	-	-	-	-	-	-	-
Washington County	25,530	16,043	-	-	-	-	14,810	-	-	-	-	-	-	-	-	-	-	-	-	-	-	-	-	-
SOUTH CAROLINA	18,795	20,541	21,638	29,105	-	14,018	18,640	-	18,422	22,734	26,969	7,253	-	26,961	17,655	10,268	-	-	-	-	-	31,053	-	15,609
Aiken County	18,772	18,299	-	-	-	-	-	-	-	-	-	-	-	-	-	-	-	-	-	-	-	-	-	-
Anderson County	18,365	19,938	-	-	-	-	-	-	-	-	-	-	-	-	-	-	-	-	-	-	-	-	-	-
Beaufort County	25,377	26,772	-	-	-	-	-	-	-	-	-	-	-	-	-	-	-	-	-	-	-	-	-	-
Berkeley County	16,879	18,308	-	-	-	-	-	-	18,421	-	-	-	-	-	-	-	-	-	-	-	-	-	-	-
Charleston County	21,393	20,671	-	26,239	-	-	17,868	-	15,006	-	-	-	-	-	-	-	-	-	-	-	-	-	-	-
Dorchester County	18,840	23,743	-	-	-	-	-	-	22,518	-	-	-	-	-	-	-	-	-	-	-	-	-	-	-
Florence County	17,876	38,297	-	-	-	-	-	-	-	-	-	-	-	-	-	-	-	-	-	-	-	-	-	-
Greenville County	22,081	22,430	-	26,669	-	-	18,688	-	19,645	-	-	-	-	-	-	-	-	-	-	-	-	-	-	18,196
Greenwood County	17,446	42,088	-	-	-	-	-	-	-	-	-	-	-	-	-	-	-	-	-	-	-	-	-	-
Horry County	19,949	21,612	-	-	-	-	-	-	-	-	-	-	-	-	-	-	-	-	-	-	-	-	-	-
Lexington County	21,063	17,232	-	25,223	-	-	12,203	-	-	-	-	-	-	-	-	-	-	-	-	-	-	-	-	-
Oconee County	18,965	31,033	-	-	-	-	-	-	-	-	-	-	-	-	-	-	-	-	-	-	-	-	-	-

Notes: Please refer to the User's Guide for an explanation of data; data is arranged alphabetically by state, then county, then city within each county; table includes counties with populations greater than 49,999 unless noted and cities with populations greater than 9,999 whose Asian and/or NHPI population rates are greater than the national average; (1) Native Hawaiian and other Pacific Islander; (2) excludes Taiwanese; (3) includes Chamorro; (4) county does not meet population threshold but is shown in order to allow inclusion of city

Place	Total population	Total Asian population	Total NHPI[1] population	Asian Indian	Bangladeshi	Cambodian	Chinese[2]	Fijian	Filipino	Guamanian[3]	Hawaiian, Native	Hmong	Indonesian	Japanese	Korean	Laotian	Malaysian	Pakistani	Samoan	Sri Lankan	Taiwanese	Thai	Tongan	Vietnamese
Pickens County	17,434	20,978	-	13,005	-	-	21,156	-	-	-	-	-	-	-	-	-	-	-	-	-	-	-	-	-
Clemson (city)	19,272	9,739	-	-	-	-	-	-	-	-	-	-	-	-	-	-	-	-	-	-	-	-	-	-
Richland County	20,794	20,845	-	32,199	-	-	18,047	-	19,217	-	-	-	-	-	15,515	-	-	-	-	-	-	-	-	15,275
Spartanburg County	18,738	14,194	-	24,261	-	-	-	-	-	-	-	7,778	-	-	-	9,883	-	-	-	-	-	-	-	-
Sumter County	15,657	16,850	-	-	-	-	-	-	-	-	-	-	-	-	-	-	-	-	-	-	-	-	-	-
York County	20,536	16,984	-	-	-	-	-	-	-	-	-	-	-	-	-	-	-	-	-	-	-	-	-	17,329
SOUTH DAKOTA	17,562	14,528	-	22,328	-	-	17,557	-	15,777	-	-	-	-	12,836	8,469	12,390	-	-	-	-	-	-	-	15,817
Minnehaha County	20,713	15,953	-	-	-	-	-	-	-	-	-	-	-	-	-	-	-	-	-	-	-	-	-	16,726
Pennington County	18,938	12,876	-	-	-	-	-	-	-	-	-	-	-	-	-	-	-	-	-	-	-	-	-	-
TENNESSEE	19,393	20,331	15,178	27,635	-	11,075	21,140	-	22,336	10,879	19,640	-	-	24,647	15,834	14,882	-	23,790	15,642	-	31,106	17,980	-	12,773
Anderson County	19,009	21,304	-	-	-	-	-	-	-	-	-	-	-	-	-	-	-	-	-	-	-	-	-	-
Blount County	19,416	24,095	-	-	-	-	-	-	-	-	-	-	-	-	-	-	-	-	-	-	-	-	-	-
Bradley County	18,108	16,665	-	-	-	-	-	-	-	-	-	-	-	-	-	-	-	-	-	-	-	-	-	-
Davidson County	23,069	17,740	10,511	23,103	-	-	17,412	-	25,463	-	-	-	-	19,900	15,492	12,442	-	-	-	-	-	-	-	11,577
Hamilton County	21,593	26,602	-	35,110	-	-	-	-	19,435	-	-	-	-	-	19,993	-	-	-	-	-	-	-	-	11,079
Knox County	21,875	21,974	-	26,636	-	-	25,865	-	-	-	-	-	-	-	10,538	-	-	-	-	-	-	-	-	14,958
Madison County	19,389	19,945	-	-	-	-	-	-	-	-	-	-	-	-	-	-	-	-	-	-	-	-	-	-
Montgomery County	17,265	10,904	-	-	-	-	-	-	-	-	-	-	-	-	8,045	-	-	-	-	-	-	-	-	-
Putnam County	16,927	15,588	-	-	-	-	-	-	-	-	-	-	-	-	-	-	-	-	-	-	-	-	-	-
Rutherford County	19,938	19,728	-	-	-	-	-	-	-	-	-	-	-	-	-	16,596	-	-	-	-	-	-	-	-
Shelby County	20,856	20,570	17,828	25,820	-	13,269	21,672	-	23,981	-	-	-	-	20,739	20,297	-	-	-	-	-	-	-	-	12,909
Germantown (city)	44,021	34,726	-	29,722	-	-	35,202	-	-	-	-	-	-	-	-	-	-	-	-	-	-	-	-	-
Sullivan County	19,202	27,329	-	-	-	-	-	-	-	-	-	-	-	-	-	-	-	-	-	-	-	-	-	-
Sumner County	21,164	28,089	-	-	-	-	-	-	-	-	-	-	-	-	-	-	-	-	-	-	-	-	-	-
Washington County	19,085	42,978	-	-	-	-	-	-	-	-	-	-	-	-	-	-	-	-	-	-	-	-	-	-
Weakley County[4]	15,408	9,149	-	-	-	-	-	-	-	-	-	-	-	-	-	-	-	-	-	-	-	-	-	-
Martin (city)	15,184	8,976	-	-	-	-	-	-	-	-	-	-	-	-	-	-	-	-	-	-	-	-	-	-
Williamson County	32,496	27,473	-	-	-	-	-	-	-	-	-	-	-	-	-	-	-	-	-	-	-	-	-	-
Wilson County	22,739	29,477	-	-	-	-	-	-	-	-	-	-	-	-	-	-	-	-	-	-	-	-	-	-
TEXAS	19,617	20,956	15,119	26,158	18,741	13,585	24,444	-	21,753	16,168	15,491	-	21,810	25,363	17,481	13,433	23,385	16,228	13,133	22,582	23,636	19,744	11,564	16,059
Anderson County	13,838	14,911	-	-	-	-	-	-	-	-	-	-	-	-	-	-	-	-	-	-	-	-	-	-
Angelina County	15,876	18,150	-	-	-	-	-	-	-	-	-	-	-	-	-	-	-	-	-	-	-	-	-	-
Bell County	17,219	17,040	15,701	30,403	-	-	-	-	16,896	17,289	-	-	-	12,281	14,992	-	-	-	-	-	-	-	-	-
Killeen (city)	15,323	15,668	14,233	-	-	-	-	-	15,243	16,823	-	-	-	-	15,721	-	-	-	-	-	-	-	-	-
Bexar County	18,363	20,089	16,707	26,680	-	-	23,321	-	17,575	-	20,905	-	-	22,288	17,007	11,514	-	-	-	-	-	19,005	-	15,693
Bowie County	17,357	26,180	-	-	-	-	-	-	-	-	-	-	-	-	-	-	-	-	-	-	-	-	-	-
Brazoria County	20,021	22,433	-	30,293	-	8,739	30,048	-	23,390	-	-	-	-	-	-	-	-	-	-	-	-	-	-	19,890
Brazos County	16,212	12,587	-	14,389	-	-	13,552	-	-	-	-	-	-	-	8,953	-	-	-	-	-	-	-	-	8,071
College Station (city)	15,170	12,251	-	15,455	-	-	13,450	-	-	-	-	-	-	-	5,034	-	-	-	-	-	-	-	-	-
Calhoun County[4]	17,125	19,472	-	-	-	-	-	-	-	-	-	-	-	-	-	-	-	-	-	-	-	-	-	7,799
Port Lavaca (city)	15,431	23,208	-	-	-	-	-	-	-	-	-	-	-	-	-	-	-	-	-	-	-	-	-	-

Notes: Please refer to the User's Guide for an explanation of data; data is arranged alphabetically by state, then county, then city within each county; table includes counties with populations greater than 49,999 unless noted and cities with populations greater than 9,999 whose Asian and/or NHPI population rates are greater than the national average; (1) Native Hawaiian and other Pacific Islander; (2) excludes Taiwanese; (3) includes Chamorro; (4) county does not meet population threshold but is shown in order to allow inclusion of city

Place	Total population	Total Asian population	Total NHPI[1] population	Asian Indian	Bangladeshi	Cambodian	Chinese[2]	Fijian	Filipino	Guamanian[3]	Hawaiian, Native	Hmong	Indonesian	Japanese	Korean	Laotian	Malaysian	Pakistani	Samoan	Sri Lankan	Taiwanese	Thai	Tongan	Vietnamese
Cameron County	10,960	32,886	-	-	-	-	-	-	27,771	-	-	-	-	-	-	-	-	-	-	-	-	-	-	-
Collin County	33,345	30,136	-	34,466	-	-	30,040	-	36,059	-	-	-	-	33,691	23,329	-	-	22,249	-	-	29,471	17,224	-	27,758
Allen (city)	28,575	21,428	-	20,767	-	-	-	-	-	-	-	-	-	-	-	-	-	-	-	-	-	-	-	22,461
Plano (city)	36,514	30,358	-	36,664	-	-	28,651	-	39,477	-	-	-	-	30,921	27,287	-	-	26,363	-	-	31,279	-	-	26,303
Comal County	21,914	27,676	-	-	-	-	-	-	-	-	-	-	-	-	-	-	-	-	-	-	-	-	-	-
Coryell County	14,410	12,440	11,951	-	-	-	-	-	-	-	-	-	-	-	8,339	-	-	-	-	-	-	-	-	-
Dallas County	22,603	20,812	18,869	24,880	17,057	14,397	25,584	-	24,058	-	-	-	-	29,170	16,386	12,253	-	14,972	-	-	28,332	27,002	-	16,534
Addison (town)	38,606	30,299	-	28,470	-	-	-	-	-	-	-	-	-	-	-	-	-	-	-	-	-	-	-	-
Coppell (city)	40,219	27,084	-	33,200	-	-	30,343	-	-	-	-	-	-	-	17,823	-	-	-	-	-	-	-	-	-
Farmers Branch (city)	24,921	29,404	-	-	-	-	-	-	-	-	-	-	-	-	-	-	-	-	-	-	-	-	-	-
Garland (city)	20,000	15,952	-	18,449	-	-	18,660	-	20,339	-	-	-	-	-	11,116	-	-	9,741	-	-	-	-	-	14,653
Grand Prairie (city)	18,978	17,749	-	19,672	-	-	-	-	20,837	-	-	-	-	-	-	9,226	-	-	-	-	-	-	-	16,160
Irving (city)	23,419	24,393	-	28,864	-	-	29,616	-	26,582	-	-	-	-	25,587	16,823	13,010	-	18,290	-	-	-	-	-	21,812
Mesquite (city)	20,890	19,808	-	20,274	-	-	-	-	21,180	-	-	-	-	-	-	-	-	-	-	-	-	-	-	-
Richardson (city)	29,551	22,397	-	22,430	-	-	23,377	-	22,699	-	-	-	-	-	16,341	-	-	20,244	-	-	-	-	-	23,390
Rowlett (city)	26,144	24,551	-	22,901	-	-	-	-	-	-	-	-	-	-	-	-	-	-	-	-	-	-	-	-
Denton County	26,895	21,784	-	24,775	-	15,691	23,781	-	24,319	-	-	-	-	16,380	20,896	-	-	20,979	-	-	-	-	-	18,354
Carrollton (city)	26,746	19,041	-	21,028	-	12,855	23,482	-	-	-	-	-	-	-	17,018	-	-	17,257	-	-	-	-	-	16,724
Lewisville (city)	24,703	25,805	-	24,907	-	-	-	-	-	-	-	-	-	-	-	-	-	-	-	-	-	-	-	22,427
Ector County	15,031	31,896	-	-	-	-	-	-	-	-	-	-	-	-	-	-	-	-	-	-	-	-	-	-
El Paso County	13,421	19,691	11,909	23,055	-	-	32,213	-	23,434	-	-	-	-	18,953	12,134	-	-	-	-	-	-	-	-	-
Ellis County	20,212	21,301	-	-	-	-	-	-	-	-	-	-	-	-	-	-	-	-	-	-	-	-	-	-
Fort Bend County	24,985	23,930	-	25,588	-	-	25,246	-	23,123	-	-	-	-	-	23,590	-	-	17,270	-	-	19,574	-	-	22,886
Cinco Ranch (cdp)	37,747	32,642	-	-	-	-	-	-	-	-	-	-	-	-	-	-	-	-	-	-	-	-	-	-
Mission Bend (cdp)	20,029	18,540	-	24,160	-	-	18,108	-	19,294	-	-	-	-	-	-	-	-	7,655	-	-	-	-	-	18,488
Missouri City (city)	27,210	25,586	-	27,950	-	-	24,032	-	26,169	-	-	-	-	-	-	-	-	-	-	-	-	-	-	29,181
New Territory (cdp)	29,341	30,674	-	32,515	-	-	31,252	-	-	-	-	-	-	-	-	-	-	-	-	-	-	-	-	-
Stafford (city)	22,803	18,564	-	14,147	-	-	21,395	-	21,175	-	-	-	-	-	-	-	-	-	-	-	-	-	-	24,298
Sugar Land (city)	33,506	25,925	-	29,478	-	-	26,383	-	24,574	-	-	-	-	-	36,667	-	-	19,986	-	-	17,939	-	-	20,488
Galveston County	21,568	17,338	-	20,359	-	-	18,031	-	23,750	-	-	-	-	-	-	-	-	-	-	-	-	-	-	13,217
Grayson County	18,862	23,917	-	-	-	-	-	-	-	-	-	-	-	-	-	-	-	-	-	-	-	-	-	-
Gregg County	18,449	28,499	-	-	-	-	-	-	-	-	-	-	-	-	-	-	-	-	-	-	-	-	-	-
Guadalupe County	18,430	15,506	-	-	-	-	-	-	-	-	-	-	-	-	-	-	-	-	-	-	-	-	-	-
Harris County	21,435	19,918	18,242	24,061	18,461	13,014	22,690	-	22,959	16,888	-	-	16,689	29,295	19,615	15,552	-	14,864	-	-	25,897	21,090	-	15,392
Bellaire (city)	46,674	38,716	-	-	-	-	40,482	-	-	-	-	-	-	-	-	-	-	-	-	-	-	-	-	-
Houston (city)	20,101	19,196	16,088	23,352	-	11,207	21,710	-	23,755	15,836	-	-	18,016	28,368	18,107	-	-	13,157	-	-	22,563	23,413	-	14,421
West University Place (city)	69,674	64,108	-	-	-	-	-	-	-	-	-	-	-	-	-	-	-	-	-	-	-	-	-	-
Hays County	19,931	22,631	-	-	-	-	-	-	-	-	-	-	-	-	-	-	-	-	-	-	-	-	-	-
Hidalgo County	9,899	29,833	-	43,717	-	-	-	-	25,170	-	-	-	-	-	-	-	-	-	-	-	-	-	-	-
Hunt County	17,554	15,302	-	-	-	-	-	-	-	-	-	-	-	-	-	-	-	-	-	-	-	-	-	-
Jefferson County	17,571	14,969	-	26,933	-	-	29,965	-	23,851	-	-	-	-	-	-	-	-	-	-	-	-	-	-	8,418

Notes: Please refer to the User's Guide for an explanation of data; data is arranged alphabetically by state, then county, then city within each county; table includes counties with populations greater than 49,999 unless noted and cities with populations greater than 9,999 whose Asian and/or NHPI population rates are greater than the national average; (1) Native Hawaiian and other Pacific Islander; (2) excludes Taiwanese; (3) includes Chamorro; (4) county does not meet population threshold but is shown in order to allow inclusion of city

Place	Total population	Total Asian population	Total NHPI[1] population	Asian Indian	Bangladeshi	Cambodian	Chinese[2]	Fijian	Filipino	Guamanian[3]	Hawaiian, Native	Hmong	Indonesian	Japanese	Korean	Laotian	Malaysian	Pakistani	Samoan	Sri Lankan	Taiwanese	Thai	Tongan	Vietnamese
Port Arthur (city)	14,183	9,187	-	-	-	-	-	-	-	-	-	-	-	-	-	-	-	-	-	-	-	-	-	7,471
Johnson County	18,400	14,021	-	-	-	-	-	-	-	-	-	-	-	-	-	-	-	-	-	-	-	-	-	-
Kaufman County	18,827	22,909	-	-	-	-	-	-	-	-	-	-	-	-	-	-	-	-	-	-	-	-	-	-
Lubbock County	17,323	21,366	-	32,689	-	-	22,002	-	-	-	-	-	-	-	-	-	-	-	-	-	-	-	-	12,702
McLennan County	17,174	18,635	-	39,881	-	-	-	-	-	-	-	-	-	-	-	-	-	-	-	-	-	-	-	-
Midland County	20,369	30,696	-	37,397	-	-	-	-	-	-	-	-	-	-	-	-	-	-	-	-	-	-	-	-
Montgomery County	24,544	34,853	-	53,606	-	-	32,389	-	22,957	-	-	-	-	-	-	-	-	-	-	-	-	-	-	-
Nacogdoches County	15,437	31,697	-	-	-	-	-	-	-	-	-	-	-	-	-	-	-	-	-	-	-	-	-	-
Nueces County	17,036	20,759	-	24,121	-	-	-	-	18,175	-	-	-	-	-	-	-	-	-	-	-	-	-	-	-
Orange County	17,554	16,974	-	-	-	-	-	-	-	-	-	-	-	-	-	-	-	-	-	-	-	-	-	12,744
Potter County	14,947	14,677	-	-	-	-	-	-	-	-	-	-	-	-	-	11,666	-	-	-	-	-	-	-	13,655
Randall County	21,840	18,006	-	-	-	-	-	-	-	-	-	-	-	-	-	-	-	-	-	-	-	-	-	-
San Patricio County	15,425	12,971	-	-	-	-	-	-	-	-	-	-	-	-	-	-	-	-	-	-	-	-	-	-
Smith County	19,072	28,594	-	-	-	-	-	-	-	-	-	-	-	-	-	-	-	-	-	-	-	-	-	-
Tarrant County	22,548	18,291	13,735	25,506	-	9,827	22,152	-	19,002	-	-	-	-	25,975	13,904	14,206	-	21,780	-	-	24,873	19,680	12,189	14,921
Arlington (city)	22,445	16,114	-	21,605	-	-	19,127	-	16,071	-	-	-	-	-	12,094	-	-	-	-	-	24,280	-	-	13,677
Euless (city)	23,764	19,317	-	26,632	-	-	-	-	-	-	-	-	-	-	-	-	-	-	-	-	-	-	-	-
Haltom City (city)	17,740	14,069	-	-	-	-	-	-	-	-	-	-	-	-	-	11,773	-	-	-	-	-	-	-	12,948
Taylor County	17,176	12,978	-	-	-	-	-	-	16,150	-	-	-	-	-	-	-	-	-	-	-	-	-	-	-
Tom Green County	17,325	14,439	-	-	-	-	-	-	-	-	-	-	-	-	-	-	-	-	-	-	-	-	-	-
Travis County	25,883	22,144	14,627	27,628	-	-	25,254	-	19,176	-	-	-	-	25,638	16,254	-	-	11,957	-	-	17,818	18,362	-	18,616
Austin (city)	24,163	21,805	17,679	28,067	-	-	24,124	-	19,099	-	-	-	-	23,832	14,630	-	-	11,122	-	-	15,436	-	-	18,650
Pflugerville (city)	26,226	19,680	-	-	-	-	-	-	-	-	-	-	-	-	-	-	-	-	-	-	-	-	-	-
Wells Branch (cdp)	27,664	20,485	-	-	-	-	-	-	-	-	-	-	-	-	-	-	-	-	-	-	-	-	-	-
Victoria County	18,379	23,267	-	-	-	-	-	-	-	-	-	-	-	-	-	-	-	-	-	-	-	-	-	-
Webb County	10,759	18,616	-	-	-	-	-	-	-	-	-	-	-	-	-	-	-	-	-	-	-	-	-	-
Wichita County	16,965	17,048	-	-	-	-	-	-	9,781	-	-	-	-	-	-	-	-	-	-	-	-	-	-	16,942
Williamson County	24,547	23,605	-	25,524	-	-	22,234	-	-	-	-	-	-	-	15,101	-	-	-	-	-	-	-	-	24,666
Brushy Creek (cdp)	28,129	25,012	-	-	-	-	-	-	-	-	-	-	-	-	-	-	-	-	-	-	-	-	-	-
Jollyville (cdp)	28,113	20,746	-	-	-	-	-	-	-	-	-	-	-	-	-	-	-	-	-	-	-	-	-	-
UTAH	18,185	16,296	10,296	16,761	-	11,753	17,118	-	17,787	-	17,422	-	-	22,837	12,627	12,526	-	14,402	10,878	-	13,099	17,462	8,881	14,468
Cache County	15,094	10,314	-	-	-	-	12,160	-	-	-	-	-	-	-	-	-	-	-	-	-	-	-	-	-
Davis County	19,506	20,041	12,903	-	-	-	-	-	23,069	-	-	-	-	23,225	19,763	-	-	-	-	-	-	-	-	-
Salt Lake County	20,190	16,973	9,861	16,949	-	12,098	19,083	-	18,355	-	20,635	-	-	26,220	13,505	12,613	-	-	10,794	-	-	-	8,736	14,447
Kearns (cdp)	14,110	14,700	9,904	-	-	-	-	-	-	-	-	-	-	-	-	-	-	-	-	-	-	-	-	-
Salt Lake City (city)	20,752	16,729	9,159	16,454	-	-	19,065	-	16,820	-	-	-	-	26,818	10,749	-	-	-	10,790	-	-	-	7,882	10,370
Sandy (city)	22,928	20,135	10,689	-	-	-	19,397	-	-	-	-	-	-	-	-	-	-	-	-	-	-	-	-	-
Taylorsville (city)	17,812	14,180	9,479	-	-	-	-	-	-	-	-	-	-	-	-	-	-	-	-	-	-	-	-	14,493
West Jordan (city)	17,221	17,746	10,924	-	-	-	-	-	-	-	-	-	-	-	-	-	-	-	-	-	-	-	10,049	-
West Valley City (city)	15,031	14,014	8,748	-	-	10,518	11,933	-	-	-	-	-	-	-	-	12,918	-	-	10,045	-	-	-	7,734	19,038
Utah County	15,557	11,814	10,589	-	-	-	11,138	-	13,704	-	12,424	-	-	11,437	9,923	-	-	-	11,507	-	-	-	10,871	-

Notes: Please refer to the User's Guide for an explanation of data; data is arranged alphabetically by state, then county, then city within each county; table includes counties with populations greater than 49,999 unless noted and cities with populations greater than 9,999 whose Asian and/or NHPI population rates are greater than the national average; (1) Native Hawaiian and other Pacific Islander; (2) excludes Taiwanese; (3) includes Chamorro; (4) county does not meet population threshold but is shown in order to allow inclusion of city

Place	Total population	Total Asian population	Total NHPI[1] population	Asian Indian	Bangladeshi	Cambodian	Chinese[2]	Fijian	Filipino	Guamanian[3]	Hawaiian, Native	Hmong	Indonesian	Japanese	Korean	Laotian	Malaysian	Pakistani	Samoan	Sri Lankan	Taiwanese	Thai	Tongan	Vietnamese
Orem (city)	16,590	15,447	12,127	-	-	-	-	-	-	-	-	-	-	-	-	-	-	-	-	-	-	-	-	-
Provo (city)	13,207	9,411	8,463	-	-	-	9,953	-	-	-	-	-	-	5,276	-	-	-	-	-	-	-	-	-	-
Washington County	15,873	8,646	9,505	-	-	-	-	-	-	-	-	-	-	-	-	-	-	-	-	-	-	-	-	-
St. George (city)	17,022	8,606	9,048	-	-	-	-	-	-	-	-	-	-	-	-	-	-	-	-	-	-	-	-	-
Weber County	18,246	17,625	-	-	-	-	-	-	-	-	-	-	-	24,937	-	-	-	-	-	-	-	-	-	-
VERMONT	20,625	13,718	-	20,888	-	-	15,048	-	18,966	-	-	-	-	14,855	7,581	-	-	-	-	-	-	-	-	10,526
Chittenden County	23,501	14,409	-	22,129	-	-	12,842	-	-	-	-	-	-	-	-	-	-	-	-	-	-	-	-	12,134
Rutland County	18,874	13,992	-	-	-	-	-	-	-	-	-	-	-	-	-	-	-	-	-	-	-	-	-	-
Washington County	21,113	14,336	-	-	-	-	-	-	-	-	-	-	-	-	-	-	-	-	-	-	-	-	-	-
Windsor County	22,369	12,843	-	-	-	-	-	-	-	-	-	-	-	-	-	-	-	-	-	-	-	-	-	-
VIRGINIA	23,975	22,790	20,761	29,811	19,768	16,278	26,107	-	21,295	22,946	25,305	-	24,383	29,901	19,725	16,234	-	14,562	16,642	19,950	29,478	20,843	-	19,977
Albemarle County	28,852	22,713	-	21,128	-	-	20,380	-	-	-	-	-	-	-	-	-	-	-	-	-	-	-	-	-
Alexandria Independent City	37,645	22,156	-	23,684	-	-	27,345	-	24,933	-	-	-	-	-	18,416	-	-	12,380	-	-	-	-	-	30,196
Arlington County	37,706	25,533	-	29,407	-	13,863	29,631	-	23,094	-	-	-	-	37,457	33,839	-	-	14,399	-	-	-	-	-	17,224
Arlington (cdp)	37,706	25,533	-	29,407	-	13,863	29,631	-	23,094	-	-	-	-	37,457	33,839	-	-	14,399	-	-	-	-	-	17,224
Bedford County	21,582	18,937	-	-	-	-	-	-	-	-	-	-	-	-	-	-	-	-	-	-	-	-	-	-
Charlottesville Independent City	16,973	8,485	-	5,510	-	-	10,794	-	-	-	-	-	-	-	-	-	-	-	-	-	-	-	-	-
Chesapeake Independent City	20,949	26,643	-	-	-	-	-	-	25,568	-	-	-	-	-	-	-	-	-	-	-	-	-	-	-
Chesterfield County	25,286	23,303	-	36,651	-	10,539	20,883	-	22,055	-	-	-	-	-	22,986	-	-	-	-	-	-	-	-	17,415
Fairfax Independent City	31,247	23,426	-	40,117	-	-	20,443	-	-	-	-	-	-	-	16,648	-	-	-	-	-	-	-	-	21,678
Fairfax County	36,888	25,528	30,029	33,329	24,035	20,145	31,023	-	26,323	-	-	-	23,871	36,453	20,921	17,028	-	14,188	-	-	37,535	21,388	-	21,883
Annandale (cdp)	31,623	22,187	-	27,481	-	-	20,437	-	29,347	-	-	-	-	-	21,204	-	-	-	-	-	-	-	-	20,647
Bailey's Crossroads (cdp)	24,091	16,858	-	-	-	-	-	-	-	-	-	-	-	-	-	-	-	8,252	-	-	-	-	-	15,615
Burke (cdp)	34,936	23,318	-	27,997	-	-	30,552	-	25,781	-	-	-	-	-	18,950	-	-	-	-	-	-	-	-	23,568
Centreville (cdp)	28,878	22,573	-	26,281	-	-	18,993	-	22,465	-	-	-	-	-	20,435	-	-	-	-	-	-	-	-	24,405
Chantilly (cdp)	36,200	27,540	-	28,819	-	-	30,414	-	-	-	-	-	-	-	23,939	-	-	-	-	-	-	-	-	24,897
Franconia (cdp)	37,134	25,965	-	24,268	-	-	-	-	30,164	-	-	-	-	-	22,382	-	-	-	-	-	-	-	-	31,905
Groveton (cdp)	27,697	19,392	-	-	-	-	-	-	-	-	-	-	-	-	-	-	-	-	-	-	-	-	-	-
Herndon (town)	26,941	21,416	-	22,468	-	-	-	-	-	-	-	-	-	-	-	-	-	-	-	-	-	-	-	22,301
Hybla Valley (cdp)	24,745	14,379	-	-	-	-	-	-	-	-	-	-	-	-	-	-	-	-	-	-	-	-	-	-
Idylwood (cdp)	34,485	30,172	-	34,334	-	-	27,374	-	-	-	-	-	-	-	-	-	-	-	-	-	-	-	-	41,304
Jefferson (cdp)	28,705	20,601	-	31,104	-	-	26,978	-	17,764	-	-	-	-	-	-	-	-	-	-	-	-	-	-	17,426
Lincolnia (cdp)	26,876	18,006	-	-	-	-	-	-	-	-	-	-	-	-	-	-	-	8,512	-	-	-	-	-	22,771
Lorton (cdp)	25,146	20,372	-	-	-	-	-	-	-	-	-	-	-	-	-	-	-	-	-	-	-	-	-	-
McLean (cdp)	63,209	48,077	-	84,047	-	-	54,484	-	35,107	-	-	-	-	34,090	29,087	-	-	-	-	-	-	-	-	-
Merrifield (cdp)	32,819	24,353	-	29,384	-	-	-	-	-	-	-	-	-	-	15,249	-	-	-	-	-	-	-	-	24,806
Mount Vernon (cdp)	29,299	18,140	-	-	-	-	-	-	-	-	-	-	-	-	17,644	-	-	-	-	-	-	-	-	-
Newington (cdp)	32,901	20,603	-	22,083	-	-	-	-	25,598	-	-	-	-	-	14,451	-	-	-	-	-	-	-	-	-
Oakton (cdp)	43,297	28,803	-	40,756	-	-	36,306	-	-	-	-	-	-	-	16,687	-	-	-	-	-	-	-	-	24,403
Reston (cdp)	42,747	29,097	-	31,809	-	-	40,382	-	25,849	-	-	-	-	-	31,256	-	-	-	-	-	-	-	-	-
Rose Hill (cdp)	34,213	23,654	-	-	-	-	-	-	-	-	-	-	-	-	-	-	-	-	-	-	-	-	-	-

Notes: Please refer to the User's Guide for an explanation of data; data is arranged alphabetically by state, then county, then city within each county; table includes counties with populations greater than 49,999 unless noted and cities with populations greater than 9,999 whose Asian and/or NHPI population rates are greater than the national average; (1) Native Hawaiian and other Pacific Islander; (2) excludes Taiwanese; (3) includes Chamorro; (4) county does not meet population threshold but is shown in order to allow inclusion of city

Place	Total population	Total Asian population	Total NHPI[1] population	Asian Indian	Bangladeshi	Cambodian	Chinese[2]	Fijian	Filipino	Guamanian[3]	Hawaiian, Native	Hmong	Indonesian	Japanese	Korean	Laotian	Malaysian	Pakistani	Samoan	Sri Lankan	Taiwanese	Thai	Tongan	Vietnamese
Springfield (cdp)	27,807	18,825	-	18,279	-	-	22,688	-	19,427	-	-	-	-	-	22,144	14,969	-	-	-	-	-	-	-	19,866
Tysons Corner (cdp)	47,292	32,259	-	42,919	-	-	28,779	-	-	-	-	-	-	-	26,855	-	-	-	-	-	-	-	-	-
Vienna (town)	37,753	24,528	-	-	-	-	-	-	-	-	-	-	-	-	-	-	-	-	-	-	-	-	-	-
West Springfield (cdp)	35,375	18,850	-	15,432	-	-	27,523	-	-	-	-	-	-	-	18,328	-	-	-	-	-	-	-	-	15,737
Wolf Trap (cdp)	56,294	38,590	-	37,207	-	-	42,662	-	-	-	-	-	-	-	-	-	-	-	-	-	-	-	-	-
Falls Church Independent City	41,051	31,194	-	-	-	-	-	-	-	-	-	-	-	-	-	-	-	-	-	-	-	-	-	-
Fauquier County	28,757	22,740	-	-	-	-	-	-	-	-	-	-	-	-	-	-	-	-	-	-	-	-	-	-
Frederick County	21,080	19,528	-	-	-	-	-	-	-	-	-	-	-	-	-	-	-	-	-	-	-	-	-	-
Hampton Independent City	19,774	19,604	-	-	-	-	-	-	17,432	-	-	-	-	-	-	-	-	-	-	-	-	-	-	15,470
Hanover County	25,120	22,327	-	-	-	-	-	-	-	-	-	-	-	-	-	-	-	-	-	-	-	-	-	-
Henrico County	26,410	21,908	-	30,404	-	14,622	20,834	-	24,760	-	-	-	-	-	19,995	-	-	-	-	-	-	-	-	14,441
Glen Allen (cdp)	25,719	19,929	-	-	-	-	-	-	-	-	-	-	-	-	-	-	-	-	-	-	-	-	-	-
Laurel (cdp)	21,893	18,356	-	-	-	-	-	-	-	-	-	-	-	-	-	-	-	-	-	-	-	-	-	-
Loudoun County	33,530	25,565	-	29,584	-	-	30,673	-	29,048	-	-	-	-	-	19,254	-	-	18,141	-	-	-	-	-	23,589
Lynchburg Independent City	18,263	16,345	-	-	-	-	-	-	-	-	-	-	-	-	-	-	-	-	-	-	-	-	-	-
Manassas Park Indep. City	21,048	17,599	-	-	-	-	-	-	-	-	-	-	-	-	-	-	-	-	-	-	-	-	-	-
Montgomery County	17,077	8,326	-	12,592	-	-	8,962	-	-	-	-	-	-	-	5,736	-	-	-	-	-	-	-	-	-
Blacksburg (town)	13,946	7,019	-	9,561	-	-	7,610	-	-	-	-	-	-	-	5,297	-	-	-	-	-	-	-	-	-
Newport News Independent City	17,843	16,210	-	-	-	-	19,020	-	14,843	-	-	-	-	-	16,484	-	-	-	-	-	-	-	-	12,229
Norfolk Independent City	17,372	15,868	-	18,305	-	-	16,646	-	15,556	-	-	-	-	-	-	-	-	-	-	-	-	-	-	11,921
Portsmouth Independent City	16,507	13,216	-	-	-	-	-	-	15,595	-	-	-	-	-	-	-	-	-	-	-	-	-	-	-
Prince William County	25,641	19,761	-	17,203	-	-	26,157	-	22,616	-	-	-	-	24,823	18,548	-	-	12,639	-	-	-	-	-	20,738
Bull Run (cdp)	22,384	26,633	-	-	-	-	-	-	-	-	-	-	-	-	-	-	-	-	-	-	-	-	-	-
Dale City (cdp)	22,363	15,641	-	13,307	-	-	-	-	14,209	-	-	-	-	-	-	-	-	11,233	-	-	-	-	-	-
Lake Ridge (cdp)	30,506	22,046	-	-	-	-	-	-	-	-	-	-	-	-	-	-	-	-	-	-	-	-	-	-
Woodbridge (cdp)	19,810	14,559	-	-	-	-	-	-	-	-	-	-	-	-	-	-	-	-	-	-	-	-	-	-
Richmond Independent City	20,337	12,808	-	16,706	-	-	-	-	14,088	-	-	-	-	-	-	-	-	-	-	-	-	-	-	-
Roanoke Independent City	18,468	13,116	-	-	-	-	-	-	-	-	-	-	-	-	-	-	-	-	-	-	-	-	-	-
Roanoke County	24,637	26,521	-	-	-	-	-	-	-	-	-	-	-	-	-	-	-	-	-	-	-	-	-	-
Spotsylvania County	22,536	14,907	-	-	-	-	-	-	-	-	-	-	-	-	-	-	-	-	-	-	-	-	-	-
Stafford County	24,762	18,799	-	-	-	-	-	-	22,848	-	-	-	-	-	-	-	-	-	-	-	-	-	-	-
Suffolk Independent City	18,836	24,140	-	-	-	-	-	-	-	-	-	-	-	-	-	-	-	-	-	-	-	-	-	-
Virginia Beach Independent City	22,365	18,197	-	28,180	-	-	20,441	-	17,693	-	-	-	-	18,106	21,931	-	-	-	-	-	-	-	-	12,344
Williamsburg Independent City	18,483	10,136	-	-	-	-	-	-	-	-	-	-	-	-	-	-	-	-	-	-	-	-	-	-
York County	24,560	19,289	-	24,773	-	-	-	-	-	-	-	-	-	-	12,050	-	-	-	-	-	-	-	-	-
WASHINGTON	22,973	20,141	15,025	27,282	-	10,584	24,822	22,380	18,930	16,809	19,765	6,445	18,320	28,307	17,349	12,911	-	18,367	11,337	24,346	22,569	16,723	13,177	14,553
Benton County	21,301	25,108	-	34,473	-	-	35,101	-	-	-	-	-	-	-	12,322	-	-	-	-	-	-	-	-	16,896
Richland (city)	25,494	29,812	-	-	-	-	42,465	-	-	-	-	-	-	-	-	-	-	-	-	-	-	-	-	-
Chelan County	19,273	15,865	-	-	-	-	-	-	-	-	-	-	-	-	-	-	-	-	-	-	-	-	-	-
Clallam County	19,517	18,072	-	-	-	-	-	-	-	-	-	-	-	-	-	-	-	-	-	-	-	-	-	-
Clark County	21,448	19,653	13,008	22,643	-	16,482	22,970	-	20,526	-	-	-	-	23,157	21,569	15,578	-	-	-	-	-	-	-	14,399

Notes: Please refer to the User's Guide for an explanation of data; data is arranged alphabetically by state, then county, then city within each county; table includes counties with populations greater than 49,999 unless noted and cities with populations greater than 9,999 whose Asian and/or NHPI population rates are greater than the national average; (1) Native Hawaiian and other Pacific Islander; (2) excludes Taiwanese; (3) includes Chamorro; (4) county does not meet population threshold but is shown in order to allow inclusion of city

Place	Total population	Total Asian population	Total NHPI[1] population	Asian Indian	Bangladeshi	Cambodian	Chinese[2]	Fijian	Filipino	Guamanian[3]	Hawaiian, Native	Hmong	Indonesian	Japanese	Korean	Laotian	Malaysian	Pakistani	Samoan	Sri Lankan	Taiwanese	Thai	Tongan	Vietnamese
Five Corners (cdp)	19,570	17,511	-	-	-	-	-	-	-	-	-	-	-	-	-	-	-	-	-	-	-	-	-	-
Orchards (cdp)	17,866	13,498	-	-	-	-	-	-	-	-	-	-	-	-	-	-	-	-	-	-	-	-	-	-
Vancouver (city)	20,192	20,345	12,744	-	-	-	26,717	-	20,287	-	-	-	-	22,803	24,966	-	-	-	-	-	-	-	-	13,766
Cowlitz County	18,583	12,746	-	-	-	5,160	-	-	-	-	-	-	-	-	-	-	-	-	-	-	-	-	-	12,230
Grant County	15,037	16,616	-	-	-	-	-	-	-	-	-	-	-	-	-	-	-	-	-	-	-	-	-	-
Grays Harbor County	16,799	14,494	-	-	-	-	-	-	-	-	-	-	-	-	-	-	-	-	-	-	-	-	-	-
Island County	21,472	13,613	-	-	-	-	-	-	13,132	-	-	-	-	13,912	-	-	-	-	-	-	-	-	-	-
Oak Harbor (city)	16,830	11,802	-	-	-	-	-	-	12,294	-	-	-	-	-	-	-	-	-	-	-	-	-	-	-
King County	29,521	22,273	15,486	30,828	-	10,191	25,918	15,851	20,298	22,182	25,666	6,950	20,822	33,263	18,683	12,840	-	18,226	11,017	-	24,150	19,750	16,341	14,572
Auburn (city)	19,630	16,786	-	-	-	-	-	-	-	-	-	-	-	-	-	-	-	-	-	-	-	-	-	-
Bellevue (city)	36,905	30,640	-	39,844	-	-	34,027	-	28,325	-	-	-	-	37,593	21,592	15,072	-	-	-	-	29,981	-	-	19,605
Bothell (city)	26,483	26,438	-	-	-	-	24,723	-	-	-	-	-	-	-	-	-	-	-	-	-	-	-	-	-
Bryn Mawr-Skyway (cdp)	23,294	23,428	-	-	-	-	-	-	19,354	-	-	-	-	47,783	-	-	-	-	-	-	-	-	-	18,544
Burien (city)	23,737	17,290	-	-	-	-	-	-	16,473	-	-	-	-	-	-	-	-	-	-	-	-	-	-	16,076
Cascade-Fairwood (cdp)	25,752	21,838	-	-	-	-	24,657	-	24,500	-	-	-	-	31,920	-	-	-	-	-	-	-	-	-	15,951
Cottage Lake (cdp)	39,763	53,066	-	-	-	-	-	-	-	-	-	-	-	-	-	-	-	-	-	-	-	-	-	-
Des Moines (city)	24,127	16,435	11,119	-	-	-	-	-	21,264	-	-	-	-	-	-	-	-	-	-	-	-	-	-	12,074
East Hill-Meridian (cdp)	23,621	20,359	-	19,734	-	-	19,526	-	19,842	-	-	-	-	-	-	-	-	-	-	-	-	-	-	18,781
Federal Way (city)	22,451	18,089	13,335	-	-	-	21,249	-	19,698	-	-	-	-	31,236	15,869	-	-	-	14,686	-	-	-	-	17,657
Inglewood-Finn Hill (cdp)	31,272	27,263	-	-	-	-	36,983	-	-	-	-	-	-	-	-	-	-	-	-	-	-	-	-	-
Issaquah (city)	34,222	27,854	-	-	-	-	-	-	-	-	-	-	-	-	-	-	-	-	-	-	-	-	-	-
Kenmore (city)	31,692	24,845	-	-	-	-	-	-	-	-	-	-	-	-	-	-	-	-	-	-	-	-	-	-
Kent (city)	21,390	17,323	-	15,227	-	-	21,705	-	18,819	-	-	-	-	29,460	13,343	-	-	-	-	-	-	-	-	14,623
Kingsgate (cdp)	26,543	18,048	-	-	-	-	28,090	-	-	-	-	-	-	-	-	-	-	-	-	-	-	-	-	-
Kirkland (city)	38,903	26,510	-	-	-	-	28,387	-	-	-	-	-	-	34,652	-	-	-	-	-	-	-	-	-	21,019
Lake Forest Park (city)	33,419	27,372	-	-	-	-	-	-	-	-	-	-	-	-	-	-	-	-	-	-	-	-	-	-
Lakeland North (cdp)	23,776	18,045	-	-	-	-	-	-	-	-	-	-	-	-	-	-	-	-	-	-	-	-	-	-
Lakeland South (cdp)	26,833	31,518	-	-	-	-	-	-	-	-	-	-	-	-	-	-	-	-	-	-	-	-	-	-
Lea Hill (cdp)	26,767	17,562	-	-	-	-	-	-	-	-	-	-	-	-	-	-	-	-	-	-	-	-	-	-
Mercer Island (city)	53,799	37,284	-	-	-	-	31,230	-	-	-	-	-	-	56,966	-	-	-	-	-	-	-	-	-	-
Redmond (city)	36,233	33,730	-	38,862	-	-	34,937	-	-	-	-	-	-	43,576	29,692	-	-	-	-	-	-	-	-	-
Renton (city)	24,346	21,559	-	-	-	-	28,356	-	20,650	-	-	-	-	29,339	-	-	-	-	-	-	-	-	-	15,888
Riverton-Boulevard Park (cdp)	18,523	13,870	-	-	-	-	-	-	-	-	-	-	-	-	-	-	-	-	-	-	-	-	-	-
Sammamish (city)	42,971	37,981	-	-	-	-	33,874	-	-	-	-	-	-	-	-	-	-	-	-	-	-	-	-	-
SeaTac (city)	19,717	16,058	21,087	15,269	-	-	-	-	18,222	-	-	-	-	-	-	-	-	-	-	-	-	-	-	11,025
Seattle (city)	30,306	19,059	13,121	29,324	-	8,371	20,242	-	18,503	-	-	-	18,036	29,239	18,578	12,336	-	-	8,774	-	15,196	18,480	-	12,375
Shoreline (city)	24,959	21,511	-	22,054	-	-	25,005	-	21,087	-	-	-	-	29,923	21,926	-	-	-	-	-	-	-	-	14,913
Tukwila (city)	22,354	17,826	17,328	-	-	-	-	-	20,583	-	-	-	-	-	-	-	-	-	-	-	-	-	-	-
Union Hill-Novelty Hill (cdp)	46,538	66,472	-	-	-	-	-	-	-	-	-	-	-	-	-	-	-	-	-	-	-	-	-	-
White Center (cdp)	17,339	10,996	-	-	-	7,823	-	-	16,316	-	-	-	-	-	-	-	-	-	-	-	-	-	-	10,188
Kitsap County	22,317	18,366	11,934	-	-	-	18,885	-	16,845	12,121	-	-	-	21,931	37,065	-	-	-	-	-	-	-	-	11,493

Notes: Please refer to the User's Guide for an explanation of data; data is arranged alphabetically by state, then county, then city within each county; table includes counties with populations greater than 49,999 unless noted and cities with populations greater than 9,999 whose Asian and/or NHPI population rates are greater than the national average; (1) Native Hawaiian and other Pacific Islander; (2) excludes Taiwanese; (3) includes Chamorro; (4) county does not meet population threshold but is shown in order to allow inclusion of city

Place	Total population	Total Asian population	Total NHPI[1] population	Asian Indian	Bangladeshi	Cambodian	Chinese[2]	Fijian	Filipino	Guamanian[3]	Hawaiian, Native	Hmong	Indonesian	Japanese	Korean	Laotian	Malaysian	Pakistani	Samoan	Sri Lankan	Taiwanese	Thai	Tongan	Vietnamese
Bremerton (city)	16,724	13,458	-	-	-	-	-	-	13,645	-	-	-	-	-	-	-	-	-	-	-	-	-	-	-
Silverdale (cdp)	21,763	17,005	-	-	-	-	-	-	17,518	-	-	-	-	-	-	-	-	-	-	-	-	-	-	-
Lewis County	17,082	12,688	-	-	-	-	-	-	-	-	-	-	-	-	-	-	-	-	-	-	-	-	-	-
Pierce County	20,948	15,936	14,259	24,305	-	8,450	25,711	-	17,858	14,974	17,975	-	-	23,168	14,593	11,807	-	-	11,007	-	-	16,769	-	12,777
Elk Plain (cdp)	19,547	16,427	-	-	-	-	-	-	-	-	-	-	-	-	-	-	-	-	-	-	-	-	-	-
Fort Lewis (cdp)	12,865	19,577	10,958	-	-	-	-	-	12,299	-	-	-	-	-	-	-	-	-	-	-	-	-	-	-
Lakewood (city)	20,569	16,047	13,983	-	-	-	-	-	14,885	-	-	-	-	24,058	16,074	-	-	-	10,881	-	-	-	-	-
Parkland (cdp)	18,649	15,388	14,893	-	-	-	-	-	-	-	-	-	-	-	13,994	-	-	-	-	-	-	-	-	-
Spanaway (cdp)	17,928	13,273	9,874	-	-	-	-	-	13,887	-	-	-	-	-	10,897	-	-	-	-	-	-	-	-	-
Tacoma (city)	19,130	14,021	15,396	-	-	8,097	25,976	-	19,803	17,841	-	-	-	18,279	13,688	11,741	-	-	10,688	-	-	-	-	10,410
University Place (city)	25,544	18,018	-	-	-	-	-	-	-	-	-	-	-	-	15,427	-	-	-	-	-	-	-	-	-
Skagit County	21,256	14,154	-	-	-	-	-	-	15,741	-	-	-	-	-	-	-	-	-	-	-	-	-	-	-
Snohomish County	23,417	19,170	22,511	23,975	-	16,108	20,709	-	18,699	-	21,237	-	-	26,120	18,095	16,248	-	16,811	-	-	-	-	-	17,432
Alderwood Manor (cdp)	24,012	20,440	-	-	-	-	-	-	-	-	-	-	-	-	-	-	-	-	-	-	-	-	-	-
Edmonds (city)	30,076	23,669	-	-	-	-	-	-	21,191	-	-	-	-	-	17,235	-	-	-	-	-	-	-	-	-
Everett (city)	20,577	15,579	-	13,729	-	10,606	-	-	17,751	-	-	-	-	-	-	-	-	-	-	-	-	-	-	14,765
Lynnwood (city)	19,971	17,518	-	-	-	-	15,698	-	19,644	-	-	-	-	-	17,864	-	-	-	-	-	-	-	-	15,947
Martha Lake (cdp)	24,721	18,287	-	-	-	-	-	-	-	-	-	-	-	-	-	-	-	-	-	-	-	-	-	-
Marysville (city)	20,414	18,732	-	-	-	-	-	-	-	-	-	-	-	-	-	-	-	-	-	-	-	-	-	-
Mill Creek (city)	36,234	22,393	-	-	-	-	-	-	-	-	-	-	-	-	21,418	-	-	-	-	-	-	-	-	-
Mountlake Terrace (city)	21,566	14,175	-	-	-	-	-	-	15,641	-	-	-	-	-	14,990	-	-	-	-	-	-	-	-	-
Mukilteo (city)	29,134	26,196	-	-	-	-	-	-	-	-	-	-	-	-	21,561	-	-	-	-	-	-	-	-	-
North Creek (cdp)	25,861	24,424	-	-	-	-	-	-	-	-	-	-	-	-	-	-	-	-	-	-	-	-	-	-
Paine Field-Lk. Stickney (cdp)	19,801	16,437	-	-	-	-	-	-	-	-	-	-	-	-	-	-	-	-	-	-	-	-	-	-
Picnic Pt.-N. Lynnwood (cdp)	24,003	16,514	-	-	-	-	-	-	17,338	-	-	-	-	-	13,219	-	-	-	-	-	-	-	-	-
Seattle Hill-Silver Firs (cdp)	26,617	23,774	-	-	-	-	-	-	15,116	-	-	-	-	-	22,524	-	-	-	-	-	-	-	-	25,957
Spokane County	19,233	14,518	14,243	29,727	-	-	16,266	-	15,358	-	-	5,209	-	15,778	10,422	-	-	-	-	-	-	-	-	11,817
Spokane (city)	18,451	12,453	16,137	-	-	-	15,592	-	14,977	-	-	4,148	-	16,018	8,845	-	-	-	-	-	-	-	-	11,477
Thurston County	22,415	17,000	16,072	21,296	-	11,488	20,692	-	18,034	18,137	-	-	-	25,411	16,224	-	-	-	-	-	-	-	-	15,028
Lacey (city)	20,224	15,758	-	-	-	-	-	-	17,148	-	-	-	-	-	11,904	-	-	-	-	-	-	-	-	13,963
Olympia (city)	22,590	17,015	-	-	-	-	-	-	-	-	-	-	-	-	-	-	-	-	-	-	-	-	-	14,524
Tumwater (city)	25,080	19,084	-	-	-	-	-	-	-	-	-	-	-	-	-	-	-	-	-	-	-	-	-	-
Walla Walla County	16,509	12,934	-	-	-	-	-	-	-	-	-	-	-	-	-	-	-	-	-	-	-	-	-	-
Whatcom County	20,025	12,040	-	9,603	-	-	16,191	-	15,740	-	-	-	-	12,046	10,549	-	-	-	-	-	-	-	-	11,987
Bellingham (city)	19,483	11,107	-	7,471	-	-	-	-	-	-	-	-	-	-	-	-	-	-	-	-	-	-	-	11,558
Whitman County[4]	15,298	8,965	-	-	-	-	12,235	-	-	-	-	-	-	6,612	-	-	-	-	-	-	-	-	-	-
Pullman (city)	13,448	9,287	-	-	-	-	13,683	-	-	-	-	-	-	6,678	-	-	-	-	-	-	-	-	-	-
Yakima County	15,606	16,188	-	-	-	-	-	-	15,688	-	-	-	-	-	-	-	-	-	-	-	-	-	-	-
WEST VIRGINIA	16,477	28,607	10,194	44,354	-	-	16,973	-	38,914	-	-	-	-	15,114	14,365	-	-	27,172	-	-	-	-	-	18,405
Cabell County	17,638	19,194	-	-	-	-	-	-	-	-	-	-	-	-	-	-	-	-	-	-	-	-	-	-
Harrison County	16,810	11,308	-	-	-	-	-	-	-	-	-	-	-	-	-	-	-	-	-	-	-	-	-	-

Notes: Please refer to the User's Guide for an explanation of data; data is arranged alphabetically by state, then county, then city within each county; table includes counties with populations greater than 49,999 unless noted and cities with populations greater than 9,999 whose Asian and/or NHPI population rates are greater than the national average; (1) Native Hawaiian and other Pacific Islander; (2) excludes Taiwanese; (3) includes Chamorro; (4) county does not meet population threshold but is shown in order to allow inclusion of city

Place	Total population	Total Asian population	Total NHPI[1] population	Asian Indian	Bangladeshi	Cambodian	Chinese[2]	Fijian	Filipino	Guamanian[3]	Hawaiian, Native	Hmong	Indonesian	Japanese	Korean	Laotian	Malaysian	Pakistani	Samoan	Sri Lankan	Taiwanese	Thai	Tongan	Vietnamese
Kanawha County	20,354	42,594	-	62,451	-	-	-	-	-	-	-	-	-	-	-	-	-	-	-	-	-	-	-	-
Monongalia County	17,106	16,007	-	20,235	-	-	13,561	-	-	-	-	-	-	-	-	-	-	-	-	-	-	-	-	-
Putnam County	20,471	21,471	-	-	-	-	-	-	-	-	-	-	-	-	-	-	-	-	-	-	-	-	-	-
Raleigh County	16,233	50,782	-	-	-	-	-	-	-	-	-	-	-	-	-	-	-	-	-	-	-	-	-	-
Wood County	18,073	41,513	-	-	-	-	-	-	-	-	-	-	-	-	-	-	-	-	-	-	-	-	-	-
WISCONSIN	21,271	14,962	15,076	27,673	-	8,346	21,249	-	27,047	18,029	15,605	6,860	15,131	23,084	14,290	10,145	-	17,464	-	-	12,998	13,486	-	15,543
Brown County	21,784	10,695	-	22,537	-	-	-	-	-	-	-	7,528	-	-	-	6,283	-	-	-	-	-	-	-	-
Chippewa County	18,243	6,629	-	-	-	-	-	-	-	-	-	3,926	-	-	-	-	-	-	-	-	-	-	-	-
Columbia County	21,014	22,848	-	-	-	-	-	-	-	-	-	-	-	-	-	-	-	-	-	-	-	-	-	-
Dane County	24,985	14,413	-	22,814	-	-	17,824	-	18,922	-	-	7,657	-	18,806	7,627	11,778	-	-	-	-	7,564	-	-	12,872
Madison (city)	23,498	13,569	-	22,629	-	-	16,931	-	16,956	-	-	7,522	-	17,024	7,759	-	-	-	-	-	7,598	-	-	10,767
Dodge County	19,574	42,971	-	-	-	-	-	-	-	-	-	-	-	-	-	-	-	-	-	-	-	-	-	-
Eau Claire County	19,250	11,881	-	-	-	-	-	-	-	-	-	6,986	-	-	-	-	-	-	-	-	-	-	-	-
Fond du Lac County	20,022	13,057	-	-	-	-	-	-	-	-	-	4,051	-	-	-	-	-	-	-	-	-	-	-	-
Jefferson County	21,236	18,373	-	-	-	-	-	-	-	-	-	-	-	-	-	-	-	-	-	-	-	-	-	-
Kenosha County	21,207	21,097	-	-	-	-	-	-	-	-	-	-	-	-	-	-	-	-	-	-	-	-	-	-
La Crosse County	19,800	12,239	-	-	-	-	-	-	-	-	-	5,626	-	-	-	-	-	-	-	-	-	-	-	-
La Crosse (city)	17,650	12,509	-	-	-	-	-	-	-	-	-	4,752	-	-	-	-	-	-	-	-	-	-	-	-
Manitowoc County	20,285	9,400	-	-	-	-	-	-	-	-	-	8,295	-	-	-	-	-	-	-	-	-	-	-	-
Marathon County	20,703	7,353	-	-	-	-	-	-	-	-	-	5,302	-	-	-	-	-	-	-	-	-	-	-	-
Wausau (city)	20,227	7,186	-	-	-	-	-	-	-	-	-	4,955	-	-	-	-	-	-	-	-	-	-	-	-
Milwaukee County	19,939	16,145	13,968	24,325	-	-	22,472	-	25,954	-	-	7,965	-	34,398	17,681	12,365	-	20,797	-	-	-	-	-	16,400
Outagamie County	21,943	9,447	-	8,441	-	-	-	-	-	-	-	7,076	-	-	-	-	-	-	-	-	-	-	-	-
Appleton (city)	22,478	8,273	-	-	-	-	-	-	-	-	-	7,036	-	-	-	-	-	-	-	-	-	-	-	-
Ozaukee County	31,947	27,456	-	-	-	-	-	-	-	-	-	-	-	-	-	-	-	-	-	-	-	-	-	-
Portage County	19,854	8,675	-	-	-	-	-	-	-	-	-	5,134	-	-	-	-	-	-	-	-	-	-	-	-
Stevens Point (city)	17,510	4,928	-	-	-	-	-	-	-	-	-	5,277	-	-	-	-	-	-	-	-	-	-	-	-
Racine County	21,772	22,030	-	-	-	-	-	-	-	-	-	-	-	-	-	-	-	-	-	-	-	-	-	-
Rock County	20,895	18,286	-	-	-	-	-	-	-	-	-	-	-	-	-	-	-	-	-	-	-	-	-	-
St. Croix County	23,937	14,739	-	-	-	-	-	-	-	-	-	-	-	-	-	-	-	-	-	-	-	-	-	-
Sauk County	19,695	20,561	-	-	-	-	-	-	-	-	-	-	-	-	-	-	-	-	-	-	-	-	-	-
Sheboygan County	21,509	8,888	-	-	-	-	-	-	-	-	-	6,973	-	-	-	-	-	-	-	-	-	-	-	-
Sheboygan (city)	19,270	8,289	-	-	-	-	-	-	-	-	-	6,868	-	-	-	-	-	-	-	-	-	-	-	-
Walworth County	21,229	19,017	-	-	-	-	-	-	-	-	-	-	-	-	-	-	-	-	-	-	-	-	-	-
Washington County	24,319	19,129	-	-	-	-	-	-	-	-	-	-	-	-	-	-	-	-	-	-	-	-	-	-
Waukesha County	29,164	32,578	-	47,426	-	-	29,841	-	39,351	-	-	-	-	-	15,596	-	-	-	-	-	-	-	-	-
Winnebago County	21,706	17,100	-	-	-	-	-	-	-	-	-	7,695	-	-	-	-	-	-	-	-	-	-	-	-
Wood County	20,203	10,700	-	-	-	-	-	-	-	-	-	4,572	-	-	-	-	-	-	-	-	-	-	-	-
WYOMING	19,134	18,464	-	20,117	-	-	14,642	-	30,138	-	-	-	-	17,342	14,529	-	-	-	-	-	-	-	-	-
Laramie County	19,634	19,244	-	-	-	-	-	-	-	-	-	-	-	-	-	-	-	-	-	-	-	-	-	-
Natrona County	18,913	36,342	-	-	-	-	-	-	-	-	-	-	-	-	-	-	-	-	-	-	-	-	-	-

Notes: Please refer to the User's Guide for an explanation of data; data is arranged alphabetically by state, then county, then city within each county; table includes counties with populations greater than 49,999 unless noted and cities with populations greater than 9,999 whose Asian and/or NHPI population rates are greater than the national average; (1) Native Hawaiian and other Pacific Islander; (2) excludes Taiwanese; (3) includes Chamorro; (4) county does not meet population threshold but is shown in order to allow inclusion of city

Poverty Status

(Universe: Population for Whom Poverty Status is Determined)

Place	Total population with income below poverty level	Asian population for whom poverty status is determined	Asians with income below poverty level	NHPI[1] population for whom poverty status is determined	NHPIs[1] with income below poverty level	Asian Indian	Bangladeshi	Cambodian	Chinese[2]	Fijian	Filipino	Guamanian[3]	Hawaiian, Native	Hmong	Indonesian	Japanese	Korean	Laotian	Malaysian	Pakistani	Samoan	Sri Lankan	Taiwanese	Thai	Tongan	Vietnamese
UNITED STATES	33,899,812 12.38	9,979,963	1,257,237 12.60 12.60 3.71	364,909	64,558 17.69 17.69 0.19	157,516 9.75 12.53 1.58 0.46	8,734 21.29 0.69 0.09 0.03	51,240 29.28 4.08 0.51 0.15	303,054 13.43 24.10 3.04 0.89	1,066 10.47 1.65 0.29 <0.01	114,849 6.25 9.14 1.15 0.34	7,292 13.75 11.30 2.00 0.02	20,840 15.58 32.28 5.71 0.06	63,633 37.78 5.06 0.64 0.19	7,650 20.92 0.61 0.08 0.02	75,540 9.72 6.01 0.76 0.22	154,688 14.77 12.30 1.55 0.46	30,604 18.51 2.43 0.31 0.09	2,618 25.04 0.21 0.03 0.01	25,406 16.47 2.02 0.25 0.07	16,629 20.18 25.76 4.56 0.05	1,933 10.36 0.15 0.02 0.01	17,523 14.73 1.39 0.18 0.05	15,548 14.35 1.24 0.16 0.05	5,310 19.48 8.23 1.46 0.02	175,924 16.05 13.99 1.76 0.52
ALABAMA	698,097 16.10	29,109	4,461 15.33 15.33 0.64	1,111	191 17.19 17.19 0.03	740 11.29 16.59 2.54 0.11	-	147 26.44 3.30 0.50 0.02	930 16.90 20.85 3.19 0.13	-	333 13.83 7.46 1.14 0.05	74 18.27 38.74 6.66 0.01	-	-	-	286 15.58 6.41 0.98 0.04	612 15.48 13.72 2.10 0.09	93 13.17 2.08 0.32 0.01	-	82 21.87 1.84 0.28 0.01	-	-	-	37 6.09 0.83 0.13 0.01	-	863 18.88 19.35 2.96 0.12
Baldwin County	14,018 10.15	526	118 22.43 22.43 0.84	-	-	-	-	-	-	-	-	-	-	-	-	-	-	-	-	-	-	-	-	-	-	-
Calhoun County	17,695 16.11	653	66 10.11 10.11 0.37	-	-	-	-	-	-	-	-	-	-	-	-	-	-	-	-	-	-	-	-	-	-	-
Etowah County	15,938 15.70	346	54 15.61 15.61 0.34	-	-	-	-	-	-	-	-	-	-	-	-	-	-	-	-	-	-	-	-	-	-	-
Houston County	13,146 15.00	490	49 10.00 10.00 0.37	-	-	-	-	-	-	-	-	-	-	-	-	-	-	-	-	-	-	-	-	-	-	-
Jefferson County	95,674 14.77	5,558	818 14.72 14.72 0.85	-	-	151 11.10 18.46 2.72 0.16	-	-	248 13.87 30.32 4.46 0.26	-	-	-	-	-	-	-	105 23.03 12.84 1.89 0.11	-	-	-	-	-	-	-	-	205 23.62 25.06 3.69 0.21
Lee County	24,119 21.81	1,797	377 20.98 20.98 1.56	-	-	-	-	-	107 17.34 28.38 5.95 0.44	-	-	-	-	-	-	-	-	-	-	-	-	-	-	-	-	-
Madison County	28,408 10.55	4,613	442 9.58 9.58 1.56	-	-	62 4.25 14.03 1.34 0.22	-	-	127 20.09 28.73 2.75 0.45	-	-	-	-	-	-	-	104 10.80 23.53 2.25 0.37	-	-	-	-	-	-	-	-	14 3.71 3.17 0.30 0.05

Notes: Please refer to the User's Guide for an explanation of data; data is arranged alphabetically by state, then county, then city within each county; table includes counties with populations greater than 49,999 unless noted and cities with populations greater than 9,999 whose Asian and/or NHPI population rates are greater than the national average; (1) Native Hawaiian and other Pacific Islander; (2) excludes Taiwanese; (3) includes Chamorro; (4) county does not meet population threshold but is shown in order to allow inclusion of city

Place	Total population with income below poverty level	Asian population for whom poverty status is determined	Asians with income below poverty level	NHPI[1] population for whom poverty status is determined	NHPIs[1] with income below poverty level	Asian Indian	Bangladeshi	Cambodian	Chinese[2]	Fijian	Filipino	Guamanian[3]	Hawaiian, Native	Hmong	Indonesian	Japanese	Korean	Laotian	Malaysian	Pakistani	Samoan	Sri Lankan	Taiwanese	Thai	Tongan	Vietnamese
Mobile County	72,549 18.51	5,187	1,203 23.19 23.19 1.66	-	-	245 43.06 20.37 4.72 0.34	-	95 24.42 7.90 1.83 0.13	114 17.46 9.48 2.20 0.16	-	55 15.15 4.57 1.06 0.08	-	-	-	-	-	-	53 16.88 4.41 1.02 0.07	-	-	-	-	-	-	-	370 18.24 30.76 7.13 0.51
Montgomery County	36,809 17.34	1,647	117 7.10 7.10 0.32	-	-	-	-	-	-	-	-	-	-	-	-	-	-	-	-	-	-	-	-	-	-	-
Morgan County	13,476 12.29	571	37 6.48 6.48 0.27	-	-	-	-	-	-	-	-	-	-	-	-	-	-	-	-	-	-	-	-	-	-	-
Shelby County	8,932 6.31	991	33 3.33 3.33 0.37	-	-	5 1.29 15.15 0.50 0.06	-	-	-	-	-	-	-	-	-	-	-	-	-	-	-	-	-	-	-	-
Tuscaloosa County	26,633 17.02	1,446	469 32.43 32.43 1.76	-	-	-	-	-	-	-	-	-	-	-	-	-	-	-	-	-	-	-	-	-	-	-
ALASKA	57,602 9.40	25,235	3,076 12.19 12.19 5.34	3,062	539 17.60 17.60 0.94	12 2.21 0.39 0.05 0.02	-	-	79 5.17 2.57 0.31 0.14	-	1,178 9.52 38.30 4.67 2.05	-	33 6.86 6.12 1.08 0.06	313 59.96 10.18 1.24 0.54	-	47 3.33 1.53 0.19 0.08	619 13.67 20.12 2.45 1.07	331 24.57 10.76 1.31 0.57	-	-	261 17.42 48.42 8.52 0.45	-	-	54 6.91 1.76 0.21 0.09	160 38.19 29.68 5.23 0.28	128 13.42 4.16 0.51 0.22
Anchorage Borough	18,682 7.35	14,097	2,042 14.49 14.49 10.93	1,999	233 11.66 11.66 1.25	6 1.92 0.29 0.04 0.03	-	-	8 0.94 0.39 0.06 0.04	-	438 8.83 21.45 3.11 2.34	-	-	313 59.96 15.33 2.22 1.68	-	18 2.06 0.88 0.13 0.10	500 14.56 24.49 3.55 2.68	317 25.48 15.52 2.25 1.70	-	-	157 13.17 67.38 7.85 0.84	-	-	49 8.49 2.40 0.35 0.26	-	113 23.74 5.53 0.80 0.60
Fairbanks North Star Borough	6,206 7.78	1,969	160 8.13 8.13 2.58	-	-	-	-	-	41 11.88 25.62 2.08 0.66	-	28 4.98 17.50 1.42 0.45	-	-	-	-	-	65 11.86 40.63 3.30 1.05	-	-	-	-	-	-	-	-	-
Juneau City and Borough	1,797 5.97	1,376	37 2.69 2.69 2.06	-	-	-	-	-	-	-	20 1.94 54.05 1.45 1.11	-	-	-	-	-	-	-	-	-	-	-	-	-	-	-
Matanuska-Susitna Borough	6,419 11.01	384	9 2.34 2.34 0.14	-	-	-	-	-	-	-	-	-	-	-	-	-	-	-	-	-	-	-	-	-	-	-

Notes: Please refer to the User's Guide for an explanation of data; data is arranged alphabetically by state, then county, then city within each county; table includes counties with populations greater than 49,999 unless noted and cities with populations greater than 9,999 whose Asian and/or NHPI population rates are greater than the national average; (1) Native Hawaiian and other Pacific Islander; (2) excludes Taiwanese; (3) includes Chamorro; (4) county does not meet population threshold but is shown in order to allow inclusion of city

Place	Total population with income below poverty level	Asian population for whom poverty status is determined	Asians with income below poverty level	NHPI[1] population for whom poverty status is determined	NHPIs[1] with income below poverty level	Asian Indian	Bangladeshi	Cambodian	Chinese[2]	Fijian	Filipino	Guamanian[3]	Hawaiian, Native	Hmong	Indonesian	Japanese	Korean	Laotian	Malaysian	Pakistani	Samoan	Sri Lankan	Taiwanese	Thai	Tongan	Vietnamese
ARIZONA	698,669 13.91	89,681	11,042 12.31 12.31 1.58	6,016	966 16.06 16.06 0.14	1,749 12.21 15.84 1.95 0.25	-	86 7.00 0.78 0.10 0.01	2,723 13.18 24.66 3.04 0.39	-	1,310 8.24 11.86 1.46 0.19	151 12.15 15.63 2.51 0.02	320 16.71 33.13 5.32 0.05	-	106 18.50 0.96 0.12 0.02	975 13.29 8.83 1.09 0.14	1,440 14.77 13.04 1.61 0.21	46 5.19 0.42 0.05 0.01	-	45 6.70 0.41 0.05 0.01	141 16.73 14.60 2.34 0.02	-	188 23.77 1.70 0.21 0.03	220 13.62 1.99 0.25 0.03	116 18.47 12.01 1.93 0.02	1,403 12.10 12.71 1.56 0.20
Cochise County	19,772 17.67	1,847	197 10.67 10.67 1.00	-	-	-	-	-	-	-	36 9.45 18.27 1.95 0.18	-	-	-	-	-	86 11.72 43.65 4.66 0.43	-	-	-	-	-	-	-	-	-
Coconino County	20,609 18.23	870	132 15.17 15.17 0.64	-	-	-	-	-	-	-	-	-	-	-	-	-	-	-	-	-	-	-	-	-	-	-
Maricopa County	355,668 11.75	65,736	7,260 11.04 11.04 2.04	3,744	566 15.12 15.12 0.16	1,123 10.00 15.47 1.71 0.32	-	86 7.29 1.18 0.13 0.02	1,864 12.12 25.67 2.84 0.52	-	831 7.02 11.45 1.26 0.23	62 9.58 10.95 1.66 0.02	180 16.64 31.80 4.81 0.05	-	72 17.48 0.99 0.11 0.02	547 11.36 7.53 0.83 0.15	867 14.45 11.94 1.32 0.24	34 5.66 0.47 0.05 0.01	-	22 4.23 0.30 0.03 0.01	48 8.68 8.48 1.28 0.01	-	93 14.49 1.28 0.14 0.03	121 10.71 1.67 0.18 0.03	116 22.01 20.49 3.10 0.03	1,140 12.90 15.70 1.73 0.32
Chandler (city)	11,632 6.64	7,460	407 5.46 5.46 3.50	-	-	16 1.03 3.93 0.21 0.14	-	-	168 8.28 41.28 2.25 1.44	-	41 3.53 10.07 0.55 0.35	-	-	-	-	-	-	-	-	-	-	-	-	-	-	37 3.88 9.09 0.50 0.32
Gilbert (town)	3,529 3.22	3,984	83 2.08 2.08 2.35	-	-	0 0.00 0.00 0.00 0.00	-	-	59 4.98 71.08 1.48 1.67	-	18 2.51 21.69 0.45 0.51	-	-	-	-	-	-	-	-	-	-	-	-	-	-	-
Mesa (city)	35,031 8.92	6,007	553 9.21 9.21 1.58	634	27 4.26 4.26 0.08	97 16.41 17.54 1.61 0.28	-	-	155 15.27 28.03 2.58 0.44	-	67 4.60 12.12 1.12 0.19	-	-	-	-	62 10.58 11.21 1.03 0.18	53 7.38 9.58 0.88 0.15	-	-	-	-	-	-	-	-	56 7.43 10.13 0.93 0.16
Phoenix (city)	205,320 15.79	25,482	3,090 12.13 12.13 1.50	1,703	260 15.27 15.27 0.13	429 9.68 13.88 1.68 0.21	-	28 5.13 0.91 0.11 0.01	645 11.58 20.87 2.53 0.31	-	475 9.46 15.37 1.86 0.23	-	95 19.59 36.54 5.58 0.05	-	-	246 15.55 7.96 0.97 0.12	250 12.69 8.09 0.98 0.12	-	-	-	-	-	-	-	-	778 17.73 25.18 3.05 0.38
Tempe (city)	21,904 14.33	7,708	1,874 24.31 24.31 8.56	-	-	398 21.61 21.24 5.16 1.82	-	-	523 27.82 27.91 6.79 2.39	-	98 16.58 5.23 1.27 0.45	-	-	-	-	175 28.93 9.34 2.27 0.80	278 40.29 14.83 3.61 1.27	-	-	-	-	-	-	-	-	146 18.79 7.79 1.89 0.67
Mohave County	21,252 13.88	921	147 15.96 15.96 0.69	-	-	-	-	-	-	-	-	-	-	-	-	-	-	-	-	-	-	-	-	-	-	-

Notes: Please refer to the User's Guide for an explanation of data; data is arranged alphabetically by state, then county, then city within each county; table includes counties with populations greater than 49,999 unless noted and cities with populations greater than 9,999 whose Asian and/or NHPI population rates are greater than the national average; (1) Native Hawaiian and other Pacific Islander; (2) excludes Taiwanese; (3) includes Chamorro; (4) county does not meet population threshold but is shown in order to allow inclusion of city

Place	Total population with income below poverty level	Asian population for whom poverty status is determined	Asians with income below poverty level	NHPI[1] population for whom poverty status is determined	NHPIs[1] with income below poverty level	Asian Indian	Bangladeshi	Cambodian	Chinese[2]	Fijian	Filipino	Guamanian[3]	Hawaiian, Native	Hmong	Indonesian	Japanese	Korean	Laotian	Malaysian	Pakistani	Samoan	Sri Lankan	Taiwanese	Thai	Tongan	Vietnamese
Pima County	120,778 14.66	16,448	2,760 16.78 16.78 2.29	1,068	177 16.57 16.57 0.15	431 22.46 15.62 2.62 0.36	-	-	763 17.04 27.64 4.64 0.63	-	273 11.78 9.89 1.66 0.23	-	65 14.22 36.72 6.09 0.05	-	-	302 20.57 10.94 1.84 0.25	387 17.83 14.02 2.35 0.32	-	-	-	-	-	-	-	-	179 7.90 6.49 1.09 0.15
Tucson (city)	86,532 18.44	11,183	2,380 21.28 21.28 2.75	718	96 13.37 13.37 0.11	422 33.25 17.73 3.77 0.49	-	-	721 24.33 30.29 6.45 0.83	-	227 13.60 9.54 2.03 0.26	-	-	-	-	261 26.91 10.97 2.33 0.30	308 25.39 12.94 2.75 0.36	-	-	-	-	-	-	-	-	146 7.86 6.13 1.31 0.17
Pinal County	27,816 16.91	810	160 19.75 19.75 0.58	-	-	-	-	-	-	-	-	-	-	-	-	-	-	-	-	-	-	-	-	-	-	-
Yavapai County	19,552 11.95	768	150 19.53 19.53 0.77	-	-	-	-	-	-	-	-	-	-	-	-	-	-	-	-	-	-	-	-	-	-	-
Yuma County	29,670 19.23	1,295	119 9.19 9.19 0.40	-	-	-	-	-	-	-	25 5.84 21.01 1.93 0.08	-	-	-	-	-	-	-	-	-	-	-	-	-	-	-
ARKANSAS	411,777 15.84	18,505	2,497 13.49 13.49 0.61	1,430	482 33.71 33.71 0.12	243 9.23 9.73 1.31 0.06	-	-	569 20.21 22.79 3.07 0.14	-	215 9.59 8.61 1.16 0.05	-	83 35.47 17.22 5.80 0.02	-	-	164 15.69 6.57 0.89 0.04	113 7.91 4.53 0.61 0.03	349 13.07 13.98 1.89 0.08	-	-	-	-	-	40 13.70 1.60 0.22 0.01	-	564 14.73 22.59 3.05 0.14
Benton County	15,201 10.07	1,474	59 4.00 4.00 0.39	-	-	0 0.00 0.00 0.00 0.00	-	-	-	-	-	-	-	-	-	-	-	-	-	-	-	-	-	-	-	0 0.00 0.00 0.00 0.00
Craighead County	12,246 15.40	437	280 64.07 64.07 2.29	-	-	-	-	-	-	-	-	-	-	-	-	-	-	-	-	-	-	-	-	-	-	-
Crawford County	7,500 14.21	631	88 13.95 13.95 1.17	-	-	-	-	-	-	-	-	-	-	-	-	-	-	-	-	-	-	-	-	-	-	-
Faulkner County	10,333 12.55	436	75 17.20 17.20 0.73	-	-	-	-	-	-	-	-	-	-	-	-	-	-	-	-	-	-	-	-	-	-	-

Notes: Please refer to the User's Guide for an explanation of data; data is arranged alphabetically by state, then county, then city within each county; table includes counties with populations greater than 49,999 unless noted and cities with populations greater than 9,999 whose Asian and/or NHPI population rates are greater than the national average; (1) Native Hawaiian and other Pacific Islander; (2) excludes Taiwanese; (3) includes Chamorro; (4) county does not meet population threshold but is shown in order to allow inclusion of city

Place	Total population with income below poverty level	Asian population for whom poverty status is determined	Asians with income below poverty level	NHPI[1] population for whom poverty status is determined	NHPIs[1] with income below poverty level	Asian Indian	Bangladeshi	Cambodian	Chinese[2]	Fijian	Filipino	Guamanian[3]	Hawaiian, Native	Hmong	Indonesian	Japanese	Korean	Laotian	Malaysian	Pakistani	Samoan	Sri Lankan	Taiwanese	Thai	Tongan	Vietnamese
Jefferson County	16,203	443	0	-	-	-	-	-	-	-	-	-	-	-	-	-	-	-	-	-	-	-	-	-	-	-
	20.53		<0.01																							
			<0.01																							
			<0.01																							
Pulaski County	47,129	4,269	497	-	-	113	-	-	59	-	72	-	-	-	-	-	-	-	-	-	-	-	-	-	-	-
	13.32		11.64			12.00			6.78		11.30															
						22.74			11.87		14.49															
			11.64			2.65			1.38		1.69															
			1.05			0.24			0.13		0.15															
Saline County	5,890	445	26	-	-	-	-	-	-	-	-	-	-	-	-	-	-	-	-	-	-	-	-	-	-	-
	7.18		5.84																							
			5.84																							
			0.44																							
Sebastian County	15,410	3,581	345	-	-	-	-	-	-	-	-	-	-	-	-	-	-	115	-	-	-	-	-	-	-	206
	13.64		9.63															9.97								11.48
																		33.33								59.71
			9.63															3.21								5.75
			2.24															0.75								1.34
Fort Smith (city)	12,409	3,277	315	-	-	-	-	-	-	-	-	-	-	-	-	-	-	95	-	-	-	-	-	-	-	206
	15.80		9.61															8.46								12.03
																		30.16								65.40
			9.61															2.90								6.29
			2.54															0.77								1.66
Washington County	22,104	2,513	567	756	290	-	-	-	271	-	-	-	-	-	-	-	-	41	-	-	-	-	-	-	-	-
	14.60		22.56		38.36				37.38									7.44								
									47.80									7.23								
			22.56		38.36				10.78									1.63								
			2.57		1.31				1.23									0.19								
Springdale (city)	5,684	739	19	694	277	-	-	-	-	-	-	-	-	-	-	-	-	0	-	-	-	-	-	-	-	-
	12.54		2.57		39.91													0.00								
																		0.00								
			2.57		39.91													0.00								
			0.33		4.87													0.00								
CALIFORNIA	4,706,130	3,634,242	466,431	111,363	17,484	27,139	330	28,680	103,787	879	58,148	1,997	2,203	36,351	2,685	25,923	50,212	18,096	225	3,057	7,822	408	8,938	5,729	2,147	79,635
	14.22		12.83		15.70	8.94	12.06	40.77	11.52	10.49	6.39	9.92	11.66	53.17	16.45	9.09	14.82	32.18	13.04	15.59	20.39	7.68	14.28	16.06	18.03	18.03
						5.82	0.07	6.15	22.25	5.03	12.47	11.42	12.60	7.79	0.58	5.56	10.77	3.88	0.05	0.66	44.74	0.09	1.92	1.23	12.28	17.07
			12.83		15.70	0.75	0.01	0.79	2.86	0.79	1.60	1.79	1.98	1.00	0.07	0.71	1.38	0.50	0.01	0.08	7.02	0.01	0.25	0.16	1.93	2.19
			9.91		0.37	0.58	0.01	0.61	2.21	0.02	1.24	0.04	0.05	0.77	0.06	0.55	1.07	0.38	<0.01	0.06	0.17	0.01	0.19	0.12	0.05	1.69
Alameda County	156,804	291,008	32,650	9,102	837	2,744	-	1,542	12,625	119	3,037	116	145	-	58	1,284	2,134	926	-	285	108	-	585	182	254	5,833
	11.04		11.22		9.20	6.59		40.01	11.95	8.16	4.38	8.93	11.44		9.09	10.52	14.89	29.65		14.46	4.50		15.06	12.79	13.92	25.05
						8.40		4.72	38.67	14.22	9.30	13.86	17.32		0.18	3.93	6.54	2.84		0.87	12.90		1.79	0.56	30.35	17.87
			11.22		9.20	0.94		0.53	4.34	1.31	1.04	1.27	1.59		0.02	0.44	0.73	0.32		0.10	1.19		0.20	0.06	2.79	2.00
			20.82		0.53	1.75		0.98	8.05	0.08	1.94	0.07	0.09		0.04	0.82	1.36	0.59		0.18	0.07		0.37	0.12	0.16	3.72
Alameda (city)	5,887	18,634	1,729	796	97	64	-	-	598	-	347	-	-	-	-	61	116	-	-	-	-	-	-	-	-	405
	8.24		9.28		12.19	6.00			8.09		5.74					8.69	9.42									31.44
						3.70			34.59		20.07					3.53	6.71									23.42
			9.28		12.19	0.34			3.21		1.86					0.33	0.62									2.17
			29.37		1.65	1.09			10.16		5.89					1.04	1.97									6.88

Notes: Please refer to the User's Guide for an explanation of data; data is arranged alphabetically by state, then county, then city within each county; table includes counties with populations greater than 49,999 unless noted and cities with populations greater than 9,999 whose Asian and/or NHPI population rates are greater than the national average; (1) Native Hawaiian and other Pacific Islander; (2) excludes Taiwanese; (3) includes Chamorro; (4) county does not meet population threshold but is shown in order to allow inclusion of city

Place	Total population with income below poverty level	Asian population for whom poverty status is determined	Asians with income below poverty level	NHPI[1] population for whom poverty status is determined	NHPIs[1] with income below poverty level	Asian Indian	Bangladeshi	Cambodian	Chinese[2]	Fijian	Filipino	Guamanian[3]	Hawaiian, Native	Hmong	Indonesian	Japanese	Korean	Laotian	Malaysian	Pakistani	Samoan	Sri Lankan	Taiwanese	Thai	Tongan	Vietnamese
Albany (city)	1,304	4,246	466	-	-	12	-	-	239	-	-	-	-	-	-	46	112	-	-	-	-	-	-	-	-	-
	7.94		10.98			3.63			11.61							7.15	21.54									
						2.58			51.29							9.87	24.03									
			10.98			0.28			5.63							1.08	2.64									
			35.74			0.92			18.33							3.53	8.59									
Ashland (cdp)	2,920	3,121	198	-	-	-	-	-	18	-	78	-	-	-	-	-	-	-	-	-	-	-	-	-	-	-
	14.28		6.34						1.87		5.88															
									9.09		39.39															
			6.34						0.58		2.50															
			6.78						0.62		2.67															
Berkeley (city)	19,495	14,889	5,955	-	-	677	-	-	2,596	-	258	-	-	-	-	489	848	-	-	-	-	-	227	-	-	419
	19.95		40.00			40.56			41.72		23.52					24.01	57.96						63.59			52.05
						11.37			43.59		4.33					8.21	14.24						3.81			7.04
			40.00			4.55			17.44		1.73					3.28	5.70						1.52			2.81
			30.55			3.47			13.32		1.32					2.51	4.35						1.16			2.15
Castro Valley (cdp)	2,519	7,275	400	-	-	27	-	-	150	-	28	-	-	-	-	39	114	-	-	-	-	-	-	-	-	-
	4.50		5.50			3.25			4.38		2.37					6.27	15.24									
						6.75			37.50		7.00					9.75	28.50									
			5.50			0.37			2.06		0.38					0.54	1.57									
			15.88			1.07			5.95		1.11					1.55	4.53									
Cherryland (cdp)	1,660	1,182	47	-	-	-	-	-	-	-	5	-	-	-	-	-	-	-	-	-	-	-	-	-	-	-
	12.28		3.98								0.80															
											10.64															
			3.98								0.42															
			2.83								0.30															
Dublin (city)	719	2,824	130	-	-	0	-	-	47	-	18	-	-	-	-	-	-	-	-	-	-	-	-	-	-	-
	2.92		4.60			0.00			5.17		2.34															
						0.00			36.15		13.85															
			4.60			0.00			1.66		0.64															
			18.08			0.00			6.54		2.50															
Fremont (city)	10,915	74,678	3,594	670	80	867	-	-	1,385	-	408	-	-	-	-	18	163	-	-	46	-	-	206	-	-	351
	5.40		4.81		11.94	4.19			5.27		3.59					1.16	4.10			4.17			8.40			8.10
						24.12			38.54		11.35					0.50	4.54			1.28			5.73			9.77
			4.81		11.94	1.16			1.85		0.55					0.02	0.22			0.06			0.28			0.47
			32.93		0.73	7.94			12.69		3.74					0.16	1.49			0.42			1.89			3.22
Hayward (city)	13,805	25,828	2,558	2,330	82	449	-	-	284	58	564	-	-	-	-	235	174	-	-	-	0	-	-	-	-	530
	10.01		9.90		3.52	12.73			7.78	6.88	4.51					19.75	21.80				0.00					20.50
						17.55			11.10	70.73	22.05					9.19	6.80				0.00					20.72
			9.90		3.52	1.74			1.10	2.49	2.18					0.91	0.67				0.00					2.05
			18.53		0.59	3.25			2.06	0.42	4.09					1.70	1.26				0.00					3.84
Livermore (city)	3,891	4,245	171	-	-	0	-	-	69	-	0	-	-	-	-	-	-	-	-	-	-	-	-	-	-	87
	5.33		4.03			0.00			9.07		0.00															18.51
						0.00			40.35		0.00															50.88
			4.03			0.00			1.63		0.00															2.05
			4.39			0.00			1.77		0.00															2.24
Newark (city)	2,323	9,249	486	-	-	66	-	-	114	-	77	-	-	-	-	-	0	-	-	-	-	-	-	-	-	184
	5.48		5.25			4.10			6.73		2.22						0.00									25.00
						13.58			23.46		15.84						0.00									37.86
			5.25			0.71			1.23		0.83						0.00									1.99
			20.92			2.84			4.91		3.31						0.00									7.92

Notes: Please refer to the User's Guide for an explanation of data; data is arranged alphabetically by state, then county, then city within each county; table includes counties with populations greater than 49,999 unless noted and cities with populations greater than 9,999 whose Asian and/or NHPI population rates are greater than the national average; (1) Native Hawaiian and other Pacific Islander; (2) excludes Taiwanese; (3) includes Chamorro; (4) county does not meet population threshold but is shown in order to allow inclusion of city

Place	Total population with income below poverty level	Asian population for whom poverty status is determined	Asians with income below poverty level	NHPI[1] population for whom poverty status is determined	NHPIs[1] with income below poverty level	Asian Indian	Bangladeshi	Cambodian	Chinese[2]	Fijian	Filipino	Guamanian[3]	Hawaiian, Native	Hmong	Indonesian	Japanese	Korean	Laotian	Malaysian	Pakistani	Samoan	Sri Lankan	Taiwanese	Thai	Tongan	Vietnamese
Oakland (city)	76,489 19.39	59,813	13,153 21.99 21.99 17.20	2,546	416 16.34 16.34 0.54	177 10.33 1.35 0.30 0.23	-	1,398 48.01 10.63 2.34 1.83	5,787 18.43 44.00 9.68 7.57	-	566 8.55 4.30 0.95 0.74	-	-	-	-	193 9.18 1.47 0.32 0.25	372 21.18 2.83 0.62 0.49	872 37.00 6.63 1.46 1.14	-	-	-	-	-	-	218 16.62 52.40 8.56 0.29	3,050 37.32 23.19 5.10 3.99
Piedmont (city)	221 2.02	1,803	53 2.94 2.94 23.98	-	-	-	-	-	37 2.72 69.81 2.05 16.74	-	-	-	-	-	-	-	-	-	-	-	-	-	-	-	-	-
Pleasanton (city)	1,619 2.56	7,392	303 4.10 4.10 18.72	-	-	49 3.10 16.17 0.66 3.03	-	-	156 5.96 51.49 2.11 9.64	-	15 1.79 4.95 0.20 0.93	-	-	-	-	0 0.00 0.00 0.00 0.00	0 0.00 0.00 0.00 0.00	-	-	-	-	-	-	-	-	-
San Leandro (city)	5,037 6.42	18,313	831 4.54 4.54 16.50	601	18 3.00 3.00 0.36	35 4.99 4.21 0.19 0.69	-	-	509 6.19 61.25 2.78 10.11	-	83 1.34 9.99 0.45 1.65	-	-	-	-	9 1.70 1.08 0.05 0.18	32 6.99 3.85 0.17 0.64	-	-	-	-	-	-	-	-	95 7.36 11.43 0.52 1.89
San Lorenzo (cdp)	1,185 5.42	3,471	134 3.86 3.86 11.31	-	-	-	-	-	60 6.18 44.78 1.73 5.06	-	9 0.65 6.72 0.26 0.76	-	-	-	-	-	-	-	-	-	-	-	-	-	-	33 11.11 24.63 0.95 2.78
Union City (city)	4,340 6.53	29,374	1,805 6.14 6.14 41.59	629	53 8.43 8.43 1.22	211 3.94 11.69 0.72 4.86	-	-	340 5.71 18.84 1.16 7.83	-	537 4.10 29.75 1.83 12.37	-	-	-	-	77 15.81 4.27 0.26 1.77	49 5.20 2.71 0.17 1.13	-	-	-	-	-	-	-	-	486 23.81 26.93 1.65 11.20
Butte County	39,148 19.79	6,402	3,202 50.02 50.02 8.18	-	-	180 41.67 5.62 2.81 0.46	-	-	178 25.76 5.56 2.78 0.45	-	35 10.09 1.09 0.55 0.09	-	-	1,952 69.52 60.96 30.49 4.99	-	175 30.59 5.47 2.73 0.45	-	390 70.78 12.18 6.09 1.00	-	-	-	-	-	-	-	-
Chico (city)	15,121 26.60	2,168	963 44.42 44.42 6.37	-	-	-	-	-	120 29.34 12.46 5.54 0.79	-	-	-	-	520 71.33 54.00 23.99 3.44	-	-	-	-	-	-	-	-	-	-	-	-
Oroville (city)	4,036 33.06	722	557 77.15 77.15 13.80	-	-	-	-	-	-	-	-	-	-	366 76.89 65.71 50.69 9.07	-	-	-	-	-	-	-	-	-	-	-	-
Contra Costa County	71,575 7.63	102,672	6,823 6.65 6.65 9.53	3,367	291 8.64 8.64 0.41	731 6.54 10.71 0.71 1.02	-	-	1,425 5.17 20.89 1.39 1.99	20 3.72 6.87 0.59 0.03	1,307 3.82 19.16 1.27 1.83	23 4.23 7.90 0.68 0.03	31 5.21 10.65 0.92 0.04	-	45 9.51 0.66 0.04 0.06	460 5.56 6.74 0.45 0.64	535 11.94 7.84 0.52 0.75	699 16.55 10.24 0.68 0.98	-	109 15.40 1.60 0.11 0.15	4 0.53 1.37 0.12 0.01	-	79 6.26 1.16 0.08 0.11	87 14.22 1.28 0.08 0.12	192 42.57 65.98 5.70 0.27	1,047 19.38 15.35 1.02 1.46

Notes: Please refer to the User's Guide for an explanation of data; data is arranged alphabetically by state, then county, then city within each county; table includes counties with populations greater than 49,999 unless noted and cities with populations greater than 9,999 whose Asian and/or NHPI population rates are greater than the national average; (1) Native Hawaiian and other Pacific Islander; (2) excludes Taiwanese; (3) includes Chamorro; (4) county does not meet population threshold but is shown in order to allow inclusion of city

Place	Total population with income below poverty level	Asian population for whom poverty status is determined	Asians with income below poverty level	NHPI[1] population for whom poverty status is determined	NHPIs[1] with income below poverty level	Asian Indian	Bangladeshi	Cambodian	Chinese[2]	Fijian	Filipino	Guamanian[3]	Hawaiian, Native	Hmong	Indonesian	Japanese	Korean	Laotian	Malaysian	Pakistani	Samoan	Sri Lankan	Taiwanese	Thai	Tongan	Vietnamese
Alamo (cdp)	572	863	25	-	-	-	-	-	-	-	-	-	-	-	-	-	-	-	-	-	-	-	-	-	-	-
	3.78		2.90																							
			2.90																							
			4.37																							
Antioch (city)	7,683	6,658	445	408	6	0	-	-	65	-	179	-	-	-	-	-	-	-	-	-	-	-	-	-	-	60
	8.53		6.68		1.47	0.00			5.80		5.11															12.63
						0.00			14.61		40.22															13.48
			6.68		1.47	0.00			0.98		2.69															0.90
			5.79		0.08	0.00			0.85		2.33															0.78
Bay Point (cdp)	3,656	2,463	167	-	-	-	-	-	-	-	28	-	-	-	-	-	-	-	-	-	-	-	-	-	-	-
	17.23		6.78								2.30															
											16.77															
			6.78								1.14															
			4.57								0.77															
Blackhawk-Camino-Tass. (cdp)	88	1,682	41	-	-	-	-	-	37	-	-	-	-	-	-	-	-	-	-	-	-	-	-	-	-	-
	0.88		2.44						3.84																	
									90.24																	
			2.44						2.20																	
			46.59						42.05																	
Clayton (city)	278	596	0	-	-	-	-	-	-	-	-	-	-	-	-	-	-	-	-	-	-	-	-	-	-	-
	2.58		<0.01																							
			<0.01																							
			<0.01																							
Concord (city)	9,151	11,039	855	464	56	127	-	-	147	-	183	-	-	-	-	20	181	-	-	-	-	-	-	-	-	126
	7.60		7.75		12.07	8.26			5.70		4.46					2.34	39.52									19.12
						14.85			17.19		21.40					2.34	21.17									14.74
			7.75		12.07	1.15			1.33		1.66					0.18	1.64									1.14
			9.34		0.61	1.39			1.61		2.00					0.22	1.98									1.38
Danville (town)	908	3,582	85	-	-	0	-	-	37	-	42	-	-	-	-	-	-	-	-	-	-	-	-	-	-	-
	2.16		2.37			0.00			2.39		9.13															
						0.00			43.53		49.41															
			2.37			0.00			1.03		1.17															
			9.36			0.00			4.07		4.63															
El Cerrito (city)	1,545	5,622	694	-	-	167	-	-	231	-	27	-	-	-	-	63	-	-	-	-	-	-	-	-	-	-
	6.68		12.34			44.53			9.38		5.65					5.11										
						24.06			33.29		3.89					9.08										
			12.34			2.97			4.11		0.48					1.12										
			44.92			10.81			14.95		1.75					4.08										
El Sobrante (cdp)	1,095	1,349	165	-	-	61	-	-	-	-	-	-	-	-	-	-	-	-	-	-	-	-	-	-	-	-
	9.48		12.23			16.90																				
						36.97																				
			12.23			4.52																				
			15.07			5.57																				
Hercules (city)	610	8,259	257	-	-	0	-	-	44	-	144	-	-	-	-	-	-	-	-	-	-	-	-	-	-	-
	3.18		3.11			0.00			2.74		2.93															
						0.00			17.12		56.03															
			3.11			0.00			0.53		1.74															
			42.13			0.00			7.21		23.61															

Notes: Please refer to the User's Guide for an explanation of data; data is arranged alphabetically by state, then county, then city within each county; table includes counties with populations greater than 49,999 unless noted and cities with populations greater than 9,999 whose Asian and/or NHPI population rates are greater than the national average; (1) Native Hawaiian and other Pacific Islander; (2) excludes Taiwanese; (3) includes Chamorro; (4) county does not meet population threshold but is shown in order to allow inclusion of city

Place	Total population with income below poverty level	Asian population for whom poverty status is determined	Asians with income below poverty level	NHPI[1] population for whom poverty status is determined	NHPIs[1] with income below poverty level	Asian Indian	Bangladeshi	Cambodian	Chinese[2]	Fijian	Filipino	Guamanian[3]	Hawaiian, Native	Hmong	Indonesian	Japanese	Korean	Laotian	Malaysian	Pakistani	Samoan	Sri Lankan	Taiwanese	Thai	Tongan	Vietnamese
	672	1,660	108	-	-	-	-	-	27	-	-	-	-	-	-	-	-	-	-	-	-	-	-	-	-	-
	2.87		6.51						3.32																	
Lafayette (city)									25.00																	
			6.51						1.63																	
			16.07						4.02																	
	1,826	2,240	100	-	-	-	-	-	48	-	6	-	-	-	-	-	-	-	-	-	-	-	-	-	-	-
	5.25		4.46						10.06		0.63															
Martinez (city)									48.00		6.00															
			4.46						2.14		0.27															
			5.48						2.63		0.33															
	437	2,057	42	-	-	-	-	-	29	-	-	-	-	-	-	-	-	-	-	-	-	-	-	-	-	-
	2.89		2.04						2.40																	
Moraga (town)									69.05																	
			2.04						1.41																	
			9.61						6.64																	
	328	1,524	55	-	-	-	-	-	28	-	-	-	-	-	-	-	-	-	-	-	-	-	-	-	-	-
	1.89		3.61						3.14																	
Orinda (city)									50.91																	
			3.61						1.84																	
			16.77						8.54																	
	954	4,095	198	-	-	-	-	-	27	-	26	-	-	-	-	-	-	-	-	-	-	-	-	-	-	-
	4.95		4.84						3.07		1.29															
Pinole (city)									13.64		13.13															
			4.84						0.66		0.63															
			20.75						2.83		2.73															
	6,480	7,241	483	554	102	111	-	-	12	-	170	-	-	-	-	-	-	-	-	-	-	-	-	-	-	-
	11.51		6.67		18.41	11.62			2.67		3.57															
Pittsburg (city)						22.98			2.48		35.20															
			6.67		18.41	1.53			0.17		2.35															
			7.45		1.57	1.71			0.19		2.62															
	1,639	3,286	333	-	-	-	-	-	88	-	44	-	-	-	-	-	115	-	-	-	-	-	-	-	-	-
	5.05		10.13						9.59		5.24						22.03									
Pleasant Hill (city)									26.43		13.21						34.53									
			10.13						2.68		1.34						3.50									
			20.32						5.37		2.68						7.02									
	15,873	12,030	1,084	394	88	84	-	-	353	-	69	-	-	-	-	29	49	360	-	-	-	-	-	-	-	82
	16.18		9.01		22.34	7.55			11.34		2.50					3.28	10.61	15.27								17.71
Richmond (city)						7.75			32.56		6.37					2.68	4.52	33.21								7.56
			9.01		22.34	0.70			2.93		0.57					0.24	0.41	2.99								0.68
			6.83		0.55	0.53			2.22		0.43					0.18	0.31	2.27								0.52
	5,331	4,894	592	-	-	50	-	-	-	-	93	-	-	-	-	-	-	203	-	-	-	-	-	-	-	202
	18.06		12.10			8.26					5.36							18.27								28.45
San Pablo (city)						8.45					15.71							34.29								34.12
			12.10			1.02					1.90							4.15								4.13
			11.10			0.94					1.74							3.81								3.79
	878	6,779	250	-	-	17	-	-	72	-	12	-	-	-	-	28	-	-	-	-	-	-	-	-	-	-
	1.98		3.69			1.23			2.69		1.28					6.21										
San Ramon (city)						6.80			28.80		4.80					11.20										
			3.69			0.25			1.06		0.18					0.41										
			28.47			1.94			8.20		1.37					3.19										

Notes: Please refer to the User's Guide for an explanation of data; data is arranged alphabetically by state, then county, then city within each county; table includes counties with populations greater than 49,999 unless noted and cities with populations greater than 9,999 whose Asian and/or NHPI population rates are greater than the national average; (1) Native Hawaiian and other Pacific Islander; (2) excludes Taiwanese; (3) includes Chamorro; (4) county does not meet population threshold but is shown in order to allow inclusion of city

Place	Total population with income below poverty level	Asian population for whom poverty status is determined	Asians with income below poverty level	NHPI[1] population for whom poverty status is determined	NHPIs[1] with income below poverty level	Asian Indian	Bangladeshi	Cambodian	Chinese[2]	Fijian	Filipino	Guamanian[3]	Hawaiian, Native	Hmong	Indonesian	Japanese	Korean	Laotian	Malaysian	Pakistani	Samoan	Sri Lankan	Taiwanese	Thai	Tongan	Vietnamese
Walnut Creek (city)	2,353 3.68	6,171	275 4.46 4.46 11.69	-	-	18 3.22 6.55 0.29 0.76	-	-	76 2.89 27.64 1.23 3.23	-	45 3.71 16.36 0.73 1.91	-	-	-	-	70 8.50 25.45 1.13 2.97	58 11.81 21.09 0.94 2.46	-	-	-	-	-	-	-	-	-
El Dorado County	11,079 7.15	3,021	123 4.07 4.07 1.11	-	-	-	-	-	-	-	66 4.86 53.66 2.18 0.60	-	-	-	-	22 4.35 17.89 0.73 0.20	-	-	-	-	-	-	-	-	-	-
El Dorado Hills (cdp)	299 1.66	658	11 1.67 1.67 3.68	-	-	-	-	-	-	-	-	-	-	-	-	-	-	-	-	-	-	-	-	-	-	-
South Lake Tahoe (city)	2,937 12.48	1,415	64 4.52 4.52 2.18	-	-	-	-	-	-	-	39 3.97 60.94 2.76 1.33	-	-	-	-	-	-	-	-	-	-	-	-	-	-	-
Fresno County	179,085 22.89	63,387	24,436 38.55 38.55 13.64	643	190 29.55 29.55 0.11	1,263 18.27 5.17 1.99 0.71	-	2,066 52.76 8.45 3.26 1.15	896 18.72 3.67 1.41 0.50	-	423 6.92 1.73 0.67 0.24	-	-	13,862 57.72 56.73 21.87 7.74	-	500 8.84 2.05 0.79 0.28	178 13.69 0.73 0.28 0.10	3,618 57.97 14.81 5.71 2.02	-	-	-	-	-	-	-	959 45.62 3.92 1.51 0.54
Clovis (city)	7,160 10.58	4,429	1,335 30.14 30.14 18.65	-	-	-	-	-	-	-	35 5.15 2.62 0.79 0.49	-	-	995 55.31 74.53 22.47 13.90	-	49 8.94 3.67 1.11 0.68	-	-	-	-	-	-	-	-	-	-
Fresno (city)	109,703 26.19	48,147	21,271 44.18 44.18 19.39	-	-	795 21.62 3.74 1.65 0.72	-	1,843 51.28 8.66 3.83 1.68	851 23.00 4.00 1.77 0.78	-	322 7.41 1.51 0.67 0.29	-	-	12,302 60.56 57.83 25.55 11.21	-	332 12.73 1.56 0.69 0.30	86 9.17 0.40 0.18 0.08	3,227 59.09 15.17 6.70 2.94	-	-	-	-	-	-	-	922 53.57 4.33 1.91 0.84
Reedley (city)	4,832 23.81	772	39 5.05 5.05 0.81	-	-	-	-	-	-	-	-	-	-	-	-	-	-	-	-	-	-	-	-	-	-	-
Humboldt County	24,059 19.53	1,834	751 40.95 40.95 3.12	-	-	-	-	-	-	-	-	-	-	-	-	78 27.27 10.39 4.25 0.32	-	-	-	-	-	-	-	-	-	-
Imperial County	29,681 22.58	2,693	399 14.82 14.82 1.34	-	-	-	-	-	80 14.36 20.05 2.97 0.27	-	108 12.40 27.07 4.01 0.36	-	-	-	-	-	77 15.62 19.30 2.86 0.26	-	-	-	-	-	-	-	-	-

Notes: Please refer to the User's Guide for an explanation of data; data is arranged alphabetically by state, then county, then city within each county; table includes counties with populations greater than 49,999 unless noted and cities with populations greater than 9,999 whose Asian and/or NHPI population rates are greater than the national average; (1) Native Hawaiian and other Pacific Islander; (2) excludes Taiwanese; (3) includes Chamorro; (4) county does not meet population threshold but is shown in order to allow inclusion of city

Place	Total population with income below poverty level	Asian population for whom poverty status is determined	Asians with income below poverty level	NHPI[1] population for whom poverty status is determined	NHPIs[1] with income below poverty level	Asian Indian	Bangladeshi	Cambodian	Chinese[2]	Fijian	Filipino	Guamanian[3]	Hawaiian, Native	Hmong	Indonesian	Japanese	Korean	Laotian	Malaysian	Pakistani	Samoan	Sri Lankan	Taiwanese	Thai	Tongan	Vietnamese
Kern County	130,949 20.76	21,296	3,142 14.75 14.75 2.40	765	116 15.16 15.16 0.09	470 11.31 14.96 2.21 0.36	-	195 45.24 6.21 0.92 0.15	192 9.50 6.11 0.90 0.15	-	1,661 15.92 52.86 7.80 1.27	-	-	-	-	120 11.55 3.82 0.56 0.09	183 14.49 5.82 0.86 0.14	-	-	-	-	-	-	-	-	115 18.79 3.66 0.54 0.09
Bakersfield (city)	43,781 17.97	10,443	1,292 12.37 12.37 2.95	468	53 11.32 11.32 0.12	330 10.48 25.54 3.16 0.75	-	-	117 7.94 9.06 1.12 0.27	-	229 8.36 17.72 2.19 0.52	-	-	-	-	83 12.79 6.42 0.79 0.19	136 14.08 10.53 1.30 0.31	-	-	-	-	-	-	-	-	104 23.69 8.05 1.00 0.24
Delano (city)	9,566 28.15	6,000	1,113 18.55 18.55 11.63	-	-	-	-	-	-	-	1,086 19.42 97.57 18.10 11.35	-	-	-	-	-	-	-	-	-	-	-	-	-	-	-
Ridgecrest (city)	3,045 12.27	1,005	104 10.35 10.35 3.42	-	-	-	-	-	-	-	42 9.03 40.38 4.18 1.38	-	-	-	-	-	-	-	-	-	-	-	-	-	-	-
Kings County	21,307 19.51	3,603	350 9.71 9.71 1.64	-	-	-	-	-	-	-	168 7.21 48.00 4.66 0.79	-	-	-	-	-	-	-	-	-	-	-	-	-	-	-
Lemoore (city)	2,592 13.36	1,434	79 5.51 5.51 3.05	-	-	-	-	-	-	-	66 6.16 83.54 4.60 2.55	-	-	-	-	-	-	-	-	-	-	-	-	-	-	-
Lake County	10,081 17.59	498	119 23.90 23.90 1.18	-	-	-	-	-	-	-	-	-	-	-	-	-	-	-	-	-	-	-	-	-	-	-
Los Angeles County	1,674,599 17.91	1,119,041	153,497 13.72 13.72 9.17	26,671	6,177 23.16 23.16 0.37	6,331 10.92 4.12 0.57 0.38	277 21.10 0.18 0.02 0.02	11,755 39.32 7.66 1.05 0.70	42,464 14.79 27.66 3.79 2.54	85 17.82 1.38 0.32 0.01	18,826 7.25 12.26 1.68 1.12	452 14.46 7.32 1.69 0.03	741 17.65 12.00 2.78 0.04	194 45.97 0.13 0.02 0.01	1,098 19.62 0.72 0.10 0.07	10,410 9.40 6.78 0.93 0.62	28,972 15.81 18.87 2.59 1.73	704 22.62 0.46 0.06 0.04	89 17.52 0.06 0.01 0.01	1,005 21.49 0.65 0.09 0.06	3,606 26.83 58.38 13.52 0.22	142 5.91 0.09 0.01 0.01	5,280 15.39 3.44 0.47 0.32	2,962 15.28 1.93 0.26 0.18	632 28.47 10.23 2.37 0.04	16,477 21.29 10.73 1.47 0.98
Agoura Hills (city)	704 3.47	1,242	21 1.69 1.69 2.98	-	-	-	-	-	-	-	-	-	-	-	-	-	-	-	-	-	-	-	-	-	-	-
Alhambra (city)	12,057 14.34	40,201	6,952 17.29 17.29 57.66	-	-	55 10.70 0.79 0.14 0.46	-	-	4,157 15.86 59.80 10.34 34.48	-	138 7.38 1.99 0.34 1.14	-	-	-	-	211 14.69 3.04 0.52 1.75	55 6.64 0.79 0.14 0.46	-	-	-	-	-	329 21.53 4.73 0.82 2.73	-	-	1,356 30.96 19.51 3.37 11.25

Notes: Please refer to the User's Guide for an explanation of data; data is arranged alphabetically by state, then county, then city within each county; table includes counties with populations greater than 49,999 unless noted and cities with populations greater than 9,999 whose Asian and/or NHPI population rates are greater than the national average; (1) Native Hawaiian and other Pacific Islander; (2) excludes Taiwanese; (3) includes Chamorro; (4) county does not meet population threshold but is shown in order to allow inclusion of city

Place	Total population with income below poverty level	Asian population for whom poverty status is determined	Asians with income below poverty level	NHPI[1] population for whom poverty status is determined	NHPIs[1] with income below poverty level	Asian Indian	Bangladeshi	Cambodian	Chinese[2]	Fijian	Filipino	Guamanian[3]	Hawaiian, Native	Hmong	Indonesian	Japanese	Korean	Laotian	Malaysian	Pakistani	Samoan	Sri Lankan	Taiwanese	Thai	Tongan	Vietnamese
Altadena (cdp)	4,404 10.58	1,733	95 5.48 5.48 2.16	-	-	-	-	-	-	-	0 0.00 0.00 0.00 0.00	-	-	-	-	15 2.47 15.79 0.87 0.34	-	-	-	-	-	-	-	-	-	-
Arcadia (city)	4,150 7.92	23,954	2,348 9.80 9.80 56.58	-	-	37 5.63 1.58 0.15 0.89	-	-	1,344 9.62 57.24 5.61 32.39	-	41 5.20 1.75 0.17 0.99	-	-	-	-	80 6.97 3.41 0.33 1.93	116 6.00 4.94 0.48 2.80	-	-	-	-	-	400 10.66 17.04 1.67 9.64	-	-	-
Artesia (city)	1,822 11.46	4,524	549 12.14 12.14 30.13	-	-	68 14.20 12.39 1.50 3.73	-	-	105 16.48 19.13 2.32 5.76	-	226 12.63 41.17 5.00 12.40	-	-	-	-	-	94 10.74 17.12 2.08 5.16	-	-	-	-	-	-	-	-	-
Avocado Heights (cdp)	2,433 16.29	1,357	231 17.02 17.02 9.49	-	-	-	-	-	-	-	-	-	-	-	-	-	-	-	-	-	-	-	-	-	-	-
Azusa (city)	7,926 18.76	2,344	298 12.71 12.71 3.76	-	-	-	-	-	-	-	95 8.13 31.88 4.05 1.20	-	-	-	-	-	-	-	-	-	-	-	-	-	-	-
Baldwin Park (city)	13,541 18.17	8,963	977 10.90 10.90 7.22	-	-	-	-	-	413 14.78 42.27 4.61 3.05	-	175 4.36 17.91 1.95 1.29	-	-	-	-	-	-	-	-	-	-	-	-	-	-	218 22.95 22.31 2.43 1.61
Bellflower (city)	11,385 15.76	7,148	944 13.21 13.21 8.29	-	-	-	-	165 30.90 17.48 2.31 1.45	-	-	249 6.87 26.38 3.48 2.19	-	-	-	-	-	239 25.73 25.32 3.34 2.10	-	-	-	-	-	-	9 2.31 0.95 0.13 0.08	-	-
Beverly Hills (city)	3,058 9.06	2,570	288 11.21 11.21 9.42	-	-	-	-	-	18 3.51 6.25 0.70 0.59	-	-	-	-	-	-	-	175 19.19 60.76 6.81 5.72	-	-	-	-	-	-	-	-	-
Burbank (city)	10,484 10.53	9,057	791 8.73 8.73 7.54	-	-	18 1.89 2.28 0.20 0.17	-	-	74 8.22 9.36 0.82 0.71	-	173 5.29 21.87 1.91 1.65	-	-	-	-	62 9.90 7.84 0.68 0.59	266 13.43 33.63 2.94 2.54	-	-	-	-	-	-	-	-	46 8.78 5.82 0.51 0.44
Calabasas (city)	663 3.32	1,652	106 6.42 6.42 15.99	-	-	-	-	-	10 1.97 9.43 0.61 1.51	-	-	-	-	-	-	-	-	-	-	-	-	-	-	-	-	-

Notes: Please refer to the User's Guide for an explanation of data; data is arranged alphabetically by state, then county, then city within each county; table includes counties with populations greater than 49,999 unless noted and cities with populations greater than 9,999 whose Asian and/or NHPI population rates are greater than the national average; (1) Native Hawaiian and other Pacific Islander; (2) excludes Taiwanese; (3) includes Chamorro; (4) county does not meet population threshold but is shown in order to allow inclusion of city

Place	Total population with income below poverty level	Asian population for whom poverty status is determined	Asians with income below poverty level	NHPI[1] population for whom poverty status is determined	NHPIs[1] with income below poverty level	Asian Indian	Bangladeshi	Cambodian	Chinese[2]	Fijian	Filipino	Guamanian[3]	Hawaiian, Native	Hmong	Indonesian	Japanese	Korean	Laotian	Malaysian	Pakistani	Samoan	Sri Lankan	Taiwanese	Thai	Tongan	Vietnamese
Carson (city)	8,216	20,067	1,083	1,929	138	-	-	-	11	-	996	-	-	-	-	15	-	-	-	-	133	-	-	-	-	7
	9.33		5.40		7.15				2.31		5.76					2.42					9.25					2.18
									1.02		91.97					1.39					96.38					0.65
			5.40		7.15				0.05		4.96					0.07					6.89					0.03
			13.18		1.68				0.13		12.12					0.18					1.62					0.09
Cerritos (city)	2,554	30,131	1,669	-	-	98	-	-	384	-	223	-	-	-	-	49	572	-	-	-	-	-	107	55	-	114
	4.97		5.54			3.33			6.66		3.91					2.45	6.48						5.97	11.80		9.05
						5.87			23.01		13.36					2.94	34.27						6.41	3.30		6.83
			5.54			0.33			1.27		0.74					0.16	1.90						0.36	0.18		0.38
			65.35			3.84			15.04		8.73					1.92	22.40						4.19	2.15		4.46
Citrus (cdp)	1,359	784	40	-	-	-	-	-	-	-	-	-	-	-	-	-	-	-	-	-	-	-	-	-	-	-
	12.82		5.10																							
			5.10																							
			2.94																							
Claremont (city)	2,328	3,122	435	-	-	48	-	-	92	-	-	-	-	-	-	-	50	-	-	-	-	-	-	-	-	-
	8.02		13.93			10.67			9.85								12.29									
						11.03			21.15								11.49									
			13.93			1.54			2.95								1.60									
			18.69			2.06			3.95								2.15									
Compton (city)	25,771	415	151	1,028	551	-	-	-	-	-	-	-	-	-	-	-	-	-	-	-	544	-	-	-	-	-
	28.05		36.39		53.60																55.45					
																					98.73					
			36.39		53.60																52.92					
			0.59		2.14																2.11					
Covina (city)	5,408	4,551	461	-	-	-	-	-	248	-	20	-	-	-	-	20	-	-	-	-	-	-	-	-	-	67
	11.60		10.13						21.25		1.48					5.01										15.16
									53.80		4.34					4.34										14.53
			10.13						5.45		0.44					0.44										1.47
			8.52						4.59		0.37					0.37										1.24
Culver City (city)	3,308	4,684	292	-	-	80	-	-	13	-	12	-	-	-	-	100	-	-	-	-	-	-	-	-	-	-
	8.59		6.23			12.88			1.68		1.22					7.45										
						27.40			4.45		4.11					34.25										
			6.23			1.71			0.28		0.26					2.13										
			8.83			2.42			0.39		0.36					3.02										
Diamond Bar (city)	3,369	23,820	1,651	-	-	193	-	-	392	-	51	-	-	-	-	8	495	-	-	-	-	-	270	-	-	0
	6.01		6.93			7.78			5.12		1.63					1.16	8.84						12.86			0.00
						11.69			23.74		3.09					0.48	29.98						16.35			0.00
			6.93			0.81			1.65		0.21					0.03	2.08						1.13			0.00
			49.01			5.73			11.64		1.51					0.24	14.69						8.01			0.00
Downey (city)	11,714	7,745	508	-	-	17	-	-	30	-	20	-	-	-	-	11	201	-	-	-	-	-	-	-	-	34
	11.10		6.56			3.77			5.98		1.04					2.99	6.34									8.44
						3.35			5.91		3.94					2.17	39.57									6.69
			6.56			0.22			0.39		0.26					0.14	2.60									0.44
			4.34			0.15			0.26		0.17					0.09	1.72									0.29
Duarte (city)	2,353	2,712	185	-	-	-	-	-	39	-	80	-	-	-	-	-	-	-	-	-	-	-	-	-	-	-
	11.25		6.82						8.88		5.70															
									21.08		43.24															
			6.82						1.44		2.95															
			7.86						1.66		3.40															

Notes: Please refer to the User's Guide for an explanation of data; data is arranged alphabetically by state, then county, then city within each county; table includes counties with populations greater than 49,999 unless noted and cities with populations greater than 9,999 whose Asian and/or NHPI population rates are greater than the national average; (1) Native Hawaiian and other Pacific Islander; (2) excludes Taiwanese; (3) includes Chamorro; (4) county does not meet population threshold but is shown in order to allow inclusion of city

Place	Total population with income below poverty level	Asian population for whom poverty status is determined	Asians with income below poverty level	NHPI[1] population for whom poverty status is determined	NHPIs[1] with income below poverty level	Asian Indian	Bangladeshi	Cambodian	Chinese[2]	Fijian	Filipino	Guamanian[3]	Hawaiian, Native	Hmong	Indonesian	Japanese	Korean	Laotian	Malaysian	Pakistani	Samoan	Sri Lankan	Taiwanese	Thai	Tongan	Vietnamese
East San Gabriel (cdp)	1,533 10.54	6,093	796 13.06 13.06 51.92	-	-	-	-	-	475 13.60 59.67 7.80 30.98	-	-	-	-	-	-	15 2.68 1.88 0.25 0.98	-	-	-	-	-	-	163 25.43 20.48 2.68 10.63	-	-	-
El Monte (city)	29,939 26.14	21,395	4,283 20.02 20.02 14.31	-	-	-	-	-	1,943 16.69 45.37 9.08 6.49	-	77 8.02 1.80 0.36 0.26	-	-	-	-	-	-	-	-	-	-	-	95 23.69 2.22 0.44 0.32	-	-	1,834 29.00 42.82 8.57 6.13
El Segundo (city)	726 4.56	1,063	10 0.94 0.94 1.38	-	-	-	-	-	-	-	-	-	-	-	-	-	-	-	-	-	-	-	-	-	-	-
Gardena (city)	8,944 15.70	15,278	1,488 9.74 9.74 16.64	-	-	-	-	-	28 3.18 1.88 0.18 0.31	-	139 7.87 9.34 0.91 1.55	-	-	-	-	480 7.34 32.26 3.14 5.37	524 14.02 35.22 3.43 5.86	-	-	-	-	-	-	-	-	226 17.61 15.19 1.48 2.53
Glendale (city)	29,927 15.50	31,800	3,090 9.72 9.72 10.33	-	-	35 3.61 1.13 0.11 0.12	-	-	265 9.88 8.58 0.83 0.89	-	713 6.20 23.07 2.24 2.38	-	-	-	-	217 13.10 7.02 0.68 0.73	1,566 12.57 50.68 4.92 5.23	-	-	-	-	-	-	59 14.05 1.91 0.19 0.20	-	94 9.98 3.04 0.30 0.31
Glendora (city)	2,856 5.86	3,217	248 7.71 7.71 8.68	-	-	30 5.63 12.10 0.93 1.05	-	-	112 12.90 45.16 3.48 3.92	-	15 1.81 6.05 0.47 0.53	-	-	-	-	-	-	-	-	-	-	-	-	-	-	-
Hacienda Heights (cdp)	4,928 9.32	19,171	2,210 11.53 11.53 44.85	-	-	-	-	-	900 9.91 40.72 4.69 18.26	-	92 6.93 4.16 0.48 1.87	-	-	-	-	76 5.71 3.44 0.40 1.54	457 17.78 20.68 2.38 9.27	-	-	-	-	-	448 15.58 20.27 2.34 9.09	-	-	71 14.73 3.21 0.37 1.44
Hawaiian Gardens (city)	3,251 22.07	1,292	354 27.40 27.40 10.89	-	-	-	-	-	-	-	-	-	-	-	-	-	233 30.86 65.82 18.03 7.17	-	-	-	-	-	-	-	-	-
Hawthorne (city)	16,870 20.33	5,930	852 14.37 14.37 5.05	546	150 27.47 27.47 0.89	115 23.91 13.50 1.94 0.68	-	-	42 7.98 4.93 0.71 0.25	-	101 4.54 11.85 1.70 0.60	-	-	-	-	51 11.36 5.99 0.86 0.30	-	-	-	-	-	-	-	-	-	344 23.29 40.38 5.80 2.04
Hermosa Beach (city)	839 4.57	861	43 4.99 4.99 5.13	-	-	-	-	-	-	-	-	-	-	-	-	-	-	-	-	-	-	-	-	-	-	-

Notes: Please refer to the User's Guide for an explanation of data; data is arranged alphabetically by state, then county, then city within each county; table includes counties with populations greater than 49,999 unless noted and cities with populations greater than 9,999 whose Asian and/or NHPI population rates are greater than the national average; (1) Native Hawaiian and other Pacific Islander; (2) excludes Taiwanese; (3) includes Chamorro; (4) county does not meet population threshold but is shown in order to allow inclusion of city

Place	Total population with income below poverty level	Asian population for whom poverty status is determined	Asians with income below poverty level	NHPI[1] population for whom poverty status is determined	NHPIs[1] with income below poverty level	Asian Indian	Bangladeshi	Cambodian	Chinese[2]	Fijian	Filipino	Guamanian[3]	Hawaiian, Native	Hmong	Indonesian	Japanese	Korean	Laotian	Malaysian	Pakistani	Samoan	Sri Lankan	Taiwanese	Thai	Tongan	Vietnamese
La Canada Flintridge (city)	862	3,890	231	-	-	-	-	-	0	-	-	-	-	-	-	15	169	-	-	-	-	-	-	-	-	-
	4.26		5.94						0.00							3.94	7.66									
									0.00							6.49	73.16									
			5.94						0.00							0.39	4.34									
			26.80						0.00							1.74	19.61									
La Crescenta-Montrose (cdp)	976	3,502	249	-	-	-	-	-	-	-	10	-	-	-	-	-	193	-	-	-	-	-	-	-	-	-
	5.32		7.11								2.87						7.77									
											4.02						77.51									
			7.11								0.29						5.51									
			25.51								1.02						19.77									
La Mirada (city)	2,542	6,854	550	-	-	60	-	-	10	-	82	-	-	-	-	38	214	-	-	-	-	-	-	-	-	-
	5.64		8.02			11.56			1.56		3.73					9.74	9.30									
						10.91			1.82		14.91					6.91	38.91									
			8.02			0.88			0.15		1.20					0.55	3.12									
			21.64			2.36			0.39		3.23					1.49	8.42									
La Puente (city)	7,656	2,873	152	-	-	-	-	-	23	-	36	-	-	-	-	-	-	-	-	-	-	-	-	-	-	-
	18.93		5.29						2.64		3.59															
									15.13		23.68															
			5.29						0.80		1.25															
			1.99						0.30		0.47															
La Verne (city)	1,464	2,346	65	-	-	-	-	-	-	-	10	-	-	-	-	-	-	-	-	-	-	-	-	-	-	-
	4.70		2.77								1.15															
											15.38															
			2.77								0.43															
			4.44								0.68															
Lakewood (city)	5,820	10,428	1,440	762	33	111	-	144	143	-	405	-	-	-	-	9	328	-	-	-	26	-	-	-	-	80
	7.37		13.81		4.33	25.75		19.67	14.16		8.48					1.24	22.71				4.35					18.10
						7.71		10.00	9.93		28.13					0.63	22.78				78.79					5.56
			13.81		4.33	1.06		1.38	1.37		3.88					0.09	3.15				3.41					0.77
			24.74		0.57	1.91		2.47	2.46		6.96					0.15	5.64				0.45					1.37
Lancaster (city)	18,239	4,277	537	-	-	75	-	-	101	-	264	-	-	-	-	-	-	-	-	-	-	-	-	-	-	-
	16.35		12.56			11.94			24.34		12.79															
						13.97			18.81		49.16															
			12.56			1.75			2.36		6.17															
			2.94			0.41			0.55		1.45															
Lawndale (city)	5,457	2,924	569	463	98	-	-	-	-	-	34	-	-	-	-	-	-	-	-	-	-	-	-	-	-	319
	17.26		19.46		21.17						5.18															24.30
											5.98															56.06
			19.46		21.17						1.16															10.91
			10.43		1.80						0.62															5.85
Lomita (city)	2,208	2,265	207	-	-	-	-	-	-	-	24	-	-	-	-	66	51	-	-	-	-	-	-	-	-	-
	11.13		9.14								5.24					10.63	9.53									
											11.59					31.88	24.64									
			9.14								1.06					2.91	2.25									
			9.38								1.09					2.99	2.31									
Long Beach (city)	103,434	54,490	13,730	5,050	1,918	272	-	8,326	520	-	1,503	-	-	-	-	477	308	156	-	-	1,488	-	-	67	-	1,281
	22.83		25.20		37.98	23.29		47.15	17.05		8.42					13.86	18.36	21.02			40.31			11.24		25.45
						1.98		60.64	3.79		10.95					3.47	2.24	1.14			77.58			0.49		9.33
			25.20		37.98	0.50		15.28	0.95		2.76					0.88	0.57	0.29			29.47			0.12		2.35
			13.27		1.85	0.26		8.05	0.50		1.45					0.46	0.30	0.15			1.44			0.06		1.24

Notes: Please refer to the User's Guide for an explanation of data; data is arranged alphabetically by state, then county, then city within each county; table includes counties with populations greater than 49,999 unless noted and cities with populations greater than 9,999 whose Asian and/or NHPI population rates are greater than the national average; (1) Native Hawaiian and other Pacific Islander; (2) excludes Taiwanese; (3) includes Chamorro; (4) county does not meet population threshold but is shown in order to allow inclusion of city

Place	Total population with income below poverty level	Asian population for whom poverty status is determined	Asians with income below poverty level	NHPI[1] population for whom poverty status is determined	NHPIs[1] with income below poverty level	Asian Indian	Bangladeshi	Cambodian	Chinese[2]	Fijian	Filipino	Guamanian[3]	Hawaiian, Native	Hmong	Indonesian	Japanese	Korean	Laotian	Malaysian	Pakistani	Samoan	Sri Lankan	Taiwanese	Thai	Tongan	Vietnamese
Los Angeles (city)	801,050	359,776	60,765	6,255	1,189	3,695	188	1,462	12,181	-	9,252	221	310	-	470	4,947	18,493	222	-	432	309	81	736	1,749	176	4,362
	22.11		16.89		19.01	15.78	22.79	35.37	21.25		9.19	19.34	20.56		26.26	13.82	20.58	33.28		26.54	15.20	6.86	24.01	19.38	51.46	22.86
						6.08	0.31	2.41	20.05		15.23	18.59	26.07		0.77	8.14	30.43	0.37		0.71	25.99	0.13	1.21	2.88	14.80	7.18
			16.89		19.01	1.03	0.05	0.41	3.39		2.57	3.53	4.96		0.13	1.38	5.14	0.06		0.12	4.94	0.02	0.20	0.49	2.81	1.21
			7.59		0.15	0.46	0.02	0.18	1.52		1.15	0.03	0.04		0.06	0.62	2.31	0.03		0.05	0.04	0.01	0.09	0.22	0.02	0.54
Manhattan Beach (city)	1,104	2,016	60	-	-	-	-	-	0	-	-	-	-	-	-	17	-	-	-	-	-	-	-	-	-	-
	3.25		2.98						0.00							2.79										
									0.00							28.33										
			2.98						0.00							0.84										
			5.43						0.00							1.54										
Monrovia (city)	4,797	2,480	216	-	-	-	-	-	66	-	81	-	-	-	-	-	-	-	-	-	-	-	-	-	-	-
	13.11		8.71						9.40		8.79															
									30.56		37.50															
			8.71						2.66		3.27															
			4.50						1.38		1.69															
Montebello (city)	10,436	7,022	461	-	-	-	-	-	207	-	24	-	-	-	-	16	95	-	-	-	-	-	-	-	-	-
	16.99		6.57						8.20		2.76					0.89	15.13									
									44.90		5.21					3.47	20.61									
			6.57						2.95		0.34					0.23	1.35									
			4.42						1.98		0.23					0.15	0.91									
Monterey Park (city)	9,310	36,457	5,927	-	-	-	-	89	3,966	-	80	-	-	-	-	195	64	-	-	-	-	-	176	-	-	905
	15.61		16.26					21.55	17.46		9.48					4.05	7.45						16.75			28.23
								1.50	66.91		1.35					3.29	1.08						2.97			15.27
			16.26					0.24	10.88		0.22					0.53	0.18						0.48			2.48
			63.66					0.96	42.60		0.86					2.09	0.69						1.89			9.72
Norwalk (city)	12,058	12,168	992	-	-	109	-	0	143	-	128	-	-	-	-	2	364	-	-	-	-	-	-	-	-	148
	11.87		8.15			8.13		0.00	15.38		2.86					0.42	14.46									17.25
						10.99		0.00	14.42		12.90					0.20	36.69									14.92
			8.15			0.90		0.00	1.18		1.05					0.02	2.99									1.22
			8.23			0.90		0.00	1.19		1.06					0.02	3.02									1.23
Palmdale (city)	18,272	4,285	219	-	-	14	-	-	-	-	93	-	-	-	-	-	-	-	-	-	-	-	-	-	-	-
	15.81		5.11			3.29					4.29															
						6.39					42.47															
			5.11			0.33					2.17															
			1.20			0.08					0.51															
Palos Verdes Estates (city)	287	2,317	165	-	-	-	-	-	32	-	-	-	-	-	-	25	26	-	-	-	-	-	-	-	-	-
	2.16		7.12						5.83							3.75	9.00									
									19.39							15.15	15.76									
			7.12						1.38							1.08	1.12									
			57.49						11.15							8.71	9.06									
Pasadena (city)	20,909	13,126	1,946	-	-	43	-	-	671	-	96	-	-	-	-	385	372	-	-	-	-	-	-	-	-	57
	15.92		14.83			5.17			16.51		3.76					17.20	26.94									7.50
						2.21			34.48		4.93					19.78	19.12									2.93
			14.83			0.33			5.11		0.73					2.93	2.83									0.43
			9.31			0.21			3.21		0.46					1.84	1.78									0.27
Pomona (city)	31,149	9,858	1,972	-	-	55	-	372	465	-	225	-	-	-	-	121	-	135	-	-	-	-	-	-	-	359
	21.61		20.00			9.93		49.14	26.66		8.24					28.61		25.33								22.51
						2.79		18.86	23.58		11.41					6.14		6.85								18.20
			20.00			0.56		3.77	4.72		2.28					1.23		1.37								3.64
			6.33			0.18		1.19	1.49		0.72					0.39		0.43								1.15

Notes: Please refer to the User's Guide for an explanation of data; data is arranged alphabetically by state, then county, then city within each county; table includes counties with populations greater than 49,999 unless noted and cities with populations greater than 9,999 whose Asian and/or NHPI population rates are greater than the national average; (1) Native Hawaiian and other Pacific Islander; (2) excludes Taiwanese; (3) includes Chamorro; (4) county does not meet population threshold but is shown in order to allow inclusion of city

Place	Total population with income below poverty level	Asian population for whom poverty status is determined	Asians with income below poverty level	NHPI[1] population for whom poverty status is determined	NHPIs[1] with income below poverty level	Asian Indian	Bangladeshi	Cambodian	Chinese[2]	Fijian	Filipino	Guamanian[3]	Hawaiian, Native	Hmong	Indonesian	Japanese	Korean	Laotian	Malaysian	Pakistani	Samoan	Sri Lankan	Taiwanese	Thai	Tongan	Vietnamese
Rancho Palos Verdes (city)	1,188	10,372	485	-	-	0	-	-	114	-	40	-	-	-	-	74	173	-	-	-	-	-	70	-	-	-
	2.90		4.68			0.00			4.31		6.83					2.42	7.12						12.96			
						0.00			23.51		8.25					15.26	35.67						14.43			
			4.68			0.00			1.10		0.39					0.71	1.67						0.67			
			40.82			0.00			9.60		3.37					6.23	14.56						5.89			
Redondo Beach (city)	3,719	5,896	224	-	-	0	-	-	41	-	11	-	-	-	-	101	29	-	-	-	-	-	-	-	-	-
	5.90		3.80			0.00			3.39		1.38					5.06	4.33									
						0.00			18.30		4.91					45.09	12.95									
			3.80			0.00			0.70		0.19					1.71	0.49									
			6.02			0.00			1.10		0.30					2.72	0.78									
Rosemead (city)	12,042	25,759	6,321	-	-	-	-	149	3,879	-	18	-	-	-	-	40	-	-	-	-	-	-	-	-	-	1,678
	22.82		24.54					19.23	26.00		2.62					5.12										28.42
								2.36	61.37		0.28					0.63										26.55
			24.54					0.58	15.06		0.07					0.16										6.51
			52.49					1.24	32.21		0.15					0.33										13.93
Rowland Heights (cdp)	5,744	24,727	3,070	-	-	67	-	-	1,677	-	177	-	-	-	-	48	449	-	-	-	-	-	409	-	-	76
	11.97		12.42			6.42			14.74		5.40					7.29	12.05						15.77			12.18
						2.18			54.63		5.77					1.56	14.63						13.32			2.48
			12.42			0.27			6.78		0.72					0.19	1.82						1.65			0.31
			53.45			1.17			29.20		3.08					0.84	7.82						7.12			1.32
San Dimas (city)	2,167	3,166	264	-	-	-	-	-	51	-	28	-	-	-	-	-	-	-	-	-	-	-	-	-	-	-
	6.32		8.34						4.26		3.64															
									19.32		10.61															
			8.34						1.61		0.88															
			12.18						2.35		1.29															
San Gabriel (city)	6,140	19,031	3,460	-	-	-	-	-	2,121	-	137	-	-	-	-	49	-	-	-	-	-	-	80	-	-	707
	15.92		18.18						18.17		11.79					7.88							10.48			26.62
									61.30		3.96					1.42							2.31			20.43
			18.18						11.14		0.72					0.26							0.42			3.71
			56.35						34.54		2.23					0.80							1.30			11.51
San Marino (city)	643	6,071	466	-	-	-	-	-	304	-	-	-	-	-	-	-	-	-	-	-	-	-	114	-	-	-
	4.96		7.68						7.77														7.47			
									65.24														24.46			
			7.68						5.01														1.88			
			72.47						47.28														17.73			
Santa Clarita (city)	9,552	7,559	483	-	-	7	-	-	65	-	176	-	-	-	-	81	77	-	-	-	-	-	-	-	-	0
	6.38		6.39			0.93			7.56		7.09					7.24	9.64									0.00
						1.45			13.46		36.44					16.77	15.94									0.00
			6.39			0.09			0.86		2.33					1.07	1.02									0.00
			5.06			0.07			0.68		1.84					0.85	0.81									0.00
Santa Monica (city)	8,636	5,929	1,031	-	-	47	-	-	205	-	58	-	-	-	-	444	140	-	-	-	-	-	-	-	-	-
	10.42		17.39			7.64			12.94		12.64					24.32	18.84									
						4.56			19.88		5.63					43.06	13.58									
			17.39			0.79			3.46		0.98					7.49	2.36									
			11.94			0.54			2.37		0.67					5.14	1.62									
Sierra Madre (city)	389	566	8	-	-	-	-	-	-	-	-	-	-	-	-	-	-	-	-	-	-	-	-	-	-	-
	3.72		1.41																							
			1.41																							
			2.06																							

Notes: Please refer to the User's Guide for an explanation of data; data is arranged alphabetically by state, then county, then city within each county; table includes counties with populations greater than 49,999 unless noted and cities with populations greater than 9,999 whose Asian and/or NHPI population rates are greater than the national average; (1) Native Hawaiian and other Pacific Islander; (2) excludes Taiwanese; (3) includes Chamorro; (4) county does not meet population threshold but is shown in order to allow inclusion of city

Place	Total population with income below poverty level	Asian population for whom poverty status is determined	Asians with income below poverty level	NHPI[1] population for whom poverty status is determined	NHPIs[1] with income below poverty level	Asian Indian	Bangladeshi	Cambodian	Chinese[2]	Fijian	Filipino	Guamanian[3]	Hawaiian, Native	Hmong	Indonesian	Japanese	Korean	Laotian	Malaysian	Pakistani	Samoan	Sri Lankan	Taiwanese	Thai	Tongan	Vietnamese
South El Monte (city)	3,957 19.04	1,591	305 19.17 19.17 7.71	-	-	-	-	-	110 16.06 36.07 6.91 2.78	-	-	-	-	-	-	-	-	-	-	-	-	-	-	-	-	135 21.36 44.26 8.49 3.41
South Pasadena (city)	1,466 6.08	6,220	376 6.05 6.05 25.65	-	-	-	-	-	116 3.49 30.85 1.86 7.91	-	-	-	-	-	-	114 11.45 30.32 1.83 7.78	33 4.92 8.78 0.53 2.25	-	-	-	-	-	-	-	-	-
South San Jose Hills (cdp)	3,658 18.49	1,241	36 2.90 2.90 0.98	-	-	-	-	-	-	-	23 3.16 63.89 1.85 0.63	-	-	-	-	-	-	-	-	-	-	-	-	-	-	-
Temple City (city)	3,069 9.32	12,905	1,506 11.67 11.67 49.07	-	-	-	-	-	929 11.79 61.69 7.20 30.27	-	18 2.77 1.20 0.14 0.59	-	-	-	-	40 6.94 2.66 0.31 1.30	29 5.78 1.93 0.22 0.94	-	-	-	-	-	249 16.25 16.53 1.93 8.11	-	-	135 15.94 8.96 1.05 4.40
Torrance (city)	8,815 6.44	39,352	2,923 7.43 7.43 33.16	-	-	162 7.35 5.54 0.41 1.84	-	-	312 5.29 10.67 0.79 3.54	-	262 7.38 8.96 0.67 2.97	-	-	-	-	551 4.09 18.85 1.40 6.25	825 9.68 28.22 2.10 9.36	-	-	123 18.75 4.21 0.31 1.40	-	-	227 17.69 7.77 0.58 2.58	-	-	253 13.82 8.66 0.64 2.87
Valinda (cdp)	2,740 12.76	1,917	114 5.95 5.95 4.16	-	-	-	-	-	-	-	75 7.58 65.79 3.91 2.74	-	-	-	-	-	-	-	-	-	-	-	-	-	-	0 0.00 0.00 0.00 0.00
Vincent (cdp)	1,476 9.83	1,093	34 3.11 3.11 2.30	-	-	-	-	-	-	-	34 5.48 100.00 3.11 2.30	-	-	-	-	-	-	-	-	-	-	-	-	-	-	-
Walnut (city)	1,942 6.49	16,836	1,245 7.39 7.39 64.11	-	-	0 0.00 0.00 0.00 0.00	-	-	544 8.63 43.69 3.23 28.01	-	37 1.08 2.97 0.22 1.91	-	-	-	-	21 4.82 1.69 0.12 1.08	259 13.74 20.80 1.54 13.34	-	-	-	-	-	226 11.73 18.15 1.34 11.64	-	-	11 1.91 0.88 0.07 0.57
West Carson (cdp)	1,937 9.51	5,030	250 4.97 4.97 12.91	-	-	-	-	-	-	-	134 6.39 53.60 2.66 6.92	-	-	-	-	27 2.43 10.80 0.54 1.39	40 4.65 16.00 0.80 2.07	-	-	-	-	-	-	-	-	-
West Covina (city)	9,400 9.03	23,695	2,010 8.48 8.48 21.38	432	98 22.69 22.69 1.04	58 11.58 2.89 0.24 0.62	-	-	789 11.94 39.25 3.33 8.39	-	526 5.24 26.17 2.22 5.60	-	-	-	-	145 20.03 7.21 0.61 1.54	56 6.11 2.79 0.24 0.60	-	-	-	-	-	113 12.00 5.62 0.48 1.20	-	-	220 10.22 10.95 0.93 2.34

Notes: Please refer to the User's Guide for an explanation of data; data is arranged alphabetically by state, then county, then city within each county; table includes counties with populations greater than 49,999 unless noted and cities with populations greater than 9,999 whose Asian and/or NHPI population rates are greater than the national average; (1) Native Hawaiian and other Pacific Islander; (2) excludes Taiwanese; (3) includes Chamorro; (4) county does not meet population threshold but is shown in order to allow inclusion of city

Place	Total population with income below poverty level	Asian population for whom poverty status is determined	Asians with income below poverty level	NHPI[1] population for whom poverty status is determined	NHPIs[1] with income below poverty level	Asian Indian	Bangladeshi	Cambodian	Chinese[2]	Fijian	Filipino	Guamanian[3]	Hawaiian, Native	Hmong	Indonesian	Japanese	Korean	Laotian	Malaysian	Pakistani	Samoan	Sri Lankan	Taiwanese	Thai	Tongan	Vietnamese
West Hollywood (city)	4,086 11.45	1,412	178 12.61 12.61 4.36	-	-	-	-	-	-	-	-	-	-	-	-	-	-	-	-	-	-	-	-	-	-	-
West Puente Valley (cdp)	2,597 11.46	1,723	227 13.17 13.17 8.74	-	-	-	-	-	-	-	6 0.83 2.64 0.35 0.23	-	-	-	-	-	-	-	-	-	-	-	-	-	-	95 20.56 41.85 5.51 3.66
Whittier (city)	8,549 10.47	3,167	256 8.08 8.08 2.99	-	-	-	-	-	121 10.25 47.27 3.82 1.42	-	8 1.28 3.13 0.25 0.09	-	-	-	-	14 3.23 5.47 0.44 0.16	12 3.52 4.69 0.38 0.14	-	-	-	-	-	-	-	-	-
Madera County	24,514 21.35	1,376	198 14.39 14.39 0.81	-	-	110 20.37 55.56 7.99 0.45	-	-	-	-	32 8.12 16.16 2.33 0.13	-	-	-	-	-	-	-	-	-	-	-	-	-	-	-
Marin County	15,601 6.57	10,661	974 9.14 9.14 6.24	-	-	73 5.09 7.49 0.68 0.47	-	-	173 5.57 17.76 1.62 1.11	-	45 3.77 4.62 0.42 0.29	-	-	-	-	111 6.88 11.40 1.04 0.71	133 12.01 13.66 1.25 0.85	-	-	-	-	-	-	-	-	386 31.20 39.63 3.62 2.47
Larkspur (city)	434 3.66	440	0 <0.01 <0.01 <0.01	-	-	-	-	-	-	-	-	-	-	-	-	-	-	-	-	-	-	-	-	-	-	-
Novato (city)	2,622 5.57	2,515	183 7.28 7.28 6.98	-	-	-	-	-	43 6.64 23.50 1.71 1.64	-	30 6.40 16.39 1.19 1.14	-	-	-	-	-	-	-	-	-	-	-	-	-	-	-
San Rafael (city)	5,587 10.23	3,077	373 12.12 12.12 6.68	-	-	40 7.83 10.72 1.30 0.72	-	-	72 7.49 19.30 2.34 1.29	-	-	-	-	-	-	-	-	-	-	-	-	-	-	-	-	197 30.03 52.82 6.40 3.53
Tamalpais-Homestead (cdp)	400 3.78	508	8 1.57 1.57 2.00	-	-	-	-	-	-	-	-	-	-	-	-	-	-	-	-	-	-	-	-	-	-	-
Mendocino County	13,505 15.94	826	181 21.91 21.91 1.34	-	-	-	-	-	-	-	-	-	-	-	-	-	-	-	-	-	-	-	-	-	-	-

Notes: Please refer to the User's Guide for an explanation of data; data is arranged alphabetically by state, then county, then city within each county; table includes counties with populations greater than 49,999 unless noted and cities with populations greater than 9,999 whose Asian and/or NHPI population rates are greater than the national average; (1) Native Hawaiian and other Pacific Islander; (2) excludes Taiwanese; (3) includes Chamorro; (4) county does not meet population threshold but is shown in order to allow inclusion of city

Place	Total population with income below poverty level	Asian population for whom poverty status is determined	Asians with income below poverty level	NHPI[1] population for whom poverty status is determined	NHPIs[1] with income below poverty level	Asian Indian	Bangladeshi	Cambodian	Chinese[2]	Fijian	Filipino	Guamanian[3]	Hawaiian, Native	Hmong	Indonesian	Japanese	Korean	Laotian	Malaysian	Pakistani	Samoan	Sri Lankan	Taiwanese	Thai	Tongan	Vietnamese
Merced County	45,059	14,376	5,574	-	-	397	-	-	62	-	135	-	-	3,782	-	59	-	647	-	-	-	-	-	-	-	-
	21.66		38.77			18.74			13.75		8.93			57.70		10.91		37.68								
						7.12			1.11		2.42			67.85		1.06		11.61								
			38.77			2.76			0.43		0.94			26.31		0.41		4.50								
			12.37			0.88			0.14		0.30			8.39		0.13		1.44								
Atwater (city)	4,261	1,228	177	-	-	-	-	-	-	-	-	-	-	102	-	-	-	-	-	-	-	-	-	-	-	-
	18.74		14.41											25.95												
														57.63												
			14.41											8.31												
			4.15											2.39												
Livingston (city)	2,595	1,553	361	-	-	308	-	-	-	-	-	-	-	-	-	-	-	-	-	-	-	-	-	-	-	-
	25.23		23.25			24.74																				
						85.32																				
			23.25			19.83																				
			13.91			11.87																				
Merced (city)	17,489	7,048	4,005	-	-	-	-	-	-	-	-	-	-	2,862	-	-	-	601	-	-	-	-	-	-	-	-
	27.86		56.82											68.09				43.30								
														71.46				15.01								
			56.82											40.61				8.53								
			22.90											16.36				3.44								
Monterey County	51,692	23,830	2,448	1,795	215	177	-	-	254	-	846	128	-	-	-	315	320	-	-	-	-	-	-	-	-	434
	13.51		10.27		11.98	14.32			12.24		7.47	18.99				9.45	11.40									22.56
						7.23			10.38		34.56	59.53				12.87	13.07									17.73
			10.27		11.98	0.74			1.07		3.55	7.13				1.32	1.34									1.82
			4.74		0.42	0.34			0.49		1.64	0.25				0.61	0.62									0.84
Marina (city)	2,518	4,139	531	492	18	-	-	-	-	-	173	-	-	-	-	18	122	-	-	-	-	-	-	-	-	124
	13.12		12.83		3.66						14.07					4.81	9.74									17.27
											32.58					3.39	22.98									23.35
			12.83		3.66						4.18					0.43	2.95									3.00
			21.09		0.71						6.87					0.71	4.85									4.92
Monterey (city)	2,105	2,217	376	-	-	-	-	-	68	-	65	-	-	-	-	173	-	-	-	-	-	-	-	-	-	-
	7.81		16.96						17.66		15.78					23.63										
									18.09		17.29					46.01										
			16.96						3.07		2.93					7.80										
			17.86						3.23		3.09					8.22										
Pacific Grove (city)	826	660	105	-	-	-	-	-	-	-	-	-	-	-	-	-	-	-	-	-	-	-	-	-	-	-
	5.38		15.91																							
			15.91																							
			12.71																							
Salinas (city)	23,676	8,980	853	531	111	28	-	-	61	-	430	-	-	-	-	35	70	-	-	-	-	-	-	-	-	168
	16.70		9.50		20.90	5.16			10.61		7.32					4.45	15.15									35.22
						3.28			7.15		50.41					4.10	8.21									19.70
			9.50		20.90	0.31			0.68		4.79					0.39	0.78									1.87
			3.60		0.47	0.12			0.26		1.82					0.15	0.30									0.71
Seaside (city)	3,808	3,328	282	-	-	-	-	-	-	-	86	-	-	-	-	34	-	-	-	-	-	-	-	-	-	111
	12.11		8.47								4.38					8.13										23.67
											30.50					12.06										39.36
			8.47								2.58					1.02										3.34
			7.41								2.26					0.89										2.91

Notes: Please refer to the User's Guide for an explanation of data; data is arranged alphabetically by state, then county, then city within each county; table includes counties with populations greater than 49,999 unless noted and cities with populations greater than 9,999 whose Asian and/or NHPI population rates are greater than the national average; (1) Native Hawaiian and other Pacific Islander; (2) excludes Taiwanese; (3) includes Chamorro; (4) county does not meet population threshold but is shown in order to allow inclusion of city

Place	Total population with income below poverty level	Asian population for whom poverty status is determined	Asians with income below poverty level	NHPI[1] population for whom poverty status is determined	NHPIs[1] with income below poverty level	Asian Indian	Bangladeshi	Cambodian	Chinese[2]	Fijian	Filipino	Guamanian[3]	Hawaiian, Native	Hmong	Indonesian	Japanese	Korean	Laotian	Malaysian	Pakistani	Samoan	Sri Lankan	Taiwanese	Thai	Tongan	Vietnamese
Napa County	9,913	3,647	137	-	-	-	-	-	58	-	39	-	-	-	-	5	-	-	-	-	-	-	-	-	-	-
	8.29		3.76						11.18		2.06					1.27										
									42.34		28.47					3.65										
			3.76						1.59		1.07					0.14										
			1.38						0.59		0.39					0.05										
Nevada County	7,332	590	85	-	-	-	-	-	-	-	-	-	-	-	-	-	-	-	-	-	-	-	-	-	-	-
	8.06		14.41																							
			14.41																							
			1.16																							
Orange County	289,475	381,091	43,906	8,439	907	1,565	-	718	5,120	-	3,317	105	93	74	402	2,155	7,345	279	-	177	288	66	1,146	497	172	19,967
	10.33		11.52		10.75	5.92		16.44	10.56		6.88	9.59	5.54	7.01	21.07	7.30	12.92	9.65		6.84	7.81	9.90	12.60	16.32	29.60	14.77
						3.56		1.64	11.66		7.55	11.58	10.25	0.17	0.92	4.91	16.73	0.64		0.40	31.75	0.15	2.61	1.13	18.96	45.48
			11.52		10.75	0.41		0.19	1.34		0.87	1.24	1.10	0.02	0.11	0.57	1.93	0.07		0.05	3.41	0.02	0.30	0.13	2.04	5.24
			15.17		0.31	0.54		0.25	1.77		1.15	0.04	0.03	0.03	0.14	0.74	2.54	0.10		0.06	0.10	0.02	0.40	0.17	0.06	6.90
Aliso Viejo (cdp)	1,114	4,377	240	-	-	40	-	-	50	-	0	-	-	-	-	8	97	-	-	-	-	-	-	-	-	0
	2.77		5.48			7.37			7.14		0.00					1.37	20.12									0.00
						16.67			20.83		0.00					3.33	40.42									0.00
			5.48			0.91			1.14		0.00					0.18	2.22									0.00
			21.54			3.59			4.49		0.00					0.72	8.71									0.00
Anaheim (city)	45,615	39,460	3,613	1,094	174	205	-	-	412	-	459	-	-	-	-	88	739	47	-	57	42	-	201	40	-	1,183
	14.10		9.16		15.90	4.98			10.61		5.94					4.01	11.24	5.90		13.44	7.57		30.04	8.77		11.20
						5.67			11.40		12.70					2.44	20.45	1.30		1.58	24.14		5.56	1.11		32.74
			9.16		15.90	0.52			1.04		1.16					0.22	1.87	0.12		0.14	3.84		0.51	0.10		3.00
			7.92		0.38	0.45			0.90		1.01					0.19	1.62	0.10		0.12	0.09		0.44	0.09		2.59
Brea (city)	1,874	3,155	146	-	-	13	-	-	0	-	24	-	-	-	-	-	89	-	-	-	-	-	-	-	-	-
	5.35		4.63			2.84			0.00		4.77						10.84									
						8.90			0.00		16.44						60.96									
			4.63			0.41			0.00		0.76						2.82									
			7.79			0.69			0.00		1.28						4.75									
Buena Park (city)	8,754	16,839	1,580	-	-	40	-	-	134	-	226	-	-	-	-	33	829	-	-	-	-	-	-	-	-	115
	11.29		9.38			2.30			9.92		4.45					4.47	15.62									11.57
						2.53			8.48		14.30					2.09	52.47									7.28
			9.38			0.24			0.80		1.34					0.20	4.92									0.68
			18.05			0.46			1.53		2.58					0.38	9.47									1.31
Costa Mesa (city)	13,393	7,817	1,386	652	117	82	-	-	171	-	114	-	-	-	-	364	186	-	-	-	-	-	-	-	-	211
	12.62		17.73		17.94	19.43			18.02		8.68					24.43	31.96									9.42
						5.92			12.34		8.23					26.26	13.42									15.22
			17.73		17.94	1.05			2.19		1.46					4.66	2.38									2.70
			10.35		0.87	0.61			1.28		0.85					2.72	1.39									1.58
Cypress (city)	2,799	9,450	778	-	-	62	-	-	85	-	80	-	-	-	-	4	249	-	-	-	-	-	165	-	-	93
	6.04		8.23			8.93			5.77		4.61					0.42	9.73						22.18			12.14
						7.97			10.93		10.28					0.51	32.01						21.21			11.95
			8.23			0.66			0.90		0.85					0.04	2.63						1.75			0.98
			27.80			2.22			3.04		2.86					0.14	8.90						5.89			3.32
Foothill Ranch (cdp)	173	1,713	0	-	-	-	-	-	-	-	-	-	-	-	-	-	-	-	-	-	-	-	-	-	-	-
	1.59		<0.01																							
			<0.01																							
			<0.01																							

Notes: Please refer to the User's Guide for an explanation of data; data is arranged alphabetically by state, then county, then city within each county; table includes counties with populations greater than 49,999 unless noted and cities with populations greater than 9,999 whose Asian and/or NHPI population rates are greater than the national average; (1) Native Hawaiian and other Pacific Islander; (2) excludes Taiwanese; (3) includes Chamorro; (4) county does not meet population threshold but is shown in order to allow inclusion of city

Place	Total population with income below poverty level	Asian population for whom poverty status is determined	Asians with income below poverty level	NHPI[1] population for whom poverty status is determined	NHPIs[1] with income below poverty level	Asian Indian	Bangladeshi	Cambodian	Chinese[2]	Fijian	Filipino	Guamanian[3]	Hawaiian, Native	Hmong	Indonesian	Japanese	Korean	Laotian	Malaysian	Pakistani	Samoan	Sri Lankan	Taiwanese	Thai	Tongan	Vietnamese
Fountain Valley (city)	2,348 4.30	14,372	938 6.53 6.53 39.95	-	-	42 5.68 4.48 0.29 1.79	-	-	157 6.45 16.74 1.09 6.69	-	16 2.70 1.71 0.11 0.68	-	-	-	-	54 3.81 5.76 0.38 2.30	63 5.92 6.72 0.44 2.68	-	-	-	-	-	49 12.34 5.22 0.34 2.09	-	-	544 7.70 58.00 3.79 23.17
Fullerton (city)	14,116 11.39	20,100	2,565 12.76 12.76 18.17	-	-	91 4.98 3.55 0.45 0.64	-	-	454 16.41 17.70 2.26 3.22	-	97 4.45 3.78 0.48 0.69	-	-	-	-	91 8.21 3.55 0.45 0.64	1,170 13.06 45.61 5.82 8.29	-	-	-	-	-	-	-	-	277 17.87 10.80 1.38 1.96
Garden Grove (city)	22,779 13.90	50,635	8,318 16.43 16.43 36.52	1,261	237 18.79 18.79 1.04	135 18.65 1.62 0.27 0.59	-	93 18.60 1.12 0.18 0.41	366 14.26 4.40 0.72 1.61	-	177 6.03 2.13 0.35 0.78	-	-	-	-	65 6.30 0.78 0.13 0.29	849 14.07 10.21 1.68 3.73	-	-	-	57 7.42 24.05 4.52 0.25	-	-	-	-	6,363 18.34 76.50 12.57 27.93
Huntington Beach (city)	12,442 6.59	17,608	1,409 8.00 8.00 11.32	354	31 8.76 8.76 0.25	13 1.29 0.92 0.07 0.10	-	-	103 3.48 7.31 0.58 0.83	-	62 3.74 4.40 0.35 0.50	-	-	-	-	143 5.01 10.15 0.81 1.15	157 9.39 11.14 0.89 1.26	-	-	-	-	-	40 7.07 2.84 0.23 0.32	-	-	818 13.94 58.06 4.65 6.57
Irvine (city)	12,379 9.11	39,079	6,381 16.33 16.33 51.55	-	-	355 8.23 5.56 0.91 2.87	-	-	1,803 17.63 28.26 4.61 14.56	-	891 30.28 13.96 2.28 7.20	-	-	-	-	631 13.05 9.89 1.61 5.10	1,520 20.09 23.82 3.89 12.28	-	-	-	-	-	328 13.15 5.14 0.84 2.65	-	-	454 9.80 7.11 1.16 3.67
La Habra (city)	7,559 12.89	3,392	332 9.79 9.79 4.39	-	-	-	-	-	39 8.18 11.75 1.15 0.52	-	32 5.45 9.64 0.94 0.42	-	-	-	-	-	173 14.20 52.11 5.10 2.29	-	-	-	-	-	-	-	-	-
La Palma (city)	736 4.88	6,569	419 6.38 6.38 56.93	-	-	30 5.00 7.16 0.46 4.08	-	-	51 5.47 12.17 0.78 6.93	-	17 1.38 4.06 0.26 2.31	-	-	-	-	40 5.56 9.55 0.61 5.43	265 11.04 63.25 4.03 36.01	-	-	-	-	-	-	-	-	-
Laguna Hills (city)	1,532 4.95	3,174	78 2.46 2.46 5.09	-	-	-	-	-	13 2.28 16.67 0.41 0.85	-	16 2.74 20.51 0.50 1.04	-	-	-	-	-	-	-	-	-	-	-	-	-	-	13 2.28 16.67 0.41 0.85
Laguna Niguel (city)	2,503 4.06	4,668	239 5.12 5.12 9.55	-	-	-	-	-	46 4.59 19.25 0.99 1.84	-	74 8.97 30.96 1.59 2.96	-	-	-	-	24 2.81 10.04 0.51 0.96	25 3.70 10.46 0.54 1.00	-	-	-	-	-	-	-	-	16 3.45 6.69 0.34 0.64
Lake Forest (city)	3,093 5.34	5,421	333 6.14 6.14 10.77	-	-	56 7.59 16.82 1.03 1.81	-	-	54 7.98 16.22 1.00 1.75	-	101 9.86 30.33 1.86 3.27	-	-	-	-	41 7.23 12.31 0.76 1.33	48 8.32 14.41 0.89 1.55	-	-	-	-	-	-	-	-	16 1.15 4.80 0.30 0.52

Notes: Please refer to the User's Guide for an explanation of data; data is arranged alphabetically by state, then county, then city within each county; table includes counties with populations greater than 49,999 unless noted and cities with populations greater than 9,999 whose Asian and/or NHPI population rates are greater than the national average; (1) Native Hawaiian and other Pacific Islander; (2) excludes Taiwanese; (3) includes Chamorro; (4) county does not meet population threshold but is shown in order to allow inclusion of city

Place	Total population with income below poverty level	Asian population for whom poverty status is determined	Asians with income below poverty level	NHPI[1] population for whom poverty status is determined	NHPIs[1] with income below poverty level	Asian Indian	Bangladeshi	Cambodian	Chinese[2]	Fijian	Filipino	Guamanian[3]	Hawaiian, Native	Hmong	Indonesian	Japanese	Korean	Laotian	Malaysian	Pakistani	Samoan	Sri Lankan	Taiwanese	Thai	Tongan	Vietnamese
Los Alamitos (city)	567 5.20	1,046	122 11.66 11.66 21.52	-	-	-	-	-	-	-	-	-	-	-	-	-	-	-	-	-	-	-	-	-	-	-
Mission Viejo (city)	3,480 3.76	7,356	230 3.13 3.13 6.61	-	-	0 0.00 0.00 0.00 0.00	-	-	9 0.70 3.91 0.12 0.26	-	45 3.02 19.57 0.61 1.29	-	-	-	-	38 3.52 16.52 0.52 1.09	36 4.49 15.65 0.49 1.03	-	-	-	-	-	-	-	-	75 5.76 32.61 1.02 2.16
Newport Beach (city)	3,075 4.44	2,632	201 7.64 7.64 6.54	-	-	-	-	-	69 10.71 34.33 2.62 2.24	-	-	-	-	-	-	58 11.81 28.86 2.20 1.89	-	-	-	-	-	-	-	-	-	-
Orange (city)	12,404 10.04	11,552	1,144 9.90 9.90 9.22	-	-	60 7.19 5.24 0.52 0.48	-	-	74 5.67 6.47 0.64 0.60	-	155 7.82 13.55 1.34 1.25	-	-	-	-	50 6.66 4.37 0.43 0.40	186 11.52 16.26 1.61 1.50	-	-	-	-	-	23 4.98 2.01 0.20 0.19	-	-	526 13.91 45.98 4.55 4.24
Placentia (city)	4,052 8.66	5,247	142 2.71 2.71 3.50	-	-	0 0.00 0.00 0.00 0.00	-	-	81 7.09 57.04 1.54 2.00	-	21 2.74 14.79 0.40 0.52	-	-	-	-	24 5.16 16.90 0.46 0.59	0 0.00 0.00 0.00 0.00	-	-	-	-	-	-	-	-	16 1.71 11.27 0.30 0.39
Rancho Santa Margarita (city)	1,367 2.87	3,831	40 1.04 1.04 2.93	-	-	-	-	-	0 0.00 0.00 0.00 0.00	-	26 2.38 65.00 0.68 1.90	-	-	-	-	-	-	-	-	-	-	-	-	-	-	7 1.33 17.50 0.18 0.51
Rossmoor (cdp)	208 2.03	514	0 <0.01 <0.01 <0.01	-	-	-	-	-	-	-	-	-	-	-	-	-	-	-	-	-	-	-	-	-	-	-
Santa Ana (city)	65,268 19.85	29,448	3,756 12.75 12.75 5.75	1,248	90 7.21 7.21 0.14	57 10.69 1.52 0.19 0.09	-	357 21.05 9.50 1.21 0.55	303 15.05 8.07 1.03 0.46	-	269 12.06 7.16 0.91 0.41	-	-	39 7.39 1.04 0.13 0.06	-	60 7.20 1.60 0.20 0.09	156 24.34 4.15 0.53 0.24	129 13.34 3.43 0.44 0.20	-	-	29 4.24 32.22 2.32 0.04	-	-	-	-	2,296 12.05 61.13 7.80 3.52
Seal Beach (city)	1,330 5.54	1,244	51 4.10 4.10 3.83	-	-	-	-	-	-	-	-	-	-	-	-	11 3.00 21.57 0.88 0.83	-	-	-	-	-	-	-	-	-	-
Stanton (city)	6,514 17.98	5,717	741 12.96 12.96 11.38	-	-	-	-	-	-	-	39 3.26 5.26 0.68 0.60	-	-	-	-	-	137 17.41 18.49 2.40 2.10	-	-	-	-	-	-	-	-	479 17.58 64.64 8.38 7.35

Notes: Please refer to the User's Guide for an explanation of data; data is arranged alphabetically by state, then county, then city within each county; table includes counties with populations greater than 49,999 unless noted and cities with populations greater than 9,999 whose Asian and/or NHPI population rates are greater than the national average; (1) Native Hawaiian and other Pacific Islander; (2) excludes Taiwanese; (3) includes Chamorro; (4) county does not meet population threshold but is shown in order to allow inclusion of city

Place	Total population with income below poverty level	Asian population for whom poverty status is determined	Asians with income below poverty level	NHPI[1] population for whom poverty status is determined	NHPIs[1] with income below poverty level	Asian Indian	Bangladeshi	Cambodian	Chinese[2]	Fijian	Filipino	Guamanian[3]	Hawaiian, Native	Hmong	Indonesian	Japanese	Korean	Laotian	Malaysian	Pakistani	Samoan	Sri Lankan	Taiwanese	Thai	Tongan	Vietnamese
	5,689	9,336	766	-	-	63	-	-	69	-	116	-	-	-	-	93	52	-	-	-		-	39	-	-	207
	8.46		8.20			4.88			5.24		6.82					13.48	4.44						8.35			12.01
Tustin (city)						8.22			9.01		15.14					12.14	6.79						5.09			27.02
			8.20			0.67			0.74		1.24					1.00	0.56						0.42			2.22
			13.46			1.11			1.21		2.04					1.63	0.91						0.69			3.64
	783	1,707	79	-	-	-	-	-	15	-	-	-	-	-	-	-	-	-	-	-	-	-	-	-	-	-
	3.27		4.63						3.08																	
Tustin Foothills (cdp)									18.99																	
			4.63						0.88																	
			10.09						1.92																	
	11,757	33,220	5,967	435	84	20	-	-	211	-	87	-	-	-	-	41	129	-	-	-	84	-	-	-	-	5,312
	13.48		17.96		19.31	4.76			13.59		6.21					4.00	18.67				22.34					19.66
Westminster (city)						0.34			3.54		1.46					0.69	2.16				100.00					89.02
			17.96		19.31	0.06			0.64		0.26					0.12	0.39				19.31					15.99
			50.75		0.71	0.17			1.79		0.74					0.35	1.10				0.71					45.18
	1,756	6,399	200	-	-	0	-	-	36	-	9	-	-	-	-	49	0	-	-	-	-	-	-	-	-	29
	3.00		3.13			0.00			2.23		0.98					5.88	0.00									4.51
Yorba Linda (city)						0.00			18.00		4.50					24.50	0.00									14.50
			3.13			0.00			0.56		0.14					0.77	0.00									0.45
			11.39			0.00			2.05		0.51					2.79	0.00									1.65
	14,272	7,227	332	-	-	36	-	-	93	-	62	-	-	-	-	51	54	-	-	-	-	-	-	-	-	20
	5.81		4.59			4.19			7.05		3.17					2.81	11.18									4.49
Placer County						10.84			28.01		18.67					15.36	16.27									6.02
			4.59			0.50			1.29		0.86					0.71	0.75									0.28
			2.33			0.25			0.65		0.43					0.36	0.38									0.14
	1,639	1,314	57	-	-	-	-	-	-	-	-	-	-	-	-	0	-	-	-	-	-	-	-	-	-	-
	4.50		4.34													0.00										
Rocklin (city)																0.00										
			4.34													0.00										
			3.48													0.00										
	3,916	3,358	200	-	-	36	-	-	60	-	32	-	-	-	-	22	-	-	-	-	-	-	-	-	-	-
	4.95		5.96			5.64			8.72		3.24					4.36										
Roseville (city)						18.00			30.00		16.00					11.00										
			5.96			1.07			1.79		0.95					0.66										
			5.11			0.92			1.53		0.82					0.56										
	214,084	52,944	7,700	3,633	419	655	-	126	1,265	-	1,347	91	43	253	-	571	968	369	-	15	115	-	115	262	-	1,238
	14.17		14.54		11.53	11.87		21.95	22.84		7.05	10.01	5.51	51.95		13.02	17.39	24.87		3.64	12.46		26.56	29.91		20.76
Riverside County						8.51		1.64	16.43		17.49	21.72	10.26	3.29		7.42	12.57	4.79		0.19	27.45		1.49	3.40		16.08
			14.54		11.53	1.24		0.24	2.39		2.54	2.50	1.18	0.48		1.08	1.83	0.70		0.03	3.17		0.22	0.49		2.34
			3.60		0.20	0.31		0.06	0.59		0.63	0.04	0.02	0.12		0.27	0.45	0.17		0.01	0.05		0.05	0.12		0.58
	4,617	1,057	410	-	-	-	-	-	-	-	-	-	-	-	-	-	-	105	-	-	-	-	-	-	-	-
	19.94		38.79															30.79								
Banning (city)																		25.61								
			38.79															9.93								
			8.88															2.27								
	10,244	9,258	493	-	-	16	-	-	67	-	73	-	-	-	-	48	148	-	-	-	-	-	-	-	-	58
	8.27		5.33			1.06			7.55		2.42					8.03	12.05									4.06
Corona (city)						3.25			13.59		14.81					9.74	30.02									11.76
			5.33			0.17			0.72		0.79					0.52	1.60									0.63
			4.81			0.16			0.65		0.71					0.47	1.44									0.57

Notes: Please refer to the User's Guide for an explanation of data; data is arranged alphabetically by state, then county, then city within each county; table includes counties with populations greater than 49,999 unless noted and cities with populations greater than 9,999 whose Asian and/or NHPI population rates are greater than the national average; (1) Native Hawaiian and other Pacific Islander; (2) excludes Taiwanese; (3) includes Chamorro; (4) county does not meet population threshold but is shown in order to allow inclusion of city

Place	Total population with income below poverty level	Asian population for whom poverty status is determined	Asians with income below poverty level	NHPI[1] population for whom poverty status is determined	NHPIs[1] with income below poverty level	Asian Indian	Bangladeshi	Cambodian	Chinese[2]	Fijian	Filipino	Guamanian[3]	Hawaiian, Native	Hmong	Indonesian	Japanese	Korean	Laotian	Malaysian	Pakistani	Samoan	Sri Lankan	Taiwanese	Thai	Tongan	Vietnamese
Moreno Valley (city)	20,141 14.23	7,953	1,055 13.27 13.27 5.24	-	-	-	-	-	85 18.36 8.06 1.07 0.42	-	263 6.67 24.93 3.31 1.31	-	-	-	-	57 11.42 5.40 0.72 0.28	84 12.43 7.96 1.06 0.42	172 35.25 16.30 2.16 0.85	-	-	-	-	-	-	-	215 35.71 20.38 2.70 1.07
Palm Springs (city)	6,402 15.09	1,748	91 5.21 5.21 1.42	-	-	-	-	-	-	-	25 2.19 27.47 1.43 0.39	-	-	-	-	-	-	-	-	-	-	-	-	-	-	-
Pedley (cdp)	946 8.68	459	36 7.84 7.84 3.81	-	-	-	-	-	-	-	-	-	-	-	-	-	-	-	-	-	-	-	-	-	-	-
Riverside (city)	39,060 15.75	13,004	3,753 28.86 28.86 9.61	1,051	151 14.37 14.37 0.39	402 28.98 10.71 3.09 1.03	-	-	943 47.82 25.13 7.25 2.41	-	505 17.36 13.46 3.88 1.29	-	-	-	-	290 26.95 7.73 2.23 0.74	440 25.88 11.72 3.38 1.13	88 25.88 2.34 0.68 0.23	-	-	-	-	-	-	-	546 25.07 14.55 4.20 1.40
Temecula (city)	3,864 6.74	2,668	111 4.16 4.16 2.87	-	-	-	-	-	0 0.00 0.00 0.00 0.00	-	47 3.41 42.34 1.76 1.22	-	-	-	-	-	-	-	-	-	-	-	-	-	-	-
Sacramento County	169,784 14.13	134,000	27,499 20.52 20.52 16.20	6,222	1,379 22.16 22.16 0.81	1,363 10.75 4.96 1.02 0.80	-	456 41.08 1.66 0.34 0.27	4,666 16.34 16.97 3.48 2.75	373 21.35 27.05 5.99 0.22	1,996 8.37 7.26 1.49 1.18	112 12.80 8.12 1.80 0.07	89 13.73 6.45 1.43 0.05	8,330 48.18 30.29 6.22 4.91	-	739 6.04 2.69 0.55 0.44	478 10.28 1.74 0.36 0.28	3,233 33.83 11.76 2.41 1.90	-	342 23.82 1.24 0.26 0.20	500 40.65 36.26 8.04 0.29	-	29 7.14 0.11 0.02 0.02	138 19.17 0.50 0.10 0.08	137 18.87 9.93 2.20 0.08	4,882 29.67 17.75 3.64 2.88
Arden-Arcade (cdp)	12,958 13.72	4,732	779 16.46 16.46 6.01	-	-	117 16.30 15.02 2.47 0.90	-	-	158 18.02 20.28 3.34 1.22	-	98 8.94 12.58 2.07 0.76	-	-	31 8.83 3.98 0.66 0.24	-	87 17.40 11.17 1.84 0.67	-	-	-	-	-	-	-	-	-	146 36.59 18.74 3.09 1.13
Elk Grove (cdp)	3,073 5.16	10,529	1,104 10.49 10.49 35.93	-	-	56 3.88 5.07 0.53 1.82	-	-	97 6.57 8.79 0.92 3.16	-	186 5.49 16.85 1.77 6.05	-	-	-	-	16 3.52 1.45 0.15 0.52	-	-	-	-	-	-	-	-	-	582 26.81 52.72 5.53 18.94
Fair Oaks (cdp)	1,790 6.46	1,196	112 9.36 9.36 6.26	-	-	-	-	-	-	-	-	-	-	-	-	-	-	-	-	-	-	-	-	-	-	-
Florin (cdp)	5,892 21.68	5,495	1,869 34.01 34.01 31.72	-	-	35 11.48 1.87 0.64 0.59	-	-	314 46.80 16.80 5.71 5.33	-	129 13.68 6.90 2.35 2.19	-	-	541 50.99 28.95 9.85 9.18	-	-	-	-	-	-	-	-	-	-	-	472 36.25 25.25 8.59 8.01

Notes: Please refer to the User's Guide for an explanation of data; data is arranged alphabetically by state, then county, then city within each county; table includes counties with populations greater than 49,999 unless noted and cities with populations greater than 9,999 whose Asian and/or NHPI population rates are greater than the national average; (1) Native Hawaiian and other Pacific Islander; (2) excludes Taiwanese; (3) includes Chamorro; (4) county does not meet population threshold but is shown in order to allow inclusion of city

Place	Total population with income below poverty level	Asian population for whom poverty status is determined	Asians with income below poverty level	NHPI[1] population for whom poverty status is determined	NHPIs[1] with income below poverty level	Asian Indian	Bangladeshi	Cambodian	Chinese[2]	Fijian	Filipino	Guamanian[3]	Hawaiian, Native	Hmong	Indonesian	Japanese	Korean	Laotian	Malaysian	Pakistani	Samoan	Sri Lankan	Taiwanese	Thai	Tongan	Vietnamese
Folsom (city)	3,541	3,569	116	-	-	53	-	-	40	-	6	-	-	-	-	-	-	-	-	-	-	-	-	-	-	-
	7.30		3.25			3.91			6.99		0.95															
						45.69			34.48		5.17															
			3.25			1.49			1.12		0.17															
			3.28			1.50			1.13		0.17															
Foothill Farms (cdp)	2,216	788	132	-	-	-	-	-	-	-	-	-	-	-	-	-	-	-	-	-	-	-	-	-	-	-
	12.83		16.75																							
			16.75																							
			5.96																							
La Riviera (cdp)	1,068	883	134	-	-	-	-	-	-	-	-	-	-	-	-	-	-	-	-	-	-	-	-	-	-	-
	10.54		15.18																							
			15.18																							
			12.55																							
Laguna (cdp)	1,481	6,223	545	-	-	0	-	-	239	-	78	-	-	-	-	0	-	-	-	-	-	-	-	-	-	188
	4.33		8.76			0.00			12.26		4.29					0.00										37.23
						0.00			43.85		14.31					0.00										34.50
			8.76			0.00			3.84		1.25					0.00										3.02
			36.80			0.00			16.14		5.27					0.00										12.69
North Highlands (cdp)	9,854	2,451	423	-	-	-	-	-	-	-	74	-	-	-	-	-	-	-	-	-	-	-	-	-	-	168
	22.79		17.26								9.06															26.21
											17.49															39.72
			17.26								3.02															6.85
			4.29								0.75															1.70
Parkway-S. Sacramento (cdp)	10,394	6,710	3,183	-	-	-	-	-	281	-	-	-	-	1,835	-	-	-	515	-	-	-	-	-	-	-	316
	28.65		47.44						53.42					66.73				37.13								28.70
									8.83					57.65				16.18								9.93
			47.44						4.19					27.35				7.68								4.71
			30.62						2.70					17.65				4.95								3.04
Rancho Cordova (cdp)	8,649	4,375	612	-	-	0	-	-	127	-	45	-	-	-	-	-	84	-	-	-	-	-	-	-	-	161
	15.99		13.99			0.00			26.19		4.44						19.63									19.17
						0.00			20.75		7.35						13.73									26.31
			13.99			0.00			2.90		1.03						1.92									3.68
			7.08			0.00			1.47		0.52						0.97									1.86
Rosemont (cdp)	2,534	2,646	342	-	-	-	-	-	-	-	94	-	-	-	-	-	45	-	-	-	-	-	-	-	-	69
	11.36		12.93								21.61						9.41									13.14
											27.49						13.16									20.18
			12.93								3.55						1.70									2.61
			13.50								3.71						1.78									2.72
Sacramento (city)	79,737	66,876	16,663	3,661	978	871	-	172	3,077	213	940	-	-	5,557	-	349	130	2,221	-	234	389	-	-	-	123	2,478
	19.99		24.92		26.71	21.55		36.13	16.30	17.23	11.69			46.14		5.23	19.17	35.59		30.04	53.07				21.73	38.48
						5.23		1.03	18.47	21.78	5.64			33.35		2.09	0.78	13.33		1.40	39.78				12.58	14.87
			24.92		26.71	1.30		0.26	4.60	5.82	1.41			8.31		0.52	0.19	3.32		0.35	10.63				3.36	3.71
			20.90		1.23	1.09		0.22	3.86	0.27	1.18			6.97		0.44	0.16	2.79		0.29	0.49				0.15	3.11
Vineyard (cdp)	318	1,618	47	-	-	-	-	-	-	-	0	-	-	-	-	-	-	-	-	-	-	-	-	-	-	-
	3.19		2.90								0.00															
											0.00															
			2.90								0.00															
			14.78								0.00															

Notes: Please refer to the User's Guide for an explanation of data; data is arranged alphabetically by state, then county, then city within each county; table includes counties with populations greater than 49,999 unless noted and cities with populations greater than 9,999 whose Asian and/or NHPI population rates are greater than the national average; (1) Native Hawaiian and other Pacific Islander; (2) excludes Taiwanese; (3) includes Chamorro; (4) county does not meet population threshold but is shown in order to allow inclusion of city

Place	Total population with income below poverty level	Asian population for whom poverty status is determined	Asians with income below poverty level	NHPI[1] population for whom poverty status is determined	NHPIs[1] with income below poverty level	Asian Indian	Bangladeshi	Cambodian	Chinese[2]	Fijian	Filipino	Guamanian[3]	Hawaiian, Native	Hmong	Indonesian	Japanese	Korean	Laotian	Malaysian	Pakistani	Samoan	Sri Lankan	Taiwanese	Thai	Tongan	Vietnamese
San Benito County	5,241	1,021	47	-	-	-	-	-	-	-	35	-	-	-	-	-	-	-	-	-	-	-	-	-	-	-
	9.95		4.60								6.68															
											74.47															
			4.60								3.43															
			0.90								0.67															
San Bernardino County	263,412	77,935	10,625	4,835	1,053	734	-	737	1,321	-	1,701	50	73	-	424	356	1,086	116	-	141	577	-	323	209	253	2,894
	15.84		13.63		21.78	9.31		43.12	12.55		6.76	4.83	12.76		12.86	8.38	15.38	26.07		20.64	29.60		15.93	12.35	31.74	28.38
						6.91		6.94	12.43		16.01	4.75	6.93		3.99	3.35	10.22	1.09		1.33	54.80		3.04	1.97	24.03	27.24
			13.63		21.78	0.94		0.95	1.70		2.18	1.03	1.51		0.54	0.46	1.39	0.15		0.18	11.93		0.41	0.27	5.23	3.71
			4.03		0.40	0.28		0.28	0.50		0.65	0.02	0.03		0.16	0.14	0.41	0.04		0.05	0.22		0.12	0.08	0.10	1.10
Chino (city)	4,976	3,228	356	-	-	-	-	-	-	-	76	-	-	-	-	-	-	-	-	-	-	-	-	-	-	74
	8.34		11.03								5.09															15.81
											21.35															20.79
			11.03								2.35															2.29
			7.15								1.53															1.49
Chino Hills (city)	3,419	14,223	759	-	-	30	-	-	156	-	154	-	-	-	-	7	50	-	-	-	-	-	136	-	-	157
	5.15		5.34			2.55			4.51		2.77					1.27	4.78						21.45			19.77
						3.95			20.55		20.29					0.92	6.59						17.92			20.69
			5.34			0.21			1.10		1.08					0.05	0.35						0.96			1.10
			22.20			0.88			4.56		4.50					0.20	1.46						3.98			4.59
Colton (city)	9,343	2,440	437	-	-	-	-	-	-	-	136	-	-	-	-	-	-	-	-	-	-	-	-	-	-	-
	19.63		17.91								23.09															
											31.12															
			17.91								5.57															
			4.68								1.46															
Fontana (city)	18,676	5,892	443	577	6	141	-	-	-	-	151	-	-	-	-	-	-	-	-	-	-	-	-	-	-	-
	14.68		7.52		1.04	21.43					5.07															
						31.83					34.09															
			7.52		1.04	2.39					2.56															
			2.37		0.03	0.75					0.81															
Grand Terrace (city)	861	586	27	-	-	-	-	-	-	-	-	-	-	-	-	-	-	-	-	-	-	-	-	-	-	-
	7.38		4.61																							
			4.61																							
			3.14																							
Highland (city)	9,523	2,820	614	-	-	-	-	-	-	-	67	-	-	-	-	-	-	-	-	-	-	-	-	-	-	249
	21.46		21.77								7.01															41.64
											10.91															40.55
			21.77								2.38															8.83
			6.45								0.70															2.61
Loma Linda (city)	2,735	4,331	677	-	-	24	-	-	83	-	111	-	-	-	51	-	170	-	-	-	-	-	-	-	-	-
	15.12		15.63			5.94			11.76		10.65				9.77		21.14									
						3.55			12.26		16.40				7.53		25.11									
			15.63			0.55			1.92		2.56				1.18		3.93									
			24.75			0.88			3.03		4.06				1.86		6.22									
Montclair (city)	5,690	2,622	585	-	-	-	-	-	-	-	-	-	-	-	-	-	-	-	-	-	-	-	-	-	-	374
	17.41		22.31																							30.71
																										63.93
			22.31																							14.26
			10.28																							6.57

Notes: Please refer to the User's Guide for an explanation of data; data is arranged alphabetically by state, then county, then city within each county; table includes counties with populations greater than 49,999 unless noted and cities with populations greater than 9,999 whose Asian and/or NHPI population rates are greater than the national average; (1) Native Hawaiian and other Pacific Islander; (2) excludes Taiwanese; (3) includes Chamorro; (4) county does not meet population threshold but is shown in order to allow inclusion of city

Place	Total population with income below poverty level	Asian population for whom poverty status is determined	Asians with income below poverty level	NHPI[1] population for whom poverty status is determined	NHPIs[1] with income below poverty level	Asian Indian	Bangladeshi	Cambodian	Chinese[2]	Fijian	Filipino	Guamanian[3]	Hawaiian, Native	Hmong	Indonesian	Japanese	Korean	Laotian	Malaysian	Pakistani	Samoan	Sri Lankan	Taiwanese	Thai	Tongan	Vietnamese
	24,133	6,080	575	544	248	14	-	-	75	-	71	-	-	-	-	-	-	-	-	-	-	-	-	-	-	233
	15.51		9.46		45.59	2.84			16.20		3.08															14.58
Ontario (city)						2.43			13.04		12.35															40.52
			9.46		45.59	0.23			1.23		1.17															3.83
			2.38		1.03	0.06			0.31		0.29															0.97
	8,955	7,309	585	-	-	24	-	-	229	-	15	-	-	-	-	10	139	-	-	-	-	-	-	-	-	100
	7.14		8.00			2.44			17.12		0.69					1.90	18.58									19.46
Rancho Cucamonga (city)						4.10			39.15		2.56					1.71	23.76									17.09
			8.00			0.33			3.13		0.21					0.14	1.90									1.37
			6.53			0.27			2.56		0.17					0.11	1.55									1.12
	6,492	3,219	330	-	-	0	-	-	51	-	29	-	-	-	-	-	68	-	-	-	-	-	-	-	-	-
	10.54		10.25			0.00			10.56		4.60						12.50									
Redlands (city)						0.00			15.45		8.79						20.61									
			10.25			0.00			1.58		0.90						2.11									
			5.08			0.00			0.79		0.45						1.05									
	15,778	1,742	118	532	30	-	-	-	-	-	27	-	-	-	-	-	-	-	-	-	-	-	-	-	-	-
	17.39		6.77		5.64						5.50															
Rialto (city)											22.88															
			6.77		5.64						1.55															
			0.75		0.19						0.17															
	49,691	7,251	2,215	709	134	250	-	225	237	-	132	-	-	-	186	-	123	-	-	-	116	-	-	-	-	643
	27.59		30.55		18.90	28.34		51.25	40.37		7.69				41.89		32.20				26.42					43.33
San Bernardino (city)						11.29		10.16	10.70		5.96				8.40		5.55				86.57					29.03
			30.55		18.90	3.45		3.10	3.27		1.82				2.57		1.70				16.36					8.87
			4.46		0.27	0.50		0.45	0.48		0.27				0.37		0.25				0.23					1.29
	8,106	4,990	1,030	-	-	28	-	-	95	-	77	-	-	-	-	-	167	-	-	-	-	-	45	-	-	470
	11.96		20.64			4.86			13.53		13.58						17.31						9.62			55.36
Upland (city)						2.72			9.22		7.48						16.21						4.37			45.63
			20.64			0.56			1.90		1.54						3.35						0.90			9.42
			12.71			0.35			1.17		0.95						2.06						0.56			5.80
	11,885	2,356	367	-	-	-	-	-	-	-	216	-	-	-	-	-	-	-	-	-	-	-	-	-	-	-
	18.71		15.58								18.14															
Victorville (city)											58.86															
			15.58								9.17															
			3.09								1.82															
	338,399	243,365	27,844	13,136	1,398	1,161	-	1,959	2,966	-	6,954	367	201	312	90	2,681	2,094	1,431	-	53	613	-	326	256	92	6,479
	12.43		11.44		10.64	12.55		46.94	10.67		5.85	8.13	9.31	23.51	18.99	14.47	19.35	20.36		9.94	12.59		14.03	19.91	21.55	19.07
San Diego County						4.17		7.04	10.65		24.97	26.25	14.38	1.12	0.32	9.63	7.52	5.14		0.19	43.85		1.17	0.92	6.58	23.27
			11.44		10.64	0.48		0.80	1.22		2.86	2.79	1.53	0.13	0.04	1.10	0.86	0.59		0.02	4.67		0.13	0.11	0.70	2.66
			8.23		0.41	0.34		0.58	0.88		2.05	0.11	0.06	0.09	0.03	0.79	0.62	0.42		0.02	0.18		0.10	0.08	0.03	1.91
	448	994	32	-	-	-	-	-	-	-	0	-	-	-	-	-	-	-	-	-	-	-	-	-	-	-
	3.74		3.22								0.00															
Bonita (cdp)											0.00															
			3.22								0.00															
			7.14								0.00															
	4,576	3,177	211	-	-	-	-	-	7	-	54	-	-	-	-	22	-	-	-	-	-	-	-	-	-	-
	5.93		6.64						0.98		8.72					4.61										
Carlsbad (city)									3.32		25.59					10.43										
			6.64						0.22		1.70					0.69										
			4.61						0.15		1.18					0.48										

Notes: Please refer to the User's Guide for an explanation of data; data is arranged alphabetically by state, then county, then city within each county; table includes counties with populations greater than 49,999 unless noted and cities with populations greater than 9,999 whose Asian and/or NHPI population rates are greater than the national average; (1) Native Hawaiian and other Pacific Islander; (2) excludes Taiwanese; (3) includes Chamorro; (4) county does not meet population threshold but is shown in order to allow inclusion of city

Place	Total population with income below poverty level	Asian population for whom poverty status is determined	Asians with income below poverty level	NHPI[1] population for whom poverty status is determined	NHPIs[1] with income below poverty level	Asian Indian	Bangladeshi	Cambodian	Chinese[2]	Fijian	Filipino	Guamanian[3]	Hawaiian, Native	Hmong	Indonesian	Japanese	Korean	Laotian	Malaysian	Pakistani	Samoan	Sri Lankan	Taiwanese	Thai	Tongan	Vietnamese
Chula Vista (city)	18,357 10.64	18,779	1,064 5.67 5.67 5.80	750	58 7.73 7.73 0.32	-	-	-	18 1.69 1.69 0.10 0.10	-	655 5.03 61.56 3.49 3.57	38 8.94 65.52 5.07 0.21	-	-	-	130 6.43 12.22 0.69 0.71	159 11.29 14.94 0.85 0.87	-	-	-	-	-	-	-	-	-
Coronado (city)	881 4.98	529	75 14.18 14.18 8.51	-	-	-	-	-	-	-	41 17.98 54.67 7.75 4.65	-	-	-	-	-	-	-	-	-	-	-	-	-	-	-
Escondido (city)	17,759 13.44	5,531	538 9.73 9.73 3.03	-	-	-	-	-	30 6.93 5.58 0.54 0.17	-	72 3.54 13.38 1.30 0.41	-	-	-	-	-	-	124 25.89 23.05 2.24 0.70	-	-	-	-	-	-	-	122 9.63 22.68 2.21 0.69
Imperial Beach (city)	5,048 18.79	1,821	229 12.58 12.58 4.54	-	-	-	-	-	-	-	186 12.35 81.22 10.21 3.68	-	-	-	-	-	-	-	-	-	-	-	-	-	-	-
La Mesa (city)	5,062 9.42	2,238	451 20.15 20.15 8.91	-	-	-	-	-	-	-	55 9.75 12.20 2.46 1.09	-	-	-	-	-	-	-	-	-	-	-	-	-	-	-
La Presa (cdp)	3,475 10.68	3,389	137 4.04 4.04 3.94	-	-	-	-	-	-	-	99 3.24 72.26 2.92 2.85	-	-	-	-	-	-	-	-	-	-	-	-	-	-	-
Lemon Grove (city)	3,375 13.73	1,432	170 11.87 11.87 5.04	-	-	-	-	-	-	-	19 2.66 11.18 1.33 0.56	-	-	-	-	-	-	-	-	-	-	-	-	-	-	62 17.13 36.47 4.33 1.84
National City (city)	11,233 21.96	9,709	1,142 11.76 11.76 10.17	-	-	-	-	-	-	-	1,012 11.38 88.62 10.42 9.01	-	-	-	-	-	-	-	-	-	-	-	-	-	-	-
Oceanside (city)	18,492 11.59	8,964	461 5.14 5.14 2.49	2,274	123 5.41 5.41 0.67	-	-	-	39 7.80 8.46 0.44 0.21	-	113 2.15 24.51 1.26 0.61	-	-	-	-	102 8.58 22.13 1.14 0.55	-	-	-	-	84 5.48 68.29 3.69 0.45	-	-	-	-	129 15.14 27.98 1.44 0.70
Poway (city)	2,044 4.28	3,442	146 4.24 4.24 7.14	-	-	-	-	-	27 3.96 18.49 0.78 1.32	-	34 2.49 23.29 0.99 1.66	-	-	-	-	-	-	-	-	-	-	-	-	-	-	-

Notes: Please refer to the User's Guide for an explanation of data; data is arranged alphabetically by state, then county, then city within each county; table includes counties with populations greater than 49,999 unless noted and cities with populations greater than 9,999 whose Asian and/or NHPI population rates are greater than the national average; (1) Native Hawaiian and other Pacific Islander; (2) excludes Taiwanese; (3) includes Chamorro; (4) county does not meet population threshold but is shown in order to allow inclusion of city

Place	Total population with income below poverty level	Asian population for whom poverty status is determined	Asians with income below poverty level	NHPI[1] population for whom poverty status is determined	NHPIs[1] with income below poverty level	Asian Indian	Bangladeshi	Cambodian	Chinese[2]	Fijian	Filipino	Guamanian[3]	Hawaiian, Native	Hmong	Indonesian	Japanese	Korean	Laotian	Malaysian	Pakistani	Samoan	Sri Lankan	Taiwanese	Thai	Tongan	Vietnamese
Rancho San Diego (cdp)	915 4.58	1,003	75 7.48 7.48 8.20	-	-	-	-	-	-	-	36 6.59 48.00 3.59 3.93	-	-	-	-	-	-	-	-	-	-	-	-	-	-	-
San Diego (city)	172,527 14.60	162,737	21,355 13.12 13.12 12.38	5,985	738 12.33 12.33 0.43	970 15.73 4.54 0.60 0.56	-	1,951 51.01 9.14 1.20 1.13	2,528 12.06 11.84 1.55 1.47	-	4,070 5.59 19.06 2.50 2.36	170 8.51 23.04 2.84 0.10	153 14.06 20.73 2.56 0.09	244 22.98 1.14 0.15 0.14	-	1,715 17.17 8.03 1.05 0.99	1,524 23.79 7.14 0.94 0.88	1,206 20.19 5.65 0.74 0.70	-	-	392 18.52 53.12 6.55 0.23	-	205 13.24 0.96 0.13 0.12	185 22.92 0.87 0.11 0.11	-	5,792 20.50 27.12 3.56 3.36
San Marcos (city)	6,592 12.03	2,463	146 5.93 5.93 2.21	-	-	-	-	-	0 0.00 0.00 0.00 0.00	-	51 4.07 34.93 2.07 0.77	-	-	-	-	-	-	-	-	-	-	-	-	-	-	-
Solana Beach (city)	856 6.69	515	50 9.71 9.71 5.84	-	-	-	-	-	-	-	-	-	-	-	-	-	-	-	-	-	-	-	-	-	-	-
Spring Valley (cdp)	2,284 8.63	1,361	91 6.69 6.69 3.98	-	-	-	-	-	-	-	27 4.29 29.67 1.98 1.18	-	-	-	-	-	-	-	-	-	-	-	-	-	-	-
Vista (city)	12,533 14.23	3,142	501 15.95 15.95 4.00	574	107 18.64 18.64 0.85	-	-	-	-	-	116 9.89 23.15 3.69 0.93	-	-	-	-	222 37.69 44.31 7.07 1.77	-	-	-	-	-	-	-	-	-	-
San Francisco County	86,585 11.31	238,054	25,485 10.71 10.71 29.43	3,494	944 27.02 27.02 1.09	643 13.42 2.52 0.27 0.74	-	173 26.78 0.68 0.07 0.20	15,271 9.94 59.92 6.41 17.64	-	2,952 7.43 11.58 1.24 3.41	-	-	-	233 26.69 0.91 0.10 0.27	1,575 14.77 6.18 0.66 1.82	1,053 14.94 4.13 0.44 1.22	-	-	42 7.55 0.16 0.02 0.05	767 34.20 81.25 21.95 0.89	-	160 21.71 0.63 0.07 0.18	357 24.44 1.40 0.15 0.41	-	2,205 21.37 8.65 0.93 2.55
San Francisco (city)	86,585 11.31	238,054	25,485 10.71 10.71 29.43	3,494	944 27.02 27.02 1.09	643 13.42 2.52 0.27 0.74	-	173 26.78 0.68 0.07 0.20	15,271 9.94 59.92 6.41 17.64	-	2,952 7.43 11.58 1.24 3.41	-	-	-	233 26.69 0.91 0.10 0.27	1,575 14.77 6.18 0.66 1.82	1,053 14.94 4.13 0.44 1.22	-	-	42 7.55 0.16 0.02 0.05	767 34.20 81.25 21.95 0.89	-	160 21.71 0.63 0.07 0.18	357 24.44 1.40 0.15 0.41	-	2,205 21.37 8.65 0.93 2.55
San Joaquin County	97,105 17.74	64,238	18,271 28.44 28.44 18.82	1,758	259 14.73 14.73 0.27	603 11.75 3.30 0.94 0.62	-	5,627 59.80 30.80 8.76 5.79	652 11.68 3.57 1.01 0.67	-	1,845 8.80 10.10 2.87 1.90	-	72 17.35 27.80 4.10 0.07	3,441 58.07 18.83 5.36 3.54	-	371 10.58 2.03 0.58 0.38	147 17.75 0.80 0.23 0.15	1,395 45.77 7.64 2.17 1.44	-	511 38.45 2.80 0.80 0.53	52 14.44 20.08 2.96 0.05	-	-	-	-	3,003 47.96 16.44 4.67 3.09
Lathrop (city)	957 9.33	1,439	57 3.96 3.96 5.96	-	-	-	-	-	-	-	57 5.49 100.00 3.96 5.96	-	-	-	-	-	-	-	-	-	-	-	-	-	-	-

Notes: Please refer to the User's Guide for an explanation of data; data is arranged alphabetically by state, then county, then city within each county; table includes counties with populations greater than 49,999 unless noted and cities with populations greater than 9,999 whose Asian and/or NHPI population rates are greater than the national average; (1) Native Hawaiian and other Pacific Islander; (2) excludes Taiwanese; (3) includes Chamorro; (4) county does not meet population threshold but is shown in order to allow inclusion of city

Place	Total population with income below poverty level	Asian population for whom poverty status is determined	Asians with income below poverty level	NHPI[1] population for whom poverty status is determined	NHPIs[1] with income below poverty level	Asian Indian	Bangladeshi	Cambodian	Chinese[2]	Fijian	Filipino	Guamanian[3]	Hawaiian, Native	Hmong	Indonesian	Japanese	Korean	Laotian	Malaysian	Pakistani	Samoan	Sri Lankan	Taiwanese	Thai	Tongan	Vietnamese
Lodi (city)	9,374 16.73	3,084	787 25.52 25.52 8.40	-	-	208 27.08 26.43 6.74 2.22	-	-	-	-	66 10.54 8.39 2.14 0.70	-	-	-	-	79 12.08 10.04 2.56 0.84	-	-	-	-	-	-	-	-	-	-
Stockton (city)	56,783 23.86	48,155	16,113 33.46 33.46 28.38	1,022	157 15.36 15.36 0.28	297 14.38 1.84 0.62 0.52	-	5,484 60.52 34.03 11.39 9.66	542 12.85 3.36 1.13 0.95	-	1,488 9.95 9.23 3.09 2.62	-	-	2,886 58.53 17.91 5.99 5.08	-	190 12.13 1.18 0.39 0.33	-	1,367 46.56 8.48 2.84 2.41	-	217 31.27 1.35 0.45 0.38	-	-	-	-	-	2,980 52.26 18.49 6.19 5.25
Tracy (city)	3,928 6.96	4,742	134 2.83 2.83 3.41	-	-	34 2.99 25.37 0.72 0.87	-	-	16 4.34 11.94 0.34 0.41	-	25 1.26 18.66 0.53 0.64	-	-	-	-	-	-	-	-	-	-	-	-	-	-	-
San Luis Obispo County	29,775 12.84	6,199	1,365 22.02 22.02 4.58	-	-	107 18.10 7.84 1.73 0.36	-	-	424 42.02 31.06 6.84 1.42	-	357 15.20 26.15 5.76 1.20	-	-	-	-	251 25.43 18.39 4.05 0.84	77 10.91 5.64 1.24 0.26	-	-	-	-	-	-	-	-	-
Baywood-Los Osos (cdp)	1,205 8.54	829	77 9.29 9.29 6.39	-	-	-	-	-	-	-	56 9.84 72.73 6.76 4.65	-	-	-	-	-	-	-	-	-	-	-	-	-	-	-
Grover Beach (city)	1,469 11.35	501	7 1.40 1.40 0.48	-	-	-	-	-	-	-	-	-	-	-	-	-	-	-	-	-	-	-	-	-	-	-
San Luis Obispo (city)	11,407 26.64	2,210	1,020 46.15 46.15 8.94	-	-	-	-	-	304 55.99 29.80 13.76 2.67	-	265 50.48 25.98 11.99 2.32	-	-	-	-	-	-	-	-	-	-	-	-	-	-	-
San Mateo County	40,692 5.83	141,274	6,779 4.80 4.80 16.66	8,441	788 9.34 9.34 1.94	735 6.66 10.84 0.52 1.81	-	-	2,534 5.36 37.38 1.79 6.23	72 6.22 9.14 0.85 0.18	1,946 3.27 28.71 1.38 4.78	0 0.00 0.00 0.00 0.00	87 10.86 11.04 1.03 0.21	-	112 14.81 1.65 0.08 0.28	447 4.75 6.59 0.32 1.10	464 10.67 6.84 0.33 1.14	-	-	-	213 14.96 27.03 2.52 0.52	-	28 3.64 0.41 0.02 0.07	27 3.85 0.40 0.02 0.07	213 5.88 27.03 2.52 0.52	213 7.70 3.14 0.15 0.52
Belmont (city)	991 4.02	3,853	196 5.09 5.09 19.78	-	-	31 4.29 15.82 0.80 3.13	-	-	98 5.85 50.00 2.54 9.89	-	5 0.80 2.55 0.13 0.50	-	-	-	-	31 7.13 15.82 0.80 3.13	-	-	-	-	-	-	-	-	-	-
Burlingame (city)	1,570 5.70	3,718	461 12.40 12.40 29.36	-	-	-	-	-	257 14.01 55.75 6.91 16.37	-	33 6.00 7.16 0.89 2.10	-	-	-	-	0 0.00 0.00 0.00 0.00	-	-	-	-	-	-	-	-	-	-

Notes: Please refer to the User's Guide for an explanation of data; data is arranged alphabetically by state, then county, then city within each county; table includes counties with populations greater than 49,999 unless noted and cities with populations greater than 9,999 whose Asian and/or NHPI population rates are greater than the national average; (1) Native Hawaiian and other Pacific Islander; (2) excludes Taiwanese; (3) includes Chamorro; (4) county does not meet population threshold but is shown in order to allow inclusion of city

Place	Total population with income below poverty level	Asian population for whom poverty status is determined	Asians with income below poverty level	NHPI[1] population for whom poverty status is determined	NHPIs[1] with income below poverty level	Asian Indian	Bangladeshi	Cambodian	Chinese[2]	Fijian	Filipino	Guamanian[3]	Hawaiian, Native	Hmong	Indonesian	Japanese	Korean	Laotian	Malaysian	Pakistani	Samoan	Sri Lankan	Taiwanese	Thai	Tongan	Vietnamese
Daly City (city)	7,265 7.08	51,984	2,549 4.90 4.90 35.09	861	66 7.67 7.67 0.91	143 13.72 5.61 0.28 1.97	-	-	635 4.64 24.91 1.22 8.74	-	1,231 3.76 48.29 2.37 16.94	-	-	-	-	92 11.21 3.61 0.18 1.27	147 18.54 5.77 0.28 2.02	-	-	-	-	-	-	-	-	85 9.33 3.33 0.16 1.17
East Palo Alto (city)	4,658 16.17	563	54 9.59 9.59 1.16	2,186	151 6.91 6.91 3.24	-	-	-	-	-	-	-	-	-	-	-	-	-	-	-	-	-	-	-	60 4.08 39.74 2.74 1.29	-
Foster City (city)	820 2.86	9,372	360 3.84 3.84 43.90	-	-	26 1.46 7.22 0.28 3.17	-	-	273 6.45 75.83 2.91 33.29	-	61 7.67 16.94 0.65 7.44	-	-	-	-	0 0.00 0.00 0.00 0.00	0 0.00 0.00 0.00 0.00	-	-	-	-	-	-	-	-	-
Hillsborough (town)	299 2.76	2,702	109 4.03 4.03 36.45	-	-	-	-	-	43 2.16 39.45 1.59 14.38	-	-	-	-	-	-	-	-	-	-	-	-	-	-	-	-	-
Menlo Park (city)	2,059 6.85	2,122	142 6.69 6.69 6.90	-	-	-	-	-	42 4.88 29.58 1.98 2.04	-	-	-	-	-	-	29 6.40 20.42 1.37 1.41	-	-	-	-	-	-	-	-	-	-
Millbrae (city)	693 3.40	5,856	249 4.25 4.25 35.93	-	-	6 1.61 2.41 0.10 0.87	-	-	171 4.48 68.67 2.92 24.68	-	18 2.79 7.23 0.31 2.60	-	-	-	-	4 0.99 1.61 0.07 0.58	33 10.31 13.25 0.56 4.76	-	-	-	-	-	-	-	-	-
Pacifica (city)	1,112 2.92	5,855	117 2.00 2.00 10.52	-	-	-	-	-	45 2.98 38.46 0.77 4.05	-	21 0.65 17.95 0.36 1.89	-	-	-	-	0 0.00 0.00 0.00 0.00	-	-	-	-	-	-	-	-	-	-
Redwood City (city)	4,418 5.99	6,833	309 4.52 4.52 6.99	566	58 10.25 10.25 1.31	73 5.84 23.62 1.07 1.65	-	-	59 2.32 19.09 0.86 1.34	-	49 3.56 15.86 0.72 1.11	-	-	-	-	26 4.37 8.41 0.38 0.59	-	-	-	-	-	-	-	-	-	-
San Bruno (city)	1,774 4.44	7,487	289 3.86 3.86 16.29	1,017	50 4.92 4.92 2.82	65 6.18 22.49 0.87 3.66	-	-	139 6.44 48.10 1.86 7.84	-	12 0.39 4.15 0.16 0.68	-	-	-	-	9 1.86 3.11 0.12 0.51	-	-	-	-	-	-	-	-	35 6.57 70.00 3.44 1.97	-
San Carlos (city)	744 2.70	1,841	51 2.77 2.77 6.85	-	-	-	-	-	44 6.27 86.27 2.39 5.91	-	-	-	-	-	-	-	-	-	-	-	-	-	-	-	-	-

Notes: Please refer to the User's Guide for an explanation of data; data is arranged alphabetically by state, then county, then city within each county; table includes counties with populations greater than 49,999 unless noted and cities with populations greater than 9,999 whose Asian and/or NHPI population rates are greater than the national average; (1) Native Hawaiian and other Pacific Islander; (2) excludes Taiwanese; (3) includes Chamorro; (4) county does not meet population threshold but is shown in order to allow inclusion of city

Place	Total population with income below poverty level	Asian population for whom poverty status is determined	Asians with income below poverty level	NHPI[1] population for whom poverty status is determined	NHPIs[1] with income below poverty level	Asian Indian	Bangladeshi	Cambodian	Chinese[2]	Fijian	Filipino	Guamanian[3]	Hawaiian, Native	Hmong	Indonesian	Japanese	Korean	Laotian	Malaysian	Pakistani	Samoan	Sri Lankan	Taiwanese	Thai	Tongan	Vietnamese
	5,608	14,140	1,071	1,360	144	175	-	-	425	-	120	-	-	-	-	155	30	-	-	-	-	-	-	-	32	110
	6.13		7.57		10.59	8.05			8.06		4.13					7.75	5.27								5.02	27.30
San Mateo (city)						16.34			39.68		11.20					14.47	2.80								22.22	10.27
			7.57		10.59	1.24			3.01		0.85					1.10	0.21								2.35	0.78
			19.10		2.57	3.12			7.58		2.14					2.76	0.53								0.57	1.96
	3,151	17,571	581	874	100	21	-	-	225	-	248	-	-	-	-	12	-	-	-	-	-	-	-	-	-	-
	5.23		3.31		11.44	2.86			4.87		2.40					2.29										
South San Francisco (city)						3.61			38.73		42.69					2.07										
			3.31		11.44	0.12			1.28		1.41					0.07										
			18.44		3.17	0.67			7.14		7.87					0.38										
	55,086	15,038	2,974	788	52	171	-	-	615	-	544	-	-	79	-	461	518	-	-	-	-	-	-	-	-	268
	14.33		19.78		6.60	20.80			25.49		11.37			22.25		20.32	32.54									22.52
Santa Barbara County						5.75			20.68		18.29			2.66		15.50	17.42									9.01
			19.78		6.60	1.14			4.09		3.62			0.53		3.07	3.44									1.78
			5.40		0.09	0.31			1.12		0.99			0.14		0.84	0.94									0.49
	3,672	3,247	463	-	-	-	-	-	135	-	34	-	-	-	-	63	-	-	-	-	-	-	-	-	-	114
	6.70		14.26						17.40		6.42					13.85										23.12
Goleta (cdp)									29.16		7.34					13.61										24.62
			14.26						4.16		1.05					1.94										3.51
			12.61						3.68		0.93					1.72										3.10
	9,630	1,767	1,274	-	-	-	-	-	397	-	-	-	-	-	-	-	320	-	-	-	-	-	-	-	-	-
	62.81		72.10						66.50								79.60									
Isla Vista (cdp)									31.16								25.12									
			72.10						22.47								18.11									
			13.23						4.12								3.32									
	5,805	1,435	174	-	-	-	-	-	-	-	26	-	-	-	-	-	-	-	-	-	-	-	-	-	-	-
	15.41		12.13								7.37															
Lompoc (city)											14.94															
			12.13								1.81															
			3.00								0.45															
	1,332	1,040	57	-	-	-	-	-	-	-	-	-	-	-	-	-	-	-	-	-	-	-	-	-	-	-
	4.64		5.48																							
Orcutt (cdp)																										
			5.48																							
			4.28																							
	14,823	3,620	435	-	-	-	-	-	-	-	230	-	-	-	-	33	-	-	-	-	-	-	-	-	-	-
	19.69		12.02								9.65					7.43										
Santa Maria (city)											52.87					7.59										
			12.02								6.35					0.91										
			2.93								1.55					0.22										
	124,470	425,961	31,820	5,704	394	3,901	13	808	6,928	32	3,690	84	49	-	80	1,187	2,385	50	-	74	145	-	474	159	-	10,959
	7.53		7.47		6.91	6.04	2.69	18.94	6.22	6.26	4.79	6.15	4.46		11.64	4.44	11.12	2.49		2.71	8.52		9.13	12.26		11.33
Santa Clara County						12.26	0.04	2.54	21.77	8.12	11.60	21.32	12.44		0.25	3.73	7.50	0.16		0.23	36.80		1.49	0.50		34.44
			7.47		6.91	0.92	<0.01	0.19	1.63	0.56	0.87	1.47	0.86		0.02	0.28	0.56	0.01		0.02	2.54		0.11	0.04		2.57
			25.56		0.32	3.13	0.01	0.65	5.57	0.03	2.96	0.07	0.04		0.06	0.95	1.92	0.04		0.06	0.12		0.38	0.13		8.80
	1,482	1,251	140	-	-	-	-	-	-	-	-	-	-	-	-	-	-	-	-	-	-	-	-	-	-	38
	10.93		11.19																							6.82
Alum Rock (cdp)																										27.14
			11.19																							3.04
			9.45																							2.56

Notes: Please refer to the User's Guide for an explanation of data; data is arranged alphabetically by state, then county, then city within each county; table includes counties with populations greater than 49,999 unless noted and cities with populations greater than 9,999 whose Asian and/or NHPI population rates are greater than the national average; (1) Native Hawaiian and other Pacific Islander; (2) excludes Taiwanese; (3) includes Chamorro; (4) county does not meet population threshold but is shown in order to allow inclusion of city

Place	Total population with income below poverty level	Asian population for whom poverty status is determined	Asians with income below poverty level	NHPI[1] population for whom poverty status is determined	NHPIs[1] with income below poverty level	Asian Indian	Bangladeshi	Cambodian	Chinese[2]	Fijian	Filipino	Guamanian[3]	Hawaiian, Native	Hmong	Indonesian	Japanese	Korean	Laotian	Malaysian	Pakistani	Samoan	Sri Lankan	Taiwanese	Thai	Tongan	Vietnamese
Campbell (city)	1,819 4.80	5,641	263 4.66 4.66 14.46	-	-	20 2.60 7.60 0.35 1.10	-	-	47 3.19 17.87 0.83 2.58	-	13 2.08 4.94 0.23 0.71	-	-	-	-	34 4.29 12.93 0.60 1.87	59 6.91 22.43 1.05 3.24	-	-	-	-	-	-	-	-	90 9.89 34.22 1.60 4.95
Cupertino (city)	2,401 4.79	22,563	1,316 5.83 5.83 54.81	-	-	142 2.98 10.79 0.63 5.91	-	-	686 6.54 52.13 3.04 28.57	-	5 1.22 0.38 0.02 0.21	-	-	-	-	78 3.23 5.93 0.35 3.25	173 7.74 13.15 0.77 7.21	-	-	-	-	-	101 12.75 7.67 0.45 4.21	-	-	108 14.90 8.21 0.48 4.50
Gilroy (city)	4,250 10.35	1,912	44 2.30 2.30 1.04	-	-	-	-	-	0 0.00 0.00 0.00 0.00	-	6 0.91 13.64 0.31 0.14	-	-	-	-	-	-	-	-	-	-	-	-	-	-	-
Los Altos (city)	647 2.38	4,132	89 2.15 2.15 13.76	-	-	7 1.34 7.87 0.17 1.08	-	-	47 2.33 52.81 1.14 7.26	-	-	-	-	-	-	13 1.92 14.61 0.31 2.01	-	-	-	-	-	-	-	-	-	-
Los Gatos (town)	1,217 4.32	2,305	97 4.21 4.21 7.97	-	-	-	-	-	26 2.88 26.80 1.13 2.14	-	-	-	-	-	-	17 3.47 17.53 0.74 1.40	-	-	-	-	-	-	-	-	-	-
Milpitas (city)	2,983 5.02	32,571	1,452 4.46 4.46 48.68	581	16 2.75 2.75 0.54	262 5.57 18.04 0.80 8.78	-	-	382 4.72 26.31 1.17 12.81	-	212 2.37 14.60 0.65 7.11	-	-	-	-	25 4.25 1.72 0.08 0.84	24 2.82 1.65 0.07 0.80	-	-	-	-	-	-	-	-	510 6.50 35.12 1.57 17.10
Morgan Hill (city)	1,558 4.70	2,086	33 1.58 1.58 2.12	-	-	-	-	-	11 2.63 33.33 0.53 0.71	-	-	-	-	-	-	0 0.00 0.00 0.00 0.00	-	-	-	-	-	-	-	-	-	-
Mountain View (city)	4,749 6.78	14,536	1,077 7.41 7.41 22.68	-	-	208 7.18 19.31 1.43 4.38	-	-	317 5.78 29.43 2.18 6.68	-	177 8.43 16.43 1.22 3.73	-	-	-	-	89 5.34 8.26 0.61 1.87	130 18.68 12.07 0.89 2.74	-	-	-	-	-	-	-	-	28 3.24 2.60 0.19 0.59
Palo Alto (city)	2,801 4.81	10,272	760 7.40 7.40 27.13	-	-	132 9.12 17.37 1.29 4.71	-	-	316 5.81 41.58 3.08 11.28	-	43 10.62 5.66 0.42 1.54	-	-	-	-	77 6.44 10.13 0.75 2.75	132 13.43 17.37 1.29 4.71	-	-	-	-	-	-	-	-	-
San Jose (city)	77,893 8.82	237,660	19,964 8.40 8.40 25.63	3,214	262 8.15 8.15 0.34	1,384 5.54 6.93 0.58 1.78	-	719 18.55 3.60 0.30 0.92	3,419 6.76 17.13 1.44 4.39	-	2,526 5.14 12.65 1.06 3.24	37 5.05 14.12 1.15 0.05	22 4.17 8.40 0.68 0.03	-	-	532 4.77 2.66 0.22 0.68	969 10.38 4.85 0.41 1.24	44 2.40 0.22 0.02 0.06	-	9 0.69 0.05 <0.01 0.01	138 11.45 52.67 4.29 0.18	-	117 5.76 0.59 0.05 0.15	55 8.97 0.28 0.02 0.07	-	9,381 12.43 46.99 3.95 12.04

Notes: Please refer to the User's Guide for an explanation of data; data is arranged alphabetically by state, then county, then city within each county; table includes counties with populations greater than 49,999 unless noted and cities with populations greater than 9,999 whose Asian and/or NHPI population rates are greater than the national average; (1) Native Hawaiian and other Pacific Islander; (2) excludes Taiwanese; (3) includes Chamorro; (4) county does not meet population threshold but is shown in order to allow inclusion of city

Place	Total population with income below poverty level	Asian population for whom poverty status is determined	Asians with income below poverty level	NHPI[1] population for whom poverty status is determined	NHPIs[1] with income below poverty level	Asian Indian	Bangladeshi	Cambodian	Chinese[2]	Fijian	Filipino	Guamanian[3]	Hawaiian, Native	Hmong	Indonesian	Japanese	Korean	Laotian	Malaysian	Pakistani	Samoan	Sri Lankan	Taiwanese	Thai	Tongan	Vietnamese
Santa Clara (city)	7,786 7.84	28,897	2,413 8.35 8.35 30.99	376	59 15.69 15.69 0.76	703 7.95 29.13 2.43 9.03	-	-	397 8.57 16.45 1.37 5.10	-	274 4.67 11.36 0.95 3.52	-	-	-	-	73 5.30 3.03 0.25 0.94	309 14.96 12.81 1.07 3.97	-	-	41 8.74 1.70 0.14 0.53	-	-	-	-	-	438 9.49 18.15 1.52 5.63
Saratoga (city)	830 2.80	8,527	356 4.17 4.17 42.89	-	-	38 3.07 10.67 0.45 4.58	-	-	117 2.35 32.87 1.37 14.10	-	-	-	-	-	-	21 3.92 5.90 0.25 2.53	115 20.83 32.30 1.35 13.86	-	-	-	-	-	62 18.67 17.42 0.73 7.47	-	-	-
Stanford (cdp)	1,518 21.38	1,887	652 34.55 34.55 42.95	-	-	123 37.16 18.87 6.52 8.10	-	-	275 30.83 42.18 14.57 18.12	-	-	-	-	-	-	-	105 51.72 16.10 5.56 6.92	-	-	-	-	-	-	-	-	-
Sunnyvale (city)	7,127 5.43	42,548	2,831 6.65 6.65 39.72	536	17 3.17 3.17 0.24	859 7.04 30.34 2.02 12.05	-	-	738 6.01 26.07 1.73 10.35	-	325 4.96 11.48 0.76 4.56	-	-	-	-	136 3.96 4.80 0.32 1.91	345 12.83 12.19 0.81 4.84	-	-	-	-	-	105 15.65 3.71 0.25 1.47	-	-	212 6.68 7.49 0.50 2.97
Santa Cruz County	29,383 11.87	7,527	839 11.15 11.15 2.86	-	-	93 10.25 11.08 1.24 0.32	-	-	196 11.59 23.36 2.60 0.67	-	111 5.94 13.23 1.47 0.38	-	-	-	-	118 6.98 14.06 1.57 0.40	57 13.54 6.79 0.76 0.19	-	-	-	-	-	-	-	-	123 34.26 14.66 1.63 0.42
Capitola (city)	706 7.03	484	82 16.94 16.94 11.61	-	-	-	-	-	-	-	-	-	-	-	-	-	-	-	-	-	-	-	-	-	-	-
Santa Cruz (city)	8,350 16.47	2,285	522 22.84 22.84 6.25	-	-	24 6.50 4.60 1.05 0.29	-	-	150 21.68 28.74 6.56 1.80	-	72 17.35 13.79 3.15 0.86	-	-	-	-	102 25.50 19.54 4.46 1.22	-	-	-	-	-	-	-	-	-	-
Scotts Valley (city)	276 2.49	655	0 <0.01 <0.01 <0.01	-	-	-	-	-	-	-	-	-	-	-	-	-	-	-	-	-	-	-	-	-	-	-
Shasta County	24,556 15.36	3,154	1,019 32.31 32.31 4.15	-	-	-	-	-	-	-	22 4.97 2.16 0.70 0.09	-	-	-	-	-	-	849 49.45 83.32 26.92 3.46	-	-	-	-	-	-	-	-
Solano County	31,344 8.28	49,266	3,142 6.38 6.38 10.02	3,041	335 11.02 11.02 1.07	200 7.14 6.37 0.41 0.64	-	-	136 4.36 4.33 0.28 0.43	-	1,719 4.84 54.71 3.49 5.48	62 4.77 18.51 2.04 0.20	55 9.40 16.42 1.81 0.18	124 30.17 3.95 0.25 0.40	-	139 7.06 4.42 0.28 0.44	99 10.80 3.15 0.20 0.32	202 27.82 6.43 0.41 0.64	-	-	137 21.92 40.90 4.51 0.44	-	-	-	-	407 29.77 12.95 0.83 1.30

Notes: Please refer to the User's Guide for an explanation of data; data is arranged alphabetically by state, then county, then city within each county; table includes counties with populations greater than 49,999 unless noted and cities with populations greater than 9,999 whose Asian and/or NHPI population rates are greater than the national average; (1) Native Hawaiian and other Pacific Islander; (2) excludes Taiwanese; (3) includes Chamorro; (4) county does not meet population threshold but is shown in order to allow inclusion of city

Place	Total population with income below poverty level	Asian population for whom poverty status is determined	Asians with income below poverty level	NHPI[1] population for whom poverty status is determined	NHPIs[1] with income below poverty level	Asian Indian	Bangladeshi	Cambodian	Chinese[2]	Fijian	Filipino	Guamanian[3]	Hawaiian, Native	Hmong	Indonesian	Japanese	Korean	Laotian	Malaysian	Pakistani	Samoan	Sri Lankan	Taiwanese	Thai	Tongan	Vietnamese
Benicia (city)	1,144 4.25	1,918	58 3.02 3.02 5.07	-	-	-	-	-	34 7.38 58.62 1.77 2.97	-	14 1.36 24.14 0.73 1.22	-	-	-	-	-	-	-	-	-	-	-	-	-	-	-
Fairfield (city)	8,496 9.26	10,347	937 9.06 9.06 11.03	982	167 17.01 17.01 1.97	55 6.04 5.87 0.53 0.65	-	-	30 3.23 3.20 0.29 0.35	-	431 7.28 46.00 4.17 5.07	29 5.50 17.37 2.95 0.34	-	-	-	91 13.00 9.71 0.88 1.07	58 17.11 6.19 0.56 0.68	103 26.48 10.99 1.00 1.21	-	-	-	-	-	-	-	-
Suisun City (city)	1,667 6.48	4,785	285 5.96 5.96 17.10	-	-	0 0.00 0.00 0.00 0.00	-	-	-	-	50 1.62 17.54 1.04 3.00	-	-	-	-	-	-	-	-	-	-	-	-	-	-	-
Vacaville (city)	4,801 6.06	3,515	249 7.08 7.08 5.19	-	-	-	-	-	-	-	185 10.02 74.30 5.26 3.85	-	-	-	-	-	-	-	-	-	-	-	-	-	-	-
Vallejo (city)	11,588 10.08	27,474	1,484 5.40 5.40 12.81	1,386	144 10.39 10.39 1.24	104 11.29 7.01 0.38 0.90	-	-	32 3.62 2.16 0.12 0.28	-	976 4.22 65.77 3.55 8.42	28 4.98 19.44 2.02 0.24	-	-	-	42 11.44 2.83 0.15 0.36	-	-	-	-	-	-	-	-	-	241 38.56 16.24 0.88 2.08
Sonoma County	36,349 8.06	13,891	1,276 9.19 9.19 3.51	739	82 11.10 11.10 0.23	152 8.79 11.91 1.09 0.42	-	227 26.90 17.79 1.63 0.62	166 6.08 13.01 1.20 0.46	-	171 6.97 13.40 1.23 0.47	-	-	-	-	173 11.30 13.56 1.25 0.48	53 5.97 4.15 0.38 0.15	140 13.08 10.97 1.01 0.39	-	-	-	-	-	-	-	49 3.64 3.84 0.35 0.13
Petaluma (city)	3,245 6.00	2,232	155 6.94 6.94 4.78	-	-	-	-	-	41 5.98 26.45 1.84 1.26	-	-	-	-	-	-	-	-	-	-	-	-	-	-	-	-	-
Rohnert Park (city)	3,279 7.99	2,419	228 9.43 9.43 6.95	-	-	-	-	-	50 11.47 21.93 2.07 1.52	-	31 4.42 13.60 1.28 0.95	-	-	-	-	-	-	-	-	-	-	-	-	-	-	-
Santa Rosa (city)	12,391 8.54	5,591	646 11.55 11.55 5.21	-	-	54 7.69 8.36 0.97 0.44	-	166 25.70 25.70 2.97 1.34	64 7.90 9.91 1.14 0.52	-	63 8.57 9.75 1.13 0.51	-	-	-	-	85 20.88 13.16 1.52 0.69	-	94 15.14 14.55 1.68 0.76	-	-	-	-	-	-	-	13 1.68 2.01 0.23 0.10
Stanislaus County	70,406 15.98	18,289	4,589 25.09 25.09 6.52	1,799	519 28.85 28.85 0.74	314 7.25 6.84 1.72 0.45	-	1,725 53.82 37.59 9.43 2.45	230 12.55 5.01 1.26 0.33	12 1.72 2.31 0.67 0.02	206 7.47 4.49 1.13 0.29	-	-	596 61.51 12.99 3.26 0.85	-	63 7.74 1.37 0.34 0.09	-	768 48.42 16.74 4.20 1.09	-	-	-	-	-	-	-	377 27.20 8.22 2.06 0.54

Notes: Please refer to the User's Guide for an explanation of data; data is arranged alphabetically by state, then county, then city within each county; table includes counties with populations greater than 49,999 unless noted and cities with populations greater than 9,999 whose Asian and/or NHPI population rates are greater than the national average; (1) Native Hawaiian and other Pacific Islander; (2) excludes Taiwanese; (3) includes Chamorro; (4) county does not meet population threshold but is shown in order to allow inclusion of city

Place	Total population with income below poverty level	Asian population for whom poverty status is determined	Asians with income below poverty level	NHPI[1] population for whom poverty status is determined	NHPIs[1] with income below poverty level	Asian Indian	Bangladeshi	Cambodian	Chinese[2]	Fijian	Filipino	Guamanian[3]	Hawaiian, Native	Hmong	Indonesian	Japanese	Korean	Laotian	Malaysian	Pakistani	Samoan	Sri Lankan	Taiwanese	Thai	Tongan	Vietnamese
Ceres (city)	4,417 12.89	1,756	218 12.41 12.41 4.94	-	-	21 2.47 9.63 1.20 0.48	-	-	-	-	-	-	-	-	-	-	-	-	-	-	-	-	-	-	-	-
Modesto (city)	29,363 15.75	11,179	3,247 29.05 29.05 11.06	1,217	392 32.21 32.21 1.34	189 9.65 5.82 1.69 0.64	-	1,363 54.13 41.98 12.19 4.64	141 12.36 4.34 1.26 0.48	4 0.81 1.02 0.33 0.01	140 9.12 4.31 1.25 0.48	-	-	230 56.65 7.08 2.06 0.78	-	22 5.67 0.68 0.20 0.07	-	589 51.62 18.14 5.27 2.01	-	-	-	-	-	-	-	315 27.78 9.70 2.82 1.07
Salida (cdp)	909 7.28	482	15 3.11 3.11 1.65	-	-	-	-	-	-	-	-	-	-	-	-	-	-	-	-	-	-	-	-	-	-	-
Turlock (city)	8,798 16.19	2,367	393 16.60 16.60 4.47	-	-	62 5.92 15.78 2.62 0.70	-	-	-	-	-	-	-	-	-	-	-	-	-	-	-	-	-	-	-	-
Sutter County	12,031 15.54	8,829	1,118 12.66 12.66 9.29	-	-	939 12.96 83.99 10.64 7.80	-	-	-	-	50 12.17 4.47 0.57 0.42	-	-	-	-	12 3.30 1.07 0.14 0.10	-	-	-	-	-	-	-	-	-	-
South Yuba City (cdp)	737 5.75	2,922	245 8.38 8.38 33.24	-	-	234 8.76 95.51 8.01 31.75	-	-	-	-	-	-	-	-	-	-	-	-	-	-	-	-	-	-	-	-
Yuba City (city)	6,432 18.05	3,047	367 12.04 12.04 5.71	-	-	266 12.16 72.48 8.73 4.14	-	-	-	-	-	-	-	-	-	-	-	-	-	-	-	-	-	-	-	-
Tehama County	9,503 17.25	388	98 25.26 25.26 1.03	-	-	-	-	-	-	-	-	-	-	-	-	-	-	-	-	-	-	-	-	-	-	-
Tulare County	86,572 23.91	12,298	3,019 24.55 24.55 3.49	-	-	240 23.23 7.95 1.95 0.28	-	-	53 7.34 1.76 0.43 0.06	-	445 9.80 14.74 3.62 0.51	-	-	654 60.17 21.66 5.32 0.76	-	33 5.56 1.09 0.27 0.04	67 18.11 2.22 0.54 0.08	1,344 42.90 44.52 10.93 1.55	-	-	-	-	-	-	-	-
Porterville (city)	9,921 25.67	2,100	441 21.00 21.00 4.45	-	-	-	-	-	-	-	103 10.36 23.36 4.90 1.04	-	-	-	-	-	-	-	-	-	-	-	-	-	-	-

Notes: Please refer to the User's Guide for an explanation of data; data is arranged alphabetically by state, then county, then city within each county; table includes counties with populations greater than 49,999 unless noted and cities with populations greater than 9,999 whose Asian and/or NHPI population rates are greater than the national average; (1) Native Hawaiian and other Pacific Islander; (2) excludes Taiwanese; (3) includes Chamorro; (4) county does not meet population threshold but is shown in order to allow inclusion of city

Place	Total population with income below poverty level	Asian population for whom poverty status is determined	Asians with income below poverty level	NHPI[1] population for whom poverty status is determined	NHPIs[1] with income below poverty level	Asian Indian	Bangladeshi	Cambodian	Chinese[2]	Fijian	Filipino	Guamanian[3]	Hawaiian, Native	Hmong	Indonesian	Japanese	Korean	Laotian	Malaysian	Pakistani	Samoan	Sri Lankan	Taiwanese	Thai	Tongan	Vietnamese
Visalia (city)	15,201 16.84	5,049	1,708 33.83 33.83 11.24	-	-	-	-	-	-	-	84 10.74 4.92 1.66 0.55	-	-	384 70.98 22.48 7.61 2.53	-	-	-	950 44.29 55.62 18.82 6.25	-	-	-	-	-	-	-	-
Tuolumne County	5,690 11.44	433	40 9.24 9.24 0.70	-	-	-	-	-	-	-	-	-	-	-	-	-	-	-	-	-	-	-	-	-	-	-
Ventura County	68,540 9.23	38,774	2,733 7.05 7.05 3.99	1,627	176 10.82 10.82 0.26	248 5.87 9.07 0.64 0.36	-	-	166 3.26 6.07 0.43 0.24	-	1,261 8.38 46.14 3.25 1.84	-	11 1.91 6.25 0.68 0.02	-	-	515 9.88 18.84 1.33 0.75	133 5.18 4.87 0.34 0.19	-	-	-	71 11.75 40.34 4.36 0.10	-	3 0.38 0.11 0.01 <0.01	-	-	312 9.76 11.42 0.80 0.46
Camarillo (city)	3,012 5.34	3,974	202 5.08 5.08 6.71	-	-	-	-	-	17 3.53 8.42 0.43 0.56	-	61 4.53 30.20 1.53 2.03	-	-	-	-	40 5.69 19.80 1.01 1.33	27 6.09 13.37 0.68 0.90	-	-	-	-	-	-	-	-	38 9.18 18.81 0.96 1.26
Moorpark (city)	2,170 6.97	1,338	23 1.72 1.72 1.06	-	-	-	-	-	-	-	-	-	-	-	-	-	-	-	-	-	-	-	-	-	-	-
Oxnard (city)	25,505 15.12	12,569	1,335 10.62 10.62 5.23	869	90 10.36 10.36 0.35	89 19.35 6.67 0.71 0.35	-	-	27 7.38 2.02 0.21 0.11	-	911 10.17 68.24 7.25 3.57	-	-	-	-	162 13.55 12.13 1.29 0.64	3 0.71 0.22 0.02 0.01	-	-	-	71 13.12 78.89 8.17 0.28	-	-	-	-	137 17.59 10.26 1.09 0.54
Port Hueneme (city)	2,541 12.22	1,234	37 3.00 3.00 1.46	-	-	-	-	-	-	-	18 1.98 48.65 1.46 0.71	-	-	-	-	-	-	-	-	-	-	-	-	-	-	-
Simi Valley (city)	6,453 5.82	6,683	264 3.95 3.95 4.09	-	-	37 2.69 14.02 0.55 0.57	-	-	39 3.79 14.77 0.58 0.60	-	46 3.64 17.42 0.69 0.71	-	-	-	-	35 4.44 13.26 0.52 0.54	7 1.22 2.65 0.10 0.11	-	-	-	-	-	-	-	-	63 6.52 23.86 0.94 0.98
Thousand Oaks (city)	5,714 4.96	6,330	234 3.70 3.70 4.10	-	-	7 0.62 2.99 0.11 0.12	-	-	31 1.68 13.25 0.49 0.54	-	55 9.91 23.50 0.87 0.96	-	-	-	-	80 9.33 34.19 1.26 1.40	30 6.22 12.82 0.47 0.53	-	-	-	-	-	-	-	-	31 6.51 13.25 0.49 0.54
Yolo County	29,787 18.37	14,353	5,985 41.70 41.70 20.09	715	145 20.28 20.28 0.49	579 35.37 9.67 4.03 1.94	-	-	2,151 42.04 35.94 14.99 7.22	105 19.96 72.41 14.69 0.35	417 27.13 6.97 2.91 1.40	-	-	449 69.61 7.50 3.13 1.51	-	292 21.77 4.88 2.03 0.98	403 42.38 6.73 2.81 1.35	370 70.61 6.18 2.58 1.24	-	-	-	-	-	-	-	757 59.89 12.65 5.27 2.54

Notes: Please refer to the User's Guide for an explanation of data; data is arranged alphabetically by state, then county, then city within each county; table includes counties with populations greater than 49,999 unless noted and cities with populations greater than 9,999 whose Asian and/or NHPI population rates are greater than the national average; (1) Native Hawaiian and other Pacific Islander; (2) excludes Taiwanese; (3) includes Chamorro; (4) county does not meet population threshold but is shown in order to allow inclusion of city

Place	Total population with income below poverty level	Asian population for whom poverty status is determined	Asians with income below poverty level	NHPI[1] population for whom poverty status is determined	NHPIs[1] with income below poverty level	Asian Indian	Bangladeshi	Cambodian	Chinese[2]	Fijian	Filipino	Guamanian[3]	Hawaiian, Native	Hmong	Indonesian	Japanese	Korean	Laotian	Malaysian	Pakistani	Samoan	Sri Lankan	Taiwanese	Thai	Tongan	Vietnamese
Davis (city)	14,101	9,170	4,428	-	-	307	-	-	2,081	-	402	-	-	-	-	228	330	-	-	-	-	-	-	-	-	712
	24.49		48.29			43.24			50.25		39.57					28.43	46.81									72.65
						6.93			47.00		9.08					5.15	7.45									16.08
			48.29			3.35			22.69		4.38					2.49	3.60									7.76
			31.40			2.18			14.76		2.85					1.62	2.34									5.05
West Sacramento (city)	6,983	2,251	1,054	-	-	149	-	-	-	-	-	-	-	416	-	-	-	-	-	-	-	-	-	-	-	-
	22.25		46.82			31.91								71.85												
						14.14								39.47												
			46.82			6.62								18.48												
			15.09			2.13								5.96												
Woodland (city)	5,787	1,770	323	-	-	112	-	-	-	-	-	-	-	-	-	-	-	-	-	-	-	-	-	-	-	-
	11.91		18.25			26.60																				
						34.67																				
			18.25			6.33																				
			5.58			1.94																				
Yuba County	12,205	4,399	1,591	-	-	-	-	-	-	-	61	-	-	1,186	-	-	-	-	-	-	-	-	-	-	-	-
	20.79		36.17								12.35			44.64												
											3.83			74.54												
			36.17								1.39			26.96												
			13.04								0.50			9.72												
Linda (cdp)	4,981	2,491	1,095	-	-	-	-	-	-	-	-	-	-	922	-	-	-	-	-	-	-	-	-	-	-	-
	37.55		43.96											46.29												
														84.20												
			43.96											37.01												
			21.98											18.51												
Marysville (city)	2,227	740	170	-	-	-	-	-	-	-	-	-	-	-	-	-	-	-	-	-	-	-	-	-	-	-
	18.94		22.97																							
			22.97																							
			7.63																							
Olivehurst (cdp)	1,994	522	175	-	-	-	-	-	-	-	-	-	-	-	-	-	-	-	-	-	-	-	-	-	-	-
	18.27		33.52																							
			33.52																							
			8.78																							
COLORADO	388,952	91,603	10,213	3,978	537	1,148	-	273	1,566	-	428	133	157	421	138	1,178	1,759	142	-	76	159	-	160	275	-	1,637
	9.26		11.15		13.50	9.82		18.71	10.64		4.67	14.94	12.03	14.01	18.55	10.16	11.76	6.22		9.66	17.97		25.24	14.54		12.13
						11.24		2.67	15.33		4.19	24.77	29.24	4.12	1.35	11.53	17.22	1.39		0.74	29.61		1.57	2.69		16.03
			11.15		13.50	1.25		0.30	1.71		0.47	3.34	3.95	0.46	0.15	1.29	1.92	0.16		0.08	4.00		0.17	0.30		1.79
			2.63		0.14	0.30		0.07	0.40		0.11	0.03	0.04	0.11	0.04	0.30	0.45	0.04		0.02	0.04		0.04	0.07		0.42
Adams County	32,036	11,412	1,052	-	-	35	-	-	182	-	3	-	-	270	-	56	58	23	-	-	-	-	-	-	-	267
	8.91		9.22			5.50			16.16		0.37			12.59		5.88	6.33	2.19								12.06
						3.33			17.30		0.29			25.67		5.32	5.51	2.19								25.38
			9.22			0.31			1.59		0.03			2.37		0.49	0.51	0.20								2.34
			3.28			0.11			0.57		0.01			0.84		0.17	0.18	0.07								0.83
Berkley (cdp)	1,124	419	11	-	-	-	-	-	-	-	-	-	-	-	-	-	-	-	-	-	-	-	-	-	-	-
	10.68		2.63																							
			2.63																							
			0.98																							

Notes: Please refer to the User's Guide for an explanation of data; data is arranged alphabetically by state, then county, then city within each county; table includes counties with populations greater than 49,999 unless noted and cities with populations greater than 9,999 whose Asian and/or NHPI population rates are greater than the national average; (1) Native Hawaiian and other Pacific Islander; (2) excludes Taiwanese; (3) includes Chamorro; (4) county does not meet population threshold but is shown in order to allow inclusion of city

Place	Total population with income below poverty level	Asian population for whom poverty status is determined	Asians with income below poverty level	NHPI[1] population for whom poverty status is determined	NHPIs[1] with income below poverty level	Asian Indian	Bangladeshi	Cambodian	Chinese[2]	Fijian	Filipino	Guamanian[3]	Hawaiian, Native	Hmong	Indonesian	Japanese	Korean	Laotian	Malaysian	Pakistani	Samoan	Sri Lankan	Taiwanese	Thai	Tongan	Vietnamese
Federal Heights (city)	1,350	740	64	-	-	-	-	-	-	-	-	-	-	-	-	-	-	-	-	-	-	-	-	-	-	-
	11.23		8.65																							
			8.65																							
			4.74																							
Westminster (city)	4,726	5,455	339	-	-	43	-	-	34	-	-	-	-	66	-	-	13	23	-	-	-	-	-	-	-	87
	4.71		6.21			9.17			5.30					6.50			2.35	3.40								10.57
						12.68			10.03					19.47			3.83	6.78								25.66
			6.21			0.79			0.62					1.21			0.24	0.42								1.59
			7.17			0.91			0.72					1.40			0.28	0.49								1.84
Arapahoe County	27,987	18,665	1,449	554	16	251	-	-	221	-	102	-	-	-	-	91	381	-	-	-	-	-	-	-	-	184
	5.80		7.76		2.89	10.57			7.22		4.68					5.26	8.54									6.72
						17.32			15.25		7.04					6.28	26.29									12.70
			7.76		2.89	1.34			1.18		0.55					0.49	2.04									0.99
			5.18		0.06	0.90			0.79		0.36					0.33	1.36									0.66
Aurora (city)	24,225	11,299	908	387	32	163	-	61	60	-	38	-	-	-	-	22	296	-	-	-	-	-	-	-	-	137
	8.87		8.04		8.27	15.66		13.83	3.70		2.58					2.15	11.82									7.19
						17.95		6.72	6.61		4.19					2.42	32.60									15.09
			8.04		8.27	1.44		0.54	0.53		0.34					0.19	2.62									1.21
			3.75		0.13	0.67		0.25	0.25		0.16					0.09	1.22									0.57
Boulder County	26,818	8,848	1,322	-		70	-	-	279	-	18	-	-	-	-	204	246	-	-	-	-	-	-	-	-	109
	9.49		14.94			6.19			11.43		4.57					15.81	21.58									15.31
						5.30			21.10		1.36					15.43	18.61									8.25
			14.94			0.79			3.15		0.20					2.31	2.78									1.23
			4.93			0.26			1.04		0.07					0.76	0.92									0.41
Boulder (city)	15,095	3,280	903	-	-	37	-	-	226	-	-	-	-	-	-	160	211	-	-	-	-	-	-	-	-	-
	17.36		27.53			9.87			25.25							32.99	30.94									
						4.10			25.03							17.72	23.37									
			27.53			1.13			6.89							4.88	6.43									
			5.98			0.25			1.50							1.06	1.40									
Broomfield (city)	1,588	1,648	183	-	-	-	-	-	55	-	-	-	-	-	-	-	-	-	-	-	-	-	-	-	-	-
	4.16		11.10						16.32																	
									30.05																	
			11.10						3.34																	
			11.52						3.46																	
Lafayette (city)	1,636	892	98	-	-	-	-	-	-	-	-	-	-	-	-	-	-	-	-	-	-	-	-	-	-	-
	7.02		10.99																							
			10.99																							
			5.99																							
Denver County	77,813	14,914	2,544	378	29	372	-	126	261	-	62	-	-	-	-	256	267	-	-	-	-	-	-	95	-	683
	14.29		17.06		7.67	18.37		31.66	12.30		6.50					13.47	21.39							23.40		15.62
						14.62		4.95	10.26		2.44					10.06	10.50							3.73		26.85
			17.06		7.67	2.49		0.84	1.75		0.42					1.72	1.79							0.64		4.58
			3.27		0.04	0.48		0.16	0.34		0.08					0.33	0.34							0.12		0.88
Douglas County	3,706	4,295	191	-	-	0	-	-	77	-	-	-	-	-	-	-	16	-	-	-	-	-	-	-	-	-
	2.12		4.45			0.00			5.99								2.63									
						0.00			40.31								8.38									
			4.45			0.00			1.79								0.37									
			5.15			0.00			2.08								0.43									

Notes: Please refer to the User's Guide for an explanation of data; data is arranged alphabetically by state, then county, then city within each county; table includes counties with populations greater than 49,999 unless noted and cities with populations greater than 9,999 whose Asian and/or NHPI population rates are greater than the national average; (1) Native Hawaiian and other Pacific Islander; (2) excludes Taiwanese; (3) includes Chamorro; (4) county does not meet population threshold but is shown in order to allow inclusion of city

Place	Total population with income below poverty level	Asian population for whom poverty status is determined	Asians with income below poverty level	NHPI[1] population for whom poverty status is determined	NHPIs[1] with income below poverty level	Asian Indian	Bangladeshi	Cambodian	Chinese[2]	Fijian	Filipino	Guamanian[3]	Hawaiian, Native	Hmong	Indonesian	Japanese	Korean	Laotian	Malaysian	Pakistani	Samoan	Sri Lankan	Taiwanese	Thai	Tongan	Vietnamese
Highlands Ranch (cdp)	1,248 1.76	2,913	71 2.44 2.44 5.69	-	-	0 0.00 0.00 0.00 0.00	-	-	20 2.15 28.17 0.69 1.60	-	-	-	-	-	-	-	-	-	-	-	-	-	-	-	-	-
El Paso County	40,318 8.04	12,790	1,333 10.42 10.42 3.31	1,196	118 9.87 9.87 0.29	176 9.13 13.20 1.38 0.44	-	-	117 11.76 8.78 0.91 0.29	-	115 4.61 8.63 0.90 0.29	51 11.16 43.22 4.26 0.13	-	-	-	84 5.82 6.30 0.66 0.21	439 11.39 32.93 3.43 1.09	-	-	-	-	-	-	-	-	131 14.90 9.83 1.02 0.32
Colorado Springs (city)	30,769 8.70	10,232	1,084 10.59 10.59 3.52	773	111 14.36 14.36 0.36	176 9.35 16.24 1.72 0.57	-	-	111 13.15 10.24 1.08 0.36	-	89 5.14 8.21 0.87 0.29	-	-	-	-	43 4.23 3.97 0.42 0.14	334 11.17 30.81 3.26 1.09	-	-	-	-	-	-	-	-	96 12.89 8.86 0.94 0.31
Jefferson County	26,821 5.16	11,663	880 7.55 7.55 3.28	408	59 14.46 14.46 0.22	75 5.19 8.52 0.64 0.28	-	-	176 9.21 20.00 1.51 0.66	-	65 6.93 7.39 0.56 0.24	-	-	0 0.00 0.00 0.00 0.00	-	122 6.50 13.86 1.05 0.45	82 5.56 9.32 0.70 0.31	14 1.54 1.59 0.12 0.05	-	-	-	-	-	-	-	212 12.33 24.09 1.82 0.79
Larimer County	22,600 9.23	3,524	603 17.11 17.11 2.67	-	-	83 13.26 13.76 2.36 0.37	-	-	146 17.08 24.21 4.14 0.65	-	-	-	-	-	-	134 24.45 22.22 3.80 0.59	165 28.50 27.36 4.68 0.73	-	-	-	-	-	-	-	-	-
Mesa County	11,651 10.23	415	63 15.18 15.18 0.54	-	-	-	-	-	-	-	-	-	-	-	-	-	-	-	-	-	-	-	-	-	-	-
Pueblo County	20,449 14.86	729	105 14.40 14.40 0.51	-	-	-	-	-	-	-	-	-	-	-	-	-	-	-	-	-	-	-	-	-	-	-
Weld County	22,019 12.52	1,386	262 18.90 18.90 1.19	-	-	-	-	-	-	-	-	-	-	-	-	40 9.07 15.27 2.89 0.18	-	-	-	-	-	-	-	-	-	-
CONNECTICUT	259,514 7.86	79,715	6,679 8.38 8.38 2.57	1,171	187 15.97 15.97 0.07	1,500 6.40 22.46 1.88 0.58	61 17.89 0.91 0.08 0.02	100 4.67 1.50 0.13 0.04	1,742 9.64 26.08 2.19 0.67	-	349 4.79 5.23 0.44 0.13	49 12.16 26.20 4.18 0.02	-	-	-	535 12.27 8.01 0.67 0.21	905 13.97 13.55 1.14 0.35	248 8.06 3.71 0.31 0.10	-	325 15.59 4.87 0.41 0.13	-	-	61 8.68 0.91 0.08 0.02	64 8.16 0.96 0.08 0.02	-	354 4.86 5.30 0.44 0.14
Fairfield County	59,689 6.90	28,142	1,861 6.61 6.61 3.12	-	-	453 5.46 24.34 1.61 0.76	-	60 4.16 3.22 0.21 0.10	477 8.34 25.63 1.69 0.80	-	118 4.89 6.34 0.42 0.20	-	-	-	-	190 7.36 10.21 0.68 0.32	211 11.25 11.34 0.75 0.35	108 10.48 5.80 0.38 0.18	-	35 6.45 1.88 0.12 0.06	-	-	-	-	-	45 1.88 2.42 0.16 0.08

Notes: Please refer to the User's Guide for an explanation of data; data is arranged alphabetically by state, then county, then city within each county; table includes counties with populations greater than 49,999 unless noted and cities with populations greater than 9,999 whose Asian and/or NHPI population rates are greater than the national average; (1) Native Hawaiian and other Pacific Islander; (2) excludes Taiwanese; (3) includes Chamorro; (4) county does not meet population threshold but is shown in order to allow inclusion of city

Place	Total population with income below poverty level	Asian population for whom poverty status is determined	Asians with income below poverty level	NHPI[1] population for whom poverty status is determined	NHPIs[1] with income below poverty level	Asian Indian	Bangladeshi	Cambodian	Chinese[2]	Fijian	Filipino	Guamanian[3]	Hawaiian, Native	Hmong	Indonesian	Japanese	Korean	Laotian	Malaysian	Pakistani	Samoan	Sri Lankan	Taiwanese	Thai	Tongan	Vietnamese
Danbury (city)	5,705 7.96	3,603	111 3.08 3.08 1.95	-	-	42 3.61 37.84 1.17 0.74	-	12 2.10 10.81 0.33 0.21	49 10.54 44.14 1.36 0.86	-	-	-	-	-	-	-	-	-	-	-	-	-	-	-	-	-
Greenwich (town)	2,436 4.02	3,259	185 5.68 5.68 7.59	-	-	0 0.00 0.00 0.00 0.00	-	-	7 1.10 3.78 0.21 0.29	-	-	-	-	-	-	130 9.40 70.27 3.99 5.34	-	-	-	-	-	-	-	-	-	-
Stamford (city)	9,194 7.94	5,735	345 6.02 6.02 3.75	-	-	196 6.83 56.81 3.42 2.13	-	-	113 9.83 32.75 1.97 1.23	-	11 1.37 3.19 0.19 0.12	-	-	-	-	-	-	-	-	-	-	-	-	-	-	-
Hartford County	77,440 9.32	20,819	1,790 8.60 8.60 2.31	-	-	441 6.60 24.64 2.12 0.57	-	-	388 10.21 21.68 1.86 0.50	-	53 3.10 2.96 0.25 0.07	-	-	-	-	63 11.65 3.52 0.30 0.08	212 14.67 11.84 1.02 0.27	121 9.96 6.76 0.58 0.16	-	144 22.02 8.04 0.69 0.19	-	-	-	-	-	203 6.46 11.34 0.98 0.26
East Hartford (town)	5,048 10.33	2,080	223 10.72 10.72 4.42	-	-	64 10.29 28.70 3.08 1.27	-	-	-	-	-	-	-	-	-	-	-	-	-	-	-	-	-	-	-	36 6.51 16.14 1.73 0.71
Farmington (town)	1,051 4.51	952	68 7.14 7.14 6.47	-	-	-	-	-	-	-	-	-	-	-	-	-	-	-	-	-	-	-	-	-	-	-
Glastonbury (town)	660 2.09	1,212	11 0.91 0.91 1.67	-	-	0 0.00 0.00 0.00 0.00	-	-	-	-	-	-	-	-	-	-	-	-	-	-	-	-	-	-	-	-
Rocky Hill (town)	492 2.90	711	0 <0.01 <0.01 <0.01	-	-	-	-	-	-	-	-	-	-	-	-	-	-	-	-	-	-	-	-	-	-	-
South Windsor (town)	437 1.80	965	43 4.46 4.46 9.84	-	-	-	-	-	-	-	-	-	-	-	-	-	-	-	-	-	-	-	-	-	-	-
West Hartford (town)	2,669 4.53	3,033	185 6.10 6.10 6.93	-	-	39 5.17 21.08 1.29 1.46	-	-	39 4.73 21.08 1.29 1.46	-	-	-	-	-	-	-	-	-	-	-	-	-	-	-	-	36 5.48 19.46 1.19 1.35

Notes: Please refer to the User's Guide for an explanation of data; data is arranged alphabetically by state, then county, then city within each county; table includes counties with populations greater than 49,999 unless noted and cities with populations greater than 9,999 whose Asian and/or NHPI population rates are greater than the national average; (1) Native Hawaiian and other Pacific Islander; (2) excludes Taiwanese; (3) includes Chamorro; (4) county does not meet population threshold but is shown in order to allow inclusion of city

Place	Total population with income below poverty level	Asian population for whom poverty status is determined	Asians with income below poverty level	NHPI[1] population for whom poverty status is determined	NHPIs[1] with income below poverty level	Asian Indian	Bangladeshi	Cambodian	Chinese[2]	Fijian	Filipino	Guamanian[3]	Hawaiian, Native	Hmong	Indonesian	Japanese	Korean	Laotian	Malaysian	Pakistani	Samoan	Sri Lankan	Taiwanese	Thai	Tongan	Vietnamese
Litchfield County	8,061 4.49	2,227	87 3.91 3.91 1.08	-	-	15 3.26 17.24 0.67 0.19	-	-	19 4.77 21.84 0.85 0.24	-	-	-	-	-	-	-	29 7.88 33.33 1.30 0.36	-	-	-	-	-	-	-	-	0 0.00 0.00 0.00 0.00
Middlesex County	6,911 4.62	2,021	186 9.20 9.20 2.69	-	-	73 12.50 39.25 3.61 1.06	-	-	56 11.24 30.11 2.77 0.81	-	-	-	-	-	-	-	-	-	-	-	-	-	-	-	-	-
New Haven County	75,733 9.49	18,506	1,910 10.32 10.32 2.52	-	-	441 7.68 23.09 2.38 0.58	-	-	516 10.25 27.02 2.79 0.68	-	62 3.91 3.25 0.34 0.08	-	-	-	-	253 31.31 13.25 1.37 0.33	336 17.21 17.59 1.82 0.44	0 0.00 0.00 0.00 0.00	-	100 15.31 5.24 0.54 0.13	-	-	-	-	-	61 7.03 3.19 0.33 0.08
New Haven (city)	27,613 24.37	3,672	802 21.84 21.84 2.90	-	-	114 16.89 14.21 3.10 0.41	-	-	285 19.28 35.54 7.76 1.03	-	-	-	-	-	-	-	185 41.76 23.07 5.04 0.67	-	-	-	-	-	-	-	-	-
New London County	15,780 6.38	4,712	322 6.83 6.83 2.04	-	-	5 0.54 1.55 0.11 0.03	-	-	77 4.98 23.91 1.63 0.49	-	95 9.57 29.50 2.02 0.60	-	-	-	-	-	-	-	-	-	-	-	-	-	-	-
Tolland County	6,952 5.55	2,637	403 15.28 15.28 5.80	-	-	66 9.15 16.38 2.50 0.95	-	-	174 19.21 43.18 6.60 2.50	-	-	-	-	-	-	-	-	-	-	-	-	-	-	-	-	-
Mansfield (town)	1,805 14.22	1,034	330 31.91 31.91 18.28	-	-	52 16.25 15.76 5.03 2.88	-	-	129 28.48 39.09 12.48 7.15	-	-	-	-	-	-	-	-	-	-	-	-	-	-	-	-	-
Storrs (cdp)	1,259 33.54	611	277 45.34 45.34 22.00	-	-	-	-	-	124 31.63 44.77 20.29 9.85	-	-	-	-	-	-	-	-	-	-	-	-	-	-	-	-	-
Windham County	8,948 8.50	651	120 18.43 18.43 1.34	-	-	-	-	-	-	-	-	-	-	-	-	-	-	-	-	-	-	-	-	-	-	-
DELAWARE	69,901 9.21	15,819	1,389 8.78 8.78 1.99	247	13 5.26 5.26 0.02	398 7.67 28.65 2.52 0.57	-	-	405 10.12 29.16 2.56 0.58	-	94 5.19 6.77 0.59 0.13	-	-	-	-	35 5.79 2.52 0.22 0.05	257 13.97 18.50 1.62 0.37	-	-	0 0.00 0.00 0.00 0.00	-	-	-	-	-	16 2.33 1.15 0.10 0.02

Notes: Please refer to the User's Guide for an explanation of data; data is arranged alphabetically by state, then county, then city within each county; table includes counties with populations greater than 49,999 unless noted and cities with populations greater than 9,999 whose Asian and/or NHPI population rates are greater than the national average; (1) Native Hawaiian and other Pacific Islander; (2) excludes Taiwanese; (3) includes Chamorro; (4) county does not meet population threshold but is shown in order to allow inclusion of city

Place	Total population with income below poverty level	Asian population for whom poverty status is determined	Asians with income below poverty level	NHPI[1] population for whom poverty status is determined	NHPIs[1] with income below poverty level	Asian Indian	Bangladeshi	Cambodian	Chinese[2]	Fijian	Filipino	Guamanian[3]	Hawaiian, Native	Hmong	Indonesian	Japanese	Korean	Laotian	Malaysian	Pakistani	Samoan	Sri Lankan	Taiwanese	Thai	Tongan	Vietnamese
Kent County	13,083 10.66	2,062	270 13.09 13.09 2.06	-	-	38 9.07 14.07 1.84 0.29	-	-	-	-	48 9.76 17.78 2.33 0.37	-	-	-	-	-	-	-	-	-	-	-	-	-	-	-
New Castle County	40,710 8.42	12,975	977 7.53 7.53 2.40	-	-	286 6.20 29.27 2.20 0.70	-	-	310 8.49 31.73 2.39 0.76	-	32 2.89 3.28 0.25 0.08	-	-	-	-	35 9.07 3.58 0.27 0.09	151 10.83 15.46 1.16 0.37	-	-	-	-	-	-	-	-	0 0.00 0.00 0.00 0.00
Hockessin (cdp)	221 1.75	837	7 0.84 0.84 3.17	-	-	-	-	-	-	-	-	-	-	-	-	-	-	-	-	-	-	-	-	-	-	-
Newark (city)	4,392 20.14	1,078	256 23.75 23.75 5.83	-	-	-	-	-	76 16.07 29.69 7.05 1.73	-	-	-	-	-	-	-	-	-	-	-	-	-	-	-	-	-
Pike Creek (cdp)	309 1.59	1,085	47 4.33 4.33 15.21	-	-	-	-	-	-	-	-	-	-	-	-	-	-	-	-	-	-	-	-	-	-	-
Sussex County	16,108 10.54	782	142 18.16 18.16 0.88	-	-	-	-	-	-	-	-	-	-	-	-	-	-	-	-	-	-	-	-	-	-	-
DISTRICT OF COLUMBIA	109,500 20.22	13,602	3,098 22.78 22.78 2.83	-	-	556 24.16 17.95 4.09 0.51	-	-	984 26.42 31.76 7.23 0.90	-	320 15.33 10.33 2.35 0.29	-	-	-	-	265 27.40 8.55 1.95 0.24	190 18.68 6.13 1.40 0.17	-	-	-	-	-	-	-	-	544 30.84 17.56 4.00 0.50
FLORIDA	1,952,629 12.51	261,321	31,860 12.19 12.19 1.63	6,440	1,131 17.56 17.56 0.06	8,515 12.72 26.73 3.26 0.44	266 21.25 0.83 0.10 0.01	247 9.13 0.78 0.09 0.01	6,167 13.86 19.36 2.36 0.32	-	3,518 6.56 11.04 1.35 0.18	497 25.33 43.94 7.72 0.03	228 12.50 20.16 3.54 0.01	-	86 9.62 0.27 0.03 <0.01	1,493 13.29 4.69 0.57 0.08	3,025 16.05 9.49 1.16 0.15	337 8.37 1.06 0.13 0.02	-	856 15.81 2.69 0.33 0.04	108 14.12 9.55 1.68 0.01	77 19.54 0.24 0.03 <0.01	328 16.34 1.03 0.13 0.02	709 10.87 2.23 0.27 0.04	-	4,824 14.59 15.14 1.85 0.25
Alachua County	46,939 22.76	7,360	2,478 33.67 33.67 5.28	-	-	660 37.39 26.63 8.97 1.41	-	-	624 31.04 25.18 8.48 1.33	-	183 18.47 7.38 2.49 0.39	-	-	-	-	155 36.38 6.26 2.11 0.33	441 45.23 17.80 5.99 0.94	-	-	-	-	-	-	-	-	179 31.85 7.22 2.43 0.38
Gainesville (city)	22,559 26.69	3,901	1,476 37.84 37.84 6.54	-	-	362 41.51 24.53 9.28 1.60	-	-	462 34.71 31.30 11.84 2.05	-	-	-	-	-	-	-	243 51.59 16.46 6.23 1.08	-	-	-	-	-	-	-	-	-

Notes: Please refer to the User's Guide for an explanation of data; data is arranged alphabetically by state, then county, then city within each county; table includes counties with populations greater than 49,999 unless noted and cities with populations greater than 9,999 whose Asian and/or NHPI population rates are greater than the national average; (1) Native Hawaiian and other Pacific Islander; (2) excludes Taiwanese; (3) includes Chamorro; (4) county does not meet population threshold but is shown in order to allow inclusion of city

Place	Total population with income below poverty level	Asian population for whom poverty status is determined	Asians with income below poverty level	NHPI[1] population for whom poverty status is determined	NHPIs[1] with income below poverty level	Asian Indian	Bangladeshi	Cambodian	Chinese[2]	Fijian	Filipino	Guamanian[3]	Hawaiian, Native	Hmong	Indonesian	Japanese	Korean	Laotian	Malaysian	Pakistani	Samoan	Sri Lankan	Taiwanese	Thai	Tongan	Vietnamese
Bay County	18,882	2,369	299	-	-	-	-	-	-	-	13	-	-	-	-	-	-	-	-	-	-	-	-	-	-	167
	13.04		12.62								2.69															25.08
											4.35															55.85
			12.62								0.55															7.05
			1.58								0.07															0.88
Callaway (city)	1,645	530	71	-	-	-	-	-	-	-	-	-	-	-	-	-	-	-	-	-	-	-	-	-	-	-
	11.57		13.40																							
			13.40																							
			4.32																							
Brevard County	44,218	7,043	826	-	-	250	-	-	156	-	50	-	-	-	-	77	98	-	-	-	-	-	-	-	-	63
	9.47		11.73			13.00			17.59		3.25					14.67	15.99									8.32
						30.27			18.89		6.05					9.32	11.86									7.63
			11.73			3.55			2.21		0.71					1.09	1.39									0.89
			1.87			0.57			0.35		0.11					0.17	0.22									0.14
Broward County	184,589	36,431	3,857	639	66	1,333	-	-	1,123	-	231	-	-	-	-	93	444	-	-	79	-	-	-	98	-	281
	11.51		10.59		10.33	10.25			13.18		4.76					8.90	19.75			7.20				16.36		9.81
						34.56			29.12		5.99					2.41	11.51			2.05				2.54		7.29
			10.59		10.33	3.66			3.08		0.63					0.26	1.22			0.22				0.27		0.77
			2.09		0.04	0.72			0.61		0.13					0.05	0.24			0.04				0.05		0.15
Cooper City (city)	888	1,241	75	-	-	75	-	-	-	-	-	-	-	-	-	-	-	-	-	-	-	-	-	-	-	-
	3.21		6.04			12.65																				
						100.00																				
			6.04			6.04																				
			8.45			8.45																				
Pembroke Pines (city)	7,291	5,004	356	-	-	119	-	-	132	-	71	-	-	-	-	-	-	-	-	-	-	-	-	-	-	-
	5.38		7.11			6.79			11.45		7.66															
						33.43			37.08		19.94															
			7.11			2.38			2.64		1.42															
			4.88			1.63			1.81		0.97															
Charlotte County	11,419	849	99	-	-	-	-	-	-	-	-	-	-	-	-	-	-	-	-	-	-	-	-	-	-	-
	8.23		11.66																							
			11.66																							
			0.87																							
Citrus County	13,541	1,116	118	-	-	-	-	-	-	-	-	-	-	-	-	-	-	-	-	-	-	-	-	-	-	-
	11.68		10.57																							
			10.57																							
			0.87																							
Clay County	9,437	2,893	258	-	-	-	-	-	-	-	28	-	-	-	-	-	-	-	-	-	-	-	-	-	-	-
	6.78		8.92								1.63															
											10.85															
			8.92								0.97															
			2.73								0.30															
Bellair-Meadowbrook Ter. (cdp)	1,218	627	33	-	-	-	-	-	-	-	-	-	-	-	-	-	-	-	-	-	-	-	-	-	-	-
	7.51		5.26																							
			5.26																							
			2.71																							

Notes: Please refer to the User's Guide for an explanation of data; data is arranged alphabetically by state, then county, then city within each county; table includes counties with populations greater than 49,999 unless noted and cities with populations greater than 9,999 whose Asian and/or NHPI population rates are greater than the national average; (1) Native Hawaiian and other Pacific Islander; (2) excludes Taiwanese; (3) includes Chamorro; (4) county does not meet population threshold but is shown in order to allow inclusion of city

Place	Total population with income below poverty level	Asian population for whom poverty status is determined	Asians with income below poverty level	NHPI[1] population for whom poverty status is determined	NHPIs[1] with income below poverty level	Asian Indian	Bangladeshi	Cambodian	Chinese[2]	Fijian	Filipino	Guamanian[3]	Hawaiian, Native	Hmong	Indonesian	Japanese	Korean	Laotian	Malaysian	Pakistani	Samoan	Sri Lankan	Taiwanese	Thai	Tongan	Vietnamese
Collier County	25,449 10.26	1,200	116 9.67 9.67 0.46	-	-	-	-	-	-	-	-	-	-	-	-	-	-	-	-	-	-	-	-	-	-	-
Columbia County	8,027 15.01	386	31 8.03 8.03 0.39	-	-	-	-	-	-	-	-	-	-	-	-	-	-	-	-	-	-	-	-	-	-	-
Duval County	90,828 11.91	20,258	1,669 8.24 8.24 1.84	481	47 9.77 9.77 0.05	220 7.98 13.18 1.09 0.24	-	69 6.93 4.13 0.34 0.08	191 11.75 11.44 0.94 0.21	-	557 5.55 33.37 2.75 0.61	-	-	-	-	72 13.36 4.31 0.36 0.08	102 10.90 6.11 0.50 0.11	-	-	-	-	-	-	-	-	370 17.70 22.17 1.83 0.41
Escambia County	41,978 15.44	6,222	873 14.03 14.03 2.08	-	-	75 14.94 8.59 1.21 0.18	-	-	67 11.53 7.67 1.08 0.16	-	195 7.58 22.34 3.13 0.46	-	-	-	-	-	-	-	-	-	-	-	-	-	-	449 29.02 51.43 7.22 1.07
Bellview (cdp)	2,125 10.17	787	105 13.34 13.34 4.94	-	-	-	-	-	-	-	24 5.83 22.86 3.05 1.13	-	-	-	-	-	-	-	-	-	-	-	-	-	-	-
Myrtle Grove (cdp)	2,174 14.24	753	139 18.46 18.46 6.39	-	-	-	-	-	-	-	6 1.38 4.32 0.80 0.28	-	-	-	-	-	-	-	-	-	-	-	-	-	-	-
Hernando County	13,307 10.33	766	72 9.40 9.40 0.54	-	-	-	-	-	-	-	-	-	-	-	-	-	-	-	-	-	-	-	-	-	-	-
Highlands County	13,065 15.22	964	98 10.17 10.17 0.75	-	-	-	-	-	-	-	0 0.00 0.00 0.00 0.00	-	-	-	-	-	-	-	-	-	-	-	-	-	-	-
Hillsborough County	122,872 12.51	21,431	2,536 11.83 11.83 2.06	428	32 7.48 7.48 0.03	640 10.91 25.24 2.99 0.52	-	-	323 12.06 12.74 1.51 0.26	-	163 5.17 6.43 0.76 0.13	-	-	-	-	127 14.92 5.01 0.59 0.10	401 14.75 15.81 1.87 0.33	-	-	-	-	-	-	74 10.95 2.92 0.35 0.06	-	690 17.28 27.21 3.22 0.56
Westchase (cdp)	261 2.35	508	26 5.12 5.12 9.96	-	-	-	-	-	-	-	-	-	-	-	-	-	-	-	-	-	-	-	-	-	-	-

Notes: Please refer to the User's Guide for an explanation of data; data is arranged alphabetically by state, then county, then city within each county; table includes counties with populations greater than 49,999 unless noted and cities with populations greater than 9,999 whose Asian and/or NHPI population rates are greater than the national average; (1) Native Hawaiian and other Pacific Islander; (2) excludes Taiwanese; (3) includes Chamorro; (4) county does not meet population threshold but is shown in order to allow inclusion of city

Place	Total population with income below poverty level	Asian population for whom poverty status is determined	Asians with income below poverty level	NHPI[1] population for whom poverty status is determined	NHPIs[1] with income below poverty level	Asian Indian	Bangladeshi	Cambodian	Chinese[2]	Fijian	Filipino	Guamanian[3]	Hawaiian, Native	Hmong	Indonesian	Japanese	Korean	Laotian	Malaysian	Pakistani	Samoan	Sri Lankan	Taiwanese	Thai	Tongan	Vietnamese
Indian River County	10,325 9.30	821	148 18.03 18.03 1.43	-	-	-	-	-	-	-	-	-	-	-	-	-	-	-	-	-	-	-	-	-	-	-
Lake County	19,907 9.63	1,415	54 3.82 3.82 0.27	-	-	-	-	-	-	-	-	-	-	-	-	-	-	-	-	-	-	-	-	-	-	-
Lee County	42,316 9.73	3,144	371 11.80 11.80 0.88	-	-	81 12.11 21.83 2.58 0.19	-	-	64 10.74 17.25 2.04 0.15	-	136 12.49 36.66 4.33 0.32	-	-	-	-	-	-	-	-	-	-	-	-	-	-	-
Leon County	41,078 18.19	4,722	732 15.50 15.50 1.78	-	-	152 10.27 20.77 3.22 0.37	-	-	81 7.62 11.07 1.72 0.20	-	89 17.28 12.16 1.88 0.22	-	-	-	-	-	136 30.49 18.58 2.88 0.33	-	-	-	-	-	-	-	-	-
Manatee County	26,104 10.08	2,217	192 8.66 8.66 0.74	-	-	-	-	-	-	-	43 7.99 22.40 1.94 0.16	-	-	-	-	-	-	-	-	-	-	-	-	-	-	-
Marion County	32,918 13.08	2,185	302 13.82 13.82 0.92	-	-	150 15.81 49.67 6.86 0.46	-	-	-	-	-	-	-	-	-	-	-	-	-	-	-	-	-	-	-	-
Martin County	10,844 8.77	697	36 5.16 5.16 0.33	-	-	-	-	-	-	-	-	-	-	-	-	-	-	-	-	-	-	-	-	-	-	-
Miami-Dade County	396,995 17.97	30,177	4,192 13.89 13.89 1.06	582	85 14.60 14.60 0.02	1,340 15.52 31.97 4.44 0.34	-	-	1,432 16.21 34.16 4.75 0.36	-	330 7.41 7.87 1.09 0.08	-	-	-	-	90 6.48 2.15 0.30 0.02	148 11.45 3.53 0.49 0.04	-	-	167 21.03 3.98 0.55 0.04	-	-	-	89 10.09 2.12 0.29 0.02	-	290 18.51 6.92 0.96 0.07
Doral (cdp)	2,404 11.74	1,186	120 10.12 10.12 4.99	-	-	-	-	-	-	-	-	-	-	-	-	-	-	-	-	-	-	-	-	-	-	-
Ives Estates (cdp)	1,487 8.57	831	68 8.18 8.18 4.57	-	-	-	-	-	-	-	-	-	-	-	-	-	-	-	-	-	-	-	-	-	-	-

Notes: Please refer to the User's Guide for an explanation of data; data is arranged alphabetically by state, then county, then city within each county; table includes counties with populations greater than 49,999 unless noted and cities with populations greater than 9,999 whose Asian and/or NHPI population rates are greater than the national average; (1) Native Hawaiian and other Pacific Islander; (2) excludes Taiwanese; (3) includes Chamorro; (4) county does not meet population threshold but is shown in order to allow inclusion of city

Place	Total population with income below poverty level	Asian population for whom poverty status is determined	Asians with income below poverty level	NHPI[1] population for whom poverty status is determined	NHPIs[1] with income below poverty level	Asian Indian	Bangladeshi	Cambodian	Chinese[2]	Fijian	Filipino	Guamanian[3]	Hawaiian, Native	Hmong	Indonesian	Japanese	Korean	Laotian	Malaysian	Pakistani	Samoan	Sri Lankan	Taiwanese	Thai	Tongan	Vietnamese
North Miami Beach (city)	8,230 20.52	1,681	537 31.95 31.95 6.52	-	-	175 44.19 32.59 10.41 2.13	-	-	160 21.80 29.80 9.52 1.94	-	-	-	-	-	-	-	-	-	-	-	-	-	-	-	-	-
Pinecrest (village)	780 4.07	884	89 10.07 10.07 11.41	-	-	-	-	-	-	-	-	-	-	-	-	-	-	-	-	-	-	-	-	-	-	-
Monroe County	7,977 10.18	549	51 9.29 9.29 0.64	-	-	-	-	-	-	-	-	-	-	-	-	-	-	-	-	-	-	-	-	-	-	-
Nassau County	5,192 9.15	422	113 26.78 26.78 2.18	-	-	-	-	-	-	-	-	-	-	-	-	-	-	-	-	-	-	-	-	-	-	-
Okaloosa County	14,562 8.84	4,368	376 8.61 8.61 2.58	-	-	-	-	-	-	-	126 7.38 33.51 2.88 0.87	-	-	-	-	-	68 9.44 18.09 1.56 0.47	-	-	-	-	-	-	50 8.14 13.30 1.14 0.34	-	43 11.03 11.44 0.98 0.30
Wright (cdp)	2,291 10.93	825	83 10.06 10.06 3.62	-	-	-	-	-	-	-	-	-	-	-	-	-	-	-	-	-	-	-	-	-	-	-
Orange County	106,233 12.11	28,640	3,323 11.60 11.60 3.13	823	136 16.52 16.52 0.13	969 12.70 29.16 3.38 0.91	-	-	367 9.22 11.04 1.28 0.35	-	371 8.29 11.16 1.30 0.35	-	-	-	-	242 20.17 7.28 0.84 0.23	440 20.51 13.24 1.54 0.41	-	-	119 13.21 3.58 0.42 0.11	-	-	-	-	-	602 9.47 18.12 2.10 0.57
Oak Ridge (cdp)	4,357 19.57	1,306	200 15.31 15.31 4.59	-	-	-	-	-	-	-	-	-	-	-	-	-	-	-	-	-	-	-	-	-	-	41 7.78 20.50 3.14 0.94
Osceola County	19,532 11.52	3,635	573 15.76 15.76 2.93	-	-	272 28.16 47.47 7.48 1.39	-	-	39 6.68 6.81 1.07 0.20	-	61 6.91 10.65 1.68 0.31	-	-	-	-	-	-	-	-	-	-	-	-	-	-	-
Palm Beach County	110,430 9.92	16,813	1,911 11.37 11.37 1.73	407	81 19.90 19.90 0.07	618 12.15 32.34 3.68 0.56	-	-	407 11.20 21.30 2.42 0.37	-	129 5.80 6.75 0.77 0.12	-	-	-	-	69 12.39 3.61 0.41 0.06	24 2.61 1.26 0.14 0.02	-	-	-	-	-	-	68 9.01 3.56 0.40 0.06	-	190 9.56 9.94 1.13 0.17

Notes: Please refer to the User's Guide for an explanation of data; data is arranged alphabetically by state, then county, then city within each county; table includes counties with populations greater than 49,999 unless noted and cities with populations greater than 9,999 whose Asian and/or NHPI population rates are greater than the national average; (1) Native Hawaiian and other Pacific Islander; (2) excludes Taiwanese; (3) includes Chamorro; (4) county does not meet population threshold but is shown in order to allow inclusion of city

Place	Total population with income below poverty level	Asian population for whom poverty status is determined	Asians with income below poverty level	NHPI[1] population for whom poverty status is determined	NHPIs[1] with income below poverty level	Asian Indian	Bangladeshi	Cambodian	Chinese[2]	Fijian	Filipino	Guamanian[3]	Hawaiian, Native	Hmong	Indonesian	Japanese	Korean	Laotian	Malaysian	Pakistani	Samoan	Sri Lankan	Taiwanese	Thai	Tongan	Vietnamese
Pasco County	36,201	3,482	307	-	-	138	-	-	99	-	11	-	-	-	-	-	-	-	-	-	-	-	-	-	-	-
	10.67		8.82			14.00			19.64		1.11															
						44.95			32.25		3.58															
			8.82			3.96			2.84		0.32															
			0.85			0.38			0.27		0.03															
Pinellas County	90,059	18,677	1,992	-	-	351	-	98	197	-	342	-	-	-	-	104	104	141	-	-	-	-	-	36	-	437
	9.97		10.67			9.65		14.16	9.47		11.30					18.74	12.18	7.60						7.38		10.38
						17.62		4.92	9.89		17.17					5.22	5.22	7.08						1.81		21.94
			10.67			1.88		0.52	1.05		1.83					0.56	0.56	0.75						0.19		2.34
			2.21			0.39		0.11	0.22		0.38					0.12	0.12	0.16						0.04		0.49
Pinellas Park (city)	4,178	1,791	190	-	-	-	-	-	-	-	-	-	-	-	-	-	-	-	-	-	-	-	-	-	-	84
	9.34		10.61																							15.97
																										44.21
			10.61																							4.69
			4.55																							2.01
Polk County	60,953	5,762	762	-	-	108	-	-	84	-	20	-	-	-	-	-	-	36	-	-	-	-	-	-	-	168
	12.94		13.22			6.36			14.12		2.22							8.98								19.47
						14.17			11.02		2.62							4.72								22.05
			13.22			1.87			1.46		0.35							0.62								2.92
			1.25			0.18			0.14		0.03							0.06								0.28
Putnam County	14,449	291	36	-	-	-	-	-	-	-	-	-	-	-	-	-	-	-	-	-	-	-	-	-	-	-
	20.87		12.37																							
			12.37																							
			0.25																							
St. Johns County	9,698	1,244	110	-	-	-	-	-	-	-	-	-	-	-	-	-	-	-	-	-	-	-	-	-	-	-
	8.02		8.84																							
			8.84																							
			1.13																							
St. Lucie County	25,464	1,879	214	-	-	-	-	-	-	-	-	-	-	-	-	-	-	-	-	-	-	-	-	-	-	-
	13.40		11.39																							
			11.39																							
			0.84																							
Santa Rosa County	11,282	1,585	98	-	-	-	-	-	-	-	11	-	-	-	-	-	-	-	-	-	-	-	-	-	-	-
	9.83		6.18								1.56															
											11.22															
			6.18								0.69															
			0.87								0.10															
Sarasota County	24,817	2,560	415	-	-	-	-	-	104	-	16	-	-	-	-	-	-	-	-	-	-	-	-	-	-	166
	7.77		16.21						24.41		2.96															25.70
									25.06		3.86															40.00
			16.21						4.06		0.63															6.48
			1.67						0.42		0.06															0.67
Seminole County	26,804	8,682	833	-	-	285	-	-	188	-	80	-	-	-	-	-	130	-	-	-	-	-	-	-	-	72
	7.41		9.59			10.25			13.57		6.09						13.32									6.77
						34.21			22.57		9.60						15.61									8.64
			9.59			3.28			2.17		0.92						1.50									0.83
			3.11			1.06			0.70		0.30						0.49									0.27

Notes: Please refer to the User's Guide for an explanation of data; data is arranged alphabetically by state, then county, then city within each county; table includes counties with populations greater than 49,999 unless noted and cities with populations greater than 9,999 whose Asian and/or NHPI population rates are greater than the national average; (1) Native Hawaiian and other Pacific Islander; (2) excludes Taiwanese; (3) includes Chamorro; (4) county does not meet population threshold but is shown in order to allow inclusion of city

Place	Total population with income below poverty level	Asian population for whom poverty status is determined	Asians with income below poverty level	NHPI[1] population for whom poverty status is determined	NHPIs[1] with income below poverty level	Asian Indian	Bangladeshi	Cambodian	Chinese[2]	Fijian	Filipino	Guamanian[3]	Hawaiian, Native	Hmong	Indonesian	Japanese	Korean	Laotian	Malaysian	Pakistani	Samoan	Sri Lankan	Taiwanese	Thai	Tongan	Vietnamese
Volusia County	49,907	4,676	814	-	-	330	-	-	128	-	46	-	-	-	-	-	103	-	-	-	-	-	-	-	-	-
	11.62		17.41			21.50			19.72		5.22						23.68									
						40.54			15.72		5.65						12.65									
			17.41			7.06			2.74		0.98						2.20									
			1.63			0.66			0.26		0.09						0.21									
GEORGIA	1,033,793	167,524	17,054	3,544	574	3,488	90	568	2,742	-	634	264	66	144	112	764	3,552	423	-	400	69	-	192	274	-	2,826
	12.99		10.18		16.20	8.07	7.16	16.49	11.03		6.27	19.72	9.62	12.05	20.36	10.40	13.01	9.12		10.34	9.52		10.56	12.48		9.74
						20.45	0.53	3.33	16.08		3.72	45.99	11.50	0.84	0.66	4.48	20.83	2.48		2.35	12.02		1.13	1.61		16.57
			10.18		16.20	2.08	0.05	0.34	1.64		0.38	7.45	1.86	0.09	0.07	0.46	2.12	0.25		0.24	1.95		0.11	0.16		1.69
			1.65		0.06	0.34	0.01	0.05	0.27		0.06	0.03	0.01	0.01	0.01	0.07	0.34	0.04		0.04	0.01		0.02	0.03		0.27
Bartow County	6,445	616	34	-	-	-	-	-	-	-	-	-	-	-	-	-	-	-	-	-	-	-	-	-	-	-
	8.58		5.52																							
			5.52																							
			0.53																							
Bibb County	28,370	1,509	224	-	-	-	-	-	-	-	-	-	-	-	-	-	-	-	-	-	-	-	-	-	-	-
	19.12		14.84																							
			14.84																							
			0.79																							
Bulloch County	12,925	560	153	-	-	-	-	-	-	-	-	-	-	-	-	-	-	-	-	-	-	-	-	-	-	-
	24.49		27.32																							
			27.32																							
			1.18																							
Carroll County	11,495	445	161	-	-	-	-	-	-	-	-	-	-	-	-	-	-	-	-	-	-	-	-	-	-	-
	13.71		36.18																							
			36.18																							
			1.40																							
Catoosa County	4,966	419	13	-	-	-	-	-	-	-	-	-	-	-	-	-	-	-	-	-	-	-	-	-	-	-
	9.44		3.10																							
			3.10																							
			0.26																							
Chatham County	35,043	3,918	569	-	-	100	-	-	143	-	-	-	-	-	-	-	155	-	-	-	-	-	-	-	-	64
	15.62		14.52			13.19			19.04								39.04									6.31
						17.57			25.13								27.24									11.25
			14.52			2.55			3.65								3.96									1.63
			1.62			0.29			0.41								0.44									0.18
Cherokee County	7,474	1,412	61	-	-	0	-	-	-	-	-	-	-	-	-	-	-	-	-	-	-	-	-	-	-	-
	5.32		4.32			0.00																				
						0.00																				
			4.32			0.00																				
			0.82			0.00																				
Clarke County	26,337	2,997	921	-	-	107	-	-	218	-	-	-	-	-	-	-	348	-	-	-	-	-	-	-	-	-
	28.27		30.73			17.17			23.42								69.88									
						11.62			23.67								37.79									
			30.73			3.57			7.27								11.61									
			3.50			0.41			0.83								1.32									

Notes: Please refer to the User's Guide for an explanation of data; data is arranged alphabetically by state, then county, then city within each county; table includes counties with populations greater than 49,999 unless noted and cities with populations greater than 9,999 whose Asian and/or NHPI population rates are greater than the national average; (1) Native Hawaiian and other Pacific Islander; (2) excludes Taiwanese; (3) includes Chamorro; (4) county does not meet population threshold but is shown in order to allow inclusion of city

Place	Total population with income below poverty level	Asian population for whom poverty status is determined	Asians with income below poverty level	NHPI[1] population for whom poverty status is determined	NHPIs[1] with income below poverty level	Asian Indian	Bangladeshi	Cambodian	Chinese[2]	Fijian	Filipino	Guamanian[3]	Hawaiian, Native	Hmong	Indonesian	Japanese	Korean	Laotian	Malaysian	Pakistani	Samoan	Sri Lankan	Taiwanese	Thai	Tongan	Vietnamese
Clayton County	23,493 10.09	10,327	854 8.27 8.27 3.64	-	-	151 11.61 17.68 1.46 0.64	-	42 4.01 4.92 0.41 0.18	237 43.73 27.75 2.29 1.01	-	-	-	-	-	-	-	-	112 8.90 13.11 1.08 0.48	-	76 18.14 8.90 0.74 0.32	-	-	-	-	-	192 4.38 22.48 1.86 0.82
Forest Park (city)	3,094 15.38	1,297	51 3.93 3.93 1.65	-	-	-	-	-	-	-	-	-	-	-	-	-	-	-	-	-	-	-	-	-	-	23 2.40 45.10 1.77 0.74
Riverdale (city)	1,529 12.52	1,020	184 18.04 18.04 12.03	-	-	-	-	-	-	-	-	-	-	-	-	-	-	-	-	-	-	-	-	-	-	56 12.17 30.43 5.49 3.66
Cobb County	38,910 6.47	18,448	1,349 7.31 7.31 3.47	-	-	279 5.18 20.68 1.51 0.72	-	-	184 5.36 13.64 1.00 0.47	-	71 5.99 5.26 0.38 0.18	-	-	-	-	31 3.12 2.30 0.17 0.08	386 12.88 28.61 2.09 0.99	-	-	8 1.24 0.59 0.04 0.02	-	-	-	-	-	57 3.44 4.23 0.31 0.15
Smyrna (city)	3,630 8.95	1,619	143 8.83 8.83 3.94	-	-	36 6.32 25.17 2.22 0.99	-	-	-	-	-	-	-	-	-	-	-	-	-	-	-	-	-	-	-	-
Columbia County	4,540 5.12	2,863	56 1.96 1.96 1.23	-	-	31 3.40 55.36 1.08 0.68	-	-	0 0.00 0.00 0.00 0.00	-	-	-	-	-	-	-	25 5.73 44.64 0.87 0.55	-	-	-	-	-	-	-	-	-
Martinez (cdp)	864 3.14	1,400	4 0.29 0.29 0.46	-	-	0 0.00 0.00 0.00 0.00	-	-	-	-	-	-	-	-	-	-	-	-	-	-	-	-	-	-	-	-
Coweta County	6,888 7.81	584	20 3.42 3.42 0.29	-	-	-	-	-	-	-	-	-	-	-	-	-	-	-	-	-	-	-	-	-	-	-
DeKalb County	70,484 10.80	25,923	3,873 14.94 14.94 5.49	-	-	834 11.79 21.53 3.22 1.18	34 6.18 0.88 0.13 0.05	172 28.20 4.44 0.66 0.24	569 15.00 14.69 2.19 0.81	-	67 10.42 1.73 0.26 0.10	-	-	-	-	156 17.49 4.03 0.60 0.22	726 22.68 18.75 2.80 1.03	-	-	-	-	-	-	-	-	919 14.31 23.73 3.55 1.30
Druid Hills (cdp)	728 7.70	465	137 29.46 29.46 18.82	-	-	-	-	-	-	-	-	-	-	-	-	-	-	-	-	-	-	-	-	-	-	-

Notes: Please refer to the User's Guide for an explanation of data; data is arranged alphabetically by state, then county, then city within each county; table includes counties with populations greater than 49,999 unless noted and cities with populations greater than 9,999 whose Asian and/or NHPI population rates are greater than the national average; (1) Native Hawaiian and other Pacific Islander; (2) excludes Taiwanese; (3) includes Chamorro; (4) county does not meet population threshold but is shown in order to allow inclusion of city

Place	Total population with income below poverty level	Asian population for whom poverty status is determined	Asians with income below poverty level	NHPI[1] population for whom poverty status is determined	NHPIs[1] with income below poverty level	Asian Indian	Bangladeshi	Cambodian	Chinese[2]	Fijian	Filipino	Guamanian[3]	Hawaiian, Native	Hmong	Indonesian	Japanese	Korean	Laotian	Malaysian	Pakistani	Samoan	Sri Lankan	Taiwanese	Thai	Tongan	Vietnamese
Dunwoody (cdp)	1,179 3.64	2,480	156 6.29 6.29 13.23	-	-	8 0.74 5.13 0.32 0.68	-	-	-	-	-	-	-	-	-	-	47 10.51 30.13 1.90 3.99	-	-	-	-	-	-	-	-	-
North Atlanta (cdp)	4,450 11.83	1,687	156 9.25 9.25 3.51	-	-	-	-	-	-	-	-	-	-	-	-	-	-	-	-	-	-	-	-	-	-	-
North Decatur (cdp)	1,202 8.16	847	235 27.74 27.74 19.55	-	-	-	-	-	-	-	-	-	-	-	-	-	-	-	-	-	-	-	-	-	-	-
North Druid Hills (cdp)	2,526 13.67	1,268	359 28.31 28.31 14.21	-	-	236 41.04 65.74 18.61 9.34	-	-	-	-	-	-	-	-	-	-	-	-	-	-	-	-	-	-	-	-
Tucker (cdp)	1,141 4.34	1,963	78 3.97 3.97 6.84	-	-	-	-	-	-	-	-	-	-	-	-	-	-	-	-	-	-	-	-	-	-	37 11.60 47.44 1.88 3.24
Dougherty County	22,974 24.76	696	128 18.39 18.39 0.56	-	-	-	-	-	-	-	-	-	-	-	-	-	-	-	-	-	-	-	-	-	-	-
Douglas County	7,080 7.79	897	79 8.81 8.81 1.12	-	-	-	-	-	-	-	-	-	-	-	-	-	-	-	-	-	-	-	-	-	-	-
Fayette County	2,386 2.63	2,071	26 1.26 1.26 1.09	-	-	-	-	-	-	-	-	-	-	-	-	18 2.85 69.23 0.87 0.75	-	-	-	-	-	-	-	-	-	-
Peachtree City (city)	726 2.29	1,263	12 0.95 0.95 1.65	-	-	-	-	-	-	-	-	-	-	-	-	12 1.99 100.00 0.95 1.65	-	-	-	-	-	-	-	-	-	-
Floyd County	12,538 14.45	1,185	45 3.80 3.80 0.36	-	-	0 0.00 0.00 0.00 0.00	-	-	-	-	-	-	-	-	-	-	-	-	-	-	-	-	-	-	-	-

Notes: Please refer to the User's Guide for an explanation of data; data is arranged alphabetically by state, then county, then city within each county; table includes counties with populations greater than 49,999 unless noted and cities with populations greater than 9,999 whose Asian and/or NHPI population rates are greater than the national average; (1) Native Hawaiian and other Pacific Islander; (2) excludes Taiwanese; (3) includes Chamorro; (4) county does not meet population threshold but is shown in order to allow inclusion of city

Place	Total population with income below poverty level	Asian population for whom poverty status is determined	Asians with income below poverty level	NHPI[1] population for whom poverty status is determined	NHPIs[1] with income below poverty level	Asian Indian	Bangladeshi	Cambodian	Chinese[2]	Fijian	Filipino	Guamanian[3]	Hawaiian, Native	Hmong	Indonesian	Japanese	Korean	Laotian	Malaysian	Pakistani	Samoan	Sri Lankan	Taiwanese	Thai	Tongan	Vietnamese
Forsyth County	5,382 5.50	756	37 4.89 4.89 0.69	-	-	-	-	-	-	-	-	-	-	-	-	-	-	-	-	-	-	-	-	-	-	-
Fulton County	124,241 15.73	22,153	2,132 9.62 9.62 1.72	-	-	477 7.67 22.37 2.15 0.38	-	-	487 9.51 22.84 2.20 0.39	-	61 7.75 2.86 0.28 0.05	-	-	-	-	70 7.93 3.28 0.32 0.06	409 10.17 19.18 1.85 0.33	-	-	-	-	-	-	-	-	411 14.13 19.28 1.86 0.33
Alpharetta (city)	1,785 5.16	1,709	80 4.68 4.68 4.48	-	-	9 1.43 11.25 0.53 0.50	-	-	61 13.03 76.25 3.57 3.42	-	-	-	-	-	-	-	-	-	-	-	-	-	-	-	-	-
Roswell (city)	4,006 5.03	2,963	158 5.33 5.33 3.94	-	-	36 4.34 22.78 1.21 0.90	-	-	51 8.70 32.28 1.72 1.27	-	-	-	-	-	-	-	71 8.28 44.94 2.40 1.77	-	-	-	-	-	-	-	-	-
Glynn County	10,120 15.15	553	58 10.49 10.49 0.57	-	-	-	-	-	-	-	-	-	-	-	-	-	-	-	-	-	-	-	-	-	-	-
Gwinnett County	33,067 5.68	40,940	3,245 7.93 7.93 9.81	499	43 8.62 8.62 0.13	656 5.97 20.22 1.60 1.98	-	248 27.83 7.64 0.61 0.75	399 7.86 12.30 0.97 1.21	-	42 3.43 1.29 0.10 0.13	-	-	-	-	154 17.78 4.75 0.38 0.47	669 7.23 20.62 1.63 2.02	15 1.37 0.46 0.04 0.05	-	115 10.07 3.54 0.28 0.35	-	-	29 6.12 0.89 0.07 0.09	-	-	660 8.89 20.34 1.61 2.00
Duluth (city)	979 4.40	2,725	88 3.23 3.23 8.99	-	-	0 0.00 0.00 0.00 0.00	-	-	0 0.00 0.00 0.00 0.00	-	-	-	-	-	-	-	44 6.40 50.00 1.61 4.49	-	-	-	-	-	-	-	-	-
Lilburn (city)	681 6.10	1,466	198 13.51 13.51 29.07	-	-	37 9.54 18.69 2.52 5.43	-	-	-	-	-	-	-	-	-	-	-	-	-	-	-	-	-	-	-	117 25.32 59.09 7.98 17.18
Mountain Park (cdp)	393 3.43	1,055	37 3.51 3.51 9.41	-	-	29 4.20 78.38 2.75 7.38	-	-	-	-	-	-	-	-	-	-	-	-	-	-	-	-	-	-	-	-
Hall County	16,980 12.41	1,812	215 11.87 11.87 1.27	-	-	-	-	-	-	-	-	-	-	-	-	-	-	-	-	-	-	-	-	-	-	181 15.10 84.19 9.99 1.07

Notes: Please refer to the User's Guide for an explanation of data; data is arranged alphabetically by state, then county, then city within each county; table includes counties with populations greater than 49,999 unless noted and cities with populations greater than 9,999 whose Asian and/or NHPI population rates are greater than the national average; (1) Native Hawaiian and other Pacific Islander; (2) excludes Taiwanese; (3) includes Chamorro; (4) county does not meet population threshold but is shown in order to allow inclusion of city

Place	Total population with income below poverty level	Asian population for whom poverty status is determined	Asians with income below poverty level	NHPI[1] population for whom poverty status is determined	NHPIs[1] with income below poverty level	Asian Indian	Bangladeshi	Cambodian	Chinese[2]	Fijian	Filipino	Guamanian[3]	Hawaiian, Native	Hmong	Indonesian	Japanese	Korean	Laotian	Malaysian	Pakistani	Samoan	Sri Lankan	Taiwanese	Thai	Tongan	Vietnamese
Henry County	5,821 4.92	2,127	161 7.57 7.57 2.77	-	-	0 0.00 0.00 0.00 0.00	-	-	-	-	-	-	-	-	-	-	-	-	-	-	-	-	-	-	-	-
Houston County	11,058 10.20	1,769	152 8.59 8.59 1.37	-	-	-	-	-	-	-	105 19.09 69.08 5.94 0.95	-	-	-	-	-	-	-	-	-	-	-	-	-	-	-
Liberty County	8,464 14.95	851	102 11.99 11.99 1.21	-	-	-	-	-	-	-	-	-	-	-	-	-	47 13.17 46.08 5.52 0.56	-	-	-	-	-	-	-	-	-
Lowndes County	15,622 18.35	799	100 12.52 12.52 0.64	-	-	-	-	-	-	-	-	-	-	-	-	-	-	-	-	-	-	-	-	-	-	-
Muscogee County	27,741 15.66	2,899	295 10.18 10.18 1.06	344	44 12.79 12.79 0.16	57 10.25 19.32 1.97 0.21	-	-	36 10.03 12.20 1.24 0.13	-	17 4.06 5.76 0.59 0.06	-	-	-	-	-	94 12.48 31.86 3.24 0.34	-	-	-	-	-	-	-	-	-
Columbus (sp. city)	27,580 15.61	2,899	295 10.18 10.18 1.07	344	44 12.79 12.79 0.16	57 10.25 19.32 1.97 0.21	-	-	36 10.03 12.20 1.24 0.13	-	17 4.06 5.76 0.59 0.06	-	-	-	-	-	94 12.48 31.86 3.24 0.34	-	-	-	-	-	-	-	-	-
Newton County	6,079 10.01	369	51 13.82 13.82 0.84	-	-	-	-	-	-	-	-	-	-	-	-	-	-	-	-	-	-	-	-	-	-	-
Richmond County	37,313 19.56	2,886	419 14.52 14.52 1.12	-	-	84 12.82 20.05 2.91 0.23	-	-	107 21.44 25.54 3.71 0.29	-	-	-	-	-	-	-	119 13.85 28.40 4.12 0.32	-	-	-	-	-	-	-	-	-
Rockdale County	5,673 8.19	1,133	22 1.94 1.94 0.39	-	-	-	-	-	-	-	-	-	-	-	-	-	-	-	-	-	-	-	-	-	-	-
Spalding County	8,856 15.46	418	113 27.03 27.03 1.28	-	-	-	-	-	-	-	-	-	-	-	-	-	-	-	-	-	-	-	-	-	-	-

Notes: Please refer to the User's Guide for an explanation of data; data is arranged alphabetically by state, then county, then city within each county; table includes counties with populations greater than 49,999 unless noted and cities with populations greater than 9,999 whose Asian and/or NHPI population rates are greater than the national average; (1) Native Hawaiian and other Pacific Islander; (2) excludes Taiwanese; (3) includes Chamorro; (4) county does not meet population threshold but is shown in order to allow inclusion of city

Place	Total population with income below poverty level	Asian population for whom poverty status is determined	Asians with income below poverty level	NHPI[1] population for whom poverty status is determined	NHPIs[1] with income below poverty level	Asian Indian	Bangladeshi	Cambodian	Chinese[2]	Fijian	Filipino	Guamanian[3]	Hawaiian, Native	Hmong	Indonesian	Japanese	Korean	Laotian	Malaysian	Pakistani	Samoan	Sri Lankan	Taiwanese	Thai	Tongan	Vietnamese
	8,491	403	59	-	-	-	-	-	-	-	-	-	-	-	-	-	-	-	-	-	-	-	-	-	-	-
	14.83		14.64																							
Troup County																										
			14.64																							
			0.69																							
	5,829	478	0	-	-	-	-	-	-	-	-	-	-	-	-	-	-	-	-	-	-	-	-	-	-	-
	9.74		<0.01																							
Walton County																										
			<0.01																							
			<0.01																							
	9,494	864	60	-	-	-	-	-	-	-	-	-	-	-	-	-	-	-	-	-	-	-	-	-	-	-
	11.47		6.94																							
Whitfield County																										
			6.94																							
			0.63																							
	126,154	496,540	35,399	110,199	23,609	147	-	47	5,061	-	11,907	319	13,421	-	-	8,778	3,868	538	-	-	3,881	-	129	248	1,490	2,247
	10.70		7.13		21.42	12.64		23.62	9.18		7.05	22.26	16.88			4.44	16.60	32.82			27.81		15.81	18.24	35.88	27.39
HAWAII						0.42		0.13	14.30		33.64	1.35	56.85			24.80	10.93	1.52			16.44		0.36	0.70	6.31	6.35
			7.13		21.42	0.03		0.01	1.02		2.40	0.29	12.18			1.77	0.78	0.11			3.52		0.03	0.05	1.35	0.45
			28.06		18.71	0.12		0.04	4.01		9.44	0.25	10.64			6.96	3.07	0.43			3.08		0.10	0.20	1.18	1.78
	22,821	38,939	2,847	15,905	4,200	-	-	-	129	-	1,201	-	2,914	-	-	1,104	178	-	-	-	99	-	-	-	-	-
	15.66		7.31		26.41				9.98		9.34		21.26			5.45	22.53				33.45					
Hawaii County									4.53		42.18		69.38			38.78	6.25				2.36					
			7.31		26.41				0.33		3.08		18.32			2.84	0.46				0.62					
			12.48		18.40				0.57		5.26		12.77			4.84	0.78				0.43					
	6,773	14,965	1,002	4,847	1,701	-	-	-	46	-	285	-	1,142	-	-	556	66	-	-	-	-	-	-	-	-	-
	17.12		6.70		35.09				9.48		14.55		27.89			5.13	16.92									
Hilo (cdp)									4.59		28.44		67.14			55.49	6.59									
			6.70		35.09				0.31		1.90		23.56			3.72	0.44									
			14.79		25.11				0.68		4.21		16.86			8.21	0.97									
	83,937	398,424	29,179	75,315	15,959	117	-	-	4,772	-	8,957	235	7,713	-	-	6,692	3,510	538	-	-	3,742	-	126	203	1,161	2,179
	9.90		7.32		21.19	12.42			9.12		7.24	18.20	15.67			4.25	16.41	33.67			27.83		16.03	18.27	38.02	28.42
Honolulu County						0.40			16.35		30.70	1.47	48.33			22.93	12.03	1.84			23.45		0.43	0.70	7.27	7.47
			7.32		21.19	0.03			1.20		2.25	0.31	10.24			1.68	0.88	0.14			4.97		0.03	0.05	1.54	0.55
			34.76		19.01	0.14			5.69		10.67	0.28	9.19			7.97	4.18	0.64			4.46		0.15	0.24	1.38	2.60
	1,430	7,134	455	1,449	300	-	-	-	-	-	329	-	156	-	-	5	-	-	-	-	144	-	-	-	-	-
	9.85		6.38		20.70						5.92		16.58			0.61					34.20					
Ewa Beach (cdp)											72.31		52.00			1.10					48.00					
			6.38		20.70						4.61		10.77			0.07					9.94					
			31.82		20.98						23.01		10.91			0.35					10.07					
	1,382	7,165	434	1,512	362	-	-	-	28	-	234	-	127	-	-	66	-	-	-	-	197	-	-	-	-	-
	10.07		6.06		23.94				3.83		8.34		17.94			2.65					29.80					
Halawa (cdp)									6.45		53.92		35.08			15.21					54.42					
			6.06		23.94				0.39		3.27		8.40			0.92					13.03					
			31.40		26.19				2.03		16.93		9.19			4.78					14.25					
	42,706	204,127	20,352	25,098	6,422	79	-	-	4,198	-	4,098	166	2,355	-	-	5,154	2,940	393	-	-	1,525	-	101	133	609	2,006
	11.76		9.97		25.59	13.74			10.90		9.61	25.38	16.79			6.15	19.25	40.23			35.63		14.49	26.55	39.09	30.80
Honolulu (cdp)						0.39			20.63		20.14	2.58	36.67			25.32	14.45	1.93			23.75		0.50	0.65	9.48	9.86
			9.97		25.59	0.04			2.06		2.01	0.66	9.38			2.52	1.44	0.19			6.08		0.05	0.07	2.43	0.98
			47.66		15.04	0.18			9.83		9.60	0.39	5.51			12.07	6.88	0.92			3.57		0.24	0.31	1.43	4.70

Notes: Please refer to the User's Guide for an explanation of data; data is arranged alphabetically by state, then county, then city within each county; table includes counties with populations greater than 49,999 unless noted and cities with populations greater than 9,999 whose Asian and/or NHPI population rates are greater than the national average; (1) Native Hawaiian and other Pacific Islander; (2) excludes Taiwanese; (3) includes Chamorro; (4) county does not meet population threshold but is shown in order to allow inclusion of city

Place	Total population with income below poverty level	Asian population for whom poverty status is determined	Asians with income below poverty level	NHPI[1] population for whom poverty status is determined	NHPIs[1] with income below poverty level	Asian Indian	Bangladeshi	Cambodian	Chinese[2]	Fijian	Filipino	Guamanian[3]	Hawaiian, Native	Hmong	Indonesian	Japanese	Korean	Laotian	Malaysian	Pakistani	Samoan	Sri Lankan	Taiwanese	Thai	Tongan	Vietnamese
Kailua (cdp)	1,972	7,872	223	2,722	159	-	-	-	17	-	37	-	133	-	-	112	6	-	-	-	-	-	-	-	-	-
	5.41		2.83		5.84				1.41		3.78		5.31			2.59	1.60									
									7.62		16.59		83.65			50.22	2.69									
			2.83		5.84				0.22		0.47		4.89			1.42	0.08									
			11.31		8.06				0.86		1.88		6.74			5.68	0.30									
Kaneohe (cdp)	2,105	13,670	395	4,023	482	-	-	-	73	-	132	-	443	-	-	87	19	-	-	-	-	-	-	-	-	-
	6.08		2.89		11.98				5.09		7.92		13.16			1.05	4.34									
									18.48		33.42		91.91			22.03	4.81									
			2.89		11.98				0.53		0.97		11.01			0.64	0.14									
			18.76		22.90				3.47		6.27		21.05			4.13	0.90									
Kaneohe Station (cdp)	544	535	98	-	-	-	-	-	-	-	-	-	-	-	-	-	-	-	-	-	-	-	-	-	-	-
	7.21		18.32																							
			18.32																							
			18.01																							
Makakilo City (cdp)	663	4,399	117	1,347	108	-	-	-	-	-	95	-	74	-	-	15	-	-	-	-	-	-	-	-	-	-
	5.06		2.66		8.02						4.05		7.53			1.54										
											81.20		68.52			12.82										
			2.66		8.02						2.16		5.49			0.34										
			17.65		16.29						14.33		11.16			2.26										
Mililani Town (cdp)	912	13,166	195	1,171	44	-	-	-	18	-	70	-	12	-	-	75	14	-	-	-	-	-	-	-	-	-
	3.21		1.48		3.76				1.85		2.25		1.38			1.06	2.82									
									9.23		35.90		27.27			38.46	7.18									
			1.48		3.76				0.14		0.53		1.02			0.57	0.11									
			21.38		4.82				1.97		7.68		1.32			8.22	1.54									
Nanakuli (cdp)	2,251	1,049	126	4,026	800	-	-	-	-	-	79	-	562	-	-	-	-	-	-	-	183	-	-	-	-	-
	21.30		12.01		19.87						12.42		18.44								24.30					
											62.70		70.25								22.88					
			12.01		19.87						7.53		13.96								4.55					
			5.60		35.54						3.51		24.97								8.13					
Pearl City (cdp)	1,751	16,638	606	1,771	223	-	-	-	39	-	272	-	154	-	-	132	28	-	-	-	-	-	-	-	-	-
	6.23		3.64		12.59				3.22		6.51		11.43			1.41	7.57									
									6.44		44.88		69.06			21.78	4.62									
			3.64		12.59				0.23		1.63		8.70			0.79	0.17									
			34.61		12.74				2.23		15.53		8.79			7.54	1.60									
Schofield Barracks (cdp)	758	331	22	-	-	-	-	-	-	-	-	-	-	-	-	-	-	-	-	-	-	-	-	-	-	-
	7.20		6.65																							
			6.65																							
			2.90																							
Wahiawa (cdp)	2,668	7,105	581	1,734	660	-	-	-	-	-	283	-	132	-	-	150	-	-	-	-	-	-	-	-	-	-
	16.74		8.18		38.06						9.91		14.09			4.66										
											48.71		20.00			25.82										
			8.18		38.06						3.98		7.61			2.11										
			21.78		24.74						10.61		4.95			5.62										
Waianae (cdp)	2,108	1,928	128	2,769	710	-	-	-	-	-	53	-	547	-	-	21	-	-	-	-	-	-	-	-	-	-
	19.84		6.64		25.64						5.22		23.14			3.80										
											41.41		77.04			16.41										
			6.64		25.64						2.75		19.75			1.09										
			6.07		33.68						2.51		25.95			1.00										

Notes: Please refer to the User's Guide for an explanation of data; data is arranged alphabetically by state, then county, then city within each county; table includes counties with populations greater than 49,999 unless noted and cities with populations greater than 9,999 whose Asian and/or NHPI population rates are greater than the national average; (1) Native Hawaiian and other Pacific Islander; (2) excludes Taiwanese; (3) includes Chamorro; (4) county does not meet population threshold but is shown in order to allow inclusion of city

Place	Total population with income below poverty level	Asian population for whom poverty status is determined	Asians with income below poverty level	NHPI[1] population for whom poverty status is determined	NHPIs[1] with income below poverty level	Asian Indian	Bangladeshi	Cambodian	Chinese[2]	Fijian	Filipino	Guamanian[3]	Hawaiian, Native	Hmong	Indonesian	Japanese	Korean	Laotian	Malaysian	Pakistani	Samoan	Sri Lankan	Taiwanese	Thai	Tongan	Vietnamese
Waimalu (cdp)	1,723	15,813	701	1,502	179	-	-	-	6	-	163	-	106	-	-	193	229	-	-	-	-	-	-	-	-	-
	5.88		4.43		11.92				0.47		4.91		11.19			2.43	18.31									
									0.86		23.25		59.22			27.53	32.67									
			4.43		11.92				0.04		1.03		7.06			1.22	1.45									
			40.68		10.39				0.35		9.46		6.15			11.20	13.29									
Waipahu (cdp)	4,478	21,324	1,717	3,963	1,530	-	-	-	54	-	1,279	-	247	-	-	236	-	-	-	-	779	-	-	-	-	-
	13.76		8.05		38.61				9.38		7.88		25.65			7.11					37.51					
									3.15		74.49		16.14			13.74					50.92					
			8.05		38.61				0.25		6.00		6.23			1.11					19.66					
			38.34		34.17				1.21		28.56		5.52			5.27					17.40					
Waipio (cdp)	471	6,479	182	627	105	-	-	-	-	-	58	-	101	-	-	55	-	-	-	-	-	-	-	-	-	-
	4.08		2.81		16.75						2.45		23.17			1.92										
											31.87		96.19			30.22										
			2.81		16.75						0.90		16.11			0.85										
			38.64		22.29						12.31		21.44			11.68										
Kauai County	6,085	20,766	1,105	5,280	907	-	-	-	63	-	668	-	794	-	-	238	-	-	-	-	-	-	-	-	-	-
	10.51		5.32		17.18				14.96		6.04		16.22			3.17										
									5.70		60.45		87.54			21.54										
			5.32		17.18				0.30		3.22		15.04			1.15										
			18.16		14.91				1.04		10.98		13.05			3.91										
Maui County	13,252	38,381	2,253	13,611	2,499	-	-	-	97	-	1,081	-	1,956	-	-	729	160	-	-	-	-	-	-	-	203	-
	10.46		5.87		18.36				8.91		5.07		16.88			5.88	16.97								25.57	
									4.31		47.98		78.27			32.36	7.10								8.12	
			5.87		18.36				0.25		2.82		14.37			1.90	0.42								1.49	
			17.00		18.86				0.73		8.16		14.76			5.50	1.21								1.53	
Kahului (cdp)	2,315	10,594	588	1,761	443	-	-	-	-	-	292	-	220	-	-	234	-	-	-	-	-	-	-	-	-	-
	11.81		5.55		25.16						4.63		15.93			6.90										
											49.66		49.66			39.80										
			5.55		25.16						2.76		12.49			2.21										
			25.40		19.14						12.61		9.50			10.11										
Kihei (cdp)	1,691	4,127	266	1,137	153	-	-	-	-	-	168	-	131	-	-	43	-	-	-	-	-	-	-	-	-	-
	10.11		6.45		13.46						5.30		16.42			9.25										
											63.16		85.62			16.17										
			6.45		13.46						4.07		11.52			1.04										
			15.73		9.05						9.93		7.75			2.54										
Wailuku (cdp)	1,380	5,045	367	1,345	245	-	-	-	-	-	66	-	239	-	-	129	-	-	-	-	-	-	-	-	-	-
	11.19		7.27		18.22						4.17		18.88			4.86										
											17.98		97.55			35.15										
			7.27		18.22						1.31		17.77			2.56										
			26.59		17.75						4.78		17.32			9.35										
IDAHO	148,732	10,902	1,153	1,185	242	82	-	-	260	-	125	-	39	-	-	270	93	14	-	-	-	-	-	-	-	228
	11.77		10.58		20.42	7.40			15.07		7.97		11.64			10.42	7.89	2.76								16.90
						7.11			22.55		10.84		16.12			23.42	8.07	1.21								19.77
			10.58		20.42	0.75			2.38		1.15		3.29			2.48	0.85	0.13								2.09
			0.78		0.16	0.06			0.17		0.08		0.03			0.18	0.06	0.01								0.15
Ada County	22,471	4,698	320	413	41	35	-	-	72	-	18	-	-	-	-	33	10	-	-	-	-	-	-	-	-	117
	7.65		6.81		9.93	5.65			10.45		3.62					4.60	2.02									12.24
						10.94			22.50		5.63					10.31	3.13									36.56
			6.81		9.93	0.74			1.53		0.38					0.70	0.21									2.49
			1.42		0.18	0.16			0.32		0.08					0.15	0.04									0.52

Notes: Please refer to the User's Guide for an explanation of data; data is arranged alphabetically by state, then county, then city within each county; table includes counties with populations greater than 49,999 unless noted and cities with populations greater than 9,999 whose Asian and/or NHPI population rates are greater than the national average; (1) Native Hawaiian and other Pacific Islander; (2) excludes Taiwanese; (3) includes Chamorro; (4) county does not meet population threshold but is shown in order to allow inclusion of city

Place	Total population with income below poverty level	Asian population for whom poverty status is determined	Asians with income below poverty level	NHPI[1] population for whom poverty status is determined	NHPIs[1] with income below poverty level	Asian Indian	Bangladeshi	Cambodian	Chinese[2]	Fijian	Filipino	Guamanian[3]	Hawaiian, Native	Hmong	Indonesian	Japanese	Korean	Laotian	Malaysian	Pakistani	Samoan	Sri Lankan	Taiwanese	Thai	Tongan	Vietnamese
	10,181	732	154	-	-	-	-	-	-	-	-	-	-	-	-	-	-	-	-	-	-	-	-	-	-	-
	13.87		21.04																							
Bannock County																										
			21.04																							
			1.51																							
	8,260	486	36	-	-	-	-	-	-	-	-	-	-	-	-	-	-	-	-	-	-	-	-	-	-	-
	10.13		7.41																							
Bonneville County																										
			7.41																							
			0.44																							
	15,438	1,071	79	-	-	-	-	-	-	-	-	-	-	-	-	11	-	-	-	-	-	-	-	-	-	-
	12.00		7.38													3.69										
Canyon County																13.92										
			7.38													1.03										
			0.51													0.07										
	11,229	581	68	-	-	-	-	-	-	-	-	-	-	-	-	-	-	-	-	-	-	-	-	-	-	-
	10.47		11.70																							
Kootenai County																										
			11.70																							
			0.61																							
	8,038	384	71	-	-	-	-	-	-	-	-	-	-	-	-	-	-	-	-	-	-	-	-	-	-	-
	12.73		18.49																							
Twin Falls County																										
			18.49																							
			0.88																							
	1,291,958	413,360	39,930	3,421	456	9,167	60	462	9,302	-	3,510	195	22	-	375	1,872	7,143	214	70	2,394	91	101	396	855	-	2,541
	10.68		9.66		13.33	7.59	7.71	13.82	13.00		4.13	25.42	2.95		41.67	9.25	14.21	4.43	12.96	15.44	12.10	18.77	12.34	15.35		13.97
ILLINOIS						22.96	0.15	1.16	23.30		8.79	42.76	4.82		0.94	4.69	17.89	0.54	0.18	6.00	19.96	0.25	0.99	2.14		6.36
			9.66		13.33	2.22	0.01	0.11	2.25		0.85	5.70	0.64		0.09	0.45	1.73	0.05	0.02	0.58	2.66	0.02	0.10	0.21		0.61
			3.09		0.04	0.71	<0.01	0.04	0.72		0.27	0.02	<0.01		0.03	0.14	0.55	0.02	0.01	0.19	0.01	0.01	0.03	0.07		0.20
	26,460	9,640	3,455	-	-	756	-	-	987	-	185	-	-	-	-	127	957	-	-	-	-	-	-	-	-	102
	16.07		35.84			36.86			34.35		33.39					26.19	47.33									15.89
Champaign County						21.88			28.57		5.35					3.68	27.70									2.95
			35.84			7.84			10.24		1.92					1.32	9.93									1.06
			13.06			2.86			3.73		0.70					0.48	3.62									0.39
	13,398	3,929	1,434	-	-	358	-	-	401	-	-	-	-	-	-	-	334	-	-	-	-	-	-	-	-	79
	22.11		36.50			35.94			41.60								46.91									19.04
Champaign (city)						24.97			27.96								23.29									5.51
			36.50			9.11			10.21								8.50									2.01
			10.70			2.67			2.99								2.49									0.59
	8,306	4,149	1,847	-	-	359	-	-	566	-	-	-	-	-	-	-	513	-	-	-	-	-	-	-	-	-
	27.34		44.52			47.36			36.63								59.58									
Urbana (city)						19.44			30.64								27.77									
			44.52			8.65			13.64								12.36									
			22.24			4.32			6.81								6.18									
	8,514	333	93	-	-	-	-	-	-	-	-	-	-	-	-	-	-	-	-	-	-	-	-	-	-	-
	17.49		27.93																							
Coles County																										
			27.93																							
			1.09																							

Notes: Please refer to the User's Guide for an explanation of data; data is arranged alphabetically by state, then county, then city within each county; table includes counties with populations greater than 49,999 unless noted and cities with populations greater than 9,999 whose Asian and/or NHPI population rates are greater than the national average; (1) Native Hawaiian and other Pacific Islander; (2) excludes Taiwanese; (3) includes Chamorro; (4) county does not meet population threshold but is shown in order to allow inclusion of city

Place	Total population with income below poverty level	Asian population for whom poverty status is determined	Asians with income below poverty level	NHPI[1] population for whom poverty status is determined	NHPIs[1] with income below poverty level	Asian Indian	Bangladeshi	Cambodian	Chinese[2]	Fijian	Filipino	Guamanian[3]	Hawaiian, Native	Hmong	Indonesian	Japanese	Korean	Laotian	Malaysian	Pakistani	Samoan	Sri Lankan	Taiwanese	Thai	Tongan	Vietnamese
Cook County	713,040	256,073	28,325	1,575	275	6,161	-	375	6,878	-	2,378	-	-	-	213	1,160	5,091	43	-	2,147	-	-	269	568	-	1,940
	13.49		11.06		17.46	9.05		17.36	14.93		4.39				47.44	8.30	14.66	3.43		20.36			17.31	14.64		17.75
						21.75		1.32	24.28		8.40				0.75	4.10	17.97	0.15		7.58			0.95	2.01		6.85
			11.06		17.46	2.41		0.15	2.69		0.93				0.08	0.45	1.99	0.02		0.84			0.11	0.22		0.76
			3.97		0.04	0.86		0.05	0.96		0.33				0.03	0.16	0.71	0.01		0.30			0.04	0.08		0.27
Arlington Heights (village)	1,878	4,660	108	-	-	0	-	-	0	-	16	-	-	-	-	57	35	-	-	-	-	-	-	-	-	-
	2.50		2.32			0.00			0.00		2.32					5.73	4.40									
						0.00			0.00		14.81					52.78	32.41									
			2.32			0.00			0.00		0.34					1.22	0.75									
			5.75			0.00			0.00		0.85					3.04	1.86									
Chicago (city)	556,791	123,370	22,160	1,049	269	4,344	-	375	5,965	-	1,975	-	-	-	-	788	3,617	-	-	1,836	-	-	149	399	-	1,720
	19.61		17.96		25.64	18.77		20.34	19.42		7.16					13.53	30.41			28.69			24.87	19.49		21.19
						19.60		1.69	26.92		8.91					3.56	16.32			8.29			0.67	1.80		7.76
			17.96		25.64	3.52		0.30	4.84		1.60					0.64	2.93			1.49			0.12	0.32		1.39
			3.98		0.05	0.78		0.07	1.07		0.35					0.14	0.65			0.33			0.03	0.07		0.31
Des Plaines (city)	2,646	4,382	148	-	-	84	-	-	12	-	9	-	-	-	-	-	-	-	-	-	-	-	-	-	-	-
	4.59		3.38			4.30			2.37		0.95															
						56.76			8.11		6.08															
			3.38			1.92			0.27		0.21															
			5.59			3.17			0.45		0.34															
Elk Grove Village (village)	684	3,311	90	-	-	0	-	-	25	-	0	-	-	-	-	31	-	-	-	-	-	-	-	-	-	-
	1.98		2.72			0.00			5.97		0.00					5.08										
						0.00			27.78		0.00					34.44										
			2.72			0.00			0.76		0.00					0.94										
			13.16			0.00			3.65		0.00					4.53										
Evanston (city)	7,518	3,427	645	-	-	165	-	-	214	-	0	-	-	-	-	12	159	-	-	-	-	-	-	-	-	-
	11.05		18.82			18.54			26.52		0.00					3.70	31.80									
						25.58			33.18		0.00					1.86	24.65									
			18.82			4.81			6.24		0.00					0.35	4.64									
			8.58			2.19			2.85		0.00					0.16	2.11									
Forest Park (village)	1,074	1,048	53	-	-	-	-	-	-	-	-	-	-	-	-	-	-	-	-	-	-	-	-	-	-	-
	6.95		5.06																							
			5.06																							
			4.93																							
Glenview (village)	840	4,212	92	-	-	0	-	-	5	-	9	-	-	-	-	18	44	-	-	-	-	-	-	-	-	-
	2.03		2.18			0.00			0.71		1.55					5.73	2.76									
						0.00			5.43		9.78					19.57	47.83									
			2.18			0.00			0.12		0.21					0.43	1.04									
			10.95			0.00			0.60		1.07					2.14	5.24									
Hanover Park (village)	2,329	4,249	76	-	-	35	-	-	-	-	12	-	-	-	-	-	-	-	-	-	-	-	-	-	-	-
	6.10		1.79			1.85					1.03															
						46.05					15.79															
			1.79			0.82					0.28															
			3.26			1.50					0.52															
Hoffman Estates (village)	2,204	7,480	458	-	-	67	-	-	52	-	16	-	-	-	-	91	112	-	-	-	-	-	-	-	-	-
	4.41		6.12			2.45			6.33		1.85					10.89	7.85									
						14.63			11.35		3.49					19.87	24.45									
			6.12			0.90			0.70		0.21					1.22	1.50									
			20.78			3.04			2.36		0.73					4.13	5.08									

Notes: Please refer to the User's Guide for an explanation of data; data is arranged alphabetically by state, then county, then city within each county; table includes counties with populations greater than 49,999 unless noted and cities with populations greater than 9,999 whose Asian and/or NHPI population rates are greater than the national average; (1) Native Hawaiian and other Pacific Islander; (2) excludes Taiwanese; (3) includes Chamorro; (4) county does not meet population threshold but is shown in order to allow inclusion of city

Place	Total population with income below poverty level	Asian population for whom poverty status is determined	Asians with income below poverty level	NHPI[1] population for whom poverty status is determined	NHPIs[1] with income below poverty level	Asian Indian	Bangladeshi	Cambodian	Chinese[2]	Fijian	Filipino	Guamanian[3]	Hawaiian, Native	Hmong	Indonesian	Japanese	Korean	Laotian	Malaysian	Pakistani	Samoan	Sri Lankan	Taiwanese	Thai	Tongan	Vietnamese
Lincolnwood (village)	357	2,623	71	-	-	47	-	-	-	-	5	-	-	-	-	-	0	-	-	-	-	-	-	-	-	-
	2.91		2.71			5.93					1.01						0.00									
						66.20					7.04						0.00									
			2.71			1.79					0.19						0.00									
			19.89			13.17					1.40						0.00									
Morton Grove (village)	595	4,931	99	-	-	63	-	-	-	-	13	-	-	-	-	-	23	-	-	-	-	-	-	-	-	-
	2.69		2.01			4.11					0.73						2.64									
						63.64					13.13						23.23									
			2.01			1.28					0.26						0.47									
			16.64			10.59					2.18						3.87									
Mount Prospect (village)	2,614	6,482	361	-	-	150	-	-	10	-	0	-	-	-	-	6	159	-	-	-	-	-	-	-	-	-
	4.62		5.57			4.75			1.70		0.00					1.35	11.00									
						41.55			2.77		0.00					1.66	44.04									
			5.57			2.31			0.15		0.00					0.09	2.45									
			13.81			5.74			0.38		0.00					0.23	6.08									
Niles (village)	1,575	3,363	132	-	-	46	-	-	-	-	0	-	-	-	-	-	86	-	-	-	-	-	-	-	-	-
	5.45		3.93			3.37					0.00						8.56									
						34.85					0.00						65.15									
			3.93			1.37					0.00						2.56									
			8.38			2.92					0.00						5.46									
Northbrook (village)	756	2,896	44	-	-	-	-	-	15	-	-	-	-	-	-	-	21	-	-	-	-	-	-	-	-	-
	2.30		1.52						3.05								1.37									
									34.09								47.73									
			1.52						0.52								0.73									
			5.82						1.98								2.78									
Oak Park (village)	2,902	2,267	203	-	-	24	-	-	12	-	-	-	-	-	-	-	-	-	-	-	-	-	-	-	-	-
	5.56		8.95			3.11			2.45																	
						11.82			5.91																	
			8.95			1.06			0.53																	
			7.00			0.83			0.41																	
Orland Park (village)	1,562	2,132	120	-	-	25	-	-	-	-	9	-	-	-	-	-	-	-	-	-	-	-	-	-	-	-
	3.08		5.63			3.86					1.33															
						20.83					7.50															
			5.63			1.17					0.42															
			7.68			1.60					0.58															
Palatine (village)	3,100	5,217	167	-	-	40	-	-	38	-	45	-	-	-	-	-	0	-	-	-	-	-	-	-	-	-
	4.78		3.20			1.81			5.60		6.34						0.00									
						23.95			22.75		26.95						0.00									
			3.20			0.77			0.73		0.86						0.00									
			5.39			1.29			1.23		1.45						0.00									
Prospect Heights (city)	756	630	7	-	-	-	-	-	-	-	-	-	-	-	-	-	-	-	-	-	-	-	-	-	-	-
	4.33		1.11																							
			1.11																							
			0.93																							
Rolling Meadows (city)	1,249	1,478	54	-	-	48	-	-	-	-	-	-	-	-	-	-	-	-	-	-	-	-	-	-	-	-
	5.14		3.65			10.50																				
						88.89																				
			3.65			3.25																				
			4.32			3.84																				

Notes: Please refer to the User's Guide for an explanation of data; data is arranged alphabetically by state, then county, then city within each county; table includes counties with populations greater than 49,999 unless noted and cities with populations greater than 9,999 whose Asian and/or NHPI population rates are greater than the national average; (1) Native Hawaiian and other Pacific Islander; (2) excludes Taiwanese; (3) includes Chamorro; (4) county does not meet population threshold but is shown in order to allow inclusion of city

Place	Total population with income below poverty level	Asian population for whom poverty status is determined	Asians with income below poverty level	NHPI[1] population for whom poverty status is determined	NHPIs[1] with income below poverty level	Asian Indian	Bangladeshi	Cambodian	Chinese[2]	Fijian	Filipino	Guamanian[3]	Hawaiian, Native	Hmong	Indonesian	Japanese	Korean	Laotian	Malaysian	Pakistani	Samoan	Sri Lankan	Taiwanese	Thai	Tongan	Vietnamese
Schaumburg (village)	2,209	10,285	544	-	-	231	-	-	72	-	30	-	-	-	-	0	200	-	-	-	-	-	-	-	-	-
	2.98		5.29			5.10			5.39		3.24					0.00	11.27									
						42.46			13.24		5.51					0.00	36.76									
			5.29			2.25			0.70		0.29					0.00	1.94									
			24.63			10.46			3.26		1.36					0.00	9.05									
Schiller Park (village)	1,084	709	42	-	-	-	-	-	-	-	-	-	-	-	-	-	-	-	-	-	-	-	-	-	-	-
	9.22		5.92																							
			5.92																							
			3.87																							
Skokie (village)	3,380	13,314	486	-	-	168	-	-	23	-	37	-	-	-	-	-	96	-	-	0	-	-	-	-	-	-
	5.43		3.65			4.37			1.39		1.20						3.81			0.00						
						34.57			4.73		7.61						19.75			0.00						
			3.65			1.26			0.17		0.28						0.72			0.00						
			14.38			4.97			0.68		1.09						2.84			0.00						
Streamwood (village)	1,093	3,314	54	-	-	17	-	-	-	-	23	-	-	-	-	-	-	-	-	-	-	-	-	-	-	-
	3.00		1.63			1.38					1.94															
						31.48					42.59															
			1.63			0.51					0.69															
			4.94			1.56					2.10															
Wheeling (village)	1,803	2,947	54	-	-	23	-	-	-	-	0	-	-	-	-	-	-	-	-	-	-	-	-	-	-	-
	5.31		1.83			1.65					0.00															
						42.59					0.00															
			1.83			0.78					0.00															
			3.00			1.28					0.00															
Wilmette (village)	623	2,214	60	-	-	-	-	-	0	-	-	-	-	-	-	20	5	-	-	-	-	-	-	-	-	-
	2.26		2.71						0.00							5.78	0.64									
									0.00							33.33	8.33									
			2.71						0.00							0.90	0.23									
			9.63						0.00							3.21	0.80									
DeKalb County	9,203	1,548	593	-	-	165	-	-	-	-	-	-	-	-	-	-	-	-	-	-	-	-	-	-	-	-
	11.36		38.31			36.75																				
						27.82																				
			38.31			10.66																				
			6.44			1.79																				
DeKalb (city)	6,682	1,237	556	-	-	165	-	-	-	-	-	-	-	-	-	-	-	-	-	-	-	-	-	-	-	-
	21.28		44.95			44.12																				
						29.68																				
			44.95			13.34																				
			8.32			2.47																				
DuPage County	32,163	70,907	2,378	-	-	984	-	-	285	-	222	-	-	-	-	60	211	-	-	131	-	-	55	32	-	161
	3.62		3.35			3.10			2.85		1.58					4.21	5.07			4.65			6.55	7.66		5.79
						41.38			11.98		9.34					2.52	8.87			5.51			2.31	1.35		6.77
			3.35			1.39			0.40		0.31					0.08	0.30			0.18			0.08	0.05		0.23
			7.39			3.06			0.89		0.69					0.19	0.66			0.41			0.17	0.10		0.50
Addison (village)	3,411	2,954	326	-	-	114	-	-	-	-	13	-	-	-	-	-	-	-	-	-	-	-	-	-	-	-
	9.59		11.04			6.90					2.59															
						34.97					3.99															
			11.04			3.86					0.44															
			9.56			3.34					0.38															

Notes: Please refer to the User's Guide for an explanation of data; data is arranged alphabetically by state, then county, then city within each county; table includes counties with populations greater than 49,999 unless noted and cities with populations greater than 9,999 whose Asian and/or NHPI population rates are greater than the national average; (1) Native Hawaiian and other Pacific Islander; (2) excludes Taiwanese; (3) includes Chamorro; (4) county does not meet population threshold but is shown in order to allow inclusion of city

Place	Total population with income below poverty level	Asian population for whom poverty status is determined	Asians with income below poverty level	NHPI[1] population for whom poverty status is determined	NHPIs[1] with income below poverty level	Asian Indian	Bangladeshi	Cambodian	Chinese[2]	Fijian	Filipino	Guamanian[3]	Hawaiian, Native	Hmong	Indonesian	Japanese	Korean	Laotian	Malaysian	Pakistani	Samoan	Sri Lankan	Taiwanese	Thai	Tongan	Vietnamese
Bartlett (village)	687 1.87	2,934	36 1.23 1.23 5.24	-	-	0 0.00 0.00 0.00 0.00	-	-	-	-	10 1.52 27.78 0.34 1.46	-	-	-	-	-	-	-	-	-	-	-	-	-	-	-
Bensenville (village)	1,303 6.50	1,242	36 2.90 2.90 2.76	-	-	26 3.44 72.22 2.09 2.00	-	-	-	-	-	-	-	-	-	-	-	-	-	-	-	-	-	-	-	-
Bloomingdale (village)	572 2.74	1,914	0 <0.01 <0.01 <0.01	-	-	0 <0.01 *** ** <0.01 <0.01	-	-	-	-	-	-	-	-	-	-	-	-	-	-	-	-	-	-	-	-
Burr Ridge (village)	283 2.82	1,032	41 3.97 3.97 14.49	-	-	35 5.49 85.37 3.39 12.37	-	-	-	-	-	-	-	-	-	-	-	-	-	-	-	-	-	-	-	-
Carol Stream (village)	1,344 3.39	4,071	48 1.18 1.18 3.57	-	-	16 0.88 33.33 0.39 1.19	-	-	-	-	5 0.47 10.42 0.12 0.37	-	-	-	-	-	-	-	-	-	-	-	-	-	-	16 3.39 33.33 0.39 1.19
Darien (city)	510 2.23	2,909	23 0.79 0.79 4.51	-	-	11 0.74 47.83 0.38 2.16	-	-	-	-	12 1.52 52.17 0.41 2.35	-	-	-	-	-	-	-	-	-	-	-	-	-	-	-
Downers Grove (village)	1,096 2.29	2,870	108 3.76 3.76 9.85	-	-	55 4.28 50.93 1.92 5.02	-	-	0 0.00 0.00 0.00 0.00	-	0 0.00 0.00 0.00 0.00	-	-	-	-	-	-	-	-	-	-	-	-	-	-	-
Glen Ellyn (village)	759 2.82	1,314	61 4.64 4.64 8.04	-	-	37 7.25 60.66 2.82 4.87	-	-	-	-	-	-	-	-	-	-	-	-	-	-	-	-	-	-	-	-
Glendale Heights (village)	1,926 6.10	6,298	188 2.99 2.99 9.76	-	-	73 2.63 38.83 1.16 3.79	-	-	-	-	60 3.44 31.91 0.95 3.12	-	-	-	-	-	-	-	-	-	-	-	-	-	-	20 2.50 10.64 0.32 1.04
Hinsdale (village)	553 3.20	866	0 <0.01 <0.01 <0.01	-	-	-	-	-	-	-	-	-	-	-	-	-	-	-	-	-	-	-	-	-	-	-

Notes: Please refer to the User's Guide for an explanation of data; data is arranged alphabetically by state, then county, then city within each county; table includes counties with populations greater than 49,999 unless noted and cities with populations greater than 9,999 whose Asian and/or NHPI population rates are greater than the national average; (1) Native Hawaiian and other Pacific Islander; (2) excludes Taiwanese; (3) includes Chamorro; (4) county does not meet population threshold but is shown in order to allow inclusion of city

Place	Total population with income below poverty level	Asian population for whom poverty status is determined	Asians with income below poverty level	NHPI[1] population for whom poverty status is determined	NHPIs[1] with income below poverty level	Asian Indian	Bangladeshi	Cambodian	Chinese[2]	Fijian	Filipino	Guamanian[3]	Hawaiian, Native	Hmong	Indonesian	Japanese	Korean	Laotian	Malaysian	Pakistani	Samoan	Sri Lankan	Taiwanese	Thai	Tongan	Vietnamese
Lisle (village)	751 3.58	2,175	21 0.97 0.97 2.80	-	-	0 0.00 0.00 0.00 0.00	-	-	8 1.20 38.10 0.37 1.07	-	-	-	-	-	-	-	-	-	-	-	-	-	-	-	-	-
Lombard (village)	1,560 3.84	2,835	168 5.93 5.93 10.77	-	-	150 11.89 89.29 5.29 9.62	-	-	-	-	6 0.90 3.57 0.21 0.38	-	-	-	-	-	-	-	-	-	-	-	-	-	-	-
Naperville (city)	2,809 2.22	11,671	388 3.32 3.32 13.81	-	-	115 2.47 29.64 0.99 4.09	-	-	100 2.48 25.77 0.86 3.56	-	0 0.00 0.00 0.00 0.00	-	-	-	-	-	68 7.82 17.53 0.58 2.42	-	-	-	-	-	44 10.21 11.34 0.38 1.57	-	-	-
Roselle (village)	463 2.00	1,816	41 2.26 2.26 8.86	-	-	0 0.00 0.00 0.00 0.00	-	-	-	-	-	-	-	-	-	-	-	-	-	-	-	-	-	-	-	-
Villa Park (village)	1,065 4.79	896	0 <0.01 <0.01 <0.01	-	-	-	-	-	-	-	-	-	-	-	-	-	-	-	-	-	-	-	-	-	-	-
Warrenville (city)	204 1.55	521	18 3.45 3.45 8.82	-	-	-	-	-	-	-	-	-	-	-	-	-	-	-	-	-	-	-	-	-	-	-
Westmont (village)	1,344 5.80	2,900	101 3.48 3.48 7.51	-	-	39 2.88 38.61 1.34 2.90	-	-	57 11.90 56.44 1.97 4.24	-	5 0.99 4.95 0.17 0.37	-	-	-	-	-	-	-	-	-	-	-	-	-	-	-
Wheaton (city)	1,847 3.58	2,602	133 5.11 5.11 7.20	-	-	25 2.65 18.80 0.96 1.35	-	-	-	-	-	-	-	-	-	-	-	-	-	-	-	-	-	-	-	0 0.00 0.00 0.00 0.00
Woodridge (village)	1,188 3.83	3,503	144 4.11 4.11 12.12	-	-	91 5.54 63.19 2.60 7.66	-	-	-	-	6 0.52 4.17 0.17 0.51	-	-	-	-	-	-	-	-	-	-	-	-	-	-	-
Jackson County	13,463 25.22	1,764	864 48.98 48.98 6.42	-	-	-	-	-	183 52.74 21.18 10.37 1.36	-	-	-	-	-	-	-	-	-	-	-	-	-	-	-	-	-

Notes: Please refer to the User's Guide for an explanation of data; data is arranged alphabetically by state, then county, then city within each county; table includes counties with populations greater than 49,999 unless noted and cities with populations greater than 9,999 whose Asian and/or NHPI population rates are greater than the national average; (1) Native Hawaiian and other Pacific Islander; (2) excludes Taiwanese; (3) includes Chamorro; (4) county does not meet population threshold but is shown in order to allow inclusion of city

Place	Total population with income below poverty level	Asian population for whom poverty status is determined	Asians with income below poverty level	NHPI[1] population for whom poverty status is determined	NHPIs[1] with income below poverty level	Asian Indian	Bangladeshi	Cambodian	Chinese[2]	Fijian	Filipino	Guamanian[3]	Hawaiian, Native	Hmong	Indonesian	Japanese	Korean	Laotian	Malaysian	Pakistani	Samoan	Sri Lankan	Taiwanese	Thai	Tongan	Vietnamese
Carbondale (city)	8,207 41.36	1,370	776 56.64 56.64 9.46	-	-	-	-	-	-	-	-	-	-	-	-	-	-	-	-	-	-	-	-	-	-	-
Kane County	26,587 6.69	7,024	340 4.84 4.84 1.28	-	-	176 10.97 51.76 2.51 0.66	-	-	14 1.64 4.12 0.20 0.05	-	33 2.52 9.71 0.47 0.12	-	-	-	-	-	26 5.43 7.65 0.37 0.10	34 3.25 10.00 0.48 0.13	-	-	-	-	-	-	-	38 7.95 11.18 0.54 0.14
South Elgin (village)	458 2.98	842	52 6.18 6.18 11.35	-	-	-	-	-	-	-	-	-	-	-	-	-	-	-	-	-	-	-	-	-	-	-
Kankakee County	11,445 11.44	725	84 11.59 11.59 0.73	-	-	-	-	-	-	-	-	-	-	-	-	-	-	-	-	-	-	-	-	-	-	-
Kendall County	1,636 3.02	664	156 23.49 23.49 9.54	-	-	-	-	-	-	-	-	-	-	-	-	-	-	-	-	-	-	-	-	-	-	-
Knox County	5,754 11.13	306	35 11.44 11.44 0.61	-	-	-	-	-	-	-	-	-	-	-	-	-	-	-	-	-	-	-	-	-	-	-
La Salle County	9,894 9.14	506	55 10.87 10.87 0.56	-	-	-	-	-	-	-	-	-	-	-	-	-	-	-	-	-	-	-	-	-	-	-
Lake County	35,714 5.72	24,635	701 2.85 2.85 1.96	-	-	140 2.48 19.97 0.57 0.39	-	-	129 2.68 18.40 0.52 0.36	-	140 2.12 19.97 0.57 0.39	-	-	-	-	36 2.45 5.14 0.15 0.10	141 3.70 20.11 0.57 0.39	-	-	0 0.00 0.00 0.00 0.00	-	-	-	-	-	59 10.79 8.42 0.24 0.17
Buffalo Grove (village)	960 2.27	3,687	23 0.62 0.62 2.40	-	-	14 1.85 60.87 0.38 1.46	-	-	0 0.00 0.00 0.00 0.00	-	0 0.00 0.00 0.00 0.00	-	-	-	-	9 1.47 39.13 0.24 0.94	0 0.00 0.00 0.00 0.00	-	-	-	-	-	-	-	-	-
Gages Lake (cdp)	307 2.96	411	0 <0.01 <0.01 <0.01	-	-	-	-	-	-	-	-	-	-	-	-	-	-	-	-	-	-	-	-	-	-	-

Notes: Please refer to the User's Guide for an explanation of data; data is arranged alphabetically by state, then county, then city within each county; table includes counties with populations greater than 49,999 unless noted and cities with populations greater than 9,999 whose Asian and/or NHPI population rates are greater than the national average; (1) Native Hawaiian and other Pacific Islander; (2) excludes Taiwanese; (3) includes Chamorro; (4) county does not meet population threshold but is shown in order to allow inclusion of city

Place	Total population with income below poverty level	Asian population for whom poverty status is determined	Asians with income below poverty level	NHPI[1] population for whom poverty status is determined	NHPIs[1] with income below poverty level	Asian Indian	Bangladeshi	Cambodian	Chinese[2]	Fijian	Filipino	Guamanian[3]	Hawaiian, Native	Hmong	Indonesian	Japanese	Korean	Laotian	Malaysian	Pakistani	Samoan	Sri Lankan	Taiwanese	Thai	Tongan	Vietnamese
Grayslake (village)	560 3.03	893	27 3.02 3.02 4.82	-	-	-	-	-	-	-	-	-	-	-	-	-	-	-	-	-	-	-	-	-	-	-
Gurnee (village)	867 3.03	2,361	58 2.46 2.46 6.69	-	-	22 3.00 37.93 0.93 2.54	-	-	0 0.00 0.00 0.00 0.00	-	9 1.17 15.52 0.38 1.04	-	-	-	-	-	-	-	-	-	-	-	-	-	-	-
Lake Zurich (village)	450 2.51	691	0 <0.01 <0.01 <0.01	-	-	-	-	-	-	-	-	-	-	-	-	-	-	-	-	-	-	-	-	-	-	-
Libertyville (village)	711 3.54	980	25 2.55 2.55 3.52	-	-	-	-	-	-	-	-	-	-	-	-	-	-	-	-	-	-	-	-	-	-	-
Mundelein (village)	1,395 4.59	2,033	50 2.46 2.46 3.58	-	-	-	-	-	39 7.20 78.00 1.92 2.80	-	7 1.13 14.00 0.34 0.50	-	-	-	-	-	-	-	-	-	-	-	-	-	-	-
Vernon Hills (village)	604 2.93	2,312	86 3.72 3.72 14.24	-	-	0 0.00 0.00 0.00 0.00	-	-	20 2.95 23.26 0.87 3.31	-	-	-	-	-	-	-	66 10.33 76.74 2.85 10.93	-	-	-	-	-	-	-	-	-
Macon County	14,316 12.89	719	80 11.13 11.13 0.56	-	-	-	-	-	-	-	-	-	-	-	-	-	-	-	-	-	-	-	-	-	-	-
Madison County	24,774 9.79	1,250	115 9.20 9.20 0.46	-	-	40 11.24 34.78 3.20 0.16	-	-	-	-	-	-	-	-	-	-	-	-	-	-	-	-	-	-	-	-
McHenry County	9,446 3.66	3,395	100 2.95 2.95 1.06	-	-	5 0.53 5.00 0.15 0.05	-	-	33 6.13 33.00 0.97 0.35	-	19 1.94 19.00 0.56 0.20	-	-	-	-	-	-	-	-	-	-	-	-	-	-	-
McLean County	13,488 9.71	2,717	317 11.67 11.67 2.35	-	-	120 10.84 37.85 4.42 0.89	-	-	37 6.55 11.67 1.36 0.27	-	-	-	-	-	-	-	-	-	-	-	-	-	-	-	-	-

Notes: Please refer to the User's Guide for an explanation of data; data is arranged alphabetically by state, then county, then city within each county; table includes counties with populations greater than 49,999 unless noted and cities with populations greater than 9,999 whose Asian and/or NHPI population rates are greater than the national average; (1) Native Hawaiian and other Pacific Islander; (2) excludes Taiwanese; (3) includes Chamorro; (4) county does not meet population threshold but is shown in order to allow inclusion of city

Place	Total population with income below poverty level	Asian population for whom poverty status is determined	Asians with income below poverty level	NHPI[1] population for whom poverty status is determined	NHPIs[1] with income below poverty level	Asian Indian	Bangladeshi	Cambodian	Chinese[2]	Fijian	Filipino	Guamanian[3]	Hawaiian, Native	Hmong	Indonesian	Japanese	Korean	Laotian	Malaysian	Pakistani	Samoan	Sri Lankan	Taiwanese	Thai	Tongan	Vietnamese
Peoria County	24,228 13.70	3,085	239 7.75 7.75 0.99	-	-	65 6.23 27.20 2.11 0.27	-	-	107 12.02 44.77 3.47 0.44	-	-	-	-	-	-	-	-	-	-	-	-	-	-	-	-	18 5.81 7.53 0.58 0.07
Rock Island County	15,523 10.74	1,441	146 10.13 10.13 0.94	-	-	73 12.46 50.00 5.07 0.47	-	-	-	-	-	-	-	-	-	-	-	-	-	-	-	-	-	-	-	-
St. Clair County	36,358 14.51	2,252	141 6.26 6.26 0.39	-	-	-	-	-	-	-	18 2.90 12.77 0.80 0.05	-	-	-	-	-	35 8.66 24.82 1.55 0.10	-	-	-	-	-	-	-	-	-
Sangamon County	17,340 9.32	1,914	271 14.16 14.16 1.56	-	-	89 13.26 32.84 4.65 0.51	-	-	86 25.00 31.73 4.49 0.50	-	-	-	-	-	-	-	-	-	-	-	-	-	-	-	-	-
Tazewell County	7,806 6.25	560	13 2.32 2.32 0.17	-	-	-	-	-	-	-	-	-	-	-	-	-	-	-	-	-	-	-	-	-	-	-
Vermilion County	10,704 13.28	511	16 3.13 3.13 0.15	-	-	-	-	-	-	-	-	-	-	-	-	-	-	-	-	-	-	-	-	-	-	-
Will County	24,225 4.92	11,195	258 2.30 2.30 1.07	-	-	55 1.90 21.32 0.49 0.23	-	-	31 2.02 12.02 0.28 0.13	-	46 1.52 17.83 0.41 0.19	-	-	-	-	-	9 1.00 3.49 0.08 0.04	-	-	0 0.00 0.00 0.00 0.00	-	-	-	-	-	48 7.75 18.60 0.43 0.20
Bolingbrook (village)	2,310 4.13	3,779	35 0.93 0.93 1.52	-	-	0 0.00 0.00 0.00 0.00	-	-	-	-	18 1.54 51.43 0.48 0.78	-	-	-	-	-	-	-	-	-	-	-	-	-	-	-
Winnebago County	26,260 9.62	4,434	337 7.60 7.60 1.28	-	-	0 0.00 0.00 0.00 0.00	-	-	-	-	29 5.33 8.61 0.65 0.11	-	-	-	-	-	44 9.76 13.06 0.99 0.17	69 5.31 20.47 1.56 0.26	-	-	-	-	-	-	-	56 9.67 16.62 1.26 0.21
INDIANA	559,484 9.49	54,270	8,582 15.81 15.81 1.53	1,563	183 11.71 11.71 0.03	1,316 9.81 15.33 2.42 0.24	-	51 9.06 0.59 0.09 0.01	2,182 19.88 25.43 4.02 0.39	-	503 7.50 5.86 0.93 0.09	67 14.82 36.61 4.29 0.01	59 9.85 32.24 3.77 0.01	-	-	698 16.01 8.13 1.29 0.12	1,853 28.02 21.59 3.41 0.33	52 5.37 0.61 0.10 0.01	-	108 16.17 1.26 0.20 0.02	-	-	147 21.43 1.71 0.27 0.03	156 18.18 1.82 0.29 0.03	-	618 13.41 7.20 1.14 0.11

Notes: Please refer to the User's Guide for an explanation of data; data is arranged alphabetically by state, then county, then city within each county; table includes counties with populations greater than 49,999 unless noted and cities with populations greater than 9,999 whose Asian and/or NHPI population rates are greater than the national average; (1) Native Hawaiian and other Pacific Islander; (2) excludes Taiwanese; (3) includes Chamorro; (4) county does not meet population threshold but is shown in order to allow inclusion of city

Place	Total population with income below poverty level	Asian population for whom poverty status is determined	Asians with income below poverty level	NHPI[1] population for whom poverty status is determined	NHPIs[1] with income below poverty level	Asian Indian	Bangladeshi	Cambodian	Chinese[2]	Fijian	Filipino	Guamanian[3]	Hawaiian, Native	Hmong	Indonesian	Japanese	Korean	Laotian	Malaysian	Pakistani	Samoan	Sri Lankan	Taiwanese	Thai	Tongan	Vietnamese
Allen County	29,807 9.13	4,447	384 8.64 8.64 1.29	-	-	34 3.33 8.85 0.76 0.11	-	-	9 1.72 2.34 0.20 0.03	-	0 0.00 0.00 0.00 0.00	-	-	-	-	-	-	-	-	-	-	-	-	-	-	41 5.07 10.68 0.92 0.14
Bartholomew County	5,164 7.35	1,182	99 8.38 8.38 1.92	-	-	31 7.28 31.31 2.62 0.60	-	-	-	-	-	-	-	-	-	-	-	-	-	-	-	-	-	-	-	-
Clark County	7,683 8.11	422	53 12.56 12.56 0.69	-	-	-	-	-	-	-	-	-	-	-	-	-	-	-	-	-	-	-	-	-	-	-
Delaware County	16,862 15.09	668	330 49.40 49.40 1.96	-	-	-	-	-	-	-	-	-	-	-	-	-	-	-	-	-	-	-	-	-	-	-
Elkhart County	14,058 7.84	1,541	147 9.54 9.54 1.05	-	-	-	-	-	-	-	-	-	-	-	-	-	-	-	-	-	-	-	-	-	-	-
Grant County	8,112 11.78	355	28 7.89 7.89 0.35	-	-	-	-	-	-	-	-	-	-	-	-	-	-	-	-	-	-	-	-	-	-	-
Hamilton County	5,300 2.93	4,114	284 6.90 6.90 5.36	-	-	0 0.00 0.00 0.00 0.00	-	-	45 5.29 15.85 1.09 0.85	-	-	-	-	-	-	-	-	-	-	-	-	-	-	-	-	-
Carmel (city)	949 2.54	1,636	239 14.61 14.61 25.18	-	-	-	-	-	-	-	-	-	-	-	-	-	-	-	-	-	-	-	-	-	-	-
Hendricks County	3,665 3.64	663	0 <0.01 <0.01 <0.01	-	-	-	-	-	-	-	-	-	-	-	-	-	-	-	-	-	-	-	-	-	-	-
Howard County	7,944 9.49	678	80 11.80 11.80 1.01	-	-	-	-	-	-	-	-	-	-	-	-	-	-	-	-	-	-	-	-	-	-	-

Notes: Please refer to the User's Guide for an explanation of data; data is arranged alphabetically by state, then county, then city within each county; table includes counties with populations greater than 49,999 unless noted and cities with populations greater than 9,999 whose Asian and/or NHPI population rates are greater than the national average; (1) Native Hawaiian and other Pacific Islander; (2) excludes Taiwanese; (3) includes Chamorro; (4) county does not meet population threshold but is shown in order to allow inclusion of city

Place	Total population with income below poverty level	Asian population for whom poverty status is determined	Asians with income below poverty level	NHPI[1] population for whom poverty status is determined	NHPIs[1] with income below poverty level	Asian Indian	Bangladeshi	Cambodian	Chinese[2]	Fijian	Filipino	Guamanian[3]	Hawaiian, Native	Hmong	Indonesian	Japanese	Korean	Laotian	Malaysian	Pakistani	Samoan	Sri Lankan	Taiwanese	Thai	Tongan	Vietnamese
Johnson County	6,337 5.63	955	51 5.34 5.34 0.80	-	-	-	-	-	-	-	-	-	-	-	-	-	-	-	-	-	-	-	-	-	-	-
Kosciusko County	4,668 6.43	378	6 1.59 1.59 0.13	-	-	-	-	-	-	-	-	-	-	-	-	-	-	-	-	-	-	-	-	-	-	-
Lake County	58,380 12.22	3,920	362 9.23 9.23 0.62	-	-	61 4.26 16.85 1.56 0.10	-	-	111 17.65 30.66 2.83 0.19	-	57 7.35 15.75 1.45 0.10	-	-	-	-	-	70 12.92 19.34 1.79 0.12	-	-	-	-	-	-	-	-	-
Munster (town)	912 4.32	952	72 7.56 7.56 7.89	-	-	0 0.00 0.00 0.00 0.00	-	-	-	-	-	-	-	-	-	-	-	-	-	-	-	-	-	-	-	-
LaPorte County	8,994 8.70	352	26 7.39 7.39 0.29	-	-	-	-	-	-	-	-	-	-	-	-	-	-	-	-	-	-	-	-	-	-	-
Madison County	11,941 9.34	491	61 12.42 12.42 0.51	-	-	-	-	-	-	-	-	-	-	-	-	-	-	-	-	-	-	-	-	-	-	-
Marion County	95,827 11.40	11,388	1,385 12.16 12.16 1.45	-	-	237 7.07 17.11 2.08 0.25	-	-	330 14.77 23.83 2.90 0.34	-	93 6.46 6.71 0.82 0.10	-	-	-	-	57 11.38 4.12 0.50 0.06	216 18.34 15.60 1.90 0.23	-	-	-	-	-	-	-	-	234 18.34 16.90 2.05 0.24
Monroe County	20,095 18.92	3,319	1,590 47.91 47.91 7.91	-	-	219 39.18 13.77 6.60 1.09	-	-	321 45.34 20.19 9.67 1.60	-	-	-	-	-	-	-	519 56.29 32.64 15.64 2.58	-	-	-	-	-	-	-	-	-
Bloomington (city)	16,385 29.62	2,865	1,578 55.08 55.08 9.63	-	-	219 50.69 13.88 7.64 1.34	-	-	321 49.01 20.34 11.20 1.96	-	-	-	-	-	-	-	507 61.60 32.13 17.70 3.09	-	-	-	-	-	-	-	-	-
Porter County	8,501 5.95	1,005	101 10.05 10.05 1.19	-	-	-	-	-	-	-	-	-	-	-	-	-	-	-	-	-	-	-	-	-	-	-

Notes: Please refer to the User's Guide for an explanation of data; data is arranged alphabetically by state, then county, then city within each county; table includes counties with populations greater than 49,999 unless noted and cities with populations greater than 9,999 whose Asian and/or NHPI population rates are greater than the national average; (1) Native Hawaiian and other Pacific Islander; (2) excludes Taiwanese; (3) includes Chamorro; (4) county does not meet population threshold but is shown in order to allow inclusion of city

Place	Total population with income below poverty level	Asian population for whom poverty status is determined	Asians with income below poverty level	NHPI[1] population for whom poverty status is determined	NHPIs[1] with income below poverty level	Asian Indian	Bangladeshi	Cambodian	Chinese[2]	Fijian	Filipino	Guamanian[3]	Hawaiian, Native	Hmong	Indonesian	Japanese	Korean	Laotian	Malaysian	Pakistani	Samoan	Sri Lankan	Taiwanese	Thai	Tongan	Vietnamese
St. Joseph County	26,226	3,292	392	-	-	39	-	-	76	-	-	-	-	-	-	-	84	-	-	-	-	-	-	-	-	-
	10.37		11.91			5.89			9.39								19.13									
						9.95			19.39								21.43									
			11.91			1.18			2.31								2.55									
			1.49			0.15			0.29								0.32									
Tippecanoe County	20,567	5,614	2,139	-	-	389	-	-	713	-	-	-	-	-	-	46	591	-	-	-	-	-	-	-	-	-
	15.41		38.10			32.20			37.85							13.61	67.47									
						18.19			33.33							2.15	27.63									
			38.10			6.93			12.70							0.82	10.53									
			10.40			1.89			3.47							0.22	2.87									
West Lafayette (city)	9,099	2,496	1,205	-	-	300	-	-	410	-	-	-	-	-	-	-	-	-	-	-	-	-	-	-	-	-
	38.30		48.28			39.68			52.50																	
						24.90			34.02																	
			48.28			12.02			16.43																	
			13.24			3.30			4.51																	
Vanderburgh County	18,414	1,496	125	-	-	-	-	-	-	-	-	-	-	-	-	-	-	-	-	-	-	-	-	-	-	-
	11.16		8.36																							
			8.36																							
			0.68																							
Vigo County	13,755	951	303	-	-	-	-	-	-	-	-	-	-	-	-	-	-	-	-	-	-	-	-	-	-	-
	14.08		31.86																							
			31.86																							
			2.20																							
Wayne County	7,804	432	85	-	-	-	-	-	-	-	-	-	-	-	-	-	-	-	-	-	-	-	-	-	-	-
	11.36		19.68																							
			19.68																							
			1.09																							
IOWA	258,008	33,531	4,755	873	170	477	-	167	980	-	289	-	-	-	-	225	1,040	305	-	36	-	-	65	47	-	630
	9.13		14.18		19.47	9.19		22.03	18.37		13.00					19.91	22.37	7.87		10.68			15.22	5.17		9.46
						10.03		3.51	20.61		6.08					4.73	21.87	6.41		0.76			1.37	0.99		13.25
			14.18		19.47	1.42		0.50	2.92		0.86					0.67	3.10	0.91		0.11			0.19	0.14		1.88
			1.84		0.07	0.18		0.06	0.38		0.11					0.09	0.40	0.12		0.01			0.03	0.02		0.24
Black Hawk County	16,050	1,259	189	-	-	-	-	-	-	-	-	-	-	-	-	-	-	-	-	-	-	-	-	-	-	-
	13.12		15.01																							
			15.01																							
			1.18																							
Buena Vista County[4]	1,991	880	130	-	-	-	-	-	-	-	-	-	-	-	-	-	-	72	-	-	-	-	-	-	-	-
	10.50		14.77															12.46								
																		55.38								
			14.77															8.18								
			6.53															3.62								
Storm Lake (city)	1,036	764	128	-	-	-	-	-	-	-	-	-	-	-	-	-	-	72	-	-	-	-	-	-	-	-
	11.59		16.75															13.66								
																		56.25								
			16.75															9.42								
			12.36															6.95								

Notes: Please refer to the User's Guide for an explanation of data; data is arranged alphabetically by state, then county, then city within each county; table includes counties with populations greater than 49,999 unless noted and cities with populations greater than 9,999 whose Asian and/or NHPI population rates are greater than the national average; (1) Native Hawaiian and other Pacific Islander; (2) excludes Taiwanese; (3) includes Chamorro; (4) county does not meet population threshold but is shown in order to allow inclusion of city

Place	Total population with income below poverty level	Asian population for whom poverty status is determined	Asians with income below poverty level	NHPI[1] population for whom poverty status is determined	NHPIs[1] with income below poverty level	Asian Indian	Bangladeshi	Cambodian	Chinese[2]	Fijian	Filipino	Guamanian[3]	Hawaiian, Native	Hmong	Indonesian	Japanese	Korean	Laotian	Malaysian	Pakistani	Samoan	Sri Lankan	Taiwanese	Thai	Tongan	Vietnamese
Johnson County	15,406 14.98	4,210	1,105 26.25 26.25 7.17	-	-	72 9.08 6.52 1.71 0.47	-	-	257 17.69 23.26 6.10 1.67	-	-	-	-	-	-	-	442 63.14 40.00 10.50 2.87	-	-	-	-	-	-	-	-	-
Coralville (city)	1,434 10.07	647	221 34.16 34.16 15.41	-	-	-	-	-	-	-	-	-	-	-	-	-	-	-	-	-	-	-	-	-	-	-
Iowa City (city)	12,234 21.73	3,299	884 26.80 26.80 7.23	-	-	63 10.82 7.13 1.91 0.51	-	-	257 20.05 29.07 7.79 2.10	-	-	-	-	-	-	-	291 61.65 32.92 8.82 2.38	-	-	-	-	-	-	-	-	-
Linn County	12,150 6.50	2,579	138 5.35 5.35 1.14	-	-	0 0.00 0.00 0.00 0.00	-	-	-	-	-	-	-	-	-	-	69 21.43 50.00 2.68 0.57	-	-	-	-	-	-	-	-	-
Polk County	29,051 7.94	9,022	853 9.45 9.45 2.94	-	-	132 10.53 15.47 1.46 0.45	-	108 25.78 12.66 1.20 0.37	83 8.00 9.73 0.92 0.29	-	-	-	-	-	-	-	38 5.22 4.45 0.42 0.13	78 4.72 9.14 0.86 0.27	-	-	-	-	-	11 3.13 1.29 0.12 0.04	-	234 9.34 27.43 2.59 0.81
Pottawattamie County	7,200 8.40	548	47 8.58 8.58 0.65	-	-	-	-	-	-	-	-	-	-	-	-	-	-	-	-	-	-	-	-	-	-	-
Scott County	16,329 10.50	2,261	275 12.16 12.16 1.68	-	-	-	-	-	-	-	-	-	-	-	-	-	-	-	-	-	-	-	-	-	-	161 16.18 58.55 7.12 0.99
Story County	9,921 14.06	3,228	1,110 34.39 34.39 11.19	-	-	109 16.98 9.82 3.38 1.10	-	-	392 37.40 35.32 12.14 3.95	-	-	-	-	-	-	-	286 42.12 25.77 8.86 2.88	-	-	-	-	-	-	-	-	-
Ames (city)	8,507 20.36	3,085	1,090 35.33 35.33 12.81	-	-	109 18.11 10.00 3.53 1.28	-	-	392 38.51 35.96 12.71 4.61	-	-	-	-	-	-	-	279 42.92 25.60 9.04 3.28	-	-	-	-	-	-	-	-	-
Woodbury County	10,434 10.30	2,368	182 7.69 7.69 1.74	-	-	-	-	-	-	-	-	-	-	-	-	-	-	-	-	-	-	-	-	-	-	89 6.23 48.90 3.76 0.85

Notes: Please refer to the User's Guide for an explanation of data; data is arranged alphabetically by state, then county, then city within each county; table includes counties with populations greater than 49,999 unless noted and cities with populations greater than 9,999 whose Asian and/or NHPI population rates are greater than the national average; (1) Native Hawaiian and other Pacific Islander; (2) excludes Taiwanese; (3) includes Chamorro; (4) county does not meet population threshold but is shown in order to allow inclusion of city

Place	Total population with income below poverty level	Asian population for whom poverty status is determined	Asians with income below poverty level	NHPI[1] population for whom poverty status is determined	NHPIs[1] with income below poverty level	Asian Indian	Bangladeshi	Cambodian	Chinese[2]	Fijian	Filipino	Guamanian[3]	Hawaiian, Native	Hmong	Indonesian	Japanese	Korean	Laotian	Malaysian	Pakistani	Samoan	Sri Lankan	Taiwanese	Thai	Tongan	Vietnamese
KANSAS	257,829 9.90	43,717	6,392 14.62 14.62 2.48	1,147	154 13.43 13.43 0.06	1,121 14.86 17.54 2.56 0.43	-	230 32.86 3.60 0.53 0.09	1,007 14.70 15.75 2.30 0.39	-	246 7.49 3.85 0.56 0.10	-	72 18.56 46.75 6.28 0.03	183 19.85 2.86 0.42 0.07	-	370 21.50 5.79 0.85 0.14	692 16.57 10.83 1.58 0.27	191 6.75 2.99 0.44 0.07	-	97 12.58 1.52 0.22 0.04	-	-	108 21.77 1.69 0.25 0.04	69 10.82 1.08 0.16 0.03	-	1,656 14.79 25.91 3.79 0.64
Cowley County[4]	4,474 12.93	527	105 19.92 19.92 2.35	-	-	-	-	-	-	-	-	-	-	-	-	-	-	10 2.87 9.52 1.90 0.22	-	-	-	-	-	-	-	-
Winfield (city)	1,536 13.83	460	90 19.57 19.57 5.86	-	-	-	-	-	-	-	-	-	-	-	-	-	-	10 2.91 11.11 2.17 0.65	-	-	-	-	-	-	-	-
Douglas County	14,486 15.85	2,940	868 29.52 29.52 5.99	-	-	91 22.09 10.48 3.10 0.63	-	-	233 27.38 26.84 7.93 1.61	-	-	-	-	-	-	-	126 27.10 14.52 4.29 0.87	-	-	-	-	-	-	-	-	-
Lawrence (city)	13,650 18.88	2,907	866 29.79 29.79 6.34	-	-	91 22.98 10.51 3.13 0.67	-	-	233 27.38 26.91 8.02 1.71	-	-	-	-	-	-	-	126 27.33 14.55 4.33 0.92	-	-	-	-	-	-	-	-	-
Johnson County	15,323 3.44	12,576	741 5.89 5.89 4.84	-	-	289 7.13 39.00 2.30 1.89	-	-	107 4.13 14.44 0.85 0.70	-	10 1.06 1.35 0.08 0.07	-	-	-	-	30 6.74 4.05 0.24 0.20	127 9.58 17.14 1.01 0.83	41 6.41 5.53 0.33 0.27	-	-	-	-	-	-	-	24 1.80 3.24 0.19 0.16
Overland Park (city)	4,730 3.21	5,666	327 5.77 5.77 6.91	-	-	116 5.86 35.47 2.05 2.45	-	-	22 1.70 6.73 0.39 0.47	-	-	-	-	-	-	-	94 15.80 28.75 1.66 1.99	-	-	-	-	-	-	-	-	24 4.07 7.34 0.42 0.51
Leavenworth County	4,128 6.65	670	33 4.93 4.93 0.80	-	-	-	-	-	-	-	-	-	-	-	-	-	-	-	-	-	-	-	-	-	-	-
Riley County	11,063 20.56	1,882	507 26.94 26.94 4.58	-	-	-	-	-	119 18.09 23.47 6.32 1.08	-	-	-	-	-	-	-	143 37.05 28.21 7.60 1.29	-	-	-	-	-	-	-	-	-
Manhattan (city)	9,475 24.18	1,660	428 25.78 25.78 4.52	-	-	-	-	-	112 17.81 26.17 6.75 1.18	-	-	-	-	-	-	-	-	-	-	-	-	-	-	-	-	-

Notes: Please refer to the User's Guide for an explanation of data; data is arranged alphabetically by state, then county, then city within each county; table includes counties with populations greater than 49,999 unless noted and cities with populations greater than 9,999 whose Asian and/or NHPI population rates are greater than the national average; (1) Native Hawaiian and other Pacific Islander; (2) excludes Taiwanese; (3) includes Chamorro; (4) county does not meet population threshold but is shown in order to allow inclusion of city

Place	Total population with income below poverty level	Asian population for whom poverty status is determined	Asians with income below poverty level	NHPI[1] population for whom poverty status is determined	NHPIs[1] with income below poverty level	Asian Indian	Bangladeshi	Cambodian	Chinese[2]	Fijian	Filipino	Guamanian[3]	Hawaiian, Native	Hmong	Indonesian	Japanese	Korean	Laotian	Malaysian	Pakistani	Samoan	Sri Lankan	Taiwanese	Thai	Tongan	Vietnamese
Saline County	4,588 8.80	834	87 10.43 10.43 1.90	-	-	-	-	-	-	-	-	-	-	-	-	-	-	-	-	-	-	-	-	-	-	40 10.75 45.98 4.80 0.87
Sedgwick County	42,605 9.54	14,062	2,361 16.79 16.79 5.54	431	50 11.60 11.60 0.12	411 31.76 17.41 2.92 0.96	-	148 32.60 6.27 1.05 0.35	257 17.83 10.89 1.83 0.60	-	62 8.99 2.63 0.44 0.15	-	-	-	-	-	108 19.35 4.57 0.77 0.25	86 8.26 3.64 0.61 0.20	-	-	-	-	-	-	-	1,016 15.14 43.03 7.23 2.38
Wichita (city)	38,018 11.21	12,581	2,260 17.96 17.96 5.94	-	-	411 33.09 18.19 3.27 1.08	-	-	257 19.15 11.37 2.04 0.68	-	59 10.99 2.61 0.47 0.16	-	-	-	-	-	108 22.50 4.78 0.86 0.28	51 7.35 2.26 0.41 0.13	-	-	-	-	-	-	-	988 15.46 43.72 7.85 2.60
Shawnee County	15,824 9.59	1,439	296 20.57 20.57 1.87	-	-	-	-	-	-	-	-	-	-	-	-	-	-	-	-	-	-	-	-	-	-	-
Wyandotte County	25,773 16.54	2,217	372 16.78 16.78 1.44	-	-	-	-	-	-	-	-	-	-	175 22.46 47.04 7.89 0.68	-	-	-	-	-	-	-	-	-	-	-	-
KENTUCKY	621,096 15.82	27,556	3,430 12.45 12.45 0.55	1,074	193 17.97 17.97 0.03	654 10.19 19.07 2.37 0.11	-	-	645 13.05 18.80 2.34 0.10	-	309 10.25 9.01 1.12 0.05	63 18.16 32.64 5.87 0.01	-	-	-	296 9.57 8.63 1.07 0.05	625 16.72 18.22 2.27 0.10	-	-	7 1.25 0.20 0.03 <0.01	-	-	-	49 14.37 1.43 0.18 0.01	-	438 13.87 12.77 1.59 0.07
Boone County	4,785 5.62	1,014	30 2.96 2.96 0.63	-	-	-	-	-	-	-	-	-	-	-	-	30 6.54 100.00 2.96 0.63	-	-	-	-	-	-	-	-	-	-
Campbell County	8,093 9.33	566	26 4.59 4.59 0.32	-	-	-	-	-	-	-	-	-	-	-	-	-	-	-	-	-	-	-	-	-	-	-
Christian County	9,935 14.99	457	71 15.54 15.54 0.71	-	-	-	-	-	-	-	-	-	-	-	-	-	-	-	-	-	-	-	-	-	-	-
Fayette County	31,963 12.87	5,231	864 16.52 16.52 2.70	-	-	258 22.26 29.86 4.93 0.81	-	-	316 19.97 36.57 6.04 0.99	-	-	-	-	-	-	104 11.69 12.04 1.99 0.33	-	-	-	-	-	-	-	-	-	-

Notes: Please refer to the User's Guide for an explanation of data; data is arranged alphabetically by state, then county, then city within each county; table includes counties with populations greater than 49,999 unless noted and cities with populations greater than 9,999 whose Asian and/or NHPI population rates are greater than the national average; (1) Native Hawaiian and other Pacific Islander; (2) excludes Taiwanese; (3) includes Chamorro; (4) county does not meet population threshold but is shown in order to allow inclusion of city

Place	Total population with income below poverty level	Asian population for whom poverty status is determined	Asians with income below poverty level	NHPI[1] population for whom poverty status is determined	NHPIs[1] with income below poverty level	Asian Indian	Bangladeshi	Cambodian	Chinese[2]	Fijian	Filipino	Guamanian[3]	Hawaiian, Native	Hmong	Indonesian	Japanese	Korean	Laotian	Malaysian	Pakistani	Samoan	Sri Lankan	Taiwanese	Thai	Tongan	Vietnamese
Hardin County	9,051 10.04	1,836	114 6.21 6.21 1.26	-	-	-	-	-	-	-	-	-	-	-	-	-	55 7.40 48.25 3.00 0.61	-	-	-	-	-	-	-	-	-
Radcliff (city)	2,709 12.49	939	85 9.05 9.05 3.14	-	-	-	-	-	-	-	-	-	-	-	-	-	-	-	-	-	-	-	-	-	-	-
Jefferson County	84,143 12.36	8,919	1,024 11.48 11.48 1.22	-	-	272 11.02 26.56 3.05 0.32	-	-	145 10.37 14.16 1.63 0.17	-	45 4.96 4.39 0.50 0.05	-	-	-	-	18 5.28 1.76 0.20 0.02	197 19.33 19.24 2.21 0.23	-	-	-	-	-	-	-	-	303 17.04 29.59 3.40 0.36
Kenton County	13,487 9.02	862	94 10.90 10.90 0.70	-	-	-	-	-	-	-	-	-	-	-	-	-	-	-	-	-	-	-	-	-	-	-
Madison County	10,952 16.75	474	12 2.53 2.53 0.11	-	-	-	-	-	-	-	-	-	-	-	-	-	-	-	-	-	-	-	-	-	-	-
Warren County	13,433 15.43	1,022	129 12.62 12.62 0.96	-	-	-	-	-	-	-	-	-	-	-	-	-	-	-	-	-	-	-	-	-	-	-
LOUISIANA	851,113 19.64	54,233	11,251 20.75 20.75 1.32	1,211	312 25.76 25.76 0.04	1,491 17.92 13.25 2.75 0.18	-	-	1,177 17.83 10.46 2.17 0.14	-	544 11.78 4.84 1.00 0.06	98 23.00 31.41 8.09 0.01	94 27.33 30.13 7.76 0.01	-	-	269 19.20 2.39 0.50 0.03	467 17.68 4.15 0.86 0.05	183 14.42 1.63 0.34 0.02	-	154 15.96 1.37 0.28 0.02	-	-	18 3.64 0.16 0.03 <0.01	57 8.84 0.51 0.11 0.01	-	6,485 26.20 57.64 11.96 0.76
Ascension Parish	9,808 12.95	314	9 2.87 2.87 0.09	-	-	-	-	-	-	-	-	-	-	-	-	-	-	-	-	-	-	-	-	-	-	-
Bossier Parish	13,184 13.74	1,139	134 11.76 11.76 1.02	-	-	-	-	-	-	-	-	-	-	-	-	-	-	-	-	-	-	-	-	-	-	-
Caddo Parish	51,903 21.11	1,914	188 9.82 9.82 0.36	-	-	38 7.69 20.21 1.99 0.07	-	-	-	-	-	-	-	-	-	-	-	-	-	-	-	-	-	-	-	-

Notes: Please refer to the User's Guide for an explanation of data; data is arranged alphabetically by state, then county, then city within each county; table includes counties with populations greater than 49,999 unless noted and cities with populations greater than 9,999 whose Asian and/or NHPI population rates are greater than the national average; (1) Native Hawaiian and other Pacific Islander; (2) excludes Taiwanese; (3) includes Chamorro; (4) county does not meet population threshold but is shown in order to allow inclusion of city

Place	Total population with income below poverty level	Asian population for whom poverty status is determined	Asians with income below poverty level	NHPI[1] population for whom poverty status is determined	NHPIs[1] with income below poverty level	Asian Indian	Bangladeshi	Cambodian	Chinese[2]	Fijian	Filipino	Guamanian[3]	Hawaiian, Native	Hmong	Indonesian	Japanese	Korean	Laotian	Malaysian	Pakistani	Samoan	Sri Lankan	Taiwanese	Thai	Tongan	Vietnamese
Calcasieu Parish	27,582 15.43	1,003	93 9.27 9.27 0.34	-	-	-	-	-	-	-	-	-	-	-	-	-	-	-	-	-	-	-	-	-	-	-
East Baton Rouge Parish	71,276 17.87	8,602	2,066 24.02 24.02 2.90	-	-	339 18.43 16.41 3.94 0.48	-	-	325 19.30 15.73 3.78 0.46	-	53 11.70 2.57 0.62 0.07	-	-	-	-	-	-	-	-	-	-	-	-	-	-	1,079 30.79 52.23 12.54 1.51
Iberia Parish	16,952 23.55	1,463	418 28.57 28.57 2.47	-	-	-	-	-	-	-	-	-	-	-	-	-	-	170 19.12 40.67 11.62 1.00	-	-	-	-	-	-	-	196 50.13 46.89 13.40 1.16
Jefferson Parish	61,608 13.65	13,783	2,029 14.72 14.72 3.29	-	-	167 9.60 8.23 1.21 0.27	-	-	277 14.36 13.65 2.01 0.45	-	102 10.42 5.03 0.74 0.17	-	-	-	-	-	64 10.56 3.15 0.46 0.10	-	-	43 9.66 2.12 0.31 0.07	-	-	-	-	-	1,228 17.77 60.52 8.91 1.99
Gretna (city)	4,017 24.19	642	192 29.91 29.91 4.78	-	-	-	-	-	-	-	-	-	-	-	-	-	-	-	-	-	-	-	-	-	-	177 47.71 92.19 27.57 4.41
Harvey (cdp)	5,217 23.68	1,147	237 20.66 20.66 4.54	-	-	-	-	-	-	-	-	-	-	-	-	-	-	-	-	-	-	-	-	-	-	149 17.45 62.87 12.99 2.86
Timberlane (cdp)	964 8.51	638	18 2.82 2.82 1.87	-	-	-	-	-	-	-	-	-	-	-	-	-	-	-	-	-	-	-	-	-	-	18 3.17 100.00 2.82 1.87
Woodmere (cdp)	1,666 12.84	711	225 31.65 31.65 13.51	-	-	-	-	-	-	-	-	-	-	-	-	-	-	-	-	-	-	-	-	-	-	108 21.47 48.00 15.19 6.48
Lafayette Parish	29,216 15.72	2,085	471 22.59 22.59 1.61	-	-	189 31.29 40.13 9.06 0.65	-	-	-	-	-	-	-	-	-	-	-	-	-	-	-	-	-	-	-	156 21.37 33.12 7.48 0.53
Lafourche Parish	14,560 16.53	525	135 25.71 25.71 0.93	-	-	-	-	-	-	-	-	-	-	-	-	-	-	-	-	-	-	-	-	-	-	-

Notes: Please refer to the User's Guide for an explanation of data; data is arranged alphabetically by state, then county, then city within each county; table includes counties with populations greater than 49,999 unless noted and cities with populations greater than 9,999 whose Asian and/or NHPI population rates are greater than the national average; (1) Native Hawaiian and other Pacific Islander; (2) excludes Taiwanese; (3) includes Chamorro; (4) county does not meet population threshold but is shown in order to allow inclusion of city

Place	Total population with income below poverty level	Asian population for whom poverty status is determined	Asians with income below poverty level	NHPI[1] population for whom poverty status is determined	NHPIs[1] with income below poverty level	Asian Indian	Bangladeshi	Cambodian	Chinese[2]	Fijian	Filipino	Guamanian[3]	Hawaiian, Native	Hmong	Indonesian	Japanese	Korean	Laotian	Malaysian	Pakistani	Samoan	Sri Lankan	Taiwanese	Thai	Tongan	Vietnamese
Orleans Parish	130,896 27.94	10,074	3,038 30.16 30.16 2.32	-	-	333 30.75 10.96 3.31 0.25	-	-	172 23.50 5.66 1.71 0.13	-	68 14.53 2.24 0.68 0.05	-	-	-	-	-	-	-	-	-	-	-	-	-	-	2,184 31.85 71.89 21.68 1.67
Ouachita Parish	29,515 20.68	771	118 15.30 15.30 0.40	-	-	-	-	-	-	-	-	-	-	-	-	-	-	-	-	-	-	-	-	-	-	-
Rapides Parish	25,097 20.54	1,078	166 15.40 15.40 0.66	-	-	-	-	-	-	-	-	-	-	-	-	-	-	-	-	-	-	-	-	-	-	-
St. Bernard Parish	8,687 13.11	1,079	193 17.89 17.89 2.22	-	-	-	-	-	-	-	-	-	-	-	-	-	-	-	-	-	-	-	-	-	-	109 21.98 56.48 10.10 1.25
St. Mary Parish	12,472 23.61	979	258 26.35 26.35 2.07	-	-	-	-	-	-	-	-	-	-	-	-	-	-	-	-	-	-	-	-	-	-	252 28.54 97.67 25.74 2.02
St. Tammany Parish	18,336 9.72	1,442	95 6.59 6.59 0.52	-	-	-	-	-	-	-	-	-	-	-	-	-	-	-	-	-	-	-	-	-	-	35 11.86 36.84 2.43 0.19
Terrebonne Parish	19,607 19.09	868	227 26.15 26.15 1.16	-	-	-	-	-	-	-	-	-	-	-	-	-	-	-	-	-	-	-	-	-	-	110 28.28 48.46 12.67 0.56
Vermilion Parish	11,681 22.11	1,031	374 36.28 36.28 3.20	-	-	-	-	-	-	-	-	-	-	-	-	-	-	-	-	-	-	-	-	-	-	342 37.17 91.44 33.17 2.93
Abbeville (city)	4,414 37.66	684	339 49.56 49.56 7.68	-	-	-	-	-	-	-	-	-	-	-	-	-	-	-	-	-	-	-	-	-	-	309 47.25 91.15 45.18 7.00
Vernon Parish	7,479 15.25	1,034	176 17.02 17.02 2.35	-	-	-	-	-	-	-	-	-	-	-	-	-	74 22.84 42.05 7.16 0.99	-	-	-	-	-	-	-	-	-

Notes: Please refer to the User's Guide for an explanation of data; data is arranged alphabetically by state, then county, then city within each county; table includes counties with populations greater than 49,999 unless noted and cities with populations greater than 9,999 whose Asian and/or NHPI population rates are greater than the national average; (1) Native Hawaiian and other Pacific Islander; (2) excludes Taiwanese; (3) includes Chamorro; (4) county does not meet population threshold but is shown in order to allow inclusion of city

Place	Total population with income below poverty level	Asian population for whom poverty status is determined	Asians with income below poverty level	NHPI[1] population for whom poverty status is determined	NHPIs[1] with income below poverty level	Asian Indian	Bangladeshi	Cambodian	Chinese[2]	Fijian	Filipino	Guamanian[3]	Hawaiian, Native	Hmong	Indonesian	Japanese	Korean	Laotian	Malaysian	Pakistani	Samoan	Sri Lankan	Taiwanese	Thai	Tongan	Vietnamese
MAINE	135,501	7,824	1,492	280	18	88	-	444	242	-	99	-	-	-	-	105	108	-	-	-	-	-	-	-	-	205
	10.92		19.07		6.43	9.78		45.08	15.45		8.73					18.95	16.41									19.19
						5.90		29.76	16.22		6.64					7.04	7.24									13.74
			19.07		6.43	1.12		5.67	3.09		1.27					1.34	1.38									2.62
			1.10		0.01	0.06		0.33	0.18		0.07					0.08	0.08									0.15
Androscoggin County	11,115	428	90	-	-	-	-	-	-	-	-	-	-	-	-	-	-	-	-	-	-	-	-	-	-	-
	11.10		21.03																							
			21.03																							
			0.81																							
Aroostook County	10,313	388	93	-	-	-	-	-	-	-	-	-	-	-	-	-	-	-	-	-	-	-	-	-	-	-
	14.33		23.97																							
			23.97																							
			0.90																							
Cumberland County	20,352	3,131	834	-	-	-	-	370	35	-	29	-	-	-	-	-	-	-	-	-	-	-	-	-	-	117
	7.89		26.64					57.36	8.62		9.63															18.57
								44.36	4.20		3.48															14.03
			26.64					11.82	1.12		0.93															3.74
			4.10					1.82	0.17		0.14															0.57
Hancock County	5,159	194	30	-	-	-	-	-	-	-	-	-	-	-	-	-	-	-	-	-	-	-	-	-	-	-
	10.24		15.46																							
			15.46																							
			0.58																							
Kennebec County	12,637	618	35	-	-	-	-	-	-	-	-	-	-	-	-	-	-	-	-	-	-	-	-	-	-	-
	11.13		5.66																							
			5.66																							
			0.28																							
Oxford County	6,353	253	24	-	-	-	-	-	-	-	-	-	-	-	-	-	-	-	-	-	-	-	-	-	-	-
	11.82		9.49																							
			9.49																							
			0.38																							
Penobscot County	18,956	952	199	-	-	-	-	-	25	-	-	-	-	-	-	-	-	-	-	-	-	-	-	-	-	-
	13.68		20.90						8.71																	
									12.56																	
			20.90						2.63																	
			1.05						0.13																	
York County	15,003	938	64	-	-	-	-	-	-	-	-	-	-	-	-	-	-	-	-	-	-	-	-	-	-	-
	8.15		6.82																							
			6.82																							
			0.43																							
MARYLAND	438,676	206,609	17,130	1,948	57	3,786	66	199	3,711	-	1,267	19	7	-	132	603	4,387	84	-	467	-	53	238	194	-	1,343
	8.49		8.29		2.93	7.69	5.48	11.69	7.96		4.85	2.78	1.41		11.91	8.92	11.35	11.41		9.19		4.78	10.44	6.86		8.15
						22.10	0.39	1.16	21.66		7.40	33.33	12.28		0.77	3.52	25.61	0.49		2.73		0.31	1.39	1.13		7.84
			8.29		2.93	1.83	0.03	0.10	1.80		0.61	0.98	0.36		0.06	0.29	2.12	0.04		0.23		0.03	0.12	0.09		0.65
			3.90		0.01	0.86	0.02	0.05	0.85		0.29	<0.01	<0.01		0.03	0.14	1.00	0.02		0.11		0.01	0.05	0.04		0.31

Notes: Please refer to the User's Guide for an explanation of data; data is arranged alphabetically by state, then county, then city within each county; table includes counties with populations greater than 49,999 unless noted and cities with populations greater than 9,999 whose Asian and/or NHPI population rates are greater than the national average; (1) Native Hawaiian and other Pacific Islander; (2) excludes Taiwanese; (3) includes Chamorro; (4) county does not meet population threshold but is shown in order to allow inclusion of city

Place	Total population with income below poverty level	Asian population for whom poverty status is determined	Asians with income below poverty level	NHPI[1] population for whom poverty status is determined	NHPIs[1] with income below poverty level	Asian Indian	Bangladeshi	Cambodian	Chinese[2]	Fijian	Filipino	Guamanian[3]	Hawaiian, Native	Hmong	Indonesian	Japanese	Korean	Laotian	Malaysian	Pakistani	Samoan	Sri Lankan	Taiwanese	Thai	Tongan	Vietnamese
Allegany County	10,149 14.77	429	29 6.76 6.76 0.29	-	-	-	-	-	-	-	-	-	-	-	-	-	-	-	-	-	-	-	-	-	-	-
Anne Arundel County	24,335 5.14	11,199	706 6.30 6.30 2.90	-	-	136 8.08 19.26 1.21 0.56	-	-	84 5.66 11.90 0.75 0.35	-	72 3.02 10.20 0.64 0.30	-	-	-	-	44 6.44 6.23 0.39 0.18	267 7.31 37.82 2.38 1.10	-	-	-	-	-	-	-	-	-
Severn (cdp)	2,263 6.47	1,624	54 3.33 3.33 2.39	-	-	-	-	-	-	-	-	-	-	-	-	-	54 7.01 100.00 3.33 2.39	-	-	-	-	-	-	-	-	-
South Gate (cdp)	1,835 6.46	1,436	158 11.00 11.00 8.61	-	-	-	-	-	-	-	-	-	-	-	-	-	124 14.52 78.48 8.64 6.76	-	-	-	-	-	-	-	-	-
Baltimore Independent City	143,514 22.92	9,368	2,842 30.34 30.34 1.98	-	-	723 36.78 25.44 7.72 0.50	-	-	688 33.32 24.21 7.34 0.48	-	218 16.10 7.67 2.33 0.15	-	-	-	-	-	550 34.61 19.35 5.87 0.38	-	-	-	-	-	-	-	-	146 18.94 5.14 1.56 0.10
Baltimore County	47,603 6.45	23,212	1,960 8.44 8.44 4.12	-	-	406 6.74 20.71 1.75 0.85	-	-	417 9.35 21.28 1.80 0.88	-	118 3.72 6.02 0.51 0.25	-	-	-	-	139 22.24 7.09 0.60 0.29	586 11.56 29.90 2.52 1.23	-	-	51 5.08 2.60 0.22 0.11	-	-	-	-	-	122 10.14 6.22 0.53 0.26
Arbutus (cdp)	1,362 6.85	970	117 12.06 12.06 8.59	-	-	-	-	-	-	-	-	-	-	-	-	-	-	-	-	-	-	-	-	-	-	-
Carney (cdp)	1,499 5.35	1,589	74 4.66 4.66 4.94	-	-	-	-	-	0 0.00 0.00 0.00 0.00	-	-	-	-	-	-	-	74 9.64 100.00 4.66 4.94	-	-	-	-	-	-	-	-	-
Cockeysville (cdp)	1,608 8.25	1,741	285 16.37 16.37 17.72	-	-	-	-	-	-	-	-	-	-	-	-	-	159 23.80 55.79 9.13 9.89	-	-	-	-	-	-	-	-	-
Lutherville-Timonium (cdp)	554 3.57	662	53 8.01 8.01 9.57	-	-	-	-	-	-	-	-	-	-	-	-	-	-	-	-	-	-	-	-	-	-	-

Notes: Please refer to the User's Guide for an explanation of data; data is arranged alphabetically by state, then county, then city within each county; table includes counties with populations greater than 49,999 unless noted and cities with populations greater than 9,999 whose Asian and/or NHPI population rates are greater than the national average; (1) Native Hawaiian and other Pacific Islander; (2) excludes Taiwanese; (3) includes Chamorro; (4) county does not meet population threshold but is shown in order to allow inclusion of city

Place	Total population with income below poverty level	Asian population for whom poverty status is determined	Asians with income below poverty level	NHPI[1] population for whom poverty status is determined	NHPIs[1] with income below poverty level	Asian Indian	Bangladeshi	Cambodian	Chinese[2]	Fijian	Filipino	Guamanian[3]	Hawaiian, Native	Hmong	Indonesian	Japanese	Korean	Laotian	Malaysian	Pakistani	Samoan	Sri Lankan	Taiwanese	Thai	Tongan	Vietnamese
Mays Chapel (cdp)	274 2.40	821	8 0.97 0.97 2.92	-	-	-	-	-	-	-	-	-	-	-	-	-	-	-	-	-	-	-	-	-	-	-
Owings Mills (cdp)	1,158 5.88	767	75 9.78 9.78 6.48	-	-	-	-	-	-	-	-	-	-	-	-	-	-	-	-	-	-	-	-	-	-	-
Perry Hall (cdp)	829 2.90	1,497	87 5.81 5.81 10.49	-	-	-	-	-	-	-	-	-	-	-	-	-	61 11.62 70.11 4.07 7.36	-	-	-	-	-	-	-	-	-
Reisterstown (cdp)	1,283 5.77	1,022	56 5.48 5.48 4.36	-	-	56 9.93 100.00 5.48 4.36	-	-	-	-	-	-	-	-	-	-	-	-	-	-	-	-	-	-	-	-
Rossville (cdp)	567 4.95	556	114 20.50 20.50 20.11	-	-	-	-	-	-	-	-	-	-	-	-	-	-	-	-	-	-	-	-	-	-	-
Towson (cdp)	3,523 7.72	1,827	222 12.15 12.15 6.30	-	-	-	-	-	33 3.90 14.86 1.81 0.94	-	-	-	-	-	-	-	-	-	-	-	-	-	-	-	-	-
Woodlawn (cdp)	2,257 6.28	2,170	187 8.62 8.62 8.29	-	-	113 12.80 60.43 5.21 5.01	-	-	-	-	-	-	-	-	-	-	-	-	-	-	-	-	-	-	-	-
Calvert County	3,235 4.38	655	9 1.37 1.37 0.28	-	-	-	-	-	-	-	-	-	-	-	-	-	-	-	-	-	-	-	-	-	-	-
Carroll County	5,617 3.82	1,188	170 14.31 14.31 3.03	-	-	-	-	-	-	-	-	-	-	-	-	-	-	-	-	-	-	-	-	-	-	-
Cecil County	6,066 7.17	564	42 7.45 7.45 0.69	-	-	-	-	-	-	-	-	-	-	-	-	-	-	-	-	-	-	-	-	-	-	-

Notes: Please refer to the User's Guide for an explanation of data; data is arranged alphabetically by state, then county, then city within each county; table includes counties with populations greater than 49,999 unless noted and cities with populations greater than 9,999 whose Asian and/or NHPI population rates are greater than the national average; (1) Native Hawaiian and other Pacific Islander; (2) excludes Taiwanese; (3) includes Chamorro; (4) county does not meet population threshold but is shown in order to allow inclusion of city

Place	Total population with income below poverty level	Asian population for whom poverty status is determined	Asians with income below poverty level	NHPI[1] population for whom poverty status is determined	NHPIs[1] with income below poverty level	Asian Indian	Bangladeshi	Cambodian	Chinese[2]	Fijian	Filipino	Guamanian[3]	Hawaiian, Native	Hmong	Indonesian	Japanese	Korean	Laotian	Malaysian	Pakistani	Samoan	Sri Lankan	Taiwanese	Thai	Tongan	Vietnamese
Charles County	6,518 5.47	1,884	62 3.29 3.29 0.95	-	-	-	-	-	-	-	8 1.69 12.90 0.42 0.12	-	-	-	-	-	-	-	-	-	-	-	-	-	-	-
Frederick County	8,550 4.48	3,227	116 3.59 3.59 1.36	-	-	33 5.49 28.45 1.02 0.39	-	-	34 4.35 29.31 1.05 0.40	-	-	-	-	-	-	-	0 0.00 0.00 0.00 0.00	-	-	-	-	-	-	-	-	-
Harford County	10,695 4.94	3,147	282 8.96 8.96 2.64	-	-	135 21.57 47.87 4.29 1.26	-	-	-	-	26 4.70 9.22 0.83 0.24	-	-	-	-	-	18 2.37 6.38 0.57 0.17	-	-	-	-	-	-	-	-	-
Howard County	9,491 3.87	18,591	1,381 7.43 7.43 14.55	-	-	286 6.02 20.71 1.54 3.01	-	-	231 6.24 16.73 1.24 2.43	-	72 5.33 5.21 0.39 0.76	-	-	-	-	-	639 10.68 46.27 3.44 6.73	-	-	48 7.36 3.48 0.26 0.51	-	-	-	-	-	64 8.80 4.63 0.34 0.67
Columbia (cdp)	4,721 5.39	6,238	541 8.67 8.67 11.46	-	-	148 8.27 27.36 2.37 3.13	-	-	114 7.26 21.07 1.83 2.41	-	13 2.69 2.40 0.21 0.28	-	-	-	-	-	191 13.21 35.30 3.06 4.05	-	-	-	-	-	-	-	-	-
Elkridge (cdp)	600 2.73	1,406	50 3.56 3.56 8.33	-	-	-	-	-	-	-	-	-	-	-	-	-	0 0.00 0.00 0.00 0.00	-	-	-	-	-	-	-	-	-
Ellicott City (cdp)	1,841 3.29	6,661	629 9.44 9.44 34.17	-	-	68 6.02 10.81 1.02 3.69	-	-	106 8.39 16.85 1.59 5.76	-	54 13.33 8.59 0.81 2.93	-	-	-	-	-	337 11.75 53.58 5.06 18.31	-	-	34 8.61 5.41 0.51 1.85	-	-	-	-	-	-
North Laurel (cdp)	707 3.44	1,390	71 5.11 5.11 10.04	-	-	10 2.40 14.08 0.72 1.41	-	-	-	-	-	-	-	-	-	-	61 14.45 85.92 4.39 8.63	-	-	-	-	-	-	-	-	-
Savage-Guilford (cdp)	615 4.90	730	13 1.78 1.78 2.11	-	-	-	-	-	-	-	-	-	-	-	-	-	-	-	-	-	-	-	-	-	-	-
Montgomery County	47,024 5.44	97,727	5,766 5.90 5.90 12.26	483	19 3.93 3.93 0.04	1,311 5.38 22.74 1.34 2.79	47 5.69 0.82 0.05 0.10	110 9.52 1.91 0.11 0.23	1,311 4.79 22.74 1.34 2.79	-	201 2.96 3.49 0.21 0.43	-	-	-	83 8.94 1.44 0.08 0.18	192 6.08 3.33 0.20 0.41	1,319 8.54 22.88 1.35 2.80	-	-	118 6.49 2.05 0.12 0.25	-	42 5.61 0.73 0.04 0.09	124 10.84 2.15 0.13 0.26	55 4.14 0.95 0.06 0.12	-	623 6.69 10.80 0.64 1.32

Notes: Please refer to the User's Guide for an explanation of data; data is arranged alphabetically by state, then county, then city within each county; table includes counties with populations greater than 49,999 unless noted and cities with populations greater than 9,999 whose Asian and/or NHPI population rates are greater than the national average; (1) Native Hawaiian and other Pacific Islander; (2) excludes Taiwanese; (3) includes Chamorro; (4) county does not meet population threshold but is shown in order to allow inclusion of city

Place	Total population with income below poverty level	Asian population for whom poverty status is determined	Asians with income below poverty level	NHPI[1] population for whom poverty status is determined	NHPIs[1] with income below poverty level	Asian Indian	Bangladeshi	Cambodian	Chinese[2]	Fijian	Filipino	Guamanian[3]	Hawaiian, Native	Hmong	Indonesian	Japanese	Korean	Laotian	Malaysian	Pakistani	Samoan	Sri Lankan	Taiwanese	Thai	Tongan	Vietnamese
Aspen Hill (cdp)	3,378	5,545	244	-	-	9	-	-	129	-	0	-	-	-	-	-	84	-	-	-	-	-	-	-	-	9
	6.78		4.40			1.30			7.20		0.00						8.40									2.09
						3.69			52.87		0.00						34.43									3.69
			4.40			0.16			2.33		0.00						1.51									0.16
			7.22			0.27			3.82		0.00						2.49									0.27
Bethesda (cdp)	1,828	4,219	298	-	-	65	-	-	64	-	33	-	-	-	-	46	60	-	-	-	-	-	-	-	-	-
	3.34		7.06			6.44			5.11		9.40					10.41	9.87									
						21.81			21.48		11.07					15.44	20.13									
			7.06			1.54			1.52		0.78					1.09	1.42									
			16.30			3.56			3.50		1.81					2.52	3.28									
Calverton (cdp)	500	2,095	204	-	-	41	-	-	-	-	-	-	-	-	-	-	89	-	-	-	-	-	-	-	-	-
	4.04		9.74			5.84											15.67									
						20.10											43.63									
			9.74			1.96											4.25									
			40.80			8.20											17.80									
Colesville (cdp)	595	3,384	112	-	-	72	-	-	12	-	-	-	-	-	-	-	8	-	-	-	-	-	-	-	-	20
	3.00		3.31			9.82			1.66								0.69									6.15
						64.29			10.71								7.14									17.86
			3.31			2.13			0.35								0.24									0.59
			18.82			12.10			2.02								1.34									3.36
Fairland (cdp)	1,137	3,328	230	-	-	27	-	-	11	-	-	-	-	-	-	-	162	-	-	-	-	-	-	-	-	-
	5.32		6.91			3.31			1.80								12.84									
						11.74			4.78								70.43									
			6.91			0.81			0.33								4.87									
			20.23			2.37			0.97								14.25									
Gaithersburg (city)	3,718	6,924	364	-	-	96	-	-	136	-	10	-	-	-	-	-	61	-	-	-	-	-	-	-	-	0
	7.11		5.26			5.68			5.57		2.28						6.67									0.00
						26.37			37.36		2.75						16.76									0.00
			5.26			1.39			1.96		0.14						0.88									0.00
			9.79			2.58			3.66		0.27						1.64									0.00
Germantown (cdp)	2,511	5,277	299	-	-	41	-	-	45	-	-	-	-	-	-	-	38	-	-	-	-	-	-	-	-	85
	4.56		5.67			1.95			4.45								9.69									16.70
						13.71			15.05								12.71									28.43
			5.67			0.78			0.85								0.72									1.61
			11.91			1.63			1.79								1.51									3.39
Montgomery Village (cdp)	1,920	4,276	316	-	-	174	-	-	43	-	32	-	-	-	-	-	-	-	-	-	-	-	-	-	-	54
	5.10		7.39			9.90			6.13		5.60															13.40
						55.06			13.61		10.13															17.09
			7.39			4.07			1.01		0.75															1.26
			16.46			9.06			2.24		1.67															2.81
North Bethesda (cdp)	2,111	4,523	302	-	-	27	-	-	12	-	46	-	-	-	-	8	117	-	-	-	-	-	-	-	-	-
	5.61		6.68			2.62			0.83		12.23					1.53	17.26									
						8.94			3.97		15.23					2.65	38.74									
			6.68			0.60			0.27		1.02					0.18	2.59									
			14.31			1.28			0.57		2.18					0.38	5.54									
North Potomac (cdp)	482	6,183	101	-	-	0	-	-	78	-	-	-	-	-	-	-	0	-	-	-	-	-	-	-	-	-
	2.10		1.63			0.00			2.40								0.00									
						0.00			77.23								0.00									
			1.63			0.00			1.26								0.00									
			20.95			0.00			16.18								0.00									

Notes: Please refer to the User's Guide for an explanation of data; data is arranged alphabetically by state, then county, then city within each county; table includes counties with populations greater than 49,999 unless noted and cities with populations greater than 9,999 whose Asian and/or NHPI population rates are greater than the national average; (1) Native Hawaiian and other Pacific Islander; (2) excludes Taiwanese; (3) includes Chamorro; (4) county does not meet population threshold but is shown in order to allow inclusion of city

Place	Total population with income below poverty level	Asian population for whom poverty status is determined	Asians with income below poverty level	NHPI[1] population for whom poverty status is determined	NHPIs[1] with income below poverty level	Asian Indian	Bangladeshi	Cambodian	Chinese[2]	Fijian	Filipino	Guamanian[3]	Hawaiian, Native	Hmong	Indonesian	Japanese	Korean	Laotian	Malaysian	Pakistani	Samoan	Sri Lankan	Taiwanese	Thai	Tongan	Vietnamese
Olney (cdp)	834	2,585	16	-	-	0	-	-	9	-	-	-	-	-	-	-	0	-	-	-	-	-	-	-	-	-
	2.65		0.62			0.00			1.42								0.00									
						0.00			56.25								0.00									
			0.62			0.00			0.35								0.00									
			1.92			0.00			1.08								0.00									
Potomac (cdp)	1,481	5,819	285	-	-	68	-	-	40	-	15	-	-	-	-	-	81	-	-	-	-	-	-	-	-	-
	3.32		4.90			4.58			2.06		4.03						7.26									
						23.86			14.04		5.26						28.42									
			4.90			1.17			0.69		0.26						1.39									
			19.24			4.59			2.70		1.01						5.47									
Redland (cdp)	931	2,909	173	-	-	37	-	-	15	-	0	-	-	-	-	-	30	-	-	-	-	-	-	-	-	-
	5.42		5.95			4.95			1.92		0.00						7.30									
						21.39			8.67		0.00						17.34									
			5.95			1.27			0.52		0.00						1.03									
			18.58			3.97			1.61		0.00						3.22									
Rockville (city)	3,555	6,652	753	-	-	35	-	-	328	-	6	-	-	-	-	29	183	-	-	-	-	-	-	-	-	4
	7.77		11.32			3.51			12.24		1.43					6.53	20.13									0.93
						4.65			43.56		0.80					3.85	24.30									0.53
			11.32			0.53			4.93		0.09					0.44	2.75									0.06
			21.18			0.98			9.23		0.17					0.82	5.15									0.11
Silver Spring (cdp)	7,072	6,254	858	-	-	325	-	25	59	-	18	-	-	-	-	-	176	-	-	-	-	-	-	-	-	174
	9.27		13.72			22.87		7.67	7.91		3.86						39.82									10.03
						37.88		2.91	6.88		2.10						20.51									20.28
			13.72			5.20		0.40	0.94		0.29						2.81									2.78
			12.13			4.60		0.35	0.83		0.25						2.49									2.46
Takoma Park (city)	1,722	689	89	-	-	-	-	-	-	-	-	-	-	-	-	-	-	-	-	-	-	-	-	-	-	-
	10.34		12.92																							
			12.92																							
			5.17																							
Wheaton-Glenmont (cdp)	4,844	7,076	421	-	-	49	-	-	154	-	18	-	-	-	-	-	46	-	-	-	-	-	-	-	-	68
	8.46		5.95			4.09			8.25		2.72						5.51									5.83
						11.64			36.58		4.28						10.93									16.15
			5.95			0.69			2.18		0.25						0.65									0.96
			8.69			1.01			3.18		0.37						0.95									1.40
White Oak (cdp)	1,594	2,505	242	-	-	78	-	-	18	-	-	-	-	-	-	-	79	-	-	-	-	-	-	-	-	58
	7.68		9.66			14.39			4.03								12.36									8.84
						32.23			7.44								32.64									23.97
			9.66			3.11			0.72								3.15									2.32
			15.18			4.89			1.13								4.96									3.64
Prince George's County	60,196	29,632	2,858	-	-	662	-	-	593	-	467	-	-	-	-	69	616	-	-	38	-	-	-	56	-	137
	7.69		9.64			9.44			12.70		5.74					10.95	17.13			5.59				16.77		5.22
						23.16			20.75		16.34					2.41	21.55			1.33				1.96		4.79
			9.64			2.23			2.00		1.58					0.23	2.08			0.13				0.19		0.46
			4.75			1.10			0.99		0.78					0.11	1.02			0.06				0.09		0.23
Adelphi (cdp)	1,329	1,392	242	-	-	-	-	-	-	-	-	-	-	-	-	-	-	-	-	-	-	-	-	-	-	-
	9.04		17.39																							
			17.39																							
			18.21																							

Notes: Please refer to the User's Guide for an explanation of data; data is arranged alphabetically by state, then county, then city within each county; table includes counties with populations greater than 49,999 unless noted and cities with populations greater than 9,999 whose Asian and/or NHPI population rates are greater than the national average; (1) Native Hawaiian and other Pacific Islander; (2) excludes Taiwanese; (3) includes Chamorro; (4) county does not meet population threshold but is shown in order to allow inclusion of city

Place	Total population with income below poverty level	Asian population for whom poverty status is determined	Asians with income below poverty level	NHPI[1] population for whom poverty status is determined	NHPIs[1] with income below poverty level	Asian Indian	Bangladeshi	Cambodian	Chinese[2]	Fijian	Filipino	Guamanian[3]	Hawaiian, Native	Hmong	Indonesian	Japanese	Korean	Laotian	Malaysian	Pakistani	Samoan	Sri Lankan	Taiwanese	Thai	Tongan	Vietnamese
Beltsville (cdp)	1,119 7.15	1,706	193 11.31 11.31 17.25	-	-	45 8.70 23.32 2.64 4.02	-	-	-	-	-	-	-	-	-	-	70 24.65 36.27 4.10 6.26	-	-	-	-	-	-	-	-	-
College Park (city)	3,154 19.92	1,572	440 27.99 27.99 13.95	-	-	220 42.07 50.00 13.99 6.98	-	-	40 8.60 9.09 2.54 1.27	-	-	-	-	-	-	-	-	-	-	-	-	-	-	-	-	-
Fort Washington (cdp)	881 3.68	2,400	210 8.75 8.75 23.84	-	-	-	-	-	-	-	187 9.74 89.05 7.79 21.23	-	-	-	-	-	-	-	-	-	-	-	-	-	-	-
Friendly (cdp)	41 0.38	657	0 <0.01 <0.01 <0.01	-	-	-	-	-	-	-	0 <0.01 ***.** <0.01 <0.01	-	-	-	-	-	-	-	-	-	-	-	-	-	-	-
Glenn Dale (cdp)	578 4.53	1,008	8 0.79 0.79 1.38	-	-	-	-	-	-	-	-	-	-	-	-	-	-	-	-	-	-	-	-	-	-	-
Greenbelt (city)	2,177 10.22	2,577	381 14.78 14.78 17.50	-	-	48 6.61 12.60 1.86 2.20	-	-	116 19.53 30.45 4.50 5.33	-	-	-	-	-	-	-	119 19.73 31.23 4.62 5.47	-	-	-	-	-	-	-	-	-
Hyattsville (city)	1,586 10.85	692	39 5.64 5.64 2.46	-	-	-	-	-	-	-	-	-	-	-	-	-	-	-	-	-	-	-	-	-	-	-
Lanham-Seabrook (cdp)	852 4.76	916	37 4.04 4.04 4.34	-	-	-	-	-	-	-	-	-	-	-	-	-	-	-	-	-	-	-	-	-	-	-
Laurel (city)	1,273 6.37	1,215	89 7.33 7.33 6.99	-	-	-	-	-	-	-	-	-	-	-	-	-	-	-	-	-	-	-	-	-	-	-
New Carrollton (city)	915 7.14	517	16 3.09 3.09 1.75	-	-	-	-	-	-	-	-	-	-	-	-	-	-	-	-	-	-	-	-	-	-	-

Notes: Please refer to the User's Guide for an explanation of data; data is arranged alphabetically by state, then county, then city within each county; table includes counties with populations greater than 49,999 unless noted and cities with populations greater than 9,999 whose Asian and/or NHPI population rates are greater than the national average; (1) Native Hawaiian and other Pacific Islander; (2) excludes Taiwanese; (3) includes Chamorro; (4) county does not meet population threshold but is shown in order to allow inclusion of city

Place	Total population with income below poverty level	Asian population for whom poverty status is determined	Asians with income below poverty level	NHPI[1] population for whom poverty status is determined	NHPIs[1] with income below poverty level	Asian Indian	Bangladeshi	Cambodian	Chinese[2]	Fijian	Filipino	Guamanian[3]	Hawaiian, Native	Hmong	Indonesian	Japanese	Korean	Laotian	Malaysian	Pakistani	Samoan	Sri Lankan	Taiwanese	Thai	Tongan	Vietnamese
South Laurel (cdp)	1,216 5.89	1,164	34 2.92 2.92 2.80	-	-	-	-	-	-	-	-	-	-	-	-	-	-	-	-	-	-	-	-	-	-	-
St. Mary's County	6,031 7.22	1,590	105 6.60 6.60 1.74	-	-	2 0.72 1.90 0.13 0.03	-	-	-	-	30 4.59 28.57 1.89 0.50	-	-	-	-	-	-	-	-	-	-	-	-	-	-	-
Lexington Park (cdp)	1,219 11.91	425	43 10.12 10.12 3.53	-	-	-	-	-	-	-	-	-	-	-	-	-	-	-	-	-	-	-	-	-	-	-
Washington County	11,697 9.52	987	125 12.66 12.66 1.07	-	-	-	-	-	-	-	-	-	-	-	-	-	-	-	-	-	-	-	-	-	-	-
Wicomico County	10,463 12.83	1,732	425 24.54 24.54 4.06	-	-	0 0.00 0.00 0.00 0.00	-	-	-	-	-	-	-	-	-	-	230 39.59 54.12 13.28 2.20	-	-	-	-	-	-	-	-	-
Salisbury (city)	5,248 23.83	988	338 34.21 34.21 6.44	-	-	-	-	-	-	-	-	-	-	-	-	-	-	-	-	-	-	-	-	-	-	-
MASSACHUSETTS	573,421 9.34	226,112	36,588 16.18 16.18 6.38	1,563	395 25.27 25.27 0.07	3,715 9.37 10.15 1.64 0.65	12 2.23 0.03 0.01 <0.01	5,124 25.62 14.00 2.27 0.89	9,954 12.74 27.21 4.40 1.74	-	791 8.95 2.16 0.35 0.14	137 32.08 34.68 8.77 0.02	19 5.07 4.81 1.22 <0.01	142 14.36 0.39 0.06 0.02	190 28.57 0.52 0.08 0.03	2,413 24.24 6.60 1.07 0.42	2,919 18.82 7.98 1.29 0.51	237 6.69 0.65 0.10 0.04	-	509 22.94 1.39 0.23 0.09	-	44 9.93 0.12 0.02 0.01	421 19.38 1.15 0.19 0.07	272 13.05 0.74 0.12 0.05	-	8,138 24.22 22.24 3.60 1.42
Barnstable County	15,021 6.89	1,342	156 11.62 11.62 1.04	-	-	-	-	-	0 0.00 0.00 0.00 0.00	-	-	-	-	-	-	-	-	-	-	-	-	-	-	-	-	-
Berkshire County	12,204 9.46	1,061	216 20.36 20.36 1.77	-	-	82 25.79 37.96 7.73 0.67	-	-	-	-	-	-	-	-	-	-	-	-	-	-	-	-	-	-	-	-
Bristol County	52,236 10.02	7,131	1,345 18.86 18.86 2.57	-	-	82 5.51 6.10 1.15 0.16	-	849 39.60 63.12 11.91 1.63	156 11.40 11.60 2.19 0.30	-	19 4.59 1.41 0.27 0.04	-	-	-	-	-	77 14.89 5.72 1.08 0.15	-	-	-	-	-	-	-	-	11 2.51 0.82 0.15 0.02

Notes: Please refer to the User's Guide for an explanation of data; data is arranged alphabetically by state, then county, then city within each county; table includes counties with populations greater than 49,999 unless noted and cities with populations greater than 9,999 whose Asian and/or NHPI population rates are greater than the national average; (1) Native Hawaiian and other Pacific Islander; (2) excludes Taiwanese; (3) includes Chamorro; (4) county does not meet population threshold but is shown in order to allow inclusion of city

Place	Total population with income below poverty level	Asian population for whom poverty status is determined	Asians with income below poverty level	NHPI[1] population for whom poverty status is determined	NHPIs[1] with income below poverty level	Asian Indian	Bangladeshi	Cambodian	Chinese[2]	Fijian	Filipino	Guamanian[3]	Hawaiian, Native	Hmong	Indonesian	Japanese	Korean	Laotian	Malaysian	Pakistani	Samoan	Sri Lankan	Taiwanese	Thai	Tongan	Vietnamese
Essex County	63,137 8.93	16,934	2,164 12.78 12.78 3.43	-	-	249 10.29 11.51 1.47 0.39	-	854 22.79 39.46 5.04 1.35	112 3.49 5.18 0.66 0.18	-	30 4.55 1.39 0.18 0.05	-	-	-	-	145 15.81 6.70 0.86 0.23	168 11.16 7.76 0.99 0.27	0 0.00 0.00 0.00 0.00	-	-	-	-	-	-	-	369 12.27 17.05 2.18 0.58
Andover (town)	1,205 3.89	2,078	61 2.94 2.94 5.06	-	-	19 3.78 31.15 0.91 1.58	-	-	0 0.00 0.00 0.00 0.00	-	-	-	-	-	-	-	-	-	-	-	-	-	-	-	-	-
Lynn (city)	14,525 16.52	5,876	1,326 22.57 22.57 9.13	-	-	206 52.28 15.54 3.51 1.42	-	780 26.01 58.82 13.27 5.37	-	-	-	-	-	-	-	-	-	-	-	-	-	-	-	-	-	171 14.54 12.90 2.91 1.18
North Andover (town)	739 2.92	1,054	59 5.60 5.60 7.98	-	-	-	-	-	12 3.49 20.34 1.14 1.62	-	-	-	-	-	-	-	-	-	-	-	-	-	-	-	-	-
Franklin County	6,634 9.45	634	124 19.56 19.56 1.87	-	-	-	-	-	-	-	-	-	-	-	-	-	-	-	-	-	-	-	-	-	-	-
Hampden County	65,024 14.74	5,890	1,020 17.32 17.32 1.57	-	-	8 1.14 0.78 0.14 0.01	-	191 42.73 18.73 3.24 0.29	165 14.49 16.18 2.80 0.25	-	-	-	-	-	-	-	32 7.17 3.14 0.54 0.05	-	-	-	-	-	-	-	-	466 24.49 45.69 7.91 0.72
Hampshire County	12,585 9.40	3,192	534 16.73 16.73 4.24	-	-	18 3.38 3.37 0.56 0.14	-	-	223 18.65 41.76 6.99 1.77	-	-	-	-	-	-	-	73 17.51 13.67 2.29 0.58	-	-	-	-	-	-	-	-	-
Amherst Center (cdp)	1,474 21.57	470	65 13.83 13.83 4.41	-	-	-	-	-	-	-	-	-	-	-	-	-	-	-	-	-	-	-	-	-	-	-
Amherst (town)	4,530 20.21	1,853	450 24.28 24.28 9.93	-	-	-	-	-	204 26.05 45.33 11.01 4.50	-	-	-	-	-	-	-	-	-	-	-	-	-	-	-	-	-
Middlesex County	92,705 6.55	86,416	9,927 11.49 11.49 10.71	-	-	1,331 6.35 13.41 1.54 1.44	-	2,457 22.69 24.75 2.84 2.65	2,368 8.45 23.85 2.74 2.55	-	205 8.51 2.07 0.24 0.22	-	-	-	-	478 13.38 4.82 0.55 0.52	965 15.58 9.72 1.12 1.04	112 6.28 1.13 0.13 0.12	-	206 37.87 2.08 0.24 0.22	-	-	124 11.46 1.25 0.14 0.13	97 11.48 0.98 0.11 0.10	-	998 15.30 10.05 1.15 1.08

Notes: Please refer to the User's Guide for an explanation of data; data is arranged alphabetically by state, then county, then city within each county; table includes counties with populations greater than 49,999 unless noted and cities with populations greater than 9,999 whose Asian and/or NHPI population rates are greater than the national average; (1) Native Hawaiian and other Pacific Islander; (2) excludes Taiwanese; (3) includes Chamorro; (4) county does not meet population threshold but is shown in order to allow inclusion of city

Place	Total population with income below poverty level	Asian population for whom poverty status is determined	Asians with income below poverty level	NHPI[1] population for whom poverty status is determined	NHPIs[1] with income below poverty level	Asian Indian	Bangladeshi	Cambodian	Chinese[2]	Fijian	Filipino	Guamanian[3]	Hawaiian, Native	Hmong	Indonesian	Japanese	Korean	Laotian	Malaysian	Pakistani	Samoan	Sri Lankan	Taiwanese	Thai	Tongan	Vietnamese
Acton (town)	590	1,813	63	-	-	25	-	-	17	-	-	-	-	-	-	-	-	-	-	-	-	-	-	-	-	-
	2.92		3.47			3.83			2.10																	
						39.68			26.98																	
			3.47			1.38			0.94																	
			10.68			4.24			2.88																	
Arlington (town)	1,714	1,982	144	-	-	-	-	-	48	-	-	-	-	-	-	-	-	-	-	-	-	-	-	-	-	-
	4.06		7.27						6.58																	
									33.33																	
			7.27						2.42																	
			8.40						2.80																	
Bedford (town)	300	789	16	-	-	-	-	-	-	-	-	-	-	-	-	-	-	-	-	-	-	-	-	-	-	-
	2.49		2.03																							
			2.03																							
			5.33																							
Belmont (cdp)	1,058	1,297	124	-	-	-	-	-	27	-	-	-	-	-	-	-	-	-	-	-	-	-	-	-	-	-
	4.43		9.56						4.81																	
									21.77																	
			9.56						2.08																	
			11.72						2.55																	
Belmont (town)	1,058	1,297	124	-	-	-	-	-	27	-	-	-	-	-	-	-	-	-	-	-	-	-	-	-	-	-
	4.43		9.56						4.81																	
									21.77																	
			9.56						2.08																	
			11.72						2.55																	
Burlington (town)	434	2,314	14	-	-	0	-	-	-	-	-	-	-	-	-	-	-	-	-	-	-	-	-	-	-	-
	1.90		0.61			0.00																				
						0.00																				
			0.61			0.00																				
			3.23			0.00																				
Cambridge (city)	11,295	8,899	1,835	-	-	291	-	-	581	-	-	-	-	-	-	262	330	-	-	-	-	-	-	-	-	-
	12.94		20.62			13.75			19.86							27.07	24.14									
						15.86			31.66							14.28	17.98									
			20.62			3.27			6.53							2.94	3.71									
			16.25			2.58			5.14							2.32	2.92									
Chelmsford (town)	938	1,538	0	-	-	0	-	-	0	-	-	-	-	-	-	-	-	-	-	-	-	-	-	-	-	-
	2.81		<0.01			<0.01			<0.01																	
						*** **			*** **																	
			<0.01			<0.01			<0.01																	
			<0.01			<0.01			<0.01																	
Framingham (town)	5,130	3,304	210	-	-	49	-	-	69	-	-	-	-	-	-	-	-	-	-	-	-	-	-	-	-	-
	8.05		6.36			3.56			6.57																	
						23.33			32.86																	
			6.36			1.48			2.09																	
			4.09			0.96			1.35																	
Lexington (town)	1,007	3,251	84	-	-	0	-	-	21	-	-	-	-	-	-	-	27	-	-	-	-	-	-	-	-	-
	3.39		2.58			0.00			1.57								5.97									
						0.00			25.00								32.14									
			2.58			0.00			0.65								0.83									
			8.34			0.00			2.09								2.68									

Notes: Please refer to the User's Guide for an explanation of data; data is arranged alphabetically by state, then county, then city within each county; table includes counties with populations greater than 49,999 unless noted and cities with populations greater than 9,999 whose Asian and/or NHPI population rates are greater than the national average; (1) Native Hawaiian and other Pacific Islander; (2) excludes Taiwanese; (3) includes Chamorro; (4) county does not meet population threshold but is shown in order to allow inclusion of city

Place	Total population with income below poverty level	Asian population for whom poverty status is determined	Asians with income below poverty level	NHPI[1] population for whom poverty status is determined	NHPIs[1] with income below poverty level	Asian Indian	Bangladeshi	Cambodian	Chinese[2]	Fijian	Filipino	Guamanian[3]	Hawaiian, Native	Hmong	Indonesian	Japanese	Korean	Laotian	Malaysian	Pakistani	Samoan	Sri Lankan	Taiwanese	Thai	Tongan	Vietnamese
	17,066	16,989	3,250	-	-	260	-	2,353	103	-	-	-	-	-	-	-	-	77	-	-	-	-	-	-	-	244
	16.78		19.13			10.22		24.81	13.83									5.25								16.84
Lowell (city)						8.00		72.40	3.17									2.37								7.51
			19.13			1.53		13.85	0.61									0.45								1.44
			19.04			1.52		13.79	0.60									0.45								1.43
	5,118	7,875	1,002	-	-	101	-	-	406	-	-	-	-	-	-	-	-	-	-	-	-	-	-	-	-	315
	9.17		12.72			9.66			9.90																	23.53
Malden (city)						10.08			40.52																	31.44
			12.72			1.28			5.16																	4.00
			19.58			1.97			7.93																	6.15
	2,455	1,601	142	-	-	50	-	-	-	-	-	-	-	-	-	-	-	-	-	-	-	-	-	-	-	-
	6.85		8.87			7.18																				
Marlborough (city)						35.21																				
			8.87			3.12																				
			5.78			2.04																				
	3,418	2,068	207	-	-	19	-	-	41	-	-	-	-	-	-	-	-	-	-	-	-	-	-	-	-	53
	6.38		10.01			5.16			5.18																	14.60
Medford (city)						9.18			19.81																	25.60
			10.01			0.92			1.98																	2.56
			6.06			0.56			1.20																	1.55
	879	1,294	43	-	-	-	-	-	17	-	-	-	-	-	-	-	-	-	-	-	-	-	-	-	-	-
	2.77		3.32						2.60																	
Natick (town)									39.53																	
			3.32						1.31																	
			4.89						1.93																	
	3,382	5,955	489	-	-	50	-	-	325	-	-	-	-	-	-	-	50	-	-	-	-	-	-	-	-	-
	4.31		8.21			8.74			8.36								9.51									
Newton (city)						10.22			66.46								10.22									
			8.21			0.84			5.46								0.84									
			14.46			1.48			9.61								1.48									
	9,395	4,698	829	-	-	144	-	-	292	-	-	-	-	-	-	-	119	-	-	-	-	-	-	-	-	-
	12.49		17.65			11.71			15.38								30.20									
Somerville (city)						17.37			35.22								14.35									
			17.65			3.07			6.22								2.53									
			8.82			1.53			3.11								1.27									
	466	615	19	-	-	-	-	-	-	-	-	-	-	-	-	-	-	-	-	-	-	-	-	-	-	-
	2.80		3.09																							
Sudbury (town)																										
			3.09																							
			4.08																							
	3,752	4,037	392	-	-	134	-	-	135	-	-	-	-	-	-	-	-	-	-	-	-	-	-	-	-	-
	7.00		9.71			7.52			10.48																	
Waltham (city)						34.18			34.44																	
			9.71			3.32			3.34																	
			10.45			3.57			3.60																	
	322	682	0	-	-	-	-	-	-	-	-	-	-	-	-	-	-	-	-	-	-	-	-	-	-	-
	2.49		<0.01																							
Wayland (town)																										
			<0.01																							
			<0.01																							

Notes: Please refer to the User's Guide for an explanation of data; data is arranged alphabetically by state, then county, then city within each county; table includes counties with populations greater than 49,999 unless noted and cities with populations greater than 9,999 whose Asian and/or NHPI population rates are greater than the national average; (1) Native Hawaiian and other Pacific Islander; (2) excludes Taiwanese; (3) includes Chamorro; (4) county does not meet population threshold but is shown in order to allow inclusion of city

Place	Total population with income below poverty level	Asian population for whom poverty status is determined	Asians with income below poverty level	NHPI[1] population for whom poverty status is determined	NHPIs[1] with income below poverty level	Asian Indian	Bangladeshi	Cambodian	Chinese[2]	Fijian	Filipino	Guamanian[3]	Hawaiian, Native	Hmong	Indonesian	Japanese	Korean	Laotian	Malaysian	Pakistani	Samoan	Sri Lankan	Taiwanese	Thai	Tongan	Vietnamese
Westford (town)	345 1.67	951	0 <0.01 <0.01 <0.01	-	-	-	-	-	0 <0.01 *** ** <0.01 <0.01	-	-	-	-	-	-	-	-	-	-	-	-	-	-	-	-	-
Weston (town)	314 2.91	894	90 10.07 10.07 28.66	-	-	-	-	-	12 3.12 13.33 1.34 3.82	-	-	-	-	-	-	-	-	-	-	-	-	-	-	-	-	-
Winchester (town)	531 2.60	794	15 1.89 1.89 2.82	-	-	-	-	-	-	-	-	-	-	-	-	-	-	-	-	-	-	-	-	-	-	-
Woburn (city)	2,269 6.12	1,827	146 7.99 7.99 6.43	-	-	79 7.88 54.11 4.32 3.48	-	-	-	-	-	-	-	-	-	-	-	-	-	-	-	-	-	-	-	-
Norfolk County	29,377 4.64	34,953	3,656 10.46 10.46 12.45	-	-	409 8.38 11.19 1.17 1.39	-	-	1,408 7.50 38.51 4.03 4.79	-	65 3.55 1.78 0.19 0.22	-	-	-	-	555 27.76 15.18 1.59 1.89	458 22.20 12.53 1.31 1.56	-	-	-	-	-	76 21.97 2.08 0.22 0.26	-	-	386 13.92 10.56 1.10 1.31
Brookline (town)	5,177 9.28	7,727	1,321 17.10 17.10 25.52	-	-	207 19.18 15.67 2.68 4.00	-	-	293 8.23 22.18 3.79 5.66	-	-	-	-	-	-	338 26.02 25.59 4.37 6.53	360 36.51 27.25 4.66 6.95	-	-	-	-	-	-	-	-	-
Needham (town)	705 2.52	1,028	28 2.72 2.72 3.97	-	-	-	-	-	0 0.00 0.00 0.00 0.00	-	-	-	-	-	-	-	-	-	-	-	-	-	-	-	-	-
Norwood (town)	1,227 4.37	1,379	134 9.72 9.72 10.92	-	-	62 8.18 46.27 4.50 5.05	-	-	-	-	-	-	-	-	-	-	-	-	-	-	-	-	-	-	-	-
Quincy (city)	6,286 7.25	13,896	1,633 11.75 11.75 25.98	-	-	104 11.23 6.37 0.75 1.65	-	-	796 8.46 48.74 5.73 12.66	-	65 7.65 3.98 0.47 1.03	-	-	-	-	-	-	-	-	-	-	-	-	-	-	331 22.81 20.27 2.38 5.27
Randolph (town)	1,245 4.06	3,152	131 4.16 4.16 10.52	-	-	-	-	-	113 7.40 86.26 3.59 9.08	-	-	-	-	-	-	-	-	-	-	-	-	-	-	-	-	0 0.00 0.00 0.00 0.00

Notes: Please refer to the User's Guide for an explanation of data; data is arranged alphabetically by state, then county, then city within each county; table includes counties with populations greater than 49,999 unless noted and cities with populations greater than 9,999 whose Asian and/or NHPI population rates are greater than the national average; (1) Native Hawaiian and other Pacific Islander; (2) excludes Taiwanese; (3) includes Chamorro; (4) county does not meet population threshold but is shown in order to allow inclusion of city

Place	Total population with income below poverty level	Asian population for whom poverty status is determined	Asians with income below poverty level	NHPI[1] population for whom poverty status is determined	NHPIs[1] with income below poverty level	Asian Indian	Bangladeshi	Cambodian	Chinese[2]	Fijian	Filipino	Guamanian[3]	Hawaiian, Native	Hmong	Indonesian	Japanese	Korean	Laotian	Malaysian	Pakistani	Samoan	Sri Lankan	Taiwanese	Thai	Tongan	Vietnamese
Sharon (town)	527 3.04	694	8 1.15 1.15 1.52	-	-	-	-	-	-	-	-	-	-	-	-	-	-	-	-	-	-	-	-	-	-	-
Wellesley (town)	885 3.82	1,011	38 3.76 3.76 4.29	-	-	-	-	-	20 3.27 52.63 1.98 2.26	-	-	-	-	-	-	-	-	-	-	-	-	-	-	-	-	-
Plymouth County	30,649 6.65	4,360	505 11.58 11.58 1.65	-	-	167 26.94 33.07 3.83 0.54	-	-	121 11.65 23.96 2.78 0.39	-	22 4.13 4.36 0.50 0.07	-	-	-	-	-	-	-	-	-	-	-	-	-	-	73 10.98 14.46 1.67 0.24
Suffolk County	124,918 18.99	45,490	13,821 30.38 30.38 11.06	-	-	864 23.10 6.25 1.90 0.69	-	604 35.57 4.37 1.33 0.48	5,010 26.17 36.25 11.01 4.01	-	370 21.55 2.68 0.81 0.30	-	-	-	-	934 47.03 6.76 2.05 0.75	963 42.35 6.97 2.12 0.77	-	-	-	-	-	194 47.67 1.40 0.43 0.16	-	-	4,152 33.86 30.04 9.13 3.32
Boston (city)	109,128 19.53	41,720	12,529 30.03 30.03 11.48	-	-	807 23.47 6.44 1.93 0.74	-	145 23.93 1.16 0.35 0.13	4,868 26.12 38.85 11.67 4.46	-	351 21.91 2.80 0.84 0.32	-	-	-	-	934 47.85 7.45 2.24 0.86	903 42.86 7.21 2.16 0.83	-	-	-	-	-	194 47.67 1.55 0.47 0.18	-	-	3,698 33.84 29.52 8.86 3.39
Chelsea (city)	7,921 23.30	1,455	383 26.32 26.32 4.84	-	-	-	-	-	-	-	-	-	-	-	-	-	-	-	-	-	-	-	-	-	-	173 23.41 45.17 11.89 2.18
Revere (city)	6,873 14.64	2,161	900 41.65 41.65 13.09	-	-		-	381 47.04 42.33 17.63 5.54	-	-	-	-	-	-	-	-	-	-	-	-	-	-	-	-	-	281 48.87 31.22 13.00 4.09
Worcester County	67,136 9.24	18,490	3,073 16.62 16.62 4.58	-	-	480 12.57 15.62 2.60 0.71	-	27 8.08 0.88 0.15 0.04	326 9.75 10.61 1.76 0.49	-	25 5.39 0.81 0.14 0.04	-	-	83 12.59 2.70 0.45 0.12	-	80 23.12 2.60 0.43 0.12	97 8.19 3.16 0.52 0.14	68 7.02 2.21 0.37 0.10	-	44 11.08 1.43 0.24 0.07	-	-	-	-	-	1,589 28.43 51.71 8.59 2.37
Fitchburg (city)	5,627 15.02	1,692	201 11.88 11.88 3.57	-	-	-	-	-	-	-	-	-	-	64 10.53 31.84 3.78 1.14	-	-	-	26 6.67 12.94 1.54 0.46	-	-	-	-	-	-	-	-
Northborough (town)	386 2.79	762	4 0.52 0.52 1.04	-	-	-	-	-	-	-	-	-	-	-	-	-	-	-	-	-	-	-	-	-	-	-

Notes: Please refer to the User's Guide for an explanation of data; data is arranged alphabetically by state, then county, then city within each county; table includes counties with populations greater than 49,999 unless noted and cities with populations greater than 9,999 whose Asian and/or NHPI population rates are greater than the national average; (1) Native Hawaiian and other Pacific Islander; (2) excludes Taiwanese; (3) includes Chamorro; (4) county does not meet population threshold but is shown in order to allow inclusion of city

Place	Total population with income below poverty level	Asian population for whom poverty status is determined	Asians with income below poverty level	NHPI[1] population for whom poverty status is determined	NHPIs[1] with income below poverty level	Asian Indian	Bangladeshi	Cambodian	Chinese[2]	Fijian	Filipino	Guamanian[3]	Hawaiian, Native	Hmong	Indonesian	Japanese	Korean	Laotian	Malaysian	Pakistani	Samoan	Sri Lankan	Taiwanese	Thai	Tongan	Vietnamese
Shrewsbury (town)	1,498 4.75	2,574	197 7.65 7.65 13.15	-	-	115 10.10 58.38 4.47 7.68	-	-	51 7.80 25.89 1.98 3.40		-	-	-	-	-	-	-	-	-	-	-	-	-	-	-	31 6.01 15.74 1.20 2.07
Westborough (town)	805 4.66	1,429	83 5.81 5.81 10.31	-	-	53 8.82 63.86 3.71 6.58	-	-	30 6.22 36.14 2.10 3.73		-	-	-	-	-	-	-	-	-	-	-	-	-	-	-	-
Worcester (city)	29,115 17.92	7,621	2,114 27.74 27.74 7.26	-	-	278 27.77 13.15 3.65 0.95	-	-	156 18.31 7.38 2.05 0.54	-	-	-	-	-	-	-	-	-	-	-	-	-	-	-	-	1,346 31.72 63.67 17.66 4.62
MICHIGAN	1,021,605 10.53	170,718	19,125 11.20 11.20 1.87	2,361	392 16.60 16.60 0.04	4,168 7.77 21.79 2.44 0.41	379 22.71 1.98 0.22 0.04	130 8.23 0.68 0.08 0.01	3,296 11.57 17.23 1.93 0.32	-	889 5.14 4.65 0.52 0.09	91 14.15 23.21 3.85 0.01	73 11.35 18.62 3.09 0.01	1,669 29.87 8.73 0.98 0.16	163 26.29 0.85 0.10 0.02	1,043 10.02 5.45 0.61 0.10	3,007 14.89 15.72 1.76 0.29	365 13.18 1.91 0.21 0.04	168 37.09 0.88 0.10 0.02	537 10.86 2.81 0.31 0.05	61 14.70 15.56 2.58 0.01	17 4.96 0.09 0.01 <0.01	286 13.02 1.50 0.17 0.03	327 21.54 1.71 0.19 0.03	-	1,354 10.59 7.08 0.79 0.13
Allegan County	7,639 7.33	569	18 3.16 3.16 0.24	-	-	-	-	-	-	-	-	-	-	-	-	-	-	-	-	-	-	-	-	-	-	-
Bay County	10,605 9.74	617	80 12.97 12.97 0.75	-	-	-	-	-	-	-	-	-	-	-	-	-	-	-	-	-	-	-	-	-	-	-
Berrien County	20,202 12.70	1,647	308 18.70 18.70 1.52	-	-	50 10.57 16.23 3.04 0.25	-	-	-	-	27 8.63 8.77 1.64 0.13	-	-	-	-	-	174 46.77 56.49 10.56 0.86	-	-	-	-	-	-	-	-	-
Calhoun County	15,094 11.25	1,457	161 11.05 11.05 1.07	-	-	-	-	-	-	-	-	-	-	-	-	31 6.95 19.25 2.13 0.21	-	-	-	-	-	-	-	-	-	-
Cass County	4,987 9.89	324	5 1.54 1.54 0.10	-	-	-	-	-	-	-	-	-	-	-	-	-	-	0 0.00 0.00 0.00 0.00	-	-	-	-	-	-	-	-
Clinton County	2,963 4.63	358	0 <0.01 <0.01 <0.01	-	-	-	-	-	-	-	-	-	-	-	-	-	-	-	-	-	-	-	-	-	-	-

Notes: Please refer to the User's Guide for an explanation of data; data is arranged alphabetically by state, then county, then city within each county; table includes counties with populations greater than 49,999 unless noted and cities with populations greater than 9,999 whose Asian and/or NHPI population rates are greater than the national average; (1) Native Hawaiian and other Pacific Islander; (2) excludes Taiwanese; (3) includes Chamorro; (4) county does not meet population threshold but is shown in order to allow inclusion of city

Place	Total population with income below poverty level	Asian population for whom poverty status is determined	Asians with income below poverty level	NHPI[1] population for whom poverty status is determined	NHPIs[1] with income below poverty level	Asian Indian	Bangladeshi	Cambodian	Chinese[2]	Fijian	Filipino	Guamanian[3]	Hawaiian, Native	Hmong	Indonesian	Japanese	Korean	Laotian	Malaysian	Pakistani	Samoan	Sri Lankan	Taiwanese	Thai	Tongan	Vietnamese
Eaton County	5,948 5.84	1,206	112 9.29 9.29 1.88	-	-	60 16.62 53.57 4.98 1.01	-	-	-	-	-	-	-	-	-	-	-	-	-	-	-	-	-	-	-	25 8.50 22.32 2.07 0.42
Genesee County	56,480 13.10	3,109	331 10.65 10.65 0.59	-	-	96 8.29 29.00 3.09 0.17	-	-	17 4.75 5.14 0.55 0.03	-	7 1.65 2.11 0.23 0.01	-	-	-	-	-	36 7.93 10.88 1.16 0.06	-	-	-	-	-	-	-	-	-
Ingham County	38,421 14.63	9,111	2,545 27.93 27.93 6.62	-	-	325 17.29 12.77 3.57 0.85	-	-	297 17.63 11.67 3.26 0.77	-	46 8.88 1.81 0.50 0.12	-	-	436 79.27 17.13 4.79 1.13	-	84 18.79 3.30 0.92 0.22	621 42.56 24.40 6.82 1.62	-	-	-	-	-	-	-	-	241 18.45 9.47 2.65 0.63
East Lansing (city)	11,317 34.85	2,963	1,117 37.70 37.70 9.87	-	-	182 29.45 16.29 6.14 1.61	-	-	204 26.63 18.26 6.88 1.80	-	-	-	-	-	-	-	314 44.73 28.11 10.60 2.77	-	-	-	-	-	-	-	-	-
Meridian charter (township)	3,631 9.42	2,453	419 17.08 17.08 11.54	-	-	96 10.63 22.91 3.91 2.64	-	-	67 12.59 15.99 2.73 1.85	-	-	-	-	-	-	-	182 47.89 43.44 7.42 5.01	-	-	-	-	-	-	-	-	-
Okemos (cdp)	2,132 9.57	1,916	301 15.71 15.71 14.12	-	-	96 12.73 31.89 5.01 4.50	-	-	7 1.88 2.33 0.37 0.33	-	-	-	-	-	-	-	-	-	-	-	-	-	-	-	-	-
Ionia County	4,858 8.74	171	39 22.81 22.81 0.80	-	-	-	-	-	-	-	-	-	-	-	-	-	-	-	-	-	-	-	-	-	-	-
Isabella County	11,687 20.38	771	283 36.71 36.71 2.42	-	-	-	-	-	-	-	-	-	-	-	-	-	-	-	-	-	-	-	-	-	-	-
Jackson County	13,417 9.04	706	73 10.34 10.34 0.54	-	-	-	-	-	-	-	-	-	-	-	-	-	-	-	-	-	-	-	-	-	-	-
Kalamazoo County	27,483 12.03	4,183	863 20.63 20.63 3.14	-	-	246 19.59 28.51 5.88 0.90	-	-	211 25.86 24.45 5.04 0.77	-	-	-	-	-	-	-	99 14.71 11.47 2.37 0.36	-	-	-	-	-	-	-	-	-

Notes: Please refer to the User's Guide for an explanation of data; data is arranged alphabetically by state, then county, then city within each county; table includes counties with populations greater than 49,999 unless noted and cities with populations greater than 9,999 whose Asian and/or NHPI population rates are greater than the national average; (1) Native Hawaiian and other Pacific Islander; (2) excludes Taiwanese; (3) includes Chamorro; (4) county does not meet population threshold but is shown in order to allow inclusion of city

Place	Total population with income below poverty level	Asian population for whom poverty status is determined	Asians with income below poverty level	NHPI[1] population for whom poverty status is determined	NHPIs[1] with income below poverty level	Asian Indian	Bangladeshi	Cambodian	Chinese[2]	Fijian	Filipino	Guamanian[3]	Hawaiian, Native	Hmong	Indonesian	Japanese	Korean	Laotian	Malaysian	Pakistani	Samoan	Sri Lankan	Taiwanese	Thai	Tongan	Vietnamese
Kent County	49,832 8.86	10,385	886 8.53 8.53 1.78	-	-	50 3.67 5.64 0.48 0.10	-	-	160 15.31 18.06 1.54 0.32	-	64 10.13 7.22 0.62 0.13	-	-	-	-	-	229 12.41 25.85 2.21 0.46	-	-	-	-	-	-	-	-	269 6.27 30.36 2.59 0.54
Kentwood (city)	2,817 6.26	2,499	286 11.44 11.44 10.15	-	-	-	-	-	-	-	-	-	-	-	-	-	102 22.92 35.66 4.08 3.62	-	-	-	-	-	-	-	-	93 7.64 32.52 3.72 3.30
Lenawee County	6,340 6.73	503	40 7.95 7.95 0.63	-	-	-	-	-	-	-	-	-	-	-	-	-	-	-	-	-	-	-	-	-	-	-
Livingston County	5,228 3.36	1,028	28 2.72 2.72 0.54	-	-	-	-	-	-	-	-	-	-	-	-	-	-	-	-	-	-	-	-	-	-	-
Macomb County	44,010 5.65	17,300	1,270 7.34 7.34 2.89	-	-	374 6.76 29.45 2.16 0.85	-	-	322 13.52 25.35 1.86 0.73	-	162 4.76 12.76 0.94 0.37	-	-	42 3.88 3.31 0.24 0.10	-	-	120 7.92 9.45 0.69 0.27	-	-	48 9.06 3.78 0.28 0.11	-	-	-	-	-	157 11.06 12.36 0.91 0.36
Sterling Heights (city)	6,480 5.24	6,510	240 3.69 3.69 3.70	-	-	42 1.74 17.50 0.65 0.65	-	-	48 4.89 20.00 0.74 0.74	-	23 1.73 9.58 0.35 0.35	-	-	-	-	-	73 11.57 30.42 1.12 1.13	-	-	-	-	-	-	-	-	29 6.47 12.08 0.45 0.45
Marquette County	6,592 10.87	251	40 15.94 15.94 0.61	-	-	-	-	-	-	-	-	-	-	-	-	-	-	-	-	-	-	-	-	-	-	-
Midland County	6,818 8.38	1,165	86 7.38 7.38 1.26	-	-	7 1.84 8.14 0.60 0.10	-	-	30 7.71 34.88 2.58 0.44	-	-	-	-	-	-	-	-	-	-	-	-	-	-	-	-	-
Monroe County	10,161 7.03	871	40 4.59 4.59 0.39	-	-	-	-	-	-	-	-	-	-	-	-	-	-	-	-	-	-	-	-	-	-	-
Muskegon County	18,752 11.42	720	28 3.89 3.89 0.15	-	-	-	-	-	-	-	-	-	-	-	-	-	-	-	-	-	-	-	-	-	-	-

Notes: Please refer to the User's Guide for an explanation of data; data is arranged alphabetically by state, then county, then city within each county; table includes counties with populations greater than 49,999 unless noted and cities with populations greater than 9,999 whose Asian and/or NHPI population rates are greater than the national average; (1) Native Hawaiian and other Pacific Islander; (2) excludes Taiwanese; (3) includes Chamorro; (4) county does not meet population threshold but is shown in order to allow inclusion of city

Place	Total population with income below poverty level	Asian population for whom poverty status is determined	Asians with income below poverty level	NHPI[1] population for whom poverty status is determined	NHPIs[1] with income below poverty level	Asian Indian	Bangladeshi	Cambodian	Chinese[2]	Fijian	Filipino	Guamanian[3]	Hawaiian, Native	Hmong	Indonesian	Japanese	Korean	Laotian	Malaysian	Pakistani	Samoan	Sri Lankan	Taiwanese	Thai	Tongan	Vietnamese
Oakland County	65,478 5.54	48,229	2,404 4.98 4.98 3.67	-	-	568 2.97 23.63 1.18 0.87	-	-	479 5.56 19.93 0.99 0.73	-	92 2.30 3.83 0.19 0.14	-	-	236 22.04 9.82 0.49 0.36	-	176 4.12 7.32 0.36 0.27	242 5.03 10.07 0.50 0.37	-	-	56 5.76 2.33 0.12 0.09	-	-	40 3.24 1.66 0.08 0.06	-	-	148 9.03 6.16 0.31 0.23
Auburn Hills (city)	1,144 6.30	1,190	89 7.48 7.48 7.78	-	-	65 9.62 73.03 5.46 5.68	-	-	-	-	-	-	-	-	-	-	-	-	-	-	-	-	-	-	-	-
Bloomfield (township)	1,078 2.52	2,717	50 1.84 1.84 4.64	-	-	0 0.00 0.00 0.00 0.00	-	-	-	-	-	-	-	-	-	-	47 8.15 94.00 1.73 4.36	-	-	-	-	-	-	-	-	-
Farmington (city)	342 3.28	1,065	0 <0.01 <0.01 <0.01	-	-	0 <0.01 *** ** <0.01 <0.01	-	-	-	-	-	-	-	-	-	-	-	-	-	-	-	-	-	-	-	-
Farmington Hills (city)	3,299 4.06	5,707	291 5.10 5.10 8.82	-	-	184 5.38 63.23 3.22 5.58	-	-	21 2.39 7.22 0.37 0.64	-	0 0.00 0.00 0.00 0.00	-	-	-	-	-	-	-	-	-	-	-	-	-	-	-
Madison Heights (city)	2,738 8.90	1,595	188 11.79 11.79 6.87	-	-	-	-	-	7 1.28 3.72 0.44 0.26	-	-	-	-	-	-	-	-	-	-	-	-	-	-	-	-	-
Novi (city)	1,054 2.23	3,991	77 1.93 1.93 7.31	-	-	4 0.36 5.19 0.10 0.38	-	-	0 0.00 0.00 0.00 0.00	-	-	-	-	-	-	51 4.44 66.23 1.28 4.84	-	-	-	-	-	-	-	-	-	-
Rochester (city)	278 2.66	549	4 0.73 0.73 1.44	-	-	-	-	-	-	-	-	-	-	-	-	-	-	-	-	-	-	-	-	-	-	-
Rochester Hills (city)	2,346 3.44	4,596	66 1.44 1.44 2.81	-	-	5 0.26 7.58 0.11 0.21	-	-	52 5.12 78.79 1.13 2.22	-	-	-	-	-	-	-	0 0.00 0.00 0.00 0.00	-	-	-	-	-	-	-	-	-
Troy (city)	2,220 2.75	10,378	358 3.45 3.45 16.13	-	-	132 2.84 36.87 1.27 5.95	-	-	124 5.43 34.64 1.19 5.59	-	0 0.00 0.00 0.00 0.00	-	-	-	-	-	49 3.98 13.69 0.47 2.21	-	-	-	-	-	20 3.58 5.59 0.19 0.90	-	-	-

Notes: Please refer to the User's Guide for an explanation of data; data is arranged alphabetically by state, then county, then city within each county; table includes counties with populations greater than 49,999 unless noted and cities with populations greater than 9,999 whose Asian and/or NHPI population rates are greater than the national average; (1) Native Hawaiian and other Pacific Islander; (2) excludes Taiwanese; (3) includes Chamorro; (4) county does not meet population threshold but is shown in order to allow inclusion of city

Place	Total population with income below poverty level	Asian population for whom poverty status is determined	Asians with income below poverty level	NHPI[1] population for whom poverty status is determined	NHPIs[1] with income below poverty level	Asian Indian	Bangladeshi	Cambodian	Chinese[2]	Fijian	Filipino	Guamanian[3]	Hawaiian, Native	Hmong	Indonesian	Japanese	Korean	Laotian	Malaysian	Pakistani	Samoan	Sri Lankan	Taiwanese	Thai	Tongan	Vietnamese
West Bloomfield (township)	1,743	4,994	100	-	-	7	-	-	0	-	19	-	-	-	-	41	0	-	-	-	-	-	-	-	-	-
	2.72		2.00			0.41			0.00		4.44					3.22	0.00									
						7.00			0.00		19.00					41.00	0.00									
			2.00			0.14			0.00		0.38					0.82	0.00									
			5.74			0.40			0.00		1.09					2.35	0.00									
Ottawa County	12,655	5,080	393	-	-	30	-	101	0	-	-	-	-	-	-	-	6	54	-	-	-	-	-	-	-	73
	5.49		7.74			6.61		9.40	0.00								1.18	4.75								10.10
						7.63		25.70	0.00								1.53	13.74								18.58
			7.74			0.59		1.99	0.00								0.12	1.06								1.44
			3.11			0.24		0.80	0.00								0.05	0.43								0.58
Holland (city)	3,430	1,230	58	-	-	-	-	-	-	-	-	-	-	-	-	-	-	-	-	-	-	-	-	-	-	-
	10.63		4.72																							
			4.72																							
			1.69																							
Saginaw County	28,603	1,741	287	-	-	25	-	-	-	-	54	-	-	-	-	-	57	-	-	-	-	-	-	-	-	-
	13.92		16.48			7.37					14.40						16.86									
						8.71					18.82						19.86									
			16.48			1.44					3.10						3.27									
			1.00			0.09					0.19						0.20									
St. Clair County	12,674	424	37	-	-	-	-	-	-	-	-	-	-	-	-	-	-	-	-	-	-	-	-	-	-	-
	7.80		8.73																							
			8.73																							
			0.29																							
St. Joseph County	6,900	287	8	-	-	-	-	-	-	-	-	-	-	-	-	-	-	-	-	-	-	-	-	-	-	-
	11.26		2.79																							
			2.79																							
			0.12																							
Washtenaw County	33,450	18,287	3,679	-	-	607	-	-	1,046	-	133	-	-	-	-	278	906	-	-	61	-	-	156	-	-	95
	11.08		20.12			14.41			19.15		15.15					17.64	26.55			13.12			33.33			21.89
						16.50			28.43		3.62					7.56	24.63			1.66			4.24			2.58
			20.12			3.32			5.72		0.73					1.52	4.95			0.33			0.85			0.52
			11.00			1.81			3.13		0.40					0.83	2.71			0.18			0.47			0.28
Ann Arbor (city)	16,922	11,756	2,856	-	-	493	-	-	836	-	123	-	-	-	-	209	724	-	-	-	-	-	150	-	-	-
	16.58		24.29			17.92			23.06		26.68					17.91	31.88						38.56			
						17.26			29.27		4.31					7.32	25.35						5.25			
			24.29			4.19			7.11		1.05					1.78	6.16						1.28			
			16.88			2.91			4.94		0.73					1.24	4.28						0.89			
Pittsfield charter (township)	2,609	2,769	244	-	-	11	-	-	65	-	-	-	-	-	-	-	82	-	-	-	-	-	-	-	-	-
	9.15		8.81			1.67			8.29								14.49									
						4.51			26.64								33.61									
			8.81			0.40			2.35								2.96									
			9.35			0.42			2.49								3.14									
Scio (township)	452	611	21	-	-	-	-	-	-	-	-	-	-	-	-	-	-	-	-	-	-	-	-	-	-	-
	2.89		3.44																							
			3.44																							
			4.65																							

Notes: Please refer to the User's Guide for an explanation of data; data is arranged alphabetically by state, then county, then city within each county; table includes counties with populations greater than 49,999 unless noted and cities with populations greater than 9,999 whose Asian and/or NHPI population rates are greater than the national average; (1) Native Hawaiian and other Pacific Islander; (2) excludes Taiwanese; (3) includes Chamorro; (4) county does not meet population threshold but is shown in order to allow inclusion of city

Place	Total population with income below poverty level	Asian population for whom poverty status is determined	Asians with income below poverty level	NHPI[1] population for whom poverty status is determined	NHPIs[1] with income below poverty level	Asian Indian	Bangladeshi	Cambodian	Chinese[2]	Fijian	Filipino	Guamanian[3]	Hawaiian, Native	Hmong	Indonesian	Japanese	Korean	Laotian	Malaysian	Pakistani	Samoan	Sri Lankan	Taiwanese	Thai	Tongan	Vietnamese
Wayne County	332,598	35,128	4,423	451	118	1,496	365	-	464	-	175	-	-	624	-	140	273	-	-	259	-	-	-	-	-	69
	16.39		12.59		26.16	10.34	31.77		9.31		4.09			34.04		13.37	15.31			11.92						5.86
						33.82	8.25		10.49		3.96			14.11		3.17	6.17			5.86						1.56
			12.59		26.16	4.26	1.04		1.32		0.50			1.78		0.40	0.78			0.74						0.20
			1.33		0.04	0.45	0.11		0.14		0.05			0.19		0.04	0.08			0.08						0.02
Brownstown (township)	1,586	925	48	-	-	-	-	-	-	-	-	-	-	-	-	-	-	-	-	-	-	-	-	-	-	-
	6.93		5.19																							
			5.19																							
			3.03																							
Canton (township)	2,841	6,569	242	-	-	98	-	-	102	-	0	-	-	-	-	-	10	-	-	-	-	-	-	-	-	-
	3.73		3.68			2.76			8.20		0.00						3.34									
						40.50			42.15		0.00						4.13									
			3.68			1.49			1.55		0.00						0.15									
			8.52			3.45			3.59		0.00						0.35									
Hamtramck (city)	5,903	2,349	597	-	-	227	273	-	-	-	-	-	-	-	-	-	-	-	-	-	-	-	-	-	-	-
	26.96		25.42			20.09	37.35																			
						38.02	45.73																			
			25.42			9.66	11.62																			
			10.11			3.85	4.62																			
Inkster (city)	5,795	1,140	120	-	-	46	-	-	-	-	-	-	-	-	-	-	-	-	-	-	-	-	-	-	-	-
	19.46		10.53			6.20																				
						38.33																				
			10.53			4.04																				
			2.07			0.79																				
Northville (township)	494	922	76	-	-	16	-	-	-	-	-	-	-	-	-	-	-	-	-	-	-	-	-	-	-	-
	2.52		8.24			3.73																				
						21.05																				
			8.24			1.74																				
			15.38			3.24																				
MINNESOTA	380,476	136,520	25,887	1,436	180	1,240	-	1,101	1,466	-	335	20	49	13,987	-	699	1,245	1,385	-	152	-	-	64	164	-	2,679
	7.94		18.96		12.53	7.76		21.81	10.08		5.86	4.84	11.42	32.72		18.17	10.03	15.57		14.41			14.00	18.02		14.75
						4.79		4.25	5.66		1.29	11.11	27.22	54.03		2.70	4.81	5.35		0.59			0.25	0.63		10.35
			18.96		12.53	0.91		0.81	1.07		0.25	1.39	3.41	10.25		0.51	0.91	1.01		0.11			0.05	0.12		1.96
			6.80		0.05	0.33		0.29	0.39		0.09	0.01	0.01	3.68		0.18	0.33	0.36		0.04			0.02	0.04		0.70
Anoka County	12,367	4,960	234	-	-	52	-	-	28	-	3	-	-	0	-	-	10	-	-	-	-	-	-	-	-	35
	4.20		4.72			5.72			6.36		0.81			0.00			1.41									3.71
						22.22			11.97		1.28			0.00			4.27									14.96
			4.72			1.05			0.56		0.06			0.00			0.20									0.71
			1.89			0.42			0.23		0.02			0.00			0.08									0.28
Columbia Heights (city)	1,173	672	24	-	-	-	-	-	-	-	-	-	-	-	-	-	-	-	-	-	-	-	-	-	-	-
	6.41		3.57																							
			3.57																							
			2.05																							
Blue Earth County	6,735	692	243	-	-	-	-	-	-	-	-	-	-	-	-	-	-	-	-	-	-	-	-	-	-	-
	12.91		35.12																							
			35.12																							
			3.61																							

Notes: Please refer to the User's Guide for an explanation of data; data is arranged alphabetically by state, then county, then city within each county; table includes counties with populations greater than 49,999 unless noted and cities with populations greater than 9,999 whose Asian and/or NHPI population rates are greater than the national average; (1) Native Hawaiian and other Pacific Islander; (2) excludes Taiwanese; (3) includes Chamorro; (4) county does not meet population threshold but is shown in order to allow inclusion of city

Place	Total population with income below poverty level	Asian population for whom poverty status is determined	Asians with income below poverty level	NHPI[1] population for whom poverty status is determined	NHPIs[1] with income below poverty level	Asian Indian	Bangladeshi	Cambodian	Chinese[2]	Fijian	Filipino	Guamanian[3]	Hawaiian, Native	Hmong	Indonesian	Japanese	Korean	Laotian	Malaysian	Pakistani	Samoan	Sri Lankan	Taiwanese	Thai	Tongan	Vietnamese
Carver County	2,391 3.45	1,012	44 4.35 4.35 1.84	-	-	-	-	-	-	-	-	-	-	-	-	-	-	-	-	-	-	-	-	-	-	-
Clay County	6,272 13.25	318	105 33.02 33.02 1.67	-	-	-	-	-	-	-	-	-	-	-	-	-	-	-	-	-	-	-	-	-	-	-
Crow Wing County	5,290 9.76	218	75 34.40 34.40 1.42	-	-	-	-	-	-	-	-	-	-	-	-	-	-	-	-	-	-	-	-	-	-	-
Dakota County	12,757 3.61	9,113	594 6.52 6.52 4.66	-	-	21 1.24 3.54 0.23 0.16	-	28 6.21 4.71 0.31 0.22	57 4.13 9.60 0.63 0.45	-	56 6.87 9.43 0.61 0.44	-	-	-	-	-	40 3.63 6.73 0.44 0.31	123 17.18 20.71 1.35 0.96	-	-	-	-	-	-	-	188 10.80 31.65 2.06 1.47
Eagan (city)	1,848 2.91	3,077	293 9.52 9.52 15.85	-	-	6 0.90 2.05 0.19 0.32	-	-	39 7.80 13.31 1.27 2.11	-	-	-	-	-	-	-	-	-	-	-	-	-	-	-	-	97 17.02 33.11 3.15 5.25
Hennepin County	90,384 8.27	52,503	9,440 17.98 17.98 10.44	569	80 14.06 14.06 0.09	636 8.26 6.74 1.21 0.70	-	390 22.18 4.13 0.74 0.43	723 12.23 7.66 1.38 0.80	-	101 5.50 1.07 0.19 0.11	-	-	4,408 33.30 46.69 8.40 4.88	-	206 12.58 2.18 0.39 0.23	603 13.01 6.39 1.15 0.67	564 12.85 5.97 1.07 0.62	-	118 28.92 1.25 0.22 0.13	-	-	-	-	-	1,209 14.92 12.81 2.30 1.34
Bloomington (city)	3,343 3.97	4,216	329 7.80 7.80 9.84	-	-	11 2.13 3.34 0.26 0.33	-	157 32.11 47.72 3.72 4.70	0 0.00 0.00 0.00 0.00	-	-	-	-	-	-	-	0 0.00 0.00 0.00 0.00	-	-	-	-	-	-	-	-	125 10.67 37.99 2.96 3.74
Brooklyn Center (city)	2,143 7.44	2,597	168 6.47 6.47 7.84	-	-	-	-	-	-	-	-	-	-	130 8.98 77.38 5.01 6.07	-	-	-	0 0.00 0.00 0.00 0.00	-	-	-	-	-	-	-	-
Brooklyn Park (city)	3,421 5.10	6,189	430 6.95 6.95 12.57	-	-	0 0.00 0.00 0.00 0.00	-	-	-	-	-	-	-	276 25.09 64.19 4.46 8.07	-	-	-	55 3.81 12.79 0.89 1.61	-	-	-	-	-	-	-	27 1.82 6.28 0.44 0.79
Eden Prairie (city)	1,910 3.49	2,786	249 8.94 8.94 13.04	-	-	33 5.63 13.25 1.18 1.73	-	-	31 4.61 12.45 1.11 1.62	-	-	-	-	-	-	-	-	-	-	-	-	-	-	-	-	70 13.21 28.11 2.51 3.66

Notes: Please refer to the User's Guide for an explanation of data; data is arranged alphabetically by state, then county, then city within each county; table includes counties with populations greater than 49,999 unless noted and cities with populations greater than 9,999 whose Asian and/or NHPI population rates are greater than the national average; (1) Native Hawaiian and other Pacific Islander; (2) excludes Taiwanese; (3) includes Chamorro; (4) county does not meet population threshold but is shown in order to allow inclusion of city

Place	Total population with income below poverty level	Asian population for whom poverty status is determined	Asians with income below poverty level	NHPI[1] population for whom poverty status is determined	NHPIs[1] with income below poverty level	Asian Indian	Bangladeshi	Cambodian	Chinese[2]	Fijian	Filipino	Guamanian[3]	Hawaiian, Native	Hmong	Indonesian	Japanese	Korean	Laotian	Malaysian	Pakistani	Samoan	Sri Lankan	Taiwanese	Thai	Tongan	Vietnamese
Hopkins (city)	1,563	964	171	-	-	85	-	-	-	-	-	-	-	-	-	-	-	-	-	-	-	-	-	-	-	-
	9.34		17.74			18.48																				
						49.71																				
			17.74			8.82																				
			10.94			5.44																				
Minneapolis (city)	62,092	23,395	7,469	-	-	390	-	136	518	-	90	-	-	3,991	-	147	390	503	-	-	-	-	-	-	-	842
	16.92		31.93			19.35		27.59	26.51		12.80			39.15		20.53	25.42	31.30								30.46
						5.22		1.82	6.94		1.20			53.43		1.97	5.22	6.73								11.27
			31.93			1.67		0.58	2.21		0.38			17.06		0.63	1.67	2.15								3.60
			12.03			0.63		0.22	0.83		0.14			6.43		0.24	0.63	0.81								1.36
Plymouth (city)	1,679	2,463	121	-	-	23	-	-	15	-	-	-	-	-	-	-	41	-	-	-	-	-	-	-	-	-
	2.59		4.91			2.50			3.51								11.36									
						19.01			12.40								33.88									
			4.91			0.93			0.61								1.66									
			7.21			1.37			0.89								2.44									
Richfield (city)	2,150	1,757	175	-	-	-	-	-	-	-	-	-	-	-	-	-	-	-	-	-	-	-	-	-	-	113
	6.29		9.96																							26.84
																										64.57
			9.96																							6.43
			8.14																							5.26
Nobles County[4]	2,390	760	141	-	-	-	-	-	-	-	-	-	-	-	-	-	-	79	-	-	-	-	-	-	-	-
	11.65		18.55															19.55								
																		56.03								
			18.55															10.39								
			5.90															3.31								
Worthington (city)	1,472	692	123	-	-	-	-	-	-	-	-	-	-	-	-	-	-	67	-	-	-	-	-	-	-	-
	13.29		17.77															18.06								
																		54.47								
			17.77															9.68								
			8.36															4.55								
Olmsted County	7,806	5,295	789	-	-	52	-	204	8	-	-	-	-	35	-	137	31	102	-	-	-	-	-	-	-	157
	6.39		14.90			5.14		28.37	1.36					8.86		32.24	6.30	24.23								21.63
						6.59		25.86	1.01					4.44		17.36	3.93	12.93								19.90
			14.90			0.98		3.85	0.15					0.66		2.59	0.59	1.93								2.97
			10.11			0.67		2.61	0.10					0.45		1.76	0.40	1.31								2.01
Rochester (city)	6,556	4,772	742	-	-	52	-	199	8	-	-	-	-	35	-	-	20	102	-	-	-	-	-	-	-	157
	7.84		15.55			5.45		35.79	1.45					8.86			5.28	24.34								22.59
						7.01		26.82	1.08					4.72			2.70	13.75								21.16
			15.55			1.09		4.17	0.17					0.73			0.42	2.14								3.29
			11.32			0.79		3.04	0.12					0.53			0.31	1.56								2.39
Otter Tail County	5,644	166	28	-	-	-	-	-	-	-	-	-	-	-	-	-	-	-	-	-	-	-	-	-	-	-
	10.13		16.87																							
			16.87																							
			0.50																							
Ramsey County	52,673	43,485	11,954	-	-	180	-	335	283	-	48	-	-	9,007	-	29	300	298	-	-	-	-	-	-	-	780
	10.63		27.49			7.93		30.82	8.28		5.47			34.02		6.09	15.81	32.18								21.86
						1.51		2.80	2.37		0.40			75.35		0.24	2.51	2.49								6.53
			27.49			0.41		0.77	0.65		0.11			20.71		0.07	0.69	0.69								1.79
			22.69			0.34		0.64	0.54		0.09			17.10		0.06	0.57	0.57								1.48

Notes: Please refer to the User's Guide for an explanation of data; data is arranged alphabetically by state, then county, then city within each county; table includes counties with populations greater than 49,999 unless noted and cities with populations greater than 9,999 whose Asian and/or NHPI population rates are greater than the national average; (1) Native Hawaiian and other Pacific Islander; (2) excludes Taiwanese; (3) includes Chamorro; (4) county does not meet population threshold but is shown in order to allow inclusion of city

Place	Total population with income below poverty level	Asian population for whom poverty status is determined	Asians with income below poverty level	NHPI[1] population for whom poverty status is determined	NHPIs[1] with income below poverty level	Asian Indian	Bangladeshi	Cambodian	Chinese[2]	Fijian	Filipino	Guamanian[3]	Hawaiian, Native	Hmong	Indonesian	Japanese	Korean	Laotian	Malaysian	Pakistani	Samoan	Sri Lankan	Taiwanese	Thai	Tongan	Vietnamese
Maplewood (city)	1,667 4.83	1,347	29 2.15 2.15 1.74	-	-	-	-	-	0 0.00 0.00 0.00 0.00	-	-	-	-	0 0.00 0.00 0.00 0.00	-	-	-	-	-	-	-	-	-	-	-	-
New Brighton (city)	1,018 4.70	902	39 4.32 4.32 3.83	-	-	-	-	-	-	-	-	-	-	-	-	-	-	-	-	-	-	-	-	-	-	-
Roseville (city)	1,353 4.20	1,617	80 4.95 4.95 5.91	-	-	-	-	-	66 9.72 82.50 4.08 4.88	-	-	-	-	-	-	-	-	-	-	-	-	-	-	-	-	-
St. Paul (city)	43,266 15.61	34,867	11,455 32.85 32.85 26.48	-	-	126 15.65 1.10 0.36 0.29	-	328 35.81 2.86 0.94 0.76	120 12.59 1.05 0.34 0.28	-	48 9.02 0.42 0.14 0.11	-	-	9,006 35.52 78.62 25.83 20.82	-	-	160 18.80 1.40 0.46 0.37	275 32.20 2.40 0.79 0.64	-	-	-	-	-	-	-	758 30.00 6.62 2.17 1.75
Vadnais Heights (city)	415 3.18	567	0 <0.01 <0.01 <0.01	-	-	-	-	-	-	-	-	-	-	-	-	-	-	-	-	-	-	-	-	-	-	-
Rice County	3,485 6.94	663	50 7.54 7.54 1.43	-	-	-	-	-	-	-	-	-	-	-	-	-	-	-	-	-	-	-	-	-	-	-
St. Louis County	23,211 12.05	1,429	311 21.76 21.76 1.34	-	-	-	-	-	-	-	-	-	-	-	-	-	26 8.02 8.36 1.82 0.11	-	-	-	-	-	-	-	-	-
Scott County	2,979 3.37	1,861	38 2.04 2.04 1.28	-	-	-	-	0 0.00 0.00 0.00 0.00	-	-	-	-	-	-	-	-	-	-	-	-	-	-	-	-	-	10 2.54 26.32 0.54 0.34
Savage (city)	480 2.27	1,101	26 2.36 2.36 5.42	-	-	-	-	-	-	-	-	-	-	-	-	-	-	-	-	-	-	-	-	-	-	-
Sherburne County	2,776 4.43	344	52 15.12 15.12 1.87	-	-	-	-	-	-	-	-	-	-	-	-	-	-	-	-	-	-	-	-	-	-	-

Notes: Please refer to the User's Guide for an explanation of data; data is arranged alphabetically by state, then county, then city within each county; table includes counties with populations greater than 49,999 unless noted and cities with populations greater than 9,999 whose Asian and/or NHPI population rates are greater than the national average; (1) Native Hawaiian and other Pacific Islander; (2) excludes Taiwanese; (3) includes Chamorro; (4) county does not meet population threshold but is shown in order to allow inclusion of city

Place	Total population with income below poverty level	Asian population for whom poverty status is determined	Asians with income below poverty level	NHPI[1] population for whom poverty status is determined	NHPIs[1] with income below poverty level	Asian Indian	Bangladeshi	Cambodian	Chinese[2]	Fijian	Filipino	Guamanian[3]	Hawaiian, Native	Hmong	Indonesian	Japanese	Korean	Laotian	Malaysian	Pakistani	Samoan	Sri Lankan	Taiwanese	Thai	Tongan	Vietnamese
Stearns County	11,037 8.73	1,579	402 25.46 25.46 3.64	-	-	-	-	-	-	-	-	-	-	-	-	-	-	-	-	-	-	-	-	-	-	65 10.78 16.17 4.12 0.59
Washington County	5,765 2.91	4,333	83 1.92 1.92 1.44	-	-	6 1.05 7.23 0.14 0.10	-	-	2 0.28 2.41 0.05 0.03	-	-	-	-	28 3.65 33.73 0.65 0.49	-	-	13 1.91 15.66 0.30 0.23	-	-	-	-	-	-	-	-	0 0.00 0.00 0.00 0.00
Woodbury (city)	772 1.68	2,376	42 1.77 1.77 5.44	-	-	6 1.41 14.29 0.25 0.78	-	-	0 0.00 0.00 0.00 0.00	-	-	-	-	0 0.00 0.00 0.00 0.00	-	-	-	-	-	-	-	-	-	-	-	-
Wright County	4,211 4.74	191	5 2.62 2.62 0.12	-	-	-	-	-	-	-	-	-	-	-	-	-	-	-	-	-	-	-	-	-	-	-
MISSISSIPPI	548,079 19.93	17,017	3,040 17.86 17.86 0.55	638	53 8.31 8.31 0.01	426 13.49 14.01 2.50 0.08	-	-	479 18.65 15.76 2.81 0.09	-	189 7.56 6.22 1.11 0.03	-	-	-	-	101 18.91 3.32 0.59 0.02	223 17.81 7.34 1.31 0.04	-	-	-	-	-	-	-	-	1,363 25.98 44.84 8.01 0.25
DeSoto County	7,571 7.11	676	39 5.77 5.77 0.52	-	-	-	-	-	-	-	-	-	-	-	-	-	-	-	-	-	-	-	-	-	-	-
Forrest County	15,089 22.46	586	362 61.77 61.77 2.40	-	-	-	-	-	-	-	-	-	-	-	-	-	-	-	-	-	-	-	-	-	-	-
Harrison County	26,597 14.59	4,821	995 20.64 20.64 3.74	-	-	-	-	-	-	-	98 12.93 9.85 2.03 0.37	-	-	-	-	-	-	-	-	-	-	-	-	-	-	829 30.12 83.32 17.20 3.12
Biloxi (city)	6,906 14.56	2,366	602 25.44 25.44 8.72	-	-	-	-	-	-	-	36 9.00 5.98 1.52 0.52	-	-	-	-	-	-	-	-	-	-	-	-	-	-	537 36.41 89.20 22.70 7.78
Hinds County	48,193 19.95	1,294	267 20.63 20.63 0.55	-	-	129 22.51 48.31 9.97 0.27	-	-	-	-	-	-	-	-	-	-	-	-	-	-	-	-	-	-	-	-

Notes: Please refer to the User's Guide for an explanation of data; data is arranged alphabetically by state, then county, then city within each county; table includes counties with populations greater than 49,999 unless noted and cities with populations greater than 9,999 whose Asian and/or NHPI population rates are greater than the national average; (1) Native Hawaiian and other Pacific Islander; (2) excludes Taiwanese; (3) includes Chamorro; (4) county does not meet population threshold but is shown in order to allow inclusion of city

Place	Total population with income below poverty level	Asian population for whom poverty status is determined	Asians with income below poverty level	NHPI[1] population for whom poverty status is determined	NHPIs[1] with income below poverty level	Asian Indian	Bangladeshi	Cambodian	Chinese[2]	Fijian	Filipino	Guamanian[3]	Hawaiian, Native	Hmong	Indonesian	Japanese	Korean	Laotian	Malaysian	Pakistani	Samoan	Sri Lankan	Taiwanese	Thai	Tongan	Vietnamese
Jackson County	16,504 12.75	1,893	190 10.04 10.04 1.15	-	-	-	-	-	-	-	-	-	-	-	-	-	-	-	-	-	-	-	-	-	-	146 13.92 76.84 7.71 0.88
Madison County	10,155 13.99	585	17 2.91 2.91 0.17	-	-	-	-	-	-	-	-	-	-	-	-	-	-	-	-	-	-	-	-	-	-	-
Oktibbeha County[4]	10,869 28.20	977	393 40.23 40.23 3.62	-	-	-	-	-	-	-	-	-	-	-	-	-	-	-	-	-	-	-	-	-	-	-
Starkville (city)	6,640 31.15	798	331 41.48 41.48 4.98	-	-	-	-	-	-	-	-	-	-	-	-	-	-	-	-	-	-	-	-	-	-	-
Rankin County	10,462 9.49	550	27 4.91 4.91 0.26	-	-	-	-	-	-	-	-	-	-	-	-	-	-	-	-	-	-	-	-	-	-	-
MISSOURI	637,891 11.74	58,758	8,537 14.53 14.53 1.34	2,922	428 14.65 14.65 0.07	1,316 11.40 15.42 2.24 0.21	-	176 20.25 2.06 0.30 0.03	2,028 16.31 23.76 3.45 0.32	-	545 7.66 6.38 0.93 0.09	38 6.59 8.88 1.30 0.01	89 14.15 20.79 3.05 0.01	-	-	627 19.17 7.34 1.07 0.10	907 14.48 10.62 1.54 0.14	117 16.39 1.37 0.20 0.02	-	77 7.40 0.90 0.13 0.01	184 18.59 42.99 6.30 0.03	-	152 15.98 1.78 0.26 0.02	254 18.84 2.98 0.43 0.04	-	1,749 17.05 20.49 2.98 0.27
Boone County	18,366 14.52	3,692	891 24.13 24.13 4.85	-	-	89 11.62 9.99 2.41 0.48	-	-	306 26.42 34.34 8.29 1.67	-	-	-	-	-	-	-	196 40.25 22.00 5.31 1.07	-	-	-	-	-	-	-	-	-
Columbia (city)	14,670 19.19	3,401	859 25.26 25.26 5.86	-	-	89 12.04 10.36 2.62 0.61	-	-	306 27.62 35.62 9.00 2.09	-	-	-	-	-	-	-	164 41.10 19.09 4.82 1.12	-	-	-	-	-	-	-	-	-
Cape Girardeau County	7,255 11.10	354	98 27.68 27.68 1.35	-	-	-	-	-	-	-	-	-	-	-	-	-	-	-	-	-	-	-	-	-	-	-
Cass County	4,664 5.77	346	9 2.60 2.60 0.19	-	-	-	-	-	-	-	-	-	-	-	-	-	-	-	-	-	-	-	-	-	-	-

Notes: Please refer to the User's Guide for an explanation of data; data is arranged alphabetically by state, then county, then city within each county; table includes counties with populations greater than 49,999 unless noted and cities with populations greater than 9,999 whose Asian and/or NHPI population rates are greater than the national average; (1) Native Hawaiian and other Pacific Islander; (2) excludes Taiwanese; (3) includes Chamorro; (4) county does not meet population threshold but is shown in order to allow inclusion of city

Place	Total population with income below poverty level	Asian population for whom poverty status is determined	Asians with income below poverty level	NHPI[1] population for whom poverty status is determined	NHPIs[1] with income below poverty level	Asian Indian	Bangladeshi	Cambodian	Chinese[2]	Fijian	Filipino	Guamanian[3]	Hawaiian, Native	Hmong	Indonesian	Japanese	Korean	Laotian	Malaysian	Pakistani	Samoan	Sri Lankan	Taiwanese	Thai	Tongan	Vietnamese
Clay County	9,898 5.46	2,155	153 7.10 7.10 1.55	-	-	36 8.89 23.53 1.67 0.36	-	-	-	-	-	-	-	-	-	-	-	-	-	-	-	-	-	-	-	26 4.21 16.99 1.21 0.26
Cole County	5,709 8.68	608	57 9.38 9.38 1.00	-	-	-	-	-	-	-	-	-	-	-	-	-	-	-	-	-	-	-	-	-	-	-
Franklin County	6,494 7.02	326	37 11.35 11.35 0.57	-	-	-	-	-	-	-	-	-	-	-	-	-	-	-	-	-	-	-	-	-	-	-
Greene County	27,630 12.07	2,123	471 22.19 22.19 1.70	-	-	-	-	-	120 36.47 25.48 5.65 0.43	-	-	-	-	-	-	-	54 15.17 11.46 2.54 0.20	-	-	-	-	-	-	-	-	45 11.03 9.55 2.12 0.16
Jackson County	76,808 11.93	8,506	1,474 17.33 17.33 1.92	919	163 17.74 17.74 0.21	187 18.24 12.69 2.20 0.24	-	-	244 19.63 16.55 2.87 0.32	-	80 6.38 5.43 0.94 0.10	-	-	-	-	72 18.05 4.88 0.85 0.09	106 18.66 7.19 1.25 0.14	-	-	-	81 17.49 49.69 8.81 0.11	-	-	-	-	501 17.51 33.99 5.89 0.65
Independence (city)	9,689 8.64	1,009	86 8.52 8.52 0.89	405	69 17.04 17.04 0.71	-	-	-	-	-	-	-	-	-	-	-	-	-	-	-	-	-	-	-	-	-
Jasper County	14,808 14.48	598	191 31.94 31.94 1.29	-	-	-	-	-	-	-	-	-	-	-	-	-	-	-	-	-	-	-	-	-	-	-
Jefferson County	13,253 6.78	745	105 14.09 14.09 0.79	-	-	-	-	-	-	-	-	-	-	-	-	-	-	-	-	-	-	-	-	-	-	-
Newton County	6,011 11.64	172	39 22.67 22.67 0.65	-	-	-	-	-	-	-	-	-	-	-	-	-	-	-	-	-	-	-	-	-	-	-
Phelps County[4]	6,129 16.42	782	261 33.38 33.38 4.26	-	-	73 23.40 27.97 9.34 1.19	-	-	-	-	-	-	-	-	-	-	-	-	-	-	-	-	-	-	-	-

Notes: Please refer to the User's Guide for an explanation of data; data is arranged alphabetically by state, then county, then city within each county; table includes counties with populations greater than 49,999 unless noted and cities with populations greater than 9,999 whose Asian and/or NHPI population rates are greater than the national average; (1) Native Hawaiian and other Pacific Islander; (2) excludes Taiwanese; (3) includes Chamorro; (4) county does not meet population threshold but is shown in order to allow inclusion of city

Place	Total population with income below poverty level	Asian population for whom poverty status is determined	Asians with income below poverty level	NHPI[1] population for whom poverty status is determined	NHPIs[1] with income below poverty level	Asian Indian	Bangladeshi	Cambodian	Chinese[2]	Fijian	Filipino	Guamanian[3]	Hawaiian, Native	Hmong	Indonesian	Japanese	Korean	Laotian	Malaysian	Pakistani	Samoan	Sri Lankan	Taiwanese	Thai	Tongan	Vietnamese
Rolla (city)	3,193 21.96	633	231 36.49 36.49 7.23	-	-	-	-	-	-	-	-	-	-	-	-	-	-	-	-	-	-	-	-	-	-	-
Platte County	3,477 4.77	1,066	20 1.88 1.88 0.58	-	-	-	-	-	-	-	-	-	-	-	-	-	-	-	-	-	-	-	-	-	-	-
St. Charles County	11,177 4.00	2,373	134 5.65 5.65 1.20	-	-	0 0.00 0.00 0.00 0.00	-	-	45 10.98 33.58 1.90 0.40	-	24 5.96 17.91 1.01 0.21	-	-	-	-	-	-	-	-	-	-	-	-	-	-	-
Saint Louis Independent City	83,388 24.57	6,939	1,574 22.68 22.68 1.89	-	-	162 24.00 10.29 2.33 0.19	-	-	350 31.99 22.24 5.04 0.42	-	42 7.66 2.67 0.61 0.05	-	-	-	-	-	-	-	-	-	-	-	-	-	-	706 21.93 44.85 10.17 0.85
St. Louis County	68,552 6.87	21,192	1,864 8.80 8.80 2.72	406	77 18.97 18.97 0.11	420 7.42 22.53 1.98 0.61	-	-	568 9.58 30.47 2.68 0.83	-	65 3.26 3.49 0.31 0.09	-	-	-	-	191 16.05 10.25 0.90 0.28	210 8.47 11.27 0.99 0.31	-	-	43 7.56 2.31 0.20 0.06	-	-	20 3.13 1.07 0.09 0.03	61 16.14 3.27 0.29 0.09	-	122 8.66 6.55 0.58 0.18
Chesterfield (city)	1,188 2.59	2,436	63 2.59 2.59 5.30	-	-	19 2.87 30.16 0.78 1.60	-	-	0 0.00 0.00 0.00 0.00	-	-	-	-	-	-	-	-	-	-	-	-	-	-	-	-	-
Clayton (city)	860 7.66	724	39 5.39 5.39 4.53	-	-	-	-	-	-	-	-	-	-	-	-	-	-	-	-	-	-	-	-	-	-	-
Creve Coeur (city)	461 2.90	872	33 3.78 3.78 7.16	-	-	-	-	-	-	-	-	-	-	-	-	-	-	-	-	-	-	-	-	-	-	-
Manchester (city)	577 3.03	935	30 3.21 3.21 5.20	-	-	-	-	-	-	-	-	-	-	-	-	-	-	-	-	-	-	-	-	-	-	-
Maryland Heights (city)	1,344 5.25	1,777	219 12.32 12.32 16.29	-	-	124 17.82 56.62 6.98 9.23	-	-	42 8.20 19.18 2.36 3.13	-	-	-	-	-	-	-	-	-	-	-	-	-	-	-	-	-

Notes: Please refer to the User's Guide for an explanation of data; data is arranged alphabetically by state, then county, then city within each county; table includes counties with populations greater than 49,999 unless noted and cities with populations greater than 9,999 whose Asian and/or NHPI population rates are greater than the national average; (1) Native Hawaiian and other Pacific Islander; (2) excludes Taiwanese; (3) includes Chamorro; (4) county does not meet population threshold but is shown in order to allow inclusion of city

Place	Total population with income below poverty level	Asian population for whom poverty status is determined	Asians with income below poverty level	NHPI[1] population for whom poverty status is determined	NHPIs[1] with income below poverty level	Asian Indian	Bangladeshi	Cambodian	Chinese[2]	Fijian	Filipino	Guamanian[3]	Hawaiian, Native	Hmong	Indonesian	Japanese	Korean	Laotian	Malaysian	Pakistani	Samoan	Sri Lankan	Taiwanese	Thai	Tongan	Vietnamese
Town and Country (city)	244 2.51	828	15 1.81 1.81 6.15	-	-	5 1.32 33.33 0.60 2.05	-	-	-	-	-	-	-	-	-	-	-	-	-	-	-	-	-	-	-	-
MONTANA	128,355 14.61	4,197	853 20.32 20.32 0.66	412	60 14.56 14.56 0.05	125 28.15 14.65 2.98 0.10	-	-	133 20.62 15.59 3.17 0.10	-	106 14.23 12.43 2.53 0.08	-	51 21.79 85.00 12.38 0.04	-	-	207 26.64 24.27 4.93 0.16	126 15.42 14.77 3.00 0.10	-	-	-	-	-	-	-	-	-
Cascade County	10,605 13.52	486	79 16.26 16.26 0.74	-	-	-	-	-	-	-	-	-	-	-	-	-	-	-	-	-	-	-	-	-	-	-
Flathead County	9,489 12.96	251	25 9.96 9.96 0.26	-	-	-	-	-	-	-	-	-	-	-	-	-	-	-	-	-	-	-	-	-	-	-
Gallatin County	8,319 12.85	631	159 25.20 25.20 1.91	-	-	-	-	-	-	-	-	-	-	-	-	-	-	-	-	-	-	-	-	-	-	-
Missoula County	13,691 14.78	881	261 29.63 29.63 1.91	-	-	-	-	-	-	-	-	-	-	-	-	-	-	-	-	-	-	-	-	-	-	-
Yellowstone County	14,032 11.11	647	69 10.66 10.66 0.49	-	-	-	-	-	-	-	-	-	-	-	-	-	-	-	-	-	-	-	-	-	-	-
NEBRASKA	161,269 9.71	20,458	2,626 12.84 12.84 1.63	578	76 13.15 13.15 0.05	415 13.58 15.80 2.03 0.26	-	-	539 19.61 20.53 2.63 0.33	-	89 4.39 3.39 0.44 0.06	-	-	-	-	301 23.50 11.46 1.47 0.19	236 10.89 8.99 1.15 0.15	33 4.26 1.26 0.16 0.02	-	-	-	-	-	125 27.23 4.76 0.61 0.08	-	561 8.50 21.36 2.74 0.35
Douglas County	44,553 9.85	7,589	1,188 15.65 15.65 2.67	-	-	248 12.91 20.88 3.27 0.56	-	-	244 18.17 20.54 3.22 0.55	-	30 3.43 2.53 0.40 0.07	-	-	-	-	238 36.90 20.03 3.14 0.53	84 10.69 7.07 1.11 0.19	-	-	-	-	-	-	-	-	128 10.13 10.77 1.69 0.29
Hall County	6,292 12.00	541	29 5.36 5.36 0.46	-	-	-	-	-	-	-	-	-	-	-	-	-	-	-	-	-	-	-	-	-	-	-

Notes: Please refer to the User's Guide for an explanation of data; data is arranged alphabetically by state, then county, then city within each county; table includes counties with populations greater than 49,999 unless noted and cities with populations greater than 9,999 whose Asian and/or NHPI population rates are greater than the national average; (1) Native Hawaiian and other Pacific Islander; (2) excludes Taiwanese; (3) includes Chamorro; (4) county does not meet population threshold but is shown in order to allow inclusion of city

Place	Total population with income below poverty level	Asian population for whom poverty status is determined	Asians with income below poverty level	NHPI[1] population for whom poverty status is determined	NHPIs[1] with income below poverty level	Asian Indian	Bangladeshi	Cambodian	Chinese[2]	Fijian	Filipino	Guamanian[3]	Hawaiian, Native	Hmong	Indonesian	Japanese	Korean	Laotian	Malaysian	Pakistani	Samoan	Sri Lankan	Taiwanese	Thai	Tongan	Vietnamese
Lancaster County	22,722 9.53	6,523	869 13.32 13.32 3.82	-	-	26 4.11 2.99 0.40 0.11	-	-	246 26.68 28.31 3.77 1.08	-	-	-	-	-	-	-	35 9.89 4.03 0.54 0.15	-	-	-	-	-	-	-	-	341 9.09 39.24 5.23 1.50
Sarpy County	5,092 4.21	2,208	148 6.70 6.70 2.91	-	-	-	-	-	-	-	10 2.08 6.76 0.45 0.20	-	-	-	-	-	34 7.42 22.97 1.54 0.67	-	-	-	-	-	-	-	-	0 0.00 0.00 0.00 0.00
NEVADA	205,685 10.48	88,131	7,293 8.28 8.28 3.55	7,732	908 11.74 11.74 0.44	360 7.45 4.94 0.41 0.18	-	52 7.27 0.71 0.06 0.03	948 7.04 13.00 1.08 0.46	-	2,600 6.48 35.65 2.95 1.26	91 7.99 10.02 1.18 0.04	361 10.80 39.76 4.67 0.18	-	-	1,052 12.71 14.42 1.19 0.51	921 12.33 12.63 1.05 0.45	116 9.99 1.59 0.13 0.06	-	29 5.45 0.40 0.03 0.01	148 9.52 16.30 1.91 0.07	-	96 16.22 1.32 0.11 0.05	226 7.59 3.10 0.26 0.11	98 12.41 10.79 1.27 0.05	476 11.86 6.53 0.54 0.23
Carson City Independent City	4,923 10.02	1,061	87 8.20 8.20 1.77	-	-	-	-	-	-	-	9 3.26 10.34 0.85 0.18	-	-	-	-	-	-	-	-	-	-	-	-	-	-	-
Clark County	145,855 10.76	70,832	5,981 8.44 8.44 4.10	5,866	549 9.36 9.36 0.38	218 7.52 3.64 0.31 0.15	-	52 7.48 0.87 0.07 0.04	694 6.49 11.60 0.98 0.48	-	2,396 7.40 40.06 3.38 1.64	56 5.85 10.20 0.95 0.04	309 10.18 56.28 5.27 0.21	-	-	684 10.35 11.44 0.97 0.47	750 11.66 12.54 1.06 0.51	104 9.05 1.74 0.15 0.07	-	-	131 11.80 23.86 2.23 0.09	-	87 20.52 1.45 0.12 0.06	222 8.47 3.71 0.31 0.15	-	392 12.05 6.55 0.55 0.27
Enterprise (cdp)	1,238 8.61	692	132 19.08 19.08 10.66	-	-	-	-	-	-	-	-	-	-	-	-	-	-	-	-	-	-	-	-	-	-	-
Henderson (city)	9,774 5.60	6,683	241 3.61 3.61 2.47	758	24 3.17 3.17 0.25	5 1.07 2.07 0.07 0.05	-	-	9 1.12 3.73 0.13 0.09	-	102 3.73 42.32 1.53 1.04	-	24 5.42 100.00 3.17 0.25	-	-	0 0.00 0.00 0.00 0.00	22 2.68 9.13 0.33 0.23	-	-	-	-	-	-	-	-	-
Las Vegas (city)	56,053 11.90	21,454	1,912 8.91 8.91 3.41	1,659	247 14.89 14.89 0.44	42 4.21 2.20 0.20 0.07	-	-	89 3.27 4.65 0.41 0.16	-	834 7.77 43.62 3.89 1.49	-	125 16.30 50.61 7.53 0.22	-	-	369 15.08 19.30 1.72 0.66	256 18.29 13.39 1.19 0.46	-	-	-	-	-	-	58 8.29 3.03 0.27 0.10	-	123 21.03 6.43 0.57 0.22
North Las Vegas (city)	16,763 14.76	3,837	126 3.28 3.28 0.75	747	91 12.18 12.18 0.54	-	-	-	-	-	82 3.74 65.08 2.14 0.49	-	-	-	-	-	-	-	-	-	-	-	-	-	-	-
Paradise (cdp)	21,749 11.83	12,387	1,519 12.26 12.26 6.98	816	97 11.89 11.89 0.45	107 16.67 7.04 0.86 0.49	-	-	295 16.21 19.42 2.38 1.36	-	628 11.21 41.34 5.07 2.89	-	68 11.72 70.10 8.33 0.31	-	-	102 7.67 6.71 0.82 0.47	181 13.61 11.92 1.46 0.83	-	-	-	-	-	-	-	-	85 14.55 5.60 0.69 0.39

Notes: Please refer to the User's Guide for an explanation of data; data is arranged alphabetically by state, then county, then city within each county; table includes counties with populations greater than 49,999 unless noted and cities with populations greater than 9,999 whose Asian and/or NHPI population rates are greater than the national average; (1) Native Hawaiian and other Pacific Islander; (2) excludes Taiwanese; (3) includes Chamorro; (4) county does not meet population threshold but is shown in order to allow inclusion of city

Place	Total population with income below poverty level	Asian population for whom poverty status is determined	Asians with income below poverty level	NHPI[1] population for whom poverty status is determined	NHPIs[1] with income below poverty level	Asian Indian	Bangladeshi	Cambodian	Chinese[2]	Fijian	Filipino	Guamanian[3]	Hawaiian, Native	Hmong	Indonesian	Japanese	Korean	Laotian	Malaysian	Pakistani	Samoan	Sri Lankan	Taiwanese	Thai	Tongan	Vietnamese
Spring Valley (cdp)	7,840 6.70	12,899	1,038 8.05 8.05 13.24	657	63 9.59 9.59 0.80	-	-	-	229 5.45 22.06 1.78 2.92	-	206 5.29 19.85 1.60 2.63	-	-	-	-	135 18.75 13.01 1.05 1.72	168 12.42 16.18 1.30 2.14	-	-	-	-	-	-	91 18.31 8.77 0.71 1.16	-	73 7.55 7.03 0.57 0.93
Sunrise Manor (cdp)	19,658 12.76	8,605	684 7.95 7.95 3.48	429	21 4.90 4.90 0.11	-	-	-	62 13.03 9.06 0.72 0.32	-	342 7.09 50.00 3.97 1.74	-	-	-	-	12 2.00 1.75 0.14 0.06	45 6.16 6.58 0.52 0.23	-	-	-	-	-	-	-	-	-
Winchester (cdp)	3,716 14.00	1,463	73 4.99 4.99 1.96	-	-	-	-	-	-	-	23 5.32 31.51 1.57 0.62	-	-	-	-	-	-	-	-	-	-	-	-	-	-	-
Washoe County	33,318 9.96	14,083	1,111 7.89 7.89 3.33	1,480	333 22.50 22.50 1.00	119 7.45 10.71 0.84 0.36	-	-	227 9.67 20.43 1.61 0.68	-	155 2.46 13.95 1.10 0.47	-	-	-	-	368 29.49 33.12 2.61 1.10	78 10.47 7.02 0.55 0.23	-	-	-	-	-	-	-	98 16.98 29.43 6.62 0.29	75 10.95 6.75 0.53 0.23
Reno (city)	22,232 12.57	9,236	980 10.61 10.61 4.41	937	209 22.31 22.31 0.94	119 12.61 12.14 1.29 0.54	-	-	205 14.02 20.92 2.22 0.92	-	114 2.73 11.63 1.23 0.51	-	-	-	-	323 35.97 32.96 3.50 1.45	67 15.06 6.84 0.73 0.30	-	-	-	-	-	-	-	-	63 14.29 6.43 0.68 0.28
Sparks (city)	5,290 8.05	3,091	86 2.78 2.78 1.63	-	-	-	-	-	22 3.36 25.58 0.71 0.42	-	15 1.04 17.44 0.49 0.28	-	-	-	-	-	-	-	-	-	-	-	-	-	-	-
NEW HAMPSHIRE	78,530 6.55	14,757	1,458 9.88 9.88 1.86	-	-	263 7.56 18.04 1.78 0.33	-	-	450 12.08 30.86 3.05 0.57	-	76 6.07 5.21 0.52 0.10	-	-	-	-	119 14.25 8.16 0.81 0.15	138 7.61 9.47 0.94 0.18	63 16.98 4.32 0.43 0.08	-	-	-	-	-	-	-	143 8.63 9.81 0.97 0.18
Belknap County	3,350 6.09	347	21 6.05 6.05 0.63	-	-	-	-	-	-	-	-	-	-	-	-	-	-	-	-	-	-	-	-	-	-	-
Cheshire County	5,550 7.95	472	67 14.19 14.19 1.21	-	-	-	-	-	-	-	-	-	-	-	-	-	-	-	-	-	-	-	-	-	-	-
Grafton County	6,462 8.57	888	119 13.40 13.40 1.84	-	-	-	-	-	54 16.67 45.38 6.08 0.84	-	-	-	-	-	-	-	-	-	-	-	-	-	-	-	-	-

Notes: Please refer to the User's Guide for an explanation of data; data is arranged alphabetically by state, then county, then city within each county; table includes counties with populations greater than 49,999 unless noted and cities with populations greater than 9,999 whose Asian and/or NHPI population rates are greater than the national average; (1) Native Hawaiian and other Pacific Islander; (2) excludes Taiwanese; (3) includes Chamorro; (4) county does not meet population threshold but is shown in order to allow inclusion of city

Place	Total population with income below poverty level	Asian population for whom poverty status is determined	Asians with income below poverty level	NHPI[1] population for whom poverty status is determined	NHPIs[1] with income below poverty level	Asian Indian	Bangladeshi	Cambodian	Chinese[2]	Fijian	Filipino	Guamanian[3]	Hawaiian, Native	Hmong	Indonesian	Japanese	Korean	Laotian	Malaysian	Pakistani	Samoan	Sri Lankan	Taiwanese	Thai	Tongan	Vietnamese
Hanover (town)	633 9.06	305	57 18.69 18.69 9.00	-	-	-	-	-	-	-	-	-	-	-	-	-	-	-	-	-	-	-	-	-	-	-
Hillsborough County	23,358 6.26	7,304	723 9.90 9.90 3.10	-	-	73 3.37 10.10 1.00 0.31	-	-	289 15.39 39.97 3.96 1.24	-	35 8.82 4.84 0.48 0.15	-	-	-	-	-	71 11.83 9.82 0.97 0.30	-	-	-	-	-	-	-	-	88 8.12 12.17 1.20 0.38
Nashua (city)	5,743 6.76	3,365	250 7.43 7.43 4.35	-	-	73 5.04 29.20 2.17 1.27	-	-	94 11.87 37.60 2.79 1.64	-	-	-	-	-	-	-	-	-	-	-	-	-	-	-	-	-
Merrimack County	7,721 5.95	1,032	174 16.86 16.86 2.25	-	-	-	-	-	-	-	-	-	-	-	-	-	-	-	-	-	-	-	-	-	-	-
Rockingham County	12,347 4.49	2,931	122 4.16 4.16 0.99	-	-	74 15.48 60.66 2.52 0.60	-	-	9 1.07 7.38 0.31 0.07	-	5 1.21 4.10 0.17 0.04	-	-	-	-	-	14 3.38 11.48 0.48 0.11	-	-	-	-	-	-	-	-	-
Strafford County	9,733 9.16	1,368	142 10.38 10.38 1.46	-	-	-	-	-	4 1.33 2.82 0.29 0.04	-	-	-	-	-	-	-	-	-	-	-	-	-	-	-	-	-
NEW JERSEY	699,668 8.50	476,236	32,475 6.82 6.82 4.64	2,461	422 17.15 17.15 0.06	10,291 6.14 31.69 2.16 1.47	483 21.52 1.49 0.10 0.07	140 21.71 0.43 0.03 0.02	5,753 6.18 17.72 1.21 0.82	-	2,918 3.33 8.99 0.61 0.42	160 26.94 37.91 6.50 0.02	122 22.55 28.91 4.96 0.02	-	129 12.65 0.40 0.03 0.02	1,056 7.80 3.25 0.22 0.15	6,549 10.33 20.17 1.38 0.94	0 0.00 0.00 0.00 0.00	-	1,429 11.54 4.40 0.30 0.20	39 6.90 9.24 1.58 0.01	90 7.03 0.28 0.02 0.01	388 6.70 1.19 0.08 0.06	140 7.80 0.43 0.03 0.02	-	1,744 11.85 5.37 0.37 0.25
Atlantic County	25,906 10.50	12,782	1,116 8.73 8.73 4.31	-	-	431 10.72 38.62 3.37 1.66	129 31.70 11.56 1.01 0.50	-	39 1.91 3.49 0.31 0.15	-	72 3.37 6.45 0.56 0.28	-	-	-	-	-	67 10.69 6.00 0.52 0.26	-	-	178 36.93 15.95 1.39 0.69	-	-	-	-	-	151 7.40 13.53 1.18 0.58
Atlantic City (city)	9,427 23.65	4,115	535 13.00 13.00 5.68	-	-	163 18.01 30.47 3.96 1.73	-	-	28 3.89 5.23 0.68 0.30	-	18 3.64 3.36 0.44 0.19	-	-	-	-	-	-	-	-	-	-	-	-	-	-	73 6.15 13.64 1.77 0.77
Brigantine (city)	1,185 9.44	780	139 17.82 17.82 11.73	-	-	-	-	-	-	-	-	-	-	-	-	-	-	-	-	-	-	-	-	-	-	-

Notes: Please refer to the User's Guide for an explanation of data; data is arranged alphabetically by state, then county, then city within each county; table includes counties with populations greater than 49,999 unless noted and cities with populations greater than 9,999 whose Asian and/or NHPI population rates are greater than the national average; (1) Native Hawaiian and other Pacific Islander; (2) excludes Taiwanese; (3) includes Chamorro; (4) county does not meet population threshold but is shown in order to allow inclusion of city

Place	Total population with income below poverty level	Asian population for whom poverty status is determined	Asians with income below poverty level	NHPI[1] population for whom poverty status is determined	NHPIs[1] with income below poverty level	Asian Indian	Bangladeshi	Cambodian	Chinese[2]	Fijian	Filipino	Guamanian[3]	Hawaiian, Native	Hmong	Indonesian	Japanese	Korean	Laotian	Malaysian	Pakistani	Samoan	Sri Lankan	Taiwanese	Thai	Tongan	Vietnamese
Egg Harbor (township)	1,637 5.36	1,683	99 5.88 5.88 6.05	-	-	-	-	-	-	-	-	-	-	-	-	-	-	-	-	-	-	-	-	-	-	-
Galloway (township)	1,907 6.58	2,556	125 4.89 4.89 6.55	-	-	63 4.92 50.40 2.46 3.30	-	-	-	-	-	-	-	-	-	-	-	-	-	-	-	-	-	-	-	-
Ventnor City (city)	894 6.96	1,027	50 4.87 4.87 5.59	-	-	-	-	-	-	-	-	-	-	-	-	-	-	-	-	-	-	-	-	-	-	-
Bergen County	43,417 4.97	93,729	7,397 7.89 7.89 17.04	-	-	802 4.64 10.84 0.86 1.85	-	-	1,082 8.34 14.63 1.15 2.49	-	543 3.66 7.34 0.58 1.25	-	-	-	-	465 6.67 6.29 0.50 1.07	4,022 11.15 54.37 4.29 9.26	-	-	167 11.17 2.26 0.18 0.38	-	-	13 1.57 0.18 0.01 0.03	77 15.65 1.04 0.08 0.18	-	27 5.45 0.37 0.03 0.06
Bergenfield (borough)	919 3.51	5,331	110 2.06 2.06 11.97	-	-	15 0.99 13.64 0.28 1.63	-	-	-	-	88 2.74 80.00 1.65 9.58	-	-	-	-	-	-	-	-	-	-	-	-	-	-	-
Cliffside Park (borough)	2,462 10.73	2,650	240 9.06 9.06 9.75	-	-	-	-	-	-	-	-	-	-	-	-	41 9.19 17.08 1.55 1.67	153 10.32 63.75 5.77 6.21	-	-	-	-	-	-	-	-	-
Dumont (borough)	459 2.63	1,897	11 0.58 0.58 2.40	-	-	0 0.00 0.00 0.00 0.00	-	-	-	-	11 1.83 100.00 0.58 2.40	-	-	-	-	-	-	-	-	-	-	-	-	-	-	-
Elmwood Park (borough)	1,212 6.41	1,638	151 9.22 9.22 12.46	-	-	100 9.84 66.23 6.11 8.25	-	-	-	-	-	-	-	-	-	-	-	-	-	-	-	-	-	-	-	-
Englewood (city)	2,295 8.89	1,388	185 13.33 13.33 8.06	-	-	-	-	-	-	-	0 0.00 0.00 0.00 0.00	-	-	-	-	-	-	-	-	-	-	-	-	-	-	-
Fair Lawn (borough)	1,161 3.69	1,821	203 11.15 11.15 17.48	-	-	66 10.11 32.51 3.62 5.68	-	-	-	-	109 20.34 53.69 5.99 9.39	-	-	-	-	-	-	-	-	-	-	-	-	-	-	-

Notes: Please refer to the User's Guide for an explanation of data; data is arranged alphabetically by state, then county, then city within each county; table includes counties with populations greater than 49,999 unless noted and cities with populations greater than 9,999 whose Asian and/or NHPI population rates are greater than the national average; (1) Native Hawaiian and other Pacific Islander; (2) excludes Taiwanese; (3) includes Chamorro; (4) county does not meet population threshold but is shown in order to allow inclusion of city

Place	Total population with income below poverty level	Asian population for whom poverty status is determined	Asians with income below poverty level	NHPI[1] population for whom poverty status is determined	NHPIs[1] with income below poverty level	Asian Indian	Bangladeshi	Cambodian	Chinese[2]	Fijian	Filipino	Guamanian[3]	Hawaiian, Native	Hmong	Indonesian	Japanese	Korean	Laotian	Malaysian	Pakistani	Samoan	Sri Lankan	Taiwanese	Thai	Tongan	Vietnamese
Fairview (borough)	1,557 11.75	673	122 18.13 18.13 7.84	-	-	-	-	-	-	-	-	-	-	-	-	-	-	-	-	-	-	-	-	-	-	-
Fort Lee (borough)	2,807 7.92	11,004	1,096 9.96 9.96 39.05	-	-	67 11.06 6.11 0.61 2.39	-	-	160 9.28 14.60 1.45 5.70	-	-	-	-	-	-	130 6.47 11.86 1.18 4.63	704 11.91 64.23 6.40 25.08	-	-	-	-	-	-	-	-	-
Franklin Lakes (borough)	331 3.18	713	18 2.52 2.52 5.44	-	-	-	-	-	-	-	-	-	-	-	-	-	-	-	-	-	-	-	-	-	-	-
Glen Rock (borough)	278 2.41	722	95 13.16 13.16 34.17	-	-	-	-	-	-	-	-	-	-	-	-	-	-	-	-	-	-	-	-	-	-	-
Hackensack (city)	3,867 9.32	3,182	346 10.87 10.87 8.95	-	-	40 4.15 11.56 1.26 1.03	-	-	-	-	10 1.40 2.89 0.31 0.26	-	-	-	-	-	86 13.46 24.86 2.70 2.22	-	-	-	-	-	-	-	-	-
Hasbrouck Heights (borough)	492 4.22	626	46 7.35 7.35 9.35	-	-	-	-	-	-	-	-	-	-	-	-	-	-	-	-	-	-	-	-	-	-	-
Hillsdale (borough)	334 3.32	515	67 13.01 13.01 20.06	-	-	-	-	-	-	-	-	-	-	-	-	-	-	-	-	-	-	-	-	-	-	-
Little Ferry (borough)	677 6.28	1,845	268 14.53 14.53 39.59	-	-	54 12.50 20.15 2.93 7.98	-	-	-	-	27 7.03 10.07 1.46 3.99	-	-	-	-	-	187 25.34 69.78 10.14 27.62	-	-	-	-	-	-	-	-	-
Lodi (borough)	1,921 8.03	2,036	198 9.72 9.72 10.31	-	-	69 6.39 34.85 3.39 3.59	-	-	-	-	27 4.78 13.64 1.33 1.41	-	-	-	-	-	-	-	-	-	-	-	-	-	-	-
Lyndhurst (township)	890 4.60	1,160	64 5.52 5.52 7.19	-	-	-	-	-	-	-	-	-	-	-	-	-	-	-	-	-	-	-	-	-	-	-

Notes: Please refer to the User's Guide for an explanation of data; data is arranged alphabetically by state, then county, then city within each county; table includes counties with populations greater than 49,999 unless noted and cities with populations greater than 9,999 whose Asian and/or NHPI population rates are greater than the national average; (1) Native Hawaiian and other Pacific Islander; (2) excludes Taiwanese; (3) includes Chamorro; (4) county does not meet population threshold but is shown in order to allow inclusion of city

Place	Total population with income below poverty level	Asian population for whom poverty status is determined	Asians with income below poverty level	NHPI[1] population for whom poverty status is determined	NHPIs[1] with income below poverty level	Asian Indian	Bangladeshi	Cambodian	Chinese[2]	Fijian	Filipino	Guamanian[3]	Hawaiian, Native	Hmong	Indonesian	Japanese	Korean	Laotian	Malaysian	Pakistani	Samoan	Sri Lankan	Taiwanese	Thai	Tongan	Vietnamese
Mahwah (township)	458 2.02	1,472	39 2.65 2.65 8.52	-	-	6 1.20 15.38 0.41 1.31	-	-	-	-	-	-	-	-	-	-	-	-	-	-	-	-	-	-	-	-
New Milford (borough)	543 3.37	2,311	27 1.17 1.17 4.97	-	-	0 0.00 0.00 0.00 0.00	-	-	-	-	0 0.00 0.00 0.00 0.00	-	-	-	-	-	-	-	-	-	-	-	-	-	-	-
North Arlington (borough)	773 5.10	828	41 4.95 4.95 5.30	-	-	-	-	-	-	-	-	-	-	-	-	-	-	-	-	-	-	-	-	-	-	-
Palisades Park (borough)	1,659 9.72	6,996	834 11.92 11.92 50.27	-	-	-	-	-	-	-	-	-	-	-	-	-	779 13.20 93.41 11.13 46.96	-	-	-	-	-	-	-	-	-
Paramus (borough)	803 3.29	4,395	154 3.50 3.50 19.18	-	-	86 6.60 55.84 1.96 10.71	-	-	32 7.03 20.78 0.73 3.99	-	21 2.54 13.64 0.48 2.62	-	-	-	-	-	15 1.09 9.74 0.34 1.87	-	-	-	-	-	-	-	-	-
Ramsey (borough)	276 1.93	818	62 7.58 7.58 22.46	-	-	-	-	-	-	-	-	-	-	-	-	-	-	-	-	-	-	-	-	-	-	-
Ridgefield (borough)	709 6.55	1,776	312 17.57 17.57 44.01	-	-	-	-	-	-	-	-	-	-	-	-	-	206 15.36 66.03 11.60 29.06	-	-	-	-	-	-	-	-	-
Ridgefield Park (village)	865 6.72	1,104	148 13.41 13.41 17.11	-	-	-	-	-	-	-	-	-	-	-	-	-	53 11.75 35.81 4.80 6.13	-	-	-	-	-	-	-	-	-
Ridgewood (village)	741 3.00	2,111	173 8.20 8.20 23.35	-	-	-	-	-	-	-	-	-	-	-	-	0 0.00 0.00 0.00 0.00	125 21.93 72.25 5.92 16.87	-	-	-	-	-	-	-	-	-
River Edge (borough)	338 3.09	1,350	135 10.00 10.00 39.94	-	-	-	-	-	-	-	-	-	-	-	-	-	96 20.30 71.11 7.11 28.40	-	-	-	-	-	-	-	-	-

Notes: Please refer to the User's Guide for an explanation of data; data is arranged alphabetically by state, then county, then city within each county; table includes counties with populations greater than 49,999 unless noted and cities with populations greater than 9,999 whose Asian and/or NHPI population rates are greater than the national average; (1) Native Hawaiian and other Pacific Islander; (2) excludes Taiwanese; (3) includes Chamorro; (4) county does not meet population threshold but is shown in order to allow inclusion of city

Place	Total population with income below poverty level	Asian population for whom poverty status is determined	Asians with income below poverty level	NHPI[1] population for whom poverty status is determined	NHPIs[1] with income below poverty level	Asian Indian	Bangladeshi	Cambodian	Chinese[2]	Fijian	Filipino	Guamanian[3]	Hawaiian, Native	Hmong	Indonesian	Japanese	Korean	Laotian	Malaysian	Pakistani	Samoan	Sri Lankan	Taiwanese	Thai	Tongan	Vietnamese
Rutherford (borough)	668 3.73	2,056	144 7.00 7.00 21.56	-	-	13 3.86 9.03 0.63 1.95	-	-	-	-	-	-	-	-	-	-	91 10.14 63.19 4.43 13.62	-	-	-	-	-	-	-	-	-
Saddle Brook (township)	434 3.33	728	52 7.14 7.14 11.98	-	-	-	-	-	-	-	-	-	-	-	-	-	-	-	-	-	-	-	-	-	-	-
Teaneck (township)	1,596 4.17	2,700	145 5.37 5.37 9.09	-	-	74 9.44 51.03 2.74 4.64	-	-	-	-	0 0.00 0.00 0.00 0.00	-	-	-	-	-	-	-	-	-	-	-	-	-	-	-
Tenafly (borough)	718 5.23	2,587	190 7.34 7.34 26.46	-	-	-	-	-	12 1.61 6.32 0.46 1.67	-	-	-	-	-	-	-	69 5.85 36.32 2.67 9.61	-	-	-	-	-	-	-	-	-
Wallington (borough)	729 6.30	546	12 2.20 2.20 1.65	-	-	-	-	-	-	-	-	-	-	-	-	-	-	-	-	-	-	-	-	-	-	-
Westwood (borough)	474 4.36	527	0 <0.01 <0.01 <0.01	-	-	-	-	-	-	-	-	-	-	-	-	-	-	-	-	-	-	-	-	-	-	-
Wyckoff (township)	290 1.80	641	14 2.18 2.18 4.83	-	-	-	-	-	-	-	-	-	-	-	-	-	-	-	-	-	-	-	-	-	-	-
Burlington County	19,280 4.71	11,070	770 6.96 6.96 3.99	-	-	175 4.70 22.73 1.58 0.91	-	-	110 7.16 14.29 0.99 0.57	-	55 2.74 7.14 0.50 0.29	-	-	-	-	52 10.63 6.75 0.47 0.27	266 13.58 34.55 2.40 1.38	-	-	-	-	-	-	-	-	15 2.82 1.95 0.14 0.08
Browns Mills (cdp)	1,241 10.97	478	120 25.10 25.10 9.67	-	-	-	-	-	-	-	-	-	-	-	-	-	95 27.14 79.17 19.87 7.66	-	-	-	-	-	-	-	-	-
Evesham (township)	1,174 2.78	1,597	73 4.57 4.57 6.22	-	-	18 5.01 24.66 1.13 1.53	-	-	28 6.25 38.36 1.75 2.39	-	-	-	-	-	-	-	-	-	-	-	-	-	-	-	-	-

Notes: Please refer to the User's Guide for an explanation of data; data is arranged alphabetically by state, then county, then city within each county; table includes counties with populations greater than 49,999 unless noted and cities with populations greater than 9,999 whose Asian and/or NHPI population rates are greater than the national average; (1) Native Hawaiian and other Pacific Islander; (2) excludes Taiwanese; (3) includes Chamorro; (4) county does not meet population threshold but is shown in order to allow inclusion of city

Place	Total population with income below poverty level	Asian population for whom poverty status is determined	Asians with income below poverty level	NHPI[1] population for whom poverty status is determined	NHPIs[1] with income below poverty level	Asian Indian	Bangladeshi	Cambodian	Chinese[2]	Fijian	Filipino	Guamanian[3]	Hawaiian, Native	Hmong	Indonesian	Japanese	Korean	Laotian	Malaysian	Pakistani	Samoan	Sri Lankan	Taiwanese	Thai	Tongan	Vietnamese
Maple Shade (township)	1,009 5.38	1,083	65 6.00 6.00 6.44	-	-	30 4.61 46.15 2.77 2.97	-	-	-	-	-	-	-	-	-	-	-	-	-	-	-	-	-	-	-	-
Marlton (cdp)	353 3.45	392	36 9.18 9.18 10.20	-	-	-	-	-	-	-	-	-	-	-	-	-	-	-	-	-	-	-	-	-	-	-
Mount Laurel (township)	1,243 3.12	1,717	96 5.59 5.59 7.72	-	-	42 7.43 43.75 2.45 3.38	-	-	12 2.44 12.50 0.70 0.97	-	-	-	-	-	-	-	-	-	-	-	-	-	-	-	-	-
Camden County	52,121 10.44	19,719	1,940 9.84 9.84 3.72	-	-	427 8.50 22.01 2.17 0.82	-	120 38.34 6.19 0.61 0.23	355 9.14 18.30 1.80 0.68	-	151 4.00 7.78 0.77 0.29	-	-	-	-	-	151 8.71 7.78 0.77 0.29	-	-	0 0.00 0.00 0.00 0.00	-	-	-	-	-	503 16.11 25.93 2.55 0.97
Barclay-Kingston (cdp)	282 2.63	883	0 <0.01 <0.01 <0.01	-	-	-	-	-	-	-	-	-	-	-	-	-	-	-	-	-	-	-	-	-	-	-
Bellmawr (borough)	446 3.97	450	40 8.89 8.89 8.97	-	-	-	-	-	-	-	-	-	-	-	-	-	-	-	-	-	-	-	-	-	-	-
Cherry Hill Mall (cdp)	629 4.80	1,291	59 4.57 4.57 9.38	-	-	-	-	-	-	-	-	-	-	-	-	-	-	-	-	-	-	-	-	-	-	-
Cherry Hill (township)	2,725 3.96	6,595	203 3.08 3.08 7.45	-	-	41 2.97 20.20 0.62 1.50	-	-	82 4.47 40.39 1.24 3.01	-	29 1.96 14.29 0.44 1.06	-	-	-	-	-	51 5.01 25.12 0.77 1.87	-	-	-	-	-	-	-	-	-
Echelon (cdp)	844 8.28	1,347	154 11.43 11.43 18.25	-	-	63 7.79 40.91 4.68 7.46	-	-	-	-	-	-	-	-	-	-	-	-	-	-	-	-	-	-	-	-
Greentree (cdp)	252 2.20	1,925	0 <0.01 <0.01 <0.01	-	-	0 <0.01 *** ** <0.01 <0.01	-	-	0 <0.01 *** ** <0.01 <0.01	-	-	-	-	-	-	-	-	-	-	-	-	-	-	-	-	-

Notes: Please refer to the User's Guide for an explanation of data; data is arranged alphabetically by state, then county, then city within each county; table includes counties with populations greater than 49,999 unless noted and cities with populations greater than 9,999 whose Asian and/or NHPI population rates are greater than the national average; (1) Native Hawaiian and other Pacific Islander; (2) excludes Taiwanese; (3) includes Chamorro; (4) county does not meet population threshold but is shown in order to allow inclusion of city

Place	Total population with income below poverty level	Asian population for whom poverty status is determined	Asians with income below poverty level	NHPI[1] population for whom poverty status is determined	NHPIs[1] with income below poverty level	Asian Indian	Bangladeshi	Cambodian	Chinese[2]	Fijian	Filipino	Guamanian[3]	Hawaiian, Native	Hmong	Indonesian	Japanese	Korean	Laotian	Malaysian	Pakistani	Samoan	Sri Lankan	Taiwanese	Thai	Tongan	Vietnamese
Pennsauken (township)	2,807 7.98	1,550	226 14.58 14.58 8.05	-	-	-	-	-	-	-	-	-	-	-	-	-	-	-	-	-	-	-	-	-	-	80 11.66 35.40 5.16 2.85
Springdale (cdp)	512 3.62	1,196	37 3.09 3.09 7.23	-	-	-	-	-	7 1.50 18.92 0.59 1.37	-	-	-	-	-	-	-	-	-	-	-	-	-	-	-	-	-
Voorhees (township)	1,551 5.69	3,069	164 5.34 5.34 10.57	-	-	73 4.13 44.51 2.38 4.71	-	-	36 5.90 21.95 1.17 2.32	-	28 6.85 17.07 0.91 1.81	-	-	-	-	-	-	-	-	-	-	-	-	-	-	-
Cape May County	8,549 8.58	615	33 5.37 5.37 0.39	-	-	-	-	-	-	-	-	-	-	-	-	-	-	-	-	-	-	-	-	-	-	-
Cumberland County	20,367 15.05	1,135	100 8.81 8.81 0.49	-	-	34 8.65 34.00 3.00 0.17	-	-	-	-	-	-	-	-	-	-	-	-	-	-	-	-	-	-	-	-
Essex County	120,006 15.55	28,988	2,211 7.63 7.63 1.84	444	55 12.39 12.39 0.05	660 7.76 29.85 2.28 0.55	-	-	373 6.18 16.87 1.29 0.31	-	293 3.73 13.25 1.01 0.24	-	-	-	-	52 8.77 2.35 0.18 0.04	238 8.75 10.76 0.82 0.20	-	-	170 27.91 7.69 0.59 0.14	-	-	13 2.79 0.59 0.04 0.01	-	-	228 22.16 10.31 0.79 0.19
Belleville (township)	2,939 8.23	4,228	439 10.38 10.38 14.94	-	-	104 11.69 23.69 2.46 3.54	-	-	-	-	106 4.98 24.15 2.51 3.61	-	-	-	-	-	-	-	-	-	-	-	-	-	-	103 24.29 23.46 2.44 3.50
Bloomfield (township)	2,772 5.87	4,047	168 4.15 4.15 6.06	-	-	66 4.39 39.29 1.63 2.38	-	-	27 5.45 16.07 0.67 0.97	-	21 1.32 12.50 0.52 0.76	-	-	-	-	-	-	-	-	-	-	-	-	-	-	-
Cedar Grove (township)	230 2.04	597	0 <0.01 <0.01 <0.01	-	-	-	-	-	-	-	-	-	-	-	-	-	-	-	-	-	-	-	-	-	-	-
Livingston (township)	480 1.76	3,968	81 2.04 2.04 16.88	-	-	28 3.76 34.57 0.71 5.83	-	-	39 2.49 48.15 0.98 8.13	-	0 0.00 0.00 0.00 0.00	-	-	-	-	-	14 1.79 17.28 0.35 2.92	-	-	-	-	-	-	-	-	-

Notes: Please refer to the User's Guide for an explanation of data; data is arranged alphabetically by state, then county, then city within each county; table includes counties with populations greater than 49,999 unless noted and cities with populations greater than 9,999 whose Asian and/or NHPI population rates are greater than the national average; (1) Native Hawaiian and other Pacific Islander; (2) excludes Taiwanese; (3) includes Chamorro; (4) county does not meet population threshold but is shown in order to allow inclusion of city

Place	Total population with income below poverty level	Asian population for whom poverty status is determined	Asians with income below poverty level	NHPI[1] population for whom poverty status is determined	NHPIs[1] with income below poverty level	Asian Indian	Bangladeshi	Cambodian	Chinese[2]	Fijian	Filipino	Guamanian[3]	Hawaiian, Native	Hmong	Indonesian	Japanese	Korean	Laotian	Malaysian	Pakistani	Samoan	Sri Lankan	Taiwanese	Thai	Tongan	Vietnamese
Millburn (township)	288 1.46	1,508	34 2.25 2.25 11.81	-	-	-	-	-	14 2.14 41.18 0.93 4.86	-	-	-	-	-	-	-	-	-	-	-	-	-	-	-	-	-
Nutley (township)	1,312 4.80	1,995	91 4.56 4.56 6.94	-	-	12 1.63 13.19 0.60 0.91	-	-	-	-	0 0.00 0.00 0.00 0.00	-	-	-	-	-	-	-	-	-	-	-	-	-	-	-
Verona (township)	441 3.26	612	0 <0.01 <0.01 <0.01	-	-	-	-	-	-	-	-	-	-	-	-	-	-	-	-	-	-	-	-	-	-	-
West Caldwell (township)	227 2.07	413	0 <0.01 <0.01 <0.01	-	-	-	-	-	-	-	-	-	-	-	-	-	-	-	-	-	-	-	-	-	-	-
West Orange (township)	2,461 5.62	3,742	147 3.93 3.93 5.97	-	-	47 4.55 31.97 1.26 1.91	-	-	52 6.72 35.37 1.39 2.11	-	12 1.25 8.16 0.32 0.49	-	-	-	-	-	18 2.85 12.24 0.48 0.73	-	-	-	-	-	-	-	-	-
Gloucester County	15,395 6.16	4,138	223 5.39 5.39 1.45	-	-	91 9.16 40.81 2.20 0.59	-	-	34 4.53 15.25 0.82 0.22	-	16 1.18 7.17 0.39 0.10	-	-	-	-	-	17 3.92 7.62 0.41 0.11	-	-	-	-	-	-	-	-	-
Hudson County	93,149 15.52	56,846	5,852 10.29 10.29 6.28	-	-	2,530 12.36 43.23 4.45 2.72	-	-	858 12.89 14.66 1.51 0.92	-	738 3.72 12.61 1.30 0.79	-	-	-	-	44 4.78 0.75 0.08 0.05	462 14.53 7.89 0.81 0.50	-	-	439 18.92 7.50 0.77 0.47	-	-	-	-	-	397 24.40 6.78 0.70 0.43
Bayonne (city)	6,262 10.14	2,599	110 4.23 4.23 1.76	-	-	9 1.69 8.18 0.35 0.14	-	-	-	-	0 0.00 0.00 0.00 0.00	-	-	-	-	-	58 19.66 52.73 2.23 0.93	-	-	-	-	-	-	-	-	-
Guttenberg (town)	1,377 13.04	743	68 9.15 9.15 4.94	-	-	-	-	-	-	-	-	-	-	-	-	-	-	-	-	-	-	-	-	-	-	-
Harrison (town)	1,791 12.43	1,759	311 17.68 17.68 17.36	-	-	-	-	-	246 18.72 79.10 13.99 13.74	-	-	-	-	-	-	-	-	-	-	-	-	-	-	-	-	-

Notes: Please refer to the User's Guide for an explanation of data; data is arranged alphabetically by state, then county, then city within each county; table includes counties with populations greater than 49,999 unless noted and cities with populations greater than 9,999 whose Asian and/or NHPI population rates are greater than the national average; (1) Native Hawaiian and other Pacific Islander; (2) excludes Taiwanese; (3) includes Chamorro; (4) county does not meet population threshold but is shown in order to allow inclusion of city

Place	Total population with income below poverty level	Asian population for whom poverty status is determined	Asians with income below poverty level	NHPI[1] population for whom poverty status is determined	NHPIs[1] with income below poverty level	Asian Indian	Bangladeshi	Cambodian	Chinese[2]	Fijian	Filipino	Guamanian[3]	Hawaiian, Native	Hmong	Indonesian	Japanese	Korean	Laotian	Malaysian	Pakistani	Samoan	Sri Lankan	Taiwanese	Thai	Tongan	Vietnamese
Hoboken (city)	4,124 10.98	1,455	49 3.37 3.37 1.19	-	-	34 6.12 69.39 2.34 0.82	-	-	0 0.00 0.00 0.00 0.00	-	-	-	-	-	-	-	-	-	-	-	-	-	-	-	-	-
Jersey City (city)	44,075 18.60	38,992	3,902 10.01 10.01 8.85	-	-	1,466 10.99 37.57 3.76 3.33	-	-	410 14.12 10.51 1.05 0.93	-	694 4.22 17.79 1.78 1.57	-	-	-	-	-	297 20.05 7.61 0.76 0.67	-	-	427 22.74 10.94 1.10 0.97	-	-	-	-	-	377 27.30 9.66 0.97 0.86
Kearny (town)	3,262 8.57	2,268	396 17.46 17.46 12.14	-	-	212 26.01 53.54 9.35 6.50	-	-	151 16.56 38.13 6.66 4.63	-	-	-	-	-	-	-	-	-	-	-	-	-	-	-	-	-
North Bergen (township)	6,397 11.14	3,516	292 8.30 8.30 4.56	-	-	266 11.25 91.10 7.57 4.16	-	-	14 4.39 4.79 0.40 0.22	-	-	-	-	-	-	-	-	-	-	-	-	-	-	-	-	-
Secaucus (town)	1,149 7.59	1,837	158 8.60 8.60 13.75	-	-	99 18.57 62.66 5.39 8.62	-	-	-	-	6 0.97 3.80 0.33 0.52	-	-	-	-	-	-	-	-	-	-	-	-	-	-	-
Weehawken (township)	1,535 11.38	608	68 11.18 11.18 4.43	-	-	-	-	-	-	-	-	-	-	-	-	-	-	-	-	-	-	-	-	-	-	-
Hunterdon County	3,027 2.57	2,566	54 2.10 2.10 1.78	-	-	9 0.85 16.67 0.35 0.30	-	-	13 1.87 24.07 0.51 0.43	-	-	-	-	-	-	-	-	-	-	-	-	-	-	-	-	-
Mercer County	28,570 8.65	16,482	1,218 7.39 7.39 4.26	-	-	470 7.26 38.59 2.85 1.65	-	-	242 5.54 19.87 1.47 0.85	-	49 4.43 4.02 0.30 0.17	-	-	-	-	72 13.51 5.91 0.44 0.25	154 8.38 12.64 0.93 0.54	-	-	111 17.13 9.11 0.67 0.39	-	-	57 11.95 4.68 0.35 0.20	-	-	-
East Windsor (township)	1,312 5.34	2,363	293 12.40 12.40 22.33	-	-	126 8.45 43.00 5.33 9.60	-	-	-	-	-	-	-	-	-	-	-	-	-	-	-	-	-	-	-	-
Hopewell (township)	173 1.14	668	0 <0.01 <0.01 <0.01	-	-	-	-	-	-	-	-	-	-	-	-	-	-	-	-	-	-	-	-	-	-	-

Notes: Please refer to the User's Guide for an explanation of data; data is arranged alphabetically by state, then county, then city within each county; table includes counties with populations greater than 49,999 unless noted and cities with populations greater than 9,999 whose Asian and/or NHPI population rates are greater than the national average; (1) Native Hawaiian and other Pacific Islander; (2) excludes Taiwanese; (3) includes Chamorro; (4) county does not meet population threshold but is shown in order to allow inclusion of city

Place	Total population with income below poverty level	Asian population for whom poverty status is determined	Asians with income below poverty level	NHPI[1] population for whom poverty status is determined	NHPIs[1] with income below poverty level	Asian Indian	Bangladeshi	Cambodian	Chinese[2]	Fijian	Filipino	Guamanian[3]	Hawaiian, Native	Hmong	Indonesian	Japanese	Korean	Laotian	Malaysian	Pakistani	Samoan	Sri Lankan	Taiwanese	Thai	Tongan	Vietnamese
Lawrence (township)	1,311 4.87	2,259	86 3.81 3.81 6.56	-	-	32 2.79 37.21 1.42 2.44	-	-	27 4.19 31.40 1.20 2.06	-	-	-	-	-	-	-	-	-	-	-	-	-	-	-	-	-
Princeton (borough)	656 9.04	271	46 16.97 16.97 7.01	-	-	-	-	-	-	-	-	-	-	-	-	-	-	-	-	-	-	-	-	-	-	-
Princeton (township)	897 5.74	1,664	127 7.63 7.63 14.16	-	-	75 18.34 59.06 4.51 8.36	-	-	52 7.20 40.94 3.13 5.80	-	-	-	-	-	-	-	-	-	-	-	-	-	-	-	-	-
West Windsor (township)	548 2.50	4,792	197 4.11 4.11 35.95	-	-	41 2.55 20.81 0.86 7.48	-	-	112 6.17 56.85 2.34 20.44	-	-	-	-	-	-	-	0 0.00 0.00 0.00 0.00	-	-	-	-	-	-	-	-	-
Middlesex County	48,205 6.59	101,863	5,453 5.35 5.35 11.31	-	-	2,533 4.74 46.45 2.49 5.25	44 11.37 0.81 0.04 0.09	-	1,216 5.88 22.30 1.19 2.52	-	285 2.33 5.23 0.28 0.59	-	-	-	48 9.84 0.88 0.05 0.10	70 10.94 1.28 0.07 0.15	633 12.99 11.61 0.62 1.31	-	-	128 4.06 2.35 0.13 0.27	-	8 1.61 0.15 0.01 0.02	121 9.14 2.22 0.12 0.25	-	-	117 5.36 2.15 0.11 0.24
Avenel (cdp)	1,426 9.57	3,287	277 8.43 8.43 19.42	-	-	175 8.02 63.18 5.32 12.27	-	-	-	-	-	-	-	-	-	-	-	-	-	-	-	-	-	-	-	-
Carteret (borough)	2,253 10.97	1,656	204 12.32 12.32 9.05	-	-	172 15.61 84.31 10.39 7.63	-	-	-	-	-	-	-	-	-	-	-	-	-	-	-	-	-	-	-	-
Colonia (cdp)	387 2.18	1,263	43 3.40 3.40 11.11	-	-	43 6.88 100.00 3.40 11.11	-	-	-	-	0 0.00 0.00 0.00 0.00	-	-	-	-	-	-	-	-	-	-	-	-	-	-	-
East Brunswick (township)	1,321 2.83	7,634	371 4.86 4.86 28.08	-	-	78 2.98 21.02 1.02 5.90	-	-	221 7.13 59.57 2.89 16.73	-	8 1.42 2.16 0.10 0.61	-	-	-	-	-	51 11.62 13.75 0.67 3.86	-	-	-	-	-	-	-	-	-
Edison (township)	4,606 4.79	28,369	1,530 5.39 5.39 33.22	-	-	748 4.58 48.89 2.64 16.24	-	-	389 6.73 25.42 1.37 8.45	-	51 1.98 3.33 0.18 1.11	-	-	-	-	-	204 16.18 13.33 0.72 4.43	-	-	0 0.00 0.00 0.00 0.00	-	-	67 10.11 4.38 0.24 1.45	-	-	-

Notes: Please refer to the User's Guide for an explanation of data; data is arranged alphabetically by state, then county, then city within each county; table includes counties with populations greater than 49,999 unless noted and cities with populations greater than 9,999 whose Asian and/or NHPI population rates are greater than the national average; (1) Native Hawaiian and other Pacific Islander; (2) excludes Taiwanese; (3) includes Chamorro; (4) county does not meet population threshold but is shown in order to allow inclusion of city

Place	Total population with income below poverty level	Asian population for whom poverty status is determined	Asians with income below poverty level	NHPI[1] population for whom poverty status is determined	NHPIs[1] with income below poverty level	Asian Indian	Bangladeshi	Cambodian	Chinese[2]	Fijian	Filipino	Guamanian[3]	Hawaiian, Native	Hmong	Indonesian	Japanese	Korean	Laotian	Malaysian	Pakistani	Samoan	Sri Lankan	Taiwanese	Thai	Tongan	Vietnamese
Fords (cdp)	512 3.39	2,371	55 2.32 2.32 10.74	-	-	34 2.96 61.82 1.43 6.64	-	-	-	-	14 2.16 25.45 0.59 2.73	-	-	-	-	-	-	-	-	-	-	-	-	-	-	-
Highland Park (borough)	1,181 8.45	1,926	246 12.77 12.77 20.83	-	-	56 8.93 22.76 2.91 4.74	-	-	89 10.32 36.18 4.62 7.54	-	-	-	-	-	-	-	-	-	-	-	-	-	-	-	-	-
Iselin (cdp)	534 3.22	3,982	112 2.81 2.81 20.97	-	-	71 2.52 63.39 1.78 13.30	-	-	10 1.96 8.93 0.25 1.87	-	-	-	-	-	-	-	-	-	-	-	-	-	-	-	-	-
Metuchen (borough)	500 3.90	941	103 10.95 10.95 20.60	-	-	-	-	-	-	-	-	-	-	-	-	-	-	-	-	-	-	-	-	-	-	-
Middlesex (borough)	499 3.65	609	38 6.24 6.24 7.62	-	-	-	-	-	-	-	-	-	-	-	-	-	-	-	-	-	-	-	-	-	-	-
New Brunswick (city)	11,454 27.05	1,885	669 35.49 35.49 5.84	-	-	280 30.50 41.85 14.85 2.44	-	-	107 37.41 15.99 5.68 0.93	-	-	-	-	-	-	-	-	-	-	-	-	-	-	-	-	-
North Brunswick (township)	1,661 4.73	5,134	186 3.62 3.62 11.20	-	-	86 2.87 46.24 1.68 5.18	-	-	63 7.60 33.87 1.23 3.79	-	0 0.00 0.00 0.00 0.00	-	-	-	-	-	26 5.59 13.98 0.51 1.57	-	-	-	-	-	-	-	-	-
Old Bridge (township)	2,547 4.25	6,482	333 5.14 5.14 13.07	-	-	135 4.78 40.54 2.08 5.30	-	-	13 1.09 3.90 0.20 0.51	-	77 6.04 23.12 1.19 3.02	-	-	-	-	-	-	-	-	75 14.26 22.52 1.16 2.94	-	-	-	-	-	-
Piscataway (township)	1,769 3.78	11,287	518 4.59 4.59 29.28	-	-	137 2.50 26.45 1.21 7.74	-	-	208 9.74 40.15 1.84 11.76	-	22 1.07 4.25 0.19 1.24	-	-	-	-	-	53 9.93 10.23 0.47 3.00	-	-	-	-	-	-	-	-	-
Plainsboro (township)	601 2.98	6,164	184 2.99 2.99 30.62	-	-	101 3.09 54.89 1.64 16.81	-	-	15 0.90 8.15 0.24 2.50	-	-	-	-	-	-	-	-	-	-	-	-	-	-	-	-	-

Notes: Please refer to the User's Guide for an explanation of data; data is arranged alphabetically by state, then county, then city within each county; table includes counties with populations greater than 49,999 unless noted and cities with populations greater than 9,999 whose Asian and/or NHPI population rates are greater than the national average; (1) Native Hawaiian and other Pacific Islander; (2) excludes Taiwanese; (3) includes Chamorro; (4) county does not meet population threshold but is shown in order to allow inclusion of city

Place	Total population with income below poverty level	Asian population for whom poverty status is determined	Asians with income below poverty level	NHPI[1] population for whom poverty status is determined	NHPIs[1] with income below poverty level	Asian Indian	Bangladeshi	Cambodian	Chinese[2]	Fijian	Filipino	Guamanian[3]	Hawaiian, Native	Hmong	Indonesian	Japanese	Korean	Laotian	Malaysian	Pakistani	Samoan	Sri Lankan	Taiwanese	Thai	Tongan	Vietnamese
Princeton Meadows (cdp)	448 3.38	3,875	142 3.66 3.66 31.70	-	-	94 4.31 66.20 2.43 20.98	-	-	0 0.00 0.00 0.00 0.00	-	-	-	-	-	-	-	-	-	-	-	-	-	-	-	-	-
Sayreville (borough)	1,905 4.75	4,184	175 4.18 4.18 9.19	-	-	118 4.72 67.43 2.82 6.19	-	-	29 4.37 16.57 0.69 1.52	-	15 2.28 8.57 0.36 0.79	-	-	-	-	-	-	-	-	-	-	-	-	-	-	-
South Brunswick (township)	1,156 3.07	6,876	159 2.31 2.31 13.75	-	-	85 2.21 53.46 1.24 7.35	-	-	6 0.42 3.77 0.09 0.52	-	0 0.00 0.00 0.00 0.00	-	-	-	-	-	-	-	-	-	-	-	-	-	-	-
South Plainfield (borough)	727 3.37	1,761	77 4.37 4.37 10.59	-	-	6 0.83 7.79 0.34 0.83	-	-	-	-	0 0.00 0.00 0.00 0.00	-	-	-	-	-	-	-	-	-	-	-	-	-	-	39 10.66 50.65 2.21 5.36
Woodbridge (township)	4,565 4.84	13,928	566 4.06 4.06 12.40	-	-	396 4.50 69.96 2.84 8.67	-	-	10 0.74 1.77 0.07 0.22	-	14 0.73 2.47 0.10 0.31	-	-	-	-	-	42 6.54 7.42 0.30 0.92	-	-	24 5.14 4.24 0.17 0.53	-	-	-	-	-	-
Monmouth County	38,242 6.31	23,997	1,121 4.67 4.67 2.93	-	-	168 2.46 14.99 0.70 0.44	-	-	477 5.14 42.55 1.99 1.25	-	91 2.73 8.12 0.38 0.24	-	-	-	-	59 16.67 5.26 0.25 0.15	136 6.88 12.13 0.57 0.36	-	-	73 17.94 6.51 0.30 0.19	-	-	-	-	-	31 4.33 2.77 0.13 0.08
Aberdeen (township)	807 4.69	943	9 0.95 0.95 1.12	-	-	0 0.00 0.00 0.00 0.00	-	-	0 0.00 0.00 0.00 0.00	-	-	-	-	-	-	-	-	-	-	-	-	-	-	-	-	-
Colts Neck (township)	308 2.77	483	5 1.04 1.04 1.62	-	-	-	-	-	-	-	-	-	-	-	-	-	-	-	-	-	-	-	-	-	-	-
Eatontown (borough)	777 5.71	1,262	89 7.05 7.05 11.45	-	-	-	-	-	-	-	-	-	-	-	-	-	-	-	-	-	-	-	-	-	-	-
Freehold (township)	1,155 3.86	1,711	35 2.05 2.05 3.03	-	-	0 0.00 0.00 0.00 0.00	-	-	20 3.67 57.14 1.17 1.73	-	0 0.00 0.00 0.00 0.00	-	-	-	-	-	-	-	-	-	-	-	-	-	-	-

Notes: Please refer to the User's Guide for an explanation of data; data is arranged alphabetically by state, then county, then city within each county; table includes counties with populations greater than 49,999 unless noted and cities with populations greater than 9,999 whose Asian and/or NHPI population rates are greater than the national average; (1) Native Hawaiian and other Pacific Islander; (2) excludes Taiwanese; (3) includes Chamorro; (4) county does not meet population threshold but is shown in order to allow inclusion of city

Place	Total population with income below poverty level	Asian population for whom poverty status is determined	Asians with income below poverty level	NHPI[1] population for whom poverty status is determined	NHPIs[1] with income below poverty level	Asian Indian	Bangladeshi	Cambodian	Chinese[2]	Fijian	Filipino	Guamanian[3]	Hawaiian, Native	Hmong	Indonesian	Japanese	Korean	Laotian	Malaysian	Pakistani	Samoan	Sri Lankan	Taiwanese	Thai	Tongan	Vietnamese
Holmdel (township)	518	2,610	96	-	-	0	-	-	58	-	-	-	-	-	-	-	-	-	-	-	-	-	-	-	-	-
	3.39		3.68			0.00			3.59																	
						0.00			60.42																	
			3.68			0.00			2.22																	
			18.53			0.00			11.20																	
Howell (township)	2,049	1,849	74	-	-	0	-	-	-	-	20	-	-	-	-	-	-	-	-	-	-	-	-	-	-	-
	4.20		4.00			0.00					4.15															
						0.00					27.03															
			4.00			0.00					1.08															
			3.61			0.00					0.98															
Manalapan (township)	1,259	1,528	29	-	-	11	-	-	18	-	-	-	-	-	-	-	-	-	-	-	-	-	-	-	-	-
	3.79		1.90			1.80			3.50																	
						37.93			62.07																	
			1.90			0.72			1.18																	
			2.30			0.87			1.43																	
Marlboro (township)	1,256	4,550	150	-	-	0	-	-	100	-	-	-	-	-	-	-	-	-	-	-	-	-	-	-	-	-
	3.47		3.30			0.00			3.81																	
						0.00			66.67																	
			3.30			0.00			2.20																	
			11.94			0.00			7.96																	
Morganville (cdp)	191	1,058	0	-	-	-	-	-	0	-	-	-	-	-	-	-	-	-	-	-	-	-	-	-	-	-
	1.72		<0.01						<0.01																	
									*** **																	
			<0.01						<0.01																	
			<0.01						<0.01																	
Ocean (township)	1,350	1,525	115	-	-	61	-	-	-	-	-	-	-	-	-	-	-	-	-	-	-	-	-	-	-	-
	5.01		7.54			10.59																				
						53.04																				
			7.54			4.00																				
			8.52			4.52																				
Tinton Falls (borough)	577	797	32	-	-	-	-	-	-	-	-	-	-	-	-	-	-	-	-	-	-	-	-	-	-	-
	3.89		4.02																							
			4.02																							
			5.55																							
West Freehold (cdp)	571	581	15	-	-	-	-	-	-	-	-	-	-	-	-	-	-	-	-	-	-	-	-	-	-	-
	4.65		2.58																							
			2.58																							
			2.63																							
Morris County	17,872	29,902	1,103	-	-	272	-	-	271	-	133	-	-	-	-	39	94	-	-	40	-	-	44	-	-	69
	3.87		3.69			2.58			2.92		4.14					5.17	3.59			5.28			6.27			9.19
						24.66			24.57		12.06					3.54	8.52			3.63			3.99			6.26
			3.69			0.91			0.91		0.44					0.13	0.31			0.13			0.15			0.23
			6.17			1.52			1.52		0.74					0.22	0.53			0.22			0.25			0.39
Chatham (township)	271	565	58	-	-	-	-	-	-	-	-	-	-	-	-	-	-	-	-	-	-	-	-	-	-	-
	2.72		10.27																							
			10.27																							
			21.40																							

Notes: Please refer to the User's Guide for an explanation of data; data is arranged alphabetically by state, then county, then city within each county; table includes counties with populations greater than 49,999 unless noted and cities with populations greater than 9,999 whose Asian and/or NHPI population rates are greater than the national average; (1) Native Hawaiian and other Pacific Islander; (2) excludes Taiwanese; (3) includes Chamorro; (4) county does not meet population threshold but is shown in order to allow inclusion of city

Place	Total population with income below poverty level	Asian population for whom poverty status is determined	Asians with income below poverty level	NHPI[1] population for whom poverty status is determined	NHPIs[1] with income below poverty level	Asian Indian	Bangladeshi	Cambodian	Chinese[2]	Fijian	Filipino	Guamanian[3]	Hawaiian, Native	Hmong	Indonesian	Japanese	Korean	Laotian	Malaysian	Pakistani	Samoan	Sri Lankan	Taiwanese	Thai	Tongan	Vietnamese
Denville (township)	436 2.80	810	0 <0.01 <0.01 <0.01	-	-	-	-	-	-	-	-	-	-	-	-	-	-	-	-	-	-	-	-	-	-	-
East Hanover (township)	192 1.69	1,243	14 1.13 1.13 7.29	-	-	-	-	-	9 1.46 64.29 0.72 4.69	-	-	-	-	-	-	-	-	-	-	-	-	-	-	-	-	-
Hanover (township)	152 1.18	1,237	0 <0.01 <0.01 <0.01	-	-	0 <0.01 ***.** <0.01 <0.01	-	-	0 <0.01 ***.** <0.01 <0.01	-	-	-	-	-	-	-	-	-	-	-	-	-	-	-	-	-
Lincoln Park (borough)	286 2.79	617	0 <0.01 <0.01 <0.01	-	-	-	-	-	-	-	-	-	-	-	-	-	-	-	-	-	-	-	-	-	-	-
Montville (township)	794 3.83	2,640	86 3.26 3.26 10.83	-	-	0 0.00 0.00 0.00 0.00	-	-	41 4.32 47.67 1.55 5.16	-	-	-	-	-	-	-	-	-	-	-	-	-	-	-	-	-
Morris (township)	802 3.83	874	26 2.97 2.97 3.24	-	-	-	-	-	-	-	-	-	-	-	-	-	-	-	-	-	-	-	-	-	-	-
Mount Olive (township)	735 3.05	1,639	118 7.20 7.20 16.05	-	-	27 3.97 22.88 1.65 3.67	-	-	-	-	-	-	-	-	-	-	-	-	-	-	-	-	-	-	-	-
Parsippany-Troy Hills (twp)	1,918 3.86	9,040	414 4.58 4.58 21.58	-	-	90 2.18 21.74 1.00 4.69	-	-	94 3.60 22.71 1.04 4.90	-	29 3.81 7.00 0.32 1.51	-	-	-	-	-	0 0.00 0.00 0.00 0.00	-	-	-	-	-	-	-	-	-
Randolph (township)	356 1.43	2,495	0 <0.01 <0.01 <0.01	-	-	0 <0.01 ***.** <0.01 <0.01	-	-	0 <0.01 ***.** <0.01 <0.01	-	-	-	-	-	-	-	-	-	-	-	-	-	-	-	-	-
Rockaway (township)	551 2.41	1,317	11 0.84 0.84 2.00	-	-	11 1.74 100.00 0.84 2.00	-	-	-	-	-	-	-	-	-	-	-	-	-	-	-	-	-	-	-	-

Notes: Please refer to the User's Guide for an explanation of data; data is arranged alphabetically by state, then county, then city within each county; table includes counties with populations greater than 49,999 unless noted and cities with populations greater than 9,999 whose Asian and/or NHPI population rates are greater than the national average; (1) Native Hawaiian and other Pacific Islander; (2) excludes Taiwanese; (3) includes Chamorro; (4) county does not meet population threshold but is shown in order to allow inclusion of city

Place	Total population with income below poverty level	Asian population for whom poverty status is determined	Asians with income below poverty level	NHPI[1] population for whom poverty status is determined	NHPIs[1] with income below poverty level	Asian Indian	Bangladeshi	Cambodian	Chinese[2]	Fijian	Filipino	Guamanian[3]	Hawaiian, Native	Hmong	Indonesian	Japanese	Korean	Laotian	Malaysian	Pakistani	Samoan	Sri Lankan	Taiwanese	Thai	Tongan	Vietnamese
Roxbury (township)	642 2.70	874	25 2.86 2.86 3.89	-	-	-	-	-	-	-	-	-	-	-	-	-	-	-	-	-	-	-	-	-	-	-
Succasunna-Kenvil (cdp)	304 2.45	521	2 0.38 0.38 0.66	-	-	-	-	-	-	-	-	-	-	-	-	-	-	-	-	-	-	-	-	-	-	-
Ocean County	34,945 6.95	6,596	470 7.13 7.13 1.34	-	-	94 5.92 20.00 1.43 0.27	-	-	88 7.77 18.72 1.33 0.25	-	112 4.57 23.83 1.70 0.32	-	-	-	-	-	47 8.74 10.00 0.71 0.13	-	-	-	-	-	-	-	-	-
Passaic County	59,072 12.28	18,374	1,782 9.70 9.70 3.02	-	-	1,015 11.27 56.96 5.52 1.72	165 30.28 9.26 0.90 0.28	-	177 9.20 9.93 0.96 0.30	-	133 3.83 7.46 0.72 0.23	-	-	-	-	-	118 7.41 6.62 0.64 0.20	-	-	-	-	-	-	-	-	-
Clifton (city)	4,932 6.30	5,410	251 4.64 4.64 5.09	-	-	157 5.37 62.55 2.90 3.18	-	-	13 3.30 5.18 0.24 0.26	-	55 4.42 21.91 1.02 1.12	-	-	-	-	-	26 8.10 10.36 0.48 0.53	-	-	-	-	-	-	-	-	-
Little Falls (township)	493 4.55	459	79 17.21 17.21 16.02	-	-	-	-	-	-	-	-	-	-	-	-	-	-	-	-	-	-	-	-	-	-	-
Passaic (city)	14,249 21.19	3,824	332 8.68 8.68 2.33	-	-	244 9.67 73.49 6.38 1.71	-	-	-	-	31 4.13 9.34 0.81 0.22	-	-	-	-	-	-	-	-	-	-	-	-	-	-	-
Wayne (township)	1,443 2.79	3,206	130 4.05 4.05 9.01	-	-	0 0.00 0.00 0.00 0.00	-	-	53 7.71 40.77 1.65 3.67	-	0 0.00 0.00 0.00 0.00	-	-	-	-	-	77 9.17 59.23 2.40 5.34	-	-	-	-	-	-	-	-	-
Salem County	5,980 9.47	370	30 8.11 8.11 0.50	-	-	-	-	-	-	-	-	-	-	-	-	-	-	-	-	-	-	-	-	-	-	-
Somerset County	11,061 3.77	25,079	586 2.34 2.34 5.30	-	-	133 1.30 22.70 0.53 1.20	-	-	195 2.65 33.28 0.78 1.76	-	40 1.30 6.83 0.16 0.36	-	-	-	-	34 5.71 5.80 0.14 0.31	29 2.09 4.95 0.12 0.26	-	-	82 10.07 13.99 0.33 0.74	-	-	3 0.55 0.51 0.01 0.03	-	-	5 1.01 0.85 0.02 0.05

Notes: Please refer to the User's Guide for an explanation of data; data is arranged alphabetically by state, then county, then city within each county; table includes counties with populations greater than 49,999 unless noted and cities with populations greater than 9,999 whose Asian and/or NHPI population rates are greater than the national average; (1) Native Hawaiian and other Pacific Islander; (2) excludes Taiwanese; (3) includes Chamorro; (4) county does not meet population threshold but is shown in order to allow inclusion of city

Place	Total population with income below poverty level	Asian population for whom poverty status is determined	Asians with income below poverty level	NHPI[1] population for whom poverty status is determined	NHPIs[1] with income below poverty level	Asian Indian	Bangladeshi	Cambodian	Chinese[2]	Fijian	Filipino	Guamanian[3]	Hawaiian, Native	Hmong	Indonesian	Japanese	Korean	Laotian	Malaysian	Pakistani	Samoan	Sri Lankan	Taiwanese	Thai	Tongan	Vietnamese
Bernards (township)	319 1.34	1,918	7 0.36 0.36 2.19	-	-	0 0.00 0.00 0.00 0.00	-	-	0 0.00 0.00 0.00 0.00	-	-	-	-	-	-	-	-	-	-	-	-	-	-	-	-	-
Branchburg (township)	282 1.94	1,065	52 4.88 4.88 18.44	-	-	0 0.00 0.00 0.00 0.00	-	-	-	-	-	-	-	-	-	-	-	-	-	-	-	-	-	-	-	-
Bridgewater (township)	885 2.10	4,713	97 2.06 2.06 10.96	-	-	7 0.36 7.22 0.15 0.79	-	-	70 4.37 72.16 1.49 7.91	-	-	-	-	-	-	-	-	-	-	-	-	-	-	-	-	-
Franklin (township)	2,535 5.06	6,404	150 2.34 2.34 5.92	-	-	78 2.36 52.00 1.22 3.08	-	-	37 2.81 24.67 0.58 1.46	-	0 0.00 0.00 0.00 0.00	-	-	-	-	-	-	-	-	-	-	-	-	-	-	-
Hillsborough (township)	1,140 3.13	2,543	75 2.95 2.95 6.58	-	-	19 1.99 25.33 0.75 1.67	-	-	0 0.00 0.00 0.00 0.00	-	-	-	-	-	-	-	-	-	-	-	-	-	-	-	-	-
Montgomery (township)	261 1.51	1,964	19 0.97 0.97 7.28	-	-	0 0.00 0.00 0.00 0.00	-	-	12 1.31 63.16 0.61 4.60	-	-	-	-	-	-	-	-	-	-	-	-	-	-	-	-	-
North Plainfield (borough)	1,340 6.40	1,059	43 4.06 4.06 3.21	-	-	-	-	-	-	-	-	-	-	-	-	-	-	-	-	-	-	-	-	-	-	-
Somerset (cdp)	1,607 7.02	1,831	115 6.28 6.28 7.16	-	-	71 9.93 61.74 3.88 4.42	-	-	22 5.33 19.13 1.20 1.37	-	0 0.00 0.00 0.00 0.00	-	-	-	-	-	-	-	-	-	-	-	-	-	-	-
Somerville (borough)	926 7.72	860	57 6.63 6.63 6.16	-	-	-	-	-	-	-	-	-	-	-	-	-	-	-	-	-	-	-	-	-	-	-
Warren (township)	299 2.11	1,602	20 1.25 1.25 6.69	-	-	0 0.00 0.00 0.00 0.00	-	-	13 2.08 65.00 0.81 4.35	-	-	-	-	-	-	-	-	-	-	-	-	-	-	-	-	-

Notes: Please refer to the User's Guide for an explanation of data; data is arranged alphabetically by state, then county, then city within each county; table includes counties with populations greater than 49,999 unless noted and cities with populations greater than 9,999 whose Asian and/or NHPI population rates are greater than the national average; (1) Native Hawaiian and other Pacific Islander; (2) excludes Taiwanese; (3) includes Chamorro; (4) county does not meet population threshold but is shown in order to allow inclusion of city

Place	Total population with income below poverty level	Asian population for whom poverty status is determined	Asians with income below poverty level	NHPI[1] population for whom poverty status is determined	NHPIs[1] with income below poverty level	Asian Indian	Bangladeshi	Cambodian	Chinese[2]	Fijian	Filipino	Guamanian[3]	Hawaiian, Native	Hmong	Indonesian	Japanese	Korean	Laotian	Malaysian	Pakistani	Samoan	Sri Lankan	Taiwanese	Thai	Tongan	Vietnamese
Sussex County	5,693 3.99	1,615	62 3.84 3.84 1.09	-	-	0 0.00 0.00 0.00 0.00	-	-	-	-	2 0.40 3.23 0.12 0.04	-	-	-	-	-	-	-	-	-	-	-	-	-	-	-
Union County	43,319 8.42	19,177	877 4.57 4.57 2.02	-	-	383 5.62 43.67 2.00 0.88	-	-	169 4.50 19.27 0.88 0.39	-	183 3.23 20.87 0.95 0.42	-	-	-	-	-	77 6.96 8.78 0.40 0.18	-	-	0 0.00 0.00 0.00 0.00	-	-	-	-	-	24 5.43 2.74 0.13 0.06
Berkeley Heights (township)	278 2.14	1,047	34 3.25 3.25 12.23	-	-	-	-	-	30 7.23 88.24 2.87 10.79	-	-	-	-	-	-	-	-	-	-	-	-	-	-	-	-	-
New Providence (borough)	212 1.80	896	5 0.56 0.56 2.36	-	-	-	-	-	0 0.00 0.00 0.00 0.00	-	-	-	-	-	-	-	-	-	-	-	-	-	-	-	-	-
Rahway (city)	1,864 7.09	1,146	84 7.33 7.33 4.51	-	-	-	-	-	-	-	27 5.26 32.14 2.36 1.45	-	-	-	-	-	-	-	-	-	-	-	-	-	-	-
Roselle Park (borough)	571 4.30	1,243	135 10.86 10.86 23.64	-	-	112 12.76 82.96 9.01 19.61	-	-	-	-	-	-	-	-	-	-	-	-	-	-	-	-	-	-	-	-
Scotch Plains (township)	674 2.98	1,581	44 2.78 2.78 6.53	-	-	13 2.05 29.55 0.82 1.93	-	-	18 3.91 40.91 1.14 2.67	-	-	-	-	-	-	-	-	-	-	-	-	-	-	-	-	-
Springfield (township)	453 3.14	559	0 <0.01 <0.01 <0.01	-	-	-	-	-	-	-	-	-	-	-	-	-	-	-	-	-	-	-	-	-	-	-
Summit (city)	895 4.24	812	50 6.16 6.16 5.59	-	-	9 2.31 18.00 1.11 1.01	-	-	-	-	-	-	-	-	-	-	-	-	-	-	-	-	-	-	-	-
Union (township)	2,212 4.18	4,153	130 3.13 3.13 5.88	-	-	87 8.44 66.92 2.09 3.93	-	-	0 0.00 0.00 0.00 0.00	-	11 0.53 8.46 0.26 0.50	-	-	-	-	-	-	-	-	-	-	-	-	-	-	-

Notes: Please refer to the User's Guide for an explanation of data; data is arranged alphabetically by state, then county, then city within each county; table includes counties with populations greater than 49,999 unless noted and cities with populations greater than 9,999 whose Asian and/or NHPI population rates are greater than the national average; (1) Native Hawaiian and other Pacific Islander; (2) excludes Taiwanese; (3) includes Chamorro; (4) county does not meet population threshold but is shown in order to allow inclusion of city

Place	Total population with income below poverty level	Asian population for whom poverty status is determined	Asians with income below poverty level	NHPI[1] population for whom poverty status is determined	NHPIs[1] with income below poverty level	Asian Indian	Bangladeshi	Cambodian	Chinese[2]	Fijian	Filipino	Guamanian[3]	Hawaiian, Native	Hmong	Indonesian	Japanese	Korean	Laotian	Malaysian	Pakistani	Samoan	Sri Lankan	Taiwanese	Thai	Tongan	Vietnamese
Westfield (town)	791 2.69	1,109	6 0.54 0.54 0.76	-	-	-	-	-	-	-	-	-	-	-	-	-	-	-	-	-	-	-	-	-	-	-
Warren County	5,492 5.44	1,193	77 6.45 6.45 1.40	-	-	39 7.18 50.65 3.27 0.71	-	-	-	-	-	-	-	-	-	-	-	-	-	-	-	-	-	-	-	-
NEW MEXICO	328,933 18.44	17,895	2,421 13.53 13.53 0.74	1,208	144 11.92 11.92 0.04	363 15.43 14.99 2.03 0.11	-	-	314 7.97 12.97 1.75 0.10	-	455 15.78 18.79 2.54 0.14	26 7.12 18.06 2.15 0.01	57 15.16 39.58 4.72 0.02	-	-	191 9.38 7.89 1.07 0.06	236 13.87 9.75 1.32 0.07	-	-	-	-	-	-	42 10.74 1.73 0.23 0.01	-	548 20.01 22.64 3.06 0.17
Bernalillo County	74,987 13.70	9,687	1,470 15.17 15.17 1.96	532	47 8.83 8.83 0.06	206 18.54 14.01 2.13 0.27	-	-	124 6.17 8.44 1.28 0.17	-	214 20.34 14.56 2.21 0.29	-	-	-	-	117 10.60 7.96 1.21 0.16	106 12.57 7.21 1.09 0.14	-	-	-	-	-	-	-	-	537 21.99 36.53 5.54 0.72
Chaves County	12,778 21.27	366	23 6.28 6.28 0.18	-	-	-	-	-	-	-	-	-	-	-	-	-	-	-	-	-	-	-	-	-	-	-
Dona Ana County	43,054 25.39	1,358	353 25.99 25.99 0.82	-	-	-	-	-	102 25.69 28.90 7.51 0.24	-	-	-	-	-	-	-	-	-	-	-	-	-	-	-	-	-
Los Alamos County[4]	534 2.93	798	6 0.75 0.75 1.12	-	-	-	-	-	-	-	-	-	-	-	-	-	-	-	-	-	-	-	-	-	-	-
Los Alamos (cdp)	429 3.63	609	6 0.99 0.99 1.40	-	-	-	-	-	-	-	-	-	-	-	-	-	-	-	-	-	-	-	-	-	-	-
Otero County	11,737 19.27	686	48 7.00 7.00 0.41	-	-	-	-	-	-	-	-	-	-	-	-	-	-	-	-	-	-	-	-	-	-	-
Sandoval County	10,847 12.13	748	56 7.49 7.49 0.52	-	-	-	-	-	-	-	46 13.86 82.14 6.15 0.42	-	-	-	-	-	-	-	-	-	-	-	-	-	-	-

Notes: Please refer to the User's Guide for an explanation of data; data is arranged alphabetically by state, then county, then city within each county; table includes counties with populations greater than 49,999 unless noted and cities with populations greater than 9,999 whose Asian and/or NHPI population rates are greater than the national average; (1) Native Hawaiian and other Pacific Islander; (2) excludes Taiwanese; (3) includes Chamorro; (4) county does not meet population threshold but is shown in order to allow inclusion of city

Place	Total population with income below poverty level	Asian population for whom poverty status is determined	Asians with income below poverty level	NHPI[1] population for whom poverty status is determined	NHPIs[1] with income below poverty level	Asian Indian	Bangladeshi	Cambodian	Chinese[2]	Fijian	Filipino	Guamanian[3]	Hawaiian, Native	Hmong	Indonesian	Japanese	Korean	Laotian	Malaysian	Pakistani	Samoan	Sri Lankan	Taiwanese	Thai	Tongan	Vietnamese
Santa Fe County	15,241 12.00	944	76 8.05 8.05 0.50	-	-	-	-	-	-	-	-	-	-	-	-	-	-	-	-	-	-	-	-	-	-	-
NEW YORK	2,692,202 14.59	1,023,083	178,217 17.42 17.42 6.62	7,537	1,951 25.89 25.89 0.07	34,347 13.99 19.27 3.36 1.28	5,621 28.18 3.15 0.55 0.21	789 27.69 0.44 0.08 0.03	86,256 21.07 48.40 8.43 3.20	-	4,292 5.02 2.41 0.42 0.16	389 23.07 19.94 5.16 0.01	328 24.68 16.81 4.35 0.01	-	418 17.36 0.23 0.04 0.02	7,103 19.52 3.99 0.69 0.26	18,456 15.77 10.36 1.80 0.69	348 11.10 0.20 0.03 0.01	263 19.23 0.15 0.03 0.01	7,135 22.33 4.00 0.70 0.27	289 20.58 14.81 3.83 0.01	488 18.34 0.27 0.05 0.02	1,354 18.16 0.76 0.13 0.05	630 9.78 0.35 0.06 0.02	-	5,260 23.28 2.95 0.51 0.20
Albany County	29,745 10.62	7,205	1,061 14.73 14.73 3.57	-	-	241 10.27 22.71 3.34 0.81	-	-	227 13.31 21.39 3.15 0.76	-	18 2.69 1.70 0.25 0.06	-	-	-	-	-	189 22.96 17.81 2.62 0.64	-	-	-	-	-	-	-	-	105 20.35 9.90 1.46 0.35
Colonie (town)	3,552 4.72	2,873	121 4.21 4.21 3.41	-	-	75 6.23 61.98 2.61 2.11	-	-	7 1.14 5.79 0.24 0.20	-	-	-	-	-	-	-	-	-	-	-	-	-	-	-	-	-
Guilderland (town)	1,321 4.08	1,238	192 15.51 15.51 14.53	-	-	38 9.18 19.79 3.07 2.88	-	-	-	-	-	-	-	-	-	-	-	-	-	-	-	-	-	-	-	-
Bronx County (Bronx)	395,263 30.68	38,392	7,820 20.37 20.37 1.98	1,035	456 44.06 44.06 0.12	3,055 20.89 39.07 7.96 0.77	633 31.78 8.09 1.65 0.16	345 42.80 4.41 0.90 0.09	1,237 19.98 15.82 3.22 0.31	-	273 5.67 3.49 0.71 0.07	-	-	-	-	184 37.17 2.35 0.48 0.05	499 14.70 6.38 1.30 0.13	-	-	179 15.93 2.29 0.47 0.05	-	-	-	-	-	1,085 36.82 13.87 2.83 0.27
Broome County	24,559 12.83	4,142	1,327 32.04 32.04 5.40	-	-	184 23.03 13.87 4.44 0.75	-	-	454 48.30 34.21 10.96 1.85	-	-	-	-	-	-	-	316 50.56 23.81 7.63 1.29	91 18.09 6.86 2.20 0.37	-	-	-	-	-	-	-	96 19.67 7.23 2.32 0.39
Johnson City (village)	2,374 15.99	815	222 27.24 27.24 9.35	-	-	-	-	-	-	-	-	-	-	-	-	-	-	-	-	-	-	-	-	-	-	-
Vestal (town)	1,487 7.09	964	256 26.56 26.56 17.22	-	-	-	-	-	66 27.27 25.78 6.85 4.44	-	-	-	-	-	-	-	-	-	-	-	-	-	-	-	-	-
Cattaraugus County	11,095 13.73	435	92 21.15 21.15 0.83	-	-	-	-	-	-	-	-	-	-	-	-	-	-	-	-	-	-	-	-	-	-	-

Notes: Please refer to the User's Guide for an explanation of data; data is arranged alphabetically by state, then county, then city within each county; table includes counties with populations greater than 49,999 unless noted and cities with populations greater than 9,999 whose Asian and/or NHPI population rates are greater than the national average; (1) Native Hawaiian and other Pacific Islander; (2) excludes Taiwanese; (3) includes Chamorro; (4) county does not meet population threshold but is shown in order to allow inclusion of city

Place	Total population with income below poverty level	Asian population for whom poverty status is determined	Asians with income below poverty level	NHPI[1] population for whom poverty status is determined	NHPIs[1] with income below poverty level	Asian Indian	Bangladeshi	Cambodian	Chinese[2]	Fijian	Filipino	Guamanian[3]	Hawaiian, Native	Hmong	Indonesian	Japanese	Korean	Laotian	Malaysian	Pakistani	Samoan	Sri Lankan	Taiwanese	Thai	Tongan	Vietnamese
Cayuga County	8,544 11.06	338	58 17.16 17.16 0.68	-	-	-	-	-	-	-	-	-	-	-	-	-	-	-	-	-	-	-	-	-	-	-
Chautauqua County	18,530 13.84	433	51 11.78 11.78 0.28	-	-	-	-	-	-	-	-	-	-	-	-	-	-	-	-	-	-	-	-	-	-	-
Chemung County	11,063 12.96	731	11 1.50 1.50 0.10	-	-	-	-	-	-	-	-	-	-	-	-	-	-	-	-	-	-	-	-	-	-	-
Chenango County	7,195 14.36	164	9 5.49 5.49 0.13	-	-	-	-	-	-	-	-	-	-	-	-	-	-	-	-	-	-	-	-	-	-	-
Clinton County	10,127 13.94	580	165 28.45 28.45 1.63	-	-	-	-	-	-	-	-	-	-	-	-	-	-	-	-	-	-	-	-	-	-	-
Columbia County	5,471 9.02	455	143 31.43 31.43 2.61	-	-	-	-	-	-	-	-	-	-	-	-	-	-	-	-	-	-	-	-	-	-	-
Dutchess County	19,858 7.53	6,692	608 9.09 9.09 3.06	-	-	251 8.93 41.28 3.75 1.26	-	-	125 6.43 20.56 1.87 0.63	-	-	-	-	-	-	-	57 8.99 9.38 0.85 0.29	-	-	-	-	-	-	-	-	-
Arlington (cdp)	1,050 10.26	609	87 14.29 14.29 8.29	-	-	-	-	-	-	-	-	-	-	-	-	-	-	-	-	-	-	-	-	-	-	-
Poughkeepsie (town)	2,156 5.72	1,658	139 8.38 8.38 6.45	-	-	110 11.85 79.14 6.63 5.10	-	-	0 0.00 0.00 0.00 0.00	-	-	-	-	-	-	-	-	-	-	-	-	-	-	-	-	-
Wappinger (town)	1,082 4.13	1,180	9 0.76 0.76 0.83	-	-	9 1.99 100.00 0.76 0.83	-	-	-	-	-	-	-	-	-	-	-	-	-	-	-	-	-	-	-	-

Notes: Please refer to the User's Guide for an explanation of data; data is arranged alphabetically by state, then county, then city within each county; table includes counties with populations greater than 49,999 unless noted and cities with populations greater than 9,999 whose Asian and/or NHPI population rates are greater than the national average; (1) Native Hawaiian and other Pacific Islander; (2) excludes Taiwanese; (3) includes Chamorro; (4) county does not meet population threshold but is shown in order to allow inclusion of city

Place	Total population with income below poverty level	Asian population for whom poverty status is determined	Asians with income below poverty level	NHPI[1] population for whom poverty status is determined	NHPIs[1] with income below poverty level	Asian Indian	Bangladeshi	Cambodian	Chinese[2]	Fijian	Filipino	Guamanian[3]	Hawaiian, Native	Hmong	Indonesian	Japanese	Korean	Laotian	Malaysian	Pakistani	Samoan	Sri Lankan	Taiwanese	Thai	Tongan	Vietnamese
Erie County	112,358 12.18	12,247	2,859 23.34 23.34 2.54	-	-	356 10.48 12.45 2.91 0.32	-	-	771 27.56 26.97 6.30 0.69	-	58 8.59 2.03 0.47 0.05	-	-	-	-	153 44.61 5.35 1.25 0.14	569 31.77 19.90 4.65 0.51	-	-	-	-	-	-	-	-	427 28.20 14.94 3.49 0.38
Amherst (town)	7,015 6.39	5,030	976 19.40 19.40 13.91	-	-	87 4.84 8.91 1.73 1.24	-	-	311 21.73 31.86 6.18 4.43	-	-	-	-	-	-	-	260 34.39 26.64 5.17 3.71	-	-	-	-	-	-	-	-	-
Herkimer County	7,921 12.53	255	69 27.06 27.06 0.87	-	-	-	-	-	-	-	-	-	-	-	-	-	-	-	-	-	-	-	-	-	-	-
Jefferson County	13,751 13.29	1,082	101 9.33 9.33 0.73	-	-	-	-	-	-	-	2 0.70 1.98 0.18 0.01	-	-	-	-	-	16 4.76 15.84 1.48 0.12	-	-	-	-	-	-	-	-	-
Kings County (Brooklyn)	610,476 25.07	184,954	48,119 26.02 26.02 7.88	1,534	345 22.49 22.49 0.06	6,817 27.64 14.17 3.69 1.12	1,642 42.02 3.41 0.89 0.27	128 26.02 0.27 0.07 0.02	31,160 25.87 64.76 16.85 5.10	-	474 6.68 0.99 0.26 0.08	60 12.27 17.39 3.91 0.01	-	-	-	656 30.33 1.36 0.35 0.11	1,216 18.14 2.53 0.66 0.20	-	-	3,536 36.75 7.35 1.91 0.58	-	-	-	-	-	916 24.05 1.90 0.50 0.15
Livingston County	6,018 10.40	461	144 31.24 31.24 2.39	-	-	-	-	-	-	-	-	-	-	-	-	-	-	-	-	-	-	-	-	-	-	-
Madison County	6,313 9.78	287	11 3.83 3.83 0.17	-	-	-	-	-	-	-	-	-	-	-	-	-	-	-	-	-	-	-	-	-	-	-
Monroe County	79,311 11.15	16,463	2,037 12.37 12.37 2.57	-	-	292 7.07 14.33 1.77 0.37	-	99 25.98 4.86 0.60 0.12	608 16.84 29.85 3.69 0.77	-	17 3.00 0.83 0.10 0.02	-	-	-	-	121 23.14 5.94 0.73 0.15	243 10.66 11.93 1.48 0.31	105 7.80 5.15 0.64 0.13	-	83 19.53 4.07 0.50 0.10	-	-	-	-	-	393 17.94 19.29 2.39 0.50
Brighton (town)	2,080 6.09	2,811	364 12.95 12.95 17.50	-	-	31 3.08 8.52 1.10 1.49	-	-	116 18.13 31.87 4.13 5.58	-	-	-	-	-	-	-	-	-	-	-	-	-	-	-	-	-
Henrietta (town)	3,045 9.10	1,410	373 26.45 26.45 12.25	-	-	111 37.00 29.76 7.87 3.65	-	-	135 42.86 36.19 9.57 4.43	-	-	-	-	-	-	-	-	-	-	-	-	-	-	-	-	-

Notes: Please refer to the User's Guide for an explanation of data; data is arranged alphabetically by state, then county, then city within each county; table includes counties with populations greater than 49,999 unless noted and cities with populations greater than 9,999 whose Asian and/or NHPI population rates are greater than the national average; (1) Native Hawaiian and other Pacific Islander; (2) excludes Taiwanese; (3) includes Chamorro; (4) county does not meet population threshold but is shown in order to allow inclusion of city

Place	Total population with income below poverty level	Asian population for whom poverty status is determined	Asians with income below poverty level	NHPI[1] population for whom poverty status is determined	NHPIs[1] with income below poverty level	Asian Indian	Bangladeshi	Cambodian	Chinese[2]	Fijian	Filipino	Guamanian[3]	Hawaiian, Native	Hmong	Indonesian	Japanese	Korean	Laotian	Malaysian	Pakistani	Samoan	Sri Lankan	Taiwanese	Thai	Tongan	Vietnamese
Pittsford (town)	727	1,251	22	-	-	0	-	-	-	-	-	-	-	-	-	-	-	-	-	-	-	-	-	-	-	-
	2.87		1.76			0.00																				
						0.00																				
			1.76			0.00																				
			3.03			0.00																				
Nassau County	68,631	62,028	2,948	401	134	866	-	-	925	-	191	-	-	-	-	152	596	-	-	49	-	-	23	10	-	12
	5.22		4.75		33.42	3.70			6.23		2.68					8.73	6.67			2.09			3.94	2.85		2.67
						29.38			31.38		6.48					5.16	20.22			1.66			0.78	0.34		0.41
			4.75		33.42	1.40			1.49		0.31					0.25	0.96			0.08			0.04	0.02		0.02
			4.30		0.20	1.26			1.35		0.28					0.22	0.87			0.07			0.03	0.01		0.02
East Meadow (cdp)	1,369	2,387	110	-	-	69	-	-	-	-	5	-	-	-	-	-	-	-	-	-	-	-	-	-	-	-
	3.81		4.61			6.18					1.44															
						62.73					4.55															
			4.61			2.89					0.21															
			8.04			5.04					0.37															
Elmont (cdp)	2,442	3,178	99	-	-	65	-	-	-	-	26	-	-	-	-	-	-	-	-	-	-	-	-	-	-	-
	7.51		3.12			3.40					4.73															
						65.66					26.26															
			3.12			2.05					0.82															
			4.05			2.66					1.06															
Franklin Square (cdp)	1,459	1,173	11	-	-	0	-	-	-	-	-	-	-	-	-	-	-	-	-	-	-	-	-	-	-	-
	4.98		0.94			0.00																				
						0.00																				
			0.94			0.00																				
			0.75			0.00																				
Glen Cove (city)	2,349	1,053	172	-	-	61	-	-	-	-	-	-	-	-	-	-	91	-	-	-	-	-	-	-	-	-
	9.06		16.33			18.77											22.86									
						35.47											52.91									
			16.33			5.79											8.64									
			7.32			2.60											3.87									
Hicksville (cdp)	1,511	3,689	47	-	-	14	-	-	26	-	0	-	-	-	-	-	-	-	-	-	-	-	-	-	-	-
	3.67		1.27			0.76			3.49		0.00															
						29.79			55.32		0.00															
			1.27			0.38			0.70		0.00															
			3.11			0.93			1.72		0.00															
Jericho (cdp)	611	1,483	125	-	-	-	-	-	-	-	-	-	-	-	-	-	111	-	-	-	-	-	-	-	-	-
	4.72		8.43														15.48									
																	88.80									
			8.43														7.48									
			20.46														18.17									
Mineola (village)	797	903	20	-	-	0	-	-	-	-	-	-	-	-	-	-	-	-	-	-	-	-	-	-	-	-
	4.16		2.21			0.00																				
						0.00																				
			2.21			0.00																				
			2.51			0.00																				
North Hempstead (town)	10,442	20,355	875	-	-	241	-	-	404	-	18	-	-	-	-	30	105	-	-	36	-	-	23	-	-	-
	4.79		4.30			3.16			7.26		1.37					3.25	3.30			5.83			8.52			
						27.54			46.17		2.06					3.43	12.00			4.11			2.63			
			4.30			1.18			1.98		0.09					0.15	0.52			0.18			0.11			
			8.38			2.31			3.87		0.17					0.29	1.01			0.34			0.22			

Notes: Please refer to the User's Guide for an explanation of data; data is arranged alphabetically by state, then county, then city within each county; table includes counties with populations greater than 49,999 unless noted and cities with populations greater than 9,999 whose Asian and/or NHPI population rates are greater than the national average; (1) Native Hawaiian and other Pacific Islander; (2) excludes Taiwanese; (3) includes Chamorro; (4) county does not meet population threshold but is shown in order to allow inclusion of city

Place	Total population with income below poverty level	Asian population for whom poverty status is determined	Asians with income below poverty level	NHPI[1] population for whom poverty status is determined	NHPIs[1] with income below poverty level	Asian Indian	Bangladeshi	Cambodian	Chinese[2]	Fijian	Filipino	Guamanian[3]	Hawaiian, Native	Hmong	Indonesian	Japanese	Korean	Laotian	Malaysian	Pakistani	Samoan	Sri Lankan	Taiwanese	Thai	Tongan	Vietnamese
North Merrick (cdp)	410 3.46	479	15 3.13 3.13 3.66	-	-	-	-	-	-	-	-	-	-	-	-	-	-	-	-	-	-	-	-	-	-	-
North New Hyde Park (cdp)	399 2.74	2,141	52 2.43 2.43 13.03	-	-	46 3.84 88.46 2.15 11.53	-	-	6 0.83 11.54 0.28 1.50	-	-	-	-	-	-	-	-	-	-	-	-	-	-	-	-	-
North Valley Stream (cdp)	575 3.69	1,464	34 2.32 2.32 5.91	-	-	3 0.47 8.82 0.20 0.52	-	-	-	-	-	-	-	-	-	-	-	-	-	-	-	-	-	-	-	-
Oyster Bay (town)	9,648 3.31	13,826	518 3.75 3.75 5.37	-	-	84 1.63 16.22 0.61 0.87	-	-	125 3.42 24.13 0.90 1.30	-	46 3.59 8.88 0.33 0.48	-	-	-	-	14 3.74 2.70 0.10 0.15	245 9.93 47.30 1.77 2.54	-	-	-	-	-	-	-	-	-
Plainview (cdp)	756 2.99	1,241	24 1.93 1.93 3.17	-	-	8 2.34 33.33 0.64 1.06	-	-	11 3.22 45.83 0.89 1.46	-	-	-	-	-	-	-	5 1.29 20.83 0.40 0.66	-	-	-	-	-	-	-	-	-
Port Washington (cdp)	706 4.69	962	21 2.18 2.18 2.97	-	-	8 3.13 38.10 0.83 1.13	-	-	-	-	-	-	-	-	-	-	-	-	-	-	-	-	-	-	-	-
Salisbury (cdp)	454 3.69	1,089	26 2.39 2.39 5.73	-	-	10 2.65 38.46 0.92 2.20	-	-	-	-	-	-	-	-	-	-	-	-	-	-	-	-	-	-	-	-
Syosset (cdp)	507 2.75	2,322	140 6.03 6.03 27.61	-	-	0 0.00 0.00 0.00 0.00	-	-	67 8.60 47.86 2.89 13.21	-	-	-	-	-	-	-	63 11.35 45.00 2.71 12.43	-	-	-	-	-	-	-	-	-
Valley Stream (village)	1,256 3.46	2,553	110 4.31 4.31 8.76	-	-	-	-	-	49 6.16 44.55 1.92 3.90	-	9 1.47 8.18 0.35 0.72	-	-	-	-	-	-	-	-	-	-	-	-	-	-	-
West Hempstead (cdp)	877 4.70	994	97 9.76 9.76 11.06	-	-	0 0.00 0.00 0.00 0.00	-	-	-	-	-	-	-	-	-	-	-	-	-	-	-	-	-	-	-	-

Notes: Please refer to the User's Guide for an explanation of data; data is arranged alphabetically by state, then county, then city within each county; table includes counties with populations greater than 49,999 unless noted and cities with populations greater than 9,999 whose Asian and/or NHPI population rates are greater than the national average; (1) Native Hawaiian and other Pacific Islander; (2) excludes Taiwanese; (3) includes Chamorro; (4) county does not meet population threshold but is shown in order to allow inclusion of city

Place	Total population with income below poverty level	Asian population for whom poverty status is determined	Asians with income below poverty level	NHPI[1] population for whom poverty status is determined	NHPIs[1] with income below poverty level	Asian Indian	Bangladeshi	Cambodian	Chinese[2]	Fijian	Filipino	Guamanian[3]	Hawaiian, Native	Hmong	Indonesian	Japanese	Korean	Laotian	Malaysian	Pakistani	Samoan	Sri Lankan	Taiwanese	Thai	Tongan	Vietnamese
Westbury (village)	751 5.29	694	40 5.76 5.76 5.33	-	-	-	-	-	-	-	-	-	-	-	-	-	-	-	-	-	-	-	-	-	-	-
Woodmere (cdp)	691 4.29	598	33 5.52 5.52 4.78	-	-	-	-	-	-	-	-	-	-	-	-	-	-	-	-	-	-	-	-	-	-	-
New York City	1,668,938 21.25	779,401	152,674 19.59 19.59 9.15	4,679	1,231 26.31 26.31 0.07	28,751 17.15 18.83 3.69 1.72	5,447 28.60 3.57 0.70 0.33	495 30.82 0.32 0.06 0.03	78,628 22.14 51.50 10.09 4.71	-	3,207 5.48 2.10 0.41 0.19	209 18.37 16.98 4.47 0.01	180 24.93 14.62 3.85 0.01	-	366 20.24 0.24 0.05 0.02	5,155 23.59 3.38 0.66 0.31	14,593 17.03 9.56 1.87 0.87	-	238 19.88 0.16 0.03 0.01	6,332 26.59 4.15 0.81 0.38	236 33.15 19.17 5.04 0.01	444 22.16 0.29 0.06 0.03	761 15.79 0.50 0.10 0.05	367 9.60 0.24 0.05 0.02	-	3,335 27.81 2.18 0.43 0.20
New York County (Manhattan)	298,231 20.00	138,744	32,549 23.46 23.46 10.91	567	193 34.04 34.04 0.06	1,823 14.61 5.60 1.31 0.61	75 9.95 0.23 0.05 0.03	-	23,460 27.97 72.08 16.91 7.87	-	736 8.49 2.26 0.53 0.25	-	-	-	-	2,511 18.25 7.71 1.81 0.84	2,244 21.45 6.89 1.62 0.75	-	-	247 23.21 0.76 0.18 0.08	-	-	239 24.77 0.73 0.17 0.08	98 11.74 0.30 0.07 0.03	-	219 16.45 0.67 0.16 0.07
Niagara County	22,834 10.59	1,118	314 28.09 28.09 1.38	-	-	126 29.23 40.13 11.27 0.55	-	-	-	-	-	-	-	-	-	-	-	-	-	-	-	-	-	-	-	-
Oneida County	28,764 13.04	2,595	388 14.95 14.95 1.35	-	-	43 7.48 11.08 1.66 0.15	-	-	19 8.19 4.90 0.73 0.07	-	-	-	-	-	-	-	-	-	-	-	-	-	-	-	-	253 23.32 65.21 9.75 0.88
Onondaga County	54,208 12.17	9,234	1,864 20.19 20.19 3.44	-	-	228 11.86 12.23 2.47 0.42	-	-	425 26.81 22.80 4.60 0.78	-	32 4.40 1.72 0.35 0.06	-	-	-	-	87 25.74 4.67 0.94 0.16	463 37.73 24.84 5.01 0.85	-	-	-	-	-	-	-	-	297 17.41 15.93 3.22 0.55
Ontario County	7,106 7.31	663	34 5.13 5.13 0.48	-	-	-	-	-	-	-	-	-	-	-	-	-	-	-	-	-	-	-	-	-	-	-
Orange County	34,672 10.54	5,155	442 8.57 8.57 1.27	-	-	130 7.68 29.41 2.52 0.37	-	-	226 18.31 51.13 4.38 0.65	-	23 3.10 5.20 0.45 0.07	-	-	-	-	-	7 1.01 1.58 0.14 0.02	-	-	-	-	-	-	-	-	-
Oswego County	16,470 13.99	479	52 10.86 10.86 0.32	-	-	-	-	-	-	-	-	-	-	-	-	-	-	-	-	-	-	-	-	-	-	-

Notes: Please refer to the User's Guide for an explanation of data; data is arranged alphabetically by state, then county, then city within each county; table includes counties with populations greater than 49,999 unless noted and cities with populations greater than 9,999 whose Asian and/or NHPI population rates are greater than the national average; (1) Native Hawaiian and other Pacific Islander; (2) excludes Taiwanese; (3) includes Chamorro; (4) county does not meet population threshold but is shown in order to allow inclusion of city

Place	Total population with income below poverty level	Asian population for whom poverty status is determined	Asians with income below poverty level	NHPI[1] population for whom poverty status is determined	NHPIs[1] with income below poverty level	Asian Indian	Bangladeshi	Cambodian	Chinese[2]	Fijian	Filipino	Guamanian[3]	Hawaiian, Native	Hmong	Indonesian	Japanese	Korean	Laotian	Malaysian	Pakistani	Samoan	Sri Lankan	Taiwanese	Thai	Tongan	Vietnamese
Otsego County	8,546	244	74	-	-	-	-	-	-	-	-	-	-	-	-	-	-	-	-	-	-	-	-	-	-	-
	14.93		30.33																							
			30.33																							
			0.87																							
Putnam County	4,110	1,162	55	-	-	0	-	-	47	-	-	-	-	-	-	-	-	-	-	-	-	-	-	-	-	-
	4.37		4.73			0.00			11.08																	
						0.00			85.45																	
			4.73			0.00			4.04																	
			1.34			0.00			1.14																	
Queens County (Queens)	321,102	392,958	62,280	1,332	180	16,427	3,097	-	22,120	-	1,601	-	-	-	277	1,771	10,397	-	61	2,351	-	244	478	222	-	1,034
	14.57		15.85		13.51	15.00	25.09		16.10		4.88				22.28	33.75	16.79		10.76	20.93		26.04	13.80	9.39		27.73
						26.38	4.97		35.52		2.57				0.44	2.84	16.69		0.10	3.77		0.39	0.77	0.36		1.66
			15.85		13.51	4.18	0.79		5.63		0.41				0.07	0.45	2.65		0.02	0.60		0.06	0.12	0.06		0.26
			19.40		0.06	5.12	0.96		6.89		0.50				0.09	0.55	3.24		0.02	0.73		0.08	0.15	0.07		0.32
Rensselaer County	14,011	2,098	618	-	-	118	-	-	397	-	-	-	-	-	-	-	57	-	-	-	-	-	-	-	-	-
	9.50		29.46			29.35			43.82								16.06									
						19.09			64.24								9.22									
			29.46			5.62			18.92								2.72									
			4.41			0.84			2.83								0.41									
Richmond Co. (Staten Island)	43,866	24,353	1,906	-	-	629	-	-	651	-	123	-	-	-	-	-	237	-	-	19	-	72	-	-	-	-
	10.05		7.83			9.83			9.03		2.37						7.37			2.46		13.66				
						33.00			34.16		6.45						12.43			1.00		3.78				
			7.83			2.58			2.67		0.51						0.97			0.08		0.30				
			4.35			1.43			1.48		0.28						0.54			0.04		0.16				
Rockland County	26,772	15,997	962	-	-	331	-	-	122	-	86	-	-	-	-	-	196	-	-	-	-	-	-	-	-	-
	9.51		6.01			5.97			6.18		1.92						10.39									
						34.41			12.68		8.94						20.37									
			6.01			2.07			0.76		0.54						1.23									
			3.59			1.24			0.46		0.32						0.73									
Clarkstown (town)	3,060	6,705	439	-	-	233	-	-	17	-	57	-	-	-	-	-	91	-	-	-	-	-	-	-	-	-
	3.78		6.55			9.73			2.14		2.61						12.62									
						53.08			3.87		12.98						20.73									
			6.55			3.48			0.25		0.85						1.36									
			14.35			7.61			0.56		1.86						2.97									
Nanuet (cdp)	861	1,559	58	-	-	0	-	-	-	-	-	-	-	-	-	-	-	-	-	-	-	-	-	-	-	-
	5.25		3.72			0.00																				
						0.00																				
			3.72			0.00																				
			6.74			0.00																				
New City (cdp)	928	2,583	244	-	-	215	-	-	-	-	16	-	-	-	-	-	-	-	-	-	-	-	-	-	-	-
	2.75		9.45			20.15					2.71															
						88.11					6.56															
			9.45			8.32					0.62															
			26.29			23.17					1.72															
Orangetown (town)	2,182	2,912	214	-	-	27	-	-	82	-	0	-	-	-	-	-	38	-	-	-	-	-	-	-	-	-
	4.76		7.35			4.10			14.41		0.00						7.00									
						12.62			38.32		0.00						17.76									
			7.35			0.93			2.82		0.00						1.30									
			9.81			1.24			3.76		0.00						1.74									

Notes: Please refer to the User's Guide for an explanation of data; data is arranged alphabetically by state, then county, then city within each county; table includes counties with populations greater than 49,999 unless noted and cities with populations greater than 9,999 whose Asian and/or NHPI population rates are greater than the national average; (1) Native Hawaiian and other Pacific Islander; (2) excludes Taiwanese; (3) includes Chamorro; (4) county does not meet population threshold but is shown in order to allow inclusion of city

Place	Total population with income below poverty level	Asian population for whom poverty status is determined	Asians with income below poverty level	NHPI[1] population for whom poverty status is determined	NHPIs[1] with income below poverty level	Asian Indian	Bangladeshi	Cambodian	Chinese[2]	Fijian	Filipino	Guamanian[3]	Hawaiian, Native	Hmong	Indonesian	Japanese	Korean	Laotian	Malaysian	Pakistani	Samoan	Sri Lankan	Taiwanese	Thai	Tongan	Vietnamese
Ramapo (town)	17,458 16.29	5,095	282 5.53 5.53 1.62	-	-	49 2.45 17.38 0.96 0.28	-	-	23 4.94 8.16 0.45 0.13	-	24 1.78 8.51 0.47 0.14	-	-	-	-	-	67 12.43 23.76 1.32 0.38	-	-	-	-	-	-	-	-	-
Spring Valley (village)	4,683 18.68	1,461	167 11.43 11.43 3.57	-	-	31 4.10 18.56 2.12 0.66	-	-	-	-	-	-	-	-	-	-	-	-	-	-	-	-	-	-	-	-
St. Lawrence County	16,976 16.85	515	149 28.93 28.93 0.88	-	-	-	-	-	-	-	-	-	-	-	-	-	-	-	-	-	-	-	-	-	-	-
Saratoga County	11,238 5.72	2,103	26 1.24 1.24 0.23	-	-	5 0.73 19.23 0.24 0.04	-	-	17 4.51 65.38 0.81 0.15	-	-	-	-	-	-	-	0 0.00 0.00 0.00 0.00	-	-	-	-	-	-	-	-	-
Schenectady County	15,560 10.93	2,636	418 15.86 15.86 2.69	-	-	127 12.29 30.38 4.82 0.82	-	-	159 19.78 38.04 6.03 1.02	-	-	-	-	-	-	-	-	-	-	-	-	-	-	-	-	-
Niskayuna (town)	636 3.18	1,175	98 8.34 8.34 15.41	-	-	79 15.22 80.61 6.72 12.42	-	-	-	-	-	-	-	-	-	-	-	-	-	-	-	-	-	-	-	-
Steuben County	12,817 13.23	799	68 8.51 8.51 0.53	-	-	-	-	-	-	-	-	-	-	-	-	-	-	-	-	-	-	-	-	-	-	-
Suffolk County	83,171 5.97	31,547	2,393 7.59 7.59 2.88	381	92 24.15 24.15 0.11	805 8.19 33.64 2.55 0.97	-	-	846 10.12 35.35 2.68 1.02	-	121 3.12 5.06 0.38 0.15	-	-	-	-	10 1.01 0.42 0.03 0.01	230 6.39 9.61 0.73 0.28	-	-	210 10.65 8.78 0.67 0.25	-	-	38 9.69 1.59 0.12 0.05	7 1.97 0.29 0.02 0.01	-	30 4.33 1.25 0.10 0.04
Coram (cdp)	1,923 5.57	1,284	59 4.60 4.60 3.07	-	-	-	-	-	44 10.28 74.58 3.43 2.29	-	-	-	-	-	-	-	-	-	-	-	-	-	-	-	-	-
Dix Hills (cdp)	747 2.88	1,947	53 2.72 2.72 7.10	-	-	34 4.09 64.15 1.75 4.55	-	-	7 1.60 13.21 0.36 0.94	-	-	-	-	-	-	-	-	-	-	-	-	-	-	-	-	-

Notes: Please refer to the User's Guide for an explanation of data; data is arranged alphabetically by state, then county, then city within each county; table includes counties with populations greater than 49,999 unless noted and cities with populations greater than 9,999 whose Asian and/or NHPI population rates are greater than the national average; (1) Native Hawaiian and other Pacific Islander; (2) excludes Taiwanese; (3) includes Chamorro; (4) county does not meet population threshold but is shown in order to allow inclusion of city

Place	Total population with income below poverty level	Asian population for whom poverty status is determined	Asians with income below poverty level	NHPI[1] population for whom poverty status is determined	NHPIs[1] with income below poverty level	Asian Indian	Bangladeshi	Cambodian	Chinese[2]	Fijian	Filipino	Guamanian[3]	Hawaiian, Native	Hmong	Indonesian	Japanese	Korean	Laotian	Malaysian	Pakistani	Samoan	Sri Lankan	Taiwanese	Thai	Tongan	Vietnamese
Elwood (cdp)	225 2.09	712	7 0.98 0.98 3.11	-	-	-	-	-	-	-	-	-	-	-	-	-	-	-	-	-	-	-	-	-	-	-
Lake Grove (village)	529 5.11	554	32 5.78 5.78 6.05	-	-	-	-	-	-	-	-	-	-	-	-	-	-	-	-	-	-	-	-	-	-	-
Melville (cdp)	570 3.99	637	56 8.79 8.79 9.82	-	-	-	-	-	-	-	-	-	-	-	-	-	-	-	-	-	-	-	-	-	-	-
Setauket-East Setauket (cdp)	646 4.05	1,477	229 15.50 15.50 35.45	-	-	-	-	-	137 20.27 59.83 9.28 21.21	-	-	-	-	-	-	-	-	-	-	-	-	-	-	-	-	-
Stony Brook (cdp)	393 2.88	802	77 9.60 9.60 19.59	-	-	-	-	-	77 18.29 100.00 9.60 19.59	-	-	-	-	-	-	-	-	-	-	-	-	-	-	-	-	-
Sullivan County	11,559 16.31	831	261 31.41 31.41 2.26	-	-	-	-	-	-	-	-	-	-	-	-	-	-	-	-	-	-	-	-	-	-	-
Tioga County	4,295 8.40	349	3 0.86 0.86 0.07	-	-	-	-	-	-	-	-	-	-	-	-	-	-	-	-	-	-	-	-	-	-	-
Tompkins County	14,905 17.63	5,562	2,314 41.60 41.60 15.52	-	-	201 23.79 8.69 3.61 1.35	-	-	976 43.38 42.18 17.55 6.55	-	-	-	-	-	-	271 51.62 11.71 4.87 1.82	398 41.37 17.20 7.16 2.67	-	-	-	-	-	-	-	-	-
Ithaca (city)	8,721 40.24	2,509	1,564 62.34 62.34 17.93	-	-	151 45.62 9.65 6.02 1.73	-	-	748 66.02 47.83 29.81 8.58	-	-	-	-	-	-	-	166 68.60 10.61 6.62 1.90	-	-	-	-	-	-	-	-	-
Lansing (town)	666 6.69	1,071	225 21.01 21.01 33.78	-	-	-	-	-	-	-	-	-	-	-	-	-	-	-	-	-	-	-	-	-	-	-

Notes: Please refer to the User's Guide for an explanation of data; data is arranged alphabetically by state, then county, then city within each county; table includes counties with populations greater than 49,999 unless noted and cities with populations greater than 9,999 whose Asian and/or NHPI population rates are greater than the national average; (1) Native Hawaiian and other Pacific Islander; (2) excludes Taiwanese; (3) includes Chamorro; (4) county does not meet population threshold but is shown in order to allow inclusion of city

Place	Total population with income below poverty level	Asian population for whom poverty status is determined	Asians with income below poverty level	NHPI[1] population for whom poverty status is determined	NHPIs[1] with income below poverty level	Asian Indian	Bangladeshi	Cambodian	Chinese[2]	Fijian	Filipino	Guamanian[3]	Hawaiian, Native	Hmong	Indonesian	Japanese	Korean	Laotian	Malaysian	Pakistani	Samoan	Sri Lankan	Taiwanese	Thai	Tongan	Vietnamese
Ulster County	19,338 11.42	1,577	352 22.32 22.32 1.82	-	-	-	-	-	104 25.30 29.55 6.59 0.54	-	-	-	-	-	-	-	-	-	-	-	-	-	-	-	-	-
New Paltz (town)	1,962 18.59	383	169 44.13 44.13 8.61	-	-	-	-	-	-	-	-	-	-	-	-	-	-	-	-	-	-	-	-	-	-	-
Warren County	6,025 9.74	487	47 9.65 9.65 0.78	-	-	-	-	-	-	-	-	-	-	-	-	-	-	-	-	-	-	-	-	-	-	-
Wayne County	7,929 8.62	390	22 5.64 5.64 0.28	-	-	-	-	-	-	-	-	-	-	-	-	-	-	-	-	-	-	-	-	-	-	-
Westchester County	78,967 8.75	41,417	2,491 6.01 6.01 3.15	-	-	767 5.32 30.79 1.85 0.97	-	-	501 7.12 20.11 1.21 0.63	-	197 4.00 7.91 0.48 0.25	-	-	-	-	605 8.14 24.29 1.46 0.77	202 4.83 8.11 0.49 0.26	-	-	94 11.16 3.77 0.23 0.12	-	-	14 4.26 0.56 0.03 0.02	29 5.03 1.16 0.07 0.04	-	-
Dobbs Ferry (village)	555 5.59	750	50 6.67 6.67 9.01	-	-	-	-	-	-	-	-	-	-	-	-	-	-	-	-	-	-	-	-	-	-	-
Eastchester (cdp)	675 3.64	1,281	122 9.52 9.52 18.07	-	-	-	-	-	-	-	-	-	-	-	-	111 20.22 90.98 8.67 16.44	-	-	-	-	-	-	-	-	-	-
Eastchester (town)	1,295 4.17	2,242	122 5.44 5.44 9.42	-	-	-	-	-	-	-	-	-	-	-	-	111 9.26 90.98 4.95 8.57	-	-	-	-	-	-	-	-	-	-
Greenburgh (town)	3,324 3.90	7,746	248 3.20 3.20 7.46	-	-	77 2.98 31.05 0.99 2.32	-	-	48 3.76 19.35 0.62 1.44	-	0 0.00 0.00 0.00 0.00	-	-	-	-	98 5.12 39.52 1.27 2.95	25 2.55 10.08 0.32 0.75	-	-	-	-	-	-	-	-	-
Harrison (village)	1,277 5.58	1,264	77 6.09 6.09 6.03	-	-	-	-	-	-	-	-	-	-	-	-	56 8.28 72.73 4.43 4.39	-	-	-	-	-	-	-	-	-	-

Notes: Please refer to the User's Guide for an explanation of data; data is arranged alphabetically by state, then county, then city within each county; table includes counties with populations greater than 49,999 unless noted and cities with populations greater than 9,999 whose Asian and/or NHPI population rates are greater than the national average; (1) Native Hawaiian and other Pacific Islander; (2) excludes Taiwanese; (3) includes Chamorro; (4) county does not meet population threshold but is shown in order to allow inclusion of city

Place	Total population with income below poverty level	Asian population for whom poverty status is determined	Asians with income below poverty level	NHPI[1] population for whom poverty status is determined	NHPIs[1] with income below poverty level	Asian Indian	Bangladeshi	Cambodian	Chinese[2]	Fijian	Filipino	Guamanian[3]	Hawaiian, Native	Hmong	Indonesian	Japanese	Korean	Laotian	Malaysian	Pakistani	Samoan	Sri Lankan	Taiwanese	Thai	Tongan	Vietnamese
New Castle (town)	601 3.46	1,014	21 2.07 2.07 3.49	-	-	21 5.20 100.00 2.07 3.49	-	-	0 0.00 0.00 0.00 0.00	-	-	-	-	-	-	-	-	-	-	-	-	-	-	-	-	-
New Rochelle (city)	7,367 10.48	2,630	150 5.70 5.70 2.04	-	-	64 5.55 42.67 2.43 0.87	-	-	42 7.89 28.00 1.60 0.57	-	-	-	-	-	-	-	-	-	-	-	-	-	-	-	-	-
North Castle (town)	325 3.00	471	5 1.06 1.06 1.54	-	-	-	-	-	-	-	-	-	-	-	-	-	-	-	-	-	-	-	-	-	-	-
Ossining (town)	2,771 8.43	1,503	59 3.93 3.93 2.13	-	-	13 1.87 22.03 0.86 0.47	-	-	-	-	-	-	-	-	-	-	-	-	-	-	-	-	-	-	-	-
Ossining (village)	2,270 10.58	930	48 5.16 5.16 2.11	-	-	13 4.26 27.08 1.40 0.57	-	-	-	-	-	-	-	-	-	-	-	-	-	-	-	-	-	-	-	-
Pelham (town)	441 3.72	454	0 <0.01 <0.01 <0.01	-	-	-	-	-	-	-	-	-	-	-	-	-	-	-	-	-	-	-	-	-	-	-
Rye (city)	374 2.50	1,075	35 3.26 3.26 9.36	-	-	-	-	-	-	-	-	-	-	-	-	27 4.19 77.14 2.51 7.22	-	-	-	-	-	-	-	-	-	-
Scarsdale (village)	496 2.78	2,225	150 6.74 6.74 30.24	-	-	21 5.06 14.00 0.94 4.23	-	-	6 1.60 4.00 0.27 1.21	-	-	-	-	-	-	93 11.86 62.00 4.18 18.75	22 5.74 14.67 0.99 4.44	-	-	-	-	-	-	-	-	-
Tarrytown (village)	495 4.67	566	18 3.18 3.18 3.64	-	-	-	-	-	-	-	-	-	-	-	-	-	-	-	-	-	-	-	-	-	-	-
White Plains (city)	5,117 9.85	2,180	137 6.28 6.28 2.68	-	-	27 3.48 19.71 1.24 0.53	-	-	56 10.11 40.88 2.57 1.09	-	-	-	-	-	-	-	-	-	-	-	-	-	-	-	-	-

Notes: Please refer to the User's Guide for an explanation of data; data is arranged alphabetically by state, then county, then city within each county; table includes counties with populations greater than 49,999 unless noted and cities with populations greater than 9,999 whose Asian and/or NHPI population rates are greater than the national average; (1) Native Hawaiian and other Pacific Islander; (2) excludes Taiwanese; (3) includes Chamorro; (4) county does not meet population threshold but is shown in order to allow inclusion of city

Place	Total population with income below poverty level	Asian population for whom poverty status is determined	Asians with income below poverty level	NHPI[1] population for whom poverty status is determined	NHPIs[1] with income below poverty level	Asian Indian	Bangladeshi	Cambodian	Chinese[2]	Fijian	Filipino	Guamanian[3]	Hawaiian, Native	Hmong	Indonesian	Japanese	Korean	Laotian	Malaysian	Pakistani	Samoan	Sri Lankan	Taiwanese	Thai	Tongan	Vietnamese
Yonkers (city)	30,089 15.53	9,530	788 8.27 8.27 2.62	-	-	353 7.53 44.80 3.70 1.17	-	-	84 9.70 10.66 0.88 0.28	-	85 4.71 10.79 0.89 0.28	-	-	-	-	-	104 9.82 13.20 1.09 0.35	-	-	-	-	-	-	-	-	-
NORTH CAROLINA	958,667 12.28	107,847	10,912 10.12 10.12 1.14	3,254	491 15.09 15.09 0.05	1,906 7.74 17.47 1.77 0.20	-	228 9.85 2.09 0.21 0.02	1,957 11.54 17.93 1.81 0.20	-	640 6.50 5.87 0.59 0.07	158 14.43 32.18 4.86 0.02	169 16.46 34.42 5.19 0.02	986 14.63 9.04 0.91 0.10	-	580 9.90 5.32 0.54 0.06	1,331 11.30 12.20 1.23 0.14	508 10.40 4.66 0.47 0.05	-	382 21.42 3.50 0.35 0.04	63 15.95 12.83 1.94 0.01	-	31 3.32 0.28 0.03 <0.01	208 13.41 1.91 0.19 0.02	-	1,579 10.30 14.47 1.46 0.16
Alamance County	14,183 11.14	1,133	132 11.65 11.65 0.93	-	-	-	-	-	-	-	-	-	-	-	-	-	-	-	-	-	-	-	-	-	-	-
Buncombe County	22,920 11.44	1,795	181 10.08 10.08 0.79	-	-	31 5.68 17.13 1.73 0.14	-	-	-	-	-	-	-	-	-	-	-	-	-	-	-	-	-	-	-	-
Burke County	9,132 10.68	3,012	222 7.37 7.37 2.43	-	-	-	-	-	-	-	-	-	-	160 7.98 72.07 5.31 1.75	-	-	-	45 9.13 20.27 1.49 0.49	-	-	-	-	-	-	-	-
Cabarrus County	9,108 7.06	1,072	73 6.81 6.81 0.80	-	-	-	-	-	-	-	-	-	-	-	-	-	-	-	-	-	-	-	-	-	-	-
Catawba County	12,688 9.08	3,775	588 15.58 15.58 4.63	-	-	-	-	-	-	-	-	-	-	317 17.84 53.91 8.40 2.50	-	-	-	158 24.31 26.87 4.19 1.25	-	-	-	-	-	-	-	21 4.17 3.57 0.56 0.17
Hickory (city)	4,102 11.30	1,599	280 17.51 17.51 6.83	-	-	-	-	-	-	-	-	-	-	148 28.14 52.86 9.26 3.61	-	-	-	-	-	-	-	-	-	-	-	-
Cleveland County	12,446 13.27	774	78 10.08 10.08 0.63	-	-	-	-	-	-	-	-	-	-	-	-	-	-	-	-	-	-	-	-	-	-	-
Craven County	11,288 13.08	1,075	112 10.42 10.42 0.99	-	-	-	-	-	-	-	15 3.31 13.39 1.40 0.13	-	-	-	-	-	-	-	-	-	-	-	-	-	-	-

Notes: Please refer to the User's Guide for an explanation of data; data is arranged alphabetically by state, then county, then city within each county; table includes counties with populations greater than 49,999 unless noted and cities with populations greater than 9,999 whose Asian and/or NHPI population rates are greater than the national average; (1) Native Hawaiian and other Pacific Islander; (2) excludes Taiwanese; (3) includes Chamorro; (4) county does not meet population threshold but is shown in order to allow inclusion of city

Place	Total population with income below poverty level	Asian population for whom poverty status is determined	Asians with income below poverty level	NHPI[1] population for whom poverty status is determined	NHPIs[1] with income below poverty level	Asian Indian	Bangladeshi	Cambodian	Chinese[2]	Fijian	Filipino	Guamanian[3]	Hawaiian, Native	Hmong	Indonesian	Japanese	Korean	Laotian	Malaysian	Pakistani	Samoan	Sri Lankan	Taiwanese	Thai	Tongan	Vietnamese
Cumberland County	36,391 12.79	5,801	515 8.88 8.88 1.42	439	120 27.33 27.33 0.33	44 7.06 8.54 0.76 0.12	-	-	-	-	46 4.97 8.93 0.79 0.13	-	-	-	-	18 4.07 3.50 0.31 0.05	200 10.16 38.83 3.45 0.55	-	-	-	-	-	-	-	-	42 5.97 8.16 0.72 0.12
Davidson County	14,636 10.07	1,259	139 11.04 11.04 0.95	-	-	-	-	75 14.51 53.96 5.96 0.51	-	-	-	-	-	-	-	-	-	-	-	-	-	-	-	-	-	-
Durham County	28,557 13.37	6,388	847 13.26 13.26 2.97	-	-	198 8.06 23.38 3.10 0.69	-	-	234 16.26 27.63 3.66 0.82	-	38 6.51 4.49 0.59 0.13	-	-	-	-	106 27.89 12.51 1.66 0.37	76 15.57 8.97 1.19 0.27	-	-	-	-	-	-	-	-	-
Forsyth County	32,699 11.05	3,120	254 8.14 8.14 0.78	-	-	64 11.35 25.20 2.05 0.20	-	-	89 9.96 35.04 2.85 0.27	-	40 14.60 15.75 1.28 0.12	-	-	-	-	-	-	-	-	-	-	-	-	-	-	10 1.94 3.94 0.32 0.03
Gaston County	20,309 10.86	1,505	78 5.18 5.18 0.38	-	-	-	-	-	-	-	-	-	-	-	-	-	-	-	-	-	-	-	-	-	-	11 2.19 14.10 0.73 0.05
Guilford County	43,227 10.59	9,212	1,327 14.41 14.41 3.07	-	-	105 6.08 7.91 1.14 0.24	-	-	157 15.44 11.83 1.70 0.36	-	36 6.65 2.71 0.39 0.08	-	-	-	-	-	45 4.82 3.39 0.49 0.10	67 13.73 5.05 0.73 0.15	-	161 40.66 12.13 1.75 0.37	-	-	-	-	-	584 19.88 44.01 6.34 1.35
Halifax County	13,295 23.90	375	69 18.40 18.40 0.52	-	-	-	-	-	-	-	-	-	-	-	-	-	-	-	-	-	-	-	-	-	-	-
Harnett County	13,129 14.90	598	172 28.76 28.76 1.31	-	-	-	-	-	-	-	-	-	-	-	-	-	-	-	-	-	-	-	-	-	-	-
Henderson County	8,526 9.72	440	16 3.64 3.64 0.19	-	-	-	-	-	-	-	-	-	-	-	-	-	-	-	-	-	-	-	-	-	-	-
Iredell County	9,894 8.16	1,110	61 5.50 5.50 0.62	-	-	-	-	-	-	-	-	-	-	-	-	-	-	-	-	-	-	-	-	-	-	-

Notes: Please refer to the User's Guide for an explanation of data; data is arranged alphabetically by state, then county, then city within each county; table includes counties with populations greater than 49,999 unless noted and cities with populations greater than 9,999 whose Asian and/or NHPI population rates are greater than the national average; (1) Native Hawaiian and other Pacific Islander; (2) excludes Taiwanese; (3) includes Chamorro; (4) county does not meet population threshold but is shown in order to allow inclusion of city

Place	Total population with income below poverty level	Asian population for whom poverty status is determined	Asians with income below poverty level	NHPI[1] population for whom poverty status is determined	NHPIs[1] with income below poverty level	Asian Indian	Bangladeshi	Cambodian	Chinese[2]	Fijian	Filipino	Guamanian[3]	Hawaiian, Native	Hmong	Indonesian	Japanese	Korean	Laotian	Malaysian	Pakistani	Samoan	Sri Lankan	Taiwanese	Thai	Tongan	Vietnamese
Johnston County	15,399 12.81	579	47 8.12 8.12 0.31	-	-	-	-	-	-	-	-	-	-	-	-	-	-	-	-	-	-	-	-	-	-	-
Lenoir County	9,622 16.57	376	11 2.93 2.93 0.11	-	-	-	-	-	-	-	-	-	-	-	-	-	-	-	-	-	-	-	-	-	-	-
Mecklenburg County	62,652 9.20	20,598	1,276 6.19 6.19 2.04	-	-	225 4.38 17.63 1.09 0.36	-	66 8.60 5.17 0.32 0.11	237 8.20 18.57 1.15 0.38	-	25 2.20 1.96 0.12 0.04	-	-	180 31.63 14.11 0.87 0.29	-	63 7.77 4.94 0.31 0.10	123 5.07 9.64 0.60 0.20	8 0.91 0.63 0.04 0.01	-	-	-	-	-	-	-	266 5.75 20.85 1.29 0.42
Nash County	11,478 13.44	407	4 0.98 0.98 0.03	-	-	-	-	-	-	-	-	-	-	-	-	-	-	-	-	-	-	-	-	-	-	-
New Hanover County	20,445 13.05	1,360	236 17.35 17.35 1.15	-	-	-	-	-	-	-	-	-	-	-	-	-	-	-	-	-	-	-	-	-	-	-
Onslow County	16,917 12.91	2,288	297 12.98 12.98 1.76	373	6 1.61 1.61 0.04	-	-	-	-	-	126 12.27 42.42 5.51 0.74	-	-	-	-	23 4.72 7.74 1.01 0.14	-	-	-	-	-	-	-	-	-	-
Orange County	15,318 14.13	4,142	873 21.08 21.08 5.70	-	-	170 28.05 19.47 4.10 1.11	-	-	245 15.24 28.06 5.92 1.60	-	-	-	-	-	-	35 7.29 4.01 0.85 0.23	241 37.25 27.61 5.82 1.57	-	-	-	-	-	-	-	-	-
Carrboro (town)	3,149 19.03	802	242 30.17 30.17 7.68	-	-	-	-	-	-	-	-	-	-	-	-	-	-	-	-	-	-	-	-	-	-	-
Chapel Hill (town)	8,573 21.59	2,823	649 22.99 22.99 7.57	-	-	158 33.55 24.35 5.60 1.84	-	-	158 13.87 24.35 5.60 1.84	-	-	-	-	-	-	-	173 41.09 26.66 6.13 2.02	-	-	-	-	-	-	-	-	-
Pitt County	26,001 20.34	1,176	231 19.64 19.64 0.89	-	-	-	-	-	-	-	-	-	-	-	-	-	-	-	-	-	-	-	-	-	-	-

Notes: Please refer to the User's Guide for an explanation of data; data is arranged alphabetically by state, then county, then city within each county; table includes counties with populations greater than 49,999 unless noted and cities with populations greater than 9,999 whose Asian and/or NHPI population rates are greater than the national average; (1) Native Hawaiian and other Pacific Islander; (2) excludes Taiwanese; (3) includes Chamorro; (4) county does not meet population threshold but is shown in order to allow inclusion of city

Place	Total population with income below poverty level	Asian population for whom poverty status is determined	Asians with income below poverty level	NHPI[1] population for whom poverty status is determined	NHPIs[1] with income below poverty level	Asian Indian	Bangladeshi	Cambodian	Chinese[2]	Fijian	Filipino	Guamanian[3]	Hawaiian, Native	Hmong	Indonesian	Japanese	Korean	Laotian	Malaysian	Pakistani	Samoan	Sri Lankan	Taiwanese	Thai	Tongan	Vietnamese
Randolph County	11,802 9.15	785	58 7.39 7.39 0.49	-	-	-	-	-	-	-	-	-	-	-	-	-	-	-	-	-	-	-	-	-	-	-
Robeson County	27,326 22.81	919	107 11.64 11.64 0.39	-	-	-	-	-	-	-	-	-	-	-	-	-	-	-	-	-	-	-	-	-	-	-
Rowan County	13,372 10.59	808	0 <0.01 <0.01 <0.01	-	-	-	-	-	-	-	-	-	-	-	-	-	-	-	-	-	-	-	-	-	-	-
Stanly County	6,030 10.71	714	150 21.01 21.01 2.49	-	-	-	-	-	-	-	-	-	-	54 17.65 36.00 7.56 0.90	-	-	-	-	-	-	-	-	-	-	-	-
Surry County	8,685 12.42	478	32 6.69 6.69 0.37	-	-	-	-	-	-	-	-	-	-	-	-	-	-	-	-	-	-	-	-	-	-	-
Union County	9,926 8.14	586	54 9.22 9.22 0.54	-	-	-	-	-	-	-	-	-	-	-	-	-	-	-	-	-	-	-	-	-	-	-
Wake County	47,685 7.82	20,247	1,289 6.37 6.37 2.70	-	-	326 4.77 25.29 1.61 0.68	-	-	312 6.48 24.20 1.54 0.65	-	11 0.95 0.85 0.05 0.02	-	-	-	-	47 5.80 3.65 0.23 0.10	294 13.91 22.81 1.45 0.62	-	-	59 13.26 4.58 0.29 0.12	-	-	-	-	-	149 6.49 11.56 0.74 0.31
Apex (town)	381 1.90	761	4 0.53 0.53 1.05	-	-	-	-	-	-	-	-	-	-	-	-	-	-	-	-	-	-	-	-	-	-	-
Cary (town)	3,226 3.43	7,514	189 2.52 2.52 5.86	-	-	68 2.01 35.98 0.90 2.11	-	-	51 2.68 26.98 0.68 1.58	-	-	-	-	-	-	0 0.00 0.00 0.00 0.00	9 1.75 4.76 0.12 0.28	-	-	-	-	-	-	-	-	26 5.73 13.76 0.35 0.81
Wayne County	15,097 13.84	1,078	78 7.24 7.24 0.52	-	-	-	-	-	-	-	-	-	-	-	-	-	-	-	-	-	-	-	-	-	-	-

Notes: Please refer to the User's Guide for an explanation of data; data is arranged alphabetically by state, then county, then city within each county; table includes counties with populations greater than 49,999 unless noted and cities with populations greater than 9,999 whose Asian and/or NHPI population rates are greater than the national average; (1) Native Hawaiian and other Pacific Islander; (2) excludes Taiwanese; (3) includes Chamorro; (4) county does not meet population threshold but is shown in order to allow inclusion of city

Place	Total population with income below poverty level	Asian population for whom poverty status is determined	Asians with income below poverty level	NHPI[1] population for whom poverty status is determined	NHPIs[1] with income below poverty level	Asian Indian	Bangladeshi	Cambodian	Chinese[2]	Fijian	Filipino	Guamanian[3]	Hawaiian, Native	Hmong	Indonesian	Japanese	Korean	Laotian	Malaysian	Pakistani	Samoan	Sri Lankan	Taiwanese	Thai	Tongan	Vietnamese
Wilkes County	7,662 11.85	332	64 19.28 19.28 0.84	-	-	-	-	-	-	-	-	-	-	-	-	-	-	-	-	-	-	-	-	-	-	-
NORTH DAKOTA	73,457 11.86	3,203	464 14.49 14.49 0.63	-	-	121 11.94 26.08 3.78 0.16	-	-	89 21.39 19.18 2.78 0.12	-	22 3.91 4.74 0.69 0.03	-	-	-	-	-	60 19.23 12.93 1.87 0.08	-	-	-	-	-	-	-	-	-
Cass County	11,987 10.06	1,385	303 21.88 21.88 2.53	-	-	55 13.29 18.15 3.97 0.46	-	-	-	-	-	-	-	-	-	-	-	-	-	-	-	-	-	-	-	-
Grand Forks County	7,622 12.34	561	72 12.83 12.83 0.94	-	-	-	-	-	-	-	-	-	-	-	-	-	-	-	-	-	-	-	-	-	-	-
Ward County	6,141 10.80	293	9 3.07 3.07 0.15	-	-	-	-	-	-	-	-	-	-	-	-	-	-	-	-	-	-	-	-	-	-	-
OHIO	1,170,698 10.60	129,446	16,558 12.79 12.79 1.41	2,466	464 18.82 18.82 0.04	3,539 9.57 21.37 2.73 0.30	48 7.41 0.29 0.04 <0.01	538 20.72 3.25 0.42 0.05	3,940 14.53 23.80 3.04 0.34	-	972 7.49 5.87 0.75 0.08	60 9.42 12.93 2.43 0.01	95 13.73 20.47 3.85 0.01	-	520 49.67 3.14 0.40 0.04	1,217 12.34 7.35 0.94 0.10	2,130 15.68 12.86 1.65 0.18	336 11.28 2.03 0.26 0.03	143 43.60 0.86 0.11 0.01	337 21.10 2.04 0.26 0.03	130 27.43 28.02 5.27 0.01	54 10.51 0.33 0.04 <0.01	331 15.51 2.00 0.26 0.03	425 23.17 2.57 0.33 0.04	-	1,363 13.27 8.23 1.05 0.12
Allen County	12,374 12.10	528	57 10.80 10.80 0.46	-	-	-	-	-	-	-	-	-	-	-	-	-	-	-	-	-	-	-	-	-	-	-
Ashtabula County	12,162 12.06	277	16 5.78 5.78 0.13	-	-	-	-	-	-	-	-	-	-	-	-	-	-	-	-	-	-	-	-	-	-	-
Athens County	14,728 27.35	996	466 46.79 46.79 3.16	-	-	-	-	-	-	-	-	-	-	-	-	-	-	-	-	-	-	-	-	-	-	-
Athens (city)	7,247 51.93	756	410 54.23 54.23 5.66	-	-	-	-	-	-	-	-	-	-	-	-	-	-	-	-	-	-	-	-	-	-	-

Notes: Please refer to the User's Guide for an explanation of data; data is arranged alphabetically by state, then county, then city within each county; table includes counties with populations greater than 49,999 unless noted and cities with populations greater than 9,999 whose Asian and/or NHPI population rates are greater than the national average; (1) Native Hawaiian and other Pacific Islander; (2) excludes Taiwanese; (3) includes Chamorro; (4) county does not meet population threshold but is shown in order to allow inclusion of city

Place	Total population with income below poverty level	Asian population for whom poverty status is determined	Asians with income below poverty level	NHPI[1] population for whom poverty status is determined	NHPIs[1] with income below poverty level	Asian Indian	Bangladeshi	Cambodian	Chinese[2]	Fijian	Filipino	Guamanian[3]	Hawaiian, Native	Hmong	Indonesian	Japanese	Korean	Laotian	Malaysian	Pakistani	Samoan	Sri Lankan	Taiwanese	Thai	Tongan	Vietnamese
Butler County	27,946 8.70	4,955	435 8.78 8.78 1.56	-	-	52 2.95 11.95 1.05 0.19	-	-	98 10.14 22.53 1.98 0.35	-	41 9.69 9.43 0.83 0.15	-	-	-	-	-	28 6.07 6.44 0.57 0.10	-	-	-	-	-	-	-	-	51 7.85 11.72 1.03 0.18
Clark County	15,054 10.67	650	54 8.31 8.31 0.36	-	-	-	-	-	-	-	-	-	-	-	-	-	-	-	-	-	-	-	-	-	-	-
Clermont County	12,462 7.08	1,078	24 2.23 2.23 0.19	-	-	0 0.00 0.00 0.00 0.00	-	-	-	-	-	-	-	-	-	-	-	-	-	-	-	-	-	-	-	-
Columbiana County	12,478 11.54	248	14 5.65 5.65 0.11	-	-	-	-	-	-	-	-	-	-	-	-	-	-	-	-	-	-	-	-	-	-	-
Cuyahoga County	179,372 13.13	25,412	3,398 13.37 13.37 1.89	-	-	829 9.32 24.40 3.26 0.46	-	105 21.69 3.09 0.41 0.06	983 16.52 28.93 3.87 0.55	-	212 7.63 6.24 0.83 0.12	-	-	-	-	201 16.56 5.92 0.79 0.11	253 14.02 7.45 1.00 0.14	-	-	-	-	-	-	-	-	444 21.29 13.07 1.75 0.25
Mayfield Heights (city)	1,216 6.33	791	32 4.05 4.05 2.63	-	-	0 0.00 0.00 0.00 0.00	-	-	-	-	-	-	-	-	-	-	-	-	-	-	-	-	-	-	-	-
Richmond Heights (city)	573 5.32	515	67 13.01 13.01 11.69	-	-	-	-	-	-	-	-	-	-	-	-	-	-	-	-	-	-	-	-	-	-	-
Solon (city)	553 2.54	1,070	51 4.77 4.77 9.22	-	-	6 1.28 11.76 0.56 1.08	-	-	0 0.00 0.00 0.00 0.00	-	-	-	-	-	-	-	-	-	-	-	-	-	-	-	-	-
Westlake (city)	765 2.49	1,349	34 2.52 2.52 4.44	-	-	0 0.00 0.00 0.00 0.00	-	-	-	-	-	-	-	-	-	-	-	-	-	-	-	-	-	-	-	-
Delaware County	4,118 3.85	1,732	51 2.94 2.94 1.24	-	-	7 1.63 13.73 0.40 0.17	-	-	22 4.05 43.14 1.27 0.53	-	-	-	-	-	-	-	-	-	-	-	-	-	-	-	-	-

Notes: Please refer to the User's Guide for an explanation of data; data is arranged alphabetically by state, then county, then city within each county; table includes counties with populations greater than 49,999 unless noted and cities with populations greater than 9,999 whose Asian and/or NHPI population rates are greater than the national average; (1) Native Hawaiian and other Pacific Islander; (2) excludes Taiwanese; (3) includes Chamorro; (4) county does not meet population threshold but is shown in order to allow inclusion of city

Place	Total population with income below poverty level	Asian population for whom poverty status is determined	Asians with income below poverty level	NHPI[1] population for whom poverty status is determined	NHPIs[1] with income below poverty level	Asian Indian	Bangladeshi	Cambodian	Chinese[2]	Fijian	Filipino	Guamanian[3]	Hawaiian, Native	Hmong	Indonesian	Japanese	Korean	Laotian	Malaysian	Pakistani	Samoan	Sri Lankan	Taiwanese	Thai	Tongan	Vietnamese
Fairfield County	7,064	869	45	-	-	-	-	-	-	-	-	-	-	-	-	-	-	-	-	-	-	-	-	-	-	-
	5.90		5.18																							
			5.18																							
			0.64																							
Franklin County	121,843	32,138	5,052	353	82	1,023	-	320	1,006	-	71	-	-		321	364	775	187	-	127	-	-	123	149	-	308
	11.65		15.72		23.23	12.72		24.45	14.17		3.99				61.38	11.67	24.17	16.53		24.76			17.96	35.48		12.87
						20.25		6.33	19.91		1.41				6.35	7.21	15.34	3.70		2.51			2.43	2.95		6.10
			15.72		23.23	3.18		1.00	3.13		0.22				1.00	1.13	2.41	0.58		0.40			0.38	0.46		0.96
			4.15		0.07	0.84		0.26	0.83		0.06				0.26	0.30	0.64	0.15		0.10			0.10	0.12		0.25
Dublin (city)	845	2,497	132	-	-	0	-	-	25	-	-	-	-	-	-	107	-	-	-	-	-	-	-	-	-	-
	2.69		5.29			0.00			4.90							13.05										
						0.00			18.94							81.06										
			5.29			0.00			1.00							4.29										
			15.62			0.00			2.96							12.66										
Hilliard (city)	514	1,001	22	-	-	-	-	-	-	-	-	-	-	-	-	-	-	-	-	-	-	-	-	-	-	-
	2.15		2.20																							
			2.20																							
			4.28																							
Geauga County	4,096	370	2	-	-	-	-	-	-	-	-	-	-	-	-	-	-	-	-	-	-	-	-	-	-	-
	4.55		0.54																							
			0.54																							
			0.05																							
Greene County	11,847	2,823	512	-	-	127	-	-	151	-	-	-	-	-	-	-	32	-	-	-	-	-	-	-	-	-
	8.46		18.14			14.61			36.56								5.69									
						24.80			29.49								6.25									
			18.14			4.50			5.35								1.13									
			4.32			1.07			1.27								0.27									
Hamilton County	97,692	12,555	1,473	-	-	353	-	79	311	-	115	-	-	-	-	63	271	-	-	-	-	-	-	-	-	54
	11.82		11.73			8.89		22.51	10.50		8.85					10.62	23.96									5.11
						23.96		5.36	21.11		7.81					4.28	18.40									3.67
			11.73			2.81		0.63	2.48		0.92					0.50	2.16									0.43
			1.51			0.36		0.08	0.32		0.12					0.06	0.28									0.06
Blue Ash (city)	588	898	87	-	-	5	-	-	-	-	-	-	-	-	-	-	-	-	-	-	-	-	-	-	-	-
	4.66		9.69			1.23																				
						5.75																				
			9.69			0.56																				
			14.80			0.85																				
Sharonville (city)	538	556	16	-	-	8	-	-	-	-	-	-	-	-	-	-	-	-	-	-	-	-	-	-	-	-
	4.02		2.88			2.04																				
						50.00																				
			2.88			1.44																				
			2.97			1.49																				
Hancock County	5,176	724	149	-	-	-	-	-	-	-	-	-	-	-	-	-	-	-	-	-	-	-	-	-	-	-
	7.45		20.58																							
			20.58																							
			2.88																							

Notes: Please refer to the User's Guide for an explanation of data; data is arranged alphabetically by state, then county, then city within each county; table includes counties with populations greater than 49,999 unless noted and cities with populations greater than 9,999 whose Asian and/or NHPI population rates are greater than the national average; (1) Native Hawaiian and other Pacific Islander; (2) excludes Taiwanese; (3) includes Chamorro; (4) county does not meet population threshold but is shown in order to allow inclusion of city

Place	Total population with income below poverty level	Asian population for whom poverty status is determined	Asians with income below poverty level	NHPI[1] population for whom poverty status is determined	NHPIs[1] with income below poverty level	Asian Indian	Bangladeshi	Cambodian	Chinese[2]	Fijian	Filipino	Guamanian[3]	Hawaiian, Native	Hmong	Indonesian	Japanese	Korean	Laotian	Malaysian	Pakistani	Samoan	Sri Lankan	Taiwanese	Thai	Tongan	Vietnamese
Lake County	11,372	2,215	193	-	-	131	-	-	62	-	-	-	-	-	-	-	-	-	-	-	-	-	-	-	-	-
	5.06		8.71			19.29			12.06																	
						67.88			32.12																	
			8.71			5.91			2.80																	
			1.70			1.15			0.55																	
Licking County	10,602	627	97	-	-	-	-	-	-	-	-	-	-	-	-	-	-	-	-	-	-	-	-	-	-	-
	7.48		15.47																							
			15.47																							
			0.91																							
Lorain County	24,809	1,610	155	-	-	9	-	-	-	-	11	-	-	-	-	-	-	-	-	-	-	-	-	-	-	-
	9.00		9.63			2.53					2.63															
						5.81					7.10															
			9.63			0.56					0.68															
			0.62			0.04					0.04															
Lucas County	62,026	5,281	931	-	-	307	-	-	298	-	45	-	-	-	-	-	74	-	-	-	-	-	-	-	-	-
	13.89		17.63			19.42			20.96		7.53						14.37									
						32.98			32.01		4.83						7.95									
			17.63			5.81			5.64		0.85						1.40									
			1.50			0.49			0.48		0.07						0.12									
Mahoning County	31,328	998	102	-	-	-	-	-	-	-	-	-	-	-	-	-	-	-	-	-	-	-	-	-	-	-
	12.50		10.22																							
			10.22																							
			0.33																							
Marion County	5,963	364	36	-	-	-	-	-	-	-	-	-	-	-	-	-	-	-	-	-	-	-	-	-	-	-
	9.71		9.89																							
			9.89																							
			0.60																							
Medina County	6,849	1,144	68	-	-	0	-	-	-	-	-	-	-	-	-	-	-	-	-	-	-	-	-	-	-	-
	4.59		5.94			0.00																				
						0.00																				
			5.94			0.00																				
			0.99			0.00																				
Miami County	6,531	839	24	-	-	-	-	-	-	-	-	-	-	-	-	-	-	-	-	-	-	-	-	-	-	-
	6.72		2.86																							
			2.86																							
			0.37																							
Montgomery County	61,440	7,120	788	-	-	148	-	-	174	-	39	-	-	-	-	73	138	-	-	-	-	-	-	-	-	149
	11.32		11.07			7.08			15.55		5.45					11.41	17.60									14.48
						18.78			22.08		4.95					9.26	17.51									18.91
			11.07			2.08			2.44		0.55					1.03	1.94									2.09
			1.28			0.24			0.28		0.06					0.12	0.22									0.24
Portage County	13,395	1,048	312	-	-	-	-	-	-	-	-	-	-	-	-	-	-	-	-	-	-	-	-	-	-	-
	9.28		29.77																							
			29.77																							
			2.33																							

Notes: Please refer to the User's Guide for an explanation of data; data is arranged alphabetically by state, then county, then city within each county; table includes counties with populations greater than 49,999 unless noted and cities with populations greater than 9,999 whose Asian and/or NHPI population rates are greater than the national average; (1) Native Hawaiian and other Pacific Islander; (2) excludes Taiwanese; (3) includes Chamorro; (4) county does not meet population threshold but is shown in order to allow inclusion of city

Place	Total population with income below poverty level	Asian population for whom poverty status is determined	Asians with income below poverty level	NHPI[1] population for whom poverty status is determined	NHPIs[1] with income below poverty level	Asian Indian	Bangladeshi	Cambodian	Chinese[2]	Fijian	Filipino	Guamanian[3]	Hawaiian, Native	Hmong	Indonesian	Japanese	Korean	Laotian	Malaysian	Pakistani	Samoan	Sri Lankan	Taiwanese	Thai	Tongan	Vietnamese
Richland County	12,941 10.58	701	10 1.43 1.43 0.08	-	-	-	-	-	-	-	-	-	-	-	-	-	-	-	-	-	-	-	-	-	-	-
Stark County	33,865 9.19	1,801	206 11.44 11.44 0.61	-	-	67 14.99 32.52 3.72 0.20	-	-	25 6.44 12.14 1.39 0.07	-	-	-	-	-	-	-	-	-	-	-	-	-	-	-	-	-
Summit County	52,991 9.94	7,684	918 11.95 11.95 1.73	-	-	172 8.54 18.74 2.24 0.32	-	-	211 12.29 22.98 2.75 0.40	-	48 9.70 5.23 0.62 0.09	-	-	-	-	79 18.33 8.61 1.03 0.15	145 15.69 15.80 1.89 0.27	66 8.80 7.19 0.86 0.12	-	-	-	-	-	-	-	126 18.61 13.73 1.64 0.24
Trumbull County	22,788 10.33	1,009	87 8.62 8.62 0.38	-	-	-	-	-	-	-	-	-	-	-	-	-	-	-	-	-	-	-	-	-	-	-
Warren County	6,425 4.23	2,160	27 1.25 1.25 0.42	-	-	6 0.89 22.22 0.28 0.09	-	-	6 1.16 22.22 0.28 0.09	-	-	-	-	-	-	-	-	-	-	-	-	-	-	-	-	-
Wayne County	8,698 8.02	699	55 7.87 7.87 0.63	-	-	-	-	-	-	-	-	-	-	-	-	-	-	-	-	-	-	-	-	-	-	-
Wood County	10,903 9.61	1,123	115 10.24 10.24 1.05	-	-	-	-	-	-	-	-	-	-	-	-	-	-	-	-	-	-	-	-	-	-	-
OKLAHOMA	491,235 14.72	43,813	7,646 17.45 17.45 1.56	1,620	293 18.09 18.09 0.06	1,159 14.27 15.16 2.65 0.24	-	29 9.45 0.38 0.07 0.01	1,754 27.20 22.94 4.00 0.36	-	378 9.52 4.94 0.86 0.08	22 6.41 7.51 1.36 <0.01	59 10.67 20.14 3.64 0.01	51 16.14 0.67 0.12 0.01	-	593 24.05 7.76 1.35 0.12	823 18.68 10.76 1.88 0.17	19 2.21 0.25 0.04 <0.01	314 61.09 4.11 0.72 0.06	333 30.55 4.36 0.76 0.07	-	-	163 49.70 2.13 0.37 0.03	167 20.82 2.18 0.38 0.03	-	1,455 12.06 19.03 3.32 0.30
Canadian County	6,751 7.94	2,176	33 1.52 1.52 0.49	-	-	28 2.32 84.85 1.29 0.41	-	-	-	-	-	-	-	-	-	-	-	-	-	-	-	-	-	-	-	0 0.00 0.00 0.00 0.00
Cleveland County	20,977 10.58	5,699	1,303 22.86 22.86 6.21	-	-	203 23.52 15.58 3.56 0.97	-	-	287 27.23 22.03 5.04 1.37	-	91 16.76 6.98 1.60 0.43	-	-	-	-	-	143 21.77 10.97 2.51 0.68	-	-	-	-	-	-	-	-	201 12.01 15.43 3.53 0.96

Notes: Please refer to the User's Guide for an explanation of data; data is arranged alphabetically by state, then county, then city within each county; table includes counties with populations greater than 49,999 unless noted and cities with populations greater than 9,999 whose Asian and/or NHPI population rates are greater than the national average; (1) Native Hawaiian and other Pacific Islander; (2) excludes Taiwanese; (3) includes Chamorro; (4) county does not meet population threshold but is shown in order to allow inclusion of city

Place	Total population with income below poverty level	Asian population for whom poverty status is determined	Asians with income below poverty level	NHPI[1] population for whom poverty status is determined	NHPIs[1] with income below poverty level	Asian Indian	Bangladeshi	Cambodian	Chinese[2]	Fijian	Filipino	Guamanian[3]	Hawaiian, Native	Hmong	Indonesian	Japanese	Korean	Laotian	Malaysian	Pakistani	Samoan	Sri Lankan	Taiwanese	Thai	Tongan	Vietnamese
Comanche County	16,276	2,228	147	-	-	-	-	-	-	-	40	-	-	-	-	-	21	-	-	-	-	-	-	-	-	-
	15.60		6.60								8.99						2.57									
											27.21						14.29									
			6.60								1.80						0.94									
			0.90								0.25						0.13									
Garfield County	7,820	499	99	-	-	-	-	-	-	-	-	-	-	-	-	-	-	-	-	-	-	-	-	-	-	-
	13.93		19.84																							
			19.84																							
			1.27																							
Muskogee County	11,846	345	22	-	-	-	-	-	-	-	-	-	-	-	-	-	-	-	-	-	-	-	-	-	-	-
	17.91		6.38																							
			6.38																							
			0.19																							
Oklahoma County	98,145	17,814	3,613	-	-	480	-	-	802	-	106	-	-	-	-	320	385	4	-	-	-	-	-	97	-	959
	15.25		20.28			16.85			36.89		8.51					38.60	32.38	0.81						25.06		14.08
						13.29			22.20		2.93					8.86	10.66	0.11						2.68		26.54
			20.28			2.69			4.50		0.60					1.80	2.16	0.02						0.54		5.38
			3.68			0.49			0.82		0.11					0.33	0.39	<0.01						0.10		0.98
Payne County	12,431	1,579	689	-	-	-	-	-	240	-	-	-	-	-	-	-	-	-	-	-	-	-	-	-	-	-
	20.25		43.64						40.00																	
									34.83																	
			43.64						15.20																	
			5.54						1.93																	
Stillwater (city)	9,088	1,542	689	-	-	-	-	-	240	-	-	-	-	-	-	-	-	-	-	-	-	-	-	-	-	-
	27.27		44.68						40.27																	
									34.83																	
			44.68						15.56																	
			7.58						2.64																	
Pottawatomie County	9,121	230	29	-	-	-	-	-	-	-	-	-	-	-	-	-	-	-	-	-	-	-	-	-	-	-
	14.61		12.61																							
			12.61																							
			0.32																							
Tulsa County	64,062	8,431	1,026	-	-	118	-	-	247	-	15	-	-	-	-	-	128	-	-	209	-	-	-	-	-	119
	11.61		12.17			6.26			16.09		3.21						15.17			38.42						5.86
						11.50			24.07		1.46						12.48			20.37						11.60
			12.17			1.40			2.93		0.18						1.52			2.48						1.41
			1.60			0.18			0.39		0.02						0.20			0.33						0.19
Wagoner County	5,086	489	42	-	-	-	-	-	-	-	-	-	-	-	-	-	-	-	-	-	-	-	-	-	-	-
	8.91		8.59																							
			8.59																							
			0.83																							
OREGON	388,740	96,776	12,095	7,437	1,350	738	-	513	2,315	39	718	190	252	41	265	2,102	1,898	397	-	59	129	-	138	491	78	1,918
	11.61		12.50		18.15	7.47		18.90	12.69	10.46	6.83	17.61	13.02	3.01	42.67	19.07	15.24	10.90		15.36	17.60		18.16	33.52	17.53	10.20
						6.10		4.24	19.14	2.89	5.94	14.07	18.67	0.34	2.19	17.38	15.69	3.28		0.49	9.56		1.14	4.06	5.78	15.86
			12.50		18.15	0.76		0.53	2.39	0.52	0.74	2.55	3.39	0.04	0.27	2.17	1.96	0.41		0.06	1.73		0.14	0.51	1.05	1.98
			3.11		0.35	0.19		0.13	0.60	0.01	0.18	0.05	0.06	0.01	0.07	0.54	0.49	0.10		0.02	0.03		0.04	0.13	0.02	0.49

Notes: Please refer to the User's Guide for an explanation of data; data is arranged alphabetically by state, then county, then city within each county; table includes counties with populations greater than 49,999 unless noted and cities with populations greater than 9,999 whose Asian and/or NHPI population rates are greater than the national average; (1) Native Hawaiian and other Pacific Islander; (2) excludes Taiwanese; (3) includes Chamorro; (4) county does not meet population threshold but is shown in order to allow inclusion of city

Place	Total population with income below poverty level	Asian population for whom poverty status is determined	Asians with income below poverty level	NHPI[1] population for whom poverty status is determined	NHPIs[1] with income below poverty level	Asian Indian	Bangladeshi	Cambodian	Chinese[2]	Fijian	Filipino	Guamanian[3]	Hawaiian, Native	Hmong	Indonesian	Japanese	Korean	Laotian	Malaysian	Pakistani	Samoan	Sri Lankan	Taiwanese	Thai	Tongan	Vietnamese
Benton County	10,665	2,986	1,146	-	-	-	-	-	312	-	-	-	-	-	-	169	265	-	-	-	-	-	-	-	-	-
	14.56		38.38						34.29							45.68	43.73									
									27.23							14.75	23.12									
			38.38						10.45							5.66	8.87									
			10.75						2.93							1.58	2.48									
Corvallis (city)	9,166	2,686	1,122	-	-	-	-	-	309	-	-	-	-	-	-	-	265	-	-	-	-	-	-	-	-	-
	20.63		41.77						35.40								52.27									
									27.54								23.62									
			41.77						11.50								9.87									
			12.24						3.37								2.89									
Clackamas County	21,969	8,092	377	599	93	31	-	-	80	-	11	-	-	-	-	66	75	-	-	-	-	-	-	-	-	49
	6.56		4.66		15.53	4.42			4.36		1.13					6.58	4.46									5.16
						8.22			21.22		2.92					17.51	19.89									13.00
			4.66		15.53	0.38			0.99		0.14					0.82	0.93									0.61
			1.72		0.42	0.14			0.36		0.05					0.30	0.34									0.22
Lake Oswego (city)	1,181	1,494	40	-	-	-	-	-	0	-	-	-	-	-	-	-	-	-	-	-	-	-	-	-	-	-
	3.37		2.68						0.00																	
									0.00																	
			2.68						0.00																	
			3.39						0.00																	
Coos County	9,257	337	57	-	-	-	-	-	-	-	-	-	-	-	-	-	-	-	-	-	-	-	-	-	-	-
	15.04		16.91																							
			16.91																							
			0.62																							
Deschutes County	10,613	615	60	-	-	-	-	-	-	-	-	-	-	-	-	-	-	-	-	-	-	-	-	-	-	-
	9.29		9.76																							
			9.76																							
			0.57																							
Douglas County	12,999	593	68	-	-	-	-	-	-	-	-	-	-	-	-	-	-	-	-	-	-	-	-	-	-	-
	13.13		11.47																							
			11.47																							
			0.52																							
Jackson County	22,269	1,330	238	-	-	-	-	-	-	-	-	-	-	-	-	-	-	-	-	-	-	-	-	-	-	-
	12.54		17.89																							
			17.89																							
			1.07																							
Josephine County	11,193	392	53	-	-	-	-	-	-	-	-	-	-	-	-	-	-	-	-	-	-	-	-	-	-	-
	15.00		13.52																							
			13.52																							
			0.47																							
Klamath County	10,515	426	46	-	-	-	-	-	-	-	-	-	-	-	-	-	-	-	-	-	-	-	-	-	-	-
	16.77		10.80																							
			10.80																							
			0.44																							

Notes: Please refer to the User's Guide for an explanation of data; data is arranged alphabetically by state, then county, then city within each county; table includes counties with populations greater than 49,999 unless noted and cities with populations greater than 9,999 whose Asian and/or NHPI population rates are greater than the national average; (1) Native Hawaiian and other Pacific Islander; (2) excludes Taiwanese; (3) includes Chamorro; (4) county does not meet population threshold but is shown in order to allow inclusion of city

Place	Total population with income below poverty level	Asian population for whom poverty status is determined	Asians with income below poverty level	NHPI[1] population for whom poverty status is determined	NHPIs[1] with income below poverty level	Asian Indian	Bangladeshi	Cambodian	Chinese[2]	Fijian	Filipino	Guamanian[3]	Hawaiian, Native	Hmong	Indonesian	Japanese	Korean	Laotian	Malaysian	Pakistani	Samoan	Sri Lankan	Taiwanese	Thai	Tongan	Vietnamese
Lane County	45,423	5,754	1,790	575	149	70	-	-	360	-	75	-	-	-	-	500	311	-	-	-	-	-	-	-	-	-
	14.37		31.11		25.91	12.03			31.25		13.69					41.46	27.43									
						3.91			20.11		4.19					27.93	17.37									
			31.11		25.91	1.22			6.26		1.30					8.69	5.40									
			3.94		0.33	0.15			0.79		0.17					1.10	0.68									
Linn County	11,618	780	70	-	-	-	-	-	-	-	-	-	-	-	-	-	-	-	-	-	-	-	-	-	-	-
	11.41		8.97																							
			8.97																							
			0.60																							
Marion County	37,104	4,497	568	757	224	19	-	-	85	-	69	-	-	-	-	147	102	-	-	-	-	-	-	-	-	61
	13.50		12.63		29.59	5.57			11.29		10.50					30.63	18.55									7.69
						3.35			14.96		12.15					25.88	17.96									10.74
			12.63		29.59	0.42			1.89		1.53					3.27	2.27									1.36
			1.53		0.60	0.05			0.23		0.19					0.40	0.27									0.16
Salem (city)	19,222	3,031	246	382	127	-	-	-	63	-	32	-	-	-	-	69	-	-	-	-	-	-	-	-	-	16
	14.98		8.12		33.25				10.10		8.40					26.54										3.39
									25.61		13.01					28.05										6.50
			8.12		33.25				2.08		1.06					2.28										0.53
			1.28		0.66				0.33		0.17					0.36										0.08
Multnomah County	81,711	36,622	4,597	2,444	339	226	-	294	926	-	188	-	56	16	-	562	397	246	-	-	-	-	-	242	53	1,276
	12.66		12.55		13.87	12.60		28.19	13.43		5.72		12.28	1.52		16.45	15.71	9.60						49.19	14.76	11.25
						4.92		6.40	20.14		4.09		16.52	0.35		12.23	8.64	5.35						5.26	15.63	27.76
			12.55		13.87	0.62		0.80	2.53		0.51		2.29	0.04		1.53	1.08	0.67						0.66	2.17	3.48
			5.63		0.41	0.28		0.36	1.13		0.23		0.07	0.02		0.69	0.49	0.30						0.30	0.06	1.56
Portland (city)	67,481	33,055	4,363	1,943	286	161	-	294	922	-	170	-	48	16	-	540	344	226	-	-	-	-	-	242	53	1,261
	13.07		13.20		14.72	10.81		28.97	14.51		6.28		14.29	1.73		18.49	16.08	9.87						53.78	15.06	11.73
						3.69		6.74	21.13		3.90		16.78	0.37		12.38	7.88	5.18						5.55	18.53	28.90
			13.20		14.72	0.49		0.89	2.79		0.51		2.47	0.05		1.63	1.04	0.68						0.73	2.73	3.81
			6.47		0.42	0.24		0.44	1.37		0.25		0.07	0.02		0.80	0.51	0.33						0.36	0.08	1.87
Polk County	6,943	741	102	-	-	-	-	-	-	-	-	-	-	-	-	-	-	-	-	-	-	-	-	-	-	-
	11.47		13.77																							
			13.77																							
			1.47																							
Umatilla County	8,524	477	31	-	-	-	-	-	-	-	-	-	-	-	-	-	-	-	-	-	-	-	-	-	-	-
	12.66		6.50																							
			6.50																							
			0.36																							
Washington County	32,575	29,712	2,502	1,392	298	251	-	72	398	-	152	-	22	-	-	347	583	76	-	-	-	-	-	-	-	430
	7.38		8.42		21.41	4.52		6.52	8.15		4.89		5.26			13.39	13.61	12.62								8.61
						10.03		2.88	15.91		6.08		7.38			13.87	23.30	3.04								17.19
			8.42		21.41	0.84		0.24	1.34		0.51		1.58			1.17	1.96	0.26								1.45
			7.68		0.91	0.77		0.22	1.22		0.47		0.07			1.07	1.79	0.23								1.32
Aloha (cdp)	3,316	3,102	286	-	-	-	-	-	-	-	9	-	-	-	-	-	-	-	-	-	-	-	-	-	-	53
	7.91		9.22								2.16															4.74
											3.15															18.53
			9.22								0.29															1.71
			8.62								0.27															1.60

Notes: Please refer to the User's Guide for an explanation of data; data is arranged alphabetically by state, then county, then city within each county; table includes counties with populations greater than 49,999 unless noted and cities with populations greater than 9,999 whose Asian and/or NHPI population rates are greater than the national average; (1) Native Hawaiian and other Pacific Islander; (2) excludes Taiwanese; (3) includes Chamorro; (4) county does not meet population threshold but is shown in order to allow inclusion of city

Place	Total population with income below poverty level	Asian population for whom poverty status is determined	Asians with income below poverty level	NHPI[1] population for whom poverty status is determined	NHPIs[1] with income below poverty level	Asian Indian	Bangladeshi	Cambodian	Chinese[2]	Fijian	Filipino	Guamanian[3]	Hawaiian, Native	Hmong	Indonesian	Japanese	Korean	Laotian	Malaysian	Pakistani	Samoan	Sri Lankan	Taiwanese	Thai	Tongan	Vietnamese
Beaverton (city)	5,845 7.78	7,444	560 7.52 7.52 9.58	-	-	96 5.51 17.14 1.29 1.64	-	28 7.84 5.00 0.38 0.48	93 9.06 16.61 1.25 1.59	-	12 1.65 2.14 0.16 0.21	-	-	-	-	53 7.82 9.46 0.71 0.91	170 13.82 30.36 2.28 2.91	-	-	-	-	-	-	-	-	59 6.44 10.54 0.79 1.01
Cedar Mill (cdp)	850 6.66	982	79 8.04 8.04 9.29	-	-	-	-	-	-	-	-	-	-	-	-	-	-	-	-	-	-	-	-	-	-	-
Hillsboro (city)	6,331 9.21	4,352	390 8.96 8.96 6.16	-	-	89 6.78 22.82 2.05 1.41	-	-	81 13.57 20.77 1.86 1.28	-	-	-	-	-	-	-	43 8.16 11.03 0.99 0.68	-	-	-	-	-	-	-	-	57 7.68 14.62 1.31 0.90
Tigard (city)	2,730 6.65	2,458	124 5.04 5.04 4.54	-	-	-	-	-	38 6.11 30.65 1.55 1.39	-	-	-	-	-	-	-	-	-	-	-	-	-	-	-	-	0 0.00 0.00 0.00 0.00
Tualatin (city)	1,248 5.54	1,007	53 5.26 5.26 4.25	-	-	-	-	-	-	-	-	-	-	-	-	-	-	-	-	-	-	-	-	-	-	-
Yamhill County	7,336 9.18	685	125 18.25 18.25 1.70	-	-	-	-	-	-	-	-	-	-	-	-	-	-	-	-	-	-	-	-	-	-	-
PENNSYLVANIA	1,304,117 10.98	208,005	34,806 16.73 16.73 2.67	3,363	667 19.83 19.83 0.05	5,306 9.79 15.24 2.55 0.41	128 18.29 0.37 0.06 0.01	3,432 39.91 9.86 1.65 0.26	8,579 18.69 24.65 4.12 0.66	-	1,138 8.06 3.27 0.55 0.09	100 13.16 14.99 2.97 0.01	229 27.83 34.33 6.81 0.02	156 20.50 0.45 0.07 0.01	192 36.71 0.55 0.09 0.01	1,622 24.16 4.66 0.78 0.12	5,151 16.26 14.80 2.48 0.39	234 10.44 0.67 0.11 0.02	-	344 11.53 0.99 0.17 0.03	121 15.09 18.14 3.60 0.01	12 3.99 0.03 0.01 <0.01	613 29.93 1.76 0.29 0.05	360 21.56 1.03 0.17 0.03	-	5,757 20.46 16.54 2.77 0.44
Adams County	6,235 7.12	585	68 11.62 11.62 1.09	-	-	-	-	-	-	-	-	-	-	-	-	-	-	-	-	-	-	-	-	-	-	-
Allegheny County	139,505 11.19	19,754	3,293 16.67 16.67 2.36	604	122 20.20 20.20 0.09	571 7.73 17.34 2.89 0.41	-	-	872 18.06 26.48 4.41 0.63	-	44 4.31 1.34 0.22 0.03	-	-	-	-	516 44.64 15.67 2.61 0.37	575 26.11 17.46 2.91 0.41	-	-	-	-	-	138 32.86 4.19 0.70 0.10	-	-	313 24.32 9.51 1.58 0.22
Muni. of Monroeville (borough)	1,897 6.58	1,165	67 5.75 5.75 3.53	-	-	0 0.00 0.00 0.00 0.00	-	-	-	-	-	-	-	-	-	-	-	-	-	-	-	-	-	-	-	-

Notes: Please refer to the User's Guide for an explanation of data; data is arranged alphabetically by state, then county, then city within each county; table includes counties with populations greater than 49,999 unless noted and cities with populations greater than 9,999 whose Asian and/or NHPI population rates are greater than the national average; (1) Native Hawaiian and other Pacific Islander; (2) excludes Taiwanese; (3) includes Chamorro; (4) county does not meet population threshold but is shown in order to allow inclusion of city

Place	Total population with income below poverty level	Asian population for whom poverty status is determined	Asians with income below poverty level	NHPI[1] population for whom poverty status is determined	NHPIs[1] with income below poverty level	Asian Indian	Bangladeshi	Cambodian	Chinese[2]	Fijian	Filipino	Guamanian[3]
Scott (township)	1,219 7.19	1,000	115 11.50 11.50 9.43	-	-	104 12.50 90.43 10.40 8.53	-	-	-	-	-	-
Scott Township (cdp)	1,219 7.19	1,000	115 11.50 11.50 9.43	-	-	104 12.50 90.43 10.40 8.53	-	-	-	-	-	-
Upper St. Clair (township)	544 2.77	779	24 3.08 3.08 4.41	-	-	0 0.00 0.00 0.00 0.00	-	-	-	-	-	-
Beaver County	16,635 9.36	431	36 8.35 8.35 0.22	-	-	-	-	-	-	-	-	-
Berks County	34,201 9.43	3,464	487 14.06 14.06 1.42	-	-	81 10.99 16.63 2.34 0.24	-	-	38 7.00 7.80 1.10 0.11	-	-	-
Blair County	15,840 12.64	526	52 9.89 9.89 0.33	-	-	-	-	-	-	-	-	-
Bradford County	7,312 11.84	197	33 16.75 16.75 0.45	-	-	-	-	-	-	-	-	-
Bucks County	26,562 4.51	14,133	1,058 7.49 7.49 3.98	-	-	446 7.58 42.16 3.16 1.68	-	-	177 8.31 16.73 1.25 0.67	-	112 7.17 10.59 0.79 0.42	-
Bensalem (township)	4,311 7.42	3,807	293 7.70 7.70 6.80	-	-	78 4.14 26.62 2.05 1.81	-	-	-	-	-	-
Lower Makefield (township)	864 2.66	1,351	70 5.18 5.18 8.10	-	-	0 0.00 0.00 0.00 0.00	-	-	-	-	-	-

Place	Hawaiian, Native	Hmong	Indonesian	Japanese	Korean	Laotian	Malaysian	Pakistani	Samoan	Sri Lankan	Taiwanese	Thai	Tongan	Vietnamese
Scott (township)	-	-	-	-	-	-	-	-	-	-	-	-	-	-
Scott Township (cdp)	-	-	-	-	-	-	-	-	-	-	-	-	-	-
Upper St. Clair (township)	-	-	-	-	-	-	-	-	-	-	-	-	-	-
Beaver County	-	-	-	-	-	-	-	-	-	-	-	-	-	-
Berks County	-	-	-	-	31 10.16 6.37 0.89 0.09	-	-	-	-	-	-	-	-	269 23.13 55.24 7.77 0.79
Blair County	-	-	-	-	-	-	-	-	-	-	-	-	-	-
Bradford County	-	-	-	-	-	-	-	-	-	-	-	-	-	-
Bucks County	-	-	-	-	235 10.73 22.21 1.66 0.88	-	-	-	-	-	-	-	-	0 0.00 0.00 0.00 0.00
Bensalem (township)	-	-	-	-	101 14.72 34.47 2.65 2.34	-	-	-	-	-	-	-	-	-
Lower Makefield (township)	-	-	-	-	-	-	-	-	-	-	-	-	-	-

Notes: Please refer to the User's Guide for an explanation of data; data is arranged alphabetically by state, then county, then city within each county; table includes counties with populations greater than 49,999 unless noted and cities with populations greater than 9,999 whose Asian and/or NHPI population rates are greater than the national average; (1) Native Hawaiian and other Pacific Islander; (2) excludes Taiwanese; (3) includes Chamorro; (4) county does not meet population threshold but is shown in order to allow inclusion of city

Place	Total population with income below poverty level	Asian population for whom poverty status is determined	Asians with income below poverty level	NHPI[1] population for whom poverty status is determined	NHPIs[1] with income below poverty level	Asian Indian	Bangladeshi	Cambodian	Chinese[2]	Fijian	Filipino	Guamanian[3]	Hawaiian, Native	Hmong	Indonesian	Japanese	Korean	Laotian	Malaysian	Pakistani	Samoan	Sri Lankan	Taiwanese	Thai	Tongan	Vietnamese
Newtown (township)	272 1.50	899	33 3.67 3.67 12.13	-	-	-	-	-	-	-	-	-	-	-	-	-	-	-	-	-	-	-	-	-	-	-
Butler County	15,269 9.08	895	71 7.93 7.93 0.46	-	-	34 7.80 47.89 3.80 0.22	-	-	-	-	-	-	-	-	-	-	-	-	-	-	-	-	-	-	-	-
Cambria County	18,111 12.49	492	57 11.59 11.59 0.31	-	-	-	-	-	-	-	-	-	-	-	-	-	-	-	-	-	-	-	-	-	-	-
Centre County	22,742 18.81	4,606	1,659 36.02 36.02 7.29	-	-	349 31.33 21.04 7.58 1.53	-	-	469 31.18 28.27 10.18 2.06	-	-	-	-	-	-	-	460 50.83 27.73 9.99 2.02	-	-	-	-	-	-	-	-	-
Ferguson (township)	1,955 13.97	1,012	186 18.38 18.38 9.51	-	-	-	-	-	-	-	-	-	-	-	-	-	-	-	-	-	-	-	-	-	-	-
Patton (township)	2,058 18.08	516	100 19.38 19.38 4.86	-	-	-	-	-	-	-	-	-	-	-	-	-	-	-	-	-	-	-	-	-	-	-
State College (borough)	12,996 46.93	2,744	1,350 49.20 49.20 10.39	-	-	333 51.95 24.67 12.14 2.56	-	-	406 43.33 30.07 14.80 3.12	-	-	-	-	-	-	-	315 68.03 23.33 11.48 2.42	-	-	-	-	-	-	-	-	-
Chester County	22,032 5.23	8,712	555 6.37 6.37 2.52	-	-	131 4.70 23.60 1.50 0.59	-	-	216 9.22 38.92 2.48 0.98	-	18 3.21 3.24 0.21 0.08	-	-	-	-	85 21.25 15.32 0.98 0.39	44 4.14 7.93 0.51 0.20	-	-	-	-	-	-	-	-	42 5.05 7.57 0.48 0.19
Tredyffrin (township)	1,068 3.69	1,694	89 5.25 5.25 8.33	-	-	42 6.47 47.19 2.48 3.93	-	-	20 3.26 22.47 1.18 1.87	-	-	-	-	-	-	-	-	-	-	-	-	-	-	-	-	-
West Goshen (township)	680 3.35	777	24 3.09 3.09 3.53	-	-	-	-	-	-	-	-	-	-	-	-	-	-	-	-	-	-	-	-	-	-	-

Notes: Please refer to the User's Guide for an explanation of data; data is arranged alphabetically by state, then county, then city within each county; table includes counties with populations greater than 49,999 unless noted and cities with populations greater than 9,999 whose Asian and/or NHPI population rates are greater than the national average; (1) Native Hawaiian and other Pacific Islander; (2) excludes Taiwanese; (3) includes Chamorro; (4) county does not meet population threshold but is shown in order to allow inclusion of city

Place	Total population with income below poverty level	Asian population for whom poverty status is determined	Asians with income below poverty level	NHPI[1] population for whom poverty status is determined	NHPIs[1] with income below poverty level	Asian Indian	Bangladeshi	Cambodian	Chinese[2]	Fijian	Filipino	Guamanian[3]	Hawaiian, Native	Hmong	Indonesian	Japanese	Korean	Laotian	Malaysian	Pakistani	Samoan	Sri Lankan	Taiwanese	Thai	Tongan	Vietnamese
West Whiteland (township)	457 2.79	608	30 4.93 4.93 6.56	-	-	-	-	-	-	-	-	-	-	-	-	-	-	-	-	-	-	-	-	-	-	-
Clearfield County	10,028 12.52	263	9 3.42 3.42 0.09	-	-	-	-	-	-	-	-	-	-	-	-	-	-	-	-	-	-	-	-	-	-	-
Columbia County	7,899 13.09	281	88 31.32 31.32 1.11	-	-	-	-	-	-	-	-	-	-	-	-	-	-	-	-	-	-	-	-	-	-	-
Crawford County	11,024 12.77	275	28 10.18 10.18 0.25	-	-	-	-	-	-	-	-	-	-	-	-	-	-	-	-	-	-	-	-	-	-	-
Cumberland County	13,102 6.57	3,339	163 4.88 4.88 1.24	-	-	5 0.49 3.07 0.15 0.04	-	-	42 8.30 25.77 1.26 0.32	-	-	-	-	-	-	-	13 1.92 7.98 0.39 0.10	-	-	-	-	-	-	-	-	7 1.22 4.29 0.21 0.05
Hampden (township)	674 2.83	889	79 8.89 8.89 11.72	-	-	-	-	-	-	-	-	-	-	-	-	-	-	-	-	-	-	-	-	-	-	-
Dauphin County	23,706 9.66	4,870	494 10.14 10.14 2.08	-	-	113 11.02 22.87 2.32 0.48	-	-	67 8.72 13.56 1.38 0.28	-	-	-	-	-	-	-	57 13.70 11.54 1.17 0.24	-	-	-	-	-	-	-	-	114 6.55 23.08 2.34 0.48
Derry (township)	971 4.74	825	67 8.12 8.12 6.90	-	-	-	-	-	-	-	-	-	-	-	-	-	-	-	-	-	-	-	-	-	-	-
Hershey (cdp)	835 6.94	486	67 13.79 13.79 8.02	-	-	-	-	-	-	-	-	-	-	-	-	-	-	-	-	-	-	-	-	-	-	-
Delaware County	42,411 7.99	17,657	2,309 13.08 13.08 5.44	-	-	363 7.20 15.72 2.06 0.86	-	-	562 16.37 24.34 3.18 1.33	-	63 5.66 2.73 0.36 0.15	-	-	-	-	120 18.60 5.20 0.68 0.28	422 12.50 18.28 2.39 1.00	-	-	103 15.97 4.46 0.58 0.24	-	-	-	-	-	305 15.95 13.21 1.73 0.72

Notes: Please refer to the User's Guide for an explanation of data; data is arranged alphabetically by state, then county, then city within each county; table includes counties with populations greater than 49,999 unless noted and cities with populations greater than 9,999 whose Asian and/or NHPI population rates are greater than the national average; (1) Native Hawaiian and other Pacific Islander; (2) excludes Taiwanese; (3) includes Chamorro; (4) county does not meet population threshold but is shown in order to allow inclusion of city

Place	Total population with income below poverty level	Asian population for whom poverty status is determined	Asians with income below poverty level	NHPI[1] population for whom poverty status is determined	NHPIs[1] with income below poverty level	Asian Indian	Bangladeshi	Cambodian	Chinese[2]	Fijian	Filipino	Guamanian[3]	Hawaiian, Native	Hmong	Indonesian	Japanese	Korean	Laotian	Malaysian	Pakistani	Samoan	Sri Lankan	Taiwanese	Thai	Tongan	Vietnamese
Broomall (cdp)	490 4.38	777	82 10.55 10.55 16.73	-	-	-	-	-	-	-	-	-	-	-	-	-	82 17.60 100.00 10.55 16.73	-	-	-	-	-	-	-	-	-
Drexel Hill (cdp)	1,445 4.94	1,138	234 20.56 20.56 16.19	-	-	-	-	-	75 21.13 32.05 6.59 5.19	-	-	-	-	-	-	-	-	-	-	-	-	-	-	-	-	-
Marple (township)	1,050 4.55	1,254	108 8.61 8.61 10.29	-	-	-	-	-	-	-	-	-	-	-	-	-	82 12.44 75.93 6.54 7.81	-	-	-	-	-	-	-	-	-
Radnor (township)	1,663 6.68	1,440	116 8.06 8.06 6.98	-	-	-	-	-	36 9.14 31.03 2.50 2.16	-	-	-	-	-	-	-	-	-	-	-	-	-	-	-	-	-
Upper Darby (township)	7,449 9.14	7,065	1,377 19.49 19.49 18.49	-	-	199 9.96 14.45 2.82 2.67	-	-	426 28.17 30.94 6.03 5.72	-	-	-	-	-	-	-	167 16.78 12.13 2.36 2.24	-	-	-	-	-	-	-	-	233 19.76 16.92 3.30 3.13
Erie County	32,108 11.99	1,716	320 18.65 18.65 1.00	-	-	125 24.08 39.06 7.28 0.39	-	-	-	-	-	-	-	-	-	-	-	-	-	-	-	-	-	-	-	-
Franklin County	9,574 7.59	854	48 5.62 5.62 0.50	-	-	-	-	-	-	-	-	-	-	-	-	-	-	-	-	-	-	-	-	-	-	-
Indiana County	14,701 17.28	601	124 20.63 20.63 0.84	-	-	-	-	-	-	-	-	-	-	-	-	-	-	-	-	-	-	-	-	-	-	-
Lackawanna County	21,802 10.55	1,715	114 6.65 6.65 0.52	-	-	23 3.46 20.18 1.34 0.11	-	-	-	-	-	-	-	-	-	-	-	-	-	-	-	-	-	-	-	-
Lancaster County	35,553 7.79	6,375	482 7.56 7.56 1.36	-	-	69 9.68 14.32 1.08 0.19	-	-	61 4.77 12.66 0.96 0.17	-	-	-	-	32 6.99 6.64 0.50 0.09	-	-	59 10.75 12.24 0.93 0.17	-	-	-	-	-	-	-	-	109 5.36 22.61 1.71 0.31

Notes: Please refer to the User's Guide for an explanation of data; data is arranged alphabetically by state, then county, then city within each county; table includes counties with populations greater than 49,999 unless noted and cities with populations greater than 9,999 whose Asian and/or NHPI population rates are greater than the national average; (1) Native Hawaiian and other Pacific Islander; (2) excludes Taiwanese; (3) includes Chamorro; (4) county does not meet population threshold but is shown in order to allow inclusion of city

Place	Total population with income below poverty level	Asian population for whom poverty status is determined	Asians with income below poverty level	NHPI[1] population for whom poverty status is determined	NHPIs[1] with income below poverty level	Asian Indian	Bangladeshi	Cambodian	Chinese[2]	Fijian	Filipino	Guamanian[3]	Hawaiian, Native	Hmong	Indonesian	Japanese	Korean	Laotian	Malaysian	Pakistani	Samoan	Sri Lankan	Taiwanese	Thai	Tongan	Vietnamese
Lawrence County	11,096 12.08	293	90 30.72 30.72 0.81	-	-	-	-	-	-	-	-	-	-	-	-	-	-	-	-	-	-	-	-	-	-	-
Lebanon County	8,728 7.51	1,102	120 10.89 10.89 1.37	-	-	-	-	-	-	-	-	-	-	-	-	-	-	-	-	-	-	-	-	-	-	-
Lehigh County	28,095 9.28	6,714	627 9.34 9.34 2.23	-	-	105 4.87 16.75 1.56 0.37	-	-	97 6.01 15.47 1.44 0.35	-	-	-	-	-	-	-	62 9.69 9.89 0.92 0.22	-	-	-	-	-	-	-	-	264 18.55 42.11 3.93 0.94
Fullerton (cdp)	1,032 7.34	687	58 8.44 8.44 5.62	-	-	-	-	-	-	-	-	-	-	-	-	-	-	-	-	-	-	-	-	-	-	-
Lower Macungie (township)	432 2.28	874	0 <0.01 <0.01 <0.01	-	-	-	-	-	0 <0.01 *** ** <0.01 <0.01	-	-	-	-	-	-	-	-	-	-	-	-	-	-	-	-	-
Upper Macungie (township)	411 3.03	627	15 2.39 2.39 3.65	-	-	-	-	-	-	-	-	-	-	-	-	-	-	-	-	-	-	-	-	-	-	-
Luzerne County	34,136 11.08	1,472	133 9.04 9.04 0.39	-	-	9 2.23 6.77 0.61 0.03	-	-	-	-	-	-	-	-	-	-	-	-	-	-	-	-	-	-	-	-
Lycoming County	13,205 11.54	477	75 15.72 15.72 0.57	-	-	-	-	-	-	-	-	-	-	-	-	-	-	-	-	-	-	-	-	-	-	-
Mercer County	13,092 11.48	605	41 6.78 6.78 0.31	-	-	-	-	-	-	-	-	-	-	-	-	-	-	-	-	-	-	-	-	-	-	-
Monroe County	12,180 9.01	1,359	207 15.23 15.23 1.70	-	-	99 23.57 47.83 7.28 0.81	-	-	-	-	-	-	-	-	-	-	-	-	-	-	-	-	-	-	-	-

Notes: Please refer to the User's Guide for an explanation of data; data is arranged alphabetically by state, then county, then city within each county; table includes counties with populations greater than 49,999 unless noted and cities with populations greater than 9,999 whose Asian and/or NHPI population rates are greater than the national average; (1) Native Hawaiian and other Pacific Islander; (2) excludes Taiwanese; (3) includes Chamorro; (4) county does not meet population threshold but is shown in order to allow inclusion of city

Place	Total population with income below poverty level	Asian population for whom poverty status is determined	Asians with income below poverty level	NHPI[1] population for whom poverty status is determined	NHPIs[1] with income below poverty level	Asian Indian	Bangladeshi	Cambodian	Chinese[2]	Fijian	Filipino	Guamanian[3]	Hawaiian, Native	Hmong	Indonesian	Japanese	Korean	Laotian	Malaysian	Pakistani	Samoan	Sri Lankan	Taiwanese	Thai	Tongan	Vietnamese
Montgomery County	32,215 4.42	28,819	2,027 7.03 7.03 6.29	-	-	343 4.77 16.92 1.19 1.06	-	-	205 3.80 10.11 0.71 0.64	-	42 2.19 2.07 0.15 0.13	-	-	-	-	65 9.92 3.21 0.23 0.20	1,058 11.62 52.20 3.67 3.28	-	-	-	-	-	-	-	-	117 4.86 5.77 0.41 0.36
Cheltenham (township)	1,803 5.07	2,353	345 14.66 14.66 19.13	-	-	-	-	-	-	-	-	-	-	-	-	-	266 24.61 77.10 11.30 14.75	-	-	-	-	-	-	-	-	-
East Norriton (township)	363 2.90	538	15 2.79 2.79 4.13	-	-	-	-	-	-	-	-	-	-	-	-	-	-	-	-	-	-	-	-	-	-	-
Hatfield (township)	646 3.92	1,819	236 12.97 12.97 36.53	-	-	83 8.53 35.17 4.56 12.85	-	-	-	-	-	-	-	-	-	-	-	-	-	-	-	-	-	-	-	-
Horsham (township)	577 2.40	1,136	9 0.79 0.79 1.56	-	-	-	-	-	-	-	-	-	-	-	-	-	0 0.00 0.00 0.00 0.00	-	-	-	-	-	-	-	-	-
King of Prussia (cdp)	586 3.19	1,895	83 4.38 4.38 14.16	-	-	30 3.91 36.14 1.58 5.12	-	-	22 5.42 26.51 1.16 3.75	-	-	-	-	-	-	-	-	-	-	-	-	-	-	-	-	-
Lansdale (borough)	883 5.63	1,316	78 5.93 5.93 8.83	-	-	7 1.56 8.97 0.53 0.79	-	-	-	-	-	-	-	-	-	-	-	-	-	-	-	-	-	-	-	-
Lower Gwynedd (township)	271 2.72	403	0 <0.01 <0.01 <0.01	-	-	-	-	-	-	-	-	-	-	-	-	-	-	-	-	-	-	-	-	-	-	-
Lower Providence (township)	912 4.45	1,014	67 6.61 6.61 7.35	-	-	-	-	-	16 3.38 23.88 1.58 1.75	-	-	-	-	-	-	-	-	-	-	-	-	-	-	-	-	-
Montgomery (township)	434 2.00	1,822	35 1.92 1.92 8.06	-	-	24 4.16 68.57 1.32 5.53	-	-	-	-	-	-	-	-	-	-	0 0.00 0.00 0.00 0.00	-	-	-	-	-	-	-	-	-

Notes: Please refer to the User's Guide for an explanation of data; data is arranged alphabetically by state, then county, then city within each county; table includes counties with populations greater than 49,999 unless noted and cities with populations greater than 9,999 whose Asian and/or NHPI population rates are greater than the national average; (1) Native Hawaiian and other Pacific Islander; (2) excludes Taiwanese; (3) includes Chamorro; (4) county does not meet population threshold but is shown in order to allow inclusion of city

Place	Total population with income below poverty level	Asian population for whom poverty status is determined	Asians with income below poverty level	NHPI[1] population for whom poverty status is determined	NHPIs[1] with income below poverty level	Asian Indian	Bangladeshi	Cambodian	Chinese[2]	Fijian	Filipino	Guamanian[3]	Hawaiian, Native	Hmong	Indonesian	Japanese	Korean	Laotian	Malaysian	Pakistani	Samoan	Sri Lankan	Taiwanese	Thai	Tongan	Vietnamese
Montgomeryville (cdp)	219 1.87	820	35 4.27 4.27 15.98	-	-	-	-	-	-	-	-	-	-	-	-	-	-	-	-	-	-	-	-	-	-	-
Plymouth (township)	678 4.29	832	76 9.13 9.13 11.21	-	-	-	-	-	-	-	-	-	-	-	-	-	55 16.57 72.37 6.61 8.11	-	-	-	-	-	-	-	-	-
Towamencin (township)	503 2.87	1,043	90 8.63 8.63 17.89	-	-	-	-	-	-	-	-	-	-	-	-	-	-	-	-	-	-	-	-	-	-	-
Upper Dublin (township)	779 3.04	1,514	64 4.23 4.23 8.22	-	-	-	-	-	-	-	-	-	-	-	-	-	40 4.82 62.50 2.64 5.13	-	-	-	-	-	-	-	-	-
Upper Gwynedd (township)	274 1.95	1,144	27 2.36 2.36 9.85	-	-	-	-	-	13 4.08 48.15 1.14 4.74	-	-	-	-	-	-	-	-	-	-	-	-	-	-	-	-	-
Upper Merion (township)	784 2.94	2,161	83 3.84 3.84 10.59	-	-	30 3.30 36.14 1.39 3.83	-	-	22 4.95 26.51 1.02 2.81	-	-	-	-	-	-	-	-	-	-	-	-	-	-	-	-	-
Whitpain (township)	585 3.15	1,247	36 2.89 2.89 6.15	-	-	-	-	-	-	-	-	-	-	-	-	-	24 4.10 66.67 1.92 4.10	-	-	-	-	-	-	-	-	-
Northampton County	20,404 7.94	3,449	452 13.11 13.11 2.22	-	-	14 1.21 3.10 0.41 0.07	-	-	88 13.17 19.47 2.55 0.43	-	-	-	-	-	-	-	126 31.19 27.88 3.65 0.62	-	-	-	-	-	-	-	-	114 24.68 25.22 3.31 0.56
Northumberland County	10,818 11.90	373	32 8.58 8.58 0.30	-	-	-	-	-	-	-	-	-	-	-	-	-	-	-	-	-	-	-	-	-	-	-
Philadelphia County	336,177 22.89	62,092	18,514 29.82 29.82 5.51	714	224 31.37 31.37 0.07	2,152 18.52 11.62 3.47 0.64	-	3,188 50.17 17.22 5.13 0.95	5,181 30.89 27.98 8.34 1.54	-	469 12.82 2.53 0.76 0.14	-	-	-	-	416 38.99 2.25 0.67 0.12	1,629 26.39 8.80 2.62 0.48	146 12.03 0.79 0.24 0.04	-	122 19.84 0.66 0.20 0.04	-	-	-	-	-	3,728 34.19 20.14 6.00 1.11

Notes: Please refer to the User's Guide for an explanation of data; data is arranged alphabetically by state, then county, then city within each county; table includes counties with populations greater than 49,999 unless noted and cities with populations greater than 9,999 whose Asian and/or NHPI population rates are greater than the national average; (1) Native Hawaiian and other Pacific Islander; (2) excludes Taiwanese; (3) includes Chamorro; (4) county does not meet population threshold but is shown in order to allow inclusion of city

Place	Total population with income below poverty level	Asian population for whom poverty status is determined	Asians with income below poverty level	NHPI[1] population for whom poverty status is determined	NHPIs[1] with income below poverty level	Asian Indian	Bangladeshi	Cambodian	Chinese[2]	Fijian	Filipino	Guamanian[3]	Hawaiian, Native	Hmong	Indonesian	Japanese	Korean	Laotian	Malaysian	Pakistani	Samoan	Sri Lankan	Taiwanese	Thai	Tongan	Vietnamese
Philadelphia (city)	336,177	62,092	18,514	714	224	2,152	-	3,188	5,181	-	469	-	-	-	-	416	1,629	146	-	122	-	-	-	-	-	3,728
	22.89		29.82		31.37	18.52		50.17	30.89		12.82					38.99	26.39	12.03		19.84						34.19
						11.62		17.22	27.98		2.53					2.25	8.80	0.79		0.66						20.14
			29.82		31.37	3.47		5.13	8.34		0.76					0.67	2.62	0.24		0.20						6.00
			5.51		0.07	0.64		0.95	1.54		0.14					0.12	0.48	0.04		0.04						1.11
Schuylkill County	13,612	466	68	-	-	-	-	-	-	-	-	-	-	-	-	-	-	-	-	-	-	-	-	-	-	-
	9.52		14.59																							
			14.59																							
			0.50																							
Washington County	19,513	607	84	-	-	-	-	-	-	-	-	-	-	-	-	-	-	-	-	-	-	-	-	-	-	-
	9.84		13.84																							
			13.84																							
			0.43																							
Westmoreland County	31,284	1,683	74	-	-	29	-	-	-	-	-	-	-	-	-	-	-	-	-	-	-	-	-	-	-	-
	8.63		4.40			6.49																				
						39.19																				
			4.40			1.72																				
			0.24			0.09																				
York County	25,269	3,118	229	-	-	0	-	-	115	-	-	-	-	-	-	-	47	-	-	-	-	-	-	-	-	16
	6.75		7.34			0.00			17.83								7.52									2.74
						0.00			50.22								20.52									6.99
			7.34			0.00			3.69								1.51									0.51
			0.91			0.00			0.46								0.19									0.06
RHODE ISLAND	120,548	21,944	4,772	396	171	436	-	1,729	725	-	131	-	-	76	-	77	499	495	-	-	-	-	-	-	-	205
	11.94		21.75		43.18	18.83		36.02	17.87		6.48			8.31		10.46	29.34	17.67								21.33
						9.14		36.23	15.19		2.75			1.59		1.61	10.46	10.37								4.30
			21.75		43.18	1.99		7.88	3.30		0.60			0.35		0.35	2.27	2.26								0.93
			3.96		0.14	0.36		1.43	0.60		0.11			0.06		0.06	0.41	0.41								0.17
Bristol County	3,009	347	48	-	-	-	-	-	-	-	-	-	-	-	-	-	-	-	-	-	-	-	-	-	-	-
	6.29		13.83																							
			13.83																							
			1.60																							
Kent County	10,862	2,174	103	-	-	-	-	-	4	-	-	-	-	-	-	-	45	-	-	-	-	-	-	-	-	-
	6.58		4.74						1.08								10.92									
									3.88								43.69									
			4.74						0.18								2.07									
			0.95						0.04								0.41									
Newport County	5,906	874	83	-	-	-	-	-	-	-	24	-	-	-	-	-	-	-	-	-	-	-	-	-	-	-
	7.12		9.50								5.62															
											28.92															
			9.50								2.75															
			1.41								0.41															
Providence County	92,164	16,822	4,327	-	-	332	-	1,709	566	-	67	-	-	76	-	-	412	495	-	-	-	-	-	-	-	205
	15.47		25.72			20.10		37.14	20.54		6.40			9.42			41.45	18.41								27.33
						7.67		39.50	13.08		1.55			1.76			9.52	11.44								4.74
			25.72			1.97		10.16	3.36		0.40			0.45			2.45	2.94								1.22
			4.69			0.36		1.85	0.61		0.07			0.08			0.45	0.54								0.22

Notes: Please refer to the User's Guide for an explanation of data; data is arranged alphabetically by state, then county, then city within each county; table includes counties with populations greater than 49,999 unless noted and cities with populations greater than 9,999 whose Asian and/or NHPI population rates are greater than the national average; (1) Native Hawaiian and other Pacific Islander; (2) excludes Taiwanese; (3) includes Chamorro; (4) county does not meet population threshold but is shown in order to allow inclusion of city

Place	Total population with income below poverty level	Asian population for whom poverty status is determined	Asians with income below poverty level	NHPI[1] population for whom poverty status is determined	NHPIs[1] with income below poverty level	Asian Indian	Bangladeshi	Cambodian	Chinese[2]	Fijian	Filipino	Guamanian[3]	Hawaiian, Native	Hmong	Indonesian	Japanese	Korean	Laotian	Malaysian	Pakistani	Samoan	Sri Lankan	Taiwanese	Thai	Tongan	Vietnamese
Providence (city)	46,688 29.14	9,624	3,270 33.98 33.98 7.00	-	-	201 26.07 6.15 2.09 0.43	-	1,480 42.26 45.26 15.38 3.17	298 27.14 9.11 3.10 0.64	-	17 3.48 0.52 0.18 0.04	-	-	76 11.69 2.32 0.79 0.16	-	-	384 67.37 11.74 3.99 0.82	365 27.53 11.16 3.79 0.78	-	-	-	-	-	-	-	-
Woonsocket (city)	8,205 19.42	1,616	404 25.00 25.00 4.92	-	-	-	-	-	-	-	-	-	-	-	-	-	-	130 14.25 32.18 8.04 1.58	-	-	-	-	-	-	-	-
Washington County	8,607 7.27	1,727	211 12.22 12.22 2.45	-	-	-	-	-	119 21.96 56.40 6.89 1.38	-	-	-	-	-	-	-	-	-	-	-	-	-	-	-	-	-
SOUTH CAROLINA	547,869 14.11	35,265	4,408 12.50 12.50 0.80	1,329	212 15.95 15.95 0.04	1,363 17.04 30.92 3.87 0.25	-	0 0.00 0.00 0.00 0.00	1,045 17.28 23.71 2.96 0.19	-	469 7.07 10.64 1.33 0.09	68 19.60 32.08 5.12 0.01	65 13.98 30.66 4.89 0.01	93 10.95 2.11 0.26 0.02	-	189 8.45 4.29 0.54 0.03	499 14.96 11.32 1.42 0.09	49 3.72 1.11 0.14 0.01	-	-	-	-	-	65 9.53 1.47 0.18 0.01	-	356 9.62 8.08 1.01 0.06
Aiken County	19,455 13.83	920	136 14.78 14.78 0.70	-	-	-	-	-	-	-	-	-	-	-	-	-	-	-	-	-	-	-	-	-	-	-
Anderson County	19,639 12.03	836	114 13.64 13.64 0.58	-	-	-	-	-	-	-	-	-	-	-	-	-	-	-	-	-	-	-	-	-	-	-
Beaufort County	12,194 10.66	853	59 6.92 6.92 0.48	-	-	-	-	-	-	-	-	-	-	-	-	-	-	-	-	-	-	-	-	-	-	-
Berkeley County	16,066 11.76	2,809	267 9.51 9.51 1.66	-	-	-	-	-	-	-	141 7.98 52.81 5.02 0.88	-	-	-	-	-	-	-	-	-	-	-	-	-	-	-
Charleston County	49,330 16.43	3,309	359 10.85 10.85 0.73	-	-	39 6.67 10.86 1.18 0.08	-	-	38 5.66 10.58 1.15 0.08	-	110 12.00 30.64 3.32 0.22	-	-	-	-	-	-	-	-	-	-	-	-	-	-	-
Dorchester County	9,108 9.66	1,254	77 6.14 6.14 0.85	-	-	-	-	-	-	-	30 4.70 38.96 2.39 0.33	-	-	-	-	-	-	-	-	-	-	-	-	-	-	-

Notes: Please refer to the User's Guide for an explanation of data; data is arranged alphabetically by state, then county, then city within each county; table includes counties with populations greater than 49,999 unless noted and cities with populations greater than 9,999 whose Asian and/or NHPI population rates are greater than the national average; (1) Native Hawaiian and other Pacific Islander; (2) excludes Taiwanese; (3) includes Chamorro; (4) county does not meet population threshold but is shown in order to allow inclusion of city

Place	Total population with income below poverty level	Asian population for whom poverty status is determined	Asians with income below poverty level	NHPI[1] population for whom poverty status is determined	NHPIs[1] with income below poverty level	Asian Indian	Bangladeshi	Cambodian	Chinese[2]	Fijian	Filipino	Guamanian[3]	Hawaiian, Native	Hmong	Indonesian	Japanese	Korean	Laotian	Malaysian	Pakistani	Samoan	Sri Lankan	Taiwanese	Thai	Tongan	Vietnamese
Florence County	20,063	1,004	130	-	-	-	-	-	-	-	-	-	-	-	-	-	-	-	-	-	-	-	-	-	-	-
	16.40		12.95																							
			12.95																							
			0.65																							
Greenville County	38,825	4,808	491	-	-	254	-	-	44	-	31	-	-	-	-	-	-	-	-	-	-	-	-	-	-	72
	10.52		10.21			17.90			6.31		5.97															6.32
						51.73			8.96		6.31															14.66
			10.21			5.28			0.92		0.64															1.50
			1.26			0.65			0.11		0.08															0.19
Greenwood County	9,080	412	6	-	-	-	-	-	-	-	-	-	-	-	-	-	-	-	-	-	-	-	-	-	-	-
	14.16		1.46																							
			1.46																							
			0.07																							
Horry County	23,356	1,548	99	-	-	-	-	-	-	-	-	-	-	-	-	-	-	-	-	-	-	-	-	-	-	-
	12.04		6.40																							
			6.40																							
			0.42																							
Lexington County	19,331	1,931	425	-	-	104	-	-	205	-	-	-	-	-	-	-	-	-	-	-	-	-	-	-	-	-
	9.05		22.01			17.28			37.14																	
						24.47			48.24																	
			22.01			5.39			10.62																	
			2.20			0.54			1.06																	
Oconee County	7,075	264	8	-	-	-	-	-	-	-	-	-	-	-	-	-	-	-	-	-	-	-	-	-	-	-
	10.77		3.03																							
			3.03																							
			0.11																							
Pickens County	14,205	1,216	479	-	-	288	-	-	98	-	-	-	-	-	-	-	-	-	-	-	-	-	-	-	-	-
	13.72		39.39			59.14			27.53																	
						60.13			20.46																	
			39.39			23.68			8.06																	
			3.37			2.03			0.69																	
Clemson (city)	3,905	598	397	-	-	-	-	-	-	-	-	-	-	-	-	-	-	-	-	-	-	-	-	-	-	-
	33.12		66.39																							
			66.39																							
			10.17																							
Richland County	40,386	5,197	980	-	-	286	-	-	221	-	67	-	-	-	-	-	288	-	-	-	-	-	-	-	-	36
	13.70		18.86			19.77			20.93		16.11						24.68									7.35
						29.18			22.55		6.84						29.39									3.67
			18.86			5.50			4.25		1.29						5.54									0.69
			2.43			0.71			0.55		0.17						0.71									0.09
Spartanburg County	30,394	4,116	210	-	-	33	-	-	-	-	-	-	-	0	-	-	-	19	-	-	-	-	-	-	-	-
	12.28		5.10			4.38								0.00				2.81								
						15.71								0.00				9.05								
			5.10			0.80								0.00				0.46								
			0.69			0.11								0.00				0.06								

Notes: Please refer to the User's Guide for an explanation of data; data is arranged alphabetically by state, then county, then city within each county; table includes counties with populations greater than 49,999 unless noted and cities with populations greater than 9,999 whose Asian and/or NHPI population rates are greater than the national average; (1) Native Hawaiian and other Pacific Islander; (2) excludes Taiwanese; (3) includes Chamorro; (4) county does not meet population threshold but is shown in order to allow inclusion of city

Place	Total population with income below poverty level	Asian population for whom poverty status is determined	Asians with income below poverty level	NHPI[1] population for whom poverty status is determined	NHPIs[1] with income below poverty level	Asian Indian	Bangladeshi	Cambodian	Chinese[2]	Fijian	Filipino	Guamanian[3]	Hawaiian, Native	Hmong	Indonesian	Japanese	Korean	Laotian	Malaysian	Pakistani	Samoan	Sri Lankan	Taiwanese	Thai	Tongan	Vietnamese
Sumter County	16,451 16.25	911	19 2.09 2.09 0.12	-	-	-	-	-	-	-	-	-	-	-	-	-	-	-	-	-	-	-	-	-	-	-
York County	16,082 10.04	1,306	98 7.50 7.50 0.61	-	-	-	-	-	-	-	-	-	-	-	-	-	-	-	-	-	-	-	-	-	-	49 11.01 50.00 3.75 0.30
SOUTH DAKOTA	95,900 13.18	4,420	530 11.99 11.99 0.55	-	-	94 16.55 17.74 2.13 0.10	-	-	130 21.42 24.53 2.94 0.14	-	38 5.56 7.17 0.86 0.04	-	-	-	-	73 21.28 13.77 1.65 0.08	22 3.17 4.15 0.50 0.02	25 11.63 4.72 0.57 0.03	-	-	-	-	-	-	-	44 6.48 8.30 1.00 0.05
Minnehaha County	10,790 7.54	1,551	97 6.25 6.25 0.90	-	-	-	-	-	-	-	-	-	-	-	-	-	-	-	-	-	-	-	-	-	-	25 4.99 25.77 1.61 0.23
Pennington County	9,967 11.53	821	110 13.40 13.40 1.10	-	-	-	-	-	-	-	-	-	-	-	-	-	-	-	-	-	-	-	-	-	-	-
TENNESSEE	746,789 13.48	52,508	6,615 12.60 12.60 0.89	1,964	293 14.92 14.92 0.04	1,177 10.19 17.79 2.24 0.16	-	125 10.81 1.89 0.24 0.02	1,185 14.82 17.91 2.26 0.16	-	296 5.72 4.47 0.56 0.04	74 13.36 25.26 3.77 0.01	98 20.00 33.45 4.99 0.01	-	-	549 14.77 8.30 1.05 0.07	1,229 18.32 18.58 2.34 0.16	416 10.38 6.29 0.79 0.06	-	187 25.07 2.83 0.36 0.03	72 14.78 24.57 3.67 0.01	-	82 16.63 1.24 0.16 0.01	161 16.81 2.43 0.31 0.02	-	777 11.16 11.75 1.48 0.10
Anderson County	9,255 13.14	513	57 11.11 11.11 0.62	-	-	-	-	-	-	-	-	-	-	-	-	-	-	-	-	-	-	-	-	-	-	-
Blount County	10,084 9.73	626	45 7.19 7.19 0.45	-	-	-	-	-	-	-	-	-	-	-	-	-	-	-	-	-	-	-	-	-	-	-
Bradley County	10,463 12.22	449	3 0.67 0.67 0.03	-	-	-	-	-	-	-	-	-	-	-	-	-	-	-	-	-	-	-	-	-	-	-
Davidson County	70,960 12.99	11,163	1,637 14.66 14.66 2.31	286	94 32.87 32.87 0.13	236 10.05 14.42 2.11 0.33	-	-	239 17.01 14.60 2.14 0.34	-	26 3.29 1.59 0.23 0.04	-	-	-	-	130 15.63 7.94 1.16 0.18	221 17.69 13.50 1.98 0.31	260 19.83 15.88 2.33 0.37	-	-	-	-	-	-	-	95 5.78 5.80 0.85 0.13

Notes: Please refer to the User's Guide for an explanation of data; data is arranged alphabetically by state, then county, then city within each county; table includes counties with populations greater than 49,999 unless noted and cities with populations greater than 9,999 whose Asian and/or NHPI population rates are greater than the national average; (1) Native Hawaiian and other Pacific Islander; (2) excludes Taiwanese; (3) includes Chamorro; (4) county does not meet population threshold but is shown in order to allow inclusion of city

Place	Total population with income below poverty level	Asian population for whom poverty status is determined	Asians with income below poverty level	NHPI[1] population for whom poverty status is determined	NHPIs[1] with income below poverty level	Asian Indian	Bangladeshi	Cambodian	Chinese[2]	Fijian	Filipino	Guamanian[3]	Hawaiian, Native	Hmong	Indonesian	Japanese	Korean	Laotian	Malaysian	Pakistani	Samoan	Sri Lankan	Taiwanese	Thai	Tongan	Vietnamese
Hamilton County	36,308 12.08	3,738	327 8.75 8.75 0.90	-	-	58 5.17 17.74 1.55 0.16	-	-	-	-	24 5.94 7.34 0.64 0.07	-	-	-	-	-	116 23.63 35.47 3.10 0.32	-	-	-	-	-	-	-	-	42 9.86 12.84 1.12 0.12
Knox County	46,572 12.59	4,391	681 15.51 15.51 1.46	-	-	147 11.50 21.59 3.35 0.32	-	-	75 8.26 11.01 1.71 0.16	-	-	-	-	-	-	-	211 41.87 30.98 4.81 0.45	-	-	-	-	-	-	-	-	34 7.19 4.99 0.77 0.07
Madison County	12,349 13.95	544	5 0.92 0.92 0.04	-	-	-	-	-	-	-	-	-	-	-	-	-	-	-	-	-	-	-	-	-	-	-
Montgomery County	12,982 9.97	2,344	258 11.01 11.01 1.99	-	-	-	-	-	-	-	-	-	-	-	-	-	47 4.29 18.22 2.01 0.36	-	-	-	-	-	-	-	-	-
Putnam County	9,828 16.44	519	174 33.53 33.53 1.77	-	-	-	-	-	-	-	-	-	-	-	-	-	-	-	-	-	-	-	-	-	-	-
Rutherford County	15,808 8.99	3,230	155 4.80 4.80 0.98	-	-	-	-	-	-	-	-	-	-	-	-	-	-	73 4.66 47.10 2.26 0.46	-	-	-	-	-	-	-	-
Shelby County	140,398 15.98	14,776	2,069 14.00 14.00 1.47	480	64 13.33 13.33 0.05	511 14.35 24.70 3.46 0.36	-	69 13.37 3.33 0.47 0.05	460 16.75 22.23 3.11 0.33	-	53 3.93 2.56 0.36 0.04	-	-	-	-	80 15.66 3.87 0.54 0.06	229 18.76 11.07 1.55 0.16	-	-	-	-	-	-	-	-	505 15.19 24.41 3.42 0.36
Germantown (city)	800 2.15	1,380	143 10.36 10.36 17.88	-	-	117 22.03 81.82 8.48 14.63	-	-	0 0.00 0.00 0.00 0.00	-	-	-	-	-	-	-	-	-	-	-	-	-	-	-	-	-
Sullivan County	19,453 12.93	571	57 9.98 9.98 0.29	-	-	-	-	-	-	-	-	-	-	-	-	-	-	-	-	-	-	-	-	-	-	-
Sumner County	10,463 8.12	877	100 11.40 11.40 0.96	-	-	-	-	-	-	-	-	-	-	-	-	-	-	-	-	-	-	-	-	-	-	-

Notes: Please refer to the User's Guide for an explanation of data; data is arranged alphabetically by state, then county, then city within each county; table includes counties with populations greater than 49,999 unless noted and cities with populations greater than 9,999 whose Asian and/or NHPI population rates are greater than the national average; (1) Native Hawaiian and other Pacific Islander; (2) excludes Taiwanese; (3) includes Chamorro; (4) county does not meet population threshold but is shown in order to allow inclusion of city

Place	Total population with income below poverty level	Asian population for whom poverty status is determined	Asians with income below poverty level	NHPI[1] population for whom poverty status is determined	NHPIs[1] with income below poverty level	Asian Indian	Bangladeshi	Cambodian	Chinese[2]	Fijian	Filipino	Guamanian[3]	Hawaiian, Native	Hmong	Indonesian	Japanese	Korean	Laotian	Malaysian	Pakistani	Samoan	Sri Lankan	Taiwanese	Thai	Tongan	Vietnamese
Washington County	14,388 13.95	635	38 5.98 5.98 0.26	-	-	-	-	-	-	-	-	-	-	-	-	-	-	-	-	-	-	-	-	-	-	-
Weakley County[4]	5,174 16.04	383	155 40.47 40.47 3.00	-	-	-	-	-	-	-	-	-	-	-	-	-	-	-	-	-	-	-	-	-	-	-
Martin (city)	2,258 27.08	346	155 44.80 44.80 6.86	-	-	-	-	-	-	-	-	-	-	-	-	-	-	-	-	-	-	-	-	-	-	-
Williamson County	5,933 4.72	1,497	102 6.81 6.81 1.72	-	-	-	-	-	-	-	-	-	-	-	-	-	-	-	-	-	-	-	-	-	-	-
Wilson County	5,847 6.66	303	7 2.31 2.31 0.12	-	-	-	-	-	-	-	-	-	-	-	-	-	-	-	-	-	-	-	-	-	-	-
TEXAS	3,117,609 15.37	548,014	65,048 11.87 11.87 2.09	11,485	1,931 16.81 16.81 0.06	12,846 10.21 19.75 2.34 0.41	367 14.31 0.56 0.07 0.01	793 10.62 1.22 0.14 0.03	11,844 12.23 18.21 2.16 0.38	-	3,720 6.47 5.72 0.68 0.12	460 14.71 23.82 4.01 0.01	771 24.61 39.93 6.71 0.02	-	402 23.00 0.62 0.07 0.01	1,654 10.56 2.54 0.30 0.05	7,117 16.30 10.94 1.30 0.23	1,018 10.43 1.56 0.19 0.03	91 13.58 0.14 0.02 <0.01	3,246 17.28 4.99 0.59 0.10	260 14.08 13.46 2.26 0.01	123 12.85 0.19 0.02 <0.01	1,026 13.50 1.58 0.19 0.03	982 14.20 1.51 0.18 0.03	21 4.30 1.09 0.18 <0.01	16,984 12.77 26.11 3.10 0.54
Anderson County	6,654 16.47	353	3 0.85 0.85 0.05	-	-	-	-	-	-	-	-	-	-	-	-	-	-	-	-	-	-	-	-	-	-	-
Angelina County	12,241 15.78	539	92 17.07 17.07 0.75	-	-	-	-	-	-	-	-	-	-	-	-	-	-	-	-	-	-	-	-	-	-	-
Bell County	27,607 12.08	5,970	624 10.45 10.45 2.26	1,257	78 6.21 6.21 0.28	30 5.38 4.81 0.50 0.11	-	-	-	-	154 9.73 24.68 2.58 0.56	37 6.21 47.44 2.94 0.13	-	-	-	46 12.04 7.37 0.77 0.17	208 8.87 33.33 3.48 0.75	-	-	-	-	-	-	-	-	-
Killeen (city)	11,139 12.91	3,794	481 12.68 12.68 4.32	1,046	48 4.59 4.59 0.43	-	-	-	-	-	149 13.55 30.98 3.93 1.34	17 3.40 35.42 1.63 0.15	-	-	-	-	147 9.40 30.56 3.87 1.32	-	-	-	-	-	-	-	-	-

Notes: Please refer to the User's Guide for an explanation of data; data is arranged alphabetically by state, then county, then city within each county; table includes counties with populations greater than 49,999 unless noted and cities with populations greater than 9,999 whose Asian and/or NHPI population rates are greater than the national average; (1) Native Hawaiian and other Pacific Islander; (2) excludes Taiwanese; (3) includes Chamorro; (4) county does not meet population threshold but is shown in order to allow inclusion of city

Place	Total population with income below poverty level	Asian population for whom poverty status is determined	Asians with income below poverty level	NHPI[1] population for whom poverty status is determined	NHPIs[1] with income below poverty level	Asian Indian	Bangladeshi	Cambodian	Chinese[2]	Fijian	Filipino	Guamanian[3]	Hawaiian, Native	Hmong	Indonesian	Japanese	Korean	Laotian	Malaysian	Pakistani	Samoan	Sri Lankan	Taiwanese	Thai	Tongan	Vietnamese
Bexar County	215,736 15.87	22,026	2,153 9.77 9.77 1.00	1,009	188 18.63 18.63 0.09	406 11.06 18.86 1.84 0.19	-	-	481 13.24 22.34 2.18 0.22	-	438 8.73 20.34 1.99 0.20	-	77 21.10 40.96 7.63 0.04	-	-	142 8.31 6.60 0.64 0.07	169 6.78 7.85 0.77 0.08	7 1.85 0.33 0.03 <0.01	-	-	-	-	-	9 1.15 0.42 0.04 <0.01	-	318 11.24 14.77 1.44 0.15
Bowie County	14,628 17.67	443	63 14.22 14.22 0.43	-	-	-	-	-	-	-	-	-	-	-	-	-	-	-	-	-	-	-	-	-	-	-
Brazoria County	23,465 10.18	4,680	387 8.27 8.27 1.65	-	-	7 0.78 1.81 0.15 0.03	-	89 24.45 23.00 1.90 0.38	0 0.00 0.00 0.00 0.00	-	37 5.48 9.56 0.79 0.16	-	-	-	-	-	-	-	-	-	-	-	-	-	-	120 9.13 31.01 2.56 0.51
Brazos County	37,417 26.90	5,825	2,055 35.28 35.28 5.49	-	-	588 36.59 28.61 10.09 1.57	-	-	382 24.46 18.59 6.56 1.02	-	-	-	-	-	-	-	437 48.99 21.27 7.50 1.17	-	-	-	-	-	-	-	-	249 56.21 12.12 4.27 0.67
College Station (city)	21,379 37.39	4,747	1,643 34.61 34.61 7.69	-	-	359 31.41 21.85 7.56 1.68	-	-	327 23.97 19.90 6.89 1.53	-	-	-	-	-	-	-	388 50.92 23.62 8.17 1.81	-	-	-	-	-	-	-	-	-
Calhoun County[4]	3,340 16.38	680	109 16.03 16.03 3.26	-	-	-	-	-	-	-	-	-	-	-	-	-	-	-	-	-	-	-	-	-	-	49 30.25 44.95 7.21 1.47
Port Lavaca (city)	2,371 20.13	493	50 10.14 10.14 2.11	-	-	-	-	-	-	-	-	-	-	-	-	-	-	-	-	-	-	-	-	-	-	-
Cameron County	109,288 33.05	1,485	139 9.36 9.36 0.13	-	-	-	-	-	-	-	46 7.88 33.09 3.10 0.04	-	-	-	-	-	-	-	-	-	-	-	-	-	-	-
Collin County	23,784 4.87	33,550	1,583 4.72 4.72 6.66	-	-	361 4.13 22.80 1.08 1.52	-	-	616 4.92 38.91 1.84 2.59	-	23 1.59 1.45 0.07 0.10	-	-	-	-	24 2.63 1.52 0.07 0.10	162 5.72 10.23 0.48 0.68	-	-	78 8.18 4.93 0.23 0.33	-	-	3 0.35 0.19 0.01 0.01	19 4.19 1.20 0.06 0.08	-	123 3.52 7.77 0.37 0.52
Allen (city)	1,314 3.03	1,639	114 6.96 6.96 8.68	-	-	4 0.89 3.51 0.24 0.30	-	-	-	-	-	-	-	-	-	-	-	-	-	-	-	-	-	-	-	82 20.71 71.93 5.00 6.24

Notes: Please refer to the User's Guide for an explanation of data; data is arranged alphabetically by state, then county, then city within each county; table includes counties with populations greater than 49,999 unless noted and cities with populations greater than 9,999 whose Asian and/or NHPI population rates are greater than the national average; (1) Native Hawaiian and other Pacific Islander; (2) excludes Taiwanese; (3) includes Chamorro; (4) county does not meet population threshold but is shown in order to allow inclusion of city

Place	Total population with income below poverty level	Asian population for whom poverty status is determined	Asians with income below poverty level	NHPI[1] population for whom poverty status is determined	NHPIs[1] with income below poverty level	Asian Indian	Bangladeshi	Cambodian	Chinese[2]	Fijian	Filipino	Guamanian[3]	Hawaiian, Native	Hmong	Indonesian	Japanese	Korean	Laotian	Malaysian	Pakistani	Samoan	Sri Lankan	Taiwanese	Thai	Tongan	Vietnamese
Plano (city)	9,500	22,425	961	-	-	188	-	-	458	-	7	-	-	-	-	15	80	-	-	0	-	-	0	-	-	30
	4.30		4.29			3.31			4.93		0.90					3.01	3.75			0.00			0.00			1.66
						19.56			47.66		0.73					1.56	8.32			0.00			0.00			3.12
			4.29			0.84			2.04		0.03					0.07	0.36			0.00			0.00			0.13
			10.12			1.98			4.82		0.07					0.16	0.84			0.00			0.00			0.32
Comal County	6,585	443	46	-	-	-	-	-	-	-	-	-	-	-	-	-	-	-	-	-	-	-	-	-	-	-
	8.57		10.38																							
			10.38																							
			0.70																							
Coryell County	5,481	1,198	155	356	36	-	-	-	-	-	-	-	-	-	-	-	107	-	-	-	-	-	-	-	-	-
	9.47		12.94		10.11												22.77									
																	69.03									
			12.94		10.11												8.93									
			2.83		0.66												1.95									
Dallas County	293,267	86,957	9,417	959	319	2,019	55	263	1,225	-	364	-	-	-	-	165	1,482	241	-	536	-	-	55	192	-	2,274
	13.43		10.83		33.26	8.54	8.17	11.34	10.55		6.10					7.48	15.94	10.39		14.52			6.91	17.38		11.49
						21.44	0.58	2.79	13.01		3.87					1.75	15.74	2.56		5.69			0.58	2.04		24.15
			10.83		33.26	2.32	0.06	0.30	1.41		0.42					0.19	1.70	0.28		0.62			0.06	0.22		2.62
			3.21		0.11	0.69	0.02	0.09	0.42		0.12					0.06	0.51	0.08		0.18			0.02	0.07		0.78
Addison (town)	1,059	1,104	116	-	-	63	-	-	-	-	-	-	-	-	-	-	-	-	-	-	-	-	-	-	-	-
	7.68		10.51			10.40																				
						54.31																				
			10.51			5.71																				
			10.95			5.95																				
Coppell (city)	680	3,444	170	-	-	46	-	-	28	-	-	-	-	-	-	-	29	-	-	-	-	-	-	-	-	-
	1.89		4.94			4.04			3.61								4.26									
						27.06			16.47								17.06									
			4.94			1.34			0.81								0.84									
			25.00			6.76			4.12								4.26									
Farmers Branch (city)	1,783	1,051	46	-	-	-	-	-	-	-	-	-	-	-	-	-	-	-	-	-	-	-	-	-	-	-
	6.34		4.38																							
			4.38																							
			2.58																							
Garland (city)	19,028	15,597	1,770	-	-	235	-	-	193	-	151	-	-	-	-	-	214	-	-	206	-	-	-	-	-	652
	8.87		11.35			7.58			11.59		13.57						18.80			24.79						10.41
						13.28			10.90		8.53						12.09			11.64						36.84
			11.35			1.51			1.24		0.97						1.37			1.32						4.18
			9.30			1.24			1.01		0.79						1.12			1.08						3.43
Grand Prairie (city)	14,018	5,290	365	-	-	29	-	-	-	-	38	-	-	-	-	-	-	42	-	-	-	-	-	-	-	158
	11.11		6.90			3.98					5.40							10.74								6.63
						7.95					10.41							11.51								43.29
			6.90			0.55					0.72							0.79								2.99
			2.60			0.21					0.27							0.30								1.13
Irving (city)	20,231	15,606	1,332	-	-	411	-	-	87	-	64	-	-	-	-	20	330	26	-	22	-	-	-	-	-	84
	10.65		8.54			6.75			5.62		8.38					2.95	13.31	5.43		5.13						5.37
						30.86			6.53		4.80					1.50	24.77	1.95		1.65						6.31
			8.54			2.63			0.56		0.41					0.13	2.11	0.17		0.14						0.54
			6.58			2.03			0.43		0.32					0.10	1.63	0.13		0.11						0.42

Notes: Please refer to the User's Guide for an explanation of data; data is arranged alphabetically by state, then county, then city within each county; table includes counties with populations greater than 49,999 unless noted and cities with populations greater than 9,999 whose Asian and/or NHPI population rates are greater than the national average; (1) Native Hawaiian and other Pacific Islander; (2) excludes Taiwanese; (3) includes Chamorro; (4) county does not meet population threshold but is shown in order to allow inclusion of city

Place	Total population with income below poverty level	Asian population for whom poverty status is determined	Asians with income below poverty level	NHPI[1] population for whom poverty status is determined	NHPIs[1] with income below poverty level	Asian Indian	Bangladeshi	Cambodian	Chinese[2]	Fijian	Filipino	Guamanian[3]	Hawaiian, Native	Hmong	Indonesian	Japanese	Korean	Laotian	Malaysian	Pakistani	Samoan	Sri Lankan	Taiwanese	Thai	Tongan	Vietnamese
Mesquite (city)	8,376 6.78	4,557	322 7.07 7.07 3.84	-	-	197 8.59 61.18 4.32 2.35	-	-	-	-	0 0.00 0.00 0.00 0.00	-	-	-	-	-	-	-	-	-	-	-	-	-	-	-
Richardson (city)	5,688 6.26	10,165	1,022 10.05 10.05 17.97	-	-	384 15.94 37.57 3.78 6.75	-	-	367 12.08 35.91 3.61 6.45	-	23 6.13 2.25 0.23 0.40	-	-	-	-	-	49 4.75 4.79 0.48 0.86	-	-	58 13.71 5.68 0.57 1.02	-	-	-	-	-	87 5.00 8.51 0.86 1.53
Rowlett (city)	1,316 3.00	1,671	0 <0.01 <0.01 <0.01	-	-	0 <0.01 *** ** <0.01 <0.01	-	-	-	-	-	-	-	-	-	-	-	-	-	-	-	-	-	-	-	-
Denton County	28,039 6.62	16,660	1,791 10.75 10.75 6.39	-	-	320 5.42 17.87 1.92 1.14	-	4 0.55 0.22 0.02 0.01	327 16.82 18.26 1.96 1.17	-	56 6.91 3.13 0.34 0.20	-	-	-	-	154 34.07 8.60 0.92 0.55	397 18.17 22.17 2.38 1.42	-	-	28 3.33 1.56 0.17 0.10	-	-	-	-	-	290 11.39 16.19 1.74 1.03
Carrollton (city)	6,057 5.58	11,415	837 7.33 7.33 13.82	-	-	221 5.04 26.40 1.94 3.65	-	29 3.55 3.46 0.25 0.48	82 12.13 9.80 0.72 1.35	-	-	-	-	-	-	-	156 14.81 18.64 1.37 2.58	-	-	76 6.52 9.08 0.67 1.25	-	-	-	-	-	210 8.74 25.09 1.84 3.47
Lewisville (city)	4,629 6.00	3,043	115 3.78 3.78 2.48	-	-	6 0.49 5.22 0.20 0.13	-	-	-	-	-	-	-	-	-	-	-	-	-	-	-	-	-	-	-	27 5.97 23.48 0.89 0.58
Ector County	22,310 18.71	880	37 4.20 4.20 0.17	-	-	-	-	-	-	-	-	-	-	-	-	-	-	-	-	-	-	-	-	-	-	-
El Paso County	158,722 23.81	6,825	836 12.25 12.25 0.53	520	78 15.00 15.00 0.05	219 21.97 26.20 3.21 0.14	-	-	85 10.61 10.17 1.25 0.05	-	119 6.80 14.23 1.74 0.07	-	-	-	-	84 10.54 10.05 1.23 0.05	166 9.82 19.86 2.43 0.10	-	-	-	-	-	-	-	-	-
Ellis County	9,401 8.60	441	8 1.81 1.81 0.09	-	-	-	-	-	-	-	-	-	-	-	-	-	-	-	-	-	-	-	-	-	-	-
Fort Bend County	24,953 7.15	38,742	2,128 5.49 5.49 8.53	-	-	580 4.54 27.26 1.50 2.32	-	-	677 6.87 31.81 1.75 2.71	-	144 3.28 6.77 0.37 0.58	-	-	-	-	-	90 7.85 4.23 0.23 0.36	-	-	240 9.83 11.28 0.62 0.96	-	-	169 13.90 7.94 0.44 0.68	-	-	183 3.52 8.60 0.47 0.73

Notes: Please refer to the User's Guide for an explanation of data; data is arranged alphabetically by state, then county, then city within each county; table includes counties with populations greater than 49,999 unless noted and cities with populations greater than 9,999 whose Asian and/or NHPI population rates are greater than the national average; (1) Native Hawaiian and other Pacific Islander; (2) excludes Taiwanese; (3) includes Chamorro; (4) county does not meet population threshold but is shown in order to allow inclusion of city

Place	Total population with income below poverty level	Asian population for whom poverty status is determined	Asians with income below poverty level	NHPI[1] population for whom poverty status is determined	NHPIs[1] with income below poverty level	Asian Indian	Bangladeshi	Cambodian	Chinese[2]	Fijian	Filipino	Guamanian[3]	Hawaiian, Native	Hmong	Indonesian	Japanese	Korean	Laotian	Malaysian	Pakistani	Samoan	Sri Lankan	Taiwanese	Thai	Tongan	Vietnamese
Cinco Ranch (cdp)	144 1.28	690	30 4.35 4.35 20.83	-	-	-	-	-	-	-	-	-	-	-	-	-	-	-	-	-	-	-	-	-	-	-
Mission Bend (cdp)	1,771 5.75	5,155	453 8.79 8.79 25.58	-	-	95 7.25 20.97 1.84 5.36	-	-	65 9.46 14.35 1.26 3.67	-	31 3.37 6.84 0.60 1.75	-	-	-	-	-	-	-	-	77 16.04 17.00 1.49 4.35	-	-	-	-	-	109 8.63 24.06 2.11 6.15
Missouri City (city)	1,742 3.32	5,746	239 4.16 4.16 13.72	-	-	46 2.39 19.25 0.80 2.64	-	-	98 7.08 41.00 1.71 5.63	-	9 0.87 3.77 0.16 0.52	-	-	-	-	-	-	-	-	-	-	-	-	-	-	58 9.91 24.27 1.01 3.33
New Territory (cdp)	259 2.01	3,236	0 <0.01 <0.01 <0.01	-	-	0 <0.01 *** ** <0.01 <0.01	-	-	0 <0.01 *** ** <0.01 <0.01	-	-	-	-	-	-	-	-	-	-	-	-	-	-	-	-	-
Stafford (city)	1,026 6.58	3,312	332 10.02 10.02 32.36	-	-	186 14.53 56.02 5.62 18.13	-	-	63 11.80 18.98 1.90 6.14	-	40 7.72 12.05 1.21 3.90	-	-	-	-	-	-	-	-	-	-	-	-	-	-	31 5.12 9.34 0.94 3.02
Sugar Land (city)	2,372 3.75	14,417	778 5.40 5.40 32.80	-	-	169 3.90 21.72 1.17 7.12	-	-	306 5.79 39.33 2.12 12.90	-	40 4.02 5.14 0.28 1.69	-	-	-	-	-	32 7.27 4.11 0.22 1.35	-	-	60 9.71 7.71 0.42 2.53	-	-	157 16.76 20.18 1.09 6.62	-	-	14 1.10 1.80 0.10 0.59
Galveston County	32,510 13.22	5,194	805 15.50 15.50 2.48	-	-	121 12.79 15.03 2.33 0.37	-	-	144 16.67 17.89 2.77 0.44	-	113 14.04 14.04 2.18 0.35	-	-	-	-	-	-	-	-	-	-	-	-	-	-	254 15.03 31.55 4.89 0.78
Grayson County	12,109 11.27	603	53 8.79 8.79 0.44	-	-	-	-	-	-	-	-	-	-	-	-	-	-	-	-	-	-	-	-	-	-	-
Gregg County	16,329 15.09	617	87 14.10 14.10 0.53	-	-	-	-	-	-	-	-	-	-	-	-	-	-	-	-	-	-	-	-	-	-	-
Guadalupe County	8,568 9.82	885	78 8.81 8.81 0.91	-	-	-	-	-	-	-	-	-	-	-	-	-	-	-	-	-	-	-	-	-	-	-

Notes: Please refer to the User's Guide for an explanation of data; data is arranged alphabetically by state, then county, then city within each county; table includes counties with populations greater than 49,999 unless noted and cities with populations greater than 9,999 whose Asian and/or NHPI population rates are greater than the national average; (1) Native Hawaiian and other Pacific Islander; (2) excludes Taiwanese; (3) includes Chamorro; (4) county does not meet population threshold but is shown in order to allow inclusion of city

Place	Total population with income below poverty level	Asian population for whom poverty status is determined	Asians with income below poverty level	NHPI[1] population for whom poverty status is determined	NHPIs[1] with income below poverty level	Asian Indian	Bangladeshi	Cambodian	Chinese[2]	Fijian	Filipino	Guamanian[3]	Hawaiian, Native	Hmong	Indonesian	Japanese	Korean	Laotian	Malaysian	Pakistani	Samoan	Sri Lankan	Taiwanese	Thai	Tongan	Vietnamese
Harris County	503,234	170,910	21,880	1,492	161	4,049	86	253	4,381	-	1,078	84	-	-	160	355	1,168	123	-	1,624	-	-	321	154	-	7,361
	14.97		12.80		10.79	11.28	12.50	12.57	14.04		6.90	13.35			23.19	9.82	14.52	10.41		22.16			14.70	11.64		13.35
						18.51	0.39	1.16	20.02		4.93	52.17			0.73	1.62	5.34	0.56		7.42			1.47	0.70		33.64
			12.80		10.79	2.37	0.05	0.15	2.56		0.63	5.63			0.09	0.21	0.68	0.07		0.95			0.19	0.09		4.31
			4.35		0.03	0.80	0.02	0.05	0.87		0.21	0.02			0.03	0.07	0.23	0.02		0.32			0.06	0.03		1.46
Bellaire (city)	407	1,052	73	-	-	-	-	-	49	-	-	-	-	-	-	-	-	-	-	-	-	-	-	-	-	-
	2.64		6.94						10.79																	
									67.12																	
			6.94						4.66																	
			17.94						12.04																	
Houston (city)	369,045	101,617	15,952	868	151	2,643	-	115	3,589	-	503	84	-	-	141	278	1,052	-	-	1,085	-	-	249	118	-	5,438
	19.17		15.70		17.40	12.97		15.91	16.57		6.62	19.00			27.27	11.76	20.51			21.71			17.14	13.55		17.21
						16.57		0.72	22.50		3.15	55.63			0.88	1.74	6.59			6.80			1.56	0.74		34.09
			15.70		17.40	2.60		0.11	3.53		0.49	9.68			0.14	0.27	1.04			1.07			0.25	0.12		5.35
			4.32		0.04	0.72		0.03	0.97		0.14	0.02			0.04	0.08	0.29			0.29			0.07	0.03		1.47
West University Place (city)	239	745	5	-	-	-	-	-	-	-	-	-	-	-	-	-	-	-	-	-	-	-	-	-	-	-
	1.68		0.67																							
			0.67																							
			2.09																							
Hays County	13,039	754	122	-	-	-	-	-	-	-	-	-	-	-	-	-	-	-	-	-	-	-	-	-	-	-
	14.26		16.18																							
			16.18																							
			0.94																							
Hidalgo County	201,865	3,148	176	-	-	19	-	-	-	-	19	-	-	-	-	-	-	-	-	-	-	-	-	-	-	-
	35.87		5.59			3.02					1.26															
						10.80					10.80															
			5.59			0.60					0.60															
			0.09			0.01					0.01															
Hunt County	9,518	441	83	-	-	-	-	-	-	-	-	-	-	-	-	-	-	-	-	-	-	-	-	-	-	-
	12.78		18.82																							
			18.82																							
			0.87																							
Jefferson County	41,142	6,889	1,627	-	-	99	-	-	118	-	17	-	-	-	-	-	-	-	-	-	-	-	-	-	-	1,310
	17.37		23.62			10.99			24.28		1.80															32.55
						6.08			7.25		1.04															80.52
			23.62			1.44			1.71		0.25															19.02
			3.95			0.24			0.29		0.04															3.18
Port Arthur (city)	14,350	3,388	1,161	-	-	-	-	-	-	-	-	-	-	-	-	-	-	-	-	-	-	-	-	-	-	1,072
	25.16		34.27																							37.89
																										92.33
			34.27																							31.64
			8.09																							7.47
Johnson County	10,921	635	55	-	-	-	-	-	-	-	-	-	-	-	-	-	-	-	-	-	-	-	-	-	-	-
	8.80		8.66																							
			8.66																							
			0.50																							

Notes: Please refer to the User's Guide for an explanation of data; data is arranged alphabetically by state, then county, then city within each county; table includes counties with populations greater than 49,999 unless noted and cities with populations greater than 9,999 whose Asian and/or NHPI population rates are greater than the national average; (1) Native Hawaiian and other Pacific Islander; (2) excludes Taiwanese; (3) includes Chamorro; (4) county does not meet population threshold but is shown in order to allow inclusion of city

Place	Total population with income below poverty level	Asian population for whom poverty status is determined	Asians with income below poverty level	NHPI[1] population for whom poverty status is determined	NHPIs[1] with income below poverty level	Asian Indian	Bangladeshi	Cambodian	Chinese[2]	Fijian	Filipino	Guamanian[3]	Hawaiian, Native	Hmong	Indonesian	Japanese	Korean	Laotian	Malaysian	Pakistani	Samoan	Sri Lankan	Taiwanese	Thai	Tongan	Vietnamese
Kaufman County	7,313	487	6	-	-	-	-	-	-	-	-	-	-	-	-	-	-	-	-	-	-	-	-	-	-	-
	10.50		1.23																							
			1.23																							
			0.08																							
Lubbock County	41,542	2,852	590	-	-	258	-	-	89	-	-	-	-	-	-	-	-	-	-	-	-	-	-	-	-	40
	17.83		20.69			34.68			15.08																	11.63
						43.73			15.08																	6.78
			20.69			9.05			3.12																	1.40
			1.42			0.62			0.21																	0.10
McLennan County	35,977	1,920	620	-	-	64	-	-	-	-	-	-	-	-	-	-	-	-	-	-	-	-	-	-	-	-
	17.61		32.29			18.55																				
						10.32																				
			32.29			3.33																				
			1.72			0.18																				
Midland County	14,758	1,065	134	-	-	8	-	-	-	-	-	-	-	-	-	-	-	-	-	-	-	-	-	-	-	-
	12.90		12.58			2.01																				
						5.97																				
			12.58			0.75																				
			0.91			0.05																				
Montgomery County	27,376	3,127	138	-	-	29	-	-	19	-	32	-	-	-	-	-	-	-	-	-	-	-	-	-	-	-
	9.39		4.41			2.98			2.77		6.87															
						21.01			13.77		23.19															
			4.41			0.93			0.61		1.02															
			0.50			0.11			0.07		0.12															
Nacogdoches County	12,743	350	51	-	-	-	-	-	-	-	-	-	-	-	-	-	-	-	-	-	-	-	-	-	-	-
	23.32		14.57																							
			14.57																							
			0.40																							
Nueces County	56,097	3,488	250	-	-	60	-	-	-	-	57	-	-	-	-	-	-	-	-	-	-	-	-	-	-	-
	18.19		7.17			9.71					3.53															
						24.00					22.80															
			7.17			1.72					1.63															
			0.45			0.11					0.10															
Orange County	11,518	697	113	-	-	-	-	-	-	-	-	-	-	-	-	-	-	-	-	-	-	-	-	-	-	72
	13.75		16.21																							19.10
																										63.72
			16.21																							10.33
			0.98																							0.63
Potter County	20,478	2,952	393	-	-	-	-	-	-	-	-	-	-	-	-	-	-	111	-	-	-	-	-	-	-	117
	19.20		13.31															10.48								11.05
																		28.24								29.77
			13.31															3.76								3.96
			1.92															0.54								0.57
Randall County	8,261	1,098	199	-	-	-	-	-	-	-	-	-	-	-	-	-	-	-	-	-	-	-	-	-	-	-
	8.07		18.12																							
			18.12																							
			2.41																							

Notes: Please refer to the User's Guide for an explanation of data; data is arranged alphabetically by state, then county, then city within each county; table includes counties with populations greater than 49,999 unless noted and cities with populations greater than 9,999 whose Asian and/or NHPI population rates are greater than the national average; (1) Native Hawaiian and other Pacific Islander; (2) excludes Taiwanese; (3) includes Chamorro; (4) county does not meet population threshold but is shown in order to allow inclusion of city

Place	Total population with income below poverty level	Asian population for whom poverty status is determined	Asians with income below poverty level	NHPI[1] population for whom poverty status is determined	NHPIs[1] with income below poverty level	Asian Indian	Bangladeshi	Cambodian	Chinese[2]	Fijian	Filipino	Guamanian[3]	Hawaiian, Native	Hmong	Indonesian	Japanese	Korean	Laotian	Malaysian	Pakistani	Samoan	Sri Lankan	Taiwanese	Thai	Tongan	Vietnamese
San Patricio County	11,804 18.02	406	39 9.61 9.61 0.33	-	-	-	-	-	-	-	-	-	-	-	-	-	-	-	-	-	-	-	-	-	-	-
Smith County	23,543 13.78	1,099	127 11.56 11.56 0.54	-	-	-	-	-	-	-	-	-	-	-	-	-	-	-	-	-	-	-	-	-	-	-
Tarrant County	150,488 10.59	50,753	6,203 12.22 12.22 4.12	1,646	446 27.10 27.10 0.30	1,105 11.78 17.81 2.18 0.73	-	48 6.18 0.77 0.09 0.03	888 16.22 14.32 1.75 0.59	-	170 4.90 2.74 0.33 0.11	-	-	-	-	98 9.99 1.58 0.19 0.07	786 24.90 12.67 1.55 0.52	349 11.03 5.63 0.69 0.23	-	212 21.50 3.42 0.42 0.14	-	-	92 13.69 1.48 0.18 0.06	174 22.45 2.81 0.34 0.12	19 5.21 4.26 1.15 0.01	1,776 9.32 28.63 3.50 1.18
Arlington (city)	32,496 9.86	19,139	2,920 15.26 15.26 8.99	-	-	454 15.42 15.55 2.37 1.40	-	-	538 19.57 18.42 2.81 1.66	-	110 9.23 3.77 0.57 0.34	-	-	-	-	-	327 36.09 11.20 1.71 1.01	-	-	-	-	-	74 17.83 2.53 0.39 0.23	-	-	853 9.48 29.21 4.46 2.62
Euless (city)	3,189 6.96	3,213	360 11.20 11.20 11.29	-	-	104 8.36 28.89 3.24 3.26	-	-	-	-	-	-	-	-	-	-	-	-	-	-	-	-	-	-	-	-
Haltom City (city)	3,906 10.03	3,106	402 12.94 12.94 10.29	-	-	-	-	-	-	-	-	-	-	-	-	-	-	83 10.22 20.65 2.67 2.12	-	-	-	-	-	-	-	260 16.50 64.68 8.37 6.66
Taylor County	17,630 14.55	1,622	260 16.03 16.03 1.47	-	-	-	-	-	-	-	45 7.77 17.31 2.77 0.26	-	-	-	-	-	-	-	-	-	-	-	-	-	-	-
Tom Green County	15,193 15.20	672	93 13.84 13.84 0.61	-	-	-	-	-	-	-	-	-	-	-	-	-	-	-	-	-	-	-	-	-	-	-
Travis County	99,388 12.53	34,462	6,038 17.52 17.52 6.08	660	144 21.82 21.82 0.14	1,419 17.55 23.50 4.12 1.43	-	-	1,406 17.01 23.29 4.08 1.41	-	212 10.00 3.51 0.62 0.21	-	-	-	-	148 12.44 2.45 0.43 0.15	1,207 30.27 19.99 3.50 1.21	-	-	190 27.78 3.15 0.55 0.19	-	-	144 20.48 2.38 0.42 0.14	47 12.95 0.78 0.14 0.05	-	875 12.16 14.49 2.54 0.88
Austin (city)	92,011 14.42	29,213	5,789 19.82 19.82 6.29	445	75 16.85 16.85 0.08	1,321 18.90 22.82 4.52 1.44	-	-	1,430 19.09 24.70 4.90 1.55	-	197 12.06 3.40 0.67 0.21	-	-	-	-	145 13.06 2.50 0.50 0.16	1,153 33.28 19.92 3.95 1.25	-	-	132 27.16 2.28 0.45 0.14	-	-	144 23.57 2.49 0.49 0.16	-	-	860 15.36 14.86 2.94 0.93

Notes: Please refer to the User's Guide for an explanation of data; data is arranged alphabetically by state, then county, then city within each county; table includes counties with populations greater than 49,999 unless noted and cities with populations greater than 9,999 whose Asian and/or NHPI population rates are greater than the national average; (1) Native Hawaiian and other Pacific Islander; (2) excludes Taiwanese; (3) includes Chamorro; (4) county does not meet population threshold but is shown in order to allow inclusion of city

Place	Total population with income below poverty level	Asian population for whom poverty status is determined	Asians with income below poverty level	NHPI[1] population for whom poverty status is determined	NHPIs[1] with income below poverty level	Asian Indian	Bangladeshi	Cambodian	Chinese[2]	Fijian	Filipino	Guamanian[3]	Hawaiian, Native	Hmong	Indonesian	Japanese	Korean	Laotian	Malaysian	Pakistani	Samoan	Sri Lankan	Taiwanese	Thai	Tongan	Vietnamese
Pflugerville (city)	278 1.72	728	0 <0.01 <0.01 <0.01	-	-	-	-	-	-	-	-	-	-	-	-	-	-	-	-	-	-	-	-	-	-	-
Wells Branch (cdp)	509 4.54	1,077	124 11.51 11.51 24.36	-	-	-	-	-	-	-	-	-	-	-	-	-	-	-	-	-	-	-	-	-	-	-
Victoria County	10,681 12.94	492	34 6.91 6.91 0.32	-	-	-	-	-	-	-	-	-	-	-	-	-	-	-	-	-	-	-	-	-	-	-
Webb County	59,339 31.17	786	71 9.03 9.03 0.12	-	-	-	-	-	-	-	-	-	-	-	-	-	-	-	-	-	-	-	-	-	-	-
Wichita County	15,896 13.19	2,286	280 12.25 12.25 1.76	-	-	-	-	-	-	-	52 10.68 18.57 2.27 0.33	-	-	-	-	-	-	-	-	-	-	-	-	-	-	52 6.63 18.57 2.27 0.33
Williamson County	11,735 4.79	6,382	342 5.36 5.36 2.91	-	-	106 6.46 30.99 1.66 0.90	-	-	136 9.62 39.77 2.13 1.16	-	-	-	-	-	-	-	24 3.42 7.02 0.38 0.20	-	-	-	-	-	-	-	-	7 0.64 2.05 0.11 0.06
Brushy Creek (cdp)	269 1.70	927	0 <0.01 <0.01 <0.01	-	-	-	-	-	-	-	-	-	-	-	-	-	-	-	-	-	-	-	-	-	-	-
Jollyville (cdp)	416 2.69	1,181	28 2.37 2.37 6.73	-	-	-	-	-	-	-	-	-	-	-	-	-	-	-	-	-	-	-	-	-	-	-
UTAH	206,328 9.40	36,025	5,415 15.03 15.03 2.62	14,087	2,190 15.55 15.55 1.06	307 9.95 5.67 0.85 0.15	-	86 6.25 1.59 0.24 0.04	1,196 16.96 22.09 3.32 0.58	-	491 13.35 9.07 1.36 0.24	-	175 13.39 7.99 1.24 0.08	-	-	1,021 17.59 18.86 2.83 0.49	766 21.95 14.15 2.13 0.37	196 8.96 3.62 0.54 0.09	-	98 24.44 1.81 0.27 0.05	588 16.07 26.85 4.17 0.28	-	127 34.32 2.35 0.35 0.06	131 19.10 2.42 0.36 0.06	1,020 15.21 46.58 7.24 0.49	565 10.38 10.43 1.57 0.27
Cache County	12,017 13.47	1,607	524 32.61 32.61 4.36	-	-	-	-	-	205 40.43 39.12 12.76 1.71	-	-	-	-	-	-	-	-	-	-	-	-	-	-	-	-	-

Notes: Please refer to the User's Guide for an explanation of data; data is arranged alphabetically by state, then county, then city within each county; table includes counties with populations greater than 49,999 unless noted and cities with populations greater than 9,999 whose Asian and/or NHPI population rates are greater than the national average; (1) Native Hawaiian and other Pacific Islander; (2) excludes Taiwanese; (3) includes Chamorro; (4) county does not meet population threshold but is shown in order to allow inclusion of city

Place	Total population with income below poverty level	Asian population for whom poverty status is determined	Asians with income below poverty level	NHPI[1] population for whom poverty status is determined	NHPIs[1] with income below poverty level	Asian Indian	Bangladeshi	Cambodian	Chinese[2]	Fijian	Filipino	Guamanian[3]	Hawaiian, Native	Hmong	Indonesian	Japanese	Korean	Laotian	Malaysian	Pakistani	Samoan	Sri Lankan	Taiwanese	Thai	Tongan	Vietnamese
Davis County	11,984 5.07	3,432	315 9.18 9.18 2.63	906	93 10.26 10.26 0.78	-	-	-	-	-	117 14.34 37.14 3.41 0.98	-	-	-	-	93 11.94 29.52 2.71 0.78	8 2.16 2.54 0.23 0.07	-	-	-	-	-	-	-	-	-
Salt Lake County	70,714 8.00	22,847	2,581 11.30 11.30 3.65	10,212	1,458 14.28 14.28 2.06	92 4.27 3.56 0.40 0.13	-	28 2.69 1.08 0.12 0.04	487 10.84 18.87 2.13 0.69	-	182 10.29 7.05 0.80 0.26	-	6 1.25 0.41 0.06 0.01	-	-	355 11.50 13.75 1.55 0.50	343 19.49 13.29 1.50 0.49	126 7.11 4.88 0.55 0.18	-	-	359 14.20 24.62 3.52 0.51	-	-	-	900 15.29 61.73 8.81 1.27	531 11.47 20.57 2.32 0.75
Kearns (cdp)	2,379 7.13	862	57 6.61 6.61 2.40	400	22 5.50 5.50 0.92	-	-	-	-	-	-	-	-	-	-	-	-	-	-	-	-	-	-	-	-	-
Salt Lake City (city)	27,305 15.32	6,325	1,128 17.83 17.83 4.13	3,309	641 19.37 19.37 2.35	75 11.65 6.65 1.19 0.27	-	-	277 18.14 24.56 4.38 1.01	-	45 8.62 3.99 0.71 0.16	-	-	-	-	97 10.22 8.60 1.53 0.36	164 35.04 14.54 2.59 0.60	-	-	-	118 26.34 18.41 3.57 0.43	-	-	-	454 18.55 70.83 13.72 1.66	273 20.46 24.20 4.32 1.00
Sandy (city)	3,347 3.82	1,535	51 3.32 3.32 1.52	383	14 3.66 3.66 0.42	-	-	-	8 1.96 15.69 0.52 0.24	-	-	-	-	-	-	-	-	-	-	-	-	-	-	-	-	-
Taylorsville (city)	3,391 5.88	1,734	101 5.82 5.82 2.98	713	69 9.68 9.68 2.03	-	-	-	-	-	-	-	-	-	-	-	-	-	-	-	-	-	-	-	-	5 0.84 4.95 0.29 0.15
West Jordan (city)	3,489 5.15	1,191	78 6.55 6.55 2.24	692	56 8.09 8.09 1.61	-	-	-	-	-	-	-	-	-	-	-	-	-	-	-	-	-	-	-	42 9.07 75.00 6.07 1.20	-
West Valley City (city)	9,351 8.69	4,669	397 8.50 8.50 4.25	3,107	436 14.03 14.03 4.66	-	-	24 4.03 6.05 0.51 0.26	79 11.52 19.90 1.69 0.84	-	-	-	-	-	-	-	-	85 18.44 21.41 1.82 0.91	-	-	45 5.29 10.32 1.45 0.48	-	-	-	306 17.02 70.18 9.85 3.27	46 3.07 11.59 0.99 0.49
Utah County	43,270 12.00	3,888	1,284 33.02 33.02 2.97	1,739	423 24.32 24.32 0.98	-	-	-	386 32.11 30.06 9.93 0.89	-	82 20.05 6.39 2.11 0.19	-	122 33.98 28.84 7.02 0.28	-	-	337 46.42 26.25 8.67 0.78	158 30.74 12.31 4.06 0.37	-	-	-	74 14.10 17.49 4.26 0.17	-	-	-	85 18.40 20.09 4.89 0.20	-
Orem (city)	7,011 8.41	1,233	320 25.95 25.95 4.56	700	203 29.00 29.00 2.90	-	-	-	-	-	-	-	-	-	-	-	-	-	-	-	-	-	-	-	-	-

Notes: Please refer to the User's Guide for an explanation of data; data is arranged alphabetically by state, then county, then city within each county; table includes counties with populations greater than 49,999 unless noted and cities with populations greater than 9,999 whose Asian and/or NHPI population rates are greater than the national average; (1) Native Hawaiian and other Pacific Islander; (2) excludes Taiwanese; (3) includes Chamorro; (4) county does not meet population threshold but is shown in order to allow inclusion of city

Place	Total population with income below poverty level	Asian population for whom poverty status is determined	Asians with income below poverty level	NHPI[1] population for whom poverty status is determined	NHPIs[1] with income below poverty level	Asian Indian	Bangladeshi	Cambodian	Chinese[2]	Fijian	Filipino	Guamanian[3]	Hawaiian, Native	Hmong	Indonesian	Japanese	Korean	Laotian	Malaysian	Pakistani	Samoan	Sri Lankan	Taiwanese	Thai	Tongan	Vietnamese
Provo (city)	26,714	1,901	846	611	177	-	-	-	240	-	-	-	-	-	-	274	-	-	-	-	-	-	-	-	-	-
	26.82		44.50		28.97				32.21							68.84										
									28.37							32.39										
			44.50		28.97				12.62							14.41										
			3.17		0.66				0.90							1.03										
Washington County	9,988	433	73	462	101	-	-	-	-	-	-	-	-	-	-	-	-	-	-	-	-	-	-	-	-	-
	11.19		16.86		21.86																					
			16.86		21.86																					
			0.73		1.01																					
St. George (city)	5,665	370	71	418	85	-	-	-	-	-	-	-	-	-	-	-	-	-	-	-	-	-	-	-	-	-
	11.56		19.19		20.33																					
			19.19		20.33																					
			1.25		1.50																					
Weber County	18,022	2,283	315	-	-	-	-	-	-	-	-	-	-	-	-	26	-	-	-	-	-	-	-	-	-	-
	9.30		13.80													4.39										
																8.25										
			13.80													1.14										
			1.75													0.14										
VERMONT	55,506	4,430	645	-	-	36	-	-	189	-	32	-	-	-	-	42	91	-	-	-	-	-	-	-	-	209
	9.44		14.56			5.61			17.18		11.43					14.33	15.35									19.92
						5.58			29.30		4.96					6.51	14.11									32.40
			14.56			0.81			4.27		0.72					0.95	2.05									4.72
			1.16			0.06			0.34		0.06					0.08	0.16									0.38
Chittenden County	12,267	2,558	448	-	-	20	-	-	159	-	-	-	-	-	-	-	-	-	-	-	-	-	-	-	-	166
	8.80		17.51			5.76			24.54																	20.39
						4.46			35.49																	37.05
			17.51			0.78			6.22																	6.49
			3.65			0.16			1.30																	1.35
Rutland County	6,715	186	30	-	-	-	-	-	-	-	-	-	-	-	-	-	-	-	-	-	-	-	-	-	-	-
	10.94		16.13																							
			16.13																							
			0.45																							
Washington County	4,442	226	32	-	-	-	-	-	-	-	-	-	-	-	-	-	-	-	-	-	-	-	-	-	-	-
	7.96		14.16																							
			14.16																							
			0.72																							
Windsor County	4,346	433	49	-	-	-	-	-	-	-	-	-	-	-	-	-	-	-	-	-	-	-	-	-	-	-
	7.67		11.32																							
			11.32																							
			1.13																							
VIRGINIA	656,641	251,611	23,027	3,314	304	3,881	274	396	2,935	-	2,536	109	84	-	113	613	5,766	239	-	1,854	56	60	135	392	-	2,759
	9.59		9.15		9.17	8.30	15.28	8.11	8.74		5.41	11.24	9.71		10.40	7.07	13.02	8.08		17.88	12.36	9.60	10.78	11.08		7.89
						16.85	1.19	1.72	12.75		11.01	35.86	27.63		0.49	2.66	25.04	1.04		8.05	18.42	0.26	0.59	1.70		11.98
			9.15		9.17	1.54	0.11	0.16	1.17		1.01	3.29	2.53		0.04	0.24	2.29	0.09		0.74	1.69	0.02	0.05	0.16		1.10
			3.51		0.05	0.59	0.04	0.06	0.45		0.39	0.02	0.01		0.02	0.09	0.88	0.04		0.28	0.01	0.01	0.02	0.06		0.42

Notes: Please refer to the User's Guide for an explanation of data; data is arranged alphabetically by state, then county, then city within each county; table includes counties with populations greater than 49,999 unless noted and cities with populations greater than 9,999 whose Asian and/or NHPI population rates are greater than the national average; (1) Native Hawaiian and other Pacific Islander; (2) excludes Taiwanese; (3) includes Chamorro; (4) county does not meet population threshold but is shown in order to allow inclusion of city

Place	Total population with income below poverty level	Asian population for whom poverty status is determined	Asians with income below poverty level	NHPI[1] population for whom poverty status is determined	NHPIs[1] with income below poverty level	Asian Indian	Bangladeshi	Cambodian	Chinese[2]	Fijian	Filipino	Guamanian[3]	Hawaiian, Native	Hmong	Indonesian	Japanese	Korean	Laotian	Malaysian	Pakistani	Samoan	Sri Lankan	Taiwanese	Thai	Tongan	Vietnamese
	5,232	2,421	295	-	-	93	-	-	96	-	-	-	-	-	-	-	-	-	-	-	-	-	-	-	-	-
	6.74		12.19			13.25			10.68																	
Albemarle County						31.53			32.54																	
			12.19			3.84			3.97																	
			5.64			1.78			1.83																	
	11,279	6,953	1,005	-	-	211	-	-	114	-	94	-	-	-	-	-	327	-	-	70	-	-	-	-	-	45
	8.92		14.45			13.35			14.50		8.68						26.27			12.20						9.30
Alexandria Independent City						21.00			11.34		9.35						32.54			6.97						4.48
			14.45			3.03			1.64		1.35						4.70			1.01						0.65
			8.91			1.87			1.01		0.83						2.90			0.62						0.40
	14,371	15,670	2,512	-	-	514	-	83	329	-	157	-	-	-	-	145	291	-	-	248	-	-	-	-	-	437
	7.76		16.03			14.83		23.51	14.14		7.66					12.76	20.98			31.35						20.34
Arlington County						20.46		3.30	13.10		6.25					5.77	11.58			9.87						17.40
			16.03			3.28		0.53	2.10		1.00					0.93	1.86			1.58						2.79
			17.48			3.58		0.58	2.29		1.09					1.01	2.02			1.73						3.04
	14,371	15,670	2,512	-	-	514	-	83	329	-	157	-	-	-	-	145	291	-	-	248	-	-	-	-	-	437
	7.76		16.03			14.83		23.51	14.14		7.66					12.76	20.98			31.35						20.34
Arlington (cdp)						20.46		3.30	13.10		6.25					5.77	11.58			9.87						17.40
			16.03			3.28		0.53	2.10		1.00					0.93	1.86			1.58						2.79
			17.48			3.58		0.58	2.29		1.09					1.01	2.02			1.73						3.04
	4,263	581	48	-	-	-	-	-	-	-	-	-	-	-	-	-	-	-	-	-	-	-	-	-	-	-
	7.11		8.26																							
Bedford County																										
			8.26																							
			1.13																							
	9,950	1,523	660	-	-	182	-	-	160	-	-	-	-	-	-	-	-	-	-	-	-	-	-	-	-	-
	25.94		43.34			61.49			29.68																	
Charlottesville Independent City						27.58			24.24																	
			43.34			11.95			10.51																	
			6.63			1.83			1.61																	
	14,259	3,435	122	-	-	-	-	-	-	-	7	-	-	-	-	-	-	-	-	-	-	-	-	-	-	-
	7.32		3.55								0.39															
Chesapeake Independent City											5.74															
			3.55								0.20															
			0.86								0.05															
	11,586	6,314	389	-	-	55	-	34	86	-	4	-	-	-	-	-	162	-	-	-	-	-	-	-	-	4
	4.54		6.16			5.28		5.16	9.10		0.57						10.89									0.54
Chesterfield County						14.14		8.74	22.11		1.03						41.65									1.03
			6.16			0.87		0.54	1.36		0.06						2.57									0.06
			3.36			0.47		0.29	0.74		0.03						1.40									0.03
	1,205	2,501	182	-	-	35	-	-	41	-	-	-	-	-	-	-	85	-	-	-	-	-	-	-	-	4
	5.73		7.28			7.07			7.98								15.48									0.97
Fairfax Independent City						19.23			22.53								46.70									2.20
			7.28			1.40			1.64								3.40									0.16
			15.10			2.90			3.40								7.05									0.33
	43,396	123,093	8,691	857	30	1,361	139	71	902	-	445	-	-	-	59	53	3,012	95	-	974	-	-	14	92	-	1,074
	4.53		7.06		3.50	5.46	15.41	3.87	5.58		3.54				9.92	1.84	10.91	6.31		15.52			1.90	6.24		5.07
Fairfax County						15.66	1.60	0.82	10.38		5.12				0.68	0.61	34.66	1.09		11.21			0.16	1.06		12.36
			7.06		3.50	1.11	0.11	0.06	0.73		0.36				0.05	0.04	2.45	0.08		0.79			0.01	0.07		0.87
			20.03		0.07	3.14	0.32	0.16	2.08		1.03				0.14	0.12	6.94	0.22		2.24			0.03	0.21		2.47

Notes: Please refer to the User's Guide for an explanation of data; data is arranged alphabetically by state, then county, then city within each county; table includes counties with populations greater than 49,999 unless noted and cities with populations greater than 9,999 whose Asian and/or NHPI population rates are greater than the national average; (1) Native Hawaiian and other Pacific Islander; (2) excludes Taiwanese; (3) includes Chamorro; (4) county does not meet population threshold but is shown in order to allow inclusion of city

Place	Total population with income below poverty level	Asian population for whom poverty status is determined	Asians with income below poverty level	NHPI[1] population for whom poverty status is determined	NHPIs[1] with income below poverty level	Asian Indian	Bangladeshi	Cambodian	Chinese[2]	Fijian	Filipino	Guamanian[3]	Hawaiian, Native	Hmong	Indonesian	Japanese	Korean	Laotian	Malaysian	Pakistani	Samoan	Sri Lankan	Taiwanese	Thai	Tongan	Vietnamese
Annandale (cdp)	3,833 7.03	10,408	1,168 11.22 11.22 30.47	-	-	27 2.36 2.31 0.26 0.70	-	-	77 7.92 6.59 0.74 2.01	-	31 4.89 2.65 0.30 0.81	-	-	-	-	-	589 17.60 50.43 5.66 15.37	-	-	-	-	-	-	-	-	284 8.54 24.32 2.73 7.41
Bailey's Crossroads (cdp)	3,035 13.33	2,492	296 11.88 11.88 9.75	-	-	-	-	-	-	-	-	-	-	-	-	-	-	-	-	15 4.18 5.07 0.60 0.49	-	-	-	-	-	143 25.09 48.31 5.74 4.71
Burke (cdp)	1,306 2.28	8,266	387 4.68 4.68 29.63	-	-	28 1.97 7.24 0.34 2.14	-	-	9 1.19 2.33 0.11 0.69	-	19 1.77 4.91 0.23 1.45	-	-	-	-	-	275 8.83 71.06 3.33 21.06	-	-	-	-	-	-	-	-	12 1.06 3.10 0.15 0.92
Centreville (cdp)	1,452 3.00	6,337	438 6.91 6.91 30.17	-	-	78 4.72 17.81 1.23 5.37	-	-	79 8.32 18.04 1.25 5.44	-	53 5.80 12.10 0.84 3.65	-	-	-	-	-	202 12.46 46.12 3.19 13.91	-	-	-	-	-	-	-	-	18 4.29 4.11 0.28 1.24
Chantilly (cdp)	944 2.31	6,460	250 3.87 3.87 26.48	-	-	79 3.78 31.60 1.22 8.37	-	-	11 1.14 4.40 0.17 1.17	-	-	-	-	-	-	-	89 7.79 35.60 1.38 9.43	-	-	-	-	-	-	-	-	71 7.22 28.40 1.10 7.52
Franconia (cdp)	902 2.83	3,142	37 1.18 1.18 4.10	-	-	0 0.00 0.00 0.00 0.00	-	-	-	-	0 0.00 0.00 0.00 0.00	-	-	-	-	-	11 1.85 29.73 0.35 1.22	-	-	-	-	-	-	-	-	0 0.00 0.00 0.00 0.00
Groveton (cdp)	1,443 6.82	1,621	191 11.78 11.78 13.24	-	-	-	-	-	-	-	-	-	-	-	-	-	-	-	-	-	-	-	-	-	-	-
Herndon (town)	1,741 8.08	3,196	212 6.63 6.63 12.18	-	-	32 3.03 15.09 1.00 1.84	-	-	-	-	-	-	-	-	-	-	-	-	-	-	-	-	-	-	-	13 3.09 6.13 0.41 0.75
Hybla Valley (cdp)	2,539 15.23	1,263	396 31.35 31.35 15.60	-	-	-	-	-	-	-	-	-	-	-	-	-	-	-	-	-	-	-	-	-	-	-
Idylwood (cdp)	924 5.76	3,183	301 9.46 9.46 32.58	-	-	25 2.51 8.31 0.79 2.71	-	-	42 7.34 13.95 1.32 4.55	-	-	-	-	-	-	-	-	-	-	-	-	-	-	-	-	36 5.54 11.96 1.13 3.90

Notes: Please refer to the User's Guide for an explanation of data; data is arranged alphabetically by state, then county, then city within each county; table includes counties with populations greater than 49,999 unless noted and cities with populations greater than 9,999 whose Asian and/or NHPI population rates are greater than the national average; (1) Native Hawaiian and other Pacific Islander; (2) excludes Taiwanese; (3) includes Chamorro; (4) county does not meet population threshold but is shown in order to allow inclusion of city

Place	Total population with income below poverty level	Asian population for whom poverty status is determined	Asians with income below poverty level	NHPI[1] population for whom poverty status is determined	NHPIs[1] with income below poverty level	Asian Indian	Bangladeshi	Cambodian	Chinese[2]	Fijian	Filipino	Guamanian[3]	Hawaiian, Native	Hmong	Indonesian	Japanese	Korean	Laotian	Malaysian	Pakistani	Samoan	Sri Lankan	Taiwanese	Thai	Tongan	Vietnamese
Jefferson (cdp)	1,310 4.81	5,246	250 4.77 4.77 19.08	-	-	115 13.63 46.00 2.19 8.78	-	-	11 2.01 4.40 0.21 0.84	-	15 2.98 6.00 0.29 1.15	-	-	-	-	-	-	-	-	-	-	-	-	-	-	93 4.07 37.20 1.77 7.10
Lincolnia (cdp)	1,856 11.80	2,297	326 14.19 14.19 17.56	-	-	-	-	-	-	-	-	-	-	-	-	-	-	-	-	229 44.29 70.25 9.97 12.34	-	-	-	-	-	16 3.19 4.91 0.70 0.86
Lorton (cdp)	995 6.62	1,381	137 9.92 9.92 13.77	-	-	-	-	-	-	-	-	-	-	-	-	-	-	-	-	-	-	-	-	-	-	-
McLean (cdp)	753 1.94	4,222	150 3.55 3.55 19.92	-	-	23 2.41 15.33 0.54 3.05	-	-	30 3.89 20.00 0.71 3.98	-	46 9.20 30.67 1.09 6.11	-	-	-	-	0 0.00 0.00 0.00 0.00	38 4.61 25.33 0.90 5.05	-	-	-	-	-	-	-	-	-
Merrifield (cdp)	821 7.41	3,156	294 9.32 9.32 35.81	-	-	29 3.41 9.86 0.92 3.53	-	-	-	-	-	-	-	-	-	-	176 20.73 59.86 5.58 21.44	-	-	-	-	-	-	-	-	17 2.42 5.78 0.54 2.07
Mount Vernon (cdp)	2,008 7.05	1,856	227 12.23 12.23 11.30	-	-	-	-	-	-	-	-	-	-	-	-	-	62 13.42 27.31 3.34 3.09	-	-	-	-	-	-	-	-	-
Newington (cdp)	410 2.09	2,141	82 3.83 3.83 20.00	-	-	16 4.28 19.51 0.75 3.90	-	-	-	-	7 1.46 8.54 0.33 1.71	-	-	-	-	-	9 1.87 10.98 0.42 2.20	-	-	-	-	-	-	-	-	-
Oakton (cdp)	1,422 4.86	4,111	446 10.85 10.85 31.36	-	-	55 5.83 12.33 1.34 3.87	-	-	82 8.18 18.39 1.99 5.77	-	-	-	-	-	-	-	231 20.52 51.79 5.62 16.24	-	-	-	-	-	-	-	-	18 3.93 4.04 0.44 1.27
Reston (cdp)	2,527 4.52	5,202	535 10.28 10.28 21.17	-	-	94 4.95 17.57 1.81 3.72	-	-	50 7.00 9.35 0.96 1.98	-	13 2.25 2.43 0.25 0.51	-	-	-	-	-	62 9.12 11.59 1.19 2.45	-	-	-	-	-	-	-	-	-
Rose Hill (cdp)	534 3.58	1,216	64 5.26 5.26 11.99	-	-	-	-	-	-	-	-	-	-	-	-	-	-	-	-	-	-	-	-	-	-	-

Notes: Please refer to the User's Guide for an explanation of data; data is arranged alphabetically by state, then county, then city within each county; table includes counties with populations greater than 49,999 unless noted and cities with populations greater than 9,999 whose Asian and/or NHPI population rates are greater than the national average; (1) Native Hawaiian and other Pacific Islander; (2) excludes Taiwanese; (3) includes Chamorro; (4) county does not meet population threshold but is shown in order to allow inclusion of city

Place	Total population with income below poverty level	Asian population for whom poverty status is determined	Asians with income below poverty level	NHPI[1] population for whom poverty status is determined	NHPIs[1] with income below poverty level	Asian Indian	Bangladeshi	Cambodian	Chinese[2]	Fijian	Filipino	Guamanian[3]	Hawaiian, Native	Hmong	Indonesian	Japanese	Korean	Laotian	Malaysian	Pakistani	Samoan	Sri Lankan	Taiwanese	Thai	Tongan	Vietnamese
Springfield (cdp)	1,531	6,573	419	-	-	94	-	-	38	-	49	-	-	-	-	-	72	66	-	-	-	-	-	-	-	35
	5.10		6.37			9.81			8.92		4.79						9.01	16.58								1.89
						22.43			9.07		11.69						17.18	15.75								8.35
			6.37			1.43			0.58		0.75						1.10	1.00								0.53
			27.37			6.14			2.48		3.20						4.70	4.31								2.29
Tysons Corner (cdp)	1,287	3,155	326	-	-	13	-	-	100	-	-	-	-	-	-	-	138	-	-	-	-	-	-	-	-	-
	6.96		10.33			1.77			15.29								17.56									
						3.99			30.67								42.33									
			10.33			0.41			3.17								4.37									
			25.33			1.01			7.77								10.72									
Vienna (town)	363	1,207	2	-	-	-	-	-	-	-	-	-	-	-	-	-	-	-	-	-	-	-	-	-	-	-
	2.50		0.17																							
			0.17																							
			0.55																							
West Springfield (cdp)	683	3,913	236	-	-	35	-	-	0	-	-	-	-	-	-	-	154	-	-	-	-	-	-	-	-	6
	2.39		6.03			7.87			0.00								11.29									0.67
						14.83			0.00								65.25									2.54
			6.03			0.89			0.00								3.94									0.15
			34.55			5.12			0.00								22.55									0.88
Wolf Trap (cdp)	137	1,247	0	-	-	0	-	-	0	-	-	-	-	-	-	-	-	-	-	-	-	-	-	-	-	-
	0.99		<0.01			<0.01			<0.01																	
						*** **			*** **																	
			<0.01			<0.01			<0.01																	
			<0.01			<0.01			<0.01																	
Falls Church Independent City	432	674	38	-	-	-	-	-	-	-	-	-	-	-	-	-	-	-	-	-	-	-	-	-	-	-
	4.20		5.64																							
			5.64																							
			8.80																							
Fauquier County	2,964	471	34	-	-	-	-	-	-	-	-	-	-	-	-	-	-	-	-	-	-	-	-	-	-	-
	5.44		7.22																							
			7.22																							
			1.15																							
Frederick County	3,727	515	58	-	-	-	-	-	-	-	-	-	-	-	-	-	-	-	-	-	-	-	-	-	-	-
	6.39		11.26																							
			11.26																							
			1.56																							
Hampton Independent City	15,088	2,393	250	-	-	-	-	-	-	-	53	-	-	-	-	-	-	-	-	-	-	-	-	-	-	40
	11.30		10.45								9.17															7.71
											21.20															16.00
			10.45								2.21															1.67
			1.66								0.35															0.27
Hanover County	3,065	532	19	-	-	-	-	-	-	-	-	-	-	-	-	-	-	-	-	-	-	-	-	-	-	-
	3.64		3.57																							
			3.57																							
			0.62																							

Notes: Please refer to the User's Guide for an explanation of data; data is arranged alphabetically by state, then county, then city within each county; table includes counties with populations greater than 49,999 unless noted and cities with populations greater than 9,999 whose Asian and/or NHPI population rates are greater than the national average; (1) Native Hawaiian and other Pacific Islander; (2) excludes Taiwanese; (3) includes Chamorro; (4) county does not meet population threshold but is shown in order to allow inclusion of city

Place	Total population with income below poverty level	Asian population for whom poverty status is determined	Asians with income below poverty level	NHPI[1] population for whom poverty status is determined	NHPIs[1] with income below poverty level	Asian Indian	Bangladeshi	Cambodian	Chinese[2]	Fijian	Filipino	Guamanian[3]	Hawaiian, Native	Hmong	Indonesian	Japanese	Korean	Laotian	Malaysian	Pakistani	Samoan	Sri Lankan	Taiwanese	Thai	Tongan	Vietnamese
Henrico County	15,917 6.17	9,262	745 8.04 8.04 4.68	-	-	165 6.13 22.15 1.78 1.04	-	0 0.00 0.00 0.00 0.00	111 6.76 14.90 1.20 0.70	-	46 6.62 6.17 0.50 0.29	-	-	-	-	-	139 15.09 18.66 1.50 0.87	-	-	-	-	-	-	-	-	110 7.48 14.77 1.19 0.69
Glen Allen (cdp)	323 2.53	467	0 <0.01 <0.01 <0.01	-	-	-	-	-	-	-	-	-	-	-	-	-	-	-	-	-	-	-	-	-	-	-
Laurel (cdp)	742 5.38	775	89 11.48 11.48 11.99	-	-	-	-	-	-	-	-	-	-	-	-	-	-	-	-	-	-	-	-	-	-	-
Loudoun County	4,637 2.75	8,918	201 2.25 2.25 4.33	-	-	6 0.32 2.99 0.07 0.13	-	-	49 4.27 24.38 0.55 1.06	-	50 4.27 24.88 0.56 1.08	-	-	-	-	-	41 3.75 20.40 0.46 0.88	-	-	0 0.00 0.00 0.00 0.00	-	-	-	-	-	7 0.40 3.48 0.08 0.15
Lynchburg Independent City	9,363 15.88	856	137 16.00 16.00 1.46	-	-	-	-	-	-	-	-	-	-	-	-	-	-	-	-	-	-	-	-	-	-	-
Manassas Park Indep. City	530 5.17	385	5 1.30 1.30 0.94	-	-	-	-	-	-	-	-	-	-	-	-	-	-	-	-	-	-	-	-	-	-	-
Montgomery County	17,341 23.24	2,534	1,226 48.38 48.38 7.07	-	-	273 54.06 22.27 10.77 1.57	-	-	193 27.03 15.74 7.62 1.11	-	-	-	-	-	-	-	387 61.82 31.57 15.27 2.23	-	-	-	-	-	-	-	-	-
Blacksburg (town)	13,386 43.23	2,287	1,213 53.04 53.04 9.06	-	-	273 59.74 22.51 11.94 2.04	-	-	193 28.55 15.91 8.44 1.44	-	-	-	-	-	-	-	387 69.60 31.90 16.92 2.89	-	-	-	-	-	-	-	-	-
Newport News Independent City	24,027 13.78	4,180	492 11.77 11.77 2.05	-	-	-	-	-	58 13.15 11.79 1.39 0.24	-	83 11.35 16.87 1.99 0.35	-	-	-	-	-	94 8.39 19.11 2.25 0.39	-	-	-	-	-	-	-	-	99 13.98 20.12 2.37 0.41
Norfolk Independent City	40,857 19.40	6,506	950 14.60 14.60 2.33	-	-	112 31.28 11.79 1.72 0.27	-	-	139 20.03 14.63 2.14 0.34	-	378 9.40 39.79 5.81 0.93	-	-	-	-	-	-	-	-	-	-	-	-	-	-	57 16.33 6.00 0.88 0.14

Notes: Please refer to the User's Guide for an explanation of data; data is arranged alphabetically by state, then county, then city within each county; table includes counties with populations greater than 49,999 unless noted and cities with populations greater than 9,999 whose Asian and/or NHPI population rates are greater than the national average; (1) Native Hawaiian and other Pacific Islander; (2) excludes Taiwanese; (3) includes Chamorro; (4) county does not meet population threshold but is shown in order to allow inclusion of city

Place	Total population with income below poverty level	Asian population for whom poverty status is determined	Asians with income below poverty level	NHPI[1] population for whom poverty status is determined	NHPIs[1] with income below poverty level	Asian Indian	Bangladeshi	Cambodian	Chinese[2]	Fijian	Filipino	Guamanian[3]	Hawaiian, Native	Hmong	Indonesian	Japanese	Korean	Laotian	Malaysian	Pakistani	Samoan	Sri Lankan	Taiwanese	Thai	Tongan	Vietnamese
Portsmouth Independent City	15,471 16.16	723	107 14.80 14.80 0.69	-	-	-	-	-	-	-	59 14.22 55.14 8.16 0.38	-	-	-	-	-	-	-	-	-	-	-	-	-	-	-
Prince William County	12,182 4.39	10,358	472 4.56 4.56 3.87	-	-	102 5.06 21.61 0.98 0.84	-	-	16 1.70 3.39 0.15 0.13	-	58 2.68 12.29 0.56 0.48	-	-	-	-	18 3.95 3.81 0.17 0.15	62 3.73 13.14 0.60 0.51	-	-	100 12.30 21.19 0.97 0.82	-	-	-	-	-	33 3.49 6.99 0.32 0.27
Bull Run (cdp)	1,073 9.48	598	48 8.03 8.03 4.47	-	-	-	-	-	-	-	-	-	-	-	-	-	-	-	-	-	-	-	-	-	-	-
Dale City (cdp)	2,452 4.39	2,858	123 4.30 4.30 5.02	-	-	25 3.97 20.33 0.87 1.02	-	-	-	-	22 3.22 17.89 0.77 0.90	-	-	-	-	-	-	-	-	64 19.75 52.03 2.24 2.61	-	-	-	-	-	-
Lake Ridge (cdp)	710 2.34	1,116	30 2.69 2.69 4.23	-	-	-	-	-	-	-	-	-	-	-	-	-	-	-	-	-	-	-	-	-	-	-
Woodbridge (cdp)	1,741 5.53	1,495	35 2.34 2.34 2.01	-	-	-	-	-	-	-	-	-	-	-	-	-	-	-	-	-	-	-	-	-	-	-
Richmond Independent City	40,185 21.36	2,190	656 29.95 29.95 1.63	-	-	131 30.97 19.97 5.98 0.33	-	-	-	-	60 15.92 9.15 2.74 0.15	-	-	-	-	-	-	-	-	-	-	-	-	-	-	-
Roanoke Independent City	14,793 15.95	997	216 21.66 21.66 1.46	-	-	-	-	-	-	-	-	-	-	-	-	-	-	-	-	-	-	-	-	-	-	-
Roanoke County	3,732 4.46	985	78 7.92 7.92 2.09	-	-	-	-	-	-	-	-	-	-	-	-	-	-	-	-	-	-	-	-	-	-	-
Spotsylvania County	4,247 4.74	1,281	136 10.62 10.62 3.20	-	-	-	-	-	-	-	-	-	-	-	-	-	-	-	-	-	-	-	-	-	-	-

Notes: Please refer to the User's Guide for an explanation of data; data is arranged alphabetically by state, then county, then city within each county; table includes counties with populations greater than 49,999 unless noted and cities with populations greater than 9,999 whose Asian and/or NHPI population rates are greater than the national average; (1) Native Hawaiian and other Pacific Islander; (2) excludes Taiwanese; (3) includes Chamorro; (4) county does not meet population threshold but is shown in order to allow inclusion of city

Place	Total population with income below poverty level	Asian population for whom poverty status is determined	Asians with income below poverty level	NHPI[1] population for whom poverty status is determined	NHPIs[1] with income below poverty level	Asian Indian	Bangladeshi	Cambodian	Chinese[2]	Fijian	Filipino	Guamanian[3]	Hawaiian, Native	Hmong	Indonesian	Japanese	Korean	Laotian	Malaysian	Pakistani	Samoan	Sri Lankan	Taiwanese	Thai	Tongan	Vietnamese
	3,138	1,452	71	-	-	-	-	-	-	-	23	-	-	-	-	-	-	-	-	-	-	-	-	-	-	-
	3.46		4.89								6.42															
Stafford County											32.39															
			4.89								1.58															
			2.26								0.73															
	8,264	533	78	-	-	-	-	-	-	-	-	-	-	-	-	-	-	-	-	-	-	-	-	-	-	-
	13.22		14.63																							
Suffolk Independent City																										
			14.63																							
			0.94																							
	27,163	20,049	1,429	-	-	147	-	-	93	-	668	-	-	-	-	25	121	-	-	-	-	-	-	-	-	293
	6.52		7.13			12.22			5.75		4.96					3.38	15.80									24.96
Virginia Beach Independent City						10.29			6.51		46.75					1.75	8.47									20.50
			7.13			0.73			0.46		3.33					0.12	0.60									1.46
			5.26			0.54			0.34		2.46					0.09	0.45									1.08
	1,361	248	45	-	-	-	-	-	-	-	-	-	-	-	-	-	-	-	-	-	-	-	-	-	-	-
	18.27		18.15																							
Williamsburg Independent City																										
			18.15																							
			3.31																							
	1,947	1,826	70	-	-	0	-	-	-	-	-	-	-	-	-	-	62	-	-	-	-	-	-	-	-	-
	3.50		3.83			0.00											11.23									
York County						0.00											88.57									
			3.83			0.00											3.40									
			3.60			0.00											3.18									
	612,370	314,880	40,409	21,092	3,266	1,961	-	3,618	5,474	101	4,083	790	435	681	319	4,331	7,833	1,362	-	93	1,373	0	549	463	44	8,169
	10.62		12.83		15.48	8.79		24.72	9.73	14.25	6.40	15.02	9.80	46.36	25.89	12.05	17.10	17.16		7.73	20.09	0.00	14.90	12.16	5.29	18.52
WASHINGTON						4.85		8.95	13.55	3.09	10.10	24.19	13.32	1.69	0.79	10.72	19.38	3.37		0.23	42.04	0.00	1.36	1.15	1.35	20.22
			12.83		15.48	0.62		1.15	1.74	0.48	1.30	3.75	2.06	0.22	0.10	1.38	2.49	0.43		0.03	6.51	0.00	0.17	0.15	0.21	2.59
			6.60		0.53	0.32		0.59	0.89	0.02	0.67	0.13	0.07	0.11	0.05	0.71	1.28	0.22		0.02	0.22	0.00	0.09	0.08	0.01	1.33
	14,517	2,923	236	-	-	46	-	-	7	-	-	-	-	-	-	-	64	-	-	-	-	-	-	-	-	14
	10.28		8.07			11.39			1.31								15.65									2.78
Benton County						19.49			2.97								27.12									5.93
			8.07			1.57			0.24								2.19									0.48
			1.63			0.32			0.05								0.44									0.10
	3,142	1,555	79	-	-	-	-	-	0	-	-	-	-	-	-	-	-	-	-	-	-	-	-	-	-	-
	8.18		5.08						0.00																	
Richland (city)									0.00																	
			5.08						0.00																	
			2.51						0.00																	
	8,147	393	80	-	-	-	-	-	-	-	-	-	-	-	-	-	-	-	-	-	-	-	-	-	-	-
	12.43		20.36																							
Chelan County																										
			20.36																							
			0.98																							
	7,825	787	93	-	-	-	-	-	-	-	-	-	-	-	-	-	-	-	-	-	-	-	-	-	-	-
	12.50		11.82																							
Clallam County																										
			11.82																							
			1.19																							

Notes: Please refer to the User's Guide for an explanation of data; data is arranged alphabetically by state, then county, then city within each county; table includes counties with populations greater than 49,999 unless noted and cities with populations greater than 9,999 whose Asian and/or NHPI population rates are greater than the national average; (1) Native Hawaiian and other Pacific Islander; (2) excludes Taiwanese; (3) includes Chamorro; (4) county does not meet population threshold but is shown in order to allow inclusion of city

Place	Total population with income below poverty level	Asian population for whom poverty status is determined	Asians with income below poverty level	NHPI[1] population for whom poverty status is determined	NHPIs[1] with income below poverty level	Asian Indian	Bangladeshi	Cambodian	Chinese[2]	Fijian	Filipino	Guamanian[3]	Hawaiian, Native	Hmong	Indonesian	Japanese	Korean	Laotian	Malaysian	Pakistani	Samoan	Sri Lankan	Taiwanese	Thai	Tongan	Vietnamese
Clark County	31,027	10,622	1,138	1,324	107	40	-	36	237	-	100	-	-	-	-	150	121	37	-	-	-	-	-	-	-	339
	9.09		10.71		8.08	5.37		8.43	14.36		5.72					11.70	9.29	8.96								14.41
						3.51		3.16	20.83		8.79					13.18	10.63	3.25								29.79
			10.71		8.08	0.38		0.34	2.23		0.94					1.41	1.14	0.35								3.19
			3.67		0.34	0.13		0.12	0.76		0.32					0.48	0.39	0.12								1.09
Five Corners (cdp)	690	585	0	-	-	-	-	-	-	-	-	-	-	-	-	-	-	-	-	-	-	-	-	-	-	-
	5.75		<0.01																							
			<0.01																							
			<0.01																							
Orchards (cdp)	1,186	768	100	-	-	-	-	-	-	-	-	-	-	-	-	-	-	-	-	-	-	-	-	-	-	-
	6.66		13.02																							
			13.02																							
			8.43																							
Vancouver (city)	17,229	6,155	758	938	68	-	-	-	116	-	16	-	-	-	-	122	65	-	-	-	-	-	-	-	-	272
	12.19		12.32		7.25				11.41		1.77					15.23	9.46									18.10
									15.30		2.11					16.09	8.58									35.88
			12.32		7.25				1.88		0.26					1.98	1.06									4.42
			4.40		0.39				0.67		0.09					0.71	0.38									1.58
Cowlitz County	12,765	1,249	319	-	-	-	-	218	-	-	-	-	-	-	-	-	-	-	-	-	-	-	-	-	-	57
	13.97		25.54					61.58																		14.39
								68.34																		17.87
			25.54					17.45																		4.56
			2.50					1.71																		0.45
Grant County	12,809	534	26	-	-	-	-	-	-	-	-	-	-	-	-	-	-	-	-	-	-	-	-	-	-	-
	17.41		4.87																							
			4.87																							
			0.20																							
Grays Harbor County	10,668	629	190	-	-	-	-	-	-	-	-	-	-	-	-	-	-	-	-	-	-	-	-	-	-	-
	16.10		30.21																							
			30.21																							
			1.78																							
Island County	4,895	2,704	240	-	-	-	-	-	-	-	151	-	-	-	-	18	-	-	-	-	-	-	-	-	-	-
	7.00		8.88								8.35					4.81										
											62.92					7.50										
			8.88								5.58					0.67										
			4.90								3.08					0.37										
Oak Harbor (city)	1,839	1,723	161	-	-	-	-	-	-	-	120	-	-	-	-	-	-	-	-	-	-	-	-	-	-	-
	9.31		9.34								8.89															
											74.53															
			9.34								6.96															
			8.75								6.53															
King County	142,546	185,158	21,197	8,119	1,302	1,110	-	1,559	3,604	86	1,836	250	96	315	228	2,423	3,349	739	-	39	721	-	375	293	15	4,699
	8.35		11.45		16.04	7.93		23.77	8.37	15.84	5.52	31.02	6.97	35.59	27.47	10.94	16.88	14.87		7.66	18.79		12.60	15.32	3.03	17.59
						5.24		7.35	17.00	6.61	8.66	19.20	7.37	1.49	1.08	11.43	15.80	3.49		0.18	55.38		1.77	1.38	1.15	22.17
			11.45		16.04	0.60		0.84	1.95	1.06	0.99	3.08	1.18	0.17	0.12	1.31	1.81	0.40		0.02	8.88		0.20	0.16	0.18	2.54
			14.87		0.91	0.78		1.09	2.53	0.06	1.29	0.18	0.07	0.22	0.16	1.70	2.35	0.52		0.03	0.51		0.26	0.21	0.01	3.30

Notes: Please refer to the User's Guide for an explanation of data; data is arranged alphabetically by state, then county, then city within each county; table includes counties with populations greater than 49,999 unless noted and cities with populations greater than 9,999 whose Asian and/or NHPI population rates are greater than the national average; (1) Native Hawaiian and other Pacific Islander; (2) excludes Taiwanese; (3) includes Chamorro; (4) county does not meet population threshold but is shown in order to allow inclusion of city

Place	Total population with income below poverty level	Asian population for whom poverty status is determined	Asians with income below poverty level	NHPI[1] population for whom poverty status is determined	NHPIs[1] with income below poverty level	Asian Indian	Bangladeshi	Cambodian	Chinese[2]	Fijian	Filipino	Guamanian[3]	Hawaiian, Native	Hmong	Indonesian	Japanese	Korean	Laotian	Malaysian	Pakistani	Samoan	Sri Lankan	Taiwanese	Thai	Tongan	Vietnamese
Auburn (city)	5,092 12.77	1,557	185 11.88 11.88 3.63	-	-	-	-	-	-	-	-	-	-	-	-	-	-	-	-	-	-	-	-	-	-	-
Bellevue (city)	6,162 5.67	18,824	1,402 7.45 7.45 22.75	-	-	152 6.28 10.84 0.81 2.47	-	-	288 4.95 20.54 1.53 4.67	-	23 2.15 1.64 0.12 0.37	-	-	-	-	281 9.42 20.04 1.49 4.56	233 9.58 16.62 1.24 3.78	0 0.00 0.00 0.00 0.00	-	-	-	-	74 7.97 5.28 0.39 1.20	-	-	238 17.76 16.98 1.26 3.86
Bothell (city)	1,495 5.05	2,293	16 0.70 0.70 1.07	-	-	-	-	-	16 2.74 100.00 0.70 1.07	-	-	-	-	-	-	-	-	-	-	-	-	-	-	-	-	-
Bryn Mawr-Skyway (cdp)	1,073 7.67	3,049	95 3.12 3.12 8.85	-	-	-	-	-	-	-	7 0.80 7.37 0.23 0.65	-	-	-	-	34 5.55 35.79 1.12 3.17	-	-	-	-	-	-	-	-	-	7 1.67 7.37 0.23 0.65
Burien (city)	2,961 9.44	2,138	180 8.42 8.42 6.08	-	-	-	-	-	-	-	31 6.05 17.22 1.45 1.05	-	-	-	-	-	-	-	-	-	-	-	-	-	-	49 12.16 27.22 2.29 1.65
Cascade-Fairwood (cdp)	2,025 5.89	4,647	315 6.78 6.78 15.56	-	-	-	-	-	51 5.65 16.19 1.10 2.52	-	38 3.09 12.06 0.82 1.88	-	-	-	-	7 1.33 2.22 0.15 0.35	-	-	-	-	-	-	-	-	-	54 7.22 17.14 1.16 2.67
Cottage Lake (cdp)	661 2.72	1,051	69 6.57 6.57 10.44	-	-	-	-	-	-	-	-	-	-	-	-	-	-	-	-	-	-	-	-	-	-	-
Des Moines (city)	2,141 7.63	2,437	269 11.04 11.04 12.56	390	71 18.21 18.21 3.32	-	-	-	-	-	19 4.09 7.06 0.78 0.89	-	-	-	-	-	-	-	-	-	-	-	-	-	-	12 2.22 4.46 0.49 0.56
East Hill-Meridian (cdp)	1,297 4.40	3,905	196 5.02 5.02 15.11	-	-	63 8.32 32.14 1.61 4.86	-	-	42 5.28 21.43 1.08 3.24	-	0 0.00 0.00 0.00 0.00	-	-	-	-	-	-	-	-	-	-	-	-	-	-	56 9.96 28.57 1.43 4.32
Federal Way (city)	7,696 9.31	10,106	1,118 11.06 11.06 14.53	895	196 21.90 21.90 2.55	-	-	-	42 4.91 3.76 0.42 0.55	-	106 5.71 9.48 1.05 1.38	-	-	-	-	46 7.42 4.11 0.46 0.60	666 15.03 59.57 6.59 8.65	-	-	-	91 18.53 46.43 10.17 1.18	-	-	-	-	218 19.21 19.50 2.16 2.83

Notes: Please refer to the User's Guide for an explanation of data; data is arranged alphabetically by state, then county, then city within each county; table includes counties with populations greater than 49,999 unless noted and cities with populations greater than 9,999 whose Asian and/or NHPI population rates are greater than the national average; (1) Native Hawaiian and other Pacific Islander; (2) excludes Taiwanese; (3) includes Chamorro; (4) county does not meet population threshold but is shown in order to allow inclusion of city

Place	Total population with income below poverty level	Asian population for whom poverty status is determined	Asians with income below poverty level	NHPI[1] population for whom poverty status is determined	NHPIs[1] with income below poverty level	Asian Indian	Bangladeshi	Cambodian	Chinese[2]	Fijian	Filipino	Guamanian[3]	Hawaiian, Native	Hmong	Indonesian	Japanese	Korean	Laotian	Malaysian	Pakistani	Samoan	Sri Lankan	Taiwanese	Thai	Tongan	Vietnamese
Inglewood-Finn Hill (cdp)	921 4.09	1,679	10 0.60 0.60 1.09	-	-	-	-	-	6 1.46 60.00 0.36 0.65	-	-	-	-	-	-	-	-	-	-	-	-	-	-	-	-	-
Issaquah (city)	525 4.75	704	24 3.41 3.41 4.57	-	-	-	-	-	-	-	-	-	-	-	-	-	-	-	-	-	-	-	-	-	-	-
Kenmore (city)	1,058 5.74	1,226	99 8.08 8.08 9.36	-	-	-	-	-	-	-	-	-	-	-	-	-	-	-	-	-	-	-	-	-	-	-
Kent (city)	9,123 11.59	7,698	868 11.28 11.28 9.51	-	-	251 16.95 28.92 3.26 2.75	-	-	82 8.19 9.45 1.07 0.90	-	101 6.29 11.64 1.31 1.11	-	-	-	-	52 9.39 5.99 0.68 0.57	86 10.35 9.91 1.12 0.94	-	-	-	-	-	-	-	-	261 18.05 30.07 3.39 2.86
Kingsgate (cdp)	583 4.89	1,499	246 16.41 16.41 42.20	-	-	-	-	-	0 0.00 0.00 0.00 0.00	-	-	-	-	-	-	-	-	-	-	-	-	-	-	-	-	-
Kirkland (city)	2,337 5.31	3,416	263 7.70 7.70 11.25	-	-	-	-	-	49 6.25 18.63 1.43 2.10	-	-	-	-	-	-	39 7.60 14.83 1.14 1.67	-	-	-	-	-	-	-	-	-	0 0.00 0.00 0.00 0.00
Lake Forest Park (city)	513 3.82	1,157	18 1.56 1.56 3.51	-	-	-	-	-	-	-	-	-	-	-	-	-	-	-	-	-	-	-	-	-	-	-
Lakeland North (cdp)	763 5.05	941	97 10.31 10.31 12.71	-	-	-	-	-	-	-	-	-	-	-	-	-	-	-	-	-	-	-	-	-	-	-
Lakeland South (cdp)	606 5.28	665	17 2.56 2.56 2.81	-	-	-	-	-	-	-	-	-	-	-	-	-	-	-	-	-	-	-	-	-	-	-
Lea Hill (cdp)	628 5.93	519	172 33.14 33.14 27.39	-	-	-	-	-	-	-	-	-	-	-	-	-	-	-	-	-	-	-	-	-	-	-

Notes: Please refer to the User's Guide for an explanation of data; data is arranged alphabetically by state, then county, then city within each county; table includes counties with populations greater than 49,999 unless noted and cities with populations greater than 9,999 whose Asian and/or NHPI population rates are greater than the national average; (1) Native Hawaiian and other Pacific Islander; (2) excludes Taiwanese; (3) includes Chamorro; (4) county does not meet population threshold but is shown in order to allow inclusion of city

Place	Total population with income below poverty level	Asian population for whom poverty status is determined	Asians with income below poverty level	NHPI[1] population for whom poverty status is determined	NHPIs[1] with income below poverty level	Asian Indian	Bangladeshi	Cambodian	Chinese[2]	Fijian	Filipino	Guamanian[3]	Hawaiian, Native	Hmong	Indonesian	Japanese	Korean	Laotian	Malaysian	Pakistani	Samoan	Sri Lankan	Taiwanese	Thai	Tongan	Vietnamese
Mercer Island (city)	695	2,427	161	-	-	-	-	-	33	-	-	-	-	-	-	5	-	-	-	-	-	-	-	-	-	-
	3.18		6.63						3.20							0.88										
									20.50							3.11										
			6.63						1.36							0.21										
			23.17						4.75							0.72										
Redmond (city)	2,362	6,007	397	-	-	11	-	-	55	-	-	-	-	-	-	82	43	-	-	-	-	-	-	-	-	-
	5.26		6.61			0.88			2.86							10.59	8.85									
						2.77			13.85							20.65	10.83									
			6.61			0.18			0.92							1.37	0.72									
			16.81			0.47			2.33							3.47	1.82									
Renton (city)	4,798	6,642	557	-	-	-	-	-	26	-	0	-	-	-	-	82	-	-	-	-	-	-	-	-	-	347
	9.71		8.39						2.15		0.00					13.02										19.53
									4.67		0.00					14.72										62.30
			8.39						0.39		0.00					1.23										5.22
			11.61						0.54		0.00					1.71										7.23
Riverton-Boulevard Park (cdp)	1,310	1,521	200	-	-	-	-	-	-	-	-	-	-	-	-	-	-	-	-	-	-	-	-	-	-	-
	11.56		13.15																							
			13.15																							
			15.27																							
Sammamish (city)	674	2,530	81	-	-	-	-	-	55	-	-	-	-	-	-	-	-	-	-	-	-	-	-	-	-	-
	1.98		3.20						4.95																	
									67.90																	
			3.20						2.17																	
			12.02						8.16																	
SeaTac (city)	2,839	2,770	211	592	45	69	-	-	-	-	52	-	-	-	-	-	-	-	-	-	-	-	-	-	-	42
	11.55		7.62		7.60	12.37					7.17															8.32
						32.70					24.64															19.91
			7.62		7.60	2.49					1.88															1.52
			7.43		1.59	2.43					1.83															1.48
Seattle (city)	64,068	71,738	11,605	2,470	626	379	-	1,016	2,427	-	1,030	-	-	-	127	1,450	1,189	533	-	-	467	-	208	241	-	2,563
	11.79		16.18		25.34	13.95		40.77	13.31		6.51				33.60	15.92	25.54	20.27			35.54		22.39	28.66		22.87
						3.27		8.75	20.91		8.88				1.09	12.49	10.25	4.59			74.60		1.79	2.08		22.09
			16.18		25.34	0.53		1.42	3.38		1.44				0.18	2.02	1.66	0.74			18.91		0.29	0.34		3.57
			18.11		0.98	0.59		1.59	3.79		1.61				0.20	2.26	1.86	0.83			0.73		0.32	0.38		4.00
Shoreline (city)	3,614	6,598	721	-	-	0	-	-	101	-	16	-	-	-	-	55	325	-	-	-	-	-	-	-	-	75
	6.91		10.93			0.00			5.75		1.37					13.58	23.88									8.55
						0.00			14.01		2.22					7.63	45.08									10.40
			10.93			0.00			1.53		0.24					0.83	4.93									1.14
			19.95			0.00			2.79		0.44					1.52	8.99									2.08
Tukwila (city)	2,167	1,780	206	332	6	-	-	-	-	-	66	-	-	-	-	-	-	-	-	-	-	-	-	-	-	-
	12.70		11.57		1.81						11.04															
											32.04															
			11.57		1.81						3.71															
			9.51		0.28						3.05															
Union Hill-Novelty Hill (cdp)	322	528	23	-	-	-	-	-	-	-	-	-	-	-	-	-	-	-	-	-	-	-	-	-	-	-
	2.88		4.36																							
			4.36																							
			7.14																							

Notes: Please refer to the User's Guide for an explanation of data; data is arranged alphabetically by state, then county, then city within each county; table includes counties with populations greater than 49,999 unless noted and cities with populations greater than 9,999 whose Asian and/or NHPI population rates are greater than the national average; (1) Native Hawaiian and other Pacific Islander; (2) excludes Taiwanese; (3) includes Chamorro; (4) county does not meet population threshold but is shown in order to allow inclusion of city

Place	Total population with income below poverty level	Asian population for whom poverty status is determined	Asians with income below poverty level	NHPI[1] population for whom poverty status is determined	NHPIs[1] with income below poverty level	Asian Indian	Bangladeshi	Cambodian	Chinese[2]	Fijian	Filipino	Guamanian[3]	Hawaiian, Native	Hmong	Indonesian	Japanese	Korean	Laotian	Malaysian	Pakistani	Samoan	Sri Lankan	Taiwanese	Thai	Tongan	Vietnamese
White Center (cdp)	3,054 14.73	4,449	911 20.48 20.48 29.83	-	-	-	-	245 20.66 26.89 5.51 8.02	-	-	27 5.81 2.96 0.61 0.88	-	-	-	-	-	-	-	-	-	-	-	-	-	-	558 27.49 61.25 12.54 18.27
Kitsap County	19,601 8.75	10,201	765 7.50 7.50 3.90	1,653	279 16.88 16.88 1.42	-	-	-	41 8.70 5.36 0.40 0.21	-	437 6.45 57.12 4.28 2.23	185 17.93 66.31 11.19 0.94	-	-	-	26 2.21 3.40 0.25 0.13	82 13.58 10.72 0.80 0.42	-	-	-	-	-	-	-	-	167 40.53 21.83 1.64 0.85
Bremerton (city)	6,653 19.39	1,928	361 18.72 18.72 5.43	-	-	-	-	-	-	-	212 15.81 58.73 11.00 3.19	-	-	-	-	-	-	-	-	-	-	-	-	-	-	-
Silverdale (cdp)	740 4.76	1,751	28 1.60 1.60 3.78	-	-	-	-	-	-	-	15 1.02 53.57 0.86 2.03	-	-	-	-	-	-	-	-	-	-	-	-	-	-	-
Lewis County	9,460 14.01	371	18 4.85 4.85 0.19	-	-	-	-	-	-	-	-	-	-	-	-	-	-	-	-	-	-	-	-	-	-	-
Pierce County	71,316 10.49	34,157	6,483 18.98 18.98 9.09	4,936	734 14.87 14.87 1.03	25 3.21 0.39 0.07 0.04	-	1,292 31.97 19.93 3.78 1.81	274 15.73 4.23 0.80 0.38	-	480 7.26 7.40 1.41 0.67	187 10.46 25.48 3.79 0.26	110 12.60 14.99 2.23 0.15	-	-	395 11.54 6.09 1.16 0.55	2,377 21.54 36.67 6.96 3.33	156 41.49 2.41 0.46 0.22	-	-	403 23.93 54.90 8.16 0.57	-	-	17 4.57 0.26 0.05 0.02	-	1,145 26.96 17.66 3.35 1.61
Elk Plain (cdp)	1,215 7.83	609	30 4.93 4.93 2.47	-	-	-	-	-	-	-	-	-	-	-	-	-	-	-	-	-	-	-	-	-	-	-
Fort Lewis (cdp)	1,066 8.21	479	0 <0.01 <0.01 <0.01	270	0 <0.01 <0.01 <0.01	-	-	-	-	-	0 <0.01 ***.** <0.01 <0.01	-	-	-	-	-	-	-	-	-	-	-	-	-	-	-
Lakewood (city)	8,931 15.77	5,149	1,145 22.24 22.24 12.82	737	118 16.01 16.01 1.32	-	-	-	-	-	232 19.08 20.26 4.51 2.60	-	-	-	-	57 8.89 4.98 1.11 0.64	724 31.09 63.23 14.06 8.11	-	-	-	101 34.47 85.59 13.70 1.13	-	-	-	-	-
Parkland (cdp)	3,451 15.39	1,528	229 14.99 14.99 6.64	415	38 9.16 9.16 1.10	-	-	-	-	-	-	-	-	-	-	-	141 18.15 61.57 9.23 4.09	-	-	-	-	-	-	-	-	-

Notes: Please refer to the User's Guide for an explanation of data; data is arranged alphabetically by state, then county, then city within each county; table includes counties with populations greater than 49,999 unless noted and cities with populations greater than 9,999 whose Asian and/or NHPI population rates are greater than the national average; (1) Native Hawaiian and other Pacific Islander; (2) excludes Taiwanese; (3) includes Chamorro; (4) county does not meet population threshold but is shown in order to allow inclusion of city

Place	Total population with income below poverty level	Asian population for whom poverty status is determined	Asians with income below poverty level	NHPI[1] population for whom poverty status is determined	NHPIs[1] with income below poverty level	Asian Indian	Bangladeshi	Cambodian	Chinese[2]	Fijian	Filipino	Guamanian[3]	Hawaiian, Native	Hmong	Indonesian	Japanese	Korean	Laotian	Malaysian	Pakistani	Samoan	Sri Lankan	Taiwanese	Thai	Tongan	Vietnamese
Spanaway (cdp)	2,300	1,275	184	578	85	-	-	-	-	-	47	-	-	-	-	-	118	-	-	-	-	-	-	-	-	-
	10.79		14.43		14.71						8.94						20.24									
											25.54						64.13									
			14.43		14.71						3.69						9.25									
			8.00		3.70						2.04						5.13									
Tacoma (city)	29,887	14,186	3,728	1,283	310	-	-	1,144	113	-	58	107	-	-	-	173	750	149	-	-	165	-	-	-	-	1,070
	15.90		26.28		24.16			36.29	15.29		2.94	26.82				19.66	24.50	50.00			27.05					34.54
								30.69	3.03		1.56	34.52				4.64	20.12	4.00			53.23					28.70
			26.28		24.16			8.06	0.80		0.41	8.34				1.22	5.29	1.05			12.86					7.54
			12.47		1.04			3.83	0.38		0.19	0.36				0.58	2.51	0.50			0.55					3.58
University Place (city)	2,176	2,296	300	-	-	-	-	-	-	-	-	-	-	-	-	-	231	-	-	-	-	-	-	-	-	-
	7.27		13.07														18.67									
																	77.00									
			13.07														10.06									
			13.79														10.62									
Skagit County	11,244	1,391	262	-	-	-	-	-	-	-	24	-	-	-	-	-	-	-	-	-	-	-	-	-	-	-
	11.11		18.84								4.96															
											9.16															
			18.84								1.73															
			2.33								0.21															
Snohomish County	41,024	35,292	3,689	1,244	80	202	-	179	474	-	368	-	38	-	-	222	1,000	102	-	22	-	-	-	-	-	786
	6.86		10.45		6.43	7.58		9.00	10.73		4.92		7.47			9.05	13.49	13.35		5.21						14.99
						5.48		4.85	12.85		9.98		47.50			6.02	27.11	2.76		0.60						21.31
			10.45		6.43	0.57		0.51	1.34		1.04		3.05			0.63	2.83	0.29		0.06						2.23
			8.99		0.20	0.49		0.44	1.16		0.90		0.09			0.54	2.44	0.25		0.05						1.92
Alderwood Manor (cdp)	540	1,245	61	-	-	-	-	-	-	-	-	-	-	-	-	-	-	-	-	-	-	-	-	-	-	-
	3.55		4.90																							
			4.90																							
			11.30																							
Edmonds (city)	1,821	2,187	292	-	-	-	-	-	-	-	15	-	-	-	-	-	112	-	-	-	-	-	-	-	-	-
	4.63		13.35								4.12						19.48									
											5.14						38.36									
			13.35								0.69						5.12									
			16.04								0.82						6.15									
Everett (city)	11,283	5,870	1,197	-	-	94	-	129	-	-	206	-	-	-	-	-	-	-	-	-	-	-	-	-	-	328
	12.85		20.39			15.96		20.51			12.34															27.59
						7.85		10.78			17.21															27.40
			20.39			1.60		2.20			3.51															5.59
			10.61			0.83		1.14			1.83															2.91
Lynnwood (city)	3,185	4,706	452	-	-	-	-	-	141	-	0	-	-	-	-	-	141	-	-	-	-	-	-	-	-	78
	9.49		9.60						22.60		0.00						13.60									7.97
									31.19		0.00						31.19									17.26
			9.60						3.00		0.00						3.00									1.66
			14.19						4.43		0.00						4.43									2.45
Martha Lake (cdp)	620	1,153	102	-	-	-	-	-	-	-	-	-	-	-	-	-	-	-	-	-	-	-	-	-	-	-
	4.92		8.85																							
			8.85																							
			16.45																							

Notes: Please refer to the User's Guide for an explanation of data; data is arranged alphabetically by state, then county, then city within each county; table includes counties with populations greater than 49,999 unless noted and cities with populations greater than 9,999 whose Asian and/or NHPI population rates are greater than the national average; (1) Native Hawaiian and other Pacific Islander; (2) excludes Taiwanese; (3) includes Chamorro; (4) county does not meet population threshold but is shown in order to allow inclusion of city

Place	Total population with income below poverty level	Asian population for whom poverty status is determined	Asians with income below poverty level	NHPI[1] population for whom poverty status is determined	NHPIs[1] with income below poverty level	Asian Indian	Bangladeshi	Cambodian	Chinese[2]	Fijian	Filipino	Guamanian[3]	Hawaiian, Native	Hmong	Indonesian	Japanese	Korean	Laotian	Malaysian	Pakistani	Samoan	Sri Lankan	Taiwanese	Thai	Tongan	Vietnamese
Marysville (city)	1,397 5.58	953	101 10.60 10.60 7.23	-	-	-	-	-	-	-	-	-	-	-	-	-	-	-	-	-	-	-	-	-	-	-
Mill Creek (city)	403 3.52	1,187	58 4.89 4.89 14.39	-	-	-	-	-	-	-	-	-	-	-	-	-	21 4.73 36.21 1.77 5.21	-	-	-	-	-	-	-	-	-
Mountlake Terrace (city)	1,625 8.04	2,347	356 15.17 15.17 21.91	-	-	-	-	-	-	-	17 3.07 4.78 0.72 1.05	-	-	-	-	-	86 14.33 24.16 3.66 5.29	-	-	-	-	-	-	-	-	-
Mukilteo (city)	613 3.40	2,092	93 4.45 4.45 15.17	-	-	-	-	-	-	-	-	-	-	-	-	-	80 7.95 86.02 3.82 13.05	-	-	-	-	-	-	-	-	-
North Creek (cdp)	1,051 4.07	1,537	89 5.79 5.79 8.47	-	-	-	-	-	-	-	-	-	-	-	-	-	-	-	-	-	-	-	-	-	-	-
Paine Field-Lk. Stickney (cdp)	2,641 10.96	1,572	66 4.20 4.20 2.50	-	-	-	-	-	-	-	-	-	-	-	-	-	-	-	-	-	-	-	-	-	-	-
Picnic Pt.-N. Lynnwood (cdp)	1,569 6.90	2,482	402 16.20 16.20 25.62	-	-	-	-	-	-	-	0 0.00 0.00 0.00 0.00	-	-	-	-	-	214 24.57 53.23 8.62 13.64	-	-	-	-	-	-	-	-	-
Seattle Hill-Silver Firs (cdp)	1,109 3.13	2,749	83 3.02 3.02 7.48	-	-	-	-	-	-	-	0 0.00 0.00 0.00 0.00	-	-	-	-	-	47 7.61 56.63 1.71 4.24	-	-	-	-	-	-	-	-	0 0.00 0.00 0.00 0.00
Spokane County	49,859 12.32	6,799	1,347 19.81 19.81 2.70	622	141 22.67 22.67 0.28	34 5.43 2.52 0.50 0.07	-	-	200 23.36 14.85 2.94 0.40	-	99 10.92 7.35 1.46 0.20	-	-	346 64.92 25.69 5.09 0.69	-	235 18.09 17.45 3.46 0.47	51 8.02 3.79 0.75 0.10	-	-	-	-	-	-	-	-	185 15.13 13.73 2.72 0.37
Spokane (city)	30,359 15.92	4,040	816 20.20 20.20 2.69	403	95 23.57 23.57 0.31	-	-	-	87 16.51 10.66 2.15 0.29	-	51 11.16 6.25 1.26 0.17	-	-	287 69.83 35.17 7.10 0.95	-	67 8.55 8.21 1.66 0.22	40 11.27 4.90 0.99 0.13	-	-	-	-	-	-	-	-	176 22.31 21.57 4.36 0.58

Notes: Please refer to the User's Guide for an explanation of data; data is arranged alphabetically by state, then county, then city within each county; table includes counties with populations greater than 49,999 unless noted and cities with populations greater than 9,999 whose Asian and/or NHPI population rates are greater than the national average; (1) Native Hawaiian and other Pacific Islander; (2) excludes Taiwanese; (3) includes Chamorro; (4) county does not meet population threshold but is shown in order to allow inclusion of city

Place	Total population with income below poverty level	Asian population for whom poverty status is determined	Asians with income below poverty level	NHPI[1] population for whom poverty status is determined	NHPIs[1] with income below poverty level	Asian Indian	Bangladeshi	Cambodian	Chinese[2]	Fijian	Filipino	Guamanian[3]	Hawaiian, Native	Hmong	Indonesian	Japanese	Korean	Laotian	Malaysian	Pakistani	Samoan	Sri Lankan	Taiwanese	Thai	Tongan	Vietnamese
Thurston County	17,992	9,289	1,262	1,167	115	39	-	279	68	-	145	31	-	-	-	106	138	-	-	-	-	-	-	-	-	387
	8.84		13.59		9.85	8.33		33.33	7.68		9.26	4.32				13.68	6.44									22.11
						3.09		22.11	5.39		11.49	26.96				8.40	10.94									30.67
			13.59		9.85	0.42		3.00	0.73		1.56	2.66				1.14	1.49									4.17
			7.01		0.64	0.22		1.55	0.38		0.81	0.17				0.59	0.77									2.15
Lacey (city)	2,798	2,472	271	-	-	-	-	-	-	-	78	-	-	-	-	-	5	-	-	-	-	-	-	-	-	119
	9.16		10.96								16.60						0.82									20.52
											28.78						1.85									43.91
			10.96								3.16						0.20									4.81
			9.69								2.79						0.18									4.25
Olympia (city)	4,982	2,326	413	-	-	-	-	-	-	-	-	-	-	-	-	-	-	-	-	-	-	-	-	-	-	241
	12.07		17.76																							34.04
																										58.35
			17.76																							10.36
			8.29																							4.84
Tumwater (city)	1,060	479	118	-	-	-	-	-	-	-	-	-	-	-	-	-	-	-	-	-	-	-	-	-	-	-
	8.46		24.63																							
			24.63																							
			11.13																							
Walla Walla County	7,567	544	89	-	-	-	-	-	-	-	-	-	-	-	-	-	-	-	-	-	-	-	-	-	-	-
	15.06		16.36																							
			16.36																							
			1.18																							
Whatcom County	23,003	4,152	1,007	-	-	270	-	-	81	-	61	-	-	-	-	193	161	-	-	-	-	-	-	-	-	81
	14.22		24.25			21.77			16.20		12.95					42.60	40.35									13.46
						26.81			8.04		6.06					19.17	15.99									8.04
			24.25			6.50			1.95		1.47					4.65	3.88									1.95
			4.38			1.17			0.35		0.27					0.84	0.70									0.35
Bellingham (city)	12,854	2,416	895	-	-	220	-	-	-	-	-	-	-	-	-	-	-	-	-	-	-	-	-	-	-	74
	20.62		37.04			36.07																				16.41
						24.58																				8.27
			37.04			9.11																				3.06
			6.96			1.71																				0.58
Whitman County[4]	9,027	1,737	887	-	-	-	-	-	236	-	-	-	-	-	-	240	-	-	-	-	-	-	-	-	-	-
	25.59		51.07						39.80							63.49										
									26.61							27.06										
			51.07						13.59							13.82										
			9.83						2.61							2.66										
Pullman (city)	7,444	1,564	844	-	-	-	-	-	193	-	-	-	-	-	-	240	-	-	-	-	-	-	-	-	-	-
	37.53		53.96						36.97							66.12										
									22.87							28.44										
			53.96						12.34							15.35										
			11.34						2.59							3.22										
Yakima County	43,070	2,156	392	-	-	-	-	-	-	-	151	-	-	-	-	-	-	-	-	-	-	-	-	-	-	-
	19.67		18.18								16.48															
											38.52															
			18.18								7.00															
			0.91								0.35															

Notes: Please refer to the User's Guide for an explanation of data; data is arranged alphabetically by state, then county, then city within each county; table includes counties with populations greater than 49,999 unless noted and cities with populations greater than 9,999 whose Asian and/or NHPI population rates are greater than the national average; (1) Native Hawaiian and other Pacific Islander; (2) excludes Taiwanese; (3) includes Chamorro; (4) county does not meet population threshold but is shown in order to allow inclusion of city

Place	Total population with income below poverty level	Asian population for whom poverty status is determined	Asians with income below poverty level	NHPI[1] population for whom poverty status is determined	NHPIs[1] with income below poverty level	Asian Indian	Bangladeshi	Cambodian	Chinese[2]	Fijian	Filipino	Guamanian[3]	Hawaiian, Native	Hmong	Indonesian	Japanese	Korean	Laotian	Malaysian	Pakistani	Samoan	Sri Lankan	Taiwanese	Thai	Tongan	Vietnamese
WEST VIRGINIA	315,794	8,948	1,624	386	52	339	-	-	377	-	147	-	-	-	-	283	144	-	-	62	-	-	-	-	-	70
	17.90		18.15		13.47	13.69			23.29		9.19					38.66	16.94			19.75						16.17
						20.87			23.21		9.05					17.43	8.87			3.82						4.31
			18.15		13.47	3.79			4.21		1.64					3.16	1.61			0.69						0.78
			0.51		0.02	0.11			0.12		0.05					0.09	0.05			0.02						0.02
Cabell County	17,983	719	179	-	-	-	-	-	-	-	-	-	-	-	-	-	-	-	-	-	-	-	-	-	-	-
	19.23		24.90																							
			24.90																							
			1.00																							
Harrison County	11,593	296	108	-	-	-	-	-	-	-	-	-	-	-	-	-	-	-	-	-	-	-	-	-	-	-
	17.20		36.49																							
			36.49																							
			0.93																							
Kanawha County	28,374	1,659	143	-	-	33	-	-	-	-	-	-	-	-	-	-	-	-	-	-	-	-	-	-	-	-
	14.38		8.62			5.83																				
						23.08																				
			8.62			1.99																				
			0.50			0.12																				
Monongalia County	17,394	1,824	651	-	-	168	-	-	208	-	-	-	-	-	-	-	-	-	-	-	-	-	-	-	-	-
	22.83		35.69			31.52			34.44																	
						25.81			31.95																	
			35.69			9.21			11.40																	
			3.74			0.97			1.20																	
Putnam County	4,785	300	48	-	-	-	-	-	-	-	-	-	-	-	-	-	-	-	-	-	-	-	-	-	-	-
	9.33		16.00																							
			16.00																							
			1.00																							
Raleigh County	14,006	608	10	-	-	-	-	-	-	-	-	-	-	-	-	-	-	-	-	-	-	-	-	-	-	-
	18.54		1.64																							
			1.64																							
			0.07																							
Wood County	11,979	384	43	-	-	-	-	-	-	-	-	-	-	-	-	-	-	-	-	-	-	-	-	-	-	-
	13.85		11.20																							
			11.20																							
			0.36																							
WISCONSIN	451,538	81,233	16,119	1,382	159	1,428	-	309	1,383	-	380	32	83	7,928	132	487	1,345	831	-	190	-	-	273	184	-	478
	8.66		19.84		11.51	12.95		50.00	14.89		7.18	8.40	23.12	25.86	33.00	17.09	20.46	20.39		20.81			41.87	21.45		12.61
						8.86		1.92	8.58		2.36	20.13	52.20	49.18	0.82	3.02	8.34	5.16		1.18			1.69	1.14		2.97
			19.84		11.51	1.76		0.38	1.70		0.47	2.32	6.01	9.76	0.16	0.60	1.66	1.02		0.23			0.34	0.23		0.59
			3.57		0.04	0.32		0.07	0.31		0.08	0.01	0.02	1.76	0.03	0.11	0.30	0.18		0.04			0.06	0.04		0.11
Brown County	15,123	4,514	1,034	-	-	49	-	-	-	-	-	-	-	662	-	-	-	134	-	-	-	-	-	-	-	-
	6.90		22.91			16.72								27.47				31.31								
						4.74								64.02				12.96								
			22.91			1.09								14.67				2.97								
			6.84			0.32								4.38				0.89								

Notes: Please refer to the User's Guide for an explanation of data; data is arranged alphabetically by state, then county, then city within each county; table includes counties with populations greater than 49,999 unless noted and cities with populations greater than 9,999 whose Asian and/or NHPI population rates are greater than the national average; (1) Native Hawaiian and other Pacific Islander; (2) excludes Taiwanese; (3) includes Chamorro; (4) county does not meet population threshold but is shown in order to allow inclusion of city

Place	Total population with income below poverty level	Asian population for whom poverty status is determined	Asians with income below poverty level	NHPI[1] population for whom poverty status is determined	NHPIs[1] with income below poverty level	Asian Indian	Bangladeshi	Cambodian	Chinese[2]	Fijian	Filipino	Guamanian[3]	Hawaiian, Native	Hmong	Indonesian	Japanese	Korean	Laotian	Malaysian	Pakistani	Samoan	Sri Lankan	Taiwanese	Thai	Tongan	Vietnamese
Chippewa County	4,442 8.23	463	192 41.47 41.47 4.32	-	-	-	-	-	-	-	-	-	-	161 44.85 83.85 34.77 3.62	-	-	-	-	-	-	-	-	-	-	-	-
Columbia County	2,656 5.23	177	8 4.52 4.52 0.30	-	-	-	-	-	-	-	-	-	-	-	-	-	-	-	-	-	-	-	-	-	-	-
Dane County	38,815 9.44	13,732	3,569 25.99 25.99 9.19	-	-	313 15.39 8.77 2.28 0.81	-	-	725 24.01 20.31 5.28 1.87	-	122 19.58 3.42 0.89 0.31	-	-	526 23.49 14.74 3.83 1.36	-	174 22.00 4.88 1.27 0.45	807 44.24 22.61 5.88 2.08	0 0.00 0.00 0.00 0.00	-	-	-	-	230 55.16 6.44 1.67 0.59	-	-	178 24.45 4.99 1.30 0.46
Madison (city)	29,287 14.99	11,115	3,338 30.03 30.03 11.40	-	-	295 22.78 8.84 2.65 1.01	-	-	725 27.51 21.72 6.52 2.48	-	112 26.48 3.36 1.01 0.38	-	-	431 24.47 12.91 3.88 1.47	-	167 24.52 5.00 1.50 0.57	776 47.96 23.25 6.98 2.65	-	-	-	-	-	230 55.56 6.89 2.07 0.79	-	-	178 28.34 5.33 1.60 0.61
Dodge County	4,295 5.35	268	35 13.06 13.06 0.81	-	-	-	-	-	-	-	-	-	-	-	-	-	-	-	-	-	-	-	-	-	-	-
Eau Claire County	9,581 10.87	2,234	452 20.23 20.23 4.72	-	-	-	-	-	-	-	-	-	-	333 24.56 73.67 14.91 3.48	-	-	-	-	-	-	-	-	-	-	-	-
Fond du Lac County	5,471 5.84	563	124 22.02 22.02 2.27	-	-	-	-	-	-	-	-	-	-	49 18.49 39.52 8.70 0.90	-	-	-	-	-	-	-	-	-	-	-	-
Jefferson County	4,111 5.69	209	33 15.79 15.79 0.80	-	-	-	-	-	-	-	-	-	-	-	-	-	-	-	-	-	-	-	-	-	-	-
Kenosha County	10,915 7.50	1,363	160 11.74 11.74 1.47	-	-	-	-	-	-	-	-	-	-	-	-	-	-	-	-	-	-	-	-	-	-	-
La Crosse County	10,841 10.65	2,764	424 15.34 15.34 3.91	-	-	-	-	-	-	-	-	-	-	320 16.82 75.47 11.58 2.95	-	-	-	-	-	-	-	-	-	-	-	-

Notes: Please refer to the User's Guide for an explanation of data; data is arranged alphabetically by state, then county, then city within each county; table includes counties with populations greater than 49,999 unless noted and cities with populations greater than 9,999 whose Asian and/or NHPI population rates are greater than the national average; (1) Native Hawaiian and other Pacific Islander; (2) excludes Taiwanese; (3) includes Chamorro; (4) county does not meet population threshold but is shown in order to allow inclusion of city

Place	Total population with income below poverty level	Asian population for whom poverty status is determined	Asians with income below poverty level	NHPI[1] population for whom poverty status is determined	NHPIs[1] with income below poverty level	Asian Indian	Bangladeshi	Cambodian	Chinese[2]	Fijian	Filipino	Guamanian[3]	Hawaiian, Native	Hmong	Indonesian	Japanese	Korean	Laotian	Malaysian	Pakistani	Samoan	Sri Lankan	Taiwanese	Thai	Tongan	Vietnamese
La Crosse (city)	8,085 17.20	1,852	349 18.84 18.84 4.32	-	-	-	-	-	-	-	-	-	-	254 19.49 72.78 13.71 3.14	-	-	-	-	-	-	-	-	-	-	-	-
Manitowoc County	4,960 6.06	1,467	371 25.29 25.29 7.48	-	-	-	-	-	-	-	-	-	-	315 33.69 84.91 21.47 6.35	-	-	-	-	-	-	-	-	-	-	-	-
Marathon County	8,163 6.58	5,088	1,557 30.60 30.60 19.07	-	-	-	-	-	-	-	-	-	-	1,441 35.57 92.55 28.32 17.65	-	-	-	-	-	-	-	-	-	-	-	-
Wausau (city)	4,227 11.35	4,130	1,528 37.00 37.00 36.15	-	-	-	-	-	-	-	-	-	-	1,417 41.58 92.74 34.31 33.52	-	-	-	-	-	-	-	-	-	-	-	-
Milwaukee County	139,747 15.26	22,111	4,053 18.33 18.33 2.90	410	54 13.17 13.17 0.04	544 14.43 13.42 2.46 0.39	-	-	395 17.87 9.75 1.79 0.28	-	90 5.75 2.22 0.41 0.06	-	-	1,519 20.44 37.48 6.87 1.09	-	90 12.24 2.22 0.41 0.06	254 19.95 6.27 1.15 0.18	501 29.16 12.36 2.27 0.36	-	91 25.63 2.25 0.41 0.07	-	-	-	-	-	133 10.43 3.28 0.60 0.10
Outagamie County	7,417 4.69	3,605	863 23.94 23.94 11.64	-	-	81 19.57 9.39 2.25 1.09	-	-	-	-	-	-	-	618 26.55 71.61 17.14 8.33	-	-	-	-	-	-	-	-	-	-	-	-
Appleton (city)	3,714 5.46	3,162	682 21.57 21.57 18.36	-	-	-	-	-	-	-	-	-	-	534 22.91 78.30 16.89 14.38	-	-	-	-	-	-	-	-	-	-	-	-
Ozaukee County	2,078 2.58	663	62 9.35 9.35 2.98	-	-	-	-	-	-	-	-	-	-	-	-	-	-	-	-	-	-	-	-	-	-	-
Portage County	6,074 9.52	1,225	336 27.43 27.43 5.53	-	-	-	-	-	-	-	-	-	-	221 25.43 65.77 18.04 3.64	-	-	-	-	-	-	-	-	-	-	-	-
Stevens Point (city)	3,687 17.26	965	276 28.60 28.60 7.49	-	-	-	-	-	-	-	-	-	-	188 24.83 68.12 19.48 5.10	-	-	-	-	-	-	-	-	-	-	-	-

Notes: Please refer to the User's Guide for an explanation of data; data is arranged alphabetically by state, then county, then city within each county; table includes counties with populations greater than 49,999 unless noted and cities with populations greater than 9,999 whose Asian and/or NHPI population rates are greater than the national average; (1) Native Hawaiian and other Pacific Islander; (2) excludes Taiwanese; (3) includes Chamorro; (4) county does not meet population threshold but is shown in order to allow inclusion of city

Place	Total population with income below poverty level	Asian population for whom poverty status is determined	Asians with income below poverty level	NHPI[1] population for whom poverty status is determined	NHPIs[1] with income below poverty level	Asian Indian	Bangladeshi	Cambodian	Chinese[2]	Fijian	Filipino	Guamanian[3]	Hawaiian, Native	Hmong	Indonesian	Japanese	Korean	Laotian	Malaysian	Pakistani	Samoan	Sri Lankan	Taiwanese	Thai	Tongan	Vietnamese
Racine County	15,491 8.40	1,277	182 14.25 14.25 1.17	-	-	-	-	-	-	-	-	-	-	-	-	-	-	-	-	-	-	-	-	-	-	-
Rock County	10,880 7.32	1,248	120 9.62 9.62 1.10	-	-	-	-	-	-	-	-	-	-	-	-	-	-	-	-	-	-	-	-	-	-	-
St. Croix County	2,493 4.01	255	40 15.69 15.69 1.60	-	-	-	-	-	-	-	-	-	-	-	-	-	-	-	-	-	-	-	-	-	-	-
Sauk County	3,928 7.22	209	2 0.96 0.96 0.05	-	-	-	-	-	-	-	-	-	-	-	-	-	-	-	-	-	-	-	-	-	-	-
Sheboygan County	5,658 5.18	3,534	696 19.69 19.69 12.30	-	-	-	-	-	-	-	-	-	-	505 20.29 72.56 14.29 8.93	-	-	-	-	-	-	-	-	-	-	-	-
Sheboygan (city)	4,107 8.27	3,271	675 20.64 20.64 16.44	-	-	-	-	-	-	-	-	-	-	505 21.18 74.81 15.44 12.30	-	-	-	-	-	-	-	-	-	-	-	-
Walworth County	7,478 8.41	513	78 15.20 15.20 1.04	-	-	-	-	-	-	-	-	-	-	-	-	-	-	-	-	-	-	-	-	-	-	-
Washington County	4,204 3.62	513	0 <0.01 <0.01 <0.01	-	-	-	-	-	-	-	-	-	-	-	-	-	-	-	-	-	-	-	-	-	-	-
Waukesha County	9,635 2.71	4,974	191 3.84 3.84 1.98	-	-	30 1.82 15.71 0.60 0.31	-	-	40 3.51 20.94 0.80 0.42	-	8 2.03 4.19 0.16 0.08	-	-	-	-	-	64 10.81 33.51 1.29 0.66	-	-	-	-	-	-	-	-	-
Winnebago County	9,940 6.68	2,401	403 16.78 16.78 4.05	-	-	-	-	-	-	-	-	-	-	347 23.46 86.10 14.45 3.49	-	-	-	-	-	-	-	-	-	-	-	-

Notes: Please refer to the User's Guide for an explanation of data; data is arranged alphabetically by state, then county, then city within each county; table includes counties with populations greater than 49,999 unless noted and cities with populations greater than 9,999 whose Asian and/or NHPI population rates are greater than the national average; (1) Native Hawaiian and other Pacific Islander; (2) excludes Taiwanese; (3) includes Chamorro; (4) county does not meet population threshold but is shown in order to allow inclusion of city

Place	Total population with income below poverty level	Asian population for whom poverty status is determined	Asians with income below poverty level	NHPI[1] population for whom poverty status is determined	NHPIs[1] with income below poverty level	Asian Indian	Bangladeshi	Cambodian	Chinese[2]	Fijian	Filipino	Guamanian[3]	Hawaiian, Native	Hmong	Indonesian	Japanese	Korean	Laotian	Malaysian	Pakistani	Samoan	Sri Lankan	Taiwanese	Thai	Tongan	Vietnamese
Wood County	4,851 6.51	1,160	147 12.67 12.67 3.03	-	-	-	-	-	-	-	-	-	-	120 20.30 81.63 10.34 2.47	-	-	-	-	-	-	-	-	-	-	-	-
WYOMING	54,777 11.42	2,815	310 11.01 11.01 0.57	-	-	33 7.80 10.65 1.17 0.06	-	-	60 10.00 19.35 2.13 0.11	-	47 9.42 15.16 1.67 0.09	-	-	-	-	31 7.42 10.00 1.10 0.06	61 13.32 19.68 2.17 0.11	-	-	-	-	-	-	-	-	-
Laramie County	7,104 9.10	781	41 5.25 5.25 0.58	-	-	-	-	-	-	-	-	-	-	-	-	-	-	-	-	-	-	-	-	-	-	-
Natrona County	7,695 11.84	409	46 11.25 11.25 0.60	-	-	-	-	-	-	-	-	-	-	-	-	-	-	-	-	-	-	-	-	-	-	-

Notes: Please refer to the User's Guide for an explanation of data; data is arranged alphabetically by state, then county, then city within each county; table includes counties with populations greater than 49,999 unless noted and cities with populations greater than 9,999 whose Asian and/or NHPI population rates are greater than the national average; (1) Native Hawaiian and other Pacific Islander; (2) excludes Taiwanese; (3) includes Chamorro; (4) county does not meet population threshold but is shown in order to allow inclusion of city

Homeownership

(Universe: Occupied Housing Units)

Place	All owner-occupied housing units	Asian-occupied housing units	Asians who own and occupy their own homes	NHPI[1]-occupied housing units	NHPIs[1] who own and occupy their own homes	Asian Indian	Bangladeshi	Cambodian	Chinese[2]	Fijian	Filipino	Guamanian[3]	Hawaiian, Native	Hmong	Indonesian	Japanese	Korean	Laotian	Malaysian	Pakistani	Samoan	Sri Lankan	Taiwanese	Thai	Tongan	Vietnamese
UNITED STATES	69,816,513	3,117,356	1,659,794	98,739	44,896	247,650	3,171	17,134	441,852	1,389	307,810	7,536	21,581	10,419	4,977	204,997	134,736	20,717	1,092	17,306	6,585	3,424	26,324	16,556	2,465	155,325
	66.19		53.24		45.47	46.87	28.17	43.59	58.08	50.38	59.98	47.57	52.22	38.74	38.55	60.84	40.08	52.37	29.70	41.65	34.36	51.07	64.75	48.06	48.14	53.22
						14.92	0.19	1.03	26.62	3.09	18.55	16.79	48.07	0.63	0.30	12.35	8.12	1.25	0.07	1.04	14.67	0.21	1.59	1.00	5.49	9.36
			53.24		45.47	7.94	0.10	0.55	14.17	1.41	9.87	7.63	21.86	0.33	0.16	6.58	4.32	0.66	0.04	0.56	6.67	0.11	0.84	0.53	2.50	4.98
			2.38		0.06	0.35	<0.01	0.02	0.63	<0.01	0.44	0.01	0.03	0.01	0.01	0.29	0.19	0.03	<0.01	0.02	0.01	<0.01	0.04	0.02	<0.01	0.22
ALABAMA	1,258,686	9,272	4,552	337	159	1,108	-	108	819	-	390	61	-	-	-	335	472	144	-	64	-	-	-	69	-	736
	72.46		49.09		47.18	48.07		68.79	40.87		54.47	39.87				51.78	46.50	68.57		52.89				37.50		58.41
						24.34		2.37	17.99		8.57	38.36				7.36	10.37	3.16		1.41				1.52		16.17
			49.09		47.18	11.95		1.16	8.83		4.21	18.10				3.61	5.09	1.55		0.69				0.74		7.94
			0.36		0.01	0.09		0.01	0.07		0.03	<0.01				0.03	0.04	0.01		0.01				0.01		0.06
Baldwin County	44,036	142	81	-	-	-	-	-	-	-	-	-	-	-	-	-	-	-	-	-	-	-	-	-	-	-
	79.58		57.04																							
			57.04																							
			0.18																							
Calhoun County	32,845	253	115	-	-	-	-	-	-	-	-	-	-	-	-	-	-	-	-	-	-	-	-	-	-	-
	72.49		45.45																							
			45.45																							
			0.35																							
Etowah County	30,957	121	61	-	-	-	-	-	-	-	-	-	-	-	-	-	-	-	-	-	-	-	-	-	-	-
	74.39		50.41																							
			50.41																							
			0.20																							
Houston County	24,893	151	98	-	-	-	-	-	-	-	-	-	-	-	-	-	-	-	-	-	-	-	-	-	-	-
	69.47		64.90																							
			64.90																							
			0.39																							
Jefferson County	174,982	2,038	745	-	-	238	-	-	179	-	-	-	-	-	-	-	61	-	-	-	-	-	-	-	-	95
	66.47		36.56			43.91			29.59								32.80									45.89
						31.95			24.03								8.19									12.75
			36.56			11.68			8.78								2.99									4.66
			0.43			0.14			0.10								0.03									0.05
Lee County	28,376	677	270	-	-	-	-	-	91	-	-	-	-	-	-	-	-	-	-	-	-	-	-	-	-	-
	62.09		39.88						32.16																	
									33.70																	
			39.88						13.44																	
			0.95						0.32																	
Madison County	76,816	1,421	741	-	-	246	-	-	114	-	-	-	-	-	-	-	140	-	-	-	-	-	-	-	-	93
	69.86		52.15			52.90			47.50								52.63									63.27
						33.20			15.38								18.89									12.55
			52.15			17.31			8.02								9.85									6.54
			0.96			0.32			0.15								0.18									0.12

Notes: Please refer to the User's Guide for an explanation of data; data is arranged alphabetically by state, then county, then city within each county; table includes counties with populations greater than 49,999 unless noted and cities with populations greater than 9,999 whose Asian and/or NHPI population rates are greater than the national average; (1) Native Hawaiian and other Pacific Islander; (2) excludes Taiwanese; (3) includes Chamorro; (4) county does not meet population threshold but is shown in order to allow inclusion of city

Place	All owner-occupied housing units	Asian-occupied housing units	Asians who own and occupy their own homes	NHPI[1]-occupied housing units	NHPIs[1] who own and occupy their own homes	Asian Indian	Bangladeshi	Cambodian	Chinese[2]	Fijian	Filipino	Guamanian[3]	Hawaiian, Native	Hmong	Indonesian	Japanese	Korean	Laotian	Malaysian	Pakistani	Samoan	Sri Lankan	Taiwanese	Thai	Tongan	Vietnamese
Mobile County	103,402 68.85	1,427	746 52.28 52.28 0.72	-	-	56 35.90 7.51 3.92 0.05	-	58 62.37 7.77 4.06 0.06	83 39.15 11.13 5.82 0.08	-	92 74.19 12.33 6.45 0.09	-	-	-	-	-	-	57 68.67 7.64 3.99 0.06	-	-	-	-	-	-	-	297 58.81 39.81 20.81 0.29
Montgomery County	55,126 64.05	587	343 58.43 58.43 0.62	-	-	-	-	-	-	-	-	-	-	-	-	-	-	-	-	-	-	-	-	-	-	-
Morgan County	31,881 73.12	136	75 55.15 55.15 0.24	-	-	-	-	-	-	-	-	-	-	-	-	-	-	-	-	-	-	-	-	-	-	-
Shelby County	44,220 80.94	334	230 68.86 68.86 0.52	-	-	95 67.86 41.30 28.44 0.21	-	-	-	-	-	-	-	-	-	-	-	-	-	-	-	-	-	-	-	-
Tuscaloosa County	40,958 63.48	557	167 29.98 29.98 0.41	-	-	-	-	-	-	-	-	-	-	-	-	-	-	-	-	-	-	-	-	-	-	-
ALASKA	138,503 62.50	6,330	3,019 47.69 47.69 2.18	760	315 41.45 41.45 0.23	54 36.00 1.79 0.85 0.04	-	-	279 58.86 9.24 4.41 0.20	-	1,269 46.65 42.03 20.05 0.92	-	104 55.03 33.02 13.68 0.08	17 23.61 0.56 0.27 0.01	-	406 75.61 13.45 6.41 0.29	547 37.91 18.12 8.64 0.39	80 26.85 2.65 1.26 0.06	-	-	108 33.64 34.29 14.21 0.08	-	-	119 69.59 3.94 1.88 0.09	42 56.76 13.33 5.53 0.03	104 50.00 3.44 1.64 0.08
Anchorage Borough	56,933 60.04	4,003	1,936 48.36 48.36 3.40	510	199 39.02 39.02 0.35	48 45.71 2.48 1.20 0.08	-	-	176 60.69 9.09 4.40 0.31	-	629 46.01 32.49 15.71 1.10	-	-	17 23.61 0.88 0.42 0.03	-	279 79.04 14.41 6.97 0.49	446 40.66 23.04 11.14 0.78	71 26.69 3.67 1.77 0.12	-	-	77 30.80 38.69 15.10 0.14	-	-	97 70.80 5.01 2.42 0.17	-	76 57.14 3.93 1.90 0.13
Fairbanks North Star Borough	16,070 53.97	513	176 34.31 34.31 1.10	-	-	-	-	-	49 51.58 27.84 9.55 0.30	-	37 32.74 21.02 7.21 0.23	-	-	-	-	-	36 18.27 20.45 7.02 0.22	-	-	-	-	-	-	-	-	-
Juneau City and Borough	7,363 63.79	393	268 68.19 68.19 3.64	-	-	-	-	-	-	-	194 69.29 72.39 49.36 2.63	-	-	-	-	-	-	-	-	-	-	-	-	-	-	-
Matanuska-Susitna Borough	16,206 78.84	55	43 78.18 78.18 0.27	-	-	-	-	-	-	-	-	-	-	-	-	-	-	-	-	-	-	-	-	-	-	-

Notes: Please refer to the User's Guide for an explanation of data; data is arranged alphabetically by state, then county, then city within each county; table includes counties with populations greater than 49,999 unless noted and cities with populations greater than 9,999 whose Asian and/or NHPI population rates are greater than the national average; (1) Native Hawaiian and other Pacific Islander; (2) excludes Taiwanese; (3) includes Chamorro; (4) county does not meet population threshold but is shown in order to allow inclusion of city

Place	All owner-occupied housing units	Asian-occupied housing units	Asians who own and occupy their own homes	NHPI[1]-occupied housing units	NHPIs[1] who own and occupy their own homes	Asian Indian	Bangladeshi	Cambodian	Chinese[2]	Fijian	Filipino	Guamanian[3]	Hawaiian, Native	Hmong	Indonesian	Japanese	Korean	Laotian	Malaysian	Pakistani	Samoan	Sri Lankan	Taiwanese	Thai	Tongan	Vietnamese
ARIZONA	1,293,637 68.04	29,135	16,596 56.96 56.96 1.28	1,715	803 46.82 46.82 0.06	2,605 52.00 15.70 8.94 0.20	-	185 63.14 1.11 0.63 0.01	4,756 63.10 28.66 16.32 0.37	-	2,668 59.63 16.08 9.16 0.21	191 51.21 23.79 11.14 0.01	268 46.13 33.37 15.63 0.02	-	127 57.73 0.77 0.44 0.01	1,753 57.18 10.56 6.02 0.14	1,192 43.79 7.18 4.09 0.09	141 60.00 0.85 0.48 0.01	-	98 40.50 0.59 0.34 0.01	141 54.23 17.56 8.22 0.01	-	168 57.53 1.01 0.58 0.01	185 36.49 1.11 0.63 0.01	101 75.94 12.58 5.89 0.01	2,076 63.76 12.51 7.13 0.16
Cochise County	29,546 67.31	530	301 56.79 56.79 1.02	-	-	-	-	-	-	-	53 45.30 17.61 10.00 0.18	-	-	-	-	-	60 59.41 19.93 11.32 0.20	-	-	-	-	-	-	-	-	-
Coconino County	24,828 61.38	243	74 30.45 30.45 0.30	-	-	-	-	-	-	-	-	-	-	-	-	-	-	-	-	-	-	-	-	-	-	-
Maricopa County	764,563 67.49	21,189	12,811 60.46 60.46 1.68	1,038	503 48.46 48.46 0.07	2,155 54.64 16.82 10.17 0.28	-	185 67.03 1.44 0.87 0.02	3,615 66.34 28.22 17.06 0.47	-	2,140 63.46 16.70 10.10 0.28	85 45.45 16.90 8.19 0.01	149 50.00 29.62 14.35 0.02	-	121 66.85 0.94 0.57 0.02	1,240 62.85 9.68 5.85 0.16	764 43.81 5.96 3.61 0.10	98 59.76 0.76 0.46 0.01	-	63 35.59 0.49 0.30 0.01	101 59.76 20.08 9.73 0.01	-	159 65.16 1.24 0.75 0.02	137 41.39 1.07 0.65 0.02	101 75.94 20.08 9.73 0.01	1,700 67.86 13.27 8.02 0.22
Chandler (city)	45,838 73.51	2,342	1,741 74.34 74.34 3.80	-	-	409 74.09 23.49 17.46 0.89	-	-	513 69.61 29.47 21.90 1.12	-	268 84.81 15.39 11.44 0.58	-	-	-	-	-	-	-	-	-	-	-	-	-	-	246 78.85 14.13 10.50 0.54
Gilbert (town)	30,078 84.88	1,065	969 90.99 90.99 3.22	-	-	196 92.45 20.23 18.40 0.65	-	-	337 100.00 34.78 31.64 1.12	-	167 96.53 17.23 15.68 0.56	-	-	-	-	-	-	-	-	-	-	-	-	-	-	-
Mesa (city)	97,625 66.53	1,888	1,192 63.14 63.14 1.22	132	95 71.97 71.97 0.10	134 59.56 11.24 7.10 0.14	-	-	209 61.65 17.53 11.07 0.21	-	271 64.83 22.73 14.35 0.28	-	-	-	-	193 73.11 16.19 10.22 0.20	93 40.79 7.80 4.93 0.10	-	-	-	-	-	-	-	-	151 87.79 12.67 8.00 0.15
Phoenix (city)	282,615 60.66	8,175	4,823 59.00 59.00 1.71	555	241 43.42 43.42 0.09	815 53.30 16.90 9.97 0.29	-	73 61.34 1.51 0.89 0.03	1,376 68.87 28.53 16.83 0.49	-	829 56.90 17.19 10.14 0.29	-	67 46.85 27.80 12.07 0.02	-	-	447 62.87 9.27 5.47 0.16	213 40.19 4.42 2.61 0.08	-	-	-	-	-	-	-	-	720 62.83 14.93 8.81 0.25
Tempe (city)	32,380 50.96	2,939	976 33.21 33.21 3.01	-	-	166 22.37 17.01 5.65 0.51	-	-	308 39.19 31.56 10.48 0.95	-	64 46.72 6.56 2.18 0.20	-	-	-	-	96 35.29 9.84 3.27 0.30	48 14.81 4.92 1.63 0.15	-	-	-	-	-	-	-	-	137 53.52 14.04 4.66 0.42
Mohave County	46,229 73.60	283	205 72.44 72.44 0.44	-	-	-	-	-	-	-	-	-	-	-	-	-	-	-	-	-	-	-	-	-	-	-

Notes: Please refer to the User's Guide for an explanation of data; data is arranged alphabetically by state, then county, then city within each county; table includes counties with populations greater than 49,999 unless noted and cities with populations greater than 9,999 whose Asian and/or NHPI population rates are greater than the national average; (1) Native Hawaiian and other Pacific Islander; (2) excludes Taiwanese; (3) includes Chamorro; (4) county does not meet population threshold but is shown in order to allow inclusion of city

Place	All owner-occupied housing units	Asian-occupied housing units	Asians who own and occupy their own homes	NHPI[1]-occupied housing units	NHPIs[1] who own and occupy their own homes	Asian Indian	Bangladeshi	Cambodian	Chinese[2]	Fijian	Filipino	Guamanian[3]	Hawaiian, Native	Hmong	Indonesian	Japanese	Korean	Laotian	Malaysian	Pakistani	Samoan	Sri Lankan	Taiwanese	Thai	Tongan	Vietnamese
Pima County	213,620 64.28	5,737	2,610 45.49 45.49 1.22	346	137 39.60 39.60 0.06	273 37.55 10.46 4.76 0.13	-	-	927 53.61 35.52 16.16 0.43	-	258 40.06 9.89 4.50 0.12	-	54 34.62 39.42 15.61 0.03	-	-	263 37.79 10.08 4.58 0.12	319 45.12 12.22 5.56 0.15	-	-	-	-	-	-	-	-	326 53.01 12.49 5.68 0.15
Tucson (city)	103,229 53.50	4,094	1,471 35.93 35.93 1.42	252	57 22.62 22.62 0.06	130 26.75 8.84 3.18 0.13	-	-	470 38.75 31.95 11.48 0.46	-	189 36.14 12.85 4.62 0.18	-	-	-	-	142 29.16 9.65 3.47 0.14	155 33.41 10.54 3.79 0.15	-	-	-	-	-	-	-	-	262 50.19 17.81 6.40 0.25
Pinal County	47,522 77.44	204	128 62.75 62.75 0.27	-	-	-	-	-	-	-	-	-	-	-	-	-	-	-	-	-	-	-	-	-	-	-
Yavapai County	51,519 73.42	270	143 52.96 52.96 0.28	-	-	-	-	-	-	-	-	-	-	-	-	-	-	-	-	-	-	-	-	-	-	-
Yuma County	38,886 72.21	414	204 49.28 49.28 0.52	-	-	-	-	-	-	-	58 59.18 28.43 14.01 0.15	-	-	-	-	-	-	-	-	-	-	-	-	-	-	-
ARKANSAS	723,458 69.38	5,713	3,072 53.77 53.77 0.42	338	131 38.76 38.76 0.02	364 38.64 11.85 6.37 0.05	-	-	476 46.17 15.49 8.33 0.07	-	297 51.47 9.67 5.20 0.04	-	63 54.78 48.09 18.64 0.01	-	-	230 55.69 7.49 4.03 0.03	201 51.54 6.54 3.52 0.03	541 70.17 17.61 9.47 0.07	-	-	-	-	-	23 39.66 0.75 0.40 <0.01	-	751 68.90 24.45 13.15 0.10
Benton County	42,028 72.20	496	262 52.82 52.82 0.62	-	-	33 18.86 12.60 6.65 0.08	-	-	-	-	-	-	-	-	-	-	-	-	-	-	-	-	-	-	-	108 87.80 41.22 21.77 0.26
Craighead County	20,649 63.93	100	43 43.00 43.00 0.21	-	-	-	-	-	-	-	-	-	-	-	-	-	-	-	-	-	-	-	-	-	-	-
Crawford County	14,949 75.88	192	163 84.90 84.90 1.09	-	-	-	-	-	-	-	-	-	-	-	-	-	-	-	-	-	-	-	-	-	-	-
Faulkner County	21,865 68.58	139	49 35.25 35.25 0.22	-	-	-	-	-	-	-	-	-	-	-	-	-	-	-	-	-	-	-	-	-	-	-

Notes: Please refer to the User's Guide for an explanation of data; data is arranged alphabetically by state, then county, then city within each county; table includes counties with populations greater than 49,999 unless noted and cities with populations greater than 9,999 whose Asian and/or NHPI population rates are greater than the national average; (1) Native Hawaiian and other Pacific Islander; (2) excludes Taiwanese; (3) includes Chamorro; (4) county does not meet population threshold but is shown in order to allow inclusion of city

Place	All owner-occupied housing units	Asian-occupied housing units	Asians who own and occupy their own homes	NHPI¹-occupied housing units	NHPIs¹ who own and occupy their own homes	Asian Indian	Bangladeshi	Cambodian	Chinese²	Fijian	Filipino	Guamanian³	Hawaiian, Native	Hmong	Indonesian	Japanese	Korean	Laotian	Malaysian	Pakistani	Samoan	Sri Lankan	Taiwanese	Thai	Tongan	Vietnamese
Jefferson County	20,209 66.14	118	48 40.68 40.68 0.24	-	-	-	-	-	-	-	-	-	-	-	-	-	-	-	-	-	-	-	-	-	-	-
Pulaski County	90,068 60.88	1,367	594 43.45 43.45 0.66	-	-	104 30.68 17.51 7.61 0.12	-	-	139 45.13 23.40 10.17 0.15	-	87 54.72 14.65 6.36 0.10	-	-	-	-	-	-	-	-	-	-	-	-	-	-	-
Saline County	25,645 80.70	97	72 74.23 74.23 0.28	-	-	-	-	-	-	-	-	-	-	-	-	-	-	-	-	-	-	-	-	-	-	-
Sebastian County	28,788 63.55	1,087	764 70.29 70.29 2.65	-	-	-	-	-	-	-	-	-	-	-	-	-	-	256 70.72 33.51 23.55 0.89	-	-	-	-	-	-	-	374 73.19 48.95 34.41 1.30
Fort Smith (city)	18,240 56.38	995	695 69.85 69.85 3.81	-	-	-	-	-	-	-	-	-	-	-	-	-	-	244 69.71 35.11 24.52 1.34	-	-	-	-	-	-	-	341 71.34 49.06 34.27 1.87
Washington County	35,748 59.43	867	263 30.33 30.33 0.74	132	30 22.73 22.73 0.08	-	-	-	62 23.94 23.57 7.15 0.17	-	-	-	-	-	-	-	-	82 50.93 31.18 9.46 0.23	-	-	-	-	-	-	-	-
Springdale (city)	9,820 60.55	205	94 45.85 45.85 0.96	123	26 21.14 21.14 0.26	-	-	-	-	-	-	-	-	-	-	-	-	56 48.70 59.57 27.32 0.57	-	-	-	-	-	-	-	-
CALIFORNIA	6,546,237 56.91	1,110,698	613,743 55.26 55.26 9.38	28,474	12,666 44.48 44.48 0.19	45,614 46.88 7.43 4.11 0.70	240 27.75 0.04 0.02 <0.01	3,977 26.97 0.65 0.36 0.06	190,458 63.32 31.03 17.15 2.91	1,075 51.04 8.49 3.78 0.02	147,977 59.51 24.11 13.32 2.26	2,967 50.18 23.42 10.42 0.05	3,487 51.61 27.53 12.25 0.05	1,618 16.44 0.26 0.15 0.02	2,480 47.95 0.40 0.22 0.04	82,446 64.12 13.43 7.42 1.26	43,876 38.10 7.15 3.95 0.67	3,701 31.73 0.60 0.33 0.06	248 45.67 0.04 0.02 <0.01	2,589 49.06 0.42 0.23 0.04	2,709 33.56 21.39 9.51 0.04	978 53.97 0.16 0.09 0.01	13,778 70.04 2.24 1.24 0.21	5,678 52.08 0.93 0.51 0.09	955 47.28 7.54 3.35 0.01	53,305 48.05 8.69 4.80 0.81
Alameda County	286,306 54.70	91,006	51,912 57.04 57.04 18.13	2,170	1,038 47.83 47.83 0.36	6,092 46.17 11.74 6.69 2.13	-	180 22.84 0.35 0.20 0.06	23,277 64.97 44.84 25.58 8.13	184 52.42 17.73 8.48 0.06	11,274 60.83 21.72 12.39 3.94	248 50.00 23.89 11.43 0.09	224 46.00 21.58 10.32 0.08	-	81 50.31 0.16 0.09 0.03	3,658 63.40 7.05 4.02 1.28	2,036 40.11 3.92 2.24 0.71	181 26.85 0.35 0.20 0.06	-	283 49.82 0.55 0.31 0.10	163 39.95 15.70 7.51 0.06	-	770 62.91 1.48 0.85 0.27	195 43.82 0.38 0.21 0.07	159 61.87 15.32 7.33 0.06	2,731 43.31 5.26 3.00 0.95
Alameda (city)	14,491 47.94	6,035	3,278 54.32 54.32 22.62	219	63 28.77 28.77 0.43	157 42.20 4.79 2.60 1.08	-	-	1,910 75.73 58.27 31.65 13.18	-	705 39.47 21.51 11.68 4.87	-	-	-	-	188 55.79 5.74 3.12 1.30	108 24.83 3.29 1.79 0.75	-	-	-	-	-	-	-	-	118 35.01 3.60 1.96 0.81

Notes: Please refer to the User's Guide for an explanation of data; data is arranged alphabetically by state, then county, then city within each county; table includes counties with populations greater than 49,999 unless noted and cities with populations greater than 9,999 whose Asian and/or NHPI population rates are greater than the national average; (1) Native Hawaiian and other Pacific Islander; (2) excludes Taiwanese; (3) includes Chamorro; (4) county does not meet population threshold but is shown in order to allow inclusion of city

Place	All owner-occupied housing units	Asian-occupied housing units	Asians who own and occupy their own homes	NHPI[1]-occupied housing units	NHPIs[1] who own and occupy their own homes	Asian Indian	Bangladeshi	Cambodian	Chinese[2]	Fijian	Filipino	Guamanian[3]	Hawaiian, Native	Hmong	Indonesian	Japanese	Korean	Laotian	Malaysian	Pakistani	Samoan	Sri Lankan	Taiwanese	Thai	Tongan	Vietnamese
Albany (city)	3,558 50.75	1,557	680 43.67 43.67 19.11	-	-	53 36.55 7.79 3.40 1.49	-	-	359 48.45 52.79 23.06 10.09	-	-	-	-	-	-	127 47.21 18.68 8.16 3.57	27 14.75 3.97 1.73 0.76	-	-	-	-	-	-	-	-	-
Ashland (cdp)	2,597 35.99	858	505 58.86 58.86 19.45	-	-	-	-	-	211 76.17 41.78 24.59 8.12	-	163 50.78 32.28 19.00 6.28	-	-	-	-	-	-	-	-	-	-	-	-	-	-	-
Berkeley (city)	19,207 42.72	6,838	1,742 25.48 25.48 9.07	-	-	108 14.88 6.20 1.58 0.56	-	-	761 26.04 43.69 11.13 3.96	-	151 29.72 8.67 2.21 0.79	-	-	-	-	512 49.09 29.39 7.49 2.67	41 5.64 2.35 0.60 0.21	-	-	-	-	-	30 17.86 1.72 0.44 0.16	-	-	51 16.40 2.93 0.75 0.27
Castro Valley (cdp)	15,064 69.57	2,286	1,818 79.53 79.53 12.07	-	-	189 64.07 10.40 8.27 1.25	-	-	1,033 91.42 56.82 45.19 6.86	-	200 62.31 11.00 8.75 1.33	-	-	-	-	166 83.84 9.13 7.26 1.10	143 65.60 7.87 6.26 0.95	-	-	-	-	-	-	-	-	-
Cherryland (cdp)	1,498 32.51	361	125 34.63 34.63 8.34	-	-	-	-	-	-	-	61 38.85 48.80 16.90 4.07	-	-	-	-	-	-	-	-	-	-	-	-	-	-	-
Dublin (city)	6,057 64.92	961	635 66.08 66.08 10.48	-	-	108 62.43 17.01 11.24 1.78	-	-	275 77.68 43.31 28.62 4.54	-	164 65.60 25.83 17.07 2.71	-	-	-	-	-	-	-	-	-	-	-	-	-	-	-
Fremont (city)	44,045 64.55	22,887	14,831 64.80 64.80 33.67	207	128 61.84 61.84 0.29	2,948 45.21 19.88 12.88 6.69	-	-	6,432 75.56 43.37 28.10 14.60	-	2,244 71.01 15.13 9.80 5.09	-	-	-	-	500 68.03 3.37 2.18 1.14	687 61.34 4.63 3.00 1.56	-	-	179 56.83 1.21 0.78 0.41	-	-	549 83.56 3.70 2.40 1.25	-	-	787 73.01 5.31 3.44 1.79
Hayward (city)	23,955 53.35	7,285	4,207 57.75 57.75 17.56	605	238 39.34 39.34 0.99	409 38.62 9.72 5.61 1.71	-	-	935 75.46 22.22 12.83 3.90	105 50.48 44.12 17.36 0.44	2,049 63.61 48.70 28.13 8.55	-	-	-	-	242 51.38 5.75 3.32 1.01	125 39.81 2.97 1.72 0.52	-	-	-	48 44.04 20.17 7.93 0.20	-	-	-	-	279 44.57 6.63 3.83 1.16
Livermore (city)	18,804 72.14	1,245	871 69.96 69.96 4.63	-	-	102 68.00 11.71 8.19 0.54	-	-	228 72.15 26.18 18.31 1.21	-	273 63.93 31.34 21.93 1.45	-	-	-	-	-	-	-	-	-	-	-	-	-	-	60 46.51 6.89 4.82 0.32
Newark (city)	9,181 70.67	2,668	1,859 69.68 69.68 20.25	-	-	372 73.08 20.01 13.94 4.05	-	-	508 75.26 27.33 19.04 5.53	-	539 64.94 28.99 20.20 5.87	-	-	-	-	-	67 55.37 3.60 2.51 0.73	-	-	-	-	-	-	-	-	105 59.32 5.65 3.94 1.14

Notes: Please refer to the User's Guide for an explanation of data; data is arranged alphabetically by state, then county, then city within each county; table includes counties with populations greater than 49,999 unless noted and cities with populations greater than 9,999 whose Asian and/or NHPI population rates are greater than the national average; (1) Native Hawaiian and other Pacific Islander; (2) excludes Taiwanese; (3) includes Chamorro; (4) county does not meet population threshold but is shown in order to allow inclusion of city

Place	All owner-occupied housing units	Asian-occupied housing units	Asians who own and occupy their own homes	NHPI[1]-occupied housing units	NHPIs[1] who own and occupy their own homes	Asian Indian	Bangladeshi	Cambodian	Chinese[2]	Fijian	Filipino	Guamanian[3]	Hawaiian, Native	Hmong	Indonesian	Japanese	Korean	Laotian	Malaysian	Pakistani	Samoan	Sri Lankan	Taiwanese	Thai	Tongan	Vietnamese
	62,482	19,569	7,959	420	209	188	-	45	5,275	-	803	-	-	-	-	683	216	62	-	-	-	-	-	-	121	547
	41.44		40.67		49.76	31.39		7.53	49.13		39.85					61.70	23.68	12.97							72.89	23.19
Oakland (city)						2.36		0.57	66.28		10.09					8.58	2.71	0.78							57.89	6.87
			40.67		49.76	0.96		0.23	26.96		4.10					3.49	1.10	0.32							28.81	2.80
			12.74		0.33	0.30		0.07	8.44		1.29					1.09	0.35	0.10							0.19	0.88
	3,450	504	475	-	-	-	-	-	348	-	-	-	-	-	-	-	-	-	-	-	-	-	-	-	-	-
	90.69		94.25						95.34																	
Piedmont (city)									73.26																	
			94.25						69.05																	
			13.77						10.09																	
	17,107	2,351	1,721	-	-	329	-	-	648	-	167	-	-	-	-	228	139	-	-	-	-	-	-	-	-	-
	73.37		73.20			54.92			83.51		67.61					82.01	70.92									
Pleasanton (city)						19.12			37.65		9.70					13.25	8.08									
			73.20			13.99			27.56		7.10					9.70	5.91									
			10.06			1.92			3.79		0.98					1.33	0.81									
	18,577	5,337	3,762	129	78	89	-	-	2,003	-	940	-	-	-	-	242	108	-	-	-	-	-	-	-	-	182
	60.68		70.49		60.47	35.32			84.84		58.10					76.10	62.79									51.70
San Leandro (city)						2.37			53.24		24.99					6.43	2.87									4.84
			70.49		60.47	1.67			37.53		17.61					4.53	2.02									3.41
			20.25		0.42	0.48			10.78		5.06					1.30	0.58									0.98
	5,971	943	754	-	-	-	-	-	230	-	290	-	-	-	-	-	-	-	-	-	-	-	-	-	-	39
	79.28		79.96						84.87		83.33															52.70
San Lorenzo (cdp)									30.50		38.46															5.17
			79.96						24.39		30.75															4.14
			12.63						3.85		4.86															0.65
	13,255	7,518	5,733	164	111	856	-	-	1,582	-	2,346	-	-	-	-	170	176	-	-	-	-	-	-	-	-	355
	71.16		76.26		67.68	61.67			88.68		76.79					86.29	61.75									72.90
Union City (city)						14.93			27.59		40.92					2.97	3.07									6.19
			76.26		67.68	11.39			21.04		31.21					2.26	2.34									4.72
			43.25		0.84	6.46			11.94		17.70					1.28	1.33									2.68
	48,333	1,583	588	-	-	70	-	-	134	-	54	-	-	55	-	145	-	36	-	-	-	-	-	-	-	-
	60.75		37.14			44.03			48.73		41.54			14.82		52.54		33.96								
Butte County						11.90			22.79		9.18			9.35		24.66		6.12								
			37.14			4.42			8.46		3.41			3.47		9.16		2.27								
			1.22			0.14			0.28		0.11			0.11		0.30		0.07								
	9,269	707	156	-	-	-	-	-	76	-	-	-	-	0	-	-	-	-	-	-	-	-	-	-	-	-
	39.66		22.07						39.79					0.00												
Chico (city)									48.72					0.00												
			22.07						10.75					0.00												
			1.68						0.82					0.00												
	2,078	122	34	-	-	-	-	-	-	-	-	-	-	13	-	-	-	-	-	-	-	-	-	-	-	-
	42.49		27.87											19.40												
Oroville (city)														38.24												
			27.87											10.66												
			1.64											0.63												
	238,413	32,179	22,879	791	493	2,191	-	-	7,977	54	6,738	113	149	-	83	2,997	816	248	-	74	84	-	411	102	56	687
	69.28		71.10		62.33	60.13			82.03	87.10	70.73	60.11	66.82		52.20	79.35	57.10	29.99		37.76	68.29		85.98	62.96	82.35	51.00
Contra Costa County						9.58			34.87	10.95	29.45	22.92	30.22		0.36	13.10	3.57	1.08		0.32	17.04		1.80	0.45	11.36	3.00
			71.10		62.33	6.81			24.79	6.83	20.94	14.29	18.84		0.26	9.31	2.54	0.77		0.23	10.62		1.28	0.32	7.08	2.13
			9.60		0.21	0.92			3.35	0.02	2.83	0.05	0.06		0.03	1.26	0.34	0.10		0.03	0.04		0.17	0.04	0.02	0.29

Notes: Please refer to the User's Guide for an explanation of data; data is arranged alphabetically by state, then county, then city within each county; table includes counties with populations greater than 49,999 unless noted and cities with populations greater than 9,999 whose Asian and/or NHPI population rates are greater than the national average; (1) Native Hawaiian and other Pacific Islander; (2) excludes Taiwanese; (3) includes Chamorro; (4) county does not meet population threshold but is shown in order to allow inclusion of city

Place	All owner-occupied housing units	Asian-occupied housing units	Asians who own and occupy their own homes	NHPI[1]-occupied housing units	NHPIs[1] who own and occupy their own homes	Asian Indian	Bangladeshi	Cambodian	Chinese[2]	Fijian	Filipino	Guamanian[3]	Hawaiian, Native	Hmong	Indonesian	Japanese	Korean	Laotian	Malaysian	Pakistani	Samoan	Sri Lankan	Taiwanese	Thai	Tongan	Vietnamese
Alamo (cdp)	4,924 93.90	252	231 91.67 91.67 4.69	-	-	-	-	-	-	-	-	-	-	-	-	-	-	-	-	-	-	-	-	-	-	-
Antioch (city)	20,808 70.86	1,880	1,508 80.21 80.21 7.25	89	64 71.91 71.91 0.31	87 91.58 5.77 4.63 0.42	-	-	382 93.86 25.33 20.32 1.84	-	711 80.25 47.15 37.82 3.42	-	-	-	-	-	-	-	-	-	-	-	-	-	-	84 63.16 5.57 4.47 0.40
Bay Point (cdp)	4,205 64.79	590	455 77.12 77.12 10.82	-	-	-	-	-	-	-	233 79.79 51.21 39.49 5.54	-	-	-	-	-	-	-	-	-	-	-	-	-	-	-
Blackhawk-Camino-Tass. (cdp)	3,153 94.74	499	499 100.00 100.00 15.83	-	-	-	-	-	282 100.00 56.51 56.51 8.94	-	-	-	-	-	-	-	-	-	-	-	-	-	-	-	-	-
Clayton (city)	3,698 94.10	186	186 100.00 100.00 5.03	-	-	-	-	-	-	-	-	-	-	-	-	-	-	-	-	-	-	-	-	-	-	-
Concord (city)	27,518 62.61	3,814	2,296 60.20 60.20 8.34	89	35 39.33 39.33 0.13	281 51.75 12.24 7.37 1.02	-	-	759 75.67 33.06 19.90 2.76	-	697 54.16 30.36 18.27 2.53	-	-	-	-	301 80.70 13.11 7.89 1.09	52 38.81 2.26 1.36 0.19	-	-	-	-	-	-	-	-	57 28.36 2.48 1.49 0.21
Danville (town)	13,427 89.35	1,167	1,054 90.32 90.32 7.85	-	-	140 89.74 13.28 12.00 1.04	-	-	463 95.66 43.93 39.67 3.45	-	95 71.97 9.01 8.14 0.71	-	-	-	-	-	-	-	-	-	-	-	-	-	-	-
El Cerrito (city)	6,239 60.91	2,114	1,394 65.94 65.94 22.34	-	-	44 28.39 3.16 2.08 0.71	-	-	693 72.79 49.71 32.78 11.11	-	83 59.29 5.95 3.93 1.33	-	-	-	-	415 76.15 29.77 19.63 6.65	-	-	-	-	-	-	-	-	-	-
El Sobrante (cdp)	2,880 63.13	395	222 56.20 56.20 7.71	-	-	49 45.79 22.07 12.41 1.70	-	-	-	-	-	-	-	-	-	-	-	-	-	-	-	-	-	-	-	-
Hercules (city)	5,369 84.18	2,328	2,093 89.91 89.91 38.98	-	-	147 91.30 7.02 6.31 2.74	-	-	544 95.10 25.99 23.37 10.13	-	1,147 88.37 54.80 49.27 21.36	-	-	-	-	-	-	-	-	-	-	-	-	-	-	-

Notes: Please refer to the User's Guide for an explanation of data; data is arranged alphabetically by state, then county, then city within each county; table includes counties with populations greater than 49,999 unless noted and cities with populations greater than 9,999 whose Asian and/or NHPI population rates are greater than the national average; (1) Native Hawaiian and other Pacific Islander; (2) excludes Taiwanese; (3) includes Chamorro; (4) county does not meet population threshold but is shown in order to allow inclusion of city

Place	All owner-occupied housing units	Asian-occupied housing units	Asians who own and occupy their own homes	NHPI[1]-occupied housing units	NHPIs[1] who own and occupy their own homes	Asian Indian	Bangladeshi	Cambodian	Chinese[2]	Fijian	Filipino	Guamanian[3]	Hawaiian, Native	Hmong	Indonesian	Japanese	Korean	Laotian	Malaysian	Pakistani	Samoan	Sri Lankan	Taiwanese	Thai	Tongan	Vietnamese
Lafayette (city)	6,846	600	373	-	-	-	-	-	189	-	-	-	-	-	-	-	-	-	-	-	-	-	-	-	-	-
	75.81		62.17						68.98																	
									50.67																	
			62.17						31.50																	
			5.45						2.76																	
Martinez (city)	9,913	782	589	-	-	-	-	-	181	-	193	-	-	-	-	-	-	-	-	-	-	-	-	-	-	-
	69.04		75.32						84.98		69.68															
									30.73		32.77															
			75.32						23.15		24.68															
			5.94						1.83		1.95															
Moraga (town)	4,833	622	522	-	-	-	-	-	333	-	-	-	-	-	-	-	-	-	-	-	-	-	-	-	-	-
	84.46		83.92						91.74																	
									63.79																	
			83.92						53.54																	
			10.80						6.89																	
Orinda (city)	6,045	483	451	-	-	-	-	-	298	-	-	-	-	-	-	-	-	-	-	-	-	-	-	-	-	-
	91.62		93.37						94.01																	
									66.08																	
			93.37						61.70																	
			7.46						4.93																	
Pinole (city)	5,076	1,221	956	-	-	-	-	-	258	-	420	-	-	-	-	-	-	-	-	-	-	-	-	-	-	-
	74.54		78.30						82.69		77.92															
									26.99		43.93															
			78.30						21.13		34.40															
			18.83						5.08		8.27															
Pittsburg (city)	11,181	1,924	1,371	132	118	199	-	-	112	-	929	-	-	-	-	-	-	-	-	-	-	-	-	-	-	-
	62.84		71.26		89.39	76.54			76.71		74.44															
						14.51			8.17		67.76															
			71.26		89.39	10.34			5.82		48.28															
			12.26		1.06	1.78			1.00		8.31															
Pleasant Hill (city)	8,770	1,090	692	-	-	-	-	-	222	-	158	-	-	-	-	-	80	-	-	-	-	-	-	-	-	-
	63.68		63.49						68.31		59.62						49.08									
									32.08		22.83						11.56									
			63.49						20.37		14.50						7.34									
			7.89						2.53		1.80						0.91									
Richmond (city)	18,528	3,806	2,329	93	38	125	-	-	852	-	575	-	-	-	-	373	81	146	-	-	-	-	-	-	-	68
	53.39		61.19		40.86	38.11			73.07		71.70					73.86	50.94	31.67								50.00
						5.37			36.58		24.69					16.02	3.48	6.27								2.92
			61.19		40.86	3.28			22.39		15.11					9.80	2.13	3.84								1.79
			12.57		0.21	0.67			4.60		3.10					2.01	0.44	0.79								0.37
San Pablo (city)	4,510	1,251	707	-	-	71	-	-	-	-	350	-	-	-	-	-	-	62	-	-	-	-	-	-	-	48
	49.80		56.51			40.80					76.09							27.07								29.63
						10.04					49.50							8.77								6.79
			56.51			5.68					27.98							4.96								3.84
			15.68			1.57					7.76							1.37								1.06
San Ramon (city)	11,945	2,113	1,554	-	-	202	-	-	669	-	207	-	-	-	-	202	-	-	-	-	-	-	-	-	-	-
	71.08		73.54			44.40			88.26		64.49					93.09										
						13.00			43.05		13.32					13.00										
			73.54			9.56			31.66		9.80					9.56										
			13.01			1.69			5.60		1.73					1.69										

Notes: Please refer to the User's Guide for an explanation of data; data is arranged alphabetically by state, then county, then city within each county; table includes counties with populations greater than 49,999 unless noted and cities with populations greater than 9,999 whose Asian and/or NHPI population rates are greater than the national average; (1) Native Hawaiian and other Pacific Islander; (2) excludes Taiwanese; (3) includes Chamorro; (4) county does not meet population threshold but is shown in order to allow inclusion of city

Place	All owner-occupied housing units	Asian-occupied housing units	Asians who own and occupy their own homes	NHPI[1]-occupied housing units	NHPIs[1] who own and occupy their own homes	Asian Indian	Bangladeshi	Cambodian	Chinese[2]	Fijian	Filipino	Guamanian[3]	Hawaiian, Native	Hmong	Indonesian	Japanese	Korean	Laotian	Malaysian	Pakistani	Samoan	Sri Lankan	Taiwanese	Thai	Tongan	Vietnamese
Walnut Creek (city)	20,654 68.08	2,407	1,562 64.89 64.89 7.56	-	-	136 54.62 8.71 5.65 0.66	-	-	787 78.08 50.38 32.70 3.81	-	142 33.33 9.09 5.90 0.69	-	-	-	-	315 75.18 20.17 13.09 1.53	102 62.58 6.53 4.24 0.49	-	-	-	-	-	-	-	-	-
El Dorado County	44,033 74.71	927	577 62.24 62.24 1.31	-	-	-	-	-	-	-	174 45.91 30.16 18.77 0.40	-	-	-	-	142 89.31 24.61 15.32 0.32	-	-	-	-	-	-	-	-	-	-
El Dorado Hills (cdp)	5,377 90.43	186	176 94.62 94.62 3.27	-	-	-	-	-	-	-	-	-	-	-	-	-	-	-	-	-	-	-	-	-	-	-
South Lake Tahoe (city)	4,081 43.22	426	142 33.33 33.33 3.48	-	-	-	-	-	-	-	56 22.67 39.44 13.15 1.37	-	-	-	-	-	-	-	-	-	-	-	-	-	-	-
Fresno County	142,856 56.48	14,821	7,000 47.23 47.23 4.90	164	37 22.56 22.56 0.03	996 58.08 14.23 6.72 0.70	-	136 19.88 1.94 0.92 0.10	1,219 71.50 17.41 8.22 0.85	-	1,090 62.82 15.57 7.35 0.76	-	-	542 16.19 7.74 3.66 0.38	-	2,046 76.29 29.23 13.80 1.43	221 52.49 3.16 1.49 0.15	214 16.58 3.06 1.44 0.15	-	-	-	-	-	-	-	260 43.05 3.71 1.75 0.18
Clovis (city)	14,707 60.67	1,034	628 60.74 60.74 4.27	-	-	-	-	-	-	-	118 76.13 18.79 11.41 0.80	-	-	52 21.85 8.28 5.03 0.35	-	197 80.08 31.37 19.05 1.34	-	-	-	-	-	-	-	-	-	-
Fresno (city)	70,915 50.67	10,784	4,164 38.61 38.61 5.87	-	-	482 48.39 11.58 4.47 0.68	-	98 16.07 2.35 0.91 0.14	937 69.98 22.50 8.69 1.32	-	730 57.48 17.53 6.77 1.03	-	-	414 14.47 9.94 3.84 0.58	-	840 66.88 20.17 7.79 1.18	154 49.04 3.70 1.43 0.22	155 13.23 3.72 1.44 0.22	-	-	-	-	-	-	-	177 36.80 4.25 1.64 0.25
Reedley (city)	3,540 61.31	256	212 82.81 82.81 5.99	-	-	-	-	-	-	-	-	-	-	-	-	-	-	-	-	-	-	-	-	-	-	-
Humboldt County	29,524 57.62	555	213 38.38 38.38 0.72	-	-	-	-	-	-	-	-	-	-	-	-	82 48.81 38.50 14.77 0.28	-	-	-	-	-	-	-	-	-	-
Imperial County	22,971 58.33	924	497 53.79 53.79 2.16	-	-	-	-	-	124 62.31 24.95 13.42 0.54	-	202 70.38 40.64 21.86 0.88	-	-	-	-	-	11 7.43 2.21 1.19 0.05	-	-	-	-	-	-	-	-	-

Notes: Please refer to the User's Guide for an explanation of data; data is arranged alphabetically by state, then county, then city within each county; table includes counties with populations greater than 49,999 unless noted and cities with populations greater than 9,999 whose Asian and/or NHPI population rates are greater than the national average; (1) Native Hawaiian and other Pacific Islander; (2) excludes Taiwanese; (3) includes Chamorro; (4) county does not meet population threshold but is shown in order to allow inclusion of city

Place	All owner-occupied housing units	Asian-occupied housing units	Asians who own and occupy their own homes	NHPI[1]-occupied housing units	NHPIs[1] who own and occupy their own homes	Asian Indian	Bangladeshi	Cambodian	Chinese[2]	Fijian	Filipino	Guamanian[3]	Hawaiian, Native	Hmong	Indonesian	Japanese	Korean	Laotian	Malaysian	Pakistani	Samoan	Sri Lankan	Taiwanese	Thai	Tongan	Vietnamese
Kern County	129,661	6,000	3,709	200	142	571	-	25	593	-	1,731	-	-	-	-	270	191	-	-	-	-	-	-	-	-	105
	62.14		61.82		71.00	59.29		29.76	71.62		61.69					68.35	50.13									61.76
						15.39		0.67	15.99		46.67					7.28	5.15									2.83
			61.82		71.00	9.52		0.42	9.88		28.85					4.50	3.18									1.75
			2.86		0.11	0.44		0.02	0.46		1.34					0.21	0.15									0.08
Bakersfield (city)	50,394	3,156	1,876	125	101	419	-	-	418	-	497	-	-	-	-	162	145	-	-	-	-	-	-	-	-	81
	60.40		59.44		80.80	57.79			71.94		55.41					67.22	47.39									62.79
						22.33			22.28		26.49					8.64	7.73									4.32
			59.44		80.80	13.28			13.24		15.75					5.13	4.59									2.57
			3.72		0.20	0.83			0.83		0.99					0.32	0.29									0.16
Delano (city)	4,999	1,452	976	-	-	-	-	-	-	-	891	-	-	-	-	-	-	-	-	-	-	-	-	-	-	-
	59.44		67.22								66.10															
											91.29															
			67.22								61.36															
			19.52								17.82															
Ridgecrest (city)	6,229	312	186	-	-	-	-	-	-	-	77	-	-	-	-	-	-	-	-	-	-	-	-	-	-	-
	63.06		59.62								60.63															
											41.40															
			59.62								24.68															
			2.99								1.24															
Kings County	19,250	1,087	631	-	-	-	-	-	-	-	407	-	-	-	-	-	-	-	-	-	-	-	-	-	-	-
	55.93		58.05								56.45															
											64.50															
			58.05								37.44															
			3.28								2.11															
Lemoore (city)	3,466	434	295	-	-	-	-	-	-	-	238	-	-	-	-	-	-	-	-	-	-	-	-	-	-	-
	53.71		67.97								69.79															
											80.68															
			67.97								54.84															
			8.51								6.87															
Lake County	16,908	206	131	-	-	-	-	-	-	-	-	-	-	-	-	-	-	-	-	-	-	-	-	-	-	-
	70.53		63.59																							
			63.59																							
			0.77																							
Los Angeles County	1,499,694	362,618	184,327	6,543	2,493	8,816	84	1,529	55,230	80	39,086	405	639	17	794	31,745	21,280	225	40	478	871	426	7,388	3,165	192	8,611
	47.86		50.83		38.10	46.34	21.05	23.92	59.36	39.60	52.49	44.90	46.10	17.17	42.41	61.52	32.74	29.22	26.14	35.94	30.67	51.76	69.43	53.53	47.06	42.93
						4.78	0.05	0.83	29.96	3.21	21.20	16.25	25.63	0.01	0.43	17.22	11.54	0.12	0.02	0.26	34.94	0.23	4.01	1.72	7.70	4.67
			50.83		38.10	2.43	0.02	0.42	15.23	1.22	10.78	6.19	9.77	<0.01	0.22	8.75	5.87	0.06	0.01	0.13	13.31	0.12	2.04	0.87	2.93	2.37
			12.29		0.17	0.59	0.01	0.10	3.68	0.01	2.61	0.03	0.04	<0.01	0.05	2.12	1.42	0.02	<0.01	0.03	0.06	0.03	0.49	0.21	0.01	0.57
Agoura Hills (city)	5,762	391	334	-	-	-	-	-	-	-	-	-	-	-	-	-	-	-	-	-	-	-	-	-	-	-
	84.01		85.42																							
			85.42																							
			5.80																							
Alhambra (city)	11,399	13,026	5,217	-	-	55	-	-	3,576	-	229	-	-	-	-	385	105	-	-	-	-	-	262	-	-	305
	39.16		40.05			31.98			41.97		38.75					55.48	35.12						47.90			24.64
						1.05			68.55		4.39					7.38	2.01						5.02			5.85
			40.05			0.42			27.45		1.76					2.96	0.81						2.01			2.34
			45.77			0.48			31.37		2.01					3.38	0.92						2.30			2.68

Notes: Please refer to the User's Guide for an explanation of data; data is arranged alphabetically by state, then county, then city within each county; table includes counties with populations greater than 49,999 unless noted and cities with populations greater than 9,999 whose Asian and/or NHPI population rates are greater than the national average; (1) Native Hawaiian and other Pacific Islander; (2) excludes Taiwanese; (3) includes Chamorro; (4) county does not meet population threshold but is shown in order to allow inclusion of city

Place	All owner-occupied housing units	Asian-occupied housing units	Asians who own and occupy their own homes	NHPI[1]-occupied housing units	NHPIs[1] who own and occupy their own homes	Asian Indian	Bangladeshi	Cambodian	Chinese[2]	Fijian	Filipino	Guamanian[3]	Hawaiian, Native	Hmong	Indonesian	Japanese	Korean	Laotian	Malaysian	Pakistani	Samoan	Sri Lankan	Taiwanese	Thai	Tongan	Vietnamese
Altadena (cdp)	10,959 74.17	619	468 75.61 75.61 4.27	-	-	-	-	-	-	-	63 72.41 13.46 10.18 0.57	-	-	-	-	227 84.07 48.50 36.67 2.07	-	-	-	-	-	-	-	-	-	-
Arcadia (city)	11,921 62.30	6,981	4,681 67.05 67.05 39.27	-	-	87 45.08 1.86 1.25 0.73	-	-	3,003 71.67 64.15 43.02 25.19	-	104 45.02 2.22 1.49 0.87	-	-	-	-	199 55.43 4.25 2.85 1.67	240 45.71 5.13 3.44 2.01	-	-	-	-	-	779 78.53 16.64 11.16 6.53	-	-	-
Artesia (city)	2,526 56.51	1,238	559 45.15 45.15 22.13	-	-	29 18.13 5.19 2.34 1.15	-	-	108 54.27 19.32 8.72 4.28	-	180 44.23 32.20 14.54 7.13	-	-	-	-	-	92 35.25 16.46 7.43 3.64	-	-	-	-	-	-	-	-	-
Avocado Heights (cdp)	2,813 74.91	395	333 84.30 84.30 11.84	-	-	-	-	-	-	-	-	-	-	-	-	-	-	-	-	-	-	-	-	-	-	-
Azusa (city)	6,264 50.36	717	344 47.98 47.98 5.49	-	-	-	-	-	-	-	185 57.28 53.78 25.80 2.95	-	-	-	-	-	-	-	-	-	-	-	-	-	-	-
Baldwin Park (city)	10,302 60.74	2,323	1,682 72.41 72.41 16.33	-	-	-	-	-	561 72.02 33.35 24.15 5.45	-	723 74.38 42.98 31.12 7.02	-	-	-	-	-	-	-	-	-	-	-	-	-	-	137 60.89 8.15 5.90 1.33
Bellflower (city)	9,410 40.32	1,976	842 42.61 42.61 8.95	-	-	-	-	55 42.97 6.53 2.78 0.58	-	-	403 43.43 47.86 20.39 4.28	-	-	-	-	-	69 22.62 8.19 3.49 0.73	-	-	-	-	-	-	73 54.07 8.67 3.69 0.78	-	-
Beverly Hills (city)	6,532 43.45	891	330 37.04 37.04 5.05	-	-	-	-	-	112 56.28 33.94 12.57 1.71	-	-	-	-	-	-	-	92 28.31 27.88 10.33 1.41	-	-	-	-	-	-	-	-	-
Burbank (city)	18,129 43.57	3,023	1,254 41.48 41.48 6.92	-	-	89 31.56 7.10 2.94 0.49	-	-	171 46.85 13.64 5.66 0.94	-	423 43.61 33.73 13.99 2.33	-	-	-	-	199 53.78 15.87 6.58 1.10	187 30.31 14.91 6.19 1.03	-	-	-	-	-	-	-	-	76 48.41 6.06 2.51 0.42
Calabasas (city)	5,862 80.58	525	426 81.14 81.14 7.27	-	-	-	-	-	154 88.00 36.15 29.33 2.63	-	-	-	-	-	-	-	-	-	-	-	-	-	-	-	-	-

Notes: Please refer to the User's Guide for an explanation of data; data is arranged alphabetically by state, then county, then city within each county; table includes counties with populations greater than 49,999 unless noted and cities with populations greater than 9,999 whose Asian and/or NHPI population rates are greater than the national average; (1) Native Hawaiian and other Pacific Islander; (2) excludes Taiwanese; (3) includes Chamorro; (4) county does not meet population threshold but is shown in order to allow inclusion of city

Place	All owner-occupied housing units	Asian-occupied housing units	Asians who own and occupy their own homes	NHPI[1]-occupied housing units	NHPIs[1] who own and occupy their own homes	Asian Indian	Bangladeshi	Cambodian	Chinese[2]	Fijian	Filipino	Guamanian[3]	Hawaiian, Native	Hmong	Indonesian	Japanese	Korean	Laotian	Malaysian	Pakistani	Samoan	Sri Lankan	Taiwanese	Thai	Tongan	Vietnamese
Carson (city)	19,197 77.96	5,159	3,815 73.95 73.95 19.87	389	233 59.90 59.90 1.21	-	-	-	137 88.39 3.59 2.66 0.71	-	3,035 72.28 79.55 58.83 15.81	-	-	-	-	311 94.24 8.15 6.03 1.62	-	-	-	-	127 47.39 54.51 32.65 0.66	-	-	-	-	71 77.17 1.86 1.38 0.37
Cerritos (city)	12,859 83.53	8,231	6,809 82.72 82.72 52.95	-	-	603 83.40 8.86 7.33 4.69	-	-	1,490 88.53 21.88 18.10 11.59	-	1,401 89.98 20.58 17.02 10.90	-	-	-	-	691 95.57 10.15 8.40 5.37	1,524 65.32 22.38 18.52 11.85	-	-	-	-	-	452 92.43 6.64 5.49 3.52	118 86.13 1.73 1.43 0.92	-	250 88.65 3.67 3.04 1.94
Citrus (cdp)	1,879 70.40	213	140 65.73 65.73 7.45	-	-	-	-	-	-	-	-	-	-	-	-	-	-	-	-	-	-	-	-	-	-	-
Claremont (city)	7,570 66.97	931	638 68.53 68.53 8.43	-	-	112 82.96 17.55 12.03 1.48	-	-	247 76.00 38.71 26.53 3.26	-	-	-	-	-	-	-	62 46.97 9.72 6.66 0.82	-	-	-	-	-	-	-	-	-
Compton (city)	12,684 56.87	127	102 80.31 80.31 0.80	167	22 13.17 13.17 0.17	-	-	-	-	-	-	-	-	-	-	-	-	-	-	-	22 14.01 100.00 13.17 0.17	-	-	-	-	-
Covina (city)	9,409 58.72	1,380	927 67.17 67.17 9.85	-	-	-	-	-	287 75.73 30.96 20.80 3.05	-	205 59.77 22.11 14.86 2.18	-	-	-	-	110 66.67 11.87 7.97 1.17	-	-	-	-	-	-	-	-	-	66 80.49 7.12 4.78 0.70
Culver City (city)	9,033 54.38	1,764	1,049 59.47 59.47 11.61	-	-	88 42.93 8.39 4.99 0.97	-	-	189 61.56 18.02 10.71 2.09	-	134 60.63 12.77 7.60 1.48	-	-	-	-	432 65.36 41.18 24.49 4.78	-	-	-	-	-	-	-	-	-	-
Diamond Bar (city)	14,596 82.72	6,681	5,458 81.69 81.69 37.39	-	-	531 83.23 9.73 7.95 3.64	-	-	1,887 86.80 34.57 28.24 12.93	-	651 82.20 11.93 9.74 4.46	-	-	-	-	254 79.87 4.65 3.80 1.74	1,148 71.44 21.03 17.18 7.87	-	-	-	-	-	520 87.10 9.53 7.78 3.56	-	-	155 95.68 2.84 2.32 1.06
Downey (city)	17,614 51.82	2,350	1,287 54.77 54.77 7.31	-	-	75 45.18 5.83 3.19 0.43	-	-	140 74.07 10.88 5.96 0.79	-	266 47.50 20.67 11.32 1.51	-	-	-	-	131 73.60 10.18 5.57 0.74	472 51.98 36.67 20.09 2.68	-	-	-	-	-	-	-	-	88 73.95 6.84 3.74 0.50
Duarte (city)	4,710 70.99	809	637 78.74 78.74 13.52	-	-	-	-	-	162 89.01 25.43 20.02 3.44	-	265 74.86 41.60 32.76 5.63	-	-	-	-	-	-	-	-	-	-	-	-	-	-	-

Notes: Please refer to the User's Guide for an explanation of data; data is arranged alphabetically by state, then county, then city within each county; table includes counties with populations greater than 49,999 unless noted and cities with populations greater than 9,999 whose Asian and/or NHPI population rates are greater than the national average; (1) Native Hawaiian and other Pacific Islander; (2) excludes Taiwanese; (3) includes Chamorro; (4) county does not meet population threshold but is shown in order to allow inclusion of city

Place	All owner-occupied housing units	Asian-occupied housing units	Asians who own and occupy their own homes	NHPI[1]-occupied housing units	NHPIs[1] who own and occupy their own homes	Asian Indian	Bangladeshi	Cambodian	Chinese[2]	Fijian	Filipino	Guamanian[3]	Hawaiian, Native	Hmong	Indonesian	Japanese	Korean	Laotian	Malaysian	Pakistani	Samoan	Sri Lankan	Taiwanese	Thai	Tongan	Vietnamese
East San Gabriel (cdp)	2,840 54.60	1,913	1,175 61.42 61.42 41.37	-	-	-	-	-	691 60.40 58.81 36.12 24.33	-	-	-	-	-	-	161 79.70 13.70 8.42 5.67	-	-	-	-	-	-	156 77.23 13.28 8.15 5.49	-	-	-
El Monte (city)	11,095 41.04	5,299	3,229 60.94 60.94 29.10	-	-	-	-	-	2,005 68.13 62.09 37.84 18.07	-	154 66.38 4.77 2.91 1.39	-	-	-	-	-	-	-	-	-	-	-	83 46.63 2.57 1.57 0.75	-	-	608 43.74 18.83 11.47 5.48
El Segundo (city)	2,945 41.88	400	137 34.25 34.25 4.65	-	-	-	-	-	-	-	-	-	-	-	-	-	-	-	-	-	-	-	-	-	-	-
Gardena (city)	9,622 47.32	6,423	3,165 49.28 49.28 32.89	-	-	-	-	-	241 73.70 7.61 3.75 2.50	-	344 59.21 10.87 5.36 3.58	-	-	-	-	2,005 56.53 63.35 31.22 20.84	339 24.76 10.71 5.28 3.52	-	-	-	-	-	-	-	-	143 49.14 4.52 2.23 1.49
Glendale (city)	27,541 38.36	10,744	4,197 39.06 39.06 15.24	-	-	146 39.14 3.48 1.36 0.53	-	-	688 69.78 16.39 6.40 2.50	-	1,224 33.27 29.16 11.39 4.44	-	-	-	-	398 47.16 9.48 3.70 1.45	1,474 36.75 35.12 13.72 5.35	-	-	-	-	-	-	48 34.29 1.14 0.45 0.17	-	127 38.96 3.03 1.18 0.46
Glendora (city)	12,385 73.47	912	691 75.77 75.77 5.58	-	-	100 79.37 14.47 10.96 0.81	-	-	198 88.00 28.65 21.71 1.60	-	195 74.43 28.22 21.38 1.57	-	-	-	-	-	-	-	-	-	-	-	-	-	-	-
Hacienda Heights (cdp)	12,715 79.51	5,751	4,290 74.60 74.60 33.74	-	-	-	-	-	2,109 75.24 49.16 36.67 16.59	-	212 63.10 4.94 3.69 1.67	-	-	-	-	523 90.96 12.19 9.09 4.11	457 58.82 10.65 7.95 3.59	-	-	-	-	-	601 79.71 14.01 10.45 4.73	-	-	42 70.00 0.98 0.73 0.33
Hawaiian Gardens (city)	1,584 45.14	447	123 27.52 27.52 7.77	-	-	-	-	-	-	-	-	-	-	-	-	-	35 12.92 28.46 7.83 2.21	-	-	-	-	-	-	-	-	-
Hawthorne (city)	7,355 25.84	1,884	741 39.33 39.33 10.07	157	31 19.75 19.75 0.42	55 33.74 7.42 2.92 0.75	-	-	90 58.82 12.15 4.78 1.22	-	265 37.54 35.76 14.07 3.60	-	-	-	-	92 48.68 12.42 4.88 1.25	-	-	-	-	-	-	-	-	-	157 35.44 21.19 8.33 2.13
Hermosa Beach (city)	4,033 42.71	430	177 41.16 41.16 4.39	-	-	-	-	-	-	-	-	-	-	-	-	-	-	-	-	-	-	-	-	-	-	-

Notes: Please refer to the User's Guide for an explanation of data; data is arranged alphabetically by state, then county, then city within each county; table includes counties with populations greater than 49,999 unless noted and cities with populations greater than 9,999 whose Asian and/or NHPI population rates are greater than the national average; (1) Native Hawaiian and other Pacific Islander; (2) excludes Taiwanese; (3) includes Chamorro; (4) county does not meet population threshold but is shown in order to allow inclusion of city

Place	All owner-occupied housing units	Asian-occupied housing units	Asians who own and occupy their own homes	NHPI[1]-occupied housing units	NHPIs[1] who own and occupy their own homes	Asian Indian	Bangladeshi	Cambodian	Chinese[2]	Fijian	Filipino	Guamanian[3]	Hawaiian, Native	Hmong	Indonesian	Japanese	Korean	Laotian	Malaysian	Pakistani	Samoan	Sri Lankan	Taiwanese	Thai	Tongan	Vietnamese
La Canada Flintridge (city)	6,126 90.01	1,069	923 86.34 86.34 15.07	-	-	-	-	-	203 95.75 21.99 18.99 3.31	-	-	-	-	-	-	145 96.67 15.71 13.56 2.37	470 81.88 50.92 43.97 7.67	-	-	-	-	-	-	-	-	-
La Crescenta-Montrose (cdp)	4,563 65.50	1,061	689 64.94 64.94 15.10	-	-	-	-	-	-	-	65 51.59 9.43 6.13 1.42	-	-	-	-	-	444 66.77 64.44 41.85 9.73	-	-	-	-	-	-	-	-	-
La Mirada (city)	11,949 81.98	2,079	1,617 77.78 77.78 13.53	-	-	117 73.58 7.24 5.63 0.98	-	-	216 96.43 13.36 10.39 1.81	-	499 91.73 30.86 24.00 4.18	-	-	-	-	123 66.85 7.61 5.92 1.03	467 64.50 28.88 22.46 3.91	-	-	-	-	-	-	-	-	-
La Puente (city)	5,757 60.84	844	469 55.57 55.57 8.15	-	-	-	-	-	164 70.69 34.97 19.43 2.85	-	146 48.34 31.13 17.30 2.54	-	-	-	-	-	-	-	-	-	-	-	-	-	-	-
La Verne (city)	8,643 78.08	642	529 82.40 82.40 6.12	-	-	-	-	-	-	-	186 86.51 35.16 28.97 2.15	-	-	-	-	-	-	-	-	-	-	-	-	-	-	-
Lakewood (city)	19,318 72.04	2,900	1,711 59.00 59.00 8.86	149	92 61.74 61.74 0.48	68 50.00 3.97 2.34 0.35	-	99 65.56 5.79 3.41 0.51	211 69.41 12.33 7.28 1.09	-	718 61.21 41.96 24.76 3.72	-	-	-	-	267 83.44 15.60 9.21 1.38	108 23.79 6.31 3.72 0.56	-	-	-	48 53.33 52.17 32.21 0.25	-	-	-	-	92 63.45 5.38 3.17 0.48
Lancaster (city)	23,394 61.23	1,337	859 64.25 64.25 3.67	-	-	88 47.83 10.24 6.58 0.38	-	-	102 77.86 11.87 7.63 0.44	-	447 67.32 52.04 33.43 1.91	-	-	-	-	-	-	-	-	-	-	-	-	-	-	-
Lawndale (city)	3,152 32.97	849	316 37.22 37.22 10.03	114	34 29.82 29.82 1.08	-	-	-	-	-	72 37.70 22.78 8.48 2.28	-	-	-	-	-	-	-	-	-	-	-	-	-	-	115 37.58 36.39 13.55 3.65
Lomita (city)	3,750 46.59	839	421 50.18 50.18 11.23	-	-	-	-	-	-	-	41 26.62 9.74 4.89 1.09	-	-	-	-	187 62.33 44.42 22.29 4.99	71 43.56 16.86 8.46 1.89	-	-	-	-	-	-	-	-	-
Long Beach (city)	66,971 41.06	15,195	5,733 37.73 37.73 8.56	1,067	280 26.24 26.24 0.42	160 42.67 2.79 1.05 0.24	-	678 17.96 11.83 4.46 1.01	496 44.29 8.65 3.26 0.74	-	2,545 51.30 44.39 16.75 3.80	-	-	-	-	926 52.49 16.15 6.09 1.38	111 15.12 1.94 0.73 0.17	16 10.46 0.28 0.11 0.02	-	-	173 23.32 61.79 16.21 0.26	-	-	63 33.33 1.10 0.41 0.09	-	438 33.01 7.64 2.88 0.65

Notes: Please refer to the User's Guide for an explanation of data; data is arranged alphabetically by state, then county, then city within each county; table includes counties with populations greater than 49,999 unless noted and cities with populations greater than 9,999 whose Asian and/or NHPI population rates are greater than the national average; (1) Native Hawaiian and other Pacific Islander; (2) excludes Taiwanese; (3) includes Chamorro; (4) county does not meet population threshold but is shown in order to allow inclusion of city

Place	All owner-occupied housing units	Asian-occupied housing units	Asians who own and occupy their own homes	NHPI[1]-occupied housing units	NHPIs[1] who own and occupy their own homes	Asian Indian	Bangladeshi	Cambodian	Chinese[2]	Fijian	Filipino	Guamanian[3]	Hawaiian, Native	Hmong	Indonesian	Japanese	Korean	Laotian	Malaysian	Pakistani	Samoan	Sri Lankan	Taiwanese	Thai	Tongan	Vietnamese
Los Angeles (city)	491,836 38.56	131,816	47,900 36.34 36.34 9.74	1,855	547 29.49 29.49 0.11	2,904 35.26 6.06 2.20 0.59	23 8.91 0.05 0.02 <0.01	109 12.63 0.23 0.08 0.02	9,201 41.83 19.21 6.98 1.87	-	12,993 41.81 27.13 9.86 2.64	87 27.27 15.90 4.69 0.02	193 37.48 35.28 10.40 0.04	-	205 28.47 0.43 0.16 0.04	9,328 50.63 19.47 7.08 1.90	7,800 21.77 16.28 5.92 1.59	14 7.37 0.03 0.01 <0.01	-	134 31.02 0.28 0.10 0.03	106 20.15 19.38 5.71 0.02	208 52.00 0.43 0.16 0.04	565 39.62 1.18 0.43 0.11	1,257 43.36 2.62 0.95 0.26	48 55.17 8.78 2.59 0.01	1,920 34.58 4.01 1.46 0.39
Manhattan Beach (city)	9,440 64.94	838	571 68.14 68.14 6.05	-	-	-	-	-	164 68.05 28.72 19.57 1.74	-	-	-	-	-	-	252 86.30 44.13 30.07 2.67	-	-	-	-	-	-	-	-	-	-
Monrovia (city)	6,471 48.00	882	531 60.20 60.20 8.21	-	-	-	-	-	160 60.38 30.13 18.14 2.47	-	138 52.08 25.99 15.65 2.13	-	-	-	-	-	-	-	-	-	-	-	-	-	-	-
Montebello (city)	8,965 47.61	2,475	1,753 70.83 70.83 19.55	-	-	-	-	-	699 78.80 39.87 28.24 7.80	-	176 59.86 10.04 7.11 1.96	-	-	-	-	622 86.39 35.48 25.13 6.94	77 40.74 4.39 3.11 0.86	-	-	-	-	-	-	-	-	-
Monterey Park (city)	10,567 54.10	11,745	6,412 54.59 54.59 60.68	-	-	-	-	5 6.58 0.08 0.04 0.05	3,730 51.03 58.17 31.76 35.30	-	129 56.09 2.01 1.10 1.22	-	-	-	-	1,753 84.20 27.34 14.93 16.59	157 57.72 2.45 1.34 1.49	-	-	-	-	-	197 58.63 3.07 1.68 1.86	-	-	110 15.63 1.72 0.94 1.04
Norwalk (city)	17,691 65.78	3,342	2,076 62.12 62.12 11.73	-	-	230 66.09 11.08 6.88 1.30	-	85 82.52 4.09 2.54 0.48	154 50.16 7.42 4.61 0.87	-	859 75.88 41.38 25.70 4.86	-	-	-	-	134 79.29 6.45 4.01 0.76	287 36.01 13.82 8.59 1.62	-	-	-	-	-	-	-	-	154 67.84 7.42 4.61 0.87
Palmdale (city)	24,412 71.08	1,128	1,009 89.45 89.45 4.13	-	-	106 100.00 10.51 9.40 0.43	-	-	-	-	473 87.76 46.88 41.93 1.94	-	-	-	-	-	-	-	-	-	-	-	-	-	-	-
Palos Verdes Estates (city)	4,517 90.47	702	574 81.77 81.77 12.71	-	-	-	-	-	179 95.21 31.18 25.50 3.96	-	-	-	-	-	-	193 84.65 33.62 27.49 4.27	72 66.06 12.54 10.26 1.59	-	-	-	-	-	-	-	-	-
Pasadena (city)	23,670 45.67	5,648	2,509 44.42 44.42 10.60	-	-	158 43.29 6.30 2.80 0.67	-	-	887 46.32 35.35 15.70 3.75	-	298 37.25 11.88 5.28 1.26	-	-	-	-	730 61.50 29.10 12.92 3.08	135 21.84 5.38 2.39 0.57	-	-	-	-	-	-	-	-	155 63.79 6.18 2.74 0.65
Pomona (city)	21,684 57.23	2,632	1,528 58.05 58.05 7.05	-	-	140 80.92 9.16 5.32 0.65	-	7 4.58 0.46 0.27 0.03	345 65.97 22.58 13.11 1.59	-	484 73.11 31.68 18.39 2.23	-	-	-	-	98 63.23 6.41 3.72 0.45	-	37 33.94 2.42 1.41 0.17	-	-	-	-	-	-	-	166 44.50 10.86 6.31 0.77

Notes: Please refer to the User's Guide for an explanation of data; data is arranged alphabetically by state, then county, then city within each county; table includes counties with populations greater than 49,999 unless noted and cities with populations greater than 9,999 whose Asian and/or NHPI population rates are greater than the national average; (1) Native Hawaiian and other Pacific Islander; (2) excludes Taiwanese; (3) includes Chamorro; (4) county does not meet population threshold but is shown in order to allow inclusion of city

Place	All owner-occupied housing units	Asian-occupied housing units	Asians who own and occupy their own homes	NHPI[1]-occupied housing units	NHPIs[1] who own and occupy their own homes	Asian Indian	Bangladeshi	Cambodian	Chinese[2]	Fijian	Filipino	Guamanian[3]	Hawaiian, Native	Hmong	Indonesian	Japanese	Korean	Laotian	Malaysian	Pakistani	Samoan	Sri Lankan	Taiwanese	Thai	Tongan	Vietnamese
Rancho Palos Verdes (city)	12,469	3,285	2,404	-	-	200	-	-	747	-	122	-	-	-	-	684	402	-	-	-	-	-	142	-	-	-
	81.86		73.18			93.90			86.06		79.74					64.47	59.82						82.56			
						8.32			31.07		5.07					28.45	16.72						5.91			
			73.18			6.09			22.74		3.71					20.82	12.24						4.32			
			19.28			1.60			5.99		0.98					5.49	3.22						1.14			
Redondo Beach (city)	14,147	2,513	1,364	-	-	102	-	-	320	-	141	-	-	-	-	590	89	-	-	-	-	-	-	-	-	-
	49.52		54.28			45.95			70.95		39.50					60.14	37.55									
						7.48			23.46		10.34					43.26	6.52									
			54.28			4.06			12.73		5.61					23.48	3.54									
			9.64			0.72			2.26		1.00					4.17	0.63									
Rosemead (city)	6,771	6,223	3,212	-	-	-	-	29	1,860	-	154	-	-	-	-	328	-	-	-	-	-	-	-	-	-	508
	48.75		51.61					21.17	54.43		71.30					82.21										36.05
								0.90	57.91		4.79					10.21										15.82
			51.61					0.47	29.89		2.47					5.27										8.16
			47.44					0.43	27.47		2.27					4.84										7.50
Rowland Heights (cdp)	9,367	7,168	4,731	-	-	147	-	-	2,427	-	543	-	-	-	-	201	423	-	-	-	-	-	585	-	-	100
	66.05		66.00			72.77			70.76		64.64					70.77	40.95						75.29			64.94
						3.11			51.30		11.48					4.25	8.94						12.37			2.11
			66.00			2.05			33.86		7.58					2.80	5.90						8.16			1.40
			50.51			1.57			25.91		5.80					2.15	4.52						6.25			1.07
San Dimas (city)	8,998	1,036	777	-	-	-	-	-	310	-	148	-	-	-	-	-	-	-	-	-	-	-	-	-	-	-
	73.56		75.00						86.59		65.78															
									39.90		19.05															
			75.00						29.92		14.29															
			8.64						3.45		1.64															
San Gabriel (city)	5,984	5,599	2,500	-	-	-	-	-	1,600	-	112	-	-	-	-	200	-	-	-	-	-	-	170	-	-	174
	47.74		44.65						47.20		33.94					70.18							62.04			25.11
									64.00		4.48					8.00							6.80			6.96
			44.65						28.58		2.00					3.57							3.04			3.11
			41.78						26.74		1.87					3.34							2.84			2.91
San Marino (city)	3,919	1,593	1,440	-	-	-	-	-	968	-	-	-	-	-	-	-	-	-	-	-	-	-	326	-	-	-
	91.59		90.40						96.51														82.95			
									67.22														22.64			
			90.40						60.77														20.46			
			36.74						24.70														8.32			
Santa Clarita (city)	37,891	2,038	1,569	-	-	145	-	-	210	-	514	-	-	-	-	279	119	-	-	-	-	-	-	-	-	123
	74.76		76.99			80.11			81.40		71.29					85.06	60.71									100.00
						9.24			13.38		32.76					17.78	7.58									7.84
			76.99			7.11			10.30		25.22					13.69	5.84									6.04
			4.14			0.38			0.55		1.36					0.74	0.31									0.32
Santa Monica (city)	13,282	2,739	1,053	-	-	123	-	-	386	-	39	-	-	-	-	318	100	-	-	-	-	-	-	-	-	-
	29.85		38.44			38.08			49.49		21.20					35.02	32.79									
						11.68			36.66		3.70					30.20	9.50									
			38.44			4.49			14.09		1.42					11.61	3.65									
			7.93			0.93			2.91		0.29					2.39	0.75									
Sierra Madre (city)	2,972	234	155	-	-	-	-	-	-	-	-	-	-	-	-	-	-	-	-	-	-	-	-	-	-	-
	62.49		66.24																							
			66.24																							
			5.22																							

Notes: Please refer to the User's Guide for an explanation of data; data is arranged alphabetically by state, then county, then city within each county; table includes counties with populations greater than 49,999 unless noted and cities with populations greater than 9,999 whose Asian and/or NHPI population rates are greater than the national average; (1) Native Hawaiian and other Pacific Islander; (2) excludes Taiwanese; (3) includes Chamorro; (4) county does not meet population threshold but is shown in order to allow inclusion of city

Place	All owner-occupied housing units	Asian-occupied housing units	Asians who own and occupy their own homes	NHPI[1]-occupied housing units	NHPIs[1] who own and occupy their own homes	Asian Indian	Bangladeshi	Cambodian	Chinese[2]	Fijian	Filipino	Guamanian[3]	Hawaiian, Native	Hmong	Indonesian	Japanese	Korean	Laotian	Malaysian	Pakistani	Samoan	Sri Lankan	Taiwanese	Thai	Tongan	Vietnamese
South El Monte (city)	2,288 49.67	364	181 49.73 49.73 7.91	-	-	-	-	-	66 45.52 36.46 18.13 2.88	-	-	-	-	-	-	-	-	-	-	-	-	-	-	-	-	47 37.60 25.97 12.91 2.05
South Pasadena (city)	4,622 44.12	2,252	1,269 56.35 56.35 27.46	-	-	-	-	-	799 65.65 62.96 35.48 17.29	-	-	-	-	-	-	258 57.21 20.33 11.46 5.58	35 15.09 2.76 1.55 0.76	-	-	-	-	-	-	-	-	-
South San Jose Hills (cdp)	3,228 82.12	298	265 88.93 88.93 8.21	-	-	-	-	-	-	-	137 80.59 51.70 45.97 4.24	-	-	-	-	-	-	-	-	-	-	-	-	-	-	-
Temple City (city)	7,178 63.00	3,674	2,728 74.25 74.25 38.01	-	-	-	-	-	1,661 75.16 60.89 45.21 23.14	-	108 66.26 3.96 2.94 1.50	-	-	-	-	198 84.98 7.26 5.39 2.76	100 68.97 3.67 2.72 1.39	-	-	-	-	-	365 83.52 13.38 9.93 5.08	-	-	103 46.82 3.78 2.80 1.43
Torrance (city)	30,528 55.98	13,713	7,509 54.76 54.76 24.60	-	-	221 26.28 2.94 1.61 0.72	-	-	1,488 70.92 19.82 10.85 4.87	-	527 48.17 7.02 3.84 1.73	-	-	-	-	3,657 65.63 48.70 26.67 11.98	948 35.22 12.62 6.91 3.11	-	-	41 24.26 0.55 0.30 0.13	-	-	236 66.11 3.14 1.72 0.77	-	-	234 50.43 3.12 1.71 0.77
Valinda (cdp)	3,709 77.72	445	343 77.08 77.08 9.25	-	-	-	-	-	-	-	190 81.20 55.39 42.70 5.12	-	-	-	-	-	-	-	-	-	-	-	-	-	-	42 51.85 12.24 9.44 1.13
Vincent (cdp)	3,077 80.59	273	203 74.36 74.36 6.60	-	-	-	-	-	-	-	117 77.48 57.64 42.86 3.80	-	-	-	-	-	-	-	-	-	-	-	-	-	-	-
Walnut (city)	7,340 88.86	4,422	3,923 88.72 88.72 53.45	-	-	139 74.33 3.54 3.14 1.89	-	-	1,657 92.57 42.24 37.47 22.57	-	820 93.61 20.90 18.54 11.17	-	-	-	-	152 87.86 3.87 3.44 2.07	345 74.84 8.79 7.80 4.70	-	-	-	-	-	416 90.04 10.60 9.41 5.67	-	-	94 87.85 2.40 2.13 1.28
West Carson (cdp)	5,367 75.00	1,677	1,260 75.13 75.13 23.48	-	-	-	-	-	-	-	461 70.17 36.59 27.49 8.59	-	-	-	-	389 84.02 30.87 23.20 7.25	196 73.68 15.56 11.69 3.65	-	-	-	-	-	-	-	-	-
West Covina (city)	20,899 66.56	6,400	4,428 69.19 69.19 21.19	100	53 53.00 53.00 0.25	120 69.36 2.71 1.88 0.57	-	-	1,456 75.87 32.88 22.75 6.97	-	1,630 66.45 36.81 25.47 7.80	-	-	-	-	254 80.38 5.74 3.97 1.22	167 51.07 3.77 2.61 0.80	-	-	-	-	-	197 73.51 4.45 3.08 0.94	-	-	309 67.76 6.98 4.83 1.48

Notes: Please refer to the User's Guide for an explanation of data; data is arranged alphabetically by state, then county, then city within each county; table includes counties with populations greater than 49,999 unless noted and cities with populations greater than 9,999 whose Asian and/or NHPI population rates are greater than the national average; (1) Native Hawaiian and other Pacific Islander; (2) excludes Taiwanese; (3) includes Chamorro; (4) county does not meet population threshold but is shown in order to allow inclusion of city

Place	All owner-occupied housing units	Asian-occupied housing units	Asians who own and occupy their own homes	NHPI[1]-occupied housing units	NHPIs[1] who own and occupy their own homes	Asian Indian	Bangladeshi	Cambodian	Chinese[2]	Fijian	Filipino	Guamanian[3]	Hawaiian, Native	Hmong	Indonesian	Japanese	Korean	Laotian	Malaysian	Pakistani	Samoan	Sri Lankan	Taiwanese	Thai	Tongan	Vietnamese
West Hollywood (city)	4,988 21.57	845	145 17.16 17.16 2.91	-	-	-	-	-	-	-	-	-	-	-	-	-	-	-	-	-	-	-	-	-	-	-
West Puente Valley (cdp)	4,024 83.24	401	316 78.80 78.80 7.85	-	-	-	-	-	-	-	123 75.46 38.92 30.67 3.06	-	-	-	-	-	-	-	-	-	-	-	-	-	-	76 80.85 24.05 18.95 1.89
Whittier (city)	16,380 57.81	978	679 69.43 69.43 4.15	-	-	-	-	-	250 77.16 36.82 25.56 1.53	-	97 52.15 14.29 9.92 0.59	-	-	-	-	123 73.65 18.11 12.58 0.75	104 83.20 15.32 10.63 0.63	-	-	-	-	-	-	-	-	-
Madera County	23,949 66.24	404	294 72.77 72.77 1.23	-	-	101 73.19 34.35 25.00 0.42	-	-	-	-	90 69.23 30.61 22.28 0.38	-	-	-	-	-	-	-	-	-	-	-	-	-	-	-
Marin County	64,018 63.60	3,889	2,236 57.50 57.50 3.49	-	-	238 39.80 10.64 6.12 0.37	-	-	950 79.50 42.49 24.43 1.48	-	176 45.71 7.87 4.53 0.27	-	-	-	-	502 67.20 22.45 12.91 0.78	173 48.32 7.74 4.45 0.27	-	-	-	-	-	-	-	-	91 26.38 4.07 2.34 0.14
Larkspur (city)	3,117 50.45	183	88 48.09 48.09 2.82	-	-	-	-	-	-	-	-	-	-	-	-	-	-	-	-	-	-	-	-	-	-	-
Novato (city)	12,512 67.54	854	555 64.99 64.99 4.44	-	-	-	-	-	227 97.42 40.90 26.58 1.81	-	48 36.36 8.65 5.62 0.38	-	-	-	-	-	-	-	-	-	-	-	-	-	-	-
San Rafael (city)	12,009 53.61	1,115	548 49.15 49.15 4.56	-	-	52 26.80 9.49 4.66 0.43	-	-	257 68.72 46.90 23.05 2.14	-	-	-	-	-	-	-	-	-	-	-	-	-	-	-	-	44 23.53 8.03 3.95 0.37
Tamalpais-Homestead (cdp)	3,463 76.33	213	172 80.75 80.75 4.97	-	-	-	-	-	-	-	-	-	-	-	-	-	-	-	-	-	-	-	-	-	-	-
Mendocino County	20,389 61.29	227	137 60.35 60.35 0.67	-	-	-	-	-	-	-	-	-	-	-	-	-	-	-	-	-	-	-	-	-	-	-

Notes: Please refer to the User's Guide for an explanation of data; data is arranged alphabetically by state, then county, then city within each county; table includes counties with populations greater than 49,999 unless noted and cities with populations greater than 9,999 whose Asian and/or NHPI population rates are greater than the national average; (1) Native Hawaiian and other Pacific Islander; (2) excludes Taiwanese; (3) includes Chamorro; (4) county does not meet population threshold but is shown in order to allow inclusion of city

Place	All owner-occupied housing units	Asian-occupied housing units	Asians who own and occupy their own homes	NHPI[1]-occupied housing units	NHPIs[1] who own and occupy their own homes	Asian Indian	Bangladeshi	Cambodian	Chinese[2]	Fijian	Filipino	Guamanian[3]	Hawaiian, Native	Hmong	Indonesian	Japanese	Korean	Laotian	Malaysian	Pakistani	Samoan	Sri Lankan	Taiwanese	Thai	Tongan	Vietnamese
Merced County	37,475 58.72	2,871	1,338 46.60 46.60 3.57	-	-	361 70.37 26.98 12.57 0.96	-	-	127 76.51 9.49 4.42 0.34	-	348 74.68 26.01 12.12 0.93	-	-	123 13.02 9.19 4.28 0.33	-	179 79.91 13.38 6.23 0.48	-	56 18.12 4.19 1.95 0.15	-	-	-	-	-	-	-	-
Atwater (city)	4,305 59.58	331	195 58.91 58.91 4.53	-	-	-	-	-	-	-	-	-	-	28 37.84 14.36 8.46 0.65	-	-	-	-	-	-	-	-	-	-	-	-
Livingston (city)	1,511 62.54	344	250 72.67 72.67 16.55	-	-	210 78.07 84.00 61.05 13.90	-	-	-	-	-	-	-	-	-	-	-	-	-	-	-	-	-	-	-	-
Merced (city)	9,469 46.24	1,206	259 21.48 21.48 2.74	-	-	-	-	-	-	-	-	-	-	61 9.62 23.55 5.06 0.64	-	-	-	43 15.99 16.60 3.57 0.45	-	-	-	-	-	-	-	-
Monterey County	66,266 54.66	7,613	4,550 59.77 59.77 6.87	488	250 51.23 51.23 0.38	107 34.29 2.35 1.41 0.16	-	-	546 59.93 12.00 7.17 0.82	-	1,984 63.16 43.60 26.06 2.99	68 43.31 27.20 13.93 0.10	-	-	-	1,103 72.33 24.24 14.49 1.66	443 49.50 9.74 5.82 0.67	-	-	-	-	-	-	-	-	179 35.59 3.93 2.35 0.27
Marina (city)	3,087 45.74	1,330	655 49.25 49.25 21.22	135	66 48.89 48.89 2.14	-	-	-	-	-	172 43.65 26.26 12.93 5.57	-	-	-	-	145 80.56 22.14 10.90 4.70	183 47.16 27.94 13.76 5.93	-	-	-	-	-	-	-	-	54 31.95 8.24 4.06 1.75
Monterey (city)	4,856 38.44	982	335 34.11 34.11 6.90	-	-	-	-	-	33 18.97 9.85 3.36 0.68	-	49 27.53 14.63 4.99 1.01	-	-	-	-	198 56.09 59.10 20.16 4.08	-	-	-	-	-	-	-	-	-	-
Pacific Grove (city)	3,578 49.04	300	142 47.33 47.33 3.97	-	-	-	-	-	-	-	-	-	-	-	-	-	-	-	-	-	-	-	-	-	-	-
Salinas (city)	19,154 50.11	2,619	1,767 67.47 67.47 9.23	120	70 58.33 58.33 0.37	65 45.77 3.68 2.48 0.34	-	-	191 79.92 10.81 7.29 1.00	-	1,108 72.94 62.71 42.31 5.78	-	-	-	-	230 61.33 13.02 8.78 1.20	71 56.80 4.02 2.71 0.37	-	-	-	-	-	-	-	-	66 47.14 3.74 2.52 0.34
Seaside (city)	4,328 43.98	975	561 57.54 57.54 12.96	-	-	-	-	-	-	-	292 54.68 52.05 29.95 6.75	-	-	-	-	180 82.95 32.09 18.46 4.16	-	-	-	-	-	-	-	-	-	9 10.34 1.60 0.92 0.21

Notes: Please refer to the User's Guide for an explanation of data; data is arranged alphabetically by state, then county, then city within each county; table includes counties with populations greater than 49,999 unless noted and cities with populations greater than 9,999 whose Asian and/or NHPI population rates are greater than the national average; (1) Native Hawaiian and other Pacific Islander; (2) excludes Taiwanese; (3) includes Chamorro; (4) county does not meet population threshold but is shown in order to allow inclusion of city

Place	All owner-occupied housing units	Asian-occupied housing units	Asians who own and occupy their own homes	NHPI[1]-occupied housing units	NHPIs[1] who own and occupy their own homes	Asian Indian	Bangladeshi	Cambodian	Chinese[2]	Fijian	Filipino	Guamanian[3]	Hawaiian, Native	Hmong	Indonesian	Japanese	Korean	Laotian	Malaysian	Pakistani	Samoan	Sri Lankan	Taiwanese	Thai	Tongan	Vietnamese
Napa County	29,564	1,118	840	-	-	-	-	-	154	-	440	-	-	-	-	84	-	-	-	-	-	-	-	-	-	-
	65.12		75.13						77.39		83.49					66.67										
									18.33		52.38					10.00										
			75.13						13.77		39.36					7.51										
			2.84						0.52		1.49					0.28										
Nevada County	27,950	266	206	-	-	-	-	-	-	-	-	-	-	-	-	-	-	-	-	-	-	-	-	-	-	-
	75.76		77.44																							
			77.44																							
			0.74																							
Orange County	574,193	109,642	64,110	2,045	1,033	4,626	-	566	11,444	-	8,200	238	335	91	361	8,841	8,543	306	-	374	278	127	2,082	573	26	16,413
	61.39		58.47		50.51	56.24		54.37	71.35		59.92	70.62	62.04	48.15	61.50	70.19	48.88	54.84		57.10	39.66	59.62	79.01	58.59	26.53	51.26
						7.22		0.88	17.85		12.79	23.04	32.43	0.14	0.56	13.79	13.33	0.48		0.58	26.91	0.20	3.25	0.89	2.52	25.60
			58.47		50.51	4.22		0.52	10.44		7.48	11.64	16.38	0.08	0.33	8.06	7.79	0.28		0.34	13.59	0.12	1.90	0.52	1.27	14.97
			11.17		0.18	0.81		0.10	1.99		1.43	0.04	0.06	0.02	0.06	1.54	1.49	0.05		0.07	0.05	0.02	0.36	0.10	<0.01	2.86
Aliso Viejo (cdp)	10,687	1,549	1,183	-	-	165	-	-	174	-	217	-	-	-	-	225	106	-	-	-	-	-	-	-	-	150
	66.21		76.37			79.33			74.36		80.07					77.05	60.57									88.24
						13.95			14.71		18.34					19.02	8.96									12.68
			76.37			10.65			11.23		14.01					14.53	6.84									9.68
			11.07			1.54			1.63		2.03					2.11	0.99									1.40
Anaheim (city)	48,476	11,495	6,215	249	82	677	-	-	892	-	1,092	-	-	-	-	743	883	92	-	55	56	-	105	61	-	1,376
	50.05		54.07		32.93	55.58			70.29		48.68					72.70	43.54	55.42		53.40	53.33		59.32	47.29		52.80
						10.89			14.35		17.57					11.95	14.21	1.48		0.88	68.29		1.69	0.98		22.14
			54.07		32.93	5.89			7.76		9.50					6.46	7.68	0.80		0.48	22.49		0.91	0.53		11.97
			12.82		0.17	1.40			1.84		2.25					1.53	1.82	0.19		0.11	0.12		0.22	0.13		2.84
Brea (city)	8,373	992	637	-	-	74	-	-	152	-	87	-	-	-	-	-	136	-	-	-	-	-	-	-	-	-
	64.33		64.21			52.86			100.00		53.05						56.67									
						11.62			23.86		13.66						21.35									
			64.21			7.46			15.32		8.77						13.71									
			7.61			0.88			1.82		1.04						1.62									
Buena Park (city)	13,301	4,703	2,679	-	-	292	-	-	326	-	912	-	-	-	-	222	514	-	-	-	-	-	-	-	-	183
	56.94		56.96			62.39			74.77		69.67					77.08	33.35									68.80
						10.90			12.17		34.04					8.29	19.19									6.83
			56.96			6.21			6.93		19.39					4.72	10.93									3.89
			20.14			2.20			2.45		6.86					1.67	3.86									1.38
Costa Mesa (city)	15,811	2,760	970	185	60	20	-	-	161	-	128	-	-	-	-	248	49	-	-	-	-	-	-	-	-	251
	40.35		35.14		32.43	11.24			38.52		30.12					36.80	20.68									39.90
						2.06			16.60		13.20					25.57	5.05									25.88
			35.14		32.43	0.72			5.83		4.64					8.99	1.78									9.09
			6.13		0.38	0.13			1.02		0.81					1.57	0.31									1.59
Cypress (city)	10,844	2,817	1,856	-	-	120	-	-	355	-	361	-	-	-	-	377	304	-	-	-	-	-	146	-	-	96
	69.31		65.89			57.42			82.94		64.58					86.07	44.77						82.49			44.86
						6.47			19.13		19.45					20.31	16.38						7.87			5.17
			65.89			4.26			12.60		12.82					13.38	10.79						5.18			3.41
			17.12			1.11			3.27		3.33					3.48	2.80						1.35			0.89
Foothill Ranch (cdp)	2,945	479	443	-	-	-	-	-	-	-	-	-	-	-	-	-	-	-	-	-	-	-	-	-	-	-
	76.61		92.48																							
			92.48																							
			15.04																							

Notes: Please refer to the User's Guide for an explanation of data; data is arranged alphabetically by state, then county, then city within each county; table includes counties with populations greater than 49,999 unless noted and cities with populations greater than 9,999 whose Asian and/or NHPI population rates are greater than the national average; (1) Native Hawaiian and other Pacific Islander; (2) excludes Taiwanese; (3) includes Chamorro; (4) county does not meet population threshold but is shown in order to allow inclusion of city

Place	All owner-occupied housing units	Asian-occupied housing units	Asians who own and occupy their own homes	NHPI¹-occupied housing units	NHPIs¹ who own and occupy their own homes	Asian Indian	Bangladeshi	Cambodian	Chinese²	Fijian	Filipino	Guamanian³	Hawaiian, Native	Hmong	Indonesian	Japanese	Korean	Laotian	Malaysian	Pakistani	Samoan	Sri Lankan	Taiwanese	Thai	Tongan	Vietnamese
Fountain Valley (city)	13,570	3,813	2,802	-	-	97	-	-	627	-	127	-	-	-	-	417	203	-	-	-	-	-	88	-	-	1,106
	74.68		73.49			48.99			87.94		69.78					87.79	58.84						70.97			69.74
						3.46			22.38		4.53					14.88	7.24						3.14			39.47
			73.49			2.54			16.44		3.33					10.94	5.32						2.31			29.01
			20.65			0.71			4.62		0.94					3.07	1.50						0.65			8.15
Fullerton (city)	23,441	6,289	3,358	-	-	233	-	-	591	-	289	-	-	-	-	327	1,474	-	-	-	-	-	-	-	-	190
	53.79		53.39			38.39			61.69		50.35					65.27	56.17									40.43
						6.94			17.60		8.61					9.74	43.90									5.66
			53.39			3.70			9.40		4.60					5.20	23.44									3.02
			14.33			0.99			2.52		1.23					1.39	6.29									0.81
Garden Grove (city)	27,340	12,475	5,712	251	105	109	-	60	425	-	495	-	-	-	-	412	778	-	-	-	30	-	-	-	-	3,173
	59.55		45.79		41.83	49.32		47.62	60.98		71.22					81.75	41.27				22.06					40.51
						1.91		1.05	7.44		8.67					7.21	13.62				28.57					55.55
			45.79		41.83	0.87		0.48	3.41		3.97					3.30	6.24				11.95					25.43
			20.89		0.38	0.40		0.22	1.55		1.81					1.51	2.85				0.11					11.61
Huntington Beach (city)	44,736	5,848	3,655	120	64	237	-	-	821	-	248	-	-	-	-	932	284	-	-	-	-	-	154	-	-	811
	60.61		62.50		53.33	59.70			74.50		44.36					76.83	53.18						87.01			52.29
						6.48			22.46		6.79					25.50	7.77						4.21			22.19
			62.50		53.33	4.05			14.04		4.24					15.94	4.86						2.63			13.87
			8.17		0.14	0.53			1.84		0.55					2.08	0.63						0.34			1.81
Irvine (city)	30,691	12,568	6,931	-	-	787	-	-	2,091	-	461	-	-	-	-	691	1,102	-	-	-	-	-	586	-	-	938
	59.96		55.15			55.82			61.79		49.57					37.62	45.82						77.31			74.56
						11.35			30.17		6.65					9.97	15.90						8.45			13.53
			55.15			6.26			16.64		3.67					5.50	8.77						4.66			7.46
			22.58			2.56			6.81		1.50					2.25	3.59						1.91			3.06
La Habra (city)	10,815	1,102	639	-	-	-	-	-	146	-	97	-	-	-	-	-	187	-	-	-	-	-	-	-	-	-
	56.80		57.99						82.95		48.50						49.21									
									22.85		15.18						29.26									
			57.99						13.25		8.80						16.97									
			5.91						1.35		0.90						1.73									
La Palma (city)	3,694	1,923	1,324	-	-	116	-	-	224	-	240	-	-	-	-	247	351	-	-	-	-	-	-	-	-	-
	74.30		68.85			72.05			75.42		73.85					95.00	49.79									
						8.76			16.92		18.13					18.66	26.51									
			68.85			6.03			11.65		12.48					12.84	18.25									
			35.84			3.14			6.06		6.50					6.69	9.50									
Laguna Hills (city)	8,371	926	723	-	-	-	-	-	152	-	87	-	-	-	-	-	-	-	-	-	-	-	-	-	-	137
	76.59		78.08						86.86		66.41															92.57
									21.02		12.03															18.95
			78.08						16.41		9.40															14.79
			8.64						1.82		1.04															1.64
Laguna Niguel (city)	17,443	1,614	1,256	-	-	-	-	-	361	-	127	-	-	-	-	290	142	-	-	-	-	-	-	-	-	125
	75.11		77.82						94.50		49.03					82.39	71.00									85.62
									28.74		10.11					23.09	11.31									9.95
			77.82						22.37		7.87					17.97	8.80									7.74
			7.20						2.07		0.73					1.66	0.81									0.72
Lake Forest (city)	14,422	1,670	1,150	-	-	84	-	-	188	-	208	-	-	-	-	169	141	-	-	-	-	-	-	-	-	283
	71.67		68.86			37.84			88.68		72.73					63.77	69.12									75.47
						7.30			16.35		18.09					14.70	12.26									24.61
			68.86			5.03			11.26		12.46					10.12	8.44									16.95
			7.97			0.58			1.30		1.44					1.17	0.98									1.96

Notes: Please refer to the User's Guide for an explanation of data; data is arranged alphabetically by state, then county, then city within each county; table includes counties with populations greater than 49,999 unless noted and cities with populations greater than 9,999 whose Asian and/or NHPI population rates are greater than the national average; (1) Native Hawaiian and other Pacific Islander; (2) excludes Taiwanese; (3) includes Chamorro; (4) county does not meet population threshold but is shown in order to allow inclusion of city

Place	All owner-occupied housing units	Asian-occupied housing units	Asians who own and occupy their own homes	NHPI[1]-occupied housing units	NHPIs[1] who own and occupy their own homes	Asian Indian	Bangladeshi	Cambodian	Chinese[2]	Fijian	Filipino	Guamanian[3]	Hawaiian, Native	Hmong	Indonesian	Japanese	Korean	Laotian	Malaysian	Pakistani	Samoan	Sri Lankan	Taiwanese	Thai	Tongan	Vietnamese
Los Alamitos (city)	1,890	332	105	-	-	-	-	-	-	-	-	-	-	-	-	-	-	-	-	-	-	-	-	-	-	-
	45.22		31.63																							
			31.63																							
			5.56																							
Mission Viejo (city)	26,332	2,083	1,806	-	-	137	-	-	388	-	257	-	-	-	-	404	172	-	-	-	-	-	-	-	-	272
	81.45		86.70			86.71			97.24		76.95					92.87	76.79									90.67
						7.59			21.48		14.23					22.37	9.52									15.06
			86.70			6.58			18.63		12.34					19.40	8.26									13.06
			6.86			0.52			1.47		0.98					1.53	0.65									1.03
Newport Beach (city)	18,382	1,024	479	-	-	-	-	-	122	-	-	-	-	-	-	140	-	-	-	-	-	-	-	-	-	-
	55.54		46.78						47.10							50.18										
									25.47							29.23										
			46.78						11.91							13.67										
			2.61						0.66							0.76										
Orange (city)	25,490	3,353	2,154	-	-	160	-	-	337	-	339	-	-	-	-	244	265	-	-	-	-	-	140	-	-	479
	62.47		64.24			64.00			73.42		66.73					79.22	46.99						100.00			55.96
						7.43			15.65		15.74					11.33	12.30						6.50			22.24
			64.24			4.77			10.05		10.11					7.28	7.90						4.18			14.29
			8.45			0.63			1.32		1.33					0.96	1.04						0.55			1.88
Placentia (city)	10,413	1,656	1,299	-	-	104	-	-	294	-	142	-	-	-	-	184	170	-	-	-	-	-	-	-	-	235
	68.79		78.44			63.41			78.61		61.21					87.20	86.73									86.40
						8.01			22.63		10.93					14.16	13.09									18.09
			78.44			6.28			17.75		8.57					11.11	10.27									14.19
			12.47			1.00			2.82		1.36					1.77	1.63									2.26
Rancho Santa Margarita (city)	12,710	1,173	987	-	-	-	-	-	190	-	231	-	-	-	-	-	-	-	-	-	-	-	-	-	-	117
	77.94		84.14						87.96		70.43															100.00
									19.25		23.40															11.85
			84.14						16.20		19.69															9.97
			7.77						1.49		1.82															0.92
Rossmoor (cdp)	3,329	166	151	-	-	-	-	-	-	-	-	-	-	-	-	-	-	-	-	-	-	-	-	-	-	-
	89.83		90.96																							
			90.96																							
			4.54																							
Santa Ana (city)	35,928	7,390	3,808	245	146	65	-	193	340	-	391	-	-	35	-	291	42	108	-	-	68	-	-	-	-	2,223
	49.30		51.53		59.59	37.14		53.91	52.55		57.25			38.04		64.52	17.36	59.67			57.14					51.93
						1.71		5.07	8.93		10.27			0.92		7.64	1.10	2.84			46.58					58.38
			51.53		59.59	0.88		2.61	4.60		5.29			0.47		3.94	0.57	1.46			27.76					30.08
			10.60		0.41	0.18		0.54	0.95		1.09			0.10		0.81	0.12	0.30			0.19					6.19
Seal Beach (city)	9,971	415	317	-	-	-	-	-	-	-	-	-	-	-	-	130	-	-	-	-	-	-	-	-	-	-
	76.20		76.39													78.31										
																41.01										
			76.39													31.33										
			3.18													1.30										
Stanton (city)	5,202	1,676	745	-	-	-	-	-	-	-	220	-	-	-	-	-	108	-	-	-	-	-	-	-	-	261
	48.58		44.45								63.77						41.06									36.40
											29.53						14.50									35.03
			44.45								13.13						6.44									15.57
			14.32								4.23						2.08									5.02

Notes: Please refer to the User's Guide for an explanation of data; data is arranged alphabetically by state, then county, then city within each county; table includes counties with populations greater than 49,999 unless noted and cities with populations greater than 9,999 whose Asian and/or NHPI population rates are greater than the national average; (1) Native Hawaiian and other Pacific Islander; (2) excludes Taiwanese; (3) includes Chamorro; (4) county does not meet population threshold but is shown in order to allow inclusion of city

Place	All owner-occupied housing units	Asian-occupied housing units	Asians who own and occupy their own homes	NHPI[1]-occupied housing units	NHPIs[1] who own and occupy their own homes	Asian Indian	Bangladeshi	Cambodian	Chinese[2]	Fijian	Filipino	Guamanian[3]	Hawaiian, Native	Hmong	Indonesian	Japanese	Korean	Laotian	Malaysian	Pakistani	Samoan	Sri Lankan	Taiwanese	Thai	Tongan	Vietnamese
Tustin (city)	11,845 49.69	3,062	1,690 55.19 55.19 14.27	-	-	173 40.52 10.24 5.65 1.46	-	-	323 60.49 19.11 10.55 2.73	-	279 49.82 16.51 9.11 2.36	-	-	-	-	173 62.23 10.24 5.65 1.46	216 56.99 12.78 7.05 1.82	-	-	-	-	-	131 78.92 7.75 4.28 1.11	-	-	277 55.51 16.39 9.05 2.34
Tustin Foothills (cdp)	7,716 93.01	472	447 94.70 94.70 5.79	-	-	-	-	-	154 100.00 34.45 32.63 2.00	-	-	-	-	-	-	-	-	-	-	-	-	-	-	-	-	-
Westminster (city)	15,897 60.28	8,132	4,143 50.95 50.95 26.06	74	26 35.14 35.14 0.16	53 47.75 1.28 0.65 0.33	-	-	318 72.94 7.68 3.91 2.00	-	250 62.81 6.03 3.07 1.57	-	-	-	-	389 88.21 9.39 4.78 2.45	140 59.57 3.38 1.72 0.88	-	-	-	18 30.51 69.23 24.32 0.11	-	-	-	-	2,783 44.87 67.17 34.22 17.51
Yorba Linda (city)	16,279 84.67	1,788	1,612 90.16 90.16 9.90	-	-	170 92.90 10.55 9.51 1.04	-	-	422 91.94 26.18 23.60 2.59	-	186 87.32 11.54 10.40 1.14	-	-	-	-	325 94.20 20.16 18.18 2.00	201 85.17 12.47 11.24 1.23	-	-	-	-	-	-	-	-	142 85.03 8.81 7.94 0.87
Placer County	68,368 73.21	2,325	1,650 70.97 70.97 2.41	-	-	131 43.67 7.94 5.63 0.19	-	-	392 74.95 23.76 16.86 0.57	-	408 75.84 24.73 17.55 0.60	-	-	-	-	548 77.84 33.21 23.57 0.80	43 53.75 2.61 1.85 0.06	-	-	-	-	-	-	-	-	72 64.86 4.36 3.10 0.11
Rocklin (city)	9,663 72.74	489	306 62.58 62.58 3.17	-	-	-	-	-	-	-	-	-	-	-	-	88 57.14 28.76 18.00 0.91	-	-	-	-	-	-	-	-	-	-
Roseville (city)	21,395 69.43	972	627 64.51 64.51 2.93	-	-	85 38.46 13.56 8.74 0.40	-	-	155 69.82 24.72 15.95 0.72	-	203 82.86 32.38 20.88 0.95	-	-	-	-	120 71.43 19.14 12.35 0.56	-	-	-	-	-	-	-	-	-	-
Riverside County	348,479 68.84	15,164	9,931 65.49 65.49 2.85	934	467 50.00 50.00 0.13	980 62.74 9.87 6.46 0.28	-	65 50.78 0.65 0.43 0.02	1,086 58.51 10.94 7.16 0.31	-	3,862 75.15 38.89 25.47 1.11	86 42.16 18.42 9.21 0.02	189 65.63 40.47 20.24 0.05	8 8.79 0.08 0.05 <0.01	-	1,221 75.14 12.29 8.05 0.35	832 51.74 8.38 5.49 0.24	227 60.70 2.29 1.50 0.07	-	71 55.91 0.71 0.47 0.02	89 39.91 19.06 9.53 0.03	-	86 57.72 0.87 0.57 0.02	153 55.04 1.54 1.01 0.04	-	977 64.74 9.84 6.44 0.28
Banning (city)	6,438 72.41	191	99 51.83 51.83 1.54	-	-	-	-	-	-	-	-	-	-	-	-	-	-	30 42.86 30.30 15.71 0.47	-	-	-	-	-	-	-	-
Corona (city)	25,501 67.42	2,486	1,989 80.01 80.01 7.80	-	-	285 74.03 14.33 11.46 1.12	-	-	187 73.33 9.40 7.52 0.73	-	689 85.80 34.64 27.72 2.70	-	-	-	-	191 89.67 9.60 7.68 0.75	240 82.19 12.07 9.65 0.94	-	-	-	-	-	-	-	-	283 77.11 14.23 11.38 1.11

Notes: Please refer to the User's Guide for an explanation of data; data is arranged alphabetically by state, then county, then city within each county; table includes counties with populations greater than 49,999 unless noted and cities with populations greater than 9,999 whose Asian and/or NHPI population rates are greater than the national average; (1) Native Hawaiian and other Pacific Islander; (2) excludes Taiwanese; (3) includes Chamorro; (4) county does not meet population threshold but is shown in order to allow inclusion of city

Place	All owner-occupied housing units	Asian-occupied housing units	Asians who own and occupy their own homes	NHPI[1]-occupied housing units	NHPIs[1] who own and occupy their own homes	Asian Indian	Bangladeshi	Cambodian	Chinese[2]	Fijian	Filipino	Guamanian[3]	Hawaiian, Native	Hmong	Indonesian	Japanese	Korean	Laotian	Malaysian	Pakistani	Samoan	Sri Lankan	Taiwanese	Thai	Tongan	Vietnamese
Moreno Valley (city)	27,955	2,099	1,560	-	-	-	-	-	124	-	782	-	-	-	-	165	97	67	-	-	-	-	-	-	-	113
	71.26		74.32						72.09		77.81					92.18	56.07	51.94								72.44
									7.95		50.13					10.58	6.22	4.29								7.24
			74.32						5.91		37.26					7.86	4.62	3.19								5.38
			5.58						0.44		2.80					0.59	0.35	0.24								0.40
Palm Springs (city)	12,463	508	319	-	-	-	-	-	-	-	205	-	-	-	-	-	-	-	-	-	-	-	-	-	-	-
	60.68		62.80								70.69															
											64.26															
			62.80								40.35															
			2.56								1.64															
Pedley (cdp)	2,544	108	85	-	-	-	-	-	-	-	-	-	-	-	-	-	-	-	-	-	-	-	-	-	-	-
	80.38		78.70																							
			78.70																							
			3.34																							
Riverside (city)	46,514	4,420	1,887	285	108	230	-	-	243	-	493	-	-	-	-	250	186	74	-	-	-	-	-	-	-	278
	56.67		42.69		37.89	46.94			34.76		50.67					57.87	30.64	70.48								45.72
						12.19			12.88		26.13					13.25	9.86	3.92								14.73
			42.69		37.89	5.20			5.50		11.15					5.66	4.21	1.67								6.29
			4.06		0.23	0.49			0.52		1.06					0.54	0.40	0.16								0.60
Temecula (city)	13,276	785	527	-	-	-	-	-	71	-	296	-	-	-	-	-	-	-	-	-	-	-	-	-	-	-
	72.87		67.13						60.68		79.14															
									13.47		56.17															
			67.13						9.04		37.71															
			3.97						0.53		2.23															
Sacramento County	263,811	39,585	22,893	1,727	789	2,007	-	94	7,079	242	4,591	118	146	444	-	4,590	713	583	-	182	67	-	96	91	62	1,764
	58.16		57.83		45.69	51.36		35.34	69.41	49.09	62.93	43.38	58.87	17.74		78.25	49.27	33.76		56.35	20.36		61.15	52.60	42.76	39.85
						8.77		0.41	30.92	30.67	20.05	14.96	18.50	1.94		20.05	3.11	2.55		0.80	8.49		0.42	0.40	7.86	7.71
			57.83		45.69	5.07		0.24	17.88	14.01	11.60	6.83	8.45	1.12		11.60	1.80	1.47		0.46	3.88		0.24	0.23	3.59	4.46
			8.68		0.30	0.76		0.04	2.68	0.09	1.74	0.04	0.06	0.17		1.74	0.27	0.22		0.07	0.03		0.04	0.03	0.02	0.67
Arden-Arcade (cdp)	20,200	2,022	607	-	-	74	-	-	191	-	69	-	-	0	-	143	-	-	-	-	-	-	-	-	-	32
	47.06		30.02			29.02			41.34		16.71			0.00		47.19										16.41
						12.19			31.47		11.37			0.00		23.56										5.27
			30.02			3.66			9.45		3.41			0.00		7.07										1.58
			3.00			0.37			0.95		0.34			0.00		0.71										0.16
Elk Grove (cdp)	15,206	2,536	2,101	-	-	289	-	-	368	-	725	-	-	-	-	172	-	-	-	-	-	-	-	-	-	301
	81.94		82.85			95.07			88.25		89.62					93.99										59.84
						13.76			17.52		34.51					8.19										14.33
			82.85			11.40			14.51		28.59					6.78										11.87
			13.82			1.90			2.42		4.77					1.13										1.98
Fair Oaks (cdp)	7,857	385	210	-	-	-	-	-	-	-	-	-	-	-	-	-	-	-	-	-	-	-	-	-	-	-
	70.13		54.55																							
			54.55																							
			2.67																							
Florin (cdp)	5,454	1,332	703	-	-	46	-	-	139	-	215	-	-	12	-	-	-	-	-	-	-	-	-	-	-	85
	59.62		52.78			58.23			68.81		70.72			8.00												28.62
						6.54			19.77		30.58			1.71												12.09
			52.78			3.45			10.44		16.14			0.90												6.38
			12.89			0.84			2.55		3.94			0.22												1.56

Notes: Please refer to the User's Guide for an explanation of data; data is arranged alphabetically by state, then county, then city within each county; table includes counties with populations greater than 49,999 unless noted and cities with populations greater than 9,999 whose Asian and/or NHPI population rates are greater than the national average; (1) Native Hawaiian and other Pacific Islander; (2) excludes Taiwanese; (3) includes Chamorro; (4) county does not meet population threshold but is shown in order to allow inclusion of city

Place	All owner-occupied housing units	Asian-occupied housing units	Asians who own and occupy their own homes	NHPI-occupied housing units	NHPIs[1] who own and occupy their own homes	Asian Indian	Bangladeshi	Cambodian	Chinese[2]	Fijian	Filipino	Guamanian[3]	Hawaiian, Native	Hmong	Indonesian	Japanese	Korean	Laotian	Malaysian	Pakistani	Samoan	Sri Lankan	Taiwanese	Thai	Tongan	Vietnamese
Folsom (city)	13,101	1,194	817	-	-	270	-	-	164	-	132	-	-	-	-	-	-	-	-	-	-	-	-	-	-	-
	76.26		68.43			61.78			82.00		71.74															
						33.05			20.07		16.16															
			68.43			22.61			13.74		11.06															
			6.24			2.06			1.25		1.01															
Foothill Farms (cdp)	3,470	297	154	-	-	-	-	-	-	-	-	-	-	-	-	-	-	-	-	-	-	-	-	-	-	-
	52.84		51.85																							
			51.85																							
			4.44																							
La Riviera (cdp)	2,458	336	188	-	-	-	-	-	-	-	-	-	-	-	-	-	-	-	-	-	-	-	-	-	-	-
	56.57		55.95																							
			55.95																							
			7.65																							
Laguna (cdp)	9,666	1,914	1,692	-	-	172	-	-	566	-	505	-	-	-	-	243	-	-	-	-	-	-	-	-	-	122
	85.10		88.40			96.09			89.98		91.16					91.70										73.05
						10.17			33.45		29.85					14.36										7.21
			88.40			8.99			29.57		26.38					12.70										6.37
			17.50			1.78			5.86		5.22					2.51										1.26
North Highlands (cdp)	7,535	742	340	-	-	-	-	-	-	-	168	-	-	-	-	-	-	-	-	-	-	-	-	-	-	30
	48.96		45.82								68.29															14.71
											49.41															8.82
			45.82								22.64															4.04
			4.51								2.23															0.40
Parkway-S. Sacramento (cdp)	5,275	1,424	399	-	-	-	-	-	89	-	-	-	-	13	-	-	-	30	-	-	-	-	-	-	-	81
	46.92		28.02						59.33					3.29				11.63								27.36
									22.31					3.26				7.52								20.30
			28.02						6.25					0.91				2.11								5.69
			7.56						1.69					0.25				0.57								1.54
Rancho Cordova (cdp)	9,894	1,413	493	-	-	22	-	-	82	-	152	-	-	-	-	-	62	-	-	-	-	-	-	-	-	64
	48.71		34.89			8.76			46.07		44.84						43.66									27.71
						4.46			16.63		30.83						12.58									12.98
			34.89			1.56			5.80		10.76						4.39									4.53
			4.98			0.22			0.83		1.54						0.63									0.65
Rosemont (cdp)	4,667	934	518	-	-	-	-	-	-	-	80	-	-	-	-	-	69	-	-	-	-	-	-	-	-	81
	55.96		55.46								47.90						38.12									48.50
											15.44						13.32									15.64
			55.46								8.57						7.39									8.67
			11.10								1.71						1.48									1.74
Sacramento (city)	77,396	19,691	10,809	913	446	533	-	29	4,566	189	1,414	-	-	364	-	2,601	86	386	-	80	33	-	-	-	45	459
	50.07		54.89		48.85	40.41		28.16	67.20	57.62	54.36			21.91		78.20	34.82	34.93		45.98	20.63				47.87	28.14
						4.93		0.27	42.24	42.38	13.08			3.37		24.06	0.80	3.57		0.74	7.40				10.09	4.25
			54.89		48.85	2.71		0.15	23.19	20.70	7.18			1.85		13.21	0.44	1.96		0.41	3.61				4.93	2.33
			13.97		0.58	0.69		0.04	5.90	0.24	1.83			0.47		3.36	0.11	0.50		0.10	0.04				0.06	0.59
Vineyard (cdp)	2,983	430	389	-	-	-	-	-	-	-	153	-	-	-	-	-	-	-	-	-	-	-	-	-	-	-
	91.28		90.47								93.29															
											39.33															
			90.47								35.58															
			13.04								5.13															

Notes: Please refer to the User's Guide for an explanation of data; data is arranged alphabetically by state, then county, then city within each county; table includes counties with populations greater than 49,999 unless noted and cities with populations greater than 9,999 whose Asian and/or NHPI population rates are greater than the national average; (1) Native Hawaiian and other Pacific Islander; (2) excludes Taiwanese; (3) includes Chamorro; (4) county does not meet population threshold but is shown in order to allow inclusion of city

Place	All owner-occupied housing units	Asian-occupied housing units	Asians who own and occupy their own homes	NHPI[1]-occupied housing units	NHPIs[1] who own and occupy their own homes	Asian Indian	Bangladeshi	Cambodian	Chinese[2]	Fijian	Filipino	Guamanian[3]	Hawaiian, Native	Hmong	Indonesian	Japanese	Korean	Laotian	Malaysian	Pakistani	Samoan	Sri Lankan	Taiwanese	Thai	Tongan	Vietnamese
San Benito County	10,824	335	272	-	-	-	-	-	-	-	117	-	-	-	-	-	-	-	-	-	-	-	-	-	-	-
	68.14		81.19								71.78															
											43.01															
			81.19								34.93															
			2.51								1.08															
San Bernardino County	341,014	22,398	14,773	1,149	606	1,426	-	160	2,541	-	5,074	130	187	-	495	1,154	1,290	49	-	149	152	-	393	350	76	1,226
	64.51		65.96		52.74	64.21		39.70	74.65		73.13	52.42	70.30		54.04	70.62	58.03	47.12		73.04	39.69		73.05	69.03	49.67	48.29
						9.65		1.08	17.20		34.35	21.45	30.86		3.35	7.81	8.73	0.33		1.01	25.08		2.66	2.37	12.54	8.30
			65.96		52.74	6.37		0.71	11.34		22.65	11.31	16.28		2.21	5.15	5.76	0.22		0.67	13.23		1.75	1.56	6.61	5.47
			4.33		0.18	0.42		0.05	0.75		1.49	0.04	0.05		0.15	0.34	0.38	0.01		0.04	0.04		0.12	0.10	0.02	0.36
Chino (city)	11,916	877	633	-	-	-	-	-	-	-	283	-	-	-	-	-	-	-	-	-	-	-	-	-	-	50
	68.58		72.18								81.56															49.50
											44.71															7.90
			72.18								32.27															5.70
			5.31								2.37															0.42
Chino Hills (city)	16,998	3,934	3,457	-	-	305	-	-	950	-	1,223	-	-	-	-	183	261	-	-	-	-	-	127	-	-	194
	84.93		87.87			89.44			90.13		86.43					89.27	81.31						83.01			100.00
						8.82			27.48		35.38					5.29	7.55						3.67			5.61
			87.87			7.75			24.15		31.09					4.65	6.63						3.23			4.93
			20.34			1.79			5.59		7.19					1.08	1.54						0.75			1.14
Colton (city)	7,628	751	432	-	-	-	-	-	-	-	106	-	-	-	-	-	-	-	-	-	-	-	-	-	-	-
	52.30		57.52								65.84															
											24.54															
			57.52								14.11															
			5.66								1.39															
Fontana (city)	23,157	1,395	1,180	125	119	131	-	-	-	-	606	-	-	-	-	-	-	-	-	-	-	-	-	-	-	-
	68.18		84.59		95.20	80.86					90.99															
						11.10					51.36															
			84.59		95.20	9.39					43.44															
			5.10		0.51	0.57					2.62															
Grand Terrace (city)	2,748	219	120	-	-	-	-	-	-	-	-	-	-	-	-	-	-	-	-	-	-	-	-	-	-	-
	65.46		54.79																							
			54.79																							
			4.37																							
Highland (city)	9,043	713	474	-	-	-	-	-	-	-	170	-	-	-	-	-	-	-	-	-	-	-	-	-	-	59
	66.78		66.48								71.43															40.69
											35.86															12.45
			66.48								23.84															8.27
			5.24								1.88															0.65
Loma Linda (city)	2,871	1,435	595	-	-	82	-	-	95	-	158	-	-	-	42	-	91	-	-	-	-	-	-	-	-	-
	38.38		41.46			58.99			44.60		47.88				34.71		30.13									
						13.78			15.97		26.55				7.06		15.29									
			41.46			5.71			6.62		11.01				2.93		6.34									
			20.72			2.86			3.31		5.50				1.46		3.17									
Montclair (city)	5,320	694	279	-	-	-	-	-	-	-	-	-	-	-	-	-	-	-	-	-	-	-	-	-	-	60
	60.46		40.20																							19.48
																										21.51
			40.20																							8.65
			5.24																							1.13

Notes: Please refer to the User's Guide for an explanation of data; data is arranged alphabetically by state, then county, then city within each county; table includes counties with populations greater than 49,999 unless noted and cities with populations greater than 9,999 whose Asian and/or NHPI population rates are greater than the national average; (1) Native Hawaiian and other Pacific Islander; (2) excludes Taiwanese; (3) includes Chamorro; (4) county does not meet population threshold but is shown in order to allow inclusion of city

Place	All owner-occupied housing units	Asian-occupied housing units	Asians who own and occupy their own homes	NHPI[1]-occupied housing units	NHPIs[1] who own and occupy their own homes	Asian Indian	Bangladeshi	Cambodian	Chinese[2]	Fijian	Filipino	Guamanian[3]	Hawaiian, Native	Hmong	Indonesian	Japanese	Korean	Laotian	Malaysian	Pakistani	Samoan	Sri Lankan	Taiwanese	Thai	Tongan	Vietnamese
Ontario (city)	25,089	1,840	1,107	102	65	73	-	-	121	-	450	-	-	-	-	-	-	-	-	-	-	-	-	-	-	217
	57.74		60.16		63.73	50.00			57.35		69.12															62.36
						6.59			10.93		40.65															19.60
			60.16		63.73	3.97			6.58		24.46															11.79
			4.41		0.26	0.29			0.48		1.79															0.86
Rancho Cucamonga (city)	28,814	2,197	1,620	-	-	212	-	-	373	-	449	-	-	-	-	166	108	-	-	-	-	-	-	-	-	104
	70.32		73.74			80.00			81.44		70.38					73.78	51.67									75.36
						13.09			23.02		27.72					10.25	6.67									6.42
			73.74			9.65			16.98		20.44					7.56	4.92									4.73
			5.62			0.74			1.29		1.56					0.58	0.37									0.36
Redlands (city)	14,258	1,118	625	-	-	56	-	-	119	-	150	-	-	-	-	-	123	-	-	-	-	-	-	-	-	-
	60.24		55.90			50.45			65.03		53.76						67.58									
						8.96			19.04		24.00						19.68									
			55.90			5.01			10.64		13.42						11.00									
			4.38			0.39			0.83		1.05						0.86									
Rialto (city)	16,732	432	323	99	45	-	-	-	-	-	122	-	-	-	-	-	-	-	-	-	-	-	-	-	-	-
	68.35		74.77		45.45						96.83															
											37.77															
			74.77		45.45						28.24															
			1.93		0.27						0.73															
San Bernardino (city)	29,478	2,039	827	185	67	65	-	21	78	-	313	-	-	-	45	-	67	-	-	-	34	-	-	-	-	117
	52.48		40.56		36.22	31.10		20.00	41.05		61.61				46.39		41.36				40.48					29.85
						7.86		2.54	9.43		37.85				5.44		8.10				50.75					14.15
			40.56		36.22	3.19		1.03	3.83		15.35				2.21		3.29				18.38					5.74
			2.81		0.23	0.22		0.07	0.26		1.06				0.15		0.23				0.12					0.40
Upland (city)	14,470	1,512	856	-	-	95	-	-	178	-	98	-	-	-	-	-	160	-	-	-	-	-	106	-	-	34
	58.92		56.61			65.07			76.39		46.01						60.38						71.62			15.96
						11.10			20.79		11.45						18.69						12.38			3.97
			56.61			6.28			11.77		6.48						10.58						7.01			2.25
			5.92			0.66			1.23		0.68						1.11						0.73			0.23
Victorville (city)	13,648	677	434	-	-	-	-	-	-	-	242	-	-	-	-	-	-	-	-	-	-	-	-	-	-	-
	64.87		64.11								74.69															
											55.76															
			64.11								35.75															
			3.18								1.77															
San Diego County	551,489	70,721	37,784	3,766	1,715	1,399	-	149	6,093	-	18,309	696	398	54	88	4,103	1,422	664	-	83	443	-	485	159	30	3,967
	55.44		53.43		45.54	42.16		16.54	63.44		58.61	48.84	49.63	28.42	49.44	52.74	36.78	41.24		47.16	41.02		69.48	40.05	29.70	43.85
						3.70		0.39	16.13		48.46	40.58	23.21	0.14	0.23	10.86	3.76	1.76		0.22	25.83		1.28	0.42	1.75	10.50
			53.43		45.54	1.98		0.21	8.62		25.89	18.48	10.57	0.08	0.12	5.80	2.01	0.94		0.12	11.76		0.69	0.22	0.80	5.61
			6.85		0.31	0.25		0.03	1.10		3.32	0.13	0.07	0.01	0.02	0.74	0.26	0.12		0.02	0.08		0.09	0.03	0.01	0.72
Bonita (cdp)	3,208	285	209	-	-	-	-	-	-	-	136	-	-	-	-	-	-	-	-	-	-	-	-	-	-	-
	78.88		73.33								92.52															
											65.07															
			73.33								47.72															
			6.51								4.24															
Carlsbad (city)	21,201	1,049	638	-	-	-	-	-	184	-	92	-	-	-	-	108	-	-	-	-	-	-	-	-	-	-
	67.33		60.82						80.35		37.70					59.67										
									28.84		14.42					16.93										
			60.82						17.54		8.77					10.30										
			3.01						0.87		0.43					0.51										

Notes: Please refer to the User's Guide for an explanation of data; data is arranged alphabetically by state, then county, then city within each county; table includes counties with populations greater than 49,999 unless noted and cities with populations greater than 9,999 whose Asian and/or NHPI population rates are greater than the national average; (1) Native Hawaiian and other Pacific Islander; (2) excludes Taiwanese; (3) includes Chamorro; (4) county does not meet population threshold but is shown in order to allow inclusion of city

Place	All owner-occupied housing units	Asian-occupied housing units	Asians who own and occupy their own homes	NHPI[1]-occupied housing units	NHPIs[1] who own and occupy their own homes	Asian Indian	Bangladeshi	Cambodian	Chinese[2]	Fijian	Filipino	Guamanian[3]	Hawaiian, Native	Hmong	Indonesian	Japanese	Korean	Laotian	Malaysian	Pakistani	Samoan	Sri Lankan	Taiwanese	Thai	Tongan	Vietnamese
Chula Vista (city)	33,195 57.50	5,471	3,620 66.17 66.17 10.91	311	199 63.99 63.99 0.60	-	-	-	272 68.86 7.51 4.97 0.82	-	2,507 73.52 69.25 45.82 7.55	97 68.31 48.74 31.19 0.29	-	-	-	422 48.39 11.66 7.71 1.27	195 44.72 5.39 3.56 0.59	-	-	-	-	-	-	-	-	-
Coronado (city)	3,996 51.46	123	45 36.59 36.59 1.13	-	-	-	-	-	-	-	9 45.00 20.00 7.32 0.23	-	-	-	-	-	-	-	-	-	-	-	-	-	-	-
Escondido (city)	23,337 53.29	1,627	954 58.64 58.64 4.09	-	-	-	-	-	126 67.38 13.21 7.74 0.54	-	314 59.58 32.91 19.30 1.35	-	-	-	-	-	-	69 58.97 7.23 4.24 0.30	-	-	-	-	-	-	-	192 55.98 20.13 11.80 0.82
Imperial Beach (city)	2,782 30.00	520	104 20.00 20.00 3.74	-	-	-	-	-	-	-	64 14.35 61.54 12.31 2.30	-	-	-	-	-	-	-	-	-	-	-	-	-	-	-
La Mesa (city)	11,376 47.10	739	182 24.63 24.63 1.60	-	-	-	-	-	-	-	41 25.31 22.53 5.55 0.36	-	-	-	-	-	-	-	-	-	-	-	-	-	-	-
La Presa (cdp)	6,559 65.97	753	480 63.75 63.75 7.32	-	-	-	-	-	-	-	405 60.45 84.38 53.78 6.17	-	-	-	-	-	-	-	-	-	-	-	-	-	-	-
Lemon Grove (city)	4,845 56.68	419	268 63.96 63.96 5.53	-	-	-	-	-	-	-	152 74.15 56.72 36.28 3.14	-	-	-	-	-	-	-	-	-	-	-	-	-	-	33 39.76 12.31 7.88 0.68
National City (city)	5,289 35.03	2,953	756 25.60 25.60 14.29	-	-	-	-	-	-	-	646 24.11 85.45 21.88 12.21	-	-	-	-	-	-	-	-	-	-	-	-	-	-	-
Oceanside (city)	35,032 62.12	2,494	1,649 66.12 66.12 4.71	539	283 52.50 52.50 0.81	-	-	-	139 63.47 8.43 5.57 0.40	-	694 59.22 42.09 27.83 1.98	-	-	-	-	352 76.19 21.35 14.11 1.00	-	-	-	-	193 56.60 68.20 35.81 0.55	-	-	-	-	215 87.40 13.04 8.62 0.61
Poway (city)	12,099 77.62	881	638 72.42 72.42 5.27	-	-	-	-	-	147 73.50 23.04 16.69 1.21	-	202 68.47 31.66 22.93 1.67	-	-	-	-	-	-	-	-	-	-	-	-	-	-	-

Notes: Please refer to the User's Guide for an explanation of data; data is arranged alphabetically by state, then county, then city within each county; table includes counties with populations greater than 49,999 unless noted and cities with populations greater than 9,999 whose Asian and/or NHPI population rates are greater than the national average; (1) Native Hawaiian and other Pacific Islander; (2) excludes Taiwanese; (3) includes Chamorro; (4) county does not meet population threshold but is shown in order to allow inclusion of city

Place	All owner-occupied housing units	Asian-occupied housing units	Asians who own and occupy their own homes	NHPI[1]-occupied housing units	NHPIs[1] who own and occupy their own homes	Asian Indian	Bangladeshi	Cambodian	Chinese[2]	Fijian	Filipino	Guamanian[3]	Hawaiian, Native	Hmong	Indonesian	Japanese	Korean	Laotian	Malaysian	Pakistani	Samoan	Sri Lankan	Taiwanese	Thai	Tongan	Vietnamese
Rancho San Diego (cdp)	5,433 76.83	261	219 83.91 83.91 4.03	-	-	-	-	-	-	-	110 84.62 50.23 42.15 2.02	-	-	-	-	-	-	-	-	-	-	-	-	-	-	-
San Diego (city)	223,275 49.54	47,235	24,448 51.76 51.76 10.95	1,612	708 43.92 43.92 0.32	813 34.29 3.33 1.72 0.36	-	105 12.93 0.43 0.22 0.05	4,357 61.14 17.82 9.22 1.95	-	11,923 62.21 48.77 25.24 5.34	313 52.52 44.21 19.42 0.14	175 43.42 24.72 10.86 0.08	44 29.73 0.18 0.09 0.02	-	2,054 48.31 8.40 4.35 0.92	763 31.04 3.12 1.62 0.34	529 38.98 2.16 1.12 0.24	-	-	132 32.35 18.64 8.19 0.06	-	307 62.78 1.26 0.65 0.14	81 28.93 0.33 0.17 0.04	-	2,970 39.83 12.15 6.29 1.33
San Marcos (city)	12,034 66.21	650	462 71.08 71.08 3.84	-	-	-	-	-	88 67.18 19.05 13.54 0.73	-	179 75.53 38.74 27.54 1.49	-	-	-	-	-	-	-	-	-	-	-	-	-	-	-
Solana Beach (city)	3,587 62.33	143	65 45.45 45.45 1.81	-	-	-	-	-	-	-	-	-	-	-	-	-	-	-	-	-	-	-	-	-	-	-
Spring Valley (cdp)	5,961 64.76	404	269 66.58 66.58 4.51	-	-	-	-	-	-	-	115 61.17 42.75 28.47 1.93	-	-	-	-	-	-	-	-	-	-	-	-	-	-	-
Vista (city)	15,620 53.88	1,090	515 47.25 47.25 3.30	150	52 34.67 34.67 0.33	-	-	-	-	-	143 41.21 27.77 13.12 0.92	-	-	-	-	107 40.23 20.78 9.82 0.69	-	-	-	-	-	-	-	-	-	-
San Francisco County	115,315 34.98	79,058	36,540 46.22 46.22 31.69	905	139 15.36 15.36 0.12	470 21.39 1.29 0.59 0.41	-	18 10.11 0.05 0.02 0.02	26,348 52.51 72.11 33.33 22.85	-	4,928 43.04 13.49 6.23 4.27	-	-	-	60 18.87 0.16 0.08 0.05	2,175 39.82 5.95 2.75 1.89	664 21.69 1.82 0.84 0.58	-	-	44 29.93 0.12 0.06 0.04	56 12.12 40.29 6.19 0.05	-	151 50.00 0.41 0.19 0.13	192 32.49 0.53 0.24 0.17	-	709 24.16 1.94 0.90 0.61
San Francisco (city)	115,315 34.98	79,058	36,540 46.22 46.22 31.69	905	139 15.36 15.36 0.12	470 21.39 1.29 0.59 0.41	-	18 10.11 0.05 0.02 0.02	26,348 52.51 72.11 33.33 22.85	-	4,928 43.04 13.49 6.23 4.27	-	-	-	60 18.87 0.16 0.08 0.05	2,175 39.82 5.95 2.75 1.89	664 21.69 1.82 0.84 0.58	-	-	44 29.93 0.12 0.06 0.04	56 12.12 40.29 6.19 0.05	-	151 50.00 0.41 0.19 0.13	192 32.49 0.53 0.24 0.17	-	709 24.16 1.94 0.90 0.61
San Joaquin County	109,671 60.38	16,719	9,401 56.23 56.23 8.57	551	216 39.20 39.20 0.20	880 72.31 9.36 5.26 0.80	-	265 14.76 2.82 1.59 0.24	1,549 76.68 16.48 9.26 1.41	-	4,161 68.96 44.26 24.89 3.79	-	85 48.02 39.35 15.43 0.08	135 15.73 1.44 0.81 0.12	-	1,357 80.73 14.43 8.12 1.24	150 50.51 1.60 0.90 0.14	99 14.98 1.05 0.59 0.09	-	132 48.35 1.40 0.79 0.12	42 36.84 19.44 7.62 0.04	-	-	-	-	473 33.47 5.03 2.83 0.43
Lathrop (city)	2,258 78.21	407	355 87.22 87.22 15.72	-	-	-	-	-	-	-	257 83.71 72.39 63.14 11.38	-	-	-	-	-	-	-	-	-	-	-	-	-	-	-

Notes: Please refer to the User's Guide for an explanation of data; data is arranged alphabetically by state, then county, then city within each county; table includes counties with populations greater than 49,999 unless noted and cities with populations greater than 9,999 whose Asian and/or NHPI population rates are greater than the national average; (1) Native Hawaiian and other Pacific Islander; (2) excludes Taiwanese; (3) includes Chamorro; (4) county does not meet population threshold but is shown in order to allow inclusion of city

Place	All owner-occupied housing units	Asian-occupied housing units	Asians who own and occupy their own homes	NHPI[1]-occupied housing units	NHPIs[1] who own and occupy their own homes	Asian Indian	Bangladeshi	Cambodian	Chinese[2]	Fijian	Filipino	Guamanian[3]	Hawaiian, Native	Hmong	Indonesian	Japanese	Korean	Laotian	Malaysian	Pakistani	Samoan	Sri Lankan	Taiwanese	Thai	Tongan	Vietnamese
Lodi (city)	11,264 54.43	977	602 61.62 61.62 5.34	-	-	99 50.77 16.45 10.13 0.88	-	-	-	-	91 46.43 15.12 9.31 0.81	-	-	-	-	256 79.26 42.52 26.20 2.27	-	-	-	-	-	-	-	-	-	-
Stockton (city)	40,761 51.91	12,259	6,030 49.19 49.19 14.79	327	88 26.91 26.91 0.22	352 68.35 5.84 2.87 0.86	-	257 14.74 4.26 2.10 0.63	1,130 74.44 18.74 9.22 2.77	-	2,848 65.31 47.23 23.23 6.99	-	-	80 10.99 1.33 0.65 0.20	-	633 78.73 10.50 5.16 1.55	-	90 14.22 1.49 0.73 0.22	-	64 43.54 1.06 0.52 0.16	-	-	-	-	-	377 29.66 6.25 3.08 0.92
Tracy (city)	12,727 72.39	1,166	948 81.30 81.30 7.45	-	-	192 80.33 20.25 16.47 1.51	-	-	103 85.12 10.86 8.83 0.81	-	404 88.99 42.62 34.65 3.17	-	-	-	-	-	-	-	-	-	-	-	-	-	-	-
San Luis Obispo County	56,992 61.45	2,122	972 45.81 45.81 1.71	-	-	121 58.17 12.45 5.70 0.21	-	-	138 33.41 14.20 6.50 0.24	-	326 47.94 33.54 15.36 0.57	-	-	-	-	282 59.49 29.01 13.29 0.49	74 38.74 7.61 3.49 0.13	-	-	-	-	-	-	-	-	-
Baywood-Los Osos (cdp)	4,050 69.22	220	155 70.45 70.45 3.83	-	-	-	-	-	-	-	107 78.10 69.03 48.64 2.64	-	-	-	-	-	-	-	-	-	-	-	-	-	-	-
Grover Beach (city)	2,539 50.68	128	59 46.09 46.09 2.32	-	-	-	-	-	-	-	-	-	-	-	-	-	-	-	-	-	-	-	-	-	-	-
San Luis Obispo (city)	7,795 41.79	880	199 22.61 22.61 2.55	-	-	-	-	-	53 22.18 26.63 6.02 0.68	-	8 4.19 4.02 0.91 0.10	-	-	-	-	-	-	-	-	-	-	-	-	-	-	-
San Mateo County	156,264 61.50	43,297	27,678 63.93 63.93 17.71	1,762	834 47.33 47.33 0.53	1,353 32.85 4.89 3.12 0.87	-	-	12,519 77.41 45.23 28.91 8.01	138 50.18 16.55 7.83 0.09	8,995 60.95 32.50 20.78 5.76	66 59.46 7.91 3.75 0.04	187 59.18 22.42 10.61 0.12	-	110 46.81 0.40 0.25 0.07	2,599 61.87 9.39 6.00 1.66	705 46.35 2.55 1.63 0.45	-	-	-	77 29.39 9.23 4.37 0.05	-	178 60.96 0.64 0.41 0.11	155 71.43 0.56 0.36 0.10	262 50.78 31.41 14.87 0.17	411 51.38 1.48 0.95 0.26
Belmont (city)	6,301 60.19	1,447	770 53.21 53.21 12.22	-	-	51 18.02 6.62 3.52 0.81	-	-	435 69.27 56.49 30.06 6.90	-	92 40.35 11.95 6.36 1.46	-	-	-	-	143 77.30 18.57 9.88 2.27	-	-	-	-	-	-	-	-	-	-
Burlingame (city)	5,955 47.65	1,428	555 38.87 38.87 9.32	-	-	-	-	-	343 48.72 61.80 24.02 5.76	-	31 15.74 5.59 2.17 0.52	-	-	-	-	70 36.84 12.61 4.90 1.18	-	-	-	-	-	-	-	-	-	-

Notes: Please refer to the User's Guide for an explanation of data; data is arranged alphabetically by state, then county, then city within each county; table includes counties with populations greater than 49,999 unless noted and cities with populations greater than 9,999 whose Asian and/or NHPI population rates are greater than the national average; (1) Native Hawaiian and other Pacific Islander; (2) excludes Taiwanese; (3) includes Chamorro; (4) county does not meet population threshold but is shown in order to allow inclusion of city

Place	All owner-occupied housing units	Asian-occupied housing units	Asians who own and occupy their own homes	NHPI[1]-occupied housing units	NHPIs[1] who own and occupy their own homes	Asian Indian	Bangladeshi	Cambodian	Chinese[2]	Fijian	Filipino	Guamanian[3]	Hawaiian, Native	Hmong	Indonesian	Japanese	Korean	Laotian	Malaysian	Pakistani	Samoan	Sri Lankan	Taiwanese	Thai	Tongan	Vietnamese
Daly City (city)	18,485	13,446	8,880	224	107	103	-	-	3,397	-	4,625	-	-	-	-	251	124	-	-	-	-	-	-	-	-	138
	60.16		66.04		47.77	28.45			81.50		61.45					58.64	42.32									61.33
						1.16			38.25		52.08					2.83	1.40									1.55
			66.04		47.77	0.77			25.26		34.40					1.87	0.92									1.03
			48.04		0.58	0.56			18.38		25.02					1.36	0.67									0.75
East Palo Alto (city)	3,002	248	125	330	155	-	-	-	-	-	-	-	-	-	-	-	-	-	-	-	-	-	-	-	100	-
	43.27		50.40		46.97																				49.26	
																									64.52	
			50.40		46.97																				30.30	
			4.16		5.16																				3.33	
Foster City (city)	7,149	3,372	1,932	-	-	168	-	-	1,168	-	168	-	-	-	-	262	64	-	-	-	-	-	-	-	-	-
	61.56		57.30			23.73			74.39		61.54					48.07	53.33									
						8.70			60.46		8.70					13.56	3.31									
			57.30			4.98			34.64		4.98					7.77	1.90									
			27.02			2.35			16.34		2.35					3.66	0.90									
Hillsborough (town)	3,528	757	706	-	-	-	-	-	527	-	-	-	-	-	-	-	-	-	-	-	-	-	-	-	-	-
	95.64		93.26						93.61																	
									74.65																	
			93.26						69.62																	
			20.01						14.94																	
Menlo Park (city)	7,077	835	342	-	-	-	-	-	187	-	-	-	-	-	-	54	-	-	-	-	-	-	-	-	-	-
	56.95		40.96						60.32							27.98										
									54.68							15.79										
			40.96						22.40							6.47										
			4.83						2.64							0.76										
Millbrae (city)	5,099	1,685	1,077	-	-	79	-	-	794	-	69	-	-	-	-	44	38	-	-	-	-	-	-	-	-	-
	64.08		63.92			62.20			74.00		41.82					33.59	37.62									
						7.34			73.72		6.41					4.09	3.53									
			63.92			4.69			47.12		4.09					2.61	2.26									
			21.12			1.55			15.57		1.35					0.86	0.75									
Pacifica (city)	9,605	1,632	1,174	-	-	-	-	-	423	-	455	-	-	-	-	130	-	-	-	-	-	-	-	-	-	-
	68.59		71.94						91.96		57.38					88.44										
									36.03		38.76					11.07										
			71.94						25.92		27.88					7.97										
			12.22						4.40		4.74					1.35										
Redwood City (city)	14,878	2,581	1,486	117	75	121	-	-	821	-	207	-	-	-	-	156	-	-	-	-	-	-	-	-	-	-
	52.96		57.57		64.10	25.26			75.88		52.27					52.70										
						8.14			55.25		13.93					10.50										
			57.57		64.10	4.69			31.81		8.02					6.04										
			9.99		0.50	0.81			5.52		1.39					1.05										
San Bruno (city)	9,148	2,538	1,710	201	73	125	-	-	658	-	568	-	-	-	-	198	-	-	-	-	-	-	-	-	37	-
	62.44		67.38		36.32	37.88			76.60		66.75					77.04									48.68	
						7.31			38.48		33.22					11.58									50.68	
			67.38		36.32	4.93			25.93		22.38					7.80									18.41	
			18.69		0.80	1.37			7.19		6.21					2.16									0.40	
San Carlos (city)	8,308	638	472	-	-	-	-	-	182	-	-	-	-	-	-	-	-	-	-	-	-	-	-	-	-	-
	73.13		73.98						77.45																	
									38.56																	
			73.98						28.53																	
			5.68						2.19																	

Notes: Please refer to the User's Guide for an explanation of data; data is arranged alphabetically by state, then county, then city within each county; table includes counties with populations greater than 49,999 unless noted and cities with populations greater than 9,999 whose Asian and/or NHPI population rates are greater than the national average; (1) Native Hawaiian and other Pacific Islander; (2) excludes Taiwanese; (3) includes Chamorro; (4) county does not meet population threshold but is shown in order to allow inclusion of city

Place	All owner-occupied housing units	Asian-occupied housing units	Asians who own and occupy their own homes	NHPI[1]-occupied housing units	NHPIs[1] who own and occupy their own homes	Asian Indian	Bangladeshi	Cambodian	Chinese[2]	Fijian	Filipino	Guamanian[3]	Hawaiian, Native	Hmong	Indonesian	Japanese	Korean	Laotian	Malaysian	Pakistani	Samoan	Sri Lankan	Taiwanese	Thai	Tongan	Vietnamese
	20,133	5,423	3,001	281	134	209	-	-	1,493	-	447	-	-	-	-	576	81	-	-	-	-	-	-	-	39	55
	53.95		55.34		47.69	25.15			68.33		51.03					62.61	34.62								45.35	52.38
San Mateo (city)						6.96			49.75		14.90					19.19	2.70								29.10	1.83
			55.34		47.69	3.85			27.53		8.24					10.62	1.49								13.88	1.01
			14.91		0.67	1.04			7.42		2.22					2.86	0.40								0.19	0.27
	12,322	4,915	3,570	259	105	98	-	-	1,334	-	1,722	-	-	-	-	226	-	-	-	-	-	-	-	-	-	-
	62.58		72.63		40.54	41.88			87.02		68.33					77.13										
South San Francisco (city)						2.75			37.37		48.24					6.33										
			72.63		40.54	1.99			27.14		35.04					4.60										
			28.97		0.85	0.80			10.83		13.98					1.83										
	76,579	4,862	2,325	211	129	140	-	-	264	-	829	-	-	16	-	560	143	-	-	-	-	-	-	-	-	193
	56.05		47.82		61.14	42.30			34.60		58.50			23.19		60.28	27.13									53.46
Santa Barbara County						6.02			11.35		35.66			0.69		24.09	6.15									8.30
			47.82		61.14	2.88			5.43		17.05			0.33		11.52	2.94									3.97
			3.04		0.17	0.18			0.34		1.08			0.02		0.73	0.19									0.25
	13,778	992	461	-	-	-	-	-	132	-	60	-	-	-	-	97	-	-	-	-	-	-	-	-	-	58
	69.38		46.47						51.97		44.44					57.06										41.73
Goleta (cdp)									28.63		13.02					21.04										12.58
			46.47						13.31		6.05					9.78										5.85
			3.35						0.96		0.44					0.70										0.42
	233	669	19	-	-	-	-	-	9	-	-	-	-	-	-	-	0	-	-	-	-	-	-	-	-	-
	4.52		2.84						3.56								0.00									
Isla Vista (cdp)									47.37								0.00									
			2.84						1.35								0.00									
			8.15						3.86								0.00									
	6,711	410	215	-	-	-	-	-	-	-	46	-	-	-	-	-	-	-	-	-	-	-	-	-	-	-
	51.37		52.44								40.35															
Lompoc (city)											21.40															
			52.44								11.22															
			3.20								0.69															
	8,691	326	275	-	-	-	-	-	-	-	-	-	-	-	-	-	-	-	-	-	-	-	-	-	-	-
	83.38		84.36																							
Orcutt (cdp)																										
			84.36																							
			3.16																							
	12,349	1,038	733	-	-	-	-	-	-	-	460	-	-	-	-	136	-	-	-	-	-	-	-	-	-	-
	55.91		70.62								71.32					83.95										
Santa Maria (city)											62.76					18.55										
			70.62								44.32					13.10										
			5.94								3.72					1.10										
	338,636	127,329	72,933	1,428	472	8,321	42	345	25,306	45	12,096	167	110	-	124	7,211	2,806	245	-	378	60	-	1,283	112	-	13,011
	59.84		57.28		33.05	37.43	28.57	38.33	67.45	35.71	66.65	51.07	30.73		57.94	62.49	41.39	60.05		52.21	15.92		68.10	32.56		54.86
Santa Clara County						11.41	0.06	0.47	34.70	9.53	16.59	35.38	23.31		0.17	9.89	3.85	0.34		0.52	12.71		1.76	0.15		17.84
			57.28		33.05	6.54	0.03	0.27	19.87	3.15	9.50	11.69	7.70		0.10	5.66	2.20	0.19		0.30	4.20		1.01	0.09		10.22
			21.54		0.14	2.46	0.01	0.10	7.47	0.01	3.57	0.05	0.03		0.04	2.13	0.83	0.07		0.11	0.02		0.38	0.03		3.84
	2,428	315	253	-	-	-	-	-	-	-	-	-	-	-	-	-	-	-	-	-	-	-	-	-	-	80
	73.33		80.32																							72.07
Alum Rock (cdp)																										31.62
			80.32																							25.40
			10.42																							3.29

Notes: Please refer to the User's Guide for an explanation of data; data is arranged alphabetically by state, then county, then city within each county; table includes counties with populations greater than 49,999 unless noted and cities with populations greater than 9,999 whose Asian and/or NHPI population rates are greater than the national average; (1) Native Hawaiian and other Pacific Islander; (2) excludes Taiwanese; (3) includes Chamorro; (4) county does not meet population threshold but is shown in order to allow inclusion of city

Place	All owner-occupied housing units	Asian-occupied housing units	Asians who own and occupy their own homes	NHPI[1]-occupied housing units	NHPIs[1] who own and occupy their own homes	Asian Indian	Bangladeshi	Cambodian	Chinese[2]	Fijian	Filipino	Guamanian[3]	Hawaiian, Native	Hmong	Indonesian	Japanese	Korean	Laotian	Malaysian	Pakistani	Samoan	Sri Lankan	Taiwanese	Thai	Tongan	Vietnamese
Campbell (city)	7,748 48.46	1,958	897 45.81 45.81 11.58	-	-	65 25.59 7.25 3.32 0.84	-	-	338 61.34 37.68 17.26 4.36	-	52 34.90 5.80 2.66 0.67	-	-	-	-	226 58.70 25.20 11.54 2.92	58 22.83 6.47 2.96 0.75	-	-	-	-	-	-	-	-	110 36.54 12.26 5.62 1.42
Cupertino (city)	11,540 63.35	6,770	4,169 61.58 61.58 36.13	-	-	675 49.93 16.19 9.97 5.85	-	-	2,441 74.85 58.55 36.06 21.15	-	76 71.70 1.82 1.12 0.66	-	-	-	-	305 37.01 7.32 4.51 2.64	221 37.84 5.30 3.26 1.92	-	-	-	-	-	224 77.24 5.37 3.31 1.94	-	-	124 62.63 2.97 1.83 1.07
Gilroy (city)	7,283 61.23	537	422 78.58 78.58 5.79	-	-	-	-	-	95 73.64 22.51 17.69 1.30	-	143 87.73 33.89 26.63 1.96	-	-	-	-	-	-	-	-	-	-	-	-	-	-	-
Los Altos (city)	8,999 85.97	1,370	1,215 88.69 88.69 13.50	-	-	140 76.09 11.52 10.22 1.56	-	-	635 95.78 52.26 46.35 7.06	-	-	-	-	-	-	205 83.33 16.87 14.96 2.28	-	-	-	-	-	-	-	-	-	-
Los Gatos (town)	7,852 65.36	799	597 74.72 74.72 7.60	-	-	-	-	-	263 82.70 44.05 32.92 3.35	-	-	-	-	-	-	131 74.43 21.94 16.40 1.67	-	-	-	-	-	-	-	-	-	-
Milpitas (city)	11,951 69.74	8,496	5,990 70.50 70.50 50.12	109	43 39.45 39.45 0.36	691 52.59 11.54 8.13 5.78	-	-	2,067 85.41 34.51 24.33 17.30	-	1,493 76.06 24.92 17.57 12.49	-	-	-	-	203 73.29 3.39 2.39 1.70	107 37.68 1.79 1.26 0.90	-	-	-	-	-	-	-	-	1,209 63.27 20.18 14.23 10.12
Morgan Hill (city)	7,911 72.84	677	535 79.03 79.03 6.76	-	-	-	-	-	119 76.77 22.24 17.58 1.50	-	-	-	-	-	-	118 83.69 22.06 17.43 1.49	-	-	-	-	-	-	-	-	-	-
Mountain View (city)	12,909 41.43	6,148	2,264 36.82 36.82 17.54	-	-	213 16.85 9.41 3.46 1.65	-	-	1,019 42.02 45.01 16.57 7.89	-	273 41.68 12.06 4.44 2.11	-	-	-	-	508 55.28 22.44 8.26 3.94	87 30.10 3.84 1.42 0.67	-	-	-	-	-	-	-	-	67 23.93 2.96 1.09 0.52
Palo Alto (city)	14,398 56.85	3,705	2,119 57.19 57.19 14.72	-	-	278 51.39 13.12 7.50 1.93	-	-	1,205 64.54 56.87 32.52 8.37	-	58 47.54 2.74 1.57 0.40	-	-	-	-	321 60.68 15.15 8.66 2.23	124 33.24 5.85 3.35 0.86	-	-	-	-	-	-	-	-	-
San Jose (city)	170,825 61.80	65,450	41,212 62.97 62.97 24.13	766	220 28.72 28.72 0.13	4,346 53.82 10.55 6.64 2.54	-	336 40.88 0.82 0.51 0.20	11,435 71.21 27.75 17.47 6.69	-	7,997 71.15 19.40 12.22 4.68	99 49.75 45.00 12.92 0.06	32 21.05 14.55 4.18 0.02	-	-	3,467 70.94 8.41 5.30 2.03	1,432 50.39 3.47 2.19 0.84	226 60.59 0.55 0.35 0.13	-	152 51.01 0.37 0.23 0.09	30 12.40 13.64 3.92 0.02	-	493 66.53 1.20 0.75 0.29	56 38.10 0.14 0.09 0.03	-	10,146 55.95 24.62 15.50 5.94

Notes: Please refer to the User's Guide for an explanation of data; data is arranged alphabetically by state, then county, then city within each county; table includes counties with populations greater than 49,999 unless noted and cities with populations greater than 9,999 whose Asian and/or NHPI population rates are greater than the national average; (1) Native Hawaiian and other Pacific Islander; (2) excludes Taiwanese; (3) includes Chamorro; (4) county does not meet population threshold but is shown in order to allow inclusion of city

Place	All owner-occupied housing units	Asian-occupied housing units	Asians who own and occupy their own homes	NHPI[1]-occupied housing units	NHPIs[1] who own and occupy their own homes	Asian Indian	Bangladeshi	Cambodian	Chinese[2]	Fijian	Filipino	Guamanian[3]	Hawaiian, Native	Hmong	Indonesian	Japanese	Korean	Laotian	Malaysian	Pakistani	Samoan	Sri Lankan	Taiwanese	Thai	Tongan	Vietnamese
Santa Clara (city)	17,760	9,728	3,314	114	24	534	-	-	855	-	708	-	-	-	-	386	165	-	-	34	-	-	-	-	-	529
	46.13		34.07		21.05	16.12			45.31		47.87					56.76	23.98			33.66						40.98
						16.11			25.80		21.36					11.65	4.98			1.03						15.96
			34.07		21.05	5.49			8.79		7.28					3.97	1.70			0.35						5.44
			18.66		0.14	3.01			4.81		3.99					2.17	0.93			0.19						2.98
Saratoga (city)	9,414	2,486	2,254	-	-	309	-	-	1,347	-	-	-	-	-	-	156	126	-	-	-	-	-	96	-	-	-
	89.97		90.67			94.50			94.20							70.59	74.56						94.12			
						13.71			59.76							6.92	5.59						4.26			
			90.67			12.43			54.18							6.28	5.07						3.86			
			23.94			3.28			14.31							1.66	1.34						1.02			
Stanford (cdp)	850	829	84	-	-	6	-	-	60	-	-	-	-	-	-	-	0	-	-	-	-	-	-	-	-	-
	27.00		10.13			4.17			14.46								0.00									
						7.14			71.43								0.00									
			10.13			0.72			7.24								0.00									
			9.88			0.71			7.06								0.00									
Sunnyvale (city)	25,032	15,495	5,584	160	72	614	-	-	2,549	-	843	-	-	-	-	641	289	-	-	-	-	-	182	-	-	309
	47.65		36.04		45.00	12.56			51.63		49.88					41.87	32.04						67.41			37.73
						11.00			45.65		15.10					11.48	5.18						3.26			5.53
			36.04		45.00	3.96			16.45		5.44					4.14	1.87						1.17			1.99
			22.31		0.29	2.45			10.18		3.37					2.56	1.15						0.73			1.23
Santa Cruz County	54,665	2,542	1,548	-	-	147	-	-	359	-	307	-	-	-	-	536	90	-	-	-	-	-	-	-	-	33
	59.98		60.90			44.41			69.84		60.91					70.90	55.56									35.11
						9.50			23.19		19.83					34.63	5.81									2.13
			60.90			5.78			14.12		12.08					21.09	3.54									1.30
			2.83			0.27			0.66		0.56					0.98	0.16									0.06
Capitola (city)	2,228	140	61	-	-	-	-	-	-	-	-	-	-	-	-	-	-	-	-	-	-	-	-	-	-	-
	46.90		43.57																							
			43.57																							
			2.74																							
Santa Cruz (city)	9,480	752	283	-	-	50	-	-	118	-	51	-	-	-	-	44	-	-	-	-	-	-	-	-	-	-
	46.48		37.63			32.89			61.46		49.04					27.33										
						17.67			41.70		18.02					15.55										
			37.63			6.65			15.69		6.78					5.85										
			2.99			0.53			1.24		0.54					0.46										
Scotts Valley (city)	3,229	202	150	-	-	-	-	-	-	-	-	-	-	-	-	-	-	-	-	-	-	-	-	-	-	-
	74.97		74.26																							
			74.26																							
			4.65																							
Shasta County	41,949	694	284	-	-	-	-	-	-	-	73	-	-	-	-	-	-	89	-	-	-	-	-	-	-	-
	66.14		40.92								56.59							33.33								
											25.70							31.34								
			40.92								10.52							12.82								
			0.68								0.17							0.21								
Solano County	84,997	13,690	9,807	995	573	523	-	-	900	-	7,008	296	155	24	-	533	150	37	-	-	40	-	-	-	-	238
	65.18		71.64		57.59	62.56			83.03		73.14	67.12	58.71	32.43		68.69	73.17	23.72			27.97					62.47
						5.33			9.18		71.46	51.66	27.05	0.24		5.43	1.53	0.38			6.98					2.43
			71.64		57.59	3.82			6.57		51.19	29.75	15.58	0.18		3.89	1.10	0.27			4.02					1.74
			11.54		0.67	0.62			1.06		8.24	0.35	0.18	0.03		0.63	0.18	0.04			0.05					0.28

Notes: Please refer to the User's Guide for an explanation of data; data is arranged alphabetically by state, then county, then city within each county; table includes counties with populations greater than 49,999 unless noted and cities with populations greater than 9,999 whose Asian and/or NHPI population rates are greater than the national average; (1) Native Hawaiian and other Pacific Islander; (2) excludes Taiwanese; (3) includes Chamorro; (4) county does not meet population threshold but is shown in order to allow inclusion of city

Place	All owner-occupied housing units	Asian-occupied housing units	Asians who own and occupy their own homes	NHPI[1]-occupied housing units	NHPIs[1] who own and occupy their own homes	Asian Indian	Bangladeshi	Cambodian	Chinese[2]	Fijian	Filipino	Guamanian[3]	Hawaiian, Native	Hmong	Indonesian	Japanese	Korean	Laotian	Malaysian	Pakistani	Samoan	Sri Lankan	Taiwanese	Thai	Tongan	Vietnamese
Benicia (city)	7,300	635	511	-	-	-	-	-	103	-	309	-	-	-	-	-		-	-	-	-	-	-	-	-	-
	70.70		80.47						79.84		80.05															
									20.16		60.47															
			80.47						16.22		48.66															
			7.00						1.41		4.23															
Fairfield (city)	18,463	3,033	2,002	377	204	173	-	-	233	-	1,134	126	-	-	-	215	65	13	-	-	-	-	-	-	-	-
	59.61		66.01		54.11	65.78			77.15		67.30	69.23				65.55	84.42	12.62								
						8.64			11.64		56.64	61.76				10.74	3.25	0.65								
			66.01		54.11	5.70			7.68		37.39	33.42				7.09	2.14	0.43								
			10.84		1.10	0.94			1.26		6.14	0.68				1.16	0.35	0.07								
Suisun City (city)	5,882	1,175	944	-	-	90	-	-	-	-	647	-	-	-	-	-	-	-	-	-	-	-	-	-	-	-
	73.63		80.34			93.75					84.24															
						9.53					68.54															
			80.34			7.66					55.06															
			16.05			1.53					11.00															
Vacaville (city)	18,738	1,029	701	-	-	-	-	-	-	-	356	-	-	-	-	-	-	-	-	-	-	-	-	-	-	-
	66.66		68.12								68.99															
											50.78															
			68.12								34.60															
			3.74								1.90															
Vallejo (city)	25,036	7,430	5,378	435	241	187	-	-	284	-	4,464	143	-	-	-	129	-	-	-	-	-	-	-	-	-	68
	63.29		72.38		55.40	61.51			83.78		73.51	67.77				67.19										47.89
						3.48			5.28		83.00	59.34				2.40										1.26
			72.38		55.40	2.52			3.82		60.08	32.87				1.74										0.92
			21.48		0.96	0.75			1.13		17.83	0.57				0.52										0.27
Sonoma County	110,511	4,269	2,587	188	93	207	-	28	655	-	447	-	-	-	-	541	179	92	-	-	-	-	-	-	-	231
	64.10		60.60		49.47	41.90		20.14	71.04		59.84					74.21	62.81	38.17								62.94
						8.00		1.08	25.32		17.28					20.91	6.92	3.56								8.93
			60.60		49.47	4.85		0.66	15.34		10.47					12.67	4.19	2.16								5.41
			2.34		0.08	0.19		0.03	0.59		0.40					0.49	0.16	0.08								0.21
Petaluma (city)	13,994	661	539	-	-	-	-	-	210	-	-	-	-	-	-	-	-	-	-	-	-	-	-	-	-	-
	70.09		81.54						89.36																	
									38.96																	
			81.54						31.77																	
			3.85						1.50																	
Rohnert Park (city)	9,040	738	365	-	-	-	-	-	53	-	120	-	-	-	-	-	-	-	-	-	-	-	-	-	-	-
	58.12		49.46						40.77		67.80															
									14.52		32.88															
			49.46						7.18		16.26															
			4.04						0.59		1.33															
Santa Rosa (city)	32,658	1,707	838	-	-	85	-	22	168	-	99	-	-	-	-	131	-	46	-	-	-	-	-	-	-	141
	58.25		49.09			41.46		23.40	57.14		39.44					58.74		32.62								63.80
						10.14		2.63	20.05		11.81					15.63		5.49								16.83
			49.09			4.98		1.29	9.84		5.80					7.67		2.69								8.26
			2.57			0.26		0.07	0.51		0.30					0.40		0.14								0.43
Stanislaus County	89,911	4,781	2,811	437	227	781	-	196	555	109	597	-	-	17	-	233	-	104	-	-	-	-	-	-	-	130
	61.95		58.80		51.95	71.00		33.68	81.86	67.70	69.26			10.49		72.81		27.59								41.40
						27.78		6.97	19.74	48.02	21.24			0.60		8.29		3.70								4.62
			58.80		51.95	16.34		4.10	11.61	24.94	12.49			0.36		4.87		2.18								2.72
			3.13		0.25	0.87		0.22	0.62	0.12	0.66			0.02		0.26		0.12								0.14

Notes: Please refer to the User's Guide for an explanation of data; data is arranged alphabetically by state, then county, then city within each county; table includes counties with populations greater than 49,999 unless noted and cities with populations greater than 9,999 whose Asian and/or NHPI population rates are greater than the national average; (1) Native Hawaiian and other Pacific Islander; (2) excludes Taiwanese; (3) includes Chamorro; (4) county does not meet population threshold but is shown in order to allow inclusion of city

Place	All owner-occupied housing units	Asian-occupied housing units	Asians who own and occupy their own homes	NHPI[1]-occupied housing units	NHPIs[1] who own and occupy their own homes	Asian Indian	Bangladeshi	Cambodian	Chinese[2]	Fijian	Filipino	Guamanian[3]	Hawaiian, Native	Hmong	Indonesian	Japanese	Korean	Laotian	Malaysian	Pakistani	Samoan	Sri Lankan	Taiwanese	Thai	Tongan	Vietnamese
Ceres (city)	6,980 66.65	394	275 69.80 69.80 3.94	-	-	121 63.35 44.00 30.71 1.73	-	-	-	-	-	-	-	-	-	-	-	-	-	-	-	-	-	-	-	-
Modesto (city)	38,316 58.85	2,890	1,566 54.19 54.19 4.09	284	115 40.49 40.49 0.30	391 79.15 24.97 13.53 1.02	-	146 29.80 9.32 5.05 0.38	344 81.32 21.97 11.90 0.90	60 57.69 52.17 21.13 0.16	333 64.53 21.26 11.52 0.87	-	-	0 0.00 0.00 0.00 0.00	-	96 59.63 6.13 3.32 0.25	-	43 17.27 2.75 1.49 0.11	-	-	-	-	-	-	-	91 38.56 5.81 3.15 0.24
Salida (cdp)	3,185 87.16	108	96 88.89 88.89 3.01	-	-	-	-	-	-	-	-	-	-	-	-	-	-	-	-	-	-	-	-	-	-	-
Turlock (city)	10,228 55.76	666	410 61.56 61.56 4.01	-	-	181 64.87 44.15 27.18 1.77	-	-	-	-	-	-	-	-	-	-	-	-	-	-	-	-	-	-	-	-
Sutter County	16,615 61.46	2,174	1,431 65.82 65.82 8.61	-	-	1,082 67.20 75.61 49.77 6.51	-	-	-	-	83 55.33 5.80 3.82 0.50	-	-	-	-	138 75.41 9.64 6.35 0.83	-	-	-	-	-	-	-	-	-	-
South Yuba City (cdp)	3,380 82.72	605	500 82.64 82.64 14.79	-	-	425 82.21 85.00 70.25 12.57	-	-	-	-	-	-	-	-	-	-	-	-	-	-	-	-	-	-	-	-
Yuba City (city)	6,283 47.33	894	419 46.87 46.87 6.67	-	-	269 47.44 64.20 30.09 4.28	-	-	-	-	-	-	-	-	-	-	-	-	-	-	-	-	-	-	-	-
Tehama County	14,222 67.68	121	70 57.85 57.85 0.49	-	-	-	-	-	-	-	-	-	-	-	-	-	-	-	-	-	-	-	-	-	-	-
Tulare County	67,904 61.52	2,969	1,645 55.41 55.41 2.42	-	-	94 42.92 5.71 3.17 0.14	-	-	235 88.01 14.29 7.92 0.35	-	839 69.45 51.00 28.26 1.24	-	-	20 13.25 1.22 0.67 0.03	-	251 74.93 15.26 8.45 0.37	44 40.37 2.67 1.48 0.06	98 18.92 5.96 3.30 0.14	-	-	-	-	-	-	-	-
Porterville (city)	6,729 56.22	487	234 48.05 48.05 3.48	-	-	-	-	-	-	-	153 65.67 65.38 31.42 2.27	-	-	-	-	-	-	-	-	-	-	-	-	-	-	-

Notes: Please refer to the User's Guide for an explanation of data; data is arranged alphabetically by state, then county, then city within each county; table includes counties with populations greater than 49,999 unless noted and cities with populations greater than 9,999 whose Asian and/or NHPI population rates are greater than the national average; (1) Native Hawaiian and other Pacific Islander; (2) excludes Taiwanese; (3) includes Chamorro; (4) county does not meet population threshold but is shown in order to allow inclusion of city

Place	All owner-occupied housing units	Asian-occupied housing units	Asians who own and occupy their own homes	NHPI-occupied housing units	NHPIs[1] who own and occupy their own homes	Asian Indian	Bangladeshi	Cambodian	Chinese[2]	Fijian	Filipino	Guamanian[3]	Hawaiian, Native	Hmong	Indonesian	Japanese	Korean	Laotian	Malaysian	Pakistani	Samoan	Sri Lankan	Taiwanese	Thai	Tongan	Vietnamese
Visalia (city)	19,428	1,114	518	-	-	-	-	-	-	-	165	-	-	14	-	-	-	88	-	-	-	-	-	-	-	-
	62.79		46.50								61.11			17.72				25.00								
											31.85			2.70				16.99								
			46.50								14.81			1.26				7.90								
			2.67								0.85			0.07				0.45								
Tuolumne County	14,961	154	84	-	-	-	-	-	-	-	-	-	-	-	-	-	-	-	-	-	-	-	-	-	-	-
	71.23		54.55																							
			54.55																							
			0.56																							
Ventura County	164,373	10,945	7,889	438	218	800	-	-	1,427	-	2,372	-	86	-	-	1,576	429	-	-	-	52	-	227	-	-	589
	67.58		72.08		49.77	61.35			83.99		66.67		47.51			77.10	64.03				40.63		91.90			74.09
						10.14			18.09		30.07		39.45			19.98	5.44				23.85		2.88			7.47
			72.08		49.77	7.31			13.04		21.67		19.63			14.40	3.92				11.87		2.07			5.38
			4.80		0.13	0.49			0.87		1.44		0.05			0.96	0.26				0.03		0.14			0.36
Camarillo (city)	15,770	1,136	849	-	-	-	-	-	168	-	273	-	-	-	-	183	60	-	-	-	-	-	-	-	-	76
	73.54		74.74						88.89		79.82					70.66	56.07									80.85
									19.79		32.16					21.55	7.07									8.95
			74.74						14.79		24.03					16.11	5.28									6.69
			5.38						1.07		1.73					1.16	0.38									0.48
Moorpark (city)	7,412	387	387	-	-	-	-	-	-	-	-	-	-	-	-	-	-	-	-	-	-	-	-	-	-	-
	82.50		100.00																							
			100.00																							
			5.22																							
Oxnard (city)	24,947	3,218	2,250	185	97	64	-	-	101	-	1,367	-	-	-	-	416	104	-	-	-	47	-	-	-	-	126
	57.18		69.92		52.43	67.37			64.74		66.88					80.31	72.22				45.19					71.19
						2.84			4.49		60.76					18.49	4.62				48.45					5.60
			69.92		52.43	1.99			3.14		42.48					12.93	3.23				25.41					3.92
			9.02		0.39	0.26			0.40		5.48					1.67	0.42				0.19					0.51
Port Hueneme (city)	3,569	383	151	-	-	-	-	-	-	-	74	-	-	-	-	-	-	-	-	-	-	-	-	-	-	-
	49.10		39.43								31.09															
											49.01															
			39.43								19.32															
			4.23								2.07															
Simi Valley (city)	28,306	1,925	1,480	-	-	272	-	-	291	-	241	-	-	-	-	238	97	-	-	-	-	-	-	-	-	185
	77.60		76.88			66.02			90.09		78.25					72.78	87.39									78.39
						18.38			19.66		16.28					16.08	6.55									12.50
			76.88			14.13			15.12		12.52					12.36	5.04									9.61
			5.23			0.96			1.03		0.85					0.84	0.34									0.65
Thousand Oaks (city)	31,546	1,949	1,511	-	-	224	-	-	484	-	103	-	-	-	-	299	80	-	-	-	-	-	-	-	-	86
	75.48		77.53			62.57			80.40		81.75					83.06	66.12									65.65
						14.82			32.03		6.82					19.79	5.29									5.69
			77.53			11.49			24.83		5.28					15.34	4.10									4.41
			4.79			0.71			1.53		0.33					0.95	0.25									0.27
Yolo County	31,509	4,904	1,529	209	64	176	-	-	559	41	204	-	-	0	-	311	73	0	-	-	-	-	-	-	-	59
	53.07		31.18		30.62	28.76			31.28	32.28	35.60			0.00		60.04	19.89	0.00								14.46
						11.51			36.56	64.06	13.34			0.00		20.34	4.77	0.00								3.86
			31.18		30.62	3.59			11.40	19.62	4.16			0.00		6.34	1.49	0.00								1.20
			4.85		0.20	0.56			1.77	0.13	0.65			0.00		0.99	0.23	0.00								0.19

Notes: Please refer to the User's Guide for an explanation of data; data is arranged alphabetically by state, then county, then city within each county; table includes counties with populations greater than 49,999 unless noted and cities with populations greater than 9,999 whose Asian and/or NHPI population rates are greater than the national average; (1) Native Hawaiian and other Pacific Islander; (2) excludes Taiwanese; (3) includes Chamorro; (4) county does not meet population threshold but is shown in order to allow inclusion of city

Place	All owner-occupied housing units	Asian-occupied housing units	Asians who own and occupy their own homes	NHPI[1]-occupied housing units	NHPIs[1] who own and occupy their own homes	Asian Indian	Bangladeshi	Cambodian	Chinese[2]	Fijian	Filipino	Guamanian[3]	Hawaiian, Native	Hmong	Indonesian	Japanese	Korean	Laotian	Malaysian	Pakistani	Samoan	Sri Lankan	Taiwanese	Thai	Tongan	Vietnamese
Davis (city)	10,199	3,362	890	-	-	59	-	-	419	-	82	-	-	-	-	177	54	-	-	-	-	-	-	-	-	16
	44.48		26.47			16.86			29.78		20.40					57.28	19.15									4.82
						6.63			47.08		9.21					19.89	6.07									1.80
			26.47			1.75			12.46		2.44					5.26	1.61									0.48
			8.73			0.58			4.11		0.80					1.74	0.53									0.16
West Sacramento (city)	6,225	594	228	-	-	63	-	-	-	-	-	-	-	0	-	-	-	-	-	-	-	-	-	-	-	-
	54.62		38.38			50.81								0.00												
						27.63								0.00												
			38.38			10.61								0.00												
			3.66			1.01								0.00												
Woodland (city)	9,761	538	301	-	-	54	-	-	-	-	-	-	-	-	-	-	-	-	-	-	-	-	-	-	-	-
	58.35		55.95			45.00																				
						17.94																				
			55.95			10.04																				
			3.08			0.55																				
Yuba County	11,088	741	266	-	-	-	-	-	-	-	85	-	-	47	-	-	-	-	-	-	-	-	-	-	-	-
	54.00		35.90								52.80			14.55												
											31.95			17.67												
			35.90								11.47			6.34												
			2.40								0.77			0.42												
Linda (cdp)	1,744	331	79	-	-	-	-	-	-	-	-	-	-	40	-	-	-	-	-	-	-	-	-	-	-	-
	42.79		23.87											15.87												
														50.63												
			23.87											12.08												
			4.53											2.29												
Marysville (city)	1,953	216	107	-	-	-	-	-	-	-	-	-	-	-	-	-	-	-	-	-	-	-	-	-	-	-
	41.57		49.54																							
			49.54																							
			5.48																							
Olivehurst (cdp)	2,278	48	28	-	-	-	-	-	-	-	-	-	-	-	-	-	-	-	-	-	-	-	-	-	-	-
	65.48		58.33																							
			58.33																							
			1.23																							
COLORADO	1,116,305	29,482	16,317	1,307	644	1,833	-	191	3,259	-	1,555	151	271	298	59	3,275	2,260	276	-	89	121	-	115	267	-	2,143
	67.32		55.35		49.27	39.88		57.36	65.49		58.20	44.94	56.11	57.64	21.53	66.93	50.20	52.27		41.01	55.25		39.93	42.79		59.41
						11.23		1.17	19.97		9.53	23.45	42.08	1.83	0.36	20.07	13.85	1.69		0.55	18.79		0.70	1.64		13.13
			55.35		49.27	6.22		0.65	11.05		5.27	11.55	20.73	1.01	0.20	11.11	7.67	0.94		0.30	9.26		0.39	0.91		7.27
			1.46		0.06	0.16		0.02	0.29		0.14	0.01	0.02	0.03	0.01	0.29	0.20	0.02		0.01	0.01		0.01	0.02		0.19
Adams County	90,448	2,988	2,039	-	-	84	-	-	219	-	167	-	-	225	-	341	179	129	-	-	-	-	-	-	-	443
	70.58		68.24			38.36			63.48		74.89			58.29		80.81	74.58	55.36								76.51
						4.12			10.74		8.19			11.03		16.72	8.78	6.33								21.73
			68.24			2.81			7.33		5.59			7.53		11.41	5.99	4.32								14.83
			2.25			0.09			0.24		0.18			0.25		0.38	0.20	0.14								0.49
Berkley (cdp)	2,676	100	56	-	-	-	-	-	-	-	-	-	-	-	-	-	-	-	-	-	-	-	-	-	-	-
	70.61		56.00																							
			56.00																							
			2.09																							

Notes: Please refer to the User's Guide for an explanation of data; data is arranged alphabetically by state, then county, then city within each county; table includes counties with populations greater than 49,999 unless noted and cities with populations greater than 9,999 whose Asian and/or NHPI population rates are greater than the national average; (1) Native Hawaiian and other Pacific Islander; (2) excludes Taiwanese; (3) includes Chamorro; (4) county does not meet population threshold but is shown in order to allow inclusion of city

Place	All owner-occupied housing units	Asian-occupied housing units	Asians who own and occupy their own homes	NHPI[1]-occupied housing units	NHPIs[1] who own and occupy their own homes	Asian Indian	Bangladeshi	Cambodian	Chinese[2]	Fijian	Filipino	Guamanian[3]	Hawaiian, Native	Hmong	Indonesian	Japanese	Korean	Laotian	Malaysian	Pakistani	Samoan	Sri Lankan	Taiwanese	Thai	Tongan	Vietnamese
Federal Heights (city)	3,022 58.75	171	92 53.80 53.80 3.04	-	-	-	-	-	-	-	-	-	-	-	-	-	-	-	-	-	-	-	-	-	-	-
Westminster (city)	26,922 70.08	1,442	966 66.99 66.99 3.59	-	-	62 36.90 6.42 4.30 0.23	-	-	146 65.77 15.11 10.12 0.54	-	-	-	-	93 52.84 9.63 6.45 0.35	-	-	137 87.82 14.18 9.50 0.51	90 56.96 9.32 6.24 0.33	-	-	-	-	-	-	-	174 83.25 18.01 12.07 0.65
Arapahoe County	129,899 68.04	5,882	3,606 61.31 61.31 2.78	174	95 54.60 54.60 0.07	396 46.86 10.98 6.73 0.30	-	-	816 79.61 22.63 13.87 0.63	-	375 69.83 10.40 6.38 0.29	-	-	-	-	487 72.58 13.51 8.28 0.37	715 50.46 19.83 12.16 0.55	-	-	-	-	-	-	-	-	448 64.93 12.42 7.62 0.34
Aurora (city)	67,447 63.93	3,525	2,195 62.27 62.27 3.25	136	43 31.62 31.62 0.06	162 51.43 7.38 4.60 0.24	-	61 64.89 2.78 1.73 0.09	426 83.04 19.41 12.09 0.63	-	274 68.84 12.48 7.77 0.41	-	-	-	-	323 78.21 14.72 9.16 0.48	348 39.86 15.85 9.87 0.52	-	-	-	-	-	-	-	-	341 67.52 15.54 9.67 0.51
Boulder County	74,249 64.74	3,091	1,507 48.75 48.75 2.03	-	-	233 43.71 15.46 7.54 0.31	-	-	509 63.31 33.78 16.47 0.69	-	48 44.04 3.19 1.55 0.06	-	-	-	-	321 60.45 21.30 10.38 0.43	96 20.78 6.37 3.11 0.13	-	-	-	-	-	-	-	-	124 54.87 8.23 4.01 0.17
Boulder (city)	19,588 49.42	1,294	364 28.13 28.13 1.86	-	-	45 27.95 12.36 3.48 0.23	-	-	170 47.62 46.70 13.14 0.87	-	-	-	-	-	-	57 26.89 15.66 4.40 0.29	29 9.32 7.97 2.24 0.15	-	-	-	-	-	-	-	-	-
Broomfield (city)	10,609 76.56	457	319 69.80 69.80 3.01	-	-	-	-	-	70 70.71 21.94 15.32 0.66	-	-	-	-	-	-	-	-	-	-	-	-	-	-	-	-	-
Lafayette (city)	6,756 76.06	284	214 75.35 75.35 3.17	-	-	-	-	-	-	-	-	-	-	-	-	-	-	-	-	-	-	-	-	-	-	-
Denver County	125,631 52.51	5,863	2,124 36.23 36.23 1.69	160	60 37.50 37.50 0.05	173 18.78 8.15 2.95 0.14	-	34 39.53 1.60 0.58 0.03	357 38.80 16.81 6.09 0.28	-	221 49.11 10.40 3.77 0.18	-	-	-	-	581 53.16 27.35 9.91 0.46	151 31.13 7.11 2.58 0.12	-	-	-	-	-	-	15 8.06 0.71 0.26 0.01	-	506 43.36 23.82 8.63 0.40
Douglas County	53,542 87.88	1,197	1,068 89.22 89.22 1.99	-	-	245 89.74 22.94 20.47 0.46	-	-	346 89.87 32.40 28.91 0.65	-	-	-	-	-	-	-	175 95.11 16.39 14.62 0.33	-	-	-	-	-	-	-	-	-

Notes: Please refer to the User's Guide for an explanation of data; data is arranged alphabetically by state, then county, then city within each county; table includes counties with populations greater than 49,999 unless noted and cities with populations greater than 9,999 whose Asian and/or NHPI population rates are greater than the national average; (1) Native Hawaiian and other Pacific Islander; (2) excludes Taiwanese; (3) includes Chamorro; (4) county does not meet population threshold but is shown in order to allow inclusion of city

Place	All owner-occupied housing units	Asian-occupied housing units	Asians who own and occupy their own homes	NHPI[1]-occupied housing units	NHPIs[1] who own and occupy their own homes	Asian Indian	Bangladeshi	Cambodian	Chinese[2]	Fijian	Filipino	Guamanian[3]	Hawaiian, Native	Hmong	Indonesian	Japanese	Korean	Laotian	Malaysian	Pakistani	Samoan	Sri Lankan	Taiwanese	Thai	Tongan	Vietnamese
Highlands Ranch (cdp)	21,452 87.46	781	729 93.34 93.34 3.40	-	-	207 100.00 28.40 26.50 0.96	-	-	244 88.09 33.47 31.24 1.14	-	-	-	-	-	-	-	-	-	-	-	-	-	-	-	-	-
El Paso County	124,443 64.68	4,077	2,007 49.23 49.23 1.61	378	157 41.53 41.53 0.13	219 25.67 10.91 5.37 0.18	-	-	256 72.52 12.76 6.28 0.21	-	342 46.72 17.04 8.39 0.27	80 42.11 50.96 21.16 0.06	-	-	-	378 67.74 18.83 9.27 0.30	516 52.12 25.71 12.66 0.41	-	-	-	-	-	-	-	-	123 47.86 6.13 3.02 0.10
Colorado Springs (city)	86,076 60.76	3,372	1,474 43.71 43.71 1.71	247	77 31.17 31.17 0.09	219 25.67 14.86 6.49 0.25	-	-	191 68.71 12.96 5.66 0.22	-	198 36.53 13.43 5.87 0.23	-	-	-	-	233 59.44 15.81 6.91 0.27	370 46.54 25.10 10.97 0.43	-	-	-	-	-	-	-	-	114 53.77 7.73 3.38 0.13
Jefferson County	149,395 72.50	3,376	2,276 67.42 67.42 1.52	170	86 50.59 50.59 0.06	311 57.81 13.66 9.21 0.21	-	-	359 70.67 15.77 10.63 0.24	-	172 63.70 7.56 5.09 0.12	-	-	33 60.00 1.45 0.98 0.02	-	545 78.64 23.95 16.14 0.36	276 68.49 12.13 8.18 0.18	116 58.59 5.10 3.44 0.08	-	-	-	-	-	-	-	324 69.08 14.24 9.60 0.22
Larimer County	65,744 67.66	1,228	631 51.38 51.38 0.96	-	-	68 35.23 10.78 5.54 0.10	-	-	165 49.85 26.15 13.44 0.25	-	-	-	-	-	-	146 64.89 23.14 11.89 0.22	63 42.28 9.98 5.13 0.10	-	-	-	-	-	-	-	-	-
Mesa County	33,306 72.68	86	38 44.19 44.19 0.11	-	-	-	-	-	-	-	-	-	-	-	-	-	-	-	-	-	-	-	-	-	-	-
Pueblo County	38,434 70.42	228	182 79.82 79.82 0.47	-	-	-	-	-	-	-	-	-	-	-	-	-	-	-	-	-	-	-	-	-	-	-
Weld County	43,428 68.66	473	287 60.68 60.68 0.66	-	-	-	-	-	-	-	-	-	-	-	-	111 59.36 38.68 23.47 0.26	-	-	-	-	-	-	-	-	-	-
CONNECTICUT	869,742 66.82	25,611	12,530 48.92 48.92 1.44	274	143 52.19 52.19 0.02	3,753 46.39 29.95 14.65 0.43	49 41.53 0.39 0.19 0.01	341 69.88 2.72 1.33 0.04	3,462 55.04 27.63 13.52 0.40	-	1,073 51.17 8.56 4.19 0.12	49 54.44 34.27 17.88 0.01	-	-	-	541 37.34 4.32 2.11 0.06	761 39.70 6.07 2.97 0.09	455 56.45 3.63 1.78 0.05	-	233 35.74 1.86 0.91 0.03	-	-	145 55.77 1.16 0.57 0.02	88 41.71 0.70 0.34 0.01	-	1,024 51.05 8.17 4.00 0.12
Fairfield County	224,509 69.24	8,683	4,839 55.73 55.73 2.16	-	-	1,525 51.36 31.51 17.56 0.68	-	240 75.24 4.96 2.76 0.11	1,328 69.49 27.44 15.29 0.59	-	363 56.02 7.50 4.18 0.16	-	-	-	-	259 36.33 5.35 2.98 0.12	278 48.69 5.74 3.20 0.12	163 61.28 3.37 1.88 0.07	-	48 30.77 0.99 0.55 0.02	-	-	-	-	-	313 53.60 6.47 3.60 0.14

Notes: Please refer to the User's Guide for an explanation of data; data is arranged alphabetically by state, then county, then city within each county; table includes counties with populations greater than 49,999 unless noted and cities with populations greater than 9,999 whose Asian and/or NHPI population rates are greater than the national average; (1) Native Hawaiian and other Pacific Islander; (2) excludes Taiwanese; (3) includes Chamorro; (4) county does not meet population threshold but is shown in order to allow inclusion of city

Place	All owner-occupied housing units	Asian-occupied housing units	Asians who own and occupy their own homes	NHPI-occupied housing units	NHPIs[1] who own and occupy their own homes	Asian Indian	Bangladeshi	Cambodian	Chinese[2]	Fijian	Filipino	Guamanian[3]	Hawaiian, Native	Hmong	Indonesian	Japanese	Korean	Laotian	Malaysian	Pakistani	Samoan	Sri Lankan	Taiwanese	Thai	Tongan	Vietnamese
Danbury (city)	15,839 58.27	1,113	640 57.50 57.50 4.04	-	-	196 48.51 30.63 17.61 1.24	-	109 81.34 17.03 9.79 0.69	100 64.10 15.63 8.98 0.63	-	-	-	-	-	-	-	-	-	-	-	-	-	-	-	-	-
Greenwich (town)	15,988 68.82	916	467 50.98 50.98 2.92	-	-	94 67.63 20.13 10.26 0.59	-	-	166 82.18 35.55 18.12 1.04	-	-	-	-	-	-	69 19.11 14.78 7.53 0.43	-	-	-	-	-	-	-	-	-	-
Stamford (city)	25,716 56.64	2,029	894 44.06 44.06 3.48	-	-	360 33.21 40.27 17.74 1.40	-	-	277 60.48 30.98 13.65 1.08	-	93 49.73 10.40 4.58 0.36	-	-	-	-	-	-	-	-	-	-	-	-	-	-	-
Hartford County	215,253 64.24	6,495	3,218 49.55 49.55 1.49	-	-	1,073 49.61 33.34 16.52 0.50	-	-	735 60.05 22.84 11.32 0.34	-	197 40.04 6.12 3.03 0.09	-	-	-	-	59 28.64 1.83 0.91 0.03	187 38.96 5.81 2.88 0.09	161 52.44 5.00 2.48 0.07	-	69 30.53 2.14 1.06 0.03	-	-	-	-	-	451 51.96 14.01 6.94 0.21
East Hartford (town)	11,652 57.67	545	294 53.94 53.94 2.52	-	-	90 52.94 30.61 16.51 0.77	-	-	-	-	-	-	-	-	-	-	-	-	-	-	-	-	-	-	-	83 65.35 28.23 15.23 0.71
Farmington (town)	7,150 75.29	298	189 63.42 63.42 2.64	-	-	-	-	-	-	-	-	-	-	-	-	-	-	-	-	-	-	-	-	-	-	-
Glastonbury (town)	10,007 81.64	376	313 83.24 83.24 3.13	-	-	118 80.82 37.70 31.38 1.18	-	-	-	-	-	-	-	-	-	-	-	-	-	-	-	-	-	-	-	-
Rocky Hill (town)	4,945 65.46	292	87 29.79 29.79 1.76	-	-	-	-	-	-	-	-	-	-	-	-	-	-	-	-	-	-	-	-	-	-	-
South Windsor (town)	7,936 89.09	280	224 80.00 80.00 2.82	-	-	-	-	-	-	-	-	-	-	-	-	-	-	-	-	-	-	-	-	-	-	-
West Hartford (town)	17,660 71.86	824	543 65.90 65.90 3.07	-	-	168 83.17 30.94 20.39 0.95	-	-	170 68.83 31.31 20.63 0.96	-	-	-	-	-	-	-	-	-	-	-	-	-	-	-	-	93 52.25 17.13 11.29 0.53

Notes: Please refer to the User's Guide for an explanation of data; data is arranged alphabetically by state, then county, then city within each county; table includes counties with populations greater than 49,999 unless noted and cities with populations greater than 9,999 whose Asian and/or NHPI population rates are greater than the national average; (1) Native Hawaiian and other Pacific Islander; (2) excludes Taiwanese; (3) includes Chamorro; (4) county does not meet population threshold but is shown in order to allow inclusion of city

Place	All owner-occupied housing units	Asian-occupied housing units	Asians who own and occupy their own homes	NHPI[1]-occupied housing units	NHPIs[1] who own and occupy their own homes	Asian Indian	Bangladeshi	Cambodian	Chinese[2]	Fijian	Filipino	Guamanian[3]	Hawaiian, Native	Hmong	Indonesian	Japanese	Korean	Laotian	Malaysian	Pakistani	Samoan	Sri Lankan	Taiwanese	Thai	Tongan	Vietnamese
Litchfield County	53,813 75.21	568	379 66.73 66.73 0.70	-	-	96 71.11 25.33 16.90 0.18	-	-	79 63.20 20.84 13.91 0.15	-	-	-	-	-	-	-	31 62.00 8.18 5.46 0.06	-	-	-	-	-	-	-	-	41 50.62 10.82 7.22 0.08
Middlesex County	44,216 72.08	610	271 44.43 44.43 0.61	-	-	60 31.75 22.14 9.84 0.14	-	-	80 47.06 29.52 13.11 0.18	-	-	-	-	-	-	-	-	-	-	-	-	-	-	-	-	-
New Haven County	201,349 63.11	6,633	2,608 39.32 39.32 1.30	-	-	721 35.07 27.65 10.87 0.36	-	-	877 44.25 33.63 13.22 0.44	-	202 41.48 7.75 3.05 0.10	-	-	-	-	150 38.86 5.75 2.26 0.07	196 32.50 7.52 2.95 0.10	64 51.20 2.45 0.96 0.03	-	68 38.42 2.61 1.03 0.03	-	-	-	-	-	136 45.79 5.21 2.05 0.07
New Haven (city)	13,918 29.55	1,673	221 13.21 13.21 1.59	-	-	32 10.49 14.48 1.91 0.23	-	-	82 11.73 37.10 4.90 0.59	-	-	-	-	-	-	-	12 5.29 5.43 0.72 0.09	-	-	-	-	-	-	-	-	-
New London County	66,548 66.66	1,493	817 54.72 54.72 1.23	-	-	135 43.27 16.52 9.04 0.20	-	-	268 59.03 32.80 17.95 0.40	-	226 65.51 27.66 15.14 0.34	-	-	-	-	-	-	-	-	-	-	-	-	-	-	-
Tolland County	36,316 73.47	873	296 33.91 33.91 0.82	-	-	130 52.85 43.92 14.89 0.36	-	-	56 17.02 18.92 6.41 0.15	-	-	-	-	-	-	-	-	-	-	-	-	-	-	-	-	-
Mansfield (town)	3,275 61.90	385	84 21.82 21.82 2.56	-	-	39 41.49 46.43 10.13 1.19	-	-	5 2.82 5.95 1.30 0.15	-	-	-	-	-	-	-	-	-	-	-	-	-	-	-	-	-
Storrs (cdp)	634 37.92	253	0 <0.01 <0.01 <0.01	-	-	-	-	-	0 <0.01 *** ** <0.01 <0.01	-	-	-	-	-	-	-	-	-	-	-	-	-	-	-	-	-
Windham County	27,738 67.42	256	102 39.84 39.84 0.37	-	-	-	-	-	-	-	-	-	-	-	-	-	-	-	-	-	-	-	-	-	-	-
DELAWARE	216,046 72.32	5,171	2,701 52.23 52.23 1.25	83	45 54.22 54.22 0.02	794 44.16 29.40 15.35 0.37	-	-	785 55.59 29.06 15.18 0.36	-	348 61.70 12.88 6.73 0.16	-	-	-	-	135 68.18 5.00 2.61 0.06	223 41.45 8.26 4.31 0.10	-	-	65 59.09 2.41 1.26 0.03	-	-	-	-	-	108 64.29 4.00 2.09 0.05

Notes: Please refer to the User's Guide for an explanation of data; data is arranged alphabetically by state, then county, then city within each county; table includes counties with populations greater than 49,999 unless noted and cities with populations greater than 9,999 whose Asian and/or NHPI population rates are greater than the national average; (1) Native Hawaiian and other Pacific Islander; (2) excludes Taiwanese; (3) includes Chamorro; (4) county does not meet population threshold but is shown in order to allow inclusion of city

Place	All owner-occupied housing units	Asian-occupied housing units	Asians who own and occupy their own homes	NHPI[1]-occupied housing units	NHPIs[1] who own and occupy their own homes	Asian Indian	Bangladeshi	Cambodian	Chinese[2]	Fijian	Filipino	Guamanian[3]	Hawaiian, Native	Hmong	Indonesian	Japanese	Korean	Laotian	Malaysian	Pakistani	Samoan	Sri Lankan	Taiwanese	Thai	Tongan	Vietnamese
Kent County	33,048	622	292	-	-	95	-	-	-	-	69	-	-	-	-	-	-	-	-	-	-	-	-	-	-	-
	69.98		46.95			54.29					43.67															
						32.53					23.63															
			46.95			15.27					11.09															
			0.88			0.29					0.21															
New Castle County	132,493	4,291	2,223	-	-	658	-	-	715	-	235	-	-	-	-	90	184	-	-	-	-	-	-	-	-	98
	70.13		51.81			41.72			55.56		67.14					58.82	46.35									67.59
						29.60			32.16		10.57					4.05	8.28									4.41
			51.81			15.33			16.66		5.48					2.10	4.29									2.28
			1.68			0.50			0.54		0.18					0.07	0.14									0.07
Hockessin (cdp)	4,030	257	244	-	-	-	-	-	-	-	-	-	-	-	-	-	-	-	-	-	-	-	-	-	-	-
	90.52		94.94																							
			94.94																							
			6.05																							
Newark (city)	4,921	409	120	-	-	-	-	-	45	-	-	-	-	-	-	-	-	-	-	-	-	-	-	-	-	-
	54.74		29.34						24.32																	
									37.50																	
			29.34						11.00																	
			2.44						0.91																	
Pike Creek (cdp)	6,073	322	199	-	-	-	-	-	-	-	-	-	-	-	-	-	-	-	-	-	-	-	-	-	-	-
	74.18		61.80																							
			61.80																							
			3.28																							
Sussex County	50,505	258	186	-	-	-	-	-	-	-	-	-	-	-	-	-	-	-	-	-	-	-	-	-	-	-
	80.71		72.09																							
			72.09																							
			0.37																							
DISTRICT OF COLUMBIA	101,216	6,445	1,588	-	-	443	-	-	501	-	176	-	-	-	-	130	102	-	-	-	-	-	-	-	-	86
	40.76		24.64			31.73			28.84		21.60					19.46	19.10									15.55
						27.90			31.55		11.08					8.19	6.42									5.42
			24.64			6.87			7.77		2.73					2.02	1.58									1.33
			1.57			0.44			0.49		0.17					0.13	0.10									0.08
FLORIDA	4,441,711	82,089	49,897	1,914	919	12,490	134	547	10,446	-	10,160	249	315	-	218	2,368	2,661	766	-	905	94	110	528	1,069	-	5,870
	70.08		60.78		48.01	55.38	33.84	78.59	65.96		66.89	44.86	48.69		53.69	58.05	47.95	68.82		55.62	47.24	62.50	71.45	56.62		63.81
						25.03	0.27	1.10	20.94		20.36	27.09	34.28		0.44	4.75	5.33	1.54		1.81	10.23	0.22	1.06	2.14		11.76
			60.78		48.01	15.22	0.16	0.67	12.73		12.38	13.01	16.46		0.27	2.88	3.24	0.93		1.10	4.91	0.13	0.64	1.30		7.15
			1.12		0.02	0.28	<0.01	0.01	0.24		0.23	0.01	0.01		<0.01	0.05	0.06	0.02		0.02	<0.01	<0.01	0.01	0.02		0.13
Alachua County	48,084	3,104	939	-	-	299	-	-	237	-	138	-	-	-	-	26	56	-	-	-	-	-	-	-	-	76
	54.95		30.25			38.48			25.93		42.86					15.48	13.93									33.93
						31.84			25.24		14.70					2.77	5.96									8.09
			30.25			9.63			7.64		4.45					0.84	1.80									2.45
			1.95			0.62			0.49		0.29					0.05	0.12									0.16
Gainesville (city)	17,791	1,765	426	-	-	135	-	-	91	-	-	-	-	-	-	-	31	-	-	-	-	-	-	-	-	-
	47.73		24.14			33.67			15.17								14.90									
						31.69			21.36								7.28									
			24.14			7.65			5.16								1.76									
			2.39			0.76			0.51								0.17									

Notes: Please refer to the User's Guide for an explanation of data; data is arranged alphabetically by state, then county, then city within each county; table includes counties with populations greater than 49,999 unless noted and cities with populations greater than 9,999 whose Asian and/or NHPI population rates are greater than the national average; (1) Native Hawaiian and other Pacific Islander; (2) excludes Taiwanese; (3) includes Chamorro; (4) county does not meet population threshold but is shown in order to allow inclusion of city

Place	All owner-occupied housing units	Asian-occupied housing units	Asians who own and occupy their own homes	NHPI[1]-occupied housing units	NHPIs[1] who own and occupy their own homes	Asian Indian	Bangladeshi	Cambodian	Chinese[2]	Fijian	Filipino	Guamanian[3]	Hawaiian, Native	Hmong	Indonesian	Japanese	Korean	Laotian	Malaysian	Pakistani	Samoan	Sri Lankan	Taiwanese	Thai	Tongan	Vietnamese
Bay County	40,892 68.61	663	348 52.49 52.49 0.85	-	-	-	-	-	-	-	38 43.68 10.92 5.73 0.09	-	-	-	-	-	-	-	-	-	-	-	-	-	-	111 58.12 31.90 16.74 0.27
Callaway (city)	3,565 63.88	158	87 55.06 55.06 2.44	-	-	-	-	-	-	-	-	-	-	-	-	-	-	-	-	-	-	-	-	-	-	-
Brevard County	147,878 74.61	2,252	1,379 61.23 61.23 0.93	-	-	379 58.85 27.48 16.83 0.26	-	-	182 55.83 13.20 8.08 0.12	-	299 62.82 21.68 13.28 0.20	-	-	-	-	112 53.85 8.12 4.97 0.08	116 67.05 8.41 5.15 0.08	-	-	-	-	-	-	-	-	156 75.73 11.31 6.93 0.11
Broward County	454,625 69.47	11,261	7,555 67.09 67.09 1.66	206	106 51.46 51.46 0.02	2,666 63.80 35.29 23.67 0.59	-	-	2,240 80.87 29.65 19.89 0.49	-	862 71.48 11.41 7.65 0.19	-	-	-	-	275 69.27 3.64 2.44 0.06	310 43.12 4.10 2.75 0.07	-	-	135 40.42 1.79 1.20 0.03	-	-	-	123 63.08 1.63 1.09 0.03	-	550 63.44 7.28 4.88 0.12
Cooper City (city)	8,381 92.24	337	301 89.32 89.32 3.59	-	-	135 78.95 44.85 40.06 1.61	-	-	-	-	-	-	-	-	-	-	-	-	-	-	-	-	-	-	-	-
Pembroke Pines (city)	41,636 80.10	1,515	1,099 72.54 72.54 2.64	-	-	345 65.84 31.39 22.77 0.83	-	-	286 78.36 26.02 18.88 0.69	-	244 85.92 22.20 16.11 0.59	-	-	-	-	-	-	-	-	-	-	-	-	-	-	-
Charlotte County	53,444 83.68	220	168 76.36 76.36 0.31	-	-	-	-	-	-	-	-	-	-	-	-	-	-	-	-	-	-	-	-	-	-	-
Citrus County	45,047 85.59	353	223 63.17 63.17 0.50	-	-	-	-	-	-	-	-	-	-	-	-	-	-	-	-	-	-	-	-	-	-	-
Clay County	39,120 77.86	691	562 81.33 81.33 1.44	-	-	-	-	-	-	-	317 81.91 56.41 45.88 0.81	-	-	-	-	-	-	-	-	-	-	-	-	-	-	-
Bellair-Meadowbrook Ter. (cdp)	3,400 52.56	187	139 74.33 74.33 4.09	-	-	-	-	-	-	-	-	-	-	-	-	-	-	-	-	-	-	-	-	-	-	-

Notes: Please refer to the User's Guide for an explanation of data; data is arranged alphabetically by state, then county, then city within each county; table includes counties with populations greater than 49,999 unless noted and cities with populations greater than 9,999 whose Asian and/or NHPI population rates are greater than the national average; (1) Native Hawaiian and other Pacific Islander; (2) excludes Taiwanese; (3) includes Chamorro; (4) county does not meet population threshold but is shown in order to allow inclusion of city

Place	All owner-occupied housing units	Asian-occupied housing units	Asians who own and occupy their own homes	NHPI[1]-occupied housing units	NHPIs[1] who own and occupy their own homes	Asian Indian	Bangladeshi	Cambodian	Chinese[2]	Fijian	Filipino	Guamanian[3]	Hawaiian, Native	Hmong	Indonesian	Japanese	Korean	Laotian	Malaysian	Pakistani	Samoan	Sri Lankan	Taiwanese	Thai	Tongan	Vietnamese
Collier County	77,829	362	156	-	-	-	-	-	-	-	-	-	-	-	-	-	-	-	-	-	-	-	-	-	-	-
	75.58		43.09																							
			43.09																							
			0.20																							
Columbia County	16,137	125	75	-	-	-	-	-	-	-	-	-	-	-	-	-	-	-	-	-	-	-	-	-	-	-
	77.12		60.00																							
			60.00																							
			0.46																							
Duval County	191,722	6,151	3,898	154	68	399	-	172	312	-	2,230	-	-	-	-	115	144	-	-	-	-	-	-	-	-	274
	63.12		63.37		44.16	38.00		74.14	53.06		77.94					64.97	55.17									46.76
						10.24		4.41	8.00		57.21					2.95	3.69									7.03
			63.37		44.16	6.49		2.80	5.07		36.25					1.87	2.34									4.45
			2.03		0.04	0.21		0.09	0.16		1.16					0.06	0.08									0.14
Escambia County	74,690	1,800	1,127	-	-	92	-	-	115	-	480	-	-	-	-	-	-	-	-	-	-	-	-	-	-	240
	67.26		62.61			67.65			61.83		64.52															57.28
						8.16			10.20		42.59															21.30
			62.61			5.11			6.39		26.67															13.33
			1.51			0.12			0.15		0.64															0.32
Bellview (cdp)	6,082	210	146	-	-	-	-	-	-	-	88	-	-	-	-	-	-	-	-	-	-	-	-	-	-	-
	75.17		69.52								73.95															
											60.27															
			69.52								41.90															
			2.40								1.45															
Myrtle Grove (cdp)	3,700	258	126	-	-	-	-	-	-	-	101	-	-	-	-	-	-	-	-	-	-	-	-	-	-	-
	58.91		48.84								58.72															
											80.16															
			48.84								39.15															
			3.41								2.73															
Hernando County	47,954	237	179	-	-	-	-	-	-	-	-	-	-	-	-	-	-	-	-	-	-	-	-	-	-	-
	86.52		75.53																							
			75.53																							
			0.37																							
Highlands County	29,854	293	195	-	-	-	-	-	-	-	88	-	-	-	-	-	-	-	-	-	-	-	-	-	-	-
	79.67		66.55								70.97															
											45.13															
			66.55								30.03															
			0.65								0.29															
Hillsborough County	251,023	6,599	3,573	120	76	944	-	-	527	-	500	-	-	-	-	190	402	-	-	-	-	-	-	144	-	576
	64.14		54.14		63.33	46.53			55.07		56.88					56.72	55.91							62.07		58.54
						26.42			14.75		13.99					5.32	11.25							4.03		16.12
			54.14		63.33	14.31			7.99		7.58					2.88	6.09							2.18		8.73
			1.42		0.03	0.38			0.21		0.20					0.08	0.16							0.06		0.23
Westchase (cdp)	3,688	148	130	-	-	-	-	-	-	-	-	-	-	-	-	-	-	-	-	-	-	-	-	-	-	-
	88.29		87.84																							
			87.84																							
			3.52																							

Notes: Please refer to the User's Guide for an explanation of data; data is arranged alphabetically by state, then county, then city within each county; table includes counties with populations greater than 49,999 unless noted and cities with populations greater than 9,999 whose Asian and/or NHPI population rates are greater than the national average; (1) Native Hawaiian and other Pacific Islander; (2) excludes Taiwanese; (3) includes Chamorro; (4) county does not meet population threshold but is shown in order to allow inclusion of city

Place	All owner-occupied housing units	Asian-occupied housing units	Asians who own and occupy their own homes	NHPI[1]-occupied housing units	NHPIs[1] who own and occupy their own homes	Asian Indian	Bangladeshi	Cambodian	Chinese[2]	Fijian	Filipino	Guamanian[3]	Hawaiian, Native	Hmong	Indonesian	Japanese	Korean	Laotian	Malaysian	Pakistani	Samoan	Sri Lankan	Taiwanese	Thai	Tongan	Vietnamese
Indian River County	38,119 77.58	237	158 66.67 66.67 0.41	-	-	-	-	-	-	-	-	-	-	-	-	-	-	-	-	-	-	-	-	-	-	-
Lake County	72,047 81.49	414	293 70.77 70.77 0.41	-	-	-	-	-	-	-	-	-	-	-	-	-	-	-	-	-	-	-	-	-	-	-
Lee County	144,256 76.49	952	588 61.76 61.76 0.41	-	-	131 57.46 22.28 13.76 0.09	-	-	178 82.79 30.27 18.70 0.12	-	203 70.73 34.52 21.32 0.14	-	-	-	-	-	-	-	-	-	-	-	-	-	-	-
Leon County	55,014 57.00	1,774	806 45.43 45.43 1.47	-	-	308 52.56 38.21 17.36 0.56	-	-	174 44.05 21.59 9.81 0.32	-	59 37.11 7.32 3.33 0.11	-	-	-	-	-	52 27.66 6.45 2.93 0.09	-	-	-	-	-	-	-	-	-
Manatee County	82,936 73.75	691	518 74.96 74.96 0.62	-	-	-	-	-	-	-	105 81.40 20.27 15.20 0.13	-	-	-	-	-	-	-	-	-	-	-	-	-	-	-
Marion County	85,171 79.78	631	460 72.90 72.90 0.54	-	-	175 62.72 38.04 27.73 0.21	-	-	-	-	-	-	-	-	-	-	-	-	-	-	-	-	-	-	-	-
Martin County	44,131 79.82	205	100 48.78 48.78 0.23	-	-	-	-	-	-	-	-	-	-	-	-	-	-	-	-	-	-	-	-	-	-	-
Miami-Dade County	449,333 57.85	10,275	6,017 58.56 58.56 1.34	133	81 60.90 60.90 0.02	1,537 50.96 25.54 14.96 0.34	-	-	2,181 68.93 36.25 21.23 0.49	-	888 59.60 14.76 8.64 0.20	-	-	-	-	271 52.02 4.50 2.64 0.06	278 60.30 4.62 2.71 0.06	-	-	166 55.33 2.76 1.62 0.04	-	-	-	123 54.42 2.04 1.20 0.03	-	186 39.41 3.09 1.81 0.04
Doral (cdp)	4,382 56.44	390	219 56.15 56.15 5.00	-	-	-	-	-	-	-	-	-	-	-	-	-	-	-	-	-	-	-	-	-	-	-
Ives Estates (cdp)	5,294 77.22	265	168 63.40 63.40 3.17	-	-	-	-	-	-	-	-	-	-	-	-	-	-	-	-	-	-	-	-	-	-	-

Notes: Please refer to the User's Guide for an explanation of data; data is arranged alphabetically by state, then county, then city within each county; table includes counties with populations greater than 49,999 unless noted and cities with populations greater than 9,999 whose Asian and/or NHPI population rates are greater than the national average; (1) Native Hawaiian and other Pacific Islander; (2) excludes Taiwanese; (3) includes Chamorro; (4) county does not meet population threshold but is shown in order to allow inclusion of city

Place	All owner-occupied housing units	Asian-occupied housing units	Asians who own and occupy their own homes	NHPI[1]-occupied housing units	NHPIs[1] who own and occupy their own homes	Asian Indian	Bangladeshi	Cambodian	Chinese[2]	Fijian	Filipino	Guamanian[3]	Hawaiian, Native	Hmong	Indonesian	Japanese	Korean	Laotian	Malaysian	Pakistani	Samoan	Sri Lankan	Taiwanese	Thai	Tongan	Vietnamese
North Miami Beach (city)	8,688 62.11	506	314 62.06 62.06 3.61	-	-	60 46.88 19.11 11.86 0.69	-	-	175 79.55 55.73 34.58 2.01	-	-	-	-	-	-	-	-	-	-	-	-	-	-	-	-	-
Pinecrest (village)	5,186 83.02	224	107 47.77 47.77 2.06	-	-	-	-	-	-	-	-	-	-	-	-	-	-	-	-	-	-	-	-	-	-	-
Monroe County	21,900 62.42	206	119 57.77 57.77 0.54	-	-	-	-	-	-	-	-	-	-	-	-	-	-	-	-	-	-	-	-	-	-	-
Nassau County	17,732 80.67	95	61 64.21 64.21 0.34	-	-	-	-	-	-	-	-	-	-	-	-	-	-	-	-	-	-	-	-	-	-	-
Okaloosa County	43,972 66.35	1,059	609 57.51 57.51 1.38	-	-	-	-	-	-	-	219 52.64 35.96 20.68 0.50	-	-	-	-	-	64 51.20 10.51 6.04 0.15	-	-	-	-	-	-	69 65.71 11.33 6.52 0.16	-	68 62.39 11.17 6.42 0.15
Wright (cdp)	4,973 54.47	218	128 58.72 58.72 2.57	-	-	-	-	-	-	-	-	-	-	-	-	-	-	-	-	-	-	-	-	-	-	-
Orange County	204,230 60.73	8,969	5,346 59.61 59.61 2.62	180	100 55.56 55.56 0.05	1,382 55.84 25.85 15.41 0.68	-	-	863 61.55 16.14 9.62 0.42	-	833 66.91 15.58 9.29 0.41	-	-	-	-	196 42.89 3.67 2.19 0.10	344 43.22 6.43 3.84 0.17	-	-	153 59.53 2.86 1.71 0.07	-	-	-	-	-	1,225 71.14 22.91 13.66 0.60
Oak Ridge (cdp)	2,776 37.47	409	228 55.75 55.75 8.21	-	-	-	-	-	-	-	-	-	-	-	-	-	-	-	-	-	-	-	-	-	-	129 88.97 56.58 31.54 4.65
Osceola County	41,315 67.76	1,171	731 62.43 62.43 1.77	-	-	149 52.28 20.38 12.72 0.36	-	-	193 73.11 26.40 16.48 0.47	-	213 78.60 29.14 18.19 0.52	-	-	-	-	-	-	-	-	-	-	-	-	-	-	-
Palm Beach County	354,024 74.66	5,569	3,626 65.11 65.11 1.02	80	15 18.75 18.75 <0.01	970 55.88 26.75 17.42 0.27	-	-	971 75.15 26.78 17.44 0.27	-	414 58.23 11.42 7.43 0.12	-	-	-	-	171 77.38 4.72 3.07 0.05	115 43.56 3.17 2.07 0.03	-	-	-	-	-	-	135 62.50 3.72 2.42 0.04	-	424 73.23 11.69 7.61 0.12

Notes: Please refer to the User's Guide for an explanation of data; data is arranged alphabetically by state, then county, then city within each county; table includes counties with populations greater than 49,999 unless noted and cities with populations greater than 9,999 whose Asian and/or NHPI population rates are greater than the national average; (1) Native Hawaiian and other Pacific Islander; (2) excludes Taiwanese; (3) includes Chamorro; (4) county does not meet population threshold but is shown in order to allow inclusion of city

Place	All owner-occupied housing units	Asian-occupied housing units	Asians who own and occupy their own homes	NHPI[1]-occupied housing units	NHPIs[1] who own and occupy their own homes	Asian Indian	Bangladeshi	Cambodian	Chinese[2]	Fijian	Filipino	Guamanian[3]	Hawaiian, Native	Hmong	Indonesian	Japanese	Korean	Laotian	Malaysian	Pakistani	Samoan	Sri Lankan	Taiwanese	Thai	Tongan	Vietnamese
Pasco County	121,548 82.37	1,034	821 79.40 79.40 0.68	-	-	199 72.36 24.24 19.25 0.16	-	-	132 82.50 16.08 12.77 0.11	-	229 76.59 27.89 22.15 0.19	-	-	-	-	-	-	-	-	-	-	-	-	-	-	-
Pinellas County	293,869 70.82	5,901	3,528 59.79 59.79 1.20	-	-	641 51.78 18.17 10.86 0.22	-	161 81.31 4.56 2.73 0.05	546 63.56 15.48 9.25 0.19	-	539 56.15 15.28 9.13 0.18	-	-	-	-	110 44.72 3.12 1.86 0.04	172 63.00 4.88 2.91 0.06	328 71.62 9.30 5.56 0.11	-	-	-	-	-	53 40.77 1.50 0.90 0.02	-	846 69.46 23.98 14.34 0.29
Pinellas Park (city)	14,530 74.65	552	387 70.11 70.11 2.66	-	-	-	-	-	-	-	-	-	-	-	-	-	-	-	-	-	-	-	-	-	-	158 80.61 40.83 28.62 1.09
Polk County	137,373 73.37	1,524	943 61.88 61.88 0.69	-	-	290 57.88 30.75 19.03 0.21	-	-	98 53.55 10.39 6.43 0.07	-	155 74.16 16.44 10.17 0.11	-	-	-	-	-	-	86 100.00 9.12 5.64 0.06	-	-	-	-	-	-	-	142 71.00 15.06 9.32 0.10
Putnam County	22,265 79.98	81	56 69.14 69.14 0.25	-	-	-	-	-	-	-	-	-	-	-	-	-	-	-	-	-	-	-	-	-	-	-
St. Johns County	37,889 76.37	380	221 58.16 58.16 0.58	-	-	-	-	-	-	-	-	-	-	-	-	-	-	-	-	-	-	-	-	-	-	-
St. Lucie County	60,035 78.04	568	405 71.30 71.30 0.67	-	-	-	-	-	-	-	-	-	-	-	-	-	-	-	-	-	-	-	-	-	-	-
Santa Rosa County	35,198 80.37	331	208 62.84 62.84 0.59	-	-	-	-	-	-	-	90 62.50 43.27 27.19 0.26	-	-	-	-	-	-	-	-	-	-	-	-	-	-	-
Sarasota County	118,538 79.06	719	501 69.68 69.68 0.42	-	-	-	-	-	94 66.67 18.76 13.07 0.08	-	51 68.00 10.18 7.09 0.04	-	-	-	-	-	-	-	-	-	-	-	-	-	-	107 69.03 21.36 14.88 0.09
Seminole County	96,956 69.47	2,770	1,821 65.74 65.74 1.88	-	-	623 67.06 34.21 22.49 0.64	-	-	326 73.59 17.90 11.77 0.34	-	282 76.63 15.49 10.18 0.29	-	-	-	-	-	85 29.82 4.67 3.07 0.09	-	-	-	-	-	-	-	-	250 81.17 13.73 9.03 0.26

Notes: Please refer to the User's Guide for an explanation of data; data is arranged alphabetically by state, then county, then city within each county; table includes counties with populations greater than 49,999 unless noted and cities with populations greater than 9,999 whose Asian and/or NHPI population rates are greater than the national average; (1) Native Hawaiian and other Pacific Islander; (2) excludes Taiwanese; (3) includes Chamorro; (4) county does not meet population threshold but is shown in order to allow inclusion of city

Place	All owner-occupied housing units	Asian-occupied housing units	Asians who own and occupy their own homes	NHPI[1]-occupied housing units	NHPIs[1] who own and occupy their own homes	Asian Indian	Bangladeshi	Cambodian	Chinese[2]	Fijian	Filipino	Guamanian[3]	Hawaiian, Native	Hmong	Indonesian	Japanese	Korean	Laotian	Malaysian	Pakistani	Samoan	Sri Lankan	Taiwanese	Thai	Tongan	Vietnamese
Volusia County	139,037	1,478	903	-	-	285	-	-	156	-	170	-	-	-	-	-	47	-	-	-	-	-	-	-	-	-
	75.27		61.10			59.87			56.73		71.13						41.96									
						31.56			17.28		18.83						5.20									
			61.10			19.28			10.55		11.50						3.18									
			0.65			0.20			0.11		0.12						0.03									
GEORGIA	2,029,293	49,630	27,433	1,189	553	6,743	123	590	5,203	-	1,624	209	136	133	60	1,189	4,160	848	-	419	125	-	456	372	-	4,646
	67.50		55.28		46.51	48.51	38.68	87.67	62.21		57.36	44.85	60.71	58.85	31.91	44.53	50.57	69.91		40.84	47.17		78.08	52.47		67.65
						24.58	0.45	2.15	18.97		5.92	37.79	24.59	0.48	0.22	4.33	15.16	3.09		1.53	22.60		1.66	1.36		16.94
			55.28		46.51	13.59	0.25	1.19	10.48		3.27	17.58	11.44	0.27	0.12	2.40	8.38	1.71		0.84	10.51		0.92	0.75		9.36
			1.35		0.03	0.33	0.01	0.03	0.26		0.08	0.01	0.01	0.01	<0.01	0.06	0.20	0.04		0.02	0.01		0.02	0.02		0.23
Bartow County	20,444	141	68	-	-	-	-	-	-	-	-	-	-	-	-	-	-	-	-	-	-	-	-	-	-	-
	75.23		48.23																							
			48.23																							
			0.33																							
Bibb County	35,086	475	190	-	-	-	-	-	-	-	-	-	-	-	-	-	-	-	-	-	-	-	-	-	-	-
	58.80		40.00																							
			40.00																							
			0.54																							
Bulloch County	12,053	209	77	-	-	-	-	-	-	-	-	-	-	-	-	-	-	-	-	-	-	-	-	-	-	-
	58.11		36.84																							
			36.84																							
			0.64																							
Carroll County	22,259	103	81	-	-	-	-	-	-	-	-	-	-	-	-	-	-	-	-	-	-	-	-	-	-	-
	70.51		78.64																							
			78.64																							
			0.36																							
Catoosa County	15,737	144	90	-	-	-	-	-	-	-	-	-	-	-	-	-	-	-	-	-	-	-	-	-	-	-
	77.05		62.50																							
			62.50																							
			0.57																							
Chatham County	54,288	1,215	710	-	-	110	-	-	197	-	-	-	-	-	-	-	57	-	-	-	-	-	-	-	-	160
	60.41		58.44			49.11			64.59								46.34									63.75
						15.49			27.75								8.03									22.54
			58.44			9.05			16.21								4.69									13.17
			1.31			0.20			0.36								0.10									0.29
Cherokee County	41,503	362	238	-	-	65	-	-	-	-	-	-	-	-	-	-	-	-	-	-	-	-	-	-	-	-
	83.85		65.75			65.00																				
						27.31																				
			65.75			17.96																				
			0.57			0.16																				
Clarke County	16,716	1,146	262	-	-	96	-	-	61	-	-	-	-	-	-	-	9	-	-	-	-	-	-	-	-	-
	42.10		22.86			37.80			15.76								5.56									
						36.64			23.28								3.44									
			22.86			8.38			5.32								0.79									
			1.57			0.57			0.36								0.05									

Notes: Please refer to the User's Guide for an explanation of data; data is arranged alphabetically by state, then county, then city within each county; table includes counties with populations greater than 49,999 unless noted and cities with populations greater than 9,999 whose Asian and/or NHPI population rates are greater than the national average; (1) Native Hawaiian and other Pacific Islander; (2) excludes Taiwanese; (3) includes Chamorro; (4) county does not meet population threshold but is shown in order to allow inclusion of city

Place	All owner-occupied housing units	Asian-occupied housing units	Asians who own and occupy their own homes	NHPI[1]-occupied housing units	NHPIs[1] who own and occupy their own homes	Asian Indian	Bangladeshi	Cambodian	Chinese[2]	Fijian	Filipino	Guamanian[3]	Hawaiian, Native	Hmong	Indonesian	Japanese	Korean	Laotian	Malaysian	Pakistani	Samoan	Sri Lankan	Taiwanese	Thai	Tongan	Vietnamese
Clayton County	49,845 60.61	2,473	1,773 71.69 71.69 3.56	-	-	203 49.39 11.45 8.21 0.41	-	174 91.58 9.81 7.04 0.35	85 52.80 4.79 3.44 0.17	-	-	-	-	-	-	-	-	243 81.82 13.71 9.83 0.49	-	24 21.82 1.35 0.97 0.05	-	-	-	-	-	873 88.09 49.24 35.30 1.75
Forest Park (city)	3,737 55.04	273	220 80.59 80.59 5.89	-	-	-	-	-	-	-	-	-	-	-	-	-	-	-	-	-	-	-	-	-	-	178 88.12 80.91 65.20 4.76
Riverdale (city)	2,156 49.16	224	129 57.59 57.59 5.98	-	-	-	-	-	-	-	-	-	-	-	-	-	-	-	-	-	-	-	-	-	-	84 85.71 65.12 37.50 3.90
Cobb County	155,075 68.17	5,825	3,333 57.22 57.22 2.15	-	-	824 44.83 24.72 14.15 0.53	-	-	917 78.24 27.51 15.74 0.59	-	187 54.36 5.61 3.21 0.12	-	-	-	-	177 52.37 5.31 3.04 0.11	552 56.85 16.56 9.48 0.36	-	-	81 50.94 2.43 1.39 0.05	-	-	-	-	-	293 75.13 8.79 5.03 0.19
Smyrna (city)	9,283 50.30	625	246 39.36 39.36 2.65	-	-	33 13.98 13.41 5.28 0.36	-	-	-	-	-	-	-	-	-	-	-	-	-	-	-	-	-	-	-	-
Columbia County	25,544 82.08	826	696 84.26 84.26 2.72	-	-	229 76.33 32.90 27.72 0.90	-	-	137 94.48 19.68 16.59 0.54	-	-	-	-	-	-	-	80 91.95 11.49 9.69 0.31	-	-	-	-	-	-	-	-	-
Martinez (cdp)	7,909 80.26	393	313 79.64 79.64 3.96	-	-	118 76.62 37.70 30.03 1.49	-	-	-	-	-	-	-	-	-	-	-	-	-	-	-	-	-	-	-	-
Coweta County	24,533 78.03	145	112 77.24 77.24 0.46	-	-	-	-	-	-	-	-	-	-	-	-	-	-	-	-	-	-	-	-	-	-	-
DeKalb County	145,821 58.48	8,199	2,966 36.18 36.18 2.03	-	-	738 29.43 24.88 9.00 0.51	38 29.69 1.28 0.46 0.03	89 84.76 3.00 1.09 0.06	629 43.96 21.21 7.67 0.43	-	82 43.16 2.76 1.00 0.06	-	-	-	-	80 23.53 2.70 0.98 0.05	310 23.56 10.45 3.78 0.21	-	-	-	-	-	-	-	-	657 46.24 22.15 8.01 0.45
Druid Hills (cdp)	2,555 55.57	135	34 25.19 25.19 1.33	-	-	-	-	-	-	-	-	-	-	-	-	-	-	-	-	-	-	-	-	-	-	-

Notes: Please refer to the User's Guide for an explanation of data; data is arranged alphabetically by state, then county, then city within each county; table includes counties with populations greater than 49,999 unless noted and cities with populations greater than 9,999 whose Asian and/or NHPI population rates are greater than the national average; (1) Native Hawaiian and other Pacific Islander; (2) excludes Taiwanese; (3) includes Chamorro; (4) county does not meet population threshold but is shown in order to allow inclusion of city

Place	All owner-occupied housing units	Asian-occupied housing units	Asians who own and occupy their own homes	NHPI¹-occupied housing units	NHPIs¹ who own and occupy their own homes	Asian Indian	Bangladeshi	Cambodian	Chinese²	Fijian	Filipino	Guamanian³	Hawaiian, Native	Hmong	Indonesian	Japanese	Korean	Laotian	Malaysian	Pakistani	Samoan	Sri Lankan	Taiwanese	Thai	Tongan	Vietnamese
Dunwoody (cdp)	9,195 66.89	889	312 35.10 35.10 3.39	-	-	100 21.79 32.05 11.25 1.09	-	-	-	-	-	-	-	-	-	-	49 32.03 15.71 5.51 0.53	-	-	-	-	-	-	-	-	-
North Atlanta (cdp)	5,845 36.85	594	108 18.18 18.18 1.85	-	-	-	-	-	-	-	-	-	-	-	-	-	-	-	-	-	-	-	-	-	-	-
North Decatur (cdp)	4,447 55.85	359	97 27.02 27.02 2.18	-	-	-	-	-	-	-	-	-	-	-	-	-	-	-	-	-	-	-	-	-	-	-
North Druid Hills (cdp)	3,691 37.82	563	56 9.95 9.95 1.52	-	-	15 5.91 26.79 2.66 0.41	-	-	-	-	-	-	-	-	-	-	-	-	-	-	-	-	-	-	-	-
Tucker (cdp)	7,794 74.58	560	397 70.89 70.89 5.09	-	-	-	-	-	-	-	-	-	-	-	-	-	-	-	-	-	-	-	-	-	-	70 66.67 17.63 12.50 0.90
Dougherty County	19,012 53.48	202	47 23.27 23.27 0.25	-	-	-	-	-	-	-	-	-	-	-	-	-	-	-	-	-	-	-	-	-	-	-
Douglas County	24,555 74.81	267	158 59.18 59.18 0.64	-	-	-	-	-	-	-	-	-	-	-	-	-	-	-	-	-	-	-	-	-	-	-
Fayette County	27,285 86.55	543	344 63.35 63.35 1.26	-	-	-	-	-	-	-	-	-	-	-	-	63 32.14 18.31 11.60 0.23	-	-	-	-	-	-	-	-	-	-
Peachtree City (city)	8,920 81.06	344	176 51.16 51.16 1.97	-	-	-	-	-	-	-	-	-	-	-	-	63 32.14 35.80 18.31 0.71	-	-	-	-	-	-	-	-	-	-
Floyd County	22,740 66.83	333	191 57.36 57.36 0.84	-	-	46 40.00 24.08 13.81 0.20	-	-	-	-	-	-	-	-	-	-	-	-	-	-	-	-	-	-	-	-

Notes: Please refer to the User's Guide for an explanation of data; data is arranged alphabetically by state, then county, then city within each county; table includes counties with populations greater than 49,999 unless noted and cities with populations greater than 9,999 whose Asian and/or NHPI population rates are greater than the national average; (1) Native Hawaiian and other Pacific Islander; (2) excludes Taiwanese; (3) includes Chamorro; (4) county does not meet population threshold but is shown in order to allow inclusion of city

Place	All owner-occupied housing units	Asian-occupied housing units	Asians who own and occupy their own homes	NHPI[1]-occupied housing units	NHPIs[1] who own and occupy their own homes	Asian Indian	Bangladeshi	Cambodian	Chinese[2]	Fijian	Filipino	Guamanian[3]	Hawaiian, Native	Hmong	Indonesian	Japanese	Korean	Laotian	Malaysian	Pakistani	Samoan	Sri Lankan	Taiwanese	Thai	Tongan	Vietnamese
Forsyth County	30,436 88.05	249	217 87.15 87.15 0.71	-	-	-	-	-	-	-	-	-	-	-	-	-	-	-	-	-	-	-	-	-	-	-
Fulton County	167,111 52.02	7,517	3,636 48.37 48.37 2.18	-	-	969 41.84 26.65 12.89 0.58	-	-	1,025 58.40 28.19 13.64 0.61	-	152 49.84 4.18 2.02 0.09	-	-	-	-	163 43.35 4.48 2.17 0.10	652 51.10 17.93 8.67 0.39	-	-	-	-	-	-	-	-	284 42.51 7.81 3.78 0.17
Alpharetta (city)	8,327 60.15	566	303 53.53 53.53 3.64	-	-	88 37.77 29.04 15.55 1.06	-	-	115 70.12 37.95 20.32 1.38	-	-	-	-	-	-	-	-	-	-	-	-	-	-	-	-	-
Roswell (city)	20,349 67.15	973	577 59.30 59.30 2.84	-	-	166 50.61 28.77 17.06 0.82	-	-	140 71.43 24.26 14.39 0.69	-	-	-	-	-	-	-	125 55.07 21.66 12.85 0.61	-	-	-	-	-	-	-	-	-
Glynn County	17,818 65.49	183	98 53.55 53.55 0.55	-	-	-	-	-	-	-	-	-	-	-	-	-	-	-	-	-	-	-	-	-	-	-
Gwinnett County	146,565 72.44	11,514	7,859 68.26 68.26 5.36	133	55 41.35 41.35 0.04	2,095 64.76 26.66 18.20 1.43	-	169 100.00 2.15 1.47 0.12	1,237 78.94 15.74 10.74 0.84	-	174 56.49 2.21 1.51 0.12	-	-	-	-	167 46.13 2.12 1.45 0.11	1,615 58.28 20.55 14.03 1.10	263 89.15 3.35 2.28 0.18	-	151 54.32 1.92 1.31 0.10	-	-	145 86.31 1.85 1.26 0.10	-	-	1,407 82.47 17.90 12.22 0.96
Duluth (city)	5,138 58.46	784	525 66.96 66.96 10.22	-	-	200 83.33 38.10 25.51 3.89	-	-	118 83.69 22.48 15.05 2.30	-	-	-	-	-	-	-	120 51.95 22.86 15.31 2.34	-	-	-	-	-	-	-	-	-
Lilburn (city)	2,732 69.84	353	300 84.99 84.99 10.98	-	-	84 90.32 28.00 23.80 3.07	-	-	-	-	-	-	-	-	-	-	-	-	-	-	-	-	-	-	-	85 90.43 28.33 24.08 3.11
Mountain Park (cdp)	3,749 87.74	265	257 96.98 96.98 6.86	-	-	165 100.00 64.20 62.26 4.40	-	-	-	-	-	-	-	-	-	-	-	-	-	-	-	-	-	-	-	-
Hall County	33,681 71.09	418	239 57.18 57.18 0.71	-	-	-	-	-	-	-	-	-	-	-	-	-	-	-	-	-	-	-	-	-	-	179 65.57 74.90 42.82 0.53

Notes: Please refer to the User's Guide for an explanation of data; data is arranged alphabetically by state, then county, then city within each county; table includes counties with populations greater than 49,999 unless noted and cities with populations greater than 9,999 whose Asian and/or NHPI population rates are greater than the national average; (1) Native Hawaiian and other Pacific Islander; (2) excludes Taiwanese; (3) includes Chamorro; (4) county does not meet population threshold but is shown in order to allow inclusion of city

Place	All owner-occupied housing units	Asian-occupied housing units	Asians who own and occupy their own homes	NHPI[1]-occupied housing units	NHPIs[1] who own and occupy their own homes	Asian Indian	Bangladeshi	Cambodian	Chinese[2]	Fijian	Filipino	Guamanian[3]	Hawaiian, Native	Hmong	Indonesian	Japanese	Korean	Laotian	Malaysian	Pakistani	Samoan	Sri Lankan	Taiwanese	Thai	Tongan	Vietnamese
Henry County	35,272	485	396	-	-	135	-	-	-	-	-	-	-	-	-	-	-	-	-	-	-	-	-	-	-	-
	85.25		81.65			69.95																				
						34.09																				
			81.65			27.84																				
			1.12			0.38																				
Houston County	28,026	468	283	-	-	-	-	-	-	-	53	-	-	-	-	-	-	-	-	-	-	-	-	-	-	-
	68.50		60.47								35.57															
											18.73															
			60.47								11.32															
			1.01								0.19															
Liberty County	9,824	205	58	-	-	-	-	-	-	-	-	-	-	-	-	-	23	-	-	-	-	-	-	-	-	-
	50.68		28.29														30.26									
																	39.66									
			28.29														11.22									
			0.59														0.23									
Lowndes County	19,865	170	105	-	-	-	-	-	-	-	-	-	-	-	-	-	-	-	-	-	-	-	-	-	-	-
	60.83		61.76																							
			61.76																							
			0.53																							
Muscogee County	39,372	836	481	99	21	77	-	-	74	-	74	-	-	-	-	-	89	-	-	-	-	-	-	-	-	-
	56.39		57.54		21.21	44.77			63.25		57.81						58.94									
						16.01			15.38		15.38						18.50									
			57.54		21.21	9.21			8.85		8.85						10.65									
			1.22		0.05	0.20			0.19		0.19						0.23									
Columbus (sp. city)	39,266	836	481	99	21	77	-	-	74	-	74	-	-	-	-	-	89	-	-	-	-	-	-	-	-	-
	56.42		57.54		21.21	44.77			63.25		57.81						58.94									
						16.01			15.38		15.38						18.50									
			57.54		21.21	9.21			8.85		8.85						10.65									
			1.22		0.05	0.20			0.19		0.19						0.23									
Newton County	17,099	90	62	-	-	-	-	-	-	-	-	-	-	-	-	-	-	-	-	-	-	-	-	-	-	-
	77.73		68.89																							
			68.89																							
			0.36																							
Richmond County	42,819	908	485	-	-	92	-	-	106	-	-	-	-	-	-	-	147	-	-	-	-	-	-	-	-	-
	57.93		53.41			37.86			73.61								62.55									
						18.97			21.86								30.31									
			53.41			10.13			11.67								16.19									
			1.13			0.21			0.25								0.34									
Rockdale County	17,923	293	125	-	-	-	-	-	-	-	-	-	-	-	-	-	-	-	-	-	-	-	-	-	-	-
	74.52		42.66																							
			42.66																							
			0.70																							
Spalding County	13,523	116	34	-	-	-	-	-	-	-	-	-	-	-	-	-	-	-	-	-	-	-	-	-	-	-
	62.84		29.31																							
			29.31																							
			0.25																							

Notes: Please refer to the User's Guide for an explanation of data; data is arranged alphabetically by state, then county, then city within each county; table includes counties with populations greater than 49,999 unless noted and cities with populations greater than 9,999 whose Asian and/or NHPI population rates are greater than the national average; (1) Native Hawaiian and other Pacific Islander; (2) excludes Taiwanese; (3) includes Chamorro; (4) county does not meet population threshold but is shown in order to allow inclusion of city

Place	All owner-occupied housing units	Asian-occupied housing units	Asians who own and occupy their own homes	NHPI[1]-occupied housing units	NHPIs[1] who own and occupy their own homes	Asian Indian	Bangladeshi	Cambodian	Chinese[2]	Fijian	Filipino	Guamanian[3]	Hawaiian, Native	Hmong	Indonesian	Japanese	Korean	Laotian	Malaysian	Pakistani	Samoan	Sri Lankan	Taiwanese	Thai	Tongan	Vietnamese
Troup County	14,132 64.47	111	56 50.45 50.45 0.40	-	-	-	-	-	-	-	-	-	-	-	-	-	-	-	-	-	-	-	-	-	-	-
Walton County	16,308 76.54	98	77 78.57 78.57 0.47	-	-	-	-	-	-	-	-	-	-	-	-	-	-	-	-	-	-	-	-	-	-	-
Whitfield County	19,862 67.59	247	116 46.96 46.96 0.58	-	-	-	-	-	-	-	-	-	-	-	-	-	-	-	-	-	-	-	-	-	-	-
HAWAII	227,783 56.49	173,037	119,676 69.16 69.16 52.54	29,580	13,635 46.10 46.10 5.99	248 51.45 0.21 0.14 0.11	-	10 43.48 0.01 0.01 <0.01	16,491 73.45 13.78 9.53 7.24	-	27,368 63.59 22.87 15.82 12.01	114 22.75 0.84 0.39 0.05	12,259 54.02 89.91 41.44 5.38	-	-	65,195 76.36 54.48 37.68 28.62	3,864 43.84 3.23 2.23 1.70	65 14.71 0.05 0.04 0.03	-	-	687 19.96 5.04 2.32 0.30	-	148 70.14 0.12 0.09 0.06	112 35.90 0.09 0.06 0.05	222 26.78 1.63 0.75 0.10	526 19.87 0.44 0.30 0.23
Hawaii County	34,166 64.48	15,277	11,755 76.95 76.95 34.41	4,592	2,414 52.57 52.57 7.07	-	-	-	481 78.47 4.09 3.15 1.41	-	2,726 71.40 23.19 17.84 7.98	-	2,298 56.25 95.19 50.04 6.73	-	-	7,698 80.72 65.49 50.39 22.53	169 66.54 1.44 1.11 0.49	-	-	-	44 40.37 1.82 0.96 0.13	-	-	-	-	-
Hilo (cdp)	8,870 60.83	6,406	4,922 76.83 76.83 55.49	1,438	674 46.87 46.87 7.60	-	-	-	206 78.63 4.19 3.22 2.32	-	414 60.79 8.41 6.46 4.67	-	661 53.14 98.07 45.97 7.45	-	-	3,938 79.78 80.01 61.47 44.40	97 69.78 1.97 1.51 1.09	-	-	-	-	-	-	-	-	-
Honolulu County	156,233 54.54	137,480	93,145 67.75 67.75 59.62	19,785	8,520 43.06 43.06 5.45	195 50.13 0.21 0.14 0.12	-	-	15,561 73.47 16.71 11.32 9.96	-	18,769 61.12 20.15 13.65 12.01	103 21.96 1.21 0.52 0.07	7,417 53.28 87.05 37.49 4.75	-	-	49,965 75.37 53.64 36.34 31.98	3,503 42.58 3.76 2.55 2.24	56 13.43 0.06 0.04 0.04	-	-	621 19.15 7.29 3.14 0.40	-	142 69.27 0.15 0.10 0.09	79 29.48 0.08 0.06 0.05	151 25.64 1.77 0.76 0.10	435 17.54 0.47 0.32 0.28
Ewa Beach (cdp)	2,272 68.74	1,620	1,304 80.49 80.49 57.39	295	164 55.59 55.59 7.22	-	-	-	-	-	933 79.40 71.55 57.59 41.07	-	110 57.29 67.07 37.29 4.84	-	-	235 93.25 18.02 14.51 10.34	-	-	-	-	38 54.29 23.17 12.88 1.67	-	-	-	-	-
Halawa (cdp)	2,663 64.06	2,162	1,808 83.63 83.63 67.89	347	99 28.53 28.53 3.72	-	-	-	220 91.67 12.17 10.18 8.26	-	486 68.64 26.88 22.48 18.25	-	90 43.06 90.91 25.94 3.38	-	-	899 93.06 49.72 41.58 33.76	-	-	-	-	6 5.41 6.06 1.73 0.23	-	-	-	-	-
Honolulu (cdp)	65,860 46.93	77,326	43,988 56.89 56.89 66.79	7,623	2,038 26.73 26.73 3.09	115 47.13 0.26 0.15 0.17	-	-	10,832 67.93 24.62 14.01 16.45	-	4,385 40.84 9.97 5.67 6.66	36 13.85 1.77 0.47 0.05	1,870 38.53 91.76 24.53 2.84	-	-	24,333 64.70 55.32 31.47 36.95	2,201 34.63 5.00 2.85 3.34	12 4.27 0.03 0.02 0.02	-	-	32 2.57 1.57 0.42 0.05	-	122 65.95 0.28 0.16 0.19	17 11.04 0.04 0.02 0.03	45 14.29 2.21 0.59 0.07	308 14.08 0.70 0.40 0.47

Notes: Please refer to the User's Guide for an explanation of data; data is arranged alphabetically by state, then county, then city within each county; table includes counties with populations greater than 49,999 unless noted and cities with populations greater than 9,999 whose Asian and/or NHPI population rates are greater than the national average; (1) Native Hawaiian and other Pacific Islander; (2) excludes Taiwanese; (3) includes Chamorro; (4) county does not meet population threshold but is shown in order to allow inclusion of city

Place	All owner-occupied housing units	Asian-occupied housing units	Asians who own and occupy their own homes	NHPI[1]-occupied housing units	NHPIs[1] who own and occupy their own homes	Asian Indian	Bangladeshi	Cambodian	Chinese[2]	Fijian	Filipino	Guamanian[3]	Hawaiian, Native	Hmong	Indonesian	Japanese	Korean	Laotian	Malaysian	Pakistani	Samoan	Sri Lankan	Taiwanese	Thai	Tongan	Vietnamese
Kailua (cdp)	8,527 69.82	2,718	2,364 86.98 86.98 27.72	786	516 65.65 65.65 6.05	-	-	-	423 95.27 17.89 15.56 4.96	-	178 57.42 7.53 6.55 2.09	-	485 66.99 93.99 61.70 5.69	-	-	1,502 90.37 63.54 55.26 17.61	107 100.00 4.53 3.94 1.25	-	-	-	-	-	-	-	-	-
Kaneohe (cdp)	7,479 68.13	4,710	4,029 85.54 85.54 53.87	960	551 57.40 57.40 7.37	-	-	-	560 87.91 13.90 11.89 7.49	-	313 70.81 7.77 6.65 4.19	-	493 59.69 89.47 51.35 6.59	-	-	2,727 87.74 67.68 57.90 36.46	115 81.56 2.85 2.44 1.54	-	-	-	-	-	-	-	-	-
Kaneohe Station (cdp)	32 1.37	85	0 <0.01 <0.01 <0.01	-	-	-	-	-	-	-	-	-	-	-	-	-	-	-	-	-	-	-	-	-	-	-
Makakilo City (cdp)	2,729 70.37	1,279	1,096 85.69 85.69 40.16	306	177 57.84 57.84 6.49	-	-	-	-	-	473 78.96 43.16 36.98 17.33	-	172 68.80 97.18 56.21 6.30	-	-	346 89.18 31.57 27.05 12.68	-	-	-	-	-	-	-	-	-	-
Mililani Town (cdp)	6,844 75.99	4,318	3,957 91.64 91.64 57.82	368	273 74.18 74.18 3.99	-	-	-	385 95.77 9.73 8.92 5.63	-	725 80.02 18.32 16.79 10.59	-	215 82.06 78.75 58.42 3.14	-	-	2,472 96.11 62.47 57.25 36.12	129 92.14 3.26 2.99 1.88	-	-	-	-	-	-	-	-	-
Nanakuli (cdp)	1,559 67.00	256	177 69.14 69.14 11.35	897	669 74.58 74.58 42.91	-	-	-	-	-	108 65.85 61.02 42.19 6.93	-	616 84.15 92.08 68.67 39.51	-	-	-	-	-	-	-	46 34.07 6.88 5.13 2.95	-	-	-	-	-
Pearl City (cdp)	6,180 69.71	5,672	4,691 82.70 82.70 75.91	380	215 56.58 56.58 3.48	-	-	-	435 89.88 9.27 7.67 7.04	-	744 68.32 15.86 13.12 12.04	-	188 62.46 87.44 49.47 3.04	-	-	3,277 88.52 69.86 57.78 53.03	88 73.33 1.88 1.55 1.42	-	-	-	-	-	-	-	-	-
Schofield Barracks (cdp)	10 0.34	42	0 <0.01 <0.01 <0.01	-	-	-	-	-	-	-	-	-	-	-	-	-	-	-	-	-	-	-	-	-	-	-
Wahiawa (cdp)	2,503 46.56	2,586	1,687 65.24 65.24 67.40	558	153 27.42 27.42 6.11	-	-	-	-	-	345 47.20 20.45 13.34 13.78	-	135 36.10 88.24 24.19 5.39	-	-	1,107 77.79 65.62 42.81 44.23	-	-	-	-	-	-	-	-	-	-
Waianae (cdp)	1,774 66.57	658	488 74.16 74.16 27.51	643	370 57.54 57.54 20.86	-	-	-	-	-	218 68.99 44.67 33.13 12.29	-	362 63.18 97.84 56.30 20.41	-	-	186 90.29 38.11 28.27 10.48	-	-	-	-	-	-	-	-	-	-

Notes: Please refer to the User's Guide for an explanation of data; data is arranged alphabetically by state, then county, then city within each county; table includes counties with populations greater than 49,999 unless noted and cities with populations greater than 9,999 whose Asian and/or NHPI population rates are greater than the national average; (1) Native Hawaiian and other Pacific Islander; (2) excludes Taiwanese; (3) includes Chamorro; (4) county does not meet population threshold but is shown in order to allow inclusion of city

Place	All owner-occupied housing units	Asian-occupied housing units	Asians who own and occupy their own homes	NHPI¹-occupied housing units	NHPIs¹ who own and occupy their own homes	Asian Indian	Bangladeshi	Cambodian	Chinese²	Fijian	Filipino	Guamanian³	Hawaiian, Native	Hmong	Indonesian	Japanese	Korean	Laotian	Malaysian	Pakistani	Samoan	Sri Lankan	Taiwanese	Thai	Tongan	Vietnamese
Waimalu (cdp)	6,502	5,489	4,365	484	177	-	-	-	519	-	553	-	111	-	-	2,737	199	-	-	-	-	-	-	-	-	-
	61.50		79.52		36.57				91.86		61.93		35.81			87.08	57.85									
									11.89		12.67		62.71			62.70	4.56									
			79.52		36.57				9.46		10.07		22.93			49.86	3.63									
			67.13		2.72				7.98		8.51		1.71			42.09	3.06									
Waipahu (cdp)	4,043	5,102	3,403	754	101	-	-	-	120	-	2,146	-	67	-	-	993	-	-	-	-	29	-	-	-	-	-
	53.54		66.70		13.40				78.43		61.38		36.61			83.66					6.87					
									3.53		63.06		66.34			29.18					28.71					
			66.70		13.40				2.35		42.06		8.89			19.46					3.85					
			84.17		2.50				2.97		53.08		1.66			24.56					0.72					
Waipio (cdp)	2,555	2,174	1,764	196	88	-	-	-	-	-	513	-	67	-	-	993	-	-	-	-	-	-	-	-	-	-
	64.37		81.14		44.90						82.48		49.26			86.50										
											29.08		76.14			56.29										
			81.14		44.90						23.60		34.18			45.68										
			69.04		3.44						20.08		2.62			38.86										
Kauai County	12,366	7,587	5,586	1,333	728	-	-	-	113	-	2,196	-	702	-	-	2,962	-	-	-	-	-	-	-	-	-	-
	61.27		73.63		54.61				55.67		68.41		56.25			80.25										
									2.02		39.31		96.43			53.03										
			73.63		54.61				1.49		28.94		52.66			39.04										
			45.17		5.89				0.91		17.76		5.68			23.95										
Maui County	25,018	12,680	9,190	3,793	1,973	-	-	-	336	-	3,677	-	1,842	-	-	4,570	160	-	-	-	-	-	-	-	67	-
	57.50		72.48		52.02				74.01		69.35		54.77			78.17	55.36								41.61	
									3.66		40.01		93.36			49.73	1.74								3.40	
			72.48		52.02				2.65		29.00		48.56			36.04	1.26								1.77	
			36.73		7.89				1.34		14.70		7.36			18.27	0.64								0.27	
Kahului (cdp)	3,182	3,341	2,354	484	101	-	-	-	-	-	960	-	101	-	-	1,237	-	-	-	-	-	-	-	-	-	-
	54.29		70.46		20.87						65.84		24.82			78.54										
											40.78		100.00			52.55										
			70.46		20.87						28.73		20.87			37.02										
			73.98		3.17						30.17		3.17			38.87										
Kihei (cdp)	3,036	1,201	754	353	173	-	-	-	-	-	511	-	126	-	-	171	-	-	-	-	-	-	-	-	-	-
	49.14		62.78		49.01						68.41		55.26			55.88										
											67.77		72.83			22.68										
			62.78		49.01						42.55		35.69			14.24										
			24.84		5.70						16.83		4.15			5.63										
Wailuku (cdp)	2,679	2,062	1,455	395	183	-	-	-	-	-	267	-	176	-	-	1,013	-	-	-	-	-	-	-	-	-	-
	58.80		70.56		46.33						65.12		46.44			74.65										
											18.35		96.17			69.62										
			70.56		46.33						12.95		44.56			49.13										
			54.31		6.83						9.97		6.57			37.81										
IDAHO	339,913	3,515	2,278	304	139	127	-	-	361	-	286	-	52	-	-	867	137	113	-	-	-	-	-	-	-	240
	72.38		64.81		45.72	37.24			60.88		64.85		34.90			75.00	55.24	88.98								62.99
						5.58			15.85		12.55		37.41			38.06	6.01	4.96								10.54
			64.81		45.72	3.61			10.27		8.14		17.11			24.67	3.90	3.21								6.83
			0.67		0.04	0.04			0.11		0.08		0.02			0.26	0.04	0.03								0.07
Ada County	80,133	1,520	998	104	57	78	-	-	156	-	127	-	-	-	-	251	64	-	-	-	-	-	-	-	-	173
	70.66		65.66		54.81	36.45			61.18		70.95					81.23	73.56									67.32
						7.82			15.63		12.73					25.15	6.41									17.33
			65.66		54.81	5.13			10.26		8.36					16.51	4.21									11.38
			1.25		0.07	0.10			0.19		0.16					0.31	0.08									0.22

Notes: Please refer to the User's Guide for an explanation of data; data is arranged alphabetically by state, then county, then city within each county; table includes counties with populations greater than 49,999 unless noted and cities with populations greater than 9,999 whose Asian and/or NHPI population rates are greater than the national average; (1) Native Hawaiian and other Pacific Islander; (2) excludes Taiwanese; (3) includes Chamorro; (4) county does not meet population threshold but is shown in order to allow inclusion of city

Place	All owner-occupied housing units	Asian-occupied housing units	Asians who own and occupy their own homes	NHPI[1]-occupied housing units	NHPIs[1] who own and occupy their own homes	Asian Indian	Bangladeshi	Cambodian	Chinese[2]	Fijian	Filipino	Guamanian[3]	Hawaiian, Native	Hmong	Indonesian	Japanese	Korean	Laotian	Malaysian	Pakistani	Samoan	Sri Lankan	Taiwanese	Thai	Tongan	Vietnamese
Bannock County	19,207 70.63	243	133 54.73 54.73 0.69	-	-	-	-	-	-	-	-	-	-	-	-	-	-	-	-	-	-	-	-	-	-	-
Bonneville County	21,477 74.69	173	128 73.99 73.99 0.60	-	-	-	-	-	-	-	-	-	-	-	-	-	-	-	-	-	-	-	-	-	-	-
Canyon County	33,010 73.33	344	278 80.81 80.81 0.84	-	-	-	-	-	-	-	-	-	-	-	-	107 74.83 38.49 31.10 0.32	-	-	-	-	-	-	-	-	-	-
Kootenai County	30,781 74.52	149	90 60.40 60.40 0.29	-	-	-	-	-	-	-	-	-	-	-	-	-	-	-	-	-	-	-	-	-	-	-
Twin Falls County	16,292 68.30	104	76 73.08 73.08 0.47	-	-	-	-	-	-	-	-	-	-	-	-	-	-	-	-	-	-	-	-	-	-	-
ILLINOIS	3,089,124 67.28	134,404	73,273 54.52 54.52 2.37	967	488 50.47 50.47 0.02	20,013 52.74 27.31 14.89 0.65	108 44.26 0.15 0.08 <0.01	437 55.88 0.60 0.33 0.01	14,000 55.05 19.11 10.42 0.45	-	17,087 66.86 23.32 12.71 0.55	108 37.89 22.13 11.17 <0.01	81 34.18 16.60 8.38 <0.01	-	95 27.07 0.13 0.07 <0.01	4,307 48.37 5.88 3.20 0.14	8,143 46.32 11.11 6.06 0.26	907 74.34 1.24 0.67 0.03	27 14.44 0.04 0.02 <0.01	1,867 44.96 2.55 1.39 0.06	125 66.49 25.61 12.93 <0.01	100 45.05 0.14 0.07 <0.01	801 56.45 1.09 0.60 0.03	988 53.46 1.35 0.74 0.03	-	2,636 50.39 3.60 1.96 0.09
Champaign County	39,334 55.72	3,982	829 20.82 20.82 2.11	-	-	120 14.53 14.48 3.01 0.31	-	-	220 19.03 26.54 5.52 0.56	-	66 30.99 7.96 1.66 0.17	-	-	-	-	48 22.43 5.79 1.21 0.12	98 10.17 11.82 2.46 0.25	-	-	-	-	-	-	-	-	153 76.88 18.46 3.84 0.39
Champaign (city)	12,853 47.35	1,692	334 19.74 19.74 2.60	-	-	62 14.42 18.56 3.66 0.48	-	-	91 20.97 27.25 5.38 0.71	-	-	-	-	-	-	-	24 6.32 7.19 1.42 0.19	-	-	-	-	-	-	-	-	104 76.47 31.14 6.15 0.81
Urbana (city)	5,247 36.80	1,767	196 11.09 11.09 3.74	-	-	7 2.34 3.57 0.40 0.13	-	-	71 11.60 36.22 4.02 1.35	-	-	-	-	-	-	-	7 1.64 3.57 0.40 0.13	-	-	-	-	-	-	-	-	-
Coles County	13,027 61.91	113	42 37.17 37.17 0.32	-	-	-	-	-	-	-	-	-	-	-	-	-	-	-	-	-	-	-	-	-	-	-

Notes: Please refer to the User's Guide for an explanation of data; data is arranged alphabetically by state, then county, then city within each county; table includes counties with populations greater than 49,999 unless noted and cities with populations greater than 9,999 whose Asian and/or NHPI population rates are greater than the national average; (1) Native Hawaiian and other Pacific Islander; (2) excludes Taiwanese; (3) includes Chamorro; (4) county does not meet population threshold but is shown in order to allow inclusion of city

Place	All owner-occupied housing units	Asian-occupied housing units	Asians who own and occupy their own homes	NHPI[1]-occupied housing units	NHPIs[1] who own and occupy their own homes	Asian Indian	Bangladeshi	Cambodian	Chinese[2]	Fijian	Filipino	Guamanian[3]	Hawaiian, Native	Hmong	Indonesian	Japanese	Korean	Laotian	Malaysian	Pakistani	Samoan	Sri Lankan	Taiwanese	Thai	Tongan	Vietnamese
Cook County	1,142,743	86,092	42,363	446	180	9,981	-	205	8,535	-	10,443	-	-	-	63	2,971	5,623	240	-	1,020	-	-	360	680	-	1,292
	57.88		49.21		40.36	46.26		42.01	50.58		62.11				32.81	46.84	43.45	73.85		35.40			43.58	51.79		40.05
						23.56		0.48	20.15		24.65				0.15	7.01	13.27	0.57		2.41			0.85	1.61		3.05
			49.21		40.36	11.59		0.24	9.91		12.13				0.07	3.45	6.53	0.28		1.18			0.42	0.79		1.50
			3.71		0.02	0.87		0.02	0.75		0.91				0.01	0.26	0.49	0.02		0.09			0.03	0.06		0.11
Arlington Heights (village)	23,565	1,638	749	-	-	99	-	-	113	-	163	-	-	-	-	93	184	-	-	-	-	-	-	-	-	-
	76.68		45.73			20.58			61.75		84.46					21.23	76.03									
						13.22			15.09		21.76					12.42	24.57									
			45.73			6.04			6.90		9.95					5.68	11.23									
			3.18			0.42			0.48		0.69					0.39	0.78									
Chicago (city)	464,912	45,129	16,555	278	88	2,312	-	129	5,029	-	4,535	-	-	-	-	1,487	1,049	-	-	409	-	-	91	244	-	744
	43.78		36.68		31.65	27.78		31.93	44.71		49.38					47.13	18.49			21.27			21.77	32.32		30.68
						13.97		0.78	30.38		27.39					8.98	6.34			2.47			0.55	1.47		4.49
			36.68		31.65	5.12		0.29	11.14		10.05					3.29	2.32			0.91			0.20	0.54		1.65
			3.56		0.02	0.50		0.03	1.08		0.98					0.32	0.23			0.09			0.02	0.05		0.16
Des Plaines (city)	17,907	1,119	949	-	-	392	-	-	90	-	203	-	-	-	-	-	-	-	-	-	-	-	-	-	-	-
	79.68		84.81			86.53			60.81		96.21															
						41.31			9.48		21.39															
			84.81			35.03			8.04		18.14															
			5.30			2.19			0.50		1.13															
Elk Grove Village (village)	10,136	1,054	719	-	-	223	-	-	135	-	151	-	-	-	-	76	-	-	-	-	-	-	-	-	-	-
	76.64		68.22			76.90			75.00		87.28					36.36										
						31.02			18.78		21.00					10.57										
			68.22			21.16			12.81		14.33					7.21										
			7.09			2.20			1.33		1.49					0.75										
Evanston (city)	15,611	1,605	366	-	-	92	-	-	65	-	106	-	-	-	-	64	7	-	-	-	-	-	-	-	-	-
	52.65		22.80			24.21			15.48		67.09					38.32	2.78									
						25.14			17.76		28.96					17.49	1.91									
			22.80			5.73			4.05		6.60					3.99	0.44									
			2.34			0.59			0.42		0.68					0.41	0.04									
Forest Park (village)	3,419	372	163	-	-	-	-	-	-	-	-	-	-	-	-	-	-	-	-	-	-	-	-	-	-	-
	44.80		43.82																							
			43.82																							
			4.77																							
Glenview (village)	13,482	1,289	1,115	-	-	160	-	-	247	-	139	-	-	-	-	65	438	-	-	-	-	-	-	-	-	-
	87.32		86.50			89.89			88.85		82.25					58.56	91.82									
						14.35			22.15		12.47					5.83	39.28									
			86.50			12.41			19.16		10.78					5.04	33.98									
			8.27			1.19			1.83		1.03					0.48	3.25									
Hanover Park (village)	9,148	1,086	960	-	-	419	-	-	-	-	284	-	-	-	-	-	-	-	-	-	-	-	-	-	-	-
	82.01		88.40			84.65					100.00															
						43.65					29.58															
			88.40			38.58					26.15															
			10.49			4.58					3.10															
Hoffman Estates (village)	13,120	2,228	1,525	-	-	548	-	-	181	-	255	-	-	-	-	81	342	-	-	-	-	-	-	-	-	-
	76.31		68.45			68.33			63.29		94.10					31.76	80.66									
						35.93			11.87		16.72					5.31	22.43									
			68.45			24.60			8.12		11.45					3.64	15.35									
			11.62			4.18			1.38		1.94					0.62	2.61									

Notes: Please refer to the User's Guide for an explanation of data; data is arranged alphabetically by state, then county, then city within each county; table includes counties with populations greater than 49,999 unless noted and cities with populations greater than 9,999 whose Asian and/or NHPI population rates are greater than the national average; (1) Native Hawaiian and other Pacific Islander; (2) excludes Taiwanese; (3) includes Chamorro; (4) county does not meet population threshold but is shown in order to allow inclusion of city

Place	All owner-occupied housing units	Asian-occupied housing units	Asians who own and occupy their own homes	NHPI[1]-occupied housing units	NHPIs[1] who own and occupy their own homes	Asian Indian	Bangladeshi	Cambodian	Chinese[2]	Fijian	Filipino	Guamanian[3]	Hawaiian, Native	Hmong	Indonesian	Japanese	Korean	Laotian	Malaysian	Pakistani	Samoan	Sri Lankan	Taiwanese	Thai	Tongan	Vietnamese
Lincolnwood (village)	4,095 91.37	678	663 97.79 97.79 16.19	-	-	171 91.94 25.79 25.22 4.18	-	-	-	-	141 100.00 21.27 20.80 3.44	-	-	-	-	-	188 100.00 28.36 27.73 4.59	-	-	-	-	-	-	-	-	-
Morton Grove (village)	7,754 94.54	1,225	1,171 95.59 95.59 15.10	-	-	337 100.00 28.78 27.51 4.35	-	-	-	-	385 92.11 32.88 31.43 4.97	-	-	-	-	-	218 93.56 18.62 17.80 2.81	-	-	-	-	-	-	-	-	-
Mount Prospect (village)	15,483 71.29	2,197	830 37.78 37.78 5.36	-	-	275 25.23 33.13 12.52 1.78	-	-	69 29.74 8.31 3.14 0.45	-	117 76.47 14.10 5.33 0.76	-	-	-	-	78 45.88 9.40 3.55 0.50	232 53.70 27.95 10.56 1.50	-	-	-	-	-	-	-	-	-
Niles (village)	9,208 76.19	1,010	693 68.61 68.61 7.53	-	-	252 77.06 36.36 24.95 2.74	-	-	-	-	98 56.98 14.14 9.70 1.06	-	-	-	-	-	216 62.61 31.17 21.39 2.35	-	-	-	-	-	-	-	-	-
Northbrook (village)	11,188 91.63	854	770 90.16 90.16 6.88	-	-	-	-	-	162 95.29 21.04 18.97 1.45	-	-	-	-	-	-	-	413 90.77 53.64 48.36 3.69	-	-	-	-	-	-	-	-	-
Oak Park (village)	12,988 56.28	909	360 39.60 39.60 2.77	-	-	119 39.40 33.06 13.09 0.92	-	-	101 60.48 28.06 11.11 0.78	-	-	-	-	-	-	-	-	-	-	-	-	-	-	-	-	-
Orland Park (village)	17,071 91.33	597	571 95.64 95.64 3.34	-	-	169 95.48 29.60 28.31 0.99	-	-	-	-	174 100.00 30.47 29.15 1.02	-	-	-	-	-	-	-	-	-	-	-	-	-	-	-
Palatine (village)	17,686 69.21	1,827	955 52.27 52.27 5.40	-	-	330 45.21 34.55 18.06 1.87	-	-	155 56.36 16.23 8.48 0.88	-	193 74.81 20.21 10.56 1.09	-	-	-	-	-	122 58.94 12.77 6.68 0.69	-	-	-	-	-	-	-	-	-
Prospect Heights (city)	4,691 72.98	189	78 41.27 41.27 1.66	-	-	-	-	-	-	-	-	-	-	-	-	-	-	-	-	-	-	-	-	-	-	-
Rolling Meadows (city)	6,786 76.83	482	271 56.22 56.22 3.99	-	-	54 36.00 19.93 11.20 0.80	-	-	-	-	-	-	-	-	-	-	-	-	-	-	-	-	-	-	-	-

Notes: Please refer to the User's Guide for an explanation of data; data is arranged alphabetically by state, then county, then city within each county; table includes counties with populations greater than 49,999 unless noted and cities with populations greater than 9,999 whose Asian and/or NHPI population rates are greater than the national average; (1) Native Hawaiian and other Pacific Islander; (2) excludes Taiwanese; (3) includes Chamorro; (4) county does not meet population threshold but is shown in order to allow inclusion of city

Place	All owner-occupied housing units	Asian-occupied housing units	Asians who own and occupy their own homes	NHPI[1]-occupied housing units	NHPIs[1] who own and occupy their own homes	Asian Indian	Bangladeshi	Cambodian	Chinese[2]	Fijian	Filipino	Guamanian[3]	Hawaiian, Native	Hmong	Indonesian	Japanese	Korean	Laotian	Malaysian	Pakistani	Samoan	Sri Lankan	Taiwanese	Thai	Tongan	Vietnamese
Schaumburg (village)	22,019 69.36	3,763	1,799 47.81 47.81 8.17	-	-	718 43.17 39.91 19.08 3.26	-	-	300 59.17 16.68 7.97 1.36	-	231 65.07 12.84 6.14 1.05	-	-	-	-	92 23.53 5.11 2.44 0.42	271 46.25 15.06 7.20 1.23	-	-	-	-	-	-	-	-	-
Schiller Park (village)	2,267 53.52	181	61 33.70 33.70 2.69	-	-	-	-	-	-	-	-	-	-	-	-	-	-	-	-	-	-	-	-	-	-	-
Skokie (village)	17,426 75.11	3,701	2,801 75.68 75.68 16.07	-	-	774 84.22 27.63 20.91 4.44	-	-	397 66.06 14.17 10.73 2.28	-	615 72.18 21.96 16.62 3.53	-	-	-	-	-	513 68.31 18.31 13.86 2.94	-	-	73 75.26 2.61 1.97 0.42	-	-	-	-	-	-
Streamwood (village)	10,876 89.48	901	846 93.90 93.90 7.78	-	-	294 91.59 34.75 32.63 2.70	-	-	-	-	280 97.22 33.10 31.08 2.57	-	-	-	-	-	-	-	-	-	-	-	-	-	-	-
Wheeling (village)	8,821 66.49	920	484 52.61 52.61 5.49	-	-	216 51.80 44.63 23.48 2.45	-	-	-	-	129 88.97 26.65 14.02 1.46	-	-	-	-	-	-	-	-	-	-	-	-	-	-	-
Wilmette (village)	8,732 86.95	663	486 73.30 73.30 5.57	-	-	-	-	-	108 78.83 22.22 16.29 1.24	-	-	-	-	-	-	46 38.98 9.47 6.94 0.53	186 77.18 38.27 28.05 2.13	-	-	-	-	-	-	-	-	-
DeKalb County	18,878 59.60	509	76 14.93 14.93 0.40	-	-	35 19.89 46.05 6.88 0.19	-	-	-	-	-	-	-	-	-	-	-	-	-	-	-	-	-	-	-	-
DeKalb (city)	5,450 41.97	425	47 11.06 11.06 0.86	-	-	32 19.16 68.09 7.53 0.59	-	-	-	-	-	-	-	-	-	-	-	-	-	-	-	-	-	-	-	-
DuPage County	248,771 76.40	21,105	14,890 70.55 70.55 5.99	-	-	6,164 65.78 41.40 29.21 2.48	-	-	2,535 77.36 17.02 12.01 1.02	-	3,190 80.07 21.42 15.11 1.28	-	-	-	-	365 54.97 2.45 1.73 0.15	843 69.84 5.66 3.99 0.34	-	-	477 69.74 3.20 2.26 0.19	-	-	243 85.87 1.63 1.15 0.10	77 57.46 0.52 0.36 0.03	-	497 67.44 3.34 2.35 0.20
Addison (village)	7,926 68.34	805	433 53.79 53.79 5.46	-	-	241 50.63 55.66 29.94 3.04	-	-	-	-	70 68.63 16.17 8.70 0.88	-	-	-	-	-	-	-	-	-	-	-	-	-	-	-

Notes: Please refer to the User's Guide for an explanation of data; data is arranged alphabetically by state, then county, then city within each county; table includes counties with populations greater than 49,999 unless noted and cities with populations greater than 9,999 whose Asian and/or NHPI population rates are greater than the national average; (1) Native Hawaiian and other Pacific Islander; (2) excludes Taiwanese; (3) includes Chamorro; (4) county does not meet population threshold but is shown in order to allow inclusion of city

Place	All owner-occupied housing units	Asian-occupied housing units	Asians who own and occupy their own homes	NHPI¹-occupied housing units	NHPIs¹ who own and occupy their own homes	Asian Indian	Bangladeshi	Cambodian	Chinese²	Fijian	Filipino	Guamanian³	Hawaiian, Native	Hmong	Indonesian	Japanese	Korean	Laotian	Malaysian	Pakistani	Samoan	Sri Lankan	Taiwanese	Thai	Tongan	Vietnamese
Bartlett (village)	11,361 93.45	762	740 97.11 97.11 6.51	-	-	365 98.12 49.32 47.90 3.21	-	-	-	-	162 97.01 21.89 21.26 1.43	-	-	-	-	-	-	-	-	-	-	-	-	-	-	-
Bensenville (village)	3,839 55.75	362	161 44.48 44.48 4.19	-	-	80 42.33 49.69 22.10 2.08	-	-	-	-	-	-	-	-	-	-	-	-	-	-	-	-	-	-	-	-
Bloomingdale (village)	5,951 72.83	587	384 65.42 65.42 6.45	-	-	171 81.82 44.53 29.13 2.87	-	-	-	-	-	-	-	-	-	-	-	-	-	-	-	-	-	-	-	-
Burr Ridge (village)	3,313 96.50	293	293 100.00 100.00 8.84	-	-	155 100.00 52.90 52.90 4.68	-	-	-	-	-	-	-	-	-	-	-	-	-	-	-	-	-	-	-	-
Carol Stream (village)	9,704 70.05	1,183	884 74.73 74.73 9.11	-	-	376 68.86 42.53 31.78 3.87	-	-	-	-	272 84.47 30.77 22.99 2.80	-	-	-	-	-	-	-	-	-	-	-	-	-	-	94 77.05 10.63 7.95 0.97
Darien (city)	7,450 85.58	845	742 87.81 87.81 9.96	-	-	360 89.55 48.52 42.60 4.83	-	-	-	-	192 78.05 25.88 22.72 2.58	-	-	-	-	-	-	-	-	-	-	-	-	-	-	-
Downers Grove (village)	14,923 78.54	867	602 69.43 69.43 4.03	-	-	241 61.64 40.03 27.80 1.61	-	-	112 65.88 18.60 12.92 0.75	-	124 89.21 20.60 14.30 0.83	-	-	-	-	-	-	-	-	-	-	-	-	-	-	-
Glen Ellyn (village)	7,992 77.96	347	173 49.86 49.86 2.16	-	-	67 46.53 38.73 19.31 0.84	-	-	-	-	-	-	-	-	-	-	-	-	-	-	-	-	-	-	-	-
Glendale Heights (village)	7,517 70.00	1,741	1,263 72.54 72.54 16.80	-	-	511 72.28 40.46 29.35 6.80	-	-	-	-	369 74.10 29.22 21.19 4.91	-	-	-	-	-	-	-	-	-	-	-	-	-	-	185 80.43 14.65 10.63 2.46
Hinsdale (village)	4,971 83.72	278	183 65.83 65.83 3.68	-	-	-	-	-	-	-	-	-	-	-	-	-	-	-	-	-	-	-	-	-	-	-

Notes: Please refer to the User's Guide for an explanation of data; data is arranged alphabetically by state, then county, then city within each county; table includes counties with populations greater than 49,999 unless noted and cities with populations greater than 9,999 whose Asian and/or NHPI population rates are greater than the national average; (1) Native Hawaiian and other Pacific Islander; (2) excludes Taiwanese; (3) includes Chamorro; (4) county does not meet population threshold but is shown in order to allow inclusion of city

Place	All owner-occupied housing units	Asian-occupied housing units	Asians who own and occupy their own homes	NHPI[1]-occupied housing units	NHPIs[1] who own and occupy their own homes	Asian Indian	Bangladeshi	Cambodian	Chinese[2]	Fijian	Filipino	Guamanian[3]	Hawaiian, Native	Hmong	Indonesian	Japanese	Korean	Laotian	Malaysian	Pakistani	Samoan	Sri Lankan	Taiwanese	Thai	Tongan	Vietnamese
Lisle (village)	4,865 56.77	730	387 53.01 53.01 7.95	-	-	126 42.00 32.56 17.26 2.59	-	-	152 69.41 39.28 20.82 3.12	-	-	-	-	-	-	-	-	-	-	-	-	-	-	-	-	-
Lombard (village)	12,315 75.02	987	573 58.05 58.05 4.65	-	-	191 43.71 33.33 19.35 1.55	-	-	-	-	178 76.72 31.06 18.03 1.45	-	-	-	-	-	-	-	-	-	-	-	-	-	-	-
Naperville (city)	34,952 79.95	3,535	2,743 77.60 77.60 7.85	-	-	1,045 69.48 38.10 29.56 2.99	-	-	1,026 86.07 37.40 29.02 2.94	-	123 75.00 4.48 3.48 0.35	-	-	-	-	-	154 78.17 5.61 4.36 0.44	-	-	-	-	-	113 81.29 4.12 3.20 0.32	-	-	-
Roselle (village)	6,848 81.25	546	416 76.19 76.19 6.07	-	-	198 83.19 47.60 36.26 2.89	-	-	-	-	-	-	-	-	-	-	-	-	-	-	-	-	-	-	-	-
Villa Park (village)	5,974 76.69	218	141 64.68 64.68 2.36	-	-	-	-	-	-	-	-	-	-	-	-	-	-	-	-	-	-	-	-	-	-	-
Warrenville (city)	4,032 82.81	154	143 92.86 92.86 3.55	-	-	-	-	-	-	-	-	-	-	-	-	-	-	-	-	-	-	-	-	-	-	-
Westmont (village)	5,385 54.66	1,013	444 43.83 43.83 8.25	-	-	127 28.80 28.60 12.54 2.36	-	-	122 60.70 27.48 12.04 2.27	-	81 49.69 18.24 8.00 1.50	-	-	-	-	-	-	-	-	-	-	-	-	-	-	-
Wheaton (city)	14,384 74.10	822	432 52.55 52.55 3.00	-	-	163 48.37 37.73 19.83 1.13	-	-	-	-	-	-	-	-	-	-	-	-	-	-	-	-	-	-	-	13 15.12 3.01 1.58 0.09
Woodridge (village)	7,640 67.20	1,105	676 61.18 61.18 8.85	-	-	266 47.42 39.35 24.07 3.48	-	-	-	-	247 84.30 36.54 22.35 3.23	-	-	-	-	-	-	-	-	-	-	-	-	-	-	-
Jackson County	12,917 53.34	858	167 19.46 19.46 1.29	-	-	-	-	-	14 8.54 8.38 1.63 0.11	-	-	-	-	-	-	-	-	-	-	-	-	-	-	-	-	-

Notes: Please refer to the User's Guide for an explanation of data; data is arranged alphabetically by state, then county, then city within each county; table includes counties with populations greater than 49,999 unless noted and cities with populations greater than 9,999 whose Asian and/or NHPI population rates are greater than the national average; (1) Native Hawaiian and other Pacific Islander; (2) excludes Taiwanese; (3) includes Chamorro; (4) county does not meet population threshold but is shown in order to allow inclusion of city

Place	All owner-occupied housing units	Asian-occupied housing units	Asians who own and occupy their own homes	NHPI[1]-occupied housing units	NHPIs[1] who own and occupy their own homes	Asian Indian	Bangladeshi	Cambodian	Chinese[2]	Fijian	Filipino	Guamanian[3]	Hawaiian, Native	Hmong	Indonesian	Japanese	Korean	Laotian	Malaysian	Pakistani	Samoan	Sri Lankan	Taiwanese	Thai	Tongan	Vietnamese
Carbondale (city)	2,828 28.37	730	98 13.42 13.42 3.47	-	-	-	-	-	-	-	-	-	-	-	-	-	-	-	-	-	-	-	-	-	-	-
Kane County	101,727 75.97	1,894	1,468 77.51 77.51 1.44	-	-	360 79.82 24.52 19.01 0.35	-	-	161 70.00 10.97 8.50 0.16	-	338 84.92 23.02 17.85 0.33	-	-	-	-	-	80 70.18 5.45 4.22 0.08	152 64.96 10.35 8.03 0.15	-	-	-	-	-	-	-	126 82.89 8.58 6.65 0.12
South Elgin (village)	4,814 88.87	188	174 92.55 92.55 3.61	-	-	-	-	-	-	-	-	-	-	-	-	-	-	-	-	-	-	-	-	-	-	-
Kankakee County	26,502 69.41	200	127 63.50 63.50 0.48	-	-	-	-	-	-	-	-	-	-	-	-	-	-	-	-	-	-	-	-	-	-	-
Kendall County	15,810 84.10	184	166 90.22 90.22 1.05	-	-	-	-	-	-	-	-	-	-	-	-	-	-	-	-	-	-	-	-	-	-	-
Knox County	15,785 71.57	83	60 72.29 72.29 0.38	-	-	-	-	-	-	-	-	-	-	-	-	-	-	-	-	-	-	-	-	-	-	-
La Salle County	32,596 75.08	182	112 61.54 61.54 0.34	-	-	-	-	-	-	-	-	-	-	-	-	-	-	-	-	-	-	-	-	-	-	-
Lake County	168,293 77.81	7,411	5,416 73.08 73.08 3.22	-	-	1,224 69.00 22.60 16.52 0.73	-	-	1,219 78.44 22.51 16.45 0.72	-	1,269 71.09 23.43 17.12 0.75	-	-	-	-	324 62.67 5.98 4.37 0.19	883 79.41 16.30 11.91 0.52	-	-	102 73.38 1.88 1.38 0.06	-	-	-	-	-	99 68.28 1.83 1.34 0.06
Buffalo Grove (village)	13,596 87.15	1,119	797 71.22 71.22 5.86	-	-	136 55.06 17.06 12.15 1.00	-	-	166 81.77 20.83 14.83 1.22	-	120 83.33 15.06 10.72 0.88	-	-	-	-	84 42.86 10.54 7.51 0.62	234 86.03 29.36 20.91 1.72	-	-	-	-	-	-	-	-	-
Gages Lake (cdp)	3,234 86.73	113	113 100.00 100.00 3.49	-	-	-	-	-	-	-	-	-	-	-	-	-	-	-	-	-	-	-	-	-	-	-

Notes: Please refer to the User's Guide for an explanation of data; data is arranged alphabetically by state, then county, then city within each county; table includes counties with populations greater than 49,999 unless noted and cities with populations greater than 9,999 whose Asian and/or NHPI population rates are greater than the national average; (1) Native Hawaiian and other Pacific Islander; (2) excludes Taiwanese; (3) includes Chamorro; (4) county does not meet population threshold but is shown in order to allow inclusion of city

Place	All owner-occupied housing units	Asian-occupied housing units	Asians who own and occupy their own homes	NHPI[1]-occupied housing units	NHPIs[1] who own and occupy their own homes	Asian Indian	Bangladeshi	Cambodian	Chinese[2]	Fijian	Filipino	Guamanian[3]	Hawaiian, Native	Hmong	Indonesian	Japanese	Korean	Laotian	Malaysian	Pakistani	Samoan	Sri Lankan	Taiwanese	Thai	Tongan	Vietnamese
Grayslake (village)	5,124 78.43	282	226 80.14 80.14 4.41	-	-	-	-	-	-	-	-	-	-	-	-	-	-	-	-	-	-	-	-	-	-	-
Gurnee (village)	8,229 78.08	710	603 84.93 84.93 7.33	-	-	183 81.33 30.35 25.77 2.22	-	-	93 67.39 15.42 13.10 1.13	-	188 94.95 31.18 26.48 2.28	-	-	-	-	-	-	-	-	-	-	-	-	-	-	-
Lake Zurich (village)	5,210 91.20	202	186 92.08 92.08 3.57	-	-	-	-	-	-	-	-	-	-	-	-	-	-	-	-	-	-	-	-	-	-	-
Libertyville (village)	5,875 80.96	346	236 68.21 68.21 4.02	-	-	-	-	-	-	-	-	-	-	-	-	-	-	-	-	-	-	-	-	-	-	-
Mundelein (village)	7,856 79.89	567	486 85.71 85.71 6.19	-	-	-	-	-	137 90.13 28.19 24.16 1.74	-	142 84.02 29.22 25.04 1.81	-	-	-	-	-	-	-	-	-	-	-	-	-	-	-
Vernon Hills (village)	6,149 79.85	722	564 78.12 78.12 9.17	-	-	127 77.44 22.52 17.59 2.07	-	-	179 87.32 31.74 24.79 2.91	-	-	-	-	-	-	-	139 73.94 24.65 19.25 2.26	-	-	-	-	-	-	-	-	-
Macon County	33,379 71.69	212	86 40.57 40.57 0.26	-	-	-	-	-	-	-	-	-	-	-	-	-	-	-	-	-	-	-	-	-	-	-
Madison County	75,235 73.79	351	211 60.11 60.11 0.28	-	-	57 48.72 27.01 16.24 0.08	-	-	-	-	-	-	-	-	-	-	-	-	-	-	-	-	-	-	-	-
McHenry County	74,324 83.13	915	729 79.67 79.67 0.98	-	-	189 74.70 25.93 20.66 0.25	-	-	123 71.51 16.87 13.44 0.17	-	205 82.00 28.12 22.40 0.28	-	-	-	-	-	-	-	-	-	-	-	-	-	-	-
McLean County	37,707 66.45	1,092	347 31.78 31.78 0.92	-	-	96 20.69 27.67 8.79 0.25	-	-	125 49.02 36.02 11.45 0.33	-	-	-	-	-	-	-	-	-	-	-	-	-	-	-	-	-

Notes: Please refer to the User's Guide for an explanation of data; data is arranged alphabetically by state, then county, then city within each county; table includes counties with populations greater than 49,999 unless noted and cities with populations greater than 9,999 whose Asian and/or NHPI population rates are greater than the national average; (1) Native Hawaiian and other Pacific Islander; (2) excludes Taiwanese; (3) includes Chamorro; (4) county does not meet population threshold but is shown in order to allow inclusion of city

Place	All owner-occupied housing units	Asian-occupied housing units	Asians who own and occupy their own homes	NHPI[1]-occupied housing units	NHPIs[1] who own and occupy their own homes	Asian Indian	Bangladeshi	Cambodian	Chinese[2]	Fijian	Filipino	Guamanian[3]	Hawaiian, Native	Hmong	Indonesian	Japanese	Korean	Laotian	Malaysian	Pakistani	Samoan	Sri Lankan	Taiwanese	Thai	Tongan	Vietnamese
Peoria County	49,297 67.78	1,106	536 48.46 48.46 1.09	-	-	156 40.10 29.10 14.10 0.32	-	-	165 52.72 30.78 14.92 0.33	-	-	-	-	-	-	-	-	-	-	-	-	-	-	-	-	67 69.07 12.50 6.06 0.14
Rock Island County	42,306 69.68	439	180 41.00 41.00 0.43	-	-	47 20.98 26.11 10.71 0.11	-	-	-	-	-	-	-	-	-	-	-	-	-	-	-	-	-	-	-	-
St. Clair County	64,860 67.00	546	313 57.33 57.33 0.48	-	-	-	-	-	-	-	112 64.00 35.78 20.51 0.17	-	-	-	-	-	37 45.68 11.82 6.78 0.06	-	-	-	-	-	-	-	-	-
Sangamon County	55,098 69.99	695	404 58.13 58.13 0.73	-	-	140 50.54 34.65 20.14 0.25	-	-	89 65.93 22.03 12.81 0.16	-	-	-	-	-	-	-	-	-	-	-	-	-	-	-	-	-
Tazewell County	38,304 76.11	138	75 54.35 54.35 0.20	-	-	-	-	-	-	-	-	-	-	-	-	-	-	-	-	-	-	-	-	-	-	-
Vermilion County	23,980 71.78	152	98 64.47 64.47 0.41	-	-	-	-	-	-	-	-	-	-	-	-	-	-	-	-	-	-	-	-	-	-	-
Will County	139,411 83.21	3,156	2,745 86.98 86.98 1.97	-	-	705 87.69 25.68 22.34 0.51	-	-	405 89.60 14.75 12.83 0.29	-	785 88.60 28.60 24.87 0.56	-	-	-	-	-	219 90.87 7.98 6.94 0.16	-	-	65 84.42 2.37 2.06 0.05	-	-	-	-	-	150 80.21 5.46 4.75 0.11
Bolingbrook (village)	14,860 85.20	999	902 90.29 90.29 6.07	-	-	259 93.84 28.71 25.93 1.74	-	-	-	-	296 89.97 32.82 29.63 1.99	-	-	-	-	-	-	-	-	-	-	-	-	-	-	-
Winnebago County	75,667 70.08	1,226	758 61.83 61.83 1.00	-	-	120 59.11 15.83 9.79 0.16	-	-	-	-	117 72.67 15.44 9.54 0.15	-	-	-	-	-	35 35.35 4.62 2.85 0.05	263 77.13 34.70 21.45 0.35	-	-	-	-	-	-	-	80 51.28 10.55 6.53 0.11
INDIANA	1,669,083 71.44	19,132	8,910 46.57 46.57 0.53	498	227 45.58 45.58 0.01	2,231 44.26 25.04 11.66 0.13	-	93 70.99 1.04 0.49 0.01	1,767 43.89 19.83 9.24 0.11	-	1,246 62.05 13.98 6.51 0.07	60 50.00 26.43 12.05 <0.01	97 59.15 42.73 19.48 0.01	-	-	675 36.63 7.58 3.53 0.04	854 37.82 9.58 4.46 0.05	184 66.43 2.07 0.96 0.01	-	117 63.59 1.31 0.61 0.01	-	-	112 31.28 1.26 0.59 0.01	133 52.78 1.49 0.70 0.01	-	984 65.30 11.04 5.14 0.06

Notes: Please refer to the User's Guide for an explanation of data; data is arranged alphabetically by state, then county, then city within each county; table includes counties with populations greater than 49,999 unless noted and cities with populations greater than 9,999 whose Asian and/or NHPI population rates are greater than the national average; (1) Native Hawaiian and other Pacific Islander; (2) excludes Taiwanese; (3) includes Chamorro; (4) county does not meet population threshold but is shown in order to allow inclusion of city

Place	All owner-occupied housing units	Asian-occupied housing units	Asians who own and occupy their own homes	NHPI[1]-occupied housing units	NHPIs[1] who own and occupy their own homes	Asian Indian	Bangladeshi	Cambodian	Chinese[2]	Fijian	Filipino	Guamanian[3]	Hawaiian, Native	Hmong	Indonesian	Japanese	Korean	Laotian	Malaysian	Pakistani	Samoan	Sri Lankan	Taiwanese	Thai	Tongan	Vietnamese
Allen County	91,394 70.99	1,552	857 55.22 55.22 0.94	-	-	225 52.69 26.25 14.50 0.25	-	-	108 67.92 12.60 6.96 0.12	-	71 50.71 8.28 4.57 0.08	-	-	-	-	-	-	-	-	-	-	-	-	-	-	158 68.70 18.44 10.18 0.17
Bartholomew County	20,738 74.23	462	167 36.15 36.15 0.81	-	-	24 12.00 14.37 5.19 0.12	-	-	-	-	-	-	-	-	-	-	-	-	-	-	-	-	-	-	-	-
Clark County	27,114 69.97	183	99 54.10 54.10 0.37	-	-	-	-	-	-	-	-	-	-	-	-	-	-	-	-	-	-	-	-	-	-	-
Delaware County	31,692 67.24	233	84 36.05 36.05 0.27	-	-	-	-	-	-	-	-	-	-	-	-	-	-	-	-	-	-	-	-	-	-	-
Elkhart County	47,792 72.24	444	279 62.84 62.84 0.58	-	-	-	-	-	-	-	-	-	-	-	-	-	-	-	-	-	-	-	-	-	-	-
Grant County	20,742 73.24	145	77 53.10 53.10 0.37	-	-	-	-	-	-	-	-	-	-	-	-	-	-	-	-	-	-	-	-	-	-	-
Hamilton County	53,344 80.91	1,267	934 73.72 73.72 1.75	-	-	255 79.19 27.30 20.13 0.48	-	-	239 83.86 25.59 18.86 0.45	-	-	-	-	-	-	-	-	-	-	-	-	-	-	-	-	-
Carmel (city)	10,801 78.96	505	386 76.44 76.44 3.57	-	-	-	-	-	-	-	-	-	-	-	-	-	-	-	-	-	-	-	-	-	-	-
Hendricks County	30,919 82.95	174	143 82.18 82.18 0.46	-	-	-	-	-	-	-	-	-	-	-	-	-	-	-	-	-	-	-	-	-	-	-
Howard County	24,954 71.71	234	95 40.60 40.60 0.38	-	-	-	-	-	-	-	-	-	-	-	-	-	-	-	-	-	-	-	-	-	-	-

Notes: Please refer to the User's Guide for an explanation of data; data is arranged alphabetically by state, then county, then city within each county; table includes counties with populations greater than 49,999 unless noted and cities with populations greater than 9,999 whose Asian and/or NHPI population rates are greater than the national average; (1) Native Hawaiian and other Pacific Islander; (2) excludes Taiwanese; (3) includes Chamorro; (4) county does not meet population threshold but is shown in order to allow inclusion of city

Place	All owner-occupied housing units	Asian-occupied housing units	Asians who own and occupy their own homes	NHPI[1]-occupied housing units	NHPIs[1] who own and occupy their own homes	Asian Indian	Bangladeshi	Cambodian	Chinese[2]	Fijian	Filipino	Guamanian[3]	Hawaiian, Native	Hmong	Indonesian	Japanese	Korean	Laotian	Malaysian	Pakistani	Samoan	Sri Lankan	Taiwanese	Thai	Tongan	Vietnamese
Johnson County	32,464 76.50	311	202 64.95 64.95 0.62	-	-	-	-	-	-	-	-	-	-	-	-	-	-	-	-	-	-	-	-	-	-	-
Kosciusko County	21,538 78.94	100	67 67.00 67.00 0.31	-	-	-	-	-	-	-	-	-	-	-	-	-	-	-	-	-	-	-	-	-	-	-
Lake County	125,323 69.00	1,274	822 64.52 64.52 0.66	-	-	252 57.67 30.66 19.78 0.20	-	-	142 86.06 17.27 11.15 0.11	-	175 71.72 21.29 13.74 0.14	-	-	-	-	-	144 56.25 17.52 11.30 0.11	-	-	-	-	-	-	-	-	-
Munster (town)	7,211 89.12	338	279 82.54 82.54 3.87	-	-	90 79.65 32.26 26.63 1.25	-	-	-	-	-	-	-	-	-	-	-	-	-	-	-	-	-	-	-	-
LaPorte County	30,866 75.19	94	75 79.79 79.79 0.24	-	-	-	-	-	-	-	-	-	-	-	-	-	-	-	-	-	-	-	-	-	-	-
Madison County	39,352 74.18	143	80 55.94 55.94 0.20	-	-	-	-	-	-	-	-	-	-	-	-	-	-	-	-	-	-	-	-	-	-	-
Marion County	208,932 59.33	4,159	1,802 43.33 43.33 0.86	-	-	482 33.97 26.75 11.59 0.23	-	-	359 44.05 19.92 8.63 0.17	-	218 50.82 12.10 5.24 0.10	-	-	-	-	78 38.81 4.33 1.88 0.04	209 47.72 11.60 5.03 0.10	-	-	-	-	-	-	-	-	265 58.37 14.71 6.37 0.13
Monroe County	25,298 53.94	1,620	320 19.75 19.75 1.26	-	-	92 29.97 28.75 5.68 0.36	-	-	91 24.66 28.44 5.62 0.36	-	-	-	-	-	-	-	41 9.93 12.81 2.53 0.16	-	-	-	-	-	-	-	-	-
Bloomington (city)	9,365 35.45	1,464	192 13.11 13.11 2.05	-	-	29 11.89 15.10 1.98 0.31	-	-	83 23.58 43.23 5.67 0.89	-	-	-	-	-	-	-	31 7.87 16.15 2.12 0.33	-	-	-	-	-	-	-	-	-
Porter County	41,867 76.61	343	217 63.27 63.27 0.52	-	-	-	-	-	-	-	-	-	-	-	-	-	-	-	-	-	-	-	-	-	-	-

Notes: Please refer to the User's Guide for an explanation of data; data is arranged alphabetically by state, then county, then city within each county; table includes counties with populations greater than 49,999 unless noted and cities with populations greater than 9,999 whose Asian and/or NHPI population rates are greater than the national average; (1) Native Hawaiian and other Pacific Islander; (2) excludes Taiwanese; (3) includes Chamorro; (4) county does not meet population threshold but is shown in order to allow inclusion of city

Place	All owner-occupied housing units	Asian-occupied housing units	Asians who own and occupy their own homes	NHPI[1]-occupied housing units	NHPIs[1] who own and occupy their own homes	Asian Indian	Bangladeshi	Cambodian	Chinese[2]	Fijian	Filipino	Guamanian[3]	Hawaiian, Native	Hmong	Indonesian	Japanese	Korean	Laotian	Malaysian	Pakistani	Samoan	Sri Lankan	Taiwanese	Thai	Tongan	Vietnamese
St. Joseph County	72,206 71.67	1,160	553 47.67 47.67 0.77	-	-	121 46.18 21.88 10.43 0.17	-	-	153 50.66 27.67 13.19 0.21	-	-	-	-	-	-	-	59 41.84 10.67 5.09 0.08	-	-	-	-	-	-	-	-	-
Tippecanoe County	30,882 55.92	2,424	399 16.46 16.46 1.29	-	-	104 21.44 26.07 4.29 0.34	-	-	99 11.07 24.81 4.08 0.32	-	-	-	-	-	-	30 18.07 7.52 1.24 0.10	27 7.50 6.77 1.11 0.09	-	-	-	-	-	-	-	-	-
West Lafayette (city)	3,457 32.95	1,162	183 15.75 15.75 5.29	-	-	66 21.09 36.07 5.68 1.91	-	-	54 13.99 29.51 4.65 1.56	-	-	-	-	-	-	-	-	-	-	-	-	-	-	-	-	-
Vanderburgh County	47,185 66.81	455	265 58.24 58.24 0.56	-	-	-	-	-	-	-	-	-	-	-	-	-	-	-	-	-	-	-	-	-	-	-
Vigo County	27,639 67.42	423	143 33.81 33.81 0.52	-	-	-	-	-	-	-	-	-	-	-	-	-	-	-	-	-	-	-	-	-	-	-
Wayne County	19,564 68.72	116	62 53.45 53.45 0.32	-	-	-	-	-	-	-	-	-	-	-	-	-	-	-	-	-	-	-	-	-	-	-
IOWA	831,427 72.34	10,093	4,507 44.65 44.65 0.54	284	100 35.21 35.21 0.01	794 40.66 17.62 7.87 0.10	-	143 72.59 3.17 1.42 0.02	677 33.66 15.02 6.71 0.08	-	332 55.33 7.37 3.29 0.04	-	-	-	-	179 39.25 3.97 1.77 0.02	256 24.88 5.68 2.54 0.03	647 64.12 14.36 6.41 0.08	-	48 44.04 1.07 0.48 0.01	-	-	70 42.42 1.55 0.69 0.01	143 52.57 3.17 1.42 0.02	-	980 57.14 21.74 9.71 0.12
Black Hawk County	34,239 68.91	417	178 42.69 42.69 0.52	-	-	-	-	-	-	-	-	-	-	-	-	-	-	-	-	-	-	-	-	-	-	-
Buena Vista County[4]	5,289 70.53	235	99 42.13 42.13 1.87	-	-	-	-	-	-	-	-	-	-	-	-	-	-	80 55.94 80.81 34.04 1.51	-	-	-	-	-	-	-	-
Storm Lake (city)	2,223 63.55	206	92 44.66 44.66 4.14	-	-	-	-	-	-	-	-	-	-	-	-	-	-	76 58.02 82.61 36.89 3.42	-	-	-	-	-	-	-	-

Notes: Please refer to the User's Guide for an explanation of data; data is arranged alphabetically by state, then county, then city within each county; table includes counties with populations greater than 49,999 unless noted and cities with populations greater than 9,999 whose Asian and/or NHPI population rates are greater than the national average; (1) Native Hawaiian and other Pacific Islander; (2) excludes Taiwanese; (3) includes Chamorro; (4) county does not meet population threshold but is shown in order to allow inclusion of city

Place	All owner-occupied housing units	Asian-occupied housing units	Asians who own and occupy their own homes	NHPI[1]-occupied housing units	NHPIs[1] who own and occupy their own homes	Asian Indian	Bangladeshi	Cambodian	Chinese[2]	Fijian	Filipino	Guamanian[3]	Hawaiian, Native	Hmong	Indonesian	Japanese	Korean	Laotian	Malaysian	Pakistani	Samoan	Sri Lankan	Taiwanese	Thai	Tongan	Vietnamese
Johnson County	24,986 56.68	1,684	408 24.23 24.23 1.63	-	-	99 31.63 24.26 5.88 0.40	-	-	110 17.35 26.96 6.53 0.44	-	-	-	-	-	-	-	14 5.38 3.43 0.83 0.06	-	-	-	-	-	-	-	-	-
Coralville (city)	3,159 48.99	240	64 26.67 26.67 2.03	-	-	-	-	-	-	-	-	-	-	-	-	-	-	-	-	-	-	-	-	-	-	-
Iowa City (city)	11,749 46.63	1,371	294 21.44 21.44 2.50	-	-	69 30.13 23.47 5.03 0.59	-	-	88 15.44 29.93 6.42 0.75	-	-	-	-	-	-	-	14 7.11 4.76 1.02 0.12	-	-	-	-	-	-	-	-	-
Linn County	55,821 72.73	789	389 49.30 49.30 0.70	-	-	101 28.06 25.96 12.80 0.18	-	-	-	-	-	-	-	-	-	-	13 20.31 3.34 1.65 0.02	-	-	-	-	-	-	-	-	-
Polk County	102,623 68.82	2,512	1,382 55.02 55.02 1.35	-	-	183 41.40 13.24 7.29 0.18	-	81 75.70 5.86 3.22 0.08	208 56.37 15.05 8.28 0.20	-	-	-	-	-	-	-	77 57.04 5.57 3.07 0.08	254 65.97 18.38 10.11 0.25	-	-	-	-	-	67 61.47 4.85 2.67 0.07	-	361 54.61 26.12 14.37 0.35
Pottawattamie County	24,052 71.07	152	79 51.97 51.97 0.33	-	-	-	-	-	-	-	-	-	-	-	-	-	-	-	-	-	-	-	-	-	-	-
Scott County	43,950 70.51	663	330 49.77 49.77 0.75	-	-	-	-	-	-	-	-	-	-	-	-	-	-	-	-	-	-	-	-	-	-	136 55.97 41.21 20.51 0.31
Story County	17,123 58.28	1,325	242 18.26 18.26 1.41	-	-	110 47.83 45.45 8.30 0.64	-	-	39 8.76 16.12 2.94 0.23	-	-	-	-	-	-	-	18 6.87 7.44 1.36 0.11	-	-	-	-	-	-	-	-	-
Ames (city)	8,326 46.14	1,278	222 17.37 17.37 2.67	-	-	99 46.48 44.59 7.75 1.19	-	-	32 7.31 14.41 2.50 0.38	-	-	-	-	-	-	-	18 7.09 8.11 1.41 0.22	-	-	-	-	-	-	-	-	-
Woodbury County	26,859 68.60	527	309 58.63 58.63 1.15	-	-	-	-	-	-	-	-	-	-	-	-	-	-	-	-	-	-	-	-	-	-	166 55.52 53.72 31.50 0.62

Notes: Please refer to the User's Guide for an explanation of data; data is arranged alphabetically by state, then county, then city within each county; table includes counties with populations greater than 49,999 unless noted and cities with populations greater than 9,999 whose Asian and/or NHPI population rates are greater than the national average; (1) Native Hawaiian and other Pacific Islander; (2) excludes Taiwanese; (3) includes Chamorro; (4) county does not meet population threshold but is shown in order to allow inclusion of city

Place	All owner-occupied housing units	Asian-occupied housing units	Asians who own and occupy their own homes	NHPI[1]-occupied housing units	NHPIs[1] who own and occupy their own homes	Asian Indian	Bangladeshi	Cambodian	Chinese[2]	Fijian	Filipino	Guamanian[3]	Hawaiian, Native	Hmong	Indonesian	Japanese	Korean	Laotian	Malaysian	Pakistani	Samoan	Sri Lankan	Taiwanese	Thai	Tongan	Vietnamese
KANSAS	718,873 69.26	14,031	7,038 50.16 50.16 0.98	395	191 48.35 48.35 0.03	1,227 44.06 17.43 8.74 0.17	-	116 58.88 1.65 0.83 0.02	1,194 47.18 16.97 8.51 0.17	-	509 49.80 7.23 3.63 0.07	-	65 44.52 34.03 16.46 0.01	107 61.49 1.52 0.76 0.01	-	389 49.49 5.53 2.77 0.05	502 43.46 7.13 3.58 0.07	584 71.05 8.30 4.16 0.08	-	94 34.43 1.34 0.67 0.01	-	-	87 43.94 1.24 0.62 0.01	73 28.29 1.04 0.52 0.01	-	1,908 62.78 27.11 13.60 0.27
Cowley County[4]	9,949 70.87	190	118 62.11 62.11 1.19	-	-	-	-	-	-	-	-	-	-	-	-	-	-	96 74.42 81.36 50.53 0.96	-	-	-	-	-	-	-	-
Winfield (city)	3,049 65.65	170	112 65.88 65.88 3.67	-	-	-	-	-	-	-	-	-	-	-	-	-	-	96 76.19 85.71 56.47 3.15	-	-	-	-	-	-	-	-
Douglas County	19,972 51.89	1,182	278 23.52 23.52 1.39	-	-	43 21.39 15.47 3.64 0.22	-	-	89 29.67 32.01 7.53 0.45	-	-	-	-	-	-	-	0 0.00 0.00 0.00 0.00	-	-	-	-	-	-	-	-	-
Lawrence (city)	14,412 45.85	1,177	278 23.62 23.62 1.93	-	-	43 21.39 15.47 3.65 0.30	-	-	89 29.67 32.01 7.56 0.62	-	-	-	-	-	-	-	0 0.00 0.00 0.00 0.00	-	-	-	-	-	-	-	-	-
Johnson County	126,231 72.31	4,141	2,094 50.57 50.57 1.66	-	-	686 46.92 32.76 16.57 0.54	-	-	562 59.66 26.84 13.57 0.45	-	146 48.50 6.97 3.53 0.12	-	-	-	-	95 45.02 4.54 2.29 0.08	198 53.23 9.46 4.78 0.16	84 50.91 4.01 2.03 0.07	-	-	-	-	-	-	-	211 64.72 10.08 5.10 0.17
Overland Park (city)	40,732 68.18	1,990	907 45.58 45.58 2.23	-	-	240 31.87 26.46 12.06 0.59	-	-	269 54.67 29.66 13.52 0.66	-	-	-	-	-	-	-	114 58.76 12.57 5.73 0.28	-	-	-	-	-	-	-	-	109 80.15 12.02 5.48 0.27
Leavenworth County	15,450 66.97	140	87 62.14 62.14 0.56	-	-	-	-	-	-	-	-	-	-	-	-	-	-	-	-	-	-	-	-	-	-	-
Riley County	10,464 47.27	639	163 25.51 25.51 1.56	-	-	-	-	-	44 17.25 26.99 6.89 0.42	-	-	-	-	-	-	-	29 25.44 17.79 4.54 0.28	-	-	-	-	-	-	-	-	-
Manhattan (city)	7,337 43.21	581	150 25.82 25.82 2.04	-	-	-	-	-	39 15.79 26.00 6.71 0.53	-	-	-	-	-	-	-	-	-	-	-	-	-	-	-	-	-

Notes: Please refer to the User's Guide for an explanation of data; data is arranged alphabetically by state, then county, then city within each county; table includes counties with populations greater than 49,999 unless noted and cities with populations greater than 9,999 whose Asian and/or NHPI population rates are greater than the national average; (1) Native Hawaiian and other Pacific Islander; (2) excludes Taiwanese; (3) includes Chamorro; (4) county does not meet population threshold but is shown in order to allow inclusion of city

Place	All owner-occupied housing units	Asian-occupied housing units	Asians who own and occupy their own homes	NHPI[1]-occupied housing units	NHPIs[1] who own and occupy their own homes	Asian Indian	Bangladeshi	Cambodian	Chinese[2]	Fijian	Filipino	Guamanian[3]	Hawaiian, Native	Hmong	Indonesian	Japanese	Korean	Laotian	Malaysian	Pakistani	Samoan	Sri Lankan	Taiwanese	Thai	Tongan	Vietnamese
Saline County	14,799 69.04	224	146 65.18 65.18 0.99	-	-	-	-	-	-	-	-	-	-	-	-	-	-	-	-	-	-	-	-	-	-	63 67.74 43.15 28.13 0.43
Sedgwick County	116,738 66.16	4,338	2,371 54.66 54.66 2.03	157	87 55.41 55.41 0.07	189 39.62 7.97 4.36 0.16	-	66 48.18 2.78 1.52 0.06	275 45.38 11.60 6.34 0.24	-	130 64.36 5.48 3.00 0.11	-	-	-	-	-	74 45.68 3.12 1.71 0.06	212 77.94 8.94 4.89 0.18	-	-	-	-	-	-	-	1,161 62.55 48.97 26.76 0.99
Wichita (city)	85,659 61.62	3,923	2,057 52.43 52.43 2.40	-	-	165 37.16 8.02 4.21 0.19	-	-	238 42.20 11.57 6.07 0.28	-	115 63.54 5.59 2.93 0.13	-	-	-	-	-	59 42.75 2.87 1.50 0.07	158 83.16 7.68 4.03 0.18	-	-	-	-	-	-	-	1,088 61.57 52.89 27.73 1.27
Shawnee County	46,522 67.50	544	284 52.21 52.21 0.61	-	-	-	-	-	-	-	-	-	-	-	-	-	-	-	-	-	-	-	-	-	-	-
Wyandotte County	37,531 62.87	711	333 46.84 46.84 0.89	-	-	-	-	-	-	-	-	-	-	89 65.44 26.73 12.52 0.24	-	-	-	-	-	-	-	-	-	-	-	-
KENTUCKY	1,125,298 70.74	9,105	3,893 42.76 42.76 0.35	292	79 27.05 27.05 0.01	971 40.31 24.94 10.66 0.09	-	-	706 40.34 18.14 7.75 0.06	-	492 55.10 12.64 5.40 0.04	27 32.93 34.18 9.25 <0.01	-	-	-	408 31.73 10.48 4.48 0.04	441 47.78 11.33 4.84 0.04	-	-	95 52.20 2.44 1.04 0.01	-	-	-	47 33.10 1.21 0.52 <0.01	-	443 54.22 11.38 4.87 0.04
Boone County	23,196 74.21	313	105 33.55 33.55 0.45	-	-	-	-	-	-	-	-	-	-	-	-	9 6.57 8.57 2.88 0.04	-	-	-	-	-	-	-	-	-	-
Campbell County	23,973 69.00	178	113 63.48 63.48 0.47	-	-	-	-	-	-	-	-	-	-	-	-	-	-	-	-	-	-	-	-	-	-	-
Christian County	13,742 55.28	137	49 35.77 35.77 0.36	-	-	-	-	-	-	-	-	-	-	-	-	-	-	-	-	-	-	-	-	-	-	-
Fayette County	59,915 55.33	2,008	643 32.02 32.02 1.07	-	-	158 31.92 24.57 7.87 0.26	-	-	157 25.99 24.42 7.82 0.26	-	-	-	-	-	-	95 28.02 14.77 4.73 0.16	-	-	-	-	-	-	-	-	-	-

Notes: Please refer to the User's Guide for an explanation of data; data is arranged alphabetically by state, then county, then city within each county; table includes counties with populations greater than 49,999 unless noted and cities with populations greater than 9,999 whose Asian and/or NHPI population rates are greater than the national average; (1) Native Hawaiian and other Pacific Islander; (2) excludes Taiwanese; (3) includes Chamorro; (4) county does not meet population threshold but is shown in order to allow inclusion of city

Place	All owner-occupied housing units	Asian-occupied housing units	Asians who own and occupy their own homes	NHPI[1]-occupied housing units	NHPIs[1] who own and occupy their own homes	Asian Indian	Bangladeshi	Cambodian	Chinese[2]	Fijian	Filipino	Guamanian[3]	Hawaiian, Native	Hmong	Indonesian	Japanese	Korean	Laotian	Malaysian	Pakistani	Samoan	Sri Lankan	Taiwanese	Thai	Tongan	Vietnamese
Hardin County	23,075 66.89	465	241 51.83 51.83 1.04	-	-	-	-	-	-	-	-	-	-	-	-	-	95 64.63 39.42 20.43 0.41	-	-	-	-	-	-	-	-	-
Radcliff (city)	4,865 57.50	261	141 54.02 54.02 2.90	-	-	-	-	-	-	-	-	-	-	-	-	-	-	-	-	-	-	-	-	-	-	-
Jefferson County	186,358 64.93	3,097	1,456 47.01 47.01 0.78	-	-	332 33.13 22.80 10.72 0.18	-	-	272 53.33 18.68 8.78 0.15	-	211 61.34 14.49 6.81 0.11	-	-	-	-	117 66.10 8.04 3.78 0.06	135 40.42 9.27 4.36 0.07	-	-	-	-	-	-	-	-	252 56.00 17.31 8.14 0.14
Kenton County	39,442 66.35	233	96 41.20 41.20 0.24	-	-	-	-	-	-	-	-	-	-	-	-	-	-	-	-	-	-	-	-	-	-	-
Madison County	16,216 59.72	157	75 47.77 47.77 0.46	-	-	-	-	-	-	-	-	-	-	-	-	-	-	-	-	-	-	-	-	-	-	-
Warren County	22,643 64.03	324	131 40.43 40.43 0.58	-	-	-	-	-	-	-	-	-	-	-	-	-	-	-	-	-	-	-	-	-	-	-
LOUISIANA	1,124,995 67.93	16,221	8,556 52.75 52.75 0.76	406	240 59.11 59.11 0.02	1,355 44.44 15.84 8.35 0.12	-	-	1,103 44.80 12.89 6.80 0.10	-	868 60.87 10.14 5.35 0.08	125 69.44 52.08 30.79 0.01	70 61.40 29.17 17.24 0.01	-	-	220 42.55 2.57 1.36 0.02	344 43.77 4.02 2.12 0.03	233 85.35 2.72 1.44 0.02	-	97 29.22 1.13 0.60 0.01	-	-	113 62.78 1.32 0.70 0.01	116 57.14 1.36 0.72 0.01	-	3,776 60.06 44.13 23.28 0.34
Ascension Parish	21,952 82.24	104	91 87.50 87.50 0.41	-	-	-	-	-	-	-	-	-	-	-	-	-	-	-	-	-	-	-	-	-	-	-
Bossier Parish	25,442 69.46	304	147 48.36 48.36 0.58	-	-	-	-	-	-	-	-	-	-	-	-	-	-	-	-	-	-	-	-	-	-	-
Caddo Parish	62,546 63.84	654	329 50.31 50.31 0.53	-	-	70 37.63 21.28 10.70 0.11	-	-	-	-	-	-	-	-	-	-	-	-	-	-	-	-	-	-	-	-

Notes: Please refer to the User's Guide for an explanation of data; data is arranged alphabetically by state, then county, then city within each county; table includes counties with populations greater than 49,999 unless noted and cities with populations greater than 9,999 whose Asian and/or NHPI population rates are greater than the national average; (1) Native Hawaiian and other Pacific Islander; (2) excludes Taiwanese; (3) includes Chamorro; (4) county does not meet population threshold but is shown in order to allow inclusion of city

Place	All owner-occupied housing units	Asian-occupied housing units	Asians who own and occupy their own homes	NHPI[1]-occupied housing units	NHPIs[1] who own and occupy their own homes	Asian Indian	Bangladeshi	Cambodian	Chinese[2]	Fijian	Filipino	Guamanian[3]	Hawaiian, Native	Hmong	Indonesian	Japanese	Korean	Laotian	Malaysian	Pakistani	Samoan	Sri Lankan	Taiwanese	Thai	Tongan	Vietnamese
Calcasieu Parish	49,085 71.54	292	138 47.26 47.26 0.28	-	-	-	-	-	-	-	-	-	-	-	-	-	-	-	-	-	-	-	-	-	-	-
East Baton Rouge Parish	96,305 61.59	2,813	1,180 41.95 41.95 1.23	-	-	303 41.56 25.68 10.77 0.31	-	-	278 43.23 23.56 9.88 0.29	-	47 37.60 3.98 1.67 0.05	-	-	-	-	-	-	-	-	-	-	-	-	-	-	420 45.50 35.59 14.93 0.44
Iberia Parish	18,628 73.39	268	229 85.45 85.45 1.23	-	-	-	-	-	-	-	-	-	-	-	-	-	-	117 84.78 51.09 43.66 0.63	-	-	-	-	-	-	-	64 87.67 27.95 23.88 0.34
Jefferson Parish	112,534 63.85	4,178	2,386 57.11 57.11 2.12	-	-	257 39.18 10.77 6.15 0.23	-	-	317 46.62 13.29 7.59 0.28	-	225 69.02 9.43 5.39 0.20	-	-	-	-	-	144 73.10 6.04 3.45 0.13	-	-	46 27.71 1.93 1.10 0.04	-	-	-	-	-	1,195 69.44 50.08 28.60 1.06
Gretna (city)	3,458 49.96	187	80 42.78 42.78 2.31	-	-	-	-	-	-	-	-	-	-	-	-	-	-	-	-	-	-	-	-	-	-	29 27.88 36.25 15.51 0.84
Harvey (cdp)	4,543 57.46	301	198 65.78 65.78 4.36	-	-	-	-	-	-	-	-	-	-	-	-	-	-	-	-	-	-	-	-	-	-	131 65.83 66.16 43.52 2.88
Timberlane (cdp)	3,025 75.27	124	107 86.29 86.29 3.54	-	-	-	-	-	-	-	-	-	-	-	-	-	-	-	-	-	-	-	-	-	-	95 84.82 88.79 76.61 3.14
Woodmere (cdp)	3,169 84.91	168	151 89.88 89.88 4.76	-	-	-	-	-	-	-	-	-	-	-	-	-	-	-	-	-	-	-	-	-	-	90 84.11 59.60 53.57 2.84
Lafayette Parish	47,803 66.05	707	309 43.71 43.71 0.65	-	-	65 28.51 21.04 9.19 0.14	-	-	-	-	-	-	-	-	-	-	-	-	-	-	-	-	-	-	-	120 65.22 38.83 16.97 0.25
Lafourche Parish	24,988 77.95	159	128 80.50 80.50 0.51	-	-	-	-	-	-	-	-	-	-	-	-	-	-	-	-	-	-	-	-	-	-	-

Notes: Please refer to the User's Guide for an explanation of data; data is arranged alphabetically by state, then county, then city within each county; table includes counties with populations greater than 49,999 unless noted and cities with populations greater than 9,999 whose Asian and/or NHPI population rates are greater than the national average; (1) Native Hawaiian and other Pacific Islander; (2) excludes Taiwanese; (3) includes Chamorro; (4) county does not meet population threshold but is shown in order to allow inclusion of city

Place	All owner-occupied housing units	Asian-occupied housing units	Asians who own and occupy their own homes	NHPI[1]-occupied housing units	NHPIs[1] who own and occupy their own homes	Asian Indian	Bangladeshi	Cambodian	Chinese[2]	Fijian	Filipino	Guamanian[3]	Hawaiian, Native	Hmong	Indonesian	Japanese	Korean	Laotian	Malaysian	Pakistani	Samoan	Sri Lankan	Taiwanese	Thai	Tongan	Vietnamese
Orleans Parish	87,535 46.50	3,066	1,350 44.03 44.03 1.54	-	-	144 34.37 10.67 4.70 0.16	-	-	127 35.57 9.41 4.14 0.15	-	60 32.43 4.44 1.96 0.07	-	-	-	-	-	-	-	-	-	-	-	-	-	-	917 54.36 67.93 29.91 1.05
Ouachita Parish	35,412 64.13	315	173 54.92 54.92 0.49	-	-	-	-	-	-	-	-	-	-	-	-	-	-	-	-	-	-	-	-	-	-	-
Rapides Parish	32,055 68.03	269	150 55.76 55.76 0.47	-	-	-	-	-	-	-	-	-	-	-	-	-	-	-	-	-	-	-	-	-	-	-
St. Bernard Parish	18,758 74.66	295	181 61.36 61.36 0.96	-	-	-	-	-	-	-	-	-	-	-	-	-	-	-	-	-	-	-	-	-	-	59 53.64 32.60 20.00 0.31
St. Mary Parish	14,275 73.90	242	172 71.07 71.07 1.20	-	-	-	-	-	-	-	-	-	-	-	-	-	-	-	-	-	-	-	-	-	-	155 71.76 90.12 64.05 1.09
St. Tammany Parish	55,732 80.48	326	240 73.62 73.62 0.43	-	-	-	-	-	-	-	-	-	-	-	-	-	-	-	-	-	-	-	-	-	-	47 58.75 19.58 14.42 0.08
Terrebonne Parish	27,193 75.54	260	188 72.31 72.31 0.69	-	-	-	-	-	-	-	-	-	-	-	-	-	-	-	-	-	-	-	-	-	-	76 59.84 40.43 29.23 0.28
Vermilion Parish	15,267 76.98	213	122 57.28 57.28 0.80	-	-	-	-	-	-	-	-	-	-	-	-	-	-	-	-	-	-	-	-	-	-	114 61.29 93.44 53.52 0.75
Abbeville (city)	2,737 60.19	125	71 56.80 56.80 2.59	-	-	-	-	-	-	-	-	-	-	-	-	-	-	-	-	-	-	-	-	-	-	71 60.17 100.00 56.80 2.59
Vernon Parish	10,360 56.74	303	107 35.31 35.31 1.03	-	-	-	-	-	-	-	-	-	-	-	-	-	48 48.48 44.86 15.84 0.46	-	-	-	-	-	-	-	-	-

Notes: Please refer to the User's Guide for an explanation of data; data is arranged alphabetically by state, then county, then city within each county; table includes counties with populations greater than 49,999 unless noted and cities with populations greater than 9,999 whose Asian and/or NHPI population rates are greater than the national average; (1) Native Hawaiian and other Pacific Islander; (2) excludes Taiwanese; (3) includes Chamorro; (4) county does not meet population threshold but is shown in order to allow inclusion of city

Place	All owner-occupied housing units	Asian-occupied housing units	Asians who own and occupy their own homes	NHPI[1]-occupied housing units	NHPIs[1] who own and occupy their own homes	Asian Indian	Bangladeshi	Cambodian	Chinese[2]	Fijian	Filipino	Guamanian[3]	Hawaiian, Native	Hmong	Indonesian	Japanese	Korean	Laotian	Malaysian	Pakistani	Samoan	Sri Lankan	Taiwanese	Thai	Tongan	Vietnamese
MAINE	370,920 71.58	2,191	987 45.05 45.05 0.27	88	49 55.68 55.68 0.01	135 47.20 13.68 6.16 0.04	-	89 37.55 9.02 4.06 0.02	242 54.75 24.52 11.05 0.07	-	161 54.58 16.31 7.35 0.04	-	-	-	-	91 52.91 9.22 4.15 0.02	63 36.21 6.38 2.88 0.02	-	-	-	-	-	-	-	-	128 37.76 12.97 5.84 0.03
Androscoggin County	26,655 63.42	87	49 56.32 56.32 0.18	-	-	-	-	-	-	-	-	-	-	-	-	-	-	-	-	-	-	-	-	-	-	-
Aroostook County	22,179 73.06	103	25 24.27 24.27 0.11	-	-	-	-	-	-	-	-	-	-	-	-	-	-	-	-	-	-	-	-	-	-	-
Cumberland County	72,066 66.73	942	367 38.96 38.96 0.51	-	-	-	-	47 27.98 12.81 4.99 0.07	59 54.63 16.08 6.26 0.08	-	72 66.06 19.62 7.64 0.10	-	-	-	-	-	-	-	-	-	-	-	-	-	-	62 29.95 16.89 6.58 0.09
Hancock County	16,532 75.61	57	33 57.89 57.89 0.20	-	-	-	-	-	-	-	-	-	-	-	-	-	-	-	-	-	-	-	-	-	-	-
Kennebec County	33,947 71.19	201	101 50.25 50.25 0.30	-	-	-	-	-	-	-	-	-	-	-	-	-	-	-	-	-	-	-	-	-	-	-
Oxford County	17,176 76.97	59	25 42.37 42.37 0.15	-	-	-	-	-	-	-	-	-	-	-	-	-	-	-	-	-	-	-	-	-	-	-
Penobscot County	40,542 69.78	273	137 50.18 50.18 0.34	-	-	-	-	-	48 58.54 35.04 17.58 0.12	-	-	-	-	-	-	-	-	-	-	-	-	-	-	-	-	-
York County	54,170 72.65	230	136 59.13 59.13 0.25	-	-	-	-	-	-	-	-	-	-	-	-	-	-	-	-	-	-	-	-	-	-	-
MARYLAND	1,341,594 67.73	63,349	38,662 61.03 61.03 2.88	466	226 48.50 48.50 0.02	9,287 58.63 24.02 14.66 0.69	196 58.86 0.51 0.31 0.01	288 63.72 0.74 0.45 0.02	10,380 67.25 26.85 16.39 0.77	-	5,103 68.60 13.20 8.06 0.38	110 60.11 48.67 23.61 0.01	71 54.62 31.42 15.24 0.01	-	159 51.29 0.41 0.25 0.01	1,203 49.63 3.11 1.90 0.09	6,361 54.82 16.45 10.04 0.47	122 60.40 0.32 0.19 0.01	-	692 52.74 1.79 1.09 0.05	-	303 74.63 0.78 0.48 0.02	501 62.24 1.30 0.79 0.04	544 64.92 1.41 0.86 0.04	-	2,646 63.67 6.84 4.18 0.20

Notes: Please refer to the User's Guide for an explanation of data; data is arranged alphabetically by state, then county, then city within each county; table includes counties with populations greater than 49,999 unless noted and cities with populations greater than 9,999 whose Asian and/or NHPI population rates are greater than the national average; (1) Native Hawaiian and other Pacific Islander; (2) excludes Taiwanese; (3) includes Chamorro; (4) county does not meet population threshold but is shown in order to allow inclusion of city

Place	All owner-occupied housing units	Asian-occupied housing units	Asians who own and occupy their own homes	NHPI[1]-occupied housing units	NHPIs[1] who own and occupy their own homes	Asian Indian	Bangladeshi	Cambodian	Chinese[2]	Fijian	Filipino	Guamanian[3]	Hawaiian, Native	Hmong	Indonesian	Japanese	Korean	Laotian	Malaysian	Pakistani	Samoan	Sri Lankan	Taiwanese	Thai	Tongan	Vietnamese
Allegany County	20,569 70.15	108	79 73.15 73.15 0.38	-	-	-	-	-	-	-	-	-	-	-	-	-	-	-	-	-	-	-	-	-	-	-
Anne Arundel County	134,922 75.51	3,124	1,807 57.84 57.84 1.34	-	-	252 46.67 13.95 8.07 0.19	-	-	315 71.59 17.43 10.08 0.23	-	469 69.28 25.95 15.01 0.35	-	-	-	-	151 68.64 8.36 4.83 0.11	458 48.52 25.35 14.66 0.34	-	-	-	-	-	-	-	-	-
Severn (cdp)	8,834 73.39	432	295 68.29 68.29 3.34	-	-	-	-	-	-	-	-	-	-	-	-	-	115 53.49 38.98 26.62 1.30	-	-	-	-	-	-	-	-	-
South Gate (cdp)	5,663 50.12	455	163 35.82 35.82 2.88	-	-	-	-	-	-	-	-	-	-	-	-	-	58 25.44 35.58 12.75 1.02	-	-	-	-	-	-	-	-	-
Baltimore Independent City	129,879 50.34	4,135	1,234 29.84 29.84 0.95	-	-	226 23.94 18.31 5.47 0.17	-	-	258 26.57 20.91 6.24 0.20	-	250 55.19 20.26 6.05 0.19	-	-	-	-	-	168 19.95 13.61 4.06 0.13	-	-	-	-	-	-	-	-	120 72.73 9.72 2.90 0.09
Baltimore County	202,574 67.55	7,307	3,954 54.11 54.11 1.95	-	-	971 49.26 24.56 13.29 0.48	-	-	800 52.91 20.23 10.95 0.39	-	752 71.69 19.02 10.29 0.37	-	-	-	-	65 27.54 1.64 0.89 0.03	796 57.23 20.13 10.89 0.39	-	-	103 35.40 2.60 1.41 0.05	-	-	-	-	-	190 61.49 4.81 2.60 0.09
Arbutus (cdp)	5,615 69.15	423	82 19.39 19.39 1.46	-	-	-	-	-	-	-	-	-	-	-	-	-	-	-	-	-	-	-	-	-	-	-
Carney (cdp)	7,230 59.89	527	258 48.96 48.96 3.57	-	-	-	-	-	43 37.07 16.67 8.16 0.59	-	-	-	-	-	-	-	84 39.44 32.56 15.94 1.16	-	-	-	-	-	-	-	-	-
Cockeysville (cdp)	3,064 33.38	629	173 27.50 27.50 5.65	-	-	-	-	-	-	-	-	-	-	-	-	-	42 18.18 24.28 6.68 1.37	-	-	-	-	-	-	-	-	-
Lutherville-Timonium (cdp)	5,346 82.63	219	183 83.56 83.56 3.42	-	-	-	-	-	-	-	-	-	-	-	-	-	-	-	-	-	-	-	-	-	-	-

Notes: Please refer to the User's Guide for an explanation of data; data is arranged alphabetically by state, then county, then city within each county; table includes counties with populations greater than 49,999 unless noted and cities with populations greater than 9,999 whose Asian and/or NHPI population rates are greater than the national average; (1) Native Hawaiian and other Pacific Islander; (2) excludes Taiwanese; (3) includes Chamorro; (4) county does not meet population threshold but is shown in order to allow inclusion of city

Place	All owner-occupied housing units	Asian-occupied housing units	Asians who own and occupy their own homes	NHPI[1]-occupied housing units	NHPIs[1] who own and occupy their own homes	Asian Indian	Bangladeshi	Cambodian	Chinese[2]	Fijian	Filipino	Guamanian[3]	Hawaiian, Native	Hmong	Indonesian	Japanese	Korean	Laotian	Malaysian	Pakistani	Samoan	Sri Lankan	Taiwanese	Thai	Tongan	Vietnamese
Mays Chapel (cdp)	4,026 86.17	248	238 95.97 95.97 5.91	-	-	-	-	-	-	-	-	-	-	-	-	-	-	-	-	-	-	-	-	-	-	-
Owings Mills (cdp)	4,283 48.29	268	100 37.31 37.31 2.33	-	-	-	-	-	-	-	-	-	-	-	-	-	-	-	-	-	-	-	-	-	-	-
Perry Hall (cdp)	8,756 77.33	417	309 74.10 74.10 3.53	-	-	-	-	-	-	-	-	-	-	-	-	-	88 63.77 28.48 21.10 1.01	-	-	-	-	-	-	-	-	-
Reisterstown (cdp)	5,613 64.48	313	186 59.42 59.42 3.31	-	-	88 51.76 47.31 28.12 1.57	-	-	-	-	-	-	-	-	-	-	-	-	-	-	-	-	-	-	-	-
Rossville (cdp)	2,287 47.11	207	73 35.27 35.27 3.19	-	-	-	-	-	-	-	-	-	-	-	-	-	-	-	-	-	-	-	-	-	-	-
Towson (cdp)	12,566 59.59	588	204 34.69 34.69 1.62	-	-	-	-	-	102 39.08 50.00 17.35 0.81	-	-	-	-	-	-	-	-	-	-	-	-	-	-	-	-	-
Woodlawn (cdp)	9,445 67.66	554	277 50.00 50.00 2.93	-	-	83 34.58 29.96 14.98 0.88	-	-	-	-	-	-	-	-	-	-	-	-	-	-	-	-	-	-	-	-
Calvert County	21,676 85.18	177	160 90.40 90.40 0.74	-	-	-	-	-	-	-	-	-	-	-	-	-	-	-	-	-	-	-	-	-	-	-
Carroll County	43,037 81.97	327	257 78.59 78.59 0.60	-	-	-	-	-	-	-	-	-	-	-	-	-	-	-	-	-	-	-	-	-	-	-
Cecil County	23,395 74.93	148	102 68.92 68.92 0.44	-	-	-	-	-	-	-	-	-	-	-	-	-	-	-	-	-	-	-	-	-	-	-

Notes: Please refer to the User's Guide for an explanation of data; data is arranged alphabetically by state, then county, then city within each county; table includes counties with populations greater than 49,999 unless noted and cities with populations greater than 9,999 whose Asian and/or NHPI population rates are greater than the national average; (1) Native Hawaiian and other Pacific Islander; (2) excludes Taiwanese; (3) includes Chamorro; (4) county does not meet population threshold but is shown in order to allow inclusion of city

Place	All owner-occupied housing units	Asian-occupied housing units	Asians who own and occupy their own homes	NHPI[1]-occupied housing units	NHPIs[1] who own and occupy their own homes	Asian Indian	Bangladeshi	Cambodian	Chinese[2]	Fijian	Filipino	Guamanian[3]	Hawaiian, Native	Hmong	Indonesian	Japanese	Korean	Laotian	Malaysian	Pakistani	Samoan	Sri Lankan	Taiwanese	Thai	Tongan	Vietnamese
Charles County	32,567 78.16	391	302 77.24 77.24 0.93	-	-	-	-	-	-	-	93 76.23 30.79 23.79 0.29	-	-	-	-	-	-	-	-	-	-	-	-	-	-	-
Frederick County	53,138 75.85	824	502 60.92 60.92 0.94	-	-	140 67.96 27.89 16.99 0.26	-	-	138 57.26 27.49 16.75 0.26	-	-	-	-	-	-	-	36 48.65 7.17 4.37 0.07	-	-	-	-	-	-	-	-	-
Harford County	62,119 77.97	730	529 72.47 72.47 0.85	-	-	114 78.62 21.55 15.62 0.18	-	-	-	-	80 61.54 15.12 10.96 0.13	-	-	-	-	-	107 59.78 20.23 14.66 0.17	-	-	-	-	-	-	-	-	-
Howard County	66,414 73.76	5,571	3,722 66.81 66.81 5.60	-	-	942 66.48 25.31 16.91 1.42	-	-	939 77.80 25.23 16.86 1.41	-	305 73.85 8.19 5.47 0.46	-	-	-	-	-	951 56.47 25.55 17.07 1.43	-	-	98 68.06 2.63 1.76 0.15	-	-	-	-	-	175 76.42 4.70 3.14 0.26
Columbia (cdp)	22,566 66.00	2,066	1,229 59.49 59.49 5.45	-	-	324 55.10 26.36 15.68 1.44	-	-	392 71.14 31.90 18.97 1.74	-	99 61.88 8.06 4.79 0.44	-	-	-	-	-	230 49.15 18.71 11.13 1.02	-	-	-	-	-	-	-	-	-
Elkridge (cdp)	6,447 77.43	399	276 69.17 69.17 4.28	-	-	-	-	-	-	-	-	-	-	-	-	-	70 64.22 25.36 17.54 1.09	-	-	-	-	-	-	-	-	-
Ellicott City (cdp)	15,114 74.71	1,919	1,240 64.62 64.62 8.20	-	-	222 65.49 17.90 11.57 1.47	-	-	310 80.10 25.00 16.15 2.05	-	87 74.36 7.02 4.53 0.58	-	-	-	-	-	421 53.63 33.95 21.94 2.79	-	-	58 64.44 4.68 3.02 0.38	-	-	-	-	-	-
North Laurel (cdp)	5,164 71.09	484	351 72.52 72.52 6.80	-	-	121 75.16 34.47 25.00 2.34	-	-	-	-	-	-	-	-	-	-	62 50.41 17.66 12.81 1.20	-	-	-	-	-	-	-	-	-
Savage-Guilford (cdp)	2,986 62.65	166	89 53.61 53.61 2.98	-	-	-	-	-	-	-	-	-	-	-	-	-	-	-	-	-	-	-	-	-	-	-
Montgomery County	223,008 68.71	30,160	20,027 66.40 66.40 8.98	119	43 36.13 36.13 0.02	5,027 64.82 25.10 16.67 2.25	155 66.52 0.77 0.51 0.07	219 69.52 1.09 0.73 0.10	6,628 73.92 33.10 21.98 2.97	-	1,142 59.82 5.70 3.79 0.51	-	-	-	128 51.41 0.64 0.42 0.06	593 47.59 2.96 1.97 0.27	3,050 63.86 15.23 10.11 1.37	-	-	314 70.09 1.57 1.04 0.14	-	205 82.66 1.02 0.68 0.09	342 86.15 1.71 1.13 0.15	299 73.11 1.49 0.99 0.13	-	1,533 62.85 7.65 5.08 0.69

Notes: Please refer to the User's Guide for an explanation of data; data is arranged alphabetically by state, then county, then city within each county; table includes counties with populations greater than 49,999 unless noted and cities with populations greater than 9,999 whose Asian and/or NHPI population rates are greater than the national average; (1) Native Hawaiian and other Pacific Islander; (2) excludes Taiwanese; (3) includes Chamorro; (4) county does not meet population threshold but is shown in order to allow inclusion of city

Place	All owner-occupied housing units	Asian-occupied housing units	Asians who own and occupy their own homes	NHPI[1]-occupied housing units	NHPIs[1] who own and occupy their own homes	Asian Indian	Bangladeshi	Cambodian	Chinese[2]	Fijian	Filipino	Guamanian[3]	Hawaiian, Native	Hmong	Indonesian	Japanese	Korean	Laotian	Malaysian	Pakistani	Samoan	Sri Lankan	Taiwanese	Thai	Tongan	Vietnamese
Aspen Hill (cdp)	12,233 67.24	1,733	1,229 70.92 70.92 10.05	-	-	145 57.77 11.80 8.37 1.19	-	-	454 80.35 36.94 26.20 3.71	-	116 69.05 9.44 6.69 0.95	-	-	-	-	-	231 62.77 18.80 13.33 1.89	-	-	-	-	-	-	-	-	59 53.64 4.80 3.40 0.48
Bethesda (cdp)	16,373 69.19	1,529	859 56.18 56.18 5.25	-	-	235 69.53 27.36 15.37 1.44	-	-	227 48.50 26.43 14.85 1.39	-	51 49.51 5.94 3.34 0.31	-	-	-	-	115 56.10 13.39 7.52 0.70	131 59.28 15.25 8.57 0.80	-	-	-	-	-	-	-	-	-
Calverton (cdp)	3,462 76.27	614	473 77.04 77.04 13.66	-	-	184 78.97 38.90 29.97 5.31	-	-	-	-	-	-	-	-	-	-	116 70.30 24.52 18.89 3.35	-	-	-	-	-	-	-	-	-
Colesville (cdp)	5,999 91.92	872	808 92.66 92.66 13.47	-	-	227 100.00 28.09 26.03 3.78	-	-	181 100.00 22.40 20.76 3.02	-	-	-	-	-	-	-	244 83.56 30.20 27.98 4.07	-	-	-	-	-	-	-	-	76 87.36 9.41 8.72 1.27
Fairland (cdp)	4,075 47.37	997	595 59.68 59.68 14.60	-	-	123 44.40 20.67 12.34 3.02	-	-	147 78.19 24.71 14.74 3.61	-	-	-	-	-	-	-	219 59.67 36.81 21.97 5.37	-	-	-	-	-	-	-	-	-
Gaithersburg (city)	10,334 52.99	2,278	1,337 58.69 58.69 12.94	-	-	225 37.82 16.83 9.88 2.18	-	-	585 68.02 43.75 25.68 5.66	-	66 54.55 4.94 2.90 0.64	-	-	-	-	-	206 67.99 15.41 9.04 1.99	-	-	-	-	-	-	-	-	111 77.08 8.30 4.87 1.07
Germantown (cdp)	14,068 67.64	1,715	1,133 66.06 66.06 8.05	-	-	437 61.46 38.57 25.48 3.11	-	-	253 69.51 22.33 14.75 1.80	-	-	-	-	-	-	-	83 59.29 7.33 4.84 0.59	-	-	-	-	-	-	-	-	130 84.97 11.47 7.58 0.92
Montgomery Village (cdp)	10,196 72.07	1,420	830 58.45 58.45 8.14	-	-	257 43.78 30.96 18.10 2.52	-	-	204 70.83 24.58 14.37 2.00	-	106 62.72 12.77 7.46 1.04	-	-	-	-	-	-	-	-	-	-	-	-	-	-	80 67.80 9.64 5.63 0.78
North Bethesda (cdp)	10,201 58.93	1,739	753 43.30 43.30 7.38	-	-	154 40.10 20.45 8.86 1.51	-	-	292 48.99 38.78 16.79 2.86	-	54 42.86 7.17 3.11 0.53	-	-	-	-	61 25.10 8.10 3.51 0.60	139 60.17 18.46 7.99 1.36	-	-	-	-	-	-	-	-	-
North Potomac (cdp)	6,320 91.79	1,729	1,598 92.42 92.42 25.28	-	-	358 95.47 22.40 20.71 5.66	-	-	822 92.78 51.44 47.54 13.01	-	-	-	-	-	-	-	248 87.94 15.52 14.34 3.92	-	-	-	-	-	-	-	-	-

Notes: Please refer to the User's Guide for an explanation of data; data is arranged alphabetically by state, then county, then city within each county; table includes counties with populations greater than 49,999 unless noted and cities with populations greater than 9,999 whose Asian and/or NHPI population rates are greater than the national average; (1) Native Hawaiian and other Pacific Islander; (2) excludes Taiwanese; (3) includes Chamorro; (4) county does not meet population threshold but is shown in order to allow inclusion of city

Place	All owner-occupied housing units	Asian-occupied housing units	Asians who own and occupy their own homes	NHPI[1]-occupied housing units	NHPIs[1] who own and occupy their own homes	Asian Indian	Bangladeshi	Cambodian	Chinese[2]	Fijian	Filipino	Guamanian[3]	Hawaiian, Native	Hmong	Indonesian	Japanese	Korean	Laotian	Malaysian	Pakistani	Samoan	Sri Lankan	Taiwanese	Thai	Tongan	Vietnamese
Olney (cdp)	9,382	681	653	-	-	175	-	-	195	-	-	-	-	-	-	-	130	-	-	-	-	-	-	-	-	-
	91.24		95.89			100.00			100.00								95.59									
						26.80			29.86								19.91									
			95.89			25.70			28.63								19.09									
			6.96			1.87			2.08								1.39									
Potomac (cdp)	13,921	1,754	1,563	-	-	403	-	-	605	-	59	-	-	-	-	-	285	-	-	-	-	-	-	-	-	-
	88.93		89.11			85.74			94.09		84.29						90.19									
						25.78			38.71		3.77						18.23									
			89.11			22.98			34.49		3.36						16.25									
			11.23			2.89			4.35		0.42						2.05									
Redland (cdp)	4,143	802	636	-	-	188	-	-	180	-	58	-	-	-	-	-	84	-	-	-	-	-	-	-	-	-
	77.63		79.30			85.07			93.75		77.33						67.74									
						29.56			28.30		9.12						13.21									
			79.30			23.44			22.44		7.23						10.47									
			15.35			4.54			4.34		1.40						2.03									
Rockville (city)	11,713	2,204	1,045	-	-	194	-	-	433	-	64	-	-	-	-	21	99	-	-	-	-	-	-	-	-	70
	67.92		47.41			51.87			48.06		46.38					12.21	34.74									65.42
						18.56			41.44		6.12					2.01	9.47									6.70
			47.41			8.80			19.65		2.90					0.95	4.49									3.18
			8.92			1.66			3.70		0.55					0.18	0.85									0.60
Silver Spring (cdp)	13,263	1,978	662	-	-	116	-	51	170	-	17	-	-	-	-	-	31	-	-	-	-	-	-	-	-	161
	43.62		33.47			28.57		69.86	52.80		10.30						14.16									35.38
						17.52		7.70	25.68		2.57						4.68									24.32
			33.47			5.86		2.58	8.59		0.86						1.57									8.14
			4.99			0.87		0.38	1.28		0.13						0.23									1.21
Takoma Park (city)	3,130	199	82	-	-	-	-	-	-	-	-	-	-	-	-	-	-	-	-	-	-	-	-	-	-	-
	45.49		41.21																							
			41.21																							
			2.62																							
Wheaton-Glenmont (cdp)	13,235	1,996	1,411	-	-	274	-	-	424	-	124	-	-	-	-	-	126	-	-	-	-	-	-	-	-	170
	67.59		70.69			77.62			76.40		71.26						53.16									57.24
						19.42			30.05		8.79						8.93									12.05
			70.69			13.73			21.24		6.21						6.31									8.52
			10.66			2.07			3.20		0.94						0.95									1.28
White Oak (cdp)	3,332	824	317	-	-	90	-	-	77	-	-	-	-	-	-	-	42	-	-	-	-	-	-	-	-	85
	42.03		38.47			43.48			48.43								19.63									49.42
						28.39			24.29								13.25									26.81
			38.47			10.92			9.34								5.10									10.32
			9.51			2.70			2.31								1.26									2.55
Prince George's County	177,206	8,594	5,027	-	-	1,158	-	-	838	-	1,628	-	-	-	-	108	553	-	-	45	-	-	-	52	-	382
	61.83		58.49			53.24			56.97		77.05					54.27	45.78			25.42				53.06		62.32
						23.04			16.67		32.39					2.15	11.00			0.90				1.03		7.60
			58.49			13.47			9.75		18.94					1.26	6.43			0.52				0.61		4.44
			2.84			0.65			0.47		0.92					0.06	0.31			0.03				0.03		0.22
Adelphi (cdp)	2,783	478	222	-	-	-	-	-	-	-	-	-	-	-	-	-	-	-	-	-	-	-	-	-	-	-
	52.17		46.44																							
			46.44																							
			7.98																							

Notes: Please refer to the User's Guide for an explanation of data; data is arranged alphabetically by state, then county, then city within each county; table includes counties with populations greater than 49,999 unless noted and cities with populations greater than 9,999 whose Asian and/or NHPI population rates are greater than the national average; (1) Native Hawaiian and other Pacific Islander; (2) excludes Taiwanese; (3) includes Chamorro; (4) county does not meet population threshold but is shown in order to allow inclusion of city

Place	All owner-occupied housing units	Asian-occupied housing units	Asians who own and occupy their own homes	NHPI[1]-occupied housing units	NHPIs[1] who own and occupy their own homes	Asian Indian	Bangladeshi	Cambodian	Chinese[2]	Fijian	Filipino	Guamanian[3]	Hawaiian, Native	Hmong	Indonesian	Japanese	Korean	Laotian	Malaysian	Pakistani	Samoan	Sri Lankan	Taiwanese	Thai	Tongan	Vietnamese
Beltsville (cdp)	3,698 65.01	511	280 54.79 54.79 7.57	-	-	82 54.67 29.29 16.05 2.22	-	-	-	-	-	-	-	-	-	-	54 43.55 19.29 10.57 1.46	-	-	-	-	-	-	-	-	-
College Park (city)	3,508 58.02	525	185 35.24 35.24 5.27	-	-	70 43.75 37.84 13.33 2.00	-	-	54 34.39 29.19 10.29 1.54	-	-	-	-	-	-	-	-	-	-	-	-	-	-	-	-	-
Fort Washington (cdp)	7,220 88.15	575	502 87.30 87.30 6.95	-	-	-	-	-	-	-	401 84.60 79.88 69.74 5.55	-	-	-	-	-	-	-	-	-	-	-	-	-	-	-
Friendly (cdp)	3,326 93.01	157	157 100.00 100.00 4.72	-	-	-	-	-	-	-	118 100.00 75.16 75.16 3.55	-	-	-	-	-	-	-	-	-	-	-	-	-	-	-
Glenn Dale (cdp)	3,012 73.73	299	258 86.29 86.29 8.57	-	-	-	-	-	-	-	-	-	-	-	-	-	-	-	-	-	-	-	-	-	-	-
Greenbelt (city)	4,293 45.95	882	309 35.03 35.03 7.20	-	-	87 34.52 28.16 9.86 2.03	-	-	71 36.04 22.98 8.05 1.65	-	-	-	-	-	-	-	86 40.00 27.83 9.75 2.00	-	-	-	-	-	-	-	-	-
Hyattsville (city)	2,808 50.80	177	70 39.55 39.55 2.49	-	-	-	-	-	-	-	-	-	-	-	-	-	-	-	-	-	-	-	-	-	-	-
Lanham-Seabrook (cdp)	4,745 76.13	249	188 75.50 75.50 3.96	-	-	-	-	-	-	-	-	-	-	-	-	-	-	-	-	-	-	-	-	-	-	-
Laurel (city)	4,493 49.93	385	144 37.40 37.40 3.20	-	-	-	-	-	-	-	-	-	-	-	-	-	-	-	-	-	-	-	-	-	-	-
New Carrollton (city)	2,523 54.90	170	69 40.59 40.59 2.73	-	-	-	-	-	-	-	-	-	-	-	-	-	-	-	-	-	-	-	-	-	-	-

Notes: Please refer to the User's Guide for an explanation of data; data is arranged alphabetically by state, then county, then city within each county; table includes counties with populations greater than 49,999 unless noted and cities with populations greater than 9,999 whose Asian and/or NHPI population rates are greater than the national average; (1) Native Hawaiian and other Pacific Islander; (2) excludes Taiwanese; (3) includes Chamorro; (4) county does not meet population threshold but is shown in order to allow inclusion of city

Place	All owner-occupied housing units	Asian-occupied housing units	Asians who own and occupy their own homes	NHPI[1]-occupied housing units	NHPIs[1] who own and occupy their own homes	Asian Indian	Bangladeshi	Cambodian	Chinese[2]	Fijian	Filipino	Guamanian[3]	Hawaiian, Native	Hmong	Indonesian	Japanese	Korean	Laotian	Malaysian	Pakistani	Samoan	Sri Lankan	Taiwanese	Thai	Tongan	Vietnamese
South Laurel (cdp)	2,847 34.23	379	166 43.80 43.80 5.83	-	-	-	-	-	-	-	-	-	-	-	-	-	-	-	-	-	-	-	-	-	-	-
St. Mary's County	22,001 71.80	477	284 59.54 59.54 1.29	-	-	54 73.97 19.01 11.32 0.25	-	-	-	-	117 60.94 41.20 24.53 0.53	-	-	-	-	-	-	-	-	-	-	-	-	-	-	-
Lexington Park (cdp)	1,147 28.64	173	80 46.24 46.24 6.97	-	-	-	-	-	-	-	-	-	-	-	-	-	-	-	-	-	-	-	-	-	-	-
Washington County	32,630 65.62	314	103 32.80 32.80 0.32	-	-	-	-	-	-	-	-	-	-	-	-	-	-	-	-	-	-	-	-	-	-	-
Wicomico County	21,413 66.46	568	315 55.46 55.46 1.47	-	-	79 62.70 25.08 13.91 0.37	-	-	-	-	-	-	-	-	-	-	77 38.69 24.44 13.56 0.36	-	-	-	-	-	-	-	-	-
Salisbury (city)	3,502 37.98	324	129 39.81 39.81 3.68	-	-	-	-	-	-	-	-	-	-	-	-	-	-	-	-	-	-	-	-	-	-	-
MASSACHUSETTS	1,508,248 61.72	72,627	29,767 40.99 40.99 1.97	495	183 36.97 36.97 0.01	5,292 36.65 17.78 7.29 0.35	41 28.67 0.14 0.06 <0.01	1,525 34.75 5.12 2.10 0.10	13,570 51.07 45.59 18.68 0.90	-	1,308 47.62 4.39 1.80 0.09	56 45.90 30.60 11.31 <0.01	40 30.08 21.86 8.08 <0.01	98 55.06 0.33 0.13 0.01	108 37.11 0.36 0.15 0.01	974 23.47 3.27 1.34 0.06	1,622 28.93 5.45 2.23 0.11	357 40.48 1.20 0.49 0.02	-	170 30.14 0.57 0.23 0.01	-	105 60.69 0.35 0.14 0.01	379 44.28 1.27 0.52 0.03	206 26.41 0.69 0.28 0.01	-	3,144 36.35 10.56 4.33 0.21
Barnstable County	73,783 77.81	396	206 52.02 52.02 0.28	-	-	-	-	-	96 76.19 46.60 24.24 0.13	-	-	-	-	-	-	-	-	-	-	-	-	-	-	-	-	-
Berkshire County	37,488 66.94	342	103 30.12 30.12 0.27	-	-	7 5.88 6.80 2.05 0.02	-	-	-	-	-	-	-	-	-	-	-	-	-	-	-	-	-	-	-	-
Bristol County	126,531 61.60	2,141	992 46.33 46.33 0.78	-	-	241 50.84 24.29 11.26 0.19	-	101 22.25 10.18 4.72 0.08	287 61.46 28.93 13.40 0.23	-	108 62.43 10.89 5.04 0.09	-	-	-	-	-	52 31.90 5.24 2.43 0.04	-	-	-	-	-	-	-	-	81 61.36 8.17 3.78 0.06

Notes: Please refer to the User's Guide for an explanation of data; data is arranged alphabetically by state, then county, then city within each county; table includes counties with populations greater than 49,999 unless noted and cities with populations greater than 9,999 whose Asian and/or NHPI population rates are greater than the national average; (1) Native Hawaiian and other Pacific Islander; (2) excludes Taiwanese; (3) includes Chamorro; (4) county does not meet population threshold but is shown in order to allow inclusion of city

Place	All owner-occupied housing units	Asian-occupied housing units	Asians who own and occupy their own homes	NHPI[1]-occupied housing units	NHPIs[1] who own and occupy their own homes	Asian Indian	Bangladeshi	Cambodian	Chinese[2]	Fijian	Filipino	Guamanian[3]	Hawaiian, Native	Hmong	Indonesian	Japanese	Korean	Laotian	Malaysian	Pakistani	Samoan	Sri Lankan	Taiwanese	Thai	Tongan	Vietnamese
	175,022	4,697	2,376	-	-	411	-	321	703	-	96	-	-	-	-	99	234	33	-	-	-	-	-	-	-	357
	63.55		50.59			48.07		39.98	68.99		56.14					32.67	51.54	51.56								47.47
Essex County						17.30		13.51	29.59		4.04					4.17	9.85	1.39								15.03
			50.59			8.75		6.83	14.97		2.04					2.11	4.98	0.70								7.60
			1.36			0.23		0.18	0.40		0.05					0.06	0.13	0.02								0.20
	8,891	641	461	-	-	109	-	-	191	-	-	-	-	-	-	-	-	-	-	-	-	-	-	-	-	-
	78.65		71.92			63.37			77.33																	
Andover (town)						23.64			41.43																	
			71.92			17.00			29.80																	
			5.19			1.23			2.15																	
	15,315	1,252	445	-	-	14	-	204	-	-	-	-	-	-	-	-	-	-	-	-	-	-	-	-	-	79
	45.63		35.54			18.18		33.55																		31.47
Lynn (city)						3.15		45.84																		17.75
			35.54			1.12		16.29																		6.31
			2.91			0.09		1.33																		0.52
	7,073	383	271	-	-	-	-	-	118	-	-	-	-	-	-	-	-	-	-	-	-	-	-	-	-	-
	72.74		70.76						83.10																	
North Andover (town)									43.54																	
			70.76						30.81																	
			3.83						1.67																	
	19,729	203	78	-	-	-	-	-	-	-	-	-	-	-	-	-	-	-	-	-	-	-	-	-	-	-
	66.96		38.42																							
Franklin County																										
			38.42																							
			0.40																							
	108,524	1,723	838	-	-	141	-	48	192	-	-	-	-	-	-	-	58	-	-	-	-	-	-	-	-	197
	61.91		48.64			61.84		38.10	55.17								44.27									40.45
Hampden County						16.83		5.73	22.91								6.92									23.51
			48.64			8.18		2.79	11.14								3.37									11.43
			0.77			0.13		0.04	0.18								0.05									0.18
	36,367	1,252	369	-	-	66	-	-	148	-	-	-	-	-	-	-	25	-	-	-	-	-	-	-	-	-
	64.95		29.47			26.83			35.92								13.74									
Hampshire County						17.89			40.11								6.78									
			29.47			5.27			11.82								2.00									
			1.01			0.18			0.41								0.07									
	1,150	207	36	-	-	-	-	-	-	-	-	-	-	-	-	-	-	-	-	-	-	-	-	-	-	-
	36.91		17.39																							
Amherst Center (cdp)																										
			17.39																							
			3.13																							
	4,128	806	185	-	-	-	-	-	100	-	-	-	-	-	-	-	-	-	-	-	-	-	-	-	-	-
	45.00		22.95						32.57																	
Amherst (town)									54.05																	
			22.95						12.41																	
			4.48						2.42																	
	346,591	27,356	12,106	-	-	2,769	-	838	5,625	-	276	-	-	-	-	376	606	161	-	18	-	-	231	86	-	720
	61.76		44.25			38.17		35.71	59.72		39.15					26.44	28.44	38.06		11.11			56.90	29.97		41.57
Middlesex County						22.87		6.92	46.46		2.28					3.11	5.01	1.33		0.15			1.91	0.71		5.95
			44.25			10.12		3.06	20.56		1.01					1.37	2.22	0.59		0.07			0.84	0.31		2.63
			3.49			0.80		0.24	1.62		0.08					0.11	0.17	0.05		0.01			0.07	0.02		0.21

Notes: Please refer to the User's Guide for an explanation of data; data is arranged alphabetically by state, then county, then city within each county; table includes counties with populations greater than 49,999 unless noted and cities with populations greater than 9,999 whose Asian and/or NHPI population rates are greater than the national average; (1) Native Hawaiian and other Pacific Islander; (2) excludes Taiwanese; (3) includes Chamorro; (4) county does not meet population threshold but is shown in order to allow inclusion of city

Place	All owner-occupied housing units	Asian-occupied housing units	Asians who own and occupy their own homes	NHPI[1]-occupied housing units	NHPIs[1] who own and occupy their own homes	Asian Indian	Bangladeshi	Cambodian	Chinese[2]	Fijian	Filipino	Guamanian[3]	Hawaiian, Native	Hmong	Indonesian	Japanese	Korean	Laotian	Malaysian	Pakistani	Samoan	Sri Lankan	Taiwanese	Thai	Tongan	Vietnamese
Acton (town)	5,700 76.05	613	406 66.23 66.23 7.12	-	-	130 52.21 32.02 21.21 2.28	-	-	184 75.41 45.32 30.02 3.23	-	-	-	-	-	-	-	-	-	-	-	-	-	-	-	-	-
Arlington (town)	11,196 58.89	714	245 34.31 34.31 2.19	-	-	-	-	-	104 43.33 42.45 14.57 0.93	-	-	-	-	-	-	-	-	-	-	-	-	-	-	-	-	-
Bedford (town)	3,706 80.20	193	173 89.64 89.64 4.67	-	-	-	-	-	-	-	-	-	-	-	-	-	-	-	-	-	-	-	-	-	-	-
Belmont (cdp)	5,924 60.87	406	187 46.06 46.06 3.16	-	-	-	-	-	112 65.88 59.89 27.59 1.89	-	-	-	-	-	-	-	-	-	-	-	-	-	-	-	-	-
Belmont (town)	5,924 60.87	406	187 46.06 46.06 3.16	-	-	-	-	-	112 65.88 59.89 27.59 1.89	-	-	-	-	-	-	-	-	-	-	-	-	-	-	-	-	-
Burlington (town)	6,591 79.52	793	388 48.93 48.93 5.89	-	-	222 42.53 57.22 27.99 3.37	-	-	-	-	-	-	-	-	-	-	-	-	-	-	-	-	-	-	-	-
Cambridge (city)	13,735 32.23	3,876	729 18.81 18.81 5.31	-	-	147 16.57 20.16 3.79 1.07	-	-	346 26.45 47.46 8.93 2.52	-	-	-	-	-	-	64 13.53 8.78 1.65 0.47	53 8.62 7.27 1.37 0.39	-	-	-	-	-	-	-	-	-
Chelmsford (town)	10,744 83.86	446	372 83.41 83.41 3.46	-	-	95 76.61 25.54 21.30 0.88	-	-	174 92.06 46.77 39.01 1.62	-	-	-	-	-	-	-	-	-	-	-	-	-	-	-	-	-
Framingham (town)	14,514 55.50	1,290	588 45.58 45.58 4.05	-	-	232 40.99 39.46 17.98 1.60	-	-	223 55.06 37.93 17.29 1.54	-	-	-	-	-	-	-	-	-	-	-	-	-	-	-	-	-
Lexington (town)	9,166 82.50	908	752 82.82 82.82 8.20	-	-	197 84.19 26.20 21.70 2.15	-	-	381 92.03 50.66 41.96 4.16	-	-	-	-	-	-	-	52 55.91 6.91 5.73 0.57	-	-	-	-	-	-	-	-	-

Notes: Please refer to the User's Guide for an explanation of data; data is arranged alphabetically by state, then county, then city within each county; table includes counties with populations greater than 49,999 unless noted and cities with populations greater than 9,999 whose Asian and/or NHPI population rates are greater than the national average; (1) Native Hawaiian and other Pacific Islander; (2) excludes Taiwanese; (3) includes Chamorro; (4) county does not meet population threshold but is shown in order to allow inclusion of city

Place	All owner-occupied housing units	Asian-occupied housing units	Asians who own and occupy their own homes	NHPI[1]-occupied housing units	NHPIs[1] who own and occupy their own homes	Asian Indian	Bangladeshi	Cambodian	Chinese[2]	Fijian	Filipino	Guamanian[3]	Hawaiian, Native	Hmong	Indonesian	Japanese	Korean	Laotian	Malaysian	Pakistani	Samoan	Sri Lankan	Taiwanese	Thai	Tongan	Vietnamese
Lowell (city)	16,330 43.10	4,175	1,145 27.43 27.43 7.01	-	-	117 14.22 10.22 2.80 0.72	-	630 30.55 55.02 15.09 3.86	68 23.61 5.94 1.63 0.42	-	-	-	-	-	-	-	-	112 32.18 9.78 2.68 0.69	-	-	-	-	-	-	-	145 38.16 12.66 3.47 0.89
Malden (city)	9,970 43.33	2,311	912 39.46 39.46 9.15	-	-	82 20.71 8.99 3.55 0.82	-	-	587 51.36 64.36 25.40 5.89	-	-	-	-	-	-	-	-	-	-	-	-	-	-	-	-	119 34.39 13.05 5.15 1.19
Marlborough (city)	8,847 61.01	565	237 41.95 41.95 2.68	-	-	97 38.96 40.93 17.17 1.10	-	-	-	-	-	-	-	-	-	-	-	-	-	-	-	-	-	-	-	-
Medford (city)	12,944 58.66	732	360 49.18 49.18 2.78	-	-	79 56.03 21.94 10.79 0.61	-	-	167 55.30 46.39 22.81 1.29	-	-	-	-	-	-	-	-	-	-	-	-	-	-	-	-	60 56.60 16.67 8.20 0.46
Natick (town)	9,306 71.15	477	289 60.59 60.59 3.11	-	-	-	-	-	181 73.88 62.63 37.95 1.94	-	-	-	-	-	-	-	-	-	-	-	-	-	-	-	-	-
Newton (city)	21,703 69.56	1,851	1,302 70.34 70.34 6.00	-	-	124 59.33 9.52 6.70 0.57	-	-	922 79.07 70.81 49.81 4.25	-	-	-	-	-	-	-	102 56.98 7.83 5.51 0.47	-	-	-	-	-	-	-	-	-
Somerville (city)	9,663 30.62	1,546	414 26.78 26.78 4.28	-	-	119 33.06 28.74 7.70 1.23	-	-	249 38.02 60.14 16.11 2.58	-	-	-	-	-	-	-	0 0.00 0.00 0.00 0.00	-	-	-	-	-	-	-	-	-
Sudbury (town)	5,060 91.93	193	188 97.41 97.41 3.72	-	-	-	-	-	-	-	-	-	-	-	-	-	-	-	-	-	-	-	-	-	-	-
Waltham (city)	10,670 45.98	1,395	407 29.18 29.18 3.81	-	-	123 22.74 30.22 8.82 1.15	-	-	218 43.00 53.56 15.63 2.04	-	-	-	-	-	-	-	-	-	-	-	-	-	-	-	-	-
Wayland (town)	4,236 91.59	189	181 95.77 95.77 4.27	-	-	-	-	-	-	-	-	-	-	-	-	-	-	-	-	-	-	-	-	-	-	-

Notes: Please refer to the User's Guide for an explanation of data; data is arranged alphabetically by state, then county, then city within each county; table includes counties with populations greater than 49,999 unless noted and cities with populations greater than 9,999 whose Asian and/or NHPI population rates are greater than the national average; (1) Native Hawaiian and other Pacific Islander; (2) excludes Taiwanese; (3) includes Chamorro; (4) county does not meet population threshold but is shown in order to allow inclusion of city

Place	All owner-occupied housing units	Asian-occupied housing units	Asians who own and occupy their own homes	NHPI[1]-occupied housing units	NHPIs[1] who own and occupy their own homes	Asian Indian	Bangladeshi	Cambodian	Chinese[2]	Fijian	Filipino	Guamanian[3]	Hawaiian, Native	Hmong	Indonesian	Japanese	Korean	Laotian	Malaysian	Pakistani	Samoan	Sri Lankan	Taiwanese	Thai	Tongan	Vietnamese
Westford (town)	6,258	279	279	-	-	-	-	-	104	-	-	-	-	-	-	-	-	-	-	-	-	-	-	-	-	-
	91.92		100.00						100.00																	
									37.28																	
			100.00						37.28																	
			4.46						1.66																	
Weston (town)	3,203	245	245	-	-	-	-	-	130	-	-	-	-	-	-	-	-	-	-	-	-	-	-	-	-	-
	86.15		100.00						100.00																	
									53.06																	
			100.00						53.06																	
			7.65						4.06																	
Winchester (town)	6,205	252	203	-	-	-	-	-	-	-	-	-	-	-	-	-	-	-	-	-	-	-	-	-	-	-
	80.43		80.56																							
			80.56																							
			3.27																							
Woburn (city)	9,175	699	139	-	-	39	-	-	-	-	-	-	-	-	-	-	-	-	-	-	-	-	-	-	-	-
	61.18		19.89			10.18																				
						28.06																				
			19.89			5.58																				
			1.51			0.43																				
Norfolk County	173,413	10,996	5,871	-	-	656	-	-	3,783	-	340	-	-	-	-	165	235	-	-	-	-	-	54	-	-	387
	69.69		53.39			34.51			67.71		61.37					21.37	32.78						54.55			51.19
						11.17			64.44		5.79					2.81	4.00						0.92			6.59
			53.39			5.97			34.40		3.09					1.50	2.14						0.49			3.52
			3.39			0.38			2.18		0.20					0.10	0.14						0.03			0.22
Brookline (town)	11,553	3,032	1,090	-	-	147	-	-	703	-	-	-	-	-	-	82	66	-	-	-	-	-	-	-	-	-
	45.18		35.95			32.52			53.75							14.91	15.57									
						13.49			64.50							7.52	6.06									
			35.95			4.85			23.19							2.70	2.18									
			9.43			1.27			6.08							0.71	0.57									
Needham (town)	8,584	250	181	-	-	-	-	-	104	-	-	-	-	-	-	-	-	-	-	-	-	-	-	-	-	-
	80.89		72.40						80.00																	
									57.46																	
			72.40						41.60																	
			2.11						1.21																	
Norwood (town)	6,648	509	102	-	-	19	-	-	-	-	-	-	-	-	-	-	-	-	-	-	-	-	-	-	-	-
	57.20		20.04			5.99																				
						18.63																				
			20.04			3.73																				
			1.53			0.29																				
Quincy (city)	19,081	4,077	2,167	-	-	42	-	-	1,744	-	138	-	-	-	-	-	-	-	-	-	-	-	-	-	-	101
	49.07		53.15			9.57			67.99		46.94															26.86
						1.94			80.48		6.37															4.66
			53.15			1.03			42.78		3.38															2.48
			11.36			0.22			9.14		0.72															0.53
Randolph (town)	8,174	848	655	-	-	-	-	-	358	-	-	-	-	-	-	-	-	-	-	-	-	-	-	-	-	146
	72.29		77.24						84.24																	81.11
									54.66																	22.29
			77.24						42.22																	17.22
			8.01						4.38																	1.79

Notes: Please refer to the User's Guide for an explanation of data; data is arranged alphabetically by state, then county, then city within each county; table includes counties with populations greater than 49,999 unless noted and cities with populations greater than 9,999 whose Asian and/or NHPI population rates are greater than the national average; (1) Native Hawaiian and other Pacific Islander; (2) excludes Taiwanese; (3) includes Chamorro; (4) county does not meet population threshold but is shown in order to allow inclusion of city

Place	All owner-occupied housing units	Asian-occupied housing units	Asians who own and occupy their own homes	NHPI¹-occupied housing units	NHPIs¹ who own and occupy their own homes	Asian Indian	Bangladeshi	Cambodian	Chinese²	Fijian	Filipino	Guamanian³	Hawaiian, Native	Hmong	Indonesian	Japanese	Korean	Laotian	Malaysian	Pakistani	Samoan	Sri Lankan	Taiwanese	Thai	Tongan	Vietnamese
Sharon (town)	5,335 89.91	207	188 90.82 90.82 3.52	-	-	-	-	-	-	-	-	-	-	-	-	-	-	-	-	-	-	-	-	-	-	-
Wellesley (town)	7,140 83.08	318	265 83.33 83.33 3.71	-	-	-	-	-	168 86.60 63.40 52.83 2.35	-	-	-	-	-	-	-	-	-	-	-	-	-	-	-	-	-
Plymouth County	127,239 75.58	1,017	696 68.44 68.44 0.55	-	-	108 67.50 15.52 10.62 0.08	-	-	173 65.04 24.86 17.01 0.14	-	97 85.84 13.94 9.54 0.08	-	-	-	-	-	-	-	-	-	-	-	-	-	-	90 64.29 12.93 8.85 0.07
Suffolk County	94,552 33.92	16,891	3,594 21.28 21.28 3.80	-	-	231 13.34 6.43 1.37 0.24	-	89 22.88 2.48 0.53 0.09	1,898 24.54 52.81 11.24 2.01	-	196 32.56 5.45 1.16 0.21	-	-	-	-	108 9.95 3.01 0.64 0.11	131 10.34 3.64 0.78 0.14	-	-	-	-	-	32 15.09 0.89 0.19 0.03	-	-	735 24.02 20.45 4.35 0.78
Boston (city)	77,209 32.23	15,920	3,276 20.58 20.58 4.24	-	-	212 13.12 6.47 1.33 0.27	-	39 22.41 1.19 0.24 0.05	1,797 23.86 54.85 11.29 2.33	-	177 30.78 5.40 1.11 0.23	-	-	-	-	108 10.03 3.30 0.68 0.14	117 9.60 3.57 0.73 0.15	-	-	-	-	-	32 15.09 0.98 0.20 0.04	-	-	652 23.46 19.90 4.10 0.84
Chelsea (city)	3,448 29.00	359	106 29.53 29.53 3.07	-	-	-	-	-	-	-	-	-	-	-	-	-	-	-	-	-	-	-	-	-	-	17 10.97 16.04 4.74 0.49
Revere (city)	9,721 49.95	567	187 32.98 32.98 1.92	-		-	-	36 22.93 19.25 6.35 0.37	-	-	-	-	-	-	-	-	-	-	-	-	-	-	-	-	-	66 52.38 35.29 11.64 0.68
Worcester County	182,097 64.14	5,567	2,524 45.34 45.34 1.39	-	-	641 45.66 25.40 11.51 0.35	-	44 52.38 1.74 0.79 0.02	601 57.02 23.81 10.80 0.33	-	67 45.89 2.65 1.20 0.04	-	-	47 43.93 1.86 0.84 0.03	-	56 40.58 2.22 1.01 0.03	205 50.25 8.12 3.68 0.11	135 48.91 5.35 2.43 0.07	-	38 40.43 1.51 0.68 0.02	-	-	-	-	-	529 36.08 20.96 9.50 0.29
Fitchburg (city)	7,698 51.52	392	171 43.62 43.62 2.22	-	-	-	-	-	-	-	-	-	-	44 48.89 25.73 11.22 0.57	-	-	-	48 46.60 28.07 12.24 0.62	-	-	-	-	-	-	-	-
Northborough (town)	4,127 84.12	223	189 84.75 84.75 4.58	-	-	-	-	-	-	-	-	-	-	-	-	-	-	-	-	-	-	-	-	-	-	-

Notes: Please refer to the User's Guide for an explanation of data; data is arranged alphabetically by state, then county, then city within each county; table includes counties with populations greater than 49,999 unless noted and cities with populations greater than 9,999 whose Asian and/or NHPI population rates are greater than the national average; (1) Native Hawaiian and other Pacific Islander; (2) excludes Taiwanese; (3) includes Chamorro; (4) county does not meet population threshold but is shown in order to allow inclusion of city

Place	All owner-occupied housing units	Asian-occupied housing units	Asians who own and occupy their own homes	NHPI[1]-occupied housing units	NHPIs[1] who own and occupy their own homes	Asian Indian	Bangladeshi	Cambodian	Chinese[2]	Fijian	Filipino	Guamanian[3]	Hawaiian, Native	Hmong	Indonesian	Japanese	Korean	Laotian	Malaysian	Pakistani	Samoan	Sri Lankan	Taiwanese	Thai	Tongan	Vietnamese
Shrewsbury (town)	9,034 73.06	819	434 52.99 52.99 4.80	-	-	177 43.07 40.78 21.61 1.96	-	-	129 61.72 29.72 15.75 1.43	-	-	-	-	-	-	-	-	-	-	-	-	-	-	-	-	88 78.57 20.28 10.74 0.97
Westborough (town)	4,211 64.45	461	190 41.21 41.21 4.51	-	-	61 29.33 32.11 13.23 1.45	-	-	81 51.92 42.63 17.57 1.92	-	-	-	-	-	-	-	-	-	-	-	-	-	-	-	-	-
Worcester (city)	29,042 43.33	2,354	703 29.86 29.86 2.42	-	-	156 40.21 22.19 6.63 0.54	-	-	79 30.86 11.24 3.36 0.27	-	-	-	-	-	-	-	-	-	-	-	-	-	-	-	-	345 30.03 49.08 14.66 1.19
MICHIGAN	2,793,346 73.79	54,445	27,093 49.76 49.76 0.97	640	323 50.47 50.47 0.01	8,695 47.15 32.09 15.97 0.31	211 47.85 0.78 0.39 0.01	223 65.40 0.82 0.41 0.01	5,354 52.51 19.76 9.83 0.19	-	3,735 67.95 13.79 6.86 0.13	79 58.09 24.46 12.34 <0.01	123 58.57 38.08 19.22 <0.01	593 59.18 2.19 1.09 0.02	67 30.88 0.25 0.12 <0.01	1,515 36.20 5.59 2.78 0.05	2,041 37.53 7.53 3.75 0.07	450 68.70 1.66 0.83 0.02	35 19.89 0.13 0.06 <0.01	643 50.83 2.37 1.18 0.02	43 36.13 13.31 6.72 <0.01	63 61.17 0.23 0.12 <0.01	533 71.35 1.97 0.98 0.02	175 28.74 0.65 0.32 0.01	-	1,974 55.70 7.29 3.63 0.07
Allegan County	31,629 82.87	119	68 57.14 57.14 0.21	-	-	-	-	-	-	-	-	-	-	-	-	-	-	-	-	-	-	-	-	-	-	-
Bay County	34,849 79.33	156	84 53.85 53.85 0.24	-	-	-	-	-	-	-	-	-	-	-	-	-	-	-	-	-	-	-	-	-	-	-
Berrien County	45,925 72.24	472	210 44.49 44.49 0.46	-	-	61 35.67 29.05 12.92 0.13	-	-	-	-	55 90.16 26.19 11.65 0.12	-	-	-	-	-	14 13.59 6.67 2.97 0.03	-	-	-	-	-	-	-	-	-
Calhoun County	39,485 72.99	565	198 35.04 35.04 0.50	-	-	-	-	-	-	-	-	-	-	-	-	30 15.00 15.15 5.31 0.08	-	-	-	-	-	-	-	-	-	-
Cass County	16,114 81.90	72	51 70.83 70.83 0.32	-	-	-	-	-	-	-	-	-	-	-	-	-	-	21 65.63 41.18 29.17 0.13	-	-	-	-	-	-	-	-
Clinton County	20,162 85.24	77	56 72.73 72.73 0.28	-	-	-	-	-	-	-	-	-	-	-	-	-	-	-	-	-	-	-	-	-	-	-

Notes: Please refer to the User's Guide for an explanation of data; data is arranged alphabetically by state, then county, then city within each county; table includes counties with populations greater than 49,999 unless noted and cities with populations greater than 9,999 whose Asian and/or NHPI population rates are greater than the national average; (1) Native Hawaiian and other Pacific Islander; (2) excludes Taiwanese; (3) includes Chamorro; (4) county does not meet population threshold but is shown in order to allow inclusion of city

Place	All owner-occupied housing units	Asian-occupied housing units	Asians who own and occupy their own homes	NHPI-occupied housing units	NHPIs[1] who own and occupy their own homes	Asian Indian	Bangladeshi	Cambodian	Chinese[2]	Fijian	Filipino	Guamanian[3]	Hawaiian, Native	Hmong	Indonesian	Japanese	Korean	Laotian	Malaysian	Pakistani	Samoan	Sri Lankan	Taiwanese	Thai	Tongan	Vietnamese
Eaton County	29,770	345	110	-	-	19	-	-	-	-	-	-	-	-	-	-	-	-	-	-	-	-	-	-	-	37
	74.12		31.88			13.38																				58.73
						17.27																				33.64
			31.88			5.51																				10.72
			0.37			0.06																				0.12
Genesee County	124,387	1,124	676	-	-	263	-	-	86	-	137	-	-	-	-	-	66	-	-	-	-	-	-	-	-	-
	73.24		60.14			55.72			52.12		79.65						64.08									
						38.91			12.72		20.27						9.76									
			60.14			23.40			7.65		12.19						5.87									
			0.54			0.21			0.07		0.11						0.05									
Ingham County	65,969	3,196	887	-	-	279	-	-	220	-	107	-	-	15	-	54	38	-	-	-	-	-	-	-	-	101
	60.75		27.75			39.35			32.02		61.14			21.74		25.35	6.50									27.52
						31.45			24.80		12.06			1.69		6.09	4.28									11.39
			27.75			8.73			6.88		3.35			0.47		1.69	1.19									3.16
			1.34			0.42			0.33		0.16			0.02		0.08	0.06									0.15
East Lansing (city)	4,644	1,337	119	-	-	49	-	-	40	-	-	-	-	-	-	-	5	-	-	-	-	-	-	-	-	-
	32.19		8.90			18.49			10.72								1.46									
						41.18			33.61								4.20									
			8.90			3.66			2.99								0.37									
			2.56			1.06			0.86								0.11									
Meridian charter (township)	10,161	874	417	-	-	156	-	-	106	-	-	-	-	-	-	-	28	-	-	-	-	-	-	-	-	-
	61.98		47.71			51.49			57.61								20.90									
						37.41			25.42								6.71									
			47.71			17.85			12.13								3.20									
			4.10			1.54			1.04								0.28									
Okemos (cdp)	5,942	665	312	-	-	110	-	-	72	-	-	-	-	-	-	-	-	-	-	-	-	-	-	-	-	-
	64.66		46.92			46.61			63.72																	
						35.26			23.08																	
			46.92			16.54			10.83																	
			5.25			1.85			1.21																	
Ionia County	16,497	47	17	-	-	-	-	-	-	-	-	-	-	-	-	-	-	-	-	-	-	-	-	-	-	-
	80.06		36.17																							
			36.17																							
			0.10																							
Isabella County	14,204	332	67	-	-	-	-	-	-	-	-	-	-	-	-	-	-	-	-	-	-	-	-	-	-	-
	63.34		20.18																							
			20.18																							
			0.47																							
Jackson County	44,502	214	103	-	-	-	-	-	-	-	-	-	-	-	-	-	-	-	-	-	-	-	-	-	-	-
	76.51		48.13																							
			48.13																							
			0.23																							
Kalamazoo County	61,484	1,466	538	-	-	159	-	-	118	-	-	-	-	-	-	-	39	-	-	-	-	-	-	-	-	-
	65.77		36.70			36.64			33.33								24.84									
						29.55			21.93								7.25									
			36.70			10.85			8.05								2.66									
			0.88			0.26			0.19								0.06									

Notes: Please refer to the User's Guide for an explanation of data; data is arranged alphabetically by state, then county, then city within each county; table includes counties with populations greater than 49,999 unless noted and cities with populations greater than 9,999 whose Asian and/or NHPI population rates are greater than the national average; (1) Native Hawaiian and other Pacific Islander; (2) excludes Taiwanese; (3) includes Chamorro; (4) county does not meet population threshold but is shown in order to allow inclusion of city

Place	All owner-occupied housing units	Asian-occupied housing units	Asians who own and occupy their own homes	NHPI[1]-occupied housing units	NHPIs[1] who own and occupy their own homes	Asian Indian	Bangladeshi	Cambodian	Chinese[2]	Fijian	Filipino	Guamanian[3]	Hawaiian, Native	Hmong	Indonesian	Japanese	Korean	Laotian	Malaysian	Pakistani	Samoan	Sri Lankan	Taiwanese	Thai	Tongan	Vietnamese
	149,719	2,819	1,576	-	-	164	-	-	183	-	100	-	-	-	-	-	142	-	-	-	-	-	-	-	-	744
	70.33		55.91			33.00			60.80		60.24						40.69									64.25
Kent County						10.41			11.61		6.35						9.01									47.21
			55.91			5.82			6.49		3.55						5.04									26.39
			1.05			0.11			0.12		0.07						0.09									0.50
	11,261	738	396	-	-	-	-	-	-	-	-	-	-	-	-	-	53	-	-	-	-	-	-	-	-	217
	61.03		53.66														46.90									63.27
Kentwood (city)																	13.38									54.80
			53.66														7.18									29.40
			3.52														0.47									1.93
	28,101	173	94	-	-	-	-	-	-	-	-	-	-	-	-	-	-	-	-	-	-	-	-	-	-	-
	78.21		54.34																							
Lenawee County																										
			54.34																							
			0.33																							
	48,780	241	195	-	-	-	-	-	-	-	-	-	-	-	-	-	-	-	-	-	-	-	-	-	-	-
	88.08		80.91																							
Livingston County																										
			80.91																							
			0.40																							
	243,887	5,137	2,972	-	-	830	-	-	424	-	773	-	-	186	-	-	126	-	-	84	-	-	-	-	-	247
	78.88		57.85			48.12			52.35		71.71			87.32			34.24			67.20						61.44
Macomb County						27.93			14.27		26.01			6.26			4.24			2.83						8.31
			57.85			16.16			8.25		15.05			3.62			2.45			1.64						4.81
			1.22			0.34			0.17		0.32			0.08			0.05			0.03						0.10
	36,574	1,949	1,303	-	-	500	-	-	191	-	327	-	-	-	-	-	46	-	-	-	-	-	-	-	-	103
	78.96		66.85			72.05			55.85		77.30						24.86									79.84
Sterling Heights (city)						38.37			14.66		25.10						3.53									7.90
			66.85			25.65			9.80		16.78						2.36									5.28
			3.56			1.37			0.52		0.89						0.13									0.28
	17,990	100	59	-	-	-	-	-	-	-	-	-	-	-	-	-	-	-	-	-	-	-	-	-	-	-
	69.82		59.00																							
Marquette County																										
			59.00																							
			0.33																							
	24,893	385	264	-	-	90	-	-	96	-	-	-	-	-	-	-	-	-	-	-	-	-	-	-	-	-
	78.36		68.57			72.00			72.18																	
Midland County						34.09			36.36																	
			68.57			23.38			24.94																	
			1.06			0.36			0.39																	
	43,519	233	107	-	-	-	-	-	-	-	-	-	-	-	-	-	-	-	-	-	-	-	-	-	-	-
	80.93		45.92																							
Monroe County																										
			45.92																							
			0.25																							
	49,238	181	97	-	-	-	-	-	-	-	-	-	-	-	-	-	-	-	-	-	-	-	-	-	-	-
	77.75		53.59																							
Muskegon County																										
			53.59																							
			0.20																							

Notes: Please refer to the User's Guide for an explanation of data; data is arranged alphabetically by state, then county, then city within each county; table includes counties with populations greater than 49,999 unless noted and cities with populations greater than 9,999 whose Asian and/or NHPI population rates are greater than the national average; (1) Native Hawaiian and other Pacific Islander; (2) excludes Taiwanese; (3) includes Chamorro; (4) county does not meet population threshold but is shown in order to allow inclusion of city

Place	All owner-occupied housing units	Asian-occupied housing units	Asians who own and occupy their own homes	NHPI-occupied housing units	NHPIs[1] who own and occupy their own homes	Asian Indian	Bangladeshi	Cambodian	Chinese[2]	Fijian	Filipino	Guamanian[3]	Hawaiian, Native	Hmong	Indonesian	Japanese	Korean	Laotian	Malaysian	Pakistani	Samoan	Sri Lankan	Taiwanese	Thai	Tongan	Vietnamese
Oakland County	352,242	15,862	8,950	-	-	3,398	-	-	1,993	-	971	-	-	135	-	513	788	-	-	152	-	-	326	-	-	249
	74.77		56.42			50.91			70.82		73.23			64.59		29.95	58.72			53.33			89.32			53.43
						37.97			22.27		10.85			1.51		5.73	8.80			1.70			3.64			2.78
			56.42			21.42			12.56		6.12			0.85		3.23	4.97			0.96			2.06			1.57
			2.54			0.96			0.57		0.28			0.04		0.15	0.22			0.04			0.09			0.07
Auburn Hills (city)	4,141	473	86	-	-	7	-	-	-	-	-	-	-	-	-	-	-	-	-	-	-	-	-	-	-	-
	51.25		18.18			2.44																				
						8.14																				
			18.18			1.48																				
			2.08			0.17																				
Bloomfield (township)	15,153	855	697	-	-	292	-	-	-	-	-	-	-	-	-	-	111	-	-	-	-	-	-	-	-	-
	90.15		81.52			83.19											73.03									
						41.89											15.93									
			81.52			34.15											12.98									
			4.60			1.93											0.73									
Farmington (city)	3,092	393	29	-	-	5	-	-	-	-	-	-	-	-	-	-	-	-	-	-	-	-	-	-	-	-
	64.08		7.38			1.56																				
						17.24																				
			7.38			1.27																				
			0.94			0.16																				
Farmington Hills (city)	22,428	2,129	871	-	-	483	-	-	226	-	55	-	-	-	-	-	-	-	-	-	-	-	-	-	-	-
	66.83		40.91			36.02			84.64		49.11															
						55.45			25.95		6.31															
			40.91			22.69			10.62		2.58															
			3.88			2.15			1.01		0.25															
Madison Heights (city)	9,328	661	155	-	-	-	-	-	47	-	-	-	-	-	-	-	-	-	-	-	-	-	-	-	-	-
	70.14		23.45						21.46																	
									30.32																	
			23.45						7.11																	
			1.66						0.50																	
Novi (city)	13,288	1,311	793	-	-	282	-	-	222	-	-	-	-	-	-	97	-	-	-	-	-	-	-	-	-	-
	70.94		60.49			82.22			94.07							21.51										
						35.56			27.99							12.23										
			60.49			21.51			16.93							7.40										
			5.97			2.12			1.67							0.73										
Rochester (city)	2,994	147	119	-	-	-	-	-	-	-	-	-	-	-	-	-	-	-	-	-	-	-	-	-	-	-
	64.15		80.95																							
			80.95																							
			3.97																							
Rochester Hills (city)	20,845	1,475	1,029	-	-	452	-	-	237	-	-	-	-	-	-	-	56	-	-	-	-	-	-	-	-	-
	79.20		69.76			69.75			75.24								61.54									
						43.93			23.03								5.44									
			69.76			30.64			16.07								3.80									
			4.94			2.17			1.14								0.27									
Troy (city)	23,220	3,211	2,148	-	-	888	-	-	563	-	208	-	-	-	-	-	173	-	-	-	-	-	153	-	-	-
	77.35		66.90			60.29			79.97		77.32						56.72						92.17			
						41.34			26.21		9.68						8.05						7.12			
			66.90			27.65			17.53		6.48						5.39						4.76			
			9.25			3.82			2.42		0.90						0.75						0.66			

Notes: Please refer to the User's Guide for an explanation of data; data is arranged alphabetically by state, then county, then city within each county; table includes counties with populations greater than 49,999 unless noted and cities with populations greater than 9,999 whose Asian and/or NHPI population rates are greater than the national average; (1) Native Hawaiian and other Pacific Islander; (2) excludes Taiwanese; (3) includes Chamorro; (4) county does not meet population threshold but is shown in order to allow inclusion of city

Place	All owner-occupied housing units	Asian-occupied housing units	Asians who own and occupy their own homes	NHPI[1]-occupied housing units	NHPIs[1] who own and occupy their own homes	Asian Indian	Bangladeshi	Cambodian	Chinese[2]	Fijian	Filipino	Guamanian[3]	Hawaiian, Native	Hmong	Indonesian	Japanese	Korean	Laotian	Malaysian	Pakistani	Samoan	Sri Lankan	Taiwanese	Thai	Tongan	Vietnamese
West Bloomfield (township)	20,326 86.89	1,509	1,047 69.38 69.38 5.15	-	-	465 93.00 44.41 30.82 2.29	-	-	184 90.20 17.57 12.19 0.91	-	122 97.60 11.65 8.08 0.60	-	-	-	-	89 20.41 8.50 5.90 0.44	91 70.00 8.69 6.03 0.45	-	-	-	-	-	-	-	-	-
Ottawa County	65,968 80.78	1,119	716 63.99 63.99 1.09	-	-	49 41.88 6.84 4.38 0.07	-	134 62.62 18.72 11.97 0.20	69 90.79 9.64 6.17 0.10	-	-	-	-	-	-	-	31 81.58 4.33 2.77 0.05	231 79.11 32.26 20.64 0.35	-	-	-	-	-	-	-	-	112 58.03 15.64 10.01 0.17
Holland (city)	8,050 67.11	295	140 47.46 47.46 1.74	-	-	-	-	-	-	-	-	-	-	-	-	-	-	-	-	-	-	-	-	-	-	-
Saginaw County	59,385 73.83	542	252 46.49 46.49 0.42	-	-	95 85.59 37.70 17.53 0.16	-	-	-	-	66 62.26 26.19 12.18 0.11	-	-	-	-	-	24 24.49 9.52 4.43 0.04	-	-	-	-	-	-	-	-	-
St. Clair County	49,404 79.59	126	97 76.98 76.98 0.20	-	-	-	-	-	-	-	-	-	-	-	-	-	-	-	-	-	-	-	-	-	-	-
St. Joseph County	17,985 76.92	88	55 62.50 62.50 0.31	-	-	-	-	-	-	-	-	-	-	-	-	-	-	-	-	-	-	-	-	-	-	-
Washtenaw County	74,846 59.72	7,145	2,232 31.24 31.24 2.98	-	-	586 33.39 26.25 8.20 0.78	-	-	802 35.14 35.93 11.22 1.07	-	158 47.16 7.08 2.21 0.21	-	-	-	-	107 16.85 4.79 1.50 0.14	288 22.77 12.90 4.03 0.38	-	-	53 45.30 2.37 0.74 0.07	-	-	100 54.05 4.48 1.40 0.13	-	-	53 47.75 2.37 0.74 0.07
Ann Arbor (city)	20,630 45.17	4,850	1,148 23.67 23.67 5.56	-	-	342 29.03 29.79 7.05 1.66	-	-	391 25.76 34.06 8.06 1.90	-	54 25.47 4.70 1.11 0.26	-	-	-	-	70 14.29 6.10 1.44 0.34	152 16.80 13.24 3.13 0.74	-	-	-	-	-	80 50.31 6.97 1.65 0.39	-	-	-
Pittsfield charter (township)	6,699 56.66	999	488 48.85 48.85 7.28	-	-	101 38.26 20.70 10.11 1.51	-	-	231 63.64 47.34 23.12 3.45	-	-	-	-	-	-	-	66 34.38 13.52 6.61 0.99	-	-	-	-	-	-	-	-	-
Scio (township)	4,763 78.88	190	133 70.00 70.00 2.79	-	-	-	-	-	-	-	-	-	-	-	-	-	-	-	-	-	-	-	-	-	-	-

Notes: Please refer to the User's Guide for an explanation of data; data is arranged alphabetically by state, then county, then city within each county; table includes counties with populations greater than 49,999 unless noted and cities with populations greater than 9,999 whose Asian and/or NHPI population rates are greater than the national average; (1) Native Hawaiian and other Pacific Islander; (2) excludes Taiwanese; (3) includes Chamorro; (4) county does not meet population threshold but is shown in order to allow inclusion of city

Place	All owner-occupied housing units	Asian-occupied housing units	Asians who own and occupy their own homes	NHPI[1]-occupied housing units	NHPIs[1] who own and occupy their own homes	Asian Indian	Bangladeshi	Cambodian	Chinese[2]	Fijian	Filipino	Guamanian[3]	Hawaiian, Native	Hmong	Indonesian	Japanese	Korean	Laotian	Malaysian	Pakistani	Samoan	Sri Lankan	Taiwanese	Thai	Tongan	Vietnamese
Wayne County	511,936 66.62	10,762	5,652 52.52 52.52 1.10	135	49 36.30 36.30 0.01	2,284 50.08 40.41 21.22 0.45	149 49.83 2.64 1.38 0.03	-	933 52.53 16.51 8.67 0.18	-	948 71.01 16.77 8.81 0.19	-	-	183 62.89 3.24 1.70 0.04	-	212 44.17 3.75 1.97 0.04	226 41.62 4.00 2.10 0.04	-	-	261 50.98 4.62 2.43 0.05	-	-	-	-	-	225 60.81 3.98 2.09 0.04
Brownstown (township)	6,296 75.65	152	118 77.63 77.63 1.87	-	-	-	-	-	-	-	-	-	-	-	-	-	-	-	-	-	-	-	-	-	-	-
Canton (township)	21,760 79.18	2,004	1,483 74.00 74.00 6.82	-	-	757 72.16 51.05 37.77 3.48	-	-	341 81.58 22.99 17.02 1.57	-	145 79.23 9.78 7.24 0.67	-	-	-	-	-	59 65.56 3.98 2.94 0.27	-	-	-	-	-	-	-	-	-
Hamtramck (city)	4,014 49.97	550	323 58.73 58.73 8.05	-	-	156 57.78 48.30 28.36 3.89	100 56.50 30.96 18.18 2.49	-	-	-	-	-	-	-	-	-	-	-	-	-	-	-	-	-	-	-
Inkster (city)	6,469 57.92	506	46 9.09 9.09 0.71	-	-	13 3.85 28.26 2.57 0.20	-	-	-	-	-	-	-	-	-	-	-	-	-	-	-	-	-	-	-	-
Northville (township)	5,974 73.58	244	131 53.69 53.69 2.19	-	-	72 75.79 54.96 29.51 1.21	-	-	-	-	-	-	-	-	-	-	-	-	-	-	-	-	-	-	-	-
MINNESOTA	1,412,724 74.55	35,297	18,452 52.28 52.28 1.31	456	251 55.04 55.04 0.02	2,682 44.96 14.54 7.60 0.19	-	806 62.14 4.37 2.28 0.06	2,885 56.15 15.64 8.17 0.20	-	934 60.73 5.06 2.65 0.07	74 71.84 29.48 16.23 0.01	87 62.14 34.66 19.08 0.01	3,810 53.94 20.65 10.79 0.27	-	707 47.29 3.83 2.00 0.05	1,024 38.07 5.55 2.90 0.07	1,273 61.03 6.90 3.61 0.09	-	156 47.13 0.85 0.44 0.01	-	-	125 76.69 0.68 0.35 0.01	140 59.83 0.76 0.40 0.01	-	3,085 56.62 16.72 8.74 0.22
Anoka County	88,776 83.41	1,016	836 82.28 82.28 0.94	-	-	215 83.33 25.72 21.16 0.24	-	-	114 89.06 13.64 11.22 0.13	-	83 96.51 9.93 8.17 0.09	-	-	67 80.72 8.01 6.59 0.08	-	-	50 56.82 5.98 4.92 0.06	-	-	-	-	-	-	-	-	169 82.84 20.22 16.63 0.19
Columbia Heights (city)	5,747 71.54	157	98 62.42 62.42 1.71	-	-	-	-	-	-	-	-	-	-	-	-	-	-	-	-	-	-	-	-	-	-	-
Blue Earth County	13,988 66.41	277	71 25.63 25.63 0.51	-	-	-	-	-	-	-	-	-	-	-	-	-	-	-	-	-	-	-	-	-	-	-

Notes: Please refer to the User's Guide for an explanation of data; data is arranged alphabetically by state, then county, then city within each county; table includes counties with populations greater than 49,999 unless noted and cities with populations greater than 9,999 whose Asian and/or NHPI population rates are greater than the national average; (1) Native Hawaiian and other Pacific Islander; (2) excludes Taiwanese; (3) includes Chamorro; (4) county does not meet population threshold but is shown in order to allow inclusion of city

Place	All owner-occupied housing units	Asian-occupied housing units	Asians who own and occupy their own homes	NHPI[1]-occupied housing units	NHPIs[1] who own and occupy their own homes	Asian Indian	Bangladeshi	Cambodian	Chinese[2]	Fijian	Filipino	Guamanian[3]	Hawaiian, Native	Hmong	Indonesian	Japanese	Korean	Laotian	Malaysian	Pakistani	Samoan	Sri Lankan	Taiwanese	Thai	Tongan	Vietnamese
Carver County	20,327 83.46	245	213 86.94 86.94 1.05	-	-	-	-	-	-	-	-	-	-	-	-	-	-	-	-	-	-	-	-	-	-	-
Clay County	13,377 71.65	101	49 48.51 48.51 0.37	-	-	-	-	-	-	-	-	-	-	-	-	-	-	-	-	-	-	-	-	-	-	-
Crow Wing County	17,719 79.64	59	16 27.12 27.12 0.09	-	-	-	-	-	-	-	-	-	-	-	-	-	-	-	-	-	-	-	-	-	-	-
Dakota County	102,549 78.19	2,499	1,572 62.91 62.91 1.53	-	-	297 45.90 18.89 11.88 0.29	-	88 80.73 5.60 3.52 0.09	346 76.38 22.01 13.85 0.34	-	100 69.93 6.36 4.00 0.10	-	-	-	-	-	100 51.55 6.36 4.00 0.10	119 74.84 7.57 4.76 0.12	-	-	-	-	-	-	-	301 67.49 19.15 12.04 0.29
Eagan (city)	17,785 74.80	873	425 48.68 48.68 2.39	-	-	78 28.26 18.35 8.93 0.44	-	-	107 60.80 25.18 12.26 0.60	-	-	-	-	-	-	-	-	-	-	-	-	-	-	-	-	92 72.44 21.65 10.54 0.52
Hennepin County	301,835 66.17	14,843	7,122 47.98 47.98 2.36	183	56 30.60 30.60 0.02	1,111 38.02 15.60 7.49 0.37	-	251 54.09 3.52 1.69 0.08	1,028 47.77 14.43 6.93 0.34	-	301 53.75 4.23 2.03 0.10	-	-	1,239 58.36 17.40 8.35 0.41	-	309 49.60 4.34 2.08 0.10	438 31.24 6.15 2.95 0.15	702 65.92 9.86 4.73 0.23	-	42 33.87 0.59 0.28 0.01	-	-	-	-	-	1,302 51.83 18.28 8.77 0.43
Bloomington (city)	25,717 70.66	1,273	758 59.54 59.54 2.95	-	-	77 36.67 10.16 6.05 0.30	-	64 52.03 8.44 5.03 0.25	182 67.16 24.01 14.30 0.71	-	-	-	-	-	-	-	95 74.22 12.53 7.46 0.37	-	-	-	-	-	-	-	-	225 66.57 29.68 17.67 0.87
Brooklyn Center (city)	7,870 68.89	492	348 70.73 70.73 4.42	-	-	-	-	-	-	-	-	-	-	178 79.82 51.15 36.18 2.26	-	-	-	58 81.69 16.67 11.79 0.74	-	-	-	-	-	-	-	-
Brooklyn Park (city)	17,894 73.24	1,440	1,079 74.93 74.93 6.03	-	-	184 67.90 17.05 12.78 1.03	-	-	-	-	-	-	-	124 81.58 11.49 8.61 0.69	-	-	-	274 86.71 25.39 19.03 1.53	-	-	-	-	-	-	-	279 72.85 25.86 19.38 1.56
Eden Prairie (city)	16,033 78.37	802	460 57.36 57.36 2.87	-	-	75 29.64 16.30 9.35 0.47	-	-	128 72.73 27.83 15.96 0.80	-	-	-	-	-	-	-	-	-	-	-	-	-	-	-	-	110 73.33 23.91 13.72 0.69

Notes: Please refer to the User's Guide for an explanation of data; data is arranged alphabetically by state, then county, then city within each county; table includes counties with populations greater than 49,999 unless noted and cities with populations greater than 9,999 whose Asian and/or NHPI population rates are greater than the national average; (1) Native Hawaiian and other Pacific Islander; (2) excludes Taiwanese; (3) includes Chamorro; (4) county does not meet population threshold but is shown in order to allow inclusion of city

Place	All owner-occupied housing units	Asian-occupied housing units	Asians who own and occupy their own homes	NHPI[1]-occupied housing units	NHPIs[1] who own and occupy their own homes	Asian Indian	Bangladeshi	Cambodian	Chinese[2]	Fijian	Filipino	Guamanian[3]	Hawaiian, Native	Hmong	Indonesian	Japanese	Korean	Laotian	Malaysian	Pakistani	Samoan	Sri Lankan	Taiwanese	Thai	Tongan	Vietnamese
Hopkins (city)	3,168	362	55	-	-	7	-	-	-	-	-	-	-	-	-	-	-	-	-	-	-	-	-	-	-	-
	38.47		15.19			4.00																				
						12.73																				
			15.19			1.93																				
			1.74			0.22																				
Minneapolis (city)	83,422	6,725	2,408	-	-	208	-	50	239	-	104	-	-	870	-	137	85	213	-	-	-	-	-	-	-	319
	51.38		35.81			26.30		41.32	26.23		45.81			52.50		37.13	11.90	50.47								31.62
						8.64		2.08	9.93		4.32			36.13		5.69	3.53	8.85								13.25
			35.81			3.09		0.74	3.55		1.55			12.94		2.04	1.26	3.17								4.74
			2.89			0.25		0.06	0.29		0.12			1.04		0.16	0.10	0.26								0.38
Plymouth (city)	19,005	758	432	-	-	174	-	-	52	-	-	-	-	-	-	-	83	-	-	-	-	-	-	-	-	-
	76.57		56.99			55.06			37.41								73.45									
						40.28			12.04								19.21									
			56.99			22.96			6.86								10.95									
			2.27			0.92			0.27								0.44									
Richfield (city)	10,174	584	283	-	-	-	-	-	-	-	-	-	-	-	-	-	-	-	-	-	-	-	-	-	-	49
	67.50		48.46																							35.51
																										17.31
			48.46																							8.39
			2.78																							0.48
Nobles County[4]	5,961	170	82	-	-	-	-	-	-	-	-	-	-	-	-	-	-	28	-	-	-	-	-	-	-	-
	75.09		48.24															41.18								
																		34.15								
			48.24															16.47								
			1.38															0.47								
Worthington (city)	2,846	157	75	-	-	-	-	-	-	-	-	-	-	-	-	-	-	25	-	-	-	-	-	-	-	-
	66.02		47.77															42.37								
																		33.33								
			47.77															15.92								
			2.64															0.88								
Olmsted County	36,311	1,678	872	-	-	163	-	86	184	-	-	-	-	46	-	30	53	29	-	-	-	-	-	-	-	152
	75.95		51.97			45.79		59.31	70.23					73.02		20.13	54.08	27.10								59.14
						18.69		9.86	21.10					5.28		3.44	6.08	3.33								17.43
			51.97			9.71		5.13	10.97					2.74		1.79	3.16	1.73								9.06
			2.40			0.45		0.24	0.51					0.13		0.08	0.15	0.08								0.42
Rochester (city)	24,094	1,572	781	-	-	152	-	60	169	-	-	-	-	46	-	-	53	29	-	-	-	-	-	-	-	137
	70.89		49.68			44.06		53.10	68.42					73.02			54.08	27.10								56.61
						19.46		7.68	21.64					5.89			6.79	3.71								17.54
			49.68			9.67		3.82	10.75					2.93			3.37	1.84								8.72
			3.24			0.63		0.25	0.70					0.19			0.22	0.12								0.57
Otter Tail County	18,140	45	27	-	-	-	-	-	-	-	-	-	-	-	-	-	-	-	-	-	-	-	-	-	-	-
	80.01		60.00																							
			60.00																							
			0.15																							
Ramsey County	127,703	9,744	4,673	-	-	435	-	171	578	-	114	-	-	2,236	-	104	118	86	-	-	-	-	-	-	-	546
	63.46		47.96			48.17		51.98	48.49		41.01			50.75		49.76	26.40	45.50								49.14
						9.31		3.66	12.37		2.44			47.85		2.23	2.53	1.84								11.68
			47.96			4.46		1.75	5.93		1.17			22.95		1.07	1.21	0.88								5.60
			3.66			0.34		0.13	0.45		0.09			1.75		0.08	0.09	0.07								0.43

Notes: Please refer to the User's Guide for an explanation of data; data is arranged alphabetically by state, then county, then city within each county; table includes counties with populations greater than 49,999 unless noted and cities with populations greater than 9,999 whose Asian and/or NHPI population rates are greater than the national average; (1) Native Hawaiian and other Pacific Islander; (2) excludes Taiwanese; (3) includes Chamorro; (4) county does not meet population threshold but is shown in order to allow inclusion of city

Place	All owner-occupied housing units	Asian-occupied housing units	Asians who own and occupy their own homes	NHPI[1]-occupied housing units	NHPIs[1] who own and occupy their own homes	Asian Indian	Bangladeshi	Cambodian	Chinese[2]	Fijian	Filipino	Guamanian[3]	Hawaiian, Native	Hmong	Indonesian	Japanese	Korean	Laotian	Malaysian	Pakistani	Samoan	Sri Lankan	Taiwanese	Thai	Tongan	Vietnamese
Maplewood (city)	10,403 75.61	376	246 65.43 65.43 2.36	-	-	-	-	-	77 81.91 31.30 20.48 0.74	-	-	-	-	53 80.30 21.54 14.10 0.51	-	-	-	-	-	-	-	-	-	-	-	-
New Brighton (city)	6,075 67.10	360	193 53.61 53.61 3.18	-	-	-	-	-	-	-	-	-	-	-	-	-	-	-	-	-	-	-	-	-	-	-
Roseville (city)	9,848 67.43	496	249 50.20 50.20 2.53	-	-	-	-	-	129 69.73 51.81 26.01 1.31	-	-	-	-	-	-	-	-	-	-	-	-	-	-	-	-	-
St. Paul (city)	61,437 54.80	7,059	3,194 45.25 45.25 5.20	-	-	109 34.49 3.41 1.54 0.18	-	138 51.11 4.32 1.95 0.22	132 36.46 4.13 1.87 0.21	-	56 33.33 1.75 0.79 0.09	-	-	2,080 49.71 65.12 29.47 3.39	-	-	33 16.34 1.03 0.47 0.05	77 45.29 2.41 1.09 0.13	-	-	-	-	-	-	-	340 43.81 10.64 4.82 0.55
Vadnais Heights (city)	4,303 85.04	112	106 94.64 94.64 2.46	-	-	-	-	-	-	-	-	-	-	-	-	-	-	-	-	-	-	-	-	-	-	-
Rice County	14,722 77.94	170	98 57.65 57.65 0.67	-	-	-	-	-	-	-	-	-	-	-	-	-	-	-	-	-	-	-	-	-	-	-
St. Louis County	61,690 74.67	380	210 55.26 55.26 0.34	-	-	-	-	-	-	-	-	-	-	-	-	-	18 52.94 8.57 4.74 0.03	-	-	-	-	-	-	-	-	-
Scott County	26,591 86.64	493	423 85.80 85.80 1.59	-	-	-	-	90 100.00 21.28 18.26 0.34	-	-	-	-	-	-	-	-	-	-	-	-	-	-	-	-	-	95 95.00 22.46 19.27 0.36
Savage (city)	6,219 91.16	270	249 92.22 92.22 4.00	-	-	-	-	-	-	-	-	-	-	-	-	-	-	-	-	-	-	-	-	-	-	-
Sherburne County	18,125 83.99	94	53 56.38 56.38 0.29	-	-	-	-	-	-	-	-	-	-	-	-	-	-	-	-	-	-	-	-	-	-	-

Notes: Please refer to the User's Guide for an explanation of data; data is arranged alphabetically by state, then county, then city within each county; table includes counties with populations greater than 49,999 unless noted and cities with populations greater than 9,999 whose Asian and/or NHPI population rates are greater than the national average; (1) Native Hawaiian and other Pacific Islander; (2) excludes Taiwanese; (3) includes Chamorro; (4) county does not meet population threshold but is shown in order to allow inclusion of city

Place	All owner-occupied housing units	Asian-occupied housing units	Asians who own and occupy their own homes	NHPI[1]-occupied housing units	NHPIs[1] who own and occupy their own homes	Asian Indian	Bangladeshi	Cambodian	Chinese[2]	Fijian	Filipino	Guamanian[3]	Hawaiian, Native	Hmong	Indonesian	Japanese	Korean	Laotian	Malaysian	Pakistani	Samoan	Sri Lankan	Taiwanese	Thai	Tongan	Vietnamese
Stearns County	35,111 73.76	547	208 38.03 38.03 0.59	-	-	-	-	-	-	-	-	-	-	-	-	-	-	-	-	-	-	-	-	-	-	103 59.88 49.52 18.83 0.29
Washington County	61,336 85.83	1,104	937 84.87 84.87 1.53	-	-	146 66.97 15.58 13.22 0.24	-	-	237 97.53 25.29 21.47 0.39	-	-	-	-	116 77.85 12.38 10.51 0.19	-	-	90 87.38 9.61 8.15 0.15	-	-	-	-	-	-	-	-	121 90.30 12.91 10.96 0.20
Woodbury (city)	14,219 85.27	651	531 81.57 81.57 3.73	-	-	98 62.42 18.46 15.05 0.69	-	-	147 100.00 27.68 22.58 1.03	-	-	-	-	42 85.71 7.91 6.45 0.30	-	-	-	-	-	-	-	-	-	-	-	-
Wright County	26,531 84.32	16	12 75.00 75.00 0.05	-	-	-	-	-	-	-	-	-	-	-	-	-	-	-	-	-	-	-	-	-	-	-
MISSISSIPPI	757,151 72.36	4,665	2,373 50.87 50.87 0.31	162	104 64.20 64.20 0.01	454 45.26 19.13 9.73 0.06	-	-	468 51.71 19.72 10.03 0.06	-	334 53.53 14.08 7.16 0.04	-	-	-	-	89 46.11 3.75 1.91 0.01	91 37.45 3.83 1.95 0.01	-	-	-	-	-	-	-	-	729 58.60 30.72 15.63 0.10
DeSoto County	30,736 79.23	143	104 72.73 72.73 0.34	-	-	-	-	-	-	-	-	-	-	-	-	-	-	-	-	-	-	-	-	-	-	-
Forrest County	16,420 60.41	211	13 6.16 6.16 0.08	-	-	-	-	-	-	-	-	-	-	-	-	-	-	-	-	-	-	-	-	-	-	-
Harrison County	44,845 62.69	1,153	575 49.87 49.87 1.28	-	-	-	-	-	-	-	76 45.51 13.22 6.59 0.17	-	-	-	-	-	-	-	-	-	-	-	-	-	-	318 54.17 55.30 27.58 0.71
Biloxi (city)	9,632 49.10	527	172 32.64 32.64 1.79	-	-	-	-	-	-	-	27 27.55 15.70 5.12 0.28	-	-	-	-	-	-	-	-	-	-	-	-	-	-	109 35.28 63.37 20.68 1.13
Hinds County	58,153 63.88	438	169 38.58 38.58 0.29	-	-	85 41.67 50.30 19.41 0.15	-	-	-	-	-	-	-	-	-	-	-	-	-	-	-	-	-	-	-	-

Notes: Please refer to the User's Guide for an explanation of data; data is arranged alphabetically by state, then county, then city within each county; table includes counties with populations greater than 49,999 unless noted and cities with populations greater than 9,999 whose Asian and/or NHPI population rates are greater than the national average; (1) Native Hawaiian and other Pacific Islander; (2) excludes Taiwanese; (3) includes Chamorro; (4) county does not meet population threshold but is shown in order to allow inclusion of city

Place	All owner-occupied housing units	Asian-occupied housing units	Asians who own and occupy their own homes	NHPI[1]-occupied housing units	NHPIs[1] who own and occupy their own homes	Asian Indian	Bangladeshi	Cambodian	Chinese[2]	Fijian	Filipino	Guamanian[3]	Hawaiian, Native	Hmong	Indonesian	Japanese	Korean	Laotian	Malaysian	Pakistani	Samoan	Sri Lankan	Taiwanese	Thai	Tongan	Vietnamese
Jackson County	35,548 74.56	468	311 66.45 66.45 0.87	-	-	-	-	-	-	-	-	-	-	-	-	-	-	-	-	-	-	-	-	-	-	217 82.51 69.77 46.37 0.61
Madison County	19,272 70.80	185	106 57.30 57.30 0.55	-	-	-	-	-	-	-	-	-	-	-	-	-	-	-	-	-	-	-	-	-	-	-
Oktibbeha County[4]	8,870 55.63	316	47 14.87 14.87 0.53	-	-	-	-	-	-	-	-	-	-	-	-	-	-	-	-	-	-	-	-	-	-	-
Starkville (city)	3,883 40.93	278	45 16.19 16.19 1.16	-	-	-	-	-	-	-	-	-	-	-	-	-	-	-	-	-	-	-	-	-	-	-
Rankin County	32,476 77.16	144	71 49.31 49.31 0.22	-	-	-	-	-	-	-	-	-	-	-	-	-	-	-	-	-	-	-	-	-	-	-
MISSOURI	1,542,310 70.28	19,836	9,289 46.83 46.83 0.60	874	406 46.45 46.45 0.03	1,955 45.43 21.05 9.86 0.13	-	122 73.05 1.31 0.62 0.01	2,007 44.88 21.61 10.12 0.13	-	1,289 55.11 13.88 6.50 0.08	79 50.97 19.46 9.04 0.01	131 61.79 32.27 14.99 0.01	-	-	659 51.09 7.09 3.32 0.04	721 36.36 7.76 3.63 0.05	153 71.50 1.65 0.77 0.01	-	98 26.70 1.06 0.49 0.01	143 49.65 35.22 16.36 0.01	-	207 50.99 2.23 1.04 0.01	190 41.85 2.05 0.96 0.01	-	1,530 54.41 16.47 7.71 0.10
Boone County	30,529 57.50	1,394	365 26.18 26.18 1.20	-	-	98 32.89 26.85 7.03 0.32	-	-	152 36.02 41.64 10.90 0.50	-	-	-	-	-	-	-	23 11.50 6.30 1.65 0.08	-	-	-	-	-	-	-	-	-
Columbia (city)	15,926 47.18	1,308	315 24.08 24.08 1.98	-	-	82 29.08 26.03 6.27 0.51	-	-	129 32.82 40.95 9.86 0.81	-	-	-	-	-	-	-	23 13.07 7.30 1.76 0.14	-	-	-	-	-	-	-	-	-
Cape Girardeau County	18,450 68.38	148	44 29.73 29.73 0.24	-	-	-	-	-	-	-	-	-	-	-	-	-	-	-	-	-	-	-	-	-	-	-
Cass County	24,002 79.56	61	47 77.05 77.05 0.20	-	-	-	-	-	-	-	-	-	-	-	-	-	-	-	-	-	-	-	-	-	-	-

Notes: Please refer to the User's Guide for an explanation of data; data is arranged alphabetically by state, then county, then city within each county; table includes counties with populations greater than 49,999 unless noted and cities with populations greater than 9,999 whose Asian and/or NHPI population rates are greater than the national average; (1) Native Hawaiian and other Pacific Islander; (2) excludes Taiwanese; (3) includes Chamorro; (4) county does not meet population threshold but is shown in order to allow inclusion of city

Place	All owner-occupied housing units	Asian-occupied housing units	Asians who own and occupy their own homes	NHPI[1]-occupied housing units	NHPIs[1] who own and occupy their own homes	Asian Indian	Bangladeshi	Cambodian	Chinese[2]	Fijian	Filipino	Guamanian[3]	Hawaiian, Native	Hmong	Indonesian	Japanese	Korean	Laotian	Malaysian	Pakistani	Samoan	Sri Lankan	Taiwanese	Thai	Tongan	Vietnamese
Clay County	51,282 70.68	729	354 48.56 48.56 0.69	-	-	60 40.54 16.95 8.23 0.12	-	-	-	-	-	-	-	-	-	-	-	-	-	-	-	-	-	-	-	111 65.29 31.36 15.23 0.22
Cole County	18,341 67.83	230	90 39.13 39.13 0.49	-	-	-	-	-	-	-	-	-	-	-	-	-	-	-	-	-	-	-	-	-	-	-
Franklin County	27,265 78.02	46	46 100.00 100.00 0.17	-	-	-	-	-	-	-	-	-	-	-	-	-	-	-	-	-	-	-	-	-	-	-
Greene County	62,284 63.65	730	286 39.18 39.18 0.46	-	-	-	-	-	33 26.61 11.54 4.52 0.05	-	-	-	-	-	-	-	18 15.13 6.29 2.47 0.03	-	-	-	-	-	-	-	-	79 79.00 27.62 10.82 0.13
Jackson County	167,435 62.88	2,656	1,191 44.84 44.84 0.71	279	146 52.33 52.33 0.09	154 42.08 12.93 5.80 0.09	-	-	132 28.21 11.08 4.97 0.08	-	191 58.59 16.04 7.19 0.11	-	-	-	-	91 43.75 7.64 3.43 0.05	59 30.73 4.95 2.22 0.04	-	-	-	83 57.24 56.85 29.75 0.05	-	-	-	-	386 50.79 32.41 14.53 0.23
Independence (city)	32,096 67.77	355	189 53.24 53.24 0.59	97	70 72.16 72.16 0.22	-	-	-	-	-	-	-	-	-	-	-	-	-	-	-	-	-	-	-	-	-
Jasper County	27,736 66.98	150	70 46.67 46.67 0.25	-	-	-	-	-	-	-	-	-	-	-	-	-	-	-	-	-	-	-	-	-	-	-
Jefferson County	59,615 83.38	188	124 65.96 65.96 0.21	-	-	-	-	-	-	-	-	-	-	-	-	-	-	-	-	-	-	-	-	-	-	-
Newton County	15,431 76.62	57	30 52.63 52.63 0.19	-	-	-	-	-	-	-	-	-	-	-	-	-	-	-	-	-	-	-	-	-	-	-
Phelps County[4]	10,289 65.61	328	78 23.78 23.78 0.76	-	-	47 43.12 60.26 14.33 0.46	-	-	-	-	-	-	-	-	-	-	-	-	-	-	-	-	-	-	-	-

Notes: Please refer to the User's Guide for an explanation of data; data is arranged alphabetically by state, then county, then city within each county; table includes counties with populations greater than 49,999 unless noted and cities with populations greater than 9,999 whose Asian and/or NHPI population rates are greater than the national average; (1) Native Hawaiian and other Pacific Islander; (2) excludes Taiwanese; (3) includes Chamorro; (4) county does not meet population threshold but is shown in order to allow inclusion of city

Place	All owner-occupied housing units	Asian-occupied housing units	Asians who own and occupy their own homes	NHPI[1]-occupied housing units	NHPIs[1] who own and occupy their own homes	Asian Indian	Bangladeshi	Cambodian	Chinese[2]	Fijian	Filipino	Guamanian[3]	Hawaiian, Native	Hmong	Indonesian	Japanese	Korean	Laotian	Malaysian	Pakistani	Samoan	Sri Lankan	Taiwanese	Thai	Tongan	Vietnamese
Rolla (city)	3,107 47.41	295	59 20.00 20.00 1.90	-	-	-	-	-	-	-	-	-	-	-	-	-	-	-	-	-	-	-	-	-	-	-
Platte County	19,744 67.44	399	232 58.15 58.15 1.18	-	-	-	-	-	-	-	-	-	-	-	-	-	-	-	-	-	-	-	-	-	-	-
St. Charles County	83,347 81.98	680	468 68.82 68.82 0.56	-	-	125 75.76 26.71 18.38 0.15	-	-	100 61.73 21.37 14.71 0.12	-	86 86.00 18.38 12.65 0.10	-	-	-	-	-	-	-	-	-	-	-	-	-	-	-
Saint Louis Independent City	68,917 46.86	2,626	892 33.97 33.97 1.29	-	-	79 21.88 8.86 3.01 0.11	-	-	110 22.54 12.33 4.19 0.16	-	70 28.34 7.85 2.67 0.10	-	-	-	-	-	-	-	-	-	-	-	-	-	-	428 46.88 47.98 16.30 0.62
St. Louis County	299,789 74.15	7,397	3,970 53.67 53.67 1.32	151	64 42.38 42.38 0.02	1,080 52.02 27.20 14.60 0.36	-	-	1,154 56.24 29.07 15.60 0.38	-	489 63.75 12.32 6.61 0.16	-	-	-	-	238 53.85 5.99 3.22 0.08	331 43.55 8.34 4.47 0.11	-	-	28 16.57 0.71 0.38 0.01	-	-	163 66.53 4.11 2.20 0.05	74 48.68 1.86 1.00 0.02	-	259 64.11 6.52 3.50 0.09
Chesterfield (city)	14,138 78.15	797	605 75.91 75.91 4.28	-	-	177 76.62 29.26 22.21 1.25	-	-	233 94.33 38.51 29.23 1.65	-	-	-	-	-	-	-	-	-	-	-	-	-	-	-	-	-
Clayton (city)	2,927 54.73	261	62 23.75 23.75 2.12	-	-	-	-	-	-	-	-	-	-	-	-	-	-	-	-	-	-	-	-	-	-	-
Creve Coeur (city)	4,924 70.69	315	173 54.92 54.92 3.51	-	-	-	-	-	-	-	-	-	-	-	-	-	-	-	-	-	-	-	-	-	-	-
Manchester (city)	5,794 80.52	257	151 58.75 58.75 2.61	-	-	-	-	-	-	-	-	-	-	-	-	-	-	-	-	-	-	-	-	-	-	-
Maryland Heights (city)	7,102 63.02	680	149 21.91 21.91 2.10	-	-	40 12.58 26.85 5.88 0.56	-	-	62 34.07 41.61 9.12 0.87	-	-	-	-	-	-	-	-	-	-	-	-	-	-	-	-	-

Notes: Please refer to the User's Guide for an explanation of data; data is arranged alphabetically by state, then county, then city within each county; table includes counties with populations greater than 49,999 unless noted and cities with populations greater than 9,999 whose Asian and/or NHPI population rates are greater than the national average; (1) Native Hawaiian and other Pacific Islander; (2) excludes Taiwanese; (3) includes Chamorro; (4) county does not meet population threshold but is shown in order to allow inclusion of city

Place	All owner-occupied housing units	Asian-occupied housing units	Asians who own and occupy their own homes	NHPI[1]-occupied housing units	NHPIs[1] who own and occupy their own homes	Asian Indian	Bangladeshi	Cambodian	Chinese[2]	Fijian	Filipino	Guamanian[3]	Hawaiian, Native	Hmong	Indonesian	Japanese	Korean	Laotian	Malaysian	Pakistani	Samoan	Sri Lankan	Taiwanese	Thai	Tongan	Vietnamese
Town and Country (city)	3,151 88.34	254	244 96.06 96.06 7.74	-	-	122 100.00 50.00 48.03 3.87	-	-	-	-	-	-	-	-	-	-	-	-	-	-	-	-	-	-	-	-
MONTANA	247,700 69.06	1,298	626 48.23 48.23 0.25	127	56 44.09 44.09 0.02	52 38.24 8.31 4.01 0.02	-	-	111 54.15 17.73 8.55 0.04	-	84 43.98 13.42 6.47 0.03	-	38 56.72 67.86 29.92 0.02	-	-	222 56.35 35.46 17.10 0.09	53 36.55 8.47 4.08 0.02	-	-	-	-	-	-	-	-	-
Cascade County	21,111 64.86	164	40 24.39 24.39 0.19	-	-	-	-	-	-	-	-	-	-	-	-	-	-	-	-	-	-	-	-	-	-	-
Flathead County	21,682 73.28	77	54 70.13 70.13 0.25	-	-	-	-	-	-	-	-	-	-	-	-	-	-	-	-	-	-	-	-	-	-	-
Gallatin County	16,435 62.44	163	43 26.38 26.38 0.26	-	-	-	-	-	-	-	-	-	-	-	-	-	-	-	-	-	-	-	-	-	-	-
Missoula County	23,793 61.90	286	129 45.10 45.10 0.54	-	-	-	-	-	-	-	-	-	-	-	-	-	-	-	-	-	-	-	-	-	-	-
Yellowstone County	36,037 69.19	182	113 62.09 62.09 0.31	-	-	-	-	-	-	-	-	-	-	-	-	-	-	-	-	-	-	-	-	-	-	-
NEBRASKA	449,306 67.44	6,138	2,594 42.26 42.26 0.58	184	72 39.13 39.13 0.02	432 37.18 16.65 7.04 0.10	-	-	318 30.40 12.26 5.18 0.07	-	279 49.73 10.76 4.55 0.06	-	-	-	-	238 43.91 9.18 3.88 0.05	163 35.59 6.28 2.66 0.04	167 73.89 6.44 2.72 0.04	-	-	-	-	-	56 34.78 2.16 0.91 0.01	-	817 53.61 31.50 13.31 0.18
Douglas County	115,199 63.23	2,511	858 34.17 34.17 0.74	-	-	247 35.44 28.79 9.84 0.21	-	-	160 33.61 18.65 6.37 0.14	-	107 38.21 12.47 4.26 0.09	-	-	-	-	75 25.17 8.74 2.99 0.07	62 31.00 7.23 2.47 0.05	-	-	-	-	-	-	-	-	153 46.36 17.83 6.09 0.13
Hall County	13,406 65.86	165	89 53.94 53.94 0.66	-	-	-	-	-	-	-	-	-	-	-	-	-	-	-	-	-	-	-	-	-	-	-

Notes: Please refer to the User's Guide for an explanation of data; data is arranged alphabetically by state, then county, then city within each county; table includes counties with populations greater than 49,999 unless noted and cities with populations greater than 9,999 whose Asian and/or NHPI population rates are greater than the national average; (1) Native Hawaiian and other Pacific Islander; (2) excludes Taiwanese; (3) includes Chamorro; (4) county does not meet population threshold but is shown in order to allow inclusion of city

Place	All owner-occupied housing units	Asian-occupied housing units	Asians who own and occupy their own homes	NHPI[1]-occupied housing units	NHPIs[1] who own and occupy their own homes	Asian Indian	Bangladeshi	Cambodian	Chinese[2]	Fijian	Filipino	Guamanian[3]	Hawaiian, Native	Hmong	Indonesian	Japanese	Korean	Laotian	Malaysian	Pakistani	Samoan	Sri Lankan	Taiwanese	Thai	Tongan	Vietnamese
Lancaster County	59,967	1,929	788	-	-	96	-	-	71	-	-	-	-	-	-	-	30	-	-	-	-	-	-	-	-	443
	60.46		40.85			37.65			18.02								23.81									54.69
						12.18			9.01								3.81									56.22
			40.85			4.98			3.68								1.56									22.97
			1.31			0.16			0.12								0.05									0.74
Sarpy County	30,058	600	320	-	-	-	-	-	-	-	76	-	-	-	-	-	60	-	-	-	-	-	-	-	-	67
	69.22		53.33								69.09						61.86									71.28
											23.75						18.75									20.94
			53.33								12.67						10.00									11.17
			1.06								0.25						0.20									0.22
NEVADA	457,245	28,132	16,562	2,265	917	859	-	121	3,439	-	6,560	180	434	-	-	2,112	1,171	210	-	65	117	-	157	444	57	742
	60.87		58.87		40.49	55.10		51.49	69.46		57.51	47.87	38.48			60.64	47.16	75.54		44.22	34.01		74.06	49.17	34.34	55.66
						5.19		0.73	20.76		39.61	19.63	47.33			12.75	7.07	1.27		0.39	12.76		0.95	2.68	6.22	4.48
			58.87		40.49	3.05		0.43	12.22		23.32	7.95	19.16			7.51	4.16	0.75		0.23	5.17		0.56	1.58	2.52	2.64
			3.62		0.20	0.19		0.03	0.75		1.43	0.04	0.09			0.46	0.26	0.05		0.01	0.03		0.03	0.10	0.01	0.16
Carson City Independent City	12,727	335	191	-	-	-	-	-	-	-	28	-	-	-	-	-	-	-	-	-	-	-	-	-	-	-
	63.10		57.01								44.44															
											14.66															
			57.01								8.36															
			1.50								0.22															
Clark County	302,842	22,846	13,788	1,834	772	558	-	110	2,867	-	5,498	176	393	-	-	1,677	1,049	210	-	-	91	-	133	397	-	646
	59.12		60.35		42.09	56.25		49.11	71.12		59.21	52.23	39.54			62.97	48.84	75.54			35.69		70.74	47.89		57.83
						4.05		0.80	20.79		39.88	22.80	50.91			12.16	7.61	1.52			11.79		0.96	2.88		4.69
			60.35		42.09	2.44		0.48	12.55		24.07	9.60	21.43			7.34	4.59	0.92			4.96		0.58	1.74		2.83
			4.55		0.25	0.18		0.04	0.95		1.82	0.06	0.13			0.55	0.35	0.07			0.03		0.04	0.13		0.21
Enterprise (cdp)	3,537	213	110	-	-	-	-	-	-	-	-	-	-	-	-	-	-	-	-	-	-	-	-	-	-	-
	61.32		51.64																							
			51.64																							
			3.11																							
Henderson (city)	46,948	2,170	1,522	274	199	101	-	-	305	-	534	-	117	-	-	175	157	-	-	-	-	-	-	-	-	-
	70.55		70.14		72.63	68.24			90.24		64.03		70.06			65.06	64.34									
						6.64			20.04		35.09		58.79			11.50	10.32									
			70.14		72.63	4.65			14.06		24.61		42.70			8.06	7.24									
			3.24		0.42	0.22			0.65		1.14		0.25			0.37	0.33									
Las Vegas (city)	104,514	6,968	4,349	552	199	195	-	-	845	-	1,802	-	84	-	-	629	267	-	-	-	-	-	-	132	-	109
	59.10		62.41		36.05	62.30			82.12		56.74		28.77			66.77	64.49							51.16		48.02
						4.48			19.43		41.43		42.21			14.46	6.14							3.04		2.51
			62.41		36.05	2.80			12.13		25.86		15.22			9.03	3.83							1.89		1.56
			4.16		0.19	0.19			0.81		1.72		0.08			0.60	0.26							0.13		0.10
North Las Vegas (city)	23,868	950	809	192	141	-	-	-	-	-	450	-	-	-	-	-	-	-	-	-	-	-	-	-	-	-
	70.18		85.16		73.44						84.91															
											55.62															
			85.16		73.44						47.37															
			3.39		0.59						1.89															
Paradise (cdp)	34,912	4,703	1,867	259	27	116	-	-	371	-	691	-	27	-	-	304	152	-	-	-	-	-	-	-	-	110
	45.12		39.70		10.42	43.61			42.89		39.17		16.07			48.72	25.89									52.63
						6.21			19.87		37.01		100.00			16.28	8.14									5.89
			39.70		10.42	2.47			7.89		14.69		10.42			6.46	3.23									2.34
			5.35		0.08	0.33			1.06		1.98		0.08			0.87	0.44									0.32

Notes: Please refer to the User's Guide for an explanation of data; data is arranged alphabetically by state, then county, then city within each county; table includes counties with populations greater than 49,999 unless noted and cities with populations greater than 9,999 whose Asian and/or NHPI population rates are greater than the national average; (1) Native Hawaiian and other Pacific Islander; (2) excludes Taiwanese; (3) includes Chamorro; (4) county does not meet population threshold but is shown in order to allow inclusion of city

Place	All owner-occupied housing units	Asian-occupied housing units	Asians who own and occupy their own homes	NHPI[1]-occupied housing units	NHPIs[1] who own and occupy their own homes	Asian Indian	Bangladeshi	Cambodian	Chinese[2]	Fijian	Filipino	Guamanian[3]	Hawaiian, Native	Hmong	Indonesian	Japanese	Korean	Laotian	Malaysian	Pakistani	Samoan	Sri Lankan	Taiwanese	Thai	Tongan	Vietnamese
Spring Valley (cdp)	27,405	4,192	2,864	233	95	-	-	-	1,042	-	766	-	-	-	-	199	280	-	-	-	-	-	-	97	-	197
	57.08		68.32		40.77				74.70		68.58					63.17	58.09							71.32		59.52
									36.38		26.75					6.95	9.78							3.39		6.88
			68.32		40.77				24.86		18.27					4.75	6.68							2.31		4.70
			10.45		0.35				3.80		2.80					0.73	1.02							0.35		0.72
Sunrise Manor (cdp)	33,171	2,313	1,670	111	48	-	-	-	133	-	971	-	-	-	-	134	94	-	-	-	-	-	-	-	-	-
	61.97		72.20		43.24				68.91		76.70					93.71	47.47									
									7.96		58.14					8.02	5.63									
			72.20		43.24				5.75		41.98					5.79	4.06									
			5.03		0.14				0.40		2.93					0.40	0.28									
Winchester (cdp)	4,919	531	144	-	-	-	-	-	-	-	34	-	-	-	-	-	-	-	-	-	-	-	-	-	-	-
	41.12		27.12								22.67															
											23.61															
			27.12								6.40															
			2.93								0.69															
Washoe County	78,318	4,350	2,227	315	96	256	-	-	477	-	830	-	-	-	-	344	77	-	-	-	-	-	-	-	49	92
	59.29		51.20		30.48	55.41			61.31		47.98					50.59	27.70								46.67	52.27
						11.50			21.42		37.27					15.45	3.46								51.04	4.13
			51.20		30.48	5.89			10.97		19.08					7.91	1.77								15.56	2.11
			2.84		0.12	0.33			0.61		1.06					0.44	0.10								0.06	0.12
Reno (city)	35,282	3,052	1,365	204	50	138	-	-	290	-	528	-	-	-	-	207	42	-	-	-	-	-	-	-	-	63
	47.66		44.72		24.51	45.39			54.00		43.28					41.40	21.88									52.94
						10.11			21.25		38.68					15.16	3.08									4.62
			44.72		24.51	4.52			9.50		17.30					6.78	1.38									2.06
			3.87		0.14	0.39			0.82		1.50					0.59	0.12									0.18
Sparks (city)	14,750	882	500	-	-	-	-	-	136	-	179	-	-	-	-	-	-	-	-	-	-	-	-	-	-	-
	59.84		56.69						71.58		49.31															
									27.20		35.80															
			56.69						15.42		20.29															
			3.39						0.92		1.21															
NEW HAMPSHIRE	330,783	4,440	1,884	-	-	435	-	-	623	-	150	-	-	-	-	101	205	33	-	-	-	-	-	-	-	166
	69.70		42.43			34.94			52.57		47.62					35.56	50.74	35.11								34.66
						23.09			33.07		7.96					5.36	10.88	1.75								8.81
			42.43			9.80			14.03		3.38					2.27	4.62	0.74								3.74
			0.57			0.13			0.19		0.05					0.03	0.06	0.01								0.05
Belknap County	16,640	72	61	-	-	-	-	-	-	-	-	-	-	-	-	-	-	-	-	-	-	-	-	-	-	-
	74.09		84.72																							
			84.72																							
			0.37																							
Cheshire County	20,057	113	55	-	-	-	-	-	-	-	-	-	-	-	-	-	-	-	-	-	-	-	-	-	-	-
	70.88		48.67																							
			48.67																							
			0.27																							
Grafton County	21,687	315	124	-	-	-	-	-	51	-	-	-	-	-	-	-	-	-	-	-	-	-	-	-	-	-
	68.63		39.37						50.50																	
									41.13																	
			39.37						16.19																	
			0.57						0.24																	

Notes: Please refer to the User's Guide for an explanation of data; data is arranged alphabetically by state, then county, then city within each county; table includes counties with populations greater than 49,999 unless noted and cities with populations greater than 9,999 whose Asian and/or NHPI population rates are greater than the national average; (1) Native Hawaiian and other Pacific Islander; (2) excludes Taiwanese; (3) includes Chamorro; (4) county does not meet population threshold but is shown in order to allow inclusion of city

Place	All owner-occupied housing units	Asian-occupied housing units	Asians who own and occupy their own homes	NHPI[1]-occupied housing units	NHPIs[1] who own and occupy their own homes	Asian Indian	Bangladeshi	Cambodian	Chinese[2]	Fijian	Filipino	Guamanian[3]	Hawaiian, Native	Hmong	Indonesian	Japanese	Korean	Laotian	Malaysian	Pakistani	Samoan	Sri Lankan	Taiwanese	Thai	Tongan	Vietnamese
Hanover (town)	1,872 66.10	113	43 38.05 38.05 2.30	-	-	-	-	-	-	-	-	-	-	-	-	-	-	-	-	-	-	-	-	-	-	-
Hillsborough County	93,820 64.95	2,248	873 38.83 38.83 0.93	-	-	242 31.19 27.72 10.77 0.26	-	-	319 51.12 36.54 14.19 0.34	-	44 35.48 5.04 1.96 0.05	-	-	-	-	-	60 54.55 6.87 2.67 0.06	-	-	-	-	-	-	-	-	92 30.56 10.54 4.09 0.10
Nashua (city)	19,700 56.91	1,194	415 34.76 34.76 2.11	-	-	148 28.30 35.66 12.40 0.75	-	-	154 47.83 37.11 12.90 0.78	-	-	-	-	-	-	-	-	-	-	-	-	-	-	-	-	-
Merrimack County	36,048 69.53	361	107 29.64 29.64 0.30	-	-	-	-	-	-	-	-	-	-	-	-	-	-	-	-	-	-	-	-	-	-	-
Rockingham County	78,999 75.58	783	441 56.32 56.32 0.56	-	-	67 38.95 15.19 8.56 0.08	-	-	168 66.14 38.10 21.46 0.21	-	36 44.44 8.16 4.60 0.05	-	-	-	-	-	59 66.29 13.38 7.54 0.07	-	-	-	-	-	-	-	-	-
Strafford County	27,426 64.41	429	172 40.09 40.09 0.63	-	-	-	-	-	27 30.68 15.70 6.29 0.10	-	-	-	-	-	-	-	-	-	-	-	-	-	-	-	-	-
NEW JERSEY	2,011,298 65.63	144,527	79,352 54.90 54.90 3.95	668	264 39.52 39.52 0.01	24,851 48.22 31.32 17.19 1.24	266 39.12 0.34 0.18 0.01	71 53.79 0.09 0.05 <0.01	20,992 69.66 26.45 14.52 1.04	-	15,583 63.68 19.64 10.78 0.77	26 21.49 9.85 3.89 <0.01	65 40.88 24.62 9.73 <0.01	-	155 45.99 0.20 0.11 0.01	2,078 38.36 2.62 1.44 0.10	7,936 41.94 10.00 5.49 0.39	32 26.67 0.04 0.02 <0.01	-	1,540 50.05 1.94 1.07 0.08	75 59.06 28.41 11.23 <0.01	226 60.92 0.28 0.16 0.01	1,517 79.26 1.91 1.05 0.08	350 58.14 0.44 0.24 0.02	-	2,212 58.03 2.79 1.53 0.11
Atlantic County	63,040 66.34	3,583	2,101 58.64 58.64 3.33	-	-	578 51.61 27.51 16.13 0.92	19 18.27 0.90 0.53 0.03	-	434 69.11 20.66 12.11 0.69	-	360 63.49 17.13 10.05 0.57	-	-	-	-	-	102 64.15 4.85 2.85 0.16	-	-	54 31.40 2.57 1.51 0.09	-	-	-	-	-	386 73.38 18.37 10.77 0.61
Atlantic City (city)	4,583 28.92	1,265	502 39.68 39.68 10.95	-	-	75 24.59 14.94 5.93 1.64	-	-	106 46.90 21.12 8.38 2.31	-	60 36.59 11.95 4.74 1.31	-	-	-	-	-	-	-	-	-	-	-	-	-	-	185 65.60 36.85 14.62 4.04
Brigantine (city)	3,483 63.64	227	107 47.14 47.14 3.07	-	-	-	-	-	-	-	-	-	-	-	-	-	-	-	-	-	-	-	-	-	-	-

Notes: Please refer to the User's Guide for an explanation of data; data is arranged alphabetically by state, then county, then city within each county; table includes counties with populations greater than 49,999 unless noted and cities with populations greater than 9,999 whose Asian and/or NHPI population rates are greater than the national average; (1) Native Hawaiian and other Pacific Islander; (2) excludes Taiwanese; (3) includes Chamorro; (4) county does not meet population threshold but is shown in order to allow inclusion of city

Place	All owner-occupied housing units	Asian-occupied housing units	Asians who own and occupy their own homes	NHPI[1]-occupied housing units	NHPIs[1] who own and occupy their own homes	Asian Indian	Bangladeshi	Cambodian	Chinese[2]	Fijian	Filipino	Guamanian[3]	Hawaiian, Native	Hmong	Indonesian	Japanese	Korean	Laotian	Malaysian	Pakistani	Samoan	Sri Lankan	Taiwanese	Thai	Tongan	Vietnamese
Egg Harbor (township)	9,444 84.65	462	355 76.84 76.84 3.76	-	-	-	-	-	-	-	-	-	-	-	-	-	-	-	-	-	-	-	-	-	-	-
Galloway (township)	7,998 74.43	674	507 75.22 75.22 6.34	-	-	233 76.39 45.96 34.57 2.91	-	-	-	-	-	-	-	-	-	-	-	-	-	-	-	-	-	-	-	-
Ventnor City (city)	3,336 60.88	264	157 59.47 59.47 4.71	-	-	-	-	-	-	-	-	-	-	-	-	-	-	-	-	-	-	-	-	-	-	-
Bergen County	222,237 67.18	28,805	14,388 49.95 49.95 6.47	-	-	2,817 54.27 19.58 9.78 1.27	-	-	3,133 71.66 21.78 10.88 1.41	-	2,732 68.16 18.99 9.48 1.23	-	-	-	-	740 28.55 5.14 2.57 0.33	3,988 36.37 27.72 13.84 1.79	-	-	193 51.19 1.34 0.67 0.09	-	-	257 93.80 1.79 0.89 0.12	93 52.84 0.65 0.32 0.04	-	61 49.19 0.42 0.21 0.03
Bergenfield (borough)	6,385 71.09	1,294	940 72.64 72.64 14.72	-	-	279 76.02 29.68 21.56 4.37	-	-	-	-	531 75.64 56.49 41.04 8.32	-	-	-	-	-	-	-	-	-	-	-	-	-	-	-
Cliffside Park (borough)	4,704 46.91	1,098	349 31.79 31.79 7.42	-	-	-	-	-	-	-	-	-	-	-	-	41 21.24 11.75 3.73 0.87	157 27.40 44.99 14.30 3.34	-	-	-	-	-	-	-	-	-
Dumont (borough)	4,740 74.41	466	381 81.76 81.76 8.04	-	-	92 85.19 24.15 19.74 1.94	-	-	-	-	125 75.76 32.81 26.82 2.64	-	-	-	-	-	-	-	-	-	-	-	-	-	-	-
Elmwood Park (borough)	4,298 60.63	460	191 41.52 41.52 4.44	-	-	125 45.79 65.45 27.17 2.91	-	-	-	-	-	-	-	-	-	-	-	-	-	-	-	-	-	-	-	-
Englewood (city)	5,497 59.28	466	237 50.86 50.86 4.31	-	-	-	-	-	-	-	76 68.47 32.07 16.31 1.38	-	-	-	-	-	-	-	-	-	-	-	-	-	-	-
Fair Lawn (borough)	9,455 80.09	550	409 74.36 74.36 4.33	-	-	162 72.97 39.61 29.45 1.71	-	-	-	-	129 90.21 31.54 23.45 1.36	-	-	-	-	-	-	-	-	-	-	-	-	-	-	-

Notes: Please refer to the User's Guide for an explanation of data; data is arranged alphabetically by state, then county, then city within each county; table includes counties with populations greater than 49,999 unless noted and cities with populations greater than 9,999 whose Asian and/or NHPI population rates are greater than the national average; (1) Native Hawaiian and other Pacific Islander; (2) excludes Taiwanese; (3) includes Chamorro; (4) county does not meet population threshold but is shown in order to allow inclusion of city

Place	All owner-occupied housing units	Asian-occupied housing units	Asians who own and occupy their own homes	NHPI[1]-occupied housing units	NHPIs[1] who own and occupy their own homes	Asian Indian	Bangladeshi	Cambodian	Chinese[2]	Fijian	Filipino	Guamanian[3]	Hawaiian, Native	Hmong	Indonesian	Japanese	Korean	Laotian	Malaysian	Pakistani	Samoan	Sri Lankan	Taiwanese	Thai	Tongan	Vietnamese
Fairview (borough)	1,683 34.62	217	30 13.82 13.82 1.78	-	-	-	-	-	-	-	-	-	-	-	-	-	-	-	-	-	-	-	-	-	-	-
Fort Lee (borough)	9,307 56.26	3,940	1,409 35.76 35.76 15.14	-	-	119 51.74 8.45 3.02 1.28	-	-	425 65.28 30.16 10.79 4.57	-	-	-	-	-	-	103 13.75 7.31 2.61 1.11	535 27.05 37.97 13.58 5.75	-	-	-	-	-	-	-	-	-
Franklin Lakes (borough)	3,160 95.12	131	131 100.00 100.00 4.15	-	-	-	-	-	-	-	-	-	-	-	-	-	-	-	-	-	-	-	-	-	-	-
Glen Rock (borough)	3,677 92.46	224	181 80.80 80.80 4.92	-	-	-	-	-	-	-	-	-	-	-	-	-	-	-	-	-	-	-	-	-	-	-
Hackensack (city)	5,873 32.42	1,240	254 20.48 20.48 4.32	-	-	32 7.67 12.60 2.58 0.54	-	-	-	-	65 29.15 25.59 5.24 1.11	-	-	-	-	-	60 24.19 23.62 4.84 1.02	-	-	-	-	-	-	-	-	-
Hasbrouck Heights (borough)	3,138 69.41	183	50 27.32 27.32 1.59	-	-	-	-	-	-	-	-	-	-	-	-	-	-	-	-	-	-	-	-	-	-	-
Hillsdale (borough)	3,115 88.95	121	94 77.69 77.69 3.02	-	-	-	-	-	-	-	-	-	-	-	-	-	-	-	-	-	-	-	-	-	-	-
Little Ferry (borough)	2,021 46.29	640	98 15.31 15.31 4.85	-	-	21 15.79 21.43 3.28 1.04	-	-	-	-	54 54.55 55.10 8.44 2.67	-	-	-	-	-	0 0.00 0.00 0.00 0.00	-	-	-	-	-	-	-	-	-
Lodi (borough)	4,015 42.14	628	145 23.09 23.09 3.61	-	-	71 20.29 48.97 11.31 1.77	-	-	-	-	35 22.88 24.14 5.57 0.87	-	-	-	-	-	-	-	-	-	-	-	-	-	-	-
Lyndhurst (township)	4,721 59.93	364	129 35.44 35.44 2.73	-	-	-	-	-	-	-	-	-	-	-	-	-	-	-	-	-	-	-	-	-	-	-

Notes: Please refer to the User's Guide for an explanation of data; data is arranged alphabetically by state, then county, then city within each county; table includes counties with populations greater than 49,999 unless noted and cities with populations greater than 9,999 whose Asian and/or NHPI population rates are greater than the national average; (1) Native Hawaiian and other Pacific Islander; (2) excludes Taiwanese; (3) includes Chamorro; (4) county does not meet population threshold but is shown in order to allow inclusion of city

Place	All owner-occupied housing units	Asian-occupied housing units	Asians who own and occupy their own homes	NHPI[1]-occupied housing units	NHPIs[1] who own and occupy their own homes	Asian Indian	Bangladeshi	Cambodian	Chinese[2]	Fijian	Filipino	Guamanian[3]	Hawaiian, Native	Hmong	Indonesian	Japanese	Korean	Laotian	Malaysian	Pakistani	Samoan	Sri Lankan	Taiwanese	Thai	Tongan	Vietnamese
Mahwah (township)	7,851 84.06	473	302 63.85 63.85 3.85	-	-	105 74.47 34.77 22.20 1.34	-	-	-	-	-	-	-	-	-	-	-	-	-	-	-	-	-	-	-	-
New Milford (borough)	4,015 63.27	715	404 56.50 56.50 10.06	-	-	99 51.30 24.50 13.85 2.47	-	-	-	-	166 63.60 41.09 23.22 4.13	-	-	-	-	-	-	-	-	-	-	-	-	-	-	-
North Arlington (borough)	3,475 54.36	302	105 34.77 34.77 3.02	-	-	-	-	-	-	-	-	-	-	-	-	-	-	-	-	-	-	-	-	-	-	-
Palisades Park (borough)	2,321 37.15	2,230	501 22.47 22.47 21.59	-	-	-	-	-	-	-	-	-	-	-	-	-	337 17.95 67.27 15.11 14.52	-	-	-	-	-	-	-	-	-
Paramus (borough)	7,327 90.66	1,109	923 83.23 83.23 12.60	-	-	288 97.30 31.20 25.97 3.93	-	-	163 92.61 17.66 14.70 2.22	-	209 95.00 22.64 18.85 2.85	-	-	-	-	-	185 62.93 20.04 16.68 2.52	-	-	-	-	-	-	-	-	-
Ramsey (borough)	4,473 84.19	266	187 70.30 70.30 4.18	-	-	-	-	-	-	-	-	-	-	-	-	-	-	-	-	-	-	-	-	-	-	-
Ridgefield (borough)	2,305 57.34	498	133 26.71 26.71 5.77	-	-	-	-	-	-	-	-	-	-	-	-	-	89 24.86 66.92 17.87 3.86	-	-	-	-	-	-	-	-	-
Ridgefield Park (village)	2,669 53.25	343	126 36.73 36.73 4.72	-	-	-	-	-	-	-	-	-	-	-	-	-	20 15.63 15.87 5.83 0.75	-	-	-	-	-	-	-	-	-
Ridgewood (village)	6,880 79.97	556	347 62.41 62.41 5.04	-	-	-	-	-	-	-	-	-	-	-	-	41 35.04 11.82 7.37 0.60	68 46.90 19.60 12.23 0.99	-	-	-	-	-	-	-	-	-
River Edge (borough)	3,095 74.31	412	196 47.57 47.57 6.33	-	-	-	-	-	-	-	-	-	-	-	-	-	21 17.80 10.71 5.10 0.68	-	-	-	-	-	-	-	-	-

Notes: Please refer to the User's Guide for an explanation of data; data is arranged alphabetically by state, then county, then city within each county; table includes counties with populations greater than 49,999 unless noted and cities with populations greater than 9,999 whose Asian and/or NHPI population rates are greater than the national average; (1) Native Hawaiian and other Pacific Islander; (2) excludes Taiwanese; (3) includes Chamorro; (4) county does not meet population threshold but is shown in order to allow inclusion of city

Place	All owner-occupied housing units	Asian-occupied housing units	Asians who own and occupy their own homes	NHPI[1]-occupied housing units	NHPIs[1] who own and occupy their own homes	Asian Indian	Bangladeshi	Cambodian	Chinese[2]	Fijian	Filipino	Guamanian[3]	Hawaiian, Native	Hmong	Indonesian	Japanese	Korean	Laotian	Malaysian	Pakistani	Samoan	Sri Lankan	Taiwanese	Thai	Tongan	Vietnamese
Rutherford (borough)	4,622 65.51	620	244 39.35 39.35 5.28	-	-	41 36.61 16.80 6.61 0.89	-	-	-	-	-	-	-	-	-	-	66 23.00 27.05 10.65 1.43	-	-	-	-	-	-	-	-	-
Saddle Brook (township)	3,771 74.50	199	117 58.79 58.79 3.10	-	-	-	-	-	-	-	-	-	-	-	-	-	-	-	-	-	-	-	-	-	-	-
Teaneck (township)	10,410 77.58	719	532 73.99 73.99 5.11	-	-	187 78.90 35.15 26.01 1.80	-	-	-	-	194 89.81 36.47 26.98 1.86	-	-	-	-	-	-	-	-	-	-	-	-	-	-	-
Tenafly (borough)	3,848 80.60	736	450 61.14 61.14 11.69	-	-	-	-	-	213 92.61 47.33 28.94 5.54	-	-	-	-	-	-	-	115 35.06 25.56 15.63 2.99	-	-	-	-	-	-	-	-	-
Wallington (borough)	1,963 41.31	179	7 3.91 3.91 0.36	-	-	-	-	-	-	-	-	-	-	-	-	-	-	-	-	-	-	-	-	-	-	-
Westwood (borough)	2,779 61.96	182	74 40.66 40.66 2.66	-	-	-	-	-	-	-	-	-	-	-	-	-	-	-	-	-	-	-	-	-	-	-
Wyckoff (township)	5,143 92.82	183	153 83.61 83.61 2.97	-	-	-	-	-	-	-	-	-	-	-	-	-	-	-	-	-	-	-	-	-	-	-
Burlington County	119,500 77.41	3,353	2,065 61.59 61.59 1.73	-	-	584 48.03 28.28 17.42 0.49	-	-	373 74.90 18.06 11.12 0.31	-	403 71.71 19.52 12.02 0.34	-	-	-	-	165 67.35 7.99 4.92 0.14	290 65.46 14.04 8.65 0.24	-	-	-	-	-	-	-	-	113 74.83 5.47 3.37 0.09
Browns Mills (cdp)	3,084 78.00	132	97 73.48 73.48 3.15	-	-	-	-	-	-	-	-	-	-	-	-	-	69 90.79 71.13 52.27 2.24	-	-	-	-	-	-	-	-	-
Evesham (township)	12,275 77.57	477	323 67.71 67.71 2.63	-	-	51 38.93 15.79 10.69 0.42	-	-	106 86.18 32.82 22.22 0.86	-	-	-	-	-	-	-	-	-	-	-	-	-	-	-	-	-

Notes: Please refer to the User's Guide for an explanation of data; data is arranged alphabetically by state, then county, then city within each county; table includes counties with populations greater than 49,999 unless noted and cities with populations greater than 9,999 whose Asian and/or NHPI population rates are greater than the national average; (1) Native Hawaiian and other Pacific Islander; (2) excludes Taiwanese; (3) includes Chamorro; (4) county does not meet population threshold but is shown in order to allow inclusion of city

Place	All owner-occupied housing units	Asian-occupied housing units	Asians who own and occupy their own homes	NHPI[1]-occupied housing units	NHPIs[1] who own and occupy their own homes	Asian Indian	Bangladeshi	Cambodian	Chinese[2]	Fijian	Filipino	Guamanian[3]	Hawaiian, Native	Hmong	Indonesian	Japanese	Korean	Laotian	Malaysian	Pakistani	Samoan	Sri Lankan	Taiwanese	Thai	Tongan	Vietnamese
Maple Shade (township)	4,216 49.82	418	19 4.55 4.55 0.45	-	-	0 0.00 0.00 0.00 0.00	-	-	-	-	-	-	-	-	-	-	-	-	-	-	-	-	-	-	-	-
Marlton (cdp)	2,792 68.21	153	59 38.56 38.56 2.11	-	-	-	-	-	-	-	-	-	-	-	-	-	-	-	-	-	-	-	-	-	-	-
Mount Laurel (township)	13,863 83.66	516	398 77.13 77.13 2.87	-	-	130 82.80 32.66 25.19 0.94	-	-	133 78.70 33.42 25.78 0.96	-	-	-	-	-	-	-	-	-	-	-	-	-	-	-	-	-
Camden County	130,007 69.99	5,707	3,739 65.52 65.52 2.88	-	-	940 60.88 25.14 16.47 0.72	-	28 50.91 0.75 0.49 0.02	809 70.04 21.64 14.18 0.62	-	865 79.07 23.13 15.16 0.67	-	-	-	-	-	315 62.01 8.42 5.52 0.24	-	-	67 62.62 1.79 1.17 0.05	-	-	-	-	-	452 58.40 12.09 7.92 0.35
Barclay-Kingston (cdp)	3,305 80.57	236	184 77.97 77.97 5.57	-	-	-	-	-	-	-	-	-	-	-	-	-	-	-	-	-	-	-	-	-	-	-
Bellmawr (borough)	3,272 73.59	138	71 51.45 51.45 2.17	-	-	-	-	-	-	-	-	-	-	-	-	-	-	-	-	-	-	-	-	-	-	-
Cherry Hill Mall (cdp)	4,110 80.43	360	225 62.50 62.50 5.47	-	-	-	-	-	-	-	-	-	-	-	-	-	-	-	-	-	-	-	-	-	-	-
Cherry Hill (township)	21,751 82.93	1,790	1,487 83.07 83.07 6.84	-	-	340 79.44 22.86 18.99 1.56	-	-	408 89.87 27.44 22.79 1.88	-	368 90.64 24.75 20.56 1.69	-	-	-	-	-	196 72.32 13.18 10.95 0.90	-	-	-	-	-	-	-	-	-
Echelon (cdp)	2,056 42.11	494	146 29.55 29.55 7.10	-	-	73 27.86 50.00 14.78 3.55	-	-	-	-	-	-	-	-	-	-	-	-	-	-	-	-	-	-	-	-
Greentree (cdp)	3,527 91.71	471	471 100.00 100.00 13.35	-	-	159 100.00 33.76 33.76 4.51	-	-	166 100.00 35.24 35.24 4.71	-	-	-	-	-	-	-	-	-	-	-	-	-	-	-	-	-

Notes: Please refer to the User's Guide for an explanation of data; data is arranged alphabetically by state, then county, then city within each county; table includes counties with populations greater than 49,999 unless noted and cities with populations greater than 9,999 whose Asian and/or NHPI population rates are greater than the national average; (1) Native Hawaiian and other Pacific Islander; (2) excludes Taiwanese; (3) includes Chamorro; (4) county does not meet population threshold but is shown in order to allow inclusion of city

Place	All owner-occupied housing units	Asian-occupied housing units	Asians who own and occupy their own homes	NHPI[1]-occupied housing units	NHPIs[1] who own and occupy their own homes	Asian Indian	Bangladeshi	Cambodian	Chinese[2]	Fijian	Filipino	Guamanian[3]	Hawaiian, Native	Hmong	Indonesian	Japanese	Korean	Laotian	Malaysian	Pakistani	Samoan	Sri Lankan	Taiwanese	Thai	Tongan	Vietnamese
Pennsauken (township)	9,966 80.49	385	296 76.88 76.88 2.97	-	-	-	-	-	-	-	-	-	-	-	-	-	-	-	-	-	-	-	-	-	-	111 74.00 37.50 28.83 1.11
Springdale (cdp)	4,628 88.80	351	321 91.45 91.45 6.94	-	-	-	-	-	110 100.00 34.27 31.34 2.38	-	-	-	-	-	-	-	-	-	-	-	-	-	-	-	-	-
Voorhees (township)	7,102 67.71	1,020	650 63.73 63.73 9.15	-	-	351 62.46 54.00 34.41 4.94	-	-	149 69.95 22.92 14.61 2.10	-	86 67.72 13.23 8.43 1.21	-	-	-	-	-	-	-	-	-	-	-	-	-	-	-
Cape May County	31,299 74.26	184	137 74.46 74.46 0.44	-	-	-	-	-	-	-	-	-	-	-	-	-	-	-	-	-	-	-	-	-	-	-
Cumberland County	33,392 67.95	388	302 77.84 77.84 0.90	-	-	47 51.09 15.56 12.11 0.14	-	-	-	-	-	-	-	-	-	-	-	-	-	-	-	-	-	-	-	-
Essex County	129,489 45.64	8,749	5,284 60.40 60.40 4.08	127	26 20.47 20.47 0.02	1,467 52.49 27.76 16.77 1.13	-	-	1,388 74.34 26.27 15.86 1.07	-	1,354 62.25 25.62 15.48 1.05	-	-	-	-	110 55.56 2.08 1.26 0.08	493 61.24 9.33 5.63 0.38	-	-	66 38.15 1.25 0.75 0.05	-	-	138 90.20 2.61 1.58 0.11	-	-	121 42.91 2.29 1.38 0.09
Belleville (township)	6,995 50.94	1,117	512 45.84 45.84 7.32	-	-	83 27.57 16.21 7.43 1.19	-	-	-	-	289 60.59 56.45 25.87 4.13	-	-	-	-	-	-	-	-	-	-	-	-	-	-	35 33.33 6.84 3.13 0.50
Bloomfield (township)	10,137 53.30	1,264	768 60.76 60.76 7.58	-	-	278 56.39 36.20 21.99 2.74	-	-	112 71.34 14.58 8.86 1.10	-	311 64.79 40.49 24.60 3.07	-	-	-	-	-	-	-	-	-	-	-	-	-	-	-
Cedar Grove (township)	3,480 79.04	174	138 79.31 79.31 3.97	-	-	-	-	-	-	-	-	-	-	-	-	-	-	-	-	-	-	-	-	-	-	-
Livingston (township)	8,719 93.75	1,120	1,041 92.95 92.95 11.94	-	-	191 87.21 18.35 17.05 2.19	-	-	464 98.10 44.57 41.43 5.32	-	130 90.28 12.49 11.61 1.49	-	-	-	-	-	179 86.47 17.20 15.98 2.05	-	-	-	-	-	-	-	-	-

Notes: Please refer to the User's Guide for an explanation of data; data is arranged alphabetically by state, then county, then city within each county; table includes counties with populations greater than 49,999 unless noted and cities with populations greater than 9,999 whose Asian and/or NHPI population rates are greater than the national average; (1) Native Hawaiian and other Pacific Islander; (2) excludes Taiwanese; (3) includes Chamorro; (4) county does not meet population threshold but is shown in order to allow inclusion of city

Place	All owner-occupied housing units	Asian-occupied housing units	Asians who own and occupy their own homes	NHPI[1]-occupied housing units	NHPIs[1] who own and occupy their own homes	Asian Indian	Bangladeshi	Cambodian	Chinese[2]	Fijian	Filipino	Guamanian[3]	Hawaiian, Native	Hmong	Indonesian	Japanese	Korean	Laotian	Malaysian	Pakistani	Samoan	Sri Lankan	Taiwanese	Thai	Tongan	Vietnamese
Millburn (township)	5,777 82.35	464	308 66.38 66.38 5.33	-	-	-	-	-	137 76.11 44.48 29.53 2.37	-	-	-	-	-	-	-	-	-	-	-	-	-	-	-	-	-
Nutley (township)	7,276 66.85	581	323 55.59 55.59 4.44	-	-	98 50.26 30.34 16.87 1.35	-	-	-	-	88 60.69 27.24 15.15 1.21	-	-	-	-	-	-	-	-	-	-	-	-	-	-	-
Verona (township)	4,306 77.10	168	137 81.55 81.55 3.18	-	-	-	-	-	-	-	-	-	-	-	-	-	-	-	-	-	-	-	-	-	-	-
West Caldwell (township)	3,440 86.22	143	115 80.42 80.42 3.34	-	-	-	-	-	-	-	-	-	-	-	-	-	-	-	-	-	-	-	-	-	-	-
West Orange (township)	11,514 70.24	1,141	805 70.55 70.55 6.99	-	-	250 65.96 31.06 21.91 2.17	-	-	175 72.92 21.74 15.34 1.52	-	222 82.84 27.58 19.46 1.93	-	-	-	-	-	102 62.20 12.67 8.94 0.89	-	-	-	-	-	-	-	-	-
Gloucester County	72,482 79.90	1,130	876 77.52 77.52 1.21	-	-	199 68.62 22.72 17.61 0.27	-	-	185 83.33 21.12 16.37 0.26	-	327 89.59 37.33 28.94 0.45	-	-	-	-	-	42 55.26 4.79 3.72 0.06	-	-	-	-	-	-	-	-	-
Hudson County	70,658 30.65	18,334	6,264 34.17 34.17 8.87	-	-	1,672 26.88 26.69 9.12 2.37	-	-	898 34.49 14.34 4.90 1.27	-	2,691 45.56 42.96 14.68 3.81	-	-	-	-	119 27.17 1.90 0.65 0.17	325 22.38 5.19 1.77 0.46	-	-	185 35.58 2.95 1.01 0.26	-	-	-	-	-	124 25.31 1.98 0.68 0.18
Bayonne (city)	10,228 40.04	680	179 26.32 26.32 1.75	-	-	34 24.29 18.99 5.00 0.33	-	-	-	-	84 27.10 46.93 12.35 0.82	-	-	-	-	-	29 23.02 16.20 4.26 0.28	-	-	-	-	-	-	-	-	-
Guttenberg (town)	1,532 34.33	328	162 49.39 49.39 10.57	-	-	-	-	-	-	-	-	-	-	-	-	-	-	-	-	-	-	-	-	-	-	-
Harrison (town)	1,645 32.03	605	127 20.99 20.99 7.72	-	-	-	-	-	113 25.57 88.98 18.68 6.87	-	-	-	-	-	-	-	-	-	-	-	-	-	-	-	-	-

Notes: Please refer to the User's Guide for an explanation of data; data is arranged alphabetically by state, then county, then city within each county; table includes counties with populations greater than 49,999 unless noted and cities with populations greater than 9,999 whose Asian and/or NHPI population rates are greater than the national average; (1) Native Hawaiian and other Pacific Islander; (2) excludes Taiwanese; (3) includes Chamorro; (4) county does not meet population threshold but is shown in order to allow inclusion of city

Place	All owner-occupied housing units	Asian-occupied housing units	Asians who own and occupy their own homes	NHPI[1]-occupied housing units	NHPIs[1] who own and occupy their own homes	Asian Indian	Bangladeshi	Cambodian	Chinese[2]	Fijian	Filipino	Guamanian[3]	Hawaiian, Native	Hmong	Indonesian	Japanese	Korean	Laotian	Malaysian	Pakistani	Samoan	Sri Lankan	Taiwanese	Thai	Tongan	Vietnamese
Hoboken (city)	4,484	701	153	-	-	55	-	-	37	-	-	-	-	-	-	-	-	-	-	-	-	-	-	-	-	-
	22.99		21.83			22.92			18.50																	
						35.95			24.18																	
			21.83			7.85			5.28																	
			3.41			1.23			0.83																	
Jersey City (city)	24,965	12,306	4,309	-	-	969	-	-	396	-	2,354	-	-	-	-	-	146	-	-	138	-	-	-	-	-	89
	28.17		35.02			24.53			33.56		47.20						20.19			32.78						21.34
						22.49			9.19		54.63						3.39			3.20						2.07
			35.02			7.87			3.22		19.13						1.19			1.12						0.72
			17.26			3.88			1.59		9.43						0.58			0.55						0.36
Kearny (town)	6,496	685	174	-	-	52	-	-	83	-	-	-	-	-	-	-	-	-	-	-	-	-	-	-	-	-
	47.98		25.40			21.85			29.33																	
						29.89			47.70																	
			25.40			7.59			12.12																	
			2.68			0.80			1.28																	
North Bergen (township)	8,013	1,083	472	-	-	274	-	-	72	-	-	-	-	-	-	-	-	-	-	-	-	-	-	-	-	-
	37.68		43.58			41.77			71.29																	
						58.05			15.25																	
			43.58			25.30			6.65																	
			5.89			3.42			0.90																	
Secaucus (town)	3,690	566	321	-	-	76	-	-	-	-	99	-	-	-	-	-	-	-	-	-	-	-	-	-	-	-
	60.24		56.71			43.43					63.87															
						23.68					30.84															
			56.71			13.43					17.49															
			8.70			2.06					2.68															
Weehawken (township)	1,865	260	78	-	-	-	-	-	-	-	-	-	-	-	-	-	-	-	-	-	-	-	-	-	-	-
	31.21		30.00																							
			30.00																							
			4.18																							
Hunterdon County	36,549	703	562	-	-	239	-	-	173	-	-	-	-	-	-	-	-	-	-	-	-	-	-	-	-	-
	83.68		79.94			80.20			78.28																	
						42.53			30.78																	
			79.94			34.00			24.61																	
			1.54			0.65			0.47																	
Mercer County	84,325	5,032	3,087	-	-	1,203	-	-	911	-	254	-	-	-	-	95	262	-	-	114	-	-	110	-	-	-
	67.03		61.35			61.16			67.23		71.75					37.85	52.72			62.64			75.34			
						38.97			29.51		8.23					3.08	8.49			3.69			3.56			
			61.35			23.91			18.10		5.05					1.89	5.21			2.27			2.19			
			3.66			1.43			1.08		0.30					0.11	0.31			0.14			0.13			
East Windsor (township)	5,777	730	333	-	-	231	-	-	-	-	-	-	-	-	-	-	-	-	-	-	-	-	-	-	-	-
	61.15		45.62			53.10																				
						69.37																				
			45.62			31.64																				
			5.76			4.00																				
Hopewell (township)	5,109	169	169	-	-	-	-	-	-	-	-	-	-	-	-	-	-	-	-	-	-	-	-	-	-	-
	92.92		100.00																							
			100.00																							
			3.31																							

Notes: Please refer to the User's Guide for an explanation of data; data is arranged alphabetically by state, then county, then city within each county; table includes counties with populations greater than 49,999 unless noted and cities with populations greater than 9,999 whose Asian and/or NHPI population rates are greater than the national average; (1) Native Hawaiian and other Pacific Islander; (2) excludes Taiwanese; (3) includes Chamorro; (4) county does not meet population threshold but is shown in order to allow inclusion of city

Place	All owner-occupied housing units	Asian-occupied housing units	Asians who own and occupy their own homes	NHPI-occupied housing units	NHPIs[1] who own and occupy their own homes	Asian Indian	Bangladeshi	Cambodian	Chinese[2]	Fijian	Filipino	Guamanian[3]	Hawaiian, Native	Hmong	Indonesian	Japanese	Korean	Laotian	Malaysian	Pakistani	Samoan	Sri Lankan	Taiwanese	Thai	Tongan	Vietnamese
	7,637	701	395	-	-	169	-	-	126	-	-	-	-	-	-	-	-	-	-	-	-	-	-	-	-	-
	70.73		56.35			53.14			60.00																	
Lawrence (township)						42.78			31.90																	
			56.35			24.11			17.97																	
			5.17			2.21			1.65																	
	1,557	129	11	-	-	-	-	-	-	-	-	-	-	-	-	-	-	-	-	-	-	-	-	-	-	-
	46.81		8.53																							
Princeton (borough)																										
			8.53																							
			0.71																							
	4,245	499	274	-	-	89	-	-	101	-	-	-	-	-	-	-	-	-	-	-	-	-	-	-	-	-
	70.23		54.91			79.46			44.30																	
Princeton (township)						32.48			36.86																	
			54.91			17.84			20.24																	
			6.45			2.10			2.38																	
	5,871	1,389	1,156	-	-	413	-	-	465	-	-	-	-	-	-	-	74	-	-	-	-	-	-	-	-	-
	80.62		83.23			88.25			95.29								53.24									
West Windsor (township)						35.73			40.22								6.40									
			83.23			29.73			33.48								5.33									
			19.69			7.03			7.92								1.26									
	177,377	31,293	16,180	-	-	7,026	29	-	4,514	-	2,352	-	-	-	41	77	666	-	-	438	-	93	308	-	-	331
	66.73		51.70			41.51	21.97		67.42		72.15				33.88	24.06	45.21			56.81		74.40	71.46			69.54
Middlesex County						43.42	0.18		27.90		14.54				0.25	0.48	4.12			2.71		0.57	1.90			2.05
			51.70			22.45	0.09		14.42		7.52				0.13	0.25	2.13			1.40		0.30	0.98			1.06
			9.12			3.96	0.02		2.54		1.33				0.02	0.04	0.38			0.25		0.05	0.17			0.19
	2,849	1,038	154	-	-	52	-	-	-	-	-	-	-	-	-	-	-	-	-	-	-	-	-	-	-	-
	54.44		14.84			6.99																				
Avenel (cdp)						33.77																				
			14.84			5.01																				
			5.41			1.83																				
	4,808	392	260	-	-	173	-	-	-	-	-	-	-	-	-	-	-	-	-	-	-	-	-	-	-	-
	68.31		66.33			60.07																				
Carteret (borough)						66.54																				
			66.33			44.13																				
			5.41			3.60																				
	5,566	302	270	-	-	128	-	-	-	-	85	-	-	-	-	-	-	-	-	-	-	-	-	-	-	-
	90.05		89.40			83.66					100.00															
Colonia (cdp)						47.41					31.48															
			89.40			42.38					28.15															
			4.85			2.30					1.53															
	13,764	2,277	1,757	-	-	548	-	-	825	-	116	-	-	-	-	-	76	-	-	-	-	-	-	-	-	-
	84.07		77.16			67.24			85.40		86.57						58.91									
East Brunswick (township)						31.19			46.96		6.60						4.33									
			77.16			24.07			36.23		5.09						3.34									
			12.77			3.98			5.99		0.84						0.55									
	22,462	8,622	4,213	-	-	1,893	-	-	1,264	-	489	-	-	-	-	-	178	-	-	105	-	-	140	-	-	-
	63.93		48.86			36.50			73.02		71.49						48.24			56.76			83.83			
Edison (township)						44.93			30.00		11.61						4.23			2.49			3.32			
			48.86			21.96			14.66		5.67						2.06			1.22			1.62			
			18.76			8.43			5.63		2.18						0.79			0.47			0.62			

Notes: Please refer to the User's Guide for an explanation of data; data is arranged alphabetically by state, then county, then city within each county; table includes counties with populations greater than 49,999 unless noted and cities with populations greater than 9,999 whose Asian and/or NHPI population rates are greater than the national average; (1) Native Hawaiian and other Pacific Islander; (2) excludes Taiwanese; (3) includes Chamorro; (4) county does not meet population threshold but is shown in order to allow inclusion of city

Place	All owner-occupied housing units	Asian-occupied housing units	Asians who own and occupy their own homes	NHPI[1]-occupied housing units	NHPIs[1] who own and occupy their own homes	Asian Indian	Bangladeshi	Cambodian	Chinese[2]	Fijian	Filipino	Guamanian[3]	Hawaiian, Native	Hmong	Indonesian	Japanese	Korean	Laotian	Malaysian	Pakistani	Samoan	Sri Lankan	Taiwanese	Thai	Tongan	Vietnamese
Fords (cdp)	4,092	761	335	-	-	99	-	-	-	-	143	-	-	-	-	-	-	-	-	-	-	-	-	-	-	-
	72.75		44.02			23.86					78.14															
						29.55					42.69															
			44.02			13.01					18.79															
			8.19			2.42					3.49															
Highland Park (borough)	2,478	742	62	-	-	0	-	-	45	-	-	-	-	-	-	-	-	-	-	-	-	-	-	-	-	-
	42.01		8.36			0.00			13.76																	
						0.00			72.58																	
			8.36			0.00			6.06																	
			2.50			0.00			1.82																	
Iselin (cdp)	4,502	1,161	523	-	-	329	-	-	86	-	-	-	-	-	-	-	-	-	-	-	-	-	-	-	-	-
	75.32		45.05			40.07			55.48																	
						62.91			16.44																	
			45.05			28.34			7.41																	
			11.62			7.31			1.91																	
Metuchen (borough)	4,028	307	201	-	-	-	-	-	-	-	-	-	-	-	-	-	-	-	-	-	-	-	-	-	-	-
	80.69		65.47																							
			65.47																							
			4.99																							
Middlesex (borough)	3,789	172	102	-	-	-	-	-	-	-	-	-	-	-	-	-	-	-	-	-	-	-	-	-	-	-
	75.06		59.30																							
			59.30																							
			2.69																							
New Brunswick (city)	3,437	651	78	-	-	39	-	-	15	-	-	-	-	-	-	-	-	-	-	-	-	-	-	-	-	-
	26.32		11.98			11.24			22.39																	
						50.00			19.23																	
			11.98			5.99			2.30																	
			2.27			1.13			0.44																	
North Brunswick (township)	8,568	1,665	1,019	-	-	521	-	-	239	-	95	-	-	-	-	-	77	-	-	-	-	-	-	-	-	-
	62.84		61.20			56.57			78.62		70.90						49.68									
						51.13			23.45		9.32						7.56									
			61.20			31.29			14.35		5.71						4.62									
			11.89			6.08			2.79		1.11						0.90									
Old Bridge (township)	14,823	1,850	1,143	-	-	456	-	-	258	-	255	-	-	-	-	-	-	-	-	65	-	-	-	-	-	-
	69.14		61.78			56.72			68.62		72.24									59.63						
						39.90			22.57		22.31									5.69						
			61.78			24.65			13.95		13.78									3.51						
			7.71			3.08			1.74		1.72									0.44						
Piscataway (township)	11,416	3,329	1,678	-	-	695	-	-	397	-	363	-	-	-	-	-	71	-	-	-	-	-	-	-	-	-
	69.19		50.41			40.43			50.64		85.61						52.99									
						41.42			23.66		21.63						4.23									
			50.41			20.88			11.93		10.90						2.13									
			14.70			6.09			3.48		3.18						0.62									
Plainsboro (township)	3,677	2,237	891	-	-	365	-	-	372	-	-	-	-	-	-	-	-	-	-	-	-	-	-	-	-	-
	42.06		39.83			31.66			61.59																	
						40.97			41.75																	
			39.83			16.32			16.63																	
			24.23			9.93			10.12																	

Notes: Please refer to the User's Guide for an explanation of data; data is arranged alphabetically by state, then county, then city within each county; table includes counties with populations greater than 49,999 unless noted and cities with populations greater than 9,999 whose Asian and/or NHPI population rates are greater than the national average; (1) Native Hawaiian and other Pacific Islander; (2) excludes Taiwanese; (3) includes Chamorro; (4) county does not meet population threshold but is shown in order to allow inclusion of city

Place	All owner-occupied housing units	Asian-occupied housing units	Asians who own and occupy their own homes	NHPI[1]-occupied housing units	NHPIs[1] who own and occupy their own homes	Asian Indian	Bangladeshi	Cambodian	Chinese[2]	Fijian	Filipino	Guamanian[3]	Hawaiian, Native	Hmong	Indonesian	Japanese	Korean	Laotian	Malaysian	Pakistani	Samoan	Sri Lankan	Taiwanese	Thai	Tongan	Vietnamese
Princeton Meadows (cdp)	2,016	1,423	464	-	-	186	-	-	188	-	-	-	-	-	-	-	-	-	-	-	-	-	-	-	-	-
	33.79		32.61			24.80			53.71																	
						40.09			40.52																	
			32.61			13.07			13.21																	
			23.02			9.23			9.33																	
Sayreville (borough)	10,120	1,348	540	-	-	237	-	-	136	-	98	-	-	-	-	-	-	-	-	-	-	-	-	-	-	-
	67.67		40.06			28.35			60.18		53.26															
						43.89			25.19		18.15															
			40.06			17.58			10.09		7.27															
			5.34			2.34			1.34		0.97															
South Brunswick (township)	10,226	2,168	1,631	-	-	882	-	-	367	-	153	-	-	-	-	-	-	-	-	-	-	-	-	-	-	-
	76.15		75.23			74.94			77.59		81.82															
						54.08			22.50		9.38															
			75.23			40.68			16.93		7.06															
			15.95			8.63			3.59		1.50															
South Plainfield (borough)	6,360	423	355	-	-	146	-	-	-	-	94	-	-	-	-	-	-	-	-	-	-	-	-	-	-	58
	88.94		83.92			90.68					100.00															59.79
						41.13					26.48															16.34
			83.92			34.52					22.22															13.71
			5.58			2.30					1.48															0.91
Woodbridge (township)	24,404	4,283	1,649	-	-	822	-	-	238	-	374	-	-	-	-	-	82	-	-	53	-	-	-	-	-	-
	70.61		38.50			28.75			58.33		67.03						43.16			54.08						
						49.85			14.43		22.68						4.97			3.21						
			38.50			19.19			5.56		8.73						1.91			1.24						
			6.76			3.37			0.98		1.53						0.34			0.22						
Monmouth County	167,273	7,234	5,193	-	-	1,309	-	-	2,383	-	700	-	-	-	-	105	295	-	-	45	-	-	-	-	-	138
	74.60		71.79			61.48			82.77		74.15					71.92	60.33			43.69						75.00
						25.21			45.89		13.48					2.02	5.68			0.87						2.66
			71.79			18.10			32.94		9.68					1.45	4.08			0.62						1.91
			3.10			0.78			1.42		0.42					0.06	0.18			0.03						0.08
Aberdeen (township)	4,973	349	198	-	-	47	-	-	115	-	-	-	-	-	-	-	-	-	-	-	-	-	-	-	-	-
	77.68		56.73			30.13			87.79																	
						23.74			58.08																	
			56.73			13.47			32.95																	
			3.98			0.95			2.31																	
Colts Neck (township)	2,896	136	124	-	-	-	-	-	-	-	-	-	-	-	-	-	-	-	-	-	-	-	-	-	-	-
	82.44		91.18																							
			91.18																							
			4.28																							
Eatontown (borough)	2,837	524	179	-	-	-	-	-	-	-	-	-	-	-	-	-	-	-	-	-	-	-	-	-	-	-
	49.11		34.16																							
			34.16																							
			6.31																							
Freehold (township)	9,431	466	430	-	-	116	-	-	140	-	112	-	-	-	-	-	-	-	-	-	-	-	-	-	-	-
	87.21		92.27			93.55			86.96		100.00															
						26.98			32.56		26.05															
			92.27			24.89			30.04		24.03															
			4.56			1.23			1.48		1.19															

Notes: Please refer to the User's Guide for an explanation of data; data is arranged alphabetically by state, then county, then city within each county; table includes counties with populations greater than 49,999 unless noted and cities with populations greater than 9,999 whose Asian and/or NHPI population rates are greater than the national average; (1) Native Hawaiian and other Pacific Islander; (2) excludes Taiwanese; (3) includes Chamorro; (4) county does not meet population threshold but is shown in order to allow inclusion of city

Place	All owner-occupied housing units	Asian-occupied housing units	Asians who own and occupy their own homes	NHPI[1]-occupied housing units	NHPIs[1] who own and occupy their own homes	Asian Indian	Bangladeshi	Cambodian	Chinese[2]	Fijian	Filipino	Guamanian[3]	Hawaiian, Native	Hmong	Indonesian	Japanese	Korean	Laotian	Malaysian	Pakistani	Samoan	Sri Lankan	Taiwanese	Thai	Tongan	Vietnamese
Holmdel (township)	4,725 95.51	719	679 94.44 94.44 14.37	-	-	126 87.50 18.56 17.52 2.67	-	-	420 96.33 61.86 58.41 8.89	-	-	-	-	-	-	-	-	-	-	-	-	-	-	-	-	-
Howell (township)	14,281 88.91	497	429 86.32 86.32 3.00	-	-	155 95.09 36.13 31.19 1.09	-	-	-	-	111 92.50 25.87 22.33 0.78	-	-	-	-	-	-	-	-	-	-	-	-	-	-	-
Manalapan (township)	10,132 93.98	365	350 95.89 95.89 3.45	-	-	143 95.97 40.86 39.18 1.41	-	-	122 96.06 34.86 33.42 1.20	-	-	-	-	-	-	-	-	-	-	-	-	-	-	-	-	-
Marlboro (township)	11,043 96.21	1,213	1,184 97.61 97.61 10.72	-	-	252 95.82 21.28 20.77 2.28	-	-	732 100.00 61.82 60.35 6.63	-	-	-	-	-	-	-	-	-	-	-	-	-	-	-	-	-
Morganville (cdp)	3,511 97.07	275	266 96.73 96.73 7.58	-	-	-	-	-	184 100.00 69.17 66.91 5.24	-	-	-	-	-	-	-	-	-	-	-	-	-	-	-	-	-
Ocean (township)	6,874 67.04	515	176 34.17 34.17 2.56	-	-	55 24.02 31.25 10.68 0.80	-	-	-	-	-	-	-	-	-	-	-	-	-	-	-	-	-	-	-	-
Tinton Falls (borough)	4,878 82.85	242	204 84.30 84.30 4.18	-	-	-	-	-	-	-	-	-	-	-	-	-	-	-	-	-	-	-	-	-	-	-
West Freehold (cdp)	4,000 86.30	153	141 92.16 92.16 3.52	-	-	-	-	-	-	-	-	-	-	-	-	-	-	-	-	-	-	-	-	-	-	-
Morris County	128,990 76.01	9,087	5,806 63.89 63.89 4.50	-	-	1,785 52.81 30.74 19.64 1.38	-	-	2,241 75.25 38.60 24.66 1.74	-	600 72.20 10.33 6.60 0.47	-	-	-	-	165 51.56 2.84 1.82 0.13	406 61.61 6.99 4.47 0.31	-	-	78 46.99 1.34 0.86 0.06	-	-	196 84.85 3.38 2.16 0.15	-	-	132 64.71 2.27 1.45 0.10
Chatham (township)	3,274 83.52	184	98 53.26 53.26 2.99	-	-	-	-	-	-	-	-	-	-	-	-	-	-	-	-	-	-	-	-	-	-	-

Notes: Please refer to the User's Guide for an explanation of data; data is arranged alphabetically by state, then county, then city within each county; table includes counties with populations greater than 49,999 unless noted and cities with populations greater than 9,999 whose Asian and/or NHPI population rates are greater than the national average; (1) Native Hawaiian and other Pacific Islander; (2) excludes Taiwanese; (3) includes Chamorro; (4) county does not meet population threshold but is shown in order to allow inclusion of city

Place	All owner-occupied housing units	Asian-occupied housing units	Asians who own and occupy their own homes	NHPI[1]-occupied housing units	NHPIs[1] who own and occupy their own homes	Asian Indian	Bangladeshi	Cambodian	Chinese[2]	Fijian	Filipino	Guamanian[3]	Hawaiian, Native	Hmong	Indonesian	Japanese	Korean	Laotian	Malaysian	Pakistani	Samoan	Sri Lankan	Taiwanese	Thai	Tongan	Vietnamese
	5,148	222	197	-	-	-	-	-	-	-	-	-	-	-	-	-	-	-	-	-	-	-	-	-	-	-
	85.94		88.74																							
Denville (township)																										
			88.74																							
			3.83																							
	3,613	355	334	-	-	-	-	-	161	-	-	-	-	-	-	-	-	-	-	-	-	-	-	-	-	-
	94.02		94.08						92.00																	
East Hanover (township)									48.20																	
			94.08						45.35																	
			9.24						4.46																	
	4,367	323	297	-	-	75	-	-	151	-	-	-	-	-	-	-	-	-	-	-	-	-	-	-	-	-
	92.03		91.95			93.75			93.21																	
Hanover (township)						25.25			50.84																	
			91.95			23.22			46.75																	
			6.80			1.72			3.46																	
	3,059	173	106	-	-	-	-	-	-	-	-	-	-	-	-	-	-	-	-	-	-	-	-	-	-	-
	75.98		61.27																							
Lincoln Park (borough)																										
			61.27																							
			3.47																							
	6,340	727	566	-	-	191	-	-	265	-	-	-	-	-	-	-	-	-	-	-	-	-	-	-	-	-
	85.91		77.85			68.46			86.60																	
Montville (township)						33.75			46.82																	
			77.85			26.27			36.45																	
			8.93			3.01			4.18																	
	6,887	332	255	-	-	-	-	-	-	-	-	-	-	-	-	-	-	-	-	-	-	-	-	-	-	-
	84.86		76.81																							
Morris (township)																										
			76.81																							
			3.70																							
	5,080	544	191	-	-	58	-	-	-	-	-	-	-	-	-	-	-	-	-	-	-	-	-	-	-	-
	56.02		35.11			21.80																				
Mount Olive (township)						30.37																				
			35.11			10.66																				
			3.76			1.14																				
	11,868	2,825	1,549	-	-	534	-	-	610	-	168	-	-	-	-	-	85	-	-	-	-	-	-	-	-	-
	60.48		54.83			40.89			70.44		80.00						55.19									
Parsippany-Troy Hills (twp)						34.47			39.38		10.85						5.49									
			54.83			18.90			21.59		5.95						3.01									
			13.05			4.50			5.14		1.42						0.72									
	6,431	787	396	-	-	121	-	-	145	-	-	-	-	-	-	-	-	-	-	-	-	-	-	-	-	-
	74.10		50.32			32.53			76.72																	
Randolph (township)						30.56			36.62																	
			50.32			15.37			18.42																	
			6.16			1.88			2.25																	
	6,870	388	306	-	-	141	-	-	-	-	-	-	-	-	-	-	-	-	-	-	-	-	-	-	-	-
	84.73		78.87			86.50																				
Rockaway (township)						46.08																				
			78.87			36.34																				
			4.45			2.05																				

Notes: Please refer to the User's Guide for an explanation of data; data is arranged alphabetically by state, then county, then city within each county; table includes counties with populations greater than 49,999 unless noted and cities with populations greater than 9,999 whose Asian and/or NHPI population rates are greater than the national average; (1) Native Hawaiian and other Pacific Islander; (2) excludes Taiwanese; (3) includes Chamorro; (4) county does not meet population threshold but is shown in order to allow inclusion of city

Place	All owner-occupied housing units	Asian-occupied housing units	Asians who own and occupy their own homes	NHPI[1]-occupied housing units	NHPIs[1] who own and occupy their own homes	Asian Indian	Bangladeshi	Cambodian	Chinese[2]	Fijian	Filipino	Guamanian[3]	Hawaiian, Native	Hmong	Indonesian	Japanese	Korean	Laotian	Malaysian	Pakistani	Samoan	Sri Lankan	Taiwanese	Thai	Tongan	Vietnamese
Roxbury (township)	7,011 83.82	210	172 81.90 81.90 2.45	-	-	-	-	-	-	-	-	-	-	-	-	-	-	-	-	-	-	-	-	-	-	-
Succasunna-Kenvil (cdp)	3,794 92.49	114	100 87.72 87.72 2.64	-	-	-	-	-	-	-	-	-	-	-	-	-	-	-	-	-	-	-	-	-	-	-
Ocean County	166,779 83.22	1,863	1,287 69.08 69.08 0.77	-	-	285 57.58 22.14 15.30 0.17	-	-	304 77.75 23.62 16.32 0.18	-	511 79.97 39.70 27.43 0.31	-	-	-	-	-	27 46.55 2.10 1.45 0.02	-	-	-	-	-	-	-	-	-
Passaic County	91,171 55.64	4,824	2,593 53.75 53.75 2.84	-	-	992 46.51 38.26 20.56 1.09	74 56.92 2.85 1.53 0.08	-	371 64.30 14.31 7.69 0.41	-	658 65.21 25.38 13.64 0.72	-	-	-	-	-	266 54.29 10.26 5.51 0.29	-	-	-	-	-	-	-	-	-
Clifton (city)	18,410 60.87	1,423	896 62.97 62.97 4.87	-	-	390 60.94 43.53 27.41 2.12	-	-	94 61.44 10.49 6.61 0.51	-	288 79.34 32.14 20.24 1.56	-	-	-	-	-	36 27.48 4.02 2.53 0.20	-	-	-	-	-	-	-	-	-
Little Falls (township)	3,251 69.36	151	77 50.99 50.99 2.37	-	-	-	-	-	-	-	-	-	-	-	-	-	-	-	-	-	-	-	-	-	-	-
Passaic (city)	5,229 26.87	976	304 31.15 31.15 5.81	-	-	131 20.28 43.09 13.42 2.51	-	-	-	-	128 66.67 42.11 13.11 2.45	-	-	-	-	-	-	-	-	-	-	-	-	-	-	-
Wayne (township)	15,411 82.13	886	612 69.07 69.07 3.97	-	-	189 67.50 30.88 21.33 1.23	-	-	162 83.51 26.47 18.28 1.05	-	54 68.35 8.82 6.09 0.35	-	-	-	-	-	169 71.31 27.61 19.07 1.10	-	-	-	-	-	-	-	-	-
Salem County	17,734 72.99	110	76 69.09 69.09 0.43	-	-	-	-	-	-	-	-	-	-	-	-	-	-	-	-	-	-	-	-	-	-	-
Somerset County	84,153 77.22	7,614	5,444 71.50 71.50 6.47	-	-	2,304 70.61 42.32 30.26 2.74	-	-	1,848 80.84 33.95 24.27 2.20	-	524 64.14 9.63 6.88 0.62	-	-	-	-	92 43.60 1.69 1.21 0.11	213 55.61 3.91 2.80 0.25	-	-	100 52.36 1.84 1.31 0.12	-	-	178 89.90 3.27 2.34 0.21	-	-	105 84.68 1.93 1.38 0.12

Notes: Please refer to the User's Guide for an explanation of data; data is arranged alphabetically by state, then county, then city within each county; table includes counties with populations greater than 49,999 unless noted and cities with populations greater than 9,999 whose Asian and/or NHPI population rates are greater than the national average; (1) Native Hawaiian and other Pacific Islander; (2) excludes Taiwanese; (3) includes Chamorro; (4) county does not meet population threshold but is shown in order to allow inclusion of city

Place	All owner-occupied housing units	Asian-occupied housing units	Asians who own and occupy their own homes	NHPI[1]-occupied housing units	NHPIs[1] who own and occupy their own homes	Asian Indian	Bangladeshi	Cambodian	Chinese[2]	Fijian	Filipino	Guamanian[3]	Hawaiian, Native	Hmong	Indonesian	Japanese	Korean	Laotian	Malaysian	Pakistani	Samoan	Sri Lankan	Taiwanese	Thai	Tongan	Vietnamese
Bernards (township)	7,999 86.55	584	513 87.84 87.84 6.41	-	-	157 86.26 30.60 26.88 1.96	-	-	263 94.27 51.27 45.03 3.29	-	-	-	-	-	-	-	-	-	-	-	-	-	-	-	-	-
Branchburg (township)	4,702 88.43	308	273 88.64 88.64 5.81	-	-	155 94.51 56.78 50.32 3.30	-	-	-	-	-	-	-	-	-	-	-	-	-	-	-	-	-	-	-	-
Bridgewater (township)	13,390 86.21	1,373	1,195 87.04 87.04 8.92	-	-	539 88.94 45.10 39.26 4.03	-	-	411 83.71 34.39 29.93 3.07	-	-	-	-	-	-	-	-	-	-	-	-	-	-	-	-	-
Franklin (township)	13,937 72.01	2,167	1,327 61.24 61.24 9.52	-	-	664 57.09 50.04 30.64 4.76	-	-	331 75.23 24.94 15.27 2.37	-	170 64.89 12.81 7.84 1.22	-	-	-	-	-	-	-	-	-	-	-	-	-	-	-
Hillsborough (township)	10,465 83.00	731	529 72.37 72.37 5.05	-	-	241 80.33 45.56 32.97 2.30	-	-	171 76.68 32.33 23.39 1.63	-	-	-	-	-	-	-	-	-	-	-	-	-	-	-	-	-
Montgomery (township)	5,033 86.79	576	488 84.72 84.72 9.70	-	-	150 85.23 30.74 26.04 2.98	-	-	243 92.40 49.80 42.19 4.83	-	-	-	-	-	-	-	-	-	-	-	-	-	-	-	-	-
North Plainfield (borough)	4,225 58.66	301	120 39.87 39.87 2.84	-	-	-	-	-	-	-	-	-	-	-	-	-	-	-	-	-	-	-	-	-	-	-
Somerset (cdp)	5,546 67.00	712	291 40.87 40.87 5.25	-	-	99 31.23 34.02 13.90 1.79	-	-	87 53.70 29.90 12.22 1.57	-	87 54.37 29.90 12.22 1.57	-	-	-	-	-	-	-	-	-	-	-	-	-	-	-
Somerville (borough)	2,316 48.52	294	89 30.27 30.27 3.84	-	-	-	-	-	-	-	-	-	-	-	-	-	-	-	-	-	-	-	-	-	-	-
Warren (township)	4,279 92.44	428	406 94.86 94.86 9.49	-	-	148 100.00 36.45 34.58 3.46	-	-	159 90.86 39.16 37.15 3.72	-	-	-	-	-	-	-	-	-	-	-	-	-	-	-	-	-

Notes: Please refer to the User's Guide for an explanation of data; data is arranged alphabetically by state, then county, then city within each county; table includes counties with populations greater than 49,999 unless noted and cities with populations greater than 9,999 whose Asian and/or NHPI population rates are greater than the national average; (1) Native Hawaiian and other Pacific Islander; (2) excludes Taiwanese; (3) includes Chamorro; (4) county does not meet population threshold but is shown in order to allow inclusion of city

Place	All owner-occupied housing units	Asian-occupied housing units	Asians who own and occupy their own homes	NHPI[1]-occupied housing units	NHPIs[1] who own and occupy their own homes	Asian Indian	Bangladeshi	Cambodian	Chinese[2]	Fijian	Filipino	Guamanian[3]	Hawaiian, Native	Hmong	Indonesian	Japanese	Korean	Laotian	Malaysian	Pakistani	Samoan	Sri Lankan	Taiwanese	Thai	Tongan	Vietnamese
Sussex County	42,019 82.66	418	353 84.45 84.45 0.84	-	-	130 91.55 36.83 31.10 0.31	-	-	-	-	96 71.11 27.20 22.97 0.23	-	-	-	-	-	-	-	-	-	-	-	-	-	-	-
Union County	114,688 61.62	5,818	3,440 59.13 59.13 3.00	-	-	1,164 54.39 33.84 20.01 1.01	-	-	858 71.62 24.94 14.75 0.75	-	986 62.64 28.66 16.95 0.86	-	-	-	-	-	146 41.48 4.24 2.51 0.13	-	-	38 53.52 1.10 0.65 0.03	-	-	-	-	-	54 38.30 1.57 0.93 0.05
Berkeley Heights (township)	4,116 91.90	293	260 88.74 88.74 6.32	-	-	-	-	-	108 81.20 41.54 36.86 2.62	-	-	-	-	-	-	-	-	-	-	-	-	-	-	-	-	-
New Providence (borough)	3,360 76.29	283	172 60.78 60.78 5.12	-	-	-	-	-	87 73.73 50.58 30.74 2.59	-	-	-	-	-	-	-	-	-	-	-	-	-	-	-	-	-
Rahway (city)	6,304 62.86	398	228 57.29 57.29 3.62	-	-	-	-	-	-	-	98 62.03 42.98 24.62 1.55	-	-	-	-	-	-	-	-	-	-	-	-	-	-	-
Roselle Park (borough)	3,022 58.83	389	134 34.45 34.45 4.43	-	-	68 26.05 50.75 17.48 2.25	-	-	-	-	-	-	-	-	-	-	-	-	-	-	-	-	-	-	-	-
Scotch Plains (township)	6,569 78.68	512	287 56.05 56.05 4.37	-	-	109 41.76 37.98 21.29 1.66	-	-	84 77.78 29.27 16.41 1.28	-	-	-	-	-	-	-	-	-	-	-	-	-	-	-	-	-
Springfield (township)	4,442 74.02	183	116 63.39 63.39 2.61	-	-	-	-	-	-	-	-	-	-	-	-	-	-	-	-	-	-	-	-	-	-	-
Summit (city)	5,371 68.01	274	128 46.72 46.72 2.38	-	-	76 51.35 59.38 27.74 1.42	-	-	-	-	-	-	-	-	-	-	-	-	-	-	-	-	-	-	-	-
Union (township)	14,945 76.51	1,043	855 81.98 81.98 5.72	-	-	194 72.93 22.69 18.60 1.30	-	-	130 84.42 15.20 12.46 0.87	-	435 90.81 50.88 41.71 2.91	-	-	-	-	-	-	-	-	-	-	-	-	-	-	-

Notes: Please refer to the User's Guide for an explanation of data; data is arranged alphabetically by state, then county, then city within each county; table includes counties with populations greater than 49,999 unless noted and cities with populations greater than 9,999 whose Asian and/or NHPI population rates are greater than the national average; (1) Native Hawaiian and other Pacific Islander; (2) excludes Taiwanese; (3) includes Chamorro; (4) county does not meet population threshold but is shown in order to allow inclusion of city

Place	All owner-occupied housing units	Asian-occupied housing units	Asians who own and occupy their own homes	NHPI[1]-occupied housing units	NHPIs[1] who own and occupy their own homes	Asian Indian	Bangladeshi	Cambodian	Chinese[2]	Fijian	Filipino	Guamanian[3]	Hawaiian, Native	Hmong	Indonesian	Japanese	Korean	Laotian	Malaysian	Pakistani	Samoan	Sri Lankan	Taiwanese	Thai	Tongan	Vietnamese
Westfield (town)	8,670	390	252	-	-	-	-	-	-	-	-	-	-	-	-	-	-	-	-	-	-	-	-	-	-	-
	81.62		64.62																							
			64.62																							
			2.91																							
Warren County	28,136	298	175	-	-	62	-	-	-	-	-	-	-	-	-	-	-	-	-	-	-	-	-	-	-	-
	72.78		58.72			49.60																				
						35.43																				
			58.72			20.81																				
			0.62			0.22																				
NEW MEXICO	474,435	5,782	3,167	381	188	521	-	-	762	-	350	44	68	-	-	635	187	-	-	-	-	-	-	39	-	452
	69.98		54.77		49.34	57.19			58.48		47.36	43.56	54.84			68.65	42.21							48.75		51.48
						16.45			24.06		11.05	23.40	36.17			20.05	5.90							1.23		14.27
			54.77		49.34	9.01			13.18		6.05	11.55	17.85			10.98	3.23							0.67		7.82
			0.67		0.04	0.11			0.16		0.07	0.01	0.01			0.13	0.04							0.01		0.10
Bernalillo County	140,605	3,283	1,779	162	85	256	-	-	395	-	126	-	-	-	-	345	103	-	-	-	-	-	-	-	-	412
	63.64		54.19		52.47	58.85			62.70		38.18					67.12	35.64									52.28
						14.39			22.20		7.08					19.39	5.79									23.16
			54.19		52.47	7.80			12.03		3.84					10.51	3.14									12.55
			1.27		0.06	0.18			0.28		0.09					0.25	0.07									0.29
Chaves County	15,986	124	92	-	-	-	-	-	-	-	-	-	-	-	-	-	-	-	-	-	-	-	-	-	-	-
	70.86		74.19																							
			74.19																							
			0.58																							
Dona Ana County	40,201	429	193	-	-	-	-	-	67	-	-	-	-	-	-	-	-	-	-	-	-	-	-	-	-	-
	67.50		44.99						42.95																	
									34.72																	
			44.99						15.62																	
			0.48						0.17																	
Los Alamos County[4]	5,895	231	130	-	-	-	-	-	-	-	-	-	-	-	-	-	-	-	-	-	-	-	-	-	-	-
	78.63		56.28																							
			56.28																							
			2.21																							
Los Alamos (cdp)	3,640	195	94	-	-	-	-	-	-	-	-	-	-	-	-	-	-	-	-	-	-	-	-	-	-	-
	71.27		48.21																							
			48.21																							
			2.58																							
Otero County	15,377	150	58	-	-	-	-	-	-	-	-	-	-	-	-	-	-	-	-	-	-	-	-	-	-	-
	66.90		38.67																							
			38.67																							
			0.38																							
Sandoval County	26,265	181	153	-	-	-	-	-	-	-	45	-	-	-	-	-	-	-	-	-	-	-	-	-	-	-
	83.62		84.53								84.91															
											29.41															
			84.53								24.86															
			0.58								0.17															

Notes: Please refer to the User's Guide for an explanation of data; data is arranged alphabetically by state, then county, then city within each county; table includes counties with populations greater than 49,999 unless noted and cities with populations greater than 9,999 whose Asian and/or NHPI population rates are greater than the national average; (1) Native Hawaiian and other Pacific Islander; (2) excludes Taiwanese; (3) includes Chamorro; (4) county does not meet population threshold but is shown in order to allow inclusion of city

Place	All owner-occupied housing units	Asian-occupied housing units	Asians who own and occupy their own homes	NHPI[1]-occupied housing units	NHPIs[1] who own and occupy their own homes	Asian Indian	Bangladeshi	Cambodian	Chinese[2]	Fijian	Filipino	Guamanian[3]	Hawaiian, Native	Hmong	Indonesian	Japanese	Korean	Laotian	Malaysian	Pakistani	Samoan	Sri Lankan	Taiwanese	Thai	Tongan	Vietnamese
Santa Fe County	35,977	316	171	-	-	-	-	-	-	-	-	-	-	-	-	-	-	-	-	-	-	-	-	-	-	-
	68.55		54.11																							
			54.11																							
			0.48																							
NEW YORK	3,739,247	318,404	126,291	2,008	577	31,356	881	252	57,137	-	12,260	65	139	-	186	3,934	10,011	397	108	2,146	126	335	1,429	1,020	-	2,135
	52.99		39.66		28.74	43.32	19.16	36.90	44.77		47.02	16.33	33.74		19.94	22.93	25.63	49.38	20.89	26.97	37.06	40.75	51.05	44.14		33.98
						24.83	0.70	0.20	45.24		9.71	11.27	24.09		0.15	3.12	7.93	0.31	0.09	1.70	21.84	0.27	1.13	0.81		1.69
			39.66		28.74	9.85	0.28	0.08	17.94		3.85	3.24	6.92		0.06	1.24	3.14	0.12	0.03	0.67	6.27	0.11	0.45	0.32		0.67
			3.38		0.02	0.84	0.02	0.01	1.53		0.33	<0.01	<0.01		<0.01	0.11	0.27	0.01	<0.01	0.06	<0.01	0.01	0.04	0.03		0.06
Albany County	69,542	2,480	874	-	-	314	-	-	214	-	126	-	-	-	-	-	20	-	-	-	-	-	-	-	-	72
	57.71		35.24			35.56			34.02		57.01						10.05									43.64
						35.93			24.49		14.42						2.29									8.24
			35.24			12.66			8.63		5.08						0.81									2.90
			1.26			0.45			0.31		0.18						0.03									0.10
Colonie (town)	22,250	854	470	-	-	198	-	-	113	-	-	-	-	-	-	-	-	-	-	-	-	-	-	-	-	-
	71.82		55.04			48.77			64.20																	
						42.13			24.04																	
			55.04			23.19			13.23																	
			2.11			0.89			0.51																	
Guilderland (town)	8,939	496	137	-	-	38	-	-	-	-	-	-	-	-	-	-	-	-	-	-	-	-	-	-	-	-
	66.60		27.62			20.65																				
						27.74																				
			27.62			7.66																				
			1.53			0.43																				
Bronx County (Bronx)	90,522	11,253	2,671	266	55	1,273	58	23	585	-	303	-	-	-	-	19	159	-	-	31	-	-	-	-	-	104
	19.54		23.74		20.68	30.22	13.00	14.47	30.23		20.12					8.02	14.01			10.10						14.86
						47.66	2.17	0.86	21.90		11.34					0.71	5.95			1.16						3.89
			23.74		20.68	11.31	0.52	0.20	5.20		2.69					0.17	1.41			0.28						0.92
			2.95		0.06	1.41	0.06	0.03	0.65		0.33					0.02	0.18			0.03						0.11
Broome County	52,570	1,426	492	-	-	137	-	-	92	-	-	-	-	-	-	-	26	50	-	-	-	-	-	-	-	61
	65.10		34.50			47.74			24.21								13.20	37.88								32.45
						27.85			18.70								5.28	10.16								12.40
			34.50			9.61			6.45								1.82	3.51								4.28
			0.94			0.26			0.18								0.05	0.10								0.12
Johnson City (village)	3,567	292	62	-	-	-	-	-	-	-	-	-	-	-	-	-	-	-	-	-	-	-	-	-	-	-
	51.09		21.23																							
			21.23																							
			1.74																							
Vestal (town)	6,709	352	154	-	-	-	-	-	37	-	-	-	-	-	-	-	-	-	-	-	-	-	-	-	-	-
	78.70		43.75						30.58																	
									24.03																	
			43.75						10.51																	
			2.30						0.55																	
Cattaraugus County	23,831	129	64	-	-	-	-	-	-	-	-	-	-	-	-	-	-	-	-	-	-	-	-	-	-	-
	74.42		49.61																							
			49.61																							
			0.27																							

Notes: Please refer to the User's Guide for an explanation of data; data is arranged alphabetically by state, then county, then city within each county; table includes counties with populations greater than 49,999 unless noted and cities with populations greater than 9,999 whose Asian and/or NHPI population rates are greater than the national average; (1) Native Hawaiian and other Pacific Islander; (2) excludes Taiwanese; (3) includes Chamorro; (4) county does not meet population threshold but is shown in order to allow inclusion of city

Place	All owner-occupied housing units	Asian-occupied housing units	Asians who own and occupy their own homes	NHPI[1]-occupied housing units	NHPIs[1] who own and occupy their own homes	Asian Indian	Bangladeshi	Cambodian	Chinese[2]	Fijian	Filipino	Guamanian[3]	Hawaiian, Native	Hmong	Indonesian	Japanese	Korean	Laotian	Malaysian	Pakistani	Samoan	Sri Lankan	Taiwanese	Thai	Tongan	Vietnamese
Cayuga County	22,005 72.01	43	22 51.16 51.16 0.10	-	-	-	-	-	-	-	-	-	-	-	-	-	-	-	-	-	-	-	-	-	-	-
Chautauqua County	37,757 69.26	130	82 63.08 63.08 0.22	-	-	-	-	-	-	-	-	-	-	-	-	-	-	-	-	-	-	-	-	-	-	-
Chemung County	24,159 68.93	201	124 61.69 61.69 0.51	-	-	-	-	-	-	-	-	-	-	-	-	-	-	-	-	-	-	-	-	-	-	-
Chenango County	15,004 75.30	55	40 72.73 72.73 0.27	-	-	-	-	-	-	-	-	-	-	-	-	-	-	-	-	-	-	-	-	-	-	-
Clinton County	20,162 68.52	183	84 45.90 45.90 0.42	-	-	-	-	-	-	-	-	-	-	-	-	-	-	-	-	-	-	-	-	-	-	-
Columbia County	17,493 70.55	131	20 15.27 15.27 0.11	-	-	-	-	-	-	-	-	-	-	-	-	-	-	-	-	-	-	-	-	-	-	-
Dutchess County	68,628 68.95	2,200	1,276 58.00 58.00 1.86	-	-	503 54.44 39.42 22.86 0.73	-	-	458 67.06 35.89 20.82 0.67	-	-	-	-	-	-	-	124 61.08 9.72 5.64 0.18	-	-	-	-	-	-	-	-	-
Arlington (cdp)	2,029 46.43	215	26 12.09 12.09 1.28	-	-	-	-	-	-	-	-	-	-	-	-	-	-	-	-	-	-	-	-	-	-	-
Poughkeepsie (town)	10,239 70.19	605	291 48.10 48.10 2.84	-	-	103 34.22 35.40 17.02 1.01	-	-	89 54.60 30.58 14.71 0.87	-	-	-	-	-	-	-	-	-	-	-	-	-	-	-	-	-
Wappinger (town)	6,433 65.58	388	177 45.62 45.62 2.75	-	-	68 46.90 38.42 17.53 1.06	-	-	-	-	-	-	-	-	-	-	-	-	-	-	-	-	-	-	-	-

Notes: Please refer to the User's Guide for an explanation of data; data is arranged alphabetically by state, then county, then city within each county; table includes counties with populations greater than 49,999 unless noted and cities with populations greater than 9,999 whose Asian and/or NHPI population rates are greater than the national average; (1) Native Hawaiian and other Pacific Islander; (2) excludes Taiwanese; (3) includes Chamorro; (4) county does not meet population threshold but is shown in order to allow inclusion of city

Place	All owner-occupied housing units	Asian-occupied housing units	Asians who own and occupy their own homes	NHPI[1]-occupied housing units	NHPIs[1] who own and occupy their own homes	Asian Indian	Bangladeshi	Cambodian	Chinese[2]	Fijian	Filipino	Guamanian[3]	Hawaiian, Native	Hmong	Indonesian	Japanese	Korean	Laotian	Malaysian	Pakistani	Samoan	Sri Lankan	Taiwanese	Thai	Tongan	Vietnamese
Erie County	248,780 65.32	4,241	1,600 37.73 37.73 0.64	-	-	568 45.33 35.50 13.39 0.23	-	-	390 33.22 24.38 9.20 0.16	-	125 69.44 7.81 2.95 0.05	-	-	-	-	39 23.64 2.44 0.92 0.02	131 23.56 8.19 3.09 0.05	-	-	-	-	-	-	-	-	173 42.51 10.81 4.08 0.07
Amherst (town)	33,368 74.03	1,777	812 45.69 45.69 2.43	-	-	396 62.46 48.77 22.28 1.19	-	-	235 40.17 28.94 13.22 0.70	-	-	-	-	-	-	-	64 27.12 7.88 3.60 0.19	-	-	-	-	-	-	-	-	-
Herkimer County	18,318 71.18	93	37 39.78 39.78 0.20	-	-	-	-	-	-	-	-	-	-	-	-	-	-	-	-	-	-	-	-	-	-	-
Jefferson County	23,950 59.77	264	80 30.30 30.30 0.33	-	-	-	-	-	-	-	14 19.72 17.50 5.30 0.06	-	-	-	-	-	23 35.94 28.75 8.71 0.10	-	-	-	-	-	-	-	-	-
Kings County (Brooklyn)	238,290 27.06	51,153	18,097 35.38 35.38 7.59	412	76 18.45 18.45 0.03	1,498 21.26 8.28 2.93 0.63	79 9.36 0.44 0.15 0.03	21 13.04 0.12 0.04 0.01	14,259 44.46 78.79 27.88 5.98	-	718 31.63 3.97 1.40 0.30	8 9.09 10.53 1.94 <0.01	-	-	-	158 15.69 0.87 0.31 0.07	342 14.07 1.89 0.67 0.14	-	-	293 12.91 1.62 0.57 0.12	-	-	-	-	-	268 25.33 1.48 0.52 0.11
Livingston County	16,509 74.53	117	84 71.79 71.79 0.51	-	-	-	-	-	-	-	-	-	-	-	-	-	-	-	-	-	-	-	-	-	-	-
Madison County	19,012 74.94	78	37 47.44 47.44 0.19	-	-	-	-	-	-	-	-	-	-	-	-	-	-	-	-	-	-	-	-	-	-	-
Monroe County	186,458 65.08	5,083	2,511 49.40 49.40 1.35	-	-	669 47.15 26.64 13.16 0.36	-	44 53.01 1.75 0.87 0.02	616 45.63 24.53 12.12 0.33	-	124 67.39 4.94 2.44 0.07	-	-	-	-	99 40.08 3.94 1.95 0.05	213 48.41 8.48 4.19 0.11	177 49.72 7.05 3.48 0.09	-	31 26.50 1.23 0.61 0.02	-	-	-	-	-	374 65.73 14.89 7.36 0.20
Brighton (town)	9,076 57.25	1,035	313 30.24 30.24 3.45	-	-	93 24.16 29.71 8.99 1.02	-	-	85 32.44 27.16 8.21 0.94	-	-	-	-	-	-	-	-	-	-	-	-	-	-	-	-	-
Henrietta (town)	9,228 71.96	452	193 42.70 42.70 2.09	-	-	45 43.27 23.32 9.96 0.49	-	-	56 43.41 29.02 12.39 0.61	-	-	-	-	-	-	-	-	-	-	-	-	-	-	-	-	-

Notes: Please refer to the User's Guide for an explanation of data; data is arranged alphabetically by state, then county, then city within each county; table includes counties with populations greater than 49,999 unless noted and cities with populations greater than 9,999 whose Asian and/or NHPI population rates are greater than the national average; (1) Native Hawaiian and other Pacific Islander; (2) excludes Taiwanese; (3) includes Chamorro; (4) county does not meet population threshold but is shown in order to allow inclusion of city

Place	All owner-occupied housing units	Asian-occupied housing units	Asians who own and occupy their own homes	NHPI[1]-occupied housing units	NHPIs[1] who own and occupy their own homes	Asian Indian	Bangladeshi	Cambodian	Chinese[2]	Fijian	Filipino	Guamanian[3]	Hawaiian, Native	Hmong	Indonesian	Japanese	Korean	Laotian	Malaysian	Pakistani	Samoan	Sri Lankan	Taiwanese	Thai	Tongan	Vietnamese
Pittsford (town)	8,209	349	279	-	-	134	-	-	-	-	-	-	-	-	-	-	-	-	-	-	-	-	-	-	-	-
	86.91		79.94			76.57																				
						48.03																				
			79.94			38.40																				
			3.40			1.63																				
Nassau County	359,257	16,182	12,735	109	64	4,799	-	-	3,824	-	1,373	-	-	-	-	289	1,382	-	-	388	-	-	140	87	-	53
	80.30		78.70		58.72	80.24			89.32		81.63					42.88	64.07			75.05			98.59	76.32		86.89
						37.68			30.03		10.78					2.27	10.85			3.05			1.10	0.68		0.42
			78.70		58.72	29.66			23.63		8.48					1.79	8.54			2.40			0.87	0.54		0.33
			3.54		0.02	1.34			1.06		0.38					0.08	0.38			0.11			0.04	0.02		0.01
East Meadow (cdp)	10,727	590	477	-	-	205	-	-	-	-	110	-	-	-	-	-	-	-	-	-	-	-	-	-	-	-
	87.92		80.85			73.74					94.83															
						42.98					23.06															
			80.85			34.75					18.64															
			4.45			1.91					1.03															
Elmont (cdp)	7,735	790	661	-	-	398	-	-	-	-	110	-	-	-	-	-	-	-	-	-	-	-	-	-	-	-
	78.12		83.67			83.26					95.65															
						60.21					16.64															
			83.67			50.38					13.92															
			8.55			5.15					1.42															
Franklin Square (cdp)	8,254	250	212	-	-	94	-	-	-	-	-	-	-	-	-	-	-	-	-	-	-	-	-	-	-	-
	81.02		84.80			97.92																				
						44.34																				
			84.80			37.60																				
			2.57			1.14																				
Glen Cove (city)	5,530	289	145	-	-	24	-	-	-	-	-	-	-	-	-	-	55	-	-	-	-	-	-	-	-	-
	58.45		50.17			29.27											56.70									
						16.55											37.93									
			50.17			8.30											19.03									
			2.62			0.43											0.99									
Hicksville (cdp)	11,722	855	727	-	-	355	-	-	194	-	103	-	-	-	-	-	-	-	-	-	-	-	-	-	-	-
	85.50		85.03			86.17			87.39		87.29															
						48.83			26.69		14.17															
			85.03			41.52			22.69		12.05															
			6.20			3.03			1.66		0.88															
Jericho (cdp)	3,885	388	274	-	-	-	-	-	-	-	-	-	-	-	-	-	104	-	-	-	-	-	-	-	-	-
	85.35		70.62														55.91									
																	37.96									
			70.62														26.80									
			7.05														2.68									
Mineola (village)	4,700	257	112	-	-	36	-	-	-	-	-	-	-	-	-	-	-	-	-	-	-	-	-	-	-	-
	62.84		43.58			35.64																				
						32.14																				
			43.58			14.01																				
			2.38			0.77																				
North Hempstead (town)	60,270	5,532	4,321	-	-	1,606	-	-	1,388	-	286	-	-	-	-	141	543	-	-	124	-	-	73	-	-	-
	78.46		78.11			81.28			89.38		80.11					38.42	65.58			79.49			97.33			
						37.17			32.12		6.62					3.26	12.57			2.87			1.69			
			78.11			29.03			25.09		5.17					2.55	9.82			2.24			1.32			
			7.17			2.66			2.30		0.47					0.23	0.90			0.21			0.12			

Notes: Please refer to the User's Guide for an explanation of data; data is arranged alphabetically by state, then county, then city within each county; table includes counties with populations greater than 49,999 unless noted and cities with populations greater than 9,999 whose Asian and/or NHPI population rates are greater than the national average; (1) Native Hawaiian and other Pacific Islander; (2) excludes Taiwanese; (3) includes Chamorro; (4) county does not meet population threshold but is shown in order to allow inclusion of city.

Place	All owner-occupied housing units	Asian-occupied housing units	Asians who own and occupy their own homes	NHPI[1]-occupied housing units	NHPIs[1] who own and occupy their own homes	Asian Indian	Bangladeshi	Cambodian	Chinese[2]	Fijian	Filipino	Guamanian[3]	Hawaiian, Native	Hmong	Indonesian	Japanese	Korean	Laotian	Malaysian	Pakistani	Samoan	Sri Lankan	Taiwanese	Thai	Tongan	Vietnamese
North Merrick (cdp)	3,692 93.16	90	76 84.44 84.44 2.06	-	-	-	-	-	-	-	-	-	-	-	-	-	-	-	-	-	-	-	-	-	-	-
North New Hyde Park (cdp)	4,713 93.66	514	478 93.00 93.00 10.14	-	-	246 94.62 51.46 47.86 5.22	-	-	182 91.92 38.08 35.41 3.86	-	-	-	-	-	-	-	-	-	-	-	-	-	-	-	-	-
North Valley Stream (cdp)	4,356 89.63	350	318 90.86 90.86 7.30	-	-	150 100.00 47.17 42.86 3.44	-	-	-	-	-	-	-	-	-	-	-	-	-	-	-	-	-	-	-	-
Oyster Bay (town)	86,345 86.91	3,521	2,902 82.42 82.42 3.36	-	-	1,087 84.92 37.46 30.87 1.26	-	-	928 90.10 31.98 26.36 1.07	-	236 83.10 8.13 6.70 0.27	-	-	-	-	60 44.78 2.07 1.70 0.07	406 68.93 13.99 11.53 0.47	-	-	-	-	-	-	-	-	-
Plainview (cdp)	7,991 93.40	316	267 84.49 84.49 3.34	-	-	81 88.04 30.34 25.63 1.01	-	-	86 84.31 32.21 27.22 1.08	-	-	-	-	-	-	-	64 83.12 23.97 20.25 0.80	-	-	-	-	-	-	-	-	-
Port Washington (cdp)	4,061 73.40	323	205 63.47 63.47 5.05	-	-	61 69.32 29.76 18.89 1.50	-	-	-	-	-	-	-	-	-	-	-	-	-	-	-	-	-	-	-	-
Salisbury (cdp)	3,687 92.18	272	257 94.49 94.49 6.97	-	-	121 100.00 47.08 44.49 3.28	-	-	-	-	-	-	-	-	-	-	-	-	-	-	-	-	-	-	-	-
Syosset (cdp)	5,816 92.60	603	542 89.88 89.88 9.32	-	-	158 89.77 29.15 26.20 2.72	-	-	215 100.00 39.67 35.66 3.70	-	-	-	-	-	-	-	112 81.75 20.66 18.57 1.93	-	-	-	-	-	-	-	-	-
Valley Stream (village)	10,038 80.36	594	512 86.20 86.20 5.10	-	-	-	-	-	207 100.00 40.43 34.85 2.06	-	114 95.00 22.27 19.19 1.14	-	-	-	-	-	-	-	-	-	-	-	-	-	-	-
West Hempstead (cdp)	5,294 87.82	249	193 77.51 77.51 3.65	-	-	69 75.82 35.75 27.71 1.30	-	-	-	-	-	-	-	-	-	-	-	-	-	-	-	-	-	-	-	-

Notes: Please refer to the User's Guide for an explanation of data; data is arranged alphabetically by state, then county, then city within each county; table includes counties with populations greater than 49,999 unless noted and cities with populations greater than 9,999 whose Asian and/or NHPI population rates are greater than the national average; (1) Native Hawaiian and other Pacific Islander; (2) excludes Taiwanese; (3) includes Chamorro; (4) county does not meet population threshold but is shown in order to allow inclusion of city

Place	All owner-occupied housing units	Asian-occupied housing units	Asians who own and occupy their own homes	NHPI[1]-occupied housing units	NHPIs[1] who own and occupy their own homes	Asian Indian	Bangladeshi	Cambodian	Chinese[2]	Fijian	Filipino	Guamanian[3]	Hawaiian, Native	Hmong	Indonesian	Japanese	Korean	Laotian	Malaysian	Pakistani	Samoan	Sri Lankan	Taiwanese	Thai	Tongan	Vietnamese
Westbury (village)	3,611 77.86	197	155 78.68 78.68 4.29	-	-	-	-	-	-	-	-	-	-	-	-	-	-	-	-	-	-	-	-	-	-	-
Woodmere (cdp)	4,844 90.56	149	134 89.93 89.93 2.77	-	-	-	-	-	-	-	-	-	-	-	-	-	-	-	-	-	-	-	-	-	-	-
New York City	912,133 30.19	246,389	85,118 34.55 34.55 9.33	1,274	300 23.55 23.55 0.03	17,284 35.28 20.31 7.01 1.89	739 17.03 0.87 0.30 0.08	80 19.95 0.09 0.03 0.01	46,358 42.26 54.46 18.81 5.08	-	7,304 38.38 8.58 2.96 0.80	37 14.23 12.33 2.90 <0.01	65 29.02 21.67 5.10 0.01	-	84 12.28 0.10 0.03 0.01	2,082 17.42 2.45 0.85 0.23	6,003 19.39 7.05 2.44 0.66	-	86 18.45 0.10 0.03 0.01	1,095 18.29 1.29 0.44 0.12	28 16.87 9.33 2.20 <0.01	209 32.45 0.25 0.08 0.02	947 48.66 1.11 0.38 0.10	485 34.28 0.57 0.20 0.05	-	822 23.87 0.97 0.33 0.09
New York County (Manhattan)	148,695 20.13	59,449	9,403 15.82 15.82 6.32	171	0 <0.01 <0.01 <0.01	1,138 18.38 12.10 1.91 0.77	0 0.00 0.00 0.00 0.00	-	4,596 14.66 48.88 7.73 3.09	-	769 18.57 8.18 1.29 0.52	-	-	-	-	1,360 17.27 14.46 2.29 0.91	919 16.09 9.77 1.55 0.62	-	-	55 12.67 0.58 0.09 0.04	-	-	117 18.99 1.24 0.20 0.08	70 18.42 0.74 0.12 0.05	-	107 16.59 1.14 0.18 0.07
Niagara County	61,394 69.89	317	117 36.91 36.91 0.19	-	-	70 54.69 59.83 22.08 0.11	-	-	-	-	-	-	-	-	-	-	-	-	-	-	-	-	-	-	-	-
Oneida County	60,808 67.19	669	284 42.45 42.45 0.47	-	-	72 58.54 25.35 10.76 0.12	-	-	52 61.90 18.31 7.77 0.09	-	-	-	-	-	-	-	-	-	-	-	-	-	-	-	-	61 22.02 21.48 9.12 0.10
Onondaga County	116,815 64.48	3,198	1,205 37.68 37.68 1.03	-	-	338 43.17 28.05 10.57 0.29	-	-	167 26.47 13.86 5.22 0.14	-	137 58.80 11.37 4.28 0.12	-	-	-	-	81 49.69 6.72 2.53 0.07	88 21.52 7.30 2.75 0.08	-	-	-	-	-	-	-	-	203 40.12 16.85 6.35 0.17
Ontario County	28,230 73.57	218	115 52.75 52.75 0.41	-	-	-	-	-	-	-	-	-	-	-	-	-	-	-	-	-	-	-	-	-	-	-
Orange County	76,948 67.03	1,349	831 61.60 61.60 1.08	-	-	267 61.24 32.13 19.79 0.35	-	-	210 64.81 25.27 15.57 0.27	-	117 56.52 14.08 8.67 0.15	-	-	-	-	-	84 60.00 10.11 6.23 0.11	-	-	-	-	-	-	-	-	-
Oswego County	33,121 72.76	135	51 37.78 37.78 0.15	-	-	-	-	-	-	-	-	-	-	-	-	-	-	-	-	-	-	-	-	-	-	-

Notes: Please refer to the User's Guide for an explanation of data; data is arranged alphabetically by state, then county, then city within each county; table includes counties with populations greater than 49,999 unless noted and cities with populations greater than 9,999 whose Asian and/or NHPI population rates are greater than the national average; (1) Native Hawaiian and other Pacific Islander; (2) excludes Taiwanese; (3) includes Chamorro; (4) county does not meet population threshold but is shown in order to allow inclusion of city

Place	All owner-occupied housing units	Asian-occupied housing units	Asians who own and occupy their own homes	NHPI[1]-occupied housing units	NHPIs[1] who own and occupy their own homes	Asian Indian	Bangladeshi	Cambodian	Chinese[2]	Fijian	Filipino	Guamanian[3]	Hawaiian, Native	Hmong	Indonesian	Japanese	Korean	Laotian	Malaysian	Pakistani	Samoan	Sri Lankan	Taiwanese	Thai	Tongan	Vietnamese
Otsego County	17,012 73.04	76	25 32.89 32.89 0.15	-	-	-	-	-	-	-	-	-	-	-	-	-	-	-	-	-	-	-	-	-	-	-
Putnam County	26,884 82.21	311	243 78.14 78.14 0.90	-	-	77 74.76 31.69 24.76 0.29	-	-	86 79.63 35.39 27.65 0.32	-	-	-	-	-	-	-	-	-	-	-	-	-	-	-	-	-
Queens County (Queens)	334,894 42.79	117,338	50,262 42.84 42.84 15.01	341	140 41.06 41.06 0.04	12,359 41.56 24.59 10.53 3.69	602 20.79 1.20 0.51 0.18	-	25,190 59.69 50.12 21.47 7.52	-	4,497 46.83 8.95 3.83 1.34	-	-	-	61 13.29 0.12 0.05 0.02	531 19.26 1.06 0.45 0.16	4,006 19.41 7.97 3.41 1.20	-	49 24.02 0.10 0.04 0.01	623 22.08 1.24 0.53 0.19	-	101 37.69 0.20 0.09 0.03	770 65.37 1.53 0.66 0.23	321 42.40 0.64 0.27 0.10	-	330 33.43 0.66 0.28 0.10
Rensselaer County	38,856 64.87	792	150 18.94 18.94 0.39	-	-	46 21.40 30.67 5.81 0.12	-	-	44 13.75 29.33 5.56 0.11	-	-	-	-	-	-	-	8 8.16 5.33 1.01 0.02	-	-	-	-	-	-	-	-	-
Richmond Co. (Staten Island)	99,732 63.79	7,196	4,685 65.11 65.11 4.70	-	-	1,016 56.32 21.69 14.12 1.02	-	-	1,728 80.48 36.88 24.01 1.73	-	1,017 67.26 21.71 14.13 1.02	-	-	-	-	-	577 55.11 12.32 8.02 0.58	-	-	93 60.78 1.99 1.29 0.09	-	66 46.15 1.41 0.92 0.07	-	-	-	-
Rockland County	66,461 71.71	4,355	3,089 70.93 70.93 4.65	-	-	1,094 70.54 35.42 25.12 1.65	-	-	422 76.59 13.66 9.69 0.63	-	924 79.45 29.91 21.22 1.39	-	-	-	-	-	396 69.35 12.82 9.09 0.60	-	-	-	-	-	-	-	-	-
Clarkstown (town)	22,716 82.02	1,737	1,394 80.25 80.25 6.14	-	-	476 83.51 34.15 27.40 2.10	-	-	213 83.86 15.28 12.26 0.94	-	453 83.43 32.50 26.08 1.99	-	-	-	-	-	158 73.83 11.33 9.10 0.70	-	-	-	-	-	-	-	-	-
Nanuet (cdp)	4,202 70.31	453	349 77.04 77.04 8.31	-	-	115 95.04 32.95 25.39 2.74	-	-	-	-	-	-	-	-	-	-	-	-	-	-	-	-	-	-	-	-
New City (cdp)	10,059 90.81	596	481 80.70 80.70 4.78	-	-	147 65.92 30.56 24.66 1.46	-	-	-	-	139 95.21 28.90 23.32 1.38	-	-	-	-	-	-	-	-	-	-	-	-	-	-	-
Orangetown (town)	12,334 71.10	861	612 71.08 71.08 4.96	-	-	167 68.72 27.29 19.40 1.35	-	-	112 70.44 18.30 13.01 0.91	-	160 80.81 26.14 18.58 1.30	-	-	-	-	-	121 71.60 19.77 14.05 0.98	-	-	-	-	-	-	-	-	-

Notes: Please refer to the User's Guide for an explanation of data; data is arranged alphabetically by state, then county, then city within each county; table includes counties with populations greater than 49,999 unless noted and cities with populations greater than 9,999 whose Asian and/or NHPI population rates are greater than the national average; (1) Native Hawaiian and other Pacific Islander; (2) excludes Taiwanese; (3) includes Chamorro; (4) county does not meet population threshold but is shown in order to allow inclusion of city

Place	All owner-occupied housing units	Asian-occupied housing units	Asians who own and occupy their own homes	NHPI[1]-occupied housing units	NHPIs[1] who own and occupy their own homes	Asian Indian	Bangladeshi	Cambodian	Chinese[2]	Fijian	Filipino	Guamanian[3]	Hawaiian, Native	Hmong	Indonesian	Japanese	Korean	Laotian	Malaysian	Pakistani	Samoan	Sri Lankan	Taiwanese	Thai	Tongan	Vietnamese
Ramapo (town)	20,193 63.98	1,357	821 60.50 60.50 4.07	-	-	355 62.83 43.24 26.16 1.76	-	-	64 65.31 7.80 4.72 0.32	-	270 72.78 32.89 19.90 1.34	-	-	-	-	-	88 55.35 10.72 6.48 0.44	-	-	-	-	-	-	-	-	-
Spring Valley (village)	2,377 31.52	439	118 26.88 26.88 4.96	-	-	54 26.09 45.76 12.30 2.27	-	-	-	-	-	-	-	-	-	-	-	-	-	-	-	-	-	-	-	-
St. Lawrence County	28,613 70.64	200	71 35.50 35.50 0.25	-	-	-	-	-	-	-	-	-	-	-	-	-	-	-	-	-	-	-	-	-	-	-
Saratoga County	56,317 72.05	616	355 57.63 57.63 0.63	-	-	148 53.05 41.69 24.03 0.26	-	-	80 65.57 22.54 12.99 0.14	-	-	-	-	-	-	-	44 70.97 12.39 7.14 0.08	-	-	-	-	-	-	-	-	-
Schenectady County	39,038 65.41	846	407 48.11 48.11 1.04	-	-	124 38.99 30.47 14.66 0.32	-	-	169 59.09 41.52 19.98 0.43	-	-	-	-	-	-	-	-	-	-	-	-	-	-	-	-	-
Niskayuna (town)	6,383 82.08	388	230 59.28 59.28 3.60	-	-	72 39.78 31.30 18.56 1.13	-	-	-	-	-	-	-	-	-	-	-	-	-	-	-	-	-	-	-	-
Steuben County	28,584 73.16	263	152 57.79 57.79 0.53	-	-	-	-	-	-	-	-	-	-	-	-	-	-	-	-	-	-	-	-	-	-	-
Suffolk County	374,371 79.77	8,575	5,775 67.35 67.35 1.54	77	61 79.22 79.22 0.02	1,771 64.07 30.67 20.65 0.47	-	-	1,705 64.98 29.52 19.88 0.46	-	804 82.55 13.92 9.38 0.21	-	-	-	-	224 67.67 3.88 2.61 0.06	543 63.07 9.40 6.33 0.15	-	-	259 64.27 4.48 3.02 0.07	-	-	67 70.53 1.16 0.78 0.02	99 100.00 1.71 1.15 0.03	-	121 73.78 2.10 1.41 0.03
Coram (cdp)	8,661 69.01	398	176 44.22 44.22 2.03	-	-	-	-	-	61 42.96 34.66 15.33 0.70	-	-	-	-	-	-	-	-	-	-	-	-	-	-	-	-	-
Dix Hills (cdp)	7,662 96.24	484	475 98.14 98.14 6.20	-	-	230 100.00 48.42 47.52 3.00	-	-	113 100.00 23.79 23.35 1.47	-	-	-	-	-	-	-	-	-	-	-	-	-	-	-	-	-

Notes: Please refer to the User's Guide for an explanation of data; data is arranged alphabetically by state, then county, then city within each county; table includes counties with populations greater than 49,999 unless noted and cities with populations greater than 9,999 whose Asian and/or NHPI population rates are greater than the national average; (1) Native Hawaiian and other Pacific Islander; (2) excludes Taiwanese; (3) includes Chamorro; (4) county does not meet population threshold but is shown in order to allow inclusion of city

Place	All owner-occupied housing units	Asian-occupied housing units	Asians who own and occupy their own homes	NHPI-occupied housing units	NHPIs[1] who own and occupy their own homes	Asian Indian	Bangladeshi	Cambodian	Chinese[2]	Fijian	Filipino	Guamanian[3]	Hawaiian, Native	Hmong	Indonesian	Japanese	Korean	Laotian	Malaysian	Pakistani	Samoan	Sri Lankan	Taiwanese	Thai	Tongan	Vietnamese
Elwood (cdp)	3,226 94.13	156	156 100.00 100.00 4.84	-	-	-	-	-	-	-	-	-	-	-	-	-	-	-	-	-	-	-	-	-	-	-
Lake Grove (village)	2,717 79.24	202	80 39.60 39.60 2.94	-	-	-	-	-	-	-	-	-	-	-	-	-	-	-	-	-	-	-	-	-	-	-
Melville (cdp)	4,245 86.09	182	133 73.08 73.08 3.13	-	-	-	-	-	-	-	-	-	-	-	-	-	-	-	-	-	-	-	-	-	-	-
Setauket-East Setauket (cdp)	4,583 83.31	544	188 34.56 34.56 4.10	-	-	-	-	-	78 23.49 41.49 14.34 1.70	-	-	-	-	-	-	-	-	-	-	-	-	-	-	-	-	-
Stony Brook (cdp)	4,389 92.15	230	186 80.87 80.87 4.24	-	-	-	-	-	103 73.05 55.38 44.78 2.35	-	-	-	-	-	-	-	-	-	-	-	-	-	-	-	-	-
Sullivan County	18,845 68.13	222	138 62.16 62.16 0.73	-	-	-	-	-	-	-	-	-	-	-	-	-	-	-	-	-	-	-	-	-	-	-
Tioga County	15,347 77.80	86	65 75.58 75.58 0.42	-	-	-	-	-	-	-	-	-	-	-	-	-	-	-	-	-	-	-	-	-	-	-
Tompkins County	19,583 53.77	2,371	338 14.26 14.26 1.73	-	-	77 20.87 22.78 3.25 0.39	-	-	163 16.14 48.22 6.87 0.83	-	-	-	-	-	-	23 9.20 6.80 0.97 0.12	34 8.76 10.06 1.43 0.17	-	-	-	-	-	-	-	-	-
Ithaca (city)	2,638 25.73	1,094	60 5.48 5.48 2.27	-	-	0 0.00 0.00 0.00 0.00	-	-	36 6.55 60.00 3.29 1.36	-	-	-	-	-	-	-	10 9.01 16.67 0.91 0.38	-	-	-	-	-	-	-	-	-
Lansing (town)	2,467 56.54	477	87 18.24 18.24 3.53	-	-	-	-	-	-	-	-	-	-	-	-	-	-	-	-	-	-	-	-	-	-	-

Notes: Please refer to the User's Guide for an explanation of data; data is arranged alphabetically by state, then county, then city within each county; table includes counties with populations greater than 49,999 unless noted and cities with populations greater than 9,999 whose Asian and/or NHPI population rates are greater than the national average; (1) Native Hawaiian and other Pacific Islander; (2) excludes Taiwanese; (3) includes Chamorro; (4) county does not meet population threshold but is shown in order to allow inclusion of city

Place	All owner-occupied housing units	Asian-occupied housing units	Asians who own and occupy their own homes	NHPI[1]-occupied housing units	NHPIs[1] who own and occupy their own homes	Asian Indian	Bangladeshi	Cambodian	Chinese[2]	Fijian	Filipino	Guamanian[3]	Hawaiian, Native	Hmong	Indonesian	Japanese	Korean	Laotian	Malaysian	Pakistani	Samoan	Sri Lankan	Taiwanese	Thai	Tongan	Vietnamese
Ulster County	45,916 68.02	481	193 40.12 40.12 0.42	-	-	-	-	-	68 51.52 35.23 14.14 0.15	-	-	-	-	-	-	-	-	-	-	-	-	-	-	-	-	-
New Paltz (town)	2,422 54.37	165	26 15.76 15.76 1.07	-	-	-	-	-	-	-	-	-	-	-	-	-	-	-	-	-	-	-	-	-	-	-
Warren County	17,974 69.87	163	134 82.21 82.21 0.75	-	-	-	-	-	-	-	-	-	-	-	-	-	-	-	-	-	-	-	-	-	-	-
Wayne County	27,093 77.61	61	54 88.52 88.52 0.20	-	-	-	-	-	-	-	-	-	-	-	-	-	-	-	-	-	-	-	-	-	-	-
Westchester County	202,765 60.14	12,857	6,778 52.72 52.72 3.34	-	-	2,416 54.35 35.64 18.79 1.19	-	-	1,575 66.91 23.24 12.25 0.78	-	789 56.72 11.64 6.14 0.39	-	-	-	-	720 29.95 10.62 5.60 0.36	666 50.88 9.83 5.18 0.33	-	-	79 39.70 1.17 0.61 0.04	-	-	71 63.96 1.05 0.55 0.04	163 83.59 2.40 1.27 0.08	-	-
Dobbs Ferry (village)	2,222 58.60	213	77 36.15 36.15 3.47	-	-	-	-	-	-	-	-	-	-	-	-	-	-	-	-	-	-	-	-	-	-	-
Eastchester (cdp)	5,998 78.03	430	193 44.88 44.88 3.22	-	-	-	-	-	-	-	-	-	-	-	-	37 20.90 19.17 8.60 0.62	-	-	-	-	-	-	-	-	-	-
Eastchester (town)	9,010 71.36	775	306 39.48 39.48 3.40	-	-	-	-	-	-	-	-	-	-	-	-	86 20.87 28.10 11.10 0.95	-	-	-	-	-	-	-	-	-	-
Greenburgh (town)	23,072 69.82	2,436	1,356 55.67 55.67 5.88	-	-	496 59.19 36.58 20.36 2.15	-	-	306 69.86 22.57 12.56 1.33	-	109 67.28 8.04 4.47 0.47	-	-	-	-	160 27.07 11.80 6.57 0.69	197 69.61 14.53 8.09 0.85	-	-	-	-	-	-	-	-	-
Harrison (village)	5,436 64.93	362	93 25.69 25.69 1.71	-	-	-	-	-	-	-	-	-	-	-	-	0 0.00 0.00 0.00 0.00	-	-	-	-	-	-	-	-	-	-

Notes: Please refer to the User's Guide for an explanation of data; data is arranged alphabetically by state, then county, then city within each county; table includes counties with populations greater than 49,999 unless noted and cities with populations greater than 9,999 whose Asian and/or NHPI population rates are greater than the national average; (1) Native Hawaiian and other Pacific Islander; (2) excludes Taiwanese; (3) includes Chamorro; (4) county does not meet population threshold but is shown in order to allow inclusion of city

Place	All owner-occupied housing units	Asian-occupied housing units	Asians who own and occupy their own homes	NHPI[1]-occupied housing units	NHPIs[1] who own and occupy their own homes	Asian Indian	Bangladeshi	Cambodian	Chinese[2]	Fijian	Filipino	Guamanian[3]	Hawaiian, Native	Hmong	Indonesian	Japanese	Korean	Laotian	Malaysian	Pakistani	Samoan	Sri Lankan	Taiwanese	Thai	Tongan	Vietnamese
New Castle (town)	5,258 91.73	288	251 87.15 87.15 4.77	-	-	105 91.30 41.83 36.46 2.00	-	-	79 87.78 31.47 27.43 1.50	-	-	-	-	-	-	-	-	-	-	-	-	-	-	-	-	-
New Rochelle (city)	13,173 50.30	836	385 46.05 46.05 2.92	-	-	162 45.38 42.08 19.38 1.23	-	-	71 42.51 18.44 8.49 0.54	-	-	-	-	-	-	-	-	-	-	-	-	-	-	-	-	-
North Castle (town)	3,118 87.02	133	113 84.96 84.96 3.62	-	-	-	-	-	-	-	-	-	-	-	-	-	-	-	-	-	-	-	-	-	-	-
Ossining (town)	7,892 63.88	492	252 51.22 51.22 3.19	-	-	130 50.00 51.59 26.42 1.65	-	-	-	-	-	-	-	-	-	-	-	-	-	-	-	-	-	-	-	-
Ossining (village)	4,287 52.11	308	105 34.09 34.09 2.45	-	-	33 25.19 31.43 10.71 0.77	-	-	-	-	-	-	-	-	-	-	-	-	-	-	-	-	-	-	-	-
Pelham (town)	3,169 76.38	123	85 69.11 69.11 2.68	-	-	-	-	-	-	-	-	-	-	-	-	-	-	-	-	-	-	-	-	-	-	-
Rye (city)	4,029 74.93	342	164 47.95 47.95 4.07	-	-	-	-	-	-	-	-	-	-	-	-	55 26.07 33.54 16.08 1.37	-	-	-	-	-	-	-	-	-	-
Scarsdale (village)	5,160 91.13	616	379 61.53 61.53 7.34	-	-	90 100.00 23.75 14.61 1.74	-	-	129 95.56 34.04 20.94 2.50	-	-	-	-	-	-	38 17.35 10.03 6.17 0.74	67 67.00 17.68 10.88 1.30	-	-	-	-	-	-	-	-	-
Tarrytown (village)	2,378 52.46	243	88 36.21 36.21 3.70	-	-	-	-	-	-	-	-	-	-	-	-	-	-	-	-	-	-	-	-	-	-	-
White Plains (city)	10,970 52.44	910	339 37.25 37.25 3.09	-	-	82 24.26 24.19 9.01 0.75	-	-	93 41.52 27.43 10.22 0.85	-	-	-	-	-	-	-	-	-	-	-	-	-	-	-	-	-

Notes: Please refer to the User's Guide for an explanation of data; data is arranged alphabetically by state, then county, then city within each county; table includes counties with populations greater than 49,999 unless noted and cities with populations greater than 9,999 whose Asian and/or NHPI population rates are greater than the national average; (1) Native Hawaiian and other Pacific Islander; (2) excludes Taiwanese; (3) includes Chamorro; (4) county does not meet population threshold but is shown in order to allow inclusion of city

Place	All owner-occupied housing units	Asian-occupied housing units	Asians who own and occupy their own homes	NHPI[1]-occupied housing units	NHPIs[1] who own and occupy their own homes	Asian Indian	Bangladeshi	Cambodian	Chinese[2]	Fijian	Filipino	Guamanian[3]	Hawaiian, Native	Hmong	Indonesian	Japanese	Korean	Laotian	Malaysian	Pakistani	Samoan	Sri Lankan	Taiwanese	Thai	Tongan	Vietnamese
Yonkers (city)	32,115 43.19	2,820	1,311 46.49 46.49 4.08	-	-	585 45.07 44.62 20.74 1.82	-	-	154 52.74 11.75 5.46 0.48	-	293 56.35 22.35 10.39 0.91	-	-	-	-	-	116 32.68 8.85 4.11 0.36	-	-	-	-	-	-	-	-	-
NORTH CAROLINA	2,172,270 69.36	31,943	16,302 51.03 51.03 0.75	907	403 44.43 44.43 0.02	3,778 45.34 23.18 11.83 0.17	-	375 68.81 2.30 1.17 0.02	3,215 55.71 19.72 10.06 0.15	-	1,386 49.48 8.50 4.34 0.06	129 45.10 32.01 14.22 0.01	135 42.86 33.50 14.88 0.01	610 53.46 3.74 1.91 0.03	-	966 48.11 5.93 3.02 0.04	1,588 44.69 9.74 4.97 0.07	612 55.18 3.75 1.92 0.03	-	236 42.52 1.45 0.74 0.01	49 37.98 12.16 5.40 <0.01	-	250 74.18 1.53 0.78 0.01	237 59.10 1.45 0.74 0.01	-	2,500 60.98 15.34 7.83 0.12
Alamance County	36,176 70.13	293	169 57.68 57.68 0.47	-	-	-	-	-	-	-	-	-	-	-	-	-	-	-	-	-	-	-	-	-	-	-
Buncombe County	60,275 70.27	476	239 50.21 50.21 0.40	-	-	78 49.68 32.64 16.39 0.13	-	-	-	-	-	-	-	-	-	-	-	-	-	-	-	-	-	-	-	-
Burke County	25,597 74.13	525	305 58.10 58.10 1.19	-	-	-	-	-	-	-	-	-	-	188 61.84 61.64 35.81 0.73	-	-	-	42 57.53 13.77 8.00 0.16	-	-	-	-	-	-	-	-
Cabarrus County	36,974 74.67	259	164 63.32 63.32 0.44	-	-	-	-	-	-	-	-	-	-	-	-	-	-	-	-	-	-	-	-	-	-	-
Catawba County	40,299 72.57	830	446 53.73 53.73 1.11	-	-	-	-	-	-	-	-	-	-	130 43.92 29.15 15.66 0.32	-	-	-	29 32.95 6.50 3.49 0.07	-	-	-	-	-	-	-	90 58.06 20.18 10.84 0.22
Hickory (city)	8,512 55.05	370	122 32.97 32.97 1.43	-	-	-	-	-	-	-	-	-	-	7 7.78 5.74 1.89 0.08	-	-	-	-	-	-	-	-	-	-	-	-
Cleveland County	27,003 72.89	177	121 68.36 68.36 0.45	-	-	-	-	-	-	-	-	-	-	-	-	-	-	-	-	-	-	-	-	-	-	-
Craven County	23,068 66.71	289	153 52.94 52.94 0.66	-	-	-	-	-	-	-	83 71.55 54.25 28.72 0.36	-	-	-	-	-	-	-	-	-	-	-	-	-	-	-

Notes: Please refer to the User's Guide for an explanation of data; data is arranged alphabetically by state, then county, then city within each county; table includes counties with populations greater than 49,999 unless noted and cities with populations greater than 9,999 whose Asian and/or NHPI population rates are greater than the national average; (1) Native Hawaiian and other Pacific Islander; (2) excludes Taiwanese; (3) includes Chamorro; (4) county does not meet population threshold but is shown in order to allow inclusion of city

Place	All owner-occupied housing units	Asian-occupied housing units	Asians who own and occupy their own homes	NHPI[1]-occupied housing units	NHPIs[1] who own and occupy their own homes	Asian Indian	Bangladeshi	Cambodian	Chinese[2]	Fijian	Filipino	Guamanian[3]	Hawaiian, Native	Hmong	Indonesian	Japanese	Korean	Laotian	Malaysian	Pakistani	Samoan	Sri Lankan	Taiwanese	Thai	Tongan	Vietnamese
Cumberland County	63,748 59.38	1,603	924 57.64 57.64 1.45	152	79 51.97 51.97 0.12	108 54.82 11.69 6.74 0.17	-	-	-	-	145 42.40 15.69 9.05 0.23	-	-	-	-	112 70.00 12.12 6.99 0.18	252 56.76 27.27 15.72 0.40	-	-	-	-	-	-	-	-	118 75.16 12.77 7.36 0.19
Davidson County	43,160 74.21	320	193 60.31 60.31 0.45	-	-	-	-	71 57.26 36.79 22.19 0.16	-	-	-	-	-	-	-	-	-	-	-	-	-	-	-	-	-	-
Durham County	48,278 54.24	2,585	805 31.14 31.14 1.67	-	-	261 27.42 32.42 10.10 0.54	-	-	204 31.63 25.34 7.89 0.42	-	117 54.42 14.53 4.53 0.24	-	-	-	-	23 13.69 2.86 0.89 0.05	52 20.55 6.46 2.01 0.11	-	-	-	-	-	-	-	-	-
Forsyth County	81,252 65.60	1,103	555 50.32 50.32 0.68	-	-	88 33.33 15.86 7.98 0.11	-	-	186 55.86 33.51 16.86 0.23	-	40 48.78 7.21 3.63 0.05	-	-	-	-	-	-	-	-	-	-	-	-	-	-	109 71.24 19.64 9.88 0.13
Gaston County	50,905 68.85	413	225 54.48 54.48 0.44	-	-	-	-	-	-	-	-	-	-	-	-	-	-	-	-	-	-	-	-	-	-	69 62.16 30.67 16.71 0.14
Guilford County	105,700 62.67	2,618	1,199 45.80 45.80 1.13	-	-	253 43.85 21.10 9.66 0.24	-	-	155 50.82 12.93 5.92 0.15	-	86 46.24 7.17 3.28 0.08	-	-	-	-	-	115 41.82 9.59 4.39 0.11	72 57.60 6.01 2.75 0.07	-	18 20.93 1.50 0.69 0.02	-	-	-	-	-	361 47.31 30.11 13.79 0.34
Halifax County	14,827 67.02	97	48 49.48 49.48 0.32	-	-	-	-	-	-	-	-	-	-	-	-	-	-	-	-	-	-	-	-	-	-	-
Harnett County	23,753 70.28	144	34 23.61 23.61 0.14	-	-	-	-	-	-	-	-	-	-	-	-	-	-	-	-	-	-	-	-	-	-	-
Henderson County	29,483 78.80	117	86 73.50 73.50 0.29	-	-	-	-	-	-	-	-	-	-	-	-	-	-	-	-	-	-	-	-	-	-	-
Iredell County	35,680 75.34	286	147 51.40 51.40 0.41	-	-	-	-	-	-	-	-	-	-	-	-	-	-	-	-	-	-	-	-	-	-	-

Notes: Please refer to the User's Guide for an explanation of data; data is arranged alphabetically by state, then county, then city within each county; table includes counties with populations greater than 49,999 unless noted and cities with populations greater than 9,999 whose Asian and/or NHPI population rates are greater than the national average; (1) Native Hawaiian and other Pacific Islander; (2) excludes Taiwanese; (3) includes Chamorro; (4) county does not meet population threshold but is shown in order to allow inclusion of city

Place	All owner-occupied housing units	Asian-occupied housing units	Asians who own and occupy their own homes	NHPI[1]-occupied housing units	NHPIs[1] who own and occupy their own homes	Asian Indian	Bangladeshi	Cambodian	Chinese[2]	Fijian	Filipino	Guamanian[3]	Hawaiian, Native	Hmong	Indonesian	Japanese	Korean	Laotian	Malaysian	Pakistani	Samoan	Sri Lankan	Taiwanese	Thai	Tongan	Vietnamese
Johnston County	34,222 73.45	102	49 48.04 48.04 0.14	-	-	-	-	-	-	-	-	-	-	-	-	-	-	-	-	-	-	-	-	-	-	-
Lenoir County	15,984 66.99	87	67 77.01 77.01 0.42	-	-	-	-	-	-	-	-	-	-	-	-	-	-	-	-	-	-	-	-	-	-	-
Mecklenburg County	170,392 62.32	5,977	3,393 56.77 56.77 1.99	-	-	830 50.58 24.46 13.89 0.49	-	132 71.74 3.89 2.21 0.08	540 65.14 15.92 9.03 0.32	-	234 65.18 6.90 3.92 0.14	-	-	80 62.99 2.36 1.34 0.05	-	131 45.80 3.86 2.19 0.08	358 47.93 10.55 5.99 0.21	125 48.83 3.68 2.09 0.07	-	-	-	-	-	-	-	787 66.64 23.19 13.17 0.46
Nash County	22,777 67.70	137	68 49.64 49.64 0.30	-	-	-	-	-	-	-	-	-	-	-	-	-	-	-	-	-	-	-	-	-	-	-
New Hanover County	44,115 64.70	489	208 42.54 42.54 0.47	-	-	-	-	-	-	-	-	-	-	-	-	-	-	-	-	-	-	-	-	-	-	-
Onslow County	27,968 58.12	596	280 46.98 46.98 1.00	79	32 40.51 40.51 0.11	-	-	-	-	-	61 25.85 21.79 10.23 0.22	-	-	-	-	84 78.50 30.00 14.09 0.30	-	-	-	-	-	-	-	-	-	-
Orange County	26,395 57.55	1,612	567 35.17 35.17 2.15	-	-	82 28.77 14.46 5.09 0.31	-	-	330 51.40 58.20 20.47 1.25	-	-	-	-	-	-	40 24.54 7.05 2.48 0.15	21 8.11 3.70 1.30 0.08	-	-	-	-	-	-	-	-	-
Carrboro (town)	2,341 31.07	305	49 16.07 16.07 2.09	-	-	-	-	-	-	-	-	-	-	-	-	-	-	-	-	-	-	-	-	-	-	-
Chapel Hill (town)	7,567 42.20	1,149	396 34.46 34.46 5.23	-	-	47 22.27 11.87 4.09 0.62	-	-	255 51.00 64.39 22.19 3.37	-	-	-	-	-	-	-	14 7.87 3.54 1.22 0.19	-	-	-	-	-	-	-	-	-
Pitt County	30,539 58.13	411	162 39.42 39.42 0.53	-	-	-	-	-	-	-	-	-	-	-	-	-	-	-	-	-	-	-	-	-	-	-

Notes: Please refer to the User's Guide for an explanation of data; data is arranged alphabetically by state, then county, then city within each county; table includes counties with populations greater than 49,999 unless noted and cities with populations greater than 9,999 whose Asian and/or NHPI population rates are greater than the national average; (1) Native Hawaiian and other Pacific Islander; (2) excludes Taiwanese; (3) includes Chamorro; (4) county does not meet population threshold but is shown in order to allow inclusion of city

Place	All owner-occupied housing units	Asian-occupied housing units	Asians who own and occupy their own homes	NHPI[1]-occupied housing units	NHPIs[1] who own and occupy their own homes	Asian Indian	Bangladeshi	Cambodian	Chinese[2]	Fijian	Filipino	Guamanian[3]	Hawaiian, Native	Hmong	Indonesian	Japanese	Korean	Laotian	Malaysian	Pakistani	Samoan	Sri Lankan	Taiwanese	Thai	Tongan	Vietnamese
Randolph County	38,793 76.58	165	107 64.85 64.85 0.28	-	-	-	-	-	-	-	-	-	-	-	-	-	-	-	-	-	-	-	-	-	-	-
Robeson County	31,779 72.76	266	159 59.77 59.77 0.50	-	-	-	-	-	-	-	-	-	-	-	-	-	-	-	-	-	-	-	-	-	-	-
Rowan County	36,737 73.56	192	123 64.06 64.06 0.33	-	-	-	-	-	-	-	-	-	-	-	-	-	-	-	-	-	-	-	-	-	-	-
Stanly County	16,945 76.25	147	68 46.26 46.26 0.40	-	-	-	-	-	-	-	-	-	-	18 30.00 26.47 12.24 0.11	-	-	-	-	-	-	-	-	-	-	-	-
Surry County	21,687 76.34	68	9 13.24 13.24 0.04	-	-	-	-	-	-	-	-	-	-	-	-	-	-	-	-	-	-	-	-	-	-	-
Union County	34,957 80.56	163	93 57.06 57.06 0.27	-	-	-	-	-	-	-	-	-	-	-	-	-	-	-	-	-	-	-	-	-	-	-
Wake County	159,456 65.88	6,664	3,554 53.33 53.33 2.23	-	-	1,138 46.85 32.02 17.08 0.71	-	-	981 60.33 27.60 14.72 0.62	-	207 52.41 5.82 3.11 0.13	-	-	-	-	119 45.95 3.35 1.79 0.07	272 42.30 7.65 4.08 0.17	-	-	78 51.66 2.19 1.17 0.05	-	-	-	-	-	469 70.21 13.20 7.04 0.29
Apex (town)	5,634 76.04	246	158 64.23 64.23 2.80	-	-	-	-	-	-	-	-	-	-	-	-	-	-	-	-	-	-	-	-	-	-	-
Cary (town)	25,512 73.13	2,438	1,557 63.86 63.86 6.10	-	-	638 59.02 40.98 26.17 2.50	-	-	451 71.02 28.97 18.50 1.77	-	-	-	-	-	-	62 50.82 3.98 2.54 0.24	82 48.81 5.27 3.36 0.32	-	-	-	-	-	-	-	-	136 81.93 8.73 5.58 0.53
Wayne County	27,826 65.30	281	156 55.52 55.52 0.56	-	-	-	-	-	-	-	-	-	-	-	-	-	-	-	-	-	-	-	-	-	-	-

Notes: Please refer to the User's Guide for an explanation of data; data is arranged alphabetically by state, then county, then city within each county; table includes counties with populations greater than 49,999 unless noted and cities with populations greater than 9,999 whose Asian and/or NHPI population rates are greater than the national average; (1) Native Hawaiian and other Pacific Islander; (2) excludes Taiwanese; (3) includes Chamorro; (4) county does not meet population threshold but is shown in order to allow inclusion of city

Place	All owner-occupied housing units	Asian-occupied housing units	Asians who own and occupy their own homes	NHPI[1]-occupied housing units	NHPIs[1] who own and occupy their own homes	Asian Indian	Bangladeshi	Cambodian	Chinese[2]	Fijian	Filipino	Guamanian[3]	Hawaiian, Native	Hmong	Indonesian	Japanese	Korean	Laotian	Malaysian	Pakistani	Samoan	Sri Lankan	Taiwanese	Thai	Tongan	Vietnamese
Wilkes County	20,773 77.95	107	23 21.50 21.50 0.11	-	-	-	-	-	-	-	-	-	-	-	-	-	-	-	-	-	-	-	-	-	-	-
NORTH DAKOTA	171,310 66.62	1,048	385 36.74 36.74 0.22	-	-	144 42.23 37.40 13.74 0.08	-	-	42 30.00 10.91 4.01 0.02	-	62 37.35 16.10 5.92 0.04	-	-	-	-	-	37 42.53 9.61 3.53 0.02	-	-	-	-	-	-	-	-	-
Cass County	27,892 54.35	497	132 26.56 26.56 0.47	-	-	52 34.21 39.39 10.46 0.19	-	-	-	-	-	-	-	-	-	-	-	-	-	-	-	-	-	-	-	-
Grand Forks County	13,655 53.69	176	43 24.43 24.43 0.31	-	-	-	-	-	-	-	-	-	-	-	-	-	-	-	-	-	-	-	-	-	-	-
Ward County	14,453 62.73	76	39 51.32 51.32 0.27	-	-	-	-	-	-	-	-	-	-	-	-	-	-	-	-	-	-	-	-	-	-	-
OHIO	3,072,514 69.11	45,070	21,305 47.27 47.27 0.69	642	335 52.18 52.18 0.01	6,041 43.54 28.35 13.40 0.20	97 44.09 0.46 0.22 <0.01	294 48.84 1.38 0.65 0.01	4,844 49.22 22.74 10.75 0.16	-	2,600 61.67 12.20 5.77 0.08	58 44.96 17.31 9.03 <0.01	134 55.14 40.00 20.87 <0.01	-	67 15.62 0.31 0.15 <0.01	1,857 45.07 8.72 4.12 0.06	1,621 36.90 7.61 3.60 0.05	468 61.02 2.20 1.04 0.02	50 43.10 0.23 0.11 <0.01	190 38.00 0.89 0.42 0.01	27 31.76 8.06 4.21 <0.01	110 58.51 0.52 0.24 <0.01	461 58.73 2.16 1.02 0.02	244 40.94 1.15 0.54 0.01	-	1,672 57.20 7.85 3.71 0.05
Allen County	29,290 72.06	180	120 66.67 66.67 0.41	-	-	-	-	-	-	-	-	-	-	-	-	-	-	-	-	-	-	-	-	-	-	-
Ashtabula County	29,187 74.08	111	63 56.76 56.76 0.22	-	-	-	-	-	-	-	-	-	-	-	-	-	-	-	-	-	-	-	-	-	-	-
Athens County	13,596 60.42	445	86 19.33 19.33 0.63	-	-	-	-	-	-	-	-	-	-	-	-	-	-	-	-	-	-	-	-	-	-	-
Athens (city)	1,817 29.00	349	46 13.18 13.18 2.53	-	-	-	-	-	-	-	-	-	-	-	-	-	-	-	-	-	-	-	-	-	-	-

Notes: Please refer to the User's Guide for an explanation of data; data is arranged alphabetically by state, then county, then city within each county; table includes counties with populations greater than 49,999 unless noted and cities with populations greater than 9,999 whose Asian and/or NHPI population rates are greater than the national average; (1) Native Hawaiian and other Pacific Islander; (2) excludes Taiwanese; (3) includes Chamorro; (4) county does not meet population threshold but is shown in order to allow inclusion of city

Place	All owner-occupied housing units	Asian-occupied housing units	Asians who own and occupy their own homes	NHPI[1]-occupied housing units	NHPIs[1] who own and occupy their own homes	Asian Indian	Bangladeshi	Cambodian	Chinese[2]	Fijian	Filipino	Guamanian[3]	Hawaiian, Native	Hmong	Indonesian	Japanese	Korean	Laotian	Malaysian	Pakistani	Samoan	Sri Lankan	Taiwanese	Thai	Tongan	Vietnamese
Butler County	88,121 71.60	1,451	906 62.44 62.44 1.03	-	-	314 59.47 34.66 21.64 0.36	-	-	209 63.72 23.07 14.40 0.24	-	96 82.76 10.60 6.62 0.11	-	-	-	-	-	77 71.30 8.50 5.31 0.09	-	-	-	-	-	-	-	-	90 52.94 9.93 6.20 0.10
Clark County	40,490 71.48	212	124 58.49 58.49 0.31	-	-	-	-	-	-	-	-	-	-	-	-	-	-	-	-	-	-	-	-	-	-	-
Clermont County	49,353 74.76	391	234 59.85 59.85 0.47	-	-	98 59.04 41.88 25.06 0.20	-	-	-	-	-	-	-	-	-	-	-	-	-	-	-	-	-	-	-	-
Columbiana County	32,656 75.99	70	41 58.57 58.57 0.13	-	-	-	-	-	-	-	-	-	-	-	-	-	-	-	-	-	-	-	-	-	-	-
Cuyahoga County	360,988 63.17	9,324	4,500 48.26 48.26 1.25	-	-	1,508 46.49 33.51 16.17 0.42	-	65 63.73 1.44 0.70 0.02	1,098 51.62 24.40 11.78 0.30	-	640 57.04 14.22 6.86 0.18	-	-	-	-	276 46.08 6.13 2.96 0.08	260 36.47 5.78 2.79 0.07	-	-	-	-	-	-	-	-	328 51.98 7.29 3.52 0.09
Mayfield Heights (city)	4,999 50.76	331	66 19.94 19.94 1.32	-	-	28 14.66 42.42 8.46 0.56	-	-	-	-	-	-	-	-	-	-	-	-	-	-	-	-	-	-	-	-
Richmond Heights (city)	3,064 62.99	226	104 46.02 46.02 3.39	-	-	-	-	-	-	-	-	-	-	-	-	-	-	-	-	-	-	-	-	-	-	-
Solon (city)	6,635 87.83	296	250 84.46 84.46 3.77	-	-	116 86.57 46.40 39.19 1.75	-	-	76 80.85 30.40 25.68 1.15	-	-	-	-	-	-	-	-	-	-	-	-	-	-	-	-	-
Westlake (city)	9,660 75.08	450	313 69.56 69.56 3.24	-	-	128 58.72 40.89 28.44 1.33	-	-	-	-	-	-	-	-	-	-	-	-	-	-	-	-	-	-	-	-
Delaware County	31,902 80.41	582	451 77.49 77.49 1.41	-	-	124 78.48 27.49 21.31 0.39	-	-	156 93.98 34.59 26.80 0.49	-	-	-	-	-	-	-	-	-	-	-	-	-	-	-	-	-

Notes: Please refer to the User's Guide for an explanation of data; data is arranged alphabetically by state, then county, then city within each county; table includes counties with populations greater than 49,999 unless noted and cities with populations greater than 9,999 whose Asian and/or NHPI population rates are greater than the national average; (1) Native Hawaiian and other Pacific Islander; (2) excludes Taiwanese; (3) includes Chamorro; (4) county does not meet population threshold but is shown in order to allow inclusion of city

Place	All owner-occupied housing units	Asian-occupied housing units	Asians who own and occupy their own homes	NHPI[1]-occupied housing units	NHPIs[1] who own and occupy their own homes	Asian Indian	Bangladeshi	Cambodian	Chinese[2]	Fijian	Filipino	Guamanian[3]	Hawaiian, Native	Hmong	Indonesian	Japanese	Korean	Laotian	Malaysian	Pakistani	Samoan	Sri Lankan	Taiwanese	Thai	Tongan	Vietnamese
Fairfield County	34,626 76.23	212	151 71.23 71.23 0.44	-	-	-	-	-	-	-	-	-	-	-	-	-	-	-	-	-	-	-	-	-	-	-
Franklin County	249,613 56.89	11,755	4,070 34.62 34.62 1.63	93	24 25.81 25.81 0.01	856 25.81 21.03 7.28 0.34	-	136 42.50 3.34 1.16 0.05	1,078 41.22 26.49 9.17 0.43	-	264 45.44 6.49 2.25 0.11	-	-	-	8 3.24 0.20 0.07 <0.01	475 38.71 11.67 4.04 0.19	208 15.73 5.11 1.77 0.08	178 52.51 4.37 1.51 0.07	-	61 45.52 1.50 0.52 0.02	-	-	134 55.37 3.29 1.14 0.05	49 35.77 1.20 0.42 0.02	-	398 58.79 9.78 3.39 0.16
Dublin (city)	8,622 77.22	816	422 51.72 51.72 4.89	-	-	142 58.92 33.65 17.40 1.65	-	-	115 75.66 27.25 14.09 1.33	-	-	-	-	-	-	82 29.93 19.43 10.05 0.95	-	-	-	-	-	-	-	-	-	-
Hilliard (city)	6,473 75.87	257	140 54.47 54.47 2.16	-	-	-	-	-	-	-	-	-	-	-	-	-	-	-	-	-	-	-	-	-	-	-
Geauga County	27,614 87.30	122	113 92.62 92.62 0.41	-	-	-	-	-	-	-	-	-	-	-	-	-	-	-	-	-	-	-	-	-	-	-
Greene County	38,523 69.65	986	478 48.48 48.48 1.24	-	-	177 57.10 37.03 17.95 0.46	-	-	68 42.24 14.23 6.90 0.18	-	-	-	-	-	-	-	62 35.23 12.97 6.29 0.16	-	-	-	-	-	-	-	-	-
Hamilton County	207,533 59.84	4,780	1,825 38.18 38.18 0.88	-	-	487 29.95 26.68 10.19 0.23	-	39 39.80 2.14 0.82 0.02	366 32.53 20.05 7.66 0.18	-	284 58.68 15.56 5.94 0.14	-	-	-	-	136 44.74 7.45 2.85 0.07	147 37.40 8.05 3.08 0.07	-	-	-	-	-	-	-	-	160 55.17 8.77 3.35 0.08
Blue Ash (city)	3,722 73.56	299	140 46.82 46.82 3.76	-	-	52 36.62 37.14 17.39 1.40	-	-	-	-	-	-	-	-	-	-	-	-	-	-	-	-	-	-	-	-
Sharonville (city)	3,980 64.31	233	78 33.48 33.48 1.96	-	-	50 29.59 64.10 21.46 1.26	-	-	-	-	-	-	-	-	-	-	-	-	-	-	-	-	-	-	-	-
Hancock County	20,404 73.14	285	141 49.47 49.47 0.69	-	-	-	-	-	-	-	-	-	-	-	-	-	-	-	-	-	-	-	-	-	-	-

Notes: Please refer to the User's Guide for an explanation of data; data is arranged alphabetically by state, then county, then city within each county; table includes counties with populations greater than 49,999 unless noted and cities with populations greater than 9,999 whose Asian and/or NHPI population rates are greater than the national average; (1) Native Hawaiian and other Pacific Islander; (2) excludes Taiwanese; (3) includes Chamorro; (4) county does not meet population threshold but is shown in order to allow inclusion of city

Place	All owner-occupied housing units	Asian-occupied housing units	Asians who own and occupy their own homes	NHPI¹-occupied housing units	NHPIs¹ who own and occupy their own homes	Asian Indian	Bangladeshi	Cambodian	Chinese²	Fijian	Filipino	Guamanian³	Hawaiian, Native	Hmong	Indonesian	Japanese	Korean	Laotian	Malaysian	Pakistani	Samoan	Sri Lankan	Taiwanese	Thai	Tongan	Vietnamese
Lake County	69,502 77.48	688	357 51.89 51.89 0.51	-	-	85 36.96 23.81 12.35 0.12	-	-	107 64.46 29.97 15.55 0.15	-	-	-	-	-	-	-	-	-	-	-	-	-	-	-	-	-
Licking County	41,397 74.44	215	146 67.91 67.91 0.35	-	-	-	-	-	-	-	-	-	-	-	-	-	-	-	-	-	-	-	-	-	-	-
Lorain County	78,472 74.14	536	343 63.99 63.99 0.44	-	-	81 72.32 23.62 15.11 0.10	-	-	-	-	88 69.29 25.66 16.42 0.11	-	-	-	-	-	-	-	-	-	-	-	-	-	-	-
Lucas County[4]	119,487 65.35	1,963	892 45.44 45.44 0.75	-	-	277 46.48 31.05 14.11 0.23	-	-	229 42.10 25.67 11.67 0.19	-	135 67.16 15.13 6.88 0.11	-	-	-	-	-	60 44.78 6.73 3.06 0.05	-	-	-	-	-	-	-	-	-
Mahoning County	74,690 72.81	266	152 57.14 57.14 0.20	-	-	-	-	-	-	-	-	-	-	-	-	-	-	-	-	-	-	-	-	-	-	-
Marion County	17,912 72.88	95	54 56.84 56.84 0.30	-	-	-	-	-	-	-	-	-	-	-	-	-	-	-	-	-	-	-	-	-	-	-
Medina County	44,302 81.23	350	244 69.71 69.71 0.55	-	-	104 67.53 42.62 29.71 0.23	-	-	-	-	-	-	-	-	-	-	-	-	-	-	-	-	-	-	-	-
Miami County	27,800 72.33	273	171 62.64 62.64 0.62	-	-	-	-	-	-	-	-	-	-	-	-	-	-	-	-	-	-	-	-	-	-	-
Montgomery County	148,254 64.68	2,422	1,271 52.48 52.48 0.86	-	-	373 49.34 29.35 15.40 0.25	-	-	262 59.82 20.61 10.82 0.18	-	123 63.73 9.68 5.08 0.08	-	-	-	-	93 34.32 7.32 3.84 0.06	90 37.50 7.08 3.72 0.06	-	-	-	-	-	-	-	-	208 72.22 16.37 8.59 0.14
Portage County	40,225 71.26	387	106 27.39 27.39 0.26	-	-	-	-	-	-	-	-	-	-	-	-	-	-	-	-	-	-	-	-	-	-	-

Notes: Please refer to the User's Guide for an explanation of data; data is arranged alphabetically by state, then county, then city within each county; table includes counties with populations greater than 49,999 unless noted and cities with populations greater than 9,999 whose Asian and/or NHPI population rates are greater than the national average; (1) Native Hawaiian and other Pacific Islander; (2) excludes Taiwanese; (3) includes Chamorro; (4) county does not meet population threshold but is shown in order to allow inclusion of city

Place	All owner-occupied housing units	Asian-occupied housing units	Asians who own and occupy their own homes	NHPI[1]-occupied housing units	NHPIs[1] who own and occupy their own homes	Asian Indian	Bangladeshi	Cambodian	Chinese[2]	Fijian	Filipino	Guamanian[3]	Hawaiian, Native	Hmong	Indonesian	Japanese	Korean	Laotian	Malaysian	Pakistani	Samoan	Sri Lankan	Taiwanese	Thai	Tongan	Vietnamese
Richland County	35,444 71.55	199	117 58.79 58.79 0.33	-	-	-	-	-	-	-	-	-	-	-	-	-	-	-	-	-	-	-	-	-	-	-
Stark County	107,397 72.41	619	392 63.33 63.33 0.37	-	-	93 63.27 23.72 15.02 0.09	-	-	108 79.41 27.55 17.45 0.10	-	-	-	-	-	-	-	-	-	-	-	-	-	-	-	-	-
Summit County	152,996 70.25	2,383	1,352 56.74 56.74 0.88	-	-	372 53.22 27.51 15.61 0.24	-	-	331 59.21 24.48 13.89 0.22	-	116 70.30 8.58 4.87 0.08	-	-	-	-	57 34.97 4.22 2.39 0.04	117 49.16 8.65 4.91 0.08	135 77.59 9.99 5.67 0.09	-	-	-	-	-	-	-	117 66.86 8.65 4.91 0.08
Trumbull County	66,104 74.26	310	185 59.68 59.68 0.28	-	-	-	-	-	-	-	-	-	-	-	-	-	-	-	-	-	-	-	-	-	-	-
Warren County	43,953 78.54	683	526 77.01 77.01 1.20	-	-	150 63.03 28.52 21.96 0.34	-	-	175 91.62 33.27 25.62 0.40	-	-	-	-	-	-	-	-	-	-	-	-	-	-	-	-	-
Wayne County	29,653 73.32	182	98 53.85 53.85 0.33	-	-	-	-	-	-	-	-	-	-	-	-	-	-	-	-	-	-	-	-	-	-	-
Wood County	31,892 70.60	390	147 37.69 37.69 0.46	-	-	-	-	-	-	-	-	-	-	-	-	-	-	-	-	-	-	-	-	-	-	-
OKLAHOMA	918,141 68.40	14,107	6,648 47.13 47.13 0.72	459	222 48.37 48.37 0.02	1,289 45.39 19.39 9.14 0.14	-	67 89.33 1.01 0.47 0.01	853 35.09 12.83 6.05 0.09	-	502 44.58 7.55 3.56 0.05	68 49.28 30.63 14.81 0.01	101 57.06 45.50 22.00 0.01	23 40.35 0.35 0.16 <0.01	-	462 47.00 6.95 3.27 0.05	620 48.48 9.33 4.39 0.07	185 75.51 2.78 1.31 0.02	38 18.10 0.57 0.27 <0.01	108 29.51 1.62 0.77 0.01	-	-	43 25.60 0.65 0.30 <0.01	112 40.58 1.68 0.79 0.01	-	2,175 64.39 32.72 15.42 0.24
Canadian County	24,854 78.94	550	531 96.55 96.55 2.14	-	-	301 95.56 56.69 54.73 1.21	-	-	-	-	-	-	-	-	-	-	-	-	-	-	-	-	-	-	-	149 96.75 28.06 27.09 0.60
Cleveland County	53,030 66.97	2,064	947 45.88 45.88 1.79	-	-	139 46.33 14.68 6.73 0.26	-	-	122 27.54 12.88 5.91 0.23	-	97 48.99 10.24 4.70 0.18	-	-	-	-	-	143 50.35 15.10 6.93 0.27	-	-	-	-	-	-	-	-	351 72.22 37.06 17.01 0.66

Notes: Please refer to the User's Guide for an explanation of data; data is arranged alphabetically by state, then county, then city within each county; table includes counties with populations greater than 49,999 unless noted and cities with populations greater than 9,999 whose Asian and/or NHPI population rates are greater than the national average; (1) Native Hawaiian and other Pacific Islander; (2) excludes Taiwanese; (3) includes Chamorro; (4) county does not meet population threshold but is shown in order to allow inclusion of city

Place	All owner-occupied housing units	Asian-occupied housing units	Asians who own and occupy their own homes	NHPI[1]-occupied housing units	NHPIs[1] who own and occupy their own homes	Asian Indian	Bangladeshi	Cambodian	Chinese[2]	Fijian	Filipino	Guamanian[3]	Hawaiian, Native	Hmong	Indonesian	Japanese	Korean	Laotian	Malaysian	Pakistani	Samoan	Sri Lankan	Taiwanese	Thai	Tongan	Vietnamese
Comanche County	24,003 60.30	620	385 62.10 62.10 1.60	-	-	-	-	-	-	-	82 56.94 21.30 13.23 0.34	-	-	-	-	-	140 58.82 36.36 22.58 0.58	-	-	-	-	-	-	-	-	-
Garfield County	16,274 70.22	185	103 55.68 55.68 0.63	-	-	-	-	-	-	-	-	-	-	-	-	-	-	-	-	-	-	-	-	-	-	-
Muskogee County	18,414 69.60	93	45 48.39 48.39 0.24	-	-	-	-	-	-	-	-	-	-	-	-	-	-	-	-	-	-	-	-	-	-	-
Oklahoma County	161,158 60.40	5,971	2,689 45.03 45.03 1.67	-	-	403 38.71 14.99 6.75 0.25	-	-	274 29.37 10.19 4.59 0.17	-	129 35.73 4.80 2.16 0.08	-	-	-	-	153 37.23 5.69 2.56 0.09	175 41.67 6.51 2.93 0.11	125 81.17 4.65 2.09 0.08	-	-	-	-	-	54 38.57 2.01 0.90 0.03	-	1,212 63.69 45.07 20.30 0.75
Payne County	14,912 55.89	661	64 9.68 9.68 0.43	-	-	-	-	-	35 14.58 54.69 5.30 0.23	-	-	-	-	-	-	-	-	-	-	-	-	-	-	-	-	-
Stillwater (city)	6,475 41.59	655	64 9.77 9.77 0.99	-	-	-	-	-	35 14.58 54.69 5.34 0.54	-	-	-	-	-	-	-	-	-	-	-	-	-	-	-	-	-
Pottawatomie County	17,711 72.17	83	19 22.89 22.89 0.11	-	-	-	-	-	-	-	-	-	-	-	-	-	-	-	-	-	-	-	-	-	-	-
Tulsa County	140,131 61.76	2,570	1,216 47.32 47.32 0.87	-	-	274 37.33 22.53 10.66 0.20	-	-	254 51.31 20.89 9.88 0.18	-	48 44.86 3.95 1.87 0.03	-	-	-	-	-	88 48.35 7.24 3.42 0.06	-	-	65 42.21 5.35 2.53 0.05	-	-	-	-	-	335 62.27 27.55 13.04 0.24
Wagoner County	17,025 81.03	116	74 63.79 63.79 0.43	-	-	-	-	-	-	-	-	-	-	-	-	-	-	-	-	-	-	-	-	-	-	-
OREGON	856,890 64.25	31,527	17,313 54.91 54.91 2.02	2,352	946 40.22 40.22 0.11	1,499 41.70 8.66 4.75 0.17	-	336 44.27 1.94 1.07 0.04	4,027 63.48 23.26 12.77 0.47	96 68.57 10.15 4.08 0.01	1,704 54.41 9.84 5.40 0.20	139 37.57 14.69 5.91 0.02	370 49.53 39.11 15.73 0.04	102 37.78 0.59 0.32 0.01	98 41.00 0.57 0.31 0.01	2,833 56.40 16.36 8.99 0.33	1,536 40.88 8.87 4.87 0.18	559 60.96 3.23 1.77 0.07	-	91 72.22 0.53 0.29 0.01	47 25.97 4.97 2.00 0.01	-	162 58.70 0.94 0.51 0.02	246 50.41 1.42 0.78 0.03	31 31.96 3.28 1.32 <0.01	3,326 64.51 19.21 10.55 0.39

Notes: Please refer to the User's Guide for an explanation of data; data is arranged alphabetically by state, then county, then city within each county; table includes counties with populations greater than 49,999 unless noted and cities with populations greater than 9,999 whose Asian and/or NHPI population rates are greater than the national average; (1) Native Hawaiian and other Pacific Islander; (2) excludes Taiwanese; (3) includes Chamorro; (4) county does not meet population threshold but is shown in order to allow inclusion of city

Place	All owner-occupied housing units	Asian-occupied housing units	Asians who own and occupy their own homes	NHPI[1]-occupied housing units	NHPIs[1] who own and occupy their own homes	Asian Indian	Bangladeshi	Cambodian	Chinese[2]	Fijian	Filipino	Guamanian[3]	Hawaiian, Native	Hmong	Indonesian	Japanese	Korean	Laotian	Malaysian	Pakistani	Samoan	Sri Lankan	Taiwanese	Thai	Tongan	Vietnamese
Benton County	17,267 57.28	1,204	400 33.22 33.22 2.32	-	-	-	-	-	142 38.48 35.50 11.79 0.82	-	-	-	-	-	-	101 53.72 25.25 8.39 0.58	28 12.67 7.00 2.33 0.16	-	-	-	-	-	-	-	-	-
Corvallis (city)	8,757 44.59	1,107	309 27.91 27.91 3.53	-	-	-	-	-	131 37.22 42.39 11.83 1.50	-	-	-	-	-	-	-	22 10.23 7.12 1.99 0.25	-	-	-	-	-	-	-	-	-
Clackamas County	91,145 71.10	2,522	1,715 68.00 68.00 1.88	197	111 56.35 56.35 0.12	116 55.50 6.76 4.60 0.13	-	-	477 79.10 27.81 18.91 0.52	-	110 43.65 6.41 4.36 0.12	-	-	-	-	381 77.28 22.22 15.11 0.42	252 54.55 14.69 9.99 0.28	-	-	-	-	-	-	-	-	176 80.73 10.26 6.98 0.19
Lake Oswego (city)	10,508 71.46	532	324 60.90 60.90 3.08	-	-	-	-	-	105 78.36 32.41 19.74 1.00	-	-	-	-	-	-	-	-	-	-	-	-	-	-	-	-	-
Coos County	17,870 68.17	108	68 62.96 62.96 0.38	-	-	-	-	-	-	-	-	-	-	-	-	-	-	-	-	-	-	-	-	-	-	-
Deschutes County	32,967 72.30	168	106 63.10 63.10 0.32	-	-	-	-	-	-	-	-	-	-	-	-	-	-	-	-	-	-	-	-	-	-	-
Douglas County	28,570 71.75	129	78 60.47 60.47 0.27	-	-	-	-	-	-	-	-	-	-	-	-	-	-	-	-	-	-	-	-	-	-	-
Jackson County	47,574 66.51	484	277 57.23 57.23 0.58	-	-	-	-	-	-	-	-	-	-	-	-	-	-	-	-	-	-	-	-	-	-	-
Josephine County	21,713 70.04	163	100 61.35 61.35 0.46	-	-	-	-	-	-	-	-	-	-	-	-	-	-	-	-	-	-	-	-	-	-	-
Klamath County	17,150 68.04	110	69 62.73 62.73 0.40	-	-	-	-	-	-	-	-	-	-	-	-	-	-	-	-	-	-	-	-	-	-	-

Notes: Please refer to the User's Guide for an explanation of data; data is arranged alphabetically by state, then county, then city within each county; table includes counties with populations greater than 49,999 unless noted and cities with populations greater than 9,999 whose Asian and/or NHPI population rates are greater than the national average; (1) Native Hawaiian and other Pacific Islander; (2) excludes Taiwanese; (3) includes Chamorro; (4) county does not meet population threshold but is shown in order to allow inclusion of city

Place	All owner-occupied housing units	Asian-occupied housing units	Asians who own and occupy their own homes	NHPI[1]-occupied housing units	NHPIs[1] who own and occupy their own homes	Asian Indian	Bangladeshi	Cambodian	Chinese[2]	Fijian	Filipino	Guamanian[3]	Hawaiian, Native	Hmong	Indonesian	Japanese	Korean	Laotian	Malaysian	Pakistani	Samoan	Sri Lankan	Taiwanese	Thai	Tongan	Vietnamese
Lane County	81,208	2,209	677	213	103	45	-	-	172	-	72	-	-	-	-	171	81	-	-	-	-	-	-	-	-	-
	62.25		30.65		48.36	24.32			33.53		55.38					29.03	22.56									
						6.65			25.41		10.64					25.26	11.96									
			30.65		48.36	2.04			7.79		3.26					7.74	3.67									
			0.83		0.13	0.06			0.21		0.09					0.21	0.10									
Linn County	26,843	206	131	-	-	-	-	-	-	-	-	-	-	-	-	-	-	-	-	-	-	-	-	-	-	-
	67.89		63.59																							
			63.59																							
			0.49																							
Marion County	63,956	1,401	835	220	54	42	-	-	206	-	149	-	-	-	-	105	57	-	-	-	-	-	-	-	-	169
	62.92		59.60		24.55	37.84			69.83		57.75					55.85	53.77									71.31
						5.03			24.67		17.84					12.57	6.83									20.24
			59.60		24.55	3.00			14.70		10.64					7.49	4.07									12.06
			1.31		0.08	0.07			0.32		0.23					0.16	0.09									0.26
Salem (city)	28,879	934	554	89	16	-	-	-	166	-	58	-	-	-	-	60	-	-	-	-	-	-	-	-	-	111
	57.02		59.31		17.98				70.34		45.31					55.56										79.86
									29.96		10.47					10.83										20.04
			59.31		17.98				17.77		6.21					6.42										11.88
			1.92		0.06				0.57		0.20					0.21										0.38
Multnomah County	154,784	11,710	6,670	759	287	364	-	94	1,571	-	672	-	90	88	-	908	328	404	-	-	-	-	-	48	21	1,845
	56.89		56.96		37.81	56.96		35.07	65.98		58.49		47.62	41.71		55.33	34.53	63.22						31.58	30.43	60.35
						5.46		1.41	23.55		10.07		31.36	1.32		13.61	4.92	6.06						0.72	7.32	27.66
			56.96		37.81	3.11		0.80	13.42		5.74		11.86	0.75		7.75	2.80	3.45						0.41	2.77	15.76
			4.31		0.19	0.24		0.06	1.01		0.43		0.06	0.06		0.59	0.21	0.26						0.03	0.01	1.19
Portland (city)	124,782	10,575	5,891	644	219	299	-	86	1,412	-	536	-	66	73	-	759	293	359	-	-	-	-	-	43	21	1,717
	55.77		55.71		34.01	54.56		33.86	64.39		56.24		40.00	38.62		52.67	35.34	65.27						29.25	30.43	58.80
						5.08		1.46	23.97		9.10		30.14	1.24		12.88	4.97	6.09						0.73	9.59	29.15
			55.71		34.01	2.83		0.81	13.35		5.07		10.25	0.69		7.18	2.77	3.39						0.41	3.26	16.24
			4.72		0.18	0.24		0.07	1.13		0.43		0.05	0.06		0.61	0.23	0.29						0.03	0.02	1.38
Polk County	15,779	213	128	-	-	-	-	-	-	-	-	-	-	-	-	-	-	-	-	-	-	-	-	-	-	-
	68.43		60.09																							
			60.09																							
			0.81																							
Umatilla County	16,343	143	81	-	-	-	-	-	-	-	-	-	-	-	-	-	-	-	-	-	-	-	-	-	-	-
	64.87		56.64																							
			56.64																							
			0.50																							
Washington County	102,424	9,749	5,290	451	193	800	-	162	1,051	-	478	-	50	-	-	569	610	91	-	-	-	-	-	-	-	1,021
	60.55		54.26		42.79	37.21		51.92	65.40		53.65		39.06			53.08	45.32	53.53								72.57
						15.12		3.06	19.87		9.04		25.91			10.76	11.53	1.72								19.30
			54.26		42.79	8.21		1.66	10.78		4.90		11.09			5.84	6.26	0.93								10.47
			5.16		0.19	0.78		0.16	1.03		0.47		0.05			0.56	0.60	0.09								1.00
Aloha (cdp)	9,626	854	646	-	-	-	-	-	-	-	76	-	-	-	-	-	-	-	-	-	-	-	-	-	-	247
	67.27		75.64								66.67															87.90
											11.76															38.24
			75.64								8.90															28.92
			6.71								0.79															2.57

Notes: Please refer to the User's Guide for an explanation of data; data is arranged alphabetically by state, then county, then city within each county; table includes counties with populations greater than 49,999 unless noted and cities with populations greater than 9,999 whose Asian and/or NHPI population rates are greater than the national average; (1) Native Hawaiian and other Pacific Islander; (2) excludes Taiwanese; (3) includes Chamorro; (4) county does not meet population threshold but is shown in order to allow inclusion of city

Place	All owner-occupied housing units	Asian-occupied housing units	Asians who own and occupy their own homes	NHPI[1]-occupied housing units	NHPIs[1] who own and occupy their own homes	Asian Indian	Bangladeshi	Cambodian	Chinese[2]	Fijian	Filipino	Guamanian[3]	Hawaiian, Native	Hmong	Indonesian	Japanese	Korean	Laotian	Malaysian	Pakistani	Samoan	Sri Lankan	Taiwanese	Thai	Tongan	Vietnamese
Beaverton (city)	14,759	2,577	998	-	-	126	-	52	162	-	109	-	-	-	-	120	153	-	-	-	-	-	-	-	-	187
	47.87		38.73			16.78		40.00	52.26		43.08					50.63	39.43									64.48
						12.63		5.21	16.23		10.92					12.02	15.33									18.74
			38.73			4.89		2.02	6.29		4.23					4.66	5.94									7.26
			6.76			0.85		0.35	1.10		0.74					0.81	1.04									1.27
Cedar Mill (cdp)	3,211	314	231	-	-	-	-	-	-	-	-	-	-	-	-	-	-	-	-	-	-	-	-	-	-	-
	67.84		73.57																							
			73.57																							
			7.19																							
Hillsboro (city)	13,118	1,650	563	-	-	105	-	-	101	-	-	-	-	-	-	-	50	-	-	-	-	-	-	-	-	129
	52.41		34.12			18.17			40.73								28.90									56.09
						18.65			17.94								8.88									22.91
			34.12			6.36			6.12								3.03									7.82
			4.29			0.80			0.77								0.38									0.98
Tigard (city)	9,654	722	491	-	-	-	-	-	153	-	-	-	-	-	-	-	-	-	-	-	-	-	-	-	-	69
	58.47		68.01						85.47																	56.10
									31.16																	14.05
			68.01						21.19																	9.56
			5.09						1.58																	0.71
Tualatin (city)	4,733	334	164	-	-	-	-	-	-	-	-	-	-	-	-	-	-	-	-	-	-	-	-	-	-	-
	54.84		49.10																							
			49.10																							
			3.47																							
Yamhill County	19,989	174	139	-	-	-	-	-	-	-	-	-	-	-	-	-	-	-	-	-	-	-	-	-	-	-
	69.57		79.89																							
			79.89																							
			0.70																							
PENNSYLVANIA	3,406,167	66,818	32,325	852	467	8,336	63	1,092	7,435	-	2,689	107	156	60	57	1,105	4,311	365	-	362	108	90	358	156	-	4,725
	71.30		48.38		54.81	45.32	25.20	57.63	47.62		60.10	58.47	64.46	52.17	31.32	38.17	43.10	64.15		43.83	62.07	54.88	37.45	25.12		61.17
						25.79	0.19	3.38	23.00		8.32	22.91	33.40	0.19	0.18	3.42	13.34	1.13		1.12	23.13	0.28	1.11	0.48		14.62
			48.38		54.81	12.48	0.09	1.63	11.13		4.02	12.56	18.31	0.09	0.09	1.65	6.45	0.55		0.54	12.68	0.13	0.54	0.23		7.07
			0.95		0.01	0.24	<0.01	0.03	0.22		0.08	<0.01	<0.01	<0.01	<0.01	0.03	0.13	0.01		0.01	<0.01	<0.01	0.01	<0.01		0.14
Adams County	25,853	175	103	-	-	-	-	-	-	-	-	-	-	-	-	-	-	-	-	-	-	-	-	-	-	-
	76.82		58.86																							
			58.86																							
			0.40																							
Allegheny County	360,021	7,950	2,663	195	87	1,044	-	-	666	-	193	-	-	-	-	97	220	-	-	-	-	-	53	-	-	157
	67.02		33.50		44.62	36.35			32.97		48.13					17.32	24.44						25.36			41.64
						39.20			25.01		7.25					3.64	8.26						1.99			5.90
			33.50		44.62	13.13			8.38		2.43					1.22	2.77						0.67			1.97
			0.74		0.02	0.29			0.18		0.05					0.03	0.06						0.01			0.04
Muni. of Monroeville (borough)	8,623	398	176	-	-	80	-	-	-	-	-	-	-	-	-	-	-	-	-	-	-	-	-	-	-	-
	69.68		44.22			37.21																				
						45.45																				
			44.22			20.10																				
			2.04			0.93																				

Notes: Please refer to the User's Guide for an explanation of data; data is arranged alphabetically by state, then county, then city within each county; table includes counties with populations greater than 49,999 unless noted and cities with populations greater than 9,999 whose Asian and/or NHPI population rates are greater than the national average; (1) Native Hawaiian and other Pacific Islander; (2) excludes Taiwanese; (3) includes Chamorro; (4) county does not meet population threshold but is shown in order to allow inclusion of city

Place	All owner-occupied housing units	Asian-occupied housing units	Asians who own and occupy their own homes	NHPI[1]-occupied housing units	NHPIs[1] who own and occupy their own homes	Asian Indian	Bangladeshi	Cambodian	Chinese[2]	Fijian	Filipino	Guamanian[3]	Hawaiian, Native	Hmong	Indonesian	Japanese	Korean	Laotian	Malaysian	Pakistani	Samoan	Sri Lankan	Taiwanese	Thai	Tongan	Vietnamese
Scott (township)	5,254 67.06	453	43 9.49 9.49 0.82	-	-	34 9.04 79.07 7.51 0.65	-	-	-	-	-	-	-	-	-	-	-	-	-	-	-	-	-	-	-	-
Scott Township (cdp)	5,254 67.06	453	43 9.49 9.49 0.82	-	-	34 9.04 79.07 7.51 0.65	-	-	-	-	-	-	-	-	-	-	-	-	-	-	-	-	-	-	-	-
Upper St. Clair (township)	6,452 92.62	218	218 100.00 100.00 3.38	-	-	130 100.00 59.63 59.63 2.01	-	-	-	-	-	-	-	-	-	-	-	-	-	-	-	-	-	-	-	-
Beaver County	54,379 74.93	157	107 68.15 68.15 0.20	-	-	-	-	-	-	-	-	-	-	-	-	-	-	-	-	-	-	-	-	-	-	-
Berks County	104,693 73.95	980	679 69.29 69.29 0.65	-	-	132 56.65 19.44 13.47 0.13	-	-	123 84.83 18.11 12.55 0.12	-	-	-	-	-	-	-	47 70.15 6.92 4.80 0.04	-	-	-	-	-	-	-	-	230 77.97 33.87 23.47 0.22
Blair County	37,561 72.91	188	108 57.45 57.45 0.29	-	-	-	-	-	-	-	-	-	-	-	-	-	-	-	-	-	-	-	-	-	-	-
Bradford County	18,457 75.48	67	20 29.85 29.85 0.11	-	-	-	-	-	-	-	-	-	-	-	-	-	-	-	-	-	-	-	-	-	-	-
Bucks County	169,177 77.35	4,119	2,442 59.29 59.29 1.44	-	-	886 50.17 36.28 21.51 0.52	-	-	419 63.29 17.16 10.17 0.25	-	321 75.18 13.14 7.79 0.19	-	-	-	-	-	349 60.17 14.29 8.47 0.21	-	-	-	-	-	-	-	-	120 73.62 4.91 2.91 0.07
Bensalem (township)	13,143 58.09	1,231	495 40.21 40.21 3.77	-	-	190 28.44 38.38 15.43 1.45	-	-	-	-	-	-	-	-	-	-	101 50.75 20.40 8.20 0.77	-	-	-	-	-	-	-	-	-
Lower Makefield (township)	10,373 88.61	399	329 82.46 82.46 3.17	-	-	163 86.70 49.54 40.85 1.57	-	-	-	-	-	-	-	-	-	-	-	-	-	-	-	-	-	-	-	-

Notes: Please refer to the User's Guide for an explanation of data; data is arranged alphabetically by state, then county, then city within each county; table includes counties with populations greater than 49,999 unless noted and cities with populations greater than 9,999 whose Asian and/or NHPI population rates are greater than the national average; (1) Native Hawaiian and other Pacific Islander; (2) excludes Taiwanese; (3) includes Chamorro; (4) county does not meet population threshold but is shown in order to allow inclusion of city

Place	All owner-occupied housing units	Asian-occupied housing units	Asians who own and occupy their own homes	NHPI[1]-occupied housing units	NHPIs[1] who own and occupy their own homes	Asian Indian	Bangladeshi	Cambodian	Chinese[2]	Fijian	Filipino	Guamanian[3]	Hawaiian, Native	Hmong	Indonesian	Japanese	Korean	Laotian	Malaysian	Pakistani	Samoan	Sri Lankan	Taiwanese	Thai	Tongan	Vietnamese
Newtown (township)	5,881 86.93	286	213 74.48 74.48 3.62	-	-	-	-	-	-	-	-	-	-	-	-	-	-	-	-	-	-	-	-	-	-	-
Butler County	51,245 77.81	297	199 67.00 67.00 0.39	-	-	100 68.97 50.25 33.67 0.20	-	-	-	-	-	-	-	-	-	-	-	-	-	-	-	-	-	-	-	-
Cambria County	45,242 74.74	145	82 56.55 56.55 0.18	-	-	-	-	-	-	-	-	-	-	-	-	-	-	-	-	-	-	-	-	-	-	-
Centre County	29,673 60.16	1,983	279 14.07 14.07 0.94	-	-	95 21.49 34.05 4.79 0.32	-	-	97 14.04 34.77 4.89 0.33	-	-	-	-	-	-	-	32 7.80 11.47 1.61 0.11	-	-	-	-	-	-	-	-	-
Ferguson (township)	3,286 59.63	368	103 27.99 27.99 3.13	-	-	-	-	-	-	-	-	-	-	-	-	-	-	-	-	-	-	-	-	-	-	-
Patton (township)	2,535 52.91	211	57 27.01 27.01 2.25	-	-	-	-	-	-	-	-	-	-	-	-	-	-	-	-	-	-	-	-	-	-	-
State College (borough)	2,736 22.75	1,279	69 5.39 5.39 2.52	-	-	15 5.62 21.74 1.17 0.55	-	-	28 6.28 40.58 2.19 1.02	-	-	-	-	-	-	-	0 0.00 0.00 0.00 0.00	-	-	-	-	-	-	-	-	-
Chester County	120,500 76.31	2,633	1,466 55.68 55.68 1.22	-	-	450 45.27 30.70 17.09 0.37	-	-	418 63.14 28.51 15.88 0.35	-	100 53.76 6.82 3.80 0.08	-	-	-	-	54 35.29 3.68 2.05 0.04	137 70.26 9.35 5.20 0.11	-	-	-	-	-	-	-	-	168 75.00 11.46 6.38 0.14
Tredyffrin (township)	9,615 78.66	473	226 47.78 47.78 2.35	-	-	75 34.56 33.19 15.86 0.78	-	-	108 61.02 47.79 22.83 1.12	-	-	-	-	-	-	-	-	-	-	-	-	-	-	-	-	-
West Goshen (township)	5,660 74.93	240	74 30.83 30.83 1.31	-	-	-	-	-	-	-	-	-	-	-	-	-	-	-	-	-	-	-	-	-	-	-

Notes: Please refer to the User's Guide for an explanation of data; data is arranged alphabetically by state, then county, then city within each county; table includes counties with populations greater than 49,999 unless noted and cities with populations greater than 9,999 whose Asian and/or NHPI population rates are greater than the national average; (1) Native Hawaiian and other Pacific Islander; (2) excludes Taiwanese; (3) includes Chamorro; (4) county does not meet population threshold but is shown in order to allow inclusion of city

Place	All owner-occupied housing units	Asian-occupied housing units	Asians who own and occupy their own homes	NHPI[1]-occupied housing units	NHPIs[1] who own and occupy their own homes	Asian Indian	Bangladeshi	Cambodian	Chinese[2]	Fijian	Filipino	Guamanian[3]	Hawaiian, Native	Hmong	Indonesian	Japanese	Korean	Laotian	Malaysian	Pakistani	Samoan	Sri Lankan	Taiwanese	Thai	Tongan	Vietnamese
West Whiteland (township)	4,532 68.48	247	124 50.20 50.20 2.74	-	-	-	-	-	-	-	-	-	-	-	-	-	-	-	-	-	-	-	-	-	-	-
Clearfield County	25,950 79.15	88	56 63.64 63.64 0.22	-	-	-	-	-	-	-	-	-	-	-	-	-	-	-	-	-	-	-	-	-	-	-
Columbia County	17,993 72.22	86	53 61.63 61.63 0.29	-	-	-	-	-	-	-	-	-	-	-	-	-	-	-	-	-	-	-	-	-	-	-
Crawford County	26,155 75.42	76	42 55.26 55.26 0.16	-	-	-	-	-	-	-	-	-	-	-	-	-	-	-	-	-	-	-	-	-	-	-
Cumberland County	60,635 73.04	920	604 65.65 65.65 1.00	-	-	213 66.15 35.26 23.15 0.35	-	-	89 61.38 14.74 9.67 0.15	-	-	-	-	-	-	-	111 69.81 18.38 12.07 0.18	-	-	-	-	-	-	-	-	105 82.03 17.38 11.41 0.17
Hampden (township)	7,662 80.04	274	199 72.63 72.63 2.60	-	-	-	-	-	-	-	-	-	-	-	-	-	-	-	-	-	-	-	-	-	-	-
Dauphin County	67,116 65.37	1,445	674 46.64 46.64 1.00	-	-	109 30.97 16.17 7.54 0.16	-	-	100 36.76 14.84 6.92 0.15	-	-	-	-	-	-	-	34 47.22 5.04 2.35 0.05	-	-	-	-	-	-	-	-	274 59.57 40.65 18.96 0.41
Derry (township)	5,524 62.34	272	122 44.85 44.85 2.21	-	-	-	-	-	-	-	-	-	-	-	-	-	-	-	-	-	-	-	-	-	-	-
Hershey (cdp)	3,055 56.21	172	71 41.28 41.28 2.32	-	-	-	-	-	-	-	-	-	-	-	-	-	-	-	-	-	-	-	-	-	-	-
Delaware County	148,293 71.88	5,430	2,883 53.09 53.09 1.94	-	-	822 50.43 28.51 15.14 0.55	-	-	629 55.81 21.82 11.58 0.42	-	159 47.60 5.52 2.93 0.11	-	-	-	-	71 27.95 2.46 1.31 0.05	508 52.75 17.62 9.36 0.34	-	-	74 48.68 2.57 1.36 0.05	-	-	-	-	-	355 67.36 12.31 6.54 0.24

Notes: Please refer to the User's Guide for an explanation of data; data is arranged alphabetically by state, then county, then city within each county; table includes counties with populations greater than 49,999 unless noted and cities with populations greater than 9,999 whose Asian and/or NHPI population rates are greater than the national average; (1) Native Hawaiian and other Pacific Islander; (2) excludes Taiwanese; (3) includes Chamorro; (4) county does not meet population threshold but is shown in order to allow inclusion of city

Place	All owner-occupied housing units	Asian-occupied housing units	Asians who own and occupy their own homes	NHPI[1]-occupied housing units	NHPIs[1] who own and occupy their own homes	Asian Indian	Bangladeshi	Cambodian	Chinese[2]	Fijian	Filipino	Guamanian[3]	Hawaiian, Native	Hmong	Indonesian	Japanese	Korean	Laotian	Malaysian	Pakistani	Samoan	Sri Lankan	Taiwanese	Thai	Tongan	Vietnamese
Broomall (cdp)	3,447 81.12	232	129 55.60 55.60 3.74	-	-	-	-	-	-	-	-	-	-	-	-	-	52 36.36 40.31 22.41 1.51	-	-	-	-	-	-	-	-	-
Drexel Hill (cdp)	7,710 65.11	405	85 20.99 20.99 1.10	-	-	-	-	-	27 22.88 31.76 6.67 0.35	-	-	-	-	-	-	-	-	-	-	-	-	-	-	-	-	-
Marple (township)	7,220 83.73	372	252 67.74 67.74 3.49	-	-	-	-	-	-	-	-	-	-	-	-	-	101 52.60 40.08 27.15 1.40	-	-	-	-	-	-	-	-	-
Radnor (township)	6,540 63.21	486	221 45.47 45.47 3.38	-	-	-	-	-	102 72.86 46.15 20.99 1.56	-	-	-	-	-	-	-	-	-	-	-	-	-	-	-	-	-
Upper Darby (township)	20,287 62.32	2,113	937 44.34 44.34 4.62	-	-	299 44.63 31.91 14.15 1.47	-	-	178 40.09 19.00 8.42 0.88	-	-	-	-	-	-	-	134 45.12 14.30 6.34 0.66	-	-	-	-	-	-	-	-	185 58.36 19.74 8.76 0.91
Erie County	73,708 69.20	589	273 46.35 46.35 0.37	-	-	61 29.90 22.34 10.36 0.08	-	-	-	-	-	-	-	-	-	-	-	-	-	-	-	-	-	-	-	-
Franklin County	37,469 74.00	210	141 67.14 67.14 0.38	-	-	-	-	-	-	-	-	-	-	-	-	-	-	-	-	-	-	-	-	-	-	-
Indiana County	24,491 71.77	260	91 35.00 35.00 0.37	-	-	-	-	-	-	-	-	-	-	-	-	-	-	-	-	-	-	-	-	-	-	-
Lackawanna County	58,284 67.60	504	252 50.00 50.00 0.43	-	-	89 45.64 35.32 17.66 0.15	-	-	-	-	-	-	-	-	-	-	-	-	-	-	-	-	-	-	-	-
Lancaster County	122,264 70.85	1,731	1,088 62.85 62.85 0.89	-	-	91 42.52 8.36 5.26 0.07	-	-	217 67.39 19.94 12.54 0.18	-	-	-	-	37 53.62 3.40 2.14 0.03	-	-	80 62.50 7.35 4.62 0.07	-	-	-	-	-	-	-	-	454 73.11 41.73 26.23 0.37

Notes: Please refer to the User's Guide for an explanation of data; data is arranged alphabetically by state, then county, then city within each county; table includes counties with populations greater than 49,999 unless noted and cities with populations greater than 9,999 whose Asian and/or NHPI population rates are greater than the national average; (1) Native Hawaiian and other Pacific Islander; (2) excludes Taiwanese; (3) includes Chamorro; (4) county does not meet population threshold but is shown in order to allow inclusion of city

Place	All owner-occupied housing units	Asian-occupied housing units	Asians who own and occupy their own homes	NHPI[1]-occupied housing units	NHPIs[1] who own and occupy their own homes	Asian Indian	Bangladeshi	Cambodian	Chinese[2]	Fijian	Filipino	Guamanian[3]	Hawaiian, Native	Hmong	Indonesian	Japanese	Korean	Laotian	Malaysian	Pakistani	Samoan	Sri Lankan	Taiwanese	Thai	Tongan	Vietnamese
Lawrence County	28,660 77.27	98	58 59.18 59.18 0.20	-	-	-	-	-	-	-	-	-	-	-	-	-	-	-	-	-	-	-	-	-	-	-
Lebanon County	33,863 72.74	299	210 70.23 70.23 0.62	-	-	-	-	-	-	-	-	-	-	-	-	-	-	-	-	-	-	-	-	-	-	-
Lehigh County	83,896 68.82	1,999	937 46.87 46.87 1.12	-	-	235 34.41 25.08 11.76 0.28	-	-	294 56.98 31.38 14.71 0.35	-	-	-	-	-	-	-	66 34.02 7.04 3.30 0.08	-	-	-	-	-	-	-	-	226 60.92 24.12 11.31 0.27
Fullerton (cdp)	3,360 54.03	255	70 27.45 27.45 2.08	-	-	-	-	-	-	-	-	-	-	-	-	-	-	-	-	-	-	-	-	-	-	-
Lower Macungie (township)	6,274 87.63	239	214 89.54 89.54 3.41	-	-	-	-	-	117 100.00 54.67 48.95 1.86	-	-	-	-	-	-	-	-	-	-	-	-	-	-	-	-	-
Upper Macungie (township)	4,354 84.91	154	112 72.73 72.73 2.57	-	-	-	-	-	-	-	-	-	-	-	-	-	-	-	-	-	-	-	-	-	-	-
Luzerne County	91,880 70.31	406	260 64.04 64.04 0.28	-	-	101 74.26 38.85 24.88 0.11	-	-	-	-	-	-	-	-	-	-	-	-	-	-	-	-	-	-	-	-
Lycoming County	32,653 69.47	121	44 36.36 36.36 0.13	-	-	-	-	-	-	-	-	-	-	-	-	-	-	-	-	-	-	-	-	-	-	-
Mercer County	35,613 76.24	178	103 57.87 57.87 0.29	-	-	-	-	-	-	-	-	-	-	-	-	-	-	-	-	-	-	-	-	-	-	-
Monroe County	38,742 78.34	328	246 75.00 75.00 0.63	-	-	87 76.99 35.37 26.52 0.22	-	-	-	-	-	-	-	-	-	-	-	-	-	-	-	-	-	-	-	-

Notes: Please refer to the User's Guide for an explanation of data; data is arranged alphabetically by state, then county, then city within each county; table includes counties with populations greater than 49,999 unless noted and cities with populations greater than 9,999 whose Asian and/or NHPI population rates are greater than the national average; (1) Native Hawaiian and other Pacific Islander; (2) excludes Taiwanese; (3) includes Chamorro; (4) county does not meet population threshold but is shown in order to allow inclusion of city

Place	All owner-occupied housing units	Asian-occupied housing units	Asians who own and occupy their own homes	NHPI¹-occupied housing units	NHPIs¹ who own and occupy their own homes	Asian Indian	Bangladeshi	Cambodian	Chinese²	Fijian	Filipino	Guamanian³	Hawaiian, Native	Hmong	Indonesian	Japanese	Korean	Laotian	Malaysian	Pakistani	Samoan	Sri Lankan	Taiwanese	Thai	Tongan	Vietnamese
Montgomery County	210,237 73.48	9,321	5,117 54.90 54.90 2.43	-	-	1,161 46.76 22.69 12.46 0.55	-	-	1,065 56.35 20.81 11.43 0.51	-	405 64.80 7.91 4.35 0.19	-	-	-	-	186 68.13 3.63 2.00 0.09	1,470 53.59 28.73 15.77 0.70	-	-	-	-	-	-	-	-	457 70.42 8.93 4.90 0.22
Cheltenham (township)	9,254 64.51	744	318 42.74 42.74 3.44	-	-	-	-	-	-	-	-	-	-	-	-	-	104 30.59 32.70 13.98 1.12	-	-	-	-	-	-	-	-	-
East Norriton (township)	3,933 76.34	230	113 49.13 49.13 2.87	-	-	-	-	-	-	-	-	-	-	-	-	-	-	-	-	-	-	-	-	-	-	-
Hatfield (township)	4,088 65.13	535	224 41.87 41.87 5.48	-	-	105 36.08 46.88 19.63 2.57	-	-	-	-	-	-	-	-	-	-	-	-	-	-	-	-	-	-	-	-
Horsham (township)	6,675 73.50	379	185 48.81 48.81 2.77	-	-	-	-	-	-	-	-	-	-	-	-	-	97 61.78 52.43 25.59 1.45	-	-	-	-	-	-	-	-	-
King of Prussia (cdp)	4,898 59.18	805	219 27.20 27.20 4.47	-	-	102 31.10 46.58 12.67 2.08	-	-	45 23.81 20.55 5.59 0.92	-	-	-	-	-	-	-	-	-	-	-	-	-	-	-	-	-
Lansdale (borough)	3,810 57.55	413	135 32.69 32.69 3.54	-	-	42 30.66 31.11 10.17 1.10	-	-	-	-	-	-	-	-	-	-	-	-	-	-	-	-	-	-	-	-
Lower Gwynedd (township)	3,115 74.58	139	120 86.33 86.33 3.85	-	-	-	-	-	-	-	-	-	-	-	-	-	-	-	-	-	-	-	-	-	-	-
Lower Providence (township)	5,949 79.62	361	192 53.19 53.19 3.23	-	-	-	-	-	86 56.21 44.79 23.82 1.45	-	-	-	-	-	-	-	-	-	-	-	-	-	-	-	-	-
Montgomery (township)	7,442 93.89	508	489 96.26 96.26 6.57	-	-	121 100.00 24.74 23.82 1.63	-	-	-	-	-	-	-	-	-	-	207 91.59 42.33 40.75 2.78	-	-	-	-	-	-	-	-	-

Notes: Please refer to the User's Guide for an explanation of data; data is arranged alphabetically by state, then county, then city within each county; table includes counties with populations greater than 49,999 unless noted and cities with populations greater than 9,999 whose Asian and/or NHPI population rates are greater than the national average; (1) Native Hawaiian and other Pacific Islander; (2) excludes Taiwanese; (3) includes Chamorro; (4) county does not meet population threshold but is shown in order to allow inclusion of city

Place	All owner-occupied housing units	Asian-occupied housing units	Asians who own and occupy their own homes	NHPI[1]-occupied housing units	NHPIs[1] who own and occupy their own homes	Asian Indian	Bangladeshi	Cambodian	Chinese[2]	Fijian	Filipino	Guamanian[3]	Hawaiian, Native	Hmong	Indonesian	Japanese	Korean	Laotian	Malaysian	Pakistani	Samoan	Sri Lankan	Taiwanese	Thai	Tongan	Vietnamese
Montgomeryville (cdp)	3,750 91.98	217	198 91.24 91.24 5.28	-	-	-	-	-	-	-	-	-	-	-	-	-	-	-	-	-	-	-	-	-	-	-
Plymouth (township)	4,634 71.16	298	149 50.00 50.00 3.22	-	-	-	-	-	-	-	-	-	-	-	-	-	41 38.68 27.52 13.76 0.88	-	-	-	-	-	-	-	-	-
Towamencin (township)	5,016 72.96	321	157 48.91 48.91 3.13	-	-	-	-	-	-	-	-	-	-	-	-	-	-	-	-	-	-	-	-	-	-	-
Upper Dublin (township)	8,150 88.84	438	366 83.56 83.56 4.49	-	-	-	-	-	-	-	-	-	-	-	-	-	182 87.50 49.73 41.55 2.23	-	-	-	-	-	-	-	-	-
Upper Gwynedd (township)	4,322 80.92	366	261 71.31 71.31 6.04	-	-	-	-	-	51 64.56 19.54 13.93 1.18	-	-	-	-	-	-	-	-	-	-	-	-	-	-	-	-	-
Upper Merion (township)	7,760 67.19	881	295 33.48 33.48 3.80	-	-	135 37.40 45.76 15.32 1.74	-	-	66 31.43 22.37 7.49 0.85	-	-	-	-	-	-	-	-	-	-	-	-	-	-	-	-	-
Whitpain (township)	5,458 78.11	434	315 72.58 72.58 5.77	-	-	-	-	-	-	-	-	-	-	-	-	-	135 77.59 42.86 31.11 2.47	-	-	-	-	-	-	-	-	-
Northampton County	74,451 73.32	941	564 59.94 59.94 0.76	-	-	247 82.06 43.79 26.25 0.33	-	-	117 45.70 20.74 12.43 0.16	-	-	-	-	-	-	-	21 23.86 3.72 2.23 0.03	-	-	-	-	-	-	-	-	86 74.14 15.25 9.14 0.12
Northumberland County	28,577 73.59	121	76 62.81 62.81 0.27	-	-	-	-	-	-	-	-	-	-	-	-	-	-	-	-	-	-	-	-	-	-	-
Philadelphia County	349,651 59.26	20,439	8,707 42.60 42.60 2.49	158	118 74.68 74.68 0.03	1,655 41.11 19.01 8.10 0.47	-	737 52.76 8.46 3.61 0.21	2,437 42.65 27.99 11.92 0.70	-	748 58.44 8.59 3.66 0.21	-	-	-	-	117 18.60 1.34 0.57 0.03	698 26.64 8.02 3.42 0.20	186 60.39 2.14 0.91 0.05	-	68 41.46 0.78 0.33 0.02	-	-	-	-	-	1,670 56.30 19.18 8.17 0.48

Notes: Please refer to the User's Guide for an explanation of data; data is arranged alphabetically by state, then county, then city within each county; table includes counties with populations greater than 49,999 unless noted and cities with populations greater than 9,999 whose Asian and/or NHPI population rates are greater than the national average; (1) Native Hawaiian and other Pacific Islander; (2) excludes Taiwanese; (3) includes Chamorro; (4) county does not meet population threshold but is shown in order to allow inclusion of city

Place	All owner-occupied housing units	Asian-occupied housing units	Asians who own and occupy their own homes	NHPI[1]-occupied housing units	NHPIs[1] who own and occupy their own homes	Asian Indian	Bangladeshi	Cambodian	Chinese[2]	Fijian	Filipino	Guamanian[3]	Hawaiian, Native	Hmong	Indonesian	Japanese	Korean	Laotian	Malaysian	Pakistani	Samoan	Sri Lankan	Taiwanese	Thai	Tongan	Vietnamese
	349,651	20,439	8,707	158	118	1,655	-	737	2,437	-	748	-	-	-	-	117	698	186	-	68	-	-	-	-	-	1,670
	59.26		42.60		74.68	41.11		52.76	42.65		58.44					18.60	26.64	60.39		41.46						56.30
Philadelphia (city)						19.01		8.46	27.99		8.59					1.34	8.02	2.14		0.78						19.18
			42.60		74.68	8.10		3.61	11.92		3.66					0.57	3.42	0.91		0.33						8.17
			2.49		0.03	0.47		0.21	0.70		0.21					0.03	0.20	0.05		0.02						0.48
	47,177	136	62	-	-	-	-	-	-	-	-	-	-	-	-	-	-	-	-	-	-	-	-	-	-	-
	77.94		45.59																							
Schuylkill County																										
			45.59																							
			0.13																							
	62,570	200	128	-	-	-	-	-	-	-	-	-	-	-	-	-	-	-	-	-	-	-	-	-	-	-
	77.12		64.00																							
Washington County																										
			64.00																							
			0.20																							
	116,847	487	371	-	-	125	-	-	-	-	-	-	-	-	-	-	-	-	-	-	-	-	-	-	-	-
	78.00		76.18			93.98																				
Westmoreland County						33.69																				
			76.18			25.67																				
			0.32			0.11																				
	112,816	805	566	-	-	108	-	-	105	-	-	-	-	-	-	-	95	-	-	-	-	-	-	-	-	113
	76.11		70.31			60.34			58.66								82.61									83.70
York County						19.08			18.55								16.78									19.96
			70.31			13.42			13.04								11.80									14.04
			0.50			0.10			0.09								0.08									0.10
	245,150	6,754	2,744	130	60	396	-	454	637	-	278	-	-	47	-	190	185	296	-	-	-	-	-	-	-	73
	60.02		40.63		46.15	42.86		37.03	45.66		44.62			38.52		55.88	30.38	39.05								28.74
RHODE ISLAND						14.43		16.55	23.21		10.13			1.71		6.92	6.74	10.79								2.66
			40.63		46.15	5.86		6.72	9.43		4.12			0.70		2.81	2.74	4.38								1.08
			1.12		0.02	0.16		0.19	0.26		0.11			0.02		0.08	0.08	0.12								0.03
	13,555	135	113	-	-	-	-	-	-	-	-	-	-	-	-	-	-	-	-	-	-	-	-	-	-	-
	71.22		83.70																							
Bristol County																										
			83.70																							
			0.83																							
	48,187	698	391	-	-	-	-	-	69	-	-	-	-	-	-	-	35	-	-	-	-	-	-	-	-	-
	71.58		56.02						55.20								37.23									
Kent County									17.65								8.95									
			56.02						9.89								5.01									
			0.81						0.14								0.07									
	21,699	255	105	-	-	-	-	-	-	-	37	-	-	-	-	-	-	-	-	-	-	-	-	-	-	-
	61.60		41.18								31.09															
Newport County											35.24															
			41.18								14.51															
			0.48								0.17															
	127,531	5,147	1,851	-	-	232	-	414	403	-	148	-	-	34	-	-	109	282	-	-	-	-	-	-	-	39
	53.15		35.96			36.31		34.91	41.80		44.31			33.33			25.35	39.06								18.40
Providence County						12.53		22.37	21.77		8.00			1.84			5.89	15.24								2.11
			35.96			4.51		8.04	7.83		2.88			0.66			2.12	5.48								0.76
			1.45			0.18		0.32	0.32		0.12			0.03			0.09	0.22								0.03

Notes: Please refer to the User's Guide for an explanation of data; data is arranged alphabetically by state, then county, then city within each county; table includes counties with populations greater than 49,999 unless noted and cities with populations greater than 9,999 whose Asian and/or NHPI population rates are greater than the national average; (1) Native Hawaiian and other Pacific Islander; (2) excludes Taiwanese; (3) includes Chamorro; (4) county does not meet population threshold but is shown in order to allow inclusion of city

Place	All owner-occupied housing units	Asian-occupied housing units	Asians who own and occupy their own homes	NHPI[1]-occupied housing units	NHPIs[1] who own and occupy their own homes	Asian Indian	Bangladeshi	Cambodian	Chinese[2]	Fijian	Filipino	Guamanian[3]	Hawaiian, Native	Hmong	Indonesian	Japanese	Korean	Laotian	Malaysian	Pakistani	Samoan	Sri Lankan	Taiwanese	Thai	Tongan	Vietnamese
Providence (city)	21,565 34.57	3,037	793 26.11 26.11 3.68	-	-	91 28.71 11.48 3.00 0.42	-	276 30.33 34.80 9.09 1.28	120 26.32 15.13 3.95 0.56	-	49 28.00 6.18 1.61 0.23	-	-	20 24.39 2.52 0.66 0.09	-	-	41 13.10 5.17 1.35 0.19	124 34.54 15.64 4.08 0.58	-	-	-	-	-	-	-	-
Woonsocket (city)	6,214 35.01	453	119 26.27 26.27 1.92	-	-	-	-	-	-	-	-	-	-	-	-	-	-	76 27.94 63.87 16.78 1.22	-	-	-	-	-	-	-	-
Washington County	34,178 72.86	519	284 54.72 54.72 0.83	-	-	-	-	-	80 48.19 28.17 15.41 0.23	-	-	-	-	-	-	-	-	-	-	-	-	-	-	-	-	-
SOUTH CAROLINA	1,107,619 72.21	10,969	5,903 53.82 53.82 0.53	408	182 44.61 44.61 0.02	1,265 48.92 21.43 11.53 0.11	-	50 56.18 0.85 0.46 <0.01	1,086 55.24 18.40 9.90 0.10	-	1,134 58.73 19.21 10.34 0.10	38 41.30 20.88 9.31 <0.01	74 46.54 40.66 18.14 0.01	75 57.25 1.27 0.68 0.01	-	474 56.29 8.03 4.32 0.04	460 41.33 7.79 4.19 0.04	248 77.74 4.20 2.26 0.02	-	-	-	-	-	107 45.73 1.81 0.98 0.01	-	736 61.80 12.47 6.71 0.07
Aiken County	42,057 75.66	254	140 55.12 55.12 0.33	-	-	-	-	-	-	-	-	-	-	-	-	-	-	-	-	-	-	-	-	-	-	-
Anderson County	50,067 76.26	249	113 45.38 45.38 0.23	-	-	-	-	-	-	-	-	-	-	-	-	-	-	-	-	-	-	-	-	-	-	-
Beaufort County	33,363 73.27	256	200 78.13 78.13 0.60	-	-	-	-	-	-	-	-	-	-	-	-	-	-	-	-	-	-	-	-	-	-	-
Berkeley County	37,042 74.20	847	605 71.43 71.43 1.63	-	-	-	-	-	-	-	420 75.95 69.42 49.59 1.13	-	-	-	-	-	-	-	-	-	-	-	-	-	-	-
Charleston County	75,291 61.05	1,236	476 38.51 38.51 0.63	-	-	67 32.21 14.08 5.42 0.09	-	-	151 54.91 31.72 12.22 0.20	-	96 30.38 20.17 7.77 0.13	-	-	-	-	-	-	-	-	-	-	-	-	-	-	-
Dorchester County	26,027 74.99	345	267 77.39 77.39 1.03	-	-	-	-	-	-	-	132 88.00 49.44 38.26 0.51	-	-	-	-	-	-	-	-	-	-	-	-	-	-	-

Notes: Please refer to the User's Guide for an explanation of data; data is arranged alphabetically by state, then county, then city within each county; table includes counties with populations greater than 49,999 unless noted and cities with populations greater than 9,999 whose Asian and/or NHPI population rates are greater than the national average; (1) Native Hawaiian and other Pacific Islander; (2) excludes Taiwanese; (3) includes Chamorro; (4) county does not meet population threshold but is shown in order to allow inclusion of city

Place	All owner-occupied housing units	Asian-occupied housing units	Asians who own and occupy their own homes	NHPI-occupied housing units	NHPIs[1] who own and occupy their own homes	Asian Indian	Bangladeshi	Cambodian	Chinese[2]	Fijian	Filipino	Guamanian[3]	Hawaiian, Native	Hmong	Indonesian	Japanese	Korean	Laotian	Malaysian	Pakistani	Samoan	Sri Lankan	Taiwanese	Thai	Tongan	Vietnamese
Florence County	34,403 72.97	370	264 71.35 71.35 0.77	-	-	-	-	-	-	-	-	-	-	-	-	-	-	-	-	-	-	-	-	-	-	-
Greenville County	101,971 68.18	1,538	718 46.68 46.68 0.70	-	-	159 35.49 22.14 10.34 0.16	-	-	104 53.61 14.48 6.76 0.10	-	70 50.72 9.75 4.55 0.07	-	-	-	-	-	-	-	-	-	-	-	-	-	-	198 51.56 27.58 12.87 0.19
Greenwood County	17,825 69.28	137	60 43.80 43.80 0.34	-	-	-	-	-	-	-	-	-	-	-	-	-	-	-	-	-	-	-	-	-	-	-
Horry County	59,699 72.98	418	304 72.73 72.73 0.51	-	-	-	-	-	-	-	-	-	-	-	-	-	-	-	-	-	-	-	-	-	-	-
Lexington County	64,274 77.22	570	341 59.82 59.82 0.53	-	-	104 57.78 30.50 18.25 0.16	-	-	77 46.67 22.58 13.51 0.12	-	-	-	-	-	-	-	-	-	-	-	-	-	-	-	-	-
Oconee County	21,380 78.36	115	90 78.26 78.26 0.42	-	-	-	-	-	-	-	-	-	-	-	-	-	-	-	-	-	-	-	-	-	-	-
Pickens County	30,325 73.42	449	113 25.17 25.17 0.37	-	-	29 20.28 25.66 6.46 0.10	-	-	32 21.48 28.32 7.13 0.11	-	-	-	-	-	-	-	-	-	-	-	-	-	-	-	-	-
Clemson (city)	2,315 45.20	210	27 12.86 12.86 1.17	-	-	-	-	-	-	-	-	-	-	-	-	-	-	-	-	-	-	-	-	-	-	-
Richland County	73,759 61.41	1,816	750 41.30 41.30 1.02	-	-	171 34.83 22.80 9.42 0.23	-	-	151 39.43 20.13 8.31 0.20	-	60 37.74 8.00 3.30 0.08	-	-	-	-	-	143 36.95 19.07 7.87 0.19	-	-	-	-	-	-	-	-	96 68.57 12.80 5.29 0.13
Spartanburg County	70,354 71.98	950	628 66.11 66.11 0.89	-	-	160 66.39 25.48 16.84 0.23	-	-	-	-	-	-	-	65 59.63 10.35 6.84 0.09	-	-	-	107 72.30 17.04 11.26 0.15	-	-	-	-	-	-	-	-

Notes: Please refer to the User's Guide for an explanation of data; data is arranged alphabetically by state, then county, then city within each county; table includes counties with populations greater than 49,999 unless noted and cities with populations greater than 9,999 whose Asian and/or NHPI population rates are greater than the national average; (1) Native Hawaiian and other Pacific Islander; (2) excludes Taiwanese; (3) includes Chamorro; (4) county does not meet population threshold but is shown in order to allow inclusion of city

Place	All owner-occupied housing units	Asian-occupied housing units	Asians who own and occupy their own homes	NHPI[1]-occupied housing units	NHPIs[1] who own and occupy their own homes	Asian Indian	Bangladeshi	Cambodian	Chinese[2]	Fijian	Filipino	Guamanian[3]	Hawaiian, Native	Hmong	Indonesian	Japanese	Korean	Laotian	Malaysian	Pakistani	Samoan	Sri Lankan	Taiwanese	Thai	Tongan	Vietnamese
Sumter County	26,207 69.46	252	151 59.92 59.92 0.58	-	-	-	-	-	-	-	-	-	-	-	-	-	-	-	-	-	-	-	-	-	-	-
York County	44,645 73.13	381	250 65.62 65.62 0.56	-	-	-	-	-	-	-	-	-	-	-	-	-	-	-	-	-	-	-	-	-	-	100 74.63 40.00 26.25 0.22
SOUTH DAKOTA	197,907 68.19	1,246	432 34.67 34.67 0.22	-	-	31 15.20 7.18 2.49 0.02	-	-	87 38.67 20.14 6.98 0.04	-	54 28.72 12.50 4.33 0.03	-	-	-	-	53 39.85 12.27 4.25 0.03	47 54.65 10.88 3.77 0.02	24 42.86 5.56 1.93 0.01	-	-	-	-	-	-	-	97 47.32 22.45 7.78 0.05
Minnehaha County	37,512 64.68	381	173 45.41 45.41 0.46	-	-	-	-	-	-	-	-	-	-	-	-	-	-	-	-	-	-	-	-	-	-	69 52.27 39.88 18.11 0.18
Pennington County	22,931 66.20	218	81 37.16 37.16 0.35	-	-	-	-	-	-	-	-	-	-	-	-	-	-	-	-	-	-	-	-	-	-	-
TENNESSEE	1,561,461 69.93	16,791	8,248 49.12 49.12 0.53	578	274 47.40 47.40 0.02	1,916 45.79 23.23 11.41 0.12	-	173 57.86 2.10 1.03 0.01	1,423 49.24 17.25 8.47 0.09	-	825 60.75 10.00 4.91 0.05	37 27.61 13.50 6.40 <0.01	113 66.86 41.24 19.55 0.01	-	-	481 33.40 5.83 2.86 0.03	785 41.49 9.52 4.68 0.05	822 73.66 9.97 4.90 0.05	-	121 65.76 1.47 0.72 0.01	59 44.03 21.53 10.21 <0.01	-	137 56.61 1.66 0.82 0.01	177 45.04 2.15 1.05 0.01	-	989 52.36 11.99 5.89 0.06
Anderson County	21,585 72.48	159	76 47.80 47.80 0.35	-	-	-	-	-	-	-	-	-	-	-	-	-	-	-	-	-	-	-	-	-	-	-
Blount County	32,382 75.89	221	73 33.03 33.03 0.23	-	-	-	-	-	-	-	-	-	-	-	-	-	-	-	-	-	-	-	-	-	-	-
Bradley County	23,501 68.55	141	73 51.77 51.77 0.31	-	-	-	-	-	-	-	-	-	-	-	-	-	-	-	-	-	-	-	-	-	-	-
Davidson County	131,384 55.34	3,881	1,577 40.63 40.63 1.20	108	35 32.41 32.41 0.03	371 39.68 23.53 9.56 0.28	-	-	198 34.62 12.56 5.10 0.15	-	124 48.06 7.86 3.20 0.09	-	-	-	-	92 28.66 5.83 2.37 0.07	107 24.54 6.79 2.76 0.08	264 76.30 16.74 6.80 0.20	-	-	-	-	-	-	-	209 50.85 13.25 5.39 0.16

Notes: Please refer to the User's Guide for an explanation of data; data is arranged alphabetically by state, then county, then city within each county; table includes counties with populations greater than 49,999 unless noted and cities with populations greater than 9,999 whose Asian and/or NHPI population rates are greater than the national average; (1) Native Hawaiian and other Pacific Islander; (2) excludes Taiwanese; (3) includes Chamorro; (4) county does not meet population threshold but is shown in order to allow inclusion of city

Place	All owner-occupied housing units	Asian-occupied housing units	Asians who own and occupy their own homes	NHPI[1]-occupied housing units	NHPIs[1] who own and occupy their own homes	Asian Indian	Bangladeshi	Cambodian	Chinese[2]	Fijian	Filipino	Guamanian[3]	Hawaiian, Native	Hmong	Indonesian	Japanese	Korean	Laotian	Malaysian	Pakistani	Samoan	Sri Lankan	Taiwanese	Thai	Tongan	Vietnamese
Hamilton County	82,055 65.94	1,229	686 55.82 55.82 0.84	-	-	224 59.89 32.65 18.23 0.27	-	-	-	-	58 53.70 8.45 4.72 0.07	-	-	-	-	-	61 35.88 8.89 4.96 0.07	-	-	-	-	-	-	-	-	68 46.90 9.91 5.53 0.08
Knox County	105,594 66.89	1,609	630 39.15 39.15 0.60	-	-	204 41.98 32.38 12.68 0.19	-	-	174 44.73 27.62 10.81 0.16	-	-	-	-	-	-	-	36 18.27 5.71 2.24 0.03	-	-	-	-	-	-	-	-	58 47.93 9.21 3.60 0.05
Madison County	23,815 66.99	137	87 63.50 63.50 0.37	-	-	-	-	-	-	-	-	-	-	-	-	-	-	-	-	-	-	-	-	-	-	-
Montgomery County	30,685 63.49	444	267 60.14 60.14 0.87	-	-	-	-	-	-	-	-	-	-	-	-	-	117 68.42 43.82 26.35 0.38	-	-	-	-	-	-	-	-	-
Putnam County	16,317 65.62	213	72 33.80 33.80 0.44	-	-	-	-	-	-	-	-	-	-	-	-	-	-	-	-	-	-	-	-	-	-	-
Rutherford County	46,408 69.85	922	615 66.70 66.70 1.33	-	-	-	-	-	-	-	-	-	-	-	-	-	-	367 78.59 59.67 39.80 0.79	-	-	-	-	-	-	-	-
Shelby County	213,444 63.08	4,808	2,345 48.77 48.77 1.10	108	50 46.30 46.30 0.02	447 34.60 19.06 9.30 0.21	-	87 62.14 3.71 1.81 0.04	545 54.61 23.24 11.34 0.26	-	288 72.00 12.28 5.99 0.13	-	-	-	-	97 40.59 4.14 2.02 0.05	206 51.76 8.78 4.28 0.10	-	-	-	-	-	-	-	-	445 51.39 18.98 9.26 0.21
Germantown (city)	11,749 88.79	384	282 73.44 73.44 2.40	-	-	93 80.17 32.98 24.22 0.79	-	-	108 89.26 38.30 28.13 0.92	-	-	-	-	-	-	-	-	-	-	-	-	-	-	-	-	-
Sullivan County	48,153 75.76	163	114 69.94 69.94 0.24	-	-	-	-	-	-	-	-	-	-	-	-	-	-	-	-	-	-	-	-	-	-	-
Sumner County	36,970 75.54	273	196 71.79 71.79 0.53	-	-	-	-	-	-	-	-	-	-	-	-	-	-	-	-	-	-	-	-	-	-	-

Notes: Please refer to the User's Guide for an explanation of data; data is arranged alphabetically by state, then county, then city within each county; table includes counties with populations greater than 49,999 unless noted and cities with populations greater than 9,999 whose Asian and/or NHPI population rates are greater than the national average; (1) Native Hawaiian and other Pacific Islander; (2) excludes Taiwanese; (3) includes Chamorro; (4) county does not meet population threshold but is shown in order to allow inclusion of city

Place	All owner-occupied housing units	Asian-occupied housing units	Asians who own and occupy their own homes	NHPI[1]-occupied housing units	NHPIs[1] who own and occupy their own homes	Asian Indian	Bangladeshi	Cambodian	Chinese[2]	Fijian	Filipino	Guamanian[3]	Hawaiian, Native	Hmong	Indonesian	Japanese	Korean	Laotian	Malaysian	Pakistani	Samoan	Sri Lankan	Taiwanese	Thai	Tongan	Vietnamese
	30,122	168	97	-	-	-	-	-	-	-	-	-	-	-	-	-	-	-	-	-	-	-	-	-	-	-
	68.16		57.74																							
Washington County																										
			57.74																							
			0.32																							
	9,362	200	63	-	-	-	-	-	-	-	-	-	-	-	-	-	-	-	-	-	-	-	-	-	-	-
	68.84		31.50																							
Weakley County[4]																										
			31.50																							
			0.67																							
	1,926	198	63	-	-	-	-	-	-	-	-	-	-	-	-	-	-	-	-	-	-	-	-	-	-	-
	51.26		31.82																							
Martin (city)																										
			31.82																							
			3.27																							
	36,437	430	274	-	-	-	-	-	-	-	-	-	-	-	-	-	-	-	-	-	-	-	-	-	-	-
	81.47		63.72																							
Williamson County																										
			63.72																							
			0.75																							
	26,705	82	48	-	-	-	-	-	-	-	-	-	-	-	-	-	-	-	-	-	-	-	-	-	-	-
	81.42		58.54																							
Wilson County																										
			58.54																							
			0.18																							
	4,717,294	175,248	92,317	3,486	1,674	20,123	229	1,221	19,752	-	9,692	548	506	-	190	2,803	5,928	1,647	82	2,090	203	147	1,831	1,061	43	22,822
	63.80		52.68		48.02	47.55	23.54	66.79	56.34		56.15	51.94	50.00		27.82	43.42	42.86	65.02	36.28	39.34	42.65	37.89	66.61	44.34	33.33	60.41
TEXAS						21.80	0.25	1.32	21.40		10.50	32.74	30.23		0.21	3.04	6.42	1.78	0.09	2.26	12.13	0.16	1.98	1.15	2.57	24.72
			52.68		48.02	11.48	0.13	0.70	11.27		5.53	15.72	14.52		0.11	1.60	3.38	0.94	0.05	1.19	5.82	0.08	1.04	0.61	1.23	13.02
			1.96		0.04	0.43	<0.01	0.03	0.42		0.21	0.01	0.01		<0.01	0.06	0.13	0.03	<0.01	0.04	<0.01	<0.01	0.04	0.02	<0.01	0.48
	11,585	82	73	-	-	-	-	-	-	-	-	-	-	-	-	-	-	-	-	-	-	-	-	-	-	-
	73.89		89.02																							
Anderson County																										
			89.02																							
			0.63																							
	20,775	187	109	-	-	-	-	-	-	-	-	-	-	-	-	-	-	-	-	-	-	-	-	-	-	-
	72.42		58.29																							
Angelina County																										
			58.29																							
			0.52																							
	47,629	1,730	902	399	207	100	-	-	-	-	272	113	-	-	-	81	312	-	-	-	-	-	-	-	-	-
	55.70		52.14		51.88	49.50					53.97	54.59				60.45	56.62									
Bell County						11.09					30.16	54.59				8.98	34.59									
			52.14		51.88	5.78					15.72	28.32				4.68	18.03									
			1.89		0.43	0.21					0.57	0.24				0.17	0.66									
	14,994	1,132	568	318	186	-	-	-	-	-	209	104	-	-	-	-	176	-	-	-	-	-	-	-	-	-
	46.20		50.18		58.49						56.33	61.90					48.35									
Killeen (city)											36.80	55.91					30.99									
			50.18		58.49						18.46	32.70					15.55									
			3.79		1.24						1.39	0.69					1.17									

Notes: Please refer to the User's Guide for an explanation of data; data is arranged alphabetically by state, then county, then city within each county; table includes counties with populations greater than 49,999 unless noted and cities with populations greater than 9,999 whose Asian and/or NHPI population rates are greater than the national average; (1) Native Hawaiian and other Pacific Islander; (2) excludes Taiwanese; (3) includes Chamorro; (4) county does not meet population threshold but is shown in order to allow inclusion of city

Place	All owner-occupied housing units	Asian-occupied housing units	Asians who own and occupy their own homes	NHPI[1]-occupied housing units	NHPIs[1] who own and occupy their own homes	Asian Indian	Bangladeshi	Cambodian	Chinese[2]	Fijian	Filipino	Guamanian[3]	Hawaiian, Native	Hmong	Indonesian	Japanese	Korean	Laotian	Malaysian	Pakistani	Samoan	Sri Lankan	Taiwanese	Thai	Tongan	Vietnamese
Bexar County	299,171	7,185	3,936	346	222	681	-	-	696	-	841	-	121	-	-	321	365	70	-	-	-	-	-	116	-	580
	61.19		54.78		64.16	54.92			54.59		54.68		70.76			47.14	52.37	65.42						41.73		64.37
						17.30			17.68		21.37		54.50			8.16	9.27	1.78						2.95		14.74
			54.78		64.16	9.48			9.69		11.70		34.97			4.47	5.08	0.97						1.61		8.07
			1.32		0.07	0.23			0.23		0.28		0.04			0.11	0.12	0.02						0.04		0.19
Bowie County	23,449	103	86	-	-	-	-	-	-	-	-	-	-	-	-	-	-	-	-	-	-	-	-	-	-	-
	70.93		83.50																							
			83.50																							
			0.37																							
Brazoria County	60,682	1,337	1,104	-	-	202	-	92	183	-	151	-	-	-	-	-	-	-	-	-	-	-	-	-	-	348
	74.04		82.57			77.39		92.00	87.56		86.29															85.71
						18.30		8.33	16.58		13.68															31.52
			82.57			15.11		6.88	13.69		11.29															26.03
			1.82			0.33		0.15	0.30		0.25															0.57
Brazos County	25,147	2,485	395	-	-	137	-	-	120	-	-	-	-	-	-	-	23	-	-	-	-	-	-	-	-	17
	45.55		15.90			21.61			18.35								5.49									9.71
						34.68			30.38								5.82									4.30
			15.90			5.51			4.83								0.93									0.68
			1.57			0.54			0.48								0.09									0.07
College Station (city)	7,573	1,986	334	-	-	114	-	-	109	-	-	-	-	-	-	-	14	-	-	-	-	-	-	-	-	-
	30.71		16.82			26.03			19.68								3.98									
						34.13			32.63								4.19									
			16.82			5.74			5.49								0.70									
			4.41			1.51			1.44								0.18									
Calhoun County[4]	5,416	215	147	-	-	-	-	-	-	-	-	-	-	-	-	-	-	-	-	-	-	-	-	-	-	39
	72.78		68.37																							81.25
																										26.53
			68.37																							18.14
			2.71																							0.72
Port Lavaca (city)	2,733	160	108	-	-	-	-	-	-	-	-	-	-	-	-	-	-	-	-	-	-	-	-	-	-	-
	65.30		67.50																							
			67.50																							
			3.95																							
Cameron County	65,854	503	248	-	-	-	-	-	-	-	94	-	-	-	-	-	-	-	-	-	-	-	-	-	-	-
	67.70		49.30								40.34															
											37.90															
			49.30								18.69															
			0.38								0.14															
Collin County	124,935	10,768	7,094	-	-	1,685	-	-	3,028	-	213	-	-	-	-	147	449	-	-	123	-	-	232	95	-	809
	68.66		65.88			55.54			75.72		49.31					45.37	55.64			44.09			96.27	90.48		78.01
						23.75			42.68		3.00					2.07	6.33			1.73			3.27	1.34		11.40
			65.88			15.65			28.12		1.98					1.37	4.17			1.14			2.15	0.88		7.51
			5.68			1.35			2.42		0.17					0.12	0.36			0.10			0.19	0.08		0.65
Allen (city)	12,184	494	412	-	-	94	-	-	-	-	-	-	-	-	-	-	-	-	-	-	-	-	-	-	-	91
	85.72		83.40			80.34																				79.82
						22.82																				22.09
			83.40			19.03																				18.42
			3.38			0.77																				0.75

Notes: Please refer to the User's Guide for an explanation of data; data is arranged alphabetically by state, then county, then city within each county; table includes counties with populations greater than 49,999 unless noted and cities with populations greater than 9,999 whose Asian and/or NHPI population rates are greater than the national average; (1) Native Hawaiian and other Pacific Islander; (2) excludes Taiwanese; (3) includes Chamorro; (4) county does not meet population threshold but is shown in order to allow inclusion of city

Place	All owner-occupied housing units	Asian-occupied housing units	Asians who own and occupy their own homes	NHPI[1]-occupied housing units	NHPIs[1] who own and occupy their own homes	Asian Indian	Bangladeshi	Cambodian	Chinese[2]	Fijian	Filipino	Guamanian[3]	Hawaiian, Native	Hmong	Indonesian	Japanese	Korean	Laotian	Malaysian	Pakistani	Samoan	Sri Lankan	Taiwanese	Thai	Tongan	Vietnamese
Plano (city)	55,725 68.87	6,831	4,992 73.08 73.08 8.96	-	-	1,239 66.72 24.82 18.14 2.22	-	-	2,294 82.91 45.95 33.58 4.12	-	94 43.72 1.88 1.38 0.17	-	-	-	-	76 50.00 1.52 1.11 0.14	363 58.83 7.27 5.31 0.65	-	-	83 52.53 1.66 1.22 0.15	-	-	146 96.05 2.92 2.14 0.26	-	-	441 82.12 8.83 6.46 0.79
Comal County	22,441 77.21	129	100 77.52 77.52 0.45	-	-	-	-	-	-	-	-	-	-	-	-	-	-	-	-	-	-	-	-	-	-	-
Coryell County	10,933 54.80	346	130 37.57 37.57 1.19	94	47 50.00 50.00 0.43	-	-	-	-	-	-	-	-	-	-	-	68 61.26 52.31 19.65 0.62	-	-	-	-	-	-	-	-	-
Dallas County	424,788 52.60	28,973	12,138 41.89 41.89 2.86	298	136 45.64 45.64 0.03	2,958 35.82 24.37 10.21 0.70	32 13.50 0.26 0.11 0.01	272 50.37 2.24 0.94 0.06	1,997 46.16 16.45 6.89 0.47	-	1,115 56.37 9.19 3.85 0.26	-	-	-	-	338 35.03 2.78 1.17 0.08	1,130 34.69 9.31 3.90 0.27	362 59.64 2.98 1.25 0.09	-	355 33.65 2.92 1.23 0.08	-	-	170 58.02 1.40 0.59 0.04	201 43.70 1.66 0.69 0.05	-	2,822 48.00 23.25 9.74 0.66
Addison (town)	1,504 19.80	538	45 8.36 8.36 2.99	-	-	19 7.12 42.22 3.53 1.26	-	-	-	-	-	-	-	-	-	-	-	-	-	-	-	-	-	-	-	-
Coppell (city)	9,401 77.19	957	677 70.74 70.74 7.20	-	-	245 70.81 36.19 25.60 2.61	-	-	196 84.85 28.95 20.48 2.08	-	-	-	-	-	-	-	116 62.70 17.13 12.12 1.23	-	-	-	-	-	-	-	-	-
Farmers Branch (city)	6,702 68.33	341	172 50.44 50.44 2.57	-	-	-	-	-	-	-	-	-	-	-	-	-	-	-	-	-	-	-	-	-	-	-
Garland (city)	48,043 65.60	4,145	2,751 66.37 66.37 5.73	-	-	537 66.21 19.52 12.96 1.12	-	-	358 76.66 13.01 8.64 0.75	-	292 81.79 10.61 7.04 0.61	-	-	-	-	-	149 47.00 5.42 3.59 0.31	-	-	117 65.00 4.25 2.82 0.24	-	-	-	-	-	1,006 61.76 36.57 24.27 2.09
Grand Prairie (city)	26,742 61.31	1,474	1,037 70.35 70.35 3.88	-	-	159 83.68 15.33 10.79 0.59	-	-	-	-	111 60.66 10.70 7.53 0.42	-	-	-	-	-	-	57 79.17 5.50 3.87 0.21	-	-	-	-	-	-	-	468 75.12 45.13 31.75 1.75
Irving (city)	28,439 37.29	5,998	1,578 26.31 26.31 5.55	-	-	516 21.57 32.70 8.60 1.81	-	-	188 27.61 11.91 3.13 0.66	-	87 34.94 5.51 1.45 0.31	-	-	-	-	43 15.52 2.72 0.72 0.15	182 20.24 11.53 3.03 0.64	68 47.89 4.31 1.13 0.24	-	38 25.50 2.41 0.63 0.13	-	-	-	-	-	280 49.65 17.74 4.67 0.98

Notes: Please refer to the User's Guide for an explanation of data; data is arranged alphabetically by state, then county, then city within each county; table includes counties with populations greater than 49,999 unless noted and cities with populations greater than 9,999 whose Asian and/or NHPI population rates are greater than the national average; (1) Native Hawaiian and other Pacific Islander; (2) excludes Taiwanese; (3) includes Chamorro; (4) county does not meet population threshold but is shown in order to allow inclusion of city

Place	All owner-occupied housing units	Asian-occupied housing units	Asians who own and occupy their own homes	NHPI[1]-occupied housing units	NHPIs[1] who own and occupy their own homes	Asian Indian	Bangladeshi	Cambodian	Chinese[2]	Fijian	Filipino	Guamanian[3]	Hawaiian, Native	Hmong	Indonesian	Japanese	Korean	Laotian	Malaysian	Pakistani	Samoan	Sri Lankan	Taiwanese	Thai	Tongan	Vietnamese
Mesquite (city)	28,882 65.53	1,203	948 78.80 78.80 3.28	-	-	520 80.75 54.85 43.23 1.80	-	-	-	-	159 79.10 16.77 13.22 0.55	-	-	-	-	-	-	-	-	-	-	-	-	-	-	-
Richardson (city)	22,614 64.54	3,365	1,617 48.05 48.05 7.15	-	-	254 30.02 15.71 7.55 1.12	-	-	574 57.34 35.50 17.06 2.54	-	104 78.20 6.43 3.09 0.46	-	-	-	-	-	152 47.50 9.40 4.52 0.67	-	-	53 36.81 3.28 1.58 0.23	-	-	-	-	-	306 61.57 18.92 9.09 1.35
Rowlett (city)	13,122 92.10	432	401 92.82 92.82 3.06	-	-	145 100.00 36.16 33.56 1.11	-	-	-	-	-	-	-	-	-	-	-	-	-	-	-	-	-	-	-	-
Denton County	102,469 64.49	5,241	3,047 58.14 58.14 2.97	-	-	1,266 67.92 41.55 24.16 1.24	-	145 100.00 4.76 2.77 0.14	376 47.96 12.34 7.17 0.37	-	141 57.32 4.63 2.69 0.14	-	-	-	-	74 31.49 2.43 1.41 0.07	319 44.68 10.47 6.09 0.31	-	-	105 60.69 3.45 2.00 0.10	-	-	-	-	-	430 65.25 14.11 8.20 0.42
Carrollton (city)	25,657 65.52	3,095	2,045 66.07 66.07 7.97	-	-	741 61.14 36.23 23.94 2.89	-	140 73.68 6.85 4.52 0.55	184 79.31 9.00 5.95 0.72	-	-	-	-	-	-	-	208 64.60 10.17 6.72 0.81	-	-	129 45.10 6.31 4.17 0.50	-	-	-	-	-	461 75.33 22.54 14.89 1.80
Lewisville (city)	16,162 53.83	937	550 58.70 58.70 3.40	-	-	223 57.03 40.55 23.80 1.38	-	-	-	-	-	-	-	-	-	-	-	-	-	-	-	-	-	-	-	81 77.88 14.73 8.64 0.50
Ector County	30,098 68.64	268	156 58.21 58.21 0.52	-	-	-	-	-	-	-	-	-	-	-	-	-	-	-	-	-	-	-	-	-	-	-
El Paso County	133,596 63.61	2,355	1,111 47.18 47.18 0.83	93	28 30.11 30.11 0.02	94 22.71 8.46 3.99 0.07	-	-	109 42.41 9.81 4.63 0.08	-	378 61.97 34.02 16.05 0.28	-	-	-	-	205 53.39 18.45 8.70 0.15	257 58.14 23.13 10.91 0.19	-	-	-	-	-	-	-	-	-
Ellis County	28,226 76.25	100	75 75.00 75.00 0.27	-	-	-	-	-	-	-	-	-	-	-	-	-	-	-	-	-	-	-	-	-	-	-
Fort Bend County	89,628 80.81	10,686	9,308 87.10 87.10 10.39	-	-	3,003 84.33 32.26 28.10 3.35	-	-	2,726 93.16 29.29 25.51 3.04	-	999 83.25 10.73 9.35 1.11	-	-	-	-	-	241 90.94 2.59 2.26 0.27	-	-	451 78.30 4.85 4.22 0.50	-	-	287 83.43 3.08 2.69 0.32	-	-	1,234 88.08 13.26 11.55 1.38

Notes: Please refer to the User's Guide for an explanation of data; data is arranged alphabetically by state, then county, then city within each county; table includes counties with populations greater than 49,999 unless noted and cities with populations greater than 9,999 whose Asian and/or NHPI population rates are greater than the national average; (1) Native Hawaiian and other Pacific Islander; (2) excludes Taiwanese; (3) includes Chamorro; (4) county does not meet population threshold but is shown in order to allow inclusion of city

Place	All owner-occupied housing units	Asian-occupied housing units	Asians who own and occupy their own homes	NHPI[1]-occupied housing units	NHPIs[1] who own and occupy their own homes	Asian Indian	Bangladeshi	Cambodian	Chinese[2]	Fijian	Filipino	Guamanian[3]	Hawaiian, Native	Hmong	Indonesian	Japanese	Korean	Laotian	Malaysian	Pakistani	Samoan	Sri Lankan	Taiwanese	Thai	Tongan	Vietnamese
Cinco Ranch (cdp)	3,151 92.70	180	170 94.44 94.44 5.40	-	-	-	-	-	-	-	-	-	-	-	-	-	-	-	-	-	-	-	-	-	-	-
Mission Bend (cdp)	7,677 85.33	1,313	1,225 93.30 93.30 15.96	-	-	373 94.91 30.45 28.41 4.86	-	-	206 100.00 16.82 15.69 2.68	-	173 89.64 14.12 13.18 2.25	-	-	-	-	-	-	-	-	61 70.93 4.98 4.65 0.79	-	-	-	-	-	326 95.32 26.61 24.83 4.25
Missouri City (city)	15,490 90.99	1,548	1,497 96.71 96.71 9.66	-	-	549 96.32 36.67 35.47 3.54	-	-	372 97.13 24.85 24.03 2.40	-	256 100.00 17.10 16.54 1.65	-	-	-	-	-	-	-	-	-	-	-	-	-	-	147 88.55 9.82 9.50 0.95
New Territory (cdp)	3,463 92.05	822	813 98.91 98.91 23.48	-	-	370 97.63 45.51 45.01 10.68	-	-	187 100.00 23.00 22.75 5.40	-	-	-	-	-	-	-	-	-	-	-	-	-	-	-	-	-
Stafford (city)	2,702 46.28	1,039	527 50.72 50.72 19.50	-	-	177 44.70 33.59 17.04 6.55	-	-	138 71.50 26.19 13.28 5.11	-	56 38.10 10.63 5.39 2.07	-	-	-	-	-	-	-	-	-	-	-	-	-	-	108 60.00 20.49 10.39 4.00
Sugar Land (city)	17,419 84.51	4,108	3,566 86.81 86.81 20.47	-	-	1,003 81.94 28.13 24.42 5.76	-	-	1,473 92.53 41.31 35.86 8.46	-	251 85.96 7.04 6.11 1.44	-	-	-	-	-	111 93.28 3.11 2.70 0.64	-	-	119 76.28 3.34 2.90 0.68	-	-	220 82.09 6.17 5.36 1.26	-	-	294 87.50 8.24 7.16 1.69
Galveston County	62,790 66.25	1,740	920 52.87 52.87 1.47	-	-	154 41.62 16.74 8.85 0.25	-	-	170 49.13 18.48 9.77 0.27	-	152 63.07 16.52 8.74 0.24	-	-	-	-	-	-	-	-	-	-	-	-	-	-	297 69.72 32.28 17.07 0.47
Grayson County	30,228 70.55	199	84 42.21 42.21 0.28	-	-	-	-	-	-	-	-	-	-	-	-	-	-	-	-	-	-	-	-	-	-	-
Gregg County	27,366 64.11	182	89 48.90 48.90 0.33	-	-	-	-	-	-	-	-	-	-	-	-	-	-	-	-	-	-	-	-	-	-	-
Guadalupe County	23,799 77.02	192	158 82.29 82.29 0.66	-	-	-	-	-	-	-	-	-	-	-	-	-	-	-	-	-	-	-	-	-	-	-

Notes: Please refer to the User's Guide for an explanation of data; data is arranged alphabetically by state, then county, then city within each county; table includes counties with populations greater than 49,999 unless noted and cities with populations greater than 9,999 whose Asian and/or NHPI population rates are greater than the national average; (1) Native Hawaiian and other Pacific Islander; (2) excludes Taiwanese; (3) includes Chamorro; (4) county does not meet population threshold but is shown in order to allow inclusion of city

Place	All owner-occupied housing units	Asian-occupied housing units	Asians who own and occupy their own homes	NHPI[1]-occupied housing units	NHPIs[1] who own and occupy their own homes	Asian Indian	Bangladeshi	Cambodian	Chinese[2]	Fijian	Filipino	Guamanian[3]	Hawaiian, Native	Hmong	Indonesian	Japanese	Korean	Laotian	Malaysian	Pakistani	Samoan	Sri Lankan	Taiwanese	Thai	Tongan	Vietnamese
Harris County	667,129 55.34	55,562	29,092 52.36 52.36 4.36	458	235 51.31 51.31 0.04	5,311 45.12 18.26 9.56 0.80	74 31.62 0.25 0.13 0.01	418 71.09 1.44 0.75 0.06	6,379 53.58 21.93 11.48 0.96	-	2,756 56.33 9.47 4.96 0.41	103 47.25 43.83 22.49 0.02	-	-	56 25.81 0.19 0.10 0.01	532 33.19 1.83 0.96 0.08	1,303 46.82 4.48 2.35 0.20	238 70.62 0.82 0.43 0.04	-	637 29.70 2.19 1.15 0.10	-	-	637 73.30 2.19 1.15 0.10	237 49.17 0.81 0.43 0.04	-	9,632 60.42 33.11 17.34 1.44
Bellaire (city)	4,970 82.74	298	271 90.94 90.94 5.45	-	-	-	-	-	119 95.20 43.91 39.93 2.39	-	-	-	-	-	-	-	-	-	-	-	-	-	-	-	-	-
Houston (city)	329,006 45.81	36,166	14,784 40.88 40.88 4.49	308	119 38.64 38.64 0.04	2,404 33.06 16.26 6.65 0.73	-	126 54.08 0.85 0.35 0.04	4,008 44.51 27.11 11.08 1.22	-	1,168 43.05 7.90 3.23 0.36	72 43.11 60.50 23.38 0.02	-	-	32 16.58 0.22 0.09 0.01	249 23.29 1.68 0.69 0.08	658 34.18 4.45 1.82 0.20	-	-	291 19.76 1.97 0.80 0.09	-	-	426 67.73 2.88 1.18 0.13	148 40.33 1.00 0.41 0.04	-	4,730 48.18 31.99 13.08 1.44
West University Place (city)	4,780 90.43	225	216 96.00 96.00 4.52	-	-	-	-	-	-	-	-	-	-	-	-	-	-	-	-	-	-	-	-	-	-	-
Hays County	21,680 64.89	211	67 31.75 31.75 0.31	-	-	-	-	-	-	-	-	-	-	-	-	-	-	-	-	-	-	-	-	-	-	-
Hidalgo County	114,570 73.06	1,023	592 57.87 57.87 0.52	-	-	146 77.25 24.66 14.27 0.13	-	-	-	-	254 55.46 42.91 24.83 0.22	-	-	-	-	-	-	-	-	-	-	-	-	-	-	-
Hunt County	20,532 71.44	120	40 33.33 33.33 0.19	-	-	-	-	-	-	-	-	-	-	-	-	-	-	-	-	-	-	-	-	-	-	-
Jefferson County	61,253 65.95	1,802	1,133 62.87 62.87 1.85	-	-	150 55.56 13.24 8.32 0.24	-	-	99 70.21 8.74 5.49 0.16	-	153 63.75 13.50 8.49 0.25	-	-	-	-	-	-	-	-	-	-	-	-	-	-	656 65.21 57.90 36.40 1.07
Port Arthur (city)	13,574 62.17	844	530 62.80 62.80 3.90	-	-	-	-	-	-	-	-	-	-	-	-	-	-	-	-	-	-	-	-	-	-	446 66.17 84.15 52.84 3.29
Johnson County	34,420 78.88	182	120 65.93 65.93 0.35	-	-	-	-	-	-	-	-	-	-	-	-	-	-	-	-	-	-	-	-	-	-	-

Notes: Please refer to the User's Guide for an explanation of data; data is arranged alphabetically by state, then county, then city within each county; table includes counties with populations greater than 49,999 unless noted and cities with populations greater than 9,999 whose Asian and/or NHPI population rates are greater than the national average; (1) Native Hawaiian and other Pacific Islander; (2) excludes Taiwanese; (3) includes Chamorro; (4) county does not meet population threshold but is shown in order to allow inclusion of city

Place	All owner-occupied housing units	Asian-occupied housing units	Asians who own and occupy their own homes	NHPI[1]-occupied housing units	NHPIs[1] who own and occupy their own homes	Asian Indian	Bangladeshi	Cambodian	Chinese[2]	Fijian	Filipino	Guamanian[3]	Hawaiian, Native	Hmong	Indonesian	Japanese	Korean	Laotian	Malaysian	Pakistani	Samoan	Sri Lankan	Taiwanese	Thai	Tongan	Vietnamese
Kaufman County	19,299 79.20	101	98 97.03 97.03 0.51	-	-	-	-	-	-	-	-	-	-	-	-	-	-	-	-	-	-	-	-	-	-	-
Lubbock County	54,763 59.19	1,060	349 32.92 32.92 0.64	-	-	109 39.49 31.23 10.28 0.20	-	-	62 23.94 17.77 5.85 0.11	-	-	-	-	-	-	-	-	-	-	-	-	-	-	-	-	29 23.97 8.31 2.74 0.05
McLennan County	47,463 60.19	668	163 24.40 24.40 0.34	-	-	37 34.58 22.70 5.54 0.08	-	-	-	-	-	-	-	-	-	-	-	-	-	-	-	-	-	-	-	-
Midland County	29,724 69.54	288	182 63.19 63.19 0.61	-	-	88 77.88 48.35 30.56 0.30	-	-	-	-	-	-	-	-	-	-	-	-	-	-	-	-	-	-	-	-
Montgomery County	80,750 78.17	950	652 68.63 68.63 0.81	-	-	237 66.20 36.35 24.95 0.29	-	-	204 93.15 31.29 21.47 0.25	-	77 77.00 11.81 8.11 0.10	-	-	-	-	-	-	-	-	-	-	-	-	-	-	-
Nacogdoches County	13,540 61.53	98	59 60.20 60.20 0.44	-	-	-	-	-	-	-	-	-	-	-	-	-	-	-	-	-	-	-	-	-	-	-
Nueces County	67,687 61.33	1,073	609 56.76 56.76 0.90	-	-	122 60.40 20.03 11.37 0.18	-	-	-	-	287 63.64 47.13 26.75 0.42	-	-	-	-	-	-	-	-	-	-	-	-	-	-	-
Orange County	24,436 77.23	190	123 64.74 64.74 0.50	-	-	-	-	-	-	-	-	-	-	-	-	-	-	-	-	-	-	-	-	-	-	78 76.47 63.41 41.05 0.32
Potter County	24,497 60.10	878	536 61.05 61.05 2.19	-	-	-	-	-	-	-	-	-	-	-	-	-	-	207 72.38 38.62 23.58 0.85	-	-	-	-	-	-	-	205 67.88 38.25 23.35 0.84
Randall County	28,988 70.29	388	184 47.42 47.42 0.63	-	-	-	-	-	-	-	-	-	-	-	-	-	-	-	-	-	-	-	-	-	-	-

Notes: Please refer to the User's Guide for an explanation of data; data is arranged alphabetically by state, then county, then city within each county; table includes counties with populations greater than 49,999 unless noted and cities with populations greater than 9,999 whose Asian and/or NHPI population rates are greater than the national average; (1) Native Hawaiian and other Pacific Islander; (2) excludes Taiwanese; (3) includes Chamorro; (4) county does not meet population threshold but is shown in order to allow inclusion of city

Place	All owner-occupied housing units	Asian-occupied housing units	Asians who own and occupy their own homes	NHPI[1]-occupied housing units	NHPIs[1] who own and occupy their own homes	Asian Indian	Bangladeshi	Cambodian	Chinese[2]	Fijian	Filipino	Guamanian[3]	Hawaiian, Native	Hmong	Indonesian	Japanese	Korean	Laotian	Malaysian	Pakistani	Samoan	Sri Lankan	Taiwanese	Thai	Tongan	Vietnamese
San Patricio County	15,072 68.22	65	27 41.54 41.54 0.18	-	-	-	-	-	-	-	-	-	-	-	-	-	-	-	-	-	-	-	-	-	-	-
Smith County	45,777 69.68	271	172 63.47 63.47 0.38	-	-	-	-	-	-	-	-	-	-	-	-	-	-	-	-	-	-	-	-	-	-	-
Tarrant County	324,754 60.83	14,879	7,636 51.32 51.32 2.35	463	161 34.77 34.77 0.05	1,194 37.89 15.64 8.02 0.37	-	88 61.54 1.15 0.59 0.03	1,051 53.57 13.76 7.06 0.32	-	515 51.81 6.74 3.46 0.16	-	-	-	-	187 49.08 2.45 1.26 0.06	392 41.70 5.13 2.63 0.12	531 70.52 6.95 3.57 0.16	-	123 37.85 1.61 0.83 0.04	-	-	120 49.38 1.57 0.81 0.04	90 36.89 1.18 0.60 0.03	38 45.78 23.60 8.21 0.01	3,014 61.61 39.47 20.26 0.93
Arlington (city)	68,309 54.70	5,563	2,789 50.13 50.13 4.08	-	-	341 35.52 12.23 6.13 0.50	-	-	479 48.68 17.17 8.61 0.70	-	171 49.00 6.13 3.07 0.25	-	-	-	-	-	96 35.42 3.44 1.73 0.14	-	-	-	-	-	59 38.82 2.12 1.06 0.09	-	-	1,453 65.75 52.10 26.12 2.13
Euless (city)	8,408 43.82	1,010	265 26.24 26.24 3.15	-	-	40 8.91 15.09 3.96 0.48	-	-	-	-	-	-	-	-	-	-	-	-	-	-	-	-	-	-	-	-
Haltom City (city)	8,882 59.14	944	428 45.34 45.34 4.82	-	-	-	-	-	-	-	-	-	-	-	-	-	-	139 71.65 32.48 14.72 1.56	-	-	-	-	-	-	-	197 41.39 46.03 20.87 2.22
Taylor County	29,091 61.54	467	196 41.97 41.97 0.67	-	-	-	-	-	-	-	70 40.94 35.71 14.99 0.24	-	-	-	-	-	-	-	-	-	-	-	-	-	-	-
Tom Green County	25,334 64.13	253	138 54.55 54.55 0.54	-	-	-	-	-	-	-	-	-	-	-	-	-	-	-	-	-	-	-	-	-	-	-
Travis County	165,123 51.48	13,132	4,628 35.24 35.24 2.80	228	65 28.51 28.51 0.04	937 26.74 20.25 7.14 0.57	-	-	1,385 39.68 29.93 10.55 0.84	-	226 32.52 4.88 1.72 0.14	-	-	-	-	143 30.43 3.09 1.09 0.09	283 20.30 6.11 2.16 0.17	-	-	57 23.55 1.23 0.43 0.03	-	-	119 38.64 2.57 0.91 0.07	54 40.91 1.17 0.41 0.03	-	1,216 55.73 26.27 9.26 0.74
Austin (city)	119,191 44.91	11,613	3,508 30.21 30.21 2.94	197	41 20.81 20.81 0.03	745 23.86 21.24 6.42 0.63	-	-	1,128 35.21 32.16 9.71 0.95	-	129 22.67 3.68 1.11 0.11	-	-	-	-	139 30.96 3.96 1.20 0.12	193 15.23 5.50 1.66 0.16	-	-	33 18.97 0.94 0.28 0.03	-	-	104 36.62 2.96 0.90 0.09	-	-	837 47.50 23.86 7.21 0.70

Notes: Please refer to the User's Guide for an explanation of data; data is arranged alphabetically by state, then county, then city within each county; table includes counties with populations greater than 49,999 unless noted and cities with populations greater than 9,999 whose Asian and/or NHPI population rates are greater than the national average; (1) Native Hawaiian and other Pacific Islander; (2) excludes Taiwanese; (3) includes Chamorro; (4) county does not meet population threshold but is shown in order to allow inclusion of city

Place	All owner-occupied housing units	Asian-occupied housing units	Asians who own and occupy their own homes	NHPI[1]-occupied housing units	NHPIs[1] who own and occupy their own homes	Asian Indian	Bangladeshi	Cambodian	Chinese[2]	Fijian	Filipino	Guamanian[3]	Hawaiian, Native	Hmong	Indonesian	Japanese	Korean	Laotian	Malaysian	Pakistani	Samoan	Sri Lankan	Taiwanese	Thai	Tongan	Vietnamese
Pflugerville (city)	4,641 89.61	143	134 93.71 93.71 2.89	-	-	-	-	-	-	-	-	-	-	-	-	-	-	-	-	-	-	-	-	-	-	-
Wells Branch (cdp)	1,785 32.63	428	121 28.27 28.27 6.78	-	-	-	-	-	-	-	-	-	-	-	-	-	-	-	-	-	-	-	-	-	-	-
Victoria County	20,257 67.36	125	71 56.80 56.80 0.35	-	-	-	-	-	-	-	-	-	-	-	-	-	-	-	-	-	-	-	-	-	-	-
Webb County	33,320 65.67	266	70 26.32 26.32 0.21	-	-	-	-	-	-	-	-	-	-	-	-	-	-	-	-	-	-	-	-	-	-	-
Wichita County	30,192 62.33	677	388 57.31 57.31 1.29	-	-	-	-	-	-	-	55 39.57 14.18 8.12 0.18	-	-	-	-	-	-	-	-	-	-	-	-	-	-	157 83.96 40.46 23.19 0.52
Williamson County	64,391 74.21	1,752	1,301 74.26 74.26 2.02	-	-	353 76.57 27.13 20.15 0.55	-	-	326 82.95 25.06 18.61 0.51	-	-	-	-	-	-	-	117 71.34 8.99 6.68 0.18	-	-	-	-	-	-	-	-	199 70.57 15.30 11.36 0.31
Brushy Creek (cdp)	4,646 94.30	259	259 100.00 100.00 5.57	-	-	-	-	-	-	-	-	-	-	-	-	-	-	-	-	-	-	-	-	-	-	-
Jollyville (cdp)	3,897 67.35	344	288 83.72 83.72 7.39	-	-	-	-	-	-	-	-	-	-	-	-	-	-	-	-	-	-	-	-	-	-	-
UTAH	501,659 71.53	10,577	6,203 58.65 58.65 1.24	3,106	1,780 57.31 57.31 0.35	328 37.49 5.29 3.10 0.07	-	221 81.55 3.56 2.09 0.04	1,236 54.88 19.93 11.69 0.25	-	547 59.52 8.82 5.17 0.11	-	175 44.87 9.83 5.63 0.03	-	-	1,734 73.47 27.95 16.39 0.35	302 32.72 4.87 2.86 0.06	366 66.55 5.90 3.46 0.07	-	56 63.64 0.90 0.53 0.01	502 54.51 28.20 16.16 0.10	-	102 62.58 1.64 0.96 0.02	90 43.06 1.45 0.85 0.02	870 69.49 48.88 28.01 0.17	970 70.49 15.64 9.17 0.19
Cache County	17,802 64.63	550	189 34.36 34.36 1.06	-	-	-	-	-	69 35.57 36.51 12.55 0.39	-	-	-	-	-	-	-	-	-	-	-	-	-	-	-	-	-

Notes: Please refer to the User's Guide for an explanation of data; data is arranged alphabetically by state, then county, then city within each county; table includes counties with populations greater than 49,999 unless noted and cities with populations greater than 9,999 whose Asian and/or NHPI population rates are greater than the national average; (1) Native Hawaiian and other Pacific Islander; (2) excludes Taiwanese; (3) includes Chamorro; (4) county does not meet population threshold but is shown in order to allow inclusion of city

Place	All owner-occupied housing units	Asian-occupied housing units	Asians who own and occupy their own homes	NHPI[1]-occupied housing units	NHPIs[1] who own and occupy their own homes	Asian Indian	Bangladeshi	Cambodian	Chinese[2]	Fijian	Filipino	Guamanian[3]	Hawaiian, Native	Hmong	Indonesian	Japanese	Korean	Laotian	Malaysian	Pakistani	Samoan	Sri Lankan	Taiwanese	Thai	Tongan	Vietnamese
Davis County	55,245 77.59	977	716 73.29 73.29 1.30	238	132 55.46 55.46 0.24	-	-	-	-	-	180 81.82 25.14 18.42 0.33	-	-	-	-	270 84.64 37.71 27.64 0.49	45 75.00 6.28 4.61 0.08	-	-	-	-	-	-	-	-	-
Salt Lake County	203,690 69.01	6,750	4,006 59.35 59.35 1.97	2,105	1,315 62.47 62.47 0.65	240 37.97 5.99 3.56 0.12	-	156 86.19 3.89 2.31 0.08	854 59.18 21.32 12.65 0.42	-	263 59.50 6.57 3.90 0.13	-	61 43.57 4.64 2.90 0.03	-	-	943 70.53 23.54 13.97 0.46	166 30.13 4.14 2.46 0.08	292 71.39 7.29 4.33 0.14	-	-	346 58.64 26.31 16.44 0.17	-	-	-	755 72.18 57.41 35.87 0.37	781 68.03 19.50 11.57 0.38
Kearns (cdp)	8,155 88.73	230	208 90.43 90.43 2.55	74	43 58.11 58.11 0.53	-	-	-	-	-	-	-	-	-	-	-	-	-	-	-	-	-	-	-	-	-
Salt Lake City (city)	36,579 51.23	2,292	909 39.66 39.66 2.49	642	394 61.37 61.37 1.08	71 31.28 7.81 3.10 0.19	-	-	203 33.44 22.33 8.86 0.55	-	64 55.17 7.04 2.79 0.17	-	-	-	-	284 58.08 31.24 12.39 0.78	29 13.49 3.19 1.27 0.08	-	-	-	69 59.48 17.51 10.75 0.19	-	-	-	301 73.59 76.40 46.88 0.82	127 37.80 13.97 5.54 0.35
Sandy (city)	21,663 84.29	442	351 79.41 79.41 1.62	56	51 91.07 91.07 0.24	-	-	-	84 89.36 23.93 19.00 0.39	-	-	-	-	-	-	-	-	-	-	-	-	-	-	-	-	-
Taylorsville (city)	13,205 71.08	442	336 76.02 76.02 2.54	173	97 56.07 56.07 0.73	-	-	-	-	-	-	-	-	-	-	-	-	-	-	-	-	-	-	-	-	131 96.32 38.99 29.64 0.99
West Jordan (city)	15,444 81.87	268	213 79.48 79.48 1.38	128	95 74.22 74.22 0.62	-	-	-	-	-	-	-	-	-	-	-	-	-	-	-	-	-	-	-	66 82.50 69.47 51.56 0.43	-
West Valley City (city)	23,422 72.60	1,091	790 72.41 72.41 3.37	621	436 70.21 70.21 1.86	-	-	113 100.00 14.30 10.36 0.48	91 79.13 11.52 8.34 0.39	-	-	-	-	-	-	-	-	88 64.23 11.14 8.07 0.38	-	-	154 78.57 35.32 24.80 0.66	-	-	-	226 79.86 51.83 36.39 0.96	296 76.49 37.47 27.13 1.26
Utah County	66,800 66.84	970	411 42.37 42.37 0.62	430	189 43.95 43.95 0.28	-	-	-	147 45.79 35.77 15.15 0.22	-	47 39.50 11.44 4.85 0.07	-	23 23.96 12.17 5.35 0.03	-	-	64 44.76 15.57 6.60 0.10	41 41.00 9.98 4.23 0.06	-	-	-	73 49.66 38.62 16.98 0.11	-	-	-	63 56.25 33.33 14.65 0.09	-
Orem (city)	15,679 67.04	306	135 44.12 44.12 0.86	174	89 51.15 51.15 0.57	-	-	-	-	-	-	-	-	-	-	-	-	-	-	-	-	-	-	-	-	-

Notes: Please refer to the User's Guide for an explanation of data; data is arranged alphabetically by state, then county, then city within each county; table includes counties with populations greater than 49,999 unless noted and cities with populations greater than 9,999 whose Asian and/or NHPI population rates are greater than the national average; (1) Native Hawaiian and other Pacific Islander; (2) excludes Taiwanese; (3) includes Chamorro; (4) county does not meet population threshold but is shown in order to allow inclusion of city

Place	All owner-occupied housing units	Asian-occupied housing units	Asians who own and occupy their own homes	NHPI[1]-occupied housing units	NHPIs[1] who own and occupy their own homes	Asian Indian	Bangladeshi	Cambodian	Chinese[2]	Fijian	Filipino	Guamanian[3]	Hawaiian, Native	Hmong	Indonesian	Japanese	Korean	Laotian	Malaysian	Pakistani	Samoan	Sri Lankan	Taiwanese	Thai	Tongan	Vietnamese
Provo (city)	12,478	551	183	155	47	-	-	-	84	-	-	-	-	-	-	31	-	-	-	-	-	-	-	-	-	-
	42.70		33.21		30.32				40.38							33.33										
									45.90							16.94										
			33.21		30.32				15.25							5.63										
			1.47		0.38				0.67							0.25										
Washington County	22,144	96	43	98	28	-	-	-	-	-	-	-	-	-	-	-	-	-	-	-	-	-	-	-	-	-
	73.96		44.79		28.57																					
			44.79		28.57																					
			0.19		0.13																					
St. George (city)	11,795	87	38	83	22	-	-	-	-	-	-	-	-	-	-	-	-	-	-	-	-	-	-	-	-	-
	67.95		43.68		26.51																					
			43.68		26.51																					
			0.32		0.19																					
Weber County	49,194	732	559	-	-	-	-	-	-	-	-	-	-	-	-	280	-	-	-	-	-	-	-	-	-	-
	74.88		76.37													96.89										
																50.09										
			76.37													38.25										
			1.14													0.57										
VERMONT	169,777	1,185	500	-	-	86	-	-	177	-	47	-	-	-	-	74	28	-	-	-	-	-	-	-	-	41
	70.55		42.19			44.56			56.91		48.96					61.67	28.00									17.52
						17.20			35.40		9.40					14.80	5.60									8.20
			42.19			7.26			14.94		3.97					6.24	2.36									3.46
			0.29			0.05			0.10		0.03					0.04	0.02									0.02
Chittenden County	37,291	726	257	-	-	36	-	-	84	-	-	-	-	-	-	-	-	-	-	-	-	-	-	-	-	35
	66.06		35.40			32.43			45.41																	16.83
						14.01			32.68																	13.62
			35.40			4.96			11.57																	4.82
			0.69			0.10			0.23																	0.09
Rutland County	17,924	60	34	-	-	-	-	-	-	-	-	-	-	-	-	-	-	-	-	-	-	-	-	-	-	-
	69.80		56.67																							
			56.67																							
			0.19																							
Washington County	16,202	61	22	-	-	-	-	-	-	-	-	-	-	-	-	-	-	-	-	-	-	-	-	-	-	-
	68.48		36.07																							
			36.07																							
			0.14																							
Windsor County	17,284	71	29	-	-	-	-	-	-	-	-	-	-	-	-	-	-	-	-	-	-	-	-	-	-	-
	71.53		40.85																							
			40.85																							
			0.17																							
VIRGINIA	1,837,958	77,765	44,185	995	468	7,055	220	817	7,060	-	9,392	119	169	-	140	1,565	7,224	534	-	1,202	36	118	303	688	-	6,418
	68.09		56.82		47.04	44.99	43.22	72.82	61.75		67.82	40.48	58.28		40.46	49.37	52.62	66.92		49.59	34.62	58.71	64.47	54.39		63.63
						15.97	0.50	1.85	15.98		21.26	25.43	36.11		0.32	3.54	16.35	1.21		2.72	7.69	0.27	0.69	1.56		14.53
			56.82		47.04	9.07	0.28	1.05	9.08		12.08	11.96	16.98		0.18	2.01	9.29	0.69		1.55	3.62	0.15	0.39	0.88		8.25
			2.40		0.03	0.38	0.01	0.04	0.38		0.51	0.01	0.01		0.01	0.09	0.39	0.03		0.07	<0.01	0.01	0.02	0.04		0.35

Notes: Please refer to the User's Guide for an explanation of data; data is arranged alphabetically by state, then county, then city within each county; table includes counties with populations greater than 49,999 unless noted and cities with populations greater than 9,999 whose Asian and/or NHPI population rates are greater than the national average; (1) Native Hawaiian and other Pacific Islander; (2) excludes Taiwanese; (3) includes Chamorro; (4) county does not meet population threshold but is shown in order to allow inclusion of city

Place	All owner-occupied housing units	Asian-occupied housing units	Asians who own and occupy their own homes	NHPI[1]-occupied housing units	NHPIs[1] who own and occupy their own homes	Asian Indian	Bangladeshi	Cambodian	Chinese[2]	Fijian	Filipino	Guamanian[3]	Hawaiian, Native	Hmong	Indonesian	Japanese	Korean	Laotian	Malaysian	Pakistani	Samoan	Sri Lankan	Taiwanese	Thai	Tongan	Vietnamese
Albemarle County	20,983	779	273	-	-	79	-	-	109	-	-	-	-	-	-	-	-	-	-	-	-	-	-	-	-	-
	65.83		35.04			39.30			36.09																	
						28.94			39.93																	
			35.04			10.14			13.99																	
			1.30			0.38			0.52																	
Alexandria Independent City	24,727	3,050	726	-	-	53	-	-	216	-	125	-	-	-	-	-	84	-	-	25	-	-	-	-	-	46
	39.95		23.80			8.28			58.06		27.47						12.57			14.88						19.09
						7.30			29.75		17.22						11.57			3.44						6.34
			23.80			1.74			7.08		4.10						2.75			0.82						1.51
			2.94			0.21			0.87		0.51						0.34			0.10						0.19
Arlington County	37,364	6,555	1,534	-	-	218	-	31	300	-	349	-	-	-	-	91	157	-	-	36	-	-	-	-	-	236
	43.27		23.40			14.11		33.70	27.99		45.80					15.58	20.71			20.57						29.84
						14.21		2.02	19.56		22.75					5.93	10.23			2.35						15.38
			23.40			3.33		0.47	4.58		5.32					1.39	2.40			0.55						3.60
			4.11			0.58		0.08	0.80		0.93					0.24	0.42			0.10						0.63
Arlington (cdp)	37,364	6,555	1,534	-	-	218	-	31	300	-	349	-	-	-	-	91	157	-	-	36	-	-	-	-	-	236
	43.27		23.40			14.11		33.70	27.99		45.80					15.58	20.71			20.57						29.84
						14.21		2.02	19.56		22.75					5.93	10.23			2.35						15.38
			23.40			3.33		0.47	4.58		5.32					1.39	2.40			0.55						3.60
			4.11			0.58		0.08	0.80		0.93					0.24	0.42			0.10						0.63
Bedford County	20,640	173	121	-	-	-	-	-	-	-	-	-	-	-	-	-	-	-	-	-	-	-	-	-	-	-
	86.58		69.94																							
			69.94																							
			0.59																							
Charlottesville Independent City	6,887	574	96	-	-	12	-	-	36	-	-	-	-	-	-	-	-	-	-	-	-	-	-	-	-	-
	40.87		16.72			12.63			16.74																	
						12.50			37.50																	
			16.72			2.09			6.27																	
			1.39			0.17			0.52																	
Chesapeake Independent City	52,323	991	752	-	-	-	-	-	-	-	476	-	-	-	-	-	-	-	-	-	-	-	-	-	-	-
	74.85		75.88								84.40															
											63.30															
			75.88								48.03															
			1.44								0.91															
Chesterfield County	75,907	1,801	1,307	-	-	270	-	110	214	-	138	-	-	-	-	-	300	-	-	-	-	-	-	-	-	162
	80.95		72.57			72.78		81.48	73.79		79.77						77.12									71.68
						20.66		8.42	16.37		10.56						22.95									12.39
			72.57			14.99		6.11	11.88		7.66						16.66									9.00
			1.72			0.36		0.14	0.28		0.18						0.40									0.21
Fairfax Independent City	5,551	747	338	-	-	32	-	-	75	-	-	-	-	-	-	-	74	-	-	-	-	-	-	-	-	87
	69.09		45.25			20.00			51.02								42.53									72.50
						9.47			22.19								21.89									25.74
			45.25			4.28			10.04								9.91									11.65
			6.09			0.58			1.35								1.33									1.57
Fairfax County	248,858	36,014	22,775	206	105	4,001	124	301	3,768	-	2,479	-	-	-	85	587	5,014	267	-	775	-	-	224	359	-	4,038
	70.96		63.24		50.97	51.03	54.39	73.06	72.42		72.06				66.93	61.27	60.18	72.95		54.89			87.84	75.26		70.59
						17.57	0.54	1.32	16.54		10.88				0.37	2.58	22.02	1.17		3.40			0.98	1.58		17.73
			63.24		50.97	11.11	0.34	0.84	10.46		6.88				0.24	1.63	13.92	0.74		2.15			0.62	1.00		11.21
			9.15		0.04	1.61	0.05	0.12	1.51		1.00				0.03	0.24	2.01	0.11		0.31			0.09	0.14		1.62

Notes: Please refer to the User's Guide for an explanation of data; data is arranged alphabetically by state, then county, then city within each county; table includes counties with populations greater than 49,999 unless noted and cities with populations greater than 9,999 whose Asian and/or NHPI population rates are greater than the national average; (1) Native Hawaiian and other Pacific Islander; (2) excludes Taiwanese; (3) includes Chamorro; (4) county does not meet population threshold but is shown in order to allow inclusion of city

Place	All owner-occupied housing units	Asian-occupied housing units	Asians who own and occupy their own homes	NHPI[1]-occupied housing units	NHPIs[1] who own and occupy their own homes	Asian Indian	Bangladeshi	Cambodian	Chinese[2]	Fijian	Filipino	Guamanian[3]	Hawaiian, Native	Hmong	Indonesian	Japanese	Korean	Laotian	Malaysian	Pakistani	Samoan	Sri Lankan	Taiwanese	Thai	Tongan	Vietnamese
Annandale (cdp)	13,411 67.38	3,166	1,561 49.31 49.31 11.64	-	-	146 35.44 9.35 4.61 1.09	-	-	165 55.93 10.57 5.21 1.23	-	146 75.26 9.35 4.61 1.09	-	-	-	-	-	345 30.80 22.10 10.90 2.57	-	-	-	-	-	-	-	-	612 68.15 39.21 19.33 4.56
Bailey's Crossroads (cdp)	3,517 41.41	878	340 38.72 38.72 9.67	-	-	-	-	-	-	-	-	-	-	-	-	-	-	-	-	7 8.05 2.06 0.80 0.20	-	-	-	-	-	84 38.18 24.71 9.57 2.39
Burke (cdp)	16,121 83.76	2,175	1,859 85.47 85.47 11.53	-	-	319 87.64 17.16 14.67 1.98	-	-	198 93.84 10.65 9.10 1.23	-	256 96.60 13.77 11.77 1.59	-	-	-	-	-	656 78.56 35.29 30.16 4.07	-	-	-	-	-	-	-	-	256 87.67 13.77 11.77 1.59
Centreville (cdp)	11,612 65.39	1,924	1,274 66.22 66.22 10.97	-	-	272 56.20 21.35 14.14 2.34	-	-	239 75.87 18.76 12.42 2.06	-	165 60.22 12.95 8.58 1.42	-	-	-	-	-	310 63.27 24.33 16.11 2.67	-	-	-	-	-	-	-	-	99 75.00 7.77 5.15 0.85
Chantilly (cdp)	10,940 73.68	1,860	1,350 72.58 72.58 12.34	-	-	290 51.88 21.48 15.59 2.65	-	-	256 89.51 18.96 13.76 2.34	-	-	-	-	-	-	-	304 84.92 22.52 16.34 2.78	-	-	-	-	-	-	-	-	201 86.27 14.89 10.81 1.84
Franconia (cdp)	9,510 71.20	906	788 86.98 86.98 8.29	-	-	110 91.67 13.96 12.14 1.16	-	-	-	-	147 71.01 18.65 16.23 1.55	-	-	-	-	-	160 91.43 20.30 17.66 1.68	-	-	-	-	-	-	-	-	132 100.00 16.75 14.57 1.39
Groveton (cdp)	4,568 56.66	424	227 53.54 53.54 4.97	-	-	-	-	-	-	-	-	-	-	-	-	-	-	-	-	-	-	-	-	-	-	-
Herndon (town)	4,586 65.86	879	515 58.59 58.59 11.23	-	-	168 52.66 32.62 19.11 3.66	-	-	-	-	-	-	-	-	-	-	-	-	-	-	-	-	-	-	-	67 62.62 13.01 7.62 1.46
Hybla Valley (cdp)	3,334 52.24	377	207 54.91 54.91 6.21	-	-	-	-	-	-	-	-	-	-	-	-	-	-	-	-	-	-	-	-	-	-	-
Idylwood (cdp)	3,347 50.94	1,125	425 37.78 37.78 12.70	-	-	72 17.73 16.94 6.40 2.15	-	-	98 48.28 23.06 8.71 2.93	-	-	-	-	-	-	-	-	-	-	-	-	-	-	-	-	151 70.56 35.53 13.42 4.51

Notes: Please refer to the User's Guide for an explanation of data; data is arranged alphabetically by state, then county, then city within each county; table includes counties with populations greater than 49,999 unless noted and cities with populations greater than 9,999 whose Asian and/or NHPI population rates are greater than the national average; (1) Native Hawaiian and other Pacific Islander; (2) excludes Taiwanese; (3) includes Chamorro; (4) county does not meet population threshold but is shown in order to allow inclusion of city

Place	All owner-occupied housing units	Asian-occupied housing units	Asians who own and occupy their own homes	NHPI[1]-occupied housing units	NHPIs[1] who own and occupy their own homes	Asian Indian	Bangladeshi	Cambodian	Chinese[2]	Fijian	Filipino	Guamanian[3]	Hawaiian, Native	Hmong	Indonesian	Japanese	Korean	Laotian	Malaysian	Pakistani	Samoan	Sri Lankan	Taiwanese	Thai	Tongan	Vietnamese
Jefferson (cdp)	6,571 65.64	1,504	719 47.81 47.81 10.94	-	-	65 21.81 9.04 4.32 0.99	-	-	89 49.17 12.38 5.92 1.35	-	78 73.58 10.85 5.19 1.19	-	-	-	-	-	-	-	-	-	-	-	-	-	-	317 50.40 44.09 21.08 4.82
Lincolnia (cdp)	2,767 53.21	599	262 43.74 43.74 9.47	-	-	-	-	-	-	-	-	-	-	-	-	-	-	-	-	4 2.76 1.53 0.67 0.14	-	-	-	-	-	76 76.77 29.01 12.69 2.75
Lorton (cdp)	3,585 63.44	401	315 78.55 78.55 8.79	-	-	-	-	-	-	-	-	-	-	-	-	-	-	-	-	-	-	-	-	-	-	-
McLean (cdp)	12,294 85.27	1,172	870 74.23 74.23 7.08	-	-	251 89.64 28.85 21.42 2.04	-	-	222 92.50 25.52 18.94 1.81	-	81 100.00 9.31 6.91 0.66	-	-	-	-	24 15.58 2.76 2.05 0.20	141 58.26 16.21 12.03 1.15	-	-	-	-	-	-	-	-	-
Merrifield (cdp)	2,220 50.48	1,030	447 43.40 43.40 20.14	-	-	108 34.84 24.16 10.49 4.86	-	-	-	-	-	-	-	-	-	-	67 24.19 14.99 6.50 3.02	-	-	-	-	-	-	-	-	136 69.39 30.43 13.20 6.13
Mount Vernon (cdp)	6,776 64.08	545	311 57.06 57.06 4.59	-	-	-	-	-	-	-	-	-	-	-	-	-	91 60.67 29.26 16.70 1.34	-	-	-	-	-	-	-	-	-
Newington (cdp)	5,258 78.78	543	461 84.90 84.90 8.77	-	-	94 100.00 20.39 17.31 1.79	-	-	-	-	89 72.36 19.31 16.39 1.69	-	-	-	-	-	79 79.00 17.14 14.55 1.50	-	-	-	-	-	-	-	-	-
Oakton (cdp)	7,333 65.81	1,317	606 46.01 46.01 8.26	-	-	109 32.44 17.99 8.28 1.49	-	-	166 55.70 27.39 12.60 2.26	-	-	-	-	-	-	-	153 40.69 25.25 11.62 2.09	-	-	-	-	-	-	-	-	91 68.42 15.02 6.91 1.24
Reston (cdp)	15,516 66.64	1,758	775 44.08 44.08 4.99	-	-	191 29.48 24.65 10.86 1.23	-	-	224 71.57 28.90 12.74 1.44	-	118 79.73 15.23 6.71 0.76	-	-	-	-	-	130 47.45 16.77 7.39 0.84	-	-	-	-	-	-	-	-	-
Rose Hill (cdp)	4,585 81.21	369	268 72.63 72.63 5.85	-	-	-	-	-	-	-	-	-	-	-	-	-	-	-	-	-	-	-	-	-	-	-

Notes: Please refer to the User's Guide for an explanation of data; data is arranged alphabetically by state, then county, then city within each county; table includes counties with populations greater than 49,999 unless noted and cities with populations greater than 9,999 whose Asian and/or NHPI population rates are greater than the national average; (1) Native Hawaiian and other Pacific Islander; (2) excludes Taiwanese; (3) includes Chamorro; (4) county does not meet population threshold but is shown in order to allow inclusion of city

Place	All owner-occupied housing units	Asian-occupied housing units	Asians who own and occupy their own homes	NHPI[1]-occupied housing units	NHPIs[1] who own and occupy their own homes	Asian Indian	Bangladeshi	Cambodian	Chinese[2]	Fijian	Filipino	Guamanian[3]	Hawaiian, Native	Hmong	Indonesian	Japanese	Korean	Laotian	Malaysian	Pakistani	Samoan	Sri Lankan	Taiwanese	Thai	Tongan	Vietnamese
Springfield (cdp)	7,400 70.73	1,576	1,167 74.05 74.05 15.77	-	-	138 57.26 11.83 8.76 1.86	-	-	108 73.47 9.25 6.85 1.46	-	145 71.08 12.43 9.20 1.96	-	-	-	-	-	157 73.36 13.45 9.96 2.12	81 91.01 6.94 5.14 1.09	-	-	-	-	-	-	-	352 83.02 30.16 22.34 4.76
Tysons Corner (cdp)	4,173 47.36	1,205	425 35.27 35.27 10.18	-	-	124 37.80 29.18 10.29 2.97	-	-	81 32.02 19.06 6.72 1.94	-	-	-	-	-	-	-	94 30.72 22.12 7.80 2.25	-	-	-	-	-	-	-	-	-
Vienna (town)	4,606 86.29	304	250 82.24 82.24 5.43	-	-	-	-	-	-	-	-	-	-	-	-	-	-	-	-	-	-	-	-	-	-	-
West Springfield (cdp)	8,501 82.63	1,006	777 77.24 77.24 9.14	-	-	98 91.59 12.61 9.74 1.15	-	-	107 96.40 13.77 10.64 1.26	-	-	-	-	-	-	-	270 68.18 34.75 26.84 3.18	-	-	-	-	-	-	-	-	129 68.62 16.60 12.82 1.52
Wolf Trap (cdp)	4,356 94.88	367	343 93.46 93.46 7.87	-	-	99 93.40 28.86 26.98 2.27	-	-	81 100.00 23.62 22.07 1.86	-	-	-	-	-	-	-	-	-	-	-	-	-	-	-	-	-
Falls Church Independent City	2,704 60.48	279	101 36.20 36.20 3.74	-	-	-	-	-	-	-	-	-	-	-	-	-	-	-	-	-	-	-	-	-	-	-
Fauquier County	15,113 76.17	112	101 90.18 90.18 0.67	-	-	-	-	-	-	-	-	-	-	-	-	-	-	-	-	-	-	-	-	-	-	-
Frederick County	17,754 80.35	129	92 71.32 71.32 0.52	-	-	-	-	-	-	-	-	-	-	-	-	-	-	-	-	-	-	-	-	-	-	-
Hampton Independent City	31,566 58.58	761	404 53.09 53.09 1.28	-	-	-	-	-	-	-	55 37.16 13.61 7.23 0.17	-	-	-	-	-	-	-	-	-	-	-	-	-	-	119 63.30 29.46 15.64 0.38
Hanover County	26,226 84.27	148	123 83.11 83.11 0.47	-	-	-	-	-	-	-	-	-	-	-	-	-	-	-	-	-	-	-	-	-	-	-

Notes: Please refer to the User's Guide for an explanation of data; data is arranged alphabetically by state, then county, then city within each county; table includes counties with populations greater than 49,999 unless noted and cities with populations greater than 9,999 whose Asian and/or NHPI population rates are greater than the national average; (1) Native Hawaiian and other Pacific Islander; (2) excludes Taiwanese; (3) includes Chamorro; (4) county does not meet population threshold but is shown in order to allow inclusion of city

Place	All owner-occupied housing units	Asian-occupied housing units	Asians who own and occupy their own homes	NHPI[1]-occupied housing units	NHPIs[1] who own and occupy their own homes	Asian Indian	Bangladeshi	Cambodian	Chinese[2]	Fijian	Filipino	Guamanian[3]	Hawaiian, Native	Hmong	Indonesian	Japanese	Korean	Laotian	Malaysian	Pakistani	Samoan	Sri Lankan	Taiwanese	Thai	Tongan	Vietnamese
Henrico County	71,089 65.75	3,100	1,566 50.52 50.52 2.20	-	-	356 33.15 22.73 11.48 0.50	-	142 92.21 9.07 4.58 0.20	334 62.66 21.33 10.77 0.47	-	89 39.38 5.68 2.87 0.13	-	-	-	-	-	161 47.08 10.28 5.19 0.23	-	-	-	-	-	-	-	-	293 66.29 18.71 9.45 0.41
Glen Allen (cdp)	4,145 80.31	141	117 82.98 82.98 2.82	-	-	-	-	-	-	-	-	-	-	-	-	-	-	-	-	-	-	-	-	-	-	-
Laurel (cdp)	3,605 58.04	274	128 46.72 46.72 3.55	-	-	-	-	-	-	-	-	-	-	-	-	-	-	-	-	-	-	-	-	-	-	-
Loudoun County	47,588 79.45	2,584	2,014 77.94 77.94 4.23	-	-	418 65.31 20.75 16.18 0.88	-	-	350 86.21 17.38 13.54 0.74	-	347 92.78 17.23 13.43 0.73	-	-	-	-	-	173 70.04 8.59 6.70 0.36	-	-	97 66.44 4.82 3.75 0.20	-	-	-	-	-	411 90.13 20.41 15.91 0.86
Lynchburg Independent City	14,903 58.50	330	102 30.91 30.91 0.68	-	-	-	-	-	-	-	-	-	-	-	-	-	-	-	-	-	-	-	-	-	-	-
Manassas Park Indep. City	2,561 78.70	109	100 91.74 91.74 3.90	-	-	-	-	-	-	-	-	-	-	-	-	-	-	-	-	-	-	-	-	-	-	-
Montgomery County	17,093 55.14	970	104 10.72 10.72 0.61	-	-	29 15.85 27.88 2.99 0.17	-	-	37 13.21 35.58 3.81 0.22	-	-	-	-	-	-	-	24 10.91 23.08 2.47 0.14	-	-	-	-	-	-	-	-	-
Blacksburg (town)	3,941 29.99	855	53 6.20 6.20 1.34	-	-	8 4.94 15.09 0.94 0.20	-	-	14 5.45 26.42 1.64 0.36	-	-	-	-	-	-	-	24 12.37 45.28 2.81 0.61	-	-	-	-	-	-	-	-	-
Newport News Independent City	36,528 52.42	1,300	701 53.92 53.92 1.92	-	-	-	-	-	62 43.06 8.84 4.77 0.17	-	107 46.12 15.26 8.23 0.29	-	-	-	-	-	202 59.06 28.82 15.54 0.55	-	-	-	-	-	-	-	-	87 46.77 12.41 6.69 0.24
Norfolk Independent City	39,271 45.55	2,119	972 45.87 45.87 2.48	-	-	38 31.15 3.91 1.79 0.10	-	-	70 27.34 7.20 3.30 0.18	-	709 58.50 72.94 33.46 1.81	-	-	-	-	-	-	-	-	-	-	-	-	-	-	70 60.87 7.20 3.30 0.18

Notes: Please refer to the User's Guide for an explanation of data; data is arranged alphabetically by state, then county, then city within each county; table includes counties with populations greater than 49,999 unless noted and cities with populations greater than 9,999 whose Asian and/or NHPI population rates are greater than the national average; (1) Native Hawaiian and other Pacific Islander; (2) excludes Taiwanese; (3) includes Chamorro; (4) county does not meet population threshold but is shown in order to allow inclusion of city

Place	All owner-occupied housing units	Asian-occupied housing units	Asians who own and occupy their own homes	NHPI[1]-occupied housing units	NHPIs[1] who own and occupy their own homes	Asian Indian	Bangladeshi	Cambodian	Chinese[2]	Fijian	Filipino	Guamanian[3]	Hawaiian, Native	Hmong	Indonesian	Japanese	Korean	Laotian	Malaysian	Pakistani	Samoan	Sri Lankan	Taiwanese	Thai	Tongan	Vietnamese
Portsmouth Independent City	22,347 58.55	234	165 70.51 70.51 0.74	-	-	-	-	-	-	-	114 72.15 69.09 48.72 0.51	-	-	-	-	-	-	-	-	-	-	-	-	-	-	-
Prince William County	67,798 71.69	2,737	1,890 69.05 69.05 2.79	-	-	301 67.19 15.93 11.00 0.44	-	-	225 70.31 11.90 8.22 0.33	-	421 71.11 22.28 15.38 0.62	-	-	-	-	83 67.48 4.39 3.03 0.12	233 60.05 12.33 8.51 0.34	-	-	147 76.96 7.78 5.37 0.22	-	-	-	-	-	215 75.70 11.38 7.86 0.32
Bull Run (cdp)	1,800 37.84	220	82 37.27 37.27 4.56	-	-	-	-	-	-	-	-	-	-	-	-	-	-	-	-	-	-	-	-	-	-	-
Dale City (cdp)	13,683 77.69	664	547 82.38 82.38 4.00	-	-	82 64.06 14.99 12.35 0.60	-	-	-	-	89 92.71 16.27 13.40 0.65	-	-	-	-	-	-	-	-	70 90.91 12.80 10.54 0.51	-	-	-	-	-	-
Lake Ridge (cdp)	7,990 72.59	287	181 63.07 63.07 2.27	-	-	-	-	-	-	-	-	-	-	-	-	-	-	-	-	-	-	-	-	-	-	-
Woodbridge (cdp)	6,307 59.08	391	251 64.19 64.19 3.98	-	-	-	-	-	-	-	-	-	-	-	-	-	-	-	-	-	-	-	-	-	-	-
Richmond Independent City	39,010 46.14	992	265 26.71 26.71 0.68	-	-	28 14.21 10.57 2.82 0.07	-	-	-	-	68 45.95 25.66 6.85 0.17	-	-	-	-	-	-	-	-	-	-	-	-	-	-	-
Roanoke Independent City	23,632 56.26	333	153 45.95 45.95 0.65	-	-	-	-	-	-	-	-	-	-	-	-	-	-	-	-	-	-	-	-	-	-	-
Roanoke County	26,753 77.13	341	232 68.04 68.04 0.87	-	-	-	-	-	-	-	-	-	-	-	-	-	-	-	-	-	-	-	-	-	-	-
Spotsylvania County	25,736 82.20	308	245 79.55 79.55 0.95	-	-	-	-	-	-	-	-	-	-	-	-	-	-	-	-	-	-	-	-	-	-	-

Notes: Please refer to the User's Guide for an explanation of data; data is arranged alphabetically by state, then county, then city within each county; table includes counties with populations greater than 49,999 unless noted and cities with populations greater than 9,999 whose Asian and/or NHPI population rates are greater than the national average; (1) Native Hawaiian and other Pacific Islander; (2) excludes Taiwanese; (3) includes Chamorro; (4) county does not meet population threshold but is shown in order to allow inclusion of city

Place	All owner-occupied housing units	Asian-occupied housing units	Asians who own and occupy their own homes	NHPI[1]-occupied housing units	NHPIs[1] who own and occupy their own homes	Asian Indian	Bangladeshi	Cambodian	Chinese[2]	Fijian	Filipino	Guamanian[3]	Hawaiian, Native	Hmong	Indonesian	Japanese	Korean	Laotian	Malaysian	Pakistani	Samoan	Sri Lankan	Taiwanese	Thai	Tongan	Vietnamese
Stafford County	24,331 80.60	393	284 72.26 72.26 1.17	-	-	-	-	-	-	-	82 79.61 28.87 20.87 0.34	-	-	-	-	-	-	-	-	-	-	-	-	-	-	-
Suffolk Independent City	16,814 72.22	178	163 91.57 91.57 0.97	-	-	-	-	-	-	-	-	-	-	-	-	-	-	-	-	-	-	-	-	-	-	-
Virginia Beach Independent City	101,265 65.56	5,724	4,169 72.83 72.83 4.12	-	-	209 55.00 5.01 3.65 0.21	-	-	351 83.77 8.42 6.13 0.35	-	2,990 77.00 71.72 52.24 2.95	-	-	-	-	115 57.79 2.76 2.01 0.11	131 55.74 3.14 2.29 0.13	-	-	-	-	-	-	-	-	163 47.80 3.91 2.85 0.16
Williamsburg Independent City	1,602 44.27	67	16 23.88 23.88 1.00	-	-	-	-	-	-	-	-	-	-	-	-	-	-	-	-	-	-	-	-	-	-	-
York County	15,160 75.80	458	292 63.76 63.76 1.93	-	-	64 73.56 21.92 13.97 0.42	-	-	-	-	-	-	-	-	-	-	49 44.14 16.78 10.70 0.32	-	-	-	-	-	-	-	-	-
WASHINGTON	1,466,985 64.59	100,963	57,520 56.97 56.97 3.92	6,140	2,626 42.77 42.77 0.18	3,551 46.68 6.17 3.52 0.24	-	1,573 45.85 2.73 1.56 0.11	13,200 66.56 22.95 13.07 0.90	88 40.37 3.35 1.43 0.01	11,802 63.64 20.52 11.69 0.80	915 54.43 34.84 14.90 0.06	752 46.80 28.64 12.25 0.05	73 32.59 0.13 0.07 <0.01	154 29.90 0.27 0.15 0.01	9,999 63.67 17.38 9.90 0.68	6,780 47.50 11.79 6.72 0.46	1,086 53.79 1.89 1.08 0.07	-	181 43.30 0.31 0.18 0.01	515 31.58 19.61 8.39 0.04	82 52.56 0.14 0.08 0.01	784 66.89 1.36 0.78 0.05	449 41.92 0.78 0.44 0.03	72 39.56 2.74 1.17 <0.01	6,053 47.45 10.52 6.00 0.41
Benton County	36,354 68.77	960	595 61.98 61.98 1.64	-	-	94 57.32 15.80 9.79 0.26	-	-	125 60.39 21.01 13.02 0.34	-	-	-	-	-	-	-	60 65.22 10.08 6.25 0.17	-	-	-	-	-	-	-	-	59 59.00 9.92 6.15 0.16
Richland (city)	10,295 66.29	567	327 57.67 57.67 3.18	-	-	-	-	-	96 58.90 29.36 16.93 0.93	-	-	-	-	-	-	-	-	-	-	-	-	-	-	-	-	-
Chelan County	16,170 64.63	132	76 57.58 57.58 0.47	-	-	-	-	-	-	-	-	-	-	-	-	-	-	-	-	-	-	-	-	-	-	-
Clallam County	19,767 72.77	209	134 64.11 64.11 0.68	-	-	-	-	-	-	-	-	-	-	-	-	-	-	-	-	-	-	-	-	-	-	-

Notes: Please refer to the User's Guide for an explanation of data; data is arranged alphabetically by state, then county, then city within each county; table includes counties with populations greater than 49,999 unless noted and cities with populations greater than 9,999 whose Asian and/or NHPI population rates are greater than the national average; (1) Native Hawaiian and other Pacific Islander; (2) excludes Taiwanese; (3) includes Chamorro; (4) county does not meet population threshold but is shown in order to allow inclusion of city

Place	All owner-occupied housing units	Asian-occupied housing units	Asians who own and occupy their own homes	NHPI[1]-occupied housing units	NHPIs[1] who own and occupy their own homes	Asian Indian	Bangladeshi	Cambodian	Chinese[2]	Fijian	Filipino	Guamanian[3]	Hawaiian, Native	Hmong	Indonesian	Japanese	Korean	Laotian	Malaysian	Pakistani	Samoan	Sri Lankan	Taiwanese	Thai	Tongan	Vietnamese
Clark County	85,551	3,368	2,172	308	100	141	-	69	446	-	423	-	-	-	-	240	270	74	-	-	-	-	-	-	-	387
	67.25		64.49		32.47	58.02		58.47	76.76		73.82					52.17	59.87	66.07								58.02
						6.49		3.18	20.53		19.48					11.05	12.43	3.41								17.82
			64.49		32.47	4.19		2.05	13.24		12.56					7.13	8.02	2.20								11.49
			2.54		0.12	0.16		0.08	0.52		0.49					0.28	0.32	0.09								0.45
Five Corners (cdp)	3,286	113	108	-	-	-	-	-	-	-	-	-	-	-	-	-	-	-	-	-	-	-	-	-	-	-
	80.56		95.58																							
			95.58																							
			3.29																							
Orchards (cdp)	4,349	183	166	-	-	-	-	-	-	-	-	-	-	-	-	-	-	-	-	-	-	-	-	-	-	-
	74.29		90.71																							
			90.71																							
			3.82																							
Vancouver (city)	30,098	2,184	1,168	199	54	-	-	-	297	-	220	-	-	-	-	118	115	-	-	-	-	-	-	-	-	216
	53.14		53.48		27.14				73.51		63.04					39.33	45.28									45.67
									25.43		18.84					10.10	9.85									18.49
			53.48		27.14				13.60		10.07					5.40	5.27									9.89
			3.88		0.18				0.99		0.73					0.39	0.38									0.72
Cowlitz County	24,252	303	128	-	-	-	-	10	-	-	-	-	-	-	-	-	-	-	-	-	-	-	-	-	-	56
	67.65		42.24					14.71																		50.45
								7.81																		43.75
			42.24					3.30																		18.48
			0.53					0.04																		0.23
Grant County	16,805	182	108	-	-	-	-	-	-	-	-	-	-	-	-	-	-	-	-	-	-	-	-	-	-	-
	66.68		59.34																							
			59.34																							
			0.64																							
Grays Harbor County	18,514	195	105	-	-	-	-	-	-	-	-	-	-	-	-	-	-	-	-	-	-	-	-	-	-	-
	69.06		53.85																							
			53.85																							
			0.57																							
Island County	19,488	733	439	-	-	-	-	-	-	-	331	-	-	-	-	44	-	-	-	-	-	-	-	-	-	-
	70.14		59.89								62.93					57.89										
											75.40					10.02										
			59.89								45.16					6.00										
			2.25								1.70					0.23										
Oak Harbor (city)	3,191	452	247	-	-	-	-	-	-	-	220	-	-	-	-	-	-	-	-	-	-	-	-	-	-	-
	43.42		54.65								59.95															
											89.07															
			54.65								48.67															
			7.74								6.89															
King County	425,451	62,109	34,621	2,329	831	2,203	-	695	10,293	68	6,088	126	293	42	96	6,368	2,776	581	-	66	226	-	646	229	60	3,444
	59.85		55.74		35.68	42.71		43.41	67.30	44.44	61.03	41.45	51.49	29.37	25.95	62.57	42.30	48.30		35.68	25.22		67.36	34.54	45.45	45.05
						6.36		2.01	29.73	8.18	17.58	15.16	35.26	0.12	0.28	18.39	8.02	1.68		0.19	27.20		1.87	0.66	7.22	9.95
			55.74		35.68	3.55		1.12	16.57	2.92	9.80	5.41	12.58	0.07	0.15	10.25	4.47	0.94		0.11	9.70		1.04	0.37	2.58	5.55
			8.14		0.20	0.52		0.16	2.42	0.02	1.43	0.03	0.07	0.01	0.02	1.50	0.65	0.14		0.02	0.05		0.15	0.05	0.01	0.81

Notes: Please refer to the User's Guide for an explanation of data; data is arranged alphabetically by state, then county, then city within each county; table includes counties with populations greater than 49,999 unless noted and cities with populations greater than 9,999 whose Asian and/or NHPI population rates are greater than the national average; (1) Native Hawaiian and other Pacific Islander; (2) excludes Taiwanese; (3) includes Chamorro; (4) county does not meet population threshold but is shown in order to allow inclusion of city

Place	All owner-occupied housing units	Asian-occupied housing units	Asians who own and occupy their own homes	NHPI[1]-occupied housing units	NHPIs[1] who own and occupy their own homes	Asian Indian	Bangladeshi	Cambodian	Chinese[2]	Fijian	Filipino	Guamanian[3]	Hawaiian, Native	Hmong	Indonesian	Japanese	Korean	Laotian	Malaysian	Pakistani	Samoan	Sri Lankan	Taiwanese	Thai	Tongan	Vietnamese
Auburn (city)	8,659	534	329	-	-	-	-	-	-	-	-	-	-	-	-	-	-	-	-	-	-	-	-	-	-	-
	53.92		61.61																							
			61.61																							
			3.80																							
Bellevue (city)	28,012	6,847	3,677	-	-	194	-	-	1,484	-	208	-	-	-	-	821	372	62	-	-	-	-	228	-	-	156
	61.31		53.70			17.81			69.97		52.79					64.19	49.40	63.27					83.82			37.96
						5.28			40.36		5.66					22.33	10.12	1.69					6.20			4.24
			53.70			2.83			21.67		3.04					11.99	5.43	0.91					3.33			2.28
			13.13			0.69			5.30		0.74					2.93	1.33	0.22					0.81			0.56
Bothell (city)	8,129	646	470	-	-	-	-	-	124	-	-	-	-	-	-	-	-	-	-	-	-	-	-	-	-	-
	68.02		72.76						70.45																	
									26.38																	
			72.76						19.20																	
			5.78						1.53																	
Bryn Mawr-Skyway (cdp)	3,675	852	712	-	-	-	-	-	-	-	187	-	-	-	-	214	-	-	-	-	-	-	-	-	-	96
	65.85		83.57								80.95					95.11										80.67
											26.26					30.06										13.48
			83.57								21.95					25.12										11.27
			19.37								5.09					5.82										2.61
Burien (city)	7,602	618	347	-	-	-	-	-	-	-	79	-	-	-	-	-	-	-	-	-	-	-	-	-	-	59
	56.58		56.15								58.96															53.15
											22.77															17.00
			56.15								12.78															9.55
			4.56								1.04															0.78
Cascade-Fairwood (cdp)	9,124	1,434	1,053	-	-	-	-	-	235	-	318	-	-	-	-	183	-	-	-	-	-	-	-	-	-	145
	69.96		73.43						85.77		80.71					66.55										81.92
									22.32		30.20					17.38										13.77
			73.43						16.39		22.18					12.76										10.11
			11.54						2.58		3.49					2.01										1.59
Cottage Lake (cdp)	7,128	345	306	-	-	-	-	-	-	-	-	-	-	-	-	-	-	-	-	-	-	-	-	-	-	-
	91.09		88.70																							
			88.70																							
			4.29																							
Des Moines (city)	6,969	724	350	121	10	-	-	-	-	-	78	-	-	-	-	-	-	-	-	-	-	-	-	-	-	58
	61.27		48.34		8.26						56.93															43.61
											22.29															16.57
			48.34		8.26						10.77															8.01
			5.02		0.14						1.12															0.83
East Hill-Meridian (cdp)	7,919	1,096	848	-	-	140	-	-	205	-	154	-	-	-	-	-	-	-	-	-	-	-	-	-	-	90
	80.51		77.37			57.85			96.70		96.25															46.15
						16.51			24.17		18.16															10.61
			77.37			12.77			18.70		14.05															8.21
			10.71			1.77			2.59		1.94															1.14
Federal Way (city)	17,695	3,108	1,733	275	109	-	-	-	213	-	343	-	-	-	-	233	581	-	-	-	37	-	-	-	-	226
	56.23		55.76		39.64				70.53		68.74					78.19	42.88				30.33					68.28
									12.29		19.79					13.44	33.53				33.94					13.04
			55.76		39.64				6.85		11.04					7.50	18.69				13.45					7.27
			9.79		0.62				1.20		1.94					1.32	3.28				0.21					1.28

Notes: Please refer to the User's Guide for an explanation of data; data is arranged alphabetically by state, then county, then city within each county; table includes counties with populations greater than 49,999 unless noted and cities with populations greater than 9,999 whose Asian and/or NHPI population rates are greater than the national average; (1) Native Hawaiian and other Pacific Islander; (2) excludes Taiwanese; (3) includes Chamorro; (4) county does not meet population threshold but is shown in order to allow inclusion of city

Place	All owner-occupied housing units	Asian-occupied housing units	Asians who own and occupy their own homes	NHPI[1]-occupied housing units	NHPIs[1] who own and occupy their own homes	Asian Indian	Bangladeshi	Cambodian	Chinese[2]	Fijian	Filipino	Guamanian[3]	Hawaiian, Native	Hmong	Indonesian	Japanese	Korean	Laotian	Malaysian	Pakistani	Samoan	Sri Lankan	Taiwanese	Thai	Tongan	Vietnamese
Inglewood-Finn Hill (cdp)	6,392 77.48	535	371 69.35 69.35 5.80	-	-	-	-	-	101 82.11 27.22 18.88 1.58	-	-	-	-	-	-	-	-	-	-	-	-	-	-	-	-	-
Issaquah (city)	2,791 58.28	243	180 74.07 74.07 6.45	-	-	-	-	-	-	-	-	-	-	-	-	-	-	-	-	-	-	-	-	-	-	-
Kenmore (city)	5,143 70.93	400	298 74.50 74.50 5.79	-	-	-	-	-	-	-	-	-	-	-	-	-	-	-	-	-	-	-	-	-	-	-
Kent (city)	15,222 48.89	2,336	1,403 60.06 60.06 9.22	-	-	221 51.28 15.75 9.46 1.45	-	-	257 68.90 18.32 11.00 1.69	-	282 61.30 20.10 12.07 1.85	-	-	-	-	161 64.40 11.48 6.89 1.06	153 61.20 10.91 6.55 1.01	-	-	-	-	-	-	-	-	209 55.44 14.90 8.95 1.37
Kingsgate (cdp)	3,322 77.71	444	272 61.26 61.26 8.19	-	-	-	-	-	138 96.50 50.74 31.08 4.15	-	-	-	-	-	-	-	-	-	-	-	-	-	-	-	-	-
Kirkland (city)	11,814 56.74	1,400	638 45.57 45.57 5.40	-	-	-	-	-	188 60.06 29.47 13.43 1.59	-	-	-	-	-	-	124 53.22 19.44 8.86 1.05	-	-	-	-	-	-	-	-	-	75 41.90 11.76 5.36 0.63
Lake Forest Park (city)	4,089 80.49	341	291 85.34 85.34 7.12	-	-	-	-	-	-	-	-	-	-	-	-	-	-	-	-	-	-	-	-	-	-	-
Lakeland North (cdp)	4,311 85.60	240	171 71.25 71.25 3.97	-	-	-	-	-	-	-	-	-	-	-	-	-	-	-	-	-	-	-	-	-	-	-
Lakeland South (cdp)	3,509 83.61	178	178 100.00 100.00 5.07	-	-	-	-	-	-	-	-	-	-	-	-	-	-	-	-	-	-	-	-	-	-	-
Lea Hill (cdp)	2,832 79.08	124	102 82.26 82.26 3.60	-	-	-	-	-	-	-	-	-	-	-	-	-	-	-	-	-	-	-	-	-	-	-

Notes: Please refer to the User's Guide for an explanation of data; data is arranged alphabetically by state, then county, then city within each county; table includes counties with populations greater than 49,999 unless noted and cities with populations greater than 9,999 whose Asian and/or NHPI population rates are greater than the national average; (1) Native Hawaiian and other Pacific Islander; (2) excludes Taiwanese; (3) includes Chamorro; (4) county does not meet population threshold but is shown in order to allow inclusion of city

Place	All owner-occupied housing units	Asian-occupied housing units	Asians who own and occupy their own homes	NHPI[1]-occupied housing units	NHPIs[1] who own and occupy their own homes	Asian Indian	Bangladeshi	Cambodian	Chinese[2]	Fijian	Filipino	Guamanian[3]	Hawaiian, Native	Hmong	Indonesian	Japanese	Korean	Laotian	Malaysian	Pakistani	Samoan	Sri Lankan	Taiwanese	Thai	Tongan	Vietnamese
Mercer Island (city)	6,783 80.40	838	622 74.22 74.22 9.17	-	-	-	-	-	266 81.10 42.77 31.74 3.92	-	-	-	-	-	-	177 81.94 28.46 21.12 2.61	-	-	-	-	-	-	-	-	-	-
Redmond (city)	10,569 55.25	2,300	1,143 49.70 49.70 10.81	-	-	140 23.97 12.25 6.09 1.32	-	-	485 64.75 42.43 21.09 4.59	-	-	-	-	-	-	185 54.09 16.19 8.04 1.75	72 51.43 6.30 3.13 0.68	-	-	-	-	-	-	-	-	-
Renton (city)	10,924 50.37	2,294	1,479 64.47 64.47 13.54	-	-	-	-	-	376 86.84 25.42 16.39 3.44	-	370 79.57 25.02 16.13 3.39	-	-	-	-	204 57.46 13.79 8.89 1.87	-	-	-	-	-	-	-	-	-	316 58.09 21.37 13.78 2.89
Riverton-Boulevard Park (cdp)	2,240 50.33	366	187 51.09 51.09 8.35	-	-	-	-	-	-	-	-	-	-	-	-	-	-	-	-	-	-	-	-	-	-	-
Sammamish (city)	10,025 89.94	740	729 98.51 98.51 7.27	-	-	-	-	-	295 96.41 40.47 39.86 2.94	-	-	-	-	-	-	-	-	-	-	-	-	-	-	-	-	-
SeaTac (city)	5,232 53.99	801	372 46.44 46.44 7.11	148	51 34.46 34.46 0.97	25 13.74 6.72 3.12 0.48	-	-	-	-	91 44.61 24.46 11.36 1.74	-	-	-	-	-	-	-	-	-	-	-	-	-	-	82 82.00 22.04 10.24 1.57
Seattle (city)	125,151 48.41	26,006	12,106 46.55 46.55 9.67	729	210 28.81 28.81 0.17	458 41.71 3.78 1.76 0.37	-	185 29.79 1.53 0.71 0.15	3,915 55.45 32.34 15.05 3.13	-	2,678 54.78 22.12 10.30 2.14	-	-	-	31 17.51 0.26 0.12 0.02	2,548 53.87 21.05 9.80 2.04	430 21.98 3.55 1.65 0.34	268 42.61 2.21 1.03 0.21	-	-	43 16.54 20.48 5.90 0.03	-	126 38.41 1.04 0.48 0.10	127 34.70 1.05 0.49 0.10	-	1,013 30.95 8.37 3.90 0.81
Shoreline (city)	14,120 68.10	2,015	1,248 61.94 61.94 8.84	-	-	105 82.03 8.41 5.21 0.74	-	-	415 87.18 33.25 20.60 2.94	-	218 63.01 17.47 10.82 1.54	-	-	-	-	105 64.42 8.41 5.21 0.74	166 37.39 13.30 8.24 1.18	-	-	-	-	-	-	-	-	92 38.02 7.37 4.57 0.65
Tukwila (city)	3,061 42.51	609	276 45.32 45.32 9.02	77	12 15.58 15.58 0.39	-	-	-	-	-	73 43.71 26.45 11.99 2.38	-	-	-	-	-	-	-	-	-	-	-	-	-	-	-
Union Hill-Novelty Hill (cdp)	3,374 94.17	172	156 90.70 90.70 4.62	-	-	-	-	-	-	-	-	-	-	-	-	-	-	-	-	-	-	-	-	-	-	-

Notes: Please refer to the User's Guide for an explanation of data; data is arranged alphabetically by state, then county, then city within each county; table includes counties with populations greater than 49,999 unless noted and cities with populations greater than 9,999 whose Asian and/or NHPI population rates are greater than the national average; (1) Native Hawaiian and other Pacific Islander; (2) excludes Taiwanese; (3) includes Chamorro; (4) county does not meet population threshold but is shown in order to allow inclusion of city

Place	All owner-occupied housing units	Asian-occupied housing units	Asians who own and occupy their own homes	NHPI[1]-occupied housing units	NHPIs[1] who own and occupy their own homes	Asian Indian	Bangladeshi	Cambodian	Chinese[2]	Fijian	Filipino	Guamanian[3]	Hawaiian, Native	Hmong	Indonesian	Japanese	Korean	Laotian	Malaysian	Pakistani	Samoan	Sri Lankan	Taiwanese	Thai	Tongan	Vietnamese
White Center (cdp)	4,291 57.06	1,103	510 46.24 46.24 11.89	-	-	-	-	87 34.66 17.06 7.89 2.03	-	-	52 52.53 10.20 4.71 1.21	-	-	-	-	-	-	-	-	-	-	-	-	-	-	223 40.33 43.73 20.22 5.20
Kitsap County	58,252 67.41	2,817	1,888 67.02 67.02 3.24	440	214 48.64 48.64 0.37	-	-	-	113 62.78 5.99 4.01 0.19	-	1,281 67.56 67.85 45.47 2.20	148 54.01 69.16 33.64 0.25	-	-	-	271 82.37 14.35 9.62 0.47	81 49.39 4.29 2.88 0.14	-	-	-	-	-	-	-	-	47 40.87 2.49 1.67 0.08
Bremerton (city)	6,127 40.62	655	255 38.93 38.93 4.16	-	-	-	-	-	-	-	193 39.39 75.69 29.47 3.15	-	-	-	-	-	-	-	-	-	-	-	-	-	-	-
Silverdale (cdp)	3,043 51.95	437	344 78.72 78.72 11.30	-	-	-	-	-	-	-	298 79.26 86.63 68.19 9.79	-	-	-	-	-	-	-	-	-	-	-	-	-	-	-
Lewis County	18,791 71.43	64	44 68.75 68.75 0.23	-	-	-	-	-	-	-	-	-	-	-	-	-	-	-	-	-	-	-	-	-	-	-
Pierce County	165,623 63.51	10,613	5,806 54.71 54.71 3.51	1,447	669 46.23 46.23 0.40	123 53.95 2.12 1.16 0.07	-	318 36.10 5.48 3.00 0.19	433 68.19 7.46 4.08 0.26	-	1,182 61.53 20.36 11.14 0.71	309 55.78 46.19 21.35 0.19	121 39.67 18.09 8.36 0.07	-	-	1,156 75.31 19.91 10.89 0.70	1,699 48.96 29.26 16.01 1.03	79 71.82 1.36 0.74 0.05	-	-	148 35.92 22.12 10.23 0.09	-	-	46 57.50 0.79 0.43 0.03	-	512 38.50 8.82 4.82 0.31
Elk Plain (cdp)	4,245 84.82	122	122 100.00 100.00 2.87	-	-	-	-	-	-	-	-	-	-	-	-	-	-	-	-	-	-	-	-	-	-	-
Fort Lewis (cdp)	30 0.86	114	0 <0.01 <0.01 <0.01	66	4 6.06 6.06 13.33	-	-	-	-	-	0 <0.01 *** ** <0.01 <0.01	-	-	-	-	-	-	-	-	-	-	-	-	-	-	-
Lakewood (city)	11,295 47.53	1,847	864 46.78 46.78 7.65	238	100 42.02 42.02 0.89	-	-	-	-	-	193 48.25 22.34 10.45 1.71	-	-	-	-	284 85.80 32.87 15.38 2.51	296 34.70 34.26 16.03 2.62	-	-	-	12 17.39 12.00 5.04 0.11	-	-	-	-	-
Parkland (cdp)	5,102 57.69	467	270 57.82 57.82 5.29	143	55 38.46 38.46 1.08	-	-	-	-	-	-	-	-	-	-	-	128 50.59 47.41 27.41 2.51	-	-	-	-	-	-	-	-	-

Notes: Please refer to the User's Guide for an explanation of data; data is arranged alphabetically by state, then county, then city within each county; table includes counties with populations greater than 49,999 unless noted and cities with populations greater than 9,999 whose Asian and/or NHPI population rates are greater than the national average; (1) Native Hawaiian and other Pacific Islander; (2) excludes Taiwanese; (3) includes Chamorro; (4) county does not meet population threshold but is shown in order to allow inclusion of city

Place	All owner-occupied housing units	Asian-occupied housing units	Asians who own and occupy their own homes	NHPI¹-occupied housing units	NHPIs¹ who own and occupy their own homes	Asian Indian	Bangladeshi	Cambodian	Chinese²	Fijian	Filipino	Guamanian³	Hawaiian, Native	Hmong	Indonesian	Japanese	Korean	Laotian	Malaysian	Pakistani	Samoan	Sri Lankan	Taiwanese	Thai	Tongan	Vietnamese
	5,424	299	234	131	108	-	-	-	-	-	67	-	-	-	-	-	102	-	-	-	-	-	-	-	-	-
	71.55		78.26		82.44						69.79						85.71									
Spanaway (cdp)											28.63						43.59									
			78.26		82.44						22.41						34.11									
			4.31		1.99						1.24						1.88									
	41,727	4,368	2,063	426	180	-	-	231	185	-	408	70	-	-	-	222	531	58	-	-	52	-	-	-	-	261
	54.82		47.23		42.25			33.67	61.06		65.38	48.95				53.49	51.25	68.24			37.96					28.65
Tacoma (city)								11.20	8.97		19.78	38.89				10.76	25.74	2.81			28.89					12.65
			47.23		42.25			5.29	4.24		9.34	16.43				5.08	12.16	1.33			12.21					5.98
			4.94		0.43			0.55	0.44		0.98	0.17				0.53	1.27	0.14			0.12					0.63
	7,054	663	407	-	-	-	-	-	-	-	-	-	-	-	-	-	191	-	-	-	-	-	-	-	-	-
	57.93		61.39														51.48									
University Place (city)																	46.93									
			61.39														28.81									
			5.77														2.71									
	27,087	405	201	-	-	-	-	-	-	-	45	-	-	-	-	-	-	-	-	-	-	-	-	-	-	-
	69.72		49.63								44.55															
Skagit County											22.39															
			49.63								11.11															
			0.74								0.17															
	152,324	10,262	6,627	422	172	493	-	336	1,002	-	1,442	-	84	-	-	655	1,317	120	-	73	-	-	-	-	-	875
	67.74		64.58		40.76	60.49		72.41	71.47		72.54		49.41			68.87	59.27	59.70		52.14						57.87
Snohomish County						7.44		5.07	15.12		21.76		48.84			9.88	19.87	1.81		1.10						13.20
			64.58		40.76	4.80		3.27	9.76		14.05		19.91			6.38	12.83	1.17		0.71						8.53
			4.35		0.11	0.32		0.22	0.66		0.95		0.06			0.43	0.86	0.08		0.05						0.57
	4,484	354	298	-	-	-	-	-	-	-	-	-	-	-	-	-	-	-	-	-	-	-	-	-	-	-
	80.16		84.18																							
Alderwood Manor (cdp)																										
			84.18																							
			6.65																							
	11,563	763	388	-	-	-	-	-	-	-	73	-	-	-	-	-	69	-	-	-	-	-	-	-	-	-
	68.27		50.85								73.74						39.20									
Edmonds (city)											18.81						17.78									
			50.85								9.57						9.04									
			3.36								0.63						0.60									
	16,703	1,800	801	-	-	62	-	55	-	-	314	-	-	-	-	-	-	-	-	-	-	-	-	-	-	139
	45.94		44.50			31.31		35.95			63.82															40.88
Everett (city)						7.74		6.87			39.20															17.35
			44.50			3.44		3.06			17.44															7.72
			4.80			0.37		0.33			1.88															0.83
	6,998	1,403	791	-	-	-	-	-	143	-	172	-	-	-	-	-	185	-	-	-	-	-	-	-	-	129
	52.77		56.38						66.20		73.82						59.11									39.81
Lynnwood (city)									18.08		21.74						23.39									16.31
			56.38						10.19		12.26						13.19									9.19
			11.30						2.04		2.46						2.64									1.84
	3,144	360	243	-	-	-	-	-	-	-	-	-	-	-	-	-	-	-	-	-	-	-	-	-	-	-
	68.33		67.50																							
Martha Lake (cdp)																										
			67.50																							
			7.73																							

Notes: Please refer to the User's Guide for an explanation of data; data is arranged alphabetically by state, then county, then city within each county; table includes counties with populations greater than 49,999 unless noted and cities with populations greater than 9,999 whose Asian and/or NHPI population rates are greater than the national average; (1) Native Hawaiian and other Pacific Islander; (2) excludes Taiwanese; (3) includes Chamorro; (4) county does not meet population threshold but is shown in order to allow inclusion of city

Place	All owner-occupied housing units	Asian-occupied housing units	Asians who own and occupy their own homes	NHPI[1]-occupied housing units	NHPIs[1] who own and occupy their own homes	Asian Indian	Bangladeshi	Cambodian	Chinese[2]	Fijian	Filipino	Guamanian[3]	Hawaiian, Native	Hmong	Indonesian	Japanese	Korean	Laotian	Malaysian	Pakistani	Samoan	Sri Lankan	Taiwanese	Thai	Tongan	Vietnamese
Marysville (city)	5,920 63.03	270	198 73.33 73.33 3.34	-	-	-	-	-	-	-	-	-	-	-	-	-	-	-	-	-	-	-	-	-	-	-
Mill Creek (city)	3,100 66.55	388	266 68.56 68.56 8.58	-	-	-	-	-	-	-	-	-	-	-	-	-	107 74.83 40.23 27.58 3.45	-	-	-	-	-	-	-	-	-
Mountlake Terrace (city)	4,709 59.60	716	406 56.70 56.70 8.62	-	-	-	-	-	-	-	104 73.24 25.62 14.53 2.21	-	-	-	-	-	78 33.77 19.21 10.89 1.66	-	-	-	-	-	-	-	-	-
Mukilteo (city)	4,629 68.47	570	405 71.05 71.05 8.75	-	-	-	-	-	-	-	-	-	-	-	-	-	162 67.50 40.00 28.42 3.50	-	-	-	-	-	-	-	-	-
North Creek (cdp)	6,951 76.02	464	422 90.95 90.95 6.07	-	-	-	-	-	-	-	-	-	-	-	-	-	-	-	-	-	-	-	-	-	-	-
Paine Field-Lk. Stickney (cdp)	4,490 44.99	443	199 44.92 44.92 4.43	-	-	-	-	-	-	-	-	-	-	-	-	-	-	-	-	-	-	-	-	-	-	-
Picnic Pt.-N. Lynnwood (cdp)	5,106 59.18	814	483 59.34 59.34 9.46	-	-	-	-	-	-	-	65 52.85 13.46 7.99 1.27	-	-	-	-	-	140 53.85 28.99 17.20 2.74	-	-	-	-	-	-	-	-	-
Seattle Hill-Silver Firs (cdp)	10,663 91.71	743	704 94.75 94.75 6.60	-	-	-	-	-	-	-	106 92.17 15.06 14.27 0.99	-	-	-	-	-	185 100.00 26.28 24.90 1.73	-	-	-	-	-	-	-	-	149 94.30 21.16 20.05 1.40
Spokane County	107,166 65.50	2,081	1,085 52.14 52.14 1.01	239	104 43.51 43.51 0.10	80 52.98 7.37 3.84 0.07	-	-	128 49.61 11.80 6.15 0.12	-	129 49.43 11.89 6.20 0.12	-	-	28 40.00 2.58 1.35 0.03	-	382 60.16 35.21 18.36 0.36	59 32.96 5.44 2.84 0.06	-	-	-	-	-	-	-	-	228 67.06 21.01 10.96 0.21
Spokane (city)	48,090 58.88	1,240	682 55.00 55.00 1.42	153	66 43.14 43.14 0.14	-	-	-	86 57.72 12.61 6.94 0.18	-	76 63.87 11.14 6.13 0.16	-	-	21 46.67 3.08 1.69 0.04	-	288 67.92 42.23 23.23 0.60	31 28.18 4.55 2.50 0.06	-	-	-	-	-	-	-	-	132 55.93 19.35 10.65 0.27

Notes: Please refer to the User's Guide for an explanation of data; data is arranged alphabetically by state, then county, then city within each county; table includes counties with populations greater than 49,999 unless noted and cities with populations greater than 9,999 whose Asian and/or NHPI population rates are greater than the national average; (1) Native Hawaiian and other Pacific Islander; (2) excludes Taiwanese; (3) includes Chamorro; (4) county does not meet population threshold but is shown in order to allow inclusion of city

Place	All owner-occupied housing units	Asian-occupied housing units	Asians who own and occupy their own homes	NHPI[1]-occupied housing units	NHPIs[1] who own and occupy their own homes	Asian Indian	Bangladeshi	Cambodian	Chinese[2]	Fijian	Filipino	Guamanian[3]	Hawaiian, Native	Hmong	Indonesian	Japanese	Korean	Laotian	Malaysian	Pakistani	Samoan	Sri Lankan	Taiwanese	Thai	Tongan	Vietnamese
Thurston County	54,364 66.60	2,668	1,574 59.00 59.00 2.90	338	230 68.05 68.05 0.42	68 40.48 4.32 2.55 0.13	-	80 42.55 5.08 3.00 0.15	171 62.41 10.86 6.41 0.31	-	365 72.71 23.19 13.68 0.67	167 75.57 72.61 49.41 0.31	-	-	-	181 63.73 11.50 6.78 0.33	278 55.05 17.66 10.42 0.51	-	-	-	-	-	-	-	-	288 53.14 18.30 10.79 0.53
Lacey (city)	6,892 55.71	668	428 64.07 64.07 6.21	-	-	-	-	-	-	-	97 82.20 22.66 14.52 1.41	-	-	-	-	-	75 53.96 17.52 11.23 1.09	-	-	-	-	-	-	-	-	108 61.36 25.23 16.17 1.57
Olympia (city)	9,458 50.63	787	375 47.65 47.65 3.96	-	-	-	-	-	-	-	-	-	-	-	-	-	-	-	-	-	-	-	-	-	-	100 41.32 26.67 12.71 1.06
Tumwater (city)	2,750 48.89	166	56 33.73 33.73 2.04	-	-	-	-	-	-	-	-	-	-	-	-	-	-	-	-	-	-	-	-	-	-	-
Walla Walla County	12,817 65.24	140	83 59.29 59.29 0.65	-	-	-	-	-	-	-	-	-	-	-	-	-	-	-	-	-	-	-	-	-	-	-
Whatcom County	40,871 63.42	1,205	584 48.46 48.46 1.43	-	-	165 53.75 28.25 13.69 0.40	-	-	124 63.92 21.23 10.29 0.30	-	62 62.63 10.62 5.15 0.15	-	-	-	-	64 40.25 10.96 5.31 0.16	20 15.04 3.42 1.66 0.05	-	-	-	-	-	-	-	-	71 37.77 12.16 5.89 0.17
Bellingham (city)	13,377 47.86	772	300 38.86 38.86 2.24	-	-	65 43.33 21.67 8.42 0.49	-	-	-	-	-	-	-	-	-	-	-	-	-	-	-	-	-	-	-	50 35.46 16.67 6.48 0.37
Whitman County[4]	7,300 47.85	735	119 16.19 16.19 1.63	-	-	-	-	-	65 24.81 54.62 8.84 0.89	-	-	-	-	-	-	10 5.21 8.40 1.36 0.14	-	-	-	-	-	-	-	-	-	-
Pullman (city)	2,716 30.74	701	97 13.84 13.84 3.57	-	-	-	-	-	53 21.20 54.64 7.56 1.95	-	-	-	-	-	-	9 4.71 9.28 1.28 0.33	-	-	-	-	-	-	-	-	-	-
Yakima County	47,687 64.45	735	506 68.84 68.84 1.06	-	-	-	-	-	-	-	224 76.98 44.27 30.48 0.47	-	-	-	-	-	-	-	-	-	-	-	-	-	-	-

Notes: Please refer to the User's Guide for an explanation of data; data is arranged alphabetically by state, then county, then city within each county; table includes counties with populations greater than 49,999 unless noted and cities with populations greater than 9,999 whose Asian and/or NHPI population rates are greater than the national average; (1) Native Hawaiian and other Pacific Islander; (2) excludes Taiwanese; (3) includes Chamorro; (4) county does not meet population threshold but is shown in order to allow inclusion of city

Place	All owner-occupied housing units	Asian-occupied housing units	Asians who own and occupy their own homes	NHPI[1]-occupied housing units	NHPIs[1] who own and occupy their own homes	Asian Indian	Bangladeshi	Cambodian	Chinese[2]	Fijian	Filipino	Guamanian[3]	Hawaiian, Native	Hmong	Indonesian	Japanese	Korean	Laotian	Malaysian	Pakistani	Samoan	Sri Lankan	Taiwanese	Thai	Tongan	Vietnamese
WEST VIRGINIA	553,626	3,117	1,523	84	47	517	-	-	202	-	417	-	-	-	-	109	82	-	-	44	-	-	-	-	-	22
	75.17		48.86		55.95	52.54			37.97		73.54					34.06	40.80			44.44						20.18
						33.95			13.26		27.38					7.16	5.38			2.89						1.44
			48.86		55.95	16.59			6.48		13.38					3.50	2.63			1.41						0.71
			0.28		0.01	0.09			0.04		0.08					0.02	0.01			0.01						<0.01
Cabell County	26,596	276	94	-	-	-	-	-	-	-	-	-	-	-	-	-	-	-	-	-	-	-	-	-	-	-
	64.58		34.06																							
			34.06																							
			0.35																							
Harrison County	20,835	109	37	-	-	-	-	-	-	-	-	-	-	-	-	-	-	-	-	-	-	-	-	-	-	-
	74.77		33.94																							
			33.94																							
			0.18																							
Kanawha County	60,616	553	334	-	-	158	-	-	-	-	-	-	-	-	-	-	-	-	-	-	-	-	-	-	-	-
	70.30		60.40			73.49																				
						47.31																				
			60.40			28.57																				
			0.55			0.26																				
Monongalia County	20,402	814	243	-	-	56	-	-	79	-	-	-	-	-	-	-	-	-	-	-	-	-	-	-	-	-
	61.00		29.85			23.63			35.11																	
						23.05			32.51																	
			29.85			6.88			9.71																	
			1.19			0.27			0.39																	
Putnam County	16,817	54	34	-	-	-	-	-	-	-	-	-	-	-	-	-	-	-	-	-	-	-	-	-	-	-
	83.97		62.96																							
			62.96																							
			0.20																							
Raleigh County	24,326	194	137	-	-	-	-	-	-	-	-	-	-	-	-	-	-	-	-	-	-	-	-	-	-	-
	76.51		70.62																							
			70.62																							
			0.56																							
Wood County	26,621	156	93	-	-	-	-	-	-	-	-	-	-	-	-	-	-	-	-	-	-	-	-	-	-	-
	73.39		59.62																							
			59.62																							
			0.35																							
WISCONSIN	1,426,660	21,184	8,757	300	175	1,428	-	42	1,444	-	764	43	61	2,472	40	527	521	482	-	65	-	-	51	78	-	514
	68.44		41.34		58.33	35.03		26.92	43.25		57.53	54.43	62.24	47.12	18.96	44.77	29.40	55.21		19.58			17.59	23.49		43.05
						16.31		0.48	16.49		8.72	24.57	34.86	28.23	0.46	6.02	5.95	5.50		0.74			0.58	0.89		5.87
			41.34		58.33	6.74		0.20	6.82		3.61	14.33	20.33	11.67	0.19	2.49	2.46	2.28		0.31			0.24	0.37		2.43
			0.61		0.01	0.10		<0.01	0.10		0.05	<0.01	<0.01	0.17	<0.01	0.04	0.04	0.03		<0.01			<0.01	0.01		0.04
Brown County	57,134	928	324	-	-	21	-	-	-	-	-	-	-	147	-	-	-	23	-	-	-	-	-	-	-	-
	65.45		34.91			18.92								33.72				32.86								
						6.48								45.37				7.10								
			34.91			2.26								15.84				2.48								
			0.57			0.04								0.26				0.04								

Notes: Please refer to the User's Guide for an explanation of data; data is arranged alphabetically by state, then county, then city within each county; table includes counties with populations greater than 49,999 unless noted and cities with populations greater than 9,999 whose Asian and/or NHPI population rates are greater than the national average; (1) Native Hawaiian and other Pacific Islander; (2) excludes Taiwanese; (3) includes Chamorro; (4) county does not meet population threshold but is shown in order to allow inclusion of city

Place	All owner-occupied housing units	Asian-occupied housing units	Asians who own and occupy their own homes	NHPI[1]-occupied housing units	NHPIs[1] who own and occupy their own homes	Asian Indian	Bangladeshi	Cambodian	Chinese[2]	Fijian	Filipino	Guamanian[3]	Hawaiian, Native	Hmong	Indonesian	Japanese	Korean	Laotian	Malaysian	Pakistani	Samoan	Sri Lankan	Taiwanese	Thai	Tongan	Vietnamese
Chippewa County	16,152 75.63	104	45 43.27 43.27 0.28	-	-	-	-	-	-	-	-	-	-	30 40.54 66.67 28.85 0.19	-	-	-	-	-	-	-	-	-	-	-	-
Columbia County	15,300 74.86	63	31 49.21 49.21 0.20	-	-	-	-	-	-	-	-	-	-	-	-	-	-	-	-	-	-	-	-	-	-	-
Dane County	99,923 57.60	4,989	1,163 23.31 23.31 1.16	-	-	171 19.08 14.70 3.43 0.17	-	-	355 27.67 30.52 7.12 0.36	-	47 34.06 4.04 0.94 0.05	-	-	195 39.63 16.77 3.91 0.20	-	150 41.10 12.90 3.01 0.15	28 4.06 2.41 0.56 0.03	10 10.10 0.86 0.20 0.01	-	-	-	-	21 10.71 1.81 0.42 0.02	-	-	65 27.66 5.59 1.30 0.07
Madison (city)	42,425 47.75	4,200	812 19.33 19.33 1.91	-	-	82 13.00 10.10 1.95 0.19	-	-	275 24.25 33.87 6.55 0.65	-	28 31.82 3.45 0.67 0.07	-	-	146 40.56 17.98 3.48 0.34	-	106 33.76 13.05 2.52 0.25	27 4.14 3.33 0.64 0.06	-	-	-	-	-	21 10.71 2.59 0.50 0.05	-	-	36 17.65 4.43 0.86 0.08
Dodge County	23,077 73.45	68	31 45.59 45.59 0.13	-	-	-	-	-	-	-	-	-	-	-	-	-	-	-	-	-	-	-	-	-	-	-
Eau Claire County	23,271 64.96	421	202 47.98 47.98 0.87	-	-	-	-	-	-	-	-	-	-	126 54.55 62.38 29.93 0.54	-	-	-	-	-	-	-	-	-	-	-	-
Fond du Lac County	26,954 72.98	137	50 36.50 36.50 0.19	-	-	-	-	-	-	-	-	-	-	34 57.63 68.00 24.82 0.13	-	-	-	-	-	-	-	-	-	-	-	-
Jefferson County	20,231 71.73	60	42 70.00 70.00 0.21	-	-	-	-	-	-	-	-	-	-	-	-	-	-	-	-	-	-	-	-	-	-	-
Kenosha County	38,733 69.10	362	194 53.59 53.59 0.50	-	-	-	-	-	-	-	-	-	-	-	-	-	-	-	-	-	-	-	-	-	-	-
La Crosse County	27,076 65.09	550	233 42.36 42.36 0.86	-	-	-	-	-	-	-	-	-	-	152 47.65 65.24 27.64 0.56	-	-	-	-	-	-	-	-	-	-	-	-

Notes: Please refer to the User's Guide for an explanation of data; data is arranged alphabetically by state, then county, then city within each county; table includes counties with populations greater than 49,999 unless noted and cities with populations greater than 9,999 whose Asian and/or NHPI population rates are greater than the national average; (1) Native Hawaiian and other Pacific Islander; (2) excludes Taiwanese; (3) includes Chamorro; (4) county does not meet population threshold but is shown in order to allow inclusion of city

Place	All owner-occupied housing units	Asian-occupied housing units	Asians who own and occupy their own homes	NHPI[1]-occupied housing units	NHPIs[1] who own and occupy their own homes	Asian Indian	Bangladeshi	Cambodian	Chinese[2]	Fijian	Filipino	Guamanian[3]	Hawaiian, Native	Hmong	Indonesian	Japanese	Korean	Laotian	Malaysian	Pakistani	Samoan	Sri Lankan	Taiwanese	Thai	Tongan	Vietnamese
La Crosse (city)	10,668 50.68	408	107 26.23 26.23 1.00	-	-	-	-	-	-	-	-	-	-	69 29.87 64.49 16.91 0.65	-	-	-	-	-	-	-	-	-	-	-	-
Manitowoc County	24,874 76.02	278	168 60.43 60.43 0.68	-	-	-	-	-	-	-	-	-	-	92 55.76 54.76 33.09 0.37	-	-	-	-	-	-	-	-	-	-	-	-
Marathon County	36,109 75.70	835	371 44.43 44.43 1.03	-	-	-	-	-	-	-	-	-	-	252 43.52 67.92 30.18 0.70	-	-	-	-	-	-	-	-	-	-	-	-
Wausau (city)	9,696 61.74	705	273 38.72 38.72 2.82	-	-	-	-	-	-	-	-	-	-	195 38.54 71.43 27.66 2.01	-	-	-	-	-	-	-	-	-	-	-	-
Milwaukee County	198,768 52.62	6,342	2,605 41.08 41.08 1.31	83	26 31.33 31.33 0.01	464 31.27 17.81 7.32 0.23	-	-	321 35.35 12.32 5.06 0.16	-	207 50.00 7.95 3.26 0.10	-	-	747 59.71 28.68 11.78 0.38	-	183 51.84 7.02 2.89 0.09	126 28.77 4.84 1.99 0.06	259 60.51 9.94 4.08 0.13	-	27 17.65 1.04 0.43 0.01	-	-	-	-	-	172 38.39 6.60 2.71 0.09
Outagamie County	43,846 72.44	700	282 40.29 40.29 0.64	-	-	15 19.74 5.32 2.14 0.03	-	-	-	-	-	-	-	132 32.51 46.81 18.86 0.30	-	-	-	-	-	-	-	-	-	-	-	-
Appleton (city)	18,430 68.82	563	233 41.39 41.39 1.26	-	-	-	-	-	-	-	-	-	-	162 40.40 69.53 28.77 0.88	-	-	-	-	-	-	-	-	-	-	-	-
Ozaukee County	23,546 76.31	195	149 76.41 76.41 0.63	-	-	-	-	-	-	-	-	-	-	-	-	-	-	-	-	-	-	-	-	-	-	-
Portage County	17,751 70.89	207	79 38.16 38.16 0.45	-	-	-	-	-	-	-	-	-	-	54 38.85 68.35 26.09 0.30	-	-	-	-	-	-	-	-	-	-	-	-
Stevens Point (city)	4,876 52.46	165	56 33.94 33.94 1.15	-	-	-	-	-	-	-	-	-	-	47 41.59 83.93 28.48 0.96	-	-	-	-	-	-	-	-	-	-	-	-

Notes: Please refer to the User's Guide for an explanation of data; data is arranged alphabetically by state, then county, then city within each county; table includes counties with populations greater than 49,999 unless noted and cities with populations greater than 9,999 whose Asian and/or NHPI population rates are greater than the national average; (1) Native Hawaiian and other Pacific Islander; (2) excludes Taiwanese; (3) includes Chamorro; (4) county does not meet population threshold but is shown in order to allow inclusion of city

Place	All owner-occupied housing units	Asian-occupied housing units	Asians who own and occupy their own homes	NHPI[1]-occupied housing units	NHPIs[1] who own and occupy their own homes	Asian Indian	Bangladeshi	Cambodian	Chinese[2]	Fijian	Filipino	Guamanian[3]	Hawaiian, Native	Hmong	Indonesian	Japanese	Korean	Laotian	Malaysian	Pakistani	Samoan	Sri Lankan	Taiwanese	Thai	Tongan	Vietnamese
Racine County	49,998 70.60	327	173 52.91 52.91 0.35	-	-	-	-	-	-	-	-	-	-	-	-	-	-	-	-	-	-	-	-	-	-	-
Rock County	41,710 71.16	349	206 59.03 59.03 0.49	-	-	-	-	-	-	-	-	-	-	-	-	-	-	-	-	-	-	-	-	-	-	-
St. Croix County	17,885 76.40	72	44 61.11 61.11 0.25	-	-	-	-	-	-	-	-	-	-	-	-	-	-	-	-	-	-	-	-	-	-	-
Sauk County	15,872 73.33	47	12 25.53 25.53 0.08	-	-	-	-	-	-	-	-	-	-	-	-	-	-	-	-	-	-	-	-	-	-	-
Sheboygan County	31,087 71.39	664	338 50.90 50.90 1.09	-	-	-	-	-	-	-	-	-	-	184 48.04 54.44 27.71 0.59	-	-	-	-	-	-	-	-	-	-	-	-
Sheboygan (city)	12,693 60.98	600	295 49.17 49.17 2.32	-	-	-	-	-	-	-	-	-	-	168 46.03 56.95 28.00 1.32	-	-	-	-	-	-	-	-	-	-	-	-
Walworth County	23,852 69.09	189	88 46.56 46.56 0.37	-	-	-	-	-	-	-	-	-	-	-	-	-	-	-	-	-	-	-	-	-	-	-
Washington County	33,310 75.98	107	71 66.36 66.36 0.21	-	-	-	-	-	-	-	-	-	-	-	-	-	-	-	-	-	-	-	-	-	-	-
Waukesha County	103,458 76.51	1,465	913 62.32 62.32 0.88	-	-	307 56.64 33.63 20.96 0.30	-	-	249 73.67 27.27 17.00 0.24	-	103 71.03 11.28 7.03 0.10	-	-	-	-	-	75 83.33 8.21 5.12 0.07	-	-	-	-	-	-	-	-	-
Winnebago County	41,558 67.95	523	298 56.98 56.98 0.72	-	-	-	-	-	-	-	-	-	-	134 52.34 44.97 25.62 0.32	-	-	-	-	-	-	-	-	-	-	-	-

Notes: Please refer to the User's Guide for an explanation of data; data is arranged alphabetically by state, then county, then city within each county; table includes counties with populations greater than 49,999 unless noted and cities with populations greater than 9,999 whose Asian and/or NHPI population rates are greater than the national average; (1) Native Hawaiian and other Pacific Islander; (2) excludes Taiwanese; (3) includes Chamorro; (4) county does not meet population threshold but is shown in order to allow inclusion of city

Place	All owner-occupied housing units	Asian-occupied housing units	Asians who own and occupy their own homes	NHPI[1]-occupied housing units	NHPIs[1] who own and occupy their own homes	Asian Indian	Bangladeshi	Cambodian	Chinese[2]	Fijian	Filipino	Guamanian[3]	Hawaiian, Native	Hmong	Indonesian	Japanese	Korean	Laotian	Malaysian	Pakistani	Samoan	Sri Lankan	Taiwanese	Thai	Tongan	Vietnamese
Wood County	22,380 74.27	193	100 51.81 51.81 0.45	-	-	-	-	-	-	-	-	-	-	39 50.00 39.00 20.21 0.17	-	-	-	-	-	-	-	-	-	-	-	-
WYOMING	135,488 69.98	799	506 63.33 63.33 0.37	-	-	94 64.83 18.58 11.76 0.07	-	-	101 62.35 19.96 12.64 0.07	-	60 65.93 11.86 7.51 0.04	-	-	-	-	138 83.64 27.27 17.27 0.10	36 34.29 7.11 4.51 0.03	-	-	-	-	-	-	-	-	-
Laramie County	22,050 69.06	175	104 59.43 59.43 0.47	-	-	-	-	-	-	-	-	-	-	-	-	-	-	-	-	-	-	-	-	-	-	-
Natrona County	18,757 69.94	107	74 69.16 69.16 0.39	-	-	-	-	-	-	-	-	-	-	-	-	-	-	-	-	-	-	-	-	-	-	-

Notes: Please refer to the User's Guide for an explanation of data; data is arranged alphabetically by state, then county, then city within each county; table includes counties with populations greater than 49,999 unless noted and cities with populations greater than 9,999 whose Asian and/or NHPI population rates are greater than the national average; (1) Native Hawaiian and other Pacific Islander; (2) excludes Taiwanese; (3) includes Chamorro; (4) county does not meet population threshold but is shown in order to allow inclusion of city

Median Gross Rent

(Universe: Specified Renter-Occupied Housing Units Paying Cash Rent)

Place	All specified renter-occupied housing units	Specified housing units rented by Asians	Specified housing units rented by NHPIs[1]	Asian Indian	Bangladeshi	Cambodian	Chinese[2]	Fijian	Filipino	Guamanian[3]	Hawaiian, Native	Hmong	Indonesian	Japanese	Korean	Laotian	Malaysian	Pakistani	Samoan	Sri Lankan	Taiwanese	Thai	Tongan	Vietnamese
UNITED STATES	602	734	690	793	721	582	689	740	730	673	687	517	722	825	796	564	662	763	701	722	763	671	740	653
ALABAMA	447	513	542	570	-	456	418	-	525	518	-	-	-	491	572	512	-	639	-	-	-	507	-	520
Baldwin County	566	444	-	-	-	-	-	-	-	-	-	-	-	-	-	-	-	-	-	-	-	-	-	-
Calhoun County	413	416	-	-	-	-	-	-	-	-	-	-	-	-	-	-	-	-	-	-	-	-	-	-
Etowah County	395	415	-	-	-	-	-	-	-	-	-	-	-	-	-	-	-	-	-	-	-	-	-	-
Houston County	413	573	-	-	-	-	-	-	-	-	-	-	-	-	-	-	-	-	-	-	-	-	-	-
Jefferson County	500	556	-	663	-	-	467	-	-	-	-	-	-	-	652	-	-	-	-	-	-	-	-	565
Lee County	449	331	-	-	-	-	279	-	-	-	-	-	-	-	-	-	-	-	-	-	-	-	-	-
Madison County	503	553	-	580	-	-	535	-	-	-	-	-	-	-	578	-	-	-	-	-	-	-	-	678
Mobile County	476	497	-	571	-	460	446	-	569	-	-	-	-	-	-	377	-	-	-	-	-	-	-	500
Montgomery County	526	569	-	-	-	-	-	-	-	-	-	-	-	-	-	-	-	-	-	-	-	-	-	-
Morgan County	429	1,069	-	-	-	-	-	-	-	-	-	-	-	-	-	-	-	-	-	-	-	-	-	-
Shelby County	635	637	-	641	-	-	-	-	-	-	-	-	-	-	-	-	-	-	-	-	-	-	-	-
Tuscaloosa County	487	377	-	-	-	-	-	-	-	-	-	-	-	-	-	-	-	-	-	-	-	-	-	-
ALASKA	720	664	729	718	-	-	703	-	683	-	733	698	-	695	618	635	-	-	783	-	-	711	814	808
Anchorage Borough	736	643	727	648	-	-	690	-	657	-	-	698	-	680	607	642	-	-	803	-	-	708	-	648
Fairbanks North Star Borough	679	646	-	-	-	-	620	-	717	-	-	-	-	-	634	-	-	-	-	-	-	-	-	-
Juneau City and Borough	863	737	-	-	-	-	-	-	743	-	-	-	-	-	-	-	-	-	-	-	-	-	-	-
Matanuska-Susitna Borough	700	725	-	-	-	-	-	-	-	-	-	-	-	-	-	-	-	-	-	-	-	-	-	-
ARIZONA	619	638	590	684	-	632	611	-	628	635	546	-	568	647	697	569	-	813	575	-	719	598	712	540
Cochise County	470	453	-	-	-	-	-	-	485	-	-	-	-	-	479	-	-	-	-	-	-	-	-	-
Coconino County	629	582	-	-	-	-	-	-	-	-	-	-	-	-	-	-	-	-	-	-	-	-	-	-
Maricopa County	666	694	626	712	-	665	708	-	679	707	643	-	657	703	750	614	-	744	594	-	707	620	712	558
Chandler (city)	795	815	-	810	-	-	784	-	820	-	-	-	-	-	-	-	-	-	-	-	-	-	-	914
Gilbert (town)	792	848	-	1,125	-	-	0	-	0	-	-	-	-	-	-	-	-	-	-	-	-	-	-	-
Mesa (city)	669	666	548	607	-	-	647	-	659	-	-	-	-	735	705	-	-	-	-	-	-	-	-	1,031
Phoenix (city)	622	681	611	721	-	614	610	-	701	-	608	-	-	724	799	-	-	-	-	-	-	-	-	526
Tempe (city)	715	673	-	687	-	-	679	-	693	-	-	-	-	667	701	-	-	-	-	-	-	-	-	638
Mohave County	559	519	-	-	-	-	-	-	-	-	-	-	-	-	-	-	-	-	-	-	-	-	-	-
Pima County	544	498	476	574	-	-	462	-	507	-	475	-	-	489	496	-	-	-	-	-	-	-	-	484
Tucson (city)	516	480	468	551	-	-	455	-	493	-	-	-	-	451	479	-	-	-	-	-	-	-	-	484
Pinal County	509	521	-	-	-	-	-	-	-	-	-	-	-	-	-	-	-	-	-	-	-	-	-	-
Yavapai County	600	544	-	-	-	-	-	-	-	-	-	-	-	-	-	-	-	-	-	-	-	-	-	-
Yuma County	508	660	-	-	-	-	-	-	520	-	-	-	-	-	-	-	-	-	-	-	-	-	-	-
ARKANSAS	453	491	471	565	-	-	476	-	529	-	486	-	-	429	548	459	-	-	-	-	-	411	-	395
Benton County	528	538	-	558	-	-	-	-	-	-	-	-	-	-	-	-	-	-	-	-	-	-	-	325
Craighead County	454	447	-	-	-	-	-	-	-	-	-	-	-	-	-	-	-	-	-	-	-	-	-	-
Crawford County	405	341	-	-	-	-	-	-	-	-	-	-	-	-	-	-	-	-	-	-	-	-	-	-

Notes: Please refer to the User's Guide for an explanation of data; data is arranged alphabetically by state, then county, then city within each county; table includes counties with populations greater than 49,999 unless noted and cities with populations greater than 9,999 whose Asian and/or NHPI population rates are greater than the national average; (1) Native Hawaiian and other Pacific Islander; (2) excludes Taiwanese; (3) includes Chamorro; (4) county does not meet population threshold but is shown in order to allow inclusion of city

Place	All specified renter-occupied housing units	Specified housing units rented by Asians	Specified housing units rented by NHPIs[1]	Asian Indian	Bangladeshi	Cambodian	Chinese[2]	Fijian	Filipino	Guamanian[3]	Hawaiian, Native	Hmong	Indonesian	Japanese	Korean	Laotian	Malaysian	Pakistani	Samoan	Sri Lankan	Taiwanese	Thai	Tongan	Vietnamese
Faulkner County	499	485	-	-	-	-	-	-	-	-	-	-	-	-	-	-	-	-	-	-	-	-	-	-
Jefferson County	463	519	-	-	-	-	-	-	-	-	-	-	-	-	-	-	-	-	-	-	-	-	-	-
Pulaski County	539	565	-	555	-	-	583	-	539	-	-	-	-	-	-	-	-	-	-	-	-	-	-	-
Saline County	525	1,076	-	-	-	-	-	-	-	-	-	-	-	-	-	-	-	-	-	-	-	-	-	-
Sebastian County	428	365	-	-	-	-	-	-	-	-	-	-	-	-	-	458	-	-	-	-	-	-	-	285
Fort Smith (city)	424	355	-	-	-	-	-	-	-	-	-	-	-	-	-	458	-	-	-	-	-	-	-	285
Washington County	490	424	486	-	-	-	393	-	-	-	-	-	-	-	-	457	-	-	-	-	-	-	-	-
Springdale (city)	505	487	489	-	-	-	-	-	-	-	-	-	-	-	-	478	-	-	-	-	-	-	-	-
CALIFORNIA	747	809	799	1,051	788	601	779	771	773	786	824	532	839	885	840	574	984	878	788	818	931	764	832	792
Alameda County	852	887	910	1,133	-	620	747	943	910	898	886	-	1,058	915	901	652	-	1,180	953	-	945	929	892	730
Alameda (city)	899	856	814	1,038	-	-	847	-	816	-	-	-	-	867	999	-	-	-	-	-	-	-	-	834
Albany (city)	947	856	-	939	-	-	867	-	-	-	-	-	-	794	693	-	-	-	-	-	-	-	-	-
Ashland (cdp)	800	829	-	-	-	-	845	-	867	-	-	-	-	-	-	-	-	-	-	-	-	-	-	-
Berkeley (city)	740	749	-	919	-	-	769	-	710	-	-	-	-	734	740	-	-	-	-	-	777	-	-	719
Castro Valley (cdp)	954	1,009	-	1,010	-	-	825	-	1,058	-	-	-	-	1,107	1,038	-	-	-	-	-	-	-	-	-
Cherryland (cdp)	836	824	-	-	-	-	-	-	775	-	-	-	-	-	-	-	-	-	-	-	-	-	-	-
Dublin (city)	1,356	1,259	-	1,199	-	-	1,361	-	1,121	-	-	-	-	-	-	-	-	-	-	-	-	-	-	-
Fremont (city)	1,196	1,185	937	1,196	-	-	1,119	-	1,173	-	-	-	-	1,492	1,293	-	-	1,211	-	-	1,318	-	-	1,089
Hayward (city)	921	956	928	1,032	-	-	964	956	919	-	-	-	-	1,130	995	-	-	-	1,069	-	-	-	-	926
Livermore (city)	1,035	907	-	894	-	-	968	-	988	-	-	-	-	-	-	-	-	-	-	-	-	-	-	371
Newark (city)	1,093	1,031	-	1,280	-	-	631	-	1,018	-	-	-	-	-	1,282	-	-	-	-	-	-	-	-	894
Oakland (city)	696	610	859	772	-	619	533	-	696	-	-	-	-	749	566	631	-	-	-	-	-	-	943	572
Piedmont (city)	1,814	942	-	-	-	-	1,375	-	-	-	-	-	-	-	-	-	-	-	-	-	-	-	-	-
Pleasanton (city)	1,219	1,270	-	1,234	-	-	1,217	-	1,277	-	-	-	-	1,125	1,318	-	-	-	-	-	-	-	-	-
San Leandro (city)	873	909	887	932	-	-	829	-	901	-	-	-	-	948	938	-	-	-	-	-	-	-	-	902
San Lorenzo (cdp)	953	816	-	-	-	-	696	-	1,045	-	-	-	-	-	-	-	-	-	-	-	-	-	-	796
Union City (city)	1,094	1,122	1,086	1,173	-	-	927	-	1,112	-	-	-	-	1,009	1,016	-	-	-	-	-	-	-	-	1,144
Butte County	563	516	-	578	-	-	626	-	575	-	-	502	-	476	-	459	-	-	-	-	-	-	-	-
Chico (city)	594	547	-	-	-	-	649	-	-	-	-	520	-	-	-	-	-	-	-	-	-	-	-	-
Oroville (city)	445	463	-	-	-	-	-	-	-	-	-	469	-	-	-	-	-	-	-	-	-	-	-	-
Contra Costa County	898	906	967	1,006	-	-	981	850	872	1,304	1,115	-	900	940	1,070	638	-	1,160	825	-	1,009	933	900	811
Alamo (cdp)	1,449	548	-	-	-	-	-	-	-	-	-	-	-	-	-	-	-	-	-	-	-	-	-	-
Antioch (city)	786	767	720	725	-	-	1,109	-	843	-	-	-	-	-	-	-	-	-	-	-	-	-	-	457
Bay Point (cdp)	721	396	-	-	-	-	-	-	530	-	-	-	-	-	-	-	-	-	-	-	-	-	-	-
Blackhawk-Camino-Tass. (cdp)	2,001	0	-	-	-	-	0	-	-	-	-	-	-	-	-	-	-	-	-	-	-	-	-	-
Clayton (city)	1,516	0	-	-	-	-	-	-	-	-	-	-	-	-	-	-	-	-	-	-	-	-	-	-
Concord (city)	880	836	1,150	929	-	-	864	-	811	-	-	-	-	832	739	-	-	-	-	-	-	-	-	715
Danville (town)	1,604	1,506	-	2,001	-	-	1,938	-	996	-	-	-	-	-	-	-	-	-	-	-	-	-	-	-
El Cerrito (city)	907	859	-	834	-	-	838	-	644	-	-	-	-	909	-	-	-	-	-	-	-	-	-	-
El Sobrante (cdp)	802	872	-	870	-	-	-	-	-	-	-	-	-	-	-	-	-	-	-	-	-	-	-	-
Hercules (city)	1,111	1,122	-	1,281	-	-	1,078	-	1,075	-	-	-	-	-	-	-	-	-	-	-	-	-	-	-

Notes: Please refer to the User's Guide for an explanation of data; data is arranged alphabetically by state, then county, then city within each county; table includes counties with populations greater than 49,999 unless noted and cities with populations greater than 9,999 whose Asian and/or NHPI population rates are greater than the national average; (1) Native Hawaiian and other Pacific Islander; (2) excludes Taiwanese; (3) includes Chamorro; (4) county does not meet population threshold but is shown in order to allow inclusion of city

Place	All specified renter-occupied housing units	Specified housing units rented by Asians	Specified housing units rented by NHPIs[1]	Asian Indian	Bangladeshi	Cambodian	Chinese[2]	Fijian	Filipino	Guamanian[3]	Hawaiian, Native	Hmong	Indonesian	Japanese	Korean	Laotian	Malaysian	Pakistani	Samoan	Sri Lankan	Taiwanese	Thai	Tongan	Vietnamese
Lafayette (city)	1,076	1,288	-	-	-	-	1,520	-	-	-	-	-	-	-	-	-	-	-	-	-	-	-	-	-
Martinez (city)	870	837	-	-	-	-	900	-	853	-	-	-	-	-	-	-	-	-	-	-	-	-	-	-
Moraga (town)	1,112	1,010	-	-	-	-	1,097	-	-	-	-	-	-	-	-	-	-	-	-	-	-	-	-	-
Orinda (city)	1,239	1,172	-	-	-	-	294	-	-	-	-	-	-	-	-	-	-	-	-	-	-	-	-	-
Pinole (city)	855	898	-	-	-	-	948	-	946	-	-	-	-	-	-	-	-	-	-	-	-	-	-	-
Pittsburg (city)	880	982	1,219	1,039	-	-	1,080	-	984	-	-	-	-	-	-	-	-	-	-	-	-	-	-	-
Pleasant Hill (city)	984	975	-	-	-	-	1,086	-	866	-	-	-	-	-	1,016	-	-	-	-	-	-	-	-	-
Richmond (city)	764	878	807	988	-	-	957	-	807	-	-	-	-	1,113	1,035	585	-	-	-	-	-	-	-	771
San Pablo (city)	687	702	-	699	-	-	-	-	714	-	-	-	-	-	-	666	-	-	-	-	-	-	-	850
San Ramon (city)	1,388	1,293	-	1,201	-	-	1,201	-	1,363	-	-	-	-	1,438	-	-	-	-	-	-	-	-	-	-
Walnut Creek (city)	1,024	962	-	964	-	-	926	-	958	-	-	-	-	1,017	1,049	-	-	-	-	-	-	-	-	-
El Dorado County	702	668	-	-	-	-	-	-	600	-	-	-	-	739	-	-	-	-	-	-	-	-	-	-
El Dorado Hills (cdp)	1,255	1,125	-	-	-	-	-	-	-	-	-	-	-	-	-	-	-	-	-	-	-	-	-	-
South Lake Tahoe (city)	642	645	-	-	-	-	-	-	590	-	-	-	-	-	-	-	-	-	-	-	-	-	-	-
Fresno County	534	498	829	572	-	457	551	-	526	-	-	494	-	512	548	442	-	-	-	-	-	-	-	528
Clovis (city)	580	541	-	-	-	-	-	-	613	-	-	569	-	444	-	-	-	-	-	-	-	-	-	-
Fresno (city)	538	492	-	609	-	449	549	-	520	-	-	485	-	525	584	438	-	-	-	-	-	-	-	532
Reedley (city)	526	612	-	-	-	-	-	-	-	-	-	-	-	-	-	-	-	-	-	-	-	-	-	-
Humboldt County	537	478	-	-	-	-	-	-	-	-	-	-	-	437	-	-	-	-	-	-	-	-	-	-
Imperial County	504	758	-	-	-	-	555	-	546	-	-	-	-	-	801	-	-	-	-	-	-	-	-	-
Kern County	518	556	489	694	-	556	622	-	517	-	-	-	-	513	683	-	-	-	-	-	-	-	-	545
Bakersfield (city)	564	588	568	721	-	-	605	-	537	-	-	-	-	552	688	-	-	-	-	-	-	-	-	675
Delano (city)	467	507	-	-	-	-	-	-	505	-	-	-	-	-	-	-	-	-	-	-	-	-	-	-
Ridgecrest (city)	500	575	-	-	-	-	-	-	593	-	-	-	-	-	-	-	-	-	-	-	-	-	-	-
Kings County	533	507	-	-	-	-	-	-	478	-	-	-	-	-	-	-	-	-	-	-	-	-	-	-
Lemoore (city)	541	477	-	-	-	-	-	-	455	-	-	-	-	-	-	-	-	-	-	-	-	-	-	-
Lake County	567	633	-	-	-	-	-	-	-	-	-	-	-	-	-	-	-	-	-	-	-	-	-	-
Los Angeles County	704	746	726	826	674	620	729	711	711	742	703	675	831	798	777	660	1,068	835	726	785	899	724	626	719
Agoura Hills (city)	1,215	1,203	-	-	-	-	-	-	-	-	-	-	-	-	-	-	-	-	-	-	-	-	-	-
Alhambra (city)	721	731	-	672	-	-	724	-	735	-	-	-	-	808	819	-	-	-	-	-	729	-	-	722
Altadena (cdp)	752	688	-	-	-	-	-	-	683	-	-	-	-	546	-	-	-	-	-	-	-	-	-	-
Arcadia (city)	830	907	-	1,021	-	-	861	-	726	-	-	-	-	1,444	987	-	-	-	-	-	1,250	-	-	-
Artesia (city)	795	781	-	725	-	-	851	-	747	-	-	-	-	-	811	-	-	-	-	-	-	-	-	-
Avocado Heights (cdp)	803	1,056	-	-	-	-	-	-	-	-	-	-	-	-	-	-	-	-	-	-	-	-	-	-
Azusa (city)	743	805	-	-	-	-	-	-	736	-	-	-	-	-	-	-	-	-	-	-	-	-	-	-
Baldwin Park (city)	724	778	-	-	-	-	765	-	778	-	-	-	-	-	-	-	-	-	-	-	-	-	-	807
Bellflower (city)	704	700	-	-	-	768	-	-	676	-	-	-	-	-	739	-	-	-	-	-	-	679	-	-
Beverly Hills (city)	1,171	1,316	-	-	-	-	991	-	-	-	-	-	-	-	1,354	-	-	-	-	-	-	-	-	-
Burbank (city)	778	876	-	884	-	-	870	-	812	-	-	-	-	797	996	-	-	-	-	-	-	-	-	849
Calabasas (city)	1,233	1,102	-	-	-	-	1,625	-	-	-	-	-	-	-	-	-	-	-	-	-	-	-	-	-
Carson (city)	754	737	738	-	-	-	836	-	746	-	-	-	-	588	-	-	-	-	728	-	-	-	-	620

Notes: Please refer to the User's Guide for an explanation of data; data is arranged alphabetically by state, then county, then city within each county; table includes counties with populations greater than 49,999 unless noted and cities with populations greater than 9,999 whose Asian and/or NHPI population rates are greater than the national average; (1) Native Hawaiian and other Pacific Islander; (2) excludes Taiwanese; (3) includes Chamorro; (4) county does not meet population threshold but is shown in order to allow inclusion of city

Place	All specified renter-occupied housing units	Specified housing units rented by Asians	Specified housing units rented by NHPIs[1]	Asian Indian	Bangladeshi	Cambodian	Chinese[2]	Fijian	Filipino	Guamanian[3]	Hawaiian, Native	Hmong	Indonesian	Japanese	Korean	Laotian	Malaysian	Pakistani	Samoan	Sri Lankan	Taiwanese	Thai	Tongan	Vietnamese
Cerritos (city)	1,260	1,270	-	983	-	-	1,255	-	1,202	-	-	-	-	957	1,301	-	-	-	-	-	1,354	679	-	1,340
Citrus (cdp)	924	907	-	-	-	-	-	-	-	-	-	-	-	-	-	-	-	-	-	-	-	-	-	-
Claremont (city)	771	835	-	896	-	-	870	-	-	-	-	-	-	-	1,007	-	-	-	-	-	-	-	-	-
Compton (city)	597	1,010	363	-	-	-	-	-	-	-	-	-	-	-	-	-	-	-	354	-	-	-	-	-
Covina (city)	742	841	-	-	-	-	802	-	877	-	-	-	-	778	-	-	-	-	-	-	-	-	-	825
Culver City (city)	887	869	-	1,022	-	-	756	-	854	-	-	-	-	812	-	-	-	-	-	-	-	-	-	-
Diamond Bar (city)	1,012	1,068	-	1,183	-	-	1,007	-	1,071	-	-	-	-	1,000	1,144	-	-	-	-	-	916	-	-	675
Downey (city)	731	768	-	738	-	-	768	-	721	-	-	-	-	698	934	-	-	-	-	-	-	-	-	681
Duarte (city)	791	746	-	-	-	-	779	-	646	-	-	-	-	-	-	-	-	-	-	-	-	-	-	-
East San Gabriel (cdp)	718	688	-	-	-	-	643	-	-	-	-	-	-	1,563	-	-	-	-	-	-	694	-	-	-
El Monte (city)	672	718	-	-	-	-	670	-	642	-	-	-	-	-	-	-	-	-	-	-	398	-	-	775
El Segundo (city)	882	876	-	-	-	-	-	-	-	-	-	-	-	-	-	-	-	-	-	-	-	-	-	-
Gardena (city)	710	716	-	-	-	-	634	-	734	-	-	-	-	706	736	-	-	-	-	-	-	-	-	709
Glendale (city)	758	843	-	850	-	-	779	-	759	-	-	-	-	778	936	-	-	-	-	-	-	675	-	768
Glendora (city)	822	937	-	650	-	-	850	-	1,017	-	-	-	-	-	-	-	-	-	-	-	-	-	-	-
Hacienda Heights (cdp)	946	885	-	-	-	-	791	-	776	-	-	-	-	986	1,011	-	-	-	-	-	995	-	-	914
Hawaiian Gardens (city)	718	661	-	-	-	-	-	-	-	-	-	-	-	-	670	-	-	-	-	-	-	-	-	-
Hawthorne (city)	636	642	613	671	-	-	592	-	651	-	-	-	-	645	-	-	-	-	-	-	-	-	-	718
Hermosa Beach (city)	1,146	1,057	-	-	-	-	-	-	-	-	-	-	-	-	-	-	-	-	-	-	-	-	-	-
La Canada Flintridge (city)	1,148	1,865	-	-	-	-	2,001	-	-	-	-	-	-	2,001	1,846	-	-	-	-	-	-	-	-	-
La Crescenta-Montrose (cdp)	789	896	-	-	-	-	-	-	868	-	-	-	-	-	988	-	-	-	-	-	-	-	-	-
La Mirada (city)	870	736	-	840	-	-	1,125	-	828	-	-	-	-	888	649	-	-	-	-	-	-	-	-	-
La Puente (city)	678	501	-	-	-	-	920	-	394	-	-	-	-	-	-	-	-	-	-	-	-	-	-	-
La Verne (city)	856	844	-	-	-	-	-	-	772	-	-	-	-	-	-	-	-	-	-	-	-	-	-	-
Lakewood (city)	886	864	1,013	867	-	727	884	-	866	-	-	-	-	807	916	-	-	-	1,011	-	-	-	-	666
Lancaster (city)	643	626	-	663	-	-	616	-	616	-	-	-	-	-	-	-	-	-	-	-	-	-	-	-
Lawndale (city)	783	773	882	-	-	-	-	-	773	-	-	-	-	-	-	-	-	-	-	-	-	-	-	924
Lomita (city)	784	766	-	-	-	-	-	-	788	-	-	-	-	713	1,058	-	-	-	-	-	-	-	-	-
Long Beach (city)	639	634	648	838	-	593	713	-	650	-	-	-	-	762	604	560	-	-	651	-	-	683	-	595
Los Angeles (city)	672	691	747	785	652	644	642	-	663	744	674	-	801	730	700	678	-	853	789	666	894	683	603	668
Manhattan Beach (city)	1,358	1,108	-	-	-	-	925	-	-	-	-	-	-	1,321	-	-	-	-	-	-	-	-	-	-
Monrovia (city)	746	696	-	-	-	-	536	-	681	-	-	-	-	-	-	-	-	-	-	-	-	-	-	-
Montebello (city)	698	772	-	-	-	-	383	-	816	-	-	-	-	725	798	-	-	-	-	-	-	-	-	-
Monterey Park (city)	722	717	-	-	-	731	712	-	691	-	-	-	-	735	786	-	-	-	-	-	773	-	-	703
Norwalk (city)	767	787	-	939	-	600	760	-	686	-	-	-	-	1,033	831	-	-	-	-	-	-	-	-	796
Palmdale (city)	630	652	-	0	-	-	-	-	636	-	-	-	-	-	-	-	-	-	-	-	-	-	-	-
Palos Verdes Estates (city)	1,351	1,761	-	-	-	-	1,375	-	-	-	-	-	-	1,986	1,409	-	-	-	-	-	-	-	-	-
Pasadena (city)	746	782	-	879	-	-	767	-	710	-	-	-	-	863	801	-	-	-	-	-	-	-	-	659
Pomona (city)	644	682	-	446	-	629	621	-	923	-	-	-	-	597	-	575	-	-	-	-	-	-	-	648
Rancho Palos Verdes (city)	1,496	1,713	-	1,203	-	-	1,482	-	1,438	-	-	-	-	2,001	1,449	-	-	-	-	-	1,625	-	-	-
Redondo Beach (city)	995	1,028	-	1,101	-	-	1,093	-	994	-	-	-	-	1,125	923	-	-	-	-	-	-	-	-	-

Notes: Please refer to the User's Guide for an explanation of data; data is arranged alphabetically by state, then county, then city within each county; table includes counties with populations greater than 49,999 unless noted and cities with populations greater than 9,999 whose Asian and/or NHPI population rates are greater than the national average; (1) Native Hawaiian and other Pacific Islander; (2) excludes Taiwanese; (3) includes Chamorro; (4) county does not meet population threshold but is shown in order to allow inclusion of city

Place	All specified renter-occupied housing units	Specified housing units rented by Asians	Specified housing units rented by NHPIs[1]	Asian Indian	Bangladeshi	Cambodian	Chinese[2]	Fijian	Filipino	Guamanian[3]	Hawaiian, Native	Hmong	Indonesian	Japanese	Korean	Laotian	Malaysian	Pakistani	Samoan	Sri Lankan	Taiwanese	Thai	Tongan	Vietnamese
Rosemead (city)	722	735	-	-	-	633	733	-	808	-	-	-	-	643	-	-	-	-	-	-	-	-	-	761
Rowland Heights (cdp)	855	881	-	771	-	-	859	-	750	-	-	-	-	1,156	905	-	-	-	-	-	929	-	-	1,017
San Dimas (city)	876	912	-	-	-	-	908	-	1,006	-	-	-	-	-	-	-	-	-	-	-	-	-	-	-
San Gabriel (city)	759	780	-	-	-	-	776	-	826	-	-	-	-	831	-	-	-	-	-	-	960	-	-	745
San Marino (city)	2,001	1,875	-	-	-	-	1,554	-	-	-	-	-	-	-	-	-	-	-	-	-	1,516	-	-	-
Santa Clarita (city)	943	923	-	1,025	-	-	1,000	-	794	-	-	-	-	965	829	-	-	-	-	-	-	-	-	0
Santa Monica (city)	792	888	-	1,081	-	-	868	-	702	-	-	-	-	913	910	-	-	-	-	-	-	-	-	-
Sierra Madre (city)	836	792	-	-	-	-	-	-	-	-	-	-	-	-	-	-	-	-	-	-	-	-	-	-
South El Monte (city)	684	811	-	-	-	-	755	-	-	-	-	-	-	-	-	-	-	-	-	-	-	-	-	888
South Pasadena (city)	833	817	-	-	-	-	753	-	-	-	-	-	-	743	932	-	-	-	-	-	-	-	-	-
South San Jose Hills (cdp)	874	1,125	-	-	-	-	-	-	1,125	-	-	-	-	-	-	-	-	-	-	-	-	-	-	-
Temple City (city)	800	863	-	-	-	-	859	-	1,077	-	-	-	-	789	982	-	-	-	-	-	746	-	-	788
Torrance (city)	903	936	-	904	-	-	898	-	842	-	-	-	-	1,014	962	-	-	872	-	-	1,000	-	-	878
Valinda (cdp)	839	861	-	-	-	-	-	-	825	-	-	-	-	-	-	-	-	-	-	-	-	-	-	1,038
Vincent (cdp)	987	880	-	-	-	-	-	-	868	-	-	-	-	-	-	-	-	-	-	-	-	-	-	-
Walnut (city)	1,223	1,299	-	1,850	-	-	1,156	-	1,319	-	-	-	-	1,375	1,258	-	-	-	-	-	990	-	-	1,125
West Carson (cdp)	872	907	-	-	-	-	-	-	912	-	-	-	-	913	897	-	-	-	-	-	-	-	-	-
West Covina (city)	828	822	597	812	-	-	789	-	829	-	-	-	-	445	865	-	-	-	-	-	794	-	-	971
West Hollywood (city)	773	827	-	-	-	-	-	-	-	-	-	-	-	-	-	-	-	-	-	-	-	-	-	-
West Puente Valley (cdp)	816	339	-	-	-	-	-	-	260	-	-	-	-	-	-	-	-	-	-	-	-	-	-	925
Whittier (city)	723	707	-	-	-	-	539	-	646	-	-	-	-	875	721	-	-	-	-	-	-	-	-	-
Madera County	562	620	-	606	-	-	-	-	627	-	-	-	-	-	-	-	-	-	-	-	-	-	-	-
Marin County	1,162	1,125	-	1,191	-	-	1,179	-	1,155	-	-	-	-	1,191	890	-	-	-	-	-	-	-	-	945
Larkspur (city)	1,321	1,488	-	-	-	-	-	-	-	-	-	-	-	-	-	-	-	-	-	-	-	-	-	-
Novato (city)	1,146	1,010	-	-	-	-	1,125	-	1,070	-	-	-	-	-	-	-	-	-	-	-	-	-	-	-
San Rafael (city)	1,040	1,158	-	1,208	-	-	1,260	-	-	-	-	-	-	-	-	-	-	-	-	-	-	-	-	1,025
Tamalpais-Homestead (cdp)	1,387	1,196	-	-	-	-	-	-	-	-	-	-	-	-	-	-	-	-	-	-	-	-	-	-
Mendocino County	600	639	-	-	-	-	-	-	-	-	-	-	-	-	-	-	-	-	-	-	-	-	-	-
Merced County	518	516	-	537	-	-	570	-	555	-	-	511	-	194	-	476	-	-	-	-	-	-	-	-
Atwater (city)	521	539	-	-	-	-	-	-	-	-	-	558	-	-	-	-	-	-	-	-	-	-	-	-
Livingston (city)	538	499	-	499	-	-	-	-	-	-	-	-	-	-	-	-	-	-	-	-	-	-	-	-
Merced (city)	509	485	-	-	-	-	-	-	-	-	-	472	-	-	-	482	-	-	-	-	-	-	-	-
Monterey County	776	775	779	915	-	-	796	-	770	785	-	-	-	782	774	-	-	-	-	-	-	-	-	703
Marina (city)	778	758	730	-	-	-	-	-	778	-	-	-	-	678	740	-	-	-	-	-	-	-	-	739
Monterey (city)	888	860	-	-	-	-	850	-	886	-	-	-	-	834	-	-	-	-	-	-	-	-	-	-
Pacific Grove (city)	962	781	-	-	-	-	-	-	-	-	-	-	-	-	-	-	-	-	-	-	-	-	-	-
Salinas (city)	725	763	734	950	-	-	680	-	767	-	-	-	-	696	692	-	-	-	-	-	-	-	-	729
Seaside (city)	810	731	-	-	-	-	-	-	743	-	-	-	-	913	-	-	-	-	-	-	-	-	-	581
Napa County	818	867	-	-	-	-	845	-	743	-	-	-	-	2,001	-	-	-	-	-	-	-	-	-	-
Nevada County	746	919	-	-	-	-	-	-	-	-	-	-	-	-	-	-	-	-	-	-	-	-	-	-
Orange County	923	903	916	929	-	851	950	-	898	873	1,016	929	935	1,111	949	788	-	870	948	908	1,052	850	730	847

Notes: Please refer to the User's Guide for an explanation of data; data is arranged alphabetically by state, then county, then city within each county; table includes counties with populations greater than 49,999 unless noted and cities with populations greater than 9,999 whose Asian and/or NHPI population rates are greater than the national average; (1) Native Hawaiian and other Pacific Islander; (2) excludes Taiwanese; (3) includes Chamorro; (4) county does not meet population threshold but is shown in order to allow inclusion of city

Place	All specified renter-occupied housing units	Specified housing units rented by Asians	Specified housing units rented by NHPIs[1]	Asian Indian	Bangladeshi	Cambodian	Chinese[2]	Fijian	Filipino	Guamanian[3]	Hawaiian, Native	Hmong	Indonesian	Japanese	Korean	Laotian	Malaysian	Pakistani	Samoan	Sri Lankan	Taiwanese	Thai	Tongan	Vietnamese
Aliso Viejo (cdp)	1,268	1,227	-	1,300	-	-	1,150	-	1,224	-	-	-	-	1,329	1,234	-	-	-	-	-	-	-	-	1,192
Anaheim (city)	818	843	844	867	-	-	850	-	820	-	-	-	-	866	844	757	-	833	806	-	747	736	-	829
Brea (city)	935	913	-	906	-	-	0	-	923	-	-	-	-	-	1,097	-	-	-	-	-	-	-	-	-
Buena Park (city)	841	871	-	782	-	-	834	-	838	-	-	-	-	910	914	-	-	-	-	-	-	-	-	783
Costa Mesa (city)	956	963	950	1,025	-	-	973	-	955	-	-	-	-	1,059	1,025	-	-	-	-	-	-	-	-	886
Cypress (city)	922	915	-	852	-	-	763	-	900	-	-	-	-	841	982	-	-	-	-	-	881	-	-	794
Foothill Ranch (cdp)	1,208	1,375	-	-	-	-	-	-	-	-	-	-	-	-	-	-	-	-	-	-	-	-	-	-
Fountain Valley (city)	1,058	1,031	-	1,029	-	-	1,057	-	1,054	-	-	-	-	1,277	1,066	-	-	-	-	-	1,279	-	-	1,010
Fullerton (city)	820	800	-	732	-	-	738	-	807	-	-	-	-	848	1,041	-	-	-	-	-	-	-	-	780
Garden Grove (city)	827	820	1,036	896	-	693	753	-	846	-	-	-	-	809	851	-	-	-	1,029	-	-	-	-	814
Huntington Beach (city)	985	965	927	992	-	-	1,076	-	964	-	-	-	-	1,016	867	-	-	-	-	-	1,680	-	-	950
Irvine (city)	1,272	1,285	-	1,293	-	-	1,192	-	1,163	-	-	-	-	1,477	1,260	-	-	-	-	-	1,300	-	-	1,228
La Habra (city)	787	868	-	-	-	-	875	-	890	-	-	-	-	-	922	-	-	-	-	-	-	-	-	-
La Palma (city)	955	951	-	959	-	-	956	-	941	-	-	-	-	1,125	949	-	-	-	-	-	-	-	-	-
Laguna Hills (city)	1,184	1,123	-	-	-	-	928	-	1,250	-	-	-	-	-	-	-	-	-	-	-	-	-	-	850
Laguna Niguel (city)	1,205	1,226	-	-	-	-	1,219	-	1,220	-	-	-	-	1,216	1,313	-	-	-	-	-	-	-	-	1,188
Lake Forest (city)	1,085	1,005	-	1,081	-	-	963	-	989	-	-	-	-	973	979	-	-	-	-	-	-	-	-	976
Los Alamitos (city)	883	902	-	-	-	-	-	-	-	-	-	-	-	-	-	-	-	-	-	-	-	-	-	-
Mission Viejo (city)	1,145	983	-	875	-	-	625	-	1,095	-	-	-	-	1,264	1,205	-	-	-	-	-	-	-	-	444
Newport Beach (city)	1,257	1,265	-	-	-	-	1,340	-	-	-	-	-	-	1,518	-	-	-	-	-	-	-	-	-	-
Orange (city)	884	839	-	952	-	-	919	-	816	-	-	-	-	815	385	-	-	-	-	-	0	-	-	864
Placentia (city)	890	862	-	1,110	-	-	714	-	844	-	-	-	-	841	1,047	-	-	-	-	-	-	-	-	741
Rancho Santa Margarita (city)	1,110	1,095	-	-	-	-	1,047	-	1,075	-	-	-	-	-	-	-	-	-	-	-	-	-	-	0
Rossmoor (cdp)	1,194	1,896	-	-	-	-	-	-	-	-	-	-	-	-	-	-	-	-	-	-	-	-	-	-
Santa Ana (city)	815	868	953	868	-	716	902	-	848	-	-	1,022	-	884	661	948	-	-	926	-	-	-	-	886
Seal Beach (city)	1,036	1,082	-	-	-	-	-	-	-	-	-	-	-	1,000	-	-	-	-	-	-	-	-	-	-
Stanton (city)	793	799	-	-	-	-	-	-	760	-	-	-	-	-	861	-	-	-	-	-	-	-	-	805
Tustin (city)	925	917	-	864	-	-	902	-	926	-	-	-	-	970	1,131	-	-	-	-	-	798	-	-	888
Tustin Foothills (cdp)	1,197	498	-	-	-	-	0	-	-	-	-	-	-	-	-	-	-	-	-	-	-	-	-	-
Westminster (city)	842	838	837	862	-	-	847	-	909	-	-	-	-	850	848	-	-	-	850	-	-	-	-	831
Yorba Linda (city)	1,191	1,153	-	1,203	-	-	1,047	-	907	-	-	-	-	1,344	1,138	-	-	-	-	-	-	-	-	1,109
Placer County	780	865	-	758	-	-	880	-	775	-	-	-	-	1,132	1,057	-	-	-	-	-	-	-	-	747
Rocklin (city)	900	906	-	-	-	-	-	-	-	-	-	-	-	1,039	-	-	-	-	-	-	-	-	-	-
Roseville (city)	809	903	-	798	-	-	965	-	926	-	-	-	-	1,477	-	-	-	-	-	-	-	-	-	-
Riverside County	660	725	695	699	-	657	722	-	733	689	642	538	-	672	807	582	-	764	679	-	663	691	-	679
Banning (city)	564	643	-	-	-	-	-	-	-	-	-	-	-	-	-	525	-	-	-	-	-	-	-	-
Corona (city)	812	927	-	934	-	-	867	-	1,018	-	-	-	-	582	1,063	-	-	-	-	-	-	-	-	907
Moreno Valley (city)	743	775	-	-	-	-	563	-	808	-	-	-	-	175	844	669	-	-	-	-	-	-	-	1,035
Palm Springs (city)	631	587	-	-	-	-	-	-	578	-	-	-	-	-	-	-	-	-	-	-	-	-	-	-
Pedley (cdp)	958	1,125	-	-	-	-	-	-	-	-	-	-	-	-	-	-	-	-	-	-	-	-	-	-
Riverside (city)	670	691	721	621	-	-	706	-	696	-	-	-	-	658	792	454	-	-	-	-	-	-	-	667

Notes: Please refer to the User's Guide for an explanation of data; data is arranged alphabetically by state, then county, then city within each county; table includes counties with populations greater than 49,999 unless noted and cities with populations greater than 9,999 whose Asian and/or NHPI population rates are greater than the national average; (1) Native Hawaiian and other Pacific Islander; (2) excludes Taiwanese; (3) includes Chamorro; (4) county does not meet population threshold but is shown in order to allow inclusion of city

Place	All specified renter-occupied housing units	Specified housing units rented by Asians	Specified housing units rented by NHPIs[1]	Asian Indian	Bangladeshi	Cambodian	Chinese[2]	Fijian	Filipino	Guamanian[3]	Hawaiian, Native	Hmong	Indonesian	Japanese	Korean	Laotian	Malaysian	Pakistani	Samoan	Sri Lankan	Taiwanese	Thai	Tongan	Vietnamese
Temecula (city)	846	758	-	-	-	-	750	-	692	-	-	-	-	-	-	-	-	-	-	-	-	-	-	-
Sacramento County	659	622	604	696	-	538	543	598	666	659	633	567	-	678	651	571	-	701	589	-	622	521	703	574
Arden-Arcade (cdp)	606	569	-	652	-	-	518	-	603	-	-	576	-	592	-	-	-	-	-	-	-	-	-	544
Elk Grove (cdp)	800	735	-	850	-	-	915	-	681	-	-	-	-	739	-	-	-	-	-	-	-	-	-	728
Fair Oaks (cdp)	710	810	-	-	-	-	-	-	-	-	-	-	-	-	-	-	-	-	-	-	-	-	-	-
Florin (cdp)	630	572	-	637	-	-	497	-	696	-	-	613	-	-	-	-	-	-	-	-	-	-	-	550
Folsom (city)	939	964	-	992	-	-	1,036	-	1,000	-	-	-	-	-	-	-	-	-	-	-	-	-	-	-
Foothill Farms (cdp)	651	759	-	-	-	-	-	-	-	-	-	-	-	-	-	-	-	-	-	-	-	-	-	-
La Riviera (cdp)	723	670	-	-	-	-	-	-	-	-	-	-	-	-	-	-	-	-	-	-	-	-	-	-
Laguna (cdp)	1,009	947	-	1,125	-	-	919	-	698	-	-	-	-	992	-	-	-	-	-	-	-	-	-	867
North Highlands (cdp)	633	567	-	-	-	-	-	-	497	-	-	-	-	-	-	-	-	-	-	-	-	-	-	511
Parkway-S. Sacramento (cdp)	565	517	-	-	-	-	476	-	-	-	-	540	-	-	-	523	-	-	-	-	-	-	-	489
Rancho Cordova (cdp)	659	655	-	735	-	-	486	-	664	-	-	-	-	-	613	-	-	-	-	-	-	-	-	574
Rosemont (cdp)	736	695	-	-	-	-	-	-	712	-	-	-	-	-	672	-	-	-	-	-	-	-	-	421
Sacramento (city)	625	592	589	646	-	615	502	596	659	-	-	574	-	667	607	569	-	625	588	-	-	-	797	551
Vineyard (cdp)	991	985	-	-	-	-	-	-	1,125	-	-	-	-	-	-	-	-	-	-	-	-	-	-	-
San Benito County	765	1,014	-	-	-	-	-	-	1,375	-	-	-	-	-	-	-	-	-	-	-	-	-	-	-
San Bernardino County	648	692	623	725	-	554	748	-	689	584	525	-	688	694	751	633	-	481	624	-	867	757	657	625
Chino (city)	769	765	-	-	-	-	-	-	819	-	-	-	-	-	-	-	-	-	-	-	-	-	-	419
Chino Hills (city)	1,035	1,061	-	900	-	-	938	-	1,103	-	-	-	-	1,167	1,163	-	-	-	-	-	930	-	-	0
Colton (city)	618	676	-	-	-	-	-	-	695	-	-	-	-	-	-	-	-	-	-	-	-	-	-	-
Fontana (city)	636	672	175	759	-	-	-	-	660	-	-	-	-	-	-	-	-	-	-	-	-	-	-	-
Grand Terrace (city)	777	768	-	-	-	-	-	-	-	-	-	-	-	-	-	-	-	-	-	-	-	-	-	-
Highland (city)	574	595	-	-	-	-	-	-	583	-	-	-	-	-	-	-	-	-	-	-	-	-	-	604
Loma Linda (city)	660	623	-	755	-	-	593	-	667	-	-	-	616	-	654	-	-	-	-	-	-	-	-	-
Montclair (city)	671	648	-	-	-	-	-	-	-	-	-	-	-	-	-	-	-	-	-	-	-	-	-	632
Ontario (city)	720	790	699	864	-	-	738	-	705	-	-	-	-	-	-	-	-	-	-	-	-	-	-	944
Rancho Cucamonga (city)	872	898	-	934	-	-	850	-	982	-	-	-	-	978	920	-	-	-	-	-	-	-	-	663
Redlands (city)	689	695	-	713	-	-	733	-	621	-	-	-	-	-	894	-	-	-	-	-	-	-	-	-
Rialto (city)	631	813	1,096	-	-	-	-	-	1,125	-	-	-	-	-	-	-	-	-	-	-	-	-	-	-
San Bernardino (city)	563	626	538	653	-	450	761	-	496	-	-	-	763	-	627	-	-	-	534	-	-	-	-	538
Upland (city)	710	709	-	701	-	-	684	-	738	-	-	-	-	-	837	-	-	-	-	-	953	-	-	623
Victorville (city)	584	583	-	-	-	-	-	-	560	-	-	-	-	-	-	-	-	-	-	-	-	-	-	-
San Diego County	761	763	801	956	-	574	850	-	722	775	851	903	886	880	910	661	-	985	854	-	804	724	788	687
Bonita (cdp)	942	873	-	-	-	-	-	-	850	-	-	-	-	-	-	-	-	-	-	-	-	-	-	-
Carlsbad (city)	989	960	-	-	-	-	1,042	-	1,026	-	-	-	-	663	-	-	-	-	-	-	-	-	-	-
Chula Vista (city)	707	798	760	-	-	-	696	-	722	447	-	-	-	1,037	996	-	-	-	-	-	-	-	-	-
Coronado (city)	1,024	1,000	-	-	-	-	-	-	892	-	-	-	-	-	-	-	-	-	-	-	-	-	-	-
Escondido (city)	746	710	-	-	-	-	578	-	653	-	-	-	-	-	-	729	-	-	-	-	-	-	-	861
Imperial Beach (city)	690	637	-	-	-	-	-	-	635	-	-	-	-	-	-	-	-	-	-	-	-	-	-	-
La Mesa (city)	759	736	-	-	-	-	-	-	691	-	-	-	-	-	-	-	-	-	-	-	-	-	-	-

Notes: Please refer to the User's Guide for an explanation of data; data is arranged alphabetically by state, then county, then city within each county; table includes counties with populations greater than 49,999 unless noted and cities with populations greater than 9,999 whose Asian and/or NHPI population rates are greater than the national average; (1) Native Hawaiian and other Pacific Islander; (2) excludes Taiwanese; (3) includes Chamorro; (4) county does not meet population threshold but is shown in order to allow inclusion of city

Place	All specified renter-occupied housing units	Specified housing units rented by Asians	Specified housing units rented by NHPIs[1]	Asian Indian	Bangladeshi	Cambodian	Chinese[2]	Fijian	Filipino	Guamanian[3]	Hawaiian, Native	Hmong	Indonesian	Japanese	Korean	Laotian	Malaysian	Pakistani	Samoan	Sri Lankan	Taiwanese	Thai	Tongan	Vietnamese
La Presa (cdp)	729	673	-	-	-	-	-	-	672	-	-	-	-	-	-	-	-	-	-	-	-	-	-	-
Lemon Grove (city)	710	722	-	-	-	-	-	-	764	-	-	-	-	-	-	-	-	-	-	-	-	-	-	800
National City (city)	573	580	-	-	-	-	-	-	580	-	-	-	-	-	-	-	-	-	-	-	-	-	-	-
Oceanside (city)	818	814	906	-	-	-	843	-	764	-	-	-	-	813	-	-	-	-	922	-	-	-	-	842
Poway (city)	910	853	-	-	-	-	777	-	807	-	-	-	-	-	-	-	-	-	-	-	-	-	-	-
Rancho San Diego (cdp)	977	943	-	-	-	-	-	-	850	-	-	-	-	-	-	-	-	-	-	-	-	-	-	-
San Diego (city)	763	788	817	985	-	571	863	-	785	817	801	846	-	916	934	649	-	-	905	-	832	723	-	674
San Marcos (city)	797	769	-	-	-	-	729	-	960	-	-	-	-	-	-	-	-	-	-	-	-	-	-	-
Solana Beach (city)	1,112	1,042	-	-	-	-	-	-	-	-	-	-	-	-	-	-	-	-	-	-	-	-	-	-
Spring Valley (cdp)	792	793	-	-	-	-	-	-	796	-	-	-	-	-	-	-	-	-	-	-	-	-	-	-
Vista (city)	788	842	857	-	-	-	-	-	843	-	-	-	-	761	-	-	-	-	-	-	-	-	-	-
San Francisco County	928	747	612	1,164	-	740	651	-	777	-	-	-	1,299	918	978	-	-	1,338	401	-	1,076	859	-	747
San Francisco (city)	928	747	612	1,164	-	740	651	-	777	-	-	-	1,299	918	978	-	-	1,338	401	-	1,076	859	-	747
San Joaquin County	617	569	679	634	-	525	553	-	582	-	756	541	-	572	639	546	-	555	725	-	-	-	-	679
Lathrop (city)	742	665	-	-	-	-	-	-	670	-	-	-	-	-	-	-	-	-	-	-	-	-	-	-
Lodi (city)	621	613	-	802	-	-	-	-	616	-	-	-	-	613	-	-	-	-	-	-	-	-	-	-
Stockton (city)	581	554	671	624	-	523	536	-	558	-	-	538	-	532	-	543	-	542	-	-	-	-	-	692
Tracy (city)	807	697	-	673	-	-	850	-	621	-	-	-	-	-	-	-	-	-	-	-	-	-	-	-
San Luis Obispo County	719	682	-	832	-	-	739	-	661	-	-	-	-	670	703	-	-	-	-	-	-	-	-	-
Baywood-Los Osos (cdp)	819	639	-	-	-	-	-	-	623	-	-	-	-	-	-	-	-	-	-	-	-	-	-	-
Grover Beach (city)	747	669	-	-	-	-	-	-	-	-	-	-	-	-	-	-	-	-	-	-	-	-	-	-
San Luis Obispo (city)	724	688	-	-	-	-	713	-	706	-	-	-	-	-	-	-	-	-	-	-	-	-	-	-
San Mateo County	1,144	1,188	1,127	1,254	-	-	1,216	957	1,097	1,549	1,298	-	1,055	1,411	1,240	-	-	-	1,182	-	1,083	1,179	1,091	1,129
Belmont (city)	1,116	1,146	-	1,167	-	-	1,065	-	1,069	-	-	-	-	1,625	-	-	-	-	-	-	-	-	-	-
Burlingame (city)	1,108	1,169	-	-	-	-	1,203	-	1,045	-	-	-	-	1,430	-	-	-	-	-	-	-	-	-	-
Daly City (city)	1,074	1,089	1,273	1,134	-	-	1,137	-	1,059	-	-	-	-	1,163	1,156	-	-	-	-	-	-	-	-	1,107
East Palo Alto (city)	854	747	971	-	-	-	-	-	-	-	-	-	-	-	-	-	-	-	-	-	-	-	1,015	-
Foster City (city)	1,620	1,515	-	1,447	-	-	1,524	-	1,460	-	-	-	-	2,001	1,491	-	-	-	-	-	-	-	-	-
Hillsborough (town)	2,001	2,001	-	-	-	-	2,001	-	-	-	-	-	-	-	-	-	-	-	-	-	-	-	-	-
Menlo Park (city)	1,319	1,493	-	-	-	-	1,319	-	-	-	-	-	-	1,813	-	-	-	-	-	-	-	-	-	-
Millbrae (city)	1,161	1,279	-	1,750	-	-	1,297	-	1,118	-	-	-	-	1,734	1,168	-	-	-	-	-	-	-	-	-
Pacifica (city)	1,261	1,308	-	-	-	-	1,250	-	1,310	-	-	-	-	1,348	-	-	-	-	-	-	-	-	-	-
Redwood City (city)	1,105	1,167	844	1,238	-	-	1,308	-	926	-	-	-	-	950	-	-	-	-	-	-	-	-	-	-
San Bruno (city)	1,162	1,165	1,159	1,195	-	-	1,152	-	1,171	-	-	-	-	1,104	-	-	-	-	-	-	-	-	1,305	-
San Carlos (city)	1,181	1,259	-	-	-	-	1,313	-	-	-	-	-	-	-	-	-	-	-	-	-	-	-	-	-
San Mateo (city)	1,168	1,172	1,219	1,208	-	-	1,097	-	1,076	-	-	-	-	1,356	1,297	-	-	-	-	-	-	-	1,057	1,147
South San Francisco (city)	1,057	1,148	1,352	1,050	-	-	1,283	-	1,157	-	-	-	-	1,117	-	-	-	-	-	-	-	-	-	-
Santa Barbara County	830	806	718	819	-	-	883	-	707	-	-	598	-	865	960	-	-	-	-	-	-	-	-	756
Goleta (cdp)	989	924	-	-	-	-	1,068	-	726	-	-	-	-	1,213	-	-	-	-	-	-	-	-	-	1,039
Isla Vista (cdp)	842	736	-	-	-	-	726	-	-	-	-	-	-	-	796	-	-	-	-	-	-	-	-	-
Lompoc (city)	639	615	-	-	-	-	-	-	541	-	-	-	-	-	-	-	-	-	-	-	-	-	-	-

Notes: Please refer to the User's Guide for an explanation of data; data is arranged alphabetically by state, then county, then city within each county; table includes counties with populations greater than 49,999 unless noted and cities with populations greater than 9,999 whose Asian and/or NHPI population rates are greater than the national average; (1) Native Hawaiian and other Pacific Islander; (2) excludes Taiwanese; (3) includes Chamorro; (4) county does not meet population threshold but is shown in order to allow inclusion of city

Place	All specified renter-occupied housing units	Specified housing units rented by Asians	Specified housing units rented by NHPIs[1]	Asian Indian	Bangladeshi	Cambodian	Chinese[2]	Fijian	Filipino	Guamanian[3]	Hawaiian, Native	Hmong	Indonesian	Japanese	Korean	Laotian	Malaysian	Pakistani	Samoan	Sri Lankan	Taiwanese	Thai	Tongan	Vietnamese
Orcutt (cdp)	868	889	-	-	-	-	-	-	-	-	-	-	-	-	-	-	-	-	-	-	-	-	-	-
Santa Maria (city)	675	684	-	-	-	-	-	-	668	-	-	-	-	648	-	-	-	-	-	-	-	-	-	-
Santa Clara County	1,185	1,217	1,281	1,341	1,258	1,039	1,171	1,128	1,129	1,288	1,371	-	1,243	1,521	1,281	1,232	-	1,395	1,302	-	1,310	1,238	-	1,008
Alum Rock (cdp)	1,100	1,087	-	-	-	-	-	-	-	-	-	-	-	-	-	-	-	-	-	-	-	-	-	741
Campbell (city)	1,154	1,120	-	1,192	-	-	1,077	-	1,163	-	-	-	-	1,233	1,038	-	-	-	-	-	-	-	-	934
Cupertino (city)	1,693	1,706	-	1,641	-	-	1,582	-	1,833	-	-	-	-	2,001	1,735	-	-	-	-	-	1,368	-	-	1,592
Gilroy (city)	936	960	-	-	-	-	711	-	983	-	-	-	-	-	-	-	-	-	-	-	-	-	-	-
Los Altos (city)	1,727	1,645	-	1,471	-	-	1,652	-	-	-	-	-	-	2,001	-	-	-	-	-	-	-	-	-	-
Los Gatos (town)	1,331	1,236	-	-	-	-	1,342	-	-	-	-	-	-	1,766	-	-	-	-	-	-	-	-	-	-
Milpitas (city)	1,279	1,241	1,646	1,280	-	-	1,248	-	1,189	-	-	-	-	1,708	1,262	-	-	-	-	-	-	-	-	1,169
Morgan Hill (city)	1,112	1,271	-	-	-	-	1,400	-	-	-	-	-	-	1,641	-	-	-	-	-	-	-	-	-	-
Mountain View (city)	1,222	1,238	-	1,317	-	-	1,226	-	1,067	-	-	-	-	1,345	1,134	-	-	-	-	-	-	-	-	985
Palo Alto (city)	1,349	1,320	-	1,384	-	-	1,215	-	947	-	-	-	-	1,454	1,548	-	-	-	-	-	-	-	-	-
San Jose (city)	1,123	1,119	1,246	1,268	-	1,012	1,104	-	1,127	1,256	1,574	-	-	1,278	1,189	1,232	-	1,313	1,253	-	1,295	1,631	-	989
Santa Clara (city)	1,238	1,273	1,317	1,351	-	-	1,207	-	1,131	-	-	-	-	1,399	1,345	-	-	1,588	-	-	-	-	-	1,003
Saratoga (city)	1,689	2,001	-	2,001	-	-	597	-	-	-	-	-	-	2,001	359	-	-	-	-	-	1,625	-	-	-
Stanford (cdp)	842	881	-	871	-	-	912	-	-	-	-	-	-	-	860	-	-	-	-	-	-	-	-	-
Sunnyvale (city)	1,270	1,299	1,028	1,374	-	-	1,161	-	1,120	-	-	-	-	1,764	1,300	-	-	-	-	-	1,395	-	-	1,101
Santa Cruz County	924	1,012	-	1,053	-	-	912	-	793	-	-	-	-	1,149	1,088	-	-	-	-	-	-	-	-	1,229
Capitola (city)	973	1,162	-	-	-	-	-	-	-	-	-	-	-	-	-	-	-	-	-	-	-	-	-	-
Santa Cruz (city)	941	981	-	992	-	-	904	-	733	-	-	-	-	1,153	-	-	-	-	-	-	-	-	-	-
Scotts Valley (city)	1,177	1,361	-	-	-	-	-	-	-	-	-	-	-	-	-	-	-	-	-	-	-	-	-	-
Shasta County	563	550	-	-	-	-	-	-	731	-	-	-	-	-	-	441	-	-	-	-	-	-	-	-
Solano County	797	771	887	876	-	-	855	-	751	808	933	684	-	680	789	597	-	-	939	-	-	-	-	764
Benicia (city)	892	925	-	-	-	-	978	-	906	-	-	-	-	-	-	-	-	-	-	-	-	-	-	-
Fairfield (city)	778	750	794	1,091	-	-	775	-	745	732	-	-	-	802	525	600	-	-	-	-	-	-	-	-
Suisun City (city)	870	807	-	1,125	-	-	-	-	802	-	-	-	-	-	-	-	-	-	-	-	-	-	-	-
Vacaville (city)	842	765	-	-	-	-	-	-	796	-	-	-	-	-	-	-	-	-	-	-	-	-	-	-
Vallejo (city)	781	760	919	774	-	-	856	-	733	906	-	-	-	543	-	-	-	-	-	-	-	-	-	886
Sonoma County	864	860	884	875	-	686	820	-	955	-	-	-	-	876	919	905	-	-	-	-	-	-	-	814
Petaluma (city)	946	1,066	-	-	-	-	1,010	-	-	-	-	-	-	-	-	-	-	-	-	-	-	-	-	-
Rohnert Park (city)	903	879	-	-	-	-	785	-	792	-	-	-	-	-	-	-	-	-	-	-	-	-	-	-
Santa Rosa (city)	862	858	-	806	-	781	824	-	1,004	-	-	-	-	794	-	939	-	-	-	-	-	-	-	795
Stanislaus County	611	587	648	595	-	560	583	495	630	-	-	559	-	620	-	469	-	-	-	-	-	-	-	826
Ceres (city)	607	605	-	611	-	-	-	-	-	-	-	-	-	-	-	-	-	-	-	-	-	-	-	-
Modesto (city)	639	596	665	833	-	516	601	560	635	-	-	525	-	675	-	464	-	-	-	-	-	-	-	840
Salida (cdp)	696	2,001	-	-	-	-	-	-	-	-	-	-	-	-	-	-	-	-	-	-	-	-	-	-
Turlock (city)	590	565	-	563	-	-	-	-	-	-	-	-	-	-	-	-	-	-	-	-	-	-	-	-
Sutter County	506	468	-	464	-	-	-	-	389	-	-	-	-	633	-	-	-	-	-	-	-	-	-	-
South Yuba City (cdp)	806	856	-	783	-	-	-	-	-	-	-	-	-	-	-	-	-	-	-	-	-	-	-	-
Yuba City (city)	496	461	-	454	-	-	-	-	-	-	-	-	-	-	-	-	-	-	-	-	-	-	-	-

Notes: Please refer to the User's Guide for an explanation of data; data is arranged alphabetically by state, then county, then city within each county; table includes counties with populations greater than 49,999 unless noted and cities with populations greater than 9,999 whose Asian and/or NHPI population rates are greater than the national average; (1) Native Hawaiian and other Pacific Islander; (2) excludes Taiwanese; (3) includes Chamorro; (4) county does not meet population threshold but is shown in order to allow inclusion of city

Place	All specified renter-occupied housing units	Specified housing units rented by Asians	Specified housing units rented by NHPIs[1]	Asian Indian	Bangladeshi	Cambodian	Chinese[2]	Fijian	Filipino	Guamanian[3]	Hawaiian, Native	Hmong	Indonesian	Japanese	Korean	Laotian	Malaysian	Pakistani	Samoan	Sri Lankan	Taiwanese	Thai	Tongan	Vietnamese
Tehama County	486	430	-	-	-	-	-	-	-	-	-	-	-	-	-	-	-	-	-	-	-	-	-	-
Tulare County	516	513	-	753	-	-	575	-	482	-	-	542	-	617	652	439	-	-	-	-	-	-	-	-
Porterville (city)	504	484	-	-	-	-	-	-	455	-	-	-	-	-	-	-	-	-	-	-	-	-	-	-
Visalia (city)	578	494	-	-	-	-	-	-	563	-	-	442	-	-	-	435	-	-	-	-	-	-	-	-
Tuolumne County	611	581	-	-	-	-	-	-	-	-	-	-	-	-	-	-	-	-	-	-	-	-	-	-
Ventura County	892	960	1,010	983	-	-	979	-	913	-	1,065	-	-	1,083	946	-	-	-	798	-	1,143	-	-	971
Camarillo (city)	975	959	-	-	-	-	870	-	967	-	-	-	-	950	932	-	-	-	-	-	-	-	-	950
Moorpark (city)	1,172	0	-	-	-	-	-	-	-	-	-	-	-	-	-	-	-	-	-	-	-	-	-	-
Oxnard (city)	780	899	800	1,125	-	-	1,045	-	911	-	-	-	-	825	900	-	-	-	790	-	-	-	-	925
Port Hueneme (city)	803	840	-	-	-	-	-	-	805	-	-	-	-	-	-	-	-	-	-	-	-	-	-	-
Simi Valley (city)	1,058	1,028	-	990	-	-	935	-	862	-	-	-	-	1,169	1,125	-	-	-	-	-	-	-	-	854
Thousand Oaks (city)	1,131	1,102	-	1,101	-	-	950	-	1,081	-	-	-	-	1,227	889	-	-	-	-	-	-	-	-	1,352
Yolo County	687	695	656	692	-	-	711	694	742	-	-	544	-	737	755	615	-	-	-	-	-	-	-	696
Davis (city)	775	741	-	724	-	-	740	-	773	-	-	-	-	807	787	-	-	-	-	-	-	-	-	706
West Sacramento (city)	525	483	-	470	-	-	-	-	-	-	-	521	-	-	-	-	-	-	-	-	-	-	-	-
Woodland (city)	655	614	-	688	-	-	-	-	-	-	-	-	-	-	-	-	-	-	-	-	-	-	-	-
Yuba County	488	441	-	-	-	-	-	-	245	-	-	436	-	-	-	-	-	-	-	-	-	-	-	-
Linda (cdp)	454	437	-	-	-	-	-	-	-	-	-	437	-	-	-	-	-	-	-	-	-	-	-	-
Marysville (city)	480	444	-	-	-	-	-	-	-	-	-	-	-	-	-	-	-	-	-	-	-	-	-	-
Olivehurst (cdp)	533	658	-	-	-	-	-	-	-	-	-	-	-	-	-	-	-	-	-	-	-	-	-	-
COLORADO	671	664	657	744	-	541	617	-	712	637	667	635	641	628	635	671	-	739	692	-	532	668	-	573
Adams County	705	662	-	740	-	-	783	-	805	-	-	603	-	626	711	661	-	-	-	-	-	-	-	608
Berkley (cdp)	693	619	-	-	-	-	-	-	-	-	-	-	-	-	-	-	-	-	-	-	-	-	-	-
Federal Heights (city)	703	767	-	-	-	-	-	-	-	-	-	-	-	-	-	-	-	-	-	-	-	-	-	-
Westminster (city)	848	769	-	864	-	-	1,061	-	-	-	-	573	-	-	950	613	-	-	-	-	-	-	-	533
Arapahoe County	735	708	646	779	-	-	648	-	842	-	-	-	-	823	679	-	-	-	-	-	-	-	-	563
Aurora (city)	700	649	594	776	-	565	651	-	770	-	-	-	-	808	634	-	-	-	-	-	-	-	-	479
Boulder County	825	716	-	798	-	-	763	-	1,108	-	-	-	-	699	646	-	-	-	-	-	-	-	-	543
Boulder (city)	818	649	-	794	-	-	632	-	-	-	-	-	-	691	614	-	-	-	-	-	-	-	-	-
Broomfield (city)	856	717	-	-	-	-	831	-	-	-	-	-	-	-	-	-	-	-	-	-	-	-	-	-
Lafayette (city)	834	871	-	-	-	-	-	-	-	-	-	-	-	-	-	-	-	-	-	-	-	-	-	-
Denver County	631	625	703	690	-	506	583	-	701	-	-	-	-	538	668	-	-	-	-	-	-	662	-	558
Douglas County	1,053	1,009	-	944	-	-	1,125	-	-	-	-	-	-	-	950	-	-	-	-	-	-	-	-	-
Highlands Ranch (cdp)	1,164	1,125	-	0	-	-	1,125	-	-	-	-	-	-	-	-	-	-	-	-	-	-	-	-	-
El Paso County	657	658	687	701	-	-	484	-	635	667	-	-	-	635	616	-	-	-	-	-	-	-	-	674
Colorado Springs (city)	652	656	673	701	-	-	482	-	639	-	-	-	-	641	600	-	-	-	-	-	-	-	-	771
Jefferson County	760	722	792	835	-	-	599	-	769	-	-	892	-	758	543	668	-	-	-	-	-	-	-	591
Larimer County	678	631	-	808	-	-	622	-	-	-	-	-	-	569	500	-	-	-	-	-	-	-	-	-
Mesa County	527	610	-	-	-	-	-	-	-	-	-	-	-	-	-	-	-	-	-	-	-	-	-	-
Pueblo County	489	497	-	-	-	-	-	-	-	-	-	-	-	-	-	-	-	-	-	-	-	-	-	-
Weld County	564	515	-	-	-	-	-	-	-	-	-	-	-	528	-	-	-	-	-	-	-	-	-	-

Notes: Please refer to the User's Guide for an explanation of data; data is arranged alphabetically by state, then county, then city within each county; table includes counties with populations greater than 49,999 unless noted and cities with populations greater than 9,999 whose Asian and/or NHPI population rates are greater than the national average; (1) Native Hawaiian and other Pacific Islander; (2) excludes Taiwanese; (3) includes Chamorro; (4) county does not meet population threshold but is shown in order to allow inclusion of city

Place	All specified renter-occupied housing units	Specified housing units rented by Asians	Specified housing units rented by NHPIs[1]	Asian Indian	Bangladeshi	Cambodian	Chinese[2]	Fijian	Filipino	Guamanian[3]	Hawaiian, Native	Hmong	Indonesian	Japanese	Korean	Laotian	Malaysian	Pakistani	Samoan	Sri Lankan	Taiwanese	Thai	Tongan	Vietnamese
CONNECTICUT	681	765	719	816	635	679	733	-	728	219	-	-	-	1,158	787	623	-	814	-	-	690	653	-	653
Fairfield County	838	1,062	-	1,105	-	878	1,040	-	900	-	-	-	-	2,001	1,077	769	-	1,164	-	-	-	-	-	753
Danbury (city)	818	880	-	936	-	922	909	-	-	-	-	-	-	-	-	-	-	-	-	-	-	-	-	-
Greenwich (town)	1,322	2,001	-	1,089	-	-	872	-	-	-	-	-	-	2,001	-	-	-	-	-	-	-	-	-	-
Stamford (city)	1,007	1,282	-	1,266	-	-	1,381	-	1,574	-	-	-	-	-	-	-	-	-	-	-	-	-	-	-
Hartford County	645	711	-	745	-	-	704	-	742	-	-	-	-	692	776	520	-	698	-	-	-	-	-	613
East Hartford (town)	621	626	-	675	-	-	-	-	-	-	-	-	-	-	-	-	-	-	-	-	-	-	-	625
Farmington (town)	860	880	-	-	-	-	-	-	-	-	-	-	-	-	-	-	-	-	-	-	-	-	-	-
Glastonbury (town)	775	973	-	930	-	-	-	-	-	-	-	-	-	-	-	-	-	-	-	-	-	-	-	-
Rocky Hill (town)	851	903	-	-	-	-	-	-	-	-	-	-	-	-	-	-	-	-	-	-	-	-	-	-
South Windsor (town)	844	1,023	-	-	-	-	-	-	-	-	-	-	-	-	-	-	-	-	-	-	-	-	-	-
West Hartford (town)	751	739	-	718	-	-	698	-	-	-	-	-	-	-	-	-	-	-	-	-	-	-	-	819
Litchfield County	660	700	-	822	-	-	875	-	-	-	-	-	-	-	484	-	-	-	-	-	-	-	-	639
Middlesex County	701	712	-	751	-	-	663	-	-	-	-	-	-	-	-	-	-	-	-	-	-	-	-	-
New Haven County	666	725	-	746	-	-	703	-	680	-	-	-	-	825	785	679	-	760	-	-	-	-	-	630
New Haven (city)	651	688	-	696	-	-	659	-	-	-	-	-	-	-	769	-	-	-	-	-	-	-	-	-
New London County	646	681	-	723	-	-	674	-	577	-	-	-	-	-	-	-	-	-	-	-	-	-	-	-
Tolland County	662	607	-	573	-	-	608	-	-	-	-	-	-	-	-	-	-	-	-	-	-	-	-	-
Mansfield (town)	626	564	-	546	-	-	567	-	-	-	-	-	-	-	-	-	-	-	-	-	-	-	-	-
Storrs (cdp)	630	564	-	-	-	-	550	-	-	-	-	-	-	-	-	-	-	-	-	-	-	-	-	-
Windham County	548	577	-	-	-	-	-	-	-	-	-	-	-	-	-	-	-	-	-	-	-	-	-	-
DELAWARE	639	685	880	704	-	-	670	-	618	-	-	-	-	638	690	-	-	1,000	-	-	-	-	-	667
Kent County	573	634	-	671	-	-	-	-	479	-	-	-	-	-	-	-	-	-	-	-	-	-	-	-
New Castle County	670	694	-	706	-	-	675	-	670	-	-	-	-	638	742	-	-	-	-	-	-	-	-	641
Hockessin (cdp)	2,001	1,625	-	-	-	-	-	-	-	-	-	-	-	-	-	-	-	-	-	-	-	-	-	-
Newark (city)	681	669	-	-	-	-	625	-	-	-	-	-	-	-	-	-	-	-	-	-	-	-	-	-
Pike Creek (cdp)	791	872	-	-	-	-	-	-	-	-	-	-	-	-	-	-	-	-	-	-	-	-	-	-
Sussex County	507	561	-	-	-	-	-	-	-	-	-	-	-	-	-	-	-	-	-	-	-	-	-	-
DISTRICT OF COLUMBIA	618	736	-	822	-	-	652	-	758	-	-	-	-	805	745	-	-	-	-	-	-	-	-	605
FLORIDA	641	685	653	740	656	448	654	-	637	635	628	-	573	706	740	688	-	781	585	775	589	686	-	594
Alachua County	553	534	-	642	-	-	421	-	525	-	-	-	-	714	569	-	-	-	-	-	-	-	-	529
Gainesville (city)	540	460	-	572	-	-	402	-	-	-	-	-	-	-	488	-	-	-	-	-	-	-	-	-
Bay County	536	556	-	-	-	-	-	-	561	-	-	-	-	-	-	-	-	-	-	-	-	-	-	497
Callaway (city)	536	548	-	-	-	-	-	-	-	-	-	-	-	-	-	-	-	-	-	-	-	-	-	-
Brevard County	604	595	-	592	-	-	588	-	580	-	-	-	-	661	629	-	-	-	-	-	-	-	-	575
Broward County	757	811	753	781	-	-	849	-	788	-	-	-	-	756	897	-	-	865	-	-	-	838	-	788
Cooper City (city)	988	750	-	750	-	-	-	-	-	-	-	-	-	-	-	-	-	-	-	-	-	-	-	-
Pembroke Pines (city)	945	913	-	922	-	-	945	-	859	-	-	-	-	-	-	-	-	-	-	-	-	-	-	-
Charlotte County	626	1,534	-	-	-	-	-	-	-	-	-	-	-	-	-	-	-	-	-	-	-	-	-	-
Citrus County	478	632	-	-	-	-	-	-	-	-	-	-	-	-	-	-	-	-	-	-	-	-	-	-
Clay County	668	559	-	-	-	-	-	-	552	-	-	-	-	-	-	-	-	-	-	-	-	-	-	-

Notes: Please refer to the User's Guide for an explanation of data; data is arranged alphabetically by state, then county, then city within each county; table includes counties with populations greater than 49,999 unless noted and cities with populations greater than 9,999 whose Asian and/or NHPI population rates are greater than the national average; (1) Native Hawaiian and other Pacific Islander; (2) excludes Taiwanese; (3) includes Chamorro; (4) county does not meet population threshold but is shown in order to allow inclusion of city

Place	All specified renter-occupied housing units	Specified housing units rented by Asians	Specified housing units rented by NHPIs[1]	Asian Indian	Bangladeshi	Cambodian	Chinese[2]	Fijian	Filipino	Guamanian[3]	Hawaiian, Native	Hmong	Indonesian	Japanese	Korean	Laotian	Malaysian	Pakistani	Samoan	Sri Lankan	Taiwanese	Thai	Tongan	Vietnamese
Bellair-Meadowbrook Ter. (cdp)	706	560	-	-	-	-	-	-	-	-	-	-	-	-	-	-	-	-	-	-	-	-	-	-
Collier County	753	778	-	-	-	-	-	-	-	-	-	-	-	-	-	-	-	-	-	-	-	-	-	-
Columbia County	448	623	-	-	-	-	-	-	-	-	-	-	-	-	-	-	-	-	-	-	-	-	-	-
Duval County	604	635	575	750	-	384	663	-	627	-	-	-	-	464	631	-	-	-	-	-	-	-	-	474
Escambia County	533	493	-	623	-	-	453	-	518	-	-	-	-	-	-	-	-	-	-	-	-	-	-	474
Bellview (cdp)	585	647	-	-	-	-	-	-	665	-	-	-	-	-	-	-	-	-	-	-	-	-	-	-
Myrtle Grove (cdp)	576	520	-	-	-	-	-	-	496	-	-	-	-	-	-	-	-	-	-	-	-	-	-	-
Hernando County	550	756	-	-	-	-	-	-	-	-	-	-	-	-	-	-	-	-	-	-	-	-	-	-
Highlands County	479	565	-	-	-	-	-	-	639	-	-	-	-	-	-	-	-	-	-	-	-	-	-	-
Hillsborough County	623	640	735	656	-	-	591	-	654	-	-	-	-	796	659	-	-	-	-	-	-	628	-	557
Westchase (cdp)	934	982	-	-	-	-	-	-	-	-	-	-	-	-	-	-	-	-	-	-	-	-	-	-
Indian River County	615	826	-	-	-	-	-	-	-	-	-	-	-	-	-	-	-	-	-	-	-	-	-	-
Lake County	534	619	-	-	-	-	-	-	-	-	-	-	-	-	-	-	-	-	-	-	-	-	-	-
Lee County	646	616	-	576	-	-	678	-	635	-	-	-	-	-	-	-	-	-	-	-	-	-	-	-
Leon County	606	554	-	541	-	-	481	-	625	-	-	-	-	-	600	-	-	-	-	-	-	-	-	-
Manatee County	637	561	-	-	-	-	-	-	613	-	-	-	-	-	-	-	-	-	-	-	-	-	-	-
Marion County	513	742	-	824	-	-	-	-	-	-	-	-	-	-	-	-	-	-	-	-	-	-	-	-
Martin County	633	664	-	-	-	-	-	-	-	-	-	-	-	-	-	-	-	-	-	-	-	-	-	-
Miami-Dade County	647	749	683	795	-	-	733	-	711	-	-	-	-	842	910	-	-	725	-	-	-	790	-	682
Doral (cdp)	968	873	-	-	-	-	-	-	-	-	-	-	-	-	-	-	-	-	-	-	-	-	-	-
Ives Estates (cdp)	776	735	-	-	-	-	-	-	-	-	-	-	-	-	-	-	-	-	-	-	-	-	-	-
North Miami Beach (city)	643	672	-	830	-	-	653	-	-	-	-	-	-	-	-	-	-	-	-	-	-	-	-	-
Pinecrest (village)	775	734	-	-	-	-	-	-	-	-	-	-	-	-	-	-	-	-	-	-	-	-	-	-
Monroe County	820	825	-	-	-	-	-	-	-	-	-	-	-	-	-	-	-	-	-	-	-	-	-	-
Nassau County	553	660	-	-	-	-	-	-	-	-	-	-	-	-	-	-	-	-	-	-	-	-	-	-
Okaloosa County	601	561	-	-	-	-	-	-	518	-	-	-	-	-	626	-	-	-	-	-	-	771	-	584
Wright (cdp)	595	758	-	-	-	-	-	-	-	-	-	-	-	-	-	-	-	-	-	-	-	-	-	-
Orange County	699	726	688	777	-	-	694	-	722	-	-	-	-	735	808	-	-	689	-	-	-	-	-	622
Oak Ridge (cdp)	671	666	-	-	-	-	-	-	-	-	-	-	-	-	-	-	-	-	-	-	-	-	-	600
Osceola County	714	712	-	675	-	-	675	-	693	-	-	-	-	-	-	-	-	-	-	-	-	-	-	-
Palm Beach County	739	764	845	830	-	-	731	-	762	-	-	-	-	566	841	-	-	-	-	-	-	850	-	595
Pasco County	518	528	-	600	-	-	423	-	452	-	-	-	-	-	-	-	-	-	-	-	-	-	-	-
Pinellas County	616	617	-	662	-	444	644	-	580	-	-	-	-	568	603	650	-	-	-	-	-	714	-	472
Pinellas Park (city)	614	605	-	-	-	-	-	-	-	-	-	-	-	-	-	-	-	-	-	-	-	-	-	603
Polk County	501	538	-	562	-	-	496	-	520	-	-	-	-	-	-	0	-	-	-	-	-	-	-	491
Putnam County	384	920	-	-	-	-	-	-	-	-	-	-	-	-	-	-	-	-	-	-	-	-	-	-
St. Johns County	724	751	-	-	-	-	-	-	-	-	-	-	-	-	-	-	-	-	-	-	-	-	-	-
St. Lucie County	621	713	-	-	-	-	-	-	-	-	-	-	-	-	-	-	-	-	-	-	-	-	-	-
Santa Rosa County	540	628	-	-	-	-	-	-	432	-	-	-	-	-	-	-	-	-	-	-	-	-	-	-
Sarasota County	711	644	-	-	-	-	622	-	597	-	-	-	-	-	-	-	-	-	-	-	-	-	-	586
Seminole County	731	782	-	839	-	-	628	-	604	-	-	-	-	-	857	-	-	-	-	-	-	-	-	742

Notes: Please refer to the User's Guide for an explanation of data; data is arranged alphabetically by state, then county, then city within each county; table includes counties with populations greater than 49,999 unless noted and cities with populations greater than 9,999 whose Asian and/or NHPI population rates are greater than the national average; (1) Native Hawaiian and other Pacific Islander; (2) excludes Taiwanese; (3) includes Chamorro; (4) county does not meet population threshold but is shown in order to allow inclusion of city

Place	All specified renter-occupied housing units	Specified housing units rented by Asians	Specified housing units rented by NHPIs[1]	Asian Indian	Bangladeshi	Cambodian	Chinese[2]	Fijian	Filipino	Guamanian[3]	Hawaiian, Native	Hmong	Indonesian	Japanese	Korean	Laotian	Malaysian	Pakistani	Samoan	Sri Lankan	Taiwanese	Thai	Tongan	Vietnamese
Volusia County	597	634	-	736	-	-	578	-	632	-	-	-	-	-	640	-	-	-	-	-	-	-	-	-
GEORGIA	613	761	619	793	715	571	705	-	702	563	642	503	804	936	818	530	-	837	636	-	733	652	-	658
Bartow County	575	665	-	-	-	-	-	-	-	-	-	-	-	-	-	-	-	-	-	-	-	-	-	-
Bibb County	474	571	-	-	-	-	-	-	-	-	-	-	-	-	-	-	-	-	-	-	-	-	-	-
Bulloch County	436	512	-	-	-	-	-	-	-	-	-	-	-	-	-	-	-	-	-	-	-	-	-	-
Carroll County	488	607	-	-	-	-	-	-	-	-	-	-	-	-	-	-	-	-	-	-	-	-	-	-
Catoosa County	482	628	-	-	-	-	-	-	-	-	-	-	-	-	-	-	-	-	-	-	-	-	-	-
Chatham County	589	603	-	611	-	-	713	-	-	-	-	-	-	-	575	-	-	-	-	-	-	-	-	575
Cherokee County	740	963	-	1,060	-	-	-	-	-	-	-	-	-	-	-	-	-	-	-	-	-	-	-	-
Clarke County	540	450	-	536	-	-	419	-	-	-	-	-	-	-	448	-	-	-	-	-	-	-	-	-
Clayton County	699	678	-	718	-	700	703	-	-	-	-	-	-	-	-	483	-	768	-	-	-	-	-	550
Forest Park (city)	621	545	-	-	-	-	-	-	-	-	-	-	-	-	-	-	-	-	-	-	-	-	-	575
Riverdale (city)	666	579	-	-	-	-	-	-	-	-	-	-	-	-	-	-	-	-	-	-	-	-	-	525
Cobb County	806	840	-	839	-	-	839	-	733	-	-	-	-	1,247	839	-	-	919	-	-	-	-	-	731
Smyrna (city)	776	827	-	911	-	-	-	-	-	-	-	-	-	-	-	-	-	-	-	-	-	-	-	-
Columbia County	620	652	-	642	-	-	625	-	-	-	-	-	-	-	715	-	-	-	-	-	-	-	-	-
Martinez (cdp)	630	613	-	495	-	-	-	-	-	-	-	-	-	-	-	-	-	-	-	-	-	-	-	-
Coweta County	628	850	-	-	-	-	-	-	-	-	-	-	-	-	-	-	-	-	-	-	-	-	-	-
DeKalb County	767	771	-	797	700	1,028	747	-	850	-	-	-	-	1,039	771	-	-	-	-	-	-	-	-	706
Druid Hills (cdp)	858	787	-	-	-	-	-	-	-	-	-	-	-	-	-	-	-	-	-	-	-	-	-	-
Dunwoody (cdp)	998	899	-	871	-	-	-	-	-	-	-	-	-	-	960	-	-	-	-	-	-	-	-	-
North Atlanta (cdp)	819	780	-	-	-	-	-	-	-	-	-	-	-	-	-	-	-	-	-	-	-	-	-	-
North Decatur (cdp)	858	822	-	-	-	-	-	-	-	-	-	-	-	-	-	-	-	-	-	-	-	-	-	-
North Druid Hills (cdp)	902	873	-	833	-	-	-	-	-	-	-	-	-	-	-	-	-	-	-	-	-	-	-	-
Tucker (cdp)	839	851	-	-	-	-	-	-	-	-	-	-	-	-	-	-	-	-	-	-	-	-	-	708
Dougherty County	469	586	-	-	-	-	-	-	-	-	-	-	-	-	-	-	-	-	-	-	-	-	-	-
Douglas County	731	838	-	-	-	-	-	-	-	-	-	-	-	-	-	-	-	-	-	-	-	-	-	-
Fayette County	890	1,094	-	-	-	-	-	-	-	-	-	-	-	1,253	-	-	-	-	-	-	-	-	-	-
Peachtree City (city)	990	1,168	-	-	-	-	-	-	-	-	-	-	-	1,253	-	-	-	-	-	-	-	-	-	-
Floyd County	476	595	-	622	-	-	-	-	-	-	-	-	-	-	-	-	-	-	-	-	-	-	-	-
Forsyth County	683	984	-	-	-	-	-	-	-	-	-	-	-	-	-	-	-	-	-	-	-	-	-	-
Fulton County	709	828	-	851	-	-	743	-	808	-	-	-	-	1,119	868	-	-	-	-	-	-	-	-	563
Alpharetta (city)	908	906	-	857	-	-	879	-	-	-	-	-	-	-	-	-	-	-	-	-	-	-	-	-
Roswell (city)	894	859	-	837	-	-	856	-	-	-	-	-	-	-	962	-	-	-	-	-	-	-	-	-
Glynn County	533	625	-	-	-	-	-	-	-	-	-	-	-	-	-	-	-	-	-	-	-	-	-	-
Gwinnett County	824	838	578	830	-	0	780	-	802	-	-	-	-	768	883	806	-	903	-	-	738	-	-	844
Duluth (city)	877	864	-	823	-	-	875	-	-	-	-	-	-	-	881	-	-	-	-	-	-	-	-	-
Lilburn (city)	767	825	-	775	-	-	-	-	-	-	-	-	-	-	-	-	-	-	-	-	-	-	-	850
Mountain Park (cdp)	878	950	-	0	-	-	-	-	-	-	-	-	-	-	-	-	-	-	-	-	-	-	-	-
Hall County	619	620	-	-	-	-	-	-	-	-	-	-	-	-	-	-	-	-	-	-	-	-	-	639
Henry County	740	813	-	850	-	-	-	-	-	-	-	-	-	-	-	-	-	-	-	-	-	-	-	-

Notes: Please refer to the User's Guide for an explanation of data; data is arranged alphabetically by state, then county, then city within each county; table includes counties with populations greater than 49,999 unless noted and cities with populations greater than 9,999 whose Asian and/or NHPI population rates are greater than the national average; (1) Native Hawaiian and other Pacific Islander; (2) excludes Taiwanese; (3) includes Chamorro; (4) county does not meet population threshold but is shown in order to allow inclusion of city

Place	All specified renter-occupied housing units	Specified housing units rented by Asians	Specified housing units rented by NHPIs[1]	Asian Indian	Bangladeshi	Cambodian	Chinese[2]	Fijian	Filipino	Guamanian[3]	Hawaiian, Native	Hmong	Indonesian	Japanese	Korean	Laotian	Malaysian	Pakistani	Samoan	Sri Lankan	Taiwanese	Thai	Tongan	Vietnamese
Houston County	558	659	-	-	-	-	-	-	700	-	-	-	-	-	-	-	-	-	-	-	-	-	-	-
Liberty County	529	549	-	-	-	-	-	-	-	-	-	-	-	-	756	-	-	-	-	-	-	-	-	-
Lowndes County	495	708	-	-	-	-	-	-	-	-	-	-	-	-	-	-	-	-	-	-	-	-	-	-
Muscogee County	500	632	564	663	-	-	623	-	544	-	-	-	-	-	638	-	-	-	-	-	-	-	-	-
Columbus (sp. city)	500	632	564	663	-	-	623	-	544	-	-	-	-	-	638	-	-	-	-	-	-	-	-	-
Newton County	597	1,083	-	-	-	-	-	-	-	-	-	-	-	-	-	-	-	-	-	-	-	-	-	-
Richmond County	505	603	-	624	-	-	447	-	-	-	-	-	-	-	708	-	-	-	-	-	-	-	-	-
Rockdale County	757	739	-	-	-	-	-	-	-	-	-	-	-	-	-	-	-	-	-	-	-	-	-	-
Spalding County	537	625	-	-	-	-	-	-	-	-	-	-	-	-	-	-	-	-	-	-	-	-	-	-
Troup County	482	511	-	-	-	-	-	-	-	-	-	-	-	-	-	-	-	-	-	-	-	-	-	-
Walton County	558	919	-	-	-	-	-	-	-	-	-	-	-	-	-	-	-	-	-	-	-	-	-	-
Whitfield County	484	807	-	-	-	-	-	-	-	-	-	-	-	-	-	-	-	-	-	-	-	-	-	-
HAWAII	779	722	702	820	-	775	694	-	717	930	707	-	-	730	744	503	-	-	672	-	950	700	766	666
Hawaii County	645	562	618	-	-	-	653	-	546	-	610	-	-	528	733	-	-	-	845	-	-	-	-	-
Hilo (cdp)	542	492	527	-	-	-	486	-	481	-	529	-	-	486	455	-	-	-	-	-	-	-	-	-
Honolulu County	802	738	722	788	-	-	693	-	749	948	745	-	-	752	745	482	-	-	670	-	950	707	785	662
Ewa Beach (cdp)	931	874	1,083	-	-	-	-	-	845	-	1,060	-	-	1,288	-	-	-	-	1,096	-	-	-	-	-
Halawa (cdp)	871	815	521	-	-	-	779	-	843	-	543	-	-	1,057	-	-	-	-	460	-	-	-	-	-
Honolulu (cdp)	760	730	683	764	-	-	683	-	747	925	694	-	-	746	734	417	-	-	604	-	950	732	746	668
Kailua (cdp)	1,111	896	846	-	-	-	1,239	-	783	-	852	-	-	933	0	-	-	-	-	-	-	-	-	-
Kaneohe (cdp)	1,075	947	950	-	-	-	793	-	1,115	-	959	-	-	929	1,125	-	-	-	-	-	-	-	-	-
Kaneohe Station (cdp)	1,012	895	-	-	-	-	-	-	-	-	-	-	-	-	-	-	-	-	-	-	-	-	-	-
Makakilo City (cdp)	1,056	1,017	984	-	-	-	-	-	1,098	-	956	-	-	792	-	-	-	-	-	-	-	-	-	-
Mililani Town (cdp)	1,174	1,104	1,263	-	-	-	1,788	-	1,010	-	1,170	-	-	1,219	646	-	-	-	-	-	-	-	-	-
Nanakuli (cdp)	749	652	875	-	-	-	-	-	667	-	928	-	-	-	-	-	-	-	860	-	-	-	-	-
Pearl City (cdp)	798	807	1,082	-	-	-	528	-	1,072	-	1,125	-	-	707	1,125	-	-	-	-	-	-	-	-	-
Schofield Barracks (cdp)	1,039	950	-	-	-	-	-	-	-	-	-	-	-	-	-	-	-	-	-	-	-	-	-	-
Wahiawa (cdp)	644	560	661	-	-	-	-	-	573	-	597	-	-	590	-	-	-	-	-	-	-	-	-	-
Waianae (cdp)	631	625	517	-	-	-	-	-	738	-	458	-	-	425	-	-	-	-	-	-	-	-	-	-
Waimalu (cdp)	962	887	1,023	-	-	-	889	-	904	-	1,038	-	-	806	1,152	-	-	-	-	-	-	-	-	-
Waipahu (cdp)	664	678	625	-	-	-	522	-	686	-	783	-	-	680	-	-	-	-	615	-	-	-	-	-
Waipio (cdp)	931	927	862	-	-	-	-	-	983	-	842	-	-	934	-	-	-	-	-	-	-	-	-	-
Kauai County	739	659	660	-	-	-	876	-	601	-	648	-	-	634	-	-	-	-	-	-	-	-	-	-
Maui County	788	675	706	-	-	-	625	-	676	-	711	-	-	631	731	-	-	-	-	-	-	-	697	-
Kahului (cdp)	642	638	645	-	-	-	-	-	660	-	666	-	-	520	-	-	-	-	-	-	-	-	-	-
Kihei (cdp)	821	758	864	-	-	-	-	-	739	-	850	-	-	769	-	-	-	-	-	-	-	-	-	-
Wailuku (cdp)	662	642	643	-	-	-	-	-	684	-	636	-	-	585	-	-	-	-	-	-	-	-	-	-
IDAHO	515	545	381	608	-	-	603	-	524	-	420	-	-	453	490	471	-	-	-	-	-	-	-	537
Ada County	617	640	585	647	-	-	719	-	594	-	-	-	-	739	552	-	-	-	-	-	-	-	-	531
Bannock County	443	481	-	-	-	-	-	-	-	-	-	-	-	-	-	-	-	-	-	-	-	-	-	-
Bonneville County	485	352	-	-	-	-	-	-	-	-	-	-	-	-	-	-	-	-	-	-	-	-	-	-

Notes: Please refer to the User's Guide for an explanation of data; data is arranged alphabetically by state, then county, then city within each county; table includes counties with populations greater than 49,999 unless noted and cities with populations greater than 9,999 whose Asian and/or NHPI population rates are greater than the national average; (1) Native Hawaiian and other Pacific Islander; (2) excludes Taiwanese; (3) includes Chamorro; (4) county does not meet population threshold but is shown in order to allow inclusion of city

Place	All specified renter-occupied housing units	Specified housing units rented by Asians	Specified housing units rented by NHPIs[1]	Asian Indian	Bangladeshi	Cambodian	Chinese[2]	Fijian	Filipino	Guamanian[3]	Hawaiian, Native	Hmong	Indonesian	Japanese	Korean	Laotian	Malaysian	Pakistani	Samoan	Sri Lankan	Taiwanese	Thai	Tongan	Vietnamese
Canyon County	509	520	-	-	-	-	-	-	-	-	-	-	-	529	-	-	-	-	-	-	-	-	-	-
Kootenai County	571	520	-	-	-	-	-	-	-	-	-	-	-	-	-	-	-	-	-	-	-	-	-	-
Twin Falls County	489	425	-	-	-	-	-	-	-	-	-	-	-	-	-	-	-	-	-	-	-	-	-	-
ILLINOIS	605	728	674	790	616	667	654	-	687	496	850	-	645	938	717	565	663	712	703	706	709	643	-	654
Champaign County	540	513	-	600	-	-	479	-	498	-	-	-	-	542	527	-	-	-	-	-	-	-	-	467
Champaign (city)	549	510	-	600	-	-	429	-	-	-	-	-	-	-	513	-	-	-	-	-	-	-	-	467
Urbana (city)	537	512	-	586	-	-	487	-	-	-	-	-	-	-	535	-	-	-	-	-	-	-	-	-
Coles County	438	461	-	-	-	-	-	-	-	-	-	-	-	-	-	-	-	-	-	-	-	-	-	-
Cook County	648	739	706	808	-	673	669	-	679	-	-	-	726	965	749	648	-	705	-	-	757	655	-	659
Arlington Heights (village)	933	970	-	912	-	-	799	-	1,029	-	-	-	-	1,322	973	-	-	-	-	-	-	-	-	-
Chicago (city)	616	666	681	742	-	676	610	-	647	-	-	-	-	731	640	-	-	680	-	-	713	686	-	642
Des Plaines (city)	764	739	-	872	-	-	640	-	1,125	-	-	-	-	-	-	-	-	-	-	-	-	-	-	-
Elk Grove Village (village)	825	887	-	846	-	-	786	-	692	-	-	-	-	1,281	-	-	-	-	-	-	-	-	-	-
Evanston (city)	856	842	-	977	-	-	783	-	712	-	-	-	-	945	846	-	-	-	-	-	-	-	-	-
Forest Park (village)	670	659	-	-	-	-	-	-	-	-	-	-	-	-	-	-	-	-	-	-	-	-	-	-
Glenview (village)	828	841	-	850	-	-	784	-	789	-	-	-	-	1,088	822	-	-	-	-	-	-	-	-	-
Hanover Park (village)	750	823	-	847	-	-	-	-	0	-	-	-	-	-	-	-	-	-	-	-	-	-	-	-
Hoffman Estates (village)	888	876	-	817	-	-	789	-	850	-	-	-	-	1,643	952	-	-	-	-	-	-	-	-	-
Lincolnwood (village)	2,001	1,266	-	1,266	-	-	-	-	0	-	-	-	-	-	0	-	-	-	-	-	-	-	-	-
Morton Grove (village)	691	814	-	0	-	-	-	-	643	-	-	-	-	-	1,516	-	-	-	-	-	-	-	-	-
Mount Prospect (village)	786	797	-	785	-	-	764	-	850	-	-	-	-	1,583	838	-	-	-	-	-	-	-	-	-
Niles (village)	747	729	-	714	-	-	-	-	732	-	-	-	-	-	763	-	-	-	-	-	-	-	-	-
Northbrook (village)	1,279	2,001	-	-	-	-	2,001	-	-	-	-	-	-	-	2,001	-	-	-	-	-	-	-	-	-
Oak Park (village)	710	713	-	732	-	-	765	-	-	-	-	-	-	-	-	-	-	-	-	-	-	-	-	-
Orland Park (village)	760	863	-	850	-	-	-	-	0	-	-	-	-	-	-	-	-	-	-	-	-	-	-	-
Palatine (village)	884	900	-	891	-	-	826	-	958	-	-	-	-	-	873	-	-	-	-	-	-	-	-	-
Prospect Heights (city)	698	854	-	-	-	-	-	-	-	-	-	-	-	-	-	-	-	-	-	-	-	-	-	-
Rolling Meadows (city)	867	879	-	881	-	-	-	-	-	-	-	-	-	-	-	-	-	-	-	-	-	-	-	-
Schaumburg (village)	981	994	-	988	-	-	882	-	986	-	-	-	-	1,323	1,063	-	-	-	-	-	-	-	-	-
Schiller Park (village)	624	592	-	-	-	-	-	-	-	-	-	-	-	-	-	-	-	-	-	-	-	-	-	-
Skokie (village)	800	820	-	783	-	-	839	-	845	-	-	-	-	-	829	-	-	685	-	-	-	-	-	-
Streamwood (village)	1,130	1,336	-	1,322	-	-	-	-	775	-	-	-	-	-	-	-	-	-	-	-	-	-	-	-
Wheeling (village)	885	935	-	943	-	-	-	-	911	-	-	-	-	-	-	-	-	-	-	-	-	-	-	-
Wilmette (village)	1,028	1,236	-	-	-	-	1,161	-	-	-	-	-	-	1,950	1,131	-	-	-	-	-	-	-	-	-
DeKalb County	577	480	-	480	-	-	-	-	-	-	-	-	-	-	-	-	-	-	-	-	-	-	-	-
DeKalb (city)	565	484	-	480	-	-	-	-	-	-	-	-	-	-	-	-	-	-	-	-	-	-	-	-
DuPage County	837	832	-	848	-	-	836	-	785	-	-	-	-	929	856	-	-	785	-	-	809	779	-	723
Addison (village)	688	617	-	587	-	-	-	-	647	-	-	-	-	-	-	-	-	-	-	-	-	-	-	-
Bartlett (village)	752	707	-	725	-	-	-	-	775	-	-	-	-	-	-	-	-	-	-	-	-	-	-	-
Bensenville (village)	798	864	-	929	-	-	-	-	-	-	-	-	-	-	-	-	-	-	-	-	-	-	-	-
Bloomingdale (village)	961	991	-	1,111	-	-	-	-	-	-	-	-	-	-	-	-	-	-	-	-	-	-	-	-

Notes: Please refer to the User's Guide for an explanation of data; data is arranged alphabetically by state, then county, then city within each county; table includes counties with populations greater than 49,999 unless noted and cities with populations greater than 9,999 whose Asian and/or NHPI population rates are greater than the national average; (1) Native Hawaiian and other Pacific Islander; (2) excludes Taiwanese; (3) includes Chamorro; (4) county does not meet population threshold but is shown in order to allow inclusion of city

Place	All specified renter-occupied housing units	Specified housing units rented by Asians	Specified housing units rented by NHPIs[1]	Asian Indian	Bangladeshi	Cambodian	Chinese[2]	Fijian	Filipino	Guamanian[3]	Hawaiian, Native	Hmong	Indonesian	Japanese	Korean	Laotian	Malaysian	Pakistani	Samoan	Sri Lankan	Taiwanese	Thai	Tongan	Vietnamese
Burr Ridge (village)	1,205	0	-	0	-	-	-	-	-	-	-	-	-	-	-	-	-	-	-	-	-	-	-	-
Carol Stream (village)	798	782	-	796	-	-	-	-	781	-	-	-	-	-	-	-	-	-	-	-	-	-	-	775
Darien (city)	763	863	-	1,297	-	-	-	-	700	-	-	-	-	-	-	-	-	-	-	-	-	-	-	-
Downers Grove (village)	768	698	-	750	-	-	806	-	675	-	-	-	-	-	-	-	-	-	-	-	-	-	-	-
Glen Ellyn (village)	736	755	-	755	-	-	-	-	-	-	-	-	-	-	-	-	-	-	-	-	-	-	-	-
Glendale Heights (village)	823	795	-	818	-	-	-	-	744	-	-	-	-	-	-	-	-	-	-	-	-	-	-	804
Hinsdale (village)	885	806	-	-	-	-	-	-	-	-	-	-	-	-	-	-	-	-	-	-	-	-	-	-
Lisle (village)	893	902	-	923	-	-	878	-	-	-	-	-	-	-	-	-	-	-	-	-	-	-	-	-
Lombard (village)	889	892	-	887	-	-	-	-	950	-	-	-	-	-	-	-	-	-	-	-	-	-	-	-
Naperville (city)	942	936	-	918	-	-	961	-	806	-	-	-	-	-	990	-	-	-	-	-	850	-	-	-
Roselle (village)	895	933	-	905	-	-	-	-	-	-	-	-	-	-	-	-	-	-	-	-	-	-	-	-
Villa Park (village)	720	775	-	-	-	-	-	-	-	-	-	-	-	-	-	-	-	-	-	-	-	-	-	-
Warrenville (city)	1,019	775	-	-	-	-	-	-	-	-	-	-	-	-	-	-	-	-	-	-	-	-	-	-
Westmont (village)	759	805	-	859	-	-	760	-	731	-	-	-	-	-	-	-	-	-	-	-	-	-	-	-
Wheaton (city)	892	908	-	954	-	-	-	-	-	-	-	-	-	-	-	-	-	-	-	-	-	-	-	675
Woodridge (village)	756	716	-	721	-	-	-	-	738	-	-	-	-	-	-	-	-	-	-	-	-	-	-	-
Jackson County	409	399	-	-	-	-	335	-	-	-	-	-	-	-	-	-	-	-	-	-	-	-	-	-
Carbondale (city)	403	395	-	-	-	-	-	-	-	-	-	-	-	-	-	-	-	-	-	-	-	-	-	-
Kane County	686	675	-	763	-	-	688	-	705	-	-	-	-	-	440	547	-	-	-	-	-	-	-	239
South Elgin (village)	765	525	-	-	-	-	-	-	-	-	-	-	-	-	-	-	-	-	-	-	-	-	-	-
Kankakee County	539	604	-	-	-	-	-	-	-	-	-	-	-	-	-	-	-	-	-	-	-	-	-	-
Kendall County	720	475	-	-	-	-	-	-	-	-	-	-	-	-	-	-	-	-	-	-	-	-	-	-
Knox County	411	386	-	-	-	-	-	-	-	-	-	-	-	-	-	-	-	-	-	-	-	-	-	-
La Salle County	474	486	-	-	-	-	-	-	-	-	-	-	-	-	-	-	-	-	-	-	-	-	-	-
Lake County	742	861	-	829	-	-	1,030	-	733	-	-	-	-	1,849	860	-	-	945	-	-	-	-	-	811
Buffalo Grove (village)	1,079	1,231	-	1,152	-	-	1,325	-	1,019	-	-	-	-	1,967	1,583	-	-	-	-	-	-	-	-	-
Gages Lake (cdp)	833	0	-	-	-	-	-	-	-	-	-	-	-	-	-	-	-	-	-	-	-	-	-	-
Grayslake (village)	820	897	-	-	-	-	-	-	-	-	-	-	-	-	-	-	-	-	-	-	-	-	-	-
Gurnee (village)	806	1,074	-	1,125	-	-	1,038	-	1,125	-	-	-	-	-	-	-	-	-	-	-	-	-	-	-
Lake Zurich (village)	786	911	-	-	-	-	-	-	-	-	-	-	-	-	-	-	-	-	-	-	-	-	-	-
Libertyville (village)	835	956	-	-	-	-	-	-	-	-	-	-	-	-	-	-	-	-	-	-	-	-	-	-
Mundelein (village)	774	702	-	-	-	-	1,375	-	240	-	-	-	-	-	-	-	-	-	-	-	-	-	-	-
Vernon Hills (village)	866	878	-	799	-	-	775	-	-	-	-	-	-	-	1,008	-	-	-	-	-	-	-	-	-
Macon County	448	527	-	-	-	-	-	-	-	-	-	-	-	-	-	-	-	-	-	-	-	-	-	-
Madison County	490	561	-	591	-	-	-	-	-	-	-	-	-	-	-	-	-	-	-	-	-	-	-	-
McHenry County	761	757	-	935	-	-	786	-	656	-	-	-	-	-	-	-	-	-	-	-	-	-	-	-
McLean County	533	576	-	579	-	-	543	-	-	-	-	-	-	-	-	-	-	-	-	-	-	-	-	-
Peoria County	490	603	-	640	-	-	546	-	-	-	-	-	-	-	-	-	-	-	-	-	-	-	-	-
Rock Island County	450	516	-	519	-	-	-	-	-	-	-	-	-	-	-	-	-	-	-	-	-	-	-	525
St. Clair County	503	538	-	-	-	-	-	-	528	-	-	-	-	-	478	-	-	-	-	-	-	-	-	-
Sangamon County	503	530	-	537	-	-	511	-	-	-	-	-	-	-	-	-	-	-	-	-	-	-	-	-

Notes: Please refer to the User's Guide for an explanation of data; data is arranged alphabetically by state, then county, then city within each county; table includes counties with populations greater than 49,999 unless noted and cities with populations greater than 9,999 whose Asian and/or NHPI population rates are greater than the national average; (1) Native Hawaiian and other Pacific Islander; (2) excludes Taiwanese; (3) includes Chamorro; (4) county does not meet population threshold but is shown in order to allow inclusion of city

Place	All specified renter-occupied housing units	Specified housing units rented by Asians	Specified housing units rented by NHPIs[1]	Asian Indian	Bangladeshi	Cambodian	Chinese[2]	Fijian	Filipino	Guamanian[3]	Hawaiian, Native	Hmong	Indonesian	Japanese	Korean	Laotian	Malaysian	Pakistani	Samoan	Sri Lankan	Taiwanese	Thai	Tongan	Vietnamese
Tazewell County	471	670	-	-	-	-	-	-	-	-	-	-	-	-	-	-	-	-	-	-	-	-	-	-
Vermilion County	420	554	-	-	-	-	-	-	-	-	-	-	-	-	-	-	-	-	-	-	-	-	-	-
Will County	630	791	-	639	-	-	692	-	755	-	-	-	-	-	1,054	-	-	850	-	-	-	-	-	868
Bolingbrook (village)	786	775	-	697	-	-	-	-	553	-	-	-	-	-	-	-	-	-	-	-	-	-	-	-
Winnebago County	514	492	-	562	-	-	-	-	433	-	-	-	-	-	704	461	-	-	-	-	-	-	-	425
INDIANA	521	565	516	608	-	563	516	-	605	510	585	-	-	626	575	537	-	698	-	-	506	487	-	511
Allen County	506	529	-	595	-	-	534	-	475	-	-	-	-	-	-	-	-	-	-	-	-	-	-	413
Bartholomew County	570	687	-	667	-	-	-	-	-	-	-	-	-	-	-	-	-	-	-	-	-	-	-	-
Clark County	511	464	-	-	-	-	-	-	-	-	-	-	-	-	-	-	-	-	-	-	-	-	-	-
Delaware County	465	469	-	-	-	-	-	-	-	-	-	-	-	-	-	-	-	-	-	-	-	-	-	-
Elkhart County	541	577	-	-	-	-	-	-	-	-	-	-	-	-	-	-	-	-	-	-	-	-	-	-
Grant County	428	511	-	-	-	-	-	-	-	-	-	-	-	-	-	-	-	-	-	-	-	-	-	-
Hamilton County	709	819	-	828	-	-	581	-	-	-	-	-	-	-	-	-	-	-	-	-	-	-	-	-
Carmel (city)	748	723	-	-	-	-	-	-	-	-	-	-	-	-	-	-	-	-	-	-	-	-	-	-
Hendricks County	644	657	-	-	-	-	-	-	-	-	-	-	-	-	-	-	-	-	-	-	-	-	-	-
Howard County	509	752	-	-	-	-	-	-	-	-	-	-	-	-	-	-	-	-	-	-	-	-	-	-
Johnson County	599	642	-	-	-	-	-	-	-	-	-	-	-	-	-	-	-	-	-	-	-	-	-	-
Kosciusko County	502	701	-	-	-	-	-	-	-	-	-	-	-	-	-	-	-	-	-	-	-	-	-	-
Lake County	544	688	-	695	-	-	732	-	666	-	-	-	-	-	690	-	-	-	-	-	-	-	-	-
Munster (town)	771	676	-	694	-	-	-	-	-	-	-	-	-	-	-	-	-	-	-	-	-	-	-	-
LaPorte County	495	463	-	-	-	-	-	-	-	-	-	-	-	-	-	-	-	-	-	-	-	-	-	-
Madison County	490	484	-	-	-	-	-	-	-	-	-	-	-	-	-	-	-	-	-	-	-	-	-	-
Marion County	567	584	-	600	-	-	511	-	629	-	-	-	-	602	652	-	-	-	-	-	-	-	-	625
Monroe County	560	542	-	582	-	-	519	-	-	-	-	-	-	-	568	-	-	-	-	-	-	-	-	-
Bloomington (city)	557	541	-	582	-	-	523	-	-	-	-	-	-	-	564	-	-	-	-	-	-	-	-	-
Porter County	625	622	-	-	-	-	-	-	-	-	-	-	-	-	-	-	-	-	-	-	-	-	-	-
St. Joseph County	535	572	-	542	-	-	527	-	-	-	-	-	-	-	625	-	-	-	-	-	-	-	-	-
Tippecanoe County	565	529	-	586	-	-	473	-	-	-	-	-	-	766	524	-	-	-	-	-	-	-	-	-
West Lafayette (city)	614	600	-	670	-	-	567	-	-	-	-	-	-	-	-	-	-	-	-	-	-	-	-	-
Vanderburgh County	458	547	-	-	-	-	-	-	-	-	-	-	-	-	-	-	-	-	-	-	-	-	-	-
Vigo County	445	417	-	-	-	-	-	-	-	-	-	-	-	-	-	-	-	-	-	-	-	-	-	-
Wayne County	446	439	-	-	-	-	-	-	-	-	-	-	-	-	-	-	-	-	-	-	-	-	-	-
IOWA	470	505	459	582	-	414	483	-	400	-	-	-	-	499	528	490	-	430	-	-	542	558	-	419
Black Hawk County	472	467	-	-	-	-	-	-	-	-	-	-	-	-	-	-	-	-	-	-	-	-	-	-
Buena Vista County[4]	417	459	-	-	-	-	-	-	-	-	-	-	-	-	-	538	-	-	-	-	-	-	-	-
Storm Lake (city)	435	456	-	-	-	-	-	-	-	-	-	-	-	-	-	552	-	-	-	-	-	-	-	-
Johnson County	564	487	-	565	-	-	455	-	-	-	-	-	-	-	502	-	-	-	-	-	-	-	-	-
Coralville (city)	561	576	-	-	-	-	-	-	-	-	-	-	-	-	-	-	-	-	-	-	-	-	-	-
Iowa City (city)	572	471	-	541	-	-	446	-	-	-	-	-	-	-	485	-	-	-	-	-	-	-	-	-
Linn County	510	570	-	606	-	-	-	-	-	-	-	-	-	-	553	-	-	-	-	-	-	-	-	-
Polk County	574	513	-	611	-	396	499	-	-	-	-	-	-	-	446	491	-	-	-	-	-	616	-	345

Notes: Please refer to the User's Guide for an explanation of data; data is arranged alphabetically by state, then county, then city within each county; table includes counties with populations greater than 49,999 unless noted and cities with populations greater than 9,999 whose Asian and/or NHPI population rates are greater than the national average; (1) Native Hawaiian and other Pacific Islander; (2) excludes Taiwanese; (3) includes Chamorro; (4) county does not meet population threshold but is shown in order to allow inclusion of city

Place	All specified renter-occupied housing units	Specified housing units rented by Asians	Specified housing units rented by NHPIs[1]	Asian Indian	Bangladeshi	Cambodian	Chinese[2]	Fijian	Filipino	Guamanian[3]	Hawaiian, Native	Hmong	Indonesian	Japanese	Korean	Laotian	Malaysian	Pakistani	Samoan	Sri Lankan	Taiwanese	Thai	Tongan	Vietnamese
Pottawattamie County	537	541	-	-	-	-	-	-	-	-	-	-	-	-	-	-	-	-	-	-	-	-	-	-
Scott County	496	539	-	-	-	-	-	-	-	-	-	-	-	-	-	-	-	-	-	-	-	-	-	394
Story County	575	541	-	660	-	-	497	-	-	-	-	-	-	-	580	-	-	-	-	-	-	-	-	-
Ames (city)	600	543	-	660	-	-	497	-	-	-	-	-	-	-	581	-	-	-	-	-	-	-	-	-
Woodbury County	494	415	-	-	-	-	-	-	-	-	-	-	-	-	-	-	-	-	-	-	-	-	-	399
KANSAS	498	509	509	623	-	401	493	-	581	-	517	465	-	557	494	446	-	511	-	-	415	555	-	420
Cowley County[4]	417	404	-	-	-	-	-	-	-	-	-	-	-	-	-	382	-	-	-	-	-	-	-	-
Winfield (city)	413	383	-	-	-	-	-	-	-	-	-	-	-	-	-	377	-	-	-	-	-	-	-	-
Douglas County	560	469	-	521	-	-	433	-	-	-	-	-	-	-	472	-	-	-	-	-	-	-	-	-
Lawrence (city)	555	470	-	521	-	-	433	-	-	-	-	-	-	-	472	-	-	-	-	-	-	-	-	-
Johnson County	702	693	-	702	-	-	691	-	735	-	-	-	-	684	740	513	-	-	-	-	-	-	-	575
Overland Park (city)	766	731	-	733	-	-	727	-	-	-	-	-	-	-	1,050	-	-	-	-	-	-	-	-	652
Leavenworth County	551	479	-	-	-	-	-	-	-	-	-	-	-	-	-	-	-	-	-	-	-	-	-	-
Riley County	475	318	-	-	-	-	288	-	-	-	-	-	-	-	341	-	-	-	-	-	-	-	-	-
Manhattan (city)	483	314	-	-	-	-	288	-	-	-	-	-	-	-	-	-	-	-	-	-	-	-	-	-
Saline County	457	418	-	-	-	-	-	-	-	-	-	-	-	-	-	-	-	-	-	-	-	-	-	332
Sedgwick County	511	421	526	498	-	398	459	-	504	-	-	-	-	-	480	348	-	-	-	-	-	-	-	400
Wichita (city)	505	413	-	481	-	-	462	-	514	-	-	-	-	-	473	322	-	-	-	-	-	-	-	395
Shawnee County	494	468	-	-	-	-	-	-	-	-	-	-	-	-	-	-	-	-	-	-	-	-	-	-
Wyandotte County	492	508	-	-	-	-	-	-	-	-	-	458	-	-	-	-	-	-	-	-	-	-	-	-
KENTUCKY	445	534	524	549	-	-	458	-	525	490	-	-	-	970	510	-	-	716	-	-	-	369	-	436
Boone County	596	1,000	-	-	-	-	-	-	-	-	-	-	-	2,000	-	-	-	-	-	-	-	-	-	-
Campbell County	512	701	-	-	-	-	-	-	-	-	-	-	-	-	-	-	-	-	-	-	-	-	-	-
Christian County	458	642	-	-	-	-	-	-	-	-	-	-	-	-	-	-	-	-	-	-	-	-	-	-
Fayette County	528	482	-	550	-	-	429	-	-	-	-	-	-	1,008	-	-	-	-	-	-	-	-	-	-
Hardin County	443	504	-	-	-	-	-	-	-	-	-	-	-	-	445	-	-	-	-	-	-	-	-	-
Radcliff (city)	433	437	-	-	-	-	-	-	-	-	-	-	-	-	-	-	-	-	-	-	-	-	-	-
Jefferson County	494	543	-	555	-	-	536	-	563	-	-	-	-	830	573	-	-	-	-	-	-	-	-	397
Kenton County	517	607	-	-	-	-	-	-	-	-	-	-	-	-	-	-	-	-	-	-	-	-	-	-
Madison County	428	630	-	-	-	-	-	-	-	-	-	-	-	-	-	-	-	-	-	-	-	-	-	-
Warren County	490	505	-	-	-	-	-	-	-	-	-	-	-	-	-	-	-	-	-	-	-	-	-	-
LOUISIANA	466	497	421	577	-	-	491	-	525	408	408	-	-	545	529	440	-	547	-	-	467	686	-	457
Ascension Parish	450	554	-	-	-	-	-	-	-	-	-	-	-	-	-	-	-	-	-	-	-	-	-	-
Bossier Parish	488	541	-	-	-	-	-	-	-	-	-	-	-	-	-	-	-	-	-	-	-	-	-	-
Caddo Parish	463	518	-	503	-	-	-	-	-	-	-	-	-	-	-	-	-	-	-	-	-	-	-	-
Calcasieu Parish	465	597	-	-	-	-	-	-	-	-	-	-	-	-	-	-	-	-	-	-	-	-	-	-
East Baton Rouge Parish	510	465	-	488	-	-	459	-	539	-	-	-	-	-	-	-	-	-	-	-	-	-	-	441
Iberia Parish	388	423	-	-	-	-	-	-	-	-	-	-	-	-	-	418	-	-	-	-	-	-	-	705
Jefferson Parish	544	536	-	653	-	-	548	-	576	-	-	-	-	-	562	-	-	538	-	-	-	-	-	455
Gretna (city)	457	474	-	-	-	-	-	-	-	-	-	-	-	-	-	-	-	-	-	-	-	-	-	448
Harvey (cdp)	488	475	-	-	-	-	-	-	-	-	-	-	-	-	-	-	-	-	-	-	-	-	-	465

Notes: Please refer to the User's Guide for an explanation of data; data is arranged alphabetically by state, then county, then city within each county; table includes counties with populations greater than 49,999 unless noted and cities with populations greater than 9,999 whose Asian and/or NHPI population rates are greater than the national average; (1) Native Hawaiian and other Pacific Islander; (2) excludes Taiwanese; (3) includes Chamorro; (4) county does not meet population threshold but is shown in order to allow inclusion of city

Place	All specified renter-occupied housing units	Specified housing units rented by Asians	Specified housing units rented by NHPIs[1]	Asian Indian	Bangladeshi	Cambodian	Chinese[2]	Fijian	Filipino	Guamanian[3]	Hawaiian, Native	Hmong	Indonesian	Japanese	Korean	Laotian	Malaysian	Pakistani	Samoan	Sri Lankan	Taiwanese	Thai	Tongan	Vietnamese
Timberlane (cdp)	610	1,375	-	-	-	-	-	-	-	-	-	-	-	-	-	-	-	-	-	-	-	-	-	1,375
Woodmere (cdp)	585	915	-	-	-	-	-	-	-	-	-	-	-	-	-	-	-	-	-	-	-	-	-	915
Lafayette Parish	475	526	-	607	-	-	-	-	-	-	-	-	-	-	-	-	-	-	-	-	-	-	-	444
Lafourche Parish	402	495	-	-	-	-	-	-	-	-	-	-	-	-	-	-	-	-	-	-	-	-	-	-
Orleans Parish	488	518	-	679	-	-	476	-	521	-	-	-	-	-	-	-	-	-	-	-	-	-	-	475
Ouachita Parish	444	426	-	-	-	-	-	-	-	-	-	-	-	-	-	-	-	-	-	-	-	-	-	-
Rapides Parish	434	407	-	-	-	-	-	-	-	-	-	-	-	-	-	-	-	-	-	-	-	-	-	-
St. Bernard Parish	489	460	-	-	-	-	-	-	-	-	-	-	-	-	-	-	-	-	-	-	-	-	-	388
St. Mary Parish	397	433	-	-	-	-	-	-	-	-	-	-	-	-	-	-	-	-	-	-	-	-	-	423
St. Tammany Parish	593	565	-	-	-	-	-	-	-	-	-	-	-	-	-	-	-	-	-	-	-	-	-	481
Terrebonne Parish	460	426	-	-	-	-	-	-	-	-	-	-	-	-	-	-	-	-	-	-	-	-	-	407
Vermilion Parish	342	375	-	-	-	-	-	-	-	-	-	-	-	-	-	-	-	-	-	-	-	-	-	375
Abbeville (city)	314	333	-	-	-	-	-	-	-	-	-	-	-	-	-	-	-	-	-	-	-	-	-	325
Vernon Parish	411	452	-	-	-	-	-	-	-	-	-	-	-	-	385	-	-	-	-	-	-	-	-	-
MAINE	497	532	831	508	-	509	563	-	603	-	-	-	-	500	638	-	-	-	-	-	-	-	-	466
Androscoggin County	433	579	-	-	-	-	-	-	-	-	-	-	-	-	-	-	-	-	-	-	-	-	-	-
Aroostook County	364	442	-	-	-	-	-	-	-	-	-	-	-	-	-	-	-	-	-	-	-	-	-	-
Cumberland County	615	542	-	-	-	503	756	-	472	-	-	-	-	-	-	-	-	-	-	-	-	-	-	470
Hancock County	514	575	-	-	-	-	-	-	-	-	-	-	-	-	-	-	-	-	-	-	-	-	-	-
Kennebec County	439	450	-	-	-	-	-	-	-	-	-	-	-	-	-	-	-	-	-	-	-	-	-	-
Oxford County	418	809	-	-	-	-	-	-	-	-	-	-	-	-	-	-	-	-	-	-	-	-	-	-
Penobscot County	468	539	-	-	-	-	569	-	-	-	-	-	-	-	-	-	-	-	-	-	-	-	-	-
York County	568	538	-	-	-	-	-	-	-	-	-	-	-	-	-	-	-	-	-	-	-	-	-	-
MARYLAND	689	788	728	800	772	721	789	-	760	769	720	-	853	954	780	786	-	769	-	685	794	819	-	765
Allegany County	381	564	-	-	-	-	-	-	-	-	-	-	-	-	-	-	-	-	-	-	-	-	-	-
Anne Arundel County	798	767	-	734	-	-	913	-	789	-	-	-	-	700	764	-	-	-	-	-	-	-	-	-
Severn (cdp)	831	724	-	-	-	-	-	-	-	-	-	-	-	-	600	-	-	-	-	-	-	-	-	-
South Gate (cdp)	711	694	-	-	-	-	-	-	-	-	-	-	-	-	745	-	-	-	-	-	-	-	-	-
Baltimore Independent City	498	575	-	627	-	-	586	-	537	-	-	-	-	-	483	-	-	-	-	-	-	-	-	610
Baltimore County	670	673	-	653	-	-	631	-	699	-	-	-	-	830	713	-	-	675	-	-	-	-	-	685
Arbutus (cdp)	609	499	-	-	-	-	-	-	-	-	-	-	-	-	-	-	-	-	-	-	-	-	-	-
Carney (cdp)	729	661	-	-	-	-	660	-	-	-	-	-	-	-	646	-	-	-	-	-	-	-	-	-
Cockeysville (cdp)	702	671	-	-	-	-	-	-	-	-	-	-	-	-	761	-	-	-	-	-	-	-	-	-
Lutherville-Timonium (cdp)	713	764	-	-	-	-	-	-	-	-	-	-	-	-	-	-	-	-	-	-	-	-	-	-
Mays Chapel (cdp)	839	1,375	-	-	-	-	-	-	-	-	-	-	-	-	-	-	-	-	-	-	-	-	-	-
Owings Mills (cdp)	783	785	-	-	-	-	-	-	-	-	-	-	-	-	-	-	-	-	-	-	-	-	-	-
Perry Hall (cdp)	793	775	-	-	-	-	-	-	-	-	-	-	-	-	736	-	-	-	-	-	-	-	-	-
Reisterstown (cdp)	640	655	-	633	-	-	-	-	-	-	-	-	-	-	-	-	-	-	-	-	-	-	-	-
Rossville (cdp)	631	644	-	-	-	-	-	-	-	-	-	-	-	-	-	-	-	-	-	-	-	-	-	-
Towson (cdp)	746	659	-	-	-	-	633	-	-	-	-	-	-	-	-	-	-	-	-	-	-	-	-	-
Woodlawn (cdp)	667	681	-	660	-	-	-	-	-	-	-	-	-	-	-	-	-	-	-	-	-	-	-	-

Notes: Please refer to the User's Guide for an explanation of data; data is arranged alphabetically by state, then county, then city within each county; table includes counties with populations greater than 49,999 unless noted and cities with populations greater than 9,999 whose Asian and/or NHPI population rates are greater than the national average; (1) Native Hawaiian and other Pacific Islander; (2) excludes Taiwanese; (3) includes Chamorro; (4) county does not meet population threshold but is shown in order to allow inclusion of city

Place	All specified renter-occupied housing units	Specified housing units rented by Asians	Specified housing units rented by NHPIs[1]	Asian Indian	Bangladeshi	Cambodian	Chinese[2]	Fijian	Filipino	Guamanian[3]	Hawaiian, Native	Hmong	Indonesian	Japanese	Korean	Laotian	Malaysian	Pakistani	Samoan	Sri Lankan	Taiwanese	Thai	Tongan	Vietnamese
Calvert County	837	1,125	-	-	-	-	-	-	-	-	-	-	-	-	-	-	-	-	-	-	-	-	-	-
Carroll County	638	717	-	-	-	-	-	-	-	-	-	-	-	-	-	-	-	-	-	-	-	-	-	-
Cecil County	617	823	-	-	-	-	-	-	-	-	-	-	-	-	-	-	-	-	-	-	-	-	-	-
Charles County	858	966	-	-	-	-	-	-	939	-	-	-	-	-	-	-	-	-	-	-	-	-	-	-
Frederick County	719	804	-	769	-	-	804	-	-	-	-	-	-	-	914	-	-	-	-	-	-	-	-	-
Harford County	648	688	-	479	-	-	-	-	647	-	-	-	-	-	759	-	-	-	-	-	-	-	-	-
Howard County	879	860	-	903	-	-	829	-	963	-	-	-	-	-	836	-	-	844	-	-	-	-	-	785
Columbia (cdp)	922	925	-	974	-	-	868	-	995	-	-	-	-	-	909	-	-	-	-	-	-	-	-	-
Elkridge (cdp)	928	924	-	-	-	-	-	-	-	-	-	-	-	-	886	-	-	-	-	-	-	-	-	-
Ellicott City (cdp)	769	776	-	766	-	-	757	-	633	-	-	-	-	-	784	-	-	792	-	-	-	-	-	-
North Laurel (cdp)	861	909	-	850	-	-	-	-	-	-	-	-	-	-	947	-	-	-	-	-	-	-	-	-
Savage-Guilford (cdp)	890	955	-	-	-	-	-	-	-	-	-	-	-	-	-	-	-	-	-	-	-	-	-	-
Montgomery County	914	883	893	898	761	875	873	-	869	-	-	-	916	1,148	913	-	-	961	-	1,170	873	861	-	768
Aspen Hill (cdp)	902	870	-	790	-	-	900	-	891	-	-	-	-	-	864	-	-	-	-	-	-	-	-	906
Bethesda (cdp)	1,013	897	-	1,038	-	-	857	-	686	-	-	-	-	1,600	928	-	-	-	-	-	-	-	-	-
Calverton (cdp)	876	877	-	893	-	-	-	-	-	-	-	-	-	-	877	-	-	-	-	-	-	-	-	-
Colesville (cdp)	1,184	1,375	-	0	-	-	0	-	-	-	-	-	-	-	1,524	-	-	-	-	-	-	-	-	908
Fairland (cdp)	914	893	-	912	-	-	866	-	-	-	-	-	-	-	900	-	-	-	-	-	-	-	-	-
Gaithersburg (city)	904	884	-	898	-	-	900	-	893	-	-	-	-	-	953	-	-	-	-	-	-	-	-	670
Germantown (cdp)	943	948	-	967	-	-	943	-	-	-	-	-	-	-	1,067	-	-	-	-	-	-	-	-	375
Montgomery Village (cdp)	937	848	-	830	-	-	833	-	1,135	-	-	-	-	-	-	-	-	-	-	-	-	-	-	956
North Bethesda (cdp)	1,047	962	-	1,063	-	-	887	-	828	-	-	-	-	1,380	929	-	-	-	-	-	-	-	-	-
North Potomac (cdp)	1,340	1,317	-	1,375	-	-	1,266	-	-	-	-	-	-	-	1,364	-	-	-	-	-	-	-	-	-
Olney (cdp)	1,113	266	-	0	-	-	0	-	-	-	-	-	-	-	675	-	-	-	-	-	-	-	-	-
Potomac (cdp)	1,179	1,591	-	2,001	-	-	736	-	1,375	-	-	-	-	-	138	-	-	-	-	-	-	-	-	-
Redland (cdp)	928	941	-	833	-	-	900	-	1,375	-	-	-	-	-	1,015	-	-	-	-	-	-	-	-	-
Rockville (city)	972	903	-	875	-	-	859	-	813	-	-	-	-	1,027	1,104	-	-	-	-	-	-	-	-	606
Silver Spring (cdp)	803	758	-	733	-	808	750	-	860	-	-	-	-	-	645	-	-	-	-	-	-	-	-	752
Takoma Park (city)	664	688	-	-	-	-	-	-	-	-	-	-	-	-	-	-	-	-	-	-	-	-	-	-
Wheaton-Glenmont (cdp)	911	791	-	850	-	-	774	-	738	-	-	-	-	-	813	-	-	-	-	-	-	-	-	613
White Oak (cdp)	873	883	-	960	-	-	860	-	-	-	-	-	-	-	864	-	-	-	-	-	-	-	-	879
Prince George's County	737	758	-	769	-	-	748	-	699	-	-	-	-	701	768	-	-	751	-	-	-	782	-	775
Adelphi (cdp)	783	761	-	-	-	-	-	-	-	-	-	-	-	-	-	-	-	-	-	-	-	-	-	-
Beltsville (cdp)	765	723	-	714	-	-	-	-	-	-	-	-	-	-	707	-	-	-	-	-	-	-	-	-
College Park (city)	806	715	-	877	-	-	692	-	-	-	-	-	-	-	-	-	-	-	-	-	-	-	-	-
Fort Washington (cdp)	764	696	-	-	-	-	-	-	696	-	-	-	-	-	-	-	-	-	-	-	-	-	-	-
Friendly (cdp)	1,106	0	-	-	-	-	-	-	0	-	-	-	-	-	-	-	-	-	-	-	-	-	-	-
Glenn Dale (cdp)	847	819	-	-	-	-	-	-	-	-	-	-	-	-	-	-	-	-	-	-	-	-	-	-
Greenbelt (city)	801	764	-	759	-	-	776	-	-	-	-	-	-	-	782	-	-	-	-	-	-	-	-	-
Hyattsville (city)	643	704	-	-	-	-	-	-	-	-	-	-	-	-	-	-	-	-	-	-	-	-	-	-
Lanham-Seabrook (cdp)	770	859	-	-	-	-	-	-	-	-	-	-	-	-	-	-	-	-	-	-	-	-	-	-

Notes: Please refer to the User's Guide for an explanation of data; data is arranged alphabetically by state, then county, then city within each county; table includes counties with populations greater than 49,999 unless noted and cities with populations greater than 9,999 whose Asian and/or NHPI population rates are greater than the national average; (1) Native Hawaiian and other Pacific Islander; (2) excludes Taiwanese; (3) includes Chamorro; (4) county does not meet population threshold but is shown in order to allow inclusion of city

Place	All specified renter-occupied housing units	Specified housing units rented by Asians	Specified housing units rented by NHPIs[1]	Asian Indian	Bangladeshi	Cambodian	Chinese[2]	Fijian	Filipino	Guamanian[3]	Hawaiian, Native	Hmong	Indonesian	Japanese	Korean	Laotian	Malaysian	Pakistani	Samoan	Sri Lankan	Taiwanese	Thai	Tongan	Vietnamese
Laurel (city)	774	749	-	-	-	-	-	-	-	-	-	-	-	-	-	-	-	-	-	-	-	-	-	-
New Carrollton (city)	768	778	-	-	-	-	-	-	-	-	-	-	-	-	-	-	-	-	-	-	-	-	-	-
South Laurel (cdp)	760	746	-	-	-	-	-	-	-	-	-	-	-	-	-	-	-	-	-	-	-	-	-	-
St. Mary's County	719	683	-	914	-	-	-	-	608	-	-	-	-	-	-	-	-	-	-	-	-	-	-	-
Lexington Park (cdp)	740	489	-	-	-	-	-	-	-	-	-	-	-	-	-	-	-	-	-	-	-	-	-	-
Washington County	482	581	-	-	-	-	-	-	-	-	-	-	-	-	-	-	-	-	-	-	-	-	-	-
Wicomico County	567	723	-	784	-	-	-	-	-	-	-	-	-	-	640	-	-	-	-	-	-	-	-	-
Salisbury (city)	574	740	-	-	-	-	-	-	-	-	-	-	-	-	-	-	-	-	-	-	-	-	-	-
MASSACHUSETTS	684	839	784	966	613	602	774	-	832	883	831	591	883	1,069	972	649	-	895	-	906	906	849	-	687
Barnstable County	723	831	-	-	-	-	912	-	-	-	-	-	-	-	-	-	-	-	-	-	-	-	-	-
Berkshire County	499	538	-	569	-	-	-	-	-	-	-	-	-	-	-	-	-	-	-	-	-	-	-	-
Bristol County	499	531	-	789	-	388	535	-	547	-	-	-	-	-	616	-	-	-	-	-	-	-	-	656
Essex County	665	731	-	846	-	625	803	-	696	-	-	-	-	940	766	654	-	-	-	-	-	-	-	663
Andover (town)	781	1,179	-	909	-	-	1,536	-	-	-	-	-	-	-	-	-	-	-	-	-	-	-	-	-
Lynn (city)	608	646	-	584	-	613	-	-	-	-	-	-	-	-	-	-	-	-	-	-	-	-	-	775
North Andover (town)	879	1,171	-	-	-	-	1,188	-	-	-	-	-	-	-	-	-	-	-	-	-	-	-	-	-
Franklin County	541	659	-	-	-	-	-	-	-	-	-	-	-	-	-	-	-	-	-	-	-	-	-	-
Hampden County	535	572	-	548	-	493	592	-	-	-	-	-	-	-	465	-	-	-	-	-	-	-	-	569
Hampshire County	631	642	-	729	-	-	609	-	-	-	-	-	-	-	764	-	-	-	-	-	-	-	-	-
Amherst Center (cdp)	654	537	-	-	-	-	-	-	-	-	-	-	-	-	-	-	-	-	-	-	-	-	-	-
Amherst (town)	687	628	-	-	-	-	575	-	-	-	-	-	-	-	-	-	-	-	-	-	-	-	-	-
Middlesex County	835	922	-	975	-	648	940	-	907	-	-	-	-	1,167	1,000	661	-	971	-	-	847	873	-	747
Acton (town)	867	886	-	877	-	-	906	-	-	-	-	-	-	-	-	-	-	-	-	-	-	-	-	-
Arlington (town)	934	952	-	-	-	-	925	-	-	-	-	-	-	-	-	-	-	-	-	-	-	-	-	-
Bedford (town)	980	655	-	-	-	-	-	-	-	-	-	-	-	-	-	-	-	-	-	-	-	-	-	-
Belmont (cdp)	1,141	1,335	-	-	-	-	1,352	-	-	-	-	-	-	-	-	-	-	-	-	-	-	-	-	-
Belmont (town)	1,141	1,335	-	-	-	-	1,352	-	-	-	-	-	-	-	-	-	-	-	-	-	-	-	-	-
Burlington (town)	1,061	961	-	947	-	-	-	-	-	-	-	-	-	-	-	-	-	-	-	-	-	-	-	-
Cambridge (city)	962	1,046	-	1,054	-	-	962	-	-	-	-	-	-	1,191	1,090	-	-	-	-	-	-	-	-	-
Chelmsford (town)	777	927	-	997	-	-	697	-	-	-	-	-	-	-	-	-	-	-	-	-	-	-	-	-
Framingham (town)	835	1,006	-	1,053	-	-	1,003	-	-	-	-	-	-	-	-	-	-	-	-	-	-	-	-	-
Lexington (town)	1,288	1,399	-	1,347	-	-	1,275	-	-	-	-	-	-	-	1,367	-	-	-	-	-	-	-	-	-
Lowell (city)	627	671	-	782	-	650	690	-	-	-	-	-	-	-	-	661	-	-	-	-	-	-	-	623
Malden (city)	777	887	-	1,077	-	-	834	-	-	-	-	-	-	-	-	-	-	-	-	-	-	-	-	724
Marlborough (city)	811	984	-	978	-	-	-	-	-	-	-	-	-	-	-	-	-	-	-	-	-	-	-	-
Medford (city)	819	936	-	1,145	-	-	920	-	-	-	-	-	-	-	-	-	-	-	-	-	-	-	-	686
Natick (town)	873	1,056	-	-	-	-	963	-	-	-	-	-	-	-	-	-	-	-	-	-	-	-	-	-
Newton (city)	1,083	1,337	-	1,375	-	-	1,250	-	-	-	-	-	-	-	1,561	-	-	-	-	-	-	-	-	-
Somerville (city)	874	977	-	949	-	-	1,026	-	-	-	-	-	-	-	871	-	-	-	-	-	-	-	-	-
Sudbury (town)	756	125	-	-	-	-	-	-	-	-	-	-	-	-	-	-	-	-	-	-	-	-	-	-
Waltham (city)	869	969	-	1,070	-	-	847	-	-	-	-	-	-	-	-	-	-	-	-	-	-	-	-	-

Notes: Please refer to the User's Guide for an explanation of data; data is arranged alphabetically by state, then county, then city within each county; table includes counties with populations greater than 49,999 unless noted and cities with populations greater than 9,999 whose Asian and/or NHPI population rates are greater than the national average; (1) Native Hawaiian and other Pacific Islander; (2) excludes Taiwanese; (3) includes Chamorro; (4) county does not meet population threshold but is shown in order to allow inclusion of city

Place	All specified renter-occupied housing units	Specified housing units rented by Asians	Specified housing units rented by NHPIs[1]	Asian Indian	Bangladeshi	Cambodian	Chinese[2]	Fijian	Filipino	Guamanian[3]	Hawaiian, Native	Hmong	Indonesian	Japanese	Korean	Laotian	Malaysian	Pakistani	Samoan	Sri Lankan	Taiwanese	Thai	Tongan	Vietnamese
Wayland (town)	821	850	-	-	-	-	-	-	-	-	-	-	-	-	-	-	-	-	-	-	-	-	-	-
Westford (town)	690	0	-	-	-	-	0	-	-	-	-	-	-	-	-	-	-	-	-	-	-	-	-	-
Weston (town)	780	0	-	-	-	-	0	-	-	-	-	-	-	-	-	-	-	-	-	-	-	-	-	-
Winchester (town)	1,031	985	-	-	-	-	-	-	-	-	-	-	-	-	-	-	-	-	-	-	-	-	-	-
Woburn (city)	881	1,018	-	1,055	-	-	-	-	-	-	-	-	-	-	-	-	-	-	-	-	-	-	-	-
Norfolk County	853	1,027	-	1,086	-	-	892	-	888	-	-	-	-	1,293	1,353	-	-	-	-	-	1,174	-	-	894
Brookline (town)	1,262	1,302	-	1,165	-	-	1,205	-	-	-	-	-	-	1,361	1,437	-	-	-	-	-	-	-	-	-
Needham (town)	1,289	1,235	-	-	-	-	1,250	-	-	-	-	-	-	-	-	-	-	-	-	-	-	-	-	-
Norwood (town)	895	1,123	-	1,116	-	-	-	-	-	-	-	-	-	-	-	-	-	-	-	-	-	-	-	-
Quincy (city)	808	879	-	1,035	-	-	780	-	853	-	-	-	-	-	-	-	-	-	-	-	-	-	-	845
Randolph (town)	863	970	-	-	-	-	290	-	-	-	-	-	-	-	-	-	-	-	-	-	-	-	-	1,057
Sharon (town)	782	275	-	-	-	-	-	-	-	-	-	-	-	-	-	-	-	-	-	-	-	-	-	-
Wellesley (town)	1,063	982	-	-	-	-	914	-	-	-	-	-	-	-	-	-	-	-	-	-	-	-	-	-
Plymouth County	679	806	-	838	-	-	802	-	625	-	-	-	-	-	-	-	-	-	-	-	-	-	-	597
Suffolk County	791	816	-	1,068	-	561	612	-	930	-	-	-	-	977	1,020	-	-	-	-	-	978	-	-	742
Boston (city)	803	824	-	1,091	-	628	617	-	936	-	-	-	-	979	1,029	-	-	-	-	-	978	-	-	747
Chelsea (city)	695	689	-	-	-	-	-	-	-	-	-	-	-	-	-	-	-	-	-	-	-	-	-	713
Revere (city)	726	678	-	-	-	532	-	-	-	-	-	-	-	-	-	-	-	-	-	-	-	-	-	717
Worcester County	580	651	-	827	-	643	681	-	630	-	-	578	-	648	723	509	-	682	-	-	-	-	-	566
Fitchburg (city)	555	581	-	-	-	-	-	-	-	-	-	583	-	-	-	534	-	-	-	-	-	-	-	-
Northborough (town)	792	879	-	-	-	-	-	-	-	-	-	-	-	-	-	-	-	-	-	-	-	-	-	-
Shrewsbury (town)	817	877	-	894	-	-	783	-	-	-	-	-	-	-	-	-	-	-	-	-	-	-	-	785
Westborough (town)	863	953	-	939	-	-	945	-	-	-	-	-	-	-	-	-	-	-	-	-	-	-	-	-
Worcester (city)	577	603	-	636	-	-	628	-	-	-	-	-	-	-	-	-	-	-	-	-	-	-	-	549
MICHIGAN	546	659	545	690	522	555	607	-	615	563	573	460	533	1,011	656	603	497	680	488	533	704	631	-	538
Allegan County	515	549	-	-	-	-	-	-	-	-	-	-	-	-	-	-	-	-	-	-	-	-	-	-
Bay County	440	483	-	-	-	-	-	-	-	-	-	-	-	-	-	-	-	-	-	-	-	-	-	-
Berrien County	476	492	-	534	-	-	-	-	375	-	-	-	-	-	482	-	-	-	-	-	-	-	-	-
Calhoun County	484	620	-	-	-	-	-	-	-	-	-	-	-	1,125	-	-	-	-	-	-	-	-	-	-
Cass County	471	619	-	-	-	-	-	-	-	-	-	-	-	-	-	619	-	-	-	-	-	-	-	-
Clinton County	511	488	-	-	-	-	-	-	-	-	-	-	-	-	-	-	-	-	-	-	-	-	-	-
Eaton County	569	594	-	620	-	-	-	-	-	-	-	-	-	-	-	-	-	-	-	-	-	-	-	625
Genesee County	507	584	-	608	-	-	470	-	634	-	-	-	-	-	534	-	-	-	-	-	-	-	-	-
Ingham County	542	506	-	595	-	-	476	-	517	-	-	338	-	601	499	-	-	-	-	-	-	-	-	439
East Lansing (city)	578	476	-	493	-	-	448	-	-	-	-	-	-	-	468	-	-	-	-	-	-	-	-	-
Meridian charter (township)	641	697	-	762	-	-	656	-	-	-	-	-	-	-	674	-	-	-	-	-	-	-	-	-
Okemos (cdp)	674	689	-	776	-	-	632	-	-	-	-	-	-	-	-	-	-	-	-	-	-	-	-	-
Ionia County	468	607	-	-	-	-	-	-	-	-	-	-	-	-	-	-	-	-	-	-	-	-	-	-
Isabella County	462	438	-	-	-	-	-	-	-	-	-	-	-	-	-	-	-	-	-	-	-	-	-	-
Jackson County	505	759	-	-	-	-	-	-	-	-	-	-	-	-	-	-	-	-	-	-	-	-	-	-
Kalamazoo County	529	509	-	547	-	-	474	-	-	-	-	-	-	-	613	-	-	-	-	-	-	-	-	-

Notes: Please refer to the User's Guide for an explanation of data; data is arranged alphabetically by state, then county, then city within each county; table includes counties with populations greater than 49,999 unless noted and cities with populations greater than 9,999 whose Asian and/or NHPI population rates are greater than the national average; (1) Native Hawaiian and other Pacific Islander; (2) excludes Taiwanese; (3) includes Chamorro; (4) county does not meet population threshold but is shown in order to allow inclusion of city

Place	All specified renter-occupied housing units	Specified housing units rented by Asians	Specified housing units rented by NHPIs[1]	Asian Indian	Bangladeshi	Cambodian	Chinese[2]	Fijian	Filipino	Guamanian[3]	Hawaiian, Native	Hmong	Indonesian	Japanese	Korean	Laotian	Malaysian	Pakistani	Samoan	Sri Lankan	Taiwanese	Thai	Tongan	Vietnamese
Kent County	554	552	-	621	-	-	565	-	547	-	-	-	-	-	550	-	-	-	-	-	-	-	-	497
Kentwood (city)	586	626	-	-	-	-	-	-	-	-	-	-	-	-	536	-	-	-	-	-	-	-	-	447
Lenawee County	517	631	-	-	-	-	-	-	-	-	-	-	-	-	-	-	-	-	-	-	-	-	-	-
Livingston County	681	640	-	-	-	-	-	-	-	-	-	-	-	-	-	-	-	-	-	-	-	-	-	-
Macomb County	603	634	-	662	-	-	629	-	591	-	-	639	-	-	649	-	-	585	-	-	-	-	-	521
Sterling Heights (city)	644	641	-	642	-	-	720	-	611	-	-	-	-	-	631	-	-	-	-	-	-	-	-	500
Marquette County	398	475	-	-	-	-	-	-	-	-	-	-	-	-	-	-	-	-	-	-	-	-	-	-
Midland County	498	444	-	684	-	-	438	-	-	-	-	-	-	-	-	-	-	-	-	-	-	-	-	-
Monroe County	549	776	-	-	-	-	-	-	-	-	-	-	-	-	-	-	-	-	-	-	-	-	-	-
Muskegon County	453	539	-	-	-	-	-	-	-	-	-	-	-	-	-	-	-	-	-	-	-	-	-	-
Oakland County	707	799	-	780	-	-	649	-	710	-	-	443	-	1,352	824	-	-	858	-	-	714	-	-	689
Auburn Hills (city)	749	760	-	748	-	-	-	-	-	-	-	-	-	-	-	-	-	-	-	-	-	-	-	-
Bloomfield (township)	905	953	-	993	-	-	-	-	-	-	-	-	-	-	950	-	-	-	-	-	-	-	-	-
Farmington (city)	734	764	-	766	-	-	-	-	-	-	-	-	-	-	-	-	-	-	-	-	-	-	-	-
Farmington Hills (city)	840	855	-	840	-	-	565	-	870	-	-	-	-	-	-	-	-	-	-	-	-	-	-	-
Madison Heights (city)	588	604	-	-	-	-	596	-	-	-	-	-	-	-	-	-	-	-	-	-	-	-	-	-
Novi (city)	817	1,305	-	950	-	-	644	-	-	-	-	-	-	1,517	-	-	-	-	-	-	-	-	-	-
Rochester (city)	633	613	-	-	-	-	-	-	-	-	-	-	-	-	-	-	-	-	-	-	-	-	-	-
Rochester Hills (city)	827	920	-	797	-	-	738	-	-	-	-	-	-	-	1,060	-	-	-	-	-	-	-	-	-
Troy (city)	808	825	-	818	-	-	763	-	871	-	-	-	-	-	913	-	-	-	-	-	791	-	-	-
West Bloomfield (township)	1,182	1,388	-	1,238	-	-	1,625	-	0	-	-	-	-	1,479	1,125	-	-	-	-	-	-	-	-	-
Ottawa County	579	592	-	631	-	575	950	-	-	-	-	-	-	-	375	604	-	-	-	-	-	-	-	571
Holland (city)	551	546	-	-	-	-	-	-	-	-	-	-	-	-	-	-	-	-	-	-	-	-	-	-
Saginaw County	497	546	-	517	-	-	-	-	619	-	-	-	-	-	544	-	-	-	-	-	-	-	-	-
St. Clair County	537	605	-	-	-	-	-	-	-	-	-	-	-	-	-	-	-	-	-	-	-	-	-	-
St. Joseph County	456	472	-	-	-	-	-	-	-	-	-	-	-	-	-	-	-	-	-	-	-	-	-	-
Washtenaw County	687	741	-	725	-	-	683	-	783	-	-	-	-	897	763	-	-	797	-	-	808	-	-	680
Ann Arbor (city)	742	769	-	757	-	-	710	-	802	-	-	-	-	992	763	-	-	-	-	-	808	-	-	-
Pittsfield charter (township)	732	745	-	734	-	-	728	-	-	-	-	-	-	-	793	-	-	-	-	-	-	-	-	-
Scio (township)	741	739	-	-	-	-	-	-	-	-	-	-	-	-	-	-	-	-	-	-	-	-	-	-
Wayne County	530	613	492	635	493	-	594	-	619	-	-	506	-	664	584	-	-	636	-	-	-	-	-	577
Brownstown (township)	535	575	-	-	-	-	-	-	-	-	-	-	-	-	-	-	-	-	-	-	-	-	-	-
Canton (township)	666	644	-	615	-	-	640	-	781	-	-	-	-	-	788	-	-	-	-	-	-	-	-	-
Hamtramck (city)	454	495	-	474	496	-	-	-	-	-	-	-	-	-	-	-	-	-	-	-	-	-	-	-
Inkster (city)	557	648	-	642	-	-	-	-	-	-	-	-	-	-	-	-	-	-	-	-	-	-	-	-
Northville (township)	835	970	-	938	-	-	-	-	-	-	-	-	-	-	-	-	-	-	-	-	-	-	-	-
MINNESOTA	566	587	584	733	-	556	589	-	669	441	588	515	-	658	616	522	-	784	-	-	396	571	-	512
Anoka County	649	570	-	499	-	-	1,125	-	475	-	-	610	-	-	579	-	-	-	-	-	-	-	-	606
Columbia Heights (city)	567	472	-	-	-	-	-	-	-	-	-	-	-	-	-	-	-	-	-	-	-	-	-	-
Blue Earth County	487	467	-	-	-	-	-	-	-	-	-	-	-	-	-	-	-	-	-	-	-	-	-	-
Carver County	637	631	-	-	-	-	-	-	-	-	-	-	-	-	-	-	-	-	-	-	-	-	-	-

Notes: Please refer to the User's Guide for an explanation of data; data is arranged alphabetically by state, then county, then city within each county; table includes counties with populations greater than 49,999 unless noted and cities with populations greater than 9,999 whose Asian and/or NHPI population rates are greater than the national average; (1) Native Hawaiian and other Pacific Islander; (2) excludes Taiwanese; (3) includes Chamorro; (4) county does not meet population threshold but is shown in order to allow inclusion of city

Place	All specified renter-occupied housing units	Specified housing units rented by Asians	Specified housing units rented by NHPIs[1]	Asian Indian	Bangladeshi	Cambodian	Chinese[2]	Fijian	Filipino	Guamanian[3]	Hawaiian, Native	Hmong	Indonesian	Japanese	Korean	Laotian	Malaysian	Pakistani	Samoan	Sri Lankan	Taiwanese	Thai	Tongan	Vietnamese
Clay County	421	212	-	-	-	-	-	-	-	-	-	-	-	-	-	-	-	-	-	-	-	-	-	-
Crow Wing County	458	555	-	-	-	-	-	-	-	-	-	-	-	-	-	-	-	-	-	-	-	-	-	-
Dakota County	722	751	-	808	-	613	699	-	879	-	-	-	-	-	689	622	-	-	-	-	-	-	-	741
Eagan (city)	806	786	-	834	-	-	685	-	-	-	-	-	-	-	-	-	-	-	-	-	-	-	-	729
Hennepin County	654	628	593	769	-	665	640	-	693	-	-	560	-	653	616	568	-	875	-	-	-	-	-	506
Bloomington (city)	753	723	-	841	-	632	726	-	-	-	-	-	-	-	591	-	-	-	-	-	-	-	-	685
Brooklyn Center (city)	636	624	-	-	-	-	-	-	-	-	-	617	-	-	-	659	-	-	-	-	-	-	-	-
Brooklyn Park (city)	663	676	-	769	-	-	-	-	-	-	-	617	-	-	-	689	-	-	-	-	-	-	-	665
Eden Prairie (city)	883	857	-	864	-	-	823	-	-	-	-	-	-	-	-	-	-	-	-	-	-	-	-	454
Hopkins (city)	710	725	-	746	-	-	-	-	-	-	-	-	-	-	-	-	-	-	-	-	-	-	-	-
Minneapolis (city)	575	534	-	602	-	625	575	-	689	-	-	551	-	579	550	517	-	-	-	-	-	-	-	339
Plymouth (city)	857	864	-	874	-	-	882	-	-	-	-	-	-	-	900	-	-	-	-	-	-	-	-	-
Richfield (city)	638	662	-	-	-	-	-	-	-	-	-	-	-	-	-	-	-	-	-	-	-	-	-	674
Nobles County[4]	388	432	-	-	-	-	-	-	-	-	-	-	-	-	-	422	-	-	-	-	-	-	-	-
Worthington (city)	396	426	-	-	-	-	-	-	-	-	-	-	-	-	-	407	-	-	-	-	-	-	-	-
Olmsted County	556	633	-	689	-	505	418	-	-	-	-	1,014	-	838	691	517	-	-	-	-	-	-	-	505
Rochester (city)	561	637	-	689	-	515	418	-	-	-	-	1,014	-	-	691	517	-	-	-	-	-	-	-	505
Otter Tail County	391	281	-	-	-	-	-	-	-	-	-	-	-	-	-	-	-	-	-	-	-	-	-	-
Ramsey County	606	534	-	698	-	459	541	-	661	-	-	495	-	681	616	394	-	-	-	-	-	-	-	508
Maplewood (city)	688	686	-	-	-	-	711	-	-	-	-	596	-	-	-	-	-	-	-	-	-	-	-	-
New Brighton (city)	663	649	-	-	-	-	-	-	-	-	-	-	-	-	-	-	-	-	-	-	-	-	-	-
Roseville (city)	688	682	-	-	-	-	656	-	-	-	-	-	-	-	-	-	-	-	-	-	-	-	-	-
St. Paul (city)	565	503	-	657	-	391	531	-	658	-	-	488	-	-	586	394	-	-	-	-	-	-	-	451
Vadnais Heights (city)	708	850	-	-	-	-	-	-	-	-	-	-	-	-	-	-	-	-	-	-	-	-	-	-
Rice County	519	575	-	-	-	-	-	-	-	-	-	-	-	-	-	-	-	-	-	-	-	-	-	-
St. Louis County	415	383	-	-	-	-	-	-	-	-	-	-	-	-	575	-	-	-	-	-	-	-	-	-
Scott County	655	814	-	-	-	0	-	-	-	-	-	-	-	-	-	-	-	-	-	-	-	-	-	525
Savage (city)	694	604	-	-	-	-	-	-	-	-	-	-	-	-	-	-	-	-	-	-	-	-	-	-
Sherburne County	570	432	-	-	-	-	-	-	-	-	-	-	-	-	-	-	-	-	-	-	-	-	-	-
Stearns County	473	434	-	-	-	-	-	-	-	-	-	-	-	-	-	-	-	-	-	-	-	-	-	527
Washington County	699	911	-	871	-	-	525	-	-	-	-	866	-	-	1,125	-	-	-	-	-	-	-	-	580
Woodbury (city)	991	939	-	643	-	-	0	-	-	-	-	1,125	-	-	-	-	-	-	-	-	-	-	-	-
Wright County	526	225	-	-	-	-	-	-	-	-	-	-	-	-	-	-	-	-	-	-	-	-	-	-
MISSISSIPPI	439	518	471	548	-	-	424	-	541	-	-	-	-	443	470	-	-	-	-	-	-	-	-	562
DeSoto County	657	689	-	-	-	-	-	-	-	-	-	-	-	-	-	-	-	-	-	-	-	-	-	-
Forrest County	438	421	-	-	-	-	-	-	-	-	-	-	-	-	-	-	-	-	-	-	-	-	-	-
Harrison County	543	555	-	-	-	-	-	-	570	-	-	-	-	-	-	-	-	-	-	-	-	-	-	566
Biloxi (city)	531	557	-	-	-	-	-	-	565	-	-	-	-	-	-	-	-	-	-	-	-	-	-	588
Hinds County	503	525	-	612	-	-	-	-	-	-	-	-	-	-	-	-	-	-	-	-	-	-	-	-
Jackson County	522	584	-	-	-	-	-	-	-	-	-	-	-	-	-	-	-	-	-	-	-	-	-	758
Madison County	590	528	-	-	-	-	-	-	-	-	-	-	-	-	-	-	-	-	-	-	-	-	-	-

Notes: Please refer to the User's Guide for an explanation of data; data is arranged alphabetically by state, then county, then city within each county; table includes counties with populations greater than 49,999 unless noted and cities with populations greater than 9,999 whose Asian and/or NHPI population rates are greater than the national average; (1) Native Hawaiian and other Pacific Islander; (2) excludes Taiwanese; (3) includes Chamorro; (4) county does not meet population threshold but is shown in order to allow inclusion of city

Place	All specified renter-occupied housing units	Specified housing units rented by Asians	Specified housing units rented by NHPIs[1]	Asian Indian	Bangladeshi	Cambodian	Chinese[2]	Fijian	Filipino	Guamanian[3]	Hawaiian, Native	Hmong	Indonesian	Japanese	Korean	Laotian	Malaysian	Pakistani	Samoan	Sri Lankan	Taiwanese	Thai	Tongan	Vietnamese
Oktibbeha County[4]	473	421	-	-	-	-	-	-	-	-	-	-	-	-	-	-	-	-	-	-	-	-	-	-
Starkville (city)	473	382	-	-	-	-	-	-	-	-	-	-	-	-	-	-	-	-	-	-	-	-	-	-
Rankin County	576	754	-	-	-	-	-	-	-	-	-	-	-	-	-	-	-	-	-	-	-	-	-	-
MISSOURI	484	540	552	613	-	545	519	-	524	548	573	-	-	557	572	456	-	700	542	-	548	553	-	436
Boone County	523	505	-	585	-	-	442	-	-	-	-	-	-	-	516	-	-	-	-	-	-	-	-	-
Columbia (city)	525	500	-	585	-	-	440	-	-	-	-	-	-	-	478	-	-	-	-	-	-	-	-	-
Cape Girardeau County	440	465	-	-	-	-	-	-	-	-	-	-	-	-	-	-	-	-	-	-	-	-	-	-
Cass County	543	508	-	-	-	-	-	-	-	-	-	-	-	-	-	-	-	-	-	-	-	-	-	-
Clay County	576	599	-	663	-	-	-	-	-	-	-	-	-	-	-	-	-	-	-	-	-	-	-	591
Cole County	441	471	-	-	-	-	-	-	-	-	-	-	-	-	-	-	-	-	-	-	-	-	-	-
Franklin County	471	0	-	-	-	-	-	-	-	-	-	-	-	-	-	-	-	-	-	-	-	-	-	-
Greene County	462	440	-	-	-	-	414	-	-	-	-	-	-	-	560	-	-	-	-	-	-	-	-	531
Jackson County	536	491	623	563	-	-	462	-	657	-	-	-	-	489	495	-	-	-	653	-	-	-	-	426
Independence (city)	518	478	445	-	-	-	-	-	-	-	-	-	-	-	-	-	-	-	-	-	-	-	-	-
Jasper County	441	428	-	-	-	-	-	-	-	-	-	-	-	-	-	-	-	-	-	-	-	-	-	-
Jefferson County	502	575	-	-	-	-	-	-	-	-	-	-	-	-	-	-	-	-	-	-	-	-	-	-
Newton County	421	662	-	-	-	-	-	-	-	-	-	-	-	-	-	-	-	-	-	-	-	-	-	-
Phelps County[4]	396	317	-	386	-	-	-	-	-	-	-	-	-	-	-	-	-	-	-	-	-	-	-	-
Rolla (city)	402	308	-	-	-	-	-	-	-	-	-	-	-	-	-	-	-	-	-	-	-	-	-	-
Platte County	640	559	-	-	-	-	-	-	-	-	-	-	-	-	-	-	-	-	-	-	-	-	-	-
St. Charles County	624	671	-	722	-	-	608	-	432	-	-	-	-	-	-	-	-	-	-	-	-	-	-	-
Saint Louis Independent City	442	484	-	563	-	-	617	-	444	-	-	-	-	-	-	-	-	-	-	-	-	-	-	380
St. Louis County	601	638	601	671	-	-	595	-	554	-	-	-	-	756	633	-	-	743	-	-	691	468	-	520
Chesterfield (city)	838	819	-	839	-	-	775	-	-	-	-	-	-	-	-	-	-	-	-	-	-	-	-	-
Clayton (city)	708	674	-	-	-	-	-	-	-	-	-	-	-	-	-	-	-	-	-	-	-	-	-	-
Creve Coeur (city)	777	773	-	-	-	-	-	-	-	-	-	-	-	-	-	-	-	-	-	-	-	-	-	-
Manchester (city)	690	689	-	-	-	-	-	-	-	-	-	-	-	-	-	-	-	-	-	-	-	-	-	-
Maryland Heights (city)	659	661	-	640	-	-	657	-	-	-	-	-	-	-	-	-	-	-	-	-	-	-	-	-
Town and Country (city)	903	675	-	0	-	-	-	-	-	-	-	-	-	-	-	-	-	-	-	-	-	-	-	-
MONTANA	447	411	513	421	-	-	433	-	368	-	429	-	-	389	414	-	-	-	-	-	-	-	-	-
Cascade County	414	367	-	-	-	-	-	-	-	-	-	-	-	-	-	-	-	-	-	-	-	-	-	-
Flathead County	484	421	-	-	-	-	-	-	-	-	-	-	-	-	-	-	-	-	-	-	-	-	-	-
Gallatin County	555	405	-	-	-	-	-	-	-	-	-	-	-	-	-	-	-	-	-	-	-	-	-	-
Missoula County	530	431	-	-	-	-	-	-	-	-	-	-	-	-	-	-	-	-	-	-	-	-	-	-
Yellowstone County	474	352	-	-	-	-	-	-	-	-	-	-	-	-	-	-	-	-	-	-	-	-	-	-
NEBRASKA	491	495	444	547	-	-	425	-	491	-	-	-	-	500	569	603	-	-	-	-	-	519	-	481
Douglas County	541	523	-	586	-	-	397	-	489	-	-	-	-	484	584	-	-	-	-	-	-	-	-	580
Hall County	456	493	-	-	-	-	-	-	-	-	-	-	-	-	-	-	-	-	-	-	-	-	-	-
Lancaster County	519	453	-	514	-	-	424	-	-	-	-	-	-	-	575	-	-	-	-	-	-	-	-	442
Sarpy County	607	530	-	-	-	-	-	-	528	-	-	-	-	-	391	-	-	-	-	-	-	-	-	583
NEVADA	699	686	699	713	-	769	697	-	678	770	676	-	-	659	720	655	-	706	839	-	710	674	560	717

Notes: Please refer to the User's Guide for an explanation of data; data is arranged alphabetically by state, then county, then city within each county; table includes counties with populations greater than 49,999 unless noted and cities with populations greater than 9,999 whose Asian and/or NHPI population rates are greater than the national average; (1) Native Hawaiian and other Pacific Islander; (2) excludes Taiwanese; (3) includes Chamorro; (4) county does not meet population threshold but is shown in order to allow inclusion of city

Place	All specified renter-occupied housing units	Specified housing units rented by Asians	Specified housing units rented by NHPIs[1]	Asian Indian	Bangladeshi	Cambodian	Chinese[2]	Fijian	Filipino	Guamanian[3]	Hawaiian, Native	Hmong	Indonesian	Japanese	Korean	Laotian	Malaysian	Pakistani	Samoan	Sri Lankan	Taiwanese	Thai	Tongan	Vietnamese
Carson City Independent City	650	689	-	-	-	-	-	-	709	-	-	-	-	-	-	-	-	-	-	-	-	-	-	-
Clark County	716	700	726	733	-	769	717	-	685	806	690	-	-	686	730	655	-	-	840	-	710	671	-	727
Enterprise (cdp)	834	788	-	-	-	-	-	-	-	-	-	-	-	-	-	-	-	-	-	-	-	-	-	-
Henderson (city)	857	840	1,010	1,005	-	-	803	-	826	-	1,090	-	-	832	881	-	-	-	-	-	-	-	-	-
Las Vegas (city)	699	673	724	689	-	-	672	-	686	-	714	-	-	669	708	-	-	-	-	-	-	589	-	597
North Las Vegas (city)	644	735	806	-	-	-	-	-	696	-	-	-	-	-	-	-	-	-	-	-	-	-	-	-
Paradise (cdp)	675	653	654	735	-	-	639	-	628	-	611	-	-	632	711	-	-	-	-	-	-	-	-	676
Spring Valley (cdp)	827	798	781	-	-	-	782	-	830	-	-	-	-	759	811	-	-	-	-	-	-	896	-	832
Sunrise Manor (cdp)	688	655	985	-	-	-	765	-	651	-	-	-	-	475	744	-	-	-	-	-	-	-	-	-
Winchester (cdp)	662	634	-	-	-	-	-	-	610	-	-	-	-	-	-	-	-	-	-	-	-	-	-	-
Washoe County	675	623	617	586	-	-	577	-	652	-	-	-	-	591	622	-	-	-	-	-	-	-	561	575
Reno (city)	650	614	588	589	-	-	551	-	646	-	-	-	-	583	615	-	-	-	-	-	-	-	-	619
Sparks (city)	716	675	-	-	-	-	667	-	672	-	-	-	-	-	-	-	-	-	-	-	-	-	-	-
NEW HAMPSHIRE	646	753	-	800	-	-	674	-	767	-	-	-	-	765	810	718	-	-	-	-	-	-	-	598
Belknap County	588	446	-	-	-	-	-	-	-	-	-	-	-	-	-	-	-	-	-	-	-	-	-	-
Cheshire County	596	715	-	-	-	-	-	-	-	-	-	-	-	-	-	-	-	-	-	-	-	-	-	-
Grafton County	560	645	-	-	-	-	680	-	-	-	-	-	-	-	-	-	-	-	-	-	-	-	-	-
Hanover (town)	857	811	-	-	-	-	-	-	-	-	-	-	-	-	-	-	-	-	-	-	-	-	-	-
Hillsborough County	694	784	-	857	-	-	727	-	757	-	-	-	-	-	948	-	-	-	-	-	-	-	-	592
Nashua (city)	757	827	-	897	-	-	784	-	-	-	-	-	-	-	-	-	-	-	-	-	-	-	-	-
Merrimack County	613	683	-	-	-	-	-	-	-	-	-	-	-	-	-	-	-	-	-	-	-	-	-	-
Rockingham County	717	802	-	772	-	-	591	-	839	-	-	-	-	-	936	-	-	-	-	-	-	-	-	-
Strafford County	623	607	-	-	-	-	513	-	-	-	-	-	-	-	-	-	-	-	-	-	-	-	-	-
NEW JERSEY	751	882	646	870	787	782	869	-	798	627	853	-	784	1,386	1,017	813	-	841	600	807	950	829	-	726
Atlantic County	677	681	-	700	663	-	695	-	700	-	-	-	-	-	852	-	-	661	-	-	-	-	-	642
Atlantic City (city)	561	646	-	668	-	-	624	-	665	-	-	-	-	-	-	-	-	-	-	-	-	-	-	628
Brigantine (city)	792	678	-	-	-	-	-	-	-	-	-	-	-	-	-	-	-	-	-	-	-	-	-	-
Egg Harbor (township)	700	742	-	-	-	-	-	-	-	-	-	-	-	-	-	-	-	-	-	-	-	-	-	-
Galloway (township)	811	827	-	809	-	-	-	-	-	-	-	-	-	-	-	-	-	-	-	-	-	-	-	-
Ventnor City (city)	729	695	-	-	-	-	-	-	-	-	-	-	-	-	-	-	-	-	-	-	-	-	-	-
Bergen County	872	999	-	881	-	-	949	-	879	-	-	-	-	1,731	1,094	-	-	890	-	-	1,514	820	-	791
Bergenfield (borough)	855	871	-	856	-	-	-	-	908	-	-	-	-	-	-	-	-	-	-	-	-	-	-	-
Cliffside Park (borough)	864	988	-	-	-	-	-	-	-	-	-	-	-	1,556	975	-	-	-	-	-	-	-	-	-
Dumont (borough)	882	966	-	1,125	-	-	-	-	1,021	-	-	-	-	-	-	-	-	-	-	-	-	-	-	-
Elmwood Park (borough)	897	928	-	915	-	-	-	-	-	-	-	-	-	-	-	-	-	-	-	-	-	-	-	-
Englewood (city)	825	974	-	-	-	-	-	-	895	-	-	-	-	-	-	-	-	-	-	-	-	-	-	-
Fair Lawn (borough)	923	1,025	-	923	-	-	-	-	1,375	-	-	-	-	-	-	-	-	-	-	-	-	-	-	-
Fairview (borough)	846	874	-	-	-	-	-	-	-	-	-	-	-	-	-	-	-	-	-	-	-	-	-	-
Fort Lee (borough)	1,101	1,354	-	1,319	-	-	1,007	-	-	-	-	-	-	1,822	1,295	-	-	-	-	-	-	-	-	-
Franklin Lakes (borough)	1,313	0	-	-	-	-	-	-	-	-	-	-	-	-	-	-	-	-	-	-	-	-	-	-
Glen Rock (borough)	1,188	2,001	-	-	-	-	-	-	-	-	-	-	-	-	-	-	-	-	-	-	-	-	-	-

Notes: Please refer to the User's Guide for an explanation of data; data is arranged alphabetically by state, then county, then city within each county; table includes counties with populations greater than 49,999 unless noted and cities with populations greater than 9,999 whose Asian and/or NHPI population rates are greater than the national average; (1) Native Hawaiian and other Pacific Islander; (2) excludes Taiwanese; (3) includes Chamorro; (4) county does not meet population threshold but is shown in order to allow inclusion of city

Place	All specified renter-occupied housing units	Specified housing units rented by Asians	Specified housing units rented by NHPIs[1]	Asian Indian	Bangladeshi	Cambodian	Chinese[2]	Fijian	Filipino	Guamanian[3]	Hawaiian, Native	Hmong	Indonesian	Japanese	Korean	Laotian	Malaysian	Pakistani	Samoan	Sri Lankan	Taiwanese	Thai	Tongan	Vietnamese
Hackensack (city)	848	904	-	943	-	-	-	-	794	-	-	-	-	-	995	-	-	-	-	-	-	-	-	-
Hasbrouck Heights (borough)	874	994	-	-	-	-	-	-	-	-	-	-	-	-	-	-	-	-	-	-	-	-	-	-
Hillsdale (borough)	926	698	-	-	-	-	-	-	-	-	-	-	-	-	-	-	-	-	-	-	-	-	-	-
Little Ferry (borough)	822	837	-	774	-	-	-	-	781	-	-	-	-	-	929	-	-	-	-	-	-	-	-	-
Lodi (borough)	811	838	-	821	-	-	-	-	800	-	-	-	-	-	-	-	-	-	-	-	-	-	-	-
Lyndhurst (township)	805	777	-	-	-	-	-	-	-	-	-	-	-	-	-	-	-	-	-	-	-	-	-	-
Mahwah (township)	1,160	1,271	-	946	-	-	-	-	-	-	-	-	-	-	-	-	-	-	-	-	-	-	-	-
New Milford (borough)	763	765	-	745	-	-	-	-	779	-	-	-	-	-	-	-	-	-	-	-	-	-	-	-
North Arlington (borough)	763	856	-	-	-	-	-	-	-	-	-	-	-	-	-	-	-	-	-	-	-	-	-	-
Palisades Park (borough)	903	1,011	-	-	-	-	-	-	-	-	-	-	-	-	1,021	-	-	-	-	-	-	-	-	-
Paramus (borough)	1,483	1,912	-	1,625	-	-	893	-	892	-	-	-	-	-	2,001	-	-	-	-	-	-	-	-	-
Ramsey (borough)	1,120	1,211	-	-	-	-	-	-	-	-	-	-	-	-	-	-	-	-	-	-	-	-	-	-
Ridgefield (borough)	903	939	-	-	-	-	-	-	-	-	-	-	-	-	953	-	-	-	-	-	-	-	-	-
Ridgefield Park (village)	848	884	-	-	-	-	-	-	-	-	-	-	-	-	896	-	-	-	-	-	-	-	-	-
Ridgewood (village)	1,220	1,730	-	-	-	-	-	-	-	-	-	-	-	2,001	1,648	-	-	-	-	-	-	-	-	-
River Edge (borough)	969	988	-	-	-	-	-	-	-	-	-	-	-	-	999	-	-	-	-	-	-	-	-	-
Rutherford (borough)	832	852	-	748	-	-	-	-	-	-	-	-	-	-	903	-	-	-	-	-	-	-	-	-
Saddle Brook (township)	887	875	-	-	-	-	-	-	-	-	-	-	-	-	-	-	-	-	-	-	-	-	-	-
Teaneck (township)	873	1,071	-	945	-	-	-	-	1,344	-	-	-	-	-	-	-	-	-	-	-	-	-	-	-
Tenafly (borough)	1,186	1,562	-	-	-	-	2,001	-	-	-	-	-	-	-	1,527	-	-	-	-	-	-	-	-	-
Wallington (borough)	756	789	-	-	-	-	-	-	-	-	-	-	-	-	-	-	-	-	-	-	-	-	-	-
Westwood (borough)	996	1,200	-	-	-	-	-	-	-	-	-	-	-	-	-	-	-	-	-	-	-	-	-	-
Wyckoff (township)	1,114	1,222	-	-	-	-	-	-	-	-	-	-	-	-	-	-	-	-	-	-	-	-	-	-
Burlington County	758	762	-	755	-	-	853	-	682	-	-	-	-	646	818	-	-	-	-	-	-	-	-	992
Browns Mills (cdp)	673	558	-	-	-	-	-	-	-	-	-	-	-	-	525	-	-	-	-	-	-	-	-	-
Evesham (township)	886	794	-	694	-	-	885	-	-	-	-	-	-	-	-	-	-	-	-	-	-	-	-	-
Maple Shade (township)	767	785	-	834	-	-	-	-	-	-	-	-	-	-	-	-	-	-	-	-	-	-	-	-
Marlton (cdp)	743	742	-	-	-	-	-	-	-	-	-	-	-	-	-	-	-	-	-	-	-	-	-	-
Mount Laurel (township)	939	964	-	844	-	-	1,125	-	-	-	-	-	-	-	-	-	-	-	-	-	-	-	-	-
Camden County	635	702	-	768	-	925	697	-	639	-	-	-	-	-	780	-	-	681	-	-	-	-	-	547
Barclay-Kingston (cdp)	800	810	-	-	-	-	-	-	-	-	-	-	-	-	-	-	-	-	-	-	-	-	-	-
Bellmawr (borough)	523	536	-	-	-	-	-	-	-	-	-	-	-	-	-	-	-	-	-	-	-	-	-	-
Cherry Hill Mall (cdp)	873	813	-	-	-	-	-	-	-	-	-	-	-	-	-	-	-	-	-	-	-	-	-	-
Cherry Hill (township)	793	811	-	738	-	-	711	-	638	-	-	-	-	-	891	-	-	-	-	-	-	-	-	-
Echelon (cdp)	833	861	-	908	-	-	-	-	-	-	-	-	-	-	-	-	-	-	-	-	-	-	-	-
Greentree (cdp)	1,320	0	-	0	-	-	0	-	-	-	-	-	-	-	-	-	-	-	-	-	-	-	-	-
Pennsauken (township)	584	593	-	-	-	-	-	-	-	-	-	-	-	-	-	-	-	-	-	-	-	-	-	572
Springdale (cdp)	394	1,803	-	-	-	-	0	-	-	-	-	-	-	-	-	-	-	-	-	-	-	-	-	-
Voorhees (township)	864	873	-	928	-	-	783	-	729	-	-	-	-	-	-	-	-	-	-	-	-	-	-	-
Cape May County	650	775	-	-	-	-	-	-	-	-	-	-	-	-	-	-	-	-	-	-	-	-	-	-
Cumberland County	616	654	-	685	-	-	-	-	-	-	-	-	-	-	-	-	-	-	-	-	-	-	-	-

Notes: Please refer to the User's Guide for an explanation of data; data is arranged alphabetically by state, then county, then city within each county; table includes counties with populations greater than 49,999 unless noted and cities with populations greater than 9,999 whose Asian and/or NHPI population rates are greater than the national average; (1) Native Hawaiian and other Pacific Islander; (2) excludes Taiwanese; (3) includes Chamorro; (4) county does not meet population threshold but is shown in order to allow inclusion of city

Place	All specified renter-occupied housing units	Specified housing units rented by Asians	Specified housing units rented by NHPIs[1]	Asian Indian	Bangladeshi	Cambodian	Chinese[2]	Fijian	Filipino	Guamanian[3]	Hawaiian, Native	Hmong	Indonesian	Japanese	Korean	Laotian	Malaysian	Pakistani	Samoan	Sri Lankan	Taiwanese	Thai	Tongan	Vietnamese
Essex County	675	806	729	821	-	-	809	-	788	-	-	-	-	790	919	-	-	711	-	-	475	-	-	725
Belleville (township)	752	780	-	798	-	-	-	-	820	-	-	-	-	-	-	-	-	-	-	-	-	-	-	743
Bloomfield (township)	768	806	-	767	-	-	848	-	798	-	-	-	-	-	-	-	-	-	-	-	-	-	-	-
Cedar Grove (township)	973	1,047	-	-	-	-	-	-	-	-	-	-	-	-	-	-	-	-	-	-	-	-	-	-
Livingston (township)	1,244	1,694	-	2,001	-	-	1,375	-	1,625	-	-	-	-	-	1,469	-	-	-	-	-	-	-	-	-
Millburn (township)	1,114	1,179	-	-	-	-	1,072	-	-	-	-	-	-	-	-	-	-	-	-	-	-	-	-	-
Nutley (township)	814	858	-	892	-	-	-	-	859	-	-	-	-	-	-	-	-	-	-	-	-	-	-	-
Verona (township)	867	907	-	-	-	-	-	-	-	-	-	-	-	-	-	-	-	-	-	-	-	-	-	-
West Caldwell (township)	1,193	1,136	-	-	-	-	-	-	-	-	-	-	-	-	-	-	-	-	-	-	-	-	-	-
West Orange (township)	857	935	-	899	-	-	876	-	797	-	-	-	-	-	1,052	-	-	-	-	-	-	-	-	-
Gloucester County	645	693	-	721	-	-	600	-	710	-	-	-	-	-	732	-	-	-	-	-	-	-	-	-
Hudson County	703	800	-	772	-	-	936	-	747	-	-	-	-	1,133	889	-	-	781	-	-	-	-	-	643
Bayonne (city)	681	809	-	830	-	-	-	-	715	-	-	-	-	-	877	-	-	-	-	-	-	-	-	-
Guttenberg (town)	794	968	-	-	-	-	-	-	-	-	-	-	-	-	-	-	-	-	-	-	-	-	-	-
Harrison (town)	723	816	-	-	-	-	799	-	-	-	-	-	-	-	-	-	-	-	-	-	-	-	-	-
Hoboken (city)	1,002	1,194	-	1,269	-	-	1,183	-	-	-	-	-	-	-	-	-	-	-	-	-	-	-	-	-
Jersey City (city)	675	781	-	766	-	-	1,160	-	739	-	-	-	-	-	863	-	-	769	-	-	-	-	-	642
Kearny (town)	769	732	-	808	-	-	717	-	-	-	-	-	-	-	-	-	-	-	-	-	-	-	-	-
North Bergen (township)	733	749	-	691	-	-	907	-	-	-	-	-	-	-	-	-	-	-	-	-	-	-	-	-
Secaucus (town)	850	983	-	827	-	-	-	-	967	-	-	-	-	-	-	-	-	-	-	-	-	-	-	-
Weehawken (township)	781	935	-	-	-	-	-	-	-	-	-	-	-	-	-	-	-	-	-	-	-	-	-	-
Hunterdon County	867	973	-	1,022	-	-	775	-	-	-	-	-	-	-	-	-	-	-	-	-	-	-	-	-
Mercer County	727	814	-	805	-	-	748	-	865	-	-	-	-	1,181	1,077	-	-	700	-	-	833	-	-	-
East Windsor (township)	791	815	-	836	-	-	-	-	-	-	-	-	-	-	-	-	-	-	-	-	-	-	-	-
Hopewell (township)	925	0	-	-	-	-	-	-	-	-	-	-	-	-	-	-	-	-	-	-	-	-	-	-
Lawrence (township)	935	1,218	-	1,380	-	-	1,000	-	-	-	-	-	-	-	-	-	-	-	-	-	-	-	-	-
Princeton (borough)	920	765	-	-	-	-	-	-	-	-	-	-	-	-	-	-	-	-	-	-	-	-	-	-
Princeton (township)	748	901	-	778	-	-	683	-	-	-	-	-	-	-	-	-	-	-	-	-	-	-	-	-
West Windsor (township)	1,198	1,423	-	1,137	-	-	1,375	-	-	-	-	-	-	-	1,375	-	-	-	-	-	-	-	-	-
Middlesex County	845	926	-	943	856	-	862	-	918	-	-	-	763	896	1,009	-	-	877	-	750	1,052	-	-	877
Avenel (cdp)	856	873	-	875	-	-	-	-	-	-	-	-	-	-	-	-	-	-	-	-	-	-	-	-
Carteret (borough)	741	786	-	781	-	-	-	-	-	-	-	-	-	-	-	-	-	-	-	-	-	-	-	-
Colonia (cdp)	753	850	-	1,271	-	-	-	-	0	-	-	-	-	-	-	-	-	-	-	-	-	-	-	-
East Brunswick (township)	877	854	-	879	-	-	763	-	875	-	-	-	-	-	867	-	-	-	-	-	-	-	-	-
Edison (township)	913	1,010	-	994	-	-	1,018	-	986	-	-	-	-	-	1,203	-	-	1,098	-	-	1,375	-	-	-
Fords (cdp)	787	821	-	806	-	-	-	-	797	-	-	-	-	-	-	-	-	-	-	-	-	-	-	-
Highland Park (borough)	848	896	-	974	-	-	857	-	-	-	-	-	-	-	-	-	-	-	-	-	-	-	-	-
Iselin (cdp)	995	1,084	-	1,093	-	-	1,005	-	-	-	-	-	-	-	-	-	-	-	-	-	-	-	-	-
Metuchen (borough)	873	1,103	-	-	-	-	-	-	-	-	-	-	-	-	-	-	-	-	-	-	-	-	-	-
Middlesex (borough)	830	933	-	-	-	-	-	-	-	-	-	-	-	-	-	-	-	-	-	-	-	-	-	-
New Brunswick (city)	837	912	-	884	-	-	811	-	-	-	-	-	-	-	-	-	-	-	-	-	-	-	-	-

Notes: Please refer to the User's Guide for an explanation of data; data is arranged alphabetically by state, then county, then city within each county; table includes counties with populations greater than 49,999 unless noted and cities with populations greater than 9,999 whose Asian and/or NHPI population rates are greater than the national average; (1) Native Hawaiian and other Pacific Islander; (2) excludes Taiwanese; (3) includes Chamorro; (4) county does not meet population threshold but is shown in order to allow inclusion of city

Place	All specified renter-occupied housing units	Specified housing units rented by Asians	Specified housing units rented by NHPIs[1]	Asian Indian	Bangladeshi	Cambodian	Chinese[2]	Fijian	Filipino	Guamanian[3]	Hawaiian, Native	Hmong	Indonesian	Japanese	Korean	Laotian	Malaysian	Pakistani	Samoan	Sri Lankan	Taiwanese	Thai	Tongan	Vietnamese
North Brunswick (township)	907	964	-	952	-	-	876	-	1,076	-	-	-	-	-	1,056	-	-	-	-	-	-	-	-	-
Old Bridge (township)	770	769	-	779	-	-	783	-	746	-	-	-	-	-	-	-	-	761	-	-	-	-	-	-
Piscataway (township)	829	818	-	874	-	-	742	-	816	-	-	-	-	-	734	-	-	-	-	-	-	-	-	-
Plainsboro (township)	942	973	-	991	-	-	948	-	-	-	-	-	-	-	-	-	-	-	-	-	-	-	-	-
Princeton Meadows (cdp)	958	1,014	-	1,036	-	-	1,032	-	-	-	-	-	-	-	-	-	-	-	-	-	-	-	-	-
Sayreville (borough)	795	856	-	867	-	-	852	-	750	-	-	-	-	-	-	-	-	-	-	-	-	-	-	-
South Brunswick (township)	969	991	-	1,008	-	-	933	-	1,125	-	-	-	-	-	-	-	-	-	-	-	-	-	-	-
South Plainfield (borough)	976	992	-	1,125	-	-	-	-	0	-	-	-	-	-	-	-	-	-	-	-	-	-	-	975
Woodbridge (township)	879	965	-	967	-	-	897	-	1,026	-	-	-	-	-	1,057	-	-	881	-	-	-	-	-	-
Monmouth County	759	802	-	811	-	-	823	-	809	-	-	-	-	733	748	-	-	958	-	-	-	-	-	631
Aberdeen (township)	817	763	-	766	-	-	664	-	-	-	-	-	-	-	-	-	-	-	-	-	-	-	-	-
Colts Neck (township)	974	0	-	-	-	-	-	-	-	-	-	-	-	-	-	-	-	-	-	-	-	-	-	-
Eatontown (borough)	766	809	-	-	-	-	-	-	-	-	-	-	-	-	-	-	-	-	-	-	-	-	-	-
Freehold (township)	904	1,542	-	1,875	-	-	1,531	-	0	-	-	-	-	-	-	-	-	-	-	-	-	-	-	-
Holmdel (township)	1,512	1,783	-	1,750	-	-	1,500	-	-	-	-	-	-	-	-	-	-	-	-	-	-	-	-	-
Howell (township)	816	1,081	-	675	-	-	-	-	1,125	-	-	-	-	-	-	-	-	-	-	-	-	-	-	-
Manalapan (township)	1,124	1,920	-	1,875	-	-	1,875	-	-	-	-	-	-	-	-	-	-	-	-	-	-	-	-	-
Marlboro (township)	1,334	1,201	-	1,375	-	-	0	-	-	-	-	-	-	-	-	-	-	-	-	-	-	-	-	-
Morganville (cdp)	1,148	1,125	-	-	-	-	0	-	-	-	-	-	-	-	-	-	-	-	-	-	-	-	-	-
Ocean (township)	689	697	-	752	-	-	-	-	-	-	-	-	-	-	-	-	-	-	-	-	-	-	-	-
Tinton Falls (borough)	1,198	1,182	-	-	-	-	-	-	-	-	-	-	-	-	-	-	-	-	-	-	-	-	-	-
West Freehold (cdp)	851	1,813	-	-	-	-	-	-	-	-	-	-	-	-	-	-	-	-	-	-	-	-	-	-
Morris County	883	892	-	861	-	-	929	-	920	-	-	-	-	1,513	1,063	-	-	895	-	-	859	-	-	827
Chatham (township)	1,371	1,288	-	-	-	-	-	-	-	-	-	-	-	-	-	-	-	-	-	-	-	-	-	-
Denville (township)	1,129	1,484	-	-	-	-	-	-	-	-	-	-	-	-	-	-	-	-	-	-	-	-	-	-
East Hanover (township)	1,504	1,125	-	-	-	-	750	-	-	-	-	-	-	-	-	-	-	-	-	-	-	-	-	-
Hanover (township)	1,098	1,150	-	2,001	-	-	2,001	-	-	-	-	-	-	-	-	-	-	-	-	-	-	-	-	-
Lincoln Park (borough)	947	990	-	-	-	-	-	-	-	-	-	-	-	-	-	-	-	-	-	-	-	-	-	-
Montville (township)	1,186	1,271	-	1,125	-	-	1,375	-	-	-	-	-	-	-	-	-	-	-	-	-	-	-	-	-
Morris (township)	1,040	1,399	-	-	-	-	-	-	-	-	-	-	-	-	-	-	-	-	-	-	-	-	-	-
Mount Olive (township)	800	825	-	789	-	-	-	-	-	-	-	-	-	-	-	-	-	-	-	-	-	-	-	-
Parsippany-Troy Hills (twp)	823	833	-	827	-	-	854	-	900	-	-	-	-	-	783	-	-	-	-	-	-	-	-	-
Randolph (township)	875	889	-	876	-	-	900	-	-	-	-	-	-	-	-	-	-	-	-	-	-	-	-	-
Rockaway (township)	948	1,031	-	946	-	-	-	-	-	-	-	-	-	-	-	-	-	-	-	-	-	-	-	-
Roxbury (township)	759	840	-	-	-	-	-	-	-	-	-	-	-	-	-	-	-	-	-	-	-	-	-	-
Succasunna-Kenvil (cdp)	1,010	1,075	-	-	-	-	-	-	-	-	-	-	-	-	-	-	-	-	-	-	-	-	-	-
Ocean County	819	863	-	825	-	-	796	-	938	-	-	-	-	-	996	-	-	-	-	-	-	-	-	-
Passaic County	747	809	-	756	880	-	752	-	793	-	-	-	-	-	958	-	-	-	-	-	-	-	-	-
Clifton (city)	784	819	-	832	-	-	638	-	727	-	-	-	-	-	937	-	-	-	-	-	-	-	-	-
Little Falls (township)	909	1,024	-	-	-	-	-	-	-	-	-	-	-	-	-	-	-	-	-	-	-	-	-	-
Passaic (city)	677	648	-	638	-	-	-	-	813	-	-	-	-	-	-	-	-	-	-	-	-	-	-	-

Notes: Please refer to the User's Guide for an explanation of data; data is arranged alphabetically by state, then county, then city within each county; table includes counties with populations greater than 49,999 unless noted and cities with populations greater than 9,999 whose Asian and/or NHPI population rates are greater than the national average; (1) Native Hawaiian and other Pacific Islander; (2) excludes Taiwanese; (3) includes Chamorro; (4) county does not meet population threshold but is shown in order to allow inclusion of city

Place	All specified renter-occupied housing units	Specified housing units rented by Asians	Specified housing units rented by NHPIs[1]	Asian Indian	Bangladeshi	Cambodian	Chinese[2]	Fijian	Filipino	Guamanian[3]	Hawaiian, Native	Hmong	Indonesian	Japanese	Korean	Laotian	Malaysian	Pakistani	Samoan	Sri Lankan	Taiwanese	Thai	Tongan	Vietnamese
Wayne (township)	943	1,119	-	1,204	-	-	1,188	-	883	-	-	-	-	-	970	-	-	-	-	-	-	-	-	-
Salem County	602	681	-	-	-	-	-	-	-	-	-	-	-	-	-	-	-	-	-	-	-	-	-	-
Somerset County	898	910	-	919	-	-	872	-	864	-	-	-	-	1,285	988	-	-	898	-	-	2,001	-	-	719
Bernards (township)	1,494	1,656	-	1,063	-	-	2,001	-	-	-	-	-	-	-	-	-	-	-	-	-	-	-	-	-
Branchburg (township)	1,036	2,001	-	1,125	-	-	-	-	-	-	-	-	-	-	-	-	-	-	-	-	-	-	-	-
Bridgewater (township)	1,096	1,135	-	1,205	-	-	798	-	-	-	-	-	-	-	-	-	-	-	-	-	-	-	-	-
Franklin (township)	897	907	-	911	-	-	868	-	1,208	-	-	-	-	-	-	-	-	-	-	-	-	-	-	-
Hillsborough (township)	931	938	-	928	-	-	845	-	-	-	-	-	-	-	-	-	-	-	-	-	-	-	-	-
Montgomery (township)	1,196	1,294	-	1,579	-	-	1,075	-	-	-	-	-	-	-	-	-	-	-	-	-	-	-	-	-
North Plainfield (borough)	828	803	-	-	-	-	-	-	-	-	-	-	-	-	-	-	-	-	-	-	-	-	-	-
Somerset (cdp)	870	888	-	885	-	-	879	-	810	-	-	-	-	-	-	-	-	-	-	-	-	-	-	-
Somerville (borough)	822	851	-	-	-	-	-	-	-	-	-	-	-	-	-	-	-	-	-	-	-	-	-	-
Warren (township)	1,135	1,268	-	0	-	-	1,375	-	-	-	-	-	-	-	-	-	-	-	-	-	-	-	-	-
Sussex County	790	795	-	925	-	-	-	-	775	-	-	-	-	-	-	-	-	-	-	-	-	-	-	-
Union County	752	881	-	905	-	-	916	-	834	-	-	-	-	-	1,002	-	-	789	-	-	-	-	-	828
Berkeley Heights (township)	1,248	1,672	-	-	-	-	1,777	-	-	-	-	-	-	-	-	-	-	-	-	-	-	-	-	-
New Providence (borough)	941	1,041	-	-	-	-	965	-	-	-	-	-	-	-	-	-	-	-	-	-	-	-	-	-
Rahway (city)	732	753	-	-	-	-	-	-	792	-	-	-	-	-	-	-	-	-	-	-	-	-	-	-
Roselle Park (borough)	785	770	-	747	-	-	-	-	-	-	-	-	-	-	-	-	-	-	-	-	-	-	-	-
Scotch Plains (township)	985	1,027	-	1,069	-	-	1,063	-	-	-	-	-	-	-	-	-	-	-	-	-	-	-	-	-
Springfield (township)	1,018	1,098	-	-	-	-	-	-	-	-	-	-	-	-	-	-	-	-	-	-	-	-	-	-
Summit (city)	1,078	981	-	1,139	-	-	-	-	-	-	-	-	-	-	-	-	-	-	-	-	-	-	-	-
Union (township)	844	974	-	1,086	-	-	756	-	1,241	-	-	-	-	-	-	-	-	-	-	-	-	-	-	-
Westfield (town)	1,048	1,174	-	-	-	-	-	-	-	-	-	-	-	-	-	-	-	-	-	-	-	-	-	-
Warren County	689	680	-	672	-	-	-	-	-	-	-	-	-	-	-	-	-	-	-	-	-	-	-	-
NEW MEXICO	503	535	583	536	-	-	556	-	569	596	534	-	-	466	625	-	-	-	-	-	-	433	-	480
Bernalillo County	560	530	570	524	-	-	588	-	595	-	-	-	-	443	611	-	-	-	-	-	-	-	-	441
Chaves County	402	625	-	-	-	-	-	-	-	-	-	-	-	-	-	-	-	-	-	-	-	-	-	-
Dona Ana County	445	515	-	-	-	-	435	-	-	-	-	-	-	-	-	-	-	-	-	-	-	-	-	-
Los Alamos County[4]	666	672	-	-	-	-	-	-	-	-	-	-	-	-	-	-	-	-	-	-	-	-	-	-
Los Alamos (cdp)	650	672	-	-	-	-	-	-	-	-	-	-	-	-	-	-	-	-	-	-	-	-	-	-
Otero County	441	429	-	-	-	-	-	-	-	-	-	-	-	-	-	-	-	-	-	-	-	-	-	-
Sandoval County	726	650	-	-	-	-	-	-	1,125	-	-	-	-	-	-	-	-	-	-	-	-	-	-	-
Santa Fe County	690	754	-	-	-	-	-	-	-	-	-	-	-	-	-	-	-	-	-	-	-	-	-	-
NEW YORK	672	792	668	827	773	675	685	-	823	736	601	-	829	1,098	931	530	786	795	577	901	849	754	-	670
Albany County	611	694	-	713	-	-	678	-	585	-	-	-	-	-	699	-	-	-	-	-	-	-	-	598
Colonie (town)	688	713	-	689	-	-	753	-	-	-	-	-	-	-	-	-	-	-	-	-	-	-	-	-
Guilderland (town)	768	774	-	758	-	-	-	-	-	-	-	-	-	-	-	-	-	-	-	-	-	-	-	-
Bronx County (Bronx)	620	695	578	688	706	618	663	-	727	-	-	-	-	705	817	-	-	718	-	-	-	-	-	690
Broome County	462	441	-	556	-	-	396	-	-	-	-	-	-	-	446	417	-	-	-	-	-	-	-	443
Johnson City (village)	468	450	-	-	-	-	-	-	-	-	-	-	-	-	-	-	-	-	-	-	-	-	-	-

Notes: Please refer to the User's Guide for an explanation of data; data is arranged alphabetically by state, then county, then city within each county; table includes counties with populations greater than 49,999 unless noted and cities with populations greater than 9,999 whose Asian and/or NHPI population rates are greater than the national average; (1) Native Hawaiian and other Pacific Islander; (2) excludes Taiwanese; (3) includes Chamorro; (4) county does not meet population threshold but is shown in order to allow inclusion of city

Place	All specified renter-occupied housing units	Specified housing units rented by Asians	Specified housing units rented by NHPIs[1]	Asian Indian	Bangladeshi	Cambodian	Chinese[2]	Fijian	Filipino	Guamanian[3]	Hawaiian, Native	Hmong	Indonesian	Japanese	Korean	Laotian	Malaysian	Pakistani	Samoan	Sri Lankan	Taiwanese	Thai	Tongan	Vietnamese
Vestal (town)	550	510	-	-	-	-	510	-	-	-	-	-	-	-	-	-	-	-	-	-	-	-	-	-
Cattaraugus County	425	486	-	-	-	-	-	-	-	-	-	-	-	-	-	-	-	-	-	-	-	-	-	-
Cayuga County	482	775	-	-	-	-	-	-	-	-	-	-	-	-	-	-	-	-	-	-	-	-	-	-
Chautauqua County	438	570	-	-	-	-	-	-	-	-	-	-	-	-	-	-	-	-	-	-	-	-	-	-
Chemung County	493	666	-	-	-	-	-	-	-	-	-	-	-	-	-	-	-	-	-	-	-	-	-	-
Chenango County	439	761	-	-	-	-	-	-	-	-	-	-	-	-	-	-	-	-	-	-	-	-	-	-
Clinton County	479	387	-	-	-	-	-	-	-	-	-	-	-	-	-	-	-	-	-	-	-	-	-	-
Columbia County	553	539	-	-	-	-	-	-	-	-	-	-	-	-	-	-	-	-	-	-	-	-	-	-
Dutchess County	707	772	-	798	-	-	726	-	-	-	-	-	-	-	804	-	-	-	-	-	-	-	-	-
Arlington (cdp)	725	770	-	-	-	-	-	-	-	-	-	-	-	-	-	-	-	-	-	-	-	-	-	-
Poughkeepsie (town)	745	775	-	795	-	-	758	-	-	-	-	-	-	-	-	-	-	-	-	-	-	-	-	-
Wappinger (town)	798	793	-	854	-	-	-	-	-	-	-	-	-	-	-	-	-	-	-	-	-	-	-	-
Erie County	516	585	-	624	-	-	581	-	664	-	-	-	-	588	635	-	-	-	-	-	-	-	-	520
Amherst (town)	681	673	-	678	-	-	641	-	-	-	-	-	-	-	756	-	-	-	-	-	-	-	-	-
Herkimer County	420	431	-	-	-	-	-	-	-	-	-	-	-	-	-	-	-	-	-	-	-	-	-	-
Jefferson County	486	653	-	-	-	-	-	-	409	-	-	-	-	-	419	-	-	-	-	-	-	-	-	-
Kings County (Brooklyn)	672	722	665	747	743	808	687	-	751	682	-	-	-	841	863	-	-	735	-	-	-	-	-	720
Livingston County	541	614	-	-	-	-	-	-	-	-	-	-	-	-	-	-	-	-	-	-	-	-	-	-
Madison County	509	563	-	-	-	-	-	-	-	-	-	-	-	-	-	-	-	-	-	-	-	-	-	-
Monroe County	612	655	-	686	-	496	624	-	542	-	-	-	-	680	659	599	-	665	-	-	-	-	-	572
Brighton (town)	708	711	-	737	-	-	719	-	-	-	-	-	-	-	-	-	-	-	-	-	-	-	-	-
Henrietta (town)	697	723	-	829	-	-	718	-	-	-	-	-	-	-	-	-	-	-	-	-	-	-	-	-
Pittsford (town)	815	1,078	-	744	-	-	-	-	-	-	-	-	-	-	-	-	-	-	-	-	-	-	-	-
Nassau County	964	1,144	810	1,079	-	-	966	-	1,062	-	-	-	-	1,832	1,314	-	-	1,224	-	-	1,125	928	-	683
East Meadow (cdp)	930	612	-	442	-	-	-	-	275	-	-	-	-	-	-	-	-	-	-	-	-	-	-	-
Elmont (cdp)	843	1,100	-	1,075	-	-	-	-	950	-	-	-	-	-	-	-	-	-	-	-	-	-	-	-
Franklin Square (cdp)	880	1,000	-	1,125	-	-	-	-	-	-	-	-	-	-	-	-	-	-	-	-	-	-	-	-
Glen Cove (city)	1,002	1,174	-	965	-	-	-	-	-	-	-	-	-	-	1,413	-	-	-	-	-	-	-	-	-
Hicksville (cdp)	1,083	1,049	-	988	-	-	975	-	1,458	-	-	-	-	-	-	-	-	-	-	-	-	-	-	-
Jericho (cdp)	1,307	1,228	-	-	-	-	-	-	-	-	-	-	-	-	1,537	-	-	-	-	-	-	-	-	-
Mineola (village)	972	1,139	-	1,122	-	-	-	-	-	-	-	-	-	-	-	-	-	-	-	-	-	-	-	-
North Hempstead (town)	1,086	1,365	-	1,201	-	-	1,104	-	1,213	-	-	-	-	1,863	1,462	-	-	1,278	-	-	1,125	-	-	-
North Merrick (cdp)	1,160	1,125	-	-	-	-	-	-	-	-	-	-	-	-	-	-	-	-	-	-	-	-	-	-
North New Hyde Park (cdp)	1,050	2,001	-	1,444	-	-	0	-	-	-	-	-	-	-	-	-	-	-	-	-	-	-	-	-
North Valley Stream (cdp)	978	904	-	0	-	-	-	-	-	-	-	-	-	-	-	-	-	-	-	-	-	-	-	-
Oyster Bay (town)	1,065	1,220	-	1,198	-	-	985	-	1,138	-	-	-	-	2,001	1,403	-	-	-	-	-	-	-	-	-
Plainview (cdp)	1,024	1,375	-	1,446	-	-	425	-	-	-	-	-	-	-	1,797	-	-	-	-	-	-	-	-	-
Port Washington (cdp)	1,161	1,889	-	1,183	-	-	-	-	-	-	-	-	-	-	-	-	-	-	-	-	-	-	-	-
Salisbury (cdp)	1,103	1,830	-	0	-	-	-	-	-	-	-	-	-	-	-	-	-	-	-	-	-	-	-	-
Syosset (cdp)	924	1,660	-	1,125	-	-	0	-	-	-	-	-	-	-	1,602	-	-	-	-	-	-	-	-	-
Valley Stream (village)	955	1,120	-	-	-	-	0	-	1,125	-	-	-	-	-	-	-	-	-	-	-	-	-	-	-

Notes: Please refer to the User's Guide for an explanation of data; data is arranged alphabetically by state, then county, then city within each county; table includes counties with populations greater than 49,999 unless noted and cities with populations greater than 9,999 whose Asian and/or NHPI population rates are greater than the national average; (1) Native Hawaiian and other Pacific Islander; (2) excludes Taiwanese; (3) includes Chamorro; (4) county does not meet population threshold but is shown in order to allow inclusion of city

Place	All specified renter-occupied housing units	Specified housing units rented by Asians	Specified housing units rented by NHPIs[1]	Asian Indian	Bangladeshi	Cambodian	Chinese[2]	Fijian	Filipino	Guamanian[3]	Hawaiian, Native	Hmong	Indonesian	Japanese	Korean	Laotian	Malaysian	Pakistani	Samoan	Sri Lankan	Taiwanese	Thai	Tongan	Vietnamese
West Hempstead (cdp)	980	1,125	-	1,214	-	-	-	-	-	-	-	-	-	-	-	-	-	-	-	-	-	-	-	-
Westbury (village)	1,050	1,375	-	-	-	-	-	-	-	-	-	-	-	-	-	-	-	-	-	-	-	-	-	-
Woodmere (cdp)	1,007	950	-	-	-	-	-	-	-	-	-	-	-	-	-	-	-	-	-	-	-	-	-	-
New York City	705	799	689	833	773	724	687	-	827	725	630	-	859	1,070	945	-	803	789	580	899	996	783	-	743
New York County (Manhattan)	796	819	875	1,247	707	-	575	-	978	-	-	-	-	1,287	1,250	-	-	928	-	-	1,504	835	-	1,070
Niagara County	479	464	-	768	-	-	-	-	-	-	-	-	-	-	-	-	-	-	-	-	-	-	-	-
Oneida County	470	438	-	705	-	-	742	-	-	-	-	-	-	-	-	-	-	-	-	-	-	-	-	412
Onondaga County	550	561	-	583	-	-	537	-	623	-	-	-	-	636	596	-	-	-	-	-	-	-	-	476
Ontario County	564	528	-	-	-	-	-	-	-	-	-	-	-	-	-	-	-	-	-	-	-	-	-	-
Orange County	714	797	-	790	-	-	779	-	954	-	-	-	-	-	773	-	-	-	-	-	-	-	-	-
Oswego County	507	542	-	-	-	-	-	-	-	-	-	-	-	-	-	-	-	-	-	-	-	-	-	-
Otsego County	485	535	-	-	-	-	-	-	-	-	-	-	-	-	-	-	-	-	-	-	-	-	-	-
Putnam County	913	889	-	1,292	-	-	850	-	-	-	-	-	-	-	-	-	-	-	-	-	-	-	-	-
Queens County (Queens)	775	849	790	854	796	-	794	-	816	-	-	-	840	876	926	-	911	841	-	896	808	782	-	775
Rensselaer County	547	600	-	625	-	-	581	-	-	-	-	-	-	-	622	-	-	-	-	-	-	-	-	-
Richmond Co. (Staten Island)	742	800	-	774	-	-	865	-	843	-	-	-	-	-	778	-	-	1,053	-	820	-	-	-	-
Rockland County	884	938	-	922	-	-	1,286	-	831	-	-	-	-	-	1,069	-	-	-	-	-	-	-	-	-
Clarkstown (town)	1,034	1,148	-	991	-	-	1,636	-	1,208	-	-	-	-	-	1,203	-	-	-	-	-	-	-	-	-
Nanuet (cdp)	1,187	1,529	-	1,375	-	-	-	-	-	-	-	-	-	-	-	-	-	-	-	-	-	-	-	-
New City (cdp)	945	1,000	-	1,000	-	-	-	-	725	-	-	-	-	-	-	-	-	-	-	-	-	-	-	-
Orangetown (town)	915	980	-	980	-	-	1,038	-	642	-	-	-	-	-	960	-	-	-	-	-	-	-	-	-
Ramapo (town)	833	865	-	884	-	-	1,352	-	798	-	-	-	-	-	1,063	-	-	-	-	-	-	-	-	-
Spring Valley (village)	815	856	-	870	-	-	-	-	-	-	-	-	-	-	-	-	-	-	-	-	-	-	-	-
St. Lawrence County	428	406	-	-	-	-	-	-	-	-	-	-	-	-	-	-	-	-	-	-	-	-	-	-
Saratoga County	638	749	-	798	-	-	729	-	-	-	-	-	-	-	363	-	-	-	-	-	-	-	-	-
Schenectady County	572	636	-	682	-	-	574	-	-	-	-	-	-	-	-	-	-	-	-	-	-	-	-	-
Niskayuna (town)	727	714	-	698	-	-	-	-	-	-	-	-	-	-	-	-	-	-	-	-	-	-	-	-
Steuben County	468	607	-	-	-	-	-	-	-	-	-	-	-	-	-	-	-	-	-	-	-	-	-	-
Suffolk County	945	961	1,063	961	-	-	870	-	953	-	-	-	-	1,213	1,127	-	-	1,024	-	-	1,143	0	-	925
Coram (cdp)	956	966	-	-	-	-	918	-	-	-	-	-	-	-	-	-	-	-	-	-	-	-	-	-
Dix Hills (cdp)	1,363	2,001	-	0	-	-	0	-	-	-	-	-	-	-	-	-	-	-	-	-	-	-	-	-
Elwood (cdp)	1,292	0	-	-	-	-	-	-	-	-	-	-	-	-	-	-	-	-	-	-	-	-	-	-
Lake Grove (village)	962	920	-	-	-	-	-	-	-	-	-	-	-	-	-	-	-	-	-	-	-	-	-	-
Melville (cdp)	1,842	1,768	-	-	-	-	-	-	-	-	-	-	-	-	-	-	-	-	-	-	-	-	-	-
Setauket-East Setauket (cdp)	843	553	-	-	-	-	440	-	-	-	-	-	-	-	-	-	-	-	-	-	-	-	-	-
Stony Brook (cdp)	1,402	2,000	-	-	-	-	2,001	-	-	-	-	-	-	-	-	-	-	-	-	-	-	-	-	-
Sullivan County	545	668	-	-	-	-	-	-	-	-	-	-	-	-	-	-	-	-	-	-	-	-	-	-
Tioga County	468	398	-	-	-	-	-	-	-	-	-	-	-	-	-	-	-	-	-	-	-	-	-	-
Tompkins County	611	660	-	660	-	-	644	-	-	-	-	-	-	687	673	-	-	-	-	-	-	-	-	-
Ithaca (city)	574	601	-	573	-	-	636	-	-	-	-	-	-	-	673	-	-	-	-	-	-	-	-	-
Lansing (town)	683	704	-	-	-	-	-	-	-	-	-	-	-	-	-	-	-	-	-	-	-	-	-	-

Notes: Please refer to the User's Guide for an explanation of data; data is arranged alphabetically by state, then county, then city within each county; table includes counties with populations greater than 49,999 unless noted and cities with populations greater than 9,999 whose Asian and/or NHPI population rates are greater than the national average; (1) Native Hawaiian and other Pacific Islander; (2) excludes Taiwanese; (3) includes Chamorro; (4) county does not meet population threshold but is shown in order to allow inclusion of city

Place	All specified renter-occupied housing units	Specified housing units rented by Asians	Specified housing units rented by NHPIs[1]	Asian Indian	Bangladeshi	Cambodian	Chinese[2]	Fijian	Filipino	Guamanian[3]	Hawaiian, Native	Hmong	Indonesian	Japanese	Korean	Laotian	Malaysian	Pakistani	Samoan	Sri Lankan	Taiwanese	Thai	Tongan	Vietnamese
Ulster County	626	724	-	-	-	-	854	-	-	-	-	-	-	-	-	-	-	-	-	-	-	-	-	-
New Paltz (town)	625	772	-	-	-	-	-	-	-	-	-	-	-	-	-	-	-	-	-	-	-	-	-	-
Warren County	557	669	-	-	-	-	-	-	-	-	-	-	-	-	-	-	-	-	-	-	-	-	-	-
Wayne County	527	471	-	-	-	-	-	-	-	-	-	-	-	-	-	-	-	-	-	-	-	-	-	-
Westchester County	839	1,071	-	901	-	-	975	-	848	-	-	-	-	2,001	1,153	-	-	1,073	-	-	1,422	931	-	-
Dobbs Ferry (village)	908	914	-	-	-	-	-	-	-	-	-	-	-	-	-	-	-	-	-	-	-	-	-	-
Eastchester (cdp)	1,054	2,001	-	-	-	-	-	-	-	-	-	-	-	2,001	-	-	-	-	-	-	-	-	-	-
Eastchester (town)	1,065	2,001	-	-	-	-	-	-	-	-	-	-	-	2,001	-	-	-	-	-	-	-	-	-	-
Greenburgh (town)	1,010	1,409	-	1,162	-	-	1,386	-	935	-	-	-	-	2,001	1,321	-	-	-	-	-	-	-	-	-
Harrison (village)	1,167	1,853	-	-	-	-	-	-	-	-	-	-	-	2,001	-	-	-	-	-	-	-	-	-	-
New Castle (town)	1,375	2,001	-	2,001	-	-	2,001	-	-	-	-	-	-	-	-	-	-	-	-	-	-	-	-	-
New Rochelle (city)	848	835	-	879	-	-	686	-	-	-	-	-	-	-	-	-	-	-	-	-	-	-	-	-
North Castle (town)	1,118	871	-	-	-	-	-	-	-	-	-	-	-	-	-	-	-	-	-	-	-	-	-	-
Ossining (town)	861	983	-	1,028	-	-	-	-	-	-	-	-	-	-	-	-	-	-	-	-	-	-	-	-
Ossining (village)	850	984	-	1,056	-	-	-	-	-	-	-	-	-	-	-	-	-	-	-	-	-	-	-	-
Pelham (town)	1,100	1,139	-	-	-	-	-	-	-	-	-	-	-	-	-	-	-	-	-	-	-	-	-	-
Rye (city)	1,329	2,001	-	-	-	-	-	-	-	-	-	-	-	2,001	-	-	-	-	-	-	-	-	-	-
Scarsdale (village)	2,001	2,001	-	0	-	-	2,001	-	-	-	-	-	-	2,001	2,001	-	-	-	-	-	-	-	-	-
Tarrytown (village)	960	1,102	-	-	-	-	-	-	-	-	-	-	-	-	-	-	-	-	-	-	-	-	-	-
White Plains (city)	879	1,044	-	1,034	-	-	971	-	-	-	-	-	-	-	-	-	-	-	-	-	-	-	-	-
Yonkers (city)	735	839	-	791	-	-	867	-	812	-	-	-	-	-	961	-	-	-	-	-	-	-	-	-
NORTH CAROLINA	548	667	571	716	-	450	661	-	636	513	638	484	-	757	714	513	-	578	542	-	858	675	-	601
Alamance County	557	608	-	-	-	-	-	-	-	-	-	-	-	-	-	-	-	-	-	-	-	-	-	-
Buncombe County	551	612	-	772	-	-	-	-	-	-	-	-	-	-	-	-	-	-	-	-	-	-	-	-
Burke County	450	434	-	-	-	-	-	-	-	-	-	411	-	-	-	411	-	-	-	-	-	-	-	-
Cabarrus County	566	674	-	-	-	-	-	-	-	-	-	-	-	-	-	-	-	-	-	-	-	-	-	-
Catawba County	525	486	-	-	-	-	-	-	-	-	-	467	-	-	-	517	-	-	-	-	-	-	-	601
Hickory (city)	540	480	-	-	-	-	-	-	-	-	-	452	-	-	-	-	-	-	-	-	-	-	-	-
Cleveland County	447	492	-	-	-	-	-	-	-	-	-	-	-	-	-	-	-	-	-	-	-	-	-	-
Craven County	501	495	-	-	-	-	-	-	372	-	-	-	-	-	-	-	-	-	-	-	-	-	-	-
Cumberland County	581	612	485	635	-	-	-	-	627	-	-	-	-	680	606	-	-	-	-	-	-	-	-	631
Davidson County	464	504	-	-	-	501	-	-	-	-	-	-	-	-	-	-	-	-	-	-	-	-	-	-
Durham County	658	720	-	743	-	-	680	-	723	-	-	-	-	838	630	-	-	-	-	-	-	-	-	-
Forsyth County	523	564	-	588	-	-	482	-	521	-	-	-	-	-	-	-	-	-	-	-	-	-	-	650
Gaston County	535	557	-	-	-	-	-	-	-	-	-	-	-	-	-	-	-	-	-	-	-	-	-	486
Guilford County	590	622	-	694	-	-	669	-	626	-	-	-	-	-	794	557	-	511	-	-	-	-	-	563
Halifax County	399	527	-	-	-	-	-	-	-	-	-	-	-	-	-	-	-	-	-	-	-	-	-	-
Harnett County	486	481	-	-	-	-	-	-	-	-	-	-	-	-	-	-	-	-	-	-	-	-	-	-
Henderson County	513	505	-	-	-	-	-	-	-	-	-	-	-	-	-	-	-	-	-	-	-	-	-	-
Iredell County	540	680	-	-	-	-	-	-	-	-	-	-	-	-	-	-	-	-	-	-	-	-	-	-
Johnston County	498	610	-	-	-	-	-	-	-	-	-	-	-	-	-	-	-	-	-	-	-	-	-	-

Notes: Please refer to the User's Guide for an explanation of data; data is arranged alphabetically by state, then county, then city within each county; table includes counties with populations greater than 49,999 unless noted and cities with populations greater than 9,999 whose Asian and/or NHPI population rates are greater than the national average; (1) Native Hawaiian and other Pacific Islander; (2) excludes Taiwanese; (3) includes Chamorro; (4) county does not meet population threshold but is shown in order to allow inclusion of city

Place	All specified renter-occupied housing units	Specified housing units rented by Asians	Specified housing units rented by NHPIs[1]	Asian Indian	Bangladeshi	Cambodian	Chinese[2]	Fijian	Filipino	Guamanian[3]	Hawaiian, Native	Hmong	Indonesian	Japanese	Korean	Laotian	Malaysian	Pakistani	Samoan	Sri Lankan	Taiwanese	Thai	Tongan	Vietnamese
Lenoir County	405	492	-	-	-	-	-	-	-	-	-	-	-	-	-	-	-	-	-	-	-	-	-	-
Mecklenburg County	693	718	-	742	-	403	700	-	692	-	-	562	-	842	749	530	-	-	-	-	-	-	-	628
Nash County	494	763	-	-	-	-	-	-	-	-	-	-	-	-	-	-	-	-	-	-	-	-	-	-
New Hanover County	631	619	-	-	-	-	-	-	-	-	-	-	-	-	-	-	-	-	-	-	-	-	-	-
Onslow County	518	560	642	-	-	-	-	-	532	-	-	-	-	563	-	-	-	-	-	-	-	-	-	-
Orange County	684	648	-	599	-	-	631	-	-	-	-	-	-	923	654	-	-	-	-	-	-	-	-	-
Carrboro (town)	697	689	-	-	-	-	-	-	-	-	-	-	-	-	-	-	-	-	-	-	-	-	-	-
Chapel Hill (town)	690	628	-	574	-	-	633	-	-	-	-	-	-	-	575	-	-	-	-	-	-	-	-	-
Pitt County	471	498	-	-	-	-	-	-	-	-	-	-	-	-	-	-	-	-	-	-	-	-	-	-
Randolph County	463	613	-	-	-	-	-	-	-	-	-	-	-	-	-	-	-	-	-	-	-	-	-	-
Robeson County	389	598	-	-	-	-	-	-	-	-	-	-	-	-	-	-	-	-	-	-	-	-	-	-
Rowan County	496	570	-	-	-	-	-	-	-	-	-	-	-	-	-	-	-	-	-	-	-	-	-	-
Stanly County	463	586	-	-	-	-	-	-	-	-	-	547	-	-	-	-	-	-	-	-	-	-	-	-
Surry County	411	416	-	-	-	-	-	-	-	-	-	-	-	-	-	-	-	-	-	-	-	-	-	-
Union County	587	556	-	-	-	-	-	-	-	-	-	-	-	-	-	-	-	-	-	-	-	-	-	-
Wake County	727	757	-	759	-	-	761	-	763	-	-	-	-	1,031	789	-	-	592	-	-	-	-	-	741
Apex (town)	838	807	-	-	-	-	-	-	-	-	-	-	-	-	-	-	-	-	-	-	-	-	-	-
Cary (town)	826	838	-	802	-	-	856	-	-	-	-	-	-	1,845	858	-	-	-	-	-	-	-	-	906
Wayne County	455	576	-	-	-	-	-	-	-	-	-	-	-	-	-	-	-	-	-	-	-	-	-	-
Wilkes County	416	525	-	-	-	-	-	-	-	-	-	-	-	-	-	-	-	-	-	-	-	-	-	-
NORTH DAKOTA	412	387	-	427	-	-	316	-	476	-	-	-	-	-	425	-	-	-	-	-	-	-	-	-
Cass County	463	329	-	331	-	-	-	-	-	-	-	-	-	-	-	-	-	-	-	-	-	-	-	-
Grand Forks County	477	485	-	-	-	-	-	-	-	-	-	-	-	-	-	-	-	-	-	-	-	-	-	-
Ward County	408	383	-	-	-	-	-	-	-	-	-	-	-	-	-	-	-	-	-	-	-	-	-	-
OHIO	515	587	539	621	660	459	533	-	592	527	575	-	679	744	614	499	468	607	583	512	557	491	-	511
Allen County	446	448	-	-	-	-	-	-	-	-	-	-	-	-	-	-	-	-	-	-	-	-	-	-
Ashtabula County	473	461	-	-	-	-	-	-	-	-	-	-	-	-	-	-	-	-	-	-	-	-	-	-
Athens County	469	508	-	-	-	-	-	-	-	-	-	-	-	-	-	-	-	-	-	-	-	-	-	-
Athens (city)	496	505	-	-	-	-	-	-	-	-	-	-	-	-	-	-	-	-	-	-	-	-	-	-
Butler County	569	645	-	688	-	-	591	-	617	-	-	-	-	-	485	-	-	-	-	-	-	-	-	763
Clark County	487	610	-	-	-	-	-	-	-	-	-	-	-	-	-	-	-	-	-	-	-	-	-	-
Clermont County	552	638	-	769	-	-	-	-	-	-	-	-	-	-	-	-	-	-	-	-	-	-	-	-
Columbiana County	421	447	-	-	-	-	-	-	-	-	-	-	-	-	-	-	-	-	-	-	-	-	-	-
Cuyahoga County	541	603	-	644	-	435	558	-	556	-	-	-	-	739	659	-	-	-	-	-	-	-	-	517
Mayfield Heights (city)	665	663	-	649	-	-	-	-	-	-	-	-	-	-	-	-	-	-	-	-	-	-	-	-
Richmond Heights (city)	557	587	-	-	-	-	-	-	-	-	-	-	-	-	-	-	-	-	-	-	-	-	-	-
Solon (city)	814	687	-	771	-	-	675	-	-	-	-	-	-	-	-	-	-	-	-	-	-	-	-	-
Westlake (city)	866	943	-	998	-	-	-	-	-	-	-	-	-	-	-	-	-	-	-	-	-	-	-	-
Delaware County	639	693	-	667	-	-	625	-	-	-	-	-	-	-	-	-	-	-	-	-	-	-	-	-
Fairfield County	550	619	-	-	-	-	-	-	-	-	-	-	-	-	-	-	-	-	-	-	-	-	-	-
Franklin County	595	613	558	636	-	442	548	-	632	-	-	-	714	924	630	552	-	598	-	-	576	533	-	529

Notes: Please refer to the User's Guide for an explanation of data; data is arranged alphabetically by state, then county, then city within each county; table includes counties with populations greater than 49,999 unless noted and cities with populations greater than 9,999 whose Asian and/or NHPI population rates are greater than the national average; (1) Native Hawaiian and other Pacific Islander; (2) excludes Taiwanese; (3) includes Chamorro; (4) county does not meet population threshold but is shown in order to allow inclusion of city

Place	All specified renter-occupied housing units	Specified housing units rented by Asians	Specified housing units rented by NHPIs[1]	Asian Indian	Bangladeshi	Cambodian	Chinese[2]	Fijian	Filipino	Guamanian[3]	Hawaiian, Native	Hmong	Indonesian	Japanese	Korean	Laotian	Malaysian	Pakistani	Samoan	Sri Lankan	Taiwanese	Thai	Tongan	Vietnamese
Dublin (city)	929	1,036	-	910	-	-	939	-	-	-	-	-	-	1,438	-	-	-	-	-	-	-	-	-	-
Hilliard (city)	772	888	-	-	-	-	-	-	-	-	-	-	-	-	-	-	-	-	-	-	-	-	-	-
Geauga County	592	925	-	-	-	-	-	-	-	-	-	-	-	-	-	-	-	-	-	-	-	-	-	-
Greene County	587	632	-	674	-	-	624	-	-	-	-	-	-	-	875	-	-	-	-	-	-	-	-	-
Hamilton County	485	542	-	567	-	448	529	-	663	-	-	-	-	654	456	-	-	-	-	-	-	-	-	510
Blue Ash (city)	816	774	-	757	-	-	-	-	-	-	-	-	-	-	-	-	-	-	-	-	-	-	-	-
Sharonville (city)	666	621	-	623	-	-	-	-	-	-	-	-	-	-	-	-	-	-	-	-	-	-	-	-
Hancock County	487	450	-	-	-	-	-	-	-	-	-	-	-	-	-	-	-	-	-	-	-	-	-	-
Lake County	623	646	-	701	-	-	618	-	-	-	-	-	-	-	-	-	-	-	-	-	-	-	-	-
Licking County	504	490	-	-	-	-	-	-	-	-	-	-	-	-	-	-	-	-	-	-	-	-	-	-
Lorain County	518	543	-	842	-	-	-	-	554	-	-	-	-	-	-	-	-	-	-	-	-	-	-	-
Lucas County	484	485	-	546	-	-	461	-	556	-	-	-	-	-	667	-	-	-	-	-	-	-	-	-
Mahoning County	446	498	-	-	-	-	-	-	-	-	-	-	-	-	-	-	-	-	-	-	-	-	-	-
Marion County	500	545	-	-	-	-	-	-	-	-	-	-	-	-	-	-	-	-	-	-	-	-	-	-
Medina County	625	604	-	535	-	-	-	-	-	-	-	-	-	-	-	-	-	-	-	-	-	-	-	-
Miami County	522	586	-	-	-	-	-	-	-	-	-	-	-	-	-	-	-	-	-	-	-	-	-	-
Montgomery County	525	629	-	634	-	-	612	-	598	-	-	-	-	701	729	-	-	-	-	-	-	-	-	541
Portage County	544	475	-	-	-	-	-	-	-	-	-	-	-	-	-	-	-	-	-	-	-	-	-	-
Richland County	451	596	-	-	-	-	-	-	-	-	-	-	-	-	-	-	-	-	-	-	-	-	-	-
Stark County	486	501	-	571	-	-	444	-	-	-	-	-	-	-	-	-	-	-	-	-	-	-	-	-
Summit County	546	563	-	546	-	-	488	-	765	-	-	-	-	995	605	509	-	-	-	-	-	-	-	474
Trumbull County	461	510	-	-	-	-	-	-	-	-	-	-	-	-	-	-	-	-	-	-	-	-	-	-
Warren County	613	836	-	831	-	-	827	-	-	-	-	-	-	-	-	-	-	-	-	-	-	-	-	-
Wayne County	492	415	-	-	-	-	-	-	-	-	-	-	-	-	-	-	-	-	-	-	-	-	-	-
Wood County	508	515	-	-	-	-	-	-	-	-	-	-	-	-	-	-	-	-	-	-	-	-	-	-
OKLAHOMA	456	456	479	493	-	775	435	-	471	553	464	575	-	475	441	525	417	464	-	-	433	471	-	455
Canadian County	510	525	-	525	-	-	-	-	-	-	-	-	-	-	-	-	-	-	-	-	-	-	-	0
Cleveland County	526	454	-	481	-	-	432	-	498	-	-	-	-	-	507	-	-	-	-	-	-	-	-	494
Comanche County	452	467	-	-	-	-	-	-	450	-	-	-	-	-	372	-	-	-	-	-	-	-	-	-
Garfield County	436	417	-	-	-	-	-	-	-	-	-	-	-	-	-	-	-	-	-	-	-	-	-	-
Muskogee County	396	431	-	-	-	-	-	-	-	-	-	-	-	-	-	-	-	-	-	-	-	-	-	-
Oklahoma County	483	456	-	483	-	-	408	-	474	-	-	-	-	484	437	475	-	-	-	-	-	561	-	434
Payne County	459	424	-	-	-	-	437	-	-	-	-	-	-	-	-	-	-	-	-	-	-	-	-	-
Stillwater (city)	468	424	-	-	-	-	437	-	-	-	-	-	-	-	-	-	-	-	-	-	-	-	-	-
Pottawatomie County	431	378	-	-	-	-	-	-	-	-	-	-	-	-	-	-	-	-	-	-	-	-	-	-
Tulsa County	520	522	-	603	-	-	483	-	603	-	-	-	-	-	450	-	-	439	-	-	-	-	-	522
Wagoner County	469	391	-	-	-	-	-	-	-	-	-	-	-	-	-	-	-	-	-	-	-	-	-	-
OREGON	620	634	599	715	-	609	620	571	626	622	656	591	531	600	646	618	-	764	667	-	580	615	590	607
Benton County	597	496	-	-	-	-	541	-	-	-	-	-	-	522	464	-	-	-	-	-	-	-	-	-
Corvallis (city)	592	497	-	-	-	-	545	-	-	-	-	-	-	-	464	-	-	-	-	-	-	-	-	-
Clackamas County	702	747	620	693	-	-	766	-	699	-	-	-	-	853	791	-	-	-	-	-	-	-	-	725

Notes: Please refer to the User's Guide for an explanation of data; data is arranged alphabetically by state, then county, then city within each county; table includes counties with populations greater than 49,999 unless noted and cities with populations greater than 9,999 whose Asian and/or NHPI population rates are greater than the national average; (1) Native Hawaiian and other Pacific Islander; (2) excludes Taiwanese; (3) includes Chamorro; (4) county does not meet population threshold but is shown in order to allow inclusion of city

Place	All specified renter-occupied housing units	Specified housing units rented by Asians	Specified housing units rented by NHPIs[1]	Asian Indian	Bangladeshi	Cambodian	Chinese[2]	Fijian	Filipino	Guamanian[3]	Hawaiian, Native	Hmong	Indonesian	Japanese	Korean	Laotian	Malaysian	Pakistani	Samoan	Sri Lankan	Taiwanese	Thai	Tongan	Vietnamese
Lake Oswego (city)	839	849	-	-	-	-	1,097	-	-	-	-	-	-	-	-	-	-	-	-	-	-	-	-	-
Coos County	499	407	-	-	-	-	-	-	-	-	-	-	-	-	-	-	-	-	-	-	-	-	-	-
Deschutes County	644	497	-	-	-	-	-	-	-	-	-	-	-	-	-	-	-	-	-	-	-	-	-	-
Douglas County	489	416	-	-	-	-	-	-	-	-	-	-	-	-	-	-	-	-	-	-	-	-	-	-
Jackson County	597	594	-	-	-	-	-	-	-	-	-	-	-	-	-	-	-	-	-	-	-	-	-	-
Josephine County	534	525	-	-	-	-	-	-	-	-	-	-	-	-	-	-	-	-	-	-	-	-	-	-
Klamath County	475	425	-	-	-	-	-	-	-	-	-	-	-	-	-	-	-	-	-	-	-	-	-	-
Lane County	604	568	803	531	-	-	559	-	464	-	-	-	-	543	600	-	-	-	-	-	-	-	-	-
Linn County	580	447	-	-	-	-	-	-	-	-	-	-	-	-	-	-	-	-	-	-	-	-	-	-
Marion County	574	490	595	492	-	-	609	-	539	-	-	-	-	482	476	-	-	-	-	-	-	-	-	441
Salem (city)	560	488	575	-	-	-	483	-	480	-	-	-	-	495	-	-	-	-	-	-	-	-	-	563
Multnomah County	633	599	586	620	-	619	597	-	593	-	661	580	-	599	624	608	-	-	-	-	-	647	823	583
Portland (city)	622	594	584	612	-	619	598	-	596	-	661	573	-	600	600	574	-	-	-	-	-	647	823	581
Polk County	565	465	-	-	-	-	-	-	-	-	-	-	-	-	-	-	-	-	-	-	-	-	-	-
Umatilla County	481	471	-	-	-	-	-	-	-	-	-	-	-	-	-	-	-	-	-	-	-	-	-	-
Washington County	720	728	649	747	-	717	689	-	690	-	670	-	-	910	713	641	-	-	-	-	-	-	-	684
Aloha (cdp)	792	764	-	-	-	-	-	-	950	-	-	-	-	-	-	-	-	-	-	-	-	-	-	811
Beaverton (city)	706	719	-	723	-	535	761	-	635	-	-	-	-	1,267	650	-	-	-	-	-	-	-	-	638
Cedar Mill (cdp)	626	686	-	-	-	-	-	-	-	-	-	-	-	-	-	-	-	-	-	-	-	-	-	-
Hillsboro (city)	782	789	-	815	-	-	709	-	-	-	-	-	-	-	777	-	-	-	-	-	-	-	-	708
Tigard (city)	673	691	-	-	-	-	475	-	-	-	-	-	-	-	-	-	-	-	-	-	-	-	-	691
Tualatin (city)	768	814	-	-	-	-	-	-	-	-	-	-	-	-	-	-	-	-	-	-	-	-	-	-
Yamhill County	623	538	-	-	-	-	-	-	-	-	-	-	-	-	-	-	-	-	-	-	-	-	-	-
PENNSYLVANIA	531	648	541	699	558	523	627	-	648	475	507	534	574	670	681	615	-	717	838	525	611	555	-	544
Adams County	509	576	-	-	-	-	-	-	-	-	-	-	-	-	-	-	-	-	-	-	-	-	-	-
Allegheny County	516	621	435	675	-	-	584	-	545	-	-	-	-	614	623	-	-	-	-	-	484	-	-	513
Muni. of Monroeville (borough)	684	705	-	709	-	-	-	-	-	-	-	-	-	-	-	-	-	-	-	-	-	-	-	-
Scott (township)	644	659	-	668	-	-	-	-	-	-	-	-	-	-	-	-	-	-	-	-	-	-	-	-
Scott Township (cdp)	644	659	-	668	-	-	-	-	-	-	-	-	-	-	-	-	-	-	-	-	-	-	-	-
Upper St. Clair (township)	1,207	0	-	0	-	-	-	-	-	-	-	-	-	-	-	-	-	-	-	-	-	-	-	-
Beaver County	438	533	-	-	-	-	-	-	-	-	-	-	-	-	-	-	-	-	-	-	-	-	-	-
Berks County	545	593	-	590	-	-	492	-	-	-	-	-	-	-	594	-	-	-	-	-	-	-	-	470
Blair County	411	594	-	-	-	-	-	-	-	-	-	-	-	-	-	-	-	-	-	-	-	-	-	-
Bradford County	414	475	-	-	-	-	-	-	-	-	-	-	-	-	-	-	-	-	-	-	-	-	-	-
Bucks County	736	699	-	681	-	-	744	-	860	-	-	-	-	-	742	-	-	-	-	-	-	-	-	631
Bensalem (township)	752	722	-	713	-	-	-	-	-	-	-	-	-	-	714	-	-	-	-	-	-	-	-	-
Lower Makefield (township)	1,167	1,241	-	1,184	-	-	-	-	-	-	-	-	-	-	-	-	-	-	-	-	-	-	-	-
Newtown (township)	1,005	1,092	-	-	-	-	-	-	-	-	-	-	-	-	-	-	-	-	-	-	-	-	-	-
Butler County	487	709	-	774	-	-	-	-	-	-	-	-	-	-	-	-	-	-	-	-	-	-	-	-
Cambria County	361	508	-	-	-	-	-	-	-	-	-	-	-	-	-	-	-	-	-	-	-	-	-	-
Centre County	565	541	-	615	-	-	525	-	-	-	-	-	-	-	525	-	-	-	-	-	-	-	-	-

Notes: Please refer to the User's Guide for an explanation of data; data is arranged alphabetically by state, then county, then city within each county; table includes counties with populations greater than 49,999 unless noted and cities with populations greater than 9,999 whose Asian and/or NHPI population rates are greater than the national average; (1) Native Hawaiian and other Pacific Islander; (2) excludes Taiwanese; (3) includes Chamorro; (4) county does not meet population threshold but is shown in order to allow inclusion of city

Place	All specified renter-occupied housing units	Specified housing units rented by Asians	Specified housing units rented by NHPIs[1]	Asian Indian	Bangladeshi	Cambodian	Chinese[2]	Fijian	Filipino	Guamanian[3]	Hawaiian, Native	Hmong	Indonesian	Japanese	Korean	Laotian	Malaysian	Pakistani	Samoan	Sri Lankan	Taiwanese	Thai	Tongan	Vietnamese
Ferguson (township)	587	538	-	-	-	-	-	-	-	-	-	-	-	-	-	-	-	-	-	-	-	-	-	-
Patton (township)	679	634	-	-	-	-	-	-	-	-	-	-	-	-	-	-	-	-	-	-	-	-	-	-
State College (borough)	595	539	-	586	-	-	519	-	-	-	-	-	-	-	537	-	-	-	-	-	-	-	-	-
Chester County	754	837	-	881	-	-	767	-	746	-	-	-	-	860	878	-	-	-	-	-	-	-	-	792
Tredyffrin (township)	928	910	-	955	-	-	782	-	-	-	-	-	-	-	-	-	-	-	-	-	-	-	-	-
West Goshen (township)	801	845	-	-	-	-	-	-	-	-	-	-	-	-	-	-	-	-	-	-	-	-	-	-
West Whiteland (township)	976	1,023	-	-	-	-	-	-	-	-	-	-	-	-	-	-	-	-	-	-	-	-	-	-
Clearfield County	376	719	-	-	-	-	-	-	-	-	-	-	-	-	-	-	-	-	-	-	-	-	-	-
Columbia County	448	370	-	-	-	-	-	-	-	-	-	-	-	-	-	-	-	-	-	-	-	-	-	-
Crawford County	406	631	-	-	-	-	-	-	-	-	-	-	-	-	-	-	-	-	-	-	-	-	-	-
Cumberland County	576	604	-	708	-	-	775	-	-	-	-	-	-	-	562	-	-	-	-	-	-	-	-	863
Hampden (township)	695	802	-	-	-	-	-	-	-	-	-	-	-	-	-	-	-	-	-	-	-	-	-	-
Dauphin County	557	595	-	663	-	-	608	-	-	-	-	-	-	-	581	-	-	-	-	-	-	-	-	348
Derry (township)	690	682	-	-	-	-	-	-	-	-	-	-	-	-	-	-	-	-	-	-	-	-	-	-
Hershey (cdp)	658	666	-	-	-	-	-	-	-	-	-	-	-	-	-	-	-	-	-	-	-	-	-	-
Delaware County	662	699	-	692	-	-	641	-	661	-	-	-	-	893	805	-	-	656	-	-	-	-	-	654
Broomall (cdp)	784	822	-	-	-	-	-	-	-	-	-	-	-	-	832	-	-	-	-	-	-	-	-	-
Drexel Hill (cdp)	702	809	-	-	-	-	787	-	-	-	-	-	-	-	-	-	-	-	-	-	-	-	-	-
Marple (township)	798	831	-	-	-	-	-	-	-	-	-	-	-	-	832	-	-	-	-	-	-	-	-	-
Radnor (township)	935	1,016	-	-	-	-	872	-	-	-	-	-	-	-	-	-	-	-	-	-	-	-	-	-
Upper Darby (township)	651	690	-	700	-	-	643	-	-	-	-	-	-	-	757	-	-	-	-	-	-	-	-	650
Erie County	445	567	-	638	-	-	-	-	-	-	-	-	-	-	-	-	-	-	-	-	-	-	-	-
Franklin County	455	642	-	-	-	-	-	-	-	-	-	-	-	-	-	-	-	-	-	-	-	-	-	-
Indiana County	426	419	-	-	-	-	-	-	-	-	-	-	-	-	-	-	-	-	-	-	-	-	-	-
Lackawanna County	440	600	-	646	-	-	-	-	-	-	-	-	-	-	-	-	-	-	-	-	-	-	-	-
Lancaster County	572	646	-	763	-	-	662	-	-	-	-	558	-	-	604	-	-	-	-	-	-	-	-	529
Lawrence County	424	546	-	-	-	-	-	-	-	-	-	-	-	-	-	-	-	-	-	-	-	-	-	-
Lebanon County	470	507	-	-	-	-	-	-	-	-	-	-	-	-	-	-	-	-	-	-	-	-	-	-
Lehigh County	586	670	-	691	-	-	669	-	-	-	-	-	-	-	622	-	-	-	-	-	-	-	-	589
Fullerton (cdp)	665	688	-	-	-	-	-	-	-	-	-	-	-	-	-	-	-	-	-	-	-	-	-	-
Lower Macungie (township)	795	608	-	-	-	-	0	-	-	-	-	-	-	-	-	-	-	-	-	-	-	-	-	-
Upper Macungie (township)	864	936	-	-	-	-	-	-	-	-	-	-	-	-	-	-	-	-	-	-	-	-	-	-
Luzerne County	434	550	-	598	-	-	-	-	-	-	-	-	-	-	-	-	-	-	-	-	-	-	-	-
Lycoming County	449	608	-	-	-	-	-	-	-	-	-	-	-	-	-	-	-	-	-	-	-	-	-	-
Mercer County	443	559	-	-	-	-	-	-	-	-	-	-	-	-	-	-	-	-	-	-	-	-	-	-
Monroe County	658	700	-	693	-	-	-	-	-	-	-	-	-	-	-	-	-	-	-	-	-	-	-	-
Montgomery County	757	796	-	796	-	-	762	-	916	-	-	-	-	888	823	-	-	-	-	-	-	-	-	633
Cheltenham (township)	742	769	-	-	-	-	-	-	-	-	-	-	-	-	754	-	-	-	-	-	-	-	-	-
East Norriton (township)	887	850	-	-	-	-	-	-	-	-	-	-	-	-	-	-	-	-	-	-	-	-	-	-
Hatfield (township)	734	696	-	718	-	-	-	-	-	-	-	-	-	-	-	-	-	-	-	-	-	-	-	-
Horsham (township)	821	799	-	-	-	-	-	-	-	-	-	-	-	-	840	-	-	-	-	-	-	-	-	-

Notes: Please refer to the User's Guide for an explanation of data; data is arranged alphabetically by state, then county, then city within each county; table includes counties with populations greater than 49,999 unless noted and cities with populations greater than 9,999 whose Asian and/or NHPI population rates are greater than the national average; (1) Native Hawaiian and other Pacific Islander; (2) excludes Taiwanese; (3) includes Chamorro; (4) county does not meet population threshold but is shown in order to allow inclusion of city

Place	All specified renter-occupied housing units	Specified housing units rented by Asians	Specified housing units rented by NHPIs[1]	Asian Indian	Bangladeshi	Cambodian	Chinese[2]	Fijian	Filipino	Guamanian[3]	Hawaiian, Native	Hmong	Indonesian	Japanese	Korean	Laotian	Malaysian	Pakistani	Samoan	Sri Lankan	Taiwanese	Thai	Tongan	Vietnamese
King of Prussia (cdp)	894	917	-	895	-	-	934	-	-	-	-	-	-	-	-	-	-	-	-	-	-	-	-	-
Lansdale (borough)	672	739	-	698	-	-	-	-	-	-	-	-	-	-	-	-	-	-	-	-	-	-	-	-
Lower Gwynedd (township)	1,209	1,238	-	-	-	-	-	-	-	-	-	-	-	-	-	-	-	-	-	-	-	-	-	-
Lower Providence (township)	807	729	-	-	-	-	718	-	-	-	-	-	-	-	-	-	-	-	-	-	-	-	-	-
Montgomery (township)	976	956	-	0	-	-	-	-	-	-	-	-	-	-	956	-	-	-	-	-	-	-	-	-
Montgomeryville (cdp)	979	956	-	-	-	-	-	-	-	-	-	-	-	-	-	-	-	-	-	-	-	-	-	-
Plymouth (township)	823	845	-	-	-	-	-	-	-	-	-	-	-	-	871	-	-	-	-	-	-	-	-	-
Towamencin (township)	838	856	-	-	-	-	-	-	-	-	-	-	-	-	-	-	-	-	-	-	-	-	-	-
Upper Dublin (township)	890	980	-	-	-	-	-	-	-	-	-	-	-	-	950	-	-	-	-	-	-	-	-	-
Upper Gwynedd (township)	922	823	-	-	-	-	767	-	-	-	-	-	-	-	-	-	-	-	-	-	-	-	-	-
Upper Merion (township)	898	917	-	895	-	-	934	-	-	-	-	-	-	-	-	-	-	-	-	-	-	-	-	-
Whitpain (township)	1,154	1,173	-	-	-	-	-	-	-	-	-	-	-	-	1,202	-	-	-	-	-	-	-	-	-
Northampton County	576	577	-	853	-	-	486	-	-	-	-	-	-	-	574	-	-	-	-	-	-	-	-	656
Northumberland County	389	528	-	-	-	-	-	-	-	-	-	-	-	-	-	-	-	-	-	-	-	-	-	-
Philadelphia County	569	606	584	671	-	519	598	-	551	-	-	-	-	643	652	607	-	625	-	-	-	-	-	531
Philadelphia (city)	569	606	584	671	-	519	598	-	551	-	-	-	-	643	652	607	-	625	-	-	-	-	-	531
Schuylkill County	379	406	-	-	-	-	-	-	-	-	-	-	-	-	-	-	-	-	-	-	-	-	-	-
Washington County	423	490	-	-	-	-	-	-	-	-	-	-	-	-	-	-	-	-	-	-	-	-	-	-
Westmoreland County	432	806	-	950	-	-	-	-	-	-	-	-	-	-	-	-	-	-	-	-	-	-	-	-
York County	531	620	-	669	-	-	623	-	-	-	-	-	-	-	689	-	-	-	-	-	-	-	-	561
RHODE ISLAND	553	590	438	688	-	517	606	-	597	-	-	525	-	751	730	500	-	-	-	-	-	-	-	599
Bristol County	578	650	-	-	-	-	-	-	-	-	-	-	-	-	-	-	-	-	-	-	-	-	-	-
Kent County	613	766	-	-	-	-	682	-	-	-	-	-	-	-	955	-	-	-	-	-	-	-	-	-
Newport County	689	711	-	-	-	-	-	-	739	-	-	-	-	-	-	-	-	-	-	-	-	-	-	-
Providence County	527	564	-	659	-	517	550	-	566	-	-	500	-	-	710	494	-	-	-	-	-	-	-	590
Providence (city)	526	570	-	672	-	510	627	-	550	-	-	492	-	-	703	506	-	-	-	-	-	-	-	-
Woonsocket (city)	483	485	-	-	-	-	-	-	-	-	-	-	-	-	-	473	-	-	-	-	-	-	-	-
Washington County	645	715	-	-	-	-	704	-	-	-	-	-	-	-	-	-	-	-	-	-	-	-	-	-
SOUTH CAROLINA	510	559	572	607	-	579	498	-	527	389	578	447	-	575	606	565	-	-	-	-	-	540	-	505
Aiken County	475	536	-	-	-	-	-	-	-	-	-	-	-	-	-	-	-	-	-	-	-	-	-	-
Anderson County	454	511	-	-	-	-	-	-	-	-	-	-	-	-	-	-	-	-	-	-	-	-	-	-
Beaufort County	690	672	-	-	-	-	-	-	-	-	-	-	-	-	-	-	-	-	-	-	-	-	-	-
Berkeley County	562	483	-	-	-	-	-	-	448	-	-	-	-	-	-	-	-	-	-	-	-	-	-	-
Charleston County	605	604	-	540	-	-	568	-	561	-	-	-	-	-	-	-	-	-	-	-	-	-	-	-
Dorchester County	568	488	-	-	-	-	-	-	441	-	-	-	-	-	-	-	-	-	-	-	-	-	-	-
Florence County	452	544	-	-	-	-	-	-	-	-	-	-	-	-	-	-	-	-	-	-	-	-	-	-
Greenville County	544	595	-	628	-	-	560	-	607	-	-	-	-	-	-	-	-	-	-	-	-	-	-	482
Greenwood County	440	515	-	-	-	-	-	-	-	-	-	-	-	-	-	-	-	-	-	-	-	-	-	-
Horry County	594	500	-	-	-	-	-	-	-	-	-	-	-	-	-	-	-	-	-	-	-	-	-	-
Lexington County	548	586	-	746	-	-	513	-	-	-	-	-	-	-	-	-	-	-	-	-	-	-	-	-
Oconee County	424	535	-	-	-	-	-	-	-	-	-	-	-	-	-	-	-	-	-	-	-	-	-	-

Notes: Please refer to the User's Guide for an explanation of data; data is arranged alphabetically by state, then county, then city within each county; table includes counties with populations greater than 49,999 unless noted and cities with populations greater than 9,999 whose Asian and/or NHPI population rates are greater than the national average; (1) Native Hawaiian and other Pacific Islander; (2) excludes Taiwanese; (3) includes Chamorro; (4) county does not meet population threshold but is shown in order to allow inclusion of city

Place	All specified renter-occupied housing units	Specified housing units rented by Asians	Specified housing units rented by NHPIs[1]	Asian Indian	Bangladeshi	Cambodian	Chinese[2]	Fijian	Filipino	Guamanian[3]	Hawaiian, Native	Hmong	Indonesian	Japanese	Korean	Laotian	Malaysian	Pakistani	Samoan	Sri Lankan	Taiwanese	Thai	Tongan	Vietnamese
Pickens County	479	435	-	538	-	-	364	-	-	-	-	-	-	-	-	-	-	-	-	-	-	-	-	-
Clemson (city)	535	490	-	-	-	-	-	-	-	-	-	-	-	-	-	-	-	-	-	-	-	-	-	-
Richland County	570	583	-	632	-	-	534	-	544	-	-	-	-	-	606	-	-	-	-	-	-	-	-	485
Spartanburg County	485	526	-	653	-	-	-	-	-	-	-	431	-	-	-	532	-	-	-	-	-	-	-	-
Sumter County	461	584	-	-	-	-	-	-	-	-	-	-	-	-	-	-	-	-	-	-	-	-	-	-
York County	581	660	-	-	-	-	-	-	-	-	-	-	-	-	-	-	-	-	-	-	-	-	-	625
SOUTH DAKOTA	426	457	-	522	-	-	394	-	481	-	-	-	-	436	483	425	-	-	-	-	-	-	-	438
Minnehaha County	516	481	-	-	-	-	-	-	-	-	-	-	-	-	-	-	-	-	-	-	-	-	-	439
Pennington County	497	483	-	-	-	-	-	-	-	-	-	-	-	-	-	-	-	-	-	-	-	-	-	-
TENNESSEE	505	601	527	635	-	558	539	-	597	525	375	-	-	779	613	559	-	648	581	-	433	607	-	497
Anderson County	450	549	-	-	-	-	-	-	-	-	-	-	-	-	-	-	-	-	-	-	-	-	-	-
Blount County	450	673	-	-	-	-	-	-	-	-	-	-	-	-	-	-	-	-	-	-	-	-	-	-
Bradley County	455	583	-	-	-	-	-	-	-	-	-	-	-	-	-	-	-	-	-	-	-	-	-	-
Davidson County	615	634	577	631	-	-	586	-	633	-	-	-	-	784	690	546	-	-	-	-	-	-	-	597
Hamilton County	510	561	-	565	-	-	-	-	528	-	-	-	-	-	544	-	-	-	-	-	-	-	-	528
Knox County	493	453	-	524	-	-	384	-	-	-	-	-	-	-	533	-	-	-	-	-	-	-	-	482
Madison County	510	967	-	-	-	-	-	-	-	-	-	-	-	-	-	-	-	-	-	-	-	-	-	-
Montgomery County	549	546	-	-	-	-	-	-	-	-	-	-	-	-	525	-	-	-	-	-	-	-	-	-
Putnam County	441	451	-	-	-	-	-	-	-	-	-	-	-	-	-	-	-	-	-	-	-	-	-	-
Rutherford County	601	655	-	-	-	-	-	-	-	-	-	-	-	-	-	600	-	-	-	-	-	-	-	-
Shelby County	566	626	528	677	-	571	613	-	684	-	-	-	-	822	581	-	-	-	-	-	-	-	-	456
Germantown (city)	929	1,100	-	907	-	-	893	-	-	-	-	-	-	-	-	-	-	-	-	-	-	-	-	-
Sullivan County	419	496	-	-	-	-	-	-	-	-	-	-	-	-	-	-	-	-	-	-	-	-	-	-
Sumner County	594	816	-	-	-	-	-	-	-	-	-	-	-	-	-	-	-	-	-	-	-	-	-	-
Washington County	446	397	-	-	-	-	-	-	-	-	-	-	-	-	-	-	-	-	-	-	-	-	-	-
Weakley County[4]	391	396	-	-	-	-	-	-	-	-	-	-	-	-	-	-	-	-	-	-	-	-	-	-
Martin (city)	408	396	-	-	-	-	-	-	-	-	-	-	-	-	-	-	-	-	-	-	-	-	-	-
Williamson County	744	971	-	-	-	-	-	-	-	-	-	-	-	-	-	-	-	-	-	-	-	-	-	-
Wilson County	567	825	-	-	-	-	-	-	-	-	-	-	-	-	-	-	-	-	-	-	-	-	-	-
TEXAS	574	627	620	690	627	555	581	-	602	583	642	-	643	758	664	523	758	710	578	609	585	567	653	556
Anderson County	456	425	-	-	-	-	-	-	-	-	-	-	-	-	-	-	-	-	-	-	-	-	-	-
Angelina County	461	570	-	-	-	-	-	-	-	-	-	-	-	-	-	-	-	-	-	-	-	-	-	-
Bell County	543	535	490	635	-	-	-	-	572	600	-	-	-	417	466	-	-	-	-	-	-	-	-	-
Killeen (city)	559	538	484	-	-	-	-	-	574	496	-	-	-	-	478	-	-	-	-	-	-	-	-	-
Bexar County	556	581	588	588	-	-	570	-	571	-	727	-	-	666	601	396	-	-	-	-	-	600	-	489
Bowie County	459	497	-	-	-	-	-	-	-	-	-	-	-	-	-	-	-	-	-	-	-	-	-	-
Brazoria County	542	547	-	713	-	625	1,309	-	463	-	-	-	-	-	-	-	-	-	-	-	-	-	-	481
Brazos County	584	481	-	559	-	-	441	-	-	-	-	-	-	-	454	-	-	-	-	-	-	-	-	576
College Station (city)	597	475	-	578	-	-	435	-	-	-	-	-	-	-	441	-	-	-	-	-	-	-	-	-
Calhoun County[4]	440	433	-	-	-	-	-	-	-	-	-	-	-	-	-	-	-	-	-	-	-	-	-	615
Port Lavaca (city)	430	413	-	-	-	-	-	-	-	-	-	-	-	-	-	-	-	-	-	-	-	-	-	-

Notes: Please refer to the User's Guide for an explanation of data; data is arranged alphabetically by state, then county, then city within each county; table includes counties with populations greater than 49,999 unless noted and cities with populations greater than 9,999 whose Asian and/or NHPI population rates are greater than the national average; (1) Native Hawaiian and other Pacific Islander; (2) excludes Taiwanese; (3) includes Chamorro; (4) county does not meet population threshold but is shown in order to allow inclusion of city

Place	All specified renter-occupied housing units	Specified housing units rented by Asians	Specified housing units rented by NHPIs[1]	Asian Indian	Bangladeshi	Cambodian	Chinese[2]	Fijian	Filipino	Guamanian[3]	Hawaiian, Native	Hmong	Indonesian	Japanese	Korean	Laotian	Malaysian	Pakistani	Samoan	Sri Lankan	Taiwanese	Thai	Tongan	Vietnamese
Cameron County	413	501	-	-	-	-	-	-	511	-	-	-	-	-	-	-	-	-	-	-	-	-	-	-
Collin County	798	799	-	788	-	-	740	-	769	-	-	-	-	1,264	964	-	-	813	-	-	875	1,125	-	781
Allen (city)	887	776	-	786	-	-	-	-	-	-	-	-	-	-	-	-	-	-	-	-	-	-	-	148
Plano (city)	862	848	-	819	-	-	817	-	763	-	-	-	-	1,129	998	-	-	1,065	-	-	850	-	-	792
Comal County	626	850	-	-	-	-	-	-	-	-	-	-	-	-	-	-	-	-	-	-	-	-	-	-
Coryell County	548	434	661	-	-	-	-	-	-	-	-	-	-	-	556	-	-	-	-	-	-	-	-	-
Dallas County	647	680	731	721	664	563	663	-	657	-	-	-	-	889	715	538	-	769	-	-	669	694	-	584
Addison (town)	738	657	-	666	-	-	-	-	-	-	-	-	-	-	-	-	-	-	-	-	-	-	-	-
Coppell (city)	946	956	-	928	-	-	738	-	-	-	-	-	-	-	991	-	-	-	-	-	-	-	-	-
Farmers Branch (city)	783	735	-	-	-	-	-	-	-	-	-	-	-	-	-	-	-	-	-	-	-	-	-	-
Garland (city)	672	597	-	625	-	-	586	-	663	-	-	-	-	-	623	-	-	681	-	-	-	-	-	578
Grand Prairie (city)	642	719	-	661	-	-	-	-	645	-	-	-	-	-	-	753	-	-	-	-	-	-	-	755
Irving (city)	714	748	-	773	-	-	701	-	886	-	-	-	-	940	724	545	-	741	-	-	-	-	-	651
Mesquite (city)	691	727	-	706	-	-	-	-	667	-	-	-	-	-	-	-	-	-	-	-	-	-	-	-
Richardson (city)	827	771	-	771	-	-	708	-	664	-	-	-	-	-	906	-	-	812	-	-	-	-	-	720
Rowlett (city)	900	832	-	0	-	-	-	-	-	-	-	-	-	-	-	-	-	-	-	-	-	-	-	-
Denton County	725	652	-	754	-	0	582	-	626	-	-	-	-	616	669	-	-	778	-	-	-	-	-	652
Carrollton (city)	781	764	-	754	-	543	900	-	-	-	-	-	-	-	785	-	-	834	-	-	-	-	-	717
Lewisville (city)	783	787	-	788	-	-	-	-	-	-	-	-	-	-	-	-	-	-	-	-	-	-	-	566
Ector County	400	507	-	-	-	-	-	-	-	-	-	-	-	-	-	-	-	-	-	-	-	-	-	-
El Paso County	468	536	570	495	-	-	475	-	491	-	-	-	-	671	649	-	-	-	-	-	-	-	-	-
Ellis County	584	1,094	-	-	-	-	-	-	-	-	-	-	-	-	-	-	-	-	-	-	-	-	-	-
Fort Bend County	730	867	-	825	-	-	888	-	895	-	-	-	-	-	863	-	-	948	-	-	971	-	-	864
Cinco Ranch (cdp)	1,016	2,001	-	-	-	-	-	-	-	-	-	-	-	-	-	-	-	-	-	-	-	-	-	-
Mission Bend (cdp)	844	805	-	688	-	-	0	-	829	-	-	-	-	-	-	-	-	874	-	-	-	-	-	325
Missouri City (city)	893	775	-	621	-	-	1,625	-	0	-	-	-	-	-	-	-	-	-	-	-	-	-	-	1,534
New Territory (cdp)	816	1,125	-	1,125	-	-	0	-	-	-	-	-	-	-	-	-	-	-	-	-	-	-	-	-
Stafford (city)	791	798	-	747	-	-	826	-	886	-	-	-	-	-	-	-	-	-	-	-	-	-	-	886
Sugar Land (city)	939	955	-	890	-	-	992	-	911	-	-	-	-	-	850	-	-	1,205	-	-	1,008	-	-	964
Galveston County	571	612	-	689	-	-	494	-	524	-	-	-	-	-	-	-	-	-	-	-	-	-	-	530
Grayson County	518	547	-	-	-	-	-	-	-	-	-	-	-	-	-	-	-	-	-	-	-	-	-	-
Gregg County	474	440	-	-	-	-	-	-	-	-	-	-	-	-	-	-	-	-	-	-	-	-	-	-
Guadalupe County	508	867	-	-	-	-	-	-	-	-	-	-	-	-	-	-	-	-	-	-	-	-	-	-
Harris County	590	602	627	661	629	509	549	-	629	669	-	-	698	869	674	501	-	663	-	-	600	514	-	538
Bellaire (city)	1,119	696	-	-	-	-	1,375	-	-	-	-	-	-	-	-	-	-	-	-	-	-	-	-	-
Houston (city)	575	594	619	662	-	509	543	-	625	672	-	-	698	861	675	-	-	662	-	-	609	523	-	526
West University Place (city)	1,418	1,625	-	-	-	-	-	-	-	-	-	-	-	-	-	-	-	-	-	-	-	-	-	-
Hays County	628	636	-	-	-	-	-	-	-	-	-	-	-	-	-	-	-	-	-	-	-	-	-	-
Hidalgo County	401	547	-	532	-	-	-	-	533	-	-	-	-	-	-	-	-	-	-	-	-	-	-	-
Hunt County	476	403	-	-	-	-	-	-	-	-	-	-	-	-	-	-	-	-	-	-	-	-	-	-
Jefferson County	477	476	-	573	-	-	293	-	516	-	-	-	-	-	-	-	-	-	-	-	-	-	-	428

Notes: Please refer to the User's Guide for an explanation of data; data is arranged alphabetically by state, then county, then city within each county; table includes counties with populations greater than 49,999 unless noted and cities with populations greater than 9,999 whose Asian and/or NHPI population rates are greater than the national average; (1) Native Hawaiian and other Pacific Islander; (2) excludes Taiwanese; (3) includes Chamorro; (4) county does not meet population threshold but is shown in order to allow inclusion of city

Place	All specified renter-occupied housing units	Specified housing units rented by Asians	Specified housing units rented by NHPIs[1]	Asian Indian	Bangladeshi	Cambodian	Chinese[2]	Fijian	Filipino	Guamanian[3]	Hawaiian, Native	Hmong	Indonesian	Japanese	Korean	Laotian	Malaysian	Pakistani	Samoan	Sri Lankan	Taiwanese	Thai	Tongan	Vietnamese
Port Arthur (city)	405	488	-	-	-	-	-	-	-	-	-	-	-	-	-	-	-	-	-	-	-	-	-	455
Johnson County	540	543	-	-	-	-	-	-	-	-	-	-	-	-	-	-	-	-	-	-	-	-	-	-
Kaufman County	533	775	-	-	-	-	-	-	-	-	-	-	-	-	-	-	-	-	-	-	-	-	-	-
Lubbock County	507	424	-	368	-	-	286	-	-	-	-	-	-	-	-	-	-	-	-	-	-	-	-	594
McLennan County	499	498	-	675	-	-	-	-	-	-	-	-	-	-	-	-	-	-	-	-	-	-	-	-
Midland County	464	467	-	541	-	-	-	-	-	-	-	-	-	-	-	-	-	-	-	-	-	-	-	-
Montgomery County	617	698	-	754	-	-	725	-	535	-	-	-	-	-	-	-	-	-	-	-	-	-	-	-
Nacogdoches County	465	950	-	-	-	-	-	-	-	-	-	-	-	-	-	-	-	-	-	-	-	-	-	-
Nueces County	548	565	-	575	-	-	-	-	584	-	-	-	-	-	-	-	-	-	-	-	-	-	-	-
Orange County	472	492	-	-	-	-	-	-	-	-	-	-	-	-	-	-	-	-	-	-	-	-	-	472
Potter County	451	441	-	-	-	-	-	-	-	-	-	-	-	-	-	357	-	-	-	-	-	-	-	383
Randall County	504	412	-	-	-	-	-	-	-	-	-	-	-	-	-	-	-	-	-	-	-	-	-	-
San Patricio County	518	559	-	-	-	-	-	-	-	-	-	-	-	-	-	-	-	-	-	-	-	-	-	-
Smith County	517	544	-	-	-	-	-	-	-	-	-	-	-	-	-	-	-	-	-	-	-	-	-	-
Tarrant County	612	570	596	620	-	465	535	-	589	-	-	-	-	557	632	567	-	701	-	-	517	519	558	522
Arlington (city)	635	545	-	569	-	-	516	-	579	-	-	-	-	-	564	-	-	-	-	-	516	-	-	556
Euless (city)	703	676	-	749	-	-	-	-	-	-	-	-	-	-	-	-	-	-	-	-	-	-	-	-
Haltom City (city)	569	492	-	-	-	-	-	-	-	-	-	-	-	-	-	468	-	-	-	-	-	-	-	478
Taylor County	472	446	-	-	-	-	-	-	450	-	-	-	-	-	-	-	-	-	-	-	-	-	-	-
Tom Green County	457	391	-	-	-	-	-	-	-	-	-	-	-	-	-	-	-	-	-	-	-	-	-	-
Travis County	727	707	801	765	-	-	642	-	702	-	-	-	-	845	679	-	-	811	-	-	647	664	-	643
Austin (city)	724	704	812	758	-	-	640	-	714	-	-	-	-	836	675	-	-	770	-	-	639	-	-	640
Pflugerville (city)	891	775	-	-	-	-	-	-	-	-	-	-	-	-	-	-	-	-	-	-	-	-	-	-
Wells Branch (cdp)	756	802	-	-	-	-	-	-	-	-	-	-	-	-	-	-	-	-	-	-	-	-	-	-
Victoria County	507	518	-	-	-	-	-	-	-	-	-	-	-	-	-	-	-	-	-	-	-	-	-	-
Webb County	449	624	-	-	-	-	-	-	-	-	-	-	-	-	-	-	-	-	-	-	-	-	-	-
Wichita County	486	472	-	-	-	-	-	-	475	-	-	-	-	-	-	-	-	-	-	-	-	-	-	473
Williamson County	787	779	-	798	-	-	786	-	-	-	-	-	-	-	788	-	-	-	-	-	-	-	-	685
Brushy Creek (cdp)	1,084	0	-	-	-	-	-	-	-	-	-	-	-	-	-	-	-	-	-	-	-	-	-	-
Jollyville (cdp)	820	564	-	-	-	-	-	-	-	-	-	-	-	-	-	-	-	-	-	-	-	-	-	-
UTAH	597	572	630	661	-	546	541	-	595	-	615	-	-	538	576	561	-	593	606	-	538	530	673	525
Cache County	509	542	-	-	-	-	552	-	-	-	-	-	-	-	-	-	-	-	-	-	-	-	-	-
Davis County	637	604	709	-	-	-	-	-	577	-	-	-	-	725	475	-	-	-	-	-	-	-	-	-
Salt Lake County	638	586	644	665	-	602	514	-	763	-	597	-	-	539	609	594	-	-	636	-	-	-	681	525
Kearns (cdp)	830	825	630	-	-	-	-	-	-	-	-	-	-	-	-	-	-	-	-	-	-	-	-	-
Salt Lake City (city)	564	511	578	645	-	-	484	-	427	-	-	-	-	490	523	-	-	-	618	-	-	-	653	413
Sandy (city)	768	699	1,375	-	-	-	508	-	-	-	-	-	-	-	-	-	-	-	-	-	-	-	-	-
Taylorsville (city)	681	620	719	-	-	-	-	-	-	-	-	-	-	-	-	-	-	-	-	-	-	-	-	525
West Jordan (city)	730	542	747	-	-	-	-	-	-	-	-	-	-	-	-	-	-	-	-	-	-	-	744	-
West Valley City (city)	643	638	638	-	-	0	650	-	-	-	-	-	-	-	-	595	-	-	617	-	-	-	768	586
Utah County	580	569	618	-	-	-	617	-	532	-	623	-	-	681	689	-	-	-	550	-	-	-	584	-

Notes: Please refer to the User's Guide for an explanation of data; data is arranged alphabetically by state, then county, then city within each county; table includes counties with populations greater than 49,999 unless noted and cities with populations greater than 9,999 whose Asian and/or NHPI population rates are greater than the national average; (1) Native Hawaiian and other Pacific Islander; (2) excludes Taiwanese; (3) includes Chamorro; (4) county does not meet population threshold but is shown in order to allow inclusion of city

Place	All specified renter-occupied housing units	Specified housing units rented by Asians	Specified housing units rented by NHPIs[1]	Asian Indian	Bangladeshi	Cambodian	Chinese[2]	Fijian	Filipino	Guamanian[3]	Hawaiian, Native	Hmong	Indonesian	Japanese	Korean	Laotian	Malaysian	Pakistani	Samoan	Sri Lankan	Taiwanese	Thai	Tongan	Vietnamese
Orem (city)	639	572	631	-	-	-	-	-	-	-	-	-	-	-	-	-	-	-	-	-	-	-	-	-
Provo (city)	521	541	581	-	-	-	519	-	-	-	-	-	-	494	-	-	-	-	-	-	-	-	-	-
Washington County	594	516	534	-	-	-	-	-	-	-	-	-	-	-	-	-	-	-	-	-	-	-	-	-
St. George (city)	591	503	506	-	-	-	-	-	-	-	-	-	-	-	-	-	-	-	-	-	-	-	-	-
Weber County	544	503	-	-	-	-	-	-	-	-	-	-	-	345	-	-	-	-	-	-	-	-	-	-
VERMONT	553	663	-	764	-	-	586	-	542	-	-	-	-	683	588	-	-	-	-	-	-	-	-	673
Chittenden County	662	672	-	743	-	-	599	-	-	-	-	-	-	-	-	-	-	-	-	-	-	-	-	692
Rutland County	517	487	-	-	-	-	-	-	-	-	-	-	-	-	-	-	-	-	-	-	-	-	-	-
Washington County	519	605	-	-	-	-	-	-	-	-	-	-	-	-	-	-	-	-	-	-	-	-	-	-
Windsor County	539	590	-	-	-	-	-	-	-	-	-	-	-	-	-	-	-	-	-	-	-	-	-	-
VIRGINIA	650	823	654	882	723	731	753	-	744	575	518	-	952	931	868	765	-	858	689	718	725	806	-	717
Albemarle County	712	592	-	667	-	-	505	-	-	-	-	-	-	-	-	-	-	-	-	-	-	-	-	-
Alexandria Independent City	861	823	-	853	-	-	855	-	799	-	-	-	-	-	781	-	-	874	-	-	-	-	-	853
Arlington County	897	855	-	869	-	792	874	-	814	-	-	-	-	1,058	896	-	-	783	-	-	-	-	-	659
Arlington (cdp)	897	855	-	869	-	792	874	-	814	-	-	-	-	1,058	896	-	-	783	-	-	-	-	-	659
Bedford County	444	389	-	-	-	-	-	-	-	-	-	-	-	-	-	-	-	-	-	-	-	-	-	-
Charlottesville Independent City	596	608	-	636	-	-	518	-	-	-	-	-	-	-	-	-	-	-	-	-	-	-	-	-
Chesapeake Independent City	642	720	-	-	-	-	-	-	647	-	-	-	-	-	-	-	-	-	-	-	-	-	-	-
Chesterfield County	717	733	-	658	-	465	758	-	803	-	-	-	-	-	939	-	-	-	-	-	-	-	-	631
Fairfax Independent City	945	960	-	955	-	-	889	-	-	-	-	-	-	-	1,095	-	-	-	-	-	-	-	-	525
Fairfax County	998	952	1,069	994	759	784	896	-	965	-	-	-	1,016	1,930	987	741	-	881	-	-	796	874	-	836
Annandale (cdp)	896	902	-	920	-	-	848	-	918	-	-	-	-	-	893	-	-	-	-	-	-	-	-	950
Bailey's Crossroads (cdp)	857	792	-	-	-	-	-	-	-	-	-	-	-	-	-	-	-	851	-	-	-	-	-	664
Burke (cdp)	1,194	1,088	-	925	-	-	641	-	1,275	-	-	-	-	-	1,128	-	-	-	-	-	-	-	-	892
Centreville (cdp)	1,043	1,069	-	1,032	-	-	900	-	1,090	-	-	-	-	-	1,134	-	-	-	-	-	-	-	-	297
Chantilly (cdp)	1,146	1,073	-	1,121	-	-	962	-	-	-	-	-	-	-	1,111	-	-	-	-	-	-	-	-	845
Franconia (cdp)	1,190	1,244	-	1,125	-	-	-	-	1,313	-	-	-	-	-	788	-	-	-	-	-	-	-	-	0
Groveton (cdp)	814	826	-	-	-	-	-	-	-	-	-	-	-	-	-	-	-	-	-	-	-	-	-	-
Herndon (town)	964	950	-	979	-	-	-	-	-	-	-	-	-	-	-	-	-	-	-	-	-	-	-	1,125
Hybla Valley (cdp)	772	725	-	-	-	-	-	-	-	-	-	-	-	-	-	-	-	-	-	-	-	-	-	-
Idylwood (cdp)	999	972	-	1,041	-	-	909	-	-	-	-	-	-	-	-	-	-	-	-	-	-	-	-	928
Jefferson (cdp)	931	914	-	1,013	-	-	867	-	1,044	-	-	-	-	-	-	-	-	-	-	-	-	-	-	843
Lincolnia (cdp)	922	895	-	-	-	-	-	-	-	-	-	-	-	-	-	-	-	893	-	-	-	-	-	912
Lorton (cdp)	932	818	-	-	-	-	-	-	-	-	-	-	-	-	-	-	-	-	-	-	-	-	-	-
McLean (cdp)	1,707	2,001	-	1,875	-	-	1,625	-	0	-	-	-	-	2,001	1,978	-	-	-	-	-	-	-	-	-
Merrifield (cdp)	1,057	1,101	-	1,089	-	-	-	-	-	-	-	-	-	-	1,105	-	-	-	-	-	-	-	-	1,162
Mount Vernon (cdp)	843	817	-	-	-	-	-	-	-	-	-	-	-	-	834	-	-	-	-	-	-	-	-	-
Newington (cdp)	1,247	1,105	-	0	-	-	-	-	1,250	-	-	-	-	-	1,138	-	-	-	-	-	-	-	-	-
Oakton (cdp)	1,053	923	-	959	-	-	800	-	-	-	-	-	-	-	888	-	-	-	-	-	-	-	-	638
Reston (cdp)	989	922	-	984	-	-	879	-	1,063	-	-	-	-	-	915	-	-	-	-	-	-	-	-	-
Rose Hill (cdp)	1,031	985	-	-	-	-	-	-	-	-	-	-	-	-	-	-	-	-	-	-	-	-	-	-

Notes: Please refer to the User's Guide for an explanation of data; data is arranged alphabetically by state, then county, then city within each county; table includes counties with populations greater than 49,999 unless noted and cities with populations greater than 9,999 whose Asian and/or NHPI population rates are greater than the national average; (1) Native Hawaiian and other Pacific Islander; (2) excludes Taiwanese; (3) includes Chamorro; (4) county does not meet population threshold but is shown in order to allow inclusion of city

Place	All specified renter-occupied housing units	Specified housing units rented by Asians	Specified housing units rented by NHPIs[1]	Asian Indian	Bangladeshi	Cambodian	Chinese[2]	Fijian	Filipino	Guamanian[3]	Hawaiian, Native	Hmong	Indonesian	Japanese	Korean	Laotian	Malaysian	Pakistani	Samoan	Sri Lankan	Taiwanese	Thai	Tongan	Vietnamese
Springfield (cdp)	1,053	783	-	782	-	-	781	-	1,071	-	-	-	-	-	783	525	-	-	-	-	-	-	-	792
Tysons Corner (cdp)	1,174	1,082	-	1,067	-	-	1,064	-	-	-	-	-	-	-	1,073	-	-	-	-	-	-	-	-	-
Vienna (town)	1,035	746	-	-	-	-	-	-	-	-	-	-	-	-	-	-	-	-	-	-	-	-	-	-
West Springfield (cdp)	1,139	1,067	-	1,125	-	-	850	-	-	-	-	-	-	-	1,142	-	-	-	-	-	-	-	-	783
Wolf Trap (cdp)	2,001	2,001	-	2,001	-	-	0	-	-	-	-	-	-	-	-	-	-	-	-	-	-	-	-	-
Falls Church Independent City	965	850	-	-	-	-	-	-	-	-	-	-	-	-	-	-	-	-	-	-	-	-	-	-
Fauquier County	705	0	-	-	-	-	-	-	-	-	-	-	-	-	-	-	-	-	-	-	-	-	-	-
Frederick County	620	675	-	-	-	-	-	-	-	-	-	-	-	-	-	-	-	-	-	-	-	-	-	-
Hampton Independent City	603	594	-	-	-	-	-	-	672	-	-	-	-	-	-	-	-	-	-	-	-	-	-	372
Hanover County	686	820	-	-	-	-	-	-	-	-	-	-	-	-	-	-	-	-	-	-	-	-	-	-
Henrico County	676	702	-	726	-	707	641	-	661	-	-	-	-	-	706	-	-	-	-	-	-	-	-	692
Glen Allen (cdp)	811	986	-	-	-	-	-	-	-	-	-	-	-	-	-	-	-	-	-	-	-	-	-	-
Laurel (cdp)	691	716	-	-	-	-	-	-	-	-	-	-	-	-	-	-	-	-	-	-	-	-	-	-
Loudoun County	954	919	-	952	-	-	822	-	850	-	-	-	-	-	886	-	-	962	-	-	-	-	-	1,161
Lynchburg Independent City	469	514	-	-	-	-	-	-	-	-	-	-	-	-	-	-	-	-	-	-	-	-	-	-
Manassas Park Indep. City	930	0	-	-	-	-	-	-	-	-	-	-	-	-	-	-	-	-	-	-	-	-	-	-
Montgomery County	535	526	-	610	-	-	482	-	-	-	-	-	-	-	607	-	-	-	-	-	-	-	-	-
Blacksburg (town)	553	523	-	610	-	-	482	-	-	-	-	-	-	-	600	-	-	-	-	-	-	-	-	-
Newport News Independent City	559	578	-	-	-	-	661	-	629	-	-	-	-	-	555	-	-	-	-	-	-	-	-	495
Norfolk Independent City	538	550	-	540	-	-	543	-	536	-	-	-	-	-	-	-	-	-	-	-	-	-	-	499
Portsmouth Independent City	540	560	-	-	-	-	-	-	565	-	-	-	-	-	-	-	-	-	-	-	-	-	-	-
Prince William County	862	802	-	789	-	-	691	-	814	-	-	-	-	768	837	-	-	695	-	-	-	-	-	825
Bull Run (cdp)	880	907	-	-	-	-	-	-	-	-	-	-	-	-	-	-	-	-	-	-	-	-	-	-
Dale City (cdp)	908	809	-	824	-	-	-	-	675	-	-	-	-	-	-	-	-	1,875	-	-	-	-	-	-
Lake Ridge (cdp)	986	852	-	-	-	-	-	-	-	-	-	-	-	-	-	-	-	-	-	-	-	-	-	-
Woodbridge (cdp)	791	763	-	-	-	-	-	-	-	-	-	-	-	-	-	-	-	-	-	-	-	-	-	-
Richmond Independent City	540	558	-	646	-	-	-	-	550	-	-	-	-	-	-	-	-	-	-	-	-	-	-	-
Roanoke Independent City	448	438	-	-	-	-	-	-	-	-	-	-	-	-	-	-	-	-	-	-	-	-	-	-
Roanoke County	575	559	-	-	-	-	-	-	-	-	-	-	-	-	-	-	-	-	-	-	-	-	-	-
Spotsylvania County	805	732	-	-	-	-	-	-	-	-	-	-	-	-	-	-	-	-	-	-	-	-	-	-
Stafford County	842	819	-	-	-	-	-	-	850	-	-	-	-	-	-	-	-	-	-	-	-	-	-	-
Suffolk Independent City	506	597	-	-	-	-	-	-	-	-	-	-	-	-	-	-	-	-	-	-	-	-	-	-
Virginia Beach Independent City	734	701	-	763	-	-	721	-	700	-	-	-	-	875	781	-	-	-	-	-	-	-	-	365
Williamsburg Independent City	616	568	-	-	-	-	-	-	-	-	-	-	-	-	-	-	-	-	-	-	-	-	-	-
York County	708	713	-	832	-	-	-	-	-	-	-	-	-	-	717	-	-	-	-	-	-	-	-	-
WASHINGTON	663	670	692	808	-	526	690	727	679	718	642	584	768	680	687	592	-	784	681	668	785	704	822	551
Benton County	566	546	-	543	-	-	508	-	-	-	-	-	-	-	495	-	-	-	-	-	-	-	-	513
Richland (city)	619	538	-	-	-	-	488	-	-	-	-	-	-	-	-	-	-	-	-	-	-	-	-	-
Chelan County	535	619	-	-	-	-	-	-	-	-	-	-	-	-	-	-	-	-	-	-	-	-	-	-
Clallam County	532	455	-	-	-	-	-	-	-	-	-	-	-	-	-	-	-	-	-	-	-	-	-	-
Clark County	684	657	816	685	-	469	686	-	721	-	-	-	-	810	634	414	-	-	-	-	-	-	-	594

Notes: Please refer to the User's Guide for an explanation of data; data is arranged alphabetically by state, then county, then city within each county; table includes counties with populations greater than 49,999 unless noted and cities with populations greater than 9,999 whose Asian and/or NHPI population rates are greater than the national average; (1) Native Hawaiian and other Pacific Islander; (2) excludes Taiwanese; (3) includes Chamorro; (4) county does not meet population threshold but is shown in order to allow inclusion of city

Place	All specified renter-occupied housing units	Specified housing units rented by Asians	Specified housing units rented by NHPIs[1]	Asian Indian	Bangladeshi	Cambodian	Chinese[2]	Fijian	Filipino	Guamanian[3]	Hawaiian, Native	Hmong	Indonesian	Japanese	Korean	Laotian	Malaysian	Pakistani	Samoan	Sri Lankan	Taiwanese	Thai	Tongan	Vietnamese
Five Corners (cdp)	850	1,125	-	-	-	-	-	-	-	-	-	-	-	-	-	-	-	-	-	-	-	-	-	-
Orchards (cdp)	803	675	-	-	-	-	-	-	-	-	-	-	-	-	-	-	-	-	-	-	-	-	-	-
Vancouver (city)	671	643	828	-	-	-	678	-	709	-	-	-	-	737	627	-	-	-	-	-	-	-	-	584
Cowlitz County	518	614	-	-	-	607	-	-	-	-	-	-	-	-	-	-	-	-	-	-	-	-	-	575
Grant County	476	620	-	-	-	-	-	-	-	-	-	-	-	-	-	-	-	-	-	-	-	-	-	-
Grays Harbor County	500	477	-	-	-	-	-	-	-	-	-	-	-	-	-	-	-	-	-	-	-	-	-	-
Island County	684	586	-	-	-	-	-	-	578	-	-	-	-	743	-	-	-	-	-	-	-	-	-	-
Oak Harbor (city)	629	574	-	-	-	-	-	-	571	-	-	-	-	-	-	-	-	-	-	-	-	-	-	-
King County	758	714	725	856	-	545	729	725	706	772	742	597	834	735	757	591	-	795	697	-	805	758	813	567
Auburn (city)	639	697	-	-	-	-	-	-	-	-	-	-	-	-	-	-	-	-	-	-	-	-	-	-
Bellevue (city)	916	891	-	904	-	-	830	-	819	-	-	-	-	1,043	999	676	-	-	-	-	1,097	-	-	682
Bothell (city)	913	892	-	-	-	-	868	-	-	-	-	-	-	-	-	-	-	-	-	-	-	-	-	-
Bryn Mawr-Skyway (cdp)	742	627	-	-	-	-	-	-	625	-	-	-	-	625	-	-	-	-	-	-	-	-	-	756
Burien (city)	666	664	-	-	-	-	-	-	693	-	-	-	-	-	-	-	-	-	-	-	-	-	-	663
Cascade-Fairwood (cdp)	853	789	-	-	-	-	907	-	630	-	-	-	-	870	-	-	-	-	-	-	-	-	-	1,083
Cottage Lake (cdp)	897	798	-	-	-	-	-	-	-	-	-	-	-	-	-	-	-	-	-	-	-	-	-	-
Des Moines (city)	705	624	705	-	-	-	-	-	709	-	-	-	-	-	-	-	-	-	-	-	-	-	-	525
East Hill-Meridian (cdp)	740	628	-	654	-	-	675	-	1,625	-	-	-	-	-	-	-	-	-	-	-	-	-	-	581
Federal Way (city)	737	727	640	-	-	-	801	-	720	-	-	-	-	638	759	-	-	-	616	-	-	-	-	542
Inglewood-Finn Hill (cdp)	919	851	-	-	-	-	850	-	-	-	-	-	-	-	-	-	-	-	-	-	-	-	-	-
Issaquah (city)	902	829	-	-	-	-	-	-	-	-	-	-	-	-	-	-	-	-	-	-	-	-	-	-
Kenmore (city)	836	823	-	-	-	-	-	-	-	-	-	-	-	-	-	-	-	-	-	-	-	-	-	-
Kent (city)	724	696	-	683	-	-	828	-	753	-	-	-	-	738	701	-	-	-	-	-	-	-	-	539
Kingsgate (cdp)	811	764	-	-	-	-	775	-	-	-	-	-	-	-	-	-	-	-	-	-	-	-	-	-
Kirkland (city)	972	937	-	-	-	-	890	-	-	-	-	-	-	952	-	-	-	-	-	-	-	-	-	892
Lake Forest Park (city)	837	675	-	-	-	-	-	-	-	-	-	-	-	-	-	-	-	-	-	-	-	-	-	-
Lakeland North (cdp)	857	577	-	-	-	-	-	-	-	-	-	-	-	-	-	-	-	-	-	-	-	-	-	-
Lakeland South (cdp)	919	0	-	-	-	-	-	-	-	-	-	-	-	-	-	-	-	-	-	-	-	-	-	-
Lea Hill (cdp)	814	900	-	-	-	-	-	-	-	-	-	-	-	-	-	-	-	-	-	-	-	-	-	-
Mercer Island (city)	1,014	942	-	-	-	-	723	-	-	-	-	-	-	1,227	-	-	-	-	-	-	-	-	-	-
Redmond (city)	1,021	1,002	-	1,046	-	-	970	-	-	-	-	-	-	1,192	897	-	-	-	-	-	-	-	-	-
Renton (city)	723	707	-	-	-	-	807	-	630	-	-	-	-	721	-	-	-	-	-	-	-	-	-	602
Riverton-Boulevard Park (cdp)	655	653	-	-	-	-	-	-	-	-	-	-	-	-	-	-	-	-	-	-	-	-	-	-
Sammamish (city)	1,121	0	-	-	-	-	0	-	-	-	-	-	-	-	-	-	-	-	-	-	-	-	-	-
SeaTac (city)	654	594	679	625	-	-	-	-	675	-	-	-	-	-	-	-	-	-	-	-	-	-	-	775
Seattle (city)	721	632	653	778	-	486	614	-	644	-	-	-	821	663	673	551	-	-	658	-	770	717	-	545
Shoreline (city)	798	761	-	748	-	-	973	-	804	-	-	-	-	711	789	-	-	-	-	-	-	-	-	779
Tukwila (city)	697	677	691	-	-	-	-	-	663	-	-	-	-	-	-	-	-	-	-	-	-	-	-	-
Union Hill-Novelty Hill (cdp)	1,199	1,000	-	-	-	-	-	-	-	-	-	-	-	-	-	-	-	-	-	-	-	-	-	-
White Center (cdp)	629	415	-	-	-	386	-	-	702	-	-	-	-	-	-	-	-	-	-	-	-	-	-	379
Kitsap County	667	566	678	-	-	-	573	-	550	710	-	-	-	595	730	-	-	-	-	-	-	-	-	393

Notes: Please refer to the User's Guide for an explanation of data; data is arranged alphabetically by state, then county, then city within each county; table includes counties with populations greater than 49,999 unless noted and cities with populations greater than 9,999 whose Asian and/or NHPI population rates are greater than the national average; (1) Native Hawaiian and other Pacific Islander; (2) excludes Taiwanese; (3) includes Chamorro; (4) county does not meet population threshold but is shown in order to allow inclusion of city

Place	All specified renter-occupied housing units	Specified housing units rented by Asians	Specified housing units rented by NHPIs[1]	Asian Indian	Bangladeshi	Cambodian	Chinese[2]	Fijian	Filipino	Guamanian[3]	Hawaiian, Native	Hmong	Indonesian	Japanese	Korean	Laotian	Malaysian	Pakistani	Samoan	Sri Lankan	Taiwanese	Thai	Tongan	Vietnamese
Bremerton (city)	554	498	-	-	-	-	-	-	513	-	-	-	-	-	-	-	-	-	-	-	-	-	-	-
Silverdale (cdp)	723	635	-	-	-	-	-	-	629	-	-	-	-	-	-	-	-	-	-	-	-	-	-	-
Lewis County	551	600	-	-	-	-	-	-	-	-	-	-	-	-	-	-	-	-	-	-	-	-	-	-
Pierce County	624	532	623	673	-	474	522	-	638	694	535	-	-	552	538	658	-	-	644	-	-	675	-	465
Elk Plain (cdp)	779	0	-	-	-	-	-	-	-	-	-	-	-	-	-	-	-	-	-	-	-	-	-	-
Fort Lewis (cdp)	650	583	725	-	-	-	-	-	597	-	-	-	-	-	-	-	-	-	-	-	-	-	-	-
Lakewood (city)	550	493	712	-	-	-	-	-	580	-	-	-	-	490	477	-	-	-	686	-	-	-	-	-
Parkland (cdp)	590	575	573	-	-	-	-	-	-	-	-	-	-	-	548	-	-	-	-	-	-	-	-	-
Spanaway (cdp)	651	434	675	-	-	-	-	-	681	-	-	-	-	-	425	-	-	-	-	-	-	-	-	-
Tacoma (city)	581	485	544	-	-	488	523	-	664	641	-	-	-	534	471	692	-	-	525	-	-	-	-	442
University Place (city)	618	622	-	-	-	-	-	-	-	-	-	-	-	-	681	-	-	-	-	-	-	-	-	-
Skagit County	668	536	-	-	-	-	-	-	750	-	-	-	-	-	-	-	-	-	-	-	-	-	-	-
Snohomish County	766	743	789	774	-	598	789	-	739	-	808	-	-	766	783	701	-	806	-	-	-	-	-	663
Alderwood Manor (cdp)	868	850	-	-	-	-	-	-	-	-	-	-	-	-	-	-	-	-	-	-	-	-	-	-
Edmonds (city)	779	731	-	-	-	-	-	-	625	-	-	-	-	-	739	-	-	-	-	-	-	-	-	-
Everett (city)	687	662	-	733	-	575	-	-	721	-	-	-	-	-	-	-	-	-	-	-	-	-	-	600
Lynnwood (city)	741	747	-	-	-	-	848	-	736	-	-	-	-	-	857	-	-	-	-	-	-	-	-	703
Martha Lake (cdp)	855	808	-	-	-	-	-	-	-	-	-	-	-	-	-	-	-	-	-	-	-	-	-	-
Marysville (city)	724	678	-	-	-	-	-	-	-	-	-	-	-	-	-	-	-	-	-	-	-	-	-	-
Mill Creek (city)	894	865	-	-	-	-	-	-	-	-	-	-	-	-	882	-	-	-	-	-	-	-	-	-
Mountlake Terrace (city)	833	793	-	-	-	-	-	-	854	-	-	-	-	-	787	-	-	-	-	-	-	-	-	-
Mukilteo (city)	849	830	-	-	-	-	-	-	-	-	-	-	-	-	900	-	-	-	-	-	-	-	-	-
North Creek (cdp)	948	961	-	-	-	-	-	-	-	-	-	-	-	-	-	-	-	-	-	-	-	-	-	-
Paine Field-Lk. Stickney (cdp)	758	752	-	-	-	-	-	-	-	-	-	-	-	-	-	-	-	-	-	-	-	-	-	-
Picnic Pt.-N. Lynnwood (cdp)	814	764	-	-	-	-	-	-	700	-	-	-	-	-	761	-	-	-	-	-	-	-	-	-
Seattle Hill-Silver Firs (cdp)	1,018	1,131	-	-	-	-	-	-	1,125	-	-	-	-	-	0	-	-	-	-	-	-	-	-	525
Spokane County	532	488	569	570	-	-	381	-	579	-	-	457	-	456	486	-	-	-	-	-	-	-	-	452
Spokane (city)	509	471	539	-	-	-	428	-	598	-	-	143	-	480	469	-	-	-	-	-	-	-	-	446
Thurston County	655	625	708	788	-	686	543	-	736	1,045	-	-	-	643	623	-	-	-	-	-	-	-	-	470
Lacey (city)	677	669	-	-	-	-	-	-	950	-	-	-	-	-	578	-	-	-	-	-	-	-	-	535
Olympia (city)	624	493	-	-	-	-	-	-	-	-	-	-	-	-	-	-	-	-	-	-	-	-	-	396
Tumwater (city)	686	712	-	-	-	-	-	-	-	-	-	-	-	-	-	-	-	-	-	-	-	-	-	-
Walla Walla County	487	588	-	-	-	-	-	-	-	-	-	-	-	-	-	-	-	-	-	-	-	-	-	-
Whatcom County	622	589	-	611	-	-	595	-	706	-	-	-	-	508	640	-	-	-	-	-	-	-	-	565
Bellingham (city)	613	569	-	617	-	-	-	-	-	-	-	-	-	-	-	-	-	-	-	-	-	-	-	572
Whitman County[4]	482	401	-	-	-	-	373	-	-	-	-	-	-	394	-	-	-	-	-	-	-	-	-	-
Pullman (city)	486	399	-	-	-	-	373	-	-	-	-	-	-	394	-	-	-	-	-	-	-	-	-	-
Yakima County	534	567	-	-	-	-	-	-	573	-	-	-	-	-	-	-	-	-	-	-	-	-	-	-
WEST VIRGINIA	401	467	713	514	-	-	419	-	469	-	-	-	-	438	432	-	-	578	-	-	-	-	-	575
Cabell County	420	410	-	-	-	-	-	-	-	-	-	-	-	-	-	-	-	-	-	-	-	-	-	-
Harrison County	398	400	-	-	-	-	-	-	-	-	-	-	-	-	-	-	-	-	-	-	-	-	-	-

Notes: Please refer to the User's Guide for an explanation of data; data is arranged alphabetically by state, then county, then city within each county; table includes counties with populations greater than 49,999 unless noted and cities with populations greater than 9,999 whose Asian and/or NHPI population rates are greater than the national average; (1) Native Hawaiian and other Pacific Islander; (2) excludes Taiwanese; (3) includes Chamorro; (4) county does not meet population threshold but is shown in order to allow inclusion of city

Place	All specified renter-occupied housing units	Specified housing units rented by Asians	Specified housing units rented by NHPIs[1]	Asian Indian	Bangladeshi	Cambodian	Chinese[2]	Fijian	Filipino	Guamanian[3]	Hawaiian, Native	Hmong	Indonesian	Japanese	Korean	Laotian	Malaysian	Pakistani	Samoan	Sri Lankan	Taiwanese	Thai	Tongan	Vietnamese
Kanawha County	444	537	-	565	-	-	-	-	-	-	-	-	-	-	-	-	-	-	-	-	-	-	-	-
Monongalia County	453	436	-	508	-	-	380	-	-	-	-	-	-	-	-	-	-	-	-	-	-	-	-	-
Putnam County	496	1,208	-	-	-	-	-	-	-	-	-	-	-	-	-	-	-	-	-	-	-	-	-	-
Raleigh County	385	499	-	-	-	-	-	-	-	-	-	-	-	-	-	-	-	-	-	-	-	-	-	-
Wood County	429	395	-	-	-	-	-	-	-	-	-	-	-	-	-	-	-	-	-	-	-	-	-	-
WISCONSIN	540	563	558	630	-	361	567	-	580	475	513	475	501	610	622	534	-	617	-	-	622	528	-	558
Brown County	520	496	-	530	-	-	-	-	-	-	-	466	-	-	-	479	-	-	-	-	-	-	-	-
Chippewa County	446	519	-	-	-	-	-	-	-	-	-	495	-	-	-	-	-	-	-	-	-	-	-	-
Columbia County	507	526	-	-	-	-	-	-	-	-	-	-	-	-	-	-	-	-	-	-	-	-	-	-
Dane County	641	605	-	632	-	-	566	-	588	-	-	528	-	594	639	613	-	-	-	-	614	-	-	606
Madison (city)	644	604	-	623	-	-	572	-	580	-	-	501	-	600	642	-	-	-	-	-	614	-	-	603
Dodge County	528	311	-	-	-	-	-	-	-	-	-	-	-	-	-	-	-	-	-	-	-	-	-	-
Eau Claire County	486	507	-	-	-	-	-	-	-	-	-	483	-	-	-	-	-	-	-	-	-	-	-	-
Fond du Lac County	500	476	-	-	-	-	-	-	-	-	-	447	-	-	-	-	-	-	-	-	-	-	-	-
Jefferson County	564	929	-	-	-	-	-	-	-	-	-	-	-	-	-	-	-	-	-	-	-	-	-	-
Kenosha County	589	533	-	-	-	-	-	-	-	-	-	-	-	-	-	-	-	-	-	-	-	-	-	-
La Crosse County	470	496	-	-	-	-	-	-	-	-	-	435	-	-	-	-	-	-	-	-	-	-	-	-
La Crosse (city)	449	489	-	-	-	-	-	-	-	-	-	432	-	-	-	-	-	-	-	-	-	-	-	-
Manitowoc County	433	473	-	-	-	-	-	-	-	-	-	425	-	-	-	-	-	-	-	-	-	-	-	-
Marathon County	484	515	-	-	-	-	-	-	-	-	-	499	-	-	-	-	-	-	-	-	-	-	-	-
Wausau (city)	473	525	-	-	-	-	-	-	-	-	-	508	-	-	-	-	-	-	-	-	-	-	-	-
Milwaukee County	555	575	565	619	-	-	564	-	584	-	-	478	-	647	594	491	-	606	-	-	-	-	-	562
Outagamie County	534	486	-	546	-	-	-	-	-	-	-	472	-	-	-	-	-	-	-	-	-	-	-	-
Appleton (city)	508	476	-	-	-	-	-	-	-	-	-	465	-	-	-	-	-	-	-	-	-	-	-	-
Ozaukee County	642	708	-	-	-	-	-	-	-	-	-	-	-	-	-	-	-	-	-	-	-	-	-	-
Portage County	477	495	-	-	-	-	-	-	-	-	-	578	-	-	-	-	-	-	-	-	-	-	-	-
Stevens Point (city)	468	399	-	-	-	-	-	-	-	-	-	556	-	-	-	-	-	-	-	-	-	-	-	-
Racine County	548	573	-	-	-	-	-	-	-	-	-	-	-	-	-	-	-	-	-	-	-	-	-	-
Rock County	543	517	-	-	-	-	-	-	-	-	-	-	-	-	-	-	-	-	-	-	-	-	-	-
St. Croix County	587	665	-	-	-	-	-	-	-	-	-	-	-	-	-	-	-	-	-	-	-	-	-	-
Sauk County	508	859	-	-	-	-	-	-	-	-	-	-	-	-	-	-	-	-	-	-	-	-	-	-
Sheboygan County	482	444	-	-	-	-	-	-	-	-	-	452	-	-	-	-	-	-	-	-	-	-	-	-
Sheboygan (city)	477	448	-	-	-	-	-	-	-	-	-	450	-	-	-	-	-	-	-	-	-	-	-	-
Walworth County	588	530	-	-	-	-	-	-	-	-	-	-	-	-	-	-	-	-	-	-	-	-	-	-
Washington County	620	852	-	-	-	-	-	-	-	-	-	-	-	-	-	-	-	-	-	-	-	-	-	-
Waukesha County	726	750	-	736	-	-	691	-	696	-	-	-	-	-	975	-	-	-	-	-	-	-	-	-
Winnebago County	500	505	-	-	-	-	-	-	-	-	-	502	-	-	-	-	-	-	-	-	-	-	-	-
Wood County	442	476	-	-	-	-	-	-	-	-	-	493	-	-	-	-	-	-	-	-	-	-	-	-
WYOMING	437	411	-	339	-	-	388	-	487	-	-	-	-	433	432	-	-	-	-	-	-	-	-	-
Laramie County	473	448	-	-	-	-	-	-	-	-	-	-	-	-	-	-	-	-	-	-	-	-	-	-
Natrona County	409	460	-	-	-	-	-	-	-	-	-	-	-	-	-	-	-	-	-	-	-	-	-	-

Notes: Please refer to the User's Guide for an explanation of data; data is arranged alphabetically by state, then county, then city within each county; table includes counties with populations greater than 49,999 unless noted and cities with populations greater than 9,999 whose Asian and/or NHPI population rates are greater than the national average; (1) Native Hawaiian and other Pacific Islander; (2) excludes Taiwanese; (3) includes Chamorro; (4) county does not meet population threshold but is shown in order to allow inclusion of city

Median Home Value

(Universe: Specified Owner-Occupied Housing Units)

Place	All specified owner-occupied housing units	Specified housing units owned and occup. by Asians	Specified housing units owned and occup. by NHPIs[1]	Asian Indian	Bangladeshi	Cambodian	Chinese[2]	Fijian	Filipino	Guamanian[3]	Hawaiian, Native	Hmong	Indonesian	Japanese	Korean	Laotian	Malaysian	Pakistani	Samoan	Sri Lankan	Taiwanese	Thai	Tongan	Vietnamese
UNITED STATES	119,600	199,300	160,500	210,200	171,000	120,800	230,700	181,000	188,100	143,500	177,100	92,600	186,300	238,300	209,500	100,500	169,700	181,400	153,200	202,000	260,700	160,900	149,100	151,400
ALABAMA	85,100	128,200	111,300	172,500	-	55,700	138,200	-	93,000	126,900	-	-	-	108,800	121,200	83,100	-	157,900	-	-	-	116,100	-	94,500
Baldwin County	122,500	98,000	-	-	-	-	-	-	-	-	-	-	-	-	-	-	-	-	-	-	-	-	-	-
Calhoun County	71,600	73,300	-	-	-	-	-	-	-	-	-	-	-	-	-	-	-	-	-	-	-	-	-	-
Etowah County	71,200	169,600	-	-	-	-	-	-	-	-	-	-	-	-	-	-	-	-	-	-	-	-	-	-
Houston County	82,000	111,500	-	-	-	-	-	-	-	-	-	-	-	-	-	-	-	-	-	-	-	-	-	-
Jefferson County	90,700	156,800	-	171,100	-	-	149,100	-	-	-	-	-	-	-	156,000	-	-	-	-	-	-	-	-	129,700
Lee County	104,100	176,700	-	-	-	-	180,100	-	-	-	-	-	-	-	-	-	-	-	-	-	-	-	-	-
Madison County	103,300	135,700	-	177,400	-	-	109,100	-	-	-	-	-	-	-	96,500	-	-	-	-	-	-	-	-	98,200
Mobile County	80,500	86,500	-	218,300	-	27,300	141,700	-	88,900	-	-	-	-	-	-	85,000	-	-	-	-	-	-	-	70,800
Montgomery County	87,700	100,000	-	-	-	-	-	-	-	-	-	-	-	-	-	-	-	-	-	-	-	-	-	-
Morgan County	88,600	155,900	-	-	-	-	-	-	-	-	-	-	-	-	-	-	-	-	-	-	-	-	-	-
Shelby County	146,700	175,000	-	237,500	-	-	-	-	-	-	-	-	-	-	-	-	-	-	-	-	-	-	-	-
Tuscaloosa County	106,600	152,600	-	-	-	-	-	-	-	-	-	-	-	-	-	-	-	-	-	-	-	-	-	-
ALASKA	144,200	151,900	142,000	194,000	-	-	170,000	-	145,200	-	137,500	137,500	-	141,000	167,200	132,500	-	-	142,800	-	-	143,100	159,400	195,300
Anchorage Borough	160,700	159,100	150,000	197,600	-	-	187,500	-	151,600	-	-	137,500	-	139,300	175,600	107,500	-	-	147,700	-	-	137,500	-	200,000
Fairbanks North Star Borough	132,700	134,000	-	-	-	-	135,400	-	121,400	-	-	-	-	-	127,500	-	-	-	-	-	-	-	-	-
Juneau City and Borough	195,100	170,900	-	-	-	-	-	-	157,100	-	-	-	-	-	-	-	-	-	-	-	-	-	-	-
Matanuska-Susitna Borough	125,800	120,000	-	-	-	-	-	-	-	-	-	-	-	-	-	-	-	-	-	-	-	-	-	-
ARIZONA	121,300	141,300	118,500	192,300	-	160,200	157,600	-	130,400	118,200	123,200	-	96,000	123,200	136,700	97,000	-	155,100	116,100	-	225,400	106,500	100,600	106,200
Cochise County	88,200	96,700	-	-	-	-	-	-	103,600	-	-	-	-	-	105,800	-	-	-	-	-	-	-	-	-
Coconino County	142,500	216,700	-	-	-	-	-	-	-	-	-	-	-	-	-	-	-	-	-	-	-	-	-	-
Maricopa County	129,200	145,900	121,000	197,100	-	160,200	166,000	-	133,800	160,900	124,300	-	95,300	126,200	139,400	107,300	-	152,900	117,300	-	225,400	107,400	100,600	113,200
Chandler (city)	137,600	167,800	-	191,700	-	-	177,100	-	144,200	-	-	-	-	-	-	-	-	-	-	-	-	-	-	139,600
Gilbert (town)	157,300	171,600	-	193,800	-	-	194,400	-	148,800	-	-	-	-	-	-	-	-	-	-	-	-	-	-	-
Mesa (city)	122,100	127,700	112,900	156,300	-	-	160,200	-	138,600	-	-	-	-	104,300	120,600	-	-	-	-	-	-	-	-	107,400
Phoenix (city)	112,600	123,500	122,400	181,400	-	123,900	132,800	-	116,800	-	116,400	-	-	120,100	119,200	-	-	-	-	-	-	-	-	90,700
Tempe (city)	132,100	150,500	-	218,200	-	-	191,700	-	129,200	-	-	-	-	147,700	156,300	-	-	-	-	-	-	-	-	101,800
Mohave County	95,300	96,300	-	-	-	-	-	-	-	-	-	-	-	-	-	-	-	-	-	-	-	-	-	-
Pima County	114,600	124,700	118,500	186,600	-	-	133,400	-	113,200	-	129,500	-	-	115,600	138,000	-	-	-	-	-	-	-	-	91,600
Tucson (city)	96,300	100,900	111,300	132,600	-	-	112,000	-	103,800	-	-	-	-	97,600	111,900	-	-	-	-	-	-	-	-	86,900
Pinal County	93,900	97,500	-	-	-	-	-	-	-	-	-	-	-	-	-	-	-	-	-	-	-	-	-	-
Yavapai County	138,000	184,100	-	-	-	-	-	-	-	-	-	-	-	-	-	-	-	-	-	-	-	-	-	-
Yuma County	85,100	89,700	-	-	-	-	-	-	116,700	-	-	-	-	-	-	-	-	-	-	-	-	-	-	-
ARKANSAS	72,800	75,500	68,000	153,600	-	-	90,500	-	95,500	-	70,700	-	-	83,600	68,800	59,000	-	-	-	-	-	67,500	-	63,400
Benton County	94,800	93,600	-	108,900	-	-	-	-	-	-	-	-	-	-	-	-	-	-	-	-	-	-	-	82,700
Craighead County	79,200	104,800	-	-	-	-	-	-	-	-	-	-	-	-	-	-	-	-	-	-	-	-	-	-
Crawford County	71,600	58,300	-	-	-	-	-	-	-	-	-	-	-	-	-	-	-	-	-	-	-	-	-	-

Notes: Please refer to the User's Guide for an explanation of data; data is arranged alphabetically by state, then county, then city within each county; table includes counties with populations greater than 49,999 unless noted and cities with populations greater than 9,999 whose Asian and/or NHPI population rates are greater than the national average; (1) Native Hawaiian and other Pacific Islander; (2) excludes Taiwanese; (3) includes Chamorro; (4) county does not meet population threshold but is shown in order to allow inclusion of city

Place	All specified owner-occupied housing units	Specified housing units owned and occup. by Asians	Specified housing units owned and occup. by NHPIs[1]	Asian Indian	Bangladeshi	Cambodian	Chinese[2]	Fijian	Filipino	Guamanian[3]	Hawaiian, Native	Hmong	Indonesian	Japanese	Korean	Laotian	Malaysian	Pakistani	Samoan	Sri Lankan	Taiwanese	Thai	Tongan	Vietnamese
Faulkner County	92,900	98,000	-	-	-	-	-	-	-	-	-	-	-	-	-	-	-	-	-	-	-	-	-	-
Jefferson County	57,600	119,900	-	-	-	-	-	-	-	-	-	-	-	-	-	-	-	-	-	-	-	-	-	-
Pulaski County	85,300	107,600	-	201,800	-	-	110,300	-	111,300	-	-	-	-	-	-	-	-	-	-	-	-	-	-	-
Saline County	93,700	63,300	-	-	-	-	-	-	-	-	-	-	-	-	-	-	-	-	-	-	-	-	-	-
Sebastian County	73,300	54,200	-	-	-	-	-	-	-	-	-	-	-	-	-	49,100	-	-	-	-	-	-	-	56,900
Fort Smith (city)	74,200	52,700	-	-	-	-	-	-	-	-	-	-	-	-	-	48,300	-	-	-	-	-	-	-	56,100
Washington County	90,100	94,300	64,500	-	-	-	98,900	-	-	-	-	-	-	-	-	82,500	-	-	-	-	-	-	-	-
Springdale (city)	87,500	94,600	65,000	-	-	-	-	-	-	-	-	-	-	-	-	85,000	-	-	-	-	-	-	-	-
CALIFORNIA	211,500	256,700	187,500	329,300	304,300	175,800	300,600	195,100	218,400	184,700	193,300	95,500	231,800	254,600	266,100	147,700	248,100	261,400	180,400	275,000	317,500	204,400	188,200	245,500
Alameda County	303,100	328,200	246,600	405,400	-	259,400	328,200	266,300	292,800	276,700	262,500	-	394,100	327,300	325,500	236,400	-	387,200	228,000	-	469,000	327,300	179,000	304,100
Alameda (city)	345,000	352,100	255,300	414,900	-	-	364,900	-	327,600	-	-	-	-	276,000	365,000	-	-	-	-	-	-	-	-	376,300
Albany (city)	334,800	337,600	-	425,000	-	-	300,000	-	-	-	-	-	-	357,000	350,000	-	-	-	-	-	-	-	-	-
Ashland (cdp)	192,800	246,500	-	-	-	-	261,700	-	232,900	-	-	-	-	-	-	-	-	-	-	-	-	-	-	-
Berkeley (city)	380,200	328,700	-	397,400	-	-	339,800	-	252,800	-	-	-	-	324,800	453,600	-	-	-	-	-	450,000	-	-	381,300
Castro Valley (cdp)	298,300	338,900	-	358,300	-	-	350,200	-	298,100	-	-	-	-	387,500	273,700	-	-	-	-	-	-	-	-	-
Cherryland (cdp)	201,400	178,300	-	-	-	-	-	-	154,200	-	-	-	-	-	-	-	-	-	-	-	-	-	-	-
Dublin (city)	330,700	354,600	-	361,500	-	-	383,800	-	330,200	-	-	-	-	-	-	-	-	-	-	-	-	-	-	-
Fremont (city)	363,400	394,700	367,500	459,300	-	-	392,300	-	358,300	-	-	-	-	373,300	346,300	-	-	413,600	-	-	496,000	-	-	370,600
Hayward (city)	237,300	262,200	245,900	292,300	-	-	250,000	269,900	257,200	-	-	-	-	248,400	297,500	-	-	-	236,400	-	-	-	-	270,600
Livermore (city)	314,600	300,800	-	370,600	-	-	318,300	-	264,300	-	-	-	-	-	-	-	-	-	-	-	-	-	-	292,900
Newark (city)	303,700	314,900	-	336,200	-	-	321,600	-	319,500	-	-	-	-	-	273,200	-	-	-	-	-	-	-	-	268,100
Oakland (city)	235,500	211,800	165,100	327,400	-	185,400	211,200	-	184,400	-	-	-	-	358,500	315,600	171,200	-	-	-	-	-	-	167,400	168,500
Piedmont (city)	760,000	610,200	-	-	-	-	600,500	-	-	-	-	-	-	-	-	-	-	-	-	-	-	-	-	-
Pleasanton (city)	435,300	456,200	-	506,900	-	-	456,900	-	422,900	-	-	-	-	380,100	498,500	-	-	-	-	-	-	-	-	-
San Leandro (city)	235,500	249,300	236,500	287,500	-	-	246,600	-	253,500	-	-	-	-	243,600	250,000	-	-	-	-	-	-	-	-	277,400
San Lorenzo (cdp)	223,300	239,600	-	-	-	-	245,900	-	251,600	-	-	-	-	-	-	-	-	-	-	-	-	-	-	221,300
Union City (city)	312,600	333,700	312,500	355,500	-	-	353,600	-	316,200	-	-	-	-	349,300	239,800	-	-	-	-	-	-	-	-	357,100
Butte County	129,800	127,600	-	112,500	-	-	170,100	-	186,400	-	-	99,400	-	146,600	-	66,400	-	-	-	-	-	-	-	-
Chico (city)	141,600	149,300	-	-	-	-	196,400	-	-	-	-	0	-	-	-	-	-	-	-	-	-	-	-	-
Oroville (city)	88,900	211,500	-	-	-	-	-	-	-	-	-	75,000	-	-	-	-	-	-	-	-	-	-	-	-
Contra Costa County	267,800	270,800	204,200	319,100	-	-	311,400	215,400	226,200	195,400	221,400	-	253,900	288,800	326,600	181,300	-	255,000	211,800	-	360,900	280,000	120,000	239,400
Alamo (cdp)	731,200	872,100	-	-	-	-	-	-	-	-	-	-	-	-	-	-	-	-	-	-	-	-	-	-
Antioch (city)	196,600	222,900	202,100	228,400	-	-	226,400	-	220,000	-	-	-	-	-	-	-	-	-	-	-	-	-	-	220,500
Bay Point (cdp)	145,500	195,300	-	-	-	-	-	-	166,800	-	-	-	-	-	-	-	-	-	-	-	-	-	-	-
Blackhawk-Camino-Tass. (cdp)	716,100	679,900	-	-	-	-	711,800	-	-	-	-	-	-	-	-	-	-	-	-	-	-	-	-	-
Clayton (city)	358,700	362,600	-	-	-	-	-	-	-	-	-	-	-	-	-	-	-	-	-	-	-	-	-	-
Concord (city)	233,700	245,800	194,900	313,300	-	-	246,900	-	227,900	-	-	-	-	237,800	229,700	-	-	-	-	-	-	-	-	223,500
Danville (town)	541,400	533,800	-	473,000	-	-	563,800	-	587,300	-	-	-	-	-	-	-	-	-	-	-	-	-	-	-
El Cerrito (city)	291,300	283,100	-	384,600	-	-	283,800	-	251,600	-	-	-	-	283,600	-	-	-	-	-	-	-	-	-	-
El Sobrante (cdp)	199,200	207,300	-	208,300	-	-	-	-	-	-	-	-	-	-	-	-	-	-	-	-	-	-	-	-
Hercules (city)	241,500	260,900	-	263,000	-	-	255,800	-	266,800	-	-	-	-	-	-	-	-	-	-	-	-	-	-	-

Notes: Please refer to the User's Guide for an explanation of data; data is arranged alphabetically by state, then county, then city within each county; table includes counties with populations greater than 49,999 unless noted and cities with populations greater than 9,999 whose Asian and/or NHPI population rates are greater than the national average; (1) Native Hawaiian and other Pacific Islander; (2) excludes Taiwanese; (3) includes Chamorro; (4) county does not meet population threshold but is shown in order to allow inclusion of city

Place	All specified owner-occupied housing units	Specified housing units owned and occup. by Asians	Specified housing units owned and occup. by NHPIs[1]	Asian Indian	Bangladeshi	Cambodian	Chinese[2]	Fijian	Filipino	Guamanian[3]	Hawaiian, Native	Hmong	Indonesian	Japanese	Korean	Laotian	Malaysian	Pakistani	Samoan	Sri Lankan	Taiwanese	Thai	Tongan	Vietnamese
Lafayette (city)	583,000	560,000	-	-	-	-	559,100	-	-	-	-	-	-	-	-	-	-	-	-	-	-	-	-	-
Martinez (city)	254,300	283,400	-	-	-	-	281,700	-	293,600	-	-	-	-	-	-	-	-	-	-	-	-	-	-	-
Moraga (town)	538,500	495,900	-	-	-	-	526,100	-	-	-	-	-	-	-	-	-	-	-	-	-	-	-	-	-
Orinda (city)	631,800	570,600	-	-	-	-	575,000	-	-	-	-	-	-	-	-	-	-	-	-	-	-	-	-	-
Pinole (city)	223,900	235,000	-	-	-	-	237,500	-	231,200	-	-	-	-	-	-	-	-	-	-	-	-	-	-	-
Pittsburg (city)	165,100	184,700	145,100	174,600	-	-	221,400	-	180,100	-	-	-	-	-	-	-	-	-	-	-	-	-	-	-
Pleasant Hill (city)	294,000	298,500	-	-	-	-	298,800	-	233,300	-	-	-	-	-	320,800	-	-	-	-	-	-	-	-	-
Richmond (city)	171,900	221,000	183,300	259,600	-	-	227,600	-	238,500	-	-	-	-	202,000	294,200	168,800	-	-	-	-	-	-	-	200,000
San Pablo (city)	146,100	171,500	-	164,100	-	-	-	-	169,800	-	-	-	-	-	-	186,400	-	-	-	-	-	-	-	181,300
San Ramon (city)	428,700	460,300	-	478,800	-	-	448,900	-	460,700	-	-	-	-	453,000	-	-	-	-	-	-	-	-	-	-
Walnut Creek (city)	391,200	416,800	-	481,800	-	-	434,000	-	380,000	-	-	-	-	356,100	427,800	-	-	-	-	-	-	-	-	-
El Dorado County	194,400	216,800	-	-	-	-	-	-	170,700	-	-	-	-	213,000	-	-	-	-	-	-	-	-	-	-
El Dorado Hills (cdp)	279,700	302,200	-	-	-	-	-	-	-	-	-	-	-	-	-	-	-	-	-	-	-	-	-	-
South Lake Tahoe (city)	157,800	170,200	-	-	-	-	-	-	166,800	-	-	-	-	-	-	-	-	-	-	-	-	-	-	-
Fresno County	104,900	119,400	82,500	119,600	-	80,200	143,000	-	114,200	-	-	86,700	-	126,100	165,300	84,700	-	-	-	-	-	-	-	132,000
Clovis (city)	125,200	130,900	-	-	-	-	-	-	137,500	-	-	117,000	-	133,400	-	-	-	-	-	-	-	-	-	-
Fresno (city)	97,300	117,100	-	129,900	-	68,800	150,700	-	111,000	-	-	82,100	-	122,500	166,100	80,800	-	-	-	-	-	-	-	133,000
Reedley (city)	104,200	119,000	-	-	-	-	-	-	-	-	-	-	-	-	-	-	-	-	-	-	-	-	-	-
Humboldt County	133,500	145,500	-	-	-	-	-	-	-	-	-	-	-	124,200	-	-	-	-	-	-	-	-	-	-
Imperial County	100,000	113,900	-	-	-	-	106,500	-	104,200	-	-	-	-	-	254,200	-	-	-	-	-	-	-	-	-
Kern County	93,300	105,400	105,300	117,400	-	85,000	124,200	-	93,100	-	-	-	-	128,800	144,600	-	-	-	-	-	-	-	-	126,300
Bakersfield (city)	106,500	128,000	108,500	126,400	-	-	128,900	-	117,500	-	-	-	-	143,600	147,100	-	-	-	-	-	-	-	-	132,600
Delano (city)	86,700	89,000	-	-	-	-	-	-	88,700	-	-	-	-	-	-	-	-	-	-	-	-	-	-	-
Ridgecrest (city)	72,400	78,500	-	-	-	-	-	-	74,000	-	-	-	-	-	-	-	-	-	-	-	-	-	-	-
Kings County	97,600	112,600	-	-	-	-	-	-	113,800	-	-	-	-	-	-	-	-	-	-	-	-	-	-	-
Lemoore (city)	110,900	123,900	-	-	-	-	-	-	127,400	-	-	-	-	-	-	-	-	-	-	-	-	-	-	-
Lake County	122,600	114,600	-	-	-	-	-	-	-	-	-	-	-	-	-	-	-	-	-	-	-	-	-	-
Los Angeles County	209,300	226,400	177,800	293,600	167,700	179,800	236,500	192,100	197,300	172,300	186,100	157,300	239,700	237,000	256,700	151,300	158,300	268,500	175,900	244,100	277,500	189,900	182,400	200,500
Agoura Hills (city)	366,600	335,700	-	-	-	-	-	-	-	-	-	-	-	-	-	-	-	-	-	-	-	-	-	-
Alhambra (city)	210,400	197,900	-	259,100	-	-	197,100	-	203,800	-	-	-	-	165,000	187,000	-	-	-	-	-	202,900	-	-	222,000
Altadena (cdp)	261,000	247,700	-	-	-	-	-	-	233,300	-	-	-	-	246,900	-	-	-	-	-	-	-	-	-	-
Arcadia (city)	393,700	384,400	-	459,100	-	-	374,400	-	270,000	-	-	-	-	372,400	383,600	-	-	-	-	-	408,200	-	-	-
Artesia (city)	192,300	190,000	-	192,900	-	-	185,800	-	186,100	-	-	-	-	-	188,800	-	-	-	-	-	-	-	-	-
Avocado Heights (cdp)	179,900	194,800	-	-	-	-	-	-	-	-	-	-	-	-	-	-	-	-	-	-	-	-	-	-
Azusa (city)	149,300	153,400	-	-	-	-	-	-	155,000	-	-	-	-	-	-	-	-	-	-	-	-	-	-	-
Baldwin Park (city)	146,400	155,200	-	-	-	-	140,700	-	158,300	-	-	-	-	-	-	-	-	-	-	-	-	-	-	165,400
Bellflower (city)	179,800	182,000	-	-	-	145,200	-	-	188,500	-	-	-	-	-	145,000	-	-	-	-	-	-	184,800	-	-
Beverly Hills (city)	1 Mil.+	968,200	-	-	-	-	991,100	-	-	-	-	-	-	-	1 Mil.+	-	-	-	-	-	-	-	-	-
Burbank (city)	256,400	259,900	-	300,000	-	-	342,200	-	246,100	-	-	-	-	218,600	259,100	-	-	-	-	-	-	-	-	291,700
Calabasas (city)	497,900	550,000	-	-	-	-	525,000	-	-	-	-	-	-	-	-	-	-	-	-	-	-	-	-	-
Carson (city)	183,200	186,100	177,400	-	-	-	188,900	-	187,200	-	-	-	-	176,800	-	-	-	-	181,400	-	-	-	-	194,300

Notes: Please refer to the User's Guide for an explanation of data; data is arranged alphabetically by state, then county, then city within each county; table includes counties with populations greater than 49,999 unless noted and cities with populations greater than 9,999 whose Asian and/or NHPI population rates are greater than the national average; (1) Native Hawaiian and other Pacific Islander; (2) excludes Taiwanese; (3) includes Chamorro; (4) county does not meet population threshold but is shown in order to allow inclusion of city

Place	All specified owner-occupied housing units	Specified housing units owned and occup. by Asians	Specified housing units owned and occup. by NHPIs[1]	Asian Indian	Bangladeshi	Cambodian	Chinese[2]	Fijian	Filipino	Guamanian[3]	Hawaiian, Native	Hmong	Indonesian	Japanese	Korean	Laotian	Malaysian	Pakistani	Samoan	Sri Lankan	Taiwanese	Thai	Tongan	Vietnamese
Cerritos (city)	281,000	283,000	-	315,900	-	-	289,000	-	280,400	-	-	-	-	285,800	268,900	-	-	-	-	-	275,300	297,300	-	283,100
Citrus (cdp)	151,800	157,800	-	-	-	-	-	-	-	-	-	-	-	-	-	-	-	-	-	-	-	-	-	-
Claremont (city)	251,000	275,800	-	283,300	-	-	272,200	-	-	-	-	-	-	-	346,200	-	-	-	-	-	-	-	-	-
Compton (city)	136,200	116,000	137,500	-	-	-	-	-	-	-	-	-	-	-	-	-	-	-	137,500	-	-	-	-	-
Covina (city)	189,500	188,800	-	-	-	-	180,300	-	193,100	-	-	-	-	185,700	-	-	-	-	-	-	-	-	-	191,700
Culver City (city)	311,100	305,900	-	354,300	-	-	312,500	-	295,200	-	-	-	-	302,400	-	-	-	-	-	-	-	-	-	-
Diamond Bar (city)	245,800	263,100	-	309,400	-	-	268,200	-	267,400	-	-	-	-	222,900	247,400	-	-	-	-	-	284,700	-	-	245,100
Downey (city)	209,700	214,900	-	203,800	-	-	235,500	-	203,700	-	-	-	-	241,400	214,000	-	-	-	-	-	-	-	-	193,900
Duarte (city)	173,500	196,800	-	-	-	-	207,900	-	196,200	-	-	-	-	-	-	-	-	-	-	-	-	-	-	-
East San Gabriel (cdp)	272,100	259,900	-	-	-	-	264,600	-	-	-	-	-	-	268,100	-	-	-	-	-	-	238,100	-	-	-
El Monte (city)	158,100	158,900	-	-	-	-	152,300	-	164,400	-	-	-	-	-	-	-	-	-	-	-	178,300	-	-	170,200
El Segundo (city)	371,900	385,500	-	-	-	-	-	-	-	-	-	-	-	-	-	-	-	-	-	-	-	-	-	-
Gardena (city)	179,500	183,100	-	-	-	-	190,300	-	178,100	-	-	-	-	182,000	196,200	-	-	-	-	-	-	-	-	188,300
Glendale (city)	325,700	299,300	-	439,600	-	-	391,400	-	252,700	-	-	-	-	335,500	275,700	-	-	-	-	-	-	378,900	-	319,700
Glendora (city)	225,000	212,200	-	305,700	-	-	240,300	-	184,600	-	-	-	-	-	-	-	-	-	-	-	-	-	-	-
Hacienda Heights (cdp)	230,800	249,900	-	-	-	-	243,800	-	260,100	-	-	-	-	245,000	256,100	-	-	-	-	-	263,100	-	-	228,600
Hawaiian Gardens (city)	139,500	120,300	-	-	-	-	-	-	-	-	-	-	-	-	131,000	-	-	-	-	-	-	-	-	-
Hawthorne (city)	183,700	182,300	243,800	171,400	-	-	258,300	-	177,500	-	-	-	-	204,200	-	-	-	-	-	-	-	-	-	167,000
Hermosa Beach (city)	519,200	451,400	-	-	-	-	-	-	-	-	-	-	-	-	-	-	-	-	-	-	-	-	-	-
La Canada Flintridge (city)	587,800	558,900	-	-	-	-	626,600	-	-	-	-	-	-	699,400	453,000	-	-	-	-	-	-	-	-	-
La Crescenta-Montrose (cdp)	294,700	269,100	-	-	-	-	-	-	235,000	-	-	-	-	-	285,000	-	-	-	-	-	-	-	-	-
La Mirada (city)	210,700	256,200	-	295,300	-	-	271,000	-	252,100	-	-	-	-	214,200	253,300	-	-	-	-	-	-	-	-	-
La Puente (city)	146,500	152,800	-	-	-	-	151,800	-	160,000	-	-	-	-	-	-	-	-	-	-	-	-	-	-	-
La Verne (city)	242,100	238,700	-	-	-	-	-	-	243,100	-	-	-	-	-	-	-	-	-	-	-	-	-	-	-
Lakewood (city)	202,800	199,800	169,600	195,200	-	225,600	195,300	-	208,500	-	-	-	-	195,800	188,200	-	-	-	156,900	-	-	-	-	187,500
Lancaster (city)	103,700	116,300	-	151,300	-	-	134,900	-	109,700	-	-	-	-	-	-	-	-	-	-	-	-	-	-	-
Lawndale (city)	178,700	186,200	162,500	-	-	-	-	-	204,200	-	-	-	-	-	-	-	-	-	-	-	-	-	-	191,500
Lomita (city)	262,100	277,600	-	-	-	-	-	-	438,600	-	-	-	-	273,100	259,600	-	-	-	-	-	-	-	-	-
Long Beach (city)	210,000	174,800	166,200	260,900	-	165,700	203,500	-	170,000	-	-	-	-	185,800	252,800	170,000	-	-	146,300	-	-	144,900	-	170,400
Los Angeles (city)	221,600	214,600	180,500	283,900	187,500	167,400	207,100	-	197,300	150,500	193,600	-	240,200	223,700	255,200	144,400	-	265,300	210,000	227,600	261,300	178,700	145,700	195,700
Manhattan Beach (city)	672,600	656,400	-	-	-	-	716,700	-	-	-	-	-	-	610,100	-	-	-	-	-	-	-	-	-	-
Monrovia (city)	229,600	216,700	-	-	-	-	201,700	-	227,000	-	-	-	-	-	-	-	-	-	-	-	-	-	-	-
Montebello (city)	199,000	246,300	-	-	-	-	262,100	-	268,900	-	-	-	-	235,500	205,600	-	-	-	-	-	-	-	-	-
Monterey Park (city)	216,500	218,500	-	-	-	225,000	217,700	-	201,000	-	-	-	-	220,800	251,900	-	-	-	-	-	197,300	-	-	257,700
Norwalk (city)	161,100	164,200	-	164,900	-	155,100	160,800	-	166,600	-	-	-	-	171,300	146,300	-	-	-	-	-	-	-	-	164,400
Palmdale (city)	116,400	129,300	-	160,000	-	-	-	-	127,400	-	-	-	-	-	-	-	-	-	-	-	-	-	-	-
Palos Verdes Estates (city)	795,600	903,500	-	-	-	-	948,300	-	-	-	-	-	-	710,400	1 Mil.+	-	-	-	-	-	-	-	-	-
Pasadena (city)	286,400	276,800	-	323,800	-	-	319,200	-	240,100	-	-	-	-	273,500	287,500	-	-	-	-	-	-	-	-	222,400
Pomona (city)	137,700	168,200	-	230,900	-	112,500	154,700	-	171,100	-	-	-	-	207,100	-	132,900	-	-	-	-	-	-	-	157,900
Rancho Palos Verdes (city)	560,500	593,200	-	610,100	-	-	597,600	-	497,500	-	-	-	-	566,400	618,500	-	-	-	-	-	690,200	-	-	-
Redondo Beach (city)	353,300	359,900	-	403,100	-	-	356,300	-	369,600	-	-	-	-	355,800	393,500	-	-	-	-	-	-	-	-	-

Notes: Please refer to the User's Guide for an explanation of data; data is arranged alphabetically by state, then county, then city within each county; table includes counties with populations greater than 49,999 unless noted and cities with populations greater than 9,999 whose Asian and/or NHPI population rates are greater than the national average; (1) Native Hawaiian and other Pacific Islander; (2) excludes Taiwanese; (3) includes Chamorro; (4) county does not meet population threshold but is shown in order to allow inclusion of city

Place	All specified owner-occupied housing units	Specified housing units owned and occup. by Asians	Specified housing units owned and occup. by NHPIs[1]	Asian Indian	Bangladeshi	Cambodian	Chinese[2]	Fijian	Filipino	Guamanian[3]	Hawaiian, Native	Hmong	Indonesian	Japanese	Korean	Laotian	Malaysian	Pakistani	Samoan	Sri Lankan	Taiwanese	Thai	Tongan	Vietnamese
Rosemead (city)	182,200	186,300	-	-	-	227,900	181,000	-	191,700	-	-	-	-	179,900	-	-	-	-	-	-	-	-	-	203,400
Rowland Heights (cdp)	221,000	249,900	-	277,800	-	-	276,700	-	197,400	-	-	-	-	238,900	197,200	-	-	-	-	-	272,500	-	-	231,300
San Dimas (city)	232,400	268,700	-	-	-	-	269,400	-	252,600	-	-	-	-	-	-	-	-	-	-	-	-	-	-	-
San Gabriel (city)	232,600	217,900	-	-	-	-	220,100	-	217,600	-	-	-	-	242,000	-	-	-	-	-	-	251,300	-	-	220,600
San Marino (city)	690,800	641,800	-	-	-	-	661,500	-	-	-	-	-	-	-	-	-	-	-	-	-	624,100	-	-	-
Santa Clarita (city)	229,200	235,700	-	252,700	-	-	232,100	-	228,300	-	-	-	-	207,400	258,700	-	-	-	-	-	-	-	-	266,400
Santa Monica (city)	625,900	517,400	-	532,900	-	-	542,900	-	805,600	-	-	-	-	448,600	546,900	-	-	-	-	-	-	-	-	-
Sierra Madre (city)	370,500	308,000	-	-	-	-	-	-	-	-	-	-	-	-	-	-	-	-	-	-	-	-	-	-
South El Monte (city)	157,100	163,700	-	-	-	-	149,200	-	-	-	-	-	-	-	-	-	-	-	-	-	-	-	-	187,500
South Pasadena (city)	383,600	391,200	-	-	-	-	412,800	-	-	-	-	-	-	382,100	450,000	-	-	-	-	-	-	-	-	-
South San Jose Hills (cdp)	141,200	166,300	-	-	-	-	-	-	167,500	-	-	-	-	-	-	-	-	-	-	-	-	-	-	-
Temple City (city)	234,800	229,300	-	-	-	-	219,900	-	262,500	-	-	-	-	237,500	247,600	-	-	-	-	-	232,800	-	-	242,400
Torrance (city)	320,700	300,200	-	342,100	-	-	310,800	-	290,200	-	-	-	-	293,200	315,300	-	-	281,000	-	-	329,200	-	-	263,000
Valinda (cdp)	158,300	161,300	-	-	-	-	-	-	166,900	-	-	-	-	-	-	-	-	-	-	-	-	-	-	164,600
Vincent (cdp)	154,100	157,300	-	-	-	-	-	-	160,200	-	-	-	-	-	-	-	-	-	-	-	-	-	-	-
Walnut (city)	279,700	285,700	-	361,400	-	-	281,700	-	277,000	-	-	-	-	260,700	311,300	-	-	-	-	-	367,300	-	-	252,100
West Carson (cdp)	198,100	208,000	-	-	-	-	-	-	215,700	-	-	-	-	214,900	194,400	-	-	-	-	-	-	-	-	-
West Covina (city)	190,200	191,100	217,900	245,400	-	-	191,600	-	190,100	-	-	-	-	182,200	163,600	-	-	-	-	-	200,900	-	-	193,200
West Hollywood (city)	406,400	196,300	-	-	-	-	-	-	-	-	-	-	-	-	-	-	-	-	-	-	-	-	-	-
West Puente Valley (cdp)	151,000	158,600	-	-	-	-	-	-	160,400	-	-	-	-	-	-	-	-	-	-	-	-	-	-	142,500
Whittier (city)	211,700	235,400	-	-	-	-	238,400	-	215,000	-	-	-	-	229,300	240,500	-	-	-	-	-	-	-	-	-
Madera County	118,800	131,900	-	127,300	-	-	-	-	117,900	-	-	-	-	-	-	-	-	-	-	-	-	-	-	-
Marin County	514,600	481,900	-	625,000	-	-	522,900	-	409,100	-	-	-	-	500,000	383,700	-	-	-	-	-	-	-	-	181,800
Larkspur (city)	663,000	580,900	-	-	-	-	-	-	-	-	-	-	-	-	-	-	-	-	-	-	-	-	-	-
Novato (city)	381,400	373,800	-	-	-	-	373,600	-	450,000	-	-	-	-	-	-	-	-	-	-	-	-	-	-	-
San Rafael (city)	477,100	420,700	-	457,100	-	-	481,100	-	-	-	-	-	-	-	-	-	-	-	-	-	-	-	-	150,000
Tamalpais-Homestead (cdp)	609,100	611,400	-	-	-	-	-	-	-	-	-	-	-	-	-	-	-	-	-	-	-	-	-	-
Mendocino County	170,200	220,500	-	-	-	-	-	-	-	-	-	-	-	-	-	-	-	-	-	-	-	-	-	-
Merced County	111,100	114,200	-	105,300	-	-	122,100	-	141,900	-	-	95,900	-	139,800	-	100,000	-	-	-	-	-	-	-	-
Atwater (city)	103,100	110,100	-	-	-	-	-	-	-	-	-	97,100	-	-	-	-	-	-	-	-	-	-	-	-
Livingston (city)	92,700	94,600	-	96,000	-	-	-	-	-	-	-	-	-	-	-	-	-	-	-	-	-	-	-	-
Merced (city)	106,400	107,300	-	-	-	-	-	-	-	-	-	95,300	-	-	-	111,600	-	-	-	-	-	-	-	-
Monterey County	265,800	248,400	211,400	300,000	-	-	255,700	-	219,600	188,000	-	-	-	275,500	289,500	-	-	-	-	-	-	-	-	279,400
Marina (city)	247,100	254,000	195,800	-	-	-	-	-	243,400	-	-	-	-	256,300	266,900	-	-	-	-	-	-	-	-	277,800
Monterey (city)	399,800	347,000	-	-	-	-	69,200	-	403,800	-	-	-	-	327,200	-	-	-	-	-	-	-	-	-	-
Pacific Grove (city)	417,400	414,600	-	-	-	-	-	-	-	-	-	-	-	-	-	-	-	-	-	-	-	-	-	-
Salinas (city)	195,700	219,600	225,000	228,600	-	-	237,800	-	203,000	-	-	-	-	225,800	258,600	-	-	-	-	-	-	-	-	250,000
Seaside (city)	237,700	245,300	-	-	-	-	-	-	246,600	-	-	-	-	259,800	-	-	-	-	-	-	-	-	-	0
Napa County	251,300	222,100	-	-	-	-	288,000	-	199,400	-	-	-	-	365,000	-	-	-	-	-	-	-	-	-	-
Nevada County	205,700	201,500	-	-	-	-	-	-	-	-	-	-	-	-	-	-	-	-	-	-	-	-	-	-
Orange County	270,000	260,400	207,900	314,800	-	207,400	296,600	-	243,900	211,200	200,300	217,900	233,100	277,100	262,700	182,000	-	268,400	201,500	250,000	333,100	243,800	171,900	232,400

Notes: Please refer to the User's Guide for an explanation of data; data is arranged alphabetically by state, then county, then city within each county; table includes counties with populations greater than 49,999 unless noted and cities with populations greater than 9,999 whose Asian and/or NHPI population rates are greater than the national average; (1) Native Hawaiian and other Pacific Islander; (2) excludes Taiwanese; (3) includes Chamorro; (4) county does not meet population threshold but is shown in order to allow inclusion of city

Place	All specified owner-occupied housing units	Specified housing units owned and occup. by Asians	Specified housing units owned and occup. by NHPIs[1]	Asian Indian	Bangladeshi	Cambodian	Chinese[2]	Fijian	Filipino	Guamanian[3]	Hawaiian, Native	Hmong	Indonesian	Japanese	Korean	Laotian	Malaysian	Pakistani	Samoan	Sri Lankan	Taiwanese	Thai	Tongan	Vietnamese
Aliso Viejo (cdp)	260,200	269,000	-	295,300	-	-	201,500	-	275,300	-	-	-	-	281,500	307,900	-	-	-	-	-	-	-	-	271,900
Anaheim (city)	213,800	223,800	206,600	339,300	-	-	237,900	-	215,900	-	-	-	-	199,900	206,200	191,300	-	237,500	200,000	-	261,500	197,900	-	219,300
Brea (city)	261,700	267,000	-	290,900	-	-	290,800	-	270,500	-	-	-	-	-	254,500	-	-	-	-	-	-	-	-	-
Buena Park (city)	199,400	210,600	-	203,400	-	-	199,400	-	213,300	-	-	-	-	187,800	221,400	-	-	-	-	-	-	-	-	229,400
Costa Mesa (city)	273,100	265,300	239,300	700,000	-	-	281,300	-	236,000	-	-	-	-	281,000	222,500	-	-	-	-	-	-	-	-	246,900
Cypress (city)	252,800	269,300	-	261,700	-	-	286,900	-	261,100	-	-	-	-	247,400	293,400	-	-	-	-	-	331,300	-	-	277,600
Foothill Ranch (cdp)	313,300	314,000	-	-	-	-	-	-	-	-	-	-	-	-	-	-	-	-	-	-	-	-	-	-
Fountain Valley (city)	289,500	288,800	-	282,700	-	-	294,400	-	274,300	-	-	-	-	292,700	285,800	-	-	-	-	-	311,400	-	-	289,200
Fullerton (city)	241,900	281,100	-	315,500	-	-	320,300	-	248,300	-	-	-	-	269,800	292,100	-	-	-	-	-	-	-	-	212,500
Garden Grove (city)	199,700	197,900	223,900	156,600	-	233,000	195,800	-	209,700	-	-	-	-	202,200	195,700	-	-	-	226,300	-	-	-	-	197,900
Huntington Beach (city)	311,800	320,400	195,200	343,000	-	-	350,800	-	292,200	-	-	-	-	306,000	357,700	-	-	-	-	-	341,700	-	-	306,500
Irvine (city)	316,800	322,700	-	354,300	-	-	331,000	-	274,000	-	-	-	-	284,200	293,600	-	-	-	-	-	349,000	-	-	335,400
La Habra (city)	199,500	279,100	-	-	-	-	307,900	-	234,700	-	-	-	-	-	446,100	-	-	-	-	-	-	-	-	-
La Palma (city)	286,900	287,400	-	319,800	-	-	281,900	-	295,400	-	-	-	-	274,500	285,200	-	-	-	-	-	-	-	-	-
Laguna Hills (city)	330,500	342,300	-	-	-	-	367,400	-	241,700	-	-	-	-	-	-	-	-	-	-	-	-	-	-	307,100
Laguna Niguel (city)	374,800	389,600	-	-	-	-	468,200	-	343,500	-	-	-	-	384,400	366,000	-	-	-	-	-	-	-	-	334,300
Lake Forest (city)	278,000	260,200	-	258,300	-	-	264,200	-	231,400	-	-	-	-	273,200	247,400	-	-	-	-	-	-	-	-	278,400
Los Alamitos (city)	307,100	295,000	-	-	-	-	-	-	-	-	-	-	-	-	-	-	-	-	-	-	-	-	-	-
Mission Viejo (city)	293,300	303,100	-	332,300	-	-	351,100	-	298,700	-	-	-	-	313,600	287,500	-	-	-	-	-	-	-	-	267,700
Newport Beach (city)	708,200	787,700	-	-	-	-	833,300	-	-	-	-	-	-	754,600	-	-	-	-	-	-	-	-	-	-
Orange (city)	256,600	277,000	-	353,300	-	-	284,800	-	251,800	-	-	-	-	243,800	337,200	-	-	-	-	-	300,000	-	-	278,000
Placentia (city)	264,500	271,400	-	278,000	-	-	277,200	-	267,600	-	-	-	-	265,800	256,400	-	-	-	-	-	-	-	-	282,900
Rancho Santa Margarita (city)	280,700	277,700	-	-	-	-	312,000	-	254,200	-	-	-	-	-	-	-	-	-	-	-	-	-	-	268,100
Rossmoor (cdp)	389,200	379,200	-	-	-	-	-	-	-	-	-	-	-	-	-	-	-	-	-	-	-	-	-	-
Santa Ana (city)	184,500	191,500	203,900	193,200	-	181,100	194,800	-	188,000	-	-	187,500	-	201,600	219,100	171,400	-	-	187,500	-	-	-	-	192,200
Seal Beach (city)	363,500	373,700	-	-	-	-	-	-	-	-	-	-	-	370,200	-	-	-	-	-	-	-	-	-	-
Stanton (city)	164,000	181,900	-	-	-	-	-	-	193,200	-	-	-	-	-	134,600	-	-	-	-	-	-	-	-	187,300
Tustin (city)	273,300	291,400	-	281,000	-	-	303,600	-	219,400	-	-	-	-	337,500	272,900	-	-	-	-	-	404,400	-	-	315,000
Tustin Foothills (cdp)	399,700	429,300	-	-	-	-	453,800	-	-	-	-	-	-	-	-	-	-	-	-	-	-	-	-	-
Westminster (city)	227,300	230,800	200,000	228,800	-	-	236,400	-	247,300	-	-	-	-	245,700	262,500	-	-	-	200,000	-	-	-	-	227,200
Yorba Linda (city)	346,100	376,400	-	390,000	-	-	383,300	-	351,500	-	-	-	-	361,100	315,000	-	-	-	-	-	-	-	-	394,400
Placer County	213,900	227,400	-	269,600	-	-	225,300	-	215,200	-	-	-	-	228,200	171,600	-	-	-	-	-	-	-	-	252,200
Rocklin (city)	213,100	233,100	-	-	-	-	-	-	-	-	-	-	-	219,300	-	-	-	-	-	-	-	-	-	-
Roseville (city)	194,900	214,700	-	223,400	-	-	216,100	-	210,800	-	-	-	-	210,400	-	-	-	-	-	-	-	-	-	-
Riverside County	146,500	166,500	145,800	182,300	-	178,100	171,200	-	163,800	136,700	158,000	70,000	-	155,500	191,300	95,900	-	128,800	125,000	-	146,900	147,500	-	170,500
Banning (city)	110,000	93,100	-	-	-	-	-	-	-	-	-	-	-	-	-	58,500	-	-	-	-	-	-	-	-
Corona (city)	194,400	208,800	-	224,600	-	-	211,500	-	198,100	-	-	-	-	202,700	218,400	-	-	-	-	-	-	-	-	216,300
Moreno Valley (city)	118,900	130,200	-	-	-	-	153,600	-	131,200	-	-	-	-	129,000	114,800	95,700	-	-	-	-	-	-	-	136,000
Palm Springs (city)	157,000	111,300	-	-	-	-	-	-	107,100	-	-	-	-	-	-	-	-	-	-	-	-	-	-	-
Pedley (cdp)	153,800	136,000	-	-	-	-	-	-	-	-	-	-	-	-	-	-	-	-	-	-	-	-	-	-
Riverside (city)	138,500	163,400	143,100	178,700	-	-	151,300	-	164,900	-	-	-	-	147,800	197,600	99,600	-	-	-	-	-	-	-	160,100

Notes: Please refer to the User's Guide for an explanation of data; data is arranged alphabetically by state, then county, then city within each county; table includes counties with populations greater than 49,999 unless noted and cities with populations greater than 9,999 whose Asian and/or NHPI population rates are greater than the national average; (1) Native Hawaiian and other Pacific Islander; (2) excludes Taiwanese; (3) includes Chamorro; (4) county does not meet population threshold but is shown in order to allow inclusion of city

Place	All specified owner-occupied housing units	Specified housing units owned and occup. by Asians	Specified housing units owned and occup. by NHPIs[1]	Asian Indian	Bangladeshi	Cambodian	Chinese[2]	Fijian	Filipino	Guamanian[3]	Hawaiian, Native	Hmong	Indonesian	Japanese	Korean	Laotian	Malaysian	Pakistani	Samoan	Sri Lankan	Taiwanese	Thai	Tongan	Vietnamese
Temecula (city)	190,100	189,400	-	-	-	-	222,800	-	185,200	-	-	-	-	-	-	-	-	-	-	-	-	-	-	-
Sacramento County	144,200	146,800	117,900	158,100	-	125,000	154,500	116,500	142,200	133,600	120,200	94,700	-	153,800	159,300	96,900	-	136,100	123,200	-	187,500	123,200	84,400	133,000
Arden-Arcade (cdp)	171,300	192,500	-	348,200	-	-	149,600	-	138,400	-	-	0	-	199,400	-	-	-	-	-	-	-	-	-	133,300
Elk Grove (cdp)	151,400	145,600	-	138,500	-	-	153,700	-	152,000	-	-	-	-	162,900	-	-	-	-	-	-	-	-	-	130,900
Fair Oaks (cdp)	223,900	281,400	-	-	-	-	-	-	-	-	-	-	-	-	-	-	-	-	-	-	-	-	-	-
Florin (cdp)	106,200	109,100	-	114,100	-	-	96,700	-	114,600	-	-	128,600	-	-	-	-	-	-	-	-	-	-	-	112,900
Folsom (city)	228,700	244,600	-	233,900	-	-	241,700	-	248,500	-	-	-	-	-	-	-	-	-	-	-	-	-	-	-
Foothill Farms (cdp)	120,200	130,000	-	-	-	-	-	-	-	-	-	-	-	-	-	-	-	-	-	-	-	-	-	-
La Riviera (cdp)	131,800	134,300	-	-	-	-	-	-	-	-	-	-	-	-	-	-	-	-	-	-	-	-	-	-
Laguna (cdp)	160,500	162,400	-	166,000	-	-	156,400	-	176,900	-	-	-	-	166,300	-	-	-	-	-	-	-	-	-	154,000
North Highlands (cdp)	95,000	96,000	-	-	-	-	-	-	95,600	-	-	-	-	-	-	-	-	-	-	-	-	-	-	105,800
Parkway-S. Sacramento (cdp)	92,000	91,500	-	-	-	-	92,200	-	-	-	-	137,500	-	-	-	112,500	-	-	-	-	-	-	-	88,300
Rancho Cordova (cdp)	116,500	123,200	-	131,300	-	-	110,200	-	143,500	-	-	-	-	-	133,800	-	-	-	-	-	-	-	-	117,400
Rosemont (cdp)	123,200	123,300	-	-	-	-	-	-	109,900	-	-	-	-	-	126,700	-	-	-	-	-	-	-	-	121,700
Sacramento (city)	128,800	141,100	109,500	134,200	-	80,300	153,100	115,100	118,400	-	-	92,100	-	157,700	165,000	94,200	-	116,100	97,200	-	-	-	83,600	126,000
Vineyard (cdp)	153,000	147,000	-	-	-	-	-	-	144,800	-	-	-	-	-	-	-	-	-	-	-	-	-	-	-
San Benito County	284,000	294,800	-	-	-	-	-	-	289,900	-	-	-	-	-	-	-	-	-	-	-	-	-	-	-
San Bernardino County	131,500	174,800	122,500	205,900	-	133,000	196,600		167,000	119,800	122,600	-	156,200	150,500	199,500	129,700	-	177,300	98,900	-	231,600	172,600	130,600	155,600
Chino (city)	173,600	180,100	-	-	-	-	-	-	172,700	-	-	-	-	-	-	-	-	-	-	-	-	-	-	177,800
Chino Hills (city)	242,600	258,500	-	274,200	-	-	249,300	-	254,700	-	-	-	-	225,000	264,500	-	-	-	-	-	314,000	-	-	287,800
Colton (city)	105,200	141,300	-	-	-	-	-	-	168,100	-	-	-	-	-	-	-	-	-	-	-	-	-	-	-
Fontana (city)	130,400	149,200	125,000	130,900	-	-	-	-	151,900	-	-	-	-	-	-	-	-	-	-	-	-	-	-	-
Grand Terrace (city)	142,600	159,700	-	-	-	-	-	-	-	-	-	-	-	-	-	-	-	-	-	-	-	-	-	-
Highland (city)	128,500	141,400	-	-	-	-	-	-	140,200	-	-	-	-	-	-	-	-	-	-	-	-	-	-	142,000
Loma Linda (city)	165,200	184,200	-	164,500	-	-	205,700	-	175,000	-	-	-	176,700	-	208,100	-	-	-	-	-	-	-	-	-
Montclair (city)	135,700	140,400	-	-	-	-	-	-	-	-	-	-	-	-	-	-	-	-	-	-	-	-	-	126,800
Ontario (city)	140,000	148,400	134,700	209,900	-	-	136,600	-	151,100	-	-	-	-	-	-	-	-	-	-	-	-	-	-	155,700
Rancho Cucamonga (city)	182,200	193,700	-	218,900	-	-	185,800	-	184,500	-	-	-	-	198,100	197,600	-	-	-	-	-	-	-	-	166,500
Redlands (city)	159,300	171,600	-	310,700	-	-	180,400	-	159,700	-	-	-	-	-	263,200	-	-	-	-	-	-	-	-	-
Rialto (city)	116,900	129,800	119,100	-	-	-	-	-	145,500	-	-	-	-	-	-	-	-	-	-	-	-	-	-	-
San Bernardino (city)	98,700	122,500	96,200	153,800	-	75,800	119,500	-	119,800	-	-	-	136,300	-	131,600	-	-	-	80,000	-	-	-	-	112,500
Upland (city)	211,000	239,700	-	242,400	-	-	219,700	-	284,600	-	-	-	-	-	268,600	-	-	-	-	-	236,300	-	-	214,300
Victorville (city)	98,700	112,400	-	-	-	-	-	-	113,100	-	-	-	-	-	-	-	-	-	-	-	-	-	-	-
San Diego County	227,200	213,800	193,500	348,700	-	205,800	283,400	-	192,900	187,700	218,400	208,800	211,500	234,600	259,500	169,600	-	303,600	169,800	-	335,100	250,800	306,300	216,700
Bonita (cdp)	296,400	315,800	-	-	-	-	-	-	286,500	-	-	-	-	-	-	-	-	-	-	-	-	-	-	-
Carlsbad (city)	330,100	392,100	-	-	-	-	429,600	-	330,800	-	-	-	-	296,300	-	-	-	-	-	-	-	-	-	-
Chula Vista (city)	197,000	238,100	223,800	-	-	-	241,200	-	238,800	181,300	-	-	-	216,500	252,100	-	-	-	-	-	-	-	-	-
Coronado (city)	683,400	587,500	-	-	-	-	-	-	525,000	-	-	-	-	-	-	-	-	-	-	-	-	-	-	-
Escondido (city)	192,600	224,200	-	-	-	-	298,200	-	237,500	-	-	-	-	-	-	177,100	-	-	-	-	-	-	-	168,400
Imperial Beach (city)	171,700	181,800	-	-	-	-	-	-	182,500	-	-	-	-	-	-	-	-	-	-	-	-	-	-	-
La Mesa (city)	198,700	195,700	-	-	-	-	-	-	247,200	-	-	-	-	-	-	-	-	-	-	-	-	-	-	-

Notes: Please refer to the User's Guide for an explanation of data; data is arranged alphabetically by state, then county, then city within each county; table includes counties with populations greater than 49,999 unless noted and cities with populations greater than 9,999 whose Asian and/or NHPI population rates are greater than the national average; (1) Native Hawaiian and other Pacific Islander; (2) excludes Taiwanese; (3) includes Chamorro; (4) county does not meet population threshold but is shown in order to allow inclusion of city

Place	All specified owner-occupied housing units	Specified housing units owned and occup. by Asians	Specified housing units owned and occup. by NHPIs[1]	Asian Indian	Bangladeshi	Cambodian	Chinese[2]	Fijian	Filipino	Guamanian[3]	Hawaiian, Native	Hmong	Indonesian	Japanese	Korean	Laotian	Malaysian	Pakistani	Samoan	Sri Lankan	Taiwanese	Thai	Tongan	Vietnamese
La Presa (cdp)	154,700	159,000	-	-	-	-	-	-	162,000	-	-	-	-	-	-	-	-	-	-	-	-	-	-	-
Lemon Grove (city)	164,900	178,700	-	-	-	-	-	-	187,300	-	-	-	-	-	-	-	-	-	-	-	-	-	-	170,800
National City (city)	141,500	149,100	-	-	-	-	-	-	151,900	-	-	-	-	-	-	-	-	-	-	-	-	-	-	-
Oceanside (city)	195,800	200,300	147,600	-	-	-	180,400	-	197,000	-	-	-	-	196,800	-	-	-	-	151,700	-	-	-	-	233,600
Poway (city)	284,200	365,700	-	-	-	-	412,500	-	243,200	-	-	-	-	-	-	-	-	-	-	-	-	-	-	-
Rancho San Diego (cdp)	279,000	254,800	-	-	-	-	-	-	246,900	-	-	-	-	-	-	-	-	-	-	-	-	-	-	-
San Diego (city)	233,100	204,100	196,100	349,300	-	177,800	284,500	-	186,400	179,200	222,600	171,600	-	241,800	271,100	163,200	-	-	165,900	-	342,300	287,500	-	216,200
San Marcos (city)	206,400	230,000	-	-	-	-	230,300	-	232,700	-	-	-	-	-	-	-	-	-	-	-	-	-	-	-
Solana Beach (city)	474,500	479,200	-	-	-	-	-	-	-	-	-	-	-	-	-	-	-	-	-	-	-	-	-	-
Spring Valley (cdp)	186,800	181,300	-	-	-	-	-	-	178,800	-	-	-	-	-	-	-	-	-	-	-	-	-	-	-
Vista (city)	201,600	230,100	134,700	-	-	-	-	-	197,000	-	-	-	-	270,800	-	-	-	-	-	-	-	-	-	-
San Francisco County	396,400	361,800	287,200	445,100	-	97,900	360,100	-	340,600	-	-	-	430,800	450,300	427,500	-	-	300,000	284,500	-	445,200	333,800	-	354,600
San Francisco (city)	396,400	361,800	287,200	445,100	-	97,900	360,100	-	340,600	-	-	-	430,800	450,300	427,500	-	-	300,000	284,500	-	445,200	333,800	-	354,600
San Joaquin County	142,400	135,300	191,700	179,800	-	111,700	124,600	-	132,900	-	178,100	93,500	-	132,600	215,000	116,300	-	97,900	240,900	-	-	-	-	155,100
Lathrop (city)	150,600	168,800	-	-	-	-	-	-	175,400	-	-	-	-	-	-	-	-	-	-	-	-	-	-	-
Lodi (city)	141,500	141,600	-	176,500	-	-	-	-	155,900	-	-	-	-	135,200	-	-	-	-	-	-	-	-	-	-
Stockton (city)	119,500	121,000	171,500	139,500	-	111,600	113,700	-	118,800	-	-	106,300	-	125,200	-	112,000	-	85,600	-	-	-	-	-	141,000
Tracy (city)	214,200	236,600	-	266,800	-	-	196,300	-	232,100	-	-	-	-	-	-	-	-	-	-	-	-	-	-	-
San Luis Obispo County	230,000	242,900	-	441,400	-	-	243,800	-	192,200	-	-	-	-	296,900	185,700	-	-	-	-	-	-	-	-	-
Baywood-Los Osos (cdp)	209,800	197,700	-	-	-	-	-	-	191,900	-	-	-	-	-	-	-	-	-	-	-	-	-	-	-
Grover Beach (city)	184,800	171,300	-	-	-	-	-	-	-	-	-	-	-	-	-	-	-	-	-	-	-	-	-	-
San Luis Obispo (city)	278,800	356,300	-	-	-	-	275,000	-	350,000	-	-	-	-	-	-	-	-	-	-	-	-	-	-	-
San Mateo County	469,200	399,500	355,000	564,800	-	-	437,700	354,700	359,800	447,900	356,300	-	496,600	432,100	452,800	-	-	-	364,300	-	541,700	340,200	337,200	387,700
Belmont (city)	593,200	596,200	-	772,300	-	-	604,800	-	411,500	-	-	-	-	622,000	-	-	-	-	-	-	-	-	-	-
Burlingame (city)	685,900	676,200	-	-	-	-	690,000	-	875,000	-	-	-	-	706,100	-	-	-	-	-	-	-	-	-	-
Daly City (city)	335,000	340,400	341,900	341,700	-	-	335,400	-	344,400	-	-	-	-	313,000	356,000	-	-	-	-	-	-	-	-	349,200
East Palo Alto (city)	302,100	283,600	277,300	-	-	-	-	-	-	-	-	-	-	-	-	-	-	-	-	-	-	-	292,600	-
Foster City (city)	566,500	567,000	-	586,200	-	-	563,500	-	541,700	-	-	-	-	551,300	669,100	-	-	-	-	-	-	-	-	-
Hillsborough (town)	1 Mil.+	1 Mil.+	-	-	-	-	1 Mil.+	-	-	-	-	-	-	-	-	-	-	-	-	-	-	-	-	-
Menlo Park (city)	778,500	837,400	-	-	-	-	880,200	-	-	-	-	-	-	716,700	-	-	-	-	-	-	-	-	-	-
Millbrae (city)	552,500	552,900	-	620,800	-	-	550,200	-	390,600	-	-	-	-	513,900	625,000	-	-	-	-	-	-	-	-	-
Pacifica (city)	367,700	364,600	-	-	-	-	383,600	-	348,000	-	-	-	-	316,100	-	-	-	-	-	-	-	-	-	-
Redwood City (city)	517,800	559,400	500,000	699,300	-	-	569,700	-	393,500	-	-	-	-	516,200	-	-	-	-	-	-	-	-	-	-
San Bruno (city)	385,100	398,500	242,900	396,400	-	-	403,800	-	411,600	-	-	-	-	360,000	-	-	-	-	-	-	-	-	347,100	-
San Carlos (city)	626,400	623,700	-	-	-	-	671,100	-	-	-	-	-	-	-	-	-	-	-	-	-	-	-	-	-
San Mateo (city)	477,300	456,600	451,300	513,700	-	-	487,300	-	431,100	-	-	-	-	381,100	526,300	-	-	-	-	-	-	-	450,000	460,300
South San Francisco (city)	352,900	365,000	347,000	369,400	-	-	363,600	-	366,900	-	-	-	-	347,800	-	-	-	-	-	-	-	-	-	-
Santa Barbara County	293,000	208,800	321,900	446,000	-	-	421,300	-	150,300	-	-	165,400	-	201,700	217,000	-	-	-	-	-	-	-	-	221,300
Goleta (cdp)	425,700	408,700	-	-	-	-	422,100	-	392,300	-	-	-	-	434,300	-	-	-	-	-	-	-	-	-	287,500
Isla Vista (cdp)	402,400	225,000	-	-	-	-	225,000	-	-	-	-	-	-	-	0	-	-	-	-	-	-	-	-	-
Lompoc (city)	148,300	162,200	-	-	-	-	-	-	154,000	-	-	-	-	-	-	-	-	-	-	-	-	-	-	-

Notes: Please refer to the User's Guide for an explanation of data; data is arranged alphabetically by state, then county, then city within each county; table includes counties with populations greater than 49,999 unless noted and cities with populations greater than 9,999 whose Asian and/or NHPI population rates are greater than the national average; (1) Native Hawaiian and other Pacific Islander; (2) excludes Taiwanese; (3) includes Chamorro; (4) county does not meet population threshold but is shown in order to allow inclusion of city

Place	All specified owner-occupied housing units	Specified housing units owned and occup. by Asians	Specified housing units owned and occup. by NHPIs[1]	Asian Indian	Bangladeshi	Cambodian	Chinese[2]	Fijian	Filipino	Guamanian[3]	Hawaiian, Native	Hmong	Indonesian	Japanese	Korean	Laotian	Malaysian	Pakistani	Samoan	Sri Lankan	Taiwanese	Thai	Tongan	Vietnamese
Orcutt (cdp)	181,100	186,900	-	-	-	-	-	-	-	-	-	-	-	-	-	-	-	-	-	-	-	-	-	-
Santa Maria (city)	145,600	153,700	-	-	-	-	-	-	143,000	-	-	-	-	179,700	-	-	-	-	-	-	-	-	-	-
Santa Clara County	446,400	427,000	378,200	522,400	520,800	331,000	479,100	419,400	363,500	367,000	373,900	-	409,100	447,800	479,400	279,700	-	453,200	298,500	-	490,800	457,100	-	366,100
Alum Rock (cdp)	276,100	277,000	-	-	-	-	-	-	-	-	-	-	-	-	-	-	-	-	-	-	-	-	-	332,100
Campbell (city)	436,800	429,900	-	491,700	-	-	404,200	-	380,800	-	-	-	-	467,800	419,400	-	-	-	-	-	-	-	-	512,800
Cupertino (city)	649,000	646,300	-	717,900	-	-	640,600	-	523,400	-	-	-	-	559,500	737,500	-	-	-	-	-	510,200	-	-	637,500
Gilroy (city)	344,100	361,500	-	-	-	-	373,900	-	351,100	-	-	-	-	-	-	-	-	-	-	-	-	-	-	-
Los Altos (city)	983,000	962,400	-	996,500	-	-	981,600	-	-	-	-	-	-	794,500	-	-	-	-	-	-	-	-	-	-
Los Gatos (town)	784,600	819,600	-	-	-	-	859,000	-	-	-	-	-	-	728,100	-	-	-	-	-	-	-	-	-	-
Milpitas (city)	372,900	388,200	395,500	415,000	-	-	389,800	-	378,100	-	-	-	-	362,000	345,000	-	-	-	-	-	-	-	-	398,700
Morgan Hill (city)	435,200	493,900	-	-	-	-	488,800	-	-	-	-	-	-	372,700	-	-	-	-	-	-	-	-	-	-
Mountain View (city)	546,900	531,700	-	575,700	-	-	525,500	-	493,800	-	-	-	-	551,900	660,700	-	-	-	-	-	-	-	-	465,000
Palo Alto (city)	811,800	759,800	-	884,100	-	-	739,000	-	493,800	-	-	-	-	728,500	850,800	-	-	-	-	-	-	-	-	-
San Jose (city)	394,000	383,500	363,900	468,300	-	328,100	415,100	-	354,600	388,200	331,300	-	-	392,400	424,100	282,700	-	393,900	286,800	-	451,300	436,800	-	356,200
Santa Clara (city)	396,500	388,100	420,000	441,800	-	-	404,000	-	368,800	-	-	-	-	385,700	397,700	-	-	440,000	-	-	-	-	-	374,300
Saratoga (city)	1 Mil.+	1 Mil.+	-	1 Mil.+	-	-	1 Mil.+	-	-	-	-	-	-	945,900	1 Mil.+	-	-	-	-	-	845,000	-	-	-
Stanford (cdp)	870,800	875,000	-	1 Mil.+	-	-	875,000	-	-	-	-	-	-	-	0	-	-	-	-	-	-	-	-	-
Sunnyvale (city)	495,200	481,300	237,500	615,300	-	-	487,900	-	369,600	-	-	-	-	505,300	458,600	-	-	-	-	-	475,800	-	-	395,100
Santa Cruz County	377,500	335,100	-	430,800	-	-	339,800	-	351,000	-	-	-	-	291,800	373,900	-	-	-	-	-	-	-	-	379,400
Capitola (city)	397,600	365,200	-	-	-	-	-	-	-	-	-	-	-	-	-	-	-	-	-	-	-	-	-	-
Santa Cruz (city)	411,900	348,600	-	350,000	-	-	315,100	-	382,000	-	-	-	-	364,300	-	-	-	-	-	-	-	-	-	-
Scotts Valley (city)	447,900	422,900	-	-	-	-	-	-	-	-	-	-	-	-	-	-	-	-	-	-	-	-	-	-
Shasta County	120,800	114,900	-	-	-	-	-	-	132,100	-	-	-	-	-	-	93,400	-	-	-	-	-	-	-	-
Solano County	178,300	192,500	166,600	202,000	-	-	195,300	-	193,000	160,500	177,800	143,800	-	174,800	185,200	232,700	-	-	256,500	-	-	-	-	193,800
Benicia (city)	274,600	293,900	-	-	-	-	274,300	-	298,700	-	-	-	-	-	-	-	-	-	-	-	-	-	-	-
Fairfield (city)	174,700	196,300	166,900	229,500	-	-	209,700	-	203,000	163,400	-	-	-	154,400	180,400	225,000	-	-	-	-	-	-	-	-
Suisun City (city)	160,700	171,700	-	168,200	-	-	-	-	180,100	-	-	-	-	-	-	-	-	-	-	-	-	-	-	-
Vacaville (city)	181,300	199,700	-	-	-	-	-	-	192,600	-	-	-	-	-	-	-	-	-	-	-	-	-	-	-
Vallejo (city)	166,400	190,300	162,500	188,500	-	-	181,700	-	190,600	158,500	-	-	-	184,200	-	-	-	-	-	-	-	-	-	197,900
Sonoma County	273,200	266,500	324,300	312,100	-	219,200	300,200	-	249,800	-	-	-	-	291,200	228,800	205,500	-	-	-	-	-	-	-	224,200
Petaluma (city)	289,500	303,700	-	-	-	-	313,600	-	-	-	-	-	-	-	-	-	-	-	-	-	-	-	-	-
Rohnert Park (city)	237,300	241,800	-	-	-	-	243,800	-	241,200	-	-	-	-	-	-	-	-	-	-	-	-	-	-	-
Santa Rosa (city)	245,000	233,100	-	233,900	-	207,700	310,000	-	244,600	-	-	-	-	243,800	-	213,600	-	-	-	-	-	-	-	192,900
Stanislaus County	125,300	137,100	114,100	137,600	-	123,200	140,800	105,500	134,700	-	-	119,300	-	162,500	-	122,300	-	-	-	-	-	-	-	145,700
Ceres (city)	119,900	142,200	-	149,400	-	-	-	-	-	-	-	-	-	-	-	-	-	-	-	-	-	-	-	-
Modesto (city)	126,000	131,600	104,100	133,400	-	113,300	134,800	97,500	127,900	-	-	0	-	183,900	-	111,500	-	-	-	-	-	-	-	149,300
Salida (cdp)	144,500	155,100	-	-	-	-	-	-	-	-	-	-	-	-	-	-	-	-	-	-	-	-	-	-
Turlock (city)	128,300	136,500	-	145,800	-	-	-	-	-	-	-	-	-	-	-	-	-	-	-	-	-	-	-	-
Sutter County	120,700	124,900	-	127,100	-	-	-	-	126,600	-	-	-	-	119,000	-	-	-	-	-	-	-	-	-	-
South Yuba City (cdp)	127,700	131,600	-	134,500	-	-	-	-	-	-	-	-	-	-	-	-	-	-	-	-	-	-	-	-
Yuba City (city)	115,700	124,900	-	122,800	-	-	-	-	-	-	-	-	-	-	-	-	-	-	-	-	-	-	-	-

Notes: Please refer to the User's Guide for an explanation of data; data is arranged alphabetically by state, then county, then city within each county; table includes counties with populations greater than 49,999 unless noted and cities with populations greater than 9,999 whose Asian and/or NHPI population rates are greater than the national average; (1) Native Hawaiian and other Pacific Islander; (2) excludes Taiwanese; (3) includes Chamorro; (4) county does not meet population threshold but is shown in order to allow inclusion of city

Place	All specified owner-occupied housing units	Specified housing units owned and occup. by Asians	Specified housing units owned and occup. by NHPIs[1]	Asian Indian	Bangladeshi	Cambodian	Chinese[2]	Fijian	Filipino	Guamanian[3]	Hawaiian, Native	Hmong	Indonesian	Japanese	Korean	Laotian	Malaysian	Pakistani	Samoan	Sri Lankan	Taiwanese	Thai	Tongan	Vietnamese
Tehama County	103,000	100,900	-	-	-	-	-	-	-	-	-	-	-	-	-	-	-	-	-	-	-	-	-	-
Tulare County	97,800	99,200	-	89,400	-	-	116,400	-	93,800	-	-	74,400	-	119,800	163,600	86,300	-	-	-	-	-	-	-	-
Porterville (city)	93,500	111,300	-	-	-	-	-	-	105,200	-	-	-	-	-	-	-	-	-	-	-	-	-	-	-
Visalia (city)	115,300	123,800	-	-	-	-	-	-	134,100	-	-	75,000	-	-	-	86,400	-	-	-	-	-	-	-	-
Tuolumne County	149,800	164,300	-	-	-	-	-	-	-	-	-	-	-	-	-	-	-	-	-	-	-	-	-	-
Ventura County	248,700	251,600	247,700	311,200	-	-	311,800	-	214,500	-	257,300	-	-	246,800	289,500	-	-	-	193,100	-	361,100	-	-	247,800
Camarillo (city)	252,100	276,700	-	-	-	-	296,300	-	257,100	-	-	-	-	294,600	281,000	-	-	-	-	-	-	-	-	291,200
Moorpark (city)	281,300	281,600	-	-	-	-	-	-	-	-	-	-	-	-	-	-	-	-	-	-	-	-	-	-
Oxnard (city)	189,400	193,400	195,500	216,100	-	-	180,600	-	194,900	-	-	-	-	183,300	198,400	-	-	-	190,900	-	-	-	-	232,300
Port Hueneme (city)	165,200	167,700	-	-	-	-	-	-	188,400	-	-	-	-	-	-	-	-	-	-	-	-	-	-	-
Simi Valley (city)	239,900	251,700	-	293,500	-	-	253,800	-	230,300	-	-	-	-	252,200	333,800	-	-	-	-	-	-	-	-	233,800
Thousand Oaks (city)	324,800	355,200	-	383,800	-	-	393,100	-	244,600	-	-	-	-	339,100	352,400	-	-	-	-	-	-	-	-	249,200
Yolo County	169,800	224,100	142,400	191,100	-	-	264,300	164,100	182,900	-	-	0	-	228,100	217,300	0	-	-	-	-	-	-	-	211,800
Davis (city)	238,500	255,000	-	232,500	-	-	271,400	-	194,200	-	-	-	-	257,700	230,800	-	-	-	-	-	-	-	-	244,400
West Sacramento (city)	113,000	144,500	-	169,400	-	-	-	-	-	-	-	0	-	-	-	-	-	-	-	-	-	-	-	-
Woodland (city)	153,100	153,600	-	165,400	-	-	-	-	-	-	-	-	-	-	-	-	-	-	-	-	-	-	-	-
Yuba County	89,700	92,900	-	-	-	-	-	-	94,800	-	-	87,100	-	-	-	-	-	-	-	-	-	-	-	-
Linda (cdp)	82,200	87,000	-	-	-	-	-	-	-	-	-	86,100	-	-	-	-	-	-	-	-	-	-	-	-
Marysville (city)	89,000	96,000	-	-	-	-	-	-	-	-	-	-	-	-	-	-	-	-	-	-	-	-	-	-
Olivehurst (cdp)	79,000	83,800	-	-	-	-	-	-	-	-	-	-	-	-	-	-	-	-	-	-	-	-	-	-
COLORADO	166,600	180,800	148,500	230,000	-	151,800	197,300	-	156,800	141,500	160,500	163,000	185,000	170,500	190,000	165,300	-	175,000	145,500	-	237,500	161,400	-	168,300
Adams County	149,800	160,500	-	214,300	-	-	175,700	-	162,100	-	-	160,600	-	131,300	205,100	155,300	-	-	-	-	-	-	-	163,800
Berkley (cdp)	143,100	153,800	-	-	-	-	-	-	-	-	-	-	-	-	-	-	-	-	-	-	-	-	-	-
Federal Heights (city)	143,100	164,900	-	-	-	-	-	-	-	-	-	-	-	-	-	-	-	-	-	-	-	-	-	-
Westminster (city)	170,400	186,400	-	234,800	-	-	190,300	-	-	-	-	178,500	-	-	213,600	175,500	-	-	-	-	-	-	-	167,900
Arapahoe County	171,700	172,900	156,800	210,900	-	-	167,900	-	158,700	-	-	-	-	159,200	190,100	-	-	-	-	-	-	-	-	173,500
Aurora (city)	144,600	149,500	115,600	166,700	-	138,800	149,000	-	144,600	-	-	-	-	138,800	155,700	-	-	-	-	-	-	-	-	159,400
Boulder County	241,900	249,300	-	311,300	-	-	262,700	-	219,400	-	-	-	-	246,100	223,800	-	-	-	-	-	-	-	-	225,000
Boulder (city)	304,700	390,700	-	417,500	-	-	430,000	-	-	-	-	-	-	365,000	500,000	-	-	-	-	-	-	-	-	-
Broomfield (city)	189,800	189,900	-	-	-	-	228,900	-	-	-	-	-	-	-	-	-	-	-	-	-	-	-	-	-
Lafayette (city)	193,700	201,900	-	-	-	-	-	-	-	-	-	-	-	-	-	-	-	-	-	-	-	-	-	-
Denver County	165,800	165,100	154,500	189,200	-	135,300	184,700	-	152,400	-	-	-	-	174,500	190,200	-	-	-	-	-	-	306,300	-	156,300
Douglas County	236,000	242,400	-	245,200	-	-	229,300	-	-	-	-	-	-	-	263,800	-	-	-	-	-	-	-	-	-
Highlands Ranch (cdp)	235,100	239,900	-	244,300	-	-	227,400	-	-	-	-	-	-	-	-	-	-	-	-	-	-	-	-	-
El Paso County	147,100	149,800	131,400	233,100	-	-	216,500	-	136,300	136,400	-	-	-	117,100	149,200	-	-	-	-	-	-	-	-	135,900
Colorado Springs (city)	147,100	163,300	114,400	233,100	-	-	208,600	-	140,900	-	-	-	-	134,100	164,900	-	-	-	-	-	-	-	-	140,800
Jefferson County	187,900	196,000	180,000	231,000	-	-	195,500	-	179,300	-	-	201,500	-	189,700	198,100	184,100	-	-	-	-	-	-	-	213,900
Larimer County	172,000	178,900	-	170,800	-	-	175,800	-	-	-	-	-	-	183,600	165,600	-	-	-	-	-	-	-	-	-
Mesa County	118,900	131,300	-	-	-	-	-	-	-	-	-	-	-	-	-	-	-	-	-	-	-	-	-	-
Pueblo County	95,200	135,100	-	-	-	-	-	-	-	-	-	-	-	-	-	-	-	-	-	-	-	-	-	-
Weld County	140,400	158,300	-	-	-	-	-	-	-	-	-	-	-	157,500	-	-	-	-	-	-	-	-	-	-

Notes: Please refer to the User's Guide for an explanation of data; data is arranged alphabetically by state, then county, then city within each county; table includes counties with populations greater than 49,999 unless noted and cities with populations greater than 9,999 whose Asian and/or NHPI population rates are greater than the national average; (1) Native Hawaiian and other Pacific Islander; (2) excludes Taiwanese; (3) includes Chamorro; (4) county does not meet population threshold but is shown in order to allow inclusion of city

Place	All specified owner-occupied housing units	Specified housing units owned and occup. by Asians	Specified housing units owned and occup. by NHPIs[1]	Asian Indian	Bangladeshi	Cambodian	Chinese[2]	Fijian	Filipino	Guamanian[3]	Hawaiian, Native	Hmong	Indonesian	Japanese	Korean	Laotian	Malaysian	Pakistani	Samoan	Sri Lankan	Taiwanese	Thai	Tongan	Vietnamese
CONNECTICUT	166,900	196,800	196,200	237,800	281,300	162,700	226,700	-	158,300	138,800	-	-	-	233,300	251,200	129,000	-	146,100	-	-	179,200	310,700	-	128,800
Fairfield County	288,900	300,700	-	349,100	-	164,900	354,300	-	228,800	-	-	-	-	463,800	463,500	144,900	-	210,700	-	-	-	-	-	139,800
Danbury (city)	186,500	168,000	-	159,600	-	162,200	204,400	-	-	-	-	-	-	-	-	-	-	-	-	-	-	-	-	-
Greenwich (town)	781,500	655,300	-	541,700	-	-	736,100	-	-	-	-	-	-	625,000	-	-	-	-	-	-	-	-	-	-
Stamford (city)	362,300	369,300	-	424,700	-	-	367,100	-	283,600	-	-	-	-	-	-	-	-	-	-	-	-	-	-	-
Hartford County	147,300	166,700	-	201,800	-	-	201,900	-	180,000	-	-	-	-	192,200	198,200	125,800	-	145,000	-	-	-	-	-	125,400
East Hartford (town)	112,800	113,700	-	113,500	-	-	-	-	-	-	-	-	-	-	-	-	-	-	-	-	-	-	-	105,400
Farmington (town)	194,300	228,100	-	-	-	-	-	-	-	-	-	-	-	-	-	-	-	-	-	-	-	-	-	-
Glastonbury (town)	218,900	252,600	-	292,400	-	-	-	-	-	-	-	-	-	-	-	-	-	-	-	-	-	-	-	-
Rocky Hill (town)	165,400	263,200	-	-	-	-	-	-	-	-	-	-	-	-	-	-	-	-	-	-	-	-	-	-
South Windsor (town)	167,500	233,900	-	-	-	-	-	-	-	-	-	-	-	-	-	-	-	-	-	-	-	-	-	-
West Hartford (town)	176,400	154,300	-	153,700	-	-	166,200	-	-	-	-	-	-	-	-	-	-	-	-	-	-	-	-	134,800
Litchfield County	156,600	193,800	-	216,100	-	-	187,500	-	-	-	-	-	-	-	122,900	-	-	-	-	-	-	-	-	134,600
Middlesex County	166,000	161,500	-	258,300	-	-	200,000	-	-	-	-	-	-	-	-	-	-	-	-	-	-	-	-	-
New Haven County	151,900	172,700	-	181,500	-	-	189,300	-	133,600	-	-	-	-	153,100	264,600	121,900	-	117,600	-	-	-	-	-	116,400
New Haven (city)	109,200	125,000	-	1 Mil.+	-	-	132,500	-	-	-	-	-	-	-	12,500	-	-	-	-	-	-	-	-	-
New London County	142,200	148,500	-	212,500	-	-	170,400	-	116,500	-	-	-	-	-	-	-	-	-	-	-	-	-	-	-
Tolland County	151,600	146,800	-	200,000	-	-	160,000	-	-	-	-	-	-	-	-	-	-	-	-	-	-	-	-	-
Mansfield (town)	146,300	187,500	-	313,600	-	-	22,500	-	-	-	-	-	-	-	-	-	-	-	-	-	-	-	-	-
Storrs (cdp)	146,400	0	-	-	-	-	0	-	-	-	-	-	-	-	-	-	-	-	-	-	-	-	-	-
Windham County	117,200	128,900	-	-	-	-	-	-	-	-	-	-	-	-	-	-	-	-	-	-	-	-	-	-
DELAWARE	130,400	173,500	133,100	196,900	-	-	172,700	-	151,600	-	-	-	-	135,700	183,500	-	-	195,800	-	-	-	-	-	186,700
Kent County	114,100	139,100	-	182,800	-	-	-	-	120,400	-	-	-	-	-	-	-	-	-	-	-	-	-	-	-
New Castle County	136,000	183,800	-	201,600	-	-	180,600	-	167,000	-	-	-	-	135,600	194,000	-	-	-	-	-	-	-	-	187,500
Hockessin (cdp)	250,800	282,400	-	-	-	-	-	-	-	-	-	-	-	-	-	-	-	-	-	-	-	-	-	-
Newark (city)	153,300	198,300	-	-	-	-	180,400	-	-	-	-	-	-	-	-	-	-	-	-	-	-	-	-	-
Pike Creek (cdp)	161,300	193,300	-	-	-	-	-	-	-	-	-	-	-	-	-	-	-	-	-	-	-	-	-	-
Sussex County	122,400	135,900	-	-	-	-	-	-	-	-	-	-	-	-	-	-	-	-	-	-	-	-	-	-
DISTRICT OF COLUMBIA	157,200	325,900	-	367,000	-	-	295,200	-	196,100	-	-	-	-	344,000	361,400	-	-	-	-	-	-	-	-	211,400
FLORIDA	105,500	119,700	92,000	142,500	117,900	88,800	131,600	-	110,400	96,800	92,600	-	112,900	114,100	135,300	77,800	-	143,200	78,000	151,000	189,600	94,400	-	91,500
Alachua County	97,300	133,700	-	130,700	-	-	131,500	-	151,600	-	-	-	-	157,000	118,400	-	-	-	-	-	-	-	-	90,000
Gainesville (city)	86,300	99,200	-	96,300	-	-	134,700	-	-	-	-	-	-	-	137,500	-	-	-	-	-	-	-	-	-
Bay County	93,500	83,500	-	-	-	-	-	-	86,500	-	-	-	-	-	-	-	-	-	-	-	-	-	-	64,100
Callaway (city)	93,100	91,900	-	-	-	-	-	-	-	-	-	-	-	-	-	-	-	-	-	-	-	-	-	-
Brevard County	94,400	107,000	-	140,700	-	-	130,200	-	87,100	-	-	-	-	101,000	88,200	-	-	-	-	-	-	-	-	98,300
Broward County	128,600	137,400	108,000	137,400	-	-	134,800	-	150,600	-	-	-	-	142,100	155,000	-	-	140,900	-	-	-	115,200	-	111,800
Cooper City (city)	154,200	156,700	-	156,700	-	-	-	-	-	-	-	-	-	-	-	-	-	-	-	-	-	-	-	-
Pembroke Pines (city)	143,200	155,500	-	146,000	-	-	159,000	-	167,400	-	-	-	-	-	-	-	-	-	-	-	-	-	-	-
Charlotte County	97,000	98,900	-	-	-	-	-	-	-	-	-	-	-	-	-	-	-	-	-	-	-	-	-	-
Citrus County	84,400	106,500	-	-	-	-	-	-	-	-	-	-	-	-	-	-	-	-	-	-	-	-	-	-
Clay County	108,400	115,600	-	-	-	-	-	-	116,500	-	-	-	-	-	-	-	-	-	-	-	-	-	-	-

Notes: Please refer to the User's Guide for an explanation of data; data is arranged alphabetically by state, then county, then city within each county; table includes counties with populations greater than 49,999 unless noted and cities with populations greater than 9,999 whose Asian and/or NHPI population rates are greater than the national average; (1) Native Hawaiian and other Pacific Islander; (2) excludes Taiwanese; (3) includes Chamorro; (4) county does not meet population threshold but is shown in order to allow inclusion of city

Place	All specified owner-occupied housing units	Specified housing units owned and occup. by Asians	Specified housing units owned and occup. by NHPIs[1]	Asian Indian	Bangladeshi	Cambodian	Chinese[2]	Fijian	Filipino	Guamanian[3]	Hawaiian, Native	Hmong	Indonesian	Japanese	Korean	Laotian	Malaysian	Pakistani	Samoan	Sri Lankan	Taiwanese	Thai	Tongan	Vietnamese
Bellair-Meadowbrook Ter. (cdp)	86,400	98,200	-	-	-	-	-	-	-	-	-	-	-	-	-	-	-	-	-	-	-	-	-	-
Collier County	168,000	223,800	-	-	-	-	-	-	-	-	-	-	-	-	-	-	-	-	-	-	-	-	-	-
Columbia County	73,600	88,600	-	-	-	-	-	-	-	-	-	-	-	-	-	-	-	-	-	-	-	-	-	-
Duval County	89,600	104,100	81,100	162,000	-	83,900	134,300	-	99,600	-	-	-	-	100,500	125,300	-	-	-	-	-	-	-	-	72,900
Escambia County	85,700	82,000	-	101,600	-	-	133,700	-	80,700	-	-	-	-	-	-	-	-	-	-	-	-	-	-	66,900
Bellview (cdp)	80,300	81,600	-	-	-	-	-	-	87,800	-	-	-	-	-	-	-	-	-	-	-	-	-	-	-
Myrtle Grove (cdp)	78,800	77,900	-	-	-	-	-	-	80,900	-	-	-	-	-	-	-	-	-	-	-	-	-	-	-
Hernando County	87,300	89,300	-	-	-	-	-	-	-	-	-	-	-	-	-	-	-	-	-	-	-	-	-	-
Highlands County	72,800	99,700	-	-	-	-	-	-	110,400	-	-	-	-	-	-	-	-	-	-	-	-	-	-	-
Hillsborough County	97,700	120,400	106,900	150,200	-	-	136,200	-	105,400	-	-	-	-	104,900	133,400	-	-	-	-	-	-	83,900	-	85,000
Westchase (cdp)	173,800	223,100	-	-	-	-	-	-	-	-	-	-	-	-	-	-	-	-	-	-	-	-	-	-
Indian River County	104,000	89,100	-	-	-	-	-	-	-	-	-	-	-	-	-	-	-	-	-	-	-	-	-	-
Lake County	100,600	127,900	-	-	-	-	-	-	-	-	-	-	-	-	-	-	-	-	-	-	-	-	-	-
Lee County	112,900	121,500	-	123,300	-	-	145,400	-	100,900	-	-	-	-	-	-	-	-	-	-	-	-	-	-	-
Leon County	110,900	137,300	-	161,400	-	-	163,300	-	79,700	-	-	-	-	-	148,800	-	-	-	-	-	-	-	-	-
Manatee County	119,400	120,500	-	-	-	-	-	-	114,300	-	-	-	-	-	-	-	-	-	-	-	-	-	-	-
Marion County	81,300	111,900	-	160,300	-	-	-	-	-	-	-	-	-	-	-	-	-	-	-	-	-	-	-	-
Martin County	152,400	210,200	-	-	-	-	-	-	-	-	-	-	-	-	-	-	-	-	-	-	-	-	-	-
Miami-Dade County	124,000	132,300	97,100	142,600	-	-	134,300	-	127,500	-	-	-	-	133,200	133,100	-	-	122,200	-	-	-	122,700	-	118,100
Doral (cdp)	178,500	159,400	-	-	-	-	-	-	-	-	-	-	-	-	-	-	-	-	-	-	-	-	-	-
Ives Estates (cdp)	102,400	101,600	-	-	-	-	-	-	-	-	-	-	-	-	-	-	-	-	-	-	-	-	-	-
North Miami Beach (city)	93,000	88,200	-	82,100	-	-	86,700	-	-	-	-	-	-	-	-	-	-	-	-	-	-	-	-	-
Pinecrest (village)	393,900	202,800	-	-	-	-	-	-	-	-	-	-	-	-	-	-	-	-	-	-	-	-	-	-
Monroe County	241,200	129,900	-	-	-	-	-	-	-	-	-	-	-	-	-	-	-	-	-	-	-	-	-	-
Nassau County	126,700	97,900	-	-	-	-	-	-	-	-	-	-	-	-	-	-	-	-	-	-	-	-	-	-
Okaloosa County	101,200	97,400	-	-	-	-	-	-	91,800	-	-	-	-	-	125,000	-	-	-	-	-	-	90,000	-	148,300
Wright (cdp)	94,500	108,900	-	-	-	-	-	-	-	-	-	-	-	-	-	-	-	-	-	-	-	-	-	-
Orange County	107,500	123,900	85,600	141,800	-	-	134,300	-	122,100	-	-	-	-	109,300	174,200	-	-	182,000	-	-	-	-	-	95,700
Oak Ridge (cdp)	81,100	83,700	-	-	-	-	-	-	-	-	-	-	-	-	-	-	-	-	-	-	-	-	-	85,900
Osceola County	99,300	112,500	-	97,600	-	-	119,900	-	111,400	-	-	-	-	-	-	-	-	-	-	-	-	-	-	-
Palm Beach County	135,200	141,000	117,000	153,300	-	-	155,900	-	143,100	-	-	-	-	154,600	154,200	-	-	-	-	-	-	104,700	-	113,100
Pasco County	79,600	117,400	-	149,300	-	-	90,000	-	118,500	-	-	-	-	-	-	-	-	-	-	-	-	-	-	-
Pinellas County	96,500	86,600	-	175,000	-	75,700	109,100	-	85,100	-	-	-	-	140,000	76,800	68,700	-	-	-	-	-	77,900	-	75,300
Pinellas Park (city)	75,500	77,900	-	-	-	-	-	-	-	-	-	-	-	-	-	-	-	-	-	-	-	-	-	80,300
Polk County	83,300	96,500	-	111,300	-	-	87,800	-	103,100	-	-	-	-	-	-	62,900	-	-	-	-	-	-	-	62,900
Putnam County	68,500	112,500	-	-	-	-	-	-	-	-	-	-	-	-	-	-	-	-	-	-	-	-	-	-
St. Johns County	158,400	155,900	-	-	-	-	-	-	-	-	-	-	-	-	-	-	-	-	-	-	-	-	-	-
St. Lucie County	86,100	94,800	-	-	-	-	-	-	-	-	-	-	-	-	-	-	-	-	-	-	-	-	-	-
Santa Rosa County	106,000	121,500	-	-	-	-	-	-	77,800	-	-	-	-	-	-	-	-	-	-	-	-	-	-	-
Sarasota County	122,000	97,800	-	-	-	-	101,000	-	102,800	-	-	-	-	-	-	-	-	-	-	-	-	-	-	79,400
Seminole County	119,900	135,000	-	163,800	-	-	136,500	-	125,400	-	-	-	-	-	171,900	-	-	-	-	-	-	-	-	118,400

Notes: Please refer to the User's Guide for an explanation of data; data is arranged alphabetically by state, then county, then city within each county; table includes counties with populations greater than 49,999 unless noted and cities with populations greater than 9,999 whose Asian and/or NHPI population rates are greater than the national average; (1) Native Hawaiian and other Pacific Islander; (2) excludes Taiwanese; (3) includes Chamorro; (4) county does not meet population threshold but is shown in order to allow inclusion of city

Place	All specified owner-occupied housing units	Specified housing units owned and occup. by Asians	Specified housing units owned and occup. by NHPIs[1]	Asian Indian	Bangladeshi	Cambodian	Chinese[2]	Fijian	Filipino	Guamanian[3]	Hawaiian, Native	Hmong	Indonesian	Japanese	Korean	Laotian	Malaysian	Pakistani	Samoan	Sri Lankan	Taiwanese	Thai	Tongan	Vietnamese
Volusia County	87,300	98,800	-	114,300	-	-	109,200	-	107,100	-	-	-	-	-	88,000	-	-	-	-	-	-	-	-	-
GEORGIA	111,200	146,000	100,200	167,700	146,700	104,300	164,500	-	118,800	95,600	100,900	125,200	161,600	139,400	163,300	98,300	-	150,800	120,000	-	176,700	128,500	-	119,400
Bartow County	99,600	127,500	-	-	-	-	-	-	-	-	-	-	-	-	-	-	-	-	-	-	-	-	-	-
Bibb County	84,400	135,000	-	-	-	-	-	-	-	-	-	-	-	-	-	-	-	-	-	-	-	-	-	-
Bulloch County	94,300	125,000	-	-	-	-	-	-	-	-	-	-	-	-	-	-	-	-	-	-	-	-	-	-
Carroll County	93,300	94,000	-	-	-	-	-	-	-	-	-	-	-	-	-	-	-	-	-	-	-	-	-	-
Catoosa County	90,800	117,500	-	-	-	-	-	-	-	-	-	-	-	-	-	-	-	-	-	-	-	-	-	-
Chatham County	95,000	106,400	-	98,000	-	-	122,300	-	-	-	-	-	-	-	79,100	-	-	-	-	-	-	-	-	95,000
Cherokee County	139,900	116,100	-	152,500	-	-	-	-	-	-	-	-	-	-	-	-	-	-	-	-	-	-	-	-
Clarke County	111,300	135,600	-	139,400	-	-	159,800	-	-	-	-	-	-	-	350,000	-	-	-	-	-	-	-	-	-
Clayton County	92,700	89,900	-	131,700	-	96,100	90,700	-	-	-	-	-	-	-	-	84,700	-	88,300	-	-	-	-	-	87,600
Forest Park (city)	69,600	76,400	-	-	-	-	-	-	-	-	-	-	-	-	-	-	-	-	-	-	-	-	-	76,100
Riverdale (city)	90,500	89,700	-	-	-	-	-	-	-	-	-	-	-	-	-	-	-	-	-	-	-	-	-	90,000
Cobb County	147,600	162,000	-	175,500	-	-	159,300	-	148,700	-	-	-	-	159,000	172,000	-	-	117,200	-	-	-	-	-	141,300
Smyrna (city)	129,700	142,600	-	194,200	-	-	-	-	-	-	-	-	-	-	-	-	-	-	-	-	-	-	-	-
Columbia County	118,000	154,900	-	187,000	-	-	146,300	-	-	-	-	-	-	-	135,000	-	-	-	-	-	-	-	-	-
Martinez (cdp)	105,200	137,500	-	160,300	-	-	-	-	-	-	-	-	-	-	-	-	-	-	-	-	-	-	-	-
Coweta County	121,700	129,200	-	-	-	-	-	-	-	-	-	-	-	-	-	-	-	-	-	-	-	-	-	-
DeKalb County	135,100	150,600	-	202,800	162,500	108,400	167,400	-	97,400	-	-	-	-	226,700	194,700	-	-	-	-	-	-	-	-	124,900
Druid Hills (cdp)	337,400	275,000	-	-	-	-	-	-	-	-	-	-	-	-	-	-	-	-	-	-	-	-	-	-
Dunwoody (cdp)	277,400	273,400	-	298,300	-	-	-	-	-	-	-	-	-	-	278,600	-	-	-	-	-	-	-	-	-
North Atlanta (cdp)	252,400	230,000	-	-	-	-	-	-	-	-	-	-	-	-	-	-	-	-	-	-	-	-	-	-
North Decatur (cdp)	194,700	242,600	-	-	-	-	-	-	-	-	-	-	-	-	-	-	-	-	-	-	-	-	-	-
North Druid Hills (cdp)	226,400	307,100	-	0	-	-	-	-	-	-	-	-	-	-	-	-	-	-	-	-	-	-	-	-
Tucker (cdp)	157,800	148,400	-	-	-	-	-	-	-	-	-	-	-	-	-	-	-	-	-	-	-	-	-	187,500
Dougherty County	73,900	171,900	-	-	-	-	-	-	-	-	-	-	-	-	-	-	-	-	-	-	-	-	-	-
Douglas County	102,700	169,100	-	-	-	-	-	-	-	-	-	-	-	-	-	-	-	-	-	-	-	-	-	-
Fayette County	171,500	175,600	-	-	-	-	-	-	-	-	-	-	-	146,600	-	-	-	-	-	-	-	-	-	-
Peachtree City (city)	190,900	176,500	-	-	-	-	-	-	-	-	-	-	-	146,600	-	-	-	-	-	-	-	-	-	-
Floyd County	83,500	152,200	-	210,700	-	-	-	-	-	-	-	-	-	-	-	-	-	-	-	-	-	-	-	-
Forsyth County	184,600	230,600	-	-	-	-	-	-	-	-	-	-	-	-	-	-	-	-	-	-	-	-	-	-
Fulton County	180,700	219,500	-	238,000	-	-	217,300	-	186,800	-	-	-	-	197,100	254,700	-	-	-	-	-	-	-	-	167,200
Alpharetta (city)	226,300	272,100	-	307,700	-	-	280,400	-	-	-	-	-	-	-	-	-	-	-	-	-	-	-	-	-
Roswell (city)	207,700	200,500	-	310,300	-	-	219,000	-	-	-	-	-	-	-	268,300	-	-	-	-	-	-	-	-	-
Glynn County	114,500	96,900	-	-	-	-	-	-	-	-	-	-	-	-	-	-	-	-	-	-	-	-	-	-
Gwinnett County	142,100	148,300	130,700	158,900	-	127,700	167,100	-	144,400	-	-	-	-	130,100	157,700	113,000	-	160,600	-	-	180,700	-	-	132,400
Duluth (city)	152,400	168,500	-	170,400	-	-	167,900	-	-	-	-	-	-	-	176,000	-	-	-	-	-	-	-	-	-
Lilburn (city)	133,300	132,100	-	143,400	-	-	-	-	-	-	-	-	-	-	-	-	-	-	-	-	-	-	-	133,700
Mountain Park (cdp)	138,300	154,600	-	179,700	-	-	-	-	-	-	-	-	-	-	-	-	-	-	-	-	-	-	-	-
Hall County	120,200	118,900	-	-	-	-	-	-	-	-	-	-	-	-	-	-	-	-	-	-	-	-	-	111,600
Henry County	122,400	141,900	-	138,100	-	-	-	-	-	-	-	-	-	-	-	-	-	-	-	-	-	-	-	-

Notes: Please refer to the User's Guide for an explanation of data; data is arranged alphabetically by state, then county, then city within each county; table includes counties with populations greater than 49,999 unless noted and cities with populations greater than 9,999 whose Asian and/or NHPI population rates are greater than the national average; (1) Native Hawaiian and other Pacific Islander; (2) excludes Taiwanese; (3) includes Chamorro; (4) county does not meet population threshold but is shown in order to allow inclusion of city

Place	All specified owner-occupied housing units	Specified housing units owned and occup. by Asians	Specified housing units owned and occup. by NHPIs[1]	Asian Indian	Bangladeshi	Cambodian	Chinese[2]	Fijian	Filipino	Guamanian[3]	Hawaiian, Native	Hmong	Indonesian	Japanese	Korean	Laotian	Malaysian	Pakistani	Samoan	Sri Lankan	Taiwanese	Thai	Tongan	Vietnamese
Houston County	88,900	111,400	-	-	-	-	-	-	64,200	-	-	-	-	-	-	-	-	-	-	-	-	-	-	-
Liberty County	79,800	65,800	-	-	-	-	-	-	-	-	-	-	-	-	65,000	-	-	-	-	-	-	-	-	-
Lowndes County	87,600	94,400	-	-	-	-	-	-	-	-	-	-	-	-	-	-	-	-	-	-	-	-	-	-
Muscogee County	84,000	102,100	86,100	167,000	-	-	145,800	-	93,300	-	-	-	-	-	70,800	-	-	-	-	-	-	-	-	-
Columbus (sp. city)	84,100	102,100	86,100	167,000	-	-	145,800	-	93,300	-	-	-	-	-	70,800	-	-	-	-	-	-	-	-	-
Newton County	101,300	104,700	-	-	-	-	-	-	-	-	-	-	-	-	-	-	-	-	-	-	-	-	-	-
Richmond County	76,800	78,600	-	123,900	-	-	83,700	-	-	-	-	-	-	-	66,800	-	-	-	-	-	-	-	-	-
Rockdale County	118,000	164,400	-	-	-	-	-	-	-	-	-	-	-	-	-	-	-	-	-	-	-	-	-	-
Spalding County	86,600	93,600	-	-	-	-	-	-	-	-	-	-	-	-	-	-	-	-	-	-	-	-	-	-
Troup County	83,700	122,200	-	-	-	-	-	-	-	-	-	-	-	-	-	-	-	-	-	-	-	-	-	-
Walton County	113,300	133,800	-	-	-	-	-	-	-	-	-	-	-	-	-	-	-	-	-	-	-	-	-	-
Whitfield County	91,800	94,600	-	-	-	-	-	-	-	-	-	-	-	-	-	-	-	-	-	-	-	-	-	-
HAWAII	272,700	280,200	213,100	296,400	-	0	348,400	-	239,200	282,400	209,300	-	-	286,900	311,100	230,000	-	-	200,000	-	568,500	234,400	255,600	249,200
Hawaii County	153,700	149,700	134,800	-	-	-	160,900	-	125,900	-	133,900	-	-	157,600	192,500	-	-	-	107,500	-	-	-	-	-
Hilo (cdp)	153,800	153,700	130,400	-	-	-	157,800	-	137,000	-	129,300	-	-	155,400	177,400	-	-	-	-	-	-	-	-	-
Honolulu County	309,000	311,100	255,100	313,200	-	-	356,400	-	264,400	280,500	256,600	-	-	321,700	331,000	262,500	-	-	209,100	-	586,300	265,600	247,200	289,200
Ewa Beach (cdp)	224,600	232,500	207,200	-	-	-	-	-	236,400	-	215,800	-	-	224,700	-	-	-	-	173,800	-	-	-	-	-
Halawa (cdp)	316,000	315,400	323,900	-	-	-	299,700	-	331,000	-	337,000	-	-	309,300	-	-	-	-	275,000	-	-	-	-	-
Honolulu (cdp)	386,700	378,400	356,900	434,600	-	-	392,800	-	341,400	330,000	358,000	-	-	378,800	407,700	0	-	-	316,700	-	645,800	875,000	248,600	317,700
Kailua (cdp)	367,100	337,000	339,200	-	-	-	351,000	-	321,700	-	342,500	-	-	330,300	327,800	-	-	-	-	-	-	-	-	-
Kaneohe (cdp)	298,700	298,500	278,400	-	-	-	319,000	-	304,100	-	276,700	-	-	294,200	341,000	-	-	-	-	-	-	-	-	-
Kaneohe Station (cdp)	202,500	0	-	-	-	-	-	-	-	-	-	-	-	-	-	-	-	-	-	-	-	-	-	-
Makakilo City (cdp)	243,300	241,900	224,400	-	-	-	-	-	228,300	-	224,400	-	-	241,000	-	-	-	-	-	-	-	-	-	-
Mililani Town (cdp)	276,700	279,600	275,000	-	-	-	289,900	-	264,000	-	282,500	-	-	285,300	261,300	-	-	-	-	-	-	-	-	-
Nanakuli (cdp)	148,600	172,600	138,700	-	-	-	-	-	190,600	-	138,400	-	-	-	-	-	-	-	122,100	-	-	-	-	-
Pearl City (cdp)	277,600	278,000	298,400	-	-	-	281,200	-	286,500	-	284,400	-	-	277,400	302,100	-	-	-	-	-	-	-	-	-
Schofield Barracks (cdp)	75,000	0	-	-	-	-	-	-	-	-	-	-	-	-	-	-	-	-	-	-	-	-	-	-
Wahiawa (cdp)	240,300	245,600	219,400	-	-	-	-	-	257,400	-	217,700	-	-	243,300	-	-	-	-	-	-	-	-	-	-
Waianae (cdp)	160,800	178,100	126,000	-	-	-	-	-	175,300	-	122,000	-	-	186,800	-	-	-	-	-	-	-	-	-	-
Waimalu (cdp)	337,300	346,000	286,600	-	-	-	358,200	-	358,400	-	345,000	-	-	346,300	173,900	-	-	-	-	-	-	-	-	-
Waipahu (cdp)	265,100	263,500	253,100	-	-	-	257,700	-	279,200	-	265,600	-	-	237,200	-	-	-	-	235,400	-	-	-	-	-
Waipio (cdp)	259,700	261,000	221,900	-	-	-	-	-	260,600	-	195,500	-	-	262,500	-	-	-	-	-	-	-	-	-	-
Kauai County	216,100	194,400	173,300	-	-	-	243,200	-	184,300	-	175,600	-	-	199,700	-	-	-	-	-	-	-	-	-	-
Maui County	249,900	233,300	185,200	-	-	-	292,900	-	228,600	-	181,800	-	-	232,900	232,200	-	-	-	-	-	-	-	260,000	-
Kahului (cdp)	226,500	225,200	205,100	-	-	-	-	-	240,500	-	205,100	-	-	212,500	-	-	-	-	-	-	-	-	-	-
Kihei (cdp)	247,200	234,700	196,900	-	-	-	-	-	229,600	-	123,500	-	-	259,500	-	-	-	-	-	-	-	-	-	-
Wailuku (cdp)	247,100	254,800	203,400	-	-	-	-	-	259,600	-	203,400	-	-	250,500	-	-	-	-	-	-	-	-	-	-
IDAHO	106,300	110,300	95,700	160,400	-	-	116,000	-	93,700	-	96,900	-	-	116,100	110,000	105,300	-	-	-	-	-	-	-	106,600
Ada County	124,700	115,000	101,600	175,000	-	-	133,700	-	94,900	-	-	-	-	120,100	107,200	-	-	-	-	-	-	-	-	105,000
Bannock County	90,000	87,600	-	-	-	-	-	-	-	-	-	-	-	-	-	-	-	-	-	-	-	-	-	-
Bonneville County	93,500	95,600	-	-	-	-	-	-	-	-	-	-	-	-	-	-	-	-	-	-	-	-	-	-

Notes: Please refer to the User's Guide for an explanation of data; data is arranged alphabetically by state, then county, then city within each county; table includes counties with populations greater than 49,999 unless noted and cities with populations greater than 9,999 whose Asian and/or NHPI population rates are greater than the national average; (1) Native Hawaiian and other Pacific Islander; (2) excludes Taiwanese; (3) includes Chamorro; (4) county does not meet population threshold but is shown in order to allow inclusion of city

Place	All specified owner-occupied housing units	Specified housing units owned and occup. by Asians	Specified housing units owned and occup. by NHPIs[1]	Asian Indian	Bangladeshi	Cambodian	Chinese[2]	Fijian	Filipino	Guamanian[3]	Hawaiian, Native	Hmong	Indonesian	Japanese	Korean	Laotian	Malaysian	Pakistani	Samoan	Sri Lankan	Taiwanese	Thai	Tongan	Vietnamese
Canyon County	96,300	93,300	-	-	-	-	-	-	-	-	-	-	-	93,800	-	-	-	-	-	-	-	-	-	-
Kootenai County	120,100	134,100	-	-	-	-	-	-	-	-	-	-	-	-	-	-	-	-	-	-	-	-	-	-
Twin Falls County	93,800	106,500	-	-	-	-	-	-	-	-	-	-	-	-	-	-	-	-	-	-	-	-	-	-
ILLINOIS	130,800	191,900	114,800	201,000	168,800	154,800	196,900	-	182,300	91,400	69,200	-	163,500	197,700	222,600	119,000	167,200	183,500	134,100	210,700	300,000	178,900	-	171,000
Champaign County	94,700	115,200	-	141,500	-	-	116,300	-	76,500	-	-	-	-	131,300	174,000	-	-	-	-	-	-	-	-	100,000
Champaign (city)	91,300	96,300	-	130,000	-	-	113,100	-	-	-	-	-	-	-	84,300	-	-	-	-	-	-	-	-	88,100
Urbana (city)	89,300	90,800	-	95,000	-	-	86,800	-	-	-	-	-	-	-	162,500	-	-	-	-	-	-	-	-	-
Coles County	71,500	187,500	-	-	-	-	-	-	-	-	-	-	-	-	-	-	-	-	-	-	-	-	-	-
Cook County	157,700	191,500	140,000	193,600	-	193,100	183,500	-	182,200	-	-	-	275,000	201,700	230,900	141,500	-	174,200	-	-	270,300	191,100	-	191,000
Arlington Heights (village)	240,600	245,800	-	194,700	-	-	275,000	-	233,200	-	-	-	-	280,200	263,500	-	-	-	-	-	-	-	-	-
Chicago (city)	132,400	169,500	135,000	178,800	-	229,200	153,700	-	169,000	-	-	-	-	176,900	199,300	-	-	120,100	-	-	95,000	174,600	-	191,400
Des Plaines (city)	184,600	186,600	-	174,200	-	-	203,800	-	197,400	-	-	-	-	-	-	-	-	-	-	-	-	-	-	-
Elk Grove Village (village)	189,400	197,300	-	197,500	-	-	191,300	-	202,200	-	-	-	-	226,600	-	-	-	-	-	-	-	-	-	-
Evanston (city)	290,800	216,400	-	232,800	-	-	285,700	-	167,500	-	-	-	-	225,000	22,500	-	-	-	-	-	-	-	-	-
Forest Park (village)	138,300	127,200	-	-	-	-	-	-	-	-	-	-	-	-	-	-	-	-	-	-	-	-	-	-
Glenview (village)	336,000	348,400	-	402,800	-	-	297,800	-	277,100	-	-	-	-	342,500	335,500	-	-	-	-	-	-	-	-	-
Hanover Park (village)	141,500	145,500	-	140,900	-	-	-	-	141,200	-	-	-	-	-	-	-	-	-	-	-	-	-	-	-
Hoffman Estates (village)	181,700	187,900	-	177,000	-	-	214,700	-	185,500	-	-	-	-	279,500	187,700	-	-	-	-	-	-	-	-	-
Lincolnwood (village)	291,400	280,400	-	294,100	-	-	-	-	278,300	-	-	-	-	-	278,000	-	-	-	-	-	-	-	-	-
Morton Grove (village)	217,100	225,100	-	241,200	-	-	-	-	207,300	-	-	-	-	-	239,700	-	-	-	-	-	-	-	-	-
Mount Prospect (village)	217,700	206,300	-	199,500	-	-	171,900	-	191,900	-	-	-	-	217,900	234,000	-	-	-	-	-	-	-	-	-
Niles (village)	204,400	188,800	-	159,200	-	-	-	-	222,000	-	-	-	-	-	191,500	-	-	-	-	-	-	-	-	-
Northbrook (village)	370,800	338,800	-	-	-	-	348,200	-	-	-	-	-	-	-	318,900	-	-	-	-	-	-	-	-	-
Oak Park (village)	231,300	200,000	-	211,500	-	-	187,500	-	-	-	-	-	-	-	-	-	-	-	-	-	-	-	-	-
Orland Park (village)	208,300	224,900	-	262,500	-	-	-	-	206,800	-	-	-	-	-	-	-	-	-	-	-	-	-	-	-
Palatine (village)	199,200	196,000	-	192,000	-	-	215,600	-	173,900	-	-	-	-	-	278,300	-	-	-	-	-	-	-	-	-
Prospect Heights (city)	243,300	182,400	-	-	-	-	-	-	-	-	-	-	-	-	-	-	-	-	-	-	-	-	-	-
Rolling Meadows (city)	176,600	243,000	-	316,700	-	-	-	-	-	-	-	-	-	-	-	-	-	-	-	-	-	-	-	-
Schaumburg (village)	178,200	192,200	-	197,100	-	-	181,500	-	183,100	-	-	-	-	296,900	187,100	-	-	-	-	-	-	-	-	-
Schiller Park (village)	161,600	189,600	-	-	-	-	-	-	-	-	-	-	-	-	-	-	-	-	-	-	-	-	-	-
Skokie (village)	217,500	205,800	-	201,500	-	-	200,500	-	206,700	-	-	-	-	-	206,100	-	-	199,000	-	-	-	-	-	-
Streamwood (village)	143,500	175,800	-	178,200	-	-	-	-	179,700	-	-	-	-	-	-	-	-	-	-	-	-	-	-	-
Wheeling (village)	160,900	210,200	-	214,400	-	-	-	-	216,900	-	-	-	-	-	-	-	-	-	-	-	-	-	-	-
Wilmette (village)	441,600	297,200	-	-	-	-	290,400	-	-	-	-	-	-	273,800	305,800	-	-	-	-	-	-	-	-	-
DeKalb County	135,900	160,800	-	159,400	-	-	-	-	-	-	-	-	-	-	-	-	-	-	-	-	-	-	-	-
DeKalb (city)	130,200	166,500	-	159,000	-	-	-	-	-	-	-	-	-	-	-	-	-	-	-	-	-	-	-	-
DuPage County	195,000	205,500	-	215,000	-	-	235,000	-	189,800	-	-	-	-	195,700	200,700	-	-	201,200	-	-	323,000	187,500	-	158,200
Addison (village)	173,200	196,300	-	198,000	-	-	-	-	207,100	-	-	-	-	-	-	-	-	-	-	-	-	-	-	-
Bartlett (village)	204,700	221,800	-	233,800	-	-	-	-	195,200	-	-	-	-	-	-	-	-	-	-	-	-	-	-	-
Bensenville (village)	155,900	122,900	-	89,700	-	-	-	-	-	-	-	-	-	-	-	-	-	-	-	-	-	-	-	-
Bloomingdale (village)	209,200	239,200	-	199,500	-	-	-	-	-	-	-	-	-	-	-	-	-	-	-	-	-	-	-	-

Notes: Please refer to the User's Guide for an explanation of data; data is arranged alphabetically by state, then county, then city within each county; table includes counties with populations greater than 49,999 unless noted and cities with populations greater than 9,999 whose Asian and/or NHPI population rates are greater than the national average; (1) Native Hawaiian and other Pacific Islander; (2) excludes Taiwanese; (3) includes Chamorro; (4) county does not meet population threshold but is shown in order to allow inclusion of city

Place	All specified owner-occupied housing units	Specified housing units owned and occup. by Asians	Specified housing units owned and occup. by NHPIs[1]	Asian Indian	Bangladeshi	Cambodian	Chinese[2]	Fijian	Filipino	Guamanian[3]	Hawaiian, Native	Hmong	Indonesian	Japanese	Korean	Laotian	Malaysian	Pakistani	Samoan	Sri Lankan	Taiwanese	Thai	Tongan	Vietnamese
Burr Ridge (village)	477,800	589,300	-	613,200	-	-	-	-	-	-	-	-	-	-	-	-	-	-	-	-	-	-	-	-
Carol Stream (village)	170,400	190,900	-	193,800	-	-	-	-	198,900	-	-	-	-	-	-	-	-	-	-	-	-	-	-	170,800
Darien (city)	214,500	239,300	-	246,300	-	-	-	-	234,400	-	-	-	-	-	-	-	-	-	-	-	-	-	-	-
Downers Grove (village)	205,900	227,700	-	226,500	-	-	216,700	-	232,000	-	-	-	-	-	-	-	-	-	-	-	-	-	-	-
Glen Ellyn (village)	274,800	158,800	-	115,400	-	-	-	-	-	-	-	-	-	-	-	-	-	-	-	-	-	-	-	-
Glendale Heights (village)	142,800	151,500	-	155,400	-	-	-	-	150,800	-	-	-	-	-	-	-	-	-	-	-	-	-	-	146,600
Hinsdale (village)	520,100	301,200	-	-	-	-	-	-	-	-	-	-	-	-	-	-	-	-	-	-	-	-	-	-
Lisle (village)	219,200	232,100	-	227,400	-	-	253,800	-	-	-	-	-	-	-	-	-	-	-	-	-	-	-	-	-
Lombard (village)	168,500	180,600	-	194,000	-	-	-	-	167,700	-	-	-	-	-	-	-	-	-	-	-	-	-	-	-
Naperville (city)	254,200	259,600	-	271,200	-	-	261,000	-	302,000	-	-	-	-	-	227,300	-	-	-	-	-	263,100	-	-	-
Roselle (village)	169,900	169,400	-	166,100	-	-	-	-	-	-	-	-	-	-	-	-	-	-	-	-	-	-	-	-
Villa Park (village)	155,900	156,300	-	-	-	-	-	-	-	-	-	-	-	-	-	-	-	-	-	-	-	-	-	-
Warrenville (city)	148,900	194,600	-	-	-	-	-	-	-	-	-	-	-	-	-	-	-	-	-	-	-	-	-	-
Westmont (village)	180,200	214,500	-	196,400	-	-	238,000	-	182,000	-	-	-	-	-	-	-	-	-	-	-	-	-	-	-
Wheaton (city)	222,100	199,100	-	223,100	-	-	-	-	-	-	-	-	-	-	-	-	-	-	-	-	-	-	-	148,200
Woodridge (village)	168,400	188,200	-	202,700	-	-	-	-	171,900	-	-	-	-	-	-	-	-	-	-	-	-	-	-	-
Jackson County	68,200	114,300	-	-	-	-	66,700	-	-	-	-	-	-	-	-	-	-	-	-	-	-	-	-	-
Carbondale (city)	73,400	79,200	-	-	-	-	-	-	-	-	-	-	-	-	-	-	-	-	-	-	-	-	-	-
Kane County	160,400	172,000	-	200,800	-	-	158,300	-	188,800	-	-	-	-	-	176,300	140,900	-	-	-	-	-	-	-	146,600
South Elgin (village)	154,000	158,300	-	-	-	-	-	-	-	-	-	-	-	-	-	-	-	-	-	-	-	-	-	-
Kankakee County	99,200	178,500	-	-	-	-	-	-	-	-	-	-	-	-	-	-	-	-	-	-	-	-	-	-
Kendall County	154,900	170,200	-	-	-	-	-	-	-	-	-	-	-	-	-	-	-	-	-	-	-	-	-	-
Knox County	63,500	118,400	-	-	-	-	-	-	-	-	-	-	-	-	-	-	-	-	-	-	-	-	-	-
La Salle County	87,000	142,900	-	-	-	-	-	-	-	-	-	-	-	-	-	-	-	-	-	-	-	-	-	-
Lake County	198,200	232,600	-	227,900	-	-	268,600	-	189,100	-	-	-	-	242,900	276,900	-	-	168,800	-	-	-	-	-	188,900
Buffalo Grove (village)	236,200	254,600	-	262,500	-	-	261,100	-	197,900	-	-	-	-	246,900	266,700	-	-	-	-	-	-	-	-	-
Gages Lake (cdp)	161,800	232,500	-	-	-	-	-	-	-	-	-	-	-	-	-	-	-	-	-	-	-	-	-	-
Grayslake (village)	192,900	212,700	-	-	-	-	-	-	-	-	-	-	-	-	-	-	-	-	-	-	-	-	-	-
Gurnee (village)	199,000	219,800	-	210,300	-	-	234,400	-	237,000	-	-	-	-	-	-	-	-	-	-	-	-	-	-	-
Lake Zurich (village)	225,100	278,400	-	-	-	-	-	-	-	-	-	-	-	-	-	-	-	-	-	-	-	-	-	-
Libertyville (village)	263,700	275,000	-	-	-	-	-	-	-	-	-	-	-	-	-	-	-	-	-	-	-	-	-	-
Mundelein (village)	164,300	219,000	-	-	-	-	244,100	-	231,800	-	-	-	-	-	-	-	-	-	-	-	-	-	-	-
Vernon Hills (village)	223,300	249,400	-	227,700	-	-	283,100	-	-	-	-	-	-	-	245,000	-	-	-	-	-	-	-	-	-
Macon County	69,800	151,000	-	-	-	-	-	-	-	-	-	-	-	-	-	-	-	-	-	-	-	-	-	-
Madison County	77,200	96,900	-	136,000	-	-	-	-	-	-	-	-	-	-	-	-	-	-	-	-	-	-	-	-
McHenry County	168,100	188,700	-	182,500	-	-	203,300	-	191,000	-	-	-	-	-	-	-	-	-	-	-	-	-	-	-
McLean County	114,800	162,100	-	141,800	-	-	156,800	-	-	-	-	-	-	-	-	-	-	-	-	-	-	-	-	-
Peoria County	85,800	130,300	-	157,800	-	-	117,800	-	-	-	-	-	-	-	-	-	-	-	-	-	-	-	-	51,300
Rock Island County	78,900	127,400	-	229,500	-	-	-	-	-	-	-	-	-	-	-	-	-	-	-	-	-	-	-	-
St. Clair County	77,700	100,600	-	-	-	-	-	-	112,500	-	-	-	-	-	75,500	-	-	-	-	-	-	-	-	-
Sangamon County	91,200	130,900	-	175,000	-	-	138,800	-	-	-	-	-	-	-	-	-	-	-	-	-	-	-	-	-

Notes: Please refer to the User's Guide for an explanation of data; data is arranged alphabetically by state, then county, then city within each county; table includes counties with populations greater than 49,999 unless noted and cities with populations greater than 9,999 whose Asian and/or NHPI population rates are greater than the national average; (1) Native Hawaiian and other Pacific Islander; (2) excludes Taiwanese; (3) includes Chamorro; (4) county does not meet population threshold but is shown in order to allow inclusion of city

Place	All specified owner-occupied housing units	Specified housing units owned and occup. by Asians	Specified housing units owned and occup. by NHPIs[1]	Asian Indian	Bangladeshi	Cambodian	Chinese[2]	Fijian	Filipino	Guamanian[3]	Hawaiian, Native	Hmong	Indonesian	Japanese	Korean	Laotian	Malaysian	Pakistani	Samoan	Sri Lankan	Taiwanese	Thai	Tongan	Vietnamese
Tazewell County	89,200	106,300	-	-	-	-	-	-	-	-	-	-	-	-	-	-	-	-	-	-	-	-	-	-
Vermilion County	56,000	143,800	-	-	-	-	-	-	-	-	-	-	-	-	-	-	-	-	-	-	-	-	-	-
Will County	154,300	191,000	-	210,000	-	-	244,500	-	171,500	-	-	-	-	-	234,400	-	-	225,000	-	-	-	-	-	183,500
Bolingbrook (village)	142,000	167,700	-	156,900	-	-	-	-	162,500	-	-	-	-	-	-	-	-	-	-	-	-	-	-	-
Winnebago County	91,900	108,900	-	174,000	-	-	-	-	110,800	-	-	-	-	-	106,300	85,800	-	-	-	-	-	-	-	89,200
INDIANA	94,300	138,300	78,500	171,000	-	104,600	146,400	-	139,700	70,500	95,500	-	-	113,100	140,700	82,400	-	124,100	-	-	202,100	123,600	-	94,500
Allen County	88,700	99,900	-	190,500	-	-	117,900	-	169,700	-	-	-	-	-	-	-	-	-	-	-	-	-	-	91,800
Bartholomew County	105,300	139,200	-	195,800	-	-	-	-	-	-	-	-	-	-	-	-	-	-	-	-	-	-	-	-
Clark County	89,900	133,100	-	-	-	-	-	-	-	-	-	-	-	-	-	-	-	-	-	-	-	-	-	-
Delaware County	75,400	89,800	-	-	-	-	-	-	-	-	-	-	-	-	-	-	-	-	-	-	-	-	-	-
Elkhart County	98,100	114,500	-	-	-	-	-	-	-	-	-	-	-	-	-	-	-	-	-	-	-	-	-	-
Grant County	68,500	116,900	-	-	-	-	-	-	-	-	-	-	-	-	-	-	-	-	-	-	-	-	-	-
Hamilton County	166,300	211,800	-	252,700	-	-	216,900	-	-	-	-	-	-	-	-	-	-	-	-	-	-	-	-	-
Carmel (city)	205,400	232,200	-	-	-	-	-	-	-	-	-	-	-	-	-	-	-	-	-	-	-	-	-	-
Hendricks County	133,300	127,700	-	-	-	-	-	-	-	-	-	-	-	-	-	-	-	-	-	-	-	-	-	-
Howard County	89,000	195,200	-	-	-	-	-	-	-	-	-	-	-	-	-	-	-	-	-	-	-	-	-	-
Johnson County	122,500	193,300	-	-	-	-	-	-	-	-	-	-	-	-	-	-	-	-	-	-	-	-	-	-
Kosciusko County	95,500	128,100	-	-	-	-	-	-	-	-	-	-	-	-	-	-	-	-	-	-	-	-	-	-
Lake County	97,500	167,900	-	213,300	-	-	184,500	-	167,400	-	-	-	-	-	138,900	-	-	-	-	-	-	-	-	-
Munster (town)	163,800	204,100	-	226,700	-	-	-	-	-	-	-	-	-	-	-	-	-	-	-	-	-	-	-	-
LaPorte County	93,500	141,200	-	-	-	-	-	-	-	-	-	-	-	-	-	-	-	-	-	-	-	-	-	-
Madison County	81,600	47,600	-	-	-	-	-	-	-	-	-	-	-	-	-	-	-	-	-	-	-	-	-	-
Marion County	99,000	116,200	-	123,200	-	-	123,200	-	114,200	-	-	-	-	82,700	136,900	-	-	-	-	-	-	-	-	93,900
Monroe County	113,100	133,300	-	137,500	-	-	145,500	-	-	-	-	-	-	-	218,200	-	-	-	-	-	-	-	-	-
Bloomington (city)	126,000	136,200	-	132,800	-	-	141,500	-	-	-	-	-	-	-	196,400	-	-	-	-	-	-	-	-	-
Porter County	127,000	182,700	-	-	-	-	-	-	-	-	-	-	-	-	-	-	-	-	-	-	-	-	-	-
St. Joseph County	85,700	130,400	-	134,800	-	-	156,600	-	-	-	-	-	-	-	130,100	-	-	-	-	-	-	-	-	-
Tippecanoe County	112,200	137,900	-	156,000	-	-	144,900	-	-	-	-	-	-	121,100	112,500	-	-	-	-	-	-	-	-	-
West Lafayette (city)	145,400	161,800	-	172,400	-	-	162,500	-	-	-	-	-	-	-	-	-	-	-	-	-	-	-	-	-
Vanderburgh County	82,400	151,900	-	-	-	-	-	-	-	-	-	-	-	-	-	-	-	-	-	-	-	-	-	-
Vigo County	72,500	162,500	-	-	-	-	-	-	-	-	-	-	-	-	-	-	-	-	-	-	-	-	-	-
Wayne County	80,300	85,000	-	-	-	-	-	-	-	-	-	-	-	-	-	-	-	-	-	-	-	-	-	-
IOWA	82,500	95,600	77,100	159,000	-	57,000	129,300	-	105,800	-	-	-	-	97,300	99,800	68,800	-	279,400	-	-	218,800	88,000	-	76,300
Black Hawk County	77,000	173,600	-	-	-	-	-	-	-	-	-	-	-	-	-	-	-	-	-	-	-	-	-	-
Buena Vista County[4]	64,900	63,800	-	-	-	-	-	-	-	-	-	-	-	-	-	61,900	-	-	-	-	-	-	-	-
Storm Lake (city)	71,300	63,600	-	-	-	-	-	-	-	-	-	-	-	-	-	61,900	-	-	-	-	-	-	-	-
Johnson County	131,500	128,800	-	138,000	-	-	138,600	-	-	-	-	-	-	-	14,400	-	-	-	-	-	-	-	-	-
Coralville (city)	127,200	103,600	-	-	-	-	-	-	-	-	-	-	-	-	-	-	-	-	-	-	-	-	-	-
Iowa City (city)	128,300	131,400	-	136,200	-	-	144,300	-	-	-	-	-	-	-	14,400	-	-	-	-	-	-	-	-	-
Linn County	99,400	129,600	-	157,300	-	-	-	-	-	-	-	-	-	-	59,300	-	-	-	-	-	-	-	-	-
Polk County	103,100	86,200	-	124,700	-	52,000	134,800	-	-	-	-	-	-	-	95,400	65,400	-	-	-	-	-	80,500	-	75,900

Notes: Please refer to the User's Guide for an explanation of data; data is arranged alphabetically by state, then county, then city within each county; table includes counties with populations greater than 49,999 unless noted and cities with populations greater than 9,999 whose Asian and/or NHPI population rates are greater than the national average; (1) Native Hawaiian and other Pacific Islander; (2) excludes Taiwanese; (3) includes Chamorro; (4) county does not meet population threshold but is shown in order to allow inclusion of city

Place	All specified owner-occupied housing units	Specified housing units owned and occup. by Asians	Specified housing units owned and occup. by NHPIs[1]	Asian Indian	Bangladeshi	Cambodian	Chinese[2]	Fijian	Filipino	Guamanian[3]	Hawaiian, Native	Hmong	Indonesian	Japanese	Korean	Laotian	Malaysian	Pakistani	Samoan	Sri Lankan	Taiwanese	Thai	Tongan	Vietnamese
Pottawattamie County	84,900	79,600	-		-	-		-	-	-	-	-	-	-	-	-	-	-	-	-	-	-	-	-
Scott County	92,400	95,700	-	-	-	-	-	-	-	-	-	-	-	-	-	-	-	-	-	-	-	-	-	68,600
Story County	115,800	181,300	-	235,700	-	-	195,800	-	-	-	-	-	-	-	145,500	-	-	-	-	-	-	-	-	-
Ames (city)	130,900	181,900	-	253,600	-	-	195,800	-	-	-	-	-	-	-	145,500	-	-	-	-	-	-	-	-	-
Woodbury County	76,400	66,100	-	-	-	-	-	-	-	-	-	-	-	-	-	-	-	-	-	-	-	-	-	62,500
KANSAS	83,500	104,800	92,400	162,900	-	70,300	134,700	-	92,700	-	103,100	61,500	-	99,600	115,300	59,100	-	148,100	-	-	131,700	117,000	-	78,600
Cowley County[4]	54,100	34,300	-	-	-	-	-	-	-	-	-	-	-	-	-	33,700	-	-	-	-	-	-	-	-
Winfield (city)	60,700	34,300	-	-	-	-	-	-	-	-	-	-	-	-	-	33,700	-	-	-	-	-	-	-	-
Douglas County	117,800	127,600	-	162,500	-	-	136,500	-	-	-	-	-	-	-	0	-	-	-	-	-	-	-	-	-
Lawrence (city)	118,400	127,600	-	162,500	-	-	136,500	-	-	-	-	-	-	-	0	-	-	-	-	-	-	-	-	-
Johnson County	150,100	159,100	-	175,100	-	-	153,000	-	188,800	-	-	-	-	172,300	158,300	100,000	-	-	-	-	-	-	-	115,200
Overland Park (city)	162,800	166,200	-	192,400	-	-	162,500	-	-	-	-	-	-	-	164,100	-	-	-	-	-	-	-	-	113,100
Leavenworth County	96,900	82,500	-	-	-	-	-	-	-	-	-	-	-	-	-	-	-	-	-	-	-	-	-	-
Riley County	93,700	98,500	-	-	-	-	111,600	-	-	-	-	-	-	-	102,100	-	-	-	-	-	-	-	-	-
Manhattan (city)	96,900	97,500	-	-	-	-	111,100	-	-	-	-	-	-	-	-	-	-	-	-	-	-	-	-	-
Saline County	85,300	94,500	-	-	-	-	-	-	-	-	-	-	-	-	-	-	-	-	-	-	-	-	-	89,000
Sedgwick County	83,600	83,100	55,000	134,900	-	77,800	110,700	-	71,200	-	-	-	-	-	109,300	55,700	-	-	-	-	-	-	-	71,100
Wichita (city)	78,900	83,900	-	133,600	-	-	115,400	-	71,000	-	-	-	-	-	107,700	58,200	-	-	-	-	-	-	-	74,800
Shawnee County	81,600	100,700	-	-	-	-	-	-	-	-	-	-	-	-	-	-	-	-	-	-	-	-	-	-
Wyandotte County	54,300	50,000	-	-	-	-	-	-	-	-	-	67,100	-	-	-	-	-	-	-	-	-	-	-	-
KENTUCKY	86,700	135,400	102,000	190,900	-	-	148,400	-	121,000	118,800	-	-	-	102,700	110,100	-	-	210,700	-	-	-	132,500	-	85,100
Boone County	131,800	143,400	-	-	-	-	-	-	-	-	-	-	-	137,500	-	-	-	-	-	-	-	-	-	-
Campbell County	101,000	128,000	-	-	-	-	-	-	-	-	-	-	-	-	-	-	-	-	-	-	-	-	-	-
Christian County	72,500	194,800	-	-	-	-	-	-	-	-	-	-	-	-	-	-	-	-	-	-	-	-	-	-
Fayette County	110,800	159,200	-	198,800	-	-	149,300	-	-	-	-	-	-	155,000	-	-	-	-	-	-	-	-	-	-
Hardin County	88,300	90,000	-	-	-	-	-	-	-	-	-	-	-	-	85,400	-	-	-	-	-	-	-	-	-
Radcliff (city)	83,500	82,900	-	-	-	-	-	-	-	-	-	-	-	-	-	-	-	-	-	-	-	-	-	-
Jefferson County	103,000	127,800	-	191,700	-	-	167,900	-	109,400	-	-	-	-	100,400	131,300	-	-	-	-	-	-	-	-	81,700
Kenton County	105,600	176,400	-	-	-	-	-	-	-	-	-	-	-	-	-	-	-	-	-	-	-	-	-	-
Madison County	93,500	139,600	-	-	-	-	-	-	-	-	-	-	-	-	-	-	-	-	-	-	-	-	-	-
Warren County	100,400	95,000	-	-	-	-	-	-	-	-	-	-	-	-	-	-	-	-	-	-	-	-	-	-
LOUISIANA	85,000	98,300	91,700	163,800	-	-	129,400	-	100,400	94,000	79,200	-	-	97,400	147,200	76,100	-	127,500	-	-	143,100	65,600	-	86,800
Ascension Parish	103,800	95,500	-	-	-	-	-	-	-	-	-	-	-	-	-	-	-	-	-	-	-	-	-	-
Bossier Parish	87,600	83,500	-	-	-	-	-	-	-	-	-	-	-	-	-	-	-	-	-	-	-	-	-	-
Caddo Parish	75,100	86,000	-	286,800	-	-	-	-	-	-	-	-	-	-	-	-	-	-	-	-	-	-	-	-
Calcasieu Parish	80,500	93,900	-	-	-	-	-	-	-	-	-	-	-	-	-	-	-	-	-	-	-	-	-	-
East Baton Rouge Parish	98,800	123,200	-	160,100	-	-	153,000	-	123,400	-	-	-	-	-	-	-	-	-	-	-	-	-	-	93,200
Iberia Parish	75,500	82,600	-	-	-	-	-	-	-	-	-	-	-	-	-	81,800	-	-	-	-	-	-	-	102,700
Jefferson Parish	105,300	102,100	-	181,300	-	-	158,400	-	101,400	-	-	-	-	-	199,100	-	-	170,800	-	-	-	-	-	87,600
Gretna (city)	75,400	90,000	-	-	-	-	-	-	-	-	-	-	-	-	-	-	-	-	-	-	-	-	-	65,600
Harvey (cdp)	86,500	97,000	-	-	-	-	-	-	-	-	-	-	-	-	-	-	-	-	-	-	-	-	-	84,200

Notes: Please refer to the User's Guide for an explanation of data; data is arranged alphabetically by state, then county, then city within each county; table includes counties with populations greater than 49,999 unless noted and cities with populations greater than 9,999 whose Asian and/or NHPI population rates are greater than the national average; (1) Native Hawaiian and other Pacific Islander; (2) excludes Taiwanese; (3) includes Chamorro; (4) county does not meet population threshold but is shown in order to allow inclusion of city

Place	All specified owner-occupied housing units	Specified housing units owned and occup. by Asians	Specified housing units owned and occup. by NHPIs[1]	Asian Indian	Bangladeshi	Cambodian	Chinese[2]	Fijian	Filipino	Guamanian[3]	Hawaiian, Native	Hmong	Indonesian	Japanese	Korean	Laotian	Malaysian	Pakistani	Samoan	Sri Lankan	Taiwanese	Thai	Tongan	Vietnamese
Timberlane (cdp)	95,300	85,000	-	-	-	-	-	-	-	-	-	-	-	-	-	-	-	-	-	-	-	-	-	85,000
Woodmere (cdp)	85,400	82,800	-	-	-	-	-	-	-	-	-	-	-	-	-	-	-	-	-	-	-	-	-	85,900
Lafayette Parish	100,500	126,100	-	183,000	-	-	-	-	-	-	-	-	-	-	-	-	-	-	-	-	-	-	-	115,000
Lafourche Parish	78,900	98,100	-	-	-	-	-	-	-	-	-	-	-	-	-	-	-	-	-	-	-	-	-	-
Orleans Parish	87,300	92,500	-	169,600	-	-	125,700	-	205,200	-	-	-	-	-	-	-	-	-	-	-	-	-	-	86,600
Ouachita Parish	80,000	95,000	-	-	-	-	-	-	-	-	-	-	-	-	-	-	-	-	-	-	-	-	-	-
Rapides Parish	74,000	92,100	-	-	-	-	-	-	-	-	-	-	-	-	-	-	-	-	-	-	-	-	-	-
St. Bernard Parish	85,200	103,100	-	-	-	-	-	-	-	-	-	-	-	-	-	-	-	-	-	-	-	-	-	135,200
St. Mary Parish	74,200	79,700	-	-	-	-	-	-	-	-	-	-	-	-	-	-	-	-	-	-	-	-	-	82,000
St. Tammany Parish	123,900	159,900	-	-	-	-	-	-	-	-	-	-	-	-	-	-	-	-	-	-	-	-	-	112,500
Terrebonne Parish	80,500	83,400	-	-	-	-	-	-	-	-	-	-	-	-	-	-	-	-	-	-	-	-	-	60,900
Vermilion Parish	68,000	59,200	-	-	-	-	-	-	-	-	-	-	-	-	-	-	-	-	-	-	-	-	-	57,900
Abbeville (city)	58,800	75,000	-	-	-	-	-	-	-	-	-	-	-	-	-	-	-	-	-	-	-	-	-	75,000
Vernon Parish	66,900	67,500	-	-	-	-	-	-	-	-	-	-	-	-	72,900	-	-	-	-	-	-	-	-	-
MAINE	98,700	106,500	34,500	184,100	-	89,200	98,500	-	97,000	-	-	-	-	110,900	142,200	-	-	-	-	-	-	-	-	94,400
Androscoggin County	89,900	95,400	-	-	-	-	-	-	-	-	-	-	-	-	-	-	-	-	-	-	-	-	-	-
Aroostook County	60,200	122,900	-	-	-	-	-	-	-	-	-	-	-	-	-	-	-	-	-	-	-	-	-	-
Cumberland County	131,200	120,300	-	-	-	88,100	168,800	-	103,200	-	-	-	-	-	-	-	-	-	-	-	-	-	-	93,100
Hancock County	108,600	95,600	-	-	-	-	-	-	-	-	-	-	-	-	-	-	-	-	-	-	-	-	-	-
Kennebec County	87,200	76,700	-	-	-	-	-	-	-	-	-	-	-	-	-	-	-	-	-	-	-	-	-	-
Oxford County	82,800	61,700	-	-	-	-	-	-	-	-	-	-	-	-	-	-	-	-	-	-	-	-	-	-
Penobscot County	82,400	128,300	-	-	-	-	126,400	-	-	-	-	-	-	-	-	-	-	-	-	-	-	-	-	-
York County	122,600	103,100	-	-	-	-	-	-	-	-	-	-	-	-	-	-	-	-	-	-	-	-	-	-
MARYLAND	146,000	184,700	139,200	218,000	196,300	167,900	194,300	-	154,800	129,900	155,200	-	153,100	178,200	195,300	115,600	-	176,300	-	190,900	264,900	156,100	-	161,800
Allegany County	71,100	211,800	-	-	-	-	-	-	-	-	-	-	-	-	-	-	-	-	-	-	-	-	-	-
Anne Arundel County	159,300	160,000	-	178,600	-	-	181,000	-	143,900	-	-	-	-	207,300	162,900	-	-	-	-	-	-	-	-	-
Severn (cdp)	159,000	156,900	-	-	-	-	-	-	-	-	-	-	-	-	177,600	-	-	-	-	-	-	-	-	-
South Gate (cdp)	133,500	143,600	-	-	-	-	-	-	-	-	-	-	-	-	148,800	-	-	-	-	-	-	-	-	-
Baltimore Independent City	69,100	84,200	-	86,800	-	-	73,400	-	88,700	-	-	-	-	-	109,700	-	-	-	-	-	-	-	-	73,400
Baltimore County	127,300	144,800	-	155,000	-	-	143,100	-	139,000	-	-	-	-	122,500	147,100	-	-	156,500	-	-	-	-	-	125,900
Arbutus (cdp)	112,700	115,800	-	-	-	-	-	-	-	-	-	-	-	-	-	-	-	-	-	-	-	-	-	-
Carney (cdp)	123,900	133,600	-	-	-	-	154,300	-	-	-	-	-	-	-	120,800	-	-	-	-	-	-	-	-	-
Cockeysville (cdp)	175,500	190,200	-	-	-	-	-	-	-	-	-	-	-	-	147,500	-	-	-	-	-	-	-	-	-
Lutherville-Timonium (cdp)	170,700	182,000	-	-	-	-	-	-	-	-	-	-	-	-	-	-	-	-	-	-	-	-	-	-
Mays Chapel (cdp)	204,600	200,000	-	-	-	-	-	-	-	-	-	-	-	-	-	-	-	-	-	-	-	-	-	-
Owings Mills (cdp)	141,700	154,000	-	-	-	-	-	-	-	-	-	-	-	-	-	-	-	-	-	-	-	-	-	-
Perry Hall (cdp)	141,300	135,600	-	-	-	-	-	-	-	-	-	-	-	-	141,300	-	-	-	-	-	-	-	-	-
Reisterstown (cdp)	123,700	128,800	-	135,700	-	-	-	-	-	-	-	-	-	-	-	-	-	-	-	-	-	-	-	-
Rossville (cdp)	118,200	69,500	-	-	-	-	-	-	-	-	-	-	-	-	-	-	-	-	-	-	-	-	-	-
Towson (cdp)	157,100	146,700	-	-	-	-	121,500	-	-	-	-	-	-	-	-	-	-	-	-	-	-	-	-	-
Woodlawn (cdp)	109,700	119,400	-	119,300	-	-	-	-	-	-	-	-	-	-	-	-	-	-	-	-	-	-	-	-

Notes: Please refer to the User's Guide for an explanation of data; data is arranged alphabetically by state, then county, then city within each county; table includes counties with populations greater than 49,999 unless noted and cities with populations greater than 9,999 whose Asian and/or NHPI population rates are greater than the national average; (1) Native Hawaiian and other Pacific Islander; (2) excludes Taiwanese; (3) includes Chamorro; (4) county does not meet population threshold but is shown in order to allow inclusion of city

Place	All specified owner-occupied housing units	Specified housing units owned and occup. by Asians	Specified housing units owned and occup. by NHPIs[1]	Asian Indian	Bangladeshi	Cambodian	Chinese[2]	Fijian	Filipino	Guamanian[3]	Hawaiian, Native	Hmong	Indonesian	Japanese	Korean	Laotian	Malaysian	Pakistani	Samoan	Sri Lankan	Taiwanese	Thai	Tongan	Vietnamese
Calvert County	169,200	226,300	-	-	-	-	-	-	-	-	-	-	-	-	-	-	-	-	-	-	-	-	-	-
Carroll County	162,500	175,700	-	-	-	-	-	-	-	-	-	-	-	-	-	-	-	-	-	-	-	-	-	-
Cecil County	132,300	162,500	-	-	-	-	-	-	-	-	-	-	-	-	-	-	-	-	-	-	-	-	-	-
Charles County	153,000	181,000	-	-	-	-	-	-	161,300	-	-	-	-	-	-	-	-	-	-	-	-	-	-	-
Frederick County	160,200	160,100	-	189,400	-	-	140,900	-	-	-	-	-	-	-	141,400	-	-	-	-	-	-	-	-	-
Harford County	149,800	136,600	-	142,200	-	-	-	-	137,500	-	-	-	-	-	131,800	-	-	-	-	-	-	-	-	-
Howard County	206,300	228,200	-	261,900	-	-	215,400	-	168,300	-	-	-	-	-	240,200	-	-	173,700	-	-	-	-	-	230,000
Columbia (cdp)	180,500	196,600	-	257,100	-	-	176,200	-	149,000	-	-	-	-	-	218,300	-	-	-	-	-	-	-	-	-
Elkridge (cdp)	158,600	173,000	-	-	-	-	-	-	-	-	-	-	-	-	137,500	-	-	-	-	-	-	-	-	-
Ellicott City (cdp)	241,800	255,000	-	279,600	-	-	248,600	-	213,300	-	-	-	-	-	241,700	-	-	191,100	-	-	-	-	-	-
North Laurel (cdp)	184,100	236,300	-	261,000	-	-	-	-	-	-	-	-	-	-	272,700	-	-	-	-	-	-	-	-	-
Savage-Guilford (cdp)	152,000	124,000	-	-	-	-	-	-	-	-	-	-	-	-	-	-	-	-	-	-	-	-	-	-
Montgomery County	221,800	220,000	213,200	251,200	225,700	166,800	222,800	-	177,900	-	-	-	164,100	233,300	239,200	-	-	190,700	-	171,200	293,200	163,500	-	171,400
Aspen Hill (cdp)	194,100	186,600	-	215,800	-	-	177,300	-	173,800	-	-	-	-	-	220,300	-	-	-	-	-	-	-	-	168,300
Bethesda (cdp)	396,400	359,900	-	419,500	-	-	333,600	-	270,200	-	-	-	-	397,900	328,900	-	-	-	-	-	-	-	-	-
Calverton (cdp)	167,600	163,700	-	159,800	-	-	-	-	-	-	-	-	-	-	157,600	-	-	-	-	-	-	-	-	-
Colesville (cdp)	244,400	262,200	-	311,800	-	-	233,100	-	-	-	-	-	-	-	261,400	-	-	-	-	-	-	-	-	212,500
Fairland (cdp)	155,600	206,500	-	143,800	-	-	148,400	-	-	-	-	-	-	-	247,200	-	-	-	-	-	-	-	-	-
Gaithersburg (city)	171,100	187,900	-	202,100	-	-	176,800	-	147,300	-	-	-	-	-	214,800	-	-	-	-	-	-	-	-	185,000
Germantown (cdp)	140,900	155,900	-	152,500	-	-	144,400	-	-	-	-	-	-	-	194,300	-	-	-	-	-	-	-	-	173,600
Montgomery Village (cdp)	145,800	151,900	-	182,200	-	-	158,500	-	121,300	-	-	-	-	-	-	-	-	-	-	-	-	-	-	118,300
North Bethesda (cdp)	288,200	250,700	-	278,600	-	-	257,100	-	180,000	-	-	-	-	258,300	237,500	-	-	-	-	-	-	-	-	-
North Potomac (cdp)	304,400	291,900	-	305,800	-	-	292,300	-	-	-	-	-	-	-	288,500	-	-	-	-	-	-	-	-	-
Olney (cdp)	243,800	243,100	-	266,700	-	-	223,700	-	-	-	-	-	-	-	252,100	-	-	-	-	-	-	-	-	-
Potomac (cdp)	450,800	446,400	-	458,200	-	-	442,100	-	615,700	-	-	-	-	-	437,200	-	-	-	-	-	-	-	-	-
Redland (cdp)	202,500	184,300	-	246,400	-	-	175,000	-	184,700	-	-	-	-	-	233,300	-	-	-	-	-	-	-	-	-
Rockville (city)	198,700	226,000	-	305,000	-	-	200,900	-	138,800	-	-	-	-	342,900	316,300	-	-	-	-	-	-	-	-	191,300
Silver Spring (cdp)	187,300	166,400	-	187,100	-	161,100	176,400	-	171,400	-	-	-	-	-	188,500	-	-	-	-	-	-	-	-	148,600
Takoma Park (city)	189,200	153,000	-	-	-	-	-	-	-	-	-	-	-	-	-	-	-	-	-	-	-	-	-	-
Wheaton-Glenmont (cdp)	163,100	164,200	-	161,600	-	-	163,000	-	161,800	-	-	-	-	-	196,200	-	-	-	-	-	-	-	-	166,300
White Oak (cdp)	204,700	190,000	-	184,200	-	-	223,800	-	-	-	-	-	-	-	186,800	-	-	-	-	-	-	-	-	187,500
Prince George's County	145,600	157,300	-	165,300	-	-	150,700	-	157,800	-	-	-	-	124,100	159,300	-	-	122,900	-	-	-	167,900	-	157,800
Adelphi (cdp)	166,800	210,000	-	-	-	-	-	-	-	-	-	-	-	-	-	-	-	-	-	-	-	-	-	-
Beltsville (cdp)	161,600	185,400	-	184,600	-	-	-	-	-	-	-	-	-	-	165,000	-	-	-	-	-	-	-	-	-
College Park (city)	141,300	141,300	-	141,700	-	-	138,200	-	-	-	-	-	-	-	-	-	-	-	-	-	-	-	-	-
Fort Washington (cdp)	172,400	167,000	-	-	-	-	-	-	166,700	-	-	-	-	-	-	-	-	-	-	-	-	-	-	-
Friendly (cdp)	161,300	166,300	-	-	-	-	-	-	175,000	-	-	-	-	-	-	-	-	-	-	-	-	-	-	-
Glenn Dale (cdp)	196,400	218,500	-	-	-	-	-	-	-	-	-	-	-	-	-	-	-	-	-	-	-	-	-	-
Greenbelt (city)	121,700	166,700	-	207,000	-	-	166,700	-	-	-	-	-	-	-	141,900	-	-	-	-	-	-	-	-	-
Hyattsville (city)	128,300	103,800	-	-	-	-	-	-	-	-	-	-	-	-	-	-	-	-	-	-	-	-	-	-
Lanham-Seabrook (cdp)	146,100	164,500	-	-	-	-	-	-	-	-	-	-	-	-	-	-	-	-	-	-	-	-	-	-

Notes: Please refer to the User's Guide for an explanation of data; data is arranged alphabetically by state, then county, then city within each county; table includes counties with populations greater than 49,999 unless noted and cities with populations greater than 9,999 whose Asian and/or NHPI population rates are greater than the national average; (1) Native Hawaiian and other Pacific Islander; (2) excludes Taiwanese; (3) includes Chamorro; (4) county does not meet population threshold but is shown in order to allow inclusion of city

Place	All specified owner-occupied housing units	Specified housing units owned and occup. by Asians	Specified housing units owned and occup. by NHPIs[1]	Asian Indian	Bangladeshi	Cambodian	Chinese[2]	Fijian	Filipino	Guamanian[3]	Hawaiian, Native	Hmong	Indonesian	Japanese	Korean	Laotian	Malaysian	Pakistani	Samoan	Sri Lankan	Taiwanese	Thai	Tongan	Vietnamese
Laurel (city)	126,400	142,600	-	-	-	-	-	-	-	-	-	-	-	-	-	-	-	-	-	-	-	-	-	-
New Carrollton (city)	143,200	142,200	-	-	-	-	-	-	-	-	-	-	-	-	-	-	-	-	-	-	-	-	-	-
South Laurel (cdp)	166,800	154,000	-	-	-	-	-	-	-	-	-	-	-	-	-	-	-	-	-	-	-	-	-	-
St. Mary's County	150,000	164,400	-	183,300	-	-	-	-	146,400	-	-	-	-	-	-	-	-	-	-	-	-	-	-	-
Lexington Park (cdp)	118,100	135,300	-	-	-	-	-	-	-	-	-	-	-	-	-	-	-	-	-	-	-	-	-	-
Washington County	115,000	142,200	-	-	-	-	-	-	-	-	-	-	-	-	-	-	-	-	-	-	-	-	-	-
Wicomico County	94,500	125,800	-	160,700	-	-	-	-	-	-	-	-	-	-	156,700	-	-	-	-	-	-	-	-	-
Salisbury (city)	81,700	77,100	-	-	-	-	-	-	-	-	-	-	-	-	-	-	-	-	-	-	-	-	-	-
MASSACHUSETTS	185,700	228,000	166,600	297,200	170,300	141,300	235,100	-	183,200	230,000	153,600	122,500	118,000	257,400	254,800	120,300	-	284,600	-	248,900	293,200	222,100	-	157,400
Barnstable County	178,800	212,900	-	-	-	-	265,000	-	-	-	-	-	-	-	-	-	-	-	-	-	-	-	-	-
Berkshire County	116,800	157,200	-	162,500	-	-	-	-	-	-	-	-	-	-	-	-	-	-	-	-	-	-	-	-
Bristol County	151,500	173,900	-	244,200	-	155,400	195,800	-	156,300	-	-	-	-	-	152,900	-	-	-	-	-	-	-	-	145,300
Essex County	220,000	226,300	-	312,400	-	93,300	214,400	-	198,600	-	-	-	-	281,800	277,100	121,200	-	-	-	-	-	-	-	152,900
Andover (town)	344,900	329,400	-	333,300	-	-	336,800	-	-	-	-	-	-	-	-	-	-	-	-	-	-	-	-	-
Lynn (city)	145,200	154,800	-	212,500	-	140,000	-	-	-	-	-	-	-	-	-	-	-	-	-	-	-	-	-	151,300
North Andover (town)	316,500	357,000	-	-	-	-	359,100	-	-	-	-	-	-	-	-	-	-	-	-	-	-	-	-	-
Franklin County	119,000	144,400	-	-	-	-	-	-	-	-	-	-	-	-	-	-	-	-	-	-	-	-	-	-
Hampden County	117,400	128,600	-	314,300	-	108,900	168,000	-	-	-	-	-	-	-	148,900	-	-	-	-	-	-	-	-	74,600
Hampshire County	142,400	154,200	-	225,000	-	-	120,200	-	-	-	-	-	-	-	167,500	-	-	-	-	-	-	-	-	-
Amherst Center (cdp)	170,100	136,400	-	-	-	-	-	-	-	-	-	-	-	-	-	-	-	-	-	-	-	-	-	-
Amherst (town)	177,000	153,000	-	-	-	-	133,600	-	-	-	-	-	-	-	-	-	-	-	-	-	-	-	-	-
Middlesex County	247,900	277,300	-	316,200	-	144,600	289,200	-	254,500	-	-	-	-	283,900	346,300	120,700	-	245,800	-	-	349,000	344,000	-	189,700
Acton (town)	332,400	375,900	-	419,100	-	-	351,800	-	-	-	-	-	-	-	-	-	-	-	-	-	-	-	-	-
Arlington (town)	283,800	276,400	-	-	-	-	242,600	-	-	-	-	-	-	-	-	-	-	-	-	-	-	-	-	-
Bedford (town)	332,200	391,700	-	-	-	-	-	-	-	-	-	-	-	-	-	-	-	-	-	-	-	-	-	-
Belmont (cdp)	450,000	443,900	-	-	-	-	416,700	-	-	-	-	-	-	-	-	-	-	-	-	-	-	-	-	-
Belmont (town)	450,000	443,900	-	-	-	-	416,700	-	-	-	-	-	-	-	-	-	-	-	-	-	-	-	-	-
Burlington (town)	244,800	254,800	-	276,300	-	-	-	-	-	-	-	-	-	-	-	-	-	-	-	-	-	-	-	-
Cambridge (city)	398,500	283,600	-	417,600	-	-	284,800	-	-	-	-	-	-	275,000	187,500	-	-	-	-	-	-	-	-	-
Chelmsford (town)	213,900	217,200	-	194,700	-	-	243,800	-	-	-	-	-	-	-	-	-	-	-	-	-	-	-	-	-
Framingham (town)	216,700	253,600	-	270,500	-	-	245,400	-	-	-	-	-	-	-	-	-	-	-	-	-	-	-	-	-
Lexington (town)	417,400	411,700	-	509,900	-	-	385,300	-	-	-	-	-	-	-	440,000	-	-	-	-	-	-	-	-	-
Lowell (city)	134,200	129,200	-	183,100	-	126,800	103,100	-	-	-	-	-	-	-	-	109,200	-	-	-	-	-	-	-	125,000
Malden (city)	176,100	173,700	-	187,500	-	-	166,800	-	-	-	-	-	-	-	-	-	-	-	-	-	-	-	-	187,500
Marlborough (city)	190,600	241,700	-	262,100	-	-	-	-	-	-	-	-	-	-	-	-	-	-	-	-	-	-	-	-
Medford (city)	226,800	200,800	-	215,000	-	-	206,700	-	-	-	-	-	-	-	-	-	-	-	-	-	-	-	-	173,800
Natick (town)	247,800	238,400	-	-	-	-	245,900	-	-	-	-	-	-	-	-	-	-	-	-	-	-	-	-	-
Newton (city)	438,400	355,900	-	378,300	-	-	343,100	-	-	-	-	-	-	-	480,000	-	-	-	-	-	-	-	-	-
Somerville (city)	214,100	202,300	-	218,800	-	-	195,000	-	-	-	-	-	-	-	0	-	-	-	-	-	-	-	-	-
Sudbury (town)	422,400	404,100	-	-	-	-	-	-	-	-	-	-	-	-	-	-	-	-	-	-	-	-	-	-
Waltham (city)	250,800	231,600	-	226,100	-	-	250,000	-	-	-	-	-	-	-	-	-	-	-	-	-	-	-	-	-

Notes: Please refer to the User's Guide for an explanation of data; data is arranged alphabetically by state, then county, then city within each county; table includes counties with populations greater than 49,999 unless noted and cities with populations greater than 9,999 whose Asian and/or NHPI population rates are greater than the national average; (1) Native Hawaiian and other Pacific Islander; (2) excludes Taiwanese; (3) includes Chamorro; (4) county does not meet population threshold but is shown in order to allow inclusion of city

Place	All specified owner-occupied housing units	Specified housing units owned and occup. by Asians	Specified housing units owned and occup. by NHPIs[1]	Asian Indian	Bangladeshi	Cambodian	Chinese[2]	Fijian	Filipino	Guamanian[3]	Hawaiian, Native	Hmong	Indonesian	Japanese	Korean	Laotian	Malaysian	Pakistani	Samoan	Sri Lankan	Taiwanese	Thai	Tongan	Vietnamese
Wayland (town)	391,100	375,000	-	-	-	-	-	-	-	-	-	-	-	-	-	-	-	-	-	-	-	-	-	-
Westford (town)	278,500	300,000	-	-	-	-	295,500	-	-	-	-	-	-	-	-	-	-	-	-	-	-	-	-	-
Weston (town)	739,200	629,500	-	-	-	-	546,100	-	-	-	-	-	-	-	-	-	-	-	-	-	-	-	-	-
Winchester (town)	421,800	374,200	-	-	-	-	-	-	-	-	-	-	-	-	-	-	-	-	-	-	-	-	-	-
Woburn (city)	218,600	210,000	-	253,800	-	-	-	-	-	-	-	-	-	-	-	-	-	-	-	-	-	-	-	-
Norfolk County	230,400	220,800	-	315,100	-	-	208,300	-	201,600	-	-	-	-	456,000	356,400	-	-	-	-	-	240,600	-	-	187,500
Brookline (town)	599,500	443,300	-	1 Mil.+	-	-	390,000	-	-	-	-	-	-	575,000	696,400	-	-	-	-	-	-	-	-	-
Needham (town)	385,600	489,600	-	-	-	-	547,300	-	-	-	-	-	-	-	-	-	-	-	-	-	-	-	-	-
Norwood (town)	219,800	226,200	-	202,500	-	-	-	-	-	-	-	-	-	-	-	-	-	-	-	-	-	-	-	-
Quincy (city)	185,700	182,200	-	219,200	-	-	180,400	-	169,100	-	-	-	-	-	-	-	-	-	-	-	-	-	-	209,200
Randolph (town)	161,200	163,000	-	-	-	-	147,300	-	-	-	-	-	-	-	-	-	-	-	-	-	-	-	-	160,400
Sharon (town)	270,600	318,800	-	-	-	-	-	-	-	-	-	-	-	-	-	-	-	-	-	-	-	-	-	-
Wellesley (town)	548,100	534,400	-	-	-	-	543,700	-	-	-	-	-	-	-	-	-	-	-	-	-	-	-	-	-
Plymouth County	179,200	163,900	-	211,800	-	-	184,400	-	144,600	-	-	-	-	-	-	-	-	-	-	-	-	-	-	142,600
Suffolk County	187,300	185,900	-	152,500	-	178,000	192,300	-	178,800	-	-	-	-	428,600	151,600	-	-	-	-	-	350,000	-	-	192,400
Boston (city)	190,600	191,100	-	145,700	-	179,700	201,000	-	193,800	-	-	-	-	428,600	151,600	-	-	-	-	-	350,000	-	-	194,000
Chelsea (city)	149,200	78,300	-	-	-	-	-	-	-	-	-	-	-	-	-	-	-	-	-	-	-	-	-	0
Revere (city)	168,200	149,000	-	-	-	187,500	-	-	-	-	-	-	-	-	-	-	-	-	-	-	-	-	-	144,500
Worcester County	146,000	176,500	-	274,100	-	139,600	219,800	-	203,600	-	-	85,000	-	98,500	204,700	119,600	-	284,600	-	-	-	-	-	126,900
Fitchburg (city)	112,100	113,100	-	-	-	-	-	-	-	-	-	85,000	-	-	-	115,000	-	-	-	-	-	-	-	-
Northborough (town)	228,300	276,600	-	-	-	-	-	-	-	-	-	-	-	-	-	-	-	-	-	-	-	-	-	-
Shrewsbury (town)	195,500	254,400	-	310,200	-	-	222,100	-	-	-	-	-	-	-	-	-	-	-	-	-	-	-	-	138,800
Westborough (town)	262,200	299,100	-	424,200	-	-	270,800	-	-	-	-	-	-	-	-	-	-	-	-	-	-	-	-	-
Worcester (city)	119,600	119,600	-	138,900	-	-	107,100	-	-	-	-	-	-	-	-	-	-	-	-	-	-	-	-	103,800
MICHIGAN	115,600	186,800	98,500	234,700	67,700	125,500	203,500	-	161,800	128,100	85,600	84,000	138,100	162,500	194,800	120,400	143,800	178,600	85,400	213,100	285,400	122,400	-	123,100
Allegan County	115,500	93,600	-	-	-	-	-	-	-	-	-	-	-	-	-	-	-	-	-	-	-	-	-	-
Bay County	84,900	117,900	-	-	-	-	-	-	-	-	-	-	-	-	-	-	-	-	-	-	-	-	-	-
Berrien County	94,700	161,500	-	162,500	-	-	-	-	180,500	-	-	-	-	-	67,500	-	-	-	-	-	-	-	-	-
Calhoun County	81,000	143,800	-	-	-	-	-	-	-	-	-	-	-	137,500	-	-	-	-	-	-	-	-	-	-
Cass County	91,800	67,100	-	-	-	-	-	-	-	-	-	-	-	-	-	65,000	-	-	-	-	-	-	-	-
Clinton County	120,500	119,200	-	-	-	-	-	-	-	-	-	-	-	-	-	-	-	-	-	-	-	-	-	-
Eaton County	113,700	130,000	-	216,100	-	-	-	-	-	-	-	-	-	-	-	-	-	-	-	-	-	-	-	128,800
Genesee County	95,000	156,400	-	179,900	-	-	133,200	-	102,500	-	-	-	-	-	120,300	-	-	-	-	-	-	-	-	-
Ingham County	98,400	148,400	-	169,200	-	-	159,200	-	137,100	-	-	60,600	-	182,200	148,800	-	-	-	-	-	-	-	-	107,800
East Lansing (city)	144,300	169,900	-	155,100	-	-	195,000	-	-	-	-	-	-	-	275,000	-	-	-	-	-	-	-	-	-
Meridian charter (township)	165,600	172,500	-	196,300	-	-	158,900	-	-	-	-	-	-	-	142,500	-	-	-	-	-	-	-	-	-
Okemos (cdp)	176,000	170,600	-	196,400	-	-	163,100	-	-	-	-	-	-	-	-	-	-	-	-	-	-	-	-	-
Ionia County	94,400	115,600	-	-	-	-	-	-	-	-	-	-	-	-	-	-	-	-	-	-	-	-	-	-
Isabella County	91,800	155,300	-	-	-	-	-	-	-	-	-	-	-	-	-	-	-	-	-	-	-	-	-	-
Jackson County	96,900	150,000	-	-	-	-	-	-	-	-	-	-	-	-	-	-	-	-	-	-	-	-	-	-
Kalamazoo County	108,000	164,100	-	185,800	-	-	164,700	-	-	-	-	-	-	-	121,900	-	-	-	-	-	-	-	-	-

Notes: Please refer to the User's Guide for an explanation of data; data is arranged alphabetically by state, then county, then city within each county; table includes counties with populations greater than 49,999 unless noted and cities with populations greater than 9,999 whose Asian and/or NHPI population rates are greater than the national average; (1) Native Hawaiian and other Pacific Islander; (2) excludes Taiwanese; (3) includes Chamorro; (4) county does not meet population threshold but is shown in order to allow inclusion of city

Place	All specified owner-occupied housing units	Specified housing units owned and occup. by Asians	Specified housing units owned and occup. by NHPIs[1]	Asian Indian	Bangladeshi	Cambodian	Chinese[2]	Fijian	Filipino	Guamanian[3]	Hawaiian, Native	Hmong	Indonesian	Japanese	Korean	Laotian	Malaysian	Pakistani	Samoan	Sri Lankan	Taiwanese	Thai	Tongan	Vietnamese
Kent County	115,100	124,400	-	234,000	-	-	112,100	-	149,000	-	-	-	-	-	137,900	-	-	-	-	-	-	-	-	109,100
Kentwood (city)	120,600	131,500	-	-	-	-	-	-	-	-	-	-	-	-	145,500	-	-	-	-	-	-	-	-	128,400
Lenawee County	109,500	154,200	-	-	-	-	-	-	-	-	-	-	-	-	-	-	-	-	-	-	-	-	-	-
Livingston County	187,500	218,800	-	-	-	-	-	-	-	-	-	-	-	-	-	-	-	-	-	-	-	-	-	-
Macomb County	139,200	161,900	-	174,500	-	-	167,200	-	165,100	-	-	121,300	-	-	200,000	-	-	147,800	-	-	-	-	-	144,100
Sterling Heights (city)	160,700	173,700	-	173,900	-	-	167,400	-	180,900	-	-	-	-	-	186,400	-	-	-	-	-	-	-	-	169,200
Marquette County	77,200	102,700	-	-	-	-	-	-	-	-	-	-	-	-	-	-	-	-	-	-	-	-	-	-
Midland County	101,800	182,100	-	201,600	-	-	169,100	-	-	-	-	-	-	-	-	-	-	-	-	-	-	-	-	-
Monroe County	132,000	119,900	-	-	-	-	-	-	-	-	-	-	-	-	-	-	-	-	-	-	-	-	-	-
Muskegon County	85,900	92,500	-	-	-	-	-	-	-	-	-	-	-	-	-	-	-	-	-	-	-	-	-	-
Oakland County	181,200	253,000	-	289,900	-	-	235,900	-	188,500	-	-	90,100	-	205,600	279,800	-	-	238,900	-	-	306,200	-	-	171,600
Auburn Hills (city)	137,200	140,100	-	0	-	-	-	-	-	-	-	-	-	-	-	-	-	-	-	-	-	-	-	-
Bloomfield (township)	356,800	415,500	-	394,900	-	-	-	-	-	-	-	-	-	-	538,200	-	-	-	-	-	-	-	-	-
Farmington (city)	173,900	178,400	-	225,000	-	-	-	-	-	-	-	-	-	-	-	-	-	-	-	-	-	-	-	-
Farmington Hills (city)	227,300	259,100	-	278,800	-	-	225,000	-	273,200	-	-	-	-	-	-	-	-	-	-	-	-	-	-	-
Madison Heights (city)	110,600	116,200	-	-	-	-	169,300	-	-	-	-	-	-	-	-	-	-	-	-	-	-	-	-	-
Novi (city)	236,300	317,100	-	353,000	-	-	312,300	-	-	-	-	-	-	246,400	-	-	-	-	-	-	-	-	-	-
Rochester (city)	260,700	266,700	-	-	-	-	-	-	-	-	-	-	-	-	-	-	-	-	-	-	-	-	-	-
Rochester Hills (city)	226,200	261,000	-	271,000	-	-	244,000	-	-	-	-	-	-	-	242,900	-	-	-	-	-	-	-	-	-
Troy (city)	219,800	246,200	-	275,300	-	-	226,600	-	180,000	-	-	-	-	-	265,000	-	-	-	-	-	296,000	-	-	-
West Bloomfield (township)	264,200	313,900	-	376,600	-	-	280,600	-	262,500	-	-	-	-	232,700	387,000	-	-	-	-	-	-	-	-	-
Ottawa County	133,000	135,500	-	165,300	-	126,700	151,600	-	-	-	-	-	-	-	164,600	134,700	-	-	-	-	-	-	-	130,400
Holland (city)	107,900	128,200	-	-	-	-	-	-	-	-	-	-	-	-	-	-	-	-	-	-	-	-	-	-
Saginaw County	85,200	169,200	-	260,900	-	-	-	-	133,700	-	-	-	-	-	165,000	-	-	-	-	-	-	-	-	-
St. Clair County	125,200	113,800	-	-	-	-	-	-	-	-	-	-	-	-	-	-	-	-	-	-	-	-	-	-
St. Joseph County	85,000	126,100	-	-	-	-	-	-	-	-	-	-	-	-	-	-	-	-	-	-	-	-	-	-
Washtenaw County	174,300	217,800	-	234,100	-	-	224,400	-	189,300	-	-	-	-	196,800	187,800	-	-	168,800	-	-	275,000	-	-	225,800
Ann Arbor (city)	181,400	193,200	-	201,300	-	-	191,900	-	196,100	-	-	-	-	195,800	174,000	-	-	-	-	-	269,000	-	-	-
Pittsfield charter (township)	220,700	230,100	-	251,700	-	-	234,800	-	-	-	-	-	-	-	197,900	-	-	-	-	-	-	-	-	-
Scio (township)	258,200	330,300	-	-	-	-	-	-	-	-	-	-	-	-	-	-	-	-	-	-	-	-	-	-
Wayne County	99,400	168,600	84,600	199,800	57,100	-	204,300	-	149,300	-	-	46,200	-	121,500	187,500	-	-	164,000	-	-	-	-	-	126,900
Brownstown (township)	147,200	170,500	-	-	-	-	-	-	-	-	-	-	-	-	-	-	-	-	-	-	-	-	-	-
Canton (township)	194,100	234,900	-	251,500	-	-	232,400	-	227,900	-	-	-	-	-	186,200	-	-	-	-	-	-	-	-	-
Hamtramck (city)	71,200	67,800	-	71,000	66,000	-	-	-	-	-	-	-	-	-	-	-	-	-	-	-	-	-	-	-
Inkster (city)	68,000	87,700	-	0	-	-	-	-	-	-	-	-	-	-	-	-	-	-	-	-	-	-	-	-
Northville (township)	282,500	309,200	-	337,500	-	-	-	-	-	-	-	-	-	-	-	-	-	-	-	-	-	-	-	-
MINNESOTA	122,400	129,400	107,700	154,600	-	119,100	160,300	-	126,400	87,500	129,000	93,000	-	141,400	153,400	113,500	-	153,300	-	-	183,900	134,900	-	132,600
Anoka County	131,300	136,900	-	120,900	-	-	147,200	-	138,000	-	-	150,500	-	-	135,600	-	-	-	-	-	-	-	-	139,300
Columbia Heights (city)	103,000	111,700	-	-	-	-	-	-	-	-	-	-	-	-	-	-	-	-	-	-	-	-	-	-
Blue Earth County	98,200	136,400	-	-	-	-	-	-	-	-	-	-	-	-	-	-	-	-	-	-	-	-	-	-
Carver County	170,200	197,300	-	-	-	-	-	-	-	-	-	-	-	-	-	-	-	-	-	-	-	-	-	-

Notes: Please refer to the User's Guide for an explanation of data; data is arranged alphabetically by state, then county, then city within each county; table includes counties with populations greater than 49,999 unless noted and cities with populations greater than 9,999 whose Asian and/or NHPI population rates are greater than the national average; (1) Native Hawaiian and other Pacific Islander; (2) excludes Taiwanese; (3) includes Chamorro; (4) county does not meet population threshold but is shown in order to allow inclusion of city

Place	All specified owner-occupied housing units	Specified housing units owned and occup. by Asians	Specified housing units owned and occup. by NHPIs[1]	Asian Indian	Bangladeshi	Cambodian	Chinese[2]	Fijian	Filipino	Guamanian[3]	Hawaiian, Native	Hmong	Indonesian	Japanese	Korean	Laotian	Malaysian	Pakistani	Samoan	Sri Lankan	Taiwanese	Thai	Tongan	Vietnamese
Clay County	85,400	185,000	-	-	-	-	-	-	-	-	-	-	-	-	-	-	-	-	-	-	-	-	-	-
Crow Wing County	107,500	115,600	-	-	-	-	-	-	-	-	-	-	-	-	-	-	-	-	-	-	-	-	-	-
Dakota County	152,400	150,200	-	148,600	-	140,900	173,000	-	147,000	-	-	-	-	-	138,800	146,400	-	-	-	-	-	-	-	149,600
Eagan (city)	164,500	141,600	-	133,300	-	-	183,700	-	-	-	-	-	-	-	-	-	-	-	-	-	-	-	-	142,700
Hennepin County	143,400	130,500	89,000	157,300	-	130,900	153,500	-	133,400	-	-	92,600	-	147,800	174,100	116,800	-	147,200	-	-	-	-	-	132,400
Bloomington (city)	147,000	144,800	-	137,500	-	138,400	160,700	-	-	-	-	-	-	-	177,800	-	-	-	-	-	-	-	-	138,100
Brooklyn Center (city)	105,600	127,400	-	-	-	-	-	-	-	-	-	125,500	-	-	-	112,500	-	-	-	-	-	-	-	-
Brooklyn Park (city)	131,000	133,700	-	163,700	-	-	-	-	-	-	-	121,900	-	-	-	132,200	-	-	-	-	-	-	-	140,000
Eden Prairie (city)	198,300	166,400	-	206,300	-	-	208,300	-	-	-	-	-	-	-	-	-	-	-	-	-	-	-	-	151,800
Hopkins (city)	132,400	100,800	-	137,500	-	-	-	-	-	-	-	-	-	-	-	-	-	-	-	-	-	-	-	-
Minneapolis (city)	113,500	91,300	-	121,800	-	96,700	112,500	-	128,300	-	-	84,500	-	116,400	171,400	87,200	-	-	-	-	-	-	-	89,700
Plymouth (city)	197,600	209,700	-	243,500	-	-	219,200	-	-	-	-	-	-	-	189,700	-	-	-	-	-	-	-	-	-
Richfield (city)	128,500	129,000	-	-	-	-	-	-	-	-	-	-	-	-	-	-	-	-	-	-	-	-	-	139,400
Nobles County[4]	61,400	52,800	-	-	-	-	-	-	-	-	-	-	-	-	-	57,800	-	-	-	-	-	-	-	-
Worthington (city)	69,900	53,300	-	-	-	-	-	-	-	-	-	-	-	-	-	59,400	-	-	-	-	-	-	-	-
Olmsted County	117,000	122,500	-	133,000	-	74,200	173,100	-	-	-	-	91,800	-	273,300	148,400	55,600	-	-	-	-	-	-	-	120,600
Rochester (city)	114,400	121,000	-	131,000	-	70,800	194,600	-	-	-	-	91,800	-	-	148,400	55,600	-	-	-	-	-	-	-	116,200
Otter Tail County	84,000	128,100	-	-	-	-	-	-	-	-	-	-	-	-	-	-	-	-	-	-	-	-	-	-
Ramsey County	126,400	109,400	-	150,700	-	99,000	158,300	-	110,200	-	-	89,200	-	149,400	148,100	95,000	-	-	-	-	-	-	-	126,500
Maplewood (city)	132,200	165,100	-	-	-	-	167,200	-	-	-	-	144,900	-	-	-	-	-	-	-	-	-	-	-	-
New Brighton (city)	144,200	141,900	-	-	-	-	-	-	-	-	-	-	-	-	-	-	-	-	-	-	-	-	-	-
Roseville (city)	143,400	161,500	-	-	-	-	162,500	-	-	-	-	-	-	-	-	-	-	-	-	-	-	-	-	-
St. Paul (city)	105,400	91,300	-	111,700	-	94,500	113,100	-	107,100	-	-	86,800	-	-	104,400	88,800	-	-	-	-	-	-	-	93,200
Vadnais Heights (city)	143,800	143,100	-	-	-	-	-	-	-	-	-	-	-	-	-	-	-	-	-	-	-	-	-	-
Rice County	123,600	108,700	-	-	-	-	-	-	-	-	-	-	-	-	-	-	-	-	-	-	-	-	-	-
St. Louis County	75,000	91,100	-	-	-	-	-	-	-	-	-	-	-	-	156,300	-	-	-	-	-	-	-	-	-
Scott County	157,300	169,900	-	-	-	133,300	-	-	-	-	-	-	-	-	-	-	-	-	-	-	-	-	-	162,500
Savage (city)	168,400	149,900	-	-	-	-	-	-	-	-	-	-	-	-	-	-	-	-	-	-	-	-	-	-
Sherburne County	137,500	136,800	-	-	-	-	-	-	-	-	-	-	-	-	-	-	-	-	-	-	-	-	-	-
Stearns County	100,300	109,900	-	-	-	-	-	-	-	-	-	-	-	-	-	-	-	-	-	-	-	-	-	106,300
Washington County	156,200	188,600	-	220,100	-	-	191,500	-	-	-	-	172,500	-	-	206,700	-	-	-	-	-	-	-	-	185,700
Woodbury (city)	174,300	213,100	-	228,700	-	-	212,300	-	-	-	-	150,000	-	-	-	-	-	-	-	-	-	-	-	-
Wright County	135,300	112,500	-	-	-	-	-	-	-	-	-	-	-	-	-	-	-	-	-	-	-	-	-	-
MISSISSIPPI	71,400	89,100	71,200	134,400	-	-	94,900	-	83,800	-	-	-	-	84,300	83,100	-	-	-	-	-	-	-	-	78,700
DeSoto County	103,100	76,800	-	-	-	-	-	-	-	-	-	-	-	-	-	-	-	-	-	-	-	-	-	-
Forrest County	69,100	0	-	-	-	-	-	-	-	-	-	-	-	-	-	-	-	-	-	-	-	-	-	-
Harrison County	87,200	84,500	-	-	-	-	-	-	106,700	-	-	-	-	-	-	-	-	-	-	-	-	-	-	77,700
Biloxi (city)	92,600	89,200	-	-	-	-	-	-	161,300	-	-	-	-	-	-	-	-	-	-	-	-	-	-	83,300
Hinds County	73,100	115,900	-	123,100	-	-	-	-	-	-	-	-	-	-	-	-	-	-	-	-	-	-	-	-
Jackson County	80,300	78,900	-	-	-	-	-	-	-	-	-	-	-	-	-	-	-	-	-	-	-	-	-	78,600
Madison County	117,000	162,500	-	-	-	-	-	-	-	-	-	-	-	-	-	-	-	-	-	-	-	-	-	-

Notes: Please refer to the User's Guide for an explanation of data; data is arranged alphabetically by state, then county, then city within each county; table includes counties with populations greater than 49,999 unless noted and cities with populations greater than 9,999 whose Asian and/or NHPI population rates are greater than the national average; (1) Native Hawaiian and other Pacific Islander; (2) excludes Taiwanese; (3) includes Chamorro; (4) county does not meet population threshold but is shown in order to allow inclusion of city

Place	All specified owner-occupied housing units	Specified housing units owned and occup. by Asians	Specified housing units owned and occup. by NHPIs[1]	Asian Indian	Bangladeshi	Cambodian	Chinese[2]	Fijian	Filipino	Guamanian[3]	Hawaiian, Native	Hmong	Indonesian	Japanese	Korean	Laotian	Malaysian	Pakistani	Samoan	Sri Lankan	Taiwanese	Thai	Tongan	Vietnamese
Oktibbeha County[4]	89,400	133,700	-	-	-	-	-	-	-	-	-	-	-	-	-	-	-	-	-	-	-	-	-	-
Starkville (city)	97,200	134,400	-	-	-	-	-	-	-	-	-	-	-	-	-	-	-	-	-	-	-	-	-	-
Rankin County	98,600	104,200	-	-	-	-	-	-	-	-	-	-	-	-	-	-	-	-	-	-	-	-	-	-
MISSOURI	89,900	129,900	88,700	166,000	-	73,100	142,200	-	127,200	149,000	110,000	-	-	95,700	149,500	58,900	-	128,400	83,500	-	240,600	103,100	-	78,400
Boone County	107,400	136,000	-	147,900	-	-	141,400	-	-	-	-	-	-	-	183,900	-	-	-	-	-	-	-	-	-
Columbia (city)	118,500	138,500	-	150,000	-	-	144,400	-	-	-	-	-	-	-	183,900	-	-	-	-	-	-	-	-	-
Cape Girardeau County	94,700	198,200	-	-	-	-	-	-	-	-	-	-	-	-	-	-	-	-	-	-	-	-	-	-
Cass County	104,200	155,100	-	-	-	-	-	-	-	-	-	-	-	-	-	-	-	-	-	-	-	-	-	-
Clay County	104,900	113,900	-	138,800	-	-	-	-	-	-	-	-	-	-	-	-	-	-	-	-	-	-	-	117,900
Cole County	97,200	131,000	-	-	-	-	-	-	-	-	-	-	-	-	-	-	-	-	-	-	-	-	-	-
Franklin County	96,400	93,000	-	-	-	-	-	-	-	-	-	-	-	-	-	-	-	-	-	-	-	-	-	-
Greene County	88,200	94,200	-	-	-	-	130,400	-	-	-	-	-	-	-	137,500	-	-	-	-	-	-	-	-	90,300
Jackson County	85,000	72,700	98,800	73,600	-	-	90,000	-	81,100	-	-	-	-	82,100	121,000	-	-	-	85,000	-	-	-	-	51,300
Independence (city)	77,000	70,300	100,000	-	-	-	-	-	-	-	-	-	-	-	-	-	-	-	-	-	-	-	-	-
Jasper County	67,700	75,000	-	-	-	-	-	-	-	-	-	-	-	-	-	-	-	-	-	-	-	-	-	-
Jefferson County	99,200	127,400	-	-	-	-	-	-	-	-	-	-	-	-	-	-	-	-	-	-	-	-	-	-
Newton County	74,200	56,000	-	-	-	-	-	-	-	-	-	-	-	-	-	-	-	-	-	-	-	-	-	-
Phelps County[4]	74,800	105,700	-	111,100	-	-	-	-	-	-	-	-	-	-	-	-	-	-	-	-	-	-	-	-
Rolla (city)	78,700	104,500	-	-	-	-	-	-	-	-	-	-	-	-	-	-	-	-	-	-	-	-	-	-
Platte County	126,700	141,100	-	-	-	-	-	-	-	-	-	-	-	-	-	-	-	-	-	-	-	-	-	-
St. Charles County	126,200	133,100	-	163,300	-	-	146,100	-	117,400	-	-	-	-	-	-	-	-	-	-	-	-	-	-	-
Saint Louis Independent City	63,900	61,700	-	98,000	-	-	64,200	-	71,000	-	-	-	-	-	-	-	-	-	-	-	-	-	-	60,100
St. Louis County	116,600	172,400	81,900	214,500	-	-	168,500	-	162,100	-	-	-	-	146,900	182,600	-	-	138,300	-	-	310,300	159,400	-	98,100
Chesterfield (city)	238,300	224,800	-	209,400	-	-	218,900	-	-	-	-	-	-	-	-	-	-	-	-	-	-	-	-	-
Clayton (city)	425,000	438,900	-	-	-	-	-	-	-	-	-	-	-	-	-	-	-	-	-	-	-	-	-	-
Creve Coeur (city)	277,400	300,000	-	-	-	-	-	-	-	-	-	-	-	-	-	-	-	-	-	-	-	-	-	-
Manchester (city)	144,800	144,400	-	-	-	-	-	-	-	-	-	-	-	-	-	-	-	-	-	-	-	-	-	-
Maryland Heights (city)	107,900	134,200	-	142,700	-	-	131,500	-	-	-	-	-	-	-	-	-	-	-	-	-	-	-	-	-
Town and Country (city)	466,700	602,300	-	591,700	-	-	-	-	-	-	-	-	-	-	-	-	-	-	-	-	-	-	-	-
MONTANA	99,500	101,200	91,700	164,300	-	-	113,200	-	95,000	-	87,500	-	-	93,800	88,800	-	-	-	-	-	-	-	-	-
Cascade County	92,500	75,700	-	-	-	-	-	-	-	-	-	-	-	-	-	-	-	-	-	-	-	-	-	-
Flathead County	125,600	87,800	-	-	-	-	-	-	-	-	-	-	-	-	-	-	-	-	-	-	-	-	-	-
Gallatin County	143,000	140,000	-	-	-	-	-	-	-	-	-	-	-	-	-	-	-	-	-	-	-	-	-	-
Missoula County	136,500	158,700	-	-	-	-	-	-	-	-	-	-	-	-	-	-	-	-	-	-	-	-	-	-
Yellowstone County	101,900	117,200	-	-	-	-	-	-	-	-	-	-	-	-	-	-	-	-	-	-	-	-	-	-
NEBRASKA	88,000	103,600	73,600	155,500	-	-	126,300	-	92,800	-	-	-	-	86,400	108,100	85,600	-	-	-	-	-	137,500	-	89,900
Douglas County	100,800	116,200	-	151,200	-	-	129,700	-	90,000	-	-	-	-	83,600	129,200	-	-	-	-	-	-	-	-	90,300
Hall County	83,700	73,500	-	-	-	-	-	-	-	-	-	-	-	-	-	-	-	-	-	-	-	-	-	-
Lancaster County	105,900	102,700	-	173,700	-	-	113,500	-	-	-	-	-	-	-	65,900	-	-	-	-	-	-	-	-	95,400
Sarpy County	112,100	117,300	-	-	-	-	-	-	116,100	-	-	-	-	-	97,800	-	-	-	-	-	-	-	-	148,200
NEVADA	142,000	146,100	132,900	161,200	-	130,900	155,000	-	141,900	126,400	137,500	-	-	150,200	148,000	130,800	-	158,500	118,400	-	127,000	138,700	118,800	146,500

Notes: Please refer to the User's Guide for an explanation of data; data is arranged alphabetically by state, then county, then city within each county; table includes counties with populations greater than 49,999 unless noted and cities with populations greater than 9,999 whose Asian and/or NHPI population rates are greater than the national average; (1) Native Hawaiian and other Pacific Islander; (2) excludes Taiwanese; (3) includes Chamorro; (4) county does not meet population threshold but is shown in order to allow inclusion of city

Place	All specified owner-occupied housing units	Specified housing units owned and occup. by Asians	Specified housing units owned and occup. by NHPIs[1]	Asian Indian	Bangladeshi	Cambodian	Chinese[2]	Fijian	Filipino	Guamanian[3]	Hawaiian, Native	Hmong	Indonesian	Japanese	Korean	Laotian	Malaysian	Pakistani	Samoan	Sri Lankan	Taiwanese	Thai	Tongan	Vietnamese
Carson City Independent City	147,500	164,000	-	-	-	-	-	-	148,100	-	-	-	-	-	-	-	-	-	-	-	-	-	-	-
Clark County	139,500	144,900	132,500	163,100	-	127,400	152,100	-	141,900	126,400	136,400	-	-	149,600	145,200	130,800	-	-	121,200	-	116,500	137,100	-	143,200
Enterprise (cdp)	211,400	117,600	-	-	-	-	-	-	-	-	-	-	-	-	-	-	-	-	-	-	-	-	-	-
Henderson (city)	156,000	164,000	127,300	220,500	-	-	179,000	-	154,500	-	128,400	-	-	140,100	203,800	-	-	-	-	-	-	-	-	-
Las Vegas (city)	137,300	147,700	127,800	168,800	-	-	155,000	-	146,200	-	131,600	-	-	164,000	150,400	-	-	-	-	-	-	125,600	-	106,100
North Las Vegas (city)	123,000	133,800	152,800	-	-	-	-	-	131,800	-	-	-	-	-	-	-	-	-	-	-	-	-	-	-
Paradise (cdp)	140,600	149,400	187,500	150,000	-	-	160,900	-	152,600	-	187,500	-	-	134,700	131,600	-	-	-	-	-	-	-	-	155,000
Spring Valley (cdp)	149,300	150,100	135,400	-	-	-	151,600	-	147,600	-	-	-	-	173,600	143,000	-	-	-	-	-	-	162,500	-	158,200
Sunrise Manor (cdp)	120,200	125,500	112,500	-	-	-	116,700	-	125,600	-	-	-	-	118,300	133,000	-	-	-	-	-	-	-	-	-
Winchester (cdp)	119,500	114,600	-	-	-	-	-	-	106,300	-	-	-	-	-	-	-	-	-	-	-	-	-	-	-
Washoe County	161,600	156,100	150,000	159,600	-	-	171,400	-	145,000	-	-	-	-	153,400	173,700	-	-	-	-	-	-	-	118,800	167,900
Reno (city)	158,700	158,000	121,700	164,500	-	-	183,900	-	147,600	-	-	-	-	146,200	155,200	-	-	-	-	-	-	-	-	165,200
Sparks (city)	143,700	142,300	-	-	-	-	164,700	-	128,500	-	-	-	-	-	-	-	-	-	-	-	-	-	-	-
NEW HAMPSHIRE	133,300	162,800	-	194,100	-	-	167,800	-	122,200	-	-	-	-	139,600	140,600	119,300	-	-	-	-	-	-	-	132,100
Belknap County	109,600	122,200	-	-	-	-	-	-	-	-	-	-	-	-	-	-	-	-	-	-	-	-	-	-
Cheshire County	105,300	142,000	-	-	-	-	-	-	-	-	-	-	-	-	-	-	-	-	-	-	-	-	-	-
Grafton County	109,500	189,200	-	-	-	-	232,500	-	-	-	-	-	-	-	-	-	-	-	-	-	-	-	-	-
Hanover (town)	262,200	236,800	-	-	-	-	-	-	-	-	-	-	-	-	-	-	-	-	-	-	-	-	-	-
Hillsborough County	139,100	164,800	-	195,900	-	-	155,000	-	128,600	-	-	-	-	-	137,500	-	-	-	-	-	-	-	-	135,400
Nashua (city)	137,500	174,800	-	199,000	-	-	163,300	-	-	-	-	-	-	-	-	-	-	-	-	-	-	-	-	-
Merrimack County	117,900	146,400	-	-	-	-	-	-	-	-	-	-	-	-	-	-	-	-	-	-	-	-	-	-
Rockingham County	164,900	164,600	-	151,600	-	-	232,100	-	153,300	-	-	-	-	-	135,700	-	-	-	-	-	-	-	-	-
Strafford County	121,000	148,300	-	-	-	-	123,400	-	-	-	-	-	-	-	-	-	-	-	-	-	-	-	-	-
NEW JERSEY	170,800	214,300	173,600	225,300	156,000	96,500	242,800	-	179,500	225,000	109,100	-	186,400	198,500	263,600	120,000	-	185,600	186,300	216,300	281,100	177,300	-	139,400
Atlantic County	122,000	116,300	-	111,300	0	-	102,500	-	134,500	-	-	-	-	-	134,300	-	-	133,600	-	-	-	-	-	96,400
Atlantic City (city)	87,500	91,700	-	88,000	-	-	79,800	-	111,800	-	-	-	-	-	-	-	-	-	-	-	-	-	-	90,800
Brigantine (city)	144,400	108,600	-	-	-	-	-	-	-	-	-	-	-	-	-	-	-	-	-	-	-	-	-	-
Egg Harbor (township)	131,300	131,800	-	-	-	-	-	-	-	-	-	-	-	-	-	-	-	-	-	-	-	-	-	-
Galloway (township)	130,000	121,700	-	114,500	-	-	-	-	-	-	-	-	-	-	-	-	-	-	-	-	-	-	-	-
Ventnor City (city)	129,700	134,300	-	-	-	-	-	-	-	-	-	-	-	-	-	-	-	-	-	-	-	-	-	-
Bergen County	250,300	268,400	-	255,500	-	-	286,300	-	218,700	-	-	-	-	272,800	308,800	-	-	231,300	-	-	341,400	327,500	-	322,400
Bergenfield (borough)	184,400	195,700	-	211,600	-	-	-	-	191,700	-	-	-	-	-	-	-	-	-	-	-	-	-	-	-
Cliffside Park (borough)	227,500	402,400	-	-	-	-	-	-	-	-	-	-	-	0	436,700	-	-	-	-	-	-	-	-	-
Dumont (borough)	195,000	222,900	-	247,200	-	-	-	-	220,200	-	-	-	-	-	-	-	-	-	-	-	-	-	-	-
Elmwood Park (borough)	184,100	181,400	-	186,800	-	-	-	-	-	-	-	-	-	-	-	-	-	-	-	-	-	-	-	-
Englewood (city)	212,400	248,000	-	-	-	-	-	-	165,400	-	-	-	-	-	-	-	-	-	-	-	-	-	-	-
Fair Lawn (borough)	218,000	229,700	-	237,300	-	-	-	-	221,500	-	-	-	-	-	-	-	-	-	-	-	-	-	-	-
Fairview (borough)	179,900	193,300	-	-	-	-	-	-	-	-	-	-	-	-	-	-	-	-	-	-	-	-	-	-
Fort Lee (borough)	287,000	293,200	-	285,400	-	-	315,600	-	-	-	-	-	-	32,500	265,600	-	-	-	-	-	-	-	-	-
Franklin Lakes (borough)	609,400	722,700	-	-	-	-	-	-	-	-	-	-	-	-	-	-	-	-	-	-	-	-	-	-
Glen Rock (borough)	316,900	295,100	-	-	-	-	-	-	-	-	-	-	-	-	-	-	-	-	-	-	-	-	-	-

Notes: Please refer to the User's Guide for an explanation of data; data is arranged alphabetically by state, then county, then city within each county; table includes counties with populations greater than 49,999 unless noted and cities with populations greater than 9,999 whose Asian and/or NHPI population rates are greater than the national average; (1) Native Hawaiian and other Pacific Islander; (2) excludes Taiwanese; (3) includes Chamorro; (4) county does not meet population threshold but is shown in order to allow inclusion of city

Place	All specified owner-occupied housing units	Specified housing units owned and occup. by Asians	Specified housing units owned and occup. by NHPIs[1]	Asian Indian	Bangladeshi	Cambodian	Chinese[2]	Fijian	Filipino	Guamanian[3]	Hawaiian, Native	Hmong	Indonesian	Japanese	Korean	Laotian	Malaysian	Pakistani	Samoan	Sri Lankan	Taiwanese	Thai	Tongan	Vietnamese
Hackensack (city)	187,300	190,200	-	243,800	-	-	-	-	195,800	-	-	-	-	-	47,100	-	-	-	-	-	-	-	-	-
Hasbrouck Heights (borough)	215,300	239,700	-	-	-	-	-	-	-	-	-	-	-	-	-	-	-	-	-	-	-	-	-	-
Hillsdale (borough)	291,800	326,700	-	-	-	-	-	-	-	-	-	-	-	-	-	-	-	-	-	-	-	-	-	-
Little Ferry (borough)	192,800	187,300	-	262,500	-	-	-	-	185,300	-	-	-	-	-	0	-	-	-	-	-	-	-	-	-
Lodi (borough)	172,600	174,100	-	167,300	-	-	-	-	187,500	-	-	-	-	-	-	-	-	-	-	-	-	-	-	-
Lyndhurst (township)	182,800	173,100	-	-	-	-	-	-	-	-	-	-	-	-	-	-	-	-	-	-	-	-	-	-
Mahwah (township)	334,100	331,300	-	361,400	-	-	-	-	-	-	-	-	-	-	-	-	-	-	-	-	-	-	-	-
New Milford (borough)	223,400	251,900	-	247,200	-	-	-	-	252,900	-	-	-	-	-	-	-	-	-	-	-	-	-	-	-
North Arlington (borough)	183,300	180,800	-	-	-	-	-	-	-	-	-	-	-	-	-	-	-	-	-	-	-	-	-	-
Palisades Park (borough)	231,700	255,900	-	-	-	-	-	-	-	-	-	-	-	-	271,900	-	-	-	-	-	-	-	-	-
Paramus (borough)	284,800	316,300	-	292,700	-	-	292,800	-	333,900	-	-	-	-	-	341,300	-	-	-	-	-	-	-	-	-
Ramsey (borough)	329,700	320,500	-	-	-	-	-	-	-	-	-	-	-	-	-	-	-	-	-	-	-	-	-	-
Ridgefield (borough)	239,100	254,000	-	-	-	-	-	-	-	-	-	-	-	-	248,100	-	-	-	-	-	-	-	-	-
Ridgefield Park (village)	171,300	168,800	-	-	-	-	-	-	-	-	-	-	-	-	23,300	-	-	-	-	-	-	-	-	-
Ridgewood (village)	387,200	321,200	-	-	-	-	-	-	-	-	-	-	-	295,000	334,600	-	-	-	-	-	-	-	-	-
River Edge (borough)	252,700	276,800	-	-	-	-	-	-	-	-	-	-	-	-	258,300	-	-	-	-	-	-	-	-	-
Rutherford (borough)	218,300	214,600	-	235,700	-	-	-	-	-	-	-	-	-	-	219,600	-	-	-	-	-	-	-	-	-
Saddle Brook (township)	198,600	200,700	-	-	-	-	-	-	-	-	-	-	-	-	-	-	-	-	-	-	-	-	-	-
Teaneck (township)	208,800	208,300	-	196,100	-	-	-	-	204,500	-	-	-	-	-	-	-	-	-	-	-	-	-	-	-
Tenafly (borough)	403,600	324,000	-	-	-	-	370,700	-	-	-	-	-	-	-	262,500	-	-	-	-	-	-	-	-	-
Wallington (borough)	201,800	225,000	-	-	-	-	-	-	-	-	-	-	-	-	-	-	-	-	-	-	-	-	-	-
Westwood (borough)	239,300	222,600	-	-	-	-	-	-	-	-	-	-	-	-	-	-	-	-	-	-	-	-	-	-
Wyckoff (township)	417,500	415,800	-	-	-	-	-	-	-	-	-	-	-	-	-	-	-	-	-	-	-	-	-	-
Burlington County	137,400	159,200	-	204,300	-	-	172,100	-	160,800	-	-	-	-	97,800	127,300	-	-	-	-	-	-	-	-	121,700
Browns Mills (cdp)	93,800	98,400	-	-	-	-	-	-	-	-	-	-	-	-	97,600	-	-	-	-	-	-	-	-	-
Evesham (township)	157,000	165,800	-	199,100	-	-	168,800	-	-	-	-	-	-	-	-	-	-	-	-	-	-	-	-	-
Maple Shade (township)	107,900	112,500	-	0	-	-	-	-	-	-	-	-	-	-	-	-	-	-	-	-	-	-	-	-
Marlton (cdp)	136,900	136,800	-	-	-	-	-	-	-	-	-	-	-	-	-	-	-	-	-	-	-	-	-	-
Mount Laurel (township)	161,900	168,500	-	220,600	-	-	150,700	-	-	-	-	-	-	-	-	-	-	-	-	-	-	-	-	-
Camden County	111,200	141,100	-	167,900	-	68,200	148,800	-	136,900	-	-	-	-	-	158,000	-	-	133,000	-	-	-	-	-	69,400
Barclay-Kingston (cdp)	148,000	142,300	-	-	-	-	-	-	-	-	-	-	-	-	-	-	-	-	-	-	-	-	-	-
Bellmawr (borough)	95,800	114,400	-	-	-	-	-	-	-	-	-	-	-	-	-	-	-	-	-	-	-	-	-	-
Cherry Hill Mall (cdp)	141,300	137,300	-	-	-	-	-	-	-	-	-	-	-	-	-	-	-	-	-	-	-	-	-	-
Cherry Hill (township)	154,900	162,500	-	172,800	-	-	162,500	-	150,500	-	-	-	-	-	170,100	-	-	-	-	-	-	-	-	-
Echelon (cdp)	126,600	127,000	-	127,500	-	-	-	-	-	-	-	-	-	-	-	-	-	-	-	-	-	-	-	-
Greentree (cdp)	179,400	183,000	-	191,100	-	-	180,300	-	-	-	-	-	-	-	-	-	-	-	-	-	-	-	-	-
Pennsauken (township)	95,300	98,100	-	-	-	-	-	-	-	-	-	-	-	-	-	-	-	-	-	-	-	-	-	81,900
Springdale (cdp)	213,300	186,600	-	-	-	-	173,900	-	-	-	-	-	-	-	-	-	-	-	-	-	-	-	-	-
Voorhees (township)	179,500	197,200	-	209,900	-	-	180,800	-	184,400	-	-	-	-	-	-	-	-	-	-	-	-	-	-	-
Cape May County	137,600	141,800	-	-	-	-	-	-	-	-	-	-	-	-	-	-	-	-	-	-	-	-	-	-
Cumberland County	91,200	103,200	-	126,800	-	-	-	-	-	-	-	-	-	-	-	-	-	-	-	-	-	-	-	-

Notes: Please refer to the User's Guide for an explanation of data; data is arranged alphabetically by state, then county, then city within each county; table includes counties with populations greater than 49,999 unless noted and cities with populations greater than 9,999 whose Asian and/or NHPI population rates are greater than the national average; (1) Native Hawaiian and other Pacific Islander; (2) excludes Taiwanese; (3) includes Chamorro; (4) county does not meet population threshold but is shown in order to allow inclusion of city

Place	All specified owner-occupied housing units	Specified housing units owned and occup. by Asians	Specified housing units owned and occup. by NHPIs[1]	Asian Indian	Bangladeshi	Cambodian	Chinese[2]	Fijian	Filipino	Guamanian[3]	Hawaiian, Native	Hmong	Indonesian	Japanese	Korean	Laotian	Malaysian	Pakistani	Samoan	Sri Lankan	Taiwanese	Thai	Tongan	Vietnamese
Essex County	208,400	215,200	275,000	225,900	-	-	259,900	-	173,700	-	-	-	-	239,300	246,800	-	-	235,500	-	-	357,800	-	-	191,900
Belleville (township)	147,500	158,500	-	155,700	-	-	-	-	161,600	-	-	-	-	-	-	-	-	-	-	-	-	-	-	158,600
Bloomfield (township)	164,800	172,600	-	177,300	-	-	190,200	-	167,000	-	-	-	-	-	-	-	-	-	-	-	-	-	-	-
Cedar Grove (township)	237,600	261,300	-	-	-	-	-	-	-	-	-	-	-	-	-	-	-	-	-	-	-	-	-	-
Livingston (township)	290,200	272,900	-	267,000	-	-	280,800	-	231,100	-	-	-	-	-	263,500	-	-	-	-	-	-	-	-	-
Millburn (township)	549,000	475,000	-	-	-	-	417,100	-	-	-	-	-	-	-	-	-	-	-	-	-	-	-	-	-
Nutley (township)	190,500	191,200	-	206,500	-	-	-	-	168,800	-	-	-	-	-	-	-	-	-	-	-	-	-	-	-
Verona (township)	237,900	220,700	-	-	-	-	-	-	-	-	-	-	-	-	-	-	-	-	-	-	-	-	-	-
West Caldwell (township)	265,900	238,400	-	-	-	-	-	-	-	-	-	-	-	-	-	-	-	-	-	-	-	-	-	-
West Orange (township)	209,200	204,000	-	219,000	-	-	259,100	-	190,700	-	-	-	-	-	161,100	-	-	-	-	-	-	-	-	-
Gloucester County	120,100	142,600	-	143,700	-	-	169,800	-	145,100	-	-	-	-	-	117,500	-	-	-	-	-	-	-	-	-
Hudson County	150,300	142,600	-	145,400	-	-	124,000	-	141,700	-	-	-	-	187,500	168,200	-	-	175,400	-	-	-	-	-	146,300
Bayonne (city)	155,600	158,900	-	178,600	-	-	-	-	150,000	-	-	-	-	-	137,500	-	-	-	-	-	-	-	-	-
Guttenberg (town)	150,200	0	-	-	-	-	-	-	-	-	-	-	-	-	-	-	-	-	-	-	-	-	-	-
Harrison (town)	135,000	115,300	-	-	-	-	120,800	-	-	-	-	-	-	-	-	-	-	-	-	-	-	-	-	-
Hoboken (city)	428,900	225,000	-	0	-	-	275,000	-	-	-	-	-	-	-	-	-	-	-	-	-	-	-	-	-
Jersey City (city)	125,000	133,800	-	128,800	-	-	109,900	-	135,000	-	-	-	-	-	158,300	-	-	166,300	-	-	-	-	-	162,500
Kearny (town)	158,200	141,100	-	97,500	-	-	145,800	-	-	-	-	-	-	-	-	-	-	-	-	-	-	-	-	-
North Bergen (township)	162,600	188,700	-	178,000	-	-	202,800	-	-	-	-	-	-	-	-	-	-	-	-	-	-	-	-	-
Secaucus (town)	209,400	207,800	-	193,800	-	-	-	-	221,100	-	-	-	-	-	-	-	-	-	-	-	-	-	-	-
Weehawken (township)	231,200	535,700	-	-	-	-	-	-	-	-	-	-	-	-	-	-	-	-	-	-	-	-	-	-
Hunterdon County	245,000	331,600	-	348,900	-	-	335,000	-	-	-	-	-	-	-	-	-	-	-	-	-	-	-	-	-
Mercer County	147,400	278,700	-	266,600	-	-	315,800	-	170,800	-	-	-	-	283,300	309,900	-	-	215,400	-	-	292,100	-	-	-
East Windsor (township)	152,600	141,800	-	143,400	-	-	-	-	-	-	-	-	-	-	-	-	-	-	-	-	-	-	-	-
Hopewell (township)	252,600	309,100	-	-	-	-	-	-	-	-	-	-	-	-	-	-	-	-	-	-	-	-	-	-
Lawrence (township)	177,900	176,600	-	171,300	-	-	262,000	-	-	-	-	-	-	-	-	-	-	-	-	-	-	-	-	-
Princeton (borough)	343,500	295,800	-	-	-	-	-	-	-	-	-	-	-	-	-	-	-	-	-	-	-	-	-	-
Princeton (township)	417,000	439,400	-	347,200	-	-	444,000	-	-	-	-	-	-	-	-	-	-	-	-	-	-	-	-	-
West Windsor (township)	333,800	366,800	-	404,600	-	-	350,400	-	-	-	-	-	-	-	364,600	-	-	-	-	-	-	-	-	-
Middlesex County	168,500	201,700	-	201,700	142,500	-	214,100	-	191,600	-	-	-	187,000	208,300	210,500	-	-	200,400	-	260,900	187,800	-	-	161,900
Avenel (cdp)	142,600	156,400	-	169,300	-	-	-	-	-	-	-	-	-	-	-	-	-	-	-	-	-	-	-	-
Carteret (borough)	135,500	136,300	-	134,500	-	-	-	-	-	-	-	-	-	-	-	-	-	-	-	-	-	-	-	-
Colonia (cdp)	180,800	193,800	-	235,300	-	-	-	-	180,700	-	-	-	-	-	-	-	-	-	-	-	-	-	-	-
East Brunswick (township)	212,800	232,200	-	234,100	-	-	243,700	-	230,000	-	-	-	-	-	208,300	-	-	-	-	-	-	-	-	-
Edison (township)	186,900	215,400	-	213,100	-	-	218,400	-	207,700	-	-	-	-	-	238,600	-	-	268,800	-	-	195,000	-	-	-
Fords (cdp)	154,700	159,400	-	163,600	-	-	-	-	164,700	-	-	-	-	-	-	-	-	-	-	-	-	-	-	-
Highland Park (borough)	183,300	150,000	-	0	-	-	19,600	-	-	-	-	-	-	-	-	-	-	-	-	-	-	-	-	-
Iselin (cdp)	151,000	154,600	-	154,000	-	-	143,800	-	-	-	-	-	-	-	-	-	-	-	-	-	-	-	-	-
Metuchen (borough)	194,900	203,500	-	-	-	-	-	-	-	-	-	-	-	-	-	-	-	-	-	-	-	-	-	-
Middlesex (borough)	164,200	181,900	-	-	-	-	-	-	-	-	-	-	-	-	-	-	-	-	-	-	-	-	-	-
New Brunswick (city)	122,600	119,300	-	113,200	-	-	126,600	-	-	-	-	-	-	-	-	-	-	-	-	-	-	-	-	-

Notes: Please refer to the User's Guide for an explanation of data; data is arranged alphabetically by state, then county, then city within each county; table includes counties with populations greater than 49,999 unless noted and cities with populations greater than 9,999 whose Asian and/or NHPI population rates are greater than the national average; (1) Native Hawaiian and other Pacific Islander; (2) excludes Taiwanese; (3) includes Chamorro; (4) county does not meet population threshold but is shown in order to allow inclusion of city

Place	All specified owner-occupied housing units	Specified housing units owned and occup. by Asians	Specified housing units owned and occup. by NHPIs[1]	Asian Indian	Bangladeshi	Cambodian	Chinese[2]	Fijian	Filipino	Guamanian[3]	Hawaiian, Native	Hmong	Indonesian	Japanese	Korean	Laotian	Malaysian	Pakistani	Samoan	Sri Lankan	Taiwanese	Thai	Tongan	Vietnamese
North Brunswick (township)	179,400	197,800	-	197,900	-	-	186,000	-	257,800	-	-	-	-	-	232,100	-	-	-	-	-	-	-	-	-
Old Bridge (township)	162,800	205,000	-	206,500	-	-	202,900	-	217,300	-	-	-	-	-	-	-	-	218,100	-	-	-	-	-	-
Piscataway (township)	170,800	194,800	-	187,800	-	-	218,800	-	195,100	-	-	-	-	-	189,100	-	-	-	-	-	-	-	-	-
Plainsboro (township)	257,100	293,100	-	346,200	-	-	259,600	-	-	-	-	-	-	-	-	-	-	-	-	-	-	-	-	-
Princeton Meadows (cdp)	212,200	256,000	-	343,500	-	-	183,200	-	-	-	-	-	-	-	-	-	-	-	-	-	-	-	-	-
Sayreville (borough)	153,400	180,100	-	174,800	-	-	177,800	-	168,200	-	-	-	-	-	-	-	-	-	-	-	-	-	-	-
South Brunswick (township)	202,000	231,600	-	256,600	-	-	217,100	-	253,700	-	-	-	-	-	-	-	-	-	-	-	-	-	-	-
South Plainfield (borough)	165,800	178,400	-	170,100	-	-	-	-	180,600	-	-	-	-	-	-	-	-	-	-	-	-	-	-	177,400
Woodbridge (township)	158,100	161,700	-	164,300	-	-	149,000	-	165,800	-	-	-	-	-	171,900	-	-	137,500	-	-	-	-	-	-
Monmouth County	203,100	255,100	-	273,300	-	-	262,100	-	221,800	-	-	-	-	211,500	247,500	-	-	187,500	-	-	-	-	-	172,100
Aberdeen (township)	160,800	175,500	-	164,800	-	-	169,200	-	-	-	-	-	-	-	-	-	-	-	-	-	-	-	-	-
Colts Neck (township)	425,500	417,300	-	-	-	-	-	-	-	-	-	-	-	-	-	-	-	-	-	-	-	-	-	-
Eatontown (borough)	178,200	162,500	-	-	-	-	-	-	-	-	-	-	-	-	-	-	-	-	-	-	-	-	-	-
Freehold (township)	227,500	258,600	-	286,800	-	-	245,500	-	256,300	-	-	-	-	-	-	-	-	-	-	-	-	-	-	-
Holmdel (township)	404,200	408,000	-	443,600	-	-	374,600	-	-	-	-	-	-	-	-	-	-	-	-	-	-	-	-	-
Howell (township)	172,400	190,000	-	197,500	-	-	-	-	191,000	-	-	-	-	-	-	-	-	-	-	-	-	-	-	-
Manalapan (township)	257,100	301,600	-	322,100	-	-	299,000	-	-	-	-	-	-	-	-	-	-	-	-	-	-	-	-	-
Marlboro (township)	286,300	314,800	-	355,600	-	-	312,300	-	-	-	-	-	-	-	-	-	-	-	-	-	-	-	-	-
Morganville (cdp)	278,600	272,200	-	-	-	-	297,900	-	-	-	-	-	-	-	-	-	-	-	-	-	-	-	-	-
Ocean (township)	198,900	196,900	-	172,900	-	-	-	-	-	-	-	-	-	-	-	-	-	-	-	-	-	-	-	-
Tinton Falls (borough)	187,900	182,500	-	-	-	-	-	-	-	-	-	-	-	-	-	-	-	-	-	-	-	-	-	-
West Freehold (cdp)	219,300	234,100	-	-	-	-	-	-	-	-	-	-	-	-	-	-	-	-	-	-	-	-	-	-
Morris County	257,400	280,300	-	279,300	-	-	302,900	-	238,600	-	-	-	-	271,900	281,600	-	-	192,500	-	-	308,000	-	-	191,800
Chatham (township)	449,000	444,800	-	-	-	-	-	-	-	-	-	-	-	-	-	-	-	-	-	-	-	-	-	-
Denville (township)	228,300	375,000	-	-	-	-	-	-	-	-	-	-	-	-	-	-	-	-	-	-	-	-	-	-
East Hanover (township)	322,800	335,600	-	-	-	-	308,800	-	-	-	-	-	-	-	-	-	-	-	-	-	-	-	-	-
Hanover (township)	286,100	311,700	-	279,200	-	-	381,800	-	-	-	-	-	-	-	-	-	-	-	-	-	-	-	-	-
Lincoln Park (borough)	194,300	205,700	-	-	-	-	-	-	-	-	-	-	-	-	-	-	-	-	-	-	-	-	-	-
Montville (township)	346,600	350,400	-	356,000	-	-	370,500	-	-	-	-	-	-	-	-	-	-	-	-	-	-	-	-	-
Morris (township)	350,400	364,400	-	-	-	-	-	-	-	-	-	-	-	-	-	-	-	-	-	-	-	-	-	-
Mount Olive (township)	197,800	264,100	-	330,300	-	-	-	-	-	-	-	-	-	-	-	-	-	-	-	-	-	-	-	-
Parsippany-Troy Hills (twp)	234,100	261,300	-	230,500	-	-	276,300	-	253,100	-	-	-	-	-	363,900	-	-	-	-	-	-	-	-	-
Randolph (township)	329,800	343,900	-	342,200	-	-	352,100	-	-	-	-	-	-	-	-	-	-	-	-	-	-	-	-	-
Rockaway (township)	206,200	226,100	-	209,000	-	-	-	-	-	-	-	-	-	-	-	-	-	-	-	-	-	-	-	-
Roxbury (township)	207,400	171,300	-	-	-	-	-	-	-	-	-	-	-	-	-	-	-	-	-	-	-	-	-	-
Succasunna-Kenvil (cdp)	229,600	166,700	-	-	-	-	-	-	-	-	-	-	-	-	-	-	-	-	-	-	-	-	-	-
Ocean County	131,300	152,500	-	212,000	-	-	155,000	-	140,800	-	-	-	-	-	156,700	-	-	-	-	-	-	-	-	-
Passaic County	190,600	191,400	-	178,400	58,800	-	240,300	-	179,600	-	-	-	-	-	338,500	-	-	-	-	-	-	-	-	-
Clifton (city)	181,600	186,300	-	172,400	-	-	195,600	-	196,900	-	-	-	-	-	308,300	-	-	-	-	-	-	-	-	-
Little Falls (township)	212,300	184,200	-	-	-	-	-	-	-	-	-	-	-	-	-	-	-	-	-	-	-	-	-	-
Passaic (city)	153,000	162,700	-	162,500	-	-	-	-	159,900	-	-	-	-	-	-	-	-	-	-	-	-	-	-	-

Notes: Please refer to the User's Guide for an explanation of data; data is arranged alphabetically by state, then county, then city within each county; table includes counties with populations greater than 49,999 unless noted and cities with populations greater than 9,999 whose Asian and/or NHPI population rates are greater than the national average; (1) Native Hawaiian and other Pacific Islander; (2) excludes Taiwanese; (3) includes Chamorro; (4) county does not meet population threshold but is shown in order to allow inclusion of city

Place	All specified owner-occupied housing units	Specified housing units owned and occup. by Asians	Specified housing units owned and occup. by NHPIs[1]	Asian Indian	Bangladeshi	Cambodian	Chinese[2]	Fijian	Filipino	Guamanian[3]	Hawaiian, Native	Hmong	Indonesian	Japanese	Korean	Laotian	Malaysian	Pakistani	Samoan	Sri Lankan	Taiwanese	Thai	Tongan	Vietnamese
Wayne (township)	284,800	306,600	-	296,900	-	-	314,800	-	174,100	-	-	-	-	-	351,900	-	-	-	-	-	-	-	-	-
Salem County	105,200	125,000	-	-	-	-	-	-	-	-	-	-	-	-	-	-	-	-	-	-	-	-	-	-
Somerset County	235,000	285,400	-	297,600	-	-	305,700	-	210,800	-	-	-	-	242,600	252,200	-	-	141,100	-	-	336,900	-	-	213,800
Bernards (township)	380,500	414,500	-	437,500	-	-	432,400	-	-	-	-	-	-	-	-	-	-	-	-	-	-	-	-	-
Branchburg (township)	278,000	284,100	-	271,600	-	-	-	-	-	-	-	-	-	-	-	-	-	-	-	-	-	-	-	-
Bridgewater (township)	268,100	316,800	-	331,100	-	-	333,600	-	-	-	-	-	-	-	-	-	-	-	-	-	-	-	-	-
Franklin (township)	169,700	170,300	-	168,400	-	-	158,900	-	207,400	-	-	-	-	-	-	-	-	-	-	-	-	-	-	-
Hillsborough (township)	238,600	256,100	-	257,200	-	-	260,600	-	-	-	-	-	-	-	-	-	-	-	-	-	-	-	-	-
Montgomery (township)	348,500	378,400	-	445,200	-	-	356,300	-	-	-	-	-	-	-	-	-	-	-	-	-	-	-	-	-
North Plainfield (borough)	150,100	155,100	-	-	-	-	-	-	-	-	-	-	-	-	-	-	-	-	-	-	-	-	-	-
Somerset (cdp)	167,500	157,600	-	138,200	-	-	154,000	-	188,400	-	-	-	-	-	-	-	-	-	-	-	-	-	-	-
Somerville (borough)	156,700	157,700	-	-	-	-	-	-	-	-	-	-	-	-	-	-	-	-	-	-	-	-	-	-
Warren (township)	427,200	527,700	-	493,200	-	-	608,200	-	-	-	-	-	-	-	-	-	-	-	-	-	-	-	-	-
Sussex County	157,700	187,100	-	226,900	-	-	-	-	165,200	-	-	-	-	-	-	-	-	-	-	-	-	-	-	-
Union County	188,800	202,700	-	217,100	-	-	242,200	-	174,000	-	-	-	-	-	230,600	-	-	220,000	-	-	-	-	-	143,800
Berkeley Heights (township)	324,900	362,900	-	-	-	-	392,900	-	-	-	-	-	-	-	-	-	-	-	-	-	-	-	-	-
New Providence (borough)	317,100	321,000	-	-	-	-	346,400	-	-	-	-	-	-	-	-	-	-	-	-	-	-	-	-	-
Rahway (city)	142,600	151,700	-	-	-	-	-	-	137,900	-	-	-	-	-	-	-	-	-	-	-	-	-	-	-
Roselle Park (borough)	157,700	178,000	-	169,600	-	-	-	-	-	-	-	-	-	-	-	-	-	-	-	-	-	-	-	-
Scotch Plains (township)	258,800	358,600	-	461,100	-	-	211,100	-	-	-	-	-	-	-	-	-	-	-	-	-	-	-	-	-
Springfield (township)	250,500	246,900	-	-	-	-	-	-	-	-	-	-	-	-	-	-	-	-	-	-	-	-	-	-
Summit (city)	469,200	462,500	-	443,300	-	-	-	-	-	-	-	-	-	-	-	-	-	-	-	-	-	-	-	-
Union (township)	172,900	181,500	-	184,500	-	-	166,100	-	184,300	-	-	-	-	-	-	-	-	-	-	-	-	-	-	-
Westfield (town)	346,000	276,700	-	-	-	-	-	-	-	-	-	-	-	-	-	-	-	-	-	-	-	-	-	-
Warren County	155,500	183,300	-	253,700	-	-	-	-	-	-	-	-	-	-	-	-	-	-	-	-	-	-	-	-
NEW MEXICO	108,100	136,400	114,800	141,300	-	-	151,100	-	118,200	132,100	79,500	-	-	137,300	124,100	-	-	-	-	-	-	56,700	-	127,900
Bernalillo County	128,300	139,700	124,600	203,800	-	-	178,900	-	117,000	-	-	-	-	131,700	124,700	-	-	-	-	-	-	-	-	129,800
Chaves County	61,000	115,200	-	-	-	-	-	-	-	-	-	-	-	-	-	-	-	-	-	-	-	-	-	-
Dona Ana County	90,900	137,500	-	-	-	-	134,400	-	-	-	-	-	-	-	-	-	-	-	-	-	-	-	-	-
Los Alamos County[4]	228,300	195,000	-	-	-	-	-	-	-	-	-	-	-	-	-	-	-	-	-	-	-	-	-	-
Los Alamos (cdp)	228,500	197,200	-	-	-	-	-	-	-	-	-	-	-	-	-	-	-	-	-	-	-	-	-	-
Otero County	78,800	103,100	-	-	-	-	-	-	-	-	-	-	-	-	-	-	-	-	-	-	-	-	-	-
Sandoval County	115,400	141,300	-	-	-	-	-	-	147,900	-	-	-	-	-	-	-	-	-	-	-	-	-	-	-
Santa Fe County	189,400	164,100	-	-	-	-	-	-	-	-	-	-	-	-	-	-	-	-	-	-	-	-	-	-
NEW YORK	148,700	227,700	175,200	230,100	253,400	72,000	229,200	-	214,300	164,100	167,500	-	193,200	243,000	275,400	63,400	219,800	233,300	140,500	226,400	246,500	190,500	-	92,400
Albany County	116,300	155,600	-	160,800	-	-	153,300	-	189,100	-	-	-	-	-	97,800	-	-	-	-	-	-	-	-	89,600
Colonie (town)	118,300	161,000	-	159,000	-	-	178,300	-	-	-	-	-	-	-	-	-	-	-	-	-	-	-	-	-
Guilderland (town)	135,300	183,600	-	185,900	-	-	-	-	-	-	-	-	-	-	-	-	-	-	-	-	-	-	-	-
Bronx County (Bronx)	190,400	190,800	158,300	184,700	0	194,600	190,500	-	200,700	-	-	-	-	325,000	257,100	-	-	187,500	-	-	-	-	-	207,400
Broome County	75,800	110,200	-	155,900	-	-	130,000	-	-	-	-	-	-	-	262,500	64,000	-	-	-	-	-	-	-	51,000
Johnson City (village)	62,500	65,000	-	-	-	-	-	-	-	-	-	-	-	-	-	-	-	-	-	-	-	-	-	-

Notes: Please refer to the User's Guide for an explanation of data; data is arranged alphabetically by state, then county, then city within each county; table includes counties with populations greater than 49,999 unless noted and cities with populations greater than 9,999 whose Asian and/or NHPI population rates are greater than the national average; (1) Native Hawaiian and other Pacific Islander; (2) excludes Taiwanese; (3) includes Chamorro; (4) county does not meet population threshold but is shown in order to allow inclusion of city

Place	All specified owner-occupied housing units	Specified housing units owned and occup. by Asians	Specified housing units owned and occup. by NHPIs[1]	Asian Indian	Bangladeshi	Cambodian	Chinese[2]	Fijian	Filipino	Guamanian[3]	Hawaiian, Native	Hmong	Indonesian	Japanese	Korean	Laotian	Malaysian	Pakistani	Samoan	Sri Lankan	Taiwanese	Thai	Tongan	Vietnamese
Vestal (town)	89,400	149,700	-	-	-	-	138,500	-	-	-	-	-	-	-	-	-	-	-	-	-	-	-	-	-
Cattaraugus County	60,800	122,500	-	-	-	-	-	-	-	-	-	-	-	-	-	-	-	-	-	-	-	-	-	-
Cayuga County	75,300	152,500	-	-	-	-	-	-	-	-	-	-	-	-	-	-	-	-	-	-	-	-	-	-
Chautauqua County	64,000	79,700	-	-	-	-	-	-	-	-	-	-	-	-	-	-	-	-	-	-	-	-	-	-
Chemung County	67,200	105,400	-	-	-	-	-	-	-	-	-	-	-	-	-	-	-	-	-	-	-	-	-	-
Chenango County	62,700	82,900	-	-	-	-	-	-	-	-	-	-	-	-	-	-	-	-	-	-	-	-	-	-
Clinton County	84,200	99,400	-	-	-	-	-	-	-	-	-	-	-	-	-	-	-	-	-	-	-	-	-	-
Columbia County	111,800	275,000	-	-	-	-	-	-	-	-	-	-	-	-	-	-	-	-	-	-	-	-	-	-
Dutchess County	154,200	193,600	-	184,000	-	-	208,200	-	-	-	-	-	-	-	262,900	-	-	-	-	-	-	-	-	-
Arlington (cdp)	130,700	168,800	-	-	-	-	-	-	-	-	-	-	-	-	-	-	-	-	-	-	-	-	-	-
Poughkeepsie (town)	142,000	178,600	-	175,500	-	-	208,000	-	-	-	-	-	-	-	-	-	-	-	-	-	-	-	-	-
Wappinger (town)	160,500	164,600	-	158,200	-	-	-	-	-	-	-	-	-	-	-	-	-	-	-	-	-	-	-	-
Erie County	90,800	140,600	-	165,400	-	-	136,400	-	137,500	-	-	-	-	134,400	148,100	-	-	-	-	-	-	-	-	38,200
Amherst (town)	120,000	152,100	-	176,300	-	-	136,700	-	-	-	-	-	-	-	166,100	-	-	-	-	-	-	-	-	-
Herkimer County	67,500	67,300	-	-	-	-	-	-	-	-	-	-	-	-	-	-	-	-	-	-	-	-	-	-
Jefferson County	68,200	84,500	-	-	-	-	-	-	220,800	-	-	-	-	-	62,900	-	-	-	-	-	-	-	-	-
Kings County (Brooklyn)	224,100	217,300	423,900	223,600	225,000	42,500	216,600	-	216,400	450,000	-	-	-	310,000	270,900	-	-	316,100	-	-	-	-	-	185,500
Livingston County	88,800	92,100	-	-	-	-	-	-	-	-	-	-	-	-	-	-	-	-	-	-	-	-	-	-
Madison County	81,500	64,300	-	-	-	-	-	-	-	-	-	-	-	-	-	-	-	-	-	-	-	-	-	-
Monroe County	98,700	116,300	-	170,200	-	43,600	132,800	-	110,500	-	-	-	-	79,400	118,800	57,500	-	107,100	-	-	-	-	-	74,600
Brighton (town)	124,300	136,500	-	169,700	-	-	136,900	-	-	-	-	-	-	-	-	-	-	-	-	-	-	-	-	-
Henrietta (town)	96,300	112,500	-	171,600	-	-	100,000	-	-	-	-	-	-	-	-	-	-	-	-	-	-	-	-	-
Pittsford (town)	183,100	236,500	-	269,800	-	-	-	-	-	-	-	-	-	-	-	-	-	-	-	-	-	-	-	-
Nassau County	242,300	273,200	185,700	280,200	-	-	271,800	-	223,800	-	-	-	-	295,700	326,000	-	-	263,200	-	-	342,900	230,800	-	233,300
East Meadow (cdp)	214,300	253,000	-	275,000	-	-	-	-	238,700	-	-	-	-	-	-	-	-	-	-	-	-	-	-	-
Elmont (cdp)	190,100	196,000	-	199,300	-	-	-	-	180,000	-	-	-	-	-	-	-	-	-	-	-	-	-	-	-
Franklin Square (cdp)	224,500	237,000	-	231,800	-	-	-	-	-	-	-	-	-	-	-	-	-	-	-	-	-	-	-	-
Glen Cove (city)	263,800	267,300	-	223,500	-	-	-	-	-	-	-	-	-	-	271,900	-	-	-	-	-	-	-	-	-
Hicksville (cdp)	208,000	231,600	-	238,300	-	-	226,000	-	221,300	-	-	-	-	-	-	-	-	-	-	-	-	-	-	-
Jericho (cdp)	386,300	348,800	-	-	-	-	-	-	-	-	-	-	-	-	346,200	-	-	-	-	-	-	-	-	-
Mineola (village)	247,200	250,800	-	271,100	-	-	-	-	-	-	-	-	-	-	-	-	-	-	-	-	-	-	-	-
North Hempstead (town)	354,100	360,000	-	343,400	-	-	376,500	-	276,800	-	-	-	-	386,000	430,400	-	-	273,700	-	-	375,000	-	-	-
North Merrick (cdp)	234,600	249,100	-	-	-	-	-	-	-	-	-	-	-	-	-	-	-	-	-	-	-	-	-	-
North New Hyde Park (cdp)	266,400	265,800	-	274,200	-	-	261,400	-	-	-	-	-	-	-	-	-	-	-	-	-	-	-	-	-
North Valley Stream (cdp)	207,400	202,200	-	219,600	-	-	-	-	-	-	-	-	-	-	-	-	-	-	-	-	-	-	-	-
Oyster Bay (town)	259,800	293,700	-	310,600	-	-	289,800	-	235,600	-	-	-	-	271,400	328,900	-	-	-	-	-	-	-	-	-
Plainview (cdp)	291,100	276,100	-	252,400	-	-	294,300	-	-	-	-	-	-	-	284,600	-	-	-	-	-	-	-	-	-
Port Washington (cdp)	416,100	440,300	-	506,900	-	-	-	-	-	-	-	-	-	-	-	-	-	-	-	-	-	-	-	-
Salisbury (cdp)	213,000	247,000	-	236,300	-	-	-	-	-	-	-	-	-	-	-	-	-	-	-	-	-	-	-	-
Syosset (cdp)	327,000	328,000	-	352,900	-	-	328,000	-	-	-	-	-	-	-	289,400	-	-	-	-	-	-	-	-	-
Valley Stream (village)	199,800	224,000	-	-	-	-	235,800	-	214,500	-	-	-	-	-	-	-	-	-	-	-	-	-	-	-

Notes: Please refer to the User's Guide for an explanation of data; data is arranged alphabetically by state, then county, then city within each county; table includes counties with populations greater than 49,999 unless noted and cities with populations greater than 9,999 whose Asian and/or NHPI population rates are greater than the national average; (1) Native Hawaiian and other Pacific Islander; (2) excludes Taiwanese; (3) includes Chamorro; (4) county does not meet population threshold but is shown in order to allow inclusion of city

Place	All specified owner-occupied housing units	Specified housing units owned and occup. by Asians	Specified housing units owned and occup. by NHPIs[1]	Asian Indian	Bangladeshi	Cambodian	Chinese[2]	Fijian	Filipino	Guamanian[3]	Hawaiian, Native	Hmong	Indonesian	Japanese	Korean	Laotian	Malaysian	Pakistani	Samoan	Sri Lankan	Taiwanese	Thai	Tongan	Vietnamese
West Hempstead (cdp)	218,300	197,900	-	262,100	-	-	-	-	-	-	-	-	-	-	-	-	-	-	-	-	-	-	-	-
Westbury (village)	224,200	235,300		-	-	-	-	-	-	-	-	-	-	-	-	-	-	-	-	-	-	-	-	-
Woodmere (cdp)	356,700	334,700	-	-	-	-	-	-	-	-	-	-	-	-	-	-		-	-	-	-	-	-	-
New York City	211,900	226,600	189,400	211,500	253,000	50,700	229,700	-	216,800	406,700	177,100	-	255,800	247,500	274,400	-	227,900	250,900	137,500	217,300	256,300	197,900	-	218,400
New York County (Manhattan)	1 Mil.+	1 Mil.+	0	1 Mil.+	0	-	650,000	-	0	-	-	-	-	1 Mil.+	1 Mil.+	-	-	0	-	-	0	0	-	75,000
Niagara County	82,600	213,200	-	236,100	-	-	-	-	-	-	-	-	-	-	-	-	-	-	-	-	-	-	-	-
Oneida County	76,500	114,600	-	189,300	-	-	95,800	-	-	-	-	-	-	-	-	-	-	-	-	-	-	-	-	56,300
Onondaga County	85,400	106,200	-	145,600	-	-	120,400	-	85,700	-	-	-	-	79,400	149,400	-	-	-	-	-	-	-	-	61,900
Ontario County	94,100	89,700	-	-	-	-	-	-	-	-	-	-	-	-	-	-	-	-	-	-	-	-	-	-
Orange County	144,500	169,000	-	151,500	-	-	177,900	-	177,700	-	-	-	-	-	153,800	-	-	-	-	-	-	-	-	-
Oswego County	74,200	117,700	-	-	-	-	-	-	-	-	-	-	-	-	-	-	-	-	-	-	-	-	-	-
Otsego County	75,900	73,600	-	-	-	-	-	-	-	-	-	-	-	-	-	-	-	-	-	-	-	-	-	-
Putnam County	206,900	255,000	-	286,100	-	-	283,300	-	-	-	-	-	-	-	-	-	-	-	-	-	-	-	-	-
Queens County (Queens)	212,600	235,300	151,600	211,700	256,300	-	243,500	-	224,100	-	-	-	285,700	243,100	286,100	-	236,800	243,700	-	228,400	254,000	226,700	-	247,400
Rensselaer County	102,900	104,600	-	109,700	-	-	107,100	-	-	-	-	-	-	-	0	-	-	-	-	-	-	-	-	-
Richmond Co. (Staten Island)	209,100	192,400	-	226,000	-	-	171,700	-	192,100	-	-	-	-	-	220,600	-	-	214,600	-	205,000	-	-	-	-
Rockland County	242,500	240,300	-	250,000	-	-	242,200	-	223,500	-	-	-	-	-	260,500	-	-	-	-	-	-	-	-	-
Clarkstown (town)	255,700	246,500	-	256,000	-	-	235,200	-	231,100	-	-	-	-	-	290,000	-	-	-	-	-	-	-	-	-
Nanuet (cdp)	232,800	238,600	-	256,500	-	-	-	-	-	-	-	-	-	-	-	-	-	-	-	-	-	-	-	-
New City (cdp)	272,100	265,700	-	280,300	-	-	-	-	245,200	-	-	-	-	-	-	-	-	-	-	-	-	-	-	-
Orangetown (town)	266,900	273,000	-	277,400	-	-	282,100	-	267,300	-	-	-	-	-	260,300	-	-	-	-	-	-	-	-	-
Ramapo (town)	229,600	215,000	-	237,000	-	-	196,100	-	187,300	-	-	-	-	-	227,900	-	-	-	-	-	-	-	-	-
Spring Valley (village)	149,300	130,000	-	130,000	-	-	-	-	-	-	-	-	-	-	-	-	-	-	-	-	-	-	-	-
St. Lawrence County	60,200	66,400	-	-	-	-	-	-	-	-	-	-	-	-	-	-	-	-	-	-	-	-	-	-
Saratoga County	120,400	142,800	-	135,700	-	-	196,100	-	-	-	-	-	-	-	142,900	-	-	-	-	-	-	-	-	-
Schenectady County	94,500	161,100	-	228,900	-	-	166,900	-	-	-	-	-	-	-	-	-	-	-	-	-	-	-	-	-
Niskayuna (town)	141,000	218,800	-	254,400	-	-	-	-	-	-	-	-	-	-	-	-	-	-	-	-	-	-	-	-
Steuben County	66,200	175,000	-	-	-	-	-	-	-	-	-	-	-	-	-	-	-	-	-	-	-	-	-	-
Suffolk County	185,200	217,900	181,300	229,300	-	-	209,800	-	215,200	-	-	-	-	173,200	258,200	-	-	215,900	-	-	256,600	165,200	-	156,300
Coram (cdp)	158,100	161,300	-	-	-	-	146,700	-	-	-	-	-	-	-	-	-	-	-	-	-	-	-	-	-
Dix Hills (cdp)	386,100	414,800	-	434,900	-	-	381,600	-	-	-	-	-	-	-	-	-	-	-	-	-	-	-	-	-
Elwood (cdp)	259,900	290,300	-	-	-	-	-	-	-	-	-	-	-	-	-	-	-	-	-	-	-	-	-	-
Lake Grove (village)	189,200	288,900	-	-	-	-	-	-	-	-	-	-	-	-	-	-	-	-	-	-	-	-	-	-
Melville (cdp)	336,800	427,400	-	-	-	-	-	-	-	-	-	-	-	-	-	-	-	-	-	-	-	-	-	-
Setauket-East Setauket (cdp)	274,600	286,800	-	-	-	-	235,700	-	-	-	-	-	-	-	-	-	-	-	-	-	-	-	-	-
Stony Brook (cdp)	237,600	234,300	-	-	-	-	240,500	-	-	-	-	-	-	-	-	-	-	-	-	-	-	-	-	-
Sullivan County	93,300	109,400	-	-	-	-	-	-	-	-	-	-	-	-	-	-	-	-	-	-	-	-	-	-
Tioga County	77,400	82,800	-	-	-	-	-	-	-	-	-	-	-	-	-	-	-	-	-	-	-	-	-	-
Tompkins County	101,600	133,400	-	149,100	-	-	130,000	-	-	-	-	-	-	255,800	118,800	-	-	-	-	-	-	-	-	-
Ithaca (city)	96,200	81,800	-	0	-	-	81,800	-	-	-	-	-	-	-	0	-	-	-	-	-	-	-	-	-
Lansing (town)	127,800	173,200	-	-	-	-	-	-	-	-	-	-	-	-	-	-	-	-	-	-	-	-	-	-

Notes: Please refer to the User's Guide for an explanation of data; data is arranged alphabetically by state, then county, then city within each county; table includes counties with populations greater than 49,999 unless noted and cities with populations greater than 9,999 whose Asian and/or NHPI population rates are greater than the national average; (1) Native Hawaiian and other Pacific Islander; (2) excludes Taiwanese; (3) includes Chamorro; (4) county does not meet population threshold but is shown in order to allow inclusion of city

Place	All specified owner-occupied housing units	Specified housing units owned and occup. by Asians	Specified housing units owned and occup. by NHPIs[1]	Asian Indian	Bangladeshi	Cambodian	Chinese[2]	Fijian	Filipino	Guamanian[3]	Hawaiian, Native	Hmong	Indonesian	Japanese	Korean	Laotian	Malaysian	Pakistani	Samoan	Sri Lankan	Taiwanese	Thai	Tongan	Vietnamese
Ulster County	113,100	144,000	-	-	-	-	138,900	-	-	-	-	-	-	-	-	-	-	-	-	-	-	-	-	-
New Paltz (town)	134,500	187,500	-	-	-	-	-	-	-	-	-	-	-	-	-	-	-	-	-	-	-	-	-	-
Warren County	97,500	123,600	-	-	-	-	-	-	-	-	-	-	-	-	-	-	-	-	-	-	-	-	-	-
Wayne County	85,700	86,300	-	-	-	-	-	-	-	-	-	-	-	-	-	-	-	-	-	-	-	-	-	-
Westchester County	325,800	343,800	-	336,800	-	-	342,100	-	241,400	-	-	-	-	412,400	455,000	-	-	559,800	-	-	445,500	200,000	-	-
Dobbs Ferry (village)	325,900	333,800	-	-	-	-	-	-	-	-	-	-	-	-	-	-	-	-	-	-	-	-	-	-
Eastchester (cdp)	368,400	347,400	-	-	-	-	-	-	-	-	-	-	-	381,600	-	-	-	-	-	-	-	-	-	-
Eastchester (town)	391,800	383,300	-	-	-	-	-	-	-	-	-	-	-	425,000	-	-	-	-	-	-	-	-	-	-
Greenburgh (town)	331,900	361,600	-	366,300	-	-	342,200	-	305,000	-	-	-	-	364,100	445,300	-	-	-	-	-	-	-	-	-
Harrison (village)	578,700	726,000	-	-	-	-	-	-	-	-	-	-	-	0	-	-	-	-	-	-	-	-	-	-
New Castle (town)	533,900	488,200	-	668,600	-	-	316,700	-	-	-	-	-	-	-	-	-	-	-	-	-	-	-	-	-
New Rochelle (city)	346,900	331,000	-	314,600	-	-	282,500	-	-	-	-	-	-	-	-	-	-	-	-	-	-	-	-	-
North Castle (town)	588,500	451,700	-	-	-	-	-	-	-	-	-	-	-	-	-	-	-	-	-	-	-	-	-	-
Ossining (town)	264,200	273,900	-	335,200	-	-	-	-	-	-	-	-	-	-	-	-	-	-	-	-	-	-	-	-
Ossining (village)	207,200	201,100	-	200,000	-	-	-	-	-	-	-	-	-	-	-	-	-	-	-	-	-	-	-	-
Pelham (town)	422,600	243,100	-	-	-	-	-	-	-	-	-	-	-	-	-	-	-	-	-	-	-	-	-	-
Rye (city)	635,700	655,400	-	-	-	-	-	-	-	-	-	-	-	548,600	-	-	-	-	-	-	-	-	-	-
Scarsdale (village)	708,000	684,600	-	738,900	-	-	613,600	-	-	-	-	-	-	400,000	712,000	-	-	-	-	-	-	-	-	-
Tarrytown (village)	299,900	306,800	-	-	-	-	-	-	-	-	-	-	-	-	-	-	-	-	-	-	-	-	-	-
White Plains (city)	344,100	411,100	-	385,700	-	-	408,300	-	-	-	-	-	-	-	-	-	-	-	-	-	-	-	-	-
Yonkers (city)	239,300	240,000	-	236,000	-	-	226,700	-	234,600	-	-	-	-	-	379,200	-	-	-	-	-	-	-	-	-
NORTH CAROLINA	108,300	137,900	93,300	176,000	-	96,200	169,300	-	121,700	91,900	95,400	94,800	-	126,800	150,800	88,600	-	137,500	101,400	-	201,900	89,900	-	109,700
Alamance County	107,200	89,700	-	-	-	-	-	-	-	-	-	-	-	-	-	-	-	-	-	-	-	-	-	-
Buncombe County	119,600	133,200	-	155,700	-	-	-	-	-	-	-	-	-	-	-	-	-	-	-	-	-	-	-	-
Burke County	85,900	82,700	-	-	-	-	-	-	-	-	-	79,800	-	-	-	73,900	-	-	-	-	-	-	-	-
Cabarrus County	118,200	162,500	-	-	-	-	-	-	-	-	-	-	-	-	-	-	-	-	-	-	-	-	-	-
Catawba County	103,000	106,900	-	-	-	-	-	-	-	-	-	104,300	-	-	-	89,700	-	-	-	-	-	-	-	109,700
Hickory (city)	125,000	136,600	-	-	-	-	-	-	-	-	-	95,000	-	-	-	-	-	-	-	-	-	-	-	-
Cleveland County	83,200	88,000	-	-	-	-	-	-	-	-	-	-	-	-	-	-	-	-	-	-	-	-	-	-
Craven County	96,600	82,100	-	-	-	-	-	-	87,800	-	-	-	-	-	-	-	-	-	-	-	-	-	-	-
Cumberland County	88,800	94,400	93,800	172,200	-	-	-	-	110,400	-	-	-	-	82,800	87,300	-	-	-	-	-	-	-	-	86,100
Davidson County	98,600	100,000	-	-	-	90,000	-	-	-	-	-	-	-	-	-	-	-	-	-	-	-	-	-	-
Durham County	129,000	140,700	-	141,500	-	-	139,300	-	138,500	-	-	-	-	104,700	181,300	-	-	-	-	-	-	-	-	-
Forsyth County	114,000	126,800	-	138,800	-	-	126,300	-	132,500	-	-	-	-	-	-	-	-	-	-	-	-	-	-	118,800
Gaston County	90,300	119,900	-	-	-	-	-	-	-	-	-	-	-	-	-	-	-	-	-	-	-	-	-	96,500
Guilford County	116,900	112,700	-	167,800	-	-	147,700	-	138,400	-	-	-	-	-	158,700	87,600	-	108,900	-	-	-	-	-	91,000
Halifax County	68,300	79,000	-	-	-	-	-	-	-	-	-	-	-	-	-	-	-	-	-	-	-	-	-	-
Harnett County	91,200	83,300	-	-	-	-	-	-	-	-	-	-	-	-	-	-	-	-	-	-	-	-	-	-
Henderson County	130,100	126,500	-	-	-	-	-	-	-	-	-	-	-	-	-	-	-	-	-	-	-	-	-	-
Iredell County	116,100	162,500	-	-	-	-	-	-	-	-	-	-	-	-	-	-	-	-	-	-	-	-	-	-
Johnston County	108,800	163,800	-	-	-	-	-	-	-	-	-	-	-	-	-	-	-	-	-	-	-	-	-	-

Notes: Please refer to the User's Guide for an explanation of data; data is arranged alphabetically by state, then county, then city within each county; table includes counties with populations greater than 49,999 unless noted and cities with populations greater than 9,999 whose Asian and/or NHPI population rates are greater than the national average; (1) Native Hawaiian and other Pacific Islander; (2) excludes Taiwanese; (3) includes Chamorro; (4) county does not meet population threshold but is shown in order to allow inclusion of city

Place	All specified owner-occupied housing units	Specified housing units owned and occup. by Asians	Specified housing units owned and occup. by NHPIs[1]	Asian Indian	Bangladeshi	Cambodian	Chinese[2]	Fijian	Filipino	Guamanian[3]	Hawaiian, Native	Hmong	Indonesian	Japanese	Korean	Laotian	Malaysian	Pakistani	Samoan	Sri Lankan	Taiwanese	Thai	Tongan	Vietnamese
Lenoir County	82,600	100,000	-	-	-	-	-	-	-	-	-	-	-	-	-	-	-	-	-	-	-	-	-	-
Mecklenburg County	141,800	130,200	-	156,900	-	102,000	166,700	-	116,700	-	-	104,000	-	171,900	163,200	104,400	-	-	-	-	-	-	-	105,900
Nash County	95,800	105,000	-	-	-	-	-	-	-	-	-	-	-	-	-	-	-	-	-	-	-	-	-	-
New Hanover County	135,600	142,500	-	-	-	-	-	-	-	-	-	-	-	-	-	-	-	-	-	-	-	-	-	-
Onslow County	85,900	90,900	92,900	-	-	-	-	-	82,300	-	-	-	-	66,900	-	-	-	-	-	-	-	-	-	-
Orange County	179,000	211,300	-	314,300	-	-	196,600	-	-	-	-	-	-	255,600	225,000	-	-	-	-	-	-	-	-	-
Carrboro (town)	172,800	111,900	-	-	-	-	-	-	-	-	-	-	-	-	-	-	-	-	-	-	-	-	-	-
Chapel Hill (town)	229,100	217,000	-	350,000	-	-	190,900	-	-	-	-	-	-	-	275,000	-	-	-	-	-	-	-	-	-
Pitt County	96,800	146,500	-	-	-	-	-	-	-	-	-	-	-	-	-	-	-	-	-	-	-	-	-	-
Randolph County	94,700	106,300	-	-	-	-	-	-	-	-	-	-	-	-	-	-	-	-	-	-	-	-	-	-
Robeson County	66,100	77,900	-	-	-	-	-	-	-	-	-	-	-	-	-	-	-	-	-	-	-	-	-	-
Rowan County	95,200	81,900	-	-	-	-	-	-	-	-	-	-	-	-	-	-	-	-	-	-	-	-	-	-
Stanly County	87,700	78,900	-	-	-	-	-	-	-	-	-	75,000	-	-	-	-	-	-	-	-	-	-	-	-
Surry County	87,500	85,000	-	-	-	-	-	-	-	-	-	-	-	-	-	-	-	-	-	-	-	-	-	-
Union County	128,500	161,400	-	-	-	-	-	-	-	-	-	-	-	-	-	-	-	-	-	-	-	-	-	-
Wake County	162,900	188,400	-	210,100	-	-	195,900	-	162,200	-	-	-	-	173,400	191,900	-	-	228,900	-	-	-	-	-	151,300
Apex (town)	178,800	191,900	-	-	-	-	-	-	-	-	-	-	-	-	-	-	-	-	-	-	-	-	-	-
Cary (town)	196,700	208,100	-	214,400	-	-	212,900	-	-	-	-	-	-	225,000	209,400	-	-	-	-	-	-	-	-	172,900
Wayne County	87,600	173,800	-	-	-	-	-	-	-	-	-	-	-	-	-	-	-	-	-	-	-	-	-	-
Wilkes County	89,200	120,300	-	-	-	-	-	-	-	-	-	-	-	-	-	-	-	-	-	-	-	-	-	-
NORTH DAKOTA	74,400	103,500	-	124,100	-	-	88,800	-	88,300	-	-	-	-	-	95,600	-	-	-	-	-	-	-	-	-
Cass County	98,400	119,200	-	137,500	-	-	-	-	-	-	-	-	-	-	-	-	-	-	-	-	-	-	-	-
Grand Forks County	92,800	130,000	-	-	-	-	-	-	-	-	-	-	-	-	-	-	-	-	-	-	-	-	-	-
Ward County	79,500	75,900	-	-	-	-	-	-	-	-	-	-	-	-	-	-	-	-	-	-	-	-	-	-
OHIO	103,700	155,300	116,300	192,700	173,200	94,400	162,200	-	133,900	98,800	121,200	-	125,000	141,700	166,400	81,800	128,600	188,300	85,700	144,400	176,100	107,100	-	99,900
Allen County	81,800	98,600	-	-	-	-	-	-	-	-	-	-	-	-	-	-	-	-	-	-	-	-	-	-
Ashtabula County	85,300	103,800	-	-	-	-	-	-	-	-	-	-	-	-	-	-	-	-	-	-	-	-	-	-
Athens County	84,300	113,800	-	-	-	-	-	-	-	-	-	-	-	-	-	-	-	-	-	-	-	-	-	-
Athens (city)	113,800	177,500	-	-	-	-	-	-	-	-	-	-	-	-	-	-	-	-	-	-	-	-	-	-
Butler County	123,200	180,100	-	200,300	-	-	178,000	-	143,800	-	-	-	-	-	194,900	-	-	-	-	-	-	-	-	171,200
Clark County	90,500	97,100	-	-	-	-	-	-	-	-	-	-	-	-	-	-	-	-	-	-	-	-	-	-
Clermont County	122,900	153,600	-	200,000	-	-	-	-	-	-	-	-	-	-	-	-	-	-	-	-	-	-	-	-
Columbiana County	79,800	111,600	-	-	-	-	-	-	-	-	-	-	-	-	-	-	-	-	-	-	-	-	-	-
Cuyahoga County	113,800	152,700	-	193,200	-	93,200	144,200	-	124,200	-	-	-	-	137,500	197,900	-	-	-	-	-	-	-	-	97,200
Mayfield Heights (city)	125,900	126,600	-	123,300	-	-	-	-	-	-	-	-	-	-	-	-	-	-	-	-	-	-	-	-
Richmond Heights (city)	140,800	133,800	-	-	-	-	-	-	-	-	-	-	-	-	-	-	-	-	-	-	-	-	-	-
Solon (city)	217,000	250,900	-	240,200	-	-	228,600	-	-	-	-	-	-	-	-	-	-	-	-	-	-	-	-	-
Westlake (city)	201,000	248,200	-	297,700	-	-	-	-	-	-	-	-	-	-	-	-	-	-	-	-	-	-	-	-
Delaware County	190,400	221,400	-	227,500	-	-	222,600	-	-	-	-	-	-	-	-	-	-	-	-	-	-	-	-	-
Fairfield County	129,500	147,200	-	-	-	-	-	-	-	-	-	-	-	-	-	-	-	-	-	-	-	-	-	-
Franklin County	116,200	148,400	118,800	186,700	-	90,000	164,000	-	141,000	-	-	-	112,500	151,300	189,600	86,300	-	180,600	-	-	287,500	109,400	-	96,300

Notes: Please refer to the User's Guide for an explanation of data; data is arranged alphabetically by state, then county, then city within each county; table includes counties with populations greater than 49,999 unless noted and cities with populations greater than 9,999 whose Asian and/or NHPI population rates are greater than the national average; (1) Native Hawaiian and other Pacific Islander; (2) excludes Taiwanese; (3) includes Chamorro; (4) county does not meet population threshold but is shown in order to allow inclusion of city

Place	All specified owner-occupied housing units	Specified housing units owned and occup. by Asians	Specified housing units owned and occup. by NHPIs[1]	Asian Indian	Bangladeshi	Cambodian	Chinese[2]	Fijian	Filipino	Guamanian[3]	Hawaiian, Native	Hmong	Indonesian	Japanese	Korean	Laotian	Malaysian	Pakistani	Samoan	Sri Lankan	Taiwanese	Thai	Tongan	Vietnamese
Dublin (city)	243,200	229,500	-	256,400	-	-	244,600	-	-	-	-	-	-	147,200	-	-	-	-	-	-	-	-	-	-
Hilliard (city)	157,600	207,700	-	-	-	-	-	-	-	-	-	-	-	-	-	-	-	-	-	-	-	-	-	-
Geauga County	182,400	220,000	-	-	-	-	-	-	-	-	-	-	-	-	-	-	-	-	-	-	-	-	-	-
Greene County	121,200	182,400	-	195,200	-	-	198,100	-	-	-	-	-	-	-	210,000	-	-	-	-	-	-	-	-	-
Hamilton County	111,400	162,300	-	194,400	-	67,100	201,700	-	141,400	-	-	-	-	133,200	201,600	-	-	-	-	-	-	-	-	93,300
Blue Ash (city)	151,400	224,200	-	204,200	-	-	-	-	-	-	-	-	-	-	-	-	-	-	-	-	-	-	-	-
Sharonville (city)	120,400	177,400	-	181,000	-	-	-	-	-	-	-	-	-	-	-	-	-	-	-	-	-	-	-	-
Hancock County	100,400	125,000	-	-	-	-	-	-	-	-	-	-	-	-	-	-	-	-	-	-	-	-	-	-
Lake County	127,900	136,800	-	146,900	-	-	170,300	-	-	-	-	-	-	-	-	-	-	-	-	-	-	-	-	-
Licking County	110,700	143,800	-	-	-	-	-	-	-	-	-	-	-	-	-	-	-	-	-	-	-	-	-	-
Lorain County	115,100	125,600	-	136,900	-	-	-	-	110,600	-	-	-	-	-	-	-	-	-	-	-	-	-	-	-
Lucas County	90,700	157,000	-	187,800	-	-	132,200	-	88,400	-	-	-	-	-	227,100	-	-	-	-	-	-	-	-	-
Mahoning County	79,700	171,900	-	-	-	-	-	-	-	-	-	-	-	-	-	-	-	-	-	-	-	-	-	-
Marion County	78,500	137,500	-	-	-	-	-	-	-	-	-	-	-	-	-	-	-	-	-	-	-	-	-	-
Medina County	144,400	178,300	-	197,200	-	-	-	-	-	-	-	-	-	-	-	-	-	-	-	-	-	-	-	-
Miami County	109,600	150,600	-	-	-	-	-	-	-	-	-	-	-	-	-	-	-	-	-	-	-	-	-	-
Montgomery County	95,900	136,400	-	168,100	-	-	138,500	-	134,700	-	-	-	-	86,500	134,400	-	-	-	-	-	-	-	-	110,900
Portage County	123,000	163,200	-	-	-	-	-	-	-	-	-	-	-	-	-	-	-	-	-	-	-	-	-	-
Richland County	88,100	123,600	-	-	-	-	-	-	-	-	-	-	-	-	-	-	-	-	-	-	-	-	-	-
Stark County	100,300	159,100	-	196,400	-	-	158,900	-	-	-	-	-	-	-	-	-	-	-	-	-	-	-	-	-
Summit County	109,100	165,000	-	220,000	-	-	159,800	-	167,800	-	-	-	-	184,900	180,100	74,100	-	-	-	-	-	-	-	64,600
Trumbull County	85,500	156,000	-	-	-	-	-	-	-	-	-	-	-	-	-	-	-	-	-	-	-	-	-	-
Warren County	142,200	181,700	-	209,200	-	-	172,700	-	-	-	-	-	-	-	-	-	-	-	-	-	-	-	-	-
Wayne County	108,100	155,500	-	-	-	-	-	-	-	-	-	-	-	-	-	-	-	-	-	-	-	-	-	-
Wood County	120,000	172,100	-	-	-	-	-	-	-	-	-	-	-	-	-	-	-	-	-	-	-	-	-	-
OKLAHOMA	70,700	90,200	85,000	124,200	-	79,000	119,000	-	86,900	96,700	83,100	99,500	-	71,800	88,400	56,200	50,000	105,600	-	-	85,000	66,900	-	78,800
Canadian County	84,600	98,100	-	100,300	-	-	-	-	-	-	-	-	-	-	-	-	-	-	-	-	-	-	-	98,300
Cleveland County	88,500	94,200	-	124,600	-	-	111,700	-	93,200	-	-	-	-	-	91,000	-	-	-	-	-	-	-	-	88,900
Comanche County	71,600	74,800	-	-	-	-	-	-	77,300	-	-	-	-	-	73,700	-	-	-	-	-	-	-	-	-
Garfield County	58,800	63,100	-	-	-	-	-	-	-	-	-	-	-	-	-	-	-	-	-	-	-	-	-	-
Muskogee County	57,700	95,700	-	-	-	-	-	-	-	-	-	-	-	-	-	-	-	-	-	-	-	-	-	-
Oklahoma County	75,800	82,600	-	160,800	-	-	121,600	-	99,300	-	-	-	-	77,700	79,600	47,500	-	-	-	-	-	66,900	-	69,400
Payne County	79,700	130,000	-	-	-	-	144,200	-	-	-	-	-	-	-	-	-	-	-	-	-	-	-	-	-
Stillwater (city)	96,700	130,000	-	-	-	-	144,200	-	-	-	-	-	-	-	-	-	-	-	-	-	-	-	-	-
Pottawatomie County	60,500	106,300	-	-	-	-	-	-	-	-	-	-	-	-	-	-	-	-	-	-	-	-	-	-
Tulsa County	87,000	104,500	-	127,000	-	-	141,800	-	105,800	-	-	-	-	-	125,000	-	-	98,100	-	-	-	-	-	78,200
Wagoner County	89,800	99,200	-	-	-	-	-	-	-	-	-	-	-	-	-	-	-	-	-	-	-	-	-	-
OREGON	152,100	167,800	150,700	226,100	-	151,100	171,900	176,000	154,100	150,900	150,500	131,500	202,500	172,000	181,500	152,900	-	180,100	143,800	-	230,200	132,800	164,800	154,000
Benton County	169,800	197,200	-	-	-	-	198,400	-	-	-	-	-	-	193,800	239,300	-	-	-	-	-	-	-	-	-
Corvallis (city)	159,600	183,500	-	-	-	-	195,300	-	-	-	-	-	-	-	239,300	-	-	-	-	-	-	-	-	-
Clackamas County	199,000	219,900	172,100	294,300	-	-	215,800	-	202,400	-	-	-	-	194,400	221,500	-	-	-	-	-	-	-	-	226,000

Notes: Please refer to the User's Guide for an explanation of data; data is arranged alphabetically by state, then county, then city within each county; table includes counties with populations greater than 49,999 unless noted and cities with populations greater than 9,999 whose Asian and/or NHPI population rates are greater than the national average; (1) Native Hawaiian and other Pacific Islander; (2) excludes Taiwanese; (3) includes Chamorro; (4) county does not meet population threshold but is shown in order to allow inclusion of city

Place	All specified owner-occupied housing units	Specified housing units owned and occup. by Asians	Specified housing units owned and occup. by NHPIs[1]	Asian Indian	Bangladeshi	Cambodian	Chinese[2]	Fijian	Filipino	Guamanian[3]	Hawaiian, Native	Hmong	Indonesian	Japanese	Korean	Laotian	Malaysian	Pakistani	Samoan	Sri Lankan	Taiwanese	Thai	Tongan	Vietnamese
Lake Oswego (city)	296,200	315,400	-	-	-	-	289,800	-	-	-	-	-	-	-	-	-	-	-	-	-	-	-	-	-
Coos County	98,900	109,600	-	-	-	-	-	-	-	-	-	-	-	-	-	-	-	-	-	-	-	-	-	-
Deschutes County	148,800	119,800	-	-	-	-	-	-	-	-	-	-	-	-	-	-	-	-	-	-	-	-	-	-
Douglas County	104,800	157,800	-	-	-	-	-	-	-	-	-	-	-	-	-	-	-	-	-	-	-	-	-	-
Jackson County	140,000	162,900	-	-	-	-	-	-	-	-	-	-	-	-	-	-	-	-	-	-	-	-	-	-
Josephine County	128,700	154,900	-	-	-	-	-	-	-	-	-	-	-	-	-	-	-	-	-	-	-	-	-	-
Klamath County	91,100	110,900	-	-	-	-	-	-	-	-	-	-	-	-	-	-	-	-	-	-	-	-	-	-
Lane County	141,000	146,900	117,800	146,400	-	-	149,400	-	135,300	-	-	-	-	161,100	137,500	-	-	-	-	-	-	-	-	-
Linn County	124,100	110,900	-	-	-	-	-	-	-	-	-	-	-	-	-	-	-	-	-	-	-	-	-	-
Marion County	132,600	126,900	138,400	156,300	-	-	109,400	-	131,400	-	-	-	-	143,500	136,700	-	-	-	-	-	-	-	-	123,800
Salem (city)	131,100	128,900	143,200	-	-	-	113,700	-	117,000	-	-	-	-	168,100	-	-	-	-	-	-	-	-	-	123,700
Multnomah County	157,900	147,100	166,600	180,900	-	153,200	150,500	-	134,600	-	181,500	132,100	-	165,100	160,200	144,000	-	-	-	-	-	126,400	173,900	140,500
Portland (city)	154,900	144,600	158,200	175,400	-	150,800	146,200	-	125,800	-	170,200	130,400	-	163,900	159,400	144,500	-	-	-	-	-	120,000	173,900	138,600
Polk County	142,700	190,000	-	-	-	-	-	-	-	-	-	-	-	-	-	-	-	-	-	-	-	-	-	-
Umatilla County	98,100	97,100	-	-	-	-	-	-	-	-	-	-	-	-	-	-	-	-	-	-	-	-	-	-
Washington County	184,800	201,200	167,100	233,700	-	168,600	213,100	-	185,200	-	142,300	-	-	199,100	195,900	193,100	-	-	-	-	-	-	-	180,100
Aloha (cdp)	156,100	161,400	-	-	-	-	-	-	157,600	-	-	-	-	-	-	-	-	-	-	-	-	-	-	165,900
Beaverton (city)	189,800	210,700	-	227,600	-	215,600	192,100	-	184,200	-	-	-	-	209,300	180,000	-	-	-	-	-	-	-	-	220,700
Cedar Mill (cdp)	269,600	402,400	-	-	-	-	-	-	-	-	-	-	-	-	-	-	-	-	-	-	-	-	-	-
Hillsboro (city)	165,200	182,100	-	208,700	-	-	169,700	-	-	-	-	-	-	-	173,400	-	-	-	-	-	-	-	-	173,800
Tigard (city)	188,600	209,500	-	-	-	-	216,000	-	-	-	-	-	-	-	-	-	-	-	-	-	-	-	-	218,300
Tualatin (city)	197,700	184,300	-	-	-	-	-	-	-	-	-	-	-	-	-	-	-	-	-	-	-	-	-	-
Yamhill County	146,200	146,400	-	-	-	-	-	-	-	-	-	-	-	-	-	-	-	-	-	-	-	-	-	-
PENNSYLVANIA	97,000	129,000	91,700	163,200	132,800	54,400	125,900	-	127,800	88,900	105,000	127,300	154,500	140,300	163,000	62,000	-	174,400	75,400	146,200	217,900	115,500	-	75,800
Adams County	110,100	127,600	-	-	-	-	-	-	-	-	-	-	-	-	-	-	-	-	-	-	-	-	-	-
Allegheny County	84,200	154,200	117,000	193,300	-	-	136,100	-	109,200	-	-	-	-	174,200	171,400	-	-	-	-	-	173,200	-	-	61,400
Muni. of Monroeville (borough)	92,000	139,100	-	140,600	-	-	-	-	-	-	-	-	-	-	-	-	-	-	-	-	-	-	-	-
Scott (township)	98,300	190,300	-	177,800	-	-	-	-	-	-	-	-	-	-	-	-	-	-	-	-	-	-	-	-
Scott Township (cdp)	98,300	190,300	-	177,800	-	-	-	-	-	-	-	-	-	-	-	-	-	-	-	-	-	-	-	-
Upper St. Clair (township)	174,900	237,500	-	221,900	-	-	-	-	-	-	-	-	-	-	-	-	-	-	-	-	-	-	-	-
Beaver County	85,000	112,500	-	-	-	-	-	-	-	-	-	-	-	-	-	-	-	-	-	-	-	-	-	-
Berks County	104,900	109,800	-	187,500	-	-	123,000	-	-	-	-	-	-	-	147,500	-	-	-	-	-	-	-	-	55,000
Blair County	73,600	200,000	-	-	-	-	-	-	-	-	-	-	-	-	-	-	-	-	-	-	-	-	-	-
Bradford County	73,900	261,100	-	-	-	-	-	-	-	-	-	-	-	-	-	-	-	-	-	-	-	-	-	-
Bucks County	163,200	181,500	-	193,000	-	-	198,800	-	156,700	-	-	-	-	-	190,600	-	-	-	-	-	-	-	-	102,300
Bensalem (township)	131,500	159,400	-	156,100	-	-	-	-	-	-	-	-	-	-	161,500	-	-	-	-	-	-	-	-	-
Lower Makefield (township)	243,100	257,900	-	294,600	-	-	-	-	-	-	-	-	-	-	-	-	-	-	-	-	-	-	-	-
Newtown (township)	188,200	205,100	-	-	-	-	-	-	-	-	-	-	-	-	-	-	-	-	-	-	-	-	-	-
Butler County	114,100	201,200	-	199,200	-	-	-	-	-	-	-	-	-	-	-	-	-	-	-	-	-	-	-	-
Cambria County	62,700	115,600	-	-	-	-	-	-	-	-	-	-	-	-	-	-	-	-	-	-	-	-	-	-
Centre County	114,900	158,900	-	171,300	-	-	152,100	-	-	-	-	-	-	-	172,900	-	-	-	-	-	-	-	-	-

Notes: Please refer to the User's Guide for an explanation of data; data is arranged alphabetically by state, then county, then city within each county; table includes counties with populations greater than 49,999 unless noted and cities with populations greater than 9,999 whose Asian and/or NHPI population rates are greater than the national average; (1) Native Hawaiian and other Pacific Islander; (2) excludes Taiwanese; (3) includes Chamorro; (4) county does not meet population threshold but is shown in order to allow inclusion of city

Place	All specified owner-occupied housing units	Specified housing units owned and occup. by Asians	Specified housing units owned and occup. by NHPIs[1]	Asian Indian	Bangladeshi	Cambodian	Chinese[2]	Fijian	Filipino	Guamanian[3]	Hawaiian, Native	Hmong	Indonesian	Japanese	Korean	Laotian	Malaysian	Pakistani	Samoan	Sri Lankan	Taiwanese	Thai	Tongan	Vietnamese
Ferguson (township)	144,900	183,000	-	-	-	-	-	-	-	-	-	-	-	-	-	-	-	-	-	-	-	-	-	-
Patton (township)	140,100	159,800	-	-	-	-	-	-	-	-	-	-	-	-	-	-	-	-	-	-	-	-	-	-
State College (borough)	154,600	86,300	-	89,400	-	-	55,000	-	-	-	-	-	-	-	0	-	-	-	-	-	-	-	-	-
Chester County	182,500	223,100	-	229,500	-	-	262,100	-	195,200	-	-	-	-	217,600	208,300	-	-	-	-	-	-	-	-	149,000
Tredyffrin (township)	269,800	276,700	-	221,900	-	-	296,800	-	-	-	-	-	-	-	-	-	-	-	-	-	-	-	-	-
West Goshen (township)	191,700	240,600	-	-	-	-	-	-	-	-	-	-	-	-	-	-	-	-	-	-	-	-	-	-
West Whiteland (township)	168,100	172,600	-	-	-	-	-	-	-	-	-	-	-	-	-	-	-	-	-	-	-	-	-	-
Clearfield County	62,600	131,300	-	-	-	-	-	-	-	-	-	-	-	-	-	-	-	-	-	-	-	-	-	-
Columbia County	87,300	162,500	-	-	-	-	-	-	-	-	-	-	-	-	-	-	-	-	-	-	-	-	-	-
Crawford County	72,800	120,800	-	-	-	-	-	-	-	-	-	-	-	-	-	-	-	-	-	-	-	-	-	-
Cumberland County	120,500	146,700	-	174,600	-	-	223,400	-	-	-	-	-	-	-	155,900	-	-	-	-	-	-	-	-	107,700
Hampden (township)	154,400	165,500	-	-	-	-	-	-	-	-	-	-	-	-	-	-	-	-	-	-	-	-	-	-
Dauphin County	99,900	99,900	-	107,500	-	-	113,900	-	-	-	-	-	-	-	240,000	-	-	-	-	-	-	-	-	73,600
Derry (township)	151,300	160,700	-	-	-	-	-	-	-	-	-	-	-	-	-	-	-	-	-	-	-	-	-	-
Hershey (cdp)	153,400	150,500	-	-	-	-	-	-	-	-	-	-	-	-	-	-	-	-	-	-	-	-	-	-
Delaware County	128,800	126,700	-	130,800	-	-	159,100	-	147,800	-	-	-	-	147,900	136,000	-	-	192,500	-	-	-	-	-	73,500
Broomall (cdp)	169,300	171,500	-	-	-	-	-	-	-	-	-	-	-	-	171,900	-	-	-	-	-	-	-	-	-
Drexel Hill (cdp)	126,100	175,900	-	-	-	-	215,900	-	-	-	-	-	-	-	-	-	-	-	-	-	-	-	-	-
Marple (township)	183,600	178,600	-	-	-	-	-	-	-	-	-	-	-	-	193,200	-	-	-	-	-	-	-	-	-
Radnor (township)	326,500	249,300	-	-	-	-	173,800	-	-	-	-	-	-	-	-	-	-	-	-	-	-	-	-	-
Upper Darby (township)	93,700	71,000	-	70,300	-	-	74,700	-	-	-	-	-	-	-	74,400	-	-	-	-	-	-	-	-	65,700
Erie County	85,300	147,900	-	156,300	-	-	-	-	-	-	-	-	-	-	-	-	-	-	-	-	-	-	-	-
Franklin County	97,800	158,500	-	-	-	-	-	-	-	-	-	-	-	-	-	-	-	-	-	-	-	-	-	-
Indiana County	72,700	156,300	-	-	-	-	-	-	-	-	-	-	-	-	-	-	-	-	-	-	-	-	-	-
Lackawanna County	93,400	140,100	-	146,600	-	-	-	-	-	-	-	-	-	-	-	-	-	-	-	-	-	-	-	-
Lancaster County	119,300	118,100	-	112,500	-	-	122,000	-	-	-	-	152,700	-	-	120,300	-	-	-	-	-	-	-	-	114,500
Lawrence County	72,200	113,400	-	-	-	-	-	-	-	-	-	-	-	-	-	-	-	-	-	-	-	-	-	-
Lebanon County	100,700	120,000	-	-	-	-	-	-	-	-	-	-	-	-	-	-	-	-	-	-	-	-	-	-
Lehigh County	113,600	143,400	-	183,800	-	-	179,700	-	-	-	-	-	-	-	132,500	-	-	-	-	-	-	-	-	101,300
Fullerton (cdp)	114,700	132,600	-	-	-	-	-	-	-	-	-	-	-	-	-	-	-	-	-	-	-	-	-	-
Lower Macungie (township)	169,000	221,500	-	-	-	-	213,000	-	-	-	-	-	-	-	-	-	-	-	-	-	-	-	-	-
Upper Macungie (township)	174,600	172,900	-	-	-	-	-	-	-	-	-	-	-	-	-	-	-	-	-	-	-	-	-	-
Luzerne County	84,800	159,400	-	192,500	-	-	-	-	-	-	-	-	-	-	-	-	-	-	-	-	-	-	-	-
Lycoming County	86,200	92,300	-	-	-	-	-	-	-	-	-	-	-	-	-	-	-	-	-	-	-	-	-	-
Mercer County	76,000	157,800	-	-	-	-	-	-	-	-	-	-	-	-	-	-	-	-	-	-	-	-	-	-
Monroe County	125,200	136,500	-	139,400	-	-	-	-	-	-	-	-	-	-	-	-	-	-	-	-	-	-	-	-
Montgomery County	160,700	187,000	-	192,400	-	-	194,400	-	167,900	-	-	-	-	160,300	201,000	-	-	-	-	-	-	-	-	149,800
Cheltenham (township)	165,000	162,200	-	-	-	-	-	-	-	-	-	-	-	-	153,700	-	-	-	-	-	-	-	-	-
East Norriton (township)	150,300	155,700	-	-	-	-	-	-	-	-	-	-	-	-	-	-	-	-	-	-	-	-	-	-
Hatfield (township)	156,800	151,800	-	148,500	-	-	-	-	-	-	-	-	-	-	-	-	-	-	-	-	-	-	-	-
Horsham (township)	167,700	170,800	-	-	-	-	-	-	-	-	-	-	-	-	187,500	-	-	-	-	-	-	-	-	-

Notes: Please refer to the User's Guide for an explanation of data; data is arranged alphabetically by state, then county, then city within each county; table includes counties with populations greater than 49,999 unless noted and cities with populations greater than 9,999 whose Asian and/or NHPI population rates are greater than the national average; (1) Native Hawaiian and other Pacific Islander; (2) excludes Taiwanese; (3) includes Chamorro; (4) county does not meet population threshold but is shown in order to allow inclusion of city

Place	All specified owner-occupied housing units	Specified housing units owned and occup. by Asians	Specified housing units owned and occup. by NHPIs[1]	Asian Indian	Bangladeshi	Cambodian	Chinese[2]	Fijian	Filipino	Guamanian[3]	Hawaiian, Native	Hmong	Indonesian	Japanese	Korean	Laotian	Malaysian	Pakistani	Samoan	Sri Lankan	Taiwanese	Thai	Tongan	Vietnamese
King of Prussia (cdp)	157,800	166,500	-	171,400	-	-	151,600	-	-	-	-	-	-	-	-	-	-	-	-	-	-	-	-	-
Lansdale (borough)	122,400	102,000	-	88,700	-	-	-	-	-	-	-	-	-	-	-	-	-	-	-	-	-	-	-	-
Lower Gwynedd (township)	252,500	318,800	-	-	-	-	-	-	-	-	-	-	-	-	-	-	-	-	-	-	-	-	-	-
Lower Providence (township)	172,100	240,200	-	-	-	-	268,300	-	-	-	-	-	-	-	-	-	-	-	-	-	-	-	-	-
Montgomery (township)	188,400	217,500	-	223,900	-	-	-	-	-	-	-	-	-	-	218,900	-	-	-	-	-	-	-	-	-
Montgomeryville (cdp)	181,400	183,900	-	-	-	-	-	-	-	-	-	-	-	-	-	-	-	-	-	-	-	-	-	-
Plymouth (township)	159,100	196,900	-	-	-	-	-	-	-	-	-	-	-	-	304,500	-	-	-	-	-	-	-	-	-
Towamencin (township)	171,600	181,700	-	-	-	-	-	-	-	-	-	-	-	-	-	-	-	-	-	-	-	-	-	-
Upper Dublin (township)	224,100	250,700	-	-	-	-	-	-	-	-	-	-	-	-	209,500	-	-	-	-	-	-	-	-	-
Upper Gwynedd (township)	176,600	179,200	-	-	-	-	182,300	-	-	-	-	-	-	-	-	-	-	-	-	-	-	-	-	-
Upper Merion (township)	165,700	172,200	-	170,200	-	-	168,000	-	-	-	-	-	-	-	-	-	-	-	-	-	-	-	-	-
Whitpain (township)	248,600	265,300	-	-	-	-	-	-	-	-	-	-	-	-	269,400	-	-	-	-	-	-	-	-	-
Northampton County	120,000	173,900	-	198,600	-	-	130,000	-	-	-	-	-	-	-	306,300	-	-	-	-	-	-	-	-	109,400
Northumberland County	69,300	80,000	-	-	-	-	-	-	-	-	-	-	-	-	-	-	-	-	-	-	-	-	-	-
Philadelphia County	59,700	59,400	62,000	91,100	-	47,900	61,400	-	67,900	-	-	-	-	75,000	66,500	49,400	-	91,900	-	-	-	-	-	47,100
Philadelphia (city)	59,700	59,400	62,000	91,100	-	47,900	61,400	-	67,900	-	-	-	-	75,000	66,500	49,400	-	91,900	-	-	-	-	-	47,100
Schuylkill County	63,300	125,800	-	-	-	-	-	-	-	-	-	-	-	-	-	-	-	-	-	-	-	-	-	-
Washington County	87,500	157,500	-	-	-	-	-	-	-	-	-	-	-	-	-	-	-	-	-	-	-	-	-	-
Westmoreland County	90,600	180,900	-	248,400	-	-	-	-	-	-	-	-	-	-	-	-	-	-	-	-	-	-	-	-
York County	110,500	123,300	-	160,200	-	-	138,900	-	-	-	-	-	-	-	161,000	-	-	-	-	-	-	-	-	99,300
RHODE ISLAND	133,000	125,400	173,200	152,500	-	96,000	135,000	-	130,000	-	-	79,600	-	160,500	136,200	107,000	-	-	-	-	-	-	-	94,600
Bristol County	164,600	203,800	-	-	-	-	-	-	-	-	-	-	-	-	-	-	-	-	-	-	-	-	-	-
Kent County	118,100	119,100	-	-	-	-	106,600	-	-	-	-	-	-	-	108,000	-	-	-	-	-	-	-	-	-
Newport County	164,100	152,300	-	-	-	-	-	-	130,000	-	-	-	-	-	-	-	-	-	-	-	-	-	-	-
Providence County	123,900	116,900	-	139,000	-	88,900	127,700	-	130,300	-	-	81,700	-	-	139,800	105,800	-	-	-	-	-	-	-	84,600
Providence (city)	101,500	94,000	-	143,500	-	86,100	139,700	-	76,700	-	-	75,000	-	-	218,800	81,900	-	-	-	-	-	-	-	-
Woonsocket (city)	112,800	109,400	-	-	-	-	-	-	-	-	-	-	-	-	-	112,500	-	-	-	-	-	-	-	-
Washington County	158,600	161,700	-	-	-	-	144,600	-	-	-	-	-	-	-	-	-	-	-	-	-	-	-	-	-
SOUTH CAROLINA	94,900	114,500	88,900	157,400	-	91,900	130,100	-	93,900	82,800	83,000	97,500	-	105,900	106,300	77,600	-	-	-	-	-	84,500	-	100,900
Aiken County	87,600	130,400	-	-	-	-	-	-	-	-	-	-	-	-	-	-	-	-	-	-	-	-	-	-
Anderson County	88,200	130,300	-	-	-	-	-	-	-	-	-	-	-	-	-	-	-	-	-	-	-	-	-	-
Beaufort County	213,900	161,900	-	-	-	-	-	-	-	-	-	-	-	-	-	-	-	-	-	-	-	-	-	-
Berkeley County	91,300	86,400	-	-	-	-	-	-	82,100	-	-	-	-	-	-	-	-	-	-	-	-	-	-	-
Charleston County	130,200	115,000	-	228,600	-	-	96,300	-	90,600	-	-	-	-	-	-	-	-	-	-	-	-	-	-	-
Dorchester County	104,600	124,600	-	-	-	-	-	-	118,100	-	-	-	-	-	-	-	-	-	-	-	-	-	-	-
Florence County	85,200	182,700	-	-	-	-	-	-	-	-	-	-	-	-	-	-	-	-	-	-	-	-	-	-
Greenville County	111,800	131,700	-	163,400	-	-	133,500	-	112,500	-	-	-	-	-	-	-	-	-	-	-	-	-	-	104,600
Greenwood County	81,200	144,800	-	-	-	-	-	-	-	-	-	-	-	-	-	-	-	-	-	-	-	-	-	-
Horry County	119,700	232,400	-	-	-	-	-	-	-	-	-	-	-	-	-	-	-	-	-	-	-	-	-	-
Lexington County	106,300	99,000	-	196,300	-	-	104,400	-	-	-	-	-	-	-	-	-	-	-	-	-	-	-	-	-
Oconee County	97,500	91,000	-	-	-	-	-	-	-	-	-	-	-	-	-	-	-	-	-	-	-	-	-	-

Notes: Please refer to the User's Guide for an explanation of data; data is arranged alphabetically by state, then county, then city within each county; table includes counties with populations greater than 49,999 unless noted and cities with populations greater than 9,999 whose Asian and/or NHPI population rates are greater than the national average; (1) Native Hawaiian and other Pacific Islander; (2) excludes Taiwanese; (3) includes Chamorro; (4) county does not meet population threshold but is shown in order to allow inclusion of city

Place	All specified owner-occupied housing units	Specified housing units owned and occup. by Asians	Specified housing units owned and occup. by NHPIs[1]	Asian Indian	Bangladeshi	Cambodian	Chinese[2]	Fijian	Filipino	Guamanian[3]	Hawaiian, Native	Hmong	Indonesian	Japanese	Korean	Laotian	Malaysian	Pakistani	Samoan	Sri Lankan	Taiwanese	Thai	Tongan	Vietnamese
Pickens County	96,100	120,000	-	126,600	-	-	130,000	-	-	-	-	-	-	-	-	-	-	-	-	-	-	-	-	-
Clemson (city)	133,000	116,300	-	-	-	-	-	-	-	-	-	-	-	-	-	-	-	-	-	-	-	-	-	-
Richland County	98,700	112,500	-	112,100	-	-	144,700	-	131,900	-	-	-	-	-	111,800	-	-	-	-	-	-	-	-	146,900
Spartanburg County	91,100	97,800	-	127,100	-	-	-	-	-	-	-	101,300	-	-	-	66,500	-	-	-	-	-	-	-	-
Sumter County	78,700	101,500	-	-	-	-	-	-	-	-	-	-	-	-	-	-	-	-	-	-	-	-	-	-
York County	119,600	145,600	-	-	-	-	-	-	-	-	-	-	-	-	-	-	-	-	-	-	-	-	-	121,900
SOUTH DAKOTA	79,600	90,300	-	104,200	-	-	100,000	-	77,700	-	-	-	-	80,000	137,500	93,000	-	-	-	-	-	-	-	82,700
Minnehaha County	101,200	86,800	-	-	-	-	-	-	-	-	-	-	-	-	-	-	-	-	-	-	-	-	-	82,100
Pennington County	90,900	99,500	-	-	-	-	-	-	-	-	-	-	-	-	-	-	-	-	-	-	-	-	-	-
TENNESSEE	93,000	128,000	98,300	170,700	-	82,300	149,400	-	127,100	110,400	107,500	-	-	127,700	119,700	97,400	-	165,200	81,700	-	170,000	103,200	-	96,600
Anderson County	87,500	175,000	-	-	-	-	-	-	-	-	-	-	-	-	-	-	-	-	-	-	-	-	-	-
Blount County	103,900	108,300	-	-	-	-	-	-	-	-	-	-	-	-	-	-	-	-	-	-	-	-	-	-
Bradley County	91,700	137,500	-	-	-	-	-	-	-	-	-	-	-	-	-	-	-	-	-	-	-	-	-	-
Davidson County	115,800	124,000	151,800	169,900	-	-	163,200	-	138,900	-	-	-	-	166,400	126,400	86,000	-	-	-	-	-	-	-	101,900
Hamilton County	94,700	116,200	-	172,500	-	-	-	-	92,500	-	-	-	-	-	66,100	-	-	-	-	-	-	-	-	95,000
Knox County	98,500	149,100	-	161,600	-	-	140,200	-	-	-	-	-	-	-	95,000	-	-	-	-	-	-	-	-	118,300
Madison County	85,100	169,400	-	-	-	-	-	-	-	-	-	-	-	-	-	-	-	-	-	-	-	-	-	-
Montgomery County	85,100	88,300	-	-	-	-	-	-	-	-	-	-	-	-	78,600	-	-	-	-	-	-	-	-	-
Putnam County	92,600	132,500	-	-	-	-	-	-	-	-	-	-	-	-	-	-	-	-	-	-	-	-	-	-
Rutherford County	113,500	124,400	-	-	-	-	-	-	-	-	-	-	-	-	-	103,900	-	-	-	-	-	-	-	-
Shelby County	92,200	119,500	70,000	192,500	-	69,400	139,100	-	125,600	-	-	-	-	90,900	139,600	-	-	-	-	-	-	-	-	85,900
Germantown (city)	216,500	256,500	-	373,100	-	-	242,300	-	-	-	-	-	-	-	-	-	-	-	-	-	-	-	-	-
Sullivan County	88,000	160,900	-	-	-	-	-	-	-	-	-	-	-	-	-	-	-	-	-	-	-	-	-	-
Sumner County	125,800	135,400	-	-	-	-	-	-	-	-	-	-	-	-	-	-	-	-	-	-	-	-	-	-
Washington County	96,700	179,400	-	-	-	-	-	-	-	-	-	-	-	-	-	-	-	-	-	-	-	-	-	-
Weakley County[4]	67,900	151,800	-	-	-	-	-	-	-	-	-	-	-	-	-	-	-	-	-	-	-	-	-	-
Martin (city)	79,900	151,800	-	-	-	-	-	-	-	-	-	-	-	-	-	-	-	-	-	-	-	-	-	-
Williamson County	208,400	210,600	-	-	-	-	-	-	-	-	-	-	-	-	-	-	-	-	-	-	-	-	-	-
Wilson County	136,600	183,300	-	-	-	-	-	-	-	-	-	-	-	-	-	-	-	-	-	-	-	-	-	-
TEXAS	82,500	113,700	84,200	145,500	127,100	77,900	138,300	-	97,200	83,100	83,400	-	160,600	106,600	120,700	63,000	132,100	147,000	85,400	153,300	148,800	94,800	92,700	89,600
Anderson County	58,900	187,500	-	-	-	-	-	-	-	-	-	-	-	-	-	-	-	-	-	-	-	-	-	-
Angelina County	63,600	89,000	-	-	-	-	-	-	-	-	-	-	-	-	-	-	-	-	-	-	-	-	-	-
Bell County	78,100	77,700	77,500	168,200	-	-	-	-	77,400	80,000	-	-	-	59,200	75,000	-	-	-	-	-	-	-	-	-
Killeen (city)	73,700	72,800	77,600	-	-	-	-	-	75,300	78,800	-	-	-	-	69,600	-	-	-	-	-	-	-	-	-
Bexar County	74,100	89,900	84,000	112,200	-	-	100,000	-	92,600	-	78,900	-	-	79,800	78,400	70,000	-	-	-	-	-	91,100	-	68,600
Bowie County	66,600	114,500	-	-	-	-	-	-	-	-	-	-	-	-	-	-	-	-	-	-	-	-	-	-
Brazoria County	88,500	150,600	-	180,800	-	50,000	156,300	-	149,200	-	-	-	-	-	-	-	-	-	-	-	-	-	-	148,500
Brazos County	96,000	133,600	-	227,300	-	-	113,200	-	-	-	-	-	-	-	137,500	-	-	-	-	-	-	-	-	68,500
College Station (city)	119,500	149,600	-	245,500	-	-	120,800	-	-	-	-	-	-	-	137,500	-	-	-	-	-	-	-	-	-
Calhoun County[4]	56,400	88,800	-	-	-	-	-	-	-	-	-	-	-	-	-	-	-	-	-	-	-	-	-	25,600
Port Lavaca (city)	56,600	93,100	-	-	-	-	-	-	-	-	-	-	-	-	-	-	-	-	-	-	-	-	-	-

Notes: Please refer to the User's Guide for an explanation of data; data is arranged alphabetically by state, then county, then city within each county; table includes counties with populations greater than 49,999 unless noted and cities with populations greater than 9,999 whose Asian and/or NHPI population rates are greater than the national average; (1) Native Hawaiian and other Pacific Islander; (2) excludes Taiwanese; (3) includes Chamorro; (4) county does not meet population threshold but is shown in order to allow inclusion of city

Place	All specified owner-occupied housing units	Specified housing units owned and occup. by Asians	Specified housing units owned and occup. by NHPIs[1]	Asian Indian	Bangladeshi	Cambodian	Chinese[2]	Fijian	Filipino	Guamanian[3]	Hawaiian, Native	Hmong	Indonesian	Japanese	Korean	Laotian	Malaysian	Pakistani	Samoan	Sri Lankan	Taiwanese	Thai	Tongan	Vietnamese
Cameron County	53,000	111,800	-	-	-	-	-	-	101,400	-	-	-	-	-	-	-	-	-	-	-	-	-	-	-
Collin County	155,500	180,300	-	199,800	-	-	179,100	-	173,100	-	-	-	-	183,800	167,400	-	-	199,200	-	-	171,200	140,400	-	173,800
Allen (city)	142,400	158,600	-	178,800	-	-	-	-	-	-	-	-	-	-	-	-	-	-	-	-	-	-	-	170,400
Plano (city)	162,300	181,800	-	203,600	-	-	180,500	-	196,400	-	-	-	-	177,500	168,300	-	-	221,300	-	-	168,900	-	-	162,200
Comal County	117,000	148,800	-	-	-	-	-	-	-	-	-	-	-	-	-	-	-	-	-	-	-	-	-	-
Coryell County	69,500	67,200	89,400	-	-	-	-	-	-	-	-	-	-	-	58,300	-	-	-	-	-	-	-	-	-
Dallas County	92,700	109,400	85,500	123,500	133,300	83,200	125,300	-	100,400	-	-	-	-	122,900	129,900	75,100	-	169,900	-	-	148,000	107,300	-	93,400
Addison (town)	222,400	201,700	-	192,500	-	-	-	-	-	-	-	-	-	-	-	-	-	-	-	-	-	-	-	-
Coppell (city)	210,700	212,000	-	196,800	-	-	212,500	-	-	-	-	-	-	-	238,400	-	-	-	-	-	-	-	-	-
Farmers Branch (city)	99,200	105,700	-	-	-	-	-	-	-	-	-	-	-	-	-	-	-	-	-	-	-	-	-	-
Garland (city)	86,400	95,400	-	101,500	-	-	104,600	-	97,900	-	-	-	-	-	94,300	-	-	84,800	-	-	-	-	-	91,700
Grand Prairie (city)	84,100	104,100	-	112,500	-	-	-	-	119,300	-	-	-	-	-	-	84,600	-	-	-	-	-	-	-	98,000
Irving (city)	94,200	124,500	-	149,300	-	-	153,100	-	95,800	-	-	-	-	278,800	123,600	86,100	-	275,000	-	-	-	-	-	84,300
Mesquite (city)	85,500	104,500	-	108,400	-	-	-	-	89,500	-	-	-	-	-	-	-	-	-	-	-	-	-	-	-
Richardson (city)	131,400	139,200	-	159,800	-	-	129,800	-	114,800	-	-	-	-	-	121,300	-	-	204,700	-	-	-	-	-	177,200
Rowlett (city)	116,900	165,800	-	181,300	-	-	-	-	-	-	-	-	-	-	-	-	-	-	-	-	-	-	-	-
Denton County	133,200	143,700	-	157,700	-	105,200	133,300	-	133,500	-	-	-	-	120,300	156,600	-	-	173,500	-	-	-	-	-	125,300
Carrollton (city)	125,900	144,200	-	157,700	-	99,300	140,000	-	-	-	-	-	-	-	151,400	-	-	203,700	-	-	-	-	-	119,400
Lewisville (city)	116,700	125,300	-	134,600	-	-	-	-	-	-	-	-	-	-	-	-	-	-	-	-	-	-	-	117,000
Ector County	47,700	90,800	-	-	-	-	-	-	-	-	-	-	-	-	-	-	-	-	-	-	-	-	-	-
El Paso County	69,600	84,500	93,800	98,600	-	-	119,200	-	91,700	-	-	-	-	68,900	85,300	-	-	-	-	-	-	-	-	-
Ellis County	91,400	132,300	-	-	-	-	-	-	-	-	-	-	-	-	-	-	-	-	-	-	-	-	-	-
Fort Bend County	115,100	144,400	-	153,100	-	-	152,800	-	117,300	-	-	-	-	-	164,300	-	-	152,100	-	-	151,200	-	-	129,700
Cinco Ranch (cdp)	199,800	197,700	-	-	-	-	-	-	-	-	-	-	-	-	-	-	-	-	-	-	-	-	-	-
Mission Bend (cdp)	84,500	92,400	-	94,600	-	-	90,900	-	81,300	-	-	-	-	-	-	-	-	72,700	-	-	-	-	-	100,000
Missouri City (city)	111,800	141,100	-	142,900	-	-	144,300	-	126,000	-	-	-	-	-	-	-	-	-	-	-	-	-	-	144,200
New Territory (cdp)	160,700	160,300	-	167,900	-	-	160,400	-	-	-	-	-	-	-	-	-	-	-	-	-	-	-	-	-
Stafford (city)	100,300	116,300	-	87,500	-	-	129,900	-	114,600	-	-	-	-	-	-	-	-	-	-	-	-	-	-	131,800
Sugar Land (city)	158,000	170,200	-	192,900	-	-	173,100	-	112,200	-	-	-	-	-	160,300	-	-	208,300	-	-	155,700	-	-	152,800
Galveston County	85,200	108,600	-	110,400	-	-	103,100	-	93,800	-	-	-	-	-	-	-	-	-	-	-	-	-	-	104,700
Grayson County	69,100	106,700	-	-	-	-	-	-	-	-	-	-	-	-	-	-	-	-	-	-	-	-	-	-
Gregg County	76,800	101,600	-	-	-	-	-	-	-	-	-	-	-	-	-	-	-	-	-	-	-	-	-	-
Guadalupe County	91,400	110,600	-	-	-	-	-	-	-	-	-	-	-	-	-	-	-	-	-	-	-	-	-	-
Harris County	87,000	94,000	83,200	114,700	77,900	64,600	111,300	-	92,800	86,800	-	-	103,100	121,900	116,400	69,400	-	96,400	-	-	129,900	86,500	-	80,900
Bellaire (city)	233,200	346,300	-	-	-	-	350,000	-	-	-	-	-	-	-	-	-	-	-	-	-	-	-	-	-
Houston (city)	79,300	86,200	82,800	105,300	-	60,500	97,900	-	83,500	87,000	-	-	121,900	155,400	110,100	-	-	93,600	-	-	122,500	89,300	-	74,600
West University Place (city)	372,800	302,100	-	-	-	-	-	-	-	-	-	-	-	-	-	-	-	-	-	-	-	-	-	-
Hays County	129,400	123,600	-	-	-	-	-	-	-	-	-	-	-	-	-	-	-	-	-	-	-	-	-	-
Hidalgo County	52,400	88,300	-	141,700	-	-	-	-	89,500	-	-	-	-	-	-	-	-	-	-	-	-	-	-	-
Hunt County	62,000	61,500	-	-	-	-	-	-	-	-	-	-	-	-	-	-	-	-	-	-	-	-	-	-
Jefferson County	59,400	59,400	-	134,700	-	-	141,300	-	96,300	-	-	-	-	-	-	-	-	-	-	-	-	-	-	42,000

Notes: Please refer to the User's Guide for an explanation of data; data is arranged alphabetically by state, then county, then city within each county; table includes counties with populations greater than 49,999 unless noted and cities with populations greater than 9,999 whose Asian and/or NHPI population rates are greater than the national average; (1) Native Hawaiian and other Pacific Islander; (2) excludes Taiwanese; (3) includes Chamorro; (4) county does not meet population threshold but is shown in order to allow inclusion of city

Place	All specified owner-occupied housing units	Specified housing units owned and occup. by Asians	Specified housing units owned and occup. by NHPIs[1]	Asian Indian	Bangladeshi	Cambodian	Chinese[2]	Fijian	Filipino	Guamanian[3]	Hawaiian, Native	Hmong	Indonesian	Japanese	Korean	Laotian	Malaysian	Pakistani	Samoan	Sri Lankan	Taiwanese	Thai	Tongan	Vietnamese
Port Arthur (city)	35,900	35,800	-	-	-	-	-	-	-	-	-	-	-	-	-	-	-	-	-	-	-	-	-	34,900
Johnson County	81,900	80,400	-	-	-	-	-	-	-	-	-	-	-	-	-	-	-	-	-	-	-	-	-	-
Kaufman County	85,700	77,800	-	-	-	-	-	-	-	-	-	-	-	-	-	-	-	-	-	-	-	-	-	-
Lubbock County	69,100	98,300	-	214,100	-	-	125,000	-	-	-	-	-	-	-	-	-	-	-	-	-	-	-	-	53,600
McLennan County	67,700	76,300	-	181,300	-	-	-	-	-	-	-	-	-	-	-	-	-	-	-	-	-	-	-	-
Midland County	73,400	140,000	-	157,500	-	-	-	-	-	-	-	-	-	-	-	-	-	-	-	-	-	-	-	-
Montgomery County	114,800	155,300	-	190,600	-	-	165,600	-	99,200	-	-	-	-	-	-	-	-	-	-	-	-	-	-	-
Nacogdoches County	73,900	81,400	-	-	-	-	-	-	-	-	-	-	-	-	-	-	-	-	-	-	-	-	-	-
Nueces County	70,100	114,800	-	147,600	-	-	-	-	103,800	-	-	-	-	-	-	-	-	-	-	-	-	-	-	-
Orange County	66,100	93,900	-	-	-	-	-	-	-	-	-	-	-	-	-	-	-	-	-	-	-	-	-	55,800
Potter County	54,400	49,300	-	-	-	-	-	-	-	-	-	-	-	-	-	48,400	-	-	-	-	-	-	-	49,000
Randall County	93,500	105,100	-	-	-	-	-	-	-	-	-	-	-	-	-	-	-	-	-	-	-	-	-	-
San Patricio County	66,000	57,900	-	-	-	-	-	-	-	-	-	-	-	-	-	-	-	-	-	-	-	-	-	-
Smith County	82,600	162,500	-	-	-	-	-	-	-	-	-	-	-	-	-	-	-	-	-	-	-	-	-	-
Tarrant County	90,300	95,900	97,200	143,900	-	34,200	110,900	-	111,600	-	-	-	-	119,100	96,300	64,900	-	167,700	-	-	140,900	75,900	90,500	86,700
Arlington (city)	96,400	94,600	-	148,900	-	-	122,800	-	88,600	-	-	-	-	-	114,800	-	-	-	-	-	148,800	-	-	86,700
Euless (city)	94,900	108,100	-	204,500	-	-	-	-	-	-	-	-	-	-	-	-	-	-	-	-	-	-	-	-
Haltom City (city)	64,400	70,400	-	-	-	-	-	-	-	-	-	-	-	-	-	67,400	-	-	-	-	-	-	-	70,900
Taylor County	61,700	85,500	-	-	-	-	-	-	85,000	-	-	-	-	-	-	-	-	-	-	-	-	-	-	-
Tom Green County	63,600	71,500	-	-	-	-	-	-	-	-	-	-	-	-	-	-	-	-	-	-	-	-	-	-
Travis County	134,700	156,100	97,900	195,200	-	-	179,800	-	122,700	-	-	-	-	187,500	140,300	-	-	162,500	-	-	187,500	107,100	-	126,000
Austin (city)	124,700	163,800	79,300	197,500	-	-	177,600	-	153,000	-	-	-	-	176,000	157,800	-	-	165,000	-	-	211,800	-	-	120,700
Pflugerville (city)	134,900	141,000	-	-	-	-	-	-	-	-	-	-	-	-	-	-	-	-	-	-	-	-	-	-
Wells Branch (cdp)	119,300	150,400	-	-	-	-	-	-	-	-	-	-	-	-	-	-	-	-	-	-	-	-	-	-
Victoria County	73,300	64,000	-	-	-	-	-	-	-	-	-	-	-	-	-	-	-	-	-	-	-	-	-	-
Webb County	74,600	126,400	-	-	-	-	-	-	-	-	-	-	-	-	-	-	-	-	-	-	-	-	-	-
Wichita County	61,500	56,800	-	-	-	-	-	-	56,800	-	-	-	-	-	-	-	-	-	-	-	-	-	-	48,100
Williamson County	125,800	153,500	-	163,900	-	-	157,700	-	-	-	-	-	-	-	126,600	-	-	-	-	-	-	-	-	127,700
Brushy Creek (cdp)	160,600	176,100	-	-	-	-	-	-	-	-	-	-	-	-	-	-	-	-	-	-	-	-	-	-
Jollyville (cdp)	134,700	135,200	-	-	-	-	-	-	-	-	-	-	-	-	-	-	-	-	-	-	-	-	-	-
UTAH	146,100	147,800	130,200	208,300	-	125,700	164,400	-	146,500	-	132,200	-	-	150,500	174,500	131,600	-	200,000	138,300	-	164,300	141,700	122,400	134,000
Cache County	131,800	137,500	-	-	-	-	165,900	-	-	-	-	-	-	-	-	-	-	-	-	-	-	-	-	-
Davis County	156,400	151,600	137,900	-	-	-	-	-	125,000	-	-	-	-	153,000	168,100	-	-	-	-	-	-	-	-	-
Salt Lake County	157,000	153,400	125,800	200,800	-	124,600	171,900	-	167,200	-	144,400	-	-	165,100	179,600	132,100	-	-	135,500	-	-	-	118,300	136,000
Kearns (cdp)	114,600	132,800	110,800	-	-	-	-	-	-	-	-	-	-	-	-	-	-	-	-	-	-	-	-	-
Salt Lake City (city)	153,300	147,100	113,400	240,300	-	-	147,500	-	165,600	-	-	-	-	158,100	116,200	-	-	-	128,000	-	-	-	108,400	129,200
Sandy (city)	183,500	187,500	150,600	-	-	-	197,200	-	-	-	-	-	-	-	-	-	-	-	-	-	-	-	-	-
Taylorsville (city)	138,100	147,800	137,000	-	-	-	-	-	-	-	-	-	-	-	-	-	-	-	-	-	-	-	-	140,500
West Jordan (city)	155,200	153,300	132,200	-	-	-	-	-	-	-	-	-	-	-	-	-	-	-	-	-	-	-	121,400	-
West Valley City (city)	128,600	137,000	125,800	-	-	120,500	147,400	-	-	-	-	-	-	-	-	134,600	-	-	131,100	-	-	-	119,400	140,500
Utah County	156,400	150,500	144,300	-	-	-	143,000	-	137,500	-	140,300	-	-	137,500	237,500	-	-	-	142,900	-	-	-	149,500	-

Notes: Please refer to the User's Guide for an explanation of data; data is arranged alphabetically by state, then county, then city within each county; table includes counties with populations greater than 49,999 unless noted and cities with populations greater than 9,999 whose Asian and/or NHPI population rates are greater than the national average; (1) Native Hawaiian and other Pacific Islander; (2) excludes Taiwanese; (3) includes Chamorro; (4) county does not meet population threshold but is shown in order to allow inclusion of city

Place	All specified owner-occupied housing units	Specified housing units owned and occup. by Asians	Specified housing units owned and occup. by NHPIs[1]	Asian Indian	Bangladeshi	Cambodian	Chinese[2]	Fijian	Filipino	Guamanian[3]	Hawaiian, Native	Hmong	Indonesian	Japanese	Korean	Laotian	Malaysian	Pakistani	Samoan	Sri Lankan	Taiwanese	Thai	Tongan	Vietnamese
Orem (city)	155,000	154,500	148,200	-	-	-	-	-	-	-	-	-	-	-	-	-	-	-	-	-	-	-	-	-
Provo (city)	149,700	143,100	139,600	-	-	-	137,500	-	-	-	-	-	-	211,400	-	-	-	-	-	-	-	-	-	-
Washington County	139,800	106,000	154,200	-	-	-	-	-	-	-	-	-	-	-	-	-	-	-	-	-	-	-	-	-
St. George (city)	143,200	104,300	150,000	-	-	-	-	-	-	-	-	-	-	-	-	-	-	-	-	-	-	-	-	-
Weber County	125,600	116,500	-	-	-	-	-	-	-	-	-	-	-	117,500	-	-	-	-	-	-	-	-	-	-
VERMONT	111,500	136,000	-	173,100	-	-	136,500	-	125,800	-	-	-	-	117,600	109,700	-	-	-	-	-	-	-	-	153,300
Chittenden County	139,000	136,600	-	228,100	-	-	139,600	-	-	-	-	-	-	-	-	-	-	-	-	-	-	-	-	153,300
Rutland County	96,000	112,500	-	-	-	-	-	-	-	-	-	-	-	-	-	-	-	-	-	-	-	-	-	-
Washington County	102,500	135,700	-	-	-	-	-	-	-	-	-	-	-	-	-	-	-	-	-	-	-	-	-	-
Windsor County	108,500	139,100	-	-	-	-	-	-	-	-	-	-	-	-	-	-	-	-	-	-	-	-	-	-
VIRGINIA	125,400	176,800	135,500	216,900	184,700	120,300	193,000	-	142,200	172,900	125,500	-	173,000	169,700	192,600	161,300	-	155,400	139,300	152,500	297,200	150,400	-	179,700
Albemarle County	161,100	212,500	-	224,100	-	-	140,300	-	-	-	-	-	-	-	-	-	-	-	-	-	-	-	-	-
Alexandria Independent City	252,800	187,700	-	173,200	-	-	188,100	-	214,600	-	-	-	-	-	258,900	-	-	112,500	-	-	-	-	-	187,500
Arlington County	262,400	212,900	-	226,100	-	148,800	261,300	-	198,700	-	-	-	-	245,800	236,500	-	-	202,800	-	-	-	-	-	200,800
Arlington (cdp)	262,400	212,900	-	226,100	-	148,800	261,300	-	198,700	-	-	-	-	245,800	236,500	-	-	202,800	-	-	-	-	-	200,800
Bedford County	127,000	183,600	-	-	-	-	-	-	-	-	-	-	-	-	-	-	-	-	-	-	-	-	-	-
Charlottesville Independent City	119,000	113,900	-	112,500	-	-	134,400	-	-	-	-	-	-	-	-	-	-	-	-	-	-	-	-	-
Chesapeake Independent City	122,300	158,900	-	-	-	-	-	-	148,700	-	-	-	-	-	-	-	-	-	-	-	-	-	-	-
Chesterfield County	120,500	149,200	-	190,000	-	88,100	162,500	-	142,300	-	-	-	-	-	130,600	-	-	-	-	-	-	-	-	143,000
Fairfax Independent City	192,100	192,700	-	171,400	-	-	339,300	-	-	-	-	-	-	-	204,200	-	-	-	-	-	-	-	-	167,600
Fairfax County	233,300	207,600	236,300	250,100	302,100	174,100	226,300	-	201,800	-	-	-	174,000	231,700	208,200	175,400	-	162,500	-	-	289,600	180,400	-	192,700
Annandale (cdp)	236,000	203,700	-	191,200	-	-	171,600	-	207,800	-	-	-	-	-	194,700	-	-	-	-	-	-	-	-	209,000
Bailey's Crossroads (cdp)	225,300	198,300	-	-	-	-	-	-	-	-	-	-	-	-	-	-	-	225,000	-	-	-	-	-	189,100
Burke (cdp)	215,100	191,900	-	212,500	-	-	237,000	-	196,200	-	-	-	-	-	180,400	-	-	-	-	-	-	-	-	149,300
Centreville (cdp)	167,000	162,500	-	191,100	-	-	157,100	-	165,800	-	-	-	-	-	167,600	-	-	-	-	-	-	-	-	174,500
Chantilly (cdp)	216,000	196,400	-	225,000	-	-	194,800	-	-	-	-	-	-	-	191,600	-	-	-	-	-	-	-	-	191,100
Franconia (cdp)	192,100	174,200	-	188,300	-	-	-	-	159,300	-	-	-	-	-	205,800	-	-	-	-	-	-	-	-	185,900
Groveton (cdp)	171,800	168,900	-	-	-	-	-	-	-	-	-	-	-	-	-	-	-	-	-	-	-	-	-	-
Herndon (town)	185,200	173,800	-	183,900	-	-	-	-	-	-	-	-	-	-	-	-	-	-	-	-	-	-	-	161,100
Hybla Valley (cdp)	240,600	190,600	-	-	-	-	-	-	-	-	-	-	-	-	-	-	-	-	-	-	-	-	-	-
Idylwood (cdp)	226,900	174,600	-	153,300	-	-	170,800	-	-	-	-	-	-	-	-	-	-	-	-	-	-	-	-	175,000
Jefferson (cdp)	188,500	185,600	-	206,000	-	-	200,900	-	180,600	-	-	-	-	-	-	-	-	-	-	-	-	-	-	184,000
Lincolnia (cdp)	217,100	210,200	-	-	-	-	-	-	-	-	-	-	-	-	-	-	-	162,500	-	-	-	-	-	239,100
Lorton (cdp)	147,600	161,700	-	-	-	-	-	-	-	-	-	-	-	-	-	-	-	-	-	-	-	-	-	-
McLean (cdp)	388,700	374,100	-	497,500	-	-	355,400	-	396,700	-	-	-	-	550,000	357,300	-	-	-	-	-	-	-	-	-
Merrifield (cdp)	193,100	185,400	-	259,000	-	-	-	-	-	-	-	-	-	-	272,700	-	-	-	-	-	-	-	-	154,300
Mount Vernon (cdp)	190,800	161,500	-	-	-	-	-	-	-	-	-	-	-	-	143,800	-	-	-	-	-	-	-	-	-
Newington (cdp)	193,600	184,800	-	186,000	-	-	-	-	211,300	-	-	-	-	-	147,600	-	-	-	-	-	-	-	-	-
Oakton (cdp)	300,600	244,200	-	368,200	-	-	270,800	-	-	-	-	-	-	-	213,600	-	-	-	-	-	-	-	-	228,100
Reston (cdp)	238,700	227,600	-	213,100	-	-	263,200	-	192,600	-	-	-	-	-	318,800	-	-	-	-	-	-	-	-	-
Rose Hill (cdp)	194,700	180,600	-	-	-	-	-	-	-	-	-	-	-	-	-	-	-	-	-	-	-	-	-	-

Notes: Please refer to the User's Guide for an explanation of data; data is arranged alphabetically by state, then county, then city within each county; table includes counties with populations greater than 49,999 unless noted and cities with populations greater than 9,999 whose Asian and/or NHPI population rates are greater than the national average; (1) Native Hawaiian and other Pacific Islander; (2) excludes Taiwanese; (3) includes Chamorro; (4) county does not meet population threshold but is shown in order to allow inclusion of city

Place	All specified owner-occupied housing units	Specified housing units owned and occup. by Asians	Specified housing units owned and occup. by NHPIs[1]	Asian Indian	Bangladeshi	Cambodian	Chinese[2]	Fijian	Filipino	Guamanian[3]	Hawaiian, Native	Hmong	Indonesian	Japanese	Korean	Laotian	Malaysian	Pakistani	Samoan	Sri Lankan	Taiwanese	Thai	Tongan	Vietnamese
Springfield (cdp)	185,700	178,700	-	193,300	-	-	166,900	-	166,100	-	-	-	-	-	181,300	182,600	-	-	-	-	-	-	-	182,500
Tysons Corner (cdp)	338,200	368,900	-	351,600	-	-	388,900	-	-	-	-	-	-	-	426,300	-	-	-	-	-	-	-	-	-
Vienna (town)	231,200	233,800	-	-	-	-	-	-	-	-	-	-	-	-	-	-	-	-	-	-	-	-	-	-
West Springfield (cdp)	206,600	199,500	-	226,400	-	-	192,300	-	-	-	-	-	-	-	198,900	-	-	-	-	-	-	-	-	204,000
Wolf Trap (cdp)	385,000	390,700	-	421,700	-	-	390,500	-	-	-	-	-	-	-	-	-	-	-	-	-	-	-	-	-
Falls Church Independent City	277,100	193,100	-	-	-	-	-	-	-	-	-	-	-	-	-	-	-	-	-	-	-	-	-	-
Fauquier County	162,700	174,500	-	-	-	-	-	-	-	-	-	-	-	-	-	-	-	-	-	-	-	-	-	-
Frederick County	118,300	178,100	-	-	-	-	-	-	-	-	-	-	-	-	-	-	-	-	-	-	-	-	-	-
Hampton Independent City	91,100	98,400	-	-	-	-	-	-	112,500	-	-	-	-	-	-	-	-	-	-	-	-	-	-	97,800
Hanover County	143,300	175,700	-	-	-	-	-	-	-	-	-	-	-	-	-	-	-	-	-	-	-	-	-	-
Henrico County	121,300	144,100	-	181,700	-	99,000	154,300	-	135,900	-	-	-	-	-	161,900	-	-	-	-	-	-	-	-	128,000
Glen Allen (cdp)	131,600	161,800	-	-	-	-	-	-	-	-	-	-	-	-	-	-	-	-	-	-	-	-	-	-
Laurel (cdp)	104,700	110,200	-	-	-	-	-	-	-	-	-	-	-	-	-	-	-	-	-	-	-	-	-	-
Loudoun County	200,500	194,300	-	204,000	-	-	177,900	-	236,200	-	-	-	-	-	262,100	-	-	165,900	-	-	-	-	-	179,000
Lynchburg Independent City	85,300	128,800	-	-	-	-	-	-	-	-	-	-	-	-	-	-	-	-	-	-	-	-	-	-
Manassas Park Indep. City	116,000	180,900	-	-	-	-	-	-	-	-	-	-	-	-	-	-	-	-	-	-	-	-	-	-
Montgomery County	114,600	172,300	-	271,700	-	-	168,300	-	-	-	-	-	-	-	144,800	-	-	-	-	-	-	-	-	-
Blacksburg (town)	144,000	149,200	-	162,500	-	-	137,500	-	-	-	-	-	-	-	144,800	-	-	-	-	-	-	-	-	-
Newport News Independent City	96,400	98,000	-	-	-	-	126,500	-	103,000	-	-	-	-	-	95,200	-	-	-	-	-	-	-	-	91,300
Norfolk Independent City	88,400	90,200	-	113,500	-	-	123,100	-	89,300	-	-	-	-	-	-	-	-	-	-	-	-	-	-	84,200
Portsmouth Independent City	81,300	88,700	-	-	-	-	-	-	93,200	-	-	-	-	-	-	-	-	-	-	-	-	-	-	-
Prince William County	149,600	140,500	-	123,700	-	-	156,300	-	150,000	-	-	-	-	146,000	144,300	-	-	125,600	-	-	-	-	-	142,700
Bull Run (cdp)	127,200	138,300	-	-	-	-	-	-	-	-	-	-	-	-	-	-	-	-	-	-	-	-	-	-
Dale City (cdp)	134,100	134,200	-	125,000	-	-	-	-	121,900	-	-	-	-	-	-	-	-	133,200	-	-	-	-	-	-
Lake Ridge (cdp)	158,100	171,400	-	-	-	-	-	-	-	-	-	-	-	-	-	-	-	-	-	-	-	-	-	-
Woodbridge (cdp)	115,500	116,200	-	-	-	-	-	-	-	-	-	-	-	-	-	-	-	-	-	-	-	-	-	-
Richmond Independent City	87,300	88,000	-	137,500	-	-	-	-	87,500	-	-	-	-	-	-	-	-	-	-	-	-	-	-	-
Roanoke Independent City	80,300	79,400	-	-	-	-	-	-	-	-	-	-	-	-	-	-	-	-	-	-	-	-	-	-
Roanoke County	118,100	151,800	-	-	-	-	-	-	-	-	-	-	-	-	-	-	-	-	-	-	-	-	-	-
Spotsylvania County	128,500	124,400	-	-	-	-	-	-	-	-	-	-	-	-	-	-	-	-	-	-	-	-	-	-
Stafford County	156,400	153,000	-	-	-	-	-	-	129,200	-	-	-	-	-	-	-	-	-	-	-	-	-	-	-
Suffolk Independent City	107,300	140,800	-	-	-	-	-	-	-	-	-	-	-	-	-	-	-	-	-	-	-	-	-	-
Virginia Beach Independent City	123,200	118,900	-	171,800	-	-	138,000	-	116,400	-	-	-	-	95,000	137,500	-	-	-	-	-	-	-	-	110,200
Williamsburg Independent City	212,000	205,600	-	-	-	-	-	-	-	-	-	-	-	-	-	-	-	-	-	-	-	-	-	-
York County	152,700	169,900	-	258,300	-	-	-	-	-	-	-	-	-	-	167,400	-	-	-	-	-	-	-	-	-
WASHINGTON	168,300	192,100	155,400	224,500	-	160,300	226,900	184,400	169,300	146,100	170,600	144,200	183,000	205,800	187,700	152,700	-	194,800	149,400	174,000	256,500	184,100	171,400	179,500
Benton County	119,900	126,300	-	170,500	-	-	168,200	-	-	-	-	-	-	-	108,700	-	-	-	-	-	-	-	-	113,000
Richland (city)	128,400	162,900	-	-	-	-	190,600	-	-	-	-	-	-	-	-	-	-	-	-	-	-	-	-	-
Chelan County	148,400	146,100	-	-	-	-	-	-	-	-	-	-	-	-	-	-	-	-	-	-	-	-	-	-
Clallam County	133,400	164,300	-	-	-	-	-	-	-	-	-	-	-	-	-	-	-	-	-	-	-	-	-	-
Clark County	156,600	148,800	149,100	152,700	-	141,500	159,700	-	141,400	-	-	-	-	179,800	170,400	144,700	-	-	-	-	-	-	-	139,800

Notes: Please refer to the User's Guide for an explanation of data; data is arranged alphabetically by state, then county, then city within each county; table includes counties with populations greater than 49,999 unless noted and cities with populations greater than 9,999 whose Asian and/or NHPI population rates are greater than the national average; (1) Native Hawaiian and other Pacific Islander; (2) excludes Taiwanese; (3) includes Chamorro; (4) county does not meet population threshold but is shown in order to allow inclusion of city

Place	All specified owner-occupied housing units	Specified housing units owned and occup. by Asians	Specified housing units owned and occup. by NHPIs[1]	Asian Indian	Bangladeshi	Cambodian	Chinese[2]	Fijian	Filipino	Guamanian[3]	Hawaiian, Native	Hmong	Indonesian	Japanese	Korean	Laotian	Malaysian	Pakistani	Samoan	Sri Lankan	Taiwanese	Thai	Tongan	Vietnamese
Five Corners (cdp)	137,900	142,300	-	-	-	-	-	-	-	-	-	-	-	-	-	-	-	-	-	-	-	-	-	-
Orchards (cdp)	135,200	131,000	-	-	-	-	-	-	-	-	-	-	-	-	-	-	-	-	-	-	-	-	-	-
Vancouver (city)	142,900	147,800	159,400	-	-	-	157,100	-	144,900	-	-	-	-	159,400	177,900	-	-	-	-	-	-	-	-	138,100
Cowlitz County	129,900	134,100	-	-	-	150,000	-	-	-	-	-	-	-	-	-	-	-	-	-	-	-	-	-	122,900
Grant County	99,500	141,100	-	-	-	-	-	-	-	-	-	-	-	-	-	-	-	-	-	-	-	-	-	-
Grays Harbor County	96,400	94,700	-	-	-	-	-	-	-	-	-	-	-	-	-	-	-	-	-	-	-	-	-	-
Island County	174,800	151,600	-	-	-	-	-	-	147,100	-	-	-	-	213,900	-	-	-	-	-	-	-	-	-	-
Oak Harbor (city)	151,600	145,400	-	-	-	-	-	-	142,700	-	-	-	-	-	-	-	-	-	-	-	-	-	-	-
King County	236,900	220,600	180,700	261,900	-	181,700	242,200	183,300	192,200	200,000	216,200	166,100	252,500	235,900	224,100	169,800	-	267,600	160,500	-	283,400	236,400	168,200	192,200
Auburn (city)	153,400	171,000	-	-	-	-	-	-	-	-	-	-	-	-	-	-	-	-	-	-	-	-	-	-
Bellevue (city)	299,400	298,200	-	301,300	-	-	312,400	-	221,200	-	-	-	-	296,900	312,300	222,500	-	-	-	-	407,900	-	-	321,800
Bothell (city)	237,700	285,900	-	-	-	-	278,100	-	-	-	-	-	-	-	-	-	-	-	-	-	-	-	-	-
Bryn Mawr-Skyway (cdp)	181,400	190,700	-	-	-	-	-	-	181,100	-	-	-	-	206,900	-	-	-	-	-	-	-	-	-	200,000
Burien (city)	175,100	179,600	-	-	-	-	-	-	158,000	-	-	-	-	-	-	-	-	-	-	-	-	-	-	185,500
Cascade-Fairwood (cdp)	192,800	207,300	-	-	-	-	196,000	-	194,300	-	-	-	-	233,100	-	-	-	-	-	-	-	-	-	236,500
Cottage Lake (cdp)	371,900	384,100	-	-	-	-	-	-	-	-	-	-	-	-	-	-	-	-	-	-	-	-	-	-
Des Moines (city)	174,700	174,800	241,700	-	-	-	-	-	184,600	-	-	-	-	-	-	-	-	-	-	-	-	-	-	174,500
East Hill-Meridian (cdp)	188,000	206,900	-	193,000	-	-	217,000	-	198,800	-	-	-	-	-	-	-	-	-	-	-	-	-	-	223,100
Federal Way (city)	171,700	186,200	164,600	-	-	-	220,600	-	181,700	-	-	-	-	178,400	182,500	-	-	-	159,200	-	-	-	-	185,800
Inglewood-Finn Hill (cdp)	240,300	240,900	-	-	-	-	281,800	-	-	-	-	-	-	-	-	-	-	-	-	-	-	-	-	-
Issaquah (city)	278,500	239,700	-	-	-	-	-	-	-	-	-	-	-	-	-	-	-	-	-	-	-	-	-	-
Kenmore (city)	246,000	240,500	-	-	-	-	-	-	-	-	-	-	-	-	-	-	-	-	-	-	-	-	-	-
Kent (city)	178,000	187,500	-	187,700	-	-	195,300	-	174,300	-	-	-	-	182,700	194,100	-	-	-	-	-	-	-	-	183,800
Kingsgate (cdp)	236,900	250,000	-	-	-	-	252,500	-	-	-	-	-	-	-	-	-	-	-	-	-	-	-	-	-
Kirkland (city)	283,100	264,700	-	-	-	-	277,000	-	-	-	-	-	-	248,500	-	-	-	-	-	-	-	-	-	248,800
Lake Forest Park (city)	263,300	245,300	-	-	-	-	-	-	-	-	-	-	-	-	-	-	-	-	-	-	-	-	-	-
Lakeland North (cdp)	172,500	189,100	-	-	-	-	-	-	-	-	-	-	-	-	-	-	-	-	-	-	-	-	-	-
Lakeland South (cdp)	174,400	200,000	-	-	-	-	-	-	-	-	-	-	-	-	-	-	-	-	-	-	-	-	-	-
Lea Hill (cdp)	210,800	230,200	-	-	-	-	-	-	-	-	-	-	-	-	-	-	-	-	-	-	-	-	-	-
Mercer Island (city)	573,900	512,100	-	-	-	-	458,600	-	-	-	-	-	-	520,300	-	-	-	-	-	-	-	-	-	-
Redmond (city)	269,400	266,000	-	296,300	-	-	261,200	-	-	-	-	-	-	252,400	320,800	-	-	-	-	-	-	-	-	-
Renton (city)	183,800	196,000	-	-	-	-	202,100	-	181,600	-	-	-	-	221,300	-	-	-	-	-	-	-	-	-	195,700
Riverton-Boulevard Park (cdp)	141,300	160,000	-	-	-	-	-	-	-	-	-	-	-	-	-	-	-	-	-	-	-	-	-	-
Sammamish (city)	362,900	365,500	-	-	-	-	402,900	-	-	-	-	-	-	-	-	-	-	-	-	-	-	-	-	-
SeaTac (city)	157,800	166,300	170,800	176,000	-	-	-	-	145,100	-	-	-	-	-	-	-	-	-	-	-	-	-	-	172,800
Seattle (city)	259,600	201,200	179,400	262,400	-	201,000	214,200	-	185,200	-	-	-	187,500	218,200	214,800	161,300	-	-	118,800	-	264,700	270,000	-	173,800
Shoreline (city)	205,300	205,800	-	217,700	-	-	197,700	-	216,000	-	-	-	-	206,500	227,300	-	-	-	-	-	-	-	-	193,000
Tukwila (city)	150,100	137,200	171,400	-	-	-	-	-	177,700	-	-	-	-	-	-	-	-	-	-	-	-	-	-	-
Union Hill-Novelty Hill (cdp)	414,800	465,200	-	-	-	-	-	-	-	-	-	-	-	-	-	-	-	-	-	-	-	-	-	-
White Center (cdp)	153,200	173,900	-	-	-	152,500	-	-	145,500	-	-	-	-	-	-	-	-	-	-	-	-	-	-	176,700
Kitsap County	152,100	141,900	131,700	-	-	-	189,600	-	136,900	137,500	-	-	-	174,100	269,100	-	-	-	-	-	-	-	-	118,100

Notes: Please refer to the User's Guide for an explanation of data; data is arranged alphabetically by state, then county, then city within each county; table includes counties with populations greater than 49,999 unless noted and cities with populations greater than 9,999 whose Asian and/or NHPI population rates are greater than the national average; (1) Native Hawaiian and other Pacific Islander; (2) excludes Taiwanese; (3) includes Chamorro; (4) county does not meet population threshold but is shown in order to allow inclusion of city

Place	All specified owner-occupied housing units	Specified housing units owned and occup. by Asians	Specified housing units owned and occup. by NHPIs[1]	Asian Indian	Bangladeshi	Cambodian	Chinese[2]	Fijian	Filipino	Guamanian[3]	Hawaiian, Native	Hmong	Indonesian	Japanese	Korean	Laotian	Malaysian	Pakistani	Samoan	Sri Lankan	Taiwanese	Thai	Tongan	Vietnamese
Bremerton (city)	103,500	94,600	-	-	-	-	-	-	92,300	-	-	-	-	-	-	-	-	-	-	-	-	-	-	-
Silverdale (cdp)	153,200	164,100	-	-	-	-	-	-	165,600	-	-	-	-	-	-	-	-	-	-	-	-	-	-	-
Lewis County	117,800	106,300	-	-	-	-	-	-	-	-	-	-	-	-	-	-	-	-	-	-	-	-	-	-
Pierce County	149,600	140,400	144,600	163,900	-	117,300	159,600	-	140,700	144,800	139,400	-	-	131,100	143,800	126,800	-	-	139,300	-	-	126,400	-	141,000
Elk Plain (cdp)	140,200	147,000	-	-	-	-	-	-	-	-	-	-	-	-	-	-	-	-	-	-	-	-	-	-
Fort Lewis (cdp)	90,800	0	0	-	-	-	-	-	0	-	-	-	-	-	-	-	-	-	-	-	-	-	-	-
Lakewood (city)	147,600	136,200	155,700	-	-	-	-	-	118,800	-	-	-	-	130,500	150,300	-	-	-	125,000	-	-	-	-	-
Parkland (cdp)	127,500	118,000	142,700	-	-	-	-	-	-	-	-	-	-	-	120,400	-	-	-	-	-	-	-	-	-
Spanaway (cdp)	132,700	132,500	151,500	-	-	-	-	-	146,400	-	-	-	-	-	128,100	-	-	-	-	-	-	-	-	-
Tacoma (city)	123,300	124,900	130,500	-	-	108,300	152,100	-	121,600	131,300	-	-	-	116,200	130,600	86,600	-	-	108,300	-	-	-	-	138,000
University Place (city)	177,000	174,700	-	-	-	-	-	-	-	-	-	-	-	-	180,900	-	-	-	-	-	-	-	-	-
Skagit County	158,100	163,500	-	-	-	-	-	-	136,100	-	-	-	-	-	-	-	-	-	-	-	-	-	-	-
Snohomish County	196,500	213,300	219,600	221,900	-	188,700	228,800	-	192,800	-	194,600	-	-	228,100	228,000	176,000	-	206,300	-	-	-	-	-	210,000
Alderwood Manor (cdp)	196,300	221,000	-	-	-	-	-	-	-	-	-	-	-	-	-	-	-	-	-	-	-	-	-	-
Edmonds (city)	238,200	228,400	-	-	-	-	-	-	216,200	-	-	-	-	-	219,300	-	-	-	-	-	-	-	-	-
Everett (city)	168,300	180,400	-	191,900	-	184,000	-	-	174,000	-	-	-	-	-	-	-	-	-	-	-	-	-	-	191,400
Lynnwood (city)	189,000	224,400	-	-	-	-	252,400	-	192,700	-	-	-	-	-	232,000	-	-	-	-	-	-	-	-	202,900
Martha Lake (cdp)	217,400	224,700	-	-	-	-	-	-	-	-	-	-	-	-	-	-	-	-	-	-	-	-	-	-
Marysville (city)	179,000	198,100	-	-	-	-	-	-	-	-	-	-	-	-	-	-	-	-	-	-	-	-	-	-
Mill Creek (city)	300,700	341,600	-	-	-	-	-	-	-	-	-	-	-	-	337,300	-	-	-	-	-	-	-	-	-
Mountlake Terrace (city)	170,000	177,000	-	-	-	-	-	-	150,800	-	-	-	-	-	204,500	-	-	-	-	-	-	-	-	-
Mukilteo (city)	272,300	278,400	-	-	-	-	-	-	-	-	-	-	-	-	271,600	-	-	-	-	-	-	-	-	-
North Creek (cdp)	221,800	216,200	-	-	-	-	-	-	-	-	-	-	-	-	-	-	-	-	-	-	-	-	-	-
Paine Field-Lk. Stickney (cdp)	158,000	173,400	-	-	-	-	-	-	-	-	-	-	-	-	-	-	-	-	-	-	-	-	-	-
Picnic Pt.-N. Lynnwood (cdp)	215,600	213,200	-	-	-	-	-	-	183,900	-	-	-	-	-	238,700	-	-	-	-	-	-	-	-	-
Seattle Hill-Silver Firs (cdp)	219,200	235,400	-	-	-	-	-	-	221,900	-	-	-	-	-	244,900	-	-	-	-	-	-	-	-	243,200
Spokane County	113,200	108,200	97,000	139,200	-	-	121,300	-	109,400	-	-	94,300	-	116,600	125,000	-	-	-	-	-	-	-	-	94,000
Spokane (city)	97,000	97,900	97,700	-	-	-	119,800	-	85,000	-	-	79,500	-	111,900	74,000	-	-	-	-	-	-	-	-	91,100
Thurston County	145,200	137,600	144,300	153,300	-	110,400	178,100	-	144,300	142,900	-	-	-	136,700	122,700	-	-	-	-	-	-	-	-	145,000
Lacey (city)	133,200	138,800	-	-	-	-	-	-	152,000	-	-	-	-	-	127,700	-	-	-	-	-	-	-	-	146,700
Olympia (city)	143,500	147,800	-	-	-	-	-	-	-	-	-	-	-	-	-	-	-	-	-	-	-	-	-	139,200
Tumwater (city)	141,000	136,500	-	-	-	-	-	-	-	-	-	-	-	-	-	-	-	-	-	-	-	-	-	-
Walla Walla County	114,300	88,000	-	-	-	-	-	-	-	-	-	-	-	-	-	-	-	-	-	-	-	-	-	-
Whatcom County	155,700	148,400	-	145,700	-	-	172,900	-	162,500	-	-	-	-	125,000	132,800	-	-	-	-	-	-	-	-	148,300
Bellingham (city)	156,100	162,500	-	159,600	-	-	-	-	-	-	-	-	-	-	-	-	-	-	-	-	-	-	-	171,600
Whitman County[4]	119,600	146,900	-	-	-	-	152,100	-	-	-	-	-	-	112,500	-	-	-	-	-	-	-	-	-	-
Pullman (city)	145,000	158,800	-	-	-	-	164,600	-	-	-	-	-	-	112,500	-	-	-	-	-	-	-	-	-	-
Yakima County	113,800	108,800	-	-	-	-	-	-	110,900	-	-	-	-	-	-	-	-	-	-	-	-	-	-	-
WEST VIRGINIA	72,800	140,400	45,000	192,600	-	-	138,600	-	118,500	-	-	-	-	81,700	119,300	-	-	130,700	-	-	-	-	-	119,200
Cabell County	76,200	97,500	-	-	-	-	-	-	-	-	-	-	-	-	-	-	-	-	-	-	-	-	-	-
Harrison County	67,600	122,500	-	-	-	-	-	-	-	-	-	-	-	-	-	-	-	-	-	-	-	-	-	-

Notes: Please refer to the User's Guide for an explanation of data; data is arranged alphabetically by state, then county, then city within each county; table includes counties with populations greater than 49,999 unless noted and cities with populations greater than 9,999 whose Asian and/or NHPI population rates are greater than the national average; (1) Native Hawaiian and other Pacific Islander; (2) excludes Taiwanese; (3) includes Chamorro; (4) county does not meet population threshold but is shown in order to allow inclusion of city

Place	All specified owner-occupied housing units	Specified housing units owned and occup. by Asians	Specified housing units owned and occup. by NHPIs[1]	Asian Indian	Bangladeshi	Cambodian	Chinese[2]	Fijian	Filipino	Guamanian[3]	Hawaiian, Native	Hmong	Indonesian	Japanese	Korean	Laotian	Malaysian	Pakistani	Samoan	Sri Lankan	Taiwanese	Thai	Tongan	Vietnamese
Kanawha County	80,700	217,100	-	246,800	-	-	-	-	-	-	-	-	-	-	-	-	-	-	-	-	-	-	-	-
Monongalia County	95,500	130,400	-	216,700	-	-	205,000	-	-	-	-	-	-	-	-	-	-	-	-	-	-	-	-	-
Putnam County	102,900	198,100	-	-	-	-	-	-	-	-	-	-	-	-	-	-	-	-	-	-	-	-	-	-
Raleigh County	69,800	188,800	-	-	-	-	-	-	-	-	-	-	-	-	-	-	-	-	-	-	-	-	-	-
Wood County	77,500	217,200	-	-	-	-	-	-	-	-	-	-	-	-	-	-	-	-	-	-	-	-	-	-
WISCONSIN	112,200	122,200	147,500	197,100	-	95,600	155,900	-	149,500	112,500	129,200	81,800	86,700	115,300	152,100	77,600	-	251,900	-	-	169,600	114,600	-	107,600
Brown County	116,100	124,500	-	163,500	-	-	-	-	-	-	-	105,100	-	-	-	77,900	-	-	-	-	-	-	-	-
Chippewa County	88,100	91,500	-	-	-	-	-	-	-	-	-	95,000	-	-	-	-	-	-	-	-	-	-	-	-
Columbia County	115,000	151,800	-	-	-	-	-	-	-	-	-	-	-	-	-	-	-	-	-	-	-	-	-	-
Dane County	146,900	147,300	-	172,400	-	-	158,100	-	157,000	-	-	131,300	-	132,800	187,500	137,500	-	-	-	-	209,600	-	-	141,000
Madison (city)	139,300	144,200	-	168,800	-	-	155,400	-	167,500	-	-	130,400	-	132,800	124,100	-	-	-	-	-	209,600	-	-	131,300
Dodge County	105,800	154,200	-	-	-	-	-	-	-	-	-	-	-	-	-	-	-	-	-	-	-	-	-	-
Eau Claire County	96,300	90,000	-	-	-	-	-	-	-	-	-	80,000	-	-	-	-	-	-	-	-	-	-	-	-
Fond du Lac County	101,000	68,100	-	-	-	-	-	-	-	-	-	65,000	-	-	-	-	-	-	-	-	-	-	-	-
Jefferson County	123,800	162,500	-	-	-	-	-	-	-	-	-	-	-	-	-	-	-	-	-	-	-	-	-	-
Kenosha County	120,900	147,600	-	-	-	-	-	-	-	-	-	-	-	-	-	-	-	-	-	-	-	-	-	-
La Crosse County	96,900	112,200	-	-	-	-	-	-	-	-	-	102,700	-	-	-	-	-	-	-	-	-	-	-	-
La Crosse (city)	85,100	104,000	-	-	-	-	-	-	-	-	-	82,700	-	-	-	-	-	-	-	-	-	-	-	-
Manitowoc County	90,900	92,100	-	-	-	-	-	-	-	-	-	82,100	-	-	-	-	-	-	-	-	-	-	-	-
Marathon County	95,800	83,300	-	-	-	-	-	-	-	-	-	75,500	-	-	-	-	-	-	-	-	-	-	-	-
Wausau (city)	85,500	80,500	-	-	-	-	-	-	-	-	-	73,300	-	-	-	-	-	-	-	-	-	-	-	-
Milwaukee County	103,200	94,500	130,000	154,300	-	-	128,000	-	123,800	-	-	64,500	-	101,900	144,100	64,300	-	190,300	-	-	-	-	-	85,200
Outagamie County	106,000	92,600	-	225,000	-	-	-	-	-	-	-	85,000	-	-	-	-	-	-	-	-	-	-	-	-
Appleton (city)	97,900	91,700	-	-	-	-	-	-	-	-	-	90,300	-	-	-	-	-	-	-	-	-	-	-	-
Ozaukee County	177,300	242,300	-	-	-	-	-	-	-	-	-	-	-	-	-	-	-	-	-	-	-	-	-	-
Portage County	98,300	90,000	-	-	-	-	-	-	-	-	-	87,900	-	-	-	-	-	-	-	-	-	-	-	-
Stevens Point (city)	80,800	77,500	-	-	-	-	-	-	-	-	-	91,400	-	-	-	-	-	-	-	-	-	-	-	-
Racine County	111,000	147,000	-	-	-	-	-	-	-	-	-	-	-	-	-	-	-	-	-	-	-	-	-	-
Rock County	98,200	107,000	-	-	-	-	-	-	-	-	-	-	-	-	-	-	-	-	-	-	-	-	-	-
St. Croix County	139,500	150,000	-	-	-	-	-	-	-	-	-	-	-	-	-	-	-	-	-	-	-	-	-	-
Sauk County	107,500	120,000	-	-	-	-	-	-	-	-	-	-	-	-	-	-	-	-	-	-	-	-	-	-
Sheboygan County	106,800	77,600	-	-	-	-	-	-	-	-	-	80,600	-	-	-	-	-	-	-	-	-	-	-	-
Sheboygan (city)	89,400	77,200	-	-	-	-	-	-	-	-	-	78,000	-	-	-	-	-	-	-	-	-	-	-	-
Walworth County	128,400	151,300	-	-	-	-	-	-	-	-	-	-	-	-	-	-	-	-	-	-	-	-	-	-
Washington County	155,000	182,100	-	-	-	-	-	-	-	-	-	-	-	-	-	-	-	-	-	-	-	-	-	-
Waukesha County	170,400	209,800	-	289,900	-	-	190,500	-	213,500	-	-	-	-	-	155,700	-	-	-	-	-	-	-	-	-
Winnebago County	97,700	147,600	-	-	-	-	-	-	-	-	-	87,200	-	-	-	-	-	-	-	-	-	-	-	-
Wood County	81,400	71,700	-	-	-	-	-	-	-	-	-	61,600	-	-	-	-	-	-	-	-	-	-	-	-
WYOMING	96,600	115,200	-	129,700	-	-	88,300	-	120,200	-	-	-	-	77,000	172,500	-	-	-	-	-	-	-	-	-
Laramie County	106,400	147,200	-	-	-	-	-	-	-	-	-	-	-	-	-	-	-	-	-	-	-	-	-	-
Natrona County	84,600	73,100	-	-	-	-	-	-	-	-	-	-	-	-	-	-	-	-	-	-	-	-	-	-

Notes: Please refer to the User's Guide for an explanation of data; data is arranged alphabetically by state, then county, then city within each county; table includes counties with populations greater than 49,999 unless noted and cities with populations greater than 9,999 whose Asian and/or NHPI population rates are greater than the national average; (1) Native Hawaiian and other Pacific Islander; (2) excludes Taiwanese; (3) includes Chamorro; (4) county does not meet population threshold but is shown in order to allow inclusion of city

Population

Total Population

***All States, Top 75 Counties, and Top 75 Places Sorted by Number*[1]**

State	Number
United States	281,421,906
California	33,871,648
Texas	20,851,820
New York	18,976,457
Florida	15,982,378
Illinois	12,419,293
Pennsylvania	12,281,054
Ohio	11,353,140
Michigan	9,938,444
New Jersey	8,414,350
Georgia	8,186,453
North Carolina	8,049,313
Virginia	7,078,515
Massachusetts	6,349,097
Indiana	6,080,485
Washington	5,894,121
Tennessee	5,689,283
Missouri	5,595,211
Wisconsin	5,363,675
Maryland	5,296,486
Arizona	5,130,632
Minnesota	4,919,479
Louisiana	4,468,976
Alabama	4,447,100
Colorado	4,301,261
Kentucky	4,041,769
South Carolina	4,012,012
Oklahoma	3,450,654
Oregon	3,421,399
Connecticut	3,405,565
Iowa	2,926,324
Mississippi	2,844,658
Kansas	2,688,418
Arkansas	2,673,400
Utah	2,233,169
Nevada	1,998,257
New Mexico	1,819,046
West Virginia	1,808,344
Nebraska	1,711,263
Idaho	1,293,953
Maine	1,274,923
New Hampshire	1,235,786
Hawaii	1,211,537
Rhode Island	1,048,319
Montana	902,195
Delaware	783,600
South Dakota	754,844
North Dakota	642,200
Alaska	626,932
Vermont	608,827
District of Columbia	572,059
Wyoming	493,782

County	Number
Los Angeles County, CA	9,519,338
Cook County, IL	5,376,741
Harris County, TX	3,400,578
Maricopa County, AZ	3,072,149
Orange County, CA	2,846,289
San Diego County, CA	2,813,833
Kings County, NY	2,465,326
Miami-Dade County, FL	2,253,362
Queens County, NY	2,229,379
Dallas County, TX	2,218,899
Wayne County, MI	2,061,162
King County, WA	1,737,034
San Bernardino County, CA	1,709,434
Santa Clara County, CA	1,682,585
Broward County, FL	1,623,018
Riverside County, CA	1,545,387
New York County, NY	1,537,195
Philadelphia County, PA	1,517,550
Middlesex County, MA	1,465,396
Tarrant County, TX	1,446,219
Alameda County, CA	1,443,741
Suffolk County, NY	1,419,369
Cuyahoga County, OH	1,393,978
Bexar County, TX	1,392,931
Clark County, NV	1,375,765
Nassau County, NY	1,334,544
Bronx County, NY	1,332,650
Allegheny County, PA	1,281,666
Sacramento County, CA	1,223,499
Oakland County, MI	1,194,156
Palm Beach County, FL	1,131,184
Hennepin County, MN	1,116,200
Franklin County, OH	1,068,978
St. Louis County, MO	1,016,315
Hillsborough County, FL	998,948
Fairfax County, VA	969,749
Erie County, NY	950,265
Contra Costa County, CA	948,816
Milwaukee County, WI	940,164
Westchester County, NY	923,459
Pinellas County, FL	921,482
DuPage County, IL	904,161
Salt Lake County, UT	898,387
Shelby County, TN	897,472
Orange County, FL	896,344
Bergen County, NJ	884,118
Fairfield County, CT	882,567
Honolulu County, HI	876,156
Montgomery County, MD	873,341
Marion County, IN	860,454
Hartford County, CT	857,183
Hamilton County, OH	845,303
Pima County, AZ	843,746
New Haven County, CT	824,008
Fulton County, GA	816,006
Travis County, TX	812,280
Prince George's County, MD	801,515
Fresno County, CA	799,407
Essex County, NJ	793,633
Macomb County, MI	788,149
Duval County, FL	778,879
San Francisco County, CA	776,733
Baltimore County, MD	754,292
Ventura County, CA	753,197
Worcester County, MA	750,963
Middlesex County, NJ	750,162
Montgomery County, PA	750,097
Monroe County, NY	735,343
Essex County, MA	723,419
San Mateo County, CA	707,161
Pierce County, WA	700,820
Mecklenburg County, NC	695,454
Jefferson County, KY	693,604
Suffolk County, MA	689,807
El Paso County, TX	679,622

Place	Number
New York, NY (city)	8,008,278
Los Angeles, CA (city) Los Angeles County	3,694,834
Chicago, IL (city) Cook County	2,895,964
Houston, TX (city) Harris County	1,954,848
Philadelphia, PA (city) Philadelphia County	1,517,550
Phoenix, AZ (city) Maricopa County	1,320,994
San Diego, CA (city) San Diego County	1,223,341
Dallas, TX (city) Dallas County	1,188,204
San Antonio, TX (city) Bexar County	1,144,554
Detroit, MI (city) Wayne County	951,270
San Jose, CA (city) Santa Clara County	893,889
Indianapolis, IN (sp. city) Marion County	782,414
San Francisco, CA (city) San Francisco County	776,733
Hempstead, NY (town) Nassau County	755,924
Jacksonville, FL (city) Duval County	735,503
Columbus, OH (city) Franklin County	711,644
Austin, TX (city) Travis County	656,302
Memphis, TN (city) Shelby County	649,845
Milwaukee, WI (city) Milwaukee County	596,956
Boston, MA (city) Suffolk County	589,141
El Paso, TX (city) El Paso County	564,280
Seattle, WA (city) King County	563,375
Denver, CO (city) Denver County	554,636
Nashville-Davidson, TN (sp. city) Davidson County	545,549
Charlotte, NC (city) Mecklenburg County	542,131
Fort Worth, TX (city) Tarrant County	535,420
Portland, OR (city) Multnomah County	529,025
Oklahoma City, OK (city) Oklahoma County	505,963
Tucson, AZ (city) Pima County	486,591
New Orleans, LA (city) Orleans Parish	484,674
Las Vegas, NV (city) Clark County	478,868
Cleveland, OH (city) Cuyahoga County	478,393
Long Beach, CA (city) Los Angeles County	461,381
Albuquerque, NM (city) Bernalillo County	448,627
Brookhaven, NY (town) Suffolk County	448,265
Kansas City, MO (city) Jackson County	441,269
Fresno, CA (city) Fresno County	427,224
Atlanta, GA (city) Fulton County	416,629
Sacramento, CA (city) Sacramento County	407,075
Oakland, CA (city) Alameda County	399,477
Mesa, AZ (city) Maricopa County	397,215
Tulsa, OK (city) Tulsa County	393,051
Omaha, NE (city) Douglas County	390,112
Minneapolis, MN (city) Hennepin County	382,452
Honolulu, HI (cdp) Honolulu County	371,619
Miami, FL (city) Miami-Dade County	362,563
Colorado Springs, CO (city) El Paso County	360,798
St. Louis, MO (city) Saint Louis Independent City	348,189
Wichita, KS (city) Sedgwick County	343,997
Santa Ana, CA (city) Orange County	337,512
Pittsburgh, PA (city) Allegheny County	334,563
Arlington, TX (city) Tarrant County	332,695
Cincinnati, OH (city) Hamilton County	330,662
Anaheim, CA (city) Orange County	327,357
Islip, NY (town) Suffolk County	322,625
Toledo, OH (city) Lucas County	313,587
Tampa, FL (city) Hillsborough County	303,512
Oyster Bay, NY (town) Nassau County	293,925
Buffalo, NY (city) Erie County	292,648
St. Paul, MN (city) Ramsey County	287,151
Corpus Christi, TX (city) Nueces County	277,569
Raleigh, NC (city) Wake County	276,579
Aurora, CO (city) Arapahoe County	275,936
Newark, NJ (city) Essex County	273,546
Lexington-Fayette, KY (sp. city) Fayette County	260,512
Louisville, KY (city) Jefferson County	256,420
Riverside, CA (city) Riverside County	255,093
St. Petersburg, FL (city) Pinellas County	247,793
Bakersfield, CA (city) Kern County	247,385
Birmingham, AL (city) Jefferson County	243,072
Stockton, CA (city) San Joaquin County	242,714
Jersey City, NJ (city) Hudson County	240,055
Baton Rouge, LA (city) East Baton Rouge Parish	227,920
Hialeah, FL (city) Miami-Dade County	226,411
Lincoln, NE (city) Lancaster County	225,442

Notes: Please refer to the User's Guide for an explanation of data; ranking tables include all places with Asian and/or NHPI populations above SF4 population thresholds; (1) tables reflect only those areas that meet SF4 population thresholds, therefore there may be less than 50 states, 75 counties or 75 places listed

Population

Asian

All States, Top 75 Counties, and Top 75 Places Sorted by Number[1]

State	Number
United States	10,171,820
California	3,682,975
New York	1,044,423
Texas	555,928
Hawaii	503,950
New Jersey	481,794
Illinois	423,440
Washington	320,979
Florida	264,377
Virginia	256,355
Massachusetts	238,246
Pennsylvania	216,631
Maryland	209,713
Michigan	174,824
Georgia	171,463
Minnesota	139,245
Ohio	132,131
North Carolina	111,292
Oregon	99,136
Colorado	93,306
Arizona	91,223
Nevada	89,121
Wisconsin	83,077
Connecticut	82,277
Missouri	60,429
Indiana	57,193
Louisiana	55,492
Tennessee	54,132
Oklahoma	45,546
Kansas	44,772
Utah	36,878
South Carolina	36,505
Iowa	35,023
Alabama	29,908
Kentucky	28,994
Alaska	25,496
Rhode Island	23,825
Nebraska	21,126
Arkansas	19,081
New Mexico	18,286
Mississippi	17,709
Delaware	16,053
New Hampshire	15,422
District of Columbia	14,762
Idaho	11,321
West Virginia	9,445
Maine	8,259
Vermont	4,851
South Dakota	4,729
Montana	4,363
North Dakota	3,342
Wyoming	2,972

County	Number
Los Angeles County, CA	1,134,263
Santa Clara County, CA	430,201
Honolulu County, HI	404,493
Queens County, NY	394,314
Orange County, CA	386,344
Alameda County, CA	293,807
Cook County, IL	260,996
San Diego County, CA	248,653
San Francisco County, CA	239,938
King County, WA	187,788
Kings County, NY	185,814
Harris County, TX	171,977
New York County, NY	144,368
San Mateo County, CA	142,162
Sacramento County, CA	134,881
Fairfax County, VA	123,612
Middlesex County, NJ	104,114
Contra Costa County, CA	103,198
Montgomery County, MD	97,994
Bergen County, NJ	94,124
Middlesex County, MA	91,645
Dallas County, TX	87,446
San Bernardino County, CA	79,103
Clark County, NV	71,495
DuPage County, IL	71,389
Maricopa County, AZ	66,294
Philadelphia County, PA	65,171
San Joaquin County, CA	65,065
Fresno County, CA	63,895
Nassau County, NY	62,536
Hudson County, NJ	57,191
Riverside County, CA	54,648
Hennepin County, MN	53,136
Tarrant County, TX	51,202
Solano County, CA	49,899
Oakland County, MI	48,378
Suffolk County, MA	48,115
Ramsey County, MN	44,030
Westchester County, NY	41,751
Gwinnett County, GA	41,021
Hawaii County, HI	39,708
Ventura County, CA	39,182
Bronx County, NY	39,076
Maui County, HI	38,790
Fort Bend County, TX	38,774
Multnomah County, OR	37,280
Broward County, FL	36,505
Norfolk County, MA	36,121
Travis County, TX	36,119
Snohomish County, WA	35,534
Wayne County, MI	35,273
Pierce County, WA	34,671
Suffolk County, NY	34,143
Collin County, TX	33,606
Franklin County, OH	32,912
Miami-Dade County, FL	30,692
Prince George's County, MD	30,390
Morris County, NJ	30,070
Washington County, OR	29,946
Essex County, NJ	29,468
Montgomery County, PA	29,431
Orange County, FL	28,748
Fairfield County, CT	28,452
DeKalb County, GA	26,537
Cuyahoga County, OH	25,831
Lake County, IL	25,305
Somerset County, NJ	25,117
Richmond County, NY	24,538
Monterey County, CA	24,221
Monmouth County, NJ	24,047
Fulton County, GA	23,763
Baltimore County, MD	23,723
Salt Lake County, UT	23,211
Bexar County, TX	22,586
Milwaukee County, WI	22,356

Place	Number
New York, NY (city)	788,110
Los Angeles, CA (city) Los Angeles County	368,644
San Francisco, CA (city) San Francisco County	239,938
San Jose, CA (city) Santa Clara County	239,465
Honolulu, HI (cdp) Honolulu County	208,028
San Diego, CA (city) San Diego County	166,326
Chicago, IL (city) Cook County	127,052
Houston, TX (city) Harris County	102,484
Fremont, CA (city) Alameda County	74,753
Seattle, WA (city) King County	73,849
Sacramento, CA (city) Sacramento County	67,400
Philadelphia, PA (city) Philadelphia County	65,171
Oakland, CA (city) Alameda County	60,110
Long Beach, CA (city) Los Angeles County	55,040
Daly City, CA (city) San Mateo County	52,289
Garden Grove, CA (city) Orange County	51,029
Stockton, CA (city) San Joaquin County	48,681
Fresno, CA (city) Fresno County	48,485
Boston, MA (city) Suffolk County	44,345
Sunnyvale, CA (city) Santa Clara County	42,604
Irvine, CA (city) Orange County	42,386
Alhambra, CA (city) Los Angeles County	40,563
Anaheim, CA (city) Orange County	39,590
Torrance, CA (city) Los Angeles County	39,445
Jersey City, NJ (city) Hudson County	39,070
Monterey Park, CA (city) Los Angeles County	36,674
St. Paul, MN (city) Ramsey County	35,316
Portland, OR (city) Multnomah County	33,683
Westminster, CA (city) Orange County	33,351
Milpitas, CA (city) Santa Clara County	32,766
Dallas, TX (city) Dallas County	32,165
Glendale, CA (city) Los Angeles County	31,944
Austin, TX (city) Travis County	30,866
Cerritos, CA (city) Los Angeles County	30,185
Santa Ana, CA (city) Orange County	29,802
Union City, CA (city) Alameda County	29,442
Santa Clara, CA (city) Santa Clara County	29,195
Edison, NJ (township) Middlesex County	28,438
Vallejo, CA (city) Solano County	27,632
Hempstead, NY (town) Nassau County	26,248
Hayward, CA (city) Alameda County	26,106
Rosemead, CA (city) Los Angeles County	25,917
Phoenix, AZ (city) Maricopa County	25,613
Rowland Heights, CA (cdp) Los Angeles County	24,773
Columbus, OH (city) Franklin County	24,743
Arcadia, CA (city) Los Angeles County	23,996
Minneapolis, MN (city) Hennepin County	23,912
Diamond Bar, CA (city) Los Angeles County	23,831
West Covina, CA (city) Los Angeles County	23,749
Cupertino, CA (city) Santa Clara County	22,599
Plano, TX (city) Collin County	22,465
Waipahu, HI (cdp) Honolulu County	21,657
Las Vegas, NV (city) Clark County	21,634
El Monte, CA (city) Los Angeles County	21,529
North Hempstead, NY (town) Nassau County	20,579
Fullerton, CA (city) Orange County	20,248
Carson, CA (city) Los Angeles County	20,156
Jacksonville, FL (city) Duval County	19,838
Arlington, TX (city) Tarrant County	19,271
Hacienda Heights, CA (cdp) Los Angeles County	19,225
San Gabriel, CA (city) Los Angeles County	19,190
Chula Vista, CA (city) San Diego County	18,851
Bellevue, WA (city) King County	18,828
Alameda, CA (city) Alameda County	18,698
San Leandro, CA (city) Alameda County	18,317
San Antonio, TX (city) Bexar County	18,085
Huntington Beach, CA (city) Orange County	17,636
South San Francisco, CA (city) San Mateo County	17,618
Charlotte, NC (city) Mecklenburg County	17,544
Oklahoma City, OK (city) Oklahoma County	17,279
Lowell, MA (city) Middlesex County	17,161
Buena Park, CA (city) Orange County	16,914
Pearl City, HI (cdp) Honolulu County	16,882
Walnut, CA (city) Los Angeles County	16,880
Berkeley, CA (city) Alameda County	16,660

Notes: Please refer to the User's Guide for an explanation of data; ranking tables include all places with Asian and/or NHPI populations above SF4 population thresholds; (1) tables reflect only those areas that meet SF4 population thresholds, therefore there may be less than 50 states, 75 counties or 75 places listed

Population

Asian

All States, Top 75 Counties, and Top 75 Places Sorted by Percent of Total Population[1]

State	Percent
Hawaii	41.60
California	10.87
New Jersey	5.73
New York	5.50
Washington	5.45
Nevada	4.46
Alaska	4.07
Maryland	3.96
Massachusetts	3.75
Virginia	3.62
United States	3.61
Illinois	3.41
Oregon	2.90
Minnesota	2.83
Texas	2.67
District of Columbia	2.58
Connecticut	2.42
Rhode Island	2.27
Colorado	2.17
Georgia	2.09
Delaware	2.05
Arizona	1.78
Michigan	1.76
Pennsylvania	1.76
Kansas	1.67
Florida	1.65
Utah	1.65
Wisconsin	1.55
North Carolina	1.38
Oklahoma	1.32
New Hampshire	1.25
Louisiana	1.24
Nebraska	1.23
Iowa	1.20
Ohio	1.16
Missouri	1.08
New Mexico	1.01
Tennessee	0.95
Indiana	0.94
South Carolina	0.91
Idaho	0.87
Vermont	0.80
Kentucky	0.72
Arkansas	0.71
Alabama	0.67
Maine	0.65
South Dakota	0.63
Mississippi	0.62
Wyoming	0.60
North Dakota	0.52
West Virginia	0.52
Montana	0.48

County	Percent
Honolulu County, HI	46.17
Kauai County, HI	35.80
San Francisco County, CA	30.89
Maui County, HI	30.28
Hawaii County, HI	26.71
Aleutians East Borough, AK	26.36
Santa Clara County, CA	25.57
Aleutians West Census Area, AK	25.31
Alameda County, CA	20.35
San Mateo County, CA	20.10
Queens County, NY	17.69
Kodiak Island Borough, AK	17.04
Middlesex County, NJ	13.88
Orange County, CA	13.57
Fairfax County, VA	12.75
Solano County, CA	12.65
Los Angeles County, CA	11.92
Fairfax Independent City, VA	11.77
San Joaquin County, CA	11.54
Sutter County, CA	11.24
Montgomery County, MD	11.22
Sacramento County, CA	11.02
Fort Bend County, TX	10.94
Contra Costa County, CA	10.88
King County, WA	10.81
Bergen County, NJ	10.65
Hudson County, NJ	9.39
New York County, NY	9.39
Yolo County, CA	9.36
San Diego County, CA	8.84
Ramsey County, MN	8.62
Somerset County, NJ	8.44
Arlington County, VA	8.32
Fresno County, CA	7.99
DuPage County, IL	7.90
Yuba County, CA	7.56
Howard County, MD	7.55
Kings County, NY	7.54
Tompkins County, NY	7.41
Suffolk County, MA	6.98
Gwinnett County, GA	6.97
Merced County, CA	6.87
Collin County, TX	6.84
Washington County, OR	6.72
Falls Church Independent City, VA	6.50
Champaign County, IL	6.46
Morris County, NJ	6.39
Middlesex County, MA	6.25
Washtenaw County, MI	6.20
Monterey County, CA	6.03
North Slope Borough, AK	6.01
Snohomish County, WA	5.86
Multnomah County, OR	5.64
Rockland County, NY	5.63
Norfolk County, MA	5.55
Richmond County, NY	5.53
Anchorage Borough, AK	5.48
Whitman County, WA	5.47
Alexandria Independent City, VA	5.44
Ketchikan Gateway Borough, AK	5.43
Loudoun County, VA	5.26
Clark County, NV	5.20
Ventura County, CA	5.20
Atlantic County, NJ	5.13
Harris County, TX	5.06
Mercer County, NJ	4.97
Pierce County, WA	4.95
Cook County, IL	4.85
Charlottesville Independent City, VA	4.82
Hennepin County, MN	4.76
Virginia Beach Independent City, VA	4.75
Nassau County, NY	4.69
San Bernardino County, CA	4.63
Juneau Borough, AK	4.55
Thurston County, WA	4.54

Place	Percent
Kaumakani, HI (cdp) Kauai County	76.11
Ewa Villages, HI (cdp) Honolulu County	73.31
Waipahu, HI (cdp) Honolulu County	65.41
Whitmore Village, HI (cdp) Honolulu County	65.11
Hanamaulu, HI (cdp) Kauai County	63.33
Eleele, HI (cdp) Kauai County	61.72
Monterey Park, CA (city) Los Angeles County	61.19
Village Park, HI (cdp) Honolulu County	58.66
Cerritos, CA (city) Los Angeles County	58.60
Aiea, HI (cdp) Honolulu County	57.38
Puhi, HI (cdp) Kauai County	56.75
Walnut, CA (city) Los Angeles County	56.26
Waipio, HI (cdp) Honolulu County	56.22
Honolulu, HI (cdp) Honolulu County	55.98
Keaau, HI (cdp) Hawaii County	55.71
Pearl City, HI (cdp) Honolulu County	54.78
Kahului, HI (cdp) Maui County	53.93
Waimalu, HI (cdp) Honolulu County	53.72
Millbourne, PA (borough) Delaware County	52.92
Pahoa, HI (cdp) Hawaii County	52.83
Lanai City, HI (cdp) Maui County	52.58
Pepeekeo, HI (cdp) Hawaii County	52.49
Milpitas, CA (city) Santa Clara County	52.25
Halawa, HI (cdp) Honolulu County	51.82
Ewa Gentry, HI (cdp) Honolulu County	51.78
Rowland Heights, CA (cdp) Los Angeles County	51.26
Waialua, HI (cdp) Honolulu County	51.16
Wainaku, HI (cdp) Hawaii County	50.69
Daly City, CA (city) San Mateo County	50.50
Papaikou, HI (cdp) Hawaii County	50.31
Ewa Beach, HI (cdp) Honolulu County	49.17
Lihue, HI (cdp) Kauai County	49.01
San Gabriel, CA (city) Los Angeles County	48.82
Rosemead, CA (city) Los Angeles County	48.64
Pahala, HI (cdp) Hawaii County	48.20
Alhambra, CA (city) Los Angeles County	47.19
San Marino, CA (city) Los Angeles County	46.80
Koloa, HI (cdp) Kauai County	46.76
Mililani Town, HI (cdp) Honolulu County	46.19
Haliimaile, HI (cdp) Maui County	46.05
Arcadia, CA (city) Los Angeles County	45.32
Waihee-Waiehu, HI (cdp) Maui County	45.28
Naalehu, HI (cdp) Hawaii County	45.21
Waikapu, HI (cdp) Maui County	44.84
Hanapepe, HI (cdp) Kauai County	44.68
Cupertino, CA (city) Santa Clara County	44.61
Waimea, HI (cdp) Kauai County	44.59
Wahiawa, HI (cdp) Honolulu County	44.54
Lahaina, HI (cdp) Maui County	44.14
Union City, CA (city) Alameda County	44.03
Honokaa, HI (cdp) Hawaii County	43.93
Kurtistown, HI (cdp) Hawaii County	43.70
Kekaha, HI (cdp) Kauai County	43.52
La Palma, CA (city) Orange County	43.45
Hercules, CA (city) Contra Costa County	42.96
South San Gabriel, CA (cdp) Los Angeles County	42.82
Diamond Bar, CA (city) Los Angeles County	42.29
East San Gabriel, CA (cdp) Los Angeles County	41.84
Paukaa, HI (cdp) Hawaii County	41.11
Palisades Park, NJ (borough) Bergen County	41.01
Heeia, HI (cdp) Honolulu County	40.87
Wailuku, HI (cdp) Maui County	40.62
Broadmoor, CA (cdp) San Mateo County	39.88
Paauilo, HI (cdp) Hawaii County	39.76
Kaneohe, HI (cdp) Honolulu County	39.46
Temple City, CA (city) Los Angeles County	38.85
Westminster, CA (city) Orange County	37.95
Hilo, HI (cdp) Hawaii County	37.62
Kealakekua, HI (cdp) Hawaii County	37.55
Halaula, HI (cdp) Hawaii County	37.48
Fremont, CA (city) Alameda County	36.75
Wailua, HI (cdp) Kauai County	36.25
Hacienda Heights, CA (cdp) Los Angeles County	36.20
Honomu, HI (cdp) Hawaii County	36.00
Ahuimanu, HI (cdp) Honolulu County	35.81

Notes: Please refer to the User's Guide for an explanation of data; ranking tables include all places with Asian and/or NHPI populations above SF4 population thresholds; (1) tables reflect only those areas that meet SF4 population thresholds, therefore there may be less than 50 states, 75 counties or 75 places listed

Population

Native Hawaiian and Other Pacific Islander

All States, Top 75 Counties, and Top 75 Places Sorted by Number[1]

State	Number
United States	378,782
California	113,858
Hawaii	112,561
Washington	21,738
Utah	14,366
Texas	12,464
New York	7,903
Nevada	7,806
Oregon	7,583
Florida	6,812
Arizona	6,166
Colorado	4,298
Georgia	3,866
Illinois	3,811
Pennsylvania	3,721
North Carolina	3,699
Virginia	3,617
Alaska	3,122
Missouri	3,071
New Jersey	2,709
Michigan	2,669
Ohio	2,641
Tennessee	2,159
Maryland	2,030
Oklahoma	1,840
Massachusetts	1,835
Indiana	1,762
Minnesota	1,724
Wisconsin	1,577
Arkansas	1,534
South Carolina	1,384
Louisiana	1,379
Connecticut	1,357
New Mexico	1,248
Idaho	1,232
Kansas	1,208
Alabama	1,187
Kentucky	1,155
Iowa	955
Mississippi	677
Nebraska	673
Montana	447
Rhode Island	441
West Virginia	405
Delaware	335
Maine	301

County	Number
Honolulu County, HI	77,175
Los Angeles County, CA	27,221
Hawaii County, HI	16,227
Maui County, HI	13,757
San Diego County, CA	13,482
Salt Lake County, UT	10,334
Alameda County, CA	9,188
San Mateo County, CA	8,533
Orange County, CA	8,530
King County, WA	8,270
Sacramento County, CA	6,269
Clark County, NV	5,918
Santa Clara County, CA	5,793
Kauai County, HI	5,314
Pierce County, WA	5,075
San Bernardino County, CA	5,019
Maricopa County, AZ	3,811
Riverside County, CA	3,719
San Francisco County, CA	3,581
Contra Costa County, CA	3,391
Solano County, CA	3,189
Multnomah County, OR	2,511
Anchorage Borough, AK	2,027
Monterey County, CA	1,823
Utah County, UT	1,805
Stanislaus County, CA	1,804
San Joaquin County, CA	1,785
Kitsap County, WA	1,698
Ventura County, CA	1,669
Tarrant County, TX	1,646
Cook County, IL	1,596
Kings County, NY	1,549
Harris County, TX	1,514
Washoe County, NV	1,502
Washington County, OR	1,399
Queens County, NY	1,394
Clark County, WA	1,329
El Paso County, CO	1,291
Bell County, TX	1,264
Snohomish County, WA	1,250
Thurston County, WA	1,205
Bexar County, TX	1,130
Bronx County, NY	1,099
Pima County, AZ	1,084
Dallas County, TX	987
Davis County, UT	928
Jackson County, MO	926
Santa Barbara County, CA	905
Fairfax County, VA	884
Orange County, FL	853
Philadelphia County, PA	790
Kern County, CA	778
Marion County, OR	761
Washington County, AR	756
Sonoma County, CA	750
Yolo County, CA	715
Spokane County, WA	695
Travis County, TX	676
Fresno County, CA	652
Allegheny County, PA	650
Broward County, FL	645
Clackamas County, OR	616
New York County, NY	612
Miami-Dade County, FL	605
Lane County, OR	588
Hennepin County, MN	583
Arapahoe County, CO	554
El Paso County, TX	554
Hillsborough County, FL	540
Bernalillo County, NM	532
Milwaukee County, WI	520
Duval County, FL	507
Gwinnett County, GA	506
Cumberland County, NC	503
Wayne County, MI	495

Place	Number
Honolulu, HI (cdp) Honolulu County	25,856
Los Angeles, CA (city) Los Angeles County	6,445
San Diego, CA (city) San Diego County	6,216
Long Beach, CA (city) Los Angeles County	5,145
Hilo, HI (cdp) Hawaii County	4,969
New York, NY (city)	4,870
Nanakuli, HI (cdp) Honolulu County	4,104
Kaneohe, HI (cdp) Honolulu County	4,046
Waipahu, HI (cdp) Honolulu County	4,026
Sacramento, CA (city) Sacramento County	3,692
San Francisco, CA (city) San Francisco County	3,581
Salt Lake City, UT (city) Salt Lake County	3,315
San Jose, CA (city) Santa Clara County	3,234
West Valley City, UT (city) Salt Lake County	3,126
Waianae, HI (cdp) Honolulu County	2,793
Kailua, HI (cdp) Honolulu County	2,743
Oakland, CA (city) Alameda County	2,581
Seattle, WA (city) King County	2,514
Hayward, CA (city) Alameda County	2,357
Oceanside, CA (city) San Diego County	2,274
East Palo Alto, CA (city) San Mateo County	2,211
Waimanalo Beach, HI (cdp) Honolulu County	2,143
Portland, OR (city) Multnomah County	2,010
Carson, CA (city) Los Angeles County	1,929
Kahului, HI (cdp) Maui County	1,834
Pearl City, HI (cdp) Honolulu County	1,791
Phoenix, AZ (city) Maricopa County	1,745
Wahiawa, HI (cdp) Honolulu County	1,734
Maili, HI (cdp) Honolulu County	1,722
Las Vegas, NV (city) Clark County	1,673
Laie, HI (cdp) Honolulu County	1,609
Waimalu, HI (cdp) Honolulu County	1,564
Makaha, HI (cdp) Honolulu County	1,541
Halawa, HI (cdp) Honolulu County	1,512
Hauula, HI (cdp) Honolulu County	1,479
Ewa Beach, HI (cdp) Honolulu County	1,456
Vallejo, CA (city) Solano County	1,396
Wailuku, HI (cdp) Maui County	1,378
San Mateo, CA (city) San Mateo County	1,369
Makakilo City, HI (cdp) Honolulu County	1,355
Tacoma, WA (city) Pierce County	1,347
Santa Ana, CA (city) Orange County	1,276
Garden Grove, CA (city) Orange County	1,266
Kailua, HI (cdp) Hawaii County	1,231
Modesto, CA (city) Stanislaus County	1,217
Mililani Town, HI (cdp) Honolulu County	1,173
Kihei, HI (cdp) Maui County	1,137
Anaheim, CA (city) Orange County	1,094
Waihee-Waiehu, HI (cdp) Maui County	1,074
Chicago, IL (city) Cook County	1,065
Riverside, CA (city) Riverside County	1,061
Killeen, TX (city) Bell County	1,046
Fairfield, CA (city) Solano County	1,037
Stockton, CA (city) San Joaquin County	1,036
Compton, CA (city) Los Angeles County	1,028
San Bruno, CA (city) San Mateo County	1,017
Anahola, HI (cdp) Kauai County	1,010
Waimea, HI (cdp) Hawaii County	970
Lahaina, HI (cdp) Maui County	958
Reno, NV (city) Washoe County	952
Vancouver, WA (city) Clark County	943
Kapaa, HI (cdp) Kauai County	914
Kualapuu, HI (cdp) Maui County	898
Federal Way, WA (city) King County	895
Houston, TX (city) Harris County	876
Waimanalo, HI (cdp) Honolulu County	875
South San Francisco, CA (city) San Mateo County	874
Oxnard, CA (city) Ventura County	869
Daly City, CA (city) San Mateo County	866
Paradise, NV (cdp) Clark County	841
Ahuimanu, HI (cdp) Honolulu County	839
Colorado Springs, CO (city) El Paso County	798
Alameda, CA (city) Alameda County	796
Philadelphia, PA (city) Philadelphia County	790
Kaunakakai, HI (cdp) Maui County	787

Notes: Please refer to the User's Guide for an explanation of data; ranking tables include all places with Asian and/or NHPI populations above SF4 population thresholds; (1) tables reflect only those areas that meet SF4 population thresholds, therefore there may be less than 50 states, 75 counties or 75 places listed

Population

Native Hawaiian and Other Pacific Islander

All States, Top 75 Counties, and Top 75 Places Sorted by Percent of Total Population[1]

State	Percent
Hawaii	9.29
Utah	0.64
Alaska	0.50
Nevada	0.39
Washington	0.37
California	0.34
Oregon	0.22
United States	0.13
Arizona	0.12
Colorado	0.10
Idaho	0.10
New Mexico	0.07
Arkansas	0.06
Texas	0.06
Georgia	0.05
Missouri	0.05
Montana	0.05
North Carolina	0.05
Oklahoma	0.05
Virginia	0.05
Connecticut	0.04
Delaware	0.04
Florida	0.04
Kansas	0.04
Maryland	0.04
Minnesota	0.04
Nebraska	0.04
New York	0.04
Rhode Island	0.04
Tennessee	0.04
Alabama	0.03
Illinois	0.03
Indiana	0.03
Iowa	0.03
Kentucky	0.03
Louisiana	0.03
Massachusetts	0.03
Michigan	0.03
New Jersey	0.03
Pennsylvania	0.03
South Carolina	0.03
Wisconsin	0.03
Maine	0.02
Mississippi	0.02
Ohio	0.02
West Virginia	0.02

County	Percent
Hawaii County, HI	10.91
Maui County, HI	10.74
Kauai County, HI	9.09
Honolulu County, HI	8.81
San Mateo County, CA	1.21
Salt Lake County, UT	1.15
Solano County, CA	0.81
Anchorage Borough, AK	0.78
Kitsap County, WA	0.73
Pierce County, WA	0.72
Alameda County, CA	0.64
Coryell County, TX	0.58
Thurston County, WA	0.58
Bell County, TX	0.53
Sacramento County, CA	0.51
Washington County, UT	0.51
Utah County, UT	0.49
King County, WA	0.48
San Diego County, CA	0.48
Washington County, AR	0.48
San Francisco County, CA	0.46
Monterey County, CA	0.45
Washoe County, NV	0.44
Clark County, NV	0.43
Yolo County, CA	0.42
Stanislaus County, CA	0.40
Davis County, UT	0.39
Clark County, WA	0.38
Multnomah County, OR	0.38
Contra Costa County, CA	0.36
Santa Clara County, CA	0.34
San Joaquin County, CA	0.32
Washington County, OR	0.31
Orange County, CA	0.30
Los Angeles County, CA	0.29
San Bernardino County, CA	0.29
Marion County, OR	0.27
Onslow County, NC	0.27
El Paso County, CO	0.25
Riverside County, CA	0.24
Santa Barbara County, CA	0.23
Ventura County, CA	0.22
Muscogee County, GA	0.21
Snohomish County, WA	0.21
Clackamas County, OR	0.18
Lane County, OR	0.18
Cumberland County, NC	0.17
Spokane County, WA	0.17
Sonoma County, CA	0.16
Ada County, ID	0.14
Jackson County, MO	0.14
Pima County, AZ	0.13
Kern County, CA	0.12
Maricopa County, AZ	0.12
Arapahoe County, CO	0.11
Tarrant County, TX	0.11
Bernalillo County, NM	0.10
Orange County, FL	0.10
Sedgwick County, KS	0.10
Fairfax County, VA	0.09
Gwinnett County, GA	0.09
Bexar County, TX	0.08
Bronx County, NY	0.08
Denver County, CO	0.08
El Paso County, TX	0.08
Fresno County, CA	0.08
Jefferson County, CO	0.08
Travis County, TX	0.08
Davidson County, TN	0.07
Duval County, FL	0.07
Essex County, NJ	0.06
Kings County, NY	0.06
Milwaukee County, WI	0.06
Montgomery County, MD	0.06
Queens County, NY	0.06

Place	Percent
Anahola, HI (cdp) Kauai County	50.88
Waimanalo Beach, HI (cdp) Honolulu County	50.55
Kualapuu, HI (cdp) Maui County	46.15
Hana, HI (cdp) Maui County	41.08
Hauula, HI (cdp) Honolulu County	40.24
Nanakuli, HI (cdp) Honolulu County	38.36
Laie, HI (cdp) Honolulu County	35.00
Pakala Village, HI (cdp) Kauai County	33.13
Kahuku, HI (cdp) Honolulu County	30.09
Kaunakakai, HI (cdp) Maui County	28.67
Maili, HI (cdp) Honolulu County	28.40
Waianae, HI (cdp) Honolulu County	26.23
Punaluu, HI (cdp) Honolulu County	24.70
Waimanalo, HI (cdp) Honolulu County	23.73
Kaaawa, HI (cdp) Honolulu County	23.49
Makaha Valley, HI (cdp) Honolulu County	22.64
Waikane, HI (cdp) Honolulu County	22.53
Makaha, HI (cdp) Honolulu County	19.96
Kahaluu, HI (cdp) Honolulu County	19.88
Waihee-Waiehu, HI (cdp) Maui County	14.81
Honaunau-Napoopoo, HI (cdp) Hawaii County	14.78
Volcano, HI (cdp) Hawaii County	14.62
Waimea, HI (cdp) Hawaii County	13.83
Hawaiian Beaches, HI (cdp) Hawaii County	13.52
Kailua, HI (cdp) Hawaii County	12.54
Pahoa, HI (cdp) Hawaii County	12.26
Kekaha, HI (cdp) Kauai County	12.20
Hilo, HI (cdp) Hawaii County	12.18
Waipahu, HI (cdp) Honolulu County	12.16
Naalehu, HI (cdp) Hawaii County	12.11
Kaneohe, HI (cdp) Honolulu County	11.57
Wailuku, HI (cdp) Maui County	11.10
Kalaoa, HI (cdp) Hawaii County	10.88
Halawa, HI (cdp) Honolulu County	10.83
Wahiawa, HI (cdp) Honolulu County	10.74
Lahaina, HI (cdp) Maui County	10.59
Hawaiian Paradise Park, HI (cdp) Hawaii County	10.57
Kapaau, HI (cdp) Hawaii County	10.44
Hawaiian Ocean View, HI (cdp) Hawaii County	10.43
Haleiwa, HI (cdp) Honolulu County	10.42
Makakilo City, HI (cdp) Honolulu County	10.30
Waimea, HI (cdp) Kauai County	10.27
Honalo, HI (cdp) Hawaii County	10.18
Ahuimanu, HI (cdp) Honolulu County	10.06
Waikoloa Village, HI (cdp) Hawaii County	9.99
Ewa Beach, HI (cdp) Honolulu County	9.94
Waikapu, HI (cdp) Maui County	9.60
Papaikou, HI (cdp) Hawaii County	9.57
Kapaa, HI (cdp) Kauai County	9.44
Paia, HI (cdp) Maui County	9.36
Captain Cook, HI (cdp) Hawaii County	9.20
Kahului, HI (cdp) Maui County	9.16
Napili-Honokowai, HI (cdp) Maui County	8.67
Makawao, HI (cdp) Maui County	8.59
Hanapepe, HI (cdp) Kauai County	8.49
Maunawili, HI (cdp) Honolulu County	7.65
East Palo Alto, CA (city) San Mateo County	7.51
Kailua, HI (cdp) Honolulu County	7.50
Whitmore Village, HI (cdp) Honolulu County	7.44
Holualoa, HI (cdp) Hawaii County	7.27
Kilauea, HI (cdp) Kauai County	6.97
Honolulu, HI (cdp) Honolulu County	6.96
Kihei, HI (cdp) Maui County	6.75
Village Park, HI (cdp) Honolulu County	6.22
Pahala, HI (cdp) Hawaii County	6.06
Pearl City, HI (cdp) Honolulu County	5.81
Waipio, HI (cdp) Honolulu County	5.39
Waimalu, HI (cdp) Honolulu County	5.30
Waialua, HI (cdp) Honolulu County	4.81
Aiea, HI (cdp) Honolulu County	4.47
Mililani Town, HI (cdp) Honolulu County	4.11
West Valley City, UT (city) Salt Lake County	2.87
Spanaway, WA (cdp) Pierce County	2.70
San Bruno, CA (city) San Mateo County	2.53
SeaTac, WA (city) King County	2.41

Notes: Please refer to the User's Guide for an explanation of data; ranking tables include all places with Asian and/or NHPI populations above SF4 population thresholds; (1) tables reflect only those areas that meet SF4 population thresholds, therefore there may be less than 50 states, 75 counties or 75 places listed

Population

Asian Indian

All States, Top 75 Counties, and Top 75 Places Sorted by Number[1]

State	Number
United States	1,645,510
California	307,105
New York	250,027
New Jersey	169,209
Texas	127,256
Illinois	123,275
Florida	67,790
Pennsylvania	56,233
Michigan	54,464
Maryland	49,766
Virginia	47,578
Georgia	44,732
Massachusetts	41,935
Ohio	37,624
North Carolina	25,350
Connecticut	23,905
Washington	22,489
Minnesota	16,278
Arizona	14,510
Indiana	14,159
Tennessee	11,956
Missouri	11,845
Colorado	11,826
Wisconsin	11,280
Oregon	10,188
Louisiana	8,641
Oklahoma	8,302
South Carolina	8,215
Kansas	7,681
Kentucky	6,734
Alabama	6,686
Iowa	5,407
Delaware	5,231
Nevada	4,860
New Hampshire	3,579
Mississippi	3,325
Nebraska	3,199
Utah	3,157
Arkansas	2,694
Rhode Island	2,548
West Virginia	2,529
New Mexico	2,424
District of Columbia	2,415
Hawaii	1,244
Idaho	1,142
North Dakota	1,042
Maine	978
Vermont	697
South Dakota	581
Alaska	546
Montana	450
Wyoming	423

County	Number
Queens County, NY	109,933
Cook County, IL	69,489
Santa Clara County, CA	65,087
Los Angeles County, CA	58,987
Middlesex County, NJ	54,163
Alameda County, CA	41,824
Harris County, TX	35,997
DuPage County, IL	31,875
Orange County, CA	26,910
Fairfax County, VA	24,955
Kings County, NY	24,795
Montgomery County, MD	24,411
Dallas County, TX	23,736
Nassau County, NY	23,475
Middlesex County, MA	21,930
Hudson County, NJ	20,604
Oakland County, MI	19,155
Bergen County, NJ	17,398
Bronx County, NY	14,743
Wayne County, MI	14,502
Westchester County, NY	14,496
New York County, NY	14,273
King County, WA	14,033
Broward County, FL	13,009
Fort Bend County, TX	12,788
Sacramento County, CA	12,742
Philadelphia County, PA	12,541
Maricopa County, AZ	11,289
Contra Costa County, CA	11,198
San Mateo County, CA	11,093
Gwinnett County, GA	11,002
Morris County, NJ	10,579
Suffolk County, NY	10,260
Somerset County, NJ	10,208
San Diego County, CA	9,626
Tarrant County, TX	9,474
Cuyahoga County, OH	9,055
Passaic County, NJ	9,015
Miami-Dade County, FL	8,938
Collin County, TX	8,746
Essex County, NJ	8,695
Travis County, TX	8,431
Fairfield County, CT	8,345
Franklin County, OH	8,240
San Bernardino County, CA	7,965
Hennepin County, MN	7,805
Orange County, FL	7,651
Allegheny County, PA	7,534
Montgomery County, PA	7,433
DeKalb County, GA	7,341
Sutter County, CA	7,281
Fulton County, GA	7,223
Prince George's County, MD	7,129
Fresno County, CA	6,965
Wake County, NC	6,941
Mercer County, NJ	6,836
Monmouth County, NJ	6,832
Union County, NJ	6,826
Hartford County, CT	6,726
Richmond County, NY	6,438
Baltimore County, MD	6,188
Denton County, TX	6,031
New Haven County, CT	5,916
Hillsborough County, FL	5,901
Bucks County, PA	5,887
St. Louis County, MO	5,699
Lake County, IL	5,669
Riverside County, CA	5,630
Rockland County, NY	5,582
Washington County, OR	5,568
Macomb County, MI	5,545
Cobb County, GA	5,389
San Joaquin County, CA	5,205
Delaware County, PA	5,188
Mecklenburg County, NC	5,165

Place	Number
New York, NY (city)	170,182
San Jose, CA (city) Santa Clara County	25,079
Chicago, IL (city) Cook County	24,208
Los Angeles, CA (city) Los Angeles County	24,129
Fremont, CA (city) Alameda County	20,690
Houston, TX (city) Harris County	20,476
Edison, NJ (township) Middlesex County	16,349
Jersey City, NJ (city) Hudson County	13,384
Philadelphia, PA (city) Philadelphia County	12,541
Sunnyvale, CA (city) Santa Clara County	12,211
Hempstead, NY (town) Nassau County	10,199
Santa Clara, CA (city) Santa Clara County	8,870
Woodbridge, NJ (township) Middlesex County	8,806
North Hempstead, NY (town) Nassau County	7,642
Dallas, TX (city) Dallas County	7,358
Austin, TX (city) Travis County	7,336
San Diego, CA (city) San Diego County	6,519
Columbus, OH (city) Franklin County	6,413
Irving, TX (city) Dallas County	6,093
Piscataway, NJ (township) Middlesex County	5,941
Plano, TX (city) Collin County	5,680
Union City, CA (city) Alameda County	5,377
Oyster Bay, NY (town) Nassau County	5,141
San Francisco, CA (city) San Francisco County	4,834
Cupertino, CA (city) Santa Clara County	4,771
Milpitas, CA (city) Santa Clara County	4,727
Yonkers, NY (city) Westchester County	4,689
Naperville, IL (city) Du Page County	4,674
Troy, MI (city) Oakland County	4,656
Irvine, CA (city) Orange County	4,652
Schaumburg, IL (village) Cook County	4,529
Phoenix, AZ (city) Maricopa County	4,433
Carrollton, TX (city) Denton County	4,384
Sugar Land, TX (city) Fort Bend County	4,338
Charlotte, NC (city) Mecklenburg County	4,316
Anaheim, CA (city) Orange County	4,125
Parsippany-Troy Hills, NJ (township) Morris County	4,120
Sacramento, CA (city) Sacramento County	4,053
Boston, MA (city) Suffolk County	4,051
South Brunswick, NJ (township) Middlesex County	3,861
Skokie, IL (village) Cook County	3,845
Fresno, CA (city) Fresno County	3,719
Hayward, CA (city) Alameda County	3,566
Canton, MI (township) Wayne County	3,556
Arlington, VA (cdp) Arlington County	3,481
Brookhaven, NY (town) Suffolk County	3,477
Farmington Hills, MI (city) Oakland County	3,421
Cary, NC (town) Wake County	3,381
San Antonio, TX (city) Bexar County	3,329
Detroit, MI (city) Wayne County	3,311
Franklin, NJ (township) Somerset County	3,311
Plainsboro, NJ (township) Middlesex County	3,266
Ann Arbor, MI (city) Washtenaw County	3,245
Oklahoma City, OK (city) Oklahoma County	3,231
Mount Prospect, IL (village) Cook County	3,155
Bakersfield, CA (city) Kern County	3,149
Indianapolis, IN (sp. city) Marion County	3,120
Garland, TX (city) Dallas County	3,102
North Brunswick, NJ (township) Middlesex County	3,010
Arlington, TX (city) Tarrant County	3,007
Cerritos, CA (city) Los Angeles County	2,946
Clifton, NJ (city) Passaic County	2,925
Mountain View, CA (city) Santa Clara County	2,906
Stamford, CT (city) Fairfield County	2,871
Old Bridge, NJ (township) Middlesex County	2,827
Iselin, NJ (cdp) Middlesex County	2,817
Glendale Heights, IL (village) Du Page County	2,780
Cambridge, MA (city) Middlesex County	2,768
Hoffman Estates, IL (village) Cook County	2,740
Jacksonville, FL (city) Duval County	2,730
Seattle, WA (city) King County	2,730
South Yuba City, CA (cdp) Sutter County	2,672
East Brunswick, NJ (township) Middlesex County	2,619
Lowell, MA (city) Middlesex County	2,594
Greenburgh, NY (town) Westchester County	2,586

Notes: Please refer to the User's Guide for an explanation of data; ranking tables include all places with Asian and/or NHPI populations above SF4 population thresholds; (1) tables reflect only those areas that meet SF4 population thresholds, therefore there may be less than 50 states, 75 counties or 75 places listed

Population

Asian Indian

All States, Top 75 Counties, and Top 75 Places Sorted by Percent of Asian Population[1]

State	Percent
New Jersey	35.12
Delaware	32.59
North Dakota	31.18
Michigan	31.15
Illinois	29.11
Connecticut	29.05
Ohio	28.47
West Virginia	26.78
Georgia	26.09
Pennsylvania	25.96
Florida	25.64
Indiana	24.76
New York	23.94
Maryland	23.73
Kentucky	23.23
New Hampshire	23.21
Texas	22.89
North Carolina	22.78
South Carolina	22.50
Alabama	22.36
Tennessee	22.09
Missouri	19.60
Mississippi	18.78
Virginia	18.56
Oklahoma	18.23
Massachusetts	17.60
Kansas	17.16
District of Columbia	16.36
United States	16.18
Arizona	15.91
Louisiana	15.57
Iowa	15.44
Nebraska	15.14
Vermont	14.37
Wyoming	14.23
Arkansas	14.12
Wisconsin	13.58
New Mexico	13.26
Colorado	12.67
South Dakota	12.29
Maine	11.84
Minnesota	11.69
Rhode Island	10.69
Montana	10.31
Oregon	10.28
Idaho	10.09
Utah	8.56
California	8.34
Washington	7.01
Nevada	5.45
Alaska	2.14
Hawaii	0.25

County	Percent
Sutter County, CA	82.09
Canadian County, OK	55.46
Middlesex County, NJ	52.02
Passaic County, NJ	48.84
Butler County, PA	47.56
DuPage County, IL	44.65
Warren County, NJ	44.47
Hinds County, MS	44.11
Marion County, FL	42.73
Bucks County, PA	41.54
Wayne County, MI	41.11
Hunterdon County, NJ	40.85
Rock Island County, IL	40.64
Somerset County, NJ	40.64
Dutchess County, NY	40.36
Schenectady County, NY	40.25
McLean County, IL	39.88
Oakland County, MI	39.59
Pickens County, SC	39.36
Mercer County, NJ	39.22
Floyd County, GA	38.94
Phelps County, MO	38.88
Shelby County, AL	38.47
Henry County, GA	38.43
Durham County, NC	38.41
Medina County, OH	38.33
Bronx County, NY	37.73
Nassau County, NY	37.54
Niagara County, NY	37.54
Midland County, TX	37.37
Madera County, CA	37.31
Lackawanna County, PA	37.10
Genesee County, MI	36.95
Lake County, IN	36.45
Allegheny County, PA	36.13
Bartholomew County, IN	36.04
Hudson County, NJ	36.03
Broward County, FL	35.64
Clermont County, OH	35.44
Cumberland County, NJ	35.35
New Castle County, DE	35.26
Denton County, TX	35.25
Butler County, OH	35.24
Union County, NJ	35.20
Morris County, NJ	35.18
Cuyahoga County, OH	35.05
Westchester County, NY	34.72
Rockland County, NY	34.61
Sangamon County, IL	34.46
Putnam County, NY	34.21
Kanawha County, WV	34.19
Peoria County, IL	33.55
Wake County, NC	33.50
Burlington County, NJ	33.49
Northampton County, PA	33.04
Volusia County, FL	33.04
Waukesha County, WI	33.01
Fort Bend County, TX	32.98
Midland County, MI	32.62
Johnson County, KS	32.22
Seminole County, FL	32.03
Hartford County, CT	31.94
Macomb County, MI	31.91
Saratoga County, NY	31.85
Chester County, PA	31.81
Columbia County, GA	31.72
Lehigh County, PA	31.55
Madison County, AL	31.45
Linn County, IA	31.43
Orange County, NY	31.43
Hamilton County, OH	31.37
Atlantic County, NJ	31.14
Albany County, NY	31.09
Montgomery County, TX	31.09
Leon County, FL	31.04

Place	Percent
Live Oak, CA (city) Sutter County	93.14
South Yuba City, CA (cdp) Sutter County	91.44
Little Flock, AR (city) Benton County	89.76
Scott Township, PA (cdp) Allegheny County	83.20
Scott, PA (township) Allegheny County	83.20
Kerman, CA (city) Fresno County	80.85
Livingston, CA (city) Merced County	80.17
Farmington, MI (city) Oakland County	77.28
Yuba City, CA (city) Sutter County	71.98
Iselin, NJ (cdp) Middlesex County	70.74
Sharonville, OH (city) Hamilton County	70.68
Roselle Park, NJ (borough) Union County	70.64
Naugatuck, CT (town) New Haven County	69.69
North Bergen, NJ (township) Hudson County	67.24
Upper St. Clair, PA (township) Allegheny County	66.75
East Lake, FL (cdp) Pinellas County	66.57
Carteret, NJ (borough) Middlesex County	66.55
Avenel, NJ (cdp) Middlesex County	66.23
Passaic, NJ (city) Passaic County	65.85
Flint, MI (township) Genesee County	65.55
Mountain Park, GA (cdp) Gwinnett County	65.40
Burlington, MA (town) Middlesex County	65.34
Inkster, MI (city) Wayne County	65.09
Plainsboro Center, NJ (cdp) Middlesex County	64.68
Tierra Buena, CA (cdp) Sutter County	64.02
Millbourne, PA (borough) Delaware County	63.53
East Windsor, NJ (township) Mercer County	63.14
Woodbridge, NJ (township) Middlesex County	63.13
Elmwood Park, NJ (borough) Bergen County	62.03
Burr Ridge, IL (village) Du Page County	61.72
Dayton, NJ (cdp) Middlesex County	61.36
Bensenville, IL (village) Du Page County	60.79
Muttontown, NY (village) Nassau County	60.21
Maple Shade, NJ (township) Burlington County	60.11
Elmont, NY (cdp) Nassau County	60.10
Echelon, NJ (cdp) Camden County	60.06
Sayreville, NJ (borough) Middlesex County	59.80
Farmington Hills, MI (city) Oakland County	59.79
Searingtown, NY (cdp) Nassau County	59.69
Elmhurst, IL (city) Du Page County	58.92
Municip. of Monroeville, PA (borough) Allegheny County	58.63
North Brunswick, NJ (township) Middlesex County	58.47
Madison Park, NJ (cdp) Middlesex County	58.11
Edison, NJ (township) Middlesex County	57.49
Voorhees, NJ (township) Camden County	57.49
New Hyde Park, NY (village) Nassau County	56.81
Paterson, NJ (city) Passaic County	56.39
Society Hill, NJ (cdp) Middlesex County	56.30
Princeton Meadows, NJ (cdp) Middlesex County	56.23
Herricks, NY (cdp) Nassau County	56.13
South Brunswick, NJ (township) Middlesex County	56.05
Addison, IL (village) Du Page County	55.92
North Royalton, OH (city) Cuyahoga County	55.92
North New Hyde Park, NY (cdp) Nassau County	55.91
Oak Brook, IL (village) Du Page County	55.42
Branchburg, NJ (township) Somerset County	55.40
Auburn Hills, MI (city) Oakland County	55.00
Addison, TX (town) Dallas County	54.89
Woburn, MA (city) Middlesex County	54.84
Norwood, MA (town) Norfolk County	54.77
Reisterstown, MD (cdp) Baltimore County	54.76
Canton, MI (township) Wayne County	54.13
Clifton, NJ (city) Passaic County	53.92
Bristol, PA (township) Bucks County	53.75
Hatfield, PA (township) Montgomery County	53.49
Southfield, MI (city) Oakland County	53.21
Lodi, NJ (borough) Bergen County	53.05
Plainsboro, NJ (township) Middlesex County	52.99
Poughkeepsie, NY (town) Dutchess County	52.70
Burlington, NJ (township) Burlington County	52.56
Spring Valley, NY (village) Rockland County	52.33
Franklin, NJ (township) Somerset County	51.70
Darien, IL (city) Du Page County	51.36
Lawrence, NJ (township) Mercer County	51.03
Bartlett, IL (village) Du Page County	50.95

Notes: Please refer to the User's Guide for an explanation of data; ranking tables include all places with Asian and/or NHPI populations above SF4 population thresholds; (1) tables reflect only those areas that meet SF4 population thresholds, therefore there may be less than 50 states, 75 counties or 75 places listed

Population

Asian Indian

All States, Top 75 Counties, and Top 75 Places Sorted by Percent of Total Population[1]

State	Percent
New Jersey	2.01
New York	1.32
Illinois	0.99
Maryland	0.94
California	0.91
Connecticut	0.70
Delaware	0.67
Virginia	0.67
Massachusetts	0.66
Texas	0.61
United States	0.58
Georgia	0.55
Michigan	0.55
Pennsylvania	0.46
District of Columbia	0.42
Florida	0.42
Washington	0.38
Minnesota	0.33
Ohio	0.33
North Carolina	0.31
Oregon	0.30
Kansas	0.29
New Hampshire	0.29
Arizona	0.28
Colorado	0.27
Nevada	0.24
Oklahoma	0.24
Rhode Island	0.24
Indiana	0.23
Missouri	0.21
Tennessee	0.21
Wisconsin	0.21
South Carolina	0.20
Louisiana	0.19
Nebraska	0.19
Iowa	0.18
Kentucky	0.17
North Dakota	0.16
Alabama	0.15
Utah	0.14
West Virginia	0.14
New Mexico	0.13
Mississippi	0.12
Vermont	0.11
Arkansas	0.10
Hawaii	0.10
Alaska	0.09
Idaho	0.09
Wyoming	0.09
Maine	0.08
South Dakota	0.08
Montana	0.05

County	Percent
Sutter County, CA	9.22
Middlesex County, NJ	7.22
Queens County, NY	4.93
Santa Clara County, CA	3.87
Fort Bend County, TX	3.61
DuPage County, IL	3.53
Somerset County, NJ	3.43
Hudson County, NJ	3.38
Alameda County, CA	2.90
Montgomery County, MD	2.80
Fairfax County, VA	2.57
Fairfax Independent City, VA	2.35
Morris County, NJ	2.25
Bergen County, NJ	1.97
Mercer County, NJ	1.95
Rockland County, NY	1.95
Howard County, MD	1.92
Gwinnett County, GA	1.87
Arlington County, VA	1.84
Passaic County, NJ	1.84
Collin County, TX	1.78
Nassau County, NY	1.76
Atlantic County, NJ	1.60
Oakland County, MI	1.60
San Mateo County, CA	1.57
Westchester County, NY	1.57
Middlesex County, MA	1.50
Washtenaw County, MI	1.47
Richmond County, NY	1.45
Denton County, TX	1.39
Canadian County, OK	1.38
Champaign County, IL	1.34
Union County, NJ	1.31
Cook County, IL	1.29
Washington County, OR	1.25
Alexandria Independent City, VA	1.23
Durham County, NC	1.21
Contra Costa County, CA	1.18
Brazos County, TX	1.17
Loudoun County, VA	1.12
Bronx County, NY	1.11
Monmouth County, NJ	1.11
Tippecanoe County, IN	1.11
Wake County, NC	1.11
Charlottesville Independent City, VA	1.10
DeKalb County, GA	1.10
Essex County, NJ	1.10
Tompkins County, NY	1.09
Dallas County, TX	1.07
Harris County, TX	1.06
Yolo County, CA	1.06
Sacramento County, CA	1.04
Travis County, TX	1.04
Henrico County, VA	1.03
Columbia County, GA	1.02
Dutchess County, NY	1.02
Merced County, CA	1.02
Kings County, NY	1.01
Bucks County, PA	0.99
Camden County, NJ	0.99
Montgomery County, PA	0.99
Stanislaus County, CA	0.97
Fairfield County, CT	0.95
Orange County, CA	0.95
Delaware County, PA	0.94
Centre County, PA	0.93
New Castle County, DE	0.93
New York County, NY	0.93
San Joaquin County, CA	0.92
Albemarle County, VA	0.91
Johnson County, KS	0.90
Alachua County, FL	0.89
Cobb County, GA	0.89
Fulton County, GA	0.89
Prince George's County, MD	0.89

Place	Percent
Millbourne, PA (borough) Delaware County	33.62
Plainsboro Center, NJ (cdp) Middlesex County	22.86
South Yuba City, CA (cdp) Sutter County	20.74
Society Hill, NJ (cdp) Middlesex County	19.43
Iselin, NJ (cdp) Middlesex County	16.97
Edison, NJ (township) Middlesex County	16.74
Princeton Meadows, NJ (cdp) Middlesex County	16.45
Plainsboro, NJ (township) Middlesex County	16.16
Dayton, NJ (cdp) Middlesex County	15.26
Searingtown, NY (cdp) Nassau County	13.90
Herricks, NY (cdp) Nassau County	12.46
Avenel, NJ (cdp) Middlesex County	12.44
Oak Brook, IL (village) Du Page County	12.16
Livingston, CA (city) Merced County	12.03
Piscataway, NJ (township) Middlesex County	11.77
New Territory, TX (cdp) Fort Bend County	11.30
Manhasset Hills, NY (cdp) Nassau County	10.90
Garden City Park, NY (cdp) Nassau County	10.75
Live Oak, CA (city) Sutter County	10.74
Muttontown, NY (village) Nassau County	10.27
Madison Park, NJ (cdp) Middlesex County	10.26
South Brunswick, NJ (township) Middlesex County	10.23
Fremont, CA (city) Alameda County	10.17
Cupertino, CA (city) Santa Clara County	9.42
Sunnyvale, CA (city) Santa Clara County	9.26
Woodbridge, NJ (township) Middlesex County	9.06
Glendale Heights, IL (village) Du Page County	8.78
Santa Clara, CA (city) Santa Clara County	8.69
North Brunswick, NJ (township) Middlesex County	8.29
North New Hyde Park, NY (cdp) Nassau County	8.23
Stafford, TX (city) Fort Bend County	8.19
Parsippany-Troy Hills, NJ (township) Morris County	8.13
New Hyde Park, NY (village) Nassau County	8.06
Union City, CA (city) Alameda County	8.04
Travilah, MD (cdp) Montgomery County	7.91
Farmington, MI (city) Oakland County	7.90
Echelon, NJ (cdp) Camden County	7.79
Merrifield, VA (cdp) Fairfax County	7.67
Fords, NJ (cdp) Middlesex County	7.58
Milpitas, CA (city) Santa Clara County	7.54
West Windsor, NJ (township) Mercer County	7.36
Emeryville, CA (city) Alameda County	7.34
Kerman, CA (city) Fresno County	7.33
Sugar Land, TX (city) Fort Bend County	6.83
Morton Grove, IL (village) Cook County	6.82
Burtonsville, MD (cdp) Montgomery County	6.77
Burlington, MA (town) Middlesex County	6.61
Roselle Park, NJ (borough) Union County	6.61
Darien, IL (city) Du Page County	6.51
Franklin, NJ (township) Somerset County	6.50
Lincolnwood, IL (village) Cook County	6.41
Voorhees, NJ (township) Camden County	6.29
Los Altos Hills, CA (town) Santa Clara County	6.26
Idylwood, VA (cdp) Fairfax County	6.21
Sayreville, NJ (borough) Middlesex County	6.20
Greenville, NY (cdp) Westchester County	6.19
Burr Ridge, IL (village) Du Page County	6.17
Foster City, CA (city) San Mateo County	6.17
Kendall Park, NJ (cdp) Middlesex County	6.15
Schaumburg, IL (village) Cook County	6.08
Skokie, IL (village) Cook County	6.07
Yuba City, CA (city) Sutter County	6.07
Mountain Park, GA (cdp) Gwinnett County	6.01
East Windsor, NJ (township) Mercer County	5.99
South Barrington, IL (village) Cook County	5.95
Tierra Buena, CA (cdp) Sutter County	5.89
Elmont, NY (cdp) Nassau County	5.85
Hatfield, PA (township) Montgomery County	5.85
Bergenfield, NJ (borough) Bergen County	5.75
Troy, MI (city) Oakland County	5.75
Cerritos, CA (city) Los Angeles County	5.72
East Brunswick, NJ (township) Middlesex County	5.60
Jersey City, NJ (city) Hudson County	5.58
Calverton, MD (cdp) Montgomery County	5.57
Mount Prospect, IL (village) Cook County	5.56

Notes: Please refer to the User's Guide for an explanation of data; ranking tables include all places with Asian and/or NHPI populations above SF4 population thresholds; (1) tables reflect only those areas that meet SF4 population thresholds, therefore there may be less than 50 states, 75 counties or 75 places listed

Population

Bangladeshi

All States, Top 75 Counties, and Top 75 Places Sorted by Number[1]

State	Number
United States	41,428
New York	20,087
California	2,748
Texas	2,574
New Jersey	2,256
Virginia	1,808
Michigan	1,683
Florida	1,260
Georgia	1,257
Maryland	1,204
Illinois	805
Pennsylvania	706
Ohio	648
Massachusetts	561
Connecticut	348

County	Number
Queens County, NY	12,402
Kings County, NY	3,928
Bronx County, NY	1,992
Los Angeles County, CA	1,325
Wayne County, MI	1,163
Fairfax County, VA	902
Montgomery County, MD	826
New York County, NY	783
Harris County, TX	688
Dallas County, TX	673
DeKalb County, GA	550
Passaic County, NJ	545
Santa Clara County, CA	484
Atlantic County, NJ	407
Middlesex County, NJ	387

Place	Number
New York, NY (city)	19,149
Los Angeles, CA (city) Los Angeles County	831
Hamtramck, MI (city) Wayne County	740
Paterson, NJ (city) Passaic County	459

Notes: Please refer to the User's Guide for an explanation of data; ranking tables include all places with Asian and/or NHPI populations above SF4 population thresholds; (1) tables reflect only those areas that meet SF4 population thresholds, therefore there may be less than 50 states, 75 counties or 75 places listed

Population

Bangladeshi

***All States, Top 75 Counties, and Top 75 Places Sorted by Percent of Asian Population*[1]**

State	Percent
New York	1.92
Michigan	0.96
Georgia	0.73
Virginia	0.71
Maryland	0.57
Ohio	0.49
Florida	0.48
New Jersey	0.47
Texas	0.46
Connecticut	0.42
United States	0.41
Pennsylvania	0.33
Massachusetts	0.24
Illinois	0.19
California	0.07

County	Percent
Bronx County, NY	5.10
Wayne County, MI	3.30
Queens County, NY	3.15
Atlantic County, NJ	3.14
Passaic County, NJ	2.95
Kings County, NY	2.11
DeKalb County, GA	2.07
Montgomery County, MD	0.84
Dallas County, TX	0.77
Fairfax County, VA	0.73
New York County, NY	0.54
Harris County, TX	0.40
Middlesex County, NJ	0.37
Los Angeles County, CA	0.12
Santa Clara County, CA	0.11

Place	Percent
Hamtramck, MI (city) Wayne County	31.38
Paterson, NJ (city) Passaic County	16.52
New York, NY (city)	2.43
Los Angeles, CA (city) Los Angeles County	0.23

Notes: Please refer to the User's Guide for an explanation of data; ranking tables include all places with Asian and/or NHPI populations above SF4 population thresholds; (1) tables reflect only those areas that meet SF4 population thresholds, therefore there may be less than 50 states, 75 counties or 75 places listed

Population

Bangladeshi

All States, Top 75 Counties, and Top 75 Places Sorted by Percent of Total Population[1]

State	Percent
New York	0.11
New Jersey	0.03
Virginia	0.03
Georgia	0.02
Maryland	0.02
Michigan	0.02
California	0.01
Connecticut	0.01
Florida	0.01
Illinois	0.01
Massachusetts	0.01
Ohio	0.01
Pennsylvania	0.01
Texas	0.01
United States	0.01

County	Percent
Queens County, NY	0.56
Atlantic County, NJ	0.16
Kings County, NY	0.16
Bronx County, NY	0.15
Passaic County, NJ	0.11
Fairfax County, VA	0.09
Montgomery County, MD	0.09
DeKalb County, GA	0.08
Wayne County, MI	0.06
Middlesex County, NJ	0.05
New York County, NY	0.05
Dallas County, TX	0.03
Santa Clara County, CA	0.03
Harris County, TX	0.02
Los Angeles County, CA	0.01

Place	Percent
Hamtramck, MI (city) Wayne County	3.22
Paterson, NJ (city) Passaic County	0.31
New York, NY (city)	0.24
Los Angeles, CA (city) Los Angeles County	0.02

Notes: Please refer to the User's Guide for an explanation of data; ranking tables include all places with Asian and/or NHPI populations above SF4 population thresholds; (1) tables reflect only those areas that meet SF4 population thresholds, therefore there may be less than 50 states, 75 counties or 75 places listed

Population

Cambodian

***All States, Top 75 Counties, and Top 75 Places Sorted by Number*[1]**

State	Number
United States	178,043
California	71,266
Massachusetts	20,370
Washington	14,766
Pennsylvania	8,696
Texas	7,603
Minnesota	5,128
Rhode Island	5,105
Virginia	4,968
Illinois	3,503
Georgia	3,479
New York	2,910
Florida	2,762
Oregon	2,749
Ohio	2,615
North Carolina	2,370
Connecticut	2,161
Maryland	1,708
Michigan	1,594
Colorado	1,478
Utah	1,457
Arizona	1,240
Tennessee	1,190
Maine	1,010
Missouri	879
Iowa	824
Nevada	738
Kansas	707
New Jersey	658
Wisconsin	627
Indiana	583
Alabama	565
South Carolina	341
Oklahoma	329
Hawaii	211

County	Number
Los Angeles County, CA	30,052
Middlesex County, MA	10,974
San Joaquin County, CA	9,469
King County, WA	6,623
Philadelphia County, PA	6,407
Providence County, RI	4,825
Orange County, CA	4,468
Santa Clara County, CA	4,399
San Diego County, CA	4,369
Pierce County, WA	4,058
Fresno County, CA	3,933
Alameda County, CA	3,903
Essex County, MA	3,754
Stanislaus County, CA	3,230
Dallas County, TX	2,357
Cook County, IL	2,227
Bristol County, MA	2,173
Harris County, TX	2,012
Snohomish County, WA	1,998
Fairfax County, VA	1,845
Hennepin County, MN	1,788
San Bernardino County, CA	1,742
Suffolk County, MA	1,718
Fairfield County, CT	1,442
Franklin County, OH	1,309
Maricopa County, AZ	1,186
Montgomery County, MD	1,161
Sacramento County, CA	1,117
Ramsey County, MN	1,110
Salt Lake County, UT	1,109
Washington County, OR	1,104
Ottawa County, MI	1,083
Multnomah County, OR	1,067
Clayton County, GA	1,048
Duval County, FL	1,001
Gwinnett County, GA	902
Sonoma County, CA	850
Thurston County, WA	837
Henrico County, VA	814
Bronx County, NY	810
Tarrant County, TX	778
Mecklenburg County, NC	767
Denton County, TX	726
Olmsted County, MN	722
Clark County, NV	718
Pinellas County, FL	718
Chesterfield County, VA	666
Cumberland County, ME	661
San Francisco County, CA	646
DeKalb County, GA	610
Riverside County, CA	600
Davidson County, NC	517
Shelby County, TN	516
Kings County, NY	501
Cuyahoga County, OH	484
Sedgwick County, KS	461
Hampden County, MA	455
Dakota County, MN	451
Kern County, CA	431
Clark County, WA	427
Polk County, IA	419
Denver County, CO	398
Worcester County, MA	395
Mobile County, AL	389
Brazoria County, TX	383
Monroe County, NY	381
Scott County, MN	362
Cowlitz County, WA	354
Arlington County, VA	353
Hamilton County, OH	351
Camden County, NJ	313

Place	Number
Long Beach, CA (city) Los Angeles County	17,711
Lowell, MA (city) Middlesex County	9,521
Stockton, CA (city) San Joaquin County	9,101
Philadelphia, PA (city) Philadelphia County	6,407
Los Angeles, CA (city) Los Angeles County	4,208
San Jose, CA (city) Santa Clara County	3,989
San Diego, CA (city) San Diego County	3,916
Fresno, CA (city) Fresno County	3,611
Providence, RI (city) Providence County	3,582
Tacoma, WA (city) Pierce County	3,157
Lynn, MA (city) Essex County	2,999
Oakland, CA (city) Alameda County	2,935
Modesto, CA (city) Stanislaus County	2,538
Seattle, WA (city) King County	2,524
Chicago, IL (city) Cook County	1,911
Santa Ana, CA (city) Orange County	1,736
New York, NY (city)	1,619
Fall River, MA (city) Bristol County	1,253
Columbus, OH (city) Franklin County	1,192
White Center, WA (cdp) King County	1,186
Dallas, TX (city) Dallas County	1,059
Portland, OR (city) Multnomah County	1,039
Jacksonville, FL (city) Duval County	1,001
St. Paul, MN (city) Ramsey County	928
Carrollton, TX (city) Denton County	818
Cranston, RI (city) Providence County	818
Revere, MA (city) Suffolk County	810
Signal Hill, CA (city) Los Angeles County	781
Rosemead, CA (city) Los Angeles County	775
Pomona, CA (city) Los Angeles County	757
Lakewood, CA (city) Los Angeles County	732
Houston, TX (city) Harris County	723
Charlotte, NC (city) Mecklenburg County	701
Attleboro, MA (city) Bristol County	692
West Valley City, UT (city) Salt Lake County	660
San Francisco, CA (city) San Francisco County	646
Santa Rosa, CA (city) Sonoma County	646
Everett, WA (city) Snohomish County	638
Boston, MA (city) Suffolk County	626
Portland, ME (city) Cumberland County	593
Danbury, CT (city) Fairfield County	572
Rochester, MN (city) Olmsted County	559
Phoenix, AZ (city) Maricopa County	553
Bellflower, CA (city) Los Angeles County	534
Bridgeport, CT (city) Fairfield County	520
St. Petersburg, FL (city) Pinellas County	516
Norwalk, CA (city) Los Angeles County	503
Garden Grove, CA (city) Orange County	500
Minneapolis, MN (city) Hennepin County	498
Bloomington, MN (city) Hennepin County	489
Sacramento, CA (city) Sacramento County	483
Memphis, TN (city) Shelby County	454
Lawrence, MA (city) Essex County	449
San Bernardino, CA (city) San Bernardino County	446
Aurora, CO (city) Arapahoe County	441
Monterey Park, CA (city) Los Angeles County	413
Denver, CO (city) Denver County	398
Lexington, NC (city) Davidson County	393
Beaverton, OR (city) Washington County	357
Arlington, VA (cdp) Arlington County	353
Silver Spring, MD (cdp) Montgomery County	326
Longview, WA (city) Cowlitz County	247

Notes: Please refer to the User's Guide for an explanation of data; ranking tables include all places with Asian and/or NHPI populations above SF4 population thresholds; (1) tables reflect only those areas that meet SF4 population thresholds, therefore there may be less than 50 states, 75 counties or 75 places listed

Population

Cambodian

All States, Top 75 Counties, and Top 75 Places Sorted by Percent of Asian Population[1]

State	Percent
Rhode Island	21.43
Maine	12.23
Massachusetts	8.55
Washington	4.60
Pennsylvania	4.01
Utah	3.95
Minnesota	3.68
Oregon	2.77
Connecticut	2.63
Iowa	2.35
Tennessee	2.20
North Carolina	2.13
Georgia	2.03
Ohio	1.98
California	1.94
Virginia	1.94
Alabama	1.89
United States	1.75
Colorado	1.58
Kansas	1.58
Missouri	1.45
Texas	1.37
Arizona	1.36
Florida	1.04
Indiana	1.02
South Carolina	0.93
Michigan	0.91
Illinois	0.83
Nevada	0.83
Maryland	0.81
Wisconsin	0.75
Oklahoma	0.72
New York	0.28
New Jersey	0.14
Hawaii	0.04

County	Percent
Davidson County, NC	40.81
Bristol County, MA	29.80
Cowlitz County, WA	28.12
Providence County, RI	26.34
Essex County, MA	21.75
Ottawa County, MI	20.91
Cumberland County, ME	19.88
Scott County, MN	19.39
Stanislaus County, CA	17.56
San Joaquin County, CA	14.55
Olmsted County, MN	13.55
Middlesex County, MA	11.97
Pierce County, WA	11.70
Chesterfield County, VA	10.47
Clayton County, GA	10.13
Philadelphia County, PA	9.83
Thurston County, WA	8.88
Henrico County, VA	8.78
Brazoria County, TX	8.11
Hampden County, MA	7.52
Mobile County, AL	7.40
Fresno County, CA	6.16
Sonoma County, CA	6.04
Snohomish County, WA	5.62
Fairfield County, CT	5.07
Dakota County, MN	4.93
Duval County, FL	4.87
Salt Lake County, UT	4.78
Polk County, IA	4.57
Denton County, TX	4.24
Clark County, WA	4.02
Franklin County, OH	3.98
Pinellas County, FL	3.82
Washington County, OR	3.69
Mecklenburg County, NC	3.68
Suffolk County, MA	3.57
King County, WA	3.53
Shelby County, TN	3.46
Hennepin County, MN	3.36
Sedgwick County, KS	3.25
Multnomah County, OR	2.86
Hamilton County, OH	2.77
Dallas County, TX	2.70
Los Angeles County, CA	2.65
Denver County, CO	2.62
Ramsey County, MN	2.52
DeKalb County, GA	2.30
Arlington County, VA	2.24
Gwinnett County, GA	2.20
San Bernardino County, CA	2.20
Monroe County, NY	2.15
Worcester County, MA	2.08
Bronx County, NY	2.07
Kern County, CA	2.00
Cuyahoga County, OH	1.87
Maricopa County, AZ	1.79
San Diego County, CA	1.76
Camden County, NJ	1.58
Tarrant County, TX	1.52
Fairfax County, VA	1.49
Alameda County, CA	1.33
Montgomery County, MD	1.18
Harris County, TX	1.17
Orange County, CA	1.16
Riverside County, CA	1.10
Santa Clara County, CA	1.02
Clark County, NV	1.00
Cook County, IL	0.85
Sacramento County, CA	0.83
Kings County, NY	0.27
San Francisco County, CA	0.27

Place	Percent
Fall River, MA (city) Bristol County	64.49
Attleboro, MA (city) Bristol County	57.19
Lowell, MA (city) Middlesex County	55.48
Lexington, NC (city) Davidson County	54.97
Lynn, MA (city) Essex County	50.84
Signal Hill, CA (city) Los Angeles County	47.42
Revere, MA (city) Suffolk County	37.48
Providence, RI (city) Providence County	33.45
Cranston, RI (city) Providence County	32.63
Long Beach, CA (city) Los Angeles County	32.18
Portland, ME (city) Cumberland County	30.77
Longview, WA (city) Cowlitz County	28.75
White Center, WA (cdp) King County	26.49
Modesto, CA (city) Stanislaus County	22.62
Tacoma, WA (city) Pierce County	22.02
Lawrence, MA (city) Essex County	21.93
Stockton, CA (city) San Joaquin County	18.70
Danbury, CT (city) Fairfield County	15.58
West Valley City, UT (city) Salt Lake County	13.85
Rochester, MN (city) Olmsted County	11.63
Bridgeport, CT (city) Fairfield County	11.58
Santa Rosa, CA (city) Sonoma County	11.52
Bloomington, MN (city) Hennepin County	11.50
Everett, WA (city) Snohomish County	10.53
Philadelphia, PA (city) Philadelphia County	9.83
St. Petersburg, FL (city) Pinellas County	7.67
Fresno, CA (city) Fresno County	7.45
Bellflower, CA (city) Los Angeles County	7.44
Carrollton, TX (city) Denton County	7.17
Pomona, CA (city) Los Angeles County	7.05
Lakewood, CA (city) Los Angeles County	7.02
San Bernardino, CA (city) San Bernardino County	5.95
Santa Ana, CA (city) Orange County	5.83
Silver Spring, MD (cdp) Montgomery County	5.17
Jacksonville, FL (city) Duval County	5.05
Oakland, CA (city) Alameda County	4.88
Columbus, OH (city) Franklin County	4.82
Beaverton, OR (city) Washington County	4.79
Memphis, TN (city) Shelby County	4.62
Norwalk, CA (city) Los Angeles County	4.13
Charlotte, NC (city) Mecklenburg County	4.00
Aurora, CO (city) Arapahoe County	3.89
Seattle, WA (city) King County	3.42
Dallas, TX (city) Dallas County	3.29
Portland, OR (city) Multnomah County	3.08
Rosemead, CA (city) Los Angeles County	2.99
St. Paul, MN (city) Ramsey County	2.63
Denver, CO (city) Denver County	2.62
San Diego, CA (city) San Diego County	2.35
Arlington, VA (cdp) Arlington County	2.24
Phoenix, AZ (city) Maricopa County	2.16
Minneapolis, MN (city) Hennepin County	2.08
San Jose, CA (city) Santa Clara County	1.67
Chicago, IL (city) Cook County	1.50
Boston, MA (city) Suffolk County	1.41
Los Angeles, CA (city) Los Angeles County	1.14
Monterey Park, CA (city) Los Angeles County	1.13
Garden Grove, CA (city) Orange County	0.98
Sacramento, CA (city) Sacramento County	0.72
Houston, TX (city) Harris County	0.71
San Francisco, CA (city) San Francisco County	0.27
New York, NY (city)	0.21

Notes: Please refer to the User's Guide for an explanation of data; ranking tables include all places with Asian and/or NHPI populations above SF4 population thresholds; (1) tables reflect only those areas that meet SF4 population thresholds, therefore there may be less than 50 states, 75 counties or 75 places listed

Population

Cambodian

All States, Top 75 Counties, and Top 75 Places Sorted by Percent of Total Population[1]

State	Percent
Rhode Island	0.49
Massachusetts	0.32
Washington	0.25
California	0.21
Minnesota	0.10
Maine	0.08
Oregon	0.08
Pennsylvania	0.07
Utah	0.07
Virginia	0.07
Connecticut	0.06
United States	0.06
Georgia	0.04
Nevada	0.04
Texas	0.04
Colorado	0.03
Illinois	0.03
Iowa	0.03
Kansas	0.03
Maryland	0.03
North Carolina	0.03
Arizona	0.02
Florida	0.02
Hawaii	0.02
Michigan	0.02
Missouri	0.02
New York	0.02
Ohio	0.02
Tennessee	0.02
Alabama	0.01
Indiana	0.01
New Jersey	0.01
Oklahoma	0.01
South Carolina	0.01
Wisconsin	0.01

County	Percent
San Joaquin County, CA	1.68
Providence County, RI	0.78
Middlesex County, MA	0.75
Stanislaus County, CA	0.72
Olmsted County, MN	0.58
Pierce County, WA	0.58
Essex County, MA	0.52
Fresno County, CA	0.49
Ottawa County, MI	0.45
Clayton County, GA	0.44
Philadelphia County, PA	0.42
Bristol County, MA	0.41
Scott County, MN	0.40
Thurston County, WA	0.40
Cowlitz County, WA	0.38
King County, WA	0.38
Davidson County, NC	0.35
Snohomish County, WA	0.33
Los Angeles County, CA	0.32
Henrico County, VA	0.31
Alameda County, CA	0.27
Chesterfield County, VA	0.26
Santa Clara County, CA	0.26
Cumberland County, ME	0.25
Suffolk County, MA	0.25
Washington County, OR	0.25
Ramsey County, MN	0.22
Arlington County, VA	0.19
Fairfax County, VA	0.19
Sonoma County, CA	0.19
Denton County, TX	0.17
Brazoria County, TX	0.16
Fairfield County, CT	0.16
Hennepin County, MN	0.16
Multnomah County, OR	0.16
Orange County, CA	0.16
San Diego County, CA	0.16
Gwinnett County, GA	0.15
Dakota County, MN	0.13
Duval County, FL	0.13
Montgomery County, MD	0.13
Clark County, WA	0.12
Franklin County, OH	0.12
Salt Lake County, UT	0.12
Dallas County, TX	0.11
Mecklenburg County, NC	0.11
Polk County, IA	0.11
Hampden County, MA	0.10
Mobile County, AL	0.10
San Bernardino County, CA	0.10
Sedgwick County, KS	0.10
DeKalb County, GA	0.09
Sacramento County, CA	0.09
Pinellas County, FL	0.08
San Francisco County, CA	0.08
Denver County, CO	0.07
Kern County, CA	0.07
Bronx County, NY	0.06
Camden County, NJ	0.06
Harris County, TX	0.06
Shelby County, TN	0.06
Clark County, NV	0.05
Monroe County, NY	0.05
Tarrant County, TX	0.05
Worcester County, MA	0.05
Cook County, IL	0.04
Hamilton County, OH	0.04
Maricopa County, AZ	0.04
Riverside County, CA	0.04
Cuyahoga County, OH	0.03
Kings County, NY	0.02

Place	Percent
Lowell, MA (city) Middlesex County	9.05
Signal Hill, CA (city) Los Angeles County	8.42
White Center, WA (cdp) King County	5.69
Long Beach, CA (city) Los Angeles County	3.84
Stockton, CA (city) San Joaquin County	3.75
Lynn, MA (city) Essex County	3.37
Providence, RI (city) Providence County	2.06
Lexington, NC (city) Davidson County	1.94
Revere, MA (city) Suffolk County	1.71
Attleboro, MA (city) Bristol County	1.64
Tacoma, WA (city) Pierce County	1.63
Rosemead, CA (city) Los Angeles County	1.45
Fall River, MA (city) Bristol County	1.36
Modesto, CA (city) Stanislaus County	1.34
Cranston, RI (city) Providence County	1.03
Lakewood, CA (city) Los Angeles County	0.92
Portland, ME (city) Cumberland County	0.92
Fresno, CA (city) Fresno County	0.85
Danbury, CT (city) Fairfield County	0.76
Carrollton, TX (city) Denton County	0.75
Bellflower, CA (city) Los Angeles County	0.73
Oakland, CA (city) Alameda County	0.73
Longview, WA (city) Cowlitz County	0.71
Everett, WA (city) Snohomish County	0.70
Monterey Park, CA (city) Los Angeles County	0.69
Rochester, MN (city) Olmsted County	0.65
Lawrence, MA (city) Essex County	0.62
West Valley City, UT (city) Salt Lake County	0.61
Bloomington, MN (city) Hennepin County	0.57
Pomona, CA (city) Los Angeles County	0.51
Santa Ana, CA (city) Orange County	0.51
Norwalk, CA (city) Los Angeles County	0.49
Beaverton, OR (city) Washington County	0.47
San Jose, CA (city) Santa Clara County	0.45
Seattle, WA (city) King County	0.45
Santa Rosa, CA (city) Sonoma County	0.44
Philadelphia, PA (city) Philadelphia County	0.42
Silver Spring, MD (cdp) Montgomery County	0.42
Bridgeport, CT (city) Fairfield County	0.37
San Diego, CA (city) San Diego County	0.32
St. Paul, MN (city) Ramsey County	0.32
Garden Grove, CA (city) Orange County	0.30
San Bernardino, CA (city) San Bernardino County	0.24
St. Petersburg, FL (city) Pinellas County	0.21
Portland, OR (city) Multnomah County	0.20
Arlington, VA (cdp) Arlington County	0.19
Columbus, OH (city) Franklin County	0.17
Aurora, CO (city) Arapahoe County	0.16
Jacksonville, FL (city) Duval County	0.14
Charlotte, NC (city) Mecklenburg County	0.13
Minneapolis, MN (city) Hennepin County	0.13
Sacramento, CA (city) Sacramento County	0.12
Boston, MA (city) Suffolk County	0.11
Los Angeles, CA (city) Los Angeles County	0.11
Dallas, TX (city) Dallas County	0.09
San Francisco, CA (city) San Francisco County	0.08
Chicago, IL (city) Cook County	0.07
Denver, CO (city) Denver County	0.07
Memphis, TN (city) Shelby County	0.07
Houston, TX (city) Harris County	0.04
Phoenix, AZ (city) Maricopa County	0.04
New York, NY (city)	0.02

Notes: Please refer to the User's Guide for an explanation of data; ranking tables include all places with Asian and/or NHPI populations above SF4 population thresholds; (1) tables reflect only those areas that meet SF4 population thresholds, therefore there may be less than 50 states, 75 counties or 75 places listed

Population

Chinese (except Taiwanese)

All States, Top 75 Counties, and Top 75 Places Sorted by Number[1]

State	Number
United States	2,300,219
California	914,033
New York	416,955
Texas	98,330
New Jersey	94,444
Massachusetts	82,051
Illinois	73,587
Washington	57,273
Hawaii	55,726
Pennsylvania	48,041
Maryland	47,202
Florida	44,867
Virginia	34,252
Michigan	29,443
Ohio	27,676
Georgia	25,436
Arizona	21,069
Connecticut	18,776
Oregon	18,514
North Carolina	17,502
Minnesota	14,917
Colorado	14,825
Nevada	13,540
Missouri	12,766
Indiana	11,537
Wisconsin	9,610
Tennessee	8,303
Utah	7,245
Kansas	7,055
Louisiana	6,792
Oklahoma	6,642
South Carolina	6,262
Alabama	5,709
Iowa	5,604
Kentucky	5,234
Rhode Island	4,562
Delaware	4,102
New Mexico	3,992
New Hampshire	3,873
District of Columbia	3,843
Arkansas	2,956
Nebraska	2,847
Mississippi	2,666
Idaho	1,804
West Virginia	1,651
Maine	1,632
Alaska	1,564
Vermont	1,136
South Dakota	679
Montana	650
Wyoming	615
North Dakota	429

County	Number
Los Angeles County, CA	291,347
San Francisco County, CA	154,490
Queens County, NY	137,739
Kings County, NY	120,803
Santa Clara County, CA	112,600
Alameda County, CA	106,960
New York County, NY	85,330
Honolulu County, HI	52,871
Orange County, CA	49,820
San Mateo County, CA	47,417
Cook County, IL	47,189
King County, WA	43,786
Harris County, TX	31,418
Middlesex County, MA	29,963
San Diego County, CA	28,936
Sacramento County, CA	28,723
Contra Costa County, CA	27,686
Montgomery County, MD	27,384
Middlesex County, NJ	21,277
Suffolk County, MA	19,925
Norfolk County, MA	19,185
Philadelphia County, PA	17,807
Fairfax County, VA	16,185
Maricopa County, AZ	15,505
Nassau County, NY	14,934
Bergen County, NJ	13,057
Collin County, TX	12,526
Dallas County, TX	11,734
Clark County, NV	10,730
San Bernardino County, CA	10,667
DuPage County, IL	10,103
Fort Bend County, TX	9,849
Suffolk County, NY	9,744
Morris County, NJ	9,306
Monmouth County, NJ	9,293
Miami-Dade County, FL	8,889
Travis County, TX	8,798
Oakland County, MI	8,697
Broward County, FL	8,556
Somerset County, NJ	7,365
Richmond County, NY	7,322
Franklin County, OH	7,261
Westchester County, NY	7,087
Multnomah County, OR	7,014
Hudson County, NJ	6,734
Bronx County, NY	6,346
Essex County, NJ	6,118
Cuyahoga County, OH	6,073
Washtenaw County, MI	6,061
Hennepin County, MN	6,042
St. Louis County, MO	6,003
Riverside County, CA	5,993
Fairfield County, CT	5,800
San Joaquin County, CA	5,648
Yolo County, CA	5,630
Tarrant County, TX	5,550
Montgomery County, PA	5,497
Fulton County, GA	5,398
New Haven County, CT	5,361
Ventura County, CA	5,096
Gwinnett County, GA	5,075
Wayne County, MI	4,985
Allegheny County, PA	4,957
Wake County, NC	4,929
Prince George's County, MD	4,918
Washington County, OR	4,906
Lake County, IL	4,851
Fresno County, CA	4,846
Pima County, AZ	4,692
Mercer County, NJ	4,616
Salt Lake County, UT	4,543
Baltimore County, MD	4,515
Snohomish County, WA	4,427
Orange County, FL	3,992
Monroe County, NY	3,976

Place	Number
New York, NY (city)	357,540
San Francisco, CA (city) San Francisco County	154,490
Los Angeles, CA (city) Los Angeles County	60,066
San Jose, CA (city) Santa Clara County	50,905
Honolulu, HI (cdp) Honolulu County	38,918
Oakland, CA (city) Alameda County	31,523
Chicago, IL (city) Cook County	31,416
Alhambra, CA (city) Los Angeles County	26,345
Fremont, CA (city) Alameda County	26,292
Monterey Park, CA (city) Los Angeles County	22,725
San Diego, CA (city) San Diego County	21,962
Houston, TX (city) Harris County	21,856
Boston, MA (city) Suffolk County	19,420
Sacramento, CA (city) Sacramento County	18,984
Seattle, WA (city) King County	18,871
Philadelphia, PA (city) Philadelphia County	17,807
Rosemead, CA (city) Los Angeles County	14,970
Arcadia, CA (city) Los Angeles County	13,992
Daly City, CA (city) San Mateo County	13,756
Sunnyvale, CA (city) Santa Clara County	12,306
San Gabriel, CA (city) Los Angeles County	11,716
El Monte, CA (city) Los Angeles County	11,701
Irvine, CA (city) Orange County	11,425
Rowland Heights, CA (cdp) Los Angeles County	11,422
Cupertino, CA (city) Santa Clara County	10,519
Quincy, MA (city) Norfolk County	9,442
Plano, TX (city) Collin County	9,305
Hacienda Heights, CA (cdp) Los Angeles County	9,122
San Leandro, CA (city) Alameda County	8,221
Milpitas, CA (city) Santa Clara County	8,104
Austin, TX (city) Travis County	8,022
Temple City, CA (city) Los Angeles County	7,912
Diamond Bar, CA (city) Los Angeles County	7,669
Alameda, CA (city) Alameda County	7,434
Berkeley, CA (city) Alameda County	7,227
West Covina, CA (city) Los Angeles County	6,611
Portland, OR (city) Multnomah County	6,471
Walnut, CA (city) Los Angeles County	6,312
Dallas, TX (city) Dallas County	6,083
Union City, CA (city) Alameda County	5,959
Torrance, CA (city) Los Angeles County	5,904
Edison, NJ (township) Middlesex County	5,826
Bellevue, WA (city) King County	5,819
Cerritos, CA (city) Los Angeles County	5,791
North Hempstead, NY (town) Nassau County	5,598
Phoenix, AZ (city) Maricopa County	5,568
Mountain View, CA (city) Santa Clara County	5,488
Palo Alto, CA (city) Santa Clara County	5,457
Hempstead, NY (town) Nassau County	5,339
San Mateo, CA (city) San Mateo County	5,293
Sugar Land, TX (city) Fort Bend County	5,287
Columbus, OH (city) Franklin County	5,147
Saratoga, CA (city) Santa Clara County	4,991
Brookhaven, NY (town) Suffolk County	4,762
Santa Clara, CA (city) Santa Clara County	4,694
South San Francisco, CA (city) San Mateo County	4,621
Davis, CA (city) Yolo County	4,444
Cambridge, MA (city) Middlesex County	4,340
Stockton, CA (city) San Joaquin County	4,285
Foster City, CA (city) San Mateo County	4,231
Spring Valley, NV (cdp) Clark County	4,222
Ann Arbor, MI (city) Washtenaw County	4,207
Pasadena, CA (city) Los Angeles County	4,179
Malden, MA (city) Middlesex County	4,107
Naperville, IL (city) Du Page County	4,044
Newton, MA (city) Middlesex County	3,948
San Marino, CA (city) Los Angeles County	3,915
Anaheim, CA (city) Orange County	3,888
Millbrae, CA (city) San Mateo County	3,826
Fresno, CA (city) Fresno County	3,722
Hayward, CA (city) Alameda County	3,674
Oyster Bay, NY (town) Nassau County	3,674
Brookline, MA (town) Norfolk County	3,585
East San Gabriel, CA (cdp) Los Angeles County	3,504
Chino Hills, CA (city) San Bernardino County	3,487

Notes: Please refer to the User's Guide for an explanation of data; ranking tables include all places with Asian and/or NHPI populations above SF4 population thresholds; (1) tables reflect only those areas that meet SF4 population thresholds, therefore there may be less than 50 states, 75 counties or 75 places listed

Population

Chinese (except Taiwanese)

All States, Top 75 Counties, and Top 75 Places Sorted by Percent of Asian Population[1]

State	Percent
New York	39.92
Massachusetts	34.44
District of Columbia	26.03
Delaware	25.55
New Hampshire	25.11
California	24.82
Vermont	23.42
Arizona	23.10
Connecticut	22.82
United States	22.61
Maryland	22.51
Pennsylvania	22.18
New Mexico	21.83
Missouri	21.13
Ohio	20.95
Wyoming	20.69
Indiana	20.17
Maine	19.76
Utah	19.65
New Jersey	19.60
Rhode Island	19.15
Alabama	19.09
Oregon	18.68
Kentucky	18.05
Washington	17.84
Texas	17.69
West Virginia	17.48
Illinois	17.38
South Carolina	17.15
Florida	16.97
Michigan	16.84
Iowa	16.00
Idaho	15.93
Colorado	15.89
Kansas	15.76
North Carolina	15.73
Arkansas	15.49
Tennessee	15.34
Nevada	15.19
Mississippi	15.05
Montana	14.90
Georgia	14.83
Oklahoma	14.58
South Dakota	14.36
Nebraska	13.48
Virginia	13.36
North Dakota	12.84
Louisiana	12.24
Wisconsin	11.57
Hawaii	11.06
Minnesota	10.71
Alaska	6.13

County	Percent
Kings County, NY	65.01
San Francisco County, CA	64.39
New York County, NY	59.11
Norfolk County, MA	53.11
Rensselaer County, NY	44.61
Tompkins County, NY	43.53
Suffolk County, MA	41.41
Monmouth County, NJ	38.65
Collin County, TX	37.27
Albemarle County, VA	36.57
Alameda County, CA	36.40
Orange County, NC	36.20
Yolo County, CA	35.65
Payne County, OK	34.99
Putnam County, NY	34.95
Queens County, NY	34.93
Tolland County, CT	34.36
Lee County, AL	34.30
Johnson County, IA	33.84
Riley County, KS	33.84
Grafton County, NH	33.73
Midland County, MI	33.39
San Mateo County, CA	33.35
Hampshire County, MA	33.24
Cache County, UT	32.89
Middlesex County, MA	32.69
Jefferson County, AL	32.66
Centre County, PA	32.52
New London County, CT	32.33
Charlottesville Independent City, VA	32.27
Story County, IA	32.24
Monongalia County, WV	32.15
Tippecanoe County, IN	31.89
Delaware County, OH	31.57
Barnstable County, MA	31.49
Boone County, MO	31.10
Morris County, NJ	30.95
Utah County, UT	30.87
Whitman County, WA	30.72
Washtenaw County, MI	30.27
Washington County, AR	30.11
Washington County, RI	29.94
Douglas County, CO	29.86
Fayette County, KY	29.86
Richmond County, NY	29.84
Ulster County, NY	29.64
Schenectady County, NY	29.54
Penobscot County, ME	29.46
Clarke County, GA	29.45
Somerset County, NJ	29.32
Broome County, NY	29.26
Dutchess County, NY	29.11
Lexington County, SC	29.10
Pickens County, SC	29.10
Marin County, CA	29.02
Douglas County, KS	29.00
Miami-Dade County, FL	28.96
Dona Ana County, NM	28.64
Rockingham County, NH	28.55
Suffolk County, NY	28.54
Forsyth County, NC	28.48
New Castle County, DE	28.46
Peoria County, IL	28.40
Benton County, OR	28.31
Champaign County, IL	28.25
Montgomery County, MD	27.94
Montgomery County, VA	27.94
St. Louis County, MO	27.88
Pima County, AZ	27.75
New Haven County, CT	27.33
Philadelphia County, PA	27.32
Hunterdon County, NJ	27.24
Alachua County, FL	27.17
Boulder County, CO	27.12
Contra Costa County, CA	26.83

Place	Percent
Piedmont, CA (city) Alameda County	75.35
Harrison, NJ (town) Hudson County	74.70
Hillsborough, CA (town) San Mateo County	73.83
Calexico, CA (city) Imperial County	70.51
Quincy, MA (city) Norfolk County	67.41
Alhambra, CA (city) Los Angeles County	64.95
Millbrae, CA (city) San Mateo County	64.87
San Marino, CA (city) Los Angeles County	64.49
San Francisco, CA (city) San Francisco County	64.39
Newton, MA (city) Middlesex County	62.44
Monterey Park, CA (city) Los Angeles County	61.96
Holmdel, NJ (township) Monmouth County	61.95
Temple City, CA (city) Los Angeles County	61.16
Morganville, NJ (cdp) Monmouth County	61.15
San Gabriel, CA (city) Los Angeles County	61.05
Falcon Heights, MN (city) Ramsey County	59.14
Orinda, CA (city) Contra Costa County	58.60
Saratoga, CA (city) Santa Clara County	58.50
Arcadia, CA (city) Los Angeles County	58.31
Rosemead, CA (city) Los Angeles County	57.76
Marlboro, NJ (township) Monmouth County	57.74
East San Gabriel, CA (cdp) Los Angeles County	57.40
Blackhawk-Camino Tass., CA (cdp) Contra Costa Co.	57.25
Needham, MA (town) Norfolk County	57.06
Moraga, CA (town) Contra Costa County	56.87
El Monte, CA (city) Los Angeles County	54.35
Kensington, CA (cdp) Contra Costa County	53.68
South Pasadena, CA (city) Los Angeles County	53.45
Palo Alto, CA (city) Santa Clara County	52.94
Westport, CT (town) Fairfield County	52.89
Stony Brook, NY (cdp) Suffolk County	52.49
North Potomac, MD (cdp) Montgomery County	52.47
Oakland, CA (city) Alameda County	52.44
Malden, MA (city) Middlesex County	52.13
Hazlet, NJ (township) Monmouth County	51.84
Highlands-Baywood Pk., CA (cdp) San Mateo County	51.77
Storrs, CT (cdp) Tolland County	51.22
Troy, NY (city) Rensselaer County	51.12
Mayflower Village, CA (cdp) Los Angeles County	51.03
South San Gabriel, CA (cdp) Los Angeles County	50.90
Wellesley, MA (town) Norfolk County	50.73
Natick, MA (town) Middlesex County	50.62
Los Altos Hills, CA (town) Santa Clara County	49.81
East Pasadena, CA (cdp) Los Angeles County	49.75
East Hanover, NJ (township) Morris County	49.48
Ithaca, NY (city) Tompkins County	49.37
Hudson, OH (city) Summit County	49.11
Burlingame, CA (city) San Mateo County	49.05
Lafayette, CA (city) Contra Costa County	49.04
Los Altos, CA (city) Santa Clara County	49.01
Bernards, NJ (township) Somerset County	48.75
Albany, CA (city) Alameda County	48.47
Randolph, MA (town) Norfolk County	48.41
Hacienda Heights, CA (cdp) Los Angeles County	47.45
Fishkill, NY (town) Dutchess County	47.35
Castro Valley, CA (cdp) Alameda County	47.16
Lower Macungie, PA (township) Lehigh County	46.80
Lower Providence, PA (township) Montgomery County	46.75
Montgomery, NJ (township) Somerset County	46.68
Cupertino, CA (city) Santa Clara County	46.55
Rowland Heights, CA (cdp) Los Angeles County	46.11
Brookline, MA (town) Norfolk County	46.04
Stanford, CA (cdp) Santa Clara County	45.92
Setauket-East Setauket, NY (cdp) Suffolk County	45.77
Hanover, NJ (township) Morris County	45.51
New York, NY (city)	45.37
Foster City, CA (city) San Mateo County	45.12
San Leandro, CA (city) Alameda County	44.88
Highland Park, NJ (borough) Middlesex County	44.76
Acton, MA (town) Middlesex County	44.73
Davis, CA (city) Yolo County	44.61
Newark, DE (city) New Castle County	44.38
Birmingham, AL (city) Jefferson County	44.13
Sammamish, WA (city) King County	43.91
Newcastle, WA (city) King County	43.87

Notes: Please refer to the User's Guide for an explanation of data; ranking tables include all places with Asian and/or NHPI populations above SF4 population thresholds; (1) tables reflect only those areas that meet SF4 population thresholds, therefore there may be less than 50 states, 75 counties or 75 places listed

Population

Chinese (except Taiwanese)

All States, Top 75 Counties, and Top 75 Places Sorted by Percent of Total Population[1]

State	Percent
Hawaii	4.60
California	2.70
New York	2.20
Massachusetts	1.29
New Jersey	1.12
Washington	0.97
Maryland	0.89
United States	0.82
Nevada	0.68
District of Columbia	0.67
Illinois	0.59
Connecticut	0.55
Oregon	0.54
Delaware	0.52
Virginia	0.48
Texas	0.47
Rhode Island	0.44
Arizona	0.41
Pennsylvania	0.39
Colorado	0.34
Utah	0.32
Georgia	0.31
New Hampshire	0.31
Michigan	0.30
Minnesota	0.30
Florida	0.28
Kansas	0.26
Alaska	0.25
Ohio	0.24
Missouri	0.23
New Mexico	0.22
North Carolina	0.22
Indiana	0.19
Iowa	0.19
Oklahoma	0.19
Vermont	0.19
Wisconsin	0.18
Nebraska	0.17
South Carolina	0.16
Louisiana	0.15
Tennessee	0.15
Idaho	0.14
Alabama	0.13
Kentucky	0.13
Maine	0.13
Wyoming	0.12
Arkansas	0.11
Mississippi	0.09
South Dakota	0.09
West Virginia	0.09
Montana	0.07
North Dakota	0.07

County	Percent
San Francisco County, CA	19.89
Alameda County, CA	7.41
San Mateo County, CA	6.71
Santa Clara County, CA	6.69
Queens County, NY	6.18
Honolulu County, HI	6.03
New York County, NY	5.55
Kings County, NY	4.90
Yolo County, CA	3.34
Tompkins County, NY	3.22
Montgomery County, MD	3.14
Los Angeles County, CA	3.06
Norfolk County, MA	2.95
Contra Costa County, CA	2.92
Suffolk County, MA	2.89
Middlesex County, NJ	2.84
Fort Bend County, TX	2.78
Collin County, TX	2.55
King County, WA	2.52
Somerset County, NJ	2.48
Fairfax Independent City, VA	2.39
Sacramento County, CA	2.35
Middlesex County, MA	2.04
Morris County, NJ	1.98
Washtenaw County, MI	1.88
Champaign County, IL	1.82
Orange County, CA	1.75
Whitman County, WA	1.68
Fairfax County, VA	1.67
Richmond County, NY	1.65
Charlottesville Independent City, VA	1.56
Monmouth County, NJ	1.51
Howard County, MD	1.49
Bergen County, NJ	1.48
Story County, IA	1.46
Tippecanoe County, IN	1.45
Orange County, NC	1.42
Johnson County, IA	1.34
Mercer County, NJ	1.32
Centre County, PA	1.29
Marin County, CA	1.29
Arlington County, VA	1.24
Benton County, OR	1.21
Philadelphia County, PA	1.17
Albemarle County, VA	1.13
DuPage County, IL	1.12
Nassau County, NY	1.12
Hudson County, NJ	1.11
Washington County, OR	1.10
Brazos County, TX	1.08
Travis County, TX	1.08
Riley County, KS	1.07
Multnomah County, OR	1.06
Hampshire County, MA	1.05
Montgomery County, VA	1.05
San Diego County, CA	1.03
San Joaquin County, CA	1.00
Alachua County, FL	0.98
Payne County, OK	0.98
Douglas County, KS	0.97
Clarke County, GA	0.94
Harris County, TX	0.92
Hawaii County, HI	0.90
Boone County, MO	0.89
Cook County, IL	0.88
Gwinnett County, GA	0.86
Boulder County, CO	0.85
Maui County, HI	0.85
Atlantic County, NJ	0.82
Solano County, CA	0.80
Santa Cruz County, CA	0.79
Tolland County, CT	0.79
Wake County, NC	0.79
Broome County, NY	0.78
Clark County, NV	0.78

Place	Percent
Monterey Park, CA (city) Los Angeles County	37.92
Alhambra, CA (city) Los Angeles County	30.65
San Marino, CA (city) Los Angeles County	30.18
San Gabriel, CA (city) Los Angeles County	29.81
Rosemead, CA (city) Los Angeles County	28.10
Arcadia, CA (city) Los Angeles County	26.42
East San Gabriel, CA (cdp) Los Angeles County	24.02
Temple City, CA (city) Los Angeles County	23.76
Rowland Heights, CA (cdp) Los Angeles County	23.63
South San Gabriel, CA (cdp) Los Angeles County	21.80
Walnut, CA (city) Los Angeles County	21.04
Cupertino, CA (city) Santa Clara County	20.77
San Francisco, CA (city) San Francisco County	19.89
Millbrae, CA (city) San Mateo County	18.46
Hillsborough, CA (town) San Mateo County	18.43
Hacienda Heights, CA (cdp) Los Angeles County	17.18
Saratoga, CA (city) Santa Clara County	16.72
Foster City, CA (city) San Mateo County	14.69
North Potomac, MD (cdp) Montgomery County	14.14
South Pasadena, CA (city) Los Angeles County	13.74
Diamond Bar, CA (city) Los Angeles County	13.61
Daly City, CA (city) San Mateo County	13.28
Fremont, CA (city) Alameda County	12.93
Milpitas, CA (city) Santa Clara County	12.92
Albany, CA (city) Alameda County	12.52
Piedmont, CA (city) Alameda County	12.42
Stanford, CA (cdp) Santa Clara County	11.94
Highlands-Baywood Pk., CA (cdp) San Mateo County	11.51
Los Altos Hills, CA (town) Santa Clara County	11.39
Cerritos, CA (city) Los Angeles County	11.24
Quincy, MA (city) Norfolk County	10.73
El Cerrito, CA (city) Contra Costa County	10.64
Honolulu, HI (cdp) Honolulu County	10.47
San Leandro, CA (city) Alameda County	10.37
Alameda, CA (city) Alameda County	10.29
Holmdel, NJ (township) Monmouth County	10.25
El Monte, CA (city) Los Angeles County	10.07
East Pasadena, CA (cdp) Los Angeles County	9.92
Blackhawk-Camino Tass., CA (cdp) Contra Costa Co.	9.66
Sunnyvale, CA (city) Santa Clara County	9.33
Palo Alto, CA (city) Santa Clara County	9.28
Falcon Heights, MN (city) Ramsey County	9.23
Harrison, NJ (town) Hudson County	9.11
Union City, CA (city) Alameda County	8.91
Emeryville, CA (city) Alameda County	8.56
Mayflower Village, CA (cdp) Los Angeles County	8.49
Sugar Land, TX (city) Fort Bend County	8.33
Hercules, CA (city) Contra Costa County	8.31
West Windsor, NJ (township) Mercer County	8.29
Plainsboro, NJ (township) Middlesex County	8.28
Newcastle, WA (city) King County	8.24
Irvine, CA (city) Orange County	7.99
Oakland, CA (city) Alameda County	7.89
Mountain View, CA (city) Santa Clara County	7.79
South San Francisco, CA (city) San Mateo County	7.61
Los Altos, CA (city) Santa Clara County	7.42
Moraga, CA (town) Contra Costa County	7.39
Davis, CA (city) Yolo County	7.36
Englewood Cliffs, NJ (borough) Bergen County	7.33
Malden, MA (city) Middlesex County	7.29
Marlboro, NJ (township) Monmouth County	7.22
Berkeley, CA (city) Alameda County	7.03
Ithaca, NY (city) Tompkins County	6.87
Laguna West-Lakeside, CA (cdp) Sacramento County	6.74
Belmont, CA (city) San Mateo County	6.73
Princeton Meadows, NJ (cdp) Middlesex County	6.72
Greentree, NJ (cdp) Camden County	6.71
East Brunswick, NJ (township) Middlesex County	6.63
La Habra Heights, CA (city) Los Angeles County	6.63
Burlingame, CA (city) San Mateo County	6.56
Ahuimanu, HI (cdp) Honolulu County	6.47
Rancho Palos Verdes, CA (city) Los Angeles County	6.40
West Covina, CA (city) Los Angeles County	6.30
Brookline, MA (town) Norfolk County	6.28
Highland Park, NJ (borough) Middlesex County	6.16

Notes: Please refer to the User's Guide for an explanation of data; ranking tables include all places with Asian and/or NHPI populations above SF4 population thresholds; (1) tables reflect only those areas that meet SF4 population thresholds, therefore there may be less than 50 states, 75 counties or 75 places listed

Population

Fijian

All States, Top 75 Counties, and Top 75 Places Sorted by Number[1]

State	Number
United States	10,265
California	8,410
Washington	709
Oregon	373

County	Number
Sacramento County, CA	1,751
Alameda County, CA	1,463
San Mateo County, CA	1,157
Stanislaus County, CA	698
King County, WA	543
Contra Costa County, CA	538
Yolo County, CA	526
Santa Clara County, CA	511
Los Angeles County, CA	493

Place	Number
Sacramento, CA (city) Sacramento County	1,240
Hayward, CA (city) Alameda County	843
Modesto, CA (city) Stanislaus County	494

Notes: Please refer to the User's Guide for an explanation of data; ranking tables include all places with Asian and/or NHPI populations above SF4 population thresholds; (1) tables reflect only those areas that meet SF4 population thresholds, therefore there may be less than 50 states, 75 counties or 75 places listed

Population

Fijian

All States, Top 75 Counties, and Top 75 Places Sorted by Percent of Native Hawaiian and Other Pacific Islander Population[1]

State	Percent
California	7.39
Oregon	4.92
Washington	3.26
United States	2.71

County	Percent
Yolo County, CA	73.57
Stanislaus County, CA	38.69
Sacramento County, CA	27.93
Alameda County, CA	15.92
Contra Costa County, CA	15.87
San Mateo County, CA	13.56
Santa Clara County, CA	8.82
King County, WA	6.57
Los Angeles County, CA	1.81

Place	Percent
Modesto, CA (city) Stanislaus County	40.59
Hayward, CA (city) Alameda County	35.77
Sacramento, CA (city) Sacramento County	33.59

Notes: Please refer to the User's Guide for an explanation of data; ranking tables include all places with Asian and/or NHPI populations above SF4 population thresholds; (1) tables reflect only those areas that meet SF4 population thresholds, therefore there may be less than 50 states, 75 counties or 75 places listed

Population

Fijian

***All States, Top 75 Counties, and Top 75 Places Sorted by Percent of Total Population*[1]**

State	Percent
California	0.02
Oregon	0.01
Washington	0.01
United States	<0.01

County	Percent
Yolo County, CA	0.31
San Mateo County, CA	0.16
Stanislaus County, CA	0.16
Sacramento County, CA	0.14
Alameda County, CA	0.10
Contra Costa County, CA	0.06
King County, WA	0.03
Santa Clara County, CA	0.03
Los Angeles County, CA	0.01

Place	Percent
Hayward, CA (city) Alameda County	0.60
Sacramento, CA (city) Sacramento County	0.30
Modesto, CA (city) Stanislaus County	0.26

Notes: Please refer to the User's Guide for an explanation of data; ranking tables include all places with Asian and/or NHPI populations above SF4 population thresholds; (1) tables reflect only those areas that meet SF4 population thresholds, therefore there may be less than 50 states, 75 counties or 75 places listed

Population

Filipino

All States, Top 75 Counties, and Top 75 Places Sorted by Number[1]

State	Number
United States	1,864,120
California	920,052
Hawaii	171,678
New Jersey	88,408
New York	86,722
Illinois	86,245
Washington	65,057
Texas	58,615
Florida	54,332
Virginia	48,016
Nevada	40,527
Maryland	26,672
Michigan	17,590
Arizona	16,205
Pennsylvania	14,713
Ohio	13,179
Alaska	12,488
Oregon	10,675
Georgia	10,436
North Carolina	10,194
Colorado	9,320
Massachusetts	9,287
Connecticut	7,511
Missouri	7,254
South Carolina	6,953
Indiana	6,892
Minnesota	5,900
Wisconsin	5,459
Tennessee	5,282
Louisiana	4,727
Oklahoma	4,184
Utah	3,705
Kansas	3,381
Kentucky	3,129
New Mexico	2,942
Mississippi	2,619
Alabama	2,441
Arkansas	2,303
Iowa	2,249
Rhode Island	2,126
District of Columbia	2,119
Nebraska	2,065
Delaware	1,825
West Virginia	1,658
Idaho	1,640
New Hampshire	1,272
Maine	1,170
Montana	785
South Dakota	704
North Dakota	577
Wyoming	523
Vermont	314

County	Number
Los Angeles County, CA	262,020
Honolulu County, HI	125,893
San Diego County, CA	120,655
Santa Clara County, CA	77,815
Alameda County, CA	69,680
San Mateo County, CA	60,114
Cook County, IL	54,595
Orange County, CA	48,920
San Francisco County, CA	40,072
Solano County, CA	35,862
Contra Costa County, CA	34,436
King County, WA	33,778
Queens County, NY	32,843
Clark County, NV	32,626
San Bernardino County, CA	25,621
Sacramento County, CA	24,045
Maui County, HI	21,552
San Joaquin County, CA	21,167
Hudson County, NJ	19,877
Riverside County, CA	19,627
Harris County, TX	15,774
Ventura County, CA	15,255
Bergen County, NJ	14,898
DuPage County, IL	14,111
Virginia Beach Independent City, VA	13,532
Hawaii County, HI	13,101
Fairfax County, VA	12,727
Middlesex County, NJ	12,499
Maricopa County, AZ	11,901
Monterey County, CA	11,517
Kauai County, HI	11,117
Kern County, CA	10,551
Duval County, FL	10,206
New York County, NY	8,831
Prince George's County, MD	8,239
Essex County, NJ	7,941
Snohomish County, WA	7,633
Nassau County, NY	7,168
Kings County, NY	7,149
Lake County, IL	6,988
Kitsap County, WA	6,972
Montgomery County, MD	6,898
Pierce County, WA	6,774
Washoe County, NV	6,422
Fresno County, CA	6,209
Dallas County, TX	5,994
Union County, NJ	5,731
Bexar County, TX	5,208
Richmond County, NY	5,189
Anchorage Borough, AK	5,036
Westchester County, NY	4,956
Bronx County, NY	4,934
Santa Barbara County, CA	4,880
Broward County, FL	4,870
Tulare County, CA	4,572
Orange County, FL	4,524
Miami-Dade County, FL	4,521
Rockland County, NY	4,505
Fort Bend County, TX	4,395
Wayne County, MI	4,298
Norfolk Independent City, VA	4,274
Suffolk County, NY	4,055
Oakland County, MI	4,002
Philadelphia County, PA	3,824
Camden County, NJ	3,783
Passaic County, NJ	3,480
Tarrant County, TX	3,480
Macomb County, MI	3,410
Monmouth County, NJ	3,340
Multnomah County, OR	3,324
Baltimore County, MD	3,270
Morris County, NJ	3,221
Hillsborough County, FL	3,203
Washington County, OR	3,130
Somerset County, NJ	3,079

Place	Number
Los Angeles, CA (city) Los Angeles County	102,003
San Diego, CA (city) San Diego County	73,785
New York, NY (city)	58,946
San Jose, CA (city) Santa Clara County	49,606
Honolulu, HI (cdp) Honolulu County	43,653
San Francisco, CA (city) San Francisco County	40,072
Daly City, CA (city) San Mateo County	32,923
Chicago, IL (city) Cook County	27,874
Vallejo, CA (city) Solano County	23,274
Long Beach, CA (city) Los Angeles County	17,962
Carson, CA (city) Los Angeles County	17,331
Waipahu, HI (cdp) Honolulu County	16,540
Jersey City, NJ (city) Hudson County	16,459
Seattle, WA (city) King County	16,226
Stockton, CA (city) San Joaquin County	15,033
Union City, CA (city) Alameda County	13,128
Chula Vista, CA (city) San Diego County	13,076
Hayward, CA (city) Alameda County	12,560
Glendale, CA (city) Los Angeles County	11,559
Fremont, CA (city) Alameda County	11,400
Las Vegas, NV (city) Clark County	10,791
South San Francisco, CA (city) San Mateo County	10,358
West Covina, CA (city) Los Angeles County	10,043
Jacksonville, FL (city) Duval County	9,783
National City, CA (city) San Diego County	9,061
Milpitas, CA (city) Santa Clara County	9,018
Oxnard, CA (city) Ventura County	9,005
Sacramento, CA (city) Sacramento County	8,185
Anaheim, CA (city) Orange County	7,741
Houston, TX (city) Harris County	7,686
Oakland, CA (city) Alameda County	6,677
Sunnyvale, CA (city) Santa Clara County	6,567
Kahului, HI (cdp) Maui County	6,417
San Leandro, CA (city) Alameda County	6,212
Fairfield, CA (city) Solano County	6,058
Alameda, CA (city) Alameda County	6,047
Salinas, CA (city) Monterey County	5,941
Santa Clara, CA (city) Santa Clara County	5,934
Cerritos, CA (city) Los Angeles County	5,725
Paradise, NV (cdp) Clark County	5,692
Delano, CA (city) Kern County	5,619
Ewa Beach, HI (cdp) Honolulu County	5,618
Chino Hills, CA (city) San Bernardino County	5,566
Oceanside, CA (city) San Diego County	5,255
Buena Park, CA (city) Orange County	5,092
Phoenix, AZ (city) Maricopa County	5,033
Hercules, CA (city) Contra Costa County	4,936
Sunrise Manor, NV (cdp) Clark County	4,830
Lakewood, CA (city) Los Angeles County	4,776
Pittsburg, CA (city) Contra Costa County	4,774
Norwalk, CA (city) Los Angeles County	4,478
Fresno, CA (city) Fresno County	4,424
Reno, NV (city) Washoe County	4,272
Pearl City, HI (cdp) Honolulu County	4,268
Concord, CA (city) Contra Costa County	4,140
Hempstead, NY (town) Nassau County	4,125
Baldwin Park, CA (city) Los Angeles County	4,067
Moreno Valley, CA (city) Riverside County	3,974
Spring Valley, NV (cdp) Clark County	3,910
Philadelphia, PA (city) Philadelphia County	3,824
San Antonio, TX (city) Bexar County	3,786
Village Park, HI (cdp) Honolulu County	3,704
Bellflower, CA (city) Los Angeles County	3,653
Torrance, CA (city) Los Angeles County	3,549
Antioch, CA (city) Contra Costa County	3,517
Newark, CA (city) Alameda County	3,475
Walnut, CA (city) Los Angeles County	3,452
Elk Grove, CA (cdp) Sacramento County	3,387
Waimalu, HI (cdp) Honolulu County	3,335
Irvine, CA (city) Orange County	3,332
Burbank, CA (city) Los Angeles County	3,301
Rowland Heights, CA (cdp) Los Angeles County	3,276
Pacifica, CA (city) San Mateo County	3,259
Bergenfield, NJ (borough) Bergen County	3,228
Riverside, CA (city) Riverside County	3,176

Notes: Please refer to the User's Guide for an explanation of data; ranking tables include all places with Asian and/or NHPI populations above SF4 population thresholds; (1) tables reflect only those areas that meet SF4 population thresholds, therefore there may be less than 50 states, 75 counties or 75 places listed

Population

Filipino

All States, Top 75 Counties, and Top 75 Places Sorted by Percent of Asian Population[1]

State	Percent
Alaska	48.98
Nevada	45.47
Hawaii	34.07
California	24.98
Florida	20.55
Illinois	20.37
Washington	20.27
South Carolina	19.05
Virginia	18.73
New Jersey	18.35
United States	18.33
Montana	17.99
Arizona	17.76
Wyoming	17.60
West Virginia	17.55
North Dakota	17.27
New Mexico	16.09
South Dakota	14.89
Mississippi	14.79
Idaho	14.49
District of Columbia	14.35
Maine	14.17
Maryland	12.72
Arkansas	12.07
Indiana	12.05
Missouri	12.00
Delaware	11.37
Kentucky	10.79
Oregon	10.77
Texas	10.54
Michigan	10.06
Utah	10.05
Colorado	9.99
Ohio	9.97
Nebraska	9.77
Tennessee	9.76
Oklahoma	9.19
North Carolina	9.16
Connecticut	9.13
Rhode Island	8.92
Louisiana	8.52
New York	8.30
New Hampshire	8.25
Alabama	8.16
Kansas	7.55
Pennsylvania	6.79
Wisconsin	6.57
Vermont	6.47
Iowa	6.42
Georgia	6.09
Minnesota	4.24
Massachusetts	3.90

County	Percent
Aleutians East Borough, AK	91.14
Kodiak Island Borough, AK	89.50
Ketchikan Gateway Borough, AK	84.82
Churchill County, NV	77.18
North Slope Borough, AK	76.35
Juneau Borough, AK	74.64
Solano County, CA	71.87
Aleutians West Census Area, AK	70.07
Valdez-Cordova Census Area, AK	68.65
Camden County, GA	67.18
Virginia Beach Independent City, VA	66.97
Kitsap County, WA	66.62
Island County, WA	66.53
Kings County, CA	65.26
Berkeley County, SC	61.75
Norfolk Independent City, VA	61.00
Clay County, FL	59.43
Portsmouth Independent City, VA	58.04
Maui County, HI	55.56
Kauai County, HI	53.12
Chesapeake Independent City, VA	52.35
San Benito County, CA	51.89
Dorchester County, SC	50.88
Napa County, CA	50.71
Kenai Peninsula Borough, AK	50.11
Duval County, FL	49.65
Kern County, CA	48.93
San Diego County, CA	48.52
Hidalgo County, TX	47.78
Monterey County, CA	47.55
Newport County, RI	46.95
Highlands County, FL	46.37
Nueces County, TX	46.02
Clark County, NV	45.63
Washoe County, NV	44.82
Onslow County, NC	44.58
El Dorado County, CA	44.48
Sandoval County, NM	44.39
Santa Rosa County, FL	43.97
Yakima County, WA	42.66
San Mateo County, CA	42.29
Craven County, NC	41.55
Escambia County, FL	41.39
St. Mary's County, MD	40.30
Okaloosa County, FL	39.31
Ventura County, CA	38.93
Cameron County, TX	38.70
Tulare County, CA	37.06
Ocean County, NJ	36.94
Riverside County, CA	35.92
San Luis Obispo County, CA	35.84
Taylor County, TX	35.58
Anchorage Borough, AK	35.30
Lee County, FL	34.95
Hudson County, NJ	34.76
Contra Costa County, CA	33.37
Skagit County, WA	33.17
Yuma County, AZ	33.16
Hawaii County, HI	32.99
Gloucester County, NJ	32.82
San Joaquin County, CA	32.53
San Bernardino County, CA	32.39
Imperial County, CA	31.25
Santa Barbara County, CA	31.22
Honolulu County, HI	31.12
Houston County, GA	30.95
Sussex County, NJ	30.65
Union County, NJ	29.55
McHenry County, IL	28.70
Fairbanks North Star Borough, AK	28.49
Pasco County, FL	28.49
Charleston County, SC	28.47
Madera County, CA	28.43
St. Clair County, IL	28.12
Rockland County, NY	27.93

Place	Percent
Poplar-Cotton Center, CA (cdp) Tulare County	100.00
Richgrove, CA (cdp) Tulare County	100.00
Earlimart, CA (cdp) Tulare County	96.91
Orosi, CA (cdp) Tulare County	96.85
Ketchikan, AK (city) Ketchikan Gateway Borough	93.37
Delano, CA (city) Kern County	93.23
Kodiak, AK (city) Kodiak Island Borough	92.89
Terra Bella, CA (cdp) Tulare County	91.73
National City, CA (city) San Diego County	90.92
La Presa, CA (cdp) San Diego County	90.31
Colmar Manor, MD (town) Prince George's County	87.05
Carson, CA (city) Los Angeles County	85.98
Ewa Villages, HI (cdp) Honolulu County	85.75
Silverdale, WA (cdp) Kitsap County	84.35
Vallejo, CA (city) Solano County	84.23
Whitmore Village, HI (cdp) Honolulu County	83.70
Imperial Beach, CA (city) San Diego County	82.75
Kaumakani, HI (cdp) Kauai County	82.68
American Canyon, CA (city) Napa County	82.46
Lemoore Station, CA (cdp) Kings County	80.22
Fort Washington, MD (cdp) Prince George's County	80.07
Hanamaulu, HI (cdp) Kauai County	79.87
Oxon Hill-Glassmanor, MD (cdp) Prince George's County	79.70
Puhi, HI (cdp) Kauai County	79.64
Friendly, MD (cdp) Prince George's County	79.60
Lanai City, HI (cdp) Maui County	78.56
Oak Harbor, WA (city) Island County	78.21
Haliimaile, HI (cdp) Maui County	78.19
Ewa Beach, HI (cdp) Honolulu County	77.98
Barrow, AK (city) North Slope Borough	77.93
Kihei, HI (cdp) Maui County	76.78
Waipahu, HI (cdp) Honolulu County	76.37
Port Hueneme, CA (city) Ventura County	75.11
Kekaha, HI (cdp) Kauai County	75.09
Naalehu, HI (cdp) Hawaii County	75.00
Lemoore, CA (city) Kings County	74.76
Maili, HI (cdp) Honolulu County	74.55
Omao, HI (cdp) Kauai County	74.22
Lahaina, HI (cdp) Maui County	74.13
Lakeside, FL (cdp) Clay County	73.39
Kilauea, HI (cdp) Kauai County	73.08
Lathrop, CA (city) San Joaquin County	72.66
Kaunakakai, HI (cdp) Maui County	72.18
Valley Cottage, NY (cdp) Rockland County	71.87
Oxnard, CA (city) Ventura County	71.24
Colma, CA (town) San Mateo County	70.88
Bremerton, WA (city) Kitsap County	70.78
Waimanalo, HI (cdp) Honolulu County	70.37
Waialua, HI (cdp) Honolulu County	70.27
Koloa, HI (cdp) Kauai County	69.82
South Lake Tahoe, CA (city) El Dorado County	69.47
Unalaska, AK (city) Aleutians West Census Area	69.45
Chula Vista, CA (city) San Diego County	69.37
Baywood-Los Osos, CA (cdp) San Luis Obispo County	69.23
Napili-Honokowai, HI (cdp) Maui County	68.90
Eleele, HI (cdp) Kauai County	67.91
Halaula, HI (cdp) Hawaii County	67.89
Paauilo, HI (cdp) Hawaii County	67.10
Pahala, HI (cdp) Hawaii County	66.81
Cathedral City, CA (city) Riverside County	66.07
Santa Maria, CA (city) Santa Barbara County	66.03
Pittsburg, CA (city) Contra Costa County	65.87
Kualapuu, HI (cdp) Maui County	65.68
Honokaa, HI (cdp) Hawaii County	65.65
Palm Springs, CA (city) Riverside County	65.43
Salinas, CA (city) Monterey County	65.35
Wainaku, HI (cdp) Hawaii County	65.11
Village Park, HI (cdp) Honolulu County	64.56
Suisun City, CA (city) Solano County	64.52
Hanford, CA (city) Kings County	64.26
Waihee-Waiehu, HI (cdp) Maui County	64.25
Los Banos, CA (city) Merced County	63.94
Paia, HI (cdp) Maui County	63.70
Rollingwood, CA (cdp) Contra Costa County	63.53
Daly City, CA (city) San Mateo County	62.96

Notes: Please refer to the User's Guide for an explanation of data; ranking tables include all places with Asian and/or NHPI populations above SF4 population thresholds; (1) tables reflect only those areas that meet SF4 population thresholds, therefore there may be less than 50 states, 75 counties or 75 places listed

Population

Filipino

All States, Top 75 Counties, and Top 75 Places Sorted by Percent of Total Population[1]

State	Percent
Hawaii	14.17
California	2.72
Nevada	2.03
Alaska	1.99
Washington	1.10
New Jersey	1.05
Illinois	0.69
Virginia	0.68
United States	0.66
Maryland	0.50
New York	0.46
District of Columbia	0.37
Florida	0.34
Arizona	0.32
Oregon	0.31
Texas	0.28
Delaware	0.23
Colorado	0.22
Connecticut	0.22
Rhode Island	0.20
Michigan	0.18
South Carolina	0.17
Utah	0.17
New Mexico	0.16
Massachusetts	0.15
Georgia	0.13
Idaho	0.13
Kansas	0.13
Missouri	0.13
North Carolina	0.13
Minnesota	0.12
Nebraska	0.12
Ohio	0.12
Oklahoma	0.12
Pennsylvania	0.12
Indiana	0.11
Louisiana	0.11
Wyoming	0.11
New Hampshire	0.10
Wisconsin	0.10
Arkansas	0.09
Maine	0.09
Mississippi	0.09
Montana	0.09
North Dakota	0.09
South Dakota	0.09
Tennessee	0.09
West Virginia	0.09
Iowa	0.08
Kentucky	0.08
Alabama	0.05
Vermont	0.05

County	Percent
Aleutians East Borough, AK	24.03
Kauai County, HI	19.02
Aleutians West Census Area, AK	17.73
Maui County, HI	16.83
Kodiak Island Borough, AK	15.25
Honolulu County, HI	14.37
Solano County, CA	9.09
Hawaii County, HI	8.81
San Mateo County, CA	8.50
San Francisco County, CA	5.16
Alameda County, CA	4.83
Santa Clara County, CA	4.62
Ketchikan Gateway Borough, AK	4.61
North Slope Borough, AK	4.59
San Diego County, CA	4.29
San Joaquin County, CA	3.76
Contra Costa County, CA	3.63
Juneau Borough, AK	3.39
Hudson County, NJ	3.26
Virginia Beach Independent City, VA	3.18
Kitsap County, WA	3.01
Monterey County, CA	2.87
Los Angeles County, CA	2.75
Island County, WA	2.65
Valdez-Cordova Census Area, AK	2.49
Clark County, NV	2.37
Churchill County, NV	2.33
Ventura County, CA	2.03
Sacramento County, CA	1.97
King County, WA	1.94
Anchorage Borough, AK	1.93
Kings County, CA	1.90
Washoe County, NV	1.89
Norfolk Independent City, VA	1.82
Orange County, CA	1.72
Bergen County, NJ	1.69
Middlesex County, NJ	1.67
Napa County, CA	1.61
Kern County, CA	1.59
Rockland County, NY	1.57
DuPage County, IL	1.56
San Bernardino County, CA	1.50
Queens County, NY	1.47
Duval County, FL	1.31
Fairfax County, VA	1.31
Berkeley County, SC	1.27
Riverside County, CA	1.27
Snohomish County, WA	1.26
Fort Bend County, TX	1.24
Tulare County, CA	1.24
Clay County, FL	1.22
Santa Barbara County, CA	1.22
Richmond County, NY	1.17
Union County, NJ	1.10
Arlington County, VA	1.08
Lake County, IL	1.08
Prince George's County, MD	1.03
Somerset County, NJ	1.03
Cook County, IL	1.02
Okaloosa County, FL	1.02
San Benito County, CA	1.01
Essex County, NJ	1.00
San Luis Obispo County, CA	1.00
Yolo County, CA	1.00
Pierce County, WA	0.97
Escambia County, FL	0.92
Chesapeake Independent City, VA	0.90
Yuba County, CA	0.88
El Dorado County, CA	0.87
Atlantic County, NJ	0.86
Alexandria Independent City, VA	0.84
Santa Cruz County, CA	0.80
Montgomery County, MD	0.79
Placer County, CA	0.79
Fresno County, CA	0.78

Place	Percent
Kaumakani, HI (cdp) Kauai County	62.93
Ewa Villages, HI (cdp) Honolulu County	62.86
Whitmore Village, HI (cdp) Honolulu County	54.49
Hanamaulu, HI (cdp) Kauai County	50.58
Waipahu, HI (cdp) Honolulu County	49.96
Puhi, HI (cdp) Kauai County	45.19
Eleele, HI (cdp) Kauai County	41.91
Lanai City, HI (cdp) Maui County	41.31
Ewa Beach, HI (cdp) Honolulu County	38.35
Village Park, HI (cdp) Honolulu County	37.87
Haliimaile, HI (cdp) Maui County	36.00
Waialua, HI (cdp) Honolulu County	35.95
Naalehu, HI (cdp) Hawaii County	33.91
Keaau, HI (cdp) Hawaii County	33.32
Wainaku, HI (cdp) Hawaii County	33.01
Pahoa, HI (cdp) Hawaii County	32.91
Lahaina, HI (cdp) Maui County	32.72
Kekaha, HI (cdp) Kauai County	32.68
Koloa, HI (cdp) Kauai County	32.65
Pahala, HI (cdp) Hawaii County	32.21
Kodiak, AK (city) Kodiak Island Borough	32.09
Kahului, HI (cdp) Maui County	32.05
Daly City, CA (city) San Mateo County	31.79
Ewa Gentry, HI (cdp) Honolulu County	29.35
Waihee-Waiehu, HI (cdp) Maui County	29.09
Honokaa, HI (cdp) Hawaii County	28.84
Pepeekeo, HI (cdp) Hawaii County	26.82
Paauilo, HI (cdp) Hawaii County	26.68
Hercules, CA (city) Contra Costa County	25.58
Halaula, HI (cdp) Hawaii County	25.44
Broadmoor, CA (cdp) San Mateo County	23.53
Papaikou, HI (cdp) Hawaii County	22.64
Unalaska, AK (city) Aleutians West Census Area	21.97
Kaunakakai, HI (cdp) Maui County	21.93
Omao, HI (cdp) Kauai County	21.41
Waipio, HI (cdp) Honolulu County	20.89
Waimanalo, HI (cdp) Honolulu County	20.80
Halawa, HI (cdp) Honolulu County	20.47
Vallejo, CA (city) Solano County	20.00
Poplar-Cotton Center, CA (cdp) Tulare County	19.83
Union City, CA (city) Alameda County	19.63
Kilauea, HI (cdp) Kauai County	19.56
Hanapepe, HI (cdp) Kauai County	19.36
Carson, CA (city) Los Angeles County	19.35
Maili, HI (cdp) Honolulu County	19.23
Kihei, HI (cdp) Maui County	18.86
Wahiawa, HI (cdp) Honolulu County	18.09
Makakilo City, HI (cdp) Honolulu County	17.97
Kahuku, HI (cdp) Honolulu County	17.74
Paia, HI (cdp) Maui County	17.19
South San Francisco, CA (city) San Mateo County	17.06
National City, CA (city) San Diego County	16.65
Kapaa, HI (cdp) Kauai County	16.45
Waikapu, HI (cdp) Maui County	16.12
Kurtistown, HI (cdp) Hawaii County	16.11
Waipio Acres, HI (cdp) Honolulu County	16.06
Colma, CA (town) San Mateo County	15.88
Lihue, HI (cdp) Kauai County	15.50
Rollingwood, CA (cdp) Contra Costa County	15.45
Aiea, HI (cdp) Honolulu County	14.70
Delano, CA (city) Kern County	14.41
Milpitas, CA (city) Santa Clara County	14.38
Pearl City, HI (cdp) Honolulu County	13.85
Waimea, HI (cdp) Kauai County	13.78
Napili-Honokowai, HI (cdp) Maui County	13.65
Colmar Manor, MD (town) Prince George's County	13.37
American Canyon, CA (city) Napa County	13.27
Wailuku, HI (cdp) Maui County	12.75
Bergenfield, NJ (borough) Bergen County	12.30
Suisun City, CA (city) Solano County	11.90
Honolulu, HI (cdp) Honolulu County	11.75
Kalaheo, HI (cdp) Kauai County	11.63
Hawi, HI (cdp) Hawaii County	11.60
Walnut, CA (city) Los Angeles County	11.51
Kualapuu, HI (cdp) Maui County	11.41

Notes: Please refer to the User's Guide for an explanation of data; ranking tables include all places with Asian and/or NHPI populations above SF4 population thresholds; (1) tables reflect only those areas that meet SF4 population thresholds, therefore there may be less than 50 states, 75 counties or 75 places listed

Population

Guamanian or Chamorro

All States, Top 75 Counties, and Top 75 Places Sorted by Number[1]

State	Number
United States	55,130
California	20,472
Washington	5,380
Texas	3,304
Florida	2,020
New York	1,759
Hawaii	1,491
Georgia	1,443
Arizona	1,265
North Carolina	1,197
Nevada	1,139
Oregon	1,110
Virginia	1,015
Colorado	1,012
Illinois	815
Pennsylvania	805
Maryland	701
Michigan	685
Ohio	666
Tennessee	619
Missouri	612
New Jersey	602
Indiana	526
Louisiana	467
Massachusetts	445
Minnesota	427
Wisconsin	425
Alabama	424
Connecticut	419
Oklahoma	400
Kentucky	368
New Mexico	365
South Carolina	359

County	Number
San Diego County, CA	4,629
Los Angeles County, CA	3,139
Pierce County, WA	1,825
Santa Clara County, CA	1,390
Solano County, CA	1,351
Honolulu County, HI	1,328
Alameda County, CA	1,311
Orange County, CA	1,103
Kitsap County, WA	1,043
San Bernardino County, CA	1,042
Clark County, NV	958
Riverside County, CA	942
Sacramento County, CA	875
King County, WA	834
Thurston County, WA	730
Monterey County, CA	674
Maricopa County, AZ	647
Harris County, TX	639
Bell County, TX	596
Contra Costa County, CA	544
El Paso County, CO	492
Kings County, NY	489
San Mateo County, CA	402

Place	Number
San Diego, CA (city) San Diego County	2,077
New York, NY (city)	1,176
Los Angeles, CA (city) Los Angeles County	1,149
San Jose, CA (city) Santa Clara County	732
Honolulu, HI (cdp) Honolulu County	677
Vallejo, CA (city) Solano County	572
Fairfield, CA (city) Solano County	541
Killeen, TX (city) Bell County	500
Houston, TX (city) Harris County	442
Tacoma, WA (city) Pierce County	436
Chula Vista, CA (city) San Diego County	425

Notes: Please refer to the User's Guide for an explanation of data; ranking tables include all places with Asian and/or NHPI populations above SF4 population thresholds; (1) tables reflect only those areas that meet SF4 population thresholds, therefore there may be less than 50 states, 75 counties or 75 places listed

Population

Guamanian or Chamorro

All States, Top 75 Counties, and Top 75 Places Sorted by Percent of Native Hawaiian and Other Pacific Islander Population[1]

State	Percent
Georgia	37.33
Alabama	35.72
Maryland	34.53
Louisiana	33.87
North Carolina	32.36
Kentucky	31.86
Connecticut	30.88
Indiana	29.85
Florida	29.65
New Mexico	29.25
Tennessee	28.67
Virginia	28.06
Wisconsin	26.95
Texas	26.51
South Carolina	25.94
Michigan	25.67
Ohio	25.22
Minnesota	24.77
Washington	24.75
Massachusetts	24.25
Colorado	23.55
New York	22.26
New Jersey	22.22
Oklahoma	21.74
Pennsylvania	21.63
Illinois	21.39
Arizona	20.52
Missouri	19.93
California	17.98
Oregon	14.64
Nevada	14.59
United States	14.55
Hawaii	1.32

County	Percent
Kitsap County, WA	61.43
Thurston County, WA	60.58
Bell County, TX	47.15
Solano County, CA	42.36
Harris County, TX	42.21
El Paso County, CO	38.11
Monterey County, CA	36.97
Pierce County, WA	35.96
San Diego County, CA	34.33
Kings County, NY	31.57
Riverside County, CA	25.33
Santa Clara County, CA	23.99
San Bernardino County, CA	20.76
Maricopa County, AZ	16.98
Clark County, NV	16.19
Contra Costa County, CA	16.04
Alameda County, CA	14.27
Sacramento County, CA	13.96
Orange County, CA	12.93
Los Angeles County, CA	11.53
King County, WA	10.08
San Mateo County, CA	4.71
Honolulu County, HI	1.72

Place	Percent
Chula Vista, CA (city) San Diego County	56.52
Fairfield, CA (city) Solano County	52.17
Houston, TX (city) Harris County	50.46
Killeen, TX (city) Bell County	47.80
Vallejo, CA (city) Solano County	40.97
San Diego, CA (city) San Diego County	33.41
Tacoma, WA (city) Pierce County	32.37
New York, NY (city)	24.15
San Jose, CA (city) Santa Clara County	22.63
Los Angeles, CA (city) Los Angeles County	17.83
Honolulu, HI (cdp) Honolulu County	2.62

Notes: Please refer to the User's Guide for an explanation of data; ranking tables include all places with Asian and/or NHPI populations above SF4 population thresholds; (1) tables reflect only those areas that meet SF4 population thresholds, therefore there may be less than 50 states, 75 counties or 75 places listed

Population

Guamanian or Chamorro

All States, Top 75 Counties, and Top 75 Places Sorted by Percent of Total Population[1]

State	Percent
Hawaii	0.12
Washington	0.09
California	0.06
Nevada	0.06
Oregon	0.03
Arizona	0.02
Colorado	0.02
Georgia	0.02
New Mexico	0.02
Texas	0.02
United States	0.02
Alabama	0.01
Connecticut	0.01
Florida	0.01
Illinois	0.01
Indiana	0.01
Kentucky	0.01
Louisiana	0.01
Maryland	0.01
Massachusetts	0.01
Michigan	0.01
Minnesota	0.01
Missouri	0.01
New Jersey	0.01
New York	0.01
North Carolina	0.01
Ohio	0.01
Oklahoma	0.01
Pennsylvania	0.01
South Carolina	0.01
Tennessee	0.01
Virginia	0.01
Wisconsin	0.01

County	Percent
Kitsap County, WA	0.45
Thurston County, WA	0.35
Solano County, CA	0.34
Pierce County, WA	0.26
Bell County, TX	0.25
Monterey County, CA	0.17
San Diego County, CA	0.16
Honolulu County, HI	0.15
El Paso County, CO	0.10
Alameda County, CA	0.09
Santa Clara County, CA	0.08
Clark County, NV	0.07
Sacramento County, CA	0.07
Contra Costa County, CA	0.06
Riverside County, CA	0.06
San Bernardino County, CA	0.06
San Mateo County, CA	0.06
King County, WA	0.05
Orange County, CA	0.04
Los Angeles County, CA	0.03
Harris County, TX	0.02
Kings County, NY	0.02
Maricopa County, AZ	0.02

Place	Percent
Killeen, TX (city) Bell County	0.58
Fairfield, CA (city) Solano County	0.56
Vallejo, CA (city) Solano County	0.49
Chula Vista, CA (city) San Diego County	0.24
Tacoma, WA (city) Pierce County	0.23
Honolulu, HI (cdp) Honolulu County	0.18
San Diego, CA (city) San Diego County	0.17
San Jose, CA (city) Santa Clara County	0.08
Los Angeles, CA (city) Los Angeles County	0.03
Houston, TX (city) Harris County	0.02
New York, NY (city)	0.01

Notes: Please refer to the User's Guide for an explanation of data; ranking tables include all places with Asian and/or NHPI populations above SF4 population thresholds; (1) tables reflect only those areas that meet SF4 population thresholds, therefore there may be less than 50 states, 75 counties or 75 places listed

Population

Hawaiian, Native

All States, Top 75 Counties, and Top 75 Places Sorted by Number[1]

State	Number
United States	139,495
Hawaii	80,965
California	19,661
Washington	4,511
Texas	3,655
Nevada	3,405
Arizona	1,985
Oregon	1,977
Florida	1,971
Colorado	1,454
New York	1,442
Utah	1,341
North Carolina	1,146
Pennsylvania	1,004
Virginia	924
Illinois	914
Georgia	814
Michigan	792
Ohio	791
Missouri	695
Oklahoma	676
Indiana	664
New Jersey	652
Minnesota	579
Tennessee	560
Maryland	515
Massachusetts	507
Alaska	499
South Carolina	496
Wisconsin	433
Louisiana	406
Kansas	404
New Mexico	394
Idaho	362
Arkansas	298
Montana	264

County	Number
Honolulu County, HI	50,284
Hawaii County, HI	13,947
Maui County, HI	11,719
Kauai County, HI	4,927
Los Angeles County, CA	4,398
Clark County, NV	3,080
San Diego County, CA	2,217
Orange County, CA	1,701
King County, WA	1,377
Alameda County, CA	1,283
Santa Clara County, CA	1,146
Maricopa County, AZ	1,109
Pierce County, WA	895
Riverside County, CA	809
San Mateo County, CA	805
Sacramento County, CA	654
Solano County, CA	654
San Bernardino County, CA	610
Contra Costa County, CA	595
Ventura County, CA	575
Snohomish County, WA	509
Salt Lake County, UT	480
Multnomah County, OR	468
Pima County, AZ	466
Washington County, OR	425
Bexar County, TX	420
San Joaquin County, CA	415
Utah County, UT	387

Place	Number
Honolulu, HI (cdp) Honolulu County	14,400
Hilo, HI (cdp) Hawaii County	4,177
Kaneohe, HI (cdp) Honolulu County	3,388
Nanakuli, HI (cdp) Honolulu County	3,086
Kailua, HI (cdp) Honolulu County	2,525
Waianae, HI (cdp) Honolulu County	2,388
Waimanalo Beach, HI (cdp) Honolulu County	2,051
Los Angeles, CA (city) Los Angeles County	1,613
Kahului, HI (cdp) Maui County	1,454
Maili, HI (cdp) Honolulu County	1,411
Pearl City, HI (cdp) Honolulu County	1,358
Makaha, HI (cdp) Honolulu County	1,323
Wailuku, HI (cdp) Maui County	1,287
San Diego, CA (city) San Diego County	1,125
Kailua, HI (cdp) Hawaii County	1,049
Waimalu, HI (cdp) Honolulu County	1,003
Makakilo City, HI (cdp) Honolulu County	991
Anahola, HI (cdp) Kauai County	980
Waipahu, HI (cdp) Honolulu County	973
Waimea, HI (cdp) Hawaii County	962
Ewa Beach, HI (cdp) Honolulu County	948
Wahiawa, HI (cdp) Honolulu County	937
Waihee-Waiehu, HI (cdp) Maui County	931
Kualapuu, HI (cdp) Maui County	887
Mililani Town, HI (cdp) Honolulu County	874
Lahaina, HI (cdp) Maui County	873
Kapaa, HI (cdp) Kauai County	841
Waimanalo, HI (cdp) Honolulu County	841
Ahuimanu, HI (cdp) Honolulu County	811
Kihei, HI (cdp) Maui County	798
Las Vegas, NV (city) Clark County	781
New York, NY (city)	776
Kaunakakai, HI (cdp) Maui County	765
Hauula, HI (cdp) Honolulu County	717
Halawa, HI (cdp) Honolulu County	708
Kalaoa, HI (cdp) Hawaii County	704
Hawaiian Paradise Park, HI (cdp) Hawaii County	684
Paradise, NV (cdp) Clark County	599
Kahaluu, HI (cdp) Honolulu County	576
Makawao, HI (cdp) Maui County	546
San Jose, CA (city) Santa Clara County	535
Phoenix, AZ (city) Maricopa County	503
Henderson, NV (city) Clark County	443
Waipio, HI (cdp) Honolulu County	436
Hawaiian Beaches, HI (cdp) Hawaii County	397
Holualoa, HI (cdp) Hawaii County	374
Aiea, HI (cdp) Honolulu County	368
Portland, OR (city) Multnomah County	348
Kekaha, HI (cdp) Kauai County	342
Laie, HI (cdp) Honolulu County	331
Honaunau-Napoopoo, HI (cdp) Hawaii County	318
Volcano, HI (cdp) Hawaii County	311
Waikoloa Village, HI (cdp) Hawaii County	298
Hana, HI (cdp) Maui County	274
Captain Cook, HI (cdp) Hawaii County	254
Kaaawa, HI (cdp) Honolulu County	233
Makaha Valley, HI (cdp) Honolulu County	220
Paia, HI (cdp) Maui County	213
Haleiwa, HI (cdp) Honolulu County	197
Kahuku, HI (cdp) Honolulu County	184
Hanapepe, HI (cdp) Kauai County	182
Hawaiian Ocean View, HI (cdp) Hawaii County	182
Waimea, HI (cdp) Kauai County	178
Pakala Village, HI (cdp) Kauai County	159
Honalo, HI (cdp) Hawaii County	158
Waikane, HI (cdp) Honolulu County	156
Punaluu, HI (cdp) Honolulu County	140
Kilauea, HI (cdp) Kauai County	139
Kapaau, HI (cdp) Hawaii County	122
Waialua, HI (cdp) Honolulu County	122
Naalehu, HI (cdp) Hawaii County	120
Pahala, HI (cdp) Hawaii County	86

Notes: Please refer to the User's Guide for an explanation of data; ranking tables include all places with Asian and/or NHPI populations above SF4 population thresholds; (1) tables reflect only those areas that meet SF4 population thresholds, therefore there may be less than 50 states, 75 counties or 75 places listed

Population

Hawaiian, Native

All States, Top 75 Counties, and Top 75 Places Sorted by Percent of Native Hawaiian and Other Pacific Islander Population[1]

State	Percent
Hawaii	71.93
Montana	59.06
Nevada	43.62
Indiana	37.68
United States	36.83
Oklahoma	36.74
South Carolina	35.84
Colorado	33.83
Minnesota	33.58
Kansas	33.44
Arizona	32.19
New Mexico	31.57
North Carolina	30.98
Ohio	29.95
Michigan	29.67
Louisiana	29.44
Idaho	29.38
Texas	29.32
Florida	28.93
Massachusetts	27.63
Wisconsin	27.46
Pennsylvania	26.98
Oregon	26.07
Tennessee	25.94
Virginia	25.55
Maryland	25.37
New Jersey	24.07
Illinois	23.98
Missouri	22.63
Georgia	21.06
Washington	20.75
Arkansas	19.43
New York	18.25
California	17.27
Alaska	15.98
Utah	9.33

County	Percent
Kauai County, HI	92.72
Hawaii County, HI	85.95
Maui County, HI	85.19
Honolulu County, HI	65.16
Clark County, NV	52.04
Pima County, AZ	42.99
Snohomish County, WA	40.72
Bexar County, TX	37.17
Ventura County, CA	34.45
Washington County, OR	30.38
Maricopa County, AZ	29.10
San Joaquin County, CA	23.25
Riverside County, CA	21.75
Utah County, UT	21.44
Solano County, CA	20.51
Orange County, CA	19.94
Santa Clara County, CA	19.78
Multnomah County, OR	18.64
Pierce County, WA	17.64
Contra Costa County, CA	17.55
King County, WA	16.65
San Diego County, CA	16.44
Los Angeles County, CA	16.16
Alameda County, CA	13.96
San Bernardino County, CA	12.15
Sacramento County, CA	10.43
San Mateo County, CA	9.43
Salt Lake County, UT	4.64

Place	Percent
Hana, HI (cdp) Maui County	100.00
Hanapepe, HI (cdp) Kauai County	100.00
Kapaau, HI (cdp) Hawaii County	100.00
Makawao, HI (cdp) Maui County	100.00
Naalehu, HI (cdp) Hawaii County	100.00
Pahala, HI (cdp) Hawaii County	100.00
Pakala Village, HI (cdp) Kauai County	100.00
Kahaluu, HI (cdp) Honolulu County	99.31
Waimea, HI (cdp) Hawaii County	99.18
Kualapuu, HI (cdp) Maui County	98.78
Kaunakakai, HI (cdp) Maui County	97.20
Anahola, HI (cdp) Kauai County	97.03
Waimea, HI (cdp) Kauai County	96.74
Ahuimanu, HI (cdp) Honolulu County	96.66
Waikane, HI (cdp) Honolulu County	96.30
Waimanalo, HI (cdp) Honolulu County	96.11
Waimanalo Beach, HI (cdp) Honolulu County	95.71
Volcano, HI (cdp) Hawaii County	95.40
Kalaoa, HI (cdp) Hawaii County	93.87
Wailuku, HI (cdp) Maui County	93.40
Kilauea, HI (cdp) Kauai County	93.29
Kailua, HI (cdp) Honolulu County	92.05
Kapaa, HI (cdp) Kauai County	92.01
Honaunau-Napoopoo, HI (cdp) Hawaii County	91.64
Aiea, HI (cdp) Honolulu County	91.32
Hawaiian Paradise Park, HI (cdp) Hawaii County	91.32
Lahaina, HI (cdp) Maui County	91.13
Paia, HI (cdp) Maui County	91.03
Kekaha, HI (cdp) Kauai County	88.37
Waihee-Waiehu, HI (cdp) Maui County	86.69
Makaha, HI (cdp) Honolulu County	85.85
Waianae, HI (cdp) Honolulu County	85.50
Kailua, HI (cdp) Hawaii County	85.22
Haleiwa, HI (cdp) Honolulu County	84.91
Captain Cook, HI (cdp) Hawaii County	84.39
Holualoa, HI (cdp) Hawaii County	84.23
Hilo, HI (cdp) Hawaii County	84.06
Kaneohe, HI (cdp) Honolulu County	83.74
Maili, HI (cdp) Honolulu County	81.94
Kahului, HI (cdp) Maui County	79.28
Hawaiian Ocean View, HI (cdp) Hawaii County	78.79
Hawaiian Beaches, HI (cdp) Hawaii County	77.39
Pearl City, HI (cdp) Honolulu County	75.82
Makaha Valley, HI (cdp) Honolulu County	75.34
Nanakuli, HI (cdp) Honolulu County	75.19
Kaaawa, HI (cdp) Honolulu County	74.92
Honalo, HI (cdp) Hawaii County	74.88
Mililani Town, HI (cdp) Honolulu County	74.51
Makakilo City, HI (cdp) Honolulu County	73.14
Paradise, NV (cdp) Clark County	71.22
Kihei, HI (cdp) Maui County	70.18
Waipio, HI (cdp) Honolulu County	69.54
Waialua, HI (cdp) Honolulu County	67.40
Punaluu, HI (cdp) Honolulu County	66.99
Ewa Beach, HI (cdp) Honolulu County	65.11
Waimalu, HI (cdp) Honolulu County	64.13
Waikoloa Village, HI (cdp) Hawaii County	61.83
Henderson, NV (city) Clark County	58.44
Honolulu, HI (cdp) Honolulu County	55.69
Wahiawa, HI (cdp) Honolulu County	54.04
Hauula, HI (cdp) Honolulu County	48.48
Halawa, HI (cdp) Honolulu County	46.83
Las Vegas, NV (city) Clark County	46.68
Kahuku, HI (cdp) Honolulu County	29.16
Phoenix, AZ (city) Maricopa County	28.83
Los Angeles, CA (city) Los Angeles County	25.03
Waipahu, HI (cdp) Honolulu County	24.17
Laie, HI (cdp) Honolulu County	20.57
San Diego, CA (city) San Diego County	18.10
Portland, OR (city) Multnomah County	17.31
San Jose, CA (city) Santa Clara County	16.54
New York, NY (city)	15.93

Notes: Please refer to the User's Guide for an explanation of data; ranking tables include all places with Asian and/or NHPI populations above SF4 population thresholds; (1) tables reflect only those areas that meet SF4 population thresholds, therefore there may be less than 50 states, 75 counties or 75 places listed

Population

Hawaiian, Native

All States, Top 75 Counties, and Top 75 Places Sorted by Percent of Total Population[1]

State	Percent
Hawaii	6.68
Nevada	0.17
Alaska	0.08
Washington	0.08
California	0.06
Oregon	0.06
Utah	0.06
United States	0.05
Arizona	0.04
Colorado	0.03
Idaho	0.03
Montana	0.03
Kansas	0.02
New Mexico	0.02
Oklahoma	0.02
Texas	0.02
Arkansas	0.01
Florida	0.01
Georgia	0.01
Illinois	0.01
Indiana	0.01
Louisiana	0.01
Maryland	0.01
Massachusetts	0.01
Michigan	0.01
Minnesota	0.01
Missouri	0.01
New Jersey	0.01
New York	0.01
North Carolina	0.01
Ohio	0.01
Pennsylvania	0.01
South Carolina	0.01
Tennessee	0.01
Virginia	0.01
Wisconsin	0.01

County	Percent
Hawaii County, HI	9.38
Maui County, HI	9.15
Kauai County, HI	8.43
Honolulu County, HI	5.74
Clark County, NV	0.22
Solano County, CA	0.17
Pierce County, WA	0.13
San Mateo County, CA	0.11
Utah County, UT	0.11
Washington County, OR	0.10
Alameda County, CA	0.09
King County, WA	0.08
San Diego County, CA	0.08
Snohomish County, WA	0.08
Ventura County, CA	0.08
Multnomah County, OR	0.07
San Joaquin County, CA	0.07
Santa Clara County, CA	0.07
Contra Costa County, CA	0.06
Orange County, CA	0.06
Pima County, AZ	0.06
Los Angeles County, CA	0.05
Riverside County, CA	0.05
Sacramento County, CA	0.05
Salt Lake County, UT	0.05
Maricopa County, AZ	0.04
San Bernardino County, CA	0.04
Bexar County, TX	0.03

Place	Percent
Anahola, HI (cdp) Kauai County	49.37
Waimanalo Beach, HI (cdp) Honolulu County	48.38
Kualapuu, HI (cdp) Maui County	45.58
Hana, HI (cdp) Maui County	41.08
Pakala Village, HI (cdp) Kauai County	33.13
Nanakuli, HI (cdp) Honolulu County	28.85
Kaunakakai, HI (cdp) Maui County	27.87
Maili, HI (cdp) Honolulu County	23.27
Waimanalo, HI (cdp) Honolulu County	22.81
Waianae, HI (cdp) Honolulu County	22.42
Waikane, HI (cdp) Honolulu County	21.70
Kahaluu, HI (cdp) Honolulu County	19.75
Hauula, HI (cdp) Honolulu County	19.51
Kaaawa, HI (cdp) Honolulu County	17.60
Makaha, HI (cdp) Honolulu County	17.14
Makaha Valley, HI (cdp) Honolulu County	17.05
Punaluu, HI (cdp) Honolulu County	16.55
Volcano, HI (cdp) Hawaii County	13.95
Waimea, HI (cdp) Hawaii County	13.72
Honaunau-Napoopoo, HI (cdp) Hawaii County	13.55
Waihee-Waiehu, HI (cdp) Maui County	12.84
Naalehu, HI (cdp) Hawaii County	12.11
Kekaha, HI (cdp) Kauai County	10.78
Kailua, HI (cdp) Hawaii County	10.68
Hawaiian Beaches, HI (cdp) Hawaii County	10.46
Kapaau, HI (cdp) Hawaii County	10.44
Wailuku, HI (cdp) Maui County	10.36
Hilo, HI (cdp) Hawaii County	10.24
Kalaoa, HI (cdp) Hawaii County	10.21
Waimea, HI (cdp) Kauai County	9.93
Ahuimanu, HI (cdp) Honolulu County	9.73
Kaneohe, HI (cdp) Honolulu County	9.69
Hawaiian Paradise Park, HI (cdp) Hawaii County	9.65
Lahaina, HI (cdp) Maui County	9.65
Haleiwa, HI (cdp) Honolulu County	8.85
Kahuku, HI (cdp) Honolulu County	8.77
Kapaa, HI (cdp) Kauai County	8.68
Makawao, HI (cdp) Maui County	8.59
Paia, HI (cdp) Maui County	8.52
Hanapepe, HI (cdp) Kauai County	8.49
Hawaiian Ocean View, HI (cdp) Hawaii County	8.22
Captain Cook, HI (cdp) Hawaii County	7.76
Honalo, HI (cdp) Hawaii County	7.63
Makakilo City, HI (cdp) Honolulu County	7.53
Kahului, HI (cdp) Maui County	7.26
Laie, HI (cdp) Honolulu County	7.20
Kailua, HI (cdp) Honolulu County	6.90
Kilauea, HI (cdp) Kauai County	6.50
Ewa Beach, HI (cdp) Honolulu County	6.47
Waikoloa Village, HI (cdp) Hawaii County	6.18
Holualoa, HI (cdp) Hawaii County	6.12
Pahala, HI (cdp) Hawaii County	6.06
Wahiawa, HI (cdp) Honolulu County	5.80
Halawa, HI (cdp) Honolulu County	5.07
Kihei, HI (cdp) Maui County	4.74
Pearl City, HI (cdp) Honolulu County	4.41
Aiea, HI (cdp) Honolulu County	4.08
Honolulu, HI (cdp) Honolulu County	3.87
Waipio, HI (cdp) Honolulu County	3.75
Waimalu, HI (cdp) Honolulu County	3.40
Waialua, HI (cdp) Honolulu County	3.24
Mililani Town, HI (cdp) Honolulu County	3.06
Waipahu, HI (cdp) Honolulu County	2.94
Paradise, NV (cdp) Clark County	0.32
Henderson, NV (city) Clark County	0.25
Las Vegas, NV (city) Clark County	0.16
San Diego, CA (city) San Diego County	0.09
Portland, OR (city) Multnomah County	0.07
San Jose, CA (city) Santa Clara County	0.06
Los Angeles, CA (city) Los Angeles County	0.04
Phoenix, AZ (city) Maricopa County	0.04
New York, NY (city)	0.01

Notes: Please refer to the User's Guide for an explanation of data; ranking tables include all places with Asian and/or NHPI populations above SF4 population thresholds; (1) tables reflect only those areas that meet SF4 population thresholds, therefore there may be less than 50 states, 75 counties or 75 places listed

Population

Hmong

All States, Top 75 Counties, and Top 75 Places Sorted by Number[1]

State	Number
United States	170,049
California	68,706
Minnesota	43,156
Wisconsin	31,010
North Carolina	6,819
Michigan	5,657
Colorado	3,014
Washington	1,494
Oregon	1,367
Georgia	1,200
Massachusetts	993
Rhode Island	961
Kansas	931
South Carolina	860
Pennsylvania	788
Alaska	522
Oklahoma	335

County	Number
Ramsey County, MN	26,620
Fresno County, CA	24,045
Sacramento County, CA	17,314
Hennepin County, MN	13,324
Milwaukee County, WI	7,484
Merced County, CA	6,585
San Joaquin County, CA	5,948
Marathon County, WI	4,107
Butte County, CA	2,824
Yuba County, CA	2,700
Sheboygan County, WI	2,492
Brown County, WI	2,417
Outagamie County, WI	2,328
Dane County, WI	2,297
Adams County, CO	2,144
Burke County, NC	2,005
La Crosse County, WI	1,941
Wayne County, MI	1,833
Catawba County, NC	1,794
Winnebago County, WI	1,493
Eau Claire County, WI	1,384
San Diego County, CA	1,375
Tulare County, CA	1,087
Macomb County, MI	1,082
Oakland County, MI	1,081
Multnomah County, OR	1,057
Orange County, CA	1,055
Stanislaus County, CA	969
Manitowoc County, WI	939
King County, WA	889
Portage County, WI	869
Providence County, RI	831
Wyandotte County, KS	779
Washington County, MN	771
Spartanburg County, SC	750
Yolo County, CA	665
Worcester County, MA	663
Ingham County, MI	595
Wood County, WI	591
Anoka County, MN	571
Mecklenburg County, NC	569
Dunn County, WI	564
Glenn County, CA	561
Spokane County, WA	533
Anchorage Borough, AK	522
Riverside County, CA	487
Lancaster County, PA	458
Los Angeles County, CA	440
Calumet County, WI	436
Jefferson County, CO	412
Solano County, CA	411
Olmsted County, MN	400
Chippewa County, WI	359
Santa Barbara County, CA	355
Stanly County, NC	318
Fond du Lac County, WI	265
Barrow County, GA	233

Place	Number
St. Paul, MN (city) Ramsey County	25,482
Fresno, CA (city) Fresno County	20,344
Sacramento, CA (city) Sacramento County	12,070
Minneapolis, MN (city) Hennepin County	10,266
Milwaukee, WI (city) Milwaukee County	7,250
Stockton, CA (city) San Joaquin County	4,953
Merced, CA (city) Merced County	4,228
Wausau, WI (city) Marathon County	3,434
Parkway-S. Sacramento, CA (cdp) Sacramento County	2,750
Sheboygan, WI (city) Sheboygan County	2,387
Appleton, WI (city) Outagamie County	2,331
Linda, CA (cdp) Yuba County	2,031
Green Bay, WI (city) Brown County	2,022
Madison, WI (city) Dane County	1,819
Clovis, CA (city) Fresno County	1,799
Detroit, MI (city) Wayne County	1,638
Brooklyn Center, MN (city) Hennepin County	1,452
Eau Claire, WI (city) Eau Claire County	1,448
La Crosse, WI (city) La Crosse County	1,342
Oshkosh, WI (city) Winnebago County	1,104
Brooklyn Park, MN (city) Hennepin County	1,100
San Diego, CA (city) San Diego County	1,092
Florin, CA (cdp) Sacramento County	1,061
Westminster, CO (city) Adams County	1,015
Portland, OR (city) Multnomah County	931
Manitowoc, WI (city) Manitowoc County	821
Kansas City, KS (city) Wyandotte County	779
Stevens Point, WI (city) Portage County	757
Warren, MI (city) Macomb County	749
Chico, CA (city) Butte County	729
Pontiac, MI (city) Oakland County	724
Providence, RI (city) Providence County	674
Lansing, MI (city) Ingham County	645
Thermalito, CA (cdp) Butte County	627
Fitchburg, MA (city) Worcester County	608
South Oroville, CA (cdp) Butte County	608
West Sacramento, CA (city) Yolo County	579
Charlotte, NC (city) Mecklenburg County	569
Willows, CA (city) Glenn County	561
Hickory, NC (city) Catawba County	543
Visalia, CA (city) Tulare County	541
Santa Ana, CA (city) Orange County	528
Wisconsin Rapids, WI (city) Wood County	520
Oroville, CA (city) Butte County	483
Spokane, WA (city) Spokane County	411
Modesto, CA (city) Stanislaus County	406
Rochester, MN (city) Olmsted County	400
Maplewood, MN (city) Ramsey County	396
Atwater, CA (city) Merced County	393
Woodbury, MN (city) Washington County	353
Arden-Arcade, CA (cdp) Sacramento County	351
Glen Alpine, NC (town) Burke County	218
Fond du Lac, WI (city) Fond du Lac County	209
Valdese, NC (town) Burke County	117
Connelly Springs, NC (town) Burke County	76

Notes: Please refer to the User's Guide for an explanation of data; ranking tables include all places with Asian and/or NHPI populations above SF4 population thresholds; (1) tables reflect only those areas that meet SF4 population thresholds, therefore there may be less than 50 states, 75 counties or 75 places listed

Population

Hmong

All States, Top 75 Counties, and Top 75 Places Sorted by Percent of Asian Population[1]

State	Percent
Wisconsin	37.33
Minnesota	30.99
North Carolina	6.13
Rhode Island	4.03
Michigan	3.24
Colorado	3.23
South Carolina	2.36
Kansas	2.08
Alaska	2.05
California	1.87
United States	1.67
Oregon	1.38
Oklahoma	0.74
Georgia	0.70
Washington	0.47
Massachusetts	0.42
Pennsylvania	0.36

County	Percent
Dunn County, WI	80.34
Marathon County, WI	79.65
Chippewa County, WI	76.55
Sheboygan County, WI	69.71
La Crosse County, WI	67.99
Portage County, WI	67.10
Burke County, NC	66.32
Outagamie County, WI	64.04
Manitowoc County, WI	63.83
Calumet County, WI	63.74
Glenn County, CA	63.32
Winnebago County, WI	60.79
Ramsey County, MN	60.46
Eau Claire County, WI	59.58
Yuba County, CA	59.33
Brown County, WI	52.59
Wood County, WI	50.95
Catawba County, NC	47.31
Merced County, CA	45.53
Fond du Lac County, WI	45.07
Butte County, CA	43.09
Stanly County, NC	42.29
Fresno County, CA	37.63
Wyandotte County, KS	35.01
Milwaukee County, WI	33.48
Hennepin County, MN	25.08
Barrow County, GA	22.43
Adams County, CO	18.63
Spartanburg County, SC	18.06
Washington County, MN	17.68
Dane County, WI	16.07
Sacramento County, CA	12.84
Anoka County, MN	11.44
San Joaquin County, CA	9.14
Tulare County, CA	8.81
Olmsted County, MN	7.51
Spokane County, WA	7.16
Lancaster County, PA	6.98
Macomb County, MI	6.23
Ingham County, MI	5.96
Stanislaus County, CA	5.27
Wayne County, MI	5.20
Providence County, RI	4.54
Yolo County, CA	4.21
Anchorage Borough, AK	3.66
Jefferson County, CO	3.51
Worcester County, MA	3.50
Multnomah County, OR	2.84
Mecklenburg County, NC	2.73
Santa Barbara County, CA	2.27
Oakland County, MI	2.23
Riverside County, CA	0.89
Solano County, CA	0.82
San Diego County, CA	0.55
King County, WA	0.47
Orange County, CA	0.27
Los Angeles County, CA	0.04

Place	Percent
Glen Alpine, NC (town) Burke County	87.90
Thermalito, CA (cdp) Butte County	84.50
Wausau, WI (city) Marathon County	82.39
Willows, CA (city) Glenn County	80.72
Linda, CA (cdp) Yuba County	79.99
Wisconsin Rapids, WI (city) Wood County	79.63
Stevens Point, WI (city) Portage County	73.14
Valdese, NC (town) Burke County	73.13
Appleton, WI (city) Outagamie County	73.03
Sheboygan, WI (city) Sheboygan County	72.58
St. Paul, MN (city) Ramsey County	72.15
Manitowoc, WI (city) Manitowoc County	70.78
La Crosse, WI (city) La Crosse County	69.07
Oshkosh, WI (city) Winnebago County	67.36
Oroville, CA (city) Butte County	66.26
Eau Claire, WI (city) Eau Claire County	65.40
Connelly Springs, NC (town) Burke County	64.41
Merced, CA (city) Merced County	59.56
South Oroville, CA (cdp) Butte County	58.52
Green Bay, WI (city) Brown County	58.32
Brooklyn Center, MN (city) Hennepin County	55.72
Fond du Lac, WI (city) Fond du Lac County	53.45
Pontiac, MI (city) Oakland County	46.95
Milwaukee, WI (city) Milwaukee County	44.99
Minneapolis, MN (city) Hennepin County	42.93
Fresno, CA (city) Fresno County	41.96
Parkway-S. Sacramento, CA (cdp) Sacramento County	40.83
Clovis, CA (city) Fresno County	40.62
Kansas City, KS (city) Wyandotte County	35.98
Fitchburg, MA (city) Worcester County	34.78
Hickory, NC (city) Catawba County	33.60
Chico, CA (city) Butte County	32.00
Atwater, CA (city) Merced County	31.74
Maplewood, MN (city) Ramsey County	29.16
West Sacramento, CA (city) Yolo County	25.72
Lansing, MI (city) Ingham County	20.11
Florin, CA (cdp) Sacramento County	19.29
Westminster, CO (city) Adams County	18.59
Sacramento, CA (city) Sacramento County	17.91
Brooklyn Park, MN (city) Hennepin County	17.74
Warren, MI (city) Macomb County	17.23
Detroit, MI (city) Wayne County	17.19
Madison, WI (city) Dane County	15.63
Woodbury, MN (city) Washington County	14.82
Visalia, CA (city) Tulare County	10.66
Stockton, CA (city) San Joaquin County	10.17
Spokane, WA (city) Spokane County	9.39
Rochester, MN (city) Olmsted County	8.32
Arden-Arcade, CA (cdp) Sacramento County	7.36
Providence, RI (city) Providence County	6.29
Modesto, CA (city) Stanislaus County	3.62
Charlotte, NC (city) Mecklenburg County	3.24
Portland, OR (city) Multnomah County	2.76
Santa Ana, CA (city) Orange County	1.77
San Diego, CA (city) San Diego County	0.66

Notes: Please refer to the User's Guide for an explanation of data; ranking tables include all places with Asian and/or NHPI populations above SF4 population thresholds; (1) tables reflect only those areas that meet SF4 population thresholds, therefore there may be less than 50 states, 75 counties or 75 places listed

Population

Hmong

All States, Top 75 Counties, and Top 75 Places Sorted by Percent of Total Population[1]

State	Percent
Minnesota	0.88
Wisconsin	0.58
California	0.20
Rhode Island	0.09
Alaska	0.08
North Carolina	0.08
Colorado	0.07
Michigan	0.06
United States	0.06
Oregon	0.04
Kansas	0.03
Washington	0.03
Massachusetts	0.02
South Carolina	0.02
Georgia	0.01
Oklahoma	0.01
Pennsylvania	0.01

County	Percent
Ramsey County, MN	5.21
Yuba County, CA	4.48
Marathon County, WI	3.26
Merced County, CA	3.13
Fresno County, CA	3.01
Burke County, NC	2.25
Sheboygan County, WI	2.21
Glenn County, CA	2.12
La Crosse County, WI	1.81
Eau Claire County, WI	1.49
Outagamie County, WI	1.45
Dunn County, WI	1.42
Sacramento County, CA	1.42
Butte County, CA	1.39
Portage County, WI	1.29
Catawba County, NC	1.27
Hennepin County, MN	1.19
Manitowoc County, WI	1.13
Brown County, WI	1.07
Calumet County, WI	1.07
San Joaquin County, CA	1.06
Winnebago County, WI	0.95
Milwaukee County, WI	0.80
Wood County, WI	0.78
Chippewa County, WI	0.65
Adams County, CO	0.59
Stanly County, NC	0.55
Dane County, WI	0.54
Barrow County, GA	0.50
Wyandotte County, KS	0.49
Yolo County, CA	0.39
Washington County, MN	0.38
Olmsted County, MN	0.32
Spartanburg County, SC	0.30
Tulare County, CA	0.30
Fond du Lac County, WI	0.27
Stanislaus County, CA	0.22
Ingham County, MI	0.21
Anchorage Borough, AK	0.20
Anoka County, MN	0.19
Multnomah County, OR	0.16
Macomb County, MI	0.14
Providence County, RI	0.13
Spokane County, WA	0.13
Lancaster County, PA	0.10
Solano County, CA	0.10
Oakland County, MI	0.09
Santa Barbara County, CA	0.09
Wayne County, MI	0.09
Worcester County, MA	0.09
Jefferson County, CO	0.08
Mecklenburg County, NC	0.08
King County, WA	0.05
San Diego County, CA	0.05
Orange County, CA	0.04
Riverside County, CA	0.03
Los Angeles County, CA	<0.01

Place	Percent
Glen Alpine, NC (town) Burke County	17.94
Linda, CA (cdp) Yuba County	15.14
Thermalito, CA (cdp) Butte County	10.37
Willows, CA (city) Glenn County	9.05
Wausau, WI (city) Marathon County	8.94
St. Paul, MN (city) Ramsey County	8.87
South Oroville, CA (cdp) Butte County	7.98
Parkway-S. Sacramento, CA (cdp) Sacramento County	7.54
Merced, CA (city) Merced County	6.61
Brooklyn Center, MN (city) Hennepin County	5.00
Fresno, CA (city) Fresno County	4.76
Sheboygan, WI (city) Sheboygan County	4.70
Connelly Springs, NC (town) Burke County	4.27
Florin, CA (cdp) Sacramento County	3.85
Oroville, CA (city) Butte County	3.72
Appleton, WI (city) Outagamie County	3.32
Stevens Point, WI (city) Portage County	3.09
Sacramento, CA (city) Sacramento County	2.97
Wisconsin Rapids, WI (city) Wood County	2.83
Minneapolis, MN (city) Hennepin County	2.68
Valdese, NC (town) Burke County	2.66
Clovis, CA (city) Fresno County	2.64
La Crosse, WI (city) La Crosse County	2.60
Manitowoc, WI (city) Manitowoc County	2.41
Eau Claire, WI (city) Eau Claire County	2.35
Stockton, CA (city) San Joaquin County	2.04
Green Bay, WI (city) Brown County	1.98
West Sacramento, CA (city) Yolo County	1.83
Oshkosh, WI (city) Winnebago County	1.75
Atwater, CA (city) Merced County	1.72
Brooklyn Park, MN (city) Hennepin County	1.63
Fitchburg, MA (city) Worcester County	1.55
Hickory, NC (city) Catawba County	1.45
Chico, CA (city) Butte County	1.23
Milwaukee, WI (city) Milwaukee County	1.21
Maplewood, MN (city) Ramsey County	1.13
Pontiac, MI (city) Oakland County	1.09
Westminster, CO (city) Adams County	1.00
Madison, WI (city) Dane County	0.88
Woodbury, MN (city) Washington County	0.76
Visalia, CA (city) Tulare County	0.59
Lansing, MI (city) Ingham County	0.54
Warren, MI (city) Macomb County	0.54
Kansas City, KS (city) Wyandotte County	0.53
Fond du Lac, WI (city) Fond du Lac County	0.49
Rochester, MN (city) Olmsted County	0.47
Providence, RI (city) Providence County	0.39
Arden-Arcade, CA (cdp) Sacramento County	0.37
Modesto, CA (city) Stanislaus County	0.21
Spokane, WA (city) Spokane County	0.21
Portland, OR (city) Multnomah County	0.18
Detroit, MI (city) Wayne County	0.17
Santa Ana, CA (city) Orange County	0.16
Charlotte, NC (city) Mecklenburg County	0.10
San Diego, CA (city) San Diego County	0.09

Notes: Please refer to the User's Guide for an explanation of data; ranking tables include all places with Asian and/or NHPI populations above SF4 population thresholds; (1) tables reflect only those areas that meet SF4 population thresholds, therefore there may be less than 50 states, 75 counties or 75 places listed

Population

Indonesian

All States, Top 75 Counties, and Top 75 Places Sorted by Number[1]

State	Number
United States	37,167
California	16,388
New York	2,433
Texas	1,771
Washington	1,242
Maryland	1,108
Virginia	1,095
Ohio	1,061
New Jersey	1,020
Illinois	956
Florida	894
Colorado	770
Massachusetts	710
Michigan	652
Oregon	641
Arizona	573
Georgia	550
Pennsylvania	536
Wisconsin	406

County	Number
Los Angeles County, CA	5,626
San Bernardino County, CA	3,301
Orange County, CA	1,908
Queens County, NY	1,243
Montgomery County, MD	928
San Francisco County, CA	873
King County, WA	830
San Mateo County, CA	756
Harris County, TX	690
Santa Clara County, CA	687
Alameda County, CA	643
Fairfax County, VA	595
Franklin County, OH	530
Cook County, IL	494
San Diego County, CA	490
Middlesex County, NJ	488
Contra Costa County, CA	473
Maricopa County, AZ	412

Place	Number
New York, NY (city)	1,816
Los Angeles, CA (city) Los Angeles County	1,790
San Francisco, CA (city) San Francisco County	873
Loma Linda, CA (city) San Bernardino County	522
Houston, TX (city) Harris County	517
Columbus, OH (city) Franklin County	514
San Bernardino, CA (city) San Bernardino County	449
Seattle, WA (city) King County	378

Notes: Please refer to the User's Guide for an explanation of data; ranking tables include all places with Asian and/or NHPI populations above SF4 population thresholds; (1) tables reflect only those areas that meet SF4 population thresholds, therefore there may be less than 50 states, 75 counties or 75 places listed

Population

Indonesian

All States, Top 75 Counties, and Top 75 Places Sorted by Percent of Asian Population[1]

State	Percent
Colorado	0.83
Ohio	0.80
Oregon	0.65
Arizona	0.63
Maryland	0.53
Wisconsin	0.49
California	0.44
Virginia	0.43
Washington	0.39
Michigan	0.37
United States	0.37
Florida	0.34
Georgia	0.32
Texas	0.32
Massachusetts	0.30
Pennsylvania	0.25
Illinois	0.23
New York	0.23
New Jersey	0.21

County	Percent
San Bernardino County, CA	4.17
Franklin County, OH	1.61
Montgomery County, MD	0.95
Maricopa County, AZ	0.62
San Mateo County, CA	0.53
Los Angeles County, CA	0.50
Orange County, CA	0.49
Fairfax County, VA	0.48
Middlesex County, NJ	0.47
Contra Costa County, CA	0.46
King County, WA	0.44
Harris County, TX	0.40
San Francisco County, CA	0.36
Queens County, NY	0.32
Alameda County, CA	0.22
San Diego County, CA	0.20
Cook County, IL	0.19
Santa Clara County, CA	0.16

Place	Percent
Loma Linda, CA (city) San Bernardino County	12.00
San Bernardino, CA (city) San Bernardino County	5.99
Columbus, OH (city) Franklin County	2.08
Seattle, WA (city) King County	0.51
Houston, TX (city) Harris County	0.50
Los Angeles, CA (city) Los Angeles County	0.49
San Francisco, CA (city) San Francisco County	0.36
New York, NY (city)	0.23

Notes: Please refer to the User's Guide for an explanation of data; ranking tables include all places with Asian and/or NHPI populations above SF4 population thresholds; (1) tables reflect only those areas that meet SF4 population thresholds, therefore there may be less than 50 states, 75 counties or 75 places listed

Population

Indonesian

All States, Top 75 Counties, and Top 75 Places Sorted by Percent of Total Population[1]

State	Percent
California	0.05
Colorado	0.02
Maryland	0.02
Oregon	0.02
Virginia	0.02
Washington	0.02
Arizona	0.01
Florida	0.01
Georgia	0.01
Illinois	0.01
Massachusetts	0.01
Michigan	0.01
New Jersey	0.01
New York	0.01
Ohio	0.01
Texas	0.01
United States	0.01
Wisconsin	0.01
Pennsylvania	<0.01

County	Percent
San Bernardino County, CA	0.19
Montgomery County, MD	0.11
San Francisco County, CA	0.11
San Mateo County, CA	0.11
Middlesex County, NJ	0.07
Orange County, CA	0.07
Fairfax County, VA	0.06
Los Angeles County, CA	0.06
Queens County, NY	0.06
Contra Costa County, CA	0.05
Franklin County, OH	0.05
King County, WA	0.05
Alameda County, CA	0.04
Santa Clara County, CA	0.04
Harris County, TX	0.02
San Diego County, CA	0.02
Cook County, IL	0.01
Maricopa County, AZ	0.01

Place	Percent
Loma Linda, CA (city) San Bernardino County	2.81
San Bernardino, CA (city) San Bernardino County	0.24
San Francisco, CA (city) San Francisco County	0.11
Columbus, OH (city) Franklin County	0.07
Seattle, WA (city) King County	0.07
Los Angeles, CA (city) Los Angeles County	0.05
Houston, TX (city) Harris County	0.03
New York, NY (city)	0.02

Notes: Please refer to the User's Guide for an explanation of data; ranking tables include all places with Asian and/or NHPI populations above SF4 population thresholds; (1) tables reflect only those areas that meet SF4 population thresholds, therefore there may be less than 50 states, 75 counties or 75 places listed

Population

Japanese

All States, Top 75 Counties, and Top 75 Places Sorted by Number[1]

State	Number
United States	795,051
California	289,155
Hawaii	200,364
New York	37,594
Washington	37,296
Illinois	20,835
Texas	16,114
New Jersey	13,780
Colorado	11,894
Oregon	11,652
Florida	11,346
Massachusetts	10,958
Michigan	10,646
Ohio	10,291
Virginia	8,854
Nevada	8,395
Georgia	7,511
Arizona	7,446
Pennsylvania	7,186
Maryland	6,921
North Carolina	6,037
Utah	5,980
Indiana	4,812
Connecticut	4,552
Minnesota	4,183
Tennessee	3,868
Missouri	3,425
Kentucky	3,177
Wisconsin	2,986
Oklahoma	2,790
Idaho	2,651
South Carolina	2,282
New Mexico	2,065
Alabama	1,892
Kansas	1,833
Alaska	1,425
Louisiana	1,425
Nebraska	1,383
Iowa	1,285
Arkansas	1,094
District of Columbia	1,037
New Hampshire	936
West Virginia	879
Montana	850
Rhode Island	785
Delaware	605
Maine	592
Mississippi	538
Wyoming	523
South Dakota	412
Vermont	376

County	Number
Honolulu County, HI	159,611
Los Angeles County, CA	112,548
Orange County, CA	29,970
Santa Clara County, CA	26,980
King County, WA	22,416
Hawaii County, HI	20,628
San Diego County, CA	18,760
Cook County, IL	14,263
New York County, NY	14,137
Maui County, HI	12,519
Alameda County, CA	12,424
Sacramento County, CA	12,307
San Francisco County, CA	10,818
San Mateo County, CA	9,467
Contra Costa County, CA	8,295
Kauai County, HI	7,591
Westchester County, NY	7,502
Bergen County, NJ	6,997
Clark County, NV	6,694
Fresno County, CA	5,719
Queens County, NY	5,283
Ventura County, CA	5,214
Maricopa County, AZ	4,875
Riverside County, CA	4,447
San Bernardino County, CA	4,313
Oakland County, MI	4,282
Middlesex County, MA	3,876
Harris County, TX	3,679
San Joaquin County, CA	3,565
Multnomah County, OR	3,551
Pierce County, WA	3,521
Monterey County, CA	3,332
Franklin County, OH	3,227
Montgomery County, MD	3,159
Salt Lake County, UT	3,126
Fairfax County, VA	2,907
Washington County, OR	2,695
Fairfield County, CT	2,641
Snohomish County, WA	2,454
Santa Barbara County, CA	2,301
Suffolk County, MA	2,269
Dallas County, TX	2,224
Kings County, NY	2,176
Norfolk County, MA	2,080
Solano County, CA	1,993
Denver County, CO	1,974
Jefferson County, CO	1,897
Placer County, CA	1,815
Nassau County, NY	1,787
Santa Cruz County, CA	1,749
Arapahoe County, CO	1,729
Bexar County, TX	1,715
Washtenaw County, MI	1,709
Hennepin County, MN	1,683
Spokane County, WA	1,668
Marin County, CA	1,613
Sonoma County, CA	1,559
Pima County, AZ	1,494
Lake County, IL	1,488
Yolo County, CA	1,484
El Paso County, CO	1,467
DuPage County, IL	1,462
Miami-Dade County, FL	1,404
Boulder County, CO	1,325
Washoe County, NV	1,284
Clark County, WA	1,282
Lane County, OR	1,281
Cuyahoga County, OH	1,266
Allegheny County, PA	1,217
Travis County, TX	1,215
St. Louis County, MO	1,211
Orange County, FL	1,200
Kitsap County, WA	1,195
Arlington County, VA	1,136
Bernalillo County, NM	1,119

Place	Number
Honolulu, HI (cdp) Honolulu County	85,585
Los Angeles, CA (city) Los Angeles County	36,755
New York, NY (city)	22,302
Torrance, CA (city) Los Angeles County	13,508
San Jose, CA (city) Santa Clara County	11,199
Hilo, HI (cdp) Hawaii County	11,092
San Francisco, CA (city) San Francisco County	10,818
San Diego, CA (city) San Diego County	10,195
Pearl City, HI (cdp) Honolulu County	9,453
Seattle, WA (city) King County	9,321
Kaneohe, HI (cdp) Honolulu County	8,412
Waimalu, HI (cdp) Honolulu County	7,933
Mililani Town, HI (cdp) Honolulu County	7,043
Sacramento, CA (city) Sacramento County	6,716
Gardena, CA (city) Los Angeles County	6,685
Chicago, IL (city) Cook County	6,043
Irvine, CA (city) Orange County	5,135
Monterey Park, CA (city) Los Angeles County	4,813
Kailua, HI (cdp) Honolulu County	4,324
Long Beach, CA (city) Los Angeles County	3,586
Sunnyvale, CA (city) Santa Clara County	3,445
Kahului, HI (cdp) Maui County	3,441
Waipahu, HI (cdp) Honolulu County	3,342
Wahiawa, HI (cdp) Honolulu County	3,240
Rancho Palos Verdes, CA (city) Los Angeles County	3,056
Portland, OR (city) Multnomah County	3,054
Bellevue, WA (city) King County	2,986
Waipio, HI (cdp) Honolulu County	2,873
Huntington Beach, CA (city) Orange County	2,857
Aiea, HI (cdp) Honolulu County	2,843
Fresno, CA (city) Fresno County	2,661
Wailuku, HI (cdp) Maui County	2,657
Halawa, HI (cdp) Honolulu County	2,498
Las Vegas, NV (city) Clark County	2,453
Cupertino, CA (city) Santa Clara County	2,417
Houston, TX (city) Harris County	2,407
Pasadena, CA (city) Los Angeles County	2,247
Boston, MA (city) Suffolk County	2,235
Anaheim, CA (city) Orange County	2,203
Berkeley, CA (city) Alameda County	2,164
Oakland, CA (city) Alameda County	2,102
Chula Vista, CA (city) San Diego County	2,022
San Mateo, CA (city) San Mateo County	2,014
Fort Lee, NJ (borough) Bergen County	2,008
Cerritos, CA (city) Los Angeles County	2,007
Redondo Beach, CA (city) Los Angeles County	1,995
Denver, CO (city) Denver County	1,974
Greenburgh, NY (town) Westchester County	1,957
Columbus, OH (city) Franklin County	1,845
Santa Monica, CA (city) Los Angeles County	1,834
Montebello, CA (city) Los Angeles County	1,790
Ahuimanu, HI (cdp) Honolulu County	1,773
Glendale, CA (city) Los Angeles County	1,682
Mountain View, CA (city) Santa Clara County	1,668
Stockton, CA (city) San Joaquin County	1,617
Lihue, HI (cdp) Kauai County	1,613
Phoenix, AZ (city) Maricopa County	1,582
Fremont, CA (city) Alameda County	1,554
Costa Mesa, CA (city) Orange County	1,509
Alhambra, CA (city) Los Angeles County	1,502
Foster City, CA (city) San Mateo County	1,496
Santa Clara, CA (city) Santa Clara County	1,447
Fountain Valley, CA (city) Orange County	1,416
Paradise, NV (cdp) Clark County	1,408
Greenwich, CT (town) Fairfield County	1,383
San Antonio, TX (city) Bexar County	1,383
Culver City, CA (city) Los Angeles County	1,374
Hacienda Heights, CA (cdp) Los Angeles County	1,330
Brookline, MA (town) Norfolk County	1,325
Ann Arbor, MI (city) Washtenaw County	1,273
West Bloomfield, MI (township) Oakland County	1,272
Hayward, CA (city) Alameda County	1,271
Heeia, HI (cdp) Honolulu County	1,268
El Cerrito, CA (city) Contra Costa County	1,232
Eastchester, NY (town) Westchester County	1,210

Notes: Please refer to the User's Guide for an explanation of data; ranking tables include all places with Asian and/or NHPI populations above SF4 population thresholds; (1) tables reflect only those areas that meet SF4 population thresholds, therefore there may be less than 50 states, 75 counties or 75 places listed

Population

Japanese

All States, Top 75 Counties, and Top 75 Places Sorted by Percent of Asian Population[1]

State	Percent
Hawaii	39.76
Idaho	23.42
Montana	19.48
Wyoming	17.60
Utah	16.22
Colorado	12.75
Oregon	11.75
Washington	11.62
New Mexico	11.29
Kentucky	10.96
Nevada	9.42
West Virginia	9.31
South Dakota	8.71
Indiana	8.41
Arizona	8.16
California	7.85
United States	7.82
Ohio	7.79
Vermont	7.75
Maine	7.17
Tennessee	7.15
District of Columbia	7.02
Nebraska	6.55
Alabama	6.33
South Carolina	6.25
Oklahoma	6.13
Michigan	6.09
New Hampshire	6.07
Arkansas	5.73
Missouri	5.67
Alaska	5.59
Connecticut	5.53
North Carolina	5.42
Illinois	4.92
Massachusetts	4.60
Georgia	4.38
Florida	4.29
Kansas	4.09
Delaware	3.77
Iowa	3.67
New York	3.60
Wisconsin	3.59
Virginia	3.45
Pennsylvania	3.32
Maryland	3.30
Rhode Island	3.29
Mississippi	3.04
Minnesota	3.00
Texas	2.90
New Jersey	2.86
Louisiana	2.57

County	Percent
Malheur County, OR	79.23
Hawaii County, HI	51.95
Boone County, KY	45.27
Honolulu County, HI	39.46
Kauai County, HI	36.27
Weld County, CO	32.29
Maui County, HI	32.27
Fayette County, GA	30.47
Calhoun County, MI	30.28
Canyon County, ID	28.17
Whitman County, WA	27.35
Weber County, UT	27.00
Placer County, CA	25.01
Davis County, UT	22.73
Spokane County, WA	22.41
Lane County, OR	20.99
Santa Cruz County, CA	20.85
Utah County, UT	19.22
Onslow County, NC	18.98
Westchester County, NY	17.97
El Dorado County, CA	16.56
Jefferson County, CO	16.14
Larimer County, CO	15.93
Fayette County, KY	15.59
Humboldt County, CA	15.38
Ada County, ID	15.13
San Luis Obispo County, CA	14.80
Marin County, CA	14.72
Santa Barbara County, CA	14.72
Boulder County, CO	14.44
Monterey County, CA	13.76
Island County, WA	13.63
Salt Lake County, UT	13.47
Ventura County, CA	13.31
Denver County, CO	13.01
Benton County, OR	12.97
Marion County, OR	12.66
Clackamas County, OR	12.36
Clark County, WA	12.07
King County, WA	11.94
El Paso County, TX	11.46
Kitsap County, WA	11.42
Bernalillo County, NM	11.34
Whatcom County, WA	11.30
Orange County, NC	11.21
El Paso County, CO	11.15
Sonoma County, CA	11.08
Napa County, CA	10.54
Pierce County, WA	10.16
Los Angeles County, CA	9.92
Franklin County, OH	9.80
New York County, NY	9.79
Butte County, CA	9.55
Multnomah County, OR	9.53
Yolo County, CA	9.40
Clark County, NV	9.36
Fairfield County, CT	9.28
Arapahoe County, CO	9.25
Sacramento County, CA	9.12
Washington County, OR	9.00
Washoe County, NV	8.96
Fresno County, CA	8.95
Montgomery County, OH	8.90
Oakland County, MI	8.85
Pima County, AZ	8.84
Douglas County, NE	8.78
Washtenaw County, MI	8.54
Thurston County, WA	8.35
Adams County, CO	8.32
Riverside County, CA	8.14
Tompkins County, NY	8.14
Olmsted County, MN	8.05
Contra Costa County, CA	8.04
Orange County, CA	7.76
Bexar County, TX	7.59

Place	Percent
Hilo, HI (cdp) Hawaii County	72.27
Lawai, HI (cdp) Kauai County	69.68
Wailua, HI (cdp) Kauai County	68.29
Captain Cook, HI (cdp) Hawaii County	67.33
Paukaa, HI (cdp) Hawaii County	64.06
Maunawili, HI (cdp) Honolulu County	64.02
Kealakekua, HI (cdp) Hawaii County	63.77
Heeia, HI (cdp) Honolulu County	63.12
Pukalani, HI (cdp) Maui County	62.98
Kaneohe, HI (cdp) Honolulu County	60.95
Rye, NY (city) Westchester County	60.00
Ahuimanu, HI (cdp) Honolulu County	59.40
Honaunau-Napoopoo, HI (cdp) Hawaii County	59.15
Kalaoa, HI (cdp) Hawaii County	57.50
Lihue, HI (cdp) Kauai County	56.38
Waimea, HI (cdp) Kauai County	56.20
Honalo, HI (cdp) Hawaii County	56.02
Pearl City, HI (cdp) Honolulu County	55.99
Wailua Homesteads, HI (cdp) Kauai County	55.16
Kalaheo, HI (cdp) Kauai County	55.15
Waikapu, HI (cdp) Maui County	54.95
Aiea, HI (cdp) Honolulu County	54.94
Kailua, HI (cdp) Honolulu County	54.93
Eastchester, NY (town) Westchester County	53.42
Mililani Town, HI (cdp) Honolulu County	53.38
Wailuku, HI (cdp) Maui County	52.67
Harrison, NY (village) Westchester County	51.87
Papaikou, HI (cdp) Hawaii County	50.83
Waimalu, HI (cdp) Honolulu County	50.05
Waimea, HI (cdp) Hawaii County	48.72
Peachtree City, GA (city) Fayette County	47.82
Makawao, HI (cdp) Maui County	45.28
Wahiawa, HI (cdp) Honolulu County	45.04
Holualoa, HI (cdp) Hawaii County	44.94
Kurtistown, HI (cdp) Hawaii County	44.29
Waipio, HI (cdp) Honolulu County	43.90
Gardena, CA (city) Los Angeles County	43.25
Eastchester, NY (cdp) Westchester County	42.46
Greenwich, CT (town) Fairfield County	42.44
Honolulu, HI (cdp) Honolulu County	41.14
Kapaau, HI (cdp) Hawaii County	40.80
Hanapepe, HI (cdp) Kauai County	40.40
Rolling Hills Estates, CA (city) Los Angeles County	40.04
Battle Creek, MI (city) Calhoun County	39.57
Pepeekeo, HI (cdp) Hawaii County	38.34
Altadena, CA (cdp) Los Angeles County	35.67
Kapaa, HI (cdp) Kauai County	35.45
Scarsdale, NY (village) Westchester County	35.24
Waipio Acres, HI (cdp) Honolulu County	35.08
Halawa, HI (cdp) Honolulu County	34.55
Torrance, CA (city) Los Angeles County	34.25
Redondo Beach, CA (city) Los Angeles County	33.84
Rocklin, CA (city) Placer County	33.56
Pahoa, HI (cdp) Hawaii County	33.53
Dublin, OH (city) Franklin County	32.84
Haleiwa, HI (cdp) Honolulu County	32.62
Greenville, NY (cdp) Westchester County	32.61
Kahului, HI (cdp) Maui County	31.87
Waikoloa Village, HI (cdp) Hawaii County	31.83
Monterey, CA (city) Monterey County	31.26
Santa Monica, CA (city) Los Angeles County	30.64
Kailua, HI (cdp) Hawaii County	30.30
Manhattan Beach, CA (city) Los Angeles County	30.15
Honokaa, HI (cdp) Hawaii County	29.47
Rancho Palos Verdes, CA (city) Los Angeles County	29.46
Wainaku, HI (cdp) Hawaii County	29.42
Ewa Gentry, HI (cdp) Honolulu County	29.39
Seal Beach, CA (city) Orange County	29.24
Watsonville, CA (city) Santa Cruz County	29.01
Culver City, CA (city) Los Angeles County	29.00
Keaau, HI (cdp) Hawaii County	28.83
Palos Verdes Estates, CA (city) Los Angeles County	28.79
Novi, MI (city) Oakland County	28.76
Waianae, HI (cdp) Honolulu County	28.63
Pullman, WA (city) Whitman County	28.21

Notes: Please refer to the User's Guide for an explanation of data; ranking tables include all places with Asian and/or NHPI populations above SF4 population thresholds; (1) tables reflect only those areas that meet SF4 population thresholds, therefore there may be less than 50 states, 75 counties or 75 places listed

Population

Japanese

All States, Top 75 Counties, and Top 75 Places Sorted by Percent of Total Population[1]

State	Percent
Hawaii	16.54
California	0.85
Washington	0.63
Nevada	0.42
Oregon	0.34
Colorado	0.28
United States	0.28
Utah	0.27
Alaska	0.23
Idaho	0.20
New York	0.20
District of Columbia	0.18
Illinois	0.17
Massachusetts	0.17
New Jersey	0.16
Arizona	0.15
Connecticut	0.13
Maryland	0.13
Virginia	0.13
Michigan	0.11
New Mexico	0.11
Wyoming	0.11
Georgia	0.09
Minnesota	0.09
Montana	0.09
Ohio	0.09
Delaware	0.08
Indiana	0.08
Kentucky	0.08
Nebraska	0.08
New Hampshire	0.08
North Carolina	0.08
Oklahoma	0.08
Texas	0.08
Florida	0.07
Kansas	0.07
Rhode Island	0.07
Tennessee	0.07
Missouri	0.06
Pennsylvania	0.06
South Carolina	0.06
Vermont	0.06
Wisconsin	0.06
Maine	0.05
South Dakota	0.05
West Virginia	0.05
Alabama	0.04
Arkansas	0.04
Iowa	0.04
Louisiana	0.03
Mississippi	0.02

County	Percent
Honolulu County, HI	18.22
Hawaii County, HI	13.87
Kauai County, HI	12.98
Maui County, HI	9.77
Santa Clara County, CA	1.60
Whitman County, WA	1.50
San Francisco County, CA	1.39
San Mateo County, CA	1.34
Malheur County, OR	1.30
King County, WA	1.29
Los Angeles County, CA	1.18
Orange County, CA	1.05
Sacramento County, CA	1.01
New York County, NY	0.92
Yolo County, CA	0.88
Contra Costa County, CA	0.87
Alameda County, CA	0.86
Monterey County, CA	0.83
Westchester County, NY	0.81
Bergen County, NJ	0.79
Placer County, CA	0.73
Fresno County, CA	0.72
Fayette County, GA	0.69
Ventura County, CA	0.69
Santa Cruz County, CA	0.68
San Diego County, CA	0.67
Marin County, CA	0.65
San Joaquin County, CA	0.63
Washington County, OR	0.61
Arlington County, VA	0.60
Tompkins County, NY	0.60
Santa Barbara County, CA	0.58
Benton County, OR	0.55
Island County, WA	0.54
Multnomah County, OR	0.54
Boone County, KY	0.53
Washtenaw County, MI	0.53
Kitsap County, WA	0.52
Solano County, CA	0.51
Pierce County, WA	0.50
Clark County, NV	0.49
Sutter County, CA	0.46
Boulder County, CO	0.45
Orange County, NC	0.44
San Luis Obispo County, CA	0.41
Lane County, OR	0.40
Snohomish County, WA	0.40
Spokane County, WA	0.40
Thurston County, WA	0.38
Washoe County, NV	0.38
Clark County, WA	0.37
Denver County, CO	0.36
Jefferson County, CO	0.36
Montgomery County, MD	0.36
Oakland County, MI	0.36
Arapahoe County, CO	0.35
Fayette County, KY	0.35
Olmsted County, MN	0.35
Salt Lake County, UT	0.35
Anchorage Borough, AK	0.34
Sonoma County, CA	0.34
Champaign County, IL	0.33
Davis County, UT	0.33
Napa County, CA	0.33
Suffolk County, MA	0.33
Calhoun County, MI	0.32
El Dorado County, CA	0.32
Norfolk County, MA	0.32
Onslow County, NC	0.32
Weber County, UT	0.32
Butte County, CA	0.31
Clackamas County, OR	0.30
Fairfax County, VA	0.30
Fairfield County, CT	0.30
Franklin County, OH	0.30

Place	Percent
Aiea, HI (cdp) Honolulu County	31.52
Pearl City, HI (cdp) Honolulu County	30.67
Lihue, HI (cdp) Kauai County	27.63
Hilo, HI (cdp) Hawaii County	27.19
Waimalu, HI (cdp) Honolulu County	26.89
Paukaa, HI (cdp) Hawaii County	26.34
Heeia, HI (cdp) Honolulu County	25.80
Papaikou, HI (cdp) Hawaii County	25.58
Waimea, HI (cdp) Kauai County	25.06
Wailua, HI (cdp) Kauai County	24.76
Waipio, HI (cdp) Honolulu County	24.68
Mililani Town, HI (cdp) Honolulu County	24.66
Waikapu, HI (cdp) Maui County	24.64
Kaneohe, HI (cdp) Honolulu County	24.05
Kealakekua, HI (cdp) Hawaii County	23.95
Honolulu, HI (cdp) Honolulu County	23.03
Wailuku, HI (cdp) Maui County	21.39
Ahuimanu, HI (cdp) Honolulu County	21.27
Captain Cook, HI (cdp) Hawaii County	20.53
Pepeekeo, HI (cdp) Hawaii County	20.13
Wahiawa, HI (cdp) Honolulu County	20.06
Lawai, HI (cdp) Kauai County	19.37
Kurtistown, HI (cdp) Hawaii County	19.35
Maunawili, HI (cdp) Honolulu County	19.22
Hanapepe, HI (cdp) Kauai County	18.05
Halawa, HI (cdp) Honolulu County	17.90
Pahoa, HI (cdp) Hawaii County	17.71
Kalaheo, HI (cdp) Kauai County	17.28
Kahului, HI (cdp) Maui County	17.19
Keaau, HI (cdp) Hawaii County	16.06
Eleele, HI (cdp) Kauai County	15.44
Ewa Gentry, HI (cdp) Honolulu County	15.22
Wainaku, HI (cdp) Hawaii County	14.91
Pukalani, HI (cdp) Maui County	13.50
Honokaa, HI (cdp) Hawaii County	12.95
Waipio Acres, HI (cdp) Honolulu County	12.26
Kailua, HI (cdp) Honolulu County	11.82
Wailua Homesteads, HI (cdp) Kauai County	11.58
Gardena, CA (city) Los Angeles County	11.56
Koloa, HI (cdp) Kauai County	11.43
Kapaau, HI (cdp) Hawaii County	11.38
Village Park, HI (cdp) Honolulu County	11.30
Waialua, HI (cdp) Honolulu County	11.09
Kapaa, HI (cdp) Kauai County	11.07
Honalo, HI (cdp) Hawaii County	11.00
Pahala, HI (cdp) Hawaii County	10.92
Waipahu, HI (cdp) Honolulu County	10.09
Honaunau-Napoopoo, HI (cdp) Hawaii County	10.06
Torrance, CA (city) Los Angeles County	9.79
South San Gabriel, CA (cdp) Los Angeles County	9.52
Lahaina, HI (cdp) Maui County	9.28
Hanamaulu, HI (cdp) Kauai County	9.26
Waihee-Waiehu, HI (cdp) Maui County	9.04
Waimea, HI (cdp) Hawaii County	8.97
Haleiwa, HI (cdp) Honolulu County	8.18
Rolling Hills Estates, CA (city) Los Angeles County	8.12
Kalaoa, HI (cdp) Hawaii County	8.07
Monterey Park, CA (city) Los Angeles County	8.03
Puhi, HI (cdp) Kauai County	7.76
Kekaha, HI (cdp) Kauai County	7.69
Rancho Palos Verdes, CA (city) Los Angeles County	7.40
Makakilo City, HI (cdp) Honolulu County	7.38
Holualoa, HI (cdp) Hawaii County	7.06
Kaunakakai, HI (cdp) Maui County	7.03
Paia, HI (cdp) Maui County	6.88
Makawao, HI (cdp) Maui County	6.42
Greenville, NY (cdp) Westchester County	6.29
Kahuku, HI (cdp) Honolulu County	6.29
Fort Lee, NJ (borough) Bergen County	5.66
Ewa Beach, HI (cdp) Honolulu County	5.60
Waikoloa Village, HI (cdp) Hawaii County	5.41
El Cerrito, CA (city) Contra Costa County	5.32
West Carson, CA (cdp) Los Angeles County	5.29
Kailua, HI (cdp) Hawaii County	5.26
Foster City, CA (city) San Mateo County	5.19

Notes: Please refer to the User's Guide for an explanation of data; ranking tables include all places with Asian and/or NHPI populations above SF4 population thresholds; (1) tables reflect only those areas that meet SF4 population thresholds, therefore there may be less than 50 states, 75 counties or 75 places listed

Population

Korean

All States, Top 75 Counties, and Top 75 Places Sorted by Number[1]

State	Number
United States	1,072,682
California	343,742
New York	120,775
New Jersey	64,328
Illinois	52,079
Washington	46,494
Virginia	45,059
Texas	44,374
Maryland	39,113
Pennsylvania	32,880
Georgia	27,708
Hawaii	23,708
Michigan	21,014
Florida	19,077
Massachusetts	17,400
Colorado	15,293
Ohio	13,886
Minnesota	12,853
Oregon	12,815
North Carolina	12,403
Arizona	9,936
Nevada	7,582
Indiana	7,099
Tennessee	6,902
Wisconsin	6,846
Connecticut	6,726
Missouri	6,507
Iowa	4,882
Oklahoma	4,626
Alaska	4,554
Kansas	4,361
Kentucky	4,041
Alabama	4,024
Utah	3,582
South Carolina	3,546
Louisiana	2,735
Nebraska	2,229
New Hampshire	1,950
Rhode Island	1,923
Delaware	1,850
New Mexico	1,737
Arkansas	1,496
Mississippi	1,378
Idaho	1,273
District of Columbia	1,168
West Virginia	894
Montana	839
South Dakota	745
Maine	735
Vermont	680
Wyoming	470
North Dakota	365

County	Number
Los Angeles County, CA	185,440
Queens County, NY	62,255
Orange County, CA	57,487
Bergen County, NJ	36,102
Cook County, IL	35,589
Fairfax County, VA	27,684
Honolulu County, HI	21,709
Santa Clara County, CA	21,673
King County, WA	20,185
Montgomery County, MD	15,458
Alameda County, CA	14,530
New York County, NY	11,419
San Diego County, CA	11,378
Pierce County, WA	11,122
Dallas County, TX	9,340
Gwinnett County, GA	9,260
Montgomery County, PA	9,203
Nassau County, NY	9,085
Harris County, TX	8,114
Snohomish County, WA	7,428
San Bernardino County, CA	7,171
San Francisco County, CA	7,134
Middlesex County, MA	7,100
Kings County, NY	6,761
Philadelphia County, PA	6,529
Clark County, NV	6,527
Maricopa County, AZ	6,047
Howard County, MD	6,013
Riverside County, CA	5,736
Middlesex County, NJ	5,351
Baltimore County, MD	5,114
Oakland County, MI	4,826
Hennepin County, MN	4,729
Sacramento County, CA	4,674
Contra Costa County, CA	4,492
Arapahoe County, CO	4,486
San Mateo County, CA	4,358
Washington County, OR	4,298
Westchester County, NY	4,228
DuPage County, IL	4,218
Travis County, TX	4,154
Fulton County, GA	4,076
El Paso County, CO	3,936
Lake County, IL	3,910
Suffolk County, NY	3,909
Prince George's County, MD	3,691
Washtenaw County, MI	3,690
Anne Arundel County, MD	3,686
Bronx County, NY	3,462
Delaware County, PA	3,455
Anchorage Borough, AK	3,448
Franklin County, OH	3,334
DeKalb County, GA	3,300
Richmond County, NY	3,242
Hudson County, NJ	3,206
Tarrant County, TX	3,190
Cobb County, GA	2,997
Monterey County, CA	2,850
Collin County, TX	2,841
Essex County, NJ	2,791
Hillsborough County, FL	2,718
Morris County, NJ	2,682
Suffolk County, MA	2,590
Ventura County, CA	2,589
Multnomah County, OR	2,582
Bexar County, TX	2,578
Champaign County, IL	2,546
St. Louis County, MO	2,546
Monroe County, NY	2,505
Mecklenburg County, NC	2,443
Bell County, TX	2,368
Denton County, TX	2,261
Broward County, FL	2,260
Allegheny County, PA	2,257
Norfolk County, MA	2,249

Place	Number
Los Angeles, CA (city) Los Angeles County	91,291
New York, NY (city)	87,139
Honolulu, HI (cdp) Honolulu County	15,451
Chicago, IL (city) Cook County	12,576
Glendale, CA (city) Los Angeles County	12,475
San Jose, CA (city) Santa Clara County	9,378
Fullerton, CA (city) Orange County	8,988
Cerritos, CA (city) Los Angeles County	8,829
Torrance, CA (city) Los Angeles County	8,532
Irvine, CA (city) Orange County	7,984
San Francisco, CA (city) San Francisco County	7,134
San Diego, CA (city) San Diego County	6,804
Anaheim, CA (city) Orange County	6,640
Philadelphia, PA (city) Philadelphia County	6,529
Garden Grove, CA (city) Orange County	6,062
Fort Lee, NJ (borough) Bergen County	5,911
Palisades Park, NJ (borough) Bergen County	5,902
Diamond Bar, CA (city) Los Angeles County	5,597
Buena Park, CA (city) Orange County	5,324
Houston, TX (city) Harris County	5,190
Seattle, WA (city) King County	4,960
Federal Way, WA (city) King County	4,435
Fremont, CA (city) Alameda County	3,981
Gardena, CA (city) Los Angeles County	3,745
Rowland Heights, CA (cdp) Los Angeles County	3,725
Austin, TX (city) Travis County	3,632
Annandale, VA (cdp) Fairfax County	3,356
Dallas, TX (city) Dallas County	3,337
North Hempstead, NY (town) Nassau County	3,248
Downey, CA (city) Los Angeles County	3,179
Burke, VA (cdp) Fairfax County	3,114
Tacoma, WA (city) Pierce County	3,075
Colorado Springs, CO (city) El Paso County	3,005
Hempstead, NY (town) Nassau County	2,931
Ellicott City, MD (cdp) Howard County	2,868
Sunnyvale, CA (city) Santa Clara County	2,697
Cypress, CA (city) Orange County	2,573
Hacienda Heights, CA (cdp) Los Angeles County	2,571
Ann Arbor, MI (city) Washtenaw County	2,525
Columbus, OH (city) Franklin County	2,524
Skokie, IL (village) Cook County	2,524
Norwalk, CA (city) Los Angeles County	2,517
Aurora, CO (city) Arapahoe County	2,509
La Crescenta-Montrose, CA (cdp) Los Angeles County	2,501
Irving, TX (city) Dallas County	2,480
Oyster Bay, NY (town) Nassau County	2,472
Bellevue, WA (city) King County	2,431
Rancho Palos Verdes, CA (city) Los Angeles County	2,430
Boston, MA (city) Suffolk County	2,423
La Palma, CA (city) Orange County	2,401
Lakewood, WA (city) Pierce County	2,337
La Mirada, CA (city) Los Angeles County	2,314
Cupertino, CA (city) Santa Clara County	2,235
La Canada Flintridge, CA (city) Los Angeles County	2,230
Portland, OR (city) Multnomah County	2,194
Plano, TX (city) Collin County	2,139
Santa Clara, CA (city) Santa Clara County	2,065
Burbank, CA (city) Los Angeles County	1,980
Phoenix, AZ (city) Maricopa County	1,977
Charlotte, NC (city) Mecklenburg County	1,952
Arcadia, CA (city) Los Angeles County	1,933
Cambridge, MA (city) Middlesex County	1,931
San Antonio, TX (city) Bexar County	1,896
Walnut, CA (city) Los Angeles County	1,892
Riverside, CA (city) Riverside County	1,853
Schaumburg, IL (village) Cook County	1,775
Oakland, CA (city) Alameda County	1,766
Long Beach, CA (city) Los Angeles County	1,736
Madison, WI (city) Dane County	1,694
El Paso, TX (city) El Paso County	1,674
Huntington Beach, CA (city) Orange County	1,672
Minneapolis, MN (city) Hennepin County	1,623
Berkeley, CA (city) Alameda County	1,621
Centreville, VA (cdp) Fairfax County	1,621
Orange, CA (city) Orange County	1,614

Notes: Please refer to the User's Guide for an explanation of data; ranking tables include all places with Asian and/or NHPI populations above SF4 population thresholds; (1) tables reflect only those areas that meet SF4 population thresholds, therefore there may be less than 50 states, 75 counties or 75 places listed

Population

Korean

All States, Top 75 Counties, and Top 75 Places Sorted by Percent of Asian Population[1]

State	Percent
Montana	19.23
Maryland	18.65
Alaska	17.86
Virginia	17.58
Colorado	16.39
Georgia	16.16
Wyoming	15.81
South Dakota	15.75
Pennsylvania	15.18
Washington	14.49
Vermont	14.02
Iowa	13.94
Kentucky	13.94
Alabama	13.45
New Jersey	13.35
Oregon	12.93
Tennessee	12.75
New Hampshire	12.64
Indiana	12.41
Illinois	12.30
Michigan	12.02
New York	11.56
Delaware	11.52
Idaho	11.24
North Carolina	11.14
North Dakota	10.92
Arizona	10.89
Missouri	10.77
Nebraska	10.55
United States	10.55
Ohio	10.51
Oklahoma	10.16
Kansas	9.74
South Carolina	9.71
Utah	9.71
New Mexico	9.50
West Virginia	9.47
California	9.33
Minnesota	9.23
Maine	8.90
Nevada	8.51
Wisconsin	8.24
Connecticut	8.17
Rhode Island	8.07
Texas	7.98
District of Columbia	7.91
Arkansas	7.84
Mississippi	7.78
Massachusetts	7.30
Florida	7.22
Louisiana	4.93
Hawaii	4.70

County	Percent
Geary County, KS	49.29
Montgomery County, TN	45.38
Pulaski County, MO	42.20
Hardin County, KY	39.64
Liberty County, GA	39.39
Cochise County, AZ	39.13
Bell County, TX	38.73
Bergen County, NJ	38.36
Coryell County, TX	35.87
Comanche County, OK	34.40
Cumberland County, NC	34.28
Dale County, AL	34.00
Wicomico County, MD	33.79
Anne Arundel County, MD	32.39
Howard County, MD	32.13
Pierce County, WA	32.08
Montgomery County, PA	31.27
Vernon Parish, LA	30.84
Jefferson County, NY	30.57
York County, VA	30.07
El Paso County, CO	29.92
Richmond County, GA	28.78
Fairbanks North Star Borough, AK	27.39
Monroe County, IN	27.35
Newport News Independent City, VA	26.61
Muscogee County, GA	26.15
El Paso County, TX	24.63
Montgomery County, VA	24.62
Anchorage Borough, AK	24.17
Harford County, MD	24.01
Arapahoe County, CO	24.00
St. Louis County, MN	24.00
Chesterfield County, VA	23.83
Berrien County, MI	23.40
Thurston County, WA	22.86
Gwinnett County, GA	22.57
Richland County, SC	22.47
Fairfax County, VA	22.40
Benton County, OR	21.95
Champaign County, IL	21.94
Fairfax Independent City, VA	21.70
Baltimore County, MD	21.56
Riley County, KS	21.29
Story County, IA	21.02
Snohomish County, WA	20.90
Clackamas County, OR	20.83
Madison County, AL	20.57
Sarpy County, NE	20.54
Saratoga County, NY	20.47
Lane County, OR	20.07
Cumberland County, PA	20.06
York County, PA	19.84
Greene County, OH	19.77
Saginaw County, MI	19.35
Centre County, PA	19.22
Kent County, RI	19.11
Delaware County, PA	18.89
Washtenaw County, MI	18.43
Kent County, MI	18.02
Alexandria Independent City, VA	17.82
St. Clair County, IL	17.81
Burlington County, NJ	17.65
Imperial County, CA	17.49
Ingham County, MI	17.49
Baltimore Independent City, MD	17.26
Fulton County, GA	17.15
Johnson County, IA	17.04
Orange County, NC	16.87
Clarke County, GA	16.86
Tompkins County, NY	16.83
Larimer County, CO	16.54
Kalamazoo County, MI	16.43
Los Angeles County, CA	16.35
Greene County, MO	16.27
Okaloosa County, FL	16.25

Place	Percent
Palisades Park, NJ (borough) Bergen County	84.29
Ridgefield, NJ (borough) Bergen County	75.51
Browns Mills, NJ (cdp) Burlington County	73.22
Norwood, NJ (borough) Bergen County	73.07
La Crescenta-Montrose, CA (cdp) Los Angeles County	70.97
Old Tappan, NJ (borough) Bergen County	62.73
Leonia, NJ (borough) Bergen County	62.35
Broomall, PA (cdp) Delaware County	59.97
South Gate, MD (cdp) Anne Arundel County	59.47
Hawaiian Gardens, CA (city) Los Angeles County	58.44
Pemberton, NJ (township) Burlington County	58.17
Closter, NJ (borough) Bergen County	57.61
Harrington Park, NJ (borough) Bergen County	57.18
La Canada Flintridge, CA (city) Los Angeles County	56.02
Cliffside Park, NJ (borough) Bergen County	55.92
Upper Dublin, PA (township) Montgomery County	54.82
Fort Lee, NJ (borough) Bergen County	53.72
University Place, WA (city) Pierce County	53.53
Alpine, NJ (borough) Bergen County	53.32
Lake Success, NY (village) Nassau County	53.17
Northbrook, IL (village) Cook County	53.01
Demarest, NJ (borough) Bergen County	52.70
Marple, PA (township) Delaware County	52.57
Edgewater, NJ (borough) Bergen County	50.88
Abington, PA (township) Montgomery County	50.56
Parkland, WA (cdp) Pierce County	50.41
Cresskill, NJ (borough) Bergen County	50.23
Jericho, NY (cdp) Nassau County	48.35
Carney, MD (cdp) Baltimore County	48.33
Mukilteo, WA (city) Snohomish County	48.09
Severn, MD (cdp) Anne Arundel County	47.41
Whitpain, PA (township) Montgomery County	46.99
Cheltenham, PA (township) Montgomery County	46.80
Spanaway, WA (cdp) Pierce County	45.73
Tenafly, NJ (borough) Bergen County	45.57
Clarksville, TN (city) Montgomery County	45.50
Lakewood, WA (city) Pierce County	45.11
Horsham, PA (township) Montgomery County	44.52
Fullerton, CA (city) Orange County	44.39
Englewood Cliffs, NJ (borough) Bergen County	43.78
Federal Way, WA (city) King County	43.64
Rutherford, NJ (borough) Bergen County	43.48
Ellicott City, MD (cdp) Howard County	43.06
Mantua, VA (cdp) Fairfax County	42.91
Hinesville, GA (city) Liberty County	42.33
Killeen, TX (city) Bell County	41.26
Ridgefield Park, NJ (village) Bergen County	40.85
Downey, CA (city) Los Angeles County	40.68
Little Ferry, NJ (borough) Bergen County	40.00
Plymouth, PA (township) Montgomery County	39.90
Montgomery, PA (township) Montgomery County	39.57
Glendale, CA (city) Los Angeles County	39.05
Sierra Vista, AZ (city) Cochise County	38.61
Cockeysville, MD (cdp) Baltimore County	38.37
Fairland, MD (cdp) Montgomery County	37.92
Glenview, IL (village) Cook County	37.92
Glen Cove, NY (city) Nassau County	37.80
Burke, VA (cdp) Fairfax County	37.67
Hedwig Village, TX (city) Harris County	37.42
Mill Creek, WA (city) Snohomish County	37.41
La Palma, CA (city) Orange County	36.52
La Habra, CA (city) Orange County	35.86
Beverly Hills, CA (city) Los Angeles County	35.49
Picnic Pt.-N. Lynnwood, WA (cdp) Snohomish County	35.09
Perry Hall, MD (cdp) Baltimore County	35.07
Wilmette, IL (village) Cook County	35.05
River Edge, NJ (borough) Bergen County	35.04
West Springfield, VA (cdp) Fairfax County	34.82
Colesville, MD (cdp) Montgomery County	34.10
Fairbanks, AK (city) Fairbanks North Star Borough	34.08
Lawton, OK (city) Comanche County	33.52
La Mirada, CA (city) Los Angeles County	33.21
Annandale, VA (cdp) Fairfax County	32.13
Paramus, NJ (borough) Bergen County	31.50
Buena Park, CA (city) Orange County	31.48

Notes: Please refer to the User's Guide for an explanation of data; ranking tables include all places with Asian and/or NHPI populations above SF4 population thresholds; (1) tables reflect only those areas that meet SF4 population thresholds, therefore there may be less than 50 states, 75 counties or 75 places listed

Population

Korean

All States, Top 75 Counties, and Top 75 Places Sorted by Percent of Total Population[1]

State	Percent
Hawaii	1.96
California	1.01
Washington	0.79
New Jersey	0.76
Maryland	0.74
Alaska	0.73
New York	0.64
Virginia	0.64
Illinois	0.42
Nevada	0.38
United States	0.38
Oregon	0.37
Colorado	0.36
Georgia	0.34
Massachusetts	0.27
Pennsylvania	0.27
Minnesota	0.26
Delaware	0.24
Michigan	0.21
Texas	0.21
Connecticut	0.20
District of Columbia	0.20
Arizona	0.19
Rhode Island	0.18
Iowa	0.17
Kansas	0.16
New Hampshire	0.16
Utah	0.16
North Carolina	0.15
Nebraska	0.13
Oklahoma	0.13
Wisconsin	0.13
Florida	0.12
Indiana	0.12
Missouri	0.12
Ohio	0.12
Tennessee	0.12
Vermont	0.11
Idaho	0.10
Kentucky	0.10
New Mexico	0.10
South Dakota	0.10
Wyoming	0.10
Alabama	0.09
Montana	0.09
South Carolina	0.09
Arkansas	0.06
Louisiana	0.06
Maine	0.06
North Dakota	0.06
Mississippi	0.05
West Virginia	0.05

County	Percent
Bergen County, NJ	4.08
Fairfax County, VA	2.85
Queens County, NY	2.79
Fairfax Independent City, VA	2.55
Honolulu County, HI	2.48
Howard County, MD	2.43
Orange County, CA	2.02
Los Angeles County, CA	1.95
Montgomery County, MD	1.77
Pierce County, WA	1.59
Gwinnett County, GA	1.57
Geary County, KS	1.50
Champaign County, IL	1.42
Anchorage Borough, AK	1.32
Santa Clara County, CA	1.29
Tompkins County, NY	1.25
Montgomery County, PA	1.23
Snohomish County, WA	1.23
King County, WA	1.16
Washtenaw County, MI	1.14
Thurston County, WA	1.04
Alameda County, CA	1.01
Bell County, TX	1.00
York County, VA	0.98
Alexandria Independent City, VA	0.97
Washington County, OR	0.97
Story County, IA	0.95
Benton County, OR	0.94
Pulaski County, MO	0.94
Arapahoe County, CO	0.92
Montgomery County, VA	0.92
San Francisco County, CA	0.92
Monroe County, IN	0.89
Montgomery County, TN	0.82
Hardin County, KY	0.80
Centre County, PA	0.76
El Paso County, CO	0.76
Anne Arundel County, MD	0.75
Maui County, HI	0.74
New York County, NY	0.74
Arlington County, VA	0.73
Comanche County, OK	0.73
Richmond County, NY	0.73
Middlesex County, NJ	0.71
Monterey County, CA	0.71
Wicomico County, MD	0.70
Cumberland County, NC	0.69
Tippecanoe County, IN	0.69
Baltimore County, MD	0.68
Johnson County, IA	0.68
Nassau County, NY	0.68
Riley County, KS	0.67
Rockland County, NY	0.67
Cook County, IL	0.66
Coryell County, TX	0.66
Fairbanks North Star Borough, AK	0.66
Orange County, NC	0.66
Vernon Parish, LA	0.66
Yolo County, CA	0.66
Cochise County, AZ	0.65
Loudoun County, VA	0.64
Delaware County, PA	0.63
Ingham County, MI	0.63
Newport News Independent City, VA	0.62
San Mateo County, CA	0.62
Lake County, IL	0.61
Liberty County, GA	0.61
Brazos County, TX	0.60
Prince William County, VA	0.60
Hawaii County, HI	0.59
Chesterfield County, VA	0.58
Collin County, TX	0.58
Morris County, NJ	0.57
Mercer County, NJ	0.56
Clarke County, GA	0.54

Place	Percent
Palisades Park, NJ (borough) Bergen County	34.57
Cerritos, CA (city) Los Angeles County	17.14
Fort Lee, NJ (borough) Bergen County	16.67
Leonia, NJ (borough) Bergen County	16.37
La Palma, CA (city) Orange County	15.87
La Crescenta-Montrose, CA (cdp) Los Angeles County	13.59
Norwood, NJ (borough) Bergen County	13.35
Englewood Cliffs, NJ (borough) Bergen County	12.70
Ridgefield, NJ (borough) Bergen County	12.38
Closter, NJ (borough) Bergen County	11.83
Edgewater, NJ (borough) Bergen County	11.74
La Canada Flintridge, CA (city) Los Angeles County	10.94
Demarest, NJ (borough) Bergen County	10.67
Alpine, NJ (borough) Bergen County	10.31
Old Tappan, NJ (borough) Bergen County	10.07
Diamond Bar, CA (city) Los Angeles County	9.93
Cresskill, NJ (borough) Bergen County	9.85
Lake Success, NY (village) Nassau County	8.69
Tenafly, NJ (borough) Bergen County	8.54
Harrington Park, NJ (borough) Bergen County	8.23
Rowland Heights, CA (cdp) Los Angeles County	7.71
Merrifield, VA (cdp) Fairfax County	7.66
Fullerton, CA (city) Orange County	7.12
Little Ferry, NJ (borough) Bergen County	6.83
Buena Park, CA (city) Orange County	6.79
Gardena, CA (city) Los Angeles County	6.48
Cliffside Park, NJ (borough) Bergen County	6.44
Glendale, CA (city) Los Angeles County	6.40
Walnut, CA (city) Los Angeles County	6.31
Torrance, CA (city) Los Angeles County	6.19
Annandale, VA (cdp) Fairfax County	6.10
Rancho Palos Verdes, CA (city) Los Angeles County	5.88
Fairland, MD (cdp) Montgomery County	5.85
Colesville, MD (cdp) Montgomery County	5.82
Mantua, VA (cdp) Fairfax County	5.70
Irvine, CA (city) Orange County	5.58
Mukilteo, WA (city) Snohomish County	5.58
Cypress, CA (city) Orange County	5.53
Jericho, NY (cdp) Nassau County	5.52
Burke, VA (cdp) Fairfax County	5.40
Paramus, NJ (borough) Bergen County	5.40
Artesia, CA (city) Los Angeles County	5.34
Federal Way, WA (city) King County	5.33
Lincolnwood, IL (village) Cook County	5.26
Hedwig Village, TX (city) Harris County	5.10
Ellicott City, MD (cdp) Howard County	5.09
Hawaiian Gardens, CA (city) Los Angeles County	5.06
Marina, CA (city) Monterey County	5.00
Rutherford, NJ (borough) Bergen County	4.99
La Mirada, CA (city) Los Angeles County	4.95
Hacienda Heights, CA (cdp) Los Angeles County	4.84
West Springfield, VA (cdp) Fairfax County	4.77
Northbrook, IL (village) Cook County	4.63
North Potomac, MD (cdp) Montgomery County	4.58
Calverton, MD (cdp) Montgomery County	4.51
Cupertino, CA (city) Santa Clara County	4.41
Loma Linda, CA (city) San Bernardino County	4.36
River Edge, NJ (borough) Bergen County	4.32
Tysons Corner, VA (cdp) Fairfax County	4.25
Waimalu, HI (cdp) Honolulu County	4.24
Broomall, PA (cdp) Delaware County	4.17
Honolulu, HI (cdp) Honolulu County	4.16
University Place, WA (city) Pierce County	4.11
West Carson, CA (cdp) Los Angeles County	4.07
Lakewood, WA (city) Pierce County	4.01
Skokie, IL (village) Cook County	3.99
North Springfield, VA (cdp) Fairfax County	3.91
Mill Creek, WA (city) Snohomish County	3.88
Morton Grove, IL (village) Cook County	3.87
Glenview, IL (village) Cook County	3.83
Oakton, VA (cdp) Fairfax County	3.83
Picnic Pt.-N. Lynnwood, WA (cdp) Snohomish County	3.82
Garden Grove, CA (city) Orange County	3.66
Arcadia, CA (city) Los Angeles County	3.65
Ridgefield Park, NJ (village) Bergen County	3.50

Notes: Please refer to the User's Guide for an explanation of data; ranking tables include all places with Asian and/or NHPI populations above SF4 population thresholds; (1) tables reflect only those areas that meet SF4 population thresholds, therefore there may be less than 50 states, 75 counties or 75 places listed

Population

Laotian

All States, Top 75 Counties, and Top 75 Places Sorted by Number[1]

State	Number
United States	167,792
California	56,896
Texas	9,862
Minnesota	8,997
Washington	8,097
North Carolina	4,966
Illinois	4,915
Georgia	4,730
Wisconsin	4,135
Florida	4,031
Tennessee	4,015
Iowa	3,968
Oregon	3,701
Massachusetts	3,647
New York	3,216
Connecticut	3,107
Virginia	3,001
Ohio	2,998
Rhode Island	2,889
Kansas	2,842
Michigan	2,787
Arkansas	2,712
Colorado	2,315
Pennsylvania	2,268
Utah	2,204
Hawaii	1,686
Alaska	1,368
South Carolina	1,324
Louisiana	1,294
Nevada	1,189
Indiana	983
Arizona	891
Oklahoma	881
Alabama	829
Nebraska	816
Maryland	736
Missouri	716
Idaho	508
New Jersey	480
New Hampshire	371
South Dakota	218

County	Number
Sacramento County, CA	9,648
San Diego County, CA	7,117
Fresno County, CA	6,270
King County, WA	5,040
Hennepin County, MN	4,409
Contra Costa County, CA	4,275
Tarrant County, TX	3,193
Alameda County, CA	3,162
Los Angeles County, CA	3,152
Tulare County, CA	3,142
San Joaquin County, CA	3,080
Orange County, CA	2,914
Providence County, RI	2,750
Multnomah County, OR	2,602
Dallas County, TX	2,337
Santa Clara County, CA	2,062
Pinellas County, FL	1,855
Middlesex County, MA	1,807
Salt Lake County, UT	1,789
Shasta County, CA	1,745
Merced County, CA	1,723
Milwaukee County, WI	1,718
Polk County, IA	1,654
Honolulu County, HI	1,645
Stanislaus County, CA	1,589
Rutherford County, TN	1,565
Fairfax County, VA	1,516
Riverside County, CA	1,488
Monroe County, NY	1,355
Davidson County, TN	1,311
Winnebago County, IL	1,299
Anchorage Borough, AK	1,265
Clayton County, GA	1,258
Cook County, IL	1,253
Hartford County, CT	1,215
Philadelphia County, PA	1,214
Harris County, TX	1,182
Clark County, NV	1,177
Sebastian County, AR	1,154
Ottawa County, MI	1,147
Franklin County, OH	1,136
Gwinnett County, GA	1,093
Sonoma County, CA	1,082
Adams County, CO	1,067
Potter County, TX	1,059
Sedgwick County, KS	1,053
Kane County, IL	1,046
Fairfield County, CT	1,031
Worcester County, MA	1,013
Ramsey County, MN	933
Jefferson County, CO	920
Iberia Parish, LA	900
Mecklenburg County, NC	876
Snohomish County, WA	764
Summit County, OH	763
Solano County, CA	754
Dakota County, MN	729
Spartanburg County, SC	678
Catawba County, NC	650
Johnson County, KS	640
Washington County, OR	622
Maricopa County, AZ	601
Buena Vista County, IA	578
Butte County, CA	551
Washington County, AR	551
Yolo County, CA	524
Broome County, NY	517
New Haven County, CT	504
Burke County, NC	496
Oklahoma County, OK	493
Guilford County, NC	488
San Bernardino County, CA	475
Habersham County, GA	472
Brown County, WI	440
Olmsted County, MN	440

Place	Number
Sacramento, CA (city) Sacramento County	6,305
San Diego, CA (city) San Diego County	6,037
Fresno, CA (city) Fresno County	5,482
Stockton, CA (city) San Joaquin County	2,968
Seattle, WA (city) King County	2,647
Oakland, CA (city) Alameda County	2,389
Richmond, CA (city) Contra Costa County	2,379
Portland, OR (city) Multnomah County	2,302
Visalia, CA (city) Tulare County	2,154
San Jose, CA (city) Santa Clara County	1,893
Minneapolis, MN (city) Hennepin County	1,627
Redding, CA (city) Shasta County	1,561
Milwaukee, WI (city) Milwaukee County	1,498
Lowell, MA (city) Middlesex County	1,467
Brooklyn Park, MN (city) Hennepin County	1,445
Merced, CA (city) Merced County	1,394
Parkway-S. Sacramento, CA (cdp) Sacramento County	1,392
Des Moines, IA (city) Polk County	1,363
Providence, RI (city) Providence County	1,326
Nashville-Davidson, TN (sp. city) Davidson County	1,311
Philadelphia, PA (city) Philadelphia County	1,214
Modesto, CA (city) Stanislaus County	1,141
St. Petersburg, FL (city) Pinellas County	1,133
Fort Smith, AR (city) Sebastian County	1,123
San Pablo, CA (city) Contra Costa County	1,116
Amarillo, TX (city) Potter County	1,061
Honolulu, HI (cdp) Honolulu County	984
Columbus, OH (city) Franklin County	979
Santa Ana, CA (city) Orange County	967
Woonsocket, RI (city) Providence County	912
Dallas, TX (city) Dallas County	908
Elgin, IL (city) Kane County	898
Rockford, IL (city) Winnebago County	898
Charlotte, NC (city) Mecklenburg County	865
St. Paul, MN (city) Ramsey County	861
Haltom City, TX (city) Tarrant County	812
Rochester, NY (city) Monroe County	805
Anaheim, CA (city) Orange County	796
Long Beach, CA (city) Los Angeles County	742
Murfreesboro, TN (city) Rutherford County	707
Wichita, KS (city) Sedgwick County	694
Los Angeles, CA (city) Los Angeles County	689
Westminster, CO (city) Adams County	676
Santa Rosa, CA (city) Sonoma County	633
Akron, OH (city) Summit County	572
Pomona, CA (city) Los Angeles County	533
Fort Worth, TX (city) Tarrant County	530
Storm Lake, IA (city) Buena Vista County	527
Oklahoma City, OK (city) Oklahoma County	506
Bridgeport, CT (city) Fairfield County	501
Moreno Valley, CA (city) Riverside County	488
Escondido, CA (city) San Diego County	479
Irving, TX (city) Dallas County	479
Arvada, CO (city) Jefferson County	478
Bellevue, WA (city) King County	464
West Valley City, UT (city) Salt Lake County	461
Rochester, MN (city) Olmsted County	438
Springdale, AR (city) Washington County	421
Springfield, VA (cdp) Fairfax County	398
Grand Prairie, TX (city) Dallas County	391
Fitchburg, MA (city) Worcester County	390
Fairfield, CA (city) Solano County	389
Green Bay, WI (city) Brown County	382
New Britain, CT (city) Hartford County	373
Worthington, MN (city) Nobles County	371
Riverside, CA (city) Riverside County	344
Winfield, KS (city) Cowley County	344
Banning, CA (city) Riverside County	341
Brooklyn Center, MN (city) Hennepin County	320
Tacoma, WA (city) Pierce County	310
Oaklawn-Sunview, KS (cdp) Sedgwick County	303
Raymond, WA (city) Pacific County	259
Warroad, MN (city) Roseau County	125

Notes: Please refer to the User's Guide for an explanation of data; ranking tables include all places with Asian and/or NHPI populations above SF4 population thresholds; (1) tables reflect only those areas that meet SF4 population thresholds, therefore there may be less than 50 states, 75 counties or 75 places listed

Population

Laotian

All States, Top 75 Counties, and Top 75 Places Sorted by Percent of Asian Population[1]

State	Percent
Arkansas	14.21
Rhode Island	12.13
Iowa	11.33
Tennessee	7.42
Minnesota	6.46
Kansas	6.35
Utah	5.98
Alaska	5.37
Wisconsin	4.98
South Dakota	4.61
Idaho	4.49
North Carolina	4.46
Nebraska	3.86
Connecticut	3.78
Oregon	3.73
South Carolina	3.63
Alabama	2.77
Georgia	2.76
Washington	2.52
Colorado	2.48
New Hampshire	2.41
Louisiana	2.33
Ohio	2.27
Oklahoma	1.93
Texas	1.77
Indiana	1.72
United States	1.65
Michigan	1.59
California	1.54
Massachusetts	1.53
Florida	1.52
Nevada	1.33
Missouri	1.18
Virginia	1.17
Illinois	1.16
Pennsylvania	1.05
Arizona	0.98
Maryland	0.35
Hawaii	0.33
New York	0.31
New Jersey	0.10

County	Percent
Pacific County, WA	69.86
Buena Vista County, IA	65.31
Cowley County, KS	63.04
Iberia Parish, LA	61.06
Roseau County, MN	60.12
Habersham County, GA	58.34
Shasta County, CA	54.21
Montgomery County, NC	53.12
Nobles County, MN	52.20
Rutherford County, TN	48.11
Dakota County, NE	44.31
Cass County, MI	44.14
Potter County, TX	35.42
Sebastian County, AR	32.23
Franklin County, WA	29.34
Winnebago County, IL	29.20
Tulare County, CA	25.47
Ottawa County, MI	22.14
Washington County, AR	21.14
Polk County, IA	18.03
Catawba County, NC	17.14
Burke County, NC	16.41
Spartanburg County, SC	16.33
Providence County, RI	15.01
Kane County, IL	14.82
Clayton County, GA	12.16
Merced County, CA	11.91
Davidson County, TN	11.21
Pinellas County, FL	9.88
Summit County, OH	9.86
Fresno County, CA	9.81
Broome County, NY	9.72
Brown County, WI	9.57
Adams County, CO	9.27
Anchorage Borough, AK	8.87
Stanislaus County, CA	8.64
Butte County, CA	8.41
Hennepin County, MN	8.30
Olmsted County, MN	8.26
Dakota County, MN	7.97
Jefferson County, CO	7.83
Salt Lake County, UT	7.71
Sonoma County, CA	7.69
Milwaukee County, WI	7.68
Monroe County, NY	7.64
Sedgwick County, KS	7.43
Sacramento County, CA	7.15
Multnomah County, OR	6.98
Polk County, FL	6.91
Tarrant County, TX	6.24
Mobile County, AL	5.97
Hartford County, CT	5.77
Worcester County, MA	5.34
Guilford County, NC	5.22
Johnson County, KS	5.09
San Joaquin County, CA	4.73
Mecklenburg County, NC	4.21
Contra Costa County, CA	4.14
Clark County, WA	3.89
Fairfield County, CT	3.62
Franklin County, OH	3.45
Yolo County, CA	3.32
San Diego County, CA	2.86
Riverside County, CA	2.72
Oklahoma County, OK	2.71
King County, WA	2.68
Dallas County, TX	2.67
Gwinnett County, GA	2.66
New Haven County, CT	2.57
Dane County, WI	2.41
Essex County, MA	2.24
Snohomish County, WA	2.15
Ramsey County, MN	2.12
Washington County, OR	2.08
Middlesex County, MA	1.97

Place	Percent
Raymond, WA (city) Pacific County	89.93
Warroad, MN (city) Roseau County	81.70
Winfield, KS (city) Cowley County	70.93
Storm Lake, IA (city) Buena Vista County	68.53
Oaklawn-Sunview, KS (cdp) Sedgwick County	60.97
Redding, CA (city) Shasta County	58.03
Springdale, AR (city) Washington County	56.97
Woonsocket, RI (city) Providence County	55.41
Worthington, MN (city) Nobles County	52.55
Visalia, CA (city) Tulare County	42.43
Murfreesboro, TN (city) Rutherford County	41.20
Fort Smith, AR (city) Sebastian County	34.27
Banning, CA (city) Riverside County	32.26
Rockford, IL (city) Winnebago County	30.28
Amarillo, TX (city) Potter County	29.09
Elgin, IL (city) Kane County	27.70
Haltom City, TX (city) Tarrant County	26.14
Brooklyn Park, MN (city) Hennepin County	23.31
San Pablo, CA (city) Contra Costa County	22.72
Fitchburg, MA (city) Worcester County	22.31
Des Moines, IA (city) Polk County	21.33
New Britain, CT (city) Hartford County	20.77
Parkway-S. Sacramento, CA (cdp) Sacramento County	20.67
Arvada, CO (city) Jefferson County	20.18
Richmond, CA (city) Contra Costa County	19.68
Merced, CA (city) Merced County	19.64
Akron, OH (city) Summit County	18.17
Rochester, NY (city) Monroe County	17.15
St. Petersburg, FL (city) Pinellas County	16.84
Providence, RI (city) Providence County	12.38
Westminster, CO (city) Adams County	12.38
Brooklyn Center, MN (city) Hennepin County	12.28
Nashville-Davidson, TN (sp. city) Davidson County	11.40
Fresno, CA (city) Fresno County	11.31
Santa Rosa, CA (city) Sonoma County	11.29
Bridgeport, CT (city) Fairfield County	11.15
Green Bay, WI (city) Brown County	11.02
Modesto, CA (city) Stanislaus County	10.17
West Valley City, UT (city) Salt Lake County	9.68
Sacramento, CA (city) Sacramento County	9.35
Milwaukee, WI (city) Milwaukee County	9.30
Rochester, MN (city) Olmsted County	9.11
Escondido, CA (city) San Diego County	8.63
Lowell, MA (city) Middlesex County	8.55
Grand Prairie, TX (city) Dallas County	7.38
Portland, OR (city) Multnomah County	6.83
Minneapolis, MN (city) Hennepin County	6.80
Moreno Valley, CA (city) Riverside County	6.10
Stockton, CA (city) San Joaquin County	6.10
Springfield, VA (cdp) Fairfax County	6.04
Wichita, KS (city) Sedgwick County	5.47
Pomona, CA (city) Los Angeles County	4.97
Charlotte, NC (city) Mecklenburg County	4.93
Oakland, CA (city) Alameda County	3.97
Columbus, OH (city) Franklin County	3.96
Fort Worth, TX (city) Tarrant County	3.83
Fairfield, CA (city) Solano County	3.67
San Diego, CA (city) San Diego County	3.63
Seattle, WA (city) King County	3.58
Santa Ana, CA (city) Orange County	3.24
Irving, TX (city) Dallas County	3.06
Oklahoma City, OK (city) Oklahoma County	2.93
Dallas, TX (city) Dallas County	2.82
Bellevue, WA (city) King County	2.46
St. Paul, MN (city) Ramsey County	2.44
Riverside, CA (city) Riverside County	2.43
Tacoma, WA (city) Pierce County	2.16
Anaheim, CA (city) Orange County	2.01
Philadelphia, PA (city) Philadelphia County	1.86
Long Beach, CA (city) Los Angeles County	1.35
San Jose, CA (city) Santa Clara County	0.79
Honolulu, HI (cdp) Honolulu County	0.47
Los Angeles, CA (city) Los Angeles County	0.19

Notes: Please refer to the User's Guide for an explanation of data; ranking tables include all places with Asian and/or NHPI populations above SF4 population thresholds; (1) tables reflect only those areas that meet SF4 population thresholds, therefore there may be less than 50 states, 75 counties or 75 places listed

Population

Laotian

All States, Top 75 Counties, and Top 75 Places Sorted by Percent of Total Population[1]

State	Percent
Rhode Island	0.28
Alaska	0.22
Minnesota	0.18
California	0.17
Hawaii	0.14
Iowa	0.14
Washington	0.14
Kansas	0.11
Oregon	0.11
Arkansas	0.10
Utah	0.10
Connecticut	0.09
Wisconsin	0.08
Tennessee	0.07
Georgia	0.06
Massachusetts	0.06
Nevada	0.06
North Carolina	0.06
United States	0.06
Colorado	0.05
Nebraska	0.05
Texas	0.05
Idaho	0.04
Illinois	0.04
Virginia	0.04
Florida	0.03
Louisiana	0.03
Michigan	0.03
New Hampshire	0.03
Ohio	0.03
Oklahoma	0.03
South Carolina	0.03
South Dakota	0.03
Alabama	0.02
Arizona	0.02
Indiana	0.02
New York	0.02
Pennsylvania	0.02
Maryland	0.01
Missouri	0.01
New Jersey	0.01

County	Percent
Buena Vista County, IA	2.83
Nobles County, MN	1.94
Pacific County, WA	1.67
Habersham County, GA	1.31
Roseau County, MN	1.27
Iberia Parish, LA	1.23
Dakota County, NE	1.10
Shasta County, CA	1.07
Sebastian County, AR	1.00
Cowley County, KS	0.96
Potter County, TX	0.93
Rutherford County, TN	0.86
Tulare County, CA	0.85
Merced County, CA	0.82
Sacramento County, CA	0.79
Fresno County, CA	0.78
Montgomery County, NC	0.73
Burke County, NC	0.56
Franklin County, WA	0.56
San Joaquin County, CA	0.55
Clayton County, GA	0.53
Anchorage Borough, AK	0.49
Ottawa County, MI	0.48
Winnebago County, IL	0.47
Catawba County, NC	0.46
Contra Costa County, CA	0.45
Polk County, IA	0.44
Providence County, RI	0.44
Hennepin County, MN	0.40
Multnomah County, OR	0.39
Stanislaus County, CA	0.36
Olmsted County, MN	0.35
Washington County, AR	0.35
Yolo County, CA	0.31
Adams County, CO	0.29
King County, WA	0.29
Cass County, MI	0.28
Butte County, CA	0.27
Spartanburg County, SC	0.27
Broome County, NY	0.26
Kane County, IL	0.26
San Diego County, CA	0.25
Sonoma County, CA	0.24
Davidson County, TN	0.23
Sedgwick County, KS	0.23
Alameda County, CA	0.22
Tarrant County, TX	0.22
Dakota County, MN	0.20
Pinellas County, FL	0.20
Salt Lake County, UT	0.20
Brown County, WI	0.19
Gwinnett County, GA	0.19
Honolulu County, HI	0.19
Solano County, CA	0.19
Milwaukee County, WI	0.18
Monroe County, NY	0.18
Ramsey County, MN	0.18
Jefferson County, CO	0.17
Fairfax County, VA	0.16
Hartford County, CT	0.14
Johnson County, KS	0.14
Summit County, OH	0.14
Washington County, OR	0.14
Mecklenburg County, NC	0.13
Snohomish County, WA	0.13
Worcester County, MA	0.13
Clark County, WA	0.12
Fairfield County, CT	0.12
Guilford County, NC	0.12
Middlesex County, MA	0.12
Santa Clara County, CA	0.12
Dallas County, TX	0.11
Franklin County, OH	0.11
Orange County, CA	0.10
Riverside County, CA	0.10

Place	Percent
Oaklawn-Sunview, KS (cdp) Sedgwick County	9.69
Raymond, WA (city) Pacific County	9.18
Warroad, MN (city) Roseau County	7.16
Storm Lake, IA (city) Buena Vista County	5.19
Parkway-S. Sacramento, CA (cdp) Sacramento County	3.81
San Pablo, CA (city) Contra Costa County	3.71
Worthington, MN (city) Nobles County	3.29
Winfield, KS (city) Cowley County	2.81
Richmond, CA (city) Contra Costa County	2.39
Visalia, CA (city) Tulare County	2.35
Merced, CA (city) Merced County	2.18
Brooklyn Park, MN (city) Hennepin County	2.14
Woonsocket, RI (city) Providence County	2.11
Haltom City, TX (city) Tarrant County	2.07
Redding, CA (city) Shasta County	1.92
Sacramento, CA (city) Sacramento County	1.55
Banning, CA (city) Riverside County	1.45
Fort Smith, AR (city) Sebastian County	1.40
Lowell, MA (city) Middlesex County	1.39
Springfield, VA (cdp) Fairfax County	1.32
Fresno, CA (city) Fresno County	1.28
Stockton, CA (city) San Joaquin County	1.22
Brooklyn Center, MN (city) Hennepin County	1.10
Murfreesboro, TN (city) Rutherford County	1.03
Fitchburg, MA (city) Worcester County	1.00
Elgin, IL (city) Kane County	0.96
Springdale, AR (city) Washington County	0.91
Providence, RI (city) Providence County	0.76
Des Moines, IA (city) Polk County	0.69
Westminster, CO (city) Adams County	0.67
Amarillo, TX (city) Potter County	0.61
Modesto, CA (city) Stanislaus County	0.60
Oakland, CA (city) Alameda County	0.60
Rockford, IL (city) Winnebago County	0.60
New Britain, CT (city) Hartford County	0.52
Rochester, MN (city) Olmsted County	0.51
San Diego, CA (city) San Diego County	0.49
Arvada, CO (city) Jefferson County	0.47
Seattle, WA (city) King County	0.47
St. Petersburg, FL (city) Pinellas County	0.46
Portland, OR (city) Multnomah County	0.44
Minneapolis, MN (city) Hennepin County	0.43
Santa Rosa, CA (city) Sonoma County	0.43
Bellevue, WA (city) King County	0.42
West Valley City, UT (city) Salt Lake County	0.42
Fairfield, CA (city) Solano County	0.40
Green Bay, WI (city) Brown County	0.37
Rochester, NY (city) Monroe County	0.37
Bridgeport, CT (city) Fairfield County	0.36
Escondido, CA (city) San Diego County	0.36
Pomona, CA (city) Los Angeles County	0.36
Moreno Valley, CA (city) Riverside County	0.34
Grand Prairie, TX (city) Dallas County	0.31
St. Paul, MN (city) Ramsey County	0.30
Santa Ana, CA (city) Orange County	0.29
Akron, OH (city) Summit County	0.26
Honolulu, HI (cdp) Honolulu County	0.26
Irving, TX (city) Dallas County	0.25
Milwaukee, WI (city) Milwaukee County	0.25
Anaheim, CA (city) Orange County	0.24
Nashville-Davidson, TN (sp. city) Davidson County	0.24
San Jose, CA (city) Santa Clara County	0.21
Wichita, KS (city) Sedgwick County	0.20
Charlotte, NC (city) Mecklenburg County	0.16
Long Beach, CA (city) Los Angeles County	0.16
Tacoma, WA (city) Pierce County	0.16
Columbus, OH (city) Franklin County	0.14
Riverside, CA (city) Riverside County	0.13
Fort Worth, TX (city) Tarrant County	0.10
Oklahoma City, OK (city) Oklahoma County	0.10
Dallas, TX (city) Dallas County	0.08
Philadelphia, PA (city) Philadelphia County	0.08
Los Angeles, CA (city) Los Angeles County	0.02

Notes: Please refer to the User's Guide for an explanation of data; ranking tables include all places with Asian and/or NHPI populations above SF4 population thresholds; (1) tables reflect only those areas that meet SF4 population thresholds, therefore there may be less than 50 states, 75 counties or 75 places listed

Population

Malaysian

***All States, Top 75 Counties, and Top 75 Places Sorted by Number*[1]**

State	Number
United States	10,711
California	1,761
New York	1,402
Texas	670
Illinois	567
Oklahoma	514
Michigan	457
Ohio	348

County	Number
Queens County, NY	567
Los Angeles County, CA	534

Place	Number
New York, NY (city)	1,197

Notes: Please refer to the User's Guide for an explanation of data; ranking tables include all places with Asian and/or NHPI populations above SF4 population thresholds; (1) tables reflect only those areas that meet SF4 population thresholds, therefore there may be less than 50 states, 75 counties or 75 places listed

Population

Malaysian

All States, Top 75 Counties, and Top 75 Places Sorted by Percent of Asian Population[1]

State	Percent
Oklahoma	1.13
Michigan	0.26
Ohio	0.26
Illinois	0.13
New York	0.13
Texas	0.12
United States	0.11
California	0.05

County	Percent
Queens County, NY	0.14
Los Angeles County, CA	0.05

Place	Percent
New York, NY (city)	0.15

Notes: Please refer to the User's Guide for an explanation of data; ranking tables include all places with Asian and/or NHPI populations above SF4 population thresholds; (1) tables reflect only those areas that meet SF4 population thresholds, therefore there may be less than 50 states, 75 counties or 75 places listed

Population

Malaysian

All States, Top 75 Counties, and Top 75 Places Sorted by Percent of Total Population[1]

State	Percent
California	0.01
New York	0.01
Oklahoma	0.01
Illinois	<0.01
Michigan	<0.01
Ohio	<0.01
Texas	<0.01
United States	<0.01

County	Percent
Queens County, NY	0.03
Los Angeles County, CA	0.01

Place	Percent
New York, NY (city)	0.01

Notes: Please refer to the User's Guide for an explanation of data; ranking tables include all places with Asian and/or NHPI populations above SF4 population thresholds; (1) tables reflect only those areas that meet SF4 population thresholds, therefore there may be less than 50 states, 75 counties or 75 places listed

Population

Pakistani

***All States, Top 75 Counties, and Top 75 Places Sorted by Number*[1]**

State	Number
United States	155,909
New York	32,123
California	19,837
Texas	18,872
Illinois	15,588
New Jersey	12,450
Virginia	10,459
Florida	5,446
Maryland	5,094
Michigan	4,978
Georgia	3,906
Pennsylvania	3,026
Massachusetts	2,356
Connecticut	2,112
North Carolina	1,874
Ohio	1,641
Washington	1,259
Oklahoma	1,122
Minnesota	1,098
Missouri	1,053
Louisiana	975
Wisconsin	927
Colorado	813
Kansas	779
Tennessee	764
Indiana	713
Arizona	672
Kentucky	563
Nevada	532
Utah	401
Iowa	390
Oregon	390
Alabama	385
Delaware	379
West Virginia	324

County	Number
Queens County, NY	11,252
Cook County, IL	10,612
Kings County, NY	9,621
Harris County, TX	7,332
Fairfax County, VA	6,289
Los Angeles County, CA	4,729
Dallas County, TX	3,713
Middlesex County, NJ	3,174
DuPage County, IL	2,815
Santa Clara County, CA	2,751
Orange County, CA	2,632
Fort Bend County, TX	2,441
Nassau County, NY	2,348
Hudson County, NJ	2,320
Wayne County, MI	2,178
Suffolk County, NY	2,007
Alameda County, CA	1,979
Montgomery County, MD	1,830
Bergen County, NJ	1,501
Sacramento County, CA	1,436
San Joaquin County, CA	1,337
Gwinnett County, GA	1,142
Bronx County, NY	1,124
Broward County, FL	1,097
New York County, NY	1,086
Baltimore County, MD	1,003
Tarrant County, TX	986
Oakland County, MI	973
Collin County, TX	958
Orange County, FL	901
Westchester County, NY	842
Denton County, TX	840
Somerset County, NJ	814
Prince William County, VA	813
Arlington County, VA	801
Miami-Dade County, FL	794
Richmond County, NY	772
Morris County, NJ	758
Travis County, TX	724
Contra Costa County, CA	708
San Bernardino County, CA	683
Prince George's County, MD	680
Hartford County, CT	668
Mercer County, NJ	660
New Haven County, CT	653
Howard County, MD	652
Cobb County, GA	647
Delaware County, PA	645
Philadelphia County, PA	629
Loudoun County, VA	627
Essex County, NJ	609
Middlesex County, MA	593
Alexandria Independent City, VA	574
St. Louis County, MO	569
San Francisco County, CA	556
Tulsa County, OK	544
Fairfield County, CT	543
San Diego County, CA	540
Macomb County, MI	530
King County, WA	526
Maricopa County, AZ	520
Lake County, IL	519
Franklin County, OH	513
Atlantic County, NJ	503
Washtenaw County, MI	465
Monroe County, NY	462
Jefferson Parish, LA	445
Wake County, NC	445
Riverside County, CA	444
Will County, IL	437
Snohomish County, WA	432
Clayton County, GA	419
Monmouth County, NJ	411
Guilford County, NC	409
Hennepin County, MN	408

Place	Number
New York, NY (city)	23,855
Chicago, IL (city) Cook County	6,437
Houston, TX (city) Harris County	4,997
Jersey City, NJ (city) Hudson County	1,878
Los Angeles, CA (city) Los Angeles County	1,676
Hempstead, NY (town) Nassau County	1,407
San Jose, CA (city) Santa Clara County	1,319
Dallas, TX (city) Dallas County	1,202
Carrollton, TX (city) Denton County	1,166
Fremont, CA (city) Alameda County	1,102
Garland, TX (city) Dallas County	831
Arlington, VA (cdp) Arlington County	801
Sacramento, CA (city) Sacramento County	779
Brookhaven, NY (town) Suffolk County	738
Stockton, CA (city) San Joaquin County	702
Edison, NJ (township) Middlesex County	674
Torrance, CA (city) Los Angeles County	656
Philadelphia, PA (city) Philadelphia County	629
North Hempstead, NY (town) Nassau County	618
Sugar Land, TX (city) Fort Bend County	618
Plano, TX (city) Collin County	604
San Francisco, CA (city) San Francisco County	556
Austin, TX (city) Travis County	526
Old Bridge, NJ (township) Middlesex County	526
Lincolnia, VA (cdp) Fairfax County	517
Skokie, IL (village) Cook County	495
Mission Bend, TX (cdp) Fort Bend County	480
Santa Clara, CA (city) Santa Clara County	469
Woodbridge, NJ (township) Middlesex County	467
Huntington, NY (town) Suffolk County	437
Irving, TX (city) Dallas County	429
Anaheim, CA (city) Orange County	424
Richardson, TX (city) Dallas County	423
Tulsa, OK (city) Tulsa County	415
Ellicott City, MD (cdp) Howard County	395
Bailey's Crossroads, VA (cdp) Fairfax County	359
Dale City, VA (cdp) Prince William County	324

Notes: Please refer to the User's Guide for an explanation of data; ranking tables include all places with Asian and/or NHPI populations above SF4 population thresholds; (1) tables reflect only those areas that meet SF4 population thresholds, therefore there may be less than 50 states, 75 counties or 75 places listed

Population

Pakistani

All States, Top 75 Counties, and Top 75 Places Sorted by Percent of Asian Population[1]

State	Percent
Virginia	4.08
Illinois	3.68
West Virginia	3.43
Texas	3.39
New York	3.08
Michigan	2.85
New Jersey	2.58
Connecticut	2.57
Oklahoma	2.46
Maryland	2.43
Delaware	2.36
Georgia	2.28
Florida	2.06
Kentucky	1.94
Louisiana	1.76
Kansas	1.74
Missouri	1.74
North Carolina	1.68
United States	1.53
Tennessee	1.41
Pennsylvania	1.40
Alabama	1.29
Indiana	1.25
Ohio	1.24
Wisconsin	1.12
Iowa	1.11
Utah	1.09
Massachusetts	0.99
Colorado	0.87
Minnesota	0.79
Arizona	0.74
Nevada	0.60
California	0.54
Oregon	0.39
Washington	0.39

County	Percent
Alexandria Independent City, VA	8.22
Prince William County, VA	7.79
Loudoun County, VA	7.02
Tulsa County, OK	6.32
Fort Bend County, TX	6.30
Wayne County, MI	6.17
Suffolk County, NY	5.88
Kings County, NY	5.18
Fairfax County, VA	5.09
Arlington County, VA	5.08
Denton County, TX	4.91
Guilford County, NC	4.38
Harris County, TX	4.26
Dallas County, TX	4.25
Baltimore County, MD	4.23
Cook County, IL	4.07
Hudson County, NJ	4.06
Clayton County, GA	4.05
DuPage County, IL	3.94
Atlantic County, NJ	3.88
Will County, IL	3.87
Mercer County, NJ	3.79
Nassau County, NY	3.75
Delaware County, PA	3.53
Cobb County, GA	3.50
Howard County, MD	3.48
New Haven County, CT	3.33
Somerset County, NJ	3.24
Jefferson Parish, LA	3.23
Hartford County, CT	3.17
Richmond County, NY	3.15
Orange County, FL	3.13
Macomb County, MI	3.05
Middlesex County, NJ	3.05
Broward County, FL	3.01
Bronx County, NY	2.88
Collin County, TX	2.85
Queens County, NY	2.85
Gwinnett County, GA	2.78
St. Louis County, MO	2.64
Monroe County, NY	2.60
Miami-Dade County, FL	2.59
Morris County, NJ	2.52
Washtenaw County, MI	2.32
Prince George's County, MD	2.24
Wake County, NC	2.15
Worcester County, MA	2.09
Essex County, NJ	2.07
Lake County, IL	2.05
San Joaquin County, CA	2.05
Westchester County, NY	2.02
Oakland County, MI	2.01
Travis County, TX	2.00
Tarrant County, TX	1.93
Fairfield County, CT	1.91
Camden County, NJ	1.89
Montgomery County, MD	1.87
Union County, NJ	1.86
Monmouth County, NJ	1.71
Bergen County, NJ	1.59
Milwaukee County, WI	1.59
Franklin County, OH	1.56
Snohomish County, WA	1.22
Sacramento County, CA	1.06
Philadelphia County, PA	0.97
San Bernardino County, CA	0.86
Riverside County, CA	0.81
Maricopa County, AZ	0.78
Hennepin County, MN	0.77
New York County, NY	0.75
Contra Costa County, CA	0.69
Orange County, CA	0.68
Alameda County, CA	0.67
Middlesex County, MA	0.65
Santa Clara County, CA	0.64

Place	Percent
Lincolnia, VA (cdp) Fairfax County	22.12
Bailey's Crossroads, VA (cdp) Fairfax County	14.35
Dale City, VA (cdp) Prince William County	11.31
Carrollton, TX (city) Denton County	10.21
Mission Bend, TX (cdp) Fort Bend County	9.28
Old Bridge, NJ (township) Middlesex County	8.11
Huntington, NY (town) Suffolk County	6.40
Tulsa, OK (city) Tulsa County	6.16
Ellicott City, MD (cdp) Howard County	5.93
Brookhaven, NY (town) Suffolk County	5.48
Hempstead, NY (town) Nassau County	5.36
Garland, TX (city) Dallas County	5.31
Arlington, VA (cdp) Arlington County	5.08
Chicago, IL (city) Cook County	5.07
Houston, TX (city) Harris County	4.88
Jersey City, NJ (city) Hudson County	4.81
Sugar Land, TX (city) Fort Bend County	4.29
Richardson, TX (city) Dallas County	4.15
Dallas, TX (city) Dallas County	3.74
Skokie, IL (village) Cook County	3.72
Woodbridge, NJ (township) Middlesex County	3.35
New York, NY (city)	3.03
North Hempstead, NY (town) Nassau County	3.00
Irving, TX (city) Dallas County	2.74
Plano, TX (city) Collin County	2.69
Edison, NJ (township) Middlesex County	2.37
Austin, TX (city) Travis County	1.70
Torrance, CA (city) Los Angeles County	1.66
Santa Clara, CA (city) Santa Clara County	1.61
Fremont, CA (city) Alameda County	1.47
Stockton, CA (city) San Joaquin County	1.44
Sacramento, CA (city) Sacramento County	1.16
Anaheim, CA (city) Orange County	1.07
Philadelphia, PA (city) Philadelphia County	0.97
San Jose, CA (city) Santa Clara County	0.55
Los Angeles, CA (city) Los Angeles County	0.45
San Francisco, CA (city) San Francisco County	0.23

Notes: Please refer to the User's Guide for an explanation of data; ranking tables include all places with Asian and/or NHPI populations above SF4 population thresholds; (1) tables reflect only those areas that meet SF4 population thresholds, therefore there may be less than 50 states, 75 counties or 75 places listed

Population

Pakistani

All States, Top 75 Counties, and Top 75 Places Sorted by Percent of Total Population[1]

State	Percent
New York	0.17
New Jersey	0.15
Virginia	0.15
Illinois	0.13
Maryland	0.10
Texas	0.09
California	0.06
Connecticut	0.06
United States	0.06
Delaware	0.05
Georgia	0.05
Michigan	0.05
Massachusetts	0.04
Florida	0.03
Kansas	0.03
Nevada	0.03
Oklahoma	0.03
Colorado	0.02
Louisiana	0.02
Minnesota	0.02
Missouri	0.02
North Carolina	0.02
Pennsylvania	0.02
Utah	0.02
Washington	0.02
West Virginia	0.02
Wisconsin	0.02
Alabama	0.01
Arizona	0.01
Indiana	0.01
Iowa	0.01
Kentucky	0.01
Ohio	0.01
Oregon	0.01
Tennessee	0.01

County	Percent
Fort Bend County, TX	0.69
Fairfax County, VA	0.65
Queens County, NY	0.50
Alexandria Independent City, VA	0.45
Arlington County, VA	0.42
Middlesex County, NJ	0.42
Kings County, NY	0.39
Hudson County, NJ	0.38
Loudoun County, VA	0.37
DuPage County, IL	0.31
Prince William County, VA	0.29
Somerset County, NJ	0.27
Howard County, MD	0.26
San Joaquin County, CA	0.24
Harris County, TX	0.22
Montgomery County, MD	0.21
Atlantic County, NJ	0.20
Cook County, IL	0.20
Collin County, TX	0.19
Denton County, TX	0.19
Gwinnett County, GA	0.19
Mercer County, NJ	0.19
Clayton County, GA	0.18
Nassau County, NY	0.18
Bergen County, NJ	0.17
Dallas County, TX	0.17
Richmond County, NY	0.17
Morris County, NJ	0.16
Santa Clara County, CA	0.16
Alameda County, CA	0.14
Suffolk County, NY	0.14
Washtenaw County, MI	0.14
Baltimore County, MD	0.13
Delaware County, PA	0.12
Sacramento County, CA	0.12
Cobb County, GA	0.11
Wayne County, MI	0.11
Guilford County, NC	0.10
Jefferson Parish, LA	0.10
Orange County, FL	0.10
Tulsa County, OK	0.10
Orange County, CA	0.09
Travis County, TX	0.09
Westchester County, NY	0.09
Will County, IL	0.09
Bronx County, NY	0.08
Essex County, NJ	0.08
Hartford County, CT	0.08
Lake County, IL	0.08
New Haven County, CT	0.08
Oakland County, MI	0.08
Prince George's County, MD	0.08
Broward County, FL	0.07
Camden County, NJ	0.07
Contra Costa County, CA	0.07
Macomb County, MI	0.07
Monmouth County, NJ	0.07
New York County, NY	0.07
San Francisco County, CA	0.07
Snohomish County, WA	0.07
Tarrant County, TX	0.07
Union County, NJ	0.07
Wake County, NC	0.07
Fairfield County, CT	0.06
Monroe County, NY	0.06
St. Louis County, MO	0.06
Franklin County, OH	0.05
Los Angeles County, CA	0.05
Worcester County, MA	0.05
Hennepin County, MN	0.04
Miami-Dade County, FL	0.04
Middlesex County, MA	0.04
Milwaukee County, WI	0.04
Philadelphia County, PA	0.04
San Bernardino County, CA	0.04

Place	Percent
Lincolnia, VA (cdp) Fairfax County	3.26
Bailey's Crossroads, VA (cdp) Fairfax County	1.57
Mission Bend, TX (cdp) Fort Bend County	1.55
Carrollton, TX (city) Denton County	1.07
Sugar Land, TX (city) Fort Bend County	0.97
Old Bridge, NJ (township) Middlesex County	0.87
Jersey City, NJ (city) Hudson County	0.78
Skokie, IL (village) Cook County	0.78
Ellicott City, MD (cdp) Howard County	0.70
Edison, NJ (township) Middlesex County	0.69
Dale City, VA (cdp) Prince William County	0.58
Fremont, CA (city) Alameda County	0.54
Torrance, CA (city) Los Angeles County	0.48
Woodbridge, NJ (township) Middlesex County	0.48
Richardson, TX (city) Dallas County	0.46
Santa Clara, CA (city) Santa Clara County	0.46
Arlington, VA (cdp) Arlington County	0.42
Garland, TX (city) Dallas County	0.38
New York, NY (city)	0.30
Stockton, CA (city) San Joaquin County	0.29
North Hempstead, NY (town) Nassau County	0.28
Plano, TX (city) Collin County	0.27
Houston, TX (city) Harris County	0.26
Chicago, IL (city) Cook County	0.22
Huntington, NY (town) Suffolk County	0.22
Irving, TX (city) Dallas County	0.22
Hempstead, NY (town) Nassau County	0.19
Sacramento, CA (city) Sacramento County	0.19
Brookhaven, NY (town) Suffolk County	0.16
San Jose, CA (city) Santa Clara County	0.15
Anaheim, CA (city) Orange County	0.13
Tulsa, OK (city) Tulsa County	0.11
Dallas, TX (city) Dallas County	0.10
Austin, TX (city) Travis County	0.08
San Francisco, CA (city) San Francisco County	0.07
Los Angeles, CA (city) Los Angeles County	0.05
Philadelphia, PA (city) Philadelphia County	0.04

Notes: Please refer to the User's Guide for an explanation of data; ranking tables include all places with Asian and/or NHPI populations above SF4 population thresholds; (1) tables reflect only those areas that meet SF4 population thresholds, therefore there may be less than 50 states, 75 counties or 75 places listed

Population

Samoan

All States, Top 75 Counties, and Top 75 Places Sorted by Number[1]

State	Number
United States	85,243
California	38,906
Hawaii	14,359
Washington	7,072
Utah	3,760
Texas	2,033
Nevada	1,567
Alaska	1,534
New York	1,439
Missouri	1,004
Colorado	916
Illinois	874
Arizona	850
Florida	849
Pennsylvania	844
Oregon	773
Georgia	762
New Jersey	639
Tennessee	540
Virginia	520
North Carolina	495
Ohio	491
Michigan	474

County	Number
Honolulu County, HI	13,847
Los Angeles County, CA	13,553
San Diego County, CA	4,954
King County, WA	3,921
Orange County, CA	3,721
Salt Lake County, UT	2,586
Alameda County, CA	2,406
San Francisco County, CA	2,279
San Bernardino County, CA	2,036
Pierce County, WA	1,729
Santa Clara County, CA	1,719
San Mateo County, CA	1,451
Sacramento County, CA	1,239
Anchorage Borough, AK	1,208
Clark County, NV	1,116
Riverside County, CA	943
Contra Costa County, CA	759
Solano County, CA	625
Ventura County, CA	612
Maricopa County, AZ	553
Utah County, UT	549
Jackson County, MO	470
San Joaquin County, CA	360
Hawaii County, HI	296

Place	Number
Honolulu, HI (cdp) Honolulu County	4,452
Long Beach, CA (city) Los Angeles County	3,733
San Francisco, CA (city) San Francisco County	2,279
San Diego, CA (city) San Diego County	2,171
Waipahu, HI (cdp) Honolulu County	2,120
Los Angeles, CA (city) Los Angeles County	2,055
Oceanside, CA (city) San Diego County	1,532
Carson, CA (city) Los Angeles County	1,438
Seattle, WA (city) King County	1,344
San Jose, CA (city) Santa Clara County	1,218
Compton, CA (city) Los Angeles County	981
West Valley City, UT (city) Salt Lake County	861
Garden Grove, CA (city) Orange County	773
Nanakuli, HI (cdp) Honolulu County	753
Sacramento, CA (city) Sacramento County	733
New York, NY (city)	729
Santa Ana, CA (city) Orange County	700
Laie, HI (cdp) Honolulu County	669
Halawa, HI (cdp) Honolulu County	661
Tacoma, WA (city) Pierce County	627
Lakewood, CA (city) Los Angeles County	598
Hayward, CA (city) Alameda County	582
Anaheim, CA (city) Orange County	555
Oxnard, CA (city) Ventura County	541
Federal Way, WA (city) King County	491
San Bernardino, CA (city) San Bernardino County	478
Salt Lake City, UT (city) Salt Lake County	454
Ewa Beach, HI (cdp) Honolulu County	421
Westminster, CA (city) Orange County	376
Lakewood, WA (city) Pierce County	293
Hauula, HI (cdp) Honolulu County	272
Kahuku, HI (cdp) Honolulu County	120

Notes: Please refer to the User's Guide for an explanation of data; ranking tables include all places with Asian and/or NHPI populations above SF4 population thresholds; (1) tables reflect only those areas that meet SF4 population thresholds, therefore there may be less than 50 states, 75 counties or 75 places listed

Population

Samoan

All States, Top 75 Counties, and Top 75 Places Sorted by Percent of Native Hawaiian and Other Pacific Islander Population[1]

State	Percent
Alaska	49.14
California	34.17
Missouri	32.69
Washington	32.53
Utah	26.17
Tennessee	25.01
New Jersey	23.59
Illinois	22.93
Pennsylvania	22.68
United States	22.50
Colorado	21.31
Nevada	20.07
Georgia	19.71
Ohio	18.59
New York	18.21
Michigan	17.76
Texas	16.31
Virginia	14.38
Arizona	13.79
North Carolina	13.38
Hawaii	12.76
Florida	12.46
Oregon	10.19

County	Percent
San Francisco County, CA	63.64
Anchorage Borough, AK	59.60
Jackson County, MO	50.76
Los Angeles County, CA	49.79
King County, WA	47.41
Orange County, CA	43.62
San Bernardino County, CA	40.57
San Diego County, CA	36.75
Ventura County, CA	36.67
Pierce County, WA	34.07
Utah County, UT	30.42
Santa Clara County, CA	29.67
Alameda County, CA	26.19
Riverside County, CA	25.36
Salt Lake County, UT	25.02
Contra Costa County, CA	22.38
San Joaquin County, CA	20.17
Sacramento County, CA	19.76
Solano County, CA	19.60
Clark County, NV	18.86
Honolulu County, HI	17.94
San Mateo County, CA	17.00
Maricopa County, AZ	14.51
Hawaii County, HI	1.82

Place	Percent
Compton, CA (city) Los Angeles County	95.43
Westminster, CA (city) Orange County	86.44
Lakewood, CA (city) Los Angeles County	78.48
Carson, CA (city) Los Angeles County	74.55
Long Beach, CA (city) Los Angeles County	72.56
Oceanside, CA (city) San Diego County	67.37
San Bernardino, CA (city) San Bernardino County	63.90
San Francisco, CA (city) San Francisco County	63.64
Oxnard, CA (city) Ventura County	62.26
Garden Grove, CA (city) Orange County	61.06
Federal Way, WA (city) King County	54.86
Santa Ana, CA (city) Orange County	54.86
Seattle, WA (city) King County	53.46
Waipahu, HI (cdp) Honolulu County	52.66
Anaheim, CA (city) Orange County	50.73
Tacoma, WA (city) Pierce County	46.55
Halawa, HI (cdp) Honolulu County	43.72
Laie, HI (cdp) Honolulu County	41.58
Lakewood, WA (city) Pierce County	39.28
San Jose, CA (city) Santa Clara County	37.66
San Diego, CA (city) San Diego County	34.93
Los Angeles, CA (city) Los Angeles County	31.89
Ewa Beach, HI (cdp) Honolulu County	28.91
West Valley City, UT (city) Salt Lake County	27.54
Hayward, CA (city) Alameda County	24.69
Sacramento, CA (city) Sacramento County	19.85
Kahuku, HI (cdp) Honolulu County	19.02
Hauula, HI (cdp) Honolulu County	18.39
Nanakuli, HI (cdp) Honolulu County	18.35
Honolulu, HI (cdp) Honolulu County	17.22
New York, NY (city)	14.97
Salt Lake City, UT (city) Salt Lake County	13.70

Notes: Please refer to the User's Guide for an explanation of data; ranking tables include all places with Asian and/or NHPI populations above SF4 population thresholds; (1) tables reflect only those areas that meet SF4 population thresholds, therefore there may be less than 50 states, 75 counties or 75 places listed

Population

Samoan

All States, Top 75 Counties, and Top 75 Places Sorted by Percent of Total Population[1]

State	Percent
Hawaii	1.19
Alaska	0.24
Utah	0.17
Washington	0.12
California	0.11
Nevada	0.08
United States	0.03
Arizona	0.02
Colorado	0.02
Missouri	0.02
Oregon	0.02
Florida	0.01
Georgia	0.01
Illinois	0.01
New Jersey	0.01
New York	0.01
North Carolina	0.01
Pennsylvania	0.01
Tennessee	0.01
Texas	0.01
Virginia	0.01
Michigan	<0.01
Ohio	<0.01

County	Percent
Honolulu County, HI	1.58
Anchorage Borough, AK	0.46
Salt Lake County, UT	0.29
San Francisco County, CA	0.29
Pierce County, WA	0.25
King County, WA	0.23
San Mateo County, CA	0.21
Hawaii County, HI	0.20
San Diego County, CA	0.18
Alameda County, CA	0.17
Solano County, CA	0.16
Utah County, UT	0.15
Los Angeles County, CA	0.14
Orange County, CA	0.13
San Bernardino County, CA	0.12
Sacramento County, CA	0.10
Santa Clara County, CA	0.10
Clark County, NV	0.08
Contra Costa County, CA	0.08
Ventura County, CA	0.08
Jackson County, MO	0.07
Riverside County, CA	0.06
San Joaquin County, CA	0.06
Maricopa County, AZ	0.02

Place	Percent
Laie, HI (cdp) Honolulu County	14.55
Hauula, HI (cdp) Honolulu County	7.40
Nanakuli, HI (cdp) Honolulu County	7.04
Waipahu, HI (cdp) Honolulu County	6.40
Kahuku, HI (cdp) Honolulu County	5.72
Halawa, HI (cdp) Honolulu County	4.74
Ewa Beach, HI (cdp) Honolulu County	2.87
Carson, CA (city) Los Angeles County	1.61
Honolulu, HI (cdp) Honolulu County	1.20
Compton, CA (city) Los Angeles County	1.05
Oceanside, CA (city) San Diego County	0.95
Long Beach, CA (city) Los Angeles County	0.81
West Valley City, UT (city) Salt Lake County	0.79
Lakewood, CA (city) Los Angeles County	0.75
Federal Way, WA (city) King County	0.59
Lakewood, WA (city) Pierce County	0.50
Garden Grove, CA (city) Orange County	0.47
Westminster, CA (city) Orange County	0.43
Hayward, CA (city) Alameda County	0.42
Oxnard, CA (city) Ventura County	0.32
Tacoma, WA (city) Pierce County	0.32
San Francisco, CA (city) San Francisco County	0.29
San Bernardino, CA (city) San Bernardino County	0.26
Salt Lake City, UT (city) Salt Lake County	0.25
Seattle, WA (city) King County	0.24
Santa Ana, CA (city) Orange County	0.21
Sacramento, CA (city) Sacramento County	0.18
San Diego, CA (city) San Diego County	0.18
Anaheim, CA (city) Orange County	0.17
San Jose, CA (city) Santa Clara County	0.14
Los Angeles, CA (city) Los Angeles County	0.06
New York, NY (city)	0.01

Notes: Please refer to the User's Guide for an explanation of data; ranking tables include all places with Asian and/or NHPI populations above SF4 population thresholds; (1) tables reflect only those areas that meet SF4 population thresholds, therefore there may be less than 50 states, 75 counties or 75 places listed

Population

Sri Lankan

All States, Top 75 Counties, and Top 75 Places Sorted by Number[1]

State	Number
United States	19,078
California	5,416
New York	2,689
New Jersey	1,335
Maryland	1,122
Texas	976
Virginia	636
Illinois	554
Ohio	514
Massachusetts	469
Washington	422
Florida	402
Michigan	356
Pennsylvania	330

County	Number
Los Angeles County, CA	2,441
Queens County, NY	937
Montgomery County, MD	748
Orange County, CA	677
Richmond County, NY	527
Middlesex County, NJ	497

Place	Number
New York, NY (city)	2,004
Los Angeles, CA (city) Los Angeles County	1,208

Notes: Please refer to the User's Guide for an explanation of data; ranking tables include all places with Asian and/or NHPI populations above SF4 population thresholds; (1) tables reflect only those areas that meet SF4 population thresholds, therefore there may be less than 50 states, 75 counties or 75 places listed

Population

Sri Lankan

All States, Top 75 Counties, and Top 75 Places Sorted by Percent of Asian Population[1]

State	Percent
Maryland	0.54
Ohio	0.39
New Jersey	0.28
New York	0.26
Virginia	0.25
Massachusetts	0.20
Michigan	0.20
United States	0.19
Texas	0.18
California	0.15
Florida	0.15
Pennsylvania	0.15
Illinois	0.13
Washington	0.13

County	Percent
Richmond County, NY	2.15
Montgomery County, MD	0.76
Middlesex County, NJ	0.48
Queens County, NY	0.24
Los Angeles County, CA	0.22
Orange County, CA	0.18

Place	Percent
Los Angeles, CA (city) Los Angeles County	0.33
New York, NY (city)	0.25

Notes: Please refer to the User's Guide for an explanation of data; ranking tables include all places with Asian and/or NHPI populations above SF4 population thresholds; (1) tables reflect only those areas that meet SF4 population thresholds, therefore there may be less than 50 states, 75 counties or 75 places listed

Population

Sri Lankan

All States, Top 75 Counties, and Top 75 Places Sorted by Percent of Total Population[1]

State	Percent
California	0.02
Maryland	0.02
New Jersey	0.02
Massachusetts	0.01
New York	0.01
United States	0.01
Virginia	0.01
Washington	0.01
Florida	<0.01
Illinois	<0.01
Michigan	<0.01
Ohio	<0.01
Pennsylvania	<0.01
Texas	<0.01

County	Percent
Richmond County, NY	0.12
Montgomery County, MD	0.09
Middlesex County, NJ	0.07
Queens County, NY	0.04
Los Angeles County, CA	0.03
Orange County, CA	0.02

Place	Percent
Los Angeles, CA (city) Los Angeles County	0.03
New York, NY (city)	0.03

Notes: Please refer to the User's Guide for an explanation of data; ranking tables include all places with Asian and/or NHPI populations above SF4 population thresholds; (1) tables reflect only those areas that meet SF4 population thresholds, therefore there may be less than 50 states, 75 counties or 75 places listed

Population

Taiwanese

All States, Top 75 Counties, and Top 75 Places Sorted by Number[1]

State	Number
United States	122,751
California	63,580
Texas	7,859
New York	7,790
New Jersey	5,851
Washington	3,788
Illinois	3,570
Massachusetts	2,536
Maryland	2,377
Michigan	2,284
Pennsylvania	2,277
Ohio	2,213
Florida	2,027
Georgia	1,844
Virginia	1,315
Missouri	972
North Carolina	971
Hawaii	821
Connecticut	819
Oregon	800
Arizona	794
Indiana	733
Colorado	680
Wisconsin	673
Nevada	597
Tennessee	580
Kansas	518
Louisiana	494
Minnesota	463
Iowa	446
Utah	370
Oklahoma	354

County	Number
Los Angeles County, CA	34,746
Orange County, CA	9,243
Santa Clara County, CA	5,298
Alameda County, CA	3,935
Queens County, NY	3,463
King County, WA	3,024
San Diego County, CA	2,362
Harris County, TX	2,223
San Bernardino County, CA	2,039
Cook County, IL	1,752
Middlesex County, NJ	1,360
Middlesex County, MA	1,272
Contra Costa County, CA	1,261
Oakland County, MI	1,259
Fort Bend County, TX	1,216
Montgomery County, MD	1,144
New York County, NY	1,051
Collin County, TX	850
DuPage County, IL	840
Travis County, TX	840
Bergen County, NJ	829
Dallas County, TX	804
Ventura County, CA	797
Honolulu County, HI	791
San Mateo County, CA	779
San Francisco County, CA	771
Franklin County, OH	756
Fairfax County, VA	738
Morris County, NJ	702
Tarrant County, TX	672
St. Louis County, MO	648
Maricopa County, AZ	642
Nassau County, NY	604
Somerset County, NJ	549
Washtenaw County, MI	520
Riverside County, CA	498
Mercer County, NJ	488
Essex County, NJ	477
Gwinnett County, GA	474
Suffolk County, MA	465
Allegheny County, PA	451
Clark County, NV	429
Suffolk County, NY	428
Dane County, WI	426
Norfolk County, MA	423
Sacramento County, CA	406
Westchester County, NY	338

Place	Number
New York, NY (city)	4,907
Arcadia, CA (city) Los Angeles County	3,753
Los Angeles, CA (city) Los Angeles County	3,326
Hacienda Heights, CA (cdp) Los Angeles County	2,875
Irvine, CA (city) Orange County	2,622
Rowland Heights, CA (cdp) Los Angeles County	2,593
Fremont, CA (city) Alameda County	2,452
Diamond Bar, CA (city) Los Angeles County	2,099
San Jose, CA (city) Santa Clara County	2,053
Walnut, CA (city) Los Angeles County	1,926
Cerritos, CA (city) Los Angeles County	1,791
San Diego, CA (city) San Diego County	1,587
Alhambra, CA (city) Los Angeles County	1,558
Temple City, CA (city) Los Angeles County	1,532
San Marino, CA (city) Los Angeles County	1,526
Houston, TX (city) Harris County	1,492
Torrance, CA (city) Los Angeles County	1,290
Monterey Park, CA (city) Los Angeles County	1,051
Seattle, WA (city) King County	977
West Covina, CA (city) Los Angeles County	948
Sugar Land, TX (city) Fort Bend County	937
Bellevue, WA (city) King County	929
Cupertino, CA (city) Santa Clara County	792
Chicago, IL (city) Cook County	776
San Francisco, CA (city) San Francisco County	771
San Gabriel, CA (city) Los Angeles County	763
Austin, TX (city) Travis County	748
Cypress, CA (city) Orange County	744
Honolulu, HI (cdp) Honolulu County	702
Sunnyvale, CA (city) Santa Clara County	671
Anaheim, CA (city) Orange County	669
Edison, NJ (township) Middlesex County	663
East San Gabriel, CA (cdp) Los Angeles County	641
Chino Hills, CA (city) San Bernardino County	634
Huntington Beach, CA (city) Orange County	577
Plano, TX (city) Collin County	564
Troy, MI (city) Oakland County	558
Rancho Palos Verdes, CA (city) Los Angeles County	540
Upland, CA (city) San Bernardino County	468
Tustin, CA (city) Orange County	467
Boston, MA (city) Suffolk County	465
Columbus, OH (city) Franklin County	463
Orange, CA (city) Orange County	462
Ann Arbor, MI (city) Washtenaw County	441
Naperville, IL (city) Du Page County	431
Madison, WI (city) Dane County	423
Arlington, TX (city) Tarrant County	415
Berkeley, CA (city) Alameda County	408
El Monte, CA (city) Los Angeles County	401
Fountain Valley, CA (city) Orange County	397
Saratoga, CA (city) Santa Clara County	332
North Hempstead, NY (town) Nassau County	283

Notes: Please refer to the User's Guide for an explanation of data; ranking tables include all places with Asian and/or NHPI populations above SF4 population thresholds; (1) tables reflect only those areas that meet SF4 population thresholds, therefore there may be less than 50 states, 75 counties or 75 places listed

Population

Taiwanese

All States, Top 75 Counties, and Top 75 Places Sorted by Percent of Asian Population[1]

State	Percent
California	1.73
Ohio	1.67
Missouri	1.61
Texas	1.41
Michigan	1.31
Indiana	1.28
Iowa	1.27
New Jersey	1.21
United States	1.21
Washington	1.18
Kansas	1.16
Maryland	1.13
Georgia	1.08
Tennessee	1.07
Massachusetts	1.06
Pennsylvania	1.05
Connecticut	1.00
Utah	1.00
Louisiana	0.89
Arizona	0.87
North Carolina	0.87
Illinois	0.84
Oregon	0.81
Wisconsin	0.81
Oklahoma	0.78
Florida	0.77
New York	0.75
Colorado	0.73
Nevada	0.67
Virginia	0.51
Minnesota	0.33
Hawaii	0.16

County	Percent
Fort Bend County, TX	3.14
Los Angeles County, CA	3.06
St. Louis County, MO	3.01
Dane County, WI	2.98
Mercer County, NJ	2.80
Oakland County, MI	2.60
Washtenaw County, MI	2.60
San Bernardino County, CA	2.58
Collin County, TX	2.53
Orange County, CA	2.39
Morris County, NJ	2.33
Travis County, TX	2.33
Franklin County, OH	2.30
Somerset County, NJ	2.19
Allegheny County, PA	2.16
Ventura County, CA	2.03
Essex County, NJ	1.62
King County, WA	1.61
Middlesex County, MA	1.39
Alameda County, CA	1.34
Middlesex County, NJ	1.31
Tarrant County, TX	1.31
Harris County, TX	1.29
Suffolk County, NY	1.25
Santa Clara County, CA	1.23
Contra Costa County, CA	1.22
DuPage County, IL	1.18
Montgomery County, MD	1.17
Norfolk County, MA	1.17
Gwinnett County, GA	1.16
Maricopa County, AZ	0.97
Nassau County, NY	0.97
Suffolk County, MA	0.97
San Diego County, CA	0.95
Dallas County, TX	0.92
Riverside County, CA	0.91
Bergen County, NJ	0.88
Queens County, NY	0.88
Westchester County, NY	0.81
New York County, NY	0.73
Cook County, IL	0.67
Clark County, NV	0.60
Fairfax County, VA	0.60
San Mateo County, CA	0.55
San Francisco County, CA	0.32
Sacramento County, CA	0.30
Honolulu County, HI	0.20

Place	Percent
San Marino, CA (city) Los Angeles County	25.14
Arcadia, CA (city) Los Angeles County	15.64
Hacienda Heights, CA (cdp) Los Angeles County	14.95
Temple City, CA (city) Los Angeles County	11.84
Walnut, CA (city) Los Angeles County	11.41
East San Gabriel, CA (cdp) Los Angeles County	10.50
Rowland Heights, CA (cdp) Los Angeles County	10.47
Upland, CA (city) San Bernardino County	9.37
Diamond Bar, CA (city) Los Angeles County	8.81
Cypress, CA (city) Orange County	7.86
Sugar Land, TX (city) Fort Bend County	6.50
Irvine, CA (city) Orange County	6.19
Cerritos, CA (city) Los Angeles County	5.93
Troy, MI (city) Oakland County	5.38
Rancho Palos Verdes, CA (city) Los Angeles County	5.21
Tustin, CA (city) Orange County	4.99
Bellevue, WA (city) King County	4.93
Chino Hills, CA (city) San Bernardino County	4.45
West Covina, CA (city) Los Angeles County	3.99
San Gabriel, CA (city) Los Angeles County	3.98
Orange, CA (city) Orange County	3.95
Saratoga, CA (city) Santa Clara County	3.89
Alhambra, CA (city) Los Angeles County	3.84
Naperville, IL (city) Du Page County	3.68
Madison, WI (city) Dane County	3.63
Cupertino, CA (city) Santa Clara County	3.50
Ann Arbor, MI (city) Washtenaw County	3.29
Fremont, CA (city) Alameda County	3.28
Huntington Beach, CA (city) Orange County	3.27
Torrance, CA (city) Los Angeles County	3.27
Monterey Park, CA (city) Los Angeles County	2.87
Fountain Valley, CA (city) Orange County	2.75
Plano, TX (city) Collin County	2.51
Berkeley, CA (city) Alameda County	2.45
Austin, TX (city) Travis County	2.42
Edison, NJ (township) Middlesex County	2.33
Arlington, TX (city) Tarrant County	2.15
Columbus, OH (city) Franklin County	1.87
El Monte, CA (city) Los Angeles County	1.86
Anaheim, CA (city) Orange County	1.69
Sunnyvale, CA (city) Santa Clara County	1.57
Houston, TX (city) Harris County	1.46
North Hempstead, NY (town) Nassau County	1.38
Seattle, WA (city) King County	1.32
Boston, MA (city) Suffolk County	1.05
San Diego, CA (city) San Diego County	0.95
Los Angeles, CA (city) Los Angeles County	0.90
San Jose, CA (city) Santa Clara County	0.86
New York, NY (city)	0.62
Chicago, IL (city) Cook County	0.61
Honolulu, HI (cdp) Honolulu County	0.34
San Francisco, CA (city) San Francisco County	0.32

Notes: Please refer to the User's Guide for an explanation of data; ranking tables include all places with Asian and/or NHPI populations above SF4 population thresholds; (1) tables reflect only those areas that meet SF4 population thresholds, therefore there may be less than 50 states, 75 counties or 75 places listed

Population

Taiwanese

All States, Top 75 Counties, and Top 75 Places Sorted by Percent of Total Population[1]

State	Percent
California	0.19
Hawaii	0.07
New Jersey	0.07
Washington	0.06
Maryland	0.04
Massachusetts	0.04
New York	0.04
Texas	0.04
United States	0.04
Illinois	0.03
Nevada	0.03
Arizona	0.02
Colorado	0.02
Connecticut	0.02
Georgia	0.02
Iowa	0.02
Kansas	0.02
Michigan	0.02
Missouri	0.02
Ohio	0.02
Oregon	0.02
Pennsylvania	0.02
Utah	0.02
Virginia	0.02
Florida	0.01
Indiana	0.01
Louisiana	0.01
Minnesota	0.01
North Carolina	0.01
Oklahoma	0.01
Tennessee	0.01
Wisconsin	0.01

County	Percent
Los Angeles County, CA	0.37
Fort Bend County, TX	0.34
Orange County, CA	0.32
Santa Clara County, CA	0.31
Alameda County, CA	0.27
Middlesex County, NJ	0.18
Somerset County, NJ	0.18
Collin County, TX	0.17
King County, WA	0.17
Queens County, NY	0.16
Washtenaw County, MI	0.16
Morris County, NJ	0.15
Mercer County, NJ	0.14
Contra Costa County, CA	0.13
Montgomery County, MD	0.13
San Bernardino County, CA	0.12
Oakland County, MI	0.11
San Mateo County, CA	0.11
Ventura County, CA	0.11
Dane County, WI	0.10
San Francisco County, CA	0.10
Travis County, TX	0.10
Bergen County, NJ	0.09
DuPage County, IL	0.09
Honolulu County, HI	0.09
Middlesex County, MA	0.09
Fairfax County, VA	0.08
Gwinnett County, GA	0.08
San Diego County, CA	0.08
Franklin County, OH	0.07
Harris County, TX	0.07
New York County, NY	0.07
Norfolk County, MA	0.07
Suffolk County, MA	0.07
Essex County, NJ	0.06
St. Louis County, MO	0.06
Nassau County, NY	0.05
Tarrant County, TX	0.05
Allegheny County, PA	0.04
Dallas County, TX	0.04
Westchester County, NY	0.04
Clark County, NV	0.03
Cook County, IL	0.03
Riverside County, CA	0.03
Sacramento County, CA	0.03
Suffolk County, NY	0.03
Maricopa County, AZ	0.02

Place	Percent
San Marino, CA (city) Los Angeles County	11.76
Arcadia, CA (city) Los Angeles County	7.09
Walnut, CA (city) Los Angeles County	6.42
Hacienda Heights, CA (cdp) Los Angeles County	5.41
Rowland Heights, CA (cdp) Los Angeles County	5.37
Temple City, CA (city) Los Angeles County	4.60
East San Gabriel, CA (cdp) Los Angeles County	4.39
Diamond Bar, CA (city) Los Angeles County	3.72
Cerritos, CA (city) Los Angeles County	3.48
San Gabriel, CA (city) Los Angeles County	1.94
Irvine, CA (city) Orange County	1.83
Alhambra, CA (city) Los Angeles County	1.81
Monterey Park, CA (city) Los Angeles County	1.75
Cypress, CA (city) Orange County	1.60
Cupertino, CA (city) Santa Clara County	1.56
Sugar Land, TX (city) Fort Bend County	1.48
Rancho Palos Verdes, CA (city) Los Angeles County	1.31
Fremont, CA (city) Alameda County	1.21
Saratoga, CA (city) Santa Clara County	1.11
Chino Hills, CA (city) San Bernardino County	0.95
Torrance, CA (city) Los Angeles County	0.94
West Covina, CA (city) Los Angeles County	0.90
Bellevue, WA (city) King County	0.85
Fountain Valley, CA (city) Orange County	0.72
Troy, MI (city) Oakland County	0.69
Tustin, CA (city) Orange County	0.69
Edison, NJ (township) Middlesex County	0.68
Upland, CA (city) San Bernardino County	0.68
Sunnyvale, CA (city) Santa Clara County	0.51
Berkeley, CA (city) Alameda County	0.40
Ann Arbor, MI (city) Washtenaw County	0.39
Orange, CA (city) Orange County	0.36
El Monte, CA (city) Los Angeles County	0.34
Naperville, IL (city) Du Page County	0.34
Huntington Beach, CA (city) Orange County	0.30
Plano, TX (city) Collin County	0.25
San Jose, CA (city) Santa Clara County	0.23
Anaheim, CA (city) Orange County	0.20
Madison, WI (city) Dane County	0.20
Honolulu, HI (cdp) Honolulu County	0.19
Seattle, WA (city) King County	0.17
North Hempstead, NY (town) Nassau County	0.13
San Diego, CA (city) San Diego County	0.13
Arlington, TX (city) Tarrant County	0.12
Austin, TX (city) Travis County	0.11
San Francisco, CA (city) San Francisco County	0.10
Los Angeles, CA (city) Los Angeles County	0.09
Boston, MA (city) Suffolk County	0.08
Houston, TX (city) Harris County	0.08
Columbus, OH (city) Franklin County	0.07
New York, NY (city)	0.06
Chicago, IL (city) Cook County	0.03

Notes: Please refer to the User's Guide for an explanation of data; ranking tables include all places with Asian and/or NHPI populations above SF4 population thresholds; (1) tables reflect only those areas that meet SF4 population thresholds, therefore there may be less than 50 states, 75 counties or 75 places listed

Population

Thai

All States, Top 75 Counties, and Top 75 Places Sorted by Number[1]

State	Number
United States	110,851
California	36,155
Texas	7,114
New York	6,597
Florida	6,572
Illinois	5,848
Washington	3,892
Virginia	3,581
Nevada	2,977
Maryland	2,854
Massachusetts	2,255
Georgia	2,250
Colorado	1,947
Ohio	1,900
New Jersey	1,845
Pennsylvania	1,798
Arizona	1,631
North Carolina	1,625
Michigan	1,604
Oregon	1,496
Hawaii	1,398
Missouri	1,372
Tennessee	995
Iowa	930
Minnesota	920
Indiana	904
Wisconsin	870
Oklahoma	823
Connecticut	784
Alaska	782
Utah	707
South Carolina	688
Kansas	650
Louisiana	645
Alabama	621
Nebraska	461
Kentucky	422
New Mexico	401
Arkansas	292

County	Number
Los Angeles County, CA	19,564
Cook County, IL	4,002
Orange County, CA	3,159
Clark County, NV	2,620
Queens County, NY	2,364
King County, WA	1,950
San Bernardino County, CA	1,705
Fairfax County, VA	1,492
San Francisco County, CA	1,461
Alameda County, CA	1,453
Santa Clara County, CA	1,334
Harris County, TX	1,333
Montgomery County, MD	1,327
San Diego County, CA	1,309
Honolulu County, HI	1,149
Maricopa County, AZ	1,146
Dallas County, TX	1,105
Middlesex County, MA	901
Miami-Dade County, FL	882
Riverside County, CA	876
New York County, NY	835
Bexar County, TX	814
Tarrant County, TX	775
Palm Beach County, FL	760
Sacramento County, CA	739
San Mateo County, CA	701
Hillsborough County, FL	676
Contra Costa County, CA	635
Okaloosa County, FL	624
Broward County, FL	599
Westchester County, NY	594
Anchorage Borough, AK	577
Bergen County, NJ	503
Multnomah County, OR	492
Pinellas County, FL	488
Collin County, TX	454
Franklin County, OH	428
DuPage County, IL	418
Denver County, CO	406
Travis County, TX	402
Oklahoma County, OK	397
Pierce County, WA	396
Suffolk County, NY	387
St. Louis County, MO	378
Nassau County, NY	376
Polk County, IA	358
Prince George's County, MD	334

Place	Number
Los Angeles, CA (city) Los Angeles County	9,083
New York, NY (city)	3,823
Chicago, IL (city) Cook County	2,144
San Francisco, CA (city) San Francisco County	1,461
Houston, TX (city) Harris County	881
Seattle, WA (city) King County	878
San Diego, CA (city) San Diego County	823
Las Vegas, NV (city) Clark County	700
San Jose, CA (city) Santa Clara County	631
Long Beach, CA (city) Los Angeles County	604
San Antonio, TX (city) Bexar County	577
Honolulu, HI (cdp) Honolulu County	535
Spring Valley, NV (cdp) Clark County	497
Cerritos, CA (city) Los Angeles County	466
Anaheim, CA (city) Orange County	456
Portland, OR (city) Multnomah County	450
Glendale, CA (city) Los Angeles County	420
Denver, CO (city) Denver County	406
Bellflower, CA (city) Los Angeles County	389
Columbus, OH (city) Franklin County	389
Des Moines, IA (city) Polk County	295

Notes: Please refer to the User's Guide for an explanation of data; ranking tables include all places with Asian and/or NHPI populations above SF4 population thresholds; (1) tables reflect only those areas that meet SF4 population thresholds, therefore there may be less than 50 states, 75 counties or 75 places listed

Population

Thai

All States, Top 75 Counties, and Top 75 Places Sorted by Percent of Asian Population[1]

State	Percent
Nevada	3.34
Alaska	3.07
Iowa	2.66
Florida	2.49
Missouri	2.27
New Mexico	2.19
Nebraska	2.18
Colorado	2.09
Alabama	2.08
Utah	1.92
South Carolina	1.88
Tennessee	1.84
Oklahoma	1.81
Arizona	1.79
Indiana	1.58
Arkansas	1.53
Oregon	1.51
Kentucky	1.46
North Carolina	1.46
Kansas	1.45
Ohio	1.44
Virginia	1.40
Illinois	1.38
Maryland	1.36
Georgia	1.31
Texas	1.28
Washington	1.21
Louisiana	1.16
United States	1.09
Wisconsin	1.05
California	0.98
Connecticut	0.95
Massachusetts	0.95
Michigan	0.92
Pennsylvania	0.83
Minnesota	0.66
New York	0.63
New Jersey	0.38
Hawaii	0.28

County	Percent
Okaloosa County, FL	14.08
Palm Beach County, FL	4.50
Anchorage Borough, AK	4.04
Polk County, IA	3.90
Clark County, NV	3.66
Bexar County, TX	3.60
Hillsborough County, FL	3.13
Miami-Dade County, FL	2.87
Denver County, CO	2.68
Pinellas County, FL	2.60
Oklahoma County, OK	2.18
San Bernardino County, CA	2.16
St. Louis County, MO	1.76
Maricopa County, AZ	1.73
Los Angeles County, CA	1.72
Broward County, FL	1.64
Riverside County, CA	1.60
Cook County, IL	1.53
Tarrant County, TX	1.51
Westchester County, NY	1.42
Collin County, TX	1.35
Montgomery County, MD	1.35
Multnomah County, OR	1.32
Franklin County, OH	1.30
Dallas County, TX	1.26
Fairfax County, VA	1.21
Pierce County, WA	1.14
Suffolk County, NY	1.13
Travis County, TX	1.11
Prince George's County, MD	1.10
King County, WA	1.04
Middlesex County, MA	0.98
Orange County, CA	0.82
Harris County, TX	0.78
Contra Costa County, CA	0.62
San Francisco County, CA	0.61
Nassau County, NY	0.60
Queens County, NY	0.60
DuPage County, IL	0.59
New York County, NY	0.58
Sacramento County, CA	0.55
Bergen County, NJ	0.53
San Diego County, CA	0.53
Alameda County, CA	0.49
San Mateo County, CA	0.49
Santa Clara County, CA	0.31
Honolulu County, HI	0.28

Place	Percent
Bellflower, CA (city) Los Angeles County	5.42
Des Moines, IA (city) Polk County	4.62
Spring Valley, NV (cdp) Clark County	3.84
Las Vegas, NV (city) Clark County	3.24
San Antonio, TX (city) Bexar County	3.19
Denver, CO (city) Denver County	2.68
Los Angeles, CA (city) Los Angeles County	2.46
Chicago, IL (city) Cook County	1.69
Columbus, OH (city) Franklin County	1.57
Cerritos, CA (city) Los Angeles County	1.54
Portland, OR (city) Multnomah County	1.34
Glendale, CA (city) Los Angeles County	1.31
Seattle, WA (city) King County	1.19
Anaheim, CA (city) Orange County	1.15
Long Beach, CA (city) Los Angeles County	1.10
Houston, TX (city) Harris County	0.86
San Francisco, CA (city) San Francisco County	0.61
New York, NY (city)	0.49
San Diego, CA (city) San Diego County	0.49
Honolulu, HI (cdp) Honolulu County	0.26
San Jose, CA (city) Santa Clara County	0.26

Notes: Please refer to the User's Guide for an explanation of data; ranking tables include all places with Asian and/or NHPI populations above SF4 population thresholds; (1) tables reflect only those areas that meet SF4 population thresholds, therefore there may be less than 50 states, 75 counties or 75 places listed

Population

Thai

All States, Top 75 Counties, and Top 75 Places Sorted by Percent of Total Population[1]

State	Percent
Nevada	0.15
Alaska	0.12
Hawaii	0.12
California	0.11
Washington	0.07
Colorado	0.05
Illinois	0.05
Maryland	0.05
Virginia	0.05
Florida	0.04
Massachusetts	0.04
Oregon	0.04
United States	0.04
Arizona	0.03
Georgia	0.03
Iowa	0.03
Nebraska	0.03
New York	0.03
Texas	0.03
Utah	0.03
Connecticut	0.02
Kansas	0.02
Michigan	0.02
Minnesota	0.02
Missouri	0.02
New Jersey	0.02
New Mexico	0.02
North Carolina	0.02
Ohio	0.02
Oklahoma	0.02
South Carolina	0.02
Tennessee	0.02
Wisconsin	0.02
Alabama	0.01
Arkansas	0.01
Indiana	0.01
Kentucky	0.01
Louisiana	0.01
Pennsylvania	0.01

County	Percent
Okaloosa County, FL	0.37
Anchorage Borough, AK	0.22
Los Angeles County, CA	0.21
Clark County, NV	0.19
San Francisco County, CA	0.19
Fairfax County, VA	0.15
Montgomery County, MD	0.15
Honolulu County, HI	0.13
King County, WA	0.11
Orange County, CA	0.11
Queens County, NY	0.11
Alameda County, CA	0.10
Polk County, IA	0.10
San Bernardino County, CA	0.10
San Mateo County, CA	0.10
Collin County, TX	0.09
Santa Clara County, CA	0.08
Contra Costa County, CA	0.07
Cook County, IL	0.07
Denver County, CO	0.07
Hillsborough County, FL	0.07
Multnomah County, OR	0.07
Palm Beach County, FL	0.07
Bergen County, NJ	0.06
Bexar County, TX	0.06
Middlesex County, MA	0.06
Oklahoma County, OK	0.06
Pierce County, WA	0.06
Riverside County, CA	0.06
Sacramento County, CA	0.06
Westchester County, NY	0.06
Dallas County, TX	0.05
DuPage County, IL	0.05
New York County, NY	0.05
Pinellas County, FL	0.05
San Diego County, CA	0.05
Tarrant County, TX	0.05
Travis County, TX	0.05
Broward County, FL	0.04
Franklin County, OH	0.04
Harris County, TX	0.04
Maricopa County, AZ	0.04
Miami-Dade County, FL	0.04
Prince George's County, MD	0.04
St. Louis County, MO	0.04
Nassau County, NY	0.03
Suffolk County, NY	0.03

Place	Percent
Cerritos, CA (city) Los Angeles County	0.90
Bellflower, CA (city) Los Angeles County	0.53
Spring Valley, NV (cdp) Clark County	0.42
Los Angeles, CA (city) Los Angeles County	0.25
Glendale, CA (city) Los Angeles County	0.22
San Francisco, CA (city) San Francisco County	0.19
Seattle, WA (city) King County	0.16
Des Moines, IA (city) Polk County	0.15
Las Vegas, NV (city) Clark County	0.15
Anaheim, CA (city) Orange County	0.14
Honolulu, HI (cdp) Honolulu County	0.14
Long Beach, CA (city) Los Angeles County	0.13
Portland, OR (city) Multnomah County	0.09
Chicago, IL (city) Cook County	0.07
Denver, CO (city) Denver County	0.07
San Diego, CA (city) San Diego County	0.07
San Jose, CA (city) Santa Clara County	0.07
Columbus, OH (city) Franklin County	0.05
Houston, TX (city) Harris County	0.05
New York, NY (city)	0.05
San Antonio, TX (city) Bexar County	0.05

Notes: Please refer to the User's Guide for an explanation of data; ranking tables include all places with Asian and/or NHPI populations above SF4 population thresholds; (1) tables reflect only those areas that meet SF4 population thresholds, therefore there may be less than 50 states, 75 counties or 75 places listed

Population

Tongan

All States, Top 75 Counties, and Top 75 Places Sorted by Number[1]

State	Number
United States	27,686
California	12,167
Utah	6,795
Hawaii	4,181
Washington	844
Nevada	790
Arizona	634
Texas	501
Oregon	445
Alaska	419

County	Number
Salt Lake County, UT	5,938
San Mateo County, CA	3,654
Honolulu County, HI	3,082
Los Angeles County, CA	2,276
Alameda County, CA	1,832
San Bernardino County, CA	810
Maui County, HI	794
Sacramento County, CA	741
Orange County, CA	581
Washoe County, NV	577
Maricopa County, AZ	527
King County, WA	502
Utah County, UT	462
Contra Costa County, CA	451
San Diego County, CA	435
Tarrant County, TX	365
Multnomah County, OR	359

Place	Number
Salt Lake City, UT (city) Salt Lake County	2,447
West Valley City, UT (city) Salt Lake County	1,806
Honolulu, HI (cdp) Honolulu County	1,558
East Palo Alto, CA (city) San Mateo County	1,494
Oakland, CA (city) Alameda County	1,312
San Mateo, CA (city) San Mateo County	638
Sacramento, CA (city) Sacramento County	574
San Bruno, CA (city) San Mateo County	533
West Jordan, UT (city) Salt Lake County	470
Hauula, HI (cdp) Honolulu County	360
Portland, OR (city) Multnomah County	352
Los Angeles, CA (city) Los Angeles County	342
Kahuku, HI (cdp) Honolulu County	237
Laie, HI (cdp) Honolulu County	225

Notes: Please refer to the User's Guide for an explanation of data; ranking tables include all places with Asian and/or NHPI populations above SF4 population thresholds; (1) tables reflect only those areas that meet SF4 population thresholds, therefore there may be less than 50 states, 75 counties or 75 places listed

Population

Tongan

All States, Top 75 Counties, and Top 75 Places Sorted by Percent of Native Hawaiian and Other Pacific Islander Population[1]

State	Percent
Utah	47.30
Alaska	13.42
California	10.69
Arizona	10.28
Nevada	10.12
United States	7.31
Oregon	5.87
Texas	4.02
Washington	3.88
Hawaii	3.71

County	Percent
Salt Lake County, UT	57.46
San Mateo County, CA	42.82
Washoe County, NV	38.42
Utah County, UT	25.60
Tarrant County, TX	22.17
Alameda County, CA	19.94
San Bernardino County, CA	16.14
Multnomah County, OR	14.30
Maricopa County, AZ	13.83
Contra Costa County, CA	13.30
Sacramento County, CA	11.82
Los Angeles County, CA	8.36
Orange County, CA	6.81
King County, WA	6.07
Maui County, HI	5.77
Honolulu County, HI	3.99
San Diego County, CA	3.23

Place	Percent
Salt Lake City, UT (city) Salt Lake County	73.82
East Palo Alto, CA (city) San Mateo County	67.57
West Jordan, UT (city) Salt Lake County	67.24
West Valley City, UT (city) Salt Lake County	57.77
San Bruno, CA (city) San Mateo County	52.41
Oakland, CA (city) Alameda County	50.83
San Mateo, CA (city) San Mateo County	46.60
Kahuku, HI (cdp) Honolulu County	37.56
Hauula, HI (cdp) Honolulu County	24.34
Portland, OR (city) Multnomah County	17.51
Sacramento, CA (city) Sacramento County	15.55
Laie, HI (cdp) Honolulu County	13.98
Honolulu, HI (cdp) Honolulu County	6.03
Los Angeles, CA (city) Los Angeles County	5.31

Notes: Please refer to the User's Guide for an explanation of data; ranking tables include all places with Asian and/or NHPI populations above SF4 population thresholds; (1) tables reflect only those areas that meet SF4 population thresholds, therefore there may be less than 50 states, 75 counties or 75 places listed

Population

Tongan

All States, Top 75 Counties, and Top 75 Places Sorted by Percent of Total Population[1]

State	Percent
Hawaii	0.35
Utah	0.30
Alaska	0.07
California	0.04
Nevada	0.04
Arizona	0.01
Oregon	0.01
United States	0.01
Washington	0.01
Texas	<0.01

County	Percent
Salt Lake County, UT	0.66
Maui County, HI	0.62
San Mateo County, CA	0.52
Honolulu County, HI	0.35
Washoe County, NV	0.17
Alameda County, CA	0.13
Utah County, UT	0.13
Sacramento County, CA	0.06
Contra Costa County, CA	0.05
Multnomah County, OR	0.05
San Bernardino County, CA	0.05
King County, WA	0.03
Tarrant County, TX	0.03
Los Angeles County, CA	0.02
Maricopa County, AZ	0.02
Orange County, CA	0.02
San Diego County, CA	0.02

Place	Percent
Kahuku, HI (cdp) Honolulu County	11.30
Hauula, HI (cdp) Honolulu County	9.80
East Palo Alto, CA (city) San Mateo County	5.07
Laie, HI (cdp) Honolulu County	4.89
West Valley City, UT (city) Salt Lake County	1.66
Salt Lake City, UT (city) Salt Lake County	1.35
San Bruno, CA (city) San Mateo County	1.33
San Mateo, CA (city) San Mateo County	0.69
West Jordan, UT (city) Salt Lake County	0.69
Honolulu, HI (cdp) Honolulu County	0.42
Oakland, CA (city) Alameda County	0.33
Sacramento, CA (city) Sacramento County	0.14
Portland, OR (city) Multnomah County	0.07
Los Angeles, CA (city) Los Angeles County	0.01

Notes: Please refer to the User's Guide for an explanation of data; ranking tables include all places with Asian and/or NHPI populations above SF4 population thresholds; (1) tables reflect only those areas that meet SF4 population thresholds, therefore there may be less than 50 states, 75 counties or 75 places listed

Population

Vietnamese

All States, Top 75 Counties, and Top 75 Places Sorted by Number[1]

State	Number
United States	1,110,207
California	446,475
Texas	134,145
Washington	44,658
Virginia	35,444
Massachusetts	34,376
Florida	33,391
Georgia	29,494
Pennsylvania	28,625
Louisiana	25,049
New York	23,176
Oregon	19,040
Illinois	18,420
Minnesota	18,384
Maryland	16,683
North Carolina	15,604
New Jersey	14,979
Colorado	13,666
Michigan	12,974
Oklahoma	12,221
Arizona	11,704
Kansas	11,293
Missouri	10,506
Ohio	10,357
Hawaii	8,345
Connecticut	7,399
Tennessee	7,061
Iowa	6,771
Nebraska	6,680
Utah	5,553
Mississippi	5,337
Indiana	4,714
Alabama	4,631
Nevada	4,095
Wisconsin	3,871
Arkansas	3,864
South Carolina	3,814
Kentucky	3,206
New Mexico	2,797
District of Columbia	1,789
New Hampshire	1,682
Idaho	1,360
Maine	1,115
Vermont	1,072
Rhode Island	1,028
Alaska	969
South Dakota	715
Delaware	686
West Virginia	442

County	Number
Orange County, CA	136,197
Santa Clara County, CA	97,419
Los Angeles County, CA	78,258
Harris County, TX	55,445
San Diego County, CA	34,496
King County, WA	27,041
Alameda County, CA	23,530
Fairfax County, VA	21,292
Dallas County, TX	19,878
Tarrant County, TX	19,171
Sacramento County, CA	16,557
Suffolk County, MA	12,459
Multnomah County, OR	11,460
Philadelphia County, PA	11,074
Cook County, IL	11,010
San Francisco County, CA	10,430
San Bernardino County, CA	10,306
Montgomery County, MD	9,384
Maricopa County, AZ	8,914
Hennepin County, MN	8,150
Honolulu County, HI	7,775
Gwinnett County, GA	7,468
Travis County, TX	7,386
Orleans Parish, LA	6,962
Jefferson Parish, LA	6,909
Oklahoma County, OK	6,842
Middlesex County, MA	6,736
Sedgwick County, KS	6,733
DeKalb County, GA	6,516
Orange County, FL	6,357
San Joaquin County, CA	6,320
Riverside County, CA	6,156
Worcester County, MA	5,645
Contra Costa County, CA	5,432
Snohomish County, WA	5,250
Fort Bend County, TX	5,208
Washington County, OR	5,019
Salt Lake County, UT	4,668
Mecklenburg County, NC	4,652
Denver County, CO	4,449
Clayton County, GA	4,391
Kent County, MI	4,315
Pierce County, WA	4,286
Pinellas County, FL	4,234
Jefferson County, TX	4,095
Hillsborough County, FL	3,993
Kings County, NY	3,830
Lancaster County, NE	3,776
Queens County, NY	3,739
Ramsey County, MN	3,601
East Baton Rouge Parish, LA	3,515
Collin County, TX	3,493
Shelby County, TN	3,342
Clark County, NV	3,292
Ventura County, CA	3,233
Saint Louis Independent City, MO	3,219
Hartford County, CT	3,201
Camden County, NJ	3,165
Essex County, MA	3,037
Bronx County, NY	2,995
Fulton County, GA	2,983
Guilford County, NC	2,966
Jackson County, MO	2,880
Bexar County, TX	2,879
Broward County, FL	2,867
DuPage County, IL	2,827
Norfolk County, MA	2,818
San Mateo County, CA	2,800
Harrison County, MS	2,797
Arapahoe County, CO	2,738
Prince George's County, MD	2,625
Denton County, TX	2,606
Polk County, IA	2,508
Bernalillo County, NM	2,479
Franklin County, OH	2,443

Place	Number
San Jose, CA (city) Santa Clara County	75,956
Garden Grove, CA (city) Orange County	35,023
Houston, TX (city) Harris County	31,820
San Diego, CA (city) San Diego County	28,549
Westminster, CA (city) Orange County	27,121
Los Angeles, CA (city) Los Angeles County	19,508
Santa Ana, CA (city) Orange County	19,211
New York, NY (city)	12,310
Seattle, WA (city) King County	11,443
Boston, MA (city) Suffolk County	11,126
Philadelphia, PA (city) Philadelphia County	11,074
Portland, OR (city) Multnomah County	10,874
Anaheim, CA (city) Orange County	10,568
San Francisco, CA (city) San Francisco County	10,430
Arlington, TX (city) Tarrant County	9,023
Oakland, CA (city) Alameda County	8,216
Chicago, IL (city) Cook County	8,179
Milpitas, CA (city) Santa Clara County	7,922
Oklahoma City, OK (city) Oklahoma County	7,914
Fountain Valley, CA (city) Orange County	7,117
Dallas, TX (city) Dallas County	7,070
New Orleans, LA (city) Orleans Parish	6,962
Honolulu, HI (cdp) Honolulu County	6,565
Sacramento, CA (city) Sacramento County	6,497
Wichita, KS (city) Sedgwick County	6,412
El Monte, CA (city) Los Angeles County	6,369
Garland, TX (city) Dallas County	6,301
Rosemead, CA (city) Los Angeles County	5,938
Huntington Beach, CA (city) Orange County	5,876
Austin, TX (city) Travis County	5,789
Stockton, CA (city) San Joaquin County	5,751
Fort Worth, TX (city) Tarrant County	5,374
Long Beach, CA (city) Los Angeles County	5,073
Irvine, CA (city) Orange County	4,852
Santa Clara, CA (city) Santa Clara County	4,638
Denver, CO (city) Denver County	4,449
Phoenix, AZ (city) Maricopa County	4,433
Alhambra, CA (city) Los Angeles County	4,395
Fremont, CA (city) Alameda County	4,345
Worcester, MA (city) Worcester County	4,287
Charlotte, NC (city) Mecklenburg County	3,834
Orange, CA (city) Orange County	3,832
Lincoln, NE (city) Lancaster County	3,769
Annandale, VA (cdp) Fairfax County	3,349
Monterey Park, CA (city) Los Angeles County	3,239
St. Louis, MO (city) Saint Louis Independent City	3,219
Sunnyvale, CA (city) Santa Clara County	3,176
Tacoma, WA (city) Pierce County	3,120
Kansas City, MO (city) Jackson County	3,067
Port Arthur, TX (city) Jefferson County	2,829
Minneapolis, MN (city) Hennepin County	2,804
Stanton, CA (city) Orange County	2,735
San Gabriel, CA (city) Los Angeles County	2,667
Hayward, CA (city) Alameda County	2,607
Baton Rouge, LA (city) East Baton Rouge Parish	2,585
Memphis, TN (city) Shelby County	2,573
St. Paul, MN (city) Ramsey County	2,553
Albuquerque, NM (city) Bernalillo County	2,406
Carrollton, TX (city) Denton County	2,404
Grand Prairie, TX (city) Dallas County	2,383
Riverside, CA (city) Riverside County	2,290
Jefferson, VA (cdp) Fairfax County	2,289
San Antonio, TX (city) Bexar County	2,272
Costa Mesa, CA (city) Orange County	2,241
Arlington, VA (cdp) Arlington County	2,189
Columbus, OH (city) Franklin County	2,181
Elk Grove, CA (cdp) Sacramento County	2,174
West Covina, CA (city) Los Angeles County	2,160
Des Moines, IA (city) Polk County	2,097
Jacksonville, FL (city) Duval County	2,051
Union City, CA (city) Alameda County	2,047
White Center, WA (cdp) King County	2,041
Greensboro, NC (city) Guilford County	1,932
Aurora, CO (city) Arapahoe County	1,915
Tucson, AZ (city) Pima County	1,858

Notes: Please refer to the User's Guide for an explanation of data; ranking tables include all places with Asian and/or NHPI populations above SF4 population thresholds; (1) tables reflect only those areas that meet SF4 population thresholds, therefore there may be less than 50 states, 75 counties or 75 places listed

Population

Vietnamese

All States, Top 75 Counties, and Top 75 Places Sorted by Percent of Asian Population[1]

State	Percent
Louisiana	45.14
Nebraska	31.62
Mississippi	30.14
Oklahoma	26.83
Kansas	25.22
Texas	24.13
Vermont	22.10
Arkansas	20.25
Iowa	19.33
Oregon	19.21
Missouri	17.39
Georgia	17.20
Alabama	15.48
New Mexico	15.30
South Dakota	15.12
Utah	15.06
Colorado	14.65
Massachusetts	14.43
North Carolina	14.02
Washington	13.91
Virginia	13.83
Maine	13.50
Pennsylvania	13.21
Minnesota	13.20
Tennessee	13.04
Arizona	12.83
Florida	12.63
California	12.12
District of Columbia	12.12
Idaho	12.01
Kentucky	11.06
New Hampshire	10.91
United States	10.91
South Carolina	10.45
Connecticut	8.99
Indiana	8.24
Maryland	7.96
Ohio	7.84
Michigan	7.42
West Virginia	4.68
Wisconsin	4.66
Nevada	4.59
Illinois	4.35
Rhode Island	4.31
Delaware	4.27
Alaska	3.80
New Jersey	3.11
New York	2.22
Hawaii	1.66

County	Percent
Ford County, KS	99.01
St. Mary Parish, LA	90.19
Vermilion Parish, LA	89.38
St. Martin Parish, LA	82.31
Matagorda County, TX	75.42
Aransas County, TX	71.30
Plaquemines Parish, LA	70.96
Adams County, NE	66.30
Orleans Parish, LA	66.29
Hall County, GA	66.26
Woodbury County, IA	60.10
Jefferson County, TX	58.23
Lancaster County, NE	56.36
Harrison County, MS	56.21
Jackson County, MS	54.50
Orange County, TX	54.09
Finney County, KS	52.53
Jefferson Parish, LA	50.10
Sebastian County, AR	50.10
Sedgwick County, KS	47.50
St. Bernard Parish, LA	45.97
Saint Louis Independent City, MO	45.50
Terrebonne Parish, LA	44.82
Scott County, IA	43.89
Saline County, KS	43.21
Clayton County, GA	42.45
Kent County, MI	41.04
East Baton Rouge Parish, LA	40.27
Oneida County, NY	39.82
Mobile County, AL	39.06
Oklahoma County, OK	37.65
Tarrant County, TX	37.44
Potter County, TX	35.55
Orange County, CA	35.25
Dauphin County, PA	34.88
Lafayette Parish, LA	34.50
Stearns County, MN	33.96
York County, SC	33.92
Gaston County, NC	33.49
Jackson County, MO	33.31
Minnehaha County, SD	33.00
Galveston County, TX	32.45
Harris County, TX	32.24
Berks County, PA	32.12
Hampden County, MA	32.03
Guilford County, NC	31.75
Cowlitz County, WA	31.45
Wichita County, TX	31.44
Lancaster County, PA	31.43
Multnomah County, OR	30.74
Chittenden County, VT	30.64
Worcester County, MA	29.77
Denver County, CO	29.32
Cleveland County, OK	28.92
Clay County, MO	28.50
Bay County, FL	28.11
Brazoria County, TX	28.05
Polk County, IA	27.34
Canadian County, OK	27.11
Iberia Parish, LA	26.53
Sarasota County, FL	26.03
Suffolk County, MA	25.89
Benton County, AR	25.69
Bernalillo County, NM	25.13
Chatham County, GA	25.05
DeKalb County, GA	24.55
Escambia County, FL	24.33
Calhoun County, TX	24.16
Eaton County, MI	24.06
Tulsa County, OK	23.81
Greenville County, SC	23.28
Dallas County, TX	22.73
Santa Clara County, CA	22.64
Pinellas County, FL	22.54
Shelby County, TN	22.39

Place	Percent
Dodge City, KS (city) Ford County	99.22
Amelia, LA (cdp) Saint Mary Parish	98.52
Henderson, LA (town) Saint Martin Parish	98.37
Palacios, TX (city) Matagorda County	98.04
Seadrift, TX (city) Calhoun County	97.20
Abbeville, LA (city) Vermilion Parish	95.61
Estelle, LA (cdp) Jefferson Parish	95.33
Avondale, LA (cdp) Jefferson Parish	94.64
Fulton, TX (town) Aransas County	90.06
Timberlane, LA (cdp) Jefferson Parish	89.03
Port Arthur, TX (city) Jefferson County	83.50
Gainesville, GA (city) Hall County	82.65
San Leon, TX (cdp) Galveston County	81.87
Westminster, CA (city) Orange County	81.32
Woodlynne, NJ (borough) Camden County	78.30
Marrero, LA (cdp) Jefferson Parish	78.00
Chamblee, GA (city) De Kalb County	74.81
Harvey, LA (cdp) Jefferson Parish	74.46
Forest Park, GA (city) Clayton County	73.86
Woodmere, LA (cdp) Jefferson Parish	70.75
Utica, NY (city) Oneida County	69.52
Wyoming, MI (city) Kent County	68.87
Hastings, NE (city) Adams County	68.66
Garden Grove, CA (city) Orange County	68.63
Ocean Springs, MS (city) Jackson County	66.42
New Orleans, LA (city) Orleans Parish	66.29
Santa Ana, CA (city) Orange County	64.46
Terrytown, LA (cdp) Jefferson Parish	64.29
Sioux City, IA (city) Woodbury County	64.01
Camden, NJ (city) Camden County	61.35
Biloxi, MS (city) Harrison County	60.51
Bayou La Batre, AL (city) Mobile County	59.17
West and East Lealman, FL (cdp) Pinellas County	58.59
Gretna, LA (city) Jefferson Parish	57.79
Harrisburg, PA (city) Dauphin County	57.57
Lincoln, NE (city) Lancaster County	56.79
Garden City, KS (city) Finney County	55.23
Davenport, IA (city) Scott County	54.98
Pine Hills, FL (cdp) Orange County	54.79
Worcester, MA (city) Worcester County	54.31
Reading, PA (city) Berks County	54.22
Fort Smith, AR (city) Sebastian County	52.27
Pearland, TX (city) Brazoria County	51.16
Chelsea, MA (city) Suffolk County	50.79
Haltom City, TX (city) Tarrant County	50.74
Wichita, KS (city) Sedgwick County	50.56
Springfield, MA (city) Hampden County	50.16
Seven Corners, VA (cdp) Fairfax County	50.00
Burlington, VT (city) Chittenden County	49.45
Fountain Valley, CA (city) Orange County	49.35
Kentwood, MI (city) Kent County	48.84
Everett, MA (city) Middlesex County	48.33
Doraville, GA (city) De Kalb County	48.18
Stanton, CA (city) Orange County	47.76
Arlington, TX (city) Tarrant County	46.82
Montclair, CA (city) San Bernardino County	46.24
Oklahoma City, OK (city) Oklahoma County	45.80
Riverdale, GA (city) Clayton County	45.63
White Center, WA (cdp) King County	45.58
St. Louis, MO (city) Saint Louis Independent City	45.50
Grand Prairie, TX (city) Dallas County	45.00
Lawndale, CA (city) Los Angeles County	44.98
Baton Rouge, LA (city) East Baton Rouge Parish	44.76
League City, TX (city) Galveston County	44.72
Pennsauken, NJ (township) Camden County	44.47
Alum Rock, CA (cdp) Santa Clara County	44.28
Jefferson, VA (cdp) Fairfax County	43.61
Manheim, PA (township) Lancaster County	42.35
Lawrence, MA (city) Essex County	42.26
Louisville, KY (city) Jefferson County	41.28
Grand Rapids, MI (city) Kent County	40.93
Lake Barcroft, VA (cdp) Fairfax County	40.85
Oak Ridge, FL (cdp) Orange County	40.35
Garland, TX (city) Dallas County	40.27
Alondra Park, CA (cdp) Los Angeles County	39.88

Notes: Please refer to the User's Guide for an explanation of data; ranking tables include all places with Asian and/or NHPI populations above SF4 population thresholds; (1) tables reflect only those areas that meet SF4 population thresholds, therefore there may be less than 50 states, 75 counties or 75 places listed

Population

Vietnamese

All States, Top 75 Counties, and Top 75 Places Sorted by Percent of Total Population[1]

State	Percent
California	1.32
Washington	0.76
Hawaii	0.69
Texas	0.64
Louisiana	0.56
Oregon	0.56
Massachusetts	0.54
Virginia	0.50
Kansas	0.42
Nebraska	0.39
United States	0.39
Minnesota	0.37
Georgia	0.36
Oklahoma	0.35
Colorado	0.32
District of Columbia	0.31
Maryland	0.31
Utah	0.25
Arizona	0.23
Iowa	0.23
Pennsylvania	0.23
Connecticut	0.22
Florida	0.21
Nevada	0.20
Mississippi	0.19
Missouri	0.19
North Carolina	0.19
New Jersey	0.18
Vermont	0.18
Alaska	0.15
Illinois	0.15
New Mexico	0.15
Arkansas	0.14
New Hampshire	0.14
Michigan	0.13
New York	0.12
Tennessee	0.12
Idaho	0.11
Alabama	0.10
Rhode Island	0.10
South Carolina	0.10
Delaware	0.09
Maine	0.09
Ohio	0.09
South Dakota	0.09
Indiana	0.08
Kentucky	0.08
Wisconsin	0.07
West Virginia	0.02

County	Percent
Santa Clara County, CA	5.79
Orange County, CA	4.79
Fairfax County, VA	2.20
Ford County, KS	2.16
Aransas County, TX	2.05
Fairfax Independent City, VA	2.01
Clayton County, GA	1.86
Suffolk County, MA	1.81
Matagorda County, TX	1.79
Multnomah County, OR	1.74
Vermilion Parish, LA	1.74
Plaquemines Parish, LA	1.69
St. Mary Parish, LA	1.65
Alameda County, CA	1.63
Harris County, TX	1.63
Jefferson County, TX	1.62
King County, WA	1.56
Sebastian County, AR	1.56
Jefferson Parish, LA	1.52
Lancaster County, NE	1.51
Sedgwick County, KS	1.49
Harrison County, MS	1.48
Fort Bend County, TX	1.47
Orleans Parish, LA	1.44
Woodbury County, IA	1.38
Adams County, NE	1.36
Sacramento County, CA	1.35
San Francisco County, CA	1.34
Tarrant County, TX	1.33
Finney County, KS	1.31
Gwinnett County, GA	1.27
San Diego County, CA	1.23
Arlington County, VA	1.16
Washington County, OR	1.13
San Joaquin County, CA	1.12
Montgomery County, MD	1.07
Oklahoma County, OK	1.04
Loudoun County, VA	1.03
DeKalb County, GA	0.98
Potter County, TX	0.94
Saint Louis Independent City, MO	0.92
Travis County, TX	0.91
Dallas County, TX	0.90
Honolulu County, HI	0.89
Snohomish County, WA	0.87
Hall County, GA	0.86
East Baton Rouge Parish, LA	0.85
Thurston County, WA	0.85
Yolo County, CA	0.83
Atlantic County, NJ	0.82
Cleveland County, OK	0.82
Los Angeles County, CA	0.82
Jackson County, MS	0.81
Calhoun County, TX	0.80
Denver County, CO	0.80
Kent County, MI	0.75
Worcester County, MA	0.75
St. Bernard Parish, LA	0.74
Hennepin County, MN	0.73
Philadelphia County, PA	0.73
Collin County, TX	0.71
Orange County, FL	0.71
Dauphin County, PA	0.70
Guilford County, NC	0.70
Ramsey County, MN	0.70
Saline County, KS	0.69
Clark County, WA	0.68
Galveston County, TX	0.68
Canadian County, OK	0.67
Mecklenburg County, NC	0.67
Polk County, IA	0.67
St. Martin Parish, LA	0.63
Scott County, IA	0.63
Adams County, CO	0.62
Camden County, NJ	0.62

Place	Percent
Westminster, CA (city) Orange County	30.86
Amelia, LA (cdp) Saint Mary Parish	23.46
Garden Grove, CA (city) Orange County	21.14
Bayou La Batre, AL (city) Mobile County	17.04
Henderson, LA (town) Saint Martin Parish	15.71
Fountain Valley, CA (city) Orange County	12.94
Milpitas, CA (city) Santa Clara County	12.63
Palacios, TX (city) Matagorda County	11.57
Rosemead, CA (city) Los Angeles County	11.14
Chamblee, GA (city) De Kalb County	11.08
Avondale, LA (cdp) Jefferson Parish	10.71
Seadrift, TX (city) Calhoun County	10.41
Woodlynne, NJ (borough) Camden County	10.19
Seven Corners, VA (cdp) Fairfax County	10.12
White Center, WA (cdp) King County	9.79
Fulton, TX (town) Aransas County	9.23
San Jose, CA (city) Santa Clara County	8.50
Jefferson, VA (cdp) Fairfax County	8.37
Stanton, CA (city) Orange County	7.41
San Leon, TX (cdp) Galveston County	7.11
San Gabriel, CA (city) Los Angeles County	6.79
Merrifield, VA (cdp) Fairfax County	6.34
Alondra Park, CA (cdp) Los Angeles County	6.24
North Springfield, VA (cdp) Fairfax County	6.23
Springfield, VA (cdp) Fairfax County	6.11
Annandale, VA (cdp) Fairfax County	6.08
Santa Ana, CA (city) Orange County	5.69
Abbeville, LA (city) Vermilion Parish	5.48
El Monte, CA (city) Los Angeles County	5.48
Monterey Park, CA (city) Los Angeles County	5.40
South San Gabriel, CA (cdp) Los Angeles County	5.16
Alhambra, CA (city) Los Angeles County	5.11
Timberlane, LA (cdp) Jefferson Parish	4.96
Port Arthur, TX (city) Jefferson County	4.90
Florin, CA (cdp) Sacramento County	4.72
Lake Barcroft, VA (cdp) Fairfax County	4.67
Santa Clara, CA (city) Santa Clara County	4.54
Forest Park, GA (city) Clayton County	4.50
Doraville, GA (city) De Kalb County	4.17
Lawndale, CA (city) Los Angeles County	4.15
Mission Bend, TX (cdp) Fort Bend County	4.09
Lilburn, GA (city) Gwinnett County	4.07
Idylwood, VA (cdp) Fairfax County	4.05
Alum Rock, CA (cdp) Santa Clara County	4.04
Haltom City, TX (city) Tarrant County	4.02
Stafford, TX (city) Fort Bend County	3.87
Harvey, LA (cdp) Jefferson Parish	3.84
Woodmere, LA (cdp) Jefferson Parish	3.84
Riverdale, GA (city) Clayton County	3.77
Montclair, CA (city) San Bernardino County	3.69
Elk Grove, CA (cdp) Sacramento County	3.61
Renton, WA (city) King County	3.56
Irvine, CA (city) Orange County	3.39
Anaheim, CA (city) Orange County	3.23
Lincolnia, VA (cdp) Fairfax County	3.16
West Springfield, VA (cdp) Fairfax County	3.15
White Oak, MD (cdp) Montgomery County	3.14
Huntington Beach, CA (city) Orange County	3.09
Union City, CA (city) Alameda County	3.06
Parkway-S. Sacramento, CA (cdp) Sacramento County	3.04
Bryn Mawr-Skyway, WA (cdp) King County	3.02
South El Monte, CA (city) Los Angeles County	3.02
Orange, CA (city) Orange County	2.98
Atlantic City, NJ (city) Atlantic County	2.93
Marina, CA (city) Monterey County	2.93
Biloxi, MS (city) Harrison County	2.92
Garland, TX (city) Dallas County	2.92
Lynnwood, WA (city) Snohomish County	2.90
Arlington, TX (city) Tarrant County	2.71
Kentwood, MI (city) Kent County	2.70
Estelle, LA (cdp) Jefferson Parish	2.68
Aloha, OR (cdp) Washington County	2.66
Tustin, CA (city) Orange County	2.55
Temple City, CA (city) Los Angeles County	2.54
Bailey's Crossroads, VA (cdp) Fairfax County	2.52

Notes: Please refer to the User's Guide for an explanation of data; ranking tables include all places with Asian and/or NHPI populations above SF4 population thresholds; (1) tables reflect only those areas that meet SF4 population thresholds, therefore there may be less than 50 states, 75 counties or 75 places listed

Median Age

Total Population

All States, Top 75 Counties, and Top 75 Places Sorted by Number[1]

State	Years
West Virginia	38.9
Florida	38.8
Maine	38.7
Pennsylvania	38.0
Montana	37.6
Vermont	37.6
Connecticut	37.5
New Hampshire	37.2
New Jersey	36.9
Rhode Island	36.8
Iowa	36.7
Massachusetts	36.6
Hawaii	36.5
Oregon	36.4
Wyoming	36.4
Ohio	36.3
Arkansas	36.2
Missouri	36.2
North Dakota	36.2
Delaware	36.1
Maryland	36.1
Wisconsin	36.1
Alabama	36.0
New York	36.0
Tennessee	36.0
Kentucky	35.9
Virginia	35.8
Michigan	35.6
Oklahoma	35.6
South Carolina	35.6
South Dakota	35.6
Minnesota	35.4
Nebraska	35.4
North Carolina	35.4
United States	35.4
Washington	35.4
Indiana	35.3
Kansas	35.3
Nevada	35.2
Illinois	34.8
District of Columbia	34.7
New Mexico	34.7
Colorado	34.4
Arizona	34.3
Louisiana	34.2
Mississippi	34.0
California	33.5
Georgia	33.5
Idaho	33.3
Alaska	32.5
Texas	32.5
Utah	27.2

County	Years
Charlotte County, FL	54.2
Citrus County, FL	52.6
Flagler County, FL	50.6
Sarasota County, FL	50.4
Highlands County, FL	50.0
Hernando County, FL	49.2
Martin County, FL	47.3
Indian River County, FL	46.9
Pacific County, WA	45.8
Lee County, FL	45.1
Lake County, FL	44.9
Pasco County, FL	44.8
Barnstable County, MA	44.6
Yavapai County, AZ	44.4
Collier County, FL	44.1
Lincoln County, OR	44.1
Marion County, FL	43.8
Clallam County, WA	43.7
Manatee County, FL	43.6
Nevada County, CA	43.2
Coos County, OR	43.1
Pinellas County, FL	43.1
Siskiyou County, CA	43.1
Josephine County, OR	43.0
Lake County, CA	43.0
Amador County, CA	42.9
Mohave County, AZ	42.8
Tuolumne County, CA	42.8
Henderson County, NC	42.7
Johnson County, NE	42.7
Aransas County, TX	42.6
Cape May County, NJ	42.6
Monroe County, FL	42.6
Volusia County, FL	42.4
St. Lucie County, FL	42.1
Palm Beach County, FL	41.8
Cottonwood County, MN	41.7
Douglas County, NV	41.7
Brevard County, FL	41.6
Delaware County, NY	41.5
Douglas County, OR	41.4
Marin County, CA	41.4
Westmoreland County, PA	41.3
Cambria County, PA	41.2
James City County, VA	41.1
Ocean County, NJ	41.1
Otter Tail County, MN	41.1
Windsor County, VT	41.1
Dorchester County, MD	41.0
Hancock County, ME	41.0
Sussex County, DE	41.0
Luzerne County, PA	40.9
Roanoke County, VA	40.9
St. Johns County, FL	40.9
Schuylkill County, PA	40.8
Washington County, PA	40.8
Wayne County, PA	40.8
Aroostook County, ME	40.7
Columbia County, NY	40.7
Beaver County, PA	40.6
Berkshire County, MA	40.6
Northumberland County, PA	40.6
Washington County, ME	40.6
Los Alamos County, NM	40.5
Putnam County, FL	40.5
Lackawanna County, PA	40.4
Lawrence County, PA	40.4
Colonial Heights Independent City, VA	40.3
Kanawha County, WV	40.3
Mason County, WA	40.3
Ohio County, WV	40.3
Washington County, OK	40.3
Oxford County, ME	40.1
Falls Church Independent City, VA	40.0
Windham County, VT	40.0

Place	Years
Monroe, NJ (township) Middlesex County	58.7
North Hills, NY (village) Nassau County	54.1
Seal Beach, CA (city) Orange County	53.7
Tamarac, FL (city) Broward County	51.9
Lake Success, NY (village) Nassau County	51.8
Beachwood, OH (city) Cuyahoga County	51.6
Paukaa, HI (cdp) Hawaii County	51.3
Palm Coast, FL (city) Flagler County	50.7
Oak Brook, IL (village) Du Page County	50.4
Poipu, HI (cdp) Kauai County	48.8
Palm Desert, CA (city) Riverside County	48.0
Prescott, AZ (city) Yavapai County	47.9
Rolling Hills, CA (city) Los Angeles County	47.8
Ormond Beach, FL (city) Volusia County	47.6
Largo, FL (city) Pinellas County	47.5
Spring Hill, FL (cdp) Hernando County	47.5
Saddle River, NJ (borough) Bergen County	47.1
Palm Springs, CA (city) Riverside County	47.0
Larkspur, CA (city) Marin County	46.9
Kensington, CA (cdp) Contra Costa County	46.8
Palos Verdes Estates, CA (city) Los Angeles County	46.7
Niles, IL (village) Cook County	46.2
Middletown, PA (township) Delaware County	46.1
Town and Country, MO (city) Saint Louis County	46.0
Los Altos Hills, CA (town) Santa Clara County	45.8
South Whitehall, PA (township) Lehigh County	45.8
Catalina Foothills, AZ (cdp) Pima County	45.4
Lincolnwood, IL (village) Cook County	45.4
Orinda, CA (city) Contra Costa County	45.4
Pikesville, MD (cdp) Baltimore County	45.4
Lutherville-Timonium, MD (cdp) Baltimore County	45.3
Oro Valley, AZ (town) Pima County	45.3
Bloomfield, MI (township) Oakland County	45.2
Kenwood, OH (cdp) Hamilton County	45.2
Atherton, CA (town) San Mateo County	45.1
Englewood Cliffs, NJ (borough) Bergen County	45.1
Hillsborough, CA (town) San Mateo County	45.1
Tiburon, CA (town) Marin County	44.9
Fulton, TX (town) Aransas County	44.8
Walnut Creek, CA (city) Contra Costa County	44.8
Palm Beach Gardens, FL (city) Palm Beach County	44.7
Chevy Chase, MD (cdp) Montgomery County	44.6
Morton Grove, IL (village) Cook County	44.6
Pacific Grove, CA (city) Monterey County	44.6
Rancho Palos Verdes, CA (city) Los Angeles County	44.6
Los Altos, CA (city) Santa Clara County	44.5
Loyola, CA (cdp) Santa Clara County	44.5
Alpine, NJ (borough) Bergen County	44.4
Hemet, CA (city) Riverside County	44.4
Westchester, IL (village) Cook County	44.4
Bunker Hill Village, TX (city) Harris County	44.3
Mantua, VA (cdp) Fairfax County	44.3
Deerfield Beach, FL (city) Broward County	44.2
Edina, MN (city) Hennepin County	44.2
Lincolnshire, IL (village) Lake County	44.2
Lower Gwynedd, PA (township) Montgomery County	44.2
Northbrook, IL (village) Cook County	44.2
Springdale, NJ (cdp) Camden County	44.2
Wethersfield, CT (town) Hartford County	44.2
Bradbury, CA (city) Los Angeles County	44.1
Watchung, NJ (borough) Somerset County	44.1
Delray Beach, FL (city) Palm Beach County	44.0
La Habra Heights, CA (city) Los Angeles County	44.0
Rolling Hills Estates, CA (city) Los Angeles County	44.0
Worthington, OH (city) Franklin County	44.0
Laguna Beach, CA (city) Orange County	43.9
Mayfield Heights, OH (city) Cuyahoga County	43.9
Mercer Island, WA (city) King County	43.9
Piedmont, CA (city) Alameda County	43.9
Wainaku, HI (cdp) Hawaii County	43.9
Hawaiian Ocean View, HI (cdp) Hawaii County	43.8
Potomac, MD (cdp) Montgomery County	43.8
Villa Park, CA (city) Orange County	43.8
Willowbrook, IL (village) Du Page County	43.8
Creve Coeur, MO (city) Saint Louis County	43.6

Notes: Please refer to the User's Guide for an explanation of data; ranking tables include all places with Asian and/or NHPI populations above SF4 population thresholds; (1) tables reflect only those areas that meet SF4 population thresholds, therefore there may be less than 50 states, 75 counties or 75 places listed

Median Age

Asian

All States, Top 75 Counties, and Top 75 Places Sorted by Number[1]

State	Years
Hawaii	42.7
Nevada	36.2
Alaska	35.0
California	34.5
Florida	34.1
Maryland	33.9
New Mexico	33.3
New York	33.3
Idaho	33.2
Washington	33.2
New Jersey	33.0
United States	33.0
Delaware	32.6
Virginia	32.6
Wyoming	32.6
Arizona	32.3
Illinois	32.0
South Carolina	31.7
Texas	31.5
Arkansas	31.4
Oregon	31.4
Colorado	31.3
Georgia	31.1
West Virginia	31.0
Alabama	30.9
Kentucky	30.9
Ohio	30.9
Connecticut	30.8
Mississippi	30.8
Louisiana	30.5
Missouri	30.5
Tennessee	30.5
Montana	30.4
Indiana	30.1
North Carolina	30.1
Pennsylvania	30.1
Oklahoma	30.0
New Hampshire	29.9
District of Columbia	29.8
Michigan	29.7
Massachusetts	29.6
North Dakota	29.6
Utah	29.5
Kansas	29.3
Nebraska	28.3
Iowa	27.9
Maine	27.9
South Dakota	27.6
Rhode Island	27.2
Vermont	24.9
Minnesota	24.8
Wisconsin	23.7

County	Years
Malheur County, OR	65.2
Box Elder County, UT	46.7
Hood River County, OR	46.5
Hawaii County, HI	45.8
Nevada County, CA	45.8
Chenango County, NY	44.3
Kauai County, HI	43.9
Columbia County, OR	43.6
Geary County, KS	43.6
Lake County, CA	43.4
Bowie County, TX	43.1
Kaufman County, TX	43.0
Madison County, MS	42.9
Geauga County, OH	42.6
Honolulu County, HI	42.3
Maui County, HI	42.2
Matanuska-Susitna Borough, AK	42.0
Cochise County, AZ	41.9
Sumner County, TN	41.5
Aleutians East Borough, AK	41.2
Lee County, IL	41.1
Hoke County, NC	41.0
Mendocino County, CA	41.0
Charlotte County, FL	40.9
Dale County, AL	40.8
Mason County, WA	40.8
Bethel Census Area, AK	40.5
Chaves County, NM	40.5
Henderson County, NC	40.5
Delaware County, NY	40.4
Cascade County, MT	40.1
Yuma County, AZ	40.1
Aleutians West Census Area, AK	40.0
Hernando County, FL	40.0
Newton County, MO	39.8
Clatsop County, OR	39.6
Clearfield County, PA	39.6
Suffolk Independent City, VA	39.6
Mohave County, AZ	39.5
Columbia County, WI	39.4
Putnam County, FL	39.4
Madera County, CA	39.3
Wayne County, PA	39.3
Citrus County, FL	39.2
Yavapai County, AZ	39.2
Comanche County, OK	39.1
Nash County, NC	39.1
Lincoln County, OR	39.0
Cape May County, NJ	38.8
Kay County, OK	38.8
Bonneville County, ID	38.7
Berkeley County, SC	38.6
San Francisco County, CA	38.6
Aiken County, SC	38.5
Columbiana County, OH	38.5
El Dorado County, CA	38.4
Marin County, CA	38.4
St. Lucie County, FL	38.4
Brevard County, FL	38.3
Clay County, FL	38.2
Natrona County, WY	38.2
Santa Rosa County, FL	38.2
Wood County, WV	38.2
Monroe County, FL	38.1
Okaloosa County, FL	38.0
Placer County, CA	38.0
San Benito County, CA	38.0
Benton County, WA	37.9
Hendricks County, IN	37.9
Marion County, FL	37.9
Cayuga County, NY	37.8
Miami County, OH	37.8
North Slope Borough, AK	37.8
Stafford County, VA	37.8
Sullivan County, NY	37.8

Place	Years
Pakala Village, HI (cdp) Kauai County	68.1
Laupahoehoe, HI (cdp) Hawaii County	66.9
Paukaa, HI (cdp) Hawaii County	57.5
East Los Angeles, CA (cdp) Los Angeles County	55.2
Honomu, HI (cdp) Hawaii County	54.3
Waimea, HI (cdp) Kauai County	51.9
Kealakekua, HI (cdp) Hawaii County	51.7
Halaula, HI (cdp) Hawaii County	51.3
Kaunakakai, HI (cdp) Maui County	51.2
Pahoa, HI (cdp) Hawaii County	50.6
Fowler, CA (city) Fresno County	50.5
Honaunau-Napoopoo, HI (cdp) Hawaii County	50.1
Pearl City, HI (cdp) Honolulu County	50.0
Kualapuu, HI (cdp) Maui County	49.9
Captain Cook, HI (cdp) Hawaii County	49.8
Kapaau, HI (cdp) Hawaii County	49.7
Bell, CA (city) Los Angeles County	49.0
Poipu, HI (cdp) Kauai County	48.9
Wahiawa, HI (cdp) Honolulu County	48.9
Aiea, HI (cdp) Honolulu County	48.7
Hilo, HI (cdp) Hawaii County	48.6
Atherton, CA (town) San Mateo County	48.5
Lihue, HI (cdp) Kauai County	48.5
Pahala, HI (cdp) Hawaii County	48.5
Kaaawa, HI (cdp) Honolulu County	48.3
Papaikou, HI (cdp) Hawaii County	48.3
Pepeekeo, HI (cdp) Hawaii County	48.3
Kahaluu, HI (cdp) Honolulu County	48.2
Mountain View, HI (cdp) Hawaii County	48.2
Sands Point, NY (village) Nassau County	48.1
Oak Brook, IL (village) Du Page County	47.9
Haiku-Pauwela, HI (cdp) Maui County	47.8
Kekaha, HI (cdp) Kauai County	47.5
Pukalani, HI (cdp) Maui County	47.5
Haliimaile, HI (cdp) Maui County	47.4
Waialua, HI (cdp) Honolulu County	47.4
Wailua, HI (cdp) Kauai County	47.4
Barstow, CA (city) San Bernardino County	47.1
Arroyo Grande, CA (city) San Luis Obispo County	47.0
Kurtistown, HI (cdp) Hawaii County	46.9
Volcano, HI (cdp) Hawaii County	46.8
Compton, CA (city) Los Angeles County	46.6
Kailua, HI (cdp) Honolulu County	46.6
Flossmoor, IL (village) Cook County	46.5
Honokaa, HI (cdp) Hawaii County	46.4
Junction City, KS (city) Geary County	46.4
Lawai, HI (cdp) Kauai County	46.4
Moorestown, NJ (township) Burlington County	46.4
Wailuku, HI (cdp) Maui County	46.4
Brookville, NY (village) Nassau County	46.2
Heeia, HI (cdp) Honolulu County	46.2
Makaha, HI (cdp) Honolulu County	46.2
Watsonville, CA (city) Santa Cruz County	46.2
Hunters Creek Village, TX (city) Harris County	46.1
Springfield, PA (township) Delaware County	46.1
Universal City, TX (city) Bexar County	46.1
Wailua Homesteads, HI (cdp) Kauai County	46.1
Evans, GA (cdp) Columbia County	46.0
Pemberton, NJ (township) Burlington County	46.0
Reedley, CA (city) Fresno County	46.0
Long Grove, IL (village) Lake County	45.9
Haleiwa, HI (cdp) Honolulu County	45.8
Richgrove, CA (cdp) Tulare County	45.8
Bainbridge Island, WA (city) Kitsap County	45.7
Town and Country, MO (city) Saint Louis County	45.6
Waller, WA (cdp) Pierce County	45.4
Hialeah, FL (city) Miami-Dade County	45.3
Kensington, CA (cdp) Contra Costa County	45.3
Browns Mills, NJ (cdp) Burlington County	45.1
Pacific Grove, CA (city) Monterey County	45.1
Kaneohe, HI (cdp) Honolulu County	45.0
Maunawili, HI (cdp) Honolulu County	45.0
Villa Park, CA (city) Orange County	45.0
Rolling Hills, CA (city) Los Angeles County	44.8
South Barrington, IL (village) Cook County	44.8

Notes: Please refer to the User's Guide for an explanation of data; ranking tables include all places with Asian and/or NHPI populations above SF4 population thresholds; (1) tables reflect only those areas that meet SF4 population thresholds, therefore there may be less than 50 states, 75 counties or 75 places listed

Median Age

Native Hawaiian and Other Pacific Islander

All States, Top 75 Counties, and Top 75 Places Sorted by Number[1]

State	Years
Maine	33.9
New Mexico	32.6
South Carolina	31.7
Montana	31.4
Maryland	30.9
Kansas	30.5
New Jersey	30.5
Minnesota	30.0
Florida	29.6
Louisiana	29.2
Nevada	29.2
New York	29.1
Tennessee	28.7
Hawaii	28.6
Massachusetts	28.5
California	28.3
Illinois	28.3
Colorado	28.1
Alabama	28.0
Virginia	27.8
Pennsylvania	27.6
United States	27.6
Georgia	27.4
Oregon	27.4
Oklahoma	27.3
Texas	27.1
Mississippi	26.8
Kentucky	26.7
Indiana	26.5
Missouri	26.5
Washington	26.5
North Carolina	26.3
Connecticut	25.8
Ohio	25.8
Michigan	25.4
Wisconsin	25.3
Nebraska	25.2
Arizona	24.9
Rhode Island	24.4
Idaho	23.8
Iowa	23.8
Delaware	23.0
West Virginia	22.4
Utah	22.0
Alaska	21.8
Arkansas	21.6

County	Years
Broward County, FL	35.5
Ventura County, CA	34.7
Arapahoe County, CO	33.3
Allegheny County, PA	33.2
Palm Beach County, FL	33.2
Shelby County, TN	33.0
Suffolk County, NY	32.8
Miami-Dade County, FL	31.6
Santa Barbara County, CA	31.5
Bernalillo County, NM	31.4
Montgomery County, MD	31.0
Solano County, CA	30.9
Essex County, NJ	30.8
Nassau County, NY	30.6
Wayne County, MI	30.5
Queens County, NY	30.4
Monterey County, CA	30.3
San Mateo County, CA	30.0
Sonoma County, CA	30.0
Clark County, NV	29.9
Hennepin County, MN	29.9
San Diego County, CA	29.6
Santa Clara County, CA	29.3
Maui County, HI	29.2
Washington County, OR	29.1
Yolo County, CA	29.1
Kauai County, HI	28.8
San Francisco County, CA	28.8
Fairfax County, VA	28.7
Hawaii County, HI	28.7
Snohomish County, WA	28.7
Thurston County, WA	28.7
Orange County, CA	28.6
Cook County, IL	28.5
El Paso County, TX	28.5
Honolulu County, HI	28.5
Bexar County, TX	28.4
Harris County, TX	28.3
New York County, NY	28.3
Riverside County, CA	28.1
Clackamas County, OR	28.0
Hillsborough County, FL	27.9
Contra Costa County, CA	27.6
Gwinnett County, GA	27.6
Spokane County, WA	27.6
Jefferson County, CO	27.5
Dallas County, TX	27.4
San Joaquin County, CA	27.3
Los Angeles County, CA	27.2
Alameda County, CA	27.0
San Bernardino County, CA	26.9
Kitsap County, WA	26.8
King County, WA	26.7
Sacramento County, CA	26.7
Jackson County, MO	26.6
El Paso County, CO	26.4
Lane County, OR	26.3
Pierce County, WA	26.3
Pima County, AZ	26.2
Sedgwick County, KS	26.1
Stanislaus County, CA	26.1
Tarrant County, TX	26.1
Milwaukee County, WI	25.9
Cumberland County, NC	25.8
Duval County, FL	25.8
Marion County, OR	25.8
Bell County, TX	25.7
Bronx County, NY	25.7
Travis County, TX	25.7
Kern County, CA	25.4
Maricopa County, AZ	25.3
Denver County, CO	25.0
Multnomah County, OR	25.0
Kings County, NY	24.8
St. Louis County, MO	24.8

Place	Years
Waimea, HI (cdp) Kauai County	39.9
Fairfield, CA (city) Solano County	37.8
Daly City, CA (city) San Mateo County	37.1
Kailua, HI (cdp) Honolulu County	36.2
Waimea, HI (cdp) Hawaii County	36.1
Haleiwa, HI (cdp) Honolulu County	35.7
Lahaina, HI (cdp) Maui County	35.7
Oxnard, CA (city) Ventura County	35.3
Santa Clara, CA (city) Santa Clara County	35.3
Union City, CA (city) Alameda County	35.2
Volcano, HI (cdp) Hawaii County	34.8
Naalehu, HI (cdp) Hawaii County	34.3
Aiea, HI (cdp) Honolulu County	34.0
Aurora, CO (city) Arapahoe County	34.0
Waimanalo Beach, HI (cdp) Honolulu County	33.7
Sunrise Manor, NV (cdp) Clark County	33.5
Chula Vista, CA (city) San Diego County	33.4
Paia, HI (cdp) Maui County	33.4
Fremont, CA (city) Alameda County	33.3
Marina, CA (city) Monterey County	33.2
Sunnyvale, CA (city) Santa Clara County	33.1
Kualapuu, HI (cdp) Maui County	32.9
Honaunau-Napoopoo, HI (cdp) Hawaii County	32.6
Kailua, HI (cdp) Hawaii County	32.6
Mililani Town, HI (cdp) Honolulu County	32.3
Halawa, HI (cdp) Honolulu County	32.1
San Mateo, CA (city) San Mateo County	32.1
Kihei, HI (cdp) Maui County	32.0
Holualoa, HI (cdp) Hawaii County	31.8
Los Angeles, CA (city) Los Angeles County	31.8
Kaaawa, HI (cdp) Honolulu County	31.5
Albuquerque, NM (city) Bernalillo County	31.4
Pearl City, HI (cdp) Honolulu County	31.4
Henderson, NV (city) Clark County	31.3
Honalo, HI (cdp) Hawaii County	30.9
Huntington Beach, CA (city) Orange County	30.9
Kahaluu, HI (cdp) Honolulu County	30.9
Village Park, HI (cdp) Honolulu County	30.9
Waialua, HI (cdp) Honolulu County	30.8
Hawthorne, CA (city) Los Angeles County	30.5
Kaneohe, HI (cdp) Honolulu County	30.4
Richmond, CA (city) Contra Costa County	30.4
Vallejo, CA (city) Solano County	30.2
Hawaiian Ocean View, HI (cdp) Hawaii County	30.0
Las Vegas, NV (city) Clark County	30.0
Maunawili, HI (cdp) Honolulu County	29.9
San Antonio, TX (city) Bexar County	29.8
Alameda, CA (city) Alameda County	29.7
Honolulu, HI (cdp) Honolulu County	29.7
Redwood City, CA (city) San Mateo County	29.5
Ewa Beach, HI (cdp) Honolulu County	29.4
Anahola, HI (cdp) Kauai County	29.0
Paradise, NV (cdp) Clark County	29.0
Waipio, HI (cdp) Honolulu County	29.0
Houston, TX (city) Harris County	28.8
North Las Vegas, NV (city) Clark County	28.8
San Diego, CA (city) San Diego County	28.8
San Francisco, CA (city) San Francisco County	28.8
Riverside, CA (city) Riverside County	28.7
South San Francisco, CA (city) San Mateo County	28.7
Santa Ana, CA (city) Orange County	28.6
Kalaoa, HI (cdp) Hawaii County	28.5
El Paso, TX (city) El Paso County	28.4
Rialto, CA (city) San Bernardino County	28.4
Waimalu, HI (cdp) Honolulu County	28.4
Chicago, IL (city) Cook County	28.3
Napili-Honokowai, HI (cdp) Maui County	28.2
Pakala Village, HI (cdp) Kauai County	28.2
Kansas City, MO (city) Jackson County	28.1
San Jose, CA (city) Santa Clara County	28.0
Makakilo City, HI (cdp) Honolulu County	27.9
Waikoloa Village, HI (cdp) Hawaii County	27.9
Hana, HI (cdp) Maui County	27.8
Dallas, TX (city) Dallas County	27.7
Waikapu, HI (cdp) Maui County	27.7

Notes: Please refer to the User's Guide for an explanation of data; ranking tables include all places with Asian and/or NHPI populations above SF4 population thresholds; (1) tables reflect only those areas that meet SF4 population thresholds, therefore there may be less than 50 states, 75 counties or 75 places listed

Median Age

Asian Indian

All States, Top 75 Counties, and Top 75 Places Sorted by Number[1]

State	Years
Hawaii	36.0
Nevada	33.7
Maryland	32.5
Florida	32.1
New Mexico	32.0
New York	31.4
Wyoming	31.2
New Jersey	31.0
West Virginia	30.9
Mississippi	30.6
Connecticut	30.5
California	30.3
Delaware	30.3
United States	30.3
Louisiana	30.2
Ohio	30.1
Texas	30.1
District of Columbia	30.0
Illinois	30.0
Arkansas	29.9
Kentucky	29.9
Georgia	29.8
Washington	29.8
Michigan	29.7
North Carolina	29.7
Pennsylvania	29.7
Tennessee	29.7
Virginia	29.7
South Carolina	29.6
Arizona	29.5
Alaska	29.4
Missouri	29.0
Alabama	28.9
Oklahoma	28.9
North Dakota	28.8
Oregon	28.8
Indiana	28.7
Massachusetts	28.7
Minnesota	28.6
Montana	28.6
Colorado	28.5
Wisconsin	28.4
New Hampshire	28.3
Kansas	28.2
Iowa	28.1
Rhode Island	27.9
Nebraska	27.6
Idaho	27.1
Utah	26.7
Maine	26.2
South Dakota	25.6
Vermont	24.3

County	Years
Columbia County, GA	41.4
Benton County, WA	41.1
St. Mary's County, MD	41.1
Kanawha County, WV	40.6
Madison County, IL	40.1
Madera County, CA	39.7
Chesterfield County, VA	39.1
Saratoga County, NY	38.5
Sussex County, NJ	37.9
Berks County, PA	37.8
York County, VA	37.5
Spartanburg County, SC	37.3
Litchfield County, CT	36.8
Clark County, NV	36.0
Honolulu County, HI	35.9
Nueces County, TX	35.9
Luzerne County, PA	35.6
Volusia County, FL	35.6
Lorain County, OH	35.5
Stark County, OH	35.1
Harford County, MD	35.0
Brevard County, FL	34.9
Anchorage Borough, AK	34.8
Winnebago County, IL	34.7
Clayton County, GA	34.6
Seminole County, FL	34.6
Putnam County, NY	34.5
Henry County, GA	34.3
Bell County, TX	34.2
Brazoria County, TX	34.2
Howard County, MD	34.2
Polk County, FL	34.2
Rockland County, NY	34.2
Pinellas County, FL	34.0
Clackamas County, OR	33.9
Montgomery County, MD	33.9
Kent County, DE	33.8
Cumberland County, PA	33.7
Fort Bend County, TX	33.7
Nassau County, NY	33.7
Lee County, FL	33.6
Palm Beach County, FL	33.6
Broward County, FL	33.5
Butler County, PA	33.5
Clermont County, OH	33.5
Camden County, NJ	33.4
Pasco County, FL	33.4
Virginia Beach Independent City, VA	33.4
Cumberland County, NJ	33.3
Hunterdon County, NJ	33.3
Kern County, CA	33.2
Montgomery County, TX	33.1
Ventura County, CA	33.1
El Paso County, TX	33.0
Bergen County, NJ	32.9
Greene County, OH	32.9
Hidalgo County, TX	32.9
Lake County, IL	32.9
Marion County, FL	32.9
Richmond County, NY	32.9
Essex County, NJ	32.8
Gloucester County, NJ	32.8
Madison County, AL	32.8
Orange County, FL	32.8
Medina County, OH	32.7
Niagara County, NY	32.7
Ocean County, NJ	32.7
Westchester County, NY	32.6
Monmouth County, NJ	32.5
Santa Cruz County, CA	32.5
Atlantic County, NJ	32.4
Saginaw County, MI	32.4
Contra Costa County, CA	32.3
Morris County, NJ	32.3
Orange County, NY	32.3

Place	Years
Oak Brook, IL (village) Du Page County	47.2
Town and Country, MO (city) Saint Louis County	46.3
South Barrington, IL (village) Cook County	45.3
Travilah, MD (cdp) Montgomery County	45.0
Beavercreek, OH (city) Greene County	44.5
Martinez, GA (cdp) Columbia County	44.1
Colesville, MD (cdp) Montgomery County	44.0
Warren, NJ (township) Somerset County	41.4
Westlake, OH (city) Cuyahoga County	41.2
Solon, OH (city) Cuyahoga County	41.0
Bloomfield, MI (township) Oakland County	40.7
Orland Park, IL (village) Cook County	40.7
Charleston, WV (city) Kanawha County	40.3
Pittsford, NY (town) Monroe County	40.2
Potomac, MD (cdp) Montgomery County	40.2
Glendora, CA (city) Los Angeles County	39.8
Burtonsville, MD (cdp) Montgomery County	39.6
Doctor Phillips, FL (cdp) Orange County	39.6
McLean, VA (cdp) Fairfax County	39.6
Holmdel, NJ (township) Monmouth County	39.3
Taylor, MI (city) Wayne County	39.1
Glenview, IL (village) Cook County	39.0
Yorba Linda, CA (city) Orange County	39.0
Los Altos, CA (city) Santa Clara County	38.8
Clifton Park, NY (town) Saratoga County	38.7
Corpus Christi, TX (city) Nueces County	38.6
Princeton, NJ (township) Mercer County	38.6
Concord, CA (city) Contra Costa County	38.5
Cooper City, FL (city) Broward County	38.5
Greenwich, CT (town) Fairfield County	38.5
Muttontown, NY (village) Nassau County	38.5
Livingston, NJ (township) Essex County	38.3
Redland, MD (cdp) Montgomery County	38.2
Teaneck, NJ (township) Bergen County	38.2
Lakeland, FL (city) Polk County	38.1
Burr Ridge, IL (village) Du Page County	38.0
Lower Makefield, PA (township) Bucks County	37.9
Glastonbury, CT (town) Hartford County	37.8
Perinton, NY (town) Monroe County	37.8
North Potomac, MD (cdp) Montgomery County	37.7
Upper St. Clair, PA (township) Allegheny County	37.7
Rancho Palos Verdes, CA (city) Los Angeles County	37.6
Sunrise, FL (city) Broward County	37.6
Wolf Trap, VA (cdp) Fairfax County	37.6
Mission Bend, TX (cdp) Fort Bend County	37.5
Loma Linda, CA (city) San Bernardino County	37.3
New Castle, NY (town) Westchester County	37.2
Salisbury, NY (cdp) Nassau County	37.2
Rockaway, NJ (township) Morris County	37.1
Saratoga, CA (city) Santa Clara County	37.0
Munster, IN (town) Lake County	36.9
Shoreline, WA (city) King County	36.9
Walnut, CA (city) Los Angeles County	36.9
Missouri City, TX (city) Fort Bend County	36.8
Rockford, IL (city) Winnebago County	36.8
West Covina, CA (city) Los Angeles County	36.8
Henderson, NV (city) Clark County	36.7
Montville, NJ (township) Morris County	36.7
Hawthorne, CA (city) Los Angeles County	36.6
Haverford, PA (township) Delaware County	36.5
Kenner, LA (city) Jefferson Parish	36.5
Rutherford, NJ (borough) Bergen County	36.5
SeaTac, WA (city) King County	36.5
South San Francisco, CA (city) San Mateo County	36.5
Washington, NJ (township) Gloucester County	36.5
Freehold, NJ (township) Monmouth County	36.4
Cherry Hill, NJ (township) Camden County	36.2
Herricks, NY (cdp) Nassau County	36.1
Scarsdale, NY (village) Westchester County	36.1
Bethesda, MD (cdp) Montgomery County	35.9
Dix Hills, NY (cdp) Suffolk County	35.9
Gloucester, NJ (township) Camden County	35.9
Olney, MD (cdp) Montgomery County	35.9
Ellicott City, MD (cdp) Howard County	35.8
Palmdale, CA (city) Los Angeles County	35.8

Notes: Please refer to the User's Guide for an explanation of data; ranking tables include all places with Asian and/or NHPI populations above SF4 population thresholds; (1) tables reflect only those areas that meet SF4 population thresholds, therefore there may be less than 50 states, 75 counties or 75 places listed

Median Age

Bangladeshi

All States, Top 75 Counties, and Top 75 Places Sorted by Number[1]

State	Years
Connecticut	33.0
Florida	33.0
Maryland	31.8
Ohio	30.9
California	30.7
Georgia	30.5
New Jersey	30.1
Texas	30.1
United States	29.7
Massachusetts	29.6
New York	29.6
Virginia	29.6
Michigan	29.1
Pennsylvania	28.7
Illinois	28.2

County	Years
Montgomery County, MD	34.3
Los Angeles County, CA	31.6
Santa Clara County, CA	31.5
Harris County, TX	31.2
DeKalb County, GA	30.5
Queens County, NY	29.9
Middlesex County, NJ	29.7
Bronx County, NY	29.2
Kings County, NY	29.2
Dallas County, TX	29.0
Fairfax County, VA	28.9
Atlantic County, NJ	28.8
Wayne County, MI	27.6
Passaic County, NJ	26.7
New York County, NY	26.6

Place	Years
Los Angeles, CA (city) Los Angeles County	31.4
New York, NY (city)	29.5
Paterson, NJ (city) Passaic County	26.3
Hamtramck, MI (city) Wayne County	23.9

Notes: Please refer to the User's Guide for an explanation of data; ranking tables include all places with Asian and/or NHPI populations above SF4 population thresholds; (1) tables reflect only those areas that meet SF4 population thresholds, therefore there may be less than 50 states, 75 counties or 75 places listed

Median Age

Cambodian

All States, Top 75 Counties, and Top 75 Places Sorted by Number[1]

State	Years
Maryland	30.6
Nevada	30.6
New Jersey	30.6
Florida	29.5
Oklahoma	29.0
Georgia	28.5
Oregon	28.4
Connecticut	27.5
Michigan	27.4
Virginia	27.4
Texas	27.2
Illinois	26.8
Kansas	26.6
Tennessee	25.5
South Carolina	25.4
North Carolina	25.0
Arizona	24.7
Minnesota	24.6
Washington	24.6
Colorado	24.5
United States	23.8
Ohio	23.7
Iowa	23.3
Indiana	22.8
Pennsylvania	22.8
Utah	22.5
New York	21.9
California	21.8
Wisconsin	21.6
Rhode Island	21.4
Massachusetts	21.0
Alabama	20.5
Missouri	20.1
Maine	19.9
Hawaii	16.9

County	Years
Shelby County, TN	34.9
DeKalb County, GA	31.6
Clark County, WA	31.4
Harris County, TX	31.3
Montgomery County, MD	30.8
Kings County, NY	30.7
Clark County, NV	30.4
Orange County, CA	30.1
Washington County, OR	30.1
Duval County, FL	28.9
Camden County, NJ	28.8
Denton County, TX	28.8
Fairfax County, VA	28.8
Scott County, MN	28.7
San Francisco County, CA	28.5
Cuyahoga County, OH	28.3
Cook County, IL	27.2
Denver County, CO	27.1
Sedgwick County, KS	27.1
Hamilton County, OH	26.8
Snohomish County, WA	26.7
Fairfield County, CT	26.6
Riverside County, CA	26.5
Dakota County, MN	26.2
Brazoria County, TX	25.8
Ramsey County, MN	25.8
Multnomah County, OR	25.4
Pinellas County, FL	25.4
Hennepin County, MN	25.0
Dallas County, TX	24.9
Worcester County, MA	24.8
Ottawa County, MI	24.7
Santa Clara County, CA	24.7
Hampden County, MA	24.6
King County, WA	24.5
Sacramento County, CA	24.3
Maricopa County, AZ	24.2
Thurston County, WA	24.2
Arlington County, VA	24.1
Los Angeles County, CA	24.1
Polk County, IA	24.0
Franklin County, OH	23.7
Clayton County, GA	23.5
Mecklenburg County, NC	23.3
Chesterfield County, VA	23.2
Davidson County, NC	22.6
Gwinnett County, GA	22.4
Henrico County, VA	22.3
Providence County, RI	21.8
Tarrant County, TX	21.8
Essex County, MA	21.6
Salt Lake County, UT	21.4
Philadelphia County, PA	21.1
Pierce County, WA	20.9
San Bernardino County, CA	20.9
Middlesex County, MA	20.8
Suffolk County, MA	20.8
San Diego County, CA	20.5
Kern County, CA	20.3
Sonoma County, CA	20.2
Monroe County, NY	19.9
Cowlitz County, WA	19.6
Alameda County, CA	19.5
Bronx County, NY	19.0
Cumberland County, ME	18.9
Bristol County, MA	18.7
Fresno County, CA	18.7
Olmsted County, MN	18.6
San Joaquin County, CA	18.3
Stanislaus County, CA	18.2
Mobile County, AL	17.5

Place	Years
Bellflower, CA (city) Los Angeles County	34.2
Memphis, TN (city) Shelby County	33.9
Houston, TX (city) Harris County	33.3
Garden Grove, CA (city) Orange County	31.6
Rosemead, CA (city) Los Angeles County	31.6
Norwalk, CA (city) Los Angeles County	30.2
Beaverton, OR (city) Washington County	30.0
Santa Ana, CA (city) Orange County	29.7
Cranston, RI (city) Providence County	29.1
Jacksonville, FL (city) Duval County	28.9
Silver Spring, MD (cdp) Montgomery County	28.7
Lakewood, CA (city) Los Angeles County	28.6
San Francisco, CA (city) San Francisco County	28.5
Chicago, IL (city) Cook County	27.6
Attleboro, MA (city) Bristol County	27.1
Denver, CO (city) Denver County	27.1
Lawrence, MA (city) Essex County	27.0
Los Angeles, CA (city) Los Angeles County	27.0
Phoenix, AZ (city) Maricopa County	26.5
Bloomington, MN (city) Hennepin County	26.3
New York, NY (city)	25.8
St. Paul, MN (city) Ramsey County	25.8
Monterey Park, CA (city) Los Angeles County	25.4
Sacramento, CA (city) Sacramento County	25.4
Carrollton, TX (city) Denton County	25.2
Boston, MA (city) Suffolk County	25.1
Portland, OR (city) Multnomah County	24.6
Danbury, CT (city) Fairfield County	24.5
San Jose, CA (city) Santa Clara County	24.5
Bridgeport, CT (city) Fairfield County	24.4
Arlington, VA (cdp) Arlington County	24.1
Seattle, WA (city) King County	23.8
Columbus, OH (city) Franklin County	23.7
Aurora, CO (city) Arapahoe County	23.2
Signal Hill, CA (city) Los Angeles County	23.2
Charlotte, NC (city) Mecklenburg County	22.9
Everett, WA (city) Snohomish County	22.7
St. Petersburg, FL (city) Pinellas County	21.4
Lynn, MA (city) Essex County	21.3
Philadelphia, PA (city) Philadelphia County	21.1
Lexington, NC (city) Davidson County	21.0
Dallas, TX (city) Dallas County	20.7
Providence, RI (city) Providence County	20.7
Long Beach, CA (city) Los Angeles County	20.4
Lowell, MA (city) Middlesex County	20.3
Tacoma, WA (city) Pierce County	20.1
Longview, WA (city) Cowlitz County	19.9
Santa Rosa, CA (city) Sonoma County	19.9
White Center, WA (cdp) King County	19.8
San Bernardino, CA (city) San Bernardino County	19.7
San Diego, CA (city) San Diego County	19.7
Revere, MA (city) Suffolk County	19.5
West Valley City, UT (city) Salt Lake County	18.9
Portland, ME (city) Cumberland County	18.8
Modesto, CA (city) Stanislaus County	18.6
Pomona, CA (city) Los Angeles County	18.6
Fresno, CA (city) Fresno County	18.4
Oakland, CA (city) Alameda County	18.4
Stockton, CA (city) San Joaquin County	18.4
Fall River, MA (city) Bristol County	18.0
Minneapolis, MN (city) Hennepin County	18.0
Rochester, MN (city) Olmsted County	17.9

Notes: Please refer to the User's Guide for an explanation of data; ranking tables include all places with Asian and/or NHPI populations above SF4 population thresholds; (1) tables reflect only those areas that meet SF4 population thresholds, therefore there may be less than 50 states, 75 counties or 75 places listed

Median Age

Chinese (except Taiwanese)

All States, Top 75 Counties, and Top 75 Places Sorted by Number[1]

State	Years
Hawaii	46.2
California	37.1
Nevada	37.0
Alaska	36.8
Florida	36.4
Maryland	35.7
New Jersey	35.7
Mississippi	35.6
New York	35.6
United States	35.6
Washington	35.5
Oregon	35.2
Arizona	34.2
Illinois	34.2
Colorado	34.1
Virginia	34.1
Texas	33.9
Massachusetts	33.7
Arkansas	33.4
Georgia	33.3
Wyoming	33.3
Delaware	33.0
Tennessee	33.0
Idaho	32.9
Louisiana	32.8
New Mexico	32.7
North Carolina	32.7
Michigan	32.3
Connecticut	32.2
Ohio	32.2
South Carolina	32.1
District of Columbia	31.8
New Hampshire	31.8
Minnesota	31.7
Kentucky	31.4
Kansas	31.3
Missouri	31.1
North Dakota	31.1
Pennsylvania	31.1
South Dakota	31.0
Utah	31.0
Indiana	30.7
Alabama	30.5
Nebraska	30.5
West Virginia	30.5
Oklahoma	30.4
Maine	30.2
Wisconsin	29.8
Montana	29.4
Iowa	28.5
Rhode Island	28.4
Vermont	26.5

County	Years
Maui County, HI	48.6
Kauai County, HI	48.3
Hawaii County, HI	47.7
Merced County, CA	47.2
Honolulu County, HI	46.1
Chatham County, GA	45.0
Tulare County, CA	44.2
Osceola County, FL	44.1
Monterey County, CA	43.2
Sangamon County, IL	42.3
San Joaquin County, CA	42.0
Kern County, CA	41.3
Solano County, CA	41.3
Putnam County, NY	41.1
San Francisco County, CA	40.6
Marin County, CA	40.5
Marion County, OR	40.1
Midland County, MI	39.9
Pierce County, WA	39.9
Ocean County, NJ	39.8
Contra Costa County, CA	39.7
Placer County, CA	39.5
Prince William County, VA	39.4
Ventura County, CA	39.3
Virginia Beach Independent City, VA	39.2
Pasco County, FL	39.0
Fresno County, CA	38.9
Anchorage Borough, AK	38.6
Kitsap County, WA	38.5
Pinellas County, FL	38.5
Brevard County, FL	38.4
Columbia County, GA	38.4
Miami-Dade County, FL	38.2
Clackamas County, OR	38.0
Nassau County, NY	38.0
Imperial County, CA	37.9
San Mateo County, CA	37.9
Sacramento County, CA	37.8
Fort Bend County, TX	37.7
Atlantic County, NJ	37.5
Westchester County, NY	37.5
Montgomery County, MD	37.4
Sonoma County, CA	37.4
Arapahoe County, CO	37.3
Broward County, FL	37.3
Cumberland County, PA	37.3
Richmond County, NY	37.3
Union County, NJ	37.3
Clark County, NV	37.1
Los Angeles County, CA	37.1
Queens County, NY	37.0
Thurston County, WA	37.0
Benton County, WA	36.9
Galveston County, TX	36.8
Monmouth County, NJ	36.8
Morris County, NJ	36.7
Bergen County, NJ	36.6
Montgomery County, TX	36.6
Seminole County, FL	36.6
Alameda County, CA	36.5
Essex County, NJ	36.5
Gwinnett County, GA	36.5
New York County, NY	36.5
Saratoga County, NY	36.5
Washoe County, NV	36.5
Bronx County, NY	36.4
Fairfax County, VA	36.4
Palm Beach County, FL	36.4
Somerset County, NJ	36.4
Stanislaus County, CA	36.4
Waukesha County, WI	36.4
Allen County, IN	36.3
Fairfax Independent City, VA	36.3
Howard County, MD	36.3
Rockingham County, NH	36.3

Place	Years
Pearl City, HI (cdp) Honolulu County	55.6
Miami, FL (city) Miami-Dade County	52.2
Kaneohe, HI (cdp) Honolulu County	51.8
Hilo, HI (cdp) Hawaii County	50.9
Rolling Hills Estates, CA (city) Los Angeles County	49.7
Mililani Town, HI (cdp) Honolulu County	49.5
Kailua, HI (cdp) Honolulu County	47.8
Waimalu, HI (cdp) Honolulu County	47.7
Tustin Foothills, CA (cdp) Orange County	46.9
Honolulu, HI (cdp) Honolulu County	46.6
Montebello, CA (city) Los Angeles County	46.2
Martinez, CA (city) Contra Costa County	45.7
Escondido, CA (city) San Diego County	45.5
Gardena, CA (city) Los Angeles County	45.3
McLean, VA (cdp) Fairfax County	45.3
Benicia, CA (city) Solano County	45.0
Waipahu, HI (cdp) Honolulu County	44.9
Savannah, GA (city) Chatham County	44.6
New Castle, NY (town) Westchester County	44.5
Glenview, IL (village) Cook County	44.4
Halawa, HI (cdp) Honolulu County	44.3
Westmont, IL (village) Du Page County	44.2
Los Altos Hills, CA (town) Santa Clara County	43.9
Carmichael, CA (cdp) Sacramento County	43.8
Downey, CA (city) Los Angeles County	43.8
Orinda, CA (city) Contra Costa County	43.7
Rancho Palos Verdes, CA (city) Los Angeles County	43.7
Moraga, CA (town) Contra Costa County	43.3
San Buenaventura (Ventura), CA (city) Ventura County	43.2
Hawthorne, CA (city) Los Angeles County	43.1
Salinas, CA (city) Monterey County	43.1
Laguna Hills, CA (city) Orange County	43.0
Novato, CA (city) Marin County	42.8
Scarsdale, NY (village) Westchester County	42.8
Walnut Creek, CA (city) Contra Costa County	42.7
Duarte, CA (city) Los Angeles County	42.6
Palos Verdes Estates, CA (city) Los Angeles County	42.5
Stockton, CA (city) San Joaquin County	42.5
Lake Oswego, OR (city) Clackamas County	42.4
West Bloomfield, MI (township) Oakland County	42.4
Lake Success, NY (village) Nassau County	42.3
Northbrook, IL (village) Cook County	42.3
Piedmont, CA (city) Alameda County	42.3
Wolf Trap, VA (cdp) Fairfax County	42.2
East Pasadena, CA (cdp) Los Angeles County	42.0
El Cerrito, CA (city) Contra Costa County	41.9
Calabasas, CA (city) Los Angeles County	41.8
Glendora, CA (city) Los Angeles County	41.8
Hillsborough, CA (town) San Mateo County	41.8
Lafayette, CA (city) Contra Costa County	41.8
Potomac, MD (cdp) Montgomery County	41.8
Los Altos, CA (city) Santa Clara County	41.7
Atlantic City, NJ (city) Atlantic County	41.5
Germantown, TN (city) Shelby County	41.5
Dix Hills, NY (cdp) Suffolk County	41.4
Gilroy, CA (city) Santa Clara County	41.4
Kensington, CA (cdp) Contra Costa County	41.4
Mercer Island, WA (city) King County	41.4
Hercules, CA (city) Contra Costa County	41.3
Vallejo, CA (city) Solano County	41.3
Burke, VA (cdp) Fairfax County	41.2
Yonkers, NY (city) Westchester County	41.2
Colesville, MD (cdp) Montgomery County	41.1
Huntington, NY (town) Suffolk County	41.1
Huntington Beach, CA (city) Orange County	41.0
North Miami Beach, FL (city) Miami-Dade County	41.0
Sacramento, CA (city) Sacramento County	41.0
South Pasadena, CA (city) Los Angeles County	40.9
Bellaire, TX (city) Harris County	40.8
Beverly Hills, CA (city) Los Angeles County	40.8
Montclair, NJ (township) Essex County	40.8
Newark, CA (city) Alameda County	40.8
Poway, CA (city) San Diego County	40.8
Cerritos, CA (city) Los Angeles County	40.7
Monterey Park, CA (city) Los Angeles County	40.7

Notes: Please refer to the User's Guide for an explanation of data; ranking tables include all places with Asian and/or NHPI populations above SF4 population thresholds; (1) tables reflect only those areas that meet SF4 population thresholds, therefore there may be less than 50 states, 75 counties or 75 places listed

Median Age

Fijian

All States, Top 75 Counties, and Top 75 Places Sorted by Number[1]

State	Years
Oregon	31.2
United States	29.3
Washington	29.2
California	28.7

County	Years
Los Angeles County, CA	37.4
San Mateo County, CA	31.2
King County, WA	30.1
Santa Clara County, CA	28.2
Sacramento County, CA	28.1
Alameda County, CA	25.7
Stanislaus County, CA	23.7
Yolo County, CA	22.5
Contra Costa County, CA	22.3

Place	Years
Sacramento, CA (city) Sacramento County	27.9
Hayward, CA (city) Alameda County	24.8
Modesto, CA (city) Stanislaus County	24.0

Notes: Please refer to the User's Guide for an explanation of data; ranking tables include all places with Asian and/or NHPI populations above SF4 population thresholds; (1) tables reflect only those areas that meet SF4 population thresholds, therefore there may be less than 50 states, 75 counties or 75 places listed

Median Age

Filipino

All States, Top 75 Counties, and Top 75 Places Sorted by Number[1]

State	Years
West Virginia	39.5
Delaware	38.6
Nebraska	37.4
Alabama	37.2
New York	37.2
Montana	36.9
District of Columbia	36.3
Florida	36.3
Hawaii	36.2
Maryland	36.1
Rhode Island	36.0
Wyoming	36.0
Iowa	35.9
Ohio	35.8
California	35.7
Virginia	35.6
New Jersey	35.5
United States	35.5
Idaho	35.2
Nevada	35.2
Oregon	35.2
Alaska	35.1
Kansas	35.1
Louisiana	35.1
Kentucky	34.9
South Dakota	34.9
Washington	34.9
Arkansas	34.8
Connecticut	34.8
Missouri	34.8
South Carolina	34.7
Illinois	34.6
Michigan	34.5
New Hampshire	34.5
Oklahoma	34.4
Pennsylvania	34.4
Massachusetts	34.2
Texas	34.2
Georgia	34.1
Maine	33.7
Indiana	33.6
Minnesota	33.6
Wisconsin	33.5
Colorado	33.4
Mississippi	33.4
Arizona	33.1
Tennessee	33.0
New Mexico	32.8
North Carolina	32.5
North Dakota	31.2
Utah	31.2
Vermont	30.4

County	Years
Dorchester County, SC	44.0
Marion County, OR	43.6
Genesee County, MI	43.0
Yakima County, WA	42.5
Kent County, DE	41.9
Aleutians West Census Area, AK	41.7
Mobile County, AL	41.5
Aleutians East Borough, AK	41.3
Clay County, FL	41.2
Galveston County, TX	41.1
Sarasota County, FL	41.1
Chesterfield County, VA	40.9
Osceola County, FL	40.8
Bristol County, MA	40.6
Gloucester County, NJ	40.6
Shasta County, CA	40.6
Berkeley County, SC	40.5
Marin County, CA	40.5
Stafford County, VA	40.3
Highlands County, FL	40.2
Merced County, CA	40.0
Santa Rosa County, FL	39.9
Sarpy County, NE	39.9
Cochise County, AZ	39.7
Lake County, IN	39.5
Sedgwick County, KS	39.5
Hawaii County, HI	39.4
Lee County, FL	39.4
St. Louis County, MO	39.4
Douglas County, NE	39.3
Pulaski County, AR	39.3
Hamilton County, TN	39.2
New York County, NY	39.1
Jefferson County, KY	39.0
Plymouth County, MA	38.8
Queens County, NY	38.8
Jefferson Parish, LA	38.6
Baltimore County, MD	38.5
Miami-Dade County, FL	38.5
Pasco County, FL	38.5
Rockland County, NY	38.5
St. Charles County, MO	38.5
Yuma County, AZ	38.5
Berrien County, MI	38.4
Brevard County, FL	38.4
Chesapeake Independent City, VA	38.4
Cuyahoga County, OH	38.4
Summit County, OH	38.4
Sutter County, CA	38.4
Lucas County, OH	38.3
Monmouth County, NJ	38.3
Polk County, FL	38.3
Brazoria County, TX	38.2
San Francisco County, CA	38.2
Lorain County, OH	38.1
Richmond County, NY	38.1
San Benito County, CA	38.0
North Slope Borough, AK	37.9
Ventura County, CA	37.9
Kauai County, HI	37.8
Montgomery County, TX	37.8
Placer County, CA	37.8
Montgomery County, OH	37.7
Broward County, FL	37.6
Passaic County, NJ	37.5
Thurston County, WA	37.5
Essex County, MA	37.4
Stanislaus County, CA	37.4
Volusia County, FL	37.4
Clark County, WA	37.3
Morris County, NJ	37.3
New London County, CT	37.3
Butte County, CA	37.2
Camden County, GA	37.2
Mercer County, NJ	37.2

Place	Years
Kealakekua, HI (cdp) Hawaii County	53.4
Bonita, CA (cdp) San Diego County	53.1
Halaula, HI (cdp) Hawaii County	51.1
Upland, CA (city) San Bernardino County	50.9
Kaunakakai, HI (cdp) Maui County	50.3
Kapaau, HI (cdp) Hawaii County	50.0
Freehold, NJ (township) Monmouth County	49.6
Honaunau-Napoopoo, HI (cdp) Hawaii County	49.2
Kualapuu, HI (cdp) Maui County	49.2
Orangetown, NY (town) Rockland County	47.4
Makaha, HI (cdp) Honolulu County	47.1
Winchester, NV (cdp) Clark County	46.3
Richgrove, CA (cdp) Tulare County	45.8
Waimea, HI (cdp) Kauai County	45.4
Pahala, HI (cdp) Hawaii County	45.1
Papaikou, HI (cdp) Hawaii County	44.7
Captain Cook, HI (cdp) Hawaii County	44.4
Kekaha, HI (cdp) Kauai County	44.4
Earlimart, CA (cdp) Tulare County	44.2
Thousand Oaks, CA (city) Ventura County	44.1
Pupukea, HI (cdp) Honolulu County	43.8
Salem, OR (city) Marion County	43.7
Florin, CA (cdp) Sacramento County	43.6
Lakeside, FL (cdp) Clay County	43.5
Waialua, HI (cdp) Honolulu County	43.5
Rosemead, CA (city) Los Angeles County	43.1
Westmont, IL (village) Du Page County	43.1
Lincolnwood, IL (village) Cook County	42.9
Washington, NJ (township) Gloucester County	42.9
Kahuku, HI (cdp) Honolulu County	42.8
Potomac, MD (cdp) Montgomery County	42.8
Haliimaile, HI (cdp) Maui County	42.6
Montebello, CA (city) Los Angeles County	42.4
Hilo, HI (cdp) Hawaii County	42.3
La Puente, CA (city) Los Angeles County	42.3
Omao, HI (cdp) Kauai County	42.3
Cupertino, CA (city) Santa Clara County	42.2
Hawaiian Beaches, HI (cdp) Hawaii County	42.2
Temple City, CA (city) Los Angeles County	42.2
Pepeekeo, HI (cdp) Hawaii County	42.1
Rancho Palos Verdes, CA (city) Los Angeles County	42.1
Lihue, HI (cdp) Kauai County	41.9
Lemoore, CA (city) Kings County	41.8
Puhi, HI (cdp) Kauai County	41.8
Simi Valley, CA (city) Ventura County	41.7
Unalaska, AK (city) Aleutians West Census Area	41.7
Bellview, FL (cdp) Escambia County	41.6
Terra Bella, CA (cdp) Tulare County	41.5
Parsippany-Troy Hills, NJ (township) Morris County	41.4
Downers Grove, IL (village) Du Page County	41.3
Security-Widefield, CO (cdp) El Paso County	41.3
Redlands, CA (city) San Bernardino County	41.2
Naalehu, HI (cdp) Hawaii County	41.1
Orosi, CA (cdp) Tulare County	41.1
South Brunswick, NJ (township) Middlesex County	41.1
Vancouver, WA (city) Clark County	41.1
Cicero, IL (town) Cook County	41.0
McLean, VA (cdp) Fairfax County	40.9
South San Jose Hills, CA (cdp) Los Angeles County	40.9
Fort Washington, MD (cdp) Prince George's County	40.8
Benicia, CA (city) Solano County	40.7
Culver City, CA (city) Los Angeles County	40.7
Pahoa, HI (cdp) Hawaii County	40.6
Huntington, NY (town) Suffolk County	40.5
Pearl City, HI (cdp) Honolulu County	40.5
Laguna Niguel, CA (city) Orange County	40.4
Walnut, CA (city) Los Angeles County	40.4
West Orange, NJ (township) Essex County	40.4
West Puente Valley, CA (cdp) Los Angeles County	40.4
Camarillo, CA (city) Ventura County	40.3
Cape Coral, FL (city) Lee County	40.3
Kailua, HI (cdp) Honolulu County	40.3
Pico Rivera, CA (city) Los Angeles County	40.3
Ridgecrest, CA (city) Kern County	40.3
Cerritos, CA (city) Los Angeles County	40.2

Notes: Please refer to the User's Guide for an explanation of data; ranking tables include all places with Asian and/or NHPI populations above SF4 population thresholds; (1) tables reflect only those areas that meet SF4 population thresholds, therefore there may be less than 50 states, 75 counties or 75 places listed

Median Age

Guamanian or Chamorro

All States, Top 75 Counties, and Top 75 Places Sorted by Number[1]

State	Years
Oklahoma	34.9
Colorado	34.0
Minnesota	33.8
Connecticut	33.0
Illinois	32.4
California	31.7
South Carolina	31.7
Missouri	31.2
Louisiana	30.8
Nevada	29.7
Maryland	29.5
Hawaii	29.3
United States	29.3
Florida	29.1
Texas	28.9
Massachusetts	28.3
North Carolina	28.0
Georgia	27.8
Ohio	27.8
Arizona	27.5
Oregon	27.4
Virginia	27.0
Washington	26.9
New York	26.5
Kentucky	26.4
New Jersey	26.4
New Mexico	26.0
Tennessee	25.2
Indiana	24.4
Alabama	24.3
Pennsylvania	24.1
Michigan	23.9
Wisconsin	23.3

County	Years
San Mateo County, CA	39.8
Solano County, CA	37.4
Bell County, TX	35.6
Orange County, CA	35.4
Thurston County, WA	33.1
San Diego County, CA	32.7
Riverside County, CA	32.4
El Paso County, CO	32.1
Contra Costa County, CA	31.5
Los Angeles County, CA	31.0
Alameda County, CA	30.8
San Bernardino County, CA	30.6
Clark County, NV	30.4
Santa Clara County, CA	30.1
Sacramento County, CA	29.6
Honolulu County, HI	29.1
Harris County, TX	28.9
Maricopa County, AZ	28.7
Monterey County, CA	27.4
Pierce County, WA	26.1
Kitsap County, WA	26.0
King County, WA	25.3
Kings County, NY	20.4

Place	Years
Fairfield, CA (city) Solano County	41.1
Killeen, TX (city) Bell County	39.2
Vallejo, CA (city) Solano County	35.6
Chula Vista, CA (city) San Diego County	34.6
San Jose, CA (city) Santa Clara County	33.6
Los Angeles, CA (city) Los Angeles County	32.1
San Diego, CA (city) San Diego County	31.8
Houston, TX (city) Harris County	28.9
Tacoma, WA (city) Pierce County	26.5
Honolulu, HI (cdp) Honolulu County	25.6
New York, NY (city)	24.8

Notes: Please refer to the User's Guide for an explanation of data; ranking tables include all places with Asian and/or NHPI populations above SF4 population thresholds; (1) tables reflect only those areas that meet SF4 population thresholds, therefore there may be less than 50 states, 75 counties or 75 places listed

Median Age

Hawaiian, Native

All States, Top 75 Counties, and Top 75 Places Sorted by Number[1]

State	Years
New Mexico	35.8
Maryland	35.4
South Carolina	35.2
Kansas	35.1
California	35.0
New York	34.0
Georgia	33.9
Tennessee	33.9
Florida	33.6
Illinois	33.6
Oklahoma	32.8
Virginia	32.6
Oregon	32.2
Missouri	32.1
Nevada	32.1
United States	31.8
Minnesota	31.5
New Jersey	31.4
Hawaii	31.3
Colorado	31.2
Louisiana	31.1
Washington	30.8
Pennsylvania	30.4
Texas	30.1
Alaska	29.8
Indiana	29.4
Wisconsin	28.8
Ohio	28.3
Michigan	26.9
Montana	26.8
Idaho	26.3
Arkansas	25.9
Utah	25.9
North Carolina	25.7
Arizona	25.5
Massachusetts	24.1

County	Years
San Mateo County, CA	39.9
Bexar County, TX	37.9
Ventura County, CA	37.2
Alameda County, CA	36.9
Contra Costa County, CA	36.9
Riverside County, CA	36.9
Solano County, CA	36.9
San Diego County, CA	35.2
Orange County, CA	35.1
Los Angeles County, CA	34.4
San Bernardino County, CA	33.5
Sacramento County, CA	32.3
Honolulu County, HI	31.9
Santa Clara County, CA	31.9
King County, WA	31.8
Clark County, NV	31.6
Snohomish County, WA	31.4
Hawaii County, HI	30.3
Maui County, HI	30.1
San Joaquin County, CA	29.9
Washington County, OR	29.9
Pierce County, WA	29.8
Kauai County, HI	28.9
Multnomah County, OR	28.9
Salt Lake County, UT	28.5
Pima County, AZ	26.2
Maricopa County, AZ	23.6
Utah County, UT	23.5

Place	Years
Halawa, HI (cdp) Honolulu County	42.1
Waimea, HI (cdp) Kauai County	40.5
Honalo, HI (cdp) Hawaii County	39.2
Holualoa, HI (cdp) Hawaii County	38.1
Kaaawa, HI (cdp) Honolulu County	38.0
Los Angeles, CA (city) Los Angeles County	36.6
Honolulu, HI (cdp) Honolulu County	36.2
Kailua, HI (cdp) Honolulu County	36.2
Waimea, HI (cdp) Hawaii County	35.9
Haleiwa, HI (cdp) Honolulu County	35.8
Lahaina, HI (cdp) Maui County	35.6
Hawaiian Ocean View, HI (cdp) Hawaii County	35.5
Honaunau-Napoopoo, HI (cdp) Hawaii County	35.0
Aiea, HI (cdp) Honolulu County	34.8
Volcano, HI (cdp) Hawaii County	34.8
Wahiawa, HI (cdp) Honolulu County	34.7
Naalehu, HI (cdp) Hawaii County	34.3
San Diego, CA (city) San Diego County	34.3
Waimanalo Beach, HI (cdp) Honolulu County	34.1
Waialua, HI (cdp) Honolulu County	33.8
Paia, HI (cdp) Maui County	33.4
Las Vegas, NV (city) Clark County	33.3
Kailua, HI (cdp) Hawaii County	33.2
Kualapuu, HI (cdp) Maui County	33.0
Mililani Town, HI (cdp) Honolulu County	32.9
Hauula, HI (cdp) Honolulu County	32.1
Nanakuli, HI (cdp) Honolulu County	32.1
Laie, HI (cdp) Honolulu County	31.9
Kihei, HI (cdp) Maui County	31.8
Waikoloa Village, HI (cdp) Hawaii County	31.8
Waipahu, HI (cdp) Honolulu County	31.8
Henderson, NV (city) Clark County	31.7
Kaneohe, HI (cdp) Honolulu County	31.4
Kahaluu, HI (cdp) Honolulu County	30.8
New York, NY (city)	30.6
Pearl City, HI (cdp) Honolulu County	30.6
Kahului, HI (cdp) Maui County	29.8
Waihee-Waiehu, HI (cdp) Maui County	29.4
Anahola, HI (cdp) Kauai County	29.3
Ewa Beach, HI (cdp) Honolulu County	29.2
San Jose, CA (city) Santa Clara County	28.9
Waimalu, HI (cdp) Honolulu County	28.8
Portland, OR (city) Multnomah County	28.4
Waianae, HI (cdp) Honolulu County	28.3
Pakala Village, HI (cdp) Kauai County	28.2
Waipio, HI (cdp) Honolulu County	28.2
Hilo, HI (cdp) Hawaii County	28.1
Hana, HI (cdp) Maui County	27.8
Kalaoa, HI (cdp) Hawaii County	27.5
Makakilo City, HI (cdp) Honolulu County	27.3
Wailuku, HI (cdp) Maui County	27.3
Makawao, HI (cdp) Maui County	26.8
Paradise, NV (cdp) Clark County	26.7
Kekaha, HI (cdp) Kauai County	26.4
Hawaiian Beaches, HI (cdp) Hawaii County	26.2
Captain Cook, HI (cdp) Hawaii County	25.8
Waimanalo, HI (cdp) Honolulu County	25.8
Punaluu, HI (cdp) Honolulu County	25.7
Phoenix, AZ (city) Maricopa County	25.6
Makaha Valley, HI (cdp) Honolulu County	25.5
Kaunakakai, HI (cdp) Maui County	24.9
Kahuku, HI (cdp) Honolulu County	24.8
Hanapepe, HI (cdp) Kauai County	24.6
Ahuimanu, HI (cdp) Honolulu County	24.5
Pahala, HI (cdp) Hawaii County	24.5
Hawaiian Paradise Park, HI (cdp) Hawaii County	24.2
Kapaa, HI (cdp) Kauai County	22.6
Maili, HI (cdp) Honolulu County	20.0
Makaha, HI (cdp) Honolulu County	20.0
Waikane, HI (cdp) Honolulu County	19.5
Kilauea, HI (cdp) Kauai County	18.5
Kapaau, HI (cdp) Hawaii County	16.8

Notes: Please refer to the User's Guide for an explanation of data; ranking tables include all places with Asian and/or NHPI populations above SF4 population thresholds; (1) tables reflect only those areas that meet SF4 population thresholds, therefore there may be less than 50 states, 75 counties or 75 places listed

Median Age

Hmong

All States, Top 75 Counties, and Top 75 Places Sorted by Number[1]

State	Years
Pennsylvania	19.8
Georgia	19.6
Oregon	19.1
Colorado	19.0
Rhode Island	17.8
Michigan	17.5
Kansas	17.0
Oklahoma	17.0
Massachusetts	16.3
North Carolina	16.3
United States	16.3
Minnesota	16.1
California	16.0
Washington	15.9
Wisconsin	15.9
South Carolina	14.9
Alaska	13.7

County	Years
Orange County, CA	22.3
Macomb County, MI	21.2
Los Angeles County, CA	19.9
Adams County, CO	19.4
Mecklenburg County, NC	19.4
Multnomah County, OR	19.4
San Diego County, CA	19.4
Jefferson County, CO	19.1
Oakland County, MI	18.3
Lancaster County, PA	18.2
Catawba County, NC	18.0
Barrow County, GA	17.7
Olmsted County, MN	17.6
Dane County, WI	17.4
Solano County, CA	17.4
Anoka County, MN	17.0
Manitowoc County, WI	17.0
Spokane County, WA	16.9
Brown County, WI	16.8
Milwaukee County, WI	16.6
Stanislaus County, CA	16.6
Providence County, RI	16.4
Glenn County, CA	16.3
Ramsey County, MN	16.2
Tulare County, CA	16.1
Outagamie County, WI	16.0
Sacramento County, CA	16.0
Chippewa County, WI	15.9
San Joaquin County, CA	15.9
Stanly County, NC	15.9
Fresno County, CA	15.8
Eau Claire County, WI	15.7
Hennepin County, MN	15.6
Riverside County, CA	15.6
Wyandotte County, KS	15.5
Yuba County, CA	15.4
La Crosse County, WI	15.3
Wood County, WI	15.3
Wayne County, MI	15.2
Washington County, MN	15.1
Butte County, CA	15.0
Merced County, CA	15.0
Winnebago County, WI	14.9
Marathon County, WI	14.8
Sheboygan County, WI	14.8
Burke County, NC	14.7
Portage County, WI	14.7
Spartanburg County, SC	14.7
Worcester County, MA	14.7
Fond du Lac County, WI	14.6
Dunn County, WI	13.9
Ingham County, MI	13.9
Anchorage Borough, AK	13.7
Santa Barbara County, CA	13.6
Yolo County, CA	13.1
Calumet County, WI	13.0
King County, WA	12.3

Place	Years
Santa Ana, CA (city) Orange County	22.6
Arden-Arcade, CA (cdp) Sacramento County	22.1
Warren, MI (city) Macomb County	21.6
Portland, OR (city) Multnomah County	19.6
Charlotte, NC (city) Mecklenburg County	19.4
Brooklyn Park, MN (city) Hennepin County	19.0
San Diego, CA (city) San Diego County	19.0
Westminster, CO (city) Adams County	18.8
Hickory, NC (city) Catawba County	17.9
Rochester, MN (city) Olmsted County	17.6
Brooklyn Center, MN (city) Hennepin County	17.4
Madison, WI (city) Dane County	17.0
Manitowoc, WI (city) Manitowoc County	16.8
Clovis, CA (city) Fresno County	16.5
Milwaukee, WI (city) Milwaukee County	16.5
Green Bay, WI (city) Brown County	16.4
Willows, CA (city) Glenn County	16.3
St. Paul, MN (city) Ramsey County	16.2
Eau Claire, WI (city) Eau Claire County	15.9
Chico, CA (city) Butte County	15.8
Sacramento, CA (city) Sacramento County	15.8
Fresno, CA (city) Fresno County	15.7
Modesto, CA (city) Stanislaus County	15.7
Pontiac, MI (city) Oakland County	15.7
Stockton, CA (city) San Joaquin County	15.7
Glen Alpine, NC (town) Burke County	15.6
Kansas City, KS (city) Wyandotte County	15.5
La Crosse, WI (city) La Crosse County	15.5
Woodbury, MN (city) Washington County	15.5
South Oroville, CA (cdp) Butte County	15.3
Detroit, MI (city) Wayne County	15.2
Atwater, CA (city) Merced County	15.1
Appleton, WI (city) Outagamie County	15.0
Wisconsin Rapids, WI (city) Wood County	15.0
Linda, CA (cdp) Yuba County	14.9
Minneapolis, MN (city) Hennepin County	14.9
Parkway-S. Sacramento, CA (cdp) Sacramento County	14.9
Sheboygan, WI (city) Sheboygan County	14.7
Maplewood, MN (city) Ramsey County	14.6
Merced, CA (city) Merced County	14.6
Spokane, WA (city) Spokane County	14.6
Wausau, WI (city) Marathon County	14.6
Stevens Point, WI (city) Portage County	14.5
Thermalito, CA (cdp) Butte County	14.4
Fitchburg, MA (city) Worcester County	14.1
Fond du Lac, WI (city) Fond du Lac County	13.9
Oshkosh, WI (city) Winnebago County	13.9
Lansing, MI (city) Ingham County	13.8
Florin, CA (cdp) Sacramento County	13.4
Connelly Springs, NC (town) Burke County	13.3
Visalia, CA (city) Tulare County	13.3
Providence, RI (city) Providence County	12.6
West Sacramento, CA (city) Yolo County	12.2
Valdese, NC (town) Burke County	11.9
Oroville, CA (city) Butte County	11.3

Notes: Please refer to the User's Guide for an explanation of data; ranking tables include all places with Asian and/or NHPI populations above SF4 population thresholds; (1) tables reflect only those areas that meet SF4 population thresholds, therefore there may be less than 50 states, 75 counties or 75 places listed

Median Age

Indonesian

***All States, Top 75 Counties, and Top 75 Places Sorted by Number*[1]**

State	Years
Florida	40.0
Arizona	34.0
New Jersey	33.0
New York	32.0
California	31.8
Illinois	31.2
Maryland	30.8
United States	30.1
Pennsylvania	29.6
Virginia	28.9
Georgia	28.8
Colorado	28.5
Texas	28.5
Washington	27.1
Michigan	25.7
Massachusetts	25.5
Oregon	25.1
Wisconsin	24.7
Ohio	23.1

County	Years
Contra Costa County, CA	39.1
Maricopa County, AZ	35.2
Orange County, CA	34.7
Santa Clara County, CA	34.3
Middlesex County, NJ	33.4
Montgomery County, MD	31.8
Queens County, NY	31.6
Los Angeles County, CA	31.5
Cook County, IL	31.3
San Diego County, CA	31.2
Alameda County, CA	30.3
Harris County, TX	30.3
San Bernardino County, CA	30.1
Fairfax County, VA	27.6
King County, WA	26.6
San Francisco County, CA	26.1
San Mateo County, CA	25.9
Franklin County, OH	22.0

Place	Years
Los Angeles, CA (city) Los Angeles County	34.1
New York, NY (city)	32.2
Houston, TX (city) Harris County	29.1
Loma Linda, CA (city) San Bernardino County	27.3
San Francisco, CA (city) San Francisco County	26.1
Seattle, WA (city) King County	24.7
Columbus, OH (city) Franklin County	21.9
San Bernardino, CA (city) San Bernardino County	19.3

Notes: Please refer to the User's Guide for an explanation of data; ranking tables include all places with Asian and/or NHPI populations above SF4 population thresholds; (1) tables reflect only those areas that meet SF4 population thresholds, therefore there may be less than 50 states, 75 counties or 75 places listed

Median Age

Japanese

All States, Top 75 Counties, and Top 75 Places Sorted by Number[1]

State	Years
Hawaii	50.4
Nevada	48.0
Arkansas	47.8
Delaware	45.1
New Mexico	44.8
Alaska	43.6
Maine	43.6
California	43.4
Idaho	43.1
Colorado	43.0
Montana	43.0
United States	42.6
Mississippi	42.5
Washington	41.6
Louisiana	41.1
Florida	41.0
Arizona	40.9
Wyoming	40.6
Rhode Island	40.0
Alabama	39.8
Illinois	39.3
South Carolina	39.2
Utah	39.0
Nebraska	38.7
Virginia	38.6
Maryland	38.4
Missouri	38.1
Oregon	37.9
Wisconsin	37.9
New Jersey	37.3
Texas	37.2
North Carolina	37.0
Ohio	36.1
Georgia	36.0
Kansas	35.8
Minnesota	35.4
Kentucky	34.9
Connecticut	34.5
New Hampshire	34.5
Michigan	34.0
Pennsylvania	33.9
New York	33.8
Oklahoma	33.2
Tennessee	33.1
Indiana	32.8
District of Columbia	32.2
Vermont	31.6
Massachusetts	30.6
Iowa	30.5
South Dakota	28.0
West Virginia	27.4

County	Years
Malheur County, OR	68.6
Burlington County, NJ	67.1
Merced County, CA	61.4
Tulare County, CA	59.1
Cumberland County, NC	56.1
Kauai County, HI	55.0
Maui County, HI	53.3
Monmouth County, NJ	53.1
Solano County, CA	53.0
Adams County, CO	52.9
Monterey County, CA	52.6
Bell County, TX	52.5
Hawaii County, HI	52.0
El Paso County, TX	51.7
Sutter County, CA	50.9
Pierce County, WA	50.8
San Joaquin County, CA	50.5
Honolulu County, HI	49.8
Weber County, UT	49.6
Fresno County, CA	49.0
Clark County, NV	48.6
Anne Arundel County, MD	47.3
El Paso County, CO	47.1
Palm Beach County, FL	47.1
Sacramento County, CA	46.8
Suffolk County, NY	46.5
Sonoma County, CA	46.4
Placer County, CA	46.2
Kitsap County, WA	46.1
Marin County, CA	46.1
Santa Cruz County, CA	46.1
Clackamas County, OR	45.9
Jackson County, MO	45.9
Jefferson County, CO	45.7
Bernalillo County, NM	45.3
Stanislaus County, CA	45.3
Brevard County, FL	45.0
El Dorado County, CA	44.8
Prince George's County, MD	44.8
Contra Costa County, CA	44.6
Canyon County, ID	44.5
Davis County, UT	44.5
Onslow County, NC	44.5
Anchorage Borough, AK	44.4
Riverside County, CA	44.2
Arapahoe County, CO	43.8
Los Angeles County, CA	43.8
Hillsborough County, FL	43.5
Santa Barbara County, CA	43.5
Prince William County, VA	43.1
Ventura County, CA	43.1
Alameda County, CA	42.8
Marion County, IN	42.7
Hamilton County, OH	42.4
San Francisco County, CA	42.4
Washoe County, NV	42.2
Bexar County, TX	42.1
San Bernardino County, CA	42.0
San Luis Obispo County, CA	42.0
Milwaukee County, WI	41.9
San Mateo County, CA	41.7
Kern County, CA	41.5
King County, WA	41.3
Salt Lake County, UT	41.3
Morris County, NJ	41.2
Santa Clara County, CA	41.2
Tarrant County, TX	41.1
Maricopa County, AZ	41.0
Orange County, CA	40.9
Essex County, NJ	40.7
Denver County, CO	40.5
Island County, WA	40.5
San Diego County, CA	40.4
DuPage County, IL	40.3
Montgomery County, OH	40.2

Place	Years
Pahoa, HI (cdp) Hawaii County	71.7
Pahala, HI (cdp) Hawaii County	71.5
Honokaa, HI (cdp) Hawaii County	71.3
Kahuku, HI (cdp) Honolulu County	71.0
Waialua, HI (cdp) Honolulu County	69.5
Watsonville, CA (city) Santa Cruz County	69.5
Lakewood, WA (city) Pierce County	69.1
Carson, CA (city) Los Angeles County	68.1
Koloa, HI (cdp) Kauai County	66.5
Seaside, CA (city) Monterey County	66.5
La Mirada, CA (city) Los Angeles County	65.1
Paukaa, HI (cdp) Hawaii County	64.3
Wainaku, HI (cdp) Hawaii County	63.8
Pepeekeo, HI (cdp) Hawaii County	62.7
Wahiawa, HI (cdp) Honolulu County	61.8
Waipahu, HI (cdp) Honolulu County	61.6
Hanamaulu, HI (cdp) Kauai County	61.1
Hanapepe, HI (cdp) Kauai County	61.1
Waimea, HI (cdp) Kauai County	60.6
Kahului, HI (cdp) Maui County	60.5
Fairfield, CA (city) Solano County	59.6
Sunrise Manor, NV (cdp) Clark County	59.3
Aiea, HI (cdp) Honolulu County	59.2
Lahaina, HI (cdp) Maui County	58.8
Haleiwa, HI (cdp) Honolulu County	58.5
Kekaha, HI (cdp) Kauai County	58.5
Keaau, HI (cdp) Hawaii County	58.1
Kaunakakai, HI (cdp) Maui County	57.7
Lihue, HI (cdp) Kauai County	57.5
Santa Maria, CA (city) Santa Barbara County	57.5
Kurtistown, HI (cdp) Hawaii County	56.8
Lodi, CA (city) San Joaquin County	56.7
Pearl City, HI (cdp) Honolulu County	56.0
Kealakekua, HI (cdp) Hawaii County	55.7
Ewa Beach, HI (cdp) Honolulu County	55.5
Monterey Park, CA (city) Los Angeles County	55.4
Papaikou, HI (cdp) Hawaii County	55.2
Wailuku, HI (cdp) Maui County	55.2
Marina, CA (city) Monterey County	54.8
Kapaa, HI (cdp) Kauai County	54.6
Kapaau, HI (cdp) Hawaii County	54.3
Paia, HI (cdp) Maui County	53.9
Norwalk, CA (city) Los Angeles County	53.7
Waianae, HI (cdp) Honolulu County	53.5
Garden Grove, CA (city) Orange County	53.3
San Leandro, CA (city) Alameda County	53.1
Gardena, CA (city) Los Angeles County	52.8
Heeia, HI (cdp) Honolulu County	52.6
South San Gabriel, CA (cdp) Los Angeles County	52.6
Westminster, CA (city) Orange County	52.6
Wailua, HI (cdp) Kauai County	52.5
La Palma, CA (city) Orange County	52.3
Captain Cook, HI (cdp) Hawaii County	52.2
Hawaiian Beaches, HI (cdp) Hawaii County	52.0
Eleele, HI (cdp) Kauai County	51.9
Hilo, HI (cdp) Hawaii County	51.9
Holualoa, HI (cdp) Hawaii County	51.9
Montebello, CA (city) Los Angeles County	51.9
Honaunau-Napoopoo, HI (cdp) Hawaii County	51.8
Oxnard, CA (city) Ventura County	51.8
Bryn Mawr-Skyway, WA (cdp) King County	51.7
Lawai, HI (cdp) Kauai County	51.5
Kailua, HI (cdp) Honolulu County	51.4
El Paso, TX (city) El Paso County	51.3
Hacienda Heights, CA (cdp) Los Angeles County	51.3
Honolulu, HI (cdp) Honolulu County	51.3
Mercer Island, WA (city) King County	51.3
Oceanside, CA (city) San Diego County	51.3
Temple City, CA (city) Los Angeles County	50.6
Pukalani, HI (cdp) Maui County	50.5
Stockton, CA (city) San Joaquin County	50.2
Pacifica, CA (city) San Mateo County	50.1
Halawa, HI (cdp) Honolulu County	50.0
Wailua Homesteads, HI (cdp) Kauai County	49.9
Puhi, HI (cdp) Kauai County	49.7

Notes: Please refer to the User's Guide for an explanation of data; ranking tables include all places with Asian and/or NHPI populations above SF4 population thresholds; (1) tables reflect only those areas that meet SF4 population thresholds, therefore there may be less than 50 states, 75 counties or 75 places listed

Median Age

Korean

All States, Top 75 Counties, and Top 75 Places Sorted by Number[1]

State	Years
Hawaii	41.9
Alaska	38.5
Nevada	37.6
Florida	35.8
California	34.9
South Carolina	34.8
Virginia	34.5
Arkansas	34.3
Delaware	34.3
Oklahoma	34.3
Washington	34.2
Georgia	33.8
Maryland	33.8
Tennessee	33.5
North Carolina	33.4
Texas	33.4
Alabama	33.3
Louisiana	33.3
New Mexico	32.8
Colorado	32.7
United States	32.7
Kentucky	32.6
Mississippi	32.6
New Jersey	32.4
Arizona	32.1
Illinois	32.0
New York	31.9
Kansas	31.8
Ohio	30.1
Missouri	30.0
Oregon	30.0
Pennsylvania	29.9
North Dakota	29.4
Indiana	29.3
Idaho	28.3
District of Columbia	28.2
Wyoming	27.4
Connecticut	27.2
West Virginia	27.0
Utah	26.7
Massachusetts	26.5
New Hampshire	25.0
Maine	24.9
Rhode Island	24.7
Michigan	24.4
Wisconsin	24.1
Nebraska	22.4
Iowa	21.0
Minnesota	20.5
Vermont	20.3
Montana	17.6
South Dakota	16.1

County	Years
Lake County, IN	48.3
Pulaski County, MO	43.9
Geary County, KS	43.7
Brevard County, FL	43.2
Dale County, AL	43.2
Comanche County, OK	43.1
Cochise County, AZ	42.5
Coryell County, TX	42.1
Newport News Independent City, VA	42.1
Honolulu County, HI	42.0
Virginia Beach Independent City, VA	42.0
Hardin County, KY	41.9
Hawaii County, HI	41.9
Bell County, TX	41.7
Jefferson Parish, LA	41.5
Montgomery County, TN	41.4
Richmond County, NY	41.3
Thurston County, WA	40.9
Washoe County, NV	40.8
Solano County, CA	40.2
Monterey County, CA	39.7
Richmond County, GA	39.7
St. Clair County, IL	39.6
Sonoma County, CA	39.6
Pierce County, WA	39.4
Palm Beach County, FL	39.3
Bexar County, TX	39.1
Vernon Parish, LA	38.9
Anchorage Borough, AK	38.8
El Paso County, CO	38.8
Pinellas County, FL	38.8
Fairbanks North Star Borough, AK	38.5
Tulare County, CA	38.5
Okaloosa County, FL	38.4
Muscogee County, GA	38.3
El Paso County, TX	38.2
Greene County, OH	37.9
Maui County, HI	37.9
Liberty County, GA	37.5
Rockland County, NY	37.5
Clark County, NV	37.3
Columbia County, GA	37.3
Adams County, CO	37.2
Hillsborough County, FL	37.2
Madison County, AL	37.2
Kitsap County, WA	37.0
Miami-Dade County, FL	37.0
San Joaquin County, CA	37.0
Fairfax Independent City, VA	36.9
Frederick County, MD	36.9
York County, VA	36.9
Cumberland County, PA	36.8
Douglas County, CO	36.6
Prince William County, VA	36.6
Cumberland County, NC	36.5
Duval County, FL	36.5
Marin County, CA	36.5
Chesterfield County, VA	36.2
Wicomico County, MD	36.2
Kern County, CA	36.1
Burlington County, NJ	36.0
Guilford County, NC	36.0
Cobb County, GA	35.9
Los Angeles County, CA	35.9
Johnson County, KS	35.8
Snohomish County, WA	35.8
Westchester County, NY	35.8
Fairfax County, VA	35.7
San Luis Obispo County, CA	35.7
Clackamas County, OR	35.5
Clark County, WA	35.5
Harford County, MD	35.5
Arapahoe County, CO	35.4
Bronx County, NY	35.4
Dallas County, TX	35.3

Place	Years
Kailua, HI (cdp) Honolulu County	54.6
Mililani Town, HI (cdp) Honolulu County	48.8
Kaneohe, HI (cdp) Honolulu County	48.3
Spanaway, WA (cdp) Pierce County	44.9
Oxnard, CA (city) Ventura County	44.7
Sierra Vista, AZ (city) Cochise County	44.4
Hawaiian Gardens, CA (city) Los Angeles County	44.3
Hilo, HI (cdp) Hawaii County	44.3
Lawton, OK (city) Comanche County	43.6
Palos Verdes Estates, CA (city) Los Angeles County	43.4
Lakewood, WA (city) Pierce County	42.8
Fairbanks, AK (city) Fairbanks North Star Borough	42.7
Mission Viejo, CA (city) Orange County	42.5
Lake Forest, CA (city) Orange County	42.4
Lincolnwood, IL (village) Cook County	42.3
Sunrise Manor, NV (cdp) Clark County	42.3
Syosset, NY (cdp) Nassau County	42.3
Fairfield, CA (city) Solano County	42.1
Niles, IL (village) Cook County	42.0
Rosemont, CA (cdp) Sacramento County	42.0
Honolulu, HI (cdp) Honolulu County	41.7
Northbrook, IL (village) Cook County	41.7
Pearl City, HI (cdp) Honolulu County	41.7
Killeen, TX (city) Bell County	41.6
Clarksville, TN (city) Montgomery County	41.3
Lake Success, NY (village) Nassau County	41.3
Potomac, MD (cdp) Montgomery County	41.3
Redmond, WA (city) King County	41.2
Waimalu, HI (cdp) Honolulu County	41.2
Westminster, CA (city) Orange County	41.2
Alpine, NJ (borough) Bergen County	41.0
Newark, CA (city) Alameda County	41.0
Saratoga, CA (city) Santa Clara County	41.0
Hinesville, GA (city) Liberty County	40.9
Lacey, WA (city) Thurston County	40.9
Pemberton, NJ (township) Burlington County	40.9
Morton Grove, IL (village) Cook County	40.8
Orange, CA (city) Orange County	40.8
Reno, NV (city) Washoe County	40.8
Santa Ana, CA (city) Orange County	40.8
Stanton, CA (city) Orange County	40.7
Parkland, WA (cdp) Pierce County	40.6
Browns Mills, NJ (cdp) Burlington County	40.4
Harrington Park, NJ (borough) Bergen County	40.2
Montgomery, PA (township) Montgomery County	40.1
Marina, CA (city) Monterey County	40.0
Marple, PA (township) Delaware County	40.0
Moreno Valley, CA (city) Riverside County	40.0
Whitpain, PA (township) Montgomery County	40.0
Sugar Land, TX (city) Fort Bend County	39.9
Bloomfield, MI (township) Oakland County	39.8
Huntington Beach, CA (city) Orange County	39.8
Rancho Palos Verdes, CA (city) Los Angeles County	39.8
Las Vegas, NV (city) Clark County	39.7
Montebello, CA (city) Los Angeles County	39.7
Mount Vernon, VA (cdp) Fairfax County	39.7
Temple City, CA (city) Los Angeles County	39.7
Augusta-Richmond Co., GA (sp. city) Richmond Co.	39.6
Tacoma, WA (city) Pierce County	39.5
Richardson, TX (city) Dallas County	39.3
Fountain Valley, CA (city) Orange County	39.2
Garden Grove, CA (city) Orange County	39.2
Jericho, NY (cdp) Nassau County	39.2
Wayne, NJ (township) Passaic County	39.1
Glen Cove, NY (city) Nassau County	39.0
Plymouth, PA (township) Montgomery County	39.0
Livingston, NJ (township) Essex County	38.9
Wilmette, IL (village) Cook County	38.9
Aurora, CO (city) Arapahoe County	38.8
Demarest, NJ (borough) Bergen County	38.8
Fayetteville, NC (city) Cumberland County	38.8
Huntsville, AL (city) Madison County	38.7
San Antonio, TX (city) Bexar County	38.7
Broomall, PA (cdp) Delaware County	38.6
West Springfield, VA (cdp) Fairfax County	38.6

Notes: Please refer to the User's Guide for an explanation of data; ranking tables include all places with Asian and/or NHPI populations above SF4 population thresholds; (1) tables reflect only those areas that meet SF4 population thresholds, therefore there may be less than 50 states, 75 counties or 75 places listed

Median Age

Laotian

All States, Top 75 Counties, and Top 75 Places Sorted by Number[1]

State	Years
Alabama	33.0
Idaho	32.7
Missouri	32.3
Maryland	32.0
Nevada	31.8
Arizona	30.9
Virginia	30.8
Connecticut	29.8
Tennessee	29.8
Florida	29.5
Indiana	29.2
Texas	29.0
Nebraska	28.8
Hawaii	28.5
Illinois	28.2
Georgia	28.1
New Hampshire	28.0
Pennsylvania	27.8
Rhode Island	27.8
Kansas	27.7
Louisiana	27.7
New York	27.5
Iowa	27.4
Washington	26.7
Oregon	26.6
New Jersey	26.5
Ohio	26.3
Oklahoma	26.1
United States	26.1
Massachusetts	25.9
Arkansas	25.8
Colorado	25.7
South Carolina	25.7
Utah	25.5
North Carolina	25.2
Minnesota	25.1
South Dakota	24.5
Michigan	24.4
California	23.3
Alaska	21.1
Wisconsin	21.1

County	Years
Essex County, MA	34.3
Dakota County, NE	33.5
Cass County, MI	32.6
Fairfax County, VA	32.3
Clark County, NV	32.2
Mecklenburg County, NC	32.2
Pierce County, WA	30.9
Rutherford County, TN	30.9
Cook County, IL	30.8
Hartford County, CT	30.8
Gwinnett County, GA	30.7
Montgomery County, NC	30.5
Tarrant County, TX	30.5
New Haven County, CT	30.4
Harris County, TX	30.2
Bexar County, TX	29.7
Pacific County, WA	29.6
Clayton County, GA	29.5
Cowley County, KS	29.5
Pinellas County, FL	29.5
Sebastian County, AR	29.5
Snohomish County, WA	29.5
Clark County, WA	29.4
Oklahoma County, OK	29.3
Winnebago County, IL	29.3
Fairfield County, CT	29.2
Orange County, CA	29.2
Guilford County, NC	29.0
Riverside County, CA	28.9
Johnson County, KS	28.8
Polk County, IA	28.6
Washington County, OR	28.4
Honolulu County, HI	28.3
Maricopa County, AZ	28.1
Monroe County, NY	28.1
Providence County, RI	28.0
Davidson County, TN	27.7
Polk County, FL	27.7
Franklin County, OH	27.6
Philadelphia County, PA	27.5
Mobile County, AL	27.3
Sonoma County, CA	27.1
Dallas County, TX	27.0
Roseau County, MN	27.0
Los Angeles County, CA	26.9
Nobles County, MN	26.6
Potter County, TX	26.6
San Diego County, CA	26.6
Hennepin County, MN	26.5
Jefferson County, CO	26.5
Dakota County, MN	26.2
Kane County, IL	26.1
Multnomah County, OR	26.1
Solano County, CA	26.1
Worcester County, MA	26.1
King County, WA	25.9
Ottawa County, MI	25.7
Iberia Parish, LA	25.6
Adams County, CO	25.4
San Bernardino County, CA	25.4
Buena Vista County, IA	25.3
Habersham County, GA	25.2
Middlesex County, MA	25.0
Salt Lake County, UT	24.9
Spartanburg County, SC	24.9
Dane County, WI	24.8
Stanislaus County, CA	24.8
Santa Clara County, CA	24.7
Contra Costa County, CA	24.4
Sedgwick County, KS	24.2
Milwaukee County, WI	23.8
Washington County, AR	23.8
Alameda County, CA	22.7
Broome County, NY	22.7
Summit County, OH	22.4

Place	Years
Tacoma, WA (city) Pierce County	32.9
Bridgeport, CT (city) Fairfield County	32.8
Charlotte, NC (city) Mecklenburg County	32.2
Honolulu, HI (cdp) Honolulu County	32.1
Brooklyn Center, MN (city) Hennepin County	32.0
Springfield, VA (cdp) Fairfax County	30.9
St. Petersburg, FL (city) Pinellas County	30.3
New Britain, CT (city) Hartford County	30.0
Elgin, IL (city) Kane County	29.8
Fort Smith, AR (city) Sebastian County	29.8
Westminster, CO (city) Adams County	29.8
Woonsocket, RI (city) Providence County	29.7
Murfreesboro, TN (city) Rutherford County	29.6
Riverside, CA (city) Riverside County	29.6
Winfield, KS (city) Cowley County	29.6
Fort Worth, TX (city) Tarrant County	29.4
Los Angeles, CA (city) Los Angeles County	29.3
Amarillo, TX (city) Potter County	29.2
Dallas, TX (city) Dallas County	29.1
Rockford, IL (city) Winnebago County	28.7
Anaheim, CA (city) Orange County	28.6
Providence, RI (city) Providence County	28.6
San Pablo, CA (city) Contra Costa County	28.6
Des Moines, IA (city) Polk County	28.5
Bellevue, WA (city) King County	28.4
Moreno Valley, CA (city) Riverside County	28.4
Oklahoma City, OK (city) Oklahoma County	28.1
Nashville-Davidson, TN (sp. city) Davidson County	27.7
Banning, CA (city) Riverside County	27.5
Haltom City, TX (city) Tarrant County	27.5
Philadelphia, PA (city) Philadelphia County	27.5
Columbus, OH (city) Franklin County	27.4
Santa Rosa, CA (city) Sonoma County	27.4
Irving, TX (city) Dallas County	27.2
Oaklawn-Sunview, KS (cdp) Sedgwick County	27.1
Worthington, MN (city) Nobles County	26.9
San Diego, CA (city) San Diego County	26.7
Portland, OR (city) Multnomah County	26.6
Springdale, AR (city) Washington County	26.5
Rochester, NY (city) Monroe County	26.2
Raymond, WA (city) Pacific County	26.1
Santa Ana, CA (city) Orange County	26.0
Brooklyn Park, MN (city) Hennepin County	25.9
Storm Lake, IA (city) Buena Vista County	25.6
Seattle, WA (city) King County	25.5
Lowell, MA (city) Middlesex County	25.2
Modesto, CA (city) Stanislaus County	24.9
West Valley City, UT (city) Salt Lake County	24.9
Fairfield, CA (city) Solano County	24.8
Minneapolis, MN (city) Hennepin County	24.4
Wichita, KS (city) Sedgwick County	24.4
San Jose, CA (city) Santa Clara County	24.3
Pomona, CA (city) Los Angeles County	23.9
Escondido, CA (city) San Diego County	23.7
Richmond, CA (city) Contra Costa County	23.7
Fitchburg, MA (city) Worcester County	23.5
Milwaukee, WI (city) Milwaukee County	22.7
Stockton, CA (city) San Joaquin County	21.8
Rochester, MN (city) Olmsted County	21.1
Fresno, CA (city) Fresno County	20.6
Merced, CA (city) Merced County	20.6
Akron, OH (city) Summit County	20.5
Oakland, CA (city) Alameda County	20.5
Arvada, CO (city) Jefferson County	20.4
Grand Prairie, TX (city) Dallas County	20.4
Long Beach, CA (city) Los Angeles County	20.4
Parkway-S. Sacramento, CA (cdp) Sacramento County	18.9
Sacramento, CA (city) Sacramento County	18.9
Visalia, CA (city) Tulare County	18.8
Warroad, MN (city) Roseau County	18.6
Redding, CA (city) Shasta County	18.2
St. Paul, MN (city) Ramsey County	16.3
Green Bay, WI (city) Brown County	16.0

Notes: Please refer to the User's Guide for an explanation of data; ranking tables include all places with Asian and/or NHPI populations above SF4 population thresholds; (1) tables reflect only those areas that meet SF4 population thresholds, therefore there may be less than 50 states, 75 counties or 75 places listed

Median Age

Malaysian

All States, Top 75 Counties, and Top 75 Places Sorted by Number [1]

State	Years
New York	36.6
California	33.3
Texas	32.6
United States	29.2
Ohio	26.0
Illinois	25.8
Michigan	23.5
Oklahoma	23.5

County	Years
Queens County, NY	38.1
Los Angeles County, CA	33.4

Place	Years
New York, NY (city)	38.0

Notes: Please refer to the User's Guide for an explanation of data; ranking tables include all places with Asian and/or NHPI populations above SF4 population thresholds; (1) tables reflect only those areas that meet SF4 population thresholds, therefore there may be less than 50 states, 75 counties or 75 places listed

Median Age

Pakistani

All States, Top 75 Counties, and Top 75 Places Sorted by Number[1]

State	Years
Delaware	33.3
Florida	32.4
Arizona	30.6
Louisiana	30.5
Georgia	30.4
Missouri	30.0
Illinois	29.8
West Virginia	29.7
Connecticut	29.3
Maryland	29.3
Minnesota	29.2
Texas	29.2
Kentucky	29.1
Michigan	28.7
New Jersey	28.7
United States	28.7
Pennsylvania	28.6
Alabama	28.4
Nevada	28.4
California	28.3
Kansas	28.3
New York	28.1
Oregon	28.1
Washington	28.1
Colorado	28.0
Indiana	27.8
Ohio	27.8
North Carolina	27.7
Virginia	26.7
Oklahoma	26.3
Utah	26.0
Wisconsin	25.6
Massachusetts	25.4
Iowa	24.3
Tennessee	23.5

County	Years
Miami-Dade County, FL	36.3
San Bernardino County, CA	35.6
Atlantic County, NJ	35.4
Jefferson Parish, LA	35.4
Cobb County, GA	34.2
Orange County, FL	32.6
Monroe County, NY	32.4
Bergen County, NJ	32.2
Tarrant County, TX	31.6
Montgomery County, MD	31.3
Philadelphia County, PA	31.3
Essex County, NJ	31.2
Bronx County, NY	31.1
Broward County, FL	31.0
Loudoun County, VA	30.8
Prince George's County, MD	30.7
St. Louis County, MO	30.7
Macomb County, MI	30.5
Maricopa County, AZ	30.4
Los Angeles County, CA	30.3
Fort Bend County, TX	30.1
Riverside County, CA	30.1
Alameda County, CA	30.0
Cook County, IL	29.9
Oakland County, MI	29.9
Collin County, TX	29.7
DuPage County, IL	29.7
Lake County, IL	29.6
Somerset County, NJ	29.6
Harris County, TX	29.5
Hennepin County, MN	29.5
Gwinnett County, GA	29.4
Milwaukee County, WI	29.4
Fairfield County, CT	29.3
Hartford County, CT	29.3
Contra Costa County, CA	29.1
Washtenaw County, MI	29.1
Delaware County, PA	29.0
Dallas County, TX	28.9
Hudson County, NJ	28.9
New Haven County, CT	28.9
New York County, NY	28.9
Orange County, CA	28.9
Camden County, NJ	28.8
Howard County, MD	28.7
Baltimore County, MD	28.6
Santa Clara County, CA	28.6
King County, WA	28.2
Queens County, NY	28.2
Westchester County, NY	28.2
Clayton County, GA	27.8
Morris County, NJ	27.8
Worcester County, MA	27.8
Alexandria Independent City, VA	27.6
Wayne County, MI	27.6
Monmouth County, NJ	27.4
Snohomish County, WA	27.4
Kings County, NY	27.2
Suffolk County, NY	27.1
Fairfax County, VA	26.9
Wake County, NC	26.9
Middlesex County, NJ	26.6
Nassau County, NY	26.6
Arlington County, VA	26.1
Richmond County, NY	26.0
Sacramento County, CA	26.0
Mercer County, NJ	25.4
Travis County, TX	25.4
Franklin County, OH	25.3
Guilford County, NC	25.3
San Diego County, CA	25.3
Prince William County, VA	25.0
Denton County, TX	24.5
Tulsa County, OK	24.2
Middlesex County, MA	24.1

Place	Years
Old Bridge, NJ (township) Middlesex County	32.4
Richardson, TX (city) Dallas County	32.1
Philadelphia, PA (city) Philadelphia County	31.3
Mission Bend, TX (cdp) Fort Bend County	31.1
Fremont, CA (city) Alameda County	31.0
Skokie, IL (village) Cook County	30.6
Chicago, IL (city) Cook County	30.5
Los Angeles, CA (city) Los Angeles County	30.1
Irving, TX (city) Dallas County	29.7
Dale City, VA (cdp) Prince William County	29.4
Dallas, TX (city) Dallas County	29.4
Plano, TX (city) Collin County	29.1
Houston, TX (city) Harris County	29.0
Jersey City, NJ (city) Hudson County	28.9
Torrance, CA (city) Los Angeles County	28.9
San Jose, CA (city) Santa Clara County	28.4
Sugar Land, TX (city) Fort Bend County	28.2
New York, NY (city)	28.0
Hempstead, NY (town) Nassau County	27.7
Brookhaven, NY (town) Suffolk County	27.2
Edison, NJ (township) Middlesex County	27.2
Garland, TX (city) Dallas County	27.0
Anaheim, CA (city) Orange County	26.3
Bailey's Crossroads, VA (cdp) Fairfax County	26.3
Santa Clara, CA (city) Santa Clara County	26.3
Arlington, VA (cdp) Arlington County	26.1
Huntington, NY (town) Suffolk County	25.5
Lincolnia, VA (cdp) Fairfax County	25.3
North Hempstead, NY (town) Nassau County	25.3
Austin, TX (city) Travis County	25.2
Sacramento, CA (city) Sacramento County	24.6
Carrollton, TX (city) Denton County	24.5
Tulsa, OK (city) Tulsa County	24.5
San Francisco, CA (city) San Francisco County	24.0
Woodbridge, NJ (township) Middlesex County	23.9
Stockton, CA (city) San Joaquin County	21.8
Ellicott City, MD (cdp) Howard County	19.8

Notes: Please refer to the User's Guide for an explanation of data; ranking tables include all places with Asian and/or NHPI populations above SF4 population thresholds; (1) tables reflect only those areas that meet SF4 population thresholds, therefore there may be less than 50 states, 75 counties or 75 places listed

Median Age

Samoan

All States, Top 75 Counties, and Top 75 Places Sorted by Number[1]

State	Years
New Jersey	34.6
Pennsylvania	30.3
Tennessee	29.3
Florida	28.9
New York	28.4
Michigan	28.1
Ohio	27.8
Arizona	27.3
Virginia	27.3
Georgia	26.5
North Carolina	25.9
Nevada	25.1
Illinois	24.9
Hawaii	24.6
Missouri	24.4
United States	24.4
Oregon	24.2
California	23.8
Washington	23.8
Texas	22.2
Colorado	21.9
Utah	21.8
Alaska	19.4

County	Years
Hawaii County, HI	36.3
San Joaquin County, CA	29.2
Santa Clara County, CA	27.5
Maricopa County, AZ	27.0
San Mateo County, CA	26.5
Ventura County, CA	25.6
San Diego County, CA	25.5
Orange County, CA	25.1
Solano County, CA	25.0
Clark County, NV	24.6
Honolulu County, HI	24.2
Jackson County, MO	24.2
King County, WA	24.0
Los Angeles County, CA	23.9
Contra Costa County, CA	23.7
Pierce County, WA	23.0
San Francisco County, CA	22.7
Salt Lake County, UT	22.4
Riverside County, CA	21.7
Utah County, UT	21.3
Sacramento County, CA	20.8
Alameda County, CA	20.7
San Bernardino County, CA	20.1
Anchorage Borough, AK	19.2

Place	Years
Kahuku, HI (cdp) Honolulu County	33.1
Los Angeles, CA (city) Los Angeles County	28.4
Anaheim, CA (city) Orange County	28.2
Hayward, CA (city) Alameda County	28.0
Santa Ana, CA (city) Orange County	28.0
Oceanside, CA (city) San Diego County	26.6
San Jose, CA (city) Santa Clara County	26.3
Lakewood, CA (city) Los Angeles County	25.5
Salt Lake City, UT (city) Salt Lake County	25.3
Honolulu, HI (cdp) Honolulu County	24.9
Oxnard, CA (city) Ventura County	24.9
Seattle, WA (city) King County	23.6
Westminster, CA (city) Orange County	23.5
Ewa Beach, HI (cdp) Honolulu County	23.4
Carson, CA (city) Los Angeles County	23.2
Garden Grove, CA (city) Orange County	23.1
New York, NY (city)	22.8
San Francisco, CA (city) San Francisco County	22.7
Hauula, HI (cdp) Honolulu County	22.4
Nanakuli, HI (cdp) Honolulu County	22.3
West Valley City, UT (city) Salt Lake County	21.9
Lakewood, WA (city) Pierce County	21.8
Long Beach, CA (city) Los Angeles County	21.8
San Diego, CA (city) San Diego County	21.8
Tacoma, WA (city) Pierce County	21.1
Laie, HI (cdp) Honolulu County	20.8
Federal Way, WA (city) King County	20.4
Sacramento, CA (city) Sacramento County	20.3
Waipahu, HI (cdp) Honolulu County	19.9
Halawa, HI (cdp) Honolulu County	19.4
Compton, CA (city) Los Angeles County	17.1
San Bernardino, CA (city) San Bernardino County	15.7

Notes: Please refer to the User's Guide for an explanation of data; ranking tables include all places with Asian and/or NHPI populations above SF4 population thresholds; (1) tables reflect only those areas that meet SF4 population thresholds, therefore there may be less than 50 states, 75 counties or 75 places listed

Median Age

Sri Lankan

All States, Top 75 Counties, and Top 75 Places Sorted by Number[1]

State	Years
Massachusetts	39.5
Florida	39.4
Maryland	38.6
California	36.7
Pennsylvania	36.7
Ohio	36.4
New York	36.0
United States	35.8
Virginia	35.6
Texas	35.1
New Jersey	35.0
Illinois	34.8
Michigan	34.8
Washington	32.7

County	Years
Richmond County, NY	42.9
Montgomery County, MD	40.1
Orange County, CA	36.5
Middlesex County, NJ	36.4
Los Angeles County, CA	36.1
Queens County, NY	32.3

Place	Years
Los Angeles, CA (city) Los Angeles County	35.7
New York, NY (city)	35.2

Notes: Please refer to the User's Guide for an explanation of data; ranking tables include all places with Asian and/or NHPI populations above SF4 population thresholds; (1) tables reflect only those areas that meet SF4 population thresholds, therefore there may be less than 50 states, 75 counties or 75 places listed

Median Age

Taiwanese

All States, Top 75 Counties, and Top 75 Places Sorted by Number[1]

State	Years
Louisiana	44.0
Nevada	43.5
Hawaii	42.2
Minnesota	39.2
New Jersey	37.3
North Carolina	36.5
Florida	36.2
California	33.8
Virginia	33.7
Michigan	33.6
Georgia	33.2
Missouri	33.2
United States	32.8
Iowa	32.7
Texas	32.7
Kansas	32.3
Colorado	32.1
Indiana	31.4
Maryland	31.3
New York	31.0
Illinois	30.7
Tennessee	30.5
Ohio	30.4
Oklahoma	30.1
Washington	30.1
Arizona	29.6
Wisconsin	29.6
Pennsylvania	29.0
Oregon	28.8
Utah	28.7
Massachusetts	27.3
Connecticut	24.3

County	Years
Clark County, NV	44.0
DuPage County, IL	43.5
Contra Costa County, CA	42.4
Sacramento County, CA	42.1
Essex County, NJ	41.7
Harris County, TX	41.6
Mercer County, NJ	41.5
Honolulu County, HI	41.4
Fairfax County, VA	40.9
Suffolk County, NY	39.8
Nassau County, NY	39.7
Morris County, NJ	38.5
Ventura County, CA	38.4
Westchester County, NY	37.4
Fort Bend County, TX	37.3
Bergen County, NJ	37.2
Oakland County, MI	37.0
Somerset County, NJ	37.0
San Bernardino County, CA	36.3
Montgomery County, MD	36.1
Queens County, NY	36.1
St. Louis County, MO	35.6
Middlesex County, NJ	34.9
Los Angeles County, CA	34.5
Gwinnett County, GA	34.4
Orange County, CA	34.3
Collin County, TX	34.1
Maricopa County, AZ	33.4
Santa Clara County, CA	33.4
Tarrant County, TX	32.0
San Diego County, CA	31.5
Alameda County, CA	31.4
Dallas County, TX	31.2
San Mateo County, CA	31.2
San Francisco County, CA	30.2
King County, WA	30.0
Cook County, IL	29.8
Dane County, WI	29.7
Middlesex County, MA	28.7
Washtenaw County, MI	28.5
Franklin County, OH	28.4
Allegheny County, PA	27.1
New York County, NY	26.6
Suffolk County, MA	26.1
Travis County, TX	24.4
Norfolk County, MA	24.0
Riverside County, CA	23.6

Place	Years
El Monte, CA (city) Los Angeles County	47.5
Orange, CA (city) Orange County	45.7
Huntington Beach, CA (city) Orange County	42.8
Honolulu, HI (cdp) Honolulu County	42.2
Upland, CA (city) San Bernardino County	41.5
North Hempstead, NY (town) Nassau County	40.8
Naperville, IL (city) Du Page County	40.5
Rancho Palos Verdes, CA (city) Los Angeles County	40.0
Sugar Land, TX (city) Fort Bend County	39.9
San Marino, CA (city) Los Angeles County	39.4
Houston, TX (city) Harris County	39.1
Monterey Park, CA (city) Los Angeles County	39.1
Cerritos, CA (city) Los Angeles County	38.0
Alhambra, CA (city) Los Angeles County	37.3
Fountain Valley, CA (city) Orange County	37.3
Edison, NJ (township) Middlesex County	37.2
Troy, MI (city) Oakland County	37.2
Walnut, CA (city) Los Angeles County	36.2
Torrance, CA (city) Los Angeles County	35.9
Hacienda Heights, CA (cdp) Los Angeles County	35.3
Temple City, CA (city) Los Angeles County	35.0
Plano, TX (city) Collin County	34.8
San Jose, CA (city) Santa Clara County	34.7
Rowland Heights, CA (cdp) Los Angeles County	34.2
West Covina, CA (city) Los Angeles County	34.2
Arcadia, CA (city) Los Angeles County	34.1
Cupertino, CA (city) Santa Clara County	34.1
Fremont, CA (city) Alameda County	33.7
Irvine, CA (city) Orange County	33.7
Sunnyvale, CA (city) Santa Clara County	33.7
Tustin, CA (city) Orange County	33.3
San Gabriel, CA (city) Los Angeles County	33.1
Diamond Bar, CA (city) Los Angeles County	32.9
Chino Hills, CA (city) San Bernardino County	32.7
Cypress, CA (city) Orange County	32.6
New York, NY (city)	31.2
Bellevue, WA (city) King County	30.8
San Diego, CA (city) San Diego County	30.6
San Francisco, CA (city) San Francisco County	30.2
Arlington, TX (city) Tarrant County	30.1
Saratoga, CA (city) Santa Clara County	30.0
Los Angeles, CA (city) Los Angeles County	29.9
Madison, WI (city) Dane County	29.6
East San Gabriel, CA (cdp) Los Angeles County	29.4
Seattle, WA (city) King County	29.0
Anaheim, CA (city) Orange County	28.2
Ann Arbor, MI (city) Washtenaw County	27.8
Columbus, OH (city) Franklin County	26.9
Chicago, IL (city) Cook County	26.4
Boston, MA (city) Suffolk County	26.1
Austin, TX (city) Travis County	23.8
Berkeley, CA (city) Alameda County	23.0

Notes: Please refer to the User's Guide for an explanation of data; ranking tables include all places with Asian and/or NHPI populations above SF4 population thresholds; (1) tables reflect only those areas that meet SF4 population thresholds, therefore there may be less than 50 states, 75 counties or 75 places listed

Median Age

Thai

***All States, Top 75 Counties, and Top 75 Places Sorted by Number*[1]**

State	Years
South Carolina	45.6
New Mexico	45.4
Florida	39.1
Nevada	38.3
Louisiana	36.7
Maryland	36.7
California	36.6
Virginia	35.9
Hawaii	35.5
Oklahoma	35.4
New York	35.1
Alabama	34.8
Texas	34.8
North Carolina	34.7
United States	34.7
New Jersey	33.8
Arkansas	33.5
Iowa	32.9
Georgia	32.4
Illinois	32.1
Washington	31.8
Alaska	31.5
Oregon	31.5
Colorado	31.4
Indiana	31.3
Arizona	31.2
Kentucky	31.2
Massachusetts	31.0
Utah	30.9
Michigan	30.6
Minnesota	30.4
Missouri	30.4
Connecticut	30.2
Ohio	30.1
Pennsylvania	30.0
Tennessee	29.9
Kansas	29.5
Nebraska	28.8
Wisconsin	27.2

County	Years
Okaloosa County, FL	48.7
Westchester County, NY	43.7
Riverside County, CA	42.4
San Bernardino County, CA	40.7
Pierce County, WA	40.4
Fairfax County, VA	40.1
Bexar County, TX	39.4
Montgomery County, MD	39.4
Los Angeles County, CA	38.7
Clark County, NV	38.5
Palm Beach County, FL	38.3
Miami-Dade County, FL	37.6
Pinellas County, FL	37.2
Broward County, FL	36.9
Dallas County, TX	36.8
Queens County, NY	36.5
Collin County, TX	36.4
Contra Costa County, CA	35.7
Hillsborough County, FL	35.4
Oklahoma County, OK	35.4
Honolulu County, HI	35.3
San Mateo County, CA	35.3
Orange County, CA	35.1
New York County, NY	34.7
Nassau County, NY	34.5
Sacramento County, CA	34.3
St. Louis County, MO	33.8
Cook County, IL	33.6
Polk County, IA	33.5
Bergen County, NJ	32.5
San Diego County, CA	31.5
Suffolk County, NY	31.3
DuPage County, IL	31.1
San Francisco County, CA	31.0
Tarrant County, TX	31.0
King County, WA	30.5
Harris County, TX	30.4
Maricopa County, AZ	30.1
Middlesex County, MA	30.0
Anchorage Borough, AK	29.8
Franklin County, OH	29.8
Multnomah County, OR	29.7
Alameda County, CA	29.6
Santa Clara County, CA	28.7
Travis County, TX	28.7
Denver County, CO	27.3
Prince George's County, MD	26.5

Place	Years
Glendale, CA (city) Los Angeles County	48.6
Cerritos, CA (city) Los Angeles County	46.9
Bellflower, CA (city) Los Angeles County	40.6
Anaheim, CA (city) Orange County	38.3
Los Angeles, CA (city) Los Angeles County	38.0
Spring Valley, NV (cdp) Clark County	36.5
San Antonio, TX (city) Bexar County	36.3
Las Vegas, NV (city) Clark County	36.2
Long Beach, CA (city) Los Angeles County	36.2
New York, NY (city)	36.1
Honolulu, HI (cdp) Honolulu County	35.2
Des Moines, IA (city) Polk County	34.0
Houston, TX (city) Harris County	31.1
San Francisco, CA (city) San Francisco County	31.0
Chicago, IL (city) Cook County	30.8
San Diego, CA (city) San Diego County	30.1
Columbus, OH (city) Franklin County	29.7
Portland, OR (city) Multnomah County	29.2
San Jose, CA (city) Santa Clara County	27.8
Denver, CO (city) Denver County	27.3
Seattle, WA (city) King County	26.9

Notes: Please refer to the User's Guide for an explanation of data; ranking tables include all places with Asian and/or NHPI populations above SF4 population thresholds; (1) tables reflect only those areas that meet SF4 population thresholds, therefore there may be less than 50 states, 75 counties or 75 places listed

Median Age

Tongan

***All States, Top 75 Counties, and Top 75 Places Sorted by Number*[1]**

State	Years
Hawaii	27.0
Washington	26.4
California	24.8
Nevada	24.8
Texas	24.7
United States	23.2
Utah	20.0
Arizona	18.7
Oregon	17.6
Alaska	15.1

County	Years
King County, WA	34.3
San Mateo County, CA	27.5
Honolulu County, HI	27.2
Maui County, HI	26.6
Sacramento County, CA	25.4
Maricopa County, AZ	24.4
Tarrant County, TX	24.4
San Diego County, CA	23.2
San Bernardino County, CA	23.1
Los Angeles County, CA	22.3
Orange County, CA	21.8
Washoe County, NV	21.4
Contra Costa County, CA	20.3
Utah County, UT	20.0
Alameda County, CA	19.8
Salt Lake County, UT	19.8
Multnomah County, OR	16.1

Place	Years
San Mateo, CA (city) San Mateo County	31.5
Honolulu, HI (cdp) Honolulu County	28.3
East Palo Alto, CA (city) San Mateo County	25.3
Laie, HI (cdp) Honolulu County	25.3
Kahuku, HI (cdp) Honolulu County	23.6
San Bruno, CA (city) San Mateo County	22.4
Los Angeles, CA (city) Los Angeles County	21.5
Sacramento, CA (city) Sacramento County	21.0
Hauula, HI (cdp) Honolulu County	19.8
West Jordan, UT (city) Salt Lake County	19.7
Salt Lake City, UT (city) Salt Lake County	17.8
West Valley City, UT (city) Salt Lake County	17.5
Oakland, CA (city) Alameda County	16.5
Portland, OR (city) Multnomah County	15.8

Notes: Please refer to the User's Guide for an explanation of data; ranking tables include all places with Asian and/or NHPI populations above SF4 population thresholds; (1) tables reflect only those areas that meet SF4 population thresholds, therefore there may be less than 50 states, 75 counties or 75 places listed

Median Age

Vietnamese

All States, Top 75 Counties, and Top 75 Places Sorted by Number[1]

State	Years
West Virginia	34.1
Nevada	33.9
Hawaii	33.6
Virginia	32.8
Delaware	32.3
California	31.6
New Mexico	31.3
Idaho	31.0
Maryland	31.0
Oregon	30.8
Arizona	30.7
Connecticut	30.5
Florida	30.5
New Jersey	30.5
Texas	30.5
United States	30.5
Washington	30.5
New Hampshire	30.4
Oklahoma	30.1
South Carolina	30.0
Pennsylvania	29.9
Minnesota	29.7
Iowa	29.6
New York	29.6
Arkansas	29.5
Colorado	29.5
Georgia	29.5
North Carolina	29.2
Illinois	29.0
Indiana	29.0
Ohio	29.0
Utah	29.0
Missouri	28.9
Wisconsin	28.8
Massachusetts	28.7
Kentucky	28.6
Michigan	28.6
Kansas	28.5
Alaska	28.2
District of Columbia	28.2
Tennessee	28.1
Louisiana	27.6
Maine	27.6
South Dakota	27.3
Alabama	27.2
Nebraska	27.2
Rhode Island	26.6
Mississippi	24.9
Vermont	23.3

County	Years
Madison County, AL	38.7
Burlington County, NJ	37.4
Fairfax Independent City, VA	36.7
Benton County, WA	36.4
Brevard County, FL	36.3
Benton County, AR	36.0
Hampton Independent City, VA	36.0
Bristol County, MA	35.4
Bexar County, TX	35.2
Arlington County, VA	34.8
Alexandria Independent City, VA	34.6
Chatham County, GA	34.4
Spokane County, WA	34.4
St. Louis County, MO	34.2
Ventura County, CA	34.2
Chester County, PA	34.1
Clark County, NV	34.1
Fairfax County, VA	34.0
Sonoma County, CA	34.0
Honolulu County, HI	33.8
Cowlitz County, WA	33.6
Sebastian County, AR	33.5
Seminole County, FL	33.5
Washoe County, NV	33.5
Marion County, OR	33.1
Monmouth County, NJ	33.1
Bucks County, PA	33.0
Union County, NJ	33.0
Palm Beach County, FL	32.9
San Francisco County, CA	32.9
Sarasota County, FL	32.9
Thurston County, WA	32.9
Fort Bend County, TX	32.8
Cumberland County, NC	32.7
Howard County, MD	32.7
Newport News Independent City, VA	32.6
Ford County, KS	32.5
Suffolk County, NY	32.5
Wichita County, TX	32.5
Los Angeles County, CA	32.4
Marin County, CA	32.4
Montgomery County, MD	32.4
Atlantic County, NJ	32.2
Cumberland County, PA	32.2
Orange County, CA	32.2
Olmsted County, MN	32.1
Santa Clara County, CA	32.1
Pinellas County, FL	31.9
New Castle County, DE	31.8
Orange County, TX	31.8
Pima County, AZ	31.8
Ada County, ID	31.7
Peoria County, IL	31.7
Harris County, TX	31.6
Lake County, IL	31.6
Loudoun County, VA	31.6
York County, PA	31.5
New Haven County, CT	31.4
Contra Costa County, CA	31.3
Fairfield County, CT	31.3
Prince William County, VA	31.3
San Mateo County, CA	31.3
Collin County, TX	31.2
Nassau County, NY	31.2
Snohomish County, WA	31.2
Somerset County, NJ	31.2
Washington County, MN	31.2
Bernalillo County, NM	31.1
Hillsborough County, FL	31.1
Oklahoma County, OK	31.1
Plaquemines Parish, LA	31.1
San Diego County, CA	31.1
Scott County, MN	31.1
Pierce County, WA	31.0
Washington County, OR	31.0

Place	Years
Carson, CA (city) Los Angeles County	44.6
Downey, CA (city) Los Angeles County	40.4
Las Vegas, NV (city) Clark County	40.1
Concord, CA (city) Contra Costa County	38.2
Glendale, CA (city) Los Angeles County	38.0
Terrytown, LA (cdp) Jefferson Parish	38.0
Pasadena, CA (city) Los Angeles County	37.9
Cupertino, CA (city) Santa Clara County	37.8
Hacienda Heights, CA (cdp) Los Angeles County	37.8
Temple City, CA (city) Los Angeles County	37.7
Alum Rock, CA (cdp) Santa Clara County	37.5
Olympia, WA (city) Thurston County	37.5
Bailey's Crossroads, VA (cdp) Fairfax County	37.3
Chino Hills, CA (city) San Bernardino County	36.6
Kirkland, WA (city) King County	36.5
Alondra Park, CA (cdp) Los Angeles County	36.2
Idylwood, VA (cdp) Fairfax County	36.0
Citrus Heights, CA (city) Sacramento County	35.8
Franconia, VA (cdp) Fairfax County	35.6
San Antonio, TX (city) Bexar County	35.6
Valinda, CA (cdp) Los Angeles County	35.6
Yorba Linda, CA (city) Orange County	35.6
Eden Prairie, MN (city) Hennepin County	35.5
Timberlane, LA (cdp) Jefferson Parish	35.5
West Puente Valley, CA (cdp) Los Angeles County	35.5
Colesville, MD (cdp) Montgomery County	35.4
Laguna Niguel, CA (city) Orange County	35.4
Orlando, FL (city) Orange County	35.4
Aspen Hill, MD (cdp) Montgomery County	35.1
Burke, VA (cdp) Fairfax County	35.1
Seven Corners, VA (cdp) Fairfax County	35.1
South San Gabriel, CA (cdp) Los Angeles County	35.1
Centreville, VA (cdp) Fairfax County	35.0
Cypress, CA (city) Orange County	34.9
Arlington, VA (cdp) Arlington County	34.8
Norwalk, CA (city) Los Angeles County	34.8
Glendale, AZ (city) Maricopa County	34.7
Santa Rosa, CA (city) Sonoma County	34.6
Simi Valley, CA (city) Ventura County	34.6
Town 'n' Country, FL (cdp) Hillsborough County	34.6
Annandale, VA (cdp) Fairfax County	34.4
Huntington Beach, CA (city) Orange County	34.4
Montgomery Village, MD (cdp) Montgomery County	34.4
Paradise, NV (cdp) Clark County	34.4
Lincolnia, VA (cdp) Fairfax County	34.3
Rowland Heights, CA (cdp) Los Angeles County	34.3
Walnut, CA (city) Los Angeles County	34.2
Aliso Viejo, CA (cdp) Orange County	34.1
Milpitas, CA (city) Santa Clara County	34.1
Livermore, CA (city) Alameda County	34.0
Missouri City, TX (city) Fort Bend County	34.0
North Springfield, VA (cdp) Fairfax County	34.0
Rancho Santa Margarita, CA (city) Orange County	34.0
Baldwin Park, CA (city) Los Angeles County	33.8
Cerritos, CA (city) Los Angeles County	33.8
Thousand Oaks, CA (city) Ventura County	33.8
Lake Forest, CA (city) Orange County	33.7
Mission Viejo, CA (city) Orange County	33.6
Sugar Land, TX (city) Fort Bend County	33.6
Laguna Hills, CA (city) Orange County	33.5
Buena Park, CA (city) Orange County	33.4
Salem, OR (city) Marion County	33.4
Springfield, VA (cdp) Fairfax County	33.4
Bellevue, WA (city) King County	33.3
St. Petersburg, FL (city) Pinellas County	33.3
Sunnyvale, CA (city) Santa Clara County	33.3
Chino, CA (city) San Bernardino County	33.2
Mission Bend, TX (cdp) Fort Bend County	33.2
Placentia, CA (city) Orange County	33.2
Salinas, CA (city) Monterey County	33.2
Santa Clara, CA (city) Santa Clara County	33.2
Torrance, CA (city) Los Angeles County	33.2
Campbell, CA (city) Santa Clara County	33.1
Fort Smith, AR (city) Sebastian County	33.1
Oceanside, CA (city) San Diego County	33.1

Notes: Please refer to the User's Guide for an explanation of data; ranking tables include all places with Asian and/or NHPI populations above SF4 population thresholds; (1) tables reflect only those areas that meet SF4 population thresholds, therefore there may be less than 50 states, 75 counties or 75 places listed

Average Household Size

Total Population

***All States, Top 75 Counties, and Top 75 Places Sorted by Number*[1]**

State	Number
Utah	3.12
Hawaii	2.91
California	2.87
Alaska	2.74
Texas	2.74
Idaho	2.69
New Jersey	2.68
Arizona	2.64
Georgia	2.64
Illinois	2.63
New Mexico	2.63
Mississippi	2.62
Louisiana	2.61
Nevada	2.61
New York	2.61
Maryland	2.60
United States	2.59
Michigan	2.56
Delaware	2.54
Virginia	2.54
Colorado	2.53
Connecticut	2.53
Indiana	2.53
New Hampshire	2.53
South Carolina	2.53
Washington	2.53
Minnesota	2.52
Kansas	2.51
Massachusetts	2.51
Oregon	2.50
South Dakota	2.50
Wisconsin	2.50
Alabama	2.49
Arkansas	2.49
Nebraska	2.49
North Carolina	2.49
Ohio	2.49
Oklahoma	2.48
Pennsylvania	2.48
Tennessee	2.48
Kentucky	2.47
Missouri	2.47
Rhode Island	2.47
Wyoming	2.47
Florida	2.46
Iowa	2.45
Montana	2.44
Vermont	2.44
North Dakota	2.40
Maine	2.39
West Virginia	2.39
District of Columbia	2.16

County	Number
Webb County, TX	3.75
Bethel Census Area, AK	3.73
Hidalgo County, TX	3.60
Utah County, UT	3.58
North Slope Borough, AK	3.44
Cameron County, TX	3.41
Imperial County, CA	3.33
Davis County, UT	3.31
San Benito County, CA	3.31
Tulare County, CA	3.28
Franklin County, WA	3.26
Merced County, CA	3.25
Cache County, UT	3.23
Box Elder County, UT	3.21
El Paso County, TX	3.18
Kings County, CA	3.18
Madera County, CA	3.18
Manassas Park Independent City, VA	3.16
San Bernardino County, CA	3.15
Monterey County, CA	3.14
Fort Bend County, TX	3.13
Fresno County, CA	3.09
Finney County, KS	3.08
Kodiak Island Borough, AK	3.06
Ventura County, CA	3.04
Kern County, CA	3.03
Stanislaus County, CA	3.03
Colusa County, CA	3.02
Stafford County, VA	3.02
Rockland County, NY	3.01
Orange County, CA	3.00
San Joaquin County, CA	3.00
Salt Lake County, UT	2.99
Los Angeles County, CA	2.98
Riverside County, CA	2.98
San Patricio County, TX	2.98
Kane County, IL	2.97
Seward County, KS	2.97
Washington County, UT	2.97
Suffolk County, NY	2.96
Yakima County, WA	2.96
Ellis County, TX	2.95
Honolulu County, HI	2.95
Weber County, UT	2.95
Prince William County, VA	2.94
Will County, IL	2.94
Nassau County, NY	2.93
Ford County, KS	2.92
Grant County, WA	2.92
Liberty County, GA	2.92
Passaic County, NJ	2.92
Santa Clara County, CA	2.92
Calvert County, MD	2.91
Coryell County, TX	2.91
Manassas Independent City, VA	2.91
Maui County, HI	2.91
Rockwall County, TX	2.91
St. Charles Parish, LA	2.91
Sherburne County, MN	2.90
Solano County, CA	2.90
Hall County, GA	2.89
Kendall County, IL	2.89
McHenry County, IL	2.89
Plaquemines Parish, LA	2.89
Fayette County, GA	2.88
Lake County, IL	2.88
Scott County, MN	2.88
Douglas County, CO	2.87
Gwinnett County, GA	2.87
Henry County, GA	2.87
Kaufman County, TX	2.87
Oconee County, GA	2.87
Rockdale County, GA	2.87
Spotsylvania County, VA	2.87
Yuba County, CA	2.87

Place	Number
South San Jose Hills, CA (cdp) Los Angeles County	5.13
Richgrove, CA (cdp) Tulare County	4.80
Nanakuli, HI (cdp) Honolulu County	4.75
West Puente Valley, CA (cdp) Los Angeles County	4.71
Waikane, HI (cdp) Honolulu County	4.70
Lynwood, CA (city) Los Angeles County	4.69
San Joaquin, CA (city) Fresno County	4.69
South El Monte, CA (city) Los Angeles County	4.64
Terra Bella, CA (cdp) Tulare County	4.56
Santa Ana, CA (city) Orange County	4.55
Valinda, CA (cdp) Los Angeles County	4.55
Waimanalo, HI (cdp) Honolulu County	4.55
Baldwin Park, CA (city) Los Angeles County	4.43
Ewa Beach, HI (cdp) Honolulu County	4.39
Poplar-Cotton Center, CA (cdp) Tulare County	4.38
La Puente, CA (city) Los Angeles County	4.34
Earlimart, CA (cdp) Tulare County	4.33
Laie, HI (cdp) Honolulu County	4.33
Whitmore Village, HI (cdp) Honolulu County	4.32
Livingston, CA (city) Merced County	4.30
Maili, HI (cdp) Honolulu County	4.29
Orosi, CA (cdp) Tulare County	4.29
Brentwood, NY (cdp) Suffolk County	4.24
El Monte, CA (city) Los Angeles County	4.24
Waimanalo Beach, HI (cdp) Honolulu County	4.23
Puhi, HI (cdp) Kauai County	4.22
Waipahu, HI (cdp) Honolulu County	4.22
East Palo Alto, CA (city) San Mateo County	4.21
Ewa Villages, HI (cdp) Honolulu County	4.20
Compton, CA (city) Los Angeles County	4.16
East Los Angeles, CA (cdp) Los Angeles County	4.16
South Gate, CA (city) Los Angeles County	4.16
Hana, HI (cdp) Maui County	4.12
Huntington Park, CA (city) Los Angeles County	4.11
Hawaiian Gardens, CA (city) Los Angeles County	4.07
Waianae, HI (cdp) Honolulu County	4.07
Bell, CA (city) Los Angeles County	4.05
Hauula, HI (cdp) Honolulu County	4.05
Home Gardens, CA (cdp) Riverside County	4.04
Pakala Village, HI (cdp) Kauai County	4.03
Alum Rock, CA (cdp) Santa Clara County	4.02
Delano, CA (city) Kern County	4.00
Citrus, CA (cdp) Los Angeles County	3.99
Avocado Heights, CA (cdp) Los Angeles County	3.98
East Porterville, CA (cdp) Tulare County	3.96
Kahuku, HI (cdp) Honolulu County	3.96
Rollingwood, CA (cdp) Contra Costa County	3.96
Calexico, CA (city) Imperial County	3.95
Fort Hood, TX (cdp) Coryell County	3.94
Paramount, CA (city) Los Angeles County	3.94
Vincent, CA (cdp) Los Angeles County	3.90
Waihee-Waiehu, HI (cdp) Maui County	3.86
Haliimaile, HI (cdp) Maui County	3.85
Oxnard, CA (city) Ventura County	3.85
Watsonville, CA (city) Santa Cruz County	3.83
Pico Rivera, CA (city) Los Angeles County	3.81
Pomona, CA (city) Los Angeles County	3.81
Norwalk, CA (city) Los Angeles County	3.78
Rosemead, CA (city) Los Angeles County	3.78
Four Corners, TX (cdp) Fort Bend County	3.77
North Fair Oaks, CA (cdp) San Mateo County	3.77
Fontana, CA (city) San Bernardino County	3.76
Fort Lewis, WA (cdp) Pierce County	3.74
South Whittier, CA (cdp) Los Angeles County	3.73
Anahola, HI (cdp) Kauai County	3.72
Fort Bragg, NC (cdp) Cumberland County	3.72
Perris, CA (city) Riverside County	3.72
Laredo, TX (city) Webb County	3.70
Rialto, CA (city) San Bernardino County	3.70
Village Park, HI (cdp) Honolulu County	3.70
Cicero, IL (town) Cook County	3.69
Monroe, NY (town) Orange County	3.68
Montclair, CA (city) San Bernardino County	3.68
Salinas, CA (city) Monterey County	3.67
Kearns, UT (cdp) Salt Lake County	3.66

Notes: Please refer to the User's Guide for an explanation of data; ranking tables include all places with Asian and/or NHPI populations above SF4 population thresholds; (1) tables reflect only those areas that meet SF4 population thresholds, therefore there may be less than 50 states, 75 counties or 75 places listed

Average Household Size

Asian

***All States, Top 75 Counties, and Top 75 Places Sorted by Number*[1]**

State	Number
Minnesota	3.62
Wisconsin	3.49
Alaska	3.30
California	3.23
New Jersey	3.22
Georgia	3.18
Louisiana	3.17
Utah	3.13
New York	3.11
Rhode Island	3.11
United States	3.08
Maryland	3.05
Virginia	3.05
North Carolina	3.04
Texas	3.01
Hawaii	3.00
Massachusetts	2.98
Mississippi	2.98
Illinois	2.96
Kansas	2.93
Maine	2.92
Pennsylvania	2.92
Washington	2.92
Connecticut	2.91
Florida	2.91
Arkansas	2.90
Vermont	2.90
Iowa	2.88
Michigan	2.88
Nevada	2.88
Nebraska	2.87
New Hampshire	2.87
Oregon	2.87
South Carolina	2.87
Tennessee	2.85
Colorado	2.81
Oklahoma	2.79
Alabama	2.77
Delaware	2.77
South Dakota	2.76
Arizona	2.73
Kentucky	2.68
Ohio	2.68
New Mexico	2.66
Missouri	2.64
North Dakota	2.63
Indiana	2.58
Idaho	2.56
West Virginia	2.55
Wyoming	2.55
Montana	2.42
District of Columbia	1.96

County	Number
Surry County, NC	7.38
Marathon County, WI	5.98
Portage County, WI	5.65
Burke County, NC	5.51
Alexander County, NC	5.48
Chisago County, MN	5.35
Chippewa County, WI	5.29
Manitowoc County, WI	5.16
La Crosse County, WI	5.15
Sheboygan County, WI	5.14
Jackson County, GA	5.11
Walton County, GA	5.10
Yuba County, CA	5.10
Eau Claire County, WI	5.09
Wood County, WI	5.06
Kodiak Island Borough, AK	4.87
Calumet County, WI	4.84
Glenn County, CA	4.84
Stanly County, NC	4.84
Merced County, CA	4.82
Iberia Parish, LA	4.78
Dunn County, WI	4.75
Seward County, KS	4.72
Washington County, WI	4.69
Outagamie County, WI	4.68
Ford County, KS	4.63
Matagorda County, TX	4.58
Wagoner County, OK	4.58
Catawba County, NC	4.52
Brown County, WI	4.47
Oconee County, GA	4.44
Coshocton County, OH	4.42
Crawford County, AR	4.39
Ramsey County, MN	4.38
Vermilion Parish, LA	4.34
Ketchikan Gateway Borough, AK	4.33
Hall County, GA	4.32
Craighead County, AR	4.31
Cass County, MO	4.30
St. Mary Parish, LA	4.27
Saline County, AR	4.27
Ellis County, TX	4.25
Fresno County, CA	4.23
Lyon County, MN	4.23
Cowley County, KS	4.21
Winnebago County, WI	4.19
Beltrami County, MN	4.17
Dakota County, NE	4.17
Chippewa County, MI	4.16
Bartow County, GA	4.13
Roseau County, MN	4.13
Barrow County, GA	4.09
St. Charles Parish, LA	4.08
Habersham County, GA	4.07
St. Martin Parish, LA	4.07
Washington County, TX	4.06
Montgomery County, NC	4.05
Adams County, NE	4.04
Tulare County, CA	4.04
Aleutians East Borough, AK	4.00
Hoke County, NC	4.00
Butte County, CA	3.98
Rowan County, NC	3.96
Shasta County, CA	3.96
Washington County, MN	3.95
Cass County, MI	3.94
Clayton County, GA	3.94
Sutter County, CA	3.92
Woodbury County, IA	3.92
McDowell County, NC	3.91
Canadian County, OK	3.90
Stanislaus County, CA	3.90
Cleveland County, NC	3.88
Davidson County, NC	3.87
Kendall County, IL	3.87

Place	Number
Newton, NC (city) Catawba County	10.93
Glen Alpine, NC (town) Burke County	8.82
East Porterville, CA (cdp) Tulare County	8.22
Thermalito, CA (cdp) Butte County	8.09
South Oroville, CA (cdp) Butte County	7.02
Linda, CA (cdp) Yuba County	6.77
Oroville, CA (city) Butte County	6.29
Garden Acres, CA (cdp) San Joaquin County	6.12
Olivehurst, CA (cdp) Yuba County	6.08
Wausau, WI (city) Marathon County	5.93
Wisconsin Rapids, WI (city) Wood County	5.93
Valdese, NC (town) Burke County	5.68
Palacios, TX (city) Matagorda County	5.67
Tulare, CA (city) Tulare County	5.59
Stevens Point, WI (city) Portage County	5.57
Brooklyn Center, MN (city) Hennepin County	5.51
Winton, CA (cdp) Merced County	5.45
Manitowoc, WI (city) Manitowoc County	5.43
Colmar Manor, MD (town) Prince George's County	5.41
Gainesville, GA (city) Hall County	5.38
Kerman, CA (city) Fresno County	5.38
Sun Valley, NV (cdp) Washoe County	5.38
Willows, CA (city) Glenn County	5.37
Merced, CA (city) Merced County	5.36
Hapeville, GA (city) Fulton County	5.34
Onalaska, WI (city) La Crosse County	5.32
Eau Claire, WI (city) Eau Claire County	5.31
Sheboygan, WI (city) Sheboygan County	5.27
Appleton, WI (city) Outagamie County	5.24
La Crosse, WI (city) La Crosse County	5.10
Green Bay, WI (city) Brown County	5.09
Berkley, CO (cdp) Adams County	5.07
Drexel, NC (town) Burke County	5.00
Fitchburg, MA (city) Worcester County	5.00
Amelia, LA (cdp) Saint Mary Parish	4.99
Fairless Hills, PA (cdp) Bucks County	4.97
Kodiak, AK (city) Kodiak Island Borough	4.92
Atwater, CA (city) Merced County	4.90
Riverdale Park, MD (town) Prince George's County	4.90
St. Paul, MN (city) Ramsey County	4.87
Maili, HI (cdp) Honolulu County	4.86
New Iberia, LA (city) Iberia Parish	4.85
Connelly Springs, NC (town) Burke County	4.83
Kearns, UT (cdp) Salt Lake County	4.82
Woodlynne, NJ (borough) Camden County	4.79
East Foothills, CA (cdp) Santa Clara County	4.78
Waimanalo, HI (cdp) Honolulu County	4.78
San Joaquin, CA (city) Fresno County	4.77
South Elgin, IL (village) Kane County	4.77
Woodmere, NY (cdp) Nassau County	4.77
Boonton, NJ (town) Morris County	4.76
Bunker Hill Village, TX (city) Harris County	4.76
Ewa Beach, HI (cdp) Honolulu County	4.75
Old Brookville, NY (village) Nassau County	4.75
Pedley, CA (cdp) Riverside County	4.75
Liberal, KS (city) Seward County	4.72
Van Buren, AR (city) Crawford County	4.71
Lynwood, CA (city) Los Angeles County	4.68
Upper Leacock, PA (township) Lancaster County	4.67
Ceres, CA (city) Stanislaus County	4.66
Brenham, TX (city) Washington County	4.64
Palmer, PA (township) Northampton County	4.64
South Whitehall, PA (township) Lehigh County	4.64
South Yuba City, CA (cdp) Sutter County	4.64
Berlin, CT (town) Hartford County	4.63
Colma, CA (town) San Mateo County	4.63
Hamtramck, MI (city) Wayne County	4.60
Nanakuli, HI (cdp) Honolulu County	4.60
Humble, TX (city) Harris County	4.57
Oshkosh, WI (city) Winnebago County	4.57
Dodge City, KS (city) Ford County	4.56
Madera, CA (city) Madera County	4.56
North Valley Stream, NY (cdp) Nassau County	4.56
Great Falls, VA (cdp) Fairfax County	4.55
Abbeville, LA (city) Vermilion Parish	4.54

Notes: Please refer to the User's Guide for an explanation of data; ranking tables include all places with Asian and/or NHPI populations above SF4 population thresholds; (1) tables reflect only those areas that meet SF4 population thresholds, therefore there may be less than 50 states, 75 counties or 75 places listed

Average Household Size

Native Hawaiian and Other Pacific Islander

All States, Top 75 Counties, and Top 75 Places Sorted by Number[1]

State	Number
Utah	4.73
West Virginia	4.73
Arkansas	4.26
Alaska	4.13
California	3.87
Hawaii	3.73
Alabama	3.62
United States	3.60
Connecticut	3.56
Montana	3.55
Pennsylvania	3.51
Washington	3.44
Nevada	3.42
Mississippi	3.39
North Carolina	3.36
Texas	3.34
Arizona	3.33
Idaho	3.33
Delaware	3.25
Missouri	3.24
Illinois	3.23
Oklahoma	3.16
Rhode Island	3.13
Minnesota	3.11
Georgia	3.10
Louisiana	3.08
Oregon	3.06
Michigan	3.05
Wisconsin	3.01
New Jersey	3.00
Ohio	2.99
Iowa	2.95
Maine	2.95
Indiana	2.94
New York	2.94
Maryland	2.93
Virginia	2.93
Florida	2.91
Colorado	2.86
Tennessee	2.86
South Carolina	2.80
Kansas	2.79
Nebraska	2.78
New Mexico	2.78
Kentucky	2.74
Massachusetts	2.62

County	Number
Washington County, AR	5.70
Washington County, UT	5.24
Salt Lake County, UT	5.03
San Mateo County, CA	4.68
Coryell County, TX	4.59
El Paso County, TX	4.49
Anchorage Borough, AK	4.36
Washoe County, NV	4.26
Utah County, UT	4.22
San Bernardino County, CA	4.20
Thurston County, WA	4.20
Gwinnett County, GA	4.09
Yolo County, CA	4.09
Los Angeles County, CA	4.06
Davis County, UT	4.03
Orange County, CA	3.95
Philadelphia County, PA	3.94
San Joaquin County, CA	3.93
Santa Clara County, CA	3.91
Suffolk County, NY	3.91
San Francisco County, CA	3.90
Alameda County, CA	3.89
Jackson County, MO	3.89
Bell County, TX	3.88
Onslow County, NC	3.87
Sonoma County, CA	3.87
Fresno County, CA	3.86
Honolulu County, HI	3.86
Contra Costa County, CA	3.80
Riverside County, CA	3.77
Marion County, OR	3.74
Solano County, CA	3.74
Clark County, WA	3.68
Pierce County, WA	3.64
Stanislaus County, CA	3.64
Ada County, ID	3.61
San Diego County, CA	3.61
Maui County, HI	3.58
Ventura County, CA	3.55
Maricopa County, AZ	3.54
Nassau County, NY	3.51
Fairfax County, VA	3.50
Muscogee County, GA	3.50
King County, WA	3.47
Hawaii County, HI	3.46
Allegheny County, PA	3.45
Sacramento County, CA	3.45
Kauai County, HI	3.44
Kings County, NY	3.44
Kern County, CA	3.42
Santa Barbara County, CA	3.41
Montgomery County, MD	3.38
El Paso County, CO	3.36
Clackamas County, OR	3.35
Lane County, OR	3.33
Monterey County, CA	3.33
Clark County, NV	3.31
Harris County, TX	3.30
Wayne County, MI	3.30
Cook County, IL	3.28
Tarrant County, TX	3.28
Multnomah County, OR	3.26
Hillsborough County, FL	3.23
Dallas County, TX	3.18
Palm Beach County, FL	3.16
Bronx County, NY	3.13
Duval County, FL	3.10
Snohomish County, WA	3.10
Travis County, TX	3.10
Bexar County, TX	3.08
Miami-Dade County, FL	3.07
Queens County, NY	3.06
Orange County, FL	3.04
Kitsap County, WA	2.95
Spokane County, WA	2.95

Place	Number
Kearns, UT (cdp) Salt Lake County	6.62
East Palo Alto, CA (city) San Mateo County	6.50
Sandy, UT (city) Salt Lake County	6.23
Whitmore Village, HI (cdp) Honolulu County	6.18
Compton, CA (city) Los Angeles County	5.95
West Jordan, UT (city) Salt Lake County	5.89
Springdale, AR (city) Washington County	5.85
Independence, MO (city) Jackson County	5.67
Pakala Village, HI (cdp) Kauai County	5.53
Rialto, CA (city) San Bernardino County	5.50
West Valley City, UT (city) Salt Lake County	5.48
Waikane, HI (cdp) Honolulu County	5.42
Kahuku, HI (cdp) Honolulu County	5.41
Milpitas, CA (city) Santa Clara County	5.41
Oakland, CA (city) Alameda County	5.39
Aiea, HI (cdp) Honolulu County	5.31
Salt Lake City, UT (city) Salt Lake County	5.25
St. George, UT (city) Washington County	5.23
Carson, CA (city) Los Angeles County	5.18
Spanaway, WA (cdp) Pierce County	5.17
Ontario, CA (city) San Bernardino County	5.16
Hana, HI (cdp) Maui County	5.12
Westminster, CA (city) Orange County	5.11
Ewa Beach, HI (cdp) Honolulu County	5.08
Kahaluu, HI (cdp) Honolulu County	5.05
Waimanalo Beach, HI (cdp) Honolulu County	5.03
Garden Grove, CA (city) Orange County	4.96
Papaikou, HI (cdp) Hawaii County	4.94
San Bruno, CA (city) San Mateo County	4.93
Nanakuli, HI (cdp) Honolulu County	4.92
Mesa, AZ (city) Maricopa County	4.89
San Mateo, CA (city) San Mateo County	4.89
Lawndale, CA (city) Los Angeles County	4.85
Waimanalo, HI (cdp) Honolulu County	4.85
Laie, HI (cdp) Honolulu County	4.82
Concord, CA (city) Contra Costa County	4.81
Captain Cook, HI (cdp) Hawaii County	4.79
Waipahu, HI (cdp) Honolulu County	4.76
Pahoa, HI (cdp) Hawaii County	4.72
Long Beach, CA (city) Los Angeles County	4.71
Oceanside, CA (city) San Diego County	4.70
North Las Vegas, NV (city) Clark County	4.69
Fort Lewis, WA (cdp) Pierce County	4.63
Hawthorne, CA (city) Los Angeles County	4.62
Waianae, HI (cdp) Honolulu County	4.62
Anaheim, CA (city) Orange County	4.59
Lakewood, CA (city) Los Angeles County	4.58
Richmond, CA (city) Contra Costa County	4.54
Orem, UT (city) Utah County	4.51
Paia, HI (cdp) Maui County	4.47
Salinas, CA (city) Monterey County	4.45
Santa Clara, CA (city) Santa Clara County	4.41
El Paso, TX (city) El Paso County	4.40
Hauula, HI (cdp) Honolulu County	4.40
Pittsburg, CA (city) Contra Costa County	4.38
Sunrise Manor, NV (cdp) Clark County	4.38
Makakilo City, HI (cdp) Honolulu County	4.37
Oxnard, CA (city) Ventura County	4.36
Santa Ana, CA (city) Orange County	4.36
Village Park, HI (cdp) Honolulu County	4.36
Maili, HI (cdp) Honolulu County	4.31
Tukwila, WA (city) King County	4.29
San Leandro, CA (city) Alameda County	4.27
Pearl City, HI (cdp) Honolulu County	4.26
Costa Mesa, CA (city) Orange County	4.25
Fontana, CA (city) San Bernardino County	4.16
Taylorsville, UT (city) Salt Lake County	4.13
Anahola, HI (cdp) Kauai County	4.09
South San Francisco, CA (city) San Mateo County	4.08
San Bernardino, CA (city) San Bernardino County	4.07
Hanapepe, HI (cdp) Kauai County	4.06
Killeen, TX (city) Bell County	4.06
Modesto, CA (city) Stanislaus County	4.06
Waikoloa Village, HI (cdp) Hawaii County	4.03
Halawa, HI (cdp) Honolulu County	4.02

Notes: Please refer to the User's Guide for an explanation of data; ranking tables include all places with Asian and/or NHPI populations above SF4 population thresholds; (1) tables reflect only those areas that meet SF4 population thresholds, therefore there may be less than 50 states, 75 counties or 75 places listed

Average Household Size

Asian Indian

All States, Top 75 Counties, and Top 75 Places Sorted by Number[1]

State	Number
New York	3.36
New Jersey	3.28
Utah	3.20
California	3.17
Illinois	3.17
Georgia	3.11
Maryland	3.08
United States	3.06
Nevada	3.01
Texas	3.01
Alaska	2.97
Florida	2.97
South Carolina	2.97
Virginia	2.96
Mississippi	2.92
Pennsylvania	2.91
Michigan	2.88
North Carolina	2.88
Alabama	2.87
Connecticut	2.85
Washington	2.84
Delaware	2.83
North Dakota	2.83
Oklahoma	2.83
Arizona	2.81
Louisiana	2.79
Wyoming	2.79
Hawaii	2.78
New Hampshire	2.77
Indiana	2.76
Tennessee	2.74
Wisconsin	2.74
Kansas	2.73
Kentucky	2.73
Minnesota	2.73
Ohio	2.71
Massachusetts	2.68
West Virginia	2.66
Arkansas	2.63
Missouri	2.63
Montana	2.62
Oregon	2.61
Vermont	2.61
Colorado	2.60
New Mexico	2.58
Rhode Island	2.57
South Dakota	2.56
Nebraska	2.54
Iowa	2.52
Maine	2.49
Idaho	2.47
District of Columbia	1.71

County	Number
Madera County, CA	4.79
Merced County, CA	4.61
Sutter County, CA	4.45
Tulare County, CA	4.37
Kern County, CA	4.27
Fresno County, CA	4.21
Cumberland County, NJ	4.14
Warren County, NJ	4.13
York County, VA	4.13
San Joaquin County, CA	4.06
Stanislaus County, CA	4.06
Whatcom County, WA	4.06
McHenry County, IL	4.05
Monroe County, PA	4.05
Canadian County, OK	4.04
St. Mary's County, MD	4.02
Passaic County, NJ	4.00
Floyd County, GA	3.98
Osceola County, FL	3.96
Escambia County, FL	3.94
Sonoma County, CA	3.94
Kane County, IL	3.88
Henry County, GA	3.87
Westmoreland County, PA	3.85
Nassau County, NY	3.84
Northampton County, PA	3.80
Medina County, OH	3.77
Prince William County, VA	3.77
Solano County, CA	3.77
Will County, IL	3.76
Atlantic County, NJ	3.73
Chatham County, GA	3.73
Fort Bend County, TX	3.73
Pasco County, FL	3.73
Niagara County, NY	3.72
Richmond County, NY	3.72
Washoe County, NV	3.70
Queens County, NY	3.68
Rockland County, NY	3.65
Oneida County, NY	3.63
Outagamie County, WI	3.63
San Bernardino County, CA	3.60
Cherokee County, GA	3.59
Harford County, MD	3.57
Mobile County, AL	3.54
Ottawa County, MI	3.54
Hamilton County, IN	3.52
St. Charles County, MO	3.51
York County, PA	3.50
Lake County, IN	3.47
Buncombe County, NC	3.46
Gloucester County, NJ	3.46
Midland County, TX	3.46
Columbia County, GA	3.45
Plymouth County, MA	3.45
Riverside County, CA	3.44
DuPage County, IL	3.43
Putnam County, NY	3.43
Gwinnett County, GA	3.41
Suffolk County, NY	3.40
Bergen County, NJ	3.39
Sacramento County, CA	3.37
Snohomish County, WA	3.37
Loudoun County, VA	3.36
Howard County, MD	3.35
Nueces County, TX	3.35
Kings County, NY	3.34
Lackawanna County, PA	3.34
Mercer County, NJ	3.34
Monmouth County, NJ	3.34
Pierce County, WA	3.34
Prince George's County, MD	3.34
Hampden County, MA	3.33
Polk County, FL	3.33
Salt Lake County, UT	3.33

Place	Number
Kerman, CA (city) Fresno County	6.84
Dumont, NJ (borough) Bergen County	5.16
South Yuba City, CA (cdp) Sutter County	5.03
South Plainfield, NJ (borough) Middlesex County	4.89
Brentwood, NY (cdp) Suffolk County	4.85
Paterson, NJ (city) Passaic County	4.84
Dale City, VA (cdp) Prince William County	4.82
North Valley Stream, NY (cdp) Nassau County	4.78
Livingston, CA (city) Merced County	4.74
Suisun City, CA (city) Solano County	4.69
West Springfield, VA (cdp) Fairfax County	4.69
Des Plaines, IL (city) Cook County	4.66
New Hyde Park, NY (village) Nassau County	4.65
Scarsdale, NY (village) Westchester County	4.63
Tracy, CA (city) San Joaquin County	4.60
Muttontown, NY (village) Nassau County	4.58
Paramus, NJ (borough) Bergen County	4.58
Laguna, CA (cdp) Sacramento County	4.53
Franklin Square, NY (cdp) Nassau County	4.51
North New Hyde Park, NY (cdp) Nassau County	4.51
Live Oak, CA (city) Sutter County	4.49
Hamtramck, MI (city) Wayne County	4.45
Ceres, CA (city) Stanislaus County	4.43
Bergenfield, NJ (borough) Bergen County	4.41
Lilburn, GA (city) Gwinnett County	4.40
Lynn, MA (city) Essex County	4.38
Lincolnwood, IL (village) Cook County	4.37
Searingtown, NY (cdp) Nassau County	4.34
Bloomingdale, IL (village) Du Page County	4.33
Elk Grove, CA (cdp) Sacramento County	4.33
Munster, IN (town) Lake County	4.33
Rowlett, TX (city) Dallas County	4.33
Morton Grove, IL (village) Cook County	4.30
Galloway, NJ (township) Atlantic County	4.29
Newington, VA (cdp) Fairfax County	4.29
Bartlett, IL (village) Du Page County	4.28
Bristol, PA (township) Bucks County	4.27
Bakersfield, CA (city) Kern County	4.25
Fair Lawn, NJ (borough) Bergen County	4.25
Palmdale, CA (city) Los Angeles County	4.23
Beltsville, MD (cdp) Prince George's County	4.21
Grand Prairie, TX (city) Dallas County	4.20
East Meadow, NY (cdp) Nassau County	4.19
Fontana, CA (city) San Bernardino County	4.19
Santa Rosa, CA (city) Sonoma County	4.19
East Lake, FL (cdp) Pinellas County	4.18
North Royalton, OH (city) Cuyahoga County	4.17
Norwalk, CA (city) Los Angeles County	4.17
Ontario, CA (city) San Bernardino County	4.17
Rowland Heights, CA (cdp) Los Angeles County	4.17
Mount Pleasant, NY (town) Westchester County	4.16
Weston, FL (city) Broward County	4.16
Clifton, NJ (city) Passaic County	4.15
Montgomery, PA (township) Montgomery County	4.13
Niles, IL (village) Cook County	4.13
West Sacramento, CA (city) Yolo County	4.13
Hercules, CA (city) Contra Costa County	4.11
Hicksville, NY (cdp) Nassau County	4.11
Nanuet, NY (cdp) Rockland County	4.11
Syosset, NY (cdp) Nassau County	4.11
Burr Ridge, IL (village) Du Page County	4.10
New Territory, TX (cdp) Fort Bend County	4.09
Orland Park, IL (village) Cook County	4.09
Bolingbrook, IL (village) Will County	4.07
Cloverly, MD (cdp) Montgomery County	4.07
Herricks, NY (cdp) Nassau County	4.07
Modesto, CA (city) Stanislaus County	4.07
Glendale Heights, IL (village) Du Page County	4.03
Herndon, VA (town) Fairfax County	4.03
Wolf Trap, VA (cdp) Fairfax County	4.03
Darien, IL (city) Du Page County	4.02
San Bernardino, CA (city) San Bernardino County	4.02
Antioch, CA (city) Contra Costa County	4.01
Broken Arrow, OK (city) Tulsa County	4.01
Dover, NJ (township) Ocean County	4.01

Notes: Please refer to the User's Guide for an explanation of data; ranking tables include all places with Asian and/or NHPI populations above SF4 population thresholds; (1) tables reflect only those areas that meet SF4 population thresholds, therefore there may be less than 50 states, 75 counties or 75 places listed

Average Household Size

Bangladeshi

All States, Top 75 Counties, and Top 75 Places Sorted by Number[1]

State	Number
New York	4.23
Georgia	3.99
Michigan	3.88
Maryland	3.72
Virginia	3.69
New Jersey	3.68
United States	3.67
Florida	3.40
Connecticut	3.36
California	3.13
Ohio	2.92
Texas	2.88
Illinois	2.87
Massachusetts	2.82
Pennsylvania	2.82

County	Number
Passaic County, NJ	4.79
DeKalb County, GA	4.50
Kings County, NY	4.41
Queens County, NY	4.23
New York County, NY	4.18
Bronx County, NY	4.06
Wayne County, MI	3.96
Atlantic County, NJ	3.87
Fairfax County, VA	3.81
Montgomery County, MD	3.58
Middlesex County, NJ	3.40
Los Angeles County, CA	3.29
Harris County, TX	3.18
Santa Clara County, CA	2.88
Dallas County, TX	2.72

Place	Number
Paterson, NJ (city) Passaic County	5.20
Hamtramck, MI (city) Wayne County	4.66
New York, NY (city)	4.25
Los Angeles, CA (city) Los Angeles County	3.24

Notes: Please refer to the User's Guide for an explanation of data; ranking tables include all places with Asian and/or NHPI populations above SF4 population thresholds; (1) tables reflect only those areas that meet SF4 population thresholds, therefore there may be less than 50 states, 75 counties or 75 places listed

Average Household Size

Cambodian

All States, Top 75 Counties, and Top 75 Places Sorted by Number[1]

State	Number
Utah	5.11
California	4.72
Iowa	4.71
Massachusetts	4.55
Missouri	4.49
Connecticut	4.47
Pennsylvania	4.47
Georgia	4.41
United States	4.41
Colorado	4.34
Illinois	4.33
North Carolina	4.30
Virginia	4.29
Washington	4.25
Oklahoma	4.21
Alabama	4.20
Tennessee	4.14
Maryland	4.13
Rhode Island	4.13
Texas	4.07
Minnesota	4.01
Arizona	4.00
Ohio	3.98
Michigan	3.97
New Jersey	3.92
Maine	3.90
New York	3.90
Florida	3.82
Indiana	3.80
Kansas	3.64
Oregon	3.63
South Carolina	3.60
Nevada	3.59
Wisconsin	3.19
Hawaii	2.87

County	Number
Fresno County, CA	5.60
Stanislaus County, CA	5.55
Henrico County, VA	5.38
Chesterfield County, VA	5.33
Salt Lake County, UT	5.19
Fairfield County, CT	5.16
Kern County, CA	5.15
Polk County, IA	5.13
Cowlitz County, WA	5.11
Denton County, TX	5.07
San Joaquin County, CA	5.06
Santa Clara County, CA	5.00
Camden County, NJ	4.95
Worcester County, MA	4.95
Bronx County, NY	4.94
Mobile County, AL	4.91
DeKalb County, GA	4.82
Sonoma County, CA	4.79
Alameda County, CA	4.78
Middlesex County, MA	4.77
Davidson County, NC	4.71
Pierce County, WA	4.67
Los Angeles County, CA	4.65
San Diego County, CA	4.64
Clayton County, GA	4.55
Essex County, MA	4.54
Philadelphia County, PA	4.54
Olmsted County, MN	4.49
Orange County, CA	4.48
Cook County, IL	4.47
Gwinnett County, GA	4.47
Brazoria County, TX	4.44
San Bernardino County, CA	4.44
Tarrant County, TX	4.36
Montgomery County, MD	4.34
Snohomish County, WA	4.33
Mecklenburg County, NC	4.32
Monroe County, NY	4.31
Riverside County, CA	4.31
Bristol County, MA	4.26
Cuyahoga County, OH	4.26
Thurston County, WA	4.21
Fairfax County, VA	4.18
Maricopa County, AZ	4.17
Dallas County, TX	4.14
Sacramento County, CA	4.12
Duval County, FL	4.11
Ottawa County, MI	4.11
Cumberland County, ME	4.10
Providence County, RI	4.09
Suffolk County, MA	4.09
Denver County, CO	4.06
King County, WA	4.05
Multnomah County, OR	4.02
Scott County, MN	4.02
Hennepin County, MN	3.96
Hampden County, MA	3.94
Pinellas County, FL	3.91
Franklin County, OH	3.88
Ramsey County, MN	3.87
Shelby County, TN	3.85
Arlington County, VA	3.82
Clark County, NV	3.72
Hamilton County, OH	3.60
Harris County, TX	3.60
Dakota County, MN	3.59
Kings County, NY	3.49
Washington County, OR	3.49
Sedgwick County, KS	3.48
San Francisco County, CA	3.31
Clark County, WA	3.26

Place	Number
Pomona, CA (city) Los Angeles County	5.90
Bridgeport, CT (city) Fairfield County	5.85
Fresno, CA (city) Fresno County	5.75
Santa Rosa, CA (city) Sonoma County	5.55
Santa Ana, CA (city) Orange County	5.41
Modesto, CA (city) Stanislaus County	5.28
Longview, WA (city) Cowlitz County	5.22
Signal Hill, CA (city) Los Angeles County	5.15
San Jose, CA (city) Santa Clara County	5.12
West Valley City, UT (city) Salt Lake County	5.10
Stockton, CA (city) San Joaquin County	5.06
Danbury, CT (city) Fairfield County	5.00
Oakland, CA (city) Alameda County	4.96
Silver Spring, MD (cdp) Montgomery County	4.90
Monterey Park, CA (city) Los Angeles County	4.85
Aurora, CO (city) Arapahoe County	4.84
Cranston, RI (city) Providence County	4.82
Lowell, MA (city) Middlesex County	4.79
Fall River, MA (city) Bristol County	4.74
Long Beach, CA (city) Los Angeles County	4.74
Tacoma, WA (city) Pierce County	4.70
San Diego, CA (city) San Diego County	4.69
San Bernardino, CA (city) San Bernardino County	4.67
Rochester, MN (city) Olmsted County	4.61
Lynn, MA (city) Essex County	4.58
Carrollton, TX (city) Denton County	4.57
Chicago, IL (city) Cook County	4.54
Philadelphia, PA (city) Philadelphia County	4.54
White Center, WA (cdp) King County	4.53
Revere, MA (city) Suffolk County	4.50
Lexington, NC (city) Davidson County	4.47
Lakewood, CA (city) Los Angeles County	4.46
Portland, ME (city) Cumberland County	4.41
Charlotte, NC (city) Mecklenburg County	4.37
Lawrence, MA (city) Essex County	4.37
Los Angeles, CA (city) Los Angeles County	4.33
Bellflower, CA (city) Los Angeles County	4.28
Sacramento, CA (city) Sacramento County	4.16
Rosemead, CA (city) Los Angeles County	4.14
Dallas, TX (city) Dallas County	4.13
Portland, OR (city) Multnomah County	4.13
Minneapolis, MN (city) Hennepin County	4.12
Jacksonville, FL (city) Duval County	4.11
Phoenix, AZ (city) Maricopa County	4.10
Denver, CO (city) Denver County	4.06
Attleboro, MA (city) Bristol County	4.05
Providence, RI (city) Providence County	4.02
Bloomington, MN (city) Hennepin County	4.01
New York, NY (city)	4.01
Seattle, WA (city) King County	3.98
St. Paul, MN (city) Ramsey County	3.95
St. Petersburg, FL (city) Pinellas County	3.95
Norwalk, CA (city) Los Angeles County	3.94
Columbus, OH (city) Franklin County	3.84
Garden Grove, CA (city) Orange County	3.83
Arlington, VA (cdp) Arlington County	3.82
Memphis, TN (city) Shelby County	3.79
Boston, MA (city) Suffolk County	3.77
Everett, WA (city) Snohomish County	3.73
Houston, TX (city) Harris County	3.33
San Francisco, CA (city) San Francisco County	3.31
Beaverton, OR (city) Washington County	2.82

Notes: Please refer to the User's Guide for an explanation of data; ranking tables include all places with Asian and/or NHPI populations above SF4 population thresholds; (1) tables reflect only those areas that meet SF4 population thresholds, therefore there may be less than 50 states, 75 counties or 75 places listed

Average Household Size

Chinese (except Taiwanese)

All States, Top 75 Counties, and Top 75 Places Sorted by Number[1]

State	Number
Wyoming	3.39
Maine	3.17
New York	3.15
New Jersey	2.99
Vermont	2.99
California	2.98
Utah	2.92
United States	2.91
Maryland	2.90
West Virginia	2.90
Massachusetts	2.88
Georgia	2.84
South Carolina	2.81
Virginia	2.79
Hawaii	2.78
Oregon	2.77
Washington	2.76
Connecticut	2.75
North Carolina	2.75
New Mexico	2.74
Nevada	2.73
New Hampshire	2.73
Pennsylvania	2.73
Illinois	2.72
Minnesota	2.72
Arkansas	2.71
Colorado	2.71
Delaware	2.71
Florida	2.71
Rhode Island	2.71
Texas	2.68
Idaho	2.67
Tennessee	2.67
Kansas	2.66
Montana	2.65
North Dakota	2.65
Alaska	2.61
Arizona	2.61
Michigan	2.61
Kentucky	2.60
Louisiana	2.56
Iowa	2.55
Ohio	2.55
Mississippi	2.53
Missouri	2.53
Alabama	2.51
Indiana	2.50
Wisconsin	2.50
Nebraska	2.38
Oklahoma	2.35
South Dakota	2.30
District of Columbia	2.02

County	Number
Ottawa County, MI	4.14
Strafford County, NH	3.81
Richmond County, GA	3.76
Clayton County, GA	3.73
Kings County, NY	3.66
Virginia Beach Independent City, VA	3.60
Lake County, IN	3.57
Plymouth County, MA	3.56
Litchfield County, CT	3.55
Brazoria County, TX	3.54
Gloucester County, NJ	3.54
Rockland County, NY	3.53
Orange County, NY	3.51
Columbia County, GA	3.50
Hampden County, MA	3.50
Washington County, MN	3.48
Nassau County, NY	3.45
Fairfax Independent City, VA	3.44
Fort Bend County, TX	3.41
Richmond County, NY	3.33
Guilford County, NC	3.32
Lancaster County, PA	3.31
Norfolk County, MA	3.29
Utah County, UT	3.28
Lake County, OH	3.27
Douglas County, CO	3.24
York County, PA	3.24
Monmouth County, NJ	3.23
Washington County, RI	3.23
Chesterfield County, VA	3.22
Queens County, NY	3.21
Camden County, NJ	3.20
Penobscot County, ME	3.19
Tulare County, CA	3.17
Somerset County, NJ	3.16
Williamson County, TX	3.15
San Bernardino County, CA	3.14
Worcester County, MA	3.14
Morris County, NJ	3.13
Will County, IL	3.13
Atlantic County, NJ	3.12
Midland County, MI	3.12
Montgomery County, TX	3.12
Rockingham County, NH	3.12
Waukesha County, WI	3.12
Berks County, PA	3.10
Howard County, MD	3.10
Anoka County, MN	3.09
Suffolk County, NY	3.09
New London County, CT	3.08
Adams County, CO	3.06
Essex County, MA	3.06
Kent County, MI	3.06
Lake County, IL	3.06
San Francisco County, CA	3.06
Burlington County, NJ	3.05
Prince George's County, MD	3.05
Saratoga County, NY	3.05
Bronx County, NY	3.04
Los Angeles County, CA	3.04
Middlesex County, NJ	3.04
Stanislaus County, CA	3.04
Collin County, TX	3.03
Fairfax County, VA	3.03
Delaware County, OH	3.01
Essex County, NJ	3.01
Northampton County, PA	3.01
Passaic County, NJ	3.01
Chittenden County, VT	3.00
Jefferson County, CO	3.00
Imperial County, CA	2.99
Seminole County, FL	2.99
Montgomery County, MD	2.98
Polk County, FL	2.98
Santa Clara County, CA	2.98

Place	Number
Laie, HI (cdp) Honolulu County	5.15
West Valley City, UT (city) Salt Lake County	4.69
South El Monte, CA (city) Los Angeles County	4.59
Springdale, NJ (cdp) Camden County	4.57
Ramapo, NY (town) Rockland County	4.49
Waipahu, HI (cdp) Honolulu County	4.36
Lake Success, NY (village) Nassau County	4.35
Garden City Park, NY (cdp) Nassau County	4.33
Rosemead, CA (city) Los Angeles County	4.26
Colesville, MD (cdp) Montgomery County	4.17
Benicia, CA (city) Solano County	4.15
Sandy, UT (city) Salt Lake County	4.15
Brockton, MA (city) Plymouth County	4.10
South San Gabriel, CA (cdp) Los Angeles County	4.03
Ahuimanu, HI (cdp) Honolulu County	4.01
Hazlet, NJ (township) Monmouth County	3.99
Hudson, OH (city) Summit County	3.92
Randolph, MA (town) Norfolk County	3.88
Carson, CA (city) Los Angeles County	3.87
El Monte, CA (city) Los Angeles County	3.86
Missouri City, TX (city) Fort Bend County	3.84
Calexico, CA (city) Imperial County	3.83
Augusta-Richmond Co., GA (sp. city) Richmond Co.	3.76
San Marino, CA (city) Los Angeles County	3.76
Shoreline, WA (city) King County	3.76
Apple Valley, MN (city) Dakota County	3.73
Dix Hills, NY (cdp) Suffolk County	3.73
La Canada Flintridge, CA (city) Los Angeles County	3.73
Orangetown, NY (town) Rockland County	3.72
Redland, MD (cdp) Montgomery County	3.70
Garden Grove, CA (city) Orange County	3.67
North New Hyde Park, NY (cdp) Nassau County	3.66
Warren, NJ (township) Somerset County	3.66
Babylon, NY (town) Suffolk County	3.65
North Hempstead, NY (town) Nassau County	3.64
Sunrise, FL (city) Broward County	3.64
Artesia, CA (city) Los Angeles County	3.63
Andover, MA (town) Essex County	3.62
Marlboro, NJ (township) Monmouth County	3.62
Needham, MA (town) Norfolk County	3.61
Montgomery, NJ (township) Somerset County	3.58
Quincy, MA (city) Norfolk County	3.58
Saratoga, CA (city) Santa Clara County	3.58
Cherry Hill, NJ (township) Camden County	3.57
Millbrae, CA (city) San Mateo County	3.57
New Territory, TX (cdp) Fort Bend County	3.57
Elk Grove, CA (cdp) Sacramento County	3.56
Halawa, HI (cdp) Honolulu County	3.56
Morganville, NJ (cdp) Monmouth County	3.56
North Potomac, MD (cdp) Montgomery County	3.56
San Leandro, CA (city) Alameda County	3.56
Mayflower Village, CA (cdp) Los Angeles County	3.55
Valley Stream, NY (village) Nassau County	3.54
West Windsor, NJ (township) Mercer County	3.54
Danville, CA (town) Contra Costa County	3.53
Holmdel, NJ (township) Monmouth County	3.53
Mundelein, IL (village) Lake County	3.53
Randolph, NJ (township) Morris County	3.53
San Lorenzo, CA (cdp) Alameda County	3.53
Weston, MA (town) Middlesex County	3.53
Malden, MA (city) Middlesex County	3.52
Walnut, CA (city) Los Angeles County	3.52
Roseville, MN (city) Ramsey County	3.51
Cerritos, CA (city) Los Angeles County	3.50
East Hanover, NJ (township) Morris County	3.50
Manalapan, NJ (township) Monmouth County	3.50
Union City, CA (city) Alameda County	3.50
Bellaire, TX (city) Harris County	3.49
College Park, MD (city) Prince George's County	3.49
Kailua, HI (cdp) Honolulu County	3.49
Olathe, KS (city) Johnson County	3.49
Santa Clarita, CA (city) Los Angeles County	3.49
Springfield, VA (cdp) Fairfax County	3.49
Burke, VA (cdp) Fairfax County	3.48
Millburn, NJ (township) Essex County	3.48

Notes: Please refer to the User's Guide for an explanation of data; ranking tables include all places with Asian and/or NHPI populations above SF4 population thresholds; (1) tables reflect only those areas that meet SF4 population thresholds, therefore there may be less than 50 states, 75 counties or 75 places listed

Average Household Size

Fijian

All States, Top 75 Counties, and Top 75 Places Sorted by Number[1]

State	Number
California	3.92
United States	3.72
Washington	3.53
Oregon	2.97

County	Number
Yolo County, CA	5.27
Contra Costa County, CA	5.21
Stanislaus County, CA	4.17
Santa Clara County, CA	4.00
San Mateo County, CA	3.87
Alameda County, CA	3.78
Sacramento County, CA	3.66
King County, WA	3.52
Los Angeles County, CA	2.86

Place	Number
Modesto, CA (city) Stanislaus County	4.55
Hayward, CA (city) Alameda County	3.73
Sacramento, CA (city) Sacramento County	3.72

Notes: Please refer to the User's Guide for an explanation of data; ranking tables include all places with Asian and/or NHPI populations above SF4 population thresholds; (1) tables reflect only those areas that meet SF4 population thresholds, therefore there may be less than 50 states, 75 counties or 75 places listed

Average Household Size

Filipino

All States, Top 75 Counties, and Top 75 Places Sorted by Number[1]

State	Number
Hawaii	4.25
Alaska	3.74
California	3.59
New Jersey	3.46
United States	3.41
Utah	3.35
South Dakota	3.31
Nevada	3.23
Washington	3.22
Virginia	3.14
Illinois	3.13
Maryland	3.11
Oregon	3.10
New York	3.01
Arizona	2.95
Florida	2.93
Texas	2.91
Georgia	2.87
Wyoming	2.85
South Carolina	2.84
Minnesota	2.83
Tennessee	2.83
Colorado	2.82
Louisiana	2.81
Michigan	2.80
New Hampshire	2.80
Pennsylvania	2.80
Delaware	2.79
Rhode Island	2.77
North Dakota	2.74
Vermont	2.74
Connecticut	2.73
Maine	2.73
Oklahoma	2.72
Wisconsin	2.72
Arkansas	2.71
Mississippi	2.71
New Mexico	2.71
North Carolina	2.71
Kentucky	2.69
Ohio	2.66
Massachusetts	2.64
West Virginia	2.63
Indiana	2.62
Iowa	2.61
Kansas	2.58
Missouri	2.57
Montana	2.55
Alabama	2.45
Nebraska	2.44
Idaho	2.42
District of Columbia	2.18

County	Number
Kodiak Island Borough, AK	5.04
Ketchikan Gateway Borough, AK	4.43
Maui County, HI	4.39
Honolulu County, HI	4.35
Aleutians East Borough, AK	4.17
Dakota County, MN	4.12
Santa Clara County, CA	4.12
Juneau Borough, AK	4.08
Napa County, CA	4.04
Rockingham County, NH	4.03
San Mateo County, CA	4.00
Valdez-Cordova Census Area, AK	3.93
Carson City Independent City, NV	3.85
Sandoval County, NM	3.84
Kauai County, HI	3.80
Ventura County, CA	3.80
Middlesex County, NJ	3.75
Nassau County, NY	3.73
Alameda County, CA	3.72
Madera County, CA	3.71
Fort Bend County, TX	3.70
Camden County, NJ	3.68
San Diego County, CA	3.68
Tulare County, CA	3.68
Solano County, CA	3.67
Craven County, NC	3.66
Union County, NJ	3.65
Saginaw County, MI	3.63
Santa Barbara County, CA	3.63
Riverside County, CA	3.62
Fairbanks North Star Borough, AK	3.61
Rockland County, NY	3.61
Contra Costa County, CA	3.60
San Bernardino County, CA	3.60
Monterey County, CA	3.58
Lake County, IL	3.57
Morris County, NJ	3.56
Prince George's County, MD	3.56
Virginia Beach Independent City, VA	3.56
Bergen County, NJ	3.55
Hawaii County, HI	3.55
Houston County, GA	3.54
Highlands County, FL	3.53
Kern County, CA	3.53
Salt Lake County, UT	3.53
Anoka County, MN	3.52
San Joaquin County, CA	3.52
Placer County, CA	3.51
Monmouth County, NJ	3.50
Snohomish County, WA	3.50
Orange County, CA	3.49
Thurston County, WA	3.49
Brazoria County, TX	3.48
Essex County, NJ	3.48
Jefferson County, NY	3.48
Gloucester County, NJ	3.47
Loudoun County, VA	3.46
North Slope Borough, AK	3.45
Atlantic County, NJ	3.44
Ocean County, NJ	3.44
Richmond County, NY	3.44
San Francisco County, CA	3.43
Lorain County, OH	3.42
Los Angeles County, CA	3.42
DuPage County, IL	3.40
Muscogee County, GA	3.40
Skagit County, WA	3.40
Somerset County, NJ	3.40
Washoe County, NV	3.40
Churchill County, NV	3.39
Anchorage Borough, AK	3.38
Suffolk County, NY	3.37
Fresno County, CA	3.36
McHenry County, IL	3.36
Santa Cruz County, CA	3.36

Place	Number
Colmar Manor, MD (town) Prince George's County	5.96
Lahaina, HI (cdp) Maui County	5.65
Maili, HI (cdp) Honolulu County	5.45
Waimanalo, HI (cdp) Honolulu County	5.45
Ewa Beach, HI (cdp) Honolulu County	5.37
Waihee-Waiehu, HI (cdp) Maui County	5.35
Makawao, HI (cdp) Maui County	5.13
Aiea, HI (cdp) Honolulu County	5.11
Colma, CA (town) San Mateo County	5.09
Kodiak, AK (city) Kodiak Island Borough	5.08
Nanakuli, HI (cdp) Honolulu County	5.08
Puhi, HI (cdp) Kauai County	5.03
Baywood-Los Osos, CA (cdp) San Luis Obispo County	4.98
Waipahu, HI (cdp) Honolulu County	4.94
Haliimaile, HI (cdp) Maui County	4.82
Kaneohe, HI (cdp) Honolulu County	4.81
Friendly, MD (cdp) Prince George's County	4.74
Whitmore Village, HI (cdp) Honolulu County	4.70
Napili-Honokowai, HI (cdp) Maui County	4.69
Ewa Villages, HI (cdp) Honolulu County	4.68
Halawa, HI (cdp) Honolulu County	4.66
Village Park, HI (cdp) Honolulu County	4.66
Valinda, CA (cdp) Los Angeles County	4.63
Kahului, HI (cdp) Maui County	4.61
Waikapu, HI (cdp) Maui County	4.56
Union City, CA (city) Alameda County	4.55
Porterville, CA (city) Tulare County	4.54
South San Jose Hills, CA (cdp) Los Angeles County	4.53
Baldwin Park, CA (city) Los Angeles County	4.51
Waikoloa Village, HI (cdp) Hawaii County	4.51
Hicksville, NY (cdp) Nassau County	4.50
Springfield, VA (cdp) Fairfax County	4.50
North Chicago, IL (city) Lake County	4.48
Omao, HI (cdp) Kauai County	4.48
Garden Grove, CA (city) Orange County	4.46
Kihei, HI (cdp) Maui County	4.46
Seattle Hill-Silver Firs, WA (cdp) Snohomish County	4.45
Bergenfield, NJ (borough) Bergen County	4.44
Daly City, CA (city) San Mateo County	4.44
Waipio, HI (cdp) Honolulu County	4.44
Ketchikan, AK (city) Ketchikan Gateway Borough	4.43
Park City, IL (city) Lake County	4.43
Makaha, HI (cdp) Honolulu County	4.42
Rollingwood, CA (cdp) Contra Costa County	4.42
Pearl City, HI (cdp) Honolulu County	4.41
Temple City, CA (city) Los Angeles County	4.39
Keaau, HI (cdp) Hawaii County	4.38
Mission Bend, TX (cdp) Fort Bend County	4.38
El Monte, CA (city) Los Angeles County	4.35
Milpitas, CA (city) Santa Clara County	4.34
Poplar-Cotton Center, CA (cdp) Tulare County	4.34
Poway, CA (city) San Diego County	4.34
Artesia, CA (city) Los Angeles County	4.33
Bay Point, CA (cdp) Contra Costa County	4.32
Gurnee, IL (village) Lake County	4.32
Hanamaulu, HI (cdp) Kauai County	4.32
San Jose, CA (city) Santa Clara County	4.32
South Plainfield, NJ (borough) Middlesex County	4.32
Vincent, CA (cdp) Los Angeles County	4.32
Levittown, NY (cdp) Nassau County	4.31
Mountlake Terrace, WA (city) Snohomish County	4.30
Rodeo, CA (cdp) Contra Costa County	4.30
Fair Lawn, NJ (borough) Bergen County	4.29
Valley Stream, NY (village) Nassau County	4.29
East Hill-Meridian, WA (cdp) King County	4.27
Kurtistown, HI (cdp) Hawaii County	4.27
West Puente Valley, CA (cdp) Los Angeles County	4.26
La Presa, CA (cdp) San Diego County	4.25
Delano, CA (city) Kern County	4.24
Union, NJ (township) Union County	4.24
Carson, CA (city) Los Angeles County	4.23
Duarte, CA (city) Los Angeles County	4.23
Makakilo City, HI (cdp) Honolulu County	4.23
East Brunswick, NJ (township) Middlesex County	4.21
Norwalk, CA (city) Los Angeles County	4.21

Notes: Please refer to the User's Guide for an explanation of data; ranking tables include all places with Asian and/or NHPI populations above SF4 population thresholds; (1) tables reflect only those areas that meet SF4 population thresholds, therefore there may be less than 50 states, 75 counties or 75 places listed

Average Household Size

Guamanian or Chamorro

All States, Top 75 Counties, and Top 75 Places Sorted by Number[1]

State	Number
Michigan	3.78
Connecticut	3.77
Ohio	3.72
Minnesota	3.66
Nevada	3.63
New Jersey	3.61
Massachusetts	3.54
Alabama	3.48
Pennsylvania	3.48
Florida	3.41
Tennessee	3.39
Washington	3.39
North Carolina	3.38
Arizona	3.37
California	3.36
Texas	3.35
Hawaii	3.33
United States	3.31
South Carolina	3.24
Virginia	3.24
Georgia	3.23
New York	3.19
Kentucky	3.17
Oregon	3.14
Louisiana	3.07
Colorado	3.05
Indiana	3.03
Wisconsin	2.99
Missouri	2.97
New Mexico	2.96
Illinois	2.87
Maryland	2.61
Oklahoma	2.32

County	Number
Kings County, NY	4.77
Thurston County, WA	4.43
Riverside County, CA	4.02
Pierce County, WA	3.82
Clark County, NV	3.70
Santa Clara County, CA	3.68
Solano County, CA	3.67
Los Angeles County, CA	3.59
San Bernardino County, CA	3.55
Bell County, TX	3.50
San Diego County, CA	3.47
Harris County, TX	3.44
Kitsap County, WA	3.44
Maricopa County, AZ	3.34
Monterey County, CA	3.31
Honolulu County, HI	3.30
San Mateo County, CA	3.26
Contra Costa County, CA	3.24
El Paso County, CO	3.17
Alameda County, CA	2.80
Sacramento County, CA	2.76
Orange County, CA	2.71
King County, WA	2.62

Place	Number
Fairfield, CA (city) Solano County	3.91
San Diego, CA (city) San Diego County	3.59
Vallejo, CA (city) Solano County	3.59
Killeen, TX (city) Bell County	3.57
Chula Vista, CA (city) San Diego County	3.56
San Jose, CA (city) Santa Clara County	3.46
Tacoma, WA (city) Pierce County	3.41
New York, NY (city)	3.31
Houston, TX (city) Harris County	3.17
Honolulu, HI (cdp) Honolulu County	3.13
Los Angeles, CA (city) Los Angeles County	3.09

Notes: Please refer to the User's Guide for an explanation of data; ranking tables include all places with Asian and/or NHPI populations above SF4 population thresholds; (1) tables reflect only those areas that meet SF4 population thresholds, therefore there may be less than 50 states, 75 counties or 75 places listed

Average Household Size

Hawaiian, Native

All States, Top 75 Counties, and Top 75 Places Sorted by Number[1]

State	Number
Montana	3.85
Alaska	3.53
Hawaii	3.53
Utah	3.43
Minnesota	3.34
Pennsylvania	3.30
Maryland	3.25
United States	3.21
Arizona	3.09
Oklahoma	3.06
Idaho	3.01
North Carolina	2.99
Louisiana	2.95
Indiana	2.93
Nevada	2.89
Texas	2.89
New Jersey	2.86
California	2.85
Michigan	2.78
Washington	2.77
Georgia	2.74
Missouri	2.73
South Carolina	2.72
Ohio	2.70
Oregon	2.68
Tennessee	2.66
Massachusetts	2.62
New York	2.58
Arkansas	2.57
Kansas	2.56
Florida	2.54
Wisconsin	2.53
Colorado	2.52
Illinois	2.49
Virginia	2.49
New Mexico	2.39

County	Number
Utah County, UT	3.65
Honolulu County, HI	3.62
San Joaquin County, CA	3.54
Maui County, HI	3.51
Maricopa County, AZ	3.44
Kauai County, HI	3.40
Hawaii County, HI	3.34
Snohomish County, WA	3.32
Ventura County, CA	3.08
Riverside County, CA	3.04
Salt Lake County, UT	3.01
Clark County, NV	2.99
Washington County, OR	2.98
Contra Costa County, CA	2.97
Solano County, CA	2.95
Los Angeles County, CA	2.93
Santa Clara County, CA	2.85
San Diego County, CA	2.83
San Bernardino County, CA	2.71
Alameda County, CA	2.69
King County, WA	2.64
Pierce County, WA	2.64
Multnomah County, OR	2.61
Pima County, AZ	2.61
Orange County, CA	2.59
Bexar County, TX	2.57
San Mateo County, CA	2.55
Sacramento County, CA	2.40

Place	Number
Pakala Village, HI (cdp) Kauai County	5.53
Waikane, HI (cdp) Honolulu County	5.42
Aiea, HI (cdp) Honolulu County	5.36
Hana, HI (cdp) Maui County	5.12
Kahaluu, HI (cdp) Honolulu County	5.05
Waimanalo Beach, HI (cdp) Honolulu County	5.04
Ewa Beach, HI (cdp) Honolulu County	4.95
Waimanalo, HI (cdp) Honolulu County	4.72
Waianae, HI (cdp) Honolulu County	4.63
Nanakuli, HI (cdp) Honolulu County	4.53
Captain Cook, HI (cdp) Hawaii County	4.49
Maili, HI (cdp) Honolulu County	4.26
Kahuku, HI (cdp) Honolulu County	4.19
Paia, HI (cdp) Maui County	4.14
Anahola, HI (cdp) Kauai County	4.08
Hanapepe, HI (cdp) Kauai County	4.06
Punaluu, HI (cdp) Honolulu County	4.03
Waipahu, HI (cdp) Honolulu County	4.00
Kaunakakai, HI (cdp) Maui County	3.96
Makakilo City, HI (cdp) Honolulu County	3.96
Naalehu, HI (cdp) Hawaii County	3.93
Honaunau-Napoopoo, HI (cdp) Hawaii County	3.92
Pearl City, HI (cdp) Honolulu County	3.88
Waikoloa Village, HI (cdp) Hawaii County	3.82
Ahuimanu, HI (cdp) Honolulu County	3.80
Wailuku, HI (cdp) Maui County	3.79
Kualapuu, HI (cdp) Maui County	3.76
Kaneohe, HI (cdp) Honolulu County	3.74
Waihee-Waiehu, HI (cdp) Maui County	3.72
Lahaina, HI (cdp) Maui County	3.71
Waialua, HI (cdp) Honolulu County	3.71
Hauula, HI (cdp) Honolulu County	3.66
Kapaau, HI (cdp) Hawaii County	3.62
Mililani Town, HI (cdp) Honolulu County	3.59
Kalaoa, HI (cdp) Hawaii County	3.57
Laie, HI (cdp) Honolulu County	3.55
Kailua, HI (cdp) Honolulu County	3.54
Haleiwa, HI (cdp) Honolulu County	3.50
Makaha, HI (cdp) Honolulu County	3.50
Henderson, NV (city) Clark County	3.42
Holualoa, HI (cdp) Hawaii County	3.41
Makaha Valley, HI (cdp) Honolulu County	3.40
Pahala, HI (cdp) Hawaii County	3.36
Kapaa, HI (cdp) Kauai County	3.31
Hawaiian Paradise Park, HI (cdp) Hawaii County	3.29
Hilo, HI (cdp) Hawaii County	3.27
Halawa, HI (cdp) Honolulu County	3.26
Hawaiian Beaches, HI (cdp) Hawaii County	3.21
Waimea, HI (cdp) Hawaii County	3.21
Kekaha, HI (cdp) Kauai County	3.19
Kahului, HI (cdp) Maui County	3.16
Kailua, HI (cdp) Hawaii County	3.16
Volcano, HI (cdp) Hawaii County	3.14
Honalo, HI (cdp) Hawaii County	3.12
Kihei, HI (cdp) Maui County	3.12
Paradise, NV (cdp) Clark County	3.11
Waimalu, HI (cdp) Honolulu County	3.08
Honolulu, HI (cdp) Honolulu County	3.07
Phoenix, AZ (city) Maricopa County	3.06
San Jose, CA (city) Santa Clara County	3.05
Kilauea, HI (cdp) Kauai County	3.00
Makawao, HI (cdp) Maui County	3.00
Los Angeles, CA (city) Los Angeles County	2.97
Kaaawa, HI (cdp) Honolulu County	2.94
Wahiawa, HI (cdp) Honolulu County	2.92
Waimea, HI (cdp) Kauai County	2.83
Hawaiian Ocean View, HI (cdp) Hawaii County	2.76
New York, NY (city)	2.65
San Diego, CA (city) San Diego County	2.65
Waipio, HI (cdp) Honolulu County	2.61
Las Vegas, NV (city) Clark County	2.52
Portland, OR (city) Multnomah County	2.19

Notes: Please refer to the User's Guide for an explanation of data; ranking tables include all places with Asian and/or NHPI populations above SF4 population thresholds; (1) tables reflect only those areas that meet SF4 population thresholds, therefore there may be less than 50 states, 75 counties or 75 places listed

Average Household Size

Hmong

All States, Top 75 Counties, and Top 75 Places Sorted by Number[1]

State	Number
South Carolina	6.84
Rhode Island	6.80
California	6.64
Pennsylvania	6.19
Oklahoma	6.14
United States	6.14
Massachusetts	6.07
Minnesota	6.05
Alaska	6.03
Wisconsin	5.86
Kansas	5.84
North Carolina	5.74
Michigan	5.58
Georgia	5.56
Washington	5.43
Colorado	5.24
Oregon	4.88

County	Number
Calumet County, WI	8.55
San Diego County, CA	7.41
Yuba County, CA	7.23
Providence County, RI	7.20
Butte County, CA	7.19
Yolo County, CA	7.10
Solano County, CA	7.08
Portage County, WI	7.06
Spartanburg County, SC	6.94
Olmsted County, MN	6.93
Fresno County, CA	6.89
La Crosse County, WI	6.87
Wood County, WI	6.86
Wayne County, MI	6.82
Glenn County, CA	6.76
Merced County, CA	6.76
Lancaster County, PA	6.72
Barrow County, GA	6.71
Jefferson County, CO	6.66
Sacramento County, CA	6.63
Worcester County, MA	6.60
Chippewa County, WI	6.59
Eau Claire County, WI	6.59
Marathon County, WI	6.58
Wyandotte County, KS	6.53
Hennepin County, MN	6.50
Burke County, NC	6.49
Tulare County, CA	6.34
San Joaquin County, CA	6.22
Orange County, CA	6.13
Anoka County, MN	6.05
Anchorage Borough, AK	6.03
Manitowoc County, WI	6.02
Milwaukee County, WI	6.02
Stanly County, NC	6.00
Winnebago County, WI	5.89
Ramsey County, MN	5.87
Santa Barbara County, CA	5.87
Riverside County, CA	5.72
Oakland County, MI	5.64
Dunn County, WI	5.61
Sheboygan County, WI	5.61
Outagamie County, WI	5.59
Ingham County, MI	5.50
Stanislaus County, CA	5.45
Catawba County, NC	5.44
King County, WA	5.44
Mecklenburg County, NC	5.35
Fond du Lac County, WI	5.32
Adams County, CO	5.31
Washington County, MN	5.28
Spokane County, WA	5.27
Macomb County, MI	5.26
Brown County, WI	5.22
Multnomah County, OR	4.93
Dane County, WI	4.76
Los Angeles County, CA	4.12

Place	Number
Thermalito, CA (cdp) Butte County	9.65
Glen Alpine, NC (town) Burke County	9.08
South Oroville, CA (cdp) Butte County	8.34
Providence, RI (city) Providence County	8.13
Oroville, CA (city) Butte County	7.69
Linda, CA (cdp) Yuba County	7.64
Fitchburg, MA (city) Worcester County	7.36
Brooklyn Park, MN (city) Hennepin County	7.32
West Sacramento, CA (city) Yolo County	7.23
Atwater, CA (city) Merced County	7.20
La Crosse, WI (city) La Crosse County	7.03
San Diego, CA (city) San Diego County	7.01
Modesto, CA (city) Stanislaus County	6.96
Santa Ana, CA (city) Orange County	6.95
Sacramento, CA (city) Sacramento County	6.94
Brooklyn Center, MN (city) Hennepin County	6.93
Rochester, MN (city) Olmsted County	6.93
Detroit, MI (city) Wayne County	6.92
Fresno, CA (city) Fresno County	6.91
Wisconsin Rapids, WI (city) Wood County	6.87
Willows, CA (city) Glenn County	6.76
Eau Claire, WI (city) Eau Claire County	6.74
Stevens Point, WI (city) Portage County	6.73
Kansas City, KS (city) Wyandotte County	6.53
Wausau, WI (city) Marathon County	6.49
Minneapolis, MN (city) Hennepin County	6.46
Parkway-S. Sacramento, CA (cdp) Sacramento County	6.46
Merced, CA (city) Merced County	6.45
Visalia, CA (city) Tulare County	6.42
Stockton, CA (city) San Joaquin County	6.34
Manitowoc, WI (city) Manitowoc County	6.30
Clovis, CA (city) Fresno County	6.27
Oshkosh, WI (city) Winnebago County	6.21
Warren, MI (city) Macomb County	6.19
Florin, CA (cdp) Sacramento County	6.14
Appleton, WI (city) Outagamie County	6.13
Milwaukee, WI (city) Milwaukee County	6.13
Pontiac, MI (city) Oakland County	6.08
Fond du Lac, WI (city) Fond du Lac County	5.97
St. Paul, MN (city) Ramsey County	5.94
Westminster, CO (city) Adams County	5.90
Spokane, WA (city) Spokane County	5.78
Valdese, NC (town) Burke County	5.67
Woodbury, MN (city) Washington County	5.63
Sheboygan, WI (city) Sheboygan County	5.58
Green Bay, WI (city) Brown County	5.49
Connelly Springs, NC (town) Burke County	5.43
Chico, CA (city) Butte County	5.36
Charlotte, NC (city) Mecklenburg County	5.35
Maplewood, MN (city) Ramsey County	5.29
Hickory, NC (city) Catawba County	5.04
Madison, WI (city) Dane County	4.81
Portland, OR (city) Multnomah County	4.70
Lansing, MI (city) Ingham County	4.38
Arden-Arcade, CA (cdp) Sacramento County	3.98

Notes: Please refer to the User's Guide for an explanation of data; ranking tables include all places with Asian and/or NHPI populations above SF4 population thresholds; (1) tables reflect only those areas that meet SF4 population thresholds, therefore there may be less than 50 states, 75 counties or 75 places listed

Average Household Size

Indonesian

All States, Top 75 Counties, and Top 75 Places Sorted by Number[1]

State	Number
Maryland	3.53
New Jersey	3.09
California	2.99
Pennsylvania	2.79
Colorado	2.75
New York	2.68
United States	2.67
Virginia	2.62
Georgia	2.49
Illinois	2.49
Arizona	2.44
Texas	2.42
Michigan	2.38
Florida	2.29
Massachusetts	2.26
Oregon	2.26
Ohio	2.25
Washington	2.12
Wisconsin	1.65

County	Number
Montgomery County, MD	3.90
San Bernardino County, CA	3.75
Middlesex County, NJ	3.72
Alameda County, CA	3.55
Fairfax County, VA	3.09
Orange County, CA	3.01
San Mateo County, CA	2.99
Los Angeles County, CA	2.91
Queens County, NY	2.86
San Diego County, CA	2.68
Santa Clara County, CA	2.57
Harris County, TX	2.56
Contra Costa County, CA	2.43
San Francisco County, CA	2.35
Maricopa County, AZ	2.33
Cook County, IL	2.17
Franklin County, OH	2.08
King County, WA	1.92

Place	Number
San Bernardino, CA (city) San Bernardino County	4.82
Loma Linda, CA (city) San Bernardino County	4.01
New York, NY (city)	2.82
Houston, TX (city) Harris County	2.66
Los Angeles, CA (city) Los Angeles County	2.40
San Francisco, CA (city) San Francisco County	2.35
Columbus, OH (city) Franklin County	2.04
Seattle, WA (city) King County	1.87

Notes: Please refer to the User's Guide for an explanation of data; ranking tables include all places with Asian and/or NHPI populations above SF4 population thresholds; (1) tables reflect only those areas that meet SF4 population thresholds, therefore there may be less than 50 states, 75 counties or 75 places listed

Average Household Size

Japanese

All States, Top 75 Counties, and Top 75 Places Sorted by Number[1]

State	Number
Rhode Island	2.77
Connecticut	2.66
Vermont	2.50
Hawaii	2.48
Utah	2.43
New Jersey	2.37
Michigan	2.36
New Hampshire	2.34
Ohio	2.31
Georgia	2.29
North Carolina	2.28
United States	2.25
California	2.24
Idaho	2.23
Illinois	2.16
Alaska	2.15
Tennessee	2.15
Minnesota	2.14
Texas	2.14
Virginia	2.14
Delaware	2.13
Kentucky	2.12
New Mexico	2.11
Florida	2.10
Maine	2.10
Colorado	2.09
Maryland	2.09
Washington	2.09
Oregon	2.08
Arizona	2.07
Indiana	2.06
Alabama	2.05
Massachusetts	2.04
Louisiana	2.03
Nevada	2.02
South Carolina	2.02
Missouri	1.98
Pennsylvania	1.98
Nebraska	1.95
New York	1.93
Oklahoma	1.93
South Dakota	1.92
Wisconsin	1.91
Iowa	1.90
Kansas	1.84
Montana	1.82
Wyoming	1.79
Arkansas	1.78
West Virginia	1.73
Mississippi	1.72
District of Columbia	1.49

County	Number
Fairfield County, CT	3.37
Utah County, UT	3.28
Fayette County, GA	3.15
Lake County, IL	3.01
Westchester County, NY	2.99
Essex County, NJ	2.78
Boone County, KY	2.77
Fairfax County, VA	2.75
Wake County, NC	2.72
Worcester County, MA	2.68
Cobb County, GA	2.64
Ventura County, CA	2.62
Oakland County, MI	2.60
Bergen County, NJ	2.59
Napa County, CA	2.57
Summit County, OH	2.57
Olmsted County, MN	2.56
Stanislaus County, CA	2.56
Chester County, PA	2.52
Honolulu County, HI	2.51
Canyon County, ID	2.49
San Bernardino County, CA	2.49
Franklin County, OH	2.48
Morris County, NJ	2.48
Kern County, CA	2.46
Calhoun County, MI	2.45
Essex County, MA	2.45
Weber County, UT	2.45
Collin County, TX	2.44
Snohomish County, WA	2.44
Clackamas County, OR	2.43
Shelby County, TN	2.42
Clark County, WA	2.40
Orange County, CA	2.40
Washington County, OR	2.40
Davis County, UT	2.39
Johnson County, KS	2.39
Mecklenburg County, NC	2.39
Contra Costa County, CA	2.38
Hawaii County, HI	2.38
Kauai County, HI	2.37
Santa Clara County, CA	2.37
Arapahoe County, CO	2.36
Nassau County, NY	2.36
Maui County, HI	2.35
Orange County, NC	2.35
Salt Lake County, UT	2.35
Fayette County, KY	2.33
Delaware County, PA	2.32
Norfolk County, MA	2.32
Placer County, CA	2.32
Virginia Beach Independent City, VA	2.30
Boulder County, CO	2.29
Gwinnett County, GA	2.29
Jefferson County, CO	2.29
Riverside County, CA	2.29
San Mateo County, CA	2.29
Harris County, TX	2.28
Onondaga County, NY	2.28
San Joaquin County, CA	2.26
San Luis Obispo County, CA	2.26
Santa Cruz County, CA	2.26
Suffolk County, NY	2.26
Larimer County, CO	2.25
Mercer County, NJ	2.25
Washtenaw County, MI	2.25
Orange County, FL	2.24
Sacramento County, CA	2.24
Alameda County, CA	2.23
Hartford County, CT	2.23
Monterey County, CA	2.23
Fresno County, CA	2.22
Montgomery County, PA	2.21
New Castle County, DE	2.21
Los Angeles County, CA	2.20

Place	Number
Scarsdale, NY (village) Westchester County	3.83
Greenwich, CT (town) Fairfield County	3.74
McLean, VA (cdp) Fairfax County	3.28
Heeia, HI (cdp) Honolulu County	3.24
West Bloomfield, MI (township) Oakland County	3.21
Dublin, OH (city) Franklin County	3.20
Harrison, NY (village) Westchester County	3.20
Rye, NY (city) Westchester County	3.18
Buffalo Grove, IL (village) Lake County	3.16
East San Gabriel, CA (cdp) Los Angeles County	3.15
Peachtree City, GA (city) Fayette County	3.15
Waihee-Waiehu, HI (cdp) Maui County	3.14
Elk Grove Village, IL (village) Cook County	3.13
Ridgewood, NJ (village) Bergen County	3.11
Millbrae, CA (city) San Mateo County	3.10
Eastchester, NY (town) Westchester County	3.07
Cerritos, CA (city) Los Angeles County	3.06
Kalaoa, HI (cdp) Hawaii County	3.05
Chino Hills, CA (city) San Bernardino County	3.04
Maunawili, HI (cdp) Honolulu County	3.02
Ahuimanu, HI (cdp) Honolulu County	3.01
Palos Verdes Estates, CA (city) Los Angeles County	3.01
Hoffman Estates, IL (village) Cook County	3.00
Rancho Palos Verdes, CA (city) Los Angeles County	3.00
Arcadia, CA (city) Los Angeles County	2.99
Mililani Town, HI (cdp) Honolulu County	2.99
Waianae, HI (cdp) Honolulu County	2.99
Glendale, AZ (city) Maricopa County	2.98
Kaneohe, HI (cdp) Honolulu County	2.98
Provo, UT (city) Utah County	2.97
Rolling Hills Estates, CA (city) Los Angeles County	2.97
Hawaiian Beaches, HI (cdp) Hawaii County	2.95
Wilmette, IL (village) Cook County	2.95
Yorba Linda, CA (city) Orange County	2.95
Cary, NC (town) Wake County	2.94
Thousand Oaks, CA (city) Ventura County	2.94
Covina, CA (city) Los Angeles County	2.92
Laguna, CA (cdp) Sacramento County	2.92
Waipahu, HI (cdp) Honolulu County	2.92
Union City, CA (city) Alameda County	2.91
Morgan Hill, CA (city) Santa Clara County	2.90
Foster City, CA (city) San Mateo County	2.88
Pleasanton, CA (city) Alameda County	2.87
Bryn Mawr-Skyway, WA (cdp) King County	2.86
Downey, CA (city) Los Angeles County	2.86
Ewa Beach, HI (cdp) Honolulu County	2.86
Greenburgh, NY (town) Westchester County	2.86
Norwalk, CA (city) Los Angeles County	2.86
Puhi, HI (cdp) Kauai County	2.85
Elk Grove, CA (cdp) Sacramento County	2.83
Fountain Valley, CA (city) Orange County	2.83
Rocklin, CA (city) Placer County	2.82
Whittier, CA (city) Los Angeles County	2.82
Bakersfield, CA (city) Kern County	2.81
Cupertino, CA (city) Santa Clara County	2.81
Temple City, CA (city) Los Angeles County	2.79
Village Park, HI (cdp) Honolulu County	2.79
Rowland Heights, CA (cdp) Los Angeles County	2.78
Kailua, HI (cdp) Honolulu County	2.77
Eastchester, NY (cdp) Westchester County	2.76
Mission Viejo, CA (city) Orange County	2.76
Beaverton, OR (city) Washington County	2.75
San Buenaventura (Ventura), CA (city) Ventura County	2.75
Waipio, HI (cdp) Honolulu County	2.74
Honalo, HI (cdp) Hawaii County	2.73
Mercer Island, WA (city) King County	2.72
Pearl City, HI (cdp) Honolulu County	2.72
South San Gabriel, CA (cdp) Los Angeles County	2.72
La Canada Flintridge, CA (city) Los Angeles County	2.71
La Palma, CA (city) Orange County	2.71
Waikapu, HI (cdp) Maui County	2.71
Camarillo, CA (city) Ventura County	2.70
Aiea, HI (cdp) Honolulu County	2.69
Hacienda Heights, CA (cdp) Los Angeles County	2.68
Mount Prospect, IL (village) Cook County	2.68

Notes: Please refer to the User's Guide for an explanation of data; ranking tables include all places with Asian and/or NHPI populations above SF4 population thresholds; (1) tables reflect only those areas that meet SF4 population thresholds, therefore there may be less than 50 states, 75 counties or 75 places listed

Average Household Size

Korean

All States, Top 75 Counties, and Top 75 Places Sorted by Number[1]

State	Number
New Jersey	3.09
Maryland	2.98
Georgia	2.93
New Hampshire	2.90
Virginia	2.88
California	2.87
New York	2.79
Washington	2.77
United States	2.76
Idaho	2.75
Louisiana	2.74
Delaware	2.72
Pennsylvania	2.71
Texas	2.68
Colorado	2.66
Mississippi	2.66
Oregon	2.64
Alaska	2.63
Illinois	2.63
Alabama	2.61
Florida	2.59
Montana	2.59
North Carolina	2.59
Connecticut	2.58
Kansas	2.58
Utah	2.57
New Mexico	2.55
Nevada	2.53
Arizona	2.51
Tennessee	2.50
Kentucky	2.48
Michigan	2.48
Hawaii	2.42
South Carolina	2.40
Massachusetts	2.39
Missouri	2.39
Ohio	2.39
Arkansas	2.37
Wisconsin	2.37
Oklahoma	2.36
Minnesota	2.35
Iowa	2.32
Wyoming	2.32
Indiana	2.22
Rhode Island	2.18
Maine	2.15
Nebraska	2.09
North Dakota	2.04
South Dakota	2.01
West Virginia	1.94
Vermont	1.78
District of Columbia	1.54

County	Number
Washington County, MN	4.31
Kent County, RI	3.88
Placer County, CA	3.85
Fort Bend County, TX	3.76
Loudoun County, VA	3.69
Nassau County, NY	3.69
Litchfield County, CT	3.64
Morris County, NJ	3.48
York County, VA	3.45
Rockland County, NY	3.44
Utah County, UT	3.43
Chester County, PA	3.38
Davis County, UT	3.37
Howard County, MD	3.37
York County, PA	3.37
Butler County, OH	3.35
Chesterfield County, VA	3.33
Snohomish County, WA	3.33
Will County, IL	3.29
Collin County, TX	3.28
Solano County, CA	3.28
Somerset County, NJ	3.28
Gwinnett County, GA	3.26
Mercer County, NJ	3.26
Jefferson Parish, LA	3.25
Kane County, IL	3.24
Lake County, IL	3.23
Prince William County, VA	3.23
Bucks County, PA	3.21
Delaware County, PA	3.21
Montgomery County, PA	3.21
Bergen County, NJ	3.20
Frederick County, MD	3.20
Imperial County, CA	3.20
Orange County, CA	3.19
Atlantic County, NJ	3.18
Camden County, NJ	3.17
Middlesex County, NJ	3.16
Riverside County, CA	3.14
Summit County, OH	3.14
Fairfax County, VA	3.13
Westchester County, NY	3.11
Montgomery County, MD	3.10
Essex County, NJ	3.08
Fairfax Independent City, VA	3.08
Wicomico County, MD	3.08
Marin County, CA	3.07
Waukesha County, WI	3.07
Queens County, NY	3.06
Baltimore County, MD	3.05
Berrien County, MI	3.05
Williamson County, TX	3.05
Olmsted County, MN	3.03
Santa Clara County, CA	3.03
Columbia County, GA	3.02
Fulton County, GA	3.02
Monmouth County, NJ	3.02
Suffolk County, NY	3.02
Ventura County, CA	3.01
Guilford County, NC	3.00
Burlington County, NJ	2.99
Anne Arundel County, MD	2.98
Sonoma County, CA	2.98
Riley County, KS	2.97
Washington County, OR	2.96
Hillsborough County, FL	2.95
San Bernardino County, CA	2.95
Tulsa County, OK	2.93
Cobb County, GA	2.92
Jefferson County, NY	2.92
Tulare County, CA	2.92
Johnson County, KS	2.91
Dakota County, MN	2.90
Polk County, IA	2.90
Richmond County, NY	2.90

Place	Number
Mukilteo, WA (city) Snohomish County	4.32
Lexington, MA (town) Middlesex County	4.24
Olney, MD (cdp) Montgomery County	4.24
Paramus, NJ (borough) Bergen County	4.16
Plainview, NY (cdp) Nassau County	4.16
Harrington Park, NJ (borough) Bergen County	4.15
Corona, CA (city) Riverside County	4.13
Scarsdale, NY (village) Westchester County	4.04
Ridgewood, NJ (village) Bergen County	4.02
Browns Mills, NJ (cdp) Burlington County	3.99
Clarkstown, NY (town) Rockland County	3.97
Englewood Cliffs, NJ (borough) Bergen County	3.94
Newark, CA (city) Alameda County	3.93
La Canada Flintridge, CA (city) Los Angeles County	3.89
Walnut, CA (city) Los Angeles County	3.89
Norwood, NJ (borough) Bergen County	3.88
Upper Dublin, PA (township) Montgomery County	3.87
Hempstead, NY (town) Nassau County	3.84
Spanaway, WA (cdp) Pierce County	3.83
Leonia, NJ (borough) Bergen County	3.79
Abington, PA (township) Montgomery County	3.76
Cerritos, CA (city) Los Angeles County	3.76
Coppell, TX (city) Dallas County	3.75
Cresskill, NJ (borough) Bergen County	3.75
Old Tappan, NJ (borough) Bergen County	3.75
Piscataway, NJ (township) Middlesex County	3.74
Buffalo Grove, IL (village) Lake County	3.73
Closter, NJ (borough) Bergen County	3.73
Hamilton, NJ (township) Mercer County	3.73
Jericho, NY (cdp) Nassau County	3.73
Newington, VA (cdp) Fairfax County	3.72
Oyster Bay, NY (town) Nassau County	3.71
Cupertino, CA (city) Santa Clara County	3.69
Simi Valley, CA (city) Ventura County	3.69
Glen Cove, NY (city) Nassau County	3.68
Lincolnwood, IL (village) Cook County	3.67
North Potomac, MD (cdp) Montgomery County	3.67
Colesville, MD (cdp) Montgomery County	3.66
Lynnwood, WA (city) Snohomish County	3.66
North Springfield, VA (cdp) Fairfax County	3.66
Kent, WA (city) King County	3.63
Commack, NY (cdp) Suffolk County	3.62
Marple, PA (township) Delaware County	3.62
North Hempstead, NY (town) Nassau County	3.62
Ridgefield, NJ (borough) Bergen County	3.61
Cypress, CA (city) Orange County	3.60
Mill Creek, WA (city) Snohomish County	3.60
Arcadia, CA (city) Los Angeles County	3.59
Cherry Hill, NJ (township) Camden County	3.58
Livingston, NJ (township) Essex County	3.58
East Brunswick, NJ (township) Middlesex County	3.57
Rancho Palos Verdes, CA (city) Los Angeles County	3.56
Burke, VA (cdp) Fairfax County	3.55
Chino Hills, CA (city) San Bernardino County	3.55
Fremont, CA (city) Alameda County	3.55
Naperville, IL (city) Du Page County	3.55
Alpine, NJ (borough) Bergen County	3.54
Greenburgh, NY (town) Westchester County	3.54
Placentia, CA (city) Orange County	3.54
Smithtown, NY (town) Suffolk County	3.54
Temple City, CA (city) Los Angeles County	3.54
Tenafly, NJ (borough) Bergen County	3.54
Carrollton, TX (city) Denton County	3.53
La Crescenta-Montrose, CA (cdp) Los Angeles County	3.52
Carney, MD (cdp) Baltimore County	3.51
Roswell, GA (city) Fulton County	3.51
West Springfield, VA (cdp) Fairfax County	3.51
Yorba Linda, CA (city) Orange County	3.51
West Orange, NJ (township) Essex County	3.50
Downey, CA (city) Los Angeles County	3.49
Waimalu, HI (cdp) Honolulu County	3.49
Demarest, NJ (borough) Bergen County	3.48
Diamond Bar, CA (city) Los Angeles County	3.48
Glenview, IL (village) Cook County	3.48
La Palma, CA (city) Orange County	3.48

Notes: Please refer to the User's Guide for an explanation of data; ranking tables include all places with Asian and/or NHPI populations above SF4 population thresholds; (1) tables reflect only those areas that meet SF4 population thresholds, therefore there may be less than 50 states, 75 counties or 75 places listed

Average Household Size

Laotian

***All States, Top 75 Counties, and Top 75 Places Sorted by Number*[1]**

State	Number
California	4.90
South Dakota	4.75
Colorado	4.70
Maryland	4.58
Wisconsin	4.57
New Jersey	4.45
Louisiana	4.44
North Carolina	4.38
Utah	4.37
Alaska	4.36
Massachusetts	4.32
United States	4.23
South Carolina	4.18
Minnesota	4.16
Washington	4.14
Oregon	4.10
Pennsylvania	4.05
Michigan	4.02
Ohio	3.99
Hawaii	3.97
Georgia	3.95
Oklahoma	3.90
Illinois	3.89
Iowa	3.89
Virginia	3.82
New Hampshire	3.81
Texas	3.81
New York	3.76
Arkansas	3.72
Connecticut	3.71
Alabama	3.70
Tennessee	3.70
Kansas	3.64
Nebraska	3.64
Idaho	3.63
Florida	3.62
Rhode Island	3.58
Missouri	3.42
Indiana	3.41
Arizona	3.35
Nevada	3.33

County	Number
Brown County, WI	6.01
Burke County, NC	6.01
Catawba County, NC	5.96
Tulare County, CA	5.94
Essex County, MA	5.57
Sacramento County, CA	5.57
Butte County, CA	5.41
Santa Clara County, CA	5.39
Shasta County, CA	5.23
Merced County, CA	5.18
Orange County, CA	5.12
Sonoma County, CA	5.12
Stanislaus County, CA	5.06
Iberia Parish, LA	5.04
Contra Costa County, CA	5.02
Jefferson County, CO	4.99
Cass County, MI	4.90
Alameda County, CA	4.87
Fresno County, CA	4.87
Ramsey County, MN	4.80
Salt Lake County, UT	4.76
Adams County, CO	4.75
Cowley County, KS	4.71
Solano County, CA	4.66
San Joaquin County, CA	4.65
Middlesex County, MA	4.60
Anchorage Borough, AK	4.56
Summit County, OH	4.53
San Diego County, CA	4.49
Snohomish County, WA	4.43
Clayton County, GA	4.34
Multnomah County, OR	4.31
Los Angeles County, CA	4.28
Nobles County, MN	4.24
San Bernardino County, CA	4.23
Broome County, NY	4.22
Philadelphia County, PA	4.22
Fairfax County, VA	4.21
Hennepin County, MN	4.21
King County, WA	4.20
Kane County, IL	4.18
Polk County, IA	4.18
Cook County, IL	4.16
Dakota County, MN	4.15
Tarrant County, TX	4.12
Yolo County, CA	4.12
Buena Vista County, IA	4.11
Milwaukee County, WI	4.10
Pacific County, WA	4.09
Worcester County, MA	4.08
Riverside County, CA	4.05
Mobile County, AL	4.01
Olmsted County, MN	4.01
Fairfield County, CT	4.00
Potter County, TX	4.00
Pinellas County, FL	3.99
Spartanburg County, SC	3.99
Habersham County, GA	3.98
Honolulu County, HI	3.98
Polk County, FL	3.98
Clark County, WA	3.94
Dakota County, NE	3.92
Franklin County, WA	3.91
Roseau County, MN	3.90
Guilford County, NC	3.86
Oklahoma County, OK	3.86
Gwinnett County, GA	3.83
Dane County, WI	3.79
Sedgwick County, KS	3.79
Ottawa County, MI	3.77
Dallas County, TX	3.76
Montgomery County, NC	3.75
Hartford County, CT	3.74
Winnebago County, IL	3.74
Monroe County, NY	3.72

Place	Number
Arvada, CO (city) Jefferson County	5.96
Escondido, CA (city) San Diego County	5.78
Visalia, CA (city) Tulare County	5.67
Green Bay, WI (city) Brown County	5.65
Sacramento, CA (city) Sacramento County	5.60
San Jose, CA (city) Santa Clara County	5.56
Santa Ana, CA (city) Orange County	5.51
Akron, OH (city) Summit County	5.45
Oakland, CA (city) Alameda County	5.35
Redding, CA (city) Shasta County	5.28
Merced, CA (city) Merced County	5.24
Santa Rosa, CA (city) Sonoma County	5.18
Modesto, CA (city) Stanislaus County	5.09
Richmond, CA (city) Contra Costa County	5.08
Pomona, CA (city) Los Angeles County	5.01
St. Paul, MN (city) Ramsey County	4.97
Grand Prairie, TX (city) Dallas County	4.96
Anaheim, CA (city) Orange County	4.94
Parkway-S. Sacramento, CA (cdp) Sacramento County	4.94
Winfield, KS (city) Cowley County	4.75
Fresno, CA (city) Fresno County	4.73
Stockton, CA (city) San Joaquin County	4.72
San Pablo, CA (city) Contra Costa County	4.66
Fitchburg, MA (city) Worcester County	4.61
Rochester, NY (city) Monroe County	4.52
Brooklyn Park, MN (city) Hennepin County	4.51
Des Moines, IA (city) Polk County	4.50
Elgin, IL (city) Kane County	4.50
Lowell, MA (city) Middlesex County	4.48
Warroad, MN (city) Roseau County	4.44
Brooklyn Center, MN (city) Hennepin County	4.43
Banning, CA (city) Riverside County	4.42
Springfield, VA (cdp) Fairfax County	4.41
West Valley City, UT (city) Salt Lake County	4.39
San Diego, CA (city) San Diego County	4.38
Fairfield, CA (city) Solano County	4.35
Raymond, WA (city) Pacific County	4.35
Bellevue, WA (city) King County	4.34
Portland, OR (city) Multnomah County	4.32
Milwaukee, WI (city) Milwaukee County	4.30
Long Beach, CA (city) Los Angeles County	4.25
Worthington, MN (city) Nobles County	4.25
Seattle, WA (city) King County	4.23
St. Petersburg, FL (city) Pinellas County	4.23
Philadelphia, PA (city) Philadelphia County	4.22
Moreno Valley, CA (city) Riverside County	4.18
Oklahoma City, OK (city) Oklahoma County	4.18
Haltom City, TX (city) Tarrant County	4.13
Westminster, CO (city) Adams County	4.07
Storm Lake, IA (city) Buena Vista County	4.06
Rochester, MN (city) Olmsted County	4.01
Oaklawn-Sunview, KS (cdp) Sedgwick County	3.97
Amarillo, TX (city) Potter County	3.95
Bridgeport, CT (city) Fairfield County	3.87
Minneapolis, MN (city) Hennepin County	3.84
Fort Worth, TX (city) Tarrant County	3.81
Honolulu, HI (cdp) Honolulu County	3.78
Los Angeles, CA (city) Los Angeles County	3.78
Riverside, CA (city) Riverside County	3.77
Rockford, IL (city) Winnebago County	3.75
Tacoma, WA (city) Pierce County	3.70
Providence, RI (city) Providence County	3.66
Nashville-Davidson, TN (sp. city) Davidson County	3.65
Dallas, TX (city) Dallas County	3.64
Wichita, KS (city) Sedgwick County	3.64
Springdale, AR (city) Washington County	3.63
Fort Smith, AR (city) Sebastian County	3.57
New Britain, CT (city) Hartford County	3.47
Woonsocket, RI (city) Providence County	3.46
Columbus, OH (city) Franklin County	3.45
Irving, TX (city) Dallas County	3.45
Charlotte, NC (city) Mecklenburg County	3.42
Murfreesboro, TN (city) Rutherford County	3.22

Notes: Please refer to the User's Guide for an explanation of data; ranking tables include all places with Asian and/or NHPI populations above SF4 population thresholds; (1) tables reflect only those areas that meet SF4 population thresholds, therefore there may be less than 50 states, 75 counties or 75 places listed

Average Household Size

Malaysian

All States, Top 75 Counties, and Top 75 Places Sorted by Number[1]

State	Number
California	2.89
Oklahoma	2.72
Michigan	2.68
Ohio	2.62
United States	2.61
New York	2.58
Texas	2.31
Illinois	2.24

County	Number
Queens County, NY	2.62
Los Angeles County, CA	2.59

Place	Number
New York, NY (city)	2.54

Notes: Please refer to the User's Guide for an explanation of data; ranking tables include all places with Asian and/or NHPI populations above SF4 population thresholds; (1) tables reflect only those areas that meet SF4 population thresholds, therefore there may be less than 50 states, 75 counties or 75 places listed

Average Household Size

Pakistani

All States, Top 75 Counties, and Top 75 Places Sorted by Number[1]

State	Number
Utah	4.75
Virginia	4.17
New York	4.11
New Jersey	4.07
Maryland	3.89
Georgia	3.85
Massachusetts	3.84
California	3.83
Michigan	3.81
United States	3.80
Illinois	3.78
Florida	3.74
Indiana	3.69
Tennessee	3.68
Texas	3.65
Connecticut	3.63
Nevada	3.60
Oklahoma	3.52
Oregon	3.50
North Carolina	3.48
Pennsylvania	3.45
Minnesota	3.44
Colorado	3.40
Delaware	3.35
Louisiana	3.30
Arizona	3.26
Alabama	3.25
Ohio	3.23
Iowa	3.21
Missouri	3.18
Washington	3.16
Kentucky	3.11
Kansas	3.10
Wisconsin	2.81
West Virginia	2.55

County	Number
Will County, IL	5.59
Guilford County, NC	5.10
Nassau County, NY	4.92
Sacramento County, CA	4.91
Union County, NJ	4.91
San Joaquin County, CA	4.64
Suffolk County, NY	4.61
Macomb County, MI	4.56
Prince William County, VA	4.47
Fort Bend County, TX	4.44
Loudoun County, VA	4.40
Richmond County, NY	4.40
Denton County, TX	4.37
Howard County, MD	4.35
Hudson County, NJ	4.35
Fairfax County, VA	4.32
Gwinnett County, GA	4.32
San Francisco County, CA	4.32
Montgomery County, MD	4.29
Morris County, NJ	4.29
Kings County, NY	4.28
Worcester County, MA	4.28
Lake County, IL	4.26
Somerset County, NJ	4.22
Queens County, NY	4.21
Monmouth County, NJ	4.19
Delaware County, PA	4.13
Arlington County, VA	4.12
Middlesex County, NJ	4.09
Orange County, FL	4.09
Bergen County, NJ	4.04
Santa Clara County, CA	4.02
Contra Costa County, CA	4.01
Cobb County, GA	3.99
DuPage County, IL	3.98
Washtenaw County, MI	3.97
Westchester County, NY	3.97
Fairfield County, CT	3.96
Orange County, CA	3.92
Mercer County, NJ	3.89
Prince George's County, MD	3.81
Wayne County, MI	3.81
Oakland County, MI	3.78
Cook County, IL	3.76
Hennepin County, MN	3.75
Maricopa County, AZ	3.75
Tulsa County, OK	3.75
Hartford County, CT	3.74
Franklin County, OH	3.73
Atlantic County, NJ	3.72
Alameda County, CA	3.69
Bronx County, NY	3.69
Snohomish County, WA	3.69
Essex County, NJ	3.64
Miami-Dade County, FL	3.64
Harris County, TX	3.62
Monroe County, NY	3.56
Los Angeles County, CA	3.54
Philadelphia County, PA	3.54
Riverside County, CA	3.53
Tarrant County, TX	3.52
Alexandria Independent City, VA	3.51
Camden County, NJ	3.50
Collin County, TX	3.49
New Haven County, CT	3.49
Broward County, FL	3.48
Dallas County, TX	3.41
Clayton County, GA	3.37
San Bernardino County, CA	3.28
Middlesex County, MA	3.23
Baltimore County, MD	3.22
Travis County, TX	3.18
St. Louis County, MO	3.11
Wake County, NC	3.10
Jefferson Parish, LA	3.02

Place	Number
Sacramento, CA (city) Sacramento County	5.61
Hempstead, NY (town) Nassau County	5.37
Mission Bend, TX (cdp) Fort Bend County	5.26
Dale City, VA (cdp) Prince William County	4.91
Santa Clara, CA (city) Santa Clara County	4.78
Huntington, NY (town) Suffolk County	4.72
Sugar Land, TX (city) Fort Bend County	4.58
Ellicott City, MD (cdp) Howard County	4.57
Woodbridge, NJ (township) Middlesex County	4.56
North Hempstead, NY (town) Nassau County	4.52
Jersey City, NJ (city) Hudson County	4.45
San Francisco, CA (city) San Francisco County	4.32
Stockton, CA (city) San Joaquin County	4.32
Lincolnia, VA (cdp) Fairfax County	4.24
Old Bridge, NJ (township) Middlesex County	4.24
Anaheim, CA (city) Orange County	4.19
Brookhaven, NY (town) Suffolk County	4.16
Arlington, VA (cdp) Arlington County	4.12
New York, NY (city)	4.09
Bailey's Crossroads, VA (cdp) Fairfax County	4.07
San Jose, CA (city) Santa Clara County	4.07
Carrollton, TX (city) Denton County	4.05
Skokie, IL (village) Cook County	4.04
Edison, NJ (township) Middlesex County	4.03
Torrance, CA (city) Los Angeles County	4.00
Fremont, CA (city) Alameda County	3.99
Garland, TX (city) Dallas County	3.89
Plano, TX (city) Collin County	3.78
Chicago, IL (city) Cook County	3.57
Philadelphia, PA (city) Philadelphia County	3.54
Richardson, TX (city) Dallas County	3.52
Houston, TX (city) Harris County	3.50
Tulsa, OK (city) Tulsa County	3.46
Los Angeles, CA (city) Los Angeles County	3.38
Irving, TX (city) Dallas County	3.05
Austin, TX (city) Travis County	2.94
Dallas, TX (city) Dallas County	2.83

Notes: Please refer to the User's Guide for an explanation of data; ranking tables include all places with Asian and/or NHPI populations above SF4 population thresholds; (1) tables reflect only those areas that meet SF4 population thresholds, therefore there may be less than 50 states, 75 counties or 75 places listed

Average Household Size

Samoan

All States, Top 75 Counties, and Top 75 Places Sorted by Number[1]

State	Number
Alaska	4.90
California	4.78
Utah	4.69
Hawaii	4.54
United States	4.33
Nevada	4.32
Pennsylvania	4.09
Washington	4.08
Missouri	4.07
Texas	3.84
Arizona	3.74
Colorado	3.62
New Jersey	3.39
North Carolina	3.38
Illinois	3.35
New York	3.25
Georgia	3.24
Ohio	3.19
Oregon	3.12
Virginia	2.98
Florida	2.60
Michigan	2.48
Tennessee	2.34

County	Number
San Mateo County, CA	5.58
Orange County, CA	5.46
Alameda County, CA	5.36
San Francisco County, CA	5.31
Solano County, CA	5.16
San Bernardino County, CA	5.10
San Joaquin County, CA	5.07
Ventura County, CA	5.07
Anchorage Borough, AK	5.05
Santa Clara County, CA	5.00
Utah County, UT	4.87
Salt Lake County, UT	4.84
Los Angeles County, CA	4.75
Jackson County, MO	4.65
Honolulu County, HI	4.56
San Diego County, CA	4.48
Contra Costa County, CA	4.44
Hawaii County, HI	4.31
Clark County, NV	4.26
Pierce County, WA	4.25
King County, WA	4.17
Maricopa County, AZ	4.12
Riverside County, CA	3.92
Sacramento County, CA	3.82

Place	Number
Nanakuli, HI (cdp) Honolulu County	7.26
Garden Grove, CA (city) Orange County	6.49
Compton, CA (city) Los Angeles County	6.24
Ewa Beach, HI (cdp) Honolulu County	6.13
Anaheim, CA (city) Orange County	6.09
Westminster, CA (city) Orange County	5.94
Kahuku, HI (cdp) Honolulu County	5.88
Halawa, HI (cdp) Honolulu County	5.74
Carson, CA (city) Los Angeles County	5.73
Oxnard, CA (city) Ventura County	5.71
Santa Ana, CA (city) Orange County	5.62
Laie, HI (cdp) Honolulu County	5.43
San Francisco, CA (city) San Francisco County	5.31
West Valley City, UT (city) Salt Lake County	5.28
Hayward, CA (city) Alameda County	5.26
Hauula, HI (cdp) Honolulu County	5.20
Oceanside, CA (city) San Diego County	5.18
San Diego, CA (city) San Diego County	5.12
Long Beach, CA (city) Los Angeles County	5.03
San Bernardino, CA (city) San Bernardino County	5.02
Lakewood, CA (city) Los Angeles County	4.95
Waipahu, HI (cdp) Honolulu County	4.95
San Jose, CA (city) Santa Clara County	4.93
Seattle, WA (city) King County	4.80
Lakewood, WA (city) Pierce County	4.62
Tacoma, WA (city) Pierce County	4.18
Salt Lake City, UT (city) Salt Lake County	4.16
Federal Way, WA (city) King County	4.04
Sacramento, CA (city) Sacramento County	4.03
Los Angeles, CA (city) Los Angeles County	3.92
Honolulu, HI (cdp) Honolulu County	3.73
New York, NY (city)	3.41

Notes: Please refer to the User's Guide for an explanation of data; ranking tables include all places with Asian and/or NHPI populations above SF4 population thresholds; (1) tables reflect only those areas that meet SF4 population thresholds, therefore there may be less than 50 states, 75 counties or 75 places listed

Average Household Size

Sri Lankan

All States, Top 75 Counties, and Top 75 Places Sorted by Number[1]

State	Number
Michigan	3.52
New Jersey	3.45
Washington	3.13
New York	3.12
California	3.10
Massachusetts	2.86
United States	2.86
Virginia	2.85
Illinois	2.83
Maryland	2.83
Texas	2.54
Ohio	2.52
Pennsylvania	2.52
Florida	2.23

County	Number
Richmond County, NY	3.96
Queens County, NY	3.82
Middlesex County, NJ	3.57
Orange County, CA	3.35
Los Angeles County, CA	3.19
Montgomery County, MD	3.11

Place	Number
New York, NY (city)	3.23
Los Angeles, CA (city) Los Angeles County	2.97

Notes: Please refer to the User's Guide for an explanation of data; ranking tables include all places with Asian and/or NHPI populations above SF4 population thresholds; (1) tables reflect only those areas that meet SF4 population thresholds, therefore there may be less than 50 states, 75 counties or 75 places listed

Average Household Size

Taiwanese

All States, Top 75 Counties, and Top 75 Places Sorted by Number[1]

State	Number
California	3.14
New Jersey	3.07
Hawaii	3.06
Washington	3.01
Georgia	2.97
United States	2.85
Minnesota	2.83
Texas	2.75
North Carolina	2.73
Maryland	2.72
Nevada	2.72
Connecticut	2.68
Michigan	2.64
Ohio	2.61
Florida	2.60
Arizona	2.56
New York	2.52
Utah	2.52
Louisiana	2.49
Oregon	2.45
Massachusetts	2.43
Virginia	2.38
Iowa	2.35
Illinois	2.32
Colorado	2.22
Missouri	2.17
Tennessee	2.12
Pennsylvania	2.06
Kansas	2.05
Wisconsin	1.91
Indiana	1.80
Oklahoma	1.75

County	Number
Fort Bend County, TX	3.64
Mercer County, NJ	3.60
Essex County, NJ	3.50
San Bernardino County, CA	3.50
Nassau County, NY	3.42
Ventura County, CA	3.38
Bergen County, NJ	3.29
Orange County, CA	3.25
Los Angeles County, CA	3.21
Collin County, TX	3.19
Montgomery County, MD	3.19
Somerset County, NJ	3.16
DuPage County, IL	3.12
Oakland County, MI	3.11
Middlesex County, NJ	3.10
Norfolk County, MA	3.10
Queens County, NY	3.10
Honolulu County, HI	3.09
Alameda County, CA	3.07
Riverside County, CA	3.05
Morris County, NJ	3.00
San Diego County, CA	3.00
King County, WA	2.98
Santa Clara County, CA	2.95
Suffolk County, NY	2.92
Contra Costa County, CA	2.87
Tarrant County, TX	2.85
Fairfax County, VA	2.83
Gwinnett County, GA	2.82
Dallas County, TX	2.70
San Mateo County, CA	2.69
Maricopa County, AZ	2.67
Middlesex County, MA	2.60
Franklin County, OH	2.59
Harris County, TX	2.55
Travis County, TX	2.50
Clark County, NV	2.46
St. Louis County, MO	2.46
Sacramento County, CA	2.34
San Francisco County, CA	2.34
Westchester County, NY	2.34
Washtenaw County, MI	2.15
Cook County, IL	2.00
Suffolk County, MA	1.92
Allegheny County, PA	1.82
Dane County, WI	1.75
New York County, NY	1.50

Place	Number
Walnut, CA (city) Los Angeles County	4.04
Edison, NJ (township) Middlesex County	4.02
Cypress, CA (city) Orange County	3.91
Hacienda Heights, CA (cdp) Los Angeles County	3.91
Chino Hills, CA (city) San Bernardino County	3.81
Arcadia, CA (city) Los Angeles County	3.73
Sugar Land, TX (city) Fort Bend County	3.72
West Covina, CA (city) Los Angeles County	3.67
Cerritos, CA (city) Los Angeles County	3.58
Saratoga, CA (city) Santa Clara County	3.56
Temple City, CA (city) Los Angeles County	3.56
Fremont, CA (city) Alameda County	3.46
San Marino, CA (city) Los Angeles County	3.44
Upland, CA (city) San Bernardino County	3.40
Bellevue, WA (city) King County	3.38
Fountain Valley, CA (city) Orange County	3.38
Diamond Bar, CA (city) Los Angeles County	3.37
Naperville, IL (city) Du Page County	3.36
Torrance, CA (city) Los Angeles County	3.35
Anaheim, CA (city) Orange County	3.28
North Hempstead, NY (town) Nassau County	3.28
Troy, MI (city) Oakland County	3.28
East San Gabriel, CA (cdp) Los Angeles County	3.26
Rowland Heights, CA (cdp) Los Angeles County	3.26
Plano, TX (city) Collin County	3.22
Cupertino, CA (city) Santa Clara County	3.14
Honolulu, HI (cdp) Honolulu County	3.14
Irvine, CA (city) Orange County	3.14
Huntington Beach, CA (city) Orange County	3.11
Rancho Palos Verdes, CA (city) Los Angeles County	3.09
Orange, CA (city) Orange County	3.02
Monterey Park, CA (city) Los Angeles County	3.00
San Gabriel, CA (city) Los Angeles County	2.98
San Jose, CA (city) Santa Clara County	2.95
Alhambra, CA (city) Los Angeles County	2.88
San Diego, CA (city) San Diego County	2.81
Tustin, CA (city) Orange County	2.81
Arlington, TX (city) Tarrant County	2.68
Sunnyvale, CA (city) Santa Clara County	2.58
New York, NY (city)	2.52
Seattle, WA (city) King County	2.48
Berkeley, CA (city) Alameda County	2.46
Austin, TX (city) Travis County	2.44
Houston, TX (city) Harris County	2.41
San Francisco, CA (city) San Francisco County	2.34
El Monte, CA (city) Los Angeles County	2.25
Los Angeles, CA (city) Los Angeles County	2.25
Columbus, OH (city) Franklin County	2.17
Ann Arbor, MI (city) Washtenaw County	2.13
Boston, MA (city) Suffolk County	1.92
Madison, WI (city) Dane County	1.75
Chicago, IL (city) Cook County	1.60

Notes: Please refer to the User's Guide for an explanation of data; ranking tables include all places with Asian and/or NHPI populations above SF4 population thresholds; (1) tables reflect only those areas that meet SF4 population thresholds, therefore there may be less than 50 states, 75 counties or 75 places listed

Average Household Size

Thai

All States, Top 75 Counties, and Top 75 Places Sorted by Number[1]

State	Number
Alaska	3.50
California	3.09
Arkansas	2.94
Maryland	2.79
Louisiana	2.73
New Jersey	2.72
Utah	2.66
Georgia	2.65
Nevada	2.65
Iowa	2.64
United States	2.64
Illinois	2.59
Connecticut	2.58
Hawaii	2.54
New York	2.52
North Carolina	2.52
Florida	2.51
Virginia	2.47
Colorado	2.46
Alabama	2.45
Minnesota	2.45
Oregon	2.41
Texas	2.40
Ohio	2.39
Washington	2.39
Massachusetts	2.35
New Mexico	2.34
Missouri	2.30
Tennessee	2.29
Nebraska	2.28
Indiana	2.19
Arizona	2.17
Oklahoma	2.07
Pennsylvania	2.07
Kentucky	2.03
Kansas	2.02
Michigan	1.92
South Carolina	1.87
Wisconsin	1.80

County	Number
Contra Costa County, CA	3.92
Collin County, TX	3.75
San Mateo County, CA	3.46
Anchorage Borough, AK	3.34
Los Angeles County, CA	3.28
Prince George's County, MD	3.28
Polk County, IA	3.26
Pinellas County, FL	3.24
Orange County, CA	3.21
Suffolk County, NY	3.16
Nassau County, NY	3.12
Riverside County, CA	3.09
San Bernardino County, CA	3.06
Queens County, NY	3.05
Broward County, FL	3.01
Pierce County, WA	2.98
Santa Clara County, CA	2.92
Palm Beach County, FL	2.89
Fairfax County, VA	2.87
Westchester County, NY	2.85
Montgomery County, MD	2.82
Franklin County, OH	2.78
Miami-Dade County, FL	2.72
Bergen County, NJ	2.71
Harris County, TX	2.71
Multnomah County, OR	2.64
Hillsborough County, FL	2.62
Cook County, IL	2.60
Alameda County, CA	2.58
St. Louis County, MO	2.55
Travis County, TX	2.53
Clark County, NV	2.52
Bexar County, TX	2.50
Honolulu County, HI	2.50
DuPage County, IL	2.44
Sacramento County, CA	2.44
San Diego County, CA	2.43
Dallas County, TX	2.34
Middlesex County, MA	2.32
Oklahoma County, OK	2.28
San Francisco County, CA	2.27
Tarrant County, TX	2.27
King County, WA	2.25
Maricopa County, AZ	2.23
Denver County, CO	2.09
Okaloosa County, FL	2.00
New York County, NY	1.84

Place	Number
Cerritos, CA (city) Los Angeles County	3.83
Des Moines, IA (city) Polk County	3.74
San Jose, CA (city) Santa Clara County	3.47
Anaheim, CA (city) Orange County	3.43
Bellflower, CA (city) Los Angeles County	3.22
Los Angeles, CA (city) Los Angeles County	3.14
Columbus, OH (city) Franklin County	2.96
Spring Valley, NV (cdp) Clark County	2.84
Glendale, CA (city) Los Angeles County	2.81
Long Beach, CA (city) Los Angeles County	2.72
Houston, TX (city) Harris County	2.63
Portland, OR (city) Multnomah County	2.60
New York, NY (city)	2.57
Las Vegas, NV (city) Clark County	2.41
San Diego, CA (city) San Diego County	2.38
San Antonio, TX (city) Bexar County	2.37
Chicago, IL (city) Cook County	2.30
San Francisco, CA (city) San Francisco County	2.27
Seattle, WA (city) King County	2.13
Denver, CO (city) Denver County	2.09
Honolulu, HI (cdp) Honolulu County	1.81

Notes: Please refer to the User's Guide for an explanation of data; ranking tables include all places with Asian and/or NHPI populations above SF4 population thresholds; (1) tables reflect only those areas that meet SF4 population thresholds, therefore there may be less than 50 states, 75 counties or 75 places listed

Average Household Size

Tongan

All States, Top 75 Counties, and Top 75 Places Sorted by Number[1]

State	Number
California	5.72
Utah	5.57
United States	5.31
Alaska	5.20
Hawaii	5.06
Arizona	4.77
Washington	4.73
Nevada	4.71
Texas	4.19
Oregon	4.17

County	Number
San Mateo County, CA	6.13
Sacramento County, CA	6.11
Alameda County, CA	6.10
Los Angeles County, CA	6.09
Salt Lake County, UT	5.79
Contra Costa County, CA	5.77
Washoe County, NV	5.59
San Diego County, CA	5.36
Honolulu County, HI	5.35
San Bernardino County, CA	5.32
Multnomah County, OR	4.98
Maricopa County, AZ	4.77
Maui County, HI	4.42
King County, WA	4.34
Orange County, CA	4.24
Tarrant County, TX	4.18
Utah County, UT	4.13

Place	Number
Oakland, CA (city) Alameda County	7.25
Sacramento, CA (city) Sacramento County	6.99
East Palo Alto, CA (city) San Mateo County	6.81
Laie, HI (cdp) Honolulu County	6.79
Kahuku, HI (cdp) Honolulu County	6.47
Salt Lake City, UT (city) Salt Lake County	6.34
West Valley City, UT (city) Salt Lake County	6.24
San Bruno, CA (city) San Mateo County	6.22
San Mateo, CA (city) San Mateo County	6.05
Hauula, HI (cdp) Honolulu County	5.88
West Jordan, UT (city) Salt Lake County	5.48
Los Angeles, CA (city) Los Angeles County	5.20
Honolulu, HI (cdp) Honolulu County	5.00
Portland, OR (city) Multnomah County	4.98

Notes: Please refer to the User's Guide for an explanation of data; ranking tables include all places with Asian and/or NHPI populations above SF4 population thresholds; (1) tables reflect only those areas that meet SF4 population thresholds, therefore there may be less than 50 states, 75 counties or 75 places listed

Average Household Size

Vietnamese

All States, Top 75 Counties, and Top 75 Places Sorted by Number[1]

State	Number
Nebraska	4.24
Georgia	4.11
California	3.97
Utah	3.96
Massachusetts	3.86
Vermont	3.84
New Jersey	3.78
Louisiana	3.76
Maryland	3.75
Rhode Island	3.73
Kentucky	3.72
Iowa	3.71
Kansas	3.71
New Hampshire	3.71
United States	3.70
South Dakota	3.68
Mississippi	3.67
Oregon	3.67
Colorado	3.58
Tennessee	3.58
North Carolina	3.55
Michigan	3.54
Connecticut	3.53
Pennsylvania	3.52
Texas	3.51
Illinois	3.50
Delaware	3.49
Virginia	3.49
Washington	3.44
Florida	3.42
Alabama	3.40
New York	3.40
Minnesota	3.39
Arkansas	3.38
Missouri	3.37
Arizona	3.36
Oklahoma	3.35
Alaska	3.33
Ohio	3.20
Idaho	3.17
Maine	3.13
New Mexico	3.12
West Virginia	3.09
South Carolina	3.06
Hawaii	3.04
Indiana	3.03
Wisconsin	3.00
Nevada	2.97
District of Columbia	2.70

County	Number
Hall County, GA	5.53
Matagorda County, TX	5.36
Iberia Parish, LA	5.13
Finney County, KS	4.86
Adams County, NE	4.72
Ford County, KS	4.66
Nassau County, NY	4.62
St. Bernard Parish, LA	4.60
Scott County, IA	4.57
Plymouth County, MA	4.56
Vermilion Parish, LA	4.53
St. Mary Parish, LA	4.52
Minnehaha County, SD	4.51
Clayton County, GA	4.44
Eaton County, MI	4.43
Lancaster County, NE	4.43
Prince George's County, MD	4.42
San Joaquin County, CA	4.39
Washington County, MN	4.38
Anoka County, MN	4.36
DeKalb County, GA	4.32
St. Martin Parish, LA	4.29
Sarpy County, NE	4.29
Camden County, NJ	4.27
Middlesex County, NJ	4.26
Gwinnett County, GA	4.24
Bronx County, NY	4.22
Aransas County, TX	4.21
Orange County, CA	4.20
Greene County, MO	4.18
Calhoun County, TX	4.17
Jefferson County, TX	4.15
Northampton County, PA	4.14
Woodbury County, IA	4.13
Santa Clara County, CA	4.11
Essex County, MA	4.10
Hampden County, MA	4.08
Jefferson County, KY	4.05
Fulton County, GA	4.02
San Bernardino County, CA	4.02
Polk County, FL	4.00
Cumberland County, PA	3.99
Salt Lake County, UT	3.99
Sarasota County, FL	3.99
Cobb County, GA	3.98
Norfolk County, MA	3.98
Chester County, PA	3.97
St. Tammany Parish, LA	3.97
Suffolk County, MA	3.96
Douglas County, NE	3.94
Guilford County, NC	3.94
Terrebonne Parish, LA	3.94
Orange County, TX	3.93
Fairfield County, CT	3.92
Harrison County, MS	3.92
Jefferson County, CO	3.90
Ventura County, CA	3.90
Jefferson County, AL	3.89
Clackamas County, OR	3.88
Gaston County, NC	3.88
Seminole County, FL	3.88
Stearns County, MN	3.87
Ingham County, MI	3.86
Baltimore County, MD	3.85
Chesterfield County, VA	3.85
Hillsborough County, NH	3.84
Los Angeles County, CA	3.84
Potter County, TX	3.84
Summit County, OH	3.84
Will County, IL	3.84
Dakota County, MN	3.83
Shelby County, TN	3.83
Escambia County, FL	3.82
Loudoun County, VA	3.82
Multnomah County, OR	3.82

Place	Number
Hacienda Heights, CA (cdp) Los Angeles County	7.36
Gainesville, GA (city) Hall County	6.23
Palacios, TX (city) Matagorda County	5.67
Walnut, CA (city) Los Angeles County	5.59
West Puente Valley, CA (cdp) Los Angeles County	5.56
Woodlynne, NJ (borough) Camden County	5.41
SeaTac, WA (city) King County	5.39
Garden City, KS (city) Finney County	5.34
Town 'n' Country, FL (cdp) Hillsborough County	5.26
Valinda, CA (cdp) Los Angeles County	5.15
Riverdale, GA (city) Clayton County	5.13
West Springfield, VA (cdp) Fairfax County	5.01
Amelia, LA (cdp) Saint Mary Parish	4.99
Covina, CA (city) Los Angeles County	4.92
Chamblee, GA (city) De Kalb County	4.85
Taylorsville, UT (city) Salt Lake County	4.85
San Lorenzo, CA (cdp) Alameda County	4.84
Alondra Park, CA (cdp) Los Angeles County	4.82
Chelsea, MA (city) Suffolk County	4.73
Hastings, NE (city) Adams County	4.72
Camarillo, CA (city) Ventura County	4.71
North Springfield, VA (cdp) Fairfax County	4.69
Lemon Grove, CA (city) San Diego County	4.68
Davenport, IA (city) Scott County	4.67
League City, TX (city) Galveston County	4.67
Lincolnia, VA (cdp) Fairfax County	4.67
West Valley City, UT (city) Salt Lake County	4.63
El Monte, CA (city) Los Angeles County	4.62
Florin, CA (cdp) Sacramento County	4.62
Dodge City, KS (city) Ford County	4.60
Everett, MA (city) Middlesex County	4.59
Herndon, VA (town) Fairfax County	4.59
Brockton, MA (city) Plymouth County	4.58
West Covina, CA (city) Los Angeles County	4.58
Baldwin Park, CA (city) Los Angeles County	4.57
Abbeville, LA (city) Vermilion Parish	4.56
Chino, CA (city) San Bernardino County	4.54
South San Gabriel, CA (cdp) Los Angeles County	4.54
Springfield, MA (city) Hampden County	4.54
Stockton, CA (city) San Joaquin County	4.54
Alum Rock, CA (cdp) Santa Clara County	4.53
Lynn, MA (city) Essex County	4.53
Randolph, MA (town) Norfolk County	4.53
Henderson, LA (town) Saint Martin Parish	4.52
Westminster, CO (city) Adams County	4.51
Reading, PA (city) Berks County	4.50
South El Monte, CA (city) Los Angeles County	4.50
Vallejo, CA (city) Solano County	4.50
Pearland, TX (city) Brazoria County	4.49
Doraville, GA (city) De Kalb County	4.48
Eagan, MN (city) Dakota County	4.48
Woodmere, LA (cdp) Jefferson Parish	4.48
Moreno Valley, CA (city) Riverside County	4.47
Cerritos, CA (city) Los Angeles County	4.46
Garden Grove, CA (city) Orange County	4.46
Seadrift, TX (city) Calhoun County	4.44
Sioux Falls, SD (city) Minnehaha County	4.44
Lincoln, NE (city) Lancaster County	4.43
Ontario, CA (city) San Bernardino County	4.41
Oxnard, CA (city) Ventura County	4.41
Bridgeport, CT (city) Fairfield County	4.40
Port Arthur, TX (city) Jefferson County	4.40
South Plainfield, NJ (borough) Middlesex County	4.40
Lewisville, TX (city) Denton County	4.39
Rosemead, CA (city) Los Angeles County	4.39
Springfield, MO (city) Greene County	4.39
Elk Grove, CA (cdp) Sacramento County	4.37
Overland Park, KS (city) Johnson County	4.37
Shrewsbury, MA (town) Worcester County	4.37
Pennsauken, NJ (township) Camden County	4.36
Akron, OH (city) Summit County	4.35
Chino Hills, CA (city) San Bernardino County	4.34
Fountain Valley, CA (city) Orange County	4.34
Revere, MA (city) Suffolk County	4.34
Simi Valley, CA (city) Ventura County	4.34

Notes: Please refer to the User's Guide for an explanation of data; ranking tables include all places with Asian and/or NHPI populations above SF4 population thresholds; (1) tables reflect only those areas that meet SF4 population thresholds, therefore there may be less than 50 states, 75 counties or 75 places listed

Language Spoken at Home: English Only

Total Population 5 Years and Over Who Speak English-Only at Home

All States, Top 75 Counties, and Top 75 Places Sorted by Number[1]

State	Number
United States	215,423,557
California	19,014,873
Texas	13,230,765
New York	12,786,189
Florida	11,569,739
Pennsylvania	10,583,054
Ohio	9,951,475
Illinois	9,326,786
Michigan	8,487,401
North Carolina	6,909,648
Georgia	6,843,038
Virginia	5,884,075
New Jersey	5,854,578
Indiana	5,295,736
Tennessee	5,059,404
Missouri	4,961,741
Massachusetts	4,838,679
Washington	4,730,512
Wisconsin	4,653,361
Maryland	4,322,329
Minnesota	4,201,503
Alabama	3,989,795
Louisiana	3,771,003
Kentucky	3,627,757
South Carolina	3,552,240
Arizona	3,523,487
Colorado	3,402,266
Oklahoma	2,977,187
Oregon	2,810,654
Connecticut	2,600,601
Iowa	2,578,477
Mississippi	2,545,931
Arkansas	2,368,450
Kansas	2,281,705
Utah	1,770,626
West Virginia	1,661,036
Nebraska	1,469,046
Nevada	1,425,748
Maine	1,110,198
Idaho	1,084,914
New Mexico	1,072,947
New Hampshire	1,064,252
Hawaii	832,226
Montana	803,031
Rhode Island	788,560
Delaware	662,845
South Dakota	658,245
North Dakota	565,130
Vermont	540,767
Alaska	496,982
District of Columbia	449,241
Wyoming	433,324

County	Number
Los Angeles County, CA	4,032,614
Cook County, IL	3,453,547
Maricopa County, AZ	2,148,696
Harris County, TX	1,992,143
San Diego County, CA	1,752,737
Wayne County, MI	1,703,518
Orange County, CA	1,542,698
Dallas County, TX	1,375,049
King County, WA	1,332,933
Kings County, NY	1,217,121
Philadelphia County, PA	1,168,463
Cuyahoga County, OH	1,158,729
Allegheny County, PA	1,131,112
Suffolk County, NY	1,094,244
Middlesex County, MA	1,093,227
Broward County, FL	1,083,041
Tarrant County, TX	1,040,888
San Bernardino County, CA	1,035,292
Oakland County, MI	973,064
Queens County, NY	968,415
Nassau County, NY	959,465
Riverside County, CA	957,094
Clark County, NV	942,435
Hennepin County, MN	909,793
Franklin County, OH	902,864
St. Louis County, MO	891,645
Sacramento County, CA	859,305
Santa Clara County, CA	854,337
Alameda County, CA	850,906
New York County, NY	849,603
Palm Beach County, FL	837,066
Erie County, NY	812,588
Shelby County, TN	774,966
Pinellas County, FL	771,726
Milwaukee County, WI	758,473
Hamilton County, OH	744,914
Marion County, IN	738,672
Hillsborough County, FL	736,750
Bexar County, TX	729,268
Salt Lake County, UT	685,701
Miami-Dade County, FL	676,347
DuPage County, IL	664,523
Fulton County, GA	658,421
Duval County, FL	654,825
Contra Costa County, CA	654,278
Macomb County, MI	645,489
Baltimore County, MD	641,282
New Haven County, CT	635,369
Montgomery County, PA	635,062
Fairfax County, VA	631,768
Hartford County, CT	628,513
Prince George's County, MD	625,419
Fairfield County, CT	623,417
Orange County, FL	622,997
Westchester County, NY	615,323
Jefferson County, KY	611,664
Monroe County, NY	605,172
Worcester County, MA	595,964
Jefferson County, AL	590,312
Honolulu County, HI	583,116
Bronx County, NY	578,996
Pierce County, WA	574,433
Pima County, AZ	572,101
Jackson County, MO	562,686
Baltimore Independent City, MD	562,065
Mecklenburg County, NC	560,787
Bergen County, NJ	560,343
Montgomery County, MD	556,682
Essex County, MA	544,872
Oklahoma County, OK	541,657
Travis County, TX	537,622
Norfolk County, MA	520,486
Essex County, NJ	517,923
Multnomah County, OR	515,735
Wake County, NC	511,976

Place	Number
New York, NY (city)	3,920,797
Chicago, IL (city) Cook County	1,726,905
Los Angeles, CA (city) Los Angeles County	1,438,573
Philadelphia, PA (city) Philadelphia County	1,168,463
Houston, TX (city) Harris County	1,053,207
Phoenix, AZ (city) Maricopa County	818,864
Detroit, MI (city) Wayne County	795,204
San Diego, CA (city) San Diego County	714,484
Dallas, TX (city) Dallas County	685,534
Indianapolis, IN (sp. city) Marion County	671,818
Jacksonville, FL (city) Duval County	616,988
Columbus, OH (city) Franklin County	593,275
San Antonio, TX (city) Bexar County	560,786
Memphis, TN (city) Shelby County	557,538
Hempstead, NY (town) Nassau County	547,956
Milwaukee, WI (city) Milwaukee County	462,414
Nashville-Davidson, TN (sp. city) Davidson County	457,993
Charlotte, NC (city) Mecklenburg County	430,392
Seattle, WA (city) King County	429,105
Austin, TX (city) Travis County	419,884
New Orleans, LA (city) Orleans Parish	414,214
Portland, OR (city) Multnomah County	412,928
Oklahoma City, OK (city) Oklahoma County	406,189
San Francisco, CA (city) San Francisco County	404,571
San Jose, CA (city) Santa Clara County	402,804
Cleveland, OH (city) Cuyahoga County	387,438
Denver, CO (city) Denver County	377,881
Boston, MA (city) Suffolk County	371,185
Kansas City, MO (city) Jackson County	370,142
Brookhaven, NY (town) Suffolk County	357,084
Atlanta, GA (city) Fulton County	347,775
Fort Worth, TX (city) Tarrant County	347,721
Tulsa, OK (city) Tulsa County	328,638
Omaha, NE (city) Douglas County	324,359
Las Vegas, NV (city) Clark County	323,798
Tucson, AZ (city) Pima County	304,940
Albuquerque, NM (city) Bernalillo County	301,429
St. Louis, MO (city) Saint Louis Independent City	296,924
Mesa, AZ (city) Maricopa County	296,298
Colorado Springs, CO (city) El Paso County	294,745
Minneapolis, MN (city) Hennepin County	288,932
Pittsburgh, PA (city) Allegheny County	287,641
Cincinnati, OH (city) Hamilton County	286,454
Wichita, KS (city) Sedgwick County	276,098
Toledo, OH (city) Lucas County	269,728
Sacramento, CA (city) Sacramento County	255,173
Buffalo, NY (city) Erie County	238,127
Long Beach, CA (city) Los Angeles County	236,221
Fresno, CA (city) Fresno County	235,220
Oakland, CA (city) Alameda County	234,737
Arlington, TX (city) Tarrant County	231,505
Oyster Bay, NY (town) Nassau County	228,112
Islip, NY (town) Suffolk County	227,229
Honolulu, HI (cdp) Honolulu County	226,630
Louisville, KY (city) Jefferson County	224,665
Lexington-Fayette, KY (sp. city) Fayette County	224,074
Raleigh, NC (city) Wake County	220,724
Tampa, FL (city) Hillsborough County	218,362
Birmingham, AL (city) Jefferson County	216,010
St. Paul, MN (city) Ramsey County	207,592
St. Petersburg, FL (city) Pinellas County	206,489
Aurora, CO (city) Arapahoe County	196,319
Baton Rouge, LA (city) East Baton Rouge Parish	193,774
Lincoln, NE (city) Lancaster County	190,802
Akron, OH (city) Summit County	189,917
Greensboro, NC (city) Guilford County	186,042
Montgomery, AL (city) Montgomery County	179,716
Shreveport, LA (city) Caddo Parish	178,714
Mobile, AL (city) Mobile County	174,361
Fort Wayne, IN (city) Allen County	173,752
Madison, WI (city) Dane County	171,925
Scottsdale, AZ (city) Maricopa County	170,555
Augusta-Richmond Co., GA (sp. city) Richmond Co.	169,245
Spokane, WA (city) Spokane County	168,044
Rochester, NY (city) Monroe County	166,643

Notes: Please refer to the User's Guide for an explanation of data; ranking tables include all places with Asian and/or NHPI populations above SF4 population thresholds; (1) tables reflect only those areas that meet SF4 population thresholds, therefore there may be less than 50 states, 75 counties or 75 places listed

Language Spoken at Home: English Only

Total Population 5 Years and Over Who Speak English-Only at Home

All States, Top 75 Counties, and Top 75 Places Sorted by Percent[1]

State	Percent
West Virginia	97.31
Mississippi	96.38
Alabama	96.09
Kentucky	96.07
Tennessee	95.17
Arkansas	95.03
Missouri	94.94
Montana	94.77
South Carolina	94.76
Iowa	94.16
Vermont	94.07
Ohio	93.88
North Dakota	93.70
Wyoming	93.63
Indiana	93.60
South Dakota	93.52
Wisconsin	92.66
Oklahoma	92.58
Maine	92.20
Nebraska	92.12
North Carolina	91.97
New Hampshire	91.72
Pennsylvania	91.58
Michigan	91.57
Minnesota	91.51
Kansas	91.26
Louisiana	90.79
Idaho	90.65
Delaware	90.51
Georgia	90.11
Virginia	88.89
Oregon	87.85
Utah	87.49
Maryland	87.41
Washington	85.99
Alaska	85.72
Colorado	84.92
District of Columbia	83.25
United States	82.11
Connecticut	81.66
Massachusetts	81.26
Illinois	80.77
Rhode Island	80.04
Florida	76.91
Nevada	76.91
New Jersey	74.52
Arizona	74.14
Hawaii	73.37
New York	72.04
Texas	68.76
New Mexico	63.49
California	60.52

County	Percent
Wood County, WV	98.06
Fayette County, WV	97.96
Putnam County, WV	97.75
Sullivan County, TN	97.69
Clearfield County, PA	97.47
Franklin County, MO	97.44
Tazewell County, IL	97.36
Clarion County, PA	97.35
Howell County, MO	97.35
Stevens County, WA	97.32
Cabell County, WV	97.25
Allegany County, MD	97.24
Bedford County, VA	97.24
Bradford County, PA	97.24
Halifax County, NC	97.24
Miami County, OH	97.11
Jefferson County, MO	97.08
Hendricks County, IN	97.07
Wilson County, TN	97.06
Houston County, AL	97.04
Licking County, OH	97.03
Ouachita Parish, LA	96.98
Clark County, OH	96.97
Etowah County, AL	96.97
Chippewa County, WI	96.96
Harrison County, WV	96.95
Marion County, OH	96.94
Saline County, AR	96.94
Butler County, PA	96.93
Blair County, PA	96.92
Madison County, IN	96.92
St. Croix County, WI	96.91
Clermont County, OH	96.89
Kanawha County, WV	96.88
Clark County, IN	96.86
Crow Wing County, MN	96.86
Campbell County, KY	96.83
Jessamine County, KY	96.83
Columbia County, PA	96.82
Cass County, MO	96.80
Goodhue County, MN	96.80
Wright County, MN	96.80
Blount County, TN	96.77
Washington County, MD	96.76
Fairfield County, OH	96.73
Macon County, IL	96.72
Madison County, IL	96.70
Anderson County, SC	96.69
Cape Girardeau County, MO	96.69
Lycoming County, PA	96.68
Shawano County, WI	96.63
Franklin County, TN	96.61
Jefferson County, AR	96.60
Washington County, TN	96.60
Allen County, OH	96.59
Hinds County, MS	96.54
Calhoun County, AL	96.53
Catoosa County, GA	96.52
Delaware County, IN	96.52
Flathead County, MT	96.52
Johnson County, IN	96.49
Chisago County, MN	96.48
Dorchester County, MD	96.47
Kenton County, KY	96.47
Columbiana County, OH	96.46
Madison County, KY	96.46
Hancock County, ME	96.42
Weakley County, TN	96.41
Anderson County, TN	96.40
Newton County, MO	96.40
Pittsburg County, OK	96.39
Sangamon County, IL	96.39
Washington County, PA	96.39
Ohio County, WV	96.37
DeSoto County, MS	96.36

Place	Percent
Monroe, LA (city) Ouachita Parish	96.94
Huntington, WV (city) Cabell County	96.61
Bartlett, TN (city) Shelby County	96.58
Macon, GA (city) Bibb County	96.48
Decatur, IL (city) Macon County	96.38
O'Fallon, MO (city) Saint Charles County	96.30
Blue Springs, MO (city) Jackson County	96.29
Plainfield, MI (township) Kent County	96.27
Jackson, MS (city) Hinds County	96.22
Evansville, IN (city) Vanderburgh County	96.20
St. Peters, MO (city) Saint Charles County	96.08
Ashwaubenon, WI (village) Brown County	95.94
Shreveport, LA (city) Caddo Parish	95.94
Springfield, IL (city) Sangamon County	95.92
Lee's Summit, MO (city) Jackson County	95.90
Montgomery, AL (city) Montgomery County	95.84
Muncie, IN (city) Delaware County	95.84
Cape Girardeau, MO (city) Cape Girardeau County	95.76
Raytown, MO (city) Jackson County	95.67
Dayton, OH (city) Montgomery County	95.64
Albany, GA (city) Dougherty County	95.63
Terre Haute, IN (city) Vigo County	95.59
Flint, MI (city) Genesee County	95.57
Alexandria, LA (city) Rapides Parish	95.41
Marshfield, WI (city) Wood County	95.41
Lakeville, MN (city) Dakota County	95.39
Kettering, OH (city) Montgomery County	95.35
Birmingham, AL (city) Jefferson County	95.31
Johnson City, TN (city) Washington County	95.27
Westerville, OH (city) Franklin County	95.27
Lewisville, NC (town) Forsyth County	95.26
Cuyahoga Falls, OH (city) Summit County	95.23
Wildwood, MO (city) Saint Louis County	95.22
Janesville, WI (city) Rock County	95.17
Springfield, MO (city) Greene County	95.14
Ensley, FL (cdp) Escambia County	95.13
Great Falls, MT (city) Cascade County	95.12
Independence, MO (city) Jackson County	95.05
North Fayette, PA (township) Allegheny County	95.00
St. Charles, MO (city) Saint Charles County	94.98
Bethel Park, PA (borough) Allegheny County	94.96
Del City, OK (city) Oklahoma County	94.96
Joplin, MO (city) Jasper County	94.92
Cascade, MI (township) Kent County	94.85
Hazelwood, MO (city) Saint Louis County	94.84
Riverside, OH (city) Montgomery County	94.83
Gulfport, MS (city) Harrison County	94.79
Elizabethtown, KY (city) Hardin County	94.78
Millcreek, PA (township) Erie County	94.78
Billings, MT (city) Yellowstone County	94.76
White Bear Lake, MN (city) Ramsey County	94.73
Knoxville, TN (city) Knox County	94.71
Sylvania, OH (city) Lucas County	94.71
Tuscaloosa, AL (city) Tuscaloosa County	94.71
Mentor, OH (city) Lake County	94.70
Medford, NJ (township) Burlington County	94.68
Findlay, OH (city) Hancock County	94.67
Bettendorf, IA (city) Scott County	94.66
Charleston, WV (city) Kanawha County	94.66
Dundalk, MD (cdp) Baltimore County	94.64
Blaine, MN (city) Anoka County	94.61
Maryville, TN (city) Blount County	94.61
Bangor, ME (city) Penobscot County	94.59
Coon Rapids, MN (city) Anoka County	94.59
Yukon, OK (city) Canadian County	94.57
Mobile, AL (city) Mobile County	94.56
Cedar Falls, IA (city) Black Hawk County	94.55
Onalaska, WI (city) La Crosse County	94.55
Missoula, MT (city) Missoula County	94.53
Council Bluffs, IA (city) Pottawattamie County	94.51
Parker, CO (town) Douglas County	94.51
Duluth, MN (city) Saint Louis County	94.49
Farragut, TN (town) Knox County	94.48
Rapid City, SD (city) Pennington County	94.46
Leawood, KS (city) Johnson County	94.45

Notes: Please refer to the User's Guide for an explanation of data; ranking tables include all places with Asian and/or NHPI populations above SF4 population thresholds; (1) tables reflect only those areas that meet SF4 population thresholds, therefore there may be less than 50 states, 75 counties or 75 places listed

Language Spoken at Home: English Only

Asians 5 Years and Over Who Speak English-Only at Home

All States, Top 75 Counties, and Top 75 Places Sorted by Number[1]

State	Number
United States	2,003,642
California	690,135
Hawaii	271,577
New York	156,745
Texas	76,530
Washington	75,843
Illinois	69,142
Florida	65,032
New Jersey	63,808
Virginia	44,004
Maryland	36,143
Massachusetts	35,268
Pennsylvania	34,784
Michigan	31,322
Ohio	25,401
Colorado	24,492
Oregon	22,860
Georgia	22,532
Arizona	22,474
Minnesota	22,211
Nevada	21,862
North Carolina	19,121
Connecticut	15,354
Wisconsin	13,053
Missouri	12,766
Indiana	12,639
Utah	9,611
Tennessee	9,340
Oklahoma	8,026
Louisiana	7,835
South Carolina	7,348
Kansas	6,875
Iowa	6,741
Alabama	5,650
Alaska	5,530
Kentucky	5,294
New Mexico	5,119
District of Columbia	4,267
Idaho	4,254
Nebraska	4,210
Arkansas	3,788
New Hampshire	3,371
Rhode Island	3,135
Mississippi	3,095
Delaware	3,037
West Virginia	2,593
Maine	2,484
Montana	2,058
South Dakota	1,402
Vermont	1,314
Wyoming	1,109
North Dakota	1,058

County	Number
Honolulu County, HI	215,686
Los Angeles County, CA	190,202
Santa Clara County, CA	66,873
Orange County, CA	58,819
San Diego County, CA	57,934
Queens County, NY	51,887
Alameda County, CA	51,624
King County, WA	42,075
Cook County, IL	39,337
San Francisco County, CA	38,722
San Mateo County, CA	32,677
Sacramento County, CA	30,174
Contra Costa County, CA	27,177
New York County, NY	24,964
Hawaii County, HI	24,399
Harris County, TX	18,894
Maui County, HI	18,673
Kings County, NY	18,266
Clark County, NV	17,278
San Bernardino County, CA	16,911
Maricopa County, AZ	15,583
Fairfax County, VA	14,947
Solano County, CA	14,309
Riverside County, CA	13,490
Middlesex County, MA	13,371
Montgomery County, MD	13,208
San Joaquin County, CA	12,915
Kauai County, HI	12,804
Broward County, FL	11,197
DuPage County, IL	11,113
Middlesex County, NJ	10,985
Fresno County, CA	10,718
Ventura County, CA	10,713
Nassau County, NY	10,684
Dallas County, TX	10,336
Bronx County, NY	9,401
Bergen County, NJ	9,041
Hennepin County, MN	8,889
Pierce County, WA	8,042
Philadelphia County, PA	7,812
Miami-Dade County, FL	7,409
Monterey County, CA	7,331
Hudson County, NJ	7,195
Multnomah County, OR	7,126
Oakland County, MI	7,118
Snohomish County, WA	7,108
Suffolk County, MA	7,009
Westchester County, NY	6,856
Suffolk County, NY	6,635
Orange County, FL	6,439
Tarrant County, TX	6,310
Travis County, TX	6,019
Bexar County, TX	5,826
Essex County, NJ	5,800
Virginia Beach Independent City, VA	5,539
Washington County, OR	5,447
Prince George's County, MD	5,445
Santa Barbara County, CA	5,280
Fairfield County, CT	5,205
Kern County, CA	5,104
Norfolk County, MA	5,072
Franklin County, OH	5,004
Salt Lake County, UT	4,979
Duval County, FL	4,871
Hillsborough County, FL	4,820
Lake County, IL	4,783
Wayne County, MI	4,584
Fort Bend County, TX	4,463
Pima County, AZ	4,446
Cuyahoga County, OH	4,405
Monmouth County, NJ	4,387
Yolo County, CA	4,303
Baltimore County, MD	4,266
Morris County, NJ	4,222
Allegheny County, PA	4,214

Place	Number
New York, NY (city)	107,879
Honolulu, HI (cdp) Honolulu County	101,064
Los Angeles, CA (city) Los Angeles County	63,722
San Francisco, CA (city) San Francisco County	38,722
San Diego, CA (city) San Diego County	34,354
San Jose, CA (city) Santa Clara County	32,844
Chicago, IL (city) Cook County	20,070
Seattle, WA (city) King County	17,555
Sacramento, CA (city) Sacramento County	14,448
Hilo, HI (cdp) Hawaii County	11,169
Pearl City, HI (cdp) Honolulu County	10,997
Waimalu, HI (cdp) Honolulu County	10,717
Kaneohe, HI (cdp) Honolulu County	10,525
Torrance, CA (city) Los Angeles County	10,339
Fremont, CA (city) Alameda County	10,017
Houston, TX (city) Harris County	9,852
Mililani Town, HI (cdp) Honolulu County	9,694
Daly City, CA (city) San Mateo County	9,662
Long Beach, CA (city) Los Angeles County	9,468
Oakland, CA (city) Alameda County	8,587
Waipahu, HI (cdp) Honolulu County	8,208
Philadelphia, PA (city) Philadelphia County	7,812
Stockton, CA (city) San Joaquin County	7,753
Irvine, CA (city) Orange County	7,575
Vallejo, CA (city) Solano County	6,994
Boston, MA (city) Suffolk County	6,601
Fresno, CA (city) Fresno County	6,573
Sunnyvale, CA (city) Santa Clara County	6,479
Portland, OR (city) Multnomah County	6,043
Las Vegas, NV (city) Clark County	5,847
Phoenix, AZ (city) Maricopa County	5,775
Kailua, HI (cdp) Honolulu County	5,733
Chula Vista, CA (city) San Diego County	5,532
Berkeley, CA (city) Alameda County	5,331
Austin, TX (city) Travis County	5,237
Anaheim, CA (city) Orange County	5,095
Hempstead, NY (town) Nassau County	5,030
Cerritos, CA (city) Los Angeles County	4,922
Kahului, HI (cdp) Maui County	4,815
Hayward, CA (city) Alameda County	4,789
Jersey City, NJ (city) Hudson County	4,788
Gardena, CA (city) Los Angeles County	4,766
Monterey Park, CA (city) Los Angeles County	4,739
Santa Clara, CA (city) Santa Clara County	4,722
Jacksonville, FL (city) Duval County	4,610
Union City, CA (city) Alameda County	4,557
Huntington Beach, CA (city) Orange County	4,454
Glendale, CA (city) Los Angeles County	4,418
San Antonio, TX (city) Bexar County	4,415
Carson, CA (city) Los Angeles County	4,269
South San Francisco, CA (city) San Mateo County	4,202
Waipio, HI (cdp) Honolulu County	4,195
Wahiawa, HI (cdp) Honolulu County	4,180
Halawa, HI (cdp) Honolulu County	4,029
Milpitas, CA (city) Santa Clara County	4,014
Dallas, TX (city) Dallas County	3,911
Denver, CO (city) Denver County	3,565
San Mateo, CA (city) San Mateo County	3,564
Alameda, CA (city) Alameda County	3,551
Columbus, OH (city) Franklin County	3,508
Bellevue, WA (city) King County	3,482
West Covina, CA (city) Los Angeles County	3,429
Mountain View, CA (city) Santa Clara County	3,376
Pasadena, CA (city) Los Angeles County	3,361
Aiea, HI (cdp) Honolulu County	3,353
Minneapolis, MN (city) Hennepin County	3,284
Riverside, CA (city) Riverside County	3,261
Wailuku, HI (cdp) Maui County	3,225
Davis, CA (city) Yolo County	3,189
Garden Grove, CA (city) Orange County	3,171
Fairfield, CA (city) Solano County	3,156
Alhambra, CA (city) Los Angeles County	3,095
Arlington, VA (cdp) Arlington County	3,075
North Hempstead, NY (town) Nassau County	3,039
Cupertino, CA (city) Santa Clara County	3,013

Notes: Please refer to the User's Guide for an explanation of data; ranking tables include all places with Asian and/or NHPI populations above SF4 population thresholds; (1) tables reflect only those areas that meet SF4 population thresholds, therefore there may be less than 50 states, 75 counties or 75 places listed

Language Spoken at Home: English Only

Asians 5 Years and Over Who Speak English-Only at Home

All States, Top 75 Counties, and Top 75 Places Sorted by Percent[1]

State	Percent
Hawaii	56.16
Montana	50.06
Idaho	39.92
Wyoming	39.49
North Dakota	33.61
South Dakota	33.03
Maine	32.91
New Mexico	30.44
District of Columbia	30.36
Vermont	30.35
West Virginia	29.37
Colorado	28.28
Utah	28.13
Arizona	26.43
Florida	26.19
Nevada	25.92
Washington	25.17
Oregon	24.83
Indiana	23.84
New Hampshire	23.78
Alaska	23.21
Missouri	22.83
South Carolina	21.60
Nebraska	21.55
Arkansas	21.32
United States	21.05
Iowa	20.91
Ohio	20.75
Delaware	20.45
Alabama	20.39
Connecticut	20.26
California	19.90
Kentucky	19.76
Michigan	19.49
Oklahoma	18.82
Mississippi	18.71
North Carolina	18.66
Tennessee	18.63
Maryland	18.44
Virginia	18.36
Minnesota	17.67
Illinois	17.51
Wisconsin	17.40
Pennsylvania	17.32
Kansas	16.63
New York	15.99
Massachusetts	15.95
Louisiana	15.24
Texas	14.84
New Jersey	14.33
Rhode Island	14.13
Georgia	14.11

County	Percent
Wright County, MN	76.80
Yellowstone County, MT	64.21
Hawaii County, HI	63.66
Kauai County, HI	63.52
Columbia County, OR	63.35
Stevens County, WA	63.13
Nevada County, CA	62.57
Malheur County, OR	62.31
Oxford County, ME	59.92
Natrona County, WY	59.10
Douglas County, NV	58.63
Flathead County, MT	57.33
Josephine County, OR	57.00
Rutland County, VT	56.83
Grant County, WA	56.59
Honolulu County, HI	55.59
Shawano County, WI	55.56
Etowah County, AL	55.52
Klamath County, OR	54.94
Bonneville County, ID	54.70
Chippewa County, MI	54.68
Kootenai County, ID	54.53
Ionia County, MI	54.29
Ward County, ND	53.33
Weld County, CO	53.22
Matanuska-Susitna Borough, AK	52.99
Monroe County, WI	52.79
Clatsop County, OR	51.81
Marquette County, MI	51.31
Oldham County, KY	51.05
Lewis County, WA	50.71
Nassau County, FL	50.62
Maui County, HI	50.34
Geauga County, OH	49.45
Crow Wing County, MN	49.00
Putnam County, WV	48.98
Douglas County, OR	48.90
San Benito County, CA	48.86
Blaine County, ID	47.98
Tuolumne County, CA	47.84
Washington County, UT	47.82
Tehama County, CA	47.77
Jackson County, OR	47.76
Box Elder County, UT	47.34
McLeod County, MN	47.09
Elko County, NV	47.08
Clallam County, WA	47.05
Gallatin County, MT	46.98
Addison County, VT	46.83
Bradford County, PA	46.77
Wood County, WV	46.76
Wayne County, NY	46.48
Penobscot County, ME	45.96
Ashtabula County, OH	45.74
Goodhue County, MN	45.68
Washington County, WI	45.68
Chenango County, NY	45.24
Johnston County, NC	45.06
St. Croix County, WI	44.63
Yamhill County, OR	44.43
Elmore County, ID	44.02
LaPorte County, IN	43.84
Muskegon County, MI	43.83
Warren County, NY	43.68
Placer County, CA	43.26
Collier County, FL	43.09
Madison County, IN	42.68
Sherburne County, MN	42.61
Cascade County, MT	42.59
Ontario County, NY	42.45
Kendall County, IL	42.20
Sauk County, WI	41.88
Davis County, UT	41.79
Jackson County, OK	41.76
Pike County, PA	41.75

Place	Percent
South Miami Heights, FL (cdp) Miami-Dade County	95.38
Kaaawa, HI (cdp) Honolulu County	88.98
Poipu, HI (cdp) Kauai County	88.02
Ahuimanu, HI (cdp) Honolulu County	86.80
Maunawili, HI (cdp) Honolulu County	84.03
Heeia, HI (cdp) Honolulu County	83.03
Anahola, HI (cdp) Kauai County	82.68
Lawai, HI (cdp) Kauai County	82.22
Kalaheo, HI (cdp) Kauai County	80.86
Kaneohe, HI (cdp) Honolulu County	78.42
Mokuleia, HI (cdp) Honolulu County	77.49
Volcano, HI (cdp) Hawaii County	77.18
Haiku-Pauwela, HI (cdp) Maui County	76.81
Lihue, HI (cdp) Kauai County	76.03
Mililani Town, HI (cdp) Honolulu County	76.03
Pukalani, HI (cdp) Maui County	75.57
Waimea, HI (cdp) Kauai County	75.38
Honaunau-Napoopoo, HI (cdp) Hawaii County	75.32
Wailua Homesteads, HI (cdp) Kauai County	75.31
Kailua, HI (cdp) Honolulu County	75.27
Hilo, HI (cdp) Hawaii County	75.04
Wailua, HI (cdp) Kauai County	73.88
Waimanalo Beach, HI (cdp) Honolulu County	70.85
Kapaa, HI (cdp) Kauai County	70.59
Pupukea, HI (cdp) Honolulu County	70.43
Pakala Village, HI (cdp) Kauai County	70.27
Kalaoa, HI (cdp) Hawaii County	70.12
Waikapu, HI (cdp) Maui County	70.11
Waimalu, HI (cdp) Honolulu County	70.11
Captain Cook, HI (cdp) Hawaii County	69.15
Makaha, HI (cdp) Honolulu County	68.49
Hawaiian Beaches, HI (cdp) Hawaii County	68.40
Aiea, HI (cdp) Honolulu County	67.68
Kealakekua, HI (cdp) Hawaii County	67.41
Waipio, HI (cdp) Honolulu County	67.29
Oro Valley, AZ (town) Pima County	67.15
Pearl City, HI (cdp) Honolulu County	67.09
Hauula, HI (cdp) Honolulu County	66.78
Kapaau, HI (cdp) Hawaii County	66.77
Laupahoehoe, HI (cdp) Hawaii County	66.30
Wailuku, HI (cdp) Maui County	66.19
Makawao, HI (cdp) Maui County	63.70
Kurtistown, HI (cdp) Hawaii County	63.54
Kahaluu, HI (cdp) Honolulu County	63.49
Hanapepe, HI (cdp) Kauai County	63.44
Paauilo, HI (cdp) Hawaii County	62.78
Hawi, HI (cdp) Hawaii County	62.60
Nanakuli, HI (cdp) Honolulu County	62.23
Makakilo City, HI (cdp) Honolulu County	61.35
Paukaa, HI (cdp) Hawaii County	60.94
Honalo, HI (cdp) Hawaii County	60.55
Koloa, HI (cdp) Kauai County	60.30
Mountain View, HI (cdp) Hawaii County	60.15
Honomu, HI (cdp) Hawaii County	60.00
Wahiawa, HI (cdp) Honolulu County	59.95
Alamo, CA (cdp) Contra Costa County	59.69
Waimea, HI (cdp) Hawaii County	59.19
Country Club, CA (cdp) San Joaquin County	58.68
Waipio Acres, HI (cdp) Honolulu County	58.50
Billings, MT (city) Yellowstone County	58.28
Halawa, HI (cdp) Honolulu County	58.15
Tamalpais-Homestead Valley, CA (cdp) Marin County	57.73
Papaikou, HI (cdp) Hawaii County	57.48
Manhattan Beach, CA (city) Los Angeles County	57.26
Clayton, CA (city) Contra Costa County	57.14
Sierra Madre, CA (city) Los Angeles County	56.70
Hermosa Beach, CA (city) Los Angeles County	55.87
Fallbrook, CA (cdp) San Diego County	55.43
Pepeekeo, HI (cdp) Hawaii County	55.27
Kailua, HI (cdp) Hawaii County	55.06
Arroyo Grande, CA (city) San Luis Obispo County	54.61
Waianae, HI (cdp) Honolulu County	54.08
Waikoloa Village, HI (cdp) Hawaii County	53.84
Ewa Gentry, HI (cdp) Honolulu County	53.74
Dana Point, CA (city) Orange County	53.67

Notes: Please refer to the User's Guide for an explanation of data; ranking tables include all places with Asian and/or NHPI populations above SF4 population thresholds; (1) tables reflect only those areas that meet SF4 population thresholds, therefore there may be less than 50 states, 75 counties or 75 places listed

Language Spoken at Home: English Only

Native Hawaiian and Other Pacific Islanders 5 Years and Over Who Speak English-Only at Home

All States, Top 75 Counties, and Top 75 Places Sorted by Number[1]

State	Number
United States	195,395
Hawaii	72,432
California	46,002
Washington	10,202
Texas	5,833
Nevada	4,553
Utah	4,449
Oregon	3,964
New York	3,913
Florida	3,558
Arizona	3,251
Colorado	2,821
Pennsylvania	2,176
Virginia	2,103
North Carolina	2,060
Illinois	1,950
Georgia	1,781
Missouri	1,758
Ohio	1,664
Michigan	1,529
New Jersey	1,216
Maryland	1,202
Indiana	1,159
Tennessee	1,159
Alaska	1,110
Oklahoma	1,055
Minnesota	981
Wisconsin	915
Massachusetts	911
Louisiana	870
Connecticut	840
Idaho	774
New Mexico	742
South Carolina	738
Kansas	715
Alabama	667
Kentucky	589
Iowa	581
Mississippi	496
Arkansas	469
Nebraska	299
Montana	290
West Virginia	209
Delaware	161
Maine	161
Rhode Island	146

County	Number
Honolulu County, HI	48,066
Hawaii County, HI	10,949
Los Angeles County, CA	9,757
Maui County, HI	9,468
San Diego County, CA	7,227
Kauai County, HI	3,890
Orange County, CA	3,812
Clark County, NV	3,796
King County, WA	3,178
Alameda County, CA	3,139
Santa Clara County, CA	2,694
Salt Lake County, UT	2,357
Pierce County, WA	2,213
San Mateo County, CA	1,970
Sacramento County, CA	1,868
Maricopa County, AZ	1,773
Riverside County, CA	1,760
Solano County, CA	1,623
San Bernardino County, CA	1,566
Contra Costa County, CA	1,365
Monterey County, CA	1,144
Multnomah County, OR	1,080
San Francisco County, CA	1,079
Kitsap County, WA	936
Utah County, UT	855
San Joaquin County, CA	853
El Paso County, CO	840
Snohomish County, WA	834
Ventura County, CA	824
Washington County, OR	804
Queens County, NY	791
Anchorage Borough, AK	696
Pima County, AZ	695
Thurston County, WA	685
Bell County, TX	680
Harris County, TX	664
Bexar County, TX	613
Clark County, WA	585
Cook County, IL	585
Tarrant County, TX	582
Kings County, NY	569
Santa Barbara County, CA	547
Davis County, UT	512
Washoe County, NV	493
Kern County, CA	485
Jackson County, MO	482
Stanislaus County, CA	464
Clackamas County, OR	452
Hillsborough County, FL	433
Dallas County, TX	426
Allegheny County, PA	406
Spokane County, WA	405
Fairfax County, VA	400
Broward County, FL	390
Bronx County, NY	380
Philadelphia County, PA	360
Fresno County, CA	354
Bernalillo County, NM	335
Sonoma County, CA	325
Denver County, CO	322
Orange County, FL	315
Jefferson County, CO	311
Travis County, TX	310
Cumberland County, NC	309
Arapahoe County, CO	303
Suffolk County, NY	277
Washington County, UT	272
Lane County, OR	269
Wayne County, MI	268
Marion County, OR	265
Miami-Dade County, FL	264
Shelby County, TN	264
Duval County, FL	260
Essex County, NJ	257
El Paso County, TX	252

Place	Number
Honolulu, HI (cdp) Honolulu County	13,980
San Diego, CA (city) San Diego County	3,512
Hilo, HI (cdp) Hawaii County	3,289
Kaneohe, HI (cdp) Honolulu County	2,976
Los Angeles, CA (city) Los Angeles County	2,772
Nanakuli, HI (cdp) Honolulu County	2,677
New York, NY (city)	2,120
Kailua, HI (cdp) Honolulu County	2,070
Waianae, HI (cdp) Honolulu County	1,968
Waimanalo Beach, HI (cdp) Honolulu County	1,811
Waipahu, HI (cdp) Honolulu County	1,651
San Jose, CA (city) Santa Clara County	1,334
Maili, HI (cdp) Honolulu County	1,314
Long Beach, CA (city) Los Angeles County	1,284
Makaha, HI (cdp) Honolulu County	1,207
Kahului, HI (cdp) Maui County	1,197
Pearl City, HI (cdp) Honolulu County	1,193
Wailuku, HI (cdp) Maui County	1,087
San Francisco, CA (city) San Francisco County	1,079
Ewa Beach, HI (cdp) Honolulu County	1,071
Waimalu, HI (cdp) Honolulu County	1,041
Las Vegas, NV (city) Clark County	1,026
Wahiawa, HI (cdp) Honolulu County	1,020
Makakilo City, HI (cdp) Honolulu County	951
Seattle, WA (city) King County	935
Kailua, HI (cdp) Hawaii County	907
Halawa, HI (cdp) Honolulu County	881
Sacramento, CA (city) Sacramento County	866
Mililani Town, HI (cdp) Honolulu County	842
Portland, OR (city) Multnomah County	827
West Valley City, UT (city) Salt Lake County	796
Hauula, HI (cdp) Honolulu County	776
Oceanside, CA (city) San Diego County	764
Waimea, HI (cdp) Hawaii County	759
Anahola, HI (cdp) Kauai County	758
Phoenix, AZ (city) Maricopa County	755
Ahuimanu, HI (cdp) Honolulu County	754
Waihee-Waiehu, HI (cdp) Maui County	745
Kihei, HI (cdp) Maui County	742
Laie, HI (cdp) Honolulu County	717
Waimanalo, HI (cdp) Honolulu County	698
Kualapuu, HI (cdp) Maui County	662
Kapaa, HI (cdp) Kauai County	659
Salt Lake City, UT (city) Salt Lake County	641
Kaunakakai, HI (cdp) Maui County	622
Lahaina, HI (cdp) Maui County	605
Carson, CA (city) Los Angeles County	586
Hayward, CA (city) Alameda County	586
Killeen, TX (city) Bell County	571
Tacoma, WA (city) Pierce County	568
Kalaoa, HI (cdp) Hawaii County	565
Vallejo, CA (city) Solano County	565
Santa Ana, CA (city) Orange County	562
Oakland, CA (city) Alameda County	558
Colorado Springs, CO (city) El Paso County	541
Henderson, NV (city) Clark County	540
Stockton, CA (city) San Joaquin County	536
Paradise, NV (cdp) Clark County	530
Fairfield, CA (city) Solano County	508
Kahaluu, HI (cdp) Honolulu County	495
Makawao, HI (cdp) Maui County	482
Riverside, CA (city) Riverside County	450
Federal Way, WA (city) King County	436
Anaheim, CA (city) Orange County	432
Tucson, AZ (city) Pima County	431
Hawaiian Paradise Park, HI (cdp) Hawaii County	418
Chula Vista, CA (city) San Diego County	415
Alameda, CA (city) Alameda County	408
North Las Vegas, NV (city) Clark County	407
Spring Valley, NV (cdp) Clark County	406
Waipio, HI (cdp) Honolulu County	402
Provo, UT (city) Utah County	394
Fremont, CA (city) Alameda County	392
San Antonio, TX (city) Bexar County	366
Philadelphia, PA (city) Philadelphia County	360

Notes: Please refer to the User's Guide for an explanation of data; ranking tables include all places with Asian and/or NHPI populations above SF4 population thresholds; (1) tables reflect only those areas that meet SF4 population thresholds, therefore there may be less than 50 states, 75 counties or 75 places listed

Language Spoken at Home: English Only

Native Hawaiian and Other Pacific Islanders 5 Years and Over Who Speak English-Only at Home

All States, Top 75 Counties, and Top 75 Places Sorted by Percent[1]

State	Percent
Mississippi	78.86
Montana	72.14
Colorado	70.83
Ohio	70.57
Indiana	70.16
Hawaii	70.04
Idaho	68.19
Louisiana	68.18
Connecticut	67.42
Iowa	64.77
Pennsylvania	64.59
Wisconsin	64.53
New Mexico	64.47
Maryland	63.10
Nevada	63.10
Virginia	63.06
Oklahoma	62.50
Kansas	62.34
Michigan	62.18
Missouri	62.03
North Carolina	60.61
Tennessee	60.36
Alabama	59.98
Minnesota	58.92
Maine	58.33
Arizona	57.36
West Virginia	57.10
United States	56.24
Oregon	55.99
Florida	55.46
Kentucky	55.36
South Carolina	55.07
Illinois	54.98
New York	53.93
Massachusetts	52.36
Washington	51.40
Texas	51.22
Georgia	50.58
Nebraska	49.34
Delaware	48.06
New Jersey	48.04
California	44.02
Alaska	40.50
Rhode Island	37.24
Arkansas	36.53
Utah	35.49

County	Percent
Hillsborough County, FL	82.79
Jefferson County, CO	81.20
Clackamas County, OR	80.57
Kauai County, HI	79.29
Maui County, HI	76.01
Denver County, CO	75.59
Hawaii County, HI	73.05
Snohomish County, WA	71.04
Pima County, AZ	69.92
Clark County, NV	69.35
El Paso County, CO	68.85
Kern County, CA	68.79
Bernalillo County, NM	68.51
Suffolk County, NY	67.89
Monterey County, CA	67.81
Honolulu County, HI	67.72
Cumberland County, NC	67.61
Washington County, UT	66.83
Spokane County, WA	66.39
Franklin County, OH	65.91
Broward County, FL	64.78
Allegheny County, PA	64.65
St. Louis County, MO	63.88
Davidson County, TN	63.49
Davis County, UT	62.59
Santa Barbara County, CA	62.09
Kitsap County, WA	61.58
Thurston County, WA	61.11
Sedgwick County, KS	60.90
Duval County, FL	60.89
Fresno County, CA	60.51
Nassau County, NY	60.12
Washington County, OR	60.09
Queens County, NY	59.83
Bexar County, TX	59.00
Wayne County, MI	58.90
San Diego County, CA	58.08
Essex County, NJ	58.01
Shelby County, TN	57.77
Milwaukee County, WI	56.76
Arapahoe County, CO	56.42
Onslow County, NC	55.47
Philadelphia County, PA	55.30
Bell County, TX	55.19
Jackson County, MO	55.02
Solano County, CA	54.68
Palm Beach County, FL	54.29
Utah County, UT	54.18
Muscogee County, GA	53.87
Ada County, ID	53.54
Ventura County, CA	53.44
Riverside County, CA	52.63
San Joaquin County, CA	51.32
Travis County, TX	51.07
Santa Clara County, CA	50.86
Clark County, WA	50.78
Maricopa County, AZ	50.56
Sonoma County, CA	49.77
Harris County, TX	49.44
Lane County, OR	49.36
Fairfax County, VA	49.26
El Paso County, TX	48.46
Gwinnett County, GA	48.40
Orange County, CA	47.53
Pierce County, WA	47.35
Dallas County, TX	46.51
Multnomah County, OR	46.06
Miami-Dade County, FL	44.07
Montgomery County, MD	43.97
Hennepin County, MN	43.76
Contra Costa County, CA	43.71
New York County, NY	43.06
King County, WA	42.10
Tarrant County, TX	41.48
Kings County, NY	40.70

Place	Percent
Kahaluu, HI (cdp) Honolulu County	96.30
Ahuimanu, HI (cdp) Honolulu County	96.05
Makawao, HI (cdp) Maui County	95.83
Waikane, HI (cdp) Honolulu County	94.52
Kapaau, HI (cdp) Hawaii County	93.75
Hana, HI (cdp) Maui County	90.87
Waimea, HI (cdp) Kauai County	88.83
Waimanalo Beach, HI (cdp) Honolulu County	88.77
Wailuku, HI (cdp) Maui County	88.45
Kaunakakai, HI (cdp) Maui County	87.85
Waimea, HI (cdp) Hawaii County	86.45
Naalehu, HI (cdp) Hawaii County	86.36
Paia, HI (cdp) Maui County	85.25
Waimanalo, HI (cdp) Honolulu County	85.23
Makaha, HI (cdp) Honolulu County	84.52
Punaluu, HI (cdp) Honolulu County	84.44
Kekaha, HI (cdp) Kauai County	83.90
Huntington Beach, CA (city) Orange County	83.82
Makaha Valley, HI (cdp) Honolulu County	83.78
Maili, HI (cdp) Honolulu County	82.64
Anahola, HI (cdp) Kauai County	82.39
Papaikou, HI (cdp) Hawaii County	80.99
Kailua, HI (cdp) Honolulu County	80.89
Kapaa, HI (cdp) Kauai County	79.98
Kalaoa, HI (cdp) Hawaii County	79.92
Kailua, HI (cdp) Hawaii County	78.94
Kaneohe, HI (cdp) Honolulu County	78.81
Waianae, HI (cdp) Honolulu County	78.81
Kualapuu, HI (cdp) Maui County	78.53
Henderson, NV (city) Clark County	78.49
Aiea, HI (cdp) Honolulu County	78.38
Kilauea, HI (cdp) Kauai County	78.03
Ewa Beach, HI (cdp) Honolulu County	76.83
Waihee-Waiehu, HI (cdp) Maui County	76.80
Haleiwa, HI (cdp) Honolulu County	76.36
Captain Cook, HI (cdp) Hawaii County	76.28
Denver, CO (city) Denver County	75.59
Mililani Town, HI (cdp) Honolulu County	75.58
Makakilo City, HI (cdp) Honolulu County	75.48
Volcano, HI (cdp) Hawaii County	75.08
Marina, CA (city) Monterey County	73.89
Honaunau-Napoopoo, HI (cdp) Hawaii County	73.15
Hanapepe, HI (cdp) Kauai County	72.62
Nanakuli, HI (cdp) Honolulu County	72.43
Waipio, HI (cdp) Honolulu County	72.43
Kaaawa, HI (cdp) Honolulu County	72.20
Colorado Springs, CO (city) El Paso County	72.13
Hilo, HI (cdp) Hawaii County	71.45
Kahului, HI (cdp) Maui County	71.33
Honalo, HI (cdp) Hawaii County	71.19
Kansas City, MO (city) Jackson County	70.94
Maunawili, HI (cdp) Honolulu County	70.74
Vista, CA (city) San Diego County	70.67
Waimalu, HI (cdp) Honolulu County	70.62
Pearl City, HI (cdp) Honolulu County	70.26
Kihei, HI (cdp) Maui County	70.20
Pahala, HI (cdp) Hawaii County	69.62
Spring Valley, NV (cdp) Clark County	69.05
Paradise, NV (cdp) Clark County	68.30
St. George, UT (city) Washington County	67.92
Waikapu, HI (cdp) Maui County	67.68
Hawaiian Beaches, HI (cdp) Hawaii County	67.32
Albuquerque, NM (city) Bernalillo County	67.01
Waialua, HI (cdp) Honolulu County	66.47
Las Vegas, NV (city) Clark County	65.73
Tucson, AZ (city) Pima County	65.20
Lahaina, HI (cdp) Maui County	64.71
Provo, UT (city) Utah County	63.86
Holualoa, HI (cdp) Hawaii County	63.80
Hawaiian Ocean View, HI (cdp) Hawaii County	63.68
Nashville-Davidson, TN (sp. city) Davidson County	63.09
Halawa, HI (cdp) Honolulu County	62.66
Wahiawa, HI (cdp) Honolulu County	62.54
Fremont, CA (city) Alameda County	61.64
San Diego, CA (city) San Diego County	61.32

Notes: Please refer to the User's Guide for an explanation of data; ranking tables include all places with Asian and/or NHPI populations above SF4 population thresholds; (1) tables reflect only those areas that meet SF4 population thresholds, therefore there may be less than 50 states, 75 counties or 75 places listed

Language Spoken at Home: English Only

Asian Indians 5 Years and Over Who Speak English-Only at Home

All States, Top 75 Counties, and Top 75 Places Sorted by Number[1]

State	Number
United States	292,374
New York	67,023
California	43,853
Florida	21,428
New Jersey	19,789
Texas	19,020
Illinois	15,677
Maryland	9,705
Pennsylvania	8,700
Michigan	7,579
Massachusetts	7,571
Virginia	7,344
Ohio	6,196
Georgia	6,087
Connecticut	4,838
North Carolina	4,319
Washington	4,170
Minnesota	4,142
Arizona	2,617
Colorado	2,613
Missouri	2,446
Indiana	2,408
Oregon	2,271
Wisconsin	1,969
Tennessee	1,806
Louisiana	1,693
South Carolina	1,492
Oklahoma	1,368
Kentucky	1,180
Iowa	1,166
Alabama	1,157
District of Columbia	1,139
Kansas	1,071
Nevada	986
Delaware	812
Utah	756
Mississippi	625
Nebraska	608
Hawaii	552
New Hampshire	542
New Mexico	514
West Virginia	511
Rhode Island	469
Arkansas	450
Maine	390
Idaho	261
Vermont	241
North Dakota	238
Alaska	206
Montana	202
Wyoming	96
South Dakota	78

County	Number
Queens County, NY	31,745
Los Angeles County, CA	10,682
Cook County, IL	8,044
Santa Clara County, CA	7,248
Bronx County, NY	6,942
Kings County, NY	6,667
Broward County, FL	5,904
Harris County, TX	5,164
New York County, NY	4,718
Alameda County, CA	4,545
Orange County, CA	4,480
Nassau County, NY	4,399
Montgomery County, MD	4,391
Middlesex County, NJ	4,366
DuPage County, IL	3,667
Middlesex County, MA	3,449
Miami-Dade County, FL	3,346
Dallas County, TX	3,270
Fairfax County, VA	3,146
Westchester County, NY	2,970
Orange County, FL	2,591
Essex County, NJ	2,318
King County, WA	2,263
Oakland County, MI	2,112
Hudson County, NJ	2,103
Bergen County, NJ	2,069
Hennepin County, MN	2,038
Philadelphia County, PA	2,012
Maricopa County, AZ	1,960
San Diego County, CA	1,949
Suffolk County, NY	1,866
San Mateo County, CA	1,724
Travis County, TX	1,715
Fort Bend County, TX	1,692
Fairfield County, CT	1,670
Sacramento County, CA	1,605
San Francisco County, CA	1,604
Contra Costa County, CA	1,576
Palm Beach County, FL	1,549
Suffolk County, MA	1,509
Prince George's County, MD	1,476
Hartford County, CT	1,394
San Bernardino County, CA	1,383
Hillsborough County, FL	1,358
Franklin County, OH	1,353
Morris County, NJ	1,352
Gwinnett County, GA	1,313
Tarrant County, TX	1,312
Cuyahoga County, OH	1,311
Wayne County, MI	1,305
Collin County, TX	1,255
Mercer County, NJ	1,243
Baltimore County, MD	1,238
Somerset County, NJ	1,217
Allegheny County, PA	1,211
Monmouth County, NJ	1,202
Rockland County, NY	1,152
St. Louis County, MO	1,146
Ventura County, CA	1,108
DeKalb County, GA	1,103
New Haven County, CT	1,094
Washtenaw County, MI	1,076
Richmond County, NY	1,067
Norfolk County, MA	1,066
Fulton County, GA	1,044
Montgomery County, PA	996
Denton County, TX	965
Lake County, IL	953
Howard County, MD	949
Union County, NJ	909
Pinellas County, FL	894
Riverside County, CA	881
Monroe County, NY	845
Wake County, NC	808
Baltimore Independent City, MD	796

Place	Number
New York, NY (city)	51,139
Los Angeles, CA (city) Los Angeles County	4,302
Chicago, IL (city) Cook County	3,627
Houston, TX (city) Harris County	2,670
San Jose, CA (city) Santa Clara County	2,574
Hempstead, NY (town) Nassau County	2,136
Philadelphia, PA (city) Philadelphia County	2,012
Fremont, CA (city) Alameda County	1,831
San Francisco, CA (city) San Francisco County	1,604
Austin, TX (city) Travis County	1,498
Boston, MA (city) Suffolk County	1,493
Jersey City, NJ (city) Hudson County	1,351
North Hempstead, NY (town) Nassau County	1,274
Edison, NJ (township) Middlesex County	1,180
San Diego, CA (city) San Diego County	1,116
Dallas, TX (city) Dallas County	1,055
Columbus, OH (city) Franklin County	1,043
Irvine, CA (city) Orange County	1,031
Sunnyvale, CA (city) Santa Clara County	1,006
Seattle, WA (city) King County	866
Cambridge, MA (city) Middlesex County	837
Irving, TX (city) Dallas County	836
Oyster Bay, NY (town) Nassau County	809
Minneapolis, MN (city) Hennepin County	780
Phoenix, AZ (city) Maricopa County	771
Hollywood, FL (city) Broward County	765
Ann Arbor, MI (city) Washtenaw County	764
Coral Springs, FL (city) Broward County	750
Santa Clara, CA (city) Santa Clara County	725
Plano, TX (city) Collin County	721
Arlington, VA (cdp) Arlington County	687
Sugar Land, TX (city) Fort Bend County	673
Brookhaven, NY (town) Suffolk County	665
Pembroke Pines, FL (city) Broward County	665
Charlotte, NC (city) Mecklenburg County	651
Yonkers, NY (city) Westchester County	625
Naperville, IL (city) Du Page County	621
Berkeley, CA (city) Alameda County	607
San Antonio, TX (city) Bexar County	598
Plantation, FL (city) Broward County	583
Stamford, CT (city) Fairfield County	580
Cupertino, CA (city) Santa Clara County	575
Anaheim, CA (city) Orange County	559
Woodbridge, NJ (township) Middlesex County	543
Clarkstown, NY (town) Rockland County	534
Denver, CO (city) Denver County	522
Greenburgh, NY (town) Westchester County	521
Carrollton, TX (city) Denton County	506
Newark, NJ (city) Essex County	500
Portland, OR (city) Multnomah County	482
Sunrise, FL (city) Broward County	481
Indianapolis, IN (sp. city) Marion County	479
Skokie, IL (village) Cook County	466
Columbia, MD (cdp) Howard County	464
Union City, CA (city) Alameda County	445
Oklahoma City, OK (city) Oklahoma County	444
Brookline, MA (town) Norfolk County	440
Nashville-Davidson, TN (sp. city) Davidson County	439
Saratoga, CA (city) Santa Clara County	439
Durham, NC (city) Durham County	437
Piscataway, NJ (township) Middlesex County	437
Jacksonville, FL (city) Duval County	436
Sacramento, CA (city) Sacramento County	420
Tallahassee, FL (city) Leon County	420
Huntington, NY (town) Suffolk County	418
Evanston, IL (city) Cook County	408
Torrance, CA (city) Los Angeles County	401
Islip, NY (town) Suffolk County	396
Thousand Oaks, CA (city) Ventura County	393
Milpitas, CA (city) Santa Clara County	388
Elmont, NY (cdp) Nassau County	384
Amherst, NY (town) Erie County	383
Mountain View, CA (city) Santa Clara County	380
Fort Worth, TX (city) Tarrant County	375
Troy, MI (city) Oakland County	374

Notes: Please refer to the User's Guide for an explanation of data; ranking tables include all places with Asian and/or NHPI populations above SF4 population thresholds; (1) tables reflect only those areas that meet SF4 population thresholds, therefore there may be less than 50 states, 75 counties or 75 places listed

Language Spoken at Home: English Only

Asian Indians 5 Years and Over Who Speak English-Only at Home

All States, Top 75 Counties, and Top 75 Places Sorted by Percent[1]

State	Percent
District of Columbia	48.00
Montana	47.31
Hawaii	45.54
Maine	42.95
Alaska	41.28
Vermont	35.65
Florida	34.05
New York	28.98
Minnesota	27.95
Utah	26.16
Oregon	24.97
North Dakota	24.71
Idaho	24.53
Colorado	24.46
Wyoming	24.43
Iowa	23.37
New Mexico	22.87
Missouri	22.45
Nevada	21.96
Connecticut	21.84
West Virginia	21.64
Maryland	20.88
Louisiana	20.70
Washington	20.34
Nebraska	20.30
Mississippi	20.12
Massachusetts	19.59
Rhode Island	19.53
South Carolina	19.53
Arizona	19.51
Wisconsin	19.41
United States	19.30
Kentucky	18.94
Alabama	18.91
Arkansas	18.63
North Carolina	18.59
Indiana	18.26
Ohio	17.88
Oklahoma	17.71
Delaware	17.00
New Hampshire	16.94
Virginia	16.80
Pennsylvania	16.67
Tennessee	16.30
Texas	16.25
South Dakota	15.98
California	15.58
Michigan	15.26
Kansas	15.16
Georgia	14.75
Illinois	13.77
New Jersey	12.81

County	Percent
Bronx County, NY	51.21
Broward County, FL	48.99
Charlottesville Independent City, VA	45.00
Honolulu County, HI	43.86
Lane County, OR	43.01
Saginaw County, MI	41.58
Leon County, FL	41.26
Anchorage Borough, AK	40.75
Putnam County, NY	40.69
Miami-Dade County, FL	39.94
Marion County, FL	39.63
Baltimore Independent City, MD	39.41
Santa Cruz County, CA	37.31
Marion County, OR	37.30
Pierce County, WA	37.08
Saint Louis Independent City, MO	36.99
Niagara County, NY	36.14
Suffolk County, MA	36.13
Orange County, FL	35.89
San Francisco County, CA	34.58
DeKalb County, IL	34.45
Forsyth County, NC	34.32
New York County, NY	34.20
Sussex County, NJ	34.14
Multnomah County, OR	33.65
Ottawa County, MI	33.25
Clackamas County, OR	32.98
Spokane County, WA	32.58
St. Joseph County, IN	32.44
Schenectady County, NY	32.42
Palm Beach County, FL	32.26
Lubbock County, TX	31.91
Queens County, NY	31.41
Santa Barbara County, CA	31.28
Monroe County, PA	31.14
Richmond Independent City, VA	30.80
York County, VA	29.86
Chittenden County, VT	29.83
Olmsted County, MN	29.67
Lorain County, OH	29.56
Kings County, NY	29.50
Norfolk Independent City, VA	29.28
Ocean County, NJ	29.17
Johnson County, IA	28.83
Ventura County, CA	28.66
Clark County, WA	28.61
Essex County, NJ	28.52
Osceola County, FL	28.47
Seminole County, FL	28.47
Tolland County, CT	28.47
Alachua County, FL	28.44
Orleans Parish, LA	28.44
Tompkins County, NY	28.41
Volusia County, FL	28.37
Brevard County, FL	28.31
Hennepin County, MN	28.27
Lancaster County, PA	27.83
Denver County, CO	27.80
Virginia Beach Independent City, VA	27.70
Oneida County, NY	27.59
Thurston County, WA	27.55
Shelby County, AL	27.51
Anoka County, MN	27.48
Douglas County, KS	27.40
Harford County, MD	27.18
Litchfield County, CT	27.05
Cumberland County, NC	27.03
Genesee County, MI	26.94
Monroe County, IN	26.84
Berrien County, MI	26.55
Jefferson County, CO	26.41
Kalamazoo County, MI	26.39
Clark County, NV	26.20
Pinellas County, FL	26.03
Buncombe County, NC	25.88

Place	Percent
Hollywood, FL (city) Broward County	67.94
Miramar, FL (city) Broward County	60.04
Oxnard, CA (city) Ventura County	57.57
Plantation, FL (city) Broward County	55.47
Sunrise, FL (city) Broward County	51.50
Hartford, CT (city) Hartford County	49.81
Scarsdale, NY (village) Westchester County	47.77
Montclair, NJ (township) Essex County	47.33
Kendall, FL (cdp) Miami-Dade County	45.13
North Miami Beach, FL (city) Miami-Dade County	44.29
The Hammocks, FL (cdp) Miami-Dade County	43.91
Coral Springs, FL (city) Broward County	43.71
Fort Lauderdale, FL (city) Broward County	42.86
Brookline, MA (town) Norfolk County	42.80
Pembroke Pines, FL (city) Broward County	42.63
Newark, NJ (city) Essex County	42.30
Tallahassee, FL (city) Leon County	42.13
Waterbury, CT (city) New Haven County	41.72
Mount Vernon, NY (city) Westchester County	40.38
Thousand Oaks, CA (city) Ventura County	40.06
Schenectady, NY (city) Schenectady County	40.04
Minneapolis, MN (city) Hennepin County	39.14
Miami, FL (city) Miami-Dade County	38.97
Boston, MA (city) Suffolk County	38.34
Wappinger, NY (town) Dutchess County	38.18
Saratoga, CA (city) Santa Clara County	37.65
St. Louis, MO (city) Saint Louis Independent City	36.99
Brooklyn Park, MN (city) Hennepin County	36.82
Elgin, IL (city) Kane County	36.59
Doctor Phillips, FL (cdp) Orange County	36.47
Honolulu, HI (cdp) Honolulu County	36.06
Palmdale, CA (city) Los Angeles County	35.80
Claremont, CA (city) Los Angeles County	35.76
Evanston, IL (city) Cook County	35.76
Berkeley, CA (city) Alameda County	35.62
Stanford, CA (cdp) Santa Clara County	35.57
Middletown, PA (township) Bucks County	35.51
DeKalb, IL (city) De Kalb County	35.19
Cortlandt, NY (town) Westchester County	34.90
San Francisco, CA (city) San Francisco County	34.58
Santa Cruz, CA (city) Santa Cruz County	34.42
Burnsville, MN (city) Dakota County	34.31
Los Altos Hills, CA (town) Santa Clara County	34.31
Lower Merion, PA (township) Montgomery County	34.28
St. Petersburg, FL (city) Pinellas County	34.16
Flower Mound, TX (town) Denton County	33.72
Portland, OR (city) Multnomah County	33.64
Winston-Salem, NC (city) Forsyth County	33.64
Seattle, WA (city) King County	33.50
Middletown, NJ (township) Monmouth County	32.60
New York, NY (city)	32.58
Scottsdale, AZ (city) Maricopa County	32.41
Ithaca, NY (city) Tompkins County	32.07
St. Paul, MN (city) Ramsey County	31.58
Wheaton-Glenmont, MD (cdp) Montgomery County	31.56
Lubbock, TX (city) Lubbock County	31.55
Cambridge, MA (city) Middlesex County	31.28
North Druid Hills, GA (cdp) De Kalb County	31.27
Milford, CT (town) New Haven County	31.12
Redondo Beach, CA (city) Los Angeles County	31.06
Warren, NJ (township) Somerset County	30.99
Loma Linda, CA (city) San Bernardino County	30.87
Freehold, NJ (township) Monmouth County	30.75
Boca Raton, FL (city) Palm Beach County	30.68
Medford, MA (city) Middlesex County	30.56
Santa Monica, CA (city) Los Angeles County	30.48
New Haven, CT (city) New Haven County	30.30
Calverton, MD (cdp) Montgomery County	30.02
North Valley Stream, NY (cdp) Nassau County	29.84
East Hartford, CT (town) Hartford County	29.67
San Rafael, CA (city) Marin County	29.65
South Plainfield, NJ (borough) Middlesex County	29.46
Glendale, AZ (city) Maricopa County	29.19
Lower Makefield, PA (township) Bucks County	29.17
North Laurel, MD (cdp) Howard County	29.15

Notes: Please refer to the User's Guide for an explanation of data; ranking tables include all places with Asian and/or NHPI populations above SF4 population thresholds; (1) tables reflect only those areas that meet SF4 population thresholds, therefore there may be less than 50 states, 75 counties or 75 places listed

Language Spoken at Home: English Only

Bangladeshis 5 Years and Over Who Speak English-Only at Home

All States, Top 75 Counties, and Top 75 Places Sorted by Number[1]

State	Number
United States	1,536
New York	742
California	116
Texas	80
Virginia	77
Illinois	66
New Jersey	54
Maryland	50
Michigan	41
Georgia	40
Massachusetts	37
Florida	32
Ohio	22
Connecticut	20
Pennsylvania	11

County	Number
Queens County, NY	366
Kings County, NY	258
Los Angeles County, CA	68
Fairfax County, VA	61
Bronx County, NY	50
Dallas County, TX	39
New York County, NY	30
Santa Clara County, CA	28
Montgomery County, MD	26
Harris County, TX	18
Middlesex County, NJ	18
Wayne County, MI	17
Passaic County, NJ	9
DeKalb County, GA	8
Atlantic County, NJ	0

Place	Number
New York, NY (city)	713
Los Angeles, CA (city) Los Angeles County	40
Paterson, NJ (city) Passaic County	9
Hamtramck, MI (city) Wayne County	7

Notes: Please refer to the User's Guide for an explanation of data; ranking tables include all places with Asian and/or NHPI populations above SF4 population thresholds; (1) tables reflect only those areas that meet SF4 population thresholds, therefore there may be less than 50 states, 75 counties or 75 places listed

Language Spoken at Home: English Only

Bangladeshis 5 Years and Over Who Speak English-Only at Home

All States, Top 75 Counties, and Top 75 Places Sorted by Percent[1]

State	Percent
Illinois	8.92
Massachusetts	7.52
Connecticut	6.13
Virginia	4.79
California	4.70
Maryland	4.43
United States	4.09
New York	4.04
Ohio	3.76
Georgia	3.56
Texas	3.50
Florida	2.80
Michigan	2.76
New Jersey	2.63
Pennsylvania	1.75

County	Percent
Fairfax County, VA	7.72
Kings County, NY	7.21
Dallas County, TX	6.96
Santa Clara County, CA	6.70
Los Angeles County, CA	5.77
Middlesex County, NJ	4.85
New York County, NY	4.14
Montgomery County, MD	3.34
Queens County, NY	3.24
Harris County, TX	2.86
Bronx County, NY	2.70
Passaic County, NJ	1.88
Wayne County, MI	1.67
DeKalb County, GA	1.57
Atlantic County, NJ	<0.01

Place	Percent
Los Angeles, CA (city) Los Angeles County	5.48
New York, NY (city)	4.07
Paterson, NJ (city) Passaic County	2.29
Hamtramck, MI (city) Wayne County	1.06

Notes: Please refer to the User's Guide for an explanation of data; ranking tables include all places with Asian and/or NHPI populations above SF4 population thresholds; (1) tables reflect only those areas that meet SF4 population thresholds, therefore there may be less than 50 states, 75 counties or 75 places listed

Language Spoken at Home: English Only

Cambodians 5 Years and Over Who Speak English-Only at Home

All States, Top 75 Counties, and Top 75 Places Sorted by Number[1]

State	Number
United States	13,874
California	4,957
Washington	1,137
Massachusetts	1,043
Texas	672
Pennsylvania	631
Virginia	567
Minnesota	392
Illinois	363
Florida	351
Georgia	341
New York	253
Oregon	242
Rhode Island	235
Ohio	225
Connecticut	216
Maryland	199
Arizona	194
Maine	185
Michigan	173
North Carolina	169
Colorado	144
Wisconsin	128
Indiana	120
Utah	100
Kansas	83
Tennessee	75
Missouri	74
Iowa	67
New Jersey	63
Alabama	54
Nevada	48
South Carolina	47
Hawaii	45
Oklahoma	36

County	Number
Los Angeles County, CA	2,048
Middlesex County, MA	588
King County, WA	527
Orange County, CA	386
Philadelphia County, PA	378
Stanislaus County, CA	348
Santa Clara County, CA	323
Pierce County, WA	301
Alameda County, CA	291
San Joaquin County, CA	288
San Diego County, CA	273
Fresno County, CA	260
San Bernardino County, CA	210
Fairfax County, VA	204
Providence County, RI	203
Cook County, IL	184
Bristol County, MA	176
Harris County, TX	175
Maricopa County, AZ	169
Gwinnett County, GA	149
Fairfield County, CT	146
Dallas County, TX	141
Tarrant County, TX	139
Suffolk County, MA	138
Franklin County, OH	132
Multnomah County, OR	122
Snohomish County, WA	115
Hennepin County, MN	113
Ramsey County, MN	112
Duval County, FL	106
Henrico County, VA	104
Washington County, OR	100
Montgomery County, MD	94
Sacramento County, CA	93
Riverside County, CA	86
Ottawa County, MI	83
Denton County, TX	75
Clayton County, GA	74
Sonoma County, CA	72
Essex County, MA	70
Mecklenburg County, NC	68
Salt Lake County, UT	60
Thurston County, WA	58
Cumberland County, ME	57
Davidson County, NC	51
Pinellas County, FL	49
Clark County, NV	45
Bronx County, NY	43
Scott County, MN	42
Cowlitz County, WA	38
Sedgwick County, KS	35
Shelby County, TN	35
Clark County, WA	34
DeKalb County, GA	33
Chesterfield County, VA	32
Cuyahoga County, OH	30
Arlington County, VA	26
Kings County, NY	25
San Francisco County, CA	25
Mobile County, AL	21
Dakota County, MN	20
Denver County, CO	20
Hamilton County, OH	14
Hampden County, MA	13
Monroe County, NY	13
Olmsted County, MN	13
Polk County, IA	13
Brazoria County, TX	12
Kern County, CA	11
Worcester County, MA	11
Camden County, NJ	5

Place	Number
Long Beach, CA (city) Los Angeles County	1,115
Lowell, MA (city) Middlesex County	485
Philadelphia, PA (city) Philadelphia County	378
Los Angeles, CA (city) Los Angeles County	311
Modesto, CA (city) Stanislaus County	307
Stockton, CA (city) San Joaquin County	277
San Jose, CA (city) Santa Clara County	261
Tacoma, WA (city) Pierce County	252
Fresno, CA (city) Fresno County	241
Seattle, WA (city) King County	212
San Diego, CA (city) San Diego County	210
Chicago, IL (city) Cook County	175
Oakland, CA (city) Alameda County	151
Providence, RI (city) Providence County	138
New York, NY (city)	135
Santa Ana, CA (city) Orange County	120
Portland, OR (city) Multnomah County	117
Attleboro, MA (city) Bristol County	106
Jacksonville, FL (city) Duval County	106
St. Paul, MN (city) Ramsey County	97
Lakewood, CA (city) Los Angeles County	96
Phoenix, AZ (city) Maricopa County	91
Carrollton, TX (city) Denton County	89
Rosemead, CA (city) Los Angeles County	89
Danbury, CT (city) Fairfield County	88
Columbus, OH (city) Franklin County	79
Boston, MA (city) Suffolk County	72
Pomona, CA (city) Los Angeles County	71
Lynn, MA (city) Essex County	70
White Center, WA (cdp) King County	70
Houston, TX (city) Harris County	67
Dallas, TX (city) Dallas County	66
Revere, MA (city) Suffolk County	66
Santa Rosa, CA (city) Sonoma County	60
Portland, ME (city) Cumberland County	57
Fall River, MA (city) Bristol County	48
West Valley City, UT (city) Salt Lake County	48
Everett, WA (city) Snohomish County	44
Minneapolis, MN (city) Hennepin County	43
Aurora, CO (city) Arapahoe County	41
St. Petersburg, FL (city) Pinellas County	41
Charlotte, NC (city) Mecklenburg County	39
Cranston, RI (city) Providence County	37
Memphis, TN (city) Shelby County	35
Norwalk, CA (city) Los Angeles County	31
Bellflower, CA (city) Los Angeles County	30
Sacramento, CA (city) Sacramento County	28
Arlington, VA (cdp) Arlington County	26
San Francisco, CA (city) San Francisco County	25
Monterey Park, CA (city) Los Angeles County	24
Garden Grove, CA (city) Orange County	23
Longview, WA (city) Cowlitz County	23
Bloomington, MN (city) Hennepin County	22
Lexington, NC (city) Davidson County	21
Denver, CO (city) Denver County	20
San Bernardino, CA (city) San Bernardino County	20
Beaverton, OR (city) Washington County	15
Bridgeport, CT (city) Fairfield County	12
Silver Spring, MD (cdp) Montgomery County	5
Rochester, MN (city) Olmsted County	4
Lawrence, MA (city) Essex County	0
Signal Hill, CA (city) Los Angeles County	0

Notes: Please refer to the User's Guide for an explanation of data; ranking tables include all places with Asian and/or NHPI populations above SF4 population thresholds; (1) tables reflect only those areas that meet SF4 population thresholds, therefore there may be less than 50 states, 75 counties or 75 places listed

Language Spoken at Home: English Only

Cambodians 5 Years and Over Who Speak English-Only at Home

All States, Top 75 Counties, and Top 75 Places Sorted by Percent[1]

State	Percent
Hawaii	29.22
Wisconsin	21.99
Indiana	21.47
Maine	20.37
Arizona	17.77
South Carolina	14.92
Kansas	13.52
Florida	13.36
Maryland	12.25
Virginia	12.08
Michigan	11.74
Oklahoma	11.50
Illinois	11.28
Connecticut	11.08
Alabama	10.74
Colorado	10.71
Georgia	10.52
New Jersey	10.03
Texas	9.59
Oregon	9.54
New York	9.43
Ohio	9.41
Missouri	9.15
Iowa	9.13
United States	8.43
Washington	8.30
Minnesota	8.24
Pennsylvania	7.98
North Carolina	7.62
California	7.48
Utah	7.19
Nevada	6.86
Tennessee	6.79
Massachusetts	5.63
Rhode Island	5.06

County	Percent
Tarrant County, TX	18.76
Gwinnett County, GA	17.57
Maricopa County, AZ	16.17
Riverside County, CA	15.55
Henrico County, VA	13.42
Scott County, MN	12.92
San Bernardino County, CA	12.79
Multnomah County, OR	12.41
Stanislaus County, CA	11.71
Fairfax County, VA	11.68
Franklin County, OH	11.37
Denton County, TX	11.28
Duval County, FL	11.22
Fairfield County, CT	11.01
Cowlitz County, WA	10.92
Ramsey County, MN	10.81
Davidson County, NC	10.78
Cumberland County, ME	9.81
Washington County, OR	9.64
Mecklenburg County, NC	9.48
Orange County, CA	9.24
Sonoma County, CA	9.18
Harris County, TX	9.14
Cook County, IL	8.92
Sacramento County, CA	8.90
Sedgwick County, KS	8.79
Bristol County, MA	8.68
Montgomery County, MD	8.59
Clark County, WA	8.56
King County, WA	8.56
Suffolk County, MA	8.41
Ottawa County, MI	8.36
Pierce County, WA	8.06
Alameda County, CA	7.98
Santa Clara County, CA	7.75
Arlington County, VA	7.67
Clayton County, GA	7.66
Los Angeles County, CA	7.34
Thurston County, WA	7.25
Pinellas County, FL	7.18
Fresno County, CA	7.11
Shelby County, TN	7.00
San Diego County, CA	6.83
Hennepin County, MN	6.74
Dallas County, TX	6.61
Clark County, NV	6.56
Philadelphia County, PA	6.49
Mobile County, AL	6.42
Snohomish County, WA	6.24
Cuyahoga County, OH	6.20
Middlesex County, MA	5.91
DeKalb County, GA	5.74
Salt Lake County, UT	5.71
Denver County, CO	5.60
Bronx County, NY	5.42
Chesterfield County, VA	5.25
Kings County, NY	5.23
Dakota County, MN	4.91
Providence County, RI	4.65
Hamilton County, OH	4.32
San Francisco County, CA	3.96
Monroe County, NY	3.80
Polk County, IA	3.60
Hampden County, MA	3.45
Brazoria County, TX	3.34
Worcester County, MA	3.31
San Joaquin County, CA	3.30
Kern County, CA	2.83
Essex County, MA	2.08
Olmsted County, MN	1.98
Camden County, NJ	1.66

Place	Percent
Phoenix, AZ (city) Maricopa County	18.57
Attleboro, MA (city) Bristol County	16.77
Danbury, CT (city) Fairfield County	16.51
Lakewood, CA (city) Los Angeles County	13.79
Modesto, CA (city) Stanislaus County	12.94
Rosemead, CA (city) Los Angeles County	12.73
Portland, OR (city) Multnomah County	12.25
Boston, MA (city) Suffolk County	11.76
Carrollton, TX (city) Denton County	11.59
St. Paul, MN (city) Ramsey County	11.25
Jacksonville, FL (city) Duval County	11.22
Portland, ME (city) Cumberland County	10.46
Pomona, CA (city) Los Angeles County	10.38
Aurora, CO (city) Arapahoe County	10.17
Santa Rosa, CA (city) Sonoma County	10.08
Chicago, IL (city) Cook County	9.74
Houston, TX (city) Harris County	9.64
Longview, WA (city) Cowlitz County	9.54
Seattle, WA (city) King County	9.07
Minneapolis, MN (city) Hennepin County	8.83
Tacoma, WA (city) Pierce County	8.71
New York, NY (city)	8.69
Revere, MA (city) Suffolk County	8.55
St. Petersburg, FL (city) Pinellas County	8.22
Memphis, TN (city) Shelby County	7.99
West Valley City, UT (city) Salt Lake County	7.86
Los Angeles, CA (city) Los Angeles County	7.83
Everett, WA (city) Snohomish County	7.71
Arlington, VA (cdp) Arlington County	7.67
Columbus, OH (city) Franklin County	7.41
Santa Ana, CA (city) Orange County	7.22
Fresno, CA (city) Fresno County	7.21
Dallas, TX (city) Dallas County	7.07
Norwalk, CA (city) Los Angeles County	6.92
San Jose, CA (city) Santa Clara County	6.88
Long Beach, CA (city) Los Angeles County	6.81
Philadelphia, PA (city) Philadelphia County	6.49
Monterey Park, CA (city) Los Angeles County	6.25
White Center, WA (cdp) King County	6.16
Lexington, NC (city) Davidson County	6.02
Sacramento, CA (city) Sacramento County	6.01
Charlotte, NC (city) Mecklenburg County	5.99
San Diego, CA (city) San Diego County	5.85
Bellflower, CA (city) Los Angeles County	5.69
Lowell, MA (city) Middlesex County	5.63
Denver, CO (city) Denver County	5.60
Oakland, CA (city) Alameda County	5.55
Cranston, RI (city) Providence County	4.86
Bloomington, MN (city) Hennepin County	4.82
Garden Grove, CA (city) Orange County	4.78
San Bernardino, CA (city) San Bernardino County	4.59
Beaverton, OR (city) Washington County	4.36
Providence, RI (city) Providence County	4.26
Fall River, MA (city) Bristol County	4.06
San Francisco, CA (city) San Francisco County	3.96
Stockton, CA (city) San Joaquin County	3.30
Bridgeport, CT (city) Fairfield County	2.63
Lynn, MA (city) Essex County	2.62
Silver Spring, MD (cdp) Montgomery County	1.65
Rochester, MN (city) Olmsted County	0.78
Lawrence, MA (city) Essex County	<0.01
Signal Hill, CA (city) Los Angeles County	<0.01

Notes: Please refer to the User's Guide for an explanation of data; ranking tables include all places with Asian and/or NHPI populations above SF4 population thresholds; (1) tables reflect only those areas that meet SF4 population thresholds, therefore there may be less than 50 states, 75 counties or 75 places listed

Language Spoken at Home: English Only

Chinese (except Taiwanese) 5 Years and Over Who Speak English-Only at Home

All States, Top 75 Counties, and Top 75 Places Sorted by Number[1]

State	Number
United States	322,586
California	134,723
New York	35,595
Hawaii	25,717
Texas	11,209
New Jersey	11,064
Washington	10,987
Massachusetts	10,322
Florida	9,153
Illinois	8,605
Maryland	5,815
Pennsylvania	5,442
Virginia	4,849
Arizona	4,022
Michigan	3,884
Ohio	3,429
Oregon	3,223
Georgia	3,113
Connecticut	3,086
Colorado	2,928
North Carolina	2,314
Nevada	2,153
Minnesota	1,859
Indiana	1,853
Missouri	1,657
Wisconsin	1,409
Louisiana	1,321
Tennessee	1,155
Utah	1,111
District of Columbia	847
Oklahoma	811
Kansas	792
New Mexico	753
South Carolina	699
New Hampshire	689
Rhode Island	653
Alabama	633
Iowa	624
Arkansas	502
Kentucky	502
Mississippi	419
Delaware	416
Idaho	381
Nebraska	379
Alaska	320
Maine	298
West Virginia	203
Vermont	198
Montana	146
Wyoming	128
South Dakota	125
North Dakota	70

County	Number
Los Angeles County, CA	33,062
Honolulu County, HI	23,812
San Francisco County, CA	17,978
Alameda County, CA	15,101
Santa Clara County, CA	14,746
Queens County, NY	9,129
San Mateo County, CA	9,078
New York County, NY	8,896
Orange County, CA	8,809
King County, WA	7,939
Contra Costa County, CA	7,201
Kings County, NY	7,039
Sacramento County, CA	6,401
San Diego County, CA	5,536
Cook County, IL	5,312
Middlesex County, MA	4,286
Harris County, TX	3,365
Montgomery County, MD	3,100
Maricopa County, AZ	2,691
Nassau County, NY	2,301
Suffolk County, MA	2,133
Fairfax County, VA	2,077
Middlesex County, NJ	2,001
Miami-Dade County, FL	1,993
Norfolk County, MA	1,852
Broward County, FL	1,848
San Bernardino County, CA	1,842
Bergen County, NJ	1,728
Philadelphia County, PA	1,686
Clark County, NV	1,638
Westchester County, NY	1,463
Yolo County, CA	1,433
Suffolk County, NY	1,425
Fresno County, CA	1,356
Dallas County, TX	1,309
Fairfield County, CT	1,306
Monmouth County, NJ	1,259
Ventura County, CA	1,254
Travis County, TX	1,229
Riverside County, CA	1,204
DuPage County, IL	1,198
Marin County, CA	1,179
Multnomah County, OR	1,118
Oakland County, MI	1,107
Pima County, AZ	1,098
San Joaquin County, CA	1,046
Solano County, CA	987
Morris County, NJ	948
Fort Bend County, TX	937
Collin County, TX	883
Snohomish County, WA	880
Somerset County, NJ	876
Essex County, NJ	849
Hawaii County, HI	830
Washington County, OR	824
Hennepin County, MN	803
Cuyahoga County, OH	792
Maui County, HI	779
Washtenaw County, MI	765
Bexar County, TX	762
Sonoma County, CA	747
Santa Barbara County, CA	736
New Haven County, CT	729
Fulton County, GA	712
Palm Beach County, FL	701
Tarrant County, TX	697
Richmond County, NY	686
Bronx County, NY	671
Salt Lake County, UT	670
Franklin County, OH	663
Hudson County, NJ	651
Orange County, FL	646
Montgomery County, PA	632
Lake County, IL	630
Kern County, CA	629

Place	Number
New York, NY (city)	26,421
San Francisco, CA (city) San Francisco County	17,978
Honolulu, HI (cdp) Honolulu County	15,280
Los Angeles, CA (city) Los Angeles County	9,756
San Jose, CA (city) Santa Clara County	5,213
Sacramento, CA (city) Sacramento County	4,334
San Diego, CA (city) San Diego County	3,721
Oakland, CA (city) Alameda County	3,692
Seattle, WA (city) King County	3,412
Chicago, IL (city) Cook County	2,929
Fremont, CA (city) Alameda County	2,485
Houston, TX (city) Harris County	2,072
Boston, MA (city) Suffolk County	2,026
Berkeley, CA (city) Alameda County	1,869
Sunnyvale, CA (city) Santa Clara County	1,741
Daly City, CA (city) San Mateo County	1,700
Philadelphia, PA (city) Philadelphia County	1,686
Monterey Park, CA (city) Los Angeles County	1,595
Irvine, CA (city) Orange County	1,582
Alhambra, CA (city) Los Angeles County	1,420
Cupertino, CA (city) Santa Clara County	1,301
Alameda, CA (city) Alameda County	1,263
Davis, CA (city) Yolo County	1,217
Kaneohe, HI (cdp) Honolulu County	1,145
Torrance, CA (city) Los Angeles County	1,097
Palo Alto, CA (city) Santa Clara County	1,096
Austin, TX (city) Travis County	1,073
Phoenix, AZ (city) Maricopa County	1,059
Mountain View, CA (city) Santa Clara County	1,050
Hempstead, NY (town) Nassau County	1,011
San Mateo, CA (city) San Mateo County	1,006
Portland, OR (city) Multnomah County	994
Bellevue, WA (city) King County	992
South San Francisco, CA (city) San Mateo County	942
Foster City, CA (city) San Mateo County	931
San Leandro, CA (city) Alameda County	895
Castro Valley, CA (cdp) Alameda County	887
Fresno, CA (city) Fresno County	885
Cambridge, MA (city) Middlesex County	867
Pasadena, CA (city) Los Angeles County	851
Kailua, HI (cdp) Honolulu County	848
Arcadia, CA (city) Los Angeles County	835
Milpitas, CA (city) Santa Clara County	779
Dallas, TX (city) Dallas County	774
San Ramon, CA (city) Contra Costa County	773
Cerritos, CA (city) Los Angeles County	760
South Pasadena, CA (city) Los Angeles County	748
Pearl City, HI (cdp) Honolulu County	715
Huntington Beach, CA (city) Orange County	711
Waimalu, HI (cdp) Honolulu County	711
Santa Clara, CA (city) Santa Clara County	701
Diamond Bar, CA (city) Los Angeles County	683
Richmond, CA (city) Contra Costa County	664
North Hempstead, NY (town) Nassau County	663
Long Beach, CA (city) Los Angeles County	652
Stockton, CA (city) San Joaquin County	647
El Monte, CA (city) Los Angeles County	633
Walnut Creek, CA (city) Contra Costa County	630
Tucson, AZ (city) Pima County	624
Hacienda Heights, CA (cdp) Los Angeles County	620
Millbrae, CA (city) San Mateo County	619
Union City, CA (city) Alameda County	611
San Antonio, TX (city) Bexar County	605
Plano, TX (city) Collin County	603
Newton, MA (city) Middlesex County	597
Concord, CA (city) Contra Costa County	593
Rosemead, CA (city) Los Angeles County	588
Pleasanton, CA (city) Alameda County	583
Brookline, MA (town) Norfolk County	575
San Gabriel, CA (city) Los Angeles County	574
Anaheim, CA (city) Orange County	573
Danville, CA (town) Contra Costa County	567
Glendale, CA (city) Los Angeles County	564
Mililani Town, HI (cdp) Honolulu County	563
Saratoga, CA (city) Santa Clara County	557

Notes: Please refer to the User's Guide for an explanation of data; ranking tables include all places with Asian and/or NHPI populations above SF4 population thresholds; (1) tables reflect only those areas that meet SF4 population thresholds, therefore there may be less than 50 states, 75 counties or 75 places listed

Language Spoken at Home: English Only

Chinese (except Taiwanese) 5 Years and Over Who Speak English-Only at Home

All States, Top 75 Counties, and Top 75 Places Sorted by Percent[1]

State	Percent
Hawaii	47.72
Montana	26.59
District of Columbia	23.81
Idaho	23.66
Alaska	23.39
Colorado	22.09
Wyoming	22.03
Florida	21.90
Maine	21.39
New Mexico	21.35
Vermont	21.18
Louisiana	21.01
Washington	20.54
Arizona	20.46
South Dakota	20.13
New Hampshire	19.29
Oregon	18.73
Arkansas	18.19
Connecticut	17.92
Indiana	17.55
North Dakota	17.20
Nevada	16.89
Mississippi	16.86
Utah	16.37
Wisconsin	16.10
California	15.55
Rhode Island	15.46
Tennessee	15.34
Virginia	15.14
United States	14.95
Nebraska	14.74
North Carolina	14.41
Missouri	14.33
Michigan	14.30
Minnesota	13.76
Massachusetts	13.50
Ohio	13.46
West Virginia	13.29
Maryland	13.27
Georgia	13.26
Oklahoma	13.07
New Jersey	12.68
Illinois	12.64
Alabama	12.55
Pennsylvania	12.35
Iowa	12.26
Kansas	12.26
Texas	12.25
South Carolina	12.18
Delaware	11.03
Kentucky	10.61
New York	9.04

County	Percent
Maui County, HI	74.55
Kauai County, HI	73.63
Hawaii County, HI	63.99
Placer County, CA	46.58
Honolulu County, HI	46.56
Marin County, CA	39.23
Lee County, FL	38.85
Merced County, CA	37.71
El Paso County, CO	36.57
Hunterdon County, NJ	35.38
Pierce County, WA	34.65
Napa County, CA	33.98
Thurston County, WA	33.45
Kitsap County, WA	32.59
Whatcom County, WA	32.14
Solano County, CA	32.08
Kern County, CA	32.04
Ada County, ID	31.74
Santa Cruz County, CA	31.19
Cumberland County, ME	30.75
San Luis Obispo County, CA	30.38
Santa Barbara County, CA	29.86
Monterey County, CA	29.80
Allen County, IN	29.50
Fresno County, CA	29.44
Tulare County, CA	29.23
Sonoma County, CA	28.83
Barnstable County, MA	27.94
Muscogee County, GA	27.94
Orleans Parish, LA	27.65
Polk County, FL	27.61
Contra Costa County, CA	27.16
Brevard County, FL	27.08
Anoka County, MN	26.99
Waukesha County, WI	26.54
Kane County, IL	26.50
Larimer County, CO	26.48
Ventura County, CA	26.31
Alexandria Independent City, VA	26.30
Anchorage Borough, AK	26.22
Yolo County, CA	26.14
Midland County, MI	25.41
Cumberland County, PA	25.26
Grafton County, NH	25.26
Anne Arundel County, MD	25.23
Jefferson County, TX	25.21
Pima County, AZ	25.20
Lake County, OH	25.17
Dona Ana County, NM	25.07
Middlesex County, CT	24.95
Ulster County, NY	24.51
Denver County, CO	24.49
Hillsborough County, FL	24.48
Clackamas County, OR	24.43
Putnam County, NY	24.41
Seminole County, FL	24.40
Fairfield County, CT	24.35
Saint Louis Independent City, MO	23.99
Sarasota County, FL	23.97
Saratoga County, NY	23.85
Miami-Dade County, FL	23.81
Dutchess County, NY	23.78
Prince William County, VA	23.62
Sacramento County, CA	23.48
Greenville County, SC	23.40
Stanislaus County, CA	23.36
Broward County, FL	23.34
Spokane County, WA	23.28
Plymouth County, MA	23.27
Penobscot County, ME	22.79
Bernalillo County, NM	22.56
Westchester County, NY	22.42
Butte County, CA	22.41
Jefferson County, CO	22.29
Rockingham County, NH	22.22

Place	Percent
Kaneohe, HI (cdp) Honolulu County	81.49
Waipahu, HI (cdp) Honolulu County	79.17
Ahuimanu, HI (cdp) Honolulu County	78.61
Kailua, HI (cdp) Honolulu County	73.17
Hilo, HI (cdp) Hawaii County	72.38
Mililani Town, HI (cdp) Honolulu County	59.45
Pearl City, HI (cdp) Honolulu County	58.04
Waimalu, HI (cdp) Honolulu County	56.83
Manhattan Beach, CA (city) Los Angeles County	56.23
Halawa, HI (cdp) Honolulu County	52.30
Westport, CT (town) Fairfield County	50.00
Roseville, CA (city) Placer County	49.67
Kendall, FL (cdp) Miami-Dade County	48.54
Orinda, CA (city) Contra Costa County	45.55
Miramar, FL (city) Broward County	45.38
Santa Barbara, CA (city) Santa Barbara County	42.86
San Carlos, CA (city) San Mateo County	42.35
Martinez, CA (city) Contra Costa County	42.03
Redlands, CA (city) San Bernardino County	41.04
Honolulu, HI (cdp) Honolulu County	40.47
Redondo Beach, CA (city) Los Angeles County	40.41
Camarillo, CA (city) Ventura County	40.27
Danville, CA (town) Contra Costa County	38.28
Salinas, CA (city) Monterey County	38.00
Menlo Park, CA (city) San Mateo County	37.07
Montclair, NJ (township) Essex County	36.62
Carson, CA (city) Los Angeles County	36.01
Tacoma, WA (city) Pierce County	35.68
Lancaster, CA (city) Los Angeles County	35.39
Lake Success, NY (village) Nassau County	35.00
Oak Park, IL (village) Cook County	34.81
Colorado Springs, CO (city) El Paso County	34.75
Laie, HI (cdp) Honolulu County	34.55
New Brunswick, NJ (city) Middlesex County	34.23
Novato, CA (city) Marin County	33.88
Temecula, CA (city) Riverside County	33.88
Santa Cruz, CA (city) Santa Cruz County	33.80
Culver City, CA (city) Los Angeles County	33.76
Mercer Island, WA (city) King County	33.23
Santa Monica, CA (city) Los Angeles County	33.00
La Habra, CA (city) Orange County	32.89
Rolling Hills Estates, CA (city) Los Angeles County	32.54
Pleasant Hill, CA (city) Contra Costa County	32.31
Laguna Niguel, CA (city) Orange County	32.28
Campbell, CA (city) Santa Clara County	32.21
Laguna Hills, CA (city) Orange County	32.11
Moraga, CA (town) Contra Costa County	32.11
Fairfield, CA (city) Solano County	31.77
Goleta, CA (cdp) Santa Barbara County	31.64
Moreno Valley, CA (city) Riverside County	31.38
San Luis Obispo, CA (city) San Luis Obispo County	31.36
Yonkers, NY (city) Westchester County	31.29
Boise City, ID (city) Ada County	31.26
Newport Beach, CA (city) Orange County	31.02
Reston, VA (cdp) Fairfax County	30.91
San Ramon, CA (city) Contra Costa County	30.80
Belmont, CA (city) San Mateo County	30.70
Fairfield, CT (town) Fairfield County	30.69
Piedmont, CA (city) Alameda County	30.56
Emeryville, CA (city) Alameda County	30.50
Blackhawk-Camino Tass., CA (cdp) Contra Costa Co.	30.37
Bothell, WA (city) King County	30.37
Hoboken, NJ (city) Hudson County	30.17
Folsom, CA (city) Sacramento County	29.87
Pacifica, CA (city) San Mateo County	29.72
Poway, CA (city) San Diego County	29.35
Laguna West-Lakeside, CA (cdp) Sacramento County	29.32
Carmichael, CA (cdp) Sacramento County	29.15
Santa Rosa, CA (city) Sonoma County	28.91
Aliso Viejo, CA (cdp) Orange County	28.86
West Springfield, VA (cdp) Fairfax County	28.62
Gilroy, CA (city) Santa Clara County	28.57
Bellaire, TX (city) Harris County	28.31
Bakersfield, CA (city) Kern County	28.28
Petaluma, CA (city) Sonoma County	28.19

Notes: Please refer to the User's Guide for an explanation of data; ranking tables include all places with Asian and/or NHPI populations above SF4 population thresholds; (1) tables reflect only those areas that meet SF4 population thresholds, therefore there may be less than 50 states, 75 counties or 75 places listed

Language Spoken at Home: English Only

Fijians 5 Years and Over Who Speak English-Only at Home

All States, Top 75 Counties, and Top 75 Places Sorted by Number[1]

State	Number
United States	1,565
California	1,163
Washington	108
Oregon	71

County	Number
Alameda County, CA	201
Sacramento County, CA	192
Los Angeles County, CA	144
San Mateo County, CA	103
Contra Costa County, CA	101
Santa Clara County, CA	75
King County, WA	61
Stanislaus County, CA	35
Yolo County, CA	31

Place	Number
Sacramento, CA (city) Sacramento County	137
Hayward, CA (city) Alameda County	113
Modesto, CA (city) Stanislaus County	0

Notes: Please refer to the User's Guide for an explanation of data; ranking tables include all places with Asian and/or NHPI populations above SF4 population thresholds; (1) tables reflect only those areas that meet SF4 population thresholds, therefore there may be less than 50 states, 75 counties or 75 places listed

Language Spoken at Home: English Only

Fijians 5 Years and Over Who Speak English-Only at Home

All States, Top 75 Counties, and Top 75 Places Sorted by Percent[1]

State	Percent
Oregon	19.45
Washington	16.39
United States	16.31
California	14.83

County	Percent
Los Angeles County, CA	30.64
Contra Costa County, CA	19.20
Santa Clara County, CA	15.24
Alameda County, CA	14.77
King County, WA	11.94
Sacramento County, CA	11.55
San Mateo County, CA	9.80
Yolo County, CA	7.19
Stanislaus County, CA	5.48

Place	Percent
Hayward, CA (city) Alameda County	14.29
Sacramento, CA (city) Sacramento County	11.58
Modesto, CA (city) Stanislaus County	<0.01

Notes: Please refer to the User's Guide for an explanation of data; ranking tables include all places with Asian and/or NHPI populations above SF4 population thresholds; (1) tables reflect only those areas that meet SF4 population thresholds, therefore there may be less than 50 states, 75 counties or 75 places listed

Language Spoken at Home: English Only

Filipinos 5 Years and Over Who Speak English-Only at Home

All States, Top 75 Counties, and Top 75 Places Sorted by Number[1]

State	Number
United States	517,234
California	240,320
Hawaii	60,376
Illinois	21,009
Washington	20,358
New York	19,000
New Jersey	18,059
Florida	16,338
Texas	15,863
Virginia	13,768
Nevada	9,762
Maryland	7,494
Arizona	5,792
Michigan	5,229
Pennsylvania	4,953
Ohio	4,527
Oregon	4,281
Colorado	4,251
North Carolina	3,651
Georgia	3,437
Massachusetts	3,405
Alaska	2,667
Indiana	2,591
South Carolina	2,429
Missouri	2,312
Wisconsin	2,233
Connecticut	2,106
Minnesota	2,079
Tennessee	1,798
Louisiana	1,517
Oklahoma	1,499
Utah	1,339
Kansas	1,174
New Mexico	1,156
Kentucky	1,093
Alabama	909
Arkansas	836
Iowa	823
Mississippi	788
Nebraska	727
Idaho	712
District of Columbia	656
West Virginia	605
Rhode Island	545
Delaware	544
Maine	521
New Hampshire	447
Montana	375
South Dakota	267
North Dakota	247
Wyoming	216
Vermont	150

County	Number
Los Angeles County, CA	55,111
Honolulu County, HI	44,123
San Diego County, CA	34,179
Santa Clara County, CA	19,439
Alameda County, CA	17,993
San Mateo County, CA	14,586
Orange County, CA	14,124
Cook County, IL	12,228
Solano County, CA	10,377
Contra Costa County, CA	9,681
King County, WA	9,633
San Francisco County, CA	9,450
Sacramento County, CA	8,515
Clark County, NV	7,812
San Bernardino County, CA	7,665
San Joaquin County, CA	6,879
Maui County, HI	6,400
Riverside County, CA	6,299
Queens County, NY	5,523
Hawaii County, HI	5,109
Kauai County, HI	4,744
Maricopa County, AZ	4,045
Virginia Beach Independent City, VA	4,002
Ventura County, CA	3,946
Monterey County, CA	3,816
DuPage County, IL	3,757
Harris County, TX	3,421
Duval County, FL	3,303
Hudson County, NJ	3,286
Fairfax County, VA	2,963
Middlesex County, NJ	2,897
New York County, NY	2,650
Pierce County, WA	2,631
Bergen County, NJ	2,586
Kern County, CA	2,541
Snohomish County, WA	2,302
Kitsap County, WA	2,209
Fresno County, CA	2,140
Prince George's County, MD	1,992
Bexar County, TX	1,847
Nassau County, NY	1,779
Santa Barbara County, CA	1,761
Lake County, IL	1,753
Dallas County, TX	1,661
Essex County, NJ	1,633
Orange County, FL	1,529
Broward County, FL	1,494
Washoe County, NV	1,405
Montgomery County, MD	1,390
Kings County, NY	1,334
Suffolk County, NY	1,296
Anchorage Borough, AK	1,233
Stanislaus County, CA	1,233
Washington County, OR	1,200
Oakland County, MI	1,182
Multnomah County, OR	1,172
Philadelphia County, PA	1,117
El Paso County, CO	1,109
Richmond County, NY	1,100
Tulare County, CA	1,080
Norfolk Independent City, VA	1,075
Tarrant County, TX	1,071
Union County, NJ	1,070
Sonoma County, CA	1,062
Pima County, AZ	1,037
Baltimore County, MD	1,035
San Luis Obispo County, CA	1,024
Hillsborough County, FL	1,013
Escambia County, FL	1,011
Camden County, NJ	1,006
Westchester County, NY	1,000
Yolo County, CA	1,000
Anne Arundel County, MD	996
Fort Bend County, TX	951
Rockland County, NY	908

Place	Number
San Diego, CA (city) San Diego County	20,457
Los Angeles, CA (city) Los Angeles County	19,701
Honolulu, HI (cdp) Honolulu County	13,245
San Jose, CA (city) Santa Clara County	11,786
New York, NY (city)	11,331
San Francisco, CA (city) San Francisco County	9,450
Daly City, CA (city) San Mateo County	6,692
Chicago, IL (city) Cook County	6,039
Vallejo, CA (city) Solano County	5,923
Waipahu, HI (cdp) Honolulu County	4,645
Stockton, CA (city) San Joaquin County	4,440
Seattle, WA (city) King County	4,316
Chula Vista, CA (city) San Diego County	4,229
Long Beach, CA (city) Los Angeles County	3,942
Fremont, CA (city) Alameda County	3,390
Carson, CA (city) Los Angeles County	3,327
Jacksonville, FL (city) Duval County	3,124
Hayward, CA (city) Alameda County	2,995
Union City, CA (city) Alameda County	2,964
Sacramento, CA (city) Sacramento County	2,730
South San Francisco, CA (city) San Mateo County	2,681
Las Vegas, NV (city) Clark County	2,655
Jersey City, NJ (city) Hudson County	2,497
Milpitas, CA (city) Santa Clara County	2,050
Oxnard, CA (city) Ventura County	2,028
Fairfield, CA (city) Solano County	1,989
Glendale, CA (city) Los Angeles County	1,986
Salinas, CA (city) Monterey County	1,962
West Covina, CA (city) Los Angeles County	1,924
Mililani Town, HI (cdp) Honolulu County	1,760
Chino Hills, CA (city) San Bernardino County	1,719
Oakland, CA (city) Alameda County	1,699
Kahului, HI (cdp) Maui County	1,684
Pearl City, HI (cdp) Honolulu County	1,669
Irvine, CA (city) Orange County	1,660
Sunnyvale, CA (city) Santa Clara County	1,648
Hercules, CA (city) Contra Costa County	1,614
Ewa Beach, HI (cdp) Honolulu County	1,612
Phoenix, AZ (city) Maricopa County	1,592
Santa Clara, CA (city) Santa Clara County	1,538
Cerritos, CA (city) Los Angeles County	1,509
Houston, TX (city) Harris County	1,457
Anaheim, CA (city) Orange County	1,449
Waimalu, HI (cdp) Honolulu County	1,424
Oceanside, CA (city) San Diego County	1,391
Fresno, CA (city) Fresno County	1,373
Alameda, CA (city) Alameda County	1,372
National City, CA (city) San Diego County	1,347
San Antonio, TX (city) Bexar County	1,321
Village Park, HI (cdp) Honolulu County	1,290
Paradise, NV (cdp) Clark County	1,279
San Leandro, CA (city) Alameda County	1,260
Makakilo City, HI (cdp) Honolulu County	1,219
Antioch, CA (city) Contra Costa County	1,213
Riverside, CA (city) Riverside County	1,151
Wahiawa, HI (cdp) Honolulu County	1,140
Moreno Valley, CA (city) Riverside County	1,135
Pittsburg, CA (city) Contra Costa County	1,132
Concord, CA (city) Contra Costa County	1,123
Philadelphia, PA (city) Philadelphia County	1,117
Lakewood, CA (city) Los Angeles County	1,095
Ewa Villages, HI (cdp) Honolulu County	1,091
Elk Grove, CA (cdp) Sacramento County	1,086
Hilo, HI (cdp) Hawaii County	1,059
Torrance, CA (city) Los Angeles County	1,056
Waipio, HI (cdp) Honolulu County	1,054
Newark, CA (city) Alameda County	1,033
Suisun City, CA (city) Solano County	1,008
Halawa, HI (cdp) Honolulu County	989
San Bruno, CA (city) San Mateo County	988
Fontana, CA (city) San Bernardino County	979
Sunrise Manor, NV (cdp) Clark County	976
Kihei, HI (cdp) Maui County	970
Portland, OR (city) Multnomah County	953
San Mateo, CA (city) San Mateo County	936

Notes: Please refer to the User's Guide for an explanation of data; ranking tables include all places with Asian and/or NHPI populations above SF4 population thresholds; (1) tables reflect only those areas that meet SF4 population thresholds, therefore there may be less than 50 states, 75 counties or 75 places listed

Language Spoken at Home: English Only

Filipinos 5 Years and Over Who Speak English-Only at Home

All States, Top 75 Counties, and Top 75 Places Sorted by Percent[1]

State	Percent
Montana	49.73
Vermont	48.08
Colorado	47.71
Maine	46.39
North Dakota	45.24
Idaho	45.03
Wyoming	44.72
Wisconsin	43.64
Oregon	42.17
New Mexico	41.39
Indiana	40.40
South Dakota	39.09
Alabama	38.83
Utah	38.83
Arkansas	38.65
West Virginia	38.63
Massachusetts	38.15
North Carolina	38.09
Arizona	37.90
Iowa	37.80
Oklahoma	37.31
Hawaii	37.21
Nebraska	37.13
Kansas	36.79
Minnesota	36.76
Kentucky	36.71
New Hampshire	36.52
South Carolina	36.52
Tennessee	36.45
Ohio	36.30
Pennsylvania	35.62
Georgia	34.59
Missouri	34.14
Louisiana	34.02
Washington	32.89
District of Columbia	32.05
Mississippi	31.88
Florida	31.41
Michigan	31.38
Delaware	31.32
Virginia	30.27
Connecticut	29.86
Maryland	29.38
United States	29.31
Texas	28.74
California	27.60
Rhode Island	27.10
Illinois	25.68
Nevada	25.62
New York	23.00
Alaska	22.70
New Jersey	21.72

County	Percent
Boulder County, CO	66.07
Yolo County, CA	60.98
San Benito County, CA	57.66
Cleveland County, OK	57.41
Allen County, IN	55.36
Utah County, UT	54.50
Champaign County, IL	53.79
Adams County, CO	53.34
Charles County, MD	51.68
Cumberland County, ME	51.57
Denver County, CO	51.56
Bristol County, MA	51.46
Yuba County, CA	50.49
Alachua County, FL	49.90
Yuma County, AZ	49.88
Lane County, OR	48.75
Jefferson County, CO	48.72
Richland County, SC	48.68
Butte County, CA	48.56
Richmond Independent City, VA	48.15
Suffolk County, MA	48.03
Charleston County, SC	47.76
Allegheny County, PA	47.67
Jefferson County, NY	47.62
Summit County, OH	47.53
Marin County, CA	47.41
Sandoval County, NM	47.11
Dane County, WI	46.97
Stanislaus County, CA	46.23
Shasta County, CA	46.10
El Paso County, CO	45.86
Worcester County, MA	45.85
Anoka County, MN	45.83
Newport News Independent City, VA	45.64
Pima County, AZ	45.46
Mobile County, AL	45.43
Cumberland County, NC	45.30
Bernalillo County, NM	45.11
Santa Cruz County, CA	45.10
Kauai County, HI	44.85
Washtenaw County, MI	44.82
Hamilton County, OH	44.76
Kent County, MI	44.72
Whatcom County, WA	44.67
Sonoma County, CA	44.58
Spokane County, WA	44.58
Fulton County, GA	44.00
DeKalb County, GA	43.79
Marion County, OR	43.75
Ada County, ID	43.50
Wake County, NC	43.35
Clackamas County, OR	43.34
San Luis Obispo County, CA	42.76
Sarasota County, FL	42.59
Ingham County, MI	42.52
Orleans Parish, LA	42.45
Anne Arundel County, MD	42.35
Travis County, TX	42.34
Onondaga County, NY	42.32
Berrien County, MI	42.05
Dorchester County, SC	41.95
Henrico County, VA	41.87
Milwaukee County, WI	41.76
Cochise County, AZ	41.75
Sussex County, NJ	41.35
Greenville County, SC	41.34
Monroe County, NY	41.17
Yakima County, WA	41.12
Baltimore Independent City, MD	41.10
Pierce County, WA	41.06
Churchill County, NV	41.03
Forsyth County, NC	40.94
Hawaii County, HI	40.88
Tulsa County, OK	40.86
Washington County, OR	40.79

Place	Percent
Kalaheo, HI (cdp) Kauai County	70.73
Davis, CA (city) Yolo County	67.10
Pukalani, HI (cdp) Maui County	63.64
Clovis, CA (city) Fresno County	63.47
Folsom, CA (city) Sacramento County	61.02
San Luis Obispo, CA (city) San Luis Obispo County	60.26
Rosemont, CA (cdp) Sacramento County	60.05
Honaunau-Napoopoo, HI (cdp) Hawaii County	58.54
Makaha, HI (cdp) Honolulu County	58.49
Ann Arbor, MI (city) Washtenaw County	58.41
Gilroy, CA (city) Santa Clara County	57.99
Mililani Town, HI (cdp) Honolulu County	57.93
Lihue, HI (cdp) Kauai County	57.55
Redondo Beach, CA (city) Los Angeles County	57.05
Hollister, CA (city) San Benito County	56.89
Kapaa, HI (cdp) Kauai County	56.67
Paauilo, HI (cdp) Hawaii County	55.78
Makakilo City, HI (cdp) Honolulu County	54.91
Makawao, HI (cdp) Maui County	54.49
Kailua, HI (cdp) Hawaii County	54.26
Santa Cruz, CA (city) Santa Cruz County	54.00
Lawai, HI (cdp) Kauai County	53.93
Kapaau, HI (cdp) Hawaii County	53.64
Hilo, HI (cdp) Hawaii County	53.57
Monterey, CA (city) Monterey County	52.87
Nanakuli, HI (cdp) Honolulu County	52.86
Fayetteville, NC (city) Cumberland County	52.51
Kaneohe, HI (cdp) Honolulu County	51.94
Seattle Hill-Silver Firs, WA (cdp) Snohomish County	51.67
Denver, CO (city) Denver County	51.56
Hawaiian Beaches, HI (cdp) Hawaii County	51.51
Kailua, HI (cdp) Honolulu County	51.36
Lemon Grove, CA (city) San Diego County	51.31
Irvine, CA (city) Orange County	51.30
Berkeley, CA (city) Alameda County	51.23
Waipio Acres, HI (cdp) Honolulu County	51.05
Koloa, HI (cdp) Kauai County	50.50
Haleiwa, HI (cdp) Honolulu County	50.41
La Mesa, CA (city) San Diego County	50.28
Boston, MA (city) Suffolk County	50.26
Waimea, HI (cdp) Kauai County	50.21
Santa Barbara, CA (city) Santa Barbara County	49.47
Victorville, CA (city) San Bernardino County	49.23
Lodi, CA (city) San Joaquin County	49.02
Waianae, HI (cdp) Honolulu County	48.88
Los Banos, CA (city) Merced County	48.80
West Bloomfield, MI (township) Oakland County	48.55
Lompoc, CA (city) Santa Barbara County	48.51
Security-Widefield, CO (cdp) El Paso County	47.81
Captain Cook, HI (cdp) Hawaii County	47.70
Kurtistown, HI (cdp) Hawaii County	47.62
Spring Valley, CA (cdp) San Diego County	47.45
Aiea, HI (cdp) Honolulu County	47.18
Cincinnati, OH (city) Hamilton County	47.03
Huntington Beach, CA (city) Orange County	46.91
Vacaville, CA (city) Solano County	46.91
Manteca, CA (city) San Joaquin County	46.38
Kealakekua, HI (cdp) Hawaii County	46.36
Burlingame, CA (city) San Mateo County	46.27
Waikapu, HI (cdp) Maui County	46.11
Waipio, HI (cdp) Honolulu County	46.09
Benicia, CA (city) Solano County	46.01
Rio Rancho, NM (city) Sandoval County	45.79
Glendale, AZ (city) Maricopa County	45.38
Poway, CA (city) San Diego County	44.93
Pleasanton, CA (city) Alameda County	44.92
Orland Park, IL (village) Cook County	44.72
Salem, OR (city) Marion County	44.56
Waimalu, HI (cdp) Honolulu County	44.42
Austin, TX (city) Travis County	44.11
Pepeekeo, HI (cdp) Hawaii County	43.93
Madison, WI (city) Dane County	43.85
Fountain Valley, CA (city) Orange County	43.81
Modesto, CA (city) Stanislaus County	43.74
Campbell, CA (city) Santa Clara County	43.67

Notes: Please refer to the User's Guide for an explanation of data; ranking tables include all places with Asian and/or NHPI populations above SF4 population thresholds; (1) tables reflect only those areas that meet SF4 population thresholds, therefore there may be less than 50 states, 75 counties or 75 places listed

Language Spoken at Home: English Only

Guamanians or Chamorros 5 Years and Over Who Speak English-Only at Home

All States, Top 75 Counties, and Top 75 Places Sorted by Number[1]

State	Number
United States	28,796
California	11,488
Washington	2,832
Texas	1,599
Arizona	858
Florida	829
New York	791
Oregon	723
Hawaii	714
Colorado	665
North Carolina	578
Nevada	576
Virginia	533
Pennsylvania	435
Ohio	422
Georgia	377
Maryland	377
Missouri	368
Louisiana	322
Illinois	312
Connecticut	292
Wisconsin	291
Indiana	287
Michigan	246
Oklahoma	214
Tennessee	208
New Mexico	203
Minnesota	202
New Jersey	186
Alabama	173
Kentucky	152
South Carolina	136
Massachusetts	122

County	Number
San Diego County, CA	2,801
Los Angeles County, CA	1,524
Pierce County, WA	896
Santa Clara County, CA	839
Alameda County, CA	792
Solano County, CA	688
Orange County, CA	683
Honolulu County, HI	664
Sacramento County, CA	554
Kitsap County, WA	511
King County, WA	478
Clark County, NV	471
Riverside County, CA	448
Maricopa County, AZ	440
San Bernardino County, CA	433
Monterey County, CA	420
Thurston County, WA	358
Bell County, TX	330
Contra Costa County, CA	324
El Paso County, CO	322
Harris County, TX	284
San Mateo County, CA	248
Kings County, NY	226

Place	Number
San Diego, CA (city) San Diego County	1,361
New York, NY (city)	552
Los Angeles, CA (city) Los Angeles County	482
San Jose, CA (city) Santa Clara County	445
Fairfield, CA (city) Solano County	294
Honolulu, HI (cdp) Honolulu County	281
Vallejo, CA (city) Solano County	269
Killeen, TX (city) Bell County	257
Tacoma, WA (city) Pierce County	254
Chula Vista, CA (city) San Diego County	216
Houston, TX (city) Harris County	165

Notes: Please refer to the User's Guide for an explanation of data; ranking tables include all places with Asian and/or NHPI populations above SF4 population thresholds; (1) tables reflect only those areas that meet SF4 population thresholds, therefore there may be less than 50 states, 75 counties or 75 places listed

Language Spoken at Home: English Only

Guamanians or Chamorros 5 Years and Over Who Speak English-Only at Home

All States, Top 75 Counties, and Top 75 Places Sorted by Percent[1]

State	Percent
Connecticut	75.06
Wisconsin	74.62
Arizona	73.71
Louisiana	73.68
Ohio	71.28
Colorado	68.28
Oregon	67.82
New Mexico	64.24
Missouri	64.11
Pennsylvania	60.75
California	60.01
Virginia	58.77
Indiana	58.10
Oklahoma	57.99
Maryland	57.82
Washington	57.18
United States	56.44
Nevada	53.68
North Carolina	53.67
Texas	52.46
Hawaii	50.46
Minnesota	48.21
New York	48.20
Alabama	47.27
Florida	43.86
Kentucky	43.18
Tennessee	42.89
Michigan	40.26
South Carolina	40.24
Illinois	40.15
New Jersey	36.19
Georgia	29.99
Massachusetts	29.05

County	Percent
Maricopa County, AZ	72.85
Sacramento County, CA	67.40
Santa Clara County, CA	67.39
El Paso County, CO	67.22
Monterey County, CA	66.56
Orange County, CA	64.56
Alameda County, CA	64.29
Contra Costa County, CA	64.03
San Diego County, CA	63.27
San Mateo County, CA	62.31
King County, WA	62.08
Bell County, TX	55.37
Kitsap County, WA	55.30
Pierce County, WA	54.20
Los Angeles County, CA	53.27
Solano County, CA	53.13
Clark County, NV	52.80
Honolulu County, HI	52.45
Harris County, TX	52.11
Riverside County, CA	51.14
Thurston County, WA	50.64
Kings County, NY	50.45
San Bernardino County, CA	43.83

Place	Percent
San Diego, CA (city) San Diego County	68.36
San Jose, CA (city) Santa Clara County	66.82
Tacoma, WA (city) Pierce County	63.34
Fairfield, CA (city) Solano County	55.58
Chula Vista, CA (city) San Diego County	52.68
Killeen, TX (city) Bell County	51.40
New York, NY (city)	49.91
Vallejo, CA (city) Solano County	48.21
Los Angeles, CA (city) Los Angeles County	46.26
Honolulu, HI (cdp) Honolulu County	43.70
Houston, TX (city) Harris County	42.20

Notes: Please refer to the User's Guide for an explanation of data; ranking tables include all places with Asian and/or NHPI populations above SF4 population thresholds; (1) tables reflect only those areas that meet SF4 population thresholds, therefore there may be less than 50 states, 75 counties or 75 places listed

Language Spoken at Home: English Only

Hawaiian Natives 5 Years and Over Who Speak English-Only at Home

All States, Top 75 Counties, and Top 75 Places Sorted by Number[1]

State	Number
United States	108,611
Hawaii	63,416
California	15,552
Washington	3,679
Nevada	2,641
Texas	2,277
Oregon	1,621
Florida	1,519
Arizona	1,360
Utah	1,149
Colorado	1,136
North Carolina	923
New York	814
Virginia	801
Illinois	718
Pennsylvania	691
Michigan	666
Georgia	637
Missouri	587
Ohio	571
Oklahoma	552
Indiana	537
Tennessee	466
New Jersey	464
Maryland	431
South Carolina	390
Minnesota	374
Kansas	358
Alaska	356
Massachusetts	351
Wisconsin	320
Idaho	319
Louisiana	316
New Mexico	276
Arkansas	253
Montana	215

County	Number
Honolulu County, HI	40,408
Hawaii County, HI	10,323
Maui County, HI	8,947
Kauai County, HI	3,679
Los Angeles County, CA	3,366
Clark County, NV	2,367
San Diego County, CA	1,955
Orange County, CA	1,282
King County, WA	1,116
Alameda County, CA	981
Santa Clara County, CA	939
Maricopa County, AZ	774
Pierce County, WA	686
Riverside County, CA	661
San Mateo County, CA	634
Sacramento County, CA	588
Solano County, CA	526
Contra Costa County, CA	518
San Bernardino County, CA	466
Snohomish County, WA	441
Multnomah County, OR	424
Ventura County, CA	391
Salt Lake County, UT	386
Utah County, UT	341
Washington County, OR	334
Bexar County, TX	309
San Joaquin County, CA	303
Pima County, AZ	300

Place	Number
Honolulu, HI (cdp) Honolulu County	11,554
Hilo, HI (cdp) Hawaii County	3,098
Kaneohe, HI (cdp) Honolulu County	2,668
Nanakuli, HI (cdp) Honolulu County	2,407
Kailua, HI (cdp) Honolulu County	1,959
Waianae, HI (cdp) Honolulu County	1,825
Waimanalo Beach, HI (cdp) Honolulu County	1,751
Maili, HI (cdp) Honolulu County	1,210
Los Angeles, CA (city) Los Angeles County	1,156
Kahului, HI (cdp) Maui County	1,097
Makaha, HI (cdp) Honolulu County	1,062
Wailuku, HI (cdp) Maui County	1,028
San Diego, CA (city) San Diego County	1,003
Pearl City, HI (cdp) Honolulu County	992
Ewa Beach, HI (cdp) Honolulu County	885
Waimalu, HI (cdp) Honolulu County	857
Makakilo City, HI (cdp) Honolulu County	838
Kailua, HI (cdp) Hawaii County	833
Waipahu, HI (cdp) Honolulu County	805
Wahiawa, HI (cdp) Honolulu County	785
Waimea, HI (cdp) Hawaii County	751
Anahola, HI (cdp) Kauai County	739
Mililani Town, HI (cdp) Honolulu County	731
Ahuimanu, HI (cdp) Honolulu County	726
Waihee-Waiehu, HI (cdp) Maui County	726
Waimanalo, HI (cdp) Honolulu County	679
Kualapuu, HI (cdp) Maui County	656
Kapaa, HI (cdp) Kauai County	636
Kihei, HI (cdp) Maui County	618
Kaunakakai, HI (cdp) Maui County	607
Lahaina, HI (cdp) Maui County	605
Las Vegas, NV (city) Clark County	591
Halawa, HI (cdp) Honolulu County	556
Hauula, HI (cdp) Honolulu County	555
Kalaoa, HI (cdp) Hawaii County	540
Kahaluu, HI (cdp) Honolulu County	491
Makawao, HI (cdp) Maui County	482
San Jose, CA (city) Santa Clara County	420
Hawaiian Paradise Park, HI (cdp) Hawaii County	407
Paradise, NV (cdp) Clark County	395
Henderson, NV (city) Clark County	368
Waipio, HI (cdp) Honolulu County	358
Phoenix, AZ (city) Maricopa County	322
Portland, OR (city) Multnomah County	312
Hawaiian Beaches, HI (cdp) Hawaii County	294
New York, NY (city)	282
Aiea, HI (cdp) Honolulu County	280
Kekaha, HI (cdp) Kauai County	261
Laie, HI (cdp) Honolulu County	257
Holualoa, HI (cdp) Hawaii County	248
Waikoloa Village, HI (cdp) Hawaii County	234
Honaunau-Napoopoo, HI (cdp) Hawaii County	231
Hana, HI (cdp) Maui County	219
Volcano, HI (cdp) Hawaii County	208
Makaha Valley, HI (cdp) Honolulu County	194
Captain Cook, HI (cdp) Hawaii County	192
Paia, HI (cdp) Maui County	177
Kaaawa, HI (cdp) Honolulu County	171
Kahuku, HI (cdp) Honolulu County	166
Haleiwa, HI (cdp) Honolulu County	157
Waimea, HI (cdp) Kauai County	153
Waikane, HI (cdp) Honolulu County	138
Punaluu, HI (cdp) Honolulu County	130
Honalo, HI (cdp) Hawaii County	126
Hawaiian Ocean View, HI (cdp) Hawaii County	124
Hanapepe, HI (cdp) Kauai County	122
Kilauea, HI (cdp) Kauai County	103
Naalehu, HI (cdp) Hawaii County	95
Kapaau, HI (cdp) Hawaii County	90
Waialua, HI (cdp) Honolulu County	90
Pahala, HI (cdp) Hawaii County	55
Pakala Village, HI (cdp) Kauai County	43

Notes: Please refer to the User's Guide for an explanation of data; ranking tables include all places with Asian and/or NHPI populations above SF4 population thresholds; (1) tables reflect only those areas that meet SF4 population thresholds, therefore there may be less than 50 states, 75 counties or 75 places listed

Language Spoken at Home: English Only

Hawaiian Natives 5 Years and Over Who Speak English-Only at Home

All States, Top 75 Counties, and Top 75 Places Sorted by Percent[1]

State	Percent
Idaho	93.82
Kansas	92.75
Virginia	90.51
Montana	89.21
Utah	89.07
Maryland	87.96
Missouri	87.61
Arkansas	86.94
Michigan	86.61
Louisiana	86.58
Tennessee	86.30
Indiana	85.78
Washington	85.54
Oklahoma	85.45
North Carolina	85.30
Oregon	84.82
Hawaii	84.41
United States	83.03
California	82.99
Colorado	82.44
Nevada	82.04
Illinois	81.96
Florida	81.54
Georgia	80.23
Wisconsin	79.40
South Carolina	79.27
Alaska	77.56
Massachusetts	74.52
New Mexico	74.19
New Jersey	74.00
Ohio	73.96
Arizona	73.51
Pennsylvania	71.61
Minnesota	67.03
Texas	66.52
New York	61.16

County	Percent
Multnomah County, OR	95.71
Sacramento County, CA	93.48
Snohomish County, WA	92.65
San Diego County, CA	92.13
Utah County, UT	91.67
Contra Costa County, CA	87.95
Honolulu County, HI	86.31
Salt Lake County, UT	85.78
Santa Clara County, CA	84.75
Riverside County, CA	84.74
Maui County, HI	83.57
San Mateo County, CA	83.31
Pierce County, WA	83.25
King County, WA	82.48
Solano County, CA	82.45
San Bernardino County, CA	82.04
Clark County, NV	81.23
Kauai County, HI	80.89
San Joaquin County, CA	80.59
Los Angeles County, CA	80.28
Orange County, CA	79.68
Hawaii County, HI	79.60
Washington County, OR	79.52
Alameda County, CA	78.99
Bexar County, TX	76.87
Ventura County, CA	74.90
Pima County, AZ	74.07
Maricopa County, AZ	72.27

Place	Percent
Waikane, HI (cdp) Honolulu County	97.87
Kahaluu, HI (cdp) Honolulu County	96.27
Ewa Beach, HI (cdp) Honolulu County	96.09
Ahuimanu, HI (cdp) Honolulu County	95.90
Makawao, HI (cdp) Maui County	95.83
Punaluu, HI (cdp) Honolulu County	95.59
San Diego, CA (city) San Diego County	94.98
Portland, OR (city) Multnomah County	94.26
Makaha Valley, HI (cdp) Honolulu County	94.17
Kapaau, HI (cdp) Hawaii County	93.75
Maili, HI (cdp) Honolulu County	92.86
Makakilo City, HI (cdp) Honolulu County	92.49
Waipio, HI (cdp) Honolulu County	92.27
Kahuku, HI (cdp) Honolulu County	91.21
Hana, HI (cdp) Maui County	90.87
Waimalu, HI (cdp) Honolulu County	90.78
Waimanalo Beach, HI (cdp) Honolulu County	89.70
Henderson, NV (city) Clark County	89.54
Waipahu, HI (cdp) Honolulu County	89.05
Wailuku, HI (cdp) Maui County	88.93
Honalo, HI (cdp) Hawaii County	88.73
Mililani Town, HI (cdp) Honolulu County	88.61
Paia, HI (cdp) Maui County	88.50
Kaunakakai, HI (cdp) Maui County	88.48
Waimea, HI (cdp) Kauai County	88.44
Wahiawa, HI (cdp) Honolulu County	87.71
Makaha, HI (cdp) Honolulu County	87.41
Hauula, HI (cdp) Honolulu County	86.85
Naalehu, HI (cdp) Hawaii County	86.36
Waimea, HI (cdp) Hawaii County	86.32
Kailua, HI (cdp) Hawaii County	86.14
Waihee-Waiehu, HI (cdp) Maui County	86.02
Waimanalo, HI (cdp) Honolulu County	85.95
Nanakuli, HI (cdp) Honolulu County	85.63
Honolulu, HI (cdp) Honolulu County	85.45
Haleiwa, HI (cdp) Honolulu County	84.86
Kaneohe, HI (cdp) Honolulu County	84.64
Waianae, HI (cdp) Honolulu County	84.49
Kilauea, HI (cdp) Kauai County	84.43
Kapaa, HI (cdp) Kauai County	84.02
Waikoloa Village, HI (cdp) Hawaii County	83.87
Kekaha, HI (cdp) Kauai County	83.12
Kailua, HI (cdp) Honolulu County	83.11
Kihei, HI (cdp) Maui County	82.95
Laie, HI (cdp) Honolulu County	82.90
Anahola, HI (cdp) Kauai County	82.85
Captain Cook, HI (cdp) Hawaii County	82.05
Aiea, HI (cdp) Honolulu County	81.40
Kalaoa, HI (cdp) Hawaii County	81.20
Halawa, HI (cdp) Honolulu County	80.81
Hawaiian Beaches, HI (cdp) Hawaii County	80.77
Kaaawa, HI (cdp) Honolulu County	80.28
San Jose, CA (city) Santa Clara County	79.70
Waialua, HI (cdp) Honolulu County	79.65
Hilo, HI (cdp) Hawaii County	79.19
Kahului, HI (cdp) Maui County	78.86
Las Vegas, NV (city) Clark County	78.59
Kualapuu, HI (cdp) Maui County	78.56
Pearl City, HI (cdp) Honolulu County	77.56
Honaunau-Napoopoo, HI (cdp) Hawaii County	77.52
Holualoa, HI (cdp) Hawaii County	75.15
Los Angeles, CA (city) Los Angeles County	75.11
Hawaiian Ocean View, HI (cdp) Hawaii County	74.25
Volcano, HI (cdp) Hawaii County	73.76
Hanapepe, HI (cdp) Kauai County	72.62
Paradise, NV (cdp) Clark County	71.30
Lahaina, HI (cdp) Maui County	71.18
Pahala, HI (cdp) Hawaii County	69.62
Phoenix, AZ (city) Maricopa County	64.79
Hawaiian Paradise Park, HI (cdp) Hawaii County	60.21
New York, NY (city)	40.23
Pakala Village, HI (cdp) Kauai County	29.25

Notes: Please refer to the User's Guide for an explanation of data; ranking tables include all places with Asian and/or NHPI populations above SF4 population thresholds; (1) tables reflect only those areas that meet SF4 population thresholds, therefore there may be less than 50 states, 75 counties or 75 places listed

Language Spoken at Home: English Only

Hmongs 5 Years and Over Who Speak English-Only at Home

All States, Top 75 Counties, and Top 75 Places Sorted by Number[1]

State	Number
United States	6,566
California	3,332
Minnesota	1,240
Wisconsin	1,031
Michigan	250
North Carolina	196
Colorado	75
Washington	61
Kansas	32
Oklahoma	27
Pennsylvania	21
Massachusetts	19
Oregon	16
Alaska	15
Georgia	13
Rhode Island	8
South Carolina	0

County	Number
Fresno County, CA	1,087
Ramsey County, MN	724
Sacramento County, CA	693
Merced County, CA	589
Hennepin County, MN	444
Milwaukee County, WI	287
Yuba County, CA	183
San Joaquin County, CA	162
Butte County, CA	117
Chippewa County, WI	102
Wayne County, MI	100
Dane County, WI	97
Orange County, CA	90
Macomb County, MI	86
Yolo County, CA	82
Adams County, CO	75
Stanislaus County, CA	72
Tulare County, CA	67
Brown County, WI	66
Catawba County, NC	64
Marathon County, WI	64
La Crosse County, WI	55
Manitowoc County, WI	55
Winnebago County, WI	53
Sheboygan County, WI	48
Eau Claire County, WI	47
Burke County, NC	46
King County, WA	46
Portage County, WI	43
San Diego County, CA	43
Solano County, CA	39
Outagamie County, WI	32
Riverside County, CA	28
Wood County, WI	27
Oakland County, MI	23
Wyandotte County, KS	23
Glenn County, CA	18
Calumet County, WI	17
Anchorage Borough, AK	15
Ingham County, MI	15
Spokane County, WA	15
Lancaster County, PA	14
Anoka County, MN	12
Dunn County, WI	11
Mecklenburg County, NC	11
Santa Barbara County, CA	11
Stanly County, NC	11
Barrow County, GA	9
Multnomah County, OR	9
Providence County, RI	8
Washington County, MN	8
Fond du Lac County, WI	4
Jefferson County, CO	0
Los Angeles County, CA	0
Olmsted County, MN	0
Spartanburg County, SC	0
Worcester County, MA	0

Place	Number
Fresno, CA (city) Fresno County	897
St. Paul, MN (city) Ramsey County	674
Sacramento, CA (city) Sacramento County	522
Merced, CA (city) Merced County	360
Minneapolis, MN (city) Hennepin County	291
Milwaukee, WI (city) Milwaukee County	261
Eau Claire, WI (city) Eau Claire County	142
Linda, CA (cdp) Yuba County	140
Stockton, CA (city) San Joaquin County	120
Detroit, MI (city) Wayne County	100
West Sacramento, CA (city) Yolo County	82
Brooklyn Park, MN (city) Hennepin County	75
Warren, MI (city) Macomb County	74
Parkway-S. Sacramento, CA (cdp) Sacramento County	71
Clovis, CA (city) Fresno County	68
Wausau, WI (city) Marathon County	64
Brooklyn Center, MN (city) Hennepin County	61
Appleton, WI (city) Outagamie County	49
Modesto, CA (city) Stanislaus County	49
Sheboygan, WI (city) Sheboygan County	47
Thermalito, CA (cdp) Butte County	45
Madison, WI (city) Dane County	41
Green Bay, WI (city) Brown County	39
Arden-Arcade, CA (cdp) Sacramento County	37
Stevens Point, WI (city) Portage County	37
Oshkosh, WI (city) Winnebago County	36
South Oroville, CA (cdp) Butte County	36
San Diego, CA (city) San Diego County	32
Santa Ana, CA (city) Orange County	29
Kansas City, KS (city) Wyandotte County	23
Visalia, CA (city) Tulare County	23
Florin, CA (cdp) Sacramento County	20
La Crosse, WI (city) La Crosse County	19
Pontiac, MI (city) Oakland County	19
Willows, CA (city) Glenn County	18
Manitowoc, WI (city) Manitowoc County	17
Maplewood, MN (city) Ramsey County	16
Lansing, MI (city) Ingham County	15
Spokane, WA (city) Spokane County	15
Charlotte, NC (city) Mecklenburg County	11
Wisconsin Rapids, WI (city) Wood County	10
Portland, OR (city) Multnomah County	9
Atwater, CA (city) Merced County	8
Woodbury, MN (city) Washington County	8
Oroville, CA (city) Butte County	5
Fond du Lac, WI (city) Fond du Lac County	4
Westminster, CO (city) Adams County	4
Connelly Springs, NC (town) Burke County	3
Valdese, NC (town) Burke County	3
Chico, CA (city) Butte County	0
Fitchburg, MA (city) Worcester County	0
Glen Alpine, NC (town) Burke County	0
Hickory, NC (city) Catawba County	0
Providence, RI (city) Providence County	0
Rochester, MN (city) Olmsted County	0

Notes: Please refer to the User's Guide for an explanation of data; ranking tables include all places with Asian and/or NHPI populations above SF4 population thresholds; (1) tables reflect only those areas that meet SF4 population thresholds, therefore there may be less than 50 states, 75 counties or 75 places listed

Language Spoken at Home: English Only

Hmongs 5 Years and Over Who Speak English-Only at Home

All States, Top 75 Counties, and Top 75 Places Sorted by Percent[1]

State	Percent
Oklahoma	9.12
California	5.48
Michigan	5.00
Washington	4.81
United States	4.39
Wisconsin	3.78
Kansas	3.76
North Carolina	3.33
Alaska	3.30
Minnesota	3.30
Colorado	2.76
Pennsylvania	2.70
Massachusetts	2.17
Oregon	1.35
Georgia	1.15
Rhode Island	0.91
South Carolina	<0.01

County	Percent
Chippewa County, WI	33.22
Yolo County, CA	13.46
Solano County, CA	10.21
Merced County, CA	10.09
Orange County, CA	9.23
Macomb County, MI	8.81
Stanislaus County, CA	7.87
Yuba County, CA	7.54
Tulare County, CA	7.03
Riverside County, CA	6.70
Manitowoc County, WI	6.48
Wayne County, MI	6.33
King County, WA	6.27
Portage County, WI	5.40
Fresno County, CA	5.08
Dane County, WI	4.88
Calumet County, WI	4.83
Wood County, WI	4.82
Butte County, CA	4.75
Sacramento County, CA	4.59
Milwaukee County, WI	4.36
Winnebago County, WI	4.16
Catawba County, NC	4.03
Barrow County, GA	4.02
Adams County, CO	3.86
Stanly County, NC	3.86
Hennepin County, MN	3.80
Santa Barbara County, CA	3.75
Eau Claire County, WI	3.67
Glenn County, CA	3.44
San Diego County, CA	3.39
La Crosse County, WI	3.36
Anchorage Borough, AK	3.30
Spokane County, WA	3.25
Wyandotte County, KS	3.23
Lancaster County, PA	3.13
Ramsey County, MN	3.13
Brown County, WI	3.09
San Joaquin County, CA	3.08
Ingham County, MI	2.82
Burke County, NC	2.68
Anoka County, MN	2.53
Oakland County, MI	2.34
Sheboygan County, WI	2.24
Dunn County, WI	2.20
Mecklenburg County, NC	2.12
Marathon County, WI	1.76
Fond du Lac County, WI	1.72
Outagamie County, WI	1.59
Washington County, MN	1.27
Providence County, RI	1.07
Multnomah County, OR	0.97
Jefferson County, CO	<0.01
Los Angeles County, CA	<0.01
Olmsted County, MN	<0.01
Spartanburg County, SC	<0.01
Worcester County, MA	<0.01

Place	Percent
West Sacramento, CA (city) Yolo County	15.50
Modesto, CA (city) Stanislaus County	13.42
Arden-Arcade, CA (cdp) Sacramento County	12.37
Warren, MI (city) Macomb County	10.66
Eau Claire, WI (city) Eau Claire County	10.61
Merced, CA (city) Merced County	9.74
Thermalito, CA (cdp) Butte County	7.99
Linda, CA (cdp) Yuba County	7.86
Brooklyn Park, MN (city) Hennepin County	7.57
Detroit, MI (city) Wayne County	7.10
South Oroville, CA (cdp) Butte County	6.74
Santa Ana, CA (city) Orange County	6.17
Stevens Point, WI (city) Portage County	5.32
Visalia, CA (city) Tulare County	5.10
Fresno, CA (city) Fresno County	4.97
Sacramento, CA (city) Sacramento County	4.95
Connelly Springs, NC (town) Burke County	4.76
Brooklyn Center, MN (city) Hennepin County	4.67
Maplewood, MN (city) Ramsey County	4.56
Spokane, WA (city) Spokane County	4.41
Clovis, CA (city) Fresno County	4.16
Milwaukee, WI (city) Milwaukee County	4.08
Oshkosh, WI (city) Winnebago County	3.87
Willows, CA (city) Glenn County	3.44
Minneapolis, MN (city) Hennepin County	3.26
Kansas City, KS (city) Wyandotte County	3.23
San Diego, CA (city) San Diego County	3.21
Valdese, NC (town) Burke County	3.06
St. Paul, MN (city) Ramsey County	3.05
Parkway-S. Sacramento, CA (cdp) Sacramento County	2.95
Pontiac, MI (city) Oakland County	2.89
Stockton, CA (city) San Joaquin County	2.75
Lansing, MI (city) Ingham County	2.66
Woodbury, MN (city) Washington County	2.61
Madison, WI (city) Dane County	2.59
Appleton, WI (city) Outagamie County	2.49
Sheboygan, WI (city) Sheboygan County	2.31
Manitowoc, WI (city) Manitowoc County	2.27
Fond du Lac, WI (city) Fond du Lac County	2.26
Green Bay, WI (city) Brown County	2.16
Atwater, CA (city) Merced County	2.15
Florin, CA (cdp) Sacramento County	2.15
Charlotte, NC (city) Mecklenburg County	2.12
Wausau, WI (city) Marathon County	2.09
Wisconsin Rapids, WI (city) Wood County	2.03
La Crosse, WI (city) La Crosse County	1.68
Oroville, CA (city) Butte County	1.21
Portland, OR (city) Multnomah County	1.11
Westminster, CO (city) Adams County	0.44
Chico, CA (city) Butte County	<0.01
Fitchburg, MA (city) Worcester County	<0.01
Glen Alpine, NC (town) Burke County	<0.01
Hickory, NC (city) Catawba County	<0.01
Providence, RI (city) Providence County	<0.01
Rochester, MN (city) Olmsted County	<0.01

Notes: Please refer to the User's Guide for an explanation of data; ranking tables include all places with Asian and/or NHPI populations above SF4 population thresholds; (1) tables reflect only those areas that meet SF4 population thresholds, therefore there may be less than 50 states, 75 counties or 75 places listed

Language Spoken at Home: English Only

Indonesians 5 Years and Over Who Speak English-Only at Home

All States, Top 75 Counties, and Top 75 Places Sorted by Number[1]

State	Number
United States	5,855
California	2,653
New York	345
Texas	293
Washington	192
Virginia	191
New Jersey	184
Massachusetts	167
Florida	126
Arizona	116
Illinois	116
Ohio	115
Oregon	112
Colorado	96
Pennsylvania	88
Maryland	86
Michigan	84
Wisconsin	69
Georgia	68

County	Number
Los Angeles County, CA	821
Orange County, CA	300
San Bernardino County, CA	255
San Mateo County, CA	160
King County, WA	141
San Francisco County, CA	139
Contra Costa County, CA	132
Alameda County, CA	120
Santa Clara County, CA	117
San Diego County, CA	88
Queens County, NY	87
Fairfax County, VA	82
Maricopa County, AZ	81
Harris County, TX	78
Cook County, IL	51
Montgomery County, MD	51
Middlesex County, NJ	44
Franklin County, OH	24

Place	Number
New York, NY (city)	245
Los Angeles, CA (city) Los Angeles County	244
San Francisco, CA (city) San Francisco County	139
Houston, TX (city) Harris County	73
San Bernardino, CA (city) San Bernardino County	61
Seattle, WA (city) King County	59
Loma Linda, CA (city) San Bernardino County	51
Columbus, OH (city) Franklin County	24

Notes: Please refer to the User's Guide for an explanation of data; ranking tables include all places with Asian and/or NHPI populations above SF4 population thresholds; (1) tables reflect only those areas that meet SF4 population thresholds, therefore there may be less than 50 states, 75 counties or 75 places listed

Language Spoken at Home: English Only

Indonesians 5 Years and Over Who Speak English-Only at Home

All States, Top 75 Counties, and Top 75 Places Sorted by Percent[1]

State	Percent
Massachusetts	24.49
Arizona	21.76
New Jersey	19.13
Oregon	18.21
Virginia	17.97
Pennsylvania	17.85
Wisconsin	17.56
Texas	17.39
California	17.28
United States	16.71
Washington	16.33
Florida	14.96
New York	14.77
Colorado	13.79
Michigan	13.73
Illinois	13.68
Georgia	13.26
Ohio	11.88
Maryland	8.50

County	Percent
Contra Costa County, CA	29.07
San Mateo County, CA	21.86
Alameda County, CA	21.13
Maricopa County, AZ	20.51
San Diego County, CA	19.38
King County, WA	18.05
Santa Clara County, CA	17.23
Orange County, CA	16.55
San Francisco County, CA	16.35
Los Angeles County, CA	15.43
Fairfax County, VA	14.39
Harris County, TX	12.52
Cook County, IL	11.31
Middlesex County, NJ	9.57
San Bernardino County, CA	8.76
Queens County, NY	7.29
Montgomery County, MD	6.03
Franklin County, OH	4.64

Place	Percent
San Francisco, CA (city) San Francisco County	16.35
Seattle, WA (city) King County	15.86
Houston, TX (city) Harris County	15.57
San Bernardino, CA (city) San Bernardino County	15.21
Los Angeles, CA (city) Los Angeles County	14.55
New York, NY (city)	14.10
Loma Linda, CA (city) San Bernardino County	10.43
Columbus, OH (city) Franklin County	4.79

Notes: Please refer to the User's Guide for an explanation of data; ranking tables include all places with Asian and/or NHPI populations above SF4 population thresholds; (1) tables reflect only those areas that meet SF4 population thresholds, therefore there may be less than 50 states, 75 counties or 75 places listed

Language Spoken at Home: English Only

Japanese 5 Years and Over Who Speak English-Only at Home

All States, Top 75 Counties, and Top 75 Places Sorted by Number[1]

State	Number
United States	405,791
California	148,375
Hawaii	148,182
Washington	19,444
Illinois	7,895
Colorado	7,050
New York	6,486
Texas	5,614
Oregon	5,593
Nevada	4,510
Florida	4,185
Utah	3,575
Arizona	3,481
Virginia	3,020
Ohio	2,945
Massachusetts	2,531
Michigan	2,441
Maryland	2,378
New Jersey	2,311
Pennsylvania	2,183
North Carolina	1,940
Georgia	1,818
Idaho	1,808
Minnesota	1,624
Missouri	1,477
Indiana	1,407
Wisconsin	1,222
New Mexico	1,183
Oklahoma	1,097
Connecticut	959
Tennessee	930
Alaska	817
Kansas	707
South Carolina	675
Nebraska	610
Alabama	525
Montana	489
Kentucky	484
Louisiana	445
Iowa	440
Arkansas	399
New Hampshire	341
Delaware	320
Maine	279
Rhode Island	264
District of Columbia	263
Wyoming	252
West Virginia	211
South Dakota	189
Mississippi	177
Vermont	150

County	Number
Honolulu County, HI	116,985
Los Angeles County, CA	54,840
Orange County, CA	15,605
Hawaii County, HI	15,324
Santa Clara County, CA	14,020
King County, WA	11,943
Maui County, HI	9,494
Sacramento County, CA	7,928
San Diego County, CA	7,774
Alameda County, CA	6,821
Kauai County, HI	6,364
Cook County, IL	5,433
Contra Costa County, CA	5,140
San Francisco County, CA	4,587
San Mateo County, CA	4,163
Fresno County, CA	3,877
Clark County, NV	3,540
Ventura County, CA	2,690
New York County, NY	2,601
San Bernardino County, CA	2,553
Maricopa County, AZ	2,424
Riverside County, CA	2,315
San Joaquin County, CA	2,267
Salt Lake County, UT	1,921
Multnomah County, OR	1,859
Pierce County, WA	1,665
Monterey County, CA	1,590
Santa Barbara County, CA	1,328
Jefferson County, CO	1,261
Snohomish County, WA	1,228
Placer County, CA	1,184
Harris County, TX	1,167
Santa Cruz County, CA	1,093
Denver County, CO	1,074
Washington County, OR	1,062
Arapahoe County, CO	1,018
Spokane County, WA	975
Solano County, CA	961
Sonoma County, CA	945
Middlesex County, MA	876
Montgomery County, MD	842
Marin County, CA	821
Fairfax County, VA	800
Bexar County, TX	797
Boulder County, CO	794
Washoe County, NV	712
Kern County, CA	708
Yolo County, CA	701
El Paso County, CO	678
Hennepin County, MN	676
Bernalillo County, NM	668
Pima County, AZ	639
Adams County, CO	628
Dallas County, TX	610
DuPage County, IL	605
Oakland County, MI	603
San Luis Obispo County, CA	601
Kings County, NY	597
Clackamas County, OR	595
Clark County, WA	587
Queens County, NY	555
Kitsap County, WA	544
Davis County, UT	530
Stanislaus County, CA	526
Bergen County, NJ	494
Lane County, OR	488
Franklin County, OH	470
Anchorage Borough, AK	466
Tarrant County, TX	466
Ada County, ID	465
Weber County, UT	462
Thurston County, WA	452
Norfolk County, MA	437
Cuyahoga County, OH	429
St. Louis County, MO	419

Place	Number
Honolulu, HI (cdp) Honolulu County	58,460
Los Angeles, CA (city) Los Angeles County	16,046
Hilo, HI (cdp) Hawaii County	8,469
Pearl City, HI (cdp) Honolulu County	7,392
Kaneohe, HI (cdp) Honolulu County	6,794
Waimalu, HI (cdp) Honolulu County	6,743
San Jose, CA (city) Santa Clara County	6,607
Torrance, CA (city) Los Angeles County	6,276
Mililani Town, HI (cdp) Honolulu County	5,924
Seattle, WA (city) King County	4,913
San Francisco, CA (city) San Francisco County	4,587
Sacramento, CA (city) Sacramento County	4,447
New York, NY (city)	3,914
San Diego, CA (city) San Diego County	3,783
Gardena, CA (city) Los Angeles County	3,506
Kailua, HI (cdp) Honolulu County	3,429
Chicago, IL (city) Cook County	3,129
Kahului, HI (cdp) Maui County	2,556
Monterey Park, CA (city) Los Angeles County	2,434
Waipahu, HI (cdp) Honolulu County	2,333
Waipio, HI (cdp) Honolulu County	2,283
Wahiawa, HI (cdp) Honolulu County	2,272
Aiea, HI (cdp) Honolulu County	2,150
Wailuku, HI (cdp) Maui County	2,145
Long Beach, CA (city) Los Angeles County	2,073
Halawa, HI (cdp) Honolulu County	2,041
Huntington Beach, CA (city) Orange County	1,856
Fresno, CA (city) Fresno County	1,722
Ahuimanu, HI (cdp) Honolulu County	1,578
Portland, OR (city) Multnomah County	1,567
Lihue, HI (cdp) Kauai County	1,348
Irvine, CA (city) Orange County	1,326
Cerritos, CA (city) Los Angeles County	1,285
Anaheim, CA (city) Orange County	1,279
Sunnyvale, CA (city) Santa Clara County	1,267
Las Vegas, NV (city) Clark County	1,248
Pasadena, CA (city) Los Angeles County	1,228
Oakland, CA (city) Alameda County	1,174
Berkeley, CA (city) Alameda County	1,156
Bellevue, WA (city) King County	1,148
Montebello, CA (city) Los Angeles County	1,142
Heeia, HI (cdp) Honolulu County	1,094
Denver, CO (city) Denver County	1,074
Redondo Beach, CA (city) Los Angeles County	1,019
Fremont, CA (city) Alameda County	1,009
Rancho Palos Verdes, CA (city) Los Angeles County	962
Stockton, CA (city) San Joaquin County	955
Santa Clara, CA (city) Santa Clara County	944
Kapaa, HI (cdp) Kauai County	928
Village Park, HI (cdp) Honolulu County	922
San Mateo, CA (city) San Mateo County	912
Mountain View, CA (city) Santa Clara County	852
Fountain Valley, CA (city) Orange County	829
Pukalani, HI (cdp) Maui County	806
Culver City, CA (city) Los Angeles County	786
Paradise, NV (cdp) Clark County	766
Maunawili, HI (cdp) Honolulu County	750
Glendale, CA (city) Los Angeles County	742
Santa Monica, CA (city) Los Angeles County	730
West Carson, CA (cdp) Los Angeles County	690
Hacienda Heights, CA (cdp) Los Angeles County	684
Alhambra, CA (city) Los Angeles County	683
Spokane, WA (city) Spokane County	678
Phoenix, AZ (city) Maricopa County	675
El Cerrito, CA (city) Contra Costa County	673
San Antonio, TX (city) Bexar County	670
Santa Clarita, CA (city) Los Angeles County	664
Makakilo City, HI (cdp) Honolulu County	661
Fullerton, CA (city) Orange County	649
Riverside, CA (city) Riverside County	649
Yorba Linda, CA (city) Orange County	639
Albuquerque, NM (city) Bernalillo County	636
Oceanside, CA (city) San Diego County	629
Ewa Beach, HI (cdp) Honolulu County	622
Aurora, CO (city) Arapahoe County	614

Notes: Please refer to the User's Guide for an explanation of data; ranking tables include all places with Asian and/or NHPI populations above SF4 population thresholds; (1) tables reflect only those areas that meet SF4 population thresholds, therefore there may be less than 50 states, 75 counties or 75 places listed

Language Spoken at Home: English Only

Japanese 5 Years and Over Who Speak English-Only at Home

All States, Top 75 Counties, and Top 75 Places Sorted by Percent[1]

State	Percent
Hawaii	75.53
Idaho	70.21
Utah	62.88
Colorado	60.52
New Mexico	60.30
Alaska	58.15
Montana	58.15
Nevada	54.40
Delaware	53.51
Washington	53.50
California	52.88
United States	52.73
Oregon	49.00
Arizona	48.57
Wyoming	48.46
South Dakota	48.09
Maine	47.13
Nebraska	45.35
Missouri	44.70
Vermont	44.64
Wisconsin	42.28
Oklahoma	41.01
Minnesota	40.65
Kansas	39.70
Illinois	39.50
Florida	38.08
New Hampshire	38.02
Arkansas	36.51
Texas	36.42
Maryland	36.31
Virginia	35.45
Rhode Island	35.06
Iowa	34.98
North Carolina	34.42
Louisiana	32.96
Mississippi	32.90
Pennsylvania	31.71
South Carolina	31.03
Indiana	30.92
Ohio	30.10
Alabama	29.02
District of Columbia	25.58
Tennessee	25.57
Georgia	25.35
Michigan	24.67
Massachusetts	24.31
West Virginia	24.20
Connecticut	23.63
New York	18.14
New Jersey	18.00
Kentucky	16.22

County	Percent
Kauai County, HI	84.72
Weld County, CO	80.00
Maui County, HI	76.79
Hawaii County, HI	75.93
Honolulu County, HI	74.93
El Dorado County, CA	73.32
Malheur County, OR	72.82
Weber County, UT	72.76
Davis County, UT	70.76
Humboldt County, CA	70.07
Merced County, CA	70.06
Kern County, CA	70.03
Canyon County, ID	69.66
Fresno County, CA	69.05
Jefferson County, CO	68.13
Ada County, ID	67.39
Stanislaus County, CA	66.75
San Joaquin County, CA	66.66
Placer County, CA	66.07
Sacramento County, CA	65.96
Adams County, CO	65.83
Salt Lake County, UT	65.50
Sutter County, CA	64.39
Santa Cruz County, CA	63.73
Contra Costa County, CA	63.45
Bernalillo County, NM	62.96
Boulder County, CO	62.82
Larimer County, CO	62.39
Tulare County, CA	61.72
San Bernardino County, CA	60.80
Sonoma County, CA	60.62
Arapahoe County, CO	60.38
Clackamas County, OR	59.80
San Luis Obispo County, CA	59.80
Spokane County, WA	59.38
Santa Barbara County, CA	58.94
Thurston County, WA	58.40
Alameda County, CA	56.66
Benton County, OR	55.50
Washoe County, NV	55.45
New Castle County, DE	55.41
Denver County, CO	55.05
King County, WA	54.67
Bell County, TX	54.26
Santa Clara County, CA	54.14
Riverside County, CA	53.90
Orange County, CA	53.84
Multnomah County, OR	53.82
Clark County, NV	53.72
Anchorage Borough, AK	53.69
Ventura County, CA	53.43
Marin County, CA	52.87
Monmouth County, NJ	52.63
Cumberland County, NC	52.58
Brevard County, FL	52.38
Snohomish County, WA	52.19
Maricopa County, AZ	51.86
Butte County, CA	51.84
Milwaukee County, WI	51.74
Solano County, CA	50.63
Prince William County, VA	50.56
Anne Arundel County, MD	50.37
Whatcom County, WA	50.21
Los Angeles County, CA	50.16
Yolo County, CA	49.23
Clark County, WA	49.04
Monterey County, CA	48.53
Ramsey County, MN	48.47
Marion County, IN	48.02
Bexar County, TX	47.72
Pierce County, WA	47.54
El Paso County, CO	47.41
Kitsap County, WA	46.94
San Mateo County, CA	46.09
Tarrant County, TX	45.51

Place	Percent
Puhi, HI (cdp) Kauai County	93.33
Ahuimanu, HI (cdp) Honolulu County	91.27
Waihee-Waiehu, HI (cdp) Maui County	89.16
Eleele, HI (cdp) Kauai County	89.00
Laguna, CA (cdp) Sacramento County	88.81
Heeia, HI (cdp) Honolulu County	88.15
Kapaa, HI (cdp) Kauai County	87.71
Lawai, HI (cdp) Kauai County	87.53
Waimalu, HI (cdp) Honolulu County	86.69
Kalaheo, HI (cdp) Kauai County	86.68
Mililani Town, HI (cdp) Honolulu County	86.23
Village Park, HI (cdp) Honolulu County	86.01
Ewa Gentry, HI (cdp) Honolulu County	85.57
Hanamaulu, HI (cdp) Kauai County	85.15
Hanapepe, HI (cdp) Kauai County	85.01
Lihue, HI (cdp) Kauai County	84.41
Kaunakakai, HI (cdp) Maui County	84.21
Waimea, HI (cdp) Kauai County	83.96
Honaunau-Napoopoo, HI (cdp) Hawaii County	83.48
Waimea, HI (cdp) Hawaii County	83.39
Maunawili, HI (cdp) Honolulu County	83.24
Waikapu, HI (cdp) Maui County	83.00
San Ramon, CA (city) Contra Costa County	82.99
Halawa, HI (cdp) Honolulu County	82.73
Kaneohe, HI (cdp) Honolulu County	82.64
Wailua Homesteads, HI (cdp) Kauai County	82.27
Koloa, HI (cdp) Kauai County	81.78
Wailua, HI (cdp) Kauai County	81.62
Waipio, HI (cdp) Honolulu County	81.51
Kailua, HI (cdp) Honolulu County	81.29
Cascade-Fairwood, WA (cdp) King County	81.18
Pukalani, HI (cdp) Maui County	81.09
Wailuku, HI (cdp) Maui County	81.07
Kalaoa, HI (cdp) Hawaii County	80.73
Norwalk, CA (city) Los Angeles County	80.13
Pearl City, HI (cdp) Honolulu County	79.18
Hilo, HI (cdp) Hawaii County	78.21
Kekaha, HI (cdp) Kauai County	77.59
Aiea, HI (cdp) Honolulu County	77.25
Morgan Hill, CA (city) Santa Clara County	77.20
Clovis, CA (city) Fresno County	77.19
Downey, CA (city) Los Angeles County	77.06
Captain Cook, HI (cdp) Hawaii County	76.93
Yorba Linda, CA (city) Orange County	76.80
Bryn Mawr-Skyway, WA (cdp) King County	76.63
Ewa Beach, HI (cdp) Honolulu County	76.41
Seal Beach, CA (city) Orange County	76.23
Paia, HI (cdp) Maui County	76.16
Santa Cruz, CA (city) Santa Cruz County	76.00
Kapaau, HI (cdp) Hawaii County	75.94
Elk Grove, CA (cdp) Sacramento County	75.73
Keaau, HI (cdp) Hawaii County	75.56
Rancho Cucamonga, CA (city) San Bernardino County	75.34
Renton, WA (city) King County	74.96
Kahului, HI (cdp) Maui County	74.93
Campbell, CA (city) Santa Clara County	74.58
Kurtistown, HI (cdp) Hawaii County	74.31
Lodi, CA (city) San Joaquin County	74.24
Kent, WA (city) King County	74.19
Manhattan Beach, CA (city) Los Angeles County	73.65
Kealakekua, HI (cdp) Hawaii County	73.58
Chino Hills, CA (city) San Bernardino County	72.95
Hawaiian Beaches, HI (cdp) Hawaii County	72.53
Papaikou, HI (cdp) Hawaii County	72.44
Honokaa, HI (cdp) Hawaii County	71.88
Bakersfield, CA (city) Kern County	71.81
Placentia, CA (city) Orange County	71.15
Wahiawa, HI (cdp) Honolulu County	70.93
Lakewood, CA (city) Los Angeles County	70.86
Makawao, HI (cdp) Maui County	70.86
West Covina, CA (city) Los Angeles County	70.67
La Palma, CA (city) Orange County	70.58
Waikoloa Village, HI (cdp) Hawaii County	70.43
Waipio Acres, HI (cdp) Honolulu County	70.11
Makakilo City, HI (cdp) Honolulu County	70.10

Notes: Please refer to the User's Guide for an explanation of data; ranking tables include all places with Asian and/or NHPI populations above SF4 population thresholds; (1) tables reflect only those areas that meet SF4 population thresholds, therefore there may be less than 50 states, 75 counties or 75 places listed

Language Spoken at Home: English Only

Koreans 5 Years and Over Who Speak English-Only at Home

All States, Top 75 Counties, and Top 75 Places Sorted by Number[1]

State	Number
United States	183,215
California	37,891
New York	15,576
Washington	9,043
Illinois	7,930
Minnesota	7,643
Michigan	7,530
Texas	7,090
New Jersey	6,823
Virginia	6,612
Pennsylvania	6,566
Hawaii	6,127
Maryland	5,626
Massachusetts	4,597
Florida	4,264
Ohio	3,827
Colorado	3,784
Oregon	3,552
Georgia	3,464
Arizona	2,772
Wisconsin	2,752
North Carolina	2,534
Missouri	2,269
Iowa	2,260
Indiana	2,012
Connecticut	1,834
Nevada	1,667
Oklahoma	1,486
Tennessee	1,446
Utah	1,119
Alabama	1,115
Kentucky	1,108
Kansas	1,093
Nebraska	1,059
South Carolina	936
Louisiana	693
Alaska	678
New Hampshire	646
New Mexico	638
Montana	523
Idaho	503
West Virginia	491
Rhode Island	478
Arkansas	425
District of Columbia	414
South Dakota	392
Delaware	388
Mississippi	379
Maine	374
Vermont	362
North Dakota	254
Wyoming	170

County	Number
Los Angeles County, CA	14,884
Honolulu County, HI	5,268
Orange County, CA	4,908
Cook County, IL	4,343
King County, WA	3,866
New York County, NY	3,482
Hennepin County, MN	2,654
Fairfax County, VA	2,652
Santa Clara County, CA	2,599
Queens County, NY	2,480
San Diego County, CA	2,364
Alameda County, CA	1,988
San Francisco County, CA	1,848
Maricopa County, AZ	1,712
Bergen County, NJ	1,594
Pierce County, WA	1,563
Montgomery County, MD	1,543
Middlesex County, MA	1,414
Clark County, NV	1,286
San Bernardino County, CA	1,197
Monroe County, NY	1,167
Oakland County, MI	1,164
Harris County, TX	1,152
Nassau County, NY	1,127
Ramsey County, MN	1,114
Suffolk County, NY	1,064
Snohomish County, WA	1,050
Multnomah County, OR	982
Kings County, NY	935
Contra Costa County, CA	928
Sacramento County, CA	921
St. Louis County, MO	905
Montgomery County, PA	900
Kent County, MI	878
Baltimore County, MD	866
El Paso County, CO	846
Philadelphia County, PA	825
Dallas County, TX	805
Suffolk County, MA	788
DuPage County, IL	786
Howard County, MD	783
Wayne County, MI	757
Riverside County, CA	741
San Mateo County, CA	737
Arapahoe County, CO	736
Franklin County, OH	735
Washtenaw County, MI	721
Gwinnett County, GA	720
Dakota County, MN	690
Travis County, TX	689
Erie County, NY	667
Pima County, AZ	666
Tarrant County, TX	662
Middlesex County, NJ	657
Washington County, OR	596
Morris County, NJ	576
Macomb County, MI	574
Allegheny County, PA	570
Bexar County, TX	557
Norfolk County, MA	554
Westchester County, NY	544
Cuyahoga County, OH	539
Hillsborough County, FL	537
Prince George's County, MD	528
Ventura County, CA	524
Broward County, FL	523
Hudson County, NJ	517
New Haven County, CT	516
Lake County, IL	512
Dane County, WI	507
Mercer County, NJ	487
Anne Arundel County, MD	485
Milwaukee County, WI	485
Arlington County, VA	480
Jefferson County, CO	469

Place	Number
New York, NY (city)	7,397
Los Angeles, CA (city) Los Angeles County	7,362
Honolulu, HI (cdp) Honolulu County	2,951
Chicago, IL (city) Cook County	2,166
San Francisco, CA (city) San Francisco County	1,848
Seattle, WA (city) King County	1,482
San Diego, CA (city) San Diego County	1,350
San Jose, CA (city) Santa Clara County	1,164
Minneapolis, MN (city) Hennepin County	846
Philadelphia, PA (city) Philadelphia County	825
Portland, OR (city) Multnomah County	790
Boston, MA (city) Suffolk County	754
Irvine, CA (city) Orange County	741
Torrance, CA (city) Los Angeles County	728
Houston, TX (city) Harris County	652
Colorado Springs, CO (city) El Paso County	633
Austin, TX (city) Travis County	606
Phoenix, AZ (city) Maricopa County	597
Cerritos, CA (city) Los Angeles County	540
Glendale, CA (city) Los Angeles County	537
St. Paul, MN (city) Ramsey County	529
Columbus, OH (city) Franklin County	519
Hempstead, NY (town) Nassau County	509
Arlington, VA (cdp) Arlington County	480
Fullerton, CA (city) Orange County	466
Anaheim, CA (city) Orange County	454
Oakland, CA (city) Alameda County	447
Las Vegas, NV (city) Clark County	410
Ann Arbor, MI (city) Washtenaw County	409
Berkeley, CA (city) Alameda County	407
Denver, CO (city) Denver County	398
San Antonio, TX (city) Bexar County	394
Madison, WI (city) Dane County	382
Long Beach, CA (city) Los Angeles County	377
Cambridge, MA (city) Middlesex County	376
Indianapolis, IN (sp. city) Marion County	365
El Paso, TX (city) El Paso County	362
North Hempstead, NY (town) Nassau County	357
Tucson, AZ (city) Pima County	357
Pasadena, CA (city) Los Angeles County	351
Dallas, TX (city) Dallas County	346
Brookhaven, NY (town) Suffolk County	343
Federal Way, WA (city) King County	342
Fremont, CA (city) Alameda County	341
Albuquerque, NM (city) Bernalillo County	337
Garden Grove, CA (city) Orange County	323
Aurora, CO (city) Arapahoe County	320
Columbia, MD (cdp) Howard County	313
Riverside, CA (city) Riverside County	303
Omaha, NE (city) Douglas County	302
Diamond Bar, CA (city) Los Angeles County	293
Lakewood, WA (city) Pierce County	293
Plano, TX (city) Collin County	292
Bellevue, WA (city) King County	286
Fort Lee, NJ (borough) Bergen County	278
Charlotte, NC (city) Mecklenburg County	273
Burke, VA (cdp) Fairfax County	271
Huntington Beach, CA (city) Orange County	269
Tulsa, OK (city) Tulsa County	268
Sunnyvale, CA (city) Santa Clara County	264
Bloomington, MN (city) Hennepin County	261
Annandale, VA (cdp) Fairfax County	259
Ellicott City, MD (cdp) Howard County	257
Grand Rapids, MI (city) Kent County	255
Waimalu, HI (cdp) Honolulu County	252
Killeen, TX (city) Bell County	248
Kailua, HI (cdp) Honolulu County	243
Mililani Town, HI (cdp) Honolulu County	240
Centreville, VA (cdp) Fairfax County	237
Tacoma, WA (city) Pierce County	237
Jersey City, NJ (city) Hudson County	235
Oklahoma City, OK (city) Oklahoma County	229
Atlanta, GA (city) Fulton County	228
Hilo, HI (cdp) Hawaii County	228
Fresno, CA (city) Fresno County	226

Notes: Please refer to the User's Guide for an explanation of data; ranking tables include all places with Asian and/or NHPI populations above SF4 population thresholds; (1) tables reflect only those areas that meet SF4 population thresholds, therefore there may be less than 50 states, 75 counties or 75 places listed

Language Spoken at Home: English Only

Koreans 5 Years and Over Who Speak English-Only at Home

All States, Top 75 Counties, and Top 75 Places Sorted by Percent[1]

State	Percent
North Dakota	70.17
Minnesota	64.63
Montana	64.41
South Dakota	61.25
Vermont	59.74
West Virginia	57.97
Maine	53.13
Nebraska	52.50
Iowa	50.79
Wisconsin	42.95
Idaho	41.16
Wyoming	40.09
New Mexico	39.75
Michigan	38.74
Missouri	37.37
District of Columbia	37.33
New Hampshire	36.54
Oklahoma	33.48
Utah	33.03
Indiana	30.77
Arizona	29.66
Oregon	29.58
Kentucky	29.44
Arkansas	29.29
Mississippi	29.29
Ohio	29.29
Connecticut	29.22
Alabama	29.06
Massachusetts	28.40
South Carolina	27.38
Louisiana	27.06
Kansas	26.61
Hawaii	26.55
Colorado	26.15
Rhode Island	26.02
Florida	23.55
Nevada	22.91
Tennessee	22.15
Delaware	22.03
North Carolina	21.40
Pennsylvania	21.21
Washington	20.39
United States	18.06
Texas	17.15
Illinois	16.12
Alaska	15.69
Virginia	15.42
Maryland	15.32
New York	13.58
Georgia	13.22
California	11.60
New Jersey	11.35

County	Percent
St. Louis County, MN	82.84
Ottawa County, MI	81.57
Linn County, IA	74.32
Saratoga County, NY	69.51
Anoka County, MN	69.25
Dakota County, MN	67.12
Bristol County, MA	66.45
Ocean County, NJ	63.69
Ramsey County, MN	62.69
Lancaster County, PA	61.54
Benton County, WA	60.79
Hennepin County, MN	60.15
Olmsted County, MN	58.40
Spokane County, WA	56.58
Genesee County, MI	54.91
Kent County, MI	53.83
Larimer County, CO	53.78
Douglas County, NE	51.91
Whatcom County, WA	51.66
Litchfield County, CT	50.83
Hawaii County, HI	50.58
Monroe County, NY	49.58
Polk County, IA	49.55
Northampton County, PA	49.20
Tulsa County, OK	48.44
Kalamazoo County, MI	48.29
Davis County, UT	48.28
Washington County, MN	47.78
Berks County, PA	47.19
Wayne County, MI	45.33
Placer County, CA	45.26
Marion County, OR	44.82
Bernalillo County, NM	44.71
Rockingham County, NH	44.53
Jackson County, MO	44.12
Waukesha County, WI	43.44
Jefferson County, AL	43.15
Lancaster County, NE	43.08
Winnebago County, IL	42.69
Macomb County, MI	41.27
Utah County, UT	40.78
Orange County, NY	40.21
Albany County, NY	40.02
Multnomah County, OR	39.66
Hillsborough County, NH	39.38
Ada County, ID	39.30
Milwaukee County, WI	39.27
Gloucester County, NJ	38.81
St. Louis County, MO	38.45
Sedgwick County, KS	36.56
Hampden County, MA	36.47
Harford County, MD	36.28
Arlington County, VA	35.96
Erie County, NY	35.94
Butler County, OH	35.46
Sarpy County, NE	35.35
Onondaga County, NY	35.10
Maui County, HI	34.76
Boulder County, CO	34.64
Jefferson County, NY	34.60
Pinellas County, FL	34.57
Palm Beach County, FL	33.99
Jefferson County, CO	33.84
Hampshire County, MA	33.60
Cumberland County, PA	33.54
Marion County, IN	33.54
Denver County, CO	33.31
York County, PA	32.99
Frederick County, MD	32.98
Dale County, AL	32.93
Chester County, PA	32.83
Saginaw County, MI	32.59
Greene County, MO	32.47
Rensselaer County, NY	32.42
Boone County, MO	32.39

Place	Percent
Kailua, HI (cdp) Honolulu County	64.63
St. Paul, MN (city) Ramsey County	64.36
Hilo, HI (cdp) Hawaii County	59.07
Spokane, WA (city) Spokane County	57.77
Bloomington, MN (city) Hennepin County	56.13
Minneapolis, MN (city) Hennepin County	54.13
Rochester, MN (city) Olmsted County	52.29
Grand Rapids, MI (city) Kent County	51.10
Omaha, NE (city) Douglas County	49.51
Kaneohe, HI (cdp) Honolulu County	49.09
Mililani Town, HI (cdp) Honolulu County	48.78
Tulsa, OK (city) Tulsa County	47.18
Albuquerque, NM (city) Bernalillo County	45.36
Milwaukee, WI (city) Milwaukee County	41.95
Lincoln, NE (city) Lancaster County	41.88
Islip, NY (town) Suffolk County	39.32
Portland, OR (city) Multnomah County	37.73
Indianapolis, IN (sp. city) Marion County	37.21
Rochester, NY (city) Monroe County	37.09
Fort Collins, CO (city) Larimer County	36.48
Whittier, CA (city) Los Angeles County	35.98
Arlington, VA (cdp) Arlington County	35.96
Pearl City, HI (cdp) Honolulu County	34.58
Kansas City, MO (city) Jackson County	33.79
Denver, CO (city) Denver County	33.31
Sacramento, CA (city) Sacramento County	32.84
Phoenix, AZ (city) Maricopa County	32.78
Springfield, MO (city) Greene County	31.99
Boston, MA (city) Suffolk County	31.91
Babylon, NY (town) Suffolk County	31.88
Smithtown, NY (town) Suffolk County	31.71
Atlanta, GA (city) Fulton County	31.49
Mesa, AZ (city) Maricopa County	31.20
Seattle, WA (city) King County	30.47
Wichita, KS (city) Sedgwick County	30.07
Bethesda, MD (cdp) Montgomery County	29.88
Tucson, AZ (city) Pima County	29.77
Las Vegas, NV (city) Clark County	29.12
Boulder, CO (city) Boulder County	28.97
Redondo Beach, CA (city) Los Angeles County	28.89
Plymouth, MN (city) Hennepin County	28.77
Lawrence, KS (city) Douglas County	28.72
Huntsville, AL (city) Madison County	28.32
West Bloomfield, MI (township) Oakland County	28.13
Columbia, MO (city) Boone County	27.55
Kentwood, MI (city) Kent County	27.30
Pasadena, CA (city) Los Angeles County	27.23
Corvallis, OR (city) Benton County	27.21
Mountain View, CA (city) Santa Clara County	26.95
Lower Merion, PA (township) Montgomery County	26.78
San Francisco, CA (city) San Francisco County	26.67
Iowa City, IA (city) Johnson County	26.65
Henderson, NV (city) Clark County	26.62
Davis, CA (city) Yolo County	26.42
Rochester Hills, MI (city) Oakland County	26.24
Oakland, CA (city) Alameda County	26.19
Camarillo, CA (city) Ventura County	25.88
Brookhaven, NY (town) Suffolk County	25.50
Laguna Niguel, CA (city) Orange County	25.42
Simi Valley, CA (city) Ventura County	25.32
Placentia, CA (city) Orange County	25.27
Berkeley, CA (city) Alameda County	25.19
Santa Monica, CA (city) Los Angeles County	25.14
Providence, RI (city) Providence County	25.04
Fresno, CA (city) Fresno County	24.73
Silver Spring, MD (cdp) Montgomery County	24.66
Evanston, IL (city) Cook County	24.60
Reston, VA (cdp) Fairfax County	24.54
Oklahoma City, OK (city) Oklahoma County	24.44
Vancouver, WA (city) Clark County	24.44
Fairfield, CA (city) Solano County	24.35
Madison, WI (city) Dane County	24.25
Durham, NC (city) Durham County	24.11
Columbus, GA (sp. city) Muscogee County	24.06
Orlando, FL (city) Orange County	24.02

Notes: Please refer to the User's Guide for an explanation of data; ranking tables include all places with Asian and/or NHPI populations above SF4 population thresholds; (1) tables reflect only those areas that meet SF4 population thresholds, therefore there may be less than 50 states, 75 counties or 75 places listed

Language Spoken at Home: English Only

Laotians 5 Years and Over Who Speak English-Only at Home

All States, Top 75 Counties, and Top 75 Places Sorted by Number[1]

State	Number
United States	11,151
California	3,524
Texas	681
Washington	641
Minnesota	554
Florida	382
Wisconsin	361
New York	293
North Carolina	293
Illinois	291
Massachusetts	286
Oregon	270
Virginia	260
Connecticut	243
Tennessee	235
Iowa	200
Arkansas	197
Indiana	178
Georgia	174
Ohio	170
Arizona	168
Pennsylvania	167
Michigan	137
Kansas	130
Colorado	121
Utah	118
New Jersey	116
Hawaii	115
Oklahoma	81
Alaska	76
Louisiana	69
Alabama	68
Nevada	65
Rhode Island	61
South Carolina	55
Idaho	51
Nebraska	50
Maryland	48
Missouri	44
South Dakota	28
New Hampshire	23

County	Number
Sacramento County, CA	636
Fresno County, CA	468
San Diego County, CA	439
King County, WA	333
Hennepin County, MN	260
Dallas County, TX	242
Santa Clara County, CA	236
San Joaquin County, CA	228
Contra Costa County, CA	225
Los Angeles County, CA	189
Tarrant County, TX	183
Alameda County, CA	160
Multnomah County, OR	159
Orange County, CA	157
Middlesex County, MA	149
Milwaukee County, WI	126
Maricopa County, AZ	116
Monroe County, NY	109
Pinellas County, FL	108
Merced County, CA	105
Sebastian County, AR	104
Davidson County, TN	102
Harris County, TX	99
Honolulu County, HI	99
Salt Lake County, UT	98
Broome County, NY	94
Fairfax County, VA	94
Snohomish County, WA	90
Hartford County, CT	86
Stanislaus County, CA	79
Riverside County, CA	76
Kane County, IL	72
Polk County, FL	71
Rutherford County, TN	71
Anchorage Borough, AK	69
Brown County, WI	69
New Haven County, CT	69
Dakota County, MN	68
Worcester County, MA	68
Clark County, NV	65
Philadelphia County, PA	63
Fairfield County, CT	61
Mobile County, AL	61
Providence County, RI	61
Shasta County, CA	61
Cook County, IL	60
Sonoma County, CA	60
Ottawa County, MI	58
Summit County, OH	58
Tulare County, CA	57
Oklahoma County, OK	54
Adams County, CO	52
Washington County, OR	52
Guilford County, NC	50
Pierce County, WA	50
Butte County, CA	47
Franklin County, OH	46
Catawba County, NC	42
Ramsey County, MN	42
Mecklenburg County, NC	41
Olmsted County, MN	39
Polk County, IA	37
Pacific County, WA	36
Johnson County, KS	31
Spartanburg County, SC	31
Clark County, WA	30
Buena Vista County, IA	29
Solano County, CA	29
Bexar County, TX	28
San Bernardino County, CA	27
Sedgwick County, KS	25
Jefferson County, CO	24
Dane County, WI	23
Clayton County, GA	22
Winnebago County, IL	22

Place	Number
Fresno, CA (city) Fresno County	451
Sacramento, CA (city) Sacramento County	428
San Diego, CA (city) San Diego County	385
Stockton, CA (city) San Joaquin County	228
San Jose, CA (city) Santa Clara County	217
Seattle, WA (city) King County	141
Milwaukee, WI (city) Milwaukee County	119
Richmond, CA (city) Contra Costa County	119
Oakland, CA (city) Alameda County	111
Fort Smith, AR (city) Sebastian County	104
Portland, OR (city) Multnomah County	103
Nashville-Davidson, TN (sp. city) Davidson County	102
Merced, CA (city) Merced County	96
Irving, TX (city) Dallas County	94
Minneapolis, MN (city) Hennepin County	93
Dallas, TX (city) Dallas County	92
Rochester, NY (city) Monroe County	87
Long Beach, CA (city) Los Angeles County	79
San Pablo, CA (city) Contra Costa County	75
Brooklyn Park, MN (city) Hennepin County	70
Philadelphia, PA (city) Philadelphia County	63
Oklahoma City, OK (city) Oklahoma County	62
Santa Ana, CA (city) Orange County	58
Visalia, CA (city) Tulare County	57
Parkway-S. Sacramento, CA (cdp) Sacramento County	55
Fitchburg, MA (city) Worcester County	54
Redding, CA (city) Shasta County	53
Akron, OH (city) Summit County	48
Haltom City, TX (city) Tarrant County	48
Green Bay, WI (city) Brown County	44
Modesto, CA (city) Stanislaus County	44
Bridgeport, CT (city) Fairfield County	43
Banning, CA (city) Riverside County	42
Lowell, MA (city) Middlesex County	42
St. Paul, MN (city) Ramsey County	42
Charlotte, NC (city) Mecklenburg County	41
Rochester, MN (city) Olmsted County	39
Des Moines, IA (city) Polk County	37
St. Petersburg, FL (city) Pinellas County	36
Los Angeles, CA (city) Los Angeles County	35
Springfield, VA (cdp) Fairfax County	35
Riverside, CA (city) Riverside County	34
Honolulu, HI (cdp) Honolulu County	33
Columbus, OH (city) Franklin County	32
Santa Rosa, CA (city) Sonoma County	31
Raymond, WA (city) Pacific County	30
Tacoma, WA (city) Pierce County	30
Providence, RI (city) Providence County	29
Fort Worth, TX (city) Tarrant County	27
Grand Prairie, TX (city) Dallas County	26
Woonsocket, RI (city) Providence County	25
Rockford, IL (city) Winnebago County	22
Fairfield, CA (city) Solano County	20
Storm Lake, IA (city) Buena Vista County	20
Westminster, CO (city) Adams County	17
Worthington, MN (city) Nobles County	17
Bellevue, WA (city) King County	15
Amarillo, TX (city) Potter County	14
Wichita, KS (city) Sedgwick County	13
Oaklawn-Sunview, KS (cdp) Sedgwick County	12
Murfreesboro, TN (city) Rutherford County	11
Pomona, CA (city) Los Angeles County	11
Anaheim, CA (city) Orange County	9
New Britain, CT (city) Hartford County	9
Brooklyn Center, MN (city) Hennepin County	8
Elgin, IL (city) Kane County	8
West Valley City, UT (city) Salt Lake County	7
Arvada, CO (city) Jefferson County	5
Escondido, CA (city) San Diego County	0
Moreno Valley, CA (city) Riverside County	0
Springdale, AR (city) Washington County	0
Warroad, MN (city) Roseau County	0
Winfield, KS (city) Cowley County	0

Notes: Please refer to the User's Guide for an explanation of data; ranking tables include all places with Asian and/or NHPI populations above SF4 population thresholds; (1) tables reflect only those areas that meet SF4 population thresholds, therefore there may be less than 50 states, 75 counties or 75 places listed

Language Spoken at Home: English Only

Laotians 5 Years and Over Who Speak English-Only at Home

All States, Top 75 Counties, and Top 75 Places Sorted by Percent[1]

State	Percent
New Jersey	24.42
Arizona	19.88
Indiana	18.90
South Dakota	13.73
Idaho	10.67
Florida	10.07
Oklahoma	9.74
Wisconsin	9.56
New York	9.55
Virginia	9.21
Alabama	8.85
Washington	8.60
Connecticut	8.53
Massachusetts	8.43
Oregon	8.03
Pennsylvania	7.99
Arkansas	7.96
Texas	7.37
United States	7.18
New Hampshire	7.03
Hawaii	6.99
Minnesota	6.81
Maryland	6.69
California	6.68
Missouri	6.64
Nebraska	6.57
North Carolina	6.44
Illinois	6.39
Tennessee	6.29
Ohio	6.24
Alaska	6.07
Utah	5.89
Nevada	5.82
Louisiana	5.75
Colorado	5.61
Iowa	5.51
Michigan	5.49
Kansas	5.01
South Carolina	4.59
Georgia	3.93
Rhode Island	2.26

County	Percent
Mobile County, AL	21.63
Maricopa County, AZ	20.07
Polk County, FL	19.19
Broome County, NY	18.58
Brown County, WI	15.68
New Haven County, CT	14.97
Snohomish County, WA	12.93
Pierce County, WA	12.53
Santa Clara County, CA	12.51
Oklahoma County, OK	11.30
Dallas County, TX	11.08
Pacific County, WA	10.91
Dakota County, MN	10.45
Guilford County, NC	10.37
Olmsted County, MN	10.16
Sebastian County, AR	9.96
Butte County, CA	9.09
Washington County, OR	9.08
Harris County, TX	8.98
Middlesex County, MA	8.83
Monroe County, NY	8.69
Summit County, OH	8.58
Davidson County, TN	8.23
San Joaquin County, CA	8.20
Fresno County, CA	8.05
Hartford County, CT	7.90
Clark County, WA	7.89
Kane County, IL	7.89
Catawba County, NC	7.88
Milwaukee County, WI	7.84
Bexar County, TX	7.71
Worcester County, MA	7.35
King County, WA	7.26
Sacramento County, CA	7.23
Dane County, WI	7.10
Multnomah County, OR	6.75
San Diego County, CA	6.66
Hennepin County, MN	6.52
San Bernardino County, CA	6.47
Fairfax County, VA	6.46
Merced County, CA	6.42
Los Angeles County, CA	6.40
Fairfield County, CT	6.38
Honolulu County, HI	6.17
Pinellas County, FL	6.17
Salt Lake County, UT	6.12
Tarrant County, TX	6.07
Anchorage Borough, AK	6.00
Clark County, NV	5.89
Orange County, CA	5.85
Sonoma County, CA	5.79
Ottawa County, MI	5.74
Philadelphia County, PA	5.71
Contra Costa County, CA	5.69
Alameda County, CA	5.48
Buena Vista County, IA	5.35
Riverside County, CA	5.31
Stanislaus County, CA	5.28
Adams County, CO	5.23
Cass County, MI	5.19
Essex County, MA	5.18
Franklin County, WA	5.15
Johnson County, KS	5.14
Mecklenburg County, NC	5.13
Spartanburg County, SC	5.06
Ramsey County, MN	5.04
Cook County, IL	4.86
Rutherford County, TN	4.85
Nobles County, MN	4.67
Franklin County, OH	4.47
Solano County, CA	4.05
Yolo County, CA	4.02
Shasta County, CA	3.71
Montgomery County, NC	3.68
Dakota County, NE	3.33

Place	Percent
Irving, TX (city) Dallas County	20.80
Fitchburg, MA (city) Worcester County	15.17
Banning, CA (city) Riverside County	13.55
Oklahoma City, OK (city) Oklahoma County	12.97
Raymond, WA (city) Pacific County	12.55
San Jose, CA (city) Santa Clara County	12.52
Long Beach, CA (city) Los Angeles County	11.99
Rochester, NY (city) Monroe County	11.65
Green Bay, WI (city) Brown County	11.52
Dallas, TX (city) Dallas County	10.76
Rochester, MN (city) Olmsted County	10.21
Fort Smith, AR (city) Sebastian County	10.13
Riverside, CA (city) Riverside County	10.12
Akron, OH (city) Summit County	9.90
Tacoma, WA (city) Pierce County	9.87
Springfield, VA (cdp) Fairfax County	9.38
Bridgeport, CT (city) Fairfield County	9.19
Fresno, CA (city) Fresno County	8.90
Stockton, CA (city) San Joaquin County	8.52
Milwaukee, WI (city) Milwaukee County	8.50
Nashville-Davidson, TN (sp. city) Davidson County	8.23
Sacramento, CA (city) Sacramento County	7.35
Grand Prairie, TX (city) Dallas County	7.22
Merced, CA (city) Merced County	7.22
San Pablo, CA (city) Contra Costa County	7.12
San Diego, CA (city) San Diego County	6.91
Santa Ana, CA (city) Orange County	6.74
Haltom City, TX (city) Tarrant County	6.54
Minneapolis, MN (city) Hennepin County	6.44
Seattle, WA (city) King County	5.76
Philadelphia, PA (city) Philadelphia County	5.71
St. Paul, MN (city) Ramsey County	5.52
Fairfield, CA (city) Solano County	5.45
Richmond, CA (city) Contra Costa County	5.40
Fort Worth, TX (city) Tarrant County	5.39
Brooklyn Park, MN (city) Hennepin County	5.34
Los Angeles, CA (city) Los Angeles County	5.25
Charlotte, NC (city) Mecklenburg County	5.20
Worthington, MN (city) Nobles County	5.09
Santa Rosa, CA (city) Sonoma County	5.08
Oakland, CA (city) Alameda County	5.00
Portland, OR (city) Multnomah County	4.91
Oaklawn-Sunview, KS (cdp) Sedgwick County	4.35
Parkway-S. Sacramento, CA (cdp) Sacramento County	4.31
Modesto, CA (city) Stanislaus County	4.09
Storm Lake, IA (city) Buena Vista County	4.07
Columbus, OH (city) Franklin County	3.64
Redding, CA (city) Shasta County	3.61
Bellevue, WA (city) King County	3.52
Honolulu, HI (cdp) Honolulu County	3.47
St. Petersburg, FL (city) Pinellas County	3.34
Lowell, MA (city) Middlesex County	3.09
Des Moines, IA (city) Polk County	3.07
Woonsocket, RI (city) Providence County	3.03
Visalia, CA (city) Tulare County	2.84
Brooklyn Center, MN (city) Hennepin County	2.74
New Britain, CT (city) Hartford County	2.63
Rockford, IL (city) Winnebago County	2.62
Westminster, CO (city) Adams County	2.58
Providence, RI (city) Providence County	2.29
Pomona, CA (city) Los Angeles County	2.24
Wichita, KS (city) Sedgwick County	2.08
West Valley City, UT (city) Salt Lake County	1.74
Murfreesboro, TN (city) Rutherford County	1.71
Amarillo, TX (city) Potter County	1.44
Anaheim, CA (city) Orange County	1.19
Arvada, CO (city) Jefferson County	1.10
Elgin, IL (city) Kane County	1.01
Escondido, CA (city) San Diego County	<0.01
Moreno Valley, CA (city) Riverside County	<0.01
Springdale, AR (city) Washington County	<0.01
Warroad, MN (city) Roseau County	<0.01
Winfield, KS (city) Cowley County	<0.01

Notes: Please refer to the User's Guide for an explanation of data; ranking tables include all places with Asian and/or NHPI populations above SF4 population thresholds; (1) tables reflect only those areas that meet SF4 population thresholds, therefore there may be less than 50 states, 75 counties or 75 places listed

Language Spoken at Home: English Only

Malaysians 5 Years and Over Who Speak English-Only at Home

All States, Top 75 Counties, and Top 75 Places Sorted by Number[1]

State	Number
United States	1,960
California	472
Texas	198
New York	139
Illinois	100
Ohio	81
Michigan	77
Oklahoma	32

County	Number
Los Angeles County, CA	83
Queens County, NY	8

Place	Number
New York, NY (city)	85

Notes: Please refer to the User's Guide for an explanation of data; ranking tables include all places with Asian and/or NHPI populations above SF4 population thresholds; (1) tables reflect only those areas that meet SF4 population thresholds, therefore there may be less than 50 states, 75 counties or 75 places listed

Language Spoken at Home: English Only

Malaysians 5 Years and Over Who Speak English-Only at Home

All States, Top 75 Counties, and Top 75 Places Sorted by Percent[1]

State	Percent
Texas	30.65
California	27.91
Ohio	23.68
United States	19.18
Illinois	18.98
Michigan	17.95
New York	10.15
Oklahoma	6.74

County	Percent
Los Angeles County, CA	15.78
Queens County, NY	1.46

Place	Percent
New York, NY (city)	7.25

Notes: Please refer to the User's Guide for an explanation of data; ranking tables include all places with Asian and/or NHPI populations above SF4 population thresholds; (1) tables reflect only those areas that meet SF4 population thresholds, therefore there may be less than 50 states, 75 counties or 75 places listed

Language Spoken at Home: English Only

Pakistanis 5 Years and Over Who Speak English-Only at Home

All States, Top 75 Counties, and Top 75 Places Sorted by Number[1]

State	Number
United States	10,887
California	1,957
New York	1,326
Texas	1,147
Illinois	1,027
New Jersey	782
Virginia	546
Florida	483
Maryland	441
Georgia	294
Pennsylvania	266
Michigan	250
Ohio	191
Connecticut	162
Colorado	143
Washington	139
North Carolina	138
Missouri	133
Massachusetts	122
Kansas	120
Wisconsin	105
Nevada	100
Delaware	93
Indiana	86
Oklahoma	75
Arizona	65
Kentucky	55
Minnesota	55
Utah	51
Louisiana	45
Alabama	42
Oregon	42
Tennessee	33
Iowa	30
West Virginia	28

County	Number
Cook County, IL	542
Los Angeles County, CA	393
Harris County, TX	321
Fairfax County, VA	319
Kings County, NY	316
DuPage County, IL	303
Orange County, CA	298
Dallas County, TX	294
Sacramento County, CA	220
Middlesex County, NJ	203
Queens County, NY	198
Montgomery County, MD	197
Alameda County, CA	181
New York County, NY	154
Santa Clara County, CA	152
Suffolk County, NY	143
San Joaquin County, CA	123
Bergen County, NJ	117
San Bernardino County, CA	112
Nassau County, NY	109
Oakland County, MI	97
Orange County, FL	93
Riverside County, CA	91
Broward County, FL	85
Cobb County, GA	84
Somerset County, NJ	80
Wake County, NC	80
Denton County, TX	79
Fort Bend County, TX	77
Hudson County, NJ	77
San Diego County, CA	76
Franklin County, OH	74
Tarrant County, TX	67
Middlesex County, MA	66
Maricopa County, AZ	62
Wayne County, MI	62
New Haven County, CT	59
Mercer County, NJ	58
Baltimore County, MD	57
Camden County, NJ	56
Bronx County, NY	54
King County, WA	52
Gwinnett County, GA	51
Fairfield County, CT	49
Howard County, MD	44
St. Louis County, MO	43
Collin County, TX	41
Essex County, NJ	41
Prince William County, VA	41
Snohomish County, WA	41
Westchester County, NY	41
Arlington County, VA	37
Hartford County, CT	37
Lake County, IL	37
Richmond County, NY	32
Philadelphia County, PA	30
Travis County, TX	30
Monmouth County, NJ	29
San Francisco County, CA	28
Morris County, NJ	27
Alexandria Independent City, VA	24
Miami-Dade County, FL	23
Tulsa County, OK	23
Hennepin County, MN	21
Macomb County, MI	20
Atlantic County, NJ	19
Prince George's County, MD	18
Worcester County, MA	17
Contra Costa County, CA	16
Monroe County, NY	16
Loudoun County, VA	15
Delaware County, PA	13
Washtenaw County, MI	12
Milwaukee County, WI	11
Will County, IL	11

Place	Number
New York, NY (city)	754
Chicago, IL (city) Cook County	268
Houston, TX (city) Harris County	183
Los Angeles, CA (city) Los Angeles County	142
Carrollton, TX (city) Denton County	128
Sacramento, CA (city) Sacramento County	114
Dallas, TX (city) Dallas County	83
San Jose, CA (city) Santa Clara County	80
Garland, TX (city) Dallas County	71
Fremont, CA (city) Alameda County	68
Jersey City, NJ (city) Hudson County	58
Edison, NJ (township) Middlesex County	55
Huntington, NY (town) Suffolk County	55
Hempstead, NY (town) Nassau County	54
Skokie, IL (village) Cook County	52
Brookhaven, NY (town) Suffolk County	46
Lincolnia, VA (cdp) Fairfax County	43
Arlington, VA (cdp) Arlington County	37
Old Bridge, NJ (township) Middlesex County	34
Stockton, CA (city) San Joaquin County	33
North Hempstead, NY (town) Nassau County	32
Austin, TX (city) Travis County	30
Philadelphia, PA (city) Philadelphia County	30
Plano, TX (city) Collin County	30
San Francisco, CA (city) San Francisco County	28
Dale City, VA (cdp) Prince William County	26
Anaheim, CA (city) Orange County	25
Tulsa, OK (city) Tulsa County	23
Torrance, CA (city) Los Angeles County	22
Woodbridge, NJ (township) Middlesex County	20
Ellicott City, MD (cdp) Howard County	16
Irving, TX (city) Dallas County	15
Santa Clara, CA (city) Santa Clara County	9
Richardson, TX (city) Dallas County	5
Bailey's Crossroads, VA (cdp) Fairfax County	0
Mission Bend, TX (cdp) Fort Bend County	0
Sugar Land, TX (city) Fort Bend County	0

Notes: Please refer to the User's Guide for an explanation of data; ranking tables include all places with Asian and/or NHPI populations above SF4 population thresholds; (1) tables reflect only those areas that meet SF4 population thresholds, therefore there may be less than 50 states, 75 counties or 75 places listed

Language Spoken at Home: English Only

Pakistanis 5 Years and Over Who Speak English-Only at Home

All States, Top 75 Counties, and Top 75 Places Sorted by Percent[1]

State	Percent
Delaware	28.01
Nevada	20.16
Colorado	19.22
Kansas	17.05
Utah	14.33
Missouri	13.87
Indiana	13.59
Ohio	13.25
Oregon	12.84
Washington	12.29
Wisconsin	12.08
Alabama	12.00
Kentucky	10.98
California	10.93
Arizona	10.45
West Virginia	9.82
Florida	9.69
Maryland	9.60
Pennsylvania	9.49
Iowa	8.96
Connecticut	8.34
Georgia	8.26
Oklahoma	8.14
North Carolina	8.05
United States	7.73
Illinois	7.21
New Jersey	6.86
Texas	6.76
Virginia	5.86
Michigan	5.74
Massachusetts	5.68
Minnesota	5.56
Louisiana	5.29
Tennessee	4.73
New York	4.57

County	Percent
Riverside County, CA	22.47
Wake County, NC	18.56
Sacramento County, CA	17.21
San Bernardino County, CA	17.10
Camden County, NJ	16.87
Franklin County, OH	16.37
San Diego County, CA	15.48
New York County, NY	15.37
Cobb County, GA	14.17
Maricopa County, AZ	13.00
Middlesex County, MA	12.92
Orange County, CA	12.53
Montgomery County, MD	11.70
Orange County, FL	11.51
DuPage County, IL	11.43
Snohomish County, WA	11.02
Oakland County, MI	11.01
King County, WA	10.77
Somerset County, NJ	10.67
Denton County, TX	10.56
San Joaquin County, CA	10.21
Alameda County, CA	10.08
Fairfield County, CT	9.78
New Haven County, CT	9.41
Mercer County, NJ	9.37
Los Angeles County, CA	9.20
Dallas County, TX	8.92
Bergen County, NJ	8.52
Monmouth County, NJ	8.38
Broward County, FL	8.23
St. Louis County, MO	8.13
Suffolk County, NY	7.90
Lake County, IL	7.86
Tarrant County, TX	7.61
Essex County, NJ	7.44
Howard County, MD	6.98
Middlesex County, NJ	6.96
Hartford County, CT	6.31
Santa Clara County, CA	6.26
Baltimore County, MD	6.18
Fairfax County, VA	5.71
Hennepin County, MN	5.68
Prince William County, VA	5.66
Cook County, IL	5.62
Westchester County, NY	5.55
Bronx County, NY	5.52
Tulsa County, OK	5.44
Arlington County, VA	5.32
San Francisco County, CA	5.32
Nassau County, NY	5.10
Philadelphia County, PA	5.01
Alexandria Independent City, VA	4.89
Harris County, TX	4.84
Collin County, TX	4.82
Gwinnett County, GA	4.80
Richmond County, NY	4.74
Travis County, TX	4.72
Worcester County, MA	4.66
Macomb County, MI	4.21
Monroe County, NY	3.93
Atlantic County, NJ	3.92
Morris County, NJ	3.90
Hudson County, NJ	3.66
Kings County, NY	3.65
Fort Bend County, TX	3.41
Wayne County, MI	3.29
Milwaukee County, WI	3.24
Washtenaw County, MI	3.18
Miami-Dade County, FL	3.16
Prince George's County, MD	3.00
Will County, IL	2.94
Clayton County, GA	2.81
Guilford County, NC	2.75
Loudoun County, VA	2.59
Contra Costa County, CA	2.57

Place	Percent
Sacramento, CA (city) Sacramento County	16.91
Huntington, NY (town) Suffolk County	14.14
Carrollton, TX (city) Denton County	11.87
Skokie, IL (village) Cook County	11.61
Garland, TX (city) Dallas County	10.03
Los Angeles, CA (city) Los Angeles County	9.31
Edison, NJ (township) Middlesex County	9.24
Lincolnia, VA (cdp) Fairfax County	9.07
Dale City, VA (cdp) Prince William County	8.64
Dallas, TX (city) Dallas County	8.10
Tulsa, OK (city) Tulsa County	7.35
Fremont, CA (city) Alameda County	6.99
Brookhaven, NY (town) Suffolk County	6.98
San Jose, CA (city) Santa Clara County	6.88
Old Bridge, NJ (township) Middlesex County	6.73
Anaheim, CA (city) Orange County	6.58
Austin, TX (city) Travis County	6.16
North Hempstead, NY (town) Nassau County	5.67
Plano, TX (city) Collin County	5.64
Arlington, VA (cdp) Arlington County	5.32
San Francisco, CA (city) San Francisco County	5.32
Stockton, CA (city) San Joaquin County	5.08
Philadelphia, PA (city) Philadelphia County	5.01
Woodbridge, NJ (township) Middlesex County	4.72
Chicago, IL (city) Cook County	4.53
Ellicott City, MD (cdp) Howard County	4.21
Hempstead, NY (town) Nassau County	4.20
Houston, TX (city) Harris County	4.12
Torrance, CA (city) Los Angeles County	4.02
Irving, TX (city) Dallas County	3.77
New York, NY (city)	3.49
Jersey City, NJ (city) Hudson County	3.39
Santa Clara, CA (city) Santa Clara County	2.27
Richardson, TX (city) Dallas County	1.23
Bailey's Crossroads, VA (cdp) Fairfax County	<0.01
Mission Bend, TX (cdp) Fort Bend County	<0.01
Sugar Land, TX (city) Fort Bend County	<0.01

Notes: Please refer to the User's Guide for an explanation of data; ranking tables include all places with Asian and/or NHPI populations above SF4 population thresholds; (1) tables reflect only those areas that meet SF4 population thresholds, therefore there may be less than 50 states, 75 counties or 75 places listed

Language Spoken at Home: English Only

Samoans 5 Years and Over Who Speak English-Only at Home

All States, Top 75 Counties, and Top 75 Places Sorted by Number[1]

State	Number
United States	27,622
California	10,730
Hawaii	4,096
Washington	1,979
Utah	1,097
New York	778
Texas	778
Nevada	745
Colorado	528
Pennsylvania	481
Missouri	466
Illinois	409
Alaska	370
Arizona	366
Florida	359
Oregon	354
Georgia	342
Ohio	295
New Jersey	276
Tennessee	276
Michigan	225
Virginia	209
North Carolina	182

County	Number
Honolulu County, HI	3,960
Los Angeles County, CA	3,262
San Diego County, CA	1,760
Orange County, CA	1,148
King County, WA	1,055
Salt Lake County, UT	608
Alameda County, CA	600
Clark County, NV	583
San Francisco County, CA	428
San Bernardino County, CA	406
Santa Clara County, CA	395
San Mateo County, CA	344
Pierce County, WA	333
Riverside County, CA	332
Anchorage Borough, AK	297
Sacramento County, CA	284
Utah County, UT	226
Solano County, CA	225
Contra Costa County, CA	197
Jackson County, MO	195
Ventura County, CA	182
Maricopa County, AZ	172
San Joaquin County, CA	122
Hawaii County, HI	78

Place	Number
Honolulu, HI (cdp) Honolulu County	877
San Diego, CA (city) San Diego County	849
Long Beach, CA (city) Los Angeles County	722
Los Angeles, CA (city) Los Angeles County	667
Waipahu, HI (cdp) Honolulu County	597
San Francisco, CA (city) San Francisco County	428
Oceanside, CA (city) San Diego County	372
New York, NY (city)	289
West Valley City, UT (city) Salt Lake County	286
Anaheim, CA (city) Orange County	283
Carson, CA (city) Los Angeles County	272
Halawa, HI (cdp) Honolulu County	264
Laie, HI (cdp) Honolulu County	262
Santa Ana, CA (city) Orange County	230
San Jose, CA (city) Santa Clara County	226
Seattle, WA (city) King County	223
Federal Way, WA (city) King County	211
Sacramento, CA (city) Sacramento County	202
Lakewood, CA (city) Los Angeles County	185
Ewa Beach, HI (cdp) Honolulu County	178
Compton, CA (city) Los Angeles County	160
Oxnard, CA (city) Ventura County	153
Nanakuli, HI (cdp) Honolulu County	122
Salt Lake City, UT (city) Salt Lake County	106
Garden Grove, CA (city) Orange County	100
Tacoma, WA (city) Pierce County	94
Hauula, HI (cdp) Honolulu County	93
Lakewood, WA (city) Pierce County	64
San Bernardino, CA (city) San Bernardino County	52
Kahuku, HI (cdp) Honolulu County	48
Westminster, CA (city) Orange County	42
Hayward, CA (city) Alameda County	39

Notes: Please refer to the User's Guide for an explanation of data; ranking tables include all places with Asian and/or NHPI populations above SF4 population thresholds; (1) tables reflect only those areas that meet SF4 population thresholds, therefore there may be less than 50 states, 75 counties or 75 places listed

Language Spoken at Home: English Only

Samoans 5 Years and Over Who Speak English-Only at Home

All States, Top 75 Counties, and Top 75 Places Sorted by Percent[1]

State	Percent
Ohio	68.13
Pennsylvania	65.44
Colorado	64.39
New York	59.34
Michigan	53.83
Nevada	52.65
Tennessee	52.57
Missouri	52.18
Illinois	49.88
Oregon	49.79
Georgia	48.65
Virginia	46.34
Arizona	45.98
Florida	45.79
New Jersey	44.16
Texas	42.33
North Carolina	39.82
United States	35.88
Utah	33.70
Hawaii	31.17
Washington	31.01
California	30.72
Alaska	27.86

County	Percent
Clark County, NV	58.53
Utah County, UT	45.84
Jackson County, MO	45.03
Solano County, CA	41.21
Riverside County, CA	40.59
San Diego County, CA	39.50
San Joaquin County, CA	34.86
Maricopa County, AZ	33.66
Orange County, CA	33.16
Ventura County, CA	32.97
Honolulu County, HI	31.34
King County, WA	30.11
Anchorage Borough, AK	28.59
Contra Costa County, CA	28.59
Alameda County, CA	27.75
Salt Lake County, UT	27.35
Hawaii County, HI	26.99
Los Angeles County, CA	26.95
Santa Clara County, CA	26.02
Sacramento County, CA	25.94
San Mateo County, CA	24.98
San Bernardino County, CA	23.69
San Francisco County, CA	20.88
Pierce County, WA	20.80

Place	Percent
Anaheim, CA (city) Orange County	55.27
Federal Way, WA (city) King County	50.48
Ewa Beach, HI (cdp) Honolulu County	46.11
Halawa, HI (cdp) Honolulu County	45.44
San Diego, CA (city) San Diego County	43.63
New York, NY (city)	43.46
Laie, HI (cdp) Honolulu County	42.67
Kahuku, HI (cdp) Honolulu County	41.38
Hauula, HI (cdp) Honolulu County	38.59
West Valley City, UT (city) Salt Lake County	37.48
Lakewood, CA (city) Los Angeles County	35.85
Los Angeles, CA (city) Los Angeles County	34.90
Santa Ana, CA (city) Orange County	33.97
Waipahu, HI (cdp) Honolulu County	31.59
Sacramento, CA (city) Sacramento County	31.37
Oxnard, CA (city) Ventura County	31.35
Oceanside, CA (city) San Diego County	27.05
Salt Lake City, UT (city) Salt Lake County	25.67
Lakewood, WA (city) Pierce County	23.44
Carson, CA (city) Los Angeles County	22.15
Long Beach, CA (city) Los Angeles County	21.66
Honolulu, HI (cdp) Honolulu County	21.60
San Francisco, CA (city) San Francisco County	20.88
San Jose, CA (city) Santa Clara County	20.56
Compton, CA (city) Los Angeles County	18.29
Seattle, WA (city) King County	17.94
Nanakuli, HI (cdp) Honolulu County	17.48
Tacoma, WA (city) Pierce County	16.10
Garden Grove, CA (city) Orange County	14.49
San Bernardino, CA (city) San Bernardino County	13.90
Westminster, CA (city) Orange County	11.67
Hayward, CA (city) Alameda County	7.21

Notes: Please refer to the User's Guide for an explanation of data; ranking tables include all places with Asian and/or NHPI populations above SF4 population thresholds; (1) tables reflect only those areas that meet SF4 population thresholds, therefore there may be less than 50 states, 75 counties or 75 places listed

Language Spoken at Home: English Only

Sri Lankans 5 Years and Over Who Speak English-Only at Home

All States, Top 75 Counties, and Top 75 Places Sorted by Number[1]

State	Number
United States	4,553
California	1,318
New York	530
New Jersey	323
Maryland	217
Texas	204
Virginia	182
Massachusetts	156
Washington	150
Ohio	141
Illinois	119
Florida	114
Michigan	112
Pennsylvania	72

County	Number
Los Angeles County, CA	496
Queens County, NY	181
Middlesex County, NJ	152
Orange County, CA	141
Montgomery County, MD	126
Richmond County, NY	68

Place	Number
New York, NY (city)	388
Los Angeles, CA (city) Los Angeles County	278

Notes: Please refer to the User's Guide for an explanation of data; ranking tables include all places with Asian and/or NHPI populations above SF4 population thresholds; (1) tables reflect only those areas that meet SF4 population thresholds, therefore there may be less than 50 states, 75 counties or 75 places listed

Language Spoken at Home: English Only

Sri Lankans 5 Years and Over Who Speak English-Only at Home

All States, Top 75 Counties, and Top 75 Places Sorted by Percent[1]

State	Percent
Washington	40.11
Massachusetts	35.45
Michigan	34.04
Florida	29.84
Virginia	29.35
Ohio	28.20
New Jersey	26.05
California	25.63
United States	25.34
Pennsylvania	23.30
Illinois	22.12
Texas	22.10
New York	20.67
Maryland	20.45

County	Percent
Middlesex County, NJ	33.55
Orange County, CA	22.27
Los Angeles County, CA	21.74
Queens County, NY	20.52
Montgomery County, MD	18.10
Richmond County, NY	13.26

Place	Percent
Los Angeles, CA (city) Los Angeles County	25.05
New York, NY (city)	20.43

Notes: Please refer to the User's Guide for an explanation of data; ranking tables include all places with Asian and/or NHPI populations above SF4 population thresholds; (1) tables reflect only those areas that meet SF4 population thresholds, therefore there may be less than 50 states, 75 counties or 75 places listed

Language Spoken at Home: English Only

Taiwanese 5 Years and Over Who Speak English-Only at Home

All States, Top 75 Counties, and Top 75 Places Sorted by Number[1]

State	Number
United States	9,368
California	3,388
New York	736
Texas	530
Illinois	418
Florida	393
Massachusetts	363
Pennsylvania	323
New Jersey	306
Washington	298
Michigan	211
Ohio	180
Maryland	168
Virginia	164
North Carolina	163
Colorado	134
Utah	112
Arizona	107
Kansas	105
Connecticut	99
Wisconsin	97
Indiana	95
Oregon	81
Tennessee	80
Minnesota	76
Missouri	76
Hawaii	75
Georgia	54
Nevada	39
Louisiana	26
Oklahoma	24
Iowa	23

County	Number
Los Angeles County, CA	1,144
Orange County, CA	515
Santa Clara County, CA	421
New York County, NY	305
Cook County, IL	291
San Diego County, CA	224
Alameda County, CA	216
Middlesex County, MA	195
King County, WA	182
Harris County, TX	130
Contra Costa County, CA	102
San Mateo County, CA	96
Queens County, NY	92
Fort Bend County, TX	91
San Bernardino County, CA	91
Suffolk County, MA	86
Washtenaw County, MI	82
Fairfax County, VA	81
Travis County, TX	81
Mercer County, NJ	79
Honolulu County, HI	75
San Francisco County, CA	71
Sacramento County, CA	69
Dallas County, TX	68
Maricopa County, AZ	68
Oakland County, MI	65
Allegheny County, PA	64
Middlesex County, NJ	62
Westchester County, NY	59
Franklin County, OH	57
Somerset County, NJ	51
Ventura County, CA	48
Nassau County, NY	46
Suffolk County, NY	46
Dane County, WI	43
St. Louis County, MO	41
Riverside County, CA	40
Clark County, NV	39
Montgomery County, MD	35
Tarrant County, TX	35
DuPage County, IL	28
Norfolk County, MA	24
Morris County, NJ	18
Gwinnett County, GA	14
Collin County, TX	11
Bergen County, NJ	7
Essex County, NJ	0

Place	Number
New York, NY (city)	430
Los Angeles, CA (city) Los Angeles County	183
Chicago, IL (city) Cook County	162
Seattle, WA (city) King County	159
Irvine, CA (city) Orange County	146
San Jose, CA (city) Santa Clara County	118
San Diego, CA (city) San Diego County	106
Rowland Heights, CA (cdp) Los Angeles County	91
Orange, CA (city) Orange County	90
Houston, TX (city) Harris County	87
Arcadia, CA (city) Los Angeles County	86
Boston, MA (city) Suffolk County	86
Austin, TX (city) Travis County	81
Berkeley, CA (city) Alameda County	76
Sugar Land, TX (city) Fort Bend County	76
Temple City, CA (city) Los Angeles County	75
San Francisco, CA (city) San Francisco County	71
San Marino, CA (city) Los Angeles County	71
Cerritos, CA (city) Los Angeles County	67
Ann Arbor, MI (city) Washtenaw County	64
Fremont, CA (city) Alameda County	61
Sunnyvale, CA (city) Santa Clara County	56
Hacienda Heights, CA (cdp) Los Angeles County	50
Cypress, CA (city) Orange County	46
Diamond Bar, CA (city) Los Angeles County	40
Honolulu, HI (cdp) Honolulu County	40
Madison, WI (city) Dane County	40
Alhambra, CA (city) Los Angeles County	31
East San Gabriel, CA (cdp) Los Angeles County	31
Torrance, CA (city) Los Angeles County	31
Walnut, CA (city) Los Angeles County	30
Fountain Valley, CA (city) Orange County	29
Naperville, IL (city) Du Page County	28
Arlington, TX (city) Tarrant County	25
Tustin, CA (city) Orange County	22
North Hempstead, NY (town) Nassau County	21
Troy, MI (city) Oakland County	20
Cupertino, CA (city) Santa Clara County	17
Columbus, OH (city) Franklin County	16
Rancho Palos Verdes, CA (city) Los Angeles County	16
Saratoga, CA (city) Santa Clara County	13
Chino Hills, CA (city) San Bernardino County	12
Monterey Park, CA (city) Los Angeles County	12
Plano, TX (city) Collin County	9
Bellevue, WA (city) King County	8
Huntington Beach, CA (city) Orange County	8
Edison, NJ (township) Middlesex County	6
El Monte, CA (city) Los Angeles County	6
San Gabriel, CA (city) Los Angeles County	5
Anaheim, CA (city) Orange County	0
Upland, CA (city) San Bernardino County	0
West Covina, CA (city) Los Angeles County	0

Notes: Please refer to the User's Guide for an explanation of data; ranking tables include all places with Asian and/or NHPI populations above SF4 population thresholds; (1) tables reflect only those areas that meet SF4 population thresholds, therefore there may be less than 50 states, 75 counties or 75 places listed

Language Spoken at Home: English Only

Taiwanese 5 Years and Over Who Speak English-Only at Home

All States, Top 75 Counties, and Top 75 Places Sorted by Percent[1]

State	Percent
Utah	32.46
Kansas	20.75
Colorado	20.40
Florida	20.01
North Carolina	17.81
Minnesota	17.08
Massachusetts	15.19
Wisconsin	15.06
Pennsylvania	14.60
Arizona	14.02
Tennessee	13.79
Indiana	13.65
Virginia	13.00
Connecticut	12.69
Illinois	12.04
Oregon	10.80
New York	9.72
Michigan	9.59
Hawaii	9.31
Ohio	8.53
Washington	8.33
Missouri	8.15
United States	7.99
Maryland	7.60
Texas	7.06
Oklahoma	6.90
Nevada	6.57
California	5.60
New Jersey	5.54
Louisiana	5.33
Iowa	5.25
Georgia	3.08

County	Percent
New York County, NY	29.50
Suffolk County, MA	19.20
Westchester County, NY	17.72
Sacramento County, CA	17.60
Cook County, IL	16.97
Mercer County, NJ	16.70
Middlesex County, MA	16.25
Washtenaw County, MI	16.17
Allegheny County, PA	15.17
San Mateo County, CA	12.83
Fairfax County, VA	11.59
Maricopa County, AZ	11.13
Suffolk County, NY	10.75
Dane County, WI	10.41
Travis County, TX	10.27
San Diego County, CA	10.25
Somerset County, NJ	9.90
Honolulu County, HI	9.66
San Francisco County, CA	9.38
Clark County, NV	9.15
Dallas County, TX	8.76
Santa Clara County, CA	8.40
Contra Costa County, CA	8.38
Riverside County, CA	8.15
Fort Bend County, TX	7.73
Nassau County, NY	7.73
Franklin County, OH	7.60
St. Louis County, MO	6.65
King County, WA	6.38
Norfolk County, MA	6.25
Ventura County, CA	6.18
Harris County, TX	6.01
Alameda County, CA	5.95
Orange County, CA	5.86
Tarrant County, TX	5.56
Oakland County, MI	5.44
Middlesex County, NJ	4.82
San Bernardino County, CA	4.74
DuPage County, IL	3.45
Los Angeles County, CA	3.45
Montgomery County, MD	3.31
Gwinnett County, GA	3.20
Morris County, NJ	2.83
Queens County, NY	2.73
Collin County, TX	1.37
Bergen County, NJ	0.91
Essex County, NJ	<0.01

Place	Percent
Chicago, IL (city) Cook County	20.88
Orange, CA (city) Orange County	19.82
Boston, MA (city) Suffolk County	19.20
Berkeley, CA (city) Alameda County	18.63
Seattle, WA (city) King County	16.39
Ann Arbor, MI (city) Washtenaw County	14.51
Austin, TX (city) Travis County	11.62
Madison, WI (city) Dane County	9.76
San Francisco, CA (city) San Francisco County	9.38
New York, NY (city)	8.97
Sunnyvale, CA (city) Santa Clara County	8.56
Sugar Land, TX (city) Fort Bend County	8.40
Fountain Valley, CA (city) Orange County	7.61
North Hempstead, NY (town) Nassau County	7.42
San Diego, CA (city) San Diego County	7.24
Naperville, IL (city) Du Page County	6.67
Cypress, CA (city) Orange County	6.65
Arlington, TX (city) Tarrant County	6.31
San Jose, CA (city) Santa Clara County	6.09
Houston, TX (city) Harris County	5.92
Honolulu, HI (cdp) Honolulu County	5.78
Irvine, CA (city) Orange County	5.69
Los Angeles, CA (city) Los Angeles County	5.65
East San Gabriel, CA (cdp) Los Angeles County	5.19
Tustin, CA (city) Orange County	5.13
Temple City, CA (city) Los Angeles County	5.05
San Marino, CA (city) Los Angeles County	4.82
Saratoga, CA (city) Santa Clara County	4.14
Cerritos, CA (city) Los Angeles County	3.88
Troy, MI (city) Oakland County	3.88
Rowland Heights, CA (cdp) Los Angeles County	3.70
Columbus, OH (city) Franklin County	3.48
Rancho Palos Verdes, CA (city) Los Angeles County	3.01
Fremont, CA (city) Alameda County	2.73
Torrance, CA (city) Los Angeles County	2.52
Arcadia, CA (city) Los Angeles County	2.40
Cupertino, CA (city) Santa Clara County	2.31
Chino Hills, CA (city) San Bernardino County	2.19
Alhambra, CA (city) Los Angeles County	2.03
Diamond Bar, CA (city) Los Angeles County	1.98
Hacienda Heights, CA (cdp) Los Angeles County	1.81
Walnut, CA (city) Los Angeles County	1.66
Plano, TX (city) Collin County	1.65
El Monte, CA (city) Los Angeles County	1.57
Huntington Beach, CA (city) Orange County	1.47
Monterey Park, CA (city) Los Angeles County	1.23
Edison, NJ (township) Middlesex County	0.97
Bellevue, WA (city) King County	0.96
San Gabriel, CA (city) Los Angeles County	0.73
Anaheim, CA (city) Orange County	<0.01
Upland, CA (city) San Bernardino County	<0.01
West Covina, CA (city) Los Angeles County	<0.01

Notes: Please refer to the User's Guide for an explanation of data; ranking tables include all places with Asian and/or NHPI populations above SF4 population thresholds; (1) tables reflect only those areas that meet SF4 population thresholds, therefore there may be less than 50 states, 75 counties or 75 places listed

Language Spoken at Home: English Only

Thais 5 Years and Over Who Speak English-Only at Home

All States, Top 75 Counties, and Top 75 Places Sorted by Number[1]

State	Number
United States	20,712
California	4,439
Texas	1,764
Florida	1,593
New York	958
Illinois	872
Virginia	856
Washington	795
Ohio	572
Arizona	529
Nevada	521
Maryland	498
Georgia	487
Pennsylvania	472
Missouri	392
Colorado	387
Massachusetts	385
North Carolina	364
Michigan	363
Hawaii	349
Oregon	316
New Jersey	279
Indiana	246
Oklahoma	225
Tennessee	219
Wisconsin	210
Louisiana	190
Connecticut	179
Minnesota	178
Nebraska	166
Alaska	163
Utah	161
Iowa	160
South Carolina	159
Alabama	152
Kansas	149
New Mexico	113
Arkansas	95
Kentucky	88

County	Number
Los Angeles County, CA	1,672
Clark County, NV	445
Cook County, IL	419
San Diego County, CA	394
Honolulu County, HI	333
Maricopa County, AZ	329
King County, WA	317
Fairfax County, VA	307
Orange County, CA	294
Bexar County, TX	275
Alameda County, CA	269
Harris County, TX	251
San Francisco County, CA	240
Dallas County, TX	233
Riverside County, CA	222
Tarrant County, TX	211
Montgomery County, MD	200
San Bernardino County, CA	193
Okaloosa County, FL	183
Santa Clara County, CA	177
Broward County, FL	170
New York County, NY	170
Miami-Dade County, FL	168
Pinellas County, FL	168
Sacramento County, CA	164
Palm Beach County, FL	159
Hillsborough County, FL	156
Middlesex County, MA	144
San Mateo County, CA	130
Pierce County, WA	118
Suffolk County, NY	112
DuPage County, IL	104
Anchorage Borough, AK	103
Contra Costa County, CA	97
Oklahoma County, OK	92
Franklin County, OH	89
Travis County, TX	86
Queens County, NY	77
Collin County, TX	73
Nassau County, NY	72
Multnomah County, OR	65
Prince George's County, MD	58
Westchester County, NY	54
Denver County, CO	37
St. Louis County, MO	36
Polk County, IA	35
Bergen County, NJ	32

Place	Number
Los Angeles, CA (city) Los Angeles County	648
New York, NY (city)	330
San Diego, CA (city) San Diego County	252
San Francisco, CA (city) San Francisco County	240
Chicago, IL (city) Cook County	216
San Antonio, TX (city) Bexar County	189
Seattle, WA (city) King County	138
Las Vegas, NV (city) Clark County	137
Houston, TX (city) Harris County	119
Honolulu, HI (cdp) Honolulu County	114
San Jose, CA (city) Santa Clara County	91
Cerritos, CA (city) Los Angeles County	88
Long Beach, CA (city) Los Angeles County	67
Portland, OR (city) Multnomah County	50
Columbus, OH (city) Franklin County	38
Denver, CO (city) Denver County	37
Des Moines, IA (city) Polk County	35
Bellflower, CA (city) Los Angeles County	34
Anaheim, CA (city) Orange County	17
Glendale, CA (city) Los Angeles County	13
Spring Valley, NV (cdp) Clark County	11

Notes: Please refer to the User's Guide for an explanation of data; ranking tables include all places with Asian and/or NHPI populations above SF4 population thresholds; (1) tables reflect only those areas that meet SF4 population thresholds, therefore there may be less than 50 states, 75 counties or 75 places listed

Language Spoken at Home: English Only

Thais 5 Years and Over Who Speak English-Only at Home

All States, Top 75 Counties, and Top 75 Places Sorted by Percent[1]

State	Percent
Nebraska	36.01
Arkansas	34.05
Arizona	33.31
Ohio	31.07
Louisiana	30.06
Missouri	29.50
Indiana	28.41
New Mexico	28.18
Oklahoma	27.37
Pennsylvania	27.10
Alabama	25.85
Hawaii	25.61
Texas	25.53
Florida	25.02
Wisconsin	24.91
Virginia	24.20
Connecticut	23.99
Kansas	23.84
Utah	23.82
North Carolina	23.50
South Carolina	23.28
Michigan	23.15
Alaska	23.02
Tennessee	22.60
Georgia	22.37
Oregon	22.24
Kentucky	21.46
Colorado	20.98
Washington	20.89
Minnesota	20.27
United States	19.23
Iowa	18.10
Nevada	18.02
Massachusetts	17.91
Maryland	17.88
New Jersey	15.93
Illinois	15.39
New York	14.98
California	12.57

County	Percent
Pinellas County, FL	35.74
Bexar County, TX	34.12
San Diego County, CA	30.95
Pierce County, WA	30.26
Suffolk County, NY	30.19
Okaloosa County, FL	29.66
Broward County, FL	29.57
Maricopa County, AZ	29.56
Honolulu County, HI	29.55
Tarrant County, TX	28.59
DuPage County, IL	26.13
Riverside County, CA	25.90
Hillsborough County, FL	23.93
Oklahoma County, OK	23.17
Sacramento County, CA	22.87
Palm Beach County, FL	22.08
Travis County, TX	21.39
Dallas County, TX	21.28
Franklin County, OH	21.04
New York County, NY	20.86
Fairfax County, VA	20.74
Nassau County, NY	20.57
Anchorage Borough, AK	20.44
Harris County, TX	19.61
Miami-Dade County, FL	19.47
Alameda County, CA	18.80
San Mateo County, CA	18.68
Prince George's County, MD	17.85
Clark County, NV	17.40
Collin County, TX	17.38
Middlesex County, MA	16.86
San Francisco County, CA	16.76
King County, WA	16.66
Contra Costa County, CA	16.55
Montgomery County, MD	15.36
Multnomah County, OR	14.81
Santa Clara County, CA	13.58
San Bernardino County, CA	11.49
Cook County, IL	10.80
Polk County, IA	9.89
St. Louis County, MO	9.52
Westchester County, NY	9.52
Orange County, CA	9.49
Denver County, CO	9.37
Los Angeles County, CA	8.74
Bergen County, NJ	6.63
Queens County, NY	3.34

Place	Percent
San Antonio, TX (city) Bexar County	32.76
San Diego, CA (city) San Diego County	31.07
Honolulu, HI (cdp) Honolulu County	21.76
Las Vegas, NV (city) Clark County	20.15
Cerritos, CA (city) Los Angeles County	18.88
San Francisco, CA (city) San Francisco County	16.76
Seattle, WA (city) King County	16.22
San Jose, CA (city) Santa Clara County	14.51
Houston, TX (city) Harris County	14.22
Portland, OR (city) Multnomah County	12.59
Des Moines, IA (city) Polk County	12.03
Long Beach, CA (city) Los Angeles County	11.17
Chicago, IL (city) Cook County	10.47
Columbus, OH (city) Franklin County	10.30
Denver, CO (city) Denver County	9.37
Bellflower, CA (city) Los Angeles County	8.88
New York, NY (city)	8.81
Los Angeles, CA (city) Los Angeles County	7.34
Anaheim, CA (city) Orange County	3.91
Glendale, CA (city) Los Angeles County	3.10
Spring Valley, NV (cdp) Clark County	2.30

Notes: Please refer to the User's Guide for an explanation of data; ranking tables include all places with Asian and/or NHPI populations above SF4 population thresholds; (1) tables reflect only those areas that meet SF4 population thresholds, therefore there may be less than 50 states, 75 counties or 75 places listed

Language Spoken at Home: English Only

Tongans 5 Years and Over Who Speak English-Only at Home

All States, Top 75 Counties, and Top 75 Places Sorted by Number[1]

State	Number
United States	4,175
California	1,411
Utah	1,284
Hawaii	502
Oregon	151
Arizona	142
Washington	139
Texas	126
Nevada	114
Alaska	42

County	Number
Salt Lake County, UT	995
Honolulu County, HI	368
San Mateo County, CA	274
Los Angeles County, CA	258
Alameda County, CA	243
Orange County, CA	133
Utah County, UT	124
Multnomah County, OR	112
San Bernardino County, CA	97
King County, WA	82
Tarrant County, TX	71
Maui County, HI	69
San Diego County, CA	68
Contra Costa County, CA	56
Sacramento County, CA	56
Washoe County, NV	46
Maricopa County, AZ	41

Place	Number
Salt Lake City, UT (city) Salt Lake County	371
West Valley City, UT (city) Salt Lake County	334
Honolulu, HI (cdp) Honolulu County	136
Oakland, CA (city) Alameda County	117
Portland, OR (city) Multnomah County	112
Hauula, HI (cdp) Honolulu County	74
San Mateo, CA (city) San Mateo County	70
Los Angeles, CA (city) Los Angeles County	53
Laie, HI (cdp) Honolulu County	46
San Bruno, CA (city) San Mateo County	40
East Palo Alto, CA (city) San Mateo County	26
Sacramento, CA (city) Sacramento County	23
Kahuku, HI (cdp) Honolulu County	16
West Jordan, UT (city) Salt Lake County	7

Notes: Please refer to the User's Guide for an explanation of data; ranking tables include all places with Asian and/or NHPI populations above SF4 population thresholds; (1) tables reflect only those areas that meet SF4 population thresholds, therefore there may be less than 50 states, 75 counties or 75 places listed

Language Spoken at Home: English Only

Tongans 5 Years and Over Who Speak English-Only at Home

All States, Top 75 Counties, and Top 75 Places Sorted by Percent[1]

State	Percent
Oregon	38.72
Texas	28.90
Arizona	23.36
Utah	21.54
Washington	19.17
United States	17.04
Nevada	16.40
Hawaii	13.43
California	13.05
Alaska	12.00

County	Percent
Multnomah County, OR	36.60
Utah County, UT	30.17
Orange County, CA	23.71
Tarrant County, TX	23.67
San Diego County, CA	20.99
Salt Lake County, UT	19.12
King County, WA	17.48
Contra Costa County, CA	15.43
Alameda County, CA	15.02
San Bernardino County, CA	14.00
Honolulu County, HI	13.11
Los Angeles County, CA	12.27
Maui County, HI	10.27
Washoe County, NV	9.27
Sacramento County, CA	8.59
San Mateo County, CA	8.37
Maricopa County, AZ	8.18

Place	Percent
Portland, OR (city) Multnomah County	37.46
Laie, HI (cdp) Honolulu County	22.89
Hauula, HI (cdp) Honolulu County	22.02
West Valley City, UT (city) Salt Lake County	21.59
Salt Lake City, UT (city) Salt Lake County	17.59
Los Angeles, CA (city) Los Angeles County	16.99
San Mateo, CA (city) San Mateo County	12.24
Oakland, CA (city) Alameda County	10.33
Honolulu, HI (cdp) Honolulu County	9.65
San Bruno, CA (city) San Mateo County	8.39
Kahuku, HI (cdp) Honolulu County	7.05
Sacramento, CA (city) Sacramento County	4.65
East Palo Alto, CA (city) San Mateo County	1.95
West Jordan, UT (city) Salt Lake County	1.60

Notes: Please refer to the User's Guide for an explanation of data; ranking tables include all places with Asian and/or NHPI populations above SF4 population thresholds; (1) tables reflect only those areas that meet SF4 population thresholds, therefore there may be less than 50 states, 75 counties or 75 places listed

Language Spoken at Home: English Only

Vietnamese 5 Years and Over Who Speak English-Only at Home

All States, Top 75 Counties, and Top 75 Places Sorted by Number[1]

State	Number
United States	71,438
California	24,519
Texas	7,280
Washington	3,096
Florida	2,713
Virginia	2,633
Massachusetts	2,243
Pennsylvania	2,125
New York	2,037
Illinois	1,459
Georgia	1,425
Maryland	1,343
New Jersey	1,324
North Carolina	1,282
Minnesota	1,274
Ohio	1,246
Michigan	1,167
Oregon	1,095
Louisiana	1,080
Arizona	1,025
Colorado	1,011
Missouri	902
Oklahoma	767
Hawaii	697
Kansas	683
Wisconsin	592
Tennessee	552
Indiana	523
Connecticut	477
Arkansas	461
Nevada	452
Alabama	404
Iowa	374
Utah	340
South Carolina	327
Nebraska	319
Kentucky	311
Mississippi	310
New Mexico	224
Maine	219
New Hampshire	196
Alaska	165
Idaho	145
District of Columbia	119
West Virginia	103
Delaware	91
Vermont	83
South Dakota	70
Rhode Island	40

County	Number
Orange County, CA	5,946
Los Angeles County, CA	4,466
Santa Clara County, CA	4,462
Harris County, TX	2,437
San Diego County, CA	2,151
King County, WA	1,792
Alameda County, CA	1,317
Sacramento County, CA	1,131
Fairfax County, VA	1,130
Dallas County, TX	1,060
Tarrant County, TX	1,010
San Francisco County, CA	884
Maricopa County, AZ	758
Cook County, IL	704
Suffolk County, MA	627
Honolulu County, HI	597
Hennepin County, MN	594
Philadelphia County, PA	560
Riverside County, CA	525
Multnomah County, OR	523
Travis County, TX	520
Montgomery County, MD	511
Contra Costa County, CA	506
San Bernardino County, CA	495
Middlesex County, MA	485
Orange County, FL	421
New York County, NY	413
San Mateo County, CA	409
Oklahoma County, OK	385
Sedgwick County, KS	367
San Joaquin County, CA	361
Mecklenburg County, NC	358
Bexar County, TX	348
Snohomish County, WA	345
Clark County, NV	326
Ventura County, CA	320
Franklin County, OH	318
Worcester County, MA	316
Gwinnett County, GA	309
Hillsborough County, FL	299
Washington County, OR	285
Kent County, MI	280
Denver County, CO	265
Broward County, FL	262
Jackson County, MO	258
Monterey County, CA	247
Saint Louis Independent City, MO	243
Kings County, NY	242
Jefferson Parish, LA	238
Pinellas County, FL	238
Cuyahoga County, OH	228
Essex County, MA	225
DeKalb County, GA	222
Queens County, NY	215
Arlington County, VA	214
Hampden County, MA	213
Norfolk County, MA	213
Collin County, TX	211
Hartford County, CT	209
Palm Beach County, FL	209
Wake County, NC	209
Lancaster County, PA	200
Miami-Dade County, FL	191
Montgomery County, PA	191
DuPage County, IL	185
Santa Barbara County, CA	185
Bernalillo County, NM	183
Camden County, NJ	182
Guilford County, NC	181
Ramsey County, MN	179
Monroe County, NY	178
Erie County, NY	177
Salt Lake County, UT	177
Pierce County, WA	176
Pima County, AZ	174

Place	Number
San Jose, CA (city) Santa Clara County	3,210
San Diego, CA (city) San Diego County	1,494
Los Angeles, CA (city) Los Angeles County	1,314
Houston, TX (city) Harris County	1,222
Garden Grove, CA (city) Orange County	1,132
New York, NY (city)	960
San Francisco, CA (city) San Francisco County	884
Seattle, WA (city) King County	743
Westminster, CA (city) Orange County	733
Santa Ana, CA (city) Orange County	615
Philadelphia, PA (city) Philadelphia County	560
Irvine, CA (city) Orange County	527
Boston, MA (city) Suffolk County	496
Portland, OR (city) Multnomah County	473
Anaheim, CA (city) Orange County	467
Chicago, IL (city) Cook County	467
Oklahoma City, OK (city) Oklahoma County	459
Sacramento, CA (city) Sacramento County	441
Austin, TX (city) Travis County	429
Honolulu, HI (cdp) Honolulu County	414
Oakland, CA (city) Alameda County	385
Arlington, TX (city) Tarrant County	369
Dallas, TX (city) Dallas County	355
Phoenix, AZ (city) Maricopa County	346
Santa Clara, CA (city) Santa Clara County	341
Wichita, KS (city) Sedgwick County	339
Huntington Beach, CA (city) Orange County	334
Fort Worth, TX (city) Tarrant County	333
Long Beach, CA (city) Los Angeles County	307
Garland, TX (city) Dallas County	277
Denver, CO (city) Denver County	265
San Gabriel, CA (city) Los Angeles County	263
Stockton, CA (city) San Joaquin County	262
Milpitas, CA (city) Santa Clara County	258
Minneapolis, MN (city) Hennepin County	257
Charlotte, NC (city) Mecklenburg County	256
Fremont, CA (city) Alameda County	256
Fountain Valley, CA (city) Orange County	255
St. Louis, MO (city) Saint Louis Independent City	243
Kansas City, MO (city) Jackson County	227
Columbus, OH (city) Franklin County	226
Orange, CA (city) Orange County	215
Arlington, VA (cdp) Arlington County	214
Sunnyvale, CA (city) Santa Clara County	209
Rosemead, CA (city) Los Angeles County	204
Springfield, MA (city) Hampden County	200
El Monte, CA (city) Los Angeles County	196
Worcester, MA (city) Worcester County	192
San Antonio, TX (city) Bexar County	189
Escondido, CA (city) San Diego County	185
Albuquerque, NM (city) Bernalillo County	183
Costa Mesa, CA (city) Orange County	173
Pomona, CA (city) Los Angeles County	173
Berkeley, CA (city) Alameda County	172
Grand Prairie, TX (city) Dallas County	172
New Orleans, LA (city) Orleans Parish	169
Elk Grove, CA (cdp) Sacramento County	167
Alhambra, CA (city) Los Angeles County	164
Buffalo, NY (city) Erie County	153
Memphis, TN (city) Shelby County	150
Fullerton, CA (city) Orange County	148
Davis, CA (city) Yolo County	147
Lake Forest, CA (city) Orange County	146
Des Moines, IA (city) Polk County	143
Irving, TX (city) Dallas County	143
Corona, CA (city) Riverside County	138
Raleigh, NC (city) Wake County	136
Daly City, CA (city) San Mateo County	135
Annandale, VA (cdp) Fairfax County	130
Fort Smith, AR (city) Sebastian County	129
Greensboro, NC (city) Guilford County	128
Kent, WA (city) King County	124
Riverside, CA (city) Riverside County	124
Jacksonville, FL (city) Duval County	123
Citrus Heights, CA (city) Sacramento County	118

Notes: Please refer to the User's Guide for an explanation of data; ranking tables include all places with Asian and/or NHPI populations above SF4 population thresholds; (1) tables reflect only those areas that meet SF4 population thresholds, therefore there may be less than 50 states, 75 counties or 75 places listed

Language Spoken at Home: English Only

Vietnamese 5 Years and Over Who Speak English-Only at Home

All States, Top 75 Counties, and Top 75 Places Sorted by Percent[1]

State	Percent
West Virginia	26.89
Maine	21.68
Alaska	18.19
Wisconsin	16.43
Delaware	14.65
Ohio	13.15
Arkansas	12.87
New Hampshire	12.20
Indiana	11.88
Nevada	11.85
South Dakota	11.76
Idaho	11.57
Kentucky	10.55
Michigan	9.80
New Jersey	9.59
Arizona	9.55
New York	9.54
Missouri	9.31
South Carolina	9.31
Alabama	9.27
Vermont	9.08
North Carolina	8.97
Hawaii	8.87
New Mexico	8.82
Florida	8.73
Maryland	8.69
Illinois	8.64
Tennessee	8.59
Pennsylvania	8.13
Colorado	8.07
Virginia	8.02
Washington	7.57
Minnesota	7.55
District of Columbia	7.13
Connecticut	7.06
Massachusetts	7.05
United States	6.94
Utah	6.78
Oklahoma	6.76
Kansas	6.60
Mississippi	6.29
Oregon	6.25
Iowa	6.01
California	5.88
Texas	5.85
Nebraska	5.26
Georgia	5.17
Louisiana	4.70
Rhode Island	4.13

County	Percent
Kitsap County, WA	31.46
Anchorage Borough, AK	30.07
New York County, NY	27.68
Lake County, IL	21.59
Hampton Independent City, VA	20.94
Sarpy County, NE	20.05
Scott County, MN	19.87
Kern County, CA	19.63
Santa Cruz County, CA	18.96
Alachua County, FL	18.87
Union County, NJ	18.54
Whatcom County, WA	18.02
Peoria County, IL	17.60
Okaloosa County, FL	17.28
Alexandria Independent City, VA	17.17
St. Tammany Parish, LA	17.14
Norfolk Independent City, VA	16.57
Jackson County, MS	16.34
Santa Barbara County, CA	15.93
Brevard County, FL	15.68
Dane County, WI	15.59
Will County, IL	15.55
San Mateo County, CA	15.52
Prince William County, VA	15.47
Morris County, NJ	15.41
Bucks County, PA	15.31
Knox County, TN	15.10
El Paso County, CO	14.90
Burlington County, NJ	14.84
Nassau County, NY	14.74
Washoe County, NV	14.56
Plaquemines Parish, LA	14.36
Franklin County, OH	14.33
Madison County, AL	14.29
Bristol County, MA	14.16
Washtenaw County, MI	14.05
Wayne County, MI	13.76
Monterey County, CA	13.65
Erie County, NY	13.54
Brazos County, TX	13.48
Bay County, FL	13.31
Hamilton County, TN	13.28
Miami-Dade County, FL	13.19
New Castle County, DE	13.06
Richland County, SC	13.06
Cumberland County, PA	13.05
Placer County, CA	12.93
St. Martin Parish, LA	12.92
Monmouth County, NJ	12.91
Montgomery County, OH	12.91
Benton County, WA	12.86
Bexar County, TX	12.77
Howard County, MD	12.50
Polk County, FL	12.45
Cuyahoga County, OH	12.08
Solano County, CA	12.06
Chester County, PA	12.03
Hampden County, MA	12.02
Yolo County, CA	11.89
Allegheny County, PA	11.62
Boulder County, CO	11.16
Matagorda County, TX	11.15
Palm Beach County, FL	11.02
York County, PA	10.97
Cobb County, GA	10.89
Oakland County, MI	10.69
Lancaster County, PA	10.65
Ventura County, CA	10.59
Clark County, NV	10.54
Newport News Independent City, VA	10.41
Galveston County, TX	10.39
Jefferson County, CO	10.31
Arlington County, VA	10.23
Broward County, FL	10.16
Allen County, IN	10.09

Place	Percent
Citrus Heights, CA (city) Sacramento County	25.88
Antioch, CA (city) Contra Costa County	21.66
Lewisville, TX (city) Denton County	20.00
Salinas, CA (city) Monterey County	19.78
Berkeley, CA (city) Alameda County	18.70
Aliso Viejo, CA (cdp) Orange County	17.93
Reno, NV (city) Washoe County	17.75
Carol Stream, IL (village) Du Page County	17.49
League City, TX (city) Galveston County	17.40
Ocean Springs, MS (city) Jackson County	17.00
Henderson, LA (town) Saint Martin Parish	16.99
Las Vegas, NV (city) Clark County	16.83
Laguna Niguel, CA (city) Orange County	16.81
Santa Clarita, CA (city) Los Angeles County	16.77
Kirkland, WA (city) King County	16.48
Colorado Springs, CO (city) El Paso County	16.32
Thousand Oaks, CA (city) Ventura County	16.02
Escondido, CA (city) San Diego County	15.49
Madison, WI (city) Dane County	15.37
Springfield, MA (city) Hampden County	15.37
Buffalo, NY (city) Erie County	15.18
Daly City, CA (city) San Mateo County	15.15
Franconia, VA (cdp) Fairfax County	14.92
Laguna Hills, CA (city) Orange County	14.79
West and East Lealman, FL (cdp) Pinellas County	14.52
Burbank, CA (city) Los Angeles County	14.46
Davis, CA (city) Yolo County	14.29
Marina, CA (city) Monterey County	14.26
Yorba Linda, CA (city) Orange County	14.15
Bryn Mawr-Skyway, WA (cdp) King County	13.67
Sterling Heights, MI (city) Macomb County	13.67
Bellingham, WA (city) Whatcom County	13.52
Concord, CA (city) Contra Costa County	13.48
Placentia, CA (city) Orange County	13.29
San Mateo, CA (city) San Mateo County	13.22
Seattle Hill-Silver Firs, WA (cdp) Snohomish County	13.19
Orlando, FL (city) Orange County	12.96
Richfield, MN (city) Hennepin County	12.56
North Richland Hills, TX (city) Tarrant County	12.23
Herndon, VA (town) Fairfax County	12.03
Goleta, CA (cdp) Santa Barbara County	11.96
Lilburn, GA (city) Gwinnett County	11.85
Rancho Santa Margarita, CA (city) Orange County	11.84
Cary, NC (town) Wake County	11.81
Pasadena, CA (city) Los Angeles County	11.64
Irvine, CA (city) Orange County	11.60
Westminster, CO (city) Adams County	11.49
Cypress, CA (city) Orange County	11.43
Columbus, OH (city) Franklin County	11.35
Allen, TX (city) Collin County	11.34
Oakton, VA (cdp) Fairfax County	11.19
Merrifield, VA (cdp) Fairfax County	11.09
Chantilly, VA (cdp) Fairfax County	11.07
Lake Forest, CA (city) Orange County	10.99
Revere, MA (city) Suffolk County	10.96
Gresham, OR (city) Multnomah County	10.86
Tempe, AZ (city) Maricopa County	10.86
Campbell, CA (city) Santa Clara County	10.85
Centreville, VA (cdp) Fairfax County	10.75
Bakersfield, CA (city) Kern County	10.72
Chelsea, MA (city) Suffolk County	10.71
Gaithersburg, MD (city) Montgomery County	10.67
Palacios, TX (city) Matagorda County	10.67
Rochester, NY (city) Monroe County	10.40
Corona, CA (city) Riverside County	10.39
San Gabriel, CA (city) Los Angeles County	10.34
Shrewsbury, MA (town) Worcester County	10.33
San Lorenzo, CA (cdp) Alameda County	10.31
Arlington, VA (cdp) Arlington County	10.23
Colesville, MD (cdp) Montgomery County	10.12
Pomona, CA (city) Los Angeles County	10.12
Irving, TX (city) Dallas County	10.10
Downey, CA (city) Los Angeles County	10.07
Raleigh, NC (city) Wake County	9.99
Livermore, CA (city) Alameda County	9.98

Notes: Please refer to the User's Guide for an explanation of data; ranking tables include all places with Asian and/or NHPI populations above SF4 population thresholds; (1) tables reflect only those areas that meet SF4 population thresholds, therefore there may be less than 50 states, 75 counties or 75 places listed

Foreign Born

Total Population

All States, Top 75 Counties, and Top 75 Places Sorted by Number[1]

State	Number
United States	31,107,889
California	8,864,255
New York	3,868,133
Texas	2,899,642
Florida	2,670,828
Illinois	1,529,058
New Jersey	1,476,327
Massachusetts	772,983
Arizona	656,183
Washington	614,457
Georgia	577,273
Virginia	570,279
Michigan	523,589
Maryland	518,315
Pennsylvania	508,291
North Carolina	430,000
Connecticut	369,967
Colorado	369,903
Ohio	339,279
Nevada	316,593
Oregon	289,702
Minnesota	260,463
Hawaii	212,229
Wisconsin	193,751
Indiana	186,534
Tennessee	159,004
Utah	158,664
Missouri	151,196
New Mexico	149,606
Kansas	134,735
Oklahoma	131,747
Rhode Island	119,277
South Carolina	115,978
Louisiana	115,885
Iowa	91,085
Alabama	87,772
Kentucky	80,271
Nebraska	74,638
Arkansas	73,690
District of Columbia	73,561
Idaho	64,080
New Hampshire	54,154
Delaware	44,898
Mississippi	39,908
Alaska	37,170
Maine	36,691
Vermont	23,245
West Virginia	19,390
Montana	16,396
South Dakota	13,495
North Dakota	12,114
Wyoming	11,205

County	Number
Los Angeles County, CA	3,449,444
Miami-Dade County, FL	1,147,765
Cook County, IL	1,064,703
Queens County, NY	1,028,339
Kings County, NY	931,769
Orange County, CA	849,899
Harris County, TX	756,548
San Diego County, CA	606,254
Santa Clara County, CA	573,130
Dallas County, TX	463,574
New York County, NY	452,440
Maricopa County, AZ	441,240
Broward County, FL	410,387
Alameda County, CA	392,656
Bronx County, NY	385,827
San Bernardino County, CA	318,647
Riverside County, CA	293,712
San Francisco County, CA	285,541
King County, WA	268,285
Clark County, NV	247,751
Nassau County, NY	238,414
Fairfax County, VA	237,677
Hudson County, NJ	234,597
Montgomery County, MD	232,996
San Mateo County, CA	228,118
Middlesex County, MA	223,465
Bergen County, NJ	222,301
Westchester County, NY	205,429
Sacramento County, CA	197,195
Palm Beach County, FL	196,852
El Paso County, TX	186,168
Tarrant County, TX	183,223
Middlesex County, NJ	181,761
Contra Costa County, CA	180,488
Suffolk County, MA	176,031
Fresno County, CA	168,717
Honolulu County, HI	168,246
Hidalgo County, TX	168,215
Essex County, NJ	168,165
Suffolk County, NY	158,525
Ventura County, CA	155,913
Bexar County, TX	151,340
Fairfield County, CT	149,038
DuPage County, IL	138,656
Wayne County, MI	137,769
Philadelphia County, PA	137,205
Union County, NJ	130,916
Passaic County, NJ	130,291
Orange County, FL	128,904
Travis County, TX	122,621
Oakland County, MI	119,218
Monterey County, CA	116,559
Hillsborough County, FL	115,151
Kern County, CA	111,944
Hennepin County, MN	110,496
Prince George's County, MD	110,481
San Joaquin County, CA	109,812
DeKalb County, GA	101,320
Hartford County, CT	100,693
Pima County, AZ	100,050
Gwinnett County, GA	99,518
Providence County, RI	96,676
Denver County, CO	96,601
Lake County, IL	95,536
Salt Lake County, UT	93,276
Cuyahoga County, OH	88,761
Pinellas County, FL	87,685
Cameron County, TX	85,723
Santa Barbara County, CA	84,826
Multnomah County, OR	83,965
Tulare County, CA	83,124
Essex County, MA	82,039
Stanislaus County, CA	81,615
Fulton County, GA	78,619
Norfolk County, MA	76,732

Place	Number
New York, NY (city)	2,871,032
Los Angeles, CA (city) Los Angeles County	1,512,720
Chicago, IL (city) Cook County	628,903
Houston, TX (city) Harris County	516,105
San Jose, CA (city) Santa Clara County	329,757
San Diego, CA (city) San Diego County	314,227
Dallas, TX (city) Dallas County	290,436
San Francisco, CA (city) San Francisco County	285,541
Phoenix, AZ (city) Maricopa County	257,325
Miami, FL (city) Miami-Dade County	215,739
Santa Ana, CA (city) Orange County	179,933
Hialeah, FL (city) Miami-Dade County	163,256
Boston, MA (city) Suffolk County	151,836
El Paso, TX (city) El Paso County	147,505
Philadelphia, PA (city) Philadelphia County	137,205
Hempstead, NY (town) Nassau County	134,598
San Antonio, TX (city) Bexar County	133,675
Long Beach, CA (city) Los Angeles County	132,168
Anaheim, CA (city) Orange County	123,976
Austin, TX (city) Travis County	109,006
Glendale, CA (city) Los Angeles County	106,119
Oakland, CA (city) Alameda County	106,116
Denver, CO (city) Denver County	96,601
Seattle, WA (city) King County	94,952
Honolulu, HI (cdp) Honolulu County	93,895
Las Vegas, NV (city) Clark County	90,656
Fort Worth, TX (city) Tarrant County	87,120
Fresno, CA (city) Fresno County	86,937
Sacramento, CA (city) Sacramento County	82,616
Jersey City, NJ (city) Hudson County	81,554
Fremont, CA (city) Alameda County	75,494
Garden Grove, CA (city) Orange County	71,351
Tucson, AZ (city) Pima County	69,476
Portland, OR (city) Multnomah County	68,976
Newark, NJ (city) Essex County	66,057
Oxnard, CA (city) Ventura County	62,902
East Los Angeles, CA (cdp) Los Angeles County	60,605
Charlotte, NC (city) Mecklenburg County	59,849
El Monte, CA (city) Los Angeles County	59,589
Stockton, CA (city) San Joaquin County	59,369
Minneapolis, MN (city) Hennepin County	55,475
North Hempstead, NY (town) Nassau County	55,357
Pomona, CA (city) Los Angeles County	54,893
Daly City, CA (city) San Mateo County	54,213
Salinas, CA (city) Monterey County	53,016
Elizabeth, NJ (city) Union County	52,975
Arlington, VA (cdp) Arlington County	52,693
Sunnyvale, CA (city) Santa Clara County	51,990
Yonkers, NY (city) Westchester County	51,687
Arlington, TX (city) Tarrant County	50,911
Riverside, CA (city) Riverside County	50,808
Irving, TX (city) Dallas County	50,696
Laredo, TX (city) Webb County	50,233
Chula Vista, CA (city) San Diego County	49,842
Paterson, NJ (city) Passaic County	48,924
Miami Beach, FL (city) Miami-Dade County	48,852
Ontario, CA (city) San Bernardino County	48,789
Hayward, CA (city) Alameda County	48,619
Columbus, OH (city) Franklin County	47,713
South Gate, CA (city) Los Angeles County	47,556
Islip, NY (town) Suffolk County	47,088
Milwaukee, WI (city) Milwaukee County	46,122
Irvine, CA (city) Orange County	45,877
Detroit, MI (city) Wayne County	45,541
Aurora, CO (city) Arapahoe County	44,692
Mesa, AZ (city) Maricopa County	44,546
Brownsville, TX (city) Cameron County	44,116
Providence, RI (city) Providence County	43,947
Jacksonville, FL (city) Duval County	43,661
Alhambra, CA (city) Los Angeles County	43,632
Garland, TX (city) Dallas County	43,588
Fountainbleau, FL (cdp) Miami-Dade County	43,496
Pasadena, CA (city) Los Angeles County	43,277
Oklahoma City, OK (city) Oklahoma County	42,885
Paradise, NV (cdp) Clark County	42,050

Notes: Please refer to the User's Guide for an explanation of data; ranking tables include all places with Asian and/or NHPI populations above SF4 population thresholds; (1) tables reflect only those areas that meet SF4 population thresholds, therefore there may be less than 50 states, 75 counties or 75 places listed

Foreign Born

Total Population

All States, Top 75 Counties, and Top 75 Places Sorted by Percent[1]

State	Percent
California	26.17
New York	20.38
New Jersey	17.55
Hawaii	17.52
Florida	16.71
Nevada	15.84
Texas	13.91
District of Columbia	12.86
Arizona	12.79
Illinois	12.31
Massachusetts	12.17
Rhode Island	11.38
United States	11.05
Connecticut	10.86
Washington	10.42
Maryland	9.79
Colorado	8.60
Oregon	8.47
New Mexico	8.22
Virginia	8.06
Utah	7.10
Georgia	7.05
Alaska	5.93
Delaware	5.73
North Carolina	5.34
Minnesota	5.29
Michigan	5.27
Kansas	5.01
Idaho	4.95
New Hampshire	4.38
Nebraska	4.36
Pennsylvania	4.14
Oklahoma	3.82
Vermont	3.82
Wisconsin	3.61
Iowa	3.11
Indiana	3.07
Ohio	2.99
South Carolina	2.89
Maine	2.88
Tennessee	2.79
Arkansas	2.76
Missouri	2.70
Louisiana	2.59
Wyoming	2.27
Kentucky	1.99
Alabama	1.97
North Dakota	1.89
Montana	1.82
South Dakota	1.79
Mississippi	1.40
West Virginia	1.07

County	Percent
Miami-Dade County, FL	50.94
Queens County, NY	46.13
Hudson County, NJ	38.52
Kings County, NY	37.79
San Francisco County, CA	36.76
Los Angeles County, CA	36.24
Santa Clara County, CA	34.06
San Mateo County, CA	32.26
Imperial County, CA	32.16
Orange County, CA	29.86
Hidalgo County, TX	29.54
New York County, NY	29.43
Monterey County, CA	29.01
Webb County, TX	29.01
Bronx County, NY	28.95
Arlington County, VA	27.81
Colusa County, CA	27.55
Seward County, KS	27.41
El Paso County, TX	27.39
Alameda County, CA	27.20
Montgomery County, MD	26.68
Passaic County, NJ	26.64
Cameron County, TX	25.57
Suffolk County, MA	25.52
Alexandria Independent City, VA	25.41
Fairfax Independent City, VA	25.36
Broward County, FL	25.29
Franklin County, WA	25.19
Bergen County, NJ	25.14
Union County, NJ	25.05
Merced County, CA	24.78
Fairfax County, VA	24.51
Middlesex County, NJ	24.23
Yuma County, AZ	24.05
Finney County, KS	22.69
Tulare County, CA	22.59
Ford County, KS	22.54
Harris County, TX	22.25
Westchester County, NY	22.25
San Diego County, CA	21.55
Aleutians West Census Area, AK	21.48
Santa Barbara County, CA	21.24
Essex County, NJ	21.19
Fresno County, CA	21.11
Dallas County, TX	20.89
Ventura County, CA	20.70
Yolo County, CA	20.26
Madera County, CA	20.11
Cook County, IL	19.80
San Joaquin County, CA	19.48
Sutter County, CA	19.29
Honolulu County, HI	19.20
Rockland County, NY	19.10
Contra Costa County, CA	19.02
Riverside County, CA	19.01
San Benito County, CA	18.83
Dona Ana County, NM	18.68
San Bernardino County, CA	18.64
Collier County, FL	18.33
Fort Bend County, TX	18.30
Aleutians East Borough, AK	18.28
Stanislaus County, CA	18.26
Santa Cruz County, CA	18.19
Eagle County, CO	18.18
Somerset County, NJ	18.13
Napa County, CA	18.09
Clark County, NV	18.01
Nassau County, NY	17.86
Glenn County, CA	17.84
Denver County, CO	17.42
Palm Beach County, FL	17.40
Grant County, WA	17.14
Kern County, CA	16.92
Gwinnett County, GA	16.91
Fairfield County, CT	16.89

Place	Percent
Fontainbleau, FL (cdp) Miami-Dade County	73.08
Hialeah, FL (city) Miami-Dade County	72.11
West New York, NJ (town) Hudson County	65.18
Langley Park, MD (cdp) Prince George's County	64.54
Chamblee, GA (city) De Kalb County	64.19
Doral, FL (cdp) Miami-Dade County	62.55
Seven Corners, VA (cdp) Fairfax County	60.01
Miami, FL (city) Miami-Dade County	59.50
Kendall West, FL (cdp) Miami-Dade County	59.41
Kendale Lakes, FL (cdp) Miami-Dade County	58.82
Union City, NJ (city) Hudson County	58.70
Millbourne, PA (borough) Delaware County	57.37
San Joaquin, CA (city) Fresno County	56.98
Palisades Park, NJ (borough) Bergen County	56.96
Rosemead, CA (city) Los Angeles County	56.35
Harrison, NJ (town) Hudson County	56.00
Huntington Park, CA (city) Los Angeles County	55.94
Miami Beach, FL (city) Miami-Dade County	55.48
Richgrove, CA (cdp) Tulare County	55.32
Bailey's Crossroads, VA (cdp) Fairfax County	54.69
Glendale, CA (city) Los Angeles County	54.41
Monterey Park, CA (city) Los Angeles County	53.58
Santa Ana, CA (city) Orange County	53.31
Bell, CA (city) Los Angeles County	53.26
Terra Bella, CA (cdp) Tulare County	53.03
Rowland Heights, CA (cdp) Los Angeles County	52.83
San Gabriel, CA (city) Los Angeles County	52.56
The Hammocks, FL (cdp) Miami-Dade County	52.44
Daly City, CA (city) San Mateo County	52.35
South El Monte, CA (city) Los Angeles County	51.88
El Monte, CA (city) Los Angeles County	51.26
Calexico, CA (city) Imperial County	51.24
Alhambra, CA (city) Los Angeles County	50.76
Forest Home, NY (cdp) Tompkins County	50.69
Sunset, FL (cdp) Miami-Dade County	50.66
North Miami Beach, FL (city) Miami-Dade County	49.67
Livingston, CA (city) Merced County	49.37
South Gate, CA (city) Los Angeles County	49.32
North Fair Oaks, CA (cdp) San Mateo County	49.28
Guttenberg, NJ (town) Hudson County	49.18
East Los Angeles, CA (cdp) Los Angeles County	48.73
North Miami, FL (city) Miami-Dade County	48.54
Fairview, NJ (borough) Bergen County	48.39
Orosi, CA (cdp) Tulare County	48.27
Earlimart, CA (cdp) Tulare County	47.77
Miami Lakes, FL (cdp) Miami-Dade County	47.59
Lincolnia, VA (cdp) Fairfax County	47.43
Milpitas, CA (city) Santa Clara County	47.27
Haliimaile, HI (cdp) Maui County	47.07
South San Jose Hills, CA (cdp) Los Angeles County	47.05
Country Club, FL (cdp) Miami-Dade County	47.02
North Bergen, NJ (township) Hudson County	46.76
Doraville, GA (city) De Kalb County	46.62
Walnut, CA (city) Los Angeles County	46.24
Artesia, CA (city) Los Angeles County	45.84
Passaic, NJ (city) Passaic County	45.83
Baldwin Park, CA (city) Los Angeles County	45.73
Hawaiian Gardens, CA (city) Los Angeles County	45.63
Richmond West, FL (cdp) Miami-Dade County	45.61
Cerritos, CA (city) Los Angeles County	45.54
Glenvar Heights, FL (cdp) Miami-Dade County	45.43
Golden Glades, FL (cdp) Miami-Dade County	45.29
Fort Lee, NJ (borough) Bergen County	44.74
Colma, CA (town) San Mateo County	44.72
Rollingwood, CA (cdp) Contra Costa County	44.37
Watsonville, CA (city) Santa Cruz County	44.20
South Miami Heights, FL (cdp) Miami-Dade County	44.12
Union City, CA (city) Alameda County	44.00
Plainsboro Center, NJ (cdp) Middlesex County	43.95
Elizabeth, NJ (city) Union County	43.94
East Palo Alto, CA (city) San Mateo County	43.82
Cicero, IL (town) Cook County	43.62
Lynwood, CA (city) Los Angeles County	43.60
Arcadia, CA (city) Los Angeles County	43.58
La Puente, CA (city) Los Angeles County	43.53

Notes: Please refer to the User's Guide for an explanation of data; ranking tables include all places with Asian and/or NHPI populations above SF4 population thresholds; (1) tables reflect only those areas that meet SF4 population thresholds, therefore there may be less than 50 states, 75 counties or 75 places listed

Foreign Born

Asian

All States, Top 75 Counties, and Top 75 Places Sorted by Number[1]

State	Number
United States	7,012,202
California	2,474,465
New York	796,943
Texas	408,383
New Jersey	360,165
Illinois	305,563
Washington	215,582
Florida	196,638
Virginia	191,051
Massachusetts	171,034
Hawaii	169,629
Pennsylvania	158,220
Maryland	156,046
Michigan	129,443
Georgia	128,879
Ohio	97,818
Minnesota	96,784
North Carolina	80,098
Oregon	66,927
Arizona	62,366
Colorado	61,603
Nevada	61,358
Connecticut	60,861
Wisconsin	55,567
Missouri	44,237
Indiana	42,626
Tennessee	40,361
Louisiana	37,072
Oklahoma	34,148
Kansas	32,808
Iowa	26,674
South Carolina	25,942
Utah	23,509
Kentucky	22,404
Alabama	21,998
Alaska	17,216
Nebraska	16,313
Rhode Island	15,724
Arkansas	13,756
Mississippi	12,439
Delaware	12,181
New Mexico	11,975
New Hampshire	11,477
District of Columbia	10,199
Idaho	6,864
West Virginia	6,843
Maine	5,863
Vermont	3,785
South Dakota	3,360
Montana	2,671
North Dakota	2,408
Wyoming	1,926

County	Number
Los Angeles County, CA	790,502
Queens County, NY	312,683
Santa Clara County, CA	304,162
Orange County, CA	270,037
Alameda County, CA	198,143
Cook County, IL	190,926
San Diego County, CA	166,843
San Francisco County, CA	166,590
Kings County, NY	142,618
Honolulu County, HI	138,211
Harris County, TX	129,827
King County, WA	125,632
New York County, NY	108,329
Fairfax County, VA	94,805
San Mateo County, CA	92,912
Middlesex County, NJ	78,566
Sacramento County, CA	78,474
Montgomery County, MD	74,639
Bergen County, NJ	72,553
Dallas County, TX	66,715
Middlesex County, MA	65,617
Contra Costa County, CA	63,111
San Bernardino County, CA	52,507
DuPage County, IL	51,487
Clark County, NV	49,190
Philadelphia County, PA	46,567
Maricopa County, AZ	45,429
Hudson County, NJ	44,974
Nassau County, NY	43,566
Hennepin County, MN	37,893
Tarrant County, TX	37,666
San Joaquin County, CA	36,632
Oakland County, MI	35,846
Fresno County, CA	35,757
Suffolk County, MA	35,573
Riverside County, CA	34,243
Westchester County, NY	31,862
Gwinnett County, GA	31,278
Solano County, CA	31,020
Bronx County, NY	30,356
Ramsey County, MN	28,335
Broward County, FL	27,766
Fort Bend County, TX	27,470
Wayne County, MI	26,600
Norfolk County, MA	25,912
Travis County, TX	25,622
Multnomah County, OR	25,326
Ventura County, CA	25,313
Franklin County, OH	25,016
Collin County, TX	24,914
Snohomish County, WA	24,593
Suffolk County, NY	24,498
Miami-Dade County, FL	23,901
Pierce County, WA	23,593
Prince George's County, MD	23,000
Morris County, NJ	22,137
Montgomery County, PA	21,920
Orange County, FL	21,638
Essex County, NJ	21,570
DeKalb County, GA	21,498
Fairfield County, CT	21,217
Washington County, OR	20,642
Cuyahoga County, OH	18,942
Baltimore County, MD	18,099
Somerset County, NJ	17,733
Lake County, IL	17,518
Richmond County, NY	17,342
Fulton County, GA	16,786
Monmouth County, NJ	16,772
St. Louis County, MO	16,133
Hillsborough County, FL	15,847
Hartford County, CT	15,647
Wake County, NC	15,551
Bexar County, TX	15,479
Mecklenburg County, NC	15,296

Place	Number
New York, NY (city)	611,328
Los Angeles, CA (city) Los Angeles County	262,570
San Jose, CA (city) Santa Clara County	170,354
San Francisco, CA (city) San Francisco County	166,590
San Diego, CA (city) San Diego County	113,278
Chicago, IL (city) Cook County	93,435
Houston, TX (city) Harris County	80,093
Honolulu, HI (cdp) Honolulu County	77,983
Fremont, CA (city) Alameda County	53,672
Seattle, WA (city) King County	49,573
Philadelphia, PA (city) Philadelphia County	46,567
Oakland, CA (city) Alameda County	41,156
Garden Grove, CA (city) Orange County	39,313
Sacramento, CA (city) Sacramento County	37,237
Daly City, CA (city) San Mateo County	35,710
Long Beach, CA (city) Los Angeles County	35,706
Boston, MA (city) Suffolk County	32,676
Sunnyvale, CA (city) Santa Clara County	32,192
Alhambra, CA (city) Los Angeles County	31,813
Jersey City, NJ (city) Hudson County	30,962
Anaheim, CA (city) Orange County	28,544
Fresno, CA (city) Fresno County	28,363
Stockton, CA (city) San Joaquin County	28,336
Irvine, CA (city) Orange County	28,025
Monterey Park, CA (city) Los Angeles County	25,665
Dallas, TX (city) Dallas County	25,247
Westminster, CA (city) Orange County	25,063
Milpitas, CA (city) Santa Clara County	24,205
Torrance, CA (city) Los Angeles County	23,793
Glendale, CA (city) Los Angeles County	23,776
Portland, OR (city) Multnomah County	23,200
Santa Ana, CA (city) Orange County	22,457
Austin, TX (city) Travis County	21,947
Santa Clara, CA (city) Santa Clara County	21,882
St. Paul, MN (city) Ramsey County	21,860
Edison, NJ (township) Middlesex County	21,742
Union City, CA (city) Alameda County	20,534
Cerritos, CA (city) Los Angeles County	19,998
Rosemead, CA (city) Los Angeles County	19,359
Columbus, OH (city) Franklin County	19,183
Rowland Heights, CA (cdp) Los Angeles County	19,029
Hempstead, NY (town) Nassau County	18,314
Arcadia, CA (city) Los Angeles County	18,206
Hayward, CA (city) Alameda County	17,960
Vallejo, CA (city) Solano County	17,906
Phoenix, AZ (city) Maricopa County	17,391
West Covina, CA (city) Los Angeles County	16,897
El Monte, CA (city) Los Angeles County	16,505
Plano, TX (city) Collin County	16,470
Diamond Bar, CA (city) Los Angeles County	16,449
Minneapolis, MN (city) Hennepin County	16,224
Cupertino, CA (city) Santa Clara County	15,916
San Gabriel, CA (city) Los Angeles County	14,866
Arlington, TX (city) Tarrant County	14,810
Las Vegas, NV (city) Clark County	14,413
North Hempstead, NY (town) Nassau County	14,152
Fullerton, CA (city) Orange County	13,997
Hacienda Heights, CA (cdp) Los Angeles County	13,976
Carson, CA (city) Los Angeles County	13,898
Jacksonville, FL (city) Duval County	13,857
Bellevue, WA (city) King County	13,292
Oklahoma City, OK (city) Oklahoma County	13,203
Charlotte, NC (city) Mecklenburg County	13,016
San Antonio, TX (city) Bexar County	12,496
Arlington, VA (cdp) Arlington County	12,485
San Leandro, CA (city) Alameda County	12,447
Irving, TX (city) Dallas County	12,388
Buena Park, CA (city) Orange County	12,325
Alameda, CA (city) Alameda County	12,298
Chula Vista, CA (city) San Diego County	11,954
Lowell, MA (city) Middlesex County	11,754
Walnut, CA (city) Los Angeles County	11,700
Garland, TX (city) Dallas County	11,621
South San Francisco, CA (city) San Mateo County	11,077
Waipahu, HI (cdp) Honolulu County	10,984

Notes: Please refer to the User's Guide for an explanation of data; ranking tables include all places with Asian and/or NHPI populations above SF4 population thresholds; (1) tables reflect only those areas that meet SF4 population thresholds, therefore there may be less than 50 states, 75 counties or 75 places listed

Foreign Born

Asian

***All States, Top 75 Counties, and Top 75 Places Sorted by Percent*[1]**

State	Percent
Vermont	78.03
Kentucky	77.27
Nebraska	77.22
New York	76.30
Iowa	76.16
Delaware	75.88
Georgia	75.16
Oklahoma	74.97
New Jersey	74.75
Tennessee	74.56
Indiana	74.53
Virginia	74.53
New Hampshire	74.42
Maryland	74.41
Florida	74.38
Michigan	74.04
Ohio	74.03
Connecticut	73.97
Alabama	73.55
Texas	73.46
Kansas	73.28
Missouri	73.20
Pennsylvania	73.04
West Virginia	72.45
Illinois	72.16
Arkansas	72.09
North Dakota	72.05
North Carolina	71.97
Massachusetts	71.79
South Carolina	71.06
South Dakota	71.05
Maine	70.99
Mississippi	70.24
Minnesota	69.51
District of Columbia	69.09
United States	68.94
Nevada	68.85
Arizona	68.37
Alaska	67.52
Oregon	67.51
California	67.19
Washington	67.16
Wisconsin	66.89
Louisiana	66.81
Colorado	66.02
Rhode Island	66.00
New Mexico	65.49
Wyoming	64.80
Utah	63.75
Montana	61.22
Idaho	60.63
Hawaii	33.66

County	Percent
Brookings County, SD	91.53
Grant County, WI	90.91
Blue Earth County, MN	89.92
Lafayette County, MS	88.64
Payne County, OK	88.46
Wright County, MN	86.73
Rankin County, MS	86.64
Cayuga County, NY	86.30
Whitfield County, GA	86.23
Lynchburg Independent City, VA	85.73
Clarion County, PA	85.63
Dougherty County, GA	85.63
Bradley County, TN	85.42
Blount County, TN	85.27
Fauquier County, VA	85.14
Stearns County, MN	85.13
Kay County, OK	84.73
Addison County, VT	84.58
Franklin County, TN	84.52
Story County, IA	84.50
Harrison County, WV	84.42
Isabella County, MI	84.36
Washington County, VT	84.35
Herkimer County, NY	84.31
Cape May County, NJ	84.23
Charlotte County, FL	84.17
Windsor County, VT	84.08
Richland County, OH	84.06
Oktibbeha County, MS	84.03
Wicomico County, MD	83.96
Rockdale County, GA	83.68
McDonough County, IL	83.61
Weakley County, TN	83.51
Jasper County, MO	83.28
Hancock County, OH	83.25
Phelps County, MO	83.25
Troup County, GA	83.13
Mower County, MN	82.95
Jackson County, MI	82.92
Mercer County, PA	82.86
Columbiana County, OH	82.77
Coles County, IL	82.69
Alexandria Independent City, VA	82.58
Adams County, NE	82.53
Henderson County, NC	82.50
Fairfax Independent City, VA	82.41
Falls Church Independent City, VA	82.34
Forrest County, MS	82.27
Chautauqua County, NY	82.25
Elkhart County, IN	82.25
Spalding County, GA	82.06
Nassau County, FL	81.99
Greene County, NY	81.97
Jefferson County, AR	81.94
Madison County, MS	81.71
Montgomery County, AL	81.68
Houston County, AL	81.60
Windham County, VT	81.57
Dakota County, NE	81.44
Warren County, KY	81.40
Lancaster County, NE	81.27
Portage County, OH	81.23
Hall County, GA	81.18
DeKalb County, GA	81.01
Wood County, OH	80.94
Albemarle County, VA	80.68
Columbia County, PA	80.68
Hernando County, FL	80.60
Goodhue County, MN	80.45
Kittitas County, WA	80.45
Roanoke County, VA	80.28
Jackson County, IL	80.27
Cheshire County, NH	80.25
Pickens County, SC	80.17
Kankakee County, IL	80.14

Place	Percent
Gainesville, GA (city) Hall County	93.51
Chamblee, GA (city) De Kalb County	92.31
Scottdale, GA (cdp) De Kalb County	92.03
Fairborn, OH (city) Greene County	91.55
Langley Park, MD (cdp) Prince George's County	91.42
Little Flock, AR (city) Benton County	91.34
Riverdale Park, MD (town) Prince George's County	90.86
Brookings, SD (city) Brookings County	90.67
Absecon, NJ (city) Atlantic County	90.57
Hopkins, MN (city) Hennepin County	90.56
College, AK (cdp) Fairbanks North Star Borough	90.52
Inver Grove Heights, MN (city) Dakota County	90.17
Mankato, MN (city) Blue Earth County	90.14
Plainsboro Center, NJ (cdp) Middlesex County	89.74
Hudson, NY (city) Columbia County	89.70
Dearborn Heights, MI (city) Wayne County	89.45
Forest Home, NY (cdp) Tompkins County	89.39
Clemson, SC (city) Pickens County	89.30
Homewood, AL (city) Jefferson County	89.30
Fairview, NJ (borough) Bergen County	89.10
Scott, PA (township) Allegheny County	88.90
Scott Township, PA (cdp) Allegheny County	88.90
Norcross, GA (city) Gwinnett County	88.76
Stillwater, OK (city) Payne County	88.60
Pine Hills, FL (cdp) Orange County	88.55
Fond du Lac, WI (city) Fond du Lac County	88.49
Lauderdale, MN (city) Ramsey County	88.48
Coralville, IA (city) Johnson County	88.41
Jeffersontown, KY (city) Jefferson County	88.30
Mount Pleasant, MI (city) Isabella County	88.17
East Rutherford, NJ (borough) Bergen County	87.86
Mamaroneck, NY (town) Westchester County	87.72
Oak Park, MI (city) Oakland County	87.66
Laurel, MD (city) Prince George's County	87.57
Palmer, PA (township) Northampton County	87.50
Ashwaubenon, WI (village) Brown County	87.47
Maryland Heights, MO (city) Saint Louis County	87.47
Maple Shade, NJ (township) Burlington County	87.44
Findlay, OH (city) Hancock County	87.35
Hatfield, PA (borough) Montgomery County	87.34
Keyport, NJ (borough) Monmouth County	87.31
Sharonville, OH (city) Hamilton County	87.23
Joplin, MO (city) Jasper County	86.99
Rolla, MO (city) Phelps County	86.99
West New York, NJ (town) Hudson County	86.97
Farmington, MI (city) Oakland County	86.95
East Patchogue, NY (cdp) Suffolk County	86.94
Bryan, TX (city) Brazos County	86.86
East Norriton, PA (township) Montgomery County	86.80
Forest Park, IL (village) Cook County	86.74
Naugatuck, CT (town) New Haven County	86.57
Highland Park, NJ (borough) Middlesex County	86.55
Bowling Green, OH (city) Wood County	86.39
Southington, CT (town) Hartford County	86.33
Sunset, FL (cdp) Miami-Dade County	86.31
Oshtemo, MI (township) Kalamazoo County	86.28
Matawan, NJ (borough) Monmouth County	86.23
Edgewater, NJ (borough) Bergen County	85.94
Dracut, MA (town) Middlesex County	85.90
Concord, NH (city) Merrimack County	85.82
Millbourne, PA (borough) Delaware County	85.77
Conroe, TX (city) Montgomery County	85.68
Rockville Centre, NY (village) Nassau County	85.61
Takoma Park, MD (city) Montgomery County	85.43
Clarkston, GA (city) De Kalb County	85.41
Neptune, NJ (township) Monmouth County	85.35
Crystal, MN (city) Hennepin County	85.34
Greenbelt, MD (city) Prince George's County	85.25
Westland, MI (city) Wayne County	85.19
Doral, FL (cdp) Miami-Dade County	85.16
Bellevue, NE (city) Sarpy County	85.12
Martin, TN (city) Weakley County	85.12
Ames, IA (city) Story County	84.99
Milford Mill, MD (cdp) Baltimore County	84.99
Randallstown, MD (cdp) Baltimore County	84.89

Notes: Please refer to the User's Guide for an explanation of data; ranking tables include all places with Asian and/or NHPI populations above SF4 population thresholds; (1) tables reflect only those areas that meet SF4 population thresholds, therefore there may be less than 50 states, 75 counties or 75 places listed

Foreign Born

Native Hawaiian and Other Pacific Islander

All States, Top 75 Counties, and Top 75 Places Sorted by Number[1]

State	Number
United States	75,477
California	29,763
Hawaii	11,353
Utah	5,118
Washington	3,743
Texas	2,669
New York	2,544
Oregon	2,232
Florida	1,771
Arizona	1,406
Nevada	1,295
Illinois	938
Georgia	855
Virginia	821
New Jersey	795
Arkansas	733
Alaska	717
Missouri	714
North Carolina	699
Colorado	531
Michigan	526
Minnesota	495
Tennessee	493
Pennsylvania	484
Maryland	483
Massachusetts	428
South Carolina	401
Oklahoma	381
Indiana	326
Ohio	311
Connecticut	224
Kansas	206
Wisconsin	202
Nebraska	186
Iowa	181
Louisiana	178
Kentucky	165
Alabama	154
Idaho	144
Delaware	119
Rhode Island	111
West Virginia	83
New Mexico	80
Maine	54
Montana	47
Mississippi	32

County	Number
Honolulu County, HI	8,950
Los Angeles County, CA	7,042
Salt Lake County, UT	4,201
San Mateo County, CA	3,925
Sacramento County, CA	2,874
Alameda County, CA	2,737
King County, WA	2,309
Orange County, CA	2,026
Santa Clara County, CA	1,464
San Diego County, CA	1,392
San Bernardino County, CA	1,353
Hawaii County, HI	1,250
San Francisco County, CA	1,111
Maricopa County, AZ	1,066
Multnomah County, OR	1,019
Maui County, HI	1,015
Contra Costa County, CA	990
Queens County, NY	787
Stanislaus County, CA	764
Riverside County, CA	706
Clark County, NV	674
Kings County, NY	612
Washoe County, NV	569
Tarrant County, TX	553
Cook County, IL	552
Pierce County, WA	547
Washington County, AR	537
Yolo County, CA	498
Anchorage Borough, AK	484
Utah County, UT	457
Marion County, OR	408
Ventura County, CA	395
Miami-Dade County, FL	394
Solano County, CA	352
Harris County, TX	348
San Joaquin County, CA	343
Hennepin County, MN	313
Monterey County, CA	301
Dallas County, TX	290
Washington County, OR	275
Bronx County, NY	252
Jackson County, MO	245
Broward County, FL	239
New York County, NY	239
Snohomish County, WA	238
Montgomery County, MD	237
Fairfax County, VA	226
Shelby County, TN	192
Davis County, UT	186
Kern County, CA	179
Travis County, TX	179
Bexar County, TX	169
Orange County, FL	166
Lane County, OR	165
Clark County, WA	158
Bell County, TX	154
Philadelphia County, PA	146
Santa Barbara County, CA	146
Sonoma County, CA	143
Pima County, AZ	140
Arapahoe County, CO	139
Kauai County, HI	138
Essex County, NJ	130
Allegheny County, PA	126
Kitsap County, WA	111
El Paso County, CO	110
Gwinnett County, GA	110
Spokane County, WA	107
Denver County, CO	106
Fresno County, CA	102
Nassau County, NY	102
Milwaukee County, WI	98
Palm Beach County, FL	94
Suffolk County, NY	93
Clackamas County, OR	88

Place	Number
Honolulu, HI (cdp) Honolulu County	4,837
Sacramento, CA (city) Sacramento County	1,932
New York, NY (city)	1,904
Los Angeles, CA (city) Los Angeles County	1,660
Salt Lake City, UT (city) Salt Lake County	1,475
Long Beach, CA (city) Los Angeles County	1,375
West Valley City, UT (city) Salt Lake County	1,286
East Palo Alto, CA (city) San Mateo County	1,263
San Francisco, CA (city) San Francisco County	1,111
Hayward, CA (city) Alameda County	885
San Jose, CA (city) Santa Clara County	885
Portland, OR (city) Multnomah County	860
Oakland, CA (city) Alameda County	854
Waipahu, HI (cdp) Honolulu County	851
San Diego, CA (city) San Diego County	649
San Mateo, CA (city) San Mateo County	637
San Bruno, CA (city) San Mateo County	619
Phoenix, AZ (city) Maricopa County	577
Modesto, CA (city) Stanislaus County	538
Springdale, AR (city) Washington County	502
Chicago, IL (city) Cook County	463
Seattle, WA (city) King County	458
Hilo, HI (cdp) Hawaii County	454
Laie, HI (cdp) Honolulu County	398
Garden Grove, CA (city) Orange County	390
Wahiawa, HI (cdp) Honolulu County	372
Reno, NV (city) Washoe County	354
Oceanside, CA (city) San Diego County	345
Lakewood, CA (city) Los Angeles County	316
Federal Way, WA (city) King County	315
Costa Mesa, CA (city) Orange County	313
Hauula, HI (cdp) Honolulu County	281
Anaheim, CA (city) Orange County	280
Riverside, CA (city) Riverside County	277
Union City, CA (city) Alameda County	267
Daly City, CA (city) San Mateo County	266
South San Francisco, CA (city) San Mateo County	263
Redwood City, CA (city) San Mateo County	258
Las Vegas, NV (city) Clark County	249
Oxnard, CA (city) Ventura County	249
Compton, CA (city) Los Angeles County	248
Taylorsville, UT (city) Salt Lake County	247
Houston, TX (city) Harris County	246
West Jordan, UT (city) Salt Lake County	242
Santa Ana, CA (city) Orange County	236
Salem, OR (city) Marion County	231
Vallejo, CA (city) Solano County	228
Fort Worth, TX (city) Tarrant County	227
Carson, CA (city) Los Angeles County	212
Des Moines, WA (city) King County	211
Concord, CA (city) Contra Costa County	209
Fontana, CA (city) San Bernardino County	209
Kahuku, HI (cdp) Honolulu County	208
Ontario, CA (city) San Bernardino County	206
Kihei, HI (cdp) Maui County	199
Napili-Honokowai, HI (cdp) Maui County	199
San Bernardino, CA (city) San Bernardino County	199
Waimalu, HI (cdp) Honolulu County	199
Tacoma, WA (city) Pierce County	193
Kahului, HI (cdp) Maui County	180
Dallas, TX (city) Dallas County	178
Fremont, CA (city) Alameda County	173
Kansas City, MO (city) Jackson County	173
SeaTac, WA (city) King County	168
Westminster, CA (city) Orange County	167
Orem, UT (city) Utah County	166
North Las Vegas, NV (city) Clark County	165
Bakersfield, CA (city) Kern County	161
Pittsburg, CA (city) Contra Costa County	160
Hawthorne, CA (city) Los Angeles County	158
Tukwila, WA (city) King County	152
Waikoloa Village, HI (cdp) Hawaii County	149
Philadelphia, PA (city) Philadelphia County	146
Stockton, CA (city) San Joaquin County	146
Provo, UT (city) Utah County	145

Notes: Please refer to the User's Guide for an explanation of data; ranking tables include all places with Asian and/or NHPI populations above SF4 population thresholds; (1) tables reflect only those areas that meet SF4 population thresholds, therefore there may be less than 50 states, 75 counties or 75 places listed

Foreign Born

Native Hawaiian and Other Pacific Islander

All States, Top 75 Counties, and Top 75 Places Sorted by Percent[1]

State	Percent
Arkansas	47.78
Utah	35.63
Delaware	35.52
New York	32.19
Oregon	29.43
New Jersey	29.35
South Carolina	28.97
Minnesota	28.71
Nebraska	27.64
California	26.14
Florida	26.00
Rhode Island	25.17
Illinois	24.61
Maryland	23.79
Massachusetts	23.32
Missouri	23.25
Alaska	22.97
Tennessee	22.83
Arizona	22.80
Virginia	22.70
Georgia	22.12
Texas	21.41
Oklahoma	20.71
West Virginia	20.49
United States	19.93
Michigan	19.71
Iowa	18.95
North Carolina	18.90
Indiana	18.50
Maine	17.94
Washington	17.22
Kansas	17.05
Nevada	16.59
Connecticut	16.51
Kentucky	14.29
Pennsylvania	13.01
Alabama	12.97
Louisiana	12.91
Wisconsin	12.81
Colorado	12.35
Ohio	11.78
Idaho	11.69
Montana	10.51
Hawaii	10.09
New Mexico	6.41
Mississippi	4.73

County	Percent
Washington County, AR	71.03
Yolo County, CA	69.65
Miami-Dade County, FL	65.12
Queens County, NY	56.46
Hennepin County, MN	53.69
Marion County, OR	53.61
Montgomery County, MD	48.47
San Mateo County, CA	46.00
Sacramento County, CA	45.84
Stanislaus County, CA	42.35
Salt Lake County, UT	40.65
Multnomah County, OR	40.58
Kings County, NY	39.51
New York County, NY	39.05
Shelby County, TN	38.95
Washoe County, NV	37.88
Broward County, FL	37.05
Cook County, IL	34.59
Tarrant County, TX	33.60
San Francisco County, CA	31.02
Alameda County, CA	29.79
Dallas County, TX	29.38
Contra Costa County, CA	29.19
Essex County, NJ	28.38
Lane County, OR	28.06
Maricopa County, AZ	27.97
King County, WA	27.92
San Bernardino County, CA	26.96
Travis County, TX	26.48
Jackson County, MO	26.46
Los Angeles County, CA	25.87
Fairfax County, VA	25.57
Utah County, UT	25.32
Santa Clara County, CA	25.27
Arapahoe County, CO	25.09
Nassau County, NY	24.88
Anchorage Borough, AK	23.88
Orange County, CA	23.75
Denver County, CO	23.71
Ventura County, CA	23.67
Kern County, CA	23.01
Harris County, TX	22.99
Bronx County, NY	22.93
Palm Beach County, FL	22.22
Suffolk County, NY	21.78
Gwinnett County, GA	21.74
Davis County, UT	20.04
Washington County, OR	19.66
Orange County, FL	19.46
Allegheny County, PA	19.38
San Joaquin County, CA	19.22
Sonoma County, CA	19.07
Snohomish County, WA	19.04
Riverside County, CA	18.98
Muscogee County, GA	18.96
Milwaukee County, WI	18.85
Philadelphia County, PA	18.48
Sedgwick County, KS	17.63
Monterey County, CA	16.51
Santa Barbara County, CA	16.13
Fresno County, CA	15.64
Spokane County, WA	15.40
Coryell County, TX	15.24
Bexar County, TX	14.96
Wayne County, MI	14.55
Clackamas County, OR	14.29
Hillsborough County, FL	14.26
Davidson County, TN	14.00
Pima County, AZ	12.92
Washington County, UT	12.77
St. Louis County, MO	12.59
Bell County, TX	12.18
Clark County, WA	11.89
Honolulu County, HI	11.60
Clark County, NV	11.39

Place	Percent
Springdale, AR (city) Washington County	72.33
San Bruno, CA (city) San Mateo County	60.87
Salem, OR (city) Marion County	60.47
East Palo Alto, CA (city) San Mateo County	57.12
Des Moines, WA (city) King County	54.10
Sacramento, CA (city) Sacramento County	52.33
Costa Mesa, CA (city) Orange County	48.01
San Mateo, CA (city) San Mateo County	46.53
Tukwila, WA (city) King County	45.78
Redwood City, CA (city) San Mateo County	45.58
Concord, CA (city) Contra Costa County	44.66
Salt Lake City, UT (city) Salt Lake County	44.49
Modesto, CA (city) Stanislaus County	44.21
Chicago, IL (city) Cook County	43.47
Portland, OR (city) Multnomah County	42.79
Union City, CA (city) Alameda County	42.11
Lakewood, CA (city) Los Angeles County	41.47
West Valley City, UT (city) Salt Lake County	41.14
Fort Worth, TX (city) Tarrant County	40.90
Kansas City, MO (city) Jackson County	40.14
New York, NY (city)	39.10
Westminster, CA (city) Orange County	38.39
Ontario, CA (city) San Bernardino County	37.87
Hayward, CA (city) Alameda County	37.55
Reno, NV (city) Washoe County	37.18
Santa Clara, CA (city) Santa Clara County	36.65
Federal Way, WA (city) King County	35.20
Taylorsville, UT (city) Salt Lake County	34.64
West Jordan, UT (city) Salt Lake County	34.62
Fontana, CA (city) San Bernardino County	34.60
Bakersfield, CA (city) Kern County	34.40
Richmond, CA (city) Contra Costa County	33.92
Napili-Honokowai, HI (cdp) Maui County	33.84
Oakland, CA (city) Alameda County	33.09
Phoenix, AZ (city) Maricopa County	33.07
Kahuku, HI (cdp) Honolulu County	32.96
Aurora, CO (city) Arapahoe County	32.04
Kearns, UT (cdp) Salt Lake County	31.53
San Francisco, CA (city) San Francisco County	31.02
Waikoloa Village, HI (cdp) Hawaii County	30.91
Garden Grove, CA (city) Orange County	30.81
Daly City, CA (city) San Mateo County	30.72
South San Francisco, CA (city) San Mateo County	30.09
Hawthorne, CA (city) Los Angeles County	28.94
Pittsburg, CA (city) Contra Costa County	28.88
Oxnard, CA (city) Ventura County	28.65
Sandy, UT (city) Salt Lake County	28.46
Houston, TX (city) Harris County	28.08
Dallas, TX (city) Dallas County	27.77
San Jose, CA (city) Santa Clara County	27.37
SeaTac, WA (city) King County	27.36
Rialto, CA (city) San Bernardino County	27.07
Sunnyvale, CA (city) Santa Clara County	26.87
Long Beach, CA (city) Los Angeles County	26.72
San Bernardino, CA (city) San Bernardino County	26.60
Riverside, CA (city) Riverside County	26.11
Fremont, CA (city) Alameda County	25.82
Los Angeles, CA (city) Los Angeles County	25.76
Anaheim, CA (city) Orange County	25.59
Laie, HI (cdp) Honolulu County	24.74
Compton, CA (city) Los Angeles County	24.12
Denver, CO (city) Denver County	23.71
Orem, UT (city) Utah County	23.71
North Las Vegas, NV (city) Clark County	22.09
Milpitas, CA (city) Santa Clara County	22.03
Independence, MO (city) Jackson County	21.73
Provo, UT (city) Utah County	21.71
Wahiawa, HI (cdp) Honolulu County	21.45
Lawndale, CA (city) Los Angeles County	21.38
Mesa, AZ (city) Maricopa County	21.33
Waipahu, HI (cdp) Honolulu County	21.14
Aiea, HI (cdp) Honolulu County	20.10
Antioch, CA (city) Contra Costa County	20.10
Salinas, CA (city) Monterey County	19.93
Fort Lewis, WA (cdp) Pierce County	19.87

Notes: Please refer to the User's Guide for an explanation of data; ranking tables include all places with Asian and/or NHPI populations above SF4 population thresholds; (1) tables reflect only those areas that meet SF4 population thresholds, therefore there may be less than 50 states, 75 counties or 75 places listed

Foreign Born

Asian Indian

***All States, Top 75 Counties, and Top 75 Places Sorted by Number*[1]**

State	Number
United States	1,240,755
California	228,246
New York	190,604
New Jersey	130,120
Texas	95,796
Illinois	90,799
Florida	51,515
Pennsylvania	41,611
Michigan	41,004
Maryland	37,464
Virginia	36,114
Georgia	33,403
Massachusetts	31,928
Ohio	28,818
North Carolina	19,112
Connecticut	18,347
Washington	17,257
Minnesota	13,036
Arizona	10,816
Indiana	10,497
Tennessee	9,070
Colorado	8,950
Wisconsin	8,630
Missouri	8,491
Oregon	7,724
Oklahoma	6,308
South Carolina	6,191
Louisiana	5,999
Kansas	5,957
Kentucky	5,238
Alabama	4,929
Iowa	4,205
Delaware	4,116
Nevada	3,691
New Hampshire	2,771
Nebraska	2,667
Mississippi	2,517
Utah	2,473
Arkansas	1,959
West Virginia	1,932
Rhode Island	1,789
New Mexico	1,743
District of Columbia	1,601
Idaho	930
Hawaii	858
North Dakota	809
Maine	709
Vermont	592
South Dakota	457
Alaska	379
Wyoming	307
Montana	276

County	Number
Queens County, NY	87,280
Cook County, IL	51,996
Santa Clara County, CA	51,554
Los Angeles County, CA	43,419
Middlesex County, NJ	42,736
Alameda County, CA	32,267
Harris County, TX	27,263
DuPage County, IL	23,316
Kings County, NY	19,416
Orange County, CA	19,366
Fairfax County, VA	19,087
Dallas County, TX	18,579
Montgomery County, MD	18,521
Middlesex County, MA	17,040
Hudson County, NJ	16,822
Nassau County, NY	16,507
Oakland County, MI	14,492
Bergen County, NJ	13,274
Bronx County, NY	11,542
Wayne County, MI	11,147
King County, WA	11,100
Westchester County, NY	10,966
Broward County, FL	10,283
Sacramento County, CA	9,370
New York County, NY	9,341
Fort Bend County, TX	9,161
San Mateo County, CA	8,752
Philadelphia County, PA	8,665
Maricopa County, AZ	8,412
Gwinnett County, GA	8,263
Contra Costa County, CA	8,213
Morris County, NJ	8,112
Suffolk County, NY	7,620
Somerset County, NJ	7,466
Tarrant County, TX	7,288
San Diego County, CA	6,967
Miami-Dade County, FL	6,825
Cuyahoga County, OH	6,814
Passaic County, NJ	6,751
Collin County, TX	6,735
Fairfield County, CT	6,669
Franklin County, OH	6,519
Essex County, NJ	6,473
Hennepin County, MN	6,466
Travis County, TX	6,196
DeKalb County, GA	6,035
Orange County, FL	5,793
Allegheny County, PA	5,749
Montgomery County, PA	5,695
Prince George's County, MD	5,610
San Bernardino County, CA	5,571
Wake County, NC	5,445
Union County, NJ	5,099
Hartford County, CT	5,034
Monmouth County, NJ	4,977
Fresno County, CA	4,824
Sutter County, CA	4,789
Baltimore County, MD	4,770
Mercer County, NJ	4,730
Fulton County, GA	4,705
Richmond County, NY	4,694
New Haven County, CT	4,452
Bucks County, PA	4,429
Washington County, OR	4,425
Denton County, TX	4,308
Macomb County, MI	4,287
St. Louis County, MO	4,252
Cobb County, GA	4,238
Hillsborough County, FL	4,182
Rockland County, NY	4,089
Palm Beach County, FL	4,074
Norfolk County, MA	4,070
Delaware County, PA	3,985
Lake County, IL	3,980
Mecklenburg County, NC	3,912

Place	Number
New York, NY (city)	132,273
San Jose, CA (city) Santa Clara County	19,146
Chicago, IL (city) Cook County	18,090
Los Angeles, CA (city) Los Angeles County	17,906
Fremont, CA (city) Alameda County	16,148
Houston, TX (city) Harris County	15,810
Edison, NJ (township) Middlesex County	13,119
Jersey City, NJ (city) Hudson County	11,080
Sunnyvale, CA (city) Santa Clara County	10,596
Philadelphia, PA (city) Philadelphia County	8,665
Santa Clara, CA (city) Santa Clara County	7,586
Hempstead, NY (town) Nassau County	7,250
Woodbridge, NJ (township) Middlesex County	7,243
Dallas, TX (city) Dallas County	6,040
Austin, TX (city) Travis County	5,458
North Hempstead, NY (town) Nassau County	5,310
Columbus, OH (city) Franklin County	5,131
Irving, TX (city) Dallas County	4,850
San Diego, CA (city) San Diego County	4,657
Piscataway, NJ (township) Middlesex County	4,604
Plano, TX (city) Collin County	4,287
Union City, CA (city) Alameda County	4,044
Milpitas, CA (city) Santa Clara County	3,685
Yonkers, NY (city) Westchester County	3,640
Oyster Bay, NY (town) Nassau County	3,595
Schaumburg, IL (village) Cook County	3,569
Troy, MI (city) Oakland County	3,544
Cupertino, CA (city) Santa Clara County	3,501
San Francisco, CA (city) San Francisco County	3,421
Parsippany-Troy Hills, NJ (township) Morris County	3,411
Naperville, IL (city) Du Page County	3,341
Charlotte, NC (city) Mecklenburg County	3,315
Phoenix, AZ (city) Maricopa County	3,279
Carrollton, TX (city) Denton County	3,239
Sugar Land, TX (city) Fort Bend County	3,109
Irvine, CA (city) Orange County	3,056
Sacramento, CA (city) Sacramento County	3,054
Anaheim, CA (city) Orange County	3,014
Hayward, CA (city) Alameda County	2,926
Arlington, VA (cdp) Arlington County	2,852
Farmington Hills, MI (city) Oakland County	2,764
South Brunswick, NJ (township) Middlesex County	2,746
Plainsboro, NJ (township) Middlesex County	2,705
Skokie, IL (village) Cook County	2,628
Boston, MA (city) Suffolk County	2,618
Canton, MI (township) Wayne County	2,607
Cary, NC (town) Wake County	2,584
Fresno, CA (city) Fresno County	2,561
Mount Prospect, IL (village) Cook County	2,558
Franklin, NJ (township) Somerset County	2,525
Mountain View, CA (city) Santa Clara County	2,519
Oklahoma City, OK (city) Oklahoma County	2,502
Detroit, MI (city) Wayne County	2,498
Brookhaven, NY (town) Suffolk County	2,492
Stamford, CT (city) Fairfield County	2,431
Arlington, TX (city) Tarrant County	2,399
North Brunswick, NJ (township) Middlesex County	2,391
Bakersfield, CA (city) Kern County	2,389
Indianapolis, IN (sp. city) Marion County	2,386
San Antonio, TX (city) Bexar County	2,346
Garland, TX (city) Dallas County	2,342
Iselin, NJ (cdp) Middlesex County	2,304
Lowell, MA (city) Middlesex County	2,207
Hoffman Estates, IL (village) Cook County	2,132
Bellevue, WA (city) King County	2,129
Clifton, NJ (city) Passaic County	2,112
Sayreville, NJ (borough) Middlesex County	2,111
Old Bridge, NJ (township) Middlesex County	2,088
Cerritos, CA (city) Los Angeles County	2,066
Seattle, WA (city) King County	2,062
East Brunswick, NJ (township) Middlesex County	2,060
Jacksonville, FL (city) Duval County	2,055
Glendale Heights, IL (village) Du Page County	2,042
Islip, NY (town) Suffolk County	2,036
Greenburgh, NY (town) Westchester County	2,002

Notes: Please refer to the User's Guide for an explanation of data; ranking tables include all places with Asian and/or NHPI populations above SF4 population thresholds; (1) tables reflect only those areas that meet SF4 population thresholds, therefore there may be less than 50 states, 75 counties or 75 places listed

Foreign Born

Asian Indian

All States, Top 75 Counties, and Top 75 Places Sorted by Percent[1]

State	Percent
Vermont	84.94
Nebraska	83.37
Idaho	81.44
Minnesota	80.08
Delaware	78.68
South Dakota	78.66
Utah	78.33
Kentucky	77.78
Iowa	77.77
North Dakota	77.64
Kansas	77.56
New Hampshire	77.42
New Jersey	76.90
Connecticut	76.75
Washington	76.74
Ohio	76.59
Wisconsin	76.51
West Virginia	76.39
New York	76.23
Massachusetts	76.14
Florida	75.99
Oklahoma	75.98
Nevada	75.95
Virginia	75.90
Tennessee	75.86
Oregon	75.81
Mississippi	75.70
Colorado	75.68
United States	75.40
North Carolina	75.39
South Carolina	75.36
Michigan	75.29
Maryland	75.28
Texas	75.28
Georgia	74.67
Arizona	74.54
California	74.32
Indiana	74.14
Pennsylvania	74.00
Alabama	73.72
Illinois	73.66
Arkansas	72.72
Wyoming	72.58
Maine	72.49
New Mexico	71.91
Missouri	71.68
Rhode Island	70.21
Louisiana	69.42
Alaska	69.41
Hawaii	68.97
District of Columbia	66.29
Montana	61.33

County	Percent
Chittenden County, VT	89.19
Eaton County, MI	88.64
Linn County, IA	88.22
Benton County, WA	87.38
Lancaster County, NE	86.92
Benton County, AR	86.87
Bartholomew County, IN	86.85
Fairfax Independent City, VA	86.36
Hamilton County, OH	86.27
Rock Island County, IL	86.26
Sedgwick County, KS	85.47
Guilford County, NC	84.43
Ada County, ID	84.17
Hinds County, MS	83.62
Monongalia County, WV	83.03
Delaware County, OH	82.99
Hennepin County, MN	82.84
Denver County, CO	82.62
Polk County, IA	82.51
McLean County, IL	82.46
El Paso County, CO	82.34
DeKalb County, GA	82.21
Arlington County, VA	81.93
Montgomery County, TX	81.83
Kent County, MI	81.73
Hudson County, NJ	81.64
Alexandria Independent City, VA	81.53
Madison County, IL	81.46
Douglas County, NE	81.31
Berrien County, MI	81.18
Kanawha County, WV	81.09
Greene County, OH	80.91
Albemarle County, VA	80.56
Forsyth County, NC	80.56
Marin County, CA	80.39
Norfolk County, MA	80.34
Phelps County, MO	80.31
Brevard County, FL	80.01
Oklahoma County, OK	80.01
Tippecanoe County, IN	80.01
Salt Lake County, UT	79.95
Fairfield County, CT	79.92
Palm Beach County, FL	79.91
Lee County, FL	79.82
New Castle County, DE	79.80
New London County, CT	79.76
Brazos County, TX	79.73
Chatham County, GA	79.68
Dauphin County, PA	79.64
Stark County, OH	79.64
Henrico County, VA	79.61
Ramsey County, MN	79.52
Washington County, OR	79.47
Gloucester County, NJ	79.46
Johnson County, KS	79.45
Cumberland County, PA	79.42
Berks County, PA	79.39
Queens County, NY	79.39
Mobile County, AL	79.31
El Paso County, TX	79.29
Lehigh County, PA	79.24
Santa Clara County, CA	79.21
Chesterfield County, VA	79.15
Franklin County, OH	79.11
Atlantic County, NJ	79.10
King County, WA	79.10
Schenectady County, NY	79.08
Broward County, FL	79.05
Pickens County, SC	78.96
Greenville County, SC	78.95
Whatcom County, WA	78.95
Middlesex County, NJ	78.90
San Mateo County, CA	78.90
Peoria County, IL	78.77
Pinellas County, FL	78.76

Place	Percent
Scott, PA (township) Allegheny County	97.12
Scott Township, PA (cdp) Allegheny County	97.12
Lansdale, PA (borough) Montgomery County	96.67
Little Flock, AR (city) Benton County	95.61
Boca Raton, FL (city) Palm Beach County	94.23
Naugatuck, CT (town) New Haven County	93.39
Hopkins, MN (city) Hennepin County	93.26
Plainsboro Center, NJ (cdp) Middlesex County	92.99
New Britain, CT (city) Hartford County	92.63
Sharonville, OH (city) Hamilton County	92.37
Bloomington, MN (city) Hennepin County	90.76
Inkster, MI (city) Wayne County	90.70
West Des Moines, IA (city) Polk County	90.63
Atlantic City, NJ (city) Atlantic County	90.50
Eden Prairie, MN (city) Hennepin County	90.44
Cincinnati, OH (city) Hamilton County	90.33
Grand Rapids, MI (city) Kent County	89.90
San Rafael, CA (city) Marin County	89.60
Quincy, MA (city) Norfolk County	89.37
Cedar Rapids, IA (city) Linn County	89.18
Parma, OH (city) Cuyahoga County	89.13
Lodi, NJ (borough) Bergen County	88.89
Redmond, WA (city) King County	88.89
Henderson, NV (city) Clark County	88.84
Artesia, CA (city) Los Angeles County	88.73
Maryland Heights, MO (city) Saint Louis County	88.65
St. Louis Park, MN (city) Hennepin County	88.54
Delta charter, MI (township) Eaton County	88.29
Manchester, CT (town) Hartford County	88.22
Farmington, MI (city) Oakland County	88.21
Highland Park, NJ (borough) Middlesex County	88.04
Maple Shade, NJ (township) Burlington County	88.02
Bellevue, WA (city) King County	87.94
Beaverton, OR (city) Washington County	87.89
Lakeland, FL (city) Polk County	87.86
Taylor, MI (city) Wayne County	87.72
Jefferson, VA (cdp) Fairfax County	87.68
Brentwood, NY (cdp) Suffolk County	87.63
Ocean, NJ (township) Monmouth County	87.15
Tempe, AZ (city) Maricopa County	87.13
Malden, MA (city) Middlesex County	87.09
Bloomington, IL (city) McLean County	87.01
Guilderland, NY (town) Albany County	86.96
Westland, MI (city) Wayne County	86.91
Columbus, IN (city) Bartholomew County	86.85
Melbourne, FL (city) Brevard County	86.78
Sunnyvale, CA (city) Santa Clara County	86.77
Millbourne, PA (borough) Delaware County	86.75
San Leandro, CA (city) Alameda County	86.75
Bristol, PA (township) Bucks County	86.74
Lincoln, NE (city) Lancaster County	86.72
Silver Spring, MD (cdp) Montgomery County	86.70
Mountain View, CA (city) Santa Clara County	86.68
King of Prussia, PA (cdp) Montgomery County	86.59
Hackensack, NJ (city) Bergen County	86.57
Southfield, MI (city) Oakland County	86.52
Addison, TX (town) Dallas County	86.47
Mesa, AZ (city) Maricopa County	86.29
Avenel, NJ (cdp) Middlesex County	86.17
Rancho Cordova, CA (cdp) Sacramento County	86.12
Boise City, ID (city) Ada County	85.80
Santa Clara, CA (city) Santa Clara County	85.52
Hawthorne, CA (city) Los Angeles County	85.45
Lakewood, CA (city) Los Angeles County	85.38
West New York, NJ (town) Hudson County	85.37
Wichita, KS (city) Sedgwick County	85.27
Norwood, MA (town) Norfolk County	85.22
Arlington Heights, IL (village) Cook County	85.19
Lowell, MA (city) Middlesex County	85.08
Dunwoody, GA (cdp) De Kalb County	85.01
Kearny, NJ (town) Hudson County	84.91
Brighton, NY (town) Monroe County	84.88
Greensboro, NC (city) Guilford County	84.83
Franklin Square, NY (cdp) Nassau County	84.80
Reston, VA (cdp) Fairfax County	84.78

Notes: Please refer to the User's Guide for an explanation of data; ranking tables include all places with Asian and/or NHPI populations above SF4 population thresholds; (1) tables reflect only those areas that meet SF4 population thresholds, therefore there may be less than 50 states, 75 counties or 75 places listed

Foreign Born

Bangladeshi

All States, Top 75 Counties, and Top 75 Places Sorted by Number[1]

State	Number
United States	34,353
New York	16,901
California	2,273
Texas	2,153
New Jersey	1,783
Virginia	1,492
Michigan	1,403
Florida	1,060
Maryland	1,020
Georgia	951
Pennsylvania	642
Illinois	567
Ohio	507
Massachusetts	440
Connecticut	299

County	Number
Queens County, NY	10,371
Kings County, NY	3,382
Bronx County, NY	1,708
Los Angeles County, CA	1,113
Wayne County, MI	1,012
Montgomery County, MD	692
Fairfax County, VA	690
New York County, NY	669
Harris County, TX	578
Dallas County, TX	560
DeKalb County, GA	470
Passaic County, NJ	435
Santa Clara County, CA	395
Atlantic County, NJ	335
Middlesex County, NJ	303

Place	Number
New York, NY (city)	16,146
Los Angeles, CA (city) Los Angeles County	715
Hamtramck, MI (city) Wayne County	657
Paterson, NJ (city) Passaic County	373

Notes: Please refer to the User's Guide for an explanation of data; ranking tables include all places with Asian and/or NHPI populations above SF4 population thresholds; (1) tables reflect only those areas that meet SF4 population thresholds, therefore there may be less than 50 states, 75 counties or 75 places listed

Foreign Born

Bangladeshi

All States, Top 75 Counties, and Top 75 Places Sorted by Percent[1]

State	Percent
Pennsylvania	90.93
Connecticut	85.92
Maryland	84.72
New York	84.14
Florida	84.13
Texas	83.64
Michigan	83.36
United States	82.92
California	82.71
Virginia	82.52
New Jersey	79.03
Massachusetts	78.43
Ohio	78.24
Georgia	75.66
Illinois	70.43

County	Percent
Wayne County, MI	87.02
Kings County, NY	86.10
Bronx County, NY	85.74
DeKalb County, GA	85.45
New York County, NY	85.44
Harris County, TX	84.01
Los Angeles County, CA	84.00
Montgomery County, MD	83.78
Queens County, NY	83.62
Dallas County, TX	83.21
Atlantic County, NJ	82.31
Santa Clara County, CA	81.61
Passaic County, NJ	79.82
Middlesex County, NJ	78.29
Fairfax County, VA	76.50

Place	Percent
Hamtramck, MI (city) Wayne County	88.78
Los Angeles, CA (city) Los Angeles County	86.04
New York, NY (city)	84.32
Paterson, NJ (city) Passaic County	81.26

Notes: Please refer to the User's Guide for an explanation of data; ranking tables include all places with Asian and/or NHPI populations above SF4 population thresholds; (1) tables reflect only those areas that meet SF4 population thresholds, therefore there may be less than 50 states, 75 counties or 75 places listed

Foreign Born

Cambodian

All States, Top 75 Counties, and Top 75 Places Sorted by Number[1]

State	Number
United States	117,164
California	45,198
Massachusetts	12,944
Washington	9,709
Pennsylvania	5,813
Texas	5,169
Virginia	3,703
Minnesota	3,543
Rhode Island	3,073
Georgia	2,497
Illinois	2,479
Florida	2,118
New York	2,019
Oregon	1,875
Ohio	1,769
North Carolina	1,654
Connecticut	1,456
Maryland	1,294
Michigan	1,112
Colorado	1,075
Utah	992
Tennessee	858
Arizona	752
Maine	637
Nevada	581
Missouri	570
New Jersey	529
Iowa	514
Kansas	459
Indiana	439
Wisconsin	365
Alabama	315
South Carolina	249
Oklahoma	198
Hawaii	175

County	Number
Los Angeles County, CA	19,526
Middlesex County, MA	6,821
San Joaquin County, CA	5,517
King County, WA	4,442
Philadelphia County, PA	4,181
Orange County, CA	3,195
Santa Clara County, CA	2,982
Providence County, RI	2,834
San Diego County, CA	2,710
Pierce County, WA	2,569
Alameda County, CA	2,422
Essex County, MA	2,354
Fresno County, CA	2,326
Stanislaus County, CA	1,777
Cook County, IL	1,591
Dallas County, TX	1,493
Harris County, TX	1,472
Bristol County, MA	1,391
Snohomish County, WA	1,374
Fairfax County, VA	1,361
Hennepin County, MN	1,308
Suffolk County, MA	1,170
San Bernardino County, CA	1,095
Fairfield County, CT	938
Montgomery County, MD	846
Franklin County, OH	842
Ramsey County, MN	784
Clayton County, GA	754
Salt Lake County, UT	752
Washington County, OR	751
Ottawa County, MI	746
Sacramento County, CA	731
Duval County, FL	725
Maricopa County, AZ	698
Multnomah County, OR	684
Henrico County, VA	658
Clark County, NV	561
Gwinnett County, GA	539
Pinellas County, FL	532
Mecklenburg County, NC	521
Tarrant County, TX	517
Thurston County, WA	511
Denton County, TX	502
Sonoma County, CA	501
Bronx County, NY	479
DeKalb County, GA	476
Olmsted County, MN	457
San Francisco County, CA	455
Chesterfield County, VA	452
Cumberland County, ME	448
Shelby County, TN	404
Kings County, NY	393
Cuyahoga County, OH	385
Riverside County, CA	325
Clark County, WA	324
Sedgwick County, KS	305
Dakota County, MN	296
Davidson County, NC	296
Arlington County, VA	282
Hampden County, MA	282
Denver County, CO	273
Monroe County, NY	273
Kern County, CA	270
Polk County, IA	268
Worcester County, MA	268
Camden County, NJ	256
Scott County, MN	247
Brazoria County, TX	233
Cowlitz County, WA	221
Hamilton County, OH	217
Mobile County, AL	186

Place	Number
Long Beach, CA (city) Los Angeles County	11,037
Lowell, MA (city) Middlesex County	5,799
Stockton, CA (city) San Joaquin County	5,362
Philadelphia, PA (city) Philadelphia County	4,181
Los Angeles, CA (city) Los Angeles County	2,909
San Jose, CA (city) Santa Clara County	2,672
San Diego, CA (city) San Diego County	2,427
Providence, RI (city) Providence County	2,204
Fresno, CA (city) Fresno County	2,103
Tacoma, WA (city) Pierce County	1,979
Lynn, MA (city) Essex County	1,893
Oakland, CA (city) Alameda County	1,732
Seattle, WA (city) King County	1,653
Modesto, CA (city) Stanislaus County	1,465
Chicago, IL (city) Cook County	1,379
Santa Ana, CA (city) Orange County	1,227
New York, NY (city)	1,097
Fall River, MA (city) Bristol County	799
Columbus, OH (city) Franklin County	783
White Center, WA (cdp) King County	747
Jacksonville, FL (city) Duval County	725
Portland, OR (city) Multnomah County	660
Dallas, TX (city) Dallas County	641
St. Paul, MN (city) Ramsey County	633
Houston, TX (city) Harris County	585
Revere, MA (city) Suffolk County	564
Rosemead, CA (city) Los Angeles County	533
Signal Hill, CA (city) Los Angeles County	530
Carrollton, TX (city) Denton County	516
Charlotte, NC (city) Mecklenburg County	475
Lakewood, CA (city) Los Angeles County	469
Pomona, CA (city) Los Angeles County	459
San Francisco, CA (city) San Francisco County	455
Everett, WA (city) Snohomish County	450
West Valley City, UT (city) Salt Lake County	443
Attleboro, MA (city) Bristol County	423
Cranston, RI (city) Providence County	407
Boston, MA (city) Suffolk County	398
Portland, ME (city) Cumberland County	394
Garden Grove, CA (city) Orange County	393
Bellflower, CA (city) Los Angeles County	391
Santa Rosa, CA (city) Sonoma County	384
Norwalk, CA (city) Los Angeles County	374
Bloomington, MN (city) Hennepin County	372
St. Petersburg, FL (city) Pinellas County	369
Sacramento, CA (city) Sacramento County	365
Memphis, TN (city) Shelby County	359
Bridgeport, CT (city) Fairfield County	356
Aurora, CO (city) Arapahoe County	355
Rochester, MN (city) Olmsted County	355
Phoenix, AZ (city) Maricopa County	345
Minneapolis, MN (city) Hennepin County	323
Danbury, CT (city) Fairfield County	321
Monterey Park, CA (city) Los Angeles County	318
Arlington, VA (cdp) Arlington County	282
Lawrence, MA (city) Essex County	280
Denver, CO (city) Denver County	273
San Bernardino, CA (city) San Bernardino County	261
Beaverton, OR (city) Washington County	253
Lexington, NC (city) Davidson County	225
Silver Spring, MD (cdp) Montgomery County	214
Longview, WA (city) Cowlitz County	173

Notes: Please refer to the User's Guide for an explanation of data; ranking tables include all places with Asian and/or NHPI populations above SF4 population thresholds; (1) tables reflect only those areas that meet SF4 population thresholds, therefore there may be less than 50 states, 75 counties or 75 places listed

Foreign Born

Cambodian

All States, Top 75 Counties, and Top 75 Places Sorted by Percent[1]

State	Percent
Hawaii	82.94
New Jersey	80.40
Nevada	78.73
Florida	76.68
Maryland	75.76
Indiana	75.30
Virginia	74.54
South Carolina	73.02
Colorado	72.73
Tennessee	72.10
Georgia	71.77
Illinois	70.77
North Carolina	69.79
Michigan	69.76
New York	69.38
Minnesota	69.09
Oregon	68.21
Utah	68.09
Texas	67.99
Ohio	67.65
Connecticut	67.38
Pennsylvania	66.85
United States	65.81
Washington	65.75
Kansas	64.92
Missouri	64.85
Massachusetts	63.54
California	63.42
Maine	63.07
Iowa	62.38
Arizona	60.65
Rhode Island	60.20
Oklahoma	60.18
Wisconsin	58.21
Alabama	55.75

County	Percent
Camden County, NJ	81.79
Henrico County, VA	80.84
Arlington County, VA	79.89
Cuyahoga County, OH	79.55
Kings County, NY	78.44
Shelby County, TN	78.29
Clark County, NV	78.13
DeKalb County, GA	78.03
Clark County, WA	75.88
Pinellas County, FL	74.09
Fairfax County, VA	73.77
Harris County, TX	73.16
Hennepin County, MN	73.15
Montgomery County, MD	72.87
Duval County, FL	72.43
Clayton County, GA	71.95
Monroe County, NY	71.65
Orange County, CA	71.51
Cook County, IL	71.44
Ramsey County, MN	70.63
San Francisco County, CA	70.43
Denton County, TX	69.15
Ottawa County, MI	68.88
Snohomish County, WA	68.77
Denver County, CO	68.59
Scott County, MN	68.23
Suffolk County, MA	68.10
Washington County, OR	68.03
Mecklenburg County, NC	67.93
Chesterfield County, VA	67.87
Worcester County, MA	67.85
Salt Lake County, UT	67.81
Santa Clara County, CA	67.79
Cumberland County, ME	67.78
King County, WA	67.07
Tarrant County, TX	66.45
Sedgwick County, KS	66.16
Dakota County, MN	65.63
Sacramento County, CA	65.44
Philadelphia County, PA	65.26
Fairfield County, CT	65.05
Los Angeles County, CA	64.97
Franklin County, OH	64.32
Multnomah County, OR	64.10
Bristol County, MA	64.01
Polk County, IA	63.96
Dallas County, TX	63.34
Pierce County, WA	63.31
Olmsted County, MN	63.30
San Bernardino County, CA	62.86
Essex County, MA	62.71
Kern County, CA	62.65
Cowlitz County, WA	62.43
Middlesex County, MA	62.16
Alameda County, CA	62.05
San Diego County, CA	62.03
Hampden County, MA	61.98
Hamilton County, OH	61.82
Thurston County, WA	61.05
Brazoria County, TX	60.84
Gwinnett County, GA	59.76
Bronx County, NY	59.14
Fresno County, CA	59.14
Sonoma County, CA	58.94
Maricopa County, AZ	58.85
Providence County, RI	58.74
San Joaquin County, CA	58.26
Davidson County, NC	57.25
Stanislaus County, CA	55.02
Riverside County, CA	54.17
Mobile County, AL	47.81

Place	Percent
Houston, TX (city) Harris County	80.91
Aurora, CO (city) Arapahoe County	80.50
Arlington, VA (cdp) Arlington County	79.89
Memphis, TN (city) Shelby County	79.07
Garden Grove, CA (city) Orange County	78.60
Monterey Park, CA (city) Los Angeles County	77.00
Bloomington, MN (city) Hennepin County	76.07
Sacramento, CA (city) Sacramento County	75.57
Norwalk, CA (city) Los Angeles County	74.35
Bellflower, CA (city) Los Angeles County	73.22
Jacksonville, FL (city) Duval County	72.43
Chicago, IL (city) Cook County	72.16
St. Petersburg, FL (city) Pinellas County	71.51
Beaverton, OR (city) Washington County	70.87
Santa Ana, CA (city) Orange County	70.68
Everett, WA (city) Snohomish County	70.53
San Francisco, CA (city) San Francisco County	70.43
Longview, WA (city) Cowlitz County	70.04
Revere, MA (city) Suffolk County	69.63
Los Angeles, CA (city) Los Angeles County	69.13
Rosemead, CA (city) Los Angeles County	68.77
Denver, CO (city) Denver County	68.59
Bridgeport, CT (city) Fairfield County	68.46
St. Paul, MN (city) Ramsey County	68.21
Signal Hill, CA (city) Los Angeles County	67.86
Charlotte, NC (city) Mecklenburg County	67.76
New York, NY (city)	67.76
West Valley City, UT (city) Salt Lake County	67.12
San Jose, CA (city) Santa Clara County	66.98
Portland, ME (city) Cumberland County	66.44
Columbus, OH (city) Franklin County	65.69
Silver Spring, MD (cdp) Montgomery County	65.64
Seattle, WA (city) King County	65.49
Philadelphia, PA (city) Philadelphia County	65.26
Minneapolis, MN (city) Hennepin County	64.86
Lakewood, CA (city) Los Angeles County	64.07
Fall River, MA (city) Bristol County	63.77
Boston, MA (city) Suffolk County	63.58
Portland, OR (city) Multnomah County	63.52
Rochester, MN (city) Olmsted County	63.51
Lynn, MA (city) Essex County	63.12
Carrollton, TX (city) Denton County	63.08
White Center, WA (cdp) King County	62.98
Tacoma, WA (city) Pierce County	62.69
Phoenix, AZ (city) Maricopa County	62.39
Lawrence, MA (city) Essex County	62.36
Long Beach, CA (city) Los Angeles County	62.32
San Diego, CA (city) San Diego County	61.98
Providence, RI (city) Providence County	61.53
Attleboro, MA (city) Bristol County	61.13
Lowell, MA (city) Middlesex County	60.91
Pomona, CA (city) Los Angeles County	60.63
Dallas, TX (city) Dallas County	60.53
Santa Rosa, CA (city) Sonoma County	59.44
Oakland, CA (city) Alameda County	59.01
Stockton, CA (city) San Joaquin County	58.92
San Bernardino, CA (city) San Bernardino County	58.52
Fresno, CA (city) Fresno County	58.24
Modesto, CA (city) Stanislaus County	57.72
Lexington, NC (city) Davidson County	57.25
Danbury, CT (city) Fairfield County	56.12
Cranston, RI (city) Providence County	49.76

Notes: Please refer to the User's Guide for an explanation of data; ranking tables include all places with Asian and/or NHPI populations above SF4 population thresholds; (1) tables reflect only those areas that meet SF4 population thresholds, therefore there may be less than 50 states, 75 counties or 75 places listed

Foreign Born

Chinese (except Taiwanese)

All States, Top 75 Counties, and Top 75 Places Sorted by Number[1]

State	Number
United States	1,621,997
California	623,398
New York	313,366
Texas	72,607
New Jersey	65,665
Massachusetts	57,471
Illinois	53,560
Washington	39,376
Pennsylvania	35,283
Maryland	34,319
Florida	33,776
Virginia	25,378
Hawaii	22,813
Michigan	21,878
Ohio	20,940
Georgia	18,911
Arizona	14,047
Connecticut	13,335
North Carolina	13,200
Oregon	12,564
Minnesota	11,293
Colorado	10,376
Missouri	9,845
Nevada	9,419
Indiana	8,944
Wisconsin	7,393
Tennessee	6,199
Kansas	5,508
Utah	5,332
Oklahoma	5,330
South Carolina	4,614
Louisiana	4,610
Iowa	4,420
Alabama	4,414
Kentucky	4,154
Delaware	3,159
Rhode Island	2,976
New Hampshire	2,777
New Mexico	2,774
District of Columbia	2,695
Nebraska	2,317
Arkansas	2,212
Mississippi	1,859
West Virginia	1,320
Idaho	1,271
Maine	1,160
Alaska	1,157
Vermont	783
South Dakota	568
Montana	455
Wyoming	418
North Dakota	358

County	Number
Los Angeles County, CA	211,034
San Francisco County, CA	107,744
Queens County, NY	106,258
Kings County, NY	91,569
Santa Clara County, CA	78,399
Alameda County, CA	71,625
New York County, NY	65,914
Cook County, IL	34,495
Orange County, CA	33,675
King County, WA	30,141
San Mateo County, CA	29,976
Harris County, TX	23,660
Honolulu County, HI	21,958
Middlesex County, MA	20,901
Montgomery County, MD	19,954
San Diego County, CA	19,240
Sacramento County, CA	16,293
Contra Costa County, CA	16,136
Middlesex County, NJ	14,873
Suffolk County, MA	14,628
Norfolk County, MA	13,058
Philadelphia County, PA	12,888
Fairfax County, VA	12,006
Maricopa County, AZ	10,598
Nassau County, NY	9,296
Collin County, TX	9,270
Bergen County, NJ	9,149
Dallas County, TX	9,026
Clark County, NV	7,542
DuPage County, IL	7,274
San Bernardino County, CA	7,222
Miami-Dade County, FL	6,951
Fort Bend County, TX	6,931
Suffolk County, NY	6,717
Morris County, NJ	6,579
Broward County, FL	6,404
Travis County, TX	6,314
Oakland County, MI	6,116
Monmouth County, NJ	6,057
Franklin County, OH	5,639
Hudson County, NJ	5,158
Somerset County, NJ	4,873
Westchester County, NY	4,856
Multnomah County, OR	4,739
Washtenaw County, MI	4,712
Bronx County, NY	4,707
Richmond County, NY	4,665
Hennepin County, MN	4,629
St. Louis County, MO	4,576
Cuyahoga County, OH	4,360
Tarrant County, TX	4,119
Essex County, NJ	4,097
Montgomery County, PA	4,078
Gwinnett County, GA	4,016
Fairfield County, CT	3,869
New Haven County, CT	3,859
Allegheny County, PA	3,836
Riverside County, CA	3,805
Wake County, NC	3,761
Wayne County, MI	3,721
Prince George's County, MD	3,685
Fulton County, GA	3,659
Baltimore County, MD	3,576
Lake County, IL	3,367
San Joaquin County, CA	3,365
Washington County, OR	3,359
Salt Lake County, UT	3,228
Yolo County, CA	3,221
Ventura County, CA	3,183
Snohomish County, WA	3,124
Mercer County, NJ	3,052
DeKalb County, GA	3,019
Orange County, FL	2,976
Pima County, AZ	2,926
Monroe County, NY	2,920

Place	Number
New York, NY (city)	273,113
San Francisco, CA (city) San Francisco County	107,744
Los Angeles, CA (city) Los Angeles County	41,487
San Jose, CA (city) Santa Clara County	36,192
Chicago, IL (city) Cook County	23,501
Oakland, CA (city) Alameda County	22,188
Alhambra, CA (city) Los Angeles County	21,005
Fremont, CA (city) Alameda County	18,898
Honolulu, HI (cdp) Honolulu County	17,992
Monterey Park, CA (city) Los Angeles County	17,396
Houston, TX (city) Harris County	17,136
San Diego, CA (city) San Diego County	14,732
Boston, MA (city) Suffolk County	14,229
Seattle, WA (city) King County	13,204
Philadelphia, PA (city) Philadelphia County	12,888
Rosemead, CA (city) Los Angeles County	11,151
Arcadia, CA (city) Los Angeles County	10,627
Sacramento, CA (city) Sacramento County	10,455
San Gabriel, CA (city) Los Angeles County	9,350
Daly City, CA (city) San Mateo County	9,157
El Monte, CA (city) Los Angeles County	9,069
Rowland Heights, CA (cdp) Los Angeles County	9,002
Sunnyvale, CA (city) Santa Clara County	8,982
Irvine, CA (city) Orange County	7,626
Cupertino, CA (city) Santa Clara County	7,131
Hacienda Heights, CA (cdp) Los Angeles County	6,845
Plano, TX (city) Collin County	6,796
Quincy, MA (city) Norfolk County	6,614
Milpitas, CA (city) Santa Clara County	6,076
Temple City, CA (city) Los Angeles County	5,990
Austin, TX (city) Travis County	5,778
San Leandro, CA (city) Alameda County	5,505
Diamond Bar, CA (city) Los Angeles County	5,463
West Covina, CA (city) Los Angeles County	4,885
Dallas, TX (city) Dallas County	4,688
Alameda, CA (city) Alameda County	4,550
Walnut, CA (city) Los Angeles County	4,508
Portland, OR (city) Multnomah County	4,443
Union City, CA (city) Alameda County	4,236
Columbus, OH (city) Franklin County	4,168
Bellevue, WA (city) King County	4,101
Edison, NJ (township) Middlesex County	4,094
Cerritos, CA (city) Los Angeles County	4,066
Torrance, CA (city) Los Angeles County	3,946
Mountain View, CA (city) Santa Clara County	3,849
Sugar Land, TX (city) Fort Bend County	3,802
Berkeley, CA (city) Alameda County	3,752
Phoenix, AZ (city) Maricopa County	3,722
Palo Alto, CA (city) Santa Clara County	3,603
Santa Clara, CA (city) Santa Clara County	3,562
Brookhaven, NY (town) Suffolk County	3,544
North Hempstead, NY (town) Nassau County	3,538
San Mateo, CA (city) San Mateo County	3,503
Ann Arbor, MI (city) Washtenaw County	3,299
Hempstead, NY (town) Nassau County	3,291
Malden, MA (city) Middlesex County	3,285
Spring Valley, NV (cdp) Clark County	3,069
Saratoga, CA (city) Santa Clara County	3,002
Pasadena, CA (city) Los Angeles County	2,892
Cambridge, MA (city) Middlesex County	2,847
Foster City, CA (city) San Mateo County	2,804
Naperville, IL (city) Du Page County	2,749
Anaheim, CA (city) Orange County	2,681
Stockton, CA (city) San Joaquin County	2,667
East San Gabriel, CA (cdp) Los Angeles County	2,603
Hayward, CA (city) Alameda County	2,577
Brookline, MA (town) Norfolk County	2,566
Millbrae, CA (city) San Mateo County	2,506
San Marino, CA (city) Los Angeles County	2,497
South San Francisco, CA (city) San Mateo County	2,475
Davis, CA (city) Yolo County	2,443
Richardson, TX (city) Dallas County	2,407
Newton, MA (city) Middlesex County	2,372
North Potomac, MD (cdp) Montgomery County	2,362
Chino Hills, CA (city) San Bernardino County	2,333

Notes: Please refer to the User's Guide for an explanation of data; ranking tables include all places with Asian and/or NHPI populations above SF4 population thresholds; (1) tables reflect only those areas that meet SF4 population thresholds, therefore there may be less than 50 states, 75 counties or 75 places listed

Foreign Born

Chinese (except Taiwanese)

All States, Top 75 Counties, and Top 75 Places Sorted by Percent[1]

State	Percent
South Dakota	83.65
North Dakota	83.45
Nebraska	81.38
Oklahoma	80.25
West Virginia	79.95
Kentucky	79.37
Iowa	78.87
Kansas	78.07
Indiana	77.52
Alabama	77.32
Missouri	77.12
Delaware	77.01
Wisconsin	76.93
Minnesota	75.71
Ohio	75.66
North Carolina	75.42
Florida	75.28
New York	75.16
Arkansas	74.83
Tennessee	74.66
Georgia	74.35
Michigan	74.31
Virginia	74.09
Alaska	73.98
Texas	73.84
South Carolina	73.68
Utah	73.60
Pennsylvania	73.44
Illinois	72.78
Maryland	72.71
New Hampshire	71.70
Maine	71.08
Connecticut	71.02
United States	70.51
Idaho	70.45
District of Columbia	70.13
Massachusetts	70.04
Montana	70.00
Colorado	69.99
Mississippi	69.73
Nevada	69.56
New Jersey	69.53
New Mexico	69.49
Vermont	68.93
Washington	68.75
California	68.20
Wyoming	67.97
Louisiana	67.87
Oregon	67.86
Arizona	66.67
Rhode Island	65.23
Hawaii	40.94

County	Percent
Lancaster County, NE	91.00
Story County, IA	90.23
Cache County, UT	89.82
Payne County, OK	88.91
Pickens County, SC	88.51
Albemarle County, VA	88.32
Clarke County, GA	86.42
Fairfax Independent City, VA	86.19
Greene County, OH	85.75
Marion County, IN	85.08
Lubbock County, TX	84.76
Jackson County, IL	84.62
Oneida County, NY	84.35
Cleveland County, OK	84.33
Lucas County, OH	84.25
Davidson County, TN	84.19
Riley County, KS	84.12
Ottawa County, MI	83.96
Lancaster County, PA	83.55
Lee County, AL	83.47
Oklahoma County, OK	83.40
Fayette County, KY	83.32
Onondaga County, NY	83.25
Dona Ana County, NM	83.12
Tippecanoe County, IN	83.12
Norfolk Independent City, VA	82.93
Tolland County, CT	82.67
Strafford County, NH	82.61
Pulaski County, AR	82.53
Cumberland County, PA	82.42
Forsyth County, NC	82.37
Sangamon County, IL	82.32
Johnson County, IA	82.23
York County, PA	82.13
Dane County, WI	81.48
Jackson County, MO	80.89
Richland County, SC	80.62
Montgomery County, VA	80.57
Fairbanks North Star Borough, AK	80.51
Mobile County, AL	80.42
Prince William County, VA	80.23
Orange County, NC	80.20
Stark County, OH	80.15
Whitman County, WA	79.71
Pinellas County, FL	79.66
Jefferson County, KY	79.63
Monroe County, IN	79.41
Sedgwick County, KS	79.40
Kalamazoo County, MI	79.39
Hamilton County, OH	79.23
Baltimore County, MD	79.20
Gwinnett County, GA	79.13
Monongalia County, WV	78.83
Denton County, TX	78.78
Osceola County, FL	78.60
Peoria County, IL	78.48
Cobb County, GA	78.28
Brevard County, FL	78.25
Miami-Dade County, FL	78.20
Genesee County, MI	78.14
St. Charles County, MO	78.07
McHenry County, IL	78.06
Douglas County, NE	78.04
Brazos County, TX	78.00
Washtenaw County, MI	77.74
Franklin County, OH	77.66
Olmsted County, MN	77.59
Boone County, MO	77.45
New Castle County, DE	77.43
Allegheny County, PA	77.39
Tulsa County, OK	77.36
DeKalb County, GA	77.27
New York County, NY	77.25
Johnson County, KS	77.15
Queens County, NY	77.14

Place	Percent
Westland, MI (city) Wayne County	93.39
Ames, IA (city) Story County	91.20
Lincoln, NE (city) Lancaster County	91.11
Toledo, OH (city) Lucas County	90.96
Drexel Hill, PA (cdp) Delaware County	90.42
Logan, UT (city) Cache County	89.60
Westmont, IL (village) Du Page County	89.56
West Valley City, UT (city) Salt Lake County	89.21
Stillwater, OK (city) Payne County	88.84
Norman, OK (city) Cleveland County	88.33
Raleigh, NC (city) Wake County	86.98
Mobile, AL (city) Mobile County	86.85
Lowell, MA (city) Middlesex County	86.43
Athens-Clarke County, GA (sp. city) Clarke County	86.39
Kendall, FL (cdp) Miami-Dade County	85.94
Orlando, FL (city) Orange County	85.57
Little Rock, AR (city) Pulaski County	85.56
Princeton, NJ (township) Mercer County	85.32
Towson, MD (cdp) Baltimore County	84.99
Indianapolis, IN (sp. city) Marion County	84.96
Setauket-East Setauket, NY (cdp) Suffolk County	84.91
Syracuse, NY (city) Onondaga County	84.83
Atlantic City, NJ (city) Atlantic County	84.72
Manhattan, KS (city) Riley County	84.65
Edmond, OK (city) Oklahoma County	84.60
Kearny, NJ (town) Hudson County	84.41
Pullman, WA (city) Whitman County	84.36
Irving, TX (city) Dallas County	84.16
Highland Park, NJ (borough) Middlesex County	84.11
Omaha, NE (city) Douglas County	84.09
Nashville-Davidson, TN (sp. city) Davidson County	84.03
East Lansing, MI (city) Ingham County	83.97
Bloomington, MN (city) Hennepin County	83.67
Kansas City, MO (city) Jackson County	83.67
Falcon Heights, MN (city) Ramsey County	83.66
Germantown, MD (cdp) Montgomery County	83.60
Allentown, PA (city) Lehigh County	83.52
Lubbock, TX (city) Lubbock County	83.51
Lexington-Fayette, KY (sp. city) Fayette County	83.32
St. Petersburg, FL (city) Pinellas County	83.17
Greenbelt, MD (city) Prince George's County	83.16
Auburn, AL (city) Lee County	83.01
Madison, WI (city) Dane County	83.01
Paramus, NJ (borough) Bergen County	83.01
Harrison, NJ (town) Hudson County	82.80
Carney, MD (cdp) Baltimore County	82.34
Iowa City, IA (city) Johnson County	82.20
Dover, NJ (township) Ocean County	82.07
Storrs, CT (cdp) Tolland County	82.02
Winston-Salem, NC (city) Forsyth County	81.98
Gainesville, FL (city) Alachua County	81.94
Newark, DE (city) New Castle County	81.89
Mansfield, CT (town) Tolland County	81.85
Rockville, MD (city) Montgomery County	81.71
Minneapolis, MN (city) Hennepin County	81.54
Chapel Hill, NC (town) Orange County	81.37
Toms River, NJ (cdp) Ocean County	81.36
Acton, MA (town) Middlesex County	81.26
Provo, UT (city) Utah County	81.18
Clinton, MI (township) Macomb County	81.17
Oklahoma City, OK (city) Oklahoma County	81.08
Arlington, MA (town) Middlesex County	81.07
Upper Darby, PA (township) Delaware County	81.02
Columbus, OH (city) Franklin County	80.98
Danbury, CT (city) Fairfield County	80.96
Akron, OH (city) Summit County	80.93
Buffalo, NY (city) Erie County	80.93
Westborough, MA (town) Worcester County	80.91
Milford, CT (town) New Haven County	80.86
West Lafayette, IN (city) Tippecanoe County	80.73
Wichita, KS (city) Sedgwick County	80.62
Hazlet, NJ (township) Monmouth County	80.58
North Bethesda, MD (cdp) Montgomery County	80.48
Palatine, IL (village) Cook County	80.35
Brighton, NY (town) Monroe County	80.31

Notes: Please refer to the User's Guide for an explanation of data; ranking tables include all places with Asian and/or NHPI populations above SF4 population thresholds; (1) tables reflect only those areas that meet SF4 population thresholds, therefore there may be less than 50 states, 75 counties or 75 places listed

Foreign Born

Fijian

All States, Top 75 Counties, and Top 75 Places Sorted by Number[1]

State	Number
United States	7,968
California	6,518
Washington	535
Oregon	269

County	Number
Sacramento County, CA	1,486
Alameda County, CA	1,070
San Mateo County, CA	779
Stanislaus County, CA	521
Santa Clara County, CA	493
Yolo County, CA	464
King County, WA	427
Los Angeles County, CA	380
Contra Costa County, CA	346

Place	Number
Sacramento, CA (city) Sacramento County	1,063
Hayward, CA (city) Alameda County	578
Modesto, CA (city) Stanislaus County	369

Notes: Please refer to the User's Guide for an explanation of data; ranking tables include all places with Asian and/or NHPI populations above SF4 population thresholds; (1) tables reflect only those areas that meet SF4 population thresholds, therefore there may be less than 50 states, 75 counties or 75 places listed

Foreign Born

Fijian

All States, Top 75 Counties, and Top 75 Places Sorted by Percent[1]

State	Percent
United States	77.62
California	77.50
Washington	75.46
Oregon	72.12

County	Percent
Santa Clara County, CA	96.48
Yolo County, CA	88.21
Sacramento County, CA	84.87
King County, WA	78.64
Los Angeles County, CA	77.08
Stanislaus County, CA	74.64
Alameda County, CA	73.14
San Mateo County, CA	67.33
Contra Costa County, CA	64.31

Place	Percent
Sacramento, CA (city) Sacramento County	85.73
Modesto, CA (city) Stanislaus County	74.70
Hayward, CA (city) Alameda County	68.56

Notes: Please refer to the User's Guide for an explanation of data; ranking tables include all places with Asian and/or NHPI populations above SF4 population thresholds; (1) tables reflect only those areas that meet SF4 population thresholds, therefore there may be less than 50 states, 75 counties or 75 places listed

Foreign Born

Filipino

All States, Top 75 Counties, and Top 75 Places Sorted by Number[1]

State	Number
United States	1,261,611
California	621,092
Hawaii	96,072
New York	65,361
New Jersey	65,201
Illinois	62,050
Washington	42,578
Texas	41,554
Florida	39,071
Virginia	33,142
Nevada	28,837
Maryland	19,434
Michigan	12,391
Arizona	10,546
Pennsylvania	9,995
Ohio	8,857
Alaska	8,444
North Carolina	7,099
Georgia	7,056
Oregon	6,572
Massachusetts	6,384
Colorado	5,694
Connecticut	5,534
Missouri	5,079
Indiana	4,656
South Carolina	4,650
Minnesota	3,995
Wisconsin	3,674
Tennessee	3,631
Louisiana	3,203
Oklahoma	2,768
Kansas	2,393
Utah	2,278
Kentucky	2,121
New Mexico	1,927
Mississippi	1,912
Alabama	1,625
Iowa	1,566
District of Columbia	1,565
Rhode Island	1,556
Arkansas	1,535
Nebraska	1,457
Delaware	1,301
West Virginia	1,101
Idaho	1,056
New Hampshire	969
Maine	869
South Dakota	490
Montana	458
North Dakota	312
Wyoming	303
Vermont	197

County	Number
Los Angeles County, CA	189,387
San Diego County, CA	80,757
Honolulu County, HI	70,751
Santa Clara County, CA	52,877
Alameda County, CA	47,048
San Mateo County, CA	40,637
Cook County, IL	40,302
Orange County, CA	32,813
San Francisco County, CA	28,397
Queens County, NY	25,655
Clark County, NV	23,057
Solano County, CA	22,952
King County, WA	22,395
Contra Costa County, CA	21,949
San Bernardino County, CA	16,539
Hudson County, NJ	15,066
Sacramento County, CA	14,445
Maui County, HI	12,919
Riverside County, CA	12,427
San Joaquin County, CA	12,228
Harris County, TX	11,470
Bergen County, NJ	11,079
Ventura County, CA	10,554
DuPage County, IL	9,900
Fairfax County, VA	9,089
Virginia Beach Independent City, VA	9,010
Middlesex County, NJ	9,003
Maricopa County, AZ	7,747
Kern County, CA	6,858
Hawaii County, HI	6,841
Duval County, FL	6,796
Monterey County, CA	6,673
New York County, NY	6,582
Prince George's County, MD	6,008
Essex County, NJ	5,985
Montgomery County, MD	5,656
Kings County, NY	5,563
Kauai County, HI	5,546
Nassau County, NY	5,297
Snohomish County, WA	4,973
Washoe County, NV	4,843
Lake County, IL	4,825
Kitsap County, WA	4,636
Dallas County, TX	4,387
Union County, NJ	4,347
Pierce County, WA	4,007
Westchester County, NY	3,928
Bronx County, NY	3,820
Fresno County, CA	3,817
Richmond County, NY	3,699
Broward County, FL	3,609
Miami-Dade County, FL	3,586
Bexar County, TX	3,458
Anchorage Borough, AK	3,361
Rockland County, NY	3,259
Wayne County, MI	3,256
Norfolk Independent City, VA	3,125
Orange County, FL	3,087
Fort Bend County, TX	3,023
Santa Barbara County, CA	2,908
Oakland County, MI	2,879
Tulare County, CA	2,827
Suffolk County, NY	2,795
Passaic County, NJ	2,647
Camden County, NJ	2,638
Philadelphia County, PA	2,541
Tarrant County, TX	2,472
Monmouth County, NJ	2,381
Morris County, NJ	2,352
Macomb County, MI	2,341
Baltimore County, MD	2,339
Pinellas County, FL	2,270
Hillsborough County, FL	2,268
Multnomah County, OR	2,232
Will County, IL	2,150

Place	Number
Los Angeles, CA (city) Los Angeles County	75,891
San Diego, CA (city) San Diego County	49,609
New York, NY (city)	45,319
San Jose, CA (city) Santa Clara County	33,966
San Francisco, CA (city) San Francisco County	28,397
Honolulu, HI (cdp) Honolulu County	26,747
Daly City, CA (city) San Mateo County	22,701
Chicago, IL (city) Cook County	20,755
Vallejo, CA (city) Solano County	15,399
Long Beach, CA (city) Los Angeles County	12,598
Jersey City, NJ (city) Hudson County	12,534
Carson, CA (city) Los Angeles County	12,245
Seattle, WA (city) King County	11,308
Waipahu, HI (cdp) Honolulu County	10,286
Union City, CA (city) Alameda County	9,073
Stockton, CA (city) San Joaquin County	9,031
Glendale, CA (city) Los Angeles County	8,932
Hayward, CA (city) Alameda County	8,360
Chula Vista, CA (city) San Diego County	8,203
Fremont, CA (city) Alameda County	7,617
Las Vegas, NV (city) Clark County	7,617
National City, CA (city) San Diego County	7,098
West Covina, CA (city) Los Angeles County	7,067
South San Francisco, CA (city) San Mateo County	6,905
Jacksonville, FL (city) Duval County	6,587
Oxnard, CA (city) Ventura County	6,342
Milpitas, CA (city) Santa Clara County	6,296
Houston, TX (city) Harris County	5,793
Anaheim, CA (city) Orange County	5,748
Sacramento, CA (city) Sacramento County	5,001
Oakland, CA (city) Alameda County	4,579
Sunnyvale, CA (city) Santa Clara County	4,518
San Leandro, CA (city) Alameda County	4,365
Alameda, CA (city) Alameda County	4,270
Paradise, NV (cdp) Clark County	4,231
Kahului, HI (cdp) Maui County	4,049
Delano, CA (city) Kern County	3,932
Santa Clara, CA (city) Santa Clara County	3,912
Cerritos, CA (city) Los Angeles County	3,789
Buena Park, CA (city) Orange County	3,755
Fairfield, CA (city) Solano County	3,683
Oceanside, CA (city) San Diego County	3,506
Sunrise Manor, NV (cdp) Clark County	3,463
Chino Hills, CA (city) San Bernardino County	3,437
Ewa Beach, HI (cdp) Honolulu County	3,347
Phoenix, AZ (city) Maricopa County	3,292
Lakewood, CA (city) Los Angeles County	3,289
Norwalk, CA (city) Los Angeles County	3,274
Reno, NV (city) Washoe County	3,225
Salinas, CA (city) Monterey County	3,216
Pittsburg, CA (city) Contra Costa County	3,151
Hempstead, NY (town) Nassau County	2,946
Hercules, CA (city) Contra Costa County	2,873
Fresno, CA (city) Fresno County	2,818
Baldwin Park, CA (city) Los Angeles County	2,747
Bellflower, CA (city) Los Angeles County	2,679
Concord, CA (city) Contra Costa County	2,671
Spring Valley, NV (cdp) Clark County	2,661
Moreno Valley, CA (city) Riverside County	2,658
Philadelphia, PA (city) Philadelphia County	2,541
Torrance, CA (city) Los Angeles County	2,510
San Antonio, TX (city) Bexar County	2,495
Burbank, CA (city) Los Angeles County	2,444
Bergenfield, NJ (borough) Bergen County	2,386
Rowland Heights, CA (cdp) Los Angeles County	2,384
Walnut, CA (city) Los Angeles County	2,292
Skokie, IL (village) Cook County	2,258
Newark, CA (city) Alameda County	2,153
Pearl City, HI (cdp) Honolulu County	2,152
La Presa, CA (cdp) San Diego County	2,117
Suisun City, CA (city) Solano County	2,089
Pasadena, CA (city) Los Angeles County	2,081
Garden Grove, CA (city) Orange County	2,075
Pacifica, CA (city) San Mateo County	2,068
Elk Grove, CA (cdp) Sacramento County	2,067

Notes: Please refer to the User's Guide for an explanation of data; ranking tables include all places with Asian and/or NHPI populations above SF4 population thresholds; (1) tables reflect only those areas that meet SF4 population thresholds, therefore there may be less than 50 states, 75 counties or 75 places listed

Foreign Born

Filipino

All States, Top 75 Counties, and Top 75 Places Sorted by Percent[1]

State	Percent
New Hampshire	76.18
New York	75.37
Maine	74.27
District of Columbia	73.86
New Jersey	73.75
Connecticut	73.68
Rhode Island	73.19
Mississippi	73.00
Maryland	72.86
Illinois	71.95
Florida	71.91
Delaware	71.29
Nevada	71.16
Texas	70.89
Kansas	70.78
Nebraska	70.56
Michigan	70.44
Missouri	70.02
North Carolina	69.64
Iowa	69.63
South Dakota	69.60
Virginia	69.02
Massachusetts	68.74
Tennessee	68.74
Pennsylvania	67.93
Kentucky	67.79
Louisiana	67.76
Minnesota	67.71
United States	67.68
Alaska	67.62
Georgia	67.61
Indiana	67.56
California	67.51
Wisconsin	67.30
Ohio	67.21
South Carolina	66.88
Arkansas	66.65
Alabama	66.57
West Virginia	66.41
Oklahoma	66.16
New Mexico	65.50
Washington	65.45
Arizona	65.08
Idaho	64.39
Vermont	62.74
Oregon	61.56
Utah	61.48
Colorado	61.09
Montana	58.34
Wyoming	57.93
Hawaii	55.96
North Dakota	54.07

County	Percent
Manatee County, FL	87.73
Sedgwick County, KS	86.52
Hillsborough County, NH	85.64
Cameron County, TX	83.39
Hidalgo County, TX	82.76
Santa Rosa County, FL	82.74
Carson City Independent City, NV	82.25
Montgomery County, MD	81.99
Sandoval County, NM	81.63
Volusia County, FL	81.04
New Haven County, CT	81.00
Atlantic County, NJ	79.51
Stafford County, VA	79.37
Miami-Dade County, FL	79.32
Westchester County, NY	79.26
Valdez-Cordova Census Area, AK	79.13
Clay County, FL	78.65
Queens County, NY	78.11
Kings County, NY	77.82
Pasco County, FL	77.57
Bronx County, NY	77.42
Alexandria Independent City, VA	77.38
Lorain County, OH	77.37
Durham County, NC	77.23
Sarpy County, NE	76.88
Providence County, RI	76.57
Sarasota County, FL	76.30
Montgomery County, TX	76.18
North Slope Borough, AK	76.11
Passaic County, NJ	76.06
Rockingham County, NH	75.85
Union County, NJ	75.85
Hudson County, NJ	75.80
Wayne County, MI	75.76
Fairfield County, CT	75.56
Waukesha County, WI	75.43
Washoe County, NV	75.41
Polk County, FL	75.39
Essex County, NJ	75.37
Arlington County, VA	75.31
Harford County, MD	75.22
Nueces County, TX	75.09
Winnebago County, IL	75.00
Pinellas County, FL	74.82
Hampton Independent City, VA	74.66
New York County, NY	74.53
Palm Beach County, FL	74.44
Bergen County, NJ	74.37
Marion County, IN	74.18
Broward County, FL	74.11
Galveston County, TX	74.08
Island County, WA	74.02
Nassau County, NY	73.90
Middlesex County, MA	73.88
Cook County, IL	73.82
Lee County, FL	73.82
Bay County, FL	73.76
Collin County, TX	73.60
Kent County, MI	73.42
Jefferson County, TX	73.38
Cuyahoga County, OH	73.22
Dallas County, TX	73.19
Norfolk Independent City, VA	73.12
Morris County, NJ	73.02
Prince George's County, MD	72.92
Jackson County, MO	72.91
Onslow County, NC	72.81
Kodiak Island Borough, AK	72.76
Harris County, TX	72.71
Montgomery County, PA	72.65
Mecklenburg County, NC	72.64
New Castle County, DE	72.60
Johnson County, KS	72.56
Houston County, GA	72.55
Rockland County, NY	72.34

Place	Percent
Rockville, MD (city) Montgomery County	93.47
Redland, MD (cdp) Montgomery County	92.56
Potomac, MD (cdp) Montgomery County	90.32
Wichita, KS (city) Sedgwick County	89.76
Elizabeth, NJ (city) Union County	86.14
Montgomery Village, MD (cdp) Montgomery County	85.29
Atlantic City, NJ (city) Atlantic County	84.93
Aspen Hill, MD (cdp) Montgomery County	84.68
Terra Bella, CA (cdp) Tulare County	84.43
Cicero, IL (town) Cook County	83.77
Bolingbrook, IL (village) Will County	82.85
Silver Spring, MD (cdp) Montgomery County	82.73
McAllen, TX (city) Hidalgo County	82.33
Passaic, NJ (city) Passaic County	81.75
San Gabriel, CA (city) Los Angeles County	81.58
Pembroke Pines, FL (city) Broward County	81.34
Rio Rancho, NM (city) Sandoval County	81.17
Park City, IL (city) Lake County	81.10
Lakeside, FL (cdp) Clay County	81.09
Monterey Park, CA (city) Los Angeles County	81.04
Little Ferry, NJ (borough) Bergen County	80.73
Tampa, FL (city) Hillsborough County	80.72
Upland, CA (city) San Bernardino County	80.60
Richardson, TX (city) Dallas County	80.53
Azusa, CA (city) Los Angeles County	80.47
Fair Lawn, NJ (borough) Bergen County	80.41
Quincy, MA (city) Norfolk County	80.33
South San Jose Hills, CA (cdp) Los Angeles County	80.25
Culver City, CA (city) Los Angeles County	80.16
Pasadena, CA (city) Los Angeles County	80.10
La Puente, CA (city) Los Angeles County	79.74
Rodeo, CA (cdp) Contra Costa County	79.61
Cupertino, CA (city) Santa Clara County	79.46
Palatine, IL (village) Cook County	79.44
Babylon, NY (town) Suffolk County	79.37
Haliimaile, HI (cdp) Maui County	79.00
Arlington Heights, IL (village) Cook County	78.96
Bloomfield, NJ (township) Essex County	78.92
South Brunswick, NJ (township) Middlesex County	78.70
Wayne, NJ (township) Passaic County	78.65
Streamwood, IL (village) Cook County	78.53
National City, CA (city) San Diego County	78.34
Hawthorne, CA (city) Los Angeles County	78.21
North Bethesda, MD (cdp) Montgomery County	78.19
Mission Bend, TX (cdp) Fort Bend County	78.07
Schaumburg, IL (village) Cook County	77.86
Dale City, VA (cdp) Prince William County	77.45
Rollingwood, CA (cdp) Contra Costa County	77.45
Providence, RI (city) Providence County	77.37
Sparks, NV (city) Washoe County	77.30
Berwyn, IL (city) Cook County	77.28
Glendale, CA (city) Los Angeles County	77.27
Hanford, CA (city) Kings County	77.17
West Carson, CA (cdp) Los Angeles County	77.13
Somerset, NJ (cdp) Somerset County	77.12
Aurora, IL (city) Kane County	77.04
Springfield, VA (cdp) Fairfax County	77.04
Kualapuu, HI (cdp) Maui County	77.03
Vincent, CA (cdp) Los Angeles County	76.94
Durham, NC (city) Durham County	76.89
New York, NY (city)	76.88
Dumont, NJ (borough) Bergen County	76.86
Gaithersburg, MD (city) Montgomery County	76.71
Oxon Hill-Glassmanor, MD (cdp) Prince George's County	76.70
West Orange, NJ (township) Essex County	76.51
Groton, CT (town) New London County	76.46
South Plainfield, NJ (borough) Middlesex County	76.29
Belleville, NJ (township) Essex County	76.28
Cathedral City, CA (city) Riverside County	76.19
Yonkers, NY (city) Westchester County	76.17
East Meadow, NY (cdp) Nassau County	76.15
Jersey City, NJ (city) Hudson County	76.15
Barrow, AK (city) North Slope Borough	76.11
Addison, IL (village) Du Page County	76.10
Hoffman Estates, IL (village) Cook County	76.07

Notes: Please refer to the User's Guide for an explanation of data; ranking tables include all places with Asian and/or NHPI populations above SF4 population thresholds; (1) tables reflect only those areas that meet SF4 population thresholds, therefore there may be less than 50 states, 75 counties or 75 places listed

Foreign Born

Guamanian or Chamorro

All States, Top 75 Counties, and Top 75 Places Sorted by Number[1]

State	Number
United States	6,842
California	1,710
New York	542
Florida	534
Georgia	415
Texas	373
Illinois	262
New Jersey	226
Michigan	217
Tennessee	190
Washington	181
Massachusetts	177
North Carolina	159
Nevada	149
Arizona	145
Indiana	133
Virginia	132
Minnesota	113
South Carolina	100
Maryland	99
Pennsylvania	93
Ohio	78
Missouri	69
Oregon	66
Hawaii	60
Alabama	59
Colorado	57
Connecticut	47
Kentucky	40
Louisiana	30
Oklahoma	25
New Mexico	8
Wisconsin	6

County	Number
Los Angeles County, CA	576
San Diego County, CA	198
Riverside County, CA	150
Kings County, NY	147
Clark County, NV	138
Orange County, CA	109
King County, WA	102
Santa Clara County, CA	90
Alameda County, CA	77
Harris County, TX	76
Honolulu County, HI	60
Maricopa County, AZ	56
San Bernardino County, CA	55
Sacramento County, CA	51
Monterey County, CA	26
Bell County, TX	18
Pierce County, WA	17
Solano County, CA	16
San Mateo County, CA	15
Contra Costa County, CA	11
El Paso County, CO	11
Thurston County, WA	11
Kitsap County, WA	0

Place	Number
New York, NY (city)	371
Los Angeles, CA (city) Los Angeles County	317
Houston, TX (city) Harris County	54
San Jose, CA (city) Santa Clara County	38
San Diego, CA (city) San Diego County	35
Honolulu, HI (cdp) Honolulu County	22
Chula Vista, CA (city) San Diego County	21
Killeen, TX (city) Bell County	18
Vallejo, CA (city) Solano County	16
Fairfield, CA (city) Solano County	0
Tacoma, WA (city) Pierce County	0

Notes: Please refer to the User's Guide for an explanation of data; ranking tables include all places with Asian and/or NHPI populations above SF4 population thresholds; (1) tables reflect only those areas that meet SF4 population thresholds, therefore there may be less than 50 states, 75 counties or 75 places listed

Foreign Born

Guamanian or Chamorro

All States, Top 75 Counties, and Top 75 Places Sorted by Percent[1]

State	Percent
Massachusetts	39.78
New Jersey	37.54
Illinois	32.15
Michigan	31.68
New York	30.81
Tennessee	30.69
Georgia	28.76
South Carolina	27.86
Minnesota	26.46
Florida	26.44
Indiana	25.29
Maryland	14.12
Alabama	13.92
North Carolina	13.28
Nevada	13.08
Virginia	13.00
United States	12.41
Ohio	11.71
Pennsylvania	11.55
Arizona	11.46
Texas	11.29
Missouri	11.27
Connecticut	11.22
Kentucky	10.87
California	8.35
Louisiana	6.42
Oklahoma	6.25
Oregon	5.95
Colorado	5.63
Hawaii	4.02
Washington	3.36
New Mexico	2.19
Wisconsin	1.41

County	Percent
Kings County, NY	30.06
Los Angeles County, CA	18.35
Riverside County, CA	15.92
Clark County, NV	14.41
King County, WA	12.23
Harris County, TX	11.89
Orange County, CA	9.88
Maricopa County, AZ	8.66
Santa Clara County, CA	6.47
Alameda County, CA	5.87
Sacramento County, CA	5.83
San Bernardino County, CA	5.28
Honolulu County, HI	4.52
San Diego County, CA	4.28
Monterey County, CA	3.86
San Mateo County, CA	3.73
Bell County, TX	3.02
El Paso County, CO	2.24
Contra Costa County, CA	2.02
Thurston County, WA	1.51
Solano County, CA	1.18
Pierce County, WA	0.93
Kitsap County, WA	0.00

Place	Percent
New York, NY (city)	31.55
Los Angeles, CA (city) Los Angeles County	27.59
Houston, TX (city) Harris County	12.22
San Jose, CA (city) Santa Clara County	5.19
Chula Vista, CA (city) San Diego County	4.94
Killeen, TX (city) Bell County	3.60
Honolulu, HI (cdp) Honolulu County	3.25
Vallejo, CA (city) Solano County	2.80
San Diego, CA (city) San Diego County	1.69
Fairfield, CA (city) Solano County	0.00
Tacoma, WA (city) Pierce County	0.00

Notes: Please refer to the User's Guide for an explanation of data; ranking tables include all places with Asian and/or NHPI populations above SF4 population thresholds; (1) tables reflect only those areas that meet SF4 population thresholds, therefore there may be less than 50 states, 75 counties or 75 places listed

Foreign Born

Hawaiian, Native

***All States, Top 75 Counties, and Top 75 Places Sorted by Number*[1]**

State	Number
United States	3,019
California	907
Hawaii	492
Texas	260
New York	231
Arizona	155
Washington	106
Minnesota	101
Florida	98
Nevada	82
Illinois	68
New Jersey	66
South Carolina	57
Maryland	41
Michigan	41
Utah	30
Missouri	27
Oklahoma	27
Georgia	25
Pennsylvania	25
Colorado	23
Virginia	23
Tennessee	18
Indiana	17
North Carolina	15
New Mexico	14
Wisconsin	14
Alaska	7
Ohio	7
Oregon	6
Arkansas	0
Idaho	0
Kansas	0
Louisiana	0
Massachusetts	0
Montana	0

County	Number
Honolulu County, HI	336
Los Angeles County, CA	225
Maricopa County, AZ	116
Hawaii County, HI	103
Ventura County, CA	78
Clark County, NV	74
Orange County, CA	69
Santa Clara County, CA	53
San Mateo County, CA	49
Maui County, HI	48
Alameda County, CA	47
King County, WA	44
Pima County, AZ	35
Contra Costa County, CA	34
San Bernardino County, CA	34
Sacramento County, CA	28
San Joaquin County, CA	22
Riverside County, CA	21
Salt Lake County, UT	20
San Diego County, CA	20
Bexar County, TX	16
Snohomish County, WA	12
Utah County, UT	10
Solano County, CA	7
Multnomah County, OR	6
Kauai County, HI	5
Pierce County, WA	0
Washington County, OR	0

Place	Number
New York, NY (city)	226
Honolulu, HI (cdp) Honolulu County	131
Los Angeles, CA (city) Los Angeles County	88
Aiea, HI (cdp) Honolulu County	81
Phoenix, AZ (city) Maricopa County	56
Las Vegas, NV (city) Clark County	45
San Jose, CA (city) Santa Clara County	33
Waimea, HI (cdp) Hawaii County	26
Waipio, HI (cdp) Honolulu County	22
Kihei, HI (cdp) Maui County	19
Paradise, NV (cdp) Clark County	19
Hilo, HI (cdp) Hawaii County	17
Kailua, HI (cdp) Hawaii County	12
Henderson, NV (city) Clark County	10
Lahaina, HI (cdp) Maui County	10
Waianae, HI (cdp) Honolulu County	10
Maili, HI (cdp) Honolulu County	9
Kaneohe, HI (cdp) Honolulu County	8
Pearl City, HI (cdp) Honolulu County	7
Laie, HI (cdp) Honolulu County	6
Makaha Valley, HI (cdp) Honolulu County	6
Nanakuli, HI (cdp) Honolulu County	6
Portland, OR (city) Multnomah County	6
Wahiawa, HI (cdp) Honolulu County	6
Mililani Town, HI (cdp) Honolulu County	4
Paia, HI (cdp) Maui County	4
Waikoloa Village, HI (cdp) Hawaii County	4
Waialua, HI (cdp) Honolulu County	3
Anahola, HI (cdp) Kauai County	2
Kualapuu, HI (cdp) Maui County	2
Kahuku, HI (cdp) Honolulu County	1
Pahala, HI (cdp) Hawaii County	1
Ahuimanu, HI (cdp) Honolulu County	0
Captain Cook, HI (cdp) Hawaii County	0
Ewa Beach, HI (cdp) Honolulu County	0
Halawa, HI (cdp) Honolulu County	0
Haleiwa, HI (cdp) Honolulu County	0
Hana, HI (cdp) Maui County	0
Hanapepe, HI (cdp) Kauai County	0
Hauula, HI (cdp) Honolulu County	0
Hawaiian Beaches, HI (cdp) Hawaii County	0
Hawaiian Ocean View, HI (cdp) Hawaii County	0
Hawaiian Paradise Park, HI (cdp) Hawaii County	0
Holualoa, HI (cdp) Hawaii County	0
Honalo, HI (cdp) Hawaii County	0
Honaunau-Napoopoo, HI (cdp) Hawaii County	0
Kaaawa, HI (cdp) Honolulu County	0
Kahaluu, HI (cdp) Honolulu County	0
Kahului, HI (cdp) Maui County	0
Kailua, HI (cdp) Honolulu County	0
Kalaoa, HI (cdp) Hawaii County	0
Kapaa, HI (cdp) Kauai County	0
Kapaau, HI (cdp) Hawaii County	0
Kaunakakai, HI (cdp) Maui County	0
Kekaha, HI (cdp) Kauai County	0
Kilauea, HI (cdp) Kauai County	0
Makaha, HI (cdp) Honolulu County	0
Makakilo City, HI (cdp) Honolulu County	0
Makawao, HI (cdp) Maui County	0
Naalehu, HI (cdp) Hawaii County	0
Pakala Village, HI (cdp) Kauai County	0
Punaluu, HI (cdp) Honolulu County	0
San Diego, CA (city) San Diego County	0
Volcano, HI (cdp) Hawaii County	0
Waihee-Waiehu, HI (cdp) Maui County	0
Waikane, HI (cdp) Honolulu County	0
Wailuku, HI (cdp) Maui County	0
Waimalu, HI (cdp) Honolulu County	0
Waimanalo Beach, HI (cdp) Honolulu County	0
Waimanalo, HI (cdp) Honolulu County	0
Waimea, HI (cdp) Kauai County	0
Waipahu, HI (cdp) Honolulu County	0

Notes: Please refer to the User's Guide for an explanation of data; ranking tables include all places with Asian and/or NHPI populations above SF4 population thresholds; (1) tables reflect only those areas that meet SF4 population thresholds, therefore there may be less than 50 states, 75 counties or 75 places listed

Foreign Born

Hawaiian, Native

***All States, Top 75 Counties, and Top 75 Places Sorted by Percent*[1]**

State	Percent
Minnesota	17.44
New York	16.02
South Carolina	11.49
New Jersey	10.12
Maryland	7.96
Arizona	7.81
Illinois	7.44
Texas	7.11
Michigan	5.18
Florida	4.97
California	4.61
Oklahoma	3.99
Missouri	3.88
New Mexico	3.55
Wisconsin	3.23
Tennessee	3.21
Georgia	3.07
Indiana	2.56
Pennsylvania	2.49
Virginia	2.49
Nevada	2.41
Washington	2.35
Utah	2.24
United States	2.16
Colorado	1.58
Alaska	1.40
North Carolina	1.31
Ohio	0.88
Hawaii	0.61
Oregon	0.30
Arkansas	0.00
Idaho	0.00
Kansas	0.00
Louisiana	0.00
Massachusetts	0.00
Montana	0.00

County	Percent
Ventura County, CA	13.57
Maricopa County, AZ	10.46
Pima County, AZ	7.51
San Mateo County, CA	6.09
Contra Costa County, CA	5.71
San Bernardino County, CA	5.57
San Joaquin County, CA	5.30
Los Angeles County, CA	5.12
Santa Clara County, CA	4.62
Sacramento County, CA	4.28
Salt Lake County, UT	4.17
Orange County, CA	4.06
Bexar County, TX	3.81
Alameda County, CA	3.66
King County, WA	3.20
Riverside County, CA	2.60
Utah County, UT	2.58
Clark County, NV	2.40
Snohomish County, WA	2.36
Multnomah County, OR	1.28
Solano County, CA	1.07
San Diego County, CA	0.90
Hawaii County, HI	0.74
Honolulu County, HI	0.67
Maui County, HI	0.41
Kauai County, HI	0.10
Pierce County, WA	0.00
Washington County, OR	0.00

Place	Percent
New York, NY (city)	29.12
Aiea, HI (cdp) Honolulu County	22.01
Phoenix, AZ (city) Maricopa County	11.13
San Jose, CA (city) Santa Clara County	6.17
Las Vegas, NV (city) Clark County	5.76
Los Angeles, CA (city) Los Angeles County	5.46
Waipio, HI (cdp) Honolulu County	5.05
Paradise, NV (cdp) Clark County	3.17
Makaha Valley, HI (cdp) Honolulu County	2.73
Waimea, HI (cdp) Hawaii County	2.70
Waialua, HI (cdp) Honolulu County	2.46
Kihei, HI (cdp) Maui County	2.38
Henderson, NV (city) Clark County	2.26
Paia, HI (cdp) Maui County	1.88
Laie, HI (cdp) Honolulu County	1.81
Portland, OR (city) Multnomah County	1.72
Waikoloa Village, HI (cdp) Hawaii County	1.34
Pahala, HI (cdp) Hawaii County	1.16
Lahaina, HI (cdp) Maui County	1.15
Kailua, HI (cdp) Hawaii County	1.14
Honolulu, HI (cdp) Honolulu County	0.91
Maili, HI (cdp) Honolulu County	0.64
Wahiawa, HI (cdp) Honolulu County	0.64
Kahuku, HI (cdp) Honolulu County	0.54
Pearl City, HI (cdp) Honolulu County	0.52
Mililani Town, HI (cdp) Honolulu County	0.46
Waianae, HI (cdp) Honolulu County	0.42
Hilo, HI (cdp) Hawaii County	0.41
Kaneohe, HI (cdp) Honolulu County	0.24
Kualapuu, HI (cdp) Maui County	0.23
Anahola, HI (cdp) Kauai County	0.20
Nanakuli, HI (cdp) Honolulu County	0.19
Ahuimanu, HI (cdp) Honolulu County	0.00
Captain Cook, HI (cdp) Hawaii County	0.00
Ewa Beach, HI (cdp) Honolulu County	0.00
Halawa, HI (cdp) Honolulu County	0.00
Haleiwa, HI (cdp) Honolulu County	0.00
Hana, HI (cdp) Maui County	0.00
Hanapepe, HI (cdp) Kauai County	0.00
Hauula, HI (cdp) Honolulu County	0.00
Hawaiian Beaches, HI (cdp) Hawaii County	0.00
Hawaiian Ocean View, HI (cdp) Hawaii County	0.00
Hawaiian Paradise Park, HI (cdp) Hawaii County	0.00
Holualoa, HI (cdp) Hawaii County	0.00
Honalo, HI (cdp) Hawaii County	0.00
Honaunau-Napoopoo, HI (cdp) Hawaii County	0.00
Kaaawa, HI (cdp) Honolulu County	0.00
Kahaluu, HI (cdp) Honolulu County	0.00
Kahului, HI (cdp) Maui County	0.00
Kailua, HI (cdp) Honolulu County	0.00
Kalaoa, HI (cdp) Hawaii County	0.00
Kapaa, HI (cdp) Kauai County	0.00
Kapaau, HI (cdp) Hawaii County	0.00
Kaunakakai, HI (cdp) Maui County	0.00
Kekaha, HI (cdp) Kauai County	0.00
Kilauea, HI (cdp) Kauai County	0.00
Makaha, HI (cdp) Honolulu County	0.00
Makakilo City, HI (cdp) Honolulu County	0.00
Makawao, HI (cdp) Maui County	0.00
Naalehu, HI (cdp) Hawaii County	0.00
Pakala Village, HI (cdp) Kauai County	0.00
Punaluu, HI (cdp) Honolulu County	0.00
San Diego, CA (city) San Diego County	0.00
Volcano, HI (cdp) Hawaii County	0.00
Waihee-Waiehu, HI (cdp) Maui County	0.00
Waikane, HI (cdp) Honolulu County	0.00
Wailuku, HI (cdp) Maui County	0.00
Waimalu, HI (cdp) Honolulu County	0.00
Waimanalo Beach, HI (cdp) Honolulu County	0.00
Waimanalo, HI (cdp) Honolulu County	0.00
Waimea, HI (cdp) Kauai County	0.00
Waipahu, HI (cdp) Honolulu County	0.00

Notes: Please refer to the User's Guide for an explanation of data; ranking tables include all places with Asian and/or NHPI populations above SF4 population thresholds; (1) tables reflect only those areas that meet SF4 population thresholds, therefore there may be less than 50 states, 75 counties or 75 places listed

Foreign Born

Hmong

***All States, Top 75 Counties, and Top 75 Places Sorted by Number*[1]**

State	Number
United States	94,583
California	37,725
Minnesota	24,551
Wisconsin	17,783
North Carolina	3,544
Michigan	3,401
Colorado	1,580
Washington	915
Oregon	645
Georgia	614
Rhode Island	606
Massachusetts	481
Pennsylvania	461
Kansas	380
South Carolina	377
Alaska	242
Oklahoma	176

County	Number
Ramsey County, MN	15,382
Fresno County, CA	13,173
Sacramento County, CA	9,678
Hennepin County, MN	7,389
Milwaukee County, WI	4,374
Merced County, CA	3,820
San Joaquin County, CA	3,063
Marathon County, WI	2,435
Butte County, CA	1,914
Brown County, WI	1,445
Sheboygan County, WI	1,406
Outagamie County, WI	1,398
Yuba County, CA	1,384
Dane County, WI	1,309
Wayne County, MI	1,222
Adams County, CO	1,174
Burke County, NC	1,055
La Crosse County, WI	1,046
Catawba County, NC	952
Winnebago County, WI	807
San Diego County, CA	752
Eau Claire County, WI	685
Oakland County, MI	665
Tulare County, CA	581
Manitowoc County, WI	572
Orange County, CA	562
Macomb County, MI	560
Providence County, RI	531
Multnomah County, OR	520
King County, WA	504
Portage County, WI	446
Glenn County, CA	387
Washington County, MN	371
Stanislaus County, CA	369
Ingham County, MI	365
Spokane County, WA	356
Anoka County, MN	342
Wood County, WI	341
Spartanburg County, SC	327
Mecklenburg County, NC	319
Yolo County, CA	317
Dunn County, WI	311
Worcester County, MA	310
Wyandotte County, KS	298
Lancaster County, PA	282
Calumet County, WI	260
Anchorage Borough, AK	242
Olmsted County, MN	226
Solano County, CA	212
Fond du Lac County, WI	206
Riverside County, CA	203
Los Angeles County, CA	188
Stanly County, NC	176
Jefferson County, CO	164
Santa Barbara County, CA	154
Barrow County, GA	126
Chippewa County, WI	116

Place	Number
St. Paul, MN (city) Ramsey County	14,875
Fresno, CA (city) Fresno County	11,388
Sacramento, CA (city) Sacramento County	6,754
Minneapolis, MN (city) Hennepin County	5,770
Milwaukee, WI (city) Milwaukee County	4,259
Stockton, CA (city) San Joaquin County	2,589
Merced, CA (city) Merced County	2,493
Wausau, WI (city) Marathon County	2,112
Parkway-S. Sacramento, CA (cdp) Sacramento County	1,621
Appleton, WI (city) Outagamie County	1,426
Sheboygan, WI (city) Sheboygan County	1,372
Green Bay, WI (city) Brown County	1,173
Linda, CA (cdp) Yuba County	1,064
Madison, WI (city) Dane County	1,047
Detroit, MI (city) Wayne County	1,044
Clovis, CA (city) Fresno County	808
La Crosse, WI (city) La Crosse County	733
Eau Claire, WI (city) Eau Claire County	680
Brooklyn Center, MN (city) Hennepin County	664
Brooklyn Park, MN (city) Hennepin County	656
Chico, CA (city) Butte County	586
San Diego, CA (city) San Diego County	576
Oshkosh, WI (city) Winnebago County	573
Manitowoc, WI (city) Manitowoc County	514
Florin, CA (cdp) Sacramento County	508
Westminster, CO (city) Adams County	499
Portland, OR (city) Multnomah County	473
Pontiac, MI (city) Oakland County	464
Providence, RI (city) Providence County	439
Thermalito, CA (cdp) Butte County	438
Lansing, MI (city) Ingham County	426
South Oroville, CA (cdp) Butte County	410
Warren, MI (city) Macomb County	403
Hickory, NC (city) Catawba County	387
Willows, CA (city) Glenn County	387
Stevens Point, WI (city) Portage County	379
Charlotte, NC (city) Mecklenburg County	319
Kansas City, KS (city) Wyandotte County	298
Santa Ana, CA (city) Orange County	298
Wisconsin Rapids, WI (city) Wood County	297
Oroville, CA (city) Butte County	290
West Sacramento, CA (city) Yolo County	269
Spokane, WA (city) Spokane County	265
Fitchburg, MA (city) Worcester County	262
Visalia, CA (city) Tulare County	250
Atwater, CA (city) Merced County	244
Rochester, MN (city) Olmsted County	226
Fond du Lac, WI (city) Fond du Lac County	186
Woodbury, MN (city) Washington County	185
Arden-Arcade, CA (cdp) Sacramento County	174
Maplewood, MN (city) Ramsey County	166
Glen Alpine, NC (town) Burke County	135
Modesto, CA (city) Stanislaus County	132
Valdese, NC (town) Burke County	52
Connelly Springs, NC (town) Burke County	40

Notes: Please refer to the User's Guide for an explanation of data; ranking tables include all places with Asian and/or NHPI populations above SF4 population thresholds; (1) tables reflect only those areas that meet SF4 population thresholds, therefore there may be less than 50 states, 75 counties or 75 places listed

Foreign Born

Hmong

All States, Top 75 Counties, and Top 75 Places Sorted by Percent[1]

State	Percent
Rhode Island	63.06
Washington	61.24
Michigan	60.12
Pennsylvania	58.50
Wisconsin	57.35
Minnesota	56.89
United States	55.62
California	54.91
Oklahoma	52.54
Colorado	52.42
North Carolina	51.97
Georgia	51.17
Massachusetts	48.44
Oregon	47.18
Alaska	46.36
South Carolina	43.84
Kansas	40.82

County	Percent
Fond du Lac County, WI	77.74
Glenn County, CA	68.98
Butte County, CA	67.78
Spokane County, WA	66.79
Wayne County, MI	66.67
Providence County, RI	63.90
Lancaster County, PA	61.57
Oakland County, MI	61.52
Ingham County, MI	61.34
Manitowoc County, WI	60.92
Outagamie County, WI	60.05
Anoka County, MN	59.89
Brown County, WI	59.78
Calumet County, WI	59.63
Marathon County, WI	59.29
Milwaukee County, WI	58.44
Merced County, CA	58.01
Ramsey County, MN	57.78
Wood County, WI	57.70
Dane County, WI	56.99
King County, WA	56.69
Olmsted County, MN	56.50
Sheboygan County, WI	56.42
Mecklenburg County, NC	56.06
Sacramento County, CA	55.90
Hennepin County, MN	55.46
Stanly County, NC	55.35
Dunn County, WI	55.14
Fresno County, CA	54.78
Adams County, CO	54.76
San Diego County, CA	54.69
Barrow County, GA	54.08
Winnebago County, WI	54.05
La Crosse County, WI	53.89
Tulare County, CA	53.45
Orange County, CA	53.27
Catawba County, NC	53.07
Burke County, NC	52.62
Macomb County, MI	51.76
Solano County, CA	51.58
San Joaquin County, CA	51.50
Portage County, WI	51.32
Yuba County, CA	51.26
Eau Claire County, WI	49.49
Multnomah County, OR	49.20
Washington County, MN	48.12
Yolo County, CA	47.67
Worcester County, MA	46.76
Anchorage Borough, AK	46.36
Spartanburg County, SC	43.60
Santa Barbara County, CA	43.38
Los Angeles County, CA	42.73
Riverside County, CA	41.68
Jefferson County, CO	39.81
Wyandotte County, KS	38.25
Stanislaus County, CA	38.08
Chippewa County, WI	32.31

Place	Percent
Fond du Lac, WI (city) Fond du Lac County	89.00
Chico, CA (city) Butte County	80.38
Hickory, NC (city) Catawba County	71.27
Thermalito, CA (cdp) Butte County	69.86
Willows, CA (city) Glenn County	68.98
South Oroville, CA (cdp) Butte County	67.43
Lansing, MI (city) Ingham County	66.05
Providence, RI (city) Providence County	65.13
Spokane, WA (city) Spokane County	64.48
Pontiac, MI (city) Oakland County	64.09
Detroit, MI (city) Wayne County	63.74
Manitowoc, WI (city) Manitowoc County	62.61
Atwater, CA (city) Merced County	62.09
Glen Alpine, NC (town) Burke County	61.93
Wausau, WI (city) Marathon County	61.50
Appleton, WI (city) Outagamie County	61.18
Oroville, CA (city) Butte County	60.04
Brooklyn Park, MN (city) Hennepin County	59.64
Merced, CA (city) Merced County	58.96
Parkway-S. Sacramento, CA (cdp) Sacramento County	58.95
Milwaukee, WI (city) Milwaukee County	58.74
St. Paul, MN (city) Ramsey County	58.37
Green Bay, WI (city) Brown County	58.01
Madison, WI (city) Dane County	57.56
Sheboygan, WI (city) Sheboygan County	57.48
Wisconsin Rapids, WI (city) Wood County	57.12
Rochester, MN (city) Olmsted County	56.50
Santa Ana, CA (city) Orange County	56.44
Minneapolis, MN (city) Hennepin County	56.20
Charlotte, NC (city) Mecklenburg County	56.06
Fresno, CA (city) Fresno County	55.98
Sacramento, CA (city) Sacramento County	55.96
La Crosse, WI (city) La Crosse County	54.62
Warren, MI (city) Macomb County	53.81
San Diego, CA (city) San Diego County	52.75
Connelly Springs, NC (town) Burke County	52.63
Woodbury, MN (city) Washington County	52.41
Linda, CA (cdp) Yuba County	52.39
Stockton, CA (city) San Joaquin County	52.27
Oshkosh, WI (city) Winnebago County	51.90
Portland, OR (city) Multnomah County	50.81
Stevens Point, WI (city) Portage County	50.07
Arden-Arcade, CA (cdp) Sacramento County	49.57
Westminster, CO (city) Adams County	49.16
Florin, CA (cdp) Sacramento County	47.88
Eau Claire, WI (city) Eau Claire County	46.96
West Sacramento, CA (city) Yolo County	46.46
Visalia, CA (city) Tulare County	46.21
Brooklyn Center, MN (city) Hennepin County	45.73
Clovis, CA (city) Fresno County	44.91
Valdese, NC (town) Burke County	44.44
Fitchburg, MA (city) Worcester County	43.09
Maplewood, MN (city) Ramsey County	41.92
Kansas City, KS (city) Wyandotte County	38.25
Modesto, CA (city) Stanislaus County	32.51

Notes: Please refer to the User's Guide for an explanation of data; ranking tables include all places with Asian and/or NHPI populations above SF4 population thresholds; (1) tables reflect only those areas that meet SF4 population thresholds, therefore there may be less than 50 states, 75 counties or 75 places listed

Foreign Born

Indonesian

All States, Top 75 Counties, and Top 75 Places Sorted by Number[1]

State	Number
United States	30,788
California	12,811
New York	1,967
Texas	1,591
Washington	1,113
Virginia	962
Ohio	925
Maryland	881
Illinois	852
New Jersey	841
Florida	801
Colorado	649
Michigan	602
Massachusetts	568
Oregon	528
Georgia	471
Arizona	469
Pennsylvania	460
Wisconsin	366

County	Number
Los Angeles County, CA	4,553
San Bernardino County, CA	2,431
Orange County, CA	1,500
Queens County, NY	1,007
San Francisco County, CA	783
King County, WA	732
Montgomery County, MD	726
Harris County, TX	651
San Mateo County, CA	605
Santa Clara County, CA	552
Franklin County, OH	517
Fairfax County, VA	506
Cook County, IL	453
Alameda County, CA	417
Middlesex County, NJ	416
Contra Costa County, CA	386
San Diego County, CA	373
Maricopa County, AZ	325

Place	Number
Los Angeles, CA (city) Los Angeles County	1,465
New York, NY (city)	1,412
San Francisco, CA (city) San Francisco County	783
Houston, TX (city) Harris County	503
Columbus, OH (city) Franklin County	501
Loma Linda, CA (city) San Bernardino County	405
Seattle, WA (city) King County	343
San Bernardino, CA (city) San Bernardino County	255

Notes: Please refer to the User's Guide for an explanation of data; ranking tables include all places with Asian and/or NHPI populations above SF4 population thresholds; (1) tables reflect only those areas that meet SF4 population thresholds, therefore there may be less than 50 states, 75 counties or 75 places listed

Foreign Born

Indonesian

All States, Top 75 Counties, and Top 75 Places Sorted by Percent[1]

State	Percent
Michigan	92.33
Wisconsin	90.15
Texas	89.84
Washington	89.61
Florida	89.60
Illinois	89.12
Virginia	87.85
Ohio	87.18
Pennsylvania	85.82
Georgia	85.64
Colorado	84.29
United States	82.84
New Jersey	82.45
Oregon	82.37
Arizona	81.85
New York	80.85
Massachusetts	80.00
Maryland	79.51
California	78.17

County	Percent
Franklin County, OH	97.55
Harris County, TX	94.35
Cook County, IL	91.70
San Francisco County, CA	89.69
King County, WA	88.19
Middlesex County, NJ	85.25
Fairfax County, VA	85.04
Contra Costa County, CA	81.61
Queens County, NY	81.01
Los Angeles County, CA	80.93
Santa Clara County, CA	80.35
San Mateo County, CA	80.03
Maricopa County, AZ	78.88
Orange County, CA	78.62
Montgomery County, MD	78.23
San Diego County, CA	76.12
San Bernardino County, CA	73.64
Alameda County, CA	64.85

Place	Percent
Columbus, OH (city) Franklin County	97.47
Houston, TX (city) Harris County	97.29
Seattle, WA (city) King County	90.74
San Francisco, CA (city) San Francisco County	89.69
Los Angeles, CA (city) Los Angeles County	81.84
New York, NY (city)	77.75
Loma Linda, CA (city) San Bernardino County	77.59
San Bernardino, CA (city) San Bernardino County	56.79

Notes: Please refer to the User's Guide for an explanation of data; ranking tables include all places with Asian and/or NHPI populations above SF4 population thresholds; (1) tables reflect only those areas that meet SF4 population thresholds, therefore there may be less than 50 states, 75 counties or 75 places listed

Foreign Born

Japanese

All States, Top 75 Counties, and Top 75 Places Sorted by Number[1]

State	Number
United States	314,178
California	104,729
New York	29,888
Hawaii	19,644
Washington	15,363
Illinois	11,467
New Jersey	10,518
Texas	10,507
Massachusetts	8,377
Michigan	8,090
Florida	7,916
Ohio	7,195
Virginia	5,956
Oregon	5,666
Georgia	5,662
Pennsylvania	5,114
Maryland	4,625
Colorado	4,253
North Carolina	4,078
Arizona	3,841
Nevada	3,627
Indiana	3,487
Connecticut	3,309
Tennessee	3,051
Kentucky	2,743
Minnesota	2,473
Missouri	2,212
Wisconsin	1,869
Oklahoma	1,840
Utah	1,840
South Carolina	1,663
Alabama	1,365
Kansas	1,251
Louisiana	997
Iowa	892
New Mexico	822
Arkansas	787
Nebraska	761
West Virginia	734
Idaho	728
District of Columbia	718
Alaska	577
New Hampshire	571
Rhode Island	510
Mississippi	444
Maine	440
Delaware	393
Montana	365
Vermont	286
Wyoming	250
South Dakota	193

County	Number
Los Angeles County, CA	39,898
Honolulu County, HI	17,257
New York County, NY	11,512
Orange County, CA	11,251
San Diego County, CA	10,263
Santa Clara County, CA	10,203
King County, WA	8,253
Cook County, IL	7,556
Westchester County, NY	6,315
Bergen County, NJ	5,865
San Francisco County, CA	5,085
Queens County, NY	4,419
San Mateo County, CA	4,043
Alameda County, CA	3,869
Oakland County, MI	3,442
Middlesex County, MA	2,912
Clark County, NV	2,851
Franklin County, OH	2,554
Sacramento County, CA	2,480
Harris County, TX	2,374
Contra Costa County, CA	2,336
Maricopa County, AZ	2,327
Montgomery County, MD	2,297
Fairfield County, CT	2,038
Fairfax County, VA	2,025
Ventura County, CA	1,992
Pierce County, WA	1,851
Riverside County, CA	1,842
Suffolk County, MA	1,825
Norfolk County, MA	1,632
Kings County, NY	1,582
Dallas County, TX	1,570
Multnomah County, OR	1,526
Nassau County, NY	1,508
Monterey County, CA	1,498
Hawaii County, HI	1,440
Washtenaw County, MI	1,435
Washington County, OR	1,413
San Bernardino County, CA	1,361
Miami-Dade County, FL	1,180
Snohomish County, WA	1,093
Allegheny County, PA	967
Bexar County, TX	958
Fresno County, CA	956
Lake County, IL	955
Hennepin County, MN	946
Solano County, CA	925
Pima County, AZ	919
Orange County, FL	911
Lane County, OR	855
Travis County, TX	850
DuPage County, IL	843
Arlington County, VA	830
Cobb County, GA	817
Salt Lake County, UT	816
Santa Barbara County, CA	812
St. Louis County, MO	803
Denver County, CO	800
El Paso County, CO	799
Fayette County, KY	794
Philadelphia County, PA	792
Oklahoma County, OK	791
Cuyahoga County, OH	763
DeKalb County, GA	754
Wayne County, MI	740
Broward County, FL	725
Hudson County, NJ	712
Suffolk County, NY	709
Essex County, MA	702
Tarrant County, TX	697
Collin County, TX	694
Maui County, HI	689
Marin County, CA	681
Fulton County, GA	675
Arapahoe County, CO	666

Place	Number
New York, NY (city)	18,017
Los Angeles, CA (city) Los Angeles County	14,534
Honolulu, HI (cdp) Honolulu County	12,356
San Diego, CA (city) San Diego County	5,888
Torrance, CA (city) Los Angeles County	5,229
San Francisco, CA (city) San Francisco County	5,085
San Jose, CA (city) Santa Clara County	3,223
Irvine, CA (city) Orange County	3,219
Seattle, WA (city) King County	3,182
Chicago, IL (city) Cook County	2,120
Sunnyvale, CA (city) Santa Clara County	1,832
Boston, MA (city) Suffolk County	1,803
Houston, TX (city) Harris County	1,745
Rancho Palos Verdes, CA (city) Los Angeles County	1,710
Gardena, CA (city) Los Angeles County	1,688
Cupertino, CA (city) Santa Clara County	1,687
Greenburgh, NY (town) Westchester County	1,685
Fort Lee, NJ (borough) Bergen County	1,682
Bellevue, WA (city) King County	1,511
Columbus, OH (city) Franklin County	1,395
Portland, OR (city) Multnomah County	1,342
Chula Vista, CA (city) San Diego County	1,236
Greenwich, CT (town) Fairfield County	1,207
Long Beach, CA (city) Los Angeles County	1,193
West Bloomfield, MI (township) Oakland County	1,180
Monterey Park, CA (city) Los Angeles County	1,128
Ann Arbor, MI (city) Washtenaw County	1,096
Brookline, MA (town) Norfolk County	1,082
Eastchester, NY (town) Westchester County	1,060
Novi, MI (city) Oakland County	971
Las Vegas, NV (city) Clark County	955
Santa Monica, CA (city) Los Angeles County	931
Cambridge, MA (city) Middlesex County	885
Huntington Beach, CA (city) Orange County	847
Arlington, VA (cdp) Arlington County	830
North Hempstead, NY (town) Nassau County	830
Sacramento, CA (city) Sacramento County	809
Glendale, CA (city) Los Angeles County	808
Pasadena, CA (city) Los Angeles County	801
Denver, CO (city) Denver County	800
Austin, TX (city) Travis County	797
Lexington-Fayette, KY (sp. city) Fayette County	794
Philadelphia, PA (city) Philadelphia County	792
Phoenix, AZ (city) Maricopa County	792
Costa Mesa, CA (city) Orange County	788
Schaumburg, IL (village) Cook County	774
San Mateo, CA (city) San Mateo County	772
Foster City, CA (city) San Mateo County	770
Arlington Heights, IL (village) Cook County	764
San Antonio, TX (city) Bexar County	746
Hoffman Estates, IL (village) Cook County	737
Redondo Beach, CA (city) Los Angeles County	734
Anaheim, CA (city) Orange County	724
Dublin, OH (city) Franklin County	715
Pittsburgh, PA (city) Allegheny County	712
Berkeley, CA (city) Alameda County	696
Arcadia, CA (city) Los Angeles County	688
Eugene, OR (city) Lane County	678
Tucson, AZ (city) Pima County	671
Mountain View, CA (city) Santa Clara County	661
Harrison, NY (village) Westchester County	648
Scarsdale, NY (village) Westchester County	637
Oakland, CA (city) Alameda County	634
Alhambra, CA (city) Los Angeles County	629
Palo Alto, CA (city) Santa Clara County	622
Pearl City, HI (cdp) Honolulu County	606
Nashville-Davidson, TN (sp. city) Davidson County	605
Fresno, CA (city) Fresno County	599
Hilo, HI (cdp) Hawaii County	587
Rye, NY (city) Westchester County	585
Dallas, TX (city) Dallas County	582
Oxnard, CA (city) Ventura County	569
Madison, WI (city) Dane County	554
El Paso, TX (city) El Paso County	552
Oceanside, CA (city) San Diego County	548

Notes: Please refer to the User's Guide for an explanation of data; ranking tables include all places with Asian and/or NHPI populations above SF4 population thresholds; (1) tables reflect only those areas that meet SF4 population thresholds, therefore there may be less than 50 states, 75 counties or 75 places listed

Foreign Born

Japanese

All States, Top 75 Counties, and Top 75 Places Sorted by Percent[1]

State	Percent
Kentucky	86.34
West Virginia	83.50
Mississippi	82.53
New York	79.50
Tennessee	78.88
Massachusetts	76.45
New Jersey	76.33
Vermont	76.06
Michigan	75.99
Georgia	75.38
Maine	74.32
South Carolina	72.87
Connecticut	72.69
Indiana	72.46
Alabama	72.15
Arkansas	71.94
Pennsylvania	71.17
Louisiana	69.96
Ohio	69.92
Florida	69.77
Iowa	69.42
District of Columbia	69.24
Kansas	68.25
North Carolina	67.55
Virginia	67.27
Maryland	66.83
Oklahoma	65.95
Texas	65.20
Rhode Island	64.97
Delaware	64.96
Missouri	64.58
Wisconsin	62.59
New Hampshire	61.00
Minnesota	59.12
Illinois	55.04
Nebraska	55.03
Arizona	51.58
Oregon	48.63
Wyoming	47.80
South Dakota	46.84
Nevada	43.20
Montana	42.94
Washington	41.19
Alaska	40.49
New Mexico	39.81
United States	39.52
California	36.22
Colorado	35.76
Utah	30.77
Idaho	27.46
Hawaii	9.80

County	Percent
Boone County, KY	94.55
Orange County, NC	88.10
Fayette County, KY	87.44
Fayette County, GA	86.69
DeKalb County, GA	84.53
Nassau County, NY	84.39
Westchester County, NY	84.18
Miami-Dade County, FL	84.05
Washtenaw County, MI	83.97
Bergen County, NJ	83.82
Queens County, NY	83.65
Olmsted County, MN	82.75
Cobb County, GA	82.19
New York County, NY	81.43
Suffolk County, MA	80.43
Oakland County, MI	80.38
Calhoun County, MI	80.04
Baltimore County, MD	79.88
Allegheny County, PA	79.46
Franklin County, OH	79.14
Durham County, NC	78.76
Oklahoma County, OK	78.71
Morris County, NJ	78.68
Norfolk County, MA	78.46
Tippecanoe County, IN	78.46
Pinellas County, FL	78.17
Fairfield County, CT	77.17
Tompkins County, NY	76.12
Hudson County, NJ	76.07
Middlesex County, NJ	75.98
Collin County, TX	75.93
Orange County, FL	75.92
Dane County, WI	75.47
Delaware County, PA	75.14
Middlesex County, MA	75.13
Worcester County, MA	74.94
Davidson County, TN	74.85
Shelby County, TN	74.56
Summit County, OH	73.55
Arlington County, VA	73.06
Ingham County, MI	72.99
El Paso County, TX	72.77
Montgomery County, MD	72.71
Kings County, NY	72.70
Bronx County, NY	72.25
Fulton County, GA	72.12
Jefferson County, KY	71.83
Philadelphia County, PA	71.67
Burlington County, NJ	71.57
Marion County, OR	70.72
Wayne County, MI	70.68
Alachua County, FL	70.67
Dallas County, TX	70.59
Hamilton County, OH	70.28
Essex County, NJ	70.17
Travis County, TX	69.96
Denton County, TX	69.87
Palm Beach County, FL	69.69
Fairfax County, VA	69.66
Broward County, FL	69.38
New Haven County, CT	69.21
Gwinnett County, GA	68.94
Essex County, MA	68.82
Bell County, TX	68.59
Prince George's County, MD	68.08
Hartford County, CT	68.02
Suffolk County, NY	67.91
Onslow County, NC	67.76
Virginia Beach Independent City, VA	67.56
Tarrant County, TX	67.47
Chester County, PA	67.25
Lane County, OR	66.74
St. Louis County, MO	66.31
Mecklenburg County, NC	66.19
Duval County, FL	65.82

Place	Percent
Greenville, NY (cdp) Westchester County	97.96
Harrison, NY (village) Westchester County	93.51
West Bloomfield, MI (township) Oakland County	92.77
Ridgewood, NJ (village) Bergen County	91.50
Eastchester, NY (cdp) Westchester County	90.89
Rye, NY (city) Westchester County	90.70
McLean, VA (cdp) Fairfax County	89.29
Hoffman Estates, IL (village) Cook County	88.16
Cliffside Park, NJ (borough) Bergen County	88.12
Buffalo Grove, IL (village) Lake County	87.73
Eastchester, NY (town) Westchester County	87.60
Lexington-Fayette, KY (sp. city) Fayette County	87.44
Greenwich, CT (town) Fairfield County	87.27
Dublin, OH (city) Franklin County	87.20
Peachtree City, GA (city) Fayette County	87.09
North Hempstead, NY (town) Nassau County	86.91
Rockville, MD (city) Montgomery County	86.49
Ann Arbor, MI (city) Washtenaw County	86.10
Greenburgh, NY (town) Westchester County	86.10
North Bethesda, MD (cdp) Montgomery County	85.82
Novi, MI (city) Oakland County	84.58
Oyster Bay, NY (town) Nassau County	84.22
Fort Lee, NJ (borough) Bergen County	83.76
Cambridge, MA (city) Middlesex County	83.25
Elk Grove Village, IL (village) Cook County	82.79
Schaumburg, IL (village) Cook County	82.34
Brookline, MA (town) Norfolk County	81.66
Scarsdale, NY (village) Westchester County	81.25
Pittsburgh, PA (city) Allegheny County	80.82
New York, NY (city)	80.79
Boston, MA (city) Suffolk County	80.67
Madison, WI (city) Dane County	80.41
Battle Creek, MI (city) Calhoun County	80.36
Bethesda, MD (cdp) Montgomery County	79.86
Oklahoma City, OK (city) Oklahoma County	79.74
Irving, TX (city) Dallas County	77.73
Arlington Heights, IL (village) Cook County	76.86
Columbus, OH (city) Franklin County	75.61
Plano, TX (city) Collin County	75.55
Hempstead, NY (town) Nassau County	75.52
Nashville-Davidson, TN (sp. city) Davidson County	73.69
El Paso, TX (city) El Paso County	73.60
Arlington, VA (cdp) Arlington County	73.06
Salem, OR (city) Marion County	72.94
Houston, TX (city) Harris County	72.50
Eugene, OR (city) Lane County	71.97
Philadelphia, PA (city) Philadelphia County	71.67
Pullman, WA (city) Whitman County	70.28
Austin, TX (city) Travis County	70.22
Minneapolis, MN (city) Hennepin County	70.21
Cupertino, CA (city) Santa Clara County	69.80
Cary, NC (town) Wake County	69.55
Charlotte, NC (city) Mecklenburg County	68.93
Beaverton, OR (city) Washington County	68.14
Wilmette, IL (village) Cook County	67.92
Dallas, TX (city) Dallas County	67.91
Tucson, AZ (city) Pima County	67.37
Brookhaven, NY (town) Suffolk County	67.15
Rolling Hills Estates, CA (city) Los Angeles County	66.77
Lakewood, WA (city) Pierce County	65.37
Evanston, IL (city) Cook County	65.16
Vista, CA (city) San Diego County	64.69
Jacksonville, FL (city) Duval County	64.60
Mount Prospect, IL (village) Cook County	64.27
Glenview, IL (village) Cook County	63.69
Omaha, NE (city) Douglas County	63.13
Irvine, CA (city) Orange County	62.69
Menlo Park, CA (city) San Mateo County	62.03
Chula Vista, CA (city) San Diego County	61.13
Arcadia, CA (city) Los Angeles County	59.93
Lake Forest, CA (city) Orange County	59.93
Provo, UT (city) Utah County	58.43
Millbrae, CA (city) San Mateo County	58.37
Seaside, CA (city) Monterey County	57.89
Burlingame, CA (city) San Mateo County	57.88

Notes: Please refer to the User's Guide for an explanation of data; ranking tables include all places with Asian and/or NHPI populations above SF4 population thresholds; (1) tables reflect only those areas that meet SF4 population thresholds, therefore there may be less than 50 states, 75 counties or 75 places listed

Foreign Born

Korean

All States, Top 75 Counties, and Top 75 Places Sorted by Number[1]

State	Number
United States	833,454
California	261,782
New York	96,184
New Jersey	50,953
Illinois	39,638
Washington	36,214
Virginia	36,120
Texas	34,378
Maryland	30,445
Pennsylvania	25,590
Georgia	21,859
Michigan	17,107
Hawaii	16,655
Florida	15,001
Massachusetts	12,979
Colorado	11,780
Minnesota	11,241
Ohio	10,873
Oregon	9,911
North Carolina	9,516
Arizona	7,698
Wisconsin	5,802
Indiana	5,798
Nevada	5,669
Tennessee	5,603
Connecticut	5,336
Missouri	5,021
Iowa	4,007
Oklahoma	3,778
Alaska	3,540
Kansas	3,324
Kentucky	3,276
Alabama	3,272
Utah	2,832
South Carolina	2,748
Louisiana	2,012
Nebraska	1,868
New Hampshire	1,557
Delaware	1,536
Rhode Island	1,317
New Mexico	1,306
Arkansas	1,134
Mississippi	1,120
Idaho	993
District of Columbia	874
West Virginia	730
Montana	713
South Dakota	604
Vermont	601
Maine	524
Wyoming	396
North Dakota	239

County	Number
Los Angeles County, CA	143,977
Queens County, NY	51,479
Orange County, CA	43,144
Bergen County, NJ	29,122
Cook County, IL	27,100
Fairfax County, VA	22,492
Santa Clara County, CA	16,838
King County, WA	15,671
Honolulu County, HI	15,303
Montgomery County, MD	11,936
Alameda County, CA	10,584
Pierce County, WA	8,736
San Diego County, CA	8,397
New York County, NY	8,020
Dallas County, TX	7,416
Gwinnett County, GA	7,313
Montgomery County, PA	7,019
Nassau County, NY	6,659
Harris County, TX	6,550
Snohomish County, WA	5,862
San Francisco County, CA	5,352
Kings County, NY	5,252
Middlesex County, MA	5,193
San Bernardino County, CA	5,033
Philadelphia County, PA	4,948
Clark County, NV	4,905
Maricopa County, AZ	4,770
Howard County, MD	4,601
Riverside County, CA	4,080
Middlesex County, NJ	4,076
Hennepin County, MN	4,072
Baltimore County, MD	3,990
Oakland County, MI	3,835
Sacramento County, CA	3,447
San Mateo County, CA	3,419
Arapahoe County, CO	3,326
Westchester County, NY	3,307
DuPage County, IL	3,251
Washington County, OR	3,237
Contra Costa County, CA	3,227
Fulton County, GA	3,120
Suffolk County, NY	3,083
El Paso County, CO	3,056
Prince George's County, MD	2,949
Bronx County, NY	2,945
Travis County, TX	2,940
DeKalb County, GA	2,868
Lake County, IL	2,839
Anne Arundel County, MD	2,819
Washtenaw County, MI	2,815
Delaware County, PA	2,688
Anchorage Borough, AK	2,648
Hudson County, NJ	2,630
Franklin County, OH	2,605
Richmond County, NY	2,590
Tarrant County, TX	2,492
Cobb County, GA	2,379
Monterey County, CA	2,141
Collin County, TX	2,103
Hillsborough County, FL	2,087
Monroe County, NY	2,083
Ventura County, CA	2,044
Essex County, NJ	2,036
Morris County, NJ	2,021
Bell County, TX	1,978
St. Louis County, MO	1,976
Suffolk County, MA	1,970
Bexar County, TX	1,955
Multnomah County, OR	1,949
Mecklenburg County, NC	1,892
Champaign County, IL	1,778
Ramsey County, MN	1,767
Allegheny County, PA	1,760
Broward County, FL	1,727
Norfolk County, MA	1,697

Place	Number
Los Angeles, CA (city) Los Angeles County	73,077
New York, NY (city)	70,286
Honolulu, HI (cdp) Honolulu County	11,399
Chicago, IL (city) Cook County	10,011
Glendale, CA (city) Los Angeles County	9,626
San Jose, CA (city) Santa Clara County	7,221
Fullerton, CA (city) Orange County	6,485
Torrance, CA (city) Los Angeles County	6,407
Cerritos, CA (city) Los Angeles County	6,200
Irvine, CA (city) Orange County	5,828
San Francisco, CA (city) San Francisco County	5,352
Anaheim, CA (city) Orange County	5,117
San Diego, CA (city) San Diego County	4,997
Palisades Park, NJ (borough) Bergen County	4,988
Philadelphia, PA (city) Philadelphia County	4,948
Fort Lee, NJ (borough) Bergen County	4,834
Garden Grove, CA (city) Orange County	4,807
Houston, TX (city) Harris County	4,200
Buena Park, CA (city) Orange County	4,118
Diamond Bar, CA (city) Los Angeles County	4,080
Seattle, WA (city) King County	3,957
Federal Way, WA (city) King County	3,435
Gardena, CA (city) Los Angeles County	3,045
Rowland Heights, CA (cdp) Los Angeles County	2,912
Annandale, VA (cdp) Fairfax County	2,869
Fremont, CA (city) Alameda County	2,763
Dallas, TX (city) Dallas County	2,723
Austin, TX (city) Travis County	2,567
Downey, CA (city) Los Angeles County	2,471
Burke, VA (cdp) Fairfax County	2,460
Tacoma, WA (city) Pierce County	2,424
Colorado Springs, CO (city) El Paso County	2,320
North Hempstead, NY (town) Nassau County	2,319
Ellicott City, MD (cdp) Howard County	2,227
Hempstead, NY (town) Nassau County	2,195
Sunnyvale, CA (city) Santa Clara County	2,124
Norwalk, CA (city) Los Angeles County	2,069
Columbus, OH (city) Franklin County	2,019
Skokie, IL (village) Cook County	2,008
La Palma, CA (city) Orange County	1,955
Irving, TX (city) Dallas County	1,939
Cypress, CA (city) Orange County	1,928
Aurora, CO (city) Arapahoe County	1,920
Ann Arbor, MI (city) Washtenaw County	1,902
Hacienda Heights, CA (cdp) Los Angeles County	1,889
Lakewood, WA (city) Pierce County	1,875
La Crescenta-Montrose, CA (cdp) Los Angeles County	1,870
Boston, MA (city) Suffolk County	1,822
La Mirada, CA (city) Los Angeles County	1,819
Rancho Palos Verdes, CA (city) Los Angeles County	1,814
Bellevue, WA (city) King County	1,813
Oyster Bay, NY (town) Nassau County	1,805
Santa Clara, CA (city) Santa Clara County	1,741
Cupertino, CA (city) Santa Clara County	1,707
Portland, OR (city) Multnomah County	1,677
Burbank, CA (city) Los Angeles County	1,547
Plano, TX (city) Collin County	1,545
Charlotte, NC (city) Mecklenburg County	1,534
San Antonio, TX (city) Bexar County	1,509
Phoenix, AZ (city) Maricopa County	1,496
Arcadia, CA (city) Los Angeles County	1,486
Madison, WI (city) Dane County	1,460
La Canada Flintridge, CA (city) Los Angeles County	1,458
Oakland, CA (city) Alameda County	1,362
Schaumburg, IL (village) Cook County	1,352
Killeen, TX (city) Bell County	1,349
Minneapolis, MN (city) Hennepin County	1,346
Centreville, VA (cdp) Fairfax County	1,318
Long Beach, CA (city) Los Angeles County	1,304
Walnut, CA (city) Los Angeles County	1,300
Jersey City, NJ (city) Hudson County	1,256
Huntington Beach, CA (city) Orange County	1,240
El Paso, TX (city) El Paso County	1,230
Cambridge, MA (city) Middlesex County	1,221
Cliffside Park, NJ (borough) Bergen County	1,216

Notes: Please refer to the User's Guide for an explanation of data; ranking tables include all places with Asian and/or NHPI populations above SF4 population thresholds; (1) tables reflect only those areas that meet SF4 population thresholds, therefore there may be less than 50 states, 75 counties or 75 places listed

Foreign Born

Korean

All States, Top 75 Counties, and Top 75 Places Sorted by Percent[1]

State	Percent
Vermont	88.38
Minnesota	87.46
Montana	84.98
Wisconsin	84.75
Wyoming	84.26
Nebraska	83.80
Delaware	83.03
Iowa	82.08
Indiana	81.67
Oklahoma	81.67
West Virginia	81.66
Michigan	81.41
Alabama	81.31
Mississippi	81.28
Tennessee	81.18
Kentucky	81.07
South Dakota	81.07
Virginia	80.16
New Hampshire	79.85
New York	79.64
Connecticut	79.33
New Jersey	79.21
Utah	79.06
Georgia	78.89
Florida	78.63
Ohio	78.30
Idaho	78.00
Washington	77.89
Maryland	77.84
Pennsylvania	77.83
Alaska	77.73
United States	77.70
South Carolina	77.50
Arizona	77.48
Texas	77.47
Oregon	77.34
Missouri	77.16
Colorado	77.03
North Carolina	76.72
Kansas	76.22
California	76.16
Illinois	76.11
Arkansas	75.80
New Mexico	75.19
District of Columbia	74.83
Nevada	74.77
Massachusetts	74.59
Louisiana	73.56
Maine	71.29
Hawaii	70.25
Rhode Island	68.49
North Dakota	65.48

County	Percent
St. Clair County, IL	98.27
Ocean County, NJ	96.84
Ottawa County, MI	95.70
Wicomico County, MD	92.54
Berks County, PA	91.40
Northampton County, PA	91.32
Alexandria Independent City, VA	90.76
Saginaw County, MI	90.53
Rensselaer County, NY	90.35
Anoka County, MN	90.25
Lancaster County, PA	90.14
Lancaster County, NE	88.98
Fairfax Independent City, VA	88.89
Ramsey County, MN	88.84
Onondaga County, NY	87.82
Saratoga County, NY	87.67
Dakota County, MN	87.33
Waukesha County, WI	87.33
Litchfield County, CT	87.23
Olmsted County, MN	87.20
Dane County, WI	86.99
DeKalb County, GA	86.91
Monroe County, IN	86.73
St. Joseph County, IN	86.71
Montgomery County, TN	86.68
Brevard County, FL	86.63
Ingham County, MI	86.38
Kitsap County, WA	86.37
Cochise County, AZ	86.18
Oklahoma County, OK	86.16
St. Louis County, MN	86.15
Hennepin County, MN	86.11
Chatham County, GA	86.06
Greene County, OH	85.96
Liberty County, GA	85.94
Lane County, OR	85.71
Geary County, KS	85.68
Imperial County, CA	85.60
Frederick County, MD	85.58
Lake County, IN	85.42
Kane County, IL	85.18
Kent County, MI	85.12
Bronx County, NY	85.07
Story County, IA	84.89
Johnson County, IA	84.69
Brazos County, TX	84.58
Fairbanks North Star Borough, AK	84.49
Jefferson Parish, LA	84.49
Fairfield County, CT	84.37
Bristol County, MA	84.34
Ada County, ID	84.26
Newport News Independent City, VA	84.21
Jefferson County, KY	84.14
Henrico County, VA	83.71
Jefferson County, AL	83.62
Winnebago County, IL	83.62
Bell County, TX	83.53
Hillsborough County, NH	83.53
Centre County, PA	83.43
Pinellas County, FL	83.37
Monroe County, NY	83.15
Milwaukee County, WI	83.06
Alachua County, FL	82.89
Comanche County, OK	82.78
Queens County, NY	82.69
Duval County, FL	82.52
Wayne County, MI	82.47
Davidson County, TN	82.46
Macomb County, MI	82.18
Douglas County, NE	82.15
Passaic County, NJ	82.06
Hudson County, NJ	82.03
Utah County, UT	81.99
Marion County, IN	81.98
Adams County, CO	81.76

Place	Percent
Dunwoody, GA (cdp) De Kalb County	95.75
Silver Spring, MD (cdp) Montgomery County	93.78
Hedwig Village, TX (city) Harris County	92.44
Salt Lake City, UT (city) Salt Lake County	91.94
St. Paul, MN (city) Ramsey County	91.89
Canton, MI (township) Wayne County	90.97
Westminster, CO (city) Adams County	90.05
Redmond, WA (city) King County	89.92
Merrifield, VA (cdp) Fairfax County	89.87
Hinesville, GA (city) Liberty County	89.24
Hackensack, NJ (city) Bergen County	88.89
Montebello, CA (city) Los Angeles County	88.85
Sierra Vista, AZ (city) Cochise County	88.74
Edgewater, NJ (borough) Bergen County	88.57
East Lansing, MI (city) Ingham County	88.48
Lincoln, NE (city) Lancaster County	88.44
Cheltenham, PA (township) Montgomery County	88.38
Bloomington, IN (city) Monroe County	87.85
Columbia, SC (city) Richland County	87.84
Oakton, VA (cdp) Fairfax County	87.57
Rochester Hills, MI (city) Oakland County	87.10
Rochester, MN (city) Olmsted County	87.07
Clarksville, TN (city) Montgomery County	86.71
Beltsville, MD (cdp) Prince George's County	86.62
McLean, VA (cdp) Fairfax County	86.42
Madison, WI (city) Dane County	86.19
South Pasadena, CA (city) Los Angeles County	86.01
Killeen, TX (city) Bell County	85.92
Niles, IL (village) Cook County	85.67
Tempe, AZ (city) Maricopa County	85.65
Eugene, OR (city) Lane County	85.59
Tysons Corner, VA (cdp) Fairfax County	85.50
Annandale, VA (cdp) Fairfax County	85.49
Ridgewood, NJ (village) Bergen County	85.44
West Springfield, VA (cdp) Fairfax County	85.34
Costa Mesa, CA (city) Orange County	85.25
Chula Vista, CA (city) San Diego County	85.23
Yonkers, NY (city) Westchester County	85.14
Milpitas, CA (city) Santa Clara County	85.06
Babylon, NY (town) Suffolk County	85.00
White Oak, MD (cdp) Montgomery County	84.98
Jersey City, NJ (city) Hudson County	84.81
Demarest, NJ (borough) Bergen County	84.72
Ames, IA (city) Story County	84.70
Indianapolis, IN (sp. city) Marion County	84.67
Lawton, OK (city) Comanche County	84.66
Bloomfield, MI (township) Oakland County	84.58
Palisades Park, NJ (borough) Bergen County	84.51
Oklahoma City, OK (city) Oklahoma County	84.31
Santa Clara, CA (city) Santa Clara County	84.31
Rockville, MD (city) Montgomery County	84.27
Greenbelt, MD (city) Prince George's County	84.08
Cary, NC (town) Wake County	84.05
Richardson, TX (city) Dallas County	84.00
Lexington, MA (town) Middlesex County	83.85
Newark, CA (city) Alameda County	83.85
Arlington, TX (city) Tarrant County	83.77
Picnic Pt.-N. Lynnwood, WA (cdp) Snohomish County	83.58
Tulsa, OK (city) Tulsa County	83.44
Bayonne, NJ (city) Hudson County	83.39
Kentwood, MI (city) Kent County	83.37
Chantilly, VA (cdp) Fairfax County	83.30
Gaithersburg, MD (city) Montgomery County	83.28
Little Ferry, NJ (borough) Bergen County	83.20
Artesia, CA (city) Los Angeles County	82.97
Minneapolis, MN (city) Hennepin County	82.93
Syracuse, NY (city) Onondaga County	82.62
Mesa, AZ (city) Maricopa County	82.59
Wayne, NJ (township) Passaic County	82.57
Spanaway, WA (cdp) Pierce County	82.50
Stanton, CA (city) Orange County	82.47
Mountlake Terrace, WA (city) Snohomish County	82.33
Paradise, NV (cdp) Clark County	82.31
Louisville, KY (city) Jefferson County	82.29
Nashville-Davidson, TN (sp. city) Davidson County	82.27

Notes: Please refer to the User's Guide for an explanation of data; ranking tables include all places with Asian and/or NHPI populations above SF4 population thresholds; (1) tables reflect only those areas that meet SF4 population thresholds, therefore there may be less than 50 states, 75 counties or 75 places listed

Foreign Born

Laotian

All States, Top 75 Counties, and Top 75 Places Sorted by Number[1]

State	Number
United States	114,300
California	37,489
Texas	6,938
Minnesota	5,756
Washington	5,457
Illinois	3,464
North Carolina	3,317
Georgia	3,239
Florida	2,992
Tennessee	2,901
Iowa	2,767
Wisconsin	2,586
New York	2,475
Massachusetts	2,467
Oregon	2,412
Connecticut	2,314
Ohio	2,159
Virginia	2,135
Rhode Island	2,061
Kansas	2,055
Arkansas	1,938
Michigan	1,771
Colorado	1,637
Pennsylvania	1,566
Utah	1,469
Hawaii	1,261
Louisiana	915
Alaska	881
South Carolina	859
Nevada	849
Indiana	722
Oklahoma	689
Alabama	620
Arizona	599
Nebraska	577
Maryland	549
Missouri	532
Idaho	393
New Jersey	277
New Hampshire	238
South Dakota	143

County	Number
Sacramento County, CA	5,707
San Diego County, CA	5,011
Fresno County, CA	4,037
King County, WA	3,379
Contra Costa County, CA	2,932
Hennepin County, MN	2,910
Los Angeles County, CA	2,179
Tarrant County, TX	2,174
Tulare County, CA	2,148
Orange County, CA	2,054
Providence County, RI	1,960
San Joaquin County, CA	1,903
Alameda County, CA	1,886
Multnomah County, OR	1,652
Dallas County, TX	1,609
Santa Clara County, CA	1,402
Pinellas County, FL	1,388
Middlesex County, MA	1,241
Honolulu County, HI	1,230
Milwaukee County, WI	1,219
Shasta County, CA	1,218
Salt Lake County, UT	1,203
Merced County, CA	1,161
Polk County, IA	1,150
Rutherford County, TN	1,102
Stanislaus County, CA	1,094
Riverside County, CA	1,045
Cook County, IL	1,044
Fairfax County, VA	1,044
Monroe County, NY	1,038
Davidson County, TN	999
Hartford County, CT	923
Winnebago County, IL	923
Sebastian County, AR	901
Clayton County, GA	878
Harris County, TX	872
Philadelphia County, PA	860
Clark County, NV	837
Franklin County, OH	828
Anchorage Borough, AK	793
Sonoma County, CA	767
Gwinnett County, GA	758
Adams County, CO	752
Fairfield County, CT	746
Ottawa County, MI	745
Potter County, TX	717
Sedgwick County, KS	691
Kane County, IL	647
Iberia Parish, LA	638
Mecklenburg County, NC	636
Worcester County, MA	636
Jefferson County, CO	612
Ramsey County, MN	597
Summit County, OH	516
Johnson County, KS	511
Dakota County, MN	492
Washington County, OR	456
Buena Vista County, IA	449
Solano County, CA	440
Snohomish County, WA	435
Butte County, CA	431
Oklahoma County, OK	429
Maricopa County, AZ	423
Spartanburg County, SC	419
Broome County, NY	394
Guilford County, NC	394
New Haven County, CT	366
Washington County, AR	357
Habersham County, GA	349
Yolo County, CA	339
Burke County, NC	336
Pierce County, WA	332
San Bernardino County, CA	332
Catawba County, NC	307
Clark County, WA	300

Place	Number
San Diego, CA (city) San Diego County	4,246
Sacramento, CA (city) Sacramento County	3,734
Fresno, CA (city) Fresno County	3,558
Stockton, CA (city) San Joaquin County	1,840
Seattle, WA (city) King County	1,754
Richmond, CA (city) Contra Costa County	1,645
Visalia, CA (city) Tulare County	1,486
Portland, OR (city) Multnomah County	1,485
Oakland, CA (city) Alameda County	1,364
San Jose, CA (city) Santa Clara County	1,278
Redding, CA (city) Shasta County	1,086
Milwaukee, WI (city) Milwaukee County	1,050
Minneapolis, MN (city) Hennepin County	1,045
Lowell, MA (city) Middlesex County	1,036
Nashville-Davidson, TN (sp. city) Davidson County	999
Merced, CA (city) Merced County	977
Des Moines, IA (city) Polk County	954
Providence, RI (city) Providence County	923
Brooklyn Park, MN (city) Hennepin County	908
St. Petersburg, FL (city) Pinellas County	898
Fort Smith, AR (city) Sebastian County	889
Philadelphia, PA (city) Philadelphia County	860
Modesto, CA (city) Stanislaus County	822
San Pablo, CA (city) Contra Costa County	803
Parkway-S. Sacramento, CA (cdp) Sacramento County	791
Amarillo, TX (city) Potter County	731
Woonsocket, RI (city) Providence County	714
Columbus, OH (city) Franklin County	692
Honolulu, HI (cdp) Honolulu County	691
Elgin, IL (city) Kane County	675
Rockford, IL (city) Winnebago County	658
Dallas, TX (city) Dallas County	641
Santa Ana, CA (city) Orange County	627
Charlotte, NC (city) Mecklenburg County	625
Anaheim, CA (city) Orange County	624
Rochester, NY (city) Monroe County	606
St. Paul, MN (city) Ramsey County	542
Haltom City, TX (city) Tarrant County	531
Westminster, CO (city) Adams County	522
Los Angeles, CA (city) Los Angeles County	507
Santa Rosa, CA (city) Sonoma County	499
Murfreesboro, TN (city) Rutherford County	471
Wichita, KS (city) Sedgwick County	458
Long Beach, CA (city) Los Angeles County	426
Storm Lake, IA (city) Buena Vista County	419
Oklahoma City, OK (city) Oklahoma County	418
Pomona, CA (city) Los Angeles County	417
Irving, TX (city) Dallas County	375
Bellevue, WA (city) King County	367
Moreno Valley, CA (city) Riverside County	364
Akron, OH (city) Summit County	363
Bridgeport, CT (city) Fairfield County	349
Fort Worth, TX (city) Tarrant County	335
Escondido, CA (city) San Diego County	318
West Valley City, UT (city) Salt Lake County	308
New Britain, CT (city) Hartford County	295
Grand Prairie, TX (city) Dallas County	278
Arvada, CO (city) Jefferson County	277
Green Bay, WI (city) Brown County	266
Rochester, MN (city) Olmsted County	264
Springdale, AR (city) Washington County	261
Fairfield, CA (city) Solano County	255
Tacoma, WA (city) Pierce County	254
Springfield, VA (cdp) Fairfax County	246
Riverside, CA (city) Riverside County	242
Winfield, KS (city) Cowley County	242
Worthington, MN (city) Nobles County	230
Brooklyn Center, MN (city) Hennepin County	211
Fitchburg, MA (city) Worcester County	206
Banning, CA (city) Riverside County	203
Oaklawn-Sunview, KS (cdp) Sedgwick County	200
Raymond, WA (city) Pacific County	184
Warroad, MN (city) Roseau County	61

Notes: Please refer to the User's Guide for an explanation of data; ranking tables include all places with Asian and/or NHPI populations above SF4 population thresholds; (1) tables reflect only those areas that meet SF4 population thresholds, therefore there may be less than 50 states, 75 counties or 75 places listed

Foreign Born

Laotian

All States, Top 75 Counties, and Top 75 Places Sorted by Percent[1]

State	Percent
Oklahoma	78.21
Idaho	77.36
New York	76.96
Alabama	74.79
Hawaii	74.79
Maryland	74.59
Connecticut	74.48
Missouri	74.30
Florida	74.22
Indiana	73.45
Kansas	72.31
Tennessee	72.25
Ohio	72.01
Arkansas	71.46
Nevada	71.40
Rhode Island	71.34
Virginia	71.14
Colorado	70.71
Louisiana	70.71
Nebraska	70.71
Illinois	70.48
Texas	70.35
Iowa	69.73
Pennsylvania	69.05
Georgia	68.48
United States	68.12
Massachusetts	67.64
Washington	67.40
Arizona	67.23
North Carolina	66.79
Utah	66.65
California	65.89
South Dakota	65.60
Oregon	65.17
South Carolina	64.88
Alaska	64.40
New Hampshire	64.15
Minnesota	63.98
Michigan	63.55
Wisconsin	62.54
New Jersey	57.71

County	Percent
Oklahoma County, OK	87.02
Cook County, IL	83.32
Guilford County, NC	80.74
Johnson County, KS	79.84
Butte County, CA	78.22
Sebastian County, AR	78.08
Pierce County, WA	77.75
Buena Vista County, IA	77.68
Cass County, MI	77.62
Bexar County, TX	76.88
Monroe County, NY	76.61
Montgomery County, NC	76.53
Broome County, NY	76.21
Davidson County, TN	76.20
Hartford County, CT	75.97
Dakota County, NE	75.68
Pinellas County, FL	74.82
Honolulu County, HI	74.77
Habersham County, GA	73.94
Harris County, TX	73.77
Washington County, OR	73.31
Franklin County, OH	72.89
Pacific County, WA	72.86
Clark County, WA	72.64
New Haven County, CT	72.62
Mecklenburg County, NC	72.60
Fairfield County, CT	72.36
Dane County, WI	71.51
Providence County, RI	71.27
Clark County, NV	71.11
Winnebago County, IL	71.05
Milwaukee County, WI	70.95
Iberia Parish, LA	70.89
Sonoma County, CA	70.89
Philadelphia County, PA	70.84
Mobile County, AL	70.70
Orange County, CA	70.49
Adams County, CO	70.48
Rutherford County, TN	70.42
San Diego County, CA	70.41
Maricopa County, AZ	70.38
Riverside County, CA	70.23
Cowley County, KS	70.11
San Bernardino County, CA	69.89
Shasta County, CA	69.80
Clayton County, GA	69.79
Polk County, IA	69.53
Essex County, MA	69.51
Gwinnett County, GA	69.35
Los Angeles County, CA	69.13
Fairfax County, VA	68.87
Dallas County, TX	68.85
Stanislaus County, CA	68.85
Middlesex County, MA	68.68
Contra Costa County, CA	68.58
Tulare County, CA	68.36
Tarrant County, TX	68.09
Polk County, FL	68.08
Santa Clara County, CA	67.99
Burke County, NC	67.74
Potter County, TX	67.71
Summit County, OH	67.63
Dakota County, MN	67.49
Merced County, CA	67.38
Salt Lake County, UT	67.24
King County, WA	67.04
Jefferson County, CO	66.52
Hennepin County, MN	66.00
Sedgwick County, KS	65.62
Ottawa County, MI	64.95
Washington County, AR	64.79
Yolo County, CA	64.69
Fresno County, CA	64.39
Ramsey County, MN	63.99
Brown County, WI	63.64

Place	Percent
Oklahoma City, OK (city) Oklahoma County	82.61
Tacoma, WA (city) Pierce County	81.94
Storm Lake, IA (city) Buena Vista County	79.51
St. Petersburg, FL (city) Pinellas County	79.26
Fort Smith, AR (city) Sebastian County	79.16
Bellevue, WA (city) King County	79.09
New Britain, CT (city) Hartford County	79.09
Santa Rosa, CA (city) Sonoma County	78.83
Anaheim, CA (city) Orange County	78.39
Irving, TX (city) Dallas County	78.29
Woonsocket, RI (city) Providence County	78.29
Pomona, CA (city) Los Angeles County	78.24
Westminster, CO (city) Adams County	77.22
Nashville-Davidson, TN (sp. city) Davidson County	76.20
Rochester, NY (city) Monroe County	75.28
Elgin, IL (city) Kane County	75.17
Moreno Valley, CA (city) Riverside County	74.59
Los Angeles, CA (city) Los Angeles County	73.58
Rockford, IL (city) Winnebago County	73.27
Charlotte, NC (city) Mecklenburg County	72.25
Modesto, CA (city) Stanislaus County	72.04
San Pablo, CA (city) Contra Costa County	71.95
Grand Prairie, TX (city) Dallas County	71.10
Raymond, WA (city) Pacific County	71.04
Philadelphia, PA (city) Philadelphia County	70.84
Columbus, OH (city) Franklin County	70.68
Lowell, MA (city) Middlesex County	70.62
Dallas, TX (city) Dallas County	70.59
Riverside, CA (city) Riverside County	70.35
Winfield, KS (city) Cowley County	70.35
San Diego, CA (city) San Diego County	70.33
Honolulu, HI (cdp) Honolulu County	70.22
Merced, CA (city) Merced County	70.09
Milwaukee, WI (city) Milwaukee County	70.09
Des Moines, IA (city) Polk County	69.99
Bridgeport, CT (city) Fairfield County	69.66
Green Bay, WI (city) Brown County	69.63
Providence, RI (city) Providence County	69.61
Redding, CA (city) Shasta County	69.57
Richmond, CA (city) Contra Costa County	69.15
Visalia, CA (city) Tulare County	68.99
Amarillo, TX (city) Potter County	68.90
San Jose, CA (city) Santa Clara County	67.51
West Valley City, UT (city) Salt Lake County	66.81
Murfreesboro, TN (city) Rutherford County	66.62
Escondido, CA (city) San Diego County	66.39
Seattle, WA (city) King County	66.26
Oaklawn-Sunview, KS (cdp) Sedgwick County	66.01
Wichita, KS (city) Sedgwick County	65.99
Brooklyn Center, MN (city) Hennepin County	65.94
Fairfield, CA (city) Solano County	65.55
Haltom City, TX (city) Tarrant County	65.39
Fresno, CA (city) Fresno County	64.90
Santa Ana, CA (city) Orange County	64.84
Portland, OR (city) Multnomah County	64.51
Minneapolis, MN (city) Hennepin County	64.23
Akron, OH (city) Summit County	63.46
Fort Worth, TX (city) Tarrant County	63.21
St. Paul, MN (city) Ramsey County	62.95
Brooklyn Park, MN (city) Hennepin County	62.84
Springdale, AR (city) Washington County	62.00
Stockton, CA (city) San Joaquin County	61.99
Worthington, MN (city) Nobles County	61.99
Springfield, VA (cdp) Fairfax County	61.81
Rochester, MN (city) Olmsted County	60.27
Banning, CA (city) Riverside County	59.53
Sacramento, CA (city) Sacramento County	59.22
Arvada, CO (city) Jefferson County	57.95
Long Beach, CA (city) Los Angeles County	57.41
Oakland, CA (city) Alameda County	57.10
Parkway-S. Sacramento, CA (cdp) Sacramento County	56.82
Fitchburg, MA (city) Worcester County	52.82
Warroad, MN (city) Roseau County	48.80

Notes: Please refer to the User's Guide for an explanation of data; ranking tables include all places with Asian and/or NHPI populations above SF4 population thresholds; (1) tables reflect only those areas that meet SF4 population thresholds, therefore there may be less than 50 states, 75 counties or 75 places listed

Foreign Born

Malaysian

All States, Top 75 Counties, and Top 75 Places Sorted by Number[1]

State	Number
United States	9,510
California	1,501
New York	1,227
Texas	599
Illinois	461
Oklahoma	453
Michigan	424
Ohio	296

County	Number
Queens County, NY	531
Los Angeles County, CA	504

Place	Number
New York, NY (city)	1,065

Notes: Please refer to the User's Guide for an explanation of data; ranking tables include all places with Asian and/or NHPI populations above SF4 population thresholds; (1) tables reflect only those areas that meet SF4 population thresholds, therefore there may be less than 50 states, 75 counties or 75 places listed

Foreign Born

Malaysian

***All States, Top 75 Counties, and Top 75 Places Sorted by Percent*[1]**

State	Percent
Michigan	92.78
Texas	89.40
United States	88.79
Oklahoma	88.13
New York	87.52
California	85.24
Ohio	85.06
Illinois	81.31

County	Percent
Los Angeles County, CA	94.38
Queens County, NY	93.65

Place	Percent
New York, NY (city)	88.97

Notes: Please refer to the User's Guide for an explanation of data; ranking tables include all places with Asian and/or NHPI populations above SF4 population thresholds; (1) tables reflect only those areas that meet SF4 population thresholds, therefore there may be less than 50 states, 75 counties or 75 places listed

Foreign Born

Pakistani

***All States, Top 75 Counties, and Top 75 Places Sorted by Number*[1]**

State	Number
United States	117,723
New York	24,909
Texas	14,288
California	14,016
Illinois	12,006
New Jersey	9,343
Virginia	7,884
Florida	3,953
Maryland	3,917
Michigan	3,696
Georgia	3,022
Pennsylvania	2,356
Massachusetts	1,827
Connecticut	1,741
North Carolina	1,508
Ohio	1,259
Washington	903
Minnesota	872
Missouri	824
Oklahoma	799
Louisiana	778
Wisconsin	718
Colorado	651
Tennessee	582
Kansas	567
Arizona	542
Indiana	491
Kentucky	435
Nevada	426
Alabama	313
Oregon	280
Utah	261
Delaware	252
Iowa	250
West Virginia	224

County	Number
Queens County, NY	9,082
Cook County, IL	8,445
Kings County, NY	7,740
Harris County, TX	5,966
Fairfax County, VA	4,676
Los Angeles County, CA	3,462
Dallas County, TX	2,679
Middlesex County, NJ	2,355
DuPage County, IL	2,032
Santa Clara County, CA	1,904
Orange County, CA	1,855
Fort Bend County, TX	1,847
Hudson County, NJ	1,742
Nassau County, NY	1,696
Wayne County, MI	1,588
Alameda County, CA	1,523
Montgomery County, MD	1,499
Suffolk County, NY	1,406
Bergen County, NJ	1,075
Sacramento County, CA	976
Bronx County, NY	899
San Joaquin County, CA	880
Gwinnett County, GA	860
Broward County, FL	837
New York County, NY	797
Baltimore County, MD	775
Tarrant County, TX	743
Oakland County, MI	713
Miami-Dade County, FL	685
Arlington County, VA	662
Collin County, TX	661
Somerset County, NJ	637
Prince William County, VA	625
Westchester County, NY	625
New Haven County, CT	615
Orange County, FL	614
Contra Costa County, CA	560
San Bernardino County, CA	548
Travis County, TX	547
Philadelphia County, PA	546
Prince George's County, MD	546
Denton County, TX	534
Delaware County, PA	531
Morris County, NJ	526
Hartford County, CT	520
Alexandria Independent City, VA	518
Howard County, MD	518
Cobb County, GA	516
St. Louis County, MO	505
Essex County, NJ	502
Richmond County, NY	491
Mercer County, NJ	490
Atlantic County, NJ	463
Loudoun County, VA	452
Middlesex County, MA	450
Fairfield County, CT	434
Macomb County, MI	430
Maricopa County, AZ	414
Franklin County, OH	399
Jefferson Parish, LA	392
Lake County, IL	372
Wake County, NC	356
King County, WA	351
San Diego County, CA	343
Guilford County, NC	342
Clayton County, GA	339
Milwaukee County, WI	339
San Francisco County, CA	335
Worcester County, MA	335
Washtenaw County, MI	330
Tulsa County, OK	329
Hennepin County, MN	325
Monmouth County, NJ	323
Snohomish County, WA	321
Monroe County, NY	287

Place	Number
New York, NY (city)	19,009
Chicago, IL (city) Cook County	5,404
Houston, TX (city) Harris County	4,081
Jersey City, NJ (city) Hudson County	1,467
Los Angeles, CA (city) Los Angeles County	1,167
Hempstead, NY (town) Nassau County	1,036
Dallas, TX (city) Dallas County	932
San Jose, CA (city) Santa Clara County	916
Fremont, CA (city) Alameda County	859
Carrollton, TX (city) Denton County	795
Arlington, VA (cdp) Arlington County	662
Sacramento, CA (city) Sacramento County	578
Philadelphia, PA (city) Philadelphia County	546
Garland, TX (city) Dallas County	519
Brookhaven, NY (town) Suffolk County	507
Torrance, CA (city) Los Angeles County	485
Edison, NJ (township) Middlesex County	452
Sugar Land, TX (city) Fort Bend County	444
Austin, TX (city) Travis County	434
Old Bridge, NJ (township) Middlesex County	409
Stockton, CA (city) San Joaquin County	409
Mission Bend, TX (cdp) Fort Bend County	402
Lincolnia, VA (cdp) Fairfax County	395
Plano, TX (city) Collin County	393
North Hempstead, NY (town) Nassau County	388
Woodbridge, NJ (township) Middlesex County	373
Skokie, IL (village) Cook County	359
Richardson, TX (city) Dallas County	347
San Francisco, CA (city) San Francisco County	335
Irving, TX (city) Dallas County	327
Ellicott City, MD (cdp) Howard County	305
Bailey's Crossroads, VA (cdp) Fairfax County	296
Anaheim, CA (city) Orange County	294
Santa Clara, CA (city) Santa Clara County	291
Huntington, NY (town) Suffolk County	288
Tulsa, OK (city) Tulsa County	279
Dale City, VA (cdp) Prince William County	255

Notes: Please refer to the User's Guide for an explanation of data; ranking tables include all places with Asian and/or NHPI populations above SF4 population thresholds; (1) tables reflect only those areas that meet SF4 population thresholds, therefore there may be less than 50 states, 75 counties or 75 places listed

Foreign Born

Pakistani

All States, Top 75 Counties, and Top 75 Places Sorted by Percent[1]

State	Percent
Connecticut	82.43
Alabama	81.30
Arizona	80.65
North Carolina	80.47
Nevada	80.08
Colorado	80.07
Louisiana	79.79
Minnesota	79.42
Missouri	78.25
Pennsylvania	77.86
Massachusetts	77.55
New York	77.54
Wisconsin	77.45
Georgia	77.37
Kentucky	77.26
Illinois	77.02
Maryland	76.89
Ohio	76.72
Tennessee	76.18
Texas	75.71
United States	75.51
Virginia	75.38
New Jersey	75.04
Michigan	74.25
Kansas	72.79
Florida	72.59
Oregon	71.79
Washington	71.72
Oklahoma	71.21
California	70.66
West Virginia	69.14
Indiana	68.86
Delaware	66.49
Utah	65.09
Iowa	64.10

County	Percent
Milwaukee County, WI	95.49
New Haven County, CT	94.18
Atlantic County, NJ	92.05
Alexandria Independent City, VA	90.24
St. Louis County, MO	88.75
Jefferson Parish, LA	88.09
Philadelphia County, PA	86.80
Miami-Dade County, FL	86.27
Worcester County, MA	84.38
Guilford County, NC	83.62
Arlington County, VA	82.65
Essex County, NJ	82.43
Delaware County, PA	82.33
Montgomery County, MD	81.91
Harris County, TX	81.37
Macomb County, MI	81.13
Clayton County, GA	80.91
Queens County, NY	80.71
Kings County, NY	80.45
Prince George's County, MD	80.29
San Bernardino County, CA	80.23
Wake County, NC	80.00
Bronx County, NY	79.98
Fairfield County, CT	79.93
Cobb County, GA	79.75
Hennepin County, MN	79.66
Maricopa County, AZ	79.62
Cook County, IL	79.58
Howard County, MD	79.45
Contra Costa County, CA	79.10
Monmouth County, NJ	78.59
Somerset County, NJ	78.26
Hartford County, CT	77.84
Franklin County, OH	77.78
Baltimore County, MD	77.27
Alameda County, CA	76.96
Prince William County, VA	76.88
Broward County, FL	76.30
Middlesex County, MA	75.89
Fort Bend County, TX	75.67
Travis County, TX	75.55
Tarrant County, TX	75.35
Gwinnett County, GA	75.31
Hudson County, NJ	75.09
Fairfax County, VA	74.35
Snohomish County, WA	74.31
Mercer County, NJ	74.24
Westchester County, NY	74.23
Middlesex County, NJ	74.20
New York County, NY	73.39
Oakland County, MI	73.28
Los Angeles County, CA	73.21
Wayne County, MI	72.91
Nassau County, NY	72.23
DuPage County, IL	72.18
Dallas County, TX	72.15
Loudoun County, VA	72.09
Lake County, IL	71.68
Bergen County, NJ	71.62
Washtenaw County, MI	70.97
Orange County, CA	70.48
Union County, NJ	70.28
Suffolk County, NY	70.05
Morris County, NJ	69.39
Santa Clara County, CA	69.21
Collin County, TX	69.00
Orange County, FL	68.15
Sacramento County, CA	67.97
King County, WA	66.73
San Joaquin County, CA	65.82
Richmond County, NY	63.60
Denton County, TX	63.57
San Diego County, CA	63.52
Riverside County, CA	63.29
Camden County, NJ	63.03

Place	Percent
Philadelphia, PA (city) Philadelphia County	86.80
Chicago, IL (city) Cook County	83.95
Mission Bend, TX (cdp) Fort Bend County	83.75
Arlington, VA (cdp) Arlington County	82.65
Austin, TX (city) Travis County	82.51
Bailey's Crossroads, VA (cdp) Fairfax County	82.45
Richardson, TX (city) Dallas County	82.03
Houston, TX (city) Harris County	81.67
Woodbridge, NJ (township) Middlesex County	79.87
New York, NY (city)	79.69
Dale City, VA (cdp) Prince William County	78.70
Jersey City, NJ (city) Hudson County	78.12
Fremont, CA (city) Alameda County	77.95
Old Bridge, NJ (township) Middlesex County	77.76
Dallas, TX (city) Dallas County	77.54
Ellicott City, MD (cdp) Howard County	77.22
Lincolnia, VA (cdp) Fairfax County	76.40
Irving, TX (city) Dallas County	76.22
Sacramento, CA (city) Sacramento County	74.20
Torrance, CA (city) Los Angeles County	73.93
Hempstead, NY (town) Nassau County	73.63
Skokie, IL (village) Cook County	72.53
Sugar Land, TX (city) Fort Bend County	71.84
Los Angeles, CA (city) Los Angeles County	69.63
San Jose, CA (city) Santa Clara County	69.45
Anaheim, CA (city) Orange County	69.34
Brookhaven, NY (town) Suffolk County	68.70
Carrollton, TX (city) Denton County	68.18
Tulsa, OK (city) Tulsa County	67.23
Edison, NJ (township) Middlesex County	67.06
Huntington, NY (town) Suffolk County	65.90
Plano, TX (city) Collin County	65.07
North Hempstead, NY (town) Nassau County	62.78
Garland, TX (city) Dallas County	62.45
Santa Clara, CA (city) Santa Clara County	62.05
San Francisco, CA (city) San Francisco County	60.25
Stockton, CA (city) San Joaquin County	58.26

Notes: Please refer to the User's Guide for an explanation of data; ranking tables include all places with Asian and/or NHPI populations above SF4 population thresholds; (1) tables reflect only those areas that meet SF4 population thresholds, therefore there may be less than 50 states, 75 counties or 75 places listed

Foreign Born

Samoan

All States, Top 75 Counties, and Top 75 Places Sorted by Number[1]

State	Number
United States	17,858
California	8,647
Hawaii	2,652
Washington	1,430
Utah	1,080
Texas	367
Alaska	323
Nevada	315
Florida	246
New York	239
Missouri	211
Arizona	204
Virginia	188
Oregon	166
North Carolina	161
Illinois	160
New Jersey	157
Tennessee	132
Georgia	113
Colorado	110
Pennsylvania	94
Michigan	57
Ohio	50

County	Number
Los Angeles County, CA	3,399
Honolulu County, HI	2,431
King County, WA	963
Orange County, CA	929
Salt Lake County, UT	838
San Francisco County, CA	654
San Bernardino County, CA	618
San Diego County, CA	555
Santa Clara County, CA	469
Pierce County, WA	348
San Mateo County, CA	305
Sacramento County, CA	293
Alameda County, CA	276
Anchorage Borough, AK	260
Clark County, NV	191
Contra Costa County, CA	177
Ventura County, CA	174
Riverside County, CA	170
Maricopa County, AZ	162
Jackson County, MO	126
Utah County, UT	116
Hawaii County, HI	96
Solano County, CA	87
San Joaquin County, CA	62

Place	Number
Long Beach, CA (city) Los Angeles County	1,002
Honolulu, HI (cdp) Honolulu County	882
San Francisco, CA (city) San Francisco County	654
Los Angeles, CA (city) Los Angeles County	466
Waipahu, HI (cdp) Honolulu County	382
San Jose, CA (city) Santa Clara County	359
West Valley City, UT (city) Salt Lake County	317
Lakewood, CA (city) Los Angeles County	289
Seattle, WA (city) King County	243
San Diego, CA (city) San Diego County	236
Compton, CA (city) Los Angeles County	215
Garden Grove, CA (city) Orange County	214
Oceanside, CA (city) San Diego County	207
Federal Way, WA (city) King County	204
Carson, CA (city) Los Angeles County	194
Oxnard, CA (city) Ventura County	169
Santa Ana, CA (city) Orange County	169
Westminster, CA (city) Orange County	167
New York, NY (city)	159
Tacoma, WA (city) Pierce County	154
Salt Lake City, UT (city) Salt Lake County	142
Laie, HI (cdp) Honolulu County	128
Sacramento, CA (city) Sacramento County	126
San Bernardino, CA (city) San Bernardino County	125
Halawa, HI (cdp) Honolulu County	82
Hayward, CA (city) Alameda County	82
Anaheim, CA (city) Orange County	78
Nanakuli, HI (cdp) Honolulu County	68
Hauula, HI (cdp) Honolulu County	66
Lakewood, WA (city) Pierce County	62
Ewa Beach, HI (cdp) Honolulu County	55
Kahuku, HI (cdp) Honolulu County	41

Notes: Please refer to the User's Guide for an explanation of data; ranking tables include all places with Asian and/or NHPI populations above SF4 population thresholds; (1) tables reflect only those areas that meet SF4 population thresholds, therefore there may be less than 50 states, 75 counties or 75 places listed

Foreign Born

Samoan

All States, Top 75 Counties, and Top 75 Places Sorted by Percent[1]

State	Percent
Virginia	36.15
North Carolina	32.53
Florida	28.98
Utah	28.72
New Jersey	24.57
Tennessee	24.44
Arizona	24.00
California	22.23
Oregon	21.47
Alaska	21.06
Missouri	21.02
United States	20.95
Washington	20.22
Nevada	20.10
Hawaii	18.47
Illinois	18.31
Texas	18.05
New York	16.61
Georgia	14.83
Michigan	12.03
Colorado	12.01
Pennsylvania	11.14
Ohio	10.18

County	Percent
Hawaii County, HI	32.43
Salt Lake County, UT	32.41
San Bernardino County, CA	30.35
Maricopa County, AZ	29.29
San Francisco County, CA	28.70
Ventura County, CA	28.43
Santa Clara County, CA	27.28
Jackson County, MO	26.81
Los Angeles County, CA	25.08
Orange County, CA	24.97
King County, WA	24.56
Sacramento County, CA	23.65
Contra Costa County, CA	23.32
Anchorage Borough, AK	21.52
Utah County, UT	21.13
San Mateo County, CA	21.02
Pierce County, WA	20.13
Riverside County, CA	18.03
Honolulu County, HI	17.56
San Joaquin County, CA	17.22
Clark County, NV	17.11
Solano County, CA	13.92
Alameda County, CA	11.47
San Diego County, CA	11.20

Place	Percent
Lakewood, CA (city) Los Angeles County	48.33
Westminster, CA (city) Orange County	44.41
Federal Way, WA (city) King County	41.55
West Valley City, UT (city) Salt Lake County	36.82
Kahuku, HI (cdp) Honolulu County	34.17
Salt Lake City, UT (city) Salt Lake County	31.28
Oxnard, CA (city) Ventura County	31.24
San Jose, CA (city) Santa Clara County	29.47
San Francisco, CA (city) San Francisco County	28.70
Garden Grove, CA (city) Orange County	27.68
Long Beach, CA (city) Los Angeles County	26.84
San Bernardino, CA (city) San Bernardino County	26.15
Tacoma, WA (city) Pierce County	24.56
Hauula, HI (cdp) Honolulu County	24.26
Santa Ana, CA (city) Orange County	24.14
Los Angeles, CA (city) Los Angeles County	22.68
Compton, CA (city) Los Angeles County	21.92
New York, NY (city)	21.81
Lakewood, WA (city) Pierce County	21.16
Honolulu, HI (cdp) Honolulu County	19.81
Laie, HI (cdp) Honolulu County	19.13
Seattle, WA (city) King County	18.08
Waipahu, HI (cdp) Honolulu County	18.02
Sacramento, CA (city) Sacramento County	17.19
Hayward, CA (city) Alameda County	14.09
Anaheim, CA (city) Orange County	14.05
Oceanside, CA (city) San Diego County	13.51
Carson, CA (city) Los Angeles County	13.49
Ewa Beach, HI (cdp) Honolulu County	13.06
Halawa, HI (cdp) Honolulu County	12.41
San Diego, CA (city) San Diego County	10.87
Nanakuli, HI (cdp) Honolulu County	9.03

Notes: Please refer to the User's Guide for an explanation of data; ranking tables include all places with Asian and/or NHPI populations above SF4 population thresholds; (1) tables reflect only those areas that meet SF4 population thresholds, therefore there may be less than 50 states, 75 counties or 75 places listed

Foreign Born

Sri Lankan

All States, Top 75 Counties, and Top 75 Places Sorted by Number[1]

State	Number
United States	15,767
California	4,437
New York	2,293
New Jersey	1,009
Maryland	959
Texas	781
Virginia	527
Illinois	493
Ohio	436
Massachusetts	384
Washington	345
Florida	326
Michigan	313
Pennsylvania	287

County	Number
Los Angeles County, CA	2,018
Queens County, NY	803
Montgomery County, MD	645
Orange County, CA	548
Richmond County, NY	447
Middlesex County, NJ	363

Place	Number
New York, NY (city)	1,722
Los Angeles, CA (city) Los Angeles County	948

Notes: Please refer to the User's Guide for an explanation of data; ranking tables include all places with Asian and/or NHPI populations above SF4 population thresholds; (1) tables reflect only those areas that meet SF4 population thresholds, therefore there may be less than 50 states, 75 counties or 75 places listed

Foreign Born

Sri Lankan

All States, Top 75 Counties, and Top 75 Places Sorted by Percent[1]

State	Percent
Illinois	88.99
Michigan	87.92
Pennsylvania	86.97
Maryland	85.47
New York	85.27
Ohio	84.82
Virginia	82.86
United States	82.64
California	81.92
Massachusetts	81.88
Washington	81.75
Florida	81.09
Texas	80.02
New Jersey	75.58

County	Percent
Montgomery County, MD	86.23
Queens County, NY	85.70
Richmond County, NY	84.82
Los Angeles County, CA	82.67
Orange County, CA	80.95
Middlesex County, NJ	73.04

Place	Percent
New York, NY (city)	85.93
Los Angeles, CA (city) Los Angeles County	78.48

Notes: Please refer to the User's Guide for an explanation of data; ranking tables include all places with Asian and/or NHPI populations above SF4 population thresholds; (1) tables reflect only those areas that meet SF4 population thresholds, therefore there may be less than 50 states, 75 counties or 75 places listed

Foreign Born

Taiwanese

All States, Top 75 Counties, and Top 75 Places Sorted by Number[1]

State	Number
United States	94,685
California	50,582
New York	6,167
Texas	5,902
New Jersey	4,360
Washington	2,895
Illinois	2,484
Maryland	1,734
Massachusetts	1,697
Ohio	1,643
Michigan	1,627
Pennsylvania	1,616
Florida	1,529
Georgia	1,342
Virginia	978
Missouri	762
North Carolina	694
Hawaii	669
Oregon	594
Indiana	590
Arizona	536
Wisconsin	529
Colorado	509
Nevada	501
Tennessee	468
Connecticut	459
Louisiana	431
Kansas	378
Iowa	369
Minnesota	349
Oklahoma	333
Utah	243

County	Number
Los Angeles County, CA	28,379
Orange County, CA	7,222
Santa Clara County, CA	4,052
Queens County, NY	3,027
Alameda County, CA	2,993
King County, WA	2,283
Harris County, TX	1,853
San Diego County, CA	1,747
San Bernardino County, CA	1,609
Cook County, IL	1,237
Contra Costa County, CA	1,055
Middlesex County, NJ	995
Fort Bend County, TX	919
Middlesex County, MA	855
Oakland County, MI	840
Montgomery County, MD	825
Honolulu County, HI	658
New York County, NY	652
Bergen County, NJ	630
San Mateo County, CA	625
DuPage County, IL	597
Dallas County, TX	593
Franklin County, OH	589
San Francisco County, CA	588
Travis County, TX	576
Fairfax County, VA	560
Ventura County, CA	560
Collin County, TX	543
Morris County, NJ	524
Tarrant County, TX	513
St. Louis County, MO	489
Nassau County, NY	439
Maricopa County, AZ	425
Riverside County, CA	418
Washtenaw County, MI	409
Somerset County, NJ	399
Essex County, NJ	388
Dane County, WI	360
Gwinnett County, GA	352
Clark County, NV	351
Mercer County, NJ	333
Suffolk County, NY	329
Suffolk County, MA	313
Sacramento County, CA	300
Allegheny County, PA	295
Norfolk County, MA	246
Westchester County, NY	236

Place	Number
New York, NY (city)	4,003
Arcadia, CA (city) Los Angeles County	3,013
Los Angeles, CA (city) Los Angeles County	2,754
Hacienda Heights, CA (cdp) Los Angeles County	2,409
Rowland Heights, CA (cdp) Los Angeles County	2,198
Irvine, CA (city) Orange County	2,072
Fremont, CA (city) Alameda County	1,923
Diamond Bar, CA (city) Los Angeles County	1,651
San Jose, CA (city) Santa Clara County	1,622
Walnut, CA (city) Los Angeles County	1,445
Cerritos, CA (city) Los Angeles County	1,416
Alhambra, CA (city) Los Angeles County	1,412
Houston, TX (city) Harris County	1,262
San Diego, CA (city) San Diego County	1,205
Temple City, CA (city) Los Angeles County	1,185
San Marino, CA (city) Los Angeles County	1,181
Torrance, CA (city) Los Angeles County	1,078
Monterey Park, CA (city) Los Angeles County	940
Seattle, WA (city) King County	804
West Covina, CA (city) Los Angeles County	725
Sugar Land, TX (city) Fort Bend County	714
Bellevue, WA (city) King County	645
Cupertino, CA (city) Santa Clara County	619
Honolulu, HI (cdp) Honolulu County	609
San Gabriel, CA (city) Los Angeles County	605
Sunnyvale, CA (city) Santa Clara County	589
San Francisco, CA (city) San Francisco County	588
Anaheim, CA (city) Orange County	556
Chicago, IL (city) Cook County	536
East San Gabriel, CA (cdp) Los Angeles County	531
Cypress, CA (city) Orange County	523
Austin, TX (city) Travis County	508
Edison, NJ (township) Middlesex County	472
Huntington Beach, CA (city) Orange County	462
Rancho Palos Verdes, CA (city) Los Angeles County	436
Chino Hills, CA (city) San Bernardino County	428
Upland, CA (city) San Bernardino County	409
Columbus, OH (city) Franklin County	406
Plano, TX (city) Collin County	377
El Monte, CA (city) Los Angeles County	373
Orange, CA (city) Orange County	370
Madison, WI (city) Dane County	360
Tustin, CA (city) Orange County	356
Ann Arbor, MI (city) Washtenaw County	355
Troy, MI (city) Oakland County	338
Arlington, TX (city) Tarrant County	326
Fountain Valley, CA (city) Orange County	322
Boston, MA (city) Suffolk County	313
Naperville, IL (city) Du Page County	285
Berkeley, CA (city) Alameda County	264
Saratoga, CA (city) Santa Clara County	222
North Hempstead, NY (town) Nassau County	191

Notes: Please refer to the User's Guide for an explanation of data; ranking tables include all places with Asian and/or NHPI populations above SF4 population thresholds; (1) tables reflect only those areas that meet SF4 population thresholds, therefore there may be less than 50 states, 75 counties or 75 places listed

Foreign Born

Taiwanese

All States, Top 75 Counties, and Top 75 Places Sorted by Percent[1]

State	Percent
Oklahoma	94.07
Louisiana	87.25
Nevada	83.92
Iowa	82.74
Hawaii	81.49
Tennessee	80.69
Indiana	80.49
California	79.56
New York	79.17
Wisconsin	78.60
Missouri	78.40
United States	77.14
Washington	76.43
Florida	75.43
Minnesota	75.38
Texas	75.10
Colorado	74.85
New Jersey	74.52
Virginia	74.37
Oregon	74.25
Ohio	74.24
Kansas	72.97
Maryland	72.95
Georgia	72.78
North Carolina	71.47
Michigan	71.23
Pennsylvania	70.97
Illinois	69.58
Arizona	67.51
Massachusetts	66.92
Utah	65.68
Connecticut	56.04

County	Percent
Queens County, NY	87.41
Dane County, WI	84.51
Riverside County, CA	83.94
Contra Costa County, CA	83.66
Harris County, TX	83.36
Honolulu County, HI	83.19
Clark County, NV	81.82
Los Angeles County, CA	81.68
Essex County, NJ	81.34
San Mateo County, CA	80.23
San Bernardino County, CA	78.91
Washtenaw County, MI	78.65
Orange County, CA	78.13
Franklin County, OH	77.91
Suffolk County, NY	76.87
Santa Clara County, CA	76.48
Tarrant County, TX	76.34
San Francisco County, CA	76.26
Alameda County, CA	76.06
Bergen County, NJ	76.00
Fairfax County, VA	75.88
Fort Bend County, TX	75.58
King County, WA	75.50
St. Louis County, MO	75.46
Morris County, NJ	74.64
Gwinnett County, GA	74.26
San Diego County, CA	73.96
Sacramento County, CA	73.89
Dallas County, TX	73.76
Middlesex County, NJ	73.16
Nassau County, NY	72.68
Somerset County, NJ	72.68
Montgomery County, MD	72.12
DuPage County, IL	71.07
Cook County, IL	70.61
Ventura County, CA	70.26
Westchester County, NY	69.82
Travis County, TX	68.57
Mercer County, NJ	68.24
Suffolk County, MA	67.31
Middlesex County, MA	67.22
Oakland County, MI	66.72
Maricopa County, AZ	66.20
Allegheny County, PA	65.41
Collin County, TX	63.88
New York County, NY	62.04
Norfolk County, MA	58.16

Place	Percent
El Monte, CA (city) Los Angeles County	93.02
Alhambra, CA (city) Los Angeles County	90.63
Monterey Park, CA (city) Los Angeles County	89.44
Sunnyvale, CA (city) Santa Clara County	87.78
Columbus, OH (city) Franklin County	87.69
Upland, CA (city) San Bernardino County	87.39
Honolulu, HI (cdp) Honolulu County	86.75
Madison, WI (city) Dane County	85.11
Rowland Heights, CA (cdp) Los Angeles County	84.77
Houston, TX (city) Harris County	84.58
Hacienda Heights, CA (cdp) Los Angeles County	83.79
Torrance, CA (city) Los Angeles County	83.57
Anaheim, CA (city) Orange County	83.11
East San Gabriel, CA (cdp) Los Angeles County	82.84
Los Angeles, CA (city) Los Angeles County	82.80
Seattle, WA (city) King County	82.29
New York, NY (city)	81.58
Fountain Valley, CA (city) Orange County	81.11
Rancho Palos Verdes, CA (city) Los Angeles County	80.74
Ann Arbor, MI (city) Washtenaw County	80.50
Arcadia, CA (city) Los Angeles County	80.28
Orange, CA (city) Orange County	80.09
Huntington Beach, CA (city) Orange County	80.07
San Gabriel, CA (city) Los Angeles County	79.29
Cerritos, CA (city) Los Angeles County	79.06
Irvine, CA (city) Orange County	79.02
San Jose, CA (city) Santa Clara County	79.01
Diamond Bar, CA (city) Los Angeles County	78.66
Arlington, TX (city) Tarrant County	78.55
Fremont, CA (city) Alameda County	78.43
Cupertino, CA (city) Santa Clara County	78.16
San Marino, CA (city) Los Angeles County	77.39
Temple City, CA (city) Los Angeles County	77.35
West Covina, CA (city) Los Angeles County	76.48
San Francisco, CA (city) San Francisco County	76.26
Tustin, CA (city) Orange County	76.23
Sugar Land, TX (city) Fort Bend County	76.20
San Diego, CA (city) San Diego County	75.93
Walnut, CA (city) Los Angeles County	75.03
Edison, NJ (township) Middlesex County	71.19
Cypress, CA (city) Orange County	70.30
Bellevue, WA (city) King County	69.43
Chicago, IL (city) Cook County	69.07
Austin, TX (city) Travis County	67.91
Chino Hills, CA (city) San Bernardino County	67.51
North Hempstead, NY (town) Nassau County	67.49
Boston, MA (city) Suffolk County	67.31
Saratoga, CA (city) Santa Clara County	66.87
Plano, TX (city) Collin County	66.84
Naperville, IL (city) Du Page County	66.13
Berkeley, CA (city) Alameda County	64.71
Troy, MI (city) Oakland County	60.57

Notes: Please refer to the User's Guide for an explanation of data; ranking tables include all places with Asian and/or NHPI populations above SF4 population thresholds; (1) tables reflect only those areas that meet SF4 population thresholds, therefore there may be less than 50 states, 75 counties or 75 places listed

Foreign Born

Thai

***All States, Top 75 Counties, and Top 75 Places Sorted by Number*[1]**

State	Number
United States	86,242
California	27,645
Florida	5,353
Texas	5,263
New York	4,900
Illinois	4,443
Washington	3,207
Virginia	2,894
Nevada	2,314
Maryland	2,259
Massachusetts	1,838
Georgia	1,686
Colorado	1,508
Ohio	1,507
Pennsylvania	1,381
New Jersey	1,377
Michigan	1,316
North Carolina	1,257
Oregon	1,256
Arizona	1,237
Hawaii	1,193
Missouri	1,034
Minnesota	766
Tennessee	750
Iowa	749
Wisconsin	729
Oklahoma	677
Indiana	669
Alaska	624
Connecticut	608
South Carolina	573
Utah	548
Alabama	536
Louisiana	509
Kansas	507
Nebraska	382
Kentucky	343
New Mexico	318
Arkansas	217

County	Number
Los Angeles County, CA	15,010
Cook County, IL	3,069
Orange County, CA	2,380
Clark County, NV	2,076
Queens County, NY	1,779
King County, WA	1,760
San Bernardino County, CA	1,366
Fairfax County, VA	1,182
San Francisco County, CA	1,177
Alameda County, CA	1,107
Montgomery County, MD	1,101
Santa Clara County, CA	1,048
Harris County, TX	1,024
San Diego County, CA	961
Honolulu County, HI	956
Maricopa County, AZ	892
Dallas County, TX	819
Miami-Dade County, FL	734
Middlesex County, MA	693
Riverside County, CA	631
Palm Beach County, FL	617
Bexar County, TX	599
New York County, NY	599
Tarrant County, TX	568
Hillsborough County, FL	561
Sacramento County, CA	551
Okaloosa County, FL	518
Contra Costa County, CA	490
Broward County, FL	470
San Mateo County, CA	461
Anchorage Borough, AK	451
Westchester County, NY	420
Multnomah County, OR	397
Bergen County, NJ	383
Pinellas County, FL	376
Franklin County, OH	367
Oklahoma County, OK	354
St. Louis County, MO	351
Collin County, TX	346
Denver County, CO	335
Pierce County, WA	310
Polk County, IA	285
DuPage County, IL	277
Nassau County, NY	268
Suffolk County, NY	258
Travis County, TX	251
Prince George's County, MD	228

Place	Number
Los Angeles, CA (city) Los Angeles County	7,028
New York, NY (city)	2,847
Chicago, IL (city) Cook County	1,637
San Francisco, CA (city) San Francisco County	1,177
Seattle, WA (city) King County	804
Houston, TX (city) Harris County	704
San Diego, CA (city) San Diego County	588
Las Vegas, NV (city) Clark County	564
San Jose, CA (city) Santa Clara County	494
Honolulu, HI (cdp) Honolulu County	455
Long Beach, CA (city) Los Angeles County	455
San Antonio, TX (city) Bexar County	420
Spring Valley, NV (cdp) Clark County	391
Portland, OR (city) Multnomah County	364
Glendale, CA (city) Los Angeles County	361
Anaheim, CA (city) Orange County	347
Denver, CO (city) Denver County	335
Columbus, OH (city) Franklin County	327
Cerritos, CA (city) Los Angeles County	325
Bellflower, CA (city) Los Angeles County	277
Des Moines, IA (city) Polk County	222

Notes: Please refer to the User's Guide for an explanation of data; ranking tables include all places with Asian and/or NHPI populations above SF4 population thresholds; (1) tables reflect only those areas that meet SF4 population thresholds, therefore there may be less than 50 states, 75 counties or 75 places listed

Foreign Born

Thai

All States, Top 75 Counties, and Top 75 Places Sorted by Percent[1]

State	Percent
Alabama	86.31
Hawaii	85.34
Oregon	83.96
Wisconsin	83.79
South Carolina	83.28
Minnesota	83.26
Nebraska	82.86
Washington	82.40
Oklahoma	82.26
Michigan	82.04
Massachusetts	81.51
Florida	81.45
Kentucky	81.28
Virginia	80.82
Iowa	80.54
Alaska	79.80
Ohio	79.32
New Mexico	79.30
Maryland	79.15
Louisiana	78.91
Kansas	78.00
United States	77.80
Nevada	77.73
Connecticut	77.55
Utah	77.51
Colorado	77.45
North Carolina	77.35
Pennsylvania	76.81
California	76.46
Illinois	75.97
Arizona	75.84
Tennessee	75.38
Missouri	75.36
Georgia	74.93
New Jersey	74.63
Arkansas	74.32
New York	74.28
Indiana	74.00
Texas	73.98

County	Percent
St. Louis County, MO	92.86
King County, WA	90.26
Oklahoma County, OK	89.17
Franklin County, OH	85.75
Miami-Dade County, FL	83.22
Honolulu County, HI	83.20
Okaloosa County, FL	83.01
Hillsborough County, FL	82.99
Montgomery County, MD	82.97
Denver County, CO	82.51
Palm Beach County, FL	81.18
Multnomah County, OR	80.69
San Francisco County, CA	80.56
San Bernardino County, CA	80.12
Polk County, IA	79.61
Clark County, NV	79.24
Fairfax County, VA	79.22
Santa Clara County, CA	78.56
Broward County, FL	78.46
Pierce County, WA	78.28
Anchorage Borough, AK	78.16
Maricopa County, AZ	77.84
Contra Costa County, CA	77.17
Pinellas County, FL	77.05
Middlesex County, MA	76.91
Harris County, TX	76.82
Los Angeles County, CA	76.72
Cook County, IL	76.69
Collin County, TX	76.21
Alameda County, CA	76.19
Bergen County, NJ	76.14
Orange County, CA	75.34
Queens County, NY	75.25
Sacramento County, CA	74.56
Dallas County, TX	74.12
Bexar County, TX	73.59
San Diego County, CA	73.41
Tarrant County, TX	73.29
Riverside County, CA	72.03
New York County, NY	71.74
Nassau County, NY	71.28
Westchester County, NY	70.71
Prince George's County, MD	68.26
Suffolk County, NY	66.67
DuPage County, IL	66.27
San Mateo County, CA	65.76
Travis County, TX	62.44

Place	Percent
Seattle, WA (city) King County	91.57
Glendale, CA (city) Los Angeles County	85.95
Honolulu, HI (cdp) Honolulu County	85.05
Columbus, OH (city) Franklin County	84.06
Denver, CO (city) Denver County	82.51
Portland, OR (city) Multnomah County	80.89
Las Vegas, NV (city) Clark County	80.57
San Francisco, CA (city) San Francisco County	80.56
Houston, TX (city) Harris County	79.91
Spring Valley, NV (cdp) Clark County	78.67
San Jose, CA (city) Santa Clara County	78.29
Los Angeles, CA (city) Los Angeles County	77.38
Chicago, IL (city) Cook County	76.35
Anaheim, CA (city) Orange County	76.10
Long Beach, CA (city) Los Angeles County	75.33
Des Moines, IA (city) Polk County	75.25
New York, NY (city)	74.47
San Antonio, TX (city) Bexar County	72.79
San Diego, CA (city) San Diego County	71.45
Bellflower, CA (city) Los Angeles County	71.21
Cerritos, CA (city) Los Angeles County	69.74

Notes: Please refer to the User's Guide for an explanation of data; ranking tables include all places with Asian and/or NHPI populations above SF4 population thresholds; (1) tables reflect only those areas that meet SF4 population thresholds, therefore there may be less than 50 states, 75 counties or 75 places listed

Foreign Born

Tongan

All States, Top 75 Counties, and Top 75 Places Sorted by Number[1]

State	Number
United States	14,221
California	6,504
Utah	3,099
Hawaii	2,302
Washington	460
Nevada	387
Arizona	324
Texas	284
Oregon	240
Alaska	183

County	Number
Salt Lake County, UT	2,812
San Mateo County, CA	2,208
Honolulu County, HI	1,741
Los Angeles County, CA	1,188
Alameda County, CA	900
Sacramento County, CA	429
Maui County, HI	404
San Bernardino County, CA	397
King County, WA	321
Maricopa County, AZ	316
Orange County, CA	287
Washoe County, NV	284
Contra Costa County, CA	202
Tarrant County, TX	199
San Diego County, CA	196
Multnomah County, OR	187
Utah County, UT	169

Place	Number
Salt Lake City, UT (city) Salt Lake County	1,201
East Palo Alto, CA (city) San Mateo County	929
Honolulu, HI (cdp) Honolulu County	914
West Valley City, UT (city) Salt Lake County	846
Oakland, CA (city) Alameda County	619
San Mateo, CA (city) San Mateo County	411
San Bruno, CA (city) San Mateo County	345
Sacramento, CA (city) Sacramento County	319
West Jordan, UT (city) Salt Lake County	188
Los Angeles, CA (city) Los Angeles County	185
Portland, OR (city) Multnomah County	180
Hauula, HI (cdp) Honolulu County	174
Kahuku, HI (cdp) Honolulu County	143
Laie, HI (cdp) Honolulu County	131

Notes: Please refer to the User's Guide for an explanation of data; ranking tables include all places with Asian and/or NHPI populations above SF4 population thresholds; (1) tables reflect only those areas that meet SF4 population thresholds, therefore there may be less than 50 states, 75 counties or 75 places listed

Foreign Born

Tongan

All States, Top 75 Counties, and Top 75 Places Sorted by Percent[1]

State	Percent
Texas	56.69
Hawaii	55.06
Washington	54.50
Oregon	53.93
California	53.46
United States	51.37
Arizona	51.10
Nevada	48.99
Utah	45.61
Alaska	43.68

County	Percent
King County, WA	63.94
San Mateo County, CA	60.43
Maricopa County, AZ	59.96
Sacramento County, CA	57.89
Honolulu County, HI	56.49
Tarrant County, TX	54.52
Los Angeles County, CA	52.20
Multnomah County, OR	52.09
Maui County, HI	50.88
Orange County, CA	49.40
Washoe County, NV	49.22
Alameda County, CA	49.13
San Bernardino County, CA	49.01
Salt Lake County, UT	47.36
San Diego County, CA	45.06
Contra Costa County, CA	44.79
Utah County, UT	36.58

Place	Percent
San Bruno, CA (city) San Mateo County	64.73
San Mateo, CA (city) San Mateo County	64.42
East Palo Alto, CA (city) San Mateo County	62.18
Kahuku, HI (cdp) Honolulu County	60.34
Honolulu, HI (cdp) Honolulu County	58.66
Laie, HI (cdp) Honolulu County	58.22
Sacramento, CA (city) Sacramento County	55.57
Los Angeles, CA (city) Los Angeles County	54.09
Portland, OR (city) Multnomah County	51.14
Salt Lake City, UT (city) Salt Lake County	49.08
Hauula, HI (cdp) Honolulu County	48.33
Oakland, CA (city) Alameda County	47.18
West Valley City, UT (city) Salt Lake County	46.84
West Jordan, UT (city) Salt Lake County	40.00

Notes: Please refer to the User's Guide for an explanation of data; ranking tables include all places with Asian and/or NHPI populations above SF4 population thresholds; (1) tables reflect only those areas that meet SF4 population thresholds, therefore there may be less than 50 states, 75 counties or 75 places listed

Foreign Born

Vietnamese

All States, Top 75 Counties, and Top 75 Places Sorted by Number[1]

State	Number
United States	844,893
California	339,401
Texas	99,579
Washington	34,853
Virginia	28,155
Massachusetts	26,341
Florida	25,753
Georgia	24,008
Pennsylvania	22,028
New York	18,493
Louisiana	16,138
Minnesota	14,565
Oregon	14,434
Illinois	14,128
Maryland	13,121
North Carolina	12,135
New Jersey	11,385
Colorado	10,134
Michigan	9,651
Oklahoma	9,246
Arizona	8,970
Kansas	8,343
Missouri	8,007
Ohio	7,828
Hawaii	6,405
Connecticut	5,804
Iowa	5,609
Tennessee	5,575
Nebraska	5,253
Utah	4,121
Indiana	3,577
Mississippi	3,308
Nevada	3,253
Alabama	3,218
South Carolina	2,950
Arkansas	2,800
Wisconsin	2,762
Kentucky	2,513
New Mexico	2,151
District of Columbia	1,557
New Hampshire	1,394
Idaho	1,032
Vermont	895
Maine	820
Rhode Island	758
Alaska	738
South Dakota	540
Delaware	481
West Virginia	287

County	Number
Orange County, CA	104,353
Santa Clara County, CA	75,662
Los Angeles County, CA	61,039
Harris County, TX	42,202
San Diego County, CA	25,985
King County, WA	21,227
Fairfax County, VA	17,312
Alameda County, CA	17,185
Dallas County, TX	15,465
Tarrant County, TX	14,302
Sacramento County, CA	11,979
Suffolk County, MA	9,861
Multnomah County, OR	8,986
Philadelphia County, PA	8,937
Cook County, IL	8,649
San Francisco County, CA	8,418
San Bernardino County, CA	7,736
Montgomery County, MD	7,704
Maricopa County, AZ	6,753
Hennepin County, MN	6,612
Honolulu County, HI	5,989
Gwinnett County, GA	5,969
DeKalb County, GA	5,469
Travis County, TX	5,349
Oklahoma County, OK	5,272
Orange County, FL	5,267
Middlesex County, MA	5,141
Sedgwick County, KS	4,887
Jefferson Parish, LA	4,468
Orleans Parish, LA	4,456
Worcester County, MA	4,207
Contra Costa County, CA	4,030
Riverside County, CA	4,004
Snohomish County, WA	3,965
San Joaquin County, CA	3,915
Clayton County, GA	3,847
Mecklenburg County, NC	3,764
Fort Bend County, TX	3,693
Washington County, OR	3,682
Salt Lake County, UT	3,578
Pierce County, WA	3,487
Denver County, CO	3,364
Kent County, MI	3,360
Pinellas County, FL	3,298
Hillsborough County, FL	3,230
Queens County, NY	3,082
Lancaster County, NE	3,023
Kings County, NY	2,988
Ramsey County, MN	2,800
Shelby County, TN	2,661
Clark County, NV	2,658
Hartford County, CT	2,618
Saint Louis Independent City, MO	2,603
East Baton Rouge Parish, LA	2,517
Collin County, TX	2,512
Camden County, NJ	2,460
Fulton County, GA	2,435
Guilford County, NC	2,435
Bronx County, NY	2,414
Ventura County, CA	2,305
Jefferson County, TX	2,243
Bexar County, TX	2,229
Essex County, MA	2,221
DuPage County, IL	2,214
Broward County, FL	2,211
Jackson County, MO	2,134
Arapahoe County, CO	2,132
Norfolk County, MA	2,124
Polk County, IA	2,122
San Mateo County, CA	2,083
Prince George's County, MD	2,037
Bernalillo County, NM	1,949
Franklin County, OH	1,882
Clark County, WA	1,860
Denton County, TX	1,849

Place	Number
San Jose, CA (city) Santa Clara County	59,187
Garden Grove, CA (city) Orange County	27,844
Houston, TX (city) Harris County	25,244
San Diego, CA (city) San Diego County	21,714
Westminster, CA (city) Orange County	21,185
Los Angeles, CA (city) Los Angeles County	15,353
Santa Ana, CA (city) Orange County	15,094
New York, NY (city)	9,828
Seattle, WA (city) King County	9,139
Philadelphia, PA (city) Philadelphia County	8,937
Boston, MA (city) Suffolk County	8,864
Portland, OR (city) Multnomah County	8,611
San Francisco, CA (city) San Francisco County	8,418
Anaheim, CA (city) Orange County	8,058
Arlington, TX (city) Tarrant County	6,946
Chicago, IL (city) Cook County	6,533
Oakland, CA (city) Alameda County	6,289
Milpitas, CA (city) Santa Clara County	6,068
Oklahoma City, OK (city) Oklahoma County	5,940
Dallas, TX (city) Dallas County	5,895
Fountain Valley, CA (city) Orange County	5,285
El Monte, CA (city) Los Angeles County	5,055
Honolulu, HI (cdp) Honolulu County	5,011
Garland, TX (city) Dallas County	4,927
Rosemead, CA (city) Los Angeles County	4,760
Wichita, KS (city) Sedgwick County	4,650
Sacramento, CA (city) Sacramento County	4,462
New Orleans, LA (city) Orleans Parish	4,456
Austin, TX (city) Travis County	4,159
Huntington Beach, CA (city) Orange County	4,145
Fort Worth, TX (city) Tarrant County	4,039
Long Beach, CA (city) Los Angeles County	3,877
Santa Clara, CA (city) Santa Clara County	3,621
Stockton, CA (city) San Joaquin County	3,583
Alhambra, CA (city) Los Angeles County	3,580
Denver, CO (city) Denver County	3,364
Phoenix, AZ (city) Maricopa County	3,282
Irvine, CA (city) Orange County	3,243
Worcester, MA (city) Worcester County	3,241
Charlotte, NC (city) Mecklenburg County	3,183
Fremont, CA (city) Alameda County	3,110
Lincoln, NE (city) Lancaster County	3,016
Annandale, VA (cdp) Fairfax County	2,821
Orange, CA (city) Orange County	2,785
Tacoma, WA (city) Pierce County	2,619
St. Louis, MO (city) Saint Louis Independent City	2,603
Sunnyvale, CA (city) Santa Clara County	2,573
Monterey Park, CA (city) Los Angeles County	2,543
Kansas City, MO (city) Jackson County	2,277
Minneapolis, MN (city) Hennepin County	2,274
Stanton, CA (city) Orange County	2,259
Memphis, TN (city) Shelby County	2,114
San Gabriel, CA (city) Los Angeles County	2,051
St. Paul, MN (city) Ramsey County	2,012
Baton Rouge, LA (city) East Baton Rouge Parish	1,951
Jefferson, VA (cdp) Fairfax County	1,904
Hayward, CA (city) Alameda County	1,896
Albuquerque, NM (city) Bernalillo County	1,883
San Antonio, TX (city) Bexar County	1,814
Carrollton, TX (city) Denton County	1,811
Costa Mesa, CA (city) Orange County	1,768
Des Moines, IA (city) Polk County	1,765
Arlington, VA (cdp) Arlington County	1,747
Columbus, OH (city) Franklin County	1,740
West Covina, CA (city) Los Angeles County	1,688
Greensboro, NC (city) Guilford County	1,657
White Center, WA (cdp) King County	1,614
Springfield, VA (cdp) Fairfax County	1,608
Grand Prairie, TX (city) Dallas County	1,603
Riverside, CA (city) Riverside County	1,564
Port Arthur, TX (city) Jefferson County	1,551
Jacksonville, FL (city) Duval County	1,535
Elk Grove, CA (cdp) Sacramento County	1,529
Aurora, CO (city) Arapahoe County	1,516
Atlanta, GA (city) Fulton County	1,463

Notes: Please refer to the User's Guide for an explanation of data; ranking tables include all places with Asian and/or NHPI populations above SF4 population thresholds; (1) tables reflect only those areas that meet SF4 population thresholds, therefore there may be less than 50 states, 75 counties or 75 places listed

Foreign Born

Vietnamese

All States, Top 75 Counties, and Top 75 Places Sorted by Percent[1]

State	Percent
District of Columbia	87.03
Vermont	83.49
New Hampshire	82.88
Iowa	82.84
Georgia	81.40
New York	79.79
Nevada	79.44
Virginia	79.44
Minnesota	79.23
Tennessee	78.95
Maryland	78.65
Nebraska	78.64
Connecticut	78.44
Kentucky	78.38
Washington	78.04
North Carolina	77.77
South Carolina	77.35
Florida	77.13
Pennsylvania	76.95
New Mexico	76.90
Hawaii	76.75
Illinois	76.70
Arizona	76.64
Massachusetts	76.63
Missouri	76.21
Alaska	76.16
United States	76.10
California	76.02
New Jersey	76.01
Idaho	75.88
Indiana	75.88
Oregon	75.81
Oklahoma	75.66
Ohio	75.58
South Dakota	75.52
Michigan	74.39
Texas	74.23
Utah	74.21
Colorado	74.15
Kansas	73.88
Rhode Island	73.74
Maine	73.54
Arkansas	72.46
Wisconsin	71.35
Delaware	70.12
Alabama	69.49
West Virginia	64.93
Louisiana	64.43
Mississippi	61.98

County	Percent
Nassau County, NY	92.89
Adams County, NE	91.53
Union County, NJ	91.18
Stearns County, MN	89.84
Alexandria Independent City, VA	89.26
Clayton County, GA	87.61
Hall County, GA	87.38
Spokane County, WA	86.90
Broome County, NY	86.55
Hampton Independent City, VA	86.53
Onondaga County, NY	85.14
Lubbock County, TX	85.05
Greenville County, SC	84.90
Marion County, IN	84.80
Hillsborough County, NH	84.76
Polk County, IA	84.61
Marin County, CA	84.28
Hamilton County, TN	84.17
DeKalb County, GA	83.93
Scott County, IA	83.27
Winnebago County, IL	83.25
Orange County, FL	82.85
Cumberland County, NC	82.80
Chatham County, GA	82.45
Queens County, NY	82.43
Guilford County, NC	82.10
Montgomery County, MD	82.10
Chittenden County, VT	82.08
Hartford County, CT	81.79
Bucks County, PA	81.75
Allen County, IN	81.71
Fulton County, GA	81.63
Jefferson County, KY	81.56
Hudson County, NJ	81.46
Bristol County, MA	81.42
Pierce County, WA	81.36
Fairfax County, VA	81.31
Erie County, NY	81.24
Finney County, KS	81.13
Hennepin County, MN	81.13
Woodbury County, IA	80.96
Mecklenburg County, NC	80.91
Hillsborough County, FL	80.89
Saint Louis Independent City, MO	80.86
Champaign County, IL	80.84
Summit County, OH	80.80
Clark County, NV	80.74
San Francisco County, CA	80.71
Philadelphia County, PA	80.70
Bronx County, NY	80.60
Dauphin County, PA	80.56
Davidson County, TN	80.37
Cumberland County, PA	80.36
Butler County, OH	80.31
Miami-Dade County, FL	80.31
Henrico County, VA	80.30
Cumberland County, ME	80.21
Lancaster County, NE	80.06
El Paso County, CO	79.98
Gwinnett County, GA	79.93
Hampden County, MA	79.89
Arlington County, VA	79.81
Hamilton County, OH	79.64
Shelby County, TN	79.62
Chester County, PA	79.50
York County, PA	79.45
Pima County, AZ	79.27
Sonoma County, CA	79.16
Suffolk County, MA	79.15
Suffolk County, NY	79.12
Clark County, WA	79.05
Ada County, ID	78.90
Monmouth County, NJ	78.87
Cobb County, GA	78.82
Tulsa County, OK	78.81

Place	Percent
Aspen Hill, MD (cdp) Montgomery County	95.59
Gainesville, GA (city) Hall County	95.51
North Highlands, CA (cdp) Sacramento County	94.07
Chamblee, GA (city) De Kalb County	92.75
Binghamton, NY (city) Broome County	92.20
Rockford, IL (city) Winnebago County	91.81
Hastings, NE (city) Adams County	91.53
Las Vegas, NV (city) Clark County	90.49
Tampa, FL (city) Hillsborough County	90.21
Carson, CA (city) Los Angeles County	89.72
Forest Park, GA (city) Clayton County	89.46
Hartford, CT (city) Hartford County	89.37
Seven Corners, VA (cdp) Fairfax County	89.09
St. Cloud, MN (city) Stearns County	89.03
Pine Hills, FL (cdp) Orange County	88.77
Doraville, GA (city) De Kalb County	88.42
Montclair, CA (city) San Bernardino County	88.06
Bloomington, MN (city) Hennepin County	87.87
Fort Wayne, IN (city) Allen County	87.64
Hacienda Heights, CA (cdp) Los Angeles County	87.34
North Springfield, VA (cdp) Fairfax County	87.24
Rosemont, CA (cdp) Sacramento County	87.04
Springfield, VA (cdp) Fairfax County	87.01
Burlington, VT (city) Chittenden County	86.84
Tucker, GA (cdp) De Kalb County	86.81
Town 'n' Country, FL (cdp) Hillsborough County	86.73
Spokane, WA (city) Spokane County	86.69
Manchester, NH (city) Hillsborough County	86.53
Riverdale, GA (city) Clayton County	86.38
Pittsburgh, PA (city) Allegheny County	86.19
Atlanta, GA (city) Fulton County	86.16
South El Monte, CA (city) Los Angeles County	86.08
Pasadena, CA (city) Los Angeles County	85.96
Greensboro, NC (city) Guilford County	85.77
White Oak, MD (cdp) Montgomery County	85.67
Rockville, MD (city) Montgomery County	85.62
Syracuse, NY (city) Onondaga County	85.61
Glendale, AZ (city) Maricopa County	85.50
Bellevue, WA (city) King County	85.45
Wheaton-Glenmont, MD (cdp) Montgomery County	85.43
Oak Ridge, FL (cdp) Orange County	85.39
Bryn Mawr-Skyway, WA (cdp) King County	85.18
Lubbock, TX (city) Lubbock County	85.05
Mountain View, CA (city) Santa Clara County	84.94
West Valley City, UT (city) Salt Lake County	84.89
South San Gabriel, CA (cdp) Los Angeles County	84.84
West Hartford, CT (town) Hartford County	84.63
Mesa, AZ (city) Maricopa County	84.62
Medford, MA (city) Middlesex County	84.57
San Rafael, CA (city) Marin County	84.40
Indianapolis, IN (sp. city) Marion County	84.39
Bailey's Crossroads, VA (cdp) Fairfax County	84.35
Alondra Park, CA (cdp) Los Angeles County	84.28
Annandale, VA (cdp) Fairfax County	84.23
Des Moines, IA (city) Polk County	84.17
Belleville, NJ (township) Essex County	83.96
Tacoma, WA (city) Pierce County	83.94
Cary, NC (town) Wake County	83.92
Dallas, TX (city) Dallas County	83.38
Davenport, IA (city) Scott County	83.35
Camden, NJ (city) Camden County	83.23
Jefferson, VA (cdp) Fairfax County	83.18
Idylwood, VA (cdp) Fairfax County	83.08
Charlotte, NC (city) Mecklenburg County	83.02
Grand Rapids, MI (city) Kent County	83.00
Buffalo, NY (city) Erie County	82.92
Paradise, NV (cdp) Clark County	82.88
Glendale, CA (city) Los Angeles County	82.77
Salt Lake City, UT (city) Salt Lake County	82.68
Stanton, CA (city) Orange County	82.60
Harrisburg, PA (city) Dauphin County	82.58
Herndon, VA (town) Fairfax County	82.55
East Hartford, CT (town) Hartford County	82.46
Lynnwood, WA (city) Snohomish County	82.23
Overland Park, KS (city) Johnson County	82.17

Notes: Please refer to the User's Guide for an explanation of data; ranking tables include all places with Asian and/or NHPI populations above SF4 population thresholds; (1) tables reflect only those areas that meet SF4 population thresholds, therefore there may be less than 50 states, 75 counties or 75 places listed

Foreign-Born Naturalized Citizens

Total Population

All States, Top 75 Counties, and Top 75 Places Sorted by Number[1]

State	Number
United States	12,542,626
California	3,473,266
New York	1,783,744
Florida	1,207,502
Texas	914,326
New Jersey	682,304
Illinois	603,521
Massachusetts	337,617
Washington	257,648
Pennsylvania	257,339
Michigan	239,955
Maryland	234,711
Virginia	232,767
Arizona	193,944
Connecticut	180,267
Ohio	169,295
Georgia	169,232
Hawaii	127,532
Colorado	116,875
Nevada	116,786
North Carolina	112,822
Oregon	97,381
Minnesota	97,308
Wisconsin	76,223
Indiana	70,983
Missouri	61,786
Rhode Island	56,184
Louisiana	56,102
Tennessee	53,185
New Mexico	52,103
Utah	48,178
Oklahoma	45,766
Kansas	44,763
South Carolina	42,983
Alabama	32,200
Iowa	29,951
Kentucky	27,569
New Hampshire	25,761
Nebraska	23,918
Arkansas	22,055
District of Columbia	22,050
Idaho	21,203
Maine	20,252
Alaska	20,011
Delaware	19,052
Mississippi	16,098
Vermont	12,451
West Virginia	10,446
Montana	9,482
South Dakota	5,452
North Dakota	5,156
Wyoming	5,121

County	Number
Los Angeles County, CA	1,311,755
Miami-Dade County, FL	535,080
Queens County, NY	466,608
Kings County, NY	439,973
Cook County, IL	420,739
Orange County, CA	322,592
San Diego County, CA	250,125
Santa Clara County, CA	235,952
Harris County, TX	223,609
Broward County, FL	183,641
New York County, NY	179,785
Alameda County, CA	169,708
San Francisco County, CA	163,426
Bronx County, NY	152,521
Nassau County, NY	132,767
San Bernardino County, CA	120,983
King County, WA	118,436
Maricopa County, AZ	114,048
Bergen County, NJ	112,882
San Mateo County, CA	111,735
Riverside County, CA	106,834
Honolulu County, HI	102,311
Dallas County, TX	102,201
Montgomery County, MD	100,658
Fairfax County, VA	98,601
Hudson County, NJ	97,376
Middlesex County, MA	91,978
Clark County, NV	90,437
Westchester County, NY	85,546
Sacramento County, CA	83,982
Palm Beach County, FL	83,681
Contra Costa County, CA	82,317
Middlesex County, NJ	77,921
El Paso County, TX	77,821
Suffolk County, NY	77,416
Essex County, NJ	73,983
Philadelphia County, PA	64,786
Suffolk County, MA	63,450
Bexar County, TX	63,432
Fairfield County, CT	62,953
Wayne County, MI	62,926
DuPage County, IL	61,601
Ventura County, CA	61,540
Oakland County, MI	58,944
Union County, NJ	58,826
Tarrant County, TX	56,074
Hartford County, CT	54,803
Passaic County, NJ	53,888
Orange County, FL	53,651
Cuyahoga County, OH	50,362
Fresno County, CA	49,397
Hidalgo County, TX	48,474
Hillsborough County, FL	47,127
Prince George's County, MD	42,817
Providence County, RI	42,285
Norfolk County, MA	42,260
Pinellas County, FL	40,786
Richmond County, NY	39,800
Pima County, AZ	39,665
San Joaquin County, CA	39,437
Macomb County, MI	36,883
New Haven County, CT	36,699
Hennepin County, MN	36,519
Bristol County, MA	36,225
Morris County, NJ	36,134
Solano County, CA	35,301
Lake County, IL	35,300
Monmouth County, NJ	34,090
Essex County, MA	33,707
Kern County, CA	33,590
Monterey County, CA	33,530
Travis County, TX	32,375
Fort Bend County, TX	30,828
Stanislaus County, CA	30,603
Gwinnett County, GA	29,838

Place	Number
New York, NY (city)	1,278,687
Los Angeles, CA (city) Los Angeles County	509,841
Chicago, IL (city) Cook County	223,984
San Francisco, CA (city) San Francisco County	163,426
San Jose, CA (city) Santa Clara County	140,542
Houston, TX (city) Harris County	136,472
San Diego, CA (city) San Diego County	134,456
Miami, FL (city) Miami-Dade County	89,727
Hempstead, NY (town) Nassau County	73,040
Hialeah, FL (city) Miami-Dade County	70,331
El Paso, TX (city) El Paso County	64,900
Philadelphia, PA (city) Philadelphia County	64,786
Boston, MA (city) Suffolk County	56,681
Dallas, TX (city) Dallas County	55,607
San Antonio, TX (city) Bexar County	54,322
Honolulu, HI (cdp) Honolulu County	53,278
Phoenix, AZ (city) Maricopa County	52,874
Glendale, CA (city) Los Angeles County	52,023
Long Beach, CA (city) Los Angeles County	45,713
Seattle, WA (city) King County	44,334
Santa Ana, CA (city) Orange County	42,269
Anaheim, CA (city) Orange County	38,125
Oakland, CA (city) Alameda County	37,783
Sacramento, CA (city) Sacramento County	34,257
Fremont, CA (city) Alameda County	33,755
Jersey City, NJ (city) Hudson County	33,609
Daly City, CA (city) San Mateo County	32,278
Las Vegas, NV (city) Clark County	30,945
North Hempstead, NY (town) Nassau County	30,865
Garden Grove, CA (city) Orange County	29,909
Austin, TX (city) Travis County	26,747
Fresno, CA (city) Fresno County	26,304
Portland, OR (city) Multnomah County	24,617
Tucson, AZ (city) Pima County	24,548
Chula Vista, CA (city) San Diego County	24,203
Fort Worth, TX (city) Tarrant County	23,713
Alhambra, CA (city) Los Angeles County	22,888
Pembroke Pines, FL (city) Broward County	22,597
Oyster Bay, NY (town) Nassau County	22,589
Yonkers, NY (city) Westchester County	22,521
Irvine, CA (city) Orange County	22,294
Denver, CO (city) Denver County	22,144
Miami Beach, FL (city) Miami-Dade County	21,744
Stockton, CA (city) San Joaquin County	21,734
Newark, NJ (city) Essex County	21,412
Oxnard, CA (city) Ventura County	20,862
Jacksonville, FL (city) Duval County	20,786
Brookhaven, NY (town) Suffolk County	20,640
Elizabeth, NJ (city) Union County	19,345
El Monte, CA (city) Los Angeles County	19,300
Islip, NY (town) Suffolk County	19,295
West Covina, CA (city) Los Angeles County	19,213
Westminster, CA (city) Orange County	19,200
Hayward, CA (city) Alameda County	19,046
Riverside, CA (city) Riverside County	18,788
Torrance, CA (city) Los Angeles County	18,711
Fountainbleau, FL (cdp) Miami-Dade County	18,348
Monterey Park, CA (city) Los Angeles County	18,086
Kendale Lakes, FL (cdp) Miami-Dade County	17,856
Paterson, NJ (city) Passaic County	17,263
Downey, CA (city) Los Angeles County	17,241
Laredo, TX (city) Webb County	17,120
Sunnyvale, CA (city) Santa Clara County	17,067
Huntington Beach, CA (city) Orange County	16,744
Charlotte, NC (city) Mecklenburg County	16,709
Kendall, FL (cdp) Miami-Dade County	16,474
Vallejo, CA (city) Solano County	16,443
Pomona, CA (city) Los Angeles County	16,417
Pasadena, CA (city) Los Angeles County	16,378
Burbank, CA (city) Los Angeles County	16,180
Hollywood, FL (city) Broward County	16,136
East Los Angeles, CA (cdp) Los Angeles County	16,059
Carson, CA (city) Los Angeles County	15,728
Union City, CA (city) Alameda County	15,600
Arlington, TX (city) Tarrant County	15,569

Notes: Please refer to the User's Guide for an explanation of data; ranking tables include all places with Asian and/or NHPI populations above SF4 population thresholds; (1) tables reflect only those areas that meet SF4 population thresholds, therefore there may be less than 50 states, 75 counties or 75 places listed

Foreign-Born Naturalized Citizens

Total Population

All States, Top 75 Counties, and Top 75 Places Sorted by Percent[1]

State	Percent
Hawaii	10.53
California	10.25
New York	9.40
New Jersey	8.11
Florida	7.56
Nevada	5.84
Rhode Island	5.36
Massachusetts	5.32
Connecticut	5.29
Illinois	4.86
United States	4.46
Maryland	4.43
Texas	4.38
Washington	4.37
District of Columbia	3.85
Arizona	3.78
Virginia	3.29
Alaska	3.19
New Mexico	2.86
Oregon	2.85
Colorado	2.72
Delaware	2.43
Michigan	2.41
Utah	2.16
Pennsylvania	2.10
New Hampshire	2.08
Georgia	2.07
Vermont	2.05
Minnesota	1.98
Kansas	1.67
Idaho	1.64
Maine	1.59
Ohio	1.49
Wisconsin	1.42
Nebraska	1.40
North Carolina	1.40
Oklahoma	1.33
Louisiana	1.26
Indiana	1.17
Missouri	1.10
South Carolina	1.07
Montana	1.05
Wyoming	1.04
Iowa	1.02
Tennessee	0.93
Arkansas	0.82
North Dakota	0.80
Alabama	0.72
South Dakota	0.72
Kentucky	0.68
West Virginia	0.58
Mississippi	0.57

County	Percent
Miami-Dade County, FL	23.75
San Francisco County, CA	21.04
Queens County, NY	20.93
Kings County, NY	17.85
Hudson County, NJ	15.99
San Mateo County, CA	15.80
Santa Clara County, CA	14.02
Los Angeles County, CA	13.78
Bergen County, NJ	12.77
Imperial County, CA	12.60
Alameda County, CA	11.75
New York County, NY	11.70
Honolulu County, HI	11.68
Montgomery County, MD	11.53
El Paso County, TX	11.45
Bronx County, NY	11.44
Orange County, CA	11.33
Broward County, FL	11.31
Union County, NJ	11.26
Passaic County, NJ	11.02
Middlesex County, NJ	10.39
Fairfax County, VA	10.17
Nassau County, NY	9.95
Maui County, HI	9.79
Webb County, TX	9.77
Rockland County, NY	9.71
Essex County, NJ	9.32
Westchester County, NY	9.26
Suffolk County, MA	9.20
Richmond County, NY	8.97
Solano County, CA	8.95
San Diego County, CA	8.89
Fairfax Independent City, VA	8.87
Cameron County, TX	8.82
Fort Bend County, TX	8.70
Contra Costa County, CA	8.68
Aleutians West Census Area, AK	8.66
Hidalgo County, TX	8.51
Somerset County, NJ	8.49
Monterey County, CA	8.35
Kodiak Island Borough, AK	8.28
Kauai County, HI	8.22
Ventura County, CA	8.17
Merced County, CA	7.98
Cook County, IL	7.83
Morris County, NJ	7.68
Arlington County, VA	7.60
Palm Beach County, FL	7.40
Alexandria Independent City, VA	7.21
Fairfield County, CT	7.13
San Bernardino County, CA	7.08
Yolo County, CA	7.06
San Joaquin County, CA	7.00
Marin County, CA	6.91
Riverside County, CA	6.91
Santa Barbara County, CA	6.88
Sacramento County, CA	6.86
Stanislaus County, CA	6.85
King County, WA	6.82
DuPage County, IL	6.81
Falls Church Independent City, VA	6.80
Providence County, RI	6.80
Bristol County, MA	6.78
Sutter County, CA	6.76
Flagler County, FL	6.73
Harris County, TX	6.58
Bristol County, RI	6.57
Clark County, NV	6.57
Colusa County, CA	6.52
Norfolk County, MA	6.50
Dona Ana County, NM	6.43
Hartford County, CT	6.39
Yuma County, AZ	6.39
Monroe County, FL	6.29
Middlesex County, MA	6.28

Place	Percent
Sunset, FL (cdp) Miami-Dade County	32.98
Miami Lakes, FL (cdp) Miami-Dade County	32.32
Kendale Lakes, FL (cdp) Miami-Dade County	31.39
Daly City, CA (city) San Mateo County	31.17
Hialeah, FL (city) Miami-Dade County	31.06
Fountainbleau, FL (cdp) Miami-Dade County	30.83
Monterey Park, CA (city) Los Angeles County	30.18
Cerritos, CA (city) Los Angeles County	28.95
Rosemead, CA (city) Los Angeles County	27.69
Broadmoor, CA (cdp) San Mateo County	27.51
Walnut, CA (city) Los Angeles County	27.38
Glendale, CA (city) Los Angeles County	26.67
Alhambra, CA (city) Los Angeles County	26.63
San Gabriel, CA (city) Los Angeles County	26.39
Lincolnwood, IL (village) Cook County	26.15
Rowland Heights, CA (cdp) Los Angeles County	25.46
Englewood Cliffs, NJ (borough) Bergen County	25.40
North Bergen, NJ (township) Hudson County	24.89
San Marino, CA (city) Los Angeles County	24.86
Miami, FL (city) Miami-Dade County	24.75
Miami Beach, FL (city) Miami-Dade County	24.69
Kendall West, FL (cdp) Miami-Dade County	24.63
Coral Gables, FL (city) Miami-Dade County	24.38
The Hammocks, FL (cdp) Miami-Dade County	24.16
West New York, NJ (town) Hudson County	24.05
Richmond West, FL (cdp) Miami-Dade County	23.91
Milpitas, CA (city) Santa Clara County	23.89
Waipahu, HI (cdp) Honolulu County	23.74
Ewa Villages, HI (cdp) Honolulu County	23.70
Beverly Hills, CA (city) Los Angeles County	23.59
Glenvar Heights, FL (cdp) Miami-Dade County	23.50
Union City, CA (city) Alameda County	23.33
Morton Grove, IL (village) Cook County	23.32
East San Gabriel, CA (cdp) Los Angeles County	23.05
Hercules, CA (city) Contra Costa County	23.02
South San Gabriel, CA (cdp) Los Angeles County	22.78
Diamond Bar, CA (city) Los Angeles County	22.71
Temple City, CA (city) Los Angeles County	22.25
Haliimaile, HI (cdp) Maui County	22.01
Kendall, FL (cdp) Miami-Dade County	21.88
Westminster, CA (city) Orange County	21.85
South San Francisco, CA (city) San Mateo County	21.84
Rollingwood, CA (cdp) Contra Costa County	21.82
Arcadia, CA (city) Los Angeles County	21.79
Millbrae, CA (city) San Mateo County	21.78
Skokie, IL (village) Cook County	21.72
Hacienda Heights, CA (cdp) Los Angeles County	21.69
Lanai City, HI (cdp) Maui County	21.58
Union City, NJ (city) Hudson County	21.56
North Valley Stream, NY (cdp) Nassau County	21.28
Niles, IL (village) Cook County	21.23
Fairview, NJ (borough) Bergen County	21.17
Hillcrest, NY (cdp) Rockland County	21.12
Fort Lee, NJ (borough) Bergen County	21.06
San Francisco, CA (city) San Francisco County	21.04
Palisades Park, NJ (borough) Bergen County	20.97
La Palma, CA (city) Orange County	20.93
Manhasset Hills, NY (cdp) Nassau County	20.87
Elmont, NY (cdp) Nassau County	20.82
North Miami Beach, FL (city) Miami-Dade County	20.82
Cliffside Park, NJ (borough) Bergen County	20.79
Village Park, HI (cdp) Honolulu County	20.69
Whitmore Village, HI (cdp) Honolulu County	20.64
Artesia, CA (city) Los Angeles County	20.62
Searingtown, NY (cdp) Nassau County	20.57
Guttenberg, NJ (town) Hudson County	20.50
East Pasadena, CA (cdp) Los Angeles County	20.44
Oak Brook, IL (village) Du Page County	20.38
Great Neck, NY (village) Nassau County	20.37
South Miami Heights, FL (cdp) Miami-Dade County	20.24
Miramar, FL (city) Broward County	20.19
Calexico, CA (city) Imperial County	20.16
West Hollywood, CA (city) Los Angeles County	20.16
North Miami, FL (city) Miami-Dade County	20.05
Country Club, FL (cdp) Miami-Dade County	19.98

Notes: Please refer to the User's Guide for an explanation of data; ranking tables include all places with Asian and/or NHPI populations above SF4 population thresholds; (1) tables reflect only those areas that meet SF4 population thresholds, therefore there may be less than 50 states, 75 counties or 75 places listed

Foreign-Born Naturalized Citizens

Asian

All States, Top 75 Counties, and Top 75 Places Sorted by Number[1]

State	Number
United States	3,502,021
California	1,368,752
New York	353,021
Texas	191,788
New Jersey	167,391
Illinois	147,868
Washington	117,072
Hawaii	107,282
Florida	99,107
Virginia	97,291
Maryland	82,219
Pennsylvania	72,517
Massachusetts	72,105
Michigan	53,383
Georgia	52,201
Minnesota	42,403
Ohio	41,939
Nevada	34,206
Oregon	32,409
North Carolina	32,092
Colorado	29,575
Arizona	28,524
Connecticut	27,408
Missouri	20,840
Wisconsin	20,437
Louisiana	18,233
Indiana	17,253
Tennessee	16,916
Oklahoma	15,804
Kansas	15,233
South Carolina	12,657
Iowa	11,527
Utah	10,311
Alabama	10,033
Alaska	9,849
Kentucky	8,732
Rhode Island	7,420
Nebraska	6,801
New Mexico	6,274
Mississippi	6,151
Delaware	5,742
Arkansas	5,729
New Hampshire	4,642
District of Columbia	3,599
West Virginia	3,516
Idaho	3,272
Maine	3,153
Vermont	2,006
South Dakota	1,611
Montana	1,545
Wyoming	1,144
North Dakota	1,038

County	Number
Los Angeles County, CA	428,680
Orange County, CA	155,731
Santa Clara County, CA	149,168
Queens County, NY	132,674
San Francisco County, CA	111,416
Alameda County, CA	104,462
San Diego County, CA	95,664
Cook County, IL	92,410
Honolulu County, HI	87,775
King County, WA	65,954
Kings County, NY	64,153
Harris County, TX	63,865
San Mateo County, CA	57,371
Fairfax County, VA	47,287
New York County, NY	43,667
Sacramento County, CA	41,775
Montgomery County, MD	39,168
Contra Costa County, CA	38,076
Middlesex County, NJ	32,067
San Bernardino County, CA	30,535
Bergen County, NJ	29,180
Clark County, NV	27,736
DuPage County, IL	25,806
Dallas County, TX	25,655
Middlesex County, MA	25,037
Nassau County, NY	24,149
Solano County, CA	21,021
Riverside County, CA	20,545
Maricopa County, AZ	20,181
Philadelphia County, PA	19,477
Hudson County, NJ	19,289
San Joaquin County, CA	17,968
Tarrant County, TX	17,224
Ventura County, CA	16,214
Fort Bend County, TX	16,090
Hennepin County, MN	15,909
Suffolk County, MA	14,763
Oakland County, MI	14,720
Fresno County, CA	14,662
Snohomish County, WA	14,242
Broward County, FL	13,921
Pierce County, WA	13,372
Norfolk County, MA	13,222
Gwinnett County, GA	13,179
Suffolk County, NY	12,799
Multnomah County, OR	12,585
Bronx County, NY	12,434
Morris County, NJ	11,903
Miami-Dade County, FL	11,851
Prince George's County, MD	11,775
Westchester County, NY	11,746
Essex County, NJ	10,998
Orange County, FL	10,922
Wayne County, MI	10,832
Ramsey County, MN	10,641
Montgomery County, PA	10,508
Collin County, TX	10,507
Travis County, TX	10,477
Richmond County, NY	10,174
Maui County, HI	9,662
Monmouth County, NJ	9,630
Virginia Beach Independent City, VA	9,500
Washington County, OR	9,456
Baltimore County, MD	9,390
Fairfield County, CT	9,292
Bexar County, TX	9,130
Somerset County, NJ	8,872
Cuyahoga County, OH	8,802
Lake County, IL	8,739
Monterey County, CA	8,311
Camden County, NJ	8,055
Duval County, FL	7,933
St. Louis County, MO	7,786
Franklin County, OH	7,770
Howard County, MD	7,507

Place	Number
New York, NY (city)	263,102
Los Angeles, CA (city) Los Angeles County	132,527
San Francisco, CA (city) San Francisco County	111,416
San Jose, CA (city) Santa Clara County	90,797
San Diego, CA (city) San Diego County	63,508
Honolulu, HI (cdp) Honolulu County	46,284
Chicago, IL (city) Cook County	44,502
Houston, TX (city) Harris County	35,425
Seattle, WA (city) King County	26,324
Fremont, CA (city) Alameda County	23,950
Daly City, CA (city) San Mateo County	23,708
Oakland, CA (city) Alameda County	22,333
Garden Grove, CA (city) Orange County	21,200
Philadelphia, PA (city) Philadelphia County	19,477
Long Beach, CA (city) Los Angeles County	19,452
Sacramento, CA (city) Sacramento County	18,545
Alhambra, CA (city) Los Angeles County	17,714
Anaheim, CA (city) Orange County	15,633
Westminster, CA (city) Orange County	15,152
Monterey Park, CA (city) Los Angeles County	14,952
Santa Ana, CA (city) Orange County	13,986
Jersey City, NJ (city) Hudson County	13,927
Irvine, CA (city) Orange County	13,670
Boston, MA (city) Suffolk County	13,531
Stockton, CA (city) San Joaquin County	13,177
Milpitas, CA (city) Santa Clara County	13,088
Cerritos, CA (city) Los Angeles County	12,578
Vallejo, CA (city) Solano County	12,075
Glendale, CA (city) Los Angeles County	12,017
Union City, CA (city) Alameda County	12,005
Portland, OR (city) Multnomah County	11,452
Rosemead, CA (city) Los Angeles County	11,380
Sunnyvale, CA (city) Santa Clara County	11,072
Torrance, CA (city) Los Angeles County	10,840
Fresno, CA (city) Fresno County	10,739
West Covina, CA (city) Los Angeles County	10,294
Hayward, CA (city) Alameda County	10,260
Hempstead, NY (town) Nassau County	10,012
El Monte, CA (city) Los Angeles County	9,791
Rowland Heights, CA (cdp) Los Angeles County	9,616
Diamond Bar, CA (city) Los Angeles County	9,358
Dallas, TX (city) Dallas County	8,886
Arcadia, CA (city) Los Angeles County	8,867
Carson, CA (city) Los Angeles County	8,748
Edison, NJ (township) Middlesex County	8,567
Austin, TX (city) Travis County	8,452
Las Vegas, NV (city) Clark County	8,304
Santa Clara, CA (city) Santa Clara County	8,125
San Gabriel, CA (city) Los Angeles County	8,082
Hacienda Heights, CA (cdp) Los Angeles County	7,693
North Hempstead, NY (town) Nassau County	7,690
Jacksonville, FL (city) Duval County	7,673
Huntington Beach, CA (city) Orange County	7,573
South San Francisco, CA (city) San Mateo County	7,528
Alameda, CA (city) Alameda County	7,423
Chula Vista, CA (city) San Diego County	7,380
San Leandro, CA (city) Alameda County	7,326
St. Paul, MN (city) Ramsey County	7,282
Waipahu, HI (cdp) Honolulu County	7,230
Phoenix, AZ (city) Maricopa County	7,205
San Antonio, TX (city) Bexar County	7,160
Fullerton, CA (city) Orange County	7,010
Plano, TX (city) Collin County	7,003
Walnut, CA (city) Los Angeles County	6,853
Fountain Valley, CA (city) Orange County	6,784
Oklahoma City, OK (city) Oklahoma County	6,371
Chino Hills, CA (city) San Bernardino County	6,332
Sugar Land, TX (city) Fort Bend County	6,257
Arlington, TX (city) Tarrant County	6,207
Cupertino, CA (city) Santa Clara County	6,072
Buena Park, CA (city) Orange County	6,021
Oxnard, CA (city) Ventura County	5,904
Bellevue, WA (city) King County	5,885
Quincy, MA (city) Norfolk County	5,798
Skokie, IL (village) Cook County	5,748

Notes: Please refer to the User's Guide for an explanation of data; ranking tables include all places with Asian and/or NHPI populations above SF4 population thresholds; (1) tables reflect only those areas that meet SF4 population thresholds, therefore there may be less than 50 states, 75 counties or 75 places listed

Foreign-Born Naturalized Citizens

Asian

All States, Top 75 Counties, and Top 75 Places Sorted by Percent[1]

State	Percent
Vermont	41.35
Maryland	39.21
Alaska	38.63
Wyoming	38.49
Nevada	38.38
Maine	38.18
Virginia	37.95
Florida	37.49
West Virginia	37.23
California	37.16
Washington	36.47
Delaware	35.77
Montana	35.41
Illinois	34.92
New Jersey	34.74
Mississippi	34.73
Oklahoma	34.70
South Carolina	34.67
Texas	34.50
Missouri	34.49
United States	34.43
New Mexico	34.31
South Dakota	34.07
Kansas	34.02
New York	33.80
Alabama	33.55
Pennsylvania	33.47
Connecticut	33.31
Iowa	32.91
Louisiana	32.86
Oregon	32.69
Nebraska	32.19
Ohio	31.74
Colorado	31.70
Arizona	31.27
Tennessee	31.25
Rhode Island	31.14
North Dakota	31.06
Michigan	30.54
Minnesota	30.45
Georgia	30.44
Massachusetts	30.26
Indiana	30.17
Kentucky	30.12
New Hampshire	30.10
Arkansas	30.02
Idaho	28.90
North Carolina	28.84
Utah	27.96
Wisconsin	24.60
District of Columbia	24.38
Hawaii	21.29

County	Percent
Kaufman County, TX	64.27
Madison County, MS	62.74
Cape May County, NJ	62.11
Flathead County, MT	60.16
Geauga County, OH	59.73
Windsor County, VT	59.64
Wright County, MN	58.67
Washington County, VT	57.25
Kankakee County, IL	55.48
Pottawattamie County, IA	54.74
Stafford County, VA	54.51
Chautauqua County, NY	54.33
Northumberland County, PA	53.89
Hoke County, NC	53.88
Guadalupe County, TX	53.46
Pulaski County, MO	53.11
Santa Rosa County, FL	53.05
Wayne County, NY	53.05
Steele County, MN	52.91
Wood County, WV	52.91
Blair County, PA	52.85
Colonial Heights Independent City, VA	52.72
Geary County, KS	52.24
St. Louis County, MN	52.19
Windham County, VT	52.16
Martin County, FL	51.93
McLeod County, MN	51.87
Chenango County, NY	51.46
Ketchikan Gateway Borough, AK	51.44
Crow Wing County, MN	50.92
Matanuska-Susitna Borough, AK	50.65
Clarion County, PA	50.63
Franklin County, MO	50.61
Rankin County, MS	50.54
Cochise County, AZ	50.15
Ontario County, NY	49.86
Laramie County, WY	49.82
Henderson County, NC	49.77
Chesapeake Independent City, VA	49.53
Columbia County, PA	49.49
Orange County, TX	49.35
Crawford County, PA	49.31
Saline County, KS	49.13
Livingston County, NY	49.05
Sumner County, TN	48.92
Clearfield County, PA	48.88
Howell County, MO	48.87
St. Joseph County, MI	48.82
Liberty County, GA	48.80
Putnam County, FL	48.80
Muskogee County, OK	48.43
Lebanon County, PA	48.38
Oldham County, KY	48.36
Pike County, PA	48.30
Sullivan County, TN	48.21
Columbia County, GA	48.12
Muskegon County, MI	48.05
Sandoval County, NM	47.99
Comanche County, OK	47.90
Wayne County, PA	47.83
Leavenworth County, KS	47.79
Okaloosa County, FL	47.72
Stark County, OH	47.71
Harford County, MD	47.59
Carroll County, GA	47.56
Aiken County, SC	47.45
Ashtabula County, OH	47.39
Clark County, OH	47.39
Linn County, OR	47.18
Kanawha County, WV	47.13
Virginia Beach Independent City, VA	47.01
Saratoga County, NY	46.95
Manatee County, FL	46.94
Wayne County, NC	46.94
Suffolk Independent City, VA	46.90

Place	Percent
Brier, WA (city) Snohomish County	66.05
Town and Country, MO (city) Saint Louis County	65.14
Palmer, PA (township) Northampton County	64.13
Springfield, PA (township) Delaware County	63.66
Camp Springs, MD (cdp) Prince George's County	62.99
Oak Brook, IL (village) Du Page County	61.13
Hillsdale, NJ (borough) Bergen County	59.61
Universal City, TX (city) Bexar County	59.50
Neptune, NJ (township) Monmouth County	59.44
Willingboro, NJ (township) Burlington County	58.70
Hunters Creek Village, TX (city) Harris County	58.64
Woodbridge, CT (town) New Haven County	58.64
Essex, VT (town) Chittenden County	58.45
Long Grove, IL (village) Lake County	58.31
Medford, NJ (township) Burlington County	58.30
Monroe, NJ (township) Middlesex County	58.08
Sands Point, NY (village) Nassau County	58.06
Old Westbury, NY (village) Nassau County	57.99
Bel Air South, MD (cdp) Harford County	57.89
San Juan Capistrano, CA (city) Orange County	57.87
Cinnaminson, NJ (township) Burlington County	57.54
East Hempfield, PA (township) Lancaster County	57.25
Burr Ridge, IL (village) Du Page County	56.98
Timberlane, LA (cdp) Jefferson Parish	56.90
Manheim, PA (township) Lancaster County	56.77
Barclay-Kingston, NJ (cdp) Camden County	56.63
South Barrington, IL (village) Cook County	56.44
Cheyenne, WY (city) Laramie County	56.24
Flossmoor, IL (village) Cook County	56.08
Junction City, KS (city) Geary County	55.85
Kemp Mill, MD (cdp) Montgomery County	55.83
Cornwall, NY (town) Orange County	55.78
East Northport, NY (cdp) Suffolk County	55.20
Perinton, NY (town) Monroe County	55.05
East Patchogue, NY (cdp) Suffolk County	55.03
Copperas Cove, TX (city) Coryell County	54.91
Summerlin South, NV (cdp) Clark County	54.89
Cheshire, CT (town) New Haven County	54.73
Tanglewilde-Thompson Pl., WA (cdp) Thurston County	54.70
Perry Hall, MD (cdp) Baltimore County	54.51
Kendale Lakes, FL (cdp) Miami-Dade County	54.45
Ferry Pass, FL (cdp) Escambia County	54.19
Oak Creek, WI (city) Milwaukee County	54.05
Friendly, MD (cdp) Prince George's County	54.03
Northampton, PA (township) Bucks County	54.01
Westwood, MA (town) Norfolk County	53.98
West Nyack, NY (cdp) Rockland County	53.94
Redford, MI (township) Wayne County	53.90
Colleyville, TX (city) Tarrant County	53.83
Broadmoor, CA (cdp) San Mateo County	53.79
Aldine, TX (cdp) Harris County	53.73
Briarcliff Manor, NY (village) Westchester County	53.66
Mayflower Village, CA (cdp) Los Angeles County	53.44
Lower Macungie, PA (township) Lehigh County	53.20
Cranbury, NJ (township) Middlesex County	53.15
Moorestown, NJ (township) Burlington County	52.90
Odenton, MD (cdp) Anne Arundel County	52.85
West Caldwell, NJ (township) Essex County	52.78
Blue Bell, PA (cdp) Montgomery County	52.73
Travilah, MD (cdp) Montgomery County	52.67
Spanaway, WA (cdp) Pierce County	52.63
Cimarron Hills, CO (cdp) El Paso County	52.62
Inver Grove Heights, MN (city) Dakota County	52.62
Sierra Vista, AZ (city) Cochise County	52.54
Garfield Heights, OH (city) Cuyahoga County	52.48
Hazlet, NJ (township) Monmouth County	52.38
Salmon Creek, WA (cdp) Clark County	52.30
Temple, TX (city) Bell County	52.30
West Lake Stevens, WA (cdp) Snohomish County	52.21
New Fairfield, CT (town) Fairfield County	52.19
Colesville, MD (cdp) Montgomery County	52.15
Beavercreek, OH (city) Greene County	52.12
Duluth, MN (city) Saint Louis County	52.11
Dunn Loring, VA (cdp) Fairfax County	52.08
Silverdale, WA (cdp) Kitsap County	52.03

Notes: Please refer to the User's Guide for an explanation of data; ranking tables include all places with Asian and/or NHPI populations above SF4 population thresholds; (1) tables reflect only those areas that meet SF4 population thresholds, therefore there may be less than 50 states, 75 counties or 75 places listed

Foreign-Born Naturalized Citizens

Native Hawaiian and Other Pacific Islander

All States, Top 75 Counties, and Top 75 Places Sorted by Number[1]

State	Number
United States	30,284
California	13,049
Hawaii	3,874
Utah	2,300
Washington	1,605
New York	1,096
Oregon	777
Texas	771
Florida	700
Nevada	512
Arizona	487
Illinois	443
Alaska	430
New Jersey	373
Virginia	323
Missouri	314
Pennsylvania	259
North Carolina	257
Georgia	234
Tennessee	233
Arkansas	225
Colorado	199
Maryland	187
Michigan	175
Oklahoma	166
Minnesota	143
Massachusetts	122
Ohio	115
Wisconsin	104
Indiana	102
South Carolina	85
Kentucky	79
Connecticut	67
Louisiana	66
Kansas	65
Idaho	54
Alabama	39
Iowa	35
Maine	33
Montana	28
West Virginia	27
Rhode Island	25
Nebraska	19
Delaware	17
New Mexico	12
Mississippi	7

County	Number
Los Angeles County, CA	3,474
Honolulu County, HI	3,217
Salt Lake County, UT	1,931
San Mateo County, CA	1,677
Sacramento County, CA	1,066
Alameda County, CA	967
King County, WA	961
Orange County, CA	933
San Diego County, CA	756
San Bernardino County, CA	652
Santa Clara County, CA	596
San Francisco County, CA	547
Contra Costa County, CA	487
Multnomah County, OR	382
Maui County, HI	363
Anchorage Borough, AK	330
Clark County, NV	327
Stanislaus County, CA	322
Maricopa County, AZ	318
Pierce County, WA	304
Queens County, NY	276
Kings County, NY	271
Ventura County, CA	269
Hawaii County, HI	267
Cook County, IL	259
Miami-Dade County, FL	220
Riverside County, CA	213
Bronx County, NY	193
Solano County, CA	189
Utah County, UT	183
Broward County, FL	176
Tarrant County, TX	174
San Joaquin County, CA	167
Washoe County, NV	167
Jackson County, MO	138
Washington County, AR	134
Monterey County, CA	125
Fairfax County, VA	118
Marion County, OR	117
Washington County, OR	116
Shelby County, TN	113
Philadelphia County, PA	110
Pima County, AZ	110
Harris County, TX	107
Santa Barbara County, CA	107
Davis County, UT	99
Montgomery County, MD	97
Hennepin County, MN	94
Dallas County, TX	87
New York County, NY	79
Spokane County, WA	79
Allegheny County, PA	69
Yolo County, CA	64
El Paso County, CO	63
Essex County, NJ	62
Kitsap County, WA	62
Bexar County, TX	61
Nassau County, NY	55
Suffolk County, NY	55
Milwaukee County, WI	54
Orange County, FL	53
Clark County, WA	48
Onslow County, NC	44
Bell County, TX	43
Lane County, OR	39
Sonoma County, CA	37
Hillsborough County, FL	34
Denver County, CO	29
St. Louis County, MO	29
Clackamas County, OR	27
Kauai County, HI	27
Snohomish County, WA	27
Sedgwick County, KS	25
Thurston County, WA	25
Washington County, UT	25

Place	Number
Honolulu, HI (cdp) Honolulu County	1,383
Long Beach, CA (city) Los Angeles County	886
New York, NY (city)	819
Los Angeles, CA (city) Los Angeles County	740
Sacramento, CA (city) Sacramento County	712
Salt Lake City, UT (city) Salt Lake County	673
San Francisco, CA (city) San Francisco County	547
West Valley City, UT (city) Salt Lake County	531
East Palo Alto, CA (city) San Mateo County	509
San Diego, CA (city) San Diego County	413
San Jose, CA (city) Santa Clara County	387
Portland, OR (city) Multnomah County	351
San Mateo, CA (city) San Mateo County	330
Oakland, CA (city) Alameda County	275
Lakewood, CA (city) Los Angeles County	255
Seattle, WA (city) King County	252
Compton, CA (city) Los Angeles County	240
Modesto, CA (city) Stanislaus County	231
Hayward, CA (city) Alameda County	227
Waipahu, HI (cdp) Honolulu County	225
Chicago, IL (city) Cook County	221
Garden Grove, CA (city) Orange County	211
Oxnard, CA (city) Ventura County	196
Federal Way, WA (city) King County	194
Laie, HI (cdp) Honolulu County	187
San Bruno, CA (city) San Mateo County	175
Phoenix, AZ (city) Maricopa County	174
South San Francisco, CA (city) San Mateo County	174
Taylorsville, UT (city) Salt Lake County	168
Daly City, CA (city) San Mateo County	159
Santa Ana, CA (city) Orange County	152
Concord, CA (city) Contra Costa County	149
Hauula, HI (cdp) Honolulu County	149
Oceanside, CA (city) San Diego County	135
Springdale, AR (city) Washington County	134
West Jordan, UT (city) Salt Lake County	130
Carson, CA (city) Los Angeles County	127
Kahuku, HI (cdp) Honolulu County	125
Waimalu, HI (cdp) Honolulu County	123
Westminster, CA (city) Orange County	123
Union City, CA (city) Alameda County	120
Fort Worth, TX (city) Tarrant County	115
Salem, OR (city) Marion County	115
Philadelphia, PA (city) Philadelphia County	110
Pittsburg, CA (city) Contra Costa County	109
Vallejo, CA (city) Solano County	109
Redwood City, CA (city) San Mateo County	108
Rialto, CA (city) San Bernardino County	107
Napili-Honokowai, HI (cdp) Maui County	100
Village Park, HI (cdp) Honolulu County	99
Las Vegas, NV (city) Clark County	98
Kihei, HI (cdp) Maui County	94
Hilo, HI (cdp) Hawaii County	90
Tacoma, WA (city) Pierce County	88
Alameda, CA (city) Alameda County	87
Lakewood, WA (city) Pierce County	86
Reno, NV (city) Washoe County	86
San Bernardino, CA (city) San Bernardino County	84
Sunnyvale, CA (city) Santa Clara County	83
Mililani Town, HI (cdp) Honolulu County	80
Tucson, AZ (city) Pima County	80
Houston, TX (city) Harris County	79
Sandy, UT (city) Salt Lake County	78
Riverside, CA (city) Riverside County	77
Anaheim, CA (city) Orange County	73
Provo, UT (city) Utah County	73
Aiea, HI (cdp) Honolulu County	70
Kansas City, MO (city) Jackson County	69
North Las Vegas, NV (city) Clark County	68
Milpitas, CA (city) Santa Clara County	66
Costa Mesa, CA (city) Orange County	65
Halawa, HI (cdp) Honolulu County	65
Ontario, CA (city) San Bernardino County	64
Paradise, NV (cdp) Clark County	64
Waianae, HI (cdp) Honolulu County	62

Notes: Please refer to the User's Guide for an explanation of data; ranking tables include all places with Asian and/or NHPI populations above SF4 population thresholds; (1) tables reflect only those areas that meet SF4 population thresholds, therefore there may be less than 50 states, 75 counties or 75 places listed

Foreign-Born Naturalized Citizens

Native Hawaiian and Other Pacific Islander

All States, Top 75 Counties, and Top 75 Places Sorted by Percent[1]

State	Percent
Utah	16.01
Arkansas	14.67
New York	13.87
Alaska	13.77
New Jersey	13.77
Illinois	11.62
California	11.46
Maine	10.96
Tennessee	10.79
Florida	10.28
Oregon	10.25
Missouri	10.22
Maryland	9.21
Oklahoma	9.02
Virginia	8.93
Minnesota	8.29
United States	8.00
Arizona	7.90
Washington	7.38
Pennsylvania	6.96
North Carolina	6.95
Kentucky	6.84
West Virginia	6.67
Massachusetts	6.65
Wisconsin	6.59
Michigan	6.56
Nevada	6.56
Montana	6.26
Texas	6.19
South Carolina	6.14
Georgia	6.05
Indiana	5.79
Rhode Island	5.67
Kansas	5.38
Delaware	5.07
Connecticut	4.94
Louisiana	4.79
Colorado	4.63
Idaho	4.38
Ohio	4.35
Iowa	3.66
Hawaii	3.44
Alabama	3.29
Nebraska	2.82
Mississippi	1.03
New Mexico	0.96

County	Percent
Miami-Dade County, FL	36.36
Broward County, FL	27.29
Shelby County, TN	22.92
Montgomery County, MD	19.84
Queens County, NY	19.80
San Mateo County, CA	19.65
Salt Lake County, UT	18.69
Stanislaus County, CA	17.85
Washington County, AR	17.72
Bronx County, NY	17.56
Kings County, NY	17.50
Sacramento County, CA	17.00
Anchorage Borough, AK	16.28
Cook County, IL	16.23
Hennepin County, MN	16.12
Ventura County, CA	16.12
Marion County, OR	15.37
San Francisco County, CA	15.28
Multnomah County, OR	15.21
Jackson County, MO	14.90
Contra Costa County, CA	14.36
Philadelphia County, PA	13.92
Essex County, NJ	13.54
Nassau County, NY	13.41
Fairfax County, VA	13.35
San Bernardino County, CA	12.99
New York County, NY	12.91
Suffolk County, NY	12.88
Los Angeles County, CA	12.76
Santa Barbara County, CA	11.82
King County, WA	11.62
Spokane County, WA	11.37
Washoe County, NV	11.12
Onslow County, NC	11.00
Orange County, CA	10.94
Davis County, UT	10.67
Allegheny County, PA	10.62
Tarrant County, TX	10.57
Alameda County, CA	10.52
Milwaukee County, WI	10.38
Santa Clara County, CA	10.29
Pima County, AZ	10.15
Utah County, UT	10.14
San Joaquin County, CA	9.36
Yolo County, CA	8.95
Dallas County, TX	8.81
Maricopa County, AZ	8.34
Washington County, OR	8.29
Harris County, TX	7.07
Monterey County, CA	6.86
St. Louis County, MO	6.64
Lane County, OR	6.63
Denver County, CO	6.49
Hillsborough County, FL	6.30
Orange County, FL	6.21
Pierce County, WA	5.99
Solano County, CA	5.93
Sedgwick County, KS	5.80
Riverside County, CA	5.73
Muscogee County, GA	5.71
San Diego County, CA	5.61
Clark County, NV	5.53
Washington County, UT	5.41
Bexar County, TX	5.40
Davidson County, TN	5.25
Sonoma County, CA	4.93
El Paso County, CO	4.88
Clackamas County, OR	4.38
Honolulu County, HI	4.17
Palm Beach County, FL	4.02
Gwinnett County, GA	3.95
El Paso County, TX	3.79
Kitsap County, WA	3.65
Arapahoe County, CO	3.61
Clark County, WA	3.61

Place	Percent
Lakewood, CA (city) Los Angeles County	33.46
Concord, CA (city) Contra Costa County	31.84
Salem, OR (city) Marion County	30.10
Westminster, CA (city) Orange County	28.28
San Mateo, CA (city) San Mateo County	24.11
Taylorsville, UT (city) Salt Lake County	23.56
Compton, CA (city) Los Angeles County	23.35
East Palo Alto, CA (city) San Mateo County	23.02
Oxnard, CA (city) Ventura County	22.55
Federal Way, WA (city) King County	21.68
Chicago, IL (city) Cook County	20.75
Fort Worth, TX (city) Tarrant County	20.72
Sandy, UT (city) Salt Lake County	20.37
Salt Lake City, UT (city) Salt Lake County	20.30
Rialto, CA (city) San Bernardino County	20.11
South San Francisco, CA (city) San Mateo County	19.91
Kahuku, HI (cdp) Honolulu County	19.81
Pittsburg, CA (city) Contra Costa County	19.68
Springdale, AR (city) Washington County	19.31
Sacramento, CA (city) Sacramento County	19.28
Redwood City, CA (city) San Mateo County	19.08
Modesto, CA (city) Stanislaus County	18.98
Union City, CA (city) Alameda County	18.93
West Jordan, UT (city) Salt Lake County	18.60
Daly City, CA (city) San Mateo County	18.36
Portland, OR (city) Multnomah County	17.46
Aiea, HI (cdp) Honolulu County	17.37
Long Beach, CA (city) Los Angeles County	17.22
San Bruno, CA (city) San Mateo County	17.21
Napili-Honokowai, HI (cdp) Maui County	17.01
West Valley City, UT (city) Salt Lake County	16.99
New York, NY (city)	16.82
Garden Grove, CA (city) Orange County	16.67
Village Park, HI (cdp) Honolulu County	16.28
Kansas City, MO (city) Jackson County	16.01
Sunnyvale, CA (city) Santa Clara County	15.49
San Francisco, CA (city) San Francisco County	15.28
Philadelphia, PA (city) Philadelphia County	13.92
Tukwila, WA (city) King County	13.55
Antioch, CA (city) Contra Costa County	12.99
Fort Lewis, WA (cdp) Pierce County	12.62
Aurora, CO (city) Arapahoe County	12.40
San Jose, CA (city) Santa Clara County	11.97
Santa Ana, CA (city) Orange County	11.91
Ontario, CA (city) San Bernardino County	11.76
Laie, HI (cdp) Honolulu County	11.62
Lakewood, WA (city) Pierce County	11.53
Los Angeles, CA (city) Los Angeles County	11.48
Des Moines, WA (city) King County	11.28
San Bernardino, CA (city) San Bernardino County	11.23
Richmond, CA (city) Contra Costa County	10.97
Alameda, CA (city) Alameda County	10.93
Provo, UT (city) Utah County	10.93
Tucson, AZ (city) Pima County	10.90
Oakland, CA (city) Alameda County	10.65
Milpitas, CA (city) Santa Clara County	10.46
Marina, CA (city) Monterey County	10.32
Kearns, UT (cdp) Salt Lake County	10.10
Hauula, HI (cdp) Honolulu County	10.07
Seattle, WA (city) King County	10.02
Costa Mesa, CA (city) Orange County	9.97
Phoenix, AZ (city) Maricopa County	9.97
Waialua, HI (cdp) Honolulu County	9.94
Hayward, CA (city) Alameda County	9.63
Independence, MO (city) Jackson County	9.63
Spokane, WA (city) Spokane County	9.48
SeaTac, WA (city) King County	9.12
North Las Vegas, NV (city) Clark County	9.10
Reno, NV (city) Washoe County	9.03
Houston, TX (city) Harris County	9.02
Salinas, CA (city) Monterey County	8.41
Mesa, AZ (city) Maricopa County	8.35
Kihei, HI (cdp) Maui County	8.27
Fontana, CA (city) San Bernardino County	7.95
Waimalu, HI (cdp) Honolulu County	7.86

Notes: Please refer to the User's Guide for an explanation of data; ranking tables include all places with Asian and/or NHPI populations above SF4 population thresholds; (1) tables reflect only those areas that meet SF4 population thresholds, therefore there may be less than 50 states, 75 counties or 75 places listed

Foreign-Born Naturalized Citizens

Asian Indian

All States, Top 75 Counties, and Top 75 Places Sorted by Number[1]

State	Number
United States	487,795
California	89,028
New York	81,517
New Jersey	52,534
Illinois	36,868
Texas	35,431
Florida	21,913
Maryland	17,794
Pennsylvania	16,255
Michigan	13,965
Virginia	13,777
Georgia	12,863
Ohio	10,665
Massachusetts	10,161
Connecticut	7,409
Washington	6,613
North Carolina	6,553
Minnesota	4,180
Indiana	3,871
Arizona	3,806
Tennessee	3,536
Missouri	3,399
Wisconsin	2,931
Oregon	2,627
South Carolina	2,559
Oklahoma	2,519
Louisiana	2,412
Colorado	2,268
Kansas	2,197
Alabama	2,157
Nevada	1,852
Kentucky	1,694
Delaware	1,456
Iowa	1,358
Mississippi	1,099
West Virginia	1,030
Utah	952
New Mexico	792
New Hampshire	776
Nebraska	747
Rhode Island	681
District of Columbia	647
Arkansas	608
Hawaii	437
Maine	372
Vermont	316
Idaho	280
North Dakota	280
Alaska	233
Wyoming	169
Montana	108
South Dakota	100

County	Number
Queens County, NY	35,512
Los Angeles County, CA	21,396
Cook County, IL	20,229
Middlesex County, NJ	14,056
Santa Clara County, CA	11,950
DuPage County, IL	10,374
Harris County, TX	10,332
Alameda County, CA	10,236
Orange County, CA	9,372
Nassau County, NY	8,834
Montgomery County, MD	8,686
Kings County, NY	7,869
Fairfax County, VA	7,156
Hudson County, NJ	6,547
Bergen County, NJ	5,607
Dallas County, TX	5,206
Bronx County, NY	5,092
Middlesex County, MA	4,987
Oakland County, MI	4,834
Fort Bend County, TX	4,778
Broward County, FL	4,500
Westchester County, NY	4,078
Contra Costa County, CA	3,772
Sacramento County, CA	3,765
Morris County, NJ	3,690
Suffolk County, NY	3,682
King County, WA	3,631
New York County, NY	3,630
Wayne County, MI	3,612
Gwinnett County, GA	3,362
Passaic County, NJ	3,210
Somerset County, NJ	3,086
Philadelphia County, PA	3,033
Cuyahoga County, OH	3,013
San Bernardino County, CA	3,010
Miami-Dade County, FL	2,962
San Mateo County, CA	2,961
Essex County, NJ	2,960
Maricopa County, AZ	2,916
San Diego County, CA	2,859
Fairfield County, CT	2,605
Orange County, FL	2,510
Tarrant County, TX	2,417
Baltimore County, MD	2,355
Richmond County, NY	2,318
Prince George's County, MD	2,285
Union County, NJ	2,254
Monmouth County, NJ	2,246
Montgomery County, PA	2,222
Hartford County, CT	2,146
Bucks County, PA	2,120
Camden County, NJ	2,095
Mercer County, NJ	2,081
Fresno County, CA	2,056
Sutter County, CA	2,022
Collin County, TX	2,020
DeKalb County, GA	2,012
Rockland County, NY	1,975
Riverside County, CA	1,947
Allegheny County, PA	1,927
Hennepin County, MN	1,860
Howard County, MD	1,830
San Joaquin County, CA	1,782
Travis County, TX	1,714
San Francisco County, CA	1,697
Lake County, IL	1,688
Wake County, NC	1,687
St. Louis County, MO	1,659
New Haven County, CT	1,636
Denton County, TX	1,580
Palm Beach County, FL	1,577
Hillsborough County, FL	1,558
Atlantic County, NJ	1,556
Fulton County, GA	1,538
Ventura County, CA	1,515

Place	Number
New York, NY (city)	54,421
Los Angeles, CA (city) Los Angeles County	7,948
San Jose, CA (city) Santa Clara County	6,266
Chicago, IL (city) Cook County	6,121
Houston, TX (city) Harris County	5,190
Fremont, CA (city) Alameda County	4,322
Jersey City, NJ (city) Hudson County	4,300
Edison, NJ (township) Middlesex County	4,185
Hempstead, NY (town) Nassau County	3,958
Philadelphia, PA (city) Philadelphia County	3,033
North Hempstead, NY (town) Nassau County	2,720
Oyster Bay, NY (town) Nassau County	1,991
Woodbridge, NJ (township) Middlesex County	1,930
Piscataway, NJ (township) Middlesex County	1,722
San Francisco, CA (city) San Francisco County	1,697
Skokie, IL (village) Cook County	1,693
Sugar Land, TX (city) Fort Bend County	1,684
San Diego, CA (city) San Diego County	1,641
Anaheim, CA (city) Orange County	1,598
Dallas, TX (city) Dallas County	1,598
Union City, CA (city) Alameda County	1,552
Austin, TX (city) Travis County	1,385
Troy, MI (city) Oakland County	1,348
Parsippany-Troy Hills, NJ (township) Morris County	1,306
Charlotte, NC (city) Mecklenburg County	1,304
Naperville, IL (city) Du Page County	1,297
Plano, TX (city) Collin County	1,280
San Antonio, TX (city) Bexar County	1,236
Irvine, CA (city) Orange County	1,220
Brookhaven, NY (town) Suffolk County	1,195
Carrollton, TX (city) Denton County	1,193
Sacramento, CA (city) Sacramento County	1,188
Cerritos, CA (city) Los Angeles County	1,184
Hayward, CA (city) Alameda County	1,160
Clifton, NJ (city) Passaic County	1,134
Phoenix, AZ (city) Maricopa County	1,106
Columbus, OH (city) Franklin County	1,102
Sunnyvale, CA (city) Santa Clara County	1,100
Schaumburg, IL (village) Cook County	1,075
Yonkers, NY (city) Westchester County	1,070
Oklahoma City, OK (city) Oklahoma County	1,015
East Brunswick, NJ (township) Middlesex County	1,009
South Brunswick, NJ (township) Middlesex County	1,001
Canton, MI (township) Wayne County	997
Fresno, CA (city) Fresno County	995
North Bergen, NJ (township) Hudson County	993
Bakersfield, CA (city) Kern County	986
Boston, MA (city) Suffolk County	977
Diamond Bar, CA (city) Los Angeles County	974
Old Bridge, NJ (township) Middlesex County	917
North Brunswick, NJ (township) Middlesex County	915
Milpitas, CA (city) Santa Clara County	912
Hoffman Estates, IL (village) Cook County	904
Passaic, NJ (city) Passaic County	885
South Yuba City, CA (cdp) Sutter County	870
Cary, NC (town) Wake County	861
Santa Clara, CA (city) Santa Clara County	860
Indianapolis, IN (sp. city) Marion County	851
Irving, TX (city) Dallas County	849
Islip, NY (town) Suffolk County	847
Missouri City, TX (city) Fort Bend County	845
Detroit, MI (city) Wayne County	837
Sterling Heights, MI (city) Macomb County	831
Franklin, NJ (township) Somerset County	829
Arlington, VA (cdp) Arlington County	825
Clarkstown, NY (town) Rockland County	820
Garland, TX (city) Dallas County	811
Huntington, NY (town) Suffolk County	807
Buena Park, CA (city) Orange County	801
Glendale Heights, IL (village) Du Page County	786
Nashville-Davidson, TN (sp. city) Davidson County	780
Greenburgh, NY (town) Westchester County	778
Des Plaines, IL (city) Cook County	776
Seattle, WA (city) King County	776
Torrance, CA (city) Los Angeles County	773

Notes: Please refer to the User's Guide for an explanation of data; ranking tables include all places with Asian and/or NHPI populations above SF4 population thresholds; (1) tables reflect only those areas that meet SF4 population thresholds, therefore there may be less than 50 states, 75 counties or 75 places listed

Foreign-Born Naturalized Citizens

Asian Indian

***All States, Top 75 Counties, and Top 75 Places Sorted by Percent*[1]**

State	Percent
Vermont	45.34
Alaska	42.67
West Virginia	40.73
Wyoming	39.95
Nevada	38.11
Maine	38.04
Maryland	35.76
Hawaii	35.13
Mississippi	33.05
New Mexico	32.67
New York	32.60
Florida	32.32
Alabama	32.26
South Carolina	31.15
New Jersey	31.05
Connecticut	30.99
Oklahoma	30.34
Utah	30.16
Illinois	29.91
United States	29.64
Tennessee	29.58
Washington	29.41
California	28.99
Virginia	28.96
Pennsylvania	28.91
Georgia	28.76
Missouri	28.70
Kansas	28.60
Ohio	28.35
Louisiana	27.91
Texas	27.84
Delaware	27.83
Indiana	27.34
North Dakota	26.87
District of Columbia	26.79
Rhode Island	26.73
Arizona	26.23
Wisconsin	25.98
North Carolina	25.85
Oregon	25.79
Minnesota	25.68
Michigan	25.64
Kentucky	25.16
Iowa	25.12
Idaho	24.52
Massachusetts	24.23
Montana	24.00
Nebraska	23.35
Arkansas	22.57
New Hampshire	21.68
Colorado	19.18
South Dakota	17.21

County	Percent
York County, VA	59.00
Floyd County, GA	50.64
Ottawa County, MI	49.68
Spokane County, WA	49.68
Shelby County, AL	49.61
Montgomery County, TX	49.59
Litchfield County, CT	48.70
Wicomico County, MD	48.18
Sussex County, NJ	47.68
Nueces County, TX	47.36
Kanawha County, WV	47.29
Columbia County, GA	46.88
Anchorage Borough, AK	45.57
Clackamas County, OR	45.51
Benton County, WA	44.80
Spartanburg County, SC	44.63
Harford County, MD	44.06
Stark County, OH	43.85
Hunterdon County, NJ	43.77
Madera County, CA	43.58
Saratoga County, NY	42.07
Chesterfield County, VA	41.79
Camden County, NJ	41.58
San Luis Obispo County, CA	41.48
Broome County, NY	41.26
Saginaw County, MI	41.00
Medina County, OH	40.72
Westmoreland County, PA	40.04
St. Charles County, MO	40.03
Luzerne County, PA	39.90
Greene County, OH	39.89
Cumberland County, PA	39.81
Clayton County, GA	39.66
Henry County, GA	39.39
Madison County, IL	39.33
Frederick County, MD	39.17
Clark County, NV	38.94
Virginia Beach Independent City, VA	38.73
Anne Arundel County, MD	38.63
Atlantic County, NJ	38.58
Escambia County, FL	38.57
Howard County, MD	38.46
Lee County, FL	38.42
Gloucester County, NJ	38.07
Baltimore County, MD	38.06
St. Mary's County, MD	37.99
San Bernardino County, CA	37.79
Marion County, OR	37.78
Multnomah County, OR	37.75
Nassau County, NY	37.63
Hamilton County, TN	37.46
McHenry County, IL	37.42
Fort Bend County, TX	37.36
Seminole County, FL	37.32
Volusia County, FL	37.30
Bexar County, TX	37.27
Albany County, NY	37.07
Tolland County, CT	36.84
Anoka County, MN	36.74
Jefferson County, AL	36.69
Phelps County, MO	36.62
Brazoria County, TX	36.60
Oneida County, NY	36.52
Clark County, WA	36.51
Washoe County, NV	36.43
Dauphin County, PA	36.40
Bell County, TX	36.36
Los Angeles County, CA	36.27
Hampden County, MA	36.26
Berks County, PA	36.11
Kane County, IL	36.08
Solano County, CA	36.04
Bucks County, PA	36.01
Richmond County, NY	36.00
Niagara County, NY	35.96

Place	Percent
North Laurel, MD (cdp) Howard County	63.70
Town and Country, MO (city) Saint Louis County	63.25
Oak Brook, IL (village) Du Page County	60.60
South Barrington, IL (village) Cook County	57.66
Gloucester, NJ (township) Camden County	55.77
Travilah, MD (cdp) Montgomery County	55.28
Colesville, MD (cdp) Montgomery County	54.30
Taylor, MI (city) Wayne County	53.96
Beavercreek, OH (city) Greene County	53.80
Mission Bend, TX (cdp) Fort Bend County	53.44
Oxnard, CA (city) Ventura County	53.42
Burr Ridge, IL (village) Du Page County	53.38
Muttontown, NY (village) Nassau County	53.16
Lower Makefield, PA (township) Bucks County	52.85
Newington, VA (cdp) Fairfax County	52.41
Rutherford, NJ (borough) Bergen County	52.30
The Woodlands, TX (cdp) Montgomery County	52.22
Santa Clarita, CA (city) Los Angeles County	51.45
Cooper City, FL (city) Broward County	51.10
Perinton, NY (town) Monroe County	49.65
Smithtown, NY (town) Suffolk County	49.62
North Potomac, MD (cdp) Montgomery County	49.10
Greentree, NJ (cdp) Camden County	48.81
Solon, OH (city) Cuyahoga County	48.72
Corpus Christi, TX (city) Nueces County	48.56
Freehold, NJ (township) Monmouth County	48.55
Martinez, GA (cdp) Columbia County	48.55
Potomac, MD (cdp) Montgomery County	48.25
Pittsford, NY (town) Monroe County	48.18
Cloverly, MD (cdp) Montgomery County	48.08
Brookfield, WI (city) Waukesha County	47.97
Salisbury, NY (cdp) Nassau County	47.88
Westlake, OH (city) Cuyahoga County	47.69
Lakewood, CA (city) Los Angeles County	47.56
Orland Park, IL (village) Cook County	47.45
Bloomfield, MI (township) Oakland County	46.94
Colonie, NY (town) Albany County	46.84
Davie, FL (town) Broward County	46.78
Altamonte Springs, FL (city) Seminole County	46.76
Redlands, CA (city) San Bernardino County	46.48
East Hartford, CT (town) Hartford County	46.46
Brea, CA (city) Orange County	46.39
Olney, MD (cdp) Montgomery County	46.34
Cherry Hill, NJ (township) Camden County	46.27
Chino Hills, CA (city) San Bernardino County	46.26
Walnut Creek, CA (city) Contra Costa County	46.15
Henderson, NV (city) Clark County	46.14
Palmdale, CA (city) Los Angeles County	46.12
Buena Park, CA (city) Orange County	46.01
Manalapan, NJ (township) Monmouth County	45.99
Rockaway, NJ (township) Morris County	45.32
Syosset, NY (cdp) Nassau County	45.13
Warren, NJ (township) Somerset County	45.00
Livingston, NJ (township) Essex County	44.97
Walnut, CA (city) Los Angeles County	44.75
North Valley Stream, NY (cdp) Nassau County	44.71
Burke, VA (cdp) Fairfax County	44.55
Huntington Beach, CA (city) Orange County	44.41
Strongsville, OH (city) Cuyahoga County	44.29
Hoover, AL (city) Jefferson County	44.11
Franklin Square, NY (cdp) Nassau County	44.05
Skokie, IL (village) Cook County	44.03
Missouri City, TX (city) Fort Bend County	43.94
Rancho Palos Verdes, CA (city) Los Angeles County	43.64
Lancaster, CA (city) Los Angeles County	43.57
Rowland Heights, CA (cdp) Los Angeles County	43.49
Franconia, VA (cdp) Fairfax County	43.24
Doctor Phillips, FL (cdp) Orange County	43.23
Las Vegas, NV (city) Clark County	43.20
Clifton Park, NY (town) Saratoga County	43.17
Fairfield, CA (city) Solano County	42.95
Bloomingdale, IL (village) Du Page County	42.90
Darien, IL (city) Du Page County	42.84
Loma Linda, CA (city) San Bernardino County	42.82
Redland, MD (cdp) Montgomery County	42.78

Notes: Please refer to the User's Guide for an explanation of data; ranking tables include all places with Asian and/or NHPI populations above SF4 population thresholds; (1) tables reflect only those areas that meet SF4 population thresholds, therefore there may be less than 50 states, 75 counties or 75 places listed

Foreign-Born Naturalized Citizens

Bangladeshi

All States, Top 75 Counties, and Top 75 Places Sorted by Number[1]

State	Number
United States	10,515
New York	4,791
New Jersey	771
Texas	717
California	693
Virginia	452
Michigan	431
Maryland	423
Georgia	413
Florida	328
Illinois	242
Pennsylvania	232
Massachusetts	157
Ohio	153
Connecticut	69

County	Number
Queens County, NY	2,862
Kings County, NY	949
Bronx County, NY	451
Montgomery County, MD	314
Los Angeles County, CA	309
Harris County, TX	285
Wayne County, MI	282
Fairfax County, VA	237
New York County, NY	217
Passaic County, NJ	197
Santa Clara County, CA	168
Atlantic County, NJ	157
DeKalb County, GA	155
Dallas County, TX	119
Middlesex County, NJ	106

Place	Number
New York, NY (city)	4,495
Hamtramck, MI (city) Wayne County	221
Los Angeles, CA (city) Los Angeles County	171
Paterson, NJ (city) Passaic County	149

Notes: Please refer to the User's Guide for an explanation of data; ranking tables include all places with Asian and/or NHPI populations above SF4 population thresholds; (1) tables reflect only those areas that meet SF4 population thresholds, therefore there may be less than 50 states, 75 counties or 75 places listed

Foreign-Born Naturalized Citizens

Bangladeshi

All States, Top 75 Counties, and Top 75 Places Sorted by Percent[1]

State	Percent
Maryland	35.13
New Jersey	34.18
Georgia	32.86
Pennsylvania	32.86
Illinois	30.06
Massachusetts	27.99
Texas	27.86
Florida	26.03
Michigan	25.61
United States	25.38
California	25.22
Virginia	25.00
New York	23.85
Ohio	23.61
Connecticut	19.83

County	Percent
Harris County, TX	41.42
Atlantic County, NJ	38.57
Montgomery County, MD	38.01
Passaic County, NJ	36.15
Santa Clara County, CA	34.71
DeKalb County, GA	28.18
New York County, NY	27.71
Middlesex County, NJ	27.39
Fairfax County, VA	26.27
Wayne County, MI	24.25
Kings County, NY	24.16
Los Angeles County, CA	23.32
Queens County, NY	23.08
Bronx County, NY	22.64
Dallas County, TX	17.68

Place	Percent
Paterson, NJ (city) Passaic County	32.46
Hamtramck, MI (city) Wayne County	29.86
New York, NY (city)	23.47
Los Angeles, CA (city) Los Angeles County	20.58

Notes: Please refer to the User's Guide for an explanation of data; ranking tables include all places with Asian and/or NHPI populations above SF4 population thresholds; (1) tables reflect only those areas that meet SF4 population thresholds, therefore there may be less than 50 states, 75 counties or 75 places listed

Foreign-Born Naturalized Citizens

Cambodian

All States, Top 75 Counties, and Top 75 Places Sorted by Number[1]

State	Number
United States	53,496
California	20,801
Massachusetts	4,346
Washington	4,286
Texas	2,588
Pennsylvania	2,462
Virginia	1,828
Minnesota	1,697
Illinois	1,402
Rhode Island	1,299
Georgia	1,234
Florida	1,171
Oregon	1,088
New York	987
Connecticut	942
Maryland	836
Ohio	762
North Carolina	697
Michigan	576
Colorado	493
Utah	472
Arizona	380
Tennessee	328
Nevada	317
New Jersey	304
Iowa	271
Maine	235
Missouri	189
Indiana	185
Kansas	185
Wisconsin	165
Oklahoma	149
Alabama	147
Hawaii	105
South Carolina	102

County	Number
Los Angeles County, CA	9,733
King County, WA	2,067
Orange County, CA	2,066
Middlesex County, MA	1,973
Philadelphia County, PA	1,571
San Joaquin County, CA	1,530
Santa Clara County, CA	1,482
Alameda County, CA	1,205
Providence County, RI	1,137
Pierce County, WA	935
Essex County, MA	898
Cook County, IL	838
Fairfax County, VA	833
San Diego County, CA	822
Harris County, TX	803
Snohomish County, WA	796
Dallas County, TX	791
Stanislaus County, CA	751
Fresno County, CA	697
Fairfield County, CT	624
San Bernardino County, CA	546
Hennepin County, MN	541
Montgomery County, MD	524
Suffolk County, MA	502
Washington County, OR	499
Sacramento County, CA	403
Ramsey County, MN	395
Salt Lake County, UT	388
Bristol County, MA	384
Multnomah County, OR	382
Ottawa County, MI	371
Franklin County, OH	351
Duval County, FL	349
Maricopa County, AZ	335
Gwinnett County, GA	316
Clark County, NV	303
Henrico County, VA	303
Clayton County, GA	294
San Francisco County, CA	281
Denton County, TX	264
Olmsted County, MN	255
Thurston County, WA	250
Riverside County, CA	222
Mecklenburg County, NC	221
Kings County, NY	216
Pinellas County, FL	203
Dakota County, MN	202
Shelby County, TN	186
Bronx County, NY	179
Sonoma County, CA	179
Polk County, IA	176
DeKalb County, GA	170
Tarrant County, TX	144
Cuyahoga County, OH	143
Cumberland County, ME	119
Sedgwick County, KS	115
Camden County, NJ	110
Hampden County, MA	105
Denver County, CO	103
Arlington County, VA	95
Chesterfield County, VA	95
Kern County, CA	92
Davidson County, NC	88
Scott County, MN	87
Hamilton County, OH	82
Clark County, WA	75
Mobile County, AL	75
Monroe County, NY	74
Worcester County, MA	74
Cowlitz County, WA	65
Brazoria County, TX	60

Place	Number
Long Beach, CA (city) Los Angeles County	4,978
Philadelphia, PA (city) Philadelphia County	1,571
Stockton, CA (city) San Joaquin County	1,492
Lowell, MA (city) Middlesex County	1,483
Los Angeles, CA (city) Los Angeles County	1,359
San Jose, CA (city) Santa Clara County	1,297
Providence, RI (city) Providence County	764
Seattle, WA (city) King County	764
Oakland, CA (city) Alameda County	756
Chicago, IL (city) Cook County	692
Lynn, MA (city) Essex County	688
Tacoma, WA (city) Pierce County	677
San Diego, CA (city) San Diego County	658
Modesto, CA (city) Stanislaus County	656
Fresno, CA (city) Fresno County	648
Santa Ana, CA (city) Orange County	638
New York, NY (city)	524
Portland, OR (city) Multnomah County	363
Jacksonville, FL (city) Duval County	349
Dallas, TX (city) Dallas County	335
Columbus, OH (city) Franklin County	322
Rosemead, CA (city) Los Angeles County	318
Lakewood, CA (city) Los Angeles County	293
Bellflower, CA (city) Los Angeles County	288
Signal Hill, CA (city) Los Angeles County	286
St. Paul, MN (city) Ramsey County	285
San Francisco, CA (city) San Francisco County	281
Cranston, RI (city) Providence County	271
Norwalk, CA (city) Los Angeles County	261
Garden Grove, CA (city) Orange County	260
Houston, TX (city) Harris County	254
Carrollton, TX (city) Denton County	244
Revere, MA (city) Suffolk County	242
West Valley City, UT (city) Salt Lake County	242
Boston, MA (city) Suffolk County	225
White Center, WA (cdp) King County	219
Bridgeport, CT (city) Fairfield County	210
Everett, WA (city) Snohomish County	208
Charlotte, NC (city) Mecklenburg County	198
Danbury, CT (city) Fairfield County	195
Sacramento, CA (city) Sacramento County	195
Phoenix, AZ (city) Maricopa County	193
Rochester, MN (city) Olmsted County	188
Fall River, MA (city) Bristol County	185
Pomona, CA (city) Los Angeles County	179
Beaverton, OR (city) Washington County	174
Attleboro, MA (city) Bristol County	170
Aurora, CO (city) Arapahoe County	155
Santa Rosa, CA (city) Sonoma County	145
Bloomington, MN (city) Hennepin County	144
Monterey Park, CA (city) Los Angeles County	142
Memphis, TN (city) Shelby County	141
Silver Spring, MD (cdp) Montgomery County	141
St. Petersburg, FL (city) Pinellas County	136
Lawrence, MA (city) Essex County	121
Denver, CO (city) Denver County	103
Portland, ME (city) Cumberland County	100
San Bernardino, CA (city) San Bernardino County	99
Arlington, VA (cdp) Arlington County	95
Minneapolis, MN (city) Hennepin County	83
Lexington, NC (city) Davidson County	65
Longview, WA (city) Cowlitz County	60

Notes: Please refer to the User's Guide for an explanation of data; ranking tables include all places with Asian and/or NHPI populations above SF4 population thresholds; (1) tables reflect only those areas that meet SF4 population thresholds, therefore there may be less than 50 states, 75 counties or 75 places listed

Foreign-Born Naturalized Citizens

Cambodian

All States, Top 75 Counties, and Top 75 Places Sorted by Percent[1]

State	Percent
Hawaii	49.76
Maryland	48.95
New Jersey	46.20
Oklahoma	45.29
Connecticut	43.59
Nevada	42.95
Florida	42.40
Illinois	40.02
Oregon	39.58
Virginia	36.80
Michigan	36.14
Georgia	35.47
Texas	34.04
New York	33.92
Colorado	33.36
Minnesota	33.09
Iowa	32.89
Utah	32.40
Indiana	31.73
Arizona	30.65
United States	30.05
South Carolina	29.91
North Carolina	29.41
California	29.19
Ohio	29.14
Washington	29.03
Pennsylvania	28.31
Tennessee	27.56
Wisconsin	26.32
Kansas	26.17
Alabama	26.02
Rhode Island	25.45
Maine	23.27
Missouri	21.50
Massachusetts	21.34

County	Percent
Orange County, CA	46.24
Washington County, OR	45.20
Fairfax County, VA	45.15
Montgomery County, MD	45.13
Dakota County, MN	44.79
San Francisco County, CA	43.50
Fairfield County, CT	43.27
Kings County, NY	43.11
Clark County, NV	42.20
Polk County, IA	42.00
Harris County, TX	39.91
Snohomish County, WA	39.84
Cook County, IL	37.63
Henrico County, VA	37.22
Riverside County, CA	37.00
Denton County, TX	36.36
Sacramento County, CA	36.08
Shelby County, TN	36.05
Multnomah County, OR	35.80
Ramsey County, MN	35.59
Olmsted County, MN	35.32
Camden County, NJ	35.14
Gwinnett County, GA	35.03
Salt Lake County, UT	34.99
Duval County, FL	34.87
Ottawa County, MI	34.26
Santa Clara County, CA	33.69
Dallas County, TX	33.56
Los Angeles County, CA	32.39
San Bernardino County, CA	31.34
King County, WA	31.21
Alameda County, CA	30.87
Hennepin County, MN	30.26
Thurston County, WA	29.87
Cuyahoga County, OH	29.55
Suffolk County, MA	29.22
Mecklenburg County, NC	28.81
Pinellas County, FL	28.27
Maricopa County, AZ	28.25
Clayton County, GA	28.05
DeKalb County, GA	27.87
Arlington County, VA	26.91
Franklin County, OH	26.81
Denver County, CO	25.88
Sedgwick County, KS	24.95
Philadelphia County, PA	24.52
Scott County, MN	24.03
Essex County, MA	23.92
Providence County, RI	23.56
Hamilton County, OH	23.36
Stanislaus County, CA	23.25
Hampden County, MA	23.08
Pierce County, WA	23.04
Bronx County, NY	22.10
Kern County, CA	21.35
Sonoma County, CA	21.06
Monroe County, NY	19.42
Mobile County, AL	19.28
San Diego County, CA	18.81
Worcester County, MA	18.73
Tarrant County, TX	18.51
Cowlitz County, WA	18.36
Cumberland County, ME	18.00
Middlesex County, MA	17.98
Fresno County, CA	17.72
Bristol County, MA	17.67
Clark County, WA	17.56
Davidson County, NC	17.02
San Joaquin County, CA	16.16
Brazoria County, TX	15.67
Chesterfield County, VA	14.26

Place	Percent
Bellflower, CA (city) Los Angeles County	53.93
Garden Grove, CA (city) Orange County	52.00
Norwalk, CA (city) Los Angeles County	51.89
Beaverton, OR (city) Washington County	48.74
San Francisco, CA (city) San Francisco County	43.50
Silver Spring, MD (cdp) Montgomery County	43.25
Rosemead, CA (city) Los Angeles County	41.03
Bridgeport, CT (city) Fairfield County	40.38
Sacramento, CA (city) Sacramento County	40.37
Lakewood, CA (city) Los Angeles County	40.03
Santa Ana, CA (city) Orange County	36.75
West Valley City, UT (city) Salt Lake County	36.67
Signal Hill, CA (city) Los Angeles County	36.62
Chicago, IL (city) Cook County	36.21
Boston, MA (city) Suffolk County	35.94
Aurora, CO (city) Arapahoe County	35.15
Houston, TX (city) Harris County	35.13
Portland, OR (city) Multnomah County	34.94
Phoenix, AZ (city) Maricopa County	34.90
Jacksonville, FL (city) Duval County	34.87
Monterey Park, CA (city) Los Angeles County	34.38
Danbury, CT (city) Fairfield County	34.09
Rochester, MN (city) Olmsted County	33.63
Cranston, RI (city) Providence County	33.13
Everett, WA (city) Snohomish County	32.60
San Jose, CA (city) Santa Clara County	32.51
New York, NY (city)	32.37
Los Angeles, CA (city) Los Angeles County	32.30
Dallas, TX (city) Dallas County	31.63
Memphis, TN (city) Shelby County	31.06
St. Paul, MN (city) Ramsey County	30.71
Seattle, WA (city) King County	30.27
Revere, MA (city) Suffolk County	29.88
Carrollton, TX (city) Denton County	29.83
Bloomington, MN (city) Hennepin County	29.45
Charlotte, NC (city) Mecklenburg County	28.25
Long Beach, CA (city) Los Angeles County	28.11
Columbus, OH (city) Franklin County	27.01
Lawrence, MA (city) Essex County	26.95
Arlington, VA (cdp) Arlington County	26.91
St. Petersburg, FL (city) Pinellas County	26.36
Denver, CO (city) Denver County	25.88
Modesto, CA (city) Stanislaus County	25.85
Oakland, CA (city) Alameda County	25.76
Attleboro, MA (city) Bristol County	24.57
Philadelphia, PA (city) Philadelphia County	24.52
Longview, WA (city) Cowlitz County	24.29
Pomona, CA (city) Los Angeles County	23.65
Lynn, MA (city) Essex County	22.94
Santa Rosa, CA (city) Sonoma County	22.45
San Bernardino, CA (city) San Bernardino County	22.20
Tacoma, WA (city) Pierce County	21.44
Providence, RI (city) Providence County	21.33
White Center, WA (cdp) King County	18.47
Fresno, CA (city) Fresno County	17.95
Portland, ME (city) Cumberland County	16.86
San Diego, CA (city) San Diego County	16.80
Minneapolis, MN (city) Hennepin County	16.67
Lexington, NC (city) Davidson County	16.54
Stockton, CA (city) San Joaquin County	16.39
Lowell, MA (city) Middlesex County	15.58
Fall River, MA (city) Bristol County	14.76

Notes: Please refer to the User's Guide for an explanation of data; ranking tables include all places with Asian and/or NHPI populations above SF4 population thresholds; (1) tables reflect only those areas that meet SF4 population thresholds, therefore there may be less than 50 states, 75 counties or 75 places listed

Foreign-Born Naturalized Citizens

Chinese (except Taiwanese)

***All States, Top 75 Counties, and Top 75 Places Sorted by Number*[1]**

State	Number
United States	857,071
California	380,526
New York	151,848
New Jersey	35,954
Texas	32,313
Massachusetts	28,392
Illinois	25,552
Washington	22,315
Maryland	17,854
Florida	17,580
Hawaii	15,982
Pennsylvania	14,784
Virginia	12,674
Georgia	8,318
Michigan	8,285
Ohio	7,995
Arizona	6,621
Oregon	6,375
Connecticut	6,334
Nevada	5,275
Colorado	5,204
North Carolina	4,804
Minnesota	4,597
Missouri	3,996
Indiana	2,695
Wisconsin	2,355
Tennessee	2,344
Kansas	2,255
Utah	2,041
South Carolina	2,004
Louisiana	1,918
Rhode Island	1,598
Kentucky	1,531
Oklahoma	1,472
Alabama	1,449
Delaware	1,327
New Hampshire	1,311
District of Columbia	1,173
Iowa	1,152
New Mexico	1,134
Mississippi	940
Arkansas	832
Alaska	688
Nebraska	635
Idaho	577
Maine	575
West Virginia	401
Vermont	373
Montana	212
South Dakota	206
Wyoming	192
North Dakota	103

County	Number
Los Angeles County, CA	123,835
San Francisco County, CA	75,337
Queens County, NY	52,997
Kings County, NY	44,109
Santa Clara County, CA	42,232
Alameda County, CA	40,041
New York County, NY	29,121
Orange County, CA	22,062
San Mateo County, CA	20,610
Cook County, IL	17,436
King County, WA	17,092
Honolulu County, HI	15,414
Montgomery County, MD	11,092
Contra Costa County, CA	10,854
Harris County, TX	10,804
San Diego County, CA	10,739
Sacramento County, CA	10,663
Middlesex County, MA	9,630
Norfolk County, MA	7,814
Middlesex County, NJ	7,574
Suffolk County, MA	6,869
Fairfax County, VA	6,592
Nassau County, NY	6,387
Philadelphia County, PA	5,123
Maricopa County, AZ	5,077
Bergen County, NJ	5,038
San Bernardino County, CA	4,310
Clark County, NV	4,197
Miami-Dade County, FL	4,020
Morris County, NJ	3,998
Fort Bend County, TX	3,947
Monmouth County, NJ	3,913
Dallas County, TX	3,852
Collin County, TX	3,849
Broward County, FL	3,658
DuPage County, IL	3,579
Suffolk County, NY	3,273
Richmond County, NY	3,054
Somerset County, NJ	3,005
Oakland County, MI	2,926
Westchester County, NY	2,749
Travis County, TX	2,484
Multnomah County, OR	2,455
Essex County, NJ	2,401
San Joaquin County, CA	2,384
Ventura County, CA	2,348
Riverside County, CA	2,272
Bronx County, NY	2,214
Fairfield County, CT	2,166
Gwinnett County, GA	2,075
St. Louis County, MO	1,987
Tarrant County, TX	1,953
Snohomish County, WA	1,886
Montgomery County, PA	1,877
Hennepin County, MN	1,790
Cuyahoga County, OH	1,787
Franklin County, OH	1,727
Union County, NJ	1,724
Prince George's County, MD	1,692
Hudson County, NJ	1,659
Washington County, OR	1,631
Yolo County, CA	1,629
Fresno County, CA	1,587
Camden County, NJ	1,580
New Haven County, CT	1,580
Howard County, MD	1,545
Mercer County, NJ	1,503
Orange County, FL	1,479
Baltimore County, MD	1,454
Lake County, IL	1,449
Hartford County, CT	1,427
Wake County, NC	1,421
Cobb County, GA	1,389
Wayne County, MI	1,388
Salt Lake County, UT	1,383

Place	Number
New York, NY (city)	131,495
San Francisco, CA (city) San Francisco County	75,337
Los Angeles, CA (city) Los Angeles County	24,725
San Jose, CA (city) Santa Clara County	20,063
Oakland, CA (city) Alameda County	12,900
Honolulu, HI (cdp) Honolulu County	12,129
Chicago, IL (city) Cook County	11,704
Alhambra, CA (city) Los Angeles County	11,593
Monterey Park, CA (city) Los Angeles County	10,432
Fremont, CA (city) Alameda County	9,207
San Diego, CA (city) San Diego County	8,035
Seattle, WA (city) King County	7,566
Houston, TX (city) Harris County	7,033
Sacramento, CA (city) Sacramento County	6,872
Rosemead, CA (city) Los Angeles County	6,788
Daly City, CA (city) San Mateo County	6,634
Boston, MA (city) Suffolk County	6,543
El Monte, CA (city) Los Angeles County	5,518
Arcadia, CA (city) Los Angeles County	5,383
Philadelphia, PA (city) Philadelphia County	5,123
San Gabriel, CA (city) Los Angeles County	5,036
Rowland Heights, CA (cdp) Los Angeles County	4,393
Irvine, CA (city) Orange County	4,176
Quincy, MA (city) Norfolk County	4,065
Hacienda Heights, CA (cdp) Los Angeles County	3,993
Sunnyvale, CA (city) Santa Clara County	3,893
Cupertino, CA (city) Santa Clara County	3,821
Milpitas, CA (city) Santa Clara County	3,331
San Leandro, CA (city) Alameda County	3,318
Temple City, CA (city) Los Angeles County	3,252
West Covina, CA (city) Los Angeles County	3,044
Alameda, CA (city) Alameda County	2,916
Plano, TX (city) Collin County	2,882
Diamond Bar, CA (city) Los Angeles County	2,857
Cerritos, CA (city) Los Angeles County	2,647
Union City, CA (city) Alameda County	2,520
Walnut, CA (city) Los Angeles County	2,426
North Hempstead, NY (town) Nassau County	2,305
Torrance, CA (city) Los Angeles County	2,291
Hempstead, NY (town) Nassau County	2,290
Sugar Land, TX (city) Fort Bend County	2,270
Portland, OR (city) Multnomah County	2,241
Bellevue, WA (city) King County	2,197
Saratoga, CA (city) Santa Clara County	2,175
Austin, TX (city) Travis County	2,165
Edison, NJ (township) Middlesex County	2,151
San Mateo, CA (city) San Mateo County	2,134
Berkeley, CA (city) Alameda County	1,954
Palo Alto, CA (city) Santa Clara County	1,933
Phoenix, AZ (city) Maricopa County	1,853
Stockton, CA (city) San Joaquin County	1,832
South San Francisco, CA (city) San Mateo County	1,804
Foster City, CA (city) San Mateo County	1,779
Millbrae, CA (city) San Mateo County	1,760
Anaheim, CA (city) Orange County	1,684
Dallas, TX (city) Dallas County	1,681
San Marino, CA (city) Los Angeles County	1,679
Spring Valley, NV (cdp) Clark County	1,673
Oyster Bay, NY (town) Nassau County	1,670
Hayward, CA (city) Alameda County	1,648
Mountain View, CA (city) Santa Clara County	1,641
East San Gabriel, CA (cdp) Los Angeles County	1,527
Santa Clara, CA (city) Santa Clara County	1,501
Malden, MA (city) Middlesex County	1,471
Chino Hills, CA (city) San Bernardino County	1,468
Davis, CA (city) Yolo County	1,441
Huntington Beach, CA (city) Orange County	1,417
Brookhaven, NY (town) Suffolk County	1,403
South Pasadena, CA (city) Los Angeles County	1,386
Pasadena, CA (city) Los Angeles County	1,374
Newton, MA (city) Middlesex County	1,365
Fresno, CA (city) Fresno County	1,327
Rancho Palos Verdes, CA (city) Los Angeles County	1,312
East Brunswick, NJ (township) Middlesex County	1,285
Baldwin Park, CA (city) Los Angeles County	1,282

Notes: Please refer to the User's Guide for an explanation of data; ranking tables include all places with Asian and/or NHPI populations above SF4 population thresholds; (1) tables reflect only those areas that meet SF4 population thresholds, therefore there may be less than 50 states, 75 counties or 75 places listed

Foreign-Born Naturalized Citizens

Chinese (except Taiwanese)

All States, Top 75 Counties, and Top 75 Places Sorted by Percent[1]

State	Percent
Alaska	43.99
California	41.63
Florida	39.18
Nevada	38.96
Washington	38.96
New Jersey	38.07
Maryland	37.82
United States	37.26
Virginia	37.00
New York	36.42
Mississippi	35.26
Maine	35.23
Colorado	35.10
Rhode Island	35.03
Illinois	34.72
Massachusetts	34.60
Oregon	34.43
New Hampshire	33.85
Connecticut	33.73
Texas	32.86
Vermont	32.83
Georgia	32.70
Montana	32.62
Delaware	32.35
South Carolina	32.00
Idaho	31.98
Kansas	31.96
Arizona	31.43
Missouri	31.30
Wyoming	31.22
Minnesota	30.82
Pennsylvania	30.77
District of Columbia	30.52
South Dakota	30.34
Kentucky	29.25
Ohio	28.89
Hawaii	28.68
New Mexico	28.41
Louisiana	28.24
Tennessee	28.23
Utah	28.17
Arkansas	28.15
Michigan	28.14
North Carolina	27.45
Alabama	25.38
Wisconsin	24.51
West Virginia	24.29
North Dakota	24.01
Indiana	23.36
Nebraska	22.30
Oklahoma	22.16
Iowa	20.56

County	Percent
Sangamon County, IL	56.91
Kent County, RI	55.01
Alexandria Independent City, VA	53.80
Lee County, FL	49.83
Anchorage Borough, AK	49.65
Columbia County, GA	49.64
Osceola County, FL	48.97
San Francisco County, CA	48.76
Kane County, IL	48.42
Virginia Beach Independent City, VA	47.48
Cumberland County, PA	47.27
Benton County, WA	46.34
Ventura County, CA	46.08
Merced County, CA	45.68
Union County, NJ	45.50
Volusia County, FL	45.44
Miami-Dade County, FL	45.22
Oneida County, NY	44.90
Anne Arundel County, MD	44.88
Pasco County, FL	44.84
Butler County, OH	44.49
Kitsap County, WA	44.37
Atlantic County, NJ	44.30
Orange County, CA	44.28
San Mateo County, CA	43.47
Douglas County, CO	43.35
Ocean County, NJ	43.32
Lancaster County, PA	43.17
Morris County, NJ	42.96
Clackamas County, OR	42.83
Nassau County, NY	42.77
Broward County, FL	42.75
Gloucester County, NJ	42.67
Snohomish County, WA	42.60
Penobscot County, ME	42.52
Los Angeles County, CA	42.50
Washington County, MN	42.49
Adams County, CO	42.45
San Luis Obispo County, CA	42.29
San Joaquin County, CA	42.21
Solano County, CA	42.20
Monmouth County, NJ	42.11
Dakota County, MN	42.07
Fairfax Independent City, VA	41.83
Thurston County, WA	41.81
Howard County, MD	41.75
Richmond County, NY	41.71
Rockland County, NY	41.55
Berks County, PA	41.28
Rockingham County, NH	41.26
Montgomery County, TX	41.24
Butte County, CA	41.23
Strafford County, NH	41.16
Gwinnett County, GA	40.89
Somerset County, NJ	40.80
Fairfax County, VA	40.73
Norfolk County, MA	40.73
Montgomery County, MD	40.51
San Bernardino County, CA	40.40
Camden County, NJ	40.33
Cobb County, GA	40.33
Chesterfield County, VA	40.32
Will County, IL	40.12
Fort Bend County, TX	40.08
Clayton County, GA	40.07
York County, PA	40.03
Saratoga County, NY	39.59
Jefferson County, TX	39.51
Pierce County, WA	39.43
Duval County, FL	39.28
Essex County, NJ	39.24
Contra Costa County, CA	39.20
Stark County, OH	39.18
Clark County, NV	39.11
King County, WA	39.04

Place	Percent
Scotch Plains, NJ (township) Union County	66.09
Northbrook, IL (village) Cook County	58.88
Lake Forest, CA (city) Orange County	56.43
Brea, CA (city) Orange County	56.35
Tustin Foothills, CA (cdp) Orange County	56.26
Santa Ana, CA (city) Orange County	56.08
Ashland, CA (cdp) Alameda County	55.96
Miami, FL (city) Miami-Dade County	55.40
Hicksville, NY (cdp) Nassau County	55.36
Los Gatos, CA (town) Santa Clara County	55.10
Montgomery Village, MD (cdp) Montgomery County	55.06
Fairland, MD (cdp) Montgomery County	54.41
Hawthorne, CA (city) Los Angeles County	54.23
Laguna Niguel, CA (city) Orange County	54.14
Greenwich, CT (town) Fairfield County	53.68
Ramapo, NY (town) Rockland County	53.49
Simi Valley, CA (city) Ventura County	53.34
Orange, CA (city) Orange County	53.33
Glenview, IL (village) Cook County	52.86
Fountain Valley, CA (city) Orange County	52.65
New Castle, NY (town) Westchester County	52.60
Yonkers, NY (city) Westchester County	52.06
Elk Grove, CA (cdp) Sacramento County	52.03
Wolf Trap, VA (cdp) Fairfax County	52.03
West Orange, NJ (township) Essex County	51.78
Escondido, CA (city) San Diego County	51.73
Lake Oswego, OR (city) Clackamas County	51.42
Lake Success, NY (village) Nassau County	51.41
La Mirada, CA (city) Los Angeles County	51.27
Radnor, PA (township) Delaware County	51.02
Voorhees, NJ (township) Camden County	50.81
Gardena, CA (city) Los Angeles County	50.62
Elk Grove Village, IL (village) Cook County	50.60
Wheaton-Glenmont, MD (cdp) Montgomery County	50.56
Morganville, NJ (cdp) Monmouth County	50.39
Dix Hills, NY (cdp) Suffolk County	50.22
East Pasadena, CA (cdp) Los Angeles County	50.08
South El Monte, CA (city) Los Angeles County	50.07
East Hill-Meridian, WA (cdp) King County	49.75
Hercules, CA (city) Contra Costa County	49.72
Hazlet, NJ (township) Monmouth County	49.61
Rancho Palos Verdes, CA (city) Los Angeles County	49.60
Colesville, MD (cdp) Montgomery County	49.45
Yorba Linda, CA (city) Orange County	49.41
East Hanover, NJ (township) Morris County	49.35
New Providence, NJ (borough) Union County	49.33
Randolph, MA (town) Norfolk County	49.28
Rolling Hills Estates, CA (city) Los Angeles County	49.09
Hanover, NJ (township) Morris County	49.02
Westminster, CA (city) Orange County	49.00
Garden Grove, CA (city) Orange County	48.93
Kendall, FL (cdp) Miami-Dade County	48.88
San Francisco, CA (city) San Francisco County	48.76
Montville, NJ (township) Morris County	48.58
North Miami Beach, FL (city) Miami-Dade County	48.58
San Dimas, CA (city) Los Angeles County	48.58
Hillsborough, CA (town) San Mateo County	48.47
Margate, FL (city) Broward County	48.43
Oxnard, CA (city) Ventura County	48.36
Daly City, CA (city) San Mateo County	48.23
Los Altos Hills, CA (town) Santa Clara County	48.19
North Brunswick, NJ (township) Middlesex County	48.14
Huntington Beach, CA (city) Orange County	47.92
Santa Clarita, CA (city) Los Angeles County	47.91
White Oak, MD (cdp) Montgomery County	47.87
Duarte, CA (city) Los Angeles County	47.84
El Cerrito, CA (city) Contra Costa County	47.79
Downey, CA (city) Los Angeles County	47.76
Potomac, MD (cdp) Montgomery County	47.69
Montebello, CA (city) Los Angeles County	47.56
Renton, WA (city) King County	47.49
Cypress, CA (city) Orange County	47.45
Sunrise, FL (city) Broward County	47.29
Lower Macungie, PA (township) Lehigh County	47.19
El Monte, CA (city) Los Angeles County	47.16

Notes: Please refer to the User's Guide for an explanation of data; ranking tables include all places with Asian and/or NHPI populations above SF4 population thresholds; (1) tables reflect only those areas that meet SF4 population thresholds, therefore there may be less than 50 states, 75 counties or 75 places listed

Foreign-Born Naturalized Citizens

Fijian

All States, Top 75 Counties, and Top 75 Places Sorted by Number[1]

State	Number
United States	2,901
California	2,291
Washington	200
Oregon	134

County	Number
Sacramento County, CA	458
San Mateo County, CA	442
Alameda County, CA	280
Stanislaus County, CA	232
Santa Clara County, CA	185
Los Angeles County, CA	179
King County, WA	168
Contra Costa County, CA	121
Yolo County, CA	44

Place	Number
Sacramento, CA (city) Sacramento County	338
Modesto, CA (city) Stanislaus County	152
Hayward, CA (city) Alameda County	140

Notes: Please refer to the User's Guide for an explanation of data; ranking tables include all places with Asian and/or NHPI populations above SF4 population thresholds; (1) tables reflect only those areas that meet SF4 population thresholds, therefore there may be less than 50 states, 75 counties or 75 places listed

Foreign-Born Naturalized Citizens

Fijian

All States, Top 75 Counties, and Top 75 Places Sorted by Percent[1]

State	Percent
Oregon	35.92
United States	28.26
Washington	28.21
California	27.24

County	Percent
San Mateo County, CA	38.20
Los Angeles County, CA	36.31
Santa Clara County, CA	36.20
Stanislaus County, CA	33.24
King County, WA	30.94
Sacramento County, CA	26.16
Contra Costa County, CA	22.49
Alameda County, CA	19.14
Yolo County, CA	8.37

Place	Percent
Modesto, CA (city) Stanislaus County	30.77
Sacramento, CA (city) Sacramento County	27.26
Hayward, CA (city) Alameda County	16.61

Notes: Please refer to the User's Guide for an explanation of data; ranking tables include all places with Asian and/or NHPI populations above SF4 population thresholds; (1) tables reflect only those areas that meet SF4 population thresholds, therefore there may be less than 50 states, 75 counties or 75 places listed

Foreign-Born Naturalized Citizens

Filipino

All States, Top 75 Counties, and Top 75 Places Sorted by Number[1]

State	Number
United States	775,400
California	392,117
Hawaii	63,468
Illinois	37,691
New Jersey	37,071
New York	34,693
Washington	28,194
Florida	23,541
Texas	22,366
Virginia	20,620
Nevada	16,410
Maryland	11,527
Michigan	7,578
Pennsylvania	6,124
Ohio	5,811
Arizona	5,409
Alaska	5,112
Georgia	4,175
North Carolina	3,933
Oregon	3,738
Colorado	3,698
Massachusetts	3,657
Missouri	3,346
South Carolina	3,080
Indiana	2,926
Connecticut	2,864
Minnesota	2,363
Wisconsin	2,269
Tennessee	2,000
Louisiana	1,949
Oklahoma	1,634
Kentucky	1,394
Kansas	1,363
New Mexico	1,164
Utah	1,162
Alabama	1,058
Rhode Island	1,049
Iowa	990
Mississippi	982
Nebraska	970
Delaware	917
Arkansas	833
West Virginia	827
Idaho	629
Maine	553
New Hampshire	504
District of Columbia	447
Montana	317
South Dakota	284
Wyoming	261
North Dakota	168
Vermont	164

County	Number
Los Angeles County, CA	115,150
San Diego County, CA	52,849
Honolulu County, HI	47,418
Santa Clara County, CA	31,256
Alameda County, CA	29,904
San Mateo County, CA	26,856
Cook County, IL	25,052
San Francisco County, CA	19,939
Orange County, CA	19,697
Solano County, CA	16,033
King County, WA	14,355
Contra Costa County, CA	14,339
Clark County, NV	13,283
Queens County, NY	13,073
San Bernardino County, CA	11,138
Sacramento County, CA	9,220
Hudson County, NJ	8,283
Maui County, HI	8,208
Riverside County, CA	7,965
San Joaquin County, CA	7,473
Ventura County, CA	7,049
Virginia Beach Independent City, VA	6,585
Bergen County, NJ	6,196
Harris County, TX	5,999
DuPage County, IL	5,887
Middlesex County, NJ	4,740
Fairfax County, VA	4,722
Duval County, FL	4,580
Monterey County, CA	4,201
Hawaii County, HI	4,184
Maricopa County, AZ	3,871
Prince George's County, MD	3,793
Kern County, CA	3,651
Kauai County, HI	3,643
New York County, NY	3,621
Kitsap County, WA	3,593
Snohomish County, WA	3,311
Essex County, NJ	3,275
Nassau County, NY	2,881
Pierce County, WA	2,843
Lake County, IL	2,809
Kings County, NY	2,805
Montgomery County, MD	2,790
Washoe County, NV	2,540
Fresno County, CA	2,513
Richmond County, NY	2,503
Dallas County, TX	2,482
Union County, NJ	2,380
Anchorage Borough, AK	2,226
Bexar County, TX	2,179
Broward County, FL	2,112
Wayne County, MI	2,104
Norfolk Independent City, VA	1,992
Camden County, NJ	1,971
Santa Barbara County, CA	1,929
Fort Bend County, TX	1,892
Miami-Dade County, FL	1,874
Oakland County, MI	1,839
Rockland County, NY	1,838
Orange County, FL	1,835
Suffolk County, NY	1,791
Westchester County, NY	1,737
Philadelphia County, PA	1,712
Baltimore County, MD	1,711
Passaic County, NJ	1,642
Tulare County, CA	1,597
Monmouth County, NJ	1,527
Morris County, NJ	1,484
Tarrant County, TX	1,479
Macomb County, MI	1,424
Bronx County, NY	1,419
Cuyahoga County, OH	1,306
Multnomah County, OR	1,305
Escambia County, FL	1,258
Will County, IL	1,178

Place	Number
Los Angeles, CA (city) Los Angeles County	43,826
San Diego, CA (city) San Diego County	32,765
New York, NY (city)	23,421
San Francisco, CA (city) San Francisco County	19,939
San Jose, CA (city) Santa Clara County	19,826
Honolulu, HI (cdp) Honolulu County	17,054
Daly City, CA (city) San Mateo County	15,067
Chicago, IL (city) Cook County	12,744
Vallejo, CA (city) Solano County	10,605
Long Beach, CA (city) Los Angeles County	7,857
Carson, CA (city) Los Angeles County	7,727
Seattle, WA (city) King County	7,045
Jersey City, NJ (city) Hudson County	6,932
Waipahu, HI (cdp) Honolulu County	6,740
Union City, CA (city) Alameda County	5,954
Chula Vista, CA (city) San Diego County	5,912
Stockton, CA (city) San Joaquin County	5,351
Hayward, CA (city) Alameda County	5,289
Glendale, CA (city) Los Angeles County	5,099
Fremont, CA (city) Alameda County	4,826
South San Francisco, CA (city) San Mateo County	4,681
West Covina, CA (city) Los Angeles County	4,485
Jacksonville, FL (city) Duval County	4,406
Las Vegas, NV (city) Clark County	4,392
Oxnard, CA (city) Ventura County	4,363
National City, CA (city) San Diego County	4,063
Milpitas, CA (city) Santa Clara County	3,694
Cerritos, CA (city) Los Angeles County	3,071
Anaheim, CA (city) Orange County	2,979
Sacramento, CA (city) Sacramento County	2,960
Houston, TX (city) Harris County	2,941
Oakland, CA (city) Alameda County	2,918
Sunnyvale, CA (city) Santa Clara County	2,756
Alameda, CA (city) Alameda County	2,732
Chino Hills, CA (city) San Bernardino County	2,556
San Leandro, CA (city) Alameda County	2,550
Kahului, HI (cdp) Maui County	2,493
Fairfield, CA (city) Solano County	2,475
Santa Clara, CA (city) Santa Clara County	2,473
Hercules, CA (city) Contra Costa County	2,296
Ewa Beach, HI (cdp) Honolulu County	2,229
Sunrise Manor, NV (cdp) Clark County	2,133
Lakewood, CA (city) Los Angeles County	2,030
Pittsburg, CA (city) Contra Costa County	2,001
Oceanside, CA (city) San Diego County	1,987
Paradise, NV (cdp) Clark County	1,970
Buena Park, CA (city) Orange County	1,968
Norwalk, CA (city) Los Angeles County	1,959
Salinas, CA (city) Monterey County	1,921
Delano, CA (city) Kern County	1,868
Fresno, CA (city) Fresno County	1,776
Walnut, CA (city) Los Angeles County	1,770
Moreno Valley, CA (city) Riverside County	1,739
Philadelphia, PA (city) Philadelphia County	1,712
Spring Valley, NV (cdp) Clark County	1,678
Baldwin Park, CA (city) Los Angeles County	1,661
Torrance, CA (city) Los Angeles County	1,643
Pearl City, HI (cdp) Honolulu County	1,600
Reno, NV (city) Washoe County	1,587
Rowland Heights, CA (cdp) Los Angeles County	1,579
San Antonio, TX (city) Bexar County	1,545
Suisun City, CA (city) Solano County	1,515
Village Park, HI (cdp) Honolulu County	1,501
Concord, CA (city) Contra Costa County	1,496
Diamond Bar, CA (city) Los Angeles County	1,491
Phoenix, AZ (city) Maricopa County	1,470
Skokie, IL (village) Cook County	1,408
Elk Grove, CA (cdp) Sacramento County	1,395
Hempstead, NY (town) Nassau County	1,391
San Bruno, CA (city) San Mateo County	1,385
Pacifica, CA (city) San Mateo County	1,338
Burbank, CA (city) Los Angeles County	1,326
La Presa, CA (cdp) San Diego County	1,322
Corona, CA (city) Riverside County	1,316
Bellflower, CA (city) Los Angeles County	1,310

Notes: Please refer to the User's Guide for an explanation of data; ranking tables include all places with Asian and/or NHPI populations above SF4 population thresholds; (1) tables reflect only those areas that meet SF4 population thresholds, therefore there may be less than 50 states, 75 counties or 75 places listed

Foreign-Born Naturalized Citizens

Filipino

All States, Top 75 Counties, and Top 75 Places Sorted by Percent[1]

State	Percent
Vermont	52.23
Delaware	50.25
Wyoming	49.90
West Virginia	49.88
Rhode Island	49.34
Maine	47.26
Nebraska	46.97
Missouri	46.13
Kentucky	44.55
South Carolina	44.30
Ohio	44.09
Iowa	44.02
Illinois	43.70
Alabama	43.34
Washington	43.34
Florida	43.33
Maryland	43.22
Michigan	43.08
Virginia	42.94
California	42.62
Indiana	42.46
New Jersey	41.93
Pennsylvania	41.62
United States	41.60
Wisconsin	41.56
Louisiana	41.23
Alaska	40.94
Nevada	40.49
Montana	40.38
South Dakota	40.34
Kansas	40.31
Minnesota	40.05
Georgia	40.01
New York	40.00
Colorado	39.68
New Hampshire	39.62
New Mexico	39.56
Massachusetts	39.38
Oklahoma	39.05
North Carolina	38.58
Idaho	38.35
Texas	38.16
Connecticut	38.13
Tennessee	37.86
Mississippi	37.50
Hawaii	36.97
Arkansas	36.17
Oregon	35.02
Arizona	33.38
Utah	31.36
North Dakota	29.12
District of Columbia	21.09

County	Percent
Stafford County, VA	61.38
Sandoval County, NM	60.54
Santa Rosa County, FL	57.99
Sarpy County, NE	57.81
Hamilton County, TN	56.14
Lorain County, OH	55.66
Chesapeake Independent City, VA	54.86
Jackson County, MO	53.95
Fairbanks North Star Borough, AK	53.33
Monroe County, NY	52.94
Baltimore County, MD	52.32
Volusia County, FL	52.21
Camden County, NJ	52.10
Albany County, NY	51.64
Kitsap County, WA	51.53
Jefferson County, KY	50.92
Waukesha County, WI	50.87
New Castle County, DE	50.67
Berkeley County, SC	50.58
Clay County, FL	50.29
Orleans Parish, LA	50.21
Ketchikan Gateway Borough, AK	50.15
Brevard County, FL	50.03
Osceola County, FL	49.83
San Francisco County, CA	49.76
Muscogee County, GA	49.67
North Slope Borough, AK	49.56
Douglas County, NE	49.49
Lucas County, OH	49.33
Gloucester County, NJ	49.19
Wayne County, MI	48.95
Kent County, DE	48.90
Sarasota County, FL	48.89
Nueces County, TX	48.82
Providence County, RI	48.77
Virginia Beach Independent City, VA	48.66
Pasco County, FL	48.39
Richmond County, NY	48.24
Montgomery County, TX	47.85
Onondaga County, NY	47.69
Hillsborough County, NH	47.61
Bristol County, MA	47.58
Polk County, FL	47.34
Plymouth County, MA	47.30
Sedgwick County, KS	47.25
Passaic County, NJ	47.18
St. Charles County, MO	47.15
Kings County, CA	47.05
Montgomery County, OH	46.93
St. Louis County, MO	46.92
Mercer County, NJ	46.88
Cuyahoga County, OH	46.83
Erie County, NY	46.81
Bucks County, PA	46.70
Galveston County, TX	46.68
Norfolk Independent City, VA	46.61
Lake County, IN	46.56
Dorchester County, SC	46.55
Howard County, MD	46.52
St. Mary's County, MD	46.48
Chesterfield County, VA	46.36
Escambia County, FL	46.30
Ventura County, CA	46.21
Cumberland County, NC	46.13
Portsmouth Independent City, VA	46.09
Morris County, NJ	46.07
Prince George's County, MD	46.04
Oakland County, MI	45.95
Cook County, IL	45.89
St. Clair County, IL	45.77
Monmouth County, NJ	45.72
Shasta County, CA	45.66
Richland County, SC	45.59
Prince William County, VA	45.49
Juneau Borough, AK	45.20

Place	Percent
Colonia, NJ (cdp) Middlesex County	62.12
Bonita, CA (cdp) San Diego County	61.67
Placentia, CA (city) Orange County	60.10
Rio Rancho, NM (city) Sandoval County	59.57
Pico Rivera, CA (city) Los Angeles County	59.14
Mission Bend, TX (cdp) Fort Bend County	58.85
Rancho Palos Verdes, CA (city) Los Angeles County	58.70
San Gabriel, CA (city) Los Angeles County	58.61
Arlington Heights, IL (village) Cook County	57.33
Darien, IL (city) Du Page County	56.42
Lathrop, CA (city) San Joaquin County	56.35
Lombard, IL (village) Du Page County	56.22
Hicksville, NY (cdp) Nassau County	55.71
Lakeside, FL (cdp) Clay County	55.69
Upland, CA (city) San Bernardino County	55.56
La Puente, CA (city) Los Angeles County	54.69
West Orange, NJ (township) Essex County	54.57
Washington, NJ (township) Gloucester County	54.41
Cherry Hill, NJ (township) Camden County	54.23
Gloucester, NJ (township) Camden County	54.17
Lincolnwood, IL (village) Cook County	54.16
Babylon, NY (town) Suffolk County	53.78
Oxon Hill-Glassmanor, MD (cdp) Prince George's County	53.69
Cerritos, CA (city) Los Angeles County	53.64
North Brunswick, NJ (township) Middlesex County	53.41
Hanford, CA (city) Kings County	53.28
El Monte, CA (city) Los Angeles County	53.15
Columbia, MD (cdp) Howard County	52.65
San Lorenzo, CA (cdp) Alameda County	52.61
Lemoore, CA (city) Kings County	52.52
Laguna Hills, CA (city) Orange County	52.48
Friendly, MD (cdp) Prince George's County	52.39
Rodeo, CA (cdp) Contra Costa County	52.38
Kualapuu, HI (cdp) Maui County	52.25
Passaic, NJ (city) Passaic County	52.12
Parsippany-Troy Hills, NJ (township) Morris County	52.10
Temple City, CA (city) Los Angeles County	52.08
Troy, MI (city) Oakland County	52.06
Santa Monica, CA (city) Los Angeles County	52.05
Huntington, NY (town) Suffolk County	51.98
Omao, HI (cdp) Kauai County	51.91
Castro Valley, CA (cdp) Alameda County	51.90
Dublin, CA (city) Alameda County	51.78
Culver City, CA (city) Los Angeles County	51.70
Oyster Bay, NY (town) Nassau County	51.68
Silverdale, WA (cdp) Kitsap County	51.52
Walnut, CA (city) Los Angeles County	51.27
Broadmoor, CA (cdp) San Mateo County	51.12
Hoffman Estates, IL (village) Cook County	50.98
Palatine, IL (village) Cook County	50.85
Aspen Hill, MD (cdp) Montgomery County	50.81
Toledo, OH (city) Lucas County	50.81
Myrtle Grove, FL (cdp) Escambia County	50.74
Ketchikan, AK (city) Ketchikan Gateway Borough	50.65
Canton, MI (township) Wayne County	50.57
Palmdale, CA (city) Los Angeles County	50.57
Bellevue, WA (city) King County	50.56
Winchester, NV (cdp) Clark County	50.56
Teaneck, NJ (township) Bergen County	50.23
Dale City, VA (cdp) Prince William County	50.22
New Orleans, LA (city) Orleans Parish	50.21
Detroit, MI (city) Wayne County	50.15
Arcadia, CA (city) Los Angeles County	50.12
Wichita, KS (city) Sedgwick County	49.91
Goose Creek, SC (city) Berkeley County	49.87
Bellview, FL (cdp) Escambia County	49.76
San Francisco, CA (city) San Francisco County	49.76
Columbus, GA (sp. city) Muscogee County	49.67
Oklahoma City, OK (city) Oklahoma County	49.67
Pembroke Pines, FL (city) Broward County	49.62
Security-Widefield, CO (cdp) El Paso County	49.62
Dumont, NJ (borough) Bergen County	49.59
Barrow, AK (city) North Slope Borough	49.56
Lakewood, WA (city) Pierce County	49.43
Voorhees, NJ (township) Camden County	49.39

Notes: Please refer to the User's Guide for an explanation of data; ranking tables include all places with Asian and/or NHPI populations above SF4 population thresholds; (1) tables reflect only those areas that meet SF4 population thresholds, therefore there may be less than 50 states, 75 counties or 75 places listed

Foreign-Born Naturalized Citizens

Guamanian or Chamorro

All States, Top 75 Counties, and Top 75 Places Sorted by Number[1]

State	Number
United States	2,308
California	552
New York	222
Tennessee	145
Georgia	104
Texas	97
Nevada	96
New Jersey	95
Illinois	86
Michigan	85
North Carolina	81
Florida	66
Arizona	60
Minnesota	46
Washington	46
Maryland	44
Pennsylvania	40
Virginia	40
Massachusetts	37
Oregon	35
Colorado	24
Alabama	22
Indiana	22
Ohio	22
Hawaii	20
Missouri	13
Connecticut	12
Kentucky	12
Oklahoma	12
Louisiana	7
New Mexico	6
Wisconsin	6
South Carolina	2

County	Number
Los Angeles County, CA	187
Clark County, NV	96
San Diego County, CA	84
Santa Clara County, CA	53
Kings County, NY	42
Sacramento County, CA	32
King County, WA	27
Honolulu County, HI	20
Orange County, CA	20
Solano County, CA	16
San Bernardino County, CA	15
San Mateo County, CA	15
Alameda County, CA	13
Contra Costa County, CA	11
El Paso County, CO	11
Harris County, TX	10
Riverside County, CA	10
Maricopa County, AZ	9
Monterey County, CA	9
Pierce County, WA	6
Thurston County, WA	5
Bell County, TX	0
Kitsap County, WA	0

Place	Number
New York, NY (city)	156
Los Angeles, CA (city) Los Angeles County	118
San Diego, CA (city) San Diego County	27
San Jose, CA (city) Santa Clara County	26
Chula Vista, CA (city) San Diego County	21
Vallejo, CA (city) Solano County	16
Houston, TX (city) Harris County	10
Fairfield, CA (city) Solano County	0
Honolulu, HI (cdp) Honolulu County	0
Killeen, TX (city) Bell County	0
Tacoma, WA (city) Pierce County	0

Notes: Please refer to the User's Guide for an explanation of data; ranking tables include all places with Asian and/or NHPI populations above SF4 population thresholds; (1) tables reflect only those areas that meet SF4 population thresholds, therefore there may be less than 50 states, 75 counties or 75 places listed

Foreign-Born Naturalized Citizens

Guamanian or Chamorro

All States, Top 75 Counties, and Top 75 Places Sorted by Percent[1]

State	Percent
Tennessee	23.42
New Jersey	15.78
New York	12.62
Michigan	12.41
Minnesota	10.77
Illinois	10.55
Nevada	8.43
Massachusetts	8.31
Georgia	7.21
North Carolina	6.77
Maryland	6.28
Alabama	5.19
Pennsylvania	4.97
Arizona	4.74
United States	4.19
Indiana	4.18
Virginia	3.94
Ohio	3.30
Florida	3.27
Kentucky	3.26
Oregon	3.15
Oklahoma	3.00
Texas	2.94
Connecticut	2.86
California	2.70
Colorado	2.37
Missouri	2.12
New Mexico	1.64
Louisiana	1.50
Wisconsin	1.41
Hawaii	1.34
Washington	0.86
South Carolina	0.56

County	Percent
Clark County, NV	10.02
Kings County, NY	8.59
Los Angeles County, CA	5.96
Santa Clara County, CA	3.81
San Mateo County, CA	3.73
Sacramento County, CA	3.66
King County, WA	3.24
El Paso County, CO	2.24
Contra Costa County, CA	2.02
Orange County, CA	1.81
San Diego County, CA	1.81
Harris County, TX	1.56
Honolulu County, HI	1.51
San Bernardino County, CA	1.44
Maricopa County, AZ	1.39
Monterey County, CA	1.34
Solano County, CA	1.18
Riverside County, CA	1.06
Alameda County, CA	0.99
Thurston County, WA	0.68
Pierce County, WA	0.33
Bell County, TX	0.00
Kitsap County, WA	0.00

Place	Percent
New York, NY (city)	13.27
Los Angeles, CA (city) Los Angeles County	10.27
Chula Vista, CA (city) San Diego County	4.94
San Jose, CA (city) Santa Clara County	3.55
Vallejo, CA (city) Solano County	2.80
Houston, TX (city) Harris County	2.26
San Diego, CA (city) San Diego County	1.30
Fairfield, CA (city) Solano County	0.00
Honolulu, HI (cdp) Honolulu County	0.00
Killeen, TX (city) Bell County	0.00
Tacoma, WA (city) Pierce County	0.00

Notes: Please refer to the User's Guide for an explanation of data; ranking tables include all places with Asian and/or NHPI populations above SF4 population thresholds; (1) tables reflect only those areas that meet SF4 population thresholds, therefore there may be less than 50 states, 75 counties or 75 places listed

Foreign-Born Naturalized Citizens

Hawaiian, Native

All States, Top 75 Counties, and Top 75 Places Sorted by Number[1]

State	Number
United States	1,459
California	507
Hawaii	383
New York	116
Texas	61
Nevada	56
Florida	41
Arizona	35
Washington	31
Georgia	25
Pennsylvania	25
Minnesota	23
New Jersey	20
Colorado	17
Virginia	17
Oklahoma	15
Maryland	13
South Carolina	13
Utah	10
Tennessee	9
Alaska	7
Michigan	7
Illinois	6
Oregon	6
Wisconsin	4
Arkansas	0
Idaho	0
Indiana	0
Kansas	0
Louisiana	0
Massachusetts	0
Missouri	0
Montana	0
New Mexico	0
North Carolina	0
Ohio	0

County	Number
Honolulu County, HI	293
Los Angeles County, CA	102
Ventura County, CA	78
Hawaii County, HI	71
Clark County, NV	48
Pima County, AZ	35
Santa Clara County, CA	34
San Mateo County, CA	29
Orange County, CA	28
Contra Costa County, CA	25
Alameda County, CA	24
San Bernardino County, CA	24
San Joaquin County, CA	17
Riverside County, CA	15
Maui County, HI	14
King County, WA	13
San Diego County, CA	12
Utah County, UT	10
Bexar County, TX	8
Sacramento County, CA	8
Solano County, CA	7
Multnomah County, OR	6
Kauai County, HI	5
Maricopa County, AZ	0
Pierce County, WA	0
Salt Lake County, UT	0
Snohomish County, WA	0
Washington County, OR	0

Place	Number
New York, NY (city)	116
Honolulu, HI (cdp) Honolulu County	107
Aiea, HI (cdp) Honolulu County	70
Los Angeles, CA (city) Los Angeles County	33
Las Vegas, NV (city) Clark County	29
Waipio, HI (cdp) Honolulu County	22
San Jose, CA (city) Santa Clara County	20
Paradise, NV (cdp) Clark County	19
Hilo, HI (cdp) Hawaii County	17
Waimea, HI (cdp) Hawaii County	12
Lahaina, HI (cdp) Maui County	10
Waianae, HI (cdp) Honolulu County	10
Kaneohe, HI (cdp) Honolulu County	8
Pearl City, HI (cdp) Honolulu County	7
Kailua, HI (cdp) Hawaii County	6
Makaha Valley, HI (cdp) Honolulu County	6
Nanakuli, HI (cdp) Honolulu County	6
Portland, OR (city) Multnomah County	6
Wahiawa, HI (cdp) Honolulu County	6
Maili, HI (cdp) Honolulu County	4
Mililani Town, HI (cdp) Honolulu County	4
Waikoloa Village, HI (cdp) Hawaii County	4
Laie, HI (cdp) Honolulu County	3
Waialua, HI (cdp) Honolulu County	3
Anahola, HI (cdp) Kauai County	2
Kualapuu, HI (cdp) Maui County	2
Paia, HI (cdp) Maui County	2
Kahuku, HI (cdp) Honolulu County	1
Ahuimanu, HI (cdp) Honolulu County	0
Captain Cook, HI (cdp) Hawaii County	0
Ewa Beach, HI (cdp) Honolulu County	0
Halawa, HI (cdp) Honolulu County	0
Haleiwa, HI (cdp) Honolulu County	0
Hana, HI (cdp) Maui County	0
Hanapepe, HI (cdp) Kauai County	0
Hauula, HI (cdp) Honolulu County	0
Hawaiian Beaches, HI (cdp) Hawaii County	0
Hawaiian Ocean View, HI (cdp) Hawaii County	0
Hawaiian Paradise Park, HI (cdp) Hawaii County	0
Henderson, NV (city) Clark County	0
Holualoa, HI (cdp) Hawaii County	0
Honalo, HI (cdp) Hawaii County	0
Honaunau-Napoopoo, HI (cdp) Hawaii County	0
Kaaawa, HI (cdp) Honolulu County	0
Kahaluu, HI (cdp) Honolulu County	0
Kahului, HI (cdp) Maui County	0
Kailua, HI (cdp) Honolulu County	0
Kalaoa, HI (cdp) Hawaii County	0
Kapaa, HI (cdp) Kauai County	0
Kapaau, HI (cdp) Hawaii County	0
Kaunakakai, HI (cdp) Maui County	0
Kekaha, HI (cdp) Kauai County	0
Kihei, HI (cdp) Maui County	0
Kilauea, HI (cdp) Kauai County	0
Makaha, HI (cdp) Honolulu County	0
Makakilo City, HI (cdp) Honolulu County	0
Makawao, HI (cdp) Maui County	0
Naalehu, HI (cdp) Hawaii County	0
Pahala, HI (cdp) Hawaii County	0
Pakala Village, HI (cdp) Kauai County	0
Phoenix, AZ (city) Maricopa County	0
Punaluu, HI (cdp) Honolulu County	0
San Diego, CA (city) San Diego County	0
Volcano, HI (cdp) Hawaii County	0
Waihee-Waiehu, HI (cdp) Maui County	0
Waikane, HI (cdp) Honolulu County	0
Wailuku, HI (cdp) Maui County	0
Waimalu, HI (cdp) Honolulu County	0
Waimanalo Beach, HI (cdp) Honolulu County	0
Waimanalo, HI (cdp) Honolulu County	0
Waimea, HI (cdp) Kauai County	0
Waipahu, HI (cdp) Honolulu County	0

Notes: Please refer to the User's Guide for an explanation of data; ranking tables include all places with Asian and/or NHPI populations above SF4 population thresholds; (1) tables reflect only those areas that meet SF4 population thresholds, therefore there may be less than 50 states, 75 counties or 75 places listed

Foreign-Born Naturalized Citizens

Hawaiian, Native

All States, Top 75 Counties, and Top 75 Places Sorted by Percent[1]

State	Percent
New York	8.04
Minnesota	3.97
Georgia	3.07
New Jersey	3.07
South Carolina	2.62
California	2.58
Maryland	2.52
Pennsylvania	2.49
Oklahoma	2.22
Florida	2.08
Virginia	1.84
Arizona	1.76
Texas	1.67
Nevada	1.64
Tennessee	1.61
Alaska	1.40
Colorado	1.17
United States	1.05
Wisconsin	0.92
Michigan	0.88
Utah	0.75
Washington	0.69
Illinois	0.66
Hawaii	0.47
Oregon	0.30
Arkansas	0.00
Idaho	0.00
Indiana	0.00
Kansas	0.00
Louisiana	0.00
Massachusetts	0.00
Missouri	0.00
Montana	0.00
New Mexico	0.00
North Carolina	0.00
Ohio	0.00

County	Percent
Ventura County, CA	13.57
Pima County, AZ	7.51
Contra Costa County, CA	4.20
San Joaquin County, CA	4.10
San Bernardino County, CA	3.93
San Mateo County, CA	3.60
Santa Clara County, CA	2.97
Utah County, UT	2.58
Los Angeles County, CA	2.32
Bexar County, TX	1.90
Alameda County, CA	1.87
Riverside County, CA	1.85
Orange County, CA	1.65
Clark County, NV	1.56
Multnomah County, OR	1.28
Sacramento County, CA	1.22
Solano County, CA	1.07
King County, WA	0.94
Honolulu County, HI	0.58
San Diego County, CA	0.54
Hawaii County, HI	0.51
Maui County, HI	0.12
Kauai County, HI	0.10
Maricopa County, AZ	0.00
Pierce County, WA	0.00
Salt Lake County, UT	0.00
Snohomish County, WA	0.00
Washington County, OR	0.00

Place	Percent
Aiea, HI (cdp) Honolulu County	19.02
New York, NY (city)	14.95
Waipio, HI (cdp) Honolulu County	5.05
San Jose, CA (city) Santa Clara County	3.74
Las Vegas, NV (city) Clark County	3.71
Paradise, NV (cdp) Clark County	3.17
Makaha Valley, HI (cdp) Honolulu County	2.73
Waialua, HI (cdp) Honolulu County	2.46
Los Angeles, CA (city) Los Angeles County	2.05
Portland, OR (city) Multnomah County	1.72
Waikoloa Village, HI (cdp) Hawaii County	1.34
Waimea, HI (cdp) Hawaii County	1.25
Lahaina, HI (cdp) Maui County	1.15
Paia, HI (cdp) Maui County	0.94
Laie, HI (cdp) Honolulu County	0.91
Honolulu, HI (cdp) Honolulu County	0.74
Wahiawa, HI (cdp) Honolulu County	0.64
Kailua, HI (cdp) Hawaii County	0.57
Kahuku, HI (cdp) Honolulu County	0.54
Pearl City, HI (cdp) Honolulu County	0.52
Mililani Town, HI (cdp) Honolulu County	0.46
Waianae, HI (cdp) Honolulu County	0.42
Hilo, HI (cdp) Hawaii County	0.41
Maili, HI (cdp) Honolulu County	0.28
Kaneohe, HI (cdp) Honolulu County	0.24
Kualapuu, HI (cdp) Maui County	0.23
Anahola, HI (cdp) Kauai County	0.20
Nanakuli, HI (cdp) Honolulu County	0.19
Ahuimanu, HI (cdp) Honolulu County	0.00
Captain Cook, HI (cdp) Hawaii County	0.00
Ewa Beach, HI (cdp) Honolulu County	0.00
Halawa, HI (cdp) Honolulu County	0.00
Haleiwa, HI (cdp) Honolulu County	0.00
Hana, HI (cdp) Maui County	0.00
Hanapepe, HI (cdp) Kauai County	0.00
Hauula, HI (cdp) Honolulu County	0.00
Hawaiian Beaches, HI (cdp) Hawaii County	0.00
Hawaiian Ocean View, HI (cdp) Hawaii County	0.00
Hawaiian Paradise Park, HI (cdp) Hawaii County	0.00
Henderson, NV (city) Clark County	0.00
Holualoa, HI (cdp) Hawaii County	0.00
Honalo, HI (cdp) Hawaii County	0.00
Honaunau-Napoopoo, HI (cdp) Hawaii County	0.00
Kaaawa, HI (cdp) Honolulu County	0.00
Kahaluu, HI (cdp) Honolulu County	0.00
Kahului, HI (cdp) Maui County	0.00
Kailua, HI (cdp) Honolulu County	0.00
Kalaoa, HI (cdp) Hawaii County	0.00
Kapaa, HI (cdp) Kauai County	0.00
Kapaau, HI (cdp) Hawaii County	0.00
Kaunakakai, HI (cdp) Maui County	0.00
Kekaha, HI (cdp) Kauai County	0.00
Kihei, HI (cdp) Maui County	0.00
Kilauea, HI (cdp) Kauai County	0.00
Makaha, HI (cdp) Honolulu County	0.00
Makakilo City, HI (cdp) Honolulu County	0.00
Makawao, HI (cdp) Maui County	0.00
Naalehu, HI (cdp) Hawaii County	0.00
Pahala, HI (cdp) Hawaii County	0.00
Pakala Village, HI (cdp) Kauai County	0.00
Phoenix, AZ (city) Maricopa County	0.00
Punaluu, HI (cdp) Honolulu County	0.00
San Diego, CA (city) San Diego County	0.00
Volcano, HI (cdp) Hawaii County	0.00
Waihee-Waiehu, HI (cdp) Maui County	0.00
Waikane, HI (cdp) Honolulu County	0.00
Wailuku, HI (cdp) Maui County	0.00
Waimalu, HI (cdp) Honolulu County	0.00
Waimanalo Beach, HI (cdp) Honolulu County	0.00
Waimanalo, HI (cdp) Honolulu County	0.00
Waimea, HI (cdp) Kauai County	0.00
Waipahu, HI (cdp) Honolulu County	0.00

Notes: Please refer to the User's Guide for an explanation of data; ranking tables include all places with Asian and/or NHPI populations above SF4 population thresholds; (1) tables reflect only those areas that meet SF4 population thresholds, therefore there may be less than 50 states, 75 counties or 75 places listed

Foreign-Born Naturalized Citizens

Hmong

All States, Top 75 Counties, and Top 75 Places Sorted by Number[1]

State	Number
United States	29,664
California	12,094
Minnesota	7,541
Wisconsin	4,813
Michigan	1,274
North Carolina	936
Colorado	689
Washington	355
Georgia	229
Kansas	218
South Carolina	167
Massachusetts	160
Rhode Island	155
Oregon	148
Alaska	113
Oklahoma	96
Pennsylvania	71

County	Number
Ramsey County, MN	4,626
Fresno County, CA	4,418
Sacramento County, CA	2,710
Hennepin County, MN	2,052
Milwaukee County, WI	1,467
Merced County, CA	1,207
San Joaquin County, CA	772
Marathon County, WI	569
Yuba County, CA	508
Adams County, CO	468
Butte County, CA	436
Dane County, WI	430
La Crosse County, WI	417
Orange County, CA	415
Wayne County, MI	410
Burke County, NC	319
Sheboygan County, WI	303
Outagamie County, WI	301
Macomb County, MI	292
Eau Claire County, WI	291
Oakland County, MI	290
San Diego County, CA	280
Brown County, WI	258
Tulare County, CA	245
Winnebago County, WI	240
Washington County, MN	219
Stanislaus County, CA	181
Catawba County, NC	180
Anoka County, MN	174
King County, WA	166
Spokane County, WA	154
Wyandotte County, KS	147
Spartanburg County, SC	140
Portage County, WI	135
Multnomah County, OR	133
Yolo County, CA	128
Riverside County, CA	127
Providence County, RI	121
Anchorage Borough, AK	113
Solano County, CA	111
Olmsted County, MN	108
Jefferson County, CO	100
Worcester County, MA	88
Manitowoc County, WI	80
Dunn County, WI	77
Glenn County, CA	62
Ingham County, MI	59
Los Angeles County, CA	58
Fond du Lac County, WI	47
Santa Barbara County, CA	45
Lancaster County, PA	44
Wood County, WI	42
Chippewa County, WI	38
Stanly County, NC	25
Calumet County, WI	24
Mecklenburg County, NC	23
Barrow County, GA	9

Place	Number
St. Paul, MN (city) Ramsey County	4,319
Fresno, CA (city) Fresno County	3,518
Sacramento, CA (city) Sacramento County	1,913
Milwaukee, WI (city) Milwaukee County	1,395
Minneapolis, MN (city) Hennepin County	1,326
Merced, CA (city) Merced County	782
Stockton, CA (city) San Joaquin County	616
Wausau, WI (city) Marathon County	453
Clovis, CA (city) Fresno County	424
Brooklyn Center, MN (city) Hennepin County	387
Madison, WI (city) Dane County	372
Linda, CA (cdp) Yuba County	370
Detroit, MI (city) Wayne County	351
Parkway-S. Sacramento, CA (cdp) Sacramento County	314
Eau Claire, WI (city) Eau Claire County	304
Sheboygan, WI (city) Sheboygan County	290
Appleton, WI (city) Outagamie County	267
Westminster, CO (city) Adams County	248
San Diego, CA (city) San Diego County	227
La Crosse, WI (city) La Crosse County	226
Santa Ana, CA (city) Orange County	215
Warren, MI (city) Macomb County	213
Pontiac, MI (city) Oakland County	194
Green Bay, WI (city) Brown County	174
Brooklyn Park, MN (city) Hennepin County	162
Oshkosh, WI (city) Winnebago County	152
Kansas City, KS (city) Wyandotte County	147
Chico, CA (city) Butte County	146
Maplewood, MN (city) Ramsey County	139
Stevens Point, WI (city) Portage County	129
Visalia, CA (city) Tulare County	125
Portland, OR (city) Multnomah County	120
Rochester, MN (city) Olmsted County	108
Florin, CA (cdp) Sacramento County	107
West Sacramento, CA (city) Yolo County	102
Oroville, CA (city) Butte County	100
Atwater, CA (city) Merced County	96
Fitchburg, MA (city) Worcester County	88
Woodbury, MN (city) Washington County	83
Lansing, MI (city) Ingham County	78
Spokane, WA (city) Spokane County	77
South Oroville, CA (cdp) Butte County	74
Providence, RI (city) Providence County	72
Glen Alpine, NC (town) Burke County	71
Modesto, CA (city) Stanislaus County	68
Manitowoc, WI (city) Manitowoc County	67
Willows, CA (city) Glenn County	62
Thermalito, CA (cdp) Butte County	48
Fond du Lac, WI (city) Fond du Lac County	47
Arden-Arcade, CA (cdp) Sacramento County	44
Wisconsin Rapids, WI (city) Wood County	33
Charlotte, NC (city) Mecklenburg County	23
Hickory, NC (city) Catawba County	7
Valdese, NC (town) Burke County	7
Connelly Springs, NC (town) Burke County	3

Notes: Please refer to the User's Guide for an explanation of data; ranking tables include all places with Asian and/or NHPI populations above SF4 population thresholds; (1) tables reflect only those areas that meet SF4 population thresholds, therefore there may be less than 50 states, 75 counties or 75 places listed

Foreign-Born Naturalized Citizens

Hmong

All States, Top 75 Counties, and Top 75 Places Sorted by Percent[1]

State	Percent
Oklahoma	28.66
Washington	23.76
Kansas	23.42
Colorado	22.86
Michigan	22.52
Alaska	21.65
South Carolina	19.42
Georgia	19.08
California	17.60
Minnesota	17.47
United States	17.44
Rhode Island	16.13
Massachusetts	16.11
Wisconsin	15.52
North Carolina	13.73
Oregon	10.83
Pennsylvania	9.01

County	Percent
Orange County, CA	39.34
Anoka County, MN	30.47
Spokane County, WA	28.89
Washington County, MN	28.40
Solano County, CA	27.01
Olmsted County, MN	27.00
Macomb County, MI	26.99
Oakland County, MI	26.83
Riverside County, CA	26.08
Jefferson County, CO	24.27
Tulare County, CA	22.54
Wayne County, MI	22.37
Adams County, CO	21.83
Anchorage Borough, AK	21.65
La Crosse County, WI	21.48
Eau Claire County, WI	21.03
San Diego County, CA	20.36
Milwaukee County, WI	19.60
Yolo County, CA	19.25
Wyandotte County, KS	18.87
Yuba County, CA	18.81
Dane County, WI	18.72
Stanislaus County, CA	18.68
King County, WA	18.67
Spartanburg County, SC	18.67
Fresno County, CA	18.37
Merced County, CA	18.33
Fond du Lac County, WI	17.74
Ramsey County, MN	17.38
Winnebago County, WI	16.08
Burke County, NC	15.91
Sacramento County, CA	15.65
Portage County, WI	15.54
Butte County, CA	15.44
Hennepin County, MN	15.40
Providence County, RI	14.56
Marathon County, WI	13.85
Dunn County, WI	13.65
Worcester County, MA	13.27
Los Angeles County, CA	13.18
San Joaquin County, CA	12.98
Outagamie County, WI	12.93
Santa Barbara County, CA	12.68
Multnomah County, OR	12.58
Sheboygan County, WI	12.16
Glenn County, CA	11.05
Brown County, WI	10.67
Chippewa County, WI	10.58
Catawba County, NC	10.03
Ingham County, MI	9.92
Lancaster County, PA	9.61
Manitowoc County, WI	8.52
Stanly County, NC	7.86
Wood County, WI	7.11
Calumet County, WI	5.50
Mecklenburg County, NC	4.04
Barrow County, GA	3.86

Place	Percent
Santa Ana, CA (city) Orange County	40.72
Maplewood, MN (city) Ramsey County	35.10
Glen Alpine, NC (town) Burke County	32.57
Warren, MI (city) Macomb County	28.44
Rochester, MN (city) Olmsted County	27.00
Pontiac, MI (city) Oakland County	26.80
Brooklyn Center, MN (city) Hennepin County	26.65
Atwater, CA (city) Merced County	24.43
Westminster, CO (city) Adams County	24.43
Clovis, CA (city) Fresno County	23.57
Woodbury, MN (city) Washington County	23.51
Visalia, CA (city) Tulare County	23.11
Fond du Lac, WI (city) Fond du Lac County	22.49
Detroit, MI (city) Wayne County	21.43
Eau Claire, WI (city) Eau Claire County	20.99
San Diego, CA (city) San Diego County	20.79
Oroville, CA (city) Butte County	20.70
Madison, WI (city) Dane County	20.45
Chico, CA (city) Butte County	20.03
Milwaukee, WI (city) Milwaukee County	19.24
Kansas City, KS (city) Wyandotte County	18.87
Spokane, WA (city) Spokane County	18.73
Merced, CA (city) Merced County	18.50
Linda, CA (cdp) Yuba County	18.22
West Sacramento, CA (city) Yolo County	17.62
Fresno, CA (city) Fresno County	17.29
Stevens Point, WI (city) Portage County	17.04
St. Paul, MN (city) Ramsey County	16.95
La Crosse, WI (city) La Crosse County	16.84
Modesto, CA (city) Stanislaus County	16.75
Sacramento, CA (city) Sacramento County	15.85
Brooklyn Park, MN (city) Hennepin County	14.73
Fitchburg, MA (city) Worcester County	14.47
Oshkosh, WI (city) Winnebago County	13.77
Wausau, WI (city) Marathon County	13.19
Minneapolis, MN (city) Hennepin County	12.92
Portland, OR (city) Multnomah County	12.89
Arden-Arcade, CA (cdp) Sacramento County	12.54
Stockton, CA (city) San Joaquin County	12.44
South Oroville, CA (cdp) Butte County	12.17
Sheboygan, WI (city) Sheboygan County	12.15
Lansing, MI (city) Ingham County	12.09
Appleton, WI (city) Outagamie County	11.45
Parkway-S. Sacramento, CA (cdp) Sacramento County	11.42
Willows, CA (city) Glenn County	11.05
Providence, RI (city) Providence County	10.68
Florin, CA (cdp) Sacramento County	10.08
Green Bay, WI (city) Brown County	8.61
Manitowoc, WI (city) Manitowoc County	8.16
Thermalito, CA (cdp) Butte County	7.66
Wisconsin Rapids, WI (city) Wood County	6.35
Valdese, NC (town) Burke County	5.98
Charlotte, NC (city) Mecklenburg County	4.04
Connelly Springs, NC (town) Burke County	3.95
Hickory, NC (city) Catawba County	1.29

Notes: Please refer to the User's Guide for an explanation of data; ranking tables include all places with Asian and/or NHPI populations above SF4 population thresholds; (1) tables reflect only those areas that meet SF4 population thresholds, therefore there may be less than 50 states, 75 counties or 75 places listed

Foreign-Born Naturalized Citizens

Indonesian

All States, Top 75 Counties, and Top 75 Places Sorted by Number[1]

State	Number
United States	7,646
California	3,787
New York	440
Florida	346
Washington	269
Virginia	262
Texas	224
Colorado	184
New Jersey	176
Massachusetts	155
Maryland	143
Arizona	138
Oregon	123
Ohio	120
Michigan	105
Georgia	91
Illinois	75
Pennsylvania	54
Wisconsin	27

County	Number
Los Angeles County, CA	1,322
San Bernardino County, CA	635
Orange County, CA	506
Queens County, NY	200
San Mateo County, CA	199
Alameda County, CA	169
King County, WA	158
Contra Costa County, CA	144
San Francisco County, CA	141
Santa Clara County, CA	139
Maricopa County, AZ	114
Montgomery County, MD	114
Fairfax County, VA	112
San Diego County, CA	102
Harris County, TX	57
Middlesex County, NJ	37
Cook County, IL	26
Franklin County, OH	16

Place	Number
Los Angeles, CA (city) Los Angeles County	419
New York, NY (city)	305
San Francisco, CA (city) San Francisco County	141
Loma Linda, CA (city) San Bernardino County	75
San Bernardino, CA (city) San Bernardino County	71
Seattle, WA (city) King County	42
Houston, TX (city) Harris County	14
Columbus, OH (city) Franklin County	0

Notes: Please refer to the User's Guide for an explanation of data; ranking tables include all places with Asian and/or NHPI populations above SF4 population thresholds; (1) tables reflect only those areas that meet SF4 population thresholds, therefore there may be less than 50 states, 75 counties or 75 places listed

Foreign-Born Naturalized Citizens

Indonesian

All States, Top 75 Counties, and Top 75 Places Sorted by Percent[1]

State	Percent
Florida	38.70
Arizona	24.08
Virginia	23.93
Colorado	23.90
California	23.11
Massachusetts	21.83
Washington	21.66
United States	20.57
Oregon	19.19
New York	18.08
New Jersey	17.25
Georgia	16.55
Michigan	16.10
Maryland	12.91
Texas	12.65
Ohio	11.31
Pennsylvania	10.07
Illinois	7.85
Wisconsin	6.65

County	Percent
Contra Costa County, CA	30.44
Maricopa County, AZ	27.67
Orange County, CA	26.52
San Mateo County, CA	26.32
Alameda County, CA	26.28
Los Angeles County, CA	23.50
San Diego County, CA	20.82
Santa Clara County, CA	20.23
San Bernardino County, CA	19.24
King County, WA	19.04
Fairfax County, VA	18.82
San Francisco County, CA	16.15
Queens County, NY	16.09
Montgomery County, MD	12.28
Harris County, TX	8.26
Middlesex County, NJ	7.58
Cook County, IL	5.26
Franklin County, OH	3.02

Place	Percent
Los Angeles, CA (city) Los Angeles County	23.41
New York, NY (city)	16.80
San Francisco, CA (city) San Francisco County	16.15
San Bernardino, CA (city) San Bernardino County	15.81
Loma Linda, CA (city) San Bernardino County	14.37
Seattle, WA (city) King County	11.11
Houston, TX (city) Harris County	2.71
Columbus, OH (city) Franklin County	0.00

Notes: Please refer to the User's Guide for an explanation of data; ranking tables include all places with Asian and/or NHPI populations above SF4 population thresholds; (1) tables reflect only those areas that meet SF4 population thresholds, therefore there may be less than 50 states, 75 counties or 75 places listed

Foreign-Born Naturalized Citizens

Japanese

All States, Top 75 Counties, and Top 75 Places Sorted by Number[1]

State	Number
United States	80,119
California	29,825
Hawaii	8,300
Washington	4,541
New York	3,251
Texas	3,247
Florida	2,972
Virginia	1,862
Illinois	1,769
Colorado	1,615
New Jersey	1,576
Arizona	1,431
Nevada	1,424
Maryland	1,253
Oregon	1,240
North Carolina	1,139
Georgia	1,120
Ohio	1,117
Pennsylvania	1,045
Massachusetts	961
Michigan	929
Missouri	744
Indiana	646
Oklahoma	600
Minnesota	524
South Carolina	524
Tennessee	486
Wisconsin	475
New Mexico	465
Alabama	445
Kentucky	444
Kansas	370
Utah	363
Louisiana	360
Connecticut	357
Arkansas	324
Idaho	293
Alaska	241
West Virginia	210
Nebraska	198
Maine	195
Delaware	191
Mississippi	171
New Hampshire	164
Rhode Island	150
Iowa	148
Montana	136
Wyoming	88
South Dakota	73
Vermont	40
District of Columbia	36

County	Number
Los Angeles County, CA	10,510
Honolulu County, HI	7,185
Orange County, CA	3,007
San Diego County, CA	2,978
King County, WA	1,818
Santa Clara County, CA	1,715
Sacramento County, CA	1,317
San Francisco County, CA	1,225
Clark County, NV	1,192
Pierce County, WA	1,116
Alameda County, CA	1,018
Cook County, IL	920
San Mateo County, CA	887
New York County, NY	882
Riverside County, CA	840
Monterey County, CA	821
Maricopa County, AZ	790
Contra Costa County, CA	697
Ventura County, CA	690
San Bernardino County, CA	644
Solano County, CA	622
Hawaii County, HI	599
Bexar County, TX	570
Fairfax County, VA	558
Queens County, NY	537
El Paso County, CO	532
Bergen County, NJ	480
Harris County, TX	438
Westchester County, NY	425
Fresno County, CA	418
Montgomery County, MD	408
Snohomish County, WA	397
El Paso County, TX	364
Middlesex County, MA	358
Santa Barbara County, CA	345
Tarrant County, TX	342
Maui County, HI	333
Pima County, AZ	325
Hillsborough County, FL	285
Multnomah County, OR	280
San Joaquin County, CA	278
Sonoma County, CA	274
Orange County, FL	271
Dallas County, TX	265
Virginia Beach Independent City, VA	265
Kitsap County, WA	248
Suffolk County, NY	244
Marin County, CA	236
Bernalillo County, NM	231
Anne Arundel County, MD	229
Cumberland County, NC	227
Washington County, OR	224
Jefferson County, CO	220
Burlington County, NJ	219
Miami-Dade County, FL	218
Arapahoe County, CO	212
Broward County, FL	205
St. Louis County, MO	199
Bell County, TX	198
Salt Lake County, UT	197
Denver County, CO	192
Oakland County, MI	188
Kings County, NY	187
Kauai County, HI	183
Anchorage Borough, AK	180
Palm Beach County, FL	179
Oklahoma County, OK	173
Travis County, TX	173
Clark County, WA	170
DuPage County, IL	168
Placer County, CA	168
Prince George's County, MD	168
Duval County, FL	163
Washoe County, NV	162
Hennepin County, MN	154

Place	Number
Honolulu, HI (cdp) Honolulu County	4,316
Los Angeles, CA (city) Los Angeles County	3,657
New York, NY (city)	1,707
San Diego, CA (city) San Diego County	1,339
San Francisco, CA (city) San Francisco County	1,225
Torrance, CA (city) Los Angeles County	1,002
San Jose, CA (city) Santa Clara County	886
Gardena, CA (city) Los Angeles County	660
Seattle, WA (city) King County	621
Monterey Park, CA (city) Los Angeles County	480
Chicago, IL (city) Cook County	463
Las Vegas, NV (city) Clark County	457
San Antonio, TX (city) Bexar County	437
Long Beach, CA (city) Los Angeles County	391
Sacramento, CA (city) Sacramento County	371
Waimalu, HI (cdp) Honolulu County	363
Pearl City, HI (cdp) Honolulu County	359
El Paso, TX (city) El Paso County	336
Irvine, CA (city) Orange County	331
Chula Vista, CA (city) San Diego County	326
Colorado Springs, CO (city) El Paso County	310
Phoenix, AZ (city) Maricopa County	303
Oxnard, CA (city) Ventura County	297
Lakewood, WA (city) Pierce County	294
Anaheim, CA (city) Orange County	292
Rancho Palos Verdes, CA (city) Los Angeles County	289
Huntington Beach, CA (city) Orange County	269
Fairfield, CA (city) Solano County	263
Portland, OR (city) Multnomah County	247
Hilo, HI (cdp) Hawaii County	243
Tucson, AZ (city) Pima County	241
Mililani Town, HI (cdp) Honolulu County	237
Oceanside, CA (city) San Diego County	237
Houston, TX (city) Harris County	225
Kaneohe, HI (cdp) Honolulu County	214
Tacoma, WA (city) Pierce County	214
Fresno, CA (city) Fresno County	211
Albuquerque, NM (city) Bernalillo County	208
Bellevue, WA (city) King County	192
Denver, CO (city) Denver County	192
Sunnyvale, CA (city) Santa Clara County	188
Cerritos, CA (city) Los Angeles County	187
Sunrise Manor, NV (cdp) Clark County	185
Alhambra, CA (city) Los Angeles County	184
Santa Monica, CA (city) Los Angeles County	183
Aurora, CO (city) Arapahoe County	178
Culver City, CA (city) Los Angeles County	178
San Mateo, CA (city) San Mateo County	171
Fountain Valley, CA (city) Orange County	168
Montebello, CA (city) Los Angeles County	161
Moreno Valley, CA (city) Riverside County	160
Seaside, CA (city) Monterey County	160
Oakland, CA (city) Alameda County	158
Jacksonville, FL (city) Duval County	154
Austin, TX (city) Travis County	151
Westminster, CA (city) Orange County	151
Paradise, NV (cdp) Clark County	150
Glendale, CA (city) Los Angeles County	149
Spring Valley, NV (cdp) Clark County	144
Halawa, HI (cdp) Honolulu County	143
Laguna Niguel, CA (city) Orange County	141
Waipahu, HI (cdp) Honolulu County	141
Salinas, CA (city) Monterey County	133
Hacienda Heights, CA (cdp) Los Angeles County	132
Wahiawa, HI (cdp) Honolulu County	132
Dallas, TX (city) Dallas County	131
Daly City, CA (city) San Mateo County	130
Fremont, CA (city) Alameda County	130
Fullerton, CA (city) Orange County	130
Garden Grove, CA (city) Orange County	130
Marina, CA (city) Monterey County	129
Santa Ana, CA (city) Orange County	125
Oklahoma City, OK (city) Oklahoma County	123
Philadelphia, PA (city) Philadelphia County	122
Stockton, CA (city) San Joaquin County	122

Notes: Please refer to the User's Guide for an explanation of data; ranking tables include all places with Asian and/or NHPI populations above SF4 population thresholds; (1) tables reflect only those areas that meet SF4 population thresholds, therefore there may be less than 50 states, 75 counties or 75 places listed

Foreign-Born Naturalized Citizens

Japanese

All States, Top 75 Counties, and Top 75 Places Sorted by Percent[1]

State	Percent
Maine	32.94
Mississippi	31.78
Delaware	31.57
Arkansas	29.62
Florida	26.19
Louisiana	25.26
West Virginia	23.89
Alabama	23.52
South Carolina	22.96
New Mexico	22.52
Missouri	21.72
Oklahoma	21.51
Virginia	21.03
Kansas	20.19
Texas	20.15
Arizona	19.22
Rhode Island	19.11
North Carolina	18.87
Maryland	18.10
South Dakota	17.72
New Hampshire	17.52
Nevada	16.96
Alaska	16.91
Wyoming	16.83
Montana	16.00
Wisconsin	15.91
Georgia	14.91
Pennsylvania	14.54
Nebraska	14.32
Kentucky	13.98
Colorado	13.58
Indiana	13.42
Tennessee	12.56
Minnesota	12.53
Washington	12.18
Iowa	11.52
New Jersey	11.44
Idaho	11.05
Ohio	10.85
Oregon	10.64
Vermont	10.64
California	10.31
United States	10.08
Massachusetts	8.77
Michigan	8.73
New York	8.65
Illinois	8.49
Connecticut	7.84
Utah	6.07
Hawaii	4.14
District of Columbia	3.47

County	Percent
Bell County, TX	51.83
Cumberland County, NC	50.33
El Paso County, TX	45.67
Burlington County, NJ	44.79
El Paso County, CO	36.26
Virginia Beach Independent City, VA	35.52
Anne Arundel County, MD	33.53
Bexar County, TX	33.24
Tarrant County, TX	33.11
Hillsborough County, FL	33.02
Pierce County, WA	31.70
Solano County, CA	31.21
Palm Beach County, FL	31.18
Onslow County, NC	30.80
Duval County, FL	29.64
Monmouth County, NJ	27.98
Jefferson County, KY	27.04
New Castle County, DE	26.42
Prince George's County, MD	26.42
Brevard County, FL	24.95
Jackson County, MO	24.75
Monterey County, CA	24.64
Suffolk County, NY	23.37
Prince William County, VA	22.81
Orange County, FL	22.58
Pinellas County, FL	22.01
Pima County, AZ	21.75
Marion County, IN	21.46
Alachua County, FL	21.02
Kitsap County, WA	20.75
Bernalillo County, NM	20.64
Anchorage Borough, AK	20.34
Broward County, FL	19.62
Milwaukee County, WI	19.52
Fairfax County, VA	19.20
Riverside County, CA	18.89
Worcester County, MA	18.16
Clark County, NV	17.81
Thurston County, WA	17.79
Sonoma County, CA	17.58
Oklahoma County, OK	17.21
Hartford County, CT	16.82
St. Louis County, MO	16.43
Monroe County, NY	16.30
Maricopa County, AZ	16.21
Snohomish County, WA	16.18
San Diego County, CA	15.87
Johnson County, KS	15.73
Miami-Dade County, FL	15.53
Island County, WA	15.46
Hamilton County, OH	15.11
Santa Barbara County, CA	14.99
San Bernardino County, CA	14.93
Marin County, CA	14.63
Travis County, TX	14.24
Denton County, TX	14.23
Summit County, OH	14.15
Adams County, CO	14.00
Butte County, CA	13.90
Morris County, NJ	13.77
Sutter County, CA	13.74
Clackamas County, OR	13.66
Tulare County, CA	13.66
Gwinnett County, GA	13.63
Clark County, WA	13.26
Chester County, PA	13.25
Ventura County, CA	13.23
Essex County, NJ	13.00
Wayne County, MI	12.99
Montgomery County, MD	12.92
Ada County, ID	12.69
Washoe County, NV	12.62
Merced County, CA	12.57
Canyon County, ID	12.38
Erie County, NY	12.30

Place	Percent
Lakewood, WA (city) Pierce County	45.87
El Paso, TX (city) El Paso County	44.80
Seaside, CA (city) Monterey County	38.28
Fairfield, CA (city) Solano County	37.57
Marina, CA (city) Monterey County	34.49
Moreno Valley, CA (city) Riverside County	32.06
San Antonio, TX (city) Bexar County	31.60
Sunrise Manor, NV (cdp) Clark County	30.78
Colorado Springs, CO (city) El Paso County	30.13
Jacksonville, FL (city) Duval County	29.00
Vallejo, CA (city) Solano County	25.34
Oxnard, CA (city) Ventura County	24.83
Tucson, AZ (city) Pima County	24.20
Oklahoma City, OK (city) Oklahoma County	23.08
Santa Maria, CA (city) Santa Barbara County	22.97
Tacoma, WA (city) Pierce County	22.53
Pacifica, CA (city) San Mateo County	22.10
Encinitas, CA (city) San Diego County	21.74
Carlsbad, CA (city) San Diego County	20.75
Albuquerque, NM (city) Bernalillo County	20.57
Spring Valley, NV (cdp) Clark County	20.00
Oceanside, CA (city) San Diego County	19.93
Phoenix, AZ (city) Maricopa County	19.15
Las Vegas, NV (city) Clark County	18.63
Shoreline, WA (city) King County	18.27
Mesa, AZ (city) Maricopa County	17.75
Aurora, CO (city) Arapahoe County	17.42
Vista, CA (city) San Diego County	17.32
Modesto, CA (city) Stanislaus County	17.27
Salinas, CA (city) Monterey County	16.92
Federal Way, WA (city) King County	16.77
San Buenaventura (Ventura), CA (city) Ventura County	16.61
South San Francisco, CA (city) San Mateo County	16.57
Mercer Island, WA (city) King County	16.55
Laguna Niguel, CA (city) Orange County	16.51
East San Gabriel, CA (cdp) Los Angeles County	16.28
Union City, CA (city) Alameda County	16.22
Chula Vista, CA (city) San Diego County	16.12
Santa Barbara, CA (city) Santa Barbara County	16.07
Scottsdale, AZ (city) Maricopa County	15.88
Daly City, CA (city) San Mateo County	15.83
Dallas, TX (city) Dallas County	15.29
Cliffside Park, NJ (borough) Bergen County	15.25
Salem, OR (city) Marion County	15.21
Arden-Arcade, CA (cdp) Sacramento County	15.19
Santa Ana, CA (city) Orange County	15.01
Brookhaven, NY (town) Suffolk County	14.98
Westminster, CA (city) Orange County	14.73
Rancho Cucamonga, CA (city) San Bernardino County	14.42
Alameda, CA (city) Alameda County	14.39
Roseville, CA (city) Placer County	14.26
Newcastle, WA (city) King County	14.24
Henderson, NV (city) Clark County	14.03
Glendale, AZ (city) Maricopa County	14.00
Norwalk, CA (city) Los Angeles County	13.81
Pomona, CA (city) Los Angeles County	13.76
Kailua, HI (cdp) Hawaii County	13.37
Austin, TX (city) Travis County	13.30
Anaheim, CA (city) Orange County	13.25
San Diego, CA (city) San Diego County	13.13
Culver City, CA (city) Los Angeles County	12.95
Bethesda, MD (cdp) Montgomery County	12.90
Lake Forest, CA (city) Orange County	12.72
Lakewood, CO (city) Jefferson County	12.60
Milpitas, CA (city) Santa Clara County	12.59
Covina, CA (city) Los Angeles County	12.53
Downey, CA (city) Los Angeles County	12.47
Garden Grove, CA (city) Orange County	12.45
San Bruno, CA (city) San Mateo County	12.42
Camarillo, CA (city) Ventura County	12.38
Seal Beach, CA (city) Orange County	12.26
Alhambra, CA (city) Los Angeles County	12.25
Belmont, CA (city) San Mateo County	12.19
Concord, CA (city) Contra Costa County	12.18
Fountain Valley, CA (city) Orange County	11.86

Notes: Please refer to the User's Guide for an explanation of data; ranking tables include all places with Asian and/or NHPI populations above SF4 population thresholds; (1) tables reflect only those areas that meet SF4 population thresholds, therefore there may be less than 50 states, 75 counties or 75 places listed

Foreign-Born Naturalized Citizens

Korean

All States, Top 75 Counties, and Top 75 Places Sorted by Number[1]

State	Number
United States	423,393
California	125,636
New York	39,957
Illinois	22,062
New Jersey	21,611
Washington	20,965
Virginia	18,627
Maryland	17,203
Texas	16,692
Pennsylvania	14,572
Hawaii	10,197
Michigan	9,583
Georgia	9,472
Minnesota	8,932
Florida	8,158
Colorado	6,877
Massachusetts	6,345
Ohio	6,083
Oregon	5,738
North Carolina	5,068
Arizona	4,198
Wisconsin	3,451
Nevada	3,422
Missouri	3,160
Indiana	3,016
Connecticut	2,936
Tennessee	2,831
Iowa	2,524
Oklahoma	2,498
Alaska	2,303
Kentucky	1,910
Kansas	1,843
Alabama	1,842
South Carolina	1,460
Nebraska	1,296
Utah	1,276
Louisiana	1,066
New Hampshire	942
New Mexico	934
Delaware	827
Mississippi	715
Rhode Island	671
Idaho	615
Arkansas	566
Montana	548
West Virginia	535
South Dakota	488
District of Columbia	456
Vermont	417
Maine	390
Wyoming	289
North Dakota	190

County	Number
Los Angeles County, CA	65,641
Orange County, CA	20,621
Queens County, NY	16,736
Cook County, IL	15,086
Fairfax County, VA	10,933
Bergen County, NJ	9,992
Honolulu County, HI	9,333
King County, WA	8,503
Santa Clara County, CA	7,240
Montgomery County, MD	6,953
Alameda County, CA	5,459
Pierce County, WA	5,091
San Diego County, CA	3,958
Montgomery County, PA	3,700
Nassau County, NY	3,648
New York County, NY	3,615
Snohomish County, WA	3,403
Harris County, TX	3,377
Hennepin County, MN	3,192
Dallas County, TX	3,098
San Francisco County, CA	3,075
San Bernardino County, CA	2,912
Clark County, NV	2,889
Gwinnett County, GA	2,673
Maricopa County, AZ	2,428
Howard County, MD	2,360
Philadelphia County, PA	2,342
Baltimore County, MD	2,335
Middlesex County, MA	2,248
Oakland County, MI	2,219
Sacramento County, CA	2,134
Riverside County, CA	2,126
San Mateo County, CA	1,991
DuPage County, IL	1,979
Kings County, NY	1,975
Suffolk County, NY	1,898
Middlesex County, NJ	1,858
El Paso County, CO	1,847
Arapahoe County, CO	1,840
Anchorage Borough, AK	1,744
Contra Costa County, CA	1,738
Washington County, OR	1,726
Westchester County, NY	1,723
Anne Arundel County, MD	1,680
Lake County, IL	1,651
Monroe County, NY	1,557
Prince George's County, MD	1,524
Delaware County, PA	1,449
Richmond County, NY	1,438
Ventura County, CA	1,430
St. Louis County, MO	1,351
Monterey County, CA	1,336
Ramsey County, MN	1,303
Multnomah County, OR	1,287
Bexar County, TX	1,286
Fulton County, GA	1,238
Bronx County, NY	1,227
Essex County, NJ	1,200
Tarrant County, TX	1,154
Cumberland County, NC	1,151
Morris County, NJ	1,129
DeKalb County, GA	1,117
Collin County, TX	1,067
Wayne County, MI	1,046
Thurston County, WA	1,041
Bucks County, PA	1,034
Monmouth County, NJ	1,025
Bell County, TX	1,021
Burlington County, NJ	1,017
Kent County, MI	1,015
Travis County, TX	994
Cobb County, GA	975
Franklin County, OH	974
Hillsborough County, FL	951
Mecklenburg County, NC	937

Place	Number
Los Angeles, CA (city) Los Angeles County	31,191
New York, NY (city)	24,991
Honolulu, HI (cdp) Honolulu County	6,546
Chicago, IL (city) Cook County	5,533
Glendale, CA (city) Los Angeles County	4,005
San Jose, CA (city) Santa Clara County	3,334
Cerritos, CA (city) Los Angeles County	3,089
San Francisco, CA (city) San Francisco County	3,075
Torrance, CA (city) Los Angeles County	2,985
Fullerton, CA (city) Orange County	2,936
Anaheim, CA (city) Orange County	2,449
Irvine, CA (city) Orange County	2,397
Philadelphia, PA (city) Philadelphia County	2,342
San Diego, CA (city) San Diego County	2,293
Seattle, WA (city) King County	2,263
Diamond Bar, CA (city) Los Angeles County	2,097
Houston, TX (city) Harris County	1,999
Garden Grove, CA (city) Orange County	1,817
Fort Lee, NJ (borough) Bergen County	1,555
Federal Way, WA (city) King County	1,506
Buena Park, CA (city) Orange County	1,471
Gardena, CA (city) Los Angeles County	1,454
Colorado Springs, CO (city) El Paso County	1,373
Tacoma, WA (city) Pierce County	1,365
Rowland Heights, CA (cdp) Los Angeles County	1,295
Palisades Park, NJ (borough) Bergen County	1,291
Fremont, CA (city) Alameda County	1,290
Burke, VA (cdp) Fairfax County	1,279
North Hempstead, NY (town) Nassau County	1,259
Skokie, IL (village) Cook County	1,241
Hempstead, NY (town) Nassau County	1,226
Dallas, TX (city) Dallas County	1,147
Portland, OR (city) Multnomah County	1,144
Downey, CA (city) Los Angeles County	1,125
Annandale, VA (cdp) Fairfax County	1,072
Aurora, CO (city) Arapahoe County	1,046
Lakewood, WA (city) Pierce County	1,033
Hacienda Heights, CA (cdp) Los Angeles County	1,024
Bellevue, WA (city) King County	1,008
Oyster Bay, NY (town) Nassau County	994
Ellicott City, MD (cdp) Howard County	976
San Antonio, TX (city) Bexar County	948
Minneapolis, MN (city) Hennepin County	924
Rancho Palos Verdes, CA (city) Los Angeles County	918
Norwalk, CA (city) Los Angeles County	875
La Crescenta-Montrose, CA (cdp) Los Angeles County	871
Huntington Beach, CA (city) Orange County	867
Sunnyvale, CA (city) Santa Clara County	862
La Mirada, CA (city) Los Angeles County	845
Cypress, CA (city) Orange County	844
La Palma, CA (city) Orange County	844
Orange, CA (city) Orange County	842
Plano, TX (city) Collin County	811
Long Beach, CA (city) Los Angeles County	798
Oakland, CA (city) Alameda County	781
Charlotte, NC (city) Mecklenburg County	776
Walnut, CA (city) Los Angeles County	770
La Canada Flintridge, CA (city) Los Angeles County	766
Austin, TX (city) Travis County	764
Glenview, IL (village) Cook County	750
Northbrook, IL (village) Cook County	730
Phoenix, AZ (city) Maricopa County	716
Burbank, CA (city) Los Angeles County	708
El Paso, TX (city) El Paso County	708
Irving, TX (city) Dallas County	705
Las Vegas, NV (city) Clark County	675
Boston, MA (city) Suffolk County	672
Santa Clara, CA (city) Santa Clara County	664
Columbia, MD (cdp) Howard County	660
Killeen, TX (city) Bell County	654
Schaumburg, IL (village) Cook County	637
Columbus, OH (city) Franklin County	634
Waimalu, HI (cdp) Honolulu County	630
Centreville, VA (cdp) Fairfax County	625
Arcadia, CA (city) Los Angeles County	622

Notes: Please refer to the User's Guide for an explanation of data; ranking tables include all places with Asian and/or NHPI populations above SF4 population thresholds; (1) tables reflect only those areas that meet SF4 population thresholds, therefore there may be less than 50 states, 75 counties or 75 places listed

Foreign-Born Naturalized Citizens

Korean

All States, Top 75 Counties, and Top 75 Places Sorted by Percent[1]

State	Percent
Minnesota	69.49
South Dakota	65.50
Montana	65.32
Wyoming	61.49
Vermont	61.32
West Virginia	59.84
Nebraska	58.14
Oklahoma	54.00
New Mexico	53.77
Maine	53.06
North Dakota	52.05
Mississippi	51.89
Iowa	51.70
Alaska	50.57
Wisconsin	50.41
Missouri	48.56
Idaho	48.31
New Hampshire	48.31
Kentucky	47.27
Alabama	45.78
Michigan	45.60
Nevada	45.13
Washington	45.09
Colorado	44.97
Oregon	44.78
Delaware	44.70
Pennsylvania	44.32
Maryland	43.98
Ohio	43.81
Connecticut	43.65
Hawaii	43.01
Florida	42.76
Indiana	42.48
Illinois	42.36
Kansas	42.26
Arizona	42.25
Virginia	41.34
South Carolina	41.17
Tennessee	41.02
North Carolina	40.86
United States	39.47
District of Columbia	39.04
Louisiana	38.98
Arkansas	37.83
Texas	37.62
California	36.55
Massachusetts	36.47
Utah	35.62
Rhode Island	34.89
Georgia	34.19
New Jersey	33.60
New York	33.08

County	Percent
Ottawa County, MI	82.99
Anoka County, MN	81.07
Ocean County, NJ	79.37
Berks County, PA	78.34
St. Louis County, MN	75.62
Dakota County, MN	73.50
Saratoga County, NY	72.20
Waukesha County, WI	72.13
Lancaster County, PA	69.72
Hennepin County, MN	67.50
Olmsted County, MN	67.28
Ramsey County, MN	65.51
Bristol County, MA	64.59
Lake County, IN	64.58
Chester County, PA	63.96
Pulaski County, MO	63.82
Linn County, IA	62.54
Monroe County, NY	62.16
St. Clair County, IL	61.39
Bernalillo County, NM	61.00
Dauphin County, PA	60.89
Harford County, MD	60.71
Richmond County, GA	60.46
Cochise County, AZ	60.37
Douglas County, CO	60.20
Washington County, MN	59.56
Hampden County, MA	59.47
Tulsa County, OK	59.46
Wayne County, MI	58.01
Orange County, NY	57.49
Ada County, ID	57.37
Virginia Beach Independent City, VA	57.22
Cumberland County, PA	57.16
Milwaukee County, WI	57.14
Polk County, IA	57.07
Dale County, AL	57.06
Comanche County, OK	56.70
Geary County, KS	56.56
Marion County, OR	56.45
Kitsap County, WA	56.16
Jefferson County, CO	56.06
Hardin County, KY	56.00
York County, PA	55.84
Liberty County, GA	55.70
Douglas County, NE	55.26
Ventura County, CA	55.23
Lancaster County, NE	55.10
Northampton County, PA	54.88
Cumberland County, NC	54.81
Will County, IL	54.80
Vernon Parish, LA	54.76
Okaloosa County, FL	54.44
Lucas County, OH	54.17
Winnebago County, IL	54.15
Genesee County, MI	53.74
Kent County, MI	53.56
Rockingham County, NH	53.19
St. Louis County, MO	53.06
Oklahoma County, OK	52.97
Kane County, IL	52.61
Gloucester County, NJ	52.53
Marion County, IN	52.24
Clark County, WA	52.15
Macomb County, MI	52.08
Montgomery County, TN	51.94
Coryell County, TX	51.92
Whatcom County, WA	51.88
Solano County, CA	51.86
Placer County, CA	51.71
Monmouth County, NJ	51.64
Burlington County, NJ	51.60
Litchfield County, CT	51.36
Benton County, WA	51.10
Cleveland County, OK	50.99
Spokane County, WA	50.89

Place	Percent
Bloomington, MN (city) Hennepin County	71.63
Oxnard, CA (city) Ventura County	65.48
Foster City, CA (city) San Mateo County	65.13
St. Paul, MN (city) Ramsey County	64.40
Sierra Vista, AZ (city) Cochise County	61.64
Rochester, MN (city) Olmsted County	61.21
Seattle Hill-Silver Firs, WA (cdp) Snohomish County	61.00
Islip, NY (town) Suffolk County	60.91
Tulsa, OK (city) Tulsa County	60.71
Augusta-Richmond Co., GA (sp. city) Richmond Co.	60.09
Spanaway, WA (cdp) Pierce County	59.18
Rochester Hills, MI (city) Oakland County	58.60
Albuquerque, NM (city) Bernalillo County	58.58
Hinesville, GA (city) Liberty County	58.57
Sunrise Manor, NV (cdp) Clark County	58.55
Lakewood, CO (city) Jefferson County	57.48
Mount Vernon, VA (cdp) Fairfax County	57.14
Lawton, OK (city) Comanche County	57.09
Minneapolis, MN (city) Hennepin County	56.93
Lacey, WA (city) Thurston County	56.37
Monterey Park, CA (city) Los Angeles County	55.76
Gaithersburg, MD (city) Montgomery County	55.74
Smithtown, NY (town) Suffolk County	55.48
Hamilton, NJ (township) Mercer County	55.40
Fayetteville, NC (city) Cumberland County	54.96
Lower Merion, PA (township) Montgomery County	53.87
Spokane, WA (city) Spokane County	53.74
Lake Forest, CA (city) Orange County	53.73
Clarksville, TN (city) Montgomery County	53.25
Canton, MI (township) Wayne County	53.18
Sugar Land, TX (city) Fort Bend County	53.18
Bethesda, MD (cdp) Montgomery County	53.13
Lincoln, NE (city) Lancaster County	52.89
West Carson, CA (cdp) Los Angeles County	52.21
Orange, CA (city) Orange County	52.17
Portland, OR (city) Multnomah County	52.14
Indianapolis, IN (sp. city) Marion County	51.88
Huntington Beach, CA (city) Orange County	51.85
Lincolnwood, IL (village) Cook County	51.85
Huntington, NY (town) Suffolk County	51.78
Milpitas, CA (city) Santa Clara County	51.76
Oklahoma City, OK (city) Oklahoma County	51.59
Reston, VA (cdp) Fairfax County	51.47
Potomac, MD (cdp) Montgomery County	51.16
Colesville, MD (cdp) Montgomery County	50.95
Laguna Niguel, CA (city) Orange County	50.89
Mission Viejo, CA (city) Orange County	50.81
Plymouth, MN (city) Hennepin County	50.69
Omaha, NE (city) Douglas County	50.60
Waimalu, HI (cdp) Honolulu County	50.36
Costa Mesa, CA (city) Orange County	50.34
Silver Spring, MD (cdp) Montgomery County	50.22
Simi Valley, CA (city) Ventura County	50.09
San Antonio, TX (city) Bexar County	50.00
Pemberton, NJ (township) Burlington County	49.63
Morton Grove, IL (village) Cook County	49.54
Tustin, CA (city) Orange County	49.49
Skokie, IL (village) Cook County	49.17
Thousand Oaks, CA (city) Ventura County	48.96
Chino Hills, CA (city) San Bernardino County	48.62
Camarillo, CA (city) Ventura County	48.53
Edmonds, WA (city) Snohomish County	48.52
Bloomfield, MI (township) Oakland County	48.01
Browns Mills, NJ (cdp) Burlington County	48.00
Montgomery, PA (township) Montgomery County	47.99
Fairfield, CA (city) Solano County	47.95
Westminster, CO (city) Adams County	47.92
North Springfield, VA (cdp) Fairfax County	47.91
Lake Success, NY (village) Nassau County	47.74
Sacramento, CA (city) Sacramento County	47.71
Horsham, PA (township) Montgomery County	47.66
Kansas City, MO (city) Jackson County	47.44
Plymouth, PA (township) Montgomery County	47.29
Northbrook, IL (village) Cook County	47.16
Vancouver, WA (city) Clark County	47.16

Notes: Please refer to the User's Guide for an explanation of data; ranking tables include all places with Asian and/or NHPI populations above SF4 population thresholds; (1) tables reflect only those areas that meet SF4 population thresholds, therefore there may be less than 50 states, 75 counties or 75 places listed

Foreign-Born Naturalized Citizens

Laotian

All States, Top 75 Counties, and Top 75 Places Sorted by Number[1]

State	Number
United States	55,076
California	16,663
Texas	4,006
Washington	2,755
Minnesota	2,419
Illinois	2,171
Tennessee	1,681
Georgia	1,582
Iowa	1,513
Florida	1,438
New York	1,438
Oregon	1,373
Virginia	1,287
North Carolina	1,256
Ohio	1,162
Connecticut	1,102
Kansas	1,083
Michigan	1,001
Rhode Island	914
Wisconsin	902
Massachusetts	892
Utah	789
Hawaii	771
Arkansas	722
Colorado	708
Pennsylvania	679
Nevada	479
Indiana	419
Maryland	409
Oklahoma	379
Louisiana	357
Alabama	352
Arizona	349
South Carolina	340
Missouri	298
Nebraska	271
Alaska	192
Idaho	176
New Jersey	154
New Hampshire	112
South Dakota	44

County	Number
San Diego County, CA	2,610
Sacramento County, CA	2,210
King County, WA	1,762
Contra Costa County, CA	1,714
Hennepin County, MN	1,445
Los Angeles County, CA	1,364
Tarrant County, TX	1,331
Fresno County, CA	1,167
Orange County, CA	1,041
Multnomah County, OR	956
Alameda County, CA	955
Providence County, RI	868
Honolulu County, HI	751
Polk County, IA	738
Santa Clara County, CA	731
Tulare County, CA	726
Rutherford County, TN	722
Cook County, IL	720
Fairfax County, VA	716
Dallas County, TX	686
Pinellas County, FL	624
Monroe County, NY	619
Salt Lake County, UT	594
Harris County, TX	581
Stanislaus County, CA	531
Merced County, CA	528
Riverside County, CA	525
Franklin County, OH	511
San Joaquin County, CA	503
Davidson County, TN	499
Winnebago County, IL	483
Clark County, NV	479
Gwinnett County, GA	466
Potter County, TX	464
Ottawa County, MI	447
Middlesex County, MA	442
Kane County, IL	428
Clayton County, GA	421
Sebastian County, AR	416
Shasta County, CA	408
Fairfield County, CT	396
Hartford County, CT	396
Sonoma County, CA	360
Milwaukee County, WI	341
Johnson County, KS	318
Sedgwick County, KS	314
Philadelphia County, PA	308
Mecklenburg County, NC	303
Dakota County, MN	295
Adams County, CO	291
Jefferson County, CO	271
Iberia Parish, LA	263
Washington County, OR	254
Snohomish County, WA	245
Worcester County, MA	242
Maricopa County, AZ	240
Summit County, OH	216
Oklahoma County, OK	209
Burke County, NC	191
San Bernardino County, CA	188
Anchorage Borough, AK	187
New Haven County, CT	183
Spartanburg County, SC	176
Buena Vista County, IA	171
Clark County, WA	164
Bexar County, TX	162
Broome County, NY	161
Ramsey County, MN	149
Guilford County, NC	141
Solano County, CA	138
Washington County, AR	134
Butte County, CA	128
Cowley County, KS	124
Pierce County, WA	121
Mobile County, AL	107

Place	Number
San Diego, CA (city) San Diego County	2,105
Sacramento, CA (city) Sacramento County	1,440
Richmond, CA (city) Contra Costa County	1,023
Fresno, CA (city) Fresno County	1,002
Portland, OR (city) Multnomah County	870
Seattle, WA (city) King County	849
San Jose, CA (city) Santa Clara County	637
Des Moines, IA (city) Polk County	607
Oakland, CA (city) Alameda County	604
Brooklyn Park, MN (city) Hennepin County	573
Visalia, CA (city) Tulare County	523
Nashville-Davidson, TN (sp. city) Davidson County	499
Stockton, CA (city) San Joaquin County	471
Amarillo, TX (city) Potter County	467
Honolulu, HI (cdp) Honolulu County	453
Merced, CA (city) Merced County	441
Elgin, IL (city) Kane County	405
Columbus, OH (city) Franklin County	404
Fort Smith, AR (city) Sebastian County	404
Rochester, NY (city) Monroe County	402
San Pablo, CA (city) Contra Costa County	391
Providence, RI (city) Providence County	380
St. Petersburg, FL (city) Pinellas County	377
Modesto, CA (city) Stanislaus County	375
Los Angeles, CA (city) Los Angeles County	372
Minneapolis, MN (city) Hennepin County	369
Santa Ana, CA (city) Orange County	354
Murfreesboro, TN (city) Rutherford County	348
Haltom City, TX (city) Tarrant County	344
Lowell, MA (city) Middlesex County	337
Redding, CA (city) Shasta County	323
Rockford, IL (city) Winnebago County	309
Philadelphia, PA (city) Philadelphia County	308
Charlotte, NC (city) Mecklenburg County	298
Dallas, TX (city) Dallas County	288
Woonsocket, RI (city) Providence County	269
Milwaukee, WI (city) Milwaukee County	266
Anaheim, CA (city) Orange County	259
Westminster, CO (city) Adams County	255
Bellevue, WA (city) King County	236
Wichita, KS (city) Sedgwick County	219
Oklahoma City, OK (city) Oklahoma County	217
Pomona, CA (city) Los Angeles County	211
Escondido, CA (city) San Diego County	201
Parkway-S. Sacramento, CA (cdp) Sacramento County	201
Santa Rosa, CA (city) Sonoma County	199
Fort Worth, TX (city) Tarrant County	184
Springfield, VA (cdp) Fairfax County	182
Long Beach, CA (city) Los Angeles County	181
Bridgeport, CT (city) Fairfield County	178
Riverside, CA (city) Riverside County	169
Storm Lake, IA (city) Buena Vista County	164
Akron, OH (city) Summit County	151
Grand Prairie, TX (city) Dallas County	128
West Valley City, UT (city) Salt Lake County	126
Winfield, KS (city) Cowley County	124
Moreno Valley, CA (city) Riverside County	119
St. Paul, MN (city) Ramsey County	111
Brooklyn Center, MN (city) Hennepin County	106
Irving, TX (city) Dallas County	102
Arvada, CO (city) Jefferson County	101
Rochester, MN (city) Olmsted County	97
Banning, CA (city) Riverside County	89
Springdale, AR (city) Washington County	87
Oaklawn-Sunview, KS (cdp) Sedgwick County	83
Fairfield, CA (city) Solano County	79
Green Bay, WI (city) Brown County	77
Tacoma, WA (city) Pierce County	76
Fitchburg, MA (city) Worcester County	73
Raymond, WA (city) Pacific County	66
New Britain, CT (city) Hartford County	65
Worthington, MN (city) Nobles County	31
Warroad, MN (city) Roseau County	25

Notes: Please refer to the User's Guide for an explanation of data; ranking tables include all places with Asian and/or NHPI populations above SF4 population thresholds; (1) tables reflect only those areas that meet SF4 population thresholds, therefore there may be less than 50 states, 75 counties or 75 places listed

Foreign-Born Naturalized Citizens

Laotian

All States, Top 75 Counties, and Top 75 Places Sorted by Percent[1]

State	Percent
Maryland	55.57
Hawaii	45.73
New York	44.71
Illinois	44.17
Oklahoma	43.02
Virginia	42.89
Indiana	42.62
Alabama	42.46
Tennessee	41.87
Missouri	41.62
Texas	40.62
Nevada	40.29
Arizona	39.17
Ohio	38.76
Iowa	38.13
Kansas	38.11
Oregon	37.10
Michigan	35.92
Utah	35.80
Florida	35.67
Connecticut	35.47
Idaho	34.65
Washington	34.02
Georgia	33.45
Nebraska	33.21
United States	32.82
New Jersey	32.08
Rhode Island	31.64
Colorado	30.58
New Hampshire	30.19
Pennsylvania	29.94
California	29.29
Louisiana	27.59
Minnesota	26.89
Arkansas	26.62
South Carolina	25.68
North Carolina	25.29
Massachusetts	24.46
Wisconsin	21.81
South Dakota	20.18
Alaska	14.04

County	Percent
Cook County, IL	57.46
Johnson County, KS	49.69
Harris County, TX	49.15
Fairfax County, VA	47.23
Rutherford County, TN	46.13
Monroe County, NY	45.68
Honolulu County, HI	45.65
Franklin County, OH	44.98
Polk County, IA	44.62
Potter County, TX	43.81
Los Angeles County, CA	43.27
Gwinnett County, GA	42.63
Oklahoma County, OK	42.39
Dakota County, NE	42.34
Bexar County, TX	42.08
Tarrant County, TX	41.68
Kane County, IL	40.92
Washington County, OR	40.84
Clark County, NV	40.70
Dakota County, MN	40.47
Contra Costa County, CA	40.09
Maricopa County, AZ	39.93
Clark County, WA	39.71
San Bernardino County, CA	39.58
Ottawa County, MI	38.97
Burke County, NC	38.51
Fairfield County, CT	38.41
Davidson County, TN	38.06
Winnebago County, IL	37.18
Multnomah County, OR	36.74
San Diego County, CA	36.67
New Haven County, CT	36.31
Sebastian County, AR	36.05
Orange County, CA	35.72
Cowley County, KS	35.63
Santa Clara County, CA	35.45
Riverside County, CA	35.28
King County, WA	34.96
Mecklenburg County, NC	34.59
Mobile County, AL	34.08
Pinellas County, FL	33.64
Clayton County, GA	33.47
Stanislaus County, CA	33.42
Sonoma County, CA	33.27
Salt Lake County, UT	33.20
Hennepin County, MN	32.77
Hartford County, CT	32.59
Snohomish County, WA	32.07
Providence County, RI	31.56
Franklin County, WA	31.41
Broome County, NY	31.14
Cass County, MI	30.77
Merced County, CA	30.64
Alameda County, CA	30.20
Sedgwick County, KS	29.82
Buena Vista County, IA	29.58
Jefferson County, CO	29.46
Dallas County, TX	29.35
Iberia Parish, LA	29.22
Guilford County, NC	28.89
Pierce County, WA	28.34
Summit County, OH	28.31
Dane County, WI	28.20
Adams County, CO	27.27
Pacific County, WA	26.86
Spartanburg County, SC	25.96
Philadelphia County, PA	25.37
Middlesex County, MA	24.46
Washington County, AR	24.32
Worcester County, MA	23.89
Shasta County, CA	23.38
Butte County, CA	23.23
Tulare County, CA	23.11
Sacramento County, CA	22.91
Olmsted County, MN	22.50

Place	Percent
Los Angeles, CA (city) Los Angeles County	53.99
Bellevue, WA (city) King County	50.86
Rochester, NY (city) Monroe County	49.94
Murfreesboro, TN (city) Rutherford County	49.22
Riverside, CA (city) Riverside County	49.13
Honolulu, HI (cdp) Honolulu County	46.04
Springfield, VA (cdp) Fairfax County	45.73
Elgin, IL (city) Kane County	45.10
Des Moines, IA (city) Polk County	44.53
Amarillo, TX (city) Potter County	44.02
Richmond, CA (city) Contra Costa County	43.00
Oklahoma City, OK (city) Oklahoma County	42.89
Haltom City, TX (city) Tarrant County	42.36
Escondido, CA (city) San Diego County	41.96
Columbus, OH (city) Franklin County	41.27
Brooklyn Park, MN (city) Hennepin County	39.65
Pomona, CA (city) Los Angeles County	39.59
Nashville-Davidson, TN (sp. city) Davidson County	38.06
Portland, OR (city) Multnomah County	37.79
Westminster, CO (city) Adams County	37.72
Santa Ana, CA (city) Orange County	36.61
Winfield, KS (city) Cowley County	36.05
Fort Smith, AR (city) Sebastian County	35.98
Bridgeport, CT (city) Fairfield County	35.53
San Pablo, CA (city) Contra Costa County	35.04
San Diego, CA (city) San Diego County	34.87
Fort Worth, TX (city) Tarrant County	34.72
Charlotte, NC (city) Mecklenburg County	34.45
Rockford, IL (city) Winnebago County	34.41
San Jose, CA (city) Santa Clara County	33.65
St. Petersburg, FL (city) Pinellas County	33.27
Brooklyn Center, MN (city) Hennepin County	33.13
Modesto, CA (city) Stanislaus County	32.87
Grand Prairie, TX (city) Dallas County	32.74
Anaheim, CA (city) Orange County	32.54
Seattle, WA (city) King County	32.07
Dallas, TX (city) Dallas County	31.72
Merced, CA (city) Merced County	31.64
Wichita, KS (city) Sedgwick County	31.56
Santa Rosa, CA (city) Sonoma County	31.44
Storm Lake, IA (city) Buena Vista County	31.12
Woonsocket, RI (city) Providence County	29.50
Providence, RI (city) Providence County	28.66
Oaklawn-Sunview, KS (cdp) Sedgwick County	27.39
West Valley City, UT (city) Salt Lake County	27.33
Akron, OH (city) Summit County	26.40
Banning, CA (city) Riverside County	26.10
Raymond, WA (city) Pacific County	25.48
Philadelphia, PA (city) Philadelphia County	25.37
Oakland, CA (city) Alameda County	25.28
Tacoma, WA (city) Pierce County	24.52
Long Beach, CA (city) Los Angeles County	24.39
Moreno Valley, CA (city) Riverside County	24.39
Visalia, CA (city) Tulare County	24.28
Lowell, MA (city) Middlesex County	22.97
Sacramento, CA (city) Sacramento County	22.84
Minneapolis, MN (city) Hennepin County	22.68
Rochester, MN (city) Olmsted County	22.15
Irving, TX (city) Dallas County	21.29
Arvada, CO (city) Jefferson County	21.13
Redding, CA (city) Shasta County	20.69
Springdale, AR (city) Washington County	20.67
Fairfield, CA (city) Solano County	20.31
Green Bay, WI (city) Brown County	20.16
Warroad, MN (city) Roseau County	20.00
Fitchburg, MA (city) Worcester County	18.72
Fresno, CA (city) Fresno County	18.28
Milwaukee, WI (city) Milwaukee County	17.76
New Britain, CT (city) Hartford County	17.43
Stockton, CA (city) San Joaquin County	15.87
Parkway-S. Sacramento, CA (cdp) Sacramento County	14.44
St. Paul, MN (city) Ramsey County	12.89
Worthington, MN (city) Nobles County	8.36

Notes: Please refer to the User's Guide for an explanation of data; ranking tables include all places with Asian and/or NHPI populations above SF4 population thresholds; (1) tables reflect only those areas that meet SF4 population thresholds, therefore there may be less than 50 states, 75 counties or 75 places listed

Foreign-Born Naturalized Citizens

Malaysian

All States, Top 75 Counties, and Top 75 Places Sorted by Number[1]

State	Number
United States	1,391
California	350
New York	246
Texas	95
Ohio	55
Michigan	32
Oklahoma	18
Illinois	13

County	Number
Los Angeles County, CA	115
Queens County, NY	83

Place	Number
New York, NY (city)	179

Notes: Please refer to the User's Guide for an explanation of data; ranking tables include all places with Asian and/or NHPI populations above SF4 population thresholds; (1) tables reflect only those areas that meet SF4 population thresholds, therefore there may be less than 50 states, 75 counties or 75 places listed

Foreign-Born Naturalized Citizens

Malaysian

All States, Top 75 Counties, and Top 75 Places Sorted by Percent[1]

State	Percent
California	19.88
New York	17.55
Ohio	15.80
Texas	14.18
United States	12.99
Michigan	7.00
Oklahoma	3.50
Illinois	2.29

County	Percent
Los Angeles County, CA	21.54
Queens County, NY	14.64

Place	Percent
New York, NY (city)	14.95

Notes: Please refer to the User's Guide for an explanation of data; ranking tables include all places with Asian and/or NHPI populations above SF4 population thresholds; (1) tables reflect only those areas that meet SF4 population thresholds, therefore there may be less than 50 states, 75 counties or 75 places listed

Foreign-Born Naturalized Citizens

Pakistani

All States, Top 75 Counties, and Top 75 Places Sorted by Number[1]

State	Number
United States	47,923
New York	9,393
California	6,615
Illinois	5,358
Texas	5,225
New Jersey	4,313
Virginia	3,138
Florida	1,810
Maryland	1,681
Michigan	1,412
Georgia	1,176
Pennsylvania	932
Connecticut	575
Massachusetts	536
North Carolina	516
Ohio	463
Missouri	456
Washington	442
Colorado	307
Louisiana	271
Nevada	260
Indiana	259
Tennessee	256
Minnesota	254
Wisconsin	250
Oklahoma	217
Arizona	212
Kansas	207
Delaware	160
Kentucky	139
Alabama	138
Utah	119
Oregon	113
Iowa	80
West Virginia	57

County	Number
Queens County, NY	3,573
Cook County, IL	3,373
Kings County, NY	2,157
Harris County, TX	2,088
Fairfax County, VA	1,836
Los Angeles County, CA	1,711
Middlesex County, NJ	1,218
DuPage County, IL	1,050
Orange County, CA	985
Dallas County, TX	910
Fort Bend County, TX	875
Santa Clara County, CA	853
Nassau County, NY	720
Hudson County, NJ	713
Suffolk County, NY	695
Montgomery County, MD	689
Wayne County, MI	596
Bergen County, NJ	546
Alameda County, CA	545
Sacramento County, CA	521
Gwinnett County, GA	381
Miami-Dade County, FL	357
Oakland County, MI	334
San Joaquin County, CA	322
Bronx County, NY	317
Morris County, NJ	307
Prince William County, VA	306
San Bernardino County, CA	300
Richmond County, NY	298
Broward County, FL	287
Orange County, FL	285
Tarrant County, TX	277
New York County, NY	269
Somerset County, NJ	268
Howard County, MD	265
St. Louis County, MO	258
Delaware County, PA	251
Baltimore County, MD	250
Westchester County, NY	244
Macomb County, MI	241
Contra Costa County, CA	234
Essex County, NJ	231
Collin County, TX	218
Loudoun County, VA	218
Denton County, TX	212
San Francisco County, CA	204
Philadelphia County, PA	203
Wake County, NC	202
Atlantic County, NJ	201
Mercer County, NJ	196
Lake County, IL	195
Will County, IL	194
Cobb County, GA	190
Fairfield County, CT	189
Prince George's County, MD	180
Arlington County, VA	165
Snohomish County, WA	163
Maricopa County, AZ	159
Jefferson Parish, LA	156
New Haven County, CT	156
King County, WA	154
Alexandria Independent City, VA	152
Hartford County, CT	152
Riverside County, CA	151
Monroe County, NY	146
San Diego County, CA	144
Franklin County, OH	125
Camden County, NJ	117
Tulsa County, OK	113
Clayton County, GA	111
Travis County, TX	110
Worcester County, MA	107
Union County, NJ	105
Monmouth County, NJ	97
Washtenaw County, MI	95

Place	Number
New York, NY (city)	6,614
Chicago, IL (city) Cook County	1,802
Houston, TX (city) Harris County	1,249
Jersey City, NJ (city) Hudson County	620
San Jose, CA (city) Santa Clara County	469
Los Angeles, CA (city) Los Angeles County	416
Hempstead, NY (town) Nassau County	392
Carrollton, TX (city) Denton County	290
Sacramento, CA (city) Sacramento County	282
Sugar Land, TX (city) Fort Bend County	263
Old Bridge, NJ (township) Middlesex County	262
Fremont, CA (city) Alameda County	249
Torrance, CA (city) Los Angeles County	246
Skokie, IL (village) Cook County	232
North Hempstead, NY (town) Nassau County	231
Dallas, TX (city) Dallas County	220
Edison, NJ (township) Middlesex County	220
Brookhaven, NY (town) Suffolk County	210
Garland, TX (city) Dallas County	207
Dale City, VA (cdp) Prince William County	205
San Francisco, CA (city) San Francisco County	204
Philadelphia, PA (city) Philadelphia County	203
Stockton, CA (city) San Joaquin County	198
Huntington, NY (town) Suffolk County	170
Woodbridge, NJ (township) Middlesex County	166
Arlington, VA (cdp) Arlington County	165
Ellicott City, MD (cdp) Howard County	141
Plano, TX (city) Collin County	141
Anaheim, CA (city) Orange County	135
Mission Bend, TX (cdp) Fort Bend County	133
Richardson, TX (city) Dallas County	125
Lincolnia, VA (cdp) Fairfax County	114
Irving, TX (city) Dallas County	96
Santa Clara, CA (city) Santa Clara County	96
Austin, TX (city) Travis County	86
Tulsa, OK (city) Tulsa County	73
Bailey's Crossroads, VA (cdp) Fairfax County	58

Notes: Please refer to the User's Guide for an explanation of data; ranking tables include all places with Asian and/or NHPI populations above SF4 population thresholds; (1) tables reflect only those areas that meet SF4 population thresholds, therefore there may be less than 50 states, 75 counties or 75 places listed

Foreign-Born Naturalized Citizens

Pakistani

All States, Top 75 Counties, and Top 75 Places Sorted by Percent[1]

State	Percent
Nevada	48.87
Missouri	43.30
Delaware	42.22
Colorado	37.76
Indiana	36.33
Alabama	35.84
Washington	35.11
New Jersey	34.64
Illinois	34.37
Tennessee	33.51
California	33.35
Florida	33.24
Maryland	33.00
Arizona	31.55
Pennsylvania	30.80
United States	30.74
Georgia	30.11
Virginia	30.00
Utah	29.68
New York	29.24
Oregon	28.97
Michigan	28.36
Ohio	28.21
Louisiana	27.79
Texas	27.69
North Carolina	27.53
Connecticut	27.23
Wisconsin	26.97
Kansas	26.57
Kentucky	24.69
Minnesota	23.13
Massachusetts	22.75
Iowa	20.51
Oklahoma	19.34
West Virginia	17.59

County	Percent
Macomb County, MI	45.47
Wake County, NC	45.39
St. Louis County, MO	45.34
Miami-Dade County, FL	44.96
Will County, IL	44.39
San Bernardino County, CA	43.92
Howard County, MD	40.64
Morris County, NJ	40.50
Atlantic County, NJ	39.96
Delaware County, PA	38.91
Richmond County, NY	38.60
Middlesex County, NJ	38.37
Essex County, NJ	37.93
Snohomish County, WA	37.73
Montgomery County, MD	37.65
Prince William County, VA	37.64
Lake County, IL	37.57
Orange County, CA	37.42
DuPage County, IL	37.30
San Francisco County, CA	36.69
Bergen County, NJ	36.38
Sacramento County, CA	36.28
Los Angeles County, CA	36.18
Fort Bend County, TX	35.85
Jefferson Parish, LA	35.06
Fairfield County, CT	34.81
Loudoun County, VA	34.77
Suffolk County, NY	34.63
Oakland County, MI	34.33
Riverside County, CA	34.01
Gwinnett County, GA	33.36
Contra Costa County, CA	33.05
Somerset County, NJ	32.92
Philadelphia County, PA	32.27
Cook County, IL	31.78
Queens County, NY	31.75
Orange County, FL	31.63
Monroe County, NY	31.60
Camden County, NJ	31.12
Santa Clara County, CA	31.01
Hudson County, NJ	30.73
Nassau County, NY	30.66
Maricopa County, AZ	30.58
Mercer County, NJ	29.70
Cobb County, GA	29.37
King County, WA	29.28
Fairfax County, VA	29.19
Union County, NJ	29.17
Westchester County, NY	28.98
Harris County, TX	28.48
Bronx County, NY	28.20
Tarrant County, TX	28.09
Alameda County, CA	27.54
Wayne County, MI	27.36
Worcester County, MA	26.95
San Diego County, CA	26.67
Clayton County, GA	26.49
Alexandria Independent City, VA	26.48
Milwaukee County, WI	26.48
Prince George's County, MD	26.47
Broward County, FL	26.16
Denton County, TX	25.24
Baltimore County, MD	24.93
New York County, NY	24.77
Dallas County, TX	24.51
Franklin County, OH	24.37
San Joaquin County, CA	24.08
New Haven County, CT	23.89
Monmouth County, NJ	23.60
Collin County, TX	22.76
Hartford County, CT	22.75
Kings County, NY	22.42
Hennepin County, MN	21.08
Tulsa County, OK	20.77
Arlington County, VA	20.60

Place	Percent
Dale City, VA (cdp) Prince William County	63.27
Old Bridge, NJ (township) Middlesex County	49.81
Skokie, IL (village) Cook County	46.87
Sugar Land, TX (city) Fort Bend County	42.56
Huntington, NY (town) Suffolk County	38.90
Torrance, CA (city) Los Angeles County	37.50
North Hempstead, NY (town) Nassau County	37.38
San Francisco, CA (city) San Francisco County	36.69
Sacramento, CA (city) Sacramento County	36.20
Ellicott City, MD (cdp) Howard County	35.70
San Jose, CA (city) Santa Clara County	35.56
Woodbridge, NJ (township) Middlesex County	35.55
Jersey City, NJ (city) Hudson County	33.01
Edison, NJ (township) Middlesex County	32.64
Philadelphia, PA (city) Philadelphia County	32.27
Anaheim, CA (city) Orange County	31.84
Richardson, TX (city) Dallas County	29.55
Brookhaven, NY (town) Suffolk County	28.46
Stockton, CA (city) San Joaquin County	28.21
Chicago, IL (city) Cook County	27.99
Hempstead, NY (town) Nassau County	27.86
New York, NY (city)	27.73
Mission Bend, TX (cdp) Fort Bend County	27.71
Houston, TX (city) Harris County	24.99
Garland, TX (city) Dallas County	24.91
Carrollton, TX (city) Denton County	24.87
Los Angeles, CA (city) Los Angeles County	24.82
Plano, TX (city) Collin County	23.34
Fremont, CA (city) Alameda County	22.60
Irving, TX (city) Dallas County	22.38
Lincolnia, VA (cdp) Fairfax County	22.05
Arlington, VA (cdp) Arlington County	20.60
Santa Clara, CA (city) Santa Clara County	20.47
Dallas, TX (city) Dallas County	18.30
Tulsa, OK (city) Tulsa County	17.59
Austin, TX (city) Travis County	16.35
Bailey's Crossroads, VA (cdp) Fairfax County	16.16

Notes: Please refer to the User's Guide for an explanation of data; ranking tables include all places with Asian and/or NHPI populations above SF4 population thresholds; (1) tables reflect only those areas that meet SF4 population thresholds, therefore there may be less than 50 states, 75 counties or 75 places listed

Foreign-Born Naturalized Citizens

Samoan

All States, Top 75 Counties, and Top 75 Places Sorted by Number[1]

State	Number
United States	10,283
California	5,324
Hawaii	1,616
Washington	808
Utah	595
Alaska	248
Florida	190
Texas	155
Nevada	139
Missouri	132
Pennsylvania	92
Virginia	88
North Carolina	82
Georgia	77
Illinois	71
New Jersey	65
Colorado	59
Tennessee	55
Oregon	51
Arizona	49
New York	46
Ohio	37
Michigan	25

County	Number
Los Angeles County, CA	2,212
Honolulu County, HI	1,512
Orange County, CA	628
King County, WA	488
Salt Lake County, UT	479
San Bernardino County, CA	445
San Francisco County, CA	400
San Diego County, CA	318
Santa Clara County, CA	247
Pierce County, WA	219
Anchorage Borough, AK	194
San Mateo County, CA	164
Alameda County, CA	160
Ventura County, CA	134
Contra Costa County, CA	121
Sacramento County, CA	118
Riverside County, CA	98
Jackson County, MO	97
Clark County, NV	93
Hawaii County, HI	44
San Joaquin County, CA	38
Utah County, UT	38
Solano County, CA	31
Maricopa County, AZ	30

Place	Number
Long Beach, CA (city) Los Angeles County	710
Honolulu, HI (cdp) Honolulu County	561
San Francisco, CA (city) San Francisco County	400
Los Angeles, CA (city) Los Angeles County	300
Lakewood, CA (city) Los Angeles County	241
Compton, CA (city) Los Angeles County	211
Seattle, WA (city) King County	168
San Diego, CA (city) San Diego County	167
San Jose, CA (city) Santa Clara County	165
Waipahu, HI (cdp) Honolulu County	161
West Valley City, UT (city) Salt Lake County	160
Federal Way, WA (city) King County	158
Garden Grove, CA (city) Orange County	153
Santa Ana, CA (city) Orange County	134
Oxnard, CA (city) Ventura County	129
Westminster, CA (city) Orange County	123
Carson, CA (city) Los Angeles County	121
Salt Lake City, UT (city) Salt Lake County	107
Oceanside, CA (city) San Diego County	86
Laie, HI (cdp) Honolulu County	74
Tacoma, WA (city) Pierce County	65
Lakewood, WA (city) Pierce County	59
San Bernardino, CA (city) San Bernardino County	53
Anaheim, CA (city) Orange County	51
Hauula, HI (cdp) Honolulu County	51
Sacramento, CA (city) Sacramento County	46
Ewa Beach, HI (cdp) Honolulu County	41
Nanakuli, HI (cdp) Honolulu County	37
Kahuku, HI (cdp) Honolulu County	33
Halawa, HI (cdp) Honolulu County	30
Hayward, CA (city) Alameda County	30
New York, NY (city)	20

Notes: Please refer to the User's Guide for an explanation of data; ranking tables include all places with Asian and/or NHPI populations above SF4 population thresholds; (1) tables reflect only those areas that meet SF4 population thresholds, therefore there may be less than 50 states, 75 counties or 75 places listed

Foreign-Born Naturalized Citizens

Samoan

All States, Top 75 Counties, and Top 75 Places Sorted by Percent[1]

State	Percent
Florida	22.38
Virginia	16.92
North Carolina	16.57
Alaska	16.17
Utah	15.82
California	13.68
Missouri	13.15
United States	12.06
Washington	11.43
Hawaii	11.25
Pennsylvania	10.90
Tennessee	10.19
New Jersey	10.17
Georgia	10.10
Nevada	8.87
Illinois	8.12
Texas	7.62
Ohio	7.54
Oregon	6.60
Colorado	6.44
Arizona	5.76
Michigan	5.27
New York	3.20

County	Percent
Ventura County, CA	21.90
San Bernardino County, CA	21.86
Jackson County, MO	20.64
Salt Lake County, UT	18.52
San Francisco County, CA	17.55
Orange County, CA	16.88
Los Angeles County, CA	16.32
Anchorage Borough, AK	16.06
Contra Costa County, CA	15.94
Hawaii County, HI	14.86
Santa Clara County, CA	14.37
Pierce County, WA	12.67
King County, WA	12.45
San Mateo County, CA	11.30
Honolulu County, HI	10.92
San Joaquin County, CA	10.56
Riverside County, CA	10.39
Sacramento County, CA	9.52
Clark County, NV	8.33
Utah County, UT	6.92
Alameda County, CA	6.65
San Diego County, CA	6.42
Maricopa County, AZ	5.42
Solano County, CA	4.96

Place	Percent
Lakewood, CA (city) Los Angeles County	40.30
Westminster, CA (city) Orange County	32.71
Federal Way, WA (city) King County	32.18
Kahuku, HI (cdp) Honolulu County	27.50
Oxnard, CA (city) Ventura County	23.84
Salt Lake City, UT (city) Salt Lake County	23.57
Compton, CA (city) Los Angeles County	21.51
Lakewood, WA (city) Pierce County	20.14
Garden Grove, CA (city) Orange County	19.79
Santa Ana, CA (city) Orange County	19.14
Long Beach, CA (city) Los Angeles County	19.02
Hauula, HI (cdp) Honolulu County	18.75
West Valley City, UT (city) Salt Lake County	18.58
San Francisco, CA (city) San Francisco County	17.55
Los Angeles, CA (city) Los Angeles County	14.60
San Jose, CA (city) Santa Clara County	13.55
Honolulu, HI (cdp) Honolulu County	12.60
Seattle, WA (city) King County	12.50
San Bernardino, CA (city) San Bernardino County	11.09
Laie, HI (cdp) Honolulu County	11.06
Tacoma, WA (city) Pierce County	10.37
Ewa Beach, HI (cdp) Honolulu County	9.74
Anaheim, CA (city) Orange County	9.19
Carson, CA (city) Los Angeles County	8.41
San Diego, CA (city) San Diego County	7.69
Waipahu, HI (cdp) Honolulu County	7.59
Sacramento, CA (city) Sacramento County	6.28
Oceanside, CA (city) San Diego County	5.61
Hayward, CA (city) Alameda County	5.15
Nanakuli, HI (cdp) Honolulu County	4.91
Halawa, HI (cdp) Honolulu County	4.54
New York, NY (city)	2.74

Notes: Please refer to the User's Guide for an explanation of data; ranking tables include all places with Asian and/or NHPI populations above SF4 population thresholds; (1) tables reflect only those areas that meet SF4 population thresholds, therefore there may be less than 50 states, 75 counties or 75 places listed

Foreign-Born Naturalized Citizens

Sri Lankan

All States, Top 75 Counties, and Top 75 Places Sorted by Number[1]

State	Number
United States	5,950
California	1,932
New York	680
New Jersey	417
Maryland	388
Texas	243
Virginia	243
Massachusetts	194
Florida	155
Illinois	155
Michigan	122
Ohio	114
Pennsylvania	112
Washington	104

County	Number
Los Angeles County, CA	812
Orange County, CA	238
Queens County, NY	231
Montgomery County, MD	226
Middlesex County, NJ	168
Richmond County, NY	134

Place	Number
New York, NY (city)	431
Los Angeles, CA (city) Los Angeles County	261

Notes: Please refer to the User's Guide for an explanation of data; ranking tables include all places with Asian and/or NHPI populations above SF4 population thresholds; (1) tables reflect only those areas that meet SF4 population thresholds, therefore there may be less than 50 states, 75 counties or 75 places listed

Foreign-Born Naturalized Citizens

Sri Lankan

All States, Top 75 Counties, and Top 75 Places Sorted by Percent[1]

State	Percent
Massachusetts	41.36
Florida	38.56
Virginia	38.21
California	35.67
Maryland	34.58
Michigan	34.27
Pennsylvania	33.94
New Jersey	31.24
United States	31.19
Illinois	27.98
New York	25.29
Texas	24.90
Washington	24.64
Ohio	22.18

County	Percent
Orange County, CA	35.16
Middlesex County, NJ	33.80
Los Angeles County, CA	33.27
Montgomery County, MD	30.21
Richmond County, NY	25.43
Queens County, NY	24.65

Place	Percent
Los Angeles, CA (city) Los Angeles County	21.61
New York, NY (city)	21.51

Notes: Please refer to the User's Guide for an explanation of data; ranking tables include all places with Asian and/or NHPI populations above SF4 population thresholds; (1) tables reflect only those areas that meet SF4 population thresholds, therefore there may be less than 50 states, 75 counties or 75 places listed

Foreign-Born Naturalized Citizens

Taiwanese

All States, Top 75 Counties, and Top 75 Places Sorted by Number[1]

State	Number
United States	52,483
California	27,328
Texas	3,502
New York	3,478
New Jersey	2,599
Washington	1,657
Illinois	1,609
Maryland	1,066
Florida	988
Michigan	983
Massachusetts	887
Pennsylvania	873
Ohio	863
Georgia	830
Virginia	618
North Carolina	465
Hawaii	413
Missouri	394
Tennessee	301
Arizona	267
Indiana	266
Nevada	262
Connecticut	257
Colorado	239
Louisiana	219
Oregon	200
Minnesota	191
Wisconsin	176
Kansas	174
Iowa	157
Utah	108
Oklahoma	67

County	Number
Los Angeles County, CA	15,073
Orange County, CA	4,114
Santa Clara County, CA	2,039
Queens County, NY	1,758
Alameda County, CA	1,475
King County, WA	1,300
Harris County, TX	1,161
San Diego County, CA	1,025
San Bernardino County, CA	800
Contra Costa County, CA	792
Cook County, IL	692
Middlesex County, NJ	563
Montgomery County, MD	561
Oakland County, MI	547
Middlesex County, MA	519
DuPage County, IL	504
Fort Bend County, TX	459
Ventura County, CA	436
Collin County, TX	431
Fairfax County, VA	408
Honolulu County, HI	405
Bergen County, NJ	403
San Mateo County, CA	386
Travis County, TX	331
Somerset County, NJ	328
New York County, NY	316
Morris County, NJ	315
Nassau County, NY	314
Dallas County, TX	309
Tarrant County, TX	282
St. Louis County, MO	279
San Francisco County, CA	275
Franklin County, OH	269
Riverside County, CA	257
Suffolk County, NY	248
Gwinnett County, GA	243
Maricopa County, AZ	221
Sacramento County, CA	220
Mercer County, NJ	205
Washtenaw County, MI	193
Clark County, NV	186
Essex County, NJ	183
Westchester County, NY	132
Norfolk County, MA	113
Allegheny County, PA	108
Dane County, WI	68
Suffolk County, MA	67

Place	Number
New York, NY (city)	2,281
Los Angeles, CA (city) Los Angeles County	1,583
Arcadia, CA (city) Los Angeles County	1,518
Hacienda Heights, CA (cdp) Los Angeles County	1,215
Irvine, CA (city) Orange County	1,093
Rowland Heights, CA (cdp) Los Angeles County	962
Diamond Bar, CA (city) Los Angeles County	908
Fremont, CA (city) Alameda County	851
San Marino, CA (city) Los Angeles County	838
Cerritos, CA (city) Los Angeles County	798
San Jose, CA (city) Santa Clara County	782
Houston, TX (city) Harris County	762
Alhambra, CA (city) Los Angeles County	749
Walnut, CA (city) Los Angeles County	677
Temple City, CA (city) Los Angeles County	670
San Diego, CA (city) San Diego County	658
Torrance, CA (city) Los Angeles County	533
Monterey Park, CA (city) Los Angeles County	496
Honolulu, HI (cdp) Honolulu County	405
West Covina, CA (city) Los Angeles County	402
Sugar Land, TX (city) Fort Bend County	400
Bellevue, WA (city) King County	381
Seattle, WA (city) King County	375
Huntington Beach, CA (city) Orange County	354
Cypress, CA (city) Orange County	324
Rancho Palos Verdes, CA (city) Los Angeles County	303
Plano, TX (city) Collin County	300
San Gabriel, CA (city) Los Angeles County	291
San Francisco, CA (city) San Francisco County	275
Troy, MI (city) Oakland County	272
Austin, TX (city) Travis County	270
Chino Hills, CA (city) San Bernardino County	269
Cupertino, CA (city) Santa Clara County	268
Anaheim, CA (city) Orange County	263
East San Gabriel, CA (cdp) Los Angeles County	241
Chicago, IL (city) Cook County	239
Orange, CA (city) Orange County	239
Edison, NJ (township) Middlesex County	227
Sunnyvale, CA (city) Santa Clara County	217
El Monte, CA (city) Los Angeles County	206
Naperville, IL (city) Du Page County	203
Tustin, CA (city) Orange County	192
Fountain Valley, CA (city) Orange County	184
Ann Arbor, MI (city) Washtenaw County	183
Saratoga, CA (city) Santa Clara County	183
Arlington, TX (city) Tarrant County	177
Upland, CA (city) San Bernardino County	174
Berkeley, CA (city) Alameda County	157
North Hempstead, NY (town) Nassau County	139
Columbus, OH (city) Franklin County	123
Madison, WI (city) Dane County	68
Boston, MA (city) Suffolk County	67

Notes: Please refer to the User's Guide for an explanation of data; ranking tables include all places with Asian and/or NHPI populations above SF4 population thresholds; (1) tables reflect only those areas that meet SF4 population thresholds, therefore there may be less than 50 states, 75 counties or 75 places listed

Foreign-Born Naturalized Citizens

Taiwanese

All States, Top 75 Counties, and Top 75 Places Sorted by Percent[1]

State	Percent
Tennessee	51.90
Hawaii	50.30
Florida	48.74
North Carolina	47.89
Virginia	47.00
Illinois	45.07
Georgia	45.01
Maryland	44.85
New York	44.65
Texas	44.56
New Jersey	44.42
Louisiana	44.33
Nevada	43.89
Washington	43.74
Michigan	43.04
California	42.98
United States	42.76
Minnesota	41.25
Missouri	40.53
Ohio	39.00
Pennsylvania	38.34
Indiana	36.29
Iowa	35.20
Colorado	35.15
Massachusetts	34.98
Arizona	33.63
Kansas	33.59
Connecticut	31.38
Utah	29.19
Wisconsin	26.15
Oregon	25.00
Oklahoma	18.93

County	Percent
Contra Costa County, CA	62.81
DuPage County, IL	60.00
Somerset County, NJ	59.74
Suffolk County, NY	57.94
Fairfax County, VA	55.28
Ventura County, CA	54.71
Sacramento County, CA	54.19
Harris County, TX	52.23
Nassau County, NY	51.99
Riverside County, CA	51.61
Gwinnett County, GA	51.27
Honolulu County, HI	51.20
Queens County, NY	50.77
Collin County, TX	50.71
San Mateo County, CA	49.55
Montgomery County, MD	49.04
Bergen County, NJ	48.61
Morris County, NJ	44.87
Orange County, CA	44.51
Oakland County, MI	43.45
San Diego County, CA	43.40
Los Angeles County, CA	43.38
Clark County, NV	43.36
St. Louis County, MO	43.06
King County, WA	42.99
Mercer County, NJ	42.01
Tarrant County, TX	41.96
Middlesex County, NJ	41.40
Middlesex County, MA	40.80
Cook County, IL	39.50
Travis County, TX	39.40
San Bernardino County, CA	39.23
Westchester County, NY	39.05
Santa Clara County, CA	38.49
Dallas County, TX	38.43
Essex County, NJ	38.36
Fort Bend County, TX	37.75
Alameda County, CA	37.48
Washtenaw County, MI	37.12
San Francisco County, CA	35.67
Franklin County, OH	35.58
Maricopa County, AZ	34.42
New York County, NY	30.07
Norfolk County, MA	26.71
Allegheny County, PA	23.95
Dane County, WI	15.96
Suffolk County, MA	14.41

Place	Percent
Huntington Beach, CA (city) Orange County	61.35
Honolulu, HI (cdp) Honolulu County	57.69
Rancho Palos Verdes, CA (city) Los Angeles County	56.11
Saratoga, CA (city) Santa Clara County	55.12
San Marino, CA (city) Los Angeles County	54.91
Plano, TX (city) Collin County	53.19
Orange, CA (city) Orange County	51.73
El Monte, CA (city) Los Angeles County	51.37
Houston, TX (city) Harris County	51.07
North Hempstead, NY (town) Nassau County	49.12
Troy, MI (city) Oakland County	48.75
Alhambra, CA (city) Los Angeles County	48.07
Los Angeles, CA (city) Los Angeles County	47.59
Monterey Park, CA (city) Los Angeles County	47.19
Naperville, IL (city) Du Page County	47.10
New York, NY (city)	46.48
Fountain Valley, CA (city) Orange County	46.35
Cerritos, CA (city) Los Angeles County	44.56
Temple City, CA (city) Los Angeles County	43.73
Cypress, CA (city) Orange County	43.55
Diamond Bar, CA (city) Los Angeles County	43.26
Sugar Land, TX (city) Fort Bend County	42.69
Arlington, TX (city) Tarrant County	42.65
Chino Hills, CA (city) San Bernardino County	42.43
West Covina, CA (city) Los Angeles County	42.41
Hacienda Heights, CA (cdp) Los Angeles County	42.26
Irvine, CA (city) Orange County	41.69
Ann Arbor, MI (city) Washtenaw County	41.50
San Diego, CA (city) San Diego County	41.46
Torrance, CA (city) Los Angeles County	41.32
Tustin, CA (city) Orange County	41.11
Bellevue, WA (city) King County	41.01
Arcadia, CA (city) Los Angeles County	40.45
Anaheim, CA (city) Orange County	39.31
Berkeley, CA (city) Alameda County	38.48
Seattle, WA (city) King County	38.38
San Gabriel, CA (city) Los Angeles County	38.14
San Jose, CA (city) Santa Clara County	38.09
East San Gabriel, CA (cdp) Los Angeles County	37.60
Upland, CA (city) San Bernardino County	37.18
Rowland Heights, CA (cdp) Los Angeles County	37.10
Austin, TX (city) Travis County	36.10
San Francisco, CA (city) San Francisco County	35.67
Walnut, CA (city) Los Angeles County	35.15
Fremont, CA (city) Alameda County	34.71
Edison, NJ (township) Middlesex County	34.24
Cupertino, CA (city) Santa Clara County	33.84
Sunnyvale, CA (city) Santa Clara County	32.34
Chicago, IL (city) Cook County	30.80
Columbus, OH (city) Franklin County	26.57
Madison, WI (city) Dane County	16.08
Boston, MA (city) Suffolk County	14.41

Notes: Please refer to the User's Guide for an explanation of data; ranking tables include all places with Asian and/or NHPI populations above SF4 population thresholds; (1) tables reflect only those areas that meet SF4 population thresholds, therefore there may be less than 50 states, 75 counties or 75 places listed

Foreign-Born Naturalized Citizens

Thai

All States, Top 75 Counties, and Top 75 Places Sorted by Number[1]

State	Number
United States	36,227
California	12,432
Florida	2,470
Texas	2,129
New York	1,787
Illinois	1,730
Washington	1,261
Virginia	1,176
Nevada	1,097
Maryland	988
Georgia	627
Colorado	586
Ohio	568
New Jersey	542
Pennsylvania	528
Arizona	516
Massachusetts	487
North Carolina	471
Oregon	470
Iowa	464
Missouri	448
Hawaii	442
Michigan	436
Minnesota	337
Alaska	318
Oklahoma	315
Indiana	306
South Carolina	306
Louisiana	273
Tennessee	262
Connecticut	239
Utah	230
Alabama	217
Kansas	210
New Mexico	200
Wisconsin	166
Nebraska	139
Arkansas	90
Kentucky	74

County	Number
Los Angeles County, CA	7,115
Cook County, IL	1,176
Orange County, CA	1,074
Clark County, NV	1,006
San Bernardino County, CA	643
King County, WA	591
Queens County, NY	557
Fairfax County, VA	483
San Diego County, CA	407
Montgomery County, MD	404
Okaloosa County, FL	389
Honolulu County, HI	382
Bexar County, TX	375
San Francisco County, CA	366
Riverside County, CA	356
Alameda County, CA	346
Maricopa County, AZ	332
Harris County, TX	331
Santa Clara County, CA	273
Hillsborough County, FL	264
Dallas County, TX	262
Palm Beach County, FL	257
Miami-Dade County, FL	256
San Mateo County, CA	236
New York County, NY	234
Sacramento County, CA	227
Tarrant County, TX	225
Contra Costa County, CA	224
Anchorage Borough, AK	213
Polk County, IA	198
Middlesex County, MA	177
Westchester County, NY	165
Broward County, FL	154
St. Louis County, MO	154
Oklahoma County, OK	153
Pierce County, WA	132
Collin County, TX	127
Suffolk County, NY	121
Nassau County, NY	114
Bergen County, NJ	109
Multnomah County, OR	107
Pinellas County, FL	97
DuPage County, IL	94
Travis County, TX	92
Franklin County, OH	87
Prince George's County, MD	86
Denver County, CO	83

Place	Number
Los Angeles, CA (city) Los Angeles County	2,946
New York, NY (city)	958
Chicago, IL (city) Cook County	468
San Francisco, CA (city) San Francisco County	366
San Diego, CA (city) San Diego County	268
San Antonio, TX (city) Bexar County	240
Houston, TX (city) Harris County	233
Seattle, WA (city) King County	220
Honolulu, HI (cdp) Honolulu County	199
Las Vegas, NV (city) Clark County	197
Long Beach, CA (city) Los Angeles County	197
Cerritos, CA (city) Los Angeles County	185
Spring Valley, NV (cdp) Clark County	165
Anaheim, CA (city) Orange County	153
Glendale, CA (city) Los Angeles County	152
Des Moines, IA (city) Polk County	143
Bellflower, CA (city) Los Angeles County	140
San Jose, CA (city) Santa Clara County	137
Portland, OR (city) Multnomah County	89
Denver, CO (city) Denver County	83
Columbus, OH (city) Franklin County	65

Notes: Please refer to the User's Guide for an explanation of data; ranking tables include all places with Asian and/or NHPI populations above SF4 population thresholds; (1) tables reflect only those areas that meet SF4 population thresholds, therefore there may be less than 50 states, 75 counties or 75 places listed

Foreign-Born Naturalized Citizens

Thai

All States, Top 75 Counties, and Top 75 Places Sorted by Percent[1]

State	Percent
Iowa	49.89
New Mexico	49.88
South Carolina	44.48
Louisiana	42.33
Alaska	40.66
Oklahoma	38.27
Florida	37.58
Nevada	36.85
Minnesota	36.63
Alabama	34.94
Maryland	34.62
California	34.39
Indiana	33.85
Virginia	32.84
United States	32.68
Missouri	32.65
Utah	32.53
Washington	32.40
Kansas	32.31
Arizona	31.64
Hawaii	31.62
Oregon	31.42
Arkansas	30.82
Connecticut	30.48
Nebraska	30.15
Colorado	30.10
Texas	29.93
Ohio	29.89
Illinois	29.58
New Jersey	29.38
Pennsylvania	29.37
North Carolina	28.98
Georgia	27.87
Michigan	27.18
New York	27.09
Tennessee	26.33
Massachusetts	21.60
Wisconsin	19.08
Kentucky	17.54

County	Percent
Okaloosa County, FL	62.34
Polk County, IA	55.31
Bexar County, TX	46.07
St. Louis County, MO	40.74
Riverside County, CA	40.64
Hillsborough County, FL	39.05
Oklahoma County, OK	38.54
Clark County, NV	38.40
San Bernardino County, CA	37.71
Anchorage Borough, AK	36.92
Los Angeles County, CA	36.37
Contra Costa County, CA	35.28
Orange County, CA	34.00
Palm Beach County, FL	33.82
San Mateo County, CA	33.67
Pierce County, WA	33.33
Honolulu County, HI	33.25
Fairfax County, VA	32.37
Suffolk County, NY	31.27
San Diego County, CA	31.09
Sacramento County, CA	30.72
Montgomery County, MD	30.44
Nassau County, NY	30.32
King County, WA	30.31
Cook County, IL	29.39
Tarrant County, TX	29.03
Miami-Dade County, FL	29.02
Maricopa County, AZ	28.97
New York County, NY	28.02
Collin County, TX	27.97
Westchester County, NY	27.78
Prince George's County, MD	25.75
Broward County, FL	25.71
San Francisco County, CA	25.05
Harris County, TX	24.83
Alameda County, CA	23.81
Dallas County, TX	23.71
Queens County, NY	23.56
Travis County, TX	22.89
DuPage County, IL	22.49
Multnomah County, OR	21.75
Bergen County, NJ	21.67
Santa Clara County, CA	20.46
Denver County, CO	20.44
Franklin County, OH	20.33
Pinellas County, FL	19.88
Middlesex County, MA	19.64

Place	Percent
Des Moines, IA (city) Polk County	48.47
San Antonio, TX (city) Bexar County	41.59
Cerritos, CA (city) Los Angeles County	39.70
Honolulu, HI (cdp) Honolulu County	37.20
Glendale, CA (city) Los Angeles County	36.19
Bellflower, CA (city) Los Angeles County	35.99
Anaheim, CA (city) Orange County	33.55
Spring Valley, NV (cdp) Clark County	33.20
Long Beach, CA (city) Los Angeles County	32.62
San Diego, CA (city) San Diego County	32.56
Los Angeles, CA (city) Los Angeles County	32.43
Las Vegas, NV (city) Clark County	28.14
Houston, TX (city) Harris County	26.45
New York, NY (city)	25.06
Seattle, WA (city) King County	25.06
San Francisco, CA (city) San Francisco County	25.05
Chicago, IL (city) Cook County	21.83
San Jose, CA (city) Santa Clara County	21.71
Denver, CO (city) Denver County	20.44
Portland, OR (city) Multnomah County	19.78
Columbus, OH (city) Franklin County	16.71

Notes: Please refer to the User's Guide for an explanation of data; ranking tables include all places with Asian and/or NHPI populations above SF4 population thresholds; (1) tables reflect only those areas that meet SF4 population thresholds, therefore there may be less than 50 states, 75 counties or 75 places listed

Foreign-Born Naturalized Citizens

Tongan

All States, Top 75 Counties, and Top 75 Places Sorted by Number[1]

State	Number
United States	5,434
California	2,175
Utah	1,377
Hawaii	1,006
Washington	170
Arizona	121
Nevada	115
Texas	111
Oregon	100
Alaska	82

County	Number
Salt Lake County, UT	1,263
San Mateo County, CA	812
Honolulu County, HI	728
Alameda County, CA	324
Los Angeles County, CA	322
Maui County, HI	215
Sacramento County, CA	210
King County, WA	126
Maricopa County, AZ	119
Tarrant County, TX	92
Contra Costa County, CA	90
Washoe County, NV	89
San Diego County, CA	84
Utah County, UT	76
San Bernardino County, CA	75
Orange County, CA	71
Multnomah County, OR	69

Place	Number
Salt Lake City, UT (city) Salt Lake County	526
East Palo Alto, CA (city) San Mateo County	404
Honolulu, HI (cdp) Honolulu County	367
West Valley City, UT (city) Salt Lake County	319
Oakland, CA (city) Alameda County	183
San Mateo, CA (city) San Mateo County	174
Sacramento, CA (city) Sacramento County	156
West Jordan, UT (city) Salt Lake County	115
Hauula, HI (cdp) Honolulu County	77
Kahuku, HI (cdp) Honolulu County	77
Portland, OR (city) Multnomah County	69
Los Angeles, CA (city) Los Angeles County	64
Laie, HI (cdp) Honolulu County	63
San Bruno, CA (city) San Mateo County	47

Notes: Please refer to the User's Guide for an explanation of data; ranking tables include all places with Asian and/or NHPI populations above SF4 population thresholds; (1) tables reflect only those areas that meet SF4 population thresholds, therefore there may be less than 50 states, 75 counties or 75 places listed

Foreign-Born Naturalized Citizens

Tongan

All States, Top 75 Counties, and Top 75 Places Sorted by Percent[1]

State	Percent
Hawaii	24.06
Oregon	22.47
Texas	22.16
Utah	20.26
Washington	20.14
United States	19.63
Alaska	19.57
Arizona	19.09
California	17.88
Nevada	14.56

County	Percent
Sacramento County, CA	28.34
Maui County, HI	27.08
Tarrant County, TX	25.21
King County, WA	25.10
Honolulu County, HI	23.62
Maricopa County, AZ	22.58
San Mateo County, CA	22.22
Salt Lake County, UT	21.27
Contra Costa County, CA	19.96
San Diego County, CA	19.31
Multnomah County, OR	19.22
Alameda County, CA	17.69
Utah County, UT	16.45
Washoe County, NV	15.42
Los Angeles County, CA	14.15
Orange County, CA	12.22
San Bernardino County, CA	9.26

Place	Percent
Kahuku, HI (cdp) Honolulu County	32.49
Laie, HI (cdp) Honolulu County	28.00
San Mateo, CA (city) San Mateo County	27.27
Sacramento, CA (city) Sacramento County	27.18
East Palo Alto, CA (city) San Mateo County	27.04
West Jordan, UT (city) Salt Lake County	24.47
Honolulu, HI (cdp) Honolulu County	23.56
Salt Lake City, UT (city) Salt Lake County	21.50
Hauula, HI (cdp) Honolulu County	21.39
Portland, OR (city) Multnomah County	19.60
Los Angeles, CA (city) Los Angeles County	18.71
West Valley City, UT (city) Salt Lake County	17.66
Oakland, CA (city) Alameda County	13.95
San Bruno, CA (city) San Mateo County	8.82

Notes: Please refer to the User's Guide for an explanation of data; ranking tables include all places with Asian and/or NHPI populations above SF4 population thresholds; (1) tables reflect only those areas that meet SF4 population thresholds, therefore there may be less than 50 states, 75 counties or 75 places listed

Foreign-Born Naturalized Citizens

Vietnamese

***All States, Top 75 Counties, and Top 75 Places Sorted by Number*[1]**

State	Number
United States	488,874
California	213,824
Texas	57,884
Washington	20,345
Virginia	18,278
Florida	13,645
Massachusetts	12,790
Pennsylvania	12,032
New York	10,404
Louisiana	8,832
Georgia	8,497
Maryland	8,490
Oregon	7,949
Illinois	7,808
Minnesota	7,739
New Jersey	6,281
Colorado	5,487
Oklahoma	5,438
North Carolina	5,284
Michigan	4,766
Ohio	4,763
Hawaii	4,573
Kansas	4,560
Arizona	4,173
Missouri	3,759
Connecticut	3,251
Utah	2,361
Iowa	2,305
Nebraska	2,289
Tennessee	2,233
Nevada	2,128
Indiana	1,930
Wisconsin	1,815
Alabama	1,769
South Carolina	1,689
Mississippi	1,666
Arkansas	1,443
New Mexico	1,165
Kentucky	1,000
Idaho	534
Vermont	520
Maine	515
District of Columbia	455
New Hampshire	447
Rhode Island	417
Delaware	345
Alaska	306
South Dakota	252
West Virginia	231

County	Number
Orange County, CA	67,030
Santa Clara County, CA	45,526
Los Angeles County, CA	40,661
Harris County, TX	25,833
San Diego County, CA	15,169
King County, WA	12,499
Fairfax County, VA	11,431
Alameda County, CA	10,289
Sacramento County, CA	7,191
Tarrant County, TX	7,011
Dallas County, TX	6,970
San Francisco County, CA	5,704
Montgomery County, MD	5,180
Cook County, IL	4,813
San Bernardino County, CA	4,530
Suffolk County, MA	4,515
Multnomah County, OR	4,465
Philadelphia County, PA	4,417
Honolulu County, HI	4,267
Hennepin County, MN	3,346
Travis County, TX	3,252
Riverside County, CA	3,069
Maricopa County, AZ	3,029
Fort Bend County, TX	2,919
Orange County, FL	2,892
Sedgwick County, KS	2,862
Jefferson Parish, LA	2,796
Oklahoma County, OK	2,795
Middlesex County, MA	2,769
Orleans Parish, LA	2,541
Snohomish County, WA	2,526
Contra Costa County, CA	2,471
Gwinnett County, GA	2,330
Washington County, OR	2,313
Salt Lake County, UT	2,076
San Joaquin County, CA	2,064
Kings County, NY	1,930
Collin County, TX	1,877
Clark County, NV	1,783
Queens County, NY	1,779
Pierce County, WA	1,755
San Mateo County, CA	1,751
Worcester County, MA	1,729
Mecklenburg County, NC	1,695
Ventura County, CA	1,678
DeKalb County, GA	1,662
Bexar County, TX	1,571
Hillsborough County, FL	1,556
Kent County, MI	1,531
Hartford County, CT	1,509
Ramsey County, MN	1,452
Arapahoe County, CO	1,391
Denver County, CO	1,366
Pinellas County, FL	1,356
Broward County, FL	1,353
Norfolk County, MA	1,337
Denton County, TX	1,334
Lancaster County, NE	1,333
Jefferson County, TX	1,300
Prince George's County, MD	1,234
Middlesex County, NJ	1,181
DuPage County, IL	1,150
Essex County, MA	1,133
Montgomery County, PA	1,130
Arlington County, VA	1,125
Monroe County, NY	1,106
East Baton Rouge Parish, LA	1,091
Camden County, NJ	1,070
Wake County, NC	1,054
Shelby County, TN	1,046
Saint Louis Independent City, MO	1,043
Bronx County, NY	1,015
Bernalillo County, NM	1,012
Franklin County, OH	1,001
Clark County, WA	973

Place	Number
San Jose, CA (city) Santa Clara County	34,500
Garden Grove, CA (city) Orange County	15,575
Houston, TX (city) Harris County	14,200
Westminster, CA (city) Orange County	12,604
San Diego, CA (city) San Diego County	12,321
Los Angeles, CA (city) Los Angeles County	10,072
Santa Ana, CA (city) Orange County	9,728
San Francisco, CA (city) San Francisco County	5,704
New York, NY (city)	5,654
Anaheim, CA (city) Orange County	5,175
Seattle, WA (city) King County	5,060
Philadelphia, PA (city) Philadelphia County	4,417
Portland, OR (city) Multnomah County	4,216
Milpitas, CA (city) Santa Clara County	4,121
Boston, MA (city) Suffolk County	4,044
Fountain Valley, CA (city) Orange County	3,952
Honolulu, HI (cdp) Honolulu County	3,488
Oklahoma City, OK (city) Oklahoma County	3,352
Chicago, IL (city) Cook County	3,316
Huntington Beach, CA (city) Orange County	3,238
Arlington, TX (city) Tarrant County	3,143
Oakland, CA (city) Alameda County	2,940
El Monte, CA (city) Los Angeles County	2,832
Irvine, CA (city) Orange County	2,796
Wichita, KS (city) Sedgwick County	2,704
Rosemead, CA (city) Los Angeles County	2,653
Austin, TX (city) Travis County	2,614
New Orleans, LA (city) Orleans Parish	2,541
Long Beach, CA (city) Los Angeles County	2,455
Sacramento, CA (city) Sacramento County	2,408
Alhambra, CA (city) Los Angeles County	2,407
Garland, TX (city) Dallas County	2,274
Dallas, TX (city) Dallas County	2,233
Santa Clara, CA (city) Santa Clara County	2,183
Fremont, CA (city) Alameda County	2,142
Fort Worth, TX (city) Tarrant County	2,012
Orange, CA (city) Orange County	1,961
Stockton, CA (city) San Joaquin County	1,785
Annandale, VA (cdp) Fairfax County	1,748
Sunnyvale, CA (city) Santa Clara County	1,673
Monterey Park, CA (city) Los Angeles County	1,540
Denver, CO (city) Denver County	1,366
Lincoln, NE (city) Lancaster County	1,333
Charlotte, NC (city) Mecklenburg County	1,332
Costa Mesa, CA (city) Orange County	1,289
Stanton, CA (city) Orange County	1,260
Jefferson, VA (cdp) Fairfax County	1,248
San Antonio, TX (city) Bexar County	1,223
San Gabriel, CA (city) Los Angeles County	1,214
West Covina, CA (city) Los Angeles County	1,205
Riverside, CA (city) Riverside County	1,174
Carrollton, TX (city) Denton County	1,136
Arlington, VA (cdp) Arlington County	1,125
Tacoma, WA (city) Pierce County	1,125
Hayward, CA (city) Alameda County	1,124
Worcester, MA (city) Worcester County	1,115
Minneapolis, MN (city) Hennepin County	1,096
Elk Grove, CA (cdp) Sacramento County	1,057
Springfield, VA (cdp) Fairfax County	1,043
St. Louis, MO (city) Saint Louis Independent City	1,043
Phoenix, AZ (city) Maricopa County	1,031
Albuquerque, NM (city) Bernalillo County	973
Tustin, CA (city) Orange County	954
Grand Prairie, TX (city) Dallas County	944
Plano, TX (city) Collin County	941
Union City, CA (city) Alameda County	936
Kansas City, MO (city) Jackson County	920
Port Arthur, TX (city) Jefferson County	918
Aurora, CO (city) Arapahoe County	906
Renton, WA (city) King County	903
Columbus, OH (city) Franklin County	891
Torrance, CA (city) Los Angeles County	888
St. Paul, MN (city) Ramsey County	887
Baton Rouge, LA (city) East Baton Rouge Parish	833
Tulsa, OK (city) Tulsa County	828

Notes: Please refer to the User's Guide for an explanation of data; ranking tables include all places with Asian and/or NHPI populations above SF4 population thresholds; (1) tables reflect only those areas that meet SF4 population thresholds, therefore there may be less than 50 states, 75 counties or 75 places listed

Foreign-Born Naturalized Citizens

Vietnamese

All States, Top 75 Counties, and Top 75 Places Sorted by Percent[1]

State	Percent
Hawaii	54.80
West Virginia	52.26
Nevada	51.97
Virginia	51.57
Maryland	50.89
Delaware	50.29
Vermont	48.51
California	47.89
Wisconsin	46.89
Maine	46.19
Ohio	45.99
Washington	45.56
New York	44.89
Oklahoma	44.50
South Carolina	44.28
United States	44.03
Connecticut	43.94
Texas	43.15
Utah	42.52
Illinois	42.39
Minnesota	42.10
Pennsylvania	42.03
New Jersey	41.93
Oregon	41.75
New Mexico	41.65
Indiana	40.94
Florida	40.86
Rhode Island	40.56
Kansas	40.38
Colorado	40.15
Idaho	39.26
Alabama	38.20
Arkansas	37.34
Massachusetts	37.21
Michigan	36.74
Missouri	35.78
Arizona	35.65
Louisiana	35.26
South Dakota	35.24
Nebraska	34.27
Iowa	34.04
North Carolina	33.86
Tennessee	31.62
Alaska	31.58
Mississippi	31.22
Kentucky	31.19
Georgia	28.81
New Hampshire	26.58
District of Columbia	25.43

County	Percent
Alexandria Independent City, VA	65.70
San Mateo County, CA	62.54
Canadian County, OK	61.08
Cumberland County, NC	59.78
Benton County, WA	59.64
Norfolk Independent City, VA	59.61
Bucks County, PA	58.86
Greene County, MO	58.51
Montgomery County, OH	58.44
Fairfax Independent City, VA	58.33
Nassau County, NY	57.78
Howard County, MD	56.81
Monmouth County, NJ	56.77
New Castle County, DE	56.34
Kern County, CA	56.09
Fort Bend County, TX	56.05
Montgomery County, MD	55.20
Honolulu County, HI	54.88
Santa Barbara County, CA	54.82
San Francisco County, CA	54.69
Hampton Independent City, VA	54.65
Albany County, NY	54.60
Bexar County, TX	54.57
Brazoria County, TX	54.38
Clark County, NV	54.16
New York County, NY	54.11
Collin County, TX	53.74
Fairfax County, VA	53.69
Brevard County, FL	53.21
Scott County, MN	52.54
Loudoun County, VA	52.49
Middlesex County, NJ	52.49
Morris County, NJ	52.45
Sonoma County, CA	52.18
Lake County, IL	52.14
Cumberland County, PA	51.98
Los Angeles County, CA	51.96
Ventura County, CA	51.90
Arlington County, VA	51.39
Denton County, TX	51.19
New Haven County, CT	51.01
Arapahoe County, CO	50.80
Chester County, PA	50.72
Kings County, NY	50.39
Broome County, NY	50.29
Dane County, WI	50.07
Cleveland County, OK	49.94
Riverside County, CA	49.85
Placer County, CA	49.66
Marin County, CA	49.61
Butler County, OH	49.38
Orange County, CA	49.22
Seminole County, FL	49.15
Milwaukee County, WI	49.12
Thurston County, WA	48.92
Monroe County, NY	48.79
Kane County, IL	48.74
Madison County, AL	48.54
Delaware County, PA	48.53
Spokane County, WA	48.39
Clackamas County, OR	48.26
Dakota County, MN	48.21
Snohomish County, WA	48.11
Somerset County, NJ	48.07
St. Tammany Parish, LA	47.90
Cumberland County, ME	47.70
Alachua County, FL	47.65
Queens County, NY	47.58
Saline County, KS	47.58
Bristol County, MA	47.57
Orange County, TX	47.48
Norfolk County, MA	47.44
Suffolk County, NY	47.44
Hamilton County, OH	47.35
Marion County, OR	47.35

Place	Percent
Carson, CA (city) Los Angeles County	83.18
Colesville, MD (cdp) Montgomery County	71.90
Pasadena, CA (city) Los Angeles County	71.13
Glendale, CA (city) Los Angeles County	70.90
Las Vegas, NV (city) Clark County	68.52
Aliso Viejo, CA (cdp) Orange County	67.06
Wheaton-Glenmont, MD (cdp) Montgomery County	66.58
Franconia, VA (cdp) Fairfax County	66.48
Herndon, VA (town) Fairfax County	66.04
Laguna Niguel, CA (city) Orange County	65.52
Cerritos, CA (city) Los Angeles County	65.32
Laguna, CA (cdp) Sacramento County	65.15
Downey, CA (city) Los Angeles County	64.32
Lakewood, CA (city) Los Angeles County	63.80
Lincolnia, VA (cdp) Fairfax County	63.15
Norwalk, CA (city) Los Angeles County	62.35
Chino Hills, CA (city) San Bernardino County	62.09
Temple City, CA (city) Los Angeles County	61.98
Stafford, TX (city) Fort Bend County	61.32
Bakersfield, CA (city) Kern County	61.05
Daly City, CA (city) San Mateo County	60.97
Montgomery Village, MD (cdp) Montgomery County	60.55
Missouri City, TX (city) Fort Bend County	60.51
Diamond Bar, CA (city) Los Angeles County	60.06
Burke, VA (cdp) Fairfax County	59.86
Rosemont, CA (cdp) Sacramento County	59.63
Rancho Santa Margarita, CA (city) Orange County	59.47
Pearland, TX (city) Brazoria County	58.77
Rowland Heights, CA (cdp) Los Angeles County	58.65
Lewisville, TX (city) Denton County	58.63
Albany, NY (city) Albany County	58.33
Santa Clarita, CA (city) Los Angeles County	58.30
San Leandro, CA (city) Alameda County	58.29
Covina, CA (city) Los Angeles County	57.92
Valinda, CA (cdp) Los Angeles County	57.81
Irvine, CA (city) Orange County	57.63
Costa Mesa, CA (city) Orange County	57.52
Chantilly, VA (cdp) Fairfax County	57.27
Alondra Park, CA (cdp) Los Angeles County	57.20
Laguna Hills, CA (city) Orange County	57.02
Paradise, NV (cdp) Clark County	56.85
Moreno Valley, CA (city) Riverside County	56.81
Campbell, CA (city) Santa Clara County	56.70
Goleta, CA (cdp) Santa Barbara County	56.59
Alum Rock, CA (cdp) Santa Clara County	56.55
Springfield, VA (cdp) Fairfax County	56.44
Sugar Land, TX (city) Fort Bend County	56.43
Antioch, CA (city) Contra Costa County	56.42
Aspen Hill, MD (cdp) Montgomery County	56.38
Walnut, CA (city) Los Angeles County	56.35
Seattle Hill-Silver Firs, WA (cdp) Snohomish County	56.24
West Covina, CA (city) Los Angeles County	55.79
Yorba Linda, CA (city) Orange County	55.68
Fountain Valley, CA (city) Orange County	55.53
White Oak, MD (cdp) Montgomery County	55.49
Placentia, CA (city) Orange County	55.40
Tustin, CA (city) Orange County	55.37
Cupertino, CA (city) Santa Clara County	55.31
Beaverton, OR (city) Washington County	55.24
North Highlands, CA (cdp) Sacramento County	55.23
Huntington Beach, CA (city) Orange County	55.11
Alhambra, CA (city) Los Angeles County	54.77
San Francisco, CA (city) San Francisco County	54.69
Springfield, MO (city) Greene County	54.64
Cary, NC (town) Wake County	54.63
Jefferson, VA (cdp) Fairfax County	54.52
Kent, WA (city) King County	54.50
Corona, CA (city) Riverside County	54.45
Terrytown, LA (cdp) Jefferson Parish	54.42
Baldwin Park, CA (city) Los Angeles County	54.21
Burien, WA (city) King County	54.09
Rancho Cucamonga, CA (city) San Bernardino County	54.08
Lawndale, CA (city) Los Angeles County	54.06
San Antonio, TX (city) Bexar County	53.83
Mountain View, CA (city) Santa Clara County	53.77

Notes: Please refer to the User's Guide for an explanation of data; ranking tables include all places with Asian and/or NHPI populations above SF4 population thresholds; (1) tables reflect only those areas that meet SF4 population thresholds, therefore there may be less than 50 states, 75 counties or 75 places listed

Educational Attainment: High School Graduates

Total Population 25 Years and Over Who are High School Graduates

All States, Top 75 Counties, and Top 75 Places Sorted by Number[1]

State	Number
United States	146,496,014
California	16,356,157
New York	9,916,212
Texas	9,676,332
Florida	8,804,697
Pennsylvania	6,770,179
Illinois	6,493,228
Ohio	6,149,655
Michigan	5,351,808
New Jersey	4,643,322
North Carolina	4,128,270
Georgia	4,074,616
Virginia	3,801,964
Massachusetts	3,622,182
Washington	3,333,171
Indiana	3,197,738
Wisconsin	2,957,461
Missouri	2,955,811
Maryland	2,930,509
Tennessee	2,843,244
Minnesota	2,783,000
Arizona	2,636,637
Colorado	2,413,593
Alabama	2,173,319
Louisiana	2,076,416
South Carolina	1,981,731
Kentucky	1,961,397
Connecticut	1,927,961
Oregon	1,916,187
Oklahoma	1,775,940
Iowa	1,632,420
Kansas	1,463,408
Arkansas	1,303,751
Mississippi	1,280,487
Nevada	1,056,802
Utah	1,050,881
Nebraska	941,380
West Virginia	927,767
New Mexico	894,820
Maine	742,605
New Hampshire	720,233
Hawaii	678,666
Idaho	667,144
Rhode Island	541,487
Montana	511,263
Delaware	425,122
South Dakota	401,179
Vermont	349,327
North Dakota	342,629
Alaska	335,274
District of Columbia	299,286
Wyoming	277,346

County	Number
Los Angeles County, CA	4,112,424
Cook County, IL	2,684,397
Maricopa County, AZ	1,596,366
Harris County, TX	1,542,977
San Diego County, CA	1,464,478
Orange County, CA	1,441,037
Queens County, NY	1,122,321
King County, WA	1,073,012
Kings County, NY	1,068,564
Dallas County, TX	1,023,752
Miami-Dade County, FL	1,012,436
Wayne County, MI	1,004,782
Santa Clara County, CA	928,258
Broward County, FL	923,268
Middlesex County, MA	890,431
New York County, NY	885,633
Suffolk County, NY	812,227
Nassau County, NY	787,955
Alameda County, CA	785,435
Allegheny County, PA	769,335
Cuyahoga County, OH	764,186
Tarrant County, TX	730,928
San Bernardino County, CA	729,679
Oakland County, MI	721,193
Clark County, NV	715,402
Riverside County, CA	701,551
Philadelphia County, PA	688,107
Palm Beach County, FL	683,553
Hennepin County, MN	671,196
Bexar County, TX	653,124
Sacramento County, CA	643,218
St. Louis County, MO	595,492
Fairfax County, VA	592,760
Franklin County, OH	579,896
Pinellas County, FL	576,396
Contra Costa County, CA	543,774
Bergen County, NJ	539,849
Montgomery County, MD	536,558
DuPage County, IL	530,429
Erie County, NY	528,556
Hillsborough County, FL	528,058
Westchester County, NY	525,485
Fairfield County, CT	503,136
Bronx County, NY	495,106
Honolulu County, HI	492,110
San Francisco County, CA	483,740
Hartford County, CT	477,537
Milwaukee County, WI	476,973
Orange County, FL	469,510
New Haven County, CT	457,905
Montgomery County, PA	456,564
Pima County, AZ	455,717
Marion County, IN	451,863
Hamilton County, OH	451,841
Shelby County, TN	450,794
Macomb County, MI	444,465
Fulton County, GA	443,368
Salt Lake County, UT	442,368
Baltimore County, MD	431,380
Prince George's County, MD	427,557
Travis County, TX	424,575
Middlesex County, NJ	423,088
San Mateo County, CA	418,121
Worcester County, MA	413,842
Duval County, FL	413,266
Norfolk County, MA	413,038
Essex County, MA	412,136
Monroe County, NY	405,547
Mecklenburg County, NC	392,470
Essex County, NJ	388,166
Pierce County, WA	384,540
Multnomah County, OR	382,235
Jefferson County, KY	380,016
Ventura County, CA	377,884
DeKalb County, GA	365,721

Place	Number
New York, NY (city)	3,814,256
Los Angeles, CA (city) Los Angeles County	1,538,715
Chicago, IL (city) Cook County	1,304,122
Houston, TX (city) Harris County	845,709
Philadelphia, PA (city) Philadelphia County	688,107
San Diego, CA (city) San Diego County	645,200
Phoenix, AZ (city) Maricopa County	609,329
San Antonio, TX (city) Bexar County	522,459
Dallas, TX (city) Dallas County	516,743
San Francisco, CA (city) San Francisco County	483,740
San Jose, CA (city) Santa Clara County	447,071
Hempstead, NY (town) Nassau County	431,485
Indianapolis, IN (sp. city) Marion County	408,362
Detroit, MI (city) Wayne County	392,726
Jacksonville, FL (city) Duval County	385,300
Columbus, OH (city) Franklin County	369,376
Seattle, WA (city) King County	366,435
Austin, TX (city) Travis County	334,626
Portland, OR (city) Multnomah County	311,725
Memphis, TN (city) Shelby County	304,512
Charlotte, NC (city) Mecklenburg County	299,462
Boston, MA (city) Suffolk County	297,945
Denver, CO (city) Denver County	295,444
Nashville-Davidson, TN (sp. city) Davidson County	292,562
Milwaukee, WI (city) Milwaukee County	264,358
Oklahoma City, OK (city) Oklahoma County	262,938
Brookhaven, NY (town) Suffolk County	251,158
Albuquerque, NM (city) Bernalillo County	250,444
Las Vegas, NV (city) Clark County	245,804
Tucson, AZ (city) Pima County	242,013
Kansas City, MO (city) Jackson County	236,729
Fort Worth, TX (city) Tarrant County	236,466
El Paso, TX (city) El Paso County	229,053
New Orleans, LA (city) Orleans Parish	224,486
Honolulu, HI (cdp) Honolulu County	223,118
Tulsa, OK (city) Tulsa County	213,667
Omaha, NE (city) Douglas County	212,560
Colorado Springs, CO (city) El Paso County	207,770
Mesa, AZ (city) Maricopa County	207,509
Minneapolis, MN (city) Hennepin County	206,788
Atlanta, GA (city) Fulton County	206,294
Cleveland, OH (city) Cuyahoga County	204,829
Long Beach, CA (city) Los Angeles County	201,578
Sacramento, CA (city) Sacramento County	197,067
Oakland, CA (city) Alameda County	193,305
Oyster Bay, NY (town) Nassau County	184,305
Wichita, KS (city) Sedgwick County	181,390
Pittsburgh, PA (city) Allegheny County	177,831
Islip, NY (town) Suffolk County	173,016
Arlington, TX (city) Tarrant County	172,717
Fresno, CA (city) Fresno County	163,456
Cincinnati, OH (city) Hamilton County	159,012
St. Louis, MO (city) Saint Louis Independent City	158,236
Toledo, OH (city) Lucas County	157,014
Raleigh, NC (city) Wake County	154,408
Tampa, FL (city) Hillsborough County	153,114
Aurora, CO (city) Arapahoe County	146,565
St. Paul, MN (city) Ramsey County	145,922
Lexington-Fayette, KY (sp. city) Fayette County	143,483
St. Petersburg, FL (city) Pinellas County	143,458
Scottsdale, AZ (city) Maricopa County	140,883
Buffalo, NY (city) Erie County	136,475
Plano, TX (city) Collin County	135,274
Anaheim, CA (city) Orange County	134,633
North Hempstead, NY (town) Nassau County	133,811
Miami, FL (city) Miami-Dade County	133,069
Corpus Christi, TX (city) Nueces County	129,104
Louisville, KY (city) Jefferson County	128,869
Lincoln, NE (city) Lancaster County	123,067
Huntington, NY (town) Suffolk County	122,366
Arlington, VA (cdp) Arlington County	121,919
Fremont, CA (city) Alameda County	120,443
Greensboro, NC (city) Guilford County	119,951
Huntington Beach, CA (city) Orange County	118,233
Madison, WI (city) Dane County	117,185

Notes: Please refer to the User's Guide for an explanation of data; ranking tables include all places with Asian and/or NHPI populations above SF4 population thresholds; (1) tables reflect only those areas that meet SF4 population thresholds, therefore there may be less than 50 states, 75 counties or 75 places listed

Educational Attainment: High School Graduates

Total Population 25 Years and Over Who are High School Graduates

All States, Top 75 Counties, and Top 75 Places Sorted by Percent[1]

State	Percent
Alaska	88.33
Minnesota	87.95
Wyoming	87.86
Utah	87.73
New Hampshire	87.41
Montana	87.15
Washington	87.08
Colorado	86.93
Nebraska	86.58
Vermont	86.42
Iowa	86.10
Kansas	86.02
Maine	85.37
Oregon	85.13
Wisconsin	85.09
Massachusetts	84.76
Idaho	84.72
Hawaii	84.57
South Dakota	84.57
Connecticut	83.98
North Dakota	83.86
Maryland	83.83
Michigan	83.41
Ohio	82.97
Delaware	82.60
Indiana	82.13
New Jersey	82.07
Pennsylvania	81.90
Virginia	81.47
Illinois	81.43
Missouri	81.32
Arizona	80.97
Nevada	80.66
Oklahoma	80.61
United States	80.40
Florida	79.86
New York	79.06
New Mexico	78.85
Georgia	78.57
North Carolina	78.14
Rhode Island	77.96
District of Columbia	77.83
California	76.79
South Carolina	76.34
Tennessee	75.92
Texas	75.65
Arkansas	75.31
Alabama	75.27
West Virginia	75.21
Louisiana	74.81
Kentucky	74.12
Mississippi	72.86

County	Percent
Douglas County, CO	96.96
Los Alamos County, NM	96.33
Falls Church Independent City, VA	95.87
Johnson County, KS	94.91
Hamilton County, IN	94.19
Washington County, MN	94.02
Riley County, KS	93.84
Johnson County, IA	93.66
Story County, IA	93.53
Albany County, WY	93.45
Gallatin County, MT	93.35
Sarpy County, NE	93.27
Dakota County, MN	93.21
Juneau Borough, AK	93.17
Benton County, OR	93.12
Howard County, MD	93.10
Delaware County, OH	92.85
Whitman County, WA	92.81
Boulder County, CO	92.80
Loudoun County, VA	92.53
Fayette County, GA	92.37
Douglas County, KS	92.36
Larimer County, CO	92.32
Davis County, UT	92.25
Dane County, WI	92.16
Island County, WA	92.10
Waukesha County, WI	91.96
Ozaukee County, WI	91.85
Fairbanks North Star Borough, AK	91.83
Jefferson County, CO	91.82
Barnstable County, MA	91.81
Collin County, TX	91.81
Platte County, MO	91.76
York County, VA	91.68
St. Croix County, WI	91.59
Douglas County, NV	91.57
Washtenaw County, MI	91.53
Hunterdon County, NJ	91.50
Livingston County, MI	91.39
Carver County, MN	91.36
Tompkins County, NY	91.36
Norfolk County, MA	91.28
El Paso County, CO	91.25
Marin County, CA	91.25
Olmsted County, MN	91.11
Scott County, MN	91.04
Anoka County, MN	91.03
Missoula County, MT	90.99
Champaign County, IL	90.98
Latah County, ID	90.98
Cass County, ND	90.90
Utah County, UT	90.87
Ada County, ID	90.79
Kitsap County, WA	90.77
Fairfax County, VA	90.74
McLean County, IL	90.72
Arapahoe County, CO	90.66
Hennepin County, MN	90.65
Chittenden County, VT	90.62
Linn County, IA	90.58
Morris County, NJ	90.58
Lancaster County, NE	90.50
Rockingham County, NH	90.49
Placer County, CA	90.45
Virginia Beach Independent City, VA	90.45
Cache County, UT	90.41
Montgomery County, MD	90.32
Nevada County, CA	90.32
Anchorage Borough, AK	90.29
King County, WA	90.26
Brookings County, SD	90.25
Blaine County, ID	90.22
Putnam County, NY	90.16
Nicollet County, MN	90.14
Cumberland County, ME	90.13

Place	Percent
Forest Home, NY (cdp) Tompkins County	100.00
Superior, CO (town) Boulder County	99.17
Stanford, CA (cdp) Santa Clara County	99.06
Tamalpais-Homestead Valley, CA (cdp) Marin County	99.03
Winnetka, IL (village) Cook County	98.99
Munsey Park, NY (village) Nassau County	98.74
Tiburon, CA (town) Marin County	98.65
West Lake Sammamish, WA (cdp) King County	98.57
Cinco Ranch, TX (cdp) Fort Bend County	98.53
Newport Coast, CA (cdp) Orange County	98.50
Alamo, CA (cdp) Contra Costa County	98.37
Palos Verdes Estates, CA (city) Los Angeles County	98.35
Sammamish, WA (city) King County	98.35
University Park, TX (city) Dallas County	98.34
Wolf Trap, VA (cdp) Fairfax County	98.28
Plainsboro Center, NJ (cdp) Middlesex County	98.23
Fishers, IN (town) Hamilton County	98.16
Castlewood, CO (cdp) Arapahoe County	98.14
Piedmont, CA (city) Alameda County	98.13
Leawood, KS (city) Johnson County	98.09
Druid Hills, GA (cdp) De Kalb County	98.06
Germantown, TN (city) Shelby County	98.05
Boxborough, MA (town) Middlesex County	98.01
Chappaqua, NY (cdp) Westchester County	97.97
West University Place, TX (city) Harris County	97.96
Upper Arlington, OH (city) Franklin County	97.93
Highlands Ranch, CO (cdp) Douglas County	97.84
Kensington, CA (cdp) Contra Costa County	97.80
Orinda, CA (city) Contra Costa County	97.77
Acton, MA (town) Middlesex County	97.76
Berkeley Lake, GA (city) Gwinnett County	97.75
Mercer Island, WA (city) King County	97.74
Northeast Ithaca, NY (cdp) Tompkins County	97.74
East Hills, NY (village) Nassau County	97.73
Lafayette, CA (city) Contra Costa County	97.68
Lake Oswego, OR (city) Clackamas County	97.66
Wellesley, MA (town) Norfolk County	97.63
Kaneohe Station, HI (cdp) Honolulu County	97.58
Bunker Hill Village, TX (city) Harris County	97.55
Clayton, CA (city) Contra Costa County	97.51
Hermosa Beach, CA (city) Los Angeles County	97.49
Pullman, WA (city) Whitman County	97.49
Gold River, CA (cdp) Sacramento County	97.46
North Star, DE (cdp) New Castle County	97.45
Shenandoah, LA (cdp) East Baton Rouge Parish	97.44
Flower Mound, TX (town) Denton County	97.40
East Ithaca, NY (cdp) Tompkins County	97.39
Brentwood, TN (city) Williamson County	97.36
Portola Hills, CA (cdp) Orange County	97.34
Hinsdale, IL (village) Du Page County	97.33
Catalina Foothills, AZ (cdp) Pima County	97.32
Great Falls, VA (cdp) Fairfax County	97.32
Montgomery, NJ (township) Somerset County	97.32
El Dorado Hills, CA (cdp) El Dorado County	97.31
Plainsboro, NJ (township) Middlesex County	97.29
Fort Rucker, AL (cdp) Dale County	97.28
Dublin, OH (city) Franklin County	97.27
Hickam Housing, HI (cdp) Honolulu County	97.26
Hudson, OH (city) Summit County	97.25
Los Altos, CA (city) Santa Clara County	97.25
Long Grove, IL (village) Lake County	97.24
Larkspur, CA (city) Marin County	97.23
South Barrington, IL (village) Cook County	97.23
Eden Prairie, MN (city) Hennepin County	97.22
Lake Forest, IL (city) Lake County	97.22
Upper St. Clair, PA (township) Allegheny County	97.21
Calabasas, CA (city) Los Angeles County	97.20
Marina del Rey, CA (cdp) Los Angeles County	97.17
Ann Arbor, MI (township) Washtenaw County	97.13
Cottage Lake, WA (cdp) King County	97.13
Fort Bragg, NC (cdp) Cumberland County	97.12
Scarsdale, NY (village) Westchester County	97.11
Bainbridge Island, WA (city) Kitsap County	97.08
McLean, VA (cdp) Fairfax County	97.07
Moraga, CA (town) Contra Costa County	97.07

Notes: Please refer to the User's Guide for an explanation of data; ranking tables include all places with Asian and/or NHPI populations above SF4 population thresholds; (1) tables reflect only those areas that meet SF4 population thresholds, therefore there may be less than 50 states, 75 counties or 75 places listed

Educational Attainment: High School Graduates

Asians 25 Years and Over Who are High School Graduates

***All States, Top 75 Counties, and Top 75 Places Sorted by Number*[1]**

State	Number
United States	5,340,921
California	1,960,603
New York	508,574
Hawaii	302,581
Texas	287,359
New Jersey	279,179
Illinois	240,406
Washington	168,561
Florida	143,001
Virginia	142,432
Maryland	118,907
Massachusetts	110,603
Pennsylvania	103,777
Michigan	91,693
Georgia	86,749
Ohio	74,335
North Carolina	53,737
Nevada	50,969
Arizona	50,210
Oregon	50,156
Colorado	49,425
Minnesota	49,024
Connecticut	44,186
Missouri	32,256
Indiana	30,624
Wisconsin	28,887
Tennessee	28,061
Louisiana	22,500
Oklahoma	21,627
Kansas	20,371
South Carolina	18,462
Utah	17,679
Kentucky	16,089
Alabama	15,404
Iowa	14,974
Alaska	12,108
New Mexico	9,959
Nebraska	9,780
Delaware	9,616
Rhode Island	8,901
Arkansas	8,819
District of Columbia	8,083
New Hampshire	8,043
Mississippi	7,894
Idaho	6,279
West Virginia	5,364
Maine	3,367
Montana	2,184
South Dakota	1,929
Vermont	1,895
North Dakota	1,726
Wyoming	1,573

County	Number
Los Angeles County, CA	637,192
Honolulu County, HI	245,141
Santa Clara County, CA	244,928
Orange County, CA	205,628
Queens County, NY	201,479
Alameda County, CA	157,804
Cook County, IL	149,516
San Diego County, CA	130,772
San Francisco County, CA	118,501
King County, WA	101,247
Harris County, TX	89,039
San Mateo County, CA	88,220
Fairfax County, VA	70,859
New York County, NY	70,174
Kings County, NY	69,539
Contra Costa County, CA	60,536
Middlesex County, NJ	60,403
Montgomery County, MD	58,509
Sacramento County, CA	58,349
Bergen County, NJ	57,437
Middlesex County, MA	46,531
Dallas County, TX	45,172
San Bernardino County, CA	42,943
DuPage County, IL	41,883
Clark County, NV	41,211
Maricopa County, AZ	37,479
Nassau County, NY	34,757
Hudson County, NJ	32,589
Oakland County, MI	29,178
Solano County, CA	27,574
Riverside County, CA	27,541
Westchester County, NY	25,752
Philadelphia County, PA	24,136
Hawaii County, HI	24,102
Ventura County, CA	23,823
Tarrant County, TX	22,951
San Joaquin County, CA	21,948
Maui County, HI	21,334
Gwinnett County, GA	21,181
Fort Bend County, TX	20,755
Collin County, TX	20,742
Hennepin County, MN	20,402
Broward County, FL	19,872
Snohomish County, WA	19,103
Travis County, TX	19,051
Norfolk County, MA	18,957
Suffolk County, MA	18,876
Fresno County, CA	18,562
Suffolk County, NY	18,410
Morris County, NJ	18,254
Wayne County, MI	17,833
Franklin County, OH	17,546
Essex County, NJ	17,521
Bronx County, NY	17,416
Washington County, OR	17,055
Pierce County, WA	16,961
Miami-Dade County, FL	16,886
Multnomah County, OR	16,858
Montgomery County, PA	16,737
Prince George's County, MD	16,550
Fairfield County, CT	15,826
Orange County, FL	15,500
Somerset County, NJ	15,402
Lake County, IL	15,074
Cuyahoga County, OH	15,035
Monmouth County, NJ	14,156
Richmond County, NY	13,769
DeKalb County, GA	13,309
Baltimore County, MD	13,080
St. Louis County, MO	13,056
Monterey County, CA	13,055
Fulton County, GA	12,965
Bexar County, TX	12,584
Kauai County, HI	11,989
Allegheny County, PA	11,954

Place	Number
New York, NY (city)	372,377
Los Angeles, CA (city) Los Angeles County	211,832
Honolulu, HI (cdp) Honolulu County	127,006
San Jose, CA (city) Santa Clara County	125,491
San Francisco, CA (city) San Francisco County	118,501
San Diego, CA (city) San Diego County	84,066
Chicago, IL (city) Cook County	69,751
Houston, TX (city) Harris County	54,429
Fremont, CA (city) Alameda County	45,807
Seattle, WA (city) King County	37,263
Daly City, CA (city) San Mateo County	30,006
Sunnyvale, CA (city) Santa Clara County	28,568
Sacramento, CA (city) Sacramento County	25,513
Torrance, CA (city) Los Angeles County	25,227
Oakland, CA (city) Alameda County	24,448
Philadelphia, PA (city) Philadelphia County	24,136
Long Beach, CA (city) Los Angeles County	22,732
Irvine, CA (city) Orange County	22,338
Garden Grove, CA (city) Orange County	21,984
Anaheim, CA (city) Orange County	21,941
Jersey City, NJ (city) Hudson County	21,923
Alhambra, CA (city) Los Angeles County	20,489
Glendale, CA (city) Los Angeles County	20,118
Monterey Park, CA (city) Los Angeles County	19,276
Milpitas, CA (city) Santa Clara County	18,646
Santa Clara, CA (city) Santa Clara County	18,355
Cerritos, CA (city) Los Angeles County	17,944
Boston, MA (city) Suffolk County	17,629
Dallas, TX (city) Dallas County	17,275
Edison, NJ (township) Middlesex County	16,835
Austin, TX (city) Travis County	16,212
Union City, CA (city) Alameda County	16,154
Vallejo, CA (city) Solano County	15,330
Portland, OR (city) Multnomah County	14,896
Rowland Heights, CA (cdp) Los Angeles County	14,575
Stockton, CA (city) San Joaquin County	14,462
Hempstead, NY (town) Nassau County	14,362
Hayward, CA (city) Alameda County	14,229
Diamond Bar, CA (city) Los Angeles County	13,873
Westminster, CA (city) Orange County	13,864
Plano, TX (city) Collin County	13,713
Phoenix, AZ (city) Maricopa County	13,615
Arcadia, CA (city) Los Angeles County	13,582
Cupertino, CA (city) Santa Clara County	13,582
Columbus, OH (city) Franklin County	13,017
Las Vegas, NV (city) Clark County	12,845
West Covina, CA (city) Los Angeles County	12,785
Santa Ana, CA (city) Orange County	12,075
Fresno, CA (city) Fresno County	12,066
Bellevue, WA (city) King County	11,847
Fullerton, CA (city) Orange County	11,658
Hacienda Heights, CA (cdp) Los Angeles County	11,489
Pearl City, HI (cdp) Honolulu County	11,468
North Hempstead, NY (town) Nassau County	11,451
Chula Vista, CA (city) San Diego County	11,264
Carson, CA (city) Los Angeles County	11,263
Huntington Beach, CA (city) Orange County	10,859
Jacksonville, FL (city) Duval County	10,604
South San Francisco, CA (city) San Mateo County	10,597
Alameda, CA (city) Alameda County	10,480
Gardena, CA (city) Los Angeles County	10,447
Waimalu, HI (cdp) Honolulu County	10,433
Waipahu, HI (cdp) Honolulu County	10,347
Hilo, HI (cdp) Hawaii County	10,337
Mountain View, CA (city) Santa Clara County	10,298
San Antonio, TX (city) Bexar County	10,255
San Leandro, CA (city) Alameda County	9,870
San Mateo, CA (city) San Mateo County	9,675
Buena Park, CA (city) Orange County	9,632
Kaneohe, HI (cdp) Honolulu County	9,549
Irving, TX (city) Dallas County	9,548
Walnut, CA (city) Los Angeles County	9,481
Arlington, VA (cdp) Arlington County	9,476
Pasadena, CA (city) Los Angeles County	9,328
San Gabriel, CA (city) Los Angeles County	8,901

Notes: Please refer to the User's Guide for an explanation of data; ranking tables include all places with Asian and/or NHPI populations above SF4 population thresholds; (1) tables reflect only those areas that meet SF4 population thresholds, therefore there may be less than 50 states, 75 counties or 75 places listed

Educational Attainment: High School Graduates

Asians 25 Years and Over Who are High School Graduates

All States, Top 75 Counties, and Top 75 Places Sorted by Percent[1]

State	Percent
West Virginia	90.35
New Jersey	88.50
Delaware	88.10
Illinois	86.88
Ohio	86.58
Indiana	86.19
Kentucky	86.19
Michigan	85.60
Maryland	85.53
Montana	85.25
Connecticut	85.01
New Hampshire	84.88
North Dakota	84.36
Virginia	84.15
Arizona	83.39
New Mexico	83.08
Wyoming	82.36
Missouri	82.22
Tennessee	82.13
Idaho	82.04
Nevada	81.97
District of Columbia	81.85
Colorado	81.80
Alabama	81.08
Texas	80.71
Florida	80.66
California	80.55
Washington	80.55
United States	80.43
Utah	79.92
Hawaii	79.90
South Carolina	79.52
Georgia	79.51
Oregon	79.46
North Carolina	79.31
Pennsylvania	78.40
Vermont	78.37
Nebraska	77.66
Oklahoma	77.21
Massachusetts	76.21
Kansas	74.82
Maine	74.61
Iowa	74.29
New York	73.33
Wisconsin	73.19
Alaska	73.05
Arkansas	72.90
Mississippi	72.49
South Dakota	72.27
Minnesota	71.11
Rhode Island	69.20
Louisiana	67.43

County	Percent
Addison County, VT	100.00
Sauk County, WI	100.00
Weakley County, TN	100.00
Newton County, GA	99.06
Monongalia County, WV	98.87
Portage County, OH	98.69
Jackson County, IL	97.75
Eagle County, CO	97.71
Washington County, TN	97.67
Story County, IA	97.51
Monroe County, IN	97.24
Orange County, NC	97.05
Charlottesville Independent City, VA	97.02
Albany County, WY	97.01
Athens County, OH	96.87
Montgomery County, VA	96.86
Geauga County, OH	96.85
Alachua County, FL	96.81
Jessamine County, KY	96.69
Oktibbeha County, MS	96.19
Tompkins County, NY	96.15
North Slope Borough, AK	96.13
Brazos County, TX	96.12
St. Croix County, WI	96.08
Centre County, PA	96.06
Putnam County, NY	95.94
Crow Wing County, MN	95.88
Anderson County, TN	95.76
Raleigh County, WV	95.64
Hancock County, OH	95.49
Payne County, OK	95.43
Warren County, OH	95.42
Hunterdon County, NJ	95.34
Bartholomew County, IN	95.24
McLean County, IL	95.14
Nacogdoches County, TX	95.11
Boone County, KY	95.04
Phelps County, MO	94.96
Washtenaw County, MI	94.95
Grant County, WI	94.94
Midland County, MI	94.83
Bristol County, RI	94.69
Jackson County, MI	94.61
Bulloch County, GA	94.59
Durham County, NC	94.51
Los Alamos County, NM	94.51
Riley County, KS	94.45
Lincoln Parish, LA	94.22
Somerset County, NJ	94.12
Isabella County, MI	94.08
Gallatin County, MT	94.01
Christian County, KY	94.00
Comal County, TX	93.93
Roanoke County, VA	93.84
Collin County, TX	93.78
Tippecanoe County, IN	93.76
Douglas County, KS	93.70
Hamilton County, IN	93.56
McDonough County, IL	93.48
Whitman County, WA	93.46
Albemarle County, VA	93.41
Houghton County, MI	93.33
DeKalb County, IL	93.32
Delaware County, OH	93.31
Kalamazoo County, MI	93.19
Pickens County, SC	93.14
Lee County, AL	93.13
Latah County, ID	93.05
Clarke County, GA	93.03
Chester County, PA	92.87
Lake County, IL	92.81
Kanawha County, WV	92.79
Forsyth County, GA	92.75
Delaware County, IN	92.73
Penobscot County, ME	92.70

Place	Percent
Algonquin, IL (village) McHenry County	100.00
Ardsley, NY (village) Westchester County	100.00
Auburn, AL (city) Lee County	100.00
Audubon, PA (cdp) Montgomery County	100.00
Boxborough, MA (town) Middlesex County	100.00
Budd Lake, NJ (cdp) Morris County	100.00
Cape Girardeau, MO (city) Cape Girardeau County	100.00
Cheney, WA (city) Spokane County	100.00
Clifton Park, NY (town) Saratoga County	100.00
Crofton, MD (cdp) Anne Arundel County	100.00
East Ithaca, NY (cdp) Tompkins County	100.00
East Moline, IL (city) Rock Island County	100.00
Forest Home, NY (cdp) Tompkins County	100.00
Franklin Lakes, NJ (borough) Bergen County	100.00
Galt, CA (city) Sacramento County	100.00
Heathcote, NJ (cdp) Middlesex County	100.00
Kent, OH (city) Portage County	100.00
Larkspur, CA (city) Marin County	100.00
Las Flores, CA (cdp) Orange County	100.00
Lauderdale, MN (city) Ramsey County	100.00
Long Grove, IL (village) Lake County	100.00
Long Hill, NJ (township) Morris County	100.00
Louisville, CO (city) Boulder County	100.00
Mansfield, CT (town) Tolland County	100.00
Marshfield, WI (city) Wood County	100.00
Martin, TN (city) Weakley County	100.00
Morgantown, WV (city) Monongalia County	100.00
Munsey Park, NY (village) Nassau County	100.00
Newport Coast, CA (cdp) Orange County	100.00
Northeast Ithaca, NY (cdp) Tompkins County	100.00
Oshtemo, MI (township) Kalamazoo County	100.00
Piermont, NY (village) Rockland County	100.00
Prospect Heights, IL (city) Cook County	100.00
Rossmoor, CA (cdp) Orange County	100.00
Scio, MI (township) Washtenaw County	100.00
Scott, PA (township) Allegheny County	100.00
Scott Township, PA (cdp) Allegheny County	100.00
Stoneham, MA (town) Middlesex County	100.00
Storrs, CT (cdp) Tolland County	100.00
Tiburon, CA (town) Marin County	100.00
Upper Macungie, PA (township) Lehigh County	100.00
Oro Valley, AZ (town) Pima County	99.70
Westford, MA (town) Middlesex County	99.34
Wildwood, MO (city) Saint Louis County	99.32
North Druid Hills, GA (cdp) De Kalb County	99.30
Marina del Rey, CA (cdp) Los Angeles County	99.16
Stanford, CA (cdp) Santa Clara County	99.13
East Lansing, MI (city) Ingham County	99.03
South Barrington, IL (village) Cook County	99.01
Somers, NY (town) Westchester County	98.99
McCandless, PA (township) Allegheny County	98.89
El Segundo, CA (city) Los Angeles County	98.88
Wayland, MA (town) Middlesex County	98.88
Plainsboro Center, NJ (cdp) Middlesex County	98.87
Valley Cottage, NY (cdp) Rockland County	98.87
Pike Creek, DE (cdp) New Castle County	98.84
Bronxville, NY (village) Westchester County	98.80
Ridgefield, CT (town) Fairfield County	98.75
Woodbridge, CT (town) New Haven County	98.75
Frisco, TX (city) Collin County	98.74
Sammamish, WA (city) King County	98.72
Laguna Beach, CA (city) Orange County	98.71
Carbondale, IL (city) Jackson County	98.68
Clayton, CA (city) Contra Costa County	98.67
Schererville, IN (town) Lake County	98.67
Newark, DE (city) New Castle County	98.64
Manchester, MO (city) Saint Louis County	98.63
Lower Makefield, PA (township) Bucks County	98.61
Randolph, NJ (township) Morris County	98.61
Fort Bragg, NC (cdp) Cumberland County	98.60
Elmwood Park, IL (village) Cook County	98.57
Huntington, VA (cdp) Fairfax County	98.54
Andover, MA (town) Essex County	98.51
Hermosa Beach, CA (city) Los Angeles County	98.50
Clayton, MO (city) Saint Louis County	98.48

Notes: Please refer to the User's Guide for an explanation of data; ranking tables include all places with Asian and/or NHPI populations above SF4 population thresholds; (1) tables reflect only those areas that meet SF4 population thresholds, therefore there may be less than 50 states, 75 counties or 75 places listed

Educational Attainment: High School Graduates

Native Hawaiian and Other Pacific Islanders 25 Years and Over Who are High School Graduates

All States, Top 75 Counties, and Top 75 Places Sorted by Number[1]

State	Number
United States	161,732
Hawaii	50,133
California	47,954
Washington	9,621
Texas	5,098
Utah	4,692
Nevada	3,670
Oregon	3,387
New York	3,238
Florida	2,930
Arizona	2,571
Colorado	1,984
Virginia	1,793
North Carolina	1,601
Pennsylvania	1,557
Illinois	1,532
Georgia	1,499
Missouri	1,366
New Jersey	1,159
Ohio	1,070
Maryland	1,003
Alaska	1,002
Michigan	995
Tennessee	942
Massachusetts	855
Minnesota	830
Oklahoma	766
Indiana	715
Louisiana	664
New Mexico	661
South Carolina	634
Kansas	633
Wisconsin	626
Connecticut	562
Kentucky	507
Alabama	451
Idaho	446
Arkansas	388
Iowa	346
Mississippi	309
Nebraska	210
Montana	200
West Virginia	161
Maine	155
Rhode Island	123
Delaware	80

County	Number
Honolulu County, HI	34,509
Los Angeles County, CA	10,732
Hawaii County, HI	7,328
San Diego County, CA	6,585
Maui County, HI	5,893
Orange County, CA	3,790
Alameda County, CA	3,667
King County, WA	3,560
San Mateo County, CA	3,341
Salt Lake County, UT	3,226
Clark County, NV	3,000
Santa Clara County, CA	2,763
Kauai County, HI	2,374
Sacramento County, CA	2,351
Pierce County, WA	2,316
San Bernardino County, CA	2,048
Riverside County, CA	1,651
Maricopa County, AZ	1,635
Solano County, CA	1,472
Contra Costa County, CA	1,455
San Francisco County, CA	1,291
Multnomah County, OR	1,010
Ventura County, CA	899
Kitsap County, WA	830
Monterey County, CA	829
Washington County, OR	766
San Joaquin County, CA	724
Harris County, TX	699
Tarrant County, TX	678
Stanislaus County, CA	644
Anchorage Borough, AK	626
El Paso County, CO	620
Utah County, UT	615
Snohomish County, WA	610
Thurston County, WA	610
Cook County, IL	600
Queens County, NY	584
Bell County, TX	558
Clark County, WA	537
Bexar County, TX	517
Kings County, NY	483
Washoe County, NV	472
Pima County, AZ	452
Fairfax County, VA	446
Jackson County, MO	419
Davis County, UT	388
Bronx County, NY	370
Santa Barbara County, CA	359
Dallas County, TX	356
Broward County, FL	346
Sonoma County, CA	341
Spokane County, WA	330
Orange County, FL	327
Allegheny County, PA	325
Hennepin County, MN	316
Kern County, CA	315
Marion County, OR	309
Arapahoe County, CO	306
Bernalillo County, NM	298
Clackamas County, OR	287
Montgomery County, MD	287
Philadelphia County, PA	286
Essex County, NJ	270
Travis County, TX	267
Yolo County, CA	257
Miami-Dade County, FL	252
Suffolk County, NY	244
Hillsborough County, FL	237
Cumberland County, NC	227
New York County, NY	227
Lane County, OR	225
Shelby County, TN	222
Duval County, FL	220
El Paso County, TX	218
Jefferson County, CO	214

Place	Number
Honolulu, HI (cdp) Honolulu County	11,854
San Diego, CA (city) San Diego County	3,011
Los Angeles, CA (city) Los Angeles County	2,963
Hilo, HI (cdp) Hawaii County	2,198
Kaneohe, HI (cdp) Honolulu County	2,047
New York, NY (city)	1,791
Long Beach, CA (city) Los Angeles County	1,708
Nanakuli, HI (cdp) Honolulu County	1,564
Kailua, HI (cdp) Honolulu County	1,529
San Jose, CA (city) Santa Clara County	1,463
San Francisco, CA (city) San Francisco County	1,291
Sacramento, CA (city) Sacramento County	1,280
Waianae, HI (cdp) Honolulu County	1,213
Waipahu, HI (cdp) Honolulu County	1,205
Waimanalo Beach, HI (cdp) Honolulu County	1,124
Oceanside, CA (city) San Diego County	1,041
Seattle, WA (city) King County	1,025
Salt Lake City, UT (city) Salt Lake County	961
Hayward, CA (city) Alameda County	945
West Valley City, UT (city) Salt Lake County	883
Pearl City, HI (cdp) Honolulu County	860
Las Vegas, NV (city) Clark County	826
Portland, OR (city) Multnomah County	804
Phoenix, AZ (city) Maricopa County	787
Waimalu, HI (cdp) Honolulu County	760
Oakland, CA (city) Alameda County	699
Carson, CA (city) Los Angeles County	696
Halawa, HI (cdp) Honolulu County	680
Mililani Town, HI (cdp) Honolulu County	679
Kahului, HI (cdp) Maui County	670
Laie, HI (cdp) Honolulu County	654
East Palo Alto, CA (city) San Mateo County	652
Makakilo City, HI (cdp) Honolulu County	650
Wahiawa, HI (cdp) Honolulu County	647
Vallejo, CA (city) Solano County	638
Ewa Beach, HI (cdp) Honolulu County	636
Kailua, HI (cdp) Hawaii County	609
Makaha, HI (cdp) Honolulu County	594
Maili, HI (cdp) Honolulu County	589
Tacoma, WA (city) Pierce County	574
Kihei, HI (cdp) Maui County	565
Fairfield, CA (city) Solano County	540
Wailuku, HI (cdp) Maui County	533
Hauula, HI (cdp) Honolulu County	521
Santa Ana, CA (city) Orange County	517
Waimea, HI (cdp) Hawaii County	511
San Mateo, CA (city) San Mateo County	488
Riverside, CA (city) Riverside County	487
Waihee-Waiehu, HI (cdp) Maui County	483
Daly City, CA (city) San Mateo County	470
San Bruno, CA (city) San Mateo County	468
Henderson, NV (city) Clark County	466
Anahola, HI (cdp) Kauai County	456
Anaheim, CA (city) Orange County	449
Lahaina, HI (cdp) Maui County	448
Oxnard, CA (city) Ventura County	447
Killeen, TX (city) Bell County	440
Modesto, CA (city) Stanislaus County	427
Waimanalo, HI (cdp) Honolulu County	425
Fremont, CA (city) Alameda County	424
Chula Vista, CA (city) San Diego County	420
Garden Grove, CA (city) Orange County	419
Kualapuu, HI (cdp) Maui County	414
Stockton, CA (city) San Joaquin County	396
Houston, TX (city) Harris County	388
South San Francisco, CA (city) San Mateo County	372
San Antonio, TX (city) Bexar County	370
Kapaa, HI (cdp) Kauai County	367
Vancouver, WA (city) Clark County	367
Alameda, CA (city) Alameda County	364
Paradise, NV (cdp) Clark County	363
Ahuimanu, HI (cdp) Honolulu County	359
Federal Way, WA (city) King County	359
Colorado Springs, CO (city) El Paso County	357
Lakewood, CA (city) Los Angeles County	357

Notes: Please refer to the User's Guide for an explanation of data; ranking tables include all places with Asian and/or NHPI populations above SF4 population thresholds; (1) tables reflect only those areas that meet SF4 population thresholds, therefore there may be less than 50 states, 75 counties or 75 places listed

Educational Attainment: High School Graduates

Native Hawaiian and Other Pacific Islanders 25 Years and Over Who are High School Graduates

All States, Top 75 Counties, and Top 75 Places Sorted by Percent[1]

State	Percent
Kansas	88.66
Virginia	88.06
West Virginia	86.10
Colorado	84.17
Arizona	83.80
Missouri	83.80
Washington	82.95
North Carolina	82.57
Oregon	82.15
Maryland	81.02
Hawaii	80.95
Maine	80.31
Connecticut	80.29
Nevada	80.27
Mississippi	80.26
Idaho	80.07
Montana	80.00
Louisiana	79.71
Wisconsin	78.74
Iowa	78.64
Ohio	78.50
Minnesota	78.30
United States	78.25
New Mexico	78.13
Kentucky	78.12
Indiana	76.96
Pennsylvania	76.74
Utah	76.72
Massachusetts	76.41
California	76.02
Alaska	75.79
Oklahoma	75.17
Texas	74.69
Michigan	73.49
Tennessee	73.08
South Carolina	72.46
Florida	71.53
Georgia	71.35
New York	70.90
Alabama	70.58
Illinois	70.53
Arkansas	69.16
New Jersey	68.74
Nebraska	61.95
Rhode Island	57.75
Delaware	53.33

County	Percent
Coryell County, TX	100.00
Fairfax County, VA	94.09
Jefferson County, CO	93.04
Allegheny County, PA	92.86
El Paso County, CO	92.54
Franklin County, OH	92.31
Washington County, UT	91.50
Onslow County, NC	91.11
Kitsap County, WA	90.91
Muscogee County, GA	90.59
Davis County, UT	89.81
Ventura County, CA	88.83
Sedgwick County, KS	88.26
Ada County, ID	88.24
Clark County, WA	86.75
Washington County, OR	86.75
Spokane County, WA	86.61
Pierce County, WA	86.19
Thurston County, WA	86.04
Montgomery County, MD	85.93
Bell County, TX	85.19
Jackson County, MO	84.99
Hennepin County, MN	84.72
Cumberland County, NC	84.70
Maricopa County, AZ	84.58
Clackamas County, OR	84.41
San Diego County, CA	84.37
Utah County, UT	83.56
Bernalillo County, NM	83.47
Snohomish County, WA	83.22
Essex County, NJ	83.08
Clark County, NV	82.49
Kauai County, HI	81.86
Hawaii County, HI	81.85
Suffolk County, NY	81.61
Honolulu County, HI	81.37
Contra Costa County, CA	81.19
Arapahoe County, CO	80.74
Multnomah County, OR	80.61
Harris County, TX	80.53
Santa Clara County, CA	80.53
Orange County, CA	80.01
St. Louis County, MO	80.00
Kern County, CA	79.75
Monterey County, CA	79.71
Orange County, FL	79.56
Pima County, AZ	79.44
King County, WA	79.32
Washington County, AR	78.95
Broward County, FL	78.82
San Bernardino County, CA	78.59
Bexar County, TX	78.10
Tarrant County, TX	78.02
Maui County, HI	77.75
Duval County, FL	76.92
Marion County, OR	76.87
San Joaquin County, CA	76.86
Sonoma County, CA	76.29
Denver County, CO	76.23
Anchorage Borough, AK	75.88
Alameda County, CA	75.28
Lane County, OR	75.25
Riverside County, CA	74.84
Philadelphia County, PA	74.67
Travis County, TX	74.58
Solano County, CA	74.53
Los Angeles County, CA	74.07
Salt Lake County, UT	73.19
Hillsborough County, FL	72.92
El Paso County, TX	72.67
Davidson County, TN	72.09
Queens County, NY	71.13
Washoe County, NV	69.93
Yolo County, CA	69.65
Santa Barbara County, CA	69.57

Place	Percent
Holualoa, HI (cdp) Hawaii County	98.62
Aiea, HI (cdp) Honolulu County	95.24
Mililani Town, HI (cdp) Honolulu County	95.23
Fremont, CA (city) Alameda County	95.07
Waipio, HI (cdp) Honolulu County	94.80
Spokane, WA (city) Spokane County	94.67
Waimanalo, HI (cdp) Honolulu County	94.03
Henderson, NV (city) Clark County	92.64
Waikane, HI (cdp) Honolulu County	92.50
Makawao, HI (cdp) Maui County	92.49
Hanapepe, HI (cdp) Kauai County	92.13
Kailua, HI (cdp) Honolulu County	91.72
Lakewood, WA (city) Pierce County	91.69
Vancouver, WA (city) Clark County	91.52
Mesa, AZ (city) Maricopa County	91.30
Spring Valley, NV (cdp) Clark County	90.78
Village Park, HI (cdp) Honolulu County	90.78
Columbus, GA (sp. city) Muscogee County	90.59
St. George, UT (city) Washington County	90.08
Ahuimanu, HI (cdp) Honolulu County	89.75
Hawaiian Paradise Park, HI (cdp) Hawaii County	89.60
Milpitas, CA (city) Santa Clara County	89.49
Kaneohe, HI (cdp) Honolulu County	89.12
Lakewood, CA (city) Los Angeles County	88.59
Spanaway, WA (cdp) Pierce County	88.54
Fort Lewis, WA (cdp) Pierce County	88.37
Makaha Valley, HI (cdp) Honolulu County	88.11
Laie, HI (cdp) Honolulu County	88.02
Kilauea, HI (cdp) Kauai County	87.72
Colorado Springs, CO (city) El Paso County	87.71
Kansas City, MO (city) Jackson County	87.65
Hawaiian Ocean View, HI (cdp) Hawaii County	87.50
Makakilo City, HI (cdp) Honolulu County	87.48
Oxnard, CA (city) Ventura County	86.80
Haleiwa, HI (cdp) Honolulu County	86.58
Oceanside, CA (city) San Diego County	86.53
Vista, CA (city) San Diego County	86.50
Huntington Beach, CA (city) Orange County	86.44
Pittsburg, CA (city) Contra Costa County	86.26
Kapaau, HI (cdp) Hawaii County	85.96
Makaha, HI (cdp) Honolulu County	85.84
Hawaiian Beaches, HI (cdp) Hawaii County	85.83
Papaikou, HI (cdp) Hawaii County	85.71
San Diego, CA (city) San Diego County	85.56
Phoenix, AZ (city) Maricopa County	85.45
Kapaa, HI (cdp) Kauai County	85.15
Waimalu, HI (cdp) Honolulu County	85.01
San Bruno, CA (city) San Mateo County	84.94
Maunawili, HI (cdp) Honolulu County	84.75
Waikapu, HI (cdp) Maui County	84.75
Hilo, HI (cdp) Hawaii County	84.47
Union City, CA (city) Alameda County	84.32
Taylorsville, UT (city) Salt Lake County	84.12
Bakersfield, CA (city) Kern County	83.78
Waikoloa Village, HI (cdp) Hawaii County	83.77
Kaaawa, HI (cdp) Honolulu County	83.72
Anahola, HI (cdp) Kauai County	83.67
Daly City, CA (city) San Mateo County	83.48
Waihee-Waiehu, HI (cdp) Maui County	83.28
Westminster, CA (city) Orange County	83.17
Waimanalo Beach, HI (cdp) Honolulu County	83.07
Provo, UT (city) Utah County	83.00
Waimea, HI (cdp) Hawaii County	82.82
Santa Clara, CA (city) Santa Clara County	82.80
Austin, TX (city) Travis County	82.66
Paia, HI (cdp) Maui County	82.52
West Jordan, UT (city) Salt Lake County	82.47
Orem, UT (city) Utah County	82.43
Waianae, HI (cdp) Honolulu County	82.35
Kailua, HI (cdp) Hawaii County	82.19
Killeen, TX (city) Bell County	81.94
Hana, HI (cdp) Maui County	81.88
Chula Vista, CA (city) San Diego County	81.87
Pearl City, HI (cdp) Honolulu County	81.59
Springdale, AR (city) Washington County	81.55

Notes: Please refer to the User's Guide for an explanation of data; ranking tables include all places with Asian and/or NHPI populations above SF4 population thresholds; (1) tables reflect only those areas that meet SF4 population thresholds, therefore there may be less than 50 states, 75 counties or 75 places listed

Educational Attainment: High School Graduates

Asian Indians 25 Years and Over Who are High School Graduates

All States, Top 75 Counties, and Top 75 Places Sorted by Number[1]

State	Number
United States	906,483
California	169,100
New York	123,734
New Jersey	95,797
Texas	70,213
Illinois	67,930
Florida	37,097
Michigan	31,318
Pennsylvania	30,570
Maryland	29,433
Virginia	27,869
Georgia	24,647
Massachusetts	24,363
Ohio	22,734
North Carolina	14,254
Connecticut	14,003
Washington	12,358
Minnesota	9,381
Arizona	8,268
Indiana	7,762
Colorado	7,267
Missouri	7,002
Tennessee	6,778
Wisconsin	6,230
Oregon	5,794
Louisiana	4,608
Kansas	4,284
Oklahoma	4,267
South Carolina	4,227
Kentucky	3,854
Alabama	3,793
Delaware	3,218
Iowa	3,022
Nevada	2,725
New Hampshire	2,217
Mississippi	1,810
Nebraska	1,806
District of Columbia	1,593
Arkansas	1,558
West Virginia	1,528
New Mexico	1,468
Utah	1,445
Rhode Island	1,269
Hawaii	886
Idaho	621
North Dakota	560
Maine	456
Vermont	318
South Dakota	288
Alaska	263
Wyoming	251
Montana	246

County	Number
Queens County, NY	50,401
Santa Clara County, CA	41,274
Cook County, IL	37,972
Los Angeles County, CA	33,497
Middlesex County, NJ	31,877
Alameda County, CA	24,110
Harris County, TX	19,776
DuPage County, IL	18,127
Montgomery County, MD	15,197
Fairfax County, VA	15,018
Orange County, CA	14,733
Dallas County, TX	13,377
Middlesex County, MA	13,247
Nassau County, NY	12,658
Oakland County, MI	12,378
Kings County, NY	11,244
Hudson County, NJ	10,481
Bergen County, NJ	10,222
Westchester County, NY	8,384
New York County, NY	8,351
King County, WA	8,298
Wayne County, MI	7,651
San Mateo County, CA	7,102
Broward County, FL	7,050
Fort Bend County, TX	6,733
Maricopa County, AZ	6,712
Morris County, NJ	6,382
Contra Costa County, CA	6,247
Somerset County, NJ	6,192
Bronx County, NY	6,115
Gwinnett County, GA	6,055
Sacramento County, CA	5,963
San Diego County, CA	5,756
Suffolk County, NY	5,587
Cuyahoga County, OH	5,549
Collin County, TX	5,518
Philadelphia County, PA	5,466
Tarrant County, TX	5,366
Fairfield County, CT	5,255
Essex County, NJ	4,942
Franklin County, OH	4,880
Allegheny County, PA	4,826
Miami-Dade County, FL	4,621
Hennepin County, MN	4,576
Travis County, TX	4,543
Montgomery County, PA	4,318
San Bernardino County, CA	4,161
Passaic County, NJ	4,110
DeKalb County, GA	4,107
Wake County, NC	4,101
Monmouth County, NJ	4,068
Fulton County, GA	4,037
Orange County, FL	4,011
Prince George's County, MD	3,918
Union County, NJ	3,905
Mercer County, NJ	3,809
Hartford County, CT	3,748
Richmond County, NY	3,642
St. Louis County, MO	3,586
Washington County, OR	3,546
Baltimore County, MD	3,521
New Haven County, CT	3,324
Bucks County, PA	3,290
Lake County, IL	3,287
Norfolk County, MA	3,277
Denton County, TX	3,263
Cobb County, GA	3,236
Hillsborough County, FL	3,170
Rockland County, NY	3,088
Mecklenburg County, NC	3,060
San Francisco County, CA	2,993
Macomb County, MI	2,982
Palm Beach County, FL	2,938
Camden County, NJ	2,897
New Castle County, DE	2,885

Place	Number
New York, NY (city)	79,753
San Jose, CA (city) Santa Clara County	14,880
Los Angeles, CA (city) Los Angeles County	13,137
Fremont, CA (city) Alameda County	12,909
Chicago, IL (city) Cook County	12,640
Houston, TX (city) Harris County	11,565
Edison, NJ (township) Middlesex County	9,784
Sunnyvale, CA (city) Santa Clara County	8,774
Jersey City, NJ (city) Hudson County	6,788
Santa Clara, CA (city) Santa Clara County	5,892
Hempstead, NY (town) Nassau County	5,513
Philadelphia, PA (city) Philadelphia County	5,466
Woodbridge, NJ (township) Middlesex County	5,419
Dallas, TX (city) Dallas County	4,330
North Hempstead, NY (town) Nassau County	4,083
Austin, TX (city) Travis County	3,993
San Diego, CA (city) San Diego County	3,893
Irving, TX (city) Dallas County	3,842
Columbus, OH (city) Franklin County	3,693
Plano, TX (city) Collin County	3,600
Piscataway, NJ (township) Middlesex County	3,413
San Francisco, CA (city) San Francisco County	2,993
Schaumburg, IL (village) Cook County	2,987
Troy, MI (city) Oakland County	2,912
Cupertino, CA (city) Santa Clara County	2,846
Oyster Bay, NY (town) Nassau County	2,829
Milpitas, CA (city) Santa Clara County	2,709
Naperville, IL (city) Du Page County	2,709
Union City, CA (city) Alameda County	2,669
Charlotte, NC (city) Mecklenburg County	2,566
Phoenix, AZ (city) Maricopa County	2,512
Irvine, CA (city) Orange County	2,421
Farmington Hills, MI (city) Oakland County	2,370
Parsippany-Troy Hills, NJ (township) Morris County	2,356
Sugar Land, TX (city) Fort Bend County	2,338
Arlington, VA (cdp) Arlington County	2,312
Yonkers, NY (city) Westchester County	2,292
Carrollton, TX (city) Denton County	2,289
South Brunswick, NJ (township) Middlesex County	2,279
Anaheim, CA (city) Orange County	2,132
Mountain View, CA (city) Santa Clara County	2,102
Plainsboro, NJ (township) Middlesex County	2,101
Franklin, NJ (township) Somerset County	2,019
Stamford, CT (city) Fairfield County	1,969
Cary, NC (town) Wake County	1,952
Canton, MI (township) Wayne County	1,935
Indianapolis, IN (sp. city) Marion County	1,925
Boston, MA (city) Suffolk County	1,884
North Brunswick, NJ (township) Middlesex County	1,866
Skokie, IL (village) Cook County	1,853
Brookhaven, NY (town) Suffolk County	1,836
Oklahoma City, OK (city) Oklahoma County	1,775
Hayward, CA (city) Alameda County	1,765
Seattle, WA (city) King County	1,756
San Antonio, TX (city) Bexar County	1,755
Bellevue, WA (city) King County	1,754
Cerritos, CA (city) Los Angeles County	1,732
Mount Prospect, IL (village) Cook County	1,719
Jacksonville, FL (city) Duval County	1,661
Greenburgh, NY (town) Westchester County	1,628
Sacramento, CA (city) Sacramento County	1,608
Arlington, TX (city) Tarrant County	1,573
Old Bridge, NJ (township) Middlesex County	1,571
Iselin, NJ (cdp) Middlesex County	1,548
Ann Arbor, MI (city) Washtenaw County	1,542
East Brunswick, NJ (township) Middlesex County	1,530
Sayreville, NJ (borough) Middlesex County	1,522
Hoffman Estates, IL (village) Cook County	1,505
Detroit, MI (city) Wayne County	1,502
Garland, TX (city) Dallas County	1,479
Durham, NC (city) Durham County	1,472
Nashville-Davidson, TN (sp. city) Davidson County	1,447
Fort Worth, TX (city) Tarrant County	1,429
Memphis, TN (city) Shelby County	1,423
Torrance, CA (city) Los Angeles County	1,417

Notes: Please refer to the User's Guide for an explanation of data; ranking tables include all places with Asian and/or NHPI populations above SF4 population thresholds; (1) tables reflect only those areas that meet SF4 population thresholds, therefore there may be less than 50 states, 75 counties or 75 places listed

Educational Attainment: High School Graduates

Asian Indians 25 Years and Over Who are High School Graduates

All States, Top 75 Counties, and Top 75 Places Sorted by Percent[1]

State	Percent
North Dakota	99.47
South Dakota	97.30
New Hampshire	97.24
Vermont	96.95
Montana	96.47
Iowa	94.73
Colorado	94.16
West Virginia	93.34
Missouri	93.31
Nebraska	93.04
District of Columbia	92.83
Ohio	92.81
Delaware	92.05
Massachusetts	91.88
Alabama	91.71
Indiana	91.66
Wyoming	91.61
New Mexico	91.52
Minnesota	90.97
Arizona	90.69
Wisconsin	90.67
Oregon	90.66
Tennessee	90.54
Maryland	90.48
Virginia	90.43
Michigan	90.04
North Carolina	89.63
Maine	89.41
Kentucky	89.34
Kansas	89.14
Hawaii	88.96
Georgia	88.75
Texas	88.32
Illinois	88.28
Pennsylvania	88.17
Connecticut	88.08
Rhode Island	88.00
Arkansas	87.97
Idaho	87.96
South Carolina	87.61
New Jersey	87.17
United States	86.69
Oklahoma	86.67
Louisiana	86.42
Florida	85.72
Mississippi	85.50
California	85.48
Alaska	84.29
Washington	83.99
Utah	82.38
Nevada	82.03
New York	78.62

County	Percent
Berkshire County, MA	100.00
Boone County, MO	100.00
Cass County, ND	100.00
Charlottesville Independent City, VA	100.00
Chittenden County, VT	100.00
Eaton County, MI	100.00
McLean County, IL	100.00
Midland County, MI	100.00
Monongalia County, WV	100.00
Montgomery County, VA	100.00
Peoria County, IL	100.00
Pickens County, SC	100.00
Putnam County, NY	100.00
Sangamon County, IL	100.00
Warren County, OH	99.53
Olmsted County, MN	98.93
St. Mary's County, MD	98.86
Rockingham County, NH	98.73
Champaign County, IL	98.64
Linn County, IA	98.57
Boulder County, CO	98.54
Tompkins County, NY	98.48
Bartholomew County, IN	98.23
Orange County, NC	98.04
Washington County, MN	98.03
Rensselaer County, NY	97.95
Kent County, DE	97.81
Hillsborough County, NH	97.75
Washington County, OR	97.71
Chester County, PA	97.66
St. Charles County, MO	97.55
Monroe County, IN	97.15
St. Joseph County, IN	97.01
Jefferson County, CO	96.93
Allegheny County, PA	96.71
Douglas County, NE	96.71
Hamilton County, IN	96.67
El Paso County, CO	96.64
Alachua County, FL	96.63
Washtenaw County, MI	96.47
Lake County, IN	96.38
Rock Island County, IL	96.38
Leon County, FL	96.13
Muscogee County, GA	96.10
Brazoria County, TX	95.92
Collin County, TX	95.88
Arapahoe County, CO	95.87
Forsyth County, NC	95.86
Genesee County, MI	95.76
Waukesha County, WI	95.73
Hamilton County, OH	95.57
Richland County, SC	95.55
Westmoreland County, PA	95.53
Saratoga County, NY	95.49
Story County, IA	95.44
Dane County, WI	95.39
Centre County, PA	95.25
Fairfax Independent City, VA	95.14
Dakota County, MN	95.05
Saint Louis Independent City, MO	95.03
Kanawha County, WV	95.02
Lorain County, OH	94.88
Brazos County, TX	94.85
Kalamazoo County, MI	94.85
Lucas County, OH	94.79
Norfolk County, MA	94.77
Oakland County, MI	94.68
St. Louis County, MO	94.64
Butler County, PA	94.61
Bernalillo County, NM	94.38
Henry County, GA	94.21
Sussex County, NJ	94.14
Erie County, PA	94.10
Denver County, CO	94.09
Durham County, NC	94.09

Place	Percent
Acton, MA (town) Middlesex County	100.00
Andover, MA (town) Essex County	100.00
Blacksburg, VA (town) Montgomery County	100.00
Bloomington, IL (city) McLean County	100.00
Blue Ash, OH (city) Hamilton County	100.00
Boulder, CO (city) Boulder County	100.00
Boxborough, MA (town) Middlesex County	100.00
Brookfield, WI (city) Waukesha County	100.00
Champaign, IL (city) Champaign County	100.00
Claremont, CA (city) Los Angeles County	100.00
Clifton Park, NY (town) Saratoga County	100.00
Columbia, MO (city) Boone County	100.00
Cortlandt, NY (town) Westchester County	100.00
Delta charter, MI (township) Eaton County	100.00
Dublin, OH (city) Franklin County	100.00
Eden Prairie, MN (city) Hennepin County	100.00
Fargo, ND (city) Cass County	100.00
Hamden, CT (town) New Haven County	100.00
Henrietta, NY (town) Monroe County	100.00
Highlands Ranch, CO (cdp) Douglas County	100.00
Lisle, IL (village) Du Page County	100.00
Los Altos, CA (city) Santa Clara County	100.00
Mansfield, CT (town) Tolland County	100.00
Midland, MI (city) Midland County	100.00
Mineola, NY (village) Nassau County	100.00
Montgomery, NJ (township) Somerset County	100.00
Munster, IN (town) Lake County	100.00
Niskayuna, NY (town) Schenectady County	100.00
Norwood, MA (town) Norfolk County	100.00
Peoria, IL (city) Peoria County	100.00
Plainsboro Center, NJ (cdp) Middlesex County	100.00
Randolph, NJ (township) Morris County	100.00
Santa Clarita, CA (city) Los Angeles County	100.00
Scott Township, PA (cdp) Allegheny County	100.00
Scott, PA (township) Allegheny County	100.00
Smyrna, GA (city) Cobb County	100.00
Springfield, IL (city) Sangamon County	100.00
Stanford, CA (cdp) Santa Clara County	100.00
The Woodlands, TX (cdp) Montgomery County	100.00
Tredyffrin, PA (township) Chester County	100.00
Tysons Corner, VA (cdp) Fairfax County	100.00
Urbana, IL (city) Champaign County	100.00
Vernon Hills, IL (village) Lake County	100.00
West Des Moines, IA (city) Polk County	100.00
Wolf Trap, VA (cdp) Fairfax County	100.00
Plymouth, MN (city) Hennepin County	99.02
Oak Brook, IL (village) Du Page County	98.89
Rochester, MN (city) Olmsted County	98.87
Idylwood, VA (cdp) Fairfax County	98.85
Saratoga, CA (city) Santa Clara County	98.84
Maryland Heights, MO (city) Saint Louis County	98.80
Lower Makefield, PA (township) Bucks County	98.71
West Lafayette, IN (city) Tippecanoe County	98.67
Yorba Linda, CA (city) Orange County	98.62
Evanston, IL (city) Cook County	98.61
Portage, MI (city) Kalamazoo County	98.59
Chandler, AZ (city) Maricopa County	98.52
North Olmsted, OH (city) Cuyahoga County	98.46
Annandale, VA (cdp) Fairfax County	98.44
Rancho Palos Verdes, CA (city) Los Angeles County	98.43
North Druid Hills, GA (cdp) De Kalb County	98.42
Lake Forest, CA (city) Orange County	98.41
Redwood City, CA (city) San Mateo County	98.41
Hillsboro, OR (city) Washington County	98.39
Lakewood, CO (city) Jefferson County	98.32
Middletown, NJ (township) Monmouth County	98.32
Redmond, WA (city) King County	98.29
Columbus, IN (city) Bartholomew County	98.23
Westlake, OH (city) Cuyahoga County	98.22
Waukesha, WI (city) Waukesha County	98.21
Cedar Rapids, IA (city) Linn County	98.18
Foster City, CA (city) San Mateo County	98.17
Lower Merion, PA (township) Montgomery County	98.09
Bloomington, IN (city) Monroe County	98.08
Oak Park, IL (village) Cook County	98.05

Notes: Please refer to the User's Guide for an explanation of data; ranking tables include all places with Asian and/or NHPI populations above SF4 population thresholds; (1) tables reflect only those areas that meet SF4 population thresholds, therefore there may be less than 50 states, 75 counties or 75 places listed

Educational Attainment: High School Graduates

Bangladeshis 25 Years and Over Who are High School Graduates

All States, Top 75 Counties, and Top 75 Places Sorted by Number[1]

State	Number
United States	19,556
New York	8,732
Texas	1,556
California	1,482
New Jersey	959
Virginia	869
Florida	678
Maryland	661
Georgia	644
Michigan	508
Ohio	409
Illinois	396
Pennsylvania	351
Massachusetts	305
Connecticut	193

County	Number
Queens County, NY	5,773
Kings County, NY	1,525
Bronx County, NY	696
Los Angeles County, CA	677
Montgomery County, MD	472
Fairfax County, VA	420
Harris County, TX	384
Dallas County, TX	357
Santa Clara County, CA	323
DeKalb County, GA	261
Wayne County, MI	249
New York County, NY	222
Middlesex County, NJ	210
Passaic County, NJ	162
Atlantic County, NJ	148

Place	Number
New York, NY (city)	8,232
Los Angeles, CA (city) Los Angeles County	433
Paterson, NJ (city) Passaic County	139
Hamtramck, MI (city) Wayne County	135

Notes: Please refer to the User's Guide for an explanation of data; ranking tables include all places with Asian and/or NHPI populations above SF4 population thresholds; (1) tables reflect only those areas that meet SF4 population thresholds, therefore there may be less than 50 states, 75 counties or 75 places listed

Educational Attainment: High School Graduates

Bangladeshis 25 Years and Over Who are High School Graduates

All States, Top 75 Counties, and Top 75 Places Sorted by Percent[1]

State	Percent
Ohio	94.68
Texas	92.73
Massachusetts	92.15
Illinois	89.59
Connecticut	88.53
California	85.52
Maryland	84.53
Georgia	83.20
Pennsylvania	83.18
Florida	80.43
Virginia	80.24
United States	78.22
New Jersey	73.71
New York	72.77
Michigan	53.31

County	Percent
Middlesex County, NJ	97.22
Santa Clara County, CA	95.00
Dallas County, TX	92.97
Harris County, TX	88.48
Montgomery County, MD	82.81
Los Angeles County, CA	81.57
Fairfax County, VA	79.55
Queens County, NY	76.20
DeKalb County, GA	75.22
Kings County, NY	67.15
Atlantic County, NJ	66.67
Bronx County, NY	62.20
Passaic County, NJ	54.73
New York County, NY	51.03
Wayne County, MI	39.09

Place	Percent
Los Angeles, CA (city) Los Angeles County	80.19
New York, NY (city)	72.10
Paterson, NJ (city) Passaic County	59.40
Hamtramck, MI (city) Wayne County	36.59

Notes: Please refer to the User's Guide for an explanation of data; ranking tables include all places with Asian and/or NHPI populations above SF4 population thresholds; (1) tables reflect only those areas that meet SF4 population thresholds, therefore there may be less than 50 states, 75 counties or 75 places listed

Educational Attainment: High School Graduates

Cambodians 25 Years and Over Who are High School Graduates

All States, Top 75 Counties, and Top 75 Places Sorted by Number[1]

State	Number
United States	40,287
California	14,622
Massachusetts	4,022
Washington	3,607
Texas	2,165
Virginia	1,535
Pennsylvania	1,523
Minnesota	1,324
Rhode Island	1,082
Illinois	1,041
Oregon	909
Georgia	908
Florida	823
New York	693
Maryland	649
Connecticut	616
Ohio	582
North Carolina	468
Arizona	416
Michigan	398
Utah	396
Colorado	329
Nevada	254
New Jersey	216
Tennessee	215
Maine	203
Kansas	185
Missouri	174
Oklahoma	117
Iowa	108
Wisconsin	108
Indiana	94
South Carolina	92
Alabama	59
Hawaii	42

County	Number
Los Angeles County, CA	6,385
Middlesex County, MA	2,148
King County, WA	1,725
Orange County, CA	1,672
Santa Clara County, CA	1,059
San Joaquin County, CA	1,023
Providence County, RI	1,007
Philadelphia County, PA	959
Alameda County, CA	813
Fairfax County, VA	807
Pierce County, WA	779
San Diego County, CA	726
Essex County, MA	713
Harris County, TX	671
Snohomish County, WA	626
Dallas County, TX	607
Cook County, IL	593
Hennepin County, MN	556
Stanislaus County, CA	550
Fresno County, CA	483
Montgomery County, MD	483
Washington County, OR	462
Bristol County, MA	434
San Bernardino County, CA	411
Fairfield County, CT	383
Maricopa County, AZ	378
Suffolk County, MA	310
Franklin County, OH	297
Denton County, TX	289
Multnomah County, OR	282
Salt Lake County, UT	282
Ottawa County, MI	267
Sacramento County, CA	253
Ramsey County, MN	251
Duval County, FL	249
Clark County, NV	240
Gwinnett County, GA	233
Mecklenburg County, NC	199
DeKalb County, GA	189
Thurston County, WA	189
Riverside County, CA	186
San Francisco County, CA	175
Pinellas County, FL	161
Clayton County, GA	150
Dakota County, MN	148
Clark County, WA	143
Sedgwick County, KS	143
Chesterfield County, VA	142
Kings County, NY	137
Sonoma County, CA	133
Bronx County, NY	124
Hampden County, MA	119
Olmsted County, MN	117
Scott County, MN	116
Henrico County, VA	109
Cuyahoga County, OH	107
Arlington County, VA	104
Cumberland County, ME	84
Kern County, CA	84
Shelby County, TN	80
Worcester County, MA	73
Hamilton County, OH	70
Tarrant County, TX	69
Camden County, NJ	68
Brazoria County, TX	60
Monroe County, NY	59
Davidson County, NC	53
Polk County, IA	49
Denver County, CO	46
Mobile County, AL	30
Cowlitz County, WA	28

Place	Number
Long Beach, CA (city) Los Angeles County	3,174
Lowell, MA (city) Middlesex County	1,733
San Jose, CA (city) Santa Clara County	970
Stockton, CA (city) San Joaquin County	962
Philadelphia, PA (city) Philadelphia County	959
Los Angeles, CA (city) Los Angeles County	833
Providence, RI (city) Providence County	662
San Diego, CA (city) San Diego County	583
Tacoma, WA (city) Pierce County	574
Seattle, WA (city) King County	528
Lynn, MA (city) Essex County	488
Chicago, IL (city) Cook County	482
Santa Ana, CA (city) Orange County	437
Fresno, CA (city) Fresno County	430
Oakland, CA (city) Alameda County	430
Modesto, CA (city) Stanislaus County	409
New York, NY (city)	398
Cranston, RI (city) Providence County	276
Portland, OR (city) Multnomah County	267
Columbus, OH (city) Franklin County	266
Jacksonville, FL (city) Duval County	249
Lakewood, CA (city) Los Angeles County	245
Dallas, TX (city) Dallas County	231
White Center, WA (cdp) King County	227
Attleboro, MA (city) Bristol County	218
Carrollton, TX (city) Denton County	217
Rosemead, CA (city) Los Angeles County	211
Phoenix, AZ (city) Maricopa County	208
Norwalk, CA (city) Los Angeles County	201
Garden Grove, CA (city) Orange County	198
St. Paul, MN (city) Ramsey County	184
Signal Hill, CA (city) Los Angeles County	183
San Francisco, CA (city) San Francisco County	175
Charlotte, NC (city) Mecklenburg County	172
Houston, TX (city) Harris County	158
Bloomington, MN (city) Hennepin County	156
Bellflower, CA (city) Los Angeles County	155
Boston, MA (city) Suffolk County	148
Beaverton, OR (city) Washington County	146
West Valley City, UT (city) Salt Lake County	138
Danbury, CT (city) Fairfield County	136
Fall River, MA (city) Bristol County	135
Sacramento, CA (city) Sacramento County	133
Pomona, CA (city) Los Angeles County	124
Lawrence, MA (city) Essex County	122
Everett, WA (city) Snohomish County	119
Revere, MA (city) Suffolk County	116
Silver Spring, MD (cdp) Montgomery County	106
Arlington, VA (cdp) Arlington County	104
St. Petersburg, FL (city) Pinellas County	103
Santa Rosa, CA (city) Sonoma County	102
Bridgeport, CT (city) Fairfield County	98
Minneapolis, MN (city) Hennepin County	84
Monterey Park, CA (city) Los Angeles County	82
Rochester, MN (city) Olmsted County	82
San Bernardino, CA (city) San Bernardino County	71
Aurora, CO (city) Arapahoe County	68
Memphis, TN (city) Shelby County	64
Portland, ME (city) Cumberland County	60
Denver, CO (city) Denver County	46
Lexington, NC (city) Davidson County	36
Longview, WA (city) Cowlitz County	28

Notes: Please refer to the User's Guide for an explanation of data; ranking tables include all places with Asian and/or NHPI populations above SF4 population thresholds; (1) tables reflect only those areas that meet SF4 population thresholds, therefore there may be less than 50 states, 75 counties or 75 places listed

Educational Attainment: High School Graduates

Cambodians 25 Years and Over Who are High School Graduates

All States, Top 75 Counties, and Top 75 Places Sorted by Percent[1]

State	Percent
Arizona	67.97
Oklahoma	64.64
Maryland	61.40
New Jersey	59.18
Virginia	58.57
Utah	58.32
Illinois	56.70
Oregon	56.49
Texas	53.88
Florida	53.55
Nevada	53.03
Connecticut	52.83
Minnesota	52.60
Hawaii	51.85
Kansas	50.27
Washington	49.59
South Carolina	49.20
New York	49.15
Georgia	48.30
Maine	47.32
Michigan	46.66
United States	46.66
Colorado	45.95
Ohio	45.79
Rhode Island	45.75
Missouri	44.05
California	43.84
Massachusetts	43.36
Wisconsin	40.91
North Carolina	39.46
Pennsylvania	36.65
Tennessee	35.54
Indiana	34.81
Iowa	28.95
Alabama	22.61

County	Percent
Fairfax County, VA	75.77
Denton County, TX	67.52
Maricopa County, AZ	65.85
Montgomery County, MD	65.27
Washington County, OR	64.98
Dakota County, MN	64.07
Orange County, CA	62.30
Hennepin County, MN	62.26
Riverside County, CA	60.59
Arlington County, VA	60.47
Sedgwick County, KS	57.89
Snohomish County, WA	57.70
Clark County, WA	56.52
Salt Lake County, UT	56.29
Harris County, TX	55.92
Gwinnett County, GA	54.95
Scott County, MN	53.70
Hampden County, MA	53.13
King County, WA	52.83
Mecklenburg County, NC	52.65
Multnomah County, OR	52.22
Dallas County, TX	51.75
Clark County, NV	51.61
Fairfield County, CT	50.93
Ottawa County, MI	50.47
Cook County, IL	50.38
San Francisco County, CA	50.14
San Bernardino County, CA	50.12
DeKalb County, GA	49.22
Santa Clara County, CA	48.91
Alameda County, CA	47.91
Franklin County, OH	47.29
Duval County, FL	46.89
Sacramento County, CA	46.85
Thurston County, WA	46.67
Bristol County, MA	46.07
Chesterfield County, VA	45.51
Providence County, RI	44.44
Pinellas County, FL	44.35
Kings County, NY	44.05
Stanislaus County, CA	43.69
Ramsey County, MN	43.65
Los Angeles County, CA	43.54
Middlesex County, MA	42.71
Kern County, CA	42.00
Cuyahoga County, OH	41.96
Essex County, MA	41.70
Pierce County, WA	41.55
Camden County, NJ	40.48
Olmsted County, MN	40.21
Suffolk County, MA	39.79
Bronx County, NY	38.04
San Diego County, CA	37.73
Worcester County, MA	37.63
Hamilton County, OH	37.23
Sonoma County, CA	36.04
Monroe County, NY	35.33
Cumberland County, ME	34.01
Philadelphia County, PA	32.39
Fresno County, CA	30.43
Brazoria County, TX	30.00
Clayton County, GA	29.53
San Joaquin County, CA	28.00
Henrico County, VA	27.46
Shelby County, TN	25.72
Polk County, IA	24.02
Davidson County, NC	22.46
Denver County, CO	22.44
Tarrant County, TX	19.49
Mobile County, AL	19.48
Cowlitz County, WA	18.54

Place	Percent
Phoenix, AZ (city) Maricopa County	72.98
Lakewood, CA (city) Los Angeles County	64.64
Norwalk, CA (city) Los Angeles County	64.42
Attleboro, MA (city) Bristol County	61.58
Beaverton, OR (city) Washington County	61.34
Bloomington, MN (city) Hennepin County	61.18
Arlington, VA (cdp) Arlington County	60.47
Cranston, RI (city) Providence County	59.35
Garden Grove, CA (city) Orange County	58.41
Silver Spring, MD (cdp) Montgomery County	54.64
Lawrence, MA (city) Essex County	54.22
Sacramento, CA (city) Sacramento County	53.85
Carrollton, TX (city) Denton County	52.93
Portland, OR (city) Multnomah County	51.74
Dallas, TX (city) Dallas County	51.56
Bellflower, CA (city) Los Angeles County	51.16
Minneapolis, MN (city) Hennepin County	50.91
Charlotte, NC (city) Mecklenburg County	50.44
San Francisco, CA (city) San Francisco County	50.14
San Jose, CA (city) Santa Clara County	49.67
Danbury, CT (city) Fairfield County	48.57
New York, NY (city)	48.01
Signal Hill, CA (city) Los Angeles County	47.91
West Valley City, UT (city) Salt Lake County	47.75
Chicago, IL (city) Cook County	47.25
Pomona, CA (city) Los Angeles County	47.15
Boston, MA (city) Suffolk County	47.13
Jacksonville, FL (city) Duval County	46.89
Columbus, OH (city) Franklin County	46.67
Rosemead, CA (city) Los Angeles County	46.27
Santa Ana, CA (city) Orange County	44.32
Seattle, WA (city) King County	43.89
White Center, WA (cdp) King County	43.40
St. Petersburg, FL (city) Pinellas County	42.39
Providence, RI (city) Providence County	40.49
Lowell, MA (city) Middlesex County	40.26
Modesto, CA (city) Stanislaus County	39.82
Tacoma, WA (city) Pierce County	39.70
Long Beach, CA (city) Los Angeles County	39.41
Monterey Park, CA (city) Los Angeles County	39.05
San Bernardino, CA (city) San Bernardino County	38.59
Bridgeport, CT (city) Fairfield County	38.58
Everett, WA (city) Snohomish County	38.39
St. Paul, MN (city) Ramsey County	37.94
Santa Rosa, CA (city) Sonoma County	37.50
Los Angeles, CA (city) Los Angeles County	37.37
Houston, TX (city) Harris County	36.83
Oakland, CA (city) Alameda County	36.23
Lynn, MA (city) Essex County	36.17
Rochester, MN (city) Olmsted County	36.12
Revere, MA (city) Suffolk County	35.80
San Diego, CA (city) San Diego County	34.38
Aurora, CO (city) Arapahoe County	33.33
Philadelphia, PA (city) Philadelphia County	32.39
Fresno, CA (city) Fresno County	29.68
Fall River, MA (city) Bristol County	29.03
Portland, ME (city) Cumberland County	27.78
Stockton, CA (city) San Joaquin County	27.37
Longview, WA (city) Cowlitz County	25.93
Memphis, TN (city) Shelby County	23.53
Denver, CO (city) Denver County	22.44
Lexington, NC (city) Davidson County	21.18

Notes: Please refer to the User's Guide for an explanation of data; ranking tables include all places with Asian and/or NHPI populations above SF4 population thresholds; (1) tables reflect only those areas that meet SF4 population thresholds, therefore there may be less than 50 states, 75 counties or 75 places listed

Educational Attainment: High School Graduates

Chinese (except Taiwanese) 25 Years and Over Who are High School Graduates

All States, Top 75 Counties, and Top 75 Places Sorted by Number[1]

State	Number
United States	1,205,190
California	486,125
New York	174,641
Texas	58,339
New Jersey	56,475
Massachusetts	40,700
Illinois	39,919
Hawaii	34,541
Washington	32,393
Maryland	27,623
Florida	24,216
Pennsylvania	23,086
Virginia	19,808
Michigan	16,817
Ohio	16,508
Georgia	14,585
Arizona	12,211
Connecticut	10,779
North Carolina	10,017
Oregon	9,436
Colorado	8,454
Minnesota	8,222
Nevada	7,520
Missouri	7,373
Indiana	6,469
Wisconsin	4,992
Tennessee	4,736
Kansas	4,073
Louisiana	3,848
Utah	3,794
Oklahoma	3,696
Alabama	3,426
South Carolina	3,248
Iowa	3,232
Kentucky	3,077
Delaware	2,535
New Mexico	2,333
New Hampshire	2,097
District of Columbia	1,961
Rhode Island	1,913
Nebraska	1,795
Arkansas	1,607
Mississippi	1,484
Idaho	1,001
West Virginia	904
Alaska	801
Maine	657
Vermont	501
South Dakota	383
Montana	330
North Dakota	268
Wyoming	241

County	Number
Los Angeles County, CA	150,074
Santa Clara County, CA	69,664
San Francisco County, CA	68,731
Queens County, NY	68,231
Alameda County, CA	54,704
Kings County, NY	39,646
Honolulu County, HI	32,662
San Mateo County, CA	29,810
Orange County, CA	29,719
New York County, NY	29,595
King County, WA	24,696
Cook County, IL	24,424
Harris County, TX	18,982
Contra Costa County, CA	18,073
Middlesex County, MA	16,898
Montgomery County, MD	16,763
San Diego County, CA	15,830
Sacramento County, CA	13,832
Middlesex County, NJ	12,511
Fairfax County, VA	9,738
Norfolk County, MA	9,501
Maricopa County, AZ	9,152
Nassau County, NY	8,373
Bergen County, NJ	8,247
Collin County, TX	7,950
Suffolk County, MA	7,844
Dallas County, TX	6,828
Philadelphia County, PA	6,395
San Bernardino County, CA	6,300
DuPage County, IL	6,251
Morris County, NJ	6,011
Clark County, NV	5,992
Fort Bend County, TX	5,773
Monmouth County, NJ	5,271
Travis County, TX	5,253
Oakland County, MI	5,174
Suffolk County, NY	4,888
Miami-Dade County, FL	4,825
Somerset County, NJ	4,617
Westchester County, NY	4,554
Hudson County, NJ	4,255
Franklin County, OH	4,244
Broward County, FL	4,202
Essex County, NJ	3,746
Fairfield County, CT	3,636
St. Louis County, MO	3,597
Richmond County, NY	3,538
Washtenaw County, MI	3,479
Hennepin County, MN	3,389
Cuyahoga County, OH	3,342
Ventura County, CA	3,296
Montgomery County, PA	3,234
Gwinnett County, GA	3,220
New Haven County, CT	3,118
Multnomah County, OR	3,092
Fulton County, GA	3,077
Washington County, OR	3,055
Wake County, NC	3,054
Wayne County, MI	3,036
Tarrant County, TX	3,016
Lake County, IL	3,005
Allegheny County, PA	2,975
Mercer County, NJ	2,942
Riverside County, CA	2,818
Prince George's County, MD	2,747
Bronx County, NY	2,655
Fresno County, CA	2,596
Snohomish County, WA	2,563
Pima County, AZ	2,556
Baltimore County, MD	2,440
San Joaquin County, CA	2,438
Salt Lake County, UT	2,369
New Castle County, DE	2,350
Union County, NJ	2,331
Orange County, FL	2,318

Place	Number
New York, NY (city)	143,665
San Francisco, CA (city) San Francisco County	68,731
San Jose, CA (city) Santa Clara County	29,873
Los Angeles, CA (city) Los Angeles County	27,634
Honolulu, HI (cdp) Honolulu County	23,224
Fremont, CA (city) Alameda County	16,273
Chicago, IL (city) Cook County	14,871
Houston, TX (city) Harris County	13,722
Alhambra, CA (city) Los Angeles County	13,090
Oakland, CA (city) Alameda County	12,161
San Diego, CA (city) San Diego County	11,545
Monterey Park, CA (city) Los Angeles County	11,287
Seattle, WA (city) King County	9,405
Sunnyvale, CA (city) Santa Clara County	8,820
Sacramento, CA (city) Sacramento County	8,476
Arcadia, CA (city) Los Angeles County	7,898
Daly City, CA (city) San Mateo County	7,622
Boston, MA (city) Suffolk County	7,600
Rowland Heights, CA (cdp) Los Angeles County	6,804
Philadelphia, PA (city) Philadelphia County	6,395
Cupertino, CA (city) Santa Clara County	6,327
Irvine, CA (city) Orange County	6,130
Plano, TX (city) Collin County	5,731
San Gabriel, CA (city) Los Angeles County	5,624
Hacienda Heights, CA (cdp) Los Angeles County	5,298
Milpitas, CA (city) Santa Clara County	4,888
Austin, TX (city) Travis County	4,719
Diamond Bar, CA (city) Los Angeles County	4,469
Rosemead, CA (city) Los Angeles County	4,310
El Monte, CA (city) Los Angeles County	4,307
Temple City, CA (city) Los Angeles County	4,120
Dallas, TX (city) Dallas County	3,970
Mountain View, CA (city) Santa Clara County	3,938
Quincy, MA (city) Norfolk County	3,922
Alameda, CA (city) Alameda County	3,900
San Leandro, CA (city) Alameda County	3,831
Torrance, CA (city) Los Angeles County	3,825
Bellevue, WA (city) King County	3,686
Palo Alto, CA (city) Santa Clara County	3,663
San Mateo, CA (city) San Mateo County	3,617
Union City, CA (city) Alameda County	3,561
Walnut, CA (city) Los Angeles County	3,561
Cerritos, CA (city) Los Angeles County	3,450
Santa Clara, CA (city) Santa Clara County	3,350
Edison, NJ (township) Middlesex County	3,278
West Covina, CA (city) Los Angeles County	3,233
Phoenix, AZ (city) Maricopa County	3,185
Sugar Land, TX (city) Fort Bend County	3,150
Columbus, OH (city) Franklin County	3,087
Hempstead, NY (town) Nassau County	3,042
North Hempstead, NY (town) Nassau County	3,015
Foster City, CA (city) San Mateo County	2,953
Saratoga, CA (city) Santa Clara County	2,923
Pasadena, CA (city) Los Angeles County	2,861
South San Francisco, CA (city) San Mateo County	2,845
Portland, OR (city) Multnomah County	2,779
Berkeley, CA (city) Alameda County	2,681
Naperville, IL (city) Du Page County	2,391
Anaheim, CA (city) Orange County	2,389
Newton, MA (city) Middlesex County	2,303
Ann Arbor, MI (city) Washtenaw County	2,263
Brookline, MA (town) Norfolk County	2,253
San Marino, CA (city) Los Angeles County	2,193
South Pasadena, CA (city) Los Angeles County	2,173
Hayward, CA (city) Alameda County	2,166
Chino Hills, CA (city) San Bernardino County	2,163
Cambridge, MA (city) Middlesex County	2,138
Oyster Bay, NY (town) Nassau County	2,121
Castro Valley, CA (cdp) Alameda County	2,097
Huntington Beach, CA (city) Orange County	2,069
Millbrae, CA (city) San Mateo County	2,063
East San Gabriel, CA (cdp) Los Angeles County	2,038
Brookhaven, NY (town) Suffolk County	2,034
Spring Valley, NV (cdp) Clark County	1,989
Richmond, CA (city) Contra Costa County	1,963

Notes: Please refer to the User's Guide for an explanation of data; ranking tables include all places with Asian and/or NHPI populations above SF4 population thresholds; (1) tables reflect only those areas that meet SF4 population thresholds, therefore there may be less than 50 states, 75 counties or 75 places listed

Educational Attainment: High School Graduates

Chinese (except Taiwanese) 25 Years and Over Who are High School Graduates

All States, Top 75 Counties, and Top 75 Places Sorted by Percent[1]

State	Percent
North Dakota	96.06
Nebraska	93.64
Montana	92.18
Iowa	92.05
Alabama	90.42
West Virginia	89.42
New Mexico	89.22
Delaware	88.39
Kentucky	88.14
Kansas	88.12
Indiana	88.11
New Jersey	87.87
Texas	87.74
North Carolina	87.58
Missouri	87.46
Ohio	87.05
Connecticut	86.85
Idaho	86.82
Wisconsin	86.37
Oklahoma	86.33
Michigan	85.83
Arizona	85.53
Minnesota	85.26
Maryland	85.06
New Hampshire	84.93
Georgia	84.86
Tennessee	84.77
Colorado	84.27
Virginia	83.71
Arkansas	83.70
Louisiana	83.42
Vermont	83.22
Washington	82.41
Utah	81.63
South Carolina	80.70
Mississippi	79.66
Illinois	79.57
Alaska	79.15
South Dakota	78.81
Hawaii	77.75
Nevada	77.61
Florida	77.01
California	76.30
United States	76.20
Rhode Island	75.85
Pennsylvania	75.84
Oregon	75.43
Massachusetts	75.24
District of Columbia	73.09
Maine	71.57
Wyoming	61.48
New York	60.87

County	Percent
Douglas County, KS	100.00
Jackson County, IL	100.00
Lee County, AL	100.00
Lubbock County, TX	100.00
Monongalia County, WV	100.00
Olmsted County, MN	100.00
Pickens County, SC	100.00
Riley County, KS	100.00
Saratoga County, NY	100.00
Story County, IA	100.00
Montgomery County, VA	98.70
Alachua County, FL	98.68
Brazos County, TX	98.50
Orange County, NC	98.49
Delaware County, OH	98.08
Champaign County, IL	98.00
Benton County, WA	97.97
Hunterdon County, NJ	97.78
Charlottesville Independent City, VA	97.77
Lancaster County, NE	97.46
Lake County, IN	97.44
Centre County, PA	97.41
Warren County, OH	97.41
Tippecanoe County, IN	97.27
Tompkins County, NY	97.14
Cleveland County, OK	96.75
Payne County, OK	96.75
Travis County, TX	96.65
Leon County, FL	96.41
Washington County, AR	96.24
Waukesha County, WI	96.18
Northampton County, PA	96.12
Yolo County, CA	96.05
Johnson County, IA	95.97
Chester County, PA	95.95
Durham County, NC	95.95
Washtenaw County, MI	95.76
El Paso County, CO	95.73
Madison County, AL	95.50
McHenry County, IL	95.39
Cache County, UT	95.24
Kalamazoo County, MI	94.96
Albemarle County, VA	94.92
Jefferson County, AL	94.81
Boulder County, CO	94.74
Collin County, TX	94.69
Jefferson County, TX	94.53
Dona Ana County, NM	94.52
Ada County, ID	94.51
El Paso County, TX	94.41
Monroe County, IN	94.32
Douglas County, NE	94.28
Fayette County, KY	94.25
Clarke County, GA	94.10
Morris County, NJ	94.07
Somerset County, NJ	94.07
Hamilton County, IN	93.83
Wake County, NC	93.80
Lake County, IL	93.27
St. Charles County, MO	93.13
Ingham County, MI	92.91
Penobscot County, ME	92.82
Hamilton County, OH	92.72
San Luis Obispo County, CA	92.55
Marin County, CA	92.54
Mercer County, NJ	92.54
East Baton Rouge Parish, LA	92.52
Davidson County, TN	92.37
DuPage County, IL	92.36
Whatcom County, WA	92.28
Lake County, OH	92.24
Greenville County, SC	91.78
Placer County, CA	91.70
Will County, IL	91.67
St. Joseph County, IN	91.62

Place	Percent
Ames, IA (city) Story County	100.00
Auburn, AL (city) Lee County	100.00
Brookfield, WI (city) Waukesha County	100.00
Calabasas, CA (city) Los Angeles County	100.00
Carlsbad, CA (city) San Diego County	100.00
Carmichael, CA (cdp) Sacramento County	100.00
Champaign, IL (city) Champaign County	100.00
Columbia, SC (city) Richland County	100.00
East Lansing, MI (city) Ingham County	100.00
Evanston, IL (city) Cook County	100.00
Falcon Heights, MN (city) Ramsey County	100.00
Fayetteville, AR (city) Washington County	100.00
Folsom, CA (city) Sacramento County	100.00
Hudson, OH (city) Summit County	100.00
Lawrence, KS (city) Douglas County	100.00
Lubbock, TX (city) Lubbock County	100.00
Manhattan, KS (city) Riley County	100.00
Mansfield, CT (town) Tolland County	100.00
Monterey, CA (city) Monterey County	100.00
Rancho Santa Margarita, CA (city) Orange County	100.00
Rochester, MN (city) Olmsted County	100.00
Sammamish, WA (city) King County	100.00
San Luis Obispo, CA (city) San Luis Obispo County	100.00
Solon, OH (city) Cuyahoga County	100.00
Somerset, NJ (cdp) Somerset County	100.00
Storrs, CT (cdp) Tolland County	100.00
Randolph, NJ (township) Morris County	99.09
Pleasant Hill, CA (city) Contra Costa County	98.93
Hanover, NJ (township) Morris County	98.89
Lake Success, NY (village) Nassau County	98.89
Germantown, TN (city) Shelby County	98.87
La Habra, CA (city) Orange County	98.82
Stanford, CA (cdp) Santa Clara County	98.76
Palos Verdes Estates, CA (city) Los Angeles County	98.72
La Canada Flintridge, CA (city) Los Angeles County	98.69
Lafayette, CA (city) Contra Costa County	98.63
Blacksburg, VA (town) Montgomery County	98.62
La Mirada, CA (city) Los Angeles County	98.52
Norman, OK (city) Cleveland County	98.41
Acton, MA (town) Middlesex County	98.39
Manhattan Beach, CA (city) Los Angeles County	98.39
Camarillo, CA (city) Ventura County	98.34
Westford, MA (town) Middlesex County	98.27
College Station, TX (city) Brazos County	98.24
Millburn, NJ (township) Essex County	98.20
Gainesville, FL (city) Alachua County	98.09
Upper Merion, PA (township) Montgomery County	98.08
Olathe, KS (city) Johnson County	98.02
Montville, NJ (township) Morris County	97.99
Scarsdale, NY (village) Westchester County	97.98
Setauket-East Setauket, NY (cdp) Suffolk County	97.95
Chapel Hill, NC (town) Orange County	97.93
New Haven, CT (city) New Haven County	97.92
King of Prussia, PA (cdp) Montgomery County	97.86
Cincinnati, OH (city) Hamilton County	97.85
Laie, HI (cdp) Honolulu County	97.78
Oak Park, IL (village) Cook County	97.69
Shrewsbury, MA (town) Worcester County	97.65
Urbana, IL (city) Champaign County	97.64
Newark, DE (city) New Castle County	97.58
Blackhawk-Camino Tass., CA (cdp) Contra Costa Co.	97.57
Princeton, NJ (township) Mercer County	97.51
Tredyffrin, PA (township) Chester County	97.47
Lincoln, NE (city) Lancaster County	97.45
Morganville, NJ (cdp) Monmouth County	97.44
Ann Arbor, MI (city) Washtenaw County	97.38
Paramus, NJ (borough) Bergen County	97.37
Richland, WA (city) Benton County	97.36
Tallahassee, FL (city) Leon County	97.35
Rolling Hills Estates, CA (city) Los Angeles County	97.25
Princeton Meadows, NJ (cdp) Middlesex County	97.23
Davis, CA (city) Yolo County	97.17
Montclair, NJ (township) Essex County	97.17
Bethlehem, PA (city) Northampton County	97.14
Lexington, MA (town) Middlesex County	97.11

Notes: Please refer to the User's Guide for an explanation of data; ranking tables include all places with Asian and/or NHPI populations above SF4 population thresholds; (1) tables reflect only those areas that meet SF4 population thresholds, therefore there may be less than 50 states, 75 counties or 75 places listed

Educational Attainment: High School Graduates

Fijians 25 Years and Over Who are High School Graduates

All States, Top 75 Counties, and Top 75 Places Sorted by Number[1]

State	Number
United States	3,914
California	3,046
Washington	288
Oregon	163

County	Number
Sacramento County, CA	632
Alameda County, CA	562
San Mateo County, CA	376
Los Angeles County, CA	245
King County, WA	229
Santa Clara County, CA	219
Stanislaus County, CA	217
Contra Costa County, CA	193
Yolo County, CA	148

Place	Number
Sacramento, CA (city) Sacramento County	454
Hayward, CA (city) Alameda County	283
Modesto, CA (city) Stanislaus County	164

Notes: Please refer to the User's Guide for an explanation of data; ranking tables include all places with Asian and/or NHPI populations above SF4 population thresholds; (1) tables reflect only those areas that meet SF4 population thresholds, therefore there may be less than 50 states, 75 counties or 75 places listed

Educational Attainment: High School Graduates

Fijians 25 Years and Over Who are High School Graduates

All States, Top 75 Counties, and Top 75 Places Sorted by Percent[1]

State	Percent
Oregon	74.09
United States	66.84
California	65.11
Washington	64.14

County	Percent
Alameda County, CA	75.13
Santa Clara County, CA	74.24
Contra Costa County, CA	73.38
Los Angeles County, CA	70.20
Stanislaus County, CA	65.96
King County, WA	65.24
Sacramento County, CA	60.77
Yolo County, CA	58.96
San Mateo County, CA	54.81

Place	Percent
Modesto, CA (city) Stanislaus County	68.62
Hayward, CA (city) Alameda County	68.19
Sacramento, CA (city) Sacramento County	62.53

Notes: Please refer to the User's Guide for an explanation of data; ranking tables include all places with Asian and/or NHPI populations above SF4 population thresholds; (1) tables reflect only those areas that meet SF4 population thresholds, therefore there may be less than 50 states, 75 counties or 75 places listed

Educational Attainment: High School Graduates

Filipinos 25 Years and Over Who are High School Graduates

All States, Top 75 Counties, and Top 75 Places Sorted by Number[1]

State	Number
United States	1,097,808
California	537,348
Hawaii	82,883
New York	57,009
Illinois	55,631
New Jersey	55,374
Washington	37,981
Texas	35,950
Florida	33,761
Virginia	29,211
Nevada	23,420
Maryland	16,518
Michigan	11,692
Arizona	9,327
Pennsylvania	9,285
Ohio	8,641
Georgia	6,314
Oregon	6,204
Alaska	6,195
Massachusetts	6,126
North Carolina	6,100
Colorado	5,709
Connecticut	4,949
Missouri	4,540
Indiana	4,284
South Carolina	3,864
Minnesota	3,507
Wisconsin	3,477
Tennessee	3,467
Louisiana	2,726
Oklahoma	2,348
Kansas	2,086
Utah	2,037
Kentucky	2,022
New Mexico	1,651
Alabama	1,571
Mississippi	1,555
District of Columbia	1,374
Iowa	1,362
Arkansas	1,306
Rhode Island	1,303
Nebraska	1,239
Delaware	1,171
West Virginia	1,117
Idaho	1,015
New Hampshire	785
Maine	681
Montana	442
South Dakota	426
North Dakota	339
Wyoming	288
Vermont	197

County	Number
Los Angeles County, CA	159,702
San Diego County, CA	67,912
Honolulu County, HI	61,702
Santa Clara County, CA	44,284
Alameda County, CA	41,572
Cook County, IL	36,115
San Mateo County, CA	35,825
Orange County, CA	29,895
San Francisco County, CA	23,842
Queens County, NY	21,176
Solano County, CA	20,677
Contra Costa County, CA	20,433
King County, WA	19,864
Clark County, NV	18,897
San Bernardino County, CA	14,970
Sacramento County, CA	13,953
Hudson County, NJ	12,316
Riverside County, CA	10,947
San Joaquin County, CA	10,366
Harris County, TX	10,039
Maui County, HI	9,595
Bergen County, NJ	9,486
Ventura County, CA	9,139
DuPage County, IL	9,106
Fairfax County, VA	8,301
Virginia Beach Independent City, VA	7,842
Middlesex County, NJ	7,613
New York County, NY	7,087
Maricopa County, AZ	7,018
Hawaii County, HI	6,075
Duval County, FL	6,003
Monterey County, CA	5,984
Kauai County, HI	5,496
Essex County, NJ	4,978
Prince George's County, MD	4,803
Kings County, NY	4,761
Montgomery County, MD	4,635
Kern County, CA	4,581
Snohomish County, WA	4,449
Nassau County, NY	4,444
Lake County, IL	4,089
Dallas County, TX	4,035
Kitsap County, WA	3,906
Pierce County, WA	3,900
Union County, NJ	3,612
Fresno County, CA	3,611
Washoe County, NV	3,603
Richmond County, NY	3,397
Westchester County, NY	3,317
Bexar County, TX	3,169
Bronx County, NY	3,141
Broward County, FL	3,117
Wayne County, MI	2,983
Miami-Dade County, FL	2,972
Rockland County, NY	2,856
Oakland County, MI	2,819
Orange County, FL	2,796
Suffolk County, NY	2,653
Anchorage Borough, AK	2,620
Santa Barbara County, CA	2,547
Fort Bend County, TX	2,469
Norfolk Independent City, VA	2,358
Philadelphia County, PA	2,293
Passaic County, NJ	2,270
Camden County, NJ	2,256
Macomb County, MI	2,222
Monmouth County, NJ	2,210
Baltimore County, MD	2,154
Tarrant County, TX	2,152
Morris County, NJ	2,116
Cuyahoga County, OH	2,046
Hillsborough County, FL	2,031
Will County, IL	2,005
Somerset County, NJ	1,984
Multnomah County, OR	1,966

Place	Number
Los Angeles, CA (city) Los Angeles County	63,567
San Diego, CA (city) San Diego County	41,658
New York, NY (city)	39,562
San Jose, CA (city) Santa Clara County	27,510
San Francisco, CA (city) San Francisco County	23,842
Honolulu, HI (cdp) Honolulu County	20,843
Daly City, CA (city) San Mateo County	19,102
Chicago, IL (city) Cook County	18,689
Vallejo, CA (city) Solano County	13,229
Jersey City, NJ (city) Hudson County	10,197
Long Beach, CA (city) Los Angeles County	10,059
Carson, CA (city) Los Angeles County	9,654
Seattle, WA (city) King County	9,363
Chula Vista, CA (city) San Diego County	7,834
Union City, CA (city) Alameda County	7,487
Glendale, CA (city) Los Angeles County	7,475
Stockton, CA (city) San Joaquin County	7,290
Hayward, CA (city) Alameda County	7,246
Waipahu, HI (cdp) Honolulu County	7,213
Fremont, CA (city) Alameda County	6,969
Las Vegas, NV (city) Clark County	6,271
South San Francisco, CA (city) San Mateo County	6,228
West Covina, CA (city) Los Angeles County	5,780
Jacksonville, FL (city) Duval County	5,771
Oxnard, CA (city) Ventura County	5,198
Milpitas, CA (city) Santa Clara County	5,156
Houston, TX (city) Harris County	5,091
Anaheim, CA (city) Orange County	4,760
Sacramento, CA (city) Sacramento County	4,541
National City, CA (city) San Diego County	4,534
Oakland, CA (city) Alameda County	4,044
Sunnyvale, CA (city) Santa Clara County	3,813
San Leandro, CA (city) Alameda County	3,790
Alameda, CA (city) Alameda County	3,674
Cerritos, CA (city) Los Angeles County	3,582
Fairfield, CA (city) Solano County	3,449
Santa Clara, CA (city) Santa Clara County	3,430
Paradise, NV (cdp) Clark County	3,317
Chino Hills, CA (city) San Bernardino County	3,213
Salinas, CA (city) Monterey County	3,184
Buena Park, CA (city) Orange County	3,026
Phoenix, AZ (city) Maricopa County	2,870
Kahului, HI (cdp) Maui County	2,789
Oceanside, CA (city) San Diego County	2,748
Hercules, CA (city) Contra Costa County	2,728
Lakewood, CA (city) Los Angeles County	2,726
Sunrise Manor, NV (cdp) Clark County	2,722
Pittsburg, CA (city) Contra Costa County	2,667
Fresno, CA (city) Fresno County	2,575
Hempstead, NY (town) Nassau County	2,458
Norwalk, CA (city) Los Angeles County	2,426
Pearl City, HI (cdp) Honolulu County	2,415
Reno, NV (city) Washoe County	2,383
Spring Valley, NV (cdp) Clark County	2,364
Torrance, CA (city) Los Angeles County	2,357
San Antonio, TX (city) Bexar County	2,348
Concord, CA (city) Contra Costa County	2,341
Philadelphia, PA (city) Philadelphia County	2,293
Ewa Beach, HI (cdp) Honolulu County	2,288
Moreno Valley, CA (city) Riverside County	2,260
Baldwin Park, CA (city) Los Angeles County	2,217
Walnut, CA (city) Los Angeles County	2,088
Delano, CA (city) Kern County	2,075
Village Park, HI (cdp) Honolulu County	2,007
Burbank, CA (city) Los Angeles County	2,000
Bellflower, CA (city) Los Angeles County	1,993
Rowland Heights, CA (cdp) Los Angeles County	1,961
Newark, CA (city) Alameda County	1,954
Mililani Town, HI (cdp) Honolulu County	1,945
San Mateo, CA (city) San Mateo County	1,939
San Bruno, CA (city) San Mateo County	1,917
Elk Grove, CA (cdp) Sacramento County	1,912
Antioch, CA (city) Contra Costa County	1,909
Diamond Bar, CA (city) Los Angeles County	1,899
Bergenfield, NJ (borough) Bergen County	1,867

Notes: Please refer to the User's Guide for an explanation of data; ranking tables include all places with Asian and/or NHPI populations above SF4 population thresholds; (1) tables reflect only those areas that meet SF4 population thresholds, therefore there may be less than 50 states, 75 counties or 75 places listed

Educational Attainment: High School Graduates

Filipinos 25 Years and Over Who are High School Graduates

All States, Top 75 Counties, and Top 75 Places Sorted by Percent[1]

State	Percent
New Jersey	94.45
New York	93.68
Connecticut	93.50
Illinois	93.45
Tennessee	93.25
Wisconsin	92.97
Michigan	92.78
Massachusetts	92.36
New Hampshire	92.14
West Virginia	91.86
Texas	91.73
Kentucky	91.49
Pennsylvania	91.41
Ohio	91.27
Indiana	90.65
Maryland	90.36
Colorado	89.99
Virginia	89.62
Wyoming	88.89
Florida	88.44
Missouri	88.43
Utah	88.41
Vermont	87.95
Georgia	87.87
Alabama	87.86
Minnesota	87.85
North Dakota	87.82
California	87.78
District of Columbia	87.74
North Carolina	87.69
United States	87.34
Washington	87.01
Delaware	87.00
New Mexico	86.99
Maine	86.86
Arizona	86.51
Nevada	86.42
Kansas	86.16
Iowa	85.34
Oregon	85.27
Nebraska	85.21
Idaho	84.72
Oklahoma	83.83
Rhode Island	83.42
South Carolina	83.13
Mississippi	82.45
South Dakota	81.92
Arkansas	80.82
Louisiana	80.18
Montana	76.74
Alaska	75.78
Hawaii	71.39

County	Percent
Chester County, PA	100.00
Durham County, NC	100.00
Hamilton County, TN	100.00
Cameron County, TX	99.50
Somerset County, NJ	99.20
Hidalgo County, TX	99.17
Jefferson County, TX	98.49
Richland County, SC	98.33
McHenry County, IL	98.28
Washtenaw County, MI	98.26
Kane County, IL	98.22
Alachua County, FL	98.16
Sussex County, NJ	97.81
Butte County, CA	97.35
Waukesha County, WI	97.33
Collin County, TX	97.28
Butler County, OH	97.14
Milwaukee County, WI	97.08
North Slope Borough, AK	96.79
New Castle County, DE	96.64
Johnson County, KS	96.60
Middlesex County, NJ	96.57
New York County, NY	96.57
Loudoun County, VA	96.52
Mercer County, NJ	96.47
Montgomery County, PA	96.28
Brazoria County, TX	96.23
Jefferson County, CO	96.17
Will County, IL	96.16
Essex County, NJ	96.04
Bergen County, NJ	96.02
Forsyth County, NC	96.02
Hamilton County, OH	96.02
Fairfield County, CT	96.01
Lorain County, OH	95.93
Comanche County, OK	95.85
Adams County, CO	95.56
Albany County, NY	95.52
Bucks County, PA	95.49
Jefferson County, NY	95.43
Suffolk County, NY	95.40
New Haven County, CT	95.37
Rockland County, NY	95.36
Monmouth County, NJ	95.34
Westchester County, NY	95.34
Leon County, FL	95.31
Morris County, NJ	95.27
Winnebago County, IL	95.10
Bronx County, NY	95.01
Denton County, TX	95.00
Essex County, MA	94.98
Oakland County, MI	94.98
Onondaga County, NY	94.98
Suffolk County, MA	94.98
Richmond County, NY	94.97
Gloucester County, NJ	94.93
Middlesex County, MA	94.88
Seminole County, FL	94.77
Hillsborough County, NH	94.70
Boulder County, CO	94.60
Portsmouth Independent City, VA	94.58
Charles County, MD	94.52
Guilford County, NC	94.50
DuPage County, IL	94.45
Wayne County, MI	94.43
Cumberland County, NC	94.41
Palm Beach County, FL	94.35
Alexandria Independent City, VA	94.22
Davidson County, TN	94.15
Genesee County, MI	94.12
Camden County, NJ	94.04
Howard County, MD	94.02
Hillsborough County, FL	93.98
Richmond Independent City, VA	93.94
Clackamas County, OR	93.91

Place	Percent
Beaumont, TX (city) Jefferson County	100.00
Bowie, MD (city) Prince George's County	100.00
Canton, MI (township) Wayne County	100.00
Des Plaines, IL (city) Cook County	100.00
Durham, NC (city) Durham County	100.00
East Brunswick, NJ (township) Middlesex County	100.00
East Meadow, NY (cdp) Nassau County	100.00
Franklin, NJ (township) Somerset County	100.00
Little Ferry, NJ (borough) Bergen County	100.00
Naperville, IL (city) Du Page County	100.00
Novato, CA (city) Marin County	100.00
Nutley, NJ (township) Essex County	100.00
Picnic Pt.-N. Lynnwood, WA (cdp) Snohomish County	100.00
Redland, MD (cdp) Montgomery County	100.00
Somerset, NJ (cdp) Somerset County	100.00
Tinley Park, IL (village) Cook County	100.00
Union City, NJ (city) Hudson County	100.00
Valley Cottage, NY (cdp) Rockland County	100.00
West Bloomfield, MI (township) Oakland County	100.00
Huntington, NY (town) Suffolk County	99.64
McAllen, TX (city) Hidalgo County	99.49
Edison, NJ (township) Middlesex County	99.42
Cupertino, CA (city) Santa Clara County	99.39
Greenburgh, NY (town) Westchester County	99.27
Aliso Viejo, CA (cdp) Orange County	99.17
Centreville, VA (cdp) Fairfax County	98.97
Monrovia, CA (city) Los Angeles County	98.90
Orland Park, IL (village) Cook County	98.87
Schaumburg, IL (village) Cook County	98.79
Plano, TX (city) Collin County	98.73
Streamwood, IL (village) Cook County	98.73
Ann Arbor, MI (city) Washtenaw County	98.62
Lincolnwood, IL (village) Cook County	98.62
Howell, NJ (township) Monmouth County	98.40
Old Bridge, NJ (township) Middlesex County	98.39
Teaneck, NJ (township) Bergen County	98.39
Clarkstown, NY (town) Rockland County	98.38
Danville, CA (town) Contra Costa County	98.34
Dumont, NJ (borough) Bergen County	98.30
Covina, CA (city) Los Angeles County	98.27
New City, NY (cdp) Rockland County	98.27
Freehold, NJ (township) Monmouth County	98.13
Livingston, NJ (township) Essex County	98.08
San Dimas, CA (city) Los Angeles County	98.07
Mount Prospect, IL (village) Cook County	98.06
Gurnee, IL (village) Lake County	98.02
Elgin, IL (city) Kane County	97.98
Park City, IL (city) Lake County	97.98
Bartlett, IL (village) Du Page County	97.86
Voorhees, NJ (township) Camden County	97.86
Costa Mesa, CA (city) Orange County	97.84
Santa Monica, CA (city) Los Angeles County	97.82
Bloomfield, NJ (township) Essex County	97.73
Burlingame, CA (city) San Mateo County	97.70
Colonia, NJ (cdp) Middlesex County	97.66
Burke, VA (cdp) Fairfax County	97.63
Bellevue, WA (city) King County	97.62
Folsom, CA (city) Sacramento County	97.62
Raleigh, NC (city) Wake County	97.62
Dover, NJ (township) Ocean County	97.59
Parsippany-Troy Hills, NJ (township) Morris County	97.59
Toms River, NJ (cdp) Ocean County	97.59
Rancho Santa Margarita, CA (city) Orange County	97.45
Lodi, NJ (borough) Bergen County	97.44
Englewood, NJ (city) Bergen County	97.39
Walnut Creek, CA (city) Contra Costa County	97.38
Aurora, IL (city) Kane County	97.37
Edmonds, WA (city) Snohomish County	97.35
Richardson, TX (city) Dallas County	97.28
Belleville, NJ (township) Essex County	97.25
Sterling Heights, MI (city) Macomb County	97.11
Rohnert Park, CA (city) Sonoma County	97.08
Franconia, VA (cdp) Fairfax County	97.03
Redondo Beach, CA (city) Los Angeles County	97.02
Stafford, TX (city) Fort Bend County	97.02

Notes: Please refer to the User's Guide for an explanation of data; ranking tables include all places with Asian and/or NHPI populations above SF4 population thresholds; (1) tables reflect only those areas that meet SF4 population thresholds, therefore there may be less than 50 states, 75 counties or 75 places listed

Educational Attainment: High School Graduates

Guamanians or Chamorros 25 Years and Over Who are High School Graduates

All States, Top 75 Counties, and Top 75 Places Sorted by Number[1]

State	Number
United States	25,286
California	10,299
Washington	2,520
Texas	1,542
Hawaii	780
Florida	745
New York	618
Arizona	579
Nevada	574
North Carolina	567
Oregon	548
Colorado	517
Virginia	497
Georgia	463
Illinois	397
Maryland	362
Missouri	294
Ohio	292
Pennsylvania	275
Oklahoma	228
Louisiana	225
Connecticut	207
Minnesota	196
Massachusetts	194
Michigan	186
New Mexico	176
New Jersey	175
Wisconsin	174
Tennessee	162
South Carolina	154
Alabama	147
Indiana	147
Kentucky	132

County	Number
San Diego County, CA	2,343
Los Angeles County, CA	1,330
Alameda County, CA	822
Pierce County, WA	785
Solano County, CA	755
Honolulu County, HI	714
Santa Clara County, CA	714
Orange County, CA	638
San Bernardino County, CA	565
Clark County, NV	517
Kitsap County, WA	472
Riverside County, CA	443
Sacramento County, CA	429
Thurston County, WA	385
King County, WA	376
Maricopa County, AZ	323
Bell County, TX	316
Monterey County, CA	308
Harris County, TX	297
Contra Costa County, CA	292
El Paso County, CO	284
San Mateo County, CA	250
Kings County, NY	121

Place	Number
San Diego, CA (city) San Diego County	1,074
Los Angeles, CA (city) Los Angeles County	496
San Jose, CA (city) Santa Clara County	427
New York, NY (city)	401
Vallejo, CA (city) Solano County	330
Honolulu, HI (cdp) Honolulu County	313
Fairfield, CA (city) Solano County	288
Killeen, TX (city) Bell County	257
Chula Vista, CA (city) San Diego County	207
Houston, TX (city) Harris County	205
Tacoma, WA (city) Pierce County	185

Notes: Please refer to the User's Guide for an explanation of data; ranking tables include all places with Asian and/or NHPI populations above SF4 population thresholds; (1) tables reflect only those areas that meet SF4 population thresholds, therefore there may be less than 50 states, 75 counties or 75 places listed

Educational Attainment: High School Graduates

Guamanians or Chamorros 25 Years and Over Who are High School Graduates

All States, Top 75 Counties, and Top 75 Places Sorted by Percent[1]

State	Percent
Hawaii	89.66
Connecticut	88.84
New Mexico	87.56
Maryland	86.60
Oregon	85.89
Washington	84.93
Arizona	84.53
Wisconsin	83.25
North Carolina	82.89
Virginia	82.70
Missouri	82.12
Nevada	81.42
Oklahoma	80.00
California	79.90
Ohio	79.78
Colorado	79.42
Texas	78.39
United States	77.85
Minnesota	77.47
Alabama	76.96
Massachusetts	73.21
Louisiana	72.58
Pennsylvania	70.88
Illinois	69.53
Kentucky	66.67
New York	66.24
South Carolina	64.17
Florida	62.87
Georgia	59.28
Michigan	59.24
Indiana	58.57
New Jersey	54.35
Tennessee	51.76

County	Percent
El Paso County, CO	94.98
Honolulu County, HI	91.89
Santa Clara County, CA	90.27
Monterey County, CA	89.80
Kitsap County, WA	88.56
Contra Costa County, CA	88.48
King County, WA	88.26
Alameda County, CA	87.45
San Mateo County, CA	87.41
Bell County, TX	87.05
San Bernardino County, CA	86.00
Thurston County, WA	85.18
Maricopa County, AZ	84.33
Clark County, NV	82.85
Pierce County, WA	82.72
Sacramento County, CA	81.40
San Diego County, CA	80.54
Orange County, CA	80.25
Harris County, TX	78.16
Solano County, CA	78.00
Los Angeles County, CA	70.07
Riverside County, CA	69.22
Kings County, NY	67.60

Place	Percent
San Jose, CA (city) Santa Clara County	90.85
Honolulu, HI (cdp) Honolulu County	87.43
Killeen, TX (city) Bell County	84.54
San Diego, CA (city) San Diego County	83.45
Vallejo, CA (city) Solano County	79.90
Fairfield, CA (city) Solano County	78.26
Tacoma, WA (city) Pierce County	74.00
Houston, TX (city) Harris County	73.21
Chula Vista, CA (city) San Diego County	72.38
New York, NY (city)	68.66
Los Angeles, CA (city) Los Angeles County	66.58

Notes: Please refer to the User's Guide for an explanation of data; ranking tables include all places with Asian and/or NHPI populations above SF4 population thresholds; (1) tables reflect only those areas that meet SF4 population thresholds, therefore there may be less than 50 states, 75 counties or 75 places listed

Educational Attainment: High School Graduates

Hawaiian Natives 25 Years and Over Who are High School Graduates

***All States, Top 75 Counties, and Top 75 Places Sorted by Number*[1]**

State	Number
United States	70,074
Hawaii	39,279
California	11,022
Washington	2,566
Nevada	1,901
Texas	1,557
Oregon	1,162
Florida	1,010
Arizona	894
New York	772
Colorado	738
Utah	625
Virginia	560
North Carolina	514
Pennsylvania	464
Illinois	418
Georgia	411
Ohio	368
Missouri	356
Indiana	332
Michigan	327
Oklahoma	326
New Jersey	321
Minnesota	315
Maryland	314
Tennessee	292
South Carolina	285
New Mexico	258
Alaska	244
Kansas	244
Massachusetts	230
Louisiana	198
Wisconsin	196
Idaho	164
Montana	126
Arkansas	107

County	Number
Honolulu County, HI	25,178
Hawaii County, HI	6,644
Maui County, HI	5,187
Los Angeles County, CA	2,318
Kauai County, HI	2,241
Clark County, NV	1,720
San Diego County, CA	1,343
Orange County, CA	1,046
King County, WA	888
Alameda County, CA	777
Santa Clara County, CA	656
Pierce County, WA	512
Maricopa County, AZ	486
San Mateo County, CA	480
Riverside County, CA	474
Ventura County, CA	370
San Bernardino County, CA	364
Sacramento County, CA	340
Solano County, CA	334
Contra Costa County, CA	328
Washington County, OR	284
Multnomah County, OR	271
Snohomish County, WA	270
Salt Lake County, UT	248
San Joaquin County, CA	228
Bexar County, TX	226
Pima County, AZ	206
Utah County, UT	114

Place	Number
Honolulu, HI (cdp) Honolulu County	7,988
Hilo, HI (cdp) Hawaii County	1,971
Kaneohe, HI (cdp) Honolulu County	1,733
Kailua, HI (cdp) Honolulu County	1,398
Nanakuli, HI (cdp) Honolulu County	1,318
Waianae, HI (cdp) Honolulu County	1,087
Waimanalo Beach, HI (cdp) Honolulu County	1,079
Los Angeles, CA (city) Los Angeles County	891
San Diego, CA (city) San Diego County	682
Pearl City, HI (cdp) Honolulu County	650
Kahului, HI (cdp) Maui County	567
Kailua, HI (cdp) Hawaii County	551
Mililani Town, HI (cdp) Honolulu County	550
Makaha, HI (cdp) Honolulu County	520
Wailuku, HI (cdp) Maui County	510
Waimea, HI (cdp) Hawaii County	503
Waimalu, HI (cdp) Honolulu County	499
Makakilo City, HI (cdp) Honolulu County	497
Las Vegas, NV (city) Clark County	463
Maili, HI (cdp) Honolulu County	457
Wahiawa, HI (cdp) Honolulu County	454
Waihee-Waiehu, HI (cdp) Maui County	450
Anahola, HI (cdp) Kauai County	443
Waipahu, HI (cdp) Honolulu County	434
Ewa Beach, HI (cdp) Honolulu County	421
Halawa, HI (cdp) Honolulu County	416
Waimanalo, HI (cdp) Honolulu County	408
Kualapuu, HI (cdp) Maui County	407
Lahaina, HI (cdp) Maui County	403
New York, NY (city)	388
Kihei, HI (cdp) Maui County	384
Ahuimanu, HI (cdp) Honolulu County	359
Kapaa, HI (cdp) Kauai County	343
Kalaoa, HI (cdp) Hawaii County	311
Kaunakakai, HI (cdp) Maui County	309
San Jose, CA (city) Santa Clara County	308
Hawaiian Paradise Park, HI (cdp) Hawaii County	304
Henderson, NV (city) Clark County	297
Hauula, HI (cdp) Honolulu County	288
Makawao, HI (cdp) Maui County	271
Holualoa, HI (cdp) Hawaii County	234
Paradise, NV (cdp) Clark County	233
Phoenix, AZ (city) Maricopa County	231
Aiea, HI (cdp) Honolulu County	229
Kahaluu, HI (cdp) Honolulu County	227
Waipio, HI (cdp) Honolulu County	216
Portland, OR (city) Multnomah County	201
Laie, HI (cdp) Honolulu County	186
Hawaiian Beaches, HI (cdp) Hawaii County	178
Waikoloa Village, HI (cdp) Hawaii County	152
Volcano, HI (cdp) Hawaii County	147
Kekaha, HI (cdp) Kauai County	132
Honaunau-Napoopoo, HI (cdp) Hawaii County	125
Hana, HI (cdp) Maui County	122
Kaaawa, HI (cdp) Honolulu County	122
Haleiwa, HI (cdp) Honolulu County	116
Paia, HI (cdp) Maui County	110
Makaha Valley, HI (cdp) Honolulu County	105
Hawaiian Ocean View, HI (cdp) Hawaii County	102
Captain Cook, HI (cdp) Hawaii County	99
Waimea, HI (cdp) Kauai County	91
Hanapepe, HI (cdp) Kauai County	82
Honalo, HI (cdp) Hawaii County	78
Kahuku, HI (cdp) Honolulu County	76
Waikane, HI (cdp) Honolulu County	70
Naalehu, HI (cdp) Hawaii County	55
Kilauea, HI (cdp) Kauai County	50
Waialua, HI (cdp) Honolulu County	50
Kapaau, HI (cdp) Hawaii County	49
Punaluu, HI (cdp) Honolulu County	48
Pakala Village, HI (cdp) Kauai County	41
Pahala, HI (cdp) Hawaii County	32

Notes: Please refer to the User's Guide for an explanation of data; ranking tables include all places with Asian and/or NHPI populations above SF4 population thresholds; (1) tables reflect only those areas that meet SF4 population thresholds, therefore there may be less than 50 states, 75 counties or 75 places listed

Educational Attainment: High School Graduates

Hawaiian Natives 25 Years and Over Who are High School Graduates

All States, Top 75 Counties, and Top 75 Places Sorted by Percent[1]

State	Percent
Massachusetts	98.29
Kansas	95.69
Virginia	94.28
Indiana	91.21
Montana	90.65
Washington	89.59
Arizona	88.69
Colorado	86.93
Oregon	86.91
Alaska	86.52
Maryland	85.79
New Mexico	85.71
Utah	85.62
Missouri	85.58
Idaho	85.42
North Carolina	84.96
Nevada	84.71
Hawaii	83.51
California	83.34
Louisiana	83.19
United States	83.17
Wisconsin	83.05
Ohio	81.96
Minnesota	79.95
New York	79.92
South Carolina	79.17
Michigan	77.67
Tennessee	77.04
Oklahoma	76.35
Florida	76.05
Pennsylvania	75.69
Illinois	73.85
New Jersey	72.13
Texas	71.13
Georgia	69.78
Arkansas	67.30

County	Percent
Ventura County, CA	93.43
King County, WA	92.02
Multnomah County, OR	91.86
Pierce County, WA	90.62
Maricopa County, AZ	89.83
Orange County, CA	89.71
San Diego County, CA	89.06
Snohomish County, WA	88.82
San Mateo County, CA	88.56
Washington County, OR	88.20
San Joaquin County, CA	88.03
Salt Lake County, UT	86.11
Clark County, NV	85.87
Santa Clara County, CA	85.31
Honolulu County, HI	84.46
Hawaii County, HI	83.93
Pima County, AZ	83.40
Alameda County, CA	83.37
Kauai County, HI	83.18
Contra Costa County, CA	82.41
Los Angeles County, CA	82.08
Riverside County, CA	80.20
San Bernardino County, CA	80.00
Maui County, HI	79.48
Sacramento County, CA	78.89
Utah County, UT	78.08
Bexar County, TX	74.59
Solano County, CA	73.89

Place	Percent
Mililani Town, HI (cdp) Honolulu County	100.00
Holualoa, HI (cdp) Hawaii County	98.32
Henderson, NV (city) Clark County	95.50
Waipio, HI (cdp) Honolulu County	95.15
Aiea, HI (cdp) Honolulu County	95.02
Laie, HI (cdp) Honolulu County	94.90
Kilauea, HI (cdp) Kauai County	94.34
Waimanalo, HI (cdp) Honolulu County	93.79
Hawaiian Paradise Park, HI (cdp) Hawaii County	93.25
Makakilo City, HI (cdp) Honolulu County	93.25
Makawao, HI (cdp) Maui County	92.49
Portland, OR (city) Multnomah County	92.20
Hanapepe, HI (cdp) Kauai County	92.13
Waikane, HI (cdp) Honolulu County	92.11
Kailua, HI (cdp) Honolulu County	91.73
San Diego, CA (city) San Diego County	91.54
Haleiwa, HI (cdp) Honolulu County	91.34
Kaneohe, HI (cdp) Honolulu County	89.89
Makaha, HI (cdp) Honolulu County	89.81
Ahuimanu, HI (cdp) Honolulu County	89.75
Waikoloa Village, HI (cdp) Hawaii County	88.37
Makaha Valley, HI (cdp) Honolulu County	88.24
Phoenix, AZ (city) Maricopa County	87.83
Hilo, HI (cdp) Hawaii County	87.52
Hawaiian Beaches, HI (cdp) Hawaii County	87.25
Kaaawa, HI (cdp) Honolulu County	87.14
Waihee-Waiehu, HI (cdp) Maui County	86.71
Waimalu, HI (cdp) Honolulu County	86.63
Hawaiian Ocean View, HI (cdp) Hawaii County	86.44
Kailua, HI (cdp) Hawaii County	86.23
Kapaau, HI (cdp) Hawaii County	85.96
Kalaoa, HI (cdp) Hawaii County	85.21
Kapaa, HI (cdp) Kauai County	84.90
San Jose, CA (city) Santa Clara County	84.85
Paia, HI (cdp) Maui County	84.62
Anahola, HI (cdp) Kauai County	83.74
Kahuku, HI (cdp) Honolulu County	83.52
Honolulu, HI (cdp) Honolulu County	83.47
Wahiawa, HI (cdp) Honolulu County	83.46
Waianae, HI (cdp) Honolulu County	83.42
Pearl City, HI (cdp) Honolulu County	82.59
Waimea, HI (cdp) Hawaii County	82.59
Waimanalo Beach, HI (cdp) Honolulu County	82.49
Volcano, HI (cdp) Hawaii County	82.12
Kihei, HI (cdp) Maui County	82.05
Hana, HI (cdp) Maui County	81.88
Las Vegas, NV (city) Clark County	81.37
Kaunakakai, HI (cdp) Maui County	80.89
Los Angeles, CA (city) Los Angeles County	80.85
Waimea, HI (cdp) Kauai County	80.53
Halawa, HI (cdp) Honolulu County	80.31
Naalehu, HI (cdp) Hawaii County	79.71
Kualapuu, HI (cdp) Maui County	78.27
Ewa Beach, HI (cdp) Honolulu County	77.53
Nanakuli, HI (cdp) Honolulu County	76.41
Waipahu, HI (cdp) Honolulu County	76.14
Captain Cook, HI (cdp) Hawaii County	75.00
Honalo, HI (cdp) Hawaii County	75.00
Lahaina, HI (cdp) Maui County	74.91
Wailuku, HI (cdp) Maui County	74.67
Pahala, HI (cdp) Hawaii County	74.42
Kekaha, HI (cdp) Kauai County	73.74
New York, NY (city)	72.93
Paradise, NV (cdp) Clark County	72.14
Hauula, HI (cdp) Honolulu County	72.00
Waialua, HI (cdp) Honolulu County	71.43
Maili, HI (cdp) Honolulu County	70.42
Kahului, HI (cdp) Maui County	68.98
Punaluu, HI (cdp) Honolulu County	66.67
Honaunau-Napoopoo, HI (cdp) Hawaii County	66.14
Kahaluu, HI (cdp) Honolulu County	65.42
Pakala Village, HI (cdp) Kauai County	48.81

Notes: Please refer to the User's Guide for an explanation of data; ranking tables include all places with Asian and/or NHPI populations above SF4 population thresholds; (1) tables reflect only those areas that meet SF4 population thresholds, therefore there may be less than 50 states, 75 counties or 75 places listed

Educational Attainment: High School Graduates

Hmongs 25 Years and Over Who are High School Graduates

All States, Top 75 Counties, and Top 75 Places Sorted by Number[1]

State	Number
United States	21,922
California	7,347
Minnesota	6,220
Wisconsin	4,002
North Carolina	929
Michigan	796
Colorado	637
Washington	239
Oregon	234
Georgia	206
Rhode Island	181
Massachusetts	165
Kansas	126
South Carolina	125
Pennsylvania	123
Oklahoma	59
Alaska	42

County	Number
Ramsey County, MN	3,947
Fresno County, CA	2,259
Sacramento County, CA	1,957
Hennepin County, MN	1,571
Milwaukee County, WI	1,097
Merced County, CA	617
San Joaquin County, CA	555
Adams County, CO	553
Dane County, WI	400
Marathon County, WI	376
Outagamie County, WI	345
Butte County, CA	292
Macomb County, MI	269
Sheboygan County, WI	269
Yuba County, CA	259
San Diego County, CA	255
Catawba County, NC	248
Eau Claire County, WI	248
La Crosse County, WI	247
Brown County, WI	243
Orange County, CA	237
Washington County, MN	228
Anoka County, MN	196
Winnebago County, WI	187
Burke County, NC	167
Multnomah County, OR	164
Providence County, RI	164
Oakland County, MI	155
Wayne County, MI	138
Manitowoc County, WI	115
Spartanburg County, SC	111
King County, WA	109
Olmsted County, MN	109
Wyandotte County, KS	108
Spokane County, WA	100
Portage County, WI	97
Yolo County, CA	95
Riverside County, CA	94
Wood County, WI	84
Stanislaus County, CA	81
Tulare County, CA	79
Santa Barbara County, CA	69
Dunn County, WI	67
Lancaster County, PA	63
Mecklenburg County, NC	58
Solano County, CA	58
Los Angeles County, CA	57
Worcester County, MA	55
Glenn County, CA	47
Ingham County, MI	44
Anchorage Borough, AK	42
Chippewa County, WI	35
Calumet County, WI	32
Stanly County, NC	31
Jefferson County, CO	29
Barrow County, GA	28
Fond du Lac County, WI	16

Place	Number
St. Paul, MN (city) Ramsey County	3,612
Fresno, CA (city) Fresno County	1,754
Sacramento, CA (city) Sacramento County	1,247
Minneapolis, MN (city) Hennepin County	1,083
Milwaukee, WI (city) Milwaukee County	1,008
Stockton, CA (city) San Joaquin County	464
Merced, CA (city) Merced County	361
Parkway-S. Sacramento, CA (cdp) Sacramento County	349
Appleton, WI (city) Outagamie County	336
Madison, WI (city) Dane County	323
Clovis, CA (city) Fresno County	302
Wausau, WI (city) Marathon County	284
Eau Claire, WI (city) Eau Claire County	250
Sheboygan, WI (city) Sheboygan County	246
Brooklyn Center, MN (city) Hennepin County	215
Westminster, CO (city) Adams County	209
San Diego, CA (city) San Diego County	190
Green Bay, WI (city) Brown County	187
Warren, MI (city) Macomb County	187
Linda, CA (cdp) Yuba County	145
Brooklyn Park, MN (city) Hennepin County	142
Maplewood, MN (city) Ramsey County	140
Portland, OR (city) Multnomah County	137
La Crosse, WI (city) La Crosse County	135
Providence, RI (city) Providence County	125
Oshkosh, WI (city) Winnebago County	122
Detroit, MI (city) Wayne County	121
Rochester, MN (city) Olmsted County	109
Kansas City, KS (city) Wyandotte County	108
Manitowoc, WI (city) Manitowoc County	100
Pontiac, MI (city) Oakland County	90
West Sacramento, CA (city) Yolo County	90
Hickory, NC (city) Catawba County	88
Stevens Point, WI (city) Portage County	87
Chico, CA (city) Butte County	86
Woodbury, MN (city) Washington County	85
Wisconsin Rapids, WI (city) Wood County	75
Florin, CA (cdp) Sacramento County	74
Arden-Arcade, CA (cdp) Sacramento County	73
Santa Ana, CA (city) Orange County	71
Spokane, WA (city) Spokane County	67
Atwater, CA (city) Merced County	62
Charlotte, NC (city) Mecklenburg County	58
Thermalito, CA (cdp) Butte County	55
Fitchburg, MA (city) Worcester County	52
Modesto, CA (city) Stanislaus County	52
Willows, CA (city) Glenn County	47
Lansing, MI (city) Ingham County	44
Oroville, CA (city) Butte County	41
South Oroville, CA (cdp) Butte County	40
Visalia, CA (city) Tulare County	31
Fond du Lac, WI (city) Fond du Lac County	16
Glen Alpine, NC (town) Burke County	12
Connelly Springs, NC (town) Burke County	10
Valdese, NC (town) Burke County	7

Notes: Please refer to the User's Guide for an explanation of data; ranking tables include all places with Asian and/or NHPI populations above SF4 population thresholds; (1) tables reflect only those areas that meet SF4 population thresholds, therefore there may be less than 50 states, 75 counties or 75 places listed

Educational Attainment: High School Graduates

Hmongs 25 Years and Over Who are High School Graduates

All States, Top 75 Counties, and Top 75 Places Sorted by Percent[1]

State	Percent
Rhode Island	62.20
Colorado	55.49
Oregon	54.93
Massachusetts	50.61
Oklahoma	48.36
Georgia	45.78
Minnesota	44.92
Washington	44.26
Michigan	43.10
North Carolina	42.93
Pennsylvania	42.41
Wisconsin	41.05
United States	40.40
Kansas	40.26
South Carolina	38.46
California	34.37
Alaska	21.76

County	Percent
Anoka County, MN	82.01
Washington County, MN	78.35
Olmsted County, MN	69.87
Santa Barbara County, CA	69.00
Providence County, RI	65.86
Adams County, CO	64.45
Riverside County, CA	61.84
Macomb County, MI	61.28
Eau Claire County, WI	58.91
Yolo County, CA	55.56
Los Angeles County, CA	55.34
Dane County, WI	55.10
Wood County, WI	53.85
Orange County, CA	51.41
Multnomah County, OR	50.93
Dunn County, WI	47.52
San Diego County, CA	45.86
Spokane County, WA	45.25
Portage County, WI	45.12
Ramsey County, MN	44.99
La Crosse County, WI	44.11
Outagamie County, WI	43.56
Milwaukee County, WI	42.85
Barrow County, GA	42.42
Winnebago County, WI	42.12
Wyandotte County, KS	42.02
Mecklenburg County, NC	39.73
Catawba County, NC	39.68
Hennepin County, MN	39.05
Solano County, CA	38.93
Oakland County, MI	38.56
Butte County, CA	38.47
King County, WA	37.72
Spartanburg County, SC	37.50
Sacramento County, CA	37.38
Lancaster County, PA	37.28
Manitowoc County, WI	34.53
Sheboygan County, WI	34.22
Chippewa County, WI	32.11
Yuba County, CA	31.43
Marathon County, WI	31.31
Brown County, WI	30.99
Merced County, CA	30.87
Stanly County, NC	30.39
Fresno County, CA	30.32
San Joaquin County, CA	29.35
Burke County, NC	29.25
Ingham County, MI	29.14
Stanislaus County, CA	28.62
Worcester County, MA	28.21
Wayne County, MI	26.54
Calumet County, WI	25.60
Jefferson County, CO	25.00
Tulare County, CA	23.94
Glenn County, CA	22.93
Anchorage Borough, AK	21.76
Fond du Lac County, WI	20.78

Place	Percent
Maplewood, MN (city) Ramsey County	84.34
Providence, RI (city) Providence County	72.67
Rochester, MN (city) Olmsted County	69.87
Woodbury, MN (city) Washington County	68.55
Arden-Arcade, CA (cdp) Sacramento County	64.04
Westminster, CO (city) Adams County	58.87
Warren, MI (city) Macomb County	58.81
Wisconsin Rapids, WI (city) Wood County	58.14
Eau Claire, WI (city) Eau Claire County	56.56
Madison, WI (city) Dane County	56.17
West Sacramento, CA (city) Yolo County	54.22
Modesto, CA (city) Stanislaus County	50.98
Portland, OR (city) Multnomah County	49.82
Clovis, CA (city) Fresno County	48.24
Brooklyn Park, MN (city) Hennepin County	48.14
Stevens Point, WI (city) Portage County	47.54
Brooklyn Center, MN (city) Hennepin County	46.84
Spokane, WA (city) Spokane County	45.89
San Diego, CA (city) San Diego County	45.35
Atwater, CA (city) Merced County	43.66
Appleton, WI (city) Outagamie County	43.35
St. Paul, MN (city) Ramsey County	43.21
Parkway-S. Sacramento, CA (cdp) Sacramento County	42.56
Oroville, CA (city) Butte County	42.27
Hickory, NC (city) Catawba County	42.11
Kansas City, KS (city) Wyandotte County	42.02
Oshkosh, WI (city) Winnebago County	41.36
Milwaukee, WI (city) Milwaukee County	41.33
Charlotte, NC (city) Mecklenburg County	39.73
Chico, CA (city) Butte County	39.63
Connelly Springs, NC (town) Burke County	38.46
Thermalito, CA (cdp) Butte County	37.16
La Crosse, WI (city) La Crosse County	35.90
Minneapolis, MN (city) Hennepin County	35.63
Manitowoc, WI (city) Manitowoc County	34.48
Sacramento, CA (city) Sacramento County	34.21
Florin, CA (cdp) Sacramento County	32.60
Sheboygan, WI (city) Sheboygan County	32.58
Pontiac, MI (city) Oakland County	31.58
Stockton, CA (city) San Joaquin County	30.51
Santa Ana, CA (city) Orange County	29.96
Fitchburg, MA (city) Worcester County	29.89
Green Bay, WI (city) Brown County	28.81
Merced, CA (city) Merced County	28.79
Wausau, WI (city) Marathon County	28.43
Fond du Lac, WI (city) Fond du Lac County	28.07
Fresno, CA (city) Fresno County	27.99
Detroit, MI (city) Wayne County	27.19
Lansing, MI (city) Ingham County	27.16
South Oroville, CA (cdp) Butte County	25.81
Linda, CA (cdp) Yuba County	25.48
Willows, CA (city) Glenn County	22.93
Visalia, CA (city) Tulare County	20.39
Glen Alpine, NC (town) Burke County	20.34
Valdese, NC (town) Burke County	19.44

Notes: Please refer to the User's Guide for an explanation of data; ranking tables include all places with Asian and/or NHPI populations above SF4 population thresholds; (1) tables reflect only those areas that meet SF4 population thresholds, therefore there may be less than 50 states, 75 counties or 75 places listed

Educational Attainment: High School Graduates

Indonesians 25 Years and Over Who are High School Graduates

All States, Top 75 Counties, and Top 75 Places Sorted by Number[1]

State	Number
United States	21,566
California	9,483
New York	1,464
Texas	1,081
Washington	730
New Jersey	686
Maryland	654
Illinois	650
Florida	647
Virginia	618
Ohio	446
Colorado	442
Arizona	349
Pennsylvania	320
Massachusetts	315
Michigan	307
Georgia	304
Oregon	295
Wisconsin	196

County	Number
Los Angeles County, CA	3,169
San Bernardino County, CA	1,885
Orange County, CA	1,110
Queens County, NY	720
Montgomery County, MD	552
King County, WA	481
San Francisco County, CA	473
Harris County, TX	448
San Mateo County, CA	415
Santa Clara County, CA	395
Contra Costa County, CA	363
Cook County, IL	344
San Diego County, CA	327
Alameda County, CA	320
Middlesex County, NJ	316
Maricopa County, AZ	283
Fairfax County, VA	278
Franklin County, OH	111

Place	Number
Los Angeles, CA (city) Los Angeles County	1,116
New York, NY (city)	1,087
San Francisco, CA (city) San Francisco County	473
Houston, TX (city) Harris County	325
Loma Linda, CA (city) San Bernardino County	279
Seattle, WA (city) King County	179
San Bernardino, CA (city) San Bernardino County	158
Columbus, OH (city) Franklin County	90

Notes: Please refer to the User's Guide for an explanation of data; ranking tables include all places with Asian and/or NHPI populations above SF4 population thresholds; (1) tables reflect only those areas that meet SF4 population thresholds, therefore there may be less than 50 states, 75 counties or 75 places listed

Educational Attainment: High School Graduates

Indonesians 25 Years and Over Who are High School Graduates

All States, Top 75 Counties, and Top 75 Places Sorted by Percent[1]

State	Percent
Wisconsin	100.00
Illinois	98.93
Texas	98.18
Ohio	97.38
Colorado	96.72
Washington	96.56
New Jersey	95.81
Florida	93.63
New York	93.07
United States	92.60
Virginia	92.10
Oregon	91.61
California	91.39
Pennsylvania	89.39
Arizona	88.58
Michigan	88.47
Maryland	87.67
Massachusetts	87.50
Georgia	81.50

County	Percent
Cook County, IL	100.00
Franklin County, OH	100.00
Contra Costa County, CA	97.84
San Diego County, CA	97.61
King County, WA	97.57
San Mateo County, CA	96.74
Middlesex County, NJ	96.34
San Francisco County, CA	95.75
Harris County, TX	95.73
Maricopa County, AZ	94.33
Queens County, NY	93.75
San Bernardino County, CA	93.69
Santa Clara County, CA	93.60
Orange County, CA	90.76
Los Angeles County, CA	89.52
Montgomery County, MD	85.71
Fairfax County, VA	85.28
Alameda County, CA	84.66

Place	Percent
Columbus, OH (city) Franklin County	100.00
Loma Linda, CA (city) San Bernardino County	100.00
Seattle, WA (city) King County	96.76
Houston, TX (city) Harris County	95.87
San Francisco, CA (city) San Francisco County	95.75
Los Angeles, CA (city) Los Angeles County	94.50
New York, NY (city)	92.12
San Bernardino, CA (city) San Bernardino County	87.29

Notes: Please refer to the User's Guide for an explanation of data; ranking tables include all places with Asian and/or NHPI populations above SF4 population thresholds; (1) tables reflect only those areas that meet SF4 population thresholds, therefore there may be less than 50 states, 75 counties or 75 places listed

Educational Attainment: High School Graduates

Japanese 25 Years and Over Who are High School Graduates

***All States, Top 75 Counties, and Top 75 Places Sorted by Number*[1]**

State	Number
United States	577,286
California	216,928
Hawaii	147,066
New York	27,401
Washington	26,520
Illinois	15,480
Texas	11,169
New Jersey	9,945
Colorado	8,754
Florida	8,143
Oregon	8,056
Michigan	7,168
Massachusetts	6,792
Ohio	6,659
Virginia	6,406
Nevada	6,072
Arizona	5,503
Georgia	5,163
Maryland	5,138
Pennsylvania	4,534
North Carolina	4,177
Utah	3,953
Indiana	3,058
Minnesota	2,873
Connecticut	2,730
Tennessee	2,425
Missouri	2,339
Wisconsin	2,131
Kentucky	2,089
Idaho	1,965
South Carolina	1,649
Oklahoma	1,646
New Mexico	1,549
Alabama	1,203
Kansas	1,185
Alaska	1,118
Nebraska	972
Louisiana	917
Iowa	786
District of Columbia	743
Arkansas	732
New Hampshire	591
Montana	552
Rhode Island	529
West Virginia	455
Delaware	421
Wyoming	394
Mississippi	374
Maine	345
Vermont	218
South Dakota	183

County	Number
Honolulu County, HI	118,013
Los Angeles County, CA	84,489
Orange County, CA	22,106
Santa Clara County, CA	20,872
King County, WA	16,761
Hawaii County, HI	14,660
San Diego County, CA	13,331
New York County, NY	11,497
Cook County, IL	10,973
Sacramento County, CA	9,729
Alameda County, CA	9,429
Maui County, HI	9,028
San Francisco County, CA	8,584
San Mateo County, CA	7,342
Contra Costa County, CA	6,363
Kauai County, HI	5,365
Bergen County, NJ	4,874
Clark County, NV	4,858
Westchester County, NY	4,858
Fresno County, CA	4,338
Ventura County, CA	3,841
Queens County, NY	3,783
Maricopa County, AZ	3,781
San Bernardino County, CA	3,239
Riverside County, CA	3,013
Oakland County, MI	2,934
Middlesex County, MA	2,749
Multnomah County, OR	2,740
San Joaquin County, CA	2,521
Pierce County, WA	2,513
Harris County, TX	2,496
Montgomery County, MD	2,490
Monterey County, CA	2,427
Salt Lake County, UT	2,241
Fairfax County, VA	2,117
Franklin County, OH	1,959
Washington County, OR	1,891
Snohomish County, WA	1,736
Dallas County, TX	1,669
Kings County, NY	1,603
Santa Barbara County, CA	1,602
Denver County, CO	1,593
Fairfield County, CT	1,534
Solano County, CA	1,463
Jefferson County, CO	1,435
Marin County, CA	1,422
Placer County, CA	1,388
Nassau County, NY	1,330
Norfolk County, MA	1,328
Santa Cruz County, CA	1,272
Arapahoe County, CO	1,253
Hennepin County, MN	1,232
DuPage County, IL	1,206
Sonoma County, CA	1,197
Bexar County, TX	1,164
Washtenaw County, MI	1,127
Suffolk County, MA	1,126
Pima County, AZ	1,025
El Paso County, CO	1,017
Lake County, IL	1,015
Arlington County, VA	989
Miami-Dade County, FL	964
Boulder County, CO	931
Clark County, WA	922
Orange County, FL	921
Spokane County, WA	906
Yolo County, CA	898
Washoe County, NV	869
Travis County, TX	866
Kitsap County, WA	862
Cuyahoga County, OH	860
St. Louis County, MO	848
Allegheny County, PA	842
Bernalillo County, NM	831
Broward County, FL	805

Place	Number
Honolulu, HI (cdp) Honolulu County	63,255
Los Angeles, CA (city) Los Angeles County	27,754
New York, NY (city)	17,426
Torrance, CA (city) Los Angeles County	9,768
San Jose, CA (city) Santa Clara County	8,768
San Francisco, CA (city) San Francisco County	8,584
Hilo, HI (cdp) Hawaii County	7,885
Pearl City, HI (cdp) Honolulu County	7,175
San Diego, CA (city) San Diego County	7,027
Seattle, WA (city) King County	6,783
Kaneohe, HI (cdp) Honolulu County	6,190
Waimalu, HI (cdp) Honolulu County	6,134
Sacramento, CA (city) Sacramento County	5,353
Gardena, CA (city) Los Angeles County	5,336
Mililani Town, HI (cdp) Honolulu County	5,177
Chicago, IL (city) Cook County	4,925
Monterey Park, CA (city) Los Angeles County	3,766
Kailua, HI (cdp) Honolulu County	3,310
Irvine, CA (city) Orange County	3,211
Sunnyvale, CA (city) Santa Clara County	2,629
Long Beach, CA (city) Los Angeles County	2,593
Portland, OR (city) Multnomah County	2,320
Waipahu, HI (cdp) Honolulu County	2,318
Kahului, HI (cdp) Maui County	2,298
Huntington Beach, CA (city) Orange County	2,238
Wahiawa, HI (cdp) Honolulu County	2,234
Bellevue, WA (city) King County	2,227
Aiea, HI (cdp) Honolulu County	2,127
Rancho Palos Verdes, CA (city) Los Angeles County	2,085
Wailuku, HI (cdp) Maui County	2,033
Waipio, HI (cdp) Honolulu County	2,024
Fresno, CA (city) Fresno County	1,986
Halawa, HI (cdp) Honolulu County	1,872
Pasadena, CA (city) Los Angeles County	1,830
Las Vegas, NV (city) Clark County	1,786
Oakland, CA (city) Alameda County	1,704
Anaheim, CA (city) Orange County	1,659
Cupertino, CA (city) Santa Clara County	1,635
Redondo Beach, CA (city) Los Angeles County	1,626
Houston, TX (city) Harris County	1,621
Denver, CO (city) Denver County	1,593
San Mateo, CA (city) San Mateo County	1,540
Berkeley, CA (city) Alameda County	1,526
Mountain View, CA (city) Santa Clara County	1,447
Chula Vista, CA (city) San Diego County	1,445
Santa Monica, CA (city) Los Angeles County	1,400
Cerritos, CA (city) Los Angeles County	1,394
Montebello, CA (city) Los Angeles County	1,384
Fort Lee, NJ (borough) Bergen County	1,316
Fremont, CA (city) Alameda County	1,279
Greenburgh, NY (town) Westchester County	1,279
Ahuimanu, HI (cdp) Honolulu County	1,262
Glendale, CA (city) Los Angeles County	1,209
Phoenix, AZ (city) Maricopa County	1,201
Santa Clara, CA (city) Santa Clara County	1,178
Lihue, HI (cdp) Kauai County	1,173
Stockton, CA (city) San Joaquin County	1,112
Alhambra, CA (city) Los Angeles County	1,106
Boston, MA (city) Suffolk County	1,098
Culver City, CA (city) Los Angeles County	1,095
Columbus, OH (city) Franklin County	1,081
Foster City, CA (city) San Mateo County	1,027
Heeia, HI (cdp) Honolulu County	1,024
Hacienda Heights, CA (cdp) Los Angeles County	1,005
Arlington, VA (cdp) Arlington County	989
Palo Alto, CA (city) Santa Clara County	955
Fountain Valley, CA (city) Orange County	951
San Antonio, TX (city) Bexar County	950
El Cerrito, CA (city) Contra Costa County	932
Oceanside, CA (city) San Diego County	920
Costa Mesa, CA (city) Orange County	914
Paradise, NV (cdp) Clark County	904
Fullerton, CA (city) Orange County	893
West Carson, CA (cdp) Los Angeles County	893
Brookline, MA (town) Norfolk County	880

Notes: Please refer to the User's Guide for an explanation of data; ranking tables include all places with Asian and/or NHPI populations above SF4 population thresholds; (1) tables reflect only those areas that meet SF4 population thresholds, therefore there may be less than 50 states, 75 counties or 75 places listed

Educational Attainment: High School Graduates

Japanese 25 Years and Over Who are High School Graduates

All States, Top 75 Counties, and Top 75 Places Sorted by Percent[1]

State	Percent
Nebraska	97.30
Vermont	96.04
New York	95.90
Illinois	95.57
Michigan	95.32
West Virginia	95.19
Minnesota	95.07
New Jersey	94.99
Massachusetts	94.95
Alaska	94.59
Oregon	94.32
Wyoming	94.03
Connecticut	93.94
District of Columbia	93.69
Kentucky	93.59
Wisconsin	93.51
Georgia	93.25
Maryland	93.18
Ohio	93.13
California	92.94
Tennessee	92.91
Indiana	92.84
Idaho	92.73
New Hampshire	92.63
Virginia	92.40
Washington	92.15
Utah	92.10
Rhode Island	92.00
Texas	91.88
Colorado	91.75
Iowa	91.50
North Carolina	91.42
Montana	91.24
United States	91.12
Arizona	91.08
South Carolina	91.05
New Mexico	90.58
Pennsylvania	90.09
Kansas	89.91
Nevada	89.49
Missouri	88.73
Alabama	88.46
Florida	88.12
Oklahoma	87.14
Hawaii	86.26
Louisiana	85.38
Mississippi	85.00
South Dakota	84.72
Arkansas	84.53
Delaware	84.20
Maine	80.05

County	Percent
Cobb County, GA	100.00
Dane County, WI	100.00
Denton County, TX	100.00
Durham County, NC	100.00
Humboldt County, CA	100.00
Olmsted County, MN	100.00
Orange County, NC	100.00
Tippecanoe County, IN	100.00
Tompkins County, NY	100.00
Whitman County, WA	100.00
Whatcom County, WA	99.65
Washtenaw County, MI	99.21
Summit County, OH	99.04
Collin County, TX	99.01
Washington County, OR	98.70
Boulder County, CO	98.62
Essex County, NJ	98.57
Westchester County, NY	98.56
Fayette County, GA	98.55
Arlington County, VA	98.41
Davidson County, TN	98.27
Bergen County, NJ	98.11
Middlesex County, MA	98.07
Marin County, CA	98.00
DuPage County, IL	97.97
Oakland County, MI	97.93
Wake County, NC	97.89
Douglas County, NE	97.69
Hudson County, NJ	97.62
Boone County, KY	97.60
Yolo County, CA	97.50
Ingham County, MI	97.49
Franklin County, OH	97.37
Ramsey County, MN	97.24
Norfolk County, MA	97.22
Worcester County, MA	97.22
Kings County, NY	97.21
DeKalb County, GA	97.12
Dallas County, TX	97.03
New York County, NY	97.00
Thurston County, WA	96.99
Champaign County, IL	96.87
Mecklenburg County, NC	96.77
Montgomery County, MD	96.74
Bronx County, NY	96.68
Alachua County, FL	96.64
Mercer County, NJ	96.54
Fairfax County, VA	96.53
Fairfield County, CT	96.36
San Luis Obispo County, CA	96.23
New Haven County, CT	96.19
Somerset County, NJ	96.18
Erie County, NY	96.09
Allegheny County, PA	95.90
Cook County, IL	95.90
Hennepin County, MN	95.88
Anchorage Borough, AK	95.87
Chester County, PA	95.71
Lake County, IL	95.66
Prince George's County, MD	95.65
Kern County, CA	95.63
Benton County, OR	95.61
Placer County, CA	95.53
Tulare County, CA	95.53
Marion County, IN	95.49
Multnomah County, OR	95.44
Suffolk County, MA	95.42
Onondaga County, NY	95.40
Ada County, ID	95.39
Gwinnett County, GA	95.17
Contra Costa County, CA	95.08
Middlesex County, NJ	95.08
Santa Clara County, CA	95.08
Montgomery County, OH	95.07
Travis County, TX	95.06

Place	Percent
Aliso Viejo, CA (cdp) Orange County	100.00
Beaverton, OR (city) Washington County	100.00
Boulder, CO (city) Boulder County	100.00
Buffalo Grove, IL (village) Lake County	100.00
Chino Hills, CA (city) San Bernardino County	100.00
Davis, CA (city) Yolo County	100.00
Eastchester, NY (cdp) Westchester County	100.00
Eastchester, NY (town) Westchester County	100.00
Elk Grove Village, IL (village) Cook County	100.00
Eugene, OR (city) Lane County	100.00
Glenview, IL (village) Cook County	100.00
Greenville, NY (cdp) Westchester County	100.00
Harrison, NY (village) Westchester County	100.00
Irving, TX (city) Dallas County	100.00
Kirkland, WA (city) King County	100.00
Madison, WI (city) Dane County	100.00
McLean, VA (cdp) Fairfax County	100.00
Mount Prospect, IL (village) Cook County	100.00
Newport Beach, CA (city) Orange County	100.00
North Bethesda, MD (cdp) Montgomery County	100.00
Pacifica, CA (city) San Mateo County	100.00
Palos Verdes Estates, CA (city) Los Angeles County	100.00
Pullman, WA (city) Whitman County	100.00
Redmond, WA (city) King County	100.00
Ridgewood, NJ (village) Bergen County	100.00
Rockville, MD (city) Montgomery County	100.00
Rolling Hills Estates, CA (city) Los Angeles County	100.00
Roseville, CA (city) Placer County	100.00
San Ramon, CA (city) Contra Costa County	100.00
Santa Cruz, CA (city) Santa Cruz County	100.00
Seal Beach, CA (city) Orange County	100.00
South Pasadena, CA (city) Los Angeles County	100.00
Thousand Oaks, CA (city) Ventura County	100.00
Walnut, CA (city) Los Angeles County	100.00
West Bloomfield, MI (township) Oakland County	100.00
Wilmette, IL (village) Cook County	100.00
Yorba Linda, CA (city) Orange County	100.00
North Hempstead, NY (town) Nassau County	99.73
Santa Clarita, CA (city) Los Angeles County	99.28
Cambridge, MA (city) Middlesex County	99.25
Arlington Heights, IL (village) Cook County	99.24
Concord, CA (city) Contra Costa County	99.14
Arcadia, CA (city) Los Angeles County	99.12
Schaumburg, IL (village) Cook County	99.11
La Palma, CA (city) Orange County	98.95
Dallas, TX (city) Dallas County	98.93
Redondo Beach, CA (city) Los Angeles County	98.91
Renton, WA (city) King County	98.90
Ann Arbor, MI (city) Washtenaw County	98.89
Kihei, HI (cdp) Maui County	98.86
Mercer Island, WA (city) King County	98.84
Pleasanton, CA (city) Alameda County	98.84
Plano, TX (city) Collin County	98.72
Santa Clara, CA (city) Santa Clara County	98.66
Walnut Creek, CA (city) Contra Costa County	98.59
Rye, NY (city) Westchester County	98.51
Fort Lee, NJ (borough) Bergen County	98.50
Peachtree City, GA (city) Fayette County	98.48
Arlington, VA (cdp) Arlington County	98.41
Newcastle, WA (city) King County	98.41
La Mirada, CA (city) Los Angeles County	98.31
Morgan Hill, CA (city) Santa Clara County	98.31
Waikoloa Village, HI (cdp) Hawaii County	98.26
Greenburgh, NY (town) Westchester County	98.23
Nashville-Davidson, TN (sp. city) Davidson County	98.18
Cupertino, CA (city) Santa Clara County	98.14
Tempe, AZ (city) Maricopa County	98.13
Brookline, MA (town) Norfolk County	98.10
Menlo Park, CA (city) San Mateo County	98.06
Bethesda, MD (cdp) Montgomery County	98.02
Millbrae, CA (city) San Mateo County	98.02
Rancho Palos Verdes, CA (city) Los Angeles County	97.98
Minneapolis, MN (city) Hennepin County	97.96
Fullerton, CA (city) Orange County	97.92
Cary, NC (town) Wake County	97.91

Notes: Please refer to the User's Guide for an explanation of data; ranking tables include all places with Asian and/or NHPI populations above SF4 population thresholds; (1) tables reflect only those areas that meet SF4 population thresholds, therefore there may be less than 50 states, 75 counties or 75 places listed

Educational Attainment: High School Graduates

Koreans 25 Years and Over Who are High School Graduates

All States, Top 75 Counties, and Top 75 Places Sorted by Number[1]

State	Number
United States	599,278
California	204,612
New York	68,335
New Jersey	36,886
Illinois	30,264
Virginia	25,936
Washington	24,900
Texas	24,572
Maryland	21,374
Pennsylvania	17,001
Georgia	15,271
Hawaii	14,333
Florida	10,830
Michigan	9,222
Massachusetts	8,629
Colorado	7,951
Ohio	7,429
North Carolina	6,863
Oregon	6,524
Arizona	5,450
Nevada	4,457
Minnesota	4,276
Tennessee	3,784
Indiana	3,729
Missouri	3,538
Connecticut	3,248
Wisconsin	2,933
Kansas	2,286
Oklahoma	2,263
Alaska	2,179
Kentucky	2,103
Alabama	2,024
South Carolina	2,010
Utah	1,825
Iowa	1,824
Louisiana	1,400
Delaware	999
Nebraska	887
New Mexico	863
Rhode Island	862
New Hampshire	824
District of Columbia	796
Arkansas	706
Mississippi	671
Idaho	595
West Virginia	386
Maine	297
Montana	268
Vermont	235
Wyoming	235
South Dakota	202
North Dakota	191

County	Number
Los Angeles County, CA	112,155
Queens County, NY	35,930
Orange County, CA	33,879
Bergen County, NJ	21,587
Cook County, IL	21,454
Fairfax County, VA	16,493
Honolulu County, HI	13,163
Santa Clara County, CA	12,876
King County, WA	11,194
Montgomery County, MD	9,131
Alameda County, CA	8,557
New York County, NY	7,991
San Diego County, CA	6,349
Pierce County, WA	5,821
Dallas County, TX	5,443
Montgomery County, PA	5,443
Harris County, TX	5,117
Gwinnett County, GA	5,064
Nassau County, NY	4,981
San Francisco County, CA	4,841
San Bernardino County, CA	4,345
Snohomish County, WA	4,236
Clark County, NV	3,904
Kings County, NY	3,844
Middlesex County, MA	3,786
Maricopa County, AZ	3,533
Howard County, MD	3,374
Philadelphia County, PA	3,285
Riverside County, CA	3,017
San Mateo County, CA	3,017
Middlesex County, NJ	2,793
Baltimore County, MD	2,740
Oakland County, MI	2,688
Westchester County, NY	2,673
Contra Costa County, CA	2,660
DuPage County, IL	2,561
Sacramento County, CA	2,430
Lake County, IL	2,409
Fulton County, GA	2,398
Washington County, OR	2,377
Arapahoe County, CO	2,275
Hudson County, NJ	2,146
Travis County, TX	2,138
Richmond County, NY	2,109
Suffolk County, NY	2,077
DeKalb County, GA	2,033
El Paso County, CO	1,996
Prince George's County, MD	1,987
Bronx County, NY	1,958
Franklin County, OH	1,928
Hennepin County, MN	1,914
Washtenaw County, MI	1,880
Delaware County, PA	1,828
Anne Arundel County, MD	1,783
Tarrant County, TX	1,782
Cobb County, GA	1,749
Anchorage Borough, AK	1,734
Essex County, NJ	1,608
Hillsborough County, FL	1,554
Collin County, TX	1,541
Monterey County, CA	1,506
Ventura County, CA	1,466
Multnomah County, OR	1,428
Suffolk County, MA	1,396
St. Louis County, MO	1,393
Morris County, NJ	1,377
Broward County, FL	1,367
Mecklenburg County, NC	1,354
Orange County, FL	1,298
Bexar County, TX	1,295
Denton County, TX	1,237
Cumberland County, NC	1,225
Bucks County, PA	1,222
Bell County, TX	1,218
Wake County, NC	1,193

Place	Number
Los Angeles, CA (city) Los Angeles County	55,698
New York, NY (city)	51,832
Honolulu, HI (cdp) Honolulu County	9,375
Glendale, CA (city) Los Angeles County	7,695
Chicago, IL (city) Cook County	7,533
San Jose, CA (city) Santa Clara County	5,374
Fullerton, CA (city) Orange County	5,271
Torrance, CA (city) Los Angeles County	5,112
Cerritos, CA (city) Los Angeles County	4,940
San Francisco, CA (city) San Francisco County	4,841
Irvine, CA (city) Orange County	4,195
Anaheim, CA (city) Orange County	4,170
Fort Lee, NJ (borough) Bergen County	3,745
San Diego, CA (city) San Diego County	3,676
Palisades Park, NJ (borough) Bergen County	3,669
Houston, TX (city) Harris County	3,333
Diamond Bar, CA (city) Los Angeles County	3,303
Philadelphia, PA (city) Philadelphia County	3,285
Buena Park, CA (city) Orange County	3,272
Garden Grove, CA (city) Orange County	3,268
Federal Way, WA (city) King County	2,589
Seattle, WA (city) King County	2,577
Gardena, CA (city) Los Angeles County	2,316
Fremont, CA (city) Alameda County	2,206
Rowland Heights, CA (cdp) Los Angeles County	2,150
Annandale, VA (cdp) Fairfax County	2,097
Dallas, TX (city) Dallas County	1,975
Downey, CA (city) Los Angeles County	1,963
Austin, TX (city) Travis County	1,810
North Hempstead, NY (town) Nassau County	1,780
Burke, VA (cdp) Fairfax County	1,764
Skokie, IL (village) Cook County	1,650
Sunnyvale, CA (city) Santa Clara County	1,605
Hempstead, NY (town) Nassau County	1,599
Ellicott City, MD (cdp) Howard County	1,574
Colorado Springs, CO (city) El Paso County	1,562
Norwalk, CA (city) Los Angeles County	1,562
Tacoma, WA (city) Pierce County	1,558
Hacienda Heights, CA (cdp) Los Angeles County	1,529
Columbus, OH (city) Franklin County	1,511
Rancho Palos Verdes, CA (city) Los Angeles County	1,481
Bellevue, WA (city) King County	1,473
La Palma, CA (city) Orange County	1,415
La Mirada, CA (city) Los Angeles County	1,412
Santa Clara, CA (city) Santa Clara County	1,398
Irving, TX (city) Dallas County	1,383
Oyster Bay, NY (town) Nassau County	1,377
Cypress, CA (city) Orange County	1,361
Lakewood, WA (city) Pierce County	1,292
Boston, MA (city) Suffolk County	1,288
La Crescenta-Montrose, CA (cdp) Los Angeles County	1,284
Aurora, CO (city) Arapahoe County	1,283
Ann Arbor, MI (city) Washtenaw County	1,219
Cupertino, CA (city) Santa Clara County	1,219
Burbank, CA (city) Los Angeles County	1,210
Portland, OR (city) Multnomah County	1,195
Plano, TX (city) Collin County	1,193
Oakland, CA (city) Alameda County	1,144
La Canada Flintridge, CA (city) Los Angeles County	1,138
Phoenix, AZ (city) Maricopa County	1,112
Charlotte, NC (city) Mecklenburg County	1,085
Walnut, CA (city) Los Angeles County	1,083
Huntington Beach, CA (city) Orange County	1,077
Arcadia, CA (city) Los Angeles County	1,066
Cambridge, MA (city) Middlesex County	1,059
Schaumburg, IL (village) Cook County	1,042
Long Beach, CA (city) Los Angeles County	1,040
San Antonio, TX (city) Bexar County	1,022
Jersey City, NJ (city) Hudson County	1,003
Pasadena, CA (city) Los Angeles County	1,003
Orange, CA (city) Orange County	996
Cliffside Park, NJ (borough) Bergen County	985
Northbrook, IL (village) Cook County	974
Centreville, VA (cdp) Fairfax County	973
Glenview, IL (village) Cook County	972

Notes: Please refer to the User's Guide for an explanation of data; ranking tables include all places with Asian and/or NHPI populations above SF4 population thresholds; (1) tables reflect only those areas that meet SF4 population thresholds, therefore there may be less than 50 states, 75 counties or 75 places listed

Educational Attainment: High School Graduates

Koreans 25 Years and Over Who are High School Graduates

All States, Top 75 Counties, and Top 75 Places Sorted by Percent[1]

State	Percent
District of Columbia	99.13
Rhode Island	92.00
Utah	91.39
Massachusetts	90.84
New Jersey	90.79
Connecticut	90.63
Wyoming	90.04
Iowa	89.94
Wisconsin	89.67
Michigan	89.44
Vermont	89.35
Nebraska	88.97
Illinois	88.65
California	88.12
Minnesota	87.39
Delaware	86.64
Indiana	86.56
Pennsylvania	86.50
Virginia	86.37
United States	86.31
New York	85.87
Oregon	85.52
Ohio	85.39
Missouri	85.31
Maryland	84.88
South Dakota	84.87
New Hampshire	84.60
Georgia	84.59
North Carolina	84.57
Arizona	84.56
Washington	83.29
Texas	83.12
Idaho	83.10
Florida	82.56
Kansas	82.26
Tennessee	81.53
Colorado	81.42
Kentucky	81.39
Maine	81.15
Nevada	80.77
West Virginia	80.58
South Carolina	80.27
New Mexico	80.20
Montana	79.53
Louisiana	79.32
Hawaii	78.40
North Dakota	77.64
Mississippi	75.90
Alabama	75.41
Oklahoma	75.18
Arkansas	73.93
Alaska	68.57

County	Percent
Berrien County, MI	100.00
Brazos County, TX	100.00
Ingham County, MI	100.00
Larimer County, CO	100.00
Olmsted County, MN	100.00
Orange County, NC	100.00
Ottawa County, MI	100.00
Tompkins County, NY	100.00
Utah County, UT	100.00
Whatcom County, WA	99.19
Yolo County, CA	98.41
Alachua County, FL	98.27
Johnson County, IA	98.13
Monroe County, IN	98.07
Benton County, OR	97.95
Champaign County, IL	97.84
Imperial County, CA	97.81
Washington County, MN	97.65
St. Louis County, MN	97.47
Boulder County, CO	97.36
Hampshire County, MA	97.25
Story County, IA	96.88
Rensselaer County, NY	96.72
Montgomery County, VA	96.64
Dane County, WI	96.54
Summit County, OH	96.28
Lake County, IL	95.94
Providence County, RI	95.88
Tippecanoe County, IN	95.72
Centre County, PA	95.70
Union County, NJ	95.66
Douglas County, NE	95.44
Tulare County, CA	95.42
Suffolk County, NY	95.23
Dauphin County, PA	95.07
Norfolk County, MA	94.90
San Mateo County, CA	94.76
New Haven County, CT	94.68
Washtenaw County, MI	94.42
Santa Barbara County, CA	94.36
Suffolk County, MA	94.32
New York County, NY	94.29
Onondaga County, NY	94.20
Seminole County, FL	94.18
Douglas County, KS	93.77
Westchester County, NY	93.69
Fulton County, GA	93.38
Durham County, NC	93.33
Middlesex County, MA	93.25
Oakland County, MI	93.20
Placer County, CA	93.19
Travis County, TX	93.16
Clarke County, GA	92.97
Dutchess County, NY	92.90
Ramsey County, MN	92.86
Allegheny County, PA	92.82
Mercer County, NJ	92.46
Rockland County, NY	92.46
Davis County, UT	92.42
Marin County, CA	92.39
Kern County, CA	92.34
Kalamazoo County, MI	92.25
Morris County, NJ	92.23
Boone County, MO	92.03
Fairfield County, CT	91.97
Guilford County, NC	91.97
Hamilton County, OH	91.97
Loudoun County, VA	91.96
Nassau County, NY	91.80
Broward County, FL	91.74
Bergen County, NJ	91.58
Shelby County, TN	91.55
Collin County, TX	91.51
Wake County, NC	91.42
Leon County, FL	91.41

Place	Percent
Blacksburg, VA (town) Montgomery County	100.00
Brookline, MA (town) Norfolk County	100.00
Chapel Hill, NC (town) Orange County	100.00
College Station, TX (city) Brazos County	100.00
Commack, NY (cdp) Suffolk County	100.00
Davis, CA (city) Yolo County	100.00
Denton, TX (city) Denton County	100.00
East Lansing, MI (city) Ingham County	100.00
Evanston, IL (city) Cook County	100.00
Fort Collins, CO (city) Larimer County	100.00
Harrington Park, NJ (borough) Bergen County	100.00
Iowa City, IA (city) Johnson County	100.00
Isla Vista, CA (cdp) Santa Barbara County	100.00
Ithaca, NY (city) Tompkins County	100.00
Meridian charter, MI (township) Ingham County	100.00
Newton, MA (city) Middlesex County	100.00
Norman, OK (city) Cleveland County	100.00
Parsippany-Troy Hills, NJ (township) Morris County	100.00
Pleasanton, CA (city) Alameda County	100.00
Plymouth, MN (city) Hennepin County	100.00
Providence, RI (city) Providence County	100.00
Rochester, MN (city) Olmsted County	100.00
Stanford, CA (cdp) Santa Clara County	100.00
State College, PA (borough) Centre County	100.00
Tempe, AZ (city) Maricopa County	100.00
Urbana, IL (city) Champaign County	100.00
Pasadena, CA (city) Los Angeles County	99.50
Mission Viejo, CA (city) Orange County	98.97
Palo Alto, CA (city) Santa Clara County	98.91
Berkeley, CA (city) Alameda County	98.75
Wilmette, IL (village) Cook County	98.74
Foster City, CA (city) San Mateo County	98.63
San Mateo, CA (city) San Mateo County	98.63
Demarest, NJ (borough) Bergen County	98.51
Huntington, NY (town) Suffolk County	98.45
Aliso Viejo, CA (cdp) Orange County	98.35
Santa Clarita, CA (city) Los Angeles County	98.33
Palatine, IL (village) Cook County	98.24
Bloomington, MN (city) Hennepin County	98.16
Mountain View, CA (city) Santa Clara County	98.12
Bloomington, IN (city) Monroe County	97.93
Pittsburgh, PA (city) Allegheny County	97.89
Cambridge, MA (city) Middlesex County	97.78
Corvallis, OR (city) Benton County	97.70
Glenview, IL (village) Cook County	97.69
Vernon Hills, IL (village) Lake County	97.67
Boulder, CO (city) Boulder County	97.56
Madison, WI (city) Dane County	97.56
Old Tappan, NJ (borough) Bergen County	97.54
Duluth, GA (city) Gwinnett County	97.32
Bellevue, WA (city) King County	97.16
Salt Lake City, UT (city) Salt Lake County	97.15
South Pasadena, CA (city) Los Angeles County	97.13
Rancho Palos Verdes, CA (city) Los Angeles County	97.05
Jericho, NY (cdp) Nassau County	96.96
Saratoga, CA (city) Santa Clara County	96.91
Ames, IA (city) Story County	96.86
Santa Monica, CA (city) Los Angeles County	96.85
Redlands, CA (city) San Bernardino County	96.77
Somerville, MA (city) Middlesex County	96.72
Englewood Cliffs, NJ (borough) Bergen County	96.70
Hackensack, NJ (city) Bergen County	96.69
Rockville, MD (city) Montgomery County	96.60
Brookhaven, NY (town) Suffolk County	96.59
Gainesville, FL (city) Alachua County	96.43
Cheltenham, PA (township) Montgomery County	96.32
Irvine, CA (city) Orange County	96.24
Champaign, IL (city) Champaign County	96.16
Orangetown, NY (town) Rockland County	96.15
Northbrook, IL (village) Cook County	96.06
Yorba Linda, CA (city) Orange County	96.02
Smithtown, NY (town) Suffolk County	95.94
Leonia, NJ (borough) Bergen County	95.92
Beverly Hills, CA (city) Los Angeles County	95.90
Brea, CA (city) Orange County	95.87

Notes: Please refer to the User's Guide for an explanation of data; ranking tables include all places with Asian and/or NHPI populations above SF4 population thresholds; (1) tables reflect only those areas that meet SF4 population thresholds, therefore there may be less than 50 states, 75 counties or 75 places listed

Educational Attainment: High School Graduates

Laotians 25 Years and Over Who are High School Graduates

All States, Top 75 Counties, and Top 75 Places Sorted by Number[1]

State	Number
United States	43,977
California	11,233
Texas	3,162
Minnesota	2,371
Washington	2,123
Illinois	1,915
Tennessee	1,616
Florida	1,443
Georgia	1,312
North Carolina	1,182
Virginia	1,159
Iowa	1,154
Oregon	1,107
Connecticut	1,075
Massachusetts	926
New York	883
Kansas	855
Ohio	825
Wisconsin	819
Utah	767
Michigan	758
Colorado	725
Rhode Island	709
Arkansas	631
Pennsylvania	588
Nevada	445
Hawaii	426
South Carolina	423
Alabama	390
Arizona	376
Indiana	345
Maryland	328
Oklahoma	258
Nebraska	252
Louisiana	187
Missouri	176
New Jersey	174
Alaska	172
Idaho	152
New Hampshire	116
South Dakota	38

County	Number
San Diego County, CA	2,048
Hennepin County, MN	1,393
Sacramento County, CA	1,291
King County, WA	1,256
Los Angeles County, CA	1,139
Tarrant County, TX	1,068
Orange County, CA	949
Contra Costa County, CA	829
Dallas County, TX	731
Multnomah County, OR	709
Rutherford County, TN	691
Providence County, RI	676
Fresno County, CA	671
Salt Lake County, UT	658
Fairfax County, VA	645
Alameda County, CA	642
Polk County, IA	627
Cook County, IL	594
Santa Clara County, CA	558
Pinellas County, FL	531
Davidson County, TN	472
San Joaquin County, CA	462
Winnebago County, IL	459
Monroe County, NY	450
Riverside County, CA	450
Clark County, NV	445
Hartford County, CT	445
Harris County, TX	435
Kane County, IL	418
Middlesex County, MA	402
Honolulu County, HI	401
Milwaukee County, WI	385
Gwinnett County, GA	377
Franklin County, OH	369
Ottawa County, MI	364
Jefferson County, CO	340
Clayton County, GA	336
Worcester County, MA	313
Snohomish County, WA	310
Stanislaus County, CA	309
Fairfield County, CT	304
Mecklenburg County, NC	292
Johnson County, KS	288
Adams County, CO	286
Maricopa County, AZ	278
Philadelphia County, PA	276
Sonoma County, CA	276
Sebastian County, AR	268
Dakota County, MN	254
Merced County, CA	252
Spartanburg County, SC	240
Sedgwick County, KS	234
Shasta County, CA	231
Potter County, TX	228
Washington County, OR	227
New Haven County, CT	215
Tulare County, CA	201
Ramsey County, MN	176
Summit County, OH	172
Oklahoma County, OK	145
Anchorage Borough, AK	142
Solano County, CA	139
Guilford County, NC	137
Washington County, AR	136
Pierce County, WA	133
Polk County, FL	132
Habersham County, GA	121
Catawba County, NC	120
Clark County, WA	114
Cowley County, KS	114
San Bernardino County, CA	110
Bexar County, TX	109
Mobile County, AL	108
Broome County, NY	97
Essex County, MA	95

Place	Number
San Diego, CA (city) San Diego County	1,684
Sacramento, CA (city) Sacramento County	777
Portland, OR (city) Multnomah County	638
Fresno, CA (city) Fresno County	561
Seattle, WA (city) King County	532
Des Moines, IA (city) Polk County	531
San Jose, CA (city) Santa Clara County	479
Richmond, CA (city) Contra Costa County	475
Nashville-Davidson, TN (sp. city) Davidson County	472
Brooklyn Park, MN (city) Hennepin County	445
Stockton, CA (city) San Joaquin County	418
Minneapolis, MN (city) Hennepin County	407
Elgin, IL (city) Kane County	360
Oakland, CA (city) Alameda County	345
St. Petersburg, FL (city) Pinellas County	343
Los Angeles, CA (city) Los Angeles County	339
Anaheim, CA (city) Orange County	332
Columbus, OH (city) Franklin County	320
Milwaukee, WI (city) Milwaukee County	319
Lowell, MA (city) Middlesex County	316
Murfreesboro, TN (city) Rutherford County	297
Providence, RI (city) Providence County	287
Charlotte, NC (city) Mecklenburg County	281
Philadelphia, PA (city) Philadelphia County	276
Rochester, NY (city) Monroe County	259
Fort Smith, AR (city) Sebastian County	256
Rockford, IL (city) Winnebago County	255
Dallas, TX (city) Dallas County	250
Westminster, CO (city) Adams County	237
Amarillo, TX (city) Potter County	236
San Pablo, CA (city) Contra Costa County	234
Modesto, CA (city) Stanislaus County	223
Haltom City, TX (city) Tarrant County	222
Fort Worth, TX (city) Tarrant County	220
Honolulu, HI (cdp) Honolulu County	217
Santa Ana, CA (city) Orange County	213
Redding, CA (city) Shasta County	201
Woonsocket, RI (city) Providence County	201
Irving, TX (city) Dallas County	196
Bellevue, WA (city) King County	193
Santa Rosa, CA (city) Sonoma County	179
Bridgeport, CT (city) Fairfield County	173
Merced, CA (city) Merced County	168
Wichita, KS (city) Sedgwick County	162
West Valley City, UT (city) Salt Lake County	160
Springfield, VA (cdp) Fairfax County	158
Oklahoma City, OK (city) Oklahoma County	157
Long Beach, CA (city) Los Angeles County	136
Parkway-S. Sacramento, CA (cdp) Sacramento County	136
Escondido, CA (city) San Diego County	134
Akron, OH (city) Summit County	132
Moreno Valley, CA (city) Riverside County	129
St. Paul, MN (city) Ramsey County	127
Riverside, CA (city) Riverside County	120
Arvada, CO (city) Jefferson County	117
Visalia, CA (city) Tulare County	114
Winfield, KS (city) Cowley County	114
Fitchburg, MA (city) Worcester County	109
Pomona, CA (city) Los Angeles County	109
Brooklyn Center, MN (city) Hennepin County	107
Springdale, AR (city) Washington County	106
Grand Prairie, TX (city) Dallas County	103
Banning, CA (city) Riverside County	97
Tacoma, WA (city) Pierce County	88
Storm Lake, IA (city) Buena Vista County	84
Oaklawn-Sunview, KS (cdp) Sedgwick County	69
Fairfield, CA (city) Solano County	66
Raymond, WA (city) Pacific County	60
Worthington, MN (city) Nobles County	55
Rochester, MN (city) Olmsted County	53
New Britain, CT (city) Hartford County	50
Green Bay, WI (city) Brown County	45
Warroad, MN (city) Roseau County	16

Notes: Please refer to the User's Guide for an explanation of data; ranking tables include all places with Asian and/or NHPI populations above SF4 population thresholds; (1) tables reflect only those areas that meet SF4 population thresholds, therefore there may be less than 50 states, 75 counties or 75 places listed

Educational Attainment: High School Graduates

Laotians 25 Years and Over Who are High School Graduates

All States, Top 75 Counties, and Top 75 Places Sorted by Percent[1]

State	Percent
Alabama	76.47
Arizona	71.48
Utah	68.79
Maryland	68.62
Tennessee	67.84
Illinois	67.55
New Jersey	67.18
Virginia	64.32
South Carolina	61.39
Colorado	59.43
Florida	59.36
Connecticut	59.16
Nevada	58.78
Indiana	58.57
Oregon	56.71
Michigan	56.57
Oklahoma	55.97
Texas	55.89
New Hampshire	55.24
Nebraska	53.85
Kansas	53.81
Iowa	53.43
Ohio	53.09
Minnesota	52.57
Georgia	50.91
United States	50.40
Washington	49.46
New York	49.11
Massachusetts	48.33
North Carolina	47.17
Pennsylvania	47.04
Wisconsin	45.88
Idaho	45.37
Arkansas	45.36
Hawaii	44.51
Rhode Island	42.23
California	41.60
Missouri	37.53
South Dakota	35.85
Alaska	29.05
Louisiana	27.02

County	Percent
Maricopa County, AZ	81.05
Snohomish County, WA	74.16
Salt Lake County, UT	73.77
New Haven County, CT	73.63
Kane County, IL	73.46
Spartanburg County, SC	71.01
Rutherford County, TN	70.65
Fairfax County, VA	70.18
Jefferson County, CO	70.10
Cook County, IL	68.75
Dakota County, MN	67.20
Johnson County, KS	66.51
Polk County, IA	66.21
Los Angeles County, CA	65.69
Mobile County, AL	64.67
Washington County, OR	64.12
Davidson County, TN	63.27
Winnebago County, IL	62.28
Harris County, TX	61.27
Ottawa County, MI	61.18
Hartford County, CT	60.30
Polk County, FL	59.46
Clark County, NV	58.78
Hennepin County, MN	58.55
Monroe County, NY	58.37
Franklin County, OH	57.84
Tarrant County, TX	57.76
Gwinnett County, GA	57.21
Dallas County, TX	57.20
Orange County, CA	55.53
Dane County, WI	55.29
Worcester County, MA	55.11
Santa Clara County, CA	55.03
Riverside County, CA	54.74
San Diego County, CA	52.99
Summit County, OH	52.92
Multnomah County, OR	52.48
Adams County, CO	52.19
Cowley County, KS	52.05
Mecklenburg County, NC	51.05
Pierce County, WA	50.96
Washington County, AR	50.56
Fairfield County, CT	50.08
Catawba County, NC	50.00
Clark County, WA	50.00
Oklahoma County, OK	49.83
Habersham County, GA	49.79
Pinellas County, FL	49.72
Clayton County, GA	49.70
Bexar County, TX	47.81
King County, WA	47.63
Sonoma County, CA	47.42
Milwaukee County, WI	46.67
Guilford County, NC	46.60
Sedgwick County, KS	46.34
Ramsey County, MN	46.19
Essex County, MA	45.45
San Bernardino County, CA	44.90
Middlesex County, MA	44.42
Dakota County, NE	43.79
Alameda County, CA	43.38
Honolulu County, HI	43.30
Sebastian County, AR	42.95
Providence County, RI	41.65
Broome County, NY	41.63
Philadelphia County, PA	41.19
Potter County, TX	40.43
Contra Costa County, CA	39.36
Stanislaus County, CA	39.16
Solano County, CA	36.20
Brown County, WI	35.82
Pacific County, WA	34.57
San Joaquin County, CA	33.48
Merced County, CA	33.11
Olmsted County, MN	32.74

Place	Percent
Los Angeles, CA (city) Los Angeles County	81.29
Springfield, VA (cdp) Fairfax County	73.49
Bellevue, WA (city) King County	73.38
Fort Worth, TX (city) Tarrant County	73.09
West Valley City, UT (city) Salt Lake County	70.18
Irving, TX (city) Dallas County	70.00
Murfreesboro, TN (city) Rutherford County	67.96
Anaheim, CA (city) Orange County	67.48
Des Moines, IA (city) Polk County	67.13
Nashville-Davidson, TN (sp. city) Davidson County	63.27
Riverside, CA (city) Riverside County	62.83
Elgin, IL (city) Kane County	61.43
Rochester, NY (city) Monroe County	61.37
Westminster, CO (city) Adams County	60.46
Akron, OH (city) Summit County	60.27
Grand Prairie, TX (city) Dallas County	60.23
Columbus, OH (city) Franklin County	59.37
Brooklyn Park, MN (city) Hennepin County	58.17
Escondido, CA (city) San Diego County	58.01
Fitchburg, MA (city) Worcester County	57.07
Brooklyn Center, MN (city) Hennepin County	55.15
Arvada, CO (city) Jefferson County	54.42
Oklahoma City, OK (city) Oklahoma County	54.33
Bridgeport, CT (city) Fairfield County	53.07
San Jose, CA (city) Santa Clara County	52.75
Banning, CA (city) Riverside County	52.72
Winfield, KS (city) Cowley County	52.53
Rockford, IL (city) Winnebago County	52.04
Portland, OR (city) Multnomah County	52.00
St. Petersburg, FL (city) Pinellas County	51.89
Haltom City, TX (city) Tarrant County	51.51
Minneapolis, MN (city) Hennepin County	51.13
San Diego, CA (city) San Diego County	50.91
Santa Rosa, CA (city) Sonoma County	50.14
Charlotte, NC (city) Mecklenburg County	50.09
Moreno Valley, CA (city) Riverside County	49.81
Wichita, KS (city) Sedgwick County	48.94
Springdale, AR (city) Washington County	48.85
Dallas, TX (city) Dallas County	48.26
Tacoma, WA (city) Pierce County	47.57
Milwaukee, WI (city) Milwaukee County	45.51
Oaklawn-Sunview, KS (cdp) Sedgwick County	45.39
Raymond, WA (city) Pacific County	44.44
Pomona, CA (city) Los Angeles County	43.60
Santa Ana, CA (city) Orange County	43.20
Lowell, MA (city) Middlesex County	42.82
Fort Smith, AR (city) Sebastian County	41.83
Philadelphia, PA (city) Philadelphia County	41.19
Richmond, CA (city) Contra Costa County	40.98
Amarillo, TX (city) Potter County	40.83
Long Beach, CA (city) Los Angeles County	40.00
San Pablo, CA (city) Contra Costa County	39.86
Seattle, WA (city) King County	39.76
Woonsocket, RI (city) Providence County	39.26
Modesto, CA (city) Stanislaus County	39.19
St. Paul, MN (city) Ramsey County	38.25
Honolulu, HI (cdp) Honolulu County	37.80
Providence, RI (city) Providence County	36.10
Green Bay, WI (city) Brown County	36.00
Fairfield, CA (city) Solano County	34.02
Oakland, CA (city) Alameda County	33.66
Redding, CA (city) Shasta County	32.37
Rochester, MN (city) Olmsted County	31.93
Stockton, CA (city) San Joaquin County	31.55
Sacramento, CA (city) Sacramento County	30.89
Storm Lake, IA (city) Buena Vista County	30.32
Warroad, MN (city) Roseau County	27.12
Merced, CA (city) Merced County	26.62
Worthington, MN (city) Nobles County	26.57
New Britain, CT (city) Hartford County	26.04
Fresno, CA (city) Fresno County	23.85
Parkway-S. Sacramento, CA (cdp) Sacramento County	22.52
Visalia, CA (city) Tulare County	13.44

Notes: Please refer to the User's Guide for an explanation of data; ranking tables include all places with Asian and/or NHPI populations above SF4 population thresholds; (1) tables reflect only those areas that meet SF4 population thresholds, therefore there may be less than 50 states, 75 counties or 75 places listed

Educational Attainment: High School Graduates

Malaysians 25 Years and Over Who are High School Graduates

All States, Top 75 Counties, and Top 75 Places Sorted by Number[1]

State	Number
United States	6,004
California	1,070
New York	756
Texas	453
Illinois	332
Ohio	187
Oklahoma	174
Michigan	161

County	Number
Queens County, NY	349
Los Angeles County, CA	303

Place	Number
New York, NY (city)	636

Notes: Please refer to the User's Guide for an explanation of data; ranking tables include all places with Asian and/or NHPI populations above SF4 population thresholds; (1) tables reflect only those areas that meet SF4 population thresholds, therefore there may be less than 50 states, 75 counties or 75 places listed

Educational Attainment: High School Graduates

Malaysians 25 Years and Over Who are High School Graduates

All States, Top 75 Counties, and Top 75 Places Sorted by Percent[1]

State	Percent
Illinois	98.52
Michigan	95.27
Oklahoma	95.08
Texas	93.98
Ohio	93.97
United States	89.05
California	87.63
New York	68.11

County	Percent
Los Angeles County, CA	86.08
Queens County, NY	71.52

Place	Percent
New York, NY (city)	65.16

Notes: Please refer to the User's Guide for an explanation of data; ranking tables include all places with Asian and/or NHPI populations above SF4 population thresholds; (1) tables reflect only those areas that meet SF4 population thresholds, therefore there may be less than 50 states, 75 counties or 75 places listed

Educational Attainment: High School Graduates

Pakistanis 25 Years and Over Who are High School Graduates

All States, Top 75 Counties, and Top 75 Places Sorted by Number[1]

State	Number
United States	71,715
New York	12,923
California	9,177
Texas	8,755
Illinois	7,609
New Jersey	5,659
Virginia	4,578
Florida	2,797
Michigan	2,419
Maryland	2,409
Georgia	1,955
Pennsylvania	1,507
Connecticut	1,113
Massachusetts	984
Ohio	846
North Carolina	813
Washington	654
Missouri	588
Minnesota	566
Oklahoma	537
Louisiana	490
Colorado	427
Kansas	414
Arizona	392
Wisconsin	378
Tennessee	354
Kentucky	329
Indiana	327
Nevada	257
Delaware	209
Oregon	206
Alabama	192
West Virginia	189
Iowa	181
Utah	156

County	Number
Cook County, IL	5,074
Queens County, NY	4,710
Harris County, TX	3,494
Kings County, NY	2,874
Fairfax County, VA	2,790
Los Angeles County, CA	2,284
Dallas County, TX	1,698
Middlesex County, NJ	1,522
Santa Clara County, CA	1,397
DuPage County, IL	1,339
Orange County, CA	1,264
Fort Bend County, TX	1,111
Alameda County, CA	1,081
Wayne County, MI	1,014
Nassau County, NY	1,009
Suffolk County, NY	947
Hudson County, NJ	945
Montgomery County, MD	916
Bergen County, NJ	707
New York County, NY	638
Broward County, FL	580
Gwinnett County, GA	536
Sacramento County, CA	504
Collin County, TX	489
Orange County, FL	480
Oakland County, MI	474
Tarrant County, TX	468
Bronx County, NY	463
Miami-Dade County, FL	446
Baltimore County, MD	414
Westchester County, NY	411
Somerset County, NJ	408
San Bernardino County, CA	387
Contra Costa County, CA	378
Prince George's County, MD	376
Prince William County, VA	368
Hartford County, CT	363
Morris County, NJ	351
Denton County, TX	347
New Haven County, CT	337
Delaware County, PA	327
St. Louis County, MO	326
Loudoun County, VA	319
Cobb County, GA	318
Richmond County, NY	317
Essex County, NJ	314
Howard County, MD	312
Maricopa County, AZ	288
Philadelphia County, PA	288
King County, WA	285
Mercer County, NJ	280
Lake County, IL	279
Fairfield County, CT	275
Arlington County, VA	273
Middlesex County, MA	267
Travis County, TX	267
Alexandria Independent City, VA	265
San Diego County, CA	260
San Joaquin County, CA	256
Macomb County, MI	252
Snohomish County, WA	233
Franklin County, OH	231
Jefferson Parish, LA	230
Atlantic County, NJ	223
Hennepin County, MN	219
Wake County, NC	219
Riverside County, CA	218
Washtenaw County, MI	217
Clayton County, GA	203
Tulsa County, OK	202
Will County, IL	202
San Francisco County, CA	199
Monroe County, NY	198
Monmouth County, NJ	191
Milwaukee County, WI	181

Place	Number
New York, NY (city)	9,002
Chicago, IL (city) Cook County	3,088
Houston, TX (city) Harris County	2,382
Jersey City, NJ (city) Hudson County	763
Los Angeles, CA (city) Los Angeles County	717
San Jose, CA (city) Santa Clara County	631
Fremont, CA (city) Alameda County	616
Dallas, TX (city) Dallas County	601
Hempstead, NY (town) Nassau County	561
Carrollton, TX (city) Denton County	430
Brookhaven, NY (town) Suffolk County	370
Torrance, CA (city) Los Angeles County	336
Garland, TX (city) Dallas County	333
Edison, NJ (township) Middlesex County	332
Sugar Land, TX (city) Fort Bend County	301
Plano, TX (city) Collin County	300
Philadelphia, PA (city) Philadelphia County	288
North Hempstead, NY (town) Nassau County	285
Old Bridge, NJ (township) Middlesex County	284
Sacramento, CA (city) Sacramento County	279
Arlington, VA (cdp) Arlington County	273
Irving, TX (city) Dallas County	243
Santa Clara, CA (city) Santa Clara County	203
Richardson, TX (city) Dallas County	199
San Francisco, CA (city) San Francisco County	199
Woodbridge, NJ (township) Middlesex County	199
Skokie, IL (village) Cook County	197
Lincolnia, VA (cdp) Fairfax County	195
Austin, TX (city) Travis County	194
Huntington, NY (town) Suffolk County	187
Anaheim, CA (city) Orange County	181
Mission Bend, TX (cdp) Fort Bend County	175
Stockton, CA (city) San Joaquin County	159
Ellicott City, MD (cdp) Howard County	158
Dale City, VA (cdp) Prince William County	147
Tulsa, OK (city) Tulsa County	144
Bailey's Crossroads, VA (cdp) Fairfax County	100

Notes: Please refer to the User's Guide for an explanation of data; ranking tables include all places with Asian and/or NHPI populations above SF4 population thresholds; (1) tables reflect only those areas that meet SF4 population thresholds, therefore there may be less than 50 states, 75 counties or 75 places listed

Educational Attainment: High School Graduates

Pakistanis 25 Years and Over Who are High School Graduates

All States, Top 75 Counties, and Top 75 Places Sorted by Percent[1]

State	Percent
Iowa	100.00
Kentucky	100.00
Arizona	98.74
Tennessee	96.99
Colorado	96.83
Delaware	96.76
Oregon	96.26
Alabama	94.12
Connecticut	94.08
West Virginia	92.20
Washington	92.11
Kansas	91.59
Missouri	91.02
Minnesota	89.27
Indiana	87.90
Pennsylvania	87.46
Ohio	87.40
Oklahoma	87.18
Michigan	86.49
Illinois	85.09
Florida	84.60
Louisiana	84.48
Maryland	83.47
California	83.31
Georgia	83.01
New Jersey	82.56
United States	82.03
Texas	81.91
Nevada	81.59
Virginia	81.42
Massachusetts	81.19
Wisconsin	78.42
Utah	77.61
North Carolina	76.41
New York	72.62

County	Percent
Hartford County, CT	98.91
Maricopa County, AZ	98.29
San Bernardino County, CA	95.56
Snohomish County, WA	95.49
Lake County, IL	94.90
San Diego County, CA	94.55
Will County, IL	94.39
King County, WA	94.37
Washtenaw County, MI	93.13
Riverside County, CA	92.37
Fairfield County, CT	92.28
Howard County, MD	92.04
Middlesex County, MA	91.75
Westchester County, NY	91.74
Monmouth County, NJ	91.39
Contra Costa County, CA	91.30
Middlesex County, NJ	90.92
Prince William County, VA	90.42
St. Louis County, MO	89.56
Franklin County, OH	89.53
New York County, NY	89.48
New Haven County, CT	88.68
Prince George's County, MD	88.47
Oakland County, MI	87.94
DuPage County, IL	87.92
Clayton County, GA	87.88
Broward County, FL	87.75
Alameda County, CA	87.60
Somerset County, NJ	87.55
Orange County, FL	87.43
Loudoun County, VA	87.40
Morris County, NJ	87.31
Hennepin County, MN	87.25
Orange County, CA	86.93
Santa Clara County, CA	86.77
Delaware County, PA	86.51
Collin County, TX	86.40
Suffolk County, NY	86.33
Wake County, NC	85.88
Montgomery County, MD	85.13
Denton County, TX	83.82
Los Angeles County, CA	83.72
Camden County, NJ	83.16
Tarrant County, TX	83.13
Wayne County, MI	83.11
Harris County, TX	82.68
Nassau County, NY	82.50
Cook County, IL	82.37
Mercer County, NJ	82.11
Miami-Dade County, FL	81.83
Fairfax County, VA	81.77
Gwinnett County, GA	81.71
Cobb County, GA	81.54
Bergen County, NJ	81.17
Richmond County, NY	80.87
Worcester County, MA	80.73
Macomb County, MI	80.51
Alexandria Independent City, VA	80.30
Dallas County, TX	80.28
Milwaukee County, WI	80.09
Union County, NJ	79.41
Fort Bend County, TX	79.36
Essex County, NJ	79.09
Tulsa County, OK	78.91
San Francisco County, CA	77.13
Philadelphia County, PA	77.01
Queens County, NY	75.60
Hudson County, NJ	75.18
Jefferson Parish, LA	74.92
Baltimore County, MD	73.53
Travis County, TX	72.36
Bronx County, NY	71.01
Atlantic County, NJ	70.79
Monroe County, NY	70.21
Sacramento County, CA	69.33

Place	Percent
North Hempstead, NY (town) Nassau County	91.94
Old Bridge, NJ (township) Middlesex County	91.91
Sugar Land, TX (city) Fort Bend County	91.49
Brookhaven, NY (town) Suffolk County	89.81
Woodbridge, NJ (township) Middlesex County	89.64
Edison, NJ (township) Middlesex County	88.06
Plano, TX (city) Collin County	87.72
Torrance, CA (city) Los Angeles County	87.05
Fremont, CA (city) Alameda County	87.01
Dale City, VA (cdp) Prince William County	86.47
Ellicott City, MD (cdp) Howard County	85.41
Irving, TX (city) Dallas County	85.26
Anaheim, CA (city) Orange County	84.58
Houston, TX (city) Harris County	84.44
Dallas, TX (city) Dallas County	83.94
Huntington, NY (town) Suffolk County	82.74
Santa Clara, CA (city) Santa Clara County	82.52
San Jose, CA (city) Santa Clara County	81.84
Chicago, IL (city) Cook County	79.16
Los Angeles, CA (city) Los Angeles County	78.02
Hempstead, NY (town) Nassau County	77.17
San Francisco, CA (city) San Francisco County	77.13
Philadelphia, PA (city) Philadelphia County	77.01
Richardson, TX (city) Dallas County	76.54
Garland, TX (city) Dallas County	75.00
Carrollton, TX (city) Denton County	74.91
Lincolnia, VA (cdp) Fairfax County	74.71
Jersey City, NJ (city) Hudson County	74.29
Austin, TX (city) Travis County	72.93
Tulsa, OK (city) Tulsa County	72.73
Sacramento, CA (city) Sacramento County	72.47
Skokie, IL (village) Cook County	70.61
Mission Bend, TX (cdp) Fort Bend County	68.90
New York, NY (city)	68.35
Arlington, VA (cdp) Arlington County	61.21
Bailey's Crossroads, VA (cdp) Fairfax County	55.25
Stockton, CA (city) San Joaquin County	52.65

Notes: Please refer to the User's Guide for an explanation of data; ranking tables include all places with Asian and/or NHPI populations above SF4 population thresholds; (1) tables reflect only those areas that meet SF4 population thresholds, therefore there may be less than 50 states, 75 counties or 75 places listed

Educational Attainment: High School Graduates

Samoans 25 Years and Over Who are High School Graduates

All States, Top 75 Counties, and Top 75 Places Sorted by Number[1]

State	Number
United States	31,625
California	14,243
Hawaii	5,249
Washington	2,542
Utah	1,300
Texas	666
Nevada	608
New York	537
Missouri	402
Alaska	397
Arizona	393
Florida	376
Colorado	372
Pennsylvania	359
Georgia	324
Oregon	308
Illinois	292
New Jersey	292
Tennessee	278
Virginia	230
North Carolina	218
Michigan	193
Ohio	188

County	Number
Honolulu County, HI	4,986
Los Angeles County, CA	4,893
San Diego County, CA	2,164
Orange County, CA	1,492
King County, WA	1,315
Salt Lake County, UT	867
Pierce County, WA	698
Santa Clara County, CA	697
Alameda County, CA	664
San Francisco County, CA	639
San Mateo County, CA	610
San Bernardino County, CA	607
Clark County, NV	433
Riverside County, CA	399
Sacramento County, CA	377
Anchorage Borough, AK	289
Contra Costa County, CA	266
Ventura County, CA	261
Maricopa County, AZ	258
Solano County, CA	250
Utah County, UT	190
Jackson County, MO	174
Hawaii County, HI	138
San Joaquin County, CA	133

Place	Number
Honolulu, HI (cdp) Honolulu County	1,616
Long Beach, CA (city) Los Angeles County	1,229
Los Angeles, CA (city) Los Angeles County	952
San Diego, CA (city) San Diego County	868
Oceanside, CA (city) San Diego County	679
San Francisco, CA (city) San Francisco County	639
Waipahu, HI (cdp) Honolulu County	567
Carson, CA (city) Los Angeles County	507
San Jose, CA (city) Santa Clara County	445
Seattle, WA (city) King County	435
Santa Ana, CA (city) Orange County	310
Lakewood, CA (city) Los Angeles County	295
Garden Grove, CA (city) Orange County	290
West Valley City, UT (city) Salt Lake County	272
Anaheim, CA (city) Orange County	233
Laie, HI (cdp) Honolulu County	233
Compton, CA (city) Los Angeles County	227
Tacoma, WA (city) Pierce County	225
Oxnard, CA (city) Ventura County	218
Nanakuli, HI (cdp) Honolulu County	216
Halawa, HI (cdp) Honolulu County	202
Hayward, CA (city) Alameda County	202
New York, NY (city)	169
Federal Way, WA (city) King County	168
Sacramento, CA (city) Sacramento County	163
Salt Lake City, UT (city) Salt Lake County	158
Ewa Beach, HI (cdp) Honolulu County	146
Westminster, CA (city) Orange County	145
Lakewood, WA (city) Pierce County	129
San Bernardino, CA (city) San Bernardino County	93
Hauula, HI (cdp) Honolulu County	83
Kahuku, HI (cdp) Honolulu County	59

Notes: Please refer to the User's Guide for an explanation of data; ranking tables include all places with Asian and/or NHPI populations above SF4 population thresholds; (1) tables reflect only those areas that meet SF4 population thresholds, therefore there may be less than 50 states, 75 counties or 75 places listed

Educational Attainment: High School Graduates

Samoans 25 Years and Over Who are High School Graduates

All States, Top 75 Counties, and Top 75 Places Sorted by Percent[1]

State	Percent
Colorado	88.36
Virginia	86.79
North Carolina	85.83
Tennessee	83.73
Georgia	82.65
Missouri	82.21
Utah	81.30
Oregon	81.05
Arizona	79.55
Nevada	77.45
Michigan	76.89
Pennsylvania	76.71
California	76.07
United States	75.81
Washington	75.50
Florida	75.35
Hawaii	74.55
Ohio	72.87
Texas	71.23
Alaska	70.89
New York	69.83
New Jersey	69.03
Illinois	66.97

County	Percent
Utah County, UT	92.23
Riverside County, CA	87.31
Pierce County, WA	86.60
San Diego County, CA	85.84
Ventura County, CA	84.19
Maricopa County, AZ	80.63
Orange County, CA	80.00
Solano County, CA	79.87
San Mateo County, CA	79.43
Clark County, NV	78.73
Salt Lake County, UT	76.79
Sacramento County, CA	76.01
Jackson County, MO	75.65
Contra Costa County, CA	75.57
Los Angeles County, CA	74.90
Honolulu County, HI	74.60
Santa Clara County, CA	74.07
San Bernardino County, CA	72.35
Anchorage Borough, AK	71.71
King County, WA	69.25
Alameda County, CA	67.76
Hawaii County, HI	66.99
San Joaquin County, CA	64.25
San Francisco County, CA	58.95

Place	Percent
Lakewood, WA (city) Pierce County	95.56
Lakewood, CA (city) Los Angeles County	92.77
Oceanside, CA (city) San Diego County	86.83
San Diego, CA (city) San Diego County	85.77
Santa Ana, CA (city) Orange County	84.01
Tacoma, WA (city) Pierce County	82.72
Laie, HI (cdp) Honolulu County	82.33
Los Angeles, CA (city) Los Angeles County	82.07
Kahuku, HI (cdp) Honolulu County	81.94
Oxnard, CA (city) Ventura County	81.65
Westminster, CA (city) Orange County	81.01
Anaheim, CA (city) Orange County	80.90
Garden Grove, CA (city) Orange County	80.33
Halawa, HI (cdp) Honolulu County	73.19
Ewa Beach, HI (cdp) Honolulu County	73.00
Honolulu, HI (cdp) Honolulu County	72.86
West Valley City, UT (city) Salt Lake County	72.34
Federal Way, WA (city) King County	72.10
Carson, CA (city) Los Angeles County	72.02
Long Beach, CA (city) Los Angeles County	71.87
San Jose, CA (city) Santa Clara County	70.97
Hauula, HI (cdp) Honolulu County	69.75
Nanakuli, HI (cdp) Honolulu County	69.68
Salt Lake City, UT (city) Salt Lake County	69.00
Seattle, WA (city) King County	68.50
Compton, CA (city) Los Angeles County	67.76
Sacramento, CA (city) Sacramento County	66.26
Hayward, CA (city) Alameda County	64.74
Waipahu, HI (cdp) Honolulu County	64.65
San Francisco, CA (city) San Francisco County	58.95
New York, NY (city)	56.52
San Bernardino, CA (city) San Bernardino County	53.45

Notes: Please refer to the User's Guide for an explanation of data; ranking tables include all places with Asian and/or NHPI populations above SF4 population thresholds; (1) tables reflect only those areas that meet SF4 population thresholds, therefore there may be less than 50 states, 75 counties or 75 places listed

Educational Attainment: High School Graduates

Sri Lankans 25 Years and Over Who are High School Graduates

All States, Top 75 Counties, and Top 75 Places Sorted by Number[1]

State	Number
United States	11,612
California	3,228
New York	1,371
New Jersey	803
Maryland	746
Texas	563
Illinois	405
Virginia	380
Ohio	349
Massachusetts	322
Florida	268
Michigan	248
Pennsylvania	232
Washington	222

County	Number
Los Angeles County, CA	1,368
Montgomery County, MD	467
Queens County, NY	448
Orange County, CA	412
Middlesex County, NJ	274
Richmond County, NY	203

Place	Number
New York, NY (city)	950
Los Angeles, CA (city) Los Angeles County	647

Notes: Please refer to the User's Guide for an explanation of data; ranking tables include all places with Asian and/or NHPI populations above SF4 population thresholds; (1) tables reflect only those areas that meet SF4 population thresholds, therefore there may be less than 50 states, 75 counties or 75 places listed

Educational Attainment: High School Graduates

Sri Lankans 25 Years and Over Who are High School Graduates

All States, Top 75 Counties, and Top 75 Places Sorted by Percent[1]

State	Percent
Pennsylvania	95.08
Michigan	94.30
Florida	93.06
Illinois	92.05
Massachusetts	92.00
Maryland	90.31
Ohio	90.18
Texas	86.88
United States	86.55
New Jersey	86.44
Washington	85.71
California	85.35
Virginia	83.89
New York	74.19

County	Percent
Orange County, CA	87.66
Montgomery County, MD	86.16
Middlesex County, NJ	85.89
Los Angeles County, CA	80.23
Queens County, NY	75.55
Richmond County, NY	62.27

Place	Percent
Los Angeles, CA (city) Los Angeles County	78.71
New York, NY (city)	70.68

Notes: Please refer to the User's Guide for an explanation of data; ranking tables include all places with Asian and/or NHPI populations above SF4 population thresholds; (1) tables reflect only those areas that meet SF4 population thresholds, therefore there may be less than 50 states, 75 counties or 75 places listed

Educational Attainment: High School Graduates

Taiwanese 25 Years and Over Who are High School Graduates

All States, Top 75 Counties, and Top 75 Places Sorted by Number[1]

State	Number
United States	75,069
California	38,659
New York	4,998
Texas	4,792
New Jersey	3,713
Illinois	2,189
Washington	2,144
Michigan	1,471
Maryland	1,439
Massachusetts	1,433
Pennsylvania	1,365
Ohio	1,310
Florida	1,289
Georgia	1,216
Virginia	866
Missouri	670
North Carolina	609
Hawaii	525
Indiana	504
Oregon	444
Arizona	441
Colorado	427
Wisconsin	378
Connecticut	376
Tennessee	330
Louisiana	328
Nevada	324
Minnesota	299
Kansas	291
Oklahoma	270
Iowa	264
Utah	220

County	Number
Los Angeles County, CA	20,831
Orange County, CA	5,551
Santa Clara County, CA	3,457
Alameda County, CA	2,476
Queens County, NY	2,313
King County, WA	1,766
Harris County, TX	1,535
San Diego County, CA	1,404
Cook County, IL	1,137
San Bernardino County, CA	1,125
Contra Costa County, CA	946
Middlesex County, NJ	869
Oakland County, MI	748
Middlesex County, MA	743
Montgomery County, MD	720
New York County, NY	699
Fort Bend County, TX	647
San Mateo County, CA	612
Bergen County, NJ	540
DuPage County, IL	527
San Francisco County, CA	524
Collin County, TX	519
Ventura County, CA	505
Honolulu County, HI	498
Fairfax County, VA	495
Dallas County, TX	489
Franklin County, OH	470
Morris County, NJ	452
St. Louis County, MO	450
Tarrant County, TX	428
Maricopa County, AZ	404
Travis County, TX	388
Somerset County, NJ	356
Gwinnett County, GA	353
Washtenaw County, MI	346
Nassau County, NY	335
Essex County, NJ	327
Mercer County, NJ	304
Suffolk County, MA	290
Suffolk County, NY	268
Sacramento County, CA	267
Allegheny County, PA	256
Westchester County, NY	231
Dane County, WI	230
Riverside County, CA	228
Clark County, NV	203
Norfolk County, MA	180

Place	Number
New York, NY (city)	3,251
Arcadia, CA (city) Los Angeles County	2,108
Los Angeles, CA (city) Los Angeles County	2,106
Hacienda Heights, CA (cdp) Los Angeles County	1,667
Fremont, CA (city) Alameda County	1,649
Rowland Heights, CA (cdp) Los Angeles County	1,501
Irvine, CA (city) Orange County	1,498
San Jose, CA (city) Santa Clara County	1,321
Diamond Bar, CA (city) Los Angeles County	1,179
Cerritos, CA (city) Los Angeles County	1,150
Walnut, CA (city) Los Angeles County	1,077
Houston, TX (city) Harris County	1,038
Alhambra, CA (city) Los Angeles County	979
San Diego, CA (city) San Diego County	953
San Marino, CA (city) Los Angeles County	899
Temple City, CA (city) Los Angeles County	822
Torrance, CA (city) Los Angeles County	805
Monterey Park, CA (city) Los Angeles County	702
West Covina, CA (city) Los Angeles County	584
Seattle, WA (city) King County	564
Cupertino, CA (city) Santa Clara County	535
San Francisco, CA (city) San Francisco County	524
Bellevue, WA (city) King County	518
Sugar Land, TX (city) Fort Bend County	496
Sunnyvale, CA (city) Santa Clara County	492
San Gabriel, CA (city) Los Angeles County	486
Honolulu, HI (cdp) Honolulu County	448
Chicago, IL (city) Cook County	437
Cypress, CA (city) Orange County	415
Huntington Beach, CA (city) Orange County	392
Rancho Palos Verdes, CA (city) Los Angeles County	382
Anaheim, CA (city) Orange County	379
Plano, TX (city) Collin County	366
Edison, NJ (township) Middlesex County	357
Chino Hills, CA (city) San Bernardino County	348
East San Gabriel, CA (cdp) Los Angeles County	342
Orange, CA (city) Orange County	334
Austin, TX (city) Travis County	327
Troy, MI (city) Oakland County	324
Tustin, CA (city) Orange County	307
Columbus, OH (city) Franklin County	295
Boston, MA (city) Suffolk County	290
Ann Arbor, MI (city) Washtenaw County	286
Arlington, TX (city) Tarrant County	267
El Monte, CA (city) Los Angeles County	267
Upland, CA (city) San Bernardino County	266
Naperville, IL (city) Du Page County	240
Fountain Valley, CA (city) Orange County	235
Madison, WI (city) Dane County	227
Saratoga, CA (city) Santa Clara County	174
North Hempstead, NY (town) Nassau County	167
Berkeley, CA (city) Alameda County	129

Notes: Please refer to the User's Guide for an explanation of data; ranking tables include all places with Asian and/or NHPI populations above SF4 population thresholds; (1) tables reflect only those areas that meet SF4 population thresholds, therefore there may be less than 50 states, 75 counties or 75 places listed

Educational Attainment: High School Graduates

Taiwanese 25 Years and Over Who are High School Graduates

All States, Top 75 Counties, and Top 75 Places Sorted by Percent[1]

State	Percent
Utah	100.00
Michigan	99.12
Connecticut	98.43
Missouri	98.10
Georgia	97.51
Indiana	97.49
Oklahoma	96.77
Tennessee	96.49
Minnesota	96.14
Illinois	95.80
Massachusetts	95.41
Colorado	95.31
Iowa	95.31
Oregon	95.28
New Jersey	94.53
Washington	94.41
Texas	93.63
Pennsylvania	93.17
Maryland	93.02
United States	93.01
Florida	92.80
California	92.57
Louisiana	92.13
Ohio	91.74
New York	91.35
Virginia	91.06
Arizona	90.74
Wisconsin	90.21
North Carolina	89.69
Kansas	85.84
Hawaii	83.73
Nevada	71.68

County	Percent
San Mateo County, CA	100.00
Suffolk County, MA	100.00
Westchester County, NY	100.00
Essex County, NJ	99.39
Oakland County, MI	99.07
New York County, NY	99.01
St. Louis County, MO	98.90
Gwinnett County, GA	98.88
Washtenaw County, MI	98.30
Mercer County, NJ	98.06
Morris County, NJ	97.84
Tarrant County, TX	97.49
Alameda County, CA	96.38
Middlesex County, MA	96.37
Cook County, IL	96.27
Allegheny County, PA	96.24
Ventura County, CA	96.19
Travis County, TX	96.04
Franklin County, OH	95.92
DuPage County, IL	95.82
Middlesex County, NJ	95.49
King County, WA	95.36
Bergen County, NJ	95.24
Collin County, TX	95.23
Somerset County, NJ	95.19
Montgomery County, MD	94.74
Suffolk County, NY	94.70
Harris County, TX	94.11
Orange County, CA	94.01
Santa Clara County, CA	93.99
San Diego County, CA	93.66
Contra Costa County, CA	93.48
San Francisco County, CA	93.40
Maricopa County, AZ	92.45
Riverside County, CA	92.31
Los Angeles County, CA	91.94
Norfolk County, MA	91.84
Dallas County, TX	89.72
Fort Bend County, TX	89.12
Fairfax County, VA	89.03
Nassau County, NY	88.86
Queens County, NY	88.38
Sacramento County, CA	87.83
San Bernardino County, CA	85.36
Dane County, WI	84.87
Honolulu County, HI	83.42
Clark County, NV	63.04

Place	Percent
Anaheim, CA (city) Orange County	100.00
Arlington, TX (city) Tarrant County	100.00
Berkeley, CA (city) Alameda County	100.00
Boston, MA (city) Suffolk County	100.00
Cerritos, CA (city) Los Angeles County	100.00
Troy, MI (city) Oakland County	100.00
Rancho Palos Verdes, CA (city) Los Angeles County	98.96
Ann Arbor, MI (city) Washtenaw County	97.95
Orange, CA (city) Orange County	97.95
Saratoga, CA (city) Santa Clara County	97.75
San Diego, CA (city) San Diego County	97.15
Cupertino, CA (city) Santa Clara County	96.92
Plano, TX (city) Collin County	96.57
Fremont, CA (city) Alameda County	96.55
Columbus, OH (city) Franklin County	96.09
Chicago, IL (city) Cook County	95.83
West Covina, CA (city) Los Angeles County	95.74
North Hempstead, NY (town) Nassau County	95.43
Austin, TX (city) Travis County	95.34
San Marino, CA (city) Los Angeles County	95.33
Bellevue, WA (city) King County	95.22
Los Angeles, CA (city) Los Angeles County	95.12
Irvine, CA (city) Orange County	95.05
Cypress, CA (city) Orange County	94.97
Sunnyvale, CA (city) Santa Clara County	94.80
East San Gabriel, CA (cdp) Los Angeles County	94.21
Seattle, WA (city) King County	94.16
Fountain Valley, CA (city) Orange County	93.63
Houston, TX (city) Harris County	93.60
San Francisco, CA (city) San Francisco County	93.40
Edison, NJ (township) Middlesex County	92.73
Arcadia, CA (city) Los Angeles County	92.66
Diamond Bar, CA (city) Los Angeles County	92.04
Torrance, CA (city) Los Angeles County	91.89
Hacienda Heights, CA (cdp) Los Angeles County	91.59
Naperville, IL (city) Du Page County	91.25
San Jose, CA (city) Santa Clara County	91.04
Walnut, CA (city) Los Angeles County	91.04
Tustin, CA (city) Orange County	90.83
New York, NY (city)	89.78
Rowland Heights, CA (cdp) Los Angeles County	89.72
Upland, CA (city) San Bernardino County	88.96
Sugar Land, TX (city) Fort Bend County	88.41
Chino Hills, CA (city) San Bernardino County	88.10
Temple City, CA (city) Los Angeles County	87.63
Monterey Park, CA (city) Los Angeles County	86.88
Huntington Beach, CA (city) Orange County	85.96
El Monte, CA (city) Los Angeles County	85.58
San Gabriel, CA (city) Los Angeles County	85.26
Madison, WI (city) Dane County	84.70
Alhambra, CA (city) Los Angeles County	84.11
Honolulu, HI (cdp) Honolulu County	82.66

Notes: Please refer to the User's Guide for an explanation of data; ranking tables include all places with Asian and/or NHPI populations above SF4 population thresholds; (1) tables reflect only those areas that meet SF4 population thresholds, therefore there may be less than 50 states, 75 counties or 75 places listed

Educational Attainment: High School Graduates

Thais 25 Years and Over Who are High School Graduates

All States, Top 75 Counties, and Top 75 Places Sorted by Number[1]

State	Number
United States	62,006
California	20,228
Texas	4,084
New York	3,860
Illinois	3,788
Florida	3,625
Virginia	2,124
Washington	2,069
Maryland	1,673
Nevada	1,535
Massachusetts	1,299
Georgia	1,205
Colorado	1,162
New Jersey	1,137
Ohio	1,000
Pennsylvania	964
Michigan	924
Oregon	897
Arizona	873
North Carolina	804
Missouri	761
Hawaii	729
Tennessee	582
Iowa	479
Indiana	442
South Carolina	436
Wisconsin	436
Minnesota	423
Louisiana	402
Oklahoma	395
Utah	390
Connecticut	364
Kansas	354
Nebraska	306
Kentucky	277
Alabama	273
Alaska	273
New Mexico	175
Arkansas	105

County	Number
Los Angeles County, CA	11,042
Cook County, IL	2,631
Orange County, CA	1,810
Clark County, NV	1,379
Queens County, NY	1,307
King County, WA	1,132
San Bernardino County, CA	971
San Francisco County, CA	969
Fairfax County, VA	934
Montgomery County, MD	860
Harris County, TX	785
San Diego County, CA	782
Santa Clara County, CA	740
Dallas County, TX	737
Alameda County, CA	727
New York County, NY	608
Maricopa County, AZ	602
Honolulu County, HI	597
Miami-Dade County, FL	571
Bexar County, TX	523
Middlesex County, MA	500
San Mateo County, CA	448
Palm Beach County, FL	438
Hillsborough County, FL	426
Riverside County, CA	426
Tarrant County, TX	388
Broward County, FL	384
Westchester County, NY	366
Sacramento County, CA	341
Bergen County, NJ	337
Contra Costa County, CA	333
Multnomah County, OR	293
Collin County, TX	291
DuPage County, IL	277
Pinellas County, FL	265
Pierce County, WA	244
Franklin County, OH	239
Okaloosa County, FL	230
Travis County, TX	225
Nassau County, NY	211
Oklahoma County, OK	210
Denver County, CO	207
St. Louis County, MO	199
Prince George's County, MD	185
Suffolk County, NY	182
Anchorage Borough, AK	170
Polk County, IA	147

Place	Number
Los Angeles, CA (city) Los Angeles County	4,777
New York, NY (city)	2,395
Chicago, IL (city) Cook County	1,424
San Francisco, CA (city) San Francisco County	969
Houston, TX (city) Harris County	563
Seattle, WA (city) King County	526
San Diego, CA (city) San Diego County	492
Las Vegas, NV (city) Clark County	404
San Antonio, TX (city) Bexar County	386
Long Beach, CA (city) Los Angeles County	360
San Jose, CA (city) Santa Clara County	340
Cerritos, CA (city) Los Angeles County	304
Honolulu, HI (cdp) Honolulu County	301
Glendale, CA (city) Los Angeles County	285
Portland, OR (city) Multnomah County	260
Anaheim, CA (city) Orange County	252
Spring Valley, NV (cdp) Clark County	252
Bellflower, CA (city) Los Angeles County	227
Columbus, OH (city) Franklin County	219
Denver, CO (city) Denver County	207
Des Moines, IA (city) Polk County	84

Notes: Please refer to the User's Guide for an explanation of data; ranking tables include all places with Asian and/or NHPI populations above SF4 population thresholds; (1) tables reflect only those areas that meet SF4 population thresholds, therefore there may be less than 50 states, 75 counties or 75 places listed

Educational Attainment: High School Graduates

Thais 25 Years and Over Who are High School Graduates

All States, Top 75 Counties, and Top 75 Places Sorted by Percent[1]

State	Percent
Illinois	93.03
Massachusetts	87.53
Kentucky	86.56
New Jersey	86.27
Tennessee	85.21
Colorado	84.26
New York	84.15
Nebraska	82.93
Oregon	82.90
Michigan	82.80
Wisconsin	82.42
Kansas	81.76
California	81.39
Pennsylvania	81.08
Virginia	80.09
Washington	79.36
Missouri	79.27
United States	79.12
Connecticut	78.96
Maryland	78.77
Texas	78.10
Ohio	77.64
Arizona	76.85
Louisiana	76.28
Utah	75.14
South Carolina	73.77
Florida	71.27
Hawaii	71.26
Iowa	70.86
North Carolina	70.65
Georgia	70.10
Indiana	69.72
Nevada	68.77
Minnesota	68.01
Oklahoma	63.81
Alabama	62.19
New Mexico	57.19
Arkansas	55.26
Alaska	51.22

County	Percent
DuPage County, IL	97.54
San Mateo County, CA	94.12
Bergen County, NJ	92.84
Cook County, IL	92.80
New York County, NY	91.02
San Francisco County, CA	89.81
Orange County, CA	87.57
Franklin County, OH	87.23
Middlesex County, MA	87.11
San Diego County, CA	86.70
Nassau County, NY	85.77
Westchester County, NY	85.71
Multnomah County, OR	85.42
Harris County, TX	85.33
Dallas County, TX	85.30
Santa Clara County, CA	85.06
Collin County, TX	84.84
King County, WA	84.23
Palm Beach County, FL	83.11
Fairfax County, VA	83.02
Miami-Dade County, FL	82.75
Montgomery County, MD	81.90
Queens County, NY	81.64
Los Angeles County, CA	81.36
Prince George's County, MD	80.43
Travis County, TX	80.36
Maricopa County, AZ	80.05
San Bernardino County, CA	79.46
Alameda County, CA	79.45
Denver County, CO	79.01
Broward County, FL	78.85
Hillsborough County, FL	78.74
Contra Costa County, CA	78.17
Pinellas County, FL	76.81
Bexar County, TX	76.24
Suffolk County, NY	75.52
Pierce County, WA	74.85
Sacramento County, CA	74.78
St. Louis County, MO	73.98
Honolulu County, HI	72.01
Tarrant County, TX	71.32
Clark County, NV	69.40
Riverside County, CA	68.60
Oklahoma County, OK	68.40
Polk County, IA	58.10
Anchorage Borough, AK	44.62
Okaloosa County, FL	43.40

Place	Percent
Chicago, IL (city) Cook County	93.62
San Diego, CA (city) San Diego County	92.13
Cerritos, CA (city) Los Angeles County	92.12
Seattle, WA (city) King County	91.96
Long Beach, CA (city) Los Angeles County	90.91
San Francisco, CA (city) San Francisco County	89.81
Houston, TX (city) Harris County	87.56
Columbus, OH (city) Franklin County	86.56
New York, NY (city)	86.46
Bellflower, CA (city) Los Angeles County	86.31
San Jose, CA (city) Santa Clara County	85.43
Glendale, CA (city) Los Angeles County	85.07
Portland, OR (city) Multnomah County	83.87
Anaheim, CA (city) Orange County	81.55
Denver, CO (city) Denver County	79.01
San Antonio, TX (city) Bexar County	78.30
Honolulu, HI (cdp) Honolulu County	76.59
Las Vegas, NV (city) Clark County	76.52
Los Angeles, CA (city) Los Angeles County	74.68
Spring Valley, NV (cdp) Clark County	70.99
Des Moines, IA (city) Polk County	44.21

Notes: Please refer to the User's Guide for an explanation of data; ranking tables include all places with Asian and/or NHPI populations above SF4 population thresholds; (1) tables reflect only those areas that meet SF4 population thresholds, therefore there may be less than 50 states, 75 counties or 75 places listed

Educational Attainment: High School Graduates

Tongans 25 Years and Over Who are High School Graduates

All States, Top 75 Counties, and Top 75 Places Sorted by Number[1]

State	Number
United States	8,559
California	3,686
Utah	1,932
Hawaii	1,421
Washington	366
Nevada	232
Arizona	188
Texas	169
Oregon	127
Alaska	82

County	Number
Salt Lake County, UT	1,647
San Mateo County, CA	1,179
Honolulu County, HI	1,053
Los Angeles County, CA	656
Alameda County, CA	522
San Bernardino County, CA	272
King County, WA	262
Maui County, HI	258
Sacramento County, CA	229
Maricopa County, AZ	182
San Diego County, CA	176
Washoe County, NV	172
Utah County, UT	171
Contra Costa County, CA	139
Tarrant County, TX	129
Orange County, CA	115
Multnomah County, OR	114

Place	Number
Salt Lake City, UT (city) Salt Lake County	606
Honolulu, HI (cdp) Honolulu County	494
West Valley City, UT (city) Salt Lake County	457
East Palo Alto, CA (city) San Mateo County	435
Oakland, CA (city) Alameda County	333
San Bruno, CA (city) San Mateo County	216
San Mateo, CA (city) San Mateo County	183
Sacramento, CA (city) Sacramento County	158
West Jordan, UT (city) Salt Lake County	153
Portland, OR (city) Multnomah County	107
Hauula, HI (cdp) Honolulu County	103
Laie, HI (cdp) Honolulu County	94
Los Angeles, CA (city) Los Angeles County	92
Kahuku, HI (cdp) Honolulu County	81

Notes: Please refer to the User's Guide for an explanation of data; ranking tables include all places with Asian and/or NHPI populations above SF4 population thresholds; (1) tables reflect only those areas that meet SF4 population thresholds, therefore there may be less than 50 states, 75 counties or 75 places listed

Educational Attainment: High School Graduates

Tongans 25 Years and Over Who are High School Graduates

All States, Top 75 Counties, and Top 75 Places Sorted by Percent[1]

State	Percent
Washington	85.51
Oregon	74.27
Arizona	73.44
Utah	70.93
Texas	68.42
United States	65.27
Hawaii	65.12
California	60.73
Nevada	59.18
Alaska	53.95

County	Percent
Multnomah County, OR	89.76
King County, WA	86.18
Utah County, UT	84.24
San Diego County, CA	84.21
Contra Costa County, CA	78.98
Tarrant County, TX	73.71
Maricopa County, AZ	73.39
San Bernardino County, CA	70.28
Salt Lake County, UT	69.26
Honolulu County, HI	65.98
Washoe County, NV	63.70
Alameda County, CA	61.63
Maui County, HI	61.28
Los Angeles County, CA	61.25
San Mateo County, CA	60.06
Sacramento County, CA	59.17
Orange County, CA	45.10

Place	Percent
San Bruno, CA (city) San Mateo County	90.38
Portland, OR (city) Multnomah County	89.17
West Jordan, UT (city) Salt Lake County	85.00
Laie, HI (cdp) Honolulu County	83.19
Kahuku, HI (cdp) Honolulu County	69.23
West Valley City, UT (city) Salt Lake County	66.81
Hauula, HI (cdp) Honolulu County	63.58
Salt Lake City, UT (city) Salt Lake County	62.60
Oakland, CA (city) Alameda County	61.21
Sacramento, CA (city) Sacramento County	60.08
Honolulu, HI (cdp) Honolulu County	59.95
Los Angeles, CA (city) Los Angeles County	58.23
East Palo Alto, CA (city) San Mateo County	57.39
San Mateo, CA (city) San Mateo County	46.10

Notes: Please refer to the User's Guide for an explanation of data; ranking tables include all places with Asian and/or NHPI populations above SF4 population thresholds; (1) tables reflect only those areas that meet SF4 population thresholds, therefore there may be less than 50 states, 75 counties or 75 places listed

Educational Attainment: High School Graduates

Vietnamese 25 Years and Over Who are High School Graduates

All States, Top 75 Counties, and Top 75 Places Sorted by Number[1]

State	Number
United States	429,134
California	181,849
Texas	52,438
Washington	17,493
Virginia	16,511
Florida	13,059
Massachusetts	11,135
Georgia	10,003
Pennsylvania	9,578
New York	8,285
Oregon	7,899
Illinois	7,475
Minnesota	7,229
Maryland	7,118
Louisiana	6,599
New Jersey	6,232
North Carolina	5,400
Michigan	4,901
Colorado	4,881
Oklahoma	4,627
Arizona	4,616
Ohio	4,338
Missouri	3,508
Kansas	3,167
Connecticut	2,898
Hawaii	2,850
Tennessee	2,427
Utah	1,927
Nevada	1,901
Iowa	1,839
Nebraska	1,838
Indiana	1,796
Wisconsin	1,581
South Carolina	1,427
Arkansas	1,351
Alabama	1,328
Kentucky	1,242
Mississippi	1,219
New Mexico	1,205
District of Columbia	610
New Hampshire	607
Idaho	462
Alaska	442
Rhode Island	389
Maine	385
Delaware	277
West Virginia	245
Vermont	227
South Dakota	147

County	Number
Orange County, CA	57,593
Santa Clara County, CA	42,976
Los Angeles County, CA	31,702
Harris County, TX	22,323
San Diego County, CA	12,907
Fairfax County, VA	10,700
King County, WA	10,397
Alameda County, CA	9,232
Dallas County, TX	7,504
Tarrant County, TX	6,412
Sacramento County, CA	5,850
Cook County, IL	4,421
Multnomah County, OR	4,407
Montgomery County, MD	4,216
San Francisco County, CA	3,774
San Bernardino County, CA	3,740
Suffolk County, MA	3,661
Maricopa County, AZ	3,606
Travis County, TX	3,302
Hennepin County, MN	3,197
Philadelphia County, PA	3,009
Gwinnett County, GA	2,745
Orange County, FL	2,713
Fort Bend County, TX	2,543
Oklahoma County, OK	2,532
Honolulu County, HI	2,524
Middlesex County, MA	2,431
Riverside County, CA	2,408
Washington County, OR	2,408
Snohomish County, WA	2,396
Contra Costa County, CA	2,272
Jefferson Parish, LA	2,236
DeKalb County, GA	2,061
Collin County, TX	1,944
Sedgwick County, KS	1,902
Worcester County, MA	1,755
Salt Lake County, UT	1,649
Hillsborough County, FL	1,628
Mecklenburg County, NC	1,623
Clark County, NV	1,611
Orleans Parish, LA	1,598
Ventura County, CA	1,584
Pierce County, WA	1,551
Pinellas County, FL	1,523
San Mateo County, CA	1,501
Kent County, MI	1,492
Queens County, NY	1,451
Bexar County, TX	1,441
Clayton County, GA	1,418
Denver County, CO	1,397
San Joaquin County, CA	1,362
Ramsey County, MN	1,344
Hartford County, CT	1,307
Kings County, NY	1,236
Broward County, FL	1,219
Norfolk County, MA	1,215
DuPage County, IL	1,162
Arapahoe County, CO	1,155
Denton County, TX	1,126
Bernalillo County, NM	1,046
Shelby County, TN	1,029
Wake County, NC	1,010
New York County, NY	1,009
Prince George's County, MD	1,007
Palm Beach County, FL	994
Saint Louis Independent City, MO	962
Franklin County, OH	944
Essex County, MA	937
Lancaster County, NE	934
Montgomery County, PA	921
Camden County, NJ	917
Monroe County, NY	898
Clark County, WA	894
Middlesex County, NJ	894
Loudoun County, VA	887

Place	Number
San Jose, CA (city) Santa Clara County	32,125
Garden Grove, CA (city) Orange County	13,797
Houston, TX (city) Harris County	12,718
Westminster, CA (city) Orange County	10,336
San Diego, CA (city) San Diego County	10,334
Los Angeles, CA (city) Los Angeles County	7,924
Santa Ana, CA (city) Orange County	7,450
Anaheim, CA (city) Orange County	4,739
New York, NY (city)	4,482
Portland, OR (city) Multnomah County	4,176
Milpitas, CA (city) Santa Clara County	4,012
Seattle, WA (city) King County	3,888
San Francisco, CA (city) San Francisco County	3,774
Fountain Valley, CA (city) Orange County	3,433
Boston, MA (city) Suffolk County	3,302
Chicago, IL (city) Cook County	3,147
Arlington, TX (city) Tarrant County	3,062
Philadelphia, PA (city) Philadelphia County	3,009
Oklahoma City, OK (city) Oklahoma County	3,005
Huntington Beach, CA (city) Orange County	2,719
Austin, TX (city) Travis County	2,613
Oakland, CA (city) Alameda County	2,520
Irvine, CA (city) Orange County	2,435
Fremont, CA (city) Alameda County	2,410
Dallas, TX (city) Dallas County	2,400
Garland, TX (city) Dallas County	2,392
Santa Clara, CA (city) Santa Clara County	2,288
Honolulu, HI (cdp) Honolulu County	1,970
El Monte, CA (city) Los Angeles County	1,942
Long Beach, CA (city) Los Angeles County	1,849
Rosemead, CA (city) Los Angeles County	1,842
Sacramento, CA (city) Sacramento County	1,805
Alhambra, CA (city) Los Angeles County	1,801
Wichita, KS (city) Sedgwick County	1,773
Annandale, VA (cdp) Fairfax County	1,724
Fort Worth, TX (city) Tarrant County	1,717
Orange, CA (city) Orange County	1,705
New Orleans, LA (city) Orleans Parish	1,598
Sunnyvale, CA (city) Santa Clara County	1,588
Phoenix, AZ (city) Maricopa County	1,427
Denver, CO (city) Denver County	1,397
Charlotte, NC (city) Mecklenburg County	1,264
Worcester, MA (city) Worcester County	1,215
San Antonio, TX (city) Bexar County	1,164
Stanton, CA (city) Orange County	1,098
Carrollton, TX (city) Denton County	1,096
Costa Mesa, CA (city) Orange County	1,096
Stockton, CA (city) San Joaquin County	1,096
Hayward, CA (city) Alameda County	1,045
Tacoma, WA (city) Pierce County	1,041
Jefferson, VA (cdp) Fairfax County	1,034
Monterey Park, CA (city) Los Angeles County	1,023
Albuquerque, NM (city) Bernalillo County	1,009
Minneapolis, MN (city) Hennepin County	969
Plano, TX (city) Collin County	963
St. Louis, MO (city) Saint Louis Independent City	962
West Covina, CA (city) Los Angeles County	942
Lincoln, NE (city) Lancaster County	927
Tustin, CA (city) Orange County	905
Springfield, VA (cdp) Fairfax County	896
Grand Prairie, TX (city) Dallas County	886
St. Paul, MN (city) Ramsey County	875
Columbus, OH (city) Franklin County	870
Kansas City, MO (city) Jackson County	869
Arlington, VA (cdp) Arlington County	863
Richardson, TX (city) Dallas County	833
Irving, TX (city) Dallas County	819
San Gabriel, CA (city) Los Angeles County	792
Corona, CA (city) Riverside County	773
Union City, CA (city) Alameda County	770
Elk Grove, CA (cdp) Sacramento County	736
Renton, WA (city) King County	730
Mission Viejo, CA (city) Orange County	727
Riverside, CA (city) Riverside County	725
Torrance, CA (city) Los Angeles County	713

Notes: Please refer to the User's Guide for an explanation of data; ranking tables include all places with Asian and/or NHPI populations above SF4 population thresholds; (1) tables reflect only those areas that meet SF4 population thresholds, therefore there may be less than 50 states, 75 counties or 75 places listed

Educational Attainment: High School Graduates

Vietnamese 25 Years and Over Who are High School Graduates

All States, Top 75 Counties, and Top 75 Places Sorted by Percent[1]

State	Percent
West Virginia	76.09
Virginia	69.05
Alaska	67.48
Ohio	66.66
Kentucky	66.13
Maryland	65.90
Wisconsin	65.90
Illinois	65.75
Oregon	65.43
Rhode Island	64.83
California	64.47
New Jersey	64.23
New Mexico	64.23
Nevada	64.01
Indiana	63.37
Connecticut	63.33
Minnesota	63.09
Michigan	63.01
Texas	62.42
Washington	62.37
Maine	62.20
Oklahoma	61.94
United States	61.88
Delaware	61.83
Florida	61.58
Arizona	61.12
Tennessee	58.94
Colorado	58.15
South Carolina	57.91
North Carolina	57.49
Utah	57.20
Arkansas	56.65
New York	56.45
District of Columbia	55.61
Massachusetts	55.16
Pennsylvania	55.10
Missouri	54.80
Georgia	54.50
New Hampshire	54.39
Idaho	53.78
Hawaii	52.65
Alabama	51.67
Nebraska	49.88
Kansas	48.74
Louisiana	48.49
Mississippi	45.90
Vermont	45.13
Iowa	41.72
South Dakota	34.67

County	Percent
Brazos County, TX	92.23
Somerset County, NJ	90.03
Scott County, MN	89.84
Collin County, TX	86.55
Seminole County, FL	85.29
Alachua County, FL	84.42
New York County, NY	84.36
Lake County, IL	84.12
Will County, IL	83.57
Monmouth County, NJ	82.79
Washtenaw County, MI	81.65
Brevard County, FL	81.24
Fairfax Independent City, VA	81.19
Placer County, CA	81.07
Nassau County, NY	80.73
Dane County, WI	79.87
Alexandria Independent City, VA	78.76
Brazoria County, TX	78.72
Loudoun County, VA	77.81
Palm Beach County, FL	77.54
San Mateo County, CA	77.49
Washington County, OR	77.48
Williamson County, TX	77.27
Fort Bend County, TX	76.18
Chester County, PA	75.46
Travis County, TX	75.23
Marion County, OR	74.77
Butler County, OH	74.72
Montgomery County, OH	74.69
Morris County, NJ	74.69
Boulder County, CO	74.56
Bucks County, PA	74.44
Yolo County, CA	74.38
Lafayette Parish, LA	73.83
Ventura County, CA	73.30
Burlington County, NJ	73.18
Cleveland County, OK	73.01
New Castle County, DE	72.88
Prince William County, VA	72.81
New Haven County, CT	72.77
Fairfax County, VA	72.69
Bexar County, TX	72.56
Essex County, NJ	72.37
Wayne County, MI	72.31
Greene County, MO	72.18
Lubbock County, TX	72.12
Ottawa County, MI	71.59
Snohomish County, WA	71.29
Denton County, TX	71.09
Hamilton County, TN	70.74
Kane County, IL	70.50
Santa Cruz County, CA	70.39
Washington County, MN	70.27
Marion County, IN	70.04
Norfolk County, MA	69.83
York County, PA	69.71
Oakland County, MI	69.66
Contra Costa County, CA	69.23
Kern County, CA	69.09
Wake County, NC	69.04
Richland County, SC	68.82
Summit County, OH	68.32
Santa Clara County, CA	68.17
Baltimore County, MD	68.12
Cumberland County, NC	67.98
Forsyth County, NC	67.60
Howard County, MD	67.60
Dakota County, MN	67.59
Benton County, WA	67.55
Riverside County, CA	67.53
Montgomery County, MD	67.43
Middlesex County, NJ	67.37
Hamilton County, OH	67.19
Canadian County, OK	67.15
Thurston County, WA	66.90

Place	Percent
Davis, CA (city) Yolo County	96.07
Laguna Niguel, CA (city) Orange County	95.48
Yorba Linda, CA (city) Orange County	95.09
Laguna Hills, CA (city) Orange County	94.61
Aliso Viejo, CA (cdp) Orange County	93.09
Downey, CA (city) Los Angeles County	92.18
Stafford, TX (city) Fort Bend County	90.87
Montgomery Village, MD (cdp) Montgomery County	90.27
Rancho Santa Margarita, CA (city) Orange County	90.27
Diamond Bar, CA (city) Los Angeles County	88.99
Irvine, CA (city) Orange County	88.19
Santa Clarita, CA (city) Los Angeles County	87.96
Franconia, VA (cdp) Fairfax County	87.93
Corona, CA (city) Riverside County	87.44
Arden-Arcade, CA (cdp) Sacramento County	86.76
Mission Viejo, CA (city) Orange County	86.75
Allen, TX (city) Collin County	86.58
Cerritos, CA (city) Los Angeles County	86.46
Laguna, CA (cdp) Sacramento County	85.85
Thousand Oaks, CA (city) Ventura County	85.71
San Mateo, CA (city) San Mateo County	85.66
Chantilly, VA (cdp) Fairfax County	85.60
Missouri City, TX (city) Fort Bend County	85.40
Fremont, CA (city) Alameda County	85.01
Burien, WA (city) King County	84.62
Plano, TX (city) Collin County	83.74
Cary, NC (town) Wake County	83.60
Tustin, CA (city) Orange County	82.95
Cupertino, CA (city) Santa Clara County	82.93
Hillsboro, OR (city) Washington County	82.37
Citrus Heights, CA (city) Sacramento County	82.30
Placentia, CA (city) Orange County	82.23
Lakewood, CA (city) Los Angeles County	81.90
Kirkland, WA (city) King County	81.49
Round Rock, TX (city) Williamson County	80.71
Cypress, CA (city) Orange County	80.68
Bakersfield, CA (city) Kern County	80.66
Merrifield, VA (cdp) Fairfax County	80.51
Gresham, OR (city) Multnomah County	80.23
Berkeley, CA (city) Alameda County	80.21
Aurora, IL (city) Kane County	80.06
Colesville, MD (cdp) Montgomery County	79.44
Seattle Hill-Silver Firs, WA (cdp) Snohomish County	79.20
Chandler, AZ (city) Maricopa County	79.14
Lincolnia, VA (cdp) Fairfax County	78.88
Beaverton, OR (city) Washington County	78.84
Richmond, CA (city) Contra Costa County	78.66
Madison, WI (city) Dane County	78.55
Federal Way, WA (city) King County	78.46
North Richland Hills, TX (city) Tarrant County	78.46
Pasadena, CA (city) Los Angeles County	78.18
Sterling Heights, MI (city) Macomb County	77.85
Mountain View, CA (city) Santa Clara County	77.59
Hacienda Heights, CA (cdp) Los Angeles County	77.20
Medford, MA (city) Middlesex County	76.88
Richardson, TX (city) Dallas County	76.85
Germantown, MD (cdp) Montgomery County	76.69
Milpitas, CA (city) Santa Clara County	76.68
Austin, TX (city) Travis County	76.38
Fountain Valley, CA (city) Orange County	76.37
Rancho Cucamonga, CA (city) San Bernardino County	76.13
Lake Forest, CA (city) Orange County	75.98
Lake Barcroft, VA (cdp) Fairfax County	75.87
Pinellas Park, FL (city) Pinellas County	75.75
Lynnwood, WA (city) Snohomish County	75.70
West Hartford, CT (town) Hartford County	75.49
Gaithersburg, MD (city) Montgomery County	75.43
Oakton, VA (cdp) Fairfax County	75.36
Norwalk, CA (city) Los Angeles County	75.29
Chino Hills, CA (city) San Bernardino County	74.95
Shoreline, WA (city) King County	74.51
Huntington Beach, CA (city) Orange County	74.49
Mesa, AZ (city) Maricopa County	74.31
Burke, VA (cdp) Fairfax County	74.16
Burbank, CA (city) Los Angeles County	74.05

Notes: Please refer to the User's Guide for an explanation of data; ranking tables include all places with Asian and/or NHPI populations above SF4 population thresholds; (1) tables reflect only those areas that meet SF4 population thresholds, therefore there may be less than 50 states, 75 counties or 75 places listed

Educational Attainment: Four-Year College Graduates

Total Population 25 Years and Over Who are Four-Year College Graduates

All States, Top 75 Counties, and Top 75 Places Sorted by Number[1]

State	Number
United States	44,462,605
California	5,669,966
New York	3,433,212
Texas	2,972,293
Florida	2,462,328
Illinois	2,078,049
Pennsylvania	1,847,631
New Jersey	1,684,861
Ohio	1,563,532
Massachusetts	1,418,295
Michigan	1,396,259
Virginia	1,374,988
Georgia	1,260,178
North Carolina	1,186,713
Maryland	1,099,360
Washington	1,061,425
Colorado	907,755
Minnesota	868,082
Missouri	784,476
Wisconsin	779,273
Arizona	766,212
Indiana	755,613
Tennessee	732,688
Connecticut	720,994
Oregon	564,566
Alabama	549,608
South Carolina	530,055
Louisiana	519,778
Kentucky	453,469
Oklahoma	446,771
Kansas	438,978
Iowa	402,090
Utah	312,963
Mississippi	297,091
Arkansas	288,428
New Mexico	266,149
Nebraska	258,140
Nevada	237,875
New Hampshire	236,104
Hawaii	210,041
Maine	198,960
West Virginia	182,960
Rhode Island	177,817
Idaho	170,615
District of Columbia	150,237
Montana	142,961
Delaware	128,917
Vermont	119,025
South Dakota	102,012
Alaska	93,807
North Dakota	89,843
Wyoming	69,162

County	Number
Los Angeles County, CA	1,462,389
Cook County, IL	968,642
Orange County, CA	558,743
Harris County, TX	556,887
New York County, NY	556,193
San Diego County, CA	523,511
Maricopa County, AZ	500,881
King County, WA	474,948
Santa Clara County, CA	450,539
Middlesex County, MA	438,733
Dallas County, TX	368,149
Queens County, NY	366,872
Fairfax County, VA	357,861
Kings County, NY	339,250
Alameda County, CA	332,954
Montgomery County, MD	324,080
Miami-Dade County, FL	323,399
Nassau County, NY	321,321
Oakland County, MI	308,723
Hennepin County, MN	289,405
Broward County, FL	276,527
San Francisco County, CA	267,992
Suffolk County, NY	258,864
Westchester County, NY	256,924
Allegheny County, PA	252,583
DuPage County, IL	245,452
St. Louis County, MO	239,729
Tarrant County, TX	239,285
Bergen County, NJ	238,381
Fairfield County, CT	237,674
Cuyahoga County, OH	235,413
Palm Beach County, FL	226,615
Wayne County, MI	224,792
Contra Costa County, CA	219,048
Fulton County, GA	218,405
Franklin County, OH	215,180
Travis County, TX	203,666
Montgomery County, PA	199,787
Norfolk County, MA	194,349
Bexar County, TX	192,454
Sacramento County, CA	191,641
San Mateo County, CA	191,277
Wake County, NC	177,029
Philadelphia County, PA	172,641
Hartford County, CT	171,651
Mecklenburg County, NC	168,957
Middlesex County, NJ	165,533
Hillsborough County, FL	164,109
Honolulu County, HI	161,646
Hamilton County, OH	159,212
Pinellas County, FL	157,235
Cobb County, GA	157,178
San Bernardino County, CA	156,581
Erie County, NY	156,512
Baltimore County, MD	156,341
DeKalb County, GA	156,089
Clark County, NV	156,083
Riverside County, CA	155,676
Lake County, IL	153,726
New Haven County, CT	152,433
Essex County, MA	152,225
Orange County, FL	150,009
Collin County, TX	149,417
Monroe County, NY	148,953
Pima County, AZ	146,108
Suffolk County, MA	144,910
Monmouth County, NJ	142,842
Morris County, NJ	142,770
Johnson County, KS	141,219
Essex County, NJ	141,167
Shelby County, TN	141,001
Marion County, IN	140,550
Milwaukee County, WI	140,460
Salt Lake County, UT	139,631
Multnomah County, OR	136,828

Place	Number
New York, NY (city)	1,446,833
Los Angeles, CA (city) Los Angeles County	589,061
Chicago, IL (city) Cook County	462,783
Houston, TX (city) Harris County	324,039
San Diego, CA (city) San Diego County	272,785
San Francisco, CA (city) San Francisco County	267,992
Dallas, TX (city) Dallas County	203,004
Seattle, WA (city) King County	193,322
Phoenix, AZ (city) Maricopa County	180,443
San Jose, CA (city) Santa Clara County	180,122
Philadelphia, PA (city) Philadelphia County	172,641
Austin, TX (city) Travis County	161,937
Hempstead, NY (town) Nassau County	158,382
San Antonio, TX (city) Bexar County	150,680
Boston, MA (city) Suffolk County	134,252
Denver, CO (city) Denver County	129,065
Charlotte, NC (city) Mecklenburg County	128,427
Columbus, OH (city) Franklin County	128,058
Indianapolis, IN (sp. city) Marion County	127,608
Portland, OR (city) Multnomah County	118,698
Nashville-Davidson, TN (sp. city) Davidson County	107,230
Jacksonville, FL (city) Duval County	98,991
Atlanta, GA (city) Fulton County	92,929
Albuquerque, NM (city) Bernalillo County	92,635
Minneapolis, MN (city) Hennepin County	91,027
Arlington, VA (cdp) Arlington County	83,613
Memphis, TN (city) Shelby County	83,219
Honolulu, HI (cdp) Honolulu County	83,207
Oakland, CA (city) Alameda County	80,777
Raleigh, NC (city) Wake County	78,216
Oklahoma City, OK (city) Oklahoma County	77,502
Oyster Bay, NY (town) Nassau County	77,489
New Orleans, LA (city) Orleans Parish	77,407
Plano, TX (city) Collin County	76,706
Colorado Springs, CO (city) El Paso County	76,702
Kansas City, MO (city) Jackson County	73,824
Fort Worth, TX (city) Tarrant County	72,313
Tulsa, OK (city) Tulsa County	71,568
Brookhaven, NY (town) Suffolk County	71,089
Omaha, NE (city) Douglas County	70,896
North Hempstead, NY (town) Nassau County	70,290
Tucson, AZ (city) Pima County	68,863
Scottsdale, AZ (city) Maricopa County	66,474
Long Beach, CA (city) Los Angeles County	66,424
Milwaukee, WI (city) Milwaukee County	64,742
Arlington, TX (city) Tarrant County	61,837
Detroit, MI (city) Wayne County	61,836
El Paso, TX (city) El Paso County	61,217
Madison, WI (city) Dane County	61,057
Sacramento, CA (city) Sacramento County	61,042
Huntington, NY (town) Suffolk County	59,888
Lexington-Fayette, KY (sp. city) Fayette County	59,615
Fremont, CA (city) Alameda County	58,796
Pittsburgh, PA (city) Allegheny County	57,267
Las Vegas, NV (city) Clark County	56,989
St. Paul, MN (city) Ramsey County	55,788
Cincinnati, OH (city) Hamilton County	55,215
Wichita, KS (city) Sedgwick County	54,692
Mesa, AZ (city) Maricopa County	52,929
Overland Park, KS (city) Johnson County	52,397
Irvine, CA (city) Orange County	51,932
Tampa, FL (city) Hillsborough County	50,471
Durham, NC (city) Durham County	49,307
Sunnyvale, CA (city) Santa Clara County	48,379
Greensboro, NC (city) Guilford County	48,264
Naperville, IL (city) Du Page County	47,805
Huntington Beach, CA (city) Orange County	47,476
Islip, NY (town) Suffolk County	45,456
Lincoln, NE (city) Lancaster County	45,370
Fresno, CA (city) Fresno County	44,999
Ann Arbor, MI (city) Washtenaw County	44,810
Glendale, CA (city) Los Angeles County	43,288
Cambridge, MA (city) Middlesex County	43,191
Jersey City, NJ (city) Hudson County	42,676
Little Rock, AR (city) Pulaski County	42,586

Notes: Please refer to the User's Guide for an explanation of data; ranking tables include all places with Asian and/or NHPI populations above SF4 population thresholds; (1) tables reflect only those areas that meet SF4 population thresholds, therefore there may be less than 50 states, 75 counties or 75 places listed

Educational Attainment: Four-Year College Graduates

Total Population 25 Years and Over Who are Four-Year College Graduates

All States, Top 75 Counties, and Top 75 Places Sorted by Percent[1]

State	Percent
District of Columbia	39.07
Massachusetts	33.19
Colorado	32.69
Maryland	31.45
Connecticut	31.41
New Jersey	29.78
Virginia	29.46
Vermont	29.45
New Hampshire	28.65
Washington	27.73
Minnesota	27.43
New York	27.37
California	26.62
Hawaii	26.17
Utah	26.13
Illinois	26.06
Kansas	25.80
Rhode Island	25.60
Oregon	25.08
Delaware	25.05
Alaska	24.71
United States	24.40
Montana	24.37
Georgia	24.30
Nebraska	23.74
Arizona	23.53
New Mexico	23.45
Texas	23.24
Maine	22.87
North Carolina	22.46
Wisconsin	22.42
Pennsylvania	22.35
Florida	22.33
North Dakota	21.99
Wyoming	21.91
Michigan	21.76
Idaho	21.67
Missouri	21.58
South Dakota	21.51
Iowa	21.21
Ohio	21.10
South Carolina	20.42
Oklahoma	20.28
Tennessee	19.56
Indiana	19.41
Alabama	19.03
Louisiana	18.73
Nevada	18.16
Kentucky	17.14
Mississippi	16.90
Arkansas	16.66
West Virginia	14.83

County	Percent
Falls Church Independent City, VA	63.75
Los Alamos County, NM	60.48
Arlington County, VA	60.22
Fairfax County, VA	54.78
Montgomery County, MD	54.56
Alexandria Independent City, VA	54.30
Howard County, MD	52.93
Boulder County, CO	52.38
Douglas County, CO	51.85
Orange County, NC	51.49
Marin County, CA	51.31
New York County, NY	49.40
Hamilton County, IN	48.87
Washtenaw County, MI	48.14
Johnson County, KS	47.74
Albemarle County, VA	47.68
Johnson County, IA	47.60
Tompkins County, NY	47.46
Benton County, OR	47.39
Collin County, TX	47.33
Loudoun County, VA	47.19
Somerset County, NJ	46.51
Fairfax Independent City, VA	45.65
Williamsburg Independent City, VA	45.02
San Francisco County, CA	44.98
Story County, IA	44.50
Williamson County, TN	44.36
Morris County, NJ	44.08
Albany County, WY	44.07
Whitman County, WA	44.04
Wake County, NC	43.88
Middlesex County, MA	43.59
Blaine County, ID	43.11
Norfolk County, MA	42.95
Douglas County, KS	42.68
Eagle County, CO	42.63
Chester County, PA	42.46
Hunterdon County, NJ	41.77
Boone County, MO	41.73
Leon County, FL	41.73
DuPage County, IL	41.66
James City County, VA	41.54
Fulton County, GA	41.39
Chittenden County, VT	41.16
Delaware County, OH	41.04
Gallatin County, MT	41.01
Latah County, ID	40.97
Westchester County, NY	40.85
Charlottesville Independent City, VA	40.77
Dane County, WI	40.64
Travis County, TX	40.62
Riley County, KS	40.52
Santa Clara County, CA	40.48
Durham County, NC	40.14
King County, WA	39.95
Fairfield County, CT	39.85
Clarke County, GA	39.82
Oconee County, GA	39.79
Cobb County, GA	39.76
Monroe County, IN	39.63
Larimer County, CO	39.53
Hennepin County, MN	39.09
San Mateo County, CA	39.01
Montgomery County, PA	38.73
Alachua County, FL	38.70
Ozaukee County, WI	38.61
Lake County, IL	38.60
Newport County, RI	38.32
Bergen County, NJ	38.23
Oakland County, MI	38.21
Champaign County, IL	37.99
Hampshire County, MA	37.95
Madison County, MS	37.94
Rockland County, NY	37.50
York County, VA	37.36

Place	Percent
Stanford, CA (cdp) Santa Clara County	94.56
Forest Home, NY (cdp) Tompkins County	91.76
Winnetka, IL (village) Cook County	84.41
East Ithaca, NY (cdp) Tompkins County	81.95
Bunker Hill Village, TX (city) Harris County	80.52
University Park, TX (city) Dallas County	80.45
Scarsdale, NY (village) Westchester County	79.83
Chappaqua, NY (cdp) Westchester County	79.69
West University Place, TX (city) Harris County	79.40
Ann Arbor, MI (township) Washtenaw County	78.95
Bethesda, MD (cdp) Montgomery County	78.88
Druid Hills, GA (cdp) De Kalb County	78.78
Los Altos Hills, CA (town) Santa Clara County	78.15
Kensington, CA (cdp) Contra Costa County	78.02
Piedmont, CA (city) Alameda County	77.85
Northeast Ithaca, NY (cdp) Tompkins County	77.84
Hanover, NH (town) Grafton County	77.66
Brookline, MA (town) Norfolk County	76.95
Wolf Trap, VA (cdp) Fairfax County	76.92
Potomac, MD (cdp) Montgomery County	76.40
Great Falls, VA (cdp) Fairfax County	76.28
Hunters Creek Village, TX (city) Harris County	76.24
Atherton, CA (town) San Mateo County	76.19
New Castle, NY (town) Westchester County	75.97
Princeton, NJ (township) Mercer County	75.90
Wellesley, MA (town) Norfolk County	75.89
Tamalpais-Homestead Valley, CA (cdp) Marin County	75.77
North Potomac, MD (cdp) Montgomery County	75.41
McLean, VA (cdp) Fairfax County	75.36
Chevy Chase, MD (cdp) Montgomery County	75.17
Weston, MA (town) Middlesex County	75.10
Lansing, NY (village) Tompkins County	74.76
Newport Coast, CA (cdp) Orange County	74.48
Travilah, MD (cdp) Montgomery County	74.43
Palo Alto, CA (city) Santa Clara County	74.38
Plainsboro Center, NJ (cdp) Middlesex County	74.25
Millburn, NJ (township) Essex County	74.03
Munsey Park, NY (village) Nassau County	73.93
West Windsor, NJ (township) Mercer County	73.92
Orinda, CA (city) Contra Costa County	73.91
Lake Forest, IL (city) Lake County	73.83
Chapel Hill, NC (town) Orange County	73.69
Bronxville, NY (village) Westchester County	73.56
East Hills, NY (village) Nassau County	73.33
Loyola, CA (cdp) Santa Clara County	73.10
Wilmette, IL (village) Cook County	72.58
Amherst Center, MA (cdp) Hampshire County	72.30
Briarcliff Manor, NY (village) Westchester County	72.22
Boxborough, MA (town) Middlesex County	72.13
Sands Point, NY (village) Nassau County	71.92
Sudbury, MA (town) Middlesex County	71.89
New Canaan, CT (town) Fairfield County	71.60
Los Altos, CA (city) Santa Clara County	71.30
Palos Verdes Estates, CA (city) Los Angeles County	70.85
Wilton, CT (town) Fairfield County	70.73
Darien, CT (town) Fairfield County	70.45
East Lansing, MI (city) Ingham County	70.39
Plainsboro, NJ (township) Middlesex County	70.27
Falcon Heights, MN (city) Ramsey County	70.26
Montgomery, NJ (township) Somerset County	70.16
Hillsborough, CA (town) San Mateo County	70.04
Tysons Corner, VA (cdp) Fairfax County	69.80
River Forest, IL (village) Cook County	69.70
West Lafayette, IN (city) Tippecanoe County	69.69
Clayton, MO (city) Saint Louis County	69.67
San Marino, CA (city) Los Angeles County	69.67
Tiburon, CA (town) Marin County	69.64
Westport, CT (town) Fairfield County	69.45
Acton, MA (town) Middlesex County	69.29
Ann Arbor, MI (city) Washtenaw County	69.29
State College, PA (borough) Centre County	69.19
Superior, CO (town) Boulder County	69.16
Laurel Hollow, NY (village) Nassau County	69.11
Mercer Island, WA (city) King County	69.10
Lexington, MA (town) Middlesex County	69.07

Notes: Please refer to the User's Guide for an explanation of data; ranking tables include all places with Asian and/or NHPI populations above SF4 population thresholds; (1) tables reflect only those areas that meet SF4 population thresholds, therefore there may be less than 50 states, 75 counties or 75 places listed

Educational Attainment: Four-Year College Graduates

Asians 25 Years and Over Who are Four-Year College Graduates

All States, Top 75 Counties, and Top 75 Places Sorted by Number[1]

State	Number
United States	2,925,743
California	1,012,851
New York	286,761
New Jersey	195,903
Texas	170,121
Illinois	159,582
Hawaii	100,682
Virginia	82,539
Washington	76,936
Maryland	76,464
Florida	72,564
Massachusetts	72,334
Michigan	65,379
Pennsylvania	65,179
Ohio	50,338
Georgia	48,368
Connecticut	29,977
North Carolina	29,733
Arizona	26,798
Colorado	25,860
Minnesota	25,023
Oregon	24,438
Indiana	20,602
Missouri	20,190
Nevada	17,608
Wisconsin	16,973
Tennessee	16,316
Louisiana	11,889
Kansas	11,020
Oklahoma	10,504
Kentucky	9,940
South Carolina	9,475
Alabama	9,173
Iowa	8,642
Utah	8,062
Delaware	6,741
District of Columbia	5,749
New Mexico	5,362
Nebraska	5,327
New Hampshire	5,174
Rhode Island	4,676
Arkansas	3,943
Mississippi	3,906
West Virginia	3,792
Alaska	3,519
Idaho	2,932
Maine	1,470
Vermont	1,128
South Dakota	1,056
Montana	1,050
North Dakota	1,000
Wyoming	694

County	Number
Los Angeles County, CA	332,020
Santa Clara County, CA	148,060
Orange County, CA	104,810
Queens County, NY	100,262
Cook County, IL	96,013
Alameda County, CA	89,420
Honolulu County, HI	85,664
San Diego County, CA	59,820
San Francisco County, CA	56,004
King County, WA	51,821
Harris County, TX	51,744
San Mateo County, CA	49,684
New York County, NY	48,244
Middlesex County, NJ	47,058
Fairfax County, VA	42,878
Montgomery County, MD	40,113
Bergen County, NJ	38,045
Middlesex County, MA	34,418
Contra Costa County, CA	33,822
DuPage County, IL	30,733
Kings County, NY	28,681
Dallas County, TX	25,966
Sacramento County, CA	24,583
Oakland County, MI	23,242
Nassau County, NY	22,638
San Bernardino County, CA	22,170
Hudson County, NJ	21,832
Maricopa County, AZ	20,670
Westchester County, NY	18,579
Collin County, TX	15,979
Morris County, NJ	13,914
Clark County, NV	13,773
Travis County, TX	13,649
Fort Bend County, TX	13,615
Ventura County, CA	12,841
Riverside County, CA	12,795
Wayne County, MI	12,768
Philadelphia County, PA	12,559
Somerset County, NJ	12,431
Franklin County, OH	12,264
Norfolk County, MA	12,260
Essex County, NJ	12,239
Suffolk County, NY	12,098
Tarrant County, TX	11,553
Gwinnett County, GA	11,197
Fairfield County, CT	11,073
Hennepin County, MN	10,956
Montgomery County, PA	10,940
Cuyahoga County, OH	10,701
Suffolk County, MA	10,561
Lake County, IL	10,516
Solano County, CA	10,482
Monmouth County, NJ	10,144
Washington County, OR	10,006
St. Louis County, MO	9,709
Allegheny County, PA	9,602
Broward County, FL	9,524
Washtenaw County, MI	9,474
Miami-Dade County, FL	9,467
Prince George's County, MD	9,301
Fulton County, GA	9,156
Bronx County, NY	9,104
Wake County, NC	8,807
Baltimore County, MD	8,478
Snohomish County, WA	8,359
DeKalb County, GA	8,157
New Haven County, CT	8,040
Mercer County, NJ	8,026
Union County, NJ	8,025
Orange County, FL	7,945
Fresno County, CA	7,708
Richmond County, NY	7,676
Howard County, MD	7,579
San Joaquin County, CA	7,359
Arlington County, VA	6,878

Place	Number
New York, NY (city)	193,967
Los Angeles, CA (city) Los Angeles County	109,300
San Jose, CA (city) Santa Clara County	64,058
San Francisco, CA (city) San Francisco County	56,004
Honolulu, HI (cdp) Honolulu County	47,388
Chicago, IL (city) Cook County	42,187
San Diego, CA (city) San Diego County	40,376
Houston, TX (city) Harris County	32,817
Fremont, CA (city) Alameda County	32,136
Sunnyvale, CA (city) Santa Clara County	21,021
Seattle, WA (city) King County	18,212
Irvine, CA (city) Orange County	15,883
Jersey City, NJ (city) Hudson County	14,554
Torrance, CA (city) Los Angeles County	13,804
Daly City, CA (city) San Mateo County	13,262
Edison, NJ (township) Middlesex County	13,256
Philadelphia, PA (city) Philadelphia County	12,559
Santa Clara, CA (city) Santa Clara County	12,209
Austin, TX (city) Travis County	11,966
Glendale, CA (city) Los Angeles County	11,842
Dallas, TX (city) Dallas County	11,125
Cupertino, CA (city) Santa Clara County	10,847
Cerritos, CA (city) Los Angeles County	10,789
Anaheim, CA (city) Orange County	10,775
Milpitas, CA (city) Santa Clara County	10,742
Plano, TX (city) Collin County	10,562
Oakland, CA (city) Alameda County	10,254
Boston, MA (city) Suffolk County	10,150
Sacramento, CA (city) Sacramento County	9,960
Alhambra, CA (city) Los Angeles County	9,553
Long Beach, CA (city) Los Angeles County	9,325
Columbus, OH (city) Franklin County	9,085
Hempstead, NY (town) Nassau County	8,625
Diamond Bar, CA (city) Los Angeles County	8,600
Arcadia, CA (city) Los Angeles County	8,385
Monterey Park, CA (city) Los Angeles County	8,352
Union City, CA (city) Alameda County	8,261
Bellevue, WA (city) King County	8,039
North Hempstead, NY (town) Nassau County	7,894
Rowland Heights, CA (cdp) Los Angeles County	7,726
Mountain View, CA (city) Santa Clara County	7,561
Phoenix, AZ (city) Maricopa County	7,150
Fullerton, CA (city) Orange County	6,942
Arlington, VA (cdp) Arlington County	6,878
West Covina, CA (city) Los Angeles County	6,717
Woodbridge, NJ (township) Middlesex County	6,685
Hayward, CA (city) Alameda County	6,496
Hacienda Heights, CA (cdp) Los Angeles County	6,334
Pasadena, CA (city) Los Angeles County	6,309
Irving, TX (city) Dallas County	6,263
Ann Arbor, MI (city) Washtenaw County	6,222
Vallejo, CA (city) Solano County	6,140
Huntington Beach, CA (city) Orange County	6,130
Garden Grove, CA (city) Orange County	6,050
Portland, OR (city) Multnomah County	5,813
Palo Alto, CA (city) Santa Clara County	5,791
San Mateo, CA (city) San Mateo County	5,789
Walnut, CA (city) Los Angeles County	5,735
Naperville, IL (city) Du Page County	5,670
South San Francisco, CA (city) San Mateo County	5,644
Chino Hills, CA (city) San Bernardino County	5,553
Oyster Bay, NY (town) Nassau County	5,462
Cambridge, MA (city) Middlesex County	5,444
Sugar Land, TX (city) Fort Bend County	5,442
Alameda, CA (city) Alameda County	5,438
Piscataway, NJ (township) Middlesex County	5,338
San Antonio, TX (city) Bexar County	5,159
Troy, MI (city) Oakland County	5,138
Chula Vista, CA (city) San Diego County	5,137
Fresno, CA (city) Fresno County	5,077
Rancho Palos Verdes, CA (city) Los Angeles County	4,992
Berkeley, CA (city) Alameda County	4,984
Skokie, IL (village) Cook County	4,839
Foster City, CA (city) San Mateo County	4,787
Buena Park, CA (city) Orange County	4,772

Notes: Please refer to the User's Guide for an explanation of data; ranking tables include all places with Asian and/or NHPI populations above SF4 population thresholds; (1) tables reflect only those areas that meet SF4 population thresholds, therefore there may be less than 50 states, 75 counties or 75 places listed

Educational Attainment: Four-Year College Graduates

Asians 25 Years and Over Who are Four-Year College Graduates

All States, Top 75 Counties, and Top 75 Places Sorted by Percent[1]

State	Percent
West Virginia	63.87
New Jersey	62.10
Delaware	61.76
Michigan	61.04
Ohio	58.63
District of Columbia	58.22
Indiana	57.99
Connecticut	57.67
Illinois	57.67
Maryland	55.00
New Hampshire	54.60
Kentucky	53.25
Missouri	51.46
Massachusetts	49.84
Pennsylvania	49.24
North Dakota	48.88
Virginia	48.77
Alabama	48.28
Texas	47.78
Tennessee	47.75
Vermont	46.65
New Mexico	44.73
Arizona	44.51
Georgia	44.33
United States	44.06
North Carolina	43.88
Wisconsin	43.00
Iowa	42.87
Colorado	42.80
Nebraska	42.30
California	41.61
New York	41.35
Montana	40.98
Florida	40.93
South Carolina	40.81
Kansas	40.47
South Dakota	39.57
Oregon	38.71
Idaho	38.31
Oklahoma	37.50
Washington	36.76
Utah	36.45
Rhode Island	36.35
Wyoming	36.34
Minnesota	36.30
Mississippi	35.87
Louisiana	35.63
Arkansas	32.59
Maine	32.57
Nevada	28.32
Hawaii	26.59
Alaska	21.23

County	Percent
Tompkins County, NY	88.58
Montgomery County, VA	85.56
McDonough County, IL	85.14
Centre County, PA	84.75
Lincoln Parish, LA	84.50
Washtenaw County, MI	82.53
Tippecanoe County, IN	82.22
Monroe County, IN	82.01
Oktibbeha County, MS	81.80
Monongalia County, WV	81.79
Latah County, ID	81.47
Brazos County, TX	81.28
Orange County, NC	80.91
Payne County, OK	80.63
Story County, IA	80.40
Adair County, MO	79.82
Champaign County, IL	79.35
Alachua County, FL	78.78
Durham County, NC	78.40
Phelps County, MO	78.24
Jackson County, IL	77.91
Albemarle County, VA	77.43
Portage County, OH	76.67
Athens County, OH	76.61
Clarke County, GA	76.43
Johnson County, IA	76.39
Los Alamos County, NM	76.08
Somerset County, NJ	75.97
Bristol County, RI	75.85
Charlottesville Independent City, VA	75.67
Midland County, MI	75.66
Houghton County, MI	75.56
Lafayette County, MS	75.49
Whitman County, WA	73.94
Allegheny County, PA	73.34
McLean County, IL	73.27
Bartholomew County, IN	73.01
Washington County, TN	72.79
Oakland County, MI	72.77
Isabella County, MI	72.67
Shelby County, AL	72.31
Collin County, TX	72.25
Mercer County, NJ	72.19
Tolland County, CT	71.98
Ozaukee County, WI	71.96
Addison County, VT	71.93
Rensselaer County, NY	71.67
Bulloch County, GA	71.62
Boone County, MO	71.50
Douglas County, KS	71.31
Hunterdon County, NJ	71.27
Delaware County, OH	70.89
Kalamazoo County, MI	70.89
Kanawha County, WV	70.89
Fayette County, WV	70.59
Middlesex County, NJ	70.47
Chester County, PA	70.40
Delaware County, IN	70.39
Riley County, KS	70.13
Morris County, NJ	70.06
Coles County, IL	69.90
Hamilton County, IN	69.85
Steuben County, NY	69.40
Ohio County, WV	69.05
Pickens County, SC	68.86
Grafton County, NH	68.84
Peoria County, IL	68.82
Anderson County, TN	68.36
Hampshire County, MA	68.22
Waukesha County, WI	68.19
Manassas Park Independent City, VA	68.05
Allegany County, NY	68.02
Fayette County, KY	68.02
Bradford County, PA	67.83
Gallatin County, MT	67.82

Place	Percent
East Ithaca, NY (cdp) Tompkins County	100.00
Forest Home, NY (cdp) Tompkins County	98.39
Northeast Ithaca, NY (cdp) Tompkins County	97.01
Stanford, CA (cdp) Santa Clara County	96.09
Boxborough, MA (town) Middlesex County	95.42
Scott Township, PA (cdp) Allegheny County	95.41
Scott, PA (township) Allegheny County	95.41
Lansing, NY (village) Tompkins County	95.19
Mansfield, CT (town) Tolland County	94.13
Falcon Heights, MN (city) Ramsey County	93.61
Little Flock, AR (city) Benton County	93.48
Storrs, CT (cdp) Tolland County	93.22
Lansing, NY (town) Tompkins County	92.22
Bunker Hill Village, TX (city) Harris County	91.85
Chappaqua, NY (cdp) Westchester County	91.72
Scio, MI (township) Washtenaw County	90.99
West Lafayette, IN (city) Tippecanoe County	90.93
Briarcliff Manor, NY (village) Westchester County	90.07
New Castle, NY (town) Westchester County	90.00
Bernards, NJ (township) Somerset County	89.47
Hopewell, NJ (township) Mercer County	89.30
Upper St. Clair, PA (township) Allegheny County	89.17
Heathcote, NJ (cdp) Middlesex County	89.04
Williamstown, MA (town) Berkshire County	88.89
State College, PA (borough) Centre County	88.69
Munsey Park, NY (village) Nassau County	88.64
Middleton, WI (city) Dane County	88.55
Dryden, NY (town) Tompkins County	88.51
East Lansing, MI (city) Ingham County	88.15
Tredyffrin, PA (township) Chester County	88.01
Acton, MA (town) Middlesex County	87.91
Macomb, IL (city) McDonough County	87.74
New Providence, NJ (borough) Union County	87.70
Oak Brook, IL (village) Du Page County	87.53
Urbana, IL (city) Champaign County	87.52
Montgomery, NJ (township) Somerset County	87.46
Ann Arbor, MI (city) Washtenaw County	87.38
Laurel Hollow, NY (village) Nassau County	87.37
Lincolnshire, IL (village) Lake County	87.25
North Druid Hills, GA (cdp) De Kalb County	87.11
McCandless, PA (township) Allegheny County	87.10
Blacksburg, VA (town) Montgomery County	87.08
Ann Arbor, MI (township) Washtenaw County	86.92
Ridgefield, CT (town) Fairfield County	86.92
Audubon, PA (cdp) Montgomery County	86.85
Sudbury, MA (town) Middlesex County	86.55
Los Altos Hills, CA (town) Santa Clara County	86.51
Savoy, IL (village) Champaign County	86.51
Athens, OH (city) Athens County	86.50
Clifton Park, NY (town) Saratoga County	86.46
Plainsboro Center, NJ (cdp) Middlesex County	86.31
Starkville, MS (city) Oktibbeha County	86.28
Travilah, MD (cdp) Montgomery County	86.20
Evanston, IL (city) Cook County	86.01
Rocky Hill, CT (town) Hartford County	85.95
Westford, MA (town) Middlesex County	85.95
Farmington, MI (city) Oakland County	85.85
Wildwood, MO (city) Saint Louis County	85.59
Longmeadow, MA (town) Hampden County	85.42
Norwood, MA (town) Norfolk County	85.34
Inkster, MI (city) Wayne County	85.24
Vestal, NY (town) Broome County	85.15
Concord, MA (town) Middlesex County	85.10
Needham, MA (town) Norfolk County	85.08
Plainsboro, NJ (township) Middlesex County	85.05
Druid Hills, GA (cdp) De Kalb County	84.95
Vestavia Hills, AL (city) Jefferson County	84.55
Oshtemo, MI (township) Kalamazoo County	84.53
Ruston, LA (city) Lincoln Parish	84.50
Princeton Meadows, NJ (cdp) Middlesex County	84.27
Kent, OH (city) Portage County	84.21
Newport Coast, CA (cdp) Orange County	84.04
Canton, MA (town) Norfolk County	83.91
Northville, MI (township) Wayne County	83.89
Dayton, NJ (cdp) Middlesex County	83.88

Notes: Please refer to the User's Guide for an explanation of data; ranking tables include all places with Asian and/or NHPI populations above SF4 population thresholds; (1) tables reflect only those areas that meet SF4 population thresholds, therefore there may be less than 50 states, 75 counties or 75 places listed

Educational Attainment: Four-Year College Graduates

Native Hawaiian and Other Pacific Islanders 25 Years and Over Who are Four-Year College Graduates

All States, Top 75 Counties, and Top 75 Places Sorted by Number[1]

State	Number
United States	28,498
California	7,925
Hawaii	7,301
Washington	1,406
Texas	1,045
New York	913
Utah	729
Florida	615
Oregon	589
Virginia	582
Arizona	545
Nevada	485
Colorado	466
Illinois	454
Pennsylvania	431
New Jersey	366
Maryland	325
Georgia	308
Missouri	300
Michigan	293
Massachusetts	266
North Carolina	258
Ohio	252
Tennessee	250
Minnesota	230
Indiana	162
New Mexico	160
Connecticut	156
Louisiana	155
Oklahoma	154
Kansas	151
Wisconsin	141
Alaska	128
South Carolina	104
Alabama	101
Kentucky	96
Iowa	94
Idaho	89
Mississippi	65
Nebraska	49
Arkansas	48
Montana	45
Maine	24
Rhode Island	20
Delaware	11
West Virginia	8

County	Number
Honolulu County, HI	5,396
Los Angeles County, CA	1,845
San Diego County, CA	990
Hawaii County, HI	975
Orange County, CA	659
Maui County, HI	654
Alameda County, CA	648
King County, WA	642
Santa Clara County, CA	581
San Mateo County, CA	526
Clark County, NV	402
Salt Lake County, UT	397
San Francisco County, CA	352
Maricopa County, AZ	315
Sacramento County, CA	314
Kauai County, HI	276
Contra Costa County, CA	257
Pierce County, WA	219
Fairfax County, VA	205
Multnomah County, OR	202
San Bernardino County, CA	202
Cook County, IL	201
Ventura County, CA	198
Harris County, TX	180
Riverside County, CA	176
Solano County, CA	167
Tarrant County, TX	165
Utah County, UT	165
Snohomish County, WA	159
Washington County, OR	152
Monterey County, CA	148
Allegheny County, PA	147
New York County, NY	142
Montgomery County, MD	131
Queens County, NY	131
Pima County, AZ	125
Essex County, NJ	117
Sonoma County, CA	113
Kings County, NY	111
Dallas County, TX	109
Anchorage Borough, AK	108
Santa Barbara County, CA	101
San Joaquin County, CA	98
Miami-Dade County, FL	88
Jefferson County, CO	85
Hennepin County, MN	83
El Paso County, CO	80
Jackson County, MO	80
Thurston County, WA	78
Hillsborough County, FL	77
Orange County, FL	76
Bexar County, TX	71
Nassau County, NY	71
Philadelphia County, PA	65
Davis County, UT	64
Stanislaus County, CA	62
Broward County, FL	60
Sedgwick County, KS	60
Lane County, OR	59
Fresno County, CA	56
Kern County, CA	56
St. Louis County, MO	55
Denver County, CO	54
Franklin County, OH	53
Washoe County, NV	53
Travis County, TX	52
Suffolk County, NY	51
Kitsap County, WA	50
Milwaukee County, WI	50
Arapahoe County, CO	49
Bernalillo County, NM	48
Clark County, WA	47
Coryell County, TX	46
Davidson County, TN	44
Duval County, FL	42

Place	Number
Honolulu, HI (cdp) Honolulu County	2,275
Los Angeles, CA (city) Los Angeles County	665
San Diego, CA (city) San Diego County	552
New York, NY (city)	447
San Francisco, CA (city) San Francisco County	352
Kaneohe, HI (cdp) Honolulu County	315
Hilo, HI (cdp) Hawaii County	307
San Jose, CA (city) Santa Clara County	291
Kailua, HI (cdp) Honolulu County	282
Seattle, WA (city) King County	256
Laie, HI (cdp) Honolulu County	193
Portland, OR (city) Multnomah County	165
Hayward, CA (city) Alameda County	164
Sacramento, CA (city) Sacramento County	157
Phoenix, AZ (city) Maricopa County	155
Salt Lake City, UT (city) Salt Lake County	155
Pearl City, HI (cdp) Honolulu County	147
Mililani Town, HI (cdp) Honolulu County	144
Makakilo City, HI (cdp) Honolulu County	136
Waimalu, HI (cdp) Honolulu County	135
Oakland, CA (city) Alameda County	134
Anaheim, CA (city) Orange County	133
Waimanalo Beach, HI (cdp) Honolulu County	119
Wailuku, HI (cdp) Maui County	106
Daly City, CA (city) San Mateo County	103
Long Beach, CA (city) Los Angeles County	103
Wahiawa, HI (cdp) Honolulu County	102
Carson, CA (city) Los Angeles County	100
Hauula, HI (cdp) Honolulu County	100
Lakewood, CA (city) Los Angeles County	100
Ahuimanu, HI (cdp) Honolulu County	94
Kailua, HI (cdp) Hawaii County	93
Las Vegas, NV (city) Clark County	90
Fremont, CA (city) Alameda County	89
Vallejo, CA (city) Solano County	88
Chicago, IL (city) Cook County	86
San Mateo, CA (city) San Mateo County	83
South San Francisco, CA (city) San Mateo County	80
Kahului, HI (cdp) Maui County	79
Provo, UT (city) Utah County	79
Waianae, HI (cdp) Honolulu County	78
Waipahu, HI (cdp) Honolulu County	78
Santa Clara, CA (city) Santa Clara County	74
Stockton, CA (city) San Joaquin County	72
Houston, TX (city) Harris County	71
Tacoma, WA (city) Pierce County	71
Henderson, NV (city) Clark County	69
Oceanside, CA (city) San Diego County	65
Philadelphia, PA (city) Philadelphia County	65
Dallas, TX (city) Dallas County	64
Makaha, HI (cdp) Honolulu County	64
Nanakuli, HI (cdp) Honolulu County	64
Kihei, HI (cdp) Maui County	60
Compton, CA (city) Los Angeles County	59
Sunnyvale, CA (city) Santa Clara County	58
Paradise, NV (cdp) Clark County	57
Chula Vista, CA (city) San Diego County	56
East Palo Alto, CA (city) San Mateo County	56
Halawa, HI (cdp) Honolulu County	56
Denver, CO (city) Denver County	54
Ewa Beach, HI (cdp) Honolulu County	54
Modesto, CA (city) Stanislaus County	54
Fort Worth, TX (city) Tarrant County	53
Austin, TX (city) Travis County	52
North Las Vegas, NV (city) Clark County	52
Union City, CA (city) Alameda County	51
Huntington Beach, CA (city) Orange County	50
Waimea, HI (cdp) Hawaii County	50
Oxnard, CA (city) Ventura County	48
Taylorsville, UT (city) Salt Lake County	48
Kahuku, HI (cdp) Honolulu County	47
Orem, UT (city) Utah County	47
Federal Way, WA (city) King County	46
Tucson, AZ (city) Pima County	46
San Antonio, TX (city) Bexar County	45

Notes: Please refer to the User's Guide for an explanation of data; ranking tables include all places with Asian and/or NHPI populations above SF4 population thresholds; (1) tables reflect only those areas that meet SF4 population thresholds, therefore there may be less than 50 states, 75 counties or 75 places listed

Educational Attainment: Four-Year College Graduates

Native Hawaiian and Other Pacific Islanders 25 Years and Over Who are Four-Year College Graduates

All States, Top 75 Counties, and Top 75 Places Sorted by Percent[1]

State	Percent
Virginia	28.59
Maryland	26.25
Massachusetts	23.77
Connecticut	22.29
New Jersey	21.71
Minnesota	21.70
Michigan	21.64
Iowa	21.36
Pennsylvania	21.24
Kansas	21.15
Illinois	20.90
New York	19.99
Colorado	19.77
Tennessee	19.39
New Mexico	18.91
Louisiana	18.61
Ohio	18.49
Missouri	18.40
Montana	18.00
Arizona	17.76
Wisconsin	17.74
Indiana	17.44
Mississippi	16.88
Idaho	15.98
Alabama	15.81
Texas	15.31
Oklahoma	15.11
Florida	15.01
Kentucky	14.79
Georgia	14.66
Nebraska	14.45
Oregon	14.29
United States	13.79
North Carolina	13.31
California	12.56
Maine	12.44
Washington	12.12
Utah	11.92
South Carolina	11.89
Hawaii	11.79
Nevada	10.61
Alaska	9.68
Rhode Island	9.39
Arkansas	8.56
Delaware	7.33
West Virginia	4.28

County	Percent
Fairfax County, VA	43.25
Allegheny County, PA	42.00
Montgomery County, MD	39.22
Jefferson County, CO	36.96
New York County, NY	36.88
Essex County, NJ	36.00
Franklin County, OH	31.36
Nassau County, NY	30.60
Sedgwick County, KS	26.09
Davidson County, TN	25.58
St. Louis County, MO	25.58
Sonoma County, CA	25.28
Denver County, CO	24.22
Coryell County, TX	23.96
Hillsborough County, FL	23.69
Miami-Dade County, FL	22.92
Utah County, UT	22.42
Hennepin County, MN	22.25
Pima County, AZ	21.97
Ada County, ID	21.93
Snohomish County, WA	21.69
Cook County, IL	21.61
Washington County, UT	20.92
Harris County, TX	20.74
Dallas County, TX	19.78
Lane County, OR	19.73
Santa Barbara County, CA	19.57
Ventura County, CA	19.57
Tarrant County, TX	18.99
Milwaukee County, WI	18.52
Orange County, FL	18.49
Fresno County, CA	18.30
San Francisco County, CA	17.56
Washington County, OR	17.21
Suffolk County, NY	17.06
Philadelphia County, PA	16.97
Santa Clara County, CA	16.93
Maricopa County, AZ	16.30
Jackson County, MO	16.23
Multnomah County, OR	16.12
Queens County, NY	15.96
Davis County, UT	14.81
Duval County, FL	14.69
Travis County, TX	14.53
Kings County, NY	14.47
Contra Costa County, CA	14.34
King County, WA	14.30
Monterey County, CA	14.23
Kern County, CA	14.18
Orange County, CA	13.91
Broward County, FL	13.67
Bernalillo County, NM	13.45
Alameda County, CA	13.30
Anchorage Borough, AK	13.09
Arapahoe County, CO	12.93
Los Angeles County, CA	12.73
Honolulu County, HI	12.72
Gwinnett County, GA	12.68
San Diego County, CA	12.68
El Paso County, CO	11.94
Clark County, NV	11.05
El Paso County, TX	11.00
Thurston County, WA	11.00
Hawaii County, HI	10.89
San Mateo County, CA	10.83
Spokane County, WA	10.76
Bexar County, TX	10.73
Muscogee County, GA	10.59
Yolo County, CA	10.57
San Joaquin County, CA	10.40
Shelby County, TN	10.05
Clackamas County, OR	10.00
Kauai County, HI	9.52
Marion County, OR	9.20
Sacramento County, CA	9.14

Place	Percent
Provo, UT (city) Utah County	31.23
Santa Clara, CA (city) Santa Clara County	29.60
Nashville-Davidson, TN (sp. city) Davidson County	28.03
Laie, HI (cdp) Honolulu County	25.98
Waikapu, HI (cdp) Maui County	25.42
Lakewood, CA (city) Los Angeles County	24.81
Denver, CO (city) Denver County	24.22
Ahuimanu, HI (cdp) Honolulu County	23.50
Anaheim, CA (city) Orange County	23.46
St. George, UT (city) Washington County	22.90
Independence, MO (city) Jackson County	21.43
Huntington Beach, CA (city) Orange County	21.19
Austin, TX (city) Travis County	20.97
Mililani Town, HI (cdp) Honolulu County	20.20
Fremont, CA (city) Alameda County	19.96
Volcano, HI (cdp) Hawaii County	19.59
Hawaiian Ocean View, HI (cdp) Hawaii County	19.53
Seattle, WA (city) King County	19.10
Makakilo City, HI (cdp) Honolulu County	18.30
Daly City, CA (city) San Mateo County	18.29
Fort Worth, TX (city) Tarrant County	18.03
Concord, CA (city) Contra Costa County	17.65
San Francisco, CA (city) San Francisco County	17.56
Dallas, TX (city) Dallas County	17.49
Sunnyvale, CA (city) Santa Clara County	17.21
Kansas City, MO (city) Jackson County	17.13
Philadelphia, PA (city) Philadelphia County	16.97
Kailua, HI (cdp) Honolulu County	16.92
Phoenix, AZ (city) Maricopa County	16.83
Los Angeles, CA (city) Los Angeles County	16.75
New York, NY (city)	16.67
Portland, OR (city) Multnomah County	16.60
Sunrise Manor, NV (cdp) Clark County	16.36
Taylorsville, UT (city) Salt Lake County	16.22
South San Francisco, CA (city) San Mateo County	16.10
Compton, CA (city) Los Angeles County	15.86
San Diego, CA (city) San Diego County	15.69
San Jose, CA (city) Santa Clara County	15.45
Bakersfield, CA (city) Kern County	15.32
Jacksonville, FL (city) Duval County	15.22
Honolulu, HI (cdp) Honolulu County	15.19
Waimalu, HI (cdp) Honolulu County	15.10
Orem, UT (city) Utah County	15.02
Kahuku, HI (cdp) Honolulu County	14.87
Wailuku, HI (cdp) Maui County	14.85
West Jordan, UT (city) Salt Lake County	14.78
Spokane, WA (city) Spokane County	14.75
Chicago, IL (city) Cook County	14.29
Salinas, CA (city) Monterey County	14.22
Pearl City, HI (cdp) Honolulu County	13.95
Holualoa, HI (cdp) Hawaii County	13.79
Union City, CA (city) Alameda County	13.78
Henderson, NV (city) Clark County	13.72
Kaneohe, HI (cdp) Honolulu County	13.71
Hauula, HI (cdp) Honolulu County	13.62
Stockton, CA (city) San Joaquin County	13.36
Houston, TX (city) Harris County	13.17
Tucson, AZ (city) Pima County	12.99
Redwood City, CA (city) San Mateo County	12.84
Kailua, HI (cdp) Hawaii County	12.55
Paradise, NV (cdp) Clark County	12.34
Hayward, CA (city) Alameda County	12.29
Kaaawa, HI (cdp) Honolulu County	12.21
Mesa, AZ (city) Maricopa County	12.17
Oakland, CA (city) Alameda County	12.16
North Las Vegas, NV (city) Clark County	12.09
Wahiawa, HI (cdp) Honolulu County	12.04
Kahaluu, HI (cdp) Honolulu County	11.97
Hawaiian Paradise Park, HI (cdp) Hawaii County	11.85
Hilo, HI (cdp) Hawaii County	11.80
Fontana, CA (city) San Bernardino County	11.59
Sandy, UT (city) Salt Lake County	11.51
Albuquerque, NM (city) Bernalillo County	11.26
Hanapepe, HI (cdp) Kauai County	11.24
Maunawili, HI (cdp) Honolulu County	11.21

Notes: Please refer to the User's Guide for an explanation of data; ranking tables include all places with Asian and/or NHPI populations above SF4 population thresholds; (1) tables reflect only those areas that meet SF4 population thresholds, therefore there may be less than 50 states, 75 counties or 75 places listed

Educational Attainment: Four-Year College Graduates

Asian Indians 25 Years and Over Who are Four-Year College Graduates

All States, Top 75 Counties, and Top 75 Places Sorted by Number[1]

State	Number
United States	668,029
California	124,573
New Jersey	74,099
New York	73,651
Texas	51,642
Illinois	50,789
Michigan	26,261
Pennsylvania	23,442
Maryland	22,624
Virginia	22,420
Florida	22,389
Massachusetts	20,871
Ohio	18,973
Georgia	18,216
Connecticut	10,874
North Carolina	10,849
Washington	8,590
Minnesota	7,720
Arizona	6,673
Indiana	6,276
Colorado	5,955
Missouri	5,545
Tennessee	5,380
Wisconsin	5,090
Oregon	4,835
Louisiana	3,591
Kansas	3,458
Kentucky	3,169
South Carolina	2,965
Alabama	2,961
Oklahoma	2,940
Delaware	2,704
Iowa	2,507
New Hampshire	1,898
Nebraska	1,630
Nevada	1,481
West Virginia	1,361
District of Columbia	1,353
Mississippi	1,209
Arkansas	1,164
New Mexico	1,121
Utah	976
Rhode Island	952
Hawaii	554
Idaho	475
North Dakota	437
Maine	359
Vermont	256
South Dakota	252
Montana	195
Wyoming	170
Alaska	154

County	Number
Santa Clara County, CA	35,658
Cook County, IL	27,104
Middlesex County, NJ	26,441
Queens County, NY	24,849
Los Angeles County, CA	23,544
Alameda County, CA	18,831
Harris County, TX	14,581
DuPage County, IL	14,096
Fairfax County, VA	12,434
Montgomery County, MD	12,164
Oakland County, MI	11,318
Middlesex County, MA	11,316
Orange County, CA	11,008
Dallas County, TX	9,327
Nassau County, NY	8,287
Bergen County, NJ	7,878
Hudson County, NJ	7,192
New York County, NY	7,138
Westchester County, NY	6,076
King County, WA	6,042
Wayne County, MI	5,896
San Mateo County, CA	5,588
Maricopa County, AZ	5,447
Kings County, NY	5,346
Somerset County, NJ	5,318
Morris County, NJ	5,188
Collin County, TX	4,792
Fort Bend County, TX	4,761
Cuyahoga County, OH	4,446
San Diego County, CA	4,440
Allegheny County, PA	4,319
Contra Costa County, CA	4,297
Franklin County, OH	4,276
Fairfield County, CT	4,261
Gwinnett County, GA	4,205
Travis County, TX	4,022
Suffolk County, NY	3,959
Tarrant County, TX	3,896
Hennepin County, MN	3,856
Wake County, NC	3,545
Essex County, NJ	3,523
Philadelphia County, PA	3,470
Montgomery County, PA	3,446
Fulton County, GA	3,395
Monmouth County, NJ	3,343
Broward County, FL	3,340
Sacramento County, CA	3,259
Washington County, OR	3,248
Mercer County, NJ	3,133
St. Louis County, MO	3,037
DeKalb County, GA	3,012
Norfolk County, MA	2,980
Union County, NJ	2,869
Cobb County, GA	2,734
Hartford County, CT	2,727
San Bernardino County, CA	2,704
Prince George's County, MD	2,677
Lake County, IL	2,676
Miami-Dade County, FL	2,676
Baltimore County, MD	2,593
New Haven County, CT	2,587
Passaic County, NJ	2,513
Bronx County, NY	2,480
New Castle County, DE	2,456
Bucks County, PA	2,446
San Francisco County, CA	2,326
Mecklenburg County, NC	2,308
Washtenaw County, MI	2,276
Howard County, MD	2,248
Orange County, FL	2,243
Johnson County, KS	2,199
Hamilton County, OH	2,189
Camden County, NJ	2,136
Hillsborough County, FL	2,119
Denton County, TX	2,072

Place	Number
New York, NY (city)	41,883
San Jose, CA (city) Santa Clara County	11,794
Fremont, CA (city) Alameda County	11,032
Los Angeles, CA (city) Los Angeles County	9,034
Chicago, IL (city) Cook County	8,885
Houston, TX (city) Harris County	8,850
Sunnyvale, CA (city) Santa Clara County	8,271
Edison, NJ (township) Middlesex County	8,037
Santa Clara, CA (city) Santa Clara County	5,214
Woodbridge, NJ (township) Middlesex County	4,673
Jersey City, NJ (city) Hudson County	4,574
Austin, TX (city) Travis County	3,575
Philadelphia, PA (city) Philadelphia County	3,470
Dallas, TX (city) Dallas County	3,260
Hempstead, NY (town) Nassau County	3,200
Plano, TX (city) Collin County	3,164
Columbus, OH (city) Franklin County	3,160
San Diego, CA (city) San Diego County	3,138
Irving, TX (city) Dallas County	3,128
North Hempstead, NY (town) Nassau County	2,863
Piscataway, NJ (township) Middlesex County	2,753
Cupertino, CA (city) Santa Clara County	2,645
Troy, MI (city) Oakland County	2,587
Schaumburg, IL (village) Cook County	2,407
Naperville, IL (city) Du Page County	2,367
San Francisco, CA (city) San Francisco County	2,326
Milpitas, CA (city) Santa Clara County	2,250
Farmington Hills, MI (city) Oakland County	2,223
Irvine, CA (city) Orange County	2,096
Oyster Bay, NY (town) Nassau County	2,055
South Brunswick, NJ (township) Middlesex County	2,047
Charlotte, NC (city) Mecklenburg County	1,962
Phoenix, AZ (city) Maricopa County	1,957
Plainsboro, NJ (township) Middlesex County	1,913
Mountain View, CA (city) Santa Clara County	1,887
Arlington, VA (cdp) Arlington County	1,852
Parsippany-Troy Hills, NJ (township) Morris County	1,837
Union City, CA (city) Alameda County	1,772
Cary, NC (town) Wake County	1,743
Sugar Land, TX (city) Fort Bend County	1,739
Stamford, CT (city) Fairfield County	1,720
Bellevue, WA (city) King County	1,619
Boston, MA (city) Suffolk County	1,618
Franklin, NJ (township) Somerset County	1,581
Canton, MI (township) Wayne County	1,562
Indianapolis, IN (sp. city) Marion County	1,518
Anaheim, CA (city) Orange County	1,516
North Brunswick, NJ (township) Middlesex County	1,480
Ann Arbor, MI (city) Washtenaw County	1,436
Yonkers, NY (city) Westchester County	1,343
Durham, NC (city) Durham County	1,337
Greenburgh, NY (town) Westchester County	1,322
Cerritos, CA (city) Los Angeles County	1,304
Sayreville, NJ (borough) Middlesex County	1,299
Carrollton, TX (city) Denton County	1,264
Iselin, NJ (cdp) Middlesex County	1,245
Jacksonville, FL (city) Duval County	1,245
Princeton Meadows, NJ (cdp) Middlesex County	1,232
Brookhaven, NY (town) Suffolk County	1,231
Memphis, TN (city) Shelby County	1,215
East Brunswick, NJ (township) Middlesex County	1,204
Overland Park, KS (city) Johnson County	1,198
Oklahoma City, OK (city) Oklahoma County	1,187
Foster City, CA (city) San Mateo County	1,177
Nashville-Davidson, TN (sp. city) Davidson County	1,173
Old Bridge, NJ (township) Middlesex County	1,172
Cambridge, MA (city) Middlesex County	1,169
Mount Prospect, IL (village) Cook County	1,165
San Antonio, TX (city) Bexar County	1,156
Skokie, IL (village) Cook County	1,154
Avenel, NJ (cdp) Middlesex County	1,149
Rochester Hills, MI (city) Oakland County	1,147
Raleigh, NC (city) Wake County	1,145
Seattle, WA (city) King County	1,140
Pittsburgh, PA (city) Allegheny County	1,137

Notes: Please refer to the User's Guide for an explanation of data; ranking tables include all places with Asian and/or NHPI populations above SF4 population thresholds; (1) tables reflect only those areas that meet SF4 population thresholds, therefore there may be less than 50 states, 75 counties or 75 places listed

Educational Attainment: Four-Year College Graduates

Asian Indians 25 Years and Over Who are Four-Year College Graduates

All States, Top 75 Counties, and Top 75 Places Sorted by Percent[1]

State	Percent
South Dakota	85.14
Nebraska	83.98
New Hampshire	83.25
West Virginia	83.14
District of Columbia	78.85
Massachusetts	78.71
Iowa	78.59
Vermont	78.05
North Dakota	77.62
Ohio	77.46
Delaware	77.35
Colorado	77.16
Montana	76.47
Oregon	75.65
Michigan	75.50
Minnesota	74.86
Indiana	74.11
Wisconsin	74.08
Missouri	73.89
Kentucky	73.46
Arizona	73.19
Virginia	72.75
Kansas	71.95
Tennessee	71.87
Alabama	71.59
Maine	70.39
New Mexico	69.89
Maryland	69.55
Connecticut	68.40
North Carolina	68.22
Pennsylvania	67.61
New Jersey	67.43
Louisiana	67.35
Idaho	67.28
Rhode Island	66.02
Illinois	66.00
Arkansas	65.73
Georgia	65.60
Texas	64.96
United States	63.89
California	62.97
Wyoming	62.04
South Carolina	61.45
Oklahoma	59.72
Washington	58.38
Mississippi	57.11
Utah	55.64
Hawaii	55.62
Florida	51.73
Alaska	49.36
New York	46.80
Nevada	44.58

County	Percent
Charlottesville Independent City, VA	100.00
Montgomery County, VA	96.00
Monongalia County, WV	95.83
Bartholomew County, IN	95.74
Tompkins County, NY	94.14
Linn County, IA	93.93
Washington County, MN	92.68
Midland County, MI	92.16
Rensselaer County, NY	91.80
Boulder County, CO	91.67
Eaton County, MI	90.37
Peoria County, IL	89.89
Lancaster County, NE	89.59
Washington County, OR	89.50
Olmsted County, MN	89.43
Champaign County, IL	89.41
Washtenaw County, MI	89.29
Rock Island County, IL	88.63
Centre County, PA	88.38
Chester County, PA	88.14
McLean County, IL	88.07
Kanawha County, WV	88.06
St. Mary's County, MD	88.00
Waukesha County, WI	87.87
Douglas County, NE	87.45
Chittenden County, VT	86.86
Oakland County, MI	86.57
Allegheny County, PA	86.55
Hampshire County, MA	86.50
Douglas County, CO	86.37
Norfolk County, MA	86.18
Hillsborough County, NH	85.89
Story County, IA	85.71
Sangamon County, IL	85.45
Orange County, NC	84.92
Erie County, NY	84.88
Tippecanoe County, IN	84.85
Benton County, AR	84.59
Santa Barbara County, CA	84.50
Durham County, NC	84.38
Muscogee County, GA	84.08
Phelps County, MO	83.89
Monroe County, IN	83.76
Brazos County, TX	83.46
Warren County, OH	83.41
Alachua County, FL	83.37
Collin County, TX	83.27
Travis County, TX	83.22
Forsyth County, NC	83.21
Douglas County, KS	83.11
Boone County, MO	82.99
Hamilton County, OH	82.92
Rockingham County, NH	82.80
Jefferson County, CO	82.52
Cass County, ND	82.38
Fairfax Independent City, VA	82.07
Clarke County, GA	82.03
Delaware County, OH	81.85
Westmoreland County, PA	81.71
Clackamas County, OR	81.55
Hamilton County, IN	81.52
Franklin County, OH	80.80
Denver County, CO	80.77
Larimer County, CO	80.75
Fayette County, KY	80.72
Erie County, PA	80.66
Santa Clara County, CA	80.53
Worcester County, MA	80.40
El Paso County, CO	80.31
East Baton Rouge Parish, LA	80.23
Henrico County, VA	80.22
Johnson County, KS	80.20
St. Louis County, MO	80.15
Saratoga County, NY	80.12
Somerset County, NJ	79.97

Place	Percent
Tredyffrin, PA (township) Chester County	100.00
Boulder, CO (city) Boulder County	97.93
Randolph, NJ (township) Morris County	97.92
Acton, MA (town) Middlesex County	97.91
Brookfield, WI (city) Waukesha County	97.62
Little Flock, AR (city) Benton County	97.59
Blacksburg, VA (town) Montgomery County	97.36
West Lafayette, IN (city) Tippecanoe County	97.33
Stanford, CA (cdp) Santa Clara County	96.91
Eden Prairie, MN (city) Hennepin County	96.69
Boxborough, MA (town) Middlesex County	96.50
Columbus, IN (city) Bartholomew County	95.74
Redmond, WA (city) King County	95.66
Scott, PA (township) Allegheny County	95.36
Scott Township, PA (cdp) Allegheny County	95.36
Highlands Ranch, CO (cdp) Douglas County	95.32
Bernards, NJ (township) Somerset County	95.24
Hillsboro, OR (city) Washington County	95.07
Urbana, IL (city) Champaign County	94.95
New Castle, NY (town) Westchester County	94.81
Mansfield, CT (town) Tolland County	94.38
Dayton, NJ (cdp) Middlesex County	94.26
Vernon Hills, IL (village) Lake County	94.08
Clifton Park, NY (town) Saratoga County	94.04
Los Altos, CA (city) Santa Clara County	93.96
Evanston, IL (city) Cook County	93.91
Norwood, MA (town) Norfolk County	93.77
Hopkins, MN (city) Hennepin County	93.59
Highland Park, NJ (borough) Middlesex County	93.52
Saratoga, CA (city) Santa Clara County	93.20
Oak Brook, IL (village) Du Page County	93.16
Woodbury, MN (city) Washington County	92.99
Lakewood, CO (city) Jefferson County	92.72
East Lansing, MI (city) Ingham County	92.66
Smyrna, GA (city) Cobb County	92.45
Maryland Heights, MO (city) Saint Louis County	92.42
Cedar Rapids, IA (city) Linn County	92.27
Midland, MI (city) Midland County	92.06
Inkster, MI (city) Wayne County	91.88
Lexington, MA (town) Middlesex County	91.88
Plymouth, MN (city) Hennepin County	91.87
Chelmsford, MA (town) Middlesex County	91.82
Waukesha, WI (city) Waukesha County	91.79
Brookline, MA (town) Norfolk County	91.68
Alpharetta, GA (city) Fulton County	91.63
Montgomery, NJ (township) Somerset County	91.49
Farmington, MI (city) Oakland County	91.41
Sunnyvale, CA (city) Santa Clara County	91.40
Farmington Hills, MI (city) Oakland County	91.33
West Bloomfield, MI (township) Oakland County	91.32
Lisle, IL (village) Du Page County	91.10
Westlake, OH (city) Cuyahoga County	91.09
Lincoln, NE (city) Lancaster County	90.86
Sandy Springs, GA (cdp) Fulton County	90.86
Tysons Corner, VA (cdp) Fairfax County	90.83
McLean, VA (cdp) Fairfax County	90.69
Ann Arbor, MI (city) Washtenaw County	90.60
Plainsboro Center, NJ (cdp) Middlesex County	90.56
Portage, MI (city) Kalamazoo County	90.49
Lower Merion, PA (township) Montgomery County	90.45
Scotch Plains, NJ (township) Union County	90.39
Rochester, MN (city) Olmsted County	90.18
Idylwood, VA (cdp) Fairfax County	90.11
Dublin, OH (city) Franklin County	90.05
Delta charter, MI (township) Eaton County	90.00
Cupertino, CA (city) Santa Clara County	89.87
Bridgewater, NJ (township) Somerset County	89.75
Foster City, CA (city) San Mateo County	89.71
Bellevue, WA (city) King County	89.70
Charleston, WV (city) Kanawha County	89.70
Sharonville, OH (city) Hamilton County	89.56
Municip. of Monroeville, PA (borough) Allegheny County	89.51
Peoria, IL (city) Peoria County	89.51
Westborough, MA (town) Worcester County	89.41
Overland Park, KS (city) Johnson County	89.27

Notes: Please refer to the User's Guide for an explanation of data; ranking tables include all places with Asian and/or NHPI populations above SF4 population thresholds; (1) tables reflect only those areas that meet SF4 population thresholds, therefore there may be less than 50 states, 75 counties or 75 places listed

Educational Attainment: Four-Year College Graduates

Bangladeshis 25 Years and Over Who are Four-Year College Graduates

All States, Top 75 Counties, and Top 75 Places Sorted by Number[1]

State	Number
United States	12,355
New York	4,729
Texas	1,101
California	1,062
Virginia	684
New Jersey	518
Maryland	462
Georgia	432
Florida	364
Ohio	333
Illinois	331
Michigan	280
Pennsylvania	271
Massachusetts	267
Connecticut	163

County	Number
Queens County, NY	3,135
Kings County, NY	682
Los Angeles County, CA	416
Bronx County, NY	397
Montgomery County, MD	357
Fairfax County, VA	344
Santa Clara County, CA	286
Dallas County, TX	275
Harris County, TX	197
DeKalb County, GA	159
Middlesex County, NJ	149
New York County, NY	136
Wayne County, MI	115
Atlantic County, NJ	75
Passaic County, NJ	39

Place	Number
New York, NY (city)	4,366
Los Angeles, CA (city) Los Angeles County	233
Hamtramck, MI (city) Wayne County	35
Paterson, NJ (city) Passaic County	34

Notes: Please refer to the User's Guide for an explanation of data; ranking tables include all places with Asian and/or NHPI populations above SF4 population thresholds; (1) tables reflect only those areas that meet SF4 population thresholds, therefore there may be less than 50 states, 75 counties or 75 places listed

Educational Attainment: Four-Year College Graduates

Bangladeshis 25 Years and Over Who are Four-Year College Graduates

All States, Top 75 Counties, and Top 75 Places Sorted by Percent[1]

State	Percent
Massachusetts	80.66
Ohio	77.08
Illinois	74.89
Connecticut	74.77
Texas	65.61
Pennsylvania	64.22
Virginia	63.16
California	61.28
Maryland	59.08
Georgia	55.81
United States	49.42
Florida	43.18
New Jersey	39.82
New York	39.41
Michigan	29.38

County	Percent
Santa Clara County, CA	84.12
Dallas County, TX	71.61
Middlesex County, NJ	68.98
Fairfax County, VA	65.15
Montgomery County, MD	62.63
Los Angeles County, CA	50.12
DeKalb County, GA	45.82
Harris County, TX	45.39
Queens County, NY	41.38
Bronx County, NY	35.48
Atlantic County, NJ	33.78
New York County, NY	31.26
Kings County, NY	30.03
Wayne County, MI	18.05
Passaic County, NJ	13.18

Place	Percent
Los Angeles, CA (city) Los Angeles County	43.15
New York, NY (city)	38.24
Paterson, NJ (city) Passaic County	14.53
Hamtramck, MI (city) Wayne County	9.49

Notes: Please refer to the User's Guide for an explanation of data; ranking tables include all places with Asian and/or NHPI populations above SF4 population thresholds; (1) tables reflect only those areas that meet SF4 population thresholds, therefore there may be less than 50 states, 75 counties or 75 places listed

Educational Attainment: Four-Year College Graduates

Cambodians 25 Years and Over Who are Four-Year College Graduates

All States, Top 75 Counties, and Top 75 Places Sorted by Number[1]

State	Number
United States	7,943
California	3,004
Massachusetts	711
Washington	478
Virginia	392
Texas	346
Illinois	332
Pennsylvania	290
Georgia	240
Rhode Island	235
Minnesota	223
Maryland	219
New York	176
Oregon	143
Arizona	137
Connecticut	118
Florida	111
Ohio	99
North Carolina	87
Michigan	65
New Jersey	57
Colorado	46
Tennessee	42
Maine	35
Indiana	30
South Carolina	30
Hawaii	28
Wisconsin	28
Oklahoma	26
Missouri	25
Nevada	23
Utah	23
Kansas	17
Iowa	3
Alabama	2

County	Number
Los Angeles County, CA	1,408
Orange County, CA	459
Middlesex County, MA	424
Fairfax County, VA	277
Providence County, RI	234
Cook County, IL	215
King County, WA	206
Alameda County, CA	204
Santa Clara County, CA	196
Montgomery County, MD	191
Philadelphia County, PA	168
Hennepin County, MN	132
Gwinnett County, GA	131
Maricopa County, AZ	124
San Joaquin County, CA	117
Snohomish County, WA	106
Harris County, TX	101
Washington County, OR	100
Pierce County, WA	98
Fairfield County, CT	96
Essex County, MA	95
San Bernardino County, CA	95
Fresno County, CA	91
San Diego County, CA	76
Dallas County, TX	64
Riverside County, CA	62
Sacramento County, CA	58
Franklin County, OH	54
Denton County, TX	48
San Francisco County, CA	46
Ottawa County, MI	45
Suffolk County, MA	44
Bristol County, MA	43
Multnomah County, OR	41
Stanislaus County, CA	39
Worcester County, MA	35
Camden County, NJ	33
Duval County, FL	32
Dakota County, MN	31
Monroe County, NY	30
Arlington County, VA	29
Ramsey County, MN	29
Tarrant County, TX	27
Clark County, NV	23
Clark County, WA	22
Mecklenburg County, NC	22
Shelby County, TN	20
Thurston County, WA	20
Hampden County, MA	19
DeKalb County, GA	16
Chesterfield County, VA	14
Cuyahoga County, OH	14
Salt Lake County, UT	14
Hamilton County, OH	13
Scott County, MN	13
Cumberland County, ME	12
Sedgwick County, KS	12
Sonoma County, CA	12
Henrico County, VA	11
Kings County, NY	10
Bronx County, NY	9
Clayton County, GA	8
Davidson County, NC	6
Pinellas County, FL	6
Kern County, CA	5
Olmsted County, MN	3
Brazoria County, TX	0
Cowlitz County, WA	0
Denver County, CO	0
Mobile County, AL	0
Polk County, IA	0

Place	Number
Long Beach, CA (city) Los Angeles County	569
Lowell, MA (city) Middlesex County	264
Los Angeles, CA (city) Los Angeles County	187
Chicago, IL (city) Cook County	183
San Jose, CA (city) Santa Clara County	178
Philadelphia, PA (city) Philadelphia County	168
Providence, RI (city) Providence County	165
Stockton, CA (city) San Joaquin County	104
Seattle, WA (city) King County	100
New York, NY (city)	99
Fresno, CA (city) Fresno County	91
Lynn, MA (city) Essex County	88
Lakewood, CA (city) Los Angeles County	87
Garden Grove, CA (city) Orange County	70
Oakland, CA (city) Alameda County	69
Santa Ana, CA (city) Orange County	63
Tacoma, WA (city) Pierce County	63
San Diego, CA (city) San Diego County	61
Phoenix, AZ (city) Maricopa County	58
Columbus, OH (city) Franklin County	54
Cranston, RI (city) Providence County	54
Norwalk, CA (city) Los Angeles County	54
Monterey Park, CA (city) Los Angeles County	49
San Francisco, CA (city) San Francisco County	46
Boston, MA (city) Suffolk County	44
Silver Spring, MD (cdp) Montgomery County	41
Rosemead, CA (city) Los Angeles County	39
Bloomington, MN (city) Hennepin County	37
Portland, OR (city) Multnomah County	36
San Bernardino, CA (city) San Bernardino County	34
Houston, TX (city) Harris County	32
Jacksonville, FL (city) Duval County	32
Arlington, VA (cdp) Arlington County	29
Attleboro, MA (city) Bristol County	27
Danbury, CT (city) Fairfield County	24
Bellflower, CA (city) Los Angeles County	22
Charlotte, NC (city) Mecklenburg County	22
Modesto, CA (city) Stanislaus County	21
Memphis, TN (city) Shelby County	20
Dallas, TX (city) Dallas County	19
Signal Hill, CA (city) Los Angeles County	19
Sacramento, CA (city) Sacramento County	18
Minneapolis, MN (city) Hennepin County	14
St. Paul, MN (city) Ramsey County	14
Beaverton, OR (city) Washington County	13
Carrollton, TX (city) Denton County	13
Portland, ME (city) Cumberland County	12
Aurora, CO (city) Arapahoe County	9
Bridgeport, CT (city) Fairfield County	9
Pomona, CA (city) Los Angeles County	8
Lexington, NC (city) Davidson County	6
St. Petersburg, FL (city) Pinellas County	6
Fall River, MA (city) Bristol County	4
Everett, WA (city) Snohomish County	3
Denver, CO (city) Denver County	0
Lawrence, MA (city) Essex County	0
Longview, WA (city) Cowlitz County	0
Revere, MA (city) Suffolk County	0
Rochester, MN (city) Olmsted County	0
Santa Rosa, CA (city) Sonoma County	0
West Valley City, UT (city) Salt Lake County	0
White Center, WA (cdp) King County	0

Notes: Please refer to the User's Guide for an explanation of data; ranking tables include all places with Asian and/or NHPI populations above SF4 population thresholds; (1) tables reflect only those areas that meet SF4 population thresholds, therefore there may be less than 50 states, 75 counties or 75 places listed

Educational Attainment: Four-Year College Graduates

Cambodians 25 Years and Over Who are Four-Year College Graduates

All States, Top 75 Counties, and Top 75 Places Sorted by Percent[1]

State	Percent
Hawaii	34.57
Arizona	22.39
Maryland	20.72
Illinois	18.08
South Carolina	16.04
New Jersey	15.62
Virginia	14.96
Oklahoma	14.36
Georgia	12.77
New York	12.48
Indiana	11.11
Wisconsin	10.61
Connecticut	10.12
Rhode Island	9.94
United States	9.20
California	9.01
Oregon	8.89
Minnesota	8.86
Texas	8.61
Maine	8.16
Ohio	7.79
Massachusetts	7.66
Michigan	7.62
North Carolina	7.34
Florida	7.22
Pennsylvania	6.98
Tennessee	6.94
Washington	6.57
Colorado	6.42
Missouri	6.33
Nevada	4.80
Kansas	4.62
Utah	3.39
Iowa	0.80
Alabama	0.77

County	Percent
Gwinnett County, GA	30.90
Fairfax County, VA	26.01
Montgomery County, MD	25.81
Maricopa County, AZ	21.60
Riverside County, CA	20.20
Camden County, NJ	19.64
Cook County, IL	18.27
Worcester County, MA	18.04
Monroe County, NY	17.96
Orange County, CA	17.10
Arlington County, VA	16.86
Hennepin County, MN	14.78
Washington County, OR	14.06
Dakota County, MN	13.42
San Francisco County, CA	13.18
Fairfield County, CT	12.77
Alameda County, CA	12.02
San Bernardino County, CA	11.59
Denton County, TX	11.21
Sacramento County, CA	10.74
Providence County, RI	10.33
Snohomish County, WA	9.77
Los Angeles County, CA	9.60
Santa Clara County, CA	9.05
Clark County, WA	8.70
Franklin County, OH	8.60
Ottawa County, MI	8.51
Hampden County, MA	8.48
Middlesex County, MA	8.43
Harris County, TX	8.42
Tarrant County, TX	7.63
Multnomah County, OR	7.59
Hamilton County, OH	6.91
Shelby County, TN	6.43
King County, WA	6.31
Duval County, FL	6.03
Scott County, MN	6.02
Mecklenburg County, NC	5.82
Fresno County, CA	5.73
Philadelphia County, PA	5.67
Suffolk County, MA	5.65
Essex County, MA	5.56
Cuyahoga County, OH	5.49
Dallas County, TX	5.46
Pierce County, WA	5.23
Ramsey County, MN	5.04
Clark County, NV	4.95
Thurston County, WA	4.94
Cumberland County, ME	4.86
Sedgwick County, KS	4.86
Bristol County, MA	4.56
Chesterfield County, VA	4.49
DeKalb County, GA	4.17
San Diego County, CA	3.95
Sonoma County, CA	3.25
Kings County, NY	3.22
San Joaquin County, CA	3.20
Stanislaus County, CA	3.10
Salt Lake County, UT	2.79
Henrico County, VA	2.77
Bronx County, NY	2.76
Davidson County, NC	2.54
Kern County, CA	2.50
Pinellas County, FL	1.65
Clayton County, GA	1.57
Olmsted County, MN	1.03
Brazoria County, TX	0.00
Cowlitz County, WA	0.00
Denver County, CO	0.00
Mobile County, AL	0.00
Polk County, IA	0.00

Place	Percent
Monterey Park, CA (city) Los Angeles County	23.33
Lakewood, CA (city) Los Angeles County	22.96
Silver Spring, MD (cdp) Montgomery County	21.13
Garden Grove, CA (city) Orange County	20.65
Phoenix, AZ (city) Maricopa County	20.35
San Bernardino, CA (city) San Bernardino County	18.48
Chicago, IL (city) Cook County	17.94
Norwalk, CA (city) Los Angeles County	17.31
Arlington, VA (cdp) Arlington County	16.86
Bloomington, MN (city) Hennepin County	14.51
Boston, MA (city) Suffolk County	14.01
San Francisco, CA (city) San Francisco County	13.18
New York, NY (city)	11.94
Cranston, RI (city) Providence County	11.61
Providence, RI (city) Providence County	10.09
Columbus, OH (city) Franklin County	9.47
San Jose, CA (city) Santa Clara County	9.11
Danbury, CT (city) Fairfield County	8.57
Rosemead, CA (city) Los Angeles County	8.55
Minneapolis, MN (city) Hennepin County	8.48
Los Angeles, CA (city) Los Angeles County	8.39
Seattle, WA (city) King County	8.31
Attleboro, MA (city) Bristol County	7.63
Houston, TX (city) Harris County	7.46
Memphis, TN (city) Shelby County	7.35
Sacramento, CA (city) Sacramento County	7.29
Bellflower, CA (city) Los Angeles County	7.26
Long Beach, CA (city) Los Angeles County	7.07
Portland, OR (city) Multnomah County	6.98
Lynn, MA (city) Essex County	6.52
Charlotte, NC (city) Mecklenburg County	6.45
Santa Ana, CA (city) Orange County	6.39
Fresno, CA (city) Fresno County	6.28
Lowell, MA (city) Middlesex County	6.13
Jacksonville, FL (city) Duval County	6.03
Oakland, CA (city) Alameda County	5.81
Philadelphia, PA (city) Philadelphia County	5.67
Portland, ME (city) Cumberland County	5.56
Beaverton, OR (city) Washington County	5.46
Signal Hill, CA (city) Los Angeles County	4.97
Aurora, CO (city) Arapahoe County	4.41
Tacoma, WA (city) Pierce County	4.36
Dallas, TX (city) Dallas County	4.24
San Diego, CA (city) San Diego County	3.60
Bridgeport, CT (city) Fairfield County	3.54
Lexington, NC (city) Davidson County	3.53
Carrollton, TX (city) Denton County	3.17
Pomona, CA (city) Los Angeles County	3.04
Stockton, CA (city) San Joaquin County	2.96
St. Paul, MN (city) Ramsey County	2.89
St. Petersburg, FL (city) Pinellas County	2.47
Modesto, CA (city) Stanislaus County	2.04
Everett, WA (city) Snohomish County	0.97
Fall River, MA (city) Bristol County	0.86
Denver, CO (city) Denver County	0.00
Lawrence, MA (city) Essex County	0.00
Longview, WA (city) Cowlitz County	0.00
Revere, MA (city) Suffolk County	0.00
Rochester, MN (city) Olmsted County	0.00
Santa Rosa, CA (city) Sonoma County	0.00
West Valley City, UT (city) Salt Lake County	0.00
White Center, WA (cdp) King County	0.00

Notes: Please refer to the User's Guide for an explanation of data; ranking tables include all places with Asian and/or NHPI populations above SF4 population thresholds; (1) tables reflect only those areas that meet SF4 population thresholds, therefore there may be less than 50 states, 75 counties or 75 places listed

Educational Attainment: Four-Year College Graduates

Chinese (except Taiwanese) 25 Years and Over Who are Four-Year College Graduates

All States, Top 75 Counties, and Top 75 Places Sorted by Number[1]

State	Number
United States	744,668
California	285,136
New York	89,028
Texas	42,278
New Jersey	41,185
Illinois	28,294
Massachusetts	27,165
Maryland	20,485
Washington	19,501
Pennsylvania	16,138
Hawaii	15,922
Virginia	14,347
Florida	13,959
Michigan	12,929
Ohio	12,561
Georgia	10,126
Connecticut	8,084
Arizona	7,441
North Carolina	6,991
Minnesota	6,065
Oregon	5,621
Colorado	5,595
Missouri	5,515
Indiana	4,934
Wisconsin	3,841
Tennessee	3,422
Nevada	3,102
Kansas	2,896
Alabama	2,720
Louisiana	2,711
Oklahoma	2,642
Iowa	2,550
Utah	2,510
Kentucky	2,273
South Carolina	2,250
Delaware	1,908
New Mexico	1,641
New Hampshire	1,517
District of Columbia	1,471
Nebraska	1,396
Rhode Island	1,253
Arkansas	1,061
Mississippi	991
West Virginia	675
Idaho	575
Alaska	400
Vermont	360
South Dakota	315
Maine	314
North Dakota	213
Montana	194
Wyoming	167

County	Number
Los Angeles County, CA	83,736
Santa Clara County, CA	51,593
Queens County, NY	32,937
Alameda County, CA	31,619
San Francisco County, CA	30,586
Orange County, CA	20,358
San Mateo County, CA	17,558
New York County, NY	16,933
Cook County, IL	15,815
Honolulu County, HI	15,209
King County, WA	15,081
Kings County, NY	13,628
Harris County, TX	13,145
Middlesex County, MA	13,016
Montgomery County, MD	12,572
Contra Costa County, CA	11,339
San Diego County, CA	11,195
Middlesex County, NJ	9,285
Fairfax County, VA	7,086
Sacramento County, CA	6,839
Collin County, TX	6,294
Bergen County, NJ	5,794
Maricopa County, AZ	5,443
Norfolk County, MA	5,372
DuPage County, IL	5,237
Nassau County, NY	5,191
Dallas County, TX	4,886
Morris County, NJ	4,751
Travis County, TX	4,474
Suffolk County, MA	4,254
Oakland County, MI	4,077
Fort Bend County, TX	4,012
Somerset County, NJ	3,861
Monmouth County, NJ	3,754
Westchester County, NY	3,600
San Bernardino County, CA	3,519
Philadelphia County, PA	3,508
Suffolk County, NY	3,448
Franklin County, OH	3,325
Washtenaw County, MI	3,153
Hudson County, NJ	3,149
St. Louis County, MO	2,810
Fairfield County, CT	2,696
Essex County, NJ	2,682
Miami-Dade County, FL	2,581
Lake County, IL	2,558
Mercer County, NJ	2,528
Fulton County, GA	2,518
New Haven County, CT	2,505
Montgomery County, PA	2,498
Wayne County, MI	2,414
Clark County, NV	2,409
Wake County, NC	2,406
Hennepin County, MN	2,372
Cuyahoga County, OH	2,356
Allegheny County, PA	2,351
Ventura County, CA	2,339
Washington County, OR	2,185
Tarrant County, TX	2,139
Gwinnett County, GA	1,975
Broward County, FL	1,960
Howard County, MD	1,936
Baltimore County, MD	1,905
DeKalb County, GA	1,874
New Castle County, DE	1,848
Prince George's County, MD	1,838
Pima County, AZ	1,782
Ramsey County, MN	1,717
Monroe County, NY	1,708
Union County, NJ	1,669
Yolo County, CA	1,655
Bronx County, NY	1,647
Salt Lake County, UT	1,637
Hamilton County, OH	1,633
Richmond County, NY	1,621

Place	Number
New York, NY (city)	66,766
San Francisco, CA (city) San Francisco County	30,586
San Jose, CA (city) Santa Clara County	20,233
Los Angeles, CA (city) Los Angeles County	16,294
Fremont, CA (city) Alameda County	11,753
Honolulu, HI (cdp) Honolulu County	11,100
Houston, TX (city) Harris County	9,532
Chicago, IL (city) Cook County	8,744
San Diego, CA (city) San Diego County	8,322
Sunnyvale, CA (city) Santa Clara County	6,703
Alhambra, CA (city) Los Angeles County	6,137
Monterey Park, CA (city) Los Angeles County	5,233
Cupertino, CA (city) Santa Clara County	5,203
Seattle, WA (city) King County	5,150
Arcadia, CA (city) Los Angeles County	4,955
Irvine, CA (city) Orange County	4,834
Plano, TX (city) Collin County	4,563
Oakland, CA (city) Alameda County	4,521
Boston, MA (city) Suffolk County	4,133
Austin, TX (city) Travis County	4,004
Sacramento, CA (city) Sacramento County	3,886
Rowland Heights, CA (cdp) Los Angeles County	3,701
Philadelphia, PA (city) Philadelphia County	3,508
Milpitas, CA (city) Santa Clara County	3,444
Daly City, CA (city) San Mateo County	3,248
Palo Alto, CA (city) Santa Clara County	3,148
Hacienda Heights, CA (cdp) Los Angeles County	3,136
Dallas, TX (city) Dallas County	3,117
Mountain View, CA (city) Santa Clara County	3,091
Diamond Bar, CA (city) Los Angeles County	2,797
Bellevue, WA (city) King County	2,724
Santa Clara, CA (city) Santa Clara County	2,676
Torrance, CA (city) Los Angeles County	2,576
Saratoga, CA (city) Santa Clara County	2,478
Edison, NJ (township) Middlesex County	2,463
Columbus, OH (city) Franklin County	2,428
San Gabriel, CA (city) Los Angeles County	2,393
San Mateo, CA (city) San Mateo County	2,283
Cerritos, CA (city) Los Angeles County	2,243
Sugar Land, TX (city) Fort Bend County	2,228
Union City, CA (city) Alameda County	2,150
Temple City, CA (city) Los Angeles County	2,139
Ann Arbor, MI (city) Washtenaw County	2,083
Alameda, CA (city) Alameda County	2,077
Pasadena, CA (city) Los Angeles County	2,073
Foster City, CA (city) San Mateo County	2,067
Walnut, CA (city) Los Angeles County	2,058
Naperville, IL (city) Du Page County	2,002
North Hempstead, NY (town) Nassau County	1,958
Berkeley, CA (city) Alameda County	1,871
Cambridge, MA (city) Middlesex County	1,770
Phoenix, AZ (city) Maricopa County	1,734
Newton, MA (city) Middlesex County	1,668
North Potomac, MD (cdp) Montgomery County	1,649
Brookline, MA (town) Norfolk County	1,632
Hempstead, NY (town) Nassau County	1,631
Brookhaven, NY (town) Suffolk County	1,613
San Marino, CA (city) Los Angeles County	1,602
San Leandro, CA (city) Alameda County	1,576
West Covina, CA (city) Los Angeles County	1,572
Rancho Palos Verdes, CA (city) Los Angeles County	1,513
South Pasadena, CA (city) Los Angeles County	1,491
Oyster Bay, NY (town) Nassau County	1,474
Quincy, MA (city) Norfolk County	1,472
Redwood City, CA (city) San Mateo County	1,466
South San Francisco, CA (city) San Mateo County	1,447
Anaheim, CA (city) Orange County	1,427
Huntington Beach, CA (city) Orange County	1,393
Fullerton, CA (city) Orange County	1,378
El Monte, CA (city) Los Angeles County	1,374
Rockville, MD (city) Montgomery County	1,357
Jersey City, NJ (city) Hudson County	1,356
Rosemead, CA (city) Los Angeles County	1,353
Portland, OR (city) Multnomah County	1,346
Pittsburgh, PA (city) Allegheny County	1,316

Notes: Please refer to the User's Guide for an explanation of data; ranking tables include all places with Asian and/or NHPI populations above SF4 population thresholds; (1) tables reflect only those areas that meet SF4 population thresholds, therefore there may be less than 50 states, 75 counties or 75 places listed

Educational Attainment: Four-Year College Graduates

Chinese (except Taiwanese) 25 Years and Over Who are Four-Year College Graduates

All States, Top 75 Counties, and Top 75 Places Sorted by Percent[1]

State	Percent
North Dakota	76.34
Nebraska	72.82
Iowa	72.63
Alabama	71.79
Indiana	67.20
West Virginia	66.77
Delaware	66.53
Wisconsin	66.45
Ohio	66.24
Michigan	65.99
Missouri	65.42
Connecticut	65.14
Kentucky	65.11
South Dakota	64.81
New Jersey	64.08
Texas	63.58
Maryland	63.08
Minnesota	62.89
New Mexico	62.75
Kansas	62.66
Oklahoma	61.71
New Hampshire	61.44
Tennessee	61.25
North Carolina	61.12
Virginia	60.63
Vermont	59.80
Georgia	58.91
Louisiana	58.77
Illinois	56.40
South Carolina	55.90
Colorado	55.77
Arkansas	55.26
District of Columbia	54.83
Montana	54.19
Utah	54.00
Mississippi	53.19
Pennsylvania	53.02
Arizona	52.12
Massachusetts	50.22
Idaho	49.87
Rhode Island	49.68
Washington	49.61
United States	47.08
Oregon	44.93
California	44.75
Florida	44.39
Wyoming	42.60
Alaska	39.53
Hawaii	35.84
Maine	34.20
Nevada	32.02
New York	31.03

County	Percent
Charlottesville Independent City, VA	95.54
Montgomery County, VA	95.45
Payne County, OK	94.81
Lubbock County, TX	93.18
Tompkins County, NY	91.69
Alachua County, FL	91.60
Monongalia County, WV	91.28
Centre County, PA	90.78
Johnson County, IA	90.23
Olmsted County, MN	89.91
Champaign County, IL	88.38
Riley County, KS	88.36
Tippecanoe County, IN	87.66
Brazos County, TX	87.00
Washtenaw County, MI	86.79
Pickens County, SC	86.52
Benton County, WA	85.57
Monroe County, IN	84.79
Douglas County, KS	84.58
Story County, IA	84.49
Albemarle County, VA	83.85
Orange County, NC	83.02
Travis County, TX	82.32
Clarke County, GA	81.69
Fayette County, KY	81.53
Tolland County, CT	81.52
Durham County, NC	81.38
Jefferson County, AL	80.75
Waukesha County, WI	80.34
Lee County, AL	80.04
Mercer County, NJ	79.52
Boone County, MO	79.45
Lake County, IL	79.39
Dona Ana County, NM	79.35
Warren County, OH	79.31
Washington County, AR	79.01
Whitman County, WA	79.01
Dane County, WI	78.75
Somerset County, NJ	78.67
Chester County, PA	78.25
Jackson County, IL	77.74
DuPage County, IL	77.38
Leon County, FL	77.29
Hampshire County, MA	77.26
Kalamazoo County, MI	77.22
Howard County, MD	77.13
Yolo County, CA	76.83
Summit County, OH	76.71
Ramsey County, MN	76.41
Hamilton County, OH	76.17
Greene County, OH	76.09
Lancaster County, NE	76.06
Brazoria County, TX	76.01
St. Charles County, MO	75.95
Douglas County, NE	75.90
Knox County, TN	75.79
Albany County, NY	75.73
Hamilton County, IN	75.64
Cache County, UT	75.56
Collin County, TX	74.96
Delaware County, OH	74.79
Boulder County, CO	74.37
Morris County, NJ	74.35
Wake County, NC	73.89
Erie County, NY	73.72
East Baton Rouge Parish, LA	73.68
Lake County, OH	73.41
Peoria County, IL	73.37
Grafton County, NH	72.89
Fulton County, GA	72.88
Davidson County, TN	72.72
New Haven County, CT	72.63
St. Joseph County, IN	72.37
McLean County, IL	72.16
Cleveland County, OK	71.64

Place	Percent
Brookfield, WI (city) Waukesha County	100.00
Stanford, CA (cdp) Santa Clara County	98.76
Falcon Heights, MN (city) Ramsey County	97.20
Blacksburg, VA (town) Montgomery County	95.16
Lubbock, TX (city) Lubbock County	95.14
Hudson, OH (city) Summit County	94.87
Mansfield, CT (town) Tolland County	94.85
Stillwater, OK (city) Payne County	94.81
Storrs, CT (cdp) Tolland County	94.01
Evanston, IL (city) Cook County	93.91
West Lafayette, IN (city) Tippecanoe County	93.43
State College, PA (borough) Centre County	93.32
Champaign, IL (city) Champaign County	92.78
Gainesville, FL (city) Alachua County	92.59
Tredyffrin, PA (township) Chester County	91.71
Princeton, NJ (township) Mercer County	91.65
Poughkeepsie, NY (town) Dutchess County	91.30
Manhattan, KS (city) Riley County	90.87
Los Altos Hills, CA (town) Santa Clara County	90.83
Iowa City, IA (city) Johnson County	90.23
Bernards, NJ (township) Somerset County	90.05
Westland, MI (city) Wayne County	90.02
Lower Providence, PA (township) Montgomery County	89.68
Ann Arbor, MI (city) Washtenaw County	89.63
Needham, MA (town) Norfolk County	89.30
Rochester, MN (city) Olmsted County	89.03
Drexel Hill, PA (cdp) Delaware County	88.97
Acton, MA (town) Middlesex County	88.01
Birmingham, AL (city) Jefferson County	87.88
New Haven, CT (city) New Haven County	87.86
Scarsdale, NY (village) Westchester County	87.85
Princeton Meadows, NJ (cdp) Middlesex County	87.79
Newark, DE (city) New Castle County	87.41
Boulder, CO (city) Boulder County	87.38
Setauket-East Setauket, NY (cdp) Suffolk County	87.30
Los Altos, CA (city) Santa Clara County	87.18
Montgomery, NJ (township) Somerset County	87.17
Dublin, OH (city) Franklin County	87.04
Westford, MA (town) Middlesex County	87.01
East Lansing, MI (city) Ingham County	86.73
Bethesda, MD (cdp) Montgomery County	86.72
Plainsboro, NJ (township) Middlesex County	86.49
Carlsbad, CA (city) San Diego County	86.13
La Canada Flintridge, CA (city) Los Angeles County	86.00
Lower Merion, PA (township) Montgomery County	85.83
Urbana, IL (city) Champaign County	85.39
Germantown, TN (city) Shelby County	85.28
Chapel Hill, NC (town) Orange County	84.91
College Station, TX (city) Brazos County	84.71
Pittsfield charter, MI (township) Washtenaw County	84.70
New Providence, NJ (borough) Union County	84.62
Potomac, MD (cdp) Montgomery County	84.62
Wilmette, IL (village) Cook County	84.59
Fayetteville, AR (city) Washington County	84.58
Lawrence, KS (city) Douglas County	84.58
Westport, CT (town) Fairfield County	84.53
Upper Arlington, OH (city) Franklin County	84.48
Tysons Corner, VA (cdp) Fairfax County	84.43
Lexington, MA (town) Middlesex County	84.26
Ames, IA (city) Story County	84.15
Hanover, NJ (township) Morris County	84.12
Lawrence, NJ (township) Mercer County	84.02
University City, MO (city) Saint Louis County	83.82
Millburn, NJ (township) Essex County	83.76
Bloomington, IN (city) Monroe County	83.70
Andover, MA (town) Essex County	83.67
Bellaire, TX (city) Harris County	83.57
Richland, WA (city) Benton County	83.50
Aurora, IL (city) Kane County	83.49
Ellicott City, MD (cdp) Howard County	83.40
Reston, VA (cdp) Fairfax County	83.30
Piedmont, CA (city) Alameda County	83.22
King of Prussia, PA (cdp) Montgomery County	83.21
Palo Alto, CA (city) Santa Clara County	83.15
Morganville, NJ (cdp) Monmouth County	83.12

Notes: Please refer to the User's Guide for an explanation of data; ranking tables include all places with Asian and/or NHPI populations above SF4 population thresholds; (1) tables reflect only those areas that meet SF4 population thresholds, therefore there may be less than 50 states, 75 counties or 75 places listed

Educational Attainment: Four-Year College Graduates

Fijians 25 Years and Over Who are Four-Year College Graduates

All States, Top 75 Counties, and Top 75 Places Sorted by Number[1]

State	Number
United States	514
California	360
Oregon	33
Washington	19

County	Number
Alameda County, CA	86
San Mateo County, CA	51
Santa Clara County, CA	44
Sacramento County, CA	35
Stanislaus County, CA	29
Los Angeles County, CA	26
Contra Costa County, CA	19
Yolo County, CA	13
King County, WA	6

Place	Number
Hayward, CA (city) Alameda County	58
Sacramento, CA (city) Sacramento County	32
Modesto, CA (city) Stanislaus County	29

Notes: Please refer to the User's Guide for an explanation of data; ranking tables include all places with Asian and/or NHPI populations above SF4 population thresholds; (1) tables reflect only those areas that meet SF4 population thresholds, therefore there may be less than 50 states, 75 counties or 75 places listed

Educational Attainment: Four-Year College Graduates

Fijians 25 Years and Over Who are Four-Year College Graduates

All States, Top 75 Counties, and Top 75 Places Sorted by Percent[1]

State	Percent
Oregon	15.00
United States	8.78
California	7.70
Washington	4.23

County	Percent
Santa Clara County, CA	14.92
Alameda County, CA	11.50
Stanislaus County, CA	8.81
Los Angeles County, CA	7.45
San Mateo County, CA	7.43
Contra Costa County, CA	7.22
Yolo County, CA	5.18
Sacramento County, CA	3.37
King County, WA	1.71

Place	Percent
Hayward, CA (city) Alameda County	13.98
Modesto, CA (city) Stanislaus County	12.13
Sacramento, CA (city) Sacramento County	4.41

Notes: Please refer to the User's Guide for an explanation of data; ranking tables include all places with Asian and/or NHPI populations above SF4 population thresholds; (1) tables reflect only those areas that meet SF4 population thresholds, therefore there may be less than 50 states, 75 counties or 75 places listed

Educational Attainment: Four-Year College Graduates

Filipinos 25 Years and Over Who are Four-Year College Graduates

All States, Top 75 Counties, and Top 75 Places Sorted by Number[1]

State	Number
United States	550,230
California	258,176
New York	39,836
New Jersey	38,639
Illinois	37,120
Texas	21,996
Hawaii	18,838
Florida	17,128
Washington	15,369
Virginia	14,917
Maryland	9,328
Nevada	8,335
Michigan	8,220
Pennsylvania	5,599
Ohio	5,140
Arizona	4,375
Massachusetts	3,936
Georgia	3,418
Connecticut	3,204
North Carolina	3,012
Colorado	2,747
Oregon	2,741
Indiana	2,713
Missouri	2,668
Wisconsin	2,063
Tennessee	1,889
Minnesota	1,685
South Carolina	1,640
Alaska	1,541
Louisiana	1,372
Kansas	1,071
Kentucky	1,022
Oklahoma	931
Utah	912
West Virginia	841
District of Columbia	835
New Mexico	754
Alabama	717
Delaware	710
Iowa	646
Rhode Island	621
Arkansas	559
Mississippi	558
Nebraska	552
New Hampshire	472
Idaho	451
Maine	277
Montana	171
South Dakota	156
Wyoming	112
Vermont	109
North Dakota	108

County	Number
Los Angeles County, CA	88,860
San Diego County, CA	26,898
Cook County, IL	24,393
Santa Clara County, CA	19,610
Alameda County, CA	19,509
San Mateo County, CA	17,642
Orange County, CA	16,713
Honolulu County, HI	15,142
Queens County, NY	14,039
San Francisco County, CA	11,136
Contra Costa County, CA	10,283
King County, WA	9,145
San Bernardino County, CA	8,333
Hudson County, NJ	8,134
Solano County, CA	7,948
Bergen County, NJ	6,708
Clark County, NV	6,680
Harris County, TX	6,441
DuPage County, IL	6,386
Sacramento County, CA	6,129
Middlesex County, NJ	5,774
New York County, NY	5,515
Riverside County, CA	5,370
Fairfax County, VA	5,280
Ventura County, CA	4,025
Essex County, NJ	3,716
Maricopa County, AZ	3,560
San Joaquin County, CA	3,410
Kings County, NY	3,327
Nassau County, NY	3,216
Virginia Beach Independent City, VA	3,036
Montgomery County, MD	2,855
Union County, NJ	2,555
Dallas County, TX	2,494
Westchester County, NY	2,475
Prince George's County, MD	2,441
Lake County, IL	2,412
Bronx County, NY	2,350
Richmond County, NY	2,289
Rockland County, NY	2,187
Duval County, FL	2,178
Oakland County, MI	2,148
Wayne County, MI	2,125
Maui County, HI	2,078
Miami-Dade County, FL	1,904
Broward County, FL	1,835
Monterey County, CA	1,818
Fort Bend County, TX	1,810
Snohomish County, WA	1,809
Suffolk County, NY	1,790
Fresno County, CA	1,587
Monmouth County, NJ	1,565
Morris County, NJ	1,562
Bexar County, TX	1,554
Orange County, FL	1,546
Kern County, CA	1,518
Passaic County, NJ	1,490
Baltimore County, MD	1,479
Somerset County, NJ	1,436
Macomb County, MI	1,423
Washoe County, NV	1,421
Camden County, NJ	1,389
Cuyahoga County, OH	1,383
Will County, IL	1,352
Middlesex County, MA	1,270
Fairfield County, CT	1,214
Pierce County, WA	1,191
Philadelphia County, PA	1,175
Kitsap County, WA	1,130
Hillsborough County, FL	1,114
Palm Beach County, FL	1,076
Tarrant County, TX	1,046
Ocean County, NJ	1,014
St. Louis County, MO	968
Montgomery County, PA	957

Place	Number
Los Angeles, CA (city) Los Angeles County	35,665
New York, NY (city)	27,520
San Diego, CA (city) San Diego County	17,093
Chicago, IL (city) Cook County	12,106
San Jose, CA (city) Santa Clara County	11,692
San Francisco, CA (city) San Francisco County	11,136
Daly City, CA (city) San Mateo County	8,423
Jersey City, NJ (city) Hudson County	6,842
Honolulu, HI (cdp) Honolulu County	5,411
Vallejo, CA (city) Solano County	5,326
Glendale, CA (city) Los Angeles County	4,683
Long Beach, CA (city) Los Angeles County	4,438
Seattle, WA (city) King County	4,314
Carson, CA (city) Los Angeles County	4,158
Fremont, CA (city) Alameda County	3,758
Chula Vista, CA (city) San Diego County	3,569
South San Francisco, CA (city) San Mateo County	3,399
West Covina, CA (city) Los Angeles County	3,262
Union City, CA (city) Alameda County	3,236
Houston, TX (city) Harris County	3,234
Hayward, CA (city) Alameda County	3,215
Anaheim, CA (city) Orange County	2,660
Milpitas, CA (city) Santa Clara County	2,486
Las Vegas, NV (city) Clark County	2,442
Stockton, CA (city) San Joaquin County	2,442
Cerritos, CA (city) Los Angeles County	2,255
Chino Hills, CA (city) San Bernardino County	2,234
Jacksonville, FL (city) Duval County	2,111
Oxnard, CA (city) Ventura County	2,018
Sacramento, CA (city) Sacramento County	1,850
Hempstead, NY (town) Nassau County	1,843
Alameda, CA (city) Alameda County	1,788
Oakland, CA (city) Alameda County	1,771
Sunnyvale, CA (city) Santa Clara County	1,766
Buena Park, CA (city) Orange County	1,624
San Leandro, CA (city) Alameda County	1,600
Waipahu, HI (cdp) Honolulu County	1,522
Torrance, CA (city) Los Angeles County	1,475
Walnut, CA (city) Los Angeles County	1,472
Hercules, CA (city) Contra Costa County	1,466
Phoenix, AZ (city) Maricopa County	1,462
Santa Clara, CA (city) Santa Clara County	1,408
Lakewood, CA (city) Los Angeles County	1,359
Norwalk, CA (city) Los Angeles County	1,283
Skokie, IL (village) Cook County	1,269
Diamond Bar, CA (city) Los Angeles County	1,260
National City, CA (city) San Diego County	1,249
Edison, NJ (township) Middlesex County	1,242
Baldwin Park, CA (city) Los Angeles County	1,209
San Antonio, TX (city) Bexar County	1,191
Bergenfield, NJ (borough) Bergen County	1,186
Moreno Valley, CA (city) Riverside County	1,180
Philadelphia, PA (city) Philadelphia County	1,175
Burbank, CA (city) Los Angeles County	1,158
Fresno, CA (city) Fresno County	1,146
Paradise, NV (cdp) Clark County	1,138
Rowland Heights, CA (cdp) Los Angeles County	1,117
Salinas, CA (city) Monterey County	1,113
Clarkstown, NY (town) Rockland County	1,112
San Mateo, CA (city) San Mateo County	1,105
Fairfield, CA (city) Solano County	1,096
Pasadena, CA (city) Los Angeles County	1,081
Pittsburg, CA (city) Contra Costa County	1,080
Santa Clarita, CA (city) Los Angeles County	1,069
San Bruno, CA (city) San Mateo County	1,062
Bellflower, CA (city) Los Angeles County	1,040
Concord, CA (city) Contra Costa County	1,035
Elk Grove, CA (cdp) Sacramento County	1,004
Pomona, CA (city) Los Angeles County	992
Corona, CA (city) Riverside County	987
Union, NJ (township) Union County	980
Reno, NV (city) Washoe County	968
La Mirada, CA (city) Los Angeles County	962
Richmond, CA (city) Contra Costa County	938
Riverside, CA (city) Riverside County	924

Notes: Please refer to the User's Guide for an explanation of data; ranking tables include all places with Asian and/or NHPI populations above SF4 population thresholds; (1) tables reflect only those areas that meet SF4 population thresholds, therefore there may be less than 50 states, 75 counties or 75 places listed

Educational Attainment: Four-Year College Graduates

Filipinos 25 Years and Over Who are Four-Year College Graduates

All States, Top 75 Counties, and Top 75 Places Sorted by Percent[1]

State	Percent
West Virginia	69.16
New Jersey	65.91
New York	65.46
Michigan	65.23
Illinois	62.36
Connecticut	60.53
Massachusetts	59.34
Indiana	57.41
Texas	56.12
New Hampshire	55.40
Wisconsin	55.16
Pennsylvania	55.12
Ohio	54.29
District of Columbia	53.32
Delaware	52.75
Missouri	51.97
Maryland	51.03
Tennessee	50.81
Vermont	48.66
Georgia	47.56
Kentucky	46.24
Virginia	45.76
Florida	44.87
Kansas	44.24
United States	43.77
Colorado	43.30
North Carolina	43.30
Minnesota	42.21
California	42.18
Arizona	40.58
Iowa	40.48
Louisiana	40.35
Alabama	40.10
Rhode Island	39.76
New Mexico	39.73
Utah	39.58
Nebraska	37.96
Oregon	37.67
Idaho	37.65
Maine	35.33
South Carolina	35.28
Washington	35.21
Arkansas	34.59
Wyoming	34.57
Oklahoma	33.24
Nevada	30.76
South Dakota	30.00
Montana	29.69
Mississippi	29.59
North Dakota	27.98
Alaska	18.85
Hawaii	16.23

County	Percent
Jefferson County, TX	86.82
Hidalgo County, TX	83.94
New York County, NY	75.15
Ingham County, MI	74.93
Cameron County, TX	74.31
Alachua County, FL	73.87
Durham County, NC	73.52
Middlesex County, NJ	73.25
Rockland County, NY	73.02
Mercer County, NJ	72.68
Oakland County, MI	72.37
Brazoria County, TX	72.12
Washtenaw County, MI	72.04
Somerset County, NJ	71.80
Loudoun County, VA	71.79
Essex County, NJ	71.70
Westchester County, NY	71.14
Bronx County, NY	71.08
Morris County, NJ	70.33
Fairfield County, CT	70.25
Middlesex County, MA	69.97
Albany County, NY	69.72
Collin County, TX	69.36
Lake County, IN	69.36
Waukesha County, WI	69.33
Fort Bend County, TX	68.85
Montgomery County, PA	68.45
Delaware County, PA	68.22
Bergen County, NJ	67.90
Monmouth County, NJ	67.52
Wayne County, MI	67.27
Nassau County, NY	67.21
Rockingham County, NH	67.05
Johnson County, KS	66.67
Howard County, MD	66.60
Orange County, NY	66.60
New Castle County, DE	66.50
Chesterfield County, VA	66.39
DuPage County, IL	66.24
Union County, NJ	65.77
Davidson County, TN	65.72
Onondaga County, NY	65.72
Kings County, NY	65.24
McHenry County, IL	65.16
New Haven County, CT	65.04
Hartford County, CT	64.89
Hamilton County, OH	64.85
Suffolk County, MA	64.85
Will County, IL	64.84
Palm Beach County, FL	64.70
Allegheny County, PA	64.61
Suffolk County, NY	64.37
Polk County, FL	64.36
Baltimore County, MD	64.33
Richmond County, NY	63.99
Leon County, FL	63.44
Cook County, IL	63.18
Chester County, PA	63.12
Ocean County, NJ	63.10
Cuyahoga County, OH	62.84
Sussex County, NJ	62.81
Berrien County, MI	62.50
Champaign County, IL	62.50
Gloucester County, NJ	62.46
Harford County, MD	62.40
Dane County, WI	62.36
St. Louis County, MO	62.25
Highlands County, FL	62.21
Fulton County, GA	62.06
Milwaukee County, WI	61.80
Winnebago County, IL	61.58
Gwinnett County, GA	61.50
Passaic County, NJ	61.39
Queens County, NY	61.34
Kane County, IL	61.33

Place	Percent
Beaumont, TX (city) Jefferson County	93.69
North Brunswick, NJ (township) Middlesex County	87.70
East Brunswick, NJ (township) Middlesex County	87.24
Franklin, NJ (township) Somerset County	85.48
East Meadow, NY (cdp) Nassau County	85.14
McAllen, TX (city) Hidalgo County	82.88
West Bloomfield, MI (township) Oakland County	82.29
Somerset, NJ (cdp) Somerset County	80.66
South Brunswick, NJ (township) Middlesex County	80.10
New City, NY (cdp) Rockland County	80.06
Glenview, IL (village) Cook County	79.71
Bloomfield, NJ (township) Essex County	78.93
Sayreville, NJ (borough) Middlesex County	78.93
Greenburgh, NY (town) Westchester County	78.78
Freehold, NJ (township) Monmouth County	78.75
Clarkstown, NY (town) Rockland County	78.20
Ellicott City, MD (cdp) Howard County	78.11
Huntington, NY (town) Suffolk County	77.94
Parsippany-Troy Hills, NJ (township) Morris County	77.87
Valley Cottage, NY (cdp) Rockland County	77.68
Lincolnwood, IL (village) Cook County	77.59
Stafford, TX (city) Fort Bend County	77.45
Orland Park, IL (village) Cook County	77.38
Mundelein, IL (village) Lake County	77.05
Elmont, NY (cdp) Nassau County	76.88
Old Bridge, NJ (township) Middlesex County	76.83
Arlington Heights, IL (village) Cook County	76.70
Lombard, IL (village) Du Page County	76.36
Troy, MI (city) Oakland County	76.11
Orangetown, NY (town) Rockland County	75.84
Voorhees, NJ (township) Camden County	75.64
Ann Arbor, MI (city) Washtenaw County	75.43
Paramus, NJ (borough) Bergen County	75.24
Englewood, NJ (city) Bergen County	74.92
Livingston, NJ (township) Essex County	74.76
Davis, CA (city) Yolo County	74.72
Darien, IL (city) Du Page County	74.55
Gurnee, IL (village) Lake County	74.45
Union, NJ (township) Union County	74.30
Franconia, VA (cdp) Fairfax County	73.97
Lodi, NJ (borough) Bergen County	73.72
Walnut Creek, CA (city) Contra Costa County	73.72
Teaneck, NJ (township) Bergen County	73.70
Danville, CA (town) Contra Costa County	73.68
Naperville, IL (city) Du Page County	73.58
Mission Bend, TX (cdp) Fort Bend County	73.54
Yonkers, NY (city) Westchester County	73.52
West Orange, NJ (township) Essex County	72.93
Dover, NJ (township) Ocean County	72.64
Toms River, NJ (cdp) Ocean County	72.64
Edison, NJ (township) Middlesex County	72.59
Elk Grove Village, IL (village) Cook County	72.52
Schaumburg, IL (village) Cook County	72.51
Aurora, IL (city) Kane County	72.02
Sugar Land, TX (city) Fort Bend County	71.80
Cupertino, CA (city) Santa Clara County	71.78
Durham, NC (city) Durham County	71.77
North Hempstead, NY (town) Nassau County	71.68
Canton, MI (township) Wayne County	71.43
Fair Lawn, NJ (borough) Bergen County	71.43
Woodbridge, NJ (township) Middlesex County	71.26
New Milford, NJ (borough) Bergen County	70.98
Downers Grove, IL (village) Du Page County	70.93
Evanston, IL (city) Cook County	70.52
Bowie, MD (city) Prince George's County	70.36
Missouri City, TX (city) Fort Bend County	70.23
Tinley Park, IL (village) Cook County	70.10
Rancho Palos Verdes, CA (city) Los Angeles County	69.84
Hempstead, NY (town) Nassau County	69.81
Wheeling, IL (village) Cook County	69.68
Montgomery Village, MD (cdp) Montgomery County	69.57
Levittown, NY (cdp) Nassau County	69.43
Belleville, NJ (township) Essex County	69.32
Rancho Santa Margarita, CA (city) Orange County	69.26
Plano, TX (city) Collin County	68.66

Notes: Please refer to the User's Guide for an explanation of data; ranking tables include all places with Asian and/or NHPI populations above SF4 population thresholds; (1) tables reflect only those areas that meet SF4 population thresholds, therefore there may be less than 50 states, 75 counties or 75 places listed

Educational Attainment: Four-Year College Graduates

Guamanians or Chamorros 25 Years and Over Who are Four-Year College Graduates

All States, Top 75 Counties, and Top 75 Places Sorted by Number[1]

State	Number
United States	4,635
California	1,540
Washington	382
Texas	262
Hawaii	187
Florida	172
Arizona	138
Virginia	138
Illinois	123
Nevada	112
New York	112
Colorado	107
Ohio	97
Minnesota	83
Georgia	78
Maryland	76
Pennsylvania	76
Michigan	72
Oregon	72
Missouri	70
Connecticut	69
North Carolina	68
Indiana	65
Oklahoma	53
Massachusetts	49
New Mexico	40
Wisconsin	39
Alabama	38
New Jersey	35
Louisiana	30
Tennessee	26
South Carolina	25
Kentucky	17

County	Number
Los Angeles County, CA	285
San Diego County, CA	274
Alameda County, CA	227
Honolulu County, HI	178
King County, WA	126
Santa Clara County, CA	122
Orange County, CA	119
Clark County, NV	91
Pierce County, WA	89
Maricopa County, AZ	83
Harris County, TX	82
Solano County, CA	74
Thurston County, WA	69
Sacramento County, CA	64
San Mateo County, CA	56
Contra Costa County, CA	51
El Paso County, CO	49
San Bernardino County, CA	48
Kitsap County, WA	29
Riverside County, CA	20
Bell County, TX	19
Monterey County, CA	7
Kings County, NY	6

Place	Number
San Diego, CA (city) San Diego County	173
Los Angeles, CA (city) Los Angeles County	129
San Jose, CA (city) Santa Clara County	82
Honolulu, HI (cdp) Honolulu County	59
Houston, TX (city) Harris County	47
New York, NY (city)	41
Fairfield, CA (city) Solano County	30
Vallejo, CA (city) Solano County	28
Tacoma, WA (city) Pierce County	18
Chula Vista, CA (city) San Diego County	12
Killeen, TX (city) Bell County	10

Notes: Please refer to the User's Guide for an explanation of data; ranking tables include all places with Asian and/or NHPI populations above SF4 population thresholds; (1) tables reflect only those areas that meet SF4 population thresholds, therefore there may be less than 50 states, 75 counties or 75 places listed

Educational Attainment: Four-Year College Graduates

Guamanians or Chamorros 25 Years and Over Who are Four-Year College Graduates

All States, Top 75 Counties, and Top 75 Places Sorted by Percent[1]

State	Percent
Minnesota	32.81
Connecticut	29.61
Ohio	26.50
Indiana	25.90
Virginia	22.96
Michigan	22.93
Illinois	21.54
Hawaii	21.49
Arizona	20.15
Alabama	19.90
New Mexico	19.90
Pennsylvania	19.59
Missouri	19.55
Wisconsin	18.66
Oklahoma	18.60
Massachusetts	18.49
Maryland	18.18
Colorado	16.44
Nevada	15.89
Florida	14.51
United States	14.27
Texas	13.32
Washington	12.87
New York	12.00
California	11.95
Oregon	11.29
New Jersey	10.87
South Carolina	10.42
Georgia	9.99
North Carolina	9.94
Louisiana	9.68
Kentucky	8.59
Tennessee	8.31

County	Percent
King County, WA	29.58
Alameda County, CA	24.15
Honolulu County, HI	22.91
Maricopa County, AZ	21.67
Harris County, TX	21.58
San Mateo County, CA	19.58
El Paso County, CO	16.39
Contra Costa County, CA	15.45
Santa Clara County, CA	15.42
Thurston County, WA	15.27
Los Angeles County, CA	15.02
Orange County, CA	14.97
Clark County, NV	14.58
Sacramento County, CA	12.14
San Diego County, CA	9.42
Pierce County, WA	9.38
Solano County, CA	7.64
San Bernardino County, CA	7.31
Kitsap County, WA	5.44
Bell County, TX	5.23
Kings County, NY	3.35
Riverside County, CA	3.13
Monterey County, CA	2.04

Place	Percent
San Jose, CA (city) Santa Clara County	17.45
Los Angeles, CA (city) Los Angeles County	17.32
Houston, TX (city) Harris County	16.79
Honolulu, HI (cdp) Honolulu County	16.48
San Diego, CA (city) San Diego County	13.44
Fairfield, CA (city) Solano County	8.15
Tacoma, WA (city) Pierce County	7.20
New York, NY (city)	7.02
Vallejo, CA (city) Solano County	6.78
Chula Vista, CA (city) San Diego County	4.20
Killeen, TX (city) Bell County	3.29

Notes: Please refer to the User's Guide for an explanation of data; ranking tables include all places with Asian and/or NHPI populations above SF4 population thresholds; (1) tables reflect only those areas that meet SF4 population thresholds, therefore there may be less than 50 states, 75 counties or 75 places listed

Educational Attainment: Four-Year College Graduates

Hawaiian Natives 25 Years and Over Who are Four-Year College Graduates

All States, Top 75 Counties, and Top 75 Places Sorted by Number[1]

State	Number
United States	12,843
Hawaii	5,948
California	2,393
Washington	471
Texas	339
Oregon	297
Nevada	261
New York	215
Arizona	205
Virginia	199
Colorado	190
Pennsylvania	181
Florida	158
Utah	150
Maryland	124
Illinois	115
Michigan	112
New Jersey	104
Massachusetts	99
North Carolina	93
Georgia	92
Ohio	92
Tennessee	92
Missouri	81
Oklahoma	78
Minnesota	73
Kansas	66
New Mexico	62
Wisconsin	48
South Carolina	43
Louisiana	40
Idaho	37
Montana	30
Indiana	29
Alaska	28
Arkansas	22

County	Number
Honolulu County, HI	4,200
Hawaii County, HI	915
Maui County, HI	566
Los Angeles County, CA	481
Kauai County, HI	267
San Diego County, CA	250
Clark County, NV	244
King County, WA	221
Orange County, CA	215
Santa Clara County, CA	202
Alameda County, CA	155
San Mateo County, CA	105
Contra Costa County, CA	102
Ventura County, CA	95
Multnomah County, OR	89
Riverside County, CA	88
Maricopa County, AZ	85
Salt Lake County, UT	71
San Joaquin County, CA	70
Washington County, OR	69
San Bernardino County, CA	67
Snohomish County, WA	65
Pierce County, WA	63
Pima County, AZ	62
Sacramento County, CA	58
Bexar County, TX	38
Solano County, CA	26
Utah County, UT	26

Place	Number
Honolulu, HI (cdp) Honolulu County	1,862
Hilo, HI (cdp) Hawaii County	286
Kaneohe, HI (cdp) Honolulu County	270
Kailua, HI (cdp) Honolulu County	223
Los Angeles, CA (city) Los Angeles County	205
San Diego, CA (city) San Diego County	166
Mililani Town, HI (cdp) Honolulu County	136
New York, NY (city)	125
Pearl City, HI (cdp) Honolulu County	119
Waimanalo Beach, HI (cdp) Honolulu County	112
Makakilo City, HI (cdp) Honolulu County	106
Waimalu, HI (cdp) Honolulu County	103
Ahuimanu, HI (cdp) Honolulu County	94
Wailuku, HI (cdp) Maui County	91
Kailua, HI (cdp) Hawaii County	87
Kahului, HI (cdp) Maui County	79
Las Vegas, NV (city) Clark County	79
Wahiawa, HI (cdp) Honolulu County	79
Waianae, HI (cdp) Honolulu County	78
Laie, HI (cdp) Honolulu County	75
San Jose, CA (city) Santa Clara County	72
Portland, OR (city) Multnomah County	67
Makaha, HI (cdp) Honolulu County	64
Nanakuli, HI (cdp) Honolulu County	64
Kihei, HI (cdp) Maui County	56
Henderson, NV (city) Clark County	55
Waimea, HI (cdp) Hawaii County	50
Anahola, HI (cdp) Kauai County	42
Hawaiian Paradise Park, HI (cdp) Hawaii County	41
Kahaluu, HI (cdp) Honolulu County	38
Paradise, NV (cdp) Clark County	38
Volcano, HI (cdp) Hawaii County	38
Kalaoa, HI (cdp) Hawaii County	34
Ewa Beach, HI (cdp) Honolulu County	32
Holualoa, HI (cdp) Hawaii County	31
Kualapuu, HI (cdp) Maui County	31
Waimanalo, HI (cdp) Honolulu County	31
Waipahu, HI (cdp) Honolulu County	31
Makawao, HI (cdp) Maui County	29
Phoenix, AZ (city) Maricopa County	29
Waipio, HI (cdp) Honolulu County	28
Aiea, HI (cdp) Honolulu County	26
Hauula, HI (cdp) Honolulu County	25
Waihee-Waiehu, HI (cdp) Maui County	22
Hawaiian Ocean View, HI (cdp) Hawaii County	21
Kapaa, HI (cdp) Kauai County	20
Kaaawa, HI (cdp) Honolulu County	18
Halawa, HI (cdp) Honolulu County	15
Paia, HI (cdp) Maui County	14
Waikoloa Village, HI (cdp) Hawaii County	14
Kahuku, HI (cdp) Honolulu County	12
Kekaha, HI (cdp) Kauai County	12
Captain Cook, HI (cdp) Hawaii County	11
Haleiwa, HI (cdp) Honolulu County	11
Kaunakakai, HI (cdp) Maui County	11
Hanapepe, HI (cdp) Kauai County	10
Lahaina, HI (cdp) Maui County	10
Makaha Valley, HI (cdp) Honolulu County	10
Waimea, HI (cdp) Kauai County	10
Hana, HI (cdp) Maui County	9
Waikane, HI (cdp) Honolulu County	8
Maili, HI (cdp) Honolulu County	7
Honaunau-Napoopoo, HI (cdp) Hawaii County	6
Punaluu, HI (cdp) Honolulu County	5
Honalo, HI (cdp) Hawaii County	4
Kilauea, HI (cdp) Kauai County	4
Naalehu, HI (cdp) Hawaii County	4
Waialua, HI (cdp) Honolulu County	4
Hawaiian Beaches, HI (cdp) Hawaii County	3
Kapaau, HI (cdp) Hawaii County	3
Pahala, HI (cdp) Hawaii County	1
Pakala Village, HI (cdp) Kauai County	0

Notes: Please refer to the User's Guide for an explanation of data; ranking tables include all places with Asian and/or NHPI populations above SF4 population thresholds; (1) tables reflect only those areas that meet SF4 population thresholds, therefore there may be less than 50 states, 75 counties or 75 places listed

Educational Attainment: Four-Year College Graduates

Hawaiian Natives 25 Years and Over Who are Four-Year College Graduates

All States, Top 75 Counties, and Top 75 Places Sorted by Percent[1]

State	Percent
Massachusetts	42.31
Maryland	33.88
Virginia	33.50
Pennsylvania	29.53
Michigan	26.60
Kansas	25.88
Tennessee	24.27
New Jersey	23.37
Colorado	22.38
New York	22.26
Oregon	22.21
Montana	21.58
New Mexico	20.60
Utah	20.55
Ohio	20.49
Arizona	20.34
Wisconsin	20.34
Illinois	20.32
Missouri	19.47
Idaho	19.27
Minnesota	18.53
Oklahoma	18.27
California	18.09
Louisiana	16.81
Washington	16.45
Georgia	15.62
Texas	15.49
North Carolina	15.37
United States	15.24
Arkansas	13.84
Hawaii	12.65
South Carolina	11.94
Florida	11.90
Nevada	11.63
Alaska	9.93
Indiana	7.97

County	Percent
Multnomah County, OR	30.17
San Joaquin County, CA	27.03
Santa Clara County, CA	26.27
Contra Costa County, CA	25.63
Pima County, AZ	25.10
Salt Lake County, UT	24.65
Ventura County, CA	23.99
King County, WA	22.90
Washington County, OR	21.43
Snohomish County, WA	21.38
San Mateo County, CA	19.37
Orange County, CA	18.44
Utah County, UT	17.81
Los Angeles County, CA	17.03
Alameda County, CA	16.63
San Diego County, CA	16.58
Maricopa County, AZ	15.71
Riverside County, CA	14.89
San Bernardino County, CA	14.73
Honolulu County, HI	14.09
Sacramento County, CA	13.46
Bexar County, TX	12.54
Clark County, NV	12.18
Hawaii County, HI	11.56
Pierce County, WA	11.15
Kauai County, HI	9.91
Maui County, HI	8.67
Solano County, CA	5.75

Place	Percent
Laie, HI (cdp) Honolulu County	38.27
Portland, OR (city) Multnomah County	30.73
Mililani Town, HI (cdp) Honolulu County	24.73
Ahuimanu, HI (cdp) Honolulu County	23.50
New York, NY (city)	23.50
San Diego, CA (city) San Diego County	22.28
Volcano, HI (cdp) Hawaii County	21.23
Makakilo City, HI (cdp) Honolulu County	19.89
San Jose, CA (city) Santa Clara County	19.83
Honolulu, HI (cdp) Honolulu County	19.46
Los Angeles, CA (city) Los Angeles County	18.60
Waimalu, HI (cdp) Honolulu County	17.88
Hawaiian Ocean View, HI (cdp) Hawaii County	17.80
Henderson, NV (city) Clark County	17.68
Pearl City, HI (cdp) Honolulu County	15.12
Kailua, HI (cdp) Honolulu County	14.63
Wahiawa, HI (cdp) Honolulu County	14.52
Kaneohe, HI (cdp) Honolulu County	14.00
Las Vegas, NV (city) Clark County	13.88
Kailua, HI (cdp) Hawaii County	13.62
Wailuku, HI (cdp) Maui County	13.32
Kahuku, HI (cdp) Honolulu County	13.19
Holualoa, HI (cdp) Hawaii County	13.03
Kaaawa, HI (cdp) Honolulu County	12.86
Hilo, HI (cdp) Hawaii County	12.70
Hawaiian Paradise Park, HI (cdp) Hawaii County	12.58
Waipio, HI (cdp) Honolulu County	12.33
Kihei, HI (cdp) Maui County	11.97
Paradise, NV (cdp) Clark County	11.76
Hanapepe, HI (cdp) Kauai County	11.24
Makaha, HI (cdp) Honolulu County	11.05
Phoenix, AZ (city) Maricopa County	11.03
Kahaluu, HI (cdp) Honolulu County	10.95
Aiea, HI (cdp) Honolulu County	10.79
Paia, HI (cdp) Maui County	10.77
Waikane, HI (cdp) Honolulu County	10.53
Makawao, HI (cdp) Maui County	9.90
Kahului, HI (cdp) Maui County	9.61
Kalaoa, HI (cdp) Hawaii County	9.32
Waimea, HI (cdp) Kauai County	8.85
Haleiwa, HI (cdp) Honolulu County	8.66
Waimanalo Beach, HI (cdp) Honolulu County	8.56
Makaha Valley, HI (cdp) Honolulu County	8.40
Captain Cook, HI (cdp) Hawaii County	8.33
Waimea, HI (cdp) Hawaii County	8.21
Waikoloa Village, HI (cdp) Hawaii County	8.14
Anahola, HI (cdp) Kauai County	7.94
Kilauea, HI (cdp) Kauai County	7.55
Waimanalo, HI (cdp) Honolulu County	7.13
Punaluu, HI (cdp) Honolulu County	6.94
Kekaha, HI (cdp) Kauai County	6.70
Hauula, HI (cdp) Honolulu County	6.25
Hana, HI (cdp) Maui County	6.04
Waianae, HI (cdp) Honolulu County	5.99
Kualapuu, HI (cdp) Maui County	5.96
Ewa Beach, HI (cdp) Honolulu County	5.89
Naalehu, HI (cdp) Hawaii County	5.80
Waialua, HI (cdp) Honolulu County	5.71
Waipahu, HI (cdp) Honolulu County	5.44
Kapaau, HI (cdp) Hawaii County	5.26
Kapaa, HI (cdp) Kauai County	4.95
Waihee-Waiehu, HI (cdp) Maui County	4.24
Honalo, HI (cdp) Hawaii County	3.85
Nanakuli, HI (cdp) Honolulu County	3.71
Honaunau-Napoopoo, HI (cdp) Hawaii County	3.17
Halawa, HI (cdp) Honolulu County	2.90
Kaunakakai, HI (cdp) Maui County	2.88
Pahala, HI (cdp) Hawaii County	2.33
Lahaina, HI (cdp) Maui County	1.86
Hawaiian Beaches, HI (cdp) Hawaii County	1.47
Maili, HI (cdp) Honolulu County	1.08
Pakala Village, HI (cdp) Kauai County	0.00

Notes: Please refer to the User's Guide for an explanation of data; ranking tables include all places with Asian and/or NHPI populations above SF4 population thresholds; (1) tables reflect only those areas that meet SF4 population thresholds, therefore there may be less than 50 states, 75 counties or 75 places listed

Educational Attainment: Four-Year College Graduates

Hmongs 25 Years and Over Who are Four-Year College Graduates

All States, Top 75 Counties, and Top 75 Places Sorted by Number[1]

State	Number
United States	4,053
California	1,398
Minnesota	1,176
Wisconsin	698
Colorado	140
Michigan	138
North Carolina	77
Washington	58
Georgia	51
Rhode Island	38
Oregon	36
Kansas	17
South Carolina	13
Massachusetts	9
Alaska	7
Oklahoma	6
Pennsylvania	5

County	Number
Ramsey County, MN	701
Fresno County, CA	502
Hennepin County, MN	301
Sacramento County, CA	284
Milwaukee County, WI	210
Adams County, CO	117
Merced County, CA	86
San Joaquin County, CA	85
Washington County, MN	83
San Diego County, CA	71
Dane County, WI	65
Sheboygan County, WI	61
Orange County, CA	57
Butte County, CA	56
Eau Claire County, WI	55
Marathon County, WI	53
Yuba County, CA	52
Winnebago County, WI	50
Outagamie County, WI	49
Macomb County, MI	43
King County, WA	38
Providence County, RI	38
La Crosse County, WI	36
Oakland County, MI	34
Yolo County, CA	32
Anoka County, MN	24
Brown County, WI	22
Ingham County, MI	20
Manitowoc County, WI	20
Catawba County, NC	18
Wayne County, MI	18
Calumet County, WI	17
Tulare County, CA	17
Olmsted County, MN	16
Chippewa County, WI	15
Jefferson County, CO	14
Multnomah County, OR	13
Santa Barbara County, CA	12
Spokane County, WA	12
Dunn County, WI	11
Stanly County, NC	11
Burke County, NC	10
Solano County, CA	9
Mecklenburg County, NC	8
Anchorage Borough, AK	7
Spartanburg County, SC	6
Wyandotte County, KS	6
Lancaster County, PA	5
Los Angeles County, CA	4
Wood County, WI	4
Portage County, WI	3
Stanislaus County, CA	2
Barrow County, GA	0
Fond du Lac County, WI	0
Glenn County, CA	0
Riverside County, CA	0
Worcester County, MA	0

Place	Number
St. Paul, MN (city) Ramsey County	592
Fresno, CA (city) Fresno County	385
Sacramento, CA (city) Sacramento County	175
Minneapolis, MN (city) Hennepin County	165
Milwaukee, WI (city) Milwaukee County	153
Brooklyn Center, MN (city) Hennepin County	98
San Diego, CA (city) San Diego County	64
Merced, CA (city) Merced County	63
Sheboygan, WI (city) Sheboygan County	61
Stockton, CA (city) San Joaquin County	60
Clovis, CA (city) Fresno County	57
Appleton, WI (city) Outagamie County	56
Madison, WI (city) Dane County	56
Eau Claire, WI (city) Eau Claire County	55
Maplewood, MN (city) Ramsey County	55
Westminster, CO (city) Adams County	48
Arden-Arcade, CA (cdp) Sacramento County	46
Providence, RI (city) Providence County	38
Wausau, WI (city) Marathon County	36
Linda, CA (cdp) Yuba County	34
Warren, MI (city) Macomb County	34
Oshkosh, WI (city) Winnebago County	32
West Sacramento, CA (city) Yolo County	27
Pontiac, MI (city) Oakland County	25
Lansing, MI (city) Ingham County	20
Woodbury, MN (city) Washington County	19
Manitowoc, WI (city) Manitowoc County	16
Rochester, MN (city) Olmsted County	16
Atwater, CA (city) Merced County	15
Santa Ana, CA (city) Orange County	15
Detroit, MI (city) Wayne County	12
Thermalito, CA (cdp) Butte County	10
Charlotte, NC (city) Mecklenburg County	8
La Crosse, WI (city) La Crosse County	8
Parkway-S. Sacramento, CA (cdp) Sacramento County	8
Chico, CA (city) Butte County	7
Green Bay, WI (city) Brown County	6
Kansas City, KS (city) Wyandotte County	6
Oroville, CA (city) Butte County	6
South Oroville, CA (cdp) Butte County	6
Spokane, WA (city) Spokane County	6
Visalia, CA (city) Tulare County	6
Brooklyn Park, MN (city) Hennepin County	5
Florin, CA (cdp) Sacramento County	4
Wisconsin Rapids, WI (city) Wood County	4
Stevens Point, WI (city) Portage County	3
Valdese, NC (town) Burke County	2
Connelly Springs, NC (town) Burke County	1
Fitchburg, MA (city) Worcester County	0
Fond du Lac, WI (city) Fond du Lac County	0
Glen Alpine, NC (town) Burke County	0
Hickory, NC (city) Catawba County	0
Modesto, CA (city) Stanislaus County	0
Portland, OR (city) Multnomah County	0
Willows, CA (city) Glenn County	0

Notes: Please refer to the User's Guide for an explanation of data; ranking tables include all places with Asian and/or NHPI populations above SF4 population thresholds; (1) tables reflect only those areas that meet SF4 population thresholds, therefore there may be less than 50 states, 75 counties or 75 places listed

Educational Attainment: Four-Year College Graduates

Hmongs 25 Years and Over Who are Four-Year College Graduates

All States, Top 75 Counties, and Top 75 Places Sorted by Percent[1]

State	Percent
Rhode Island	13.06
Colorado	12.20
Georgia	11.33
Washington	10.74
Minnesota	8.49
Oregon	8.45
Michigan	7.47
United States	7.47
Wisconsin	7.16
California	6.54
Kansas	5.43
Oklahoma	4.92
South Carolina	4.00
Alaska	3.63
North Carolina	3.56
Massachusetts	2.76
Pennsylvania	1.72

County	Percent
Washington County, MN	28.52
Yolo County, CA	18.71
Providence County, RI	15.26
Chippewa County, WI	13.76
Adams County, CO	13.64
Calumet County, WI	13.60
Ingham County, MI	13.25
King County, WA	13.15
Eau Claire County, WI	13.06
San Diego County, CA	12.77
Orange County, CA	12.36
Jefferson County, CO	12.07
Santa Barbara County, CA	12.00
Winnebago County, WI	11.26
Stanly County, NC	10.78
Olmsted County, MN	10.26
Anoka County, MN	10.04
Macomb County, MI	9.79
Dane County, WI	8.95
Oakland County, MI	8.46
Milwaukee County, WI	8.20
Ramsey County, MN	7.99
Dunn County, WI	7.80
Sheboygan County, WI	7.76
Hennepin County, MN	7.48
Butte County, CA	7.38
Fresno County, CA	6.74
La Crosse County, WI	6.43
Yuba County, CA	6.31
Outagamie County, WI	6.19
Solano County, CA	6.04
Manitowoc County, WI	6.01
Mecklenburg County, NC	5.48
Sacramento County, CA	5.43
Spokane County, WA	5.43
Tulare County, CA	5.15
San Joaquin County, CA	4.49
Marathon County, WI	4.41
Merced County, CA	4.30
Multnomah County, OR	4.04
Los Angeles County, CA	3.88
Anchorage Borough, AK	3.63
Wayne County, MI	3.46
Lancaster County, PA	2.96
Catawba County, NC	2.88
Brown County, WI	2.81
Wood County, WI	2.56
Wyandotte County, KS	2.33
Spartanburg County, SC	2.03
Burke County, NC	1.75
Portage County, WI	1.40
Stanislaus County, CA	0.71
Barrow County, GA	0.00
Fond du Lac County, WI	0.00
Glenn County, CA	0.00
Riverside County, CA	0.00
Worcester County, MA	0.00

Place	Percent
Arden-Arcade, CA (cdp) Sacramento County	40.35
Maplewood, MN (city) Ramsey County	33.13
Providence, RI (city) Providence County	22.09
Brooklyn Center, MN (city) Hennepin County	21.35
West Sacramento, CA (city) Yolo County	16.27
Woodbury, MN (city) Washington County	15.32
San Diego, CA (city) San Diego County	15.27
Westminster, CO (city) Adams County	13.52
Eau Claire, WI (city) Eau Claire County	12.44
Lansing, MI (city) Ingham County	12.35
Oshkosh, WI (city) Winnebago County	10.85
Warren, MI (city) Macomb County	10.69
Atwater, CA (city) Merced County	10.56
Rochester, MN (city) Olmsted County	10.26
Madison, WI (city) Dane County	9.74
Clovis, CA (city) Fresno County	9.11
Pontiac, MI (city) Oakland County	8.77
Sheboygan, WI (city) Sheboygan County	8.08
Appleton, WI (city) Outagamie County	7.23
St. Paul, MN (city) Ramsey County	7.08
Thermalito, CA (cdp) Butte County	6.76
Santa Ana, CA (city) Orange County	6.33
Milwaukee, WI (city) Milwaukee County	6.27
Oroville, CA (city) Butte County	6.19
Fresno, CA (city) Fresno County	6.14
Linda, CA (cdp) Yuba County	5.98
Valdese, NC (town) Burke County	5.56
Manitowoc, WI (city) Manitowoc County	5.52
Charlotte, NC (city) Mecklenburg County	5.48
Minneapolis, MN (city) Hennepin County	5.43
Merced, CA (city) Merced County	5.02
Sacramento, CA (city) Sacramento County	4.80
Spokane, WA (city) Spokane County	4.11
Visalia, CA (city) Tulare County	3.95
Stockton, CA (city) San Joaquin County	3.94
South Oroville, CA (cdp) Butte County	3.87
Connelly Springs, NC (town) Burke County	3.85
Wausau, WI (city) Marathon County	3.60
Chico, CA (city) Butte County	3.23
Wisconsin Rapids, WI (city) Wood County	3.10
Detroit, MI (city) Wayne County	2.70
Kansas City, KS (city) Wyandotte County	2.33
La Crosse, WI (city) La Crosse County	2.13
Florin, CA (cdp) Sacramento County	1.76
Brooklyn Park, MN (city) Hennepin County	1.69
Stevens Point, WI (city) Portage County	1.64
Parkway-S. Sacramento, CA (cdp) Sacramento County	0.98
Green Bay, WI (city) Brown County	0.92
Fitchburg, MA (city) Worcester County	0.00
Fond du Lac, WI (city) Fond du Lac County	0.00
Glen Alpine, NC (town) Burke County	0.00
Hickory, NC (city) Catawba County	0.00
Modesto, CA (city) Stanislaus County	0.00
Portland, OR (city) Multnomah County	0.00
Willows, CA (city) Glenn County	0.00

Notes: Please refer to the User's Guide for an explanation of data; ranking tables include all places with Asian and/or NHPI populations above SF4 population thresholds; (1) tables reflect only those areas that meet SF4 population thresholds, therefore there may be less than 50 states, 75 counties or 75 places listed

Educational Attainment: Four-Year College Graduates

Indonesians 25 Years and Over Who are Four-Year College Graduates

All States, Top 75 Counties, and Top 75 Places Sorted by Number[1]

State	Number
United States	10,852
California	4,333
Texas	722
New York	698
Illinois	408
Washington	379
New Jersey	373
Maryland	321
Virginia	318
Ohio	297
Florida	269
Michigan	246
Colorado	240
Arizona	186
Massachusetts	172
Oregon	169
Pennsylvania	160
Georgia	147
Wisconsin	137

County	Number
Los Angeles County, CA	1,542
San Bernardino County, CA	834
Orange County, CA	394
Queens County, NY	332
San Francisco County, CA	305
Harris County, TX	263
King County, WA	263
Montgomery County, MD	243
Cook County, IL	240
Santa Clara County, CA	218
San Mateo County, CA	203
Alameda County, CA	192
Contra Costa County, CA	176
San Diego County, CA	163
Middlesex County, NJ	148
Maricopa County, AZ	147
Fairfax County, VA	105
Franklin County, OH	66

Place	Number
Los Angeles, CA (city) Los Angeles County	531
New York, NY (city)	461
San Francisco, CA (city) San Francisco County	305
Houston, TX (city) Harris County	234
Seattle, WA (city) King County	133
Loma Linda, CA (city) San Bernardino County	129
Columbus, OH (city) Franklin County	59
San Bernardino, CA (city) San Bernardino County	49

Notes: Please refer to the User's Guide for an explanation of data; ranking tables include all places with Asian and/or NHPI populations above SF4 population thresholds; (1) tables reflect only those areas that meet SF4 population thresholds, therefore there may be less than 50 states, 75 counties or 75 places listed

Educational Attainment: Four-Year College Graduates

Indonesians 25 Years and Over Who are Four-Year College Graduates

All States, Top 75 Counties, and Top 75 Places Sorted by Percent[1]

State	Percent
Michigan	70.89
Wisconsin	69.90
Texas	65.58
Ohio	64.85
Illinois	62.10
Colorado	52.52
Oregon	52.48
New Jersey	52.09
Washington	50.13
Massachusetts	47.78
Virginia	47.39
Arizona	47.21
United States	46.60
Pennsylvania	44.69
New York	44.37
Maryland	43.03
California	41.76
Georgia	39.41
Florida	38.93

County	Percent
Cook County, IL	69.77
San Francisco County, CA	61.74
Franklin County, OH	59.46
Harris County, TX	56.20
King County, WA	53.35
Santa Clara County, CA	51.66
Alameda County, CA	50.79
Maricopa County, AZ	49.00
San Diego County, CA	48.66
Contra Costa County, CA	47.44
San Mateo County, CA	47.32
Middlesex County, NJ	45.12
Los Angeles County, CA	43.56
Queens County, NY	43.23
San Bernardino County, CA	41.45
Montgomery County, MD	37.73
Orange County, CA	32.22
Fairfax County, VA	32.21

Place	Percent
Seattle, WA (city) King County	71.89
Houston, TX (city) Harris County	69.03
Columbus, OH (city) Franklin County	65.56
San Francisco, CA (city) San Francisco County	61.74
Loma Linda, CA (city) San Bernardino County	46.24
Los Angeles, CA (city) Los Angeles County	44.96
New York, NY (city)	39.07
San Bernardino, CA (city) San Bernardino County	27.07

Notes: Please refer to the User's Guide for an explanation of data; ranking tables include all places with Asian and/or NHPI populations above SF4 population thresholds; (1) tables reflect only those areas that meet SF4 population thresholds, therefore there may be less than 50 states, 75 counties or 75 places listed

Educational Attainment: Four-Year College Graduates

Japanese 25 Years and Over Who are Four-Year College Graduates

All States, Top 75 Counties, and Top 75 Places Sorted by Number[1]

State	Number
United States	265,248
California	101,844
Hawaii	53,422
New York	17,358
Washington	12,423
Illinois	8,161
New Jersey	5,999
Texas	5,350
Massachusetts	4,851
Michigan	4,421
Colorado	4,121
Oregon	3,924
Virginia	3,549
Maryland	3,381
Ohio	3,257
Florida	2,928
Georgia	2,672
Pennsylvania	2,605
Arizona	2,345
North Carolina	1,894
Connecticut	1,813
Indiana	1,624
Minnesota	1,593
Nevada	1,583
Utah	1,540
Tennessee	1,321
Wisconsin	1,133
Missouri	1,120
Kentucky	1,047
New Mexico	735
Idaho	712
Kansas	601
District of Columbia	599
South Carolina	575
Oklahoma	552
Alaska	539
Alabama	510
Iowa	465
Louisiana	397
Nebraska	325
New Hampshire	321
Rhode Island	279
Montana	212
Arkansas	201
West Virginia	193
Maine	170
Mississippi	127
Delaware	126
Vermont	115
Wyoming	112
South Dakota	78

County	Number
Honolulu County, HI	44,309
Los Angeles County, CA	37,577
Santa Clara County, CA	11,636
Orange County, CA	11,145
King County, WA	8,749
New York County, NY	7,848
San Diego County, CA	5,797
Cook County, IL	5,627
Alameda County, CA	5,171
Hawaii County, HI	4,727
San Francisco County, CA	4,445
Sacramento County, CA	4,155
San Mateo County, CA	4,101
Contra Costa County, CA	3,505
Westchester County, NY	3,380
Bergen County, NJ	3,078
Maui County, HI	2,878
Middlesex County, MA	2,055
Queens County, NY	2,033
Oakland County, MI	1,914
Montgomery County, MD	1,899
Ventura County, CA	1,894
Fresno County, CA	1,891
Maricopa County, AZ	1,702
Kauai County, HI	1,508
Harris County, TX	1,430
Fairfax County, VA	1,417
Multnomah County, OR	1,409
San Bernardino County, CA	1,262
Clark County, NV	1,187
Riverside County, CA	1,181
Washington County, OR	1,083
Fairfield County, CT	1,050
Norfolk County, MA	1,038
Franklin County, OH	1,003
Washtenaw County, MI	969
Kings County, NY	968
Dallas County, TX	944
Salt Lake County, UT	936
Marin County, CA	928
Suffolk County, MA	895
Snohomish County, WA	888
San Joaquin County, CA	834
Nassau County, NY	798
Monterey County, CA	791
DuPage County, IL	777
Jefferson County, CO	743
Pierce County, WA	741
Arlington County, VA	730
Denver County, CO	730
Hennepin County, MN	712
Boulder County, CO	659
Santa Barbara County, CA	641
Arapahoe County, CO	620
Hudson County, NJ	593
Placer County, CA	584
Allegheny County, PA	583
DeKalb County, GA	544
Lake County, IL	535
St. Louis County, MO	535
Yolo County, CA	528
Santa Cruz County, CA	519
Cuyahoga County, OH	513
Travis County, TX	513
Miami-Dade County, FL	511
Sonoma County, CA	497
Philadelphia County, PA	480
New Haven County, CT	451
Fulton County, GA	446
Dane County, WI	439
Wayne County, MI	434
Collin County, TX	429
Pima County, AZ	428
Bernalillo County, NM	425
Lane County, OR	423

Place	Number
Honolulu, HI (cdp) Honolulu County	24,030
Los Angeles, CA (city) Los Angeles County	11,180
New York, NY (city)	11,154
Torrance, CA (city) Los Angeles County	4,718
San Jose, CA (city) Santa Clara County	4,540
San Francisco, CA (city) San Francisco County	4,445
San Diego, CA (city) San Diego County	3,579
Seattle, WA (city) King County	3,563
Hilo, HI (cdp) Hawaii County	2,952
Waimalu, HI (cdp) Honolulu County	2,548
Chicago, IL (city) Cook County	2,470
Kaneohe, HI (cdp) Honolulu County	2,281
Mililani Town, HI (cdp) Honolulu County	2,270
Sacramento, CA (city) Sacramento County	2,230
Irvine, CA (city) Orange County	2,044
Pearl City, HI (cdp) Honolulu County	1,952
Sunnyvale, CA (city) Santa Clara County	1,595
Gardena, CA (city) Los Angeles County	1,485
Kailua, HI (cdp) Honolulu County	1,474
Rancho Palos Verdes, CA (city) Los Angeles County	1,435
Bellevue, WA (city) King County	1,330
Monterey Park, CA (city) Los Angeles County	1,281
Portland, OR (city) Multnomah County	1,230
Huntington Beach, CA (city) Orange County	1,218
Oakland, CA (city) Alameda County	1,135
Long Beach, CA (city) Los Angeles County	1,082
Pasadena, CA (city) Los Angeles County	1,074
Cupertino, CA (city) Santa Clara County	1,044
Houston, TX (city) Harris County	1,038
Fresno, CA (city) Fresno County	987
Redondo Beach, CA (city) Los Angeles County	972
Greenburgh, NY (town) Westchester County	926
Berkeley, CA (city) Alameda County	922
Waipio, HI (cdp) Honolulu County	911
Fort Lee, NJ (borough) Bergen County	907
Mountain View, CA (city) Santa Clara County	882
Boston, MA (city) Suffolk County	878
Aiea, HI (cdp) Honolulu County	874
Santa Monica, CA (city) Los Angeles County	802
Brookline, MA (town) Norfolk County	765
Arlington, VA (cdp) Arlington County	730
Denver, CO (city) Denver County	730
Fremont, CA (city) Alameda County	728
San Mateo, CA (city) San Mateo County	713
Foster City, CA (city) San Mateo County	709
Cambridge, MA (city) Middlesex County	708
Ann Arbor, MI (city) Washtenaw County	707
Anaheim, CA (city) Orange County	681
Wailuku, HI (cdp) Maui County	669
Glendale, CA (city) Los Angeles County	657
Cerritos, CA (city) Los Angeles County	654
Santa Clara, CA (city) Santa Clara County	646
Palo Alto, CA (city) Santa Clara County	628
Montebello, CA (city) Los Angeles County	623
Columbus, OH (city) Franklin County	613
Wahiawa, HI (cdp) Honolulu County	604
Kahului, HI (cdp) Maui County	562
El Cerrito, CA (city) Contra Costa County	551
Phoenix, AZ (city) Maricopa County	537
Eastchester, NY (town) Westchester County	533
Ahuimanu, HI (cdp) Honolulu County	532
Chula Vista, CA (city) San Diego County	532
Halawa, HI (cdp) Honolulu County	529
Alhambra, CA (city) Los Angeles County	524
Greenwich, CT (town) Fairfield County	522
South Pasadena, CA (city) Los Angeles County	522
Novi, MI (city) Oakland County	521
West Bloomfield, MI (township) Oakland County	516
Hacienda Heights, CA (cdp) Los Angeles County	509
Arlington Heights, IL (village) Cook County	499
Culver City, CA (city) Los Angeles County	484
Philadelphia, PA (city) Philadelphia County	480
Thousand Oaks, CA (city) Ventura County	478
Arcadia, CA (city) Los Angeles County	477
Austin, TX (city) Travis County	475

Notes: Please refer to the User's Guide for an explanation of data; ranking tables include all places with Asian and/or NHPI populations above SF4 population thresholds; (1) tables reflect only those areas that meet SF4 population thresholds, therefore there may be less than 50 states, 75 counties or 75 places listed

Educational Attainment: Four-Year College Graduates

Japanese 25 Years and Over Who are Four-Year College Graduates

All States, Top 75 Counties, and Top 75 Places Sorted by Percent[1]

State	Percent
District of Columbia	75.54
Massachusetts	67.82
Connecticut	62.39
Maryland	61.32
New York	60.75
Michigan	58.79
New Jersey	57.30
Iowa	54.13
Minnesota	52.71
Pennsylvania	51.76
Virginia	51.19
Vermont	50.66
Tennessee	50.61
Illinois	50.39
New Hampshire	50.31
Wisconsin	49.71
Indiana	49.30
Rhode Island	48.52
Georgia	48.26
Kentucky	46.91
Oregon	45.94
Alaska	45.60
Kansas	45.60
Ohio	45.55
Texas	44.01
California	43.63
Colorado	43.19
Washington	43.17
New Mexico	42.98
Missouri	42.49
United States	41.87
North Carolina	41.45
West Virginia	40.38
Maine	39.44
Arizona	38.81
Alabama	37.50
Louisiana	36.96
South Dakota	36.11
Utah	35.88
Montana	35.04
Idaho	33.60
Nebraska	32.53
South Carolina	31.75
Florida	31.68
Hawaii	31.33
Oklahoma	29.22
Mississippi	28.86
Wyoming	26.73
Delaware	25.20
Nevada	23.33
Arkansas	23.21

County	Percent
Tompkins County, NY	85.32
Washtenaw County, MI	85.30
Tippecanoe County, IN	83.85
Champaign County, IL	81.48
Orange County, NC	81.44
Hudson County, NJ	78.54
Norfolk County, MA	75.99
Olmsted County, MN	75.93
Suffolk County, MA	75.85
New Haven County, CT	74.67
DeKalb County, GA	74.62
Montgomery County, MD	73.78
Middlesex County, MA	73.31
Ingham County, MI	72.91
Arlington County, VA	72.64
Mercer County, NJ	71.82
Durham County, NC	70.87
Dane County, WI	70.47
Boulder County, CO	69.81
Whitman County, WA	69.35
Onondaga County, NY	68.97
Westchester County, NY	68.57
Napa County, CA	67.41
Allegheny County, PA	66.40
Middlesex County, NJ	66.34
New York County, NY	66.21
Fairfield County, CT	65.95
Fulton County, GA	65.49
Boone County, KY	64.67
Fairfax County, VA	64.61
Morris County, NJ	64.57
Somerset County, NJ	64.54
Wake County, NC	64.15
Benton County, OR	64.04
Marin County, CA	63.96
Baltimore County, MD	63.91
Oakland County, MI	63.89
DuPage County, IL	63.12
Davidson County, TN	63.04
Bergen County, NJ	61.96
Collin County, TX	60.59
Ramsey County, MN	60.05
Montgomery County, PA	59.34
Delaware County, PA	59.08
Philadelphia County, PA	59.04
Kings County, NY	58.70
Cobb County, GA	58.54
Yolo County, CA	57.33
Hamilton County, OH	56.85
Cuyahoga County, OH	56.69
St. Louis County, MO	56.55
Washington County, OR	56.52
Travis County, TX	56.31
Nassau County, NY	56.24
Summit County, OH	55.91
Bronx County, NY	55.69
Monroe County, NY	55.69
Hennepin County, MN	55.41
Dallas County, TX	54.88
Harris County, TX	54.11
Lane County, OR	53.27
Santa Clara County, CA	53.00
San Mateo County, CA	52.64
Mecklenburg County, NC	52.55
Contra Costa County, CA	52.38
Wayne County, MI	51.73
Gwinnett County, GA	51.58
Alameda County, CA	51.54
Johnson County, KS	51.40
Erie County, NY	50.49
Lake County, IL	50.42
Queens County, NY	50.26
Alachua County, FL	50.00
Franklin County, OH	49.85
Shelby County, TN	49.33

Place	Percent
North Bethesda, MD (cdp) Montgomery County	89.91
Cambridge, MA (city) Middlesex County	88.39
Ann Arbor, MI (city) Washtenaw County	86.96
Ridgewood, NJ (village) Bergen County	86.46
Brookline, MA (town) Norfolk County	85.28
Palos Verdes Estates, CA (city) Los Angeles County	83.83
Boulder, CO (city) Boulder County	82.89
Rockville, MD (city) Montgomery County	81.48
McLean, VA (cdp) Fairfax County	81.36
San Ramon, CA (city) Contra Costa County	80.35
Eastchester, NY (cdp) Westchester County	79.71
Bethesda, MD (cdp) Montgomery County	79.04
Davis, CA (city) Yolo County	77.58
Boston, MA (city) Suffolk County	76.22
La Canada Flintridge, CA (city) Los Angeles County	76.05
Greenville, NY (cdp) Westchester County	75.47
Cary, NC (town) Wake County	74.48
Rye, NY (city) Westchester County	73.63
Pittsburgh, PA (city) Allegheny County	73.48
Madison, WI (city) Dane County	73.10
Arlington, VA (cdp) Arlington County	72.64
Evanston, IL (city) Cook County	72.16
Beaverton, OR (city) Washington County	71.37
Greenburgh, NY (town) Westchester County	71.12
Scarsdale, NY (village) Westchester County	70.10
Saratoga, CA (city) Santa Clara County	70.00
Greenwich, CT (town) Fairfield County	69.79
Pullman, WA (city) Whitman County	69.04
Albany, CA (city) Alameda County	68.62
Harrison, NY (village) Westchester County	68.47
Irving, TX (city) Dallas County	68.41
Wilmette, IL (village) Cook County	67.94
Fort Lee, NJ (borough) Bergen County	67.89
Rancho Palos Verdes, CA (city) Los Angeles County	67.43
Novi, MI (city) Oakland County	67.40
South Pasadena, CA (city) Los Angeles County	67.27
Newcastle, WA (city) King County	67.06
Eastchester, NY (town) Westchester County	66.63
Thousand Oaks, CA (city) Ventura County	66.57
Foster City, CA (city) San Mateo County	66.51
West Bloomfield, MI (township) Oakland County	65.57
Menlo Park, CA (city) San Mateo County	65.00
Millbrae, CA (city) San Mateo County	64.82
Rolling Hills Estates, CA (city) Los Angeles County	64.54
Manhattan Beach, CA (city) Los Angeles County	64.53
Arlington Heights, IL (village) Cook County	63.57
Nashville-Davidson, TN (sp. city) Davidson County	63.02
Palo Alto, CA (city) Santa Clara County	62.74
Cupertino, CA (city) Santa Clara County	62.67
Belmont, CA (city) San Mateo County	62.20
Irvine, CA (city) Orange County	62.18
Walnut Creek, CA (city) Contra Costa County	62.11
Houston, TX (city) Harris County	62.01
Seal Beach, CA (city) Orange County	61.81
New York, NY (city)	61.56
Elk Grove, CA (cdp) Sacramento County	61.37
North Hempstead, NY (town) Nassau County	61.17
Plano, TX (city) Collin County	61.13
Oakland, CA (city) Alameda County	60.86
Mercer Island, WA (city) King County	60.23
Oyster Bay, NY (town) Nassau County	60.07
Eugene, OR (city) Lane County	59.92
Aliso Viejo, CA (cdp) Orange County	59.83
Cliffside Park, NJ (borough) Bergen County	59.77
Arcadia, CA (city) Los Angeles County	59.70
Dallas, TX (city) Dallas County	59.65
Arden-Arcade, CA (cdp) Sacramento County	59.42
Elk Grove Village, IL (village) Cook County	59.29
Redondo Beach, CA (city) Los Angeles County	59.12
Buffalo Grove, IL (village) Lake County	59.09
Philadelphia, PA (city) Philadelphia County	59.04
Laguna Niguel, CA (city) Orange County	59.03
Minneapolis, MN (city) Hennepin County	59.01
Redmond, WA (city) King County	58.56
Bellevue, WA (city) King County	58.46

Notes: Please refer to the User's Guide for an explanation of data; ranking tables include all places with Asian and/or NHPI populations above SF4 population thresholds; (1) tables reflect only those areas that meet SF4 population thresholds, therefore there may be less than 50 states, 75 counties or 75 places listed

Educational Attainment: Four-Year College Graduates

Koreans 25 Years and Over Who are Four-Year College Graduates

All States, Top 75 Counties, and Top 75 Places Sorted by Number[1]

State	Number
United States	304,272
California	105,673
New York	36,570
New Jersey	21,558
Illinois	17,948
Virginia	12,394
Texas	11,444
Maryland	10,822
Washington	9,917
Pennsylvania	9,130
Georgia	6,388
Massachusetts	6,366
Michigan	5,777
Florida	4,715
Hawaii	4,445
Ohio	4,394
Colorado	3,199
Oregon	2,853
North Carolina	2,784
Arizona	2,385
Indiana	2,349
Minnesota	2,112
Connecticut	2,044
Missouri	1,950
Wisconsin	1,830
Tennessee	1,679
Nevada	1,317
Iowa	1,038
Kentucky	982
Kansas	974
Utah	916
South Carolina	911
Oklahoma	887
Alabama	842
District of Columbia	664
Rhode Island	656
Louisiana	610
Alaska	553
Delaware	468
New Hampshire	416
New Mexico	379
Nebraska	370
Idaho	297
Mississippi	261
West Virginia	230
Arkansas	209
Montana	135
Vermont	107
Maine	98
South Dakota	92
Wyoming	69
North Dakota	65

County	Number
Los Angeles County, CA	55,604
Orange County, CA	18,112
Queens County, NY	15,069
Bergen County, NJ	12,600
Cook County, IL	12,552
Fairfax County, VA	8,054
Santa Clara County, CA	7,895
New York County, NY	6,727
King County, WA	5,541
Montgomery County, MD	5,224
Alameda County, CA	4,790
Honolulu County, HI	4,090
San Diego County, CA	3,582
Nassau County, NY	3,216
San Francisco County, CA	2,985
Middlesex County, MA	2,946
Montgomery County, PA	2,802
Harris County, TX	2,494
Dallas County, TX	2,277
San Bernardino County, CA	2,244
Gwinnett County, GA	2,029
Kings County, NY	2,013
San Mateo County, CA	1,850
Philadelphia County, PA	1,823
Snohomish County, WA	1,746
Westchester County, NY	1,746
Middlesex County, NJ	1,727
Howard County, MD	1,694
Oakland County, MI	1,694
Maricopa County, AZ	1,633
Lake County, IL	1,570
Washtenaw County, MI	1,562
DuPage County, IL	1,500
Travis County, TX	1,482
Pierce County, WA	1,464
Contra Costa County, CA	1,463
Franklin County, OH	1,383
Hudson County, NJ	1,330
Riverside County, CA	1,309
Baltimore County, MD	1,301
Suffolk County, NY	1,231
Clark County, NV	1,182
Fulton County, GA	1,182
Suffolk County, MA	1,175
DeKalb County, GA	1,107
Essex County, NJ	1,084
Richmond County, NY	1,071
Champaign County, IL	1,070
Sacramento County, CA	1,000
Hennepin County, MN	999
Washington County, OR	997
Bronx County, NY	995
Norfolk County, MA	943
Collin County, TX	935
St. Louis County, MO	923
Prince George's County, MD	905
Allegheny County, PA	895
Dane County, WI	881
Tarrant County, TX	867
Morris County, NJ	865
Delaware County, PA	853
Arapahoe County, CO	852
Ventura County, CA	805
Cuyahoga County, OH	778
Hillsborough County, FL	768
Arlington County, VA	757
Cobb County, GA	753
Ingham County, MI	750
Erie County, NY	714
Rockland County, NY	712
Wake County, NC	694
Multnomah County, OR	682
Mercer County, NJ	666
New Haven County, CT	665
Fairfield County, CT	645

Place	Number
Los Angeles, CA (city) Los Angeles County	26,067
New York, NY (city)	25,875
Chicago, IL (city) Cook County	4,396
Glendale, CA (city) Los Angeles County	4,101
San Jose, CA (city) Santa Clara County	3,059
Honolulu, HI (cdp) Honolulu County	3,029
Fullerton, CA (city) Orange County	3,023
San Francisco, CA (city) San Francisco County	2,985
Irvine, CA (city) Orange County	2,948
Cerritos, CA (city) Los Angeles County	2,685
Torrance, CA (city) Los Angeles County	2,400
Fort Lee, NJ (borough) Bergen County	2,357
San Diego, CA (city) San Diego County	2,341
Anaheim, CA (city) Orange County	1,991
Diamond Bar, CA (city) Los Angeles County	1,936
Philadelphia, PA (city) Philadelphia County	1,823
Palisades Park, NJ (borough) Bergen County	1,682
Houston, TX (city) Harris County	1,654
Seattle, WA (city) King County	1,548
Buena Park, CA (city) Orange County	1,494
Austin, TX (city) Travis County	1,286
North Hempstead, NY (town) Nassau County	1,251
Boston, MA (city) Suffolk County	1,136
Garden Grove, CA (city) Orange County	1,135
Columbus, OH (city) Franklin County	1,119
Fremont, CA (city) Alameda County	1,107
Ann Arbor, MI (city) Washtenaw County	1,082
Sunnyvale, CA (city) Santa Clara County	1,032
Cambridge, MA (city) Middlesex County	995
Rowland Heights, CA (cdp) Los Angeles County	977
Dallas, TX (city) Dallas County	955
Rancho Palos Verdes, CA (city) Los Angeles County	950
Federal Way, WA (city) King County	929
Skokie, IL (village) Cook County	923
Oyster Bay, NY (town) Nassau County	921
Hempstead, NY (town) Nassau County	905
Burke, VA (cdp) Fairfax County	852
Madison, WI (city) Dane County	844
Pasadena, CA (city) Los Angeles County	839
Bellevue, WA (city) King County	803
La Mirada, CA (city) Los Angeles County	800
Santa Clara, CA (city) Santa Clara County	800
Cupertino, CA (city) Santa Clara County	794
Downey, CA (city) Los Angeles County	792
Annandale, VA (cdp) Fairfax County	777
Arlington, VA (cdp) Arlington County	757
Gardena, CA (city) Los Angeles County	756
La Canada Flintridge, CA (city) Los Angeles County	754
Plano, TX (city) Collin County	752
Hacienda Heights, CA (cdp) Los Angeles County	734
La Crescenta-Montrose, CA (cdp) Los Angeles County	704
Northbrook, IL (village) Cook County	693
Oakland, CA (city) Alameda County	693
Cypress, CA (city) Orange County	687
Burbank, CA (city) Los Angeles County	685
La Palma, CA (city) Orange County	677
Norwalk, CA (city) Los Angeles County	671
Ellicott City, MD (cdp) Howard County	663
Glenview, IL (village) Cook County	620
Walnut, CA (city) Los Angeles County	620
Cliffside Park, NJ (borough) Bergen County	610
Palo Alto, CA (city) Santa Clara County	608
Huntington Beach, CA (city) Orange County	607
Jersey City, NJ (city) Hudson County	598
Portland, OR (city) Multnomah County	597
Arcadia, CA (city) Los Angeles County	590
Schaumburg, IL (village) Cook County	562
Brookline, MA (town) Norfolk County	546
Brookhaven, NY (town) Suffolk County	538
Berkeley, CA (city) Alameda County	536
Columbia, MD (cdp) Howard County	531
Leonia, NJ (borough) Bergen County	518
Pittsburgh, PA (city) Allegheny County	510
Orange, CA (city) Orange County	506
Edison, NJ (township) Middlesex County	505

Notes: Please refer to the User's Guide for an explanation of data; ranking tables include all places with Asian and/or NHPI populations above SF4 population thresholds; (1) tables reflect only those areas that meet SF4 population thresholds, therefore there may be less than 50 states, 75 counties or 75 places listed

Educational Attainment: Four-Year College Graduates

Koreans 25 Years and Over Who are Four-Year College Graduates

***All States, Top 75 Counties, and Top 75 Places Sorted by Percent*[1]**

State	Percent
District of Columbia	82.69
Rhode Island	70.01
Massachusetts	67.02
Connecticut	57.03
Michigan	56.03
Wisconsin	55.95
Indiana	54.53
New Jersey	53.06
Illinois	52.57
Iowa	51.18
Ohio	50.51
West Virginia	48.02
Missouri	47.02
Pennsylvania	46.45
New York	45.96
Utah	45.87
California	45.51
United States	43.82
Minnesota	43.16
Maryland	42.98
New Hampshire	42.71
Idaho	41.48
Virginia	41.27
Vermont	40.68
Delaware	40.59
Montana	40.06
Texas	38.71
South Dakota	38.66
Kentucky	38.00
Oregon	37.40
Nebraska	37.11
Arizona	37.01
South Carolina	36.38
Tennessee	36.18
Florida	35.94
Georgia	35.38
New Mexico	35.22
Kansas	35.05
Louisiana	34.56
North Carolina	34.31
Washington	33.17
Colorado	32.76
Alabama	31.37
Mississippi	29.52
Oklahoma	29.47
Maine	26.78
Wyoming	26.44
North Dakota	26.42
Hawaii	24.31
Nevada	23.87
Arkansas	21.88
Alaska	17.40

County	Percent
Tompkins County, NY	98.17
Brazos County, TX	93.18
Orange County, NC	92.50
Champaign County, IL	88.72
Dane County, WI	87.06
Hampshire County, MA	86.26
Tippecanoe County, IN	86.00
Johnson County, IA	85.56
Ingham County, MI	84.27
Story County, IA	81.04
Monroe County, IN	80.53
Centre County, PA	79.63
Suffolk County, MA	79.39
New York County, NY	79.37
Benton County, OR	78.65
Washtenaw County, MI	78.45
Norfolk County, MA	77.61
Durham County, NC	77.46
Montgomery County, VA	76.45
Rensselaer County, NY	76.23
Boulder County, CO	75.84
Erie County, NY	75.56
Berrien County, MI	74.33
Alachua County, FL	73.40
Dutchess County, NY	73.33
Onondaga County, NY	73.04
Douglas County, KS	72.89
Middlesex County, MA	72.56
Clarke County, GA	71.88
Arlington County, VA	71.55
Boone County, MO	71.01
Summit County, OH	70.76
Yolo County, CA	70.39
Northampton County, PA	70.00
Allegheny County, PA	69.87
Providence County, RI	69.42
Olmsted County, MN	68.78
Kalamazoo County, MI	66.55
Somerset County, NJ	65.22
Franklin County, OH	64.93
Kent County, RI	64.79
Knox County, TN	64.60
Travis County, TX	64.58
Albany County, NY	62.57
Lake County, IL	62.52
Hamilton County, OH	62.25
New Haven County, CT	62.03
Essex County, NJ	61.56
Westchester County, NY	61.20
Larimer County, CO	60.16
Saratoga County, NY	59.51
Nassau County, NY	59.27
Cuyahoga County, OH	59.12
Fairfield County, CT	58.85
Ottawa County, MI	58.76
Oakland County, MI	58.74
Ramsey County, MN	58.70
St. Louis County, MO	58.60
Rockland County, NY	58.36
San Mateo County, CA	58.10
Morris County, NJ	57.94
Mercer County, NJ	57.71
Jefferson County, AL	57.50
Passaic County, NJ	57.35
Leon County, FL	56.75
Suffolk County, NY	56.44
Middlesex County, NJ	56.14
Collin County, TX	55.52
Essex County, MA	55.26
Santa Clara County, CA	55.03
Riley County, KS	54.92
Hudson County, NJ	54.78
Williamson County, TX	54.65
Hartford County, CT	54.62
Broome County, NY	54.30

Place	Percent
Stanford, CA (cdp) Santa Clara County	100.00
Urbana, IL (city) Champaign County	98.34
College Station, TX (city) Brazos County	96.61
Ithaca, NY (city) Tompkins County	96.10
Chapel Hill, NC (town) Orange County	94.78
Palo Alto, CA (city) Santa Clara County	94.56
Cambridge, MA (city) Middlesex County	91.87
Brookline, MA (town) Norfolk County	90.55
Madison, WI (city) Dane County	89.69
Providence, RI (city) Providence County	88.61
State College, PA (borough) Centre County	88.04
East Lansing, MI (city) Ingham County	87.08
Boulder, CO (city) Boulder County	85.56
Iowa City, IA (city) Johnson County	85.43
Amherst, NY (town) Erie County	85.24
Blacksburg, VA (town) Montgomery County	84.78
Ann Arbor, MI (city) Washtenaw County	84.66
Corvallis, OR (city) Benton County	84.54
Berkeley, CA (city) Alameda County	84.01
Champaign, IL (city) Champaign County	83.45
Pasadena, CA (city) Los Angeles County	83.23
Bloomington, IN (city) Monroe County	83.05
Pittsburgh, PA (city) Allegheny County	82.93
Boston, MA (city) Suffolk County	82.80
New Haven, CT (city) New Haven County	82.35
Evanston, IL (city) Cook County	82.22
Newton, MA (city) Middlesex County	82.01
Ames, IA (city) Story County	81.68
Syracuse, NY (city) Onondaga County	81.35
West Windsor, NJ (township) Mercer County	79.84
Palos Verdes Estates, CA (city) Los Angeles County	79.69
Davis, CA (city) Yolo County	79.43
Albany, CA (city) Alameda County	79.13
Bloomfield, MI (township) Oakland County	78.01
Rochester, MN (city) Olmsted County	77.38
Brea, CA (city) Orange County	77.30
West Bloomfield, MI (township) Oakland County	76.98
Gainesville, FL (city) Alachua County	76.79
Brookhaven, NY (town) Suffolk County	76.53
Durham, NC (city) Durham County	75.77
Louisville, KY (city) Jefferson County	75.21
Salt Lake City, UT (city) Salt Lake County	74.64
Columbia, MO (city) Boone County	74.50
Rockville, MD (city) Montgomery County	74.42
Lower Merion, PA (township) Montgomery County	74.36
Meridian charter, MI (township) Ingham County	74.23
Alpine, NJ (borough) Bergen County	73.58
Lawrence, KS (city) Douglas County	73.43
South Pasadena, CA (city) Los Angeles County	73.37
Ridgewood, NJ (village) Bergen County	73.24
Somerville, MA (city) Middlesex County	73.22
Mountain View, CA (city) Santa Clara County	73.12
Lake Success, NY (village) Nassau County	73.03
Wilmette, IL (village) Cook County	72.80
Pleasanton, CA (city) Alameda County	72.75
Clarkstown, NY (town) Rockland County	72.30
Hackensack, NJ (city) Bergen County	72.05
Athens-Clarke County, GA (sp. city) Clarke County	71.88
North Potomac, MD (cdp) Montgomery County	71.86
Arlington, VA (cdp) Arlington County	71.55
Closter, NJ (borough) Bergen County	71.28
Bethesda, MD (cdp) Montgomery County	71.18
Greenburgh, NY (town) Westchester County	70.48
Englewood Cliffs, NJ (borough) Bergen County	69.82
Pittsfield charter, MI (township) Washtenaw County	68.97
Whittier, CA (city) Los Angeles County	68.94
Edgewater, NJ (borough) Bergen County	68.84
Harrington Park, NJ (borough) Bergen County	68.38
Northbrook, IL (village) Cook County	68.34
Jericho, NY (cdp) Nassau County	68.22
Thousand Oaks, CA (city) Ventura County	68.21
Wayne, NJ (township) Passaic County	68.19
Columbus, OH (city) Franklin County	67.90
Irvine, CA (city) Orange County	67.63
Potomac, MD (cdp) Montgomery County	66.80

Notes: Please refer to the User's Guide for an explanation of data; ranking tables include all places with Asian and/or NHPI populations above SF4 population thresholds; (1) tables reflect only those areas that meet SF4 population thresholds, therefore there may be less than 50 states, 75 counties or 75 places listed

Educational Attainment: Four-Year College Graduates

Laotians 25 Years and Over Who are Four-Year College Graduates

All States, Top 75 Counties, and Top 75 Places Sorted by Number[1]

State	Number
United States	6,722
California	1,555
Texas	493
Minnesota	417
Illinois	331
Tennessee	323
Florida	262
Iowa	224
Washington	215
Virginia	205
Wisconsin	191
New York	190
Michigan	177
Oregon	172
Connecticut	170
Rhode Island	159
Georgia	157
Massachusetts	129
Pennsylvania	115
Colorado	110
Indiana	93
Ohio	91
Arizona	89
Nevada	85
Utah	76
Hawaii	73
Maryland	71
Kansas	70
Alabama	69
North Carolina	57
South Carolina	53
Arkansas	38
Louisiana	34
Missouri	32
New Jersey	31
Oklahoma	28
Alaska	26
New Hampshire	24
South Dakota	21
Idaho	13
Nebraska	13

County	Number
San Diego County, CA	332
Hennepin County, MN	219
Los Angeles County, CA	195
Cook County, IL	183
Tarrant County, TX	174
Sacramento County, CA	155
Providence County, RI	146
Fairfax County, VA	126
Alameda County, CA	122
Orange County, CA	120
Rutherford County, TN	118
King County, WA	115
Santa Clara County, CA	110
Dallas County, TX	101
Davidson County, TN	101
Milwaukee County, WI	92
Multnomah County, OR	92
Monroe County, NY	91
New Haven County, CT	89
Polk County, IA	87
Clark County, NV	85
Maricopa County, AZ	82
Contra Costa County, CA	75
Honolulu County, HI	73
Philadelphia County, PA	73
Salt Lake County, UT	67
Washington County, OR	65
Fresno County, CA	62
Dakota County, MN	61
San Joaquin County, CA	61
Jefferson County, CO	59
Ottawa County, MI	58
Ramsey County, MN	55
Harris County, TX	53
Worcester County, MA	53
Winnebago County, IL	52
Franklin County, OH	49
Pinellas County, FL	47
Riverside County, CA	47
Stanislaus County, CA	47
Gwinnett County, GA	46
Johnson County, KS	44
Clayton County, GA	43
Spartanburg County, SC	42
Hartford County, CT	37
Buena Vista County, IA	35
Middlesex County, MA	34
Snohomish County, WA	34
Pierce County, WA	33
Tulare County, CA	31
Broome County, NY	30
Bexar County, TX	29
Kane County, IL	29
Fairfield County, CT	27
Anchorage Borough, AK	26
Shasta County, CA	25
Polk County, FL	23
Potter County, TX	23
Sonoma County, CA	23
San Bernardino County, CA	20
Mobile County, AL	19
Dane County, WI	18
Olmsted County, MN	18
Adams County, CO	16
Mecklenburg County, NC	16
Summit County, OH	15
Merced County, CA	13
Nobles County, MN	13
Oklahoma County, OK	13
Sebastian County, AR	13
Solano County, CA	12
Washington County, AR	11
Iberia Parish, LA	9
Catawba County, NC	8
Essex County, MA	8

Place	Number
San Diego, CA (city) San Diego County	301
San Jose, CA (city) Santa Clara County	110
Nashville-Davidson, TN (sp. city) Davidson County	101
Portland, OR (city) Multnomah County	92
Murfreesboro, TN (city) Rutherford County	84
Sacramento, CA (city) Sacramento County	81
Los Angeles, CA (city) Los Angeles County	77
Philadelphia, PA (city) Philadelphia County	73
Brooklyn Park, MN (city) Hennepin County	70
Milwaukee, WI (city) Milwaukee County	70
Providence, RI (city) Providence County	67
Des Moines, IA (city) Polk County	65
Richmond, CA (city) Contra Costa County	60
Stockton, CA (city) San Joaquin County	57
Rochester, NY (city) Monroe County	50
Fresno, CA (city) Fresno County	45
Bellevue, WA (city) King County	44
Elgin, IL (city) Kane County	44
Columbus, OH (city) Franklin County	43
Anaheim, CA (city) Orange County	42
Dallas, TX (city) Dallas County	41
Springfield, VA (cdp) Fairfax County	39
St. Paul, MN (city) Ramsey County	35
Storm Lake, IA (city) Buena Vista County	35
Oakland, CA (city) Alameda County	34
Seattle, WA (city) King County	34
Arvada, CO (city) Jefferson County	31
Riverside, CA (city) Riverside County	31
Visalia, CA (city) Tulare County	31
Tacoma, WA (city) Pierce County	30
Honolulu, HI (cdp) Honolulu County	28
Irving, TX (city) Dallas County	27
Woonsocket, RI (city) Providence County	27
St. Petersburg, FL (city) Pinellas County	26
Modesto, CA (city) Stanislaus County	25
Redding, CA (city) Shasta County	25
Lowell, MA (city) Middlesex County	22
Santa Ana, CA (city) Orange County	22
Haltom City, TX (city) Tarrant County	21
Minneapolis, MN (city) Hennepin County	20
Rockford, IL (city) Winnebago County	20
Fitchburg, MA (city) Worcester County	19
Amarillo, TX (city) Potter County	18
Long Beach, CA (city) Los Angeles County	18
Santa Rosa, CA (city) Sonoma County	18
Oklahoma City, OK (city) Oklahoma County	17
Charlotte, NC (city) Mecklenburg County	16
Rochester, MN (city) Olmsted County	16
Westminster, CO (city) Adams County	16
Fort Worth, TX (city) Tarrant County	15
Parkway-S. Sacramento, CA (cdp) Sacramento County	15
Fort Smith, AR (city) Sebastian County	13
Grand Prairie, TX (city) Dallas County	13
Merced, CA (city) Merced County	13
Worthington, MN (city) Nobles County	13
Moreno Valley, CA (city) Riverside County	12
Springdale, AR (city) Washington County	12
Akron, OH (city) Summit County	7
Pomona, CA (city) Los Angeles County	7
Escondido, CA (city) San Diego County	6
Raymond, WA (city) Pacific County	6
West Valley City, UT (city) Salt Lake County	6
Fairfield, CA (city) Solano County	5
Banning, CA (city) Riverside County	4
Brooklyn Center, MN (city) Hennepin County	4
San Pablo, CA (city) Contra Costa County	4
Bridgeport, CT (city) Fairfield County	0
Green Bay, WI (city) Brown County	0
New Britain, CT (city) Hartford County	0
Oaklawn-Sunview, KS (cdp) Sedgwick County	0
Warroad, MN (city) Roseau County	0
Wichita, KS (city) Sedgwick County	0
Winfield, KS (city) Cowley County	0

Notes: Please refer to the User's Guide for an explanation of data; ranking tables include all places with Asian and/or NHPI populations above SF4 population thresholds; (1) tables reflect only those areas that meet SF4 population thresholds, therefore there may be less than 50 states, 75 counties or 75 places listed

Educational Attainment: Four-Year College Graduates

Laotians 25 Years and Over Who are Four-Year College Graduates

All States, Top 75 Counties, and Top 75 Places Sorted by Percent[1]

State	Percent
South Dakota	19.81
Arizona	16.92
Indiana	15.79
Maryland	14.85
Tennessee	13.56
Alabama	13.53
Michigan	13.21
New Jersey	11.97
Illinois	11.68
New Hampshire	11.43
Virginia	11.38
Nevada	11.23
Florida	10.78
Wisconsin	10.70
New York	10.57
Iowa	10.37
Rhode Island	9.47
Connecticut	9.36
Minnesota	9.25
Pennsylvania	9.20
Colorado	9.02
Oregon	8.81
Texas	8.71
United States	7.70
South Carolina	7.69
Hawaii	7.63
Missouri	6.82
Utah	6.82
Massachusetts	6.73
Georgia	6.09
Oklahoma	6.07
Ohio	5.86
California	5.76
Washington	5.01
Louisiana	4.91
Kansas	4.41
Alaska	4.39
Idaho	3.88
Nebraska	2.78
Arkansas	2.73
North Carolina	2.27

County	Percent
New Haven County, CT	30.48
Maricopa County, AZ	23.91
Cook County, IL	21.18
Washington County, OR	18.36
Dakota County, MN	16.14
Ramsey County, MN	14.44
Fairfax County, VA	13.71
Davidson County, TN	13.54
Broome County, NY	12.88
Bexar County, TX	12.72
Pierce County, WA	12.64
Spartanburg County, SC	12.43
Jefferson County, CO	12.16
Rutherford County, TN	12.07
Buena Vista County, IA	11.86
Monroe County, NY	11.80
Mobile County, AL	11.38
Los Angeles County, CA	11.25
Clark County, NV	11.23
Milwaukee County, WI	11.15
Philadelphia County, PA	10.90
Santa Clara County, CA	10.85
Olmsted County, MN	10.71
Dane County, WI	10.59
Polk County, FL	10.36
Johnson County, KS	10.16
Ottawa County, MI	9.75
Tarrant County, TX	9.41
Worcester County, MA	9.33
Hennepin County, MN	9.21
Polk County, IA	9.19
Providence County, RI	9.00
San Diego County, CA	8.59
Alameda County, CA	8.24
San Bernardino County, CA	8.16
Snohomish County, WA	8.13
Dallas County, TX	7.90
Honolulu County, HI	7.88
Franklin County, OH	7.68
Salt Lake County, UT	7.51
Harris County, TX	7.46
Winnebago County, IL	7.06
Orange County, CA	7.02
Gwinnett County, GA	6.98
Multnomah County, OR	6.81
Clayton County, GA	6.36
Cass County, MI	6.10
Stanislaus County, CA	5.96
Nobles County, MN	5.88
Riverside County, CA	5.72
Franklin County, WA	5.38
Kane County, IL	5.10
Hartford County, CT	5.01
Anchorage Borough, AK	4.74
Summit County, OH	4.62
Oklahoma County, OK	4.47
Fairfield County, CT	4.45
San Joaquin County, CA	4.42
Pinellas County, FL	4.40
King County, WA	4.36
Washington County, AR	4.09
Potter County, TX	4.08
Sonoma County, CA	3.95
Sacramento County, CA	3.90
Essex County, MA	3.83
Middlesex County, MA	3.76
Roseau County, MN	3.67
Contra Costa County, CA	3.56
Shasta County, CA	3.54
Catawba County, NC	3.33
Pacific County, WA	3.19
Solano County, CA	3.13
Adams County, CO	2.92
Mecklenburg County, NC	2.80
Guilford County, NC	2.72

Place	Percent
Murfreesboro, TN (city) Rutherford County	19.22
Los Angeles, CA (city) Los Angeles County	18.47
Springfield, VA (cdp) Fairfax County	18.14
Bellevue, WA (city) King County	16.73
Riverside, CA (city) Riverside County	16.23
Tacoma, WA (city) Pierce County	16.22
Arvada, CO (city) Jefferson County	14.42
Nashville-Davidson, TN (sp. city) Davidson County	13.54
Storm Lake, IA (city) Buena Vista County	12.64
San Jose, CA (city) Santa Clara County	12.11
Rochester, NY (city) Monroe County	11.85
Philadelphia, PA (city) Philadelphia County	10.90
St. Paul, MN (city) Ramsey County	10.54
Milwaukee, WI (city) Milwaukee County	9.99
Fitchburg, MA (city) Worcester County	9.95
Irving, TX (city) Dallas County	9.64
Rochester, MN (city) Olmsted County	9.64
Brooklyn Park, MN (city) Hennepin County	9.15
San Diego, CA (city) San Diego County	9.10
Anaheim, CA (city) Orange County	8.54
Providence, RI (city) Providence County	8.43
Des Moines, IA (city) Polk County	8.22
Columbus, OH (city) Franklin County	7.98
Dallas, TX (city) Dallas County	7.92
Grand Prairie, TX (city) Dallas County	7.60
Elgin, IL (city) Kane County	7.51
Portland, OR (city) Multnomah County	7.50
Worthington, MN (city) Nobles County	6.28
Oklahoma City, OK (city) Oklahoma County	5.88
Springdale, AR (city) Washington County	5.53
Long Beach, CA (city) Los Angeles County	5.29
Woonsocket, RI (city) Providence County	5.27
Richmond, CA (city) Contra Costa County	5.18
Santa Rosa, CA (city) Sonoma County	5.04
Fort Worth, TX (city) Tarrant County	4.98
Honolulu, HI (cdp) Honolulu County	4.88
Haltom City, TX (city) Tarrant County	4.87
Moreno Valley, CA (city) Riverside County	4.63
Santa Ana, CA (city) Orange County	4.46
Raymond, WA (city) Pacific County	4.44
Modesto, CA (city) Stanislaus County	4.39
Stockton, CA (city) San Joaquin County	4.30
Rockford, IL (city) Winnebago County	4.08
Westminster, CO (city) Adams County	4.08
Redding, CA (city) Shasta County	4.03
St. Petersburg, FL (city) Pinellas County	3.93
Visalia, CA (city) Tulare County	3.66
Oakland, CA (city) Alameda County	3.32
Sacramento, CA (city) Sacramento County	3.22
Akron, OH (city) Summit County	3.20
Amarillo, TX (city) Potter County	3.11
Lowell, MA (city) Middlesex County	2.98
Charlotte, NC (city) Mecklenburg County	2.85
Pomona, CA (city) Los Angeles County	2.80
West Valley City, UT (city) Salt Lake County	2.63
Escondido, CA (city) San Diego County	2.60
Fairfield, CA (city) Solano County	2.58
Seattle, WA (city) King County	2.54
Minneapolis, MN (city) Hennepin County	2.51
Parkway-S. Sacramento, CA (cdp) Sacramento County	2.48
Banning, CA (city) Riverside County	2.17
Fort Smith, AR (city) Sebastian County	2.12
Brooklyn Center, MN (city) Hennepin County	2.06
Merced, CA (city) Merced County	2.06
Fresno, CA (city) Fresno County	1.91
San Pablo, CA (city) Contra Costa County	0.68
Bridgeport, CT (city) Fairfield County	0.00
Green Bay, WI (city) Brown County	0.00
New Britain, CT (city) Hartford County	0.00
Oaklawn-Sunview, KS (cdp) Sedgwick County	0.00
Warroad, MN (city) Roseau County	0.00
Wichita, KS (city) Sedgwick County	0.00
Winfield, KS (city) Cowley County	0.00

Notes: Please refer to the User's Guide for an explanation of data; ranking tables include all places with Asian and/or NHPI populations above SF4 population thresholds; (1) tables reflect only those areas that meet SF4 population thresholds, therefore there may be less than 50 states, 75 counties or 75 places listed

Educational Attainment: Four-Year College Graduates

Malaysians 25 Years and Over Who are Four-Year College Graduates

All States, Top 75 Counties, and Top 75 Places Sorted by Number[1]

State	Number
United States	3,607
California	597
Texas	325
New York	279
Illinois	269
Oklahoma	150
Ohio	142
Michigan	132

County	Number
Los Angeles County, CA	180
Queens County, NY	121

Place	Number
New York, NY (city)	202

Notes: Please refer to the User's Guide for an explanation of data; ranking tables include all places with Asian and/or NHPI populations above SF4 population thresholds; (1) tables reflect only those areas that meet SF4 population thresholds, therefore there may be less than 50 states, 75 counties or 75 places listed

Educational Attainment: Four-Year College Graduates

Malaysians 25 Years and Over Who are Four-Year College Graduates

All States, Top 75 Counties, and Top 75 Places Sorted by Percent[1]

State	Percent
Oklahoma	81.97
Illinois	79.82
Michigan	78.11
Ohio	71.36
Texas	67.43
United States	53.50
California	48.89
New York	25.14

County	Percent
Los Angeles County, CA	51.14
Queens County, NY	24.80

Place	Percent
New York, NY (city)	20.70

Notes: Please refer to the User's Guide for an explanation of data; ranking tables include all places with Asian and/or NHPI populations above SF4 population thresholds; (1) tables reflect only those areas that meet SF4 population thresholds, therefore there may be less than 50 states, 75 counties or 75 places listed

Educational Attainment: Four-Year College Graduates

Pakistanis 25 Years and Over Who are Four-Year College Graduates

All States, Top 75 Counties, and Top 75 Places Sorted by Number[1]

State	Number
United States	47,470
New York	7,580
California	6,230
Texas	6,066
Illinois	5,082
New Jersey	3,837
Virginia	2,663
Michigan	1,888
Florida	1,784
Maryland	1,626
Georgia	1,116
Pennsylvania	945
Connecticut	837
Massachusetts	698
Ohio	672
North Carolina	532
Washington	466
Minnesota	425
Missouri	423
Louisiana	399
Colorado	349
Oklahoma	305
Kansas	304
Arizona	288
Kentucky	284
Indiana	268
Wisconsin	248
Tennessee	240
West Virginia	163
Iowa	159
Alabama	158
Delaware	158
Nevada	150
Oregon	147
Utah	66

County	Number
Cook County, IL	3,283
Queens County, NY	2,793
Harris County, TX	2,458
Fairfax County, VA	1,573
Los Angeles County, CA	1,481
Dallas County, TX	1,232
Kings County, NY	1,125
Middlesex County, NJ	1,124
Santa Clara County, CA	1,110
DuPage County, IL	903
Orange County, CA	890
Alameda County, CA	841
Wayne County, MI	814
Fort Bend County, TX	699
Nassau County, NY	696
Montgomery County, MD	631
Hudson County, NJ	575
Suffolk County, NY	566
Bergen County, NJ	508
New York County, NY	473
Oakland County, MI	382
Collin County, TX	373
Gwinnett County, GA	358
Broward County, FL	355
Orange County, FL	326
Westchester County, NY	319
Miami-Dade County, FL	308
Tarrant County, TX	292
Hartford County, CT	284
Somerset County, NJ	272
San Bernardino County, CA	268
Morris County, NJ	267
St. Louis County, MO	265
Baltimore County, MD	246
Bronx County, NY	243
New Haven County, CT	241
Contra Costa County, CA	240
Howard County, MD	237
Prince George's County, MD	227
King County, WA	225
Loudoun County, VA	225
San Diego County, CA	224
Denton County, TX	222
Jefferson Parish, LA	209
Delaware County, PA	207
Mercer County, NJ	207
Fairfield County, CT	204
Maricopa County, AZ	201
Sacramento County, CA	200
Essex County, NJ	195
Richmond County, NY	192
Travis County, TX	188
Franklin County, OH	187
Prince William County, VA	183
Middlesex County, MA	180
Wake County, NC	174
Washtenaw County, MI	168
Hennepin County, MN	165
Will County, IL	164
Alexandria Independent City, VA	158
Lake County, IL	154
Macomb County, MI	145
Snohomish County, WA	143
Arlington County, VA	136
Riverside County, CA	135
Cobb County, GA	133
Philadelphia County, PA	133
Monroe County, NY	130
San Francisco County, CA	121
Monmouth County, NJ	118
Camden County, NJ	114
Milwaukee County, WI	114
Worcester County, MA	104
Atlantic County, NJ	95
San Joaquin County, CA	95

Place	Number
New York, NY (city)	4,826
Chicago, IL (city) Cook County	1,852
Houston, TX (city) Harris County	1,770
Fremont, CA (city) Alameda County	504
Dallas, TX (city) Dallas County	483
San Jose, CA (city) Santa Clara County	465
Los Angeles, CA (city) Los Angeles County	435
Jersey City, NJ (city) Hudson County	433
Hempstead, NY (town) Nassau County	357
Edison, NJ (township) Middlesex County	269
Brookhaven, NY (town) Suffolk County	254
Carrollton, TX (city) Denton County	231
North Hempstead, NY (town) Nassau County	223
Plano, TX (city) Collin County	211
Old Bridge, NJ (township) Middlesex County	207
Garland, TX (city) Dallas County	205
Sugar Land, TX (city) Fort Bend County	203
Torrance, CA (city) Los Angeles County	200
Irving, TX (city) Dallas County	187
Santa Clara, CA (city) Santa Clara County	175
Richardson, TX (city) Dallas County	152
Austin, TX (city) Travis County	144
Arlington, VA (cdp) Arlington County	136
Anaheim, CA (city) Orange County	135
Philadelphia, PA (city) Philadelphia County	133
San Francisco, CA (city) San Francisco County	121
Ellicott City, MD (cdp) Howard County	117
Sacramento, CA (city) Sacramento County	113
Skokie, IL (village) Cook County	111
Huntington, NY (town) Suffolk County	108
Woodbridge, NJ (township) Middlesex County	99
Mission Bend, TX (cdp) Fort Bend County	92
Lincolnia, VA (cdp) Fairfax County	81
Tulsa, OK (city) Tulsa County	69
Bailey's Crossroads, VA (cdp) Fairfax County	49
Dale City, VA (cdp) Prince William County	46
Stockton, CA (city) San Joaquin County	45

Notes: Please refer to the User's Guide for an explanation of data; ranking tables include all places with Asian and/or NHPI populations above SF4 population thresholds; (1) tables reflect only those areas that meet SF4 population thresholds, therefore there may be less than 50 states, 75 counties or 75 places listed

Educational Attainment: Four-Year College Graduates

Pakistanis 25 Years and Over Who are Four-Year College Graduates

All States, Top 75 Counties, and Top 75 Places Sorted by Percent[1]

State	Percent
Iowa	87.85
Kentucky	86.32
West Virginia	79.51
Colorado	79.14
Alabama	77.45
Delaware	73.15
Arizona	72.54
Indiana	72.04
Connecticut	70.75
Ohio	69.42
Louisiana	68.79
Oregon	68.69
Michigan	67.50
Kansas	67.26
Minnesota	67.03
Tennessee	65.75
Washington	65.63
Missouri	65.48
Massachusetts	57.59
Illinois	56.83
Texas	56.75
California	56.56
Maryland	56.34
New Jersey	55.98
Pennsylvania	54.85
United States	54.30
Florida	53.96
Wisconsin	51.45
North Carolina	50.00
Oklahoma	49.51
Nevada	47.62
Georgia	47.39
Virginia	47.36
New York	42.59
Utah	32.84

County	Percent
San Diego County, CA	81.45
Hartford County, CT	77.38
Will County, IL	76.64
King County, WA	74.50
St. Louis County, MO	72.80
Franklin County, OH	72.48
Washtenaw County, MI	72.10
Westchester County, NY	71.21
Oakland County, MI	70.87
Howard County, MD	69.91
Santa Clara County, CA	68.94
Maricopa County, AZ	68.60
Fairfield County, CT	68.46
Wake County, NC	68.24
Alameda County, CA	68.15
Jefferson Parish, LA	68.08
Middlesex County, NJ	67.14
Wayne County, MI	66.72
Morris County, NJ	66.42
New York County, NY	66.34
San Bernardino County, CA	66.17
Collin County, TX	65.90
Hennepin County, MN	65.74
New Haven County, CT	63.42
Middlesex County, MA	61.86
Loudoun County, VA	61.64
Orange County, CA	61.21
Mercer County, NJ	60.70
Orange County, FL	59.38
DuPage County, IL	59.29
Montgomery County, MD	58.64
Snohomish County, WA	58.61
Somerset County, NJ	58.37
Bergen County, NJ	58.32
Dallas County, TX	58.25
Camden County, NJ	58.16
Harris County, TX	58.16
Contra Costa County, CA	57.97
Riverside County, CA	57.20
Nassau County, NY	56.91
Miami-Dade County, FL	56.51
Monmouth County, NJ	56.46
Delaware County, PA	54.76
Gwinnett County, GA	54.57
Los Angeles County, CA	54.29
Broward County, FL	53.71
Denton County, TX	53.62
Prince George's County, MD	53.41
Cook County, IL	53.30
Lake County, IL	52.38
Tarrant County, TX	51.87
Suffolk County, NY	51.60
Travis County, TX	50.95
Milwaukee County, WI	50.44
Fort Bend County, TX	49.93
Essex County, NJ	49.12
Richmond County, NY	48.98
Alexandria Independent City, VA	47.88
Worcester County, MA	47.71
San Francisco County, CA	46.90
Macomb County, MI	46.33
Fairfax County, VA	46.10
Monroe County, NY	46.10
Union County, NJ	45.88
Hudson County, NJ	45.74
Prince William County, VA	44.96
Queens County, NY	44.83
Baltimore County, MD	43.69
Clayton County, GA	40.69
Bronx County, NY	37.27
Philadelphia County, PA	35.56
Guilford County, NC	34.47
Cobb County, GA	34.10
Tulsa County, OK	33.98
Arlington County, VA	30.49

Place	Percent
North Hempstead, NY (town) Nassau County	71.94
Edison, NJ (township) Middlesex County	71.35
Fremont, CA (city) Alameda County	71.19
Santa Clara, CA (city) Santa Clara County	71.14
Dallas, TX (city) Dallas County	67.46
Old Bridge, NJ (township) Middlesex County	66.99
Irving, TX (city) Dallas County	65.61
Ellicott City, MD (cdp) Howard County	63.24
Anaheim, CA (city) Orange County	63.08
Houston, TX (city) Harris County	62.74
Plano, TX (city) Collin County	61.70
Sugar Land, TX (city) Fort Bend County	61.70
Brookhaven, NY (town) Suffolk County	61.65
San Jose, CA (city) Santa Clara County	60.31
Richardson, TX (city) Dallas County	58.46
Austin, TX (city) Travis County	54.14
Torrance, CA (city) Los Angeles County	51.81
Hempstead, NY (town) Nassau County	49.11
Huntington, NY (town) Suffolk County	47.79
Chicago, IL (city) Cook County	47.48
Los Angeles, CA (city) Los Angeles County	47.33
San Francisco, CA (city) San Francisco County	46.90
Garland, TX (city) Dallas County	46.17
Woodbridge, NJ (township) Middlesex County	44.59
Jersey City, NJ (city) Hudson County	42.16
Carrollton, TX (city) Denton County	40.24
Skokie, IL (village) Cook County	39.78
New York, NY (city)	36.64
Mission Bend, TX (cdp) Fort Bend County	36.22
Philadelphia, PA (city) Philadelphia County	35.56
Tulsa, OK (city) Tulsa County	34.85
Lincolnia, VA (cdp) Fairfax County	31.03
Arlington, VA (cdp) Arlington County	30.49
Sacramento, CA (city) Sacramento County	29.35
Bailey's Crossroads, VA (cdp) Fairfax County	27.07
Dale City, VA (cdp) Prince William County	27.06
Stockton, CA (city) San Joaquin County	14.90

Notes: Please refer to the User's Guide for an explanation of data; ranking tables include all places with Asian and/or NHPI populations above SF4 population thresholds; (1) tables reflect only those areas that meet SF4 population thresholds, therefore there may be less than 50 states, 75 counties or 75 places listed

Educational Attainment: Four-Year College Graduates

Samoans 25 Years and Over Who are Four-Year College Graduates

All States, Top 75 Counties, and Top 75 Places Sorted by Number[1]

State	Number
United States	4,369
California	1,713
Hawaii	480
Washington	231
New York	179
Utah	168
Texas	164
New Jersey	130
Missouri	93
Arizona	84
Illinois	84
Florida	72
Tennessee	71
Georgia	68
Pennsylvania	63
Colorado	62
Virginia	59
Ohio	42
Alaska	41
North Carolina	40
Michigan	34
Nevada	34
Oregon	19

County	Number
Los Angeles County, CA	582
Honolulu County, HI	459
San Diego County, CA	276
Orange County, CA	182
King County, WA	137
San Francisco County, CA	114
San Mateo County, CA	103
Salt Lake County, UT	74
Santa Clara County, CA	71
Alameda County, CA	62
Maricopa County, AZ	58
Utah County, UT	57
Solano County, CA	45
Anchorage Borough, AK	38
Ventura County, CA	38
Pierce County, WA	37
Sacramento County, CA	32
Riverside County, CA	31
Jackson County, MO	30
Contra Costa County, CA	29
San Bernardino County, CA	24
Clark County, NV	14
San Joaquin County, CA	4
Hawaii County, HI	2

Place	Number
Los Angeles, CA (city) Los Angeles County	156
Honolulu, HI (cdp) Honolulu County	151
San Francisco, CA (city) San Francisco County	114
Lakewood, CA (city) Los Angeles County	95
San Diego, CA (city) San Diego County	84
Anaheim, CA (city) Orange County	68
Seattle, WA (city) King County	66
Carson, CA (city) Los Angeles County	61
San Jose, CA (city) Santa Clara County	59
Oceanside, CA (city) San Diego County	49
Compton, CA (city) Los Angeles County	46
Laie, HI (cdp) Honolulu County	44
Long Beach, CA (city) Los Angeles County	39
New York, NY (city)	35
Garden Grove, CA (city) Orange County	28
Waipahu, HI (cdp) Honolulu County	27
Federal Way, WA (city) King County	23
Oxnard, CA (city) Ventura County	23
Halawa, HI (cdp) Honolulu County	20
Westminster, CA (city) Orange County	17
Salt Lake City, UT (city) Salt Lake County	15
San Bernardino, CA (city) San Bernardino County	14
Santa Ana, CA (city) Orange County	14
Ewa Beach, HI (cdp) Honolulu County	13
Tacoma, WA (city) Pierce County	13
Kahuku, HI (cdp) Honolulu County	10
Lakewood, WA (city) Pierce County	9
West Valley City, UT (city) Salt Lake County	9
Hayward, CA (city) Alameda County	8
Sacramento, CA (city) Sacramento County	6
Hauula, HI (cdp) Honolulu County	5
Nanakuli, HI (cdp) Honolulu County	0

Notes: Please refer to the User's Guide for an explanation of data; ranking tables include all places with Asian and/or NHPI populations above SF4 population thresholds; (1) tables reflect only those areas that meet SF4 population thresholds, therefore there may be less than 50 states, 75 counties or 75 places listed

Educational Attainment: Four-Year College Graduates

Samoans 25 Years and Over Who are Four-Year College Graduates

***All States, Top 75 Counties, and Top 75 Places Sorted by Percent*[1]**

State	Percent
New Jersey	30.73
New York	23.28
Virginia	22.26
Tennessee	21.39
Illinois	19.27
Missouri	19.02
Texas	17.54
Georgia	17.35
Arizona	17.00
Ohio	16.28
North Carolina	15.75
Colorado	14.73
Florida	14.43
Michigan	13.55
Pennsylvania	13.46
Utah	10.51
United States	10.47
California	9.15
Alaska	7.32
Washington	6.86
Hawaii	6.82
Oregon	5.00
Nevada	4.33

County	Percent
Utah County, UT	27.67
Maricopa County, AZ	18.13
Solano County, CA	14.38
San Mateo County, CA	13.41
Jackson County, MO	13.04
Ventura County, CA	12.26
San Diego County, CA	10.95
San Francisco County, CA	10.52
Orange County, CA	9.76
Anchorage Borough, AK	9.43
Los Angeles County, CA	8.91
Contra Costa County, CA	8.24
Santa Clara County, CA	7.55
King County, WA	7.21
Honolulu County, HI	6.87
Riverside County, CA	6.78
Salt Lake County, UT	6.55
Sacramento County, CA	6.45
Alameda County, CA	6.33
Pierce County, WA	4.59
San Bernardino County, CA	2.86
Clark County, NV	2.55
San Joaquin County, CA	1.93
Hawaii County, HI	0.97

Place	Percent
Lakewood, CA (city) Los Angeles County	29.87
Anaheim, CA (city) Orange County	23.61
Laie, HI (cdp) Honolulu County	15.55
Kahuku, HI (cdp) Honolulu County	13.89
Compton, CA (city) Los Angeles County	13.73
Los Angeles, CA (city) Los Angeles County	13.45
New York, NY (city)	11.71
San Francisco, CA (city) San Francisco County	10.52
Seattle, WA (city) King County	10.39
Federal Way, WA (city) King County	9.87
Westminster, CA (city) Orange County	9.50
San Jose, CA (city) Santa Clara County	9.41
Carson, CA (city) Los Angeles County	8.66
Oxnard, CA (city) Ventura County	8.61
San Diego, CA (city) San Diego County	8.30
San Bernardino, CA (city) San Bernardino County	8.05
Garden Grove, CA (city) Orange County	7.76
Halawa, HI (cdp) Honolulu County	7.25
Honolulu, HI (cdp) Honolulu County	6.81
Lakewood, WA (city) Pierce County	6.67
Salt Lake City, UT (city) Salt Lake County	6.55
Ewa Beach, HI (cdp) Honolulu County	6.50
Oceanside, CA (city) San Diego County	6.27
Tacoma, WA (city) Pierce County	4.78
Hauula, HI (cdp) Honolulu County	4.20
Santa Ana, CA (city) Orange County	3.79
Waipahu, HI (cdp) Honolulu County	3.08
Hayward, CA (city) Alameda County	2.56
Sacramento, CA (city) Sacramento County	2.44
West Valley City, UT (city) Salt Lake County	2.39
Long Beach, CA (city) Los Angeles County	2.28
Nanakuli, HI (cdp) Honolulu County	0.00

Notes: Please refer to the User's Guide for an explanation of data; ranking tables include all places with Asian and/or NHPI populations above SF4 population thresholds; (1) tables reflect only those areas that meet SF4 population thresholds, therefore there may be less than 50 states, 75 counties or 75 places listed

Educational Attainment: Four-Year College Graduates

Sri Lankans 25 Years and Over Who are Four-Year College Graduates

All States, Top 75 Counties, and Top 75 Places Sorted by Number[1]

State	Number
United States	6,849
California	1,506
New York	733
New Jersey	552
Maryland	458
Texas	390
Illinois	291
Ohio	247
Michigan	197
Virginia	195
Florida	194
Massachusetts	187
Pennsylvania	165
Washington	136

County	Number
Los Angeles County, CA	460
Montgomery County, MD	243
Middlesex County, NJ	202
Orange County, CA	200
Queens County, NY	136
Richmond County, NY	103

Place	Number
New York, NY (city)	447
Los Angeles, CA (city) Los Angeles County	191

Notes: Please refer to the User's Guide for an explanation of data; ranking tables include all places with Asian and/or NHPI populations above SF4 population thresholds; (1) tables reflect only those areas that meet SF4 population thresholds, therefore there may be less than 50 states, 75 counties or 75 places listed

Educational Attainment: Four-Year College Graduates

Sri Lankans 25 Years and Over Who are Four-Year College Graduates

All States, Top 75 Counties, and Top 75 Places Sorted by Percent[1]

State	Percent
Michigan	74.90
Pennsylvania	67.62
Florida	67.36
Illinois	66.14
Ohio	63.82
Texas	60.19
New Jersey	59.42
Maryland	55.45
Massachusetts	53.43
Washington	52.51
United States	51.05
Virginia	43.05
California	39.82
New York	39.66

County	Percent
Middlesex County, NJ	63.32
Montgomery County, MD	44.83
Orange County, CA	42.55
Richmond County, NY	31.60
Los Angeles County, CA	26.98
Queens County, NY	22.93

Place	Percent
New York, NY (city)	33.26
Los Angeles, CA (city) Los Angeles County	23.24

Notes: Please refer to the User's Guide for an explanation of data; ranking tables include all places with Asian and/or NHPI populations above SF4 population thresholds; (1) tables reflect only those areas that meet SF4 population thresholds, therefore there may be less than 50 states, 75 counties or 75 places listed

Educational Attainment: Four-Year College Graduates

Taiwanese 25 Years and Over Who are Four-Year College Graduates

All States, Top 75 Counties, and Top 75 Places Sorted by Number[1]

State	Number
United States	54,160
California	25,927
New York	3,712
Texas	3,643
New Jersey	3,042
Illinois	1,841
Washington	1,516
Michigan	1,276
Massachusetts	1,219
Maryland	1,189
Pennsylvania	1,163
Ohio	974
Georgia	868
Florida	821
Virginia	713
Missouri	565
North Carolina	478
Indiana	449
Colorado	341
Arizona	333
Oregon	307
Connecticut	306
Wisconsin	306
Hawaii	300
Tennessee	268
Minnesota	257
Louisiana	236
Kansas	231
Iowa	216
Oklahoma	184
Utah	154
Nevada	128

County	Number
Los Angeles County, CA	12,774
Orange County, CA	3,792
Santa Clara County, CA	2,927
Alameda County, CA	1,799
Queens County, NY	1,499
King County, WA	1,305
Harris County, TX	1,141
San Diego County, CA	1,062
Cook County, IL	957
Middlesex County, NJ	761
San Bernardino County, CA	751
Contra Costa County, CA	674
Oakland County, MI	666
New York County, NY	639
Middlesex County, MA	629
Montgomery County, MD	605
San Mateo County, CA	552
Collin County, TX	467
DuPage County, IL	466
Bergen County, NJ	439
Fairfax County, VA	416
Ventura County, CA	415
Fort Bend County, TX	414
San Francisco County, CA	378
St. Louis County, MO	370
Dallas County, TX	360
Franklin County, OH	351
Morris County, NJ	335
Tarrant County, TX	324
Somerset County, NJ	317
Maricopa County, AZ	314
Travis County, TX	307
Washtenaw County, MI	301
Nassau County, NY	296
Honolulu County, HI	284
Mercer County, NJ	265
Suffolk County, MA	254
Gwinnett County, GA	249
Essex County, NJ	232
Allegheny County, PA	208
Dane County, WI	205
Westchester County, NY	191
Riverside County, CA	161
Suffolk County, NY	161
Norfolk County, MA	159
Sacramento County, CA	155
Clark County, NV	47

Place	Number
New York, NY (city)	2,288
Los Angeles, CA (city) Los Angeles County	1,577
Arcadia, CA (city) Los Angeles County	1,328
Fremont, CA (city) Alameda County	1,215
San Jose, CA (city) Santa Clara County	1,112
Irvine, CA (city) Orange County	1,062
Hacienda Heights, CA (cdp) Los Angeles County	916
Rowland Heights, CA (cdp) Los Angeles County	823
Houston, TX (city) Harris County	795
Cerritos, CA (city) Los Angeles County	753
San Diego, CA (city) San Diego County	745
Diamond Bar, CA (city) Los Angeles County	688
San Marino, CA (city) Los Angeles County	687
Walnut, CA (city) Los Angeles County	615
Alhambra, CA (city) Los Angeles County	548
Torrance, CA (city) Los Angeles County	516
Temple City, CA (city) Los Angeles County	500
Cupertino, CA (city) Santa Clara County	459
Seattle, WA (city) King County	418
Sunnyvale, CA (city) Santa Clara County	413
Monterey Park, CA (city) Los Angeles County	411
Bellevue, WA (city) King County	383
Chicago, IL (city) Cook County	380
San Francisco, CA (city) San Francisco County	378
Edison, NJ (township) Middlesex County	317
Plano, TX (city) Collin County	314
Sugar Land, TX (city) Fort Bend County	308
San Gabriel, CA (city) Los Angeles County	305
Huntington Beach, CA (city) Orange County	300
Anaheim, CA (city) Orange County	296
West Covina, CA (city) Los Angeles County	294
Troy, MI (city) Oakland County	293
Honolulu, HI (cdp) Honolulu County	284
Chino Hills, CA (city) San Bernardino County	283
Austin, TX (city) Travis County	275
Rancho Palos Verdes, CA (city) Los Angeles County	266
Boston, MA (city) Suffolk County	254
Cypress, CA (city) Orange County	254
Ann Arbor, MI (city) Washtenaw County	249
Columbus, OH (city) Franklin County	241
Tustin, CA (city) Orange County	231
Orange, CA (city) Orange County	215
Naperville, IL (city) Du Page County	213
Arlington, TX (city) Tarrant County	206
Madison, WI (city) Dane County	202
East San Gabriel, CA (cdp) Los Angeles County	168
Upland, CA (city) San Bernardino County	156
Saratoga, CA (city) Santa Clara County	154
North Hempstead, NY (town) Nassau County	138
Fountain Valley, CA (city) Orange County	131
Berkeley, CA (city) Alameda County	121
El Monte, CA (city) Los Angeles County	87

Notes: Please refer to the User's Guide for an explanation of data; ranking tables include all places with Asian and/or NHPI populations above SF4 population thresholds; (1) tables reflect only those areas that meet SF4 population thresholds, therefore there may be less than 50 states, 75 counties or 75 places listed

Educational Attainment: Four-Year College Graduates

Taiwanese 25 Years and Over Who are Four-Year College Graduates

All States, Top 75 Counties, and Top 75 Places Sorted by Percent[1]

State	Percent
Indiana	86.85
Michigan	85.98
Missouri	82.72
Minnesota	82.64
Massachusetts	81.16
Illinois	80.57
Connecticut	80.10
Pennsylvania	79.39
Tennessee	78.36
Iowa	77.98
New Jersey	77.44
Maryland	76.86
Colorado	76.12
Virginia	74.97
Wisconsin	73.03
Texas	71.18
North Carolina	70.40
Utah	70.00
Georgia	69.61
Arizona	68.52
Ohio	68.21
Kansas	68.14
New York	67.85
United States	67.11
Washington	66.75
Louisiana	66.29
Oklahoma	65.95
Oregon	65.88
California	62.08
Florida	59.11
Hawaii	47.85
Nevada	28.32

County	Percent
New York County, NY	90.51
San Mateo County, CA	90.20
Oakland County, MI	88.21
Suffolk County, MA	87.59
Collin County, TX	85.69
Washtenaw County, MI	85.51
Mercer County, NJ	85.48
Somerset County, NJ	84.76
DuPage County, IL	84.73
Middlesex County, NJ	83.63
Westchester County, NY	82.68
Middlesex County, MA	81.58
St. Louis County, MO	81.32
Norfolk County, MA	81.12
Cook County, IL	81.03
Montgomery County, MD	79.61
Santa Clara County, CA	79.58
Ventura County, CA	79.05
Nassau County, NY	78.51
Allegheny County, PA	78.20
Bergen County, NJ	77.43
Travis County, TX	75.99
Dane County, WI	75.65
Fairfax County, VA	74.82
Tarrant County, TX	73.80
Morris County, NJ	72.51
Maricopa County, AZ	71.85
Franklin County, OH	71.63
San Diego County, CA	70.85
Essex County, NJ	70.52
King County, WA	70.46
Alameda County, CA	70.03
Harris County, TX	69.96
Gwinnett County, GA	69.75
San Francisco County, CA	67.38
Contra Costa County, CA	66.60
Dallas County, TX	66.06
Riverside County, CA	65.18
Orange County, CA	64.22
Queens County, NY	57.28
Fort Bend County, TX	57.02
San Bernardino County, CA	56.98
Suffolk County, NY	56.89
Los Angeles County, CA	56.38
Sacramento County, CA	50.99
Honolulu County, HI	47.57
Clark County, NV	14.60

Place	Percent
Berkeley, CA (city) Alameda County	93.80
Troy, MI (city) Oakland County	90.43
Boston, MA (city) Suffolk County	87.59
Saratoga, CA (city) Santa Clara County	86.52
Ann Arbor, MI (city) Washtenaw County	85.27
Chicago, IL (city) Cook County	83.33
Cupertino, CA (city) Santa Clara County	83.15
Plano, TX (city) Collin County	82.85
Edison, NJ (township) Middlesex County	82.34
Naperville, IL (city) Du Page County	80.99
Austin, TX (city) Travis County	80.17
Sunnyvale, CA (city) Santa Clara County	79.58
North Hempstead, NY (town) Nassau County	78.86
Columbus, OH (city) Franklin County	78.50
Anaheim, CA (city) Orange County	78.10
Arlington, TX (city) Tarrant County	77.15
San Jose, CA (city) Santa Clara County	76.64
San Diego, CA (city) San Diego County	75.94
Madison, WI (city) Dane County	75.37
San Marino, CA (city) Los Angeles County	72.85
Houston, TX (city) Harris County	71.69
Chino Hills, CA (city) San Bernardino County	71.65
Los Angeles, CA (city) Los Angeles County	71.23
Fremont, CA (city) Alameda County	71.14
Bellevue, WA (city) King County	70.40
Seattle, WA (city) King County	69.78
Rancho Palos Verdes, CA (city) Los Angeles County	68.91
Tustin, CA (city) Orange County	68.34
Irvine, CA (city) Orange County	67.39
San Francisco, CA (city) San Francisco County	67.38
Huntington Beach, CA (city) Orange County	65.79
Cerritos, CA (city) Los Angeles County	65.48
New York, NY (city)	63.19
Orange, CA (city) Orange County	63.05
Torrance, CA (city) Los Angeles County	58.90
Arcadia, CA (city) Los Angeles County	58.37
Cypress, CA (city) Orange County	58.12
Sugar Land, TX (city) Fort Bend County	54.90
Diamond Bar, CA (city) Los Angeles County	53.71
San Gabriel, CA (city) Los Angeles County	53.51
Temple City, CA (city) Los Angeles County	53.30
Honolulu, HI (cdp) Honolulu County	52.40
Fountain Valley, CA (city) Orange County	52.19
Upland, CA (city) San Bernardino County	52.17
Walnut, CA (city) Los Angeles County	51.99
Monterey Park, CA (city) Los Angeles County	50.87
Hacienda Heights, CA (cdp) Los Angeles County	50.33
Rowland Heights, CA (cdp) Los Angeles County	49.19
West Covina, CA (city) Los Angeles County	48.20
Alhambra, CA (city) Los Angeles County	47.08
East San Gabriel, CA (cdp) Los Angeles County	46.28
El Monte, CA (city) Los Angeles County	27.88

Notes: Please refer to the User's Guide for an explanation of data; ranking tables include all places with Asian and/or NHPI populations above SF4 population thresholds; (1) tables reflect only those areas that meet SF4 population thresholds, therefore there may be less than 50 states, 75 counties or 75 places listed

Educational Attainment: Four-Year College Graduates

Thais 25 Years and Over Who are Four-Year College Graduates

All States, Top 75 Counties, and Top 75 Places Sorted by Number[1]

State	Number
United States	30,219
California	9,574
Illinois	2,389
Texas	2,081
New York	1,871
Florida	1,336
Washington	974
Virginia	911
Maryland	904
Massachusetts	779
Georgia	660
Pennsylvania	659
New Jersey	624
Colorado	601
Ohio	550
Michigan	533
Oregon	436
Missouri	434
Nevada	410
Arizona	387
Tennessee	381
North Carolina	331
Wisconsin	317
Hawaii	256
Connecticut	243
Minnesota	237
Kentucky	218
Indiana	214
Kansas	208
Nebraska	188
South Carolina	184
Oklahoma	177
Iowa	176
Utah	150
Louisiana	138
Alabama	106
Alaska	44
New Mexico	44
Arkansas	17

County	Number
Los Angeles County, CA	4,859
Cook County, IL	1,684
Orange County, CA	939
King County, WA	602
San Francisco County, CA	565
Queens County, NY	540
Dallas County, TX	534
Montgomery County, MD	518
Santa Clara County, CA	487
San Diego County, CA	476
Alameda County, CA	448
San Bernardino County, CA	432
Harris County, TX	423
Middlesex County, MA	393
Clark County, NV	361
New York County, NY	355
Fairfax County, VA	346
Maricopa County, AZ	299
Miami-Dade County, FL	280
Bexar County, TX	233
DuPage County, IL	232
San Mateo County, CA	222
Hillsborough County, FL	221
Honolulu County, HI	214
Bergen County, NJ	195
Collin County, TX	190
Riverside County, CA	179
Tarrant County, TX	176
Broward County, FL	168
Franklin County, OH	161
Westchester County, NY	160
Palm Beach County, FL	140
Denver County, CO	135
St. Louis County, MO	130
Contra Costa County, CA	121
Travis County, TX	121
Nassau County, NY	120
Multnomah County, OR	116
Sacramento County, CA	114
Oklahoma County, OK	91
Pinellas County, FL	85
Pierce County, WA	73
Suffolk County, NY	73
Prince George's County, MD	70
Polk County, IA	30
Okaloosa County, FL	10
Anchorage Borough, AK	7

Place	Number
Los Angeles, CA (city) Los Angeles County	2,038
New York, NY (city)	1,189
Chicago, IL (city) Cook County	829
San Francisco, CA (city) San Francisco County	565
Houston, TX (city) Harris County	350
San Diego, CA (city) San Diego County	343
Seattle, WA (city) King County	302
San Jose, CA (city) Santa Clara County	202
San Antonio, TX (city) Bexar County	185
Columbus, OH (city) Franklin County	150
Cerritos, CA (city) Los Angeles County	149
Honolulu, HI (cdp) Honolulu County	136
Denver, CO (city) Denver County	135
Long Beach, CA (city) Los Angeles County	135
Anaheim, CA (city) Orange County	107
Las Vegas, NV (city) Clark County	106
Glendale, CA (city) Los Angeles County	102
Bellflower, CA (city) Los Angeles County	85
Portland, OR (city) Multnomah County	83
Spring Valley, NV (cdp) Clark County	81
Des Moines, IA (city) Polk County	13

Notes: Please refer to the User's Guide for an explanation of data; ranking tables include all places with Asian and/or NHPI populations above SF4 population thresholds; (1) tables reflect only those areas that meet SF4 population thresholds, therefore there may be less than 50 states, 75 counties or 75 places listed

Educational Attainment: Four-Year College Graduates

Thais 25 Years and Over Who are Four-Year College Graduates

All States, Top 75 Counties, and Top 75 Places Sorted by Percent[1]

State	Percent
Kentucky	68.13
Wisconsin	59.92
Illinois	58.67
Tennessee	55.78
Pennsylvania	55.42
Connecticut	52.71
Massachusetts	52.49
Nebraska	50.95
Kansas	48.04
Michigan	47.76
New Jersey	47.34
Missouri	45.21
Colorado	43.58
Ohio	42.70
Maryland	42.56
New York	40.79
Oregon	40.30
Texas	39.80
United States	38.56
California	38.52
Georgia	38.39
Minnesota	38.10
Washington	37.36
Virginia	34.35
Arizona	34.07
Indiana	33.75
South Carolina	31.13
North Carolina	29.09
Utah	28.90
Oklahoma	28.59
Florida	26.27
Louisiana	26.19
Iowa	26.04
Hawaii	25.02
Alabama	24.15
Nevada	18.37
New Mexico	14.38
Arkansas	8.95
Alaska	8.26

County	Percent
DuPage County, IL	81.69
Middlesex County, MA	68.47
Dallas County, TX	61.81
Cook County, IL	59.40
Franklin County, OH	58.76
Santa Clara County, CA	55.98
Collin County, TX	55.39
Bergen County, NJ	53.72
New York County, NY	53.14
San Diego County, CA	52.77
San Francisco County, CA	52.36
Denver County, CO	51.53
Montgomery County, MD	49.33
Alameda County, CA	48.96
Nassau County, NY	48.78
St. Louis County, MO	48.33
San Mateo County, CA	46.64
Harris County, TX	45.98
Orange County, CA	45.43
King County, WA	44.79
Travis County, TX	43.21
Hillsborough County, FL	40.85
Miami-Dade County, FL	40.58
Maricopa County, AZ	39.76
Westchester County, NY	37.47
Los Angeles County, CA	35.80
San Bernardino County, CA	35.35
Broward County, FL	34.50
Bexar County, TX	33.97
Multnomah County, OR	33.82
Queens County, NY	33.73
Tarrant County, TX	32.35
Fairfax County, VA	30.76
Prince George's County, MD	30.43
Suffolk County, NY	30.29
Oklahoma County, OK	29.64
Riverside County, CA	28.82
Contra Costa County, CA	28.40
Palm Beach County, FL	26.57
Honolulu County, HI	25.81
Sacramento County, CA	25.00
Pinellas County, FL	24.64
Pierce County, WA	22.39
Clark County, NV	18.17
Polk County, IA	11.86
Okaloosa County, FL	1.89
Anchorage Borough, AK	1.84

Place	Percent
San Diego, CA (city) San Diego County	64.23
Columbus, OH (city) Franklin County	59.29
Chicago, IL (city) Cook County	54.50
Houston, TX (city) Harris County	54.43
Seattle, WA (city) King County	52.80
San Francisco, CA (city) San Francisco County	52.36
Denver, CO (city) Denver County	51.53
San Jose, CA (city) Santa Clara County	50.75
Cerritos, CA (city) Los Angeles County	45.15
New York, NY (city)	42.92
San Antonio, TX (city) Bexar County	37.53
Anaheim, CA (city) Orange County	34.63
Honolulu, HI (cdp) Honolulu County	34.61
Long Beach, CA (city) Los Angeles County	34.09
Bellflower, CA (city) Los Angeles County	32.32
Los Angeles, CA (city) Los Angeles County	31.86
Glendale, CA (city) Los Angeles County	30.45
Portland, OR (city) Multnomah County	26.77
Spring Valley, NV (cdp) Clark County	22.82
Las Vegas, NV (city) Clark County	20.08
Des Moines, IA (city) Polk County	6.84

Notes: Please refer to the User's Guide for an explanation of data; ranking tables include all places with Asian and/or NHPI populations above SF4 population thresholds; (1) tables reflect only those areas that meet SF4 population thresholds, therefore there may be less than 50 states, 75 counties or 75 places listed

Educational Attainment: Four-Year College Graduates

Tongans 25 Years and Over Who are Four-Year College Graduates

All States, Top 75 Counties, and Top 75 Places Sorted by Number[1]

State	Number
United States	1,133
California	432
Utah	304
Hawaii	212
Washington	55
Alaska	20
Arizona	15
Nevada	13
Texas	13
Oregon	9

County	Number
Salt Lake County, UT	216
Honolulu County, HI	172
San Mateo County, CA	151
Los Angeles County, CA	69
Utah County, UT	67
King County, WA	55
San Diego County, CA	54
Sacramento County, CA	33
Orange County, CA	26
San Bernardino County, CA	25
Contra Costa County, CA	24
Alameda County, CA	19
Maui County, HI	17
Maricopa County, AZ	15
Washoe County, NV	10
Multnomah County, OR	9
Tarrant County, TX	0

Place	Number
Salt Lake City, UT (city) Salt Lake County	118
East Palo Alto, CA (city) San Mateo County	56
Hauula, HI (cdp) Honolulu County	49
Honolulu, HI (cdp) Honolulu County	36
West Jordan, UT (city) Salt Lake County	36
Sacramento, CA (city) Sacramento County	33
San Mateo, CA (city) San Mateo County	29
West Valley City, UT (city) Salt Lake County	29
Laie, HI (cdp) Honolulu County	28
Kahuku, HI (cdp) Honolulu County	20
San Bruno, CA (city) San Mateo County	14
Portland, OR (city) Multnomah County	9
Los Angeles, CA (city) Los Angeles County	6
Oakland, CA (city) Alameda County	5

Notes: Please refer to the User's Guide for an explanation of data; ranking tables include all places with Asian and/or NHPI populations above SF4 population thresholds; (1) tables reflect only those areas that meet SF4 population thresholds, therefore there may be less than 50 states, 75 counties or 75 places listed

Educational Attainment: Four-Year College Graduates

Tongans 25 Years and Over Who are Four-Year College Graduates

All States, Top 75 Counties, and Top 75 Places Sorted by Percent[1]

State	Percent
Alaska	13.16
Washington	12.85
Utah	11.16
Hawaii	9.72
United States	8.64
California	7.12
Arizona	5.86
Oregon	5.26
Texas	5.26
Nevada	3.32

County	Percent
Utah County, UT	33.00
San Diego County, CA	25.84
King County, WA	18.09
Contra Costa County, CA	13.64
Honolulu County, HI	10.78
Orange County, CA	10.20
Salt Lake County, UT	9.08
Sacramento County, CA	8.53
San Mateo County, CA	7.69
Multnomah County, OR	7.09
San Bernardino County, CA	6.46
Los Angeles County, CA	6.44
Maricopa County, AZ	6.05
Maui County, HI	4.04
Washoe County, NV	3.70
Alameda County, CA	2.24
Tarrant County, TX	0.00

Place	Percent
Hauula, HI (cdp) Honolulu County	30.25
Laie, HI (cdp) Honolulu County	24.78
West Jordan, UT (city) Salt Lake County	20.00
Kahuku, HI (cdp) Honolulu County	17.09
Sacramento, CA (city) Sacramento County	12.55
Salt Lake City, UT (city) Salt Lake County	12.19
Portland, OR (city) Multnomah County	7.50
East Palo Alto, CA (city) San Mateo County	7.39
San Mateo, CA (city) San Mateo County	7.30
San Bruno, CA (city) San Mateo County	5.86
Honolulu, HI (cdp) Honolulu County	4.37
West Valley City, UT (city) Salt Lake County	4.24
Los Angeles, CA (city) Los Angeles County	3.80
Oakland, CA (city) Alameda County	0.92

Notes: Please refer to the User's Guide for an explanation of data; ranking tables include all places with Asian and/or NHPI populations above SF4 population thresholds; (1) tables reflect only those areas that meet SF4 population thresholds, therefore there may be less than 50 states, 75 counties or 75 places listed

Educational Attainment: Four-Year College Graduates

Vietnamese 25 Years and Over Who are Four-Year College Graduates

All States, Top 75 Counties, and Top 75 Places Sorted by Number[1]

State	Number
United States	134,820
California	59,035
Texas	17,783
Virginia	6,262
Washington	4,414
Florida	4,165
New York	3,207
Massachusetts	3,111
Pennsylvania	3,085
Maryland	2,788
Illinois	2,688
New Jersey	2,372
Georgia	2,289
Oregon	2,010
Minnesota	1,931
Louisiana	1,862
Michigan	1,535
North Carolina	1,505
Colorado	1,408
Ohio	1,408
Arizona	1,182
Oklahoma	1,147
Connecticut	985
Missouri	886
Kansas	677
Tennessee	650
Indiana	586
Hawaii	573
Nebraska	457
Nevada	446
Wisconsin	442
Alabama	404
South Carolina	403
Utah	386
New Mexico	366
Mississippi	345
Iowa	332
Kentucky	300
Arkansas	254
District of Columbia	237
Delaware	192
Rhode Island	156
New Hampshire	124
Idaho	121
Vermont	87
Maine	58
Alaska	54
West Virginia	49
South Dakota	19

County	Number
Orange County, CA	18,296
Santa Clara County, CA	13,744
Los Angeles County, CA	10,564
Harris County, TX	7,408
San Diego County, CA	4,159
Fairfax County, VA	4,127
Alameda County, CA	3,580
King County, WA	2,705
Dallas County, TX	2,485
Tarrant County, TX	1,887
Montgomery County, MD	1,710
Cook County, IL	1,585
Sacramento County, CA	1,519
Travis County, TX	1,320
San Francisco County, CA	1,239
Collin County, TX	1,178
San Bernardino County, CA	1,085
Fort Bend County, TX	1,076
Middlesex County, MA	1,004
Orange County, FL	998
Philadelphia County, PA	956
Maricopa County, AZ	934
Riverside County, CA	829
Multnomah County, OR	828
Contra Costa County, CA	806
Washington County, OR	793
New York County, NY	775
Hennepin County, MN	774
Suffolk County, MA	766
Snohomish County, WA	747
San Mateo County, CA	729
Jefferson Parish, LA	719
Gwinnett County, GA	641
Ventura County, CA	636
Queens County, NY	527
Oklahoma County, OK	515
Honolulu County, HI	497
Orleans Parish, LA	472
Arapahoe County, CO	457
DeKalb County, GA	453
Hartford County, CT	446
Broward County, FL	440
Wake County, NC	433
Mecklenburg County, NC	429
Ramsey County, MN	428
Arlington County, VA	423
Kings County, NY	419
Palm Beach County, FL	404
Norfolk County, MA	391
San Joaquin County, CA	383
Worcester County, MA	375
Sedgwick County, KS	370
Denton County, TX	367
Clark County, NV	352
Middlesex County, NJ	348
Prince George's County, MD	348
DuPage County, IL	343
Montgomery County, PA	342
Hillsborough County, FL	341
Bexar County, TX	338
Kent County, MI	326
Delaware County, PA	322
Franklin County, OH	319
Brazoria County, TX	317
Pinellas County, FL	311
Salt Lake County, UT	311
Essex County, MA	306
Loudoun County, VA	302
Shelby County, TN	300
Cuyahoga County, OH	298
Denver County, CO	284
Fulton County, GA	284
Cleveland County, OK	281
Pierce County, WA	273
East Baton Rouge Parish, LA	271

Place	Number
San Jose, CA (city) Santa Clara County	9,263
Houston, TX (city) Harris County	4,233
San Diego, CA (city) San Diego County	3,316
Los Angeles, CA (city) Los Angeles County	3,201
Garden Grove, CA (city) Orange County	2,979
Westminster, CA (city) Orange County	2,534
New York, NY (city)	1,980
Santa Ana, CA (city) Orange County	1,934
Anaheim, CA (city) Orange County	1,619
Milpitas, CA (city) Santa Clara County	1,615
Fountain Valley, CA (city) Orange County	1,458
Irvine, CA (city) Orange County	1,348
San Francisco, CA (city) San Francisco County	1,239
Huntington Beach, CA (city) Orange County	1,169
Fremont, CA (city) Alameda County	1,161
Austin, TX (city) Travis County	1,091
Chicago, IL (city) Cook County	992
Philadelphia, PA (city) Philadelphia County	956
Dallas, TX (city) Dallas County	919
Arlington, TX (city) Tarrant County	886
Seattle, WA (city) King County	877
Santa Clara, CA (city) Santa Clara County	823
Oklahoma City, OK (city) Oklahoma County	753
Portland, OR (city) Multnomah County	752
Oakland, CA (city) Alameda County	747
Orange, CA (city) Orange County	743
Boston, MA (city) Suffolk County	736
Garland, TX (city) Dallas County	697
Annandale, VA (cdp) Fairfax County	668
Sunnyvale, CA (city) Santa Clara County	610
Alhambra, CA (city) Los Angeles County	548
Plano, TX (city) Collin County	513
Fort Worth, TX (city) Tarrant County	477
New Orleans, LA (city) Orleans Parish	472
Long Beach, CA (city) Los Angeles County	462
Tustin, CA (city) Orange County	458
Rosemead, CA (city) Los Angeles County	426
Arlington, VA (cdp) Arlington County	423
Richardson, TX (city) Dallas County	423
Sacramento, CA (city) Sacramento County	416
Cerritos, CA (city) Los Angeles County	373
Jefferson, VA (cdp) Fairfax County	366
Costa Mesa, CA (city) Orange County	361
Wichita, KS (city) Sedgwick County	352
El Monte, CA (city) Los Angeles County	337
Irving, TX (city) Dallas County	336
Honolulu, HI (cdp) Honolulu County	334
Mission Viejo, CA (city) Orange County	333
Phoenix, AZ (city) Maricopa County	332
Charlotte, NC (city) Mecklenburg County	327
Union City, CA (city) Alameda County	327
Hayward, CA (city) Alameda County	321
Lake Forest, CA (city) Orange County	306
West Covina, CA (city) Los Angeles County	304
Torrance, CA (city) Los Angeles County	303
Chantilly, VA (cdp) Fairfax County	300
Stockton, CA (city) San Joaquin County	285
Denver, CO (city) Denver County	284
Columbus, OH (city) Franklin County	283
Placentia, CA (city) Orange County	279
Elk Grove, CA (cdp) Sacramento County	275
Minneapolis, MN (city) Hennepin County	275
San Antonio, TX (city) Bexar County	275
Bellevue, WA (city) King County	273
Renton, WA (city) King County	266
Grand Prairie, TX (city) Dallas County	264
Corona, CA (city) Riverside County	262
Riverside, CA (city) Riverside County	256
Carrollton, TX (city) Denton County	253
Springfield, VA (cdp) Fairfax County	252
Sugar Land, TX (city) Fort Bend County	248
Albuquerque, NM (city) Bernalillo County	246
Pasadena, CA (city) Los Angeles County	245
Fullerton, CA (city) Orange County	240
Burke, VA (cdp) Fairfax County	239

Notes: Please refer to the User's Guide for an explanation of data; ranking tables include all places with Asian and/or NHPI populations above SF4 population thresholds; (1) tables reflect only those areas that meet SF4 population thresholds, therefore there may be less than 50 states, 75 counties or 75 places listed

Educational Attainment: Four-Year College Graduates

Vietnamese 25 Years and Over Who are Four-Year College Graduates

All States, Top 75 Counties, and Top 75 Places Sorted by Percent[1]

State	Percent
Delaware	42.86
Virginia	26.19
Rhode Island	26.00
Maryland	25.81
New Jersey	24.45
Illinois	23.64
New York	21.85
Ohio	21.63
District of Columbia	21.60
Connecticut	21.53
Texas	21.17
California	20.93
Indiana	20.68
Michigan	19.74
Florida	19.64
New Mexico	19.51
United States	19.44
Wisconsin	18.42
Pennsylvania	17.75
Vermont	17.30
Minnesota	16.85
Colorado	16.77
Oregon	16.65
South Carolina	16.36
North Carolina	16.02
Kentucky	15.97
Tennessee	15.78
Washington	15.74
Alabama	15.72
Arizona	15.65
Massachusetts	15.41
Oklahoma	15.35
West Virginia	15.22
Nevada	15.02
Idaho	14.09
Missouri	13.84
Louisiana	13.68
Mississippi	12.99
Georgia	12.47
Nebraska	12.40
Utah	11.46
New Hampshire	11.11
Arkansas	10.65
Hawaii	10.59
Kansas	10.42
Maine	9.37
Alaska	8.24
Iowa	7.53
South Dakota	4.48

County	Percent
Washtenaw County, MI	66.06
Alachua County, FL	65.73
New York County, NY	64.80
Somerset County, NJ	54.98
Collin County, TX	52.45
New Castle County, DE	51.98
Monmouth County, NJ	51.64
Lake County, IL	44.91
Fairfax Independent City, VA	44.88
Alexandria Independent City, VA	42.75
Madison County, AL	41.38
Howard County, MD	39.80
Brazoria County, TX	39.67
Placer County, CA	39.64
San Mateo County, CA	37.64
Clackamas County, OR	35.28
Santa Cruz County, CA	35.20
Greene County, MO	34.96
Yolo County, CA	34.69
Nassau County, NY	33.94
Bergen County, NJ	33.68
Morris County, NJ	33.40
Scott County, MN	33.33
Brazos County, TX	33.01
Dane County, WI	32.90
Fort Bend County, TX	32.23
Kern County, CA	31.95
Palm Beach County, FL	31.51
Essex County, NJ	30.94
Canadian County, OK	30.26
Travis County, TX	30.08
Chester County, PA	30.05
Cleveland County, OK	29.86
Butler County, OH	29.75
Wake County, NC	29.60
Ventura County, CA	29.43
Okaloosa County, FL	29.20
Washington County, MN	28.83
Wayne County, MI	28.48
Prince William County, VA	28.25
Will County, IL	28.24
Marion County, IN	28.06
Fairfax County, VA	28.04
Seminole County, FL	28.01
Union County, NJ	27.81
New Haven County, CT	27.56
Montgomery County, MD	27.35
Arlington County, VA	26.94
Chesterfield County, VA	26.91
Delaware County, PA	26.86
Albany County, NY	26.74
Summit County, OH	26.73
Loudoun County, VA	26.49
Brevard County, FL	26.39
Williamson County, TX	26.36
Middlesex County, NJ	26.22
Forsyth County, NC	26.17
Washington County, OR	25.51
Oakland County, MI	25.46
Suffolk County, NY	25.46
Alameda County, CA	25.18
Burlington County, NJ	25.06
Middlesex County, MA	24.86
Jefferson County, CO	24.71
Arapahoe County, CO	24.68
Contra Costa County, CA	24.56
Miami-Dade County, FL	24.47
Hudson County, NJ	24.02
Broward County, FL	23.62
Lubbock County, TX	23.56
York County, PA	23.53
Cook County, IL	23.46
Richland County, SC	23.30
Montgomery County, PA	23.27
Riverside County, CA	23.25

Place	Percent
Laguna Niguel, CA (city) Orange County	63.55
Allen, TX (city) Collin County	60.61
Aliso Viejo, CA (cdp) Orange County	57.54
Laguna Hills, CA (city) Orange County	56.59
Cary, NC (town) Wake County	54.34
Yorba Linda, CA (city) Orange County	54.01
Cupertino, CA (city) Santa Clara County	49.67
Irvine, CA (city) Orange County	48.82
Thousand Oaks, CA (city) Ventura County	48.38
Chantilly, VA (cdp) Fairfax County	46.95
Santa Clarita, CA (city) Los Angeles County	46.82
Downey, CA (city) Los Angeles County	45.93
Cerritos, CA (city) Los Angeles County	45.49
Placentia, CA (city) Orange County	45.07
Plano, TX (city) Collin County	44.61
Rancho Santa Margarita, CA (city) Orange County	43.36
Seattle Hill-Silver Firs, WA (cdp) Snohomish County	43.12
Pasadena, CA (city) Los Angeles County	42.10
Missouri City, TX (city) Fort Bend County	42.08
Chino Hills, CA (city) San Bernardino County	42.07
Tustin, CA (city) Orange County	41.98
Berkeley, CA (city) Alameda County	41.95
Franconia, VA (cdp) Fairfax County	41.21
Fremont, CA (city) Alameda County	40.95
Camarillo, CA (city) Ventura County	40.33
Montgomery Village, MD (cdp) Montgomery County	40.08
Mission Viejo, CA (city) Orange County	39.74
Davis, CA (city) Yolo County	39.33
Diamond Bar, CA (city) Los Angeles County	39.22
Mountain View, CA (city) Santa Clara County	39.21
Richardson, TX (city) Dallas County	39.02
Stafford, TX (city) Fort Bend County	38.58
Cypress, CA (city) Orange County	38.45
Gaithersburg, MD (city) Montgomery County	38.44
Sterling Heights, MI (city) Macomb County	37.46
Ocean Springs, MS (city) Jackson County	36.46
Pearland, TX (city) Brazoria County	36.39
Colesville, MD (cdp) Montgomery County	35.51
Oakton, VA (cdp) Fairfax County	34.64
Lake Forest, CA (city) Orange County	34.34
Germantown, MD (cdp) Montgomery County	33.45
Bakersfield, CA (city) Kern County	33.21
Springfield, MO (city) Greene County	33.02
Herndon, VA (town) Fairfax County	32.94
Aurora, IL (city) Kane County	32.82
Sugar Land, TX (city) Fort Bend County	32.50
Fountain Valley, CA (city) Orange County	32.44
Madison, WI (city) Dane County	32.42
Huntington Beach, CA (city) Orange County	32.03
Burke, VA (cdp) Fairfax County	31.99
Austin, TX (city) Travis County	31.89
Chandler, AZ (city) Maricopa County	31.60
Orange, CA (city) Orange County	31.43
Metairie, LA (cdp) Jefferson Parish	31.40
Laguna, CA (cdp) Sacramento County	31.38
Burbank, CA (city) Los Angeles County	31.33
Campbell, CA (city) Santa Clara County	31.30
North Richland Hills, TX (city) Tarrant County	30.89
Milpitas, CA (city) Santa Clara County	30.87
Medford, MA (city) Middlesex County	30.65
West Hartford, CT (town) Hartford County	30.58
Bellevue, WA (city) King County	30.57
Irving, TX (city) Dallas County	29.79
Corona, CA (city) Riverside County	29.64
Rowland Heights, CA (cdp) Los Angeles County	29.46
Belleville, NJ (township) Essex County	29.43
Daly City, CA (city) San Mateo County	29.25
West Springfield, VA (cdp) Fairfax County	29.21
Torrance, CA (city) Los Angeles County	29.19
Indianapolis, IN (sp. city) Marion County	29.00
Albany, NY (city) Albany County	28.93
Newark, CA (city) Alameda County	28.81
Lake Barcroft, VA (cdp) Fairfax County	28.32
Rockville, MD (city) Montgomery County	28.25
Sunnyvale, CA (city) Santa Clara County	28.07

Notes: Please refer to the User's Guide for an explanation of data; ranking tables include all places with Asian and/or NHPI populations above SF4 population thresholds; (1) tables reflect only those areas that meet SF4 population thresholds, therefore there may be less than 50 states, 75 counties or 75 places listed

Median Household Income

Total Population

All States, Top 75 Counties, and Top 75 Places Sorted by Number[1]

State	Dollars
New Jersey	55,146
Connecticut	53,935
Maryland	52,868
Alaska	51,571
Massachusetts	50,502
Hawaii	49,820
New Hampshire	49,467
California	47,493
Delaware	47,381
Colorado	47,203
Minnesota	47,111
Virginia	46,677
Illinois	46,590
Washington	45,776
Utah	45,726
Michigan	44,667
Nevada	44,581
Wisconsin	43,791
New York	43,393
Georgia	42,433
Rhode Island	42,090
United States	41,994
Indiana	41,567
Ohio	40,956
Oregon	40,916
Vermont	40,856
Kansas	40,624
Arizona	40,558
District of Columbia	40,127
Pennsylvania	40,106
Texas	39,927
Iowa	39,469
Nebraska	39,250
North Carolina	39,184
Florida	38,819
Missouri	37,934
Wyoming	37,892
Idaho	37,572
Maine	37,240
South Carolina	37,082
Tennessee	36,360
South Dakota	35,282
North Dakota	34,604
Alabama	34,135
New Mexico	34,133
Kentucky	33,672
Oklahoma	33,400
Montana	33,024
Louisiana	32,566
Arkansas	32,182
Mississippi	31,330
West Virginia	29,696

County	Dollars
Douglas County, CO	82,929
Fairfax County, VA	81,050
Loudoun County, VA	80,648
Hunterdon County, NJ	79,888
Los Alamos County, NM	78,993
Morris County, NJ	77,340
Somerset County, NJ	76,933
Falls Church Independent City, VA	74,924
Santa Clara County, CA	74,335
Howard County, MD	74,167
Putnam County, NY	72,279
Nassau County, NY	72,030
Montgomery County, MD	71,551
Marin County, CA	71,306
Fayette County, GA	71,227
Hamilton County, IN	71,026
Collin County, TX	70,835
San Mateo County, CA	70,819
Williamson County, TN	69,104
Forsyth County, GA	68,890
Rockland County, NY	67,971
DuPage County, IL	67,887
Fairfax Independent City, VA	67,642
Livingston County, MI	67,400
Delaware County, OH	67,258
Lake County, IL	66,973
Stafford County, VA	66,809
Scott County, MN	66,612
Washington County, MN	66,305
Prince William County, VA	65,960
Calvert County, MD	65,945
Carver County, MN	65,540
Chester County, PA	65,295
Suffolk County, NY	65,288
Sussex County, NJ	65,266
Fairfield County, CT	65,249
Bergen County, NJ	65,241
Rockwall County, TX	65,164
McHenry County, IL	64,826
Kendall County, IL	64,625
Monmouth County, NJ	64,271
Fort Bend County, TX	63,831
Contra Costa County, CA	63,675
Westchester County, NY	63,582
Norfolk County, MA	63,432
Oldham County, KY	63,229
North Slope Borough, AK	63,173
Arlington County, VA	63,001
Waukesha County, WI	62,839
Ozaukee County, WI	62,745
Eagle County, CO	62,682
Will County, IL	62,238
Charles County, MD	62,199
Juneau Borough, AK	62,034
Fauquier County, VA	61,999
Oakland County, MI	61,907
Dakota County, MN	61,863
Anne Arundel County, MD	61,768
Johnson County, KS	61,455
Middlesex County, NJ	61,446
Aleutians West Census Area, AK	61,406
Cherokee County, GA	60,896
Montgomery County, PA	60,829
Middlesex County, MA	60,821
Manassas Park Independent City, VA	60,794
Williamson County, TX	60,642
Gwinnett County, GA	60,537
Manassas Independent City, VA	60,409
Frederick County, MD	60,276
Geauga County, OH	60,200
Carroll County, MD	60,021
Bucks County, PA	59,727
Ventura County, CA	59,666
Kane County, IL	59,351
Hanover County, VA	59,223

Place	Dollars
Atherton, CA (town) San Mateo County	200,000+
Brookville, NY (village) Nassau County	200,000+
Laurel Hollow, NY (village) Nassau County	200,000+
Oyster Bay Cove, NY (village) Nassau County	200,000+
Rolling Hills, CA (city) Los Angeles County	200,000+
Sands Point, NY (village) Nassau County	200,000+
Hillsborough, CA (town) San Mateo County	193,157
Muttontown, NY (village) Nassau County	184,386
Scarsdale, NY (village) Westchester County	182,792
Bunker Hill Village, TX (city) Harris County	177,274
Los Altos Hills, CA (town) Santa Clara County	173,570
Hunters Creek Village, TX (city) Harris County	171,294
South Barrington, IL (village) Cook County	170,755
Winnetka, IL (village) Cook County	167,458
Newport Coast, CA (cdp) Orange County	164,653
Chappaqua, NY (cdp) Westchester County	163,201
Travilah, MD (cdp) Montgomery County	160,323
Great Falls, VA (cdp) Fairfax County	159,695
New Castle, NY (town) Westchester County	159,691
Old Westbury, NY (village) Nassau County	155,749
Blackhawk-Camino Tass., CA (cdp) Contra Costa Co.	154,598
Weston, MA (town) Middlesex County	153,918
East Hills, NY (village) Nassau County	149,726
North Hills, NY (village) Nassau County	149,122
Munsey Park, NY (village) Nassau County	149,100
Long Grove, IL (village) Lake County	148,150
Darien, CT (town) Fairfield County	146,755
Oak Brook, IL (village) Du Page County	146,537
Bronxville, NY (village) Westchester County	144,940
New Canaan, CT (town) Fairfield County	141,788
Wilton, CT (town) Fairfield County	141,428
Loyola, CA (cdp) Santa Clara County	140,617
Town and Country, MO (city) Saint Louis County	139,967
Saratoga, CA (city) Santa Clara County	139,895
Alamo, CA (cdp) Contra Costa County	137,105
Lake Forest, IL (city) Lake County	136,462
Wolf Trap, VA (cdp) Fairfax County	135,782
Lake Success, NY (village) Nassau County	134,383
Saddle River, NJ (borough) Bergen County	134,289
Piedmont, CA (city) Alameda County	134,270
Lincolnshire, IL (village) Lake County	134,259
Briarcliff Manor, NY (village) Westchester County	133,272
Old Brookville, NY (village) Nassau County	133,192
Franklin Lakes, NJ (borough) Bergen County	132,373
Southlake, TX (city) Tarrant County	131,549
Millburn, NJ (township) Essex County	130,848
Alpine, NJ (borough) Bergen County	130,740
West University Place, TX (city) Harris County	130,721
Burr Ridge, IL (village) Du Page County	129,507
Potomac, MD (cdp) Montgomery County	128,936
Los Altos, CA (city) Santa Clara County	126,740
Palos Verdes Estates, CA (city) Los Angeles County	123,534
Woodbury, NY (cdp) Nassau County	122,643
Flower Hill, NY (village) Nassau County	121,999
McLean, VA (cdp) Fairfax County	121,138
Searingtown, NY (cdp) Nassau County	120,546
Westport, CT (town) Fairfield County	119,872
Montgomery, NJ (township) Somerset County	118,850
Sudbury, MA (town) Middlesex County	118,579
North Castle, NY (town) Westchester County	117,815
Orinda, CA (city) Contra Costa County	117,637
Colleyville, TX (city) Tarrant County	117,419
San Marino, CA (city) Los Angeles County	117,267
West Windsor, NJ (township) Mercer County	116,335
Villa Park, CA (city) Orange County	116,203
Danville, CA (town) Contra Costa County	114,064
Wellesley, MA (town) Norfolk County	113,686
Holmdel, NJ (township) Monmouth County	112,879
Brentwood, TN (city) Williamson County	111,819
Cranbury, NJ (township) Middlesex County	111,680
Cinco Ranch, TX (cdp) Fort Bend County	111,517
Rye, NY (city) Westchester County	110,894
North Star, DE (cdp) New Castle County	110,616
La Canada Flintridge, CA (city) Los Angeles County	109,989
Berkeley Lake, GA (city) Gwinnett County	109,401

Notes: Please refer to the User's Guide for an explanation of data; ranking tables include all places with Asian and/or NHPI populations above SF4 population thresholds; (1) tables reflect only those areas that meet SF4 population thresholds, therefore there may be less than 50 states, 75 counties or 75 places listed

Median Household Income

Asian

All States, Top 75 Counties, and Top 75 Places Sorted by Number[1]

State	Dollars
New Jersey	72,224
Delaware	65,190
Connecticut	61,587
Maryland	59,589
Michigan	57,966
Virginia	57,420
Illinois	57,333
New Hampshire	56,344
California	55,366
Hawaii	54,232
United States	51,908
Massachusetts	51,273
West Virginia	50,658
Georgia	50,496
Texas	50,049
North Carolina	49,497
Ohio	49,266
Colorado	48,619
Washington	47,517
Alaska	47,121
Oregon	46,955
Nevada	46,328
Kentucky	46,225
Arizona	45,802
Idaho	45,746
Minnesota	45,520
Tennessee	45,497
New York	45,402
Florida	44,780
Pennsylvania	44,205
South Carolina	43,915
Indiana	42,933
Kansas	42,767
Utah	42,219
New Mexico	42,010
Alabama	42,007
Nebraska	41,945
Missouri	41,075
Mississippi	40,427
Iowa	40,348
Wyoming	40,293
Wisconsin	39,847
Vermont	39,630
South Dakota	38,346
Maine	37,873
Arkansas	37,841
Rhode Island	36,473
Louisiana	36,115
District of Columbia	36,031
North Dakota	35,441
Oklahoma	34,547
Montana	24,419

County	Dollars
Raleigh County, WV	131,870
Chemung County, NY	129,226
Westmoreland County, PA	127,242
Vermilion County, IL	101,808
Somerset County, NJ	101,349
Hunterdon County, NJ	95,454
Oldham County, KY	94,473
Geauga County, OH	94,327
Calvert County, MD	93,352
Amador County, CA	92,778
Monmouth County, NJ	92,164
Oconee County, GA	91,102
Morris County, NJ	90,386
Putnam County, NY	90,169
Forsyth County, GA	89,554
Bristol County, RI	89,451
Livingston County, MI	88,177
Midland County, MI	87,855
Westchester County, NY	86,892
Douglas County, CO	85,037
Washington County, MN	84,223
Delaware County, OH	84,131
Nassau County, NY	83,948
Williamson County, TN	83,452
Warren County, OH	83,432
Mercer County, NJ	83,288
Clearfield County, PA	83,193
Allegany County, MD	83,100
Santa Clara County, CA	82,804
Washington County, TN	82,566
Lake County, IL	81,889
Rockwall County, TX	81,482
Fayette County, GA	81,210
Bureau County, IL	81,185
Hamilton County, IN	80,076
Waukesha County, WI	79,762
Rockland County, NY	79,562
Fairfield County, CT	79,191
Loudoun County, VA	79,032
Collin County, TX	78,545
San Mateo County, CA	78,263
Middlesex County, NJ	77,613
Essex County, NJ	77,066
Ozaukee County, WI	76,919
Carver County, MN	76,638
Fort Bend County, TX	76,627
Porter County, IN	76,601
Oakland County, MI	76,579
Will County, IL	76,517
Addison County, VT	76,115
Matanuska-Susitna Borough, AK	75,942
Montgomery County, TX	75,673
Chester County, PA	75,576
DuPage County, IL	75,334
Sussex County, NJ	75,104
Union County, NJ	75,082
Franklin County, PA	75,000
North Slope Borough, AK	74,318
St. Clair County, MI	73,750
Steuben County, NY	73,125
Beaufort County, SC	72,905
Union County, PA	72,875
Boone County, KY	72,794
McHenry County, IL	72,763
Monroe County, PA	72,609
Montgomery County, NY	72,292
Gloucester County, NJ	72,083
Ventura County, CA	71,851
Cape May County, NJ	71,548
Williamson County, TX	71,295
Putnam County, WV	71,250
Lincoln County, OR	71,136
Carroll County, MD	71,094
Suffolk County, NY	71,059
New Castle County, DE	71,025

Place	Dollars
Bunker Hill Village, TX (city) Harris County	200,000+
Muttontown, NY (village) Nassau County	200,000+
Newport Coast, CA (cdp) Orange County	200,000+
Oak Brook, IL (village) Du Page County	200,000+
Oyster Bay Cove, NY (village) Nassau County	200,000+
Rolling Hills, CA (city) Los Angeles County	200,000+
Sands Point, NY (village) Nassau County	200,000+
South Barrington, IL (village) Cook County	200,000+
Town and Country, MO (city) Saint Louis County	200,000+
Los Altos Hills, CA (town) Santa Clara County	194,789
Saddle River, NJ (borough) Bergen County	194,640
Laurel Hollow, NY (village) Nassau County	192,979
Briarcliff Manor, NY (village) Westchester County	187,303
Lincolnshire, IL (village) Lake County	186,316
Burr Ridge, IL (village) Du Page County	184,734
Moorestown, NJ (township) Burlington County	184,586
Munsey Park, NY (village) Nassau County	184,324
Atherton, CA (town) San Mateo County	182,016
Longmeadow, MA (town) Hampden County	178,082
Wilton, CT (town) Fairfield County	176,601
North Hills, NY (village) Nassau County	171,052
Cornwall, NY (town) Orange County	166,639
Rye, NY (city) Westchester County	165,155
Loyola, CA (cdp) Santa Clara County	162,669
Grosse Pointe Woods, MI (city) Wayne County	162,500
New Castle, NY (town) Westchester County	162,255
Cranbury, NJ (township) Middlesex County	161,769
Old Westbury, NY (village) Nassau County	161,602
Hillsborough, CA (town) San Mateo County	161,576
Chappaqua, NY (cdp) Westchester County	160,850
Darien, CT (town) Fairfield County	159,201
Warren, NJ (township) Somerset County	158,816
Union Hill-Novelty Hill, WA (cdp) King County	155,737
Los Altos, CA (city) Santa Clara County	155,651
Saratoga, CA (city) Santa Clara County	155,207
Bloomfield, MI (township) Oakland County	154,306
Searingtown, NY (cdp) Nassau County	153,911
North Castle, NY (town) Westchester County	153,354
Westport, CT (town) Fairfield County	152,552
Upper St. Clair, PA (township) Allegheny County	151,569
Weston, MA (town) Middlesex County	151,010
Muni. of Murrysville, PA (borough) Westmoreland Co.	150,196
Flower Hill, NY (village) Nassau County	150,000
Old Brookville, NY (village) Nassau County	150,000
Simsbury, CT (town) Hartford County	145,732
Bronxville, NY (village) Westchester County	145,315
Sharon, MA (town) Norfolk County	145,183
Ardsley, NY (village) Westchester County	143,660
Woodbury, NY (cdp) Nassau County	143,126
Scarsdale, NY (village) Westchester County	143,001
Southlake, TX (city) Tarrant County	142,113
Newtown, CT (town) Fairfield County	139,629
Travilah, MD (cdp) Montgomery County	138,765
Brookville, NY (village) Nassau County	137,845
Lake Forest, IL (city) Lake County	136,461
Montgomery, NJ (township) Somerset County	136,301
Highlands-Baywood Pk., CA (cdp) San Mateo County	136,176
Alamo, CA (cdp) Contra Costa County	134,432
Bernards, NJ (township) Somerset County	132,683
Hockessin, DE (cdp) New Castle County	132,562
Piedmont, CA (city) Alameda County	132,304
Wyckoff, NJ (township) Bergen County	132,300
Sudbury, MA (town) Middlesex County	131,455
Green Brook, NJ (township) Somerset County	130,889
Bradbury, CA (city) Los Angeles County	130,846
Blackhawk-Camino Tass., CA (cdp) Contra Costa Co.	130,793
Port Washington North, NY (village) Nassau County	130,047
Hopewell, NJ (township) Mercer County	129,801
Holmdel, NJ (township) Monmouth County	129,322
Potomac, MD (cdp) Montgomery County	129,295
Danville, IL (city) Vermilion County	129,083
Berkeley Heights, NJ (township) Union County	128,361
West Windsor, NJ (township) Mercer County	128,100
Raritan, NJ (borough) Somerset County	128,075
Hunters Creek Village, TX (city) Harris County	127,715

Notes: Please refer to the User's Guide for an explanation of data; ranking tables include all places with Asian and/or NHPI populations above SF4 population thresholds; (1) tables reflect only those areas that meet SF4 population thresholds, therefore there may be less than 50 states, 75 counties or 75 places listed

Median Household Income

Native Hawaiian and Other Pacific Islander

All States, Top 75 Counties, and Top 75 Places Sorted by Number[1]

State	Dollars
Delaware	66,250
Connecticut	60,536
South Carolina	56,833
New Jersey	56,080
Maryland	55,288
Virginia	51,553
Mississippi	50,446
California	48,650
Minnesota	48,214
Maine	48,000
Wisconsin	47,670
Georgia	46,303
Utah	43,575
Nevada	43,086
Louisiana	42,875
United States	42,717
New Mexico	42,716
Pennsylvania	42,656
Hawaii	41,779
Washington	41,656
Illinois	41,276
Texas	41,072
Ohio	40,718
Colorado	39,729
Arizona	39,688
Oregon	39,218
Montana	39,063
Florida	39,050
Alaska	38,258
Oklahoma	37,957
Kansas	37,788
North Carolina	37,778
Alabama	37,583
Idaho	36,429
Michigan	35,903
Indiana	35,625
Iowa	35,568
Massachusetts	34,891
Tennessee	34,441
Nebraska	34,120
Missouri	32,773
Rhode Island	29,423
West Virginia	29,375
Kentucky	29,135
New York	28,713
Arkansas	28,322

County	Dollars
Fairfax County, VA	90,000
Santa Barbara County, CA	66,467
San Mateo County, CA	65,510
Santa Clara County, CA	65,275
Contra Costa County, CA	63,589
Ventura County, CA	62,054
Jefferson County, CO	59,688
Gwinnett County, GA	59,655
Sonoma County, CA	59,188
Arapahoe County, CO	58,438
Solano County, CA	57,125
Thurston County, WA	56,926
Montgomery County, MD	56,731
Miami-Dade County, FL	56,719
Alameda County, CA	54,231
Orange County, CA	53,929
Bell County, TX	50,224
Suffolk County, NY	49,792
Davis County, UT	49,545
Palm Beach County, FL	48,750
Milwaukee County, WI	47,891
San Diego County, CA	47,097
Snohomish County, WA	47,092
Bernalillo County, NM	46,250
Harris County, TX	45,688
San Bernardino County, CA	45,134
King County, WA	45,104
Utah County, UT	45,000
Coryell County, TX	44,583
Hillsborough County, FL	44,531
Clackamas County, OR	44,479
El Paso County, CO	44,423
San Joaquin County, CA	44,356
Kern County, CA	43,846
Monterey County, CA	43,839
Maui County, HI	43,813
Honolulu County, HI	43,442
Clark County, NV	43,250
Salt Lake County, UT	43,219
Washoe County, NV	42,981
Jackson County, MO	42,955
Orange County, FL	42,609
Hennepin County, MN	42,500
Los Angeles County, CA	42,363
Anchorage Borough, AK	41,875
Riverside County, CA	41,815
Maricopa County, AZ	41,295
Kauai County, HI	41,217
Washington County, OR	41,196
Sacramento County, CA	41,047
Broward County, FL	40,819
Pierce County, WA	40,647
Onslow County, NC	40,625
Clark County, WA	40,357
Duval County, FL	40,294
Franklin County, OH	40,048
Multnomah County, OR	39,861
Dallas County, TX	39,438
Shelby County, TN	38,977
Queens County, NY	38,854
Washington County, UT	38,611
Ada County, ID	37,279
Bexar County, TX	37,222
Stanislaus County, CA	37,167
Cook County, IL	37,153
Tarrant County, TX	36,146
Sedgwick County, KS	35,694
Hawaii County, HI	35,596
Travis County, TX	35,357
Essex County, NJ	34,712
Spokane County, WA	34,219
Marion County, OR	33,750
San Francisco County, CA	33,750
Kitsap County, WA	33,152
Wayne County, MI	32,054

Place	Dollars
Aiea, HI (cdp) Honolulu County	94,712
Mililani Town, HI (cdp) Honolulu County	87,188
Pittsburg, CA (city) Contra Costa County	78,677
San Bruno, CA (city) San Mateo County	77,561
Maunawili, HI (cdp) Honolulu County	76,999
Makakilo City, HI (cdp) Honolulu County	75,435
Kilauea, HI (cdp) Kauai County	75,000
Pearl City, HI (cdp) Honolulu County	72,543
Fremont, CA (city) Alameda County	71,705
Milpitas, CA (city) Santa Clara County	70,417
Sunnyvale, CA (city) Santa Clara County	70,179
Santa Clara, CA (city) Santa Clara County	68,438
East Palo Alto, CA (city) San Mateo County	68,333
Union City, CA (city) Alameda County	67,188
Mesa, AZ (city) Maricopa County	66,875
Village Park, HI (cdp) Honolulu County	66,250
San Mateo, CA (city) San Mateo County	65,859
Kailua, HI (cdp) Honolulu County	64,505
Captain Cook, HI (cdp) Hawaii County	63,214
West Jordan, UT (city) Salt Lake County	61,563
Hana, HI (cdp) Maui County	61,250
Fontana, CA (city) San Bernardino County	60,833
Kearns, UT (cdp) Salt Lake County	60,417
Tukwila, WA (city) King County	60,250
Paia, HI (cdp) Maui County	59,167
South San Francisco, CA (city) San Mateo County	59,107
Independence, MO (city) Jackson County	58,690
San Jose, CA (city) Santa Clara County	58,173
Makawao, HI (cdp) Maui County	58,000
Waimanalo Beach, HI (cdp) Honolulu County	57,125
Sandy, UT (city) Salt Lake County	57,019
Waikapu, HI (cdp) Maui County	57,000
Kaneohe, HI (cdp) Honolulu County	56,917
Fairfield, CA (city) Solano County	56,875
Lakewood, CA (city) Los Angeles County	56,250
Hayward, CA (city) Alameda County	55,250
Kalaoa, HI (cdp) Hawaii County	55,147
Kaaawa, HI (cdp) Honolulu County	55,000
Rialto, CA (city) San Bernardino County	54,500
Vallejo, CA (city) Solano County	54,167
Lahaina, HI (cdp) Maui County	54,097
Ahuimanu, HI (cdp) Honolulu County	54,000
Anaheim, CA (city) Orange County	53,750
Waikane, HI (cdp) Honolulu County	53,750
Carson, CA (city) Los Angeles County	53,487
Halawa, HI (cdp) Honolulu County	53,409
Holualoa, HI (cdp) Hawaii County	53,194
Kahaluu, HI (cdp) Honolulu County	52,500
Killeen, TX (city) Bell County	51,763
Oceanside, CA (city) San Diego County	51,759
Chula Vista, CA (city) San Diego County	51,630
Antioch, CA (city) Contra Costa County	51,607
North Las Vegas, NV (city) Clark County	51,023
Alameda, CA (city) Alameda County	50,982
Spanaway, WA (cdp) Pierce County	50,893
SeaTac, WA (city) King County	50,865
Costa Mesa, CA (city) Orange County	50,476
Oxnard, CA (city) Ventura County	50,208
Daly City, CA (city) San Mateo County	49,911
San Leandro, CA (city) Alameda County	49,500
Sunrise Manor, NV (cdp) Clark County	49,464
Waihee-Waiehu, HI (cdp) Maui County	49,342
Orem, UT (city) Utah County	49,000
Lakewood, WA (city) Pierce County	48,125
Honaunau-Napoopoo, HI (cdp) Hawaii County	48,056
Laie, HI (cdp) Honolulu County	47,813
Pakala Village, HI (cdp) Kauai County	47,813
Westminster, CA (city) Orange County	47,750
Ewa Beach, HI (cdp) Honolulu County	47,639
Haleiwa, HI (cdp) Honolulu County	47,500
Redwood City, CA (city) San Mateo County	47,212
San Diego, CA (city) San Diego County	47,165
Henderson, NV (city) Clark County	45,446
Marina, CA (city) Monterey County	44,844
West Valley City, UT (city) Salt Lake County	44,732

Notes: Please refer to the User's Guide for an explanation of data; ranking tables include all places with Asian and/or NHPI populations above SF4 population thresholds; (1) tables reflect only those areas that meet SF4 population thresholds, therefore there may be less than 50 states, 75 counties or 75 places listed

Median Household Income

Asian Indian

All States, Top 75 Counties, and Top 75 Places Sorted by Number[1]

State	Dollars
Delaware	76,392
New Jersey	75,677
West Virginia	72,813
California	72,130
New Hampshire	71,415
Maryland	71,336
Massachusetts	71,265
Virginia	70,392
Michigan	70,011
Oregon	67,191
Connecticut	66,903
Illinois	64,969
Arizona	64,122
Colorado	63,891
United States	63,669
Minnesota	62,146
Ohio	62,119
Hawaii	61,523
Washington	60,846
North Carolina	60,188
Texas	60,173
Iowa	60,145
Kentucky	59,817
Pennsylvania	59,643
Georgia	59,378
New Mexico	57,759
Arkansas	56,833
Indiana	56,630
Missouri	55,833
Nebraska	55,530
Kansas	55,306
Louisiana	54,461
North Dakota	54,286
New York	54,150
Alabama	54,113
Idaho	53,600
Tennessee	53,508
Wisconsin	52,344
Vermont	51,932
South Carolina	51,250
South Dakota	51,042
Florida	50,390
Maine	49,943
Mississippi	48,846
Utah	48,431
Oklahoma	48,333
Rhode Island	47,227
District of Columbia	47,011
Alaska	45,417
Nevada	42,326
Montana	33,438
Wyoming	25,313

County	Dollars
Westmoreland County, PA	134,883
York County, VA	115,437
Washington County, MN	112,435
Putnam County, NY	107,596
Hunterdon County, NJ	106,398
Waukesha County, WI	104,699
Delaware County, OH	103,983
Clackamas County, OR	103,321
Somerset County, NJ	103,249
Douglas County, CO	101,958
Brazoria County, TX	100,243
Monmouth County, NJ	99,955
Kanawha County, WV	99,647
Saginaw County, MI	97,325
St. Mary's County, MD	95,981
Saratoga County, NY	95,342
Hamilton County, IN	94,784
Sussex County, NJ	94,500
Clermont County, OH	94,304
Santa Clara County, CA	93,374
Stark County, OH	92,318
Morris County, NJ	91,882
Butler County, PA	91,583
Northampton County, PA	90,432
Chester County, PA	90,087
Cherokee County, GA	90,000
Nassau County, NY	89,657
Essex County, MA	89,301
Montgomery County, TX	87,805
Hidalgo County, TX	87,131
Ventura County, CA	86,227
Midland County, MI	86,203
Oakland County, MI	85,233
Westchester County, NY	84,791
Mercer County, NJ	84,779
Benton County, WA	84,605
Fairfax County, VA	84,084
Fort Bend County, TX	83,834
San Mateo County, CA	83,621
Montgomery County, MD	82,753
Oneida County, NY	82,699
Howard County, MD	82,457
Will County, IL	81,721
Genesee County, MI	81,489
Greene County, OH	81,283
Luzerne County, PA	81,194
Lake County, IL	81,090
Warren County, OH	80,766
Alameda County, CA	80,674
Collin County, TX	80,446
Kent County, DE	80,412
Hampden County, MA	80,402
Rockland County, NY	80,070
Butler County, OH	80,065
Bristol County, MA	79,775
Bergen County, NJ	79,161
Fairfield County, CT	78,837
Middlesex County, NJ	78,504
Norfolk County, MA	78,066
Loudoun County, VA	77,933
New Castle County, DE	76,883
McHenry County, IL	76,783
Lake County, IN	76,755
Hillsborough County, NH	76,711
McLennan County, TX	76,637
DuPage County, IL	76,555
Williamson County, TX	76,403
Orange County, CA	76,211
Suffolk County, NY	75,893
Middlesex County, MA	75,871
Placer County, CA	75,781
Tolland County, CT	75,302
Union County, NJ	75,230
Richmond County, NY	74,688
Jefferson County, CO	73,869

Place	Dollars
Brookfield, WI (city) Waukesha County	200,000+
Los Altos Hills, CA (town) Santa Clara County	200,000+
Los Altos, CA (city) Santa Clara County	200,000+
Muttontown, NY (village) Nassau County	200,000+
New Castle, NY (town) Westchester County	200,000+
Oak Brook, IL (village) Du Page County	200,000+
Scarsdale, NY (village) Westchester County	200,000+
South Barrington, IL (village) Cook County	200,000+
Town and Country, MO (city) Saint Louis County	200,000+
Upper St. Clair, PA (township) Allegheny County	186,873
Warren, NJ (township) Somerset County	176,569
Saratoga, CA (city) Santa Clara County	176,313
Searingtown, NY (cdp) Nassau County	171,148
Bloomfield, MI (township) Oakland County	167,536
Danville, CA (town) Contra Costa County	163,809
Burr Ridge, IL (village) Du Page County	161,233
Manhasset Hills, NY (cdp) Nassau County	159,057
Bernards, NJ (township) Somerset County	156,915
Potomac, MD (cdp) Montgomery County	155,091
Montgomery, NJ (township) Somerset County	153,791
Glenview, IL (village) Cook County	150,000
West Windsor, NJ (township) Mercer County	146,885
Travilah, MD (cdp) Montgomery County	146,858
Bridgewater, NJ (township) Somerset County	145,490
Port Washington, NY (cdp) Nassau County	142,846
Lexington, MA (town) Middlesex County	140,393
McLean, VA (cdp) Fairfax County	134,952
Solon, OH (city) Cuyahoga County	134,386
Wolf Trap, VA (cdp) Fairfax County	133,711
Boxborough, MA (town) Middlesex County	132,601
Newton, MA (city) Middlesex County	131,348
Cortlandt, NY (town) Westchester County	130,655
Pittsford, NY (town) Monroe County	129,814
Mahwah, NJ (township) Bergen County	129,690
Charleston, WV (city) Kanawha County	127,227
Scotch Plains, NJ (township) Union County	126,618
Wayne, NJ (township) Passaic County	126,503
Palmdale, CA (city) Los Angeles County	126,216
Germantown, TN (city) Shelby County	126,177
Plainview, NY (cdp) Nassau County	126,123
Rancho Palos Verdes, CA (city) Los Angeles County	125,973
Marlboro, NJ (township) Monmouth County	125,271
Northville, MI (township) Wayne County	125,000
Montville, NJ (township) Morris County	123,454
Holmdel, NJ (township) Monmouth County	123,283
Cupertino, CA (city) Santa Clara County	122,832
Novi, MI (city) Oakland County	122,776
Livingston, NJ (township) Essex County	119,226
Munster, IN (town) Lake County	119,134
Mount Pleasant, NY (town) Westchester County	119,072
Dix Hills, NY (cdp) Suffolk County	119,053
Syosset, NY (cdp) Nassau County	117,909
Branchburg, NJ (township) Somerset County	117,786
West Bloomfield, MI (township) Oakland County	116,703
Orland Park, IL (village) Cook County	115,985
Howell, NJ (township) Monmouth County	115,175
Manalapan, NJ (township) Monmouth County	114,288
Freehold, NJ (township) Monmouth County	114,070
Woodbury, MN (city) Washington County	111,815
Bethesda, MD (cdp) Montgomery County	110,306
Andover, MA (town) Essex County	109,819
Glastonbury, CT (town) Hartford County	109,563
Kendall Park, NJ (cdp) Middlesex County	109,069
North Potomac, MD (cdp) Montgomery County	108,893
Huntington, NY (town) Suffolk County	108,452
Newington, VA (cdp) Fairfax County	108,302
Strongsville, OH (city) Cuyahoga County	107,297
Thousand Oaks, CA (city) Ventura County	106,869
South Brunswick, NJ (township) Middlesex County	106,753
West Hempstead, NY (cdp) Nassau County	106,749
Nanuet, NY (cdp) Rockland County	105,611
Rockaway, NJ (township) Morris County	105,412
Summit, NJ (city) Union County	104,733
Oyster Bay, NY (town) Nassau County	104,560
Colesville, MD (cdp) Montgomery County	104,364

Notes: Please refer to the User's Guide for an explanation of data; ranking tables include all places with Asian and/or NHPI populations above SF4 population thresholds; (1) tables reflect only those areas that meet SF4 population thresholds, therefore there may be less than 50 states, 75 counties or 75 places listed

Median Household Income

Bangladeshi

All States, Top 75 Counties, and Top 75 Places Sorted by Number[1]

State	Dollars
Ohio	53,000
Maryland	51,534
Illinois	50,625
Connecticut	48,750
California	46,488
Virginia	45,893
New Jersey	45,324
Texas	43,897
Massachusetts	43,214
Georgia	41,947
Michigan	40,179
United States	39,321
Florida	36,570
Pennsylvania	35,179
New York	34,136

County	Dollars
Santa Clara County, CA	92,942
Montgomery County, MD	60,417
Fairfax County, VA	51,691
Middlesex County, NJ	46,125
Dallas County, TX	45,833
Atlantic County, NJ	45,563
Harris County, TX	40,938
DeKalb County, GA	37,115
Queens County, NY	35,890
Los Angeles County, CA	35,769
Wayne County, MI	33,750
New York County, NY	33,523
Passaic County, NJ	31,413
Kings County, NY	25,741
Bronx County, NY	25,430

Place	Dollars
New York, NY (city)	33,071
Los Angeles, CA (city) Los Angeles County	33,036
Paterson, NJ (city) Passaic County	32,411
Hamtramck, MI (city) Wayne County	30,625

Notes: Please refer to the User's Guide for an explanation of data; ranking tables include all places with Asian and/or NHPI populations above SF4 population thresholds; (1) tables reflect only those areas that meet SF4 population thresholds, therefore there may be less than 50 states, 75 counties or 75 places listed

Median Household Income

Cambodian

All States, Top 75 Counties, and Top 75 Places Sorted by Number[1]

State	Dollars
Connecticut	69,688
New Jersey	59,773
Michigan	58,972
Virginia	57,179
Illinois	55,817
Colorado	55,481
Georgia	54,241
Arizona	53,958
Maryland	53,056
Utah	51,458
Texas	50,036
Kansas	45,833
Oklahoma	42,969
Indiana	42,344
Tennessee	41,944
Oregon	40,417
Florida	40,345
Minnesota	39,858
North Carolina	39,643
Nevada	39,327
Iowa	39,286
New York	39,205
Missouri	38,207
Massachusetts	37,058
Ohio	36,750
United States	36,155
Washington	36,127
Alabama	28,661
California	27,579
Rhode Island	27,212
South Carolina	26,667
Pennsylvania	26,536
Maine	26,378
Wisconsin	21,985
Hawaii	12,917

County	Dollars
Fairfield County, CT	75,961
Fairfax County, VA	73,750
DeKalb County, GA	66,648
Denton County, TX	65,817
Worcester County, MA	65,682
Ottawa County, MI	59,335
Montgomery County, MD	58,162
Scott County, MN	57,552
Clayton County, GA	57,440
Riverside County, CA	56,750
Cook County, IL	55,233
Chesterfield County, VA	53,900
Santa Clara County, CA	53,482
Maricopa County, AZ	53,449
Denver County, CO	52,639
Salt Lake County, UT	52,596
Dallas County, TX	52,426
Henrico County, VA	52,283
Snohomish County, WA	51,652
Orange County, CA	51,188
Sedgwick County, KS	47,202
Clark County, WA	47,125
Gwinnett County, GA	45,909
Dakota County, MN	45,750
Cuyahoga County, OH	45,625
Washington County, OR	44,250
Hennepin County, MN	42,452
Duval County, FL	42,292
Middlesex County, MA	41,701
Tarrant County, TX	41,518
Kern County, CA	41,250
Harris County, TX	40,655
Shelby County, TN	40,000
Clark County, NV	39,856
Polk County, IA	39,107
Camden County, NJ	39,063
Arlington County, VA	38,971
Multnomah County, OR	38,885
Mecklenburg County, NC	37,500
Essex County, MA	36,779
Hampden County, MA	36,429
Monroe County, NY	35,938
Brazoria County, TX	35,536
San Bernardino County, CA	35,216
Kings County, NY	35,078
Pinellas County, FL	34,602
King County, WA	34,344
Hamilton County, OH	33,571
Pierce County, WA	31,712
San Francisco County, CA	31,458
Franklin County, OH	31,346
Ramsey County, MN	31,250
Davidson County, NC	31,000
Sacramento County, CA	30,795
Bronx County, NY	30,789
Thurston County, WA	30,000
Alameda County, CA	29,483
Olmsted County, MN	27,315
Los Angeles County, CA	26,779
San Diego County, CA	26,436
Suffolk County, MA	26,286
Stanislaus County, CA	25,781
Sonoma County, CA	25,357
Providence County, RI	25,288
Cumberland County, ME	25,000
Mobile County, AL	22,679
Bristol County, MA	21,439
Philadelphia County, PA	20,746
Fresno County, CA	20,682
Cowlitz County, WA	20,417
San Joaquin County, CA	17,377

Place	Dollars
Bridgeport, CT (city) Fairfield County	81,354
Norwalk, CA (city) Los Angeles County	79,229
Danbury, CT (city) Fairfield County	70,750
Silver Spring, MD (cdp) Montgomery County	60,114
Aurora, CO (city) Arapahoe County	59,375
Carrollton, TX (city) Denton County	56,667
Lakewood, CA (city) Los Angeles County	53,958
Phoenix, AZ (city) Maricopa County	53,438
Denver, CO (city) Denver County	52,639
Chicago, IL (city) Cook County	52,500
West Valley City, UT (city) Salt Lake County	52,500
San Jose, CA (city) Santa Clara County	52,319
Cranston, RI (city) Providence County	50,662
Dallas, TX (city) Dallas County	48,393
Garden Grove, CA (city) Orange County	47,679
Santa Ana, CA (city) Orange County	43,125
Jacksonville, FL (city) Duval County	42,292
Bloomington, MN (city) Hennepin County	41,250
Lowell, MA (city) Middlesex County	39,929
Bellflower, CA (city) Los Angeles County	39,821
Arlington, VA (cdp) Arlington County	38,971
Portland, OR (city) Multnomah County	38,378
Charlotte, NC (city) Mecklenburg County	37,750
New York, NY (city)	37,422
Memphis, TN (city) Shelby County	37,292
Signal Hill, CA (city) Los Angeles County	36,875
Lynn, MA (city) Essex County	36,667
Attleboro, MA (city) Bristol County	34,539
St. Petersburg, FL (city) Pinellas County	34,261
Houston, TX (city) Harris County	33,618
Santa Rosa, CA (city) Sonoma County	33,393
Lawrence, MA (city) Essex County	32,024
San Francisco, CA (city) San Francisco County	31,458
Columbus, OH (city) Franklin County	31,382
Everett, WA (city) Snohomish County	31,250
Sacramento, CA (city) Sacramento County	31,250
Tacoma, WA (city) Pierce County	31,250
Lexington, NC (city) Davidson County	31,000
White Center, WA (cdp) King County	29,844
Beaverton, OR (city) Washington County	29,688
St. Paul, MN (city) Ramsey County	26,964
Minneapolis, MN (city) Hennepin County	26,477
Los Angeles, CA (city) Los Angeles County	26,406
Revere, MA (city) Suffolk County	26,250
Rochester, MN (city) Olmsted County	26,111
San Diego, CA (city) San Diego County	25,441
Boston, MA (city) Suffolk County	24,886
Oakland, CA (city) Alameda County	24,453
Providence, RI (city) Providence County	23,297
Fresno, CA (city) Fresno County	22,768
Long Beach, CA (city) Los Angeles County	22,673
Pomona, CA (city) Los Angeles County	21,657
Rosemead, CA (city) Los Angeles County	21,250
Modesto, CA (city) Stanislaus County	20,938
San Bernardino, CA (city) San Bernardino County	20,865
Philadelphia, PA (city) Philadelphia County	20,746
Longview, WA (city) Cowlitz County	20,714
Seattle, WA (city) King County	20,069
Monterey Park, CA (city) Los Angeles County	19,279
Stockton, CA (city) San Joaquin County	17,264
Fall River, MA (city) Bristol County	15,938
Portland, ME (city) Cumberland County	14,643

Notes: Please refer to the User's Guide for an explanation of data; ranking tables include all places with Asian and/or NHPI populations above SF4 population thresholds; (1) tables reflect only those areas that meet SF4 population thresholds, therefore there may be less than 50 states, 75 counties or 75 places listed

Median Household Income

Chinese (except Taiwanese)

***All States, Top 75 Counties, and Top 75 Places Sorted by Number*[1]**

State	Dollars
New Jersey	80,310
Connecticut	63,762
Maryland	61,042
New Hampshire	60,750
Delaware	60,694
Virginia	59,524
Alaska	58,375
California	57,457
North Carolina	55,710
Hawaii	53,405
Michigan	52,888
Washington	52,555
Georgia	51,814
Massachusetts	51,669
Minnesota	51,542
Colorado	51,481
United States	51,321
Texas	50,812
Nevada	50,568
Illinois	50,519
Idaho	50,500
Vermont	48,125
New Mexico	48,103
Oregon	47,213
Arizona	46,576
Tennessee	46,238
Ohio	44,380
South Carolina	44,178
Wisconsin	43,151
Kansas	41,497
South Dakota	41,369
Kentucky	41,092
Florida	40,680
Arkansas	40,275
Wyoming	40,227
Pennsylvania	40,072
Missouri	39,473
New York	39,243
Maine	38,977
Utah	38,822
Mississippi	37,420
Rhode Island	37,262
Indiana	37,120
West Virginia	36,875
Louisiana	36,090
Iowa	35,363
North Dakota	34,167
Alabama	33,281
District of Columbia	31,611
Montana	30,720
Nebraska	30,115
Oklahoma	25,127

County	Dollars
Somerset County, NJ	109,693
Washington County, MN	102,679
Hunterdon County, NJ	97,948
Monmouth County, NJ	96,560
Warren County, OH	96,272
Delaware County, OH	95,489
Morris County, NJ	95,268
Midland County, MI	94,755
Essex County, NJ	94,282
Lake County, IL	94,146
Santa Clara County, CA	92,516
Berks County, PA	91,715
Loudoun County, VA	91,681
Mercer County, NJ	91,269
Westchester County, NY	90,665
Chester County, PA	90,629
Hamilton County, IN	89,788
Saratoga County, NY	89,554
Rockingham County, NH	89,251
Anoka County, MN	88,676
Putnam County, NY	88,065
DuPage County, IL	87,952
Kane County, IL	87,019
Brazoria County, TX	86,856
Ventura County, CA	86,639
Rockland County, NY	86,311
Marin County, CA	86,034
Fairfield County, CT	85,952
Will County, IL	84,350
Waukesha County, WI	83,440
Douglas County, CO	81,441
Nassau County, NY	81,338
Collin County, TX	80,992
Ocean County, NJ	80,935
Middlesex County, NJ	80,575
Montgomery County, TX	79,796
San Mateo County, CA	79,671
Fairfax County, VA	77,408
Napa County, CA	76,944
Union County, NJ	76,818
Fort Bend County, TX	76,238
Bucks County, PA	75,955
Bergen County, NJ	75,583
Burlington County, NJ	75,275
Sonoma County, CA	75,199
Contra Costa County, CA	75,113
Williamson County, TX	74,000
Benton County, WA	73,750
Butler County, OH	73,750
Lake County, OH	73,333
Gloucester County, NJ	72,625
Lehigh County, PA	72,198
Oakland County, MI	72,009
Howard County, MD	71,964
Ottawa County, MI	71,375
Dutchess County, NY	70,903
Wake County, NC	70,822
New London County, CT	70,677
Montgomery County, MD	70,418
Montgomery County, PA	70,240
Cumberland County, PA	69,861
Schenectady County, NY	69,464
Hillsborough County, NH	68,393
Passaic County, NJ	68,214
Orange County, CA	67,965
Middlesex County, MA	67,038
Washington County, OR	66,831
Alexandria Independent City, VA	66,500
Peoria County, IL	66,250
Clackamas County, OR	66,172
Placer County, CA	66,118
Plymouth County, MA	66,042
Litchfield County, CT	65,682
New Castle County, DE	65,417
Lake County, IN	65,139

Place	Dollars
Englewood Cliffs, NJ (borough) Bergen County	200,000+
Westport, CT (town) Fairfield County	200,000+
Los Altos Hills, CA (town) Santa Clara County	200,000
Los Altos, CA (city) Santa Clara County	165,961
Highlands-Baywood Pk., CA (cdp) San Mateo Co.	159,402
Saratoga, CA (city) Santa Clara County	158,514
Calabasas, CA (city) Los Angeles County	155,292
Hillsborough, CA (town) San Mateo County	154,640
Piedmont, CA (city) Alameda County	151,126
West Bloomfield, MI (township) Oakland County	151,123
San Carlos, CA (city) San Mateo County	148,885
Westford, MA (town) Middlesex County	145,096
Warren, NJ (township) Somerset County	142,984
Holmdel, NJ (township) Monmouth County	139,211
Potomac, MD (cdp) Montgomery County	138,500
Montgomery, NJ (township) Somerset County	134,367
La Canada Flintridge, CA (city) Los Angeles County	133,375
West Windsor, NJ (township) Mercer County	132,330
Hanover, NJ (township) Morris County	130,918
Bernards, NJ (township) Somerset County	130,561
Weston, MA (town) Middlesex County	130,239
Rolling Hills Estates, CA (city) Los Angeles County	129,859
Colesville, MD (cdp) Montgomery County	127,961
Lisle, IL (village) Du Page County	127,681
Scarsdale, NY (village) Westchester County	127,232
Laguna Hills, CA (city) Orange County	127,021
Bridgewater, NJ (township) Somerset County	125,597
New Castle, NY (town) Westchester County	124,081
Danville, CA (town) Contra Costa County	123,183
Montville, NJ (township) Morris County	120,500
Manhattan Beach, CA (city) Los Angeles County	119,220
North Andover, MA (town) Essex County	118,985
Blackhawk-Camino Tass., CA (cdp) Contra Costa Co.	118,693
Dublin, OH (city) Franklin County	118,591
Greenwich, CT (town) Fairfield County	117,714
Needham, MA (town) Norfolk County	117,657
Marlboro, NJ (township) Monmouth County	117,303
Wolf Trap, VA (cdp) Fairfax County	115,590
Berkeley Heights, NJ (township) Union County	115,068
Lake Success, NY (village) Nassau County	115,043
Livingston, NJ (township) Essex County	113,944
Kensington, CA (cdp) Contra Costa County	113,507
Greenburgh, NY (town) Westchester County	113,220
Vernon Hills, IL (village) Lake County	113,180
East Hanover, NJ (township) Morris County	112,671
West Orange, NJ (township) Essex County	111,683
New Providence, NJ (borough) Union County	111,618
Novi, MI (city) Oakland County	111,146
Palos Verdes Estates, CA (city) Los Angeles County	110,260
Lexington, MA (town) Middlesex County	110,008
Woodbury, MN (city) Washington County	109,671
Orinda, CA (city) Contra Costa County	109,341
Cupertino, CA (city) Santa Clara County	109,207
Acton, MA (town) Middlesex County	108,801
San Ramon, CA (city) Contra Costa County	107,900
Morganville, NJ (cdp) Monmouth County	107,148
Hudson, OH (city) Summit County	106,977
Andover, MA (town) Essex County	106,024
Lower Macungie, PA (township) Lehigh County	105,976
Pleasanton, CA (city) Alameda County	105,441
Tustin Foothills, CA (cdp) Orange County	104,925
Lower Providence, PA (township) Montgomery County	104,905
San Marino, CA (city) Los Angeles County	104,762
North Potomac, MD (cdp) Montgomery County	104,728
Mundelein, IL (village) Lake County	104,592
Los Gatos, CA (town) Santa Clara County	104,469
Carlsbad, CA (city) San Diego County	104,230
Dix Hills, NY (cdp) Suffolk County	103,986
Chesterfield, MO (city) Saint Louis County	103,903
North New Hyde Park, NY (cdp) Nassau County	103,622
Wellesley, MA (town) Norfolk County	103,013
Naperville, IL (city) Du Page County	102,958
Millburn, NJ (township) Essex County	102,752
Paramus, NJ (borough) Bergen County	102,747
Wayne, NJ (township) Passaic County	102,565

Notes: Please refer to the User's Guide for an explanation of data; ranking tables include all places with Asian and/or NHPI populations above SF4 population thresholds; (1) tables reflect only those areas that meet SF4 population thresholds, therefore there may be less than 50 states, 75 counties or 75 places listed

Median Household Income

Fijian

All States, Top 75 Counties, and Top 75 Places Sorted by Number[1]

State	Dollars
Oregon	45,694
California	45,656
United States	45,420
Washington	40,625

County	Dollars
Contra Costa County, CA	85,000
Santa Clara County, CA	61,339
San Mateo County, CA	60,313
Alameda County, CA	52,054
King County, WA	41,953
Stanislaus County, CA	39,167
Los Angeles County, CA	38,487
Sacramento County, CA	35,179
Yolo County, CA	28,676

Place	Dollars
Hayward, CA (city) Alameda County	52,083
Modesto, CA (city) Stanislaus County	38,000
Sacramento, CA (city) Sacramento County	33,365

Notes: Please refer to the User's Guide for an explanation of data; ranking tables include all places with Asian and/or NHPI populations above SF4 population thresholds; (1) tables reflect only those areas that meet SF4 population thresholds, therefore there may be less than 50 states, 75 counties or 75 places listed

Median Household Income

Filipino

All States, Top 75 Counties, and Top 75 Places Sorted by Number[1]

State	Dollars
New Jersey	80,946
West Virginia	76,919
New York	72,850
Michigan	70,486
Illinois	67,293
Maryland	65,512
Wyoming	63,393
Connecticut	62,614
California	62,143
Delaware	61,250
United States	60,570
Virginia	59,873
Wisconsin	58,851
Massachusetts	57,400
Minnesota	56,750
Hawaii	55,305
Texas	54,970
Indiana	54,324
Ohio	53,909
Alaska	53,507
Pennsylvania	53,083
Maine	52,813
Tennessee	52,396
Washington	52,393
Florida	52,039
New Hampshire	51,667
Missouri	50,908
Georgia	50,064
Colorado	49,500
Utah	49,327
Nevada	48,692
Kansas	47,847
South Dakota	47,778
Kentucky	47,569
Arizona	47,237
Mississippi	47,045
Alabama	46,429
North Carolina	46,372
Nebraska	46,307
Vermont	46,042
Rhode Island	45,648
Oregon	45,000
South Carolina	44,793
North Dakota	43,625
Louisiana	42,571
New Mexico	41,875
Idaho	41,071
Iowa	39,279
District of Columbia	35,887
Arkansas	35,765
Montana	35,556
Oklahoma	35,295

County	Dollars
Waukesha County, WI	106,001
Loudoun County, VA	98,407
Rockland County, NY	96,988
Morris County, NJ	94,969
Monmouth County, NJ	94,607
Nassau County, NY	93,280
Middlesex County, NJ	92,326
Highlands County, FL	91,662
Passaic County, NJ	90,530
Suffolk County, NY	90,391
Brazoria County, TX	87,940
Bergen County, NJ	87,226
Gloucester County, NJ	86,246
Essex County, NJ	86,197
Westchester County, NY	85,623
Marin County, CA	85,530
McHenry County, IL	85,355
Union County, NJ	84,567
Fort Bend County, TX	84,297
Santa Clara County, CA	81,884
Somerset County, NJ	81,424
Richmond County, NY	80,661
Ocean County, NJ	80,365
Summit County, OH	79,238
Fairfax County, VA	78,943
San Mateo County, CA	77,763
North Slope Borough, AK	77,433
Lake County, IL	77,418
DuPage County, IL	77,082
Dakota County, MN	76,593
Atlantic County, NJ	76,552
Baltimore County, MD	75,879
Fairfield County, CT	75,754
Kane County, IL	75,707
Washtenaw County, MI	75,645
Wayne County, MI	75,193
Genesee County, MI	74,464
New Castle County, DE	74,286
Napa County, CA	74,229
Norfolk County, MA	74,180
Chesapeake Independent City, VA	73,587
Oakland County, MI	73,500
Mercer County, NJ	73,438
Carson City Independent City, NV	72,750
Dorchester County, SC	72,727
Will County, IL	72,614
Macomb County, MI	72,453
Bronx County, NY	72,013
Contra Costa County, CA	71,906
Montgomery County, PA	71,719
Albany County, NY	71,563
Orange County, NY	71,563
Chesterfield County, VA	71,434
Queens County, NY	71,291
Juneau Borough, AK	71,094
Howard County, MD	70,817
Alameda County, CA	70,645
San Benito County, CA	70,625
Camden County, NJ	70,568
Kings County, NY	70,316
Collin County, TX	70,139
Broward County, FL	69,201
Berrien County, MI	68,942
Solano County, CA	68,615
Mecklenburg County, NC	68,289
Montgomery County, MD	67,875
Orange County, CA	67,818
Burlington County, NJ	67,386
Winnebago County, IL	67,361
Prince George's County, MD	67,034
San Bernardino County, CA	66,944
Sussex County, NJ	66,875
Johnson County, KS	66,518
Ventura County, CA	66,461
Plymouth County, MA	66,250

Place	Dollars
Orangetown, NY (town) Rockland County	124,458
McLean, VA (cdp) Fairfax County	118,814
Livingston, NJ (township) Essex County	117,601
Hicksville, NY (cdp) Nassau County	117,280
Howell, NJ (township) Monmouth County	109,992
Naperville, IL (city) Du Page County	109,761
North Brunswick, NJ (township) Middlesex County	109,672
Danville, CA (town) Contra Costa County	108,866
Paramus, NJ (borough) Bergen County	108,116
Levittown, NY (cdp) Nassau County	107,066
Newington, VA (cdp) Fairfax County	104,805
San Ramon, CA (city) Contra Costa County	104,190
New City, NY (cdp) Rockland County	102,806
Clifton, NJ (city) Passaic County	102,672
North Hempstead, NY (town) Nassau County	102,601
Dumont, NJ (borough) Bergen County	102,526
Washington, NJ (township) Gloucester County	102,134
Hillcrest, NY (cdp) Rockland County	102,026
Wayne, NJ (township) Passaic County	101,949
Babylon, NY (town) Suffolk County	101,850
West Bloomfield, MI (township) Oakland County	101,739
Valley Cottage, NY (cdp) Rockland County	101,523
Canton, MI (township) Wayne County	101,457
Clarkstown, NY (town) Rockland County	101,218
Union, NJ (township) Union County	101,179
West Orange, NJ (township) Essex County	100,991
East Brunswick, NJ (township) Middlesex County	100,863
Oyster Bay, NY (town) Nassau County	100,529
Piscataway, NJ (township) Middlesex County	100,000
Fairview, CA (cdp) Alameda County	99,687
Freehold, NJ (township) Monmouth County	99,090
Mundelein, IL (village) Lake County	98,932
Edison, NJ (township) Middlesex County	98,827
Redland, MD (cdp) Montgomery County	98,246
Little Ferry, NJ (borough) Bergen County	97,804
Orland Park, IL (village) Cook County	97,711
Huntington, NY (town) Suffolk County	97,477
Lakewood, NJ (township) Ocean County	96,639
Mission Viejo, CA (city) Orange County	96,489
Yonkers, NY (city) Westchester County	96,335
Yorba Linda, CA (city) Orange County	95,894
Gurnee, IL (village) Lake County	95,181
Walnut, CA (city) Los Angeles County	94,984
Ellicott City, MD (cdp) Howard County	94,877
Elmont, NY (cdp) Nassau County	94,779
Chino Hills, CA (city) San Bernardino County	94,700
La Palma, CA (city) Orange County	94,288
Cupertino, CA (city) Santa Clara County	93,911
Springfield, VA (cdp) Fairfax County	93,599
Pleasanton, CA (city) Alameda County	93,593
Old Bridge, NJ (township) Middlesex County	93,469
New Milford, NJ (borough) Bergen County	93,337
Burke, VA (cdp) Fairfax County	92,638
Hempstead, NY (town) Nassau County	92,539
Morton Grove, IL (village) Cook County	92,310
Valley Stream, NY (village) Nassau County	92,281
Sugar Land, TX (city) Fort Bend County	91,286
East Meadow, NY (cdp) Nassau County	91,195
Rancho Palos Verdes, CA (city) Los Angeles County	91,156
Bergenfield, NJ (borough) Bergen County	91,125
Fords, NJ (cdp) Middlesex County	91,118
Glenview, IL (village) Cook County	91,021
Skokie, IL (village) Cook County	90,930
Dublin, CA (city) Alameda County	90,784
Darien, IL (city) Du Page County	90,728
Cerritos, CA (city) Los Angeles County	90,525
Secaucus, NJ (town) Hudson County	90,444
Downers Grove, IL (village) Du Page County	90,442
Missouri City, TX (city) Fort Bend County	90,276
Montebello, CA (city) Los Angeles County	90,263
Palatine, IL (village) Cook County	90,255
Milpitas, CA (city) Santa Clara County	89,964
Des Plaines, IL (city) Cook County	89,828
Bloomfield, NJ (township) Essex County	89,547
Nutley, NJ (township) Essex County	89,529

Notes: Please refer to the User's Guide for an explanation of data; ranking tables include all places with Asian and/or NHPI populations above SF4 population thresholds; (1) tables reflect only those areas that meet SF4 population thresholds, therefore there may be less than 50 states, 75 counties or 75 places listed

Median Household Income

Guamanian or Chamorro

All States, Top 75 Counties, and Top 75 Places Sorted by Number[1]

State	Dollars
South Carolina	87,720
Minnesota	76,050
Michigan	68,750
Connecticut	65,625
Wisconsin	65,313
Maryland	64,167
New Mexico	52,500
California	52,475
Nevada	50,598
New Jersey	50,313
Arizona	47,663
Washington	47,287
Georgia	47,235
United States	46,306
Pennsylvania	46,202
Louisiana	45,833
Virginia	44,524
Missouri	43,750
Ohio	43,155
Oregon	42,043
Texas	40,795
Colorado	40,054
Florida	39,929
Oklahoma	39,853
North Carolina	38,500
Indiana	38,365
Alabama	37,625
Hawaii	36,767
Massachusetts	35,481
Kentucky	33,594
Illinois	31,607
Tennessee	27,083
New York	25,163

County	Dollars
Solano County, CA	72,813
Santa Clara County, CA	68,750
Contra Costa County, CA	67,614
San Bernardino County, CA	62,024
Alameda County, CA	61,654
Thurston County, WA	60,000
San Mateo County, CA	58,750
Orange County, CA	57,188
Sacramento County, CA	52,813
Los Angeles County, CA	52,321
Clark County, NV	52,063
Riverside County, CA	51,250
El Paso County, CO	50,132
Bell County, TX	49,712
Pierce County, WA	47,235
San Diego County, CA	46,875
Harris County, TX	44,861
Honolulu County, HI	41,875
Monterey County, CA	41,667
Maricopa County, AZ	40,833
Kitsap County, WA	40,250
Kings County, NY	37,697
King County, WA	37,257

Place	Dollars
Fairfield, CA (city) Solano County	77,912
Vallejo, CA (city) Solano County	73,417
San Jose, CA (city) Santa Clara County	69,706
Chula Vista, CA (city) San Diego County	52,500
Killeen, TX (city) Bell County	51,382
Houston, TX (city) Harris County	46,389
San Diego, CA (city) San Diego County	45,769
Los Angeles, CA (city) Los Angeles County	42,083
Tacoma, WA (city) Pierce County	41,719
Honolulu, HI (cdp) Honolulu County	35,278
New York, NY (city)	22,708

Notes: Please refer to the User's Guide for an explanation of data; ranking tables include all places with Asian and/or NHPI populations above SF4 population thresholds; (1) tables reflect only those areas that meet SF4 population thresholds, therefore there may be less than 50 states, 75 counties or 75 places listed

Median Household Income

Hawaiian, Native

All States, Top 75 Counties, and Top 75 Places Sorted by Number[1]

State	Dollars
New Jersey	68,611
Virginia	57,206
South Carolina	55,000
Georgia	54,773
Maryland	53,906
Pennsylvania	52,941
Alaska	51,625
California	50,395
Ohio	50,313
Wisconsin	46,875
Hawaii	45,486
Oregon	44,896
United States	44,554
Utah	44,271
Minnesota	43,500
New Mexico	43,125
Nevada	42,436
Tennessee	42,083
Indiana	41,250
Washington	40,870
Illinois	40,667
Kansas	40,000
Oklahoma	38,250
Colorado	37,838
Michigan	37,250
Montana	36,250
Arizona	36,033
Texas	35,788
Idaho	35,688
North Carolina	35,583
Massachusetts	35,509
Missouri	35,208
Florida	34,479
New York	32,614
Louisiana	29,643
Arkansas	22,143

County	Dollars
Ventura County, CA	68,563
Contra Costa County, CA	66,174
Santa Clara County, CA	65,260
Solano County, CA	60,952
Multnomah County, OR	60,893
San Joaquin County, CA	58,942
Orange County, CA	56,406
San Mateo County, CA	56,125
Riverside County, CA	55,865
King County, WA	52,557
Alameda County, CA	51,667
Washington County, OR	50,417
Honolulu County, HI	50,019
San Diego County, CA	49,667
San Bernardino County, CA	48,906
Bexar County, TX	47,768
Snohomish County, WA	46,549
Utah County, UT	45,417
Los Angeles County, CA	44,148
Maui County, HI	44,053
Clark County, NV	42,013
Kauai County, HI	41,118
Maricopa County, AZ	39,395
Sacramento County, CA	39,167
Salt Lake County, UT	38,333
Hawaii County, HI	37,068
Pierce County, WA	26,761
Pima County, AZ	24,155

Place	Dollars
Aiea, HI (cdp) Honolulu County	100,543
Mililani Town, HI (cdp) Honolulu County	90,776
Makakilo City, HI (cdp) Honolulu County	77,007
Pearl City, HI (cdp) Honolulu County	72,563
Kilauea, HI (cdp) Kauai County	69,375
San Jose, CA (city) Santa Clara County	65,000
Kailua, HI (cdp) Honolulu County	64,565
Captain Cook, HI (cdp) Hawaii County	63,750
Hana, HI (cdp) Maui County	61,250
Paia, HI (cdp) Maui County	58,750
Kaaawa, HI (cdp) Honolulu County	58,333
Makawao, HI (cdp) Maui County	58,000
Waimanalo Beach, HI (cdp) Honolulu County	57,438
Halawa, HI (cdp) Honolulu County	56,827
Laie, HI (cdp) Honolulu County	56,250
Waikoloa Village, HI (cdp) Hawaii County	55,893
Kalaoa, HI (cdp) Hawaii County	55,221
Ewa Beach, HI (cdp) Honolulu County	54,583
Ahuimanu, HI (cdp) Honolulu County	54,000
Kaneohe, HI (cdp) Honolulu County	53,750
Waikane, HI (cdp) Honolulu County	53,750
Lahaina, HI (cdp) Maui County	53,194
Kahaluu, HI (cdp) Honolulu County	52,500
Waipio, HI (cdp) Honolulu County	51,184
Portland, OR (city) Multnomah County	50,625
Kahuku, HI (cdp) Honolulu County	50,313
Holualoa, HI (cdp) Hawaii County	50,000
Waihee-Waiehu, HI (cdp) Maui County	49,803
San Diego, CA (city) San Diego County	48,889
Honaunau-Napoopoo, HI (cdp) Hawaii County	48,333
Pakala Village, HI (cdp) Kauai County	47,813
Haleiwa, HI (cdp) Honolulu County	47,500
Waipahu, HI (cdp) Honolulu County	47,031
Waimalu, HI (cdp) Honolulu County	46,250
Makaha Valley, HI (cdp) Honolulu County	44,375
Honolulu, HI (cdp) Honolulu County	43,418
Paradise, NV (cdp) Clark County	43,309
Punaluu, HI (cdp) Honolulu County	43,125
Wailuku, HI (cdp) Maui County	43,073
Honalo, HI (cdp) Hawaii County	42,813
Waimea, HI (cdp) Hawaii County	42,656
Los Angeles, CA (city) Los Angeles County	41,976
Nanakuli, HI (cdp) Honolulu County	41,625
Henderson, NV (city) Clark County	41,198
Waianae, HI (cdp) Honolulu County	40,167
Volcano, HI (cdp) Hawaii County	39,911
Kualapuu, HI (cdp) Maui County	39,821
Anahola, HI (cdp) Kauai County	39,792
Waimanalo, HI (cdp) Honolulu County	39,375
Waimea, HI (cdp) Kauai County	39,375
Kihei, HI (cdp) Maui County	39,150
Hauula, HI (cdp) Honolulu County	38,750
Las Vegas, NV (city) Clark County	38,229
Wahiawa, HI (cdp) Honolulu County	37,589
Kahului, HI (cdp) Maui County	37,000
Hanapepe, HI (cdp) Kauai County	36,250
Kekaha, HI (cdp) Kauai County	35,833
Phoenix, AZ (city) Maricopa County	35,417
Makaha, HI (cdp) Honolulu County	34,821
New York, NY (city)	34,432
Kapaau, HI (cdp) Hawaii County	34,375
Kailua, HI (cdp) Hawaii County	33,864
Hilo, HI (cdp) Hawaii County	32,625
Maili, HI (cdp) Honolulu County	30,529
Waialua, HI (cdp) Honolulu County	29,375
Hawaiian Beaches, HI (cdp) Hawaii County	28,750
Naalehu, HI (cdp) Hawaii County	28,750
Kaunakakai, HI (cdp) Maui County	28,125
Kapaa, HI (cdp) Kauai County	27,177
Hawaiian Ocean View, HI (cdp) Hawaii County	27,125
Pahala, HI (cdp) Hawaii County	23,750
Hawaiian Paradise Park, HI (cdp) Hawaii County	23,631

Notes: Please refer to the User's Guide for an explanation of data; ranking tables include all places with Asian and/or NHPI populations above SF4 population thresholds; (1) tables reflect only those areas that meet SF4 population thresholds, therefore there may be less than 50 states, 75 counties or 75 places listed

Median Household Income

Hmong

All States, Top 75 Counties, and Top 75 Places Sorted by Number[1]

State	Dollars
Georgia	54,000
Colorado	50,058
Massachusetts	47,153
South Carolina	45,268
Rhode Island	45,156
Pennsylvania	43,889
Kansas	43,750
North Carolina	42,544
Oklahoma	39,844
Michigan	37,868
Oregon	36,836
Wisconsin	35,898
Minnesota	35,864
United States	32,076
Washington	29,375
Alaska	25,179
California	24,542

County	Dollars
Anoka County, MN	79,545
Barrow County, GA	75,898
Orange County, CA	71,397
Mecklenburg County, NC	65,313
Washington County, MN	59,750
Adams County, CO	52,180
Macomb County, MI	52,065
Olmsted County, MN	50,774
Lancaster County, PA	48,214
Oakland County, MI	47,708
Spartanburg County, SC	46,607
Multnomah County, OR	45,938
Wyandotte County, KS	45,917
Worcester County, MA	45,750
Burke County, NC	43,056
Sheboygan County, WI	42,656
Jefferson County, CO	41,607
Providence County, RI	40,938
Stanly County, NC	40,625
Milwaukee County, WI	40,272
Outagamie County, WI	38,958
San Diego County, CA	38,947
Catawba County, NC	37,019
Portage County, WI	36,875
Eau Claire County, WI	36,786
King County, WA	36,250
La Crosse County, WI	36,250
Manitowoc County, WI	35,870
Hennepin County, MN	35,041
Dane County, WI	35,000
Ramsey County, MN	34,801
Winnebago County, WI	34,565
Brown County, WI	33,750
Santa Barbara County, CA	33,750
Wayne County, MI	33,382
Solano County, CA	32,778
Calumet County, WI	32,431
Glenn County, CA	31,875
Yuba County, CA	30,668
Marathon County, WI	29,611
Wood County, WI	29,483
Chippewa County, WI	29,453
Dunn County, WI	27,604
Sacramento County, CA	27,474
Los Angeles County, CA	26,094
San Joaquin County, CA	25,979
Tulare County, CA	25,521
Anchorage Borough, AK	25,179
Fresno County, CA	23,168
Merced County, CA	21,031
Stanislaus County, CA	20,938
Yolo County, CA	18,750
Butte County, CA	17,778
Riverside County, CA	16,750
Ingham County, MI	15,625
Spokane County, WA	14,904
Fond du Lac County, WI	11,750

Place	Dollars
Woodbury, MN (city) Washington County	78,730
Santa Ana, CA (city) Orange County	74,000
Glen Alpine, NC (town) Burke County	72,500
Charlotte, NC (city) Mecklenburg County	65,313
Warren, MI (city) Macomb County	56,136
Brooklyn Center, MN (city) Hennepin County	54,545
Fitchburg, MA (city) Worcester County	53,500
Westminster, CO (city) Adams County	52,407
Rochester, MN (city) Olmsted County	50,774
Maplewood, MN (city) Ramsey County	50,143
Pontiac, MI (city) Oakland County	49,038
Kansas City, KS (city) Wyandotte County	45,917
Portland, OR (city) Multnomah County	43,000
Brooklyn Park, MN (city) Hennepin County	42,083
Sheboygan, WI (city) Sheboygan County	41,992
Appleton, WI (city) Outagamie County	41,765
Milwaukee, WI (city) Milwaukee County	39,691
San Diego, CA (city) San Diego County	39,474
Valdese, NC (town) Burke County	39,063
Fond du Lac, WI (city) Fond du Lac County	38,036
Stevens Point, WI (city) Portage County	37,596
Providence, RI (city) Providence County	37,361
Arden-Arcade, CA (cdp) Sacramento County	36,652
Madison, WI (city) Dane County	36,429
Green Bay, WI (city) Brown County	35,909
Manitowoc, WI (city) Manitowoc County	35,707
St. Paul, MN (city) Ramsey County	34,046
Connelly Springs, NC (town) Burke County	33,750
Willows, CA (city) Glenn County	31,875
Eau Claire, WI (city) Eau Claire County	31,453
Oshkosh, WI (city) Winnebago County	31,250
Detroit, MI (city) Wayne County	30,769
La Crosse, WI (city) La Crosse County	30,565
Hickory, NC (city) Catawba County	30,417
Linda, CA (cdp) Yuba County	30,060
Wisconsin Rapids, WI (city) Wood County	29,397
Atwater, CA (city) Merced County	29,286
Minneapolis, MN (city) Hennepin County	28,772
Sacramento, CA (city) Sacramento County	28,405
Wausau, WI (city) Marathon County	27,237
Stockton, CA (city) San Joaquin County	25,448
Florin, CA (cdp) Sacramento County	25,268
Modesto, CA (city) Stanislaus County	24,583
Clovis, CA (city) Fresno County	24,203
Fresno, CA (city) Fresno County	22,663
Parkway-S. Sacramento, CA (cdp) Sacramento County	20,915
South Oroville, CA (cdp) Butte County	20,500
Merced, CA (city) Merced County	20,226
Lansing, MI (city) Ingham County	19,423
West Sacramento, CA (city) Yolo County	18,403
Thermalito, CA (cdp) Butte County	17,788
Visalia, CA (city) Tulare County	17,031
Chico, CA (city) Butte County	13,917
Oroville, CA (city) Butte County	13,846
Spokane, WA (city) Spokane County	13,580

Notes: Please refer to the User's Guide for an explanation of data; ranking tables include all places with Asian and/or NHPI populations above SF4 population thresholds; (1) tables reflect only those areas that meet SF4 population thresholds, therefore there may be less than 50 states, 75 counties or 75 places listed

Median Household Income

Indonesian

***All States, Top 75 Counties, and Top 75 Places Sorted by Number*[1]**

State	Dollars
Virginia	57,344
New Jersey	54,000
Maryland	48,750
Texas	46,094
California	44,538
Pennsylvania	43,462
New York	40,566
United States	38,175
Florida	38,167
Georgia	35,500
Wisconsin	33,281
Washington	31,776
Arizona	28,125
Michigan	27,092
Colorado	26,125
Illinois	21,667
Oregon	19,531
Massachusetts	16,500
Ohio	12,159

County	Dollars
Alameda County, CA	85,155
San Mateo County, CA	62,891
Santa Clara County, CA	62,019
Contra Costa County, CA	57,344
Fairfax County, VA	56,406
Middlesex County, NJ	51,705
Orange County, CA	50,122
San Diego County, CA	50,000
Montgomery County, MD	49,833
Harris County, TX	48,875
San Bernardino County, CA	46,898
San Francisco County, CA	40,801
Queens County, NY	40,726
Los Angeles County, CA	37,304
King County, WA	28,984
Maricopa County, AZ	28,125
Cook County, IL	19,375
Franklin County, OH	3,125

Place	Dollars
Houston, TX (city) Harris County	50,000
Loma Linda, CA (city) San Bernardino County	42,237
San Francisco, CA (city) San Francisco County	40,801
New York, NY (city)	39,338
Los Angeles, CA (city) Los Angeles County	27,759
Seattle, WA (city) King County	27,578
San Bernardino, CA (city) San Bernardino County	27,321
Columbus, OH (city) Franklin County	3,208

Notes: Please refer to the User's Guide for an explanation of data; ranking tables include all places with Asian and/or NHPI populations above SF4 population thresholds; (1) tables reflect only those areas that meet SF4 population thresholds, therefore there may be less than 50 states, 75 counties or 75 places listed

Median Household Income

Japanese

***All States, Top 75 Counties, and Top 75 Places Sorted by Number*[1]**

State	Dollars
Connecticut	70,871
New Jersey	70,292
Rhode Island	61,417
Michigan	60,317
Hawaii	57,134
California	55,577
Illinois	53,750
Maryland	53,185
Virginia	52,475
United States	52,060
Alaska	51,898
Ohio	51,854
Kentucky	51,488
Vermont	50,125
Delaware	49,167
Washington	47,438
Texas	46,312
Indiana	45,341
New York	44,927
Idaho	44,856
Colorado	44,842
Georgia	44,757
Alabama	44,524
Arizona	44,227
North Carolina	43,272
Utah	42,989
Minnesota	41,364
New Hampshire	40,815
Nevada	40,757
Tennessee	40,645
Oregon	40,199
New Mexico	40,000
District of Columbia	39,224
Massachusetts	38,033
South Carolina	35,991
Wyoming	35,417
Florida	34,663
Missouri	34,423
Louisiana	32,734
Wisconsin	32,446
Arkansas	31,310
Pennsylvania	29,397
Kansas	29,250
Maine	29,141
South Dakota	27,750
Nebraska	25,592
Iowa	22,500
Mississippi	22,083
Oklahoma	20,714
Montana	16,680
West Virginia	7,813

County	Dollars
Fairfield County, CT	121,599
Westchester County, NY	104,489
Fayette County, GA	100,386
Morris County, NJ	99,531
Somerset County, NJ	91,883
Collin County, TX	89,728
Boone County, KY	84,616
Mercer County, NJ	84,544
Fairfax County, VA	84,127
Lake County, IL	82,053
Santa Clara County, CA	80,162
Bergen County, NJ	78,049
Oakland County, MI	77,268
Stanislaus County, CA	75,308
Wake County, NC	74,345
Nassau County, NY	72,120
Anne Arundel County, MD	70,938
San Mateo County, CA	70,694
Fulton County, GA	70,329
Napa County, CA	69,444
Montgomery County, MD	68,405
Cobb County, GA	66,719
Contra Costa County, CA	66,064
Jefferson County, CO	65,924
El Dorado County, CA	65,806
Orange County, CA	65,477
Ventura County, CA	64,439
Suffolk County, NY	63,400
Mecklenburg County, NC	63,348
DuPage County, IL	62,986
Marin County, CA	62,670
Calhoun County, MI	60,991
Boulder County, CO	60,972
Honolulu County, HI	60,748
Summit County, OH	60,515
Snohomish County, WA	60,227
Washington County, OR	56,641
Sacramento County, CA	56,352
Alameda County, CA	56,333
Essex County, NJ	56,250
Hudson County, NJ	56,250
Clackamas County, OR	55,781
Santa Cruz County, CA	55,727
Ada County, ID	55,417
Franklin County, OH	54,956
Placer County, CA	54,358
Montgomery County, PA	54,000
Cook County, IL	53,886
Dallas County, TX	53,357
Harris County, TX	52,979
Broward County, FL	52,917
Chester County, PA	52,679
Arlington County, VA	52,361
San Bernardino County, CA	52,355
Riverside County, CA	52,167
King County, WA	52,156
Jefferson County, KY	52,019
Travis County, TX	51,992
New Castle County, DE	51,750
Los Angeles County, CA	51,736
Tippecanoe County, IN	51,719
Middlesex County, MA	51,696
Prince William County, VA	51,667
Wayne County, MI	51,500
Clark County, WA	51,284
DeKalb County, GA	51,250
Kern County, CA	50,982
Weber County, UT	50,893
Anchorage Borough, AK	50,625
Bernalillo County, NM	50,345
Ramsey County, MN	50,167
Virginia Beach Independent City, VA	50,000
Cuyahoga County, OH	49,861
Maui County, HI	49,729
Marion County, IN	49,712

Place	Dollars
Saratoga, CA (city) Santa Clara County	177,278
Rye, NY (city) Westchester County	172,971
La Canada Flintridge, CA (city) Los Angeles County	161,585
Harrison, NY (village) Westchester County	152,015
Palos Verdes Estates, CA (city) Los Angeles County	130,014
Rancho Palos Verdes, CA (city) Los Angeles County	126,440
West Bloomfield, MI (township) Oakland County	123,905
Ridgewood, NJ (village) Bergen County	123,293
Scarsdale, NY (village) Westchester County	121,839
Rolling Hills Estates, CA (city) Los Angeles County	119,590
Manhattan Beach, CA (city) Los Angeles County	112,207
Eastchester, NY (town) Westchester County	110,772
Greenwich, CT (town) Fairfield County	109,944
Eastchester, NY (cdp) Westchester County	108,728
McLean, VA (cdp) Fairfax County	108,684
Foster City, CA (city) San Mateo County	108,026
Wilmette, IL (village) Cook County	106,933
Los Altos, CA (city) Santa Clara County	105,461
Millbrae, CA (city) San Mateo County	104,727
Mercer Island, WA (city) King County	104,686
Cupertino, CA (city) Santa Clara County	104,074
San Ramon, CA (city) Contra Costa County	103,014
Greenville, NY (cdp) Westchester County	101,071
Peachtree City, GA (city) Fayette County	100,386
Hoffman Estates, IL (village) Cook County	100,146
Thousand Oaks, CA (city) Ventura County	97,419
Bethesda, MD (cdp) Montgomery County	96,786
Yorba Linda, CA (city) Orange County	96,088
Modesto, CA (city) Stanislaus County	94,218
Seal Beach, CA (city) Orange County	93,796
Cary, NC (town) Wake County	92,562
Glenview, IL (village) Cook County	91,985
Greenburgh, NY (town) Westchester County	91,717
Heeia, HI (cdp) Honolulu County	91,617
Redmond, WA (city) King County	90,706
Mission Viejo, CA (city) Orange County	90,533
Maunawili, HI (cdp) Honolulu County	89,934
Fremont, CA (city) Alameda County	89,474
Milpitas, CA (city) Santa Clara County	88,074
Laguna Niguel, CA (city) Orange County	87,979
Rancho Cucamonga, CA (city) San Bernardino County	87,500
Redondo Beach, CA (city) Los Angeles County	85,818
Buffalo Grove, IL (village) Lake County	85,598
Cerritos, CA (city) Los Angeles County	85,066
Mililani Town, HI (cdp) Honolulu County	84,567
Newport Beach, CA (city) Orange County	84,280
Morgan Hill, CA (city) Santa Clara County	84,257
North Hempstead, NY (town) Nassau County	83,201
Kailua, HI (cdp) Honolulu County	82,773
Plano, TX (city) Collin County	82,610
Laguna, CA (cdp) Sacramento County	82,569
Pleasanton, CA (city) Alameda County	82,439
Ahuimanu, HI (cdp) Honolulu County	82,324
La Palma, CA (city) Orange County	81,990
Sunnyvale, CA (city) Santa Clara County	81,931
Simi Valley, CA (city) Ventura County	81,843
Burlingame, CA (city) San Mateo County	81,813
Dublin, OH (city) Franklin County	80,830
Diamond Bar, CA (city) Los Angeles County	80,810
Arcadia, CA (city) Los Angeles County	80,381
Aliso Viejo, CA (cdp) Orange County	80,325
Palo Alto, CA (city) Santa Clara County	80,061
Elk Grove, CA (cdp) Sacramento County	79,336
Elk Grove Village, IL (village) Cook County	79,246
Beaverton, OR (city) Washington County	78,889
Oyster Bay, NY (town) Nassau County	78,685
Placentia, CA (city) Orange County	78,664
East San Gabriel, CA (cdp) Los Angeles County	77,177
Los Gatos, CA (town) Santa Clara County	77,064
Bryn Mawr-Skyway, WA (cdp) King County	76,666
Waipio, HI (cdp) Honolulu County	76,393
San Jose, CA (city) Santa Clara County	76,327
Encinitas, CA (city) San Diego County	76,213
Irvine, CA (city) Orange County	76,149
Lake Forest, CA (city) Orange County	76,089

Notes: Please refer to the User's Guide for an explanation of data; ranking tables include all places with Asian and/or NHPI populations above SF4 population thresholds; (1) tables reflect only those areas that meet SF4 population thresholds, therefore there may be less than 50 states, 75 counties or 75 places listed

Median Household Income

Korean

All States, Top 75 Counties, and Top 75 Places Sorted by Number[1]

State	Dollars
New Jersey	53,502
Virginia	47,871
Maryland	47,085
New Hampshire	46,422
Connecticut	43,194
Illinois	42,258
Wyoming	42,024
California	40,758
Colorado	40,206
Massachusetts	40,056
United States	40,037
Nevada	40,016
New York	39,267
Georgia	39,085
North Carolina	38,662
Oregon	36,934
Washington	36,670
Pennsylvania	36,585
Florida	36,368
Idaho	35,577
South Dakota	35,568
District of Columbia	35,500
Michigan	35,326
Texas	34,870
Arizona	34,528
Minnesota	34,457
Ohio	34,067
Missouri	33,983
Kentucky	33,702
Hawaii	33,365
Kansas	33,107
Mississippi	32,143
South Carolina	31,616
Alabama	31,445
Delaware	31,216
Maine	31,161
New Mexico	31,136
West Virginia	30,455
Alaska	30,442
Nebraska	30,208
Tennessee	28,793
Utah	28,000
Arkansas	26,625
Oklahoma	25,250
Louisiana	24,028
Wisconsin	23,167
Montana	22,583
Indiana	21,824
North Dakota	20,625
Vermont	20,625
Iowa	19,477
Rhode Island	17,344

County	Dollars
Berks County, PA	94,714
Somerset County, NJ	82,775
Will County, IL	81,131
Lake County, IL	77,190
Westchester County, NY	74,904
Morris County, NJ	74,083
Butler County, OH	73,750
Dutchess County, NY	72,083
Nassau County, NY	71,474
Fort Bend County, TX	71,179
Mercer County, NJ	68,810
Kane County, IL	68,750
Loudoun County, VA	68,472
Douglas County, CO	67,292
Davis County, UT	66,250
Oakland County, MI	65,515
Santa Clara County, CA	65,417
Gloucester County, NJ	65,000
Saratoga County, NY	63,239
Collin County, TX	62,472
San Mateo County, CA	62,443
Ada County, ID	61,563
DuPage County, IL	61,522
York County, PA	61,000
Washington County, MN	60,536
Rockland County, NY	60,347
Norfolk County, MA	60,221
Union County, NJ	59,423
Essex County, NJ	59,250
Rockingham County, NH	58,929
Monmouth County, NJ	58,250
Marin County, CA	57,981
Chester County, PA	57,721
Waukesha County, WI	57,639
Contra Costa County, CA	56,897
Montgomery County, MD	56,685
Passaic County, NJ	56,042
Suffolk County, NY	55,848
Sonoma County, CA	55,833
Fairfax County, VA	55,336
Johnson County, KS	54,875
Cumberland County, PA	54,833
Jefferson County, CO	54,167
Prince William County, VA	53,750
Sarpy County, NE	53,281
Imperial County, CA	53,250
Olmsted County, MN	52,321
Middlesex County, NJ	52,125
Fairfield County, CT	52,076
Ventura County, CA	51,875
Mecklenburg County, NC	51,833
Bergen County, NJ	51,724
Howard County, MD	51,631
Columbia County, GA	51,500
Lake County, IN	51,250
Henrico County, VA	50,781
Atlantic County, NJ	50,625
Solano County, CA	49,750
Hillsborough County, FL	49,722
Williamson County, TX	49,500
Adams County, CO	49,375
Lehigh County, PA	49,318
Fresno County, CA	49,211
Clark County, WA	48,917
Dale County, AL	48,750
Kitsap County, WA	48,750
Delaware County, PA	48,636
Fulton County, GA	48,208
Gwinnett County, GA	47,569
Orange County, CA	47,374
Summit County, OH	47,321
New York County, NY	47,231
Cobb County, GA	47,200
Richmond County, NY	47,188
Worcester County, MA	47,135

Place	Dollars
Alpine, NJ (borough) Bergen County	171,479
Scarsdale, NY (village) Westchester County	170,098
Bloomfield, MI (township) Oakland County	132,124
Palos Verdes Estates, CA (city) Los Angeles County	109,957
Englewood Cliffs, NJ (borough) Bergen County	108,831
Lake Success, NY (village) Nassau County	108,819
Foster City, CA (city) San Mateo County	106,881
Greenburgh, NY (town) Westchester County	105,965
Demarest, NJ (borough) Bergen County	100,000
Norwood, NJ (borough) Bergen County	98,646
West Windsor, NJ (township) Mercer County	96,481
Newton, MA (city) Middlesex County	94,770
West Orange, NJ (township) Essex County	92,491
La Canada Flintridge, CA (city) Los Angeles County	90,942
Rochester Hills, MI (city) Oakland County	90,383
McLean, VA (cdp) Fairfax County	87,826
Pleasanton, CA (city) Alameda County	87,461
North Hempstead, NY (town) Nassau County	86,969
Potomac, MD (cdp) Montgomery County	86,907
Saratoga, CA (city) Santa Clara County	83,434
Closter, NJ (borough) Bergen County	83,352
Buffalo Grove, IL (village) Lake County	83,219
Old Tappan, NJ (borough) Bergen County	82,840
Parsippany-Troy Hills, NJ (township) Morris County	82,046
Cupertino, CA (city) Santa Clara County	81,424
North Potomac, MD (cdp) Montgomery County	81,086
Redland, MD (cdp) Montgomery County	81,071
Mill Creek, WA (city) Snohomish County	80,761
Franconia, VA (cdp) Fairfax County	80,730
Mission Viejo, CA (city) Orange County	80,513
Plainview, NY (cdp) Nassau County	78,077
Rancho Palos Verdes, CA (city) Los Angeles County	77,798
Olney, MD (cdp) Montgomery County	77,167
Germantown, MD (cdp) Montgomery County	76,628
Sugar Land, TX (city) Fort Bend County	74,375
Tustin, CA (city) Orange County	74,205
Oyster Bay, NY (town) Nassau County	73,194
Walnut, CA (city) Los Angeles County	72,829
Islip, NY (town) Suffolk County	72,740
Placentia, CA (city) Orange County	72,688
Lincolnwood, IL (village) Cook County	72,604
Northbrook, IL (village) Cook County	72,500
Syosset, NY (cdp) Nassau County	72,250
Cresskill, NJ (borough) Bergen County	71,875
Fremont, CA (city) Alameda County	71,711
Corona, CA (city) Riverside County	71,544
Paramus, NJ (borough) Bergen County	71,151
Plano, TX (city) Collin County	71,129
Glenview, IL (village) Cook County	70,987
Henderson, NV (city) Clark County	70,982
Yorba Linda, CA (city) Orange County	70,677
Chino Hills, CA (city) San Bernardino County	70,511
Cary, NC (town) Wake County	70,250
Seattle Hill-Silver Firs, WA (cdp) Snohomish County	70,197
Walnut Creek, CA (city) Contra Costa County	70,156
Piscataway, NJ (township) Middlesex County	69,659
Kentwood, MI (city) Kent County	69,464
Livingston, NJ (township) Essex County	69,250
Whittier, CA (city) Los Angeles County	69,083
Arlington Heights, IL (village) Cook County	68,036
Whitpain, PA (township) Montgomery County	67,813
Jericho, NY (cdp) Nassau County	67,692
Plymouth, MN (city) Hennepin County	67,639
Hoffman Estates, IL (village) Cook County	67,500
Duluth, GA (city) Gwinnett County	67,159
Vernon Hills, IL (village) Lake County	66,875
Millbrae, CA (city) San Mateo County	66,719
West Bloomfield, MI (township) Oakland County	66,719
San Jose, CA (city) Santa Clara County	66,379
Simi Valley, CA (city) Ventura County	66,250
Montgomery, PA (township) Montgomery County	66,111
San Mateo, CA (city) San Mateo County	65,789
Colesville, MD (cdp) Montgomery County	64,688
Kailua, HI (cdp) Honolulu County	64,583
Milpitas, CA (city) Santa Clara County	64,500

Notes: Please refer to the User's Guide for an explanation of data; ranking tables include all places with Asian and/or NHPI populations above SF4 population thresholds; (1) tables reflect only those areas that meet SF4 population thresholds, therefore there may be less than 50 states, 75 counties or 75 places listed

Median Household Income

Laotian

All States, Top 75 Counties, and Top 75 Places Sorted by Number[1]

State	Dollars
New Jersey	63,594
Connecticut	60,112
Illinois	58,098
Virginia	58,092
Colorado	55,245
Maryland	54,119
Oregon	52,102
Tennessee	51,684
Ohio	51,339
Michigan	51,042
Georgia	50,992
Idaho	50,865
Indiana	50,455
Massachusetts	50,030
Arizona	49,375
Nevada	49,149
Pennsylvania	48,163
New Hampshire	46,190
Kansas	46,138
Texas	45,787
Oklahoma	45,778
Iowa	45,469
Nebraska	45,078
North Carolina	44,354
South Carolina	44,100
South Dakota	43,333
Utah	43,191
United States	42,978
Washington	42,887
Florida	42,808
Minnesota	42,454
Louisiana	42,237
New York	41,744
Rhode Island	41,667
Wisconsin	40,985
Alabama	37,500
Arkansas	36,906
Missouri	31,944
Alaska	31,563
California	31,353
Hawaii	24,792

County	Dollars
Santa Clara County, CA	72,941
Orange County, CA	66,161
Snohomish County, WA	65,625
Kane County, IL	64,706
Fairfield County, CT	63,403
Maricopa County, AZ	63,281
Rutherford County, TN	61,364
Fairfax County, VA	61,250
Polk County, FL	61,150
Hartford County, CT	61,029
Cook County, IL	60,347
Clayton County, GA	59,688
Cass County, MI	59,375
Gwinnett County, GA	58,382
Winnebago County, IL	58,375
New Haven County, CT	57,917
Jefferson County, CO	56,912
Ottawa County, MI	56,667
Summit County, OH	56,184
Essex County, MA	55,000
Hennepin County, MN	54,063
Buena Vista County, IA	53,375
Adams County, CO	52,031
Middlesex County, MA	51,583
Worcester County, MA	51,354
Multnomah County, OR	51,307
Clark County, WA	50,938
Harris County, TX	50,341
Tarrant County, TX	49,732
Clark County, NV	49,149
Mecklenburg County, NC	49,118
Polk County, IA	48,984
Salt Lake County, UT	48,750
Iberia Parish, LA	48,500
Johnson County, KS	47,955
Washington County, OR	47,368
Roseau County, MN	47,083
Dakota County, NE	46,932
Potter County, TX	46,429
Cowley County, KS	46,250
Sedgwick County, KS	46,042
Philadelphia County, PA	45,741
Davidson County, TN	45,469
Monroe County, NY	45,313
Franklin County, OH	45,294
Catawba County, NC	45,234
Oklahoma County, OK	44,688
Dakota County, MN	44,167
Franklin County, WA	43,750
King County, WA	43,750
Pinellas County, FL	43,561
Guilford County, NC	43,077
Spartanburg County, SC	42,102
Burke County, NC	41,563
Providence County, RI	41,500
Dallas County, TX	41,471
Washington County, AR	41,339
Solano County, CA	40,938
Montgomery County, NC	40,625
Riverside County, CA	39,706
San Diego County, CA	39,527
Dane County, WI	39,297
Brown County, WI	38,250
Contra Costa County, CA	38,095
Los Angeles County, CA	38,007
Habersham County, GA	37,273
Milwaukee County, WI	36,500
Alameda County, CA	35,603
Sonoma County, CA	33,750
Pacific County, WA	33,000
Bexar County, TX	32,500
Broome County, NY	32,344
Mobile County, AL	32,344
San Bernardino County, CA	31,806
Sebastian County, AR	31,779

Place	Dollars
Elgin, IL (city) Kane County	85,703
Anaheim, CA (city) Orange County	82,492
Escondido, CA (city) San Diego County	79,544
San Jose, CA (city) Santa Clara County	73,897
Springfield, VA (cdp) Fairfax County	68,077
Brooklyn Park, MN (city) Hennepin County	64,250
Brooklyn Center, MN (city) Hennepin County	63,542
Bellevue, WA (city) King County	61,125
Santa Ana, CA (city) Orange County	60,938
Bridgeport, CT (city) Fairfield County	57,625
Murfreesboro, TN (city) Rutherford County	57,031
Arvada, CO (city) Jefferson County	57,019
Akron, OH (city) Summit County	56,400
Storm Lake, IA (city) Buena Vista County	53,938
Warroad, MN (city) Roseau County	53,750
Rockford, IL (city) Winnebago County	53,125
Portland, OR (city) Multnomah County	52,250
Des Moines, IA (city) Polk County	49,844
Lowell, MA (city) Middlesex County	49,734
West Valley City, UT (city) Salt Lake County	49,444
Banning, CA (city) Riverside County	48,750
Charlotte, NC (city) Mecklenburg County	48,750
St. Petersburg, FL (city) Pinellas County	48,092
Dallas, TX (city) Dallas County	47,969
Winfield, KS (city) Cowley County	47,917
Fort Worth, TX (city) Tarrant County	46,875
Westminster, CO (city) Adams County	46,765
Oaklawn-Sunview, KS (cdp) Sedgwick County	46,250
Amarillo, TX (city) Potter County	46,071
Philadelphia, PA (city) Philadelphia County	45,741
Wichita, KS (city) Sedgwick County	45,550
Nashville-Davidson, TN (sp. city) Davidson County	45,469
Seattle, WA (city) King County	44,917
Grand Prairie, TX (city) Dallas County	44,531
Oklahoma City, OK (city) Oklahoma County	43,906
New Britain, CT (city) Hartford County	42,917
Pomona, CA (city) Los Angeles County	42,875
Springdale, AR (city) Washington County	42,396
Fairfield, CA (city) Solano County	41,719
Woonsocket, RI (city) Providence County	41,447
Fitchburg, MA (city) Worcester County	41,094
Irving, TX (city) Dallas County	39,821
Columbus, OH (city) Franklin County	39,565
Haltom City, TX (city) Tarrant County	39,464
Richmond, CA (city) Contra Costa County	39,444
Rochester, NY (city) Monroe County	37,841
San Diego, CA (city) San Diego County	37,419
Riverside, CA (city) Riverside County	36,146
Los Angeles, CA (city) Los Angeles County	34,313
San Pablo, CA (city) Contra Costa County	33,750
Green Bay, WI (city) Brown County	32,500
Fort Smith, AR (city) Sebastian County	32,163
Minneapolis, MN (city) Hennepin County	31,767
Moreno Valley, CA (city) Riverside County	30,682
Parkway-S. Sacramento, CA (cdp) Sacramento County	30,208
Santa Rosa, CA (city) Sonoma County	28,333
Providence, RI (city) Providence County	27,688
Milwaukee, WI (city) Milwaukee County	27,350
Raymond, WA (city) Pacific County	27,188
Sacramento, CA (city) Sacramento County	26,929
Oakland, CA (city) Alameda County	26,364
Rochester, MN (city) Olmsted County	25,625
St. Paul, MN (city) Ramsey County	24,931
Worthington, MN (city) Nobles County	24,250
Long Beach, CA (city) Los Angeles County	23,819
Merced, CA (city) Merced County	23,795
Redding, CA (city) Shasta County	23,718
Stockton, CA (city) San Joaquin County	22,932
Visalia, CA (city) Tulare County	22,792
Honolulu, HI (cdp) Honolulu County	22,188
Tacoma, WA (city) Pierce County	21,250
Modesto, CA (city) Stanislaus County	17,750
Fresno, CA (city) Fresno County	16,497

Notes: Please refer to the User's Guide for an explanation of data; ranking tables include all places with Asian and/or NHPI populations above SF4 population thresholds; (1) tables reflect only those areas that meet SF4 population thresholds, therefore there may be less than 50 states, 75 counties or 75 places listed

Median Household Income

Malaysian

All States, Top 75 Counties, and Top 75 Places Sorted by Number[1]

State	Dollars
California	62,404
Texas	42,292
Illinois	37,000
United States	35,767
New York	34,005
Ohio	33,393
Michigan	22,031
Oklahoma	5,583

County	Dollars
Los Angeles County, CA	50,694
Queens County, NY	29,214

Place	Dollars
New York, NY (city)	33,929

Notes: Please refer to the User's Guide for an explanation of data; ranking tables include all places with Asian and/or NHPI populations above SF4 population thresholds; (1) tables reflect only those areas that meet SF4 population thresholds, therefore there may be less than 50 states, 75 counties or 75 places listed

Median Household Income

Pakistani

All States, Top 75 Counties, and Top 75 Places Sorted by Number[1]

State	Dollars
Delaware	98,964
Iowa	93,358
Utah	72,788
Oregon	72,778
Indiana	67,941
Kentucky	66,250
West Virginia	64,722
Arizona	63,214
Tennessee	62,679
Minnesota	62,159
Michigan	58,987
New Jersey	56,566
Washington	55,139
Connecticut	52,868
California	52,393
Alabama	51,875
Nevada	50,781
Pennsylvania	50,707
Georgia	50,260
Florida	50,150
Maryland	47,389
United States	47,241
Kansas	46,797
Illinois	46,179
North Carolina	45,089
Massachusetts	45,087
Virginia	44,063
New York	41,675
Ohio	41,595
Texas	41,148
Colorado	40,769
Missouri	39,838
Louisiana	37,955
Wisconsin	34,274
Oklahoma	31,875

County	Dollars
Will County, IL	98,099
Santa Clara County, CA	92,530
Washtenaw County, MI	87,136
Lake County, IL	82,759
Bergen County, NJ	75,947
Loudoun County, VA	75,208
Nassau County, NY	73,750
Westchester County, NY	71,719
San Francisco County, CA	70,461
Mercer County, NJ	69,583
Oakland County, MI	69,038
Alameda County, CA	68,594
Montgomery County, MD	67,292
Orange County, FL	65,515
Morris County, NJ	65,481
Denton County, TX	64,000
Franklin County, OH	63,365
Maricopa County, AZ	62,679
Wake County, NC	62,279
Fort Bend County, TX	61,563
San Diego County, CA	61,500
Fairfield County, CT	61,406
Hennepin County, MN	61,339
DuPage County, IL	60,833
Monmouth County, NJ	60,750
Howard County, MD	60,000
Middlesex County, NJ	59,635
Collin County, TX	59,375
Orange County, CA	58,938
Snohomish County, WA	58,281
Cobb County, GA	57,868
Camden County, NJ	57,574
Prince George's County, MD	55,833
Suffolk County, NY	55,380
Somerset County, NJ	52,037
Wayne County, MI	51,875
New York County, NY	51,473
Richmond County, NY	51,406
Sacramento County, CA	50,962
Prince William County, VA	50,946
Hartford County, CT	48,750
Riverside County, CA	48,750
New Haven County, CT	48,553
Gwinnett County, GA	48,472
King County, WA	48,438
Macomb County, MI	47,450
Delaware County, PA	46,875
Essex County, NJ	46,875
Fairfax County, VA	46,574
Union County, NJ	45,208
San Bernardino County, CA	44,500
Alexandria Independent City, VA	43,828
Clayton County, GA	43,438
Miami-Dade County, FL	42,917
Broward County, FL	41,875
Los Angeles County, CA	41,563
Worcester County, MA	40,313
Queens County, NY	40,102
Hudson County, NJ	39,625
Cook County, IL	39,464
Arlington County, VA	39,414
St. Louis County, MO	39,410
Dallas County, TX	38,425
Contra Costa County, CA	37,578
Jefferson Parish, LA	37,321
Harris County, TX	35,833
Tarrant County, TX	35,500
Bronx County, NY	34,712
Milwaukee County, WI	33,813
Middlesex County, MA	33,125
Tulsa County, OK	32,031
San Joaquin County, CA	31,406
Philadelphia County, PA	30,417
Kings County, NY	29,375
Baltimore County, MD	29,135

Place	Dollars
Santa Clara, CA (city) Santa Clara County	97,831
Fremont, CA (city) Alameda County	83,398
Ellicott City, MD (cdp) Howard County	82,894
Sugar Land, TX (city) Fort Bend County	81,006
Skokie, IL (village) Cook County	78,844
San Jose, CA (city) Santa Clara County	77,046
North Hempstead, NY (town) Nassau County	76,005
Hempstead, NY (town) Nassau County	73,750
San Francisco, CA (city) San Francisco County	70,461
Edison, NJ (township) Middlesex County	68,295
Old Bridge, NJ (township) Middlesex County	66,750
Plano, TX (city) Collin County	66,518
Huntington, NY (town) Suffolk County	58,542
Woodbridge, NJ (township) Middlesex County	51,944
Dale City, VA (cdp) Prince William County	50,568
Richardson, TX (city) Dallas County	50,461
Brookhaven, NY (town) Suffolk County	46,458
Carrollton, TX (city) Denton County	45,368
Anaheim, CA (city) Orange County	42,308
Torrance, CA (city) Los Angeles County	41,094
Arlington, VA (cdp) Arlington County	39,414
Sacramento, CA (city) Sacramento County	37,656
Irving, TX (city) Dallas County	37,500
Los Angeles, CA (city) Los Angeles County	37,201
Jersey City, NJ (city) Hudson County	37,171
New York, NY (city)	37,093
Mission Bend, TX (cdp) Fort Bend County	36,979
Stockton, CA (city) San Joaquin County	36,776
Garland, TX (city) Dallas County	35,903
Dallas, TX (city) Dallas County	35,404
Houston, TX (city) Harris County	33,281
Philadelphia, PA (city) Philadelphia County	30,417
Chicago, IL (city) Cook County	28,981
Austin, TX (city) Travis County	25,263
Bailey's Crossroads, VA (cdp) Fairfax County	24,565
Lincolnia, VA (cdp) Fairfax County	22,198
Tulsa, OK (city) Tulsa County	16,518

Notes: Please refer to the User's Guide for an explanation of data; ranking tables include all places with Asian and/or NHPI populations above SF4 population thresholds; (1) tables reflect only those areas that meet SF4 population thresholds, therefore there may be less than 50 states, 75 counties or 75 places listed

Median Household Income

Samoan

***All States, Top 75 Counties, and Top 75 Places Sorted by Number*[1]**

State	Dollars
Colorado	58,882
New Jersey	56,042
Virginia	52,000
Illinois	50,682
Utah	47,542
North Carolina	47,292
New York	46,071
Texas	45,347
California	45,169
Arizona	43,152
Florida	40,956
Alaska	40,750
Ohio	40,673
United States	40,620
Nevada	40,048
Washington	39,614
Georgia	37,727
Tennessee	35,833
Missouri	35,000
Oregon	32,083
Hawaii	31,477
Pennsylvania	30,625
Michigan	22,056

County	Dollars
San Mateo County, CA	86,781
Santa Clara County, CA	63,125
Utah County, UT	63,125
Alameda County, CA	58,000
Orange County, CA	57,206
Contra Costa County, CA	56,705
Solano County, CA	51,250
Maricopa County, AZ	50,268
San Diego County, CA	48,906
San Joaquin County, CA	48,750
Ventura County, CA	46,528
Salt Lake County, UT	46,406
Jackson County, MO	43,594
Los Angeles County, CA	40,885
Anchorage Borough, AK	39,934
King County, WA	39,844
Pierce County, WA	38,984
Clark County, NV	37,361
Riverside County, CA	37,350
San Bernardino County, CA	34,853
Hawaii County, HI	34,167
Sacramento County, CA	34,044
Honolulu County, HI	31,250
San Francisco County, CA	25,469

Place	Dollars
Anaheim, CA (city) Orange County	68,839
Garden Grove, CA (city) Orange County	67,500
Carson, CA (city) Los Angeles County	55,139
San Jose, CA (city) Santa Clara County	54,643
Santa Ana, CA (city) Orange County	53,750
Oceanside, CA (city) San Diego County	51,759
Lakewood, CA (city) Los Angeles County	51,750
Federal Way, WA (city) King County	50,938
Westminster, CA (city) Orange County	49,625
Lakewood, WA (city) Pierce County	49,531
Nanakuli, HI (cdp) Honolulu County	47,321
San Diego, CA (city) San Diego County	46,635
Hayward, CA (city) Alameda County	45,938
Kahuku, HI (cdp) Honolulu County	43,750
Oxnard, CA (city) Ventura County	42,708
Ewa Beach, HI (cdp) Honolulu County	42,188
West Valley City, UT (city) Salt Lake County	40,938
Salt Lake City, UT (city) Salt Lake County	39,286
Los Angeles, CA (city) Los Angeles County	38,438
New York, NY (city)	35,313
Tacoma, WA (city) Pierce County	35,250
San Bernardino, CA (city) San Bernardino County	33,882
Hauula, HI (cdp) Honolulu County	31,181
Long Beach, CA (city) Los Angeles County	30,400
Seattle, WA (city) King County	30,000
Laie, HI (cdp) Honolulu County	29,375
Sacramento, CA (city) Sacramento County	29,250
Compton, CA (city) Los Angeles County	27,900
San Francisco, CA (city) San Francisco County	25,469
Honolulu, HI (cdp) Honolulu County	25,302
Waipahu, HI (cdp) Honolulu County	23,536
Halawa, HI (cdp) Honolulu County	21,447

Notes: Please refer to the User's Guide for an explanation of data; ranking tables include all places with Asian and/or NHPI populations above SF4 population thresholds; (1) tables reflect only those areas that meet SF4 population thresholds, therefore there may be less than 50 states, 75 counties or 75 places listed

Median Household Income

Sri Lankan

All States, Top 75 Counties, and Top 75 Places Sorted by Number[1]

State	Dollars
New Jersey	76,930
Pennsylvania	70,729
Maryland	63,906
California	61,731
Illinois	57,000
United States	52,661
Massachusetts	50,714
Michigan	49,583
New York	48,587
Ohio	47,857
Virginia	47,670
Washington	47,063
Texas	46,346
Florida	23,750

County	Dollars
Middlesex County, NJ	81,586
Montgomery County, MD	63,047
Los Angeles County, CA	60,116
Orange County, CA	54,509
Richmond County, NY	42,639
Queens County, NY	34,896

Place	Dollars
Los Angeles, CA (city) Los Angeles County	42,733
New York, NY (city)	42,069

Notes: Please refer to the User's Guide for an explanation of data; ranking tables include all places with Asian and/or NHPI populations above SF4 population thresholds; (1) tables reflect only those areas that meet SF4 population thresholds, therefore there may be less than 50 states, 75 counties or 75 places listed

Median Household Income

Taiwanese

All States, Top 75 Counties, and Top 75 Places Sorted by Number[1]

State	Dollars
New Jersey	84,297
Georgia	74,583
Minnesota	74,414
Michigan	70,260
Maryland	65,417
Virginia	64,539
Tennessee	61,103
North Carolina	60,000
Massachusetts	58,281
California	56,986
Connecticut	55,625
United States	54,928
Arizona	54,911
Missouri	52,266
New York	52,088
Texas	52,065
Illinois	51,486
Washington	50,691
Hawaii	47,500
Ohio	46,635
Florida	45,583
Nevada	43,712
Louisiana	39,107
Iowa	32,353
Kansas	31,429
Colorado	30,921
Utah	28,229
Indiana	26,382
Pennsylvania	26,250
Oregon	25,250
Wisconsin	8,661
Oklahoma	7,604

County	Dollars
DuPage County, IL	131,110
Somerset County, NJ	117,355
Mercer County, NJ	107,803
Collin County, TX	101,912
Montgomery County, MD	100,119
Ventura County, CA	100,000
Fairfax County, VA	97,621
Morris County, NJ	96,657
Suffolk County, NY	95,997
Santa Clara County, CA	90,763
Middlesex County, MA	88,971
Essex County, NJ	86,299
Westchester County, NY	83,050
Gwinnett County, GA	82,072
Oakland County, MI	80,000
Bergen County, NJ	79,249
Middlesex County, NJ	76,100
Nassau County, NY	73,611
San Mateo County, CA	71,071
Alameda County, CA	70,595
St. Louis County, MO	66,932
Contra Costa County, CA	65,859
San Francisco County, CA	63,203
San Diego County, CA	61,544
New York County, NY	61,458
Maricopa County, AZ	61,250
Orange County, CA	58,553
Tarrant County, TX	56,333
King County, WA	55,446
Fort Bend County, TX	54,919
Queens County, NY	52,695
Los Angeles County, CA	50,925
Honolulu County, HI	50,446
Harris County, TX	50,184
Dallas County, TX	49,076
Washtenaw County, MI	46,250
San Bernardino County, CA	43,750
Clark County, NV	43,144
Franklin County, OH	41,484
Cook County, IL	38,125
Travis County, TX	36,458
Riverside County, CA	35,987
Norfolk County, MA	33,750
Sacramento County, CA	31,818
Suffolk County, MA	21,591
Allegheny County, PA	13,750
Dane County, WI	4,360

Place	Dollars
Saratoga, CA (city) Santa Clara County	153,050
Plano, TX (city) Collin County	103,208
San Marino, CA (city) Los Angeles County	100,334
Naperville, IL (city) Du Page County	97,763
Edison, NJ (township) Middlesex County	95,163
Sunnyvale, CA (city) Santa Clara County	89,777
Fremont, CA (city) Alameda County	87,735
Troy, MI (city) Oakland County	84,507
San Jose, CA (city) Santa Clara County	83,806
Cupertino, CA (city) Santa Clara County	78,945
Huntington Beach, CA (city) Orange County	76,158
North Hempstead, NY (town) Nassau County	73,333
Walnut, CA (city) Los Angeles County	71,458
Cerritos, CA (city) Los Angeles County	66,518
Irvine, CA (city) Orange County	64,900
San Francisco, CA (city) San Francisco County	63,203
San Diego, CA (city) San Diego County	61,507
Bellevue, WA (city) King County	59,048
Arcadia, CA (city) Los Angeles County	58,319
Hacienda Heights, CA (cdp) Los Angeles County	56,875
Tustin, CA (city) Orange County	56,827
Diamond Bar, CA (city) Los Angeles County	56,691
Torrance, CA (city) Los Angeles County	55,962
Sugar Land, TX (city) Fort Bend County	54,597
Chino Hills, CA (city) San Bernardino County	53,750
West Covina, CA (city) Los Angeles County	53,646
Orange, CA (city) Orange County	53,269
New York, NY (city)	52,123
Honolulu, HI (cdp) Honolulu County	51,339
Rowland Heights, CA (cdp) Los Angeles County	50,893
Arlington, TX (city) Tarrant County	50,875
Rancho Palos Verdes, CA (city) Los Angeles County	50,625
Upland, CA (city) San Bernardino County	50,000
Anaheim, CA (city) Orange County	45,781
Temple City, CA (city) Los Angeles County	44,688
Fountain Valley, CA (city) Orange County	42,813
East San Gabriel, CA (cdp) Los Angeles County	42,188
Cypress, CA (city) Orange County	41,023
Houston, TX (city) Harris County	40,486
San Gabriel, CA (city) Los Angeles County	40,395
Monterey Park, CA (city) Los Angeles County	39,948
Alhambra, CA (city) Los Angeles County	37,426
Ann Arbor, MI (city) Washtenaw County	37,045
Los Angeles, CA (city) Los Angeles County	35,029
Austin, TX (city) Travis County	34,464
Chicago, IL (city) Cook County	30,938
Seattle, WA (city) King County	25,313
Boston, MA (city) Suffolk County	21,591
Columbus, OH (city) Franklin County	21,146
El Monte, CA (city) Los Angeles County	20,833
Berkeley, CA (city) Alameda County	8,864
Madison, WI (city) Dane County	4,360

Notes: Please refer to the User's Guide for an explanation of data; ranking tables include all places with Asian and/or NHPI populations above SF4 population thresholds; (1) tables reflect only those areas that meet SF4 population thresholds, therefore there may be less than 50 states, 75 counties or 75 places listed

Median Household Income

Thai

All States, Top 75 Counties, and Top 75 Places Sorted by Number[1]

State	Dollars
New Jersey	58,021
Alaska	52,125
Maryland	51,974
New York	47,677
Illinois	46,735
Iowa	45,781
California	45,533
Massachusetts	43,631
Utah	41,346
Washington	40,435
United States	40,329
Nevada	40,313
Connecticut	40,227
Colorado	40,171
Louisiana	39,750
Georgia	39,457
Tennessee	39,375
Virginia	39,063
South Carolina	38,958
New Mexico	38,750
North Carolina	37,222
Florida	37,139
Kansas	37,054
Minnesota	35,125
Hawaii	34,531
Texas	34,500
Nebraska	34,018
Missouri	33,917
Indiana	32,756
Oregon	29,688
Arizona	29,336
Ohio	26,833
Alabama	26,406
Arkansas	26,250
Michigan	25,766
Oklahoma	25,066
Kentucky	24,167
Wisconsin	21,122
Pennsylvania	18,510

County	Dollars
Nassau County, NY	86,648
Contra Costa County, CA	83,433
Suffolk County, NY	74,531
Westchester County, NY	72,000
DuPage County, IL	70,750
Collin County, TX	70,294
San Mateo County, CA	69,773
Santa Clara County, CA	60,441
Fairfax County, VA	56,413
Bergen County, NJ	56,250
Montgomery County, MD	54,531
Orange County, CA	52,599
St. Louis County, MO	50,000
Anchorage Borough, AK	49,286
Queens County, NY	47,817
Cook County, IL	46,490
Pierce County, WA	46,161
Broward County, FL	46,058
Middlesex County, MA	45,833
Polk County, IA	45,781
Los Angeles County, CA	45,325
San Bernardino County, CA	44,942
Dallas County, TX	42,125
Prince George's County, MD	41,750
Miami-Dade County, FL	41,699
Alameda County, CA	41,450
Pinellas County, FL	41,250
San Francisco County, CA	40,363
King County, WA	39,167
New York County, NY	38,672
Travis County, TX	38,194
Bexar County, TX	37,098
Clark County, NV	36,604
Okaloosa County, FL	34,464
Tarrant County, TX	34,375
Oklahoma County, OK	33,750
Palm Beach County, FL	33,750
Sacramento County, CA	32,679
Honolulu County, HI	32,045
San Diego County, CA	31,354
Harris County, TX	31,336
Hillsborough County, FL	30,972
Riverside County, CA	30,667
Maricopa County, AZ	29,583
Denver County, CO	28,125
Multnomah County, OR	22,061
Franklin County, OH	21,250

Place	Dollars
San Jose, CA (city) Santa Clara County	85,192
Cerritos, CA (city) Los Angeles County	69,464
Bellflower, CA (city) Los Angeles County	51,058
Glendale, CA (city) Los Angeles County	50,357
New York, NY (city)	46,897
Anaheim, CA (city) Orange County	43,214
Des Moines, IA (city) Polk County	42,500
Spring Valley, NV (cdp) Clark County	41,146
San Francisco, CA (city) San Francisco County	40,363
Chicago, IL (city) Cook County	39,479
Los Angeles, CA (city) Los Angeles County	37,769
San Antonio, TX (city) Bexar County	36,071
Las Vegas, NV (city) Clark County	35,350
Long Beach, CA (city) Los Angeles County	31,215
Houston, TX (city) Harris County	30,388
Denver, CO (city) Denver County	28,125
Seattle, WA (city) King County	27,100
Honolulu, HI (cdp) Honolulu County	25,694
San Diego, CA (city) San Diego County	25,500
Portland, OR (city) Multnomah County	21,892
Columbus, OH (city) Franklin County	16,125

Notes: Please refer to the User's Guide for an explanation of data; ranking tables include all places with Asian and/or NHPI populations above SF4 population thresholds; (1) tables reflect only those areas that meet SF4 population thresholds, therefore there may be less than 50 states, 75 counties or 75 places listed

Median Household Income

Tongan

***All States, Top 75 Counties, and Top 75 Places Sorted by Number*[1]**

State	Dollars
Washington	65,388
California	49,470
Alaska	48,167
Arizona	46,964
Utah	46,648
United States	45,700
Nevada	44,904
Hawaii	38,365
Texas	38,125
Oregon	35,000

County	Dollars
San Mateo County, CA	75,074
Contra Costa County, CA	70,500
King County, WA	67,069
Sacramento County, CA	66,094
Salt Lake County, UT	50,526
Tarrant County, TX	49,750
Maui County, HI	49,153
Alameda County, CA	47,596
Maricopa County, AZ	46,964
San Diego County, CA	46,250
Multnomah County, OR	45,667
Washoe County, NV	44,327
Utah County, UT	42,625
Los Angeles County, CA	39,861
Honolulu County, HI	34,375
San Bernardino County, CA	30,625
Orange County, CA	24,375

Place	Dollars
San Mateo, CA (city) San Mateo County	100,718
Laie, HI (cdp) Honolulu County	82,375
San Bruno, CA (city) San Mateo County	78,135
East Palo Alto, CA (city) San Mateo County	70,625
Sacramento, CA (city) Sacramento County	65,781
West Jordan, UT (city) Salt Lake County	64,018
West Valley City, UT (city) Salt Lake County	51,875
Oakland, CA (city) Alameda County	51,000
Portland, OR (city) Multnomah County	45,667
Salt Lake City, UT (city) Salt Lake County	43,382
Kahuku, HI (cdp) Honolulu County	40,972
Los Angeles, CA (city) Los Angeles County	37,083
Hauula, HI (cdp) Honolulu County	31,786
Honolulu, HI (cdp) Honolulu County	23,750

Notes: Please refer to the User's Guide for an explanation of data; ranking tables include all places with Asian and/or NHPI populations above SF4 population thresholds; (1) tables reflect only those areas that meet SF4 population thresholds, therefore there may be less than 50 states, 75 counties or 75 places listed

Median Household Income

Vietnamese

All States, Top 75 Counties, and Top 75 Places Sorted by Number[1]

State	Dollars
Delaware	92,565
Virginia	56,972
Alaska	55,455
New Jersey	54,745
Maryland	54,557
Connecticut	53,378
New Hampshire	52,269
Oregon	51,349
Michigan	51,276
West Virginia	51,023
Nebraska	48,594
California	48,443
Georgia	47,849
Utah	46,420
Texas	45,947
Minnesota	45,884
United States	45,085
Kansas	45,000
Colorado	44,719
Iowa	44,237
Illinois	44,177
Nevada	43,929
Rhode Island	43,409
Massachusetts	42,570
South Dakota	42,500
Arizona	42,308
North Carolina	41,875
Ohio	41,433
Indiana	41,099
Washington	40,113
Kentucky	40,030
Oklahoma	39,850
South Carolina	39,444
Tennessee	39,268
Idaho	39,007
Florida	38,877
Alabama	38,750
Pennsylvania	38,549
Wisconsin	38,510
Arkansas	38,102
New York	37,194
New Mexico	35,938
District of Columbia	35,660
Missouri	33,784
Mississippi	31,694
Louisiana	30,807
Vermont	30,000
Maine	28,611
Hawaii	26,389

County	Dollars
Bergen County, NJ	127,674
Somerset County, NJ	103,511
New Castle County, DE	95,127
Placer County, CA	90,470
Monmouth County, NJ	88,372
Collin County, TX	85,269
Loudoun County, VA	79,866
San Mateo County, CA	79,314
Scott County, MN	78,364
Nassau County, NY	77,428
Fairfax Independent City, VA	75,426
Will County, IL	74,583
Prince William County, VA	71,563
Adams County, NE	71,250
Williamson County, TX	71,083
Cumberland County, PA	71,063
Seminole County, FL	70,521
Santa Clara County, CA	68,797
Ventura County, CA	68,750
Washington County, MN	68,500
Fairfield County, CT	68,050
Middlesex County, NJ	67,500
Fort Bend County, TX	66,731
Fairfax County, VA	66,696
Suffolk County, NY	66,477
Chester County, PA	65,694
Morris County, NJ	65,625
Canadian County, OK	65,417
Clackamas County, OR	65,000
Anoka County, MN	64,844
Eaton County, MI	64,097
Madison County, AL	63,750
New York County, NY	62,292
DuPage County, IL	62,222
Ottawa County, MI	62,083
Sarpy County, NE	61,953
Saline County, KS	61,750
Richland County, SC	61,607
Oakland County, MI	61,528
Howard County, MD	61,346
Montgomery County, PA	60,950
Litchfield County, CT	60,938
Hillsborough County, NH	60,875
Washington County, OR	60,526
Prince George's County, MD	60,508
Wake County, NC	60,302
Wayne County, MI	60,179
Marion County, OR	59,000
Burlington County, NJ	58,929
Montgomery County, MD	58,884
Bristol County, MA	58,750
Arapahoe County, CO	57,228
Gwinnett County, GA	56,958
Benton County, WA	56,917
York County, PA	56,806
Middlesex County, MA	56,000
Dakota County, MN	55,938
Okaloosa County, FL	55,795
Lancaster County, PA	55,607
Denton County, TX	55,433
Sonoma County, CA	55,000
Chesterfield County, VA	54,773
Brazoria County, TX	54,722
St. Louis County, MO	54,300
Finney County, KS	54,091
Snohomish County, WA	53,834
Cleveland County, OK	53,669
Solano County, CA	53,553
Cobb County, GA	53,491
Essex County, MA	53,480
Gaston County, NC	53,125
Washtenaw County, MI	52,813
Alexandria Independent City, VA	52,083
Atlantic County, NJ	51,875
Travis County, TX	51,817

Place	Dollars
Camarillo, CA (city) Ventura County	121,279
Laguna Hills, CA (city) Orange County	100,401
Laguna Niguel, CA (city) Orange County	98,474
Walnut, CA (city) Los Angeles County	97,790
Irvine, CA (city) Orange County	95,768
Franconia, VA (cdp) Fairfax County	93,787
Fremont, CA (city) Alameda County	93,544
Hacienda Heights, CA (cdp) Los Angeles County	93,496
Mission Viejo, CA (city) Orange County	93,461
Chino Hills, CA (city) San Bernardino County	91,714
Rancho Santa Margarita, CA (city) Orange County	91,238
Lincolnia, VA (cdp) Fairfax County	90,927
Milpitas, CA (city) Santa Clara County	90,700
Placentia, CA (city) Orange County	89,868
Yorba Linda, CA (city) Orange County	89,310
Cerritos, CA (city) Los Angeles County	87,732
North Springfield, VA (cdp) Fairfax County	87,653
Burke, VA (cdp) Fairfax County	86,179
Diamond Bar, CA (city) Los Angeles County	86,058
Allen, TX (city) Collin County	85,248
Plano, TX (city) Collin County	84,195
Aliso Viejo, CA (cdp) Orange County	83,636
Herndon, VA (town) Fairfax County	81,634
Chantilly, VA (cdp) Fairfax County	81,156
Shrewsbury, MA (town) Worcester County	80,850
West Springfield, VA (cdp) Fairfax County	79,702
Oakton, VA (cdp) Fairfax County	79,430
Cary, NC (town) Wake County	78,230
Ocean Springs, MS (city) Jackson County	77,527
Cupertino, CA (city) Santa Clara County	76,996
Montgomery Village, MD (cdp) Montgomery County	76,363
Santa Clara, CA (city) Santa Clara County	75,104
Lake Forest, CA (city) Orange County	74,643
Corona, CA (city) Riverside County	74,338
Springfield, VA (cdp) Fairfax County	73,958
Simi Valley, CA (city) Ventura County	73,224
Mountain View, CA (city) Santa Clara County	73,092
Aloha, OR (cdp) Washington County	72,738
Union City, CA (city) Alameda County	72,639
Round Rock, TX (city) Williamson County	72,333
Stafford, TX (city) Fort Bend County	72,250
Hastings, NE (city) Adams County	71,250
Tustin, CA (city) Orange County	71,094
Gaithersburg, MD (city) Montgomery County	71,071
Seattle Hill-Silver Firs, WA (cdp) Snohomish County	70,721
Cascade-Fairwood, WA (cdp) King County	70,643
Santa Clarita, CA (city) Los Angeles County	70,625
Alondra Park, CA (cdp) Los Angeles County	70,385
Eagan, MN (city) Dakota County	70,250
League City, TX (city) Galveston County	70,083
Missouri City, TX (city) Fort Bend County	69,219
Daly City, CA (city) San Mateo County	69,167
Fountain Valley, CA (city) Orange County	69,120
Glendale Heights, IL (village) Du Page County	68,026
Downey, CA (city) Los Angeles County	67,813
Sugar Land, TX (city) Fort Bend County	67,778
Richardson, TX (city) Dallas County	67,569
Bridgeport, CT (city) Fairfield County	67,500
Aspen Hill, MD (cdp) Montgomery County	67,167
Sunnyvale, CA (city) Santa Clara County	66,926
Salem, OR (city) Marion County	66,875
Merrifield, VA (cdp) Fairfax County	66,800
San Jose, CA (city) Santa Clara County	66,711
Orange, CA (city) Orange County	66,196
San Mateo, CA (city) San Mateo County	65,893
Bryn Mawr-Skyway, WA (cdp) King County	65,792
Centreville, VA (cdp) Fairfax County	65,500
Oceanside, CA (city) San Diego County	65,288
South Plainfield, NJ (borough) Middlesex County	65,288
Annandale, VA (cdp) Fairfax County	65,054
West Hartford, CT (town) Hartford County	65,000
Manheim, PA (township) Lancaster County	64,167
Chino, CA (city) San Bernardino County	64,028
Rancho Cucamonga, CA (city) San Bernardino County	63,333
SeaTac, WA (city) King County	63,056

Notes: Please refer to the User's Guide for an explanation of data; ranking tables include all places with Asian and/or NHPI populations above SF4 population thresholds; (1) tables reflect only those areas that meet SF4 population thresholds, therefore there may be less than 50 states, 75 counties or 75 places listed

Per Capita Income

Total Population

All States, Top 75 Counties, and Top 75 Places Sorted by Number[1]

State	Dollars
Connecticut	28,766
District of Columbia	28,659
New Jersey	27,006
Massachusetts	25,952
Maryland	25,614
Colorado	24,049
Virginia	23,975
New Hampshire	23,844
New York	23,389
Delaware	23,305
Minnesota	23,198
Illinois	23,104
Washington	22,973
California	22,711
Alaska	22,660
Michigan	22,168
Nevada	21,989
Rhode Island	21,688
United States	21,587
Florida	21,557
Hawaii	21,525
Wisconsin	21,271
Georgia	21,154
Ohio	21,003
Oregon	20,940
Pennsylvania	20,880
Vermont	20,625
Kansas	20,506
Indiana	20,397
North Carolina	20,307
Arizona	20,275
Missouri	19,936
Iowa	19,674
Texas	19,617
Nebraska	19,613
Maine	19,533
Tennessee	19,393
Wyoming	19,134
South Carolina	18,795
Alabama	18,189
Utah	18,185
Kentucky	18,093
Idaho	17,841
North Dakota	17,769
Oklahoma	17,646
South Dakota	17,562
New Mexico	17,261
Montana	17,151
Louisiana	16,912
Arkansas	16,904
West Virginia	16,477
Mississippi	15,853

County	Dollars
Marin County, CA	44,962
New York County, NY	42,922
Falls Church Independent City, VA	41,051
Fairfield County, CT	38,350
Somerset County, NJ	37,970
Arlington County, VA	37,706
Alexandria Independent City, VA	37,645
Morris County, NJ	36,964
Fairfax County, VA	36,888
Westchester County, NY	36,726
Hunterdon County, NJ	36,370
San Mateo County, CA	36,045
Montgomery County, MD	35,684
Douglas County, CO	34,848
Los Alamos County, NM	34,646
San Francisco County, CA	34,556
Bergen County, NJ	33,638
Loudoun County, VA	33,530
Collin County, TX	33,345
Hamilton County, IN	33,109
Santa Clara County, CA	32,795
Oakland County, MI	32,534
Williamson County, TN	32,496
Norfolk County, MA	32,484
Howard County, MD	32,402
Nassau County, NY	32,151
Lake County, IL	32,102
Eagle County, CO	32,011
Ozaukee County, WI	31,947
Chester County, PA	31,627
Delaware County, OH	31,600
Blaine County, ID	31,346
DuPage County, IL	31,315
Fairfax Independent City, VA	31,247
Middlesex County, MA	31,199
Collier County, FL	31,195
Monmouth County, NJ	31,149
Johnson County, KS	30,919
Montgomery County, PA	30,898
Contra Costa County, CA	30,615
Putnam County, NY	30,127
Fulton County, GA	30,003
Martin County, FL	29,584
King County, WA	29,521
Fayette County, GA	29,464
James City County, VA	29,256
Waukesha County, WI	29,164
Forsyth County, GA	29,114
Boulder County, CO	28,976
Albemarle County, VA	28,852
Palm Beach County, FL	28,801
Hennepin County, MN	28,789
Fauquier County, VA	28,757
St. Johns County, FL	28,674
Rockwall County, TX	28,573
Carver County, MN	28,486
Litchfield County, CT	28,408
Sarasota County, FL	28,326
Middlesex County, CT	28,251
Washington County, MN	28,148
Arapahoe County, CO	28,147
Rockland County, NY	28,082
Livingston County, MI	28,069
Jefferson County, CO	28,066
Placer County, CA	27,963
Geauga County, OH	27,944
Mercer County, NJ	27,914
Cobb County, GA	27,863
St. Louis County, MO	27,595
Anne Arundel County, MD	27,578
Bucks County, PA	27,430
Mecklenburg County, NC	27,352
Douglas County, NV	27,288
Indian River County, FL	27,227
Shelby County, AL	27,176

Place	Dollars
Atherton, CA (town) San Mateo County	112,408
Rolling Hills, CA (city) Los Angeles County	111,031
Oyster Bay Cove, NY (village) Nassau County	103,203
North Hills, NY (village) Nassau County	100,093
Newport Coast, CA (cdp) Orange County	98,770
Hillsborough, CA (town) San Mateo County	98,643
Sands Point, NY (village) Nassau County	95,647
Los Altos Hills, CA (town) Santa Clara County	92,840
Scarsdale, NY (village) Westchester County	89,907
Bronxville, NY (village) Westchester County	89,483
Hunters Creek Village, TX (city) Harris County	88,821
Muttontown, NY (village) Nassau County	88,020
Bunker Hill Village, TX (city) Harris County	86,434
Tiburon, CA (town) Marin County	85,966
Saddle River, NJ (borough) Bergen County	85,934
Brookville, NY (village) Nassau County	84,375
Winnetka, IL (village) Cook County	84,134
Laurel Hollow, NY (village) Nassau County	83,366
New Canaan, CT (town) Fairfield County	82,049
Weston, MA (town) Middlesex County	79,640
Great Falls, VA (cdp) Fairfax County	78,149
Old Brookville, NY (village) Nassau County	77,874
Chappaqua, NY (cdp) Westchester County	77,835
Darien, CT (town) Fairfield County	77,519
Travilah, MD (cdp) Montgomery County	77,129
Lake Forest, IL (city) Lake County	77,092
Alpine, NJ (borough) Bergen County	76,995
Millburn, NJ (township) Essex County	76,796
Oak Brook, IL (village) Du Page County	76,668
Rye, NY (city) Westchester County	76,566
South Barrington, IL (village) Cook County	76,078
Greenwich, CT (town) Fairfield County	74,346
New Castle, NY (town) Westchester County	73,888
Westport, CT (town) Fairfield County	73,664
Piedmont, CA (city) Alameda County	70,539
Old Westbury, NY (village) Nassau County	70,089
West University Place, TX (city) Harris County	69,674
Town and Country, MO (city) Saint Louis County	69,347
Palos Verdes Estates, CA (city) Los Angeles County	69,040
Loyola, CA (cdp) Santa Clara County	68,730
Blackhawk-Camino Tass., CA (cdp) Contra Costa Co.	66,972
Los Altos, CA (city) Santa Clara County	66,776
Munsey Park, NY (village) Nassau County	66,772
Wilton, CT (town) Fairfield County	65,806
Alamo, CA (cdp) Contra Costa County	65,705
Beverly Hills, CA (city) Los Angeles County	65,507
Chatham, NJ (township) Morris County	65,497
Orinda, CA (city) Contra Costa County	65,428
Saratoga, CA (city) Santa Clara County	65,400
Flower Hill, NY (village) Nassau County	64,997
Potomac, MD (cdp) Montgomery County	64,875
Hinsdale, IL (village) Du Page County	63,765
University Park, TX (city) Dallas County	63,414
McLean, VA (cdp) Fairfax County	63,209
Newport Beach, CA (city) Orange County	63,015
Bloomfield, MI (township) Oakland County	62,716
Summit, NJ (city) Union County	62,598
Long Grove, IL (village) Lake County	62,185
Greenville, NY (cdp) Westchester County	61,785
Manhattan Beach, CA (city) Los Angeles County	61,136
Chevy Chase, MD (cdp) Montgomery County	60,893
North Castle, NY (town) Westchester County	60,628
Lincolnshire, IL (village) Lake County	60,115
Franklin Lakes, NJ (borough) Bergen County	59,763
East Hills, NY (village) Nassau County	59,297
San Marino, CA (city) Los Angeles County	59,150
Laguna Beach, CA (city) Orange County	58,732
Watchung, NJ (borough) Somerset County	58,653
Briarcliff Manor, NY (village) Westchester County	58,646
Marina del Rey, CA (cdp) Los Angeles County	58,530
Burr Ridge, IL (village) Du Page County	58,518
Bethesda, MD (cdp) Montgomery County	58,479
Woodbury, NY (cdp) Nassau County	58,316
Lake Success, NY (village) Nassau County	58,002
Mamaroneck, NY (town) Westchester County	57,822

Notes: Please refer to the User's Guide for an explanation of data; ranking tables include all places with Asian and/or NHPI populations above SF4 population thresholds; (1) tables reflect only those areas that meet SF4 population thresholds, therefore there may be less than 50 states, 75 counties or 75 places listed

Per Capita Income

Asian

All States, Top 75 Counties, and Top 75 Places Sorted by Number[1]

State	Dollars
West Virginia	28,607
Delaware	28,411
Connecticut	27,948
New Jersey	27,581
District of Columbia	27,162
Ohio	24,912
Michigan	24,581
Kentucky	24,349
Illinois	24,137
Maryland	24,025
Hawaii	22,884
Virginia	22,790
Indiana	22,421
California	22,050
Arizona	21,876
United States	21,823
New Hampshire	21,538
Massachusetts	21,452
New Mexico	21,435
Missouri	21,297
North Dakota	21,265
Colorado	20,958
Texas	20,956
New York	20,618
South Carolina	20,541
Alabama	20,488
Florida	20,429
Tennessee	20,331
Georgia	20,155
Idaho	20,143
Washington	20,141
Pennsylvania	20,096
Nevada	20,018
North Carolina	19,815
Oregon	19,790
Wyoming	18,464
Iowa	18,279
Kansas	18,182
Mississippi	17,504
Nebraska	16,739
Alaska	16,694
Arkansas	16,494
Louisiana	16,304
Utah	16,296
Oklahoma	15,691
Minnesota	15,389
Rhode Island	15,010
Wisconsin	14,962
Maine	14,592
South Dakota	14,528
Montana	14,464
Vermont	13,718

County	Dollars
Amador County, CA	58,692
Raleigh County, WV	50,782
Porter County, IN	49,691
Calvert County, MD	46,295
Washington County, TN	42,978
Dodge County, WI	42,971
Miami County, OH	42,809
Kanawha County, WV	42,594
Herkimer County, NY	42,294
Greenwood County, SC	42,088
Wood County, WV	41,513
Clearfield County, PA	41,419
St. Johns County, FL	40,366
Shelby County, AL	40,140
Malheur County, OR	39,948
Knox County, IL	39,912
Klamath County, OR	39,437
La Salle County, IL	39,317
Forsyth County, GA	38,507
Florence County, SC	38,297
Blair County, PA	37,964
Butler County, PA	37,632
Black Hawk County, IA	37,428
Marin County, CA	37,371
Steuben County, NY	37,357
Vermilion County, IL	37,289
Somerset County, NJ	37,092
Fairfield County, CT	37,087
Westchester County, NY	36,944
Marion County, OH	36,776
Bureau County, IL	36,524
Natrona County, WY	36,342
Chemung County, NY	36,102
Genesee County, MI	36,055
Hood River County, OR	35,084
Westmoreland County, PA	34,887
Boone County, KY	34,855
Montgomery County, TX	34,853
Citrus County, FL	34,576
Midland County, MI	34,555
Delaware County, OH	34,378
Los Alamos County, NM	34,231
Bethel Census Area, AK	34,226
St. Clair County, MI	33,931
Collier County, FL	33,926
Morris County, NJ	33,772
Mahoning County, OH	33,705
Clermont County, OH	33,175
Oakland County, MI	32,992
Hamilton County, IN	32,978
Monmouth County, NJ	32,951
Cameron County, TX	32,886
Putnam County, FL	32,782
Montgomery County, NY	32,725
Livingston County, MI	32,592
Waukesha County, WI	32,578
Geauga County, OH	32,547
Hunterdon County, NJ	32,445
Lake County, IN	32,442
Allegany County, MD	32,378
Medina County, OH	32,289
Mercer County, NJ	32,224
Wayne County, PA	32,031
Ector County, TX	31,896
Wayne County, NC	31,860
Nacogdoches County, TX	31,697
Warren County, OH	31,611
Lee County, IL	31,385
Webster County, IA	31,236
Falls Church Independent City, VA	31,194
Oconee County, SC	31,033
Bristol County, RI	30,989
Johnson County, IN	30,853
Midland County, TX	30,696
Cape May County, NJ	30,638

Place	Dollars
Tiburon, CA (town) Marin County	114,534
Atherton, CA (town) San Mateo County	113,641
Oyster Bay Cove, NY (village) Nassau County	104,543
Saddle River, NJ (borough) Bergen County	101,616
Rolling Hills, CA (city) Los Angeles County	91,790
Muttontown, NY (village) Nassau County	88,928
Loyola, CA (cdp) Santa Clara County	84,559
Newport Coast, CA (cdp) Orange County	84,091
Oak Brook, IL (village) Du Page County	84,054
Sands Point, NY (village) Nassau County	83,122
South Barrington, IL (village) Cook County	82,372
Los Altos Hills, CA (town) Santa Clara County	78,858
Town and Country, MO (city) Saint Louis County	78,526
Old Westbury, NY (village) Nassau County	77,912
Briarcliff Manor, NY (village) Westchester County	76,275
Westport, CT (town) Fairfield County	73,573
Laurel Hollow, NY (village) Nassau County	72,351
Rye, NY (city) Westchester County	69,806
Hockessin, DE (cdp) New Castle County	67,211
Hillsborough, CA (town) San Mateo County	66,556
Union Hill-Novelty Hill, WA (cdp) King County	66,472
Hunters Creek Village, TX (city) Harris County	65,625
North Hills, NY (village) Nassau County	65,050
West University Place, TX (city) Harris County	64,108
Elizabethtown, KY (city) Hardin County	63,871
Bloomfield, MI (township) Oakland County	62,343
Moorestown, NJ (township) Burlington County	62,102
Longmeadow, MA (town) Hampden County	61,585
Wilton, CT (town) Fairfield County	60,921
Los Altos, CA (city) Santa Clara County	60,680
Sharon, MA (town) Norfolk County	60,619
Upper St. Clair, PA (township) Allegheny County	60,605
Woodbridge, CT (town) New Haven County	59,770
Laguna Beach, CA (city) Orange County	59,578
Munsey Park, NY (village) Nassau County	59,410
Pinecrest, FL (village) Miami-Dade County	58,647
Flower Hill, NY (village) Nassau County	58,316
Watchung, NJ (borough) Somerset County	58,038
Colts Neck, NJ (township) Monmouth County	57,788
Chappaqua, NY (cdp) Westchester County	57,646
Hopewell, NJ (township) Mercer County	57,581
Mamaroneck, NY (town) Westchester County	57,327
Bunker Hill Village, TX (city) Harris County	57,084
Alpine, NJ (borough) Bergen County	56,747
Burr Ridge, IL (village) Du Page County	56,585
Lincolnshire, IL (village) Lake County	56,032
San Carlos, CA (city) San Mateo County	55,839
Greenwich, CT (town) Fairfield County	55,416
Lake Forest, IL (city) Lake County	54,345
Tamalpais-Homestead Valley, CA (cdp) Marin County	54,189
Ardsley, NY (village) Westchester County	54,171
Hermosa Beach, CA (city) Los Angeles County	54,068
Darien, CT (town) Fairfield County	53,822
New Castle, NY (town) Westchester County	53,580
Creve Coeur, MO (city) Saint Louis County	53,566
Scarsdale, NY (village) Westchester County	53,178
Cottage Lake, WA (cdp) King County	53,066
Palos Verdes Estates, CA (city) Los Angeles County	52,830
Chatham, NJ (township) Morris County	52,506
Woodbury, NY (cdp) Nassau County	51,727
East Foothills, CA (cdp) Santa Clara County	51,488
Guttenberg, NJ (town) Hudson County	51,251
McCandless, PA (township) Allegheny County	51,156
Alamo, CA (cdp) Contra Costa County	51,021
Grosse Pointe Woods, MI (city) Wayne County	50,911
Bernards, NJ (township) Somerset County	50,892
Cedar Mill, OR (cdp) Washington County	50,850
Menlo Park, CA (city) San Mateo County	50,785
Villa Park, CA (city) Orange County	50,606
Highland Park, IL (city) Lake County	50,311
Cornwall, NY (town) Orange County	50,274
Saratoga, CA (city) Santa Clara County	50,043
Charleston, WV (city) Kanawha County	49,761
Searingtown, NY (cdp) Nassau County	49,152
Potomac, MD (cdp) Montgomery County	49,146

Notes: Please refer to the User's Guide for an explanation of data; ranking tables include all places with Asian and/or NHPI populations above SF4 population thresholds; (1) tables reflect only those areas that meet SF4 population thresholds, therefore there may be less than 50 states, 75 counties or 75 places listed

Per Capita Income

Native Hawaiian and Other Pacific Islander

All States, Top 75 Counties, and Top 75 Places Sorted by Number[1]

State	Dollars
New Jersey	23,745
South Carolina	21,638
Iowa	21,436
Virginia	20,761
Mississippi	19,794
Maryland	19,600
Nevada	18,652
Connecticut	18,345
Kansas	17,272
Massachusetts	16,948
Minnesota	16,948
New Mexico	16,738
Michigan	16,378
Maine	16,353
Colorado	16,314
Delaware	16,281
California	15,610
Illinois	15,523
Oregon	15,516
Indiana	15,504
Georgia	15,333
Florida	15,251
Arizona	15,224
Tennessee	15,178
Texas	15,119
Wisconsin	15,076
United States	15,054
Washington	15,025
Pennsylvania	15,003
Louisiana	14,975
North Carolina	14,703
Hawaii	14,375
Alabama	14,089
Missouri	14,012
Nebraska	13,670
Alaska	13,557
New York	13,485
Ohio	12,919
Kentucky	12,710
Idaho	12,666
Oklahoma	11,963
Montana	11,373
Rhode Island	10,327
Utah	10,296
West Virginia	10,194
Arkansas	8,267

County	Dollars
Fairfax County, VA	30,029
Snohomish County, WA	22,511
Arapahoe County, CO	22,295
Essex County, NJ	21,839
Jefferson County, CO	21,412
Montgomery County, MD	21,258
New York County, NY	21,147
Santa Clara County, CA	21,014
San Joaquin County, CA	20,236
Wayne County, MI	19,981
Hennepin County, MN	19,761
Fresno County, CA	19,634
Broward County, FL	19,375
Contra Costa County, CA	19,330
Sonoma County, CA	19,283
Santa Barbara County, CA	19,145
Clackamas County, OR	18,912
Dallas County, TX	18,869
Ventura County, CA	18,766
Clark County, NV	18,425
Harris County, TX	18,242
Shelby County, TN	17,828
Riverside County, CA	17,415
Bernalillo County, NM	17,343
Palm Beach County, FL	17,329
Hillsborough County, FL	17,270
Gwinnett County, GA	17,184
Solano County, CA	17,089
San Diego County, CA	17,080
Sedgwick County, KS	16,739
Washington County, OR	16,716
Bexar County, TX	16,707
Alameda County, CA	16,584
Miami-Dade County, FL	16,570
San Mateo County, CA	16,470
Orange County, CA	16,373
Maricopa County, AZ	16,360
Thurston County, WA	16,072
Multnomah County, OR	16,024
Cook County, IL	15,820
Bell County, TX	15,701
King County, WA	15,486
Duval County, FL	15,447
Franklin County, OH	15,327
Monterey County, CA	15,253
Allegheny County, PA	15,186
El Paso County, CO	15,113
Honolulu County, HI	14,748
Travis County, TX	14,627
Maui County, HI	14,547
Kern County, CA	14,320
Pierce County, WA	14,259
Spokane County, WA	14,243
Milwaukee County, WI	13,968
Suffolk County, NY	13,948
Kauai County, HI	13,939
Orange County, FL	13,933
Sacramento County, CA	13,768
Tarrant County, TX	13,735
Ada County, ID	13,398
Los Angeles County, CA	13,344
Anchorage Borough, AK	13,251
Jackson County, MO	13,013
Clark County, WA	13,008
Kings County, NY	12,972
Queens County, NY	12,957
Davis County, UT	12,903
Denver County, CO	12,867
Pima County, AZ	12,678
Hawaii County, HI	12,619
San Bernardino County, CA	12,580
San Francisco County, CA	12,476
Lane County, OR	12,407
Washoe County, NV	12,222
Coryell County, TX	11,951

Place	Dollars
Chula Vista, CA (city) San Diego County	28,340
Alameda, CA (city) Alameda County	28,163
Fremont, CA (city) Alameda County	27,061
Las Vegas, NV (city) Clark County	26,250
Mililani Town, HI (cdp) Honolulu County	24,563
Maunawili, HI (cdp) Honolulu County	23,135
Sunnyvale, CA (city) Santa Clara County	22,385
Pittsburg, CA (city) Contra Costa County	21,716
SeaTac, WA (city) King County	21,087
Union City, CA (city) Alameda County	20,783
Waikapu, HI (cdp) Maui County	20,583
Redwood City, CA (city) San Mateo County	20,505
Huntington Beach, CA (city) Orange County	20,270
Holualoa, HI (cdp) Hawaii County	19,934
Santa Clara, CA (city) Santa Clara County	19,571
Village Park, HI (cdp) Honolulu County	19,257
Waimalu, HI (cdp) Honolulu County	19,163
Fairfield, CA (city) Solano County	19,132
San Jose, CA (city) Santa Clara County	19,130
Milpitas, CA (city) Santa Clara County	19,092
Volcano, HI (cdp) Hawaii County	18,923
Kailua, HI (cdp) Honolulu County	18,908
Haleiwa, HI (cdp) Honolulu County	18,815
Kilauea, HI (cdp) Kauai County	18,743
Waipio, HI (cdp) Honolulu County	18,607
South San Francisco, CA (city) San Mateo County	18,598
Lahaina, HI (cdp) Maui County	18,381
Kaaawa, HI (cdp) Honolulu County	18,267
Aiea, HI (cdp) Honolulu County	18,149
Austin, TX (city) Travis County	17,679
Tukwila, WA (city) King County	17,328
Makakilo City, HI (cdp) Honolulu County	17,141
San Antonio, TX (city) Bexar County	17,080
Makawao, HI (cdp) Maui County	17,045
Dallas, TX (city) Dallas County	17,008
Vista, CA (city) San Diego County	16,883
Aurora, CO (city) Arapahoe County	16,872
Phoenix, AZ (city) Maricopa County	16,855
Albuquerque, NM (city) Bernalillo County	16,693
Kaneohe, HI (cdp) Honolulu County	16,670
Oxnard, CA (city) Ventura County	16,649
Marina, CA (city) Monterey County	16,644
Daly City, CA (city) San Mateo County	16,635
Pearl City, HI (cdp) Honolulu County	16,538
Paia, HI (cdp) Maui County	16,502
Henderson, NV (city) Clark County	16,424
San Bruno, CA (city) San Mateo County	16,384
Honolulu, HI (cdp) Honolulu County	16,382
Honalo, HI (cdp) Hawaii County	16,248
Spring Valley, NV (cdp) Clark County	16,166
Sunrise Manor, NV (cdp) Clark County	16,146
Spokane, WA (city) Spokane County	16,137
Kualapuu, HI (cdp) Maui County	16,096
Houston, TX (city) Harris County	16,088
Los Angeles, CA (city) Los Angeles County	16,038
Portland, OR (city) Multnomah County	15,905
San Diego, CA (city) San Diego County	15,854
Vallejo, CA (city) Solano County	15,821
Stockton, CA (city) San Joaquin County	15,730
Honaunau-Napoopoo, HI (cdp) Hawaii County	15,640
Kansas City, MO (city) Jackson County	15,483
Tacoma, WA (city) Pierce County	15,396
Waimea, HI (cdp) Kauai County	15,378
Fontana, CA (city) San Bernardino County	15,326
Ahuimanu, HI (cdp) Honolulu County	15,218
Kihei, HI (cdp) Maui County	15,172
Hayward, CA (city) Alameda County	15,138
Hanapepe, HI (cdp) Kauai County	15,019
Waimea, HI (cdp) Hawaii County	14,986
Jacksonville, FL (city) Duval County	14,953
Wailuku, HI (cdp) Maui County	14,952
Waikoloa Village, HI (cdp) Hawaii County	14,901
Parkland, WA (cdp) Pierce County	14,893
Paradise, NV (cdp) Clark County	14,830
Fort Worth, TX (city) Tarrant County	14,826

Notes: Please refer to the User's Guide for an explanation of data; ranking tables include all places with Asian and/or NHPI populations above SF4 population thresholds; (1) tables reflect only those areas that meet SF4 population thresholds, therefore there may be less than 50 states, 75 counties or 75 places listed

Per Capita Income

Asian Indian

All States, Top 75 Counties, and Top 75 Places Sorted by Number[1]

State	Dollars
West Virginia	44,354
District of Columbia	41,209
Kentucky	35,162
Iowa	34,605
Connecticut	33,234
Delaware	33,056
Missouri	32,027
Ohio	31,900
Massachusetts	31,702
New Mexico	31,264
Michigan	31,216
Arizona	31,036
Oregon	30,723
Colorado	30,580
North Dakota	30,528
Virginia	29,811
Hawaii	29,742
Indiana	29,602
California	29,232
South Carolina	29,105
New Jersey	28,828
Alabama	28,786
Maryland	28,509
New Hampshire	27,991
Nebraska	27,837
Wisconsin	27,673
Tennessee	27,635
Louisiana	27,624
United States	27,514
Washington	27,282
North Carolina	27,265
Minnesota	27,156
Kansas	26,686
Pennsylvania	26,600
Arkansas	26,458
Texas	26,158
Illinois	26,094
Mississippi	25,253
Idaho	25,191
Georgia	24,917
Florida	24,363
Oklahoma	23,169
Rhode Island	23,030
New York	23,028
South Dakota	22,328
Maine	21,863
Vermont	20,888
Nevada	20,849
Wyoming	20,117
Alaska	18,295
Utah	16,761
Montana	13,398

County	Dollars
Shelby County, AL	62,543
Kanawha County, WV	62,451
Caddo Parish, LA	61,737
Montgomery County, TX	53,606
Genesee County, MI	53,544
New York County, NY	53,013
Westmoreland County, PA	50,327
Medina County, OH	47,997
Waukesha County, WI	47,426
Saginaw County, MI	47,365
Kent County, DE	46,421
Butler County, PA	45,619
Hamilton County, IN	45,525
Fairfield County, CT	45,228
Hidalgo County, TX	43,717
Santa Cruz County, CA	43,616
St. Mary's County, MD	42,322
Boulder County, CO	41,322
Hampden County, MA	41,072
San Francisco County, CA	40,986
Lake County, IN	40,903
Hinds County, MS	40,563
Saratoga County, NY	40,371
Sussex County, NJ	40,361
Greene County, OH	40,267
Stark County, OH	40,249
Midland County, MI	40,152
Fairfax Independent City, VA	40,117
San Mateo County, CA	39,943
Bristol County, MA	39,881
McLennan County, TX	39,881
Madison County, IL	39,699
Somerset County, NJ	39,465
Rock Island County, IL	39,398
St. Charles County, MO	39,300
Linn County, IA	38,929
Jefferson County, CO	38,761
Oakland County, MI	38,716
Santa Clara County, CA	38,619
Washington County, MN	38,363
Marin County, CA	38,155
Clermont County, OH	38,095
Peoria County, IL	37,932
St. Louis County, MO	37,875
Cass County, ND	37,466
Norfolk County, MA	37,442
Midland County, TX	37,397
Monmouth County, NJ	37,363
Westchester County, NY	37,127
Hunterdon County, NJ	37,069
Essex County, MA	36,905
Douglas County, CO	36,835
Chesterfield County, VA	36,651
Delaware County, OH	36,477
Allen County, IN	36,276
Washington County, OR	36,158
Allegheny County, PA	35,919
Morris County, NJ	35,825
Northampton County, PA	35,512
Hamilton County, TN	35,110
Chester County, PA	34,893
Benton County, WA	34,473
Collin County, TX	34,466
Luzerne County, PA	34,394
Boone County, MO	33,971
McHenry County, IL	33,904
New London County, CT	33,833
Monroe County, NY	33,785
Erie County, NY	33,649
Ocean County, NJ	33,608
Fairfax County, VA	33,329
Maricopa County, AZ	33,277
Jefferson Parish, LA	33,272
Putnam County, NY	33,182
Clackamas County, OR	33,118

Place	Dollars
Town and Country, MO (city) Saint Louis County	114,911
Muttontown, NY (village) Nassau County	110,041
Los Altos Hills, CA (town) Santa Clara County	98,875
Greenwich, CT (town) Fairfield County	93,678
Scarsdale, NY (village) Westchester County	89,444
Oak Brook, IL (village) Du Page County	88,710
McLean, VA (cdp) Fairfax County	84,047
Los Altos, CA (city) Santa Clara County	83,270
South Barrington, IL (village) Cook County	77,731
New Castle, NY (town) Westchester County	71,684
Bloomfield, MI (township) Oakland County	71,576
Bernards, NJ (township) Somerset County	67,934
Flint, MI (township) Genesee County	66,500
The Woodlands, TX (cdp) Montgomery County	65,670
Charleston, WV (city) Kanawha County	64,205
Brookfield, WI (city) Waukesha County	62,216
Munster, IN (town) Lake County	61,671
Shreveport, LA (city) Caddo Parish	59,442
Potomac, MD (cdp) Montgomery County	59,404
Port Washington, NY (cdp) Nassau County	58,821
Orland Park, IL (village) Cook County	58,181
Montville, NJ (township) Morris County	58,050
Searingtown, NY (cdp) Nassau County	56,329
Upper St. Clair, PA (township) Allegheny County	56,045
Saratoga, CA (city) Santa Clara County	56,009
Warren, NJ (township) Somerset County	55,959
Westlake, OH (city) Cuyahoga County	55,467
Manhasset Hills, NY (cdp) Nassau County	54,926
Foster City, CA (city) San Mateo County	54,315
Montgomery, NJ (township) Somerset County	54,172
Scotch Plains, NJ (township) Union County	53,428
Rancho Palos Verdes, CA (city) Los Angeles County	53,260
Claremont, CA (city) Los Angeles County	52,618
Newton, MA (city) Middlesex County	52,375
Pittsford, NY (town) Monroe County	52,366
Greenville, NY (cdp) Westchester County	50,360
Livingston, NJ (township) Essex County	50,008
Wheaton, IL (city) Du Page County	49,501
Boxborough, MA (town) Middlesex County	49,246
Acton, MA (town) Middlesex County	49,138
Palo Alto, CA (city) Santa Clara County	48,456
Andover, MA (town) Essex County	48,406
Gilbert, AZ (town) Maricopa County	48,228
Danville, CA (town) Contra Costa County	48,080
West Bloomfield, MI (township) Oakland County	47,579
Holmdel, NJ (township) Monmouth County	47,531
Bethesda, MD (cdp) Montgomery County	47,375
Milford, CT (town) New Haven County	47,206
Solon, OH (city) Cuyahoga County	47,197
Glenview, IL (village) Cook County	47,032
Chelmsford, MA (town) Middlesex County	46,651
Lexington, MA (town) Middlesex County	46,360
Ossining, NY (town) Westchester County	46,263
Randolph, NJ (township) Morris County	46,150
Pittsfield charter, MI (township) Washtenaw County	45,845
Princeton, NJ (township) Mercer County	45,741
Cortlandt, NY (town) Westchester County	45,687
Santa Cruz, CA (city) Santa Cruz County	45,553
Northville, MI (township) Wayne County	45,454
Bridgewater, NJ (township) Somerset County	45,291
Dix Hills, NY (cdp) Suffolk County	45,282
Mountain View, CA (city) Santa Clara County	45,209
Mahwah, NJ (township) Bergen County	44,158
West Windsor, NJ (township) Mercer County	43,969
Mount Pleasant, NY (town) Westchester County	43,934
North Potomac, MD (cdp) Montgomery County	43,906
Folsom, CA (city) Sacramento County	43,883
Pleasanton, CA (city) Alameda County	43,736
Walnut Creek, CA (city) Contra Costa County	43,568
Greenburgh, NY (town) Westchester County	43,432
Mount Laurel, NJ (township) Burlington County	43,265
Travilah, MD (cdp) Montgomery County	43,251
Tysons Corner, VA (cdp) Fairfax County	42,919
Wayne, NJ (township) Passaic County	42,725
Amherst, NY (town) Erie County	42,602

Notes: Please refer to the User's Guide for an explanation of data; ranking tables include all places with Asian and/or NHPI populations above SF4 population thresholds; (1) tables reflect only those areas that meet SF4 population thresholds, therefore there may be less than 50 states, 75 counties or 75 places listed

Per Capita Income

Bangladeshi

All States, Top 75 Counties, and Top 75 Places Sorted by Number[1]

State	Dollars
Maryland	23,182
Ohio	20,613
Connecticut	20,172
Virginia	19,768
Texas	18,741
Massachusetts	18,694
California	18,496
Pennsylvania	18,415
Illinois	18,007
Georgia	15,316
New Jersey	14,400
United States	13,971
Michigan	12,217
Florida	11,343
New York	10,899

County	Dollars
Santa Clara County, CA	34,979
Montgomery County, MD	27,231
Fairfax County, VA	24,035
Harris County, TX	18,461
Middlesex County, NJ	17,069
Dallas County, TX	17,057
DeKalb County, GA	15,366
Los Angeles County, CA	13,324
New York County, NY	12,293
Queens County, NY	11,291
Atlantic County, NJ	10,319
Kings County, NY	9,001
Passaic County, NJ	8,834
Wayne County, MI	8,771
Bronx County, NY	6,466

Place	Dollars
Los Angeles, CA (city) Los Angeles County	12,064
New York, NY (city)	10,364
Paterson, NJ (city) Passaic County	8,171
Hamtramck, MI (city) Wayne County	6,694

Notes: Please refer to the User's Guide for an explanation of data; ranking tables include all places with Asian and/or NHPI populations above SF4 population thresholds; (1) tables reflect only those areas that meet SF4 population thresholds, therefore there may be less than 50 states, 75 counties or 75 places listed

Per Capita Income

Cambodian

All States, Top 75 Counties, and Top 75 Places Sorted by Number[1]

State	Dollars
Connecticut	17,016
Virginia	16,278
Arizona	15,637
Maryland	15,594
New Jersey	14,827
Indiana	14,662
Ohio	14,136
Michigan	14,121
South Carolina	14,018
Georgia	13,843
Texas	13,585
Illinois	13,431
Nevada	12,874
Florida	12,325
Colorado	12,241
New York	12,096
Oregon	12,079
Utah	11,753
Minnesota	11,432
Iowa	11,204
Kansas	11,174
North Carolina	11,109
Tennessee	11,075
Oklahoma	11,062
Alabama	10,633
Washington	10,584
United States	10,366
Massachusetts	10,306
Missouri	10,068
California	8,534
Maine	8,362
Wisconsin	8,346
Rhode Island	8,252
Pennsylvania	8,025
Hawaii	6,649

County	Dollars
Fairfax County, VA	20,145
Franklin County, OH	17,145
Fairfield County, CT	16,893
Montgomery County, MD	16,721
Clark County, WA	16,482
Snohomish County, WA	16,108
Denton County, TX	15,691
San Francisco County, CA	15,481
DeKalb County, GA	15,339
Maricopa County, AZ	15,003
Henrico County, VA	14,622
Washington County, OR	14,452
Kings County, NY	14,446
Dallas County, TX	14,397
Scott County, MN	14,085
Ottawa County, MI	13,892
Arlington County, VA	13,863
Orange County, CA	13,710
Clayton County, GA	13,505
Shelby County, TN	13,269
Worcester County, MA	13,107
Harris County, TX	13,014
Clark County, NV	12,902
Dakota County, MN	12,735
Hennepin County, MN	12,711
San Bernardino County, CA	12,555
Sedgwick County, KS	12,544
Santa Clara County, CA	12,334
Cook County, IL	12,331
Salt Lake County, UT	12,098
Riverside County, CA	11,989
Duval County, FL	11,706
Cuyahoga County, OH	11,647
Gwinnett County, GA	11,536
Thurston County, WA	11,488
Mecklenburg County, NC	11,251
Olmsted County, MN	11,003
Camden County, NJ	10,977
Multnomah County, OR	10,666
Polk County, IA	10,609
Middlesex County, MA	10,583
Pinellas County, FL	10,582
Chesterfield County, VA	10,539
Essex County, MA	10,347
King County, WA	10,191
Hampden County, MA	9,831
Tarrant County, TX	9,827
Hamilton County, OH	9,644
Denver County, CO	9,316
Monroe County, NY	9,025
Davidson County, NC	8,890
Ramsey County, MN	8,859
Brazoria County, TX	8,739
Suffolk County, MA	8,699
Kern County, CA	8,698
Bronx County, NY	8,645
Alameda County, CA	8,503
Pierce County, WA	8,450
Los Angeles County, CA	8,373
Providence County, RI	8,247
Sacramento County, CA	8,219
Bristol County, MA	7,781
San Diego County, CA	7,721
Sonoma County, CA	7,250
Philadelphia County, PA	6,675
Stanislaus County, CA	6,225
Cumberland County, ME	6,147
Mobile County, AL	5,926
Cowlitz County, WA	5,160
San Joaquin County, CA	5,107
Fresno County, CA	4,558

Place	Dollars
Columbus, OH (city) Franklin County	17,681
Norwalk, CA (city) Los Angeles County	17,043
Beaverton, OR (city) Washington County	16,788
Aurora, CO (city) Arapahoe County	15,516
San Francisco, CA (city) San Francisco County	15,481
Bridgeport, CT (city) Fairfield County	15,011
Silver Spring, MD (cdp) Montgomery County	14,909
Phoenix, AZ (city) Maricopa County	13,910
Arlington, VA (cdp) Arlington County	13,863
Danbury, CT (city) Fairfield County	13,770
New York, NY (city)	13,582
Memphis, TN (city) Shelby County	13,310
Bellflower, CA (city) Los Angeles County	12,966
Carrollton, TX (city) Denton County	12,855
Dallas, TX (city) Dallas County	12,178
Cranston, RI (city) Providence County	12,143
San Jose, CA (city) Santa Clara County	12,034
Bloomington, MN (city) Hennepin County	11,991
Garden Grove, CA (city) Orange County	11,917
Jacksonville, FL (city) Duval County	11,706
Lakewood, CA (city) Los Angeles County	11,695
Chicago, IL (city) Cook County	11,594
Boston, MA (city) Suffolk County	11,274
Charlotte, NC (city) Mecklenburg County	11,247
Houston, TX (city) Harris County	11,207
Lawrence, MA (city) Essex County	11,141
Santa Ana, CA (city) Orange County	10,875
Everett, WA (city) Snohomish County	10,606
West Valley City, UT (city) Salt Lake County	10,518
Lynn, MA (city) Essex County	10,275
Attleboro, MA (city) Bristol County	10,225
Portland, OR (city) Multnomah County	10,104
Lowell, MA (city) Middlesex County	9,727
Rosemead, CA (city) Los Angeles County	9,626
Denver, CO (city) Denver County	9,316
St. Petersburg, FL (city) Pinellas County	9,283
Minneapolis, MN (city) Hennepin County	9,176
Pomona, CA (city) Los Angeles County	8,861
Los Angeles, CA (city) Los Angeles County	8,718
Lexington, NC (city) Davidson County	8,584
Monterey Park, CA (city) Los Angeles County	8,568
Seattle, WA (city) King County	8,371
Signal Hill, CA (city) Los Angeles County	8,278
St. Paul, MN (city) Ramsey County	8,255
Tacoma, WA (city) Pierce County	8,097
Sacramento, CA (city) Sacramento County	8,045
White Center, WA (cdp) King County	7,823
San Diego, CA (city) San Diego County	7,251
Providence, RI (city) Providence County	7,237
Rochester, MN (city) Olmsted County	7,192
Philadelphia, PA (city) Philadelphia County	6,675
Long Beach, CA (city) Los Angeles County	6,670
Santa Rosa, CA (city) Sonoma County	6,515
Revere, MA (city) Suffolk County	6,330
Oakland, CA (city) Alameda County	6,246
Longview, WA (city) Cowlitz County	6,241
Fall River, MA (city) Bristol County	6,014
Modesto, CA (city) Stanislaus County	5,986
San Bernardino, CA (city) San Bernardino County	5,584
Stockton, CA (city) San Joaquin County	4,945
Portland, ME (city) Cumberland County	4,940
Fresno, CA (city) Fresno County	4,573

Notes: Please refer to the User's Guide for an explanation of data; ranking tables include all places with Asian and/or NHPI populations above SF4 population thresholds; (1) tables reflect only those areas that meet SF4 population thresholds, therefore there may be less than 50 states, 75 counties or 75 places listed

Per Capita Income

Chinese (except Taiwanese)

All States, Top 75 Counties, and Top 75 Places Sorted by Number[1]

State	Dollars
New Jersey	32,113
Connecticut	30,673
Delaware	28,813
District of Columbia	27,447
Hawaii	27,259
Maryland	26,431
Virginia	26,107
Nevada	25,777
California	25,485
New Mexico	25,135
New Hampshire	24,960
Michigan	24,906
Washington	24,822
Texas	24,444
Illinois	24,016
Ohio	23,961
Minnesota	23,935
North Carolina	23,914
Colorado	23,898
Arizona	23,789
United States	23,642
Massachusetts	23,101
Idaho	22,853
North Dakota	22,751
Georgia	22,718
Alaska	22,128
Florida	21,313
Wisconsin	21,249
Tennessee	21,140
Oregon	20,884
Kentucky	20,882
Alabama	20,768
Louisiana	20,664
Pennsylvania	19,938
Indiana	19,791
Kansas	19,708
Mississippi	19,600
Missouri	19,597
Iowa	19,273
South Carolina	18,640
Nebraska	18,160
New York	17,784
South Dakota	17,557
Arkansas	17,303
Rhode Island	17,150
Utah	17,118
West Virginia	16,973
Oklahoma	15,900
Montana	15,506
Vermont	15,048
Maine	14,666
Wyoming	14,642

County	Dollars
Napa County, CA	60,000
Marin County, CA	48,210
Fairfield County, CT	45,523
Saratoga County, NY	41,904
Westchester County, NY	39,793
Somerset County, NJ	39,393
Morris County, NJ	38,953
Warren County, OH	38,059
Santa Clara County, CA	37,128
Olmsted County, MN	36,833
Kane County, IL	36,229
Mercer County, NJ	36,218
San Mateo County, CA	35,969
Dutchess County, NY	35,647
Union County, NJ	35,360
Benton County, WA	35,101
Ventura County, CA	35,070
Lee County, AL	35,014
Hunterdon County, NJ	34,648
Washington County, MN	34,567
Lake County, IL	34,374
Delaware County, OH	34,242
Monmouth County, NJ	34,139
DuPage County, IL	34,020
Midland County, MI	33,872
Bergen County, NJ	33,835
Hamilton County, IN	33,726
Chester County, PA	33,400
Essex County, NJ	33,097
Osceola County, FL	33,080
Contra Costa County, CA	32,985
Orleans Parish, LA	32,780
Maui County, HI	32,721
Placer County, CA	32,575
Ada County, ID	32,547
Montgomery County, TX	32,389
El Paso County, TX	32,213
Nassau County, NY	32,115
Putnam County, NY	31,843
Fairfax County, VA	31,023
Sonoma County, CA	30,998
Loudoun County, VA	30,673
Oakland County, MI	30,346
New Castle County, DE	30,219
Brazoria County, TX	30,048
Collin County, TX	30,040
Jefferson County, TX	29,965
Bucks County, PA	29,867
Waukesha County, WI	29,841
Montgomery County, MD	29,778
Arlington County, VA	29,631
Butler County, OH	29,354
Middlesex County, NJ	29,295
Douglas County, CO	29,127
Ocean County, NJ	29,107
Hudson County, NJ	28,796
Orange County, CA	28,732
Peoria County, IL	28,389
Middlesex County, MA	28,322
Wayne County, MI	28,251
Howard County, MD	28,187
Hillsborough County, NH	28,169
Hartford County, CT	28,168
Kauai County, HI	28,145
Essex County, MA	28,082
Lehigh County, PA	27,951
Rockingham County, NH	27,675
Genesee County, MI	27,673
Montgomery County, PA	27,591
Washington County, OR	27,547
Anoka County, MN	27,497
Wake County, NC	27,413
Alexandria Independent City, VA	27,345
Honolulu County, HI	27,288
Clark County, NV	27,286

Place	Dollars
Westport, CT (town) Fairfield County	97,214
Los Altos Hills, CA (town) Santa Clara County	67,555
Rolling Hills Estates, CA (city) Los Angeles County	65,025
Hillsborough, CA (town) San Mateo County	63,717
Manhattan Beach, CA (city) Los Angeles County	63,372
Englewood Cliffs, NJ (borough) Bergen County	61,036
Poughkeepsie, NY (town) Dutchess County	60,914
Calabasas, CA (city) Los Angeles County	59,680
Menlo Park, CA (city) San Mateo County	58,014
San Carlos, CA (city) San Mateo County	56,493
Highlands-Baywood Pk., CA (cdp) San Mateo County	56,023
Greenwich, CT (town) Fairfield County	55,836
Scarsdale, NY (village) Westchester County	55,691
Los Altos, CA (city) Santa Clara County	55,655
McLean, VA (cdp) Fairfax County	54,484
Westford, MA (town) Middlesex County	54,309
Morgan Hill, CA (city) Santa Clara County	53,129
Laguna Niguel, CA (city) Orange County	52,135
La Canada Flintridge, CA (city) Los Angeles County	52,100
Palos Verdes Estates, CA (city) Los Angeles County	51,508
Lawrence, NJ (township) Mercer County	51,123
Palo Alto, CA (city) Santa Clara County	50,977
Potomac, MD (cdp) Montgomery County	50,969
Carmichael, CA (cdp) Sacramento County	50,749
Tustin Foothills, CA (cdp) Orange County	50,133
Los Gatos, CA (town) Santa Clara County	49,034
New Providence, NJ (borough) Union County	48,735
Piedmont, CA (city) Alameda County	48,684
Saratoga, CA (city) Santa Clara County	48,623
Beverly Hills, CA (city) Los Angeles County	48,299
West Bloomfield, MI (township) Oakland County	48,152
Blackhawk-Camino Tass., CA (cdp) Contra Costa Co.	48,096
Stamford, CT (city) Fairfield County	47,953
Bridgewater, NJ (township) Somerset County	47,897
Plainview, NY (cdp) Nassau County	47,866
Bernards, NJ (township) Somerset County	47,784
Montclair, NJ (township) Essex County	47,224
North Andover, MA (town) Essex County	47,069
Needham, MA (town) Norfolk County	46,730
Tredyffrin, PA (township) Chester County	46,713
Lafayette, CA (city) Contra Costa County	46,178
Northbrook, IL (village) Cook County	46,018
Redwood City, CA (city) San Mateo County	45,592
Poway, CA (city) San Diego County	45,230
Lisle, IL (village) Du Page County	45,114
Norwalk, CT (city) Fairfield County	44,997
Montville, NJ (township) Morris County	44,624
East Pasadena, CA (cdp) Los Angeles County	44,526
Belmont, CA (city) San Mateo County	44,447
Fairfield, CT (town) Fairfield County	44,295
Lake Success, NY (village) Nassau County	44,156
Rancho Palos Verdes, CA (city) Los Angeles County	43,677
Woodbury, MN (city) Washington County	42,889
Wolf Trap, VA (cdp) Fairfax County	42,662
Richland, WA (city) Benton County	42,465
Laguna Hills, CA (city) Orange County	42,198
Orinda, CA (city) Contra Costa County	42,138
Holmdel, NJ (township) Monmouth County	41,902
Thousand Oaks, CA (city) Ventura County	41,835
Las Vegas, NV (city) Clark County	41,789
San Marino, CA (city) Los Angeles County	41,316
Cupertino, CA (city) Santa Clara County	41,012
Greenburgh, NY (town) Westchester County	40,941
Bellaire, TX (city) Harris County	40,482
Acton, MA (town) Middlesex County	40,437
Redondo Beach, CA (city) Los Angeles County	40,408
Reston, VA (cdp) Fairfax County	40,382
San Mateo, CA (city) San Mateo County	40,312
Dublin, CA (city) Alameda County	40,273
Sunnyvale, CA (city) Santa Clara County	40,002
Walnut Creek, CA (city) Contra Costa County	39,871
Kensington, CA (cdp) Contra Costa County	39,824
Hollywood, FL (city) Broward County	39,812
New Castle, NY (town) Westchester County	39,683
Millburn, NJ (township) Essex County	39,629

Notes: Please refer to the User's Guide for an explanation of data; ranking tables include all places with Asian and/or NHPI populations above SF4 population thresholds; (1) tables reflect only those areas that meet SF4 population thresholds, therefore there may be less than 50 states, 75 counties or 75 places listed

Per Capita Income

Fijian

All States, Top 75 Counties, and Top 75 Places Sorted by Number[1]

State	Dollars
Washington	22,380
Oregon	18,604
United States	14,745
California	13,586

County	Dollars
Santa Clara County, CA	19,301
San Mateo County, CA	16,743
King County, WA	15,851
Alameda County, CA	14,584
Los Angeles County, CA	14,291
Contra Costa County, CA	13,739
Sacramento County, CA	11,112
Stanislaus County, CA	9,538
Yolo County, CA	6,557

Place	Dollars
Hayward, CA (city) Alameda County	14,616
Sacramento, CA (city) Sacramento County	10,153
Modesto, CA (city) Stanislaus County	9,358

Notes: Please refer to the User's Guide for an explanation of data; ranking tables include all places with Asian and/or NHPI populations above SF4 population thresholds; (1) tables reflect only those areas that meet SF4 population thresholds, therefore there may be less than 50 states, 75 counties or 75 places listed

Per Capita Income

Filipino

All States, Top 75 Counties, and Top 75 Places Sorted by Number[1]

State	Dollars
West Virginia	38,914
Delaware	32,429
Wyoming	30,138
Michigan	28,788
New York	28,130
Wisconsin	27,047
New Jersey	26,970
Connecticut	26,690
Ohio	26,272
Massachusetts	26,109
Pennsylvania	25,848
Illinois	25,616
Kentucky	24,954
Alabama	24,946
Indiana	24,631
Maryland	23,754
Missouri	23,686
District of Columbia	23,532
Kansas	22,824
Montana	22,382
Tennessee	22,336
Texas	21,753
Minnesota	21,393
Virginia	21,295
United States	21,267
Georgia	20,910
Florida	20,901
Maine	20,578
California	20,543
Rhode Island	20,428
Idaho	20,278
Colorado	20,037
North Carolina	19,636
North Dakota	19,543
Iowa	19,451
Mississippi	19,272
Vermont	18,966
Washington	18,930
Arizona	18,758
Louisiana	18,460
South Carolina	18,422
New Hampshire	18,245
Nevada	18,029
Nebraska	17,915
New Mexico	17,825
Utah	17,787
Oregon	17,697
Oklahoma	17,480
Arkansas	17,458
Hawaii	16,426
Alaska	16,084
South Dakota	15,777

County	Dollars
New York County, NY	40,799
Waukesha County, WI	39,351
Summit County, OH	38,788
New Castle County, DE	37,700
Collin County, TX	36,059
Lorain County, OH	35,018
Washtenaw County, MI	34,948
Marin County, CA	34,157
Ada County, ID	33,309
St. Louis County, MO	33,176
Oakland County, MI	32,748
Onondaga County, NY	32,559
Montgomery County, PA	32,370
Monmouth County, NJ	31,924
Highlands County, FL	31,556
Delaware County, PA	31,442
Genesee County, MI	31,221
Suffolk County, NY	31,203
Rockland County, NY	31,171
Howard County, MD	31,104
Burlington County, NJ	31,062
Westchester County, NY	31,022
Lake County, IN	30,840
Norfolk County, MA	30,648
San Benito County, CA	30,473
Chester County, PA	30,403
Baltimore County, MD	30,226
Somerset County, NJ	30,222
Johnson County, KS	30,038
Morris County, NJ	29,723
Kings County, NY	29,716
Worcester County, MA	29,488
Orange County, NY	29,365
Hartford County, CT	29,295
Wayne County, MI	29,087
Loudoun County, VA	29,048
Harford County, MD	28,706
Bergen County, NJ	28,654
Gloucester County, NJ	28,388
Franklin County, OH	28,017
Marion County, IN	27,932
Fairfield County, CT	27,866
Essex County, NJ	27,823
Cameron County, TX	27,771
Middlesex County, NJ	27,717
DuPage County, IL	27,709
Kane County, IL	27,590
Nassau County, NY	27,506
Mercer County, NJ	27,411
Bristol County, MA	27,109
Will County, IL	27,029
Bronx County, NY	26,925
Winnebago County, IL	26,909
Richmond County, NY	26,890
Union County, NJ	26,890
Macomb County, MI	26,885
Jefferson County, KY	26,806
Cuyahoga County, OH	26,745
Essex County, MA	26,729
Mecklenburg County, NC	26,652
Ocean County, NJ	26,571
Fulton County, GA	26,468
Durham County, NC	26,393
Guilford County, NC	26,383
Sussex County, NJ	26,337
Berrien County, MI	26,328
Fairfax County, VA	26,323
Palm Beach County, FL	26,303
Middlesex County, MA	26,282
Hamilton County, OH	26,251
Passaic County, NJ	26,140
El Dorado County, CA	25,980
Milwaukee County, WI	25,954
Seminole County, FL	25,876
Wake County, NC	25,792

Place	Dollars
Huntington, NY (town) Suffolk County	52,453
Danville, CA (town) Contra Costa County	43,211
New City, NY (cdp) Rockland County	42,877
Freehold, NJ (township) Monmouth County	41,349
Santa Monica, CA (city) Los Angeles County	40,566
Upland, CA (city) San Bernardino County	39,987
Plano, TX (city) Collin County	39,477
North Hempstead, NY (town) Nassau County	38,800
Secaucus, NJ (town) Hudson County	38,309
Ellicott City, MD (cdp) Howard County	38,141
Redondo Beach, CA (city) Los Angeles County	37,976
Orangetown, NY (town) Rockland County	37,602
Burlingame, CA (city) San Mateo County	37,572
Schaumburg, IL (village) Cook County	37,440
Castro Valley, CA (cdp) Alameda County	37,374
Rancho Palos Verdes, CA (city) Los Angeles County	37,245
North Brunswick, NJ (township) Middlesex County	36,775
Cupertino, CA (city) Santa Clara County	36,393
Glenview, IL (village) Cook County	35,960
Greenburgh, NY (town) Westchester County	35,692
Folsom, CA (city) Sacramento County	35,141
McLean, VA (cdp) Fairfax County	35,107
Troy, MI (city) Oakland County	34,817
Palatine, IL (village) Cook County	34,352
Pleasanton, CA (city) Alameda County	34,196
San Ramon, CA (city) Contra Costa County	33,883
Lodi, CA (city) San Joaquin County	33,539
Redwood City, CA (city) San Mateo County	33,439
Dover, NJ (township) Ocean County	33,426
Toms River, NJ (cdp) Ocean County	33,426
Lombard, IL (village) Du Page County	33,356
Canton, MI (township) Wayne County	33,159
Hollister, CA (city) San Benito County	32,553
Clarkstown, NY (town) Rockland County	32,491
Babylon, NY (town) Suffolk County	32,182
Ann Arbor, MI (city) Washtenaw County	32,120
Franklin, NJ (township) Somerset County	32,064
Washington, NJ (township) Gloucester County	31,941
Lincolnwood, IL (village) Cook County	31,924
La Crescenta-Montrose, CA (cdp) Los Angeles County	31,737
Naperville, IL (city) Du Page County	31,584
El Cerrito, CA (city) Contra Costa County	31,561
Walnut Creek, CA (city) Contra Costa County	31,400
Martinez, CA (city) Contra Costa County	31,329
Aliso Viejo, CA (cdp) Orange County	31,078
Carlsbad, CA (city) San Diego County	30,731
Darien, IL (city) Du Page County	30,665
Sterling Heights, MI (city) Macomb County	30,633
Paramus, NJ (borough) Bergen County	30,621
Arlington Heights, IL (village) Cook County	30,558
West Bloomfield, MI (township) Oakland County	30,533
Benicia, CA (city) Solano County	30,518
La Verne, CA (city) Los Angeles County	30,465
Orland Park, IL (village) Cook County	30,372
Huntington Beach, CA (city) Orange County	30,304
Franconia, VA (cdp) Fairfax County	30,164
South Brunswick, NJ (township) Middlesex County	30,093
Park City, IL (city) Lake County	30,083
Palo Alto, CA (city) Santa Clara County	29,960
Teaneck, NJ (township) Bergen County	29,950
West Orange, NJ (township) Essex County	29,902
Columbus, OH (city) Franklin County	29,897
Parsippany-Troy Hills, NJ (township) Morris County	29,830
Bowie, MD (city) Prince George's County	29,646
Dumont, NJ (borough) Bergen County	29,493
Valley Cottage, NY (cdp) Rockland County	29,467
Edison, NJ (township) Middlesex County	29,463
Redland, MD (cdp) Montgomery County	29,462
Downers Grove, IL (village) Du Page County	29,359
Annandale, VA (cdp) Fairfax County	29,347
Gilroy, CA (city) Santa Clara County	29,288
Wayne, NJ (township) Passaic County	29,275
Nutley, NJ (township) Essex County	29,248
Foster City, CA (city) San Mateo County	29,149
San Mateo, CA (city) San Mateo County	29,123

Notes: Please refer to the User's Guide for an explanation of data; ranking tables include all places with Asian and/or NHPI populations above SF4 population thresholds; (1) tables reflect only those areas that meet SF4 population thresholds, therefore there may be less than 50 states, 75 counties or 75 places listed

Per Capita Income

Guamanian or Chamorro

All States, Top 75 Counties, and Top 75 Places Sorted by Number[1]

State	Dollars
Virginia	22,946
South Carolina	22,734
Maryland	20,891
California	19,930
Connecticut	19,263
Minnesota	19,113
New Jersey	18,139
Wisconsin	18,029
United States	17,583
Nevada	17,541
Illinois	17,353
Oklahoma	17,228
Arizona	17,047
Missouri	16,965
Washington	16,809
Hawaii	16,745
Georgia	16,385
Colorado	16,276
Texas	16,168
Oregon	15,924
Massachusetts	15,809
Louisiana	15,597
North Carolina	15,410
Kentucky	15,390
Ohio	15,310
Michigan	15,127
Alabama	14,678
Florida	14,108
New Mexico	13,814
Pennsylvania	13,512
Indiana	12,699
New York	11,480
Tennessee	10,879

County	Dollars
Contra Costa County, CA	28,706
Alameda County, CA	25,970
Orange County, CA	24,232
Santa Clara County, CA	23,186
San Mateo County, CA	22,367
King County, WA	22,182
Solano County, CA	20,049
Sacramento County, CA	19,964
Maricopa County, AZ	19,186
El Paso County, CO	18,682
San Diego County, CA	18,508
Clark County, NV	18,397
San Bernardino County, CA	18,350
Thurston County, WA	18,137
Riverside County, CA	17,590
Bell County, TX	17,289
Honolulu County, HI	17,120
Harris County, TX	16,888
Los Angeles County, CA	16,790
Monterey County, CA	15,216
Pierce County, WA	14,974
Kitsap County, WA	12,121
Kings County, NY	11,490

Place	Dollars
Chula Vista, CA (city) San Diego County	29,771
San Jose, CA (city) Santa Clara County	26,048
Fairfield, CA (city) Solano County	22,266
Vallejo, CA (city) Solano County	20,313
Tacoma, WA (city) Pierce County	17,841
Killeen, TX (city) Bell County	16,823
Los Angeles, CA (city) Los Angeles County	16,317
San Diego, CA (city) San Diego County	16,127
Houston, TX (city) Harris County	15,836
Honolulu, HI (cdp) Honolulu County	13,227
New York, NY (city)	11,529

Notes: Please refer to the User's Guide for an explanation of data; ranking tables include all places with Asian and/or NHPI populations above SF4 population thresholds; (1) tables reflect only those areas that meet SF4 population thresholds, therefore there may be less than 50 states, 75 counties or 75 places listed

Per Capita Income

Hawaiian, Native

All States, Top 75 Counties, and Top 75 Places Sorted by Number[1]

State	Dollars
New Jersey	35,864
South Carolina	26,969
Alaska	25,817
Virginia	25,305
Nevada	24,912
Maryland	23,647
California	22,404
Oregon	21,517
New Mexico	21,473
Kansas	20,457
Washington	19,765
Tennessee	19,640
Michigan	19,340
Colorado	18,272
Georgia	17,974
North Carolina	17,923
Illinois	17,849
United States	17,697
Pennsylvania	17,552
Utah	17,422
Indiana	17,121
Massachusetts	16,939
Hawaii	16,071
Florida	16,057
Minnesota	16,050
New York	15,882
Missouri	15,832
Ohio	15,678
Wisconsin	15,605
Idaho	15,524
Texas	15,491
Arizona	13,851
Oklahoma	13,559
Arkansas	12,391
Louisiana	11,370
Montana	10,578

County	Dollars
Contra Costa County, CA	31,594
Alameda County, CA	28,556
Orange County, CA	26,073
Riverside County, CA	25,722
King County, WA	25,666
Ventura County, CA	24,314
Santa Clara County, CA	23,784
San Mateo County, CA	23,455
Sacramento County, CA	23,429
San Diego County, CA	23,391
Multnomah County, OR	23,193
San Bernardino County, CA	22,071
San Joaquin County, CA	21,687
Solano County, CA	21,597
Clark County, NV	21,412
Snohomish County, WA	21,237
Bexar County, TX	20,905
Washington County, OR	20,728
Salt Lake County, UT	20,635
Los Angeles County, CA	19,095
Pierce County, WA	17,975
Honolulu County, HI	17,279
Maui County, HI	14,721
Kauai County, HI	14,269
Hawaii County, HI	13,516
Maricopa County, AZ	13,023
Utah County, UT	12,424
Pima County, AZ	10,811

Place	Dollars
Las Vegas, NV (city) Clark County	37,112
Mililani Town, HI (cdp) Honolulu County	27,001
Portland, OR (city) Multnomah County	23,391
San Diego, CA (city) San Diego County	23,322
Honolulu, HI (cdp) Honolulu County	22,392
San Jose, CA (city) Santa Clara County	22,027
Kaaawa, HI (cdp) Honolulu County	21,686
Waimalu, HI (cdp) Honolulu County	21,039
Honalo, HI (cdp) Hawaii County	20,299
Holualoa, HI (cdp) Hawaii County	20,105
Volcano, HI (cdp) Hawaii County	19,769
Waipio, HI (cdp) Honolulu County	19,725
Aiea, HI (cdp) Honolulu County	19,316
Haleiwa, HI (cdp) Honolulu County	18,879
Makakilo City, HI (cdp) Honolulu County	18,649
Kailua, HI (cdp) Honolulu County	18,612
Kilauea, HI (cdp) Kauai County	18,512
Los Angeles, CA (city) Los Angeles County	18,260
Waikoloa Village, HI (cdp) Hawaii County	17,877
Pearl City, HI (cdp) Honolulu County	17,521
Halawa, HI (cdp) Honolulu County	17,239
New York, NY (city)	17,095
Makawao, HI (cdp) Maui County	17,045
Honaunau-Napoopoo, HI (cdp) Hawaii County	16,399
Paia, HI (cdp) Maui County	16,296
Kahului, HI (cdp) Maui County	16,254
Kualapuu, HI (cdp) Maui County	16,119
Kaneohe, HI (cdp) Honolulu County	16,080
Henderson, NV (city) Clark County	16,029
Laie, HI (cdp) Honolulu County	15,822
Ahuimanu, HI (cdp) Honolulu County	15,744
Kailua, HI (cdp) Hawaii County	15,673
Wahiawa, HI (cdp) Honolulu County	15,538
Paradise, NV (cdp) Clark County	15,474
Lahaina, HI (cdp) Maui County	15,387
Waimea, HI (cdp) Kauai County	15,365
Wailuku, HI (cdp) Maui County	15,058
Waimea, HI (cdp) Hawaii County	15,026
Hanapepe, HI (cdp) Kauai County	15,019
Waihee-Waiehu, HI (cdp) Maui County	14,657
Kalaoa, HI (cdp) Hawaii County	14,503
Makaha Valley, HI (cdp) Honolulu County	13,795
Kahaluu, HI (cdp) Honolulu County	13,791
Kihei, HI (cdp) Maui County	13,750
Captain Cook, HI (cdp) Hawaii County	13,654
Hauula, HI (cdp) Honolulu County	13,278
Waimanalo Beach, HI (cdp) Honolulu County	13,090
Phoenix, AZ (city) Maricopa County	12,797
Hawaiian Ocean View, HI (cdp) Hawaii County	12,731
Kapaa, HI (cdp) Kauai County	12,691
Kahuku, HI (cdp) Honolulu County	12,685
Anahola, HI (cdp) Kauai County	12,634
Kekaha, HI (cdp) Kauai County	12,305
Hawaiian Paradise Park, HI (cdp) Hawaii County	12,304
Waimanalo, HI (cdp) Honolulu County	12,210
Waialua, HI (cdp) Honolulu County	12,205
Hana, HI (cdp) Maui County	12,166
Punaluu, HI (cdp) Honolulu County	12,131
Naalehu, HI (cdp) Hawaii County	12,054
Maili, HI (cdp) Honolulu County	11,713
Hilo, HI (cdp) Hawaii County	11,688
Nanakuli, HI (cdp) Honolulu County	11,595
Waikane, HI (cdp) Honolulu County	11,215
Waianae, HI (cdp) Honolulu County	10,830
Ewa Beach, HI (cdp) Honolulu County	10,764
Makaha, HI (cdp) Honolulu County	10,525
Waipahu, HI (cdp) Honolulu County	10,227
Kaunakakai, HI (cdp) Maui County	9,365
Pahala, HI (cdp) Hawaii County	8,952
Pakala Village, HI (cdp) Kauai County	8,944
Kapaau, HI (cdp) Hawaii County	8,212
Hawaiian Beaches, HI (cdp) Hawaii County	8,122

Notes: Please refer to the User's Guide for an explanation of data; ranking tables include all places with Asian and/or NHPI populations above SF4 population thresholds; (1) tables reflect only those areas that meet SF4 population thresholds, therefore there may be less than 50 states, 75 counties or 75 places listed

Per Capita Income

Hmong

All States, Top 75 Counties, and Top 75 Places Sorted by Number[1]

State	Dollars
Georgia	10,712
Colorado	10,400
North Carolina	9,358
Oregon	8,802
Massachusetts	8,472
Pennsylvania	8,432
Kansas	7,769
Michigan	7,696
South Carolina	7,253
Minnesota	7,210
Wisconsin	6,860
Rhode Island	6,664
Oklahoma	6,644
United States	6,600
Washington	6,445
California	5,263
Alaska	4,572

County	Dollars
Mecklenburg County, NC	31,970
Washington County, MN	15,276
Anoka County, MN	13,137
Macomb County, MI	11,946
Orange County, CA	11,417
Jefferson County, CO	11,037
Adams County, CO	10,841
Barrow County, GA	10,318
Oakland County, MI	10,256
Multnomah County, OR	9,485
Lancaster County, PA	8,771
Manitowoc County, WI	8,295
Catawba County, NC	8,151
Milwaukee County, WI	7,965
Spartanburg County, SC	7,778
Olmsted County, MN	7,772
Winnebago County, WI	7,695
Dane County, WI	7,657
Brown County, WI	7,528
Ramsey County, MN	7,222
San Diego County, CA	7,141
Outagamie County, WI	7,076
Eau Claire County, WI	6,986
Sheboygan County, WI	6,973
Los Angeles County, CA	6,956
King County, WA	6,950
Wyandotte County, KS	6,946
Worcester County, MA	6,916
Burke County, NC	6,899
Santa Barbara County, CA	6,722
Hennepin County, MN	6,365
Calumet County, WI	6,364
Yuba County, CA	6,358
Providence County, RI	6,123
Stanly County, NC	5,999
Sacramento County, CA	5,937
Wayne County, MI	5,691
La Crosse County, WI	5,626
Marathon County, WI	5,302
Spokane County, WA	5,209
Portage County, WI	5,134
San Joaquin County, CA	4,984
Solano County, CA	4,815
Anchorage Borough, AK	4,572
Wood County, WI	4,572
Dunn County, WI	4,538
Riverside County, CA	4,483
Fresno County, CA	4,445
Stanislaus County, CA	4,376
Glenn County, CA	4,355
Merced County, CA	4,178
Fond du Lac County, WI	4,051
Chippewa County, WI	3,926
Tulare County, CA	3,833
Butte County, CA	3,433
Yolo County, CA	3,251
Ingham County, MI	2,213

Place	Dollars
Charlotte, NC (city) Mecklenburg County	31,970
Woodbury, MN (city) Washington County	20,353
Arden-Arcade, CA (cdp) Sacramento County	11,530
Westminster, CO (city) Adams County	10,945
Warren, MI (city) Macomb County	10,879
Santa Ana, CA (city) Orange County	9,958
Pontiac, MI (city) Oakland County	9,766
Florin, CA (cdp) Sacramento County	9,741
Brooklyn Center, MN (city) Hennepin County	9,347
Portland, OR (city) Multnomah County	9,303
Maplewood, MN (city) Ramsey County	9,096
Manitowoc, WI (city) Manitowoc County	7,879
Rochester, MN (city) Olmsted County	7,772
Milwaukee, WI (city) Milwaukee County	7,733
Madison, WI (city) Dane County	7,522
Glen Alpine, NC (town) Burke County	7,432
San Diego, CA (city) San Diego County	7,327
Green Bay, WI (city) Brown County	7,228
Brooklyn Park, MN (city) Hennepin County	7,047
Appleton, WI (city) Outagamie County	7,036
St. Paul, MN (city) Ramsey County	6,996
Valdese, NC (town) Burke County	6,955
Kansas City, KS (city) Wyandotte County	6,946
Sheboygan, WI (city) Sheboygan County	6,868
Fitchburg, MA (city) Worcester County	6,828
Linda, CA (cdp) Yuba County	6,701
Hickory, NC (city) Catawba County	6,640
Oshkosh, WI (city) Winnebago County	6,577
Parkway-S. Sacramento, CA (cdp) Sacramento County	6,449
Eau Claire, WI (city) Eau Claire County	6,236
Connelly Springs, NC (town) Burke County	5,995
Minneapolis, MN (city) Hennepin County	5,500
Providence, RI (city) Providence County	5,496
Detroit, MI (city) Wayne County	5,466
Clovis, CA (city) Fresno County	5,317
Stevens Point, WI (city) Portage County	5,277
Atwater, CA (city) Merced County	5,142
Wausau, WI (city) Marathon County	4,955
Stockton, CA (city) San Joaquin County	4,932
Sacramento, CA (city) Sacramento County	4,885
La Crosse, WI (city) La Crosse County	4,752
Fond du Lac, WI (city) Fond du Lac County	4,528
Wisconsin Rapids, WI (city) Wood County	4,494
Willows, CA (city) Glenn County	4,355
Fresno, CA (city) Fresno County	4,328
Spokane, WA (city) Spokane County	4,148
Modesto, CA (city) Stanislaus County	4,094
Merced, CA (city) Merced County	3,917
Lansing, MI (city) Ingham County	3,907
South Oroville, CA (cdp) Butte County	3,347
Visalia, CA (city) Tulare County	3,308
West Sacramento, CA (city) Yolo County	3,085
Chico, CA (city) Butte County	2,880
Oroville, CA (city) Butte County	2,598
Thermalito, CA (cdp) Butte County	2,565

Notes: Please refer to the User's Guide for an explanation of data; ranking tables include all places with Asian and/or NHPI populations above SF4 population thresholds; (1) tables reflect only those areas that meet SF4 population thresholds, therefore there may be less than 50 states, 75 counties or 75 places listed

Per Capita Income

Indonesian

All States, Top 75 Counties, and Top 75 Places Sorted by Number[1]

State	Dollars
New Jersey	26,385
Virginia	24,383
Texas	21,810
Florida	20,935
California	19,544
United States	18,932
Washington	18,320
New York	18,044
Pennsylvania	17,168
Maryland	16,208
Ohio	15,888
Arizona	15,306
Massachusetts	15,264
Wisconsin	15,131
Michigan	14,904
Colorado	14,208
Oregon	13,912
Georgia	13,792
Illinois	12,594

County	Dollars
Santa Clara County, CA	30,430
San Mateo County, CA	27,521
Alameda County, CA	24,372
Contra Costa County, CA	23,976
Fairfax County, VA	23,871
Middlesex County, NJ	23,436
San Diego County, CA	21,078
King County, WA	20,822
Maricopa County, AZ	18,569
San Francisco County, CA	17,975
Orange County, CA	17,904
Los Angeles County, CA	16,839
Harris County, TX	16,689
Queens County, NY	16,291
San Bernardino County, CA	15,762
Montgomery County, MD	15,695
Cook County, IL	14,824
Franklin County, OH	9,726

Place	Dollars
Seattle, WA (city) King County	18,036
Houston, TX (city) Harris County	18,016
San Francisco, CA (city) San Francisco County	17,975
New York, NY (city)	17,028
Los Angeles, CA (city) Los Angeles County	16,385
Loma Linda, CA (city) San Bernardino County	13,205
Columbus, OH (city) Franklin County	9,661
San Bernardino, CA (city) San Bernardino County	7,845

Notes: Please refer to the User's Guide for an explanation of data; ranking tables include all places with Asian and/or NHPI populations above SF4 population thresholds; (1) tables reflect only those areas that meet SF4 population thresholds, therefore there may be less than 50 states, 75 counties or 75 places listed

Per Capita Income

Japanese

All States, Top 75 Counties, and Top 75 Places Sorted by Number[1]

State	Dollars
New Jersey	37,964
New York	37,011
Connecticut	35,833
Illinois	33,059
District of Columbia	32,873
California	32,745
Maryland	32,588
United States	30,075
Virginia	29,901
Hawaii	29,257
Michigan	29,197
Kentucky	28,544
New Mexico	28,344
Washington	28,307
Colorado	27,528
Ohio	27,470
South Carolina	26,961
Idaho	26,461
Rhode Island	26,409
Oregon	26,217
Georgia	25,799
Arizona	25,787
Alaska	25,421
Texas	25,363
Tennessee	24,647
North Carolina	23,879
Indiana	23,767
Minnesota	23,586
Massachusetts	23,302
Wisconsin	23,084
Utah	22,837
Nevada	22,756
Alabama	22,150
Florida	22,113
Delaware	21,235
Kansas	20,556
Arkansas	20,286
Pennsylvania	20,241
Missouri	19,581
Nebraska	18,593
New Hampshire	17,712
Louisiana	17,392
Wyoming	17,342
Mississippi	15,612
Iowa	15,325
Oklahoma	15,250
West Virginia	15,114
Vermont	14,855
Montana	14,220
Maine	14,154
South Dakota	12,836

County	Dollars
New York County, NY	48,981
Miami-Dade County, FL	47,220
Nassau County, NY	45,071
DuPage County, IL	44,250
Marin County, CA	43,768
Santa Clara County, CA	43,273
Westchester County, NY	43,036
Somerset County, NJ	43,008
Bergen County, NJ	41,917
Morris County, NJ	41,511
Malheur County, OR	41,334
Napa County, CA	40,802
Cobb County, GA	40,265
San Mateo County, CA	39,382
Anne Arundel County, MD	39,047
Fairfield County, CT	38,952
Montgomery County, MD	38,480
Arlington County, VA	37,457
Hudson County, NJ	37,369
Hartford County, CT	37,285
Mercer County, NJ	36,899
Summit County, OH	36,608
Monmouth County, NJ	36,514
Mecklenburg County, NC	36,489
Fairfax County, VA	36,453
San Francisco County, CA	36,223
Contra Costa County, CA	36,171
Tippecanoe County, IN	35,963
Oakland County, MI	35,824
Clackamas County, OR	35,776
Ventura County, CA	35,749
Milwaukee County, WI	34,398
Cook County, IL	34,130
Orange County, CA	34,027
Stanislaus County, CA	34,017
Jefferson County, CO	33,972
Lake County, IL	33,796
Collin County, TX	33,691
Alameda County, CA	33,645
Bernalillo County, NM	33,520
King County, WA	33,263
Jefferson County, KY	32,764
Sacramento County, CA	32,700
El Dorado County, CA	32,573
Santa Cruz County, CA	32,364
Marion County, IN	32,144
Burlington County, NJ	31,851
Placer County, CA	31,738
Ada County, ID	31,670
New Haven County, CT	31,402
Fulton County, GA	31,348
Johnson County, KS	31,222
Los Angeles County, CA	31,213
Montgomery County, OH	31,211
Hamilton County, OH	31,019
Arapahoe County, CO	30,989
DeKalb County, GA	30,896
Fayette County, GA	30,814
Wake County, NC	30,623
Solano County, CA	30,132
Suffolk County, NY	30,012
Wayne County, MI	29,990
Boone County, KY	29,936
Honolulu County, HI	29,928
Multnomah County, OR	29,619
Boulder County, CO	29,381
Harris County, TX	29,295
Middlesex County, MA	29,225
Dallas County, TX	29,170
Essex County, NJ	28,900
Maui County, HI	28,791
Fresno County, CA	28,726
Washington County, OR	28,637
Montgomery County, PA	28,432
Chester County, PA	28,272

Place	Dollars
La Canada Flintridge, CA (city) Los Angeles County	73,265
Glenview, IL (village) Cook County	70,887
Oyster Bay, NY (town) Nassau County	66,261
Saratoga, CA (city) Santa Clara County	65,996
Milpitas, CA (city) Santa Clara County	61,066
Palos Verdes Estates, CA (city) Los Angeles County	58,912
Rye, NY (city) Westchester County	57,629
Encinitas, CA (city) San Diego County	57,313
Newport Beach, CA (city) Orange County	57,139
Mercer Island, WA (city) King County	56,966
Los Altos, CA (city) Santa Clara County	55,318
Thousand Oaks, CA (city) Ventura County	54,147
Manhattan Beach, CA (city) Los Angeles County	53,314
Cliffside Park, NJ (borough) Bergen County	51,674
Buffalo Grove, IL (village) Lake County	51,519
Greenburgh, NY (town) Westchester County	50,784
Greenville, NY (cdp) Westchester County	50,331
Rancho Palos Verdes, CA (city) Los Angeles County	49,798
Palo Alto, CA (city) Santa Clara County	49,163
Ridgewood, NJ (village) Bergen County	48,407
San Ramon, CA (city) Contra Costa County	48,400
Laguna Niguel, CA (city) Orange County	48,256
Bryn Mawr-Skyway, WA (cdp) King County	47,783
Mountain View, CA (city) Santa Clara County	47,222
Burlingame, CA (city) San Mateo County	47,107
Elk Grove, CA (cdp) Sacramento County	46,432
Bethesda, MD (cdp) Montgomery County	46,233
Fremont, CA (city) Alameda County	45,120
North Hempstead, NY (town) Nassau County	44,889
Eastchester, NY (cdp) Westchester County	44,199
Redwood City, CA (city) San Mateo County	44,011
Redmond, WA (city) King County	43,576
Rolling Hills Estates, CA (city) Los Angeles County	43,475
Pleasanton, CA (city) Alameda County	43,345
Belmont, CA (city) San Mateo County	43,318
Wilmette, IL (village) Cook County	42,897
Fort Lee, NJ (borough) Bergen County	42,503
Santa Clara, CA (city) Santa Clara County	42,265
Seal Beach, CA (city) Orange County	42,179
Walnut, CA (city) Los Angeles County	41,452
Foster City, CA (city) San Mateo County	41,221
Sunnyvale, CA (city) Santa Clara County	40,917
Cupertino, CA (city) Santa Clara County	40,885
Lake Forest, CA (city) Orange County	40,875
South Pasadena, CA (city) Los Angeles County	40,661
Redondo Beach, CA (city) Los Angeles County	40,627
Eastchester, NY (town) Westchester County	40,102
Cypress, CA (city) Orange County	39,509
San Jose, CA (city) Santa Clara County	39,489
Arlington Heights, IL (village) Cook County	39,086
Walnut Creek, CA (city) Contra Costa County	38,783
Charlotte, NC (city) Mecklenburg County	38,692
New York, NY (city)	38,572
Orange, CA (city) Orange County	38,559
Laguna, CA (cdp) Sacramento County	37,940
Pasadena, CA (city) Los Angeles County	37,836
Glendale, CA (city) Los Angeles County	37,818
Diamond Bar, CA (city) Los Angeles County	37,754
Bellevue, WA (city) King County	37,593
Harrison, NY (village) Westchester County	37,554
Oakland, CA (city) Alameda County	37,488
Arlington, VA (cdp) Arlington County	37,457
South San Francisco, CA (city) San Mateo County	37,434
Simi Valley, CA (city) Ventura County	37,398
Morgan Hill, CA (city) Santa Clara County	37,184
Cary, NC (town) Wake County	36,930
Scarsdale, NY (village) Westchester County	36,925
Maunawili, HI (cdp) Honolulu County	36,623
Heeia, HI (cdp) Honolulu County	36,329
San Mateo, CA (city) San Mateo County	36,297
West Bloomfield, MI (township) Oakland County	36,297
San Francisco, CA (city) San Francisco County	36,223
Burbank, CA (city) Los Angeles County	36,036
Mission Viejo, CA (city) Orange County	36,032
Hacienda Heights, CA (cdp) Los Angeles County	36,031

Notes: Please refer to the User's Guide for an explanation of data; ranking tables include all places with Asian and/or NHPI populations above SF4 population thresholds; (1) tables reflect only those areas that meet SF4 population thresholds, therefore there may be less than 50 states, 75 counties or 75 places listed

Per Capita Income

Korean

All States, Top 75 Counties, and Top 75 Places Sorted by Number[1]

State	Dollars
District of Columbia	27,307
Connecticut	23,528
Delaware	22,575
New Jersey	21,384
Nevada	21,187
Illinois	21,179
Ohio	20,209
Massachusetts	19,827
Virginia	19,725
California	19,643
Maryland	19,623
New York	19,160
United States	18,805
Hawaii	18,447
Colorado	18,076
South Carolina	17,655
North Carolina	17,560
Missouri	17,552
Texas	17,481
Pennsylvania	17,434
Washington	17,349
Georgia	17,180
Arizona	17,120
Indiana	16,802
Rhode Island	16,737
Alaska	16,689
Oregon	16,657
Florida	16,577
Kentucky	16,352
New Mexico	16,296
Michigan	16,109
Tennessee	15,834
Louisiana	15,814
Alabama	15,228
Kansas	14,539
Wyoming	14,529
West Virginia	14,365
Wisconsin	14,290
New Hampshire	14,026
Mississippi	13,374
Minnesota	13,081
Arkansas	12,637
Utah	12,627
Oklahoma	12,410
North Dakota	11,826
Iowa	11,389
Maine	10,952
Idaho	10,875
Nebraska	10,162
South Dakota	8,469
Montana	7,704
Vermont	7,581

County	Dollars
New York County, NY	43,744
Berks County, PA	42,579
Fairfield County, CT	38,901
Kitsap County, WA	37,065
Lake County, IN	34,497
Westchester County, NY	33,966
Arlington County, VA	33,839
Imperial County, CA	32,890
San Mateo County, CA	32,099
Dutchess County, NY	31,783
San Francisco County, CA	30,471
Mercer County, NJ	30,040
Lake County, IL	29,801
Somerset County, NJ	29,458
Hudson County, NJ	27,456
Santa Clara County, CA	27,255
Douglas County, CO	27,189
Oakland County, MI	27,171
Cumberland County, PA	26,552
DuPage County, IL	26,421
Essex County, NJ	26,276
New Castle County, DE	26,179
Ventura County, CA	25,763
Marin County, CA	25,501
Norfolk County, MA	25,252
Allegheny County, PA	24,932
Cuyahoga County, OH	24,117
Morris County, NJ	24,069
Multnomah County, OR	24,005
Fort Bend County, TX	23,590
Collin County, TX	23,329
Contra Costa County, CA	23,280
Will County, IL	23,188
Denver County, CO	23,103
Chesterfield County, VA	22,986
Lucas County, OH	22,878
Nassau County, NY	22,844
Montgomery County, MD	22,812
San Joaquin County, CA	22,633
Chester County, PA	22,390
Pima County, AZ	22,172
Palm Beach County, FL	22,165
Washoe County, NV	22,120
Mecklenburg County, NC	22,097
Cobb County, GA	22,056
Sonoma County, CA	21,963
Virginia Beach Independent City, VA	21,931
Fresno County, CA	21,767
Union County, NJ	21,759
Monterey County, CA	21,607
Clark County, WA	21,569
Fulton County, GA	21,569
Clark County, NV	21,463
St. Louis County, MO	21,159
Cook County, IL	21,140
Rockland County, NY	21,025
Alameda County, CA	21,022
Bergen County, NJ	21,012
Fairfax County, VA	20,921
Denton County, TX	20,896
Washington County, MN	20,894
Essex County, MA	20,799
Passaic County, NJ	20,478
Richmond County, NY	20,390
Arapahoe County, CO	20,357
Middlesex County, MA	20,341
Shelby County, TN	20,297
Madison County, AL	20,265
Clackamas County, OR	20,149
Baltimore County, MD	20,142
Johnson County, KS	20,093
Bucks County, PA	20,040
Worcester County, MA	20,018
Henrico County, VA	19,995
Hamilton County, TN	19,993

Place	Dollars
Alpine, NJ (borough) Bergen County	62,822
Palos Verdes Estates, CA (city) Los Angeles County	56,187
Bloomfield, MI (township) Oakland County	54,346
Palo Alto, CA (city) Santa Clara County	52,382
Scarsdale, NY (village) Westchester County	48,602
Saratoga, CA (city) Santa Clara County	44,579
Lake Success, NY (village) Nassau County	42,903
Foster City, CA (city) San Mateo County	41,613
Beverly Hills, CA (city) Los Angeles County	41,264
West Windsor, NJ (township) Mercer County	40,483
Greenburgh, NY (town) Westchester County	39,625
Potomac, MD (cdp) Montgomery County	38,849
Mountain View, CA (city) Santa Clara County	37,352
Sugar Land, TX (city) Fort Bend County	36,667
Parsippany-Troy Hills, NJ (township) Morris County	36,333
Rancho Palos Verdes, CA (city) Los Angeles County	35,417
Demarest, NJ (borough) Bergen County	35,036
Santa Monica, CA (city) Los Angeles County	34,760
Thousand Oaks, CA (city) Ventura County	34,510
Norwood, NJ (borough) Bergen County	33,996
Arlington, VA (cdp) Arlington County	33,839
San Mateo, CA (city) San Mateo County	33,425
Englewood Cliffs, NJ (borough) Bergen County	32,835
Northbrook, IL (village) Cook County	32,694
Pleasanton, CA (city) Alameda County	31,431
Tustin, CA (city) Orange County	31,420
Brookline, MA (town) Norfolk County	31,325
Reston, VA (cdp) Fairfax County	31,256
San Francisco, CA (city) San Francisco County	30,471
Simi Valley, CA (city) Ventura County	30,442
North Bethesda, MD (cdp) Montgomery County	30,241
Newton, MA (city) Middlesex County	29,795
Redmond, WA (city) King County	29,692
Lower Merion, PA (township) Montgomery County	29,181
McLean, VA (cdp) Fairfax County	29,087
Kailua, HI (cdp) Honolulu County	28,733
Walnut Creek, CA (city) Contra Costa County	28,443
West Bloomfield, MI (township) Oakland County	28,268
Buffalo Grove, IL (village) Lake County	28,119
Bethesda, MD (cdp) Montgomery County	27,745
Henderson, NV (city) Clark County	27,733
Glenview, IL (village) Cook County	27,676
Edgewater, NJ (borough) Bergen County	27,641
Placentia, CA (city) Orange County	27,625
Plymouth, PA (township) Montgomery County	27,488
La Canada Flintridge, CA (city) Los Angeles County	27,373
Plano, TX (city) Collin County	27,287
North Hempstead, NY (town) Nassau County	27,269
Mission Viejo, CA (city) Orange County	26,954
Tysons Corner, VA (cdp) Fairfax County	26,855
Closter, NJ (borough) Bergen County	26,661
Old Tappan, NJ (borough) Bergen County	26,594
Millbrae, CA (city) San Mateo County	26,333
Chino Hills, CA (city) San Bernardino County	26,305
Whittier, CA (city) Los Angeles County	26,167
Huntsville, AL (city) Madison County	26,102
Milpitas, CA (city) Santa Clara County	26,072
Lincolnwood, IL (village) Cook County	26,025
Jersey City, NJ (city) Hudson County	25,957
Las Vegas, NV (city) Clark County	25,847
Redondo Beach, CA (city) Los Angeles County	25,521
Castro Valley, CA (cdp) Alameda County	25,225
Laguna Niguel, CA (city) Orange County	25,222
West Orange, NJ (township) Essex County	25,116
West Carson, CA (cdp) Los Angeles County	25,001
Vancouver, WA (city) Clark County	24,966
Huntington Beach, CA (city) Orange County	24,857
Aspen Hill, MD (cdp) Montgomery County	24,822
Commack, NY (cdp) Suffolk County	24,785
Sunnyvale, CA (city) Santa Clara County	24,754
Overland Park, KS (city) Johnson County	24,675
San Jose, CA (city) Santa Clara County	24,535
Kaneohe, HI (cdp) Honolulu County	24,475
Fresno, CA (city) Fresno County	24,421
Wilmette, IL (village) Cook County	24,224

Notes: Please refer to the User's Guide for an explanation of data; ranking tables include all places with Asian and/or NHPI populations above SF4 population thresholds; (1) tables reflect only those areas that meet SF4 population thresholds, therefore there may be less than 50 states, 75 counties or 75 places listed

Per Capita Income

Laotian

All States, Top 75 Counties, and Top 75 Places Sorted by Number[1]

State	Dollars
Indiana	19,344
Michigan	16,755
Illinois	16,398
Maryland	16,308
Idaho	16,303
Virginia	16,234
Missouri	16,214
Connecticut	16,180
New Hampshire	16,022
Arizona	15,583
Tennessee	14,882
Ohio	14,405
Georgia	14,323
Massachusetts	14,299
New Jersey	14,294
Nevada	14,026
Colorado	14,002
Kansas	13,877
New York	13,761
Pennsylvania	13,555
Texas	13,433
Oregon	13,299
Rhode Island	13,278
Florida	13,014
Washington	12,911
Iowa	12,775
Minnesota	12,640
Utah	12,526
Nebraska	12,523
South Dakota	12,390
Alabama	11,932
United States	11,830
Oklahoma	11,433
North Carolina	11,179
Louisiana	10,847
Arkansas	10,590
South Carolina	10,268
Wisconsin	10,145
California	8,745
Hawaii	8,669
Alaska	8,522

County	Dollars
Cook County, IL	20,582
Gwinnett County, GA	18,913
Ottawa County, MI	18,180
Maricopa County, AZ	17,853
Fairfield County, CT	17,244
Santa Clara County, CA	17,129
Fairfax County, VA	17,028
Polk County, FL	16,796
Rutherford County, TN	16,596
Summit County, OH	16,422
Snohomish County, WA	16,248
Kane County, IL	16,242
New Haven County, CT	15,626
Clark County, WA	15,578
Harris County, TX	15,552
Middlesex County, MA	15,515
Hartford County, CT	15,406
Johnson County, KS	15,405
Washington County, OR	15,383
Winnebago County, IL	15,245
Mecklenburg County, NC	14,922
Hennepin County, MN	14,584
Orange County, CA	14,297
Tarrant County, TX	14,206
Dakota County, NE	14,200
Clark County, NV	14,160
Jefferson County, CO	14,096
Worcester County, MA	14,035
Dakota County, MN	13,960
Cowley County, KS	13,709
Clayton County, GA	13,695
Adams County, CO	13,642
Franklin County, OH	13,426
Essex County, MA	13,354
Washington County, AR	13,319
Providence County, RI	13,311
Guilford County, NC	13,260
Polk County, IA	13,254
Philadelphia County, PA	12,947
King County, WA	12,840
Monroe County, NY	12,801
Salt Lake County, UT	12,613
Multnomah County, OR	12,596
Roseau County, MN	12,542
Davidson County, TN	12,442
Sedgwick County, KS	12,402
Milwaukee County, WI	12,365
Dallas County, TX	12,253
Cass County, MI	12,224
Mobile County, AL	11,894
Pierce County, WA	11,807
Dane County, WI	11,778
Sonoma County, CA	11,746
Potter County, TX	11,666
Pinellas County, FL	11,534
Bexar County, TX	11,514
San Diego County, CA	11,448
Franklin County, WA	11,382
Buena Vista County, IA	11,213
Habersham County, GA	11,172
Oklahoma County, OK	11,054
Los Angeles County, CA	10,738
Alameda County, CA	10,543
Olmsted County, MN	9,940
Spartanburg County, SC	9,883
Riverside County, CA	9,803
Iberia Parish, LA	9,488
Sebastian County, AR	9,468
San Bernardino County, CA	9,269
Montgomery County, NC	9,091
Contra Costa County, CA	9,082
Broome County, NY	8,946
Pacific County, WA	8,783
Burke County, NC	8,552
Solano County, CA	8,357

Place	Dollars
Elgin, IL (city) Kane County	19,355
San Jose, CA (city) Santa Clara County	16,772
Bridgeport, CT (city) Fairfield County	16,511
Anaheim, CA (city) Orange County	16,010
Murfreesboro, TN (city) Rutherford County	15,851
Lowell, MA (city) Middlesex County	15,844
Brooklyn Park, MN (city) Hennepin County	15,326
Bellevue, WA (city) King County	15,072
Brooklyn Center, MN (city) Hennepin County	15,005
Springfield, VA (cdp) Fairfax County	14,969
Charlotte, NC (city) Mecklenburg County	14,355
Fort Worth, TX (city) Tarrant County	14,304
Rockford, IL (city) Winnebago County	13,998
Winfield, KS (city) Cowley County	13,741
Woonsocket, RI (city) Providence County	13,413
Westminster, CO (city) Adams County	13,396
Springdale, AR (city) Washington County	13,381
Oaklawn-Sunview, KS (cdp) Sedgwick County	13,374
Dallas, TX (city) Dallas County	13,299
Escondido, CA (city) San Diego County	13,271
Irving, TX (city) Dallas County	13,010
Columbus, OH (city) Franklin County	12,990
Philadelphia, PA (city) Philadelphia County	12,947
Arvada, CO (city) Jefferson County	12,937
West Valley City, UT (city) Salt Lake County	12,918
Portland, OR (city) Multnomah County	12,755
Nashville-Davidson, TN (sp. city) Davidson County	12,442
St. Petersburg, FL (city) Pinellas County	12,356
Des Moines, IA (city) Polk County	12,354
Seattle, WA (city) King County	12,336
Warroad, MN (city) Roseau County	12,321
Santa Rosa, CA (city) Sonoma County	12,306
Santa Ana, CA (city) Orange County	12,295
Wichita, KS (city) Sedgwick County	12,224
Amarillo, TX (city) Potter County	11,782
Haltom City, TX (city) Tarrant County	11,773
Tacoma, WA (city) Pierce County	11,741
New Britain, CT (city) Hartford County	11,669
Akron, OH (city) Summit County	11,528
Fitchburg, MA (city) Worcester County	11,417
Storm Lake, IA (city) Buena Vista County	11,258
Milwaukee, WI (city) Milwaukee County	11,135
Rochester, NY (city) Monroe County	11,127
San Diego, CA (city) San Diego County	11,036
Oklahoma City, OK (city) Oklahoma County	10,823
Minneapolis, MN (city) Hennepin County	10,817
Providence, RI (city) Providence County	10,469
Riverside, CA (city) Riverside County	10,160
Los Angeles, CA (city) Los Angeles County	10,066
Rochester, MN (city) Olmsted County	9,839
Fort Smith, AR (city) Sebastian County	9,673
Fairfield, CA (city) Solano County	9,638
Grand Prairie, TX (city) Dallas County	9,226
Banning, CA (city) Riverside County	9,090
Pomona, CA (city) Los Angeles County	8,687
San Pablo, CA (city) Contra Costa County	8,646
Raymond, WA (city) Pacific County	8,588
Richmond, CA (city) Contra Costa County	8,062
Worthington, MN (city) Nobles County	7,667
Oakland, CA (city) Alameda County	7,522
Stockton, CA (city) San Joaquin County	7,318
Moreno Valley, CA (city) Riverside County	7,267
Parkway-S. Sacramento, CA (cdp) Sacramento County	7,082
Long Beach, CA (city) Los Angeles County	6,921
Modesto, CA (city) Stanislaus County	6,687
Green Bay, WI (city) Brown County	6,575
St. Paul, MN (city) Ramsey County	6,328
Sacramento, CA (city) Sacramento County	6,265
Honolulu, HI (cdp) Honolulu County	6,125
Visalia, CA (city) Tulare County	5,151
Merced, CA (city) Merced County	5,134
Redding, CA (city) Shasta County	4,825
Fresno, CA (city) Fresno County	4,223

Notes: Please refer to the User's Guide for an explanation of data; ranking tables include all places with Asian and/or NHPI populations above SF4 population thresholds; (1) tables reflect only those areas that meet SF4 population thresholds, therefore there may be less than 50 states, 75 counties or 75 places listed

Per Capita Income

Malaysian

All States, Top 75 Counties, and Top 75 Places Sorted by Number[1]

State	Dollars
California	24,535
Texas	23,385
Illinois	21,426
United States	19,895
New York	17,889
Ohio	17,259
Michigan	14,191
Oklahoma	6,229

County	Dollars
Los Angeles County, CA	22,298
Queens County, NY	15,569

Place	Dollars
New York, NY (city)	16,545

Notes: Please refer to the User's Guide for an explanation of data; ranking tables include all places with Asian and/or NHPI populations above SF4 population thresholds; (1) tables reflect only those areas that meet SF4 population thresholds, therefore there may be less than 50 states, 75 counties or 75 places listed

Per Capita Income

Pakistani

All States, Top 75 Counties, and Top 75 Places Sorted by Number[1]

State	Dollars
Kentucky	50,931
Iowa	48,604
Alabama	31,172
Delaware	30,615
Kansas	29,412
Indiana	28,822
Minnesota	27,195
West Virginia	27,172
Oregon	26,386
Arizona	25,063
Ohio	24,819
Tennessee	23,790
Michigan	22,883
Connecticut	22,521
Georgia	20,927
Florida	20,603
New Jersey	20,291
Pennsylvania	19,794
Colorado	19,396
California	19,254
Washington	18,367
United States	18,096
North Carolina	17,839
Illinois	17,792
Missouri	17,647
Wisconsin	17,464
Nevada	16,824
Maryland	16,518
Texas	16,228
Massachusetts	14,809
Louisiana	14,767
Virginia	14,562
New York	14,535
Utah	14,402
Oklahoma	12,274

County	Dollars
Santa Clara County, CA	32,141
Wake County, NC	31,332
Lake County, IL	31,170
Oakland County, MI	30,793
Mercer County, NJ	30,655
Essex County, NJ	28,261
San Francisco County, CA	27,818
New York County, NY	27,661
Monmouth County, NJ	26,356
Somerset County, NJ	25,715
Westchester County, NY	24,481
Hennepin County, MN	23,567
Orange County, FL	23,458
DuPage County, IL	23,227
Will County, IL	22,340
Collin County, TX	22,249
Washtenaw County, MI	22,061
Alameda County, CA	21,978
San Diego County, CA	21,960
Nassau County, NY	21,860
Tarrant County, TX	21,780
Fairfield County, CT	21,761
Bergen County, NJ	21,657
Orange County, CA	21,482
Denton County, TX	20,979
Milwaukee County, WI	20,797
Maricopa County, AZ	20,581
Hartford County, CT	20,195
San Bernardino County, CA	19,806
Miami-Dade County, FL	19,747
Middlesex County, NJ	19,699
Montgomery County, MD	19,589
Cobb County, GA	19,416
Morris County, NJ	18,792
King County, WA	18,226
Loudoun County, VA	18,141
Wayne County, MI	18,064
Riverside County, CA	17,881
Franklin County, OH	17,769
Fort Bend County, TX	17,270
Howard County, MD	17,234
Gwinnett County, GA	17,195
New Haven County, CT	16,992
Snohomish County, WA	16,811
St. Louis County, MO	16,187
Worcester County, MA	16,063
Camden County, NJ	16,002
Prince George's County, MD	15,996
Suffolk County, NY	15,863
Jefferson Parish, LA	15,756
Richmond County, NY	15,235
Contra Costa County, CA	15,173
Dallas County, TX	14,972
Harris County, TX	14,864
Los Angeles County, CA	14,608
Macomb County, MI	14,589
Cook County, IL	14,513
Delaware County, PA	14,450
Arlington County, VA	14,399
Clayton County, GA	14,256
Fairfax County, VA	14,188
Middlesex County, MA	13,983
Broward County, FL	13,943
Hudson County, NJ	13,912
Prince William County, VA	12,639
Queens County, NY	12,559
Alexandria Independent City, VA	12,380
Baltimore County, MD	12,315
Philadelphia County, PA	12,004
Travis County, TX	11,957
Monroe County, NY	11,914
Union County, NJ	11,608
Atlantic County, NJ	11,289
Bronx County, NY	11,160
Sacramento County, CA	10,211

Place	Dollars
Santa Clara, CA (city) Santa Clara County	41,617
San Francisco, CA (city) San Francisco County	27,818
Fremont, CA (city) Alameda County	26,966
Plano, TX (city) Collin County	26,363
Edison, NJ (township) Middlesex County	24,735
North Hempstead, NY (town) Nassau County	24,302
San Jose, CA (city) Santa Clara County	23,206
Skokie, IL (village) Cook County	22,213
Huntington, NY (town) Suffolk County	21,819
Richardson, TX (city) Dallas County	20,244
Sugar Land, TX (city) Fort Bend County	19,986
Ellicott City, MD (cdp) Howard County	19,633
Hempstead, NY (town) Nassau County	19,393
Old Bridge, NJ (township) Middlesex County	18,890
Anaheim, CA (city) Orange County	18,457
Irving, TX (city) Dallas County	18,290
Carrollton, TX (city) Denton County	17,257
Brookhaven, NY (town) Suffolk County	15,627
Arlington, VA (cdp) Arlington County	14,399
Houston, TX (city) Harris County	13,157
Jersey City, NJ (city) Hudson County	12,578
Dallas, TX (city) Dallas County	12,507
New York, NY (city)	12,108
Torrance, CA (city) Los Angeles County	12,070
Philadelphia, PA (city) Philadelphia County	12,004
Los Angeles, CA (city) Los Angeles County	11,898
Chicago, IL (city) Cook County	11,816
Woodbridge, NJ (township) Middlesex County	11,505
Dale City, VA (cdp) Prince William County	11,233
Austin, TX (city) Travis County	11,122
Tulsa, OK (city) Tulsa County	10,370
Garland, TX (city) Dallas County	9,741
Stockton, CA (city) San Joaquin County	8,920
Sacramento, CA (city) Sacramento County	8,564
Lincolnia, VA (cdp) Fairfax County	8,512
Bailey's Crossroads, VA (cdp) Fairfax County	8,252
Mission Bend, TX (cdp) Fort Bend County	7,655

Notes: Please refer to the User's Guide for an explanation of data; ranking tables include all places with Asian and/or NHPI populations above SF4 population thresholds; (1) tables reflect only those areas that meet SF4 population thresholds, therefore there may be less than 50 states, 75 counties or 75 places listed

Per Capita Income

Samoan

***All States, Top 75 Counties, and Top 75 Places Sorted by Number*[1]**

State	Dollars
New Jersey	26,074
Arizona	25,291
Virginia	16,642
Tennessee	15,642
Pennsylvania	15,630
Florida	15,628
New York	15,292
Colorado	14,292
Georgia	13,243
Texas	13,133
Illinois	12,728
Missouri	12,563
United States	12,160
Alaska	11,614
California	11,558
Oregon	11,526
North Carolina	11,365
Michigan	11,358
Washington	11,337
Nevada	11,245
Utah	10,878
Hawaii	10,537
Ohio	9,826

County	Dollars
Maricopa County, AZ	30,842
San Mateo County, CA	16,179
Contra Costa County, CA	15,601
Santa Clara County, CA	14,744
San Joaquin County, CA	13,376
Jackson County, MO	13,235
Ventura County, CA	13,158
Hawaii County, HI	12,741
San Diego County, CA	12,711
Orange County, CA	12,701
Solano County, CA	12,546
Alameda County, CA	11,759
Utah County, UT	11,507
Clark County, NV	11,440
Los Angeles County, CA	11,106
King County, WA	11,017
Pierce County, WA	11,007
Salt Lake County, UT	10,794
Riverside County, CA	10,557
Honolulu County, HI	10,373
Sacramento County, CA	9,608
Anchorage Borough, AK	9,323
San Bernardino County, CA	7,924
San Francisco County, CA	7,359

Place	Dollars
Los Angeles, CA (city) Los Angeles County	15,065
Federal Way, WA (city) King County	14,686
Anaheim, CA (city) Orange County	14,152
Oceanside, CA (city) San Diego County	14,011
Lakewood, CA (city) Los Angeles County	13,875
New York, NY (city)	13,721
Garden Grove, CA (city) Orange County	12,798
Oxnard, CA (city) Ventura County	11,872
San Jose, CA (city) Santa Clara County	11,597
Santa Ana, CA (city) Orange County	11,319
Carson, CA (city) Los Angeles County	11,053
Hayward, CA (city) Alameda County	10,882
Lakewood, WA (city) Pierce County	10,881
Salt Lake City, UT (city) Salt Lake County	10,790
Tacoma, WA (city) Pierce County	10,688
Kahuku, HI (cdp) Honolulu County	10,596
San Diego, CA (city) San Diego County	10,467
West Valley City, UT (city) Salt Lake County	10,045
Honolulu, HI (cdp) Honolulu County	9,698
Ewa Beach, HI (cdp) Honolulu County	9,163
Nanakuli, HI (cdp) Honolulu County	8,883
Seattle, WA (city) King County	8,774
Halawa, HI (cdp) Honolulu County	8,686
San Bernardino, CA (city) San Bernardino County	8,430
Laie, HI (cdp) Honolulu County	8,389
Westminster, CA (city) Orange County	8,125
Long Beach, CA (city) Los Angeles County	7,416
San Francisco, CA (city) San Francisco County	7,359
Sacramento, CA (city) Sacramento County	7,161
Waipahu, HI (cdp) Honolulu County	6,664
Hauula, HI (cdp) Honolulu County	5,905
Compton, CA (city) Los Angeles County	4,983

Notes: Please refer to the User's Guide for an explanation of data; ranking tables include all places with Asian and/or NHPI populations above SF4 population thresholds; (1) tables reflect only those areas that meet SF4 population thresholds, therefore there may be less than 50 states, 75 counties or 75 places listed

Per Capita Income

Sri Lankan

All States, Top 75 Counties, and Top 75 Places Sorted by Number[1]

State	Dollars
Florida	43,144
Pennsylvania	37,754
Illinois	30,961
New Jersey	30,753
California	28,482
Maryland	27,876
United States	27,478
New York	24,983
Washington	24,346
Ohio	24,167
Michigan	24,031
Massachusetts	23,204
Texas	22,582
Virginia	19,950

County	Dollars
Richmond County, NY	30,431
Middlesex County, NJ	28,666
Montgomery County, MD	26,199
Los Angeles County, CA	24,099
Orange County, CA	22,609
Queens County, NY	14,907

Place	Dollars
Los Angeles, CA (city) Los Angeles County	22,726
New York, NY (city)	21,876

Notes: Please refer to the User's Guide for an explanation of data; ranking tables include all places with Asian and/or NHPI populations above SF4 population thresholds; (1) tables reflect only those areas that meet SF4 population thresholds, therefore there may be less than 50 states, 75 counties or 75 places listed

Per Capita Income

Taiwanese

All States, Top 75 Counties, and Top 75 Places Sorted by Number[1]

State	Dollars
Florida	40,339
Georgia	35,996
Missouri	35,060
Illinois	32,430
Minnesota	31,856
New Jersey	31,184
Tennessee	31,106
Ohio	30,126
Michigan	29,836
Virginia	29,478
New York	28,698
North Carolina	28,053
Indiana	27,881
Massachusetts	26,526
Hawaii	26,021
Kansas	25,962
United States	25,890
Maryland	25,611
Pennsylvania	25,031
California	24,408
Louisiana	23,830
Texas	23,636
Arizona	23,225
Washington	22,569
Iowa	22,219
Colorado	21,721
Oregon	20,251
Connecticut	19,531
Nevada	17,802
Utah	13,099
Wisconsin	12,998
Oklahoma	11,139

County	Dollars
New York County, NY	61,900
Westchester County, NY	57,896
Gwinnett County, GA	57,843
San Mateo County, CA	49,502
DuPage County, IL	45,231
Somerset County, NJ	42,561
St. Louis County, MO	41,750
Fairfax County, VA	37,535
Franklin County, OH	35,973
Bergen County, NJ	35,756
Santa Clara County, CA	35,291
Montgomery County, MD	33,599
Oakland County, MI	32,874
Morris County, NJ	32,378
Contra Costa County, CA	32,328
Essex County, NJ	32,249
Middlesex County, MA	29,949
Ventura County, CA	29,587
Collin County, TX	29,471
Mercer County, NJ	29,092
San Francisco County, CA	28,898
Nassau County, NY	28,651
Middlesex County, NJ	28,526
Dallas County, TX	28,332
Alameda County, CA	27,995
Washtenaw County, MI	26,708
San Diego County, CA	26,687
Cook County, IL	26,272
Harris County, TX	25,897
Honolulu County, HI	25,706
Maricopa County, AZ	25,412
Tarrant County, TX	24,873
Suffolk County, NY	24,805
King County, WA	24,150
Sacramento County, CA	23,841
Los Angeles County, CA	22,113
Orange County, CA	22,009
Queens County, NY	21,933
Clark County, NV	19,970
Allegheny County, PA	19,668
Fort Bend County, TX	19,574
Suffolk County, MA	18,845
San Bernardino County, CA	18,562
Travis County, TX	17,818
Norfolk County, MA	15,070
Riverside County, CA	11,811
Dane County, WI	7,564

Place	Dollars
Saratoga, CA (city) Santa Clara County	37,878
Sunnyvale, CA (city) Santa Clara County	37,861
Orange, CA (city) Orange County	36,324
San Marino, CA (city) Los Angeles County	36,291
Naperville, IL (city) Du Page County	35,047
Troy, MI (city) Oakland County	34,534
San Jose, CA (city) Santa Clara County	33,215
Torrance, CA (city) Los Angeles County	32,702
Fremont, CA (city) Alameda County	31,906
Plano, TX (city) Collin County	31,279
New York, NY (city)	30,329
Bellevue, WA (city) King County	29,981
Cerritos, CA (city) Los Angeles County	29,492
Tustin, CA (city) Orange County	29,218
San Francisco, CA (city) San Francisco County	28,898
Cupertino, CA (city) Santa Clara County	28,848
San Diego, CA (city) San Diego County	28,668
Huntington Beach, CA (city) Orange County	28,092
North Hempstead, NY (town) Nassau County	27,918
Ann Arbor, MI (city) Washtenaw County	27,877
Honolulu, HI (cdp) Honolulu County	27,409
Rancho Palos Verdes, CA (city) Los Angeles County	27,161
Columbus, OH (city) Franklin County	26,570
Edison, NJ (township) Middlesex County	25,150
Arlington, TX (city) Tarrant County	24,280
Diamond Bar, CA (city) Los Angeles County	23,538
Chino Hills, CA (city) San Bernardino County	22,912
Los Angeles, CA (city) Los Angeles County	22,757
Irvine, CA (city) Orange County	22,703
Houston, TX (city) Harris County	22,563
Upland, CA (city) San Bernardino County	21,595
Chicago, IL (city) Cook County	20,133
Arcadia, CA (city) Los Angeles County	19,917
Walnut, CA (city) Los Angeles County	19,709
Rowland Heights, CA (cdp) Los Angeles County	18,959
Boston, MA (city) Suffolk County	18,845
West Covina, CA (city) Los Angeles County	18,667
Sugar Land, TX (city) Fort Bend County	17,939
Monterey Park, CA (city) Los Angeles County	17,186
Temple City, CA (city) Los Angeles County	16,747
San Gabriel, CA (city) Los Angeles County	16,546
Hacienda Heights, CA (cdp) Los Angeles County	16,425
Fountain Valley, CA (city) Orange County	16,187
Anaheim, CA (city) Orange County	15,732
Cypress, CA (city) Orange County	15,647
Alhambra, CA (city) Los Angeles County	15,548
Austin, TX (city) Travis County	15,436
East San Gabriel, CA (cdp) Los Angeles County	15,370
Seattle, WA (city) King County	15,196
El Monte, CA (city) Los Angeles County	14,463
Berkeley, CA (city) Alameda County	8,985
Madison, WI (city) Dane County	7,598

Notes: Please refer to the User's Guide for an explanation of data; ranking tables include all places with Asian and/or NHPI populations above SF4 population thresholds; (1) tables reflect only those areas that meet SF4 population thresholds, therefore there may be less than 50 states, 75 counties or 75 places listed

Per Capita Income

Thai

All States, Top 75 Counties, and Top 75 Places Sorted by Number[1]

State	Dollars
Indiana	32,579
South Carolina	31,053
Minnesota	25,672
New Jersey	23,932
Georgia	23,004
Maryland	22,898
Illinois	22,438
New York	21,540
Virginia	20,843
Nebraska	20,796
Connecticut	20,725
Iowa	20,238
Michigan	19,980
Massachusetts	19,885
Missouri	19,771
Texas	19,744
Nevada	19,255
Kansas	19,173
United States	19,066
California	18,477
Kentucky	18,459
Alaska	18,371
Tennessee	17,980
Utah	17,462
Florida	17,104
Pennsylvania	16,940
Washington	16,723
Arizona	16,476
Louisiana	16,331
Colorado	16,202
North Carolina	16,170
Oregon	15,819
New Mexico	14,374
Alabama	13,700
Oklahoma	13,687
Ohio	13,662
Wisconsin	13,486
Hawaii	13,263
Arkansas	10,283

County	Dollars
Dallas County, TX	27,002
New York County, NY	26,820
Bergen County, NJ	26,346
Nassau County, NY	25,711
San Mateo County, CA	25,038
San Francisco County, CA	24,511
St. Louis County, MO	23,860
Westchester County, NY	23,705
Cook County, IL	22,807
DuPage County, IL	22,729
Santa Clara County, CA	22,578
Suffolk County, NY	21,922
Contra Costa County, CA	21,825
Fairfax County, VA	21,388
Montgomery County, MD	21,235
Harris County, TX	21,090
Orange County, CA	20,811
King County, WA	19,750
Tarrant County, TX	19,680
Clark County, NV	19,629
Middlesex County, MA	19,501
Miami-Dade County, FL	19,015
Bexar County, TX	19,005
San Diego County, CA	18,667
Travis County, TX	18,362
Queens County, NY	18,175
Los Angeles County, CA	18,034
Prince George's County, MD	17,912
Alameda County, CA	17,880
Collin County, TX	17,224
Hillsborough County, FL	17,085
Pinellas County, FL	16,847
Pierce County, WA	16,769
Maricopa County, AZ	16,733
Broward County, FL	16,263
San Bernardino County, CA	15,847
Polk County, IA	15,344
Oklahoma County, OK	14,624
Denver County, CO	14,595
Palm Beach County, FL	14,587
Sacramento County, CA	14,432
Anchorage Borough, AK	14,151
Honolulu County, HI	12,782
Franklin County, OH	11,804
Multnomah County, OR	11,644
Okaloosa County, FL	11,397
Riverside County, CA	11,277

Place	Dollars
Las Vegas, NV (city) Clark County	25,999
Glendale, CA (city) Los Angeles County	24,885
Cerritos, CA (city) Los Angeles County	24,844
San Francisco, CA (city) San Francisco County	24,511
Houston, TX (city) Harris County	23,413
New York, NY (city)	22,566
San Jose, CA (city) Santa Clara County	21,393
San Diego, CA (city) San Diego County	20,688
San Antonio, TX (city) Bexar County	20,394
Chicago, IL (city) Cook County	20,073
Long Beach, CA (city) Los Angeles County	19,930
Bellflower, CA (city) Los Angeles County	19,081
Seattle, WA (city) King County	18,480
Anaheim, CA (city) Orange County	18,314
Spring Valley, NV (cdp) Clark County	16,895
Los Angeles, CA (city) Los Angeles County	16,742
Honolulu, HI (cdp) Honolulu County	14,792
Denver, CO (city) Denver County	14,595
Des Moines, IA (city) Polk County	12,973
Portland, OR (city) Multnomah County	10,911
Columbus, OH (city) Franklin County	10,742

Notes: Please refer to the User's Guide for an explanation of data; ranking tables include all places with Asian and/or NHPI populations above SF4 population thresholds; (1) tables reflect only those areas that meet SF4 population thresholds, therefore there may be less than 50 states, 75 counties or 75 places listed

Per Capita Income

Tongan

All States, Top 75 Counties, and Top 75 Places Sorted by Number[1]

State	Dollars
Washington	13,177
Nevada	12,155
Hawaii	11,953
Texas	11,564
California	11,198
United States	10,680
Utah	8,881
Arizona	8,683
Oregon	8,321
Alaska	7,725

County	Dollars
King County, WA	16,341
Maui County, HI	15,322
San Mateo County, CA	14,039
Tarrant County, TX	12,189
Sacramento County, CA	11,942
Honolulu County, HI	11,428
Contra Costa County, CA	10,882
Utah County, UT	10,871
Washoe County, NV	10,787
Maricopa County, AZ	10,446
Los Angeles County, CA	9,711
San Diego County, CA	9,661
Alameda County, CA	9,543
San Bernardino County, CA	8,750
Salt Lake County, UT	8,736
Multnomah County, OR	8,537
Orange County, CA	5,883

Place	Dollars
Laie, HI (cdp) Honolulu County	36,188
San Mateo, CA (city) San Mateo County	13,738
East Palo Alto, CA (city) San Mateo County	11,806
San Bruno, CA (city) San Mateo County	10,657
West Jordan, UT (city) Salt Lake County	10,049
Sacramento, CA (city) Sacramento County	9,665
Oakland, CA (city) Alameda County	8,674
Honolulu, HI (cdp) Honolulu County	8,358
Portland, OR (city) Multnomah County	7,961
Kahuku, HI (cdp) Honolulu County	7,952
Salt Lake City, UT (city) Salt Lake County	7,882
Hauula, HI (cdp) Honolulu County	7,745
West Valley City, UT (city) Salt Lake County	7,734
Los Angeles, CA (city) Los Angeles County	7,663

Notes: Please refer to the User's Guide for an explanation of data; ranking tables include all places with Asian and/or NHPI populations above SF4 population thresholds; (1) tables reflect only those areas that meet SF4 population thresholds, therefore there may be less than 50 states, 75 counties or 75 places listed

Per Capita Income

Vietnamese

All States, Top 75 Counties, and Top 75 Places Sorted by Number[1]

State	Dollars
Delaware	21,857
District of Columbia	20,618
Alaska	20,204
Virginia	19,977
Nevada	18,879
New Jersey	18,492
West Virginia	18,405
Maryland	17,981
New Hampshire	17,582
Connecticut	17,396
Ohio	17,099
Michigan	17,020
Illinois	16,764
Arizona	16,729
Minnesota	16,509
Oregon	16,132
Texas	16,059
California	16,000
South Dakota	15,817
New York	15,805
Indiana	15,726
United States	15,655
South Carolina	15,609
Wisconsin	15,543
Colorado	15,395
Florida	14,962
Washington	14,553
Utah	14,468
Arkansas	14,447
North Carolina	14,235
Missouri	14,208
Pennsylvania	14,052
Georgia	14,029
Oklahoma	14,018
Kansas	13,896
Massachusetts	13,522
Rhode Island	13,505
Iowa	13,480
Alabama	13,468
New Mexico	13,405
Kentucky	13,349
Nebraska	13,242
Idaho	12,857
Tennessee	12,773
Maine	12,425
Hawaii	12,124
Mississippi	11,715
Louisiana	11,162
Vermont	10,526

County	Dollars
Bergen County, NJ	40,802
New York County, NY	35,376
Will County, IL	34,182
Nassau County, NY	32,126
Monmouth County, NJ	31,510
Alexandria Independent City, VA	30,196
Somerset County, NJ	28,933
Summit County, OH	28,770
Wayne County, MI	28,621
Collin County, TX	27,758
San Mateo County, CA	27,197
Broome County, NY	25,561
New Castle County, DE	25,206
Peoria County, IL	25,105
Williamson County, TX	24,666
Madison County, AL	24,351
Union County, NJ	23,633
Loudoun County, VA	23,589
Stanislaus County, CA	23,558
Fort Bend County, TX	22,886
Placer County, CA	22,747
Bristol County, MA	22,373
Morris County, NJ	22,368
St. Louis County, MO	22,016
Fairfax County, VA	21,883
Fairfax Independent City, VA	21,678
Scott County, MN	21,538
Chester County, PA	21,169
Arapahoe County, CO	21,141
Cumberland County, PA	21,066
Seminole County, FL	21,038
Bucks County, PA	20,993
Greene County, MO	20,809
Howard County, MD	20,784
Prince William County, VA	20,738
New Haven County, CT	20,634
Santa Cruz County, CA	20,569
Suffolk County, NY	20,409
Montgomery County, PA	20,316
Burlington County, NJ	20,292
Clark County, NV	20,105
Washington County, MN	20,035
Santa Clara County, CA	19,908
Brazoria County, TX	19,890
Forsyth County, NC	19,850
Wake County, NC	19,838
DuPage County, IL	19,820
Washington County, OR	19,766
Ventura County, CA	19,638
Montgomery County, MD	18,990
Anoka County, MN	18,927
Travis County, TX	18,616
Johnson County, KS	18,520
Oakland County, MI	18,511
Anchorage Borough, AK	18,489
Fairfield County, CT	18,419
Prince George's County, MD	18,395
Denton County, TX	18,354
Hudson County, NJ	18,326
Greenville County, SC	18,196
Ottawa County, MI	18,188
York County, PA	18,113
Broward County, FL	18,109
Lake County, IL	17,924
Clackamas County, OR	17,874
Maricopa County, AZ	17,820
Cuyahoga County, OH	17,773
Marion County, IN	17,748
Hillsborough County, NH	17,652
Brevard County, FL	17,474
Orange County, FL	17,443
Snohomish County, WA	17,432
Macomb County, MI	17,431
Okaloosa County, FL	17,425
Chesterfield County, VA	17,415

Place	Dollars
Idylwood, VA (cdp) Fairfax County	41,304
Aliso Viejo, CA (cdp) Orange County	37,489
Binghamton, NY (city) Broome County	35,330
Franconia, VA (cdp) Fairfax County	31,905
Laguna Niguel, CA (city) Orange County	31,448
Laguna Hills, CA (city) Orange County	30,799
Round Rock, TX (city) Williamson County	30,759
Cary, NC (town) Wake County	30,099
Missouri City, TX (city) Fort Bend County	29,181
Akron, OH (city) Summit County	27,728
Fremont, CA (city) Alameda County	27,259
Yorba Linda, CA (city) Orange County	27,200
Tustin, CA (city) Orange County	26,912
Rancho Santa Margarita, CA (city) Orange County	26,696
Irvine, CA (city) Orange County	26,518
Plano, TX (city) Collin County	26,303
Cupertino, CA (city) Santa Clara County	26,094
Seattle Hill-Silver Firs, WA (cdp) Snohomish County	25,957
Lake Forest, CA (city) Orange County	25,800
Aurora, IL (city) Kane County	25,551
Diamond Bar, CA (city) Los Angeles County	25,492
Chantilly, VA (cdp) Fairfax County	24,897
Sunnyvale, CA (city) Santa Clara County	24,879
Merrifield, VA (cdp) Fairfax County	24,806
Placentia, CA (city) Orange County	24,804
Sterling Heights, MI (city) Macomb County	24,701
Centreville, VA (cdp) Fairfax County	24,405
Oakton, VA (cdp) Fairfax County	24,403
Cerritos, CA (city) Los Angeles County	24,359
Stafford, TX (city) Fort Bend County	24,298
Mountain View, CA (city) Santa Clara County	23,835
Mission Viejo, CA (city) Orange County	23,705
Santa Clara, CA (city) Santa Clara County	23,642
Milpitas, CA (city) Santa Clara County	23,581
Chandler, AZ (city) Maricopa County	23,574
Burke, VA (cdp) Fairfax County	23,568
Richardson, TX (city) Dallas County	23,390
Las Vegas, NV (city) Clark County	22,843
Santa Clarita, CA (city) Los Angeles County	22,800
Lincolnia, VA (cdp) Fairfax County	22,771
Thousand Oaks, CA (city) Ventura County	22,727
Gaithersburg, MD (city) Montgomery County	22,704
Allen, TX (city) Collin County	22,461
Lewisville, TX (city) Denton County	22,427
Herndon, VA (town) Fairfax County	22,301
Modesto, CA (city) Stanislaus County	22,147
Camarillo, CA (city) Ventura County	21,965
Bloomington, MN (city) Hennepin County	21,822
Irving, TX (city) Dallas County	21,812
Huntington Beach, CA (city) Orange County	21,697
Overland Park, KS (city) Johnson County	21,682
Glendale, CA (city) Los Angeles County	21,212
Rowland Heights, CA (cdp) Los Angeles County	21,074
Chino Hills, CA (city) San Bernardino County	21,059
San Leandro, CA (city) Alameda County	21,056
Kirkland, WA (city) King County	21,019
Corona, CA (city) Riverside County	20,980
Terrytown, LA (cdp) Jefferson Parish	20,912
Daly City, CA (city) San Mateo County	20,902
Beaverton, OR (city) Washington County	20,795
Colesville, MD (cdp) Montgomery County	20,750
Annandale, VA (cdp) Fairfax County	20,647
San Mateo, CA (city) San Mateo County	20,614
Glendale Heights, IL (village) Du Page County	20,530
Sugar Land, TX (city) Fort Bend County	20,488
Orlando, FL (city) Orange County	20,441
Burbank, CA (city) Los Angeles County	20,210
Union City, CA (city) Alameda County	20,154
Springfield, VA (cdp) Fairfax County	19,866
Parkway-S. Sacramento, CA (cdp) Sacramento County	19,838
Ocean Springs, MS (city) Jackson County	19,819
Rancho Cucamonga, CA (city) San Bernardino County	19,695
Salem, OR (city) Marion County	19,628
Bellevue, WA (city) King County	19,605
Campbell, CA (city) Santa Clara County	19,565

Notes: Please refer to the User's Guide for an explanation of data; ranking tables include all places with Asian and/or NHPI populations above SF4 population thresholds; (1) tables reflect only those areas that meet SF4 population thresholds, therefore there may be less than 50 states, 75 counties or 75 places listed

Poverty Status

Total Population with Income Below Poverty Level

All States, Top 75 Counties, and Top 75 Places Sorted by Number[1]

State	Number
United States	33,899,812
California	4,706,130
Texas	3,117,609
New York	2,692,202
Florida	1,952,629
Pennsylvania	1,304,117
Illinois	1,291,958
Ohio	1,170,698
Georgia	1,033,793
Michigan	1,021,605
North Carolina	958,667
Louisiana	851,113
Tennessee	746,789
New Jersey	699,668
Arizona	698,669
Alabama	698,097
Virginia	656,641
Missouri	637,891
Kentucky	621,096
Washington	612,370
Massachusetts	573,421
Indiana	559,484
Mississippi	548,079
South Carolina	547,869
Oklahoma	491,235
Wisconsin	451,538
Maryland	438,676
Arkansas	411,777
Colorado	388,952
Oregon	388,740
Minnesota	380,476
New Mexico	328,933
West Virginia	315,794
Connecticut	259,514
Iowa	258,008
Kansas	257,829
Utah	206,328
Nevada	205,685
Nebraska	161,269
Idaho	148,732
Maine	135,501
Montana	128,355
Hawaii	126,154
Rhode Island	120,548
District of Columbia	109,500
South Dakota	95,900
New Hampshire	78,530
North Dakota	73,457
Delaware	69,901
Alaska	57,602
Vermont	55,506
Wyoming	54,777

County	Number
Los Angeles County, CA	1,674,599
Cook County, IL	713,040
Kings County, NY	610,476
Harris County, TX	503,234
Miami-Dade County, FL	396,995
Bronx County, NY	395,263
Maricopa County, AZ	355,668
San Diego County, CA	338,399
Philadelphia County, PA	336,177
Wayne County, MI	332,598
Queens County, NY	321,102
New York County, NY	298,231
Dallas County, TX	293,267
Orange County, CA	289,475
San Bernardino County, CA	263,412
Bexar County, TX	215,736
Riverside County, CA	214,084
Hidalgo County, TX	201,865
Broward County, FL	184,589
Cuyahoga County, OH	179,372
Fresno County, CA	179,085
Sacramento County, CA	169,784
El Paso County, TX	158,722
Alameda County, CA	156,804
Tarrant County, TX	150,488
Clark County, NV	145,855
Baltimore Independent City, MD	143,514
King County, WA	142,546
Shelby County, TN	140,398
Milwaukee County, WI	139,747
Allegheny County, PA	139,505
Kern County, CA	130,949
Orleans Parish, LA	130,896
Suffolk County, MA	124,918
Santa Clara County, CA	124,470
Fulton County, GA	124,241
Hillsborough County, FL	122,872
Franklin County, OH	121,843
Pima County, AZ	120,778
Essex County, NJ	120,006
Erie County, NY	112,358
Palm Beach County, FL	110,430
Cameron County, TX	109,288
Orange County, FL	106,233
Travis County, TX	99,388
Oklahoma County, OK	98,145
Hamilton County, OH	97,692
San Joaquin County, CA	97,105
Marion County, IN	95,827
Jefferson County, AL	95,674
Hudson County, NJ	93,149
Middlesex County, MA	92,705
Providence County, RI	92,164
Duval County, FL	90,828
Hennepin County, MN	90,384
Pinellas County, FL	90,059
San Francisco County, CA	86,585
Tulare County, CA	86,572
Jefferson County, KY	84,143
Honolulu County, HI	83,937
Saint Louis Independent City, MO	83,388
Suffolk County, NY	83,171
Multnomah County, OR	81,711
Monroe County, NY	79,311
Westchester County, NY	78,967
Denver County, CO	77,813
Hartford County, CT	77,440
Jackson County, MO	76,808
New Haven County, CT	75,733
Bernalillo County, NM	74,987
Mobile County, AL	72,549
Contra Costa County, CA	71,575
Pierce County, WA	71,316
East Baton Rouge Parish, LA	71,276
Davidson County, TN	70,960

Place	Number
New York, NY (city)	1,668,938
Los Angeles, CA (city) Los Angeles County	801,050
Chicago, IL (city) Cook County	556,791
Houston, TX (city) Harris County	369,045
Philadelphia, PA (city) Philadelphia County	336,177
Detroit, MI (city) Wayne County	243,153
Dallas, TX (city) Dallas County	207,493
Phoenix, AZ (city) Maricopa County	205,320
San Antonio, TX (city) Bexar County	193,731
San Diego, CA (city) San Diego County	172,527
New Orleans, LA (city) Orleans Parish	130,896
Memphis, TN (city) Shelby County	130,009
El Paso, TX (city) El Paso County	124,281
Milwaukee, WI (city) Milwaukee County	123,664
Cleveland, OH (city) Cuyahoga County	122,479
Fresno, CA (city) Fresno County	109,703
Boston, MA (city) Suffolk County	109,128
Long Beach, CA (city) Los Angeles County	103,434
Columbus, OH (city) Franklin County	102,723
Miami, FL (city) Miami-Dade County	100,405
Atlanta, GA (city) Fulton County	95,743
Austin, TX (city) Travis County	92,011
Indianapolis, IN (sp. city) Marion County	90,560
Jacksonville, FL (city) Duval County	87,691
San Francisco, CA (city) San Francisco County	86,585
Tucson, AZ (city) Pima County	86,532
St. Louis, MO (city) Saint Louis Independent City	83,388
Fort Worth, TX (city) Tarrant County	82,953
Sacramento, CA (city) Sacramento County	79,737
Oklahoma City, OK (city) Oklahoma County	79,084
San Jose, CA (city) Santa Clara County	77,893
Denver, CO (city) Denver County	77,813
Oakland, CA (city) Alameda County	76,489
Buffalo, NY (city) Erie County	75,120
Newark, NJ (city) Essex County	74,263
Cincinnati, OH (city) Hamilton County	69,722
Nashville-Davidson, TN (sp. city) Davidson County	69,247
Portland, OR (city) Multnomah County	67,481
Santa Ana, CA (city) Orange County	65,268
Seattle, WA (city) King County	64,068
Pittsburgh, PA (city) Allegheny County	63,866
Minneapolis, MN (city) Hennepin County	62,092
Kansas City, MO (city) Jackson County	61,958
Albuquerque, NM (city) Bernalillo County	59,641
Birmingham, AL (city) Jefferson County	58,339
Stockton, CA (city) San Joaquin County	56,783
Charlotte, NC (city) Mecklenburg County	56,330
Las Vegas, NV (city) Clark County	56,053
Toledo, OH (city) Lucas County	54,903
Rochester, NY (city) Monroe County	54,713
Tulsa, OK (city) Tulsa County	54,121
Louisville, KY (city) Jefferson County	53,799
Tampa, FL (city) Hillsborough County	53,425
Baton Rouge, LA (city) East Baton Rouge Parish	51,824
Laredo, TX (city) Webb County	51,493
Brownsville, TX (city) Cameron County	49,701
San Bernardino, CA (city) San Bernardino County	49,691
Corpus Christi, TX (city) Nueces County	47,842
Providence, RI (city) Providence County	46,688
Anaheim, CA (city) Orange County	45,615
Shreveport, LA (city) Caddo Parish	44,505
Jersey City, NJ (city) Hudson County	44,075
Bakersfield, CA (city) Kern County	43,781
St. Paul, MN (city) Ramsey County	43,266
Omaha, NE (city) Douglas County	43,037
Hempstead, NY (town) Nassau County	42,958
Honolulu, HI (cdp) Honolulu County	42,706
Jackson, MS (city) Hinds County	41,775
Hialeah, FL (city) Miami-Dade County	41,537
Mobile, AL (city) Mobile County	40,864
Riverside, CA (city) Riverside County	39,060
Wichita, KS (city) Sedgwick County	38,018
Syracuse, NY (city) Onondaga County	37,485
Akron, OH (city) Summit County	36,975
Augusta-Richmond Co., GA (sp. city) Richmond Co.	36,605

Notes: Please refer to the User's Guide for an explanation of data; ranking tables include all places with Asian and/or NHPI populations above SF4 population thresholds; (1) tables reflect only those areas that meet SF4 population thresholds, therefore there may be less than 50 states, 75 counties or 75 places listed

Poverty Status

Total Population with Income Below Poverty Level

All States, Top 75 Counties, and Top 75 Places Sorted by Percent[1]

State	Percent
District of Columbia	20.22
Mississippi	19.93
Louisiana	19.64
New Mexico	18.44
West Virginia	17.90
Alabama	16.10
Arkansas	15.84
Kentucky	15.82
Texas	15.37
Oklahoma	14.72
Montana	14.61
New York	14.59
California	14.22
South Carolina	14.11
Arizona	13.91
Tennessee	13.48
South Dakota	13.18
Georgia	12.99
Florida	12.51
United States	12.38
North Carolina	12.28
Rhode Island	11.94
North Dakota	11.86
Idaho	11.77
Missouri	11.74
Oregon	11.61
Wyoming	11.42
Pennsylvania	10.98
Maine	10.92
Hawaii	10.70
Illinois	10.68
Washington	10.62
Ohio	10.60
Michigan	10.53
Nevada	10.48
Kansas	9.90
Nebraska	9.71
Virginia	9.59
Indiana	9.49
Vermont	9.44
Alaska	9.40
Utah	9.40
Massachusetts	9.34
Colorado	9.26
Delaware	9.21
Iowa	9.13
Wisconsin	8.66
New Jersey	8.50
Maryland	8.49
Minnesota	7.94
Connecticut	7.86
New Hampshire	6.55

County	Percent
Hidalgo County, TX	35.87
Cameron County, TX	33.05
Webb County, TX	31.17
Bronx County, NY	30.68
Harrisonburg Independent City, VA	30.11
Clarke County, GA	28.27
Oktibbeha County, MS	28.20
Orleans Parish, LA	27.94
Athens County, OH	27.35
Brazos County, TX	26.90
Lincoln Parish, LA	26.48
Charlottesville Independent City, VA	25.94
Whitman County, WA	25.59
Dona Ana County, NM	25.39
Jackson County, IL	25.22
Kings County, NY	25.07
Dougherty County, GA	24.76
Saint Louis Independent City, MO	24.57
Bulloch County, GA	24.49
Tulare County, CA	23.91
Halifax County, NC	23.90
El Paso County, TX	23.81
St. Mary Parish, LA	23.61
Iberia Parish, LA	23.55
Nacogdoches County, TX	23.32
Adair County, MO	23.31
Montgomery County, VA	23.24
Baltimore Independent City, MD	22.92
Fresno County, CA	22.89
Philadelphia County, PA	22.89
Monongalia County, WV	22.83
Robeson County, NC	22.81
Alachua County, FL	22.76
Imperial County, CA	22.58
Forrest County, MS	22.46
Vermilion Parish, LA	22.11
Aleutians East Borough, AK	21.83
Lee County, AL	21.81
Fayette County, WV	21.66
Merced County, CA	21.66
St. Martin Parish, LA	21.55
Richmond Independent City, VA	21.36
Madera County, CA	21.35
Okanogan County, WA	21.34
Chaves County, NM	21.27
Lafayette County, MS	21.26
Caddo Parish, LA	21.11
Albany County, WY	21.00
Putnam County, FL	20.87
Yuba County, CA	20.79
Kern County, CA	20.76
Ouachita Parish, LA	20.68
Bethel Census Area, AK	20.61
Riley County, KS	20.56
Rapides Parish, LA	20.54
Jefferson County, AR	20.53
Isabella County, MI	20.38
Pitt County, NC	20.34
Payne County, OK	20.25
Del Norte County, CA	20.17
New York County, NY	20.00
Hinds County, MS	19.95
Aransas County, TX	19.91
Butte County, CA	19.79
McDonough County, IL	19.78
Yakima County, WA	19.67
Kittitas County, WA	19.64
Richmond County, GA	19.56
Humboldt County, CA	19.53
Kings County, CA	19.51
Norfolk Independent City, VA	19.40
Otero County, NM	19.27
Cabell County, WV	19.23
Yuma County, AZ	19.23
Franklin County, WA	19.21

Place	Percent
Isla Vista, CA (cdp) Santa Barbara County	62.81
Athens, OH (city) Athens County	51.93
State College, PA (borough) Centre County	46.93
Pakala Village, HI (cdp) Kauai County	43.75
Oxford, OH (city) Butler County	43.66
Blacksburg, VA (town) Montgomery County	43.23
Earlimart, CA (cdp) Tulare County	41.92
Carbondale, IL (city) Jackson County	41.36
Ithaca, NY (city) Tompkins County	40.24
Terra Bella, CA (cdp) Tulare County	39.64
East Porterville, CA (cdp) Tulare County	38.63
Morgantown, WV (city) Monongalia County	38.40
West Lafayette, IN (city) Tippecanoe County	38.30
Auburn, AL (city) Lee County	38.07
Abbeville, LA (city) Vermilion Parish	37.66
Linda, CA (cdp) Yuba County	37.55
Pullman, WA (city) Whitman County	37.53
College Station, TX (city) Brazos County	37.39
Mount Pleasant, MI (city) Isabella County	37.19
New Paltz, NY (village) Ulster County	36.93
Richgrove, CA (cdp) Tulare County	36.92
Houghton, MI (city) Houghton County	36.90
Makaha Valley, HI (cdp) Honolulu County	36.57
Brownsville, TX (city) Cameron County	35.97
Camden, NJ (city) Camden County	35.52
East Lansing, MI (city) Ingham County	34.85
South Oroville, CA (cdp) Butte County	34.84
San Joaquin, CA (city) Fresno County	34.59
Ellensburg, WA (city) Kittitas County	34.26
North Amherst, MA (cdp) Hampshire County	33.58
Storrs, CT (cdp) Tolland County	33.54
Clemson, SC (city) Pickens County	33.12
Oroville, CA (city) Butte County	33.06
Madera, CA (city) Madera County	32.48
Amelia, LA (cdp) Saint Mary Parish	32.47
Monroe, LA (city) Ouachita Parish	32.30
Ruston, LA (city) Lincoln Parish	32.11
Bridge City, LA (cdp) Jefferson Parish	32.00
University, FL (cdp) Hillsborough County	31.34
Poplar-Cotton Center, CA (cdp) Tulare County	31.20
Starkville, MS (city) Oktibbeha County	31.15
Cheney, WA (city) Spokane County	30.92
Orosi, CA (cdp) Tulare County	30.85
Hartford, CT (city) Hartford County	30.61
Kirksville, MO (city) Adair County	30.56
Mountain View, HI (cdp) Hawaii County	30.35
Live Oak, CA (city) Sutter County	30.23
Bloomington, IN (city) Monroe County	29.62
Laredo, TX (city) Webb County	29.58
New Iberia, LA (city) Iberia Parish	29.55
Henderson, LA (town) Saint Martin Parish	29.50
Providence, RI (city) Providence County	29.14
Macomb, IL (city) McDonough County	29.08
Monroe, NY (town) Orange County	29.06
Winton, CA (cdp) Merced County	28.82
Parkway-S. Sacramento, CA (cdp) Sacramento County	28.65
Hawaiian Beaches, HI (cdp) Hawaii County	28.56
Athens-Clarke County, GA (sp. city) Clarke County	28.55
Miami, FL (city) Miami-Dade County	28.45
Newark, NJ (city) Essex County	28.40
Bayou La Batre, AL (city) Mobile County	28.16
Delano, CA (city) Kern County	28.15
Compton, CA (city) Los Angeles County	28.05
New Orleans, LA (city) Orleans Parish	27.94
Thermalito, CA (cdp) Butte County	27.91
Merced, CA (city) Merced County	27.86
Orchidlands Estates, HI (cdp) Hawaii County	27.59
San Bernardino, CA (city) San Bernardino County	27.59
Alexandria, LA (city) Rapides Parish	27.45
Urbana, IL (city) Champaign County	27.34
Syracuse, NY (city) Onondaga County	27.31
Stillwater, OK (city) Payne County	27.27
East Los Angeles, CA (cdp) Los Angeles County	27.23
Martin, TN (city) Weakley County	27.08
Albany, GA (city) Dougherty County	27.06

Notes: Please refer to the User's Guide for an explanation of data; ranking tables include all places with Asian and/or NHPI populations above SF4 population thresholds; (1) tables reflect only those areas that meet SF4 population thresholds, therefore there may be less than 50 states, 75 counties or 75 places listed

Poverty Status

Asians with Income Below Poverty Level

All States, Top 75 Counties, and Top 75 Places Sorted by Number[1]

State	Number
United States	1,257,237
California	466,431
New York	178,217
Texas	65,048
Washington	40,409
Illinois	39,930
Massachusetts	36,588
Hawaii	35,399
Pennsylvania	34,806
New Jersey	32,475
Florida	31,860
Minnesota	25,887
Virginia	23,027
Michigan	19,125
Maryland	17,130
Georgia	17,054
Ohio	16,558
Wisconsin	16,119
Oregon	12,095
Louisiana	11,251
Arizona	11,042
North Carolina	10,912
Colorado	10,213
Indiana	8,582
Missouri	8,537
Oklahoma	7,646
Nevada	7,293
Connecticut	6,679
Tennessee	6,615
Kansas	6,392
Utah	5,415
Rhode Island	4,772
Iowa	4,755
Alabama	4,461
South Carolina	4,408
Kentucky	3,430
District of Columbia	3,098
Alaska	3,076
Mississippi	3,040
Nebraska	2,626
Arkansas	2,497
New Mexico	2,421
West Virginia	1,624
Maine	1,492
New Hampshire	1,458
Delaware	1,389
Idaho	1,153
Montana	853
Vermont	645
South Dakota	530
North Dakota	464
Wyoming	310

County	Number
Los Angeles County, CA	153,497
Queens County, NY	62,280
Kings County, NY	48,119
Orange County, CA	43,906
Alameda County, CA	32,650
New York County, NY	32,549
Santa Clara County, CA	31,820
Honolulu County, HI	29,179
Cook County, IL	28,325
San Diego County, CA	27,844
Sacramento County, CA	27,499
San Francisco County, CA	25,485
Fresno County, CA	24,436
Harris County, TX	21,880
King County, WA	21,197
Philadelphia County, PA	18,514
San Joaquin County, CA	18,271
Suffolk County, MA	13,821
Ramsey County, MN	11,954
San Bernardino County, CA	10,625
Middlesex County, MA	9,927
Hennepin County, MN	9,440
Dallas County, TX	9,417
Fairfax County, VA	8,691
Bronx County, NY	7,820
Riverside County, CA	7,700
Bergen County, NJ	7,397
Maricopa County, AZ	7,260
Contra Costa County, CA	6,823
San Mateo County, CA	6,779
Pierce County, WA	6,483
Tarrant County, TX	6,203
Travis County, TX	6,038
Yolo County, CA	5,985
Clark County, NV	5,981
Hudson County, NJ	5,852
Montgomery County, MD	5,766
Merced County, CA	5,574
Middlesex County, NJ	5,453
Franklin County, OH	5,052
Multnomah County, OR	4,597
Stanislaus County, CA	4,589
Wayne County, MI	4,423
Providence County, RI	4,327
Miami-Dade County, FL	4,192
Milwaukee County, WI	4,053
DeKalb County, GA	3,873
Broward County, FL	3,857
Snohomish County, WA	3,689
Washtenaw County, MI	3,679
Norfolk County, MA	3,656
Oklahoma County, OK	3,613
Dane County, WI	3,569
Champaign County, IL	3,455
Cuyahoga County, OH	3,398
Orange County, FL	3,323
Allegheny County, PA	3,293
Gwinnett County, GA	3,245
Butte County, CA	3,202
Kern County, CA	3,142
Solano County, CA	3,142
Worcester County, MA	3,073
Orleans Parish, LA	3,038
Tulare County, CA	3,019
Santa Barbara County, CA	2,974
Nassau County, NY	2,948
Erie County, NY	2,859
Prince George's County, MD	2,858
Hawaii County, HI	2,847
Baltimore Independent City, MD	2,842
Pima County, AZ	2,760
Ventura County, CA	2,733
Salt Lake County, UT	2,581
Ingham County, MI	2,545
Denver County, CO	2,544

Place	Number
New York, NY (city)	152,674
Los Angeles, CA (city) Los Angeles County	60,765
San Francisco, CA (city) San Francisco County	25,485
Chicago, IL (city) Cook County	22,160
San Diego, CA (city) San Diego County	21,355
Fresno, CA (city) Fresno County	21,271
Honolulu, HI (cdp) Honolulu County	20,352
San Jose, CA (city) Santa Clara County	19,964
Philadelphia, PA (city) Philadelphia County	18,514
Sacramento, CA (city) Sacramento County	16,663
Stockton, CA (city) San Joaquin County	16,113
Houston, TX (city) Harris County	15,952
Long Beach, CA (city) Los Angeles County	13,730
Oakland, CA (city) Alameda County	13,153
Boston, MA (city) Suffolk County	12,529
Seattle, WA (city) King County	11,605
St. Paul, MN (city) Ramsey County	11,455
Garden Grove, CA (city) Orange County	8,318
Minneapolis, MN (city) Hennepin County	7,469
Alhambra, CA (city) Los Angeles County	6,952
Irvine, CA (city) Orange County	6,381
Rosemead, CA (city) Los Angeles County	6,321
Westminster, CA (city) Orange County	5,967
Berkeley, CA (city) Alameda County	5,955
Monterey Park, CA (city) Los Angeles County	5,927
Austin, TX (city) Travis County	5,789
Columbus, OH (city) Franklin County	4,482
Davis, CA (city) Yolo County	4,428
Dallas, TX (city) Dallas County	4,421
Portland, OR (city) Multnomah County	4,363
El Monte, CA (city) Los Angeles County	4,283
Merced, CA (city) Merced County	4,005
Jersey City, NJ (city) Hudson County	3,902
Santa Ana, CA (city) Orange County	3,756
Riverside, CA (city) Riverside County	3,753
Tacoma, WA (city) Pierce County	3,728
Anaheim, CA (city) Orange County	3,613
Fremont, CA (city) Alameda County	3,594
Milwaukee, WI (city) Milwaukee County	3,552
San Gabriel, CA (city) Los Angeles County	3,460
Madison, WI (city) Dane County	3,338
Providence, RI (city) Providence County	3,270
Lowell, MA (city) Middlesex County	3,250
Modesto, CA (city) Stanislaus County	3,247
Parkway-S. Sacramento, CA (cdp) Sacramento County	3,183
Glendale, CA (city) Los Angeles County	3,090
Phoenix, AZ (city) Maricopa County	3,090
Rowland Heights, CA (cdp) Los Angeles County	3,070
New Orleans, LA (city) Orleans Parish	3,038
Torrance, CA (city) Los Angeles County	2,923
Arlington, TX (city) Tarrant County	2,920
Ann Arbor, MI (city) Washtenaw County	2,856
Sunnyvale, CA (city) Santa Clara County	2,831
Oklahoma City, OK (city) Oklahoma County	2,830
Fullerton, CA (city) Orange County	2,565
Hayward, CA (city) Alameda County	2,558
Daly City, CA (city) San Mateo County	2,549
Denver, CO (city) Denver County	2,544
Arlington, VA (cdp) Arlington County	2,512
Detroit, MI (city) Wayne County	2,473
Santa Clara, CA (city) Santa Clara County	2,413
Pittsburgh, PA (city) Allegheny County	2,409
Tucson, AZ (city) Pima County	2,380
Arcadia, CA (city) Los Angeles County	2,348
Wichita, KS (city) Sedgwick County	2,260
San Bernardino, CA (city) San Bernardino County	2,215
Hacienda Heights, CA (cdp) Los Angeles County	2,210
Worcester, MA (city) Worcester County	2,114
San Antonio, TX (city) Bexar County	2,033
West Covina, CA (city) Los Angeles County	2,010
Pomona, CA (city) Los Angeles County	1,972
Pasadena, CA (city) Los Angeles County	1,946
Las Vegas, NV (city) Clark County	1,912
Fort Worth, TX (city) Tarrant County	1,877
Tempe, AZ (city) Maricopa County	1,874

Notes: Please refer to the User's Guide for an explanation of data; ranking tables include all places with Asian and/or NHPI populations above SF4 population thresholds; (1) tables reflect only those areas that meet SF4 population thresholds, therefore there may be less than 50 states, 75 counties or 75 places listed

Poverty Status

Asians with Income Below Poverty Level

All States, Top 75 Counties, and Top 75 Places Sorted by Percent[1]

State	Percent
District of Columbia	22.78
Rhode Island	21.75
Louisiana	20.75
Montana	20.32
Wisconsin	19.84
Maine	19.07
Minnesota	18.96
West Virginia	18.15
Mississippi	17.86
Oklahoma	17.45
New York	17.42
Pennsylvania	16.73
Massachusetts	16.18
Indiana	15.81
Alabama	15.33
Utah	15.03
Kansas	14.62
Vermont	14.56
Missouri	14.53
North Dakota	14.49
Iowa	14.18
New Mexico	13.53
Arkansas	13.49
Nebraska	12.84
California	12.83
Washington	12.83
Ohio	12.79
Tennessee	12.60
United States	12.60
Oregon	12.50
South Carolina	12.50
Kentucky	12.45
Arizona	12.31
Alaska	12.19
Florida	12.19
South Dakota	11.99
Texas	11.87
Michigan	11.20
Colorado	11.15
Wyoming	11.01
Idaho	10.58
Georgia	10.18
North Carolina	10.12
New Hampshire	9.88
Illinois	9.66
Virginia	9.15
Delaware	8.78
Connecticut	8.38
Maryland	8.29
Nevada	8.28
Hawaii	7.13
New Jersey	6.82

County	Percent
Craighead County, AR	64.07
Forrest County, MS	61.77
Dunn County, WI	60.34
Siskiyou County, CA	58.11
Adair County, MO	57.79
Del Norte County, CA	54.04
Whitman County, WA	51.07
Glenn County, CA	50.79
Butte County, CA	50.02
Delaware County, IN	49.40
Jackson County, IL	48.98
Chisago County, MN	48.85
Montgomery County, VA	48.38
Monroe County, IN	47.91
McDonough County, IL	47.09
Athens County, OH	46.79
Matagorda County, TX	46.62
Aransas County, TX	45.75
Payne County, OK	43.64
Jessamine County, KY	43.53
Charlottesville Independent City, VA	43.34
Yolo County, CA	41.70
Tompkins County, NY	41.60
Chippewa County, WI	41.47
Aleutians East Borough, AK	41.18
Humboldt County, CA	40.95
Kittitas County, WA	40.63
Weakley County, TN	40.47
Oktibbeha County, MS	40.23
Pickens County, SC	39.39
Merced County, CA	38.77
Fresno County, CA	38.55
Benton County, OR	38.38
DeKalb County, IL	38.31
Tippecanoe County, IN	38.10
Lyon County, KS	37.50
Isabella County, MI	36.71
Harrison County, WV	36.49
Vermilion Parish, LA	36.28
Carroll County, GA	36.18
Yuba County, CA	36.17
Centre County, PA	36.02
Champaign County, IL	35.84
Monongalia County, WV	35.69
Johnson County, MO	35.32
Brazos County, TX	35.28
Blue Earth County, MN	35.12
Crow Wing County, MN	34.40
Story County, IA	34.39
Alachua County, FL	33.67
Putnam County, TN	33.53
Lincoln Parish, LA	33.46
Phelps County, MO	33.38
Clay County, MN	33.02
Utah County, UT	33.02
Lyon County, MN	32.95
Cache County, UT	32.61
Tuscaloosa County, AL	32.43
Shasta County, CA	32.31
McLennan County, TX	32.29
Ohio County, WV	32.13
Grant County, WI	32.08
Broome County, NY	32.04
Jasper County, MO	31.94
Vigo County, IN	31.86
Columbia County, NY	31.43
Sullivan County, NY	31.41
Columbia County, PA	31.32
Livingston County, NY	31.24
Lane County, OR	31.11
Albany County, WY	30.73
Clarke County, GA	30.73
Lawrence County, PA	30.72
Marathon County, WI	30.60
Suffolk County, MA	30.38

Place	Percent
Menomonie, WI (city) Dunn County	84.85
Cheney, WA (city) Spokane County	84.56
Oroville, CA (city) Butte County	77.15
South Oroville, CA (cdp) Butte County	76.61
Wheatland, CA (city) Yuba County	75.94
Thermalito, CA (cdp) Butte County	74.76
East Porterville, CA (cdp) Tulare County	72.92
Isla Vista, CA (cdp) Santa Barbara County	72.10
Clemson, SC (city) Pickens County	66.39
New Paltz, NY (village) Ulster County	62.85
Ithaca, NY (city) Tompkins County	62.34
Kirksville, MO (city) Adair County	59.64
Muncie, IN (city) Delaware County	59.26
Morgantown, WV (city) Monongalia County	59.06
Bridge City, LA (cdp) Jefferson Parish	57.10
Willows, CA (city) Glenn County	56.83
Merced, CA (city) Merced County	56.82
Carbondale, IL (city) Jackson County	56.64
Bloomington, IN (city) Monroe County	55.08
Athens, OH (city) Athens County	54.23
Macomb, IL (city) McDonough County	54.09
Ellensburg, WA (city) Kittitas County	54.00
Pullman, WA (city) Whitman County	53.96
Blacksburg, VA (town) Montgomery County	53.04
Terre Haute, IN (city) Vigo County	52.54
Oxford, OH (city) Butler County	52.39
Abbeville, LA (city) Vermilion Parish	49.56
State College, PA (borough) Centre County	49.20
Palacios, TX (city) Matagorda County	48.94
Davis, CA (city) Yolo County	48.29
West Lafayette, IN (city) Tippecanoe County	48.28
Waco, TX (city) McLennan County	48.20
Parkway-S. Sacramento, CA (cdp) Sacramento County	47.44
Binghamton, NY (city) Broome County	47.38
West Sacramento, CA (city) Yolo County	46.82
Warrensburg, MO (city) Johnson County	46.61
San Luis Obispo, CA (city) San Luis Obispo County	46.15
Eureka, CA (city) Humboldt County	46.04
Ypsilanti, MI (city) Washtenaw County	45.98
Kalamazoo, MI (city) Kalamazoo County	45.59
Denton, TX (city) Denton County	45.42
Storrs, CT (cdp) Tolland County	45.34
DeKalb, IL (city) De Kalb County	44.95
Martin, TN (city) Weakley County	44.80
Henderson, LA (town) Saint Martin Parish	44.72
Stillwater, OK (city) Payne County	44.68
Urbana, IL (city) Champaign County	44.52
Provo, UT (city) Utah County	44.50
Chico, CA (city) Butte County	44.42
Fresno, CA (city) Fresno County	44.18
New Paltz, NY (town) Ulster County	44.13
Kent, OH (city) Portage County	44.09
Linda, CA (cdp) Yuba County	43.96
Fall River, MA (city) Bristol County	43.85
Oronoko charter, MI (township) Berrien County	43.74
Cookeville, TN (city) Putnam County	43.73
Winona, MN (city) Winona County	42.22
Fairborn, OH (city) Greene County	42.16
Troy, NY (city) Rensselaer County	42.01
Corvallis, OR (city) Benton County	41.77
Revere, MA (city) Suffolk County	41.65
Starkville, MS (city) Oktibbeha County	41.48
Mount Pleasant, MI (city) Isabella County	41.25
Berkeley, CA (city) Alameda County	40.00
Huntington, WV (city) Cabell County	39.50
Bryan, TX (city) Brazos County	39.24
Portland, ME (city) Cumberland County	38.97
Banning, CA (city) Riverside County	38.79
Eugene, OR (city) Lane County	38.61
Edmond, OK (city) Oklahoma County	38.56
Ocala, FL (city) Marion County	37.93
Seadrift, TX (city) Calhoun County	37.86
Gainesville, FL (city) Alachua County	37.84
Missoula, MT (city) Missoula County	37.79
East Lansing, MI (city) Ingham County	37.70

Notes: Please refer to the User's Guide for an explanation of data; ranking tables include all places with Asian and/or NHPI populations above SF4 population thresholds; (1) tables reflect only those areas that meet SF4 population thresholds, therefore there may be less than 50 states, 75 counties or 75 places listed

Poverty Status

Native Hawaiian and Other Pacific Islanders with Income Below Poverty Level

All States, Top 75 Counties, and Top 75 Places Sorted by Number[1]

State	Number
United States	64,558
Hawaii	23,609
California	17,484
Washington	3,266
Utah	2,190
New York	1,951
Texas	1,931
Oregon	1,350
Florida	1,131
Arizona	966
Nevada	908
Pennsylvania	667
Georgia	574
Alaska	539
Colorado	537
North Carolina	491
Arkansas	482
Ohio	464
Illinois	456
Missouri	428
New Jersey	422
Massachusetts	395
Michigan	392
Louisiana	312
Virginia	304
Oklahoma	293
Tennessee	293
Idaho	242
South Carolina	212
Kentucky	193
Alabama	191
Connecticut	187
Indiana	183
Minnesota	180
Rhode Island	171
Iowa	170
Wisconsin	159
Kansas	154
New Mexico	144
Nebraska	76
Montana	60
Maryland	57
Mississippi	53
West Virginia	52
Maine	18
Delaware	13

County	Number
Honolulu County, HI	15,959
Los Angeles County, CA	6,177
Hawaii County, HI	4,200
Maui County, HI	2,499
Salt Lake County, UT	1,458
San Diego County, CA	1,398
Sacramento County, CA	1,379
King County, WA	1,302
San Bernardino County, CA	1,053
San Francisco County, CA	944
Kauai County, HI	907
Orange County, CA	907
Alameda County, CA	837
San Mateo County, CA	788
Pierce County, WA	734
Maricopa County, AZ	566
Clark County, NV	549
Stanislaus County, CA	519
Bronx County, NY	456
Tarrant County, TX	446
Utah County, UT	423
Riverside County, CA	419
Santa Clara County, CA	394
Kings County, NY	345
Multnomah County, OR	339
Solano County, CA	335
Washoe County, NV	333
Dallas County, TX	319
Washington County, OR	298
Contra Costa County, CA	291
Washington County, AR	290
Kitsap County, WA	279
Cook County, IL	275
San Joaquin County, CA	259
Anchorage Borough, AK	233
Marion County, OR	224
Philadelphia County, PA	224
Monterey County, CA	215
New York County, NY	193
Fresno County, CA	190
Bexar County, TX	188
Queens County, NY	180
Pima County, AZ	177
Ventura County, CA	176
Jackson County, MO	163
Harris County, TX	161
Lane County, OR	149
Yolo County, CA	145
Travis County, TX	144
Spokane County, WA	141
Orange County, FL	136
Nassau County, NY	134
Allegheny County, PA	122
Cumberland County, NC	120
El Paso County, CO	118
Wayne County, MI	118
Kern County, CA	116
Thurston County, WA	115
Clark County, WA	107
Washington County, UT	101
Davidson County, TN	94
Clackamas County, OR	93
Davis County, UT	93
Suffolk County, NY	92
Miami-Dade County, FL	85
Franklin County, OH	82
Sonoma County, CA	82
Palm Beach County, FL	81
Hennepin County, MN	80
Snohomish County, WA	80
Bell County, TX	78
El Paso County, TX	78
St. Louis County, MO	77
Broward County, FL	66
Shelby County, TN	64

Place	Number
Honolulu, HI (cdp) Honolulu County	6,422
Long Beach, CA (city) Los Angeles County	1,918
Hilo, HI (cdp) Hawaii County	1,701
Waipahu, HI (cdp) Honolulu County	1,530
New York, NY (city)	1,231
Los Angeles, CA (city) Los Angeles County	1,189
Sacramento, CA (city) Sacramento County	978
San Francisco, CA (city) San Francisco County	944
Nanakuli, HI (cdp) Honolulu County	800
San Diego, CA (city) San Diego County	738
Waianae, HI (cdp) Honolulu County	710
Wahiawa, HI (cdp) Honolulu County	660
Salt Lake City, UT (city) Salt Lake County	641
Seattle, WA (city) King County	626
Compton, CA (city) Los Angeles County	551
Maili, HI (cdp) Honolulu County	525
Kaneohe, HI (cdp) Honolulu County	482
Kahului, HI (cdp) Maui County	443
West Valley City, UT (city) Salt Lake County	436
Oakland, CA (city) Alameda County	416
Modesto, CA (city) Stanislaus County	392
Hauula, HI (cdp) Honolulu County	367
Halawa, HI (cdp) Honolulu County	362
Laie, HI (cdp) Honolulu County	336
Tacoma, WA (city) Pierce County	310
Hawaiian Paradise Park, HI (cdp) Hawaii County	303
Ewa Beach, HI (cdp) Honolulu County	300
Portland, OR (city) Multnomah County	286
Springdale, AR (city) Washington County	277
Chicago, IL (city) Cook County	269
Makaha, HI (cdp) Honolulu County	267
San Jose, CA (city) Santa Clara County	262
Phoenix, AZ (city) Maricopa County	260
Kaunakakai, HI (cdp) Maui County	256
Ontario, CA (city) San Bernardino County	248
Las Vegas, NV (city) Clark County	247
Wailuku, HI (cdp) Maui County	245
Dallas, TX (city) Dallas County	244
Garden Grove, CA (city) Orange County	237
Philadelphia, PA (city) Philadelphia County	224
Pearl City, HI (cdp) Honolulu County	223
Hawaiian Beaches, HI (cdp) Hawaii County	214
Waimanalo Beach, HI (cdp) Honolulu County	211
Reno, NV (city) Washoe County	209
Orem, UT (city) Utah County	203
Waihee-Waiehu, HI (cdp) Maui County	198
Federal Way, WA (city) King County	196
Kapaa, HI (cdp) Kauai County	195
Anahola, HI (cdp) Kauai County	184
Waimalu, HI (cdp) Honolulu County	179
Provo, UT (city) Utah County	177
Anaheim, CA (city) Orange County	174
Fairfield, CA (city) Solano County	167
Kailua, HI (cdp) Honolulu County	159
Stockton, CA (city) San Joaquin County	157
Kihei, HI (cdp) Maui County	153
East Palo Alto, CA (city) San Mateo County	151
Houston, TX (city) Harris County	151
Riverside, CA (city) Riverside County	151
Hawthorne, CA (city) Los Angeles County	150
Kailua, HI (cdp) Hawaii County	147
Fort Worth, TX (city) Tarrant County	144
San Mateo, CA (city) San Mateo County	144
Vallejo, CA (city) Solano County	144
Kualapuu, HI (cdp) Maui County	143
Kalaoa, HI (cdp) Hawaii County	140
Kahuku, HI (cdp) Honolulu County	139
Carson, CA (city) Los Angeles County	138
Makaha Valley, HI (cdp) Honolulu County	137
San Bernardino, CA (city) San Bernardino County	134
San Antonio, TX (city) Bexar County	129
Salem, OR (city) Marion County	127
Oceanside, CA (city) San Diego County	123
Napili-Honokowai, HI (cdp) Maui County	119
Lakewood, WA (city) Pierce County	118

Notes: Please refer to the User's Guide for an explanation of data; ranking tables include all places with Asian and/or NHPI populations above SF4 population thresholds; (1) tables reflect only those areas that meet SF4 population thresholds, therefore there may be less than 50 states, 75 counties or 75 places listed

Poverty Status

Native Hawaiian and Other Pacific Islanders with Income Below Poverty Level

All States, Top 75 Counties, and Top 75 Places Sorted by Percent[1]

State	Percent
Rhode Island	43.18
Arkansas	33.71
New York	25.89
Louisiana	25.76
Massachusetts	25.27
Hawaii	21.42
Idaho	20.42
Pennsylvania	19.83
Iowa	19.47
Ohio	18.82
Oregon	18.15
Oklahoma	18.09
Kentucky	17.97
United States	17.69
Alaska	17.60
Florida	17.56
Alabama	17.19
New Jersey	17.15
Texas	16.81
Michigan	16.60
Georgia	16.20
Arizona	16.06
Connecticut	15.97
South Carolina	15.95
California	15.70
Utah	15.55
Washington	15.48
North Carolina	15.09
Tennessee	14.92
Missouri	14.65
Montana	14.56
Colorado	13.50
West Virginia	13.47
Kansas	13.43
Illinois	13.33
Nebraska	13.15
Minnesota	12.53
New Mexico	11.92
Nevada	11.74
Indiana	11.71
Wisconsin	11.51
Virginia	9.17
Mississippi	8.31
Maine	6.43
Delaware	5.26
Maryland	2.93

County	Percent
Bronx County, NY	44.06
Washington County, AR	38.36
New York County, NY	34.04
Nassau County, NY	33.42
Dallas County, TX	33.26
Davidson County, TN	32.87
Philadelphia County, PA	31.37
Marion County, OR	29.59
Fresno County, CA	29.55
Stanislaus County, CA	28.85
Cumberland County, NC	27.33
Tarrant County, TX	27.10
San Francisco County, CA	27.02
Hawaii County, HI	26.41
Wayne County, MI	26.16
Lane County, OR	25.91
Utah County, UT	24.32
Suffolk County, NY	24.15
Franklin County, OH	23.23
Los Angeles County, CA	23.16
Spokane County, WA	22.67
Washoe County, NV	22.50
Kings County, NY	22.49
Sacramento County, CA	22.16
Washington County, UT	21.86
Travis County, TX	21.82
San Bernardino County, CA	21.78
Washington County, OR	21.41
Honolulu County, HI	21.19
Yolo County, CA	20.28
Allegheny County, PA	20.20
Palm Beach County, FL	19.90
St. Louis County, MO	18.97
Bexar County, TX	18.63
Maui County, HI	18.36
Jackson County, MO	17.74
Cook County, IL	17.46
Kauai County, HI	17.18
Kitsap County, WA	16.88
Pima County, AZ	16.57
Orange County, FL	16.52
King County, WA	16.04
Clackamas County, OR	15.53
Kern County, CA	15.16
Maricopa County, AZ	15.12
El Paso County, TX	15.00
Pierce County, WA	14.87
San Joaquin County, CA	14.73
Miami-Dade County, FL	14.60
Jefferson County, CO	14.46
Salt Lake County, UT	14.28
Hennepin County, MN	14.06
Multnomah County, OR	13.87
Queens County, NY	13.51
Shelby County, TN	13.33
Milwaukee County, WI	13.17
Muscogee County, GA	12.79
Essex County, NJ	12.39
Monterey County, CA	11.98
Anchorage Borough, AK	11.66
Sedgwick County, KS	11.60
Riverside County, CA	11.53
Sonoma County, CA	11.10
Solano County, CA	11.02
Ventura County, CA	10.82
Harris County, TX	10.79
Orange County, CA	10.75
San Diego County, CA	10.64
Broward County, FL	10.33
Davis County, UT	10.26
Coryell County, TX	10.11
Ada County, ID	9.93
El Paso County, CO	9.87
Thurston County, WA	9.85
Duval County, FL	9.77

Place	Percent
Compton, CA (city) Los Angeles County	53.60
Pakala Village, HI (cdp) Kauai County	47.80
Makaha Valley, HI (cdp) Honolulu County	47.08
Ontario, CA (city) San Bernardino County	45.59
Hawaiian Beaches, HI (cdp) Hawaii County	42.54
Hawaiian Paradise Park, HI (cdp) Hawaii County	40.45
Springdale, AR (city) Washington County	39.91
Dallas, TX (city) Dallas County	39.17
Naalehu, HI (cdp) Hawaii County	39.17
Waipahu, HI (cdp) Honolulu County	38.61
Wahiawa, HI (cdp) Honolulu County	38.06
Long Beach, CA (city) Los Angeles County	37.98
Pahala, HI (cdp) Hawaii County	37.35
Whitmore Village, HI (cdp) Honolulu County	36.75
Hilo, HI (cdp) Hawaii County	35.09
Nashville-Davidson, TN (sp. city) Davidson County	34.69
Salem, OR (city) Marion County	33.25
Waialua, HI (cdp) Honolulu County	32.96
Kaunakakai, HI (cdp) Maui County	32.69
Modesto, CA (city) Stanislaus County	32.21
Philadelphia, PA (city) Philadelphia County	31.37
Maili, HI (cdp) Honolulu County	30.97
Honalo, HI (cdp) Hawaii County	29.76
Orem, UT (city) Utah County	29.00
Provo, UT (city) Utah County	28.97
Pahoa, HI (cdp) Hawaii County	28.21
Kaaawa, HI (cdp) Honolulu County	27.65
Hawthorne, CA (city) Los Angeles County	27.47
Punaluu, HI (cdp) Honolulu County	27.27
San Francisco, CA (city) San Francisco County	27.02
Sacramento, CA (city) Sacramento County	26.71
New York, NY (city)	26.31
Papaikou, HI (cdp) Hawaii County	26.28
Fort Worth, TX (city) Tarrant County	25.95
Waikane, HI (cdp) Honolulu County	25.66
Chicago, IL (city) Cook County	25.64
Waianae, HI (cdp) Honolulu County	25.64
Honolulu, HI (cdp) Honolulu County	25.59
Seattle, WA (city) King County	25.34
Hauula, HI (cdp) Honolulu County	25.19
Kahului, HI (cdp) Maui County	25.16
Tacoma, WA (city) Pierce County	24.16
Halawa, HI (cdp) Honolulu County	23.94
Spokane, WA (city) Spokane County	23.57
Hawaiian Ocean View, HI (cdp) Hawaii County	22.94
Kahuku, HI (cdp) Honolulu County	22.90
West Covina, CA (city) Los Angeles County	22.69
Richmond, CA (city) Contra Costa County	22.34
Reno, NV (city) Washoe County	22.31
Laie, HI (cdp) Honolulu County	22.08
Federal Way, WA (city) King County	21.90
Kapaa, HI (cdp) Kauai County	21.33
Lawndale, CA (city) Los Angeles County	21.17
Salinas, CA (city) Monterey County	20.90
Ewa Beach, HI (cdp) Honolulu County	20.70
St. George, UT (city) Washington County	20.33
Napili-Honokowai, HI (cdp) Maui County	20.24
Nanakuli, HI (cdp) Honolulu County	19.87
Salt Lake City, UT (city) Salt Lake County	19.37
Westminster, CA (city) Orange County	19.31
Waimea, HI (cdp) Kauai County	19.02
Los Angeles, CA (city) Los Angeles County	19.01
San Bernardino, CA (city) San Bernardino County	18.90
San Antonio, TX (city) Bexar County	18.86
Kalaoa, HI (cdp) Hawaii County	18.84
Garden Grove, CA (city) Orange County	18.79
Vista, CA (city) San Diego County	18.64
Waihee-Waiehu, HI (cdp) Maui County	18.57
Pittsburg, CA (city) Contra Costa County	18.41
Anahola, HI (cdp) Kauai County	18.29
Wailuku, HI (cdp) Maui County	18.22
Des Moines, WA (city) King County	18.21
Costa Mesa, CA (city) Orange County	17.94
Captain Cook, HI (cdp) Hawaii County	17.63
Makaha, HI (cdp) Honolulu County	17.61

Notes: Please refer to the User's Guide for an explanation of data; ranking tables include all places with Asian and/or NHPI populations above SF4 population thresholds; (1) tables reflect only those areas that meet SF4 population thresholds, therefore there may be less than 50 states, 75 counties or 75 places listed

Poverty Status

Asian Indians with Income Below Poverty Level

All States, Top 75 Counties, and Top 75 Places Sorted by Number[1]

State	Number
United States	157,516
New York	34,347
California	27,139
Texas	12,846
New Jersey	10,291
Illinois	9,167
Florida	8,515
Pennsylvania	5,306
Michigan	4,168
Virginia	3,881
Maryland	3,786
Massachusetts	3,715
Ohio	3,539
Georgia	3,488
Washington	1,961
North Carolina	1,906
Arizona	1,749
Connecticut	1,500
Louisiana	1,491
Wisconsin	1,428
South Carolina	1,363
Indiana	1,316
Missouri	1,316
Minnesota	1,240
Tennessee	1,177
Oklahoma	1,159
Colorado	1,148
Kansas	1,121
Alabama	740
Oregon	738
Kentucky	654
District of Columbia	556
Iowa	477
Rhode Island	436
Mississippi	426
Nebraska	415
Delaware	398
New Mexico	363
Nevada	360
West Virginia	339
Utah	307
New Hampshire	263
Arkansas	243
Hawaii	147
Montana	125
North Dakota	121
South Dakota	94
Maine	88
Idaho	82
Vermont	36
Wyoming	33
Alaska	12

County	Number
Queens County, NY	16,427
Kings County, NY	6,817
Los Angeles County, CA	6,331
Cook County, IL	6,161
Harris County, TX	4,049
Santa Clara County, CA	3,901
Bronx County, NY	3,055
Alameda County, CA	2,744
Middlesex County, NJ	2,533
Hudson County, NJ	2,530
Philadelphia County, PA	2,152
Dallas County, TX	2,019
New York County, NY	1,823
Orange County, CA	1,565
Wayne County, MI	1,496
Travis County, TX	1,419
Sacramento County, CA	1,363
Fairfax County, VA	1,361
Miami-Dade County, FL	1,340
Broward County, FL	1,333
Middlesex County, MA	1,331
Montgomery County, MD	1,311
Fresno County, CA	1,263
San Diego County, CA	1,161
Maricopa County, AZ	1,123
King County, WA	1,110
Tarrant County, TX	1,105
Franklin County, OH	1,023
Passaic County, NJ	1,015
DuPage County, IL	984
Orange County, FL	969
Sutter County, CA	939
Nassau County, NY	866
Suffolk County, MA	864
DeKalb County, GA	834
Cuyahoga County, OH	829
Suffolk County, NY	805
Bergen County, NJ	802
Westchester County, NY	767
Champaign County, IL	756
San Mateo County, CA	735
San Bernardino County, CA	734
Contra Costa County, CA	731
Baltimore Independent City, MD	723
Prince George's County, MD	662
Alachua County, FL	660
Essex County, NJ	660
Gwinnett County, GA	656
Riverside County, CA	655
San Francisco County, CA	643
Hillsborough County, FL	640
Hennepin County, MN	636
Richmond County, NY	629
Palm Beach County, FL	618
Washtenaw County, MI	607
San Joaquin County, CA	603
Brazos County, TX	588
Fort Bend County, TX	580
Yolo County, CA	579
Allegheny County, PA	571
Oakland County, MI	568
Milwaukee County, WI	544
Arlington County, VA	514
Shelby County, TN	511
Oklahoma County, OK	480
Worcester County, MA	480
Fulton County, GA	477
Kern County, CA	470
Mercer County, NJ	470
Fairfield County, CT	453
Bucks County, PA	446
Hartford County, CT	441
New Haven County, CT	441
Atlantic County, NJ	431
Pima County, AZ	431

Place	Number
New York, NY (city)	28,751
Chicago, IL (city) Cook County	4,344
Los Angeles, CA (city) Los Angeles County	3,695
Houston, TX (city) Harris County	2,643
Philadelphia, PA (city) Philadelphia County	2,152
Jersey City, NJ (city) Hudson County	1,466
San Jose, CA (city) Santa Clara County	1,384
Austin, TX (city) Travis County	1,321
San Diego, CA (city) San Diego County	970
Columbus, OH (city) Franklin County	948
Sacramento, CA (city) Sacramento County	871
Fremont, CA (city) Alameda County	867
Sunnyvale, CA (city) Santa Clara County	859
Boston, MA (city) Suffolk County	807
Fresno, CA (city) Fresno County	795
Detroit, MI (city) Wayne County	782
Edison, NJ (township) Middlesex County	748
Dallas, TX (city) Dallas County	726
Santa Clara, CA (city) Santa Clara County	703
Berkeley, CA (city) Alameda County	677
San Francisco, CA (city) San Francisco County	643
Arlington, VA (cdp) Arlington County	514
Paterson, NJ (city) Passaic County	499
Ann Arbor, MI (city) Washtenaw County	493
Hempstead, NY (town) Nassau County	469
Cleveland, OH (city) Cuyahoga County	463
Arlington, TX (city) Tarrant County	454
Hayward, CA (city) Alameda County	449
Phoenix, AZ (city) Maricopa County	429
Tucson, AZ (city) Pima County	422
Oklahoma City, OK (city) Oklahoma County	421
Irving, TX (city) Dallas County	411
Wichita, KS (city) Sedgwick County	411
San Antonio, TX (city) Bexar County	403
Riverside, CA (city) Riverside County	402
Tempe, AZ (city) Maricopa County	398
Woodbridge, NJ (township) Middlesex County	396
Minneapolis, MN (city) Hennepin County	390
Fort Worth, TX (city) Tarrant County	389
Richardson, TX (city) Dallas County	384
Seattle, WA (city) King County	379
Denver, CO (city) Denver County	372
Islip, NY (town) Suffolk County	372
Milwaukee, WI (city) Milwaukee County	368
Gainesville, FL (city) Alachua County	362
College Station, TX (city) Brazos County	359
Urbana, IL (city) Champaign County	359
Champaign, IL (city) Champaign County	358
Irvine, CA (city) Orange County	355
Yonkers, NY (city) Westchester County	353
New Orleans, LA (city) Orleans Parish	333
State College, PA (borough) Centre County	333
Bakersfield, CA (city) Kern County	330
Baton Rouge, LA (city) East Baton Rouge Parish	330
Atlanta, GA (city) Fulton County	328
Cincinnati, OH (city) Hamilton County	327
Silver Spring, MD (cdp) Montgomery County	325
Pittsburgh, PA (city) Allegheny County	323
Memphis, TN (city) Shelby County	322
Livingston, CA (city) Merced County	308
Davis, CA (city) Yolo County	307
West Lafayette, IN (city) Tippecanoe County	300
Stockton, CA (city) San Joaquin County	297
Madison, WI (city) Dane County	295
Cambridge, MA (city) Middlesex County	291
New Brunswick, NJ (city) Middlesex County	280
Worcester, MA (city) Worcester County	278
Blacksburg, VA (town) Montgomery County	273
Long Beach, CA (city) Los Angeles County	272
North Bergen, NJ (township) Hudson County	266
Yuba City, CA (city) Sutter County	266
Columbia, SC (city) Richland County	265
Milpitas, CA (city) Santa Clara County	262
Lowell, MA (city) Middlesex County	260
Lexington-Fayette, KY (sp. city) Fayette County	258

Notes: Please refer to the User's Guide for an explanation of data; ranking tables include all places with Asian and/or NHPI populations above SF4 population thresholds; (1) tables reflect only those areas that meet SF4 population thresholds, therefore there may be less than 50 states, 75 counties or 75 places listed

Poverty Status

Asian Indians with Income Below Poverty Level

All States, Top 75 Counties, and Top 75 Places Sorted by Percent[1]

State	Percent
Montana	28.15
District of Columbia	24.16
Rhode Island	18.83
Louisiana	17.92
South Carolina	17.04
South Dakota	16.55
New Mexico	15.43
Kansas	14.86
Oklahoma	14.27
New York	13.99
West Virginia	13.69
Nebraska	13.58
Mississippi	13.49
Wisconsin	12.95
Florida	12.72
Hawaii	12.64
Arizona	12.21
North Dakota	11.94
Missouri	11.40
Alabama	11.29
Texas	10.21
Kentucky	10.19
Tennessee	10.19
Utah	9.95
Colorado	9.82
Indiana	9.81
Pennsylvania	9.79
Maine	9.78
United States	9.75
Ohio	9.57
Massachusetts	9.37
Arkansas	9.23
Iowa	9.19
California	8.94
Washington	8.79
Virginia	8.30
Georgia	8.07
Wyoming	7.80
Michigan	7.77
Minnesota	7.76
North Carolina	7.74
Maryland	7.69
Delaware	7.67
Illinois	7.59
New Hampshire	7.56
Oregon	7.47
Nevada	7.45
Idaho	7.40
Connecticut	6.40
New Jersey	6.14
Vermont	5.61
Alaska	2.21

County	Percent
Charlottesville Independent City, VA	61.49
Pickens County, SC	59.14
Montgomery County, VA	54.06
Mobile County, AL	43.06
Butte County, CA	41.67
Monroe County, IN	39.18
Alachua County, FL	37.39
Champaign County, IL	36.86
Baltimore Independent City, MD	36.78
DeKalb County, IL	36.75
Brazos County, TX	36.59
Yolo County, CA	35.37
Lubbock County, TX	34.68
Tippecanoe County, IN	32.20
Sedgwick County, KS	31.76
Monongalia County, WV	31.52
Centre County, PA	31.33
Lafayette Parish, LA	31.29
Norfolk Independent City, VA	31.28
Richmond Independent City, VA	30.97
Orleans Parish, LA	30.75
Rensselaer County, NY	29.35
Niagara County, NY	29.23
Osceola County, FL	28.16
Orange County, NC	28.05
Kings County, NY	27.64
Plymouth County, MA	26.94
Berkshire County, MA	25.79
Erie County, PA	24.08
Saint Louis Independent City, MO	24.00
Tompkins County, NY	23.79
Monroe County, PA	23.57
Cleveland County, OK	23.52
Phelps County, MO	23.40
Tulare County, CA	23.23
Suffolk County, MA	23.10
Broome County, NY	23.03
Hinds County, MS	22.51
Pima County, AZ	22.46
Fayette County, KY	22.26
Douglas County, KS	22.09
El Paso County, TX	21.97
Whatcom County, WA	21.77
Harford County, MD	21.57
Volusia County, FL	21.50
Bronx County, NY	20.89
Santa Barbara County, CA	20.80
Madera County, CA	20.37
Providence County, RI	20.10
Richland County, SC	19.77
Kalamazoo County, MI	19.59
Outagamie County, WI	19.57
Lucas County, OH	19.42
Lake County, OH	19.29
Merced County, CA	18.74
McLennan County, TX	18.55
Bernalillo County, NM	18.54
Philadelphia County, PA	18.52
East Baton Rouge Parish, LA	18.43
Denver County, CO	18.37
Fresno County, CA	18.27
Jackson County, MO	18.24
San Luis Obispo County, CA	18.10
Greenville County, SC	17.90
Travis County, TX	17.55
Ingham County, MI	17.29
Lexington County, SC	17.28
Clarke County, GA	17.17
Story County, IA	16.98
Oklahoma County, OK	16.85
Brown County, WI	16.72
Eaton County, MI	16.62
Marion County, FL	15.81
Miami-Dade County, FL	15.52
Rockingham County, NH	15.48

Place	Percent
Blacksburg, VA (town) Montgomery County	59.74
Lynn, MA (city) Essex County	52.28
State College, PA (borough) Centre County	51.95
Bloomington, IN (city) Monroe County	50.69
Mobile, AL (city) Mobile County	49.29
Kalamazoo, MI (city) Kalamazoo County	49.17
Urbana, IL (city) Champaign County	47.36
Ithaca, NY (city) Tompkins County	45.62
Columbia, SC (city) Richland County	45.53
El Cerrito, CA (city) Contra Costa County	44.53
North Miami Beach, FL (city) Miami-Dade County	44.19
DeKalb, IL (city) De Kalb County	44.12
Cleveland, OH (city) Cuyahoga County	43.84
Davis, CA (city) Yolo County	43.24
College Park, MD (city) Prince George's County	42.07
Gainesville, FL (city) Alachua County	41.51
North Druid Hills, GA (cdp) De Kalb County	41.04
Berkeley, CA (city) Alameda County	40.56
West Lafayette, IN (city) Tippecanoe County	39.68
Brentwood, NY (cdp) Suffolk County	38.39
Stanford, CA (cdp) Santa Clara County	37.16
Lafayette, LA (city) Lafayette Parish	37.07
Henrietta, NY (town) Monroe County	37.00
Denton, TX (city) Denton County	36.66
Bellingham, WA (city) Whatcom County	36.07
Champaign, IL (city) Champaign County	35.94
Lubbock, TX (city) Lubbock County	34.67
Baton Rouge, LA (city) East Baton Rouge Parish	34.66
Buffalo, NY (city) Erie County	34.32
Chapel Hill, NC (town) Orange County	33.55
Tucson, AZ (city) Pima County	33.25
Wichita, KS (city) Sedgwick County	33.09
East Lake, FL (cdp) Pinellas County	32.55
West Sacramento, CA (city) Yolo County	31.91
Paterson, NJ (city) Passaic County	31.84
College Station, TX (city) Brazos County	31.41
Louisville, KY (city) Jefferson County	31.07
New Orleans, LA (city) Orleans Parish	30.75
New Brunswick, NJ (city) Middlesex County	30.50
Knoxville, TN (city) Knox County	30.06
Toledo, OH (city) Lucas County	30.00
Norman, OK (city) Cleveland County	29.59
East Lansing, MI (city) Ingham County	29.45
Riverside, CA (city) Riverside County	28.98
Syracuse, NY (city) Onondaga County	28.48
San Bernardino, CA (city) San Bernardino County	28.34
West Haven, CT (city) New Haven County	28.30
Akron, OH (city) Summit County	28.02
Albany, NY (city) Albany County	27.89
Worcester, MA (city) Worcester County	27.77
Lodi, CA (city) San Joaquin County	27.08
Fort Lauderdale, FL (city) Broward County	26.78
Woodland, CA (city) Yolo County	26.60
Providence, RI (city) Providence County	26.07
Kearny, NJ (town) Hudson County	26.01
West New York, NJ (town) Hudson County	25.91
Lakewood, CA (city) Los Angeles County	25.75
Livingston, CA (city) Merced County	24.74
Miami, FL (city) Miami-Dade County	24.33
Savannah, GA (city) Chatham County	24.33
Cleveland Heights, OH (city) Cuyahoga County	24.23
St. Louis, MO (city) Saint Louis Independent City	24.00
Hawthorne, CA (city) Los Angeles County	23.91
Des Moines, IA (city) Polk County	23.81
Detroit, MI (city) Wayne County	23.81
Boston, MA (city) Suffolk County	23.47
Long Beach, CA (city) Los Angeles County	23.29
Boca Raton, FL (city) Palm Beach County	23.18
Lawrence, KS (city) Douglas County	22.98
Silver Spring, MD (cdp) Montgomery County	22.87
Madison, WI (city) Dane County	22.78
Herricks, NY (cdp) Nassau County	22.64
El Paso, TX (city) El Paso County	22.62
Lexington-Fayette, KY (sp. city) Fayette County	22.26
Galveston, TX (city) Galveston County	22.16

Notes: Please refer to the User's Guide for an explanation of data; ranking tables include all places with Asian and/or NHPI populations above SF4 population thresholds; (1) tables reflect only those areas that meet SF4 population thresholds, therefore there may be less than 50 states, 75 counties or 75 places listed

Poverty Status

Bangladeshis with Income Below Poverty Level

All States, Top 75 Counties, and Top 75 Places Sorted by Number[1]

State	Number
United States	8,734
New York	5,621
New Jersey	483
Michigan	379
Texas	367
California	330
Virginia	274
Florida	266
Pennsylvania	128
Georgia	90
Maryland	66
Connecticut	61
Illinois	60
Ohio	48
Massachusetts	12

County	Number
Queens County, NY	3,097
Kings County, NY	1,642
Bronx County, NY	633
Wayne County, MI	365
Los Angeles County, CA	277
Passaic County, NJ	165
Fairfax County, VA	139
Atlantic County, NJ	129
Harris County, TX	86
New York County, NY	75
Dallas County, TX	55
Montgomery County, MD	47
Middlesex County, NJ	44
DeKalb County, GA	34
Santa Clara County, CA	13

Place	Number
New York, NY (city)	5,447
Hamtramck, MI (city) Wayne County	273
Los Angeles, CA (city) Los Angeles County	188
Paterson, NJ (city) Passaic County	165

Notes: Please refer to the User's Guide for an explanation of data; ranking tables include all places with Asian and/or NHPI populations above SF4 population thresholds; (1) tables reflect only those areas that meet SF4 population thresholds, therefore there may be less than 50 states, 75 counties or 75 places listed

Poverty Status

Bangladeshis with Income Below Poverty Level

All States, Top 75 Counties, and Top 75 Places Sorted by Percent[1]

State	Percent
New York	28.18
Michigan	22.71
New Jersey	21.52
United States	21.29
Florida	21.25
Pennsylvania	18.29
Connecticut	17.89
Virginia	15.28
Texas	14.31
California	12.06
Illinois	7.71
Ohio	7.41
Georgia	7.16
Maryland	5.48
Massachusetts	2.23

County	Percent
Kings County, NY	42.02
Bronx County, NY	31.78
Wayne County, MI	31.77
Atlantic County, NJ	31.70
Passaic County, NJ	30.28
Queens County, NY	25.09
Los Angeles County, CA	21.10
Fairfax County, VA	15.41
Harris County, TX	12.50
Middlesex County, NJ	11.37
New York County, NY	9.95
Dallas County, TX	8.17
DeKalb County, GA	6.18
Montgomery County, MD	5.69
Santa Clara County, CA	2.69

Place	Percent
Hamtramck, MI (city) Wayne County	37.35
Paterson, NJ (city) Passaic County	35.95
New York, NY (city)	28.60
Los Angeles, CA (city) Los Angeles County	22.79

Notes: Please refer to the User's Guide for an explanation of data; ranking tables include all places with Asian and/or NHPI populations above SF4 population thresholds; (1) tables reflect only those areas that meet SF4 population thresholds, therefore there may be less than 50 states, 75 counties or 75 places listed

Poverty Status

Cambodians with Income Below Poverty Level

All States, Top 75 Counties, and Top 75 Places Sorted by Number[1]

State	Number
United States	51,240
California	28,680
Massachusetts	5,124
Washington	3,618
Pennsylvania	3,432
Rhode Island	1,729
Minnesota	1,101
Texas	793
New York	789
Georgia	568
Ohio	538
Oregon	513
Illinois	462
Maine	444
Virginia	396
Wisconsin	309
Colorado	273
Florida	247
Kansas	230
North Carolina	228
Maryland	199
Missouri	176
Iowa	167
Alabama	147
New Jersey	140
Michigan	130
Tennessee	125
Connecticut	100
Arizona	86
Utah	86
Nevada	52
Indiana	51
Hawaii	47
Oklahoma	29
South Carolina	0

County	Number
Los Angeles County, CA	11,755
San Joaquin County, CA	5,627
Philadelphia County, PA	3,188
Middlesex County, MA	2,457
Fresno County, CA	2,066
San Diego County, CA	1,959
Stanislaus County, CA	1,725
Providence County, RI	1,709
King County, WA	1,559
Alameda County, CA	1,542
Pierce County, WA	1,292
Essex County, MA	854
Bristol County, MA	849
Santa Clara County, CA	808
San Bernardino County, CA	737
Orange County, CA	718
Suffolk County, MA	604
Sacramento County, CA	456
Hennepin County, MN	390
Cook County, IL	375
Cumberland County, ME	370
Bronx County, NY	345
Ramsey County, MN	335
Franklin County, OH	320
Multnomah County, OR	294
Thurston County, WA	279
Dallas County, TX	263
Harris County, TX	253
Gwinnett County, GA	248
Sonoma County, CA	227
Cowlitz County, WA	218
Olmsted County, MN	204
Kern County, CA	195
Hampden County, MA	191
Snohomish County, WA	179
San Francisco County, CA	173
DeKalb County, GA	172
Sedgwick County, KS	148
Kings County, NY	128
Denver County, CO	126
Riverside County, CA	126
Camden County, NJ	120
Montgomery County, MD	110
Polk County, IA	108
Cuyahoga County, OH	105
Ottawa County, MI	101
Monroe County, NY	99
Pinellas County, FL	98
Mobile County, AL	95
Brazoria County, TX	89
Maricopa County, AZ	86
Arlington County, VA	83
Hamilton County, OH	79
Davidson County, NC	75
Washington County, OR	72
Fairfax County, VA	71
Duval County, FL	69
Shelby County, TN	69
Mecklenburg County, NC	66
Fairfield County, CT	60
Clark County, NV	52
Tarrant County, TX	48
Clayton County, GA	42
Clark County, WA	36
Chesterfield County, VA	34
Dakota County, MN	28
Salt Lake County, UT	28
Worcester County, MA	27
Denton County, TX	4
Henrico County, VA	0
Scott County, MN	0

Place	Number
Long Beach, CA (city) Los Angeles County	8,326
Stockton, CA (city) San Joaquin County	5,484
Philadelphia, PA (city) Philadelphia County	3,188
Lowell, MA (city) Middlesex County	2,353
San Diego, CA (city) San Diego County	1,951
Fresno, CA (city) Fresno County	1,843
Providence, RI (city) Providence County	1,480
Los Angeles, CA (city) Los Angeles County	1,462
Oakland, CA (city) Alameda County	1,398
Modesto, CA (city) Stanislaus County	1,363
Tacoma, WA (city) Pierce County	1,144
Seattle, WA (city) King County	1,016
Lynn, MA (city) Essex County	780
San Jose, CA (city) Santa Clara County	719
Fall River, MA (city) Bristol County	717
New York, NY (city)	495
Revere, MA (city) Suffolk County	381
Chicago, IL (city) Cook County	375
Pomona, CA (city) Los Angeles County	372
Portland, ME (city) Cumberland County	370
Santa Ana, CA (city) Orange County	357
Signal Hill, CA (city) Los Angeles County	354
St. Paul, MN (city) Ramsey County	328
Portland, OR (city) Multnomah County	294
Columbus, OH (city) Franklin County	291
White Center, WA (cdp) King County	245
San Bernardino, CA (city) San Bernardino County	225
Rochester, MN (city) Olmsted County	199
Dallas, TX (city) Dallas County	196
San Francisco, CA (city) San Francisco County	173
Sacramento, CA (city) Sacramento County	172
Santa Rosa, CA (city) Sonoma County	166
Bellflower, CA (city) Los Angeles County	165
Bloomington, MN (city) Hennepin County	157
Rosemead, CA (city) Los Angeles County	149
Boston, MA (city) Suffolk County	145
Lakewood, CA (city) Los Angeles County	144
Minneapolis, MN (city) Hennepin County	136
Everett, WA (city) Snohomish County	129
Denver, CO (city) Denver County	126
Longview, WA (city) Cowlitz County	122
Houston, TX (city) Harris County	115
Garden Grove, CA (city) Orange County	93
Attleboro, MA (city) Bristol County	91
Monterey Park, CA (city) Los Angeles County	89
Arlington, VA (cdp) Arlington County	83
St. Petersburg, FL (city) Pinellas County	81
Lexington, NC (city) Davidson County	75
Lawrence, MA (city) Essex County	74
Jacksonville, FL (city) Duval County	69
Memphis, TN (city) Shelby County	69
Aurora, CO (city) Arapahoe County	61
Charlotte, NC (city) Mecklenburg County	61
Cranston, RI (city) Providence County	39
Carrollton, TX (city) Denton County	29
Beaverton, OR (city) Washington County	28
Phoenix, AZ (city) Maricopa County	28
Silver Spring, MD (cdp) Montgomery County	25
West Valley City, UT (city) Salt Lake County	24
Bridgeport, CT (city) Fairfield County	16
Danbury, CT (city) Fairfield County	12
Norwalk, CA (city) Los Angeles County	0

Notes: Please refer to the User's Guide for an explanation of data; ranking tables include all places with Asian and/or NHPI populations above SF4 population thresholds; (1) tables reflect only those areas that meet SF4 population thresholds, therefore there may be less than 50 states, 75 counties or 75 places listed

Poverty Status

Cambodians with Income Below Poverty Level

***All States, Top 75 Counties, and Top 75 Places Sorted by Percent*[1]**

State	Percent
Wisconsin	50.00
Maine	45.08
California	40.77
Pennsylvania	39.91
Rhode Island	36.02
Kansas	32.86
United States	29.28
New York	27.69
Alabama	26.44
Massachusetts	25.62
Washington	24.72
Hawaii	23.62
Iowa	22.03
Minnesota	21.81
New Jersey	21.71
Ohio	20.72
Missouri	20.25
Oregon	18.90
Colorado	18.71
Georgia	16.49
Illinois	13.82
Maryland	11.69
Tennessee	10.81
Texas	10.62
North Carolina	9.85
Oklahoma	9.45
Florida	9.13
Indiana	9.06
Michigan	8.23
Virginia	8.11
Nevada	7.27
Arizona	7.00
Utah	6.25
Connecticut	4.67
South Carolina	0.00

County	Percent
Cowlitz County, WA	61.58
San Joaquin County, CA	59.80
Cumberland County, ME	57.36
Stanislaus County, CA	53.82
Fresno County, CA	52.76
Philadelphia County, PA	50.17
San Diego County, CA	46.94
Kern County, CA	45.24
San Bernardino County, CA	43.12
Bronx County, NY	42.80
Hampden County, MA	42.73
Sacramento County, CA	41.08
Alameda County, CA	40.01
Bristol County, MA	39.60
Los Angeles County, CA	39.32
Camden County, NJ	38.34
Providence County, RI	37.14
Suffolk County, MA	35.57
Thurston County, WA	33.33
Sedgwick County, KS	32.60
Pierce County, WA	31.97
Denver County, CO	31.66
Ramsey County, MN	30.82
Olmsted County, MN	28.37
DeKalb County, GA	28.20
Multnomah County, OR	28.19
Gwinnett County, GA	27.83
Sonoma County, CA	26.90
San Francisco County, CA	26.78
Kings County, NY	26.02
Monroe County, NY	25.98
Polk County, IA	25.78
Brazoria County, TX	24.45
Franklin County, OH	24.45
Mobile County, AL	24.42
King County, WA	23.77
Arlington County, VA	23.51
Essex County, MA	22.79
Middlesex County, MA	22.69
Hamilton County, OH	22.51
Hennepin County, MN	22.18
Riverside County, CA	21.95
Cuyahoga County, OH	21.69
Santa Clara County, CA	18.94
Cook County, IL	17.36
Orange County, CA	16.44
Davidson County, NC	14.51
Pinellas County, FL	14.16
Shelby County, TN	13.37
Harris County, TX	12.57
Dallas County, TX	11.34
Montgomery County, MD	9.52
Ottawa County, MI	9.40
Snohomish County, WA	9.00
Mecklenburg County, NC	8.60
Clark County, WA	8.43
Worcester County, MA	8.08
Clark County, NV	7.48
Maricopa County, AZ	7.29
Duval County, FL	6.93
Washington County, OR	6.52
Dakota County, MN	6.21
Tarrant County, TX	6.18
Chesterfield County, VA	5.16
Fairfield County, CT	4.16
Clayton County, GA	4.01
Fairfax County, VA	3.87
Salt Lake County, UT	2.69
Denton County, TX	0.55
Henrico County, VA	0.00
Scott County, MN	0.00

Place	Percent
Portland, ME (city) Cumberland County	64.12
Stockton, CA (city) San Joaquin County	60.52
Fall River, MA (city) Bristol County	57.22
Modesto, CA (city) Stanislaus County	54.13
Fresno, CA (city) Fresno County	51.28
San Bernardino, CA (city) San Bernardino County	51.25
San Diego, CA (city) San Diego County	51.01
Philadelphia, PA (city) Philadelphia County	50.17
Longview, WA (city) Cowlitz County	49.39
Pomona, CA (city) Los Angeles County	49.14
Oakland, CA (city) Alameda County	48.01
Long Beach, CA (city) Los Angeles County	47.15
Revere, MA (city) Suffolk County	47.04
Signal Hill, CA (city) Los Angeles County	45.33
Providence, RI (city) Providence County	42.26
Seattle, WA (city) King County	40.77
Tacoma, WA (city) Pierce County	36.29
Sacramento, CA (city) Sacramento County	36.13
St. Paul, MN (city) Ramsey County	35.81
Rochester, MN (city) Olmsted County	35.79
Los Angeles, CA (city) Los Angeles County	35.37
Bloomington, MN (city) Hennepin County	32.11
Denver, CO (city) Denver County	31.66
Bellflower, CA (city) Los Angeles County	30.90
New York, NY (city)	30.82
Portland, OR (city) Multnomah County	28.97
Minneapolis, MN (city) Hennepin County	27.59
San Francisco, CA (city) San Francisco County	26.78
Lynn, MA (city) Essex County	26.01
Santa Rosa, CA (city) Sonoma County	25.70
Lowell, MA (city) Middlesex County	24.81
Columbus, OH (city) Franklin County	24.41
Boston, MA (city) Suffolk County	23.93
Arlington, VA (cdp) Arlington County	23.51
Monterey Park, CA (city) Los Angeles County	21.55
Santa Ana, CA (city) Orange County	21.05
White Center, WA (cdp) King County	20.66
Everett, WA (city) Snohomish County	20.51
Chicago, IL (city) Cook County	20.34
Lakewood, CA (city) Los Angeles County	19.67
Rosemead, CA (city) Los Angeles County	19.23
Lexington, NC (city) Davidson County	19.08
Dallas, TX (city) Dallas County	18.99
Garden Grove, CA (city) Orange County	18.60
San Jose, CA (city) Santa Clara County	18.55
St. Petersburg, FL (city) Pinellas County	16.53
Lawrence, MA (city) Essex County	16.48
Houston, TX (city) Harris County	15.91
Memphis, TN (city) Shelby County	15.20
Aurora, CO (city) Arapahoe County	13.83
Attleboro, MA (city) Bristol County	13.15
Charlotte, NC (city) Mecklenburg County	8.70
Beaverton, OR (city) Washington County	7.84
Silver Spring, MD (cdp) Montgomery County	7.67
Jacksonville, FL (city) Duval County	6.93
Cranston, RI (city) Providence County	5.60
Phoenix, AZ (city) Maricopa County	5.13
West Valley City, UT (city) Salt Lake County	4.03
Carrollton, TX (city) Denton County	3.55
Bridgeport, CT (city) Fairfield County	3.08
Danbury, CT (city) Fairfield County	2.10
Norwalk, CA (city) Los Angeles County	0.00

Notes: Please refer to the User's Guide for an explanation of data; ranking tables include all places with Asian and/or NHPI populations above SF4 population thresholds; (1) tables reflect only those areas that meet SF4 population thresholds, therefore there may be less than 50 states, 75 counties or 75 places listed

Poverty Status

Chinese (except Taiwanese) with Income Below Poverty Level

All States, Top 75 Counties, and Top 75 Places Sorted by Number[1]

State	Number
United States	303,054
California	103,787
New York	86,256
Texas	11,844
Massachusetts	9,954
Illinois	9,302
Pennsylvania	8,579
Florida	6,167
New Jersey	5,753
Washington	5,474
Hawaii	5,061
Ohio	3,940
Maryland	3,711
Michigan	3,296
Virginia	2,935
Georgia	2,742
Arizona	2,723
Oregon	2,315
Indiana	2,182
Missouri	2,028
North Carolina	1,957
Oklahoma	1,754
Connecticut	1,742
Colorado	1,566
Minnesota	1,466
Wisconsin	1,383
Utah	1,196
Tennessee	1,185
Louisiana	1,177
South Carolina	1,045
Kansas	1,007
District of Columbia	984
Iowa	980
Nevada	948
Alabama	930
Rhode Island	725
Kentucky	645
Arkansas	569
Nebraska	539
Mississippi	479
New Hampshire	450
Delaware	405
West Virginia	377
New Mexico	314
Idaho	260
Maine	242
Vermont	189
Montana	133
South Dakota	130
North Dakota	89
Alaska	79
Wyoming	60

County	Number
Los Angeles County, CA	42,464
Kings County, NY	31,160
New York County, NY	23,460
Queens County, NY	22,120
San Francisco County, CA	15,271
Alameda County, CA	12,625
Santa Clara County, CA	6,928
Cook County, IL	6,878
Philadelphia County, PA	5,181
Orange County, CA	5,120
Suffolk County, MA	5,010
Honolulu County, HI	4,772
Sacramento County, CA	4,666
Harris County, TX	4,381
King County, WA	3,604
San Diego County, CA	2,966
San Mateo County, CA	2,534
Middlesex County, MA	2,368
Yolo County, CA	2,151
Maricopa County, AZ	1,864
Miami-Dade County, FL	1,432
Contra Costa County, CA	1,425
Norfolk County, MA	1,408
Travis County, TX	1,406
San Bernardino County, CA	1,321
Montgomery County, MD	1,311
Riverside County, CA	1,265
Bronx County, NY	1,237
Dallas County, TX	1,225
Middlesex County, NJ	1,216
Broward County, FL	1,123
Bergen County, NJ	1,082
Washtenaw County, MI	1,046
Franklin County, OH	1,006
Champaign County, IL	987
Cuyahoga County, OH	983
Tompkins County, NY	976
Multnomah County, OR	926
Nassau County, NY	925
Fairfax County, VA	902
Fresno County, CA	896
Tarrant County, TX	888
Allegheny County, PA	872
Hudson County, NJ	858
Suffolk County, NY	846
Oklahoma County, OK	802
Erie County, NY	771
Pima County, AZ	763
Dane County, WI	725
Hennepin County, MN	723
Tippecanoe County, IN	713
Clark County, NV	694
Baltimore Independent City, MD	688
Fort Bend County, TX	677
San Joaquin County, CA	652
Richmond County, NY	651
Alachua County, FL	624
Collin County, TX	616
Santa Barbara County, CA	615
Monroe County, NY	608
Prince George's County, MD	593
DeKalb County, GA	569
St. Louis County, MO	568
Providence County, RI	566
Delaware County, PA	562
New Haven County, CT	516
Westchester County, NY	501
Fulton County, GA	487
Salt Lake County, UT	487
Bexar County, TX	481
Oakland County, MI	479
Fairfield County, CT	477
Monmouth County, NJ	477
Snohomish County, WA	474
Centre County, PA	469

Place	Number
New York, NY (city)	78,628
San Francisco, CA (city) San Francisco County	15,271
Los Angeles, CA (city) Los Angeles County	12,181
Chicago, IL (city) Cook County	5,965
Oakland, CA (city) Alameda County	5,787
Philadelphia, PA (city) Philadelphia County	5,181
Boston, MA (city) Suffolk County	4,868
Honolulu, HI (cdp) Honolulu County	4,198
Alhambra, CA (city) Los Angeles County	4,157
Monterey Park, CA (city) Los Angeles County	3,966
Rosemead, CA (city) Los Angeles County	3,879
Houston, TX (city) Harris County	3,589
San Jose, CA (city) Santa Clara County	3,419
Sacramento, CA (city) Sacramento County	3,077
Berkeley, CA (city) Alameda County	2,596
San Diego, CA (city) San Diego County	2,528
Seattle, WA (city) King County	2,427
San Gabriel, CA (city) Los Angeles County	2,121
Davis, CA (city) Yolo County	2,081
El Monte, CA (city) Los Angeles County	1,943
Irvine, CA (city) Orange County	1,803
Rowland Heights, CA (cdp) Los Angeles County	1,677
Austin, TX (city) Travis County	1,430
Fremont, CA (city) Alameda County	1,385
Arcadia, CA (city) Los Angeles County	1,344
Riverside, CA (city) Riverside County	943
Temple City, CA (city) Los Angeles County	929
Portland, OR (city) Multnomah County	922
Hacienda Heights, CA (cdp) Los Angeles County	900
Fresno, CA (city) Fresno County	851
Columbus, OH (city) Franklin County	843
Ann Arbor, MI (city) Washtenaw County	836
Quincy, MA (city) Norfolk County	796
West Covina, CA (city) Los Angeles County	789
Ithaca, NY (city) Tompkins County	748
Sunnyvale, CA (city) Santa Clara County	738
Madison, WI (city) Dane County	725
Tucson, AZ (city) Pima County	721
Cupertino, CA (city) Santa Clara County	686
Pasadena, CA (city) Los Angeles County	671
Phoenix, AZ (city) Maricopa County	645
Daly City, CA (city) San Mateo County	635
Pittsburgh, PA (city) Allegheny County	622
Dallas, TX (city) Dallas County	609
Alameda, CA (city) Alameda County	598
Cambridge, MA (city) Middlesex County	581
Urbana, IL (city) Champaign County	566
Walnut, CA (city) Los Angeles County	544
Stockton, CA (city) San Joaquin County	542
Arlington, TX (city) Tarrant County	538
Tempe, AZ (city) Maricopa County	523
Long Beach, CA (city) Los Angeles County	520
Minneapolis, MN (city) Hennepin County	518
San Leandro, CA (city) Alameda County	509
Brookhaven, NY (town) Suffolk County	480
East San Gabriel, CA (cdp) Los Angeles County	475
Pomona, CA (city) Los Angeles County	465
Gainesville, FL (city) Alachua County	462
Plano, TX (city) Collin County	458
Fullerton, CA (city) Orange County	454
San Antonio, TX (city) Bexar County	450
Cleveland, OH (city) Cuyahoga County	448
Upper Darby, PA (township) Delaware County	426
San Mateo, CA (city) San Mateo County	425
Oklahoma City, OK (city) Oklahoma County	418
Baldwin Park, CA (city) Los Angeles County	413
Anaheim, CA (city) Orange County	412
Jersey City, NJ (city) Hudson County	410
West Lafayette, IN (city) Tippecanoe County	410
Malden, MA (city) Middlesex County	406
State College, PA (borough) Centre County	406
North Hempstead, NY (town) Nassau County	404
Champaign, IL (city) Champaign County	401
Buffalo, NY (city) Erie County	399
Isla Vista, CA (cdp) Santa Barbara County	397

Notes: Please refer to the User's Guide for an explanation of data; ranking tables include all places with Asian and/or NHPI populations above SF4 population thresholds; (1) tables reflect only those areas that meet SF4 population thresholds, therefore there may be less than 50 states, 75 counties or 75 places listed

Poverty Status

Chinese (except Taiwanese) with Income Below Poverty Level

All States, Top 75 Counties, and Top 75 Places Sorted by Percent[1]

State	Percent
Oklahoma	27.20
District of Columbia	26.42
West Virginia	23.29
South Dakota	21.42
North Dakota	21.39
New York	21.07
Montana	20.62
Arkansas	20.21
Indiana	19.88
Nebraska	19.61
Pennsylvania	18.69
Mississippi	18.65
Iowa	18.37
Rhode Island	17.87
Louisiana	17.83
South Carolina	17.28
Vermont	17.18
Utah	16.96
Alabama	16.90
Missouri	16.31
Maine	15.45
Idaho	15.07
Wisconsin	14.89
Tennessee	14.82
Kansas	14.70
Ohio	14.53
Florida	13.86
United States	13.43
Arizona	13.18
Kentucky	13.05
Illinois	13.00
Massachusetts	12.74
Oregon	12.69
Texas	12.23
New Hampshire	12.08
Michigan	11.57
North Carolina	11.54
California	11.52
Georgia	11.03
Colorado	10.64
Delaware	10.12
Minnesota	10.08
Wyoming	10.00
Washington	9.73
Connecticut	9.64
Hawaii	9.18
Virginia	8.74
New Mexico	7.97
Maryland	7.96
Nevada	7.04
New Jersey	6.18
Alaska	5.17

County	Percent
Jackson County, IL	52.74
Broome County, NY	48.30
Monroe County, IN	45.34
Rensselaer County, NY	43.82
Clayton County, GA	43.73
Tompkins County, NY	43.38
Yolo County, CA	42.04
San Luis Obispo County, CA	42.02
Cache County, UT	40.43
Payne County, OK	40.00
Whitman County, WA	39.80
Tippecanoe County, IN	37.85
Story County, IA	37.40
Washington County, AR	37.38
Lexington County, SC	37.14
Oklahoma County, OK	36.89
Greene County, OH	36.56
Greene County, MO	36.47
Monongalia County, WV	34.44
Champaign County, IL	34.35
Benton County, OR	34.29
Baltimore Independent City, MD	33.32
Utah County, UT	32.11
Saint Louis Independent City, MO	31.99
Lane County, OR	31.25
Centre County, PA	31.18
Alachua County, FL	31.04
Philadelphia County, PA	30.89
Charlottesville Independent City, VA	29.68
New York County, NY	27.97
Erie County, NY	27.56
Pickens County, SC	27.53
Douglas County, KS	27.38
Cleveland County, OK	27.23
Montgomery County, VA	27.03
Onondaga County, NY	26.81
Lancaster County, NE	26.68
Boone County, MO	26.42
Suffolk County, MA	26.17
Kings County, NY	25.87
Kalamazoo County, MI	25.86
Butte County, CA	25.76
Dona Ana County, NM	25.69
Santa Barbara County, CA	25.49
Ulster County, NY	25.30
Sangamon County, IL	25.00
Chittenden County, VT	24.54
Brazos County, TX	24.46
Sarasota County, FL	24.41
Jefferson County, TX	24.28
Dane County, WI	24.01
Orleans Parish, LA	23.50
Clarke County, GA	23.42
Spokane County, WA	23.36
Riverside County, CA	22.84
Washington County, RI	21.96
Richmond County, GA	21.44
Lucas County, OH	20.96
Richland County, SC	20.93
Providence County, RI	20.54
Madison County, AL	20.09
Norfolk Independent City, VA	20.03
Bronx County, NY	19.98
Fayette County, KY	19.97
Schenectady County, NY	19.78
Volusia County, FL	19.72
Pasco County, FL	19.64
Jackson County, MO	19.63
East Baton Rouge Parish, LA	19.30
Tolland County, CT	19.21
Washtenaw County, MI	19.15
Chatham County, GA	19.04
Fresno County, CA	18.72
Hampshire County, MA	18.65
Orange County, NY	18.31

Place	Percent
Isla Vista, CA (cdp) Santa Barbara County	66.50
Ithaca, NY (city) Tompkins County	66.02
San Luis Obispo, CA (city) San Luis Obispo County	55.99
Troy, NY (city) Rensselaer County	55.73
Edmond, OK (city) Oklahoma County	54.23
Parkway-S. Sacramento, CA (cdp) Sacramento County	53.42
West Lafayette, IN (city) Tippecanoe County	52.50
Buffalo, NY (city) Erie County	51.75
Davis, CA (city) Yolo County	50.25
Logan, UT (city) Cache County	49.04
Bloomington, IN (city) Monroe County	49.01
Riverside, CA (city) Riverside County	47.82
Florin, CA (cdp) Sacramento County	46.80
Syracuse, NY (city) Onondaga County	46.11
Fayetteville, AR (city) Washington County	43.53
State College, PA (borough) Centre County	43.33
Henrietta, NY (town) Monroe County	42.86
Berkeley, CA (city) Alameda County	41.72
Champaign, IL (city) Champaign County	41.60
San Bernardino, CA (city) San Bernardino County	40.37
Stillwater, OK (city) Payne County	40.27
Denton, TX (city) Denton County	38.93
Ames, IA (city) Story County	38.51
University City, MO (city) Saint Louis County	38.28
New Brunswick, NJ (city) Middlesex County	37.41
Pullman, WA (city) Whitman County	36.97
Urbana, IL (city) Champaign County	36.63
Greensboro, NC (city) Guilford County	36.56
Corvallis, OR (city) Benton County	35.40
Eugene, OR (city) Lane County	35.38
Gainesville, FL (city) Alachua County	34.71
Birmingham, AL (city) Jefferson County	33.08
Norman, OK (city) Cleveland County	32.73
Provo, UT (city) Utah County	32.21
St. Louis, MO (city) Saint Louis Independent City	31.99
Miami, FL (city) Miami-Dade County	31.98
Storrs, CT (cdp) Tolland County	31.63
Albany, NY (city) Albany County	31.62
Manchester, NH (city) Hillsborough County	31.47
Philadelphia, PA (city) Philadelphia County	30.89
Stanford, CA (cdp) Santa Clara County	30.83
Rochester, NY (city) Monroe County	29.98
Louisville, KY (city) Jefferson County	29.44
Chico, CA (city) Butte County	29.34
Blacksburg, VA (town) Montgomery County	28.55
Mansfield, CT (town) Tolland County	28.48
Toledo, OH (city) Lucas County	28.17
Upper Darby, PA (township) Delaware County	28.17
Bridgeport, CT (city) Fairfield County	28.07
Tempe, AZ (city) Maricopa County	27.82
Columbia, MO (city) Boone County	27.62
Madison, WI (city) Dane County	27.51
Emeryville, CA (city) Alameda County	27.50
Milwaukee, WI (city) Milwaukee County	27.39
Lawrence, KS (city) Douglas County	27.38
Vestal, NY (town) Broome County	27.27
Providence, RI (city) Providence County	27.14
Lincoln, NE (city) Lancaster County	27.00
Pomona, CA (city) Los Angeles County	26.66
East Lansing, MI (city) Ingham County	26.63
Oklahoma City, OK (city) Oklahoma County	26.54
Evanston, IL (city) Cook County	26.52
Minneapolis, MN (city) Hennepin County	26.51
Rancho Cordova, CA (cdp) Sacramento County	26.19
Boston, MA (city) Suffolk County	26.12
Amherst, MA (town) Hampshire County	26.05
Rosemead, CA (city) Los Angeles County	26.00
Pittsburgh, PA (city) Allegheny County	25.54
Boulder, CO (city) Boulder County	25.25
Huntsville, AL (city) Madison County	24.78
Baton Rouge, LA (city) East Baton Rouge Parish	24.71
Lancaster, CA (city) Los Angeles County	24.34
Tucson, AZ (city) Pima County	24.33
College Station, TX (city) Brazos County	23.97
Carmichael, CA (cdp) Sacramento County	23.62

Notes: Please refer to the User's Guide for an explanation of data; ranking tables include all places with Asian and/or NHPI populations above SF4 population thresholds; (1) tables reflect only those areas that meet SF4 population thresholds, therefore there may be less than 50 states, 75 counties or 75 places listed

Poverty Status

Fijians with Income Below Poverty Level

All States, Top 75 Counties, and Top 75 Places Sorted by Number[1]

State	Number
United States	1,066
California	879
Washington	101
Oregon	39

County	Number
Sacramento County, CA	373
Alameda County, CA	119
Yolo County, CA	105
King County, WA	86
Los Angeles County, CA	85
San Mateo County, CA	72
Santa Clara County, CA	32
Contra Costa County, CA	20
Stanislaus County, CA	12

Place	Number
Sacramento, CA (city) Sacramento County	213
Hayward, CA (city) Alameda County	58
Modesto, CA (city) Stanislaus County	4

Notes: Please refer to the User's Guide for an explanation of data; ranking tables include all places with Asian and/or NHPI populations above SF4 population thresholds; (1) tables reflect only those areas that meet SF4 population thresholds, therefore there may be less than 50 states, 75 counties or 75 places listed

Poverty Status

Fijians with Income Below Poverty Level

***All States, Top 75 Counties, and Top 75 Places Sorted by Percent*[1]**

State	Percent
Washington	14.25
California	10.49
United States	10.47
Oregon	10.46

County	Percent
Sacramento County, CA	21.35
Yolo County, CA	19.96
Los Angeles County, CA	17.82
King County, WA	15.84
Alameda County, CA	8.16
Santa Clara County, CA	6.26
San Mateo County, CA	6.22
Contra Costa County, CA	3.72
Stanislaus County, CA	1.72

Place	Percent
Sacramento, CA (city) Sacramento County	17.23
Hayward, CA (city) Alameda County	6.88
Modesto, CA (city) Stanislaus County	0.81

Notes: Please refer to the User's Guide for an explanation of data; ranking tables include all places with Asian and/or NHPI populations above SF4 population thresholds; (1) tables reflect only those areas that meet SF4 population thresholds, therefore there may be less than 50 states, 75 counties or 75 places listed

Poverty Status

Filipinos with Income Below Poverty Level

All States, Top 75 Counties, and Top 75 Places Sorted by Number[1]

State	Number
United States	114,849
California	58,148
Hawaii	11,907
New York	4,292
Washington	4,083
Texas	3,720
Florida	3,518
Illinois	3,510
New Jersey	2,918
Nevada	2,600
Virginia	2,536
Arizona	1,310
Maryland	1,267
Alaska	1,178
Pennsylvania	1,138
Ohio	972
Michigan	889
Massachusetts	791
Oregon	718
North Carolina	640
Georgia	634
Missouri	545
Louisiana	544
Indiana	503
Utah	491
South Carolina	469
New Mexico	455
Colorado	428
Wisconsin	380
Oklahoma	378
Connecticut	349
Minnesota	335
Alabama	333
District of Columbia	320
Kentucky	309
Tennessee	296
Iowa	289
Kansas	246
Arkansas	215
Mississippi	189
West Virginia	147
Rhode Island	131
Idaho	125
Montana	106
Maine	99
Delaware	94
Nebraska	89
New Hampshire	76
Wyoming	47
South Dakota	38
Vermont	32
North Dakota	22

County	Number
Los Angeles County, CA	18,826
Honolulu County, HI	8,957
San Diego County, CA	6,954
Santa Clara County, CA	3,690
Orange County, CA	3,317
Alameda County, CA	3,037
San Francisco County, CA	2,952
Clark County, NV	2,396
Cook County, IL	2,378
Sacramento County, CA	1,996
San Mateo County, CA	1,946
San Joaquin County, CA	1,845
King County, WA	1,836
Solano County, CA	1,719
San Bernardino County, CA	1,701
Kern County, CA	1,661
Queens County, NY	1,601
Riverside County, CA	1,347
Contra Costa County, CA	1,307
Ventura County, CA	1,261
Hawaii County, HI	1,201
Maui County, HI	1,081
Harris County, TX	1,078
Monterey County, CA	846
Maricopa County, AZ	831
Hudson County, NJ	738
New York County, NY	736
Kauai County, HI	668
Virginia Beach Independent City, VA	668
Duval County, FL	557
Santa Barbara County, CA	544
Bergen County, NJ	543
Pierce County, WA	480
Kings County, NY	474
Philadelphia County, PA	469
Prince George's County, MD	467
Fairfax County, VA	445
Tulare County, CA	445
Anchorage Borough, AK	438
Bexar County, TX	438
Kitsap County, WA	437
Fresno County, CA	423
Yolo County, CA	417
Norfolk Independent City, VA	378
Orange County, FL	371
Suffolk County, MA	370
Snohomish County, WA	368
Dallas County, TX	364
San Luis Obispo County, CA	357
Pinellas County, FL	342
Miami-Dade County, FL	330
Essex County, NJ	293
Middlesex County, NJ	285
Aleutians East Borough, AK	273
Bronx County, NY	273
Pima County, AZ	273
Broward County, FL	231
DuPage County, IL	222
Baltimore Independent City, MD	218
Bernalillo County, NM	214
Cuyahoga County, OH	212
Travis County, TX	212
Stanislaus County, CA	206
Aleutians West Census Area, AK	205
Middlesex County, MA	205
Montgomery County, MD	201
Westchester County, NY	197
Escambia County, FL	195
Nassau County, NY	191
Multnomah County, OR	188
Champaign County, IL	185
Alachua County, FL	183
Union County, NJ	183
Salt Lake County, UT	182
Wayne County, MI	175

Place	Number
Los Angeles, CA (city) Los Angeles County	9,252
Honolulu, HI (cdp) Honolulu County	4,098
San Diego, CA (city) San Diego County	4,070
New York, NY (city)	3,207
San Francisco, CA (city) San Francisco County	2,952
San Jose, CA (city) Santa Clara County	2,526
Chicago, IL (city) Cook County	1,975
Long Beach, CA (city) Los Angeles County	1,503
Stockton, CA (city) San Joaquin County	1,488
Waipahu, HI (cdp) Honolulu County	1,279
Daly City, CA (city) San Mateo County	1,231
Delano, CA (city) Kern County	1,086
Seattle, WA (city) King County	1,030
National City, CA (city) San Diego County	1,012
Carson, CA (city) Los Angeles County	996
Vallejo, CA (city) Solano County	976
Sacramento, CA (city) Sacramento County	940
Oxnard, CA (city) Ventura County	911
Irvine, CA (city) Orange County	891
Las Vegas, NV (city) Clark County	834
Glendale, CA (city) Los Angeles County	713
Jersey City, NJ (city) Hudson County	694
Chula Vista, CA (city) San Diego County	655
Paradise, NV (cdp) Clark County	628
Oakland, CA (city) Alameda County	566
Hayward, CA (city) Alameda County	564
Jacksonville, FL (city) Duval County	543
Union City, CA (city) Alameda County	537
West Covina, CA (city) Los Angeles County	526
Riverside, CA (city) Riverside County	505
Houston, TX (city) Harris County	503
Phoenix, AZ (city) Maricopa County	475
Philadelphia, PA (city) Philadelphia County	469
Anaheim, CA (city) Orange County	459
Fairfield, CA (city) Solano County	431
Salinas, CA (city) Monterey County	430
Fremont, CA (city) Alameda County	408
Lakewood, CA (city) Los Angeles County	405
Davis, CA (city) Yolo County	402
San Antonio, TX (city) Bexar County	394
Boston, MA (city) Suffolk County	351
Alameda, CA (city) Alameda County	347
Sunrise Manor, NV (cdp) Clark County	342
Ewa Beach, HI (cdp) Honolulu County	329
Sunnyvale, CA (city) Santa Clara County	325
Fresno, CA (city) Fresno County	322
Kahului, HI (cdp) Maui County	292
Hilo, HI (cdp) Hawaii County	285
Wahiawa, HI (cdp) Honolulu County	283
Santa Clara, CA (city) Santa Clara County	274
Pearl City, HI (cdp) Honolulu County	272
Santa Ana, CA (city) Orange County	269
San Luis Obispo, CA (city) San Luis Obispo County	265
Lancaster, CA (city) Los Angeles County	264
Moreno Valley, CA (city) Riverside County	263
Torrance, CA (city) Los Angeles County	262
Berkeley, CA (city) Alameda County	258
Bellflower, CA (city) Los Angeles County	249
South San Francisco, CA (city) San Mateo County	248
Halawa, HI (cdp) Honolulu County	234
Lakewood, WA (city) Pierce County	232
Santa Maria, CA (city) Santa Barbara County	230
Bakersfield, CA (city) Kern County	229
Tucson, AZ (city) Pima County	227
Artesia, CA (city) Los Angeles County	226
Buena Park, CA (city) Orange County	226
Pomona, CA (city) Los Angeles County	225
Cerritos, CA (city) Los Angeles County	223
Victorville, CA (city) San Bernardino County	216
Ewa Villages, HI (cdp) Honolulu County	213
Bremerton, WA (city) Kitsap County	212
Milpitas, CA (city) Santa Clara County	212
Everett, WA (city) Snohomish County	206
Spring Valley, NV (cdp) Clark County	206
Unalaska, AK (city) Aleutians West Census Area	203

Notes: Please refer to the User's Guide for an explanation of data; ranking tables include all places with Asian and/or NHPI populations above SF4 population thresholds; (1) tables reflect only those areas that meet SF4 population thresholds, therefore there may be less than 50 states, 75 counties or 75 places listed

Poverty Status

Filipinos with Income Below Poverty Level

All States, Top 75 Counties, and Top 75 Places Sorted by Percent[1]

State	Percent
New Mexico	15.78
District of Columbia	15.33
Montana	14.23
Alabama	13.83
Utah	13.35
Iowa	13.00
Louisiana	11.78
Vermont	11.43
Kentucky	10.25
Arkansas	9.59
Alaska	9.52
Oklahoma	9.52
Wyoming	9.42
West Virginia	9.19
Massachusetts	8.95
Maine	8.73
Arizona	8.24
Pennsylvania	8.06
Idaho	7.97
Missouri	7.66
Mississippi	7.56
Indiana	7.50
Kansas	7.49
Ohio	7.49
Wisconsin	7.18
South Carolina	7.07
Hawaii	7.05
Oregon	6.83
Florida	6.56
North Carolina	6.50
Nevada	6.48
Rhode Island	6.48
Texas	6.47
Washington	6.40
California	6.39
Georgia	6.27
United States	6.25
New Hampshire	6.07
Minnesota	5.86
Tennessee	5.72
South Dakota	5.56
Virginia	5.41
Delaware	5.19
Michigan	5.14
New York	5.02
Maryland	4.85
Connecticut	4.79
Colorado	4.67
Nebraska	4.39
Illinois	4.13
North Dakota	3.91
New Jersey	3.33

County	Percent
Aleutians East Borough, AK	42.26
Champaign County, IL	33.39
Yolo County, CA	27.13
Suffolk County, MA	21.55
Aleutians West Census Area, AK	21.16
Bernalillo County, NM	20.34
Utah County, UT	20.05
Dane County, WI	19.58
Houston County, GA	19.09
Alachua County, FL	18.47
Leon County, FL	17.28
Cleveland County, OK	16.76
Yakima County, WA	16.48
Richland County, SC	16.11
Baltimore Independent City, MD	16.10
Kern County, CA	15.92
Richmond Independent City, VA	15.92
San Luis Obispo County, CA	15.20
Mobile County, AL	15.15
Washtenaw County, MI	15.15
Forsyth County, NC	14.60
Orleans Parish, LA	14.53
Saginaw County, MI	14.40
Davis County, UT	14.34
Portsmouth Independent City, VA	14.22
Galveston County, TX	14.04
Sandoval County, NM	13.86
Lane County, OR	13.69
Whatcom County, WA	12.95
Harrison County, MS	12.93
Philadelphia County, PA	12.82
Lee County, FL	12.49
Imperial County, CA	12.40
Yuba County, CA	12.35
Onslow County, NC	12.27
Sutter County, CA	12.17
Charleston County, SC	12.00
Pima County, AZ	11.78
East Baton Rouge Parish, LA	11.70
Santa Barbara County, CA	11.37
Newport News Independent City, VA	11.35
Pinellas County, FL	11.30
Pulaski County, AR	11.30
Spokane County, WA	10.92
Wichita County, TX	10.68
Marion County, OR	10.50
DeKalb County, GA	10.42
Jefferson Parish, LA	10.42
Salt Lake County, UT	10.29
Kent County, MI	10.13
Butte County, CA	10.09
Travis County, TX	10.00
Tulare County, CA	9.80
Kent County, DE	9.76
Bell County, TX	9.73
Summit County, OH	9.70
Butler County, OH	9.69
Cumberland County, ME	9.63
New London County, CT	9.57
Cochise County, AZ	9.45
Norfolk Independent City, VA	9.40
Hawaii County, HI	9.34
Thurston County, WA	9.26
Hampton Independent City, VA	9.17
Comanche County, OK	8.99
Sedgwick County, KS	8.99
Merced County, CA	8.93
Ingham County, MI	8.88
Hamilton County, OH	8.85
Anchorage Borough, AK	8.83
Hillsborough County, NH	8.82
San Joaquin County, CA	8.80
Bexar County, TX	8.73
Alexandria Independent City, VA	8.68
Berrien County, MI	8.63

Place	Percent
San Luis Obispo, CA (city) San Luis Obispo County	50.48
Davis, CA (city) Yolo County	39.57
Clearfield, UT (city) Davis County	31.04
Irvine, CA (city) Orange County	30.28
Ann Arbor, MI (city) Washtenaw County	26.68
Madison, WI (city) Dane County	26.48
Pupukea, HI (cdp) Honolulu County	24.68
Richgrove, CA (cdp) Tulare County	24.10
Indio, CA (city) Riverside County	23.53
Berkeley, CA (city) Alameda County	23.52
Colton, CA (city) San Bernardino County	23.09
Paramount, CA (city) Los Angeles County	22.95
Boston, MA (city) Suffolk County	21.91
Rosemont, CA (cdp) Sacramento County	21.61
Unalaska, AK (city) Aleutians West Census Area	21.57
Fair Lawn, NJ (borough) Bergen County	20.34
Terra Bella, CA (cdp) Tulare County	19.67
Delano, CA (city) Kern County	19.42
Albuquerque, NM (city) Bernalillo County	19.40
Lakewood, WA (city) Pierce County	19.08
Victorville, CA (city) San Bernardino County	18.14
Coronado, CA (city) San Diego County	17.98
Riverside, CA (city) Riverside County	17.36
Santa Cruz, CA (city) Santa Cruz County	17.35
Earlimart, CA (cdp) Tulare County	17.33
Lacey, WA (city) Thurston County	16.60
Tempe, AZ (city) Maricopa County	16.58
Naalehu, HI (cdp) Hawaii County	16.07
Groton, CT (town) New London County	16.06
Bremerton, WA (city) Kitsap County	15.81
Monterey, CA (city) Monterey County	15.78
Waimanalo, HI (cdp) Honolulu County	14.78
Hilo, HI (cdp) Hawaii County	14.55
New Orleans, LA (city) Orleans Parish	14.53
Hawaiian Beaches, HI (cdp) Hawaii County	14.52
Santa Barbara, CA (city) Santa Barbara County	14.29
North Charleston, SC (city) Charleston County	14.21
Rio Rancho, NM (city) Sandoval County	14.20
Jacksonville, NC (city) Onslow County	14.14
Marina, CA (city) Monterey County	14.07
Florin, CA (cdp) Sacramento County	13.68
Goose Creek, SC (city) Berkeley County	13.68
Tucson, AZ (city) Pima County	13.60
Upland, CA (city) San Bernardino County	13.58
Garland, TX (city) Dallas County	13.57
Killeen, TX (city) Bell County	13.55
Haleiwa, HI (cdp) Honolulu County	13.41
Inglewood, CA (city) Los Angeles County	13.39
Ellicott City, MD (cdp) Howard County	13.33
Keaau, HI (cdp) Hawaii County	13.02
Philadelphia, PA (city) Philadelphia County	12.82
Minneapolis, MN (city) Hennepin County	12.80
Lancaster, CA (city) Los Angeles County	12.79
Santa Monica, CA (city) Los Angeles County	12.64
Artesia, CA (city) Los Angeles County	12.63
Nanakuli, HI (cdp) Honolulu County	12.42
Imperial Beach, CA (city) San Diego County	12.35
Everett, WA (city) Snohomish County	12.34
North Bethesda, MD (cdp) Montgomery County	12.23
Kualapuu, HI (cdp) Maui County	12.16
Austin, TX (city) Travis County	12.06
Santa Ana, CA (city) Orange County	12.06
Cape Coral, FL (city) Lee County	11.86
San Gabriel, CA (city) Los Angeles County	11.79
Sacramento, CA (city) Sacramento County	11.69
Cincinnati, OH (city) Hamilton County	11.49
National City, CA (city) San Diego County	11.38
Kilauea, HI (cdp) Kauai County	11.30
Paradise, NV (cdp) Clark County	11.21
Wichita Falls, TX (city) Wichita County	11.18
Spokane, WA (city) Spokane County	11.16
Orlando, FL (city) Orange County	11.13
Santee, CA (city) San Diego County	11.11
Kaumakani, HI (cdp) Kauai County	11.05
Tukwila, WA (city) King County	11.04

Notes: Please refer to the User's Guide for an explanation of data; ranking tables include all places with Asian and/or NHPI populations above SF4 population thresholds; (1) tables reflect only those areas that meet SF4 population thresholds, therefore there may be less than 50 states, 75 counties or 75 places listed

Poverty Status

Guamanians or Chamorros with Income Below Poverty Level

All States, Top 75 Counties, and Top 75 Places Sorted by Number[1]

State	Number
United States	7,292
California	1,997
Washington	790
Florida	497
Texas	460
New York	389
Hawaii	319
Georgia	264
Illinois	195
Oregon	190
New Jersey	160
North Carolina	158
Arizona	151
Massachusetts	137
Colorado	133
Virginia	109
Pennsylvania	100
Louisiana	98
Michigan	91
Nevada	91
Alabama	74
Tennessee	74
South Carolina	68
Indiana	67
Kentucky	63
Ohio	60
Connecticut	49
Missouri	38
Wisconsin	32
New Mexico	26
Oklahoma	22
Minnesota	20
Maryland	19

County	Number
Los Angeles County, CA	452
San Diego County, CA	367
King County, WA	250
Honolulu County, HI	235
Pierce County, WA	187
Kitsap County, WA	185
Monterey County, CA	128
Alameda County, CA	116
Sacramento County, CA	112
Orange County, CA	105
Riverside County, CA	91
Harris County, TX	84
Santa Clara County, CA	84
Maricopa County, AZ	62
Solano County, CA	62
Kings County, NY	60
Clark County, NV	56
El Paso County, CO	51
San Bernardino County, CA	50
Bell County, TX	37
Thurston County, WA	31
Contra Costa County, CA	23
San Mateo County, CA	0

Place	Number
Los Angeles, CA (city) Los Angeles County	221
New York, NY (city)	209
San Diego, CA (city) San Diego County	170
Honolulu, HI (cdp) Honolulu County	166
Tacoma, WA (city) Pierce County	107
Houston, TX (city) Harris County	84
Chula Vista, CA (city) San Diego County	38
San Jose, CA (city) Santa Clara County	37
Fairfield, CA (city) Solano County	29
Vallejo, CA (city) Solano County	28
Killeen, TX (city) Bell County	17

Notes: Please refer to the User's Guide for an explanation of data; ranking tables include all places with Asian and/or NHPI populations above SF4 population thresholds; (1) tables reflect only those areas that meet SF4 population thresholds, therefore there may be less than 50 states, 75 counties or 75 places listed

Poverty Status

Guamanians or Chamorros with Income Below Poverty Level

***All States, Top 75 Counties, and Top 75 Places Sorted by Percent*[1]**

State	Percent
Massachusetts	32.08
New Jersey	26.94
Illinois	25.42
Florida	25.33
New York	23.07
Louisiana	23.00
Hawaii	22.26
Georgia	19.72
South Carolina	19.60
Alabama	18.27
Kentucky	18.16
Oregon	17.61
Washington	15.02
Colorado	14.94
Indiana	14.82
Texas	14.71
North Carolina	14.43
Michigan	14.15
United States	13.75
Tennessee	13.36
Pennsylvania	13.16
Connecticut	12.16
Arizona	12.15
Virginia	11.24
California	9.92
Ohio	9.42
Wisconsin	8.40
Nevada	7.99
New Mexico	7.12
Missouri	6.59
Oklahoma	6.41
Minnesota	4.84
Maryland	2.78

County	Percent
King County, WA	31.02
Monterey County, CA	18.99
Honolulu County, HI	18.20
Kitsap County, WA	17.93
Los Angeles County, CA	14.46
Harris County, TX	13.35
Sacramento County, CA	12.80
Kings County, NY	12.27
El Paso County, CO	11.16
Pierce County, WA	10.46
Riverside County, CA	10.01
Orange County, CA	9.59
Maricopa County, AZ	9.58
Alameda County, CA	8.93
San Diego County, CA	8.13
Bell County, TX	6.21
Santa Clara County, CA	6.15
Clark County, NV	5.85
San Bernardino County, CA	4.83
Solano County, CA	4.77
Thurston County, WA	4.32
Contra Costa County, CA	4.23
San Mateo County, CA	0.00

Place	Percent
Tacoma, WA (city) Pierce County	26.82
Honolulu, HI (cdp) Honolulu County	25.38
Los Angeles, CA (city) Los Angeles County	19.34
Houston, TX (city) Harris County	19.00
New York, NY (city)	18.37
Chula Vista, CA (city) San Diego County	8.94
San Diego, CA (city) San Diego County	8.51
Fairfield, CA (city) Solano County	5.50
San Jose, CA (city) Santa Clara County	5.05
Vallejo, CA (city) Solano County	4.98
Killeen, TX (city) Bell County	3.40

Notes: Please refer to the User's Guide for an explanation of data; ranking tables include all places with Asian and/or NHPI populations above SF4 population thresholds; (1) tables reflect only those areas that meet SF4 population thresholds, therefore there may be less than 50 states, 75 counties or 75 places listed

Poverty Status

Hawaiian Natives with Income Below Poverty Level

All States, Top 75 Counties, and Top 75 Places Sorted by Number[1]

State	Number
United States	20,840
Hawaii	13,421
California	2,203
Texas	771
Washington	435
Nevada	361
New York	328
Arizona	320
Oregon	252
Pennsylvania	229
Florida	228
Utah	175
North Carolina	169
Colorado	157
New Jersey	122
Tennessee	98
Ohio	95
Louisiana	94
Missouri	89
Virginia	84
Arkansas	83
Wisconsin	83
Michigan	73
Kansas	72
Georgia	66
South Carolina	65
Indiana	59
Oklahoma	59
New Mexico	57
Montana	51
Minnesota	49
Idaho	39
Alaska	33
Illinois	22
Massachusetts	19
Maryland	7

County	Number
Honolulu County, HI	7,713
Hawaii County, HI	2,914
Maui County, HI	1,956
Kauai County, HI	794
Los Angeles County, CA	741
Clark County, NV	309
San Diego County, CA	201
Maricopa County, AZ	180
Alameda County, CA	145
Utah County, UT	122
Pierce County, WA	110
King County, WA	96
Orange County, CA	93
Sacramento County, CA	89
San Mateo County, CA	87
Bexar County, TX	77
San Bernardino County, CA	73
San Joaquin County, CA	72
Pima County, AZ	65
Multnomah County, OR	56
Solano County, CA	55
Santa Clara County, CA	49
Riverside County, CA	43
Snohomish County, WA	38
Contra Costa County, CA	31
Washington County, OR	22
Ventura County, CA	11
Salt Lake County, UT	6

Place	Number
Honolulu, HI (cdp) Honolulu County	2,355
Hilo, HI (cdp) Hawaii County	1,142
Nanakuli, HI (cdp) Honolulu County	562
Waianae, HI (cdp) Honolulu County	547
Maili, HI (cdp) Honolulu County	470
Kaneohe, HI (cdp) Honolulu County	443
Los Angeles, CA (city) Los Angeles County	310
Makaha, HI (cdp) Honolulu County	267
Hawaiian Paradise Park, HI (cdp) Hawaii County	258
Waipahu, HI (cdp) Honolulu County	247
Kaunakakai, HI (cdp) Maui County	243
Wailuku, HI (cdp) Maui County	239
Kahului, HI (cdp) Maui County	220
Waimanalo Beach, HI (cdp) Honolulu County	211
Kapaa, HI (cdp) Kauai County	195
New York, NY (city)	180
Anahola, HI (cdp) Kauai County	167
Ewa Beach, HI (cdp) Honolulu County	156
Hauula, HI (cdp) Honolulu County	155
Pearl City, HI (cdp) Honolulu County	154
San Diego, CA (city) San Diego County	153
Kualapuu, HI (cdp) Maui County	143
Kalaoa, HI (cdp) Hawaii County	140
Kailua, HI (cdp) Honolulu County	133
Wahiawa, HI (cdp) Honolulu County	132
Kihei, HI (cdp) Maui County	131
Hawaiian Beaches, HI (cdp) Hawaii County	128
Halawa, HI (cdp) Honolulu County	127
Las Vegas, NV (city) Clark County	125
Waimalu, HI (cdp) Honolulu County	106
Waipio, HI (cdp) Honolulu County	101
Makaha Valley, HI (cdp) Honolulu County	100
Phoenix, AZ (city) Maricopa County	95
Waihee-Waiehu, HI (cdp) Maui County	92
Waimea, HI (cdp) Hawaii County	92
Pakala Village, HI (cdp) Kauai County	76
Makakilo City, HI (cdp) Honolulu County	74
Waimanalo, HI (cdp) Honolulu County	71
Paradise, NV (cdp) Clark County	68
Kaaawa, HI (cdp) Honolulu County	64
Kailua, HI (cdp) Hawaii County	61
Lahaina, HI (cdp) Maui County	58
Makawao, HI (cdp) Maui County	55
Portland, OR (city) Multnomah County	48
Waialua, HI (cdp) Honolulu County	48
Naalehu, HI (cdp) Hawaii County	47
Kahaluu, HI (cdp) Honolulu County	41
Kekaha, HI (cdp) Kauai County	40
Waikane, HI (cdp) Honolulu County	37
Waimea, HI (cdp) Kauai County	35
Hawaiian Ocean View, HI (cdp) Hawaii County	34
Haleiwa, HI (cdp) Honolulu County	31
Pahala, HI (cdp) Hawaii County	31
Laie, HI (cdp) Honolulu County	30
Captain Cook, HI (cdp) Hawaii County	27
Kahuku, HI (cdp) Honolulu County	26
Hana, HI (cdp) Maui County	25
Henderson, NV (city) Clark County	24
Kilauea, HI (cdp) Kauai County	24
Holualoa, HI (cdp) Hawaii County	22
San Jose, CA (city) Santa Clara County	22
Honalo, HI (cdp) Hawaii County	20
Waikoloa Village, HI (cdp) Hawaii County	19
Kapaau, HI (cdp) Hawaii County	18
Paia, HI (cdp) Maui County	18
Punaluu, HI (cdp) Honolulu County	18
Volcano, HI (cdp) Hawaii County	16
Honaunau-Napoopoo, HI (cdp) Hawaii County	15
Mililani Town, HI (cdp) Honolulu County	12
Ahuimanu, HI (cdp) Honolulu County	8
Aiea, HI (cdp) Honolulu County	7
Hanapepe, HI (cdp) Kauai County	3

Notes: Please refer to the User's Guide for an explanation of data; ranking tables include all places with Asian and/or NHPI populations above SF4 population thresholds; (1) tables reflect only those areas that meet SF4 population thresholds, therefore there may be less than 50 states, 75 counties or 75 places listed

Poverty Status

Hawaiian Natives with Income Below Poverty Level

All States, Top 75 Counties, and Top 75 Places Sorted by Percent[1]

State	Percent
Arkansas	35.47
Pennsylvania	27.83
Louisiana	27.33
New York	24.68
Texas	24.61
Wisconsin	23.12
New Jersey	22.55
Montana	21.79
Tennessee	20.00
Kansas	18.56
Hawaii	16.88
Arizona	16.71
North Carolina	16.46
United States	15.58
New Mexico	15.16
Missouri	14.15
South Carolina	13.98
Ohio	13.73
Utah	13.39
Oregon	13.02
Florida	12.50
Colorado	12.03
California	11.66
Idaho	11.64
Minnesota	11.42
Michigan	11.35
Nevada	10.80
Oklahoma	10.67
Indiana	9.85
Washington	9.80
Virginia	9.71
Georgia	9.62
Alaska	6.86
Massachusetts	5.07
Illinois	2.95
Maryland	1.41

County	Percent
Utah County, UT	33.98
Hawaii County, HI	21.26
Bexar County, TX	21.10
Los Angeles County, CA	17.65
San Joaquin County, CA	17.35
Maui County, HI	16.88
Maricopa County, AZ	16.64
Kauai County, HI	16.22
Honolulu County, HI	15.67
Pima County, AZ	14.22
Sacramento County, CA	13.73
San Bernardino County, CA	12.76
Pierce County, WA	12.60
Multnomah County, OR	12.28
Alameda County, CA	11.44
San Mateo County, CA	10.86
Clark County, NV	10.18
Solano County, CA	9.40
San Diego County, CA	9.31
Snohomish County, WA	7.47
King County, WA	6.97
Orange County, CA	5.54
Riverside County, CA	5.51
Washington County, OR	5.26
Contra Costa County, CA	5.21
Santa Clara County, CA	4.46
Ventura County, CA	1.91
Salt Lake County, UT	1.25

Place	Percent
Pakala Village, HI (cdp) Kauai County	47.80
Makaha Valley, HI (cdp) Honolulu County	45.66
Waialua, HI (cdp) Honolulu County	39.34
Naalehu, HI (cdp) Hawaii County	39.17
Hawaiian Paradise Park, HI (cdp) Hawaii County	37.72
Pahala, HI (cdp) Hawaii County	37.35
Maili, HI (cdp) Honolulu County	33.50
Hawaiian Beaches, HI (cdp) Hawaii County	33.07
Kaunakakai, HI (cdp) Maui County	31.93
Hilo, HI (cdp) Hawaii County	27.89
Kaaawa, HI (cdp) Honolulu County	27.47
Waipahu, HI (cdp) Honolulu County	25.65
Waikane, HI (cdp) Honolulu County	25.34
New York, NY (city)	24.93
Kapaa, HI (cdp) Kauai County	23.19
Waipio, HI (cdp) Honolulu County	23.17
Waianae, HI (cdp) Honolulu County	23.14
Hauula, HI (cdp) Honolulu County	21.62
Makaha, HI (cdp) Honolulu County	20.57
Los Angeles, CA (city) Los Angeles County	20.56
Kalaoa, HI (cdp) Hawaii County	19.89
Waimea, HI (cdp) Kauai County	19.66
Phoenix, AZ (city) Maricopa County	19.59
Wailuku, HI (cdp) Maui County	18.88
Hawaiian Ocean View, HI (cdp) Hawaii County	18.68
Nanakuli, HI (cdp) Honolulu County	18.44
Halawa, HI (cdp) Honolulu County	17.94
Kilauea, HI (cdp) Kauai County	17.27
Anahola, HI (cdp) Kauai County	17.09
Honolulu, HI (cdp) Honolulu County	16.79
Ewa Beach, HI (cdp) Honolulu County	16.58
Kihei, HI (cdp) Maui County	16.42
Las Vegas, NV (city) Clark County	16.30
Kualapuu, HI (cdp) Maui County	16.12
Kahului, HI (cdp) Maui County	15.93
Haleiwa, HI (cdp) Honolulu County	15.90
Kahuku, HI (cdp) Honolulu County	15.85
Kapaau, HI (cdp) Hawaii County	14.75
Portland, OR (city) Multnomah County	14.29
Wahiawa, HI (cdp) Honolulu County	14.09
San Diego, CA (city) San Diego County	14.06
Honalo, HI (cdp) Hawaii County	13.16
Kaneohe, HI (cdp) Honolulu County	13.16
Punaluu, HI (cdp) Honolulu County	12.86
Paradise, NV (cdp) Clark County	11.72
Kekaha, HI (cdp) Kauai County	11.70
Pearl City, HI (cdp) Honolulu County	11.43
Waimalu, HI (cdp) Honolulu County	11.19
Captain Cook, HI (cdp) Hawaii County	10.76
Waimanalo Beach, HI (cdp) Honolulu County	10.48
Makawao, HI (cdp) Maui County	10.07
Waihee-Waiehu, HI (cdp) Maui County	9.97
Waimea, HI (cdp) Hawaii County	9.56
Hana, HI (cdp) Maui County	9.23
Laie, HI (cdp) Honolulu County	9.09
Waimanalo, HI (cdp) Honolulu County	8.51
Paia, HI (cdp) Maui County	8.45
Makakilo City, HI (cdp) Honolulu County	7.53
Kahaluu, HI (cdp) Honolulu County	7.12
Lahaina, HI (cdp) Maui County	6.64
Waikoloa Village, HI (cdp) Hawaii County	6.38
Holualoa, HI (cdp) Hawaii County	6.23
Kailua, HI (cdp) Hawaii County	6.07
Volcano, HI (cdp) Hawaii County	5.93
Henderson, NV (city) Clark County	5.42
Kailua, HI (cdp) Honolulu County	5.31
Honaunau-Napoopoo, HI (cdp) Hawaii County	4.75
San Jose, CA (city) Santa Clara County	4.17
Aiea, HI (cdp) Honolulu County	1.90
Hanapepe, HI (cdp) Kauai County	1.65
Mililani Town, HI (cdp) Honolulu County	1.38
Ahuimanu, HI (cdp) Honolulu County	0.99

Notes: Please refer to the User's Guide for an explanation of data; ranking tables include all places with Asian and/or NHPI populations above SF4 population thresholds; (1) tables reflect only those areas that meet SF4 population thresholds, therefore there may be less than 50 states, 75 counties or 75 places listed

Poverty Status

Hmongs with Income Below Poverty Level

All States, Top 75 Counties, and Top 75 Places Sorted by Number[1]

State	Number
United States	63,633
California	36,351
Minnesota	13,987
Wisconsin	7,928
Michigan	1,669
North Carolina	986
Washington	681
Colorado	421
Alaska	313
Kansas	183
Pennsylvania	156
Georgia	144
Massachusetts	142
South Carolina	93
Rhode Island	76
Oklahoma	51
Oregon	41

County	Number
Fresno County, CA	13,862
Ramsey County, MN	9,007
Sacramento County, CA	8,330
Hennepin County, MN	4,408
Merced County, CA	3,782
San Joaquin County, CA	3,441
Butte County, CA	1,952
Milwaukee County, WI	1,519
Marathon County, WI	1,441
Yuba County, CA	1,186
Brown County, WI	662
Tulare County, CA	654
Wayne County, MI	624
Outagamie County, WI	618
Stanislaus County, CA	596
Dane County, WI	526
Sheboygan County, WI	505
Yolo County, CA	449
Ingham County, MI	436
Dunn County, WI	360
Winnebago County, WI	347
Spokane County, WA	346
Eau Claire County, WI	333
La Crosse County, WI	320
Catawba County, NC	317
King County, WA	315
Manitowoc County, WI	315
Anchorage Borough, AK	313
San Diego County, CA	312
Glenn County, CA	306
Adams County, CO	270
Riverside County, CA	253
Oakland County, MI	236
Portage County, WI	221
Los Angeles County, CA	194
Mecklenburg County, NC	180
Wyandotte County, KS	175
Chippewa County, WI	161
Burke County, NC	160
Solano County, CA	124
Wood County, WI	120
Worcester County, MA	83
Santa Barbara County, CA	79
Providence County, RI	76
Orange County, CA	74
Calumet County, WI	58
Stanly County, NC	54
Fond du Lac County, WI	49
Barrow County, GA	44
Macomb County, MI	42
Olmsted County, MN	35
Lancaster County, PA	32
Washington County, MN	28
Multnomah County, OR	16
Anoka County, MN	0
Jefferson County, CO	0
Spartanburg County, SC	0

Place	Number
Fresno, CA (city) Fresno County	12,302
St. Paul, MN (city) Ramsey County	9,006
Sacramento, CA (city) Sacramento County	5,557
Minneapolis, MN (city) Hennepin County	3,991
Stockton, CA (city) San Joaquin County	2,886
Merced, CA (city) Merced County	2,862
Parkway-S. Sacramento, CA (cdp) Sacramento County	1,835
Milwaukee, WI (city) Milwaukee County	1,519
Wausau, WI (city) Marathon County	1,417
Clovis, CA (city) Fresno County	995
Linda, CA (cdp) Yuba County	922
Detroit, MI (city) Wayne County	624
Green Bay, WI (city) Brown County	581
Florin, CA (cdp) Sacramento County	541
Appleton, WI (city) Outagamie County	534
South Oroville, CA (cdp) Butte County	526
Chico, CA (city) Butte County	520
Sheboygan, WI (city) Sheboygan County	505
Thermalito, CA (cdp) Butte County	499
Eau Claire, WI (city) Eau Claire County	491
Lansing, MI (city) Ingham County	436
Madison, WI (city) Dane County	431
West Sacramento, CA (city) Yolo County	416
Visalia, CA (city) Tulare County	384
Oroville, CA (city) Butte County	366
Willows, CA (city) Glenn County	306
Manitowoc, WI (city) Manitowoc County	301
Oshkosh, WI (city) Winnebago County	296
Spokane, WA (city) Spokane County	287
Brooklyn Park, MN (city) Hennepin County	276
La Crosse, WI (city) La Crosse County	254
San Diego, CA (city) San Diego County	244
Modesto, CA (city) Stanislaus County	230
Stevens Point, WI (city) Portage County	188
Charlotte, NC (city) Mecklenburg County	180
Kansas City, KS (city) Wyandotte County	175
Hickory, NC (city) Catawba County	148
Pontiac, MI (city) Oakland County	139
Brooklyn Center, MN (city) Hennepin County	130
Atwater, CA (city) Merced County	102
Wisconsin Rapids, WI (city) Wood County	91
Providence, RI (city) Providence County	76
Westminster, CO (city) Adams County	66
Fitchburg, MA (city) Worcester County	64
Connelly Springs, NC (town) Burke County	44
Warren, MI (city) Macomb County	42
Santa Ana, CA (city) Orange County	39
Rochester, MN (city) Olmsted County	35
Arden-Arcade, CA (cdp) Sacramento County	31
Portland, OR (city) Multnomah County	16
Glen Alpine, NC (town) Burke County	15
Fond du Lac, WI (city) Fond du Lac County	8
Maplewood, MN (city) Ramsey County	0
Valdese, NC (town) Burke County	0
Woodbury, MN (city) Washington County	0

Notes: Please refer to the User's Guide for an explanation of data; ranking tables include all places with Asian and/or NHPI populations above SF4 population thresholds; (1) tables reflect only those areas that meet SF4 population thresholds, therefore there may be less than 50 states, 75 counties or 75 places listed

Poverty Status

Hmongs with Income Below Poverty Level

All States, Top 75 Counties, and Top 75 Places Sorted by Percent[1]

State	Percent
Alaska	59.96
California	53.17
Washington	46.36
United States	37.78
Minnesota	32.72
Michigan	29.87
Wisconsin	25.86
Pennsylvania	20.50
Kansas	19.85
Oklahoma	16.14
North Carolina	14.63
Massachusetts	14.36
Colorado	14.01
Georgia	12.05
South Carolina	10.95
Rhode Island	8.31
Oregon	3.01

County	Percent
Ingham County, MI	79.27
Yolo County, CA	69.61
Butte County, CA	69.52
Spokane County, WA	64.92
Dunn County, WI	63.83
Stanislaus County, CA	61.51
Tulare County, CA	60.17
Anchorage Borough, AK	59.96
San Joaquin County, CA	58.07
Fresno County, CA	57.72
Merced County, CA	57.70
Glenn County, CA	54.55
Riverside County, CA	51.95
Sacramento County, CA	48.18
Los Angeles County, CA	45.97
Chippewa County, WI	44.85
Yuba County, CA	44.64
King County, WA	35.59
Marathon County, WI	35.57
Wayne County, MI	34.04
Ramsey County, MN	34.02
Manitowoc County, WI	33.69
Hennepin County, MN	33.30
Mecklenburg County, NC	31.63
Solano County, CA	30.17
Brown County, WI	27.47
Outagamie County, WI	26.55
Portage County, WI	25.43
Eau Claire County, WI	24.56
San Diego County, CA	23.51
Dane County, WI	23.49
Winnebago County, WI	23.46
Wyandotte County, KS	22.46
Santa Barbara County, CA	22.25
Oakland County, MI	22.04
Milwaukee County, WI	20.44
Wood County, WI	20.30
Sheboygan County, WI	20.29
Barrow County, GA	18.88
Fond du Lac County, WI	18.49
Catawba County, NC	17.84
Stanly County, NC	17.65
La Crosse County, WI	16.82
Calumet County, WI	13.30
Adams County, CO	12.59
Worcester County, MA	12.59
Providence County, RI	9.42
Olmsted County, MN	8.86
Burke County, NC	7.98
Orange County, CA	7.01
Lancaster County, PA	6.99
Macomb County, MI	3.88
Washington County, MN	3.65
Multnomah County, OR	1.52
Anoka County, MN	0.00
Jefferson County, CO	0.00
Spartanburg County, SC	0.00

Place	Percent
South Oroville, CA (cdp) Butte County	86.51
Thermalito, CA (cdp) Butte County	80.74
Oroville, CA (city) Butte County	76.89
West Sacramento, CA (city) Yolo County	71.85
Chico, CA (city) Butte County	71.33
Visalia, CA (city) Tulare County	70.98
Spokane, WA (city) Spokane County	69.83
Merced, CA (city) Merced County	68.09
Lansing, MI (city) Ingham County	67.60
Parkway-S. Sacramento, CA (cdp) Sacramento County	66.73
Fresno, CA (city) Fresno County	60.56
Stockton, CA (city) San Joaquin County	58.53
Connelly Springs, NC (town) Burke County	57.89
Modesto, CA (city) Stanislaus County	56.65
Clovis, CA (city) Fresno County	55.31
Willows, CA (city) Glenn County	54.55
Florin, CA (cdp) Sacramento County	50.99
Linda, CA (cdp) Yuba County	46.29
Sacramento, CA (city) Sacramento County	46.14
Wausau, WI (city) Marathon County	41.58
Minneapolis, MN (city) Hennepin County	39.15
Detroit, MI (city) Wayne County	38.10
Manitowoc, WI (city) Manitowoc County	36.84
St. Paul, MN (city) Ramsey County	35.52
Eau Claire, WI (city) Eau Claire County	34.26
Charlotte, NC (city) Mecklenburg County	31.63
Green Bay, WI (city) Brown County	28.83
Hickory, NC (city) Catawba County	28.14
Oshkosh, WI (city) Winnebago County	27.16
Atwater, CA (city) Merced County	25.95
Brooklyn Park, MN (city) Hennepin County	25.09
Stevens Point, WI (city) Portage County	24.83
Madison, WI (city) Dane County	24.47
San Diego, CA (city) San Diego County	22.98
Appleton, WI (city) Outagamie County	22.91
Kansas City, KS (city) Wyandotte County	22.46
Sheboygan, WI (city) Sheboygan County	21.18
Milwaukee, WI (city) Milwaukee County	21.11
La Crosse, WI (city) La Crosse County	19.49
Pontiac, MI (city) Oakland County	19.20
Wisconsin Rapids, WI (city) Wood County	17.50
Providence, RI (city) Providence County	11.69
Fitchburg, MA (city) Worcester County	10.53
Brooklyn Center, MN (city) Hennepin County	8.98
Rochester, MN (city) Olmsted County	8.86
Arden-Arcade, CA (cdp) Sacramento County	8.83
Santa Ana, CA (city) Orange County	7.39
Glen Alpine, NC (town) Burke County	6.88
Westminster, CO (city) Adams County	6.50
Warren, MI (city) Macomb County	5.61
Fond du Lac, WI (city) Fond du Lac County	3.83
Portland, OR (city) Multnomah County	1.73
Maplewood, MN (city) Ramsey County	0.00
Valdese, NC (town) Burke County	0.00
Woodbury, MN (city) Washington County	0.00

Notes: Please refer to the User's Guide for an explanation of data; ranking tables include all places with Asian and/or NHPI populations above SF4 population thresholds; (1) tables reflect only those areas that meet SF4 population thresholds, therefore there may be less than 50 states, 75 counties or 75 places listed

Poverty Status

Indonesians with Income Below Poverty Level

***All States, Top 75 Counties, and Top 75 Places Sorted by Number*[1]**

State	Number
United States	7,650
California	2,685
Ohio	520
New York	418
Texas	402
Illinois	375
Washington	319
Oregon	265
Pennsylvania	192
Massachusetts	190
Michigan	163
Colorado	138
Maryland	132
Wisconsin	132
New Jersey	129
Virginia	113
Georgia	112
Arizona	106
Florida	86

County	Number
Los Angeles County, CA	1,098
San Bernardino County, CA	424
Orange County, CA	402
Franklin County, OH	321
Queens County, NY	277
San Francisco County, CA	233
King County, WA	228
Cook County, IL	213
Harris County, TX	160
San Mateo County, CA	112
San Diego County, CA	90
Montgomery County, MD	83
Santa Clara County, CA	80
Maricopa County, AZ	72
Fairfax County, VA	59
Alameda County, CA	58
Middlesex County, NJ	48
Contra Costa County, CA	45

Place	Number
Los Angeles, CA (city) Los Angeles County	470
New York, NY (city)	366
Columbus, OH (city) Franklin County	321
San Francisco, CA (city) San Francisco County	233
San Bernardino, CA (city) San Bernardino County	186
Houston, TX (city) Harris County	141
Seattle, WA (city) King County	127
Loma Linda, CA (city) San Bernardino County	51

Notes: Please refer to the User's Guide for an explanation of data; ranking tables include all places with Asian and/or NHPI populations above SF4 population thresholds; (1) tables reflect only those areas that meet SF4 population thresholds, therefore there may be less than 50 states, 75 counties or 75 places listed

Poverty Status

Indonesians with Income Below Poverty Level

All States, Top 75 Counties, and Top 75 Places Sorted by Percent[1]

State	Percent
Ohio	49.67
Oregon	42.67
Illinois	41.67
Pennsylvania	36.71
Wisconsin	33.00
Massachusetts	28.57
Michigan	26.29
Washington	25.89
Texas	23.00
United States	20.92
Georgia	20.36
Colorado	18.55
Arizona	18.50
New York	17.36
California	16.45
New Jersey	12.65
Maryland	11.91
Virginia	10.40
Florida	9.62

County	Percent
Franklin County, OH	61.38
Cook County, IL	47.44
King County, WA	27.47
San Francisco County, CA	26.69
Harris County, TX	23.19
Queens County, NY	22.28
Orange County, CA	21.07
Los Angeles County, CA	19.62
San Diego County, CA	18.99
Maricopa County, AZ	17.48
San Mateo County, CA	14.81
San Bernardino County, CA	12.86
Santa Clara County, CA	11.64
Fairfax County, VA	9.92
Middlesex County, NJ	9.84
Contra Costa County, CA	9.51
Alameda County, CA	9.09
Montgomery County, MD	8.94

Place	Percent
Columbus, OH (city) Franklin County	63.31
San Bernardino, CA (city) San Bernardino County	41.89
Seattle, WA (city) King County	33.60
Houston, TX (city) Harris County	27.27
San Francisco, CA (city) San Francisco County	26.69
Los Angeles, CA (city) Los Angeles County	26.26
New York, NY (city)	20.24
Loma Linda, CA (city) San Bernardino County	9.77

Notes: Please refer to the User's Guide for an explanation of data; ranking tables include all places with Asian and/or NHPI populations above SF4 population thresholds; (1) tables reflect only those areas that meet SF4 population thresholds, therefore there may be less than 50 states, 75 counties or 75 places listed

Poverty Status

Japanese with Income Below Poverty Level

All States, Top 75 Counties, and Top 75 Places Sorted by Number[1]

State	Number
United States	75,540
California	25,923
Hawaii	8,778
New York	7,103
Washington	4,331
Massachusetts	2,413
Oregon	2,102
Illinois	1,872
Texas	1,654
Pennsylvania	1,622
Florida	1,493
Ohio	1,217
Colorado	1,178
New Jersey	1,056
Nevada	1,052
Michigan	1,043
Utah	1,021
Arizona	975
Georgia	764
Minnesota	699
Indiana	698
Missouri	627
Virginia	613
Maryland	603
Oklahoma	593
North Carolina	580
Tennessee	549
Connecticut	535
Wisconsin	487
Kansas	370
Nebraska	301
Kentucky	296
Alabama	286
West Virginia	283
Idaho	270
Louisiana	269
District of Columbia	265
Iowa	225
Montana	207
New Mexico	191
South Carolina	189
Arkansas	164
New Hampshire	119
Maine	105
Mississippi	101
Rhode Island	77
South Dakota	73
Alaska	47
Vermont	42
Delaware	35
Wyoming	31

County	Number
Los Angeles County, CA	10,410
Honolulu County, HI	6,692
San Diego County, CA	2,681
New York County, NY	2,511
King County, WA	2,423
Orange County, CA	2,155
Queens County, NY	1,771
San Francisco County, CA	1,575
Alameda County, CA	1,284
Santa Clara County, CA	1,187
Cook County, IL	1,160
Hawaii County, HI	1,104
Suffolk County, MA	934
Sacramento County, CA	739
Maui County, HI	729
Clark County, NV	684
Kings County, NY	656
Westchester County, NY	605
Riverside County, CA	571
Multnomah County, OR	562
Norfolk County, MA	555
Maricopa County, AZ	547
Allegheny County, PA	516
Ventura County, CA	515
Fresno County, CA	500
Lane County, OR	500
Middlesex County, MA	478
Bergen County, NJ	465
Santa Barbara County, CA	461
Contra Costa County, CA	460
San Mateo County, CA	447
Philadelphia County, PA	416
Pierce County, WA	395
San Joaquin County, CA	371
Washoe County, NV	368
Franklin County, OH	364
San Bernardino County, CA	356
Harris County, TX	355
Salt Lake County, UT	355
Washington County, OR	347
Utah County, UT	337
Oklahoma County, OK	320
Monterey County, CA	315
Pima County, AZ	302
Yolo County, CA	292
Washtenaw County, MI	278
Tompkins County, NY	271
Denver County, CO	256
New Haven County, CT	253
San Luis Obispo County, CA	251
Orange County, FL	242
Whitman County, WA	240
Douglas County, NE	238
Kauai County, HI	238
Spokane County, WA	235
Snohomish County, WA	222
Hennepin County, MN	206
Boulder County, CO	204
Cuyahoga County, OH	201
Whatcom County, WA	193
Montgomery County, MD	192
St. Louis County, MO	191
Fairfield County, CT	190
Bronx County, NY	184
Oakland County, MI	176
Butte County, CA	175
Dane County, WI	174
Sonoma County, CA	173
Benton County, OR	169
Dallas County, TX	165
DeKalb County, GA	156
Alachua County, FL	155
Denton County, TX	154
Gwinnett County, GA	154
Erie County, NY	153

Place	Number
New York, NY (city)	5,155
Honolulu, HI (cdp) Honolulu County	5,154
Los Angeles, CA (city) Los Angeles County	4,947
San Diego, CA (city) San Diego County	1,715
San Francisco, CA (city) San Francisco County	1,575
Seattle, WA (city) King County	1,450
Boston, MA (city) Suffolk County	934
Chicago, IL (city) Cook County	788
Irvine, CA (city) Orange County	631
Hilo, HI (cdp) Hawaii County	556
Torrance, CA (city) Los Angeles County	551
Portland, OR (city) Multnomah County	540
San Jose, CA (city) Santa Clara County	532
Berkeley, CA (city) Alameda County	489
Gardena, CA (city) Los Angeles County	480
Long Beach, CA (city) Los Angeles County	477
Pittsburgh, PA (city) Allegheny County	461
Eugene, OR (city) Lane County	460
Santa Monica, CA (city) Los Angeles County	444
Philadelphia, PA (city) Philadelphia County	416
Pasadena, CA (city) Los Angeles County	385
Las Vegas, NV (city) Clark County	369
Costa Mesa, CA (city) Orange County	364
Sacramento, CA (city) Sacramento County	349
Brookline, MA (town) Norfolk County	338
Fresno, CA (city) Fresno County	332
Reno, NV (city) Washoe County	323
Riverside, CA (city) Riverside County	290
Bellevue, WA (city) King County	281
Houston, TX (city) Harris County	278
Provo, UT (city) Utah County	274
Cambridge, MA (city) Middlesex County	262
Tucson, AZ (city) Pima County	261
Denver, CO (city) Denver County	256
Phoenix, AZ (city) Maricopa County	246
Pullman, WA (city) Whitman County	240
Waipahu, HI (cdp) Honolulu County	236
Hayward, CA (city) Alameda County	235
Kahului, HI (cdp) Maui County	234
Omaha, NE (city) Douglas County	234
Columbus, OH (city) Franklin County	232
Davis, CA (city) Yolo County	228
Vista, CA (city) San Diego County	222
Glendale, CA (city) Los Angeles County	217
Alhambra, CA (city) Los Angeles County	211
Ann Arbor, MI (city) Washtenaw County	209
Oklahoma City, OK (city) Oklahoma County	209
Monterey Park, CA (city) Los Angeles County	195
Oakland, CA (city) Alameda County	193
Waimalu, HI (cdp) Honolulu County	193
Stockton, CA (city) San Joaquin County	190
Tempe, AZ (city) Maricopa County	175
Monterey, CA (city) Monterey County	173
Tacoma, WA (city) Pierce County	173
Madison, WI (city) Dane County	167
Oxnard, CA (city) Ventura County	162
Boulder, CO (city) Boulder County	160
San Mateo, CA (city) San Mateo County	155
Wahiawa, HI (cdp) Honolulu County	150
Minneapolis, MN (city) Hennepin County	147
Arlington, VA (cdp) Arlington County	145
Austin, TX (city) Travis County	145
Santa Barbara, CA (city) Santa Barbara County	145
West Covina, CA (city) Los Angeles County	145
Huntington Beach, CA (city) Orange County	143
Sunnyvale, CA (city) Santa Clara County	136
San Antonio, TX (city) Bexar County	135
Spring Valley, NV (cdp) Clark County	135
Pearl City, HI (cdp) Honolulu County	132
Chula Vista, CA (city) San Diego County	130
Fort Lee, NJ (borough) Bergen County	130
Greenwich, CT (town) Fairfield County	130
Nashville-Davidson, TN (sp. city) Davidson County	130
Wailuku, HI (cdp) Maui County	129
Fort Collins, CO (city) Larimer County	126

Notes: Please refer to the User's Guide for an explanation of data; ranking tables include all places with Asian and/or NHPI populations above SF4 population thresholds; (1) tables reflect only those areas that meet SF4 population thresholds, therefore there may be less than 50 states, 75 counties or 75 places listed

Poverty Status

Japanese with Income Below Poverty Level

All States, Top 75 Counties, and Top 75 Places Sorted by Percent[1]

State	Percent
West Virginia	38.66
District of Columbia	27.40
Montana	26.64
Massachusetts	24.24
Pennsylvania	24.16
Oklahoma	24.05
Nebraska	23.50
Kansas	21.50
South Dakota	21.28
Iowa	19.91
New York	19.52
Louisiana	19.20
Missouri	19.17
Oregon	19.07
Maine	18.95
Mississippi	18.91
Minnesota	18.17
Utah	17.59
Wisconsin	17.09
Indiana	16.01
Arkansas	15.69
Alabama	15.58
Tennessee	14.77
Vermont	14.33
New Hampshire	14.25
Arizona	13.29
Florida	13.29
Nevada	12.71
Ohio	12.34
Connecticut	12.27
Washington	12.05
Texas	10.56
Rhode Island	10.46
Idaho	10.42
Georgia	10.40
Colorado	10.16
Michigan	10.02
North Carolina	9.90
United States	9.72
Kentucky	9.57
New Mexico	9.38
Illinois	9.25
California	9.09
Maryland	8.92
South Carolina	8.45
New Jersey	7.80
Wyoming	7.42
Virginia	7.07
Delaware	5.79
Hawaii	4.44
Alaska	3.33

County	Percent
Whitman County, WA	63.49
Tompkins County, NY	51.62
Suffolk County, MA	47.03
Utah County, UT	46.42
Benton County, OR	45.68
Allegheny County, PA	44.64
Erie County, NY	44.61
Whatcom County, WA	42.60
Lane County, OR	41.46
Philadelphia County, PA	38.99
Oklahoma County, OK	38.60
Bronx County, NY	37.17
Douglas County, NE	36.90
Alachua County, FL	36.38
Denton County, TX	34.07
Queens County, NY	33.75
Olmsted County, MN	32.24
New Haven County, CT	31.31
Marion County, OR	30.63
Butte County, CA	30.59
Kings County, NY	30.33
Washoe County, NV	29.49
Durham County, NC	27.89
Norfolk County, MA	27.76
Humboldt County, CA	27.27
Champaign County, IL	26.19
Onondaga County, NY	25.74
San Luis Obispo County, CA	25.43
Larimer County, CO	24.45
Monroe County, NY	23.14
Worcester County, MA	23.12
Baltimore County, MD	22.24
Dane County, WI	22.00
Yolo County, CA	21.77
Chester County, PA	21.25
Pima County, AZ	20.57
Santa Barbara County, CA	20.32
Orange County, FL	20.17
Ingham County, MI	18.79
Pinellas County, FL	18.74
Delaware County, PA	18.60
Summit County, OH	18.33
New York County, NY	18.25
Spokane County, WA	18.09
Jackson County, MO	18.05
Gwinnett County, GA	17.78
Washtenaw County, MI	17.64
DeKalb County, GA	17.49
Monmouth County, NJ	16.67
Cuyahoga County, OH	16.56
Multnomah County, OR	16.45
St. Louis County, MO	16.05
Boulder County, CO	15.81
Essex County, MA	15.81
Shelby County, TN	15.66
Davidson County, TN	15.63
Hillsborough County, FL	14.92
San Francisco County, CA	14.77
Brevard County, FL	14.67
San Diego County, CA	14.47
Thurston County, WA	13.68
Tippecanoe County, IN	13.61
Mercer County, NJ	13.51
Denver County, CO	13.47
Washington County, OR	13.39
Middlesex County, MA	13.38
Wayne County, MI	13.37
Duval County, FL	13.36
Riverside County, CA	13.02
Arlington County, VA	12.76
Hennepin County, MN	12.58
Travis County, TX	12.44
Palm Beach County, FL	12.39
Milwaukee County, WI	12.24
Bell County, TX	12.04

Place	Percent
Provo, UT (city) Utah County	68.84
Pullman, WA (city) Whitman County	66.12
Pittsburgh, PA (city) Allegheny County	55.95
Eugene, OR (city) Lane County	53.06
Boston, MA (city) Suffolk County	47.85
Omaha, NE (city) Douglas County	43.01
Oklahoma City, OK (city) Oklahoma County	40.43
Philadelphia, PA (city) Philadelphia County	38.99
Fort Collins, CO (city) Larimer County	38.30
Vista, CA (city) San Diego County	37.69
Reno, NV (city) Washoe County	35.97
Santa Barbara, CA (city) Santa Barbara County	34.77
Boulder, CO (city) Boulder County	32.99
Tempe, AZ (city) Maricopa County	28.93
Pomona, CA (city) Los Angeles County	28.61
Davis, CA (city) Yolo County	28.43
Cambridge, MA (city) Middlesex County	27.07
Riverside, CA (city) Riverside County	26.95
Tucson, AZ (city) Pima County	26.91
Salem, OR (city) Marion County	26.54
Brookline, MA (town) Norfolk County	26.02
Hempstead, NY (town) Nassau County	25.74
Santa Cruz, CA (city) Santa Cruz County	25.50
Madison, WI (city) Dane County	24.52
Costa Mesa, CA (city) Orange County	24.43
Santa Monica, CA (city) Los Angeles County	24.32
Berkeley, CA (city) Alameda County	24.01
Monterey, CA (city) Monterey County	23.63
New York, NY (city)	23.59
Santa Rosa, CA (city) Sonoma County	20.88
Minneapolis, MN (city) Hennepin County	20.53
Eastchester, NY (cdp) Westchester County	20.22
West Covina, CA (city) Los Angeles County	20.03
Hayward, CA (city) Alameda County	19.75
Tacoma, WA (city) Pierce County	19.66
Pahala, HI (cdp) Hawaii County	18.79
Spring Valley, NV (cdp) Clark County	18.75
Portland, OR (city) Multnomah County	18.49
Ann Arbor, MI (city) Washtenaw County	17.91
San Buenaventura (Ventura), CA (city) Ventura County	17.51
Arden-Arcade, CA (cdp) Sacramento County	17.40
Pasadena, CA (city) Los Angeles County	17.20
San Diego, CA (city) San Diego County	17.17
Hawaiian Beaches, HI (cdp) Hawaii County	16.30
Nashville-Davidson, TN (sp. city) Davidson County	16.21
Lakewood, CO (city) Jefferson County	16.10
Seattle, WA (city) King County	15.92
Union City, CA (city) Alameda County	15.81
Phoenix, AZ (city) Maricopa County	15.55
Vancouver, WA (city) Clark County	15.23
Las Vegas, NV (city) Clark County	15.08
San Francisco, CA (city) San Francisco County	14.77
Alhambra, CA (city) Los Angeles County	14.69
Long Beach, CA (city) Los Angeles County	13.86
Goleta, CA (cdp) Santa Barbara County	13.85
Jacksonville, FL (city) Duval County	13.85
Los Angeles, CA (city) Los Angeles County	13.82
Shoreline, WA (city) King County	13.58
Oxnard, CA (city) Ventura County	13.55
Chicago, IL (city) Cook County	13.53
Tustin, CA (city) Orange County	13.48
Denver, CO (city) Denver County	13.47
Columbus, OH (city) Franklin County	13.35
Glendale, CA (city) Los Angeles County	13.10
Austin, TX (city) Travis County	13.06
Dublin, OH (city) Franklin County	13.05
Irvine, CA (city) Orange County	13.05
Renton, WA (city) King County	13.02
Fairfield, CA (city) Solano County	13.00
Bakersfield, CA (city) Kern County	12.79
Arlington, VA (cdp) Arlington County	12.76
Fresno, CA (city) Fresno County	12.73
Stockton, CA (city) San Joaquin County	12.13
Lodi, CA (city) San Joaquin County	12.08
Scarsdale, NY (village) Westchester County	11.86

Notes: Please refer to the User's Guide for an explanation of data; ranking tables include all places with Asian and/or NHPI populations above SF4 population thresholds; (1) tables reflect only those areas that meet SF4 population thresholds, therefore there may be less than 50 states, 75 counties or 75 places listed

Poverty Status

Koreans with Income Below Poverty Level

***All States, Top 75 Counties, and Top 75 Places Sorted by Number*[1]**

State	Number
United States	154,688
California	50,212
New York	18,456
Washington	7,833
Illinois	7,143
Texas	7,117
New Jersey	6,549
Virginia	5,766
Pennsylvania	5,151
Maryland	4,387
Hawaii	3,868
Georgia	3,552
Florida	3,025
Michigan	3,007
Massachusetts	2,919
Ohio	2,130
Oregon	1,898
Indiana	1,853
Colorado	1,759
Arizona	1,440
Wisconsin	1,345
North Carolina	1,331
Minnesota	1,245
Tennessee	1,229
Iowa	1,040
Nevada	921
Missouri	907
Connecticut	905
Oklahoma	823
Utah	766
Kansas	692
Kentucky	625
Alaska	619
Alabama	612
Rhode Island	499
South Carolina	499
Louisiana	467
Delaware	257
Nebraska	236
New Mexico	236
Mississippi	223
District of Columbia	190
West Virginia	144
New Hampshire	138
Montana	126
Arkansas	113
Maine	108
Idaho	93
Vermont	91
Wyoming	61
North Dakota	60
South Dakota	22

County	Number
Los Angeles County, CA	28,972
Queens County, NY	10,397
Orange County, CA	7,345
Cook County, IL	5,091
Bergen County, NJ	4,022
Honolulu County, HI	3,510
King County, WA	3,349
Fairfax County, VA	3,012
Santa Clara County, CA	2,385
Pierce County, WA	2,377
New York County, NY	2,244
Alameda County, CA	2,134
San Diego County, CA	2,094
Philadelphia County, PA	1,629
Dallas County, TX	1,482
Montgomery County, MD	1,319
Kings County, NY	1,216
Travis County, TX	1,207
Harris County, TX	1,168
San Bernardino County, CA	1,086
Montgomery County, PA	1,058
San Francisco County, CA	1,053
Snohomish County, WA	1,000
Riverside County, CA	968
Middlesex County, MA	965
Suffolk County, MA	963
Champaign County, IL	957
Washtenaw County, MI	906
Maricopa County, AZ	867
Dane County, WI	807
Tarrant County, TX	786
Franklin County, OH	775
Clark County, NV	750
DeKalb County, GA	726
Gwinnett County, GA	669
Howard County, MD	639
Middlesex County, NJ	633
Ingham County, MI	621
Prince George's County, MD	616
Hennepin County, MN	603
Nassau County, NY	596
Tippecanoe County, IN	591
Baltimore County, MD	586
Washington County, OR	583
Allegheny County, PA	575
Erie County, NY	569
Baltimore Independent City, MD	550
Contra Costa County, CA	535
Monroe County, IN	519
Santa Barbara County, CA	518
Anchorage Borough, AK	500
Bronx County, NY	499
Sacramento County, CA	478
San Mateo County, CA	464
Onondaga County, NY	463
Hudson County, NJ	462
Centre County, PA	460
Norfolk County, MA	458
Broward County, FL	444
Johnson County, IA	442
Alachua County, FL	441
Orange County, FL	440
El Paso County, CO	439
Brazos County, TX	437
Delaware County, PA	422
Providence County, RI	412
Fulton County, GA	409
Yolo County, CA	403
Hillsborough County, FL	401
Tompkins County, NY	398
Denton County, TX	397
Multnomah County, OR	397
Montgomery County, VA	387
Pima County, AZ	387
Cobb County, GA	386

Place	Number
Los Angeles, CA (city) Los Angeles County	18,493
New York, NY (city)	14,593
Chicago, IL (city) Cook County	3,617
Honolulu, HI (cdp) Honolulu County	2,940
Philadelphia, PA (city) Philadelphia County	1,629
Glendale, CA (city) Los Angeles County	1,566
San Diego, CA (city) San Diego County	1,524
Irvine, CA (city) Orange County	1,520
Seattle, WA (city) King County	1,189
Fullerton, CA (city) Orange County	1,170
Austin, TX (city) Travis County	1,153
San Francisco, CA (city) San Francisco County	1,053
Houston, TX (city) Harris County	1,052
San Jose, CA (city) Santa Clara County	969
Boston, MA (city) Suffolk County	903
Garden Grove, CA (city) Orange County	849
Berkeley, CA (city) Alameda County	848
Buena Park, CA (city) Orange County	829
Torrance, CA (city) Los Angeles County	825
Palisades Park, NJ (borough) Bergen County	779
Madison, WI (city) Dane County	776
Tacoma, WA (city) Pierce County	750
Dallas, TX (city) Dallas County	740
Anaheim, CA (city) Orange County	739
Ann Arbor, MI (city) Washtenaw County	724
Lakewood, WA (city) Pierce County	724
Fort Lee, NJ (borough) Bergen County	704
Columbus, OH (city) Franklin County	688
Federal Way, WA (city) King County	666
Annandale, VA (cdp) Fairfax County	589
Cerritos, CA (city) Los Angeles County	572
Gardena, CA (city) Los Angeles County	524
Urbana, IL (city) Champaign County	513
Bloomington, IN (city) Monroe County	507
Diamond Bar, CA (city) Los Angeles County	495
Hacienda Heights, CA (cdp) Los Angeles County	457
Rowland Heights, CA (cdp) Los Angeles County	449
Pittsburgh, PA (city) Allegheny County	441
Riverside, CA (city) Riverside County	440
Minneapolis, MN (city) Hennepin County	390
College Station, TX (city) Brazos County	388
Blacksburg, VA (town) Montgomery County	387
Providence, RI (city) Providence County	384
Oakland, CA (city) Alameda County	372
Pasadena, CA (city) Los Angeles County	372
Norwalk, CA (city) Los Angeles County	364
Brookline, MA (town) Norfolk County	360
Leonia, NJ (borough) Bergen County	354
Athens-Clarke County, GA (sp. city) Clarke County	348
Sunnyvale, CA (city) Santa Clara County	345
Portland, OR (city) Multnomah County	344
Ellicott City, MD (cdp) Howard County	337
Champaign, IL (city) Champaign County	334
Colorado Springs, CO (city) El Paso County	334
Fort Worth, TX (city) Tarrant County	334
Cambridge, MA (city) Middlesex County	330
Davis, CA (city) Yolo County	330
Irving, TX (city) Dallas County	330
Lakewood, CA (city) Los Angeles County	328
Arlington, TX (city) Tarrant County	327
Shoreline, WA (city) King County	325
Isla Vista, CA (cdp) Santa Barbara County	320
State College, PA (borough) Centre County	315
East Lansing, MI (city) Ingham County	314
Santa Clara, CA (city) Santa Clara County	309
Long Beach, CA (city) Los Angeles County	308
Tucson, AZ (city) Pima County	308
Jersey City, NJ (city) Hudson County	297
Aurora, CO (city) Arapahoe County	296
Arlington, VA (cdp) Arlington County	291
Iowa City, IA (city) Johnson County	291
Tampa, FL (city) Hillsborough County	291
Oklahoma City, OK (city) Oklahoma County	281
Denton, TX (city) Denton County	280
Ames, IA (city) Story County	279

Notes: Please refer to the User's Guide for an explanation of data; ranking tables include all places with Asian and/or NHPI populations above SF4 population thresholds; (1) tables reflect only those areas that meet SF4 population thresholds, therefore there may be less than 50 states, 75 counties or 75 places listed

Poverty Status

Koreans with Income Below Poverty Level

All States, Top 75 Counties, and Top 75 Places Sorted by Percent[1]

State	Percent
Rhode Island	29.34
Indiana	28.02
Iowa	22.37
Utah	21.95
Wisconsin	20.46
North Dakota	19.23
Massachusetts	18.82
District of Columbia	18.68
Oklahoma	18.68
Tennessee	18.32
Mississippi	17.81
Louisiana	17.68
Washington	17.10
West Virginia	16.94
Kentucky	16.72
Hawaii	16.60
Kansas	16.57
Maine	16.41
Texas	16.30
Pennsylvania	16.26
Florida	16.05
New York	15.77
Ohio	15.68
Alabama	15.48
Montana	15.42
Vermont	15.35
Oregon	15.24
South Carolina	14.96
Michigan	14.89
California	14.82
Arizona	14.77
United States	14.77
Missouri	14.48
Illinois	14.21
Connecticut	13.97
Delaware	13.97
New Mexico	13.87
Alaska	13.67
Wyoming	13.32
Virginia	13.02
Georgia	13.01
Nevada	12.33
Colorado	11.76
Maryland	11.35
North Carolina	11.30
Nebraska	10.89
New Jersey	10.33
Minnesota	10.03
Arkansas	7.91
Idaho	7.89
New Hampshire	7.61
South Dakota	3.17

County	Percent
Clarke County, GA	69.88
Tippecanoe County, IN	67.47
Johnson County, IA	63.14
Montgomery County, VA	61.82
Monroe County, IN	56.29
Centre County, PA	50.83
Broome County, NY	50.56
Brazos County, TX	48.99
Champaign County, IL	47.33
Berrien County, MI	46.77
Alachua County, FL	45.23
Dane County, WI	44.24
Benton County, OR	43.73
Ingham County, MI	42.56
Yolo County, CA	42.38
Suffolk County, MA	42.35
Story County, IA	42.12
Knox County, TN	41.87
Providence County, RI	41.45
Tompkins County, NY	41.37
Whatcom County, WA	40.35
Boone County, MO	40.25
Wicomico County, MD	39.59
Chatham County, GA	39.04
Onondaga County, NY	37.73
Orange County, NC	37.25
Riley County, KS	37.05
Baltimore Independent City, MD	34.61
Santa Barbara County, CA	32.54
Oklahoma County, OK	32.38
Erie County, NY	31.77
Northampton County, PA	31.19
Utah County, UT	30.74
Leon County, FL	30.49
Travis County, TX	30.27
Larimer County, CO	28.50
Lane County, OR	27.43
Douglas County, KS	27.10
Washtenaw County, MI	26.55
Philadelphia County, PA	26.39
Alexandria Independent City, VA	26.27
Allegheny County, PA	26.11
Tarrant County, TX	24.90
Richland County, SC	24.68
Franklin County, OH	24.17
Hamilton County, OH	23.96
Volusia County, FL	23.68
Hamilton County, TN	23.63
Jefferson County, AL	23.03
Albany County, NY	22.96
Vernon Parish, LA	22.84
Coryell County, TX	22.77
DeKalb County, GA	22.68
Hawaii County, HI	22.53
Norfolk County, MA	22.20
Cleveland County, OK	21.77
Boulder County, CO	21.58
Pierce County, WA	21.54
New York County, NY	21.45
Linn County, IA	21.43
Denver County, CO	21.39
Arlington County, VA	20.98
Orange County, FL	20.51
Milwaukee County, WI	19.95
Broward County, FL	19.75
Salt Lake County, UT	19.49
San Diego County, CA	19.35
Sedgwick County, KS	19.35
Jefferson County, KY	19.33
St. Joseph County, IN	19.13
Shelby County, TN	18.76
Jackson County, MO	18.66
Marion County, OR	18.55
Marion County, IN	18.34
Denton County, TX	18.17

Place	Percent
Isla Vista, CA (cdp) Santa Barbara County	79.60
Athens-Clarke County, GA (sp. city) Clarke County	69.88
Blacksburg, VA (town) Montgomery County	69.60
Ithaca, NY (city) Tompkins County	68.60
State College, PA (borough) Centre County	68.03
Providence, RI (city) Providence County	67.37
Iowa City, IA (city) Johnson County	61.65
Bloomington, IN (city) Monroe County	61.60
Urbana, IL (city) Champaign County	59.58
Berkeley, CA (city) Alameda County	57.96
Denton, TX (city) Denton County	57.49
Syracuse, NY (city) Onondaga County	52.29
Corvallis, OR (city) Benton County	52.27
Stanford, CA (cdp) Santa Clara County	51.72
Gainesville, FL (city) Alachua County	51.59
College Station, TX (city) Brazos County	50.92
Madison, WI (city) Dane County	47.96
Meridian charter, MI (township) Ingham County	47.89
Champaign, IL (city) Champaign County	46.91
Davis, CA (city) Yolo County	46.81
East Lansing, MI (city) Ingham County	44.73
Ames, IA (city) Story County	42.92
Pittsburgh, PA (city) Allegheny County	42.90
Boston, MA (city) Suffolk County	42.86
Columbia, SC (city) Richland County	42.59
New Haven, CT (city) New Haven County	41.76
Columbia, MO (city) Boone County	41.10
Chapel Hill, NC (town) Orange County	41.09
Tempe, AZ (city) Maricopa County	40.29
Silver Spring, MD (cdp) Montgomery County	39.82
Concord, CA (city) Contra Costa County	39.52
Fort Collins, CO (city) Larimer County	38.89
Louisville, KY (city) Jefferson County	36.57
Brookline, MA (town) Norfolk County	36.51
Norman, OK (city) Cleveland County	36.18
Arlington, TX (city) Tarrant County	36.09
Salt Lake City, UT (city) Salt Lake County	35.04
Amherst, NY (town) Erie County	34.39
Austin, TX (city) Travis County	33.28
San Bernardino, CA (city) San Bernardino County	32.20
Costa Mesa, CA (city) Orange County	31.96
Ann Arbor, MI (city) Washtenaw County	31.88
Evanston, IL (city) Cook County	31.80
Milwaukee, WI (city) Milwaukee County	31.38
Fort Worth, TX (city) Tarrant County	31.19
Lakewood, WA (city) Pierce County	31.09
Boulder, CO (city) Boulder County	30.94
Hawaiian Gardens, CA (city) Los Angeles County	30.86
Memphis, TN (city) Shelby County	30.42
Chicago, IL (city) Cook County	30.41
Tampa, FL (city) Hillsborough County	30.22
Somerville, MA (city) Middlesex County	30.20
Oklahoma City, OK (city) Oklahoma County	29.42
Columbus, OH (city) Franklin County	28.64
Eugene, OR (city) Lane County	27.89
Lawrence, KS (city) Douglas County	27.33
Browns Mills, NJ (cdp) Burlington County	27.14
Pasadena, CA (city) Los Angeles County	26.94
Philadelphia, PA (city) Philadelphia County	26.39
Riverside, CA (city) Riverside County	25.88
Bellflower, CA (city) Los Angeles County	25.73
Seattle, WA (city) King County	25.54
Minneapolis, MN (city) Hennepin County	25.42
Atlanta, GA (city) Fulton County	25.40
Tucson, AZ (city) Pima County	25.39
Little Ferry, NJ (borough) Bergen County	25.34
Beltsville, MD (cdp) Prince George's County	24.65
Cheltenham, PA (township) Montgomery County	24.61
Picnic Pt.-N. Lynnwood, WA (cdp) Snohomish County	24.57
Tacoma, WA (city) Pierce County	24.50
Santa Ana, CA (city) Orange County	24.34
Leonia, NJ (borough) Bergen County	24.26
Cambridge, MA (city) Middlesex County	24.14
Shoreline, WA (city) King County	23.88
Cockeysville, MD (cdp) Baltimore County	23.80

Notes: Please refer to the User's Guide for an explanation of data; ranking tables include all places with Asian and/or NHPI populations above SF4 population thresholds; (1) tables reflect only those areas that meet SF4 population thresholds, therefore there may be less than 50 states, 75 counties or 75 places listed

Poverty Status

Laotians with Income Below Poverty Level

All States, Top 75 Counties, and Top 75 Places Sorted by Number[1]

State	Number
United States	30,604
California	18,096
Minnesota	1,385
Washington	1,362
Texas	1,018
Wisconsin	831
Hawaii	538
North Carolina	508
Rhode Island	495
Georgia	423
Tennessee	416
Oregon	397
Michigan	365
Arkansas	349
New York	348
Florida	337
Ohio	336
Alaska	331
Iowa	305
Connecticut	248
Virginia	239
Massachusetts	237
Pennsylvania	234
Illinois	214
Utah	196
Kansas	191
Louisiana	183
Colorado	142
Missouri	117
Nevada	116
Alabama	93
Maryland	84
New Hampshire	63
Indiana	52
South Carolina	49
Arizona	46
Nebraska	33
South Dakota	25
Oklahoma	19
Idaho	14
New Jersey	0

County	Number
Fresno County, CA	3,618
Sacramento County, CA	3,233
San Diego County, CA	1,431
San Joaquin County, CA	1,395
Tulare County, CA	1,344
Alameda County, CA	926
Shasta County, CA	849
Stanislaus County, CA	768
King County, WA	739
Los Angeles County, CA	704
Contra Costa County, CA	699
Merced County, CA	647
Hennepin County, MN	564
Honolulu County, HI	538
Milwaukee County, WI	501
Providence County, RI	495
Butte County, CA	390
Yolo County, CA	370
Riverside County, CA	369
Tarrant County, TX	349
Anchorage Borough, AK	317
Ramsey County, MN	298
Orange County, CA	279
Davidson County, TN	260
Multnomah County, OR	246
Dallas County, TX	241
Solano County, CA	202
Franklin County, OH	187
Iberia Parish, LA	170
Catawba County, NC	158
Pierce County, WA	156
Philadelphia County, PA	146
Pinellas County, FL	141
Sonoma County, CA	140
Brown County, WI	134
Salt Lake County, UT	126
Dakota County, MN	123
Harris County, TX	123
Hartford County, CT	121
San Bernardino County, CA	116
Sebastian County, AR	115
Clayton County, GA	112
Middlesex County, MA	112
Potter County, TX	111
Fairfield County, CT	108
Monroe County, NY	105
Clark County, NV	104
Olmsted County, MN	102
Snohomish County, WA	102
Fairfax County, VA	95
Broome County, NY	91
Pacific County, WA	91
Sedgwick County, KS	86
Nobles County, MN	79
Polk County, IA	78
Washington County, OR	76
Rutherford County, TN	73
Buena Vista County, IA	72
Winnebago County, IL	69
Worcester County, MA	68
Guilford County, NC	67
Summit County, OH	66
Habersham County, GA	60
Ottawa County, MI	54
Mobile County, AL	53
Santa Clara County, CA	50
Burke County, NC	45
Cook County, IL	43
Johnson County, KS	41
Washington County, AR	41
Clark County, WA	37
Polk County, FL	36
Franklin County, WA	35
Kane County, IL	34
Maricopa County, AZ	34

Place	Number
Fresno, CA (city) Fresno County	3,227
Sacramento, CA (city) Sacramento County	2,221
Stockton, CA (city) San Joaquin County	1,367
San Diego, CA (city) San Diego County	1,206
Visalia, CA (city) Tulare County	950
Oakland, CA (city) Alameda County	872
Redding, CA (city) Shasta County	780
Merced, CA (city) Merced County	601
Modesto, CA (city) Stanislaus County	589
Seattle, WA (city) King County	533
Parkway-S. Sacramento, CA (cdp) Sacramento County	515
Minneapolis, MN (city) Hennepin County	503
Milwaukee, WI (city) Milwaukee County	501
Honolulu, HI (cdp) Honolulu County	393
Providence, RI (city) Providence County	365
Richmond, CA (city) Contra Costa County	360
St. Paul, MN (city) Ramsey County	275
Nashville-Davidson, TN (sp. city) Davidson County	260
Portland, OR (city) Multnomah County	226
Los Angeles, CA (city) Los Angeles County	222
San Pablo, CA (city) Contra Costa County	203
Columbus, OH (city) Franklin County	187
Moreno Valley, CA (city) Riverside County	172
Long Beach, CA (city) Los Angeles County	156
Tacoma, WA (city) Pierce County	149
Philadelphia, PA (city) Philadelphia County	146
Pomona, CA (city) Los Angeles County	135
Green Bay, WI (city) Brown County	134
Woonsocket, RI (city) Providence County	130
Santa Ana, CA (city) Orange County	129
Escondido, CA (city) San Diego County	124
Dallas, TX (city) Dallas County	117
Amarillo, TX (city) Potter County	111
Bridgeport, CT (city) Fairfield County	108
Banning, CA (city) Riverside County	105
Fort Worth, TX (city) Tarrant County	104
Fairfield, CA (city) Solano County	103
Rochester, MN (city) Olmsted County	102
Fort Smith, AR (city) Sebastian County	95
Santa Rosa, CA (city) Sonoma County	94
Riverside, CA (city) Riverside County	88
Raymond, WA (city) Pacific County	86
West Valley City, UT (city) Salt Lake County	85
Haltom City, TX (city) Tarrant County	83
Des Moines, IA (city) Polk County	78
Lowell, MA (city) Middlesex County	77
Rochester, NY (city) Monroe County	77
New Britain, CT (city) Hartford County	72
Storm Lake, IA (city) Buena Vista County	72
Worthington, MN (city) Nobles County	67
Akron, OH (city) Summit County	66
Murfreesboro, TN (city) Rutherford County	66
Springfield, VA (cdp) Fairfax County	66
Rockford, IL (city) Winnebago County	65
Brooklyn Park, MN (city) Hennepin County	55
Wichita, KS (city) Sedgwick County	51
St. Petersburg, FL (city) Pinellas County	49
Anaheim, CA (city) Orange County	47
San Jose, CA (city) Santa Clara County	44
Grand Prairie, TX (city) Dallas County	42
Oaklawn-Sunview, KS (cdp) Sedgwick County	35
Fitchburg, MA (city) Worcester County	26
Irving, TX (city) Dallas County	26
Westminster, CO (city) Adams County	23
Warroad, MN (city) Roseau County	12
Winfield, KS (city) Cowley County	10
Charlotte, NC (city) Mecklenburg County	8
Arvada, CO (city) Jefferson County	7
Oklahoma City, OK (city) Oklahoma County	4
Bellevue, WA (city) King County	0
Brooklyn Center, MN (city) Hennepin County	0
Elgin, IL (city) Kane County	0
Springdale, AR (city) Washington County	0

Notes: Please refer to the User's Guide for an explanation of data; ranking tables include all places with Asian and/or NHPI populations above SF4 population thresholds; (1) tables reflect only those areas that meet SF4 population thresholds, therefore there may be less than 50 states, 75 counties or 75 places listed

Poverty Status

Laotians with Income Below Poverty Level

***All States, Top 75 Counties, and Top 75 Places Sorted by Percent*[1]**

State	Percent
Hawaii	32.82
California	32.18
Alaska	24.57
Wisconsin	20.39
United States	18.51
Rhode Island	17.67
Washington	17.16
New Hampshire	16.98
Missouri	16.39
Minnesota	15.57
Louisiana	14.42
Michigan	13.18
Alabama	13.17
Arkansas	13.07
South Dakota	11.63
Maryland	11.41
Ohio	11.28
New York	11.10
Oregon	10.90
Pennsylvania	10.44
Texas	10.43
North Carolina	10.40
Tennessee	10.38
Nevada	9.99
Georgia	9.12
Utah	8.96
Florida	8.37
Virginia	8.08
Connecticut	8.06
Iowa	7.87
Kansas	6.75
Massachusetts	6.69
Colorado	6.22
Indiana	5.37
Arizona	5.19
Illinois	4.43
Nebraska	4.26
South Carolina	3.72
Idaho	2.76
Oklahoma	2.21
New Jersey	0.00

County	Percent
Butte County, CA	70.78
Yolo County, CA	70.61
Fresno County, CA	57.97
Shasta County, CA	49.45
Stanislaus County, CA	48.42
San Joaquin County, CA	45.77
Tulare County, CA	42.90
Pierce County, WA	41.49
Merced County, CA	37.68
Sacramento County, CA	33.83
Honolulu County, HI	33.67
Ramsey County, MN	32.18
Brown County, WI	31.31
Alameda County, CA	29.65
Milwaukee County, WI	29.16
Solano County, CA	27.82
Pacific County, WA	26.45
San Bernardino County, CA	26.07
Anchorage Borough, AK	25.48
Riverside County, CA	24.87
Catawba County, NC	24.31
Olmsted County, MN	24.23
Los Angeles County, CA	22.62
San Diego County, CA	20.36
Davidson County, TN	19.83
Nobles County, MN	19.55
Iberia Parish, LA	19.12
Providence County, RI	18.41
Broome County, NY	18.09
Dakota County, MN	17.18
Mobile County, AL	16.88
Contra Costa County, CA	16.55
Franklin County, OH	16.53
King County, WA	14.87
Guilford County, NC	13.73
Snohomish County, WA	13.35
Montgomery County, NC	13.33
Habersham County, GA	13.10
Sonoma County, CA	13.08
Hennepin County, MN	12.85
Franklin County, WA	12.64
Washington County, OR	12.62
Buena Vista County, IA	12.46
Philadelphia County, PA	12.03
Tarrant County, TX	11.03
Fairfield County, CT	10.48
Potter County, TX	10.48
Harris County, TX	10.41
Dallas County, TX	10.39
Sebastian County, AR	9.97
Hartford County, CT	9.96
Orange County, CA	9.65
Multnomah County, OR	9.60
Burke County, NC	9.13
Clark County, NV	9.05
Polk County, FL	8.98
Clark County, WA	8.96
Clayton County, GA	8.90
Summit County, OH	8.80
Sedgwick County, KS	8.26
Monroe County, NY	7.80
Roseau County, MN	7.80
Pinellas County, FL	7.60
Washington County, AR	7.44
Salt Lake County, UT	7.11
Worcester County, MA	7.02
Johnson County, KS	6.41
Fairfax County, VA	6.31
Middlesex County, MA	6.28
Maricopa County, AZ	5.66
Winnebago County, IL	5.31
Ottawa County, MI	4.75
Polk County, IA	4.72
Rutherford County, TN	4.66
Dakota County, NE	4.50

Place	Percent
Fresno, CA (city) Fresno County	59.09
Modesto, CA (city) Stanislaus County	51.62
Redding, CA (city) Shasta County	50.88
Tacoma, WA (city) Pierce County	50.00
Stockton, CA (city) San Joaquin County	46.56
Visalia, CA (city) Tulare County	44.29
Merced, CA (city) Merced County	43.30
Honolulu, HI (cdp) Honolulu County	40.23
Parkway-S. Sacramento, CA (cdp) Sacramento County	37.13
Oakland, CA (city) Alameda County	37.00
Sacramento, CA (city) Sacramento County	35.59
Moreno Valley, CA (city) Riverside County	35.25
Green Bay, WI (city) Brown County	35.08
Milwaukee, WI (city) Milwaukee County	33.44
Los Angeles, CA (city) Los Angeles County	33.28
Raymond, WA (city) Pacific County	33.20
St. Paul, MN (city) Ramsey County	32.20
Minneapolis, MN (city) Hennepin County	31.30
Banning, CA (city) Riverside County	30.79
Providence, RI (city) Providence County	27.53
Fairfield, CA (city) Solano County	26.48
Escondido, CA (city) San Diego County	25.89
Riverside, CA (city) Riverside County	25.88
Pomona, CA (city) Los Angeles County	25.33
Rochester, MN (city) Olmsted County	24.34
Bridgeport, CT (city) Fairfield County	21.56
Long Beach, CA (city) Los Angeles County	21.02
Seattle, WA (city) King County	20.27
San Diego, CA (city) San Diego County	20.19
Fort Worth, TX (city) Tarrant County	19.96
Nashville-Davidson, TN (sp. city) Davidson County	19.83
New Britain, CT (city) Hartford County	19.30
Columbus, OH (city) Franklin County	19.10
West Valley City, UT (city) Salt Lake County	18.44
San Pablo, CA (city) Contra Costa County	18.27
Worthington, MN (city) Nobles County	18.06
Springfield, VA (cdp) Fairfax County	16.58
Richmond, CA (city) Contra Costa County	15.27
Santa Rosa, CA (city) Sonoma County	15.14
Woonsocket, RI (city) Providence County	14.25
Storm Lake, IA (city) Buena Vista County	13.66
Santa Ana, CA (city) Orange County	13.34
Dallas, TX (city) Dallas County	12.89
Philadelphia, PA (city) Philadelphia County	12.03
Akron, OH (city) Summit County	11.81
Oaklawn-Sunview, KS (cdp) Sedgwick County	11.67
Grand Prairie, TX (city) Dallas County	10.74
Amarillo, TX (city) Potter County	10.46
Haltom City, TX (city) Tarrant County	10.22
Portland, OR (city) Multnomah County	9.87
Warroad, MN (city) Roseau County	9.60
Rochester, NY (city) Monroe County	9.57
Murfreesboro, TN (city) Rutherford County	9.34
Fort Smith, AR (city) Sebastian County	8.46
Wichita, KS (city) Sedgwick County	7.35
Rockford, IL (city) Winnebago County	7.24
Fitchburg, MA (city) Worcester County	6.67
Anaheim, CA (city) Orange County	5.90
Des Moines, IA (city) Polk County	5.72
Irving, TX (city) Dallas County	5.43
Lowell, MA (city) Middlesex County	5.25
St. Petersburg, FL (city) Pinellas County	4.32
Brooklyn Park, MN (city) Hennepin County	3.81
Westminster, CO (city) Adams County	3.40
Winfield, KS (city) Cowley County	2.91
San Jose, CA (city) Santa Clara County	2.40
Arvada, CO (city) Jefferson County	1.46
Charlotte, NC (city) Mecklenburg County	0.92
Oklahoma City, OK (city) Oklahoma County	0.79
Bellevue, WA (city) King County	0.00
Brooklyn Center, MN (city) Hennepin County	0.00
Elgin, IL (city) Kane County	0.00
Springdale, AR (city) Washington County	0.00

Notes: Please refer to the User's Guide for an explanation of data; ranking tables include all places with Asian and/or NHPI populations above SF4 population thresholds; (1) tables reflect only those areas that meet SF4 population thresholds, therefore there may be less than 50 states, 75 counties or 75 places listed

Poverty Status

Malaysians with Income Below Poverty Level

All States, Top 75 Counties, and Top 75 Places Sorted by Number[1]

State	Number
United States	2,618
Oklahoma	314
New York	263
California	225
Michigan	168
Ohio	143
Texas	91
Illinois	70

County	Number
Los Angeles County, CA	89
Queens County, NY	61

Place	Number
New York, NY (city)	238

Notes: Please refer to the User's Guide for an explanation of data; ranking tables include all places with Asian and/or NHPI populations above SF4 population thresholds; (1) tables reflect only those areas that meet SF4 population thresholds, therefore there may be less than 50 states, 75 counties or 75 places listed

Poverty Status

Malaysians with Income Below Poverty Level

All States, Top 75 Counties, and Top 75 Places Sorted by Percent[1]

State	Percent
Oklahoma	61.09
Ohio	43.60
Michigan	37.09
United States	25.04
New York	19.23
Texas	13.58
California	13.04
Illinois	12.96

County	Percent
Los Angeles County, CA	17.52
Queens County, NY	10.76

Place	Percent
New York, NY (city)	19.88

Notes: Please refer to the User's Guide for an explanation of data; ranking tables include all places with Asian and/or NHPI populations above SF4 population thresholds; (1) tables reflect only those areas that meet SF4 population thresholds, therefore there may be less than 50 states, 75 counties or 75 places listed

Poverty Status

Pakistanis with Income Below Poverty Level

All States, Top 75 Counties, and Top 75 Places Sorted by Number[1]

State	Number
United States	25,406
New York	7,135
Texas	3,246
California	3,057
Illinois	2,394
Virginia	1,854
New Jersey	1,429
Florida	856
Michigan	537
Massachusetts	509
Maryland	467
Georgia	400
North Carolina	382
Pennsylvania	344
Ohio	337
Oklahoma	333
Connecticut	325
Wisconsin	190
Tennessee	187
Louisiana	154
Minnesota	152
Indiana	108
Utah	98
Kansas	97
Washington	93
Alabama	82
Missouri	77
Colorado	76
West Virginia	62
Oregon	59
Arizona	45
Iowa	36
Nevada	29
Kentucky	7
Delaware	0

County	Number
Kings County, NY	3,536
Queens County, NY	2,351
Cook County, IL	2,147
Harris County, TX	1,624
Los Angeles County, CA	1,005
Fairfax County, VA	974
Dallas County, TX	536
San Joaquin County, CA	511
Hudson County, NJ	439
Sacramento County, CA	342
Alameda County, CA	285
Wayne County, MI	259
Arlington County, VA	248
New York County, NY	247
Fort Bend County, TX	240
Tarrant County, TX	212
Suffolk County, NY	210
Tulsa County, OK	209
Middlesex County, MA	206
Travis County, TX	190
Bronx County, NY	179
Atlantic County, NJ	178
Orange County, CA	177
Essex County, NJ	170
Bergen County, NJ	167
Miami-Dade County, FL	167
Guilford County, NC	161
Hartford County, CT	144
San Bernardino County, CA	141
DuPage County, IL	131
Middlesex County, NJ	128
Franklin County, OH	127
Philadelphia County, PA	122
Orange County, FL	119
Hennepin County, MN	118
Montgomery County, MD	118
Gwinnett County, GA	115
Mercer County, NJ	111
Contra Costa County, CA	109
Delaware County, PA	103
New Haven County, CT	100
Prince William County, VA	100
Westchester County, NY	94
Milwaukee County, WI	91
Monroe County, NY	83
Somerset County, NJ	82
Broward County, FL	79
Collin County, TX	78
Clayton County, GA	76
Santa Clara County, CA	74
Monmouth County, NJ	73
Alexandria Independent City, VA	70
Washtenaw County, MI	61
Wake County, NC	59
Oakland County, MI	56
San Diego County, CA	53
Baltimore County, MD	51
Nassau County, NY	49
Howard County, MD	48
Macomb County, MI	48
Worcester County, MA	44
Jefferson Parish, LA	43
St. Louis County, MO	43
San Francisco County, CA	42
Morris County, NJ	40
King County, WA	39
Prince George's County, MD	38
Fairfield County, CT	35
Denton County, TX	28
Maricopa County, AZ	22
Snohomish County, WA	22
Richmond County, NY	19
Riverside County, CA	15
Cobb County, GA	8
Camden County, NJ	0

Place	Number
New York, NY (city)	6,332
Chicago, IL (city) Cook County	1,836
Houston, TX (city) Harris County	1,085
Los Angeles, CA (city) Los Angeles County	432
Jersey City, NJ (city) Hudson County	427
Arlington, VA (cdp) Arlington County	248
Sacramento, CA (city) Sacramento County	234
Lincolnia, VA (cdp) Fairfax County	229
Stockton, CA (city) San Joaquin County	217
Tulsa, OK (city) Tulsa County	209
Garland, TX (city) Dallas County	206
Dallas, TX (city) Dallas County	203
Austin, TX (city) Travis County	132
Torrance, CA (city) Los Angeles County	123
Philadelphia, PA (city) Philadelphia County	122
Mission Bend, TX (cdp) Fort Bend County	77
Carrollton, TX (city) Denton County	76
Old Bridge, NJ (township) Middlesex County	75
Brookhaven, NY (town) Suffolk County	64
Dale City, VA (cdp) Prince William County	64
Sugar Land, TX (city) Fort Bend County	60
Richardson, TX (city) Dallas County	58
Anaheim, CA (city) Orange County	57
Fremont, CA (city) Alameda County	46
San Francisco, CA (city) San Francisco County	42
Santa Clara, CA (city) Santa Clara County	41
North Hempstead, NY (town) Nassau County	36
Ellicott City, MD (cdp) Howard County	34
Huntington, NY (town) Suffolk County	24
Woodbridge, NJ (township) Middlesex County	24
Irving, TX (city) Dallas County	22
Bailey's Crossroads, VA (cdp) Fairfax County	15
Hempstead, NY (town) Nassau County	9
San Jose, CA (city) Santa Clara County	9
Edison, NJ (township) Middlesex County	0
Plano, TX (city) Collin County	0
Skokie, IL (village) Cook County	0

Notes: Please refer to the User's Guide for an explanation of data; ranking tables include all places with Asian and/or NHPI populations above SF4 population thresholds; (1) tables reflect only those areas that meet SF4 population thresholds, therefore there may be less than 50 states, 75 counties or 75 places listed

Poverty Status

Pakistanis with Income Below Poverty Level

All States, Top 75 Counties, and Top 75 Places Sorted by Percent[1]

State	Percent
Oklahoma	30.55
Tennessee	25.07
Utah	24.44
Massachusetts	22.94
New York	22.33
Alabama	21.87
North Carolina	21.42
Ohio	21.10
Wisconsin	20.81
West Virginia	19.75
Virginia	17.88
Texas	17.28
United States	16.47
Indiana	16.17
Louisiana	15.96
Florida	15.81
California	15.59
Connecticut	15.59
Illinois	15.44
Oregon	15.36
Minnesota	14.41
Kansas	12.58
New Jersey	11.54
Pennsylvania	11.53
Michigan	10.86
Iowa	10.68
Georgia	10.34
Colorado	9.66
Maryland	9.19
Washington	7.73
Missouri	7.40
Arizona	6.70
Nevada	5.45
Kentucky	1.25
Delaware	0.00

County	Percent
Guilford County, NC	40.66
San Joaquin County, CA	38.45
Tulsa County, OK	38.42
Middlesex County, MA	37.87
Atlantic County, NJ	36.93
Kings County, NY	36.75
Arlington County, VA	31.35
Hennepin County, MN	28.92
Essex County, NJ	27.91
Travis County, TX	27.78
Milwaukee County, WI	25.63
Franklin County, OH	24.76
Sacramento County, CA	23.82
New York County, NY	23.21
Harris County, TX	22.16
Hartford County, CT	22.02
Tarrant County, TX	21.50
Los Angeles County, CA	21.49
Miami-Dade County, FL	21.03
Queens County, NY	20.93
San Bernardino County, CA	20.64
Cook County, IL	20.36
Philadelphia County, PA	19.84
Monroe County, NY	19.53
Hudson County, NJ	18.92
Clayton County, GA	18.14
Monmouth County, NJ	17.94
Mercer County, NJ	17.13
Delaware County, PA	15.97
Bronx County, NY	15.93
Fairfax County, VA	15.52
Contra Costa County, CA	15.40
New Haven County, CT	15.31
Dallas County, TX	14.52
Alameda County, CA	14.46
Wake County, NC	13.26
Orange County, FL	13.21
Washtenaw County, MI	13.12
Prince William County, VA	12.30
Alexandria Independent City, VA	12.20
Wayne County, MI	11.92
Bergen County, NJ	11.17
Westchester County, NY	11.16
Worcester County, MA	11.08
Suffolk County, NY	10.65
Gwinnett County, GA	10.07
Somerset County, NJ	10.07
San Diego County, CA	9.94
Fort Bend County, TX	9.83
Jefferson Parish, LA	9.66
Macomb County, MI	9.06
Collin County, TX	8.18
King County, WA	7.66
St. Louis County, MO	7.56
San Francisco County, CA	7.55
Howard County, MD	7.36
Broward County, FL	7.20
Orange County, CA	6.84
Montgomery County, MD	6.49
Fairfield County, CT	6.45
Oakland County, MI	5.76
Prince George's County, MD	5.59
Morris County, NJ	5.28
Snohomish County, WA	5.21
Baltimore County, MD	5.08
DuPage County, IL	4.65
Maricopa County, AZ	4.23
Middlesex County, NJ	4.06
Riverside County, CA	3.64
Denton County, TX	3.33
Santa Clara County, CA	2.71
Richmond County, NY	2.46
Nassau County, NY	2.09
Cobb County, GA	1.24
Camden County, NJ	0.00

Place	Percent
Tulsa, OK (city) Tulsa County	50.36
Lincolnia, VA (cdp) Fairfax County	44.29
Arlington, VA (cdp) Arlington County	31.35
Stockton, CA (city) San Joaquin County	31.27
Sacramento, CA (city) Sacramento County	30.04
Chicago, IL (city) Cook County	28.69
Austin, TX (city) Travis County	27.16
New York, NY (city)	26.59
Los Angeles, CA (city) Los Angeles County	26.54
Garland, TX (city) Dallas County	24.79
Jersey City, NJ (city) Hudson County	22.74
Houston, TX (city) Harris County	21.71
Philadelphia, PA (city) Philadelphia County	19.84
Dale City, VA (cdp) Prince William County	19.75
Torrance, CA (city) Los Angeles County	18.75
Dallas, TX (city) Dallas County	17.20
Mission Bend, TX (cdp) Fort Bend County	16.04
Old Bridge, NJ (township) Middlesex County	14.26
Richardson, TX (city) Dallas County	13.71
Anaheim, CA (city) Orange County	13.44
Sugar Land, TX (city) Fort Bend County	9.71
Brookhaven, NY (town) Suffolk County	8.94
Santa Clara, CA (city) Santa Clara County	8.74
Ellicott City, MD (cdp) Howard County	8.61
San Francisco, CA (city) San Francisco County	7.55
Carrollton, TX (city) Denton County	6.52
North Hempstead, NY (town) Nassau County	5.83
Huntington, NY (town) Suffolk County	5.49
Woodbridge, NJ (township) Middlesex County	5.14
Irving, TX (city) Dallas County	5.13
Bailey's Crossroads, VA (cdp) Fairfax County	4.18
Fremont, CA (city) Alameda County	4.17
San Jose, CA (city) Santa Clara County	0.69
Hempstead, NY (town) Nassau County	0.64
Edison, NJ (township) Middlesex County	0.00
Plano, TX (city) Collin County	0.00
Skokie, IL (village) Cook County	0.00

Notes: Please refer to the User's Guide for an explanation of data; ranking tables include all places with Asian and/or NHPI populations above SF4 population thresholds; (1) tables reflect only those areas that meet SF4 population thresholds, therefore there may be less than 50 states, 75 counties or 75 places listed

Poverty Status

Samoans with Income Below Poverty Level

All States, Top 75 Counties, and Top 75 Places Sorted by Number[1]

State	Number
United States	16,629
California	7,822
Hawaii	3,881
Washington	1,373
Utah	588
New York	289
Alaska	261
Texas	260
Missouri	184
Colorado	159
Nevada	148
Arizona	141
Ohio	130
Oregon	129
Pennsylvania	121
Florida	108
Illinois	91
Tennessee	72
Georgia	69
North Carolina	63
Michigan	61
Virginia	56
New Jersey	39

County	Number
Honolulu County, HI	3,742
Los Angeles County, CA	3,606
San Francisco County, CA	767
King County, WA	721
San Diego County, CA	613
San Bernardino County, CA	577
Sacramento County, CA	500
Pierce County, WA	403
Salt Lake County, UT	359
Orange County, CA	288
San Mateo County, CA	213
Anchorage Borough, AK	157
Santa Clara County, CA	145
Solano County, CA	137
Clark County, NV	131
Riverside County, CA	115
Alameda County, CA	108
Hawaii County, HI	99
Jackson County, MO	81
Utah County, UT	74
Ventura County, CA	71
San Joaquin County, CA	52
Maricopa County, AZ	48
Contra Costa County, CA	4

Place	Number
Honolulu, HI (cdp) Honolulu County	1,525
Long Beach, CA (city) Los Angeles County	1,488
Waipahu, HI (cdp) Honolulu County	779
San Francisco, CA (city) San Francisco County	767
Compton, CA (city) Los Angeles County	544
Seattle, WA (city) King County	467
San Diego, CA (city) San Diego County	392
Sacramento, CA (city) Sacramento County	389
Los Angeles, CA (city) Los Angeles County	309
New York, NY (city)	236
Halawa, HI (cdp) Honolulu County	197
Nanakuli, HI (cdp) Honolulu County	183
Laie, HI (cdp) Honolulu County	167
Tacoma, WA (city) Pierce County	165
Ewa Beach, HI (cdp) Honolulu County	144
San Jose, CA (city) Santa Clara County	138
Carson, CA (city) Los Angeles County	133
Salt Lake City, UT (city) Salt Lake County	118
San Bernardino, CA (city) San Bernardino County	116
Lakewood, WA (city) Pierce County	101
Federal Way, WA (city) King County	91
Oceanside, CA (city) San Diego County	84
Westminster, CA (city) Orange County	84
Oxnard, CA (city) Ventura County	71
Hauula, HI (cdp) Honolulu County	63
Garden Grove, CA (city) Orange County	57
West Valley City, UT (city) Salt Lake County	45
Anaheim, CA (city) Orange County	42
Santa Ana, CA (city) Orange County	29
Lakewood, CA (city) Los Angeles County	26
Kahuku, HI (cdp) Honolulu County	19
Hayward, CA (city) Alameda County	0

Notes: Please refer to the User's Guide for an explanation of data; ranking tables include all places with Asian and/or NHPI populations above SF4 population thresholds; (1) tables reflect only those areas that meet SF4 population thresholds, therefore there may be less than 50 states, 75 counties or 75 places listed

Poverty Status

Samoans with Income Below Poverty Level

All States, Top 75 Counties, and Top 75 Places Sorted by Percent[1]

State	Percent
Hawaii	27.81
Ohio	27.43
New York	20.58
California	20.39
United States	20.18
Washington	20.09
Missouri	18.59
Colorado	17.97
Oregon	17.60
Alaska	17.42
Arizona	16.73
Utah	16.07
North Carolina	15.95
Pennsylvania	15.09
Tennessee	14.78
Michigan	14.70
Florida	14.12
Texas	14.08
Virginia	12.36
Illinois	12.10
Georgia	9.52
Nevada	9.52
New Jersey	6.90

County	Percent
Sacramento County, CA	40.65
San Francisco County, CA	34.20
Hawaii County, HI	33.45
San Bernardino County, CA	29.60
Honolulu County, HI	27.83
Los Angeles County, CA	26.83
Pierce County, WA	23.93
Solano County, CA	21.92
King County, WA	18.79
Jackson County, MO	17.49
San Mateo County, CA	14.96
San Joaquin County, CA	14.44
Salt Lake County, UT	14.20
Utah County, UT	14.10
Anchorage Borough, AK	13.17
San Diego County, CA	12.59
Riverside County, CA	12.46
Clark County, NV	11.80
Ventura County, CA	11.75
Maricopa County, AZ	8.68
Santa Clara County, CA	8.52
Orange County, CA	7.81
Alameda County, CA	4.50
Contra Costa County, CA	0.53

Place	Percent
Compton, CA (city) Los Angeles County	55.45
Sacramento, CA (city) Sacramento County	53.07
Long Beach, CA (city) Los Angeles County	40.31
Waipahu, HI (cdp) Honolulu County	37.51
Honolulu, HI (cdp) Honolulu County	35.63
Seattle, WA (city) King County	35.54
Lakewood, WA (city) Pierce County	34.47
Ewa Beach, HI (cdp) Honolulu County	34.20
San Francisco, CA (city) San Francisco County	34.20
New York, NY (city)	33.15
Halawa, HI (cdp) Honolulu County	29.80
Tacoma, WA (city) Pierce County	27.05
San Bernardino, CA (city) San Bernardino County	26.42
Salt Lake City, UT (city) Salt Lake County	26.34
Laie, HI (cdp) Honolulu County	26.05
Hauula, HI (cdp) Honolulu County	25.20
Nanakuli, HI (cdp) Honolulu County	24.30
Westminster, CA (city) Orange County	22.34
Federal Way, WA (city) King County	18.53
San Diego, CA (city) San Diego County	18.52
Kahuku, HI (cdp) Honolulu County	15.83
Los Angeles, CA (city) Los Angeles County	15.20
Oxnard, CA (city) Ventura County	13.12
San Jose, CA (city) Santa Clara County	11.45
Carson, CA (city) Los Angeles County	9.25
Anaheim, CA (city) Orange County	7.57
Garden Grove, CA (city) Orange County	7.42
Oceanside, CA (city) San Diego County	5.48
West Valley City, UT (city) Salt Lake County	5.29
Lakewood, CA (city) Los Angeles County	4.35
Santa Ana, CA (city) Orange County	4.24
Hayward, CA (city) Alameda County	0.00

Notes: Please refer to the User's Guide for an explanation of data; ranking tables include all places with Asian and/or NHPI populations above SF4 population thresholds; (1) tables reflect only those areas that meet SF4 population thresholds, therefore there may be less than 50 states, 75 counties or 75 places listed

Poverty Status

Sri Lankans with Income Below Poverty Level

All States, Top 75 Counties, and Top 75 Places Sorted by Number[1]

State	Number
United States	1,933
New York	488
California	408
Texas	123
Illinois	101
New Jersey	90
Florida	77
Virginia	60
Ohio	54
Maryland	53
Massachusetts	44
Michigan	17
Pennsylvania	12
Washington	0

County	Number
Queens County, NY	244
Los Angeles County, CA	142
Richmond County, NY	72
Orange County, CA	66
Montgomery County, MD	42
Middlesex County, NJ	8

Place	Number
New York, NY (city)	444
Los Angeles, CA (city) Los Angeles County	81

Notes: Please refer to the User's Guide for an explanation of data; ranking tables include all places with Asian and/or NHPI populations above SF4 population thresholds; (1) tables reflect only those areas that meet SF4 population thresholds, therefore there may be less than 50 states, 75 counties or 75 places listed

Poverty Status

Sri Lankans with Income Below Poverty Level

All States, Top 75 Counties, and Top 75 Places Sorted by Percent[1]

State	Percent
Florida	19.54
Illinois	18.77
New York	18.34
Texas	12.85
Ohio	10.51
United States	10.36
Massachusetts	9.93
Virginia	9.60
California	7.68
New Jersey	7.03
Michigan	4.96
Maryland	4.78
Pennsylvania	3.99
Washington	0.00

County	Percent
Queens County, NY	26.04
Richmond County, NY	13.66
Orange County, CA	9.90
Los Angeles County, CA	5.91
Montgomery County, MD	5.61
Middlesex County, NJ	1.61

Place	Percent
New York, NY (city)	22.16
Los Angeles, CA (city) Los Angeles County	6.86

Notes: Please refer to the User's Guide for an explanation of data; ranking tables include all places with Asian and/or NHPI populations above SF4 population thresholds; (1) tables reflect only those areas that meet SF4 population thresholds, therefore there may be less than 50 states, 75 counties or 75 places listed

Poverty Status

Taiwanese with Income Below Poverty Level

All States, Top 75 Counties, and Top 75 Places Sorted by Number[1]

State	Number
United States	17,523
California	8,938
New York	1,354
Texas	1,026
Pennsylvania	613
Washington	549
Massachusetts	421
Illinois	396
New Jersey	388
Ohio	331
Florida	328
Michigan	286
Wisconsin	273
Maryland	238
Georgia	192
Arizona	188
Oklahoma	163
Colorado	160
Missouri	152
Indiana	147
Oregon	138
Virginia	135
Hawaii	129
Utah	127
Kansas	108
Nevada	96
Tennessee	82
Iowa	65
Minnesota	64
Connecticut	61
North Carolina	31
Louisiana	18

County	Number
Los Angeles County, CA	5,280
Orange County, CA	1,146
Alameda County, CA	585
Queens County, NY	478
Santa Clara County, CA	474
King County, WA	375
San Diego County, CA	326
San Bernardino County, CA	323
Harris County, TX	321
Cook County, IL	269
New York County, NY	239
Dane County, WI	230
Suffolk County, MA	194
Fort Bend County, TX	169
San Francisco County, CA	160
Washtenaw County, MI	156
Travis County, TX	144
Allegheny County, PA	138
Honolulu County, HI	126
Middlesex County, MA	124
Montgomery County, MD	124
Franklin County, OH	123
Middlesex County, NJ	121
Riverside County, CA	115
Maricopa County, AZ	93
Tarrant County, TX	92
Clark County, NV	87
Contra Costa County, CA	79
Norfolk County, MA	76
Mercer County, NJ	57
Dallas County, TX	55
DuPage County, IL	55
Morris County, NJ	44
Oakland County, MI	40
Suffolk County, NY	38
Gwinnett County, GA	29
Sacramento County, CA	29
San Mateo County, CA	28
Nassau County, NY	23
St. Louis County, MO	20
Fairfax County, VA	14
Westchester County, NY	14
Bergen County, NJ	13
Essex County, NJ	13
Collin County, TX	3
Somerset County, NJ	3
Ventura County, CA	3

Place	Number
New York, NY (city)	761
Los Angeles, CA (city) Los Angeles County	736
Hacienda Heights, CA (cdp) Los Angeles County	448
Rowland Heights, CA (cdp) Los Angeles County	409
Arcadia, CA (city) Los Angeles County	400
Alhambra, CA (city) Los Angeles County	329
Irvine, CA (city) Orange County	328
Diamond Bar, CA (city) Los Angeles County	270
Houston, TX (city) Harris County	249
Temple City, CA (city) Los Angeles County	249
Madison, WI (city) Dane County	230
Berkeley, CA (city) Alameda County	227
Torrance, CA (city) Los Angeles County	227
Walnut, CA (city) Los Angeles County	226
Seattle, WA (city) King County	208
Fremont, CA (city) Alameda County	206
San Diego, CA (city) San Diego County	205
Anaheim, CA (city) Orange County	201
Boston, MA (city) Suffolk County	194
Monterey Park, CA (city) Los Angeles County	176
Cypress, CA (city) Orange County	165
East San Gabriel, CA (cdp) Los Angeles County	163
San Francisco, CA (city) San Francisco County	160
Sugar Land, TX (city) Fort Bend County	157
Ann Arbor, MI (city) Washtenaw County	150
Chicago, IL (city) Cook County	149
Austin, TX (city) Travis County	144
Chino Hills, CA (city) San Bernardino County	136
Columbus, OH (city) Franklin County	123
San Jose, CA (city) Santa Clara County	117
San Marino, CA (city) Los Angeles County	114
West Covina, CA (city) Los Angeles County	113
Cerritos, CA (city) Los Angeles County	107
Sunnyvale, CA (city) Santa Clara County	105
Cupertino, CA (city) Santa Clara County	101
Honolulu, HI (cdp) Honolulu County	101
El Monte, CA (city) Los Angeles County	95
San Gabriel, CA (city) Los Angeles County	80
Arlington, TX (city) Tarrant County	74
Bellevue, WA (city) King County	74
Rancho Palos Verdes, CA (city) Los Angeles County	70
Edison, NJ (township) Middlesex County	67
Saratoga, CA (city) Santa Clara County	62
Fountain Valley, CA (city) Orange County	49
Upland, CA (city) San Bernardino County	45
Naperville, IL (city) Du Page County	44
Huntington Beach, CA (city) Orange County	40
Tustin, CA (city) Orange County	39
North Hempstead, NY (town) Nassau County	23
Orange, CA (city) Orange County	23
Troy, MI (city) Oakland County	20
Plano, TX (city) Collin County	0

Notes: Please refer to the User's Guide for an explanation of data; ranking tables include all places with Asian and/or NHPI populations above SF4 population thresholds; (1) tables reflect only those areas that meet SF4 population thresholds, therefore there may be less than 50 states, 75 counties or 75 places listed

Poverty Status

Taiwanese with Income Below Poverty Level

All States, Top 75 Counties, and Top 75 Places Sorted by Percent[1]

State	Percent
Oklahoma	49.70
Wisconsin	41.87
Utah	34.32
Pennsylvania	29.93
Colorado	25.24
Arizona	23.77
Kansas	21.77
Indiana	21.43
Massachusetts	19.38
New York	18.16
Oregon	18.16
Tennessee	16.63
Florida	16.34
Nevada	16.22
Missouri	15.98
Hawaii	15.81
Ohio	15.51
Iowa	15.22
Washington	14.90
United States	14.73
California	14.28
Minnesota	14.00
Texas	13.50
Michigan	13.02
Illinois	12.34
Virginia	10.78
Georgia	10.56
Maryland	10.44
Connecticut	8.68
New Jersey	6.70
Louisiana	3.64
North Carolina	3.32

County	Percent
Dane County, WI	55.16
Suffolk County, MA	47.67
Washtenaw County, MI	33.33
Allegheny County, PA	32.86
Riverside County, CA	26.56
New York County, NY	24.77
Norfolk County, MA	21.97
San Francisco County, CA	21.71
Clark County, NV	20.52
Travis County, TX	20.48
Franklin County, OH	17.96
Cook County, IL	17.31
Honolulu County, HI	16.03
San Bernardino County, CA	15.93
Los Angeles County, CA	15.39
Alameda County, CA	15.06
Harris County, TX	14.70
Maricopa County, AZ	14.49
San Diego County, CA	14.03
Fort Bend County, TX	13.90
Queens County, NY	13.80
Tarrant County, TX	13.69
King County, WA	12.60
Orange County, CA	12.60
Mercer County, NJ	11.95
Middlesex County, MA	11.46
Montgomery County, MD	10.84
Suffolk County, NY	9.69
Middlesex County, NJ	9.14
Santa Clara County, CA	9.13
Sacramento County, CA	7.14
Dallas County, TX	6.91
DuPage County, IL	6.55
Morris County, NJ	6.27
Contra Costa County, CA	6.26
Gwinnett County, GA	6.12
Westchester County, NY	4.26
Nassau County, NY	3.94
San Mateo County, CA	3.64
Oakland County, MI	3.24
St. Louis County, MO	3.13
Essex County, NJ	2.79
Fairfax County, VA	1.90
Bergen County, NJ	1.57
Somerset County, NJ	0.55
Ventura County, CA	0.38
Collin County, TX	0.35

Place	Percent
Berkeley, CA (city) Alameda County	63.59
Madison, WI (city) Dane County	55.56
Boston, MA (city) Suffolk County	47.67
Ann Arbor, MI (city) Washtenaw County	38.56
Columbus, OH (city) Franklin County	30.90
Anaheim, CA (city) Orange County	30.04
East San Gabriel, CA (cdp) Los Angeles County	25.43
Chicago, IL (city) Cook County	24.87
Los Angeles, CA (city) Los Angeles County	24.01
El Monte, CA (city) Los Angeles County	23.69
Austin, TX (city) Travis County	23.57
Seattle, WA (city) King County	22.39
Cypress, CA (city) Orange County	22.18
San Francisco, CA (city) San Francisco County	21.71
Alhambra, CA (city) Los Angeles County	21.53
Chino Hills, CA (city) San Bernardino County	21.45
Saratoga, CA (city) Santa Clara County	18.67
Arlington, TX (city) Tarrant County	17.83
Torrance, CA (city) Los Angeles County	17.69
Houston, TX (city) Harris County	17.14
Sugar Land, TX (city) Fort Bend County	16.76
Monterey Park, CA (city) Los Angeles County	16.75
Temple City, CA (city) Los Angeles County	16.25
New York, NY (city)	15.79
Rowland Heights, CA (cdp) Los Angeles County	15.77
Sunnyvale, CA (city) Santa Clara County	15.65
Hacienda Heights, CA (cdp) Los Angeles County	15.58
Honolulu, HI (cdp) Honolulu County	14.49
San Diego, CA (city) San Diego County	13.24
Irvine, CA (city) Orange County	13.15
Rancho Palos Verdes, CA (city) Los Angeles County	12.96
Diamond Bar, CA (city) Los Angeles County	12.86
Cupertino, CA (city) Santa Clara County	12.75
Fountain Valley, CA (city) Orange County	12.34
West Covina, CA (city) Los Angeles County	12.00
Walnut, CA (city) Los Angeles County	11.73
Arcadia, CA (city) Los Angeles County	10.66
San Gabriel, CA (city) Los Angeles County	10.48
Naperville, IL (city) Du Page County	10.21
Edison, NJ (township) Middlesex County	10.11
Upland, CA (city) San Bernardino County	9.62
North Hempstead, NY (town) Nassau County	8.52
Fremont, CA (city) Alameda County	8.40
Tustin, CA (city) Orange County	8.35
Bellevue, WA (city) King County	7.97
San Marino, CA (city) Los Angeles County	7.47
Huntington Beach, CA (city) Orange County	7.07
Cerritos, CA (city) Los Angeles County	5.97
San Jose, CA (city) Santa Clara County	5.76
Orange, CA (city) Orange County	4.98
Troy, MI (city) Oakland County	3.58
Plano, TX (city) Collin County	0.00

Notes: Please refer to the User's Guide for an explanation of data; ranking tables include all places with Asian and/or NHPI populations above SF4 population thresholds; (1) tables reflect only those areas that meet SF4 population thresholds, therefore there may be less than 50 states, 75 counties or 75 places listed

Poverty Status

Thais with Income Below Poverty Level

All States, Top 75 Counties, and Top 75 Places Sorted by Number[1]

State	Number
United States	15,548
California	5,729
Texas	982
Illinois	855
Florida	709
New York	630
Oregon	491
Washington	463
Ohio	425
Virginia	392
Pennsylvania	360
Michigan	327
Colorado	275
Georgia	274
Massachusetts	272
Missouri	254
Hawaii	248
Nevada	226
Arizona	220
North Carolina	208
Maryland	194
Wisconsin	184
Oklahoma	167
Minnesota	164
Tennessee	161
Indiana	156
New Jersey	140
Utah	131
Nebraska	125
Kansas	69
South Carolina	65
Connecticut	64
Louisiana	57
Alaska	54
Kentucky	49
Iowa	47
New Mexico	42
Arkansas	40
Alabama	37

County	Number
Los Angeles County, CA	2,962
Cook County, IL	568
Orange County, CA	497
San Francisco County, CA	357
King County, WA	293
Riverside County, CA	262
San Diego County, CA	256
Multnomah County, OR	242
Clark County, NV	222
Queens County, NY	222
San Bernardino County, CA	209
Honolulu County, HI	203
Dallas County, TX	192
Alameda County, CA	182
Tarrant County, TX	174
Santa Clara County, CA	159
Harris County, TX	154
Franklin County, OH	149
Sacramento County, CA	138
Maricopa County, AZ	121
Broward County, FL	98
New York County, NY	98
Middlesex County, MA	97
Oklahoma County, OK	97
Denver County, CO	95
Fairfax County, VA	92
Miami-Dade County, FL	89
Contra Costa County, CA	87
Bergen County, NJ	77
Hillsborough County, FL	74
Palm Beach County, FL	68
St. Louis County, MO	61
Prince George's County, MD	56
Montgomery County, MD	55
Okaloosa County, FL	50
Anchorage Borough, AK	49
Travis County, TX	47
Pinellas County, FL	36
DuPage County, IL	32
Westchester County, NY	29
San Mateo County, CA	27
Collin County, TX	19
Pierce County, WA	17
Polk County, IA	11
Nassau County, NY	10
Bexar County, TX	9
Suffolk County, NY	7

Place	Number
Los Angeles, CA (city) Los Angeles County	1,749
Chicago, IL (city) Cook County	399
New York, NY (city)	367
San Francisco, CA (city) San Francisco County	357
Portland, OR (city) Multnomah County	242
Seattle, WA (city) King County	241
San Diego, CA (city) San Diego County	185
Honolulu, HI (cdp) Honolulu County	133
Columbus, OH (city) Franklin County	128
Houston, TX (city) Harris County	118
Denver, CO (city) Denver County	95
Spring Valley, NV (cdp) Clark County	91
Long Beach, CA (city) Los Angeles County	67
Glendale, CA (city) Los Angeles County	59
Las Vegas, NV (city) Clark County	58
Cerritos, CA (city) Los Angeles County	55
San Jose, CA (city) Santa Clara County	55
Anaheim, CA (city) Orange County	40
Des Moines, IA (city) Polk County	11
Bellflower, CA (city) Los Angeles County	9
San Antonio, TX (city) Bexar County	9

Notes: Please refer to the User's Guide for an explanation of data; ranking tables include all places with Asian and/or NHPI populations above SF4 population thresholds; (1) tables reflect only those areas that meet SF4 population thresholds, therefore there may be less than 50 states, 75 counties or 75 places listed

Poverty Status

Thais with Income Below Poverty Level

All States, Top 75 Counties, and Top 75 Places Sorted by Percent[1]

State	Percent
Oregon	33.52
Nebraska	27.23
Ohio	23.17
Pennsylvania	21.56
Michigan	21.54
Wisconsin	21.45
Oklahoma	20.82
Utah	19.10
Missouri	18.84
Hawaii	18.24
Indiana	18.18
Minnesota	18.02
Tennessee	16.81
California	16.06
Illinois	15.35
Colorado	14.54
Kentucky	14.37
United States	14.35
Texas	14.20
Arkansas	13.70
Arizona	13.62
North Carolina	13.41
Massachusetts	13.05
Georgia	12.48
Washington	12.16
Virginia	11.08
Florida	10.87
Kansas	10.82
New Mexico	10.74
New York	9.78
South Carolina	9.53
Louisiana	8.84
Connecticut	8.16
New Jersey	7.80
Nevada	7.59
Alaska	6.91
Maryland	6.86
Alabama	6.09
Iowa	5.17

County	Percent
Multnomah County, OR	49.19
Franklin County, OH	35.48
Riverside County, CA	29.91
Oklahoma County, OK	25.06
San Francisco County, CA	24.44
Denver County, CO	23.40
Tarrant County, TX	22.45
San Diego County, CA	19.91
Sacramento County, CA	19.17
Honolulu County, HI	18.27
Dallas County, TX	17.38
Prince George's County, MD	16.77
Broward County, FL	16.36
Orange County, CA	16.32
St. Louis County, MO	16.14
Bergen County, NJ	15.65
King County, WA	15.32
Los Angeles County, CA	15.28
Cook County, IL	14.64
Contra Costa County, CA	14.22
Travis County, TX	12.95
Alameda County, CA	12.79
San Bernardino County, CA	12.35
Santa Clara County, CA	12.26
New York County, NY	11.74
Harris County, TX	11.64
Middlesex County, MA	11.48
Hillsborough County, FL	10.95
Maricopa County, AZ	10.71
Miami-Dade County, FL	10.09
Queens County, NY	9.39
Palm Beach County, FL	9.01
Anchorage Borough, AK	8.49
Clark County, NV	8.47
Okaloosa County, FL	8.14
DuPage County, IL	7.66
Pinellas County, FL	7.38
Fairfax County, VA	6.24
Westchester County, NY	5.03
Pierce County, WA	4.57
Collin County, TX	4.19
Montgomery County, MD	4.14
San Mateo County, CA	3.85
Polk County, IA	3.13
Nassau County, NY	2.85
Suffolk County, NY	1.97
Bexar County, TX	1.15

Place	Percent
Portland, OR (city) Multnomah County	53.78
Columbus, OH (city) Franklin County	33.60
Seattle, WA (city) King County	28.66
Honolulu, HI (cdp) Honolulu County	26.55
San Francisco, CA (city) San Francisco County	24.44
Denver, CO (city) Denver County	23.40
San Diego, CA (city) San Diego County	22.92
Chicago, IL (city) Cook County	19.49
Los Angeles, CA (city) Los Angeles County	19.38
Spring Valley, NV (cdp) Clark County	18.31
Glendale, CA (city) Los Angeles County	14.05
Houston, TX (city) Harris County	13.55
Cerritos, CA (city) Los Angeles County	11.80
Long Beach, CA (city) Los Angeles County	11.24
New York, NY (city)	9.60
San Jose, CA (city) Santa Clara County	8.97
Anaheim, CA (city) Orange County	8.77
Las Vegas, NV (city) Clark County	8.29
Des Moines, IA (city) Polk County	3.82
Bellflower, CA (city) Los Angeles County	2.31
San Antonio, TX (city) Bexar County	1.64

Notes: Please refer to the User's Guide for an explanation of data; ranking tables include all places with Asian and/or NHPI populations above SF4 population thresholds; (1) tables reflect only those areas that meet SF4 population thresholds, therefore there may be less than 50 states, 75 counties or 75 places listed

Poverty Status

Tongans with Income Below Poverty Level

All States, Top 75 Counties, and Top 75 Places Sorted by Number[1]

State	Number
United States	5,310
California	2,147
Hawaii	1,490
Utah	1,020
Alaska	160
Arizona	116
Nevada	98
Oregon	78
Washington	44
Texas	21

County	Number
Honolulu County, HI	1,161
Salt Lake County, UT	900
Los Angeles County, CA	632
Alameda County, CA	254
San Bernardino County, CA	253
San Mateo County, CA	213
Maui County, HI	203
Contra Costa County, CA	192
Orange County, CA	172
Sacramento County, CA	137
Maricopa County, AZ	116
Washoe County, NV	98
San Diego County, CA	92
Utah County, UT	85
Multnomah County, OR	53
Tarrant County, TX	19
King County, WA	15

Place	Number
Honolulu, HI (cdp) Honolulu County	609
Salt Lake City, UT (city) Salt Lake County	454
West Valley City, UT (city) Salt Lake County	306
Oakland, CA (city) Alameda County	218
Los Angeles, CA (city) Los Angeles County	176
Hauula, HI (cdp) Honolulu County	139
Sacramento, CA (city) Sacramento County	123
East Palo Alto, CA (city) San Mateo County	60
Kahuku, HI (cdp) Honolulu County	54
Portland, OR (city) Multnomah County	53
Laie, HI (cdp) Honolulu County	51
West Jordan, UT (city) Salt Lake County	42
San Bruno, CA (city) San Mateo County	35
San Mateo, CA (city) San Mateo County	32

Notes: Please refer to the User's Guide for an explanation of data; ranking tables include all places with Asian and/or NHPI populations above SF4 population thresholds; (1) tables reflect only those areas that meet SF4 population thresholds, therefore there may be less than 50 states, 75 counties or 75 places listed

Poverty Status

Tongans with Income Below Poverty Level

All States, Top 75 Counties, and Top 75 Places Sorted by Percent[1]

State	Percent
Alaska	38.19
Hawaii	35.88
United States	19.48
Arizona	18.47
California	18.03
Oregon	17.53
Utah	15.21
Nevada	12.41
Washington	5.29
Texas	4.30

County	Percent
Contra Costa County, CA	42.57
Honolulu County, HI	38.02
San Bernardino County, CA	31.74
Orange County, CA	29.60
Los Angeles County, CA	28.47
Maui County, HI	25.57
Maricopa County, AZ	22.01
San Diego County, CA	21.55
Sacramento County, CA	18.87
Utah County, UT	18.40
Washoe County, NV	16.98
Salt Lake County, UT	15.29
Multnomah County, OR	14.76
Alameda County, CA	13.92
San Mateo County, CA	5.88
Tarrant County, TX	5.21
King County, WA	3.03

Place	Percent
Los Angeles, CA (city) Los Angeles County	51.46
Honolulu, HI (cdp) Honolulu County	39.09
Hauula, HI (cdp) Honolulu County	38.61
Laie, HI (cdp) Honolulu County	24.88
Kahuku, HI (cdp) Honolulu County	22.98
Sacramento, CA (city) Sacramento County	21.73
Salt Lake City, UT (city) Salt Lake County	18.55
West Valley City, UT (city) Salt Lake County	17.02
Oakland, CA (city) Alameda County	16.62
Portland, OR (city) Multnomah County	15.06
West Jordan, UT (city) Salt Lake County	9.07
San Bruno, CA (city) San Mateo County	6.57
San Mateo, CA (city) San Mateo County	5.02
East Palo Alto, CA (city) San Mateo County	4.08

Notes: Please refer to the User's Guide for an explanation of data; ranking tables include all places with Asian and/or NHPI populations above SF4 population thresholds; (1) tables reflect only those areas that meet SF4 population thresholds, therefore there may be less than 50 states, 75 counties or 75 places listed

Poverty Status

Vietnamese with Income Below Poverty Level

All States, Top 75 Counties, and Top 75 Places Sorted by Number[1]

State	Number
United States	175,924
California	79,635
Texas	16,984
Washington	8,169
Massachusetts	8,138
Louisiana	6,485
Pennsylvania	5,757
New York	5,260
Florida	4,824
Georgia	2,826
Virginia	2,759
Minnesota	2,679
Illinois	2,541
Hawaii	2,247
Oregon	1,918
Missouri	1,749
New Jersey	1,744
Kansas	1,656
Colorado	1,637
North Carolina	1,579
Oklahoma	1,455
Arizona	1,403
Mississippi	1,363
Ohio	1,363
Michigan	1,354
Maryland	1,343
Alabama	863
Tennessee	777
Iowa	630
Indiana	618
Utah	565
Arkansas	564
Nebraska	561
New Mexico	548
District of Columbia	544
Wisconsin	478
Nevada	476
Kentucky	438
South Carolina	356
Connecticut	354
Idaho	228
Vermont	209
Maine	205
Rhode Island	205
New Hampshire	143
Alaska	128
West Virginia	70
South Dakota	44
Delaware	16

County	Number
Orange County, CA	19,967
Los Angeles County, CA	16,477
Santa Clara County, CA	10,959
Harris County, TX	7,361
San Diego County, CA	6,479
Alameda County, CA	5,833
Sacramento County, CA	4,882
King County, WA	4,699
Suffolk County, MA	4,152
Philadelphia County, PA	3,728
San Joaquin County, CA	3,003
San Bernardino County, CA	2,894
Dallas County, TX	2,274
San Francisco County, CA	2,205
Orleans Parish, LA	2,184
Honolulu County, HI	2,179
Cook County, IL	1,940
Tarrant County, TX	1,776
Worcester County, MA	1,589
Jefferson County, TX	1,310
Multnomah County, OR	1,276
Riverside County, CA	1,238
Jefferson Parish, LA	1,228
Hennepin County, MN	1,209
Pierce County, WA	1,145
Maricopa County, AZ	1,140
Bronx County, NY	1,085
East Baton Rouge Parish, LA	1,079
Fairfax County, VA	1,074
Contra Costa County, CA	1,047
Queens County, NY	1,034
Sedgwick County, KS	1,016
Middlesex County, MA	998
Fresno County, CA	959
Oklahoma County, OK	959
DeKalb County, GA	919
Kings County, NY	916
Travis County, TX	875
Harrison County, MS	829
Snohomish County, WA	786
Ramsey County, MN	780
Yolo County, CA	757
Saint Louis Independent City, MO	706
Hillsborough County, FL	690
Denver County, CO	683
Gwinnett County, GA	660
Montgomery County, MD	623
Orange County, FL	602
Guilford County, NC	584
Bernalillo County, NM	537
Salt Lake County, UT	531
Shelby County, TN	505
Camden County, NJ	503
Jackson County, MO	501
Hampden County, MA	466
Escambia County, FL	449
Cuyahoga County, OH	444
Arlington County, VA	437
Pinellas County, FL	437
Monterey County, CA	434
Washington County, OR	430
Erie County, NY	427
Fulton County, GA	411
Solano County, CA	407
Hudson County, NJ	397
Monroe County, NY	393
Clark County, NV	392
Thurston County, WA	387
Marin County, CA	386
Norfolk County, MA	386
Matagorda County, TX	380
Stanislaus County, CA	377
Duval County, FL	370
Mobile County, AL	370
Essex County, MA	369

Place	Number
San Jose, CA (city) Santa Clara County	9,381
Garden Grove, CA (city) Orange County	6,363
San Diego, CA (city) San Diego County	5,792
Houston, TX (city) Harris County	5,438
Westminster, CA (city) Orange County	5,312
Los Angeles, CA (city) Los Angeles County	4,362
Philadelphia, PA (city) Philadelphia County	3,728
Boston, MA (city) Suffolk County	3,698
New York, NY (city)	3,335
Oakland, CA (city) Alameda County	3,050
Stockton, CA (city) San Joaquin County	2,980
Seattle, WA (city) King County	2,563
Sacramento, CA (city) Sacramento County	2,478
Santa Ana, CA (city) Orange County	2,296
San Francisco, CA (city) San Francisco County	2,205
New Orleans, LA (city) Orleans Parish	2,184
Honolulu, HI (cdp) Honolulu County	2,006
El Monte, CA (city) Los Angeles County	1,834
Chicago, IL (city) Cook County	1,720
Rosemead, CA (city) Los Angeles County	1,678
Alhambra, CA (city) Los Angeles County	1,356
Worcester, MA (city) Worcester County	1,346
Long Beach, CA (city) Los Angeles County	1,281
Portland, OR (city) Multnomah County	1,261
Dallas, TX (city) Dallas County	1,216
Anaheim, CA (city) Orange County	1,183
Port Arthur, TX (city) Jefferson County	1,072
Tacoma, WA (city) Pierce County	1,070
Oklahoma City, OK (city) Oklahoma County	1,028
Wichita, KS (city) Sedgwick County	988
Fresno, CA (city) Fresno County	922
Monterey Park, CA (city) Los Angeles County	905
Austin, TX (city) Travis County	860
Arlington, TX (city) Tarrant County	853
Minneapolis, MN (city) Hennepin County	842
Huntington Beach, CA (city) Orange County	818
Baton Rouge, LA (city) East Baton Rouge Parish	798
Phoenix, AZ (city) Maricopa County	778
St. Paul, MN (city) Ramsey County	758
Davis, CA (city) Yolo County	712
San Gabriel, CA (city) Los Angeles County	707
St. Louis, MO (city) Saint Louis Independent City	706
Denver, CO (city) Denver County	683
Garland, TX (city) Dallas County	652
San Bernardino, CA (city) San Bernardino County	643
Elk Grove, CA (cdp) Sacramento County	582
White Center, WA (cdp) King County	558
Riverside, CA (city) Riverside County	546
Fountain Valley, CA (city) Orange County	544
Albuquerque, NM (city) Bernalillo County	537
Biloxi, MS (city) Harrison County	537
Hayward, CA (city) Alameda County	530
Orange, CA (city) Orange County	526
Milpitas, CA (city) Santa Clara County	510
Union City, CA (city) Alameda County	486
Stanton, CA (city) Orange County	479
Florin, CA (cdp) Sacramento County	472
Fort Worth, TX (city) Tarrant County	470
Upland, CA (city) San Bernardino County	470
Kansas City, MO (city) Jackson County	463
Irvine, CA (city) Orange County	454
Santa Clara, CA (city) Santa Clara County	438
Arlington, VA (cdp) Arlington County	437
Memphis, TN (city) Shelby County	428
Berkeley, CA (city) Alameda County	419
Alameda, CA (city) Alameda County	405
Greensboro, NC (city) Guilford County	389
Jersey City, NJ (city) Hudson County	377
Montclair, CA (city) San Bernardino County	374
Springfield, MA (city) Hampden County	373
Pomona, CA (city) Los Angeles County	359
Fremont, CA (city) Alameda County	351
Jacksonville, FL (city) Duval County	347
Renton, WA (city) King County	347
Camden, NJ (city) Camden County	346

Notes: Please refer to the User's Guide for an explanation of data; ranking tables include all places with Asian and/or NHPI populations above SF4 population thresholds; (1) tables reflect only those areas that meet SF4 population thresholds, therefore there may be less than 50 states, 75 counties or 75 places listed

Poverty Status

Vietnamese with Income Below Poverty Level

All States, Top 75 Counties, and Top 75 Places Sorted by Percent[1]

State	Percent
District of Columbia	30.84
Hawaii	27.39
Louisiana	26.20
Mississippi	25.98
Massachusetts	24.22
New York	23.28
Rhode Island	21.33
Pennsylvania	20.46
New Mexico	20.01
Vermont	19.92
Maine	19.19
Alabama	18.88
Washington	18.52
California	18.03
Missouri	17.05
Idaho	16.90
West Virginia	16.17
United States	16.05
Kansas	14.79
Minnesota	14.75
Arkansas	14.73
Florida	14.59
Illinois	13.97
Kentucky	13.87
Alaska	13.42
Indiana	13.41
Ohio	13.27
Texas	12.77
Wisconsin	12.61
Colorado	12.13
Arizona	12.10
Oklahoma	12.06
Nevada	11.86
New Jersey	11.85
Tennessee	11.16
Michigan	10.59
Utah	10.38
North Carolina	10.30
Oregon	10.20
Georgia	9.74
South Carolina	9.62
Iowa	9.46
New Hampshire	8.63
Nebraska	8.50
Maryland	8.15
Virginia	7.89
South Dakota	6.48
Connecticut	4.86
Delaware	2.33

County	Percent
Yolo County, CA	59.89
Brazos County, TX	56.21
Matagorda County, TX	55.80
Iberia Parish, LA	50.13
San Joaquin County, CA	47.96
Aransas County, TX	47.07
Fresno County, CA	45.62
Kitsap County, WA	40.53
Vermilion Parish, LA	37.17
Bronx County, NY	36.82
St. Martin Parish, LA	35.18
Santa Cruz County, CA	34.26
Philadelphia County, PA	34.19
Suffolk County, MA	33.86
Plaquemines Parish, LA	33.73
Jefferson County, TX	32.55
Alachua County, FL	31.85
Orleans Parish, LA	31.85
Marin County, CA	31.20
East Baton Rouge Parish, LA	30.79
Calhoun County, TX	30.25
Harrison County, MS	30.12
Solano County, CA	29.77
Sacramento County, CA	29.67
Escambia County, FL	29.02
St. Mary Parish, LA	28.54
Worcester County, MA	28.43
Honolulu County, HI	28.42
San Bernardino County, CA	28.38
Terrebonne Parish, LA	28.28
Erie County, NY	28.20
Queens County, NY	27.73
Providence County, RI	27.33
Stanislaus County, CA	27.20
Ford County, KS	27.07
Pierce County, WA	26.96
Sarasota County, FL	25.70
Bay County, FL	25.08
Alameda County, CA	25.05
Virginia Beach Independent City, VA	24.96
Northampton County, PA	24.68
Hampden County, MA	24.49
Dane County, WI	24.45
Hudson County, NJ	24.40
Allegheny County, PA	24.32
Kings County, NY	24.05
Anchorage Borough, AK	23.74
Jefferson County, AL	23.62
Oneida County, NY	23.32
Berks County, PA	23.13
Monterey County, CA	22.56
Santa Barbara County, CA	22.52
Essex County, NJ	22.16
Thurston County, WA	22.11
Bernalillo County, NM	21.99
St. Bernard Parish, LA	21.98
Saint Louis Independent City, MO	21.93
Washtenaw County, MI	21.89
Ramsey County, MN	21.86
Olmsted County, MN	21.63
Lafayette Parish, LA	21.37
San Francisco County, CA	21.37
Cuyahoga County, OH	21.29
Los Angeles County, CA	21.29
Riverside County, CA	20.76
Chittenden County, VT	20.39
Albany County, NY	20.35
Arlington County, VA	20.34
Guilford County, NC	19.88
Broome County, NY	19.67
Polk County, FL	19.47
Contra Costa County, CA	19.38
Orange County, TX	19.10
San Diego County, CA	19.07
Baltimore Independent City, MD	18.94

Place	Percent
Davis, CA (city) Yolo County	72.65
Upland, CA (city) San Bernardino County	55.36
Fresno, CA (city) Fresno County	53.57
Stockton, CA (city) San Joaquin County	52.26
Berkeley, CA (city) Alameda County	52.05
Palacios, TX (city) Matagorda County	49.92
Revere, MA (city) Suffolk County	48.87
Gretna, LA (city) Jefferson Parish	47.71
Abbeville, LA (city) Vermilion Parish	47.25
Henderson, LA (town) Saint Martin Parish	44.63
San Bernardino, CA (city) San Bernardino County	43.33
Pittsburgh, PA (city) Allegheny County	42.86
Highland, CA (city) San Bernardino County	41.64
Vallejo, CA (city) Solano County	38.56
Sacramento, CA (city) Sacramento County	38.48
Amelia, LA (cdp) Saint Mary Parish	38.01
Port Arthur, TX (city) Jefferson County	37.89
South San Gabriel, CA (cdp) Los Angeles County	37.65
Oakland, CA (city) Alameda County	37.32
Laguna, CA (cdp) Sacramento County	37.23
Arden-Arcade, CA (cdp) Sacramento County	36.59
Biloxi, MS (city) Harrison County	36.41
Arvada, CO (city) Jefferson County	36.27
Florin, CA (cdp) Sacramento County	36.25
Seadrift, TX (city) Calhoun County	36.03
Moreno Valley, CA (city) Riverside County	35.71
Salinas, CA (city) Monterey County	35.22
Everett, MA (city) Middlesex County	34.97
Tacoma, WA (city) Pierce County	34.54
Philadelphia, PA (city) Philadelphia County	34.19
Olympia, WA (city) Thurston County	34.04
Boston, MA (city) Suffolk County	33.84
Fulton, TX (town) Aransas County	33.79
San Leon, TX (cdp) Galveston County	32.57
New Orleans, LA (city) Orleans Parish	31.85
Worcester, MA (city) Worcester County	31.72
Alameda, CA (city) Alameda County	31.44
Alhambra, CA (city) Los Angeles County	30.96
Baton Rouge, LA (city) East Baton Rouge Parish	30.87
Reading, PA (city) Berks County	30.87
Honolulu, HI (cdp) Honolulu County	30.80
Montclair, CA (city) San Bernardino County	30.71
Minneapolis, MN (city) Hennepin County	30.46
San Rafael, CA (city) Marin County	30.03
St. Paul, MN (city) Ramsey County	30.00
El Monte, CA (city) Los Angeles County	29.00
Parkway-S. Sacramento, CA (cdp) Sacramento County	28.70
San Pablo, CA (city) Contra Costa County	28.45
Rosemead, CA (city) Los Angeles County	28.42
Cleveland, OH (city) Cuyahoga County	28.36
Madison, WI (city) Dane County	28.34
Monterey Park, CA (city) Los Angeles County	28.23
New York, NY (city)	27.81
Chamblee, GA (city) De Kalb County	27.80
Modesto, CA (city) Stanislaus County	27.78
Everett, WA (city) Snohomish County	27.59
White Center, WA (cdp) King County	27.49
Jersey City, NJ (city) Hudson County	27.30
San Mateo, CA (city) San Mateo County	27.30
Richfield, MN (city) Hennepin County	26.84
Elk Grove, CA (cdp) Sacramento County	26.81
San Gabriel, CA (city) Los Angeles County	26.62
Springfield, MA (city) Hampden County	26.59
North Highlands, CA (cdp) Sacramento County	26.21
Gainesville, GA (city) Hall County	26.17
Dodge City, KS (city) Ford County	25.79
Lafayette, LA (city) Lafayette Parish	25.45
Long Beach, CA (city) Los Angeles County	25.45
Lilburn, GA (city) Gwinnett County	25.32
Bailey's Crossroads, VA (cdp) Fairfax County	25.09
Riverside, CA (city) Riverside County	25.07
Newark, CA (city) Alameda County	25.00
Beaumont, TX (city) Jefferson County	24.83
Camden, NJ (city) Camden County	24.82
High Point, NC (city) Guilford County	24.75

Notes: Please refer to the User's Guide for an explanation of data; ranking tables include all places with Asian and/or NHPI populations above SF4 population thresholds; (1) tables reflect only those areas that meet SF4 population thresholds, therefore there may be less than 50 states, 75 counties or 75 places listed

Homeownership

Total Population Who Own Their Own Homes

All States, Top 75 Counties, and Top 75 Places Sorted by Number[1]

State	Number
United States	69,816,513
California	6,546,237
Texas	4,717,294
Florida	4,441,711
New York	3,739,247
Pennsylvania	3,406,167
Illinois	3,089,124
Ohio	3,072,514
Michigan	2,793,346
North Carolina	2,172,270
Georgia	2,029,293
New Jersey	2,011,298
Virginia	1,837,958
Indiana	1,669,083
Tennessee	1,561,461
Missouri	1,542,310
Massachusetts	1,508,248
Washington	1,466,985
Wisconsin	1,426,660
Minnesota	1,412,724
Maryland	1,341,594
Arizona	1,293,637
Alabama	1,258,686
Kentucky	1,125,298
Louisiana	1,124,995
Colorado	1,116,305
South Carolina	1,107,619
Oklahoma	918,141
Connecticut	869,742
Oregon	856,890
Iowa	831,427
Mississippi	757,151
Arkansas	723,458
Kansas	718,873
West Virginia	553,626
Utah	501,659
New Mexico	474,435
Nevada	457,245
Nebraska	449,306
Maine	370,920
Idaho	339,913
New Hampshire	330,783
Montana	247,700
Rhode Island	245,150
Hawaii	227,783
Delaware	216,046
South Dakota	197,907
North Dakota	171,310
Vermont	169,777
Alaska	138,503
Wyoming	135,488
District of Columbia	101,216

County	Number
Los Angeles County, CA	1,499,694
Cook County, IL	1,142,743
Maricopa County, AZ	764,563
Harris County, TX	667,129
Orange County, CA	574,193
San Diego County, CA	551,489
Wayne County, MI	511,936
Broward County, FL	454,625
Miami-Dade County, FL	449,333
King County, WA	425,451
Dallas County, TX	424,788
Suffolk County, NY	374,371
Cuyahoga County, OH	360,988
Allegheny County, PA	360,021
Nassau County, NY	359,257
Palm Beach County, FL	354,024
Oakland County, MI	352,242
Philadelphia County, PA	349,651
Riverside County, CA	348,479
Middlesex County, MA	346,591
San Bernardino County, CA	341,014
Santa Clara County, CA	338,636
Queens County, NY	334,894
Tarrant County, TX	324,754
Clark County, NV	302,842
Hennepin County, MN	301,835
St. Louis County, MO	299,789
Bexar County, TX	299,171
Pinellas County, FL	293,869
Alameda County, CA	286,306
Sacramento County, CA	263,811
Hillsborough County, FL	251,023
Franklin County, OH	249,613
Fairfax County, VA	248,858
Erie County, NY	248,780
DuPage County, IL	248,771
Macomb County, MI	243,887
Contra Costa County, CA	238,413
Kings County, NY	238,290
Fairfield County, CT	224,509
Montgomery County, MD	223,008
Bergen County, NJ	222,237
Hartford County, CT	215,253
Pima County, AZ	213,620
Shelby County, TN	213,444
Montgomery County, PA	210,237
Marion County, IN	208,932
Hamilton County, OH	207,533
Orange County, FL	204,230
Salt Lake County, UT	203,690
Westchester County, NY	202,765
Baltimore County, MD	202,574
New Haven County, CT	201,349
Milwaukee County, WI	198,768
Duval County, FL	191,722
Monroe County, NY	186,458
Jefferson County, KY	186,358
Worcester County, MA	182,097
Middlesex County, NJ	177,377
Prince George's County, MD	177,206
Essex County, MA	175,022
Jefferson County, AL	174,982
Norfolk County, MA	173,413
Mecklenburg County, NC	170,392
Bucks County, PA	169,177
Lake County, IL	168,293
Jackson County, MO	167,435
Monmouth County, NJ	167,273
Fulton County, GA	167,111
Ocean County, NJ	166,779
Pierce County, WA	165,623
Travis County, TX	165,123
Ventura County, CA	164,373
Oklahoma County, OK	161,158
Wake County, NC	159,456

Place	Number
New York, NY (city)	912,133
Los Angeles, CA (city) Los Angeles County	491,836
Chicago, IL (city) Cook County	464,912
Philadelphia, PA (city) Philadelphia County	349,651
Houston, TX (city) Harris County	329,006
Phoenix, AZ (city) Maricopa County	282,615
San Antonio, TX (city) Bexar County	235,584
San Diego, CA (city) San Diego County	223,275
Hempstead, NY (town) Nassau County	199,148
Dallas, TX (city) Dallas County	195,227
Indianapolis, IN (sp. city) Marion County	187,846
Detroit, MI (city) Wayne County	184,672
Jacksonville, FL (city) Duval County	179,782
San Jose, CA (city) Santa Clara County	170,825
Columbus, OH (city) Franklin County	148,315
Memphis, TN (city) Shelby County	140,083
Denver, CO (city) Denver County	125,631
Seattle, WA (city) King County	125,151
Portland, OR (city) Multnomah County	124,782
Charlotte, NC (city) Mecklenburg County	124,057
Nashville-Davidson, TN (sp. city) Davidson County	124,041
Oklahoma City, OK (city) Oklahoma County	121,602
Austin, TX (city) Travis County	119,191
Brookhaven, NY (town) Suffolk County	115,894
San Francisco, CA (city) San Francisco County	115,315
El Paso, TX (city) El Paso County	111,808
Albuquerque, NM (city) Bernalillo County	110,782
Fort Worth, TX (city) Tarrant County	109,152
Kansas City, MO (city) Jackson County	106,078
Milwaukee, WI (city) Milwaukee County	105,186
Las Vegas, NV (city) Clark County	104,514
Tucson, AZ (city) Pima County	103,229
Mesa, AZ (city) Maricopa County	97,625
Omaha, NE (city) Douglas County	93,430
Cleveland, OH (city) Cuyahoga County	92,498
Tulsa, OK (city) Tulsa County	92,157
New Orleans, LA (city) Orleans Parish	87,535
Oyster Bay, NY (town) Nassau County	86,345
Colorado Springs, CO (city) El Paso County	86,076
Wichita, KS (city) Sedgwick County	85,659
Minneapolis, MN (city) Hennepin County	83,422
Islip, NY (town) Suffolk County	77,830
Sacramento, CA (city) Sacramento County	77,396
Boston, MA (city) Suffolk County	77,209
Toledo, OH (city) Lucas County	77,028
Pittsburgh, PA (city) Allegheny County	74,930
Atlanta, GA (city) Fulton County	73,475
Fresno, CA (city) Fresno County	70,915
St. Petersburg, FL (city) Pinellas County	69,697
St. Louis, MO (city) Saint Louis Independent City	68,917
Tampa, FL (city) Hillsborough County	68,753
Arlington, TX (city) Tarrant County	68,309
Aurora, CO (city) Arapahoe County	67,447
Long Beach, CA (city) Los Angeles County	66,971
Honolulu, HI (cdp) Honolulu County	65,860
Scottsdale, AZ (city) Maricopa County	63,098
Oakland, CA (city) Alameda County	62,482
St. Paul, MN (city) Ramsey County	61,437
North Hempstead, NY (town) Nassau County	60,270
Lexington-Fayette, KY (sp. city) Fayette County	59,915
Corpus Christi, TX (city) Nueces County	58,918
Louisville, KY (city) Jefferson County	58,481
Raleigh, NC (city) Wake County	58,032
Cincinnati, OH (city) Hamilton County	57,655
Huntington, NY (town) Suffolk County	56,219
Plano, TX (city) Collin County	55,725
Akron, OH (city) Summit County	53,441
Buffalo, NY (city) Erie County	53,339
Birmingham, AL (city) Jefferson County	52,886
Lincoln, NE (city) Lancaster County	52,432
Babylon, NY (town) Suffolk County	52,110
Des Moines, IA (city) Polk County	52,101
Fort Wayne, IN (city) Allen County	51,316
Bakersfield, CA (city) Kern County	50,394
Glendale, AZ (city) Maricopa County	49,168

Notes: Please refer to the User's Guide for an explanation of data; ranking tables include all places with Asian and/or NHPI populations above SF4 population thresholds; (1) tables reflect only those areas that meet SF4 population thresholds, therefore there may be less than 50 states, 75 counties or 75 places listed

Homeownership

Total Population Who Own Their Own Homes

All States, Top 75 Counties, and Top 75 Places Sorted by Percent[1]

State	Percent
West Virginia	75.17
Minnesota	74.55
Michigan	73.79
Alabama	72.46
Idaho	72.38
Mississippi	72.36
Iowa	72.34
Delaware	72.32
South Carolina	72.21
Maine	71.58
Utah	71.53
Indiana	71.44
Pennsylvania	71.30
Kentucky	70.74
Vermont	70.55
Missouri	70.28
Florida	70.08
New Mexico	69.98
Wyoming	69.98
Tennessee	69.93
New Hampshire	69.70
Arkansas	69.38
North Carolina	69.36
Kansas	69.26
Ohio	69.11
Montana	69.06
Wisconsin	68.44
Oklahoma	68.40
South Dakota	68.19
Virginia	68.09
Arizona	68.04
Louisiana	67.93
Maryland	67.73
Georgia	67.50
Nebraska	67.44
Colorado	67.32
Illinois	67.28
Connecticut	66.82
North Dakota	66.62
United States	66.19
New Jersey	65.63
Washington	64.59
Oregon	64.25
Texas	63.80
Alaska	62.50
Massachusetts	61.72
Nevada	60.87
Rhode Island	60.02
California	56.91
Hawaii	56.49
New York	52.99
District of Columbia	40.76

County	Percent
Livingston County, MI	88.08
Forsyth County, GA	88.05
Douglas County, CO	87.88
Geauga County, OH	87.30
Chisago County, MN	87.05
Oldham County, KY	86.75
Scott County, MN	86.64
Bedford County, VA	86.58
Fayette County, GA	86.55
Hernando County, FL	86.52
Washington County, MN	85.83
Citrus County, FL	85.59
Henry County, GA	85.25
Clinton County, MI	85.24
Calvert County, MD	85.18
Pike County, PA	84.82
Wright County, MN	84.32
Hanover County, VA	84.27
Roseau County, MN	84.14
Kendall County, IL	84.10
Flagler County, FL	84.06
Sherburne County, MN	83.99
Putnam County, WV	83.97
Cherokee County, GA	83.85
Charlotte County, FL	83.68
Hunterdon County, NJ	83.68
Sandoval County, NM	83.62
Carver County, MN	83.46
Anoka County, MN	83.41
Jefferson County, MO	83.38
Ocean County, NJ	83.22
Will County, IL	83.21
McHenry County, IL	83.13
Hendricks County, IN	82.95
Allegan County, MI	82.87
Rockwall County, TX	82.66
Sussex County, NJ	82.66
Pasco County, FL	82.37
Ascension Parish, LA	82.24
Putnam County, NY	82.21
Spotsylvania County, VA	82.20
Columbia County, GA	82.08
St. Charles County, MO	81.98
Carroll County, MD	81.97
Cass County, MI	81.90
St. Martin Parish, LA	81.69
Lake County, FL	81.49
Williamson County, TN	81.47
St. Charles Parish, LA	81.42
Wilson County, TN	81.42
Medina County, OH	81.23
Wagoner County, OK	81.03
Chesterfield County, VA	80.95
Shelby County, AL	80.94
Monroe County, MI	80.93
Hamilton County, IN	80.91
Fort Bend County, TX	80.81
Ottawa County, MI	80.78
Sussex County, DE	80.71
Saline County, AR	80.70
Nassau County, FL	80.67
Stafford County, VA	80.60
Union County, NC	80.56
Alexander County, NC	80.51
Wayne County, PA	80.50
St. Tammany Parish, LA	80.48
Delaware County, OH	80.41
Cottonwood County, MN	80.39
Calumet County, WI	80.38
Santa Rosa County, FL	80.37
Frederick County, VA	80.35
Nassau County, NY	80.30
Oconee County, GA	80.21
Steele County, MN	80.21
Ionia County, MI	80.06

Place	Percent
South Barrington, IL (village) Cook County	98.69
Oakland charter, MI (township) Oakland County	98.39
Manhasset Hills, NY (cdp) Nassau County	98.37
Atherton, CA (town) San Mateo County	98.34
Newport Coast, CA (cdp) Orange County	97.87
Searingtown, NY (cdp) Nassau County	97.60
Granger, IN (cdp) Saint Joseph County	97.52
Bunker Hill Village, TX (city) Harris County	97.47
Highland Heights, OH (city) Cuyahoga County	97.30
North Star, DE (cdp) New Castle County	97.26
Lake Success, NY (village) Nassau County	97.24
Oak Brook, IL (village) Du Page County	97.17
Lincolnshire, IL (village) Lake County	97.11
Hunters Creek Village, TX (city) Harris County	97.08
East Hills, NY (village) Nassau County	97.07
Morganville, NJ (cdp) Monmouth County	97.07
Long Grove, IL (village) Lake County	97.04
Colleyville, TX (city) Tarrant County	96.80
Sands Point, NY (village) Nassau County	96.74
Southlake, TX (city) Tarrant County	96.69
Macomb, MI (township) Macomb County	96.61
Burr Ridge, IL (village) Du Page County	96.50
Cinnaminson, NJ (township) Burlington County	96.26
Dix Hills, NY (cdp) Suffolk County	96.24
Marlboro, NJ (township) Monmouth County	96.21
Washington, NJ (township) Bergen County	96.05
Travilah, MD (cdp) Montgomery County	95.98
Brentwood, TN (city) Williamson County	95.97
Herricks, NY (cdp) Nassau County	95.70
Hillsborough, CA (town) San Mateo County	95.64
Holmdel, NJ (township) Monmouth County	95.51
White Meadow Lake, NJ (cdp) Morris County	95.47
Murphy, TX (city) Collin County	95.42
Great Falls, VA (cdp) Fairfax County	95.38
Muttontown, NY (village) Nassau County	95.23
Villa Park, CA (city) Orange County	95.23
Forest Hills, MI (cdp) Kent County	95.16
North Hills, NY (village) Nassau County	95.13
Franklin Lakes, NJ (borough) Bergen County	95.12
Munsey Park, NY (village) Nassau County	95.10
Haworth, NJ (borough) Bergen County	94.97
Wolf Trap, VA (cdp) Fairfax County	94.88
Monroe, NJ (township) Middlesex County	94.80
Grosse Pointe Woods, MI (city) Wayne County	94.76
Blackhawk-Camino Tass., CA (cdp) Contra Costa Co.	94.74
Berkeley Lake, GA (city) Gwinnett County	94.73
Bradbury, CA (city) Los Angeles County	94.72
Merrick, NY (cdp) Nassau County	94.63
Morton Grove, IL (village) Cook County	94.54
Brookville, NY (village) Nassau County	94.50
Brushy Creek, TX (cdp) Williamson County	94.30
La Habra Heights, CA (city) Los Angeles County	94.19
Harrington Park, NJ (borough) Bergen County	94.18
Union Hill-Novelty Hill, WA (cdp) King County	94.17
Meadows Place, TX (city) Fort Bend County	94.15
Elwood, NY (cdp) Suffolk County	94.13
Rolling Hills, CA (city) Los Angeles County	94.11
Clayton, CA (city) Contra Costa County	94.10
East Hanover, NJ (township) Morris County	94.02
Manalapan, NJ (township) Monmouth County	93.98
Alamo, CA (cdp) Contra Costa County	93.90
Montgomery, PA (township) Montgomery County	93.89
Richmond West, FL (cdp) Miami-Dade County	93.84
Westchester, IL (village) Cook County	93.81
Livingston, NJ (township) Essex County	93.75
Somers, NY (town) Westchester County	93.75
Laurel Hollow, NY (village) Nassau County	93.69
Flossmoor, IL (village) Cook County	93.66
North New Hyde Park, NY (cdp) Nassau County	93.66
Lake in the Hills, IL (village) McHenry County	93.54
Old Tappan, NJ (borough) Bergen County	93.48
Oyster Bay Cove, NY (village) Nassau County	93.47
Bartlett, IL (village) Du Page County	93.45
New Fairfield, CT (town) Fairfield County	93.45
Plainview, NY (cdp) Nassau County	93.40

Notes: Please refer to the User's Guide for an explanation of data; ranking tables include all places with Asian and/or NHPI populations above SF4 population thresholds; (1) tables reflect only those areas that meet SF4 population thresholds, therefore there may be less than 50 states, 75 counties or 75 places listed

Homeownership

Asians Who Own Their Own Homes

All States, Top 75 Counties, and Top 75 Places Sorted by Number[1]

State	Number
United States	1,659,794
California	613,743
New York	126,291
Hawaii	119,676
Texas	92,317
New Jersey	79,352
Illinois	73,273
Washington	57,520
Florida	49,897
Virginia	44,185
Maryland	38,662
Pennsylvania	32,325
Massachusetts	29,767
Georgia	27,433
Michigan	27,093
Ohio	21,305
Minnesota	18,452
Oregon	17,313
Arizona	16,596
Nevada	16,562
Colorado	16,317
North Carolina	16,302
Connecticut	12,530
Missouri	9,289
Indiana	8,910
Wisconsin	8,757
Louisiana	8,556
Tennessee	8,248
Kansas	7,038
Oklahoma	6,648
Utah	6,203
South Carolina	5,903
Alabama	4,552
Iowa	4,507
Kentucky	3,893
New Mexico	3,167
Arkansas	3,072
Alaska	3,019
Rhode Island	2,744
Delaware	2,701
Nebraska	2,594
Mississippi	2,373
Idaho	2,278
New Hampshire	1,884
District of Columbia	1,588
West Virginia	1,523
Maine	987
Montana	626
Wyoming	506
Vermont	500
South Dakota	432
North Dakota	385

County	Number
Los Angeles County, CA	184,327
Honolulu County, HI	93,145
Santa Clara County, CA	72,933
Orange County, CA	64,110
Alameda County, CA	51,912
Queens County, NY	50,262
Cook County, IL	42,363
San Diego County, CA	37,784
San Francisco County, CA	36,540
King County, WA	34,621
Harris County, TX	29,092
San Mateo County, CA	27,678
Sacramento County, CA	22,893
Contra Costa County, CA	22,879
Fairfax County, VA	22,775
Montgomery County, MD	20,027
Kings County, NY	18,097
Middlesex County, NJ	16,180
DuPage County, IL	14,890
San Bernardino County, CA	14,773
Bergen County, NJ	14,388
Clark County, NV	13,788
Maricopa County, AZ	12,811
Nassau County, NY	12,735
Dallas County, TX	12,138
Middlesex County, MA	12,106
Hawaii County, HI	11,755
Riverside County, CA	9,931
Solano County, CA	9,807
New York County, NY	9,403
San Joaquin County, CA	9,401
Fort Bend County, TX	9,308
Maui County, HI	9,190
Oakland County, MI	8,950
Philadelphia County, PA	8,707
Ventura County, CA	7,889
Gwinnett County, GA	7,859
Tarrant County, TX	7,636
Broward County, FL	7,555
Hennepin County, MN	7,122
Collin County, TX	7,094
Fresno County, CA	7,000
Westchester County, NY	6,778
Multnomah County, OR	6,670
Snohomish County, WA	6,627
Hudson County, NJ	6,264
Miami-Dade County, FL	6,017
Norfolk County, MA	5,871
Morris County, NJ	5,806
Pierce County, WA	5,806
Suffolk County, NY	5,775
Wayne County, MI	5,652
Kauai County, HI	5,586
Somerset County, NJ	5,444
Lake County, IL	5,416
Orange County, FL	5,346
Washington County, OR	5,290
Essex County, NJ	5,284
Monmouth County, NJ	5,193
Montgomery County, PA	5,117
Prince George's County, MD	5,027
Fairfield County, CT	4,839
Richmond County, NY	4,685
Ramsey County, MN	4,673
Travis County, TX	4,628
Monterey County, CA	4,550
Cuyahoga County, OH	4,500
Virginia Beach Independent City, VA	4,169
Franklin County, OH	4,070
Salt Lake County, UT	4,006
St. Louis County, MO	3,970
Baltimore County, MD	3,954
Bexar County, TX	3,936
Duval County, FL	3,898
Camden County, NJ	3,739

Place	Number
New York, NY (city)	85,118
Los Angeles, CA (city) Los Angeles County	47,900
Honolulu, HI (cdp) Honolulu County	43,988
San Jose, CA (city) Santa Clara County	41,212
San Francisco, CA (city) San Francisco County	36,540
San Diego, CA (city) San Diego County	24,448
Chicago, IL (city) Cook County	16,555
Fremont, CA (city) Alameda County	14,831
Houston, TX (city) Harris County	14,784
Seattle, WA (city) King County	12,106
Sacramento, CA (city) Sacramento County	10,809
Daly City, CA (city) San Mateo County	8,880
Philadelphia, PA (city) Philadelphia County	8,707
Oakland, CA (city) Alameda County	7,959
Torrance, CA (city) Los Angeles County	7,509
Irvine, CA (city) Orange County	6,931
Cerritos, CA (city) Los Angeles County	6,809
Monterey Park, CA (city) Los Angeles County	6,412
Anaheim, CA (city) Orange County	6,215
Stockton, CA (city) San Joaquin County	6,030
Milpitas, CA (city) Santa Clara County	5,990
Portland, OR (city) Multnomah County	5,891
Long Beach, CA (city) Los Angeles County	5,733
Union City, CA (city) Alameda County	5,733
Garden Grove, CA (city) Orange County	5,712
Sunnyvale, CA (city) Santa Clara County	5,584
Diamond Bar, CA (city) Los Angeles County	5,458
Vallejo, CA (city) Solano County	5,378
Hempstead, NY (town) Nassau County	5,235
Alhambra, CA (city) Los Angeles County	5,217
Plano, TX (city) Collin County	4,992
Hilo, HI (cdp) Hawaii County	4,922
Phoenix, AZ (city) Maricopa County	4,823
Rowland Heights, CA (cdp) Los Angeles County	4,731
Pearl City, HI (cdp) Honolulu County	4,691
Arcadia, CA (city) Los Angeles County	4,681
West Covina, CA (city) Los Angeles County	4,428
Waimalu, HI (cdp) Honolulu County	4,365
Las Vegas, NV (city) Clark County	4,349
North Hempstead, NY (town) Nassau County	4,321
Jersey City, NJ (city) Hudson County	4,309
Hacienda Heights, CA (cdp) Los Angeles County	4,290
Edison, NJ (township) Middlesex County	4,213
Hayward, CA (city) Alameda County	4,207
Glendale, CA (city) Los Angeles County	4,197
Cupertino, CA (city) Santa Clara County	4,169
Fresno, CA (city) Fresno County	4,164
Westminster, CA (city) Orange County	4,143
Kaneohe, HI (cdp) Honolulu County	4,029
Mililani Town, HI (cdp) Honolulu County	3,957
Walnut, CA (city) Los Angeles County	3,923
Carson, CA (city) Los Angeles County	3,815
Santa Ana, CA (city) Orange County	3,808
San Leandro, CA (city) Alameda County	3,762
Jacksonville, FL (city) Duval County	3,753
Bellevue, WA (city) King County	3,677
Huntington Beach, CA (city) Orange County	3,655
Chula Vista, CA (city) San Diego County	3,620
South San Francisco, CA (city) San Mateo County	3,570
Sugar Land, TX (city) Fort Bend County	3,566
Austin, TX (city) Travis County	3,508
Chino Hills, CA (city) San Bernardino County	3,457
Waipahu, HI (cdp) Honolulu County	3,403
Dallas, TX (city) Dallas County	3,365
Fullerton, CA (city) Orange County	3,358
Santa Clara, CA (city) Santa Clara County	3,314
Alameda, CA (city) Alameda County	3,278
Boston, MA (city) Suffolk County	3,276
El Monte, CA (city) Los Angeles County	3,229
Rosemead, CA (city) Los Angeles County	3,212
St. Paul, MN (city) Ramsey County	3,194
San Antonio, TX (city) Bexar County	3,179
Gardena, CA (city) Los Angeles County	3,165
San Mateo, CA (city) San Mateo County	3,001
Oklahoma City, OK (city) Oklahoma County	2,940

Notes: Please refer to the User's Guide for an explanation of data; ranking tables include all places with Asian and/or NHPI populations above SF4 population thresholds; (1) tables reflect only those areas that meet SF4 population thresholds, therefore there may be less than 50 states, 75 counties or 75 places listed

Homeownership

Asians Who Own Their Own Homes

All States, Top 75 Counties, and Top 75 Places Sorted by Percent[1]

State	Percent
Hawaii	69.16
Idaho	64.81
Wyoming	63.33
Maryland	61.03
Florida	60.78
Nevada	58.87
Utah	58.65
Washington	56.97
Arizona	56.96
Virginia	56.82
Colorado	55.35
Georgia	55.28
California	55.26
Oregon	54.91
New Jersey	54.90
New Mexico	54.77
Illinois	54.52
South Carolina	53.82
Arkansas	53.77
United States	53.24
Louisiana	52.75
Texas	52.68
Minnesota	52.28
Delaware	52.23
North Carolina	51.03
Mississippi	50.87
Kansas	50.16
Michigan	49.76
Tennessee	49.12
Alabama	49.09
Connecticut	48.92
West Virginia	48.86
Pennsylvania	48.38
Montana	48.23
Alaska	47.69
Ohio	47.27
Oklahoma	47.13
Missouri	46.83
Indiana	46.57
Maine	45.05
Iowa	44.65
Kentucky	42.76
New Hampshire	42.43
Nebraska	42.26
Vermont	42.19
Wisconsin	41.34
Massachusetts	40.99
Rhode Island	40.63
New York	39.66
North Dakota	36.74
South Dakota	34.67
District of Columbia	24.64

County	Percent
Chisago County, MN	100.00
Coshocton County, OH	100.00
Franklin County, MO	100.00
Kaufman County, TX	97.03
Canadian County, OK	96.55
Washington County, TX	96.18
Jackson County, GA	95.83
St. Martin Parish, LA	95.35
Pike County, PA	92.86
Amador County, CA	92.75
Geauga County, OH	92.62
Prince George County, VA	91.80
Manassas Park Independent City, VA	91.74
Suffolk Independent City, VA	91.57
Calvert County, MD	90.40
Oldham County, KY	90.32
Kendall County, IL	90.22
Fauquier County, VA	90.18
McDowell County, NC	89.86
Douglas County, CO	89.22
Anderson County, TX	89.02
Box Elder County, UT	88.73
Wayne County, NY	88.52
Roseau County, MN	87.84
Ascension Parish, LA	87.50
Forsyth County, GA	87.15
Fort Bend County, TX	87.10
Will County, IL	86.98
Carver County, MN	86.94
Cottonwood County, MN	86.36
Yell County, AR	86.36
Scott County, MN	85.80
Iberia Parish, LA	85.45
Lincoln County, OR	85.29
Crawford County, AR	84.90
Washington County, MN	84.87
Dakota County, NE	84.85
Belknap County, NH	84.72
Sandoval County, NM	84.53
Sussex County, NJ	84.45
Columbia County, GA	84.26
St. Charles Parish, LA	83.91
Bristol County, RI	83.70
Bowie County, TX	83.50
Hanover County, VA	83.11
Elko County, NV	82.69
Oconee County, GA	82.69
Brazoria County, TX	82.57
Guadalupe County, TX	82.29
Anoka County, MN	82.28
Warren County, NY	82.21
Hendricks County, IN	82.18
Henry County, GA	81.65
Manassas Independent City, VA	81.53
Monroe County, WI	81.40
Clay County, FL	81.33
Malheur County, OR	81.33
San Benito County, CA	81.19
Livingston County, MI	80.91
Canyon County, ID	80.81
Lafourche Parish, LA	80.50
Colusa County, CA	80.00
Rockwall County, TX	80.00
Hunterdon County, NJ	79.94
Yamhill County, OR	79.89
Pueblo County, CO	79.82
LaPorte County, IN	79.79
McHenry County, IL	79.67
Spotsylvania County, VA	79.55
Pasco County, FL	79.40
Flagler County, FL	79.31
Franklin County, WA	78.99
Ford County, KS	78.74
Nassau County, NY	78.70
Carroll County, GA	78.64

Place	Percent
Acworth, GA (city) Cobb County	100.00
Algonquin, IL (village) McHenry County	100.00
Bartlett, TN (city) Shelby County	100.00
Blackhawk-Camino Tass., CA (cdp) Contra Costa Co.	100.00
Bradbury, CA (city) Los Angeles County	100.00
Brier, WA (city) Snohomish County	100.00
Brushy Creek, TX (cdp) Williamson County	100.00
Bunker Hill Village, TX (city) Harris County	100.00
Burr Ridge, IL (village) Du Page County	100.00
Clayton, CA (city) Contra Costa County	100.00
Colleyville, TX (city) Tarrant County	100.00
Colmar Manor, MD (town) Prince George's County	100.00
Columbine, CO (cdp) Jefferson County	100.00
Cranbury, NJ (township) Middlesex County	100.00
East Hills, NY (village) Nassau County	100.00
Elk Plain, WA (cdp) Pierce County	100.00
Elwood, NY (cdp) Suffolk County	100.00
Flossmoor, IL (village) Cook County	100.00
Forest Hills, MI (cdp) Kent County	100.00
Four Corners, TX (cdp) Fort Bend County	100.00
Franklin Lakes, NJ (borough) Bergen County	100.00
Friendly, MD (cdp) Prince George's County	100.00
Frisco, TX (city) Collin County	100.00
Gages Lake, IL (cdp) Lake County	100.00
Granite Bay, CA (cdp) Placer County	100.00
Greentree, NJ (cdp) Camden County	100.00
Highland Heights, OH (city) Cuyahoga County	100.00
Hopewell, NJ (township) Mercer County	100.00
Hunters Creek Village, TX (city) Harris County	100.00
Keller, TX (city) Tarrant County	100.00
Lakeland South, WA (cdp) King County	100.00
Longmeadow, MA (town) Hampden County	100.00
Macomb, MI (township) Macomb County	100.00
Mansfield, TX (city) Tarrant County	100.00
Moorpark, CA (city) Ventura County	100.00
Murphy, TX (city) Collin County	100.00
Newport Coast, CA (cdp) Orange County	100.00
Newtown, CT (town) Fairfield County	100.00
North Marysville, WA (cdp) Snohomish County	100.00
Oak Brook, IL (village) Du Page County	100.00
Oakland charter, MI (township) Oakland County	100.00
Old Brookville, NY (village) Nassau County	100.00
Old Westbury, NY (village) Nassau County	100.00
Portola Hills, CA (cdp) Orange County	100.00
Redford, MI (township) Wayne County	100.00
Rolling Hills, CA (city) Los Angeles County	100.00
San Juan Capistrano, CA (city) Orange County	100.00
Sands Point, NY (village) Nassau County	100.00
Shenandoah, LA (cdp) East Baton Rouge Parish	100.00
South Barrington, IL (village) Cook County	100.00
South Kensington, MD (cdp) Montgomery County	100.00
Summerlin South, NV (cdp) Clark County	100.00
Upper St. Clair, PA (township) Allegheny County	100.00
Villa Park, CA (city) Orange County	100.00
West Lake Stevens, WA (cdp) Snohomish County	100.00
Westford, MA (town) Middlesex County	100.00
Weston, MA (town) Middlesex County	100.00
Yukon, OK (city) Canadian County	100.00
Heeia, HI (cdp) Honolulu County	98.97
New Territory, TX (cdp) Fort Bend County	98.91
Sammamish, WA (city) King County	98.51
Dix Hills, NY (cdp) Suffolk County	98.14
Atherton, CA (town) San Mateo County	97.92
Blaine, MN (city) Anoka County	97.86
Lincolnwood, IL (village) Cook County	97.79
Marlboro, NJ (township) Monmouth County	97.61
Searingtown, NY (cdp) Nassau County	97.53
Sudbury, MA (town) Middlesex County	97.41
East Fishkill, NY (town) Dutchess County	97.40
Wildwood, MO (city) Saint Louis County	97.30
Bartlett, IL (village) Du Page County	97.11
Mountain Park, GA (cdp) Gwinnett County	96.98
Berkeley Lake, GA (city) Gwinnett County	96.88
Morganville, NJ (cdp) Monmouth County	96.73
Missouri City, TX (city) Fort Bend County	96.71

Notes: Please refer to the User's Guide for an explanation of data; ranking tables include all places with Asian and/or NHPI populations above SF4 population thresholds; (1) tables reflect only those areas that meet SF4 population thresholds, therefore there may be less than 50 states, 75 counties or 75 places listed

Homeownership

Native Hawaiian and Other Pacific Islanders Who Own Their Own Homes

All States, Top 75 Counties, and Top 75 Places Sorted by Number[1]

State	Number
United States	44,896
Hawaii	13,635
California	12,666
Washington	2,626
Utah	1,780
Texas	1,674
Oregon	946
Florida	919
Nevada	917
Arizona	803
Colorado	644
New York	577
Georgia	553
Illinois	488
Virginia	468
Pennsylvania	467
Missouri	406
North Carolina	403
Ohio	335
Michigan	323
Alaska	315
Tennessee	274
New Jersey	264
Minnesota	251
Louisiana	240
Indiana	227
Maryland	226
Oklahoma	222
Kansas	191
New Mexico	188
Massachusetts	183
South Carolina	182
Wisconsin	175
Alabama	159
Connecticut	143
Idaho	139
Arkansas	131
Mississippi	104
Iowa	100
Kentucky	79
Nebraska	72
Rhode Island	60
Montana	56
Maine	49
West Virginia	47
Delaware	45

County	Number
Honolulu County, HI	8,520
Los Angeles County, CA	2,493
Hawaii County, HI	2,414
Maui County, HI	1,973
San Diego County, CA	1,715
Salt Lake County, UT	1,315
Alameda County, CA	1,038
Orange County, CA	1,033
San Mateo County, CA	834
King County, WA	831
Sacramento County, CA	789
Clark County, NV	772
Kauai County, HI	728
Pierce County, WA	669
San Bernardino County, CA	606
Solano County, CA	573
Maricopa County, AZ	503
Contra Costa County, CA	493
Santa Clara County, CA	472
Riverside County, CA	467
Multnomah County, OR	287
Monterey County, CA	250
Harris County, TX	235
Thurston County, WA	230
Stanislaus County, CA	227
Bexar County, TX	222
Ventura County, CA	218
San Joaquin County, CA	216
Kitsap County, WA	214
Bell County, TX	207
Anchorage Borough, AK	199
Washington County, OR	193
Utah County, UT	189
Cook County, IL	180
Snohomish County, WA	172
Tarrant County, TX	161
El Paso County, CO	157
Jackson County, MO	146
Kern County, CA	142
Queens County, NY	140
San Francisco County, CA	139
Pima County, AZ	137
Dallas County, TX	136
Davis County, UT	132
Santa Barbara County, CA	129
Philadelphia County, PA	118
Clackamas County, OR	111
Broward County, FL	106
Fairfax County, VA	105
Spokane County, WA	104
Lane County, OR	103
Clark County, WA	100
Orange County, FL	100
Washoe County, NV	96
Arapahoe County, CO	95
Sonoma County, CA	93
Allegheny County, PA	87
Sedgwick County, KS	87
Jefferson County, CO	86
Bernalillo County, NM	85
Miami-Dade County, FL	81
Cumberland County, NC	79
Hillsborough County, FL	76
Kings County, NY	76
Duval County, FL	68
Travis County, TX	65
Nassau County, NY	64
St. Louis County, MO	64
Yolo County, CA	64
Suffolk County, NY	61
Denver County, CO	60
Ada County, ID	57
Hennepin County, MN	56
Bronx County, NY	55
Gwinnett County, GA	55

Place	Number
Honolulu, HI (cdp) Honolulu County	2,038
San Diego, CA (city) San Diego County	708
Hilo, HI (cdp) Hawaii County	674
Nanakuli, HI (cdp) Honolulu County	669
Kaneohe, HI (cdp) Honolulu County	551
Los Angeles, CA (city) Los Angeles County	547
Kailua, HI (cdp) Honolulu County	516
Waimanalo Beach, HI (cdp) Honolulu County	453
Sacramento, CA (city) Sacramento County	446
West Valley City, UT (city) Salt Lake County	436
Salt Lake City, UT (city) Salt Lake County	394
Waianae, HI (cdp) Honolulu County	370
New York, NY (city)	300
Oceanside, CA (city) San Diego County	283
Long Beach, CA (city) Los Angeles County	280
Mililani Town, HI (cdp) Honolulu County	273
Phoenix, AZ (city) Maricopa County	241
Vallejo, CA (city) Solano County	241
Anahola, HI (cdp) Kauai County	238
Hayward, CA (city) Alameda County	238
Carson, CA (city) Los Angeles County	233
San Jose, CA (city) Santa Clara County	220
Portland, OR (city) Multnomah County	219
Pearl City, HI (cdp) Honolulu County	215
Seattle, WA (city) King County	210
Oakland, CA (city) Alameda County	209
Waihee-Waiehu, HI (cdp) Maui County	208
Kualapuu, HI (cdp) Maui County	206
Fairfield, CA (city) Solano County	204
Waimea, HI (cdp) Hawaii County	201
Chula Vista, CA (city) San Diego County	199
Henderson, NV (city) Clark County	199
Las Vegas, NV (city) Clark County	199
Killeen, TX (city) Bell County	186
Wailuku, HI (cdp) Maui County	183
Tacoma, WA (city) Pierce County	180
Makakilo City, HI (cdp) Honolulu County	177
Waimalu, HI (cdp) Honolulu County	177
Kailua, HI (cdp) Hawaii County	173
Kihei, HI (cdp) Maui County	173
Ewa Beach, HI (cdp) Honolulu County	164
Hauula, HI (cdp) Honolulu County	162
Maili, HI (cdp) Honolulu County	158
East Palo Alto, CA (city) San Mateo County	155
Wahiawa, HI (cdp) Honolulu County	153
Laie, HI (cdp) Honolulu County	147
Santa Ana, CA (city) Orange County	146
North Las Vegas, NV (city) Clark County	141
San Francisco, CA (city) San Francisco County	139
San Mateo, CA (city) San Mateo County	134
Kalaoa, HI (cdp) Hawaii County	131
Fremont, CA (city) Alameda County	128
Kaunakakai, HI (cdp) Maui County	123
Lahaina, HI (cdp) Maui County	122
Makaha, HI (cdp) Honolulu County	122
Waimanalo, HI (cdp) Honolulu County	121
Fontana, CA (city) San Bernardino County	119
Houston, TX (city) Harris County	119
Philadelphia, PA (city) Philadelphia County	118
Pittsburg, CA (city) Contra Costa County	118
San Antonio, TX (city) Bexar County	117
Modesto, CA (city) Stanislaus County	115
Union City, CA (city) Alameda County	111
Federal Way, WA (city) King County	109
Riverside, CA (city) Riverside County	108
Spanaway, WA (cdp) Pierce County	108
Daly City, CA (city) San Mateo County	107
Garden Grove, CA (city) Orange County	105
Kapaa, HI (cdp) Kauai County	105
South San Francisco, CA (city) San Mateo County	105
Bakersfield, CA (city) Kern County	101
Kahului, HI (cdp) Maui County	101
Waipahu, HI (cdp) Honolulu County	101
Lakewood, WA (city) Pierce County	100
Ahuimanu, HI (cdp) Honolulu County	99

Notes: Please refer to the User's Guide for an explanation of data; ranking tables include all places with Asian and/or NHPI populations above SF4 population thresholds; (1) tables reflect only those areas that meet SF4 population thresholds, therefore there may be less than 50 states, 75 counties or 75 places listed

Homeownership

Native Hawaiian and Other Pacific Islanders Who Own Their Own Homes

All States, Top 75 Counties, and Top 75 Places Sorted by Percent[1]

State	Percent
Mississippi	64.20
Louisiana	59.11
Wisconsin	58.33
Utah	57.31
West Virginia	55.95
Maine	55.68
Minnesota	55.04
Pennsylvania	54.81
Delaware	54.22
Connecticut	52.19
Ohio	52.18
Illinois	50.47
Michigan	50.47
New Mexico	49.34
Colorado	49.27
Maryland	48.50
Oklahoma	48.37
Kansas	48.35
Texas	48.02
Florida	48.01
Tennessee	47.40
Alabama	47.18
Virginia	47.04
Arizona	46.82
Georgia	46.51
Missouri	46.45
Rhode Island	46.15
Hawaii	46.10
Idaho	45.72
Indiana	45.58
United States	45.47
South Carolina	44.61
California	44.48
North Carolina	44.43
Montana	44.09
Washington	42.77
Alaska	41.45
Nevada	40.49
Oregon	40.22
New Jersey	39.52
Nebraska	39.13
Arkansas	38.76
Massachusetts	36.97
Iowa	35.21
New York	28.74
Kentucky	27.05

County	Percent
Suffolk County, NY	79.22
Philadelphia County, PA	74.68
Kern County, CA	71.00
Thurston County, WA	68.05
Bexar County, TX	64.16
Hillsborough County, FL	63.33
Salt Lake County, UT	62.47
Contra Costa County, CA	62.33
Santa Barbara County, CA	61.14
Miami-Dade County, FL	60.90
Nassau County, NY	58.72
Solano County, CA	57.59
Clackamas County, OR	56.35
Orange County, FL	55.56
Davis County, UT	55.46
Sedgwick County, KS	55.41
Ada County, ID	54.81
Kauai County, HI	54.61
Arapahoe County, CO	54.60
San Bernardino County, CA	52.74
Hawaii County, HI	52.57
Bernalillo County, NM	52.47
Jackson County, MO	52.33
Maui County, HI	52.02
Cumberland County, NC	51.97
Stanislaus County, CA	51.95
Bell County, TX	51.88
Broward County, FL	51.46
Harris County, TX	51.31
Monterey County, CA	51.23
Fairfax County, VA	50.97
Jefferson County, CO	50.59
Orange County, CA	50.51
Coryell County, TX	50.00
Riverside County, CA	50.00
Ventura County, CA	49.77
Sonoma County, CA	49.47
Kitsap County, WA	48.64
Maricopa County, AZ	48.46
Lane County, OR	48.36
Alameda County, CA	47.83
San Mateo County, CA	47.33
Shelby County, TN	46.30
Pierce County, WA	46.23
Sacramento County, CA	45.69
Dallas County, TX	45.64
San Diego County, CA	45.54
Allegheny County, PA	44.62
Duval County, FL	44.16
Utah County, UT	43.95
Spokane County, WA	43.51
Honolulu County, HI	43.06
Washington County, OR	42.79
St. Louis County, MO	42.38
Clark County, NV	42.09
El Paso County, CO	41.53
Gwinnett County, GA	41.35
Queens County, NY	41.06
Snohomish County, WA	40.76
Onslow County, NC	40.51
Cook County, IL	40.36
Pima County, AZ	39.60
San Joaquin County, CA	39.20
Anchorage Borough, AK	39.02
Los Angeles County, CA	38.10
Multnomah County, OR	37.81
Denver County, CO	37.50
Wayne County, MI	36.30
Montgomery County, MD	36.13
King County, WA	35.68
Tarrant County, TX	34.77
Santa Clara County, CA	33.05
Clark County, WA	32.47
Davidson County, TN	32.41
Milwaukee County, WI	31.33

Place	Percent
Fontana, CA (city) San Bernardino County	95.20
Sandy, UT (city) Salt Lake County	91.07
Waimanalo Beach, HI (cdp) Honolulu County	90.60
Pittsburg, CA (city) Contra Costa County	89.39
Anahola, HI (cdp) Kauai County	88.48
Hana, HI (cdp) Maui County	88.14
Waihee-Waiehu, HI (cdp) Maui County	84.90
Kualapuu, HI (cdp) Maui County	84.08
Spanaway, WA (cdp) Pierce County	82.44
Bakersfield, CA (city) Kern County	80.80
Kapaau, HI (cdp) Hawaii County	77.42
Maunawili, HI (cdp) Honolulu County	75.56
Philadelphia, PA (city) Philadelphia County	74.68
Nanakuli, HI (cdp) Honolulu County	74.58
West Jordan, UT (city) Salt Lake County	74.22
Mililani Town, HI (cdp) Honolulu County	74.18
North Las Vegas, NV (city) Clark County	73.44
Henderson, NV (city) Clark County	72.63
Kahuku, HI (cdp) Honolulu County	72.22
Independence, MO (city) Jackson County	72.16
Mesa, AZ (city) Maricopa County	71.97
Antioch, CA (city) Contra Costa County	71.91
Paia, HI (cdp) Maui County	70.59
Papaikou, HI (cdp) Hawaii County	70.27
West Valley City, UT (city) Salt Lake County	70.21
Kahaluu, HI (cdp) Honolulu County	68.84
Volcano, HI (cdp) Hawaii County	68.75
Union City, CA (city) Alameda County	67.68
Kalaoa, HI (cdp) Hawaii County	66.84
Hawaiian Beaches, HI (cdp) Hawaii County	66.07
Waikane, HI (cdp) Honolulu County	65.79
Kailua, HI (cdp) Honolulu County	65.65
Kilauea, HI (cdp) Kauai County	65.22
Redwood City, CA (city) San Mateo County	64.10
Captain Cook, HI (cdp) Hawaii County	64.06
Chula Vista, CA (city) San Diego County	63.99
Ontario, CA (city) San Bernardino County	63.73
Hawaiian Ocean View, HI (cdp) Hawaii County	62.96
Naalehu, HI (cdp) Hawaii County	62.50
Waimea, HI (cdp) Hawaii County	62.23
Hanapepe, HI (cdp) Kauai County	62.00
Fremont, CA (city) Alameda County	61.84
Lakewood, CA (city) Los Angeles County	61.74
Salt Lake City, UT (city) Salt Lake County	61.37
Honaunau-Napoopoo, HI (cdp) Hawaii County	60.87
Kekaha, HI (cdp) Kauai County	60.53
San Leandro, CA (city) Alameda County	60.47
Ahuimanu, HI (cdp) Honolulu County	60.37
Carson, CA (city) Los Angeles County	59.90
Santa Ana, CA (city) Orange County	59.59
Holualoa, HI (cdp) Hawaii County	59.38
Aiea, HI (cdp) Honolulu County	59.09
Killeen, TX (city) Bell County	58.49
Salinas, CA (city) Monterey County	58.33
Kearns, UT (cdp) Salt Lake County	58.11
Makakilo City, HI (cdp) Honolulu County	57.84
Waianae, HI (cdp) Honolulu County	57.54
Kaneohe, HI (cdp) Honolulu County	57.40
Kaaawa, HI (cdp) Honolulu County	57.14
Pearl City, HI (cdp) Honolulu County	56.58
Taylorsville, UT (city) Salt Lake County	56.07
Kaunakakai, HI (cdp) Maui County	55.91
Ewa Beach, HI (cdp) Honolulu County	55.59
Vallejo, CA (city) Solano County	55.40
Fairfield, CA (city) Solano County	54.11
Haleiwa, HI (cdp) Honolulu County	53.33
Huntington Beach, CA (city) Orange County	53.33
West Covina, CA (city) Los Angeles County	53.00
Oceanside, CA (city) San Diego County	52.50
Oxnard, CA (city) Ventura County	52.43
Hauula, HI (cdp) Honolulu County	52.26
Waimanalo, HI (cdp) Honolulu County	51.27
Orem, UT (city) Utah County	51.15
Waimea, HI (cdp) Kauai County	51.02
Kapaa, HI (cdp) Kauai County	50.97

Notes: Please refer to the User's Guide for an explanation of data; ranking tables include all places with Asian and/or NHPI populations above SF4 population thresholds; (1) tables reflect only those areas that meet SF4 population thresholds, therefore there may be less than 50 states, 75 counties or 75 places listed

Homeownership

Asian Indians Who Own Their Own Homes

All States, Top 75 Counties, and Top 75 Places Sorted by Number[1]

State	Number
United States	247,650
California	45,614
New York	31,356
New Jersey	24,851
Texas	20,123
Illinois	20,013
Florida	12,490
Maryland	9,287
Michigan	8,695
Pennsylvania	8,336
Virginia	7,055
Georgia	6,743
Ohio	6,041
Massachusetts	5,292
North Carolina	3,778
Connecticut	3,753
Washington	3,551
Minnesota	2,682
Arizona	2,605
Indiana	2,231
Missouri	1,955
Tennessee	1,916
Colorado	1,833
Oregon	1,499
Wisconsin	1,428
Louisiana	1,355
Oklahoma	1,289
South Carolina	1,265
Kansas	1,227
Alabama	1,108
Kentucky	971
Nevada	859
Delaware	794
Iowa	794
New Mexico	521
West Virginia	517
Mississippi	454
District of Columbia	443
New Hampshire	435
Nebraska	432
Rhode Island	396
Arkansas	364
Utah	328
Hawaii	248
North Dakota	144
Maine	135
Idaho	127
Wyoming	94
Vermont	86
Alaska	54
Montana	52
South Dakota	31

County	Number
Queens County, NY	12,359
Cook County, IL	9,981
Los Angeles County, CA	8,816
Santa Clara County, CA	8,321
Middlesex County, NJ	7,026
DuPage County, IL	6,164
Alameda County, CA	6,092
Harris County, TX	5,311
Montgomery County, MD	5,027
Nassau County, NY	4,799
Orange County, CA	4,626
Fairfax County, VA	4,001
Oakland County, MI	3,398
Fort Bend County, TX	3,003
Dallas County, TX	2,958
Bergen County, NJ	2,817
Middlesex County, MA	2,769
Broward County, FL	2,666
Westchester County, NY	2,416
Somerset County, NJ	2,304
Wayne County, MI	2,284
King County, WA	2,203
Contra Costa County, CA	2,191
Maricopa County, AZ	2,155
Gwinnett County, GA	2,095
Sacramento County, CA	2,007
Morris County, NJ	1,785
Suffolk County, NY	1,771
Collin County, TX	1,685
Hudson County, NJ	1,672
Philadelphia County, PA	1,655
Miami-Dade County, FL	1,537
Fairfield County, CT	1,525
Cuyahoga County, OH	1,508
Kings County, NY	1,498
Essex County, NJ	1,467
San Bernardino County, CA	1,426
San Diego County, CA	1,399
Orange County, FL	1,382
San Mateo County, CA	1,353
Monmouth County, NJ	1,309
Bronx County, NY	1,273
Denton County, TX	1,266
Lake County, IL	1,224
Mercer County, NJ	1,203
Tarrant County, TX	1,194
Union County, NJ	1,164
Montgomery County, PA	1,161
Prince George's County, MD	1,158
New York County, NY	1,138
Wake County, NC	1,138
Hennepin County, MN	1,111
Rockland County, NY	1,094
Sutter County, CA	1,082
St. Louis County, MO	1,080
Hartford County, CT	1,073
Allegheny County, PA	1,044
Richmond County, NY	1,016
Fresno County, CA	996
Passaic County, NJ	992
Riverside County, CA	980
Baltimore County, MD	971
Palm Beach County, FL	970
Fulton County, GA	969
Hillsborough County, FL	944
Howard County, MD	942
Camden County, NJ	940
Travis County, TX	937
Bucks County, PA	886
San Joaquin County, CA	880
Franklin County, OH	856
Macomb County, MI	830
Mecklenburg County, NC	830
Cobb County, GA	824
Delaware County, PA	822

Place	Number
New York, NY (city)	17,284
San Jose, CA (city) Santa Clara County	4,346
Fremont, CA (city) Alameda County	2,948
Los Angeles, CA (city) Los Angeles County	2,904
Houston, TX (city) Harris County	2,404
Chicago, IL (city) Cook County	2,312
Hempstead, NY (town) Nassau County	2,063
Edison, NJ (township) Middlesex County	1,893
Philadelphia, PA (city) Philadelphia County	1,655
North Hempstead, NY (town) Nassau County	1,606
Plano, TX (city) Collin County	1,239
Oyster Bay, NY (town) Nassau County	1,087
Naperville, IL (city) Du Page County	1,045
Sugar Land, TX (city) Fort Bend County	1,003
Jersey City, NJ (city) Hudson County	969
Troy, MI (city) Oakland County	888
South Brunswick, NJ (township) Middlesex County	882
Union City, CA (city) Alameda County	856
Woodbridge, NJ (township) Middlesex County	822
Phoenix, AZ (city) Maricopa County	815
San Diego, CA (city) San Diego County	813
Irvine, CA (city) Orange County	787
Skokie, IL (village) Cook County	774
Canton, MI (township) Wayne County	757
Austin, TX (city) Travis County	745
Carrollton, TX (city) Denton County	741
Schaumburg, IL (village) Cook County	718
Piscataway, NJ (township) Middlesex County	695
Milpitas, CA (city) Santa Clara County	691
Anaheim, CA (city) Orange County	677
Cupertino, CA (city) Santa Clara County	675
Charlotte, NC (city) Mecklenburg County	670
Dallas, TX (city) Dallas County	665
Franklin, NJ (township) Somerset County	664
Cary, NC (town) Wake County	638
Sunnyvale, CA (city) Santa Clara County	614
Cerritos, CA (city) Los Angeles County	603
San Antonio, TX (city) Bexar County	598
Yonkers, NY (city) Westchester County	585
Brookhaven, NY (town) Suffolk County	557
Missouri City, TX (city) Fort Bend County	549
East Brunswick, NJ (township) Middlesex County	548
Hoffman Estates, IL (village) Cook County	548
Bridgewater, NJ (township) Somerset County	539
Garland, TX (city) Dallas County	537
Parsippany-Troy Hills, NJ (township) Morris County	534
Santa Clara, CA (city) Santa Clara County	534
Sacramento, CA (city) Sacramento County	533
Oklahoma City, OK (city) Oklahoma County	532
Diamond Bar, CA (city) Los Angeles County	531
North Brunswick, NJ (township) Middlesex County	521
Mesquite, TX (city) Dallas County	520
Irving, TX (city) Dallas County	516
Columbus, OH (city) Franklin County	513
Glendale Heights, IL (village) Du Page County	511
Sterling Heights, MI (city) Macomb County	500
Greenburgh, NY (town) Westchester County	496
Farmington Hills, MI (city) Oakland County	483
Fresno, CA (city) Fresno County	482
Clarkstown, NY (town) Rockland County	476
Huntington, NY (town) Suffolk County	476
San Francisco, CA (city) San Francisco County	470
West Bloomfield, MI (township) Oakland County	465
Indianapolis, IN (sp. city) Marion County	461
Seattle, WA (city) King County	458
Old Bridge, NJ (township) Middlesex County	456
Rochester Hills, MI (city) Oakland County	452
Detroit, MI (city) Wayne County	448
Germantown, MD (cdp) Montgomery County	437
South Yuba City, CA (cdp) Sutter County	425
Bakersfield, CA (city) Kern County	419
Hanover Park, IL (village) Cook County	419
West Windsor, NJ (township) Mercer County	413
Chandler, AZ (city) Maricopa County	409
Hayward, CA (city) Alameda County	409

Notes: Please refer to the User's Guide for an explanation of data; ranking tables include all places with Asian and/or NHPI populations above SF4 population thresholds; (1) tables reflect only those areas that meet SF4 population thresholds, therefore there may be less than 50 states, 75 counties or 75 places listed

Homeownership

Asian Indians Who Own Their Own Homes

All States, Top 75 Counties, and Top 75 Places Sorted by Percent[1]

State	Percent
Wyoming	64.83
Maryland	58.63
New Mexico	57.19
Florida	55.38
Nevada	55.10
Illinois	52.74
West Virginia	52.54
Arizona	52.00
Hawaii	51.45
South Carolina	48.92
Georgia	48.51
New Jersey	48.22
Alabama	48.07
Texas	47.55
Maine	47.20
Michigan	47.15
California	46.88
United States	46.87
Washington	46.68
Connecticut	46.39
Tennessee	45.79
Missouri	45.43
Oklahoma	45.39
North Carolina	45.34
Pennsylvania	45.32
Mississippi	45.26
Virginia	44.99
Minnesota	44.96
Vermont	44.56
Louisiana	44.44
Indiana	44.26
Delaware	44.16
Kansas	44.06
Ohio	43.54
New York	43.32
Rhode Island	42.86
North Dakota	42.23
Oregon	41.70
Iowa	40.66
Kentucky	40.31
Colorado	39.88
Arkansas	38.64
Montana	38.24
Utah	37.49
Idaho	37.24
Nebraska	37.18
Massachusetts	36.65
Alaska	36.00
Wisconsin	35.03
New Hampshire	34.94
District of Columbia	31.73
South Dakota	15.20

County	Percent
Canadian County, OK	95.56
Westmoreland County, PA	93.98
Sussex County, NJ	91.55
Douglas County, CO	89.74
Will County, IL	87.69
Saginaw County, MI	85.59
Fort Bend County, TX	84.33
Anoka County, MN	83.33
Northampton County, PA	82.06
Nassau County, NY	80.24
Hunterdon County, NJ	80.20
Kane County, IL	79.82
Hamilton County, IN	79.19
Harford County, MD	78.62
Delaware County, OH	78.48
Midland County, TX	77.88
Brazoria County, TX	77.39
Hidalgo County, TX	77.25
Monroe County, PA	76.99
Williamson County, TX	76.57
Columbia County, GA	76.33
St. Charles County, MO	75.76
Putnam County, NY	74.76
McHenry County, IL	74.70
Luzerne County, PA	74.26
St. Mary's County, MD	73.97
York County, VA	73.56
Kanawha County, WV	73.49
Madera County, CA	73.19
Chesterfield County, VA	72.78
Pasco County, FL	72.36
Lorain County, OH	72.32
San Joaquin County, CA	72.31
Midland County, MI	72.00
Litchfield County, CT	71.11
Stanislaus County, CA	71.00
Somerset County, NJ	70.61
Rockland County, NY	70.54
Merced County, CA	70.37
Henry County, GA	69.95
Lake County, IL	69.00
Butler County, PA	68.97
Gloucester County, NJ	68.62
Frederick County, MD	67.96
Denton County, TX	67.92
Shelby County, AL	67.86
Escambia County, FL	67.65
Medina County, OH	67.53
Plymouth County, MA	67.50
Sutter County, CA	67.20
Prince William County, VA	67.19
Seminole County, FL	67.06
Washington County, MN	66.97
Howard County, MD	66.48
Spartanburg County, SC	66.39
Montgomery County, TX	66.20
Cumberland County, PA	66.15
DuPage County, IL	65.78
Loudoun County, VA	65.31
Cherokee County, GA	65.00
Montgomery County, MD	64.82
Gwinnett County, GA	64.76
San Bernardino County, CA	64.21
Suffolk County, NY	64.07
Broward County, FL	63.80
Stark County, OH	63.27
Warren County, OH	63.03
Riverside County, CA	62.74
Marion County, FL	62.72
Wicomico County, MD	62.70
Solano County, CA	62.56
Hampden County, MA	61.84
Monmouth County, NJ	61.48
Ventura County, CA	61.35
Orange County, NY	61.24

Place	Percent
Brookfield, WI (city) Waukesha County	100.00
Burr Ridge, IL (village) Du Page County	100.00
Burtonsville, MD (cdp) Montgomery County	100.00
Cloverly, MD (cdp) Montgomery County	100.00
Colesville, MD (cdp) Montgomery County	100.00
Dix Hills, NY (cdp) Suffolk County	100.00
Greentree, NJ (cdp) Camden County	100.00
Herricks, NY (cdp) Nassau County	100.00
Highlands Ranch, CO (cdp) Douglas County	100.00
Manhasset Hills, NY (cdp) Nassau County	100.00
Montgomery, PA (township) Montgomery County	100.00
Morton Grove, IL (village) Cook County	100.00
Mountain Park, GA (cdp) Gwinnett County	100.00
Newington, VA (cdp) Fairfax County	100.00
North Valley Stream, NY (cdp) Nassau County	100.00
Oak Brook, IL (village) Du Page County	100.00
Olney, MD (cdp) Montgomery County	100.00
Palmdale, CA (city) Los Angeles County	100.00
Rowlett, TX (city) Dallas County	100.00
Salisbury, NY (cdp) Nassau County	100.00
Scarsdale, NY (village) Westchester County	100.00
Searingtown, NY (cdp) Nassau County	100.00
South Barrington, IL (village) Cook County	100.00
Town and Country, MO (city) Saint Louis County	100.00
Travilah, MD (cdp) Montgomery County	100.00
Upper St. Clair, PA (township) Allegheny County	100.00
Warren, NJ (township) Somerset County	100.00
Bartlett, IL (village) Du Page County	98.12
Franklin Square, NY (cdp) Nassau County	97.92
New Territory, TX (cdp) Fort Bend County	97.63
Paramus, NJ (borough) Bergen County	97.30
Missouri City, TX (city) Fort Bend County	96.32
Laguna, CA (cdp) Sacramento County	96.09
Manalapan, NJ (township) Monmouth County	95.97
Marlboro, NJ (township) Monmouth County	95.82
Orland Park, IL (village) Cook County	95.48
North Potomac, MD (cdp) Montgomery County	95.47
Howell, NJ (township) Monmouth County	95.09
Elk Grove, CA (cdp) Sacramento County	95.07
Nanuet, NY (cdp) Rockland County	95.04
Mission Bend, TX (cdp) Fort Bend County	94.91
Flower Mound, TX (town) Denton County	94.62
North New Hyde Park, NY (cdp) Nassau County	94.62
Branchburg, NJ (township) Somerset County	94.51
Saratoga, CA (city) Santa Clara County	94.50
Rancho Palos Verdes, CA (city) Los Angeles County	93.90
Bolingbrook, IL (village) Will County	93.84
Hanover, NJ (township) Morris County	93.75
Suisun City, CA (city) Solano County	93.75
Freehold, NJ (township) Monmouth County	93.55
Wolf Trap, VA (cdp) Fairfax County	93.40
West Bloomfield, MI (township) Oakland County	93.00
Yorba Linda, CA (city) Orange County	92.90
Los Altos Hills, CA (town) Santa Clara County	92.80
Gilbert, AZ (town) Maricopa County	92.45
Muttontown, NY (village) Nassau County	92.00
Lincolnwood, IL (village) Cook County	91.94
Franconia, VA (cdp) Fairfax County	91.67
Streamwood, IL (village) Cook County	91.59
West Springfield, VA (cdp) Fairfax County	91.59
Antioch, CA (city) Contra Costa County	91.58
Hercules, CA (city) Contra Costa County	91.30
New Castle, NY (town) Westchester County	91.30
South Plainfield, NJ (borough) Middlesex County	90.68
Lilburn, GA (city) Gwinnett County	90.32
Glenview, IL (village) Cook County	89.89
Syosset, NY (cdp) Nassau County	89.77
Danville, CA (town) Contra Costa County	89.74
McLean, VA (cdp) Fairfax County	89.64
Darien, IL (city) Du Page County	89.55
Chino Hills, CA (city) San Bernardino County	89.44
Bridgewater, NJ (township) Somerset County	88.94
West Windsor, NJ (township) Mercer County	88.25
Elgin, IL (city) Kane County	88.13
Plainview, NY (cdp) Nassau County	88.04

Notes: Please refer to the User's Guide for an explanation of data; ranking tables include all places with Asian and/or NHPI populations above SF4 population thresholds; (1) tables reflect only those areas that meet SF4 population thresholds, therefore there may be less than 50 states, 75 counties or 75 places listed

Homeownership

Bangladeshis Who Own Their Own Homes

***All States, Top 75 Counties, and Top 75 Places Sorted by Number*[1]**

State	Number
United States	3,171
New York	881
New Jersey	266
California	240
Texas	229
Virginia	220
Michigan	211
Maryland	196
Florida	134
Georgia	123
Illinois	108
Ohio	97
Pennsylvania	63
Connecticut	49
Massachusetts	41

County	Number
Queens County, NY	602
Montgomery County, MD	155
Wayne County, MI	149
Fairfax County, VA	124
Los Angeles County, CA	84
Kings County, NY	79
Harris County, TX	74
Passaic County, NJ	74
Bronx County, NY	58
Santa Clara County, CA	42
DeKalb County, GA	38
Dallas County, TX	32
Middlesex County, NJ	29
Atlantic County, NJ	19
New York County, NY	0

Place	Number
New York, NY (city)	739
Hamtramck, MI (city) Wayne County	100
Paterson, NJ (city) Passaic County	48
Los Angeles, CA (city) Los Angeles County	23

Notes: Please refer to the User's Guide for an explanation of data; ranking tables include all places with Asian and/or NHPI populations above SF4 population thresholds; (1) tables reflect only those areas that meet SF4 population thresholds, therefore there may be less than 50 states, 75 counties or 75 places listed

Homeownership

Bangladeshis Who Own Their Own Homes

All States, Top 75 Counties, and Top 75 Places Sorted by Percent[1]

State	Percent
Maryland	58.86
Michigan	47.85
Illinois	44.26
Ohio	44.09
Virginia	43.22
Connecticut	41.53
New Jersey	39.12
Georgia	38.68
Florida	33.84
Massachusetts	28.67
United States	28.17
California	27.75
Pennsylvania	25.20
Texas	23.54
New York	19.16

County	Percent
Montgomery County, MD	66.52
Passaic County, NJ	56.92
Fairfax County, VA	54.39
Wayne County, MI	49.83
Harris County, TX	31.62
DeKalb County, GA	29.69
Santa Clara County, CA	28.57
Middlesex County, NJ	21.97
Los Angeles County, CA	21.05
Queens County, NY	20.79
Atlantic County, NJ	18.27
Dallas County, TX	13.50
Bronx County, NY	13.00
Kings County, NY	9.36
New York County, NY	0.00

Place	Percent
Hamtramck, MI (city) Wayne County	56.50
Paterson, NJ (city) Passaic County	48.48
New York, NY (city)	17.03
Los Angeles, CA (city) Los Angeles County	8.91

Notes: Please refer to the User's Guide for an explanation of data; ranking tables include all places with Asian and/or NHPI populations above SF4 population thresholds; (1) tables reflect only those areas that meet SF4 population thresholds, therefore there may be less than 50 states, 75 counties or 75 places listed

Homeownership

Cambodians Who Own Their Own Homes

All States, Top 75 Counties, and Top 75 Places Sorted by Number[1]

State	Number
United States	17,134
California	3,977
Washington	1,573
Massachusetts	1,525
Texas	1,221
Pennsylvania	1,092
Virginia	817
Minnesota	806
Georgia	590
Florida	547
Rhode Island	454
Illinois	437
North Carolina	375
Connecticut	341
Oregon	336
Ohio	294
Maryland	288
New York	252
Michigan	223
Utah	221
Colorado	191
Arizona	185
Tennessee	173
Iowa	143
Missouri	122
Nevada	121
Kansas	116
Alabama	108
Indiana	93
Maine	89
New Jersey	71
Oklahoma	67
South Carolina	50
Wisconsin	42
Hawaii	10

County	Number
Los Angeles County, CA	1,529
Middlesex County, MA	838
Philadelphia County, PA	737
King County, WA	695
Orange County, CA	566
Harris County, TX	418
Providence County, RI	414
Santa Clara County, CA	345
Snohomish County, WA	336
Essex County, MA	321
Pierce County, WA	318
Fairfax County, VA	301
Dallas County, TX	272
San Joaquin County, CA	265
Hennepin County, MN	251
Fairfield County, CT	240
Montgomery County, MD	219
Cook County, IL	205
Stanislaus County, CA	196
Maricopa County, AZ	185
Alameda County, CA	180
Clayton County, GA	174
Duval County, FL	172
Ramsey County, MN	171
Gwinnett County, GA	169
Washington County, OR	162
Pinellas County, FL	161
San Bernardino County, CA	160
Salt Lake County, UT	156
San Diego County, CA	149
Denton County, TX	145
Henrico County, VA	142
Franklin County, OH	136
Fresno County, CA	136
Ottawa County, MI	134
Mecklenburg County, NC	132
Chesterfield County, VA	110
Clark County, NV	110
Bristol County, MA	101
Multnomah County, OR	94
Sacramento County, CA	94
Brazoria County, TX	92
Scott County, MN	90
DeKalb County, GA	89
Suffolk County, MA	89
Dakota County, MN	88
Tarrant County, TX	88
Shelby County, TN	87
Olmsted County, MN	86
Polk County, IA	81
Thurston County, WA	80
Davidson County, NC	71
Clark County, WA	69
Sedgwick County, KS	66
Cuyahoga County, OH	65
Riverside County, CA	65
Mobile County, AL	58
Hampden County, MA	48
Cumberland County, ME	47
Monroe County, NY	44
Worcester County, MA	44
Hamilton County, OH	39
Denver County, CO	34
Arlington County, VA	31
Camden County, NJ	28
Sonoma County, CA	28
Kern County, CA	25
Bronx County, NY	23
Kings County, NY	21
San Francisco County, CA	18
Cowlitz County, WA	10

Place	Number
Philadelphia, PA (city) Philadelphia County	737
Long Beach, CA (city) Los Angeles County	678
Lowell, MA (city) Middlesex County	630
San Jose, CA (city) Santa Clara County	336
Providence, RI (city) Providence County	276
Stockton, CA (city) San Joaquin County	257
Tacoma, WA (city) Pierce County	231
Lynn, MA (city) Essex County	204
Santa Ana, CA (city) Orange County	193
Seattle, WA (city) King County	185
Jacksonville, FL (city) Duval County	172
Modesto, CA (city) Stanislaus County	146
Carrollton, TX (city) Denton County	140
St. Paul, MN (city) Ramsey County	138
Chicago, IL (city) Cook County	129
Houston, TX (city) Harris County	126
Columbus, OH (city) Franklin County	125
St. Petersburg, FL (city) Pinellas County	118
West Valley City, UT (city) Salt Lake County	113
Charlotte, NC (city) Mecklenburg County	111
Danbury, CT (city) Fairfield County	109
Los Angeles, CA (city) Los Angeles County	109
Cranston, RI (city) Providence County	108
San Diego, CA (city) San Diego County	105
Lakewood, CA (city) Los Angeles County	99
Fresno, CA (city) Fresno County	98
White Center, WA (cdp) King County	87
Portland, OR (city) Multnomah County	86
Norwalk, CA (city) Los Angeles County	85
New York, NY (city)	80
Memphis, TN (city) Shelby County	74
Phoenix, AZ (city) Maricopa County	73
Lawrence, MA (city) Essex County	71
Dallas, TX (city) Dallas County	70
Bloomington, MN (city) Hennepin County	64
Aurora, CO (city) Arapahoe County	61
Garden Grove, CA (city) Orange County	60
Rochester, MN (city) Olmsted County	60
Attleboro, MA (city) Bristol County	55
Bellflower, CA (city) Los Angeles County	55
Everett, WA (city) Snohomish County	55
Lexington, NC (city) Davidson County	53
Beaverton, OR (city) Washington County	52
Silver Spring, MD (cdp) Montgomery County	51
Minneapolis, MN (city) Hennepin County	50
Bridgeport, CT (city) Fairfield County	46
Oakland, CA (city) Alameda County	45
Boston, MA (city) Suffolk County	39
Revere, MA (city) Suffolk County	36
Signal Hill, CA (city) Los Angeles County	36
Denver, CO (city) Denver County	34
Arlington, VA (cdp) Arlington County	31
Fall River, MA (city) Bristol County	29
Rosemead, CA (city) Los Angeles County	29
Sacramento, CA (city) Sacramento County	29
Portland, ME (city) Cumberland County	26
Santa Rosa, CA (city) Sonoma County	22
San Bernardino, CA (city) San Bernardino County	21
San Francisco, CA (city) San Francisco County	18
Longview, WA (city) Cowlitz County	10
Pomona, CA (city) Los Angeles County	7
Monterey Park, CA (city) Los Angeles County	5

Notes: Please refer to the User's Guide for an explanation of data; ranking tables include all places with Asian and/or NHPI populations above SF4 population thresholds; (1) tables reflect only those areas that meet SF4 population thresholds, therefore there may be less than 50 states, 75 counties or 75 places listed

Homeownership

Cambodians Who Own Their Own Homes

All States, Top 75 Counties, and Top 75 Places Sorted by Percent[1]

State	Percent
Oklahoma	89.33
Georgia	87.67
Utah	81.55
Florida	78.59
Missouri	73.05
Virginia	72.82
Iowa	72.59
Indiana	70.99
Connecticut	69.88
North Carolina	68.81
Alabama	68.79
Texas	66.79
Michigan	65.40
Maryland	63.72
Arizona	63.14
Minnesota	62.14
Kansas	58.88
Tennessee	57.86
Pennsylvania	57.63
Colorado	57.36
South Carolina	56.18
Illinois	55.88
New Jersey	53.79
Nevada	51.49
Ohio	48.84
Washington	45.85
Oregon	44.27
United States	43.59
Hawaii	43.48
Maine	37.55
Rhode Island	37.03
New York	36.90
Massachusetts	34.75
California	26.97
Wisconsin	26.92

County	Percent
Denton County, TX	100.00
Gwinnett County, GA	100.00
Scott County, MN	100.00
Henrico County, VA	92.21
Brazoria County, TX	92.00
Clayton County, GA	91.58
Salt Lake County, UT	86.19
DeKalb County, GA	84.76
Chesterfield County, VA	81.48
Pinellas County, FL	81.31
Dakota County, MN	80.73
Polk County, IA	75.70
Fairfield County, CT	75.24
Duval County, FL	74.14
Fairfax County, VA	73.06
Snohomish County, WA	72.41
Mecklenburg County, NC	71.74
Harris County, TX	71.09
Montgomery County, MD	69.52
Maricopa County, AZ	67.03
Cuyahoga County, OH	63.73
Ottawa County, MI	62.62
Mobile County, AL	62.37
Shelby County, TN	62.14
Tarrant County, TX	61.54
Olmsted County, MN	59.31
Clark County, WA	58.47
Davidson County, NC	57.26
Orange County, CA	54.37
Hennepin County, MN	54.09
Monroe County, NY	53.01
Philadelphia County, PA	52.76
Worcester County, MA	52.38
Ramsey County, MN	51.98
Washington County, OR	51.92
Camden County, NJ	50.91
Riverside County, CA	50.78
Dallas County, TX	50.37
Clark County, NV	49.11
Sedgwick County, KS	48.18
King County, WA	43.41
Thurston County, WA	42.55
Franklin County, OH	42.50
Cook County, IL	42.01
Essex County, MA	39.98
Hamilton County, OH	39.80
San Bernardino County, CA	39.70
Denver County, CO	39.53
Santa Clara County, CA	38.33
Hampden County, MA	38.10
Pierce County, WA	36.10
Middlesex County, MA	35.71
Sacramento County, CA	35.34
Multnomah County, OR	35.07
Providence County, RI	34.91
Arlington County, VA	33.70
Stanislaus County, CA	33.68
Kern County, CA	29.76
Cumberland County, ME	27.98
Los Angeles County, CA	23.92
Suffolk County, MA	22.88
Alameda County, CA	22.84
Bristol County, MA	22.25
Sonoma County, CA	20.14
Fresno County, CA	19.88
San Diego County, CA	16.54
San Joaquin County, CA	14.76
Cowlitz County, WA	14.71
Bronx County, NY	14.47
Kings County, NY	13.04
San Francisco County, CA	10.11

Place	Percent
West Valley City, UT (city) Salt Lake County	100.00
Norwalk, CA (city) Los Angeles County	82.52
St. Petersburg, FL (city) Pinellas County	82.52
Danbury, CT (city) Fairfield County	81.34
Jacksonville, FL (city) Duval County	74.14
Carrollton, TX (city) Denton County	73.68
Silver Spring, MD (cdp) Montgomery County	69.86
Charlotte, NC (city) Mecklenburg County	68.10
Lakewood, CA (city) Los Angeles County	65.56
Aurora, CO (city) Arapahoe County	64.89
Phoenix, AZ (city) Maricopa County	61.34
Cranston, RI (city) Providence County	59.34
Memphis, TN (city) Shelby County	58.27
Lawrence, MA (city) Essex County	54.20
Houston, TX (city) Harris County	54.08
Santa Ana, CA (city) Orange County	53.91
Rochester, MN (city) Olmsted County	53.10
Philadelphia, PA (city) Philadelphia County	52.76
Bloomington, MN (city) Hennepin County	52.03
St. Paul, MN (city) Ramsey County	51.11
Bridgeport, CT (city) Fairfield County	50.00
Lexington, NC (city) Davidson County	50.00
Garden Grove, CA (city) Orange County	47.62
Bellflower, CA (city) Los Angeles County	42.97
Columbus, OH (city) Franklin County	42.96
Minneapolis, MN (city) Hennepin County	41.32
San Jose, CA (city) Santa Clara County	40.88
Beaverton, OR (city) Washington County	40.00
Denver, CO (city) Denver County	39.53
Everett, WA (city) Snohomish County	35.95
White Center, WA (cdp) King County	34.66
Attleboro, MA (city) Bristol County	34.59
Portland, OR (city) Multnomah County	33.86
Arlington, VA (cdp) Arlington County	33.70
Tacoma, WA (city) Pierce County	33.67
Lynn, MA (city) Essex County	33.55
Chicago, IL (city) Cook County	31.93
Lowell, MA (city) Middlesex County	30.55
Dallas, TX (city) Dallas County	30.43
Providence, RI (city) Providence County	30.33
Modesto, CA (city) Stanislaus County	29.80
Seattle, WA (city) King County	29.79
Sacramento, CA (city) Sacramento County	28.16
Signal Hill, CA (city) Los Angeles County	23.84
Santa Rosa, CA (city) Sonoma County	23.40
Revere, MA (city) Suffolk County	22.93
Boston, MA (city) Suffolk County	22.41
Rosemead, CA (city) Los Angeles County	21.17
San Bernardino, CA (city) San Bernardino County	20.00
New York, NY (city)	19.95
Longview, WA (city) Cowlitz County	19.23
Portland, ME (city) Cumberland County	18.71
Long Beach, CA (city) Los Angeles County	17.96
Fresno, CA (city) Fresno County	16.07
Stockton, CA (city) San Joaquin County	14.74
San Diego, CA (city) San Diego County	12.93
Los Angeles, CA (city) Los Angeles County	12.63
Fall River, MA (city) Bristol County	12.34
San Francisco, CA (city) San Francisco County	10.11
Oakland, CA (city) Alameda County	7.53
Monterey Park, CA (city) Los Angeles County	6.58
Pomona, CA (city) Los Angeles County	4.58

Notes: Please refer to the User's Guide for an explanation of data; ranking tables include all places with Asian and/or NHPI populations above SF4 population thresholds; (1) tables reflect only those areas that meet SF4 population thresholds, therefore there may be less than 50 states, 75 counties or 75 places listed

Homeownership

Chinese (except Taiwanese) Who Own Their Own Homes

All States, Top 75 Counties, and Top 75 Places Sorted by Number[1]

State	Number
United States	441,852
California	190,458
New York	57,137
New Jersey	20,992
Texas	19,752
Hawaii	16,491
Illinois	14,000
Massachusetts	13,570
Washington	13,200
Florida	10,446
Maryland	10,380
Pennsylvania	7,435
Virginia	7,060
Michigan	5,354
Georgia	5,203
Ohio	4,844
Arizona	4,756
Oregon	4,027
Connecticut	3,462
Nevada	3,439
Colorado	3,259
North Carolina	3,215
Minnesota	2,885
Missouri	2,007
Indiana	1,767
Wisconsin	1,444
Tennessee	1,423
Utah	1,236
Kansas	1,194
Louisiana	1,103
South Carolina	1,086
Oklahoma	853
Alabama	819
Delaware	785
New Mexico	762
Kentucky	706
Iowa	677
Rhode Island	637
New Hampshire	623
District of Columbia	501
Arkansas	476
Mississippi	468
Idaho	361
Nebraska	318
Alaska	279
Maine	242
West Virginia	202
Vermont	177
Montana	111
Wyoming	101
South Dakota	87
North Dakota	42

County	Number
Los Angeles County, CA	55,230
San Francisco County, CA	26,348
Santa Clara County, CA	25,306
Queens County, NY	25,190
Alameda County, CA	23,277
Honolulu County, HI	15,561
Kings County, NY	14,259
San Mateo County, CA	12,519
Orange County, CA	11,444
King County, WA	10,293
Cook County, IL	8,535
Contra Costa County, CA	7,977
Sacramento County, CA	7,079
Montgomery County, MD	6,628
Harris County, TX	6,379
San Diego County, CA	6,093
Middlesex County, MA	5,625
New York County, NY	4,596
Middlesex County, NJ	4,514
Nassau County, NY	3,824
Norfolk County, MA	3,783
Fairfax County, VA	3,768
Maricopa County, AZ	3,615
Bergen County, NJ	3,133
Collin County, TX	3,028
Clark County, NV	2,867
Fort Bend County, TX	2,726
San Bernardino County, CA	2,541
DuPage County, IL	2,535
Philadelphia County, PA	2,437
Monmouth County, NJ	2,383
Morris County, NJ	2,241
Broward County, FL	2,240
Miami-Dade County, FL	2,181
Dallas County, TX	1,997
Oakland County, MI	1,993
Suffolk County, MA	1,898
Somerset County, NJ	1,848
Richmond County, NY	1,728
Suffolk County, NY	1,705
Westchester County, NY	1,575
Multnomah County, OR	1,571
San Joaquin County, CA	1,549
Ventura County, CA	1,427
Essex County, NJ	1,388
Travis County, TX	1,385
Fairfield County, CT	1,328
Gwinnett County, GA	1,237
Fresno County, CA	1,219
Lake County, IL	1,219
St. Louis County, MO	1,154
Cuyahoga County, OH	1,098
Riverside County, CA	1,086
Franklin County, OH	1,078
Montgomery County, PA	1,065
Tarrant County, TX	1,051
Washington County, OR	1,051
Hennepin County, MN	1,028
Fulton County, GA	1,025
Snohomish County, WA	1,002
Wake County, NC	981
Palm Beach County, FL	971
Marin County, CA	950
Howard County, MD	939
Wayne County, MI	933
Pima County, AZ	927
Cobb County, GA	917
Mercer County, NJ	911
Solano County, CA	900
Hudson County, NJ	898
New Haven County, CT	877
Orange County, FL	863
Union County, NJ	858
Salt Lake County, UT	854
Prince George's County, MD	838

Place	Number
New York, NY (city)	46,358
San Francisco, CA (city) San Francisco County	26,348
San Jose, CA (city) Santa Clara County	11,435
Honolulu, HI (cdp) Honolulu County	10,832
Los Angeles, CA (city) Los Angeles County	9,201
Fremont, CA (city) Alameda County	6,432
Oakland, CA (city) Alameda County	5,275
Chicago, IL (city) Cook County	5,029
Sacramento, CA (city) Sacramento County	4,566
San Diego, CA (city) San Diego County	4,357
Houston, TX (city) Harris County	4,008
Seattle, WA (city) King County	3,915
Monterey Park, CA (city) Los Angeles County	3,730
Alhambra, CA (city) Los Angeles County	3,576
Daly City, CA (city) San Mateo County	3,397
Arcadia, CA (city) Los Angeles County	3,003
Sunnyvale, CA (city) Santa Clara County	2,549
Cupertino, CA (city) Santa Clara County	2,441
Philadelphia, PA (city) Philadelphia County	2,437
Rowland Heights, CA (cdp) Los Angeles County	2,427
Plano, TX (city) Collin County	2,294
Hacienda Heights, CA (cdp) Los Angeles County	2,109
Irvine, CA (city) Orange County	2,091
Milpitas, CA (city) Santa Clara County	2,067
El Monte, CA (city) Los Angeles County	2,005
San Leandro, CA (city) Alameda County	2,003
Alameda, CA (city) Alameda County	1,910
Diamond Bar, CA (city) Los Angeles County	1,887
Rosemead, CA (city) Los Angeles County	1,860
Boston, MA (city) Suffolk County	1,797
Quincy, MA (city) Norfolk County	1,744
Temple City, CA (city) Los Angeles County	1,661
Walnut, CA (city) Los Angeles County	1,657
San Gabriel, CA (city) Los Angeles County	1,600
Union City, CA (city) Alameda County	1,582
San Mateo, CA (city) San Mateo County	1,493
Cerritos, CA (city) Los Angeles County	1,490
Torrance, CA (city) Los Angeles County	1,488
Bellevue, WA (city) King County	1,484
Sugar Land, TX (city) Fort Bend County	1,473
West Covina, CA (city) Los Angeles County	1,456
Hempstead, NY (town) Nassau County	1,417
Portland, OR (city) Multnomah County	1,412
North Hempstead, NY (town) Nassau County	1,388
Phoenix, AZ (city) Maricopa County	1,376
Saratoga, CA (city) Santa Clara County	1,347
South San Francisco, CA (city) San Mateo County	1,334
Edison, NJ (township) Middlesex County	1,264
Palo Alto, CA (city) Santa Clara County	1,205
Foster City, CA (city) San Mateo County	1,168
Stockton, CA (city) San Joaquin County	1,130
Austin, TX (city) Travis County	1,128
Spring Valley, NV (cdp) Clark County	1,042
Castro Valley, CA (cdp) Alameda County	1,033
Naperville, IL (city) Du Page County	1,026
Mountain View, CA (city) Santa Clara County	1,019
San Marino, CA (city) Los Angeles County	968
Chino Hills, CA (city) San Bernardino County	950
Fresno, CA (city) Fresno County	937
Hayward, CA (city) Alameda County	935
Oyster Bay, NY (town) Nassau County	928
Newton, MA (city) Middlesex County	922
Anaheim, CA (city) Orange County	892
Pasadena, CA (city) Los Angeles County	887
Dallas, TX (city) Dallas County	884
Santa Clara, CA (city) Santa Clara County	855
Richmond, CA (city) Contra Costa County	852
Las Vegas, NV (city) Clark County	845
East Brunswick, NJ (township) Middlesex County	825
North Potomac, MD (cdp) Montgomery County	822
Huntington Beach, CA (city) Orange County	821
Redwood City, CA (city) San Mateo County	821
South Pasadena, CA (city) Los Angeles County	799
Millbrae, CA (city) San Mateo County	794
Walnut Creek, CA (city) Contra Costa County	787

Notes: Please refer to the User's Guide for an explanation of data; ranking tables include all places with Asian and/or NHPI populations above SF4 population thresholds; (1) tables reflect only those areas that meet SF4 population thresholds, therefore there may be less than 50 states, 75 counties or 75 places listed

Homeownership

Chinese (except Taiwanese) Who Own Their Own Homes

All States, Top 75 Counties, and Top 75 Places Sorted by Percent[1]

State	Percent
Hawaii	73.45
New Jersey	69.66
Nevada	69.46
Maryland	67.25
Washington	66.56
Florida	65.96
Colorado	65.49
Oregon	63.48
California	63.32
Arizona	63.10
Wyoming	62.35
Georgia	62.21
Virginia	61.75
Idaho	60.88
Alaska	58.86
New Mexico	58.48
United States	58.08
Vermont	56.91
Texas	56.34
Minnesota	56.15
North Carolina	55.71
Delaware	55.59
South Carolina	55.24
Illinois	55.05
Connecticut	55.04
Utah	54.88
Maine	54.75
Montana	54.15
New Hampshire	52.57
Michigan	52.51
Mississippi	51.71
Massachusetts	51.07
Tennessee	49.24
Ohio	49.22
Pennsylvania	47.62
Kansas	47.18
Arkansas	46.17
Rhode Island	45.66
Missouri	44.88
Louisiana	44.80
New York	44.77
Indiana	43.89
Wisconsin	43.25
Alabama	40.87
Kentucky	40.34
South Dakota	38.67
West Virginia	37.97
Oklahoma	35.09
Iowa	33.66
Nebraska	30.40
North Dakota	30.00
District of Columbia	28.84

County	Percent
Washington County, MN	97.53
Columbia County, GA	94.48
Delaware County, OH	93.98
Fort Bend County, TX	93.16
Montgomery County, TX	93.15
Warren County, OH	91.62
Ottawa County, MI	90.79
Douglas County, CO	89.87
Will County, IL	89.60
Nassau County, NY	89.32
Anoka County, MN	89.06
Tulare County, CA	88.01
Brazoria County, TX	87.56
Loudoun County, VA	86.21
Lake County, IN	86.06
Berks County, PA	84.83
Ventura County, CA	83.99
Hamilton County, IN	83.86
Virginia Beach Independent City, VA	83.77
Gloucester County, NJ	83.33
Solano County, CA	83.03
Williamson County, TX	82.95
Lee County, FL	82.79
Monmouth County, NJ	82.77
Pasco County, FL	82.50
Contra Costa County, CA	82.03
Stanislaus County, CA	81.86
Broward County, FL	80.87
Somerset County, NJ	80.84
Richmond County, NY	80.48
Putnam County, NY	79.63
Arapahoe County, CO	79.61
Marin County, CA	79.50
Stark County, OH	79.41
Clackamas County, OR	79.10
Gwinnett County, GA	78.94
Hawaii County, HI	78.47
Lake County, IL	78.44
Hunterdon County, NJ	78.28
Cobb County, GA	78.24
Howard County, MD	77.80
Ocean County, NJ	77.75
San Mateo County, CA	77.41
Napa County, CA	77.39
DuPage County, IL	77.36
Clark County, WA	76.76
San Joaquin County, CA	76.68
Rockland County, NY	76.59
Merced County, CA	76.51
Dakota County, MN	76.38
Barnstable County, MA	76.19
Collin County, TX	75.72
Morris County, NJ	75.25
Palm Beach County, FL	75.15
Placer County, CA	74.95
Burlington County, NJ	74.90
San Bernardino County, CA	74.65
Essex County, NJ	74.34
Maui County, HI	74.01
Montgomery County, MD	73.92
Chesterfield County, VA	73.79
Waukesha County, WI	73.67
Richmond County, GA	73.61
Seminole County, FL	73.59
Honolulu County, HI	73.47
Osceola County, FL	73.11
El Paso County, CO	72.52
Fairfax County, VA	72.42
Midland County, MI	72.18
Bergen County, NJ	71.66
Kern County, CA	71.62
Union County, NJ	71.62
Anne Arundel County, MD	71.59
McHenry County, IL	71.51
Fresno County, CA	71.50

Place	Percent
Ahuimanu, HI (cdp) Honolulu County	100.00
Blackhawk-Camino Tass., CA (cdp) Contra Costa Co.	100.00
Brea, CA (city) Orange County	100.00
Brookfield, WI (city) Waukesha County	100.00
Colesville, MD (cdp) Montgomery County	100.00
Dix Hills, NY (cdp) Suffolk County	100.00
Englewood Cliffs, NJ (borough) Bergen County	100.00
Garden City Park, NY (cdp) Nassau County	100.00
Gilbert, AZ (town) Maricopa County	100.00
Greentree, NJ (cdp) Camden County	100.00
Kensington, CA (cdp) Contra Costa County	100.00
Los Altos Hills, CA (town) Santa Clara County	100.00
Lower Macungie, PA (township) Lehigh County	100.00
Marlboro, NJ (township) Monmouth County	100.00
Mission Bend, TX (cdp) Fort Bend County	100.00
Morganville, NJ (cdp) Monmouth County	100.00
New Territory, TX (cdp) Fort Bend County	100.00
Olney, MD (cdp) Montgomery County	100.00
Rolling Hills Estates, CA (city) Los Angeles County	100.00
Springdale, NJ (cdp) Camden County	100.00
Syosset, NY (cdp) Nassau County	100.00
Tustin Foothills, CA (cdp) Orange County	100.00
Valley Stream, NY (village) Nassau County	100.00
Westford, MA (town) Middlesex County	100.00
Weston, MA (town) Middlesex County	100.00
Wolf Trap, VA (cdp) Fairfax County	100.00
Woodbury, MN (city) Washington County	100.00
Livingston, NJ (township) Essex County	98.10
Novato, CA (city) Marin County	97.42
Mission Viejo, CA (city) Orange County	97.24
Missouri City, TX (city) Fort Bend County	97.13
East Hill-Meridian, WA (cdp) King County	96.70
San Marino, CA (city) Los Angeles County	96.51
Kingsgate, WA (cdp) King County	96.50
La Mirada, CA (city) Los Angeles County	96.43
Sammamish, WA (city) King County	96.41
West Springfield, VA (cdp) Fairfax County	96.40
Holmdel, NJ (township) Monmouth County	96.33
Manalapan, NJ (township) Monmouth County	96.06
Los Altos, CA (city) Santa Clara County	95.78
Mililani Town, HI (cdp) Honolulu County	95.77
La Canada Flintridge, CA (city) Los Angeles County	95.75
Danville, CA (town) Contra Costa County	95.66
Scarsdale, NY (village) Westchester County	95.56
Piedmont, CA (city) Alameda County	95.34
Northbrook, IL (village) Cook County	95.29
West Windsor, NJ (township) Mercer County	95.29
Kailua, HI (cdp) Honolulu County	95.27
Palos Verdes Estates, CA (city) Los Angeles County	95.21
Bellaire, TX (city) Harris County	95.20
Hercules, CA (city) Contra Costa County	95.10
Laguna Niguel, CA (city) Orange County	94.50
Chesterfield, MO (city) Saint Louis County	94.33
Bernards, NJ (township) Somerset County	94.27
Saratoga, CA (city) Santa Clara County	94.20
Potomac, MD (cdp) Montgomery County	94.09
Novi, MI (city) Oakland County	94.07
Orinda, CA (city) Contra Costa County	94.01
Antioch, CA (city) Contra Costa County	93.86
Burke, VA (cdp) Fairfax County	93.84
Highlands-Baywood Pk., CA (cdp) San Mateo County	93.84
Redland, MD (cdp) Montgomery County	93.75
Hillsborough, CA (town) San Mateo County	93.61
Laguna West-Lakeside, CA (cdp) Sacramento County	93.55
Hanover, NJ (township) Morris County	93.21
North Potomac, MD (cdp) Montgomery County	92.78
Paramus, NJ (borough) Bergen County	92.61
Tenafly, NJ (borough) Bergen County	92.61
Walnut, CA (city) Los Angeles County	92.57
Sugar Land, TX (city) Fort Bend County	92.53
McLean, VA (cdp) Fairfax County	92.50
Montgomery, NJ (township) Somerset County	92.40
Chelmsford, MA (town) Middlesex County	92.06
Lexington, MA (town) Middlesex County	92.03
East Hanover, NJ (township) Morris County	92.00

Notes: Please refer to the User's Guide for an explanation of data; ranking tables include all places with Asian and/or NHPI populations above SF4 population thresholds; (1) tables reflect only those areas that meet SF4 population thresholds, therefore there may be less than 50 states, 75 counties or 75 places listed

Homeownership

Fijians Who Own Their Own Homes

All States, Top 75 Counties, and Top 75 Places Sorted by Number[1]

State	Number
United States	1,389
California	1,075
Oregon	96
Washington	88

County	Number
Sacramento County, CA	242
Alameda County, CA	184
San Mateo County, CA	138
Stanislaus County, CA	109
Los Angeles County, CA	80
King County, WA	68
Contra Costa County, CA	54
Santa Clara County, CA	45
Yolo County, CA	41

Place	Number
Sacramento, CA (city) Sacramento County	189
Hayward, CA (city) Alameda County	105
Modesto, CA (city) Stanislaus County	60

Notes: Please refer to the User's Guide for an explanation of data; ranking tables include all places with Asian and/or NHPI populations above SF4 population thresholds; (1) tables reflect only those areas that meet SF4 population thresholds, therefore there may be less than 50 states, 75 counties or 75 places listed

Homeownership

Fijians Who Own Their Own Homes

All States, Top 75 Counties, and Top 75 Places Sorted by Percent[1]

State	Percent
Oregon	68.57
California	51.04
United States	50.38
Washington	40.37

County	Percent
Contra Costa County, CA	87.10
Stanislaus County, CA	67.70
Alameda County, CA	52.42
San Mateo County, CA	50.18
Sacramento County, CA	49.09
King County, WA	44.44
Los Angeles County, CA	39.60
Santa Clara County, CA	35.71
Yolo County, CA	32.28

Place	Percent
Modesto, CA (city) Stanislaus County	57.69
Sacramento, CA (city) Sacramento County	57.62
Hayward, CA (city) Alameda County	50.48

Notes: Please refer to the User's Guide for an explanation of data; ranking tables include all places with Asian and/or NHPI populations above SF4 population thresholds; (1) tables reflect only those areas that meet SF4 population thresholds, therefore there may be less than 50 states, 75 counties or 75 places listed

Homeownership

Filipinos Who Own Their Own Homes

All States, Top 75 Counties, and Top 75 Places Sorted by Number[1]

State	Number
United States	307,810
California	147,977
Hawaii	27,368
Illinois	17,087
New Jersey	15,583
New York	12,260
Washington	11,802
Florida	10,160
Texas	9,692
Virginia	9,392
Nevada	6,560
Maryland	5,103
Michigan	3,735
Pennsylvania	2,689
Arizona	2,668
Ohio	2,600
Oregon	1,704
Georgia	1,624
Colorado	1,555
North Carolina	1,386
Massachusetts	1,308
Missouri	1,289
Alaska	1,269
Indiana	1,246
South Carolina	1,134
Connecticut	1,073
Minnesota	934
Louisiana	868
Tennessee	825
Wisconsin	764
Utah	547
Kansas	509
Oklahoma	502
Kentucky	492
West Virginia	417
Alabama	390
New Mexico	350
Delaware	348
Mississippi	334
Iowa	332
Arkansas	297
Idaho	286
Nebraska	279
Rhode Island	278
District of Columbia	176
Maine	161
New Hampshire	150
Montana	84
North Dakota	62
Wyoming	60
South Dakota	54
Vermont	47

County	Number
Los Angeles County, CA	39,086
Honolulu County, HI	18,769
San Diego County, CA	18,309
Santa Clara County, CA	12,096
Alameda County, CA	11,274
Cook County, IL	10,443
San Mateo County, CA	8,995
Orange County, CA	8,200
Solano County, CA	7,008
Contra Costa County, CA	6,738
King County, WA	6,088
Clark County, NV	5,498
San Bernardino County, CA	5,074
San Francisco County, CA	4,928
Sacramento County, CA	4,591
Queens County, NY	4,497
San Joaquin County, CA	4,161
Riverside County, CA	3,862
Maui County, HI	3,677
DuPage County, IL	3,190
Virginia Beach Independent City, VA	2,990
Harris County, TX	2,756
Bergen County, NJ	2,732
Hawaii County, HI	2,726
Hudson County, NJ	2,691
Fairfax County, VA	2,479
Ventura County, CA	2,372
Middlesex County, NJ	2,352
Duval County, FL	2,230
Kauai County, HI	2,196
Maricopa County, AZ	2,140
Monterey County, CA	1,984
Kern County, CA	1,731
Prince George's County, MD	1,628
Snohomish County, WA	1,442
Nassau County, NY	1,373
Essex County, NJ	1,354
Kitsap County, WA	1,281
Lake County, IL	1,269
Pierce County, WA	1,182
Montgomery County, MD	1,142
Dallas County, TX	1,115
Fresno County, CA	1,090
Richmond County, NY	1,017
Fort Bend County, TX	999
Union County, NJ	986
Oakland County, MI	971
Wayne County, MI	948
Rockland County, NY	924
Miami-Dade County, FL	888
Camden County, NJ	865
Broward County, FL	862
Bexar County, TX	841
Tulare County, CA	839
Orange County, FL	833
Washoe County, NV	830
Santa Barbara County, CA	829
Suffolk County, NY	804
Westchester County, NY	789
Will County, IL	785
Macomb County, MI	773
New York County, NY	769
Baltimore County, MD	752
Philadelphia County, PA	748
Kings County, NY	718
Norfolk Independent City, VA	709
Monmouth County, NJ	700
Multnomah County, OR	672
Passaic County, NJ	658
Cuyahoga County, OH	640
Anchorage Borough, AK	629
Morris County, NJ	600
Stanislaus County, CA	597
Pinellas County, FL	539
Somerset County, NJ	524

Place	Number
Los Angeles, CA (city) Los Angeles County	12,993
San Diego, CA (city) San Diego County	11,923
San Jose, CA (city) Santa Clara County	7,997
New York, NY (city)	7,304
San Francisco, CA (city) San Francisco County	4,928
Daly City, CA (city) San Mateo County	4,625
Chicago, IL (city) Cook County	4,535
Vallejo, CA (city) Solano County	4,464
Honolulu, HI (cdp) Honolulu County	4,385
Carson, CA (city) Los Angeles County	3,035
Stockton, CA (city) San Joaquin County	2,848
Seattle, WA (city) King County	2,678
Long Beach, CA (city) Los Angeles County	2,545
Chula Vista, CA (city) San Diego County	2,507
Jersey City, NJ (city) Hudson County	2,354
Union City, CA (city) Alameda County	2,346
Fremont, CA (city) Alameda County	2,244
Waipahu, HI (cdp) Honolulu County	2,146
Jacksonville, FL (city) Duval County	2,124
Hayward, CA (city) Alameda County	2,049
Las Vegas, NV (city) Clark County	1,802
South San Francisco, CA (city) San Mateo County	1,722
West Covina, CA (city) Los Angeles County	1,630
Milpitas, CA (city) Santa Clara County	1,493
Sacramento, CA (city) Sacramento County	1,414
Cerritos, CA (city) Los Angeles County	1,401
Oxnard, CA (city) Ventura County	1,367
Glendale, CA (city) Los Angeles County	1,224
Chino Hills, CA (city) San Bernardino County	1,223
Houston, TX (city) Harris County	1,168
Hercules, CA (city) Contra Costa County	1,147
Fairfield, CA (city) Solano County	1,134
Salinas, CA (city) Monterey County	1,108
Anaheim, CA (city) Orange County	1,092
Sunrise Manor, NV (cdp) Clark County	971
Kahului, HI (cdp) Maui County	960
San Leandro, CA (city) Alameda County	940
Ewa Beach, HI (cdp) Honolulu County	933
Pittsburg, CA (city) Contra Costa County	929
Buena Park, CA (city) Orange County	912
Delano, CA (city) Kern County	891
Norwalk, CA (city) Los Angeles County	859
Sunnyvale, CA (city) Santa Clara County	843
Phoenix, AZ (city) Maricopa County	829
Walnut, CA (city) Los Angeles County	820
Hempstead, NY (town) Nassau County	811
Oakland, CA (city) Alameda County	803
Moreno Valley, CA (city) Riverside County	782
Spring Valley, NV (cdp) Clark County	766
Philadelphia, PA (city) Philadelphia County	748
Pearl City, HI (cdp) Honolulu County	744
Fresno, CA (city) Fresno County	730
Elk Grove, CA (cdp) Sacramento County	725
Mililani Town, HI (cdp) Honolulu County	725
Baldwin Park, CA (city) Los Angeles County	723
Lakewood, CA (city) Los Angeles County	718
Village Park, HI (cdp) Honolulu County	712
Antioch, CA (city) Contra Costa County	711
Santa Clara, CA (city) Santa Clara County	708
Alameda, CA (city) Alameda County	705
Concord, CA (city) Contra Costa County	697
Oceanside, CA (city) San Diego County	694
Paradise, NV (cdp) Clark County	691
Corona, CA (city) Riverside County	689
Diamond Bar, CA (city) Los Angeles County	651
Suisun City, CA (city) Solano County	647
National City, CA (city) San Diego County	646
Skokie, IL (village) Cook County	615
Fontana, CA (city) San Bernardino County	606
San Antonio, TX (city) Bexar County	602
Richmond, CA (city) Contra Costa County	575
San Bruno, CA (city) San Mateo County	568
Ewa Villages, HI (cdp) Honolulu County	559
Waimalu, HI (cdp) Honolulu County	553
Rowland Heights, CA (cdp) Los Angeles County	543

Notes: Please refer to the User's Guide for an explanation of data; ranking tables include all places with Asian and/or NHPI populations above SF4 population thresholds; (1) tables reflect only those areas that meet SF4 population thresholds, therefore there may be less than 50 states, 75 counties or 75 places listed

Homeownership

Filipinos Who Own Their Own Homes

All States, Top 75 Counties, and Top 75 Places Sorted by Percent[1]

State	Percent
West Virginia	73.54
Maryland	68.60
Michigan	67.95
Virginia	67.82
Florida	66.89
Illinois	66.86
Wyoming	65.93
Idaho	64.85
New Jersey	63.68
Washington	63.64
Hawaii	63.59
Indiana	62.05
Delaware	61.70
Ohio	61.67
Louisiana	60.87
Tennessee	60.75
Minnesota	60.73
Pennsylvania	60.10
United States	59.98
Arizona	59.63
Utah	59.52
California	59.51
South Carolina	58.73
Colorado	58.20
Wisconsin	57.53
Nevada	57.51
Georgia	57.36
Texas	56.15
Iowa	55.33
Missouri	55.11
Kentucky	55.10
Maine	54.58
Alabama	54.47
Oregon	54.41
Mississippi	53.53
Arkansas	51.47
Connecticut	51.17
Kansas	49.80
Nebraska	49.73
North Carolina	49.48
Vermont	48.96
Massachusetts	47.62
New Hampshire	47.62
New Mexico	47.36
New York	47.02
Alaska	46.65
Rhode Island	44.62
Oklahoma	44.58
Montana	43.98
North Dakota	37.35
South Dakota	28.72
District of Columbia	21.60

County	Percent
Anoka County, MN	96.51
Loudoun County, VA	92.78
Berrien County, MI	90.16
Gloucester County, NJ	89.59
Will County, IL	88.60
Dorchester County, SC	88.00
Brazoria County, TX	86.29
St. Charles County, MO	86.00
Plymouth County, MA	85.84
Kane County, IL	84.92
Sandoval County, NM	84.91
Chesapeake Independent City, VA	84.40
Napa County, CA	83.49
Fort Bend County, TX	83.25
Butler County, OH	82.76
Suffolk County, NY	82.55
McHenry County, IL	82.00
Clay County, FL	81.91
Davis County, UT	81.82
Nassau County, NY	81.63
Manatee County, FL	81.40
DuPage County, IL	80.07
Ocean County, NJ	79.97
Chesterfield County, VA	79.77
Genesee County, MI	79.65
Stafford County, VA	79.61
Rockland County, NY	79.45
Camden County, NJ	79.07
Osceola County, FL	78.60
Duval County, FL	77.94
Prince George's County, MD	77.05
Montgomery County, TX	77.00
Virginia Beach Independent City, VA	77.00
Yakima County, WA	76.98
Seminole County, FL	76.63
Pasco County, FL	76.59
Charles County, MD	76.23
Berkeley County, SC	75.95
Placer County, CA	75.84
Bucks County, PA	75.18
Riverside County, CA	75.15
Adams County, CO	74.89
Merced County, CA	74.68
Mobile County, AL	74.19
Polk County, FL	74.16
Monmouth County, NJ	74.15
Howard County, MD	73.85
Clark County, WA	73.82
Oakland County, MI	73.23
Solano County, CA	73.14
San Bernardino County, CA	73.13
Thurston County, WA	72.71
Winnebago County, IL	72.67
Snohomish County, WA	72.54
Morris County, NJ	72.20
Middlesex County, NJ	72.15
Portsmouth Independent City, VA	72.15
Fairfax County, VA	72.06
Shelby County, TN	72.00
San Benito County, CA	71.78
Mercer County, NJ	71.75
Lake County, IN	71.72
Burlington County, NJ	71.71
Macomb County, MI	71.71
Baltimore County, MD	71.69
Craven County, NC	71.55
Broward County, FL	71.48
Hawaii County, HI	71.40
Volusia County, FL	71.13
Prince William County, VA	71.11
Sussex County, NJ	71.11
Lake County, IL	71.09
Waukesha County, WI	71.03
Wayne County, MI	71.01
Highlands County, FL	70.97

Place	Percent
Colmar Manor, MD (town) Prince George's County	100.00
Colonia, NJ (cdp) Middlesex County	100.00
Fairview, CA (cdp) Alameda County	100.00
Freehold, NJ (township) Monmouth County	100.00
Friendly, MD (cdp) Prince George's County	100.00
Hanover Park, IL (village) Cook County	100.00
Lincolnwood, IL (village) Cook County	100.00
McLean, VA (cdp) Fairfax County	100.00
Missouri City, TX (city) Fort Bend County	100.00
Orland Park, IL (village) Cook County	100.00
South Plainfield, NJ (borough) Middlesex County	100.00
West Bloomfield, MI (township) Oakland County	97.60
Streamwood, IL (village) Cook County	97.22
Bartlett, IL (village) Du Page County	97.01
Rialto, CA (city) San Bernardino County	96.83
Burke, VA (cdp) Fairfax County	96.60
Gilbert, AZ (town) Maricopa County	96.53
East Hill-Meridian, WA (cdp) King County	96.25
American Canyon, CA (city) Napa County	96.23
Des Plaines, IL (city) Cook County	96.21
Waikapu, HI (cdp) Maui County	95.92
Murrieta, CA (city) Riverside County	95.67
Elmont, NY (cdp) Nassau County	95.65
New City, NY (cdp) Rockland County	95.21
Miramar, FL (city) Broward County	95.00
Paramus, NJ (borough) Bergen County	95.00
Valley Stream, NY (village) Nassau County	95.00
Gurnee, IL (village) Lake County	94.95
Los Banos, CA (city) Merced County	94.92
East Meadow, NY (cdp) Nassau County	94.83
Paauilo, HI (cdp) Hawaii County	94.55
Hoffman Estates, IL (village) Cook County	94.10
Security-Widefield, CO (cdp) El Paso County	93.88
Levittown, NY (cdp) Nassau County	93.62
Walnut, CA (city) Los Angeles County	93.61
Vineyard, CA (cdp) Sacramento County	93.29
Tinley Park, IL (village) Cook County	93.02
Pupukea, HI (cdp) Honolulu County	92.86
Dale City, VA (cdp) Prince William County	92.71
Washington, NJ (township) Gloucester County	92.61
Bonita, CA (cdp) San Diego County	92.52
Howell, NJ (township) Monmouth County	92.50
Seattle Hill-Silver Firs, WA (cdp) Snohomish County	92.17
Morton Grove, IL (village) Cook County	92.11
La Mirada, CA (city) Los Angeles County	91.73
Laguna, CA (cdp) Sacramento County	91.16
Fontana, CA (city) San Bernardino County	90.99
Union, NJ (township) Union County	90.81
Pico Rivera, CA (city) Los Angeles County	90.75
Pepeekeo, HI (cdp) Hawaii County	90.74
Pahala, HI (cdp) Hawaii County	90.73
Cherry Hill, NJ (township) Camden County	90.64
Huntington, NY (town) Suffolk County	90.40
Livingston, NJ (township) Essex County	90.28
Fair Lawn, NJ (borough) Bergen County	90.21
Babylon, NY (town) Suffolk County	90.14
Aurora, IL (city) Kane County	90.07
Cerritos, CA (city) Los Angeles County	89.98
Bolingbrook, IL (village) Will County	89.97
Teaneck, NJ (township) Bergen County	89.81
Valley Cottage, NY (cdp) Rockland County	89.74
Mission Bend, TX (cdp) Fort Bend County	89.64
Elk Grove, CA (cdp) Sacramento County	89.62
Downers Grove, IL (village) Du Page County	89.21
Cathedral City, CA (city) Riverside County	89.01
Tracy, CA (city) San Joaquin County	88.99
Wheeling, IL (village) Cook County	88.97
Waihee-Waiehu, HI (cdp) Maui County	88.56
Hercules, CA (city) Contra Costa County	88.37
Bowie, MD (city) Prince George's County	88.24
Palmdale, CA (city) Los Angeles County	87.76
Gilroy, CA (city) Santa Clara County	87.73
Peoria, AZ (city) Maricopa County	87.73
Yorba Linda, CA (city) Orange County	87.32
Hicksville, NY (cdp) Nassau County	87.29

Notes: Please refer to the User's Guide for an explanation of data; ranking tables include all places with Asian and/or NHPI populations above SF4 population thresholds; (1) tables reflect only those areas that meet SF4 population thresholds, therefore there may be less than 50 states, 75 counties or 75 places listed

Homeownership

Guamanians or Chamorros Who Own Their Own Homes

All States, Top 75 Counties, and Top 75 Places Sorted by Number[1]

State	Number
United States	7,536
California	2,967
Washington	915
Texas	548
Florida	249
Georgia	209
Arizona	191
Nevada	180
Colorado	151
Oregon	139
North Carolina	129
Louisiana	125
Virginia	119
Hawaii	114
Maryland	110
Illinois	108
Pennsylvania	107
Michigan	79
Missouri	79
Minnesota	74
Oklahoma	68
New York	65
Alabama	61
Indiana	60
Ohio	58
Massachusetts	56
Connecticut	49
New Mexico	44
Wisconsin	43
South Carolina	38
Tennessee	37
Kentucky	27
New Jersey	26

County	Number
San Diego County, CA	696
Los Angeles County, CA	405
Pierce County, WA	309
Solano County, CA	296
Alameda County, CA	248
Orange County, CA	238
Clark County, NV	176
Santa Clara County, CA	167
Thurston County, WA	167
Kitsap County, WA	148
San Bernardino County, CA	130
King County, WA	126
Sacramento County, CA	118
Bell County, TX	113
Contra Costa County, CA	113
Harris County, TX	103
Honolulu County, HI	103
Riverside County, CA	86
Maricopa County, AZ	85
El Paso County, CO	80
Monterey County, CA	68
San Mateo County, CA	66
Kings County, NY	8

Place	Number
San Diego, CA (city) San Diego County	313
Vallejo, CA (city) Solano County	143
Fairfield, CA (city) Solano County	126
Killeen, TX (city) Bell County	104
San Jose, CA (city) Santa Clara County	99
Chula Vista, CA (city) San Diego County	97
Los Angeles, CA (city) Los Angeles County	87
Houston, TX (city) Harris County	72
Tacoma, WA (city) Pierce County	70
New York, NY (city)	37
Honolulu, HI (cdp) Honolulu County	36

Notes: Please refer to the User's Guide for an explanation of data; ranking tables include all places with Asian and/or NHPI populations above SF4 population thresholds; (1) tables reflect only those areas that meet SF4 population thresholds, therefore there may be less than 50 states, 75 counties or 75 places listed

Homeownership

Guamanians or Chamorros Who Own Their Own Homes

All States, Top 75 Counties, and Top 75 Places Sorted by Percent[1]

State	Percent
Minnesota	71.84
Louisiana	69.44
Maryland	60.11
Pennsylvania	58.47
Michigan	58.09
Connecticut	54.44
Washington	54.43
Wisconsin	54.43
Texas	51.94
Arizona	51.21
Missouri	50.97
California	50.18
Indiana	50.00
Oklahoma	49.28
Nevada	47.87
United States	47.57
Massachusetts	45.90
North Carolina	45.10
Ohio	44.96
Colorado	44.94
Florida	44.86
Georgia	44.85
New Mexico	43.56
South Carolina	41.30
Virginia	40.48
Alabama	39.87
Illinois	37.89
Oregon	37.57
Kentucky	32.93
Tennessee	27.61
Hawaii	22.75
New Jersey	21.49
New York	16.33

County	Percent
Thurston County, WA	75.57
Orange County, CA	70.62
Solano County, CA	67.12
Contra Costa County, CA	60.11
San Mateo County, CA	59.46
Pierce County, WA	55.78
Bell County, TX	54.59
Kitsap County, WA	54.01
San Bernardino County, CA	52.42
Clark County, NV	52.23
Santa Clara County, CA	51.07
Alameda County, CA	50.00
San Diego County, CA	48.84
Harris County, TX	47.25
Maricopa County, AZ	45.45
Los Angeles County, CA	44.90
Sacramento County, CA	43.38
Monterey County, CA	43.31
Riverside County, CA	42.16
El Paso County, CO	42.11
King County, WA	41.45
Honolulu County, HI	21.96
Kings County, NY	9.09

Place	Percent
Fairfield, CA (city) Solano County	69.23
Chula Vista, CA (city) San Diego County	68.31
Vallejo, CA (city) Solano County	67.77
Killeen, TX (city) Bell County	61.90
San Diego, CA (city) San Diego County	52.52
San Jose, CA (city) Santa Clara County	49.75
Tacoma, WA (city) Pierce County	48.95
Houston, TX (city) Harris County	43.11
Los Angeles, CA (city) Los Angeles County	27.27
New York, NY (city)	14.23
Honolulu, HI (cdp) Honolulu County	13.85

Notes: Please refer to the User's Guide for an explanation of data; ranking tables include all places with Asian and/or NHPI populations above SF4 population thresholds; (1) tables reflect only those areas that meet SF4 population thresholds, therefore there may be less than 50 states, 75 counties or 75 places listed

Homeownership

Hawaiian Natives Who Own Their Own Homes

All States, Top 75 Counties, and Top 75 Places Sorted by Number[1]

State	Number
United States	21,581
Hawaii	12,259
California	3,487
Washington	752
Texas	506
Nevada	434
Oregon	370
Florida	315
Colorado	271
Arizona	268
Utah	175
Virginia	169
Pennsylvania	156
New York	139
Georgia	136
North Carolina	135
Ohio	134
Missouri	131
Michigan	123
Tennessee	113
Alaska	104
Oklahoma	101
Indiana	97
Minnesota	87
Illinois	81
South Carolina	74
Maryland	71
Louisiana	70
New Mexico	68
Kansas	65
New Jersey	65
Arkansas	63
Wisconsin	61
Idaho	52
Massachusetts	40
Montana	38

County	Number
Honolulu County, HI	7,417
Hawaii County, HI	2,298
Maui County, HI	1,842
Kauai County, HI	702
Los Angeles County, CA	639
San Diego County, CA	398
Clark County, NV	393
Orange County, CA	335
King County, WA	293
Alameda County, CA	224
Riverside County, CA	189
San Bernardino County, CA	187
San Mateo County, CA	187
Solano County, CA	155
Contra Costa County, CA	149
Maricopa County, AZ	149
Sacramento County, CA	146
Bexar County, TX	121
Pierce County, WA	121
Santa Clara County, CA	110
Multnomah County, OR	90
Ventura County, CA	86
San Joaquin County, CA	85
Snohomish County, WA	84
Salt Lake County, UT	61
Pima County, AZ	54
Washington County, OR	50
Utah County, UT	23

Place	Number
Honolulu, HI (cdp) Honolulu County	1,870
Hilo, HI (cdp) Hawaii County	661
Nanakuli, HI (cdp) Honolulu County	616
Kaneohe, HI (cdp) Honolulu County	493
Kailua, HI (cdp) Honolulu County	485
Waimanalo Beach, HI (cdp) Honolulu County	453
Waianae, HI (cdp) Honolulu County	362
Anahola, HI (cdp) Kauai County	236
Mililani Town, HI (cdp) Honolulu County	215
Kualapuu, HI (cdp) Maui County	204
Waihee-Waiehu, HI (cdp) Maui County	204
Waimea, HI (cdp) Hawaii County	201
Los Angeles, CA (city) Los Angeles County	193
Pearl City, HI (cdp) Honolulu County	188
Wailuku, HI (cdp) Maui County	176
San Diego, CA (city) San Diego County	175
Makakilo City, HI (cdp) Honolulu County	172
Kailua, HI (cdp) Hawaii County	155
Wahiawa, HI (cdp) Honolulu County	135
Kihei, HI (cdp) Maui County	126
Kalaoa, HI (cdp) Hawaii County	124
Kaunakakai, HI (cdp) Maui County	123
Lahaina, HI (cdp) Maui County	122
Hauula, HI (cdp) Honolulu County	119
Maili, HI (cdp) Honolulu County	118
Henderson, NV (city) Clark County	117
Waimanalo, HI (cdp) Honolulu County	117
Waimalu, HI (cdp) Honolulu County	111
Ewa Beach, HI (cdp) Honolulu County	110
Kapaa, HI (cdp) Kauai County	105
Makaha, HI (cdp) Honolulu County	105
Kahului, HI (cdp) Maui County	101
Ahuimanu, HI (cdp) Honolulu County	99
Kahaluu, HI (cdp) Honolulu County	95
Halawa, HI (cdp) Honolulu County	90
Las Vegas, NV (city) Clark County	84
Makawao, HI (cdp) Maui County	82
Holualoa, HI (cdp) Hawaii County	76
Hawaiian Paradise Park, HI (cdp) Hawaii County	73
Hawaiian Beaches, HI (cdp) Hawaii County	70
Phoenix, AZ (city) Maricopa County	67
Waipahu, HI (cdp) Honolulu County	67
Waipio, HI (cdp) Honolulu County	67
Portland, OR (city) Multnomah County	66
Volcano, HI (cdp) Hawaii County	66
New York, NY (city)	65
Kekaha, HI (cdp) Kauai County	62
Honaunau-Napoopoo, HI (cdp) Hawaii County	56
Waikoloa Village, HI (cdp) Hawaii County	55
Aiea, HI (cdp) Honolulu County	52
Hana, HI (cdp) Maui County	52
Laie, HI (cdp) Honolulu County	45
Paia, HI (cdp) Maui County	44
Kaaawa, HI (cdp) Honolulu County	43
Hawaiian Ocean View, HI (cdp) Hawaii County	39
Captain Cook, HI (cdp) Hawaii County	33
Haleiwa, HI (cdp) Honolulu County	32
San Jose, CA (city) Santa Clara County	32
Hanapepe, HI (cdp) Kauai County	31
Paradise, NV (cdp) Clark County	27
Waikane, HI (cdp) Honolulu County	25
Waimea, HI (cdp) Kauai County	25
Kapaau, HI (cdp) Hawaii County	24
Kahuku, HI (cdp) Honolulu County	23
Naalehu, HI (cdp) Hawaii County	20
Honalo, HI (cdp) Hawaii County	17
Pahala, HI (cdp) Hawaii County	17
Kilauea, HI (cdp) Kauai County	15
Punaluu, HI (cdp) Honolulu County	13
Makaha Valley, HI (cdp) Honolulu County	9
Waialua, HI (cdp) Honolulu County	9
Pakala Village, HI (cdp) Kauai County	0

Notes: Please refer to the User's Guide for an explanation of data; ranking tables include all places with Asian and/or NHPI populations above SF4 population thresholds; (1) tables reflect only those areas that meet SF4 population thresholds, therefore there may be less than 50 states, 75 counties or 75 places listed

Homeownership

Hawaiian Natives Who Own Their Own Homes

All States, Top 75 Counties, and Top 75 Places Sorted by Percent[1]

State	Percent
Tennessee	66.86
Pennsylvania	64.46
Wisconsin	62.24
Minnesota	62.14
Missouri	61.79
Louisiana	61.40
Georgia	60.71
Indiana	59.15
Michigan	58.57
Virginia	58.28
Oklahoma	57.06
Montana	56.72
Colorado	56.11
Ohio	55.14
Alaska	55.03
New Mexico	54.84
Arkansas	54.78
Maryland	54.62
Hawaii	54.02
United States	52.22
California	51.61
Texas	50.00
Oregon	49.53
Florida	48.69
Washington	46.80
South Carolina	46.54
Arizona	46.13
Utah	44.87
Kansas	44.52
North Carolina	42.86
New Jersey	40.88
Nevada	38.48
Idaho	34.90
Illinois	34.18
New York	33.74
Massachusetts	30.08

County	Percent
Bexar County, TX	70.76
San Bernardino County, CA	70.30
Contra Costa County, CA	66.82
Riverside County, CA	65.63
Orange County, CA	62.04
San Mateo County, CA	59.18
Sacramento County, CA	58.87
Solano County, CA	58.71
Hawaii County, HI	56.25
Kauai County, HI	56.25
Maui County, HI	54.77
Honolulu County, HI	53.28
King County, WA	51.49
Maricopa County, AZ	50.00
San Diego County, CA	49.63
Snohomish County, WA	49.41
San Joaquin County, CA	48.02
Multnomah County, OR	47.62
Ventura County, CA	47.51
Los Angeles County, CA	46.10
Alameda County, CA	46.00
Salt Lake County, UT	43.57
Pierce County, WA	39.67
Clark County, NV	39.54
Washington County, OR	39.06
Pima County, AZ	34.62
Santa Clara County, CA	30.73
Utah County, UT	23.96

Place	Percent
Waimanalo Beach, HI (cdp) Honolulu County	91.52
Anahola, HI (cdp) Kauai County	89.06
Waihee-Waiehu, HI (cdp) Maui County	88.31
Hana, HI (cdp) Maui County	88.14
Kualapuu, HI (cdp) Maui County	84.65
Nanakuli, HI (cdp) Honolulu County	84.15
Mililani Town, HI (cdp) Honolulu County	82.06
Kapaau, HI (cdp) Hawaii County	77.42
Holualoa, HI (cdp) Hawaii County	76.00
Kilauea, HI (cdp) Kauai County	71.43
Volcano, HI (cdp) Hawaii County	70.97
Henderson, NV (city) Clark County	70.06
Hawaiian Beaches, HI (cdp) Hawaii County	69.31
Kahaluu, HI (cdp) Honolulu County	68.84
Makakilo City, HI (cdp) Honolulu County	68.80
Paia, HI (cdp) Maui County	68.75
Kalaoa, HI (cdp) Hawaii County	68.13
Kailua, HI (cdp) Honolulu County	66.99
Waikane, HI (cdp) Honolulu County	65.79
Hawaiian Ocean View, HI (cdp) Hawaii County	65.00
Aiea, HI (cdp) Honolulu County	64.20
Kaaawa, HI (cdp) Honolulu County	64.18
Haleiwa, HI (cdp) Honolulu County	64.00
Kahuku, HI (cdp) Honolulu County	63.89
Waianae, HI (cdp) Honolulu County	63.18
Naalehu, HI (cdp) Hawaii County	62.50
Pearl City, HI (cdp) Honolulu County	62.46
Waimea, HI (cdp) Hawaii County	62.23
Honaunau-Napoopoo, HI (cdp) Hawaii County	62.22
Hanapepe, HI (cdp) Kauai County	62.00
Kekaha, HI (cdp) Kauai County	62.00
Hauula, HI (cdp) Honolulu County	61.66
Captain Cook, HI (cdp) Hawaii County	61.11
Ahuimanu, HI (cdp) Honolulu County	60.37
Kaneohe, HI (cdp) Honolulu County	59.69
Ewa Beach, HI (cdp) Honolulu County	57.29
Kaunakakai, HI (cdp) Maui County	57.21
Kihei, HI (cdp) Maui County	55.26
Kapaa, HI (cdp) Kauai County	54.40
Kailua, HI (cdp) Hawaii County	54.39
Waikoloa Village, HI (cdp) Hawaii County	53.92
Waimanalo, HI (cdp) Honolulu County	53.92
Hilo, HI (cdp) Hawaii County	53.14
Laie, HI (cdp) Honolulu County	52.94
Waimea, HI (cdp) Kauai County	52.08
Lahaina, HI (cdp) Maui County	50.62
Makawao, HI (cdp) Maui County	49.70
Waipio, HI (cdp) Honolulu County	49.26
Pahala, HI (cdp) Hawaii County	47.22
Phoenix, AZ (city) Maricopa County	46.85
Wailuku, HI (cdp) Maui County	46.44
San Diego, CA (city) San Diego County	43.42
Halawa, HI (cdp) Honolulu County	43.06
Portland, OR (city) Multnomah County	40.00
Maili, HI (cdp) Honolulu County	39.73
Honolulu, HI (cdp) Honolulu County	38.53
Hawaiian Paradise Park, HI (cdp) Hawaii County	38.02
Los Angeles, CA (city) Los Angeles County	37.48
Waipahu, HI (cdp) Honolulu County	36.61
Wahiawa, HI (cdp) Honolulu County	36.10
Waimalu, HI (cdp) Honolulu County	35.81
Makaha, HI (cdp) Honolulu County	35.00
Honalo, HI (cdp) Hawaii County	30.36
New York, NY (city)	29.02
Las Vegas, NV (city) Clark County	28.77
Punaluu, HI (cdp) Honolulu County	27.66
Waialua, HI (cdp) Honolulu County	26.47
Kahului, HI (cdp) Maui County	24.82
San Jose, CA (city) Santa Clara County	21.05
Paradise, NV (cdp) Clark County	16.07
Makaha Valley, HI (cdp) Honolulu County	12.68
Pakala Village, HI (cdp) Kauai County	0.00

Notes: Please refer to the User's Guide for an explanation of data; ranking tables include all places with Asian and/or NHPI populations above SF4 population thresholds; (1) tables reflect only those areas that meet SF4 population thresholds, therefore there may be less than 50 states, 75 counties or 75 places listed

Homeownership

Hmongs Who Own Their Own Homes

All States, Top 75 Counties, and Top 75 Places Sorted by Number[1]

State	Number
United States	10,419
Minnesota	3,810
Wisconsin	2,472
California	1,618
North Carolina	610
Michigan	593
Colorado	298
Georgia	133
Kansas	107
Oregon	102
Massachusetts	98
South Carolina	75
Washington	73
Pennsylvania	60
Rhode Island	47
Oklahoma	23
Alaska	17

County	Number
Ramsey County, MN	2,236
Hennepin County, MN	1,239
Milwaukee County, WI	747
Fresno County, CA	542
Sacramento County, CA	444
Marathon County, WI	252
Adams County, CO	225
Dane County, WI	195
Burke County, NC	188
Macomb County, MI	186
Sheboygan County, WI	184
Wayne County, MI	183
La Crosse County, WI	152
Brown County, WI	147
Oakland County, MI	135
San Joaquin County, CA	135
Winnebago County, WI	134
Outagamie County, WI	132
Catawba County, NC	130
Eau Claire County, WI	126
Merced County, CA	123
Washington County, MN	116
Manitowoc County, WI	92
Orange County, CA	91
Wyandotte County, KS	89
Multnomah County, OR	88
Mecklenburg County, NC	80
Anoka County, MN	67
Spartanburg County, SC	65
Butte County, CA	55
Portage County, WI	54
San Diego County, CA	54
Worcester County, MA	47
Yuba County, CA	47
Olmsted County, MN	46
Dunn County, WI	45
King County, WA	42
Wood County, WI	39
Calumet County, WI	38
Lancaster County, PA	37
Fond du Lac County, WI	34
Providence County, RI	34
Jefferson County, CO	33
Chippewa County, WI	30
Spokane County, WA	28
Solano County, CA	24
Barrow County, GA	21
Tulare County, CA	20
Stanly County, NC	18
Anchorage Borough, AK	17
Los Angeles County, CA	17
Stanislaus County, CA	17
Santa Barbara County, CA	16
Ingham County, MI	15
Riverside County, CA	8
Glenn County, CA	5
Yolo County, CA	0

Place	Number
St. Paul, MN (city) Ramsey County	2,080
Minneapolis, MN (city) Hennepin County	870
Milwaukee, WI (city) Milwaukee County	711
Fresno, CA (city) Fresno County	414
Sacramento, CA (city) Sacramento County	364
Wausau, WI (city) Marathon County	195
Brooklyn Center, MN (city) Hennepin County	178
Sheboygan, WI (city) Sheboygan County	168
Appleton, WI (city) Outagamie County	162
Madison, WI (city) Dane County	146
Detroit, MI (city) Wayne County	143
Eau Claire, WI (city) Eau Claire County	132
Warren, MI (city) Macomb County	129
Brooklyn Park, MN (city) Hennepin County	124
Green Bay, WI (city) Brown County	96
Westminster, CO (city) Adams County	93
Pontiac, MI (city) Oakland County	91
Kansas City, KS (city) Wyandotte County	89
Manitowoc, WI (city) Manitowoc County	81
Charlotte, NC (city) Mecklenburg County	80
Stockton, CA (city) San Joaquin County	80
Oshkosh, WI (city) Winnebago County	79
Portland, OR (city) Multnomah County	73
La Crosse, WI (city) La Crosse County	69
Merced, CA (city) Merced County	61
Maplewood, MN (city) Ramsey County	53
Clovis, CA (city) Fresno County	52
Stevens Point, WI (city) Portage County	47
Rochester, MN (city) Olmsted County	46
Fitchburg, MA (city) Worcester County	44
San Diego, CA (city) San Diego County	44
Woodbury, MN (city) Washington County	42
Linda, CA (cdp) Yuba County	40
Santa Ana, CA (city) Orange County	35
Wisconsin Rapids, WI (city) Wood County	35
Fond du Lac, WI (city) Fond du Lac County	30
Atwater, CA (city) Merced County	28
Thermalito, CA (cdp) Butte County	28
Spokane, WA (city) Spokane County	21
Providence, RI (city) Providence County	20
Glen Alpine, NC (town) Burke County	18
Lansing, MI (city) Ingham County	15
Visalia, CA (city) Tulare County	14
Oroville, CA (city) Butte County	13
Parkway-S. Sacramento, CA (cdp) Sacramento County	13
Florin, CA (cdp) Sacramento County	12
Connelly Springs, NC (town) Burke County	8
Hickory, NC (city) Catawba County	7
Valdese, NC (town) Burke County	6
Willows, CA (city) Glenn County	5
Arden-Arcade, CA (cdp) Sacramento County	0
Chico, CA (city) Butte County	0
Modesto, CA (city) Stanislaus County	0
South Oroville, CA (cdp) Butte County	0
West Sacramento, CA (city) Yolo County	0

Notes: Please refer to the User's Guide for an explanation of data; ranking tables include all places with Asian and/or NHPI populations above SF4 population thresholds; (1) tables reflect only those areas that meet SF4 population thresholds, therefore there may be less than 50 states, 75 counties or 75 places listed

Homeownership

Hmongs Who Own Their Own Homes

All States, Top 75 Counties, and Top 75 Places Sorted by Percent[1]

State	Percent
Kansas	61.49
Michigan	59.18
Georgia	58.85
Colorado	57.64
South Carolina	57.25
Massachusetts	55.06
Minnesota	53.94
North Carolina	53.46
Pennsylvania	52.17
Wisconsin	47.12
Oklahoma	40.35
United States	38.74
Rhode Island	38.52
Oregon	37.78
Washington	32.59
Alaska	23.61
California	16.44

County	Percent
Macomb County, MI	87.32
Anoka County, MN	80.72
Washington County, MN	77.85
Olmsted County, MN	73.02
Wyandotte County, KS	65.44
Oakland County, MI	64.59
Mecklenburg County, NC	62.99
Wayne County, MI	62.89
Burke County, NC	61.84
Jefferson County, CO	60.00
Milwaukee County, WI	59.71
Spartanburg County, SC	59.63
Hennepin County, MN	58.36
Adams County, CO	58.29
Fond du Lac County, WI	57.63
Manitowoc County, WI	55.76
Eau Claire County, WI	54.55
Lancaster County, PA	53.62
Winnebago County, WI	52.34
Calumet County, WI	51.35
Ramsey County, MN	50.75
Barrow County, GA	50.00
Wood County, WI	50.00
Dunn County, WI	49.45
Orange County, CA	48.15
Sheboygan County, WI	48.04
La Crosse County, WI	47.65
Worcester County, MA	43.93
Catawba County, NC	43.92
Marathon County, WI	43.52
Multnomah County, OR	41.71
Chippewa County, WI	40.54
Spokane County, WA	40.00
Dane County, WI	39.63
Portage County, WI	38.85
Brown County, WI	33.72
Providence County, RI	33.33
Outagamie County, WI	32.51
Solano County, CA	32.43
Stanly County, NC	30.00
King County, WA	29.37
San Diego County, CA	28.42
Anchorage Borough, AK	23.61
Santa Barbara County, CA	23.19
Ingham County, MI	21.74
Sacramento County, CA	17.74
Los Angeles County, CA	17.17
Fresno County, CA	16.19
San Joaquin County, CA	15.73
Butte County, CA	14.82
Yuba County, CA	14.55
Tulare County, CA	13.25
Merced County, CA	13.02
Stanislaus County, CA	10.49
Riverside County, CA	8.79
Glenn County, CA	7.25
Yolo County, CA	0.00

Place	Percent
Warren, MI (city) Macomb County	100.00
Woodbury, MN (city) Washington County	85.71
Glen Alpine, NC (town) Burke County	81.82
Brooklyn Park, MN (city) Hennepin County	81.58
Maplewood, MN (city) Ramsey County	80.30
Brooklyn Center, MN (city) Hennepin County	79.82
Rochester, MN (city) Olmsted County	73.02
Pontiac, MI (city) Oakland County	67.91
Kansas City, KS (city) Wyandotte County	65.44
Fond du Lac, WI (city) Fond du Lac County	63.83
Charlotte, NC (city) Mecklenburg County	62.99
Milwaukee, WI (city) Milwaukee County	59.05
Connelly Springs, NC (town) Burke County	57.14
Detroit, MI (city) Wayne County	56.97
Manitowoc, WI (city) Manitowoc County	54.73
Westminster, CO (city) Adams County	52.84
Minneapolis, MN (city) Hennepin County	52.50
Wisconsin Rapids, WI (city) Wood County	50.72
Eau Claire, WI (city) Eau Claire County	50.57
St. Paul, MN (city) Ramsey County	49.71
Fitchburg, MA (city) Worcester County	48.89
Spokane, WA (city) Spokane County	46.67
Sheboygan, WI (city) Sheboygan County	46.03
Oshkosh, WI (city) Winnebago County	44.38
Stevens Point, WI (city) Portage County	41.59
Thermalito, CA (cdp) Butte County	40.58
Madison, WI (city) Dane County	40.56
Appleton, WI (city) Outagamie County	40.40
Portland, OR (city) Multnomah County	38.62
Wausau, WI (city) Marathon County	38.54
Santa Ana, CA (city) Orange County	38.04
Atwater, CA (city) Merced County	37.84
Valdese, NC (town) Burke County	33.33
La Crosse, WI (city) La Crosse County	29.87
San Diego, CA (city) San Diego County	29.73
Green Bay, WI (city) Brown County	28.49
Providence, RI (city) Providence County	24.39
Sacramento, CA (city) Sacramento County	21.91
Clovis, CA (city) Fresno County	21.85
Oroville, CA (city) Butte County	19.40
Visalia, CA (city) Tulare County	17.72
Lansing, MI (city) Ingham County	16.13
Linda, CA (cdp) Yuba County	15.87
Fresno, CA (city) Fresno County	14.47
Stockton, CA (city) San Joaquin County	10.99
Merced, CA (city) Merced County	9.62
Florin, CA (cdp) Sacramento County	8.00
Hickory, NC (city) Catawba County	7.78
Willows, CA (city) Glenn County	7.25
Parkway-S. Sacramento, CA (cdp) Sacramento County	3.29
Arden-Arcade, CA (cdp) Sacramento County	0.00
Chico, CA (city) Butte County	0.00
Modesto, CA (city) Stanislaus County	0.00
South Oroville, CA (cdp) Butte County	0.00
West Sacramento, CA (city) Yolo County	0.00

Notes: Please refer to the User's Guide for an explanation of data; ranking tables include all places with Asian and/or NHPI populations above SF4 population thresholds; (1) tables reflect only those areas that meet SF4 population thresholds, therefore there may be less than 50 states, 75 counties or 75 places listed

Homeownership

Indonesians Who Own Their Own Homes

All States, Top 75 Counties, and Top 75 Places Sorted by Number[1]

State	Number
United States	4,977
California	2,480
Florida	218
Texas	190
New York	186
Maryland	159
New Jersey	155
Washington	154
Virginia	140
Arizona	127
Massachusetts	108
Oregon	98
Illinois	95
Michigan	67
Ohio	67
Georgia	60
Colorado	59
Pennsylvania	57
Wisconsin	40

County	Number
Los Angeles County, CA	794
San Bernardino County, CA	495
Orange County, CA	361
Montgomery County, MD	128
Santa Clara County, CA	124
Maricopa County, AZ	121
San Mateo County, CA	110
King County, WA	96
San Diego County, CA	88
Fairfax County, VA	85
Contra Costa County, CA	83
Alameda County, CA	81
Cook County, IL	63
Queens County, NY	61
San Francisco County, CA	60
Harris County, TX	56
Middlesex County, NJ	41
Franklin County, OH	8

Place	Number
Los Angeles, CA (city) Los Angeles County	205
New York, NY (city)	84
San Francisco, CA (city) San Francisco County	60
San Bernardino, CA (city) San Bernardino County	45
Loma Linda, CA (city) San Bernardino County	42
Houston, TX (city) Harris County	32
Seattle, WA (city) King County	31
Columbus, OH (city) Franklin County	0

Notes: Please refer to the User's Guide for an explanation of data; ranking tables include all places with Asian and/or NHPI populations above SF4 population thresholds; (1) tables reflect only those areas that meet SF4 population thresholds, therefore there may be less than 50 states, 75 counties or 75 places listed

Homeownership

Indonesians Who Own Their Own Homes

***All States, Top 75 Counties, and Top 75 Places Sorted by Percent*[1]**

State	Percent
Arizona	57.73
Florida	53.69
Maryland	51.29
California	47.95
New Jersey	45.99
Oregon	41.00
Virginia	40.46
United States	38.55
Massachusetts	37.11
Georgia	31.91
Pennsylvania	31.32
Michigan	30.88
Washington	29.90
Texas	27.82
Illinois	27.07
Colorado	21.53
New York	19.94
Wisconsin	18.96
Ohio	15.62

County	Percent
Fairfax County, VA	66.93
Maricopa County, AZ	66.85
Orange County, CA	61.50
Santa Clara County, CA	57.94
San Bernardino County, CA	54.04
Contra Costa County, CA	52.20
Montgomery County, MD	51.41
Alameda County, CA	50.31
San Diego County, CA	49.44
San Mateo County, CA	46.81
Los Angeles County, CA	42.41
Middlesex County, NJ	33.88
Cook County, IL	32.81
King County, WA	25.95
Harris County, TX	25.81
San Francisco County, CA	18.87
Queens County, NY	13.29
Franklin County, OH	3.24

Place	Percent
San Bernardino, CA (city) San Bernardino County	46.39
Loma Linda, CA (city) San Bernardino County	34.71
Los Angeles, CA (city) Los Angeles County	28.47
San Francisco, CA (city) San Francisco County	18.87
Seattle, WA (city) King County	17.51
Houston, TX (city) Harris County	16.58
New York, NY (city)	12.28
Columbus, OH (city) Franklin County	0.00

Notes: Please refer to the User's Guide for an explanation of data; ranking tables include all places with Asian and/or NHPI populations above SF4 population thresholds; (1) tables reflect only those areas that meet SF4 population thresholds, therefore there may be less than 50 states, 75 counties or 75 places listed

Homeownership

Japanese Who Own Their Own Homes

All States, Top 75 Counties, and Top 75 Places Sorted by Number[1]

State	Number
United States	204,997
California	82,446
Hawaii	65,195
Washington	9,999
Illinois	4,307
New York	3,934
Colorado	3,275
Oregon	2,833
Texas	2,803
Florida	2,368
Nevada	2,112
New Jersey	2,078
Ohio	1,857
Arizona	1,753
Utah	1,734
Virginia	1,565
Michigan	1,515
Maryland	1,203
Georgia	1,189
Pennsylvania	1,105
Massachusetts	974
North Carolina	966
Idaho	867
Minnesota	707
Indiana	675
Missouri	659
New Mexico	635
Connecticut	541
Wisconsin	527
Tennessee	481
South Carolina	474
Oklahoma	462
Kentucky	408
Alaska	406
Kansas	389
Alabama	335
Nebraska	238
Arkansas	230
Montana	222
Louisiana	220
Rhode Island	190
Iowa	179
Wyoming	138
Delaware	135
District of Columbia	130
West Virginia	109
New Hampshire	101
Maine	91
Mississippi	89
Vermont	74
South Dakota	53

County	Number
Honolulu County, HI	49,965
Los Angeles County, CA	31,745
Orange County, CA	8,841
Hawaii County, HI	7,698
Santa Clara County, CA	7,211
King County, WA	6,368
Sacramento County, CA	4,590
Maui County, HI	4,570
San Diego County, CA	4,103
Alameda County, CA	3,658
Contra Costa County, CA	2,997
Cook County, IL	2,971
Kauai County, HI	2,962
San Mateo County, CA	2,599
San Francisco County, CA	2,175
Fresno County, CA	2,046
Clark County, NV	1,677
Ventura County, CA	1,576
New York County, NY	1,360
San Joaquin County, CA	1,357
Maricopa County, AZ	1,240
Riverside County, CA	1,221
Pierce County, WA	1,156
San Bernardino County, CA	1,154
Monterey County, CA	1,103
Salt Lake County, UT	943
Multnomah County, OR	908
Bergen County, NJ	740
Westchester County, NY	720
Snohomish County, WA	655
Montgomery County, MD	593
Fairfax County, VA	587
Denver County, CO	581
Washington County, OR	569
Santa Barbara County, CA	560
Placer County, CA	548
Jefferson County, CO	545
Sonoma County, CA	541
Santa Cruz County, CA	536
Solano County, CA	533
Harris County, TX	532
Queens County, NY	531
Oakland County, MI	513
Marin County, CA	502
Arapahoe County, CO	487
Franklin County, OH	475
Spokane County, WA	382
Clackamas County, OR	381
El Paso County, CO	378
Middlesex County, MA	376
DuPage County, IL	365
Bernalillo County, NM	345
Washoe County, NV	344
Adams County, CO	341
Dallas County, TX	338
Lake County, IL	324
Bexar County, TX	321
Boulder County, CO	321
Yolo County, CA	311
Hennepin County, MN	309
Nassau County, NY	289
San Luis Obispo County, CA	282
Weber County, UT	280
Anchorage Borough, AK	279
Cuyahoga County, OH	276
Broward County, FL	275
Kitsap County, WA	271
Miami-Dade County, FL	271
Davis County, UT	270
Kern County, CA	270
Pima County, AZ	263
Fairfield County, CT	259
Ada County, ID	251
Tulare County, CA	251
Clark County, WA	240

Place	Number
Honolulu, HI (cdp) Honolulu County	24,333
Los Angeles, CA (city) Los Angeles County	9,328
Hilo, HI (cdp) Hawaii County	3,938
Torrance, CA (city) Los Angeles County	3,657
San Jose, CA (city) Santa Clara County	3,467
Pearl City, HI (cdp) Honolulu County	3,277
Waimalu, HI (cdp) Honolulu County	2,737
Kaneohe, HI (cdp) Honolulu County	2,727
Sacramento, CA (city) Sacramento County	2,601
Seattle, WA (city) King County	2,548
Mililani Town, HI (cdp) Honolulu County	2,472
San Francisco, CA (city) San Francisco County	2,175
New York, NY (city)	2,082
San Diego, CA (city) San Diego County	2,054
Gardena, CA (city) Los Angeles County	2,005
Monterey Park, CA (city) Los Angeles County	1,753
Kailua, HI (cdp) Honolulu County	1,502
Chicago, IL (city) Cook County	1,487
Kahului, HI (cdp) Maui County	1,237
Wahiawa, HI (cdp) Honolulu County	1,107
Aiea, HI (cdp) Honolulu County	1,059
Wailuku, HI (cdp) Maui County	1,013
Waipahu, HI (cdp) Honolulu County	993
Waipio, HI (cdp) Honolulu County	993
Huntington Beach, CA (city) Orange County	932
Long Beach, CA (city) Los Angeles County	926
Halawa, HI (cdp) Honolulu County	899
Fresno, CA (city) Fresno County	840
Bellevue, WA (city) King County	821
Portland, OR (city) Multnomah County	759
Anaheim, CA (city) Orange County	743
Pasadena, CA (city) Los Angeles County	730
Cerritos, CA (city) Los Angeles County	691
Irvine, CA (city) Orange County	691
Rancho Palos Verdes, CA (city) Los Angeles County	684
Oakland, CA (city) Alameda County	683
Lihue, HI (cdp) Kauai County	646
Sunnyvale, CA (city) Santa Clara County	641
Stockton, CA (city) San Joaquin County	633
Las Vegas, NV (city) Clark County	629
Montebello, CA (city) Los Angeles County	622
Redondo Beach, CA (city) Los Angeles County	590
Ahuimanu, HI (cdp) Honolulu County	588
Denver, CO (city) Denver County	581
San Mateo, CA (city) San Mateo County	576
Hacienda Heights, CA (cdp) Los Angeles County	523
Berkeley, CA (city) Alameda County	512
Mountain View, CA (city) Santa Clara County	508
Fremont, CA (city) Alameda County	500
Heeia, HI (cdp) Honolulu County	461
Phoenix, AZ (city) Maricopa County	447
Culver City, CA (city) Los Angeles County	432
Chula Vista, CA (city) San Diego County	422
Fountain Valley, CA (city) Orange County	417
Oxnard, CA (city) Ventura County	416
El Cerrito, CA (city) Contra Costa County	415
Garden Grove, CA (city) Orange County	412
Mission Viejo, CA (city) Orange County	404
Glendale, CA (city) Los Angeles County	398
Village Park, HI (cdp) Honolulu County	395
Kapaa, HI (cdp) Kauai County	393
West Carson, CA (cdp) Los Angeles County	389
Westminster, CA (city) Orange County	389
Santa Clara, CA (city) Santa Clara County	386
Alhambra, CA (city) Los Angeles County	385
Cypress, CA (city) Orange County	377
Richmond, CA (city) Contra Costa County	373
Pukalani, HI (cdp) Maui County	368
Lahaina, HI (cdp) Maui County	367
Oceanside, CA (city) San Diego County	352
Makakilo City, HI (cdp) Honolulu County	346
Rosemead, CA (city) Los Angeles County	328
Fullerton, CA (city) Orange County	327
Albuquerque, NM (city) Bernalillo County	326
Yorba Linda, CA (city) Orange County	325

Notes: Please refer to the User's Guide for an explanation of data; ranking tables include all places with Asian and/or NHPI populations above SF4 population thresholds; (1) tables reflect only those areas that meet SF4 population thresholds, therefore there may be less than 50 states, 75 counties or 75 places listed

Homeownership

Japanese Who Own Their Own Homes

All States, Top 75 Counties, and Top 75 Places Sorted by Percent[1]

State	Percent
Wyoming	83.64
Hawaii	76.36
Alaska	75.61
Idaho	75.00
Utah	73.47
New Mexico	68.65
Delaware	68.18
Colorado	66.93
California	64.12
Washington	63.67
Vermont	61.67
United States	60.84
Nevada	60.64
Florida	58.05
Arizona	57.18
Oregon	56.40
Montana	56.35
South Carolina	56.29
Rhode Island	55.88
Arkansas	55.69
Maine	52.91
Alabama	51.78
Missouri	51.09
Maryland	49.63
Kansas	49.49
Virginia	49.37
Illinois	48.37
North Carolina	48.11
Minnesota	47.29
Oklahoma	47.00
Mississippi	46.11
Ohio	45.07
Wisconsin	44.77
Georgia	44.53
Nebraska	43.91
Texas	43.42
Louisiana	42.55
South Dakota	39.85
Iowa	39.25
New Jersey	38.36
Pennsylvania	38.17
Connecticut	37.34
Indiana	36.63
Michigan	36.20
New Hampshire	35.56
West Virginia	34.06
Tennessee	33.40
Kentucky	31.73
Massachusetts	23.47
New York	22.93
District of Columbia	19.46

County	Percent
Weber County, UT	96.89
El Dorado County, CA	89.31
Malheur County, OR	88.60
Davis County, UT	84.64
Kitsap County, WA	82.37
Ada County, ID	81.23
Adams County, CO	80.81
San Joaquin County, CA	80.73
Hawaii County, HI	80.72
Kauai County, HI	80.25
Merced County, CA	79.91
Contra Costa County, CA	79.35
Anchorage Borough, AK	79.04
Jefferson County, CO	78.64
Onslow County, NC	78.50
Sacramento County, CA	78.25
Maui County, HI	78.17
Placer County, CA	77.84
Palm Beach County, FL	77.38
Clackamas County, OR	77.28
Ventura County, CA	77.10
Fresno County, CA	76.29
Sutter County, CA	75.41
Honolulu County, HI	75.37
Pierce County, WA	75.31
Riverside County, CA	75.14
Tulare County, CA	74.93
Canyon County, ID	74.83
Sonoma County, CA	74.21
Stanislaus County, CA	72.81
Arapahoe County, CO	72.58
Monterey County, CA	72.33
Monmouth County, NJ	71.92
Santa Cruz County, CA	70.90
San Bernardino County, CA	70.62
Salt Lake County, UT	70.53
Orange County, CA	70.19
Cumberland County, NC	70.00
Broward County, FL	69.27
Snohomish County, WA	68.87
Solano County, CA	68.69
Anne Arundel County, MD	68.64
Kern County, CA	68.35
Montgomery County, PA	68.13
El Paso County, CO	67.74
Suffolk County, NY	67.67
Prince William County, VA	67.48
Burlington County, NJ	67.35
Marin County, CA	67.20
Bernalillo County, NM	67.12
Napa County, CA	66.67
Jefferson County, KY	66.10
Duval County, FL	64.97
Larimer County, CO	64.89
Thurston County, WA	63.73
Alameda County, CA	63.40
Clark County, NV	62.97
Maricopa County, AZ	62.85
Lake County, IL	62.67
King County, WA	62.57
Santa Clara County, CA	62.49
San Mateo County, CA	61.87
Los Angeles County, CA	61.52
Fairfax County, VA	61.27
Bell County, TX	60.45
Boulder County, CO	60.45
Santa Barbara County, CA	60.28
Spokane County, WA	60.16
Yolo County, CA	60.04
San Luis Obispo County, CA	59.49
Weld County, CO	59.36
New Castle County, DE	58.82
Island County, WA	57.89
Virginia Beach Independent City, VA	57.79
Hillsborough County, FL	56.72

Place	Percent
Heeia, HI (cdp) Honolulu County	100.00
Kekaha, HI (cdp) Kauai County	96.97
Paukaa, HI (cdp) Hawaii County	96.83
La Canada Flintridge, CA (city) Los Angeles County	96.67
Paia, HI (cdp) Maui County	96.39
Mililani Town, HI (cdp) Honolulu County	96.11
Maunawili, HI (cdp) Honolulu County	95.72
Cerritos, CA (city) Los Angeles County	95.57
Bryn Mawr-Skyway, WA (cdp) King County	95.11
La Palma, CA (city) Orange County	95.00
Village Park, HI (cdp) Honolulu County	94.72
South San Gabriel, CA (cdp) Los Angeles County	94.46
Carson, CA (city) Los Angeles County	94.24
Yorba Linda, CA (city) Orange County	94.20
Elk Grove, CA (cdp) Sacramento County	93.99
Lawai, HI (cdp) Kauai County	93.97
Sunrise Manor, NV (cdp) Clark County	93.71
Aiea, HI (cdp) Honolulu County	93.30
Ewa Beach, HI (cdp) Honolulu County	93.25
San Ramon, CA (city) Contra Costa County	93.09
Halawa, HI (cdp) Honolulu County	93.06
Mission Viejo, CA (city) Orange County	92.87
Moreno Valley, CA (city) Riverside County	92.18
Ahuimanu, HI (cdp) Honolulu County	92.16
Laguna, CA (cdp) Sacramento County	91.70
Waikapu, HI (cdp) Maui County	90.99
Hacienda Heights, CA (cdp) Los Angeles County	90.96
Hawaiian Beaches, HI (cdp) Hawaii County	90.80
Kailua, HI (cdp) Honolulu County	90.37
Waianae, HI (cdp) Honolulu County	90.29
Pahoa, HI (cdp) Hawaii County	90.00
Pukalani, HI (cdp) Maui County	89.98
Eleele, HI (cdp) Kauai County	89.93
Ewa Gentry, HI (cdp) Honolulu County	89.88
Corona, CA (city) Riverside County	89.67
Chino Hills, CA (city) San Bernardino County	89.27
Makakilo City, HI (cdp) Honolulu County	89.18
Lahaina, HI (cdp) Maui County	88.65
Pearl City, HI (cdp) Honolulu County	88.52
Pacifica, CA (city) San Mateo County	88.44
Westminster, CA (city) Orange County	88.21
Wainaku, HI (cdp) Hawaii County	88.12
Waihee-Waiehu, HI (cdp) Maui County	88.11
Pahala, HI (cdp) Hawaii County	87.95
Pepeekeo, HI (cdp) Hawaii County	87.93
Walnut, CA (city) Los Angeles County	87.86
Wailua Homesteads, HI (cdp) Kauai County	87.85
Fountain Valley, CA (city) Orange County	87.79
Waialua, HI (cdp) Honolulu County	87.77
Kaneohe, HI (cdp) Honolulu County	87.74
Placentia, CA (city) Orange County	87.20
Waimalu, HI (cdp) Honolulu County	87.08
Keaau, HI (cdp) Hawaii County	87.04
Waipio, HI (cdp) Honolulu County	86.50
Montebello, CA (city) Los Angeles County	86.39
Waipio Acres, HI (cdp) Honolulu County	86.35
Manhattan Beach, CA (city) Los Angeles County	86.30
Union City, CA (city) Alameda County	86.29
Cypress, CA (city) Orange County	86.07
Lakewood, WA (city) Pierce County	85.80
Kalaoa, HI (cdp) Hawaii County	85.65
Kapaa, HI (cdp) Kauai County	85.62
Santa Clarita, CA (city) Los Angeles County	85.06
Temple City, CA (city) Los Angeles County	84.98
Palos Verdes Estates, CA (city) Los Angeles County	84.65
Holualoa, HI (cdp) Hawaii County	84.58
Watsonville, CA (city) Santa Cruz County	84.43
Monterey Park, CA (city) Los Angeles County	84.20
Altadena, CA (cdp) Los Angeles County	84.07
West Carson, CA (cdp) Los Angeles County	84.02
Captain Cook, HI (cdp) Hawaii County	84.00
Honaunau-Napoopoo, HI (cdp) Hawaii County	83.96
Santa Maria, CA (city) Santa Barbara County	83.95
Papaikou, HI (cdp) Hawaii County	83.87
Castro Valley, CA (cdp) Alameda County	83.84

Notes: Please refer to the User's Guide for an explanation of data; ranking tables include all places with Asian and/or NHPI populations above SF4 population thresholds; (1) tables reflect only those areas that meet SF4 population thresholds, therefore there may be less than 50 states, 75 counties or 75 places listed

Homeownership

Koreans Who Own Their Own Homes

All States, Top 75 Counties, and Top 75 Places Sorted by Number[1]

State	Number
United States	134,736
California	43,876
New York	10,011
Illinois	8,143
New Jersey	7,936
Virginia	7,224
Washington	6,780
Maryland	6,361
Texas	5,928
Pennsylvania	4,311
Georgia	4,160
Hawaii	3,864
Florida	2,661
Colorado	2,260
Michigan	2,041
Massachusetts	1,622
Ohio	1,621
North Carolina	1,588
Oregon	1,536
Arizona	1,192
Nevada	1,171
Minnesota	1,024
Indiana	854
Tennessee	785
Connecticut	761
Missouri	721
Oklahoma	620
Alaska	547
Wisconsin	521
Kansas	502
Alabama	472
South Carolina	460
Kentucky	441
Louisiana	344
Utah	302
Iowa	256
Delaware	223
New Hampshire	205
Arkansas	201
New Mexico	187
Rhode Island	185
Nebraska	163
Idaho	137
District of Columbia	102
Mississippi	91
West Virginia	82
Maine	63
Montana	53
South Dakota	47
North Dakota	37
Wyoming	36
Vermont	28

County	Number
Los Angeles County, CA	21,280
Orange County, CA	8,543
Cook County, IL	5,623
Fairfax County, VA	5,014
Queens County, NY	4,006
Bergen County, NJ	3,988
Honolulu County, HI	3,503
Montgomery County, MD	3,050
Santa Clara County, CA	2,806
King County, WA	2,776
Alameda County, CA	2,036
Pierce County, WA	1,699
Gwinnett County, GA	1,615
Montgomery County, PA	1,470
San Diego County, CA	1,422
Nassau County, NY	1,382
Snohomish County, WA	1,317
Harris County, TX	1,303
San Bernardino County, CA	1,290
Dallas County, TX	1,130
Clark County, NV	1,049
Howard County, MD	951
New York County, NY	919
Lake County, IL	883
DuPage County, IL	843
Riverside County, CA	832
Contra Costa County, CA	816
Baltimore County, MD	796
Oakland County, MI	788
Maricopa County, AZ	764
Arapahoe County, CO	715
Sacramento County, CA	713
San Mateo County, CA	705
Philadelphia County, PA	698
Middlesex County, NJ	666
Westchester County, NY	666
San Francisco County, CA	664
Fulton County, GA	652
Washington County, OR	610
Middlesex County, MA	606
Richmond County, NY	577
Prince George's County, MD	553
Cobb County, GA	552
Suffolk County, NY	543
El Paso County, CO	516
Delaware County, PA	508
Essex County, NJ	493
Anne Arundel County, MD	458
Collin County, TX	449
Anchorage Borough, AK	446
Monterey County, CA	443
Hennepin County, MN	438
Ventura County, CA	429
Morris County, NJ	406
Hillsborough County, FL	402
Rockland County, NY	396
Tarrant County, TX	392
Bexar County, TX	365
Mecklenburg County, NC	358
Bucks County, PA	349
Orange County, FL	344
Kings County, NY	342
St. Louis County, MO	331
Multnomah County, OR	328
Hudson County, NJ	325
Denton County, TX	319
Pima County, AZ	319
Camden County, NJ	315
Bell County, TX	312
Broward County, FL	310
DeKalb County, GA	310
Chesterfield County, VA	300
Monmouth County, NJ	295
Burlington County, NJ	290
Washtenaw County, MI	288

Place	Number
Los Angeles, CA (city) Los Angeles County	7,800
New York, NY (city)	6,003
Honolulu, HI (cdp) Honolulu County	2,201
Cerritos, CA (city) Los Angeles County	1,524
Fullerton, CA (city) Orange County	1,474
Glendale, CA (city) Los Angeles County	1,474
San Jose, CA (city) Santa Clara County	1,432
Diamond Bar, CA (city) Los Angeles County	1,148
Irvine, CA (city) Orange County	1,102
Chicago, IL (city) Cook County	1,049
Torrance, CA (city) Los Angeles County	948
Anaheim, CA (city) Orange County	883
Garden Grove, CA (city) Orange County	778
San Diego, CA (city) San Diego County	763
Philadelphia, PA (city) Philadelphia County	698
Fremont, CA (city) Alameda County	687
San Francisco, CA (city) San Francisco County	664
Houston, TX (city) Harris County	658
Burke, VA (cdp) Fairfax County	656
Federal Way, WA (city) King County	581
North Hempstead, NY (town) Nassau County	543
Fort Lee, NJ (borough) Bergen County	535
Tacoma, WA (city) Pierce County	531
Buena Park, CA (city) Orange County	514
Skokie, IL (village) Cook County	513
Downey, CA (city) Los Angeles County	472
La Canada Flintridge, CA (city) Los Angeles County	470
La Mirada, CA (city) Los Angeles County	467
Hacienda Heights, CA (cdp) Los Angeles County	457
La Crescenta-Montrose, CA (cdp) Los Angeles County	444
Glenview, IL (village) Cook County	438
Seattle, WA (city) King County	430
Rowland Heights, CA (cdp) Los Angeles County	423
Ellicott City, MD (cdp) Howard County	421
Northbrook, IL (village) Cook County	413
Oyster Bay, NY (town) Nassau County	406
Rancho Palos Verdes, CA (city) Los Angeles County	402
Bellevue, WA (city) King County	372
Colorado Springs, CO (city) El Paso County	370
Hempstead, NY (town) Nassau County	369
Plano, TX (city) Collin County	363
La Palma, CA (city) Orange County	351
Aurora, CO (city) Arapahoe County	348
Annandale, VA (cdp) Fairfax County	345
Walnut, CA (city) Los Angeles County	345
Hoffman Estates, IL (village) Cook County	342
Gardena, CA (city) Los Angeles County	339
Palisades Park, NJ (borough) Bergen County	337
Centreville, VA (cdp) Fairfax County	310
Dallas, TX (city) Dallas County	307
Chantilly, VA (cdp) Fairfax County	304
Cypress, CA (city) Orange County	304
Lakewood, WA (city) Pierce County	296
Portland, OR (city) Multnomah County	293
Sunnyvale, CA (city) Santa Clara County	289
Norwalk, CA (city) Los Angeles County	287
Potomac, MD (cdp) Montgomery County	285
Huntington Beach, CA (city) Orange County	284
Spring Valley, NV (cdp) Clark County	280
Schaumburg, IL (village) Cook County	271
West Springfield, VA (cdp) Fairfax County	270
Las Vegas, NV (city) Clark County	267
Orange, CA (city) Orange County	265
Chino Hills, CA (city) San Bernardino County	261
El Paso, TX (city) El Paso County	257
North Potomac, MD (cdp) Montgomery County	248
Colesville, MD (cdp) Montgomery County	244
Charlotte, NC (city) Mecklenburg County	242
Arcadia, CA (city) Los Angeles County	240
Corona, CA (city) Riverside County	240
San Antonio, TX (city) Bexar County	240
Buffalo Grove, IL (village) Lake County	234
Mount Prospect, IL (village) Cook County	232
Aspen Hill, MD (cdp) Montgomery County	231
Columbia, MD (cdp) Howard County	230

Notes: Please refer to the User's Guide for an explanation of data; ranking tables include all places with Asian and/or NHPI populations above SF4 population thresholds; (1) tables reflect only those areas that meet SF4 population thresholds, therefore there may be less than 50 states, 75 counties or 75 places listed

Homeownership

Koreans Who Own Their Own Homes

All States, Top 75 Counties, and Top 75 Places Sorted by Percent[1]

State	Percent
Idaho	55.24
Maryland	54.82
South Dakota	54.65
Virginia	52.62
Arkansas	51.54
New Hampshire	50.74
Georgia	50.57
Colorado	50.20
Oklahoma	48.48
Florida	47.95
Kentucky	47.78
Washington	47.50
Nevada	47.16
Alabama	46.50
Illinois	46.32
North Carolina	44.69
Hawaii	43.84
Arizona	43.79
Louisiana	43.77
Kansas	43.46
Pennsylvania	43.10
Texas	42.86
North Dakota	42.53
New Mexico	42.21
New Jersey	41.94
Tennessee	41.49
Delaware	41.45
South Carolina	41.33
Oregon	40.88
West Virginia	40.80
United States	40.08
Connecticut	39.70
California	38.10
Minnesota	38.07
Alaska	37.91
Indiana	37.82
Michigan	37.53
Mississippi	37.45
Ohio	36.90
Montana	36.55
Missouri	36.36
Maine	36.21
Nebraska	35.59
Wyoming	34.29
Utah	32.72
Rhode Island	30.38
Wisconsin	29.40
Massachusetts	28.93
Vermont	28.00
New York	25.63
Iowa	24.88
District of Columbia	19.10

County	Percent
Douglas County, CO	95.11
Columbia County, GA	91.95
Fort Bend County, TX	90.94
Will County, IL	90.87
Washington County, MN	87.38
Waukesha County, WI	83.33
York County, PA	82.61
Ottawa County, MI	81.58
Lake County, IL	79.41
Chesterfield County, VA	77.12
Davis County, UT	75.00
Adams County, CO	74.58
Geary County, KS	73.81
Ada County, ID	73.56
Solano County, CA	73.17
Jefferson Parish, LA	73.10
Williamson County, TX	71.34
Butler County, OH	71.30
Saratoga County, NY	70.97
Dale County, AL	70.59
Chester County, PA	70.26
Kane County, IL	70.18
Berks County, PA	70.15
Loudoun County, VA	70.04
DuPage County, IL	69.84
Cumberland County, PA	69.81
Rockland County, NY	69.35
Jefferson County, CO	68.49
Montgomery County, TN	68.42
Brevard County, FL	67.05
Hawaii County, HI	66.54
Rockingham County, NH	66.29
Burlington County, NJ	65.46
Benton County, WA	65.22
Hardin County, KY	64.63
Atlantic County, NJ	64.15
Genesee County, MI	64.08
Nassau County, NY	64.07
Ventura County, CA	64.03
Montgomery County, MD	63.86
Suffolk County, NY	63.07
Pinellas County, FL	63.00
Sonoma County, CA	62.81
Richmond County, GA	62.55
Lancaster County, PA	62.50
Camden County, NJ	62.01
Litchfield County, CT	62.00
Sarpy County, NE	61.86
Morris County, NJ	61.61
Coryell County, TX	61.26
Essex County, NJ	61.24
Dutchess County, NY	61.08
Monmouth County, NJ	60.33
Miami-Dade County, FL	60.30
Fairfax County, VA	60.18
Bucks County, PA	60.17
Prince William County, VA	60.05
Orange County, NY	60.00
Clark County, WA	59.87
Harford County, MD	59.78
Cochise County, AZ	59.41
Snohomish County, WA	59.27
Newport News Independent City, VA	59.06
Muscogee County, GA	58.94
Comanche County, OK	58.82
Oakland County, MI	58.72
Gwinnett County, GA	58.28
El Paso County, TX	58.14
San Bernardino County, CA	58.03
Baltimore County, MD	57.23
Contra Costa County, CA	57.10
Polk County, IA	57.04
Cobb County, GA	56.85
Anoka County, MN	56.82
Cumberland County, NC	56.76

Place	Percent
Kailua, HI (cdp) Honolulu County	100.00
Lincolnwood, IL (village) Cook County	100.00
Old Tappan, NJ (borough) Bergen County	100.00
Seattle Hill-Silver Firs, WA (cdp) Snohomish County	100.00
Lake Success, NY (village) Nassau County	97.10
Olney, MD (cdp) Montgomery County	95.59
Harrington Park, NJ (borough) Bergen County	94.12
Morton Grove, IL (village) Cook County	93.56
Sugar Land, TX (city) Fort Bend County	93.28
Mililani Town, HI (cdp) Honolulu County	92.14
Glenview, IL (village) Cook County	91.82
Montgomery, PA (township) Montgomery County	91.59
Franconia, VA (cdp) Fairfax County	91.43
Browns Mills, NJ (cdp) Burlington County	90.79
Northbrook, IL (village) Cook County	90.77
Alpine, NJ (borough) Bergen County	90.32
Potomac, MD (cdp) Montgomery County	90.19
North Potomac, MD (cdp) Montgomery County	87.94
Westminster, CO (city) Adams County	87.82
Upper Dublin, PA (township) Montgomery County	87.50
Simi Valley, CA (city) Ventura County	87.39
Placentia, CA (city) Orange County	86.73
Livingston, NJ (township) Essex County	86.47
Buffalo Grove, IL (village) Lake County	86.03
Spanaway, WA (cdp) Pierce County	85.71
Yorba Linda, CA (city) Orange County	85.17
Chantilly, VA (cdp) Fairfax County	84.92
Fairfield, CA (city) Solano County	84.42
Colesville, MD (cdp) Montgomery County	83.56
Whittier, CA (city) Los Angeles County	83.20
Plainview, NY (cdp) Nassau County	83.12
Corona, CA (city) Riverside County	82.19
La Canada Flintridge, CA (city) Los Angeles County	81.88
Syosset, NY (cdp) Nassau County	81.75
Kaneohe, HI (cdp) Honolulu County	81.56
Chino Hills, CA (city) San Bernardino County	81.31
Englewood Cliffs, NJ (borough) Bergen County	81.22
Hoffman Estates, IL (village) Cook County	80.66
Newington, VA (cdp) Fairfax County	79.00
Burke, VA (cdp) Fairfax County	78.56
Naperville, IL (city) Du Page County	78.17
Whitpain, PA (township) Montgomery County	77.59
Wilmette, IL (village) Cook County	77.18
Mission Viejo, CA (city) Orange County	76.79
Arlington Heights, IL (village) Cook County	76.03
Pemberton, NJ (township) Burlington County	75.00
Walnut, CA (city) Los Angeles County	74.84
Mill Creek, WA (city) Snohomish County	74.83
Saratoga, CA (city) Santa Clara County	74.56
Bloomington, MN (city) Hennepin County	74.22
Vernon Hills, IL (village) Lake County	73.94
Clarkstown, NY (town) Rockland County	73.83
West Carson, CA (cdp) Los Angeles County	73.68
Plymouth, MN (city) Hennepin County	73.45
Springfield, VA (cdp) Fairfax County	73.36
Pearl City, HI (cdp) Honolulu County	73.33
Cresskill, NJ (borough) Bergen County	73.23
Smithtown, NY (town) Suffolk County	73.21
Bloomfield, MI (township) Oakland County	73.03
Cherry Hill, NJ (township) Camden County	72.32
Oxnard, CA (city) Ventura County	72.22
Orangetown, NY (town) Rockland County	71.60
Diamond Bar, CA (city) Los Angeles County	71.44
Wayne, NJ (township) Passaic County	71.31
Laguna Niguel, CA (city) Orange County	71.00
Pleasanton, CA (city) Alameda County	70.92
Hamilton, NJ (township) Mercer County	70.59
North Springfield, VA (cdp) Fairfax County	70.40
Calverton, MD (cdp) Montgomery County	70.30
West Bloomfield, MI (township) Oakland County	70.00
Hilo, HI (cdp) Hawaii County	69.78
Greenburgh, NY (town) Westchester County	69.61
Lakewood, CO (city) Jefferson County	69.30
Lake Forest, CA (city) Orange County	69.12
Temple City, CA (city) Los Angeles County	68.97

Notes: Please refer to the User's Guide for an explanation of data; ranking tables include all places with Asian and/or NHPI populations above SF4 population thresholds; (1) tables reflect only those areas that meet SF4 population thresholds, therefore there may be less than 50 states, 75 counties or 75 places listed

Homeownership

Laotians Who Own Their Own Homes

***All States, Top 75 Counties, and Top 75 Places Sorted by Number*[1]**

State	Number
United States	20,717
California	3,701
Texas	1,647
Minnesota	1,273
Washington	1,086
Illinois	907
Georgia	848
Tennessee	822
Florida	766
Iowa	647
North Carolina	612
Kansas	584
Oregon	559
Arkansas	541
Virginia	534
Wisconsin	482
Ohio	468
Connecticut	455
Michigan	450
New York	397
Utah	366
Pennsylvania	365
Massachusetts	357
Rhode Island	296
Colorado	276
South Carolina	248
Louisiana	233
Nevada	210
Oklahoma	185
Indiana	184
Nebraska	167
Missouri	153
Alabama	144
Arizona	141
Maryland	122
Idaho	113
Alaska	80
Hawaii	65
New Hampshire	33
New Jersey	32
South Dakota	24

County	Number
Hennepin County, MN	702
San Diego County, CA	664
Sacramento County, CA	583
King County, WA	581
Tarrant County, TX	531
Multnomah County, OR	404
Rutherford County, TN	367
Dallas County, TX	362
Pinellas County, FL	328
Orange County, CA	306
Salt Lake County, UT	292
Providence County, RI	282
Fairfax County, VA	267
Davidson County, TN	264
Gwinnett County, GA	263
Winnebago County, IL	263
Milwaukee County, WI	259
Sebastian County, AR	256
Polk County, IA	254
Contra Costa County, CA	248
Santa Clara County, CA	245
Clayton County, GA	243
Cook County, IL	240
Harris County, TX	238
Ottawa County, MI	231
Riverside County, CA	227
Los Angeles County, CA	225
Fresno County, CA	214
Sedgwick County, KS	212
Clark County, NV	210
Potter County, TX	207
Philadelphia County, PA	186
Alameda County, CA	181
Franklin County, OH	178
Monroe County, NY	177
Fairfield County, CT	163
Hartford County, CT	161
Middlesex County, MA	161
Kane County, IL	152
Summit County, OH	135
Worcester County, MA	135
Adams County, CO	129
Mecklenburg County, NC	125
Oklahoma County, OK	125
Snohomish County, WA	120
Dakota County, MN	119
Iberia Parish, LA	117
Jefferson County, CO	116
Spartanburg County, SC	107
Stanislaus County, CA	104
San Joaquin County, CA	99
Maricopa County, AZ	98
Tulare County, CA	98
Cowley County, KS	96
Sonoma County, CA	92
Washington County, OR	91
Shasta County, CA	89
Polk County, FL	86
Ramsey County, MN	86
Johnson County, KS	84
Habersham County, GA	83
Washington County, AR	82
Buena Vista County, IA	80
Pierce County, WA	79
Clark County, WA	74
Guilford County, NC	72
Anchorage Borough, AK	71
Bexar County, TX	70
Franklin County, WA	67
New Haven County, CT	64
Mobile County, AL	57
Honolulu County, HI	56
Merced County, CA	56
Montgomery County, NC	56
Pacific County, WA	54

Place	Number
San Diego, CA (city) San Diego County	529
Sacramento, CA (city) Sacramento County	386
Portland, OR (city) Multnomah County	359
Brooklyn Park, MN (city) Hennepin County	274
Seattle, WA (city) King County	268
Nashville-Davidson, TN (sp. city) Davidson County	264
Fort Smith, AR (city) Sebastian County	244
San Jose, CA (city) Santa Clara County	226
St. Petersburg, FL (city) Pinellas County	219
Milwaukee, WI (city) Milwaukee County	216
Des Moines, IA (city) Polk County	214
Minneapolis, MN (city) Hennepin County	213
Amarillo, TX (city) Potter County	204
Rockford, IL (city) Winnebago County	193
Philadelphia, PA (city) Philadelphia County	186
Wichita, KS (city) Sedgwick County	158
Fresno, CA (city) Fresno County	155
Columbus, OH (city) Franklin County	151
Richmond, CA (city) Contra Costa County	146
Murfreesboro, TN (city) Rutherford County	143
Haltom City, TX (city) Tarrant County	139
Elgin, IL (city) Kane County	137
Dallas, TX (city) Dallas County	131
Providence, RI (city) Providence County	124
Rochester, NY (city) Monroe County	122
Charlotte, NC (city) Mecklenburg County	117
Oklahoma City, OK (city) Oklahoma County	117
Lowell, MA (city) Middlesex County	112
Santa Ana, CA (city) Orange County	108
Akron, OH (city) Summit County	96
Winfield, KS (city) Cowley County	96
Fort Worth, TX (city) Tarrant County	93
Anaheim, CA (city) Orange County	92
Stockton, CA (city) San Joaquin County	90
Westminster, CO (city) Adams County	90
Visalia, CA (city) Tulare County	88
West Valley City, UT (city) Salt Lake County	88
Springfield, VA (cdp) Fairfax County	81
St. Paul, MN (city) Ramsey County	77
Storm Lake, IA (city) Buena Vista County	76
Woonsocket, RI (city) Providence County	76
Riverside, CA (city) Riverside County	74
Bridgeport, CT (city) Fairfield County	72
Escondido, CA (city) San Diego County	69
Irving, TX (city) Dallas County	68
Moreno Valley, CA (city) Riverside County	67
Bellevue, WA (city) King County	62
Oakland, CA (city) Alameda County	62
San Pablo, CA (city) Contra Costa County	62
Redding, CA (city) Shasta County	59
Brooklyn Center, MN (city) Hennepin County	58
Tacoma, WA (city) Pierce County	58
Grand Prairie, TX (city) Dallas County	57
Springdale, AR (city) Washington County	56
Arvada, CO (city) Jefferson County	55
New Britain, CT (city) Hartford County	49
Fitchburg, MA (city) Worcester County	48
Santa Rosa, CA (city) Sonoma County	46
Merced, CA (city) Merced County	43
Modesto, CA (city) Stanislaus County	43
Oaklawn-Sunview, KS (cdp) Sedgwick County	41
Pomona, CA (city) Los Angeles County	37
Raymond, WA (city) Pacific County	37
Banning, CA (city) Riverside County	30
Parkway-S. Sacramento, CA (cdp) Sacramento County	30
Rochester, MN (city) Olmsted County	29
Worthington, MN (city) Nobles County	25
Warroad, MN (city) Roseau County	20
Green Bay, WI (city) Brown County	19
Long Beach, CA (city) Los Angeles County	16
Los Angeles, CA (city) Los Angeles County	14
Fairfield, CA (city) Solano County	13
Honolulu, HI (cdp) Honolulu County	12

Notes: Please refer to the User's Guide for an explanation of data; ranking tables include all places with Asian and/or NHPI populations above SF4 population thresholds; (1) tables reflect only those areas that meet SF4 population thresholds, therefore there may be less than 50 states, 75 counties or 75 places listed

Homeownership

Laotians Who Own Their Own Homes

All States, Top 75 Counties, and Top 75 Places Sorted by Percent[1]

State	Percent
Idaho	88.98
Louisiana	85.35
South Carolina	77.74
Nevada	75.54
Oklahoma	75.51
Illinois	74.34
Nebraska	73.89
Tennessee	73.66
Missouri	71.50
Kansas	71.05
Arkansas	70.17
Georgia	69.91
Florida	68.82
Michigan	68.70
Alabama	68.57
Virginia	66.92
Utah	66.55
Indiana	66.43
Texas	65.02
Pennsylvania	64.15
Iowa	64.12
Minnesota	61.03
Ohio	61.02
Oregon	60.96
Maryland	60.40
Arizona	60.00
Connecticut	56.45
Wisconsin	55.21
North Carolina	55.18
Washington	53.79
United States	52.37
Colorado	52.27
New York	49.38
South Dakota	42.86
Massachusetts	40.48
Rhode Island	39.05
New Hampshire	35.11
California	31.73
Alaska	26.85
New Jersey	26.67
Hawaii	14.71

County	Percent
Polk County, FL	100.00
Franklin County, WA	89.33
Gwinnett County, GA	89.15
Roseau County, MN	85.11
Iberia Parish, LA	84.78
Clayton County, GA	81.82
Dakota County, NE	81.54
Oklahoma County, OK	81.17
Ottawa County, MI	79.11
Montgomery County, NC	78.87
Rutherford County, TN	78.59
Sedgwick County, KS	77.94
Summit County, OH	77.59
Winnebago County, IL	77.13
Davidson County, TN	76.30
Clark County, NV	75.54
Dakota County, MN	74.84
Cowley County, KS	74.42
Cook County, IL	73.85
Habersham County, GA	73.45
Fairfax County, VA	72.95
Potter County, TX	72.38
Spartanburg County, SC	72.30
Pierce County, WA	71.82
Pinellas County, FL	71.62
Salt Lake County, UT	71.39
Sebastian County, AR	70.72
Harris County, TX	70.62
Tarrant County, TX	70.52
Mobile County, AL	68.67
Clark County, WA	66.07
Polk County, IA	65.97
Hennepin County, MN	65.92
Cass County, MI	65.63
Bexar County, TX	65.42
Kane County, IL	64.96
Multnomah County, OR	63.22
Fairfield County, CT	61.28
Riverside County, CA	60.70
Milwaukee County, WI	60.51
Philadelphia County, PA	60.39
Santa Clara County, CA	60.05
Maricopa County, AZ	59.76
Snohomish County, WA	59.70
Dallas County, TX	59.64
Jefferson County, CO	58.59
Guilford County, NC	57.60
Burke County, NC	57.53
Buena Vista County, IA	55.94
Adams County, CO	55.36
Orange County, CA	54.84
Pacific County, WA	54.00
Washington County, OR	53.53
Franklin County, OH	52.51
Hartford County, CT	52.44
Essex County, MA	51.56
New Haven County, CT	51.20
Washington County, AR	50.93
Johnson County, KS	50.91
Monroe County, NY	49.72
Worcester County, MA	48.91
Mecklenburg County, NC	48.83
King County, WA	48.30
San Bernardino County, CA	47.12
Ramsey County, MN	45.50
San Diego County, CA	41.24
Nobles County, MN	41.18
Providence County, RI	39.06
Sonoma County, CA	38.17
Middlesex County, MA	38.06
Broome County, NY	37.88
Butte County, CA	33.96
Sacramento County, CA	33.76
Shasta County, CA	33.33
Catawba County, NC	32.95

Place	Percent
Springfield, VA (cdp) Fairfax County	91.01
Brooklyn Park, MN (city) Hennepin County	86.71
Akron, OH (city) Summit County	86.49
Wichita, KS (city) Sedgwick County	83.16
Oklahoma City, OK (city) Oklahoma County	82.98
Brooklyn Center, MN (city) Hennepin County	81.69
St. Petersburg, FL (city) Pinellas County	79.64
Grand Prairie, TX (city) Dallas County	79.17
Rockford, IL (city) Winnebago County	76.59
Nashville-Davidson, TN (sp. city) Davidson County	76.30
Winfield, KS (city) Cowley County	76.19
Warroad, MN (city) Roseau County	74.07
Elgin, IL (city) Kane County	73.26
Amarillo, TX (city) Potter County	72.08
Des Moines, IA (city) Polk County	71.81
Haltom City, TX (city) Tarrant County	71.65
Riverside, CA (city) Riverside County	70.48
Fort Smith, AR (city) Sebastian County	69.71
Tacoma, WA (city) Pierce County	68.24
Fort Worth, TX (city) Tarrant County	65.96
Portland, OR (city) Multnomah County	65.27
West Valley City, UT (city) Salt Lake County	64.23
Rochester, NY (city) Monroe County	64.21
Murfreesboro, TN (city) Rutherford County	63.84
Bellevue, WA (city) King County	63.27
Milwaukee, WI (city) Milwaukee County	61.02
San Jose, CA (city) Santa Clara County	60.59
Arvada, CO (city) Jefferson County	60.44
Philadelphia, PA (city) Philadelphia County	60.39
Santa Ana, CA (city) Orange County	59.67
Oaklawn-Sunview, KS (cdp) Sedgwick County	59.42
Escondido, CA (city) San Diego County	58.97
Storm Lake, IA (city) Buena Vista County	58.02
Westminster, CO (city) Adams County	56.96
Anaheim, CA (city) Orange County	55.42
Bridgeport, CT (city) Fairfield County	54.55
Dallas, TX (city) Dallas County	52.61
Moreno Valley, CA (city) Riverside County	51.94
Columbus, OH (city) Franklin County	50.50
Minneapolis, MN (city) Hennepin County	50.47
Springdale, AR (city) Washington County	48.70
Irving, TX (city) Dallas County	47.89
Charlotte, NC (city) Mecklenburg County	47.18
New Britain, CT (city) Hartford County	47.12
Raymond, WA (city) Pacific County	46.84
Fitchburg, MA (city) Worcester County	46.60
St. Paul, MN (city) Ramsey County	45.29
Banning, CA (city) Riverside County	42.86
Seattle, WA (city) King County	42.61
Worthington, MN (city) Nobles County	42.37
San Diego, CA (city) San Diego County	38.98
Sacramento, CA (city) Sacramento County	34.93
Providence, RI (city) Providence County	34.54
Pomona, CA (city) Los Angeles County	33.94
Santa Rosa, CA (city) Sonoma County	32.62
Lowell, MA (city) Middlesex County	32.18
Richmond, CA (city) Contra Costa County	31.67
Green Bay, WI (city) Brown County	28.79
Woonsocket, RI (city) Providence County	27.94
Redding, CA (city) Shasta County	27.31
Rochester, MN (city) Olmsted County	27.10
San Pablo, CA (city) Contra Costa County	27.07
Visalia, CA (city) Tulare County	25.00
Modesto, CA (city) Stanislaus County	17.27
Merced, CA (city) Merced County	15.99
Stockton, CA (city) San Joaquin County	14.22
Fresno, CA (city) Fresno County	13.23
Oakland, CA (city) Alameda County	12.97
Fairfield, CA (city) Solano County	12.62
Parkway-S. Sacramento, CA (cdp) Sacramento County	11.63
Long Beach, CA (city) Los Angeles County	10.46
Los Angeles, CA (city) Los Angeles County	7.37
Honolulu, HI (cdp) Honolulu County	4.27

Notes: Please refer to the User's Guide for an explanation of data; ranking tables include all places with Asian and/or NHPI populations above SF4 population thresholds; (1) tables reflect only those areas that meet SF4 population thresholds, therefore there may be less than 50 states, 75 counties or 75 places listed

Homeownership

Malaysians Who Own Their Own Homes

All States, Top 75 Counties, and Top 75 Places Sorted by Number[1]

State	Number
United States	1,092
California	248
New York	108
Texas	82
Ohio	50
Oklahoma	38
Michigan	35
Illinois	27

County	Number
Queens County, NY	49
Los Angeles County, CA	40

Place	Number
New York, NY (city)	86

Notes: Please refer to the User's Guide for an explanation of data; ranking tables include all places with Asian and/or NHPI populations above SF4 population thresholds; (1) tables reflect only those areas that meet SF4 population thresholds, therefore there may be less than 50 states, 75 counties or 75 places listed

Homeownership

Malaysians Who Own Their Own Homes

All States, Top 75 Counties, and Top 75 Places Sorted by Percent[1]

State	Percent
California	45.67
Ohio	43.10
Texas	36.28
United States	29.70
New York	20.89
Michigan	19.89
Oklahoma	18.10
Illinois	14.44

County	Percent
Los Angeles County, CA	26.14
Queens County, NY	24.02

Place	Percent
New York, NY (city)	18.45

Notes: Please refer to the User's Guide for an explanation of data; ranking tables include all places with Asian and/or NHPI populations above SF4 population thresholds; (1) tables reflect only those areas that meet SF4 population thresholds, therefore there may be less than 50 states, 75 counties or 75 places listed

Homeownership

Pakistanis Who Own Their Own Homes

All States, Top 75 Counties, and Top 75 Places Sorted by Number[1]

State	Number
United States	17,306
California	2,589
New York	2,146
Texas	2,090
Illinois	1,867
New Jersey	1,540
Virginia	1,202
Florida	905
Maryland	692
Michigan	643
Georgia	419
Pennsylvania	362
North Carolina	236
Connecticut	233
Ohio	190
Washington	181
Massachusetts	170
Minnesota	156
Tennessee	121
Indiana	117
Oklahoma	108
Arizona	98
Missouri	98
Louisiana	97
Kentucky	95
Kansas	94
Oregon	91
Colorado	89
Delaware	65
Nevada	65
Wisconsin	65
Alabama	64
Utah	56
Iowa	48
West Virginia	44

County	Number
Cook County, IL	1,020
Fairfax County, VA	775
Harris County, TX	637
Queens County, NY	623
Los Angeles County, CA	478
DuPage County, IL	477
Fort Bend County, TX	451
Middlesex County, NJ	438
Nassau County, NY	388
Santa Clara County, CA	378
Orange County, CA	374
Dallas County, TX	355
Montgomery County, MD	314
Kings County, NY	293
Alameda County, CA	283
Wayne County, MI	261
Suffolk County, NY	259
Bergen County, NJ	193
Hudson County, NJ	185
Sacramento County, CA	182
Miami-Dade County, FL	166
Orange County, FL	153
Oakland County, MI	152
Gwinnett County, GA	151
San Bernardino County, CA	149
Prince William County, VA	147
Broward County, FL	135
San Joaquin County, CA	132
Collin County, TX	123
Tarrant County, TX	123
Mercer County, NJ	114
Denton County, TX	105
Baltimore County, MD	103
Lake County, IL	102
Somerset County, NJ	100
Howard County, MD	98
Loudoun County, VA	97
Richmond County, NY	93
Macomb County, MI	84
San Diego County, CA	83
Cobb County, GA	81
Westchester County, NY	79
Morris County, NJ	78
Wake County, NC	78
Contra Costa County, CA	74
Delaware County, PA	74
Snohomish County, WA	73
Riverside County, CA	71
Hartford County, CT	69
New Haven County, CT	68
Philadelphia County, PA	68
Camden County, NJ	67
Essex County, NJ	66
King County, WA	66
Tulsa County, OK	65
Will County, IL	65
Maricopa County, AZ	63
Franklin County, OH	61
Travis County, TX	57
New York County, NY	55
Atlantic County, NJ	54
Washtenaw County, MI	53
Fairfield County, CT	48
Jefferson Parish, LA	46
Monmouth County, NJ	45
Prince George's County, MD	45
San Francisco County, CA	44
Hennepin County, MN	42
Union County, NJ	38
Worcester County, MA	38
Arlington County, VA	36
Bronx County, NY	31
Monroe County, NY	31
St. Louis County, MO	28
Milwaukee County, WI	27

Place	Number
New York, NY (city)	1,095
Chicago, IL (city) Cook County	409
Houston, TX (city) Harris County	291
Hempstead, NY (town) Nassau County	219
Fremont, CA (city) Alameda County	179
San Jose, CA (city) Santa Clara County	152
Jersey City, NJ (city) Hudson County	138
Los Angeles, CA (city) Los Angeles County	134
Carrollton, TX (city) Denton County	129
North Hempstead, NY (town) Nassau County	124
Sugar Land, TX (city) Fort Bend County	119
Garland, TX (city) Dallas County	117
Edison, NJ (township) Middlesex County	105
Plano, TX (city) Collin County	83
Sacramento, CA (city) Sacramento County	80
Brookhaven, NY (town) Suffolk County	75
Skokie, IL (village) Cook County	73
Huntington, NY (town) Suffolk County	71
Dale City, VA (cdp) Prince William County	70
Philadelphia, PA (city) Philadelphia County	68
Old Bridge, NJ (township) Middlesex County	65
Stockton, CA (city) San Joaquin County	64
Mission Bend, TX (cdp) Fort Bend County	61
Ellicott City, MD (cdp) Howard County	58
Anaheim, CA (city) Orange County	55
Richardson, TX (city) Dallas County	53
Woodbridge, NJ (township) Middlesex County	53
San Francisco, CA (city) San Francisco County	44
Tulsa, OK (city) Tulsa County	44
Dallas, TX (city) Dallas County	42
Torrance, CA (city) Los Angeles County	41
Irving, TX (city) Dallas County	38
Arlington, VA (cdp) Arlington County	36
Santa Clara, CA (city) Santa Clara County	34
Austin, TX (city) Travis County	33
Bailey's Crossroads, VA (cdp) Fairfax County	7
Lincolnia, VA (cdp) Fairfax County	4

Notes: Please refer to the User's Guide for an explanation of data; ranking tables include all places with Asian and/or NHPI populations above SF4 population thresholds; (1) tables reflect only those areas that meet SF4 population thresholds, therefore there may be less than 50 states, 75 counties or 75 places listed

Homeownership

Pakistanis Who Own Their Own Homes

All States, Top 75 Counties, and Top 75 Places Sorted by Percent[1]

State	Percent
Oregon	72.22
Tennessee	65.76
Utah	63.64
Indiana	63.59
Delaware	59.09
Florida	55.62
Alabama	52.89
Maryland	52.74
Kentucky	52.20
Michigan	50.83
New Jersey	50.05
Virginia	49.59
California	49.06
Minnesota	47.13
Illinois	44.96
West Virginia	44.44
Nevada	44.22
Iowa	44.04
Pennsylvania	43.83
Washington	43.30
North Carolina	42.52
United States	41.65
Colorado	41.01
Georgia	40.84
Arizona	40.50
Texas	39.34
Ohio	38.00
Connecticut	35.74
Kansas	34.43
Massachusetts	30.14
Oklahoma	29.51
Louisiana	29.22
New York	26.97
Missouri	26.70
Wisconsin	19.58

County	Percent
Will County, IL	84.42
Fort Bend County, TX	78.30
Prince William County, VA	76.96
Nassau County, NY	75.05
Lake County, IL	73.38
San Bernardino County, CA	73.04
Montgomery County, MD	70.09
DuPage County, IL	69.74
Howard County, MD	68.06
Macomb County, MI	67.20
Loudoun County, VA	66.44
Suffolk County, NY	64.27
Mercer County, NJ	62.64
Camden County, NJ	62.62
Richmond County, NY	60.78
Denton County, TX	60.69
Orange County, FL	59.53
Orange County, CA	57.10
Middlesex County, NJ	56.81
Sacramento County, CA	56.35
Riverside County, CA	55.91
Miami-Dade County, FL	55.33
Fairfax County, VA	54.89
Gwinnett County, GA	54.32
Union County, NJ	53.52
Oakland County, MI	53.33
Somerset County, NJ	52.36
Santa Clara County, CA	52.21
Snohomish County, WA	52.14
Wake County, NC	51.66
Bergen County, NJ	51.19
Wayne County, MI	50.98
Cobb County, GA	50.94
Alameda County, CA	49.82
Delaware County, PA	48.68
San Joaquin County, CA	48.35
San Diego County, CA	47.16
Morris County, NJ	46.99
Franklin County, OH	45.52
Washtenaw County, MI	45.30
Collin County, TX	44.09
Monmouth County, NJ	43.69
Tulsa County, OK	42.21
Philadelphia County, PA	41.46
Worcester County, MA	40.43
Broward County, FL	40.42
Westchester County, NY	39.70
New Haven County, CT	38.42
Essex County, NJ	38.15
Tarrant County, TX	37.85
Contra Costa County, CA	37.76
Los Angeles County, CA	35.94
King County, WA	35.68
Maricopa County, AZ	35.59
Hudson County, NJ	35.58
Baltimore County, MD	35.40
Cook County, IL	35.40
Hennepin County, MN	33.87
Dallas County, TX	33.65
Atlantic County, NJ	31.40
Fairfield County, CT	30.77
Hartford County, CT	30.53
San Francisco County, CA	29.93
Harris County, TX	29.70
Jefferson Parish, LA	27.71
Monroe County, NY	26.50
Prince George's County, MD	25.42
Travis County, TX	23.55
Queens County, NY	22.08
Clayton County, GA	21.82
Guilford County, NC	20.93
Arlington County, VA	20.57
Milwaukee County, WI	17.65
St. Louis County, MO	16.57
Alexandria Independent City, VA	14.88

Place	Percent
Dale City, VA (cdp) Prince William County	90.91
North Hempstead, NY (town) Nassau County	79.49
Huntington, NY (town) Suffolk County	76.34
Sugar Land, TX (city) Fort Bend County	76.28
Hempstead, NY (town) Nassau County	75.78
Skokie, IL (village) Cook County	75.26
Mission Bend, TX (cdp) Fort Bend County	70.93
Garland, TX (city) Dallas County	65.00
Ellicott City, MD (cdp) Howard County	64.44
Old Bridge, NJ (township) Middlesex County	59.63
Fremont, CA (city) Alameda County	56.83
Edison, NJ (township) Middlesex County	56.76
Woodbridge, NJ (township) Middlesex County	54.08
Anaheim, CA (city) Orange County	53.40
Plano, TX (city) Collin County	52.53
San Jose, CA (city) Santa Clara County	51.01
Brookhaven, NY (town) Suffolk County	49.67
Sacramento, CA (city) Sacramento County	45.98
Carrollton, TX (city) Denton County	45.10
Stockton, CA (city) San Joaquin County	43.54
Philadelphia, PA (city) Philadelphia County	41.46
Richardson, TX (city) Dallas County	36.81
Santa Clara, CA (city) Santa Clara County	33.66
Tulsa, OK (city) Tulsa County	33.08
Jersey City, NJ (city) Hudson County	32.78
Los Angeles, CA (city) Los Angeles County	31.02
San Francisco, CA (city) San Francisco County	29.93
Irving, TX (city) Dallas County	25.50
Torrance, CA (city) Los Angeles County	24.26
Chicago, IL (city) Cook County	21.27
Arlington, VA (cdp) Arlington County	20.57
Houston, TX (city) Harris County	19.76
Austin, TX (city) Travis County	18.97
New York, NY (city)	18.29
Dallas, TX (city) Dallas County	12.14
Bailey's Crossroads, VA (cdp) Fairfax County	8.05
Lincolnia, VA (cdp) Fairfax County	2.76

Notes: Please refer to the User's Guide for an explanation of data; ranking tables include all places with Asian and/or NHPI populations above SF4 population thresholds; (1) tables reflect only those areas that meet SF4 population thresholds, therefore there may be less than 50 states, 75 counties or 75 places listed

Homeownership

Samoans Who Own Their Own Homes

All States, Top 75 Counties, and Top 75 Places Sorted by Number[1]

State	Number
United States	6,585
California	2,709
Hawaii	687
Washington	515
Utah	502
Texas	203
Missouri	143
Arizona	141
New York	126
Georgia	125
Illinois	125
Colorado	121
Nevada	117
Alaska	108
Pennsylvania	108
Florida	94
New Jersey	75
Tennessee	59
North Carolina	49
Oregon	47
Michigan	43
Virginia	36
Ohio	27

County	Number
Los Angeles County, CA	871
Honolulu County, HI	621
San Diego County, CA	443
Salt Lake County, UT	346
Orange County, CA	278
King County, WA	226
Alameda County, CA	163
San Bernardino County, CA	152
Pierce County, WA	148
Maricopa County, AZ	101
Clark County, NV	91
Riverside County, CA	89
Contra Costa County, CA	84
Jackson County, MO	83
Anchorage Borough, AK	77
San Mateo County, CA	77
Utah County, UT	73
Sacramento County, CA	67
Santa Clara County, CA	60
San Francisco County, CA	56
Ventura County, CA	52
Hawaii County, HI	44
San Joaquin County, CA	42
Solano County, CA	40

Place	Number
Oceanside, CA (city) San Diego County	193
Long Beach, CA (city) Los Angeles County	173
West Valley City, UT (city) Salt Lake County	154
San Diego, CA (city) San Diego County	132
Carson, CA (city) Los Angeles County	127
Los Angeles, CA (city) Los Angeles County	106
Salt Lake City, UT (city) Salt Lake County	69
Santa Ana, CA (city) Orange County	68
Laie, HI (cdp) Honolulu County	57
Anaheim, CA (city) Orange County	56
San Francisco, CA (city) San Francisco County	56
Tacoma, WA (city) Pierce County	52
Hayward, CA (city) Alameda County	48
Lakewood, CA (city) Los Angeles County	48
Oxnard, CA (city) Ventura County	47
Nanakuli, HI (cdp) Honolulu County	46
Seattle, WA (city) King County	43
Ewa Beach, HI (cdp) Honolulu County	38
Federal Way, WA (city) King County	37
San Bernardino, CA (city) San Bernardino County	34
Sacramento, CA (city) Sacramento County	33
Honolulu, HI (cdp) Honolulu County	32
Garden Grove, CA (city) Orange County	30
San Jose, CA (city) Santa Clara County	30
Waipahu, HI (cdp) Honolulu County	29
New York, NY (city)	28
Kahuku, HI (cdp) Honolulu County	25
Compton, CA (city) Los Angeles County	22
Hauula, HI (cdp) Honolulu County	18
Westminster, CA (city) Orange County	18
Lakewood, WA (city) Pierce County	12
Halawa, HI (cdp) Honolulu County	6

Notes: Please refer to the User's Guide for an explanation of data; ranking tables include all places with Asian and/or NHPI populations above SF4 population thresholds; (1) tables reflect only those areas that meet SF4 population thresholds, therefore there may be less than 50 states, 75 counties or 75 places listed

Homeownership

Samoans Who Own Their Own Homes

All States, Top 75 Counties, and Top 75 Places Sorted by Percent[1]

State	Percent
Illinois	66.49
Pennsylvania	62.07
New Jersey	59.06
Colorado	55.25
Utah	54.51
Arizona	54.23
Missouri	49.65
Florida	47.24
Georgia	47.17
Tennessee	44.03
Texas	42.65
North Carolina	37.98
New York	37.06
Michigan	36.13
Virginia	34.62
United States	34.36
Nevada	34.01
Alaska	33.64
California	33.56
Ohio	31.76
Washington	31.58
Oregon	25.97
Hawaii	19.96

County	Percent
Contra Costa County, CA	68.29
Maricopa County, AZ	59.76
Salt Lake County, UT	58.64
Jackson County, MO	57.24
Utah County, UT	49.66
San Diego County, CA	41.02
Ventura County, CA	40.63
Hawaii County, HI	40.37
Alameda County, CA	39.95
Riverside County, CA	39.91
San Bernardino County, CA	39.69
Orange County, CA	39.66
San Joaquin County, CA	36.84
Pierce County, WA	35.92
Clark County, NV	35.69
Anchorage Borough, AK	30.80
Los Angeles County, CA	30.67
San Mateo County, CA	29.39
Solano County, CA	27.97
King County, WA	25.22
Sacramento County, CA	20.36
Honolulu County, HI	19.15
Santa Clara County, CA	15.92
San Francisco County, CA	12.12

Place	Percent
West Valley City, UT (city) Salt Lake County	78.57
Kahuku, HI (cdp) Honolulu County	65.79
Salt Lake City, UT (city) Salt Lake County	59.48
Santa Ana, CA (city) Orange County	57.14
Oceanside, CA (city) San Diego County	56.60
Ewa Beach, HI (cdp) Honolulu County	54.29
Anaheim, CA (city) Orange County	53.33
Lakewood, CA (city) Los Angeles County	53.33
Carson, CA (city) Los Angeles County	47.39
Oxnard, CA (city) Ventura County	45.19
Hayward, CA (city) Alameda County	44.04
Laie, HI (cdp) Honolulu County	43.51
San Bernardino, CA (city) San Bernardino County	40.48
Tacoma, WA (city) Pierce County	37.96
Hauula, HI (cdp) Honolulu County	36.00
Nanakuli, HI (cdp) Honolulu County	34.07
San Diego, CA (city) San Diego County	32.35
Westminster, CA (city) Orange County	30.51
Federal Way, WA (city) King County	30.33
Long Beach, CA (city) Los Angeles County	23.32
Garden Grove, CA (city) Orange County	22.06
Sacramento, CA (city) Sacramento County	20.63
Los Angeles, CA (city) Los Angeles County	20.15
Lakewood, WA (city) Pierce County	17.39
New York, NY (city)	16.87
Seattle, WA (city) King County	16.54
Compton, CA (city) Los Angeles County	14.01
San Jose, CA (city) Santa Clara County	12.40
San Francisco, CA (city) San Francisco County	12.12
Waipahu, HI (cdp) Honolulu County	6.87
Halawa, HI (cdp) Honolulu County	5.41
Honolulu, HI (cdp) Honolulu County	2.57

Notes: Please refer to the User's Guide for an explanation of data; ranking tables include all places with Asian and/or NHPI populations above SF4 population thresholds; (1) tables reflect only those areas that meet SF4 population thresholds, therefore there may be less than 50 states, 75 counties or 75 places listed

Homeownership

Sri Lankans Who Own Their Own Homes

All States, Top 75 Counties, and Top 75 Places Sorted by Number[1]

State	Number
United States	3,424
California	978
New York	335
Maryland	303
New Jersey	226
Texas	147
Virginia	118
Florida	110
Ohio	110
Massachusetts	105
Illinois	100
Pennsylvania	90
Washington	82
Michigan	63

County	Number
Los Angeles County, CA	426
Montgomery County, MD	205
Orange County, CA	127
Queens County, NY	101
Middlesex County, NJ	93
Richmond County, NY	66

Place	Number
New York, NY (city)	209
Los Angeles, CA (city) Los Angeles County	208

Notes: Please refer to the User's Guide for an explanation of data; ranking tables include all places with Asian and/or NHPI populations above SF4 population thresholds; (1) tables reflect only those areas that meet SF4 population thresholds, therefore there may be less than 50 states, 75 counties or 75 places listed

Homeownership

Sri Lankans Who Own Their Own Homes

All States, Top 75 Counties, and Top 75 Places Sorted by Percent[1]

State	Percent
Maryland	74.63
Florida	62.50
Michigan	61.17
New Jersey	60.92
Massachusetts	60.69
Virginia	58.71
Ohio	58.51
Pennsylvania	54.88
California	53.97
Washington	52.56
United States	51.07
Illinois	45.05
New York	40.75
Texas	37.89

County	Percent
Montgomery County, MD	82.66
Middlesex County, NJ	74.40
Orange County, CA	59.62
Los Angeles County, CA	51.76
Richmond County, NY	46.15
Queens County, NY	37.69

Place	Percent
Los Angeles, CA (city) Los Angeles County	52.00
New York, NY (city)	32.45

Notes: Please refer to the User's Guide for an explanation of data; ranking tables include all places with Asian and/or NHPI populations above SF4 population thresholds; (1) tables reflect only those areas that meet SF4 population thresholds, therefore there may be less than 50 states, 75 counties or 75 places listed

Homeownership

Taiwanese Who Own Their Own Homes

All States, Top 75 Counties, and Top 75 Places Sorted by Number[1]

State	Number
United States	26,324
California	13,778
Texas	1,831
New Jersey	1,517
New York	1,429
Illinois	801
Washington	784
Michigan	533
Florida	528
Maryland	501
Ohio	461
Georgia	456
Massachusetts	379
Pennsylvania	358
Virginia	303
North Carolina	250
Missouri	207
Arizona	168
Oregon	162
Nevada	157
Hawaii	148
Connecticut	145
Tennessee	137
Minnesota	125
Colorado	115
Louisiana	113
Indiana	112
Utah	102
Kansas	87
Iowa	70
Wisconsin	51
Oklahoma	43

County	Number
Los Angeles County, CA	7,388
Orange County, CA	2,082
Santa Clara County, CA	1,283
Alameda County, CA	770
Queens County, NY	770
King County, WA	646
Harris County, TX	637
San Diego County, CA	485
Contra Costa County, CA	411
San Bernardino County, CA	393
Cook County, IL	360
Montgomery County, MD	342
Oakland County, MI	326
Middlesex County, NJ	308
Fort Bend County, TX	287
Bergen County, NJ	257
DuPage County, IL	243
Collin County, TX	232
Middlesex County, MA	231
Ventura County, CA	227
Fairfax County, VA	224
Morris County, NJ	196
San Mateo County, CA	178
Somerset County, NJ	178
Dallas County, TX	170
St. Louis County, MO	163
Maricopa County, AZ	159
San Francisco County, CA	151
Gwinnett County, GA	145
Honolulu County, HI	142
Nassau County, NY	140
Essex County, NJ	138
Franklin County, OH	134
Clark County, NV	133
Tarrant County, TX	120
Travis County, TX	119
New York County, NY	117
Mercer County, NJ	110
Washtenaw County, MI	100
Sacramento County, CA	96
Riverside County, CA	86
Westchester County, NY	71
Suffolk County, NY	67
Norfolk County, MA	54
Allegheny County, PA	53
Suffolk County, MA	32
Dane County, WI	21

Place	Number
New York, NY (city)	947
Arcadia, CA (city) Los Angeles County	779
Hacienda Heights, CA (cdp) Los Angeles County	601
Irvine, CA (city) Orange County	586
Rowland Heights, CA (cdp) Los Angeles County	585
Los Angeles, CA (city) Los Angeles County	565
Fremont, CA (city) Alameda County	549
Diamond Bar, CA (city) Los Angeles County	520
San Jose, CA (city) Santa Clara County	493
Cerritos, CA (city) Los Angeles County	452
Houston, TX (city) Harris County	426
Walnut, CA (city) Los Angeles County	416
Temple City, CA (city) Los Angeles County	365
San Marino, CA (city) Los Angeles County	326
San Diego, CA (city) San Diego County	307
Alhambra, CA (city) Los Angeles County	262
Torrance, CA (city) Los Angeles County	236
Bellevue, WA (city) King County	228
Cupertino, CA (city) Santa Clara County	224
Sugar Land, TX (city) Fort Bend County	220
Monterey Park, CA (city) Los Angeles County	197
West Covina, CA (city) Los Angeles County	197
Sunnyvale, CA (city) Santa Clara County	182
San Gabriel, CA (city) Los Angeles County	170
East San Gabriel, CA (cdp) Los Angeles County	156
Huntington Beach, CA (city) Orange County	154
Troy, MI (city) Oakland County	153
San Francisco, CA (city) San Francisco County	151
Cypress, CA (city) Orange County	146
Plano, TX (city) Collin County	146
Rancho Palos Verdes, CA (city) Los Angeles County	142
Edison, NJ (township) Middlesex County	140
Orange, CA (city) Orange County	140
Tustin, CA (city) Orange County	131
Chino Hills, CA (city) San Bernardino County	127
Seattle, WA (city) King County	126
Honolulu, HI (cdp) Honolulu County	122
Naperville, IL (city) Du Page County	113
Upland, CA (city) San Bernardino County	106
Anaheim, CA (city) Orange County	105
Austin, TX (city) Travis County	104
Saratoga, CA (city) Santa Clara County	96
Chicago, IL (city) Cook County	91
Fountain Valley, CA (city) Orange County	88
El Monte, CA (city) Los Angeles County	83
Ann Arbor, MI (city) Washtenaw County	80
North Hempstead, NY (town) Nassau County	73
Arlington, TX (city) Tarrant County	59
Columbus, OH (city) Franklin County	50
Boston, MA (city) Suffolk County	32
Berkeley, CA (city) Alameda County	30
Madison, WI (city) Dane County	21

Notes: Please refer to the User's Guide for an explanation of data; ranking tables include all places with Asian and/or NHPI populations above SF4 population thresholds; (1) tables reflect only those areas that meet SF4 population thresholds, therefore there may be less than 50 states, 75 counties or 75 places listed

Homeownership

Taiwanese Who Own Their Own Homes

All States, Top 75 Counties, and Top 75 Places Sorted by Percent[1]

State	Percent
New Jersey	79.26
Georgia	78.08
Minnesota	76.69
North Carolina	74.18
Nevada	74.06
Florida	71.45
Michigan	71.35
Hawaii	70.14
California	70.04
Washington	66.89
Texas	66.61
United States	64.75
Virginia	64.47
Louisiana	62.78
Utah	62.58
Maryland	62.24
Ohio	58.73
Oregon	58.70
Arizona	57.53
Tennessee	56.61
Illinois	56.45
Connecticut	55.77
New York	51.05
Missouri	50.99
Massachusetts	44.28
Kansas	43.94
Iowa	42.42
Colorado	39.93
Pennsylvania	37.45
Indiana	31.28
Oklahoma	25.60
Wisconsin	17.59

County	Percent
Nassau County, NY	98.59
Collin County, TX	96.27
Bergen County, NJ	93.80
Ventura County, CA	91.90
Essex County, NJ	90.20
Somerset County, NJ	89.90
Oakland County, MI	89.32
Fairfax County, VA	87.84
Gwinnett County, GA	86.31
Montgomery County, MD	86.15
Contra Costa County, CA	85.98
DuPage County, IL	85.87
Morris County, NJ	84.85
Fort Bend County, TX	83.43
Orange County, CA	79.01
Mercer County, NJ	75.34
Harris County, TX	73.30
San Bernardino County, CA	73.05
Middlesex County, NJ	71.46
Clark County, NV	70.74
Suffolk County, NY	70.53
San Diego County, CA	69.48
Los Angeles County, CA	69.43
Honolulu County, HI	69.27
Santa Clara County, CA	68.10
King County, WA	67.36
St. Louis County, MO	66.53
Queens County, NY	65.37
Maricopa County, AZ	65.16
Westchester County, NY	63.96
Alameda County, CA	62.91
Sacramento County, CA	61.15
San Mateo County, CA	60.96
Dallas County, TX	58.02
Riverside County, CA	57.72
Middlesex County, MA	56.90
Franklin County, OH	55.37
Norfolk County, MA	54.55
Washtenaw County, MI	54.05
San Francisco County, CA	50.00
Tarrant County, TX	49.38
Cook County, IL	43.58
Travis County, TX	38.64
Allegheny County, PA	25.36
New York County, NY	18.99
Suffolk County, MA	15.09
Dane County, WI	10.71

Place	Percent
Orange, CA (city) Orange County	100.00
North Hempstead, NY (town) Nassau County	97.33
Plano, TX (city) Collin County	96.05
Saratoga, CA (city) Santa Clara County	94.12
Cerritos, CA (city) Los Angeles County	92.43
Troy, MI (city) Oakland County	92.17
Walnut, CA (city) Los Angeles County	90.04
Diamond Bar, CA (city) Los Angeles County	87.10
Huntington Beach, CA (city) Orange County	87.01
Edison, NJ (township) Middlesex County	83.83
Bellevue, WA (city) King County	83.82
Fremont, CA (city) Alameda County	83.56
Temple City, CA (city) Los Angeles County	83.52
Chino Hills, CA (city) San Bernardino County	83.01
San Marino, CA (city) Los Angeles County	82.95
Rancho Palos Verdes, CA (city) Los Angeles County	82.56
Cypress, CA (city) Orange County	82.49
Sugar Land, TX (city) Fort Bend County	82.09
Naperville, IL (city) Du Page County	81.29
Hacienda Heights, CA (cdp) Los Angeles County	79.71
Tustin, CA (city) Orange County	78.92
Arcadia, CA (city) Los Angeles County	78.53
Irvine, CA (city) Orange County	77.31
Cupertino, CA (city) Santa Clara County	77.24
East San Gabriel, CA (cdp) Los Angeles County	77.23
Rowland Heights, CA (cdp) Los Angeles County	75.29
West Covina, CA (city) Los Angeles County	73.51
Upland, CA (city) San Bernardino County	71.62
Fountain Valley, CA (city) Orange County	70.97
Houston, TX (city) Harris County	67.73
Sunnyvale, CA (city) Santa Clara County	67.41
San Jose, CA (city) Santa Clara County	66.53
Torrance, CA (city) Los Angeles County	66.11
Honolulu, HI (cdp) Honolulu County	65.95
San Diego, CA (city) San Diego County	62.78
San Gabriel, CA (city) Los Angeles County	62.04
Anaheim, CA (city) Orange County	59.32
Monterey Park, CA (city) Los Angeles County	58.63
Ann Arbor, MI (city) Washtenaw County	50.31
San Francisco, CA (city) San Francisco County	50.00
New York, NY (city)	48.66
Alhambra, CA (city) Los Angeles County	47.90
El Monte, CA (city) Los Angeles County	46.63
Los Angeles, CA (city) Los Angeles County	39.62
Arlington, TX (city) Tarrant County	38.82
Seattle, WA (city) King County	38.41
Austin, TX (city) Travis County	36.62
Columbus, OH (city) Franklin County	31.65
Chicago, IL (city) Cook County	21.77
Berkeley, CA (city) Alameda County	17.86
Boston, MA (city) Suffolk County	15.09
Madison, WI (city) Dane County	10.71

Notes: Please refer to the User's Guide for an explanation of data; ranking tables include all places with Asian and/or NHPI populations above SF4 population thresholds; (1) tables reflect only those areas that meet SF4 population thresholds, therefore there may be less than 50 states, 75 counties or 75 places listed

Homeownership

Thais Who Own Their Own Homes

All States, Top 75 Counties, and Top 75 Places Sorted by Number[1]

State	Number
United States	16,556
California	5,678
Florida	1,069
Texas	1,061
New York	1,020
Illinois	988
Virginia	688
Maryland	544
Washington	449
Nevada	444
Georgia	372
New Jersey	350
Colorado	267
Oregon	246
Ohio	244
North Carolina	237
Massachusetts	206
Missouri	190
Arizona	185
Tennessee	177
Michigan	175
Pennsylvania	156
Iowa	143
Minnesota	140
Indiana	133
Alaska	119
Louisiana	116
Hawaii	112
Oklahoma	112
South Carolina	107
Utah	90
Connecticut	88
Wisconsin	78
Kansas	73
Alabama	69
Nebraska	56
Kentucky	47
New Mexico	39
Arkansas	23

County	Number
Los Angeles County, CA	3,165
Cook County, IL	680
Orange County, CA	573
Clark County, NV	397
Fairfax County, VA	359
San Bernardino County, CA	350
Queens County, NY	321
Montgomery County, MD	299
Harris County, TX	237
King County, WA	229
Dallas County, TX	201
Alameda County, CA	195
San Francisco County, CA	192
Westchester County, NY	163
San Diego County, CA	159
San Mateo County, CA	155
Riverside County, CA	153
Hillsborough County, FL	144
Maricopa County, AZ	137
Palm Beach County, FL	135
Broward County, FL	123
Miami-Dade County, FL	123
Bexar County, TX	116
Santa Clara County, CA	112
Contra Costa County, CA	102
Suffolk County, NY	99
Anchorage Borough, AK	97
Collin County, TX	95
Bergen County, NJ	93
Sacramento County, CA	91
Tarrant County, TX	90
Nassau County, NY	87
Middlesex County, MA	86
Honolulu County, HI	79
DuPage County, IL	77
St. Louis County, MO	74
New York County, NY	70
Okaloosa County, FL	69
Polk County, IA	67
Oklahoma County, OK	54
Travis County, TX	54
Pinellas County, FL	53
Prince George's County, MD	52
Franklin County, OH	49
Multnomah County, OR	48
Pierce County, WA	46
Denver County, CO	15

Place	Number
Los Angeles, CA (city) Los Angeles County	1,257
New York, NY (city)	485
Chicago, IL (city) Cook County	244
San Francisco, CA (city) San Francisco County	192
Houston, TX (city) Harris County	148
Las Vegas, NV (city) Clark County	132
Seattle, WA (city) King County	127
Cerritos, CA (city) Los Angeles County	118
San Antonio, TX (city) Bexar County	102
Spring Valley, NV (cdp) Clark County	97
San Diego, CA (city) San Diego County	81
Bellflower, CA (city) Los Angeles County	73
Long Beach, CA (city) Los Angeles County	63
Anaheim, CA (city) Orange County	61
Des Moines, IA (city) Polk County	58
San Jose, CA (city) Santa Clara County	56
Glendale, CA (city) Los Angeles County	48
Portland, OR (city) Multnomah County	43
Columbus, OH (city) Franklin County	41
Honolulu, HI (cdp) Honolulu County	17
Denver, CO (city) Denver County	15

Notes: Please refer to the User's Guide for an explanation of data; ranking tables include all places with Asian and/or NHPI populations above SF4 population thresholds; (1) tables reflect only those areas that meet SF4 population thresholds, therefore there may be less than 50 states, 75 counties or 75 places listed

Homeownership

Thais Who Own Their Own Homes

All States, Top 75 Counties, and Top 75 Places Sorted by Percent[1]

State	Percent
Alaska	69.59
Maryland	64.92
Minnesota	59.83
North Carolina	59.10
New Jersey	58.14
Louisiana	57.14
Florida	56.62
Virginia	54.39
Illinois	53.46
Indiana	52.78
Iowa	52.57
Georgia	52.47
California	52.08
Oregon	50.41
Nevada	49.17
New Mexico	48.75
United States	48.06
South Carolina	45.73
Tennessee	45.04
Texas	44.34
New York	44.14
Utah	43.06
Colorado	42.79
Washington	41.92
Missouri	41.85
Connecticut	41.71
Ohio	40.94
Oklahoma	40.58
Arkansas	39.66
Alabama	37.50
Arizona	36.49
Hawaii	35.90
Nebraska	34.78
Kentucky	33.10
Michigan	28.74
Kansas	28.29
Massachusetts	26.41
Pennsylvania	25.12
Wisconsin	23.49

County	Percent
Suffolk County, NY	100.00
Collin County, TX	90.48
Westchester County, NY	83.59
Nassau County, NY	76.32
Fairfax County, VA	75.26
Montgomery County, MD	73.11
San Mateo County, CA	71.43
Anchorage Borough, AK	70.80
San Bernardino County, CA	69.03
Okaloosa County, FL	65.71
Broward County, FL	63.08
Contra Costa County, CA	62.96
Palm Beach County, FL	62.50
Hillsborough County, FL	62.07
Polk County, IA	61.47
Orange County, CA	58.59
Pierce County, WA	57.50
DuPage County, IL	57.46
Riverside County, CA	55.04
Miami-Dade County, FL	54.42
Los Angeles County, CA	53.53
Prince George's County, MD	53.06
Bergen County, NJ	52.84
Sacramento County, CA	52.60
Cook County, IL	51.79
Harris County, TX	49.17
St. Louis County, MO	48.68
Clark County, NV	47.89
Alameda County, CA	43.82
Dallas County, TX	43.70
Queens County, NY	42.40
Bexar County, TX	41.73
Maricopa County, AZ	41.39
Travis County, TX	40.91
Pinellas County, FL	40.77
San Diego County, CA	40.05
Oklahoma County, OK	38.57
Tarrant County, TX	36.89
Franklin County, OH	35.77
King County, WA	34.54
Santa Clara County, CA	32.56
San Francisco County, CA	32.49
Multnomah County, OR	31.58
Middlesex County, MA	29.97
Honolulu County, HI	29.48
New York County, NY	18.42
Denver County, CO	8.06

Place	Percent
Cerritos, CA (city) Los Angeles County	86.13
Spring Valley, NV (cdp) Clark County	71.32
Des Moines, IA (city) Polk County	70.73
Bellflower, CA (city) Los Angeles County	54.07
Las Vegas, NV (city) Clark County	51.16
Anaheim, CA (city) Orange County	47.29
Los Angeles, CA (city) Los Angeles County	43.36
San Antonio, TX (city) Bexar County	42.50
Houston, TX (city) Harris County	40.33
San Jose, CA (city) Santa Clara County	38.10
Seattle, WA (city) King County	34.70
Glendale, CA (city) Los Angeles County	34.29
New York, NY (city)	34.28
Long Beach, CA (city) Los Angeles County	33.33
San Francisco, CA (city) San Francisco County	32.49
Chicago, IL (city) Cook County	32.32
Columbus, OH (city) Franklin County	31.78
Portland, OR (city) Multnomah County	29.25
San Diego, CA (city) San Diego County	28.93
Honolulu, HI (cdp) Honolulu County	11.04
Denver, CO (city) Denver County	8.06

Notes: Please refer to the User's Guide for an explanation of data; ranking tables include all places with Asian and/or NHPI populations above SF4 population thresholds; (1) tables reflect only those areas that meet SF4 population thresholds, therefore there may be less than 50 states, 75 counties or 75 places listed

Homeownership

Tongans Who Own Their Own Homes

All States, Top 75 Counties, and Top 75 Places Sorted by Number[1]

State	Number
United States	2,465
California	955
Utah	870
Hawaii	222
Arizona	101
Washington	72
Nevada	57
Texas	43
Alaska	42
Oregon	31

County	Number
Salt Lake County, UT	755
San Mateo County, CA	262
Los Angeles County, CA	192
Alameda County, CA	159
Honolulu County, HI	151
Maricopa County, AZ	101
San Bernardino County, CA	76
Maui County, HI	67
Utah County, UT	63
Sacramento County, CA	62
King County, WA	60
Contra Costa County, CA	56
Washoe County, NV	49
Tarrant County, TX	38
San Diego County, CA	30
Orange County, CA	26
Multnomah County, OR	21

Place	Number
Salt Lake City, UT (city) Salt Lake County	301
West Valley City, UT (city) Salt Lake County	226
Oakland, CA (city) Alameda County	121
East Palo Alto, CA (city) San Mateo County	100
West Jordan, UT (city) Salt Lake County	66
Los Angeles, CA (city) Los Angeles County	48
Honolulu, HI (cdp) Honolulu County	45
Sacramento, CA (city) Sacramento County	45
San Mateo, CA (city) San Mateo County	39
Kahuku, HI (cdp) Honolulu County	37
San Bruno, CA (city) San Mateo County	37
Laie, HI (cdp) Honolulu County	21
Portland, OR (city) Multnomah County	21
Hauula, HI (cdp) Honolulu County	14

Notes: Please refer to the User's Guide for an explanation of data; ranking tables include all places with Asian and/or NHPI populations above SF4 population thresholds; (1) tables reflect only those areas that meet SF4 population thresholds, therefore there may be less than 50 states, 75 counties or 75 places listed

Homeownership

Tongans Who Own Their Own Homes

All States, Top 75 Counties, and Top 75 Places Sorted by Percent[1]

State	Percent
Arizona	75.94
Utah	69.49
Alaska	56.76
United States	48.14
California	47.28
Washington	39.56
Nevada	34.34
Texas	33.33
Oregon	31.96
Hawaii	26.78

County	Percent
Contra Costa County, CA	82.35
Maricopa County, AZ	75.94
Salt Lake County, UT	72.18
Alameda County, CA	61.87
Utah County, UT	56.25
San Mateo County, CA	50.78
San Bernardino County, CA	49.67
Los Angeles County, CA	47.06
Washoe County, NV	46.67
Tarrant County, TX	45.78
King County, WA	45.45
Sacramento County, CA	42.76
Maui County, HI	41.61
Multnomah County, OR	30.43
San Diego County, CA	29.70
Orange County, CA	26.53
Honolulu County, HI	25.64

Place	Percent
Kahuku, HI (cdp) Honolulu County	84.09
West Jordan, UT (city) Salt Lake County	82.50
West Valley City, UT (city) Salt Lake County	79.86
Salt Lake City, UT (city) Salt Lake County	73.59
Oakland, CA (city) Alameda County	72.89
Los Angeles, CA (city) Los Angeles County	55.17
Laie, HI (cdp) Honolulu County	51.22
East Palo Alto, CA (city) San Mateo County	49.26
San Bruno, CA (city) San Mateo County	48.68
Sacramento, CA (city) Sacramento County	47.87
San Mateo, CA (city) San Mateo County	45.35
Portland, OR (city) Multnomah County	30.43
Hauula, HI (cdp) Honolulu County	29.17
Honolulu, HI (cdp) Honolulu County	14.29

Notes: Please refer to the User's Guide for an explanation of data; ranking tables include all places with Asian and/or NHPI populations above SF4 population thresholds; (1) tables reflect only those areas that meet SF4 population thresholds, therefore there may be less than 50 states, 75 counties or 75 places listed

Homeownership

Vietnamese Who Own Their Own Homes

All States, Top 75 Counties, and Top 75 Places Sorted by Number[1]

State	Number
United States	155,325
California	53,305
Texas	22,822
Virginia	6,418
Washington	6,053
Florida	5,870
Pennsylvania	4,725
Georgia	4,646
Louisiana	3,776
Oregon	3,326
Massachusetts	3,144
Minnesota	3,085
Maryland	2,646
Illinois	2,636
North Carolina	2,500
New Jersey	2,212
Oklahoma	2,175
Colorado	2,143
New York	2,135
Arizona	2,076
Michigan	1,974
Kansas	1,908
Ohio	1,672
Missouri	1,530
Connecticut	1,024
Tennessee	989
Indiana	984
Iowa	980
Utah	970
Nebraska	817
Arkansas	751
Nevada	742
Alabama	736
South Carolina	736
Mississippi	729
Hawaii	526
Wisconsin	514
New Mexico	452
Kentucky	443
Idaho	240
New Hampshire	166
Maine	128
Delaware	108
Alaska	104
South Dakota	97
District of Columbia	86
Rhode Island	73
Vermont	41
West Virginia	22

County	Number
Orange County, CA	16,413
Santa Clara County, CA	13,011
Harris County, TX	9,632
Los Angeles County, CA	8,611
Fairfax County, VA	4,038
San Diego County, CA	3,967
King County, WA	3,444
Tarrant County, TX	3,014
Dallas County, TX	2,822
Alameda County, CA	2,731
Multnomah County, OR	1,845
Sacramento County, CA	1,764
Maricopa County, AZ	1,700
Philadelphia County, PA	1,670
Montgomery County, MD	1,533
Gwinnett County, GA	1,407
Hennepin County, MN	1,302
Cook County, IL	1,292
Fort Bend County, TX	1,234
San Bernardino County, CA	1,226
Orange County, FL	1,225
Travis County, TX	1,216
Oklahoma County, OK	1,212
Jefferson Parish, LA	1,195
Sedgwick County, KS	1,161
Washington County, OR	1,021
Riverside County, CA	977
Orleans Parish, LA	917
Snohomish County, WA	875
Clayton County, GA	873
Pinellas County, FL	846
Collin County, TX	809
Mecklenburg County, NC	787
Salt Lake County, UT	781
Kent County, MI	744
Suffolk County, MA	735
Middlesex County, MA	720
San Francisco County, CA	709
Contra Costa County, CA	687
DeKalb County, GA	657
Jefferson County, TX	656
Clark County, NV	646
Ventura County, CA	589
Bexar County, TX	580
Hillsborough County, FL	576
Broward County, FL	550
Ramsey County, MN	546
Worcester County, MA	529
Pierce County, WA	512
Denver County, CO	506
DuPage County, IL	497
San Joaquin County, CA	473
Wake County, NC	469
Montgomery County, PA	457
Lancaster County, PA	454
Camden County, NJ	452
Hartford County, CT	451
Arapahoe County, CO	448
Shelby County, TN	445
Adams County, CO	443
Lancaster County, NE	443
Honolulu County, HI	435
Denton County, TX	430
Saint Louis Independent City, MO	428
Palm Beach County, FL	424
East Baton Rouge Parish, LA	420
Bernalillo County, NM	412
Loudoun County, VA	411
San Mateo County, CA	411
Franklin County, OH	398
Clark County, WA	387
Norfolk County, MA	387
Atlantic County, NJ	386
Jackson County, MO	386
Prince George's County, MD	382

Place	Number
San Jose, CA (city) Santa Clara County	10,146
Houston, TX (city) Harris County	4,730
Garden Grove, CA (city) Orange County	3,173
San Diego, CA (city) San Diego County	2,970
Westminster, CA (city) Orange County	2,783
Santa Ana, CA (city) Orange County	2,223
Los Angeles, CA (city) Los Angeles County	1,920
Portland, OR (city) Multnomah County	1,717
Philadelphia, PA (city) Philadelphia County	1,670
Oklahoma City, OK (city) Oklahoma County	1,492
Arlington, TX (city) Tarrant County	1,453
Anaheim, CA (city) Orange County	1,376
Milpitas, CA (city) Santa Clara County	1,209
Fountain Valley, CA (city) Orange County	1,106
Wichita, KS (city) Sedgwick County	1,088
Seattle, WA (city) King County	1,013
Garland, TX (city) Dallas County	1,006
Irvine, CA (city) Orange County	938
New Orleans, LA (city) Orleans Parish	917
Austin, TX (city) Travis County	837
New York, NY (city)	822
Huntington Beach, CA (city) Orange County	811
Fremont, CA (city) Alameda County	787
Chicago, IL (city) Cook County	744
Fort Worth, TX (city) Tarrant County	733
Phoenix, AZ (city) Maricopa County	720
San Francisco, CA (city) San Francisco County	709
Boston, MA (city) Suffolk County	652
Charlotte, NC (city) Mecklenburg County	638
Annandale, VA (cdp) Fairfax County	612
El Monte, CA (city) Los Angeles County	608
Dallas, TX (city) Dallas County	560
Oakland, CA (city) Alameda County	547
Santa Clara, CA (city) Santa Clara County	529
Rosemead, CA (city) Los Angeles County	508
Denver, CO (city) Denver County	506
San Antonio, TX (city) Bexar County	485
Orange, CA (city) Orange County	479
Grand Prairie, TX (city) Dallas County	468
Carrollton, TX (city) Denton County	461
Sacramento, CA (city) Sacramento County	459
Port Arthur, TX (city) Jefferson County	446
Lincoln, NE (city) Lancaster County	443
Plano, TX (city) Collin County	441
Long Beach, CA (city) Los Angeles County	438
St. Louis, MO (city) Saint Louis Independent City	428
Kansas City, MO (city) Jackson County	419
Albuquerque, NM (city) Bernalillo County	404
Stockton, CA (city) San Joaquin County	377
Columbus, OH (city) Franklin County	359
Union City, CA (city) Alameda County	355
Springfield, VA (cdp) Fairfax County	352
Worcester, MA (city) Worcester County	345
Aurora, CO (city) Arapahoe County	341
Fort Smith, AR (city) Sebastian County	341
St. Paul, MN (city) Ramsey County	340
Mission Bend, TX (cdp) Fort Bend County	326
Minneapolis, MN (city) Hennepin County	319
Jefferson, VA (cdp) Fairfax County	317
Renton, WA (city) King County	316
Sunnyvale, CA (city) Santa Clara County	309
West Covina, CA (city) Los Angeles County	309
Honolulu, HI (cdp) Honolulu County	308
Richardson, TX (city) Dallas County	306
Alhambra, CA (city) Los Angeles County	305
Elk Grove, CA (cdp) Sacramento County	301
West Valley City, UT (city) Salt Lake County	296
Sugar Land, TX (city) Fort Bend County	294
Baton Rouge, LA (city) East Baton Rouge Parish	289
Corona, CA (city) Riverside County	283
Lake Forest, CA (city) Orange County	283
Memphis, TN (city) Shelby County	282
Irving, TX (city) Dallas County	280
Brooklyn Park, MN (city) Hennepin County	279
Hayward, CA (city) Alameda County	279

Notes: Please refer to the User's Guide for an explanation of data; ranking tables include all places with Asian and/or NHPI populations above SF4 population thresholds; (1) tables reflect only those areas that meet SF4 population thresholds, therefore there may be less than 50 states, 75 counties or 75 places listed

Homeownership

Vietnamese Who Own Their Own Homes

All States, Top 75 Counties, and Top 75 Places Sorted by Percent[1]

State	Percent
Utah	70.49
Arkansas	68.90
Georgia	67.65
Indiana	65.30
Oregon	64.51
Oklahoma	64.39
Delaware	64.29
Florida	63.81
Arizona	63.76
Maryland	63.67
Virginia	63.63
Idaho	62.99
Kansas	62.78
South Carolina	61.80
Pennsylvania	61.17
North Carolina	60.98
Texas	60.41
Louisiana	60.06
Colorado	59.41
Mississippi	58.60
Alabama	58.41
New Jersey	58.03
Ohio	57.20
Iowa	57.14
Minnesota	56.62
Michigan	55.70
Nevada	55.66
Missouri	54.41
Kentucky	54.22
Nebraska	53.61
United States	53.22
Tennessee	52.36
New Mexico	51.48
Connecticut	51.05
Illinois	50.39
Alaska	50.00
California	48.05
Washington	47.45
South Dakota	47.32
Wisconsin	43.05
Maine	37.76
Massachusetts	36.35
New Hampshire	34.66
New York	33.98
Rhode Island	28.74
West Virginia	20.18
Hawaii	19.87
Vermont	17.52
District of Columbia	15.55

County	Percent
Canadian County, OK	96.75
Scott County, MN	95.00
St. Martin Parish, LA	94.44
Matagorda County, TX	92.70
Washington County, MN	90.30
Loudoun County, VA	90.13
Clayton County, GA	88.09
Fort Bend County, TX	88.08
Benton County, AR	87.80
Iberia Parish, LA	87.67
Nassau County, NY	86.89
Brazoria County, TX	85.71
Somerset County, NJ	84.68
Aransas County, TX	83.96
Wichita County, TX	83.96
York County, PA	83.70
Kane County, IL	82.89
Anoka County, MN	82.84
Jackson County, MS	82.51
Gwinnett County, GA	82.47
Cumberland County, PA	82.03
Calhoun County, TX	81.25
Seminole County, FL	81.17
Clackamas County, OR	80.73
Will County, IL	80.21
Greene County, MO	79.00
Ford County, KS	78.36
Plaquemines Parish, LA	78.15
Collin County, TX	78.01
Berks County, PA	77.97
Champaign County, IL	76.88
Adams County, CO	76.51
Orange County, TX	76.47
Howard County, MD	76.42
Brevard County, FL	75.73
Prince William County, VA	75.70
Cumberland County, NC	75.16
Cobb County, GA	75.13
Chester County, PA	75.00
Monmouth County, NJ	75.00
Burlington County, NJ	74.83
York County, SC	74.63
Northampton County, PA	74.14
Ventura County, CA	74.09
Suffolk County, NY	73.78
Bucks County, PA	73.62
Atlantic County, NJ	73.38
Palm Beach County, FL	73.23
Sebastian County, AR	73.19
Lancaster County, PA	73.11
Baltimore Independent City, MD	72.73
Washington County, OR	72.57
Fairfax Independent City, VA	72.50
Cleveland County, OK	72.22
Montgomery County, OH	72.22
St. Mary Parish, LA	71.76
Chesterfield County, VA	71.68
Marion County, OR	71.31
Sarpy County, NE	71.28
Forsyth County, NC	71.24
Orange County, FL	71.14
Polk County, FL	71.00
Fairfax County, VA	70.59
Williamson County, TX	70.57
Montgomery County, PA	70.42
Wake County, NC	70.21
Galveston County, TX	69.72
Middlesex County, NJ	69.54
Pinellas County, FL	69.46
Jefferson Parish, LA	69.44
Jefferson County, CO	69.08
Peoria County, IL	69.07
Sarasota County, FL	69.03
Allen County, IN	68.70
Richland County, SC	68.57

Place	Percent
Chino Hills, CA (city) San Bernardino County	100.00
Franconia, VA (cdp) Fairfax County	100.00
Pearland, TX (city) Brazoria County	100.00
Rancho Santa Margarita, CA (city) Orange County	100.00
Santa Clarita, CA (city) Los Angeles County	100.00
Taylorsville, UT (city) Salt Lake County	96.32
Diamond Bar, CA (city) Los Angeles County	95.68
Mission Bend, TX (cdp) Fort Bend County	95.32
League City, TX (city) Galveston County	94.70
Seattle Hill-Silver Firs, WA (cdp) Snohomish County	94.30
Doraville, GA (city) De Kalb County	92.86
Laguna Hills, CA (city) Orange County	92.57
Henderson, LA (town) Saint Martin Parish	92.45
Palacios, TX (city) Matagorda County	91.38
Mission Viejo, CA (city) Orange County	90.67
Avondale, LA (cdp) Jefferson Parish	90.52
Lilburn, GA (city) Gwinnett County	90.43
Gresham, OR (city) Multnomah County	90.11
Town 'n' Country, FL (cdp) Hillsborough County	89.54
Aurora, IL (city) Kane County	88.98
Oak Ridge, FL (cdp) Orange County	88.97
Cerritos, CA (city) Los Angeles County	88.65
Missouri City, TX (city) Fort Bend County	88.55
Aliso Viejo, CA (cdp) Orange County	88.24
Forest Park, GA (city) Clayton County	88.12
North Springfield, VA (cdp) Fairfax County	88.00
Aloha, OR (cdp) Washington County	87.90
Walnut, CA (city) Los Angeles County	87.85
Mesa, AZ (city) Maricopa County	87.79
Burke, VA (cdp) Fairfax County	87.67
Sugar Land, TX (city) Fort Bend County	87.50
Oceanside, CA (city) San Diego County	87.40
Colesville, MD (cdp) Montgomery County	87.36
Placentia, CA (city) Orange County	86.40
Chantilly, VA (cdp) Fairfax County	86.27
Estelle, LA (cdp) Jefferson Parish	86.24
Riverdale, GA (city) Clayton County	85.71
Laguna Niguel, CA (city) Orange County	85.62
Yorba Linda, CA (city) Orange County	85.03
Germantown, MD (cdp) Montgomery County	84.97
Timberlane, LA (cdp) Jefferson Parish	84.82
Marrero, LA (cdp) Jefferson Parish	84.53
Woodmere, LA (cdp) Jefferson Parish	84.11
Amelia, LA (cdp) Saint Mary Parish	84.03
Wichita Falls, TX (city) Wichita County	83.96
Fulton, TX (town) Aransas County	83.87
Westminster, CO (city) Adams County	83.25
Springfield, VA (cdp) Fairfax County	83.02
Plano, TX (city) Collin County	82.12
SeaTac, WA (city) King County	82.00
Cary, NC (town) Wake County	81.93
Cascade-Fairwood, WA (cdp) King County	81.92
Ocean Springs, MS (city) Jackson County	81.48
Randolph, MA (town) Norfolk County	81.11
Camarillo, CA (city) Ventura County	80.85
West Puente Valley, CA (cdp) Los Angeles County	80.85
Bryn Mawr-Skyway, WA (cdp) King County	80.67
Pinellas Park, FL (city) Pinellas County	80.61
Covina, CA (city) Los Angeles County	80.49
Round Rock, TX (city) Williamson County	80.47
Glendale Heights, IL (village) Du Page County	80.43
Overland Park, KS (city) Johnson County	80.15
Salem, OR (city) Marion County	79.86
Sterling Heights, MI (city) Macomb County	79.84
Allen, TX (city) Collin County	79.82
Woodlynne, NJ (borough) Camden County	79.66
Garden City, KS (city) Finney County	79.00
Chandler, AZ (city) Maricopa County	78.85
Shrewsbury, MA (town) Worcester County	78.57
Simi Valley, CA (city) Ventura County	78.39
Seadrift, TX (city) Calhoun County	78.05
Lewisville, TX (city) Denton County	77.88
Carson, CA (city) Los Angeles County	77.17
Citrus Heights, CA (city) Sacramento County	77.17
Corona, CA (city) Riverside County	77.11

Notes: Please refer to the User's Guide for an explanation of data; ranking tables include all places with Asian and/or NHPI populations above SF4 population thresholds; (1) tables reflect only those areas that meet SF4 population thresholds, therefore there may be less than 50 states, 75 counties or 75 places listed

Median Gross Rent

All Specified Renter-Occupied Housing Units

All States, Top 75 Counties, and Top 75 Places Sorted by Number[1]

State	Dollars/Month
Hawaii	779
New Jersey	751
California	747
Alaska	720
Nevada	699
Maryland	689
Massachusetts	684
Connecticut	681
New York	672
Colorado	671
Washington	663
Virginia	650
New Hampshire	646
Florida	641
Delaware	639
Oregon	620
Arizona	619
District of Columbia	618
Georgia	613
Illinois	605
United States	602
Utah	597
Texas	574
Minnesota	566
Rhode Island	553
Vermont	553
North Carolina	548
Michigan	546
Wisconsin	540
Pennsylvania	531
Indiana	521
Idaho	515
Ohio	515
South Carolina	510
Tennessee	505
New Mexico	503
Kansas	498
Maine	497
Nebraska	491
Missouri	484
Iowa	470
Louisiana	466
Oklahoma	456
Arkansas	453
Alabama	447
Montana	447
Kentucky	445
Mississippi	439
Wyoming	437
South Dakota	426
North Dakota	412
West Virginia	401

County	Dollars/Month
Santa Clara County, CA	1,185
Marin County, CA	1,162
San Mateo County, CA	1,144
Douglas County, CO	1,053
Eagle County, CO	1,007
Fairfax County, VA	998
Falls Church Independent City, VA	965
Nassau County, NY	964
Loudoun County, VA	954
Fairfax Independent City, VA	945
Suffolk County, NY	945
Manassas Park Independent City, VA	930
San Francisco County, CA	928
Santa Cruz County, CA	924
Orange County, CA	923
Montgomery County, MD	914
Putnam County, NY	913
North Slope Borough, AK	902
Contra Costa County, CA	898
Somerset County, NJ	898
Arlington County, VA	897
Aleutians West Census Area, AK	892
Ventura County, CA	892
Fayette County, GA	890
Rockland County, NY	884
Morris County, NJ	883
Howard County, MD	879
Bergen County, NJ	872
Hunterdon County, NJ	867
Sonoma County, CA	864
Juneau Borough, AK	863
Prince William County, VA	862
Alexandria Independent City, VA	861
Charles County, MD	858
Norfolk County, MA	853
Alameda County, CA	852
Middlesex County, NJ	845
Stafford County, VA	842
Westchester County, NY	839
Fairfield County, CT	838
Calvert County, MD	837
DuPage County, IL	837
Middlesex County, MA	835
Santa Barbara County, CA	830
Boulder County, CO	825
Gwinnett County, GA	824
Monroe County, FL	820
Ocean County, NJ	819
Napa County, CA	818
Bethel Census Area, AK	814
Cobb County, GA	806
Spotsylvania County, VA	805
Honolulu County, HI	802
Manassas Independent City, VA	801
Anne Arundel County, MD	798
Collin County, TX	798
Solano County, CA	797
New York County, NY	796
Kodiak Island Borough, AK	791
Suffolk County, MA	791
Sussex County, NJ	790
Maui County, HI	788
Williamson County, TX	787
Douglas County, NV	780
Placer County, CA	780
Monterey County, CA	776
Ketchikan Gateway Borough, AK	775
Queens County, NY	775
DeKalb County, GA	767
Snohomish County, WA	766
San Benito County, CA	765
McHenry County, IL	761
San Diego County, CA	761
Jefferson County, CO	760
Monmouth County, NJ	759

Place	Dollars/Month
Atherton, CA (town) San Mateo County	2,000+
Blackhawk-Camino Tass., CA (cdp) Contra Costa Co.	2,000+
Bunker Hill Village, TX (city) Harris County	2,000+
Demarest, NJ (borough) Bergen County	2,000+
Englewood Cliffs, NJ (borough) Bergen County	2,000+
Great Falls, VA (cdp) Fairfax County	2,000+
Highlands-Baywood Pk., CA (cdp) San Mateo County	2,000+
Hillsborough, CA (town) San Mateo County	2,000+
Hockessin, DE (cdp) New Castle County	2,000+
Lake Success, NY (village) Nassau County	2,000+
Lincolnwood, IL (village) Cook County	2,000+
Loyola, CA (cdp) Santa Clara County	2,000+
Manhasset Hills, NY (cdp) Nassau County	2,000+
Munsey Park, NY (village) Nassau County	2,000+
Newport Coast, CA (cdp) Orange County	2,000+
North Hills, NY (village) Nassau County	2,000+
Rolling Hills, CA (city) Los Angeles County	2,000+
Rolling Hills Estates, CA (city) Los Angeles County	2,000+
San Marino, CA (city) Los Angeles County	2,000+
Scarsdale, NY (village) Westchester County	2,000+
South Barrington, IL (village) Cook County	2,000+
Wolf Trap, VA (cdp) Fairfax County	2,000+
Washington, NJ (township) Bergen County	1,909
Bronxville, NY (village) Westchester County	1,899
Chevy Chase, MD (cdp) Montgomery County	1,895
Alpine, NJ (borough) Bergen County	1,844
Melville, NY (cdp) Suffolk County	1,842
Piedmont, CA (city) Alameda County	1,814
Los Altos Hills, CA (town) Santa Clara County	1,810
Travilah, MD (cdp) Montgomery County	1,800
Allendale, NJ (borough) Bergen County	1,778
Ardsley, NY (village) Westchester County	1,736
Herricks, NY (cdp) Nassau County	1,729
Los Altos, CA (city) Santa Clara County	1,727
McLean, VA (cdp) Fairfax County	1,707
Cupertino, CA (city) Santa Clara County	1,693
Saratoga, CA (city) Santa Clara County	1,689
Old Westbury, NY (village) Nassau County	1,642
Roslyn, NY (village) Nassau County	1,637
Heeia, HI (cdp) Honolulu County	1,636
Haworth, NJ (borough) Bergen County	1,625
Sands Point, NY (village) Nassau County	1,625
Foster City, CA (city) San Mateo County	1,620
Maunawili, HI (cdp) Honolulu County	1,612
Danville, CA (town) Contra Costa County	1,604
Garden City, NY (village) Nassau County	1,604
Oyster Bay Cove, NY (village) Nassau County	1,594
Cresskill, NJ (borough) Bergen County	1,571
Kensington, CA (cdp) Contra Costa County	1,559
Tiburon, CA (town) Marin County	1,557
Dunn Loring, VA (cdp) Fairfax County	1,539
Broadmoor, CA (cdp) San Mateo County	1,536
Clayton, CA (city) Contra Costa County	1,516
Holmdel, NJ (township) Monmouth County	1,512
Chappaqua, NY (cdp) Westchester County	1,504
East Hanover, NJ (township) Morris County	1,504
Rancho Palos Verdes, CA (city) Los Angeles County	1,496
Bernards, NJ (township) Somerset County	1,494
Paramus, NJ (borough) Bergen County	1,483
Manorhaven, NY (village) Nassau County	1,476
Bradbury, CA (city) Los Angeles County	1,469
Marina del Rey, CA (cdp) Los Angeles County	1,453
Saddle River, NJ (borough) Bergen County	1,451
Somers, NY (town) Westchester County	1,451
Alamo, CA (cdp) Contra Costa County	1,449
Bedminster, NJ (township) Somerset County	1,430
West University Place, TX (city) Harris County	1,418
Stony Brook, NY (cdp) Suffolk County	1,402
East Foothills, CA (cdp) Santa Clara County	1,394
San Ramon, CA (city) Contra Costa County	1,388
Tamalpais-Homestead Valley, CA (cdp) Marin County	1,387
South Kensington, MD (cdp) Montgomery County	1,381
New Canaan, CT (town) Fairfield County	1,379
New Castle, NY (town) Westchester County	1,375
Woodbury, NY (cdp) Nassau County	1,375

Notes: Please refer to the User's Guide for an explanation of data; ranking tables include all places with Asian and/or NHPI populations above SF4 population thresholds; (1) tables reflect only those areas that meet SF4 population thresholds, therefore there may be less than 50 states, 75 counties or 75 places listed

Median Gross Rent

Specified Housing Units Rented by Asians

All States, Top 75 Counties, and Top 75 Places Sorted by Number[1]

State	Dollars/Month
New Jersey	882
Massachusetts	839
Virginia	823
California	809
New York	792
Maryland	788
Connecticut	765
Georgia	761
New Hampshire	753
District of Columbia	736
United States	734
Illinois	728
Hawaii	722
Nevada	686
Delaware	685
Florida	685
Washington	670
North Carolina	667
Alaska	664
Colorado	664
Vermont	663
Michigan	659
Pennsylvania	648
Arizona	638
Oregon	634
Texas	627
Tennessee	601
Rhode Island	590
Minnesota	587
Ohio	587
Utah	572
Indiana	565
Wisconsin	563
South Carolina	559
Idaho	545
Missouri	540
New Mexico	535
Kentucky	534
Maine	532
Mississippi	518
Alabama	513
Kansas	509
Iowa	505
Louisiana	497
Nebraska	495
Arkansas	491
West Virginia	467
South Dakota	457
Oklahoma	456
Montana	411
Wyoming	411
North Dakota	387

County	Dollars/Month
Charlotte County, FL	1,534
Santa Clara County, CA	1,217
Putnam County, WV	1,208
San Mateo County, CA	1,188
Nassau County, NY	1,144
Calvert County, MD	1,125
Marin County, CA	1,125
Chippewa County, MI	1,094
Ellis County, TX	1,094
Fayette County, GA	1,094
Newton County, GA	1,083
Saline County, AR	1,076
Westchester County, NY	1,071
Morgan County, AL	1,069
Fairfield County, CT	1,062
North Slope Borough, AK	1,035
Norfolk County, MA	1,027
San Benito County, CA	1,014
Santa Cruz County, CA	1,012
Douglas County, CO	1,009
Boone County, KY	1,000
Bergen County, NJ	999
Forsyth County, GA	984
Hunterdon County, NJ	973
Williamson County, TN	971
Madison County, TN	967
Charles County, MD	966
Cherokee County, GA	963
Suffolk County, NY	961
Fairfax Independent City, VA	960
Ventura County, CA	960
Fairfax County, VA	952
Nacogdoches County, TX	950
Rockland County, NY	938
Jefferson County, WI	929
Middlesex County, NJ	926
Eagle County, CO	925
Geauga County, OH	925
Bethel Census Area, AK	924
Middlesex County, MA	922
Putnam County, FL	920
Loudoun County, VA	919
Nevada County, CA	919
Walton County, GA	919
Amador County, CA	917
Washington County, MN	911
Somerset County, NJ	910
Contra Costa County, CA	906
Orange County, CA	903
Morris County, NJ	892
Putnam County, NY	889
Alameda County, CA	887
Montgomery County, MD	883
Union County, NJ	881
Fort Bend County, TX	867
Guadalupe County, TX	867
Napa County, CA	867
Placer County, CA	865
Ocean County, NJ	863
Lake County, IL	861
Howard County, MD	860
Sonoma County, CA	860
Sauk County, WI	859
Arlington County, VA	855
Washington County, WI	852
Comal County, TX	850
Coweta County, GA	850
Falls Church Independent City, VA	850
Pike County, PA	850
Queens County, NY	849
Cobb County, GA	840
Douglas County, GA	838
Gwinnett County, GA	838
Chester County, PA	837
Warren County, OH	836

Place	Dollars/Month
Allendale, NJ (borough) Bergen County	2,000+
Alpine, NJ (borough) Bergen County	2,000+
Ardsley, NY (village) Westchester County	2,000+
Atherton, CA (town) San Mateo County	2,000+
Branchburg, NJ (township) Somerset County	2,000+
Briarcliff Manor, NY (village) Westchester County	2,000+
Bronxville, NY (village) Westchester County	2,000+
Chappaqua, NY (cdp) Westchester County	2,000+
Cinco Ranch, TX (cdp) Fort Bend County	2,000+
Darien, CT (town) Fairfield County	2,000+
Dedham, MA (town) Norfolk County	2,000+
Deerfield, IL (village) Lake County	2,000+
Demarest, NJ (borough) Bergen County	2,000+
Dix Hills, NY (cdp) Suffolk County	2,000+
Eastchester, NY (cdp) Westchester County	2,000+
Eastchester, NY (town) Westchester County	2,000+
Emerson, NJ (borough) Bergen County	2,000+
Englewood Cliffs, NJ (borough) Bergen County	2,000+
Garden City, NY (village) Nassau County	2,000+
Glen Rock, NJ (borough) Bergen County	2,000+
Greenwich, CT (town) Fairfield County	2,000+
Harrington Park, NJ (borough) Bergen County	2,000+
Hillsborough, CA (town) San Mateo County	2,000+
Lake Success, NY (village) Nassau County	2,000+
Lincolnshire, IL (village) Lake County	2,000+
Loyola, CA (cdp) Santa Clara County	2,000+
Manhasset Hills, NY (cdp) Nassau County	2,000+
Maple Glen, PA (cdp) Montgomery County	2,000+
Maunawili, HI (cdp) Honolulu County	2,000+
McLean, VA (cdp) Fairfax County	2,000+
Munsey Park, NY (village) Nassau County	2,000+
Muttontown, NY (village) Nassau County	2,000+
New Castle, NY (town) Westchester County	2,000+
North New Hyde Park, NY (cdp) Nassau County	2,000+
North Star, DE (cdp) New Castle County	2,000+
Northbrook, IL (village) Cook County	2,000+
Oradell, NJ (borough) Bergen County	2,000+
Oyster Bay Cove, NY (village) Nassau County	2,000+
Ridgefield, CT (town) Fairfield County	2,000+
Rolling Hills Estates, CA (city) Los Angeles County	2,000+
Rye, NY (city) Westchester County	2,000+
Saddle River, NJ (borough) Bergen County	2,000+
Salida, CA (cdp) Stanislaus County	2,000+
Saratoga, CA (city) Santa Clara County	2,000+
Scarsdale, NY (village) Westchester County	2,000+
Tiburon, CA (town) Marin County	2,000+
University Gardens, NY (cdp) Nassau County	2,000+
West Lake Sammamish, WA (cdp) King County	2,000+
Wilton, CT (town) Fairfield County	2,000+
Wolf Trap, VA (cdp) Fairfax County	2,000+
Stony Brook, NY (cdp) Suffolk County	2,000
Washington, NJ (township) Bergen County	2,000
Herricks, NY (cdp) Nassau County	1,982
Cresskill, NJ (borough) Bergen County	1,974
Somers, NY (town) Westchester County	1,958
Manalapan, NJ (township) Monmouth County	1,920
Paramus, NJ (borough) Bergen County	1,912
Rossmoor, CA (cdp) Orange County	1,896
Greenville, NY (cdp) Westchester County	1,890
Port Washington, NY (cdp) Nassau County	1,889
Granger, IN (cdp) Saint Joseph County	1,875
New Canaan, CT (town) Fairfield County	1,875
San Marino, CA (city) Los Angeles County	1,875
Tappan, NY (cdp) Rockland County	1,875
Waldwick, NJ (borough) Bergen County	1,867
La Canada Flintridge, CA (city) Los Angeles County	1,865
Harrison, NY (village) Westchester County	1,853
Bedminster, NJ (township) Somerset County	1,839
Salisbury, NY (cdp) Nassau County	1,830
Albertson, NY (cdp) Nassau County	1,813
West Freehold, NJ (cdp) Monmouth County	1,813
Kensington, CA (cdp) Contra Costa County	1,804
Springdale, NJ (cdp) Camden County	1,803
Oakland, NJ (borough) Bergen County	1,798
Holmdel, NJ (township) Monmouth County	1,783

Notes: Please refer to the User's Guide for an explanation of data; ranking tables include all places with Asian and/or NHPI populations above SF4 population thresholds; (1) tables reflect only those areas that meet SF4 population thresholds, therefore there may be less than 50 states, 75 counties or 75 places listed

Median Gross Rent

Specified Housing Units Rented by Native Hawaiian and Other Pacific Islanders

All States, Top 75 Counties, and Top 75 Places Sorted by Number[1]

State	Dollars/Month
Delaware	880
Maine	831
California	799
Massachusetts	784
Alaska	729
Maryland	728
Connecticut	719
West Virginia	713
Hawaii	702
Nevada	699
Washington	692
United States	690
Illinois	674
New York	668
Colorado	657
Virginia	654
Florida	653
New Jersey	646
Utah	630
Texas	620
Georgia	619
Oregon	599
Arizona	590
Minnesota	584
New Mexico	583
South Carolina	572
North Carolina	571
Wisconsin	558
Missouri	552
Michigan	545
Alabama	542
Pennsylvania	541
Ohio	539
Tennessee	527
Kentucky	524
Indiana	516
Montana	513
Kansas	509
Oklahoma	479
Arkansas	471
Mississippi	471
Iowa	459
Nebraska	444
Rhode Island	438
Louisiana	421
Idaho	381

County	Dollars/Month
Santa Clara County, CA	1,281
San Mateo County, CA	1,127
Fairfax County, VA	1,069
Suffolk County, NY	1,063
Ventura County, CA	1,010
Contra Costa County, CA	967
Orange County, CA	916
Alameda County, CA	910
Montgomery County, MD	893
Solano County, CA	887
Sonoma County, CA	884
New York County, NY	875
Palm Beach County, FL	845
Fresno County, CA	829
Clark County, WA	816
Nassau County, NY	810
Lane County, OR	803
San Diego County, CA	801
Travis County, TX	801
Jefferson County, CO	792
Queens County, NY	790
Snohomish County, WA	789
Monterey County, CA	779
Broward County, FL	753
Hillsborough County, FL	735
Dallas County, TX	731
Essex County, NJ	729
Anchorage Borough, AK	727
Clark County, NV	726
Los Angeles County, CA	726
King County, WA	725
Honolulu County, HI	722
Santa Barbara County, CA	718
Davis County, UT	709
Thurston County, WA	708
Cook County, IL	706
Maui County, HI	706
Denver County, CO	703
Riverside County, CA	695
Orange County, FL	688
El Paso County, CO	687
Miami-Dade County, FL	683
San Joaquin County, CA	679
Kitsap County, WA	678
Kings County, NY	665
Coryell County, TX	661
Kauai County, HI	660
Yolo County, CA	656
Washington County, OR	649
Stanislaus County, CA	648
Arapahoe County, CO	646
Salt Lake County, UT	644
Onslow County, NC	642
Harris County, TX	627
Maricopa County, AZ	626
Jackson County, MO	623
Pierce County, WA	623
San Bernardino County, CA	623
Clackamas County, OR	620
Hawaii County, HI	618
Utah County, UT	618
Washoe County, NV	617
San Francisco County, CA	612
Sacramento County, CA	604
St. Louis County, MO	601
Tarrant County, TX	596
Marion County, OR	595
Hennepin County, MN	593
Bexar County, TX	588
Multnomah County, OR	586
Ada County, ID	585
Philadelphia County, PA	584
Bronx County, NY	578
Gwinnett County, GA	578
Davidson County, TN	577

Place	Dollars/Month
Milpitas, CA (city) Santa Clara County	1,646
Maunawili, HI (cdp) Honolulu County	1,375
Sandy, UT (city) Salt Lake County	1,375
South San Francisco, CA (city) San Mateo County	1,352
Santa Clara, CA (city) Santa Clara County	1,317
Daly City, CA (city) San Mateo County	1,273
Mililani Town, HI (cdp) Honolulu County	1,263
San Jose, CA (city) Santa Clara County	1,246
Pittsburg, CA (city) Contra Costa County	1,219
San Mateo, CA (city) San Mateo County	1,219
San Bruno, CA (city) San Mateo County	1,159
Concord, CA (city) Contra Costa County	1,150
Rialto, CA (city) San Bernardino County	1,096
Kalaoa, HI (cdp) Hawaii County	1,093
Union City, CA (city) Alameda County	1,086
Ewa Beach, HI (cdp) Honolulu County	1,083
Pearl City, HI (cdp) Honolulu County	1,082
Garden Grove, CA (city) Orange County	1,036
Sunnyvale, CA (city) Santa Clara County	1,028
Waimalu, HI (cdp) Honolulu County	1,023
Village Park, HI (cdp) Honolulu County	1,016
Lakewood, CA (city) Los Angeles County	1,013
Henderson, NV (city) Clark County	1,010
Sunrise Manor, NV (cdp) Clark County	985
Makakilo City, HI (cdp) Honolulu County	984
Kahaluu, HI (cdp) Honolulu County	973
East Palo Alto, CA (city) San Mateo County	971
Santa Ana, CA (city) Orange County	953
Costa Mesa, CA (city) Orange County	950
Kaneohe, HI (cdp) Honolulu County	950
Whitmore Village, HI (cdp) Honolulu County	950
Fremont, CA (city) Alameda County	937
Laie, HI (cdp) Honolulu County	932
Hayward, CA (city) Alameda County	928
Huntington Beach, CA (city) Orange County	927
Vallejo, CA (city) Solano County	919
Lahaina, HI (cdp) Maui County	915
Aiea, HI (cdp) Honolulu County	907
Oceanside, CA (city) San Diego County	906
San Leandro, CA (city) Alameda County	887
Lawndale, CA (city) Los Angeles County	882
Nanakuli, HI (cdp) Honolulu County	875
Kihei, HI (cdp) Maui County	864
Waipio, HI (cdp) Honolulu County	862
Oakland, CA (city) Alameda County	859
Waikapu, HI (cdp) Maui County	858
Vista, CA (city) San Diego County	857
Kaaawa, HI (cdp) Honolulu County	850
Paia, HI (cdp) Maui County	850
Kailua, HI (cdp) Honolulu County	846
Anaheim, CA (city) Orange County	844
Redwood City, CA (city) San Mateo County	844
Hauula, HI (cdp) Honolulu County	842
Westminster, CA (city) Orange County	837
Waimea, HI (cdp) Hawaii County	829
Vancouver, WA (city) Clark County	828
San Diego, CA (city) San Diego County	817
Alameda, CA (city) Alameda County	814
Austin, TX (city) Travis County	812
Richmond, CA (city) Contra Costa County	807
North Las Vegas, NV (city) Clark County	806
Makawao, HI (cdp) Maui County	803
Oxnard, CA (city) Ventura County	800
Hanapepe, HI (cdp) Kauai County	795
Fairfield, CA (city) Solano County	794
Waikoloa Village, HI (cdp) Hawaii County	790
Kilauea, HI (cdp) Kauai County	783
Holualoa, HI (cdp) Hawaii County	781
Spring Valley, NV (cdp) Clark County	781
Hana, HI (cdp) Maui County	775
Maili, HI (cdp) Honolulu County	764
Chula Vista, CA (city) San Diego County	760
Los Angeles, CA (city) Los Angeles County	747
West Jordan, UT (city) Salt Lake County	747
Carson, CA (city) Los Angeles County	738

Notes: Please refer to the User's Guide for an explanation of data; ranking tables include all places with Asian and/or NHPI populations above SF4 population thresholds; (1) tables reflect only those areas that meet SF4 population thresholds, therefore there may be less than 50 states, 75 counties or 75 places listed

Median Gross Rent

Specified Housing Units Rented by Asian Indians

***All States, Top 75 Counties, and Top 75 Places Sorted by Number*[1]**

State	Dollars/Month
California	1,051
Massachusetts	966
Virginia	882
New Jersey	870
New York	827
District of Columbia	822
Hawaii	820
Connecticut	816
Washington	808
Maryland	800
New Hampshire	800
Georgia	793
United States	793
Illinois	790
Vermont	764
Colorado	744
Florida	740
Minnesota	733
Alaska	718
North Carolina	716
Oregon	715
Nevada	713
Delaware	704
Pennsylvania	699
Michigan	690
Texas	690
Rhode Island	688
Arizona	684
Utah	661
Tennessee	635
Wisconsin	630
Kansas	623
Ohio	621
Missouri	613
Idaho	608
Indiana	608
South Carolina	607
Iowa	582
Louisiana	577
Alabama	570
Arkansas	565
Kentucky	549
Mississippi	548
Nebraska	547
New Mexico	536
South Dakota	522
West Virginia	514
Maine	508
Oklahoma	493
North Dakota	427
Montana	421
Wyoming	339

County	Dollars/Month
Santa Clara County, CA	1,341
Putnam County, NY	1,292
San Mateo County, CA	1,254
New York County, NY	1,247
Marin County, CA	1,191
San Francisco County, CA	1,164
Alameda County, CA	1,133
Fairfield County, CT	1,105
Norfolk County, MA	1,086
Nassau County, NY	1,079
Suffolk County, MA	1,068
Cherokee County, GA	1,060
Santa Cruz County, CA	1,053
Hunterdon County, NJ	1,022
Contra Costa County, CA	1,006
Fairfax County, VA	994
Ventura County, CA	983
Middlesex County, MA	975
Suffolk County, NY	961
San Diego County, CA	956
Fairfax Independent City, VA	955
Loudoun County, VA	952
Westmoreland County, PA	950
Douglas County, CO	944
Middlesex County, NJ	943
McHenry County, IL	935
Orange County, CA	929
Sussex County, NJ	925
Rockland County, NY	922
Somerset County, NJ	919
Monterey County, CA	915
St. Mary's County, MD	914
Union County, NJ	905
Howard County, MD	903
Westchester County, NY	901
Montgomery County, MD	898
Bergen County, NJ	881
Chester County, PA	881
Solano County, CA	876
Sonoma County, CA	875
Washington County, MN	871
Arlington County, VA	869
Morris County, NJ	861
Hillsborough County, NH	857
King County, WA	856
Queens County, NY	854
Alexandria Independent City, VA	853
Northampton County, PA	853
Fulton County, GA	851
Henry County, GA	850
DuPage County, IL	848
Essex County, MA	846
Lorain County, OH	842
Cobb County, GA	839
Seminole County, FL	839
Plymouth County, MA	838
Jefferson County, CO	835
San Luis Obispo County, CA	832
York County, VA	832
Warren County, OH	831
Gwinnett County, GA	830
Palm Beach County, FL	830
Lake County, IL	829
Hamilton County, IN	828
Worcester County, MA	827
Los Angeles County, CA	826
Fort Bend County, TX	825
Ocean County, NJ	825
Marion County, FL	824
Litchfield County, CT	822
Essex County, NJ	821
Santa Barbara County, CA	819
Monmouth County, NJ	811
Cook County, IL	808
Dakota County, MN	808

Place	Dollars/Month
Danville, CA (town) Contra Costa County	2,000+
Hanover, NJ (township) Morris County	2,000+
Livingston, NJ (township) Essex County	2,000+
Muttontown, NY (village) Nassau County	2,000+
New Castle, NY (town) Westchester County	2,000+
Potomac, MD (cdp) Montgomery County	2,000+
Saratoga, CA (city) Santa Clara County	2,000+
Wolf Trap, VA (cdp) Fairfax County	2,000+
Freehold, NJ (township) Monmouth County	1,875
Los Altos Hills, CA (town) Santa Clara County	1,875
Manalapan, NJ (township) Monmouth County	1,875
McLean, VA (cdp) Fairfax County	1,875
Walnut, CA (city) Los Angeles County	1,850
Holmdel, NJ (township) Monmouth County	1,750
Millbrae, CA (city) San Mateo County	1,750
Cupertino, CA (city) Santa Clara County	1,641
Paramus, NJ (borough) Bergen County	1,625
Montgomery, NJ (township) Somerset County	1,579
Smithtown, NY (town) Suffolk County	1,521
Los Altos, CA (city) Santa Clara County	1,471
Foster City, CA (city) San Mateo County	1,447
Plainview, NY (cdp) Nassau County	1,446
North New Hyde Park, NY (cdp) Nassau County	1,444
Palo Alto, CA (city) Santa Clara County	1,384
Lawrence, NJ (township) Mercer County	1,380
Commack, NY (cdp) Suffolk County	1,375
Marlboro, NJ (township) Monmouth County	1,375
Nanuet, NY (cdp) Rockland County	1,375
Newton, MA (city) Middlesex County	1,375
North Potomac, MD (cdp) Montgomery County	1,375
Sunnyvale, CA (city) Santa Clara County	1,374
Santa Clara, CA (city) Santa Clara County	1,351
Lexington, MA (town) Middlesex County	1,347
Streamwood, IL (village) Cook County	1,322
Fort Lee, NJ (borough) Bergen County	1,319
Elmhurst, IL (city) Du Page County	1,317
Mountain View, CA (city) Santa Clara County	1,317
Aliso Viejo, CA (cdp) Orange County	1,300
Darien, IL (city) Du Page County	1,297
Irvine, CA (city) Orange County	1,293
Hercules, CA (city) Contra Costa County	1,281
Milpitas, CA (city) Santa Clara County	1,280
Newark, CA (city) Alameda County	1,280
Colonia, NJ (cdp) Middlesex County	1,271
Hoboken, NJ (city) Hudson County	1,269
San Jose, CA (city) Santa Clara County	1,268
Lincolnwood, IL (village) Cook County	1,266
Stamford, CT (city) Fairfield County	1,266
Huntington, NY (town) Suffolk County	1,259
Redwood City, CA (city) San Mateo County	1,238
West Bloomfield, MI (township) Oakland County	1,238
Pleasanton, CA (city) Alameda County	1,234
West Hempstead, NY (cdp) Nassau County	1,214
San Mateo, CA (city) San Mateo County	1,208
San Rafael, CA (city) Marin County	1,208
Bridgewater, NJ (township) Somerset County	1,205
Wayne, NJ (township) Passaic County	1,204
Rancho Palos Verdes, CA (city) Los Angeles County	1,203
Yorba Linda, CA (city) Orange County	1,203
North Hempstead, NY (town) Nassau County	1,201
San Ramon, CA (city) Contra Costa County	1,201
Dublin, CA (city) Alameda County	1,199
Oyster Bay, NY (town) Nassau County	1,198
Fremont, CA (city) Alameda County	1,196
San Bruno, CA (city) San Mateo County	1,195
Campbell, CA (city) Santa Clara County	1,192
Lower Makefield, PA (township) Bucks County	1,184
Diamond Bar, CA (city) Los Angeles County	1,183
Port Washington, NY (cdp) Nassau County	1,183
Society Hill, NJ (cdp) Middlesex County	1,173
Union City, CA (city) Alameda County	1,173
Greenville, NY (cdp) Westchester County	1,170
Belmont, CA (city) San Mateo County	1,167
Brookline, MA (town) Norfolk County	1,165
San Francisco, CA (city) San Francisco County	1,164

Notes: Please refer to the User's Guide for an explanation of data; ranking tables include all places with Asian and/or NHPI populations above SF4 population thresholds; (1) tables reflect only those areas that meet SF4 population thresholds, therefore there may be less than 50 states, 75 counties or 75 places listed

Median Gross Rent

Specified Housing Units Rented by Bangladeshis

All States, Top 75 Counties, and Top 75 Places Sorted by Number[1]

State	Dollars/Month
California	788
New Jersey	787
New York	773
Maryland	772
Virginia	723
United States	721
Georgia	715
Ohio	660
Florida	656
Connecticut	635
Texas	627
Illinois	616
Massachusetts	613
Pennsylvania	558
Michigan	522

County	Dollars/Month
Santa Clara County, CA	1,258
Passaic County, NJ	880
Middlesex County, NJ	856
Queens County, NY	796
Montgomery County, MD	761
Fairfax County, VA	759
Kings County, NY	743
New York County, NY	707
Bronx County, NY	706
DeKalb County, GA	700
Los Angeles County, CA	674
Dallas County, TX	664
Atlantic County, NJ	663
Harris County, TX	629
Wayne County, MI	493

Place	Dollars/Month
Paterson, NJ (city) Passaic County	863
New York, NY (city)	773
Los Angeles, CA (city) Los Angeles County	652
Hamtramck, MI (city) Wayne County	496

Notes: Please refer to the User's Guide for an explanation of data; ranking tables include all places with Asian and/or NHPI populations above SF4 population thresholds; (1) tables reflect only those areas that meet SF4 population thresholds, therefore there may be less than 50 states, 75 counties or 75 places listed

Median Gross Rent

Specified Housing Units Rented by Cambodians

All States, Top 75 Counties, and Top 75 Places Sorted by Number[1]

State	Dollars/Month
New Jersey	782
Hawaii	775
Oklahoma	775
Nevada	769
Virginia	731
Maryland	721
Connecticut	679
New York	675
Illinois	667
Arizona	632
Oregon	609
Massachusetts	602
California	601
United States	582
South Carolina	579
Georgia	571
Indiana	563
Tennessee	558
Minnesota	556
Michigan	555
Texas	555
Utah	546
Missouri	545
Colorado	541
Washington	526
Pennsylvania	523
Rhode Island	517
Maine	509
Ohio	459
Alabama	456
North Carolina	450
Florida	448
Iowa	414
Kansas	401
Wisconsin	361

County	Dollars/Month
Santa Clara County, CA	1,039
DeKalb County, GA	1,028
Camden County, NJ	925
Fairfield County, CT	878
Montgomery County, MD	875
Orange County, CA	851
Kings County, NY	808
Arlington County, VA	792
Fairfax County, VA	784
Clark County, NV	769
San Francisco County, CA	740
Washington County, OR	717
Henrico County, VA	707
Clayton County, GA	700
Sonoma County, CA	686
Thurston County, WA	686
Cook County, IL	673
Hennepin County, MN	665
Maricopa County, AZ	665
Riverside County, CA	657
Middlesex County, MA	648
Worcester County, MA	643
Brazoria County, TX	625
Essex County, MA	625
Alameda County, CA	620
Los Angeles County, CA	620
Multnomah County, OR	619
Bronx County, NY	618
Dakota County, MN	613
Cowlitz County, WA	607
Salt Lake County, UT	602
Snohomish County, WA	598
Ottawa County, MI	575
San Diego County, CA	574
Shelby County, TN	571
Dallas County, TX	563
Suffolk County, MA	561
Stanislaus County, CA	560
Kern County, CA	556
San Bernardino County, CA	554
King County, WA	545
Sacramento County, CA	538
San Joaquin County, CA	525
Philadelphia County, PA	519
Providence County, RI	517
Harris County, TX	509
Denver County, CO	506
Olmsted County, MN	505
Cumberland County, ME	503
Davidson County, NC	501
Monroe County, NY	496
Hampden County, MA	493
Pierce County, WA	474
Clark County, WA	469
Chesterfield County, VA	465
Tarrant County, TX	465
Mobile County, AL	460
Ramsey County, MN	459
Fresno County, CA	457
Hamilton County, OH	448
Pinellas County, FL	444
Franklin County, OH	442
Cuyahoga County, OH	435
Mecklenburg County, NC	403
Sedgwick County, KS	398
Polk County, IA	396
Bristol County, MA	388
Duval County, FL	384
Denton County, TX	0
Gwinnett County, GA	0
Scott County, MN	0

Place	Dollars/Month
San Jose, CA (city) Santa Clara County	1,012
Danbury, CT (city) Fairfield County	922
Bridgeport, CT (city) Fairfield County	863
Silver Spring, MD (cdp) Montgomery County	808
Arlington, VA (cdp) Arlington County	792
Santa Rosa, CA (city) Sonoma County	781
Bellflower, CA (city) Los Angeles County	768
San Francisco, CA (city) San Francisco County	740
Monterey Park, CA (city) Los Angeles County	731
Lakewood, CA (city) Los Angeles County	727
New York, NY (city)	724
Santa Ana, CA (city) Orange County	716
Garden Grove, CA (city) Orange County	693
Signal Hill, CA (city) Los Angeles County	678
Chicago, IL (city) Cook County	676
Longview, WA (city) Cowlitz County	675
Lowell, MA (city) Middlesex County	650
Lawrence, MA (city) Essex County	646
Los Angeles, CA (city) Los Angeles County	644
Rosemead, CA (city) Los Angeles County	633
Bloomington, MN (city) Hennepin County	632
Pomona, CA (city) Los Angeles County	629
Boston, MA (city) Suffolk County	628
Minneapolis, MN (city) Hennepin County	625
Oakland, CA (city) Alameda County	619
Portland, OR (city) Multnomah County	619
Sacramento, CA (city) Sacramento County	615
Phoenix, AZ (city) Maricopa County	614
Lynn, MA (city) Essex County	613
Norwalk, CA (city) Los Angeles County	600
Long Beach, CA (city) Los Angeles County	593
Everett, WA (city) Snohomish County	575
Memphis, TN (city) Shelby County	571
San Diego, CA (city) San Diego County	571
Aurora, CO (city) Arapahoe County	565
Cranston, RI (city) Providence County	556
Carrollton, TX (city) Denton County	543
Beaverton, OR (city) Washington County	535
Revere, MA (city) Suffolk County	532
Stockton, CA (city) San Joaquin County	523
Philadelphia, PA (city) Philadelphia County	519
Modesto, CA (city) Stanislaus County	516
Rochester, MN (city) Olmsted County	515
Dallas, TX (city) Dallas County	510
Providence, RI (city) Providence County	510
Houston, TX (city) Harris County	509
Attleboro, MA (city) Bristol County	508
Denver, CO (city) Denver County	506
Lexington, NC (city) Davidson County	501
Tacoma, WA (city) Pierce County	488
Seattle, WA (city) King County	486
Portland, ME (city) Cumberland County	485
St. Petersburg, FL (city) Pinellas County	467
San Bernardino, CA (city) San Bernardino County	450
Fresno, CA (city) Fresno County	449
Columbus, OH (city) Franklin County	445
Charlotte, NC (city) Mecklenburg County	403
St. Paul, MN (city) Ramsey County	391
White Center, WA (cdp) King County	386
Jacksonville, FL (city) Duval County	384
Fall River, MA (city) Bristol County	371
West Valley City, UT (city) Salt Lake County	0

Notes: Please refer to the User's Guide for an explanation of data; ranking tables include all places with Asian and/or NHPI populations above SF4 population thresholds; (1) tables reflect only those areas that meet SF4 population thresholds, therefore there may be less than 50 states, 75 counties or 75 places listed

Median Gross Rent

Specified Housing Units Rented by Chinese (except Taiwanese)

All States, Top 75 Counties, and Top 75 Places Sorted by Number[1]

State	Dollars/Month
New Jersey	869
Maryland	789
California	779
Massachusetts	774
Virginia	753
Connecticut	733
Georgia	705
Alaska	703
Nevada	697
Hawaii	694
Washington	690
United States	689
New York	685
New Hampshire	674
Delaware	670
North Carolina	661
Florida	654
Illinois	654
District of Columbia	652
Pennsylvania	627
Oregon	620
Colorado	617
Arizona	611
Michigan	607
Rhode Island	606
Idaho	603
Minnesota	589
Vermont	586
Texas	581
Wisconsin	567
Maine	563
New Mexico	556
Utah	541
Tennessee	539
Ohio	533
Missouri	519
Indiana	516
South Carolina	498
Kansas	493
Louisiana	491
Iowa	483
Arkansas	476
Kentucky	458
Oklahoma	435
Montana	433
Nebraska	425
Mississippi	424
West Virginia	419
Alabama	418
South Dakota	394
Wyoming	388
North Dakota	316

County	Dollars/Month
Brazoria County, TX	1,309
Rockland County, NY	1,286
San Mateo County, CA	1,216
Marin County, CA	1,179
Santa Clara County, CA	1,171
Anoka County, MN	1,125
Douglas County, CO	1,125
Fairfield County, CT	1,040
Lake County, IL	1,030
Contra Costa County, CA	981
Ventura County, CA	979
Westchester County, NY	975
Nassau County, NY	966
Orange County, CA	950
Ottawa County, MI	950
Bergen County, NJ	949
Middlesex County, MA	940
Hudson County, NJ	936
Morris County, NJ	929
Union County, NJ	916
Anne Arundel County, MD	913
Barnstable County, MA	912
Santa Cruz County, CA	912
Fairfax County, VA	896
Norfolk County, MA	892
Fairfax Independent City, VA	889
Fort Bend County, TX	888
Santa Barbara County, CA	883
Placer County, CA	880
Kauai County, HI	876
Litchfield County, CT	875
Arlington County, VA	874
Montgomery County, MD	873
Somerset County, NJ	872
Suffolk County, NY	870
Richmond County, NY	865
Middlesex County, NJ	862
Alexandria Independent City, VA	855
Solano County, CA	855
Ulster County, NY	854
Burlington County, NJ	853
Putnam County, NY	850
San Diego County, CA	850
Broward County, FL	849
Napa County, CA	845
Cobb County, GA	839
DuPage County, IL	836
Howard County, MD	829
Warren County, OH	827
Monmouth County, NJ	823
Loudoun County, VA	822
Sonoma County, CA	820
Essex County, NJ	809
Frederick County, MD	804
Essex County, MA	803
Plymouth County, MA	802
Monterey County, CA	796
Ocean County, NJ	796
Queens County, NY	794
Snohomish County, WA	789
McHenry County, IL	786
Williamson County, TX	786
Adams County, CO	783
Gwinnett County, GA	780
Orange County, NY	779
Cumberland County, PA	775
Hunterdon County, NJ	775
Chester County, PA	767
Clackamas County, OR	766
Boulder County, CO	763
Montgomery County, PA	762
Wake County, NC	761
Chesterfield County, VA	758
Cumberland County, ME	756
Passaic County, NJ	752

Place	Dollars/Month
Bernards, NJ (township) Somerset County	2,000+
Hanover, NJ (township) Morris County	2,000+
Hillsborough, CA (town) San Mateo County	2,000+
La Canada Flintridge, CA (city) Los Angeles County	2,000+
Lake Success, NY (village) Nassau County	2,000+
New Castle, NY (town) Westchester County	2,000+
Northbrook, IL (village) Cook County	2,000+
Scarsdale, NY (village) Westchester County	2,000+
Stony Brook, NY (cdp) Suffolk County	2,000+
Tenafly, NJ (borough) Bergen County	2,000+
Danville, CA (town) Contra Costa County	1,938
Manalapan, NJ (township) Monmouth County	1,875
Mililani Town, HI (cdp) Honolulu County	1,788
Berkeley Heights, NJ (township) Union County	1,777
Highlands-Baywood Pk., CA (cdp) San Mateo County	1,725
Los Altos, CA (city) Santa Clara County	1,652
Clarkstown, NY (town) Rockland County	1,636
Calabasas, CA (city) Los Angeles County	1,625
McLean, VA (cdp) Fairfax County	1,625
Missouri City, TX (city) Fort Bend County	1,625
West Bloomfield, MI (township) Oakland County	1,625
Cupertino, CA (city) Santa Clara County	1,582
San Marino, CA (city) Los Angeles County	1,554
Andover, MA (town) Essex County	1,536
Freehold, NJ (township) Monmouth County	1,531
Foster City, CA (city) San Mateo County	1,524
Lafayette, CA (city) Contra Costa County	1,520
Holmdel, NJ (township) Monmouth County	1,500
Rancho Palos Verdes, CA (city) Los Angeles County	1,482
Morgan Hill, CA (city) Santa Clara County	1,400
Toms River, NJ (cdp) Ocean County	1,393
Greenburgh, NY (town) Westchester County	1,386
Stamford, CT (city) Fairfield County	1,381
Bellaire, TX (city) Harris County	1,375
Livingston, NJ (township) Essex County	1,375
Montville, NJ (township) Morris County	1,375
Mundelein, IL (village) Lake County	1,375
Palos Verdes Estates, CA (city) Los Angeles County	1,375
Piedmont, CA (city) Alameda County	1,375
Warren, NJ (township) Somerset County	1,375
West Windsor, NJ (township) Mercer County	1,375
Dublin, CA (city) Alameda County	1,361
Belmont, MA (cdp) Middlesex County	1,352
Belmont, MA (town) Middlesex County	1,352
Ramapo, NY (town) Rockland County	1,352
Los Gatos, CA (town) Santa Clara County	1,342
Newport Beach, CA (city) Orange County	1,340
Buffalo Grove, IL (village) Lake County	1,325
Menlo Park, CA (city) San Mateo County	1,319
San Carlos, CA (city) San Mateo County	1,313
Redwood City, CA (city) San Mateo County	1,308
Millbrae, CA (city) San Mateo County	1,297
South San Francisco, CA (city) San Mateo County	1,283
Lexington, MA (town) Middlesex County	1,275
Santa Barbara, CA (city) Santa Barbara County	1,275
North Potomac, MD (cdp) Montgomery County	1,266
Hudson, OH (city) Summit County	1,264
San Rafael, CA (city) Marin County	1,260
Cerritos, CA (city) Los Angeles County	1,255
Needham, MA (town) Norfolk County	1,250
Newton, MA (city) Middlesex County	1,250
Pacifica, CA (city) San Mateo County	1,250
Milpitas, CA (city) Santa Clara County	1,248
Kailua, HI (cdp) Honolulu County	1,239
Dover, NJ (township) Ocean County	1,232
Mountain View, CA (city) Santa Clara County	1,226
Laguna Niguel, CA (city) Orange County	1,219
Pleasanton, CA (city) Alameda County	1,217
Palo Alto, CA (city) Santa Clara County	1,215
Santa Clara, CA (city) Santa Clara County	1,207
Brookline, MA (town) Norfolk County	1,205
Burlingame, CA (city) San Mateo County	1,203
San Ramon, CA (city) Contra Costa County	1,201
Irvine, CA (city) Orange County	1,192
North Andover, MA (town) Essex County	1,188

Notes: Please refer to the User's Guide for an explanation of data; ranking tables include all places with Asian and/or NHPI populations above SF4 population thresholds; (1) tables reflect only those areas that meet SF4 population thresholds, therefore there may be less than 50 states, 75 counties or 75 places listed

Median Gross Rent

Specified Housing Units Rented by Fijians

All States, Top 75 Counties, and Top 75 Places Sorted by Number[1]

State	Dollars/Month
California	771
United States	740
Washington	727
Oregon	571

County	Dollars/Month
Santa Clara County, CA	1,128
San Mateo County, CA	957
Alameda County, CA	943
Contra Costa County, CA	850
King County, WA	725
Los Angeles County, CA	711
Yolo County, CA	694
Sacramento County, CA	598
Stanislaus County, CA	495

Place	Dollars/Month
Hayward, CA (city) Alameda County	956
Sacramento, CA (city) Sacramento County	596
Modesto, CA (city) Stanislaus County	560

Notes: Please refer to the User's Guide for an explanation of data; ranking tables include all places with Asian and/or NHPI populations above SF4 population thresholds; (1) tables reflect only those areas that meet SF4 population thresholds, therefore there may be less than 50 states, 75 counties or 75 places listed

Median Gross Rent

Specified Housing Units Rented by Filipinos

All States, Top 75 Counties, and Top 75 Places Sorted by Number[1]

State	Dollars/Month
Massachusetts	832
New York	823
New Jersey	798
California	773
New Hampshire	767
Maryland	760
District of Columbia	758
Virginia	744
United States	730
Connecticut	728
Hawaii	717
Colorado	712
Georgia	702
Illinois	687
Alaska	683
Washington	679
Nevada	678
Minnesota	669
Pennsylvania	648
Florida	637
North Carolina	636
Arizona	628
Oregon	626
Delaware	618
Michigan	615
Indiana	605
Maine	603
Texas	602
Rhode Island	597
Tennessee	597
Utah	595
Ohio	592
Kansas	581
Wisconsin	580
New Mexico	569
Vermont	542
Mississippi	541
Arkansas	529
South Carolina	527
Alabama	525
Kentucky	525
Louisiana	525
Idaho	524
Missouri	524
Nebraska	491
Wyoming	487
South Dakota	481
North Dakota	476
Oklahoma	471
West Virginia	469
Iowa	400
Montana	368

County	Dollars/Month
San Benito County, CA	1,375
Marin County, CA	1,155
Santa Clara County, CA	1,129
Sandoval County, NM	1,125
Boulder County, CO	1,108
San Mateo County, CA	1,097
Nassau County, NY	1,062
North Slope Borough, AK	1,018
New York County, NY	978
Fairfax County, VA	965
Howard County, MD	963
Sonoma County, CA	955
Orange County, NY	954
Suffolk County, NY	953
Charles County, MD	939
Ocean County, NJ	938
Suffolk County, MA	930
Morris County, NJ	920
Middlesex County, NJ	918
Montgomery County, PA	916
Ventura County, CA	913
Alameda County, CA	910
Middlesex County, MA	907
Fairfield County, CT	900
Orange County, CA	898
Fort Bend County, TX	895
Norfolk County, MA	888
Bergen County, NJ	879
Dakota County, MN	879
Contra Costa County, CA	872
Montgomery County, MD	869
Mercer County, NJ	865
Somerset County, NJ	864
Bucks County, PA	860
DeKalb County, GA	850
Loudoun County, VA	850
Stafford County, VA	850
Westchester County, NY	848
Richmond County, NY	843
Arapahoe County, CO	842
Rockingham County, NH	839
Union County, NJ	834
Rockland County, NY	831
Queens County, NY	816
Arlington County, VA	814
Prince William County, VA	814
Monmouth County, NJ	809
Fulton County, GA	808
Adams County, CO	805
Chesterfield County, VA	803
Gwinnett County, GA	802
Alexandria Independent City, VA	799
Passaic County, NJ	793
Santa Cruz County, CA	793
Anne Arundel County, MD	789
Broward County, FL	788
Essex County, NJ	788
DuPage County, IL	785
Washtenaw County, MI	783
San Francisco County, CA	777
Placer County, CA	775
Sussex County, NJ	775
Monterey County, CA	770
Collin County, TX	769
Jefferson County, CO	769
Summit County, OH	765
Salt Lake County, UT	763
Wake County, NC	763
Palm Beach County, FL	762
Hillsborough County, NH	757
Will County, IL	755
Ketchikan Gateway Borough, AK	754
Kings County, NY	751
Solano County, CA	751
Skagit County, WA	750

Place	Dollars/Month
Babylon, NY (town) Suffolk County	2,000+
Huntington, NY (town) Suffolk County	2,000+
Cupertino, CA (city) Santa Clara County	1,833
Broadmoor, CA (cdp) San Mateo County	1,641
East Hill-Meridian, WA (cdp) King County	1,625
Levittown, NY (cdp) Nassau County	1,625
Livingston, NJ (township) Essex County	1,625
Los Banos, CA (city) Merced County	1,625
Stamford, CT (city) Fairfield County	1,574
Hollister, CA (city) San Benito County	1,523
Hillcrest, NY (cdp) Rockland County	1,508
Foster City, CA (city) San Mateo County	1,460
Hicksville, NY (cdp) Nassau County	1,458
Rancho Palos Verdes, CA (city) Los Angeles County	1,438
Fair Lawn, NJ (borough) Bergen County	1,375
Miramar, FL (city) Broward County	1,375
Potomac, MD (cdp) Montgomery County	1,375
Redland, MD (cdp) Montgomery County	1,375
San Ramon, CA (city) Contra Costa County	1,363
Teaneck, NJ (township) Bergen County	1,344
Walnut, CA (city) Los Angeles County	1,319
Franconia, VA (cdp) Fairfax County	1,313
Pacifica, CA (city) San Mateo County	1,310
Pleasanton, CA (city) Alameda County	1,277
Burke, VA (cdp) Fairfax County	1,275
Laguna Hills, CA (city) Orange County	1,250
Newington, VA (cdp) Fairfax County	1,250
Union, NJ (township) Union County	1,241
Aliso Viejo, CA (cdp) Orange County	1,224
Laguna Niguel, CA (city) Orange County	1,220
North Hempstead, NY (town) Nassau County	1,213
Clarkstown, NY (town) Rockland County	1,208
Franklin, NJ (township) Somerset County	1,208
Cerritos, CA (city) Los Angeles County	1,202
Milpitas, CA (city) Santa Clara County	1,189
Fremont, CA (city) Alameda County	1,173
San Bruno, CA (city) San Mateo County	1,171
Campbell, CA (city) Santa Clara County	1,163
Irvine, CA (city) Orange County	1,163
South San Francisco, CA (city) San Mateo County	1,157
Oyster Bay, NY (town) Nassau County	1,138
Montgomery Village, MD (cdp) Montgomery County	1,135
Santa Clara, CA (city) Santa Clara County	1,131
San Jose, CA (city) Santa Clara County	1,127
Des Plaines, IL (city) Cook County	1,125
Gurnee, IL (village) Lake County	1,125
Howell, NJ (township) Monmouth County	1,125
Murrieta, CA (city) Riverside County	1,125
Rialto, CA (city) San Bernardino County	1,125
Rio Rancho, NM (city) Sandoval County	1,125
Seattle Hill-Silver Firs, WA (cdp) Snohomish County	1,125
South Brunswick, NJ (township) Middlesex County	1,125
South San Jose Hills, CA (cdp) Los Angeles County	1,125
Valley Stream, NY (village) Nassau County	1,125
Vineyard, CA (cdp) Sacramento County	1,125
Dublin, CA (city) Alameda County	1,121
Sunnyvale, CA (city) Santa Clara County	1,120
Millbrae, CA (city) San Mateo County	1,118
Kaneohe, HI (cdp) Honolulu County	1,115
Union City, CA (city) Alameda County	1,112
South Whittier, CA (cdp) Los Angeles County	1,104
Chino Hills, CA (city) San Bernardino County	1,103
Makakilo City, HI (cdp) Honolulu County	1,098
Mission Viejo, CA (city) Orange County	1,095
Centreville, VA (cdp) Fairfax County	1,090
Thousand Oaks, CA (city) Ventura County	1,081
Temple City, CA (city) Los Angeles County	1,077
North Brunswick, NJ (township) Middlesex County	1,076
San Mateo, CA (city) San Mateo County	1,076
Hercules, CA (city) Contra Costa County	1,075
Rancho Santa Margarita, CA (city) Orange County	1,075
Pearl City, HI (cdp) Honolulu County	1,072
Diamond Bar, CA (city) Los Angeles County	1,071
Dover, NJ (township) Ocean County	1,071
Springfield, VA (cdp) Fairfax County	1,071

Notes: Please refer to the User's Guide for an explanation of data; ranking tables include all places with Asian and/or NHPI populations above SF4 population thresholds; (1) tables reflect only those areas that meet SF4 population thresholds, therefore there may be less than 50 states, 75 counties or 75 places listed

Median Gross Rent

Specified Housing Units Rented by Guamanians or Chamorros

All States, Top 75 Counties, and Top 75 Places Sorted by Number[1]

State	Dollars/Month
Hawaii	930
Massachusetts	883
California	786
Nevada	770
Maryland	769
New York	736
Washington	718
United States	673
Colorado	637
Arizona	635
Florida	635
New Jersey	627
Oregon	622
New Mexico	596
Texas	583
Virginia	575
Georgia	563
Michigan	563
Oklahoma	553
Missouri	548
Ohio	527
Tennessee	525
Alabama	518
North Carolina	513
Indiana	510
Illinois	496
Kentucky	490
Pennsylvania	475
Wisconsin	475
Minnesota	441
Louisiana	408
South Carolina	389
Connecticut	219

County	Dollars/Month
San Mateo County, CA	1,549
Contra Costa County, CA	1,304
Santa Clara County, CA	1,288
Thurston County, WA	1,045
Honolulu County, HI	948
Alameda County, CA	898
Orange County, CA	873
Solano County, CA	808
Clark County, NV	806
Monterey County, CA	785
San Diego County, CA	775
King County, WA	772
Los Angeles County, CA	742
Kitsap County, WA	710
Maricopa County, AZ	707
Pierce County, WA	694
Riverside County, CA	689
Kings County, NY	682
Harris County, TX	669
El Paso County, CO	667
Sacramento County, CA	659
Bell County, TX	600
San Bernardino County, CA	584

Place	Dollars/Month
San Jose, CA (city) Santa Clara County	1,256
Honolulu, HI (cdp) Honolulu County	925
Vallejo, CA (city) Solano County	906
San Diego, CA (city) San Diego County	817
Los Angeles, CA (city) Los Angeles County	744
Fairfield, CA (city) Solano County	732
New York, NY (city)	725
Houston, TX (city) Harris County	672
Tacoma, WA (city) Pierce County	641
Killeen, TX (city) Bell County	496
Chula Vista, CA (city) San Diego County	447

Notes: Please refer to the User's Guide for an explanation of data; ranking tables include all places with Asian and/or NHPI populations above SF4 population thresholds; (1) tables reflect only those areas that meet SF4 population thresholds, therefore there may be less than 50 states, 75 counties or 75 places listed

Median Gross Rent

Specified Housing Units Rented by Hawaiian Natives

All States, Top 75 Counties, and Top 75 Places Sorted by Number[1]

State	Dollars/Month
New Jersey	853
Illinois	850
Massachusetts	831
California	824
Alaska	733
Maryland	720
Hawaii	707
United States	687
Nevada	676
Colorado	667
Oregon	656
Georgia	642
Texas	642
Washington	642
North Carolina	638
Florida	628
Utah	615
New York	601
Minnesota	588
Indiana	585
South Carolina	578
Ohio	575
Michigan	573
Missouri	573
Arizona	546
New Mexico	534
Virginia	518
Kansas	517
Wisconsin	513
Pennsylvania	507
Arkansas	486
Oklahoma	464
Montana	429
Idaho	420
Louisiana	408
Tennessee	375

County	Dollars/Month
Santa Clara County, CA	1,371
San Mateo County, CA	1,298
Contra Costa County, CA	1,115
Ventura County, CA	1,065
Orange County, CA	1,016
Solano County, CA	933
Alameda County, CA	886
San Diego County, CA	851
Snohomish County, WA	808
San Joaquin County, CA	756
Honolulu County, HI	745
King County, WA	742
Bexar County, TX	727
Maui County, HI	711
Los Angeles County, CA	703
Clark County, NV	690
Washington County, OR	670
Multnomah County, OR	661
Kauai County, HI	648
Maricopa County, AZ	643
Riverside County, CA	642
Sacramento County, CA	633
Utah County, UT	623
Hawaii County, HI	610
Salt Lake County, UT	597
Pierce County, WA	535
San Bernardino County, CA	525
Pima County, AZ	475

Place	Dollars/Month
San Jose, CA (city) Santa Clara County	1,574
Mililani Town, HI (cdp) Honolulu County	1,170
Pearl City, HI (cdp) Honolulu County	1,125
Henderson, NV (city) Clark County	1,090
Kalaoa, HI (cdp) Hawaii County	1,087
Ewa Beach, HI (cdp) Honolulu County	1,060
Waimalu, HI (cdp) Honolulu County	1,038
Kahaluu, HI (cdp) Honolulu County	973
Kaneohe, HI (cdp) Honolulu County	959
Makakilo City, HI (cdp) Honolulu County	956
Nanakuli, HI (cdp) Honolulu County	928
Lahaina, HI (cdp) Maui County	906
Aiea, HI (cdp) Honolulu County	857
Kailua, HI (cdp) Honolulu County	852
Kihei, HI (cdp) Maui County	850
Paia, HI (cdp) Maui County	850
Waipio, HI (cdp) Honolulu County	842
Waimea, HI (cdp) Hawaii County	829
Laie, HI (cdp) Honolulu County	808
Makawao, HI (cdp) Maui County	803
San Diego, CA (city) San Diego County	801
Hauula, HI (cdp) Honolulu County	800
Hanapepe, HI (cdp) Kauai County	795
Waikoloa Village, HI (cdp) Hawaii County	785
Waipahu, HI (cdp) Honolulu County	783
Hana, HI (cdp) Maui County	775
Kilauea, HI (cdp) Kauai County	775
Holualoa, HI (cdp) Hawaii County	763
Makaha, HI (cdp) Honolulu County	728
Las Vegas, NV (city) Clark County	714
Volcano, HI (cdp) Hawaii County	713
Waimea, HI (cdp) Kauai County	713
Punaluu, HI (cdp) Honolulu County	710
Ahuimanu, HI (cdp) Honolulu County	706
Honolulu, HI (cdp) Honolulu County	694
Kaaawa, HI (cdp) Honolulu County	694
Maili, HI (cdp) Honolulu County	681
Waialua, HI (cdp) Honolulu County	675
Los Angeles, CA (city) Los Angeles County	674
Hawaiian Paradise Park, HI (cdp) Hawaii County	672
Waihee-Waiehu, HI (cdp) Maui County	672
Kahului, HI (cdp) Maui County	666
Portland, OR (city) Multnomah County	661
Kapaau, HI (cdp) Hawaii County	658
Kailua, HI (cdp) Hawaii County	645
Captain Cook, HI (cdp) Hawaii County	638
Wailuku, HI (cdp) Maui County	636
Waimanalo, HI (cdp) Honolulu County	632
New York, NY (city)	630
Haleiwa, HI (cdp) Honolulu County	613
Paradise, NV (cdp) Clark County	611
Phoenix, AZ (city) Maricopa County	608
Kualapuu, HI (cdp) Maui County	606
Anahola, HI (cdp) Kauai County	600
Makaha Valley, HI (cdp) Honolulu County	600
Waimanalo Beach, HI (cdp) Honolulu County	600
Hawaiian Beaches, HI (cdp) Hawaii County	597
Wahiawa, HI (cdp) Honolulu County	597
Kapaa, HI (cdp) Kauai County	594
Waikane, HI (cdp) Honolulu County	575
Kekaha, HI (cdp) Kauai County	564
Kaunakakai, HI (cdp) Maui County	556
Halawa, HI (cdp) Honolulu County	543
Hilo, HI (cdp) Hawaii County	529
Honalo, HI (cdp) Hawaii County	500
Waianae, HI (cdp) Honolulu County	458
Kahuku, HI (cdp) Honolulu County	438
Honaunau-Napoopoo, HI (cdp) Hawaii County	433
Naalehu, HI (cdp) Hawaii County	417
Hawaiian Ocean View, HI (cdp) Hawaii County	405
Pahala, HI (cdp) Hawaii County	296
Pakala Village, HI (cdp) Kauai County	169

Notes: Please refer to the User's Guide for an explanation of data; ranking tables include all places with Asian and/or NHPI populations above SF4 population thresholds; (1) tables reflect only those areas that meet SF4 population thresholds, therefore there may be less than 50 states, 75 counties or 75 places listed

Median Gross Rent

Specified Housing Units Rented by Hmongs

All States, Top 75 Counties, and Top 75 Places Sorted by Number[1]

State	Dollars/Month
Alaska	698
Colorado	635
Massachusetts	591
Oregon	591
Washington	584
Oklahoma	575
Pennsylvania	534
California	532
Rhode Island	525
United States	517
Minnesota	515
Georgia	503
North Carolina	484
Wisconsin	475
Kansas	465
Michigan	460
South Carolina	447

County	Dollars/Month
Olmsted County, MN	1,014
Orange County, CA	929
San Diego County, CA	903
Jefferson County, CO	892
Washington County, MN	866
Barrow County, GA	752
Anchorage Borough, AK	698
Solano County, CA	684
Los Angeles County, CA	675
Macomb County, MI	639
Anoka County, MN	610
Adams County, CO	603
Santa Barbara County, CA	598
King County, WA	597
Multnomah County, OR	580
Portage County, WI	578
Worcester County, MA	578
Sacramento County, CA	567
Mecklenburg County, NC	562
Hennepin County, MN	560
Stanislaus County, CA	559
Lancaster County, PA	558
Stanly County, NC	547
Yolo County, CA	544
Tulare County, CA	542
San Joaquin County, CA	541
Riverside County, CA	538
Dane County, WI	528
Merced County, CA	511
Wayne County, MI	506
Glenn County, CA	503
Butte County, CA	502
Winnebago County, WI	502
Providence County, RI	500
Marathon County, WI	499
Chippewa County, WI	495
Ramsey County, MN	495
Fresno County, CA	494
Wood County, WI	493
Eau Claire County, WI	483
Milwaukee County, WI	478
Calumet County, WI	475
Outagamie County, WI	472
Catawba County, NC	467
Brown County, WI	466
Wyandotte County, KS	458
Spokane County, WA	457
Sheboygan County, WI	452
Fond du Lac County, WI	447
Oakland County, MI	443
Yuba County, CA	436
La Crosse County, WI	435
Spartanburg County, SC	431
Manitowoc County, WI	425
Burke County, NC	411
Dunn County, WI	375
Ingham County, MI	338

Place	Dollars/Month
Woodbury, MN (city) Washington County	1,125
Santa Ana, CA (city) Orange County	1,022
Rochester, MN (city) Olmsted County	1,014
San Diego, CA (city) San Diego County	846
Brooklyn Center, MN (city) Hennepin County	617
Brooklyn Park, MN (city) Hennepin County	617
Florin, CA (cdp) Sacramento County	613
Maplewood, MN (city) Ramsey County	596
Fitchburg, MA (city) Worcester County	583
Arden-Arcade, CA (cdp) Sacramento County	576
Fond du Lac, WI (city) Fond du Lac County	575
Sacramento, CA (city) Sacramento County	574
Portland, OR (city) Multnomah County	573
Westminster, CO (city) Adams County	573
Clovis, CA (city) Fresno County	569
Charlotte, NC (city) Mecklenburg County	562
Atwater, CA (city) Merced County	558
Stevens Point, WI (city) Portage County	556
Minneapolis, MN (city) Hennepin County	551
Parkway-S. Sacramento, CA (cdp) Sacramento County	540
Stockton, CA (city) San Joaquin County	538
Modesto, CA (city) Stanislaus County	525
South Oroville, CA (cdp) Butte County	523
West Sacramento, CA (city) Yolo County	521
Chico, CA (city) Butte County	520
Wausau, WI (city) Marathon County	508
Detroit, MI (city) Wayne County	506
Oshkosh, WI (city) Winnebago County	503
Willows, CA (city) Glenn County	503
Madison, WI (city) Dane County	501
Glen Alpine, NC (town) Burke County	500
Eau Claire, WI (city) Eau Claire County	496
Providence, RI (city) Providence County	492
St. Paul, MN (city) Ramsey County	488
Wisconsin Rapids, WI (city) Wood County	486
Fresno, CA (city) Fresno County	485
Milwaukee, WI (city) Milwaukee County	483
Green Bay, WI (city) Brown County	482
Merced, CA (city) Merced County	472
Oroville, CA (city) Butte County	469
Appleton, WI (city) Outagamie County	465
Thermalito, CA (cdp) Butte County	461
Kansas City, KS (city) Wyandotte County	458
Hickory, NC (city) Catawba County	452
Sheboygan, WI (city) Sheboygan County	450
Visalia, CA (city) Tulare County	442
Linda, CA (cdp) Yuba County	437
La Crosse, WI (city) La Crosse County	432
Manitowoc, WI (city) Manitowoc County	431
Connelly Springs, NC (town) Burke County	413
Pontiac, MI (city) Oakland County	395
Lansing, MI (city) Ingham County	373
Valdese, NC (town) Burke County	370
Spokane, WA (city) Spokane County	143
Warren, MI (city) Macomb County	0

Notes: Please refer to the User's Guide for an explanation of data; ranking tables include all places with Asian and/or NHPI populations above SF4 population thresholds; (1) tables reflect only those areas that meet SF4 population thresholds, therefore there may be less than 50 states, 75 counties or 75 places listed

Median Gross Rent

Specified Housing Units Rented by Indonesians

All States, Top 75 Counties, and Top 75 Places Sorted by Number[1]

State	Dollars/Month
Virginia	952
Massachusetts	883
Maryland	853
California	839
New York	829
Georgia	804
New Jersey	784
Washington	768
United States	722
Ohio	679
Illinois	645
Texas	643
Colorado	641
Pennsylvania	574
Florida	573
Arizona	568
Michigan	533
Oregon	531
Wisconsin	501

County	Dollars/Month
San Francisco County, CA	1,299
Santa Clara County, CA	1,243
Alameda County, CA	1,058
San Mateo County, CA	1,055
Fairfax County, VA	1,016
Orange County, CA	935
Montgomery County, MD	916
Contra Costa County, CA	900
San Diego County, CA	886
Queens County, NY	840
King County, WA	834
Los Angeles County, CA	831
Middlesex County, NJ	763
Cook County, IL	726
Franklin County, OH	714
Harris County, TX	698
San Bernardino County, CA	688
Maricopa County, AZ	657

Place	Dollars/Month
San Francisco, CA (city) San Francisco County	1,299
New York, NY (city)	859
Seattle, WA (city) King County	821
Los Angeles, CA (city) Los Angeles County	801
San Bernardino, CA (city) San Bernardino County	763
Columbus, OH (city) Franklin County	712
Houston, TX (city) Harris County	698
Loma Linda, CA (city) San Bernardino County	616

Notes: Please refer to the User's Guide for an explanation of data; ranking tables include all places with Asian and/or NHPI populations above SF4 population thresholds; (1) tables reflect only those areas that meet SF4 population thresholds, therefore there may be less than 50 states, 75 counties or 75 places listed

Median Gross Rent

Specified Housing Units Rented by Japanese

All States, Top 75 Counties, and Top 75 Places Sorted by Number[1]

State	Dollars/Month
New Jersey	1,386
Connecticut	1,158
New York	1,098
Massachusetts	1,069
Michigan	1,011
Kentucky	970
Maryland	954
Illinois	938
Georgia	936
Virginia	931
California	885
United States	825
District of Columbia	805
Tennessee	779
New Hampshire	765
Texas	758
North Carolina	757
Rhode Island	751
Ohio	744
Hawaii	730
Florida	706
Alaska	695
Vermont	683
Washington	680
Pennsylvania	670
Nevada	659
Minnesota	658
Arizona	647
Delaware	638
Colorado	628
Indiana	626
Wisconsin	610
Oregon	600
South Carolina	575
Kansas	557
Missouri	557
Louisiana	545
Utah	538
Maine	500
Nebraska	500
Iowa	499
Alabama	491
Oklahoma	475
New Mexico	466
Idaho	453
Mississippi	443
West Virginia	438
South Dakota	436
Wyoming	433
Arkansas	429
Montana	389

County	Dollars/Month
Fairfield County, CT	2,000+
Napa County, CA	2,000+
Westchester County, NY	2,000+
Boone County, KY	2,000
Fairfax County, VA	1,930
Lake County, IL	1,849
Nassau County, NY	1,832
Bergen County, NJ	1,731
Santa Clara County, CA	1,521
Morris County, NJ	1,513
San Mateo County, CA	1,411
Oakland County, MI	1,352
Norfolk County, MA	1,293
New York County, NY	1,287
Somerset County, NJ	1,285
Collin County, TX	1,264
Fayette County, GA	1,253
Cobb County, GA	1,247
Suffolk County, NY	1,213
Marin County, CA	1,191
Mercer County, NJ	1,181
Middlesex County, MA	1,167
Santa Cruz County, CA	1,149
Montgomery County, MD	1,148
Hudson County, NJ	1,133
Placer County, CA	1,132
Calhoun County, MI	1,125
Fulton County, GA	1,119
Orange County, CA	1,111
Ventura County, CA	1,083
Arlington County, VA	1,058
DeKalb County, GA	1,039
Wake County, NC	1,031
Fayette County, KY	1,008
Summit County, OH	995
Suffolk County, MA	977
Cook County, IL	965
Contra Costa County, CA	940
Essex County, MA	940
DuPage County, IL	929
Franklin County, OH	924
Orange County, NC	923
San Francisco County, CA	918
Alameda County, CA	915
Washington County, OR	910
Washtenaw County, MI	897
Middlesex County, NJ	896
Delaware County, PA	893
Dallas County, TX	889
Montgomery County, PA	888
San Diego County, CA	880
Queens County, NY	876
Sonoma County, CA	876
Virginia Beach Independent City, VA	875
Harris County, TX	869
Santa Barbara County, CA	865
Chester County, PA	860
Clackamas County, OR	853
Travis County, TX	845
Mecklenburg County, NC	842
Miami-Dade County, FL	842
Kings County, NY	841
Durham County, NC	838
Olmsted County, MN	838
Baltimore County, MD	830
Jefferson County, KY	830
New Haven County, CT	825
Arapahoe County, CO	823
Shelby County, TN	822
Clark County, WA	810
Los Angeles County, CA	798
Hillsborough County, FL	796
Essex County, NJ	790
Davidson County, TN	784
Monterey County, CA	782

Place	Dollars/Month
Cupertino, CA (city) Santa Clara County	2,000+
Eastchester, NY (cdp) Westchester County	2,000+
Eastchester, NY (town) Westchester County	2,000+
Foster City, CA (city) San Mateo County	2,000+
Greenburgh, NY (town) Westchester County	2,000+
Greenville, NY (cdp) Westchester County	2,000+
Greenwich, CT (town) Fairfield County	2,000+
Harrison, NY (village) Westchester County	2,000+
La Canada Flintridge, CA (city) Los Angeles County	2,000+
Los Altos, CA (city) Santa Clara County	2,000+
Maunawili, HI (cdp) Honolulu County	2,000+
McLean, VA (cdp) Fairfax County	2,000+
Oyster Bay, NY (town) Nassau County	2,000+
Rancho Palos Verdes, CA (city) Los Angeles County	2,000+
Ridgewood, NJ (village) Bergen County	2,000+
Rolling Hills Estates, CA (city) Los Angeles County	2,000+
Rye, NY (city) Westchester County	2,000+
Saratoga, CA (city) Santa Clara County	2,000+
Scarsdale, NY (village) Westchester County	2,000+
Palos Verdes Estates, CA (city) Los Angeles County	1,986
Buffalo Grove, IL (village) Lake County	1,967
Wilmette, IL (village) Cook County	1,950
North Hempstead, NY (town) Nassau County	1,863
Cary, NC (town) Wake County	1,845
Fort Lee, NJ (borough) Bergen County	1,822
Menlo Park, CA (city) San Mateo County	1,813
Pukalani, HI (cdp) Maui County	1,795
Los Gatos, CA (town) Santa Clara County	1,766
Sunnyvale, CA (city) Santa Clara County	1,764
Millbrae, CA (city) San Mateo County	1,734
Milpitas, CA (city) Santa Clara County	1,708
Hoffman Estates, IL (village) Cook County	1,643
Morgan Hill, CA (city) Santa Clara County	1,641
Belmont, CA (city) San Mateo County	1,625
Bethesda, MD (cdp) Montgomery County	1,600
Mount Prospect, IL (village) Cook County	1,583
East San Gabriel, CA (cdp) Los Angeles County	1,563
Cliffside Park, NJ (borough) Bergen County	1,556
Newport Beach, CA (city) Orange County	1,518
Novi, MI (city) Oakland County	1,517
Fremont, CA (city) Alameda County	1,492
West Bloomfield, MI (township) Oakland County	1,479
Irvine, CA (city) Orange County	1,477
Roseville, CA (city) Placer County	1,477
Palo Alto, CA (city) Santa Clara County	1,454
Arcadia, CA (city) Los Angeles County	1,444
Dublin, OH (city) Franklin County	1,438
San Ramon, CA (city) Contra Costa County	1,438
Burlingame, CA (city) San Mateo County	1,430
Santa Clara, CA (city) Santa Clara County	1,399
North Bethesda, MD (cdp) Montgomery County	1,380
Paia, HI (cdp) Maui County	1,375
Village Park, HI (cdp) Honolulu County	1,375
Walnut, CA (city) Los Angeles County	1,375
Brookline, MA (town) Norfolk County	1,361
San Mateo, CA (city) San Mateo County	1,356
Pacifica, CA (city) San Mateo County	1,348
Mountain View, CA (city) Santa Clara County	1,345
Yorba Linda, CA (city) Orange County	1,344
Aliso Viejo, CA (cdp) Orange County	1,329
Schaumburg, IL (village) Cook County	1,323
Arlington Heights, IL (village) Cook County	1,322
Manhattan Beach, CA (city) Los Angeles County	1,321
Brookhaven, NY (town) Suffolk County	1,292
Ewa Beach, HI (cdp) Honolulu County	1,288
Elk Grove Village, IL (village) Cook County	1,281
San Jose, CA (city) Santa Clara County	1,278
Fountain Valley, CA (city) Orange County	1,277
Beaverton, OR (city) Washington County	1,267
Mission Viejo, CA (city) Orange County	1,264
Peachtree City, GA (city) Fayette County	1,253
Campbell, CA (city) Santa Clara County	1,233
Mercer Island, WA (city) King County	1,227
Thousand Oaks, CA (city) Ventura County	1,227
Mililani Town, HI (cdp) Honolulu County	1,219

Notes: Please refer to the User's Guide for an explanation of data; ranking tables include all places with Asian and/or NHPI populations above SF4 population thresholds; (1) tables reflect only those areas that meet SF4 population thresholds, therefore there may be less than 50 states, 75 counties or 75 places listed

Median Gross Rent

Specified Housing Units Rented by Koreans

All States, Top 75 Counties, and Top 75 Places Sorted by Number[1]

State	Dollars/Month
New Jersey	1,017
Massachusetts	972
New York	931
Virginia	868
California	840
Georgia	818
New Hampshire	810
United States	796
Connecticut	787
Maryland	780
District of Columbia	745
Hawaii	744
Florida	740
Rhode Island	730
Nevada	720
Illinois	717
North Carolina	714
Arizona	697
Delaware	690
Washington	687
Pennsylvania	681
Texas	664
Michigan	656
Oregon	646
Maine	638
Colorado	635
New Mexico	625
Wisconsin	622
Alaska	618
Minnesota	616
Ohio	614
Tennessee	613
South Carolina	606
Vermont	588
Utah	576
Indiana	575
Alabama	572
Missouri	572
Nebraska	569
Arkansas	548
Louisiana	529
Iowa	528
Kentucky	510
Kansas	494
Idaho	490
South Dakota	483
Mississippi	470
Oklahoma	441
West Virginia	432
Wyoming	432
North Dakota	425
Montana	414

County	Dollars/Month
Norfolk County, MA	1,353
Nassau County, NY	1,314
Santa Clara County, CA	1,281
New York County, NY	1,250
San Mateo County, CA	1,240
Westchester County, NY	1,153
Suffolk County, NY	1,127
Washington County, MN	1,125
Fairfax Independent City, VA	1,095
Bergen County, NJ	1,094
Santa Cruz County, CA	1,088
Fairfield County, CT	1,077
Mercer County, NJ	1,077
Contra Costa County, CA	1,070
Rockland County, NY	1,069
Morris County, NJ	1,063
Placer County, CA	1,057
Will County, IL	1,054
Suffolk County, MA	1,020
Middlesex County, NJ	1,009
Union County, NJ	1,002
Middlesex County, MA	1,000
Ocean County, NJ	996
Somerset County, NJ	988
Fairfax County, VA	987
San Francisco County, CA	978
Waukesha County, WI	975
Collin County, TX	964
Santa Barbara County, CA	960
Passaic County, NJ	958
Kent County, RI	955
Douglas County, CO	950
Orange County, CA	949
Hillsborough County, NH	948
Ventura County, CA	946
Chesterfield County, VA	939
Rockingham County, NH	936
Queens County, NY	926
Essex County, NJ	919
Sonoma County, CA	919
Frederick County, MD	914
Montgomery County, MD	913
Miami-Dade County, FL	910
San Diego County, CA	910
Alameda County, CA	901
Broward County, FL	897
Arlington County, VA	896
Marin County, CA	890
Hudson County, NJ	889
Loudoun County, VA	886
Gwinnett County, GA	883
Chester County, PA	878
Greene County, OH	875
Fulton County, GA	868
Fort Bend County, TX	863
Kings County, NY	863
Lake County, IL	860
Seminole County, FL	857
DuPage County, IL	856
Atlantic County, NJ	852
Palm Beach County, FL	841
Cobb County, GA	839
Prince William County, VA	837
Howard County, MD	836
Oakland County, MI	824
Montgomery County, PA	823
Burlington County, NJ	818
Bronx County, NY	817
Orange County, FL	808
Riverside County, CA	807
Delaware County, PA	805
Dutchess County, NY	804
Imperial County, CA	801
Guilford County, NC	794
Clackamas County, OR	791

Place	Dollars/Month
Alpine, NJ (borough) Bergen County	2,000+
Demarest, NJ (borough) Bergen County	2,000+
Englewood Cliffs, NJ (borough) Bergen County	2,000+
Harrington Park, NJ (borough) Bergen County	2,000+
Lake Success, NY (village) Nassau County	2,000+
Northbrook, IL (village) Cook County	2,000+
Paramus, NJ (borough) Bergen County	2,000+
Scarsdale, NY (village) Westchester County	2,000+
McLean, VA (cdp) Fairfax County	1,978
Cresskill, NJ (borough) Bergen County	1,875
La Canada Flintridge, CA (city) Los Angeles County	1,846
Plainview, NY (cdp) Nassau County	1,797
Cupertino, CA (city) Santa Clara County	1,735
Ridgewood, NJ (village) Bergen County	1,648
Smithtown, NY (town) Suffolk County	1,625
Syosset, NY (cdp) Nassau County	1,602
Buffalo Grove, IL (village) Lake County	1,583
Newton, MA (city) Middlesex County	1,561
Palo Alto, CA (city) Santa Clara County	1,548
Jericho, NY (cdp) Nassau County	1,537
Tenafly, NJ (borough) Bergen County	1,527
Colesville, MD (cdp) Montgomery County	1,524
Morton Grove, IL (village) Cook County	1,516
Norwood, NJ (borough) Bergen County	1,500
Foster City, CA (city) San Mateo County	1,491
Livingston, NJ (township) Essex County	1,469
Closter, NJ (borough) Bergen County	1,463
North Hempstead, NY (town) Nassau County	1,462
Rancho Palos Verdes, CA (city) Los Angeles County	1,449
Commack, NY (cdp) Suffolk County	1,448
Brookline, MA (town) Norfolk County	1,437
Huntington, NY (town) Suffolk County	1,429
Glen Cove, NY (city) Nassau County	1,413
Palos Verdes Estates, CA (city) Los Angeles County	1,409
Oyster Bay, NY (town) Nassau County	1,403
West Windsor, NJ (township) Mercer County	1,375
Lexington, MA (town) Middlesex County	1,367
North Potomac, MD (cdp) Montgomery County	1,364
Beverly Hills, CA (city) Los Angeles County	1,354
Santa Clara, CA (city) Santa Clara County	1,345
Edgewater, NJ (borough) Bergen County	1,329
Greenburgh, NY (town) Westchester County	1,321
Pleasanton, CA (city) Alameda County	1,318
Laguna Niguel, CA (city) Orange County	1,313
Cerritos, CA (city) Los Angeles County	1,301
Sunnyvale, CA (city) Santa Clara County	1,300
San Mateo, CA (city) San Mateo County	1,297
Fort Lee, NJ (borough) Bergen County	1,295
Fremont, CA (city) Alameda County	1,293
Newark, CA (city) Alameda County	1,282
Milpitas, CA (city) Santa Clara County	1,262
Irvine, CA (city) Orange County	1,260
Walnut, CA (city) Los Angeles County	1,258
Aliso Viejo, CA (cdp) Orange County	1,234
Mission Viejo, CA (city) Orange County	1,205
Clarkstown, NY (town) Rockland County	1,203
Edison, NJ (township) Middlesex County	1,203
Whitpain, PA (township) Montgomery County	1,202
San Jose, CA (city) Santa Clara County	1,189
Millbrae, CA (city) San Mateo County	1,168
Chino Hills, CA (city) San Bernardino County	1,163
Daly City, CA (city) San Mateo County	1,156
Waimalu, HI (cdp) Honolulu County	1,152
Diamond Bar, CA (city) Los Angeles County	1,144
West Springfield, VA (cdp) Fairfax County	1,142
Newington, VA (cdp) Fairfax County	1,138
Yorba Linda, CA (city) Orange County	1,138
Centreville, VA (cdp) Fairfax County	1,134
Mountain View, CA (city) Santa Clara County	1,134
Tustin, CA (city) Orange County	1,131
Wilmette, IL (village) Cook County	1,131
Burke, VA (cdp) Fairfax County	1,128
Kaneohe, HI (cdp) Honolulu County	1,125
Pearl City, HI (cdp) Honolulu County	1,125
Simi Valley, CA (city) Ventura County	1,125

Notes: Please refer to the User's Guide for an explanation of data; ranking tables include all places with Asian and/or NHPI populations above SF4 population thresholds; (1) tables reflect only those areas that meet SF4 population thresholds, therefore there may be less than 50 states, 75 counties or 75 places listed

Median Gross Rent

Specified Housing Units Rented by Laotians

All States, Top 75 Counties, and Top 75 Places Sorted by Number[1]

State	Dollars/Month
New Jersey	813
Maryland	786
Virginia	765
New Hampshire	718
Florida	688
Colorado	671
Nevada	655
Massachusetts	649
Alaska	635
Connecticut	623
Oregon	618
Pennsylvania	615
Michigan	603
Nebraska	603
Washington	592
California	574
Arizona	569
Illinois	565
South Carolina	565
United States	564
Utah	561
Tennessee	559
Indiana	537
Wisconsin	534
Georgia	530
New York	530
Oklahoma	525
Texas	523
Minnesota	522
North Carolina	513
Alabama	512
Hawaii	503
Rhode Island	500
Ohio	499
Iowa	490
Idaho	471
Arkansas	459
Missouri	456
Kansas	446
Louisiana	440
South Dakota	425

County	Dollars/Month
Santa Clara County, CA	1,232
Franklin County, WA	1,050
Sonoma County, CA	905
Gwinnett County, GA	806
Orange County, CA	788
Fairfield County, CT	769
Fairfax County, VA	741
Snohomish County, WA	701
New Haven County, CT	679
Jefferson County, CO	668
Adams County, CO	661
Middlesex County, MA	661
San Diego County, CA	661
Los Angeles County, CA	660
Pierce County, WA	658
Clark County, NV	655
Essex County, MA	654
Alameda County, CA	652
Pinellas County, FL	650
Cook County, IL	648
Anchorage Borough, AK	642
Washington County, OR	641
Contra Costa County, CA	638
San Bernardino County, CA	633
Dakota County, MN	622
Cass County, MI	619
Yolo County, CA	615
Maricopa County, AZ	614
Dakota County, NE	613
Dane County, WI	613
Multnomah County, OR	608
Philadelphia County, PA	607
Ottawa County, MI	604
Rutherford County, TN	600
Monroe County, NY	599
Solano County, CA	597
Salt Lake County, UT	594
King County, WA	591
Riverside County, CA	582
Pacific County, WA	571
Sacramento County, CA	571
Hennepin County, MN	568
Tarrant County, TX	567
Guilford County, NC	557
Franklin County, OH	552
Kane County, IL	547
Davidson County, TN	546
San Joaquin County, CA	546
Buena Vista County, IA	538
Dallas County, TX	538
Spartanburg County, SC	532
Habersham County, GA	531
Mecklenburg County, NC	530
Hartford County, CT	520
Catawba County, NC	517
Olmsted County, MN	517
Johnson County, KS	513
Summit County, OH	509
Worcester County, MA	509
Harris County, TX	501
Montgomery County, NC	495
Providence County, RI	494
Milwaukee County, WI	491
Polk County, IA	491
Clayton County, GA	483
Honolulu County, HI	482
Brown County, WI	479
Merced County, CA	476
Oklahoma County, OK	475
Stanislaus County, CA	469
Winnebago County, IL	461
Butte County, CA	459
Sebastian County, AR	458
Washington County, AR	457
Fresno County, CA	442

Place	Dollars/Month
San Jose, CA (city) Santa Clara County	1,232
Santa Ana, CA (city) Orange County	948
Santa Rosa, CA (city) Sonoma County	939
Anaheim, CA (city) Orange County	757
Grand Prairie, TX (city) Dallas County	753
Escondido, CA (city) San Diego County	729
Arvada, CO (city) Jefferson County	721
St. Petersburg, FL (city) Pinellas County	708
Tacoma, WA (city) Pierce County	692
Bridgeport, CT (city) Fairfield County	689
Brooklyn Park, MN (city) Hennepin County	689
Los Angeles, CA (city) Los Angeles County	678
Bellevue, WA (city) King County	676
Moreno Valley, CA (city) Riverside County	669
San Pablo, CA (city) Contra Costa County	666
Lowell, MA (city) Middlesex County	661
Brooklyn Center, MN (city) Hennepin County	659
San Diego, CA (city) San Diego County	649
Elgin, IL (city) Kane County	644
Oakland, CA (city) Alameda County	631
Westminster, CO (city) Adams County	613
Philadelphia, PA (city) Philadelphia County	607
Fairfield, CA (city) Solano County	600
Murfreesboro, TN (city) Rutherford County	597
West Valley City, UT (city) Salt Lake County	595
Raymond, WA (city) Pacific County	586
Richmond, CA (city) Contra Costa County	585
Pomona, CA (city) Los Angeles County	575
Portland, OR (city) Multnomah County	574
Sacramento, CA (city) Sacramento County	569
Fort Worth, TX (city) Tarrant County	567
Oaklawn-Sunview, KS (cdp) Sedgwick County	567
Long Beach, CA (city) Los Angeles County	560
Columbus, OH (city) Franklin County	553
Storm Lake, IA (city) Buena Vista County	552
Seattle, WA (city) King County	551
Rochester, NY (city) Monroe County	550
Nashville-Davidson, TN (sp. city) Davidson County	546
Irving, TX (city) Dallas County	545
Stockton, CA (city) San Joaquin County	543
Fitchburg, MA (city) Worcester County	534
Charlotte, NC (city) Mecklenburg County	530
Banning, CA (city) Riverside County	525
Springfield, VA (cdp) Fairfax County	525
Dallas, TX (city) Dallas County	523
Parkway-S. Sacramento, CA (cdp) Sacramento County	523
Minneapolis, MN (city) Hennepin County	517
Rochester, MN (city) Olmsted County	517
Providence, RI (city) Providence County	506
New Britain, CT (city) Hartford County	493
Merced, CA (city) Merced County	482
Green Bay, WI (city) Brown County	479
Springdale, AR (city) Washington County	478
Woonsocket, RI (city) Providence County	473
Haltom City, TX (city) Tarrant County	468
Redding, CA (city) Shasta County	467
Rockford, IL (city) Winnebago County	466
Modesto, CA (city) Stanislaus County	464
Des Moines, IA (city) Polk County	462
Fort Smith, AR (city) Sebastian County	458
Milwaukee, WI (city) Milwaukee County	454
Riverside, CA (city) Riverside County	454
Oklahoma City, OK (city) Oklahoma County	450
Fresno, CA (city) Fresno County	438
Visalia, CA (city) Tulare County	435
Honolulu, HI (cdp) Honolulu County	417
Worthington, MN (city) Nobles County	407
St. Paul, MN (city) Ramsey County	394
Winfield, KS (city) Cowley County	377
Amarillo, TX (city) Potter County	357
Wichita, KS (city) Sedgwick County	322
Akron, OH (city) Summit County	247
Warroad, MN (city) Roseau County	213

Notes: Please refer to the User's Guide for an explanation of data; ranking tables include all places with Asian and/or NHPI populations above SF4 population thresholds; (1) tables reflect only those areas that meet SF4 population thresholds, therefore there may be less than 50 states, 75 counties or 75 places listed

Median Gross Rent

Specified Housing Units Rented by Malaysians

All States, Top 75 Counties, and Top 75 Places Sorted by Number[1]

State	Dollars/Month
California	984
New York	786
Texas	758
Illinois	663
United States	662
Michigan	497
Ohio	468
Oklahoma	417

County	Dollars/Month
Los Angeles County, CA	1,068
Queens County, NY	911

Place	Dollars/Month
New York, NY (city)	803

Notes: Please refer to the User's Guide for an explanation of data; ranking tables include all places with Asian and/or NHPI populations above SF4 population thresholds; (1) tables reflect only those areas that meet SF4 population thresholds, therefore there may be less than 50 states, 75 counties or 75 places listed

Median Gross Rent

Specified Housing Units Rented by Pakistanis

All States, Top 75 Counties, and Top 75 Places Sorted by Number[1]

State	Dollars/Month
Delaware	1,000
Massachusetts	895
California	878
Virginia	858
New Jersey	841
Georgia	837
Connecticut	814
Arizona	813
New York	795
Minnesota	784
Washington	784
Florida	781
Maryland	769
Oregon	764
United States	763
Colorado	739
Pennsylvania	717
Kentucky	716
Illinois	712
Texas	710
Nevada	706
Missouri	700
Indiana	698
Michigan	680
Tennessee	648
Alabama	639
Wisconsin	617
Ohio	607
Utah	593
North Carolina	578
West Virginia	578
Louisiana	547
Kansas	511
Oklahoma	464
Iowa	430

County	Dollars/Month
Santa Clara County, CA	1,395
San Francisco County, CA	1,338
Nassau County, NY	1,224
Alameda County, CA	1,180
Fairfield County, CT	1,164
Contra Costa County, CA	1,160
Westchester County, NY	1,073
Richmond County, NY	1,053
Suffolk County, NY	1,024
San Diego County, CA	985
Middlesex County, MA	971
Loudoun County, VA	962
Montgomery County, MD	961
Monmouth County, NJ	958
Fort Bend County, TX	948
Lake County, IL	945
New York County, NY	928
Cobb County, GA	919
Gwinnett County, GA	903
Somerset County, NJ	898
Morris County, NJ	895
Bergen County, NJ	890
Fairfax County, VA	881
Middlesex County, NJ	877
Hennepin County, MN	875
Alexandria Independent City, VA	874
Orange County, CA	870
Broward County, FL	865
Oakland County, MI	858
Will County, IL	850
Howard County, MD	844
Queens County, NY	841
Los Angeles County, CA	835
Collin County, TX	813
Travis County, TX	811
Snohomish County, WA	806
Washtenaw County, MI	797
King County, WA	795
Union County, NJ	789
DuPage County, IL	785
Arlington County, VA	783
Hudson County, NJ	781
Denton County, TX	778
Dallas County, TX	769
Clayton County, GA	768
Riverside County, CA	764
New Haven County, CT	760
Prince George's County, MD	751
Maricopa County, AZ	744
St. Louis County, MO	743
Kings County, NY	735
Miami-Dade County, FL	725
Bronx County, NY	718
Essex County, NJ	711
Cook County, IL	705
Sacramento County, CA	701
Tarrant County, TX	701
Mercer County, NJ	700
Hartford County, CT	698
Prince William County, VA	695
Orange County, FL	689
Worcester County, MA	682
Camden County, NJ	681
Baltimore County, MD	675
Monroe County, NY	665
Harris County, TX	663
Atlantic County, NJ	661
Delaware County, PA	656
Wayne County, MI	636
Philadelphia County, PA	625
Milwaukee County, WI	606
Franklin County, OH	598
Wake County, NC	592
Macomb County, MI	585
San Joaquin County, CA	555

Place	Dollars/Month
Dale City, VA (cdp) Prince William County	1,875
Santa Clara, CA (city) Santa Clara County	1,588
San Francisco, CA (city) San Francisco County	1,338
San Jose, CA (city) Santa Clara County	1,313
North Hempstead, NY (town) Nassau County	1,278
Hempstead, NY (town) Nassau County	1,250
Fremont, CA (city) Alameda County	1,211
Sugar Land, TX (city) Fort Bend County	1,205
Edison, NJ (township) Middlesex County	1,098
Plano, TX (city) Collin County	1,065
Brookhaven, NY (town) Suffolk County	1,051
Huntington, NY (town) Suffolk County	950
Lincolnia, VA (cdp) Fairfax County	893
Woodbridge, NJ (township) Middlesex County	881
Mission Bend, TX (cdp) Fort Bend County	874
Torrance, CA (city) Los Angeles County	872
Los Angeles, CA (city) Los Angeles County	853
Bailey's Crossroads, VA (cdp) Fairfax County	851
Carrollton, TX (city) Denton County	834
Anaheim, CA (city) Orange County	833
Richardson, TX (city) Dallas County	812
Ellicott City, MD (cdp) Howard County	792
New York, NY (city)	789
Arlington, VA (cdp) Arlington County	783
Austin, TX (city) Travis County	770
Jersey City, NJ (city) Hudson County	769
Old Bridge, NJ (township) Middlesex County	761
Irving, TX (city) Dallas County	741
Dallas, TX (city) Dallas County	709
Skokie, IL (village) Cook County	685
Garland, TX (city) Dallas County	681
Chicago, IL (city) Cook County	680
Houston, TX (city) Harris County	662
Philadelphia, PA (city) Philadelphia County	625
Sacramento, CA (city) Sacramento County	625
Stockton, CA (city) San Joaquin County	542
Tulsa, OK (city) Tulsa County	439

Notes: Please refer to the User's Guide for an explanation of data; ranking tables include all places with Asian and/or NHPI populations above SF4 population thresholds; (1) tables reflect only those areas that meet SF4 population thresholds, therefore there may be less than 50 states, 75 counties or 75 places listed

Median Gross Rent

Specified Housing Units Rented by Samoans

All States, Top 75 Counties, and Top 75 Places Sorted by Number[1]

State	Dollars/Month
Nevada	839
Pennsylvania	838
California	788
Alaska	783
Illinois	703
United States	701
Colorado	692
Virginia	689
Washington	681
Hawaii	672
Oregon	667
Georgia	636
Utah	606
New Jersey	600
Florida	585
Ohio	583
Tennessee	581
Texas	578
New York	577
Arizona	575
Missouri	542
North Carolina	542
Michigan	488

County	Dollars/Month
Santa Clara County, CA	1,302
San Mateo County, CA	1,182
Alameda County, CA	953
Orange County, CA	948
Solano County, CA	939
San Diego County, CA	854
Hawaii County, HI	845
Clark County, NV	840
Contra Costa County, CA	825
Anchorage Borough, AK	803
Ventura County, CA	798
Los Angeles County, CA	726
San Joaquin County, CA	725
King County, WA	697
Riverside County, CA	679
Honolulu County, HI	670
Jackson County, MO	653
Pierce County, WA	644
Salt Lake County, UT	636
San Bernardino County, CA	624
Maricopa County, AZ	594
Sacramento County, CA	589
Utah County, UT	550
San Francisco County, CA	401

Place	Dollars/Month
Kahuku, HI (cdp) Honolulu County	1,268
San Jose, CA (city) Santa Clara County	1,253
Ewa Beach, HI (cdp) Honolulu County	1,096
Hayward, CA (city) Alameda County	1,069
Hauula, HI (cdp) Honolulu County	1,050
Garden Grove, CA (city) Orange County	1,029
Lakewood, CA (city) Los Angeles County	1,011
Laie, HI (cdp) Honolulu County	965
Santa Ana, CA (city) Orange County	926
Oceanside, CA (city) San Diego County	922
San Diego, CA (city) San Diego County	905
Nanakuli, HI (cdp) Honolulu County	860
Westminster, CA (city) Orange County	850
Anaheim, CA (city) Orange County	806
Oxnard, CA (city) Ventura County	790
Los Angeles, CA (city) Los Angeles County	789
Carson, CA (city) Los Angeles County	728
Lakewood, WA (city) Pierce County	686
Seattle, WA (city) King County	658
Long Beach, CA (city) Los Angeles County	651
Salt Lake City, UT (city) Salt Lake County	618
West Valley City, UT (city) Salt Lake County	617
Federal Way, WA (city) King County	616
Waipahu, HI (cdp) Honolulu County	615
Honolulu, HI (cdp) Honolulu County	604
Sacramento, CA (city) Sacramento County	588
New York, NY (city)	580
San Bernardino, CA (city) San Bernardino County	534
Tacoma, WA (city) Pierce County	525
Halawa, HI (cdp) Honolulu County	460
San Francisco, CA (city) San Francisco County	401
Compton, CA (city) Los Angeles County	354

Notes: Please refer to the User's Guide for an explanation of data; ranking tables include all places with Asian and/or NHPI populations above SF4 population thresholds; (1) tables reflect only those areas that meet SF4 population thresholds, therefore there may be less than 50 states, 75 counties or 75 places listed

Median Gross Rent

Specified Housing Units Rented by Sri Lankans

All States, Top 75 Counties, and Top 75 Places Sorted by Number[1]

State	Dollars/Month
Massachusetts	906
New York	901
California	818
New Jersey	807
Florida	775
United States	722
Virginia	718
Illinois	706
Maryland	685
Washington	668
Texas	609
Michigan	533
Pennsylvania	525
Ohio	512

County	Dollars/Month
Montgomery County, MD	1,170
Orange County, CA	908
Queens County, NY	896
Richmond County, NY	820
Los Angeles County, CA	785
Middlesex County, NJ	750

Place	Dollars/Month
New York, NY (city)	899
Los Angeles, CA (city) Los Angeles County	666

Notes: Please refer to the User's Guide for an explanation of data; ranking tables include all places with Asian and/or NHPI populations above SF4 population thresholds; (1) tables reflect only those areas that meet SF4 population thresholds, therefore there may be less than 50 states, 75 counties or 75 places listed

Median Gross Rent

Specified Housing Units Rented by Taiwanese

All States, Top 75 Counties, and Top 75 Places Sorted by Number[1]

State	Dollars/Month
Hawaii	950
New Jersey	950
California	931
Massachusetts	906
North Carolina	858
New York	849
Maryland	794
Washington	785
United States	763
Georgia	733
Virginia	725
Arizona	719
Nevada	710
Illinois	709
Michigan	704
Connecticut	690
Wisconsin	622
Pennsylvania	611
Florida	589
Texas	585
Oregon	580
Ohio	557
Missouri	548
Iowa	542
Utah	538
Colorado	532
Indiana	506
Louisiana	467
Oklahoma	433
Tennessee	433
Kansas	415
Minnesota	396

County	Dollars/Month
Somerset County, NJ	2,000+
Bergen County, NJ	1,514
New York County, NY	1,504
Westchester County, NY	1,422
Santa Clara County, CA	1,310
Norfolk County, MA	1,174
Suffolk County, NY	1,143
Ventura County, CA	1,143
Nassau County, NY	1,125
San Mateo County, CA	1,083
San Francisco County, CA	1,076
Middlesex County, NJ	1,052
Orange County, CA	1,052
Contra Costa County, CA	1,009
Suffolk County, MA	978
Fort Bend County, TX	971
Honolulu County, HI	950
Alameda County, CA	945
Los Angeles County, CA	899
Collin County, TX	875
Montgomery County, MD	873
San Bernardino County, CA	867
Morris County, NJ	859
Middlesex County, MA	847
Mercer County, NJ	833
DuPage County, IL	809
Queens County, NY	808
Washtenaw County, MI	808
King County, WA	805
San Diego County, CA	804
Fairfax County, VA	796
Cook County, IL	757
Gwinnett County, GA	738
Oakland County, MI	714
Clark County, NV	710
Maricopa County, AZ	707
St. Louis County, MO	691
Dallas County, TX	669
Riverside County, CA	663
Travis County, TX	647
Sacramento County, CA	622
Dane County, WI	614
Harris County, TX	600
Franklin County, OH	576
Tarrant County, TX	517
Allegheny County, PA	484
Essex County, NJ	475

Place	Dollars/Month
Huntington Beach, CA (city) Orange County	1,680
Rancho Palos Verdes, CA (city) Los Angeles County	1,625
Saratoga, CA (city) Santa Clara County	1,625
San Marino, CA (city) Los Angeles County	1,516
Sunnyvale, CA (city) Santa Clara County	1,395
Edison, NJ (township) Middlesex County	1,375
Cupertino, CA (city) Santa Clara County	1,368
Cerritos, CA (city) Los Angeles County	1,354
Fremont, CA (city) Alameda County	1,318
Irvine, CA (city) Orange County	1,300
San Jose, CA (city) Santa Clara County	1,295
Fountain Valley, CA (city) Orange County	1,279
Arcadia, CA (city) Los Angeles County	1,250
North Hempstead, NY (town) Nassau County	1,125
Bellevue, WA (city) King County	1,097
San Francisco, CA (city) San Francisco County	1,076
Sugar Land, TX (city) Fort Bend County	1,008
Torrance, CA (city) Los Angeles County	1,000
New York, NY (city)	996
Hacienda Heights, CA (cdp) Los Angeles County	995
Walnut, CA (city) Los Angeles County	990
Boston, MA (city) Suffolk County	978
San Gabriel, CA (city) Los Angeles County	960
Upland, CA (city) San Bernardino County	953
Honolulu, HI (cdp) Honolulu County	950
Chino Hills, CA (city) San Bernardino County	930
Rowland Heights, CA (cdp) Los Angeles County	929
Diamond Bar, CA (city) Los Angeles County	916
Los Angeles, CA (city) Los Angeles County	894
Cypress, CA (city) Orange County	881
Naperville, IL (city) Du Page County	850
Plano, TX (city) Collin County	850
San Diego, CA (city) San Diego County	832
Ann Arbor, MI (city) Washtenaw County	808
Tustin, CA (city) Orange County	798
West Covina, CA (city) Los Angeles County	794
Troy, MI (city) Oakland County	791
Berkeley, CA (city) Alameda County	777
Monterey Park, CA (city) Los Angeles County	773
Seattle, WA (city) King County	770
Anaheim, CA (city) Orange County	747
Temple City, CA (city) Los Angeles County	746
Alhambra, CA (city) Los Angeles County	729
Chicago, IL (city) Cook County	713
East San Gabriel, CA (cdp) Los Angeles County	694
Austin, TX (city) Travis County	639
Madison, WI (city) Dane County	614
Houston, TX (city) Harris County	609
Columbus, OH (city) Franklin County	576
Arlington, TX (city) Tarrant County	516
El Monte, CA (city) Los Angeles County	398
Orange, CA (city) Orange County	0

Notes: Please refer to the User's Guide for an explanation of data; ranking tables include all places with Asian and/or NHPI populations above SF4 population thresholds; (1) tables reflect only those areas that meet SF4 population thresholds, therefore there may be less than 50 states, 75 counties or 75 places listed

Median Gross Rent

Specified Housing Units Rented by Thais

All States, Top 75 Counties, and Top 75 Places Sorted by Number[1]

State	Dollars/Month
Massachusetts	849
New Jersey	829
Maryland	819
Virginia	806
California	764
New York	754
Alaska	711
Washington	704
Hawaii	700
Florida	686
Louisiana	686
North Carolina	675
Nevada	674
United States	671
Colorado	668
Connecticut	653
Georgia	652
Illinois	643
Michigan	631
Oregon	615
Tennessee	607
Arizona	598
Minnesota	571
Texas	567
Iowa	558
Kansas	555
Pennsylvania	555
Missouri	553
South Carolina	540
Utah	530
Wisconsin	528
Nebraska	519
Alabama	507
Ohio	491
Indiana	487
Oklahoma	471
New Mexico	433
Arkansas	411
Kentucky	369

County	Dollars/Month
Santa Clara County, CA	1,238
San Mateo County, CA	1,179
Collin County, TX	1,125
Contra Costa County, CA	933
Westchester County, NY	931
Alameda County, CA	929
Nassau County, NY	928
Fairfax County, VA	874
Middlesex County, MA	873
Montgomery County, MD	861
San Francisco County, CA	859
Orange County, CA	850
Palm Beach County, FL	850
Broward County, FL	838
New York County, NY	835
Bergen County, NJ	820
Miami-Dade County, FL	790
Prince George's County, MD	782
Queens County, NY	782
DuPage County, IL	779
Okaloosa County, FL	771
King County, WA	758
San Bernardino County, CA	757
Los Angeles County, CA	724
San Diego County, CA	724
Pinellas County, FL	714
Anchorage Borough, AK	708
Honolulu County, HI	707
Dallas County, TX	694
Riverside County, CA	691
Pierce County, WA	675
Clark County, NV	671
Travis County, TX	664
Denver County, CO	662
Cook County, IL	655
Multnomah County, OR	647
Hillsborough County, FL	628
Maricopa County, AZ	620
Polk County, IA	616
Bexar County, TX	600
Oklahoma County, OK	561
Franklin County, OH	533
Sacramento County, CA	521
Tarrant County, TX	519
Harris County, TX	514
St. Louis County, MO	468
Suffolk County, NY	0

Place	Dollars/Month
San Jose, CA (city) Santa Clara County	1,631
Spring Valley, NV (cdp) Clark County	896
San Francisco, CA (city) San Francisco County	859
New York, NY (city)	783
Anaheim, CA (city) Orange County	736
Honolulu, HI (cdp) Honolulu County	732
San Diego, CA (city) San Diego County	723
Seattle, WA (city) King County	717
Chicago, IL (city) Cook County	686
Long Beach, CA (city) Los Angeles County	683
Los Angeles, CA (city) Los Angeles County	683
Bellflower, CA (city) Los Angeles County	679
Cerritos, CA (city) Los Angeles County	679
Glendale, CA (city) Los Angeles County	675
Denver, CO (city) Denver County	662
Portland, OR (city) Multnomah County	647
San Antonio, TX (city) Bexar County	623
Las Vegas, NV (city) Clark County	589
Columbus, OH (city) Franklin County	533
Houston, TX (city) Harris County	523
Des Moines, IA (city) Polk County	493

Notes: Please refer to the User's Guide for an explanation of data; ranking tables include all places with Asian and/or NHPI populations above SF4 population thresholds; (1) tables reflect only those areas that meet SF4 population thresholds, therefore there may be less than 50 states, 75 counties or 75 places listed

Median Gross Rent

Specified Housing Units Rented by Tongans

All States, Top 75 Counties, and Top 75 Places Sorted by Number[1]

State	Dollars/Month
California	832
Washington	822
Alaska	814
Hawaii	766
United States	740
Arizona	712
Utah	673
Texas	653
Oregon	590
Nevada	560

County	Dollars/Month
San Mateo County, CA	1,091
Contra Costa County, CA	900
Alameda County, CA	892
Multnomah County, OR	823
King County, WA	813
San Diego County, CA	788
Honolulu County, HI	785
Orange County, CA	730
Maricopa County, AZ	712
Sacramento County, CA	703
Maui County, HI	697
Salt Lake County, UT	681
San Bernardino County, CA	657
Los Angeles County, CA	626
Utah County, UT	584
Washoe County, NV	561
Tarrant County, TX	558

Place	Dollars/Month
San Bruno, CA (city) San Mateo County	1,305
San Mateo, CA (city) San Mateo County	1,057
East Palo Alto, CA (city) San Mateo County	1,015
Oakland, CA (city) Alameda County	943
Portland, OR (city) Multnomah County	823
Sacramento, CA (city) Sacramento County	797
Hauula, HI (cdp) Honolulu County	775
West Valley City, UT (city) Salt Lake County	768
Honolulu, HI (cdp) Honolulu County	746
West Jordan, UT (city) Salt Lake County	744
Laie, HI (cdp) Honolulu County	675
Salt Lake City, UT (city) Salt Lake County	653
Los Angeles, CA (city) Los Angeles County	603
Kahuku, HI (cdp) Honolulu County	413

Notes: Please refer to the User's Guide for an explanation of data; ranking tables include all places with Asian and/or NHPI populations above SF4 population thresholds; (1) tables reflect only those areas that meet SF4 population thresholds, therefore there may be less than 50 states, 75 counties or 75 places listed

Median Gross Rent

Specified Housing Units Rented by Vietnamese

All States, Top 75 Counties, and Top 75 Places Sorted by Number[1]

State	Dollars/Month
Alaska	808
California	792
Maryland	765
New Jersey	726
Nevada	717
Virginia	717
Massachusetts	687
Vermont	673
New York	670
Delaware	667
Hawaii	666
Georgia	658
Illinois	654
Connecticut	653
United States	653
Oregon	607
District of Columbia	605
North Carolina	601
Rhode Island	599
New Hampshire	598
Florida	594
West Virginia	575
Colorado	573
Mississippi	562
Wisconsin	558
Texas	556
Washington	551
Pennsylvania	544
Arizona	540
Michigan	538
Idaho	537
Utah	525
Alabama	520
Minnesota	512
Indiana	511
Ohio	511
South Carolina	505
Tennessee	497
Nebraska	481
New Mexico	480
Maine	466
Louisiana	457
Oklahoma	455
South Dakota	438
Kentucky	436
Missouri	436
Kansas	420
Iowa	419
Arkansas	395

County	Dollars/Month
Santa Cruz County, CA	1,229
Loudoun County, VA	1,161
San Mateo County, CA	1,129
New York County, NY	1,070
Santa Clara County, CA	1,008
Burlington County, NJ	992
Ventura County, CA	971
Marin County, CA	945
Suffolk County, NY	925
Norfolk County, MA	894
Middlesex County, NJ	877
Will County, IL	868
Fort Bend County, TX	864
Cumberland County, PA	863
Alexandria Independent City, VA	853
Orange County, CA	847
Gwinnett County, GA	844
Fairfax County, VA	836
Union County, NJ	828
Morris County, NJ	827
Stanislaus County, CA	826
Prince William County, VA	825
Sonoma County, CA	814
Contra Costa County, CA	811
Lake County, IL	811
Chester County, PA	792
Bergen County, NJ	791
Broward County, FL	788
Howard County, MD	785
Collin County, TX	781
Prince George's County, MD	775
Queens County, NY	775
Montgomery County, MD	768
Solano County, CA	764
Butler County, OH	763
Jackson County, MS	758
Santa Barbara County, CA	756
Fairfield County, CT	753
Middlesex County, MA	747
Placer County, CA	747
San Francisco County, CA	747
Seminole County, FL	742
Suffolk County, MA	742
Dakota County, MN	741
Wake County, NC	741
Cobb County, GA	731
Alameda County, CA	730
Clark County, NV	727
Clackamas County, OR	725
Essex County, NJ	725
DuPage County, IL	723
Kings County, NY	720
Los Angeles County, CA	719
Somerset County, NJ	719
DeKalb County, GA	706
Iberia Parish, LA	705
Monterey County, CA	703
Yolo County, CA	696
Chittenden County, VT	692
Henrico County, VA	692
Bronx County, NY	690
Oakland County, MI	689
San Diego County, CA	687
Baltimore County, MD	685
Williamson County, TX	685
Washington County, OR	684
Nassau County, NY	683
Miami-Dade County, FL	682
Washtenaw County, MI	680
Riverside County, CA	679
San Joaquin County, CA	679
Madison County, AL	678
El Paso County, CO	674
Essex County, MA	663
Snohomish County, WA	663

Place	Dollars/Month
Cupertino, CA (city) Santa Clara County	1,592
Missouri City, TX (city) Fort Bend County	1,534
Timberlane, LA (cdp) Jefferson Parish	1,375
Thousand Oaks, CA (city) Ventura County	1,352
Cerritos, CA (city) Los Angeles County	1,340
Irvine, CA (city) Orange County	1,228
Aliso Viejo, CA (cdp) Orange County	1,192
Laguna Niguel, CA (city) Orange County	1,188
Milpitas, CA (city) Santa Clara County	1,169
Merrifield, VA (cdp) Fairfax County	1,162
San Mateo, CA (city) San Mateo County	1,147
Union City, CA (city) Alameda County	1,144
Herndon, VA (town) Fairfax County	1,125
League City, TX (city) Galveston County	1,125
Walnut, CA (city) Los Angeles County	1,125
Yorba Linda, CA (city) Orange County	1,109
Daly City, CA (city) San Mateo County	1,107
Sunnyvale, CA (city) Santa Clara County	1,101
Fremont, CA (city) Alameda County	1,089
Cascade-Fairwood, WA (cdp) King County	1,083
Randolph, MA (town) Norfolk County	1,057
Goleta, CA (cdp) Santa Barbara County	1,039
Valinda, CA (cdp) Los Angeles County	1,038
Moreno Valley, CA (city) Riverside County	1,035
Aurora, IL (city) Kane County	1,031
Mesa, AZ (city) Maricopa County	1,031
San Rafael, CA (city) Marin County	1,025
Rowland Heights, CA (cdp) Los Angeles County	1,017
Fountain Valley, CA (city) Orange County	1,010
Santa Clara, CA (city) Santa Clara County	1,003
San Jose, CA (city) Santa Clara County	989
Mountain View, CA (city) Santa Clara County	985
Lake Forest, CA (city) Orange County	976
South Plainfield, NJ (borough) Middlesex County	975
West Covina, CA (city) Los Angeles County	971
Sugar Land, TX (city) Fort Bend County	964
Montgomery Village, MD (cdp) Montgomery County	956
Annandale, VA (cdp) Fairfax County	950
Camarillo, CA (city) Ventura County	950
Doraville, GA (city) De Kalb County	950
Huntington Beach, CA (city) Orange County	950
Ontario, CA (city) San Bernardino County	944
Campbell, CA (city) Santa Clara County	934
Idylwood, VA (cdp) Fairfax County	928
Hayward, CA (city) Alameda County	926
Oxnard, CA (city) Ventura County	925
West Puente Valley, CA (cdp) Los Angeles County	925
Lawndale, CA (city) Los Angeles County	924
Woodmere, LA (cdp) Jefferson Parish	915
Chandler, AZ (city) Maricopa County	914
Hacienda Heights, CA (cdp) Los Angeles County	914
Woodlynne, NJ (borough) Camden County	914
Lincolnia, VA (cdp) Fairfax County	912
Colesville, MD (cdp) Montgomery County	908
Corona, CA (city) Riverside County	907
Aspen Hill, MD (cdp) Montgomery County	906
Cary, NC (town) Wake County	906
San Leandro, CA (city) Alameda County	902
Newark, CA (city) Alameda County	894
Burke, VA (cdp) Fairfax County	892
Kirkland, WA (city) King County	892
South El Monte, CA (city) Los Angeles County	888
Tustin, CA (city) Orange County	888
Costa Mesa, CA (city) Orange County	886
Santa Ana, CA (city) Orange County	886
Stafford, TX (city) Fort Bend County	886
Vallejo, CA (city) Solano County	886
White Oak, MD (cdp) Montgomery County	879
Torrance, CA (city) Los Angeles County	878
Laguna, CA (cdp) Sacramento County	867
Orange, CA (city) Orange County	864
Escondido, CA (city) San Diego County	861
Simi Valley, CA (city) Ventura County	854
Laguna Hills, CA (city) Orange County	850
Lilburn, GA (city) Gwinnett County	850

Notes: Please refer to the User's Guide for an explanation of data; ranking tables include all places with Asian and/or NHPI populations above SF4 population thresholds; (1) tables reflect only those areas that meet SF4 population thresholds, therefore there may be less than 50 states, 75 counties or 75 places listed

Median Home Value

All Specified Owner-Occupied Housing Units

All States, Top 75 Counties, and Top 75 Places Sorted by Number[1]

State	Dollars
Hawaii	272,700
California	211,500
Massachusetts	185,700
New Jersey	170,800
Washington	168,300
Connecticut	166,900
Colorado	166,600
District of Columbia	157,200
Oregon	152,100
New York	148,700
Utah	146,100
Maryland	146,000
Alaska	144,200
Nevada	142,000
New Hampshire	133,300
Rhode Island	133,000
Illinois	130,800
Delaware	130,400
Virginia	125,400
Minnesota	122,400
Arizona	121,300
United States	119,600
Michigan	115,600
Wisconsin	112,200
Vermont	111,500
Georgia	111,200
North Carolina	108,300
New Mexico	108,100
Idaho	106,300
Florida	105,500
Ohio	103,700
Montana	99,500
Maine	98,700
Pennsylvania	97,000
Wyoming	96,600
South Carolina	94,900
Indiana	94,300
Tennessee	93,000
Missouri	89,900
Nebraska	88,000
Kentucky	86,700
Alabama	85,100
Louisiana	85,000
Kansas	83,500
Iowa	82,500
Texas	82,500
South Dakota	79,600
North Dakota	74,400
Arkansas	72,800
West Virginia	72,800
Mississippi	71,400
Oklahoma	70,700

County	Dollars
New York County, NY	1 mil.+
Marin County, CA	514,600
San Mateo County, CA	469,200
Santa Clara County, CA	446,400
San Francisco County, CA	396,400
Santa Cruz County, CA	377,500
Eagle County, CO	369,100
Westchester County, NY	325,800
Honolulu County, HI	309,000
Alameda County, CA	303,100
Santa Barbara County, CA	293,000
Fairfield County, CT	288,900
Blaine County, ID	288,800
San Benito County, CA	284,000
Falls Church Independent City, VA	277,100
Sonoma County, CA	273,200
Orange County, CA	270,000
Contra Costa County, CA	267,800
Monterey County, CA	265,800
Arlington County, VA	262,400
Morris County, NJ	257,400
Alexandria Independent City, VA	252,800
Napa County, CA	251,300
Bergen County, NJ	250,300
Maui County, HI	249,900
Ventura County, CA	248,700
Middlesex County, MA	247,900
Hunterdon County, NJ	245,000
Rockland County, NY	242,500
Nassau County, NY	242,300
Boulder County, CO	241,900
Monroe County, FL	241,200
King County, WA	236,900
Douglas County, CO	236,000
Somerset County, NJ	235,000
Fairfax County, VA	233,300
Norfolk County, MA	230,400
San Luis Obispo County, CA	230,000
Los Alamos County, NM	228,300
San Diego County, CA	227,200
Kings County, NY	224,100
Montgomery County, MD	221,800
Essex County, MA	220,000
Kauai County, HI	216,100
Beaufort County, SC	213,900
Placer County, CA	213,900
Queens County, NY	212,600
Williamsburg Independent City, VA	212,000
Los Angeles County, CA	209,300
Richmond County, NY	209,100
Essex County, NJ	208,400
Williamson County, TN	208,400
Putnam County, NY	206,900
Howard County, MD	206,300
Nevada County, CA	205,700
Monmouth County, NJ	203,100
Loudoun County, VA	200,500
Clackamas County, OR	199,000
Lake County, IL	198,200
Snohomish County, WA	196,500
Juneau Borough, AK	195,100
DuPage County, IL	195,000
El Dorado County, CA	194,400
Fairfax Independent City, VA	192,100
Passaic County, NJ	190,600
Bronx County, NY	190,400
Delaware County, OH	190,400
Santa Fe County, NM	189,400
Union County, NJ	188,800
Jefferson County, CO	187,900
Livingston County, MI	187,500
Suffolk County, MA	187,300
Suffolk County, NY	185,200
Washington County, OR	184,800
Forsyth County, GA	184,600

Place	Dollars
Alpine, NJ (borough) Bergen County	1 mil.+
Atherton, CA (town) San Mateo County	1 mil.+
Beverly Hills, CA (city) Los Angeles County	1 mil.+
Brookville, NY (village) Nassau County	1 mil.+
Hillsborough, CA (town) San Mateo County	1 mil.+
Los Altos Hills, CA (town) Santa Clara County	1 mil.+
Loyola, CA (cdp) Santa Clara County	1 mil.+
Old Westbury, NY (village) Nassau County	1 mil.+
Rolling Hills, CA (city) Los Angeles County	1 mil.+
Sands Point, NY (village) Nassau County	1 mil.+
Saratoga, CA (city) Santa Clara County	1 mil.+
Tiburon, CA (town) Marin County	1 mil.+
Newport Coast, CA (cdp) Orange County	987,000
Los Altos, CA (city) Santa Clara County	983,000
Oyster Bay Cove, NY (village) Nassau County	974,900
Old Brookville, NY (village) Nassau County	972,100
Saddle River, NJ (borough) Bergen County	970,100
Bronxville, NY (village) Westchester County	959,600
Laurel Hollow, NY (village) Nassau County	897,200
Stanford, CA (cdp) Santa Clara County	870,800
Muttontown, NY (village) Nassau County	831,100
New Canaan, CT (town) Fairfield County	831,000
Palo Alto, CA (city) Santa Clara County	811,800
Palos Verdes Estates, CA (city) Los Angeles County	795,600
Los Gatos, CA (town) Santa Clara County	784,600
Greenwich, CT (town) Fairfield County	781,500
Menlo Park, CA (city) San Mateo County	778,500
Piedmont, CA (city) Alameda County	760,000
Winnetka, IL (village) Cook County	756,500
Weston, MA (town) Middlesex County	739,200
Strawberry, CA (cdp) Marin County	737,300
Alamo, CA (cdp) Contra Costa County	731,200
Blackhawk-Camino Tass., CA (cdp) Contra Costa Co.	716,100
Darien, CT (town) Fairfield County	711,000
Newport Beach, CA (city) Orange County	708,200
Scarsdale, NY (village) Westchester County	708,000
Munsey Park, NY (village) Nassau County	702,300
San Marino, CA (city) Los Angeles County	690,800
Burlingame, CA (city) San Mateo County	685,900
Coronado, CA (city) San Diego County	683,400
South Barrington, IL (village) Cook County	678,800
Manhattan Beach, CA (city) Los Angeles County	672,600
Larkspur, CA (city) Marin County	663,000
Lake Forest, IL (city) Lake County	662,400
Lake Success, NY (village) Nassau County	661,300
North Hills, NY (village) Nassau County	659,100
Laguna Beach, CA (city) Orange County	653,900
Cupertino, CA (city) Santa Clara County	649,000
Highlands-Baywood Pk., CA (cdp) San Mateo County	646,000
Bradbury, CA (city) Los Angeles County	644,900
Flower Hill, NY (village) Nassau County	643,500
Rolling Hills Estates, CA (city) Los Angeles County	637,800
Rye, NY (city) Westchester County	635,700
Oak Brook, IL (village) Du Page County	635,400
Orinda, CA (city) Contra Costa County	631,800
Travilah, MD (cdp) Montgomery County	630,100
San Carlos, CA (city) San Mateo County	626,400
Santa Monica, CA (city) Los Angeles County	625,900
Westport, CT (town) Fairfield County	625,800
Franklin Lakes, NJ (borough) Bergen County	609,400
Tamalpais-Homestead Valley, CA (cdp) Marin County	609,100
Brookline, MA (town) Norfolk County	599,500
Villa Park, CA (city) Orange County	596,500
Great Falls, VA (cdp) Fairfax County	596,100
Makaha Valley, HI (cdp) Honolulu County	593,800
Belmont, CA (city) San Mateo County	593,200
North Castle, NY (town) Westchester County	588,500
La Canada Flintridge, CA (city) Los Angeles County	587,800
East Hills, NY (village) Nassau County	586,900
Lafayette, CA (city) Contra Costa County	583,000
Harrison, NY (village) Westchester County	578,700
Greenville, NY (cdp) Westchester County	575,300
Mercer Island, WA (city) King County	573,900
Woodbury, NY (cdp) Nassau County	569,800
Hunters Creek Village, TX (city) Harris County	567,300

Notes: Please refer to the User's Guide for an explanation of data; ranking tables include all places with Asian and/or NHPI populations above SF4 population thresholds; (1) tables reflect only those areas that meet SF4 population thresholds, therefore there may be less than 50 states, 75 counties or 75 places listed

Median Home Value

Specified Housing Units Owned and Occupied by Asians

All States, Top 75 Counties, and Top 75 Places Sorted by Number[1]

State	Dollars
District of Columbia	325,900
Hawaii	280,200
California	256,700
Massachusetts	228,000
New York	227,700
New Jersey	214,300
United States	199,300
Connecticut	196,800
Washington	192,100
Illinois	191,900
Michigan	186,800
Maryland	184,700
Colorado	180,800
Virginia	176,800
Delaware	173,500
Oregon	167,800
New Hampshire	162,800
Ohio	155,300
Alaska	151,900
Utah	147,800
Nevada	146,100
Georgia	146,000
Arizona	141,300
West Virginia	140,400
Indiana	138,300
North Carolina	137,900
New Mexico	136,400
Vermont	136,000
Kentucky	135,400
Missouri	129,900
Minnesota	129,400
Pennsylvania	129,000
Alabama	128,200
Tennessee	128,000
Rhode Island	125,400
Wisconsin	122,200
Florida	119,700
Wyoming	115,200
South Carolina	114,500
Texas	113,700
Idaho	110,300
Maine	106,500
Kansas	104,800
Nebraska	103,600
North Dakota	103,500
Montana	101,200
Louisiana	98,300
Iowa	95,600
South Dakota	90,300
Oklahoma	90,200
Mississippi	89,100
Arkansas	75,500

County	Dollars
New York County, NY	1 mil.+
Marin County, CA	481,900
Goodhue County, MN	450,000
Blaine County, ID	433,300
Santa Clara County, CA	427,000
San Mateo County, CA	399,500
Eagle County, CO	368,200
San Francisco County, CA	361,800
Westchester County, NY	343,800
Santa Cruz County, CA	335,100
Hunterdon County, NJ	331,600
Alameda County, CA	328,200
Honolulu County, HI	311,100
Elmore County, ID	310,000
Fairfield County, CT	300,700
San Benito County, CA	294,800
Somerset County, NJ	285,400
Morris County, NJ	280,300
Mercer County, NJ	278,700
Middlesex County, MA	277,300
Columbia County, NY	275,000
Nassau County, NY	273,200
Contra Costa County, CA	270,800
Bergen County, NJ	268,400
Sonoma County, CA	266,500
Bradford County, PA	261,100
Orange County, CA	260,400
Monmouth County, NJ	255,100
Putnam County, NY	255,000
Oakland County, MI	253,000
Ventura County, CA	251,600
Boulder County, CO	249,300
Monterey County, CA	248,400
San Luis Obispo County, CA	242,900
Douglas County, CO	242,400
Ozaukee County, WI	242,300
Rockland County, NY	240,300
Queens County, NY	235,300
Maui County, HI	233,300
Lake County, IL	232,600
Horry County, SC	232,400
Forsyth County, GA	230,600
Howard County, MD	228,200
Placer County, CA	227,400
Los Angeles County, CA	226,400
Calvert County, MD	226,300
Essex County, MA	226,300
Aleutians West Census Area, AK	225,000
Plaquemines Parish, LA	225,000
Yolo County, CA	224,100
Collier County, FL	223,800
Chester County, PA	223,100
Napa County, CA	222,100
Delaware County, OH	221,400
Norfolk County, MA	220,800
King County, WA	220,600
Mendocino County, CA	220,500
Geauga County, OH	220,000
Montgomery County, MD	220,000
Clackamas County, OR	219,900
Fulton County, GA	219,500
Livingston County, MI	218,800
Suffolk County, NY	217,900
Washtenaw County, MI	217,800
Kings County, NY	217,300
Wood County, WV	217,200
Kanawha County, WV	217,100
El Dorado County, CA	216,800
Coconino County, AZ	216,700
Essex County, NJ	215,200
San Diego County, CA	213,800
Snohomish County, WA	213,300
Niagara County, NY	213,200
Arlington County, VA	212,900
Barnstable County, MA	212,900

Place	Dollars
Alpine, NJ (borough) Bergen County	1 mil.+
Atherton, CA (town) San Mateo County	1 mil.+
Hillsborough, CA (town) San Mateo County	1 mil.+
Los Altos Hills, CA (town) Santa Clara County	1 mil.+
Loyola, CA (cdp) Santa Clara County	1 mil.+
Newport Coast, CA (cdp) Orange County	1 mil.+
Old Brookville, NY (village) Nassau County	1 mil.+
Oyster Bay Cove, NY (village) Nassau County	1 mil.+
Rolling Hills, CA (city) Los Angeles County	1 mil.+
Saddle River, NJ (borough) Bergen County	1 mil.+
Sands Point, NY (village) Nassau County	1 mil.+
Saratoga, CA (city) Santa Clara County	1 mil.+
Tiburon, CA (town) Marin County	1 mil.+
Beverly Hills, CA (city) Los Angeles County	968,200
Los Altos, CA (city) Santa Clara County	962,400
Brookville, NY (village) Nassau County	916,700
Palos Verdes Estates, CA (city) Los Angeles County	903,500
Laurel Hollow, NY (village) Nassau County	886,400
Stanford, CA (cdp) Santa Clara County	875,000
Alamo, CA (cdp) Contra Costa County	872,100
North Hills, NY (village) Nassau County	868,800
Winnetka, IL (village) Cook County	852,300
Menlo Park, CA (city) San Mateo County	837,400
Los Gatos, CA (town) Santa Clara County	819,600
New Canaan, CT (town) Fairfield County	812,500
South Barrington, IL (village) Cook County	801,300
Munsey Park, NY (village) Nassau County	791,700
Newport Beach, CA (city) Orange County	787,700
Oak Brook, IL (village) Du Page County	773,300
Palo Alto, CA (city) Santa Clara County	759,800
Rolling Hills Estates, CA (city) Los Angeles County	758,300
Harrison, NY (village) Westchester County	726,000
Franklin Lakes, NJ (borough) Bergen County	722,700
Bradbury, CA (city) Los Angeles County	718,800
Lake Forest, IL (city) Lake County	684,700
Scarsdale, NY (village) Westchester County	684,600
Blackhawk-Camino Tass., CA (cdp) Contra Costa Co.	679,900
Muttontown, NY (village) Nassau County	679,400
Travilah, MD (cdp) Montgomery County	679,100
Burlingame, CA (city) San Mateo County	676,200
Strawberry, CA (cdp) Marin County	675,000
Hunters Creek Village, TX (city) Harris County	671,100
Highlands-Baywood Pk., CA (cdp) San Mateo County	668,500
Bronxville, NY (village) Westchester County	664,800
Manhattan Beach, CA (city) Los Angeles County	656,400
Rye, NY (city) Westchester County	655,400
Greenwich, CT (town) Fairfield County	655,300
Old Westbury, NY (village) Nassau County	649,300
Cupertino, CA (city) Santa Clara County	646,300
San Marino, CA (city) Los Angeles County	641,800
Corte Madera, CA (town) Marin County	635,000
Lake Success, NY (village) Nassau County	634,300
Weston, MA (town) Middlesex County	629,500
San Carlos, CA (city) San Mateo County	623,700
Bunker Hill Village, TX (city) Harris County	619,600
Mamaroneck, NY (town) Westchester County	617,600
Laguna Beach, CA (city) Orange County	615,400
Tamalpais-Homestead Valley, CA (cdp) Marin County	611,400
Piedmont, CA (city) Alameda County	610,200
Town and Country, MO (city) Saint Louis County	602,300
Belmont, CA (city) San Mateo County	596,200
Rancho Palos Verdes, CA (city) Los Angeles County	593,200
Burr Ridge, IL (village) Du Page County	589,300
Coronado, CA (city) San Diego County	587,500
Flower Hill, NY (village) Nassau County	586,400
Villa Park, CA (city) Orange County	585,700
Larkspur, CA (city) Marin County	580,900
Darien, CT (town) Fairfield County	577,100
Orinda, CA (city) Contra Costa County	570,600
Westport, CT (town) Fairfield County	567,900
Foster City, CA (city) San Mateo County	567,000
Woodbury, NY (cdp) Nassau County	562,500
Lafayette, CA (city) Contra Costa County	560,000
Redwood City, CA (city) San Mateo County	559,400
La Canada Flintridge, CA (city) Los Angeles County	558,900

Notes: Please refer to the User's Guide for an explanation of data; ranking tables include all places with Asian and/or NHPI populations above SF4 population thresholds; (1) tables reflect only those areas that meet SF4 population thresholds, therefore there may be less than 50 states, 75 counties or 75 places listed

Median Home Value

Specified Housing Units Owned and Occupied by Native Hawaiian and Other Pacific Islanders

All States, Top 75 Counties, and Top 75 Places Sorted by Number[1]

State	Dollars
Hawaii	213,100
Connecticut	196,200
California	187,500
New York	175,200
New Jersey	173,600
Rhode Island	173,200
Massachusetts	166,600
United States	160,500
Washington	155,400
Oregon	150,700
Colorado	148,500
Wisconsin	147,500
Alaska	142,000
Maryland	139,200
Virginia	135,500
Delaware	133,100
Nevada	132,900
Utah	130,200
Arizona	118,500
Ohio	116,300
Illinois	114,800
New Mexico	114,800
Alabama	111,300
Minnesota	107,700
Kentucky	102,000
Georgia	100,200
Michigan	98,500
Tennessee	98,300
Idaho	95,700
North Carolina	93,300
Kansas	92,400
Florida	92,000
Louisiana	91,700
Montana	91,700
Pennsylvania	91,700
South Carolina	88,900
Missouri	88,700
Oklahoma	85,000
Texas	84,200
Indiana	78,500
Iowa	77,100
Nebraska	73,600
Mississippi	71,200
Arkansas	68,000
West Virginia	45,000
Maine	34,500

County	Dollars
Kings County, NY	423,900
Santa Clara County, CA	378,200
San Mateo County, CA	355,000
Sonoma County, CA	324,300
Santa Barbara County, CA	321,900
San Francisco County, CA	287,200
Essex County, NJ	275,000
Honolulu County, HI	255,100
Ventura County, CA	247,700
Alameda County, CA	246,600
Fairfax County, VA	236,300
Snohomish County, WA	219,600
Montgomery County, MD	213,200
Monterey County, CA	211,400
Orange County, CA	207,900
Contra Costa County, CA	204,200
San Diego County, CA	193,500
San Joaquin County, CA	191,700
Nassau County, NY	185,700
Maui County, HI	185,200
Suffolk County, NY	181,300
King County, WA	180,700
Jefferson County, CO	180,000
Los Angeles County, CA	177,800
Kauai County, HI	173,300
Clackamas County, OR	172,100
Washington County, OR	167,100
Multnomah County, OR	166,600
Solano County, CA	166,600
Bronx County, NY	158,300
Arapahoe County, CO	156,800
Denver County, CO	154,500
Washington County, UT	154,200
Davidson County, TN	151,800
Queens County, NY	151,600
Anchorage Borough, AK	150,000
Washoe County, NV	150,000
Clark County, WA	149,100
Riverside County, CA	145,800
Pierce County, WA	144,600
Thurston County, WA	144,300
Utah County, UT	144,300
Yolo County, CA	142,400
Cook County, IL	140,000
Marion County, OR	138,400
Davis County, UT	137,900
Hawaii County, HI	134,800
Clark County, NV	132,500
Kitsap County, WA	131,700
El Paso County, CO	131,400
Gwinnett County, GA	130,700
Milwaukee County, WI	130,000
Salt Lake County, UT	125,800
Bernalillo County, NM	124,600
San Bernardino County, CA	122,500
Maricopa County, AZ	121,000
Franklin County, OH	118,800
Pima County, AZ	118,500
Sacramento County, CA	117,900
Lane County, OR	117,800
Allegheny County, PA	117,000
Palm Beach County, FL	117,000
Stanislaus County, CA	114,100
Broward County, FL	108,000
Hillsborough County, FL	106,900
Kern County, CA	105,300
Ada County, ID	101,600
Jackson County, MO	98,800
Travis County, TX	97,900
Tarrant County, TX	97,200
Miami-Dade County, FL	97,100
Spokane County, WA	97,000
Cumberland County, NC	93,800
El Paso County, TX	93,800
Onslow County, NC	92,900

Place	Dollars
Redwood City, CA (city) San Mateo County	500,000
San Mateo, CA (city) San Mateo County	451,300
Makaha Valley, HI (cdp) Honolulu County	450,000
Santa Clara, CA (city) Santa Clara County	420,000
Punaluu, HI (cdp) Honolulu County	410,000
Kahaluu, HI (cdp) Honolulu County	400,000
Milpitas, CA (city) Santa Clara County	395,500
Waikane, HI (cdp) Honolulu County	387,500
Fremont, CA (city) Alameda County	367,500
San Jose, CA (city) Santa Clara County	363,900
Honolulu, HI (cdp) Honolulu County	356,900
Maunawili, HI (cdp) Honolulu County	355,800
South San Francisco, CA (city) San Mateo County	347,000
Daly City, CA (city) San Mateo County	341,900
Kailua, HI (cdp) Honolulu County	339,200
Halawa, HI (cdp) Honolulu County	323,900
Haleiwa, HI (cdp) Honolulu County	320,000
Union City, CA (city) Alameda County	312,500
Aiea, HI (cdp) Honolulu County	307,100
Laie, HI (cdp) Honolulu County	305,900
Ahuimanu, HI (cdp) Honolulu County	303,000
Pearl City, HI (cdp) Honolulu County	298,400
Village Park, HI (cdp) Honolulu County	289,800
Kaaawa, HI (cdp) Honolulu County	289,100
San Francisco, CA (city) San Francisco County	287,200
Waimalu, HI (cdp) Honolulu County	286,600
Waialua, HI (cdp) Honolulu County	281,300
Kaneohe, HI (cdp) Honolulu County	278,400
East Palo Alto, CA (city) San Mateo County	277,300
Mililani Town, HI (cdp) Honolulu County	275,000
Captain Cook, HI (cdp) Hawaii County	256,300
Alameda, CA (city) Alameda County	255,300
Waipahu, HI (cdp) Honolulu County	253,100
Hayward, CA (city) Alameda County	245,900
Hawthorne, CA (city) Los Angeles County	243,800
San Bruno, CA (city) San Mateo County	242,900
Napili-Honokowai, HI (cdp) Maui County	242,700
Des Moines, WA (city) King County	241,700
Costa Mesa, CA (city) Orange County	239,300
Sunnyvale, CA (city) Santa Clara County	237,500
San Leandro, CA (city) Alameda County	236,500
Makawao, HI (cdp) Maui County	235,100
Salinas, CA (city) Monterey County	225,000
Makakilo City, HI (cdp) Honolulu County	224,400
Garden Grove, CA (city) Orange County	223,900
Chula Vista, CA (city) San Diego County	223,800
Waipio, HI (cdp) Honolulu County	221,900
Wahiawa, HI (cdp) Honolulu County	219,400
West Covina, CA (city) Los Angeles County	217,900
Kapaa, HI (cdp) Kauai County	209,700
Ewa Beach, HI (cdp) Honolulu County	207,200
Hauula, HI (cdp) Honolulu County	206,700
Anaheim, CA (city) Orange County	206,600
Kahului, HI (cdp) Maui County	205,100
Santa Ana, CA (city) Orange County	203,900
Wailuku, HI (cdp) Maui County	203,400
Paia, HI (cdp) Maui County	202,300
Antioch, CA (city) Contra Costa County	202,100
Westminster, CA (city) Orange County	200,000
Kahuku, HI (cdp) Honolulu County	198,000
Kihei, HI (cdp) Maui County	196,900
Hana, HI (cdp) Maui County	196,400
San Diego, CA (city) San Diego County	196,100
Marina, CA (city) Monterey County	195,800
Whitmore Village, HI (cdp) Honolulu County	195,800
Oxnard, CA (city) Ventura County	195,500
Huntington Beach, CA (city) Orange County	195,200
Concord, CA (city) Contra Costa County	194,900
Hanapepe, HI (cdp) Kauai County	190,300
New York, NY (city)	189,400
Honalo, HI (cdp) Hawaii County	187,500
Paradise, NV (cdp) Clark County	187,500
Kalaoa, HI (cdp) Hawaii County	185,900
Lahaina, HI (cdp) Maui County	183,400
Richmond, CA (city) Contra Costa County	183,300

Notes: Please refer to the User's Guide for an explanation of data; ranking tables include all places with Asian and/or NHPI populations above SF4 population thresholds; (1) tables reflect only those areas that meet SF4 population thresholds, therefore there may be less than 50 states, 75 counties or 75 places listed

Median Home Value

Specified Housing Units Owned and Occupied by Asian Indians

All States, Top 75 Counties, and Top 75 Places Sorted by Number[1]

State	Dollars
District of Columbia	367,000
California	329,300
Massachusetts	297,200
Hawaii	296,400
Connecticut	237,800
Michigan	234,700
New York	230,100
Colorado	230,000
Oregon	226,100
New Jersey	225,300
Washington	224,500
Maryland	218,000
Virginia	216,900
United States	210,200
Utah	208,300
Illinois	201,000
Wisconsin	197,100
Delaware	196,900
New Hampshire	194,100
Alaska	194,000
Ohio	192,700
West Virginia	192,600
Arizona	192,300
Kentucky	190,900
Maine	184,100
North Carolina	176,000
Vermont	173,100
Alabama	172,500
Indiana	171,000
Tennessee	170,700
Georgia	167,700
Missouri	166,000
Montana	164,300
Louisiana	163,800
Pennsylvania	163,200
Kansas	162,900
Nevada	161,200
Idaho	160,400
Iowa	159,000
South Carolina	157,400
Nebraska	155,500
Minnesota	154,600
Arkansas	153,600
Rhode Island	152,500
Texas	145,500
Florida	142,500
New Mexico	141,300
Mississippi	134,400
Wyoming	129,700
Oklahoma	124,200
North Dakota	124,100
South Dakota	104,200

County	Dollars
New York County, NY	1 mil.+
Marin County, CA	625,000
San Mateo County, CA	564,800
Santa Clara County, CA	522,400
Santa Barbara County, CA	446,000
San Francisco County, CA	445,100
San Luis Obispo County, CA	441,400
Santa Cruz County, CA	430,800
Alameda County, CA	405,400
Fairfield County, CT	349,100
Hunterdon County, NJ	348,900
San Diego County, CA	348,700
Westchester County, NY	336,800
Contra Costa County, CA	319,100
Middlesex County, MA	316,200
Norfolk County, MA	315,100
Orange County, CA	314,800
Hampden County, MA	314,300
Orange County, NC	314,300
Honolulu County, HI	313,200
Essex County, MA	312,400
Sonoma County, CA	312,100
Boulder County, CO	311,300
Ventura County, CA	311,200
Monterey County, CA	300,000
Somerset County, NJ	297,600
Clackamas County, OR	294,300
Los Angeles County, CA	293,600
Oakland County, MI	289,900
Waukesha County, WI	289,900
Caddo Parish, LA	286,800
Putnam County, NY	286,100
Nassau County, NY	280,200
Morris County, NJ	279,300
Worcester County, MA	274,100
Monmouth County, NJ	273,300
Montgomery County, VA	271,700
Placer County, CA	269,600
Mercer County, NJ	266,600
Howard County, MD	261,900
King County, WA	261,900
Saginaw County, MI	260,900
Middlesex County, CT	258,300
York County, VA	258,300
Bergen County, NJ	255,500
Warren County, NJ	253,700
Hamilton County, IN	252,700
Montgomery County, MD	251,200
Fairfax County, VA	250,100
Rockland County, NY	250,000
Westmoreland County, PA	248,400
Kanawha County, WV	246,800
Douglas County, CO	245,200
Bristol County, MA	244,200
Fulton County, GA	238,000
Shelby County, AL	237,500
Niagara County, NY	236,100
Story County, IA	235,700
Washtenaw County, MI	234,100
Kent County, MI	234,000
Washington County, OR	233,700
El Paso County, CO	233,100
Jefferson County, CO	231,000
Chester County, PA	229,500
Rock Island County, IL	229,500
Suffolk County, NY	229,300
Schenectady County, NY	228,900
Charleston County, SC	228,600
Chittenden County, VT	228,100
Lake County, IL	227,900
Delaware County, OH	227,500
Brazos County, TX	227,300
Sussex County, NJ	226,900
Arlington County, VA	226,100
Richmond County, NY	226,000

Place	Dollars
Brookline, MA (town) Norfolk County	1 mil.+
Los Altos Hills, CA (town) Santa Clara County	1 mil.+
New Haven, CT (city) New Haven County	1 mil.+
Saratoga, CA (city) Santa Clara County	1 mil.+
Stanford, CA (cdp) Santa Clara County	1 mil.+
West New York, NJ (town) Hudson County	1 mil.+
Los Altos, CA (city) Santa Clara County	996,500
Palo Alto, CA (city) Santa Clara County	884,100
Oak Brook, IL (village) Du Page County	856,100
South Barrington, IL (village) Cook County	830,400
Belmont, CA (city) San Mateo County	772,300
Muttontown, NY (village) Nassau County	772,100
Scarsdale, NY (village) Westchester County	738,900
Cupertino, CA (city) Santa Clara County	717,900
Costa Mesa, CA (city) Orange County	700,000
Redwood City, CA (city) San Mateo County	699,300
Travilah, MD (cdp) Montgomery County	693,800
New Castle, NY (town) Westchester County	668,600
Millbrae, CA (city) San Mateo County	620,800
Greenville, NY (cdp) Westchester County	616,100
Sunnyvale, CA (city) Santa Clara County	615,300
Burr Ridge, IL (village) Du Page County	613,200
Rancho Palos Verdes, CA (city) Los Angeles County	610,100
Town and Country, MO (city) Saint Louis County	591,700
Foster City, CA (city) San Mateo County	586,200
Mountain View, CA (city) Santa Clara County	575,700
Mount Pleasant, NY (town) Westchester County	548,600
Greenwich, CT (town) Fairfield County	541,700
Searingtown, NY (cdp) Nassau County	535,900
Santa Monica, CA (city) Los Angeles County	532,900
Shelby charter, MI (township) Macomb County	520,800
San Mateo, CA (city) San Mateo County	513,700
Lexington, MA (town) Middlesex County	509,900
Pleasanton, CA (city) Alameda County	506,900
Port Washington, NY (cdp) Nassau County	506,900
McLean, VA (cdp) Fairfax County	497,500
Warren, NJ (township) Somerset County	493,200
Campbell, CA (city) Santa Clara County	491,700
Manhasset Hills, NY (cdp) Nassau County	490,800
Walnut Creek, CA (city) Contra Costa County	481,800
San Ramon, CA (city) Contra Costa County	478,800
Danville, CA (town) Contra Costa County	473,000
San Jose, CA (city) Santa Clara County	468,300
Scotch Plains, NJ (township) Union County	461,100
Fremont, CA (city) Alameda County	459,300
Arcadia, CA (city) Los Angeles County	459,100
Potomac, MD (cdp) Montgomery County	458,200
San Rafael, CA (city) Marin County	457,100
Montgomery, NJ (township) Somerset County	445,200
San Francisco, CA (city) San Francisco County	445,100
Holmdel, NJ (township) Monmouth County	443,600
Summit, NJ (city) Union County	443,300
Santa Clara, CA (city) Santa Clara County	441,800
Glendale, CA (city) Los Angeles County	439,600
Bernards, NJ (township) Somerset County	437,500
Dix Hills, NY (cdp) Suffolk County	434,900
Honolulu, HI (cdp) Honolulu County	434,600
Albany, CA (city) Alameda County	425,000
Stamford, CT (city) Fairfield County	424,700
Westborough, MA (town) Worcester County	424,200
Wolf Trap, VA (cdp) Fairfax County	421,700
Bethesda, MD (cdp) Montgomery County	419,500
Acton, MA (town) Middlesex County	419,100
Cambridge, MA (city) Middlesex County	417,600
Boulder, CO (city) Boulder County	417,500
Milpitas, CA (city) Santa Clara County	415,000
Alameda, CA (city) Alameda County	414,900
Boxborough, MA (town) Middlesex County	411,900
West Windsor, NJ (township) Mercer County	404,600
Redondo Beach, CA (city) Los Angeles County	403,100
Glenview, IL (village) Cook County	402,800
Berkeley, CA (city) Alameda County	397,400
San Bruno, CA (city) San Mateo County	396,400
Bloomfield, MI (township) Oakland County	394,900
Yorba Linda, CA (city) Orange County	390,000

Notes: Please refer to the User's Guide for an explanation of data; ranking tables include all places with Asian and/or NHPI populations above SF4 population thresholds; (1) tables reflect only those areas that meet SF4 population thresholds, therefore there may be less than 50 states, 75 counties or 75 places listed

Median Home Value

Specified Housing Units Owned and Occupied by Bangladeshis

All States, Top 75 Counties, and Top 75 Places Sorted by Number[1]

State	Dollars
California	304,300
Connecticut	281,300
New York	253,400
Maryland	196,300
Virginia	184,700
Ohio	173,200
United States	171,000
Massachusetts	170,300
Illinois	168,800
New Jersey	156,000
Georgia	146,700
Pennsylvania	132,800
Texas	127,100
Florida	117,900
Michigan	67,700

County	Dollars
Santa Clara County, CA	520,800
Fairfax County, VA	302,100
Queens County, NY	256,300
Montgomery County, MD	225,700
Kings County, NY	225,000
Los Angeles County, CA	167,700
DeKalb County, GA	162,500
Middlesex County, NJ	142,500
Dallas County, TX	133,300
Harris County, TX	77,900
Passaic County, NJ	58,800
Wayne County, MI	57,100
Atlantic County, NJ	0
Bronx County, NY	0
New York County, NY	0

Place	Dollars
New York, NY (city)	253,000
Los Angeles, CA (city) Los Angeles County	187,500
Hamtramck, MI (city) Wayne County	66,000
Paterson, NJ (city) Passaic County	56,600

Notes: Please refer to the User's Guide for an explanation of data; ranking tables include all places with Asian and/or NHPI populations above SF4 population thresholds; (1) tables reflect only those areas that meet SF4 population thresholds, therefore there may be less than 50 states, 75 counties or 75 places listed

Median Home Value

Specified Housing Units Owned and Occupied by Cambodians

All States, Top 75 Counties, and Top 75 Places Sorted by Number[1]

State	Dollars
California	175,800
Maryland	167,900
Connecticut	162,700
Washington	160,300
Arizona	160,200
Illinois	154,800
Colorado	151,800
Oregon	151,100
Massachusetts	141,300
Nevada	130,900
Utah	125,700
Michigan	125,500
United States	120,800
Virginia	120,300
Minnesota	119,100
Indiana	104,600
Georgia	104,300
New Jersey	96,500
North Carolina	96,200
Rhode Island	96,000
Wisconsin	95,600
Ohio	94,400
South Carolina	91,900
Maine	89,200
Florida	88,800
Tennessee	82,300
Oklahoma	79,000
Texas	77,900
Missouri	73,100
New York	72,000
Kansas	70,300
Iowa	57,000
Alabama	55,700
Pennsylvania	54,400
Hawaii	0

County	Dollars
Santa Clara County, CA	331,000
Alameda County, CA	259,400
Sonoma County, CA	219,200
Orange County, CA	207,400
San Diego County, CA	205,800
Bronx County, NY	194,600
Cook County, IL	193,100
Snohomish County, WA	188,700
King County, WA	181,700
Los Angeles County, CA	179,800
Riverside County, CA	178,100
Suffolk County, MA	178,000
Fairfax County, VA	174,100
Washington County, OR	168,600
Montgomery County, MD	166,800
Fairfield County, CT	164,900
Maricopa County, AZ	160,200
Bristol County, MA	155,400
Multnomah County, OR	153,200
Cowlitz County, WA	150,000
Arlington County, VA	148,800
Middlesex County, MA	144,600
Clark County, WA	141,500
Dakota County, MN	140,900
Worcester County, MA	139,600
Denver County, CO	135,300
Scott County, MN	133,300
San Bernardino County, CA	133,000
Hennepin County, MN	130,900
Gwinnett County, GA	127,700
Clark County, NV	127,400
Ottawa County, MI	126,700
Sacramento County, CA	125,000
Salt Lake County, UT	124,600
Stanislaus County, CA	123,200
Pierce County, WA	117,300
San Joaquin County, CA	111,700
Thurston County, WA	110,400
Hampden County, MA	108,900
DeKalb County, GA	108,400
Denton County, TX	105,200
Mecklenburg County, NC	102,000
Henrico County, VA	99,000
Ramsey County, MN	99,000
San Francisco County, CA	97,900
Clayton County, GA	96,100
Essex County, MA	93,300
Cuyahoga County, OH	93,200
Davidson County, NC	90,000
Franklin County, OH	90,000
Providence County, RI	88,900
Chesterfield County, VA	88,100
Cumberland County, ME	88,100
Kern County, CA	85,000
Duval County, FL	83,900
Dallas County, TX	83,200
Fresno County, CA	80,200
Sedgwick County, KS	77,800
Pinellas County, FL	75,700
Olmsted County, MN	74,200
Shelby County, TN	69,400
Camden County, NJ	68,200
Hamilton County, OH	67,100
Harris County, TX	64,600
Polk County, IA	52,000
Brazoria County, TX	50,000
Philadelphia County, PA	47,900
Monroe County, NY	43,600
Kings County, NY	42,500
Tarrant County, TX	34,200
Mobile County, AL	27,300

Place	Dollars
San Jose, CA (city) Santa Clara County	328,100
Signal Hill, CA (city) Los Angeles County	235,700
Garden Grove, CA (city) Orange County	233,000
Chicago, IL (city) Cook County	229,200
Rosemead, CA (city) Los Angeles County	227,900
Lakewood, CA (city) Los Angeles County	225,600
Monterey Park, CA (city) Los Angeles County	225,000
Beaverton, OR (city) Washington County	215,600
Santa Rosa, CA (city) Sonoma County	207,700
Seattle, WA (city) King County	201,000
Revere, MA (city) Suffolk County	187,500
Oakland, CA (city) Alameda County	185,400
Everett, WA (city) Snohomish County	184,000
Santa Ana, CA (city) Orange County	181,100
Boston, MA (city) Suffolk County	179,700
San Diego, CA (city) San Diego County	177,800
Los Angeles, CA (city) Los Angeles County	167,400
Long Beach, CA (city) Los Angeles County	165,700
Danbury, CT (city) Fairfield County	162,200
Silver Spring, MD (cdp) Montgomery County	161,100
Norwalk, CA (city) Los Angeles County	155,100
White Center, WA (cdp) King County	152,500
Portland, OR (city) Multnomah County	150,800
Longview, WA (city) Cowlitz County	150,000
Arlington, VA (cdp) Arlington County	148,800
Bellflower, CA (city) Los Angeles County	145,200
Lynn, MA (city) Essex County	140,000
Aurora, CO (city) Arapahoe County	138,800
Bloomington, MN (city) Hennepin County	138,400
Denver, CO (city) Denver County	135,300
Bridgeport, CT (city) Fairfield County	133,100
Lowell, MA (city) Middlesex County	126,800
Phoenix, AZ (city) Maricopa County	123,900
West Valley City, UT (city) Salt Lake County	120,500
Attleboro, MA (city) Bristol County	119,400
Modesto, CA (city) Stanislaus County	113,300
Pomona, CA (city) Los Angeles County	112,500
Stockton, CA (city) San Joaquin County	111,600
Tacoma, WA (city) Pierce County	108,300
Cranston, RI (city) Providence County	106,000
Charlotte, NC (city) Mecklenburg County	99,700
Carrollton, TX (city) Denton County	99,300
San Francisco, CA (city) San Francisco County	97,900
Minneapolis, MN (city) Hennepin County	96,700
Lexington, NC (city) Davidson County	96,300
St. Paul, MN (city) Ramsey County	94,500
Columbus, OH (city) Franklin County	88,000
Dallas, TX (city) Dallas County	86,300
Providence, RI (city) Providence County	86,100
Jacksonville, FL (city) Duval County	83,900
Sacramento, CA (city) Sacramento County	80,300
San Bernardino, CA (city) San Bernardino County	75,800
St. Petersburg, FL (city) Pinellas County	72,700
Lawrence, MA (city) Essex County	72,200
Rochester, MN (city) Olmsted County	70,800
Fresno, CA (city) Fresno County	68,800
Memphis, TN (city) Shelby County	65,600
Portland, ME (city) Cumberland County	65,000
Houston, TX (city) Harris County	60,500
New York, NY (city)	50,700
Philadelphia, PA (city) Philadelphia County	47,900
Fall River, MA (city) Bristol County	17,500

Notes: Please refer to the User's Guide for an explanation of data; ranking tables include all places with Asian and/or NHPI populations above SF4 population thresholds; (1) tables reflect only those areas that meet SF4 population thresholds, therefore there may be less than 50 states, 75 counties or 75 places listed

Median Home Value

Specified Housing Units Owned and Occupied by Chinese (except Taiwanese)

All States, Top 75 Counties, and Top 75 Places Sorted by Number[1]

State	Dollars
Hawaii	348,400
California	300,600
District of Columbia	295,200
New Jersey	242,800
Massachusetts	235,100
United States	230,700
New York	229,200
Washington	226,900
Connecticut	226,700
Michigan	203,500
Colorado	197,300
Illinois	196,900
Maryland	194,300
Virginia	193,000
Delaware	172,700
Oregon	171,900
Alaska	170,000
North Carolina	169,300
New Hampshire	167,800
Georgia	164,500
Utah	164,400
Ohio	162,200
Minnesota	160,300
Arizona	157,600
Wisconsin	155,900
Nevada	155,000
New Mexico	151,100
Tennessee	149,400
Kentucky	148,400
Indiana	146,400
Missouri	142,200
West Virginia	138,600
Texas	138,300
Alabama	138,200
Vermont	136,500
Rhode Island	135,000
Kansas	134,700
Florida	131,600
South Carolina	130,100
Louisiana	129,400
Iowa	129,300
Nebraska	126,300
Pennsylvania	125,900
Oklahoma	119,000
Idaho	116,000
Montana	113,200
South Dakota	100,000
Maine	98,500
Mississippi	94,900
Arkansas	90,500
North Dakota	88,800
Wyoming	88,300

County	Dollars
New York County, NY	650,000
Marin County, CA	522,900
Santa Clara County, CA	479,100
San Mateo County, CA	437,700
Santa Barbara County, CA	421,300
San Francisco County, CA	360,100
Honolulu County, HI	356,400
Fairfield County, CT	354,300
Westchester County, NY	342,100
Santa Cruz County, CA	339,800
Fairfax Independent City, VA	339,300
Hunterdon County, NJ	335,000
Alameda County, CA	328,200
Mercer County, NJ	315,800
Ventura County, CA	311,800
Contra Costa County, CA	311,400
Somerset County, NJ	305,700
Morris County, NJ	302,900
Sonoma County, CA	300,200
Orange County, CA	296,600
Maui County, HI	292,900
Middlesex County, MA	289,200
Napa County, CA	288,000
Bergen County, NJ	286,300
San Diego County, CA	283,400
Putnam County, NY	283,300
Nassau County, NY	271,800
Lake County, IL	268,600
Barnstable County, MA	265,000
Yolo County, CA	264,300
Boulder County, CO	262,700
Chester County, PA	262,100
Monmouth County, NJ	262,100
Arlington County, VA	261,300
Essex County, NJ	259,900
Monterey County, CA	255,700
Will County, IL	244,500
San Luis Obispo County, CA	243,800
Queens County, NY	243,500
Kauai County, HI	243,200
King County, WA	242,200
Rockland County, NY	242,200
Union County, NJ	242,200
Passaic County, NJ	240,300
Los Angeles County, CA	236,500
Oakland County, MI	235,900
DuPage County, IL	235,000
Grafton County, NH	232,500
Rockingham County, NH	232,100
Douglas County, CO	229,300
Snohomish County, WA	228,800
Fairfax County, VA	226,300
Placer County, CA	225,300
Washtenaw County, MI	224,400
Cumberland County, PA	223,400
Montgomery County, MD	222,800
Delaware County, OH	222,600
Worcester County, MA	219,800
Fulton County, GA	217,300
Hamilton County, IN	216,900
Kings County, NY	216,600
El Paso County, CO	216,500
Clackamas County, OR	215,800
Howard County, MD	215,400
Essex County, MA	214,400
Middlesex County, NJ	214,100
Washington County, OR	213,100
Suffolk County, NY	209,800
Norfolk County, MA	208,300
Dutchess County, NY	208,200
Monongalia County, WV	205,000
Wayne County, MI	204,300
McHenry County, IL	203,300
Hartford County, CT	201,900
Hamilton County, OH	201,700

Place	Dollars
Hillsborough, CA (town) San Mateo County	1 mil.+
Los Altos Hills, CA (town) Santa Clara County	1 mil.+
Saratoga, CA (city) Santa Clara County	1 mil.+
Beverly Hills, CA (city) Los Angeles County	991,100
Los Altos, CA (city) Santa Clara County	981,600
Palos Verdes Estates, CA (city) Los Angeles County	948,300
Menlo Park, CA (city) San Mateo County	880,200
Stanford, CA (cdp) Santa Clara County	875,000
Los Gatos, CA (town) Santa Clara County	859,000
Newport Beach, CA (city) Orange County	833,300
Rolling Hills Estates, CA (city) Los Angeles County	803,800
Palo Alto, CA (city) Santa Clara County	739,000
Greenwich, CT (town) Fairfield County	736,100
Manhattan Beach, CA (city) Los Angeles County	716,700
Blackhawk-Camino Tass., CA (cdp) Contra Costa Co.	711,800
Burlingame, CA (city) San Mateo County	690,000
San Carlos, CA (city) San Mateo County	671,100
San Marino, CA (city) Los Angeles County	661,500
Cupertino, CA (city) Santa Clara County	640,600
Highlands-Baywood Pk., CA (cdp) San Mateo County	628,800
La Canada Flintridge, CA (city) Los Angeles County	626,600
Santa Barbara, CA (city) Santa Barbara County	625,000
Lake Success, NY (village) Nassau County	616,100
Scarsdale, NY (village) Westchester County	613,600
Warren, NJ (township) Somerset County	608,200
Belmont, CA (city) San Mateo County	604,800
Piedmont, CA (city) Alameda County	600,500
Rancho Palos Verdes, CA (city) Los Angeles County	597,600
Orinda, CA (city) Contra Costa County	575,000
Redwood City, CA (city) San Mateo County	569,700
Danville, CA (town) Contra Costa County	563,800
Foster City, CA (city) San Mateo County	563,500
Englewood Cliffs, NJ (borough) Bergen County	562,500
Lafayette, CA (city) Contra Costa County	559,100
Millbrae, CA (city) San Mateo County	550,200
Needham, MA (town) Norfolk County	547,300
Weston, MA (town) Middlesex County	546,100
Wellesley, MA (town) Norfolk County	543,700
Santa Monica, CA (city) Los Angeles County	542,900
Westport, CT (town) Fairfield County	532,100
Moraga, CA (town) Contra Costa County	526,100
Mountain View, CA (city) Santa Clara County	525,500
Calabasas, CA (city) Los Angeles County	525,000
Morgan Hill, CA (city) Santa Clara County	488,800
Sunnyvale, CA (city) Santa Clara County	487,900
San Mateo, CA (city) San Mateo County	487,300
San Rafael, CA (city) Marin County	481,100
Laguna Niguel, CA (city) Orange County	468,200
La Habra Heights, CA (city) Los Angeles County	461,800
Mercer Island, WA (city) King County	458,600
Kensington, CA (cdp) Contra Costa County	458,300
Pleasanton, CA (city) Alameda County	456,900
Tustin Foothills, CA (cdp) Orange County	453,800
San Ramon, CA (city) Contra Costa County	448,900
Princeton, NJ (township) Mercer County	444,000
Potomac, MD (cdp) Montgomery County	442,100
Walnut Creek, CA (city) Contra Costa County	434,000
Bernards, NJ (township) Somerset County	432,400
Boulder, CO (city) Boulder County	430,000
Carlsbad, CA (city) San Diego County	429,600
Goleta, CA (cdp) Santa Barbara County	422,100
Millburn, NJ (township) Essex County	417,100
Belmont, MA (cdp) Middlesex County	416,700
Belmont, MA (town) Middlesex County	416,700
San Jose, CA (city) Santa Clara County	415,100
South Pasadena, CA (city) Los Angeles County	412,800
Poway, CA (city) San Diego County	412,500
White Plains, NY (city) Westchester County	408,300
Campbell, CA (city) Santa Clara County	404,200
Santa Clara, CA (city) Santa Clara County	404,000
San Bruno, CA (city) San Mateo County	403,800
Sammamish, WA (city) King County	402,900
Thousand Oaks, CA (city) Ventura County	393,100
Berkeley Heights, NJ (township) Union County	392,900
Honolulu, HI (cdp) Honolulu County	392,800

Notes: Please refer to the User's Guide for an explanation of data; ranking tables include all places with Asian and/or NHPI populations above SF4 population thresholds; (1) tables reflect only those areas that meet SF4 population thresholds, therefore there may be less than 50 states, 75 counties or 75 places listed

Median Home Value

Specified Housing Units Owned and Occupied by Fijians

All States, Top 75 Counties, and Top 75 Places Sorted by Number[1]

State	Dollars
California	195,100
Washington	184,400
United States	181,000
Oregon	176,000

County	Dollars
Santa Clara County, CA	419,400
San Mateo County, CA	354,700
Alameda County, CA	266,300
Contra Costa County, CA	215,400
Los Angeles County, CA	192,100
King County, WA	183,300
Yolo County, CA	164,100
Sacramento County, CA	116,500
Stanislaus County, CA	105,500

Place	Dollars
Hayward, CA (city) Alameda County	269,900
Sacramento, CA (city) Sacramento County	115,100
Modesto, CA (city) Stanislaus County	97,500

Notes: Please refer to the User's Guide for an explanation of data; ranking tables include all places with Asian and/or NHPI populations above SF4 population thresholds; (1) tables reflect only those areas that meet SF4 population thresholds, therefore there may be less than 50 states, 75 counties or 75 places listed

Median Home Value

Specified Housing Units Owned and Occupied by Filipinos

All States, Top 75 Counties, and Top 75 Places Sorted by Number[1]

State	Dollars
Hawaii	239,200
California	218,400
New York	214,300
District of Columbia	196,100
United States	188,100
Massachusetts	183,200
Illinois	182,300
New Jersey	179,500
Washington	169,300
Michigan	161,800
Connecticut	158,300
Colorado	156,800
Maryland	154,800
Oregon	154,100
Delaware	151,600
Wisconsin	149,500
Utah	146,500
Alaska	145,200
Virginia	142,200
Nevada	141,900
Indiana	139,700
Ohio	133,900
Arizona	130,400
Rhode Island	130,000
Pennsylvania	127,800
Missouri	127,200
Tennessee	127,100
Minnesota	126,400
Vermont	125,800
New Hampshire	122,200
North Carolina	121,700
Kentucky	121,000
Wyoming	120,200
Georgia	118,800
West Virginia	118,500
New Mexico	118,200
Florida	110,400
Iowa	105,800
Louisiana	100,400
Texas	97,200
Maine	97,000
Arkansas	95,500
Montana	95,000
South Carolina	93,900
Idaho	93,700
Alabama	93,000
Nebraska	92,800
Kansas	92,700
North Dakota	88,300
Oklahoma	86,900
Mississippi	83,800
South Dakota	77,700

County	Dollars
Marin County, CA	409,100
Santa Clara County, CA	363,500
San Mateo County, CA	359,800
Santa Cruz County, CA	351,000
San Francisco County, CA	340,600
Alameda County, CA	292,800
San Benito County, CA	289,900
Honolulu County, HI	264,400
Middlesex County, MA	254,500
Sonoma County, CA	249,800
Orange County, CA	243,900
Westchester County, NY	241,400
Morris County, NJ	238,600
Loudoun County, VA	236,200
Fairfield County, CT	228,800
Maui County, HI	228,600
Contra Costa County, CA	226,200
Aleutians West Census Area, AK	225,000
Queens County, NY	224,100
Nassau County, NY	223,800
Rockland County, NY	223,500
Monmouth County, NJ	221,800
Jefferson County, NY	220,800
Monterey County, CA	219,600
Boulder County, CO	219,400
Bergen County, NJ	218,700
Kings County, NY	216,400
Placer County, CA	215,200
Suffolk County, NY	215,200
Alexandria Independent City, VA	214,600
Ventura County, CA	214,500
Waukesha County, WI	213,500
Somerset County, NJ	210,800
Orleans Parish, LA	205,200
Worcester County, MA	203,600
Clackamas County, OR	202,400
Fairfax County, VA	201,800
Norfolk County, MA	201,600
Bronx County, NY	200,700
Napa County, CA	199,400
Arlington County, VA	198,700
Essex County, MA	198,600
Los Angeles County, CA	197,300
Chester County, PA	195,200
Solano County, CA	193,000
San Diego County, CA	192,900
Snohomish County, WA	192,800
King County, WA	192,200
San Luis Obispo County, CA	192,200
Richmond County, NY	192,100
Middlesex County, NJ	191,600
McHenry County, IL	191,000
DuPage County, IL	189,800
Washtenaw County, MI	189,300
Albany County, NY	189,100
Lake County, IL	189,100
Johnson County, KS	188,800
Kane County, IL	188,800
Oakland County, MI	188,500
Fulton County, GA	186,800
Butte County, CA	186,400
Washington County, OR	185,200
Kauai County, HI	184,300
Yolo County, CA	182,900
Cook County, IL	182,200
Berrien County, MI	180,500
Hartford County, CT	180,000
Passaic County, NJ	179,600
Jefferson County, CO	179,300
Suffolk County, MA	178,800
Montgomery County, MD	177,900
Orange County, NY	177,700
Union County, NJ	174,000
Essex County, NJ	173,700
Collin County, TX	173,100

Place	Dollars
Burlingame, CA (city) San Mateo County	875,000
Santa Monica, CA (city) Los Angeles County	805,600
Potomac, MD (cdp) Montgomery County	615,700
Danville, CA (town) Contra Costa County	587,300
Foster City, CA (city) San Mateo County	541,700
Coronado, CA (city) San Diego County	525,000
Cupertino, CA (city) Santa Clara County	523,400
Rancho Palos Verdes, CA (city) Los Angeles County	497,500
Mountain View, CA (city) Santa Clara County	493,800
Palo Alto, CA (city) Santa Clara County	493,800
San Ramon, CA (city) Contra Costa County	460,700
Novato, CA (city) Marin County	450,000
Lomita, CA (city) Los Angeles County	438,600
San Mateo, CA (city) San Mateo County	431,100
Pleasanton, CA (city) Alameda County	422,900
San Bruno, CA (city) San Mateo County	411,600
Belmont, CA (city) San Mateo County	411,500
Monterey, CA (city) Monterey County	403,800
McLean, VA (cdp) Fairfax County	396,700
Redwood City, CA (city) San Mateo County	393,500
Goleta, CA (cdp) Santa Barbara County	392,300
Millbrae, CA (city) San Mateo County	390,600
Santa Cruz, CA (city) Santa Cruz County	382,000
Campbell, CA (city) Santa Clara County	380,800
Walnut Creek, CA (city) Contra Costa County	380,000
Milpitas, CA (city) Santa Clara County	378,100
Redondo Beach, CA (city) Los Angeles County	369,600
Sunnyvale, CA (city) Santa Clara County	369,600
Santa Clara, CA (city) Santa Clara County	368,800
South San Francisco, CA (city) San Mateo County	366,900
Waimalu, HI (cdp) Honolulu County	358,400
Fremont, CA (city) Alameda County	358,300
San Jose, CA (city) Santa Clara County	354,600
Yorba Linda, CA (city) Orange County	351,500
Gilroy, CA (city) Santa Clara County	351,100
San Luis Obispo, CA (city) San Luis Obispo County	350,000
Pacifica, CA (city) San Mateo County	348,000
Daly City, CA (city) San Mateo County	344,400
Laguna Niguel, CA (city) Orange County	343,500
Honolulu, HI (cdp) Honolulu County	341,400
Aiea, HI (cdp) Honolulu County	340,800
San Francisco, CA (city) San Francisco County	340,600
Huntington, NY (town) Suffolk County	335,200
Paramus, NJ (borough) Bergen County	333,900
Halawa, HI (cdp) Honolulu County	331,000
Carlsbad, CA (city) San Diego County	330,800
Dublin, CA (city) Alameda County	330,200
Alameda, CA (city) Alameda County	327,600
Omao, HI (cdp) Kauai County	326,700
Kailua, HI (cdp) Honolulu County	321,700
Newark, CA (city) Alameda County	319,500
Broadmoor, CA (cdp) San Mateo County	319,400
Colma, CA (town) San Mateo County	316,700
Union City, CA (city) Alameda County	316,200
Greenburgh, NY (town) Westchester County	305,000
Kaneohe, HI (cdp) Honolulu County	304,100
Naperville, IL (city) Du Page County	302,000
Fairview, CA (cdp) Alameda County	300,000
Benicia, CA (city) Solano County	298,700
Mission Viejo, CA (city) Orange County	298,700
Castro Valley, CA (cdp) Alameda County	298,100
Santa Barbara, CA (city) Santa Barbara County	298,100
La Palma, CA (city) Orange County	295,400
Culver City, CA (city) Los Angeles County	295,200
Martinez, CA (city) Contra Costa County	293,600
Huntington Beach, CA (city) Orange County	292,200
Torrance, CA (city) Los Angeles County	290,200
Bonita, CA (cdp) San Diego County	286,500
Pearl City, HI (cdp) Honolulu County	286,500
Upland, CA (city) San Bernardino County	284,600
Hollister, CA (city) San Benito County	284,500
Stamford, CT (city) Fairfield County	283,600
Cerritos, CA (city) Los Angeles County	280,400
Waipahu, HI (cdp) Honolulu County	279,200
Lincolnwood, IL (village) Cook County	278,300

Notes: Please refer to the User's Guide for an explanation of data; ranking tables include all places with Asian and/or NHPI populations above SF4 population thresholds; (1) tables reflect only those areas that meet SF4 population thresholds, therefore there may be less than 50 states, 75 counties or 75 places listed

Median Home Value

Specified Housing Units Owned and Occupied by Guamanians or Chamorros

All States, Top 75 Counties, and Top 75 Places Sorted by Number[1]

State	Dollars
Hawaii	282,400
Massachusetts	230,000
New Jersey	225,000
California	184,700
Virginia	172,900
New York	164,100
Oregon	150,900
Missouri	149,000
Washington	146,100
United States	143,500
Colorado	141,500
Connecticut	138,800
New Mexico	132,100
Maryland	129,900
Michigan	128,100
Alabama	126,900
Nevada	126,400
Kentucky	118,800
Arizona	118,200
Wisconsin	112,500
Tennessee	110,400
Ohio	98,800
Florida	96,800
Oklahoma	96,700
Georgia	95,600
Louisiana	94,000
North Carolina	91,900
Illinois	91,400
Pennsylvania	88,900
Minnesota	87,500
Texas	83,100
South Carolina	82,800
Indiana	70,500

County	Dollars
Kings County, NY	450,000
San Mateo County, CA	447,900
Santa Clara County, CA	367,000
Honolulu County, HI	280,500
Alameda County, CA	276,700
Orange County, CA	211,200
King County, WA	200,000
Contra Costa County, CA	195,400
Monterey County, CA	188,000
San Diego County, CA	187,700
Los Angeles County, CA	172,300
Maricopa County, AZ	160,900
Solano County, CA	160,500
Pierce County, WA	144,800
Thurston County, WA	142,900
Kitsap County, WA	137,500
Riverside County, CA	136,700
El Paso County, CO	136,400
Sacramento County, CA	133,600
Clark County, NV	126,400
San Bernardino County, CA	119,800
Harris County, TX	86,800
Bell County, TX	80,000

Place	Dollars
New York, NY (city)	406,700
San Jose, CA (city) Santa Clara County	388,200
Honolulu, HI (cdp) Honolulu County	330,000
Chula Vista, CA (city) San Diego County	181,300
San Diego, CA (city) San Diego County	179,200
Fairfield, CA (city) Solano County	163,400
Vallejo, CA (city) Solano County	158,500
Los Angeles, CA (city) Los Angeles County	150,500
Tacoma, WA (city) Pierce County	131,300
Houston, TX (city) Harris County	87,000
Killeen, TX (city) Bell County	78,800

Notes: Please refer to the User's Guide for an explanation of data; ranking tables include all places with Asian and/or NHPI populations above SF4 population thresholds; (1) tables reflect only those areas that meet SF4 population thresholds, therefore there may be less than 50 states, 75 counties or 75 places listed

Median Home Value

Specified Housing Units Owned and Occupied by Hawaiian Natives

All States, Top 75 Counties, and Top 75 Places Sorted by Number[1]

State	Dollars
Hawaii	209,300
California	193,300
United States	177,100
Washington	170,600
New York	167,500
Colorado	160,500
Maryland	155,200
Massachusetts	153,600
Oregon	150,500
Alaska	137,500
Nevada	137,500
Utah	132,200
Wisconsin	129,200
Minnesota	129,000
Virginia	125,500
Arizona	123,200
Ohio	121,200
Missouri	110,000
New Jersey	109,100
Tennessee	107,500
Pennsylvania	105,000
Kansas	103,100
Georgia	100,900
Idaho	96,900
Indiana	95,500
North Carolina	95,400
Florida	92,600
Montana	87,500
Michigan	85,600
Texas	83,400
Oklahoma	83,100
South Carolina	83,000
New Mexico	79,500
Louisiana	79,200
Arkansas	70,700
Illinois	69,200

County	Dollars
Santa Clara County, CA	373,900
San Mateo County, CA	356,300
Alameda County, CA	262,500
Ventura County, CA	257,300
Honolulu County, HI	256,600
Contra Costa County, CA	221,400
San Diego County, CA	218,400
King County, WA	216,200
Orange County, CA	200,300
Snohomish County, WA	194,600
Los Angeles County, CA	186,100
Maui County, HI	181,800
Multnomah County, OR	181,500
San Joaquin County, CA	178,100
Solano County, CA	177,800
Kauai County, HI	175,600
Riverside County, CA	158,000
Salt Lake County, UT	144,400
Washington County, OR	142,300
Utah County, UT	140,300
Pierce County, WA	139,400
Clark County, NV	136,400
Hawaii County, HI	133,900
Pima County, AZ	129,500
Maricopa County, AZ	124,300
San Bernardino County, CA	122,600
Sacramento County, CA	120,200
Bexar County, TX	78,900

Place	Dollars
Makaha Valley, HI (cdp) Honolulu County	450,000
Punaluu, HI (cdp) Honolulu County	410,000
Kahaluu, HI (cdp) Honolulu County	400,000
Waikane, HI (cdp) Honolulu County	387,500
Honolulu, HI (cdp) Honolulu County	358,000
Waimalu, HI (cdp) Honolulu County	345,000
Kailua, HI (cdp) Honolulu County	342,500
Halawa, HI (cdp) Honolulu County	337,000
San Jose, CA (city) Santa Clara County	331,300
Haleiwa, HI (cdp) Honolulu County	320,000
Aiea, HI (cdp) Honolulu County	307,100
Ahuimanu, HI (cdp) Honolulu County	303,000
Laie, HI (cdp) Honolulu County	292,900
Kaaawa, HI (cdp) Honolulu County	284,400
Pearl City, HI (cdp) Honolulu County	284,400
Mililani Town, HI (cdp) Honolulu County	282,500
Kaneohe, HI (cdp) Honolulu County	276,700
Waipahu, HI (cdp) Honolulu County	265,600
Waialua, HI (cdp) Honolulu County	262,500
Captain Cook, HI (cdp) Hawaii County	256,300
Makawao, HI (cdp) Maui County	235,100
Makakilo City, HI (cdp) Honolulu County	224,400
San Diego, CA (city) San Diego County	222,600
Wahiawa, HI (cdp) Honolulu County	217,700
Ewa Beach, HI (cdp) Honolulu County	215,800
Kapaa, HI (cdp) Kauai County	209,700
Hauula, HI (cdp) Honolulu County	208,900
Paia, HI (cdp) Maui County	207,500
Kahului, HI (cdp) Maui County	205,100
Wailuku, HI (cdp) Maui County	203,400
Kalaoa, HI (cdp) Hawaii County	196,900
Hana, HI (cdp) Maui County	196,400
Waipio, HI (cdp) Honolulu County	195,500
Los Angeles, CA (city) Los Angeles County	193,600
Kahuku, HI (cdp) Honolulu County	192,500
Hanapepe, HI (cdp) Kauai County	190,300
Honalo, HI (cdp) Hawaii County	187,500
Paradise, NV (cdp) Clark County	187,500
Lahaina, HI (cdp) Maui County	183,400
Maili, HI (cdp) Honolulu County	182,800
Waimanalo, HI (cdp) Honolulu County	181,400
Waimanalo Beach, HI (cdp) Honolulu County	178,200
Waimea, HI (cdp) Kauai County	178,100
New York, NY (city)	177,100
Holualoa, HI (cdp) Hawaii County	172,800
Portland, OR (city) Multnomah County	170,200
Waihee-Waiehu, HI (cdp) Maui County	168,200
Kekaha, HI (cdp) Kauai County	165,600
Waikoloa Village, HI (cdp) Hawaii County	163,200
Kilauea, HI (cdp) Kauai County	162,500
Kapaau, HI (cdp) Hawaii County	160,700
Waimea, HI (cdp) Hawaii County	156,900
Makaha, HI (cdp) Honolulu County	146,900
Kaunakakai, HI (cdp) Maui County	146,000
Honaunau-Napoopoo, HI (cdp) Hawaii County	141,700
Nanakuli, HI (cdp) Honolulu County	138,400
Las Vegas, NV (city) Clark County	131,600
Hilo, HI (cdp) Hawaii County	129,300
Kailua, HI (cdp) Hawaii County	129,200
Henderson, NV (city) Clark County	128,400
Kihei, HI (cdp) Maui County	123,500
Waianae, HI (cdp) Honolulu County	122,000
Kualapuu, HI (cdp) Maui County	117,600
Phoenix, AZ (city) Maricopa County	116,400
Anahola, HI (cdp) Kauai County	112,200
Hawaiian Paradise Park, HI (cdp) Hawaii County	109,200
Volcano, HI (cdp) Hawaii County	87,400
Hawaiian Ocean View, HI (cdp) Hawaii County	83,300
Pahala, HI (cdp) Hawaii County	83,100
Hawaiian Beaches, HI (cdp) Hawaii County	75,900
Naalehu, HI (cdp) Hawaii County	63,300
Pakala Village, HI (cdp) Kauai County	0

Notes: Please refer to the User's Guide for an explanation of data; ranking tables include all places with Asian and/or NHPI populations above SF4 population thresholds; (1) tables reflect only those areas that meet SF4 population thresholds, therefore there may be less than 50 states, 75 counties or 75 places listed

Median Home Value

Specified Housing Units Owned and Occupied by Hmongs

All States, Top 75 Counties, and Top 75 Places Sorted by Number[1]

State	Dollars
Colorado	163,000
Washington	144,200
Alaska	137,500
Oregon	131,500
Pennsylvania	127,300
Georgia	125,200
Massachusetts	122,500
Oklahoma	99,500
South Carolina	97,500
California	95,500
North Carolina	94,800
Minnesota	93,000
United States	92,600
Michigan	84,000
Wisconsin	81,800
Rhode Island	79,600
Kansas	61,500

County	Dollars
Orange County, CA	217,900
San Diego County, CA	208,800
Jefferson County, CO	201,500
Washington County, MN	172,500
King County, WA	166,100
Santa Barbara County, CA	165,400
Adams County, CO	160,600
Los Angeles County, CA	157,300
Lancaster County, PA	152,700
Anoka County, MN	150,500
Calumet County, WI	145,500
Solano County, CA	143,800
Anchorage Borough, AK	137,500
Barrow County, GA	134,100
Multnomah County, OR	132,100
Dane County, WI	131,300
Macomb County, MI	121,300
Stanislaus County, CA	119,300
Brown County, WI	105,100
Catawba County, NC	104,300
Mecklenburg County, NC	104,000
La Crosse County, WI	102,700
Spartanburg County, SC	101,300
Butte County, CA	99,400
Merced County, CA	95,900
Chippewa County, WI	95,000
Sacramento County, CA	94,700
Spokane County, WA	94,300
San Joaquin County, CA	93,500
Hennepin County, MN	92,600
Olmsted County, MN	91,800
Oakland County, MI	90,100
Ramsey County, MN	89,200
Portage County, WI	87,900
Winnebago County, WI	87,200
Yuba County, CA	87,100
Fresno County, CA	86,700
Glenn County, CA	85,000
Outagamie County, WI	85,000
Worcester County, MA	85,000
Manitowoc County, WI	82,100
Providence County, RI	81,700
Sheboygan County, WI	80,600
Eau Claire County, WI	80,000
Burke County, NC	79,800
Dunn County, WI	75,900
Marathon County, WI	75,500
Stanly County, NC	75,000
Tulare County, CA	74,400
Riverside County, CA	70,000
Wyandotte County, KS	67,100
Fond du Lac County, WI	65,000
Milwaukee County, WI	64,500
Wood County, WI	61,600
Ingham County, MI	60,600
Wayne County, MI	46,200
Yolo County, CA	0

Place	Dollars
Santa Ana, CA (city) Orange County	187,500
Westminster, CO (city) Adams County	178,500
San Diego, CA (city) San Diego County	171,600
Woodbury, MN (city) Washington County	150,000
Maplewood, MN (city) Ramsey County	144,900
Parkway-S. Sacramento, CA (cdp) Sacramento Co.	137,500
Madison, WI (city) Dane County	130,400
Portland, OR (city) Multnomah County	130,400
Florin, CA (cdp) Sacramento County	128,600
Brooklyn Center, MN (city) Hennepin County	125,500
Warren, MI (city) Macomb County	125,300
Brooklyn Park, MN (city) Hennepin County	121,900
Clovis, CA (city) Fresno County	117,000
Stockton, CA (city) San Joaquin County	106,300
Charlotte, NC (city) Mecklenburg County	104,000
Atwater, CA (city) Merced County	97,100
Merced, CA (city) Merced County	95,300
Hickory, NC (city) Catawba County	95,000
Thermalito, CA (cdp) Butte County	95,000
Sacramento, CA (city) Sacramento County	92,100
Rochester, MN (city) Olmsted County	91,800
Stevens Point, WI (city) Portage County	91,400
Pontiac, MI (city) Oakland County	90,900
Appleton, WI (city) Outagamie County	90,300
Connelly Springs, NC (town) Burke County	88,300
St. Paul, MN (city) Ramsey County	86,800
Green Bay, WI (city) Brown County	86,600
Linda, CA (cdp) Yuba County	86,100
Manitowoc, WI (city) Manitowoc County	85,700
Oshkosh, WI (city) Winnebago County	85,200
Fitchburg, MA (city) Worcester County	85,000
Willows, CA (city) Glenn County	85,000
Minneapolis, MN (city) Hennepin County	84,500
La Crosse, WI (city) La Crosse County	82,700
Eau Claire, WI (city) Eau Claire County	82,500
Fresno, CA (city) Fresno County	82,100
Spokane, WA (city) Spokane County	79,500
Glen Alpine, NC (town) Burke County	78,800
Sheboygan, WI (city) Sheboygan County	78,000
Oroville, CA (city) Butte County	75,000
Providence, RI (city) Providence County	75,000
Visalia, CA (city) Tulare County	75,000
Wausau, WI (city) Marathon County	73,300
Valdese, NC (town) Burke County	67,500
Kansas City, KS (city) Wyandotte County	67,100
Fond du Lac, WI (city) Fond du Lac County	65,000
Milwaukee, WI (city) Milwaukee County	62,700
Wisconsin Rapids, WI (city) Wood County	61,600
Lansing, MI (city) Ingham County	60,600
Detroit, MI (city) Wayne County	51,000
Arden-Arcade, CA (cdp) Sacramento County	0
Chico, CA (city) Butte County	0
Modesto, CA (city) Stanislaus County	0
South Oroville, CA (cdp) Butte County	0
West Sacramento, CA (city) Yolo County	0

Notes: Please refer to the User's Guide for an explanation of data; ranking tables include all places with Asian and/or NHPI populations above SF4 population thresholds; (1) tables reflect only those areas that meet SF4 population thresholds, therefore there may be less than 50 states, 75 counties or 75 places listed

Median Home Value

Specified Housing Units Owned and Occupied by Indonesians

All States, Top 75 Counties, and Top 75 Places Sorted by Number[1]

State	Dollars
California	231,800
Oregon	202,500
New York	193,200
New Jersey	186,400
United States	186,300
Colorado	185,000
Washington	183,000
Virginia	173,000
Illinois	163,500
Georgia	161,600
Texas	160,600
Pennsylvania	154,500
Maryland	153,100
Michigan	138,100
Ohio	125,000
Massachusetts	118,000
Florida	112,900
Arizona	96,000
Wisconsin	86,700

County	Dollars
San Mateo County, CA	496,600
San Francisco County, CA	430,800
Santa Clara County, CA	409,100
Alameda County, CA	394,100
Queens County, NY	285,700
Cook County, IL	275,000
Contra Costa County, CA	253,900
King County, WA	252,500
Los Angeles County, CA	239,700
Orange County, CA	233,100
San Diego County, CA	211,500
Middlesex County, NJ	187,000
Fairfax County, VA	174,000
Montgomery County, MD	164,100
San Bernardino County, CA	156,200
Franklin County, OH	112,500
Harris County, TX	103,100
Maricopa County, AZ	95,300

Place	Dollars
San Francisco, CA (city) San Francisco County	430,800
New York, NY (city)	255,800
Los Angeles, CA (city) Los Angeles County	240,200
Seattle, WA (city) King County	187,500
Loma Linda, CA (city) San Bernardino County	176,700
San Bernardino, CA (city) San Bernardino County	136,300
Houston, TX (city) Harris County	121,900
Columbus, OH (city) Franklin County	0

Notes: Please refer to the User's Guide for an explanation of data; ranking tables include all places with Asian and/or NHPI populations above SF4 population thresholds; (1) tables reflect only those areas that meet SF4 population thresholds, therefore there may be less than 50 states, 75 counties or 75 places listed

Median Home Value

Specified Housing Units Owned and Occupied by Japanese

All States, Top 75 Counties, and Top 75 Places Sorted by Number[1]

State	Dollars
District of Columbia	344,000
Hawaii	286,900
Massachusetts	257,400
California	254,600
New York	243,000
United States	238,300
Connecticut	233,300
Washington	205,800
New Jersey	198,500
Illinois	197,700
Maryland	178,200
Oregon	172,000
Colorado	170,500
Virginia	169,700
Michigan	162,500
Rhode Island	160,500
Utah	150,500
Nevada	150,200
Ohio	141,700
Minnesota	141,400
Alaska	141,000
Pennsylvania	140,300
New Hampshire	139,600
Georgia	139,400
New Mexico	137,300
Delaware	135,700
Tennessee	127,700
North Carolina	126,800
Arizona	123,200
Vermont	117,600
Idaho	116,100
Wisconsin	115,300
Florida	114,100
Indiana	113,100
Maine	110,900
Alabama	108,800
Texas	106,600
South Carolina	105,900
Kentucky	102,700
Kansas	99,600
Louisiana	97,400
Iowa	97,300
Missouri	95,700
Montana	93,800
Nebraska	86,400
Mississippi	84,300
Arkansas	83,600
West Virginia	81,700
South Dakota	80,000
Wyoming	77,000
Oklahoma	71,800

County	Dollars
New York County, NY	1 mil.+
Marin County, CA	500,000
Fairfield County, CT	463,800
Norfolk County, MA	456,000
San Francisco County, CA	450,300
Santa Clara County, CA	447,800
San Mateo County, CA	432,100
Suffolk County, MA	428,600
Westchester County, NY	412,400
Napa County, CA	365,000
Alameda County, CA	327,300
Bronx County, NY	325,000
Honolulu County, HI	321,700
Kings County, NY	310,000
San Luis Obispo County, CA	296,900
Nassau County, NY	295,700
Santa Cruz County, CA	291,800
Sonoma County, CA	291,200
Contra Costa County, CA	288,800
Middlesex County, MA	283,900
Mercer County, NJ	283,300
Essex County, MA	281,800
Orange County, CA	277,100
Monterey County, CA	275,500
Olmsted County, MN	273,300
Bergen County, NJ	272,800
Morris County, NJ	271,900
Tompkins County, NY	255,800
Orange County, NC	255,600
Ventura County, CA	246,800
Boulder County, CO	246,100
Arlington County, VA	245,800
Queens County, NY	243,100
Lake County, IL	242,900
Somerset County, NJ	242,600
Essex County, NJ	239,300
Los Angeles County, CA	237,000
King County, WA	235,900
San Diego County, CA	234,600
Montgomery County, MD	233,300
Maui County, HI	232,900
Fairfax County, VA	231,700
Placer County, CA	228,200
Snohomish County, WA	228,100
Yolo County, CA	228,100
DeKalb County, GA	226,700
Chester County, PA	217,600
Island County, WA	213,900
El Dorado County, CA	213,000
Monmouth County, NJ	211,500
Middlesex County, NJ	208,300
Anne Arundel County, MD	207,300
Oakland County, MI	205,600
Cook County, IL	201,700
Santa Barbara County, CA	201,700
Kauai County, HI	199,700
Washington County, OR	199,100
Fulton County, GA	197,100
Washtenaw County, MI	196,800
DuPage County, IL	195,700
Clackamas County, OR	194,400
Benton County, OR	193,800
Hartford County, CT	192,200
Jefferson County, CO	189,700
Hudson County, NJ	187,500
Travis County, TX	187,500
Summit County, OH	184,900
Collin County, TX	183,800
Larimer County, CO	183,600
Ingham County, MI	182,200
Clark County, WA	179,800
Solano County, CA	174,800
Denver County, CO	174,500
Allegheny County, PA	174,200
Kitsap County, WA	174,100

Place	Dollars
Saratoga, CA (city) Santa Clara County	945,900
Los Altos, CA (city) Santa Clara County	794,500
Newport Beach, CA (city) Orange County	754,600
Palo Alto, CA (city) Santa Clara County	728,500
Los Gatos, CA (town) Santa Clara County	728,100
Menlo Park, CA (city) San Mateo County	716,700
Palos Verdes Estates, CA (city) Los Angeles County	710,400
Burlingame, CA (city) San Mateo County	706,100
La Canada Flintridge, CA (city) Los Angeles County	699,400
Rolling Hills Estates, CA (city) Los Angeles County	658,500
Greenville, NY (cdp) Westchester County	625,000
Greenwich, CT (town) Fairfield County	625,000
Belmont, CA (city) San Mateo County	622,000
Manhattan Beach, CA (city) Los Angeles County	610,100
Brookline, MA (town) Norfolk County	575,000
Rancho Palos Verdes, CA (city) Los Angeles County	566,400
Cupertino, CA (city) Santa Clara County	559,500
Mountain View, CA (city) Santa Clara County	551,900
Foster City, CA (city) San Mateo County	551,300
McLean, VA (cdp) Fairfax County	550,000
Rye, NY (city) Westchester County	548,600
Mercer Island, WA (city) King County	520,300
Redwood City, CA (city) San Mateo County	516,200
Millbrae, CA (city) San Mateo County	513,900
Sunnyvale, CA (city) Santa Clara County	505,300
Campbell, CA (city) Santa Clara County	467,800
San Ramon, CA (city) Contra Costa County	453,000
San Francisco, CA (city) San Francisco County	450,300
Santa Barbara, CA (city) Santa Barbara County	450,000
Santa Monica, CA (city) Los Angeles County	448,600
Goleta, CA (cdp) Santa Barbara County	434,300
Boston, MA (city) Suffolk County	428,600
Eastchester, NY (town) Westchester County	425,000
Scarsdale, NY (village) Westchester County	400,000
Bethesda, MD (cdp) Montgomery County	397,900
San Jose, CA (city) Santa Clara County	392,400
Castro Valley, CA (cdp) Alameda County	387,500
North Hempstead, NY (town) Nassau County	386,000
Santa Clara, CA (city) Santa Clara County	385,700
Laguna Niguel, CA (city) Orange County	384,400
South Pasadena, CA (city) Los Angeles County	382,100
Eastchester, NY (cdp) Westchester County	381,600
San Mateo, CA (city) San Mateo County	381,100
Pleasanton, CA (city) Alameda County	380,100
Honolulu, HI (cdp) Honolulu County	378,800
Fremont, CA (city) Alameda County	373,300
Morgan Hill, CA (city) Santa Clara County	372,700
Arcadia, CA (city) Los Angeles County	372,400
Seal Beach, CA (city) Orange County	370,200
Boulder, CO (city) Boulder County	365,000
Santa Cruz, CA (city) Santa Cruz County	364,300
Greenburgh, NY (town) Westchester County	364,100
Milpitas, CA (city) Santa Clara County	362,000
Yorba Linda, CA (city) Orange County	361,100
San Bruno, CA (city) San Mateo County	360,000
Oakland, CA (city) Alameda County	358,500
Albany, CA (city) Alameda County	357,000
Walnut Creek, CA (city) Contra Costa County	356,100
Redondo Beach, CA (city) Los Angeles County	355,800
Maunawili, HI (cdp) Honolulu County	352,600
Union City, CA (city) Alameda County	349,300
South San Francisco, CA (city) San Mateo County	347,800
Waimalu, HI (cdp) Honolulu County	346,300
Rockville, MD (city) Montgomery County	342,900
Glenview, IL (village) Cook County	342,500
Thousand Oaks, CA (city) Ventura County	339,100
Tustin, CA (city) Orange County	337,500
Glendale, CA (city) Los Angeles County	335,500
Aiea, HI (cdp) Honolulu County	335,000
Heeia, HI (cdp) Honolulu County	334,400
Kailua, HI (cdp) Honolulu County	330,300
Monterey, CA (city) Monterey County	327,200
Berkeley, CA (city) Alameda County	324,800
Pacifica, CA (city) San Mateo County	316,100
Encinitas, CA (city) San Diego County	314,700

Notes: Please refer to the User's Guide for an explanation of data; ranking tables include all places with Asian and/or NHPI populations above SF4 population thresholds; (1) tables reflect only those areas that meet SF4 population thresholds, therefore there may be less than 50 states, 75 counties or 75 places listed

Median Home Value

Specified Housing Units Owned and Occupied by Koreans

All States, Top 75 Counties, and Top 75 Places Sorted by Number[1]

State	Dollars
District of Columbia	361,400
Hawaii	311,100
New York	275,400
California	266,100
New Jersey	263,600
Massachusetts	254,800
Connecticut	251,200
Illinois	222,600
United States	209,500
Maryland	195,300
Michigan	194,800
Virginia	192,600
Colorado	190,000
Washington	187,700
Delaware	183,500
Oregon	181,500
Utah	174,500
Wyoming	172,500
Alaska	167,200
Ohio	166,400
Georgia	163,300
Pennsylvania	163,000
Minnesota	153,400
Wisconsin	152,100
North Carolina	150,800
Missouri	149,500
Nevada	148,000
Louisiana	147,200
Maine	142,200
Indiana	140,700
New Hampshire	140,600
South Dakota	137,500
Arizona	136,700
Rhode Island	136,200
Florida	135,300
New Mexico	124,100
Alabama	121,200
Texas	120,700
Tennessee	119,700
West Virginia	119,300
Kansas	115,300
Kentucky	110,100
Idaho	110,000
Vermont	109,700
Nebraska	108,100
South Carolina	106,300
Iowa	99,800
North Dakota	95,600
Montana	88,800
Oklahoma	88,400
Mississippi	83,100
Arkansas	68,800

County	Dollars
New York County, NY	1 mil.+
Santa Clara County, CA	479,400
Fairfield County, CT	463,500
Westchester County, NY	455,000
San Mateo County, CA	452,800
San Francisco County, CA	427,500
Marin County, CA	383,700
Santa Cruz County, CA	373,900
Norfolk County, MA	356,400
Clarke County, GA	350,000
Middlesex County, MA	346,300
Passaic County, NJ	338,500
Honolulu County, HI	331,000
Contra Costa County, CA	326,600
Nassau County, NY	326,000
Alameda County, CA	325,500
Mercer County, NJ	309,900
Bergen County, NJ	308,800
Northampton County, PA	306,300
Monterey County, CA	289,500
Ventura County, CA	289,500
Queens County, NY	286,100
Morris County, NJ	281,600
Oakland County, MI	279,800
Essex County, MA	277,100
Lake County, IL	276,900
Kings County, NY	270,900
Kitsap County, WA	269,100
New Haven County, CT	264,600
Douglas County, CO	263,800
Dutchess County, NY	262,900
Orange County, CA	262,700
Broome County, NY	262,500
Loudoun County, VA	262,100
Rockland County, NY	260,500
San Diego County, CA	259,500
Alexandria Independent City, VA	258,900
Suffolk County, NY	258,200
Bronx County, NY	257,100
Los Angeles County, CA	256,700
Fulton County, GA	254,700
Imperial County, CA	254,200
Somerset County, NJ	252,200
Monmouth County, NJ	247,500
Essex County, NJ	246,800
Howard County, MD	240,200
Dauphin County, PA	240,000
Benton County, OR	239,300
Montgomery County, MD	239,200
Utah County, UT	237,500
Arlington County, VA	236,500
Will County, IL	234,400
Maui County, HI	232,200
Cook County, IL	230,900
Union County, NJ	230,600
Sonoma County, CA	228,800
Snohomish County, WA	228,000
Lucas County, OH	227,100
Orange County, NC	225,000
King County, WA	224,100
Boulder County, CO	223,800
Clackamas County, OR	221,500
Richmond County, NY	220,600
Monroe County, IN	218,200
Yolo County, CA	217,300
Santa Barbara County, CA	217,000
San Joaquin County, CA	215,000
Middlesex County, NJ	210,500
Greene County, OH	210,000
Chester County, PA	208,300
Fairfax County, VA	208,200
Washington County, MN	206,700
Adams County, CO	205,100
Worcester County, MA	204,700
Fairfax Independent City, VA	204,200

Place	Dollars
Alpine, NJ (borough) Bergen County	1 mil.+
Beverly Hills, CA (city) Los Angeles County	1 mil.+
Palos Verdes Estates, CA (city) Los Angeles County	1 mil.+
Saratoga, CA (city) Santa Clara County	1 mil.+
Hedwig Village, TX (city) Harris County	875,000
Palo Alto, CA (city) Santa Clara County	850,800
Cupertino, CA (city) Santa Clara County	737,500
Scarsdale, NY (village) Westchester County	712,000
Brookline, MA (town) Norfolk County	696,400
Foster City, CA (city) San Mateo County	669,100
Mountain View, CA (city) Santa Clara County	660,700
Lake Success, NY (village) Nassau County	652,300
Millbrae, CA (city) San Mateo County	625,000
Rancho Palos Verdes, CA (city) Los Angeles County	618,500
Santa Monica, CA (city) Los Angeles County	546,900
Bloomfield, MI (township) Oakland County	538,200
San Mateo, CA (city) San Mateo County	526,300
Boulder, CO (city) Boulder County	500,000
Pleasanton, CA (city) Alameda County	498,500
Englewood Cliffs, NJ (borough) Bergen County	494,200
Newton, MA (city) Middlesex County	480,000
Sunnyvale, CA (city) Santa Clara County	458,600
Berkeley, CA (city) Alameda County	453,600
La Canada Flintridge, CA (city) Los Angeles County	453,000
Demarest, NJ (borough) Bergen County	450,000
South Pasadena, CA (city) Los Angeles County	450,000
La Habra, CA (city) Orange County	446,100
Greenburgh, NY (town) Westchester County	445,300
Lexington, MA (town) Middlesex County	440,000
Potomac, MD (cdp) Montgomery County	437,200
Cliffside Park, NJ (borough) Bergen County	436,700
North Hempstead, NY (town) Nassau County	430,400
Old Tappan, NJ (borough) Bergen County	430,000
Walnut Creek, CA (city) Contra Costa County	427,800
San Francisco, CA (city) San Francisco County	427,500
Tysons Corner, VA (cdp) Fairfax County	426,300
San Jose, CA (city) Santa Clara County	424,100
Atlanta, GA (city) Fulton County	420,000
Campbell, CA (city) Santa Clara County	419,400
Lower Merion, PA (township) Montgomery County	410,000
Honolulu, HI (cdp) Honolulu County	407,700
Santa Clara, CA (city) Santa Clara County	397,700
Redondo Beach, CA (city) Los Angeles County	393,500
West Bloomfield, MI (township) Oakland County	387,000
Arcadia, CA (city) Los Angeles County	383,600
Yonkers, NY (city) Westchester County	379,200
Norwood, NJ (borough) Bergen County	367,600
Laguna Niguel, CA (city) Orange County	366,000
Alameda, CA (city) Alameda County	365,000
West Windsor, NJ (township) Mercer County	364,600
Parsippany-Troy Hills, NJ (township) Morris County	363,900
Huntington Beach, CA (city) Orange County	357,700
McLean, VA (cdp) Fairfax County	357,300
Daly City, CA (city) San Mateo County	356,000
Thousand Oaks, CA (city) Ventura County	352,400
Wayne, NJ (township) Passaic County	351,900
Albany, CA (city) Alameda County	350,000
Athens-Clarke County, GA (sp. city) Clarke County	350,000
Fremont, CA (city) Alameda County	346,300
Claremont, CA (city) Los Angeles County	346,200
Jericho, NY (cdp) Nassau County	346,200
Milpitas, CA (city) Santa Clara County	345,000
Paramus, NJ (borough) Bergen County	341,300
Kaneohe, HI (cdp) Honolulu County	341,000
Harrington Park, NJ (borough) Bergen County	339,700
Leonia, NJ (borough) Bergen County	337,500
Mill Creek, WA (city) Snohomish County	337,300
Orange, CA (city) Orange County	337,200
Glenview, IL (village) Cook County	335,500
Ridgewood, NJ (village) Bergen County	334,600
Simi Valley, CA (city) Ventura County	333,800
Bethesda, MD (cdp) Montgomery County	328,900
Oyster Bay, NY (town) Nassau County	328,900
Kailua, HI (cdp) Honolulu County	327,800
Pleasant Hill, CA (city) Contra Costa County	320,800

Notes: Please refer to the User's Guide for an explanation of data; ranking tables include all places with Asian and/or NHPI populations above SF4 population thresholds; (1) tables reflect only those areas that meet SF4 population thresholds, therefore there may be less than 50 states, 75 counties or 75 places listed

Median Home Value

Specified Housing Units Owned and Occupied by Laotians

All States, Top 75 Counties, and Top 75 Places Sorted by Number[1]

State	Dollars
Hawaii	230,000
Colorado	165,300
Virginia	161,300
Oregon	152,900
Washington	152,700
California	147,700
Alaska	132,500
Utah	131,600
Nevada	130,800
Connecticut	129,000
Michigan	120,400
Massachusetts	120,300
New Jersey	120,000
New Hampshire	119,300
Illinois	119,000
Maryland	115,600
Minnesota	113,500
Rhode Island	107,000
Idaho	105,300
United States	100,500
Georgia	98,300
Tennessee	97,400
Arizona	97,000
South Dakota	93,000
North Carolina	88,600
Nebraska	85,600
Alabama	83,100
Indiana	82,400
Ohio	81,800
Florida	77,800
South Carolina	77,600
Wisconsin	77,600
Louisiana	76,100
Iowa	68,800
New York	63,400
Texas	63,000
Pennsylvania	62,000
Kansas	59,100
Arkansas	59,000
Missouri	58,900
Oklahoma	56,200

County	Dollars
Santa Clara County, CA	279,700
Honolulu County, HI	262,500
Alameda County, CA	236,400
Solano County, CA	232,700
Sonoma County, CA	205,500
Washington County, OR	193,100
Jefferson County, CO	184,100
Orange County, CA	182,000
Contra Costa County, CA	181,300
Snohomish County, WA	176,000
Fairfax County, VA	175,400
King County, WA	169,800
San Diego County, CA	169,600
Adams County, CO	155,300
Montgomery County, NC	151,800
Los Angeles County, CA	151,300
Dakota County, MN	146,400
Fairfield County, CT	144,900
Clark County, WA	144,700
Multnomah County, OR	144,000
Cook County, IL	141,500
Kane County, IL	140,900
Dane County, WI	137,500
Ottawa County, MI	134,700
Salt Lake County, UT	132,100
Clark County, NV	130,800
San Bernardino County, CA	129,700
Pierce County, WA	126,800
Hartford County, CT	125,800
Stanislaus County, CA	122,300
New Haven County, CT	121,900
Essex County, MA	121,200
Middlesex County, MA	120,700
Worcester County, MA	119,600
Dakota County, NE	117,600
Hennepin County, MN	116,800
San Joaquin County, CA	116,300
Gwinnett County, GA	113,000
Anchorage Borough, AK	107,500
Maricopa County, AZ	107,300
Providence County, RI	105,800
Mecklenburg County, NC	104,400
Rutherford County, TN	103,900
Johnson County, KS	100,000
Merced County, CA	100,000
Sacramento County, CA	96,900
Riverside County, CA	95,900
Ramsey County, MN	95,000
Shasta County, CA	93,400
Catawba County, NC	89,700
Guilford County, NC	87,600
Franklin County, OH	86,300
Tulare County, CA	86,300
Davidson County, TN	86,000
Winnebago County, IL	85,800
Mobile County, AL	85,000
Clayton County, GA	84,700
Fresno County, CA	84,700
Washington County, AR	82,500
Iberia Parish, LA	81,800
Roseau County, MN	81,700
Brown County, WI	77,900
Franklin County, WA	77,900
Dallas County, TX	75,100
Summit County, OH	74,100
Burke County, NC	73,900
Bexar County, TX	70,000
Harris County, TX	69,400
Pinellas County, FL	68,700
Spartanburg County, SC	66,500
Butte County, CA	66,400
Polk County, IA	65,400
Cass County, MI	65,000
Tarrant County, TX	64,900
Milwaukee County, WI	64,300

Place	Dollars
San Jose, CA (city) Santa Clara County	282,700
Fairfield, CA (city) Solano County	225,000
Bellevue, WA (city) King County	222,500
Santa Rosa, CA (city) Sonoma County	213,600
Anaheim, CA (city) Orange County	191,300
San Pablo, CA (city) Contra Costa County	186,400
Springfield, VA (cdp) Fairfax County	182,600
Escondido, CA (city) San Diego County	177,100
Westminster, CO (city) Adams County	175,500
Santa Ana, CA (city) Orange County	171,400
Oakland, CA (city) Alameda County	171,200
Long Beach, CA (city) Los Angeles County	170,000
Richmond, CA (city) Contra Costa County	168,800
Arvada, CO (city) Jefferson County	163,800
San Diego, CA (city) San Diego County	163,200
Seattle, WA (city) King County	161,300
Elgin, IL (city) Kane County	149,700
Portland, OR (city) Multnomah County	144,500
Los Angeles, CA (city) Los Angeles County	144,400
West Valley City, UT (city) Salt Lake County	134,600
Pomona, CA (city) Los Angeles County	132,900
Brooklyn Park, MN (city) Hennepin County	132,200
Fitchburg, MA (city) Worcester County	115,000
Brooklyn Center, MN (city) Hennepin County	112,500
Parkway-S. Sacramento, CA (cdp) Sacramento Co.	112,500
Woonsocket, RI (city) Providence County	112,500
Stockton, CA (city) San Joaquin County	112,000
Merced, CA (city) Merced County	111,600
Modesto, CA (city) Stanislaus County	111,500
Lowell, MA (city) Middlesex County	109,200
Charlotte, NC (city) Mecklenburg County	103,100
Riverside, CA (city) Riverside County	99,600
Moreno Valley, CA (city) Riverside County	95,700
Murfreesboro, TN (city) Rutherford County	95,600
Redding, CA (city) Shasta County	95,000
Sacramento, CA (city) Sacramento County	94,200
New Britain, CT (city) Hartford County	90,000
St. Paul, MN (city) Ramsey County	88,800
Minneapolis, MN (city) Hennepin County	87,200
Bridgeport, CT (city) Fairfield County	86,700
Tacoma, WA (city) Pierce County	86,600
Visalia, CA (city) Tulare County	86,400
Irving, TX (city) Dallas County	86,100
Nashville-Davidson, TN (sp. city) Davidson County	86,000
Springdale, AR (city) Washington County	85,000
Grand Prairie, TX (city) Dallas County	84,600
Columbus, OH (city) Franklin County	83,600
Rockford, IL (city) Winnebago County	82,400
Providence, RI (city) Providence County	81,900
Warroad, MN (city) Roseau County	81,700
Fresno, CA (city) Fresno County	80,800
Akron, OH (city) Summit County	76,200
Green Bay, WI (city) Brown County	75,000
St. Petersburg, FL (city) Pinellas County	68,400
Haltom City, TX (city) Tarrant County	67,400
Storm Lake, IA (city) Buena Vista County	61,900
Milwaukee, WI (city) Milwaukee County	61,000
Dallas, TX (city) Dallas County	59,800
Des Moines, IA (city) Polk County	59,400
Worthington, MN (city) Nobles County	59,400
Banning, CA (city) Riverside County	58,500
Wichita, KS (city) Sedgwick County	58,200
Raymond, WA (city) Pacific County	57,300
Rochester, MN (city) Olmsted County	55,600
Fort Worth, TX (city) Tarrant County	53,900
Rochester, NY (city) Monroe County	51,400
Oklahoma City, OK (city) Oklahoma County	50,000
Philadelphia, PA (city) Philadelphia County	49,400
Fort Smith, AR (city) Sebastian County	48,300
Amarillo, TX (city) Potter County	48,200
Winfield, KS (city) Cowley County	33,700
Oaklawn-Sunview, KS (cdp) Sedgwick County	22,100
Honolulu, HI (cdp) Honolulu County	0

Notes: Please refer to the User's Guide for an explanation of data; ranking tables include all places with Asian and/or NHPI populations above SF4 population thresholds; (1) tables reflect only those areas that meet SF4 population thresholds, therefore there may be less than 50 states, 75 counties or 75 places listed

Median Home Value

Specified Housing Units Owned and Occupied by Malaysians

All States, Top 75 Counties, and Top 75 Places Sorted by Number[1]

State	Dollars
California	248,100
New York	219,800
United States	169,700
Illinois	167,200
Michigan	143,800
Texas	132,100
Ohio	128,600
Oklahoma	50,000

County	Dollars
Queens County, NY	236,800
Los Angeles County, CA	158,300

Place	Dollars
New York, NY (city)	227,900

Notes: Please refer to the User's Guide for an explanation of data; ranking tables include all places with Asian and/or NHPI populations above SF4 population thresholds; (1) tables reflect only those areas that meet SF4 population thresholds, therefore there may be less than 50 states, 75 counties or 75 places listed

Median Home Value

Specified Housing Units Owned and Occupied by Pakistanis

All States, Top 75 Counties, and Top 75 Places Sorted by Number[1]

State	Dollars
Massachusetts	284,600
Iowa	279,400
California	261,400
Wisconsin	251,900
New York	233,300
Kentucky	210,700
Utah	200,000
Delaware	195,800
Washington	194,800
Ohio	188,300
New Jersey	185,600
Illinois	183,500
United States	181,400
Oregon	180,100
Michigan	178,600
Maryland	176,300
Colorado	175,000
Pennsylvania	174,400
Tennessee	165,200
Nevada	158,500
Alabama	157,900
Virginia	155,400
Arizona	155,100
Minnesota	153,300
Georgia	150,800
Kansas	148,100
Texas	147,000
Connecticut	146,100
Florida	143,200
North Carolina	137,500
West Virginia	130,700
Missouri	128,400
Louisiana	127,500
Indiana	124,100
Oklahoma	105,600

County	Dollars
Westchester County, NY	559,800
Santa Clara County, CA	453,200
Alameda County, CA	387,200
Kings County, NY	316,100
San Diego County, CA	303,600
San Francisco County, CA	300,000
Worcester County, MA	284,600
Los Angeles County, CA	268,500
Orange County, CA	268,400
King County, WA	267,600
Nassau County, NY	263,200
Contra Costa County, CA	255,000
Middlesex County, MA	245,800
Queens County, NY	243,700
Oakland County, MI	238,900
Essex County, NJ	235,500
Bergen County, NJ	231,300
Wake County, NC	228,900
Will County, IL	225,000
Union County, NJ	220,000
Suffolk County, NY	215,900
Mercer County, NJ	215,400
Richmond County, NY	214,600
Fairfield County, CT	210,700
Snohomish County, WA	206,300
Arlington County, VA	202,800
DuPage County, IL	201,200
Middlesex County, NJ	200,400
Collin County, TX	199,200
Delaware County, PA	192,500
Morris County, NJ	192,500
Montgomery County, MD	190,700
Milwaukee County, WI	190,300
Bronx County, NY	187,500
Monmouth County, NJ	187,500
Orange County, FL	182,000
Franklin County, OH	180,600
San Bernardino County, CA	177,300
Hudson County, NJ	175,400
Cook County, IL	174,200
Howard County, MD	173,700
Denton County, TX	173,500
Jefferson Parish, LA	170,800
Dallas County, TX	169,900
Lake County, IL	168,800
Washtenaw County, MI	168,800
Tarrant County, TX	167,700
Loudoun County, VA	165,900
Wayne County, MI	164,000
Fairfax County, VA	162,500
Travis County, TX	162,500
Gwinnett County, GA	160,600
Baltimore County, MD	156,500
Maricopa County, AZ	152,900
Fort Bend County, TX	152,100
Macomb County, MI	147,800
Hennepin County, MN	147,200
Hartford County, CT	145,000
Somerset County, NJ	141,100
Broward County, FL	140,900
St. Louis County, MO	138,300
Sacramento County, CA	136,100
Atlantic County, NJ	133,600
Camden County, NJ	133,000
Riverside County, CA	128,800
Prince William County, VA	125,600
Prince George's County, MD	122,900
Miami-Dade County, FL	122,200
New Haven County, CT	117,600
Cobb County, GA	117,200
Alexandria Independent City, VA	112,500
Guilford County, NC	108,900
Monroe County, NY	107,100
Tulsa County, OK	98,100
San Joaquin County, CA	97,900

Place	Dollars
Santa Clara, CA (city) Santa Clara County	440,000
Fremont, CA (city) Alameda County	413,600
San Jose, CA (city) Santa Clara County	393,900
San Francisco, CA (city) San Francisco County	300,000
Torrance, CA (city) Los Angeles County	281,000
Irving, TX (city) Dallas County	275,000
North Hempstead, NY (town) Nassau County	273,700
Edison, NJ (township) Middlesex County	268,800
Los Angeles, CA (city) Los Angeles County	265,300
Hempstead, NY (town) Nassau County	263,600
New York, NY (city)	250,900
Huntington, NY (town) Suffolk County	246,100
Anaheim, CA (city) Orange County	237,500
Bailey's Crossroads, VA (cdp) Fairfax County	225,000
Plano, TX (city) Collin County	221,300
Old Bridge, NJ (township) Middlesex County	218,100
Sugar Land, TX (city) Fort Bend County	208,300
Richardson, TX (city) Dallas County	204,700
Carrollton, TX (city) Denton County	203,700
Arlington, VA (cdp) Arlington County	202,800
Skokie, IL (village) Cook County	199,000
Ellicott City, MD (cdp) Howard County	191,100
Brookhaven, NY (town) Suffolk County	171,600
Jersey City, NJ (city) Hudson County	166,300
Austin, TX (city) Travis County	165,000
Dallas, TX (city) Dallas County	165,000
Lincolnia, VA (cdp) Fairfax County	162,500
Woodbridge, NJ (township) Middlesex County	137,500
Dale City, VA (cdp) Prince William County	133,200
Chicago, IL (city) Cook County	120,100
Sacramento, CA (city) Sacramento County	116,100
Tulsa, OK (city) Tulsa County	95,000
Houston, TX (city) Harris County	93,600
Philadelphia, PA (city) Philadelphia County	91,900
Stockton, CA (city) San Joaquin County	85,600
Garland, TX (city) Dallas County	84,800
Mission Bend, TX (cdp) Fort Bend County	72,700

Notes: Please refer to the User's Guide for an explanation of data; ranking tables include all places with Asian and/or NHPI populations above SF4 population thresholds; (1) tables reflect only those areas that meet SF4 population thresholds, therefore there may be less than 50 states, 75 counties or 75 places listed

Median Home Value

Specified Housing Units Owned and Occupied by Samoans

All States, Top 75 Counties, and Top 75 Places Sorted by Number[1]

State	Dollars
Hawaii	200,000
New Jersey	186,300
California	180,400
United States	153,200
Washington	149,400
Colorado	145,500
Oregon	143,800
Alaska	142,800
New York	140,500
Virginia	139,300
Utah	138,300
Illinois	134,100
Georgia	120,000
Nevada	118,400
Arizona	116,100
North Carolina	101,400
Ohio	85,700
Michigan	85,400
Texas	85,400
Missouri	83,500
Tennessee	81,700
Florida	78,000
Pennsylvania	75,400

County	Dollars
San Mateo County, CA	364,300
Santa Clara County, CA	298,500
San Francisco County, CA	284,500
Solano County, CA	256,500
San Joaquin County, CA	240,900
Alameda County, CA	228,000
Contra Costa County, CA	211,800
Honolulu County, HI	209,100
Orange County, CA	201,500
Ventura County, CA	193,100
Los Angeles County, CA	175,900
San Diego County, CA	169,800
King County, WA	160,500
Anchorage Borough, AK	147,700
Utah County, UT	142,900
Pierce County, WA	139,300
Salt Lake County, UT	135,500
Riverside County, CA	125,000
Sacramento County, CA	123,200
Clark County, NV	121,200
Maricopa County, AZ	117,300
Hawaii County, HI	107,500
San Bernardino County, CA	98,900
Jackson County, MO	85,000

Place	Dollars
Honolulu, HI (cdp) Honolulu County	316,700
San Jose, CA (city) Santa Clara County	286,800
San Francisco, CA (city) San Francisco County	284,500
Laie, HI (cdp) Honolulu County	281,800
Halawa, HI (cdp) Honolulu County	275,000
Hayward, CA (city) Alameda County	236,400
Waipahu, HI (cdp) Honolulu County	235,400
Garden Grove, CA (city) Orange County	226,300
Los Angeles, CA (city) Los Angeles County	210,000
Anaheim, CA (city) Orange County	200,000
Westminster, CA (city) Orange County	200,000
Kahuku, HI (cdp) Honolulu County	192,900
Oxnard, CA (city) Ventura County	190,900
Hauula, HI (cdp) Honolulu County	189,300
Santa Ana, CA (city) Orange County	187,500
Carson, CA (city) Los Angeles County	181,400
Ewa Beach, HI (cdp) Honolulu County	173,800
San Diego, CA (city) San Diego County	165,900
Federal Way, WA (city) King County	159,200
Lakewood, CA (city) Los Angeles County	156,900
Oceanside, CA (city) San Diego County	151,700
Long Beach, CA (city) Los Angeles County	146,300
Compton, CA (city) Los Angeles County	137,500
New York, NY (city)	137,500
West Valley City, UT (city) Salt Lake County	131,100
Salt Lake City, UT (city) Salt Lake County	128,000
Lakewood, WA (city) Pierce County	125,000
Nanakuli, HI (cdp) Honolulu County	122,100
Seattle, WA (city) King County	118,800
Tacoma, WA (city) Pierce County	108,300
Sacramento, CA (city) Sacramento County	97,200
San Bernardino, CA (city) San Bernardino County	80,000

Notes: Please refer to the User's Guide for an explanation of data; ranking tables include all places with Asian and/or NHPI populations above SF4 population thresholds; (1) tables reflect only those areas that meet SF4 population thresholds, therefore there may be less than 50 states, 75 counties or 75 places listed

Median Home Value

Specified Housing Units Owned and Occupied by Sri Lankans

All States, Top 75 Counties, and Top 75 Places Sorted by Number[1]

State	Dollars
California	275,000
Massachusetts	248,900
New York	226,400
New Jersey	216,300
Michigan	213,100
Illinois	210,700
United States	**202,000**
Maryland	190,900
Washington	174,000
Texas	153,300
Virginia	152,500
Florida	151,000
Pennsylvania	146,200
Ohio	144,400

County	Dollars
Middlesex County, NJ	260,900
Orange County, CA	250,000
Los Angeles County, CA	244,100
Queens County, NY	228,400
Richmond County, NY	205,000
Montgomery County, MD	171,200

Place	Dollars
Los Angeles, CA (city) Los Angeles County	227,600
New York, NY (city)	217,300

Notes: Please refer to the User's Guide for an explanation of data; ranking tables include all places with Asian and/or NHPI populations above SF4 population thresholds; (1) tables reflect only those areas that meet SF4 population thresholds, therefore there may be less than 50 states, 75 counties or 75 places listed

Median Home Value

Specified Housing Units Owned and Occupied by Taiwanese

All States, Top 75 Counties, and Top 75 Places Sorted by Number[1]

State	Dollars
Hawaii	568,500
California	317,500
Illinois	300,000
Virginia	297,200
Massachusetts	293,200
Michigan	285,400
New Jersey	281,100
Maryland	264,900
United States	260,700
Washington	256,500
New York	246,500
Missouri	240,600
Colorado	237,500
Oregon	230,200
Arizona	225,400
Iowa	218,800
Pennsylvania	217,900
Indiana	202,100
North Carolina	201,900
Florida	189,600
Minnesota	183,900
Connecticut	179,200
Georgia	176,700
Ohio	176,100
Tennessee	170,000
Wisconsin	169,600
Utah	164,300
Texas	148,800
Louisiana	143,100
Kansas	131,700
Nevada	127,000
Oklahoma	85,000

County	Dollars
Honolulu County, HI	586,300
San Mateo County, CA	541,700
Santa Clara County, CA	490,800
Alameda County, CA	469,000
Westchester County, NY	445,500
San Francisco County, CA	445,200
Ventura County, CA	361,100
Contra Costa County, CA	360,900
Essex County, NJ	357,800
Suffolk County, MA	350,000
Middlesex County, MA	349,000
Nassau County, NY	342,900
Bergen County, NJ	341,400
Somerset County, NJ	336,900
San Diego County, CA	335,100
Orange County, CA	333,100
DuPage County, IL	323,000
St. Louis County, MO	310,300
Morris County, NJ	308,000
Oakland County, MI	306,200
Montgomery County, MD	293,200
Mercer County, NJ	292,100
Fairfax County, VA	289,600
Franklin County, OH	287,500
King County, WA	283,400
Los Angeles County, CA	277,500
Washtenaw County, MI	275,000
Cook County, IL	270,300
Suffolk County, NY	256,600
Queens County, NY	254,000
Norfolk County, MA	240,600
San Bernardino County, CA	231,600
Maricopa County, AZ	225,400
Dane County, WI	209,600
Middlesex County, NJ	187,800
Sacramento County, CA	187,500
Travis County, TX	187,500
Gwinnett County, GA	180,700
Allegheny County, PA	173,200
Collin County, TX	171,200
Fort Bend County, TX	151,200
Dallas County, TX	148,000
Riverside County, CA	146,900
Tarrant County, TX	140,900
Harris County, TX	129,900
Clark County, NV	116,500
New York County, NY	0

Place	Dollars
Saratoga, CA (city) Santa Clara County	845,000
Rancho Palos Verdes, CA (city) Los Angeles County	690,200
Honolulu, HI (cdp) Honolulu County	645,800
San Marino, CA (city) Los Angeles County	624,100
Cupertino, CA (city) Santa Clara County	510,200
Fremont, CA (city) Alameda County	496,000
Sunnyvale, CA (city) Santa Clara County	475,800
San Jose, CA (city) Santa Clara County	451,300
Berkeley, CA (city) Alameda County	450,000
San Francisco, CA (city) San Francisco County	445,200
Arcadia, CA (city) Los Angeles County	408,200
Bellevue, WA (city) King County	407,900
Tustin, CA (city) Orange County	404,400
North Hempstead, NY (town) Nassau County	375,000
Walnut, CA (city) Los Angeles County	367,300
Boston, MA (city) Suffolk County	350,000
Irvine, CA (city) Orange County	349,000
San Diego, CA (city) San Diego County	342,300
Huntington Beach, CA (city) Orange County	341,700
Cypress, CA (city) Orange County	331,300
Torrance, CA (city) Los Angeles County	329,200
Chino Hills, CA (city) San Bernardino County	314,000
Fountain Valley, CA (city) Orange County	311,400
Orange, CA (city) Orange County	300,000
Troy, MI (city) Oakland County	296,000
Diamond Bar, CA (city) Los Angeles County	284,700
Cerritos, CA (city) Los Angeles County	275,300
Rowland Heights, CA (cdp) Los Angeles County	272,500
Ann Arbor, MI (city) Washtenaw County	269,000
Seattle, WA (city) King County	264,700
Hacienda Heights, CA (cdp) Los Angeles County	263,100
Naperville, IL (city) Du Page County	263,100
Anaheim, CA (city) Orange County	261,500
Los Angeles, CA (city) Los Angeles County	261,300
New York, NY (city)	256,300
San Gabriel, CA (city) Los Angeles County	251,300
Columbus, OH (city) Franklin County	245,000
East San Gabriel, CA (cdp) Los Angeles County	238,100
Upland, CA (city) San Bernardino County	236,300
Temple City, CA (city) Los Angeles County	232,800
Austin, TX (city) Travis County	211,800
Madison, WI (city) Dane County	209,600
Alhambra, CA (city) Los Angeles County	202,900
West Covina, CA (city) Los Angeles County	200,900
Monterey Park, CA (city) Los Angeles County	197,300
Edison, NJ (township) Middlesex County	195,000
El Monte, CA (city) Los Angeles County	178,300
Plano, TX (city) Collin County	168,900
Sugar Land, TX (city) Fort Bend County	155,700
Arlington, TX (city) Tarrant County	148,800
Houston, TX (city) Harris County	122,500
Chicago, IL (city) Cook County	95,000

Notes: Please refer to the User's Guide for an explanation of data; ranking tables include all places with Asian and/or NHPI populations above SF4 population thresholds; (1) tables reflect only those areas that meet SF4 population thresholds, therefore there may be less than 50 states, 75 counties or 75 places listed

Median Home Value

Specified Housing Units Owned and Occupied by Thais

All States, Top 75 Counties, and Top 75 Places Sorted by Number[1]

State	Dollars
Connecticut	310,700
Hawaii	234,400
Massachusetts	222,100
California	204,400
New York	190,500
Washington	184,100
Illinois	178,900
New Jersey	177,300
Colorado	161,400
United States	160,900
Maryland	156,100
Virginia	150,400
Alaska	143,100
Utah	141,700
Nevada	138,700
Nebraska	137,500
Minnesota	134,900
Oregon	132,800
Kentucky	132,500
Georgia	128,500
Indiana	123,600
Michigan	122,400
Kansas	117,000
Alabama	116,100
Pennsylvania	115,500
Wisconsin	114,600
Ohio	107,100
Arizona	106,500
Tennessee	103,200
Missouri	103,100
Texas	94,800
Florida	94,400
North Carolina	89,900
Iowa	88,000
South Carolina	84,500
Arkansas	67,500
Oklahoma	66,900
Louisiana	65,600
New Mexico	56,700

County	Dollars
Santa Clara County, CA	457,100
Middlesex County, MA	344,000
San Mateo County, CA	340,200
San Francisco County, CA	333,800
Bergen County, NJ	327,500
Alameda County, CA	327,300
Denver County, CO	306,300
Contra Costa County, CA	280,000
Honolulu County, HI	265,600
San Diego County, CA	250,800
Orange County, CA	243,800
King County, WA	236,400
Nassau County, NY	230,800
Queens County, NY	226,700
Westchester County, NY	200,000
Cook County, IL	191,100
Los Angeles County, CA	189,900
DuPage County, IL	187,500
Fairfax County, VA	180,400
San Bernardino County, CA	172,600
Prince George's County, MD	167,900
Suffolk County, NY	165,200
Montgomery County, MD	163,500
St. Louis County, MO	159,400
Riverside County, CA	147,500
Collin County, TX	140,400
Anchorage Borough, AK	137,500
Clark County, NV	137,100
Multnomah County, OR	126,400
Pierce County, WA	126,400
Sacramento County, CA	123,200
Miami-Dade County, FL	122,700
Broward County, FL	115,200
Franklin County, OH	109,400
Maricopa County, AZ	107,400
Dallas County, TX	107,300
Travis County, TX	107,100
Palm Beach County, FL	104,700
Bexar County, TX	91,100
Okaloosa County, FL	90,000
Harris County, TX	86,500
Hillsborough County, FL	83,900
Polk County, IA	80,500
Pinellas County, FL	77,900
Tarrant County, TX	75,900
Oklahoma County, OK	66,900
New York County, NY	0

Place	Dollars
Honolulu, HI (cdp) Honolulu County	875,000
San Jose, CA (city) Santa Clara County	436,800
Glendale, CA (city) Los Angeles County	378,900
San Francisco, CA (city) San Francisco County	333,800
Denver, CO (city) Denver County	306,300
Cerritos, CA (city) Los Angeles County	297,300
San Diego, CA (city) San Diego County	287,500
Seattle, WA (city) King County	270,000
Anaheim, CA (city) Orange County	197,900
New York, NY (city)	197,900
Bellflower, CA (city) Los Angeles County	184,800
Los Angeles, CA (city) Los Angeles County	178,700
Chicago, IL (city) Cook County	174,600
Spring Valley, NV (cdp) Clark County	162,500
Long Beach, CA (city) Los Angeles County	144,900
Las Vegas, NV (city) Clark County	125,600
Portland, OR (city) Multnomah County	120,000
Columbus, OH (city) Franklin County	119,100
Houston, TX (city) Harris County	89,300
San Antonio, TX (city) Bexar County	86,700
Des Moines, IA (city) Polk County	63,300

Notes: Please refer to the User's Guide for an explanation of data; ranking tables include all places with Asian and/or NHPI populations above SF4 population thresholds; (1) tables reflect only those areas that meet SF4 population thresholds, therefore there may be less than 50 states, 75 counties or 75 places listed

Median Home Value

Specified Housing Units Owned and Occupied by Tongans

All States, Top 75 Counties, and Top 75 Places Sorted by Number[1]

State	Dollars
Hawaii	255,600
California	188,200
Washington	171,400
Oregon	164,800
Alaska	159,400
United States	149,100
Utah	122,400
Nevada	118,800
Arizona	100,600
Texas	92,700

County	Dollars
San Mateo County, CA	337,200
San Diego County, CA	306,300
Maui County, HI	260,000
Honolulu County, HI	247,200
Los Angeles County, CA	182,400
Alameda County, CA	179,000
Multnomah County, OR	173,900
Orange County, CA	171,900
King County, WA	168,200
Utah County, UT	149,500
San Bernardino County, CA	130,600
Contra Costa County, CA	120,000
Washoe County, NV	118,800
Salt Lake County, UT	118,300
Maricopa County, AZ	100,600
Tarrant County, TX	90,500
Sacramento County, CA	84,400

Place	Dollars
San Mateo, CA (city) San Mateo County	450,000
Laie, HI (cdp) Honolulu County	350,000
San Bruno, CA (city) San Mateo County	347,100
East Palo Alto, CA (city) San Mateo County	292,600
Honolulu, HI (cdp) Honolulu County	248,600
Kahuku, HI (cdp) Honolulu County	225,000
Portland, OR (city) Multnomah County	173,900
Oakland, CA (city) Alameda County	167,400
Hauula, HI (cdp) Honolulu County	162,500
Los Angeles, CA (city) Los Angeles County	145,700
West Jordan, UT (city) Salt Lake County	121,400
West Valley City, UT (city) Salt Lake County	119,400
Salt Lake City, UT (city) Salt Lake County	108,400
Sacramento, CA (city) Sacramento County	83,600

Notes: Please refer to the User's Guide for an explanation of data; ranking tables include all places with Asian and/or NHPI populations above SF4 population thresholds; (1) tables reflect only those areas that meet SF4 population thresholds, therefore there may be less than 50 states, 75 counties or 75 places listed

Median Home Value

Specified Housing Units Owned and Occupied by Vietnamese

All States, Top 75 Counties, and Top 75 Places Sorted by Number[1]

State	Dollars
Hawaii	249,200
California	245,500
District of Columbia	211,400
Alaska	195,300
Delaware	186,700
Virginia	179,700
Washington	179,500
Illinois	171,000
Colorado	168,300
Maryland	161,800
Massachusetts	157,400
Oregon	154,000
Vermont	153,300
United States	151,400
Nevada	146,500
New Jersey	139,400
Utah	134,000
Minnesota	132,600
New Hampshire	132,100
Connecticut	128,800
New Mexico	127,900
Michigan	123,100
Georgia	119,400
West Virginia	119,200
North Carolina	109,700
Wisconsin	107,600
Idaho	106,600
Arizona	106,200
South Carolina	100,900
Ohio	99,900
Tennessee	96,600
Rhode Island	94,600
Alabama	94,500
Indiana	94,500
Maine	94,400
New York	92,400
Florida	91,500
Nebraska	89,900
Texas	89,600
Louisiana	86,800
Kentucky	85,100
South Dakota	82,700
Oklahoma	78,800
Mississippi	78,700
Kansas	78,600
Missouri	78,400
Iowa	76,300
Pennsylvania	75,800
Arkansas	63,400

County	Dollars
San Mateo County, CA	387,700
Santa Cruz County, CA	379,400
Santa Clara County, CA	366,100
San Francisco County, CA	354,600
Bergen County, NJ	322,400
Alameda County, CA	304,100
Honolulu County, HI	289,200
Monterey County, CA	279,400
Placer County, CA	252,200
Ventura County, CA	247,800
Queens County, NY	247,400
Contra Costa County, CA	239,400
Nassau County, NY	233,300
Orange County, CA	232,400
Howard County, MD	230,000
Clackamas County, OR	226,000
Washtenaw County, MI	225,800
Boulder County, CO	225,000
Sonoma County, CA	224,200
Santa Barbara County, CA	221,300
San Diego County, CA	216,700
Jefferson County, CO	213,900
Somerset County, NJ	213,800
Yolo County, CA	211,800
Snohomish County, WA	210,000
Bronx County, NY	207,400
Arlington County, VA	200,800
Los Angeles County, CA	200,500
Anchorage Borough, AK	200,000
Solano County, CA	193,800
Fairfax County, VA	192,700
Suffolk County, MA	192,400
King County, WA	192,200
Essex County, NJ	191,900
Morris County, NJ	191,800
Cook County, IL	191,000
Middlesex County, MA	189,700
Lake County, IL	188,900
Alexandria Independent City, VA	187,500
New Castle County, DE	187,500
Norfolk County, MA	187,500
Washington County, MN	185,700
Kings County, NY	185,500
Will County, IL	183,500
Marin County, CA	181,800
Washington County, OR	180,100
Loudoun County, VA	179,000
Collin County, TX	173,800
Arapahoe County, CO	173,500
Monmouth County, NJ	172,100
Oakland County, MI	171,600
Montgomery County, MD	171,400
Butler County, OH	171,200
Riverside County, CA	170,500
Washoe County, NV	167,900
Fairfax Independent City, VA	167,600
Fulton County, GA	167,200
Adams County, CO	163,800
Scott County, MN	162,500
Middlesex County, NJ	161,900
Plaquemines Parish, LA	160,000
Matagorda County, TX	158,800
DuPage County, IL	158,200
Prince George's County, MD	157,800
Denver County, CO	156,300
Suffolk County, NY	156,300
San Bernardino County, CA	155,600
San Joaquin County, CA	155,100
Chittenden County, VT	153,300
Essex County, MA	152,900
Wake County, NC	151,300
Montgomery County, PA	149,800
Dakota County, MN	149,600
Chester County, PA	149,000
Brazoria County, TX	148,500

Place	Dollars
Cupertino, CA (city) Santa Clara County	637,500
Campbell, CA (city) Santa Clara County	512,800
Mountain View, CA (city) Santa Clara County	465,000
San Mateo, CA (city) San Mateo County	460,300
Milpitas, CA (city) Santa Clara County	398,700
Sunnyvale, CA (city) Santa Clara County	395,100
Yorba Linda, CA (city) Orange County	394,400
Berkeley, CA (city) Alameda County	381,300
Alameda, CA (city) Alameda County	376,300
Santa Clara, CA (city) Santa Clara County	374,300
Fremont, CA (city) Alameda County	370,600
Union City, CA (city) Alameda County	357,100
San Jose, CA (city) Santa Clara County	356,200
San Francisco, CA (city) San Francisco County	354,600
Daly City, CA (city) San Mateo County	349,200
Irvine, CA (city) Orange County	335,400
Laguna Niguel, CA (city) Orange County	334,300
Alum Rock, CA (cdp) Santa Clara County	332,100
Bellevue, WA (city) King County	321,800
Glendale, CA (city) Los Angeles County	319,700
Honolulu, HI (cdp) Honolulu County	317,700
Tustin, CA (city) Orange County	315,000
Laguna Hills, CA (city) Orange County	307,100
Huntington Beach, CA (city) Orange County	306,500
Livermore, CA (city) Alameda County	292,900
Burbank, CA (city) Los Angeles County	291,700
Camarillo, CA (city) Ventura County	291,200
Fountain Valley, CA (city) Orange County	289,200
Chino Hills, CA (city) San Bernardino County	287,800
Goleta, CA (cdp) Santa Barbara County	287,500
Cerritos, CA (city) Los Angeles County	283,100
Placentia, CA (city) Orange County	282,900
Lake Forest, CA (city) Orange County	278,400
Orange, CA (city) Orange County	278,000
Marina, CA (city) Monterey County	277,800
Cypress, CA (city) Orange County	277,600
San Leandro, CA (city) Alameda County	277,400
Aliso Viejo, CA (cdp) Orange County	271,900
Lake Barcroft, VA (cdp) Fairfax County	271,700
Hayward, CA (city) Alameda County	270,600
Newark, CA (city) Alameda County	268,100
Rancho Santa Margarita, CA (city) Orange County	268,100
Mission Viejo, CA (city) Orange County	267,700
Santa Clarita, CA (city) Los Angeles County	266,400
Torrance, CA (city) Los Angeles County	263,000
Monterey Park, CA (city) Los Angeles County	257,700
Walnut, CA (city) Los Angeles County	252,100
Salinas, CA (city) Monterey County	250,000
Thousand Oaks, CA (city) Ventura County	249,200
Kirkland, WA (city) King County	248,800
Costa Mesa, CA (city) Orange County	246,900
Diamond Bar, CA (city) Los Angeles County	245,100
Davis, CA (city) Yolo County	244,400
Seattle Hill-Silver Firs, WA (cdp) Snohomish County	243,200
Temple City, CA (city) Los Angeles County	242,400
Lincolnia, VA (cdp) Fairfax County	239,100
Cascade-Fairwood, WA (cdp) King County	236,500
Simi Valley, CA (city) Ventura County	233,800
Oceanside, CA (city) San Diego County	233,600
Oxnard, CA (city) Ventura County	232,300
Rowland Heights, CA (cdp) Los Angeles County	231,300
Buena Park, CA (city) Orange County	229,400
Hacienda Heights, CA (cdp) Los Angeles County	228,600
Oakton, VA (cdp) Fairfax County	228,100
Westminster, CA (city) Orange County	227,200
Alondra Park, CA (cdp) Los Angeles County	225,000
Concord, CA (city) Contra Costa County	223,500
East Hill-Meridian, WA (cdp) King County	223,100
Pasadena, CA (city) Los Angeles County	222,400
Alhambra, CA (city) Los Angeles County	222,000
San Lorenzo, CA (cdp) Alameda County	221,300
Beaverton, OR (city) Washington County	220,700
San Gabriel, CA (city) Los Angeles County	220,600
Antioch, CA (city) Contra Costa County	220,500
Anaheim, CA (city) Orange County	219,300

Notes: Please refer to the User's Guide for an explanation of data; ranking tables include all places with Asian and/or NHPI populations above SF4 population thresholds; (1) tables reflect only those areas that meet SF4 population thresholds, therefore there may be less than 50 states, 75 counties or 75 places listed

City Finder List

Abbeville, LA (city)	Vermilion Parish
Aberdeen, NJ (township)	Monmouth County
Acton, MA (town)	Middlesex County
Addison, TX (town)	Dallas County
Addison, IL (village)	Du Page County
Adelphi, MD (cdp)	Prince George's County
Agoura Hills, CA (city)	Los Angeles County
Alameda, CA (city)	Alameda County
Alamo, CA (cdp)	Contra Costa County
Albany, CA (city)	Alameda County
Alderwood Manor, WA (cdp)	Snohomish County
Alexandria, VA (city)	Alexandria Independent City
Alhambra, CA (city)	Los Angeles County
Aliso Viejo, CA (cdp)	Orange County
Allen, TX (city)	Collin County
Aloha, OR (cdp)	Washington County
Alpharetta, GA (city)	Fulton County
Altadena, CA (cdp)	Los Angeles County
Alum Rock, CA (cdp)	Santa Clara County
Ames, IA (city)	Story County
Amherst Center, MA (cdp)	Hampshire County
Amherst, MA (town)	Hampshire County
Amherst, NY (town)	Erie County
Anaheim, CA (city)	Orange County
Andover, MA (town)	Essex County
Ann Arbor, MI (city)	Washtenaw County
Annandale, VA (cdp)	Fairfax County
Antioch, CA (city)	Contra Costa County
Apex, NC (town)	Wake County
Appleton, WI (city)	Outagamie County
Arbutus, MD (cdp)	Baltimore County
Arcadia, CA (city)	Los Angeles County
Arden-Arcade, CA (cdp)	Sacramento County
Arlington, NY (cdp)	Dutchess County
Arlington, VA (cdp)	Arlington County
Arlington Heights, IL (village)	Cook County
Arlington, TX (city)	Tarrant County
Arlington, MA (town)	Middlesex County
Artesia, CA (city)	Los Angeles County
Ashland, CA (cdp)	Alameda County
Aspen Hill, MD (cdp)	Montgomery County
Athens, OH (city)	Athens County
Atlantic City, NJ (city)	Atlantic County
Atwater, CA (city)	Merced County
Auburn Hills, MI (city)	Oakland County
Auburn, WA (city)	King County
Aurora, CO (city)	Arapahoe County
Austin, TX (city)	Travis County
Avenel, NJ (cdp)	Middlesex County
Avocado Heights, CA (cdp)	Los Angeles County
Azusa, CA (city)	Los Angeles County
Bailey's Crossroads, VA (cdp)	Fairfax County
Bakersfield, CA (city)	Kern County
Baldwin Park, CA (city)	Los Angeles County
Baltimore, MD (city)	Baltimore Independent City
Banning, CA (city)	Riverside County
Barclay-Kingston, NJ (cdp)	Camden County
Bartlett, IL (village)	Du Page County
Bay Point, CA (cdp)	Contra Costa County
Bayonne, NJ (city)	Hudson County
Baywood-Los Osos, CA (cdp)	San Luis Obispo County
Beaverton, OR (city)	Washington County
Bedford, MA (town)	Middlesex County
Bellair-Meadowbrook Terr., FL (cdp)	Clay County
Bellaire, TX (city)	Harris County
Belleville, NJ (township)	Essex County
Bellevue, WA (city)	King County
Bellflower, CA (city)	Los Angeles County
Bellingham, WA (city)	Whatcom County
Bellmawr, NJ (borough)	Camden County
Bellview, FL (cdp)	Escambia County
Belmont, MA (cdp)	Middlesex County
Belmont, CA (city)	San Mateo County
Belmont, MA (town)	Middlesex County
Beltsville, MD (cdp)	Prince George's County
Benicia, CA (city)	Solano County
Bensalem, PA (township)	Bucks County
Bensenville, IL (village)	Du Page County
Bergenfield, NJ (borough)	Bergen County
Berkeley Heights, NJ (township)	Union County
Berkeley, CA (city)	Alameda County
Berkley, CO (cdp)	Adams County
Bernards, NJ (township)	Somerset County
Bethesda, MD (cdp)	Montgomery County
Beverly Hills, CA (city)	Los Angeles County
Biloxi, MS (city)	Harrison County
Blackhawk-Camino Tassajara, CA (cdp)	Contra Costa County
Blacksburg, VA (town)	Montgomery County
Bloomfield, MI (township)	Oakland County
Bloomfield, NJ (township)	Essex County
Bloomingdale, IL (village)	Du Page County
Bloomington, IN (city)	Monroe County
Bloomington, MN (city)	Hennepin County
Blue Ash, OH (city)	Hamilton County
Bolingbrook, IL (village)	Will County
Bonita, CA (cdp)	San Diego County
Boston, MA (city)	Suffolk County
Bothell, WA (city)	King County
Boulder, CO (city)	Boulder County
Branchburg, NJ (township)	Somerset County
Brea, CA (city)	Orange County
Bremerton, WA (city)	Kitsap County
Bridgewater, NJ (township)	Somerset County
Brigantine, NJ (city)	Atlantic County
Brighton, NY (town)	Monroe County
Bronx, NY (borough)	Bronx County
Brookline, MA (town)	Norfolk County
Brooklyn Center, MN (city)	Hennepin County
Brooklyn Park, MN (city)	Hennepin County
Brooklyn, NY (borough)	Kings County
Broomall, PA (cdp)	Delaware County
Broomfield, CO (city)	Boulder County
Browns Mills, NJ (cdp)	Burlington County
Brownstown, MI (township)	Wayne County
Brushy Creek, TX (cdp)	Williamson County
Bryn Mawr-Skyway, WA (cdp)	King County
Buena Park, CA (city)	Orange County
Buffalo Grove, IL (village)	Lake County
Bull Run, VA (cdp)	Prince William County
Burbank, CA (city)	Los Angeles County
Burien, WA (city)	King County
Burke, VA (cdp)	Fairfax County
Burlingame, CA (city)	San Mateo County
Burlington, MA (town)	Middlesex County
Burr Ridge, IL (village)	Du Page County
Calabasas, CA (city)	Los Angeles County
Callaway, FL (city)	Bay County
Calverton, MD (cdp)	Montgomery County
Camarillo, CA (city)	Ventura County
Cambridge, MA (city)	Middlesex County
Campbell, CA (city)	Santa Clara County
Canton, MI (township)	Wayne County

Capitola, CA (city)	Santa Cruz County
Carbondale, IL (city)	Jackson County
Carlsbad, CA (city)	San Diego County
Carmel, IN (city)	Hamilton County
Carney, MD (cdp)	Baltimore County
Carol Stream, IL (village)	Du Page County
Carrboro, NC (town)	Orange County
Carrollton, TX (city)	Denton County
Carson City, NV (special city)	Carson City Independent City
Carson, CA (city)	Los Angeles County
Carteret, NJ (borough)	Middlesex County
Cary, NC (town)	Wake County
Cascade-Fairwood, WA (cdp)	King County
Castro Valley, CA (cdp)	Alameda County
Cedar Grove, NJ (township)	Essex County
Cedar Mill, OR (cdp)	Washington County
Centreville, VA (cdp)	Fairfax County
Ceres, CA (city)	Stanislaus County
Cerritos, CA (city)	Los Angeles County
Champaign, IL (city)	Champaign County
Chandler, AZ (city)	Maricopa County
Chantilly, VA (cdp)	Fairfax County
Chapel Hill, NC (town)	Orange County
Charlottesville, VA (city)	Charlottesville Independent City
Chatham, NJ (township)	Morris County
Chelmsford, MA (town)	Middlesex County
Chelsea, MA (city)	Suffolk County
Cheltenham, PA (township)	Montgomery County
Cherry Hill Mall, NJ (cdp)	Camden County
Cherry Hill, NJ (township)	Camden County
Cherryland, CA (cdp)	Alameda County
Chesapeake, VA (city)	Chesapeake Independent City
Chesterfield, MO (city)	Saint Louis County
Chicago, IL (city)	Cook County
Chico, CA (city)	Butte County
Chino Hills, CA (city)	San Bernardino County
Chino, CA (city)	San Bernardino County
Chula Vista, CA (city)	San Diego County
Cinco Ranch, TX (cdp)	Fort Bend County
Citrus, CA (cdp)	Los Angeles County
Claremont, CA (city)	Los Angeles County
Clarkstown, NY (town)	Rockland County
Clayton, CA (city)	Contra Costa County
Clayton, MO (city)	Saint Louis County
Clemson, SC (city)	Pickens County
Cliffside Park, NJ (borough)	Bergen County
Clifton, NJ (city)	Passaic County
Clovis, CA (city)	Fresno County
Cockeysville, MD (cdp)	Baltimore County
Colesville, MD (cdp)	Montgomery County
College Park, MD (city)	Prince George's County
College Station, TX (city)	Brazos County
Colonia, NJ (cdp)	Middlesex County
Colonie, NY (town)	Albany County
Colorado Springs, CO (city)	El Paso County
Colton, CA (city)	San Bernardino County
Colts Neck, NJ (township)	Monmouth County
Columbia, MD (cdp)	Howard County
Columbia Heights, MN (city)	Anoka County
Columbia, MO (city)	Boone County
Columbus, GA (spec. city)	Muscogee County
Compton, CA (city)	Los Angeles County
Concord, CA (city)	Contra Costa County
Cooper City, FL (city)	Broward County
Coppell, TX (city)	Dallas County
Coralville, IA (city)	Johnson County
Coram, NY (cdp)	Suffolk County
Corona, CA (city)	Riverside County
Coronado, CA (city)	San Diego County
Corvallis, OR (city)	Benton County
Costa Mesa, CA (city)	Orange County
Cottage Lake, WA (cdp)	King County
Covina, CA (city)	Los Angeles County
Creve Coeur, MO (city)	Saint Louis County
Culver City, CA (city)	Los Angeles County
Cupertino, CA (city)	Santa Clara County
Cypress, CA (city)	Orange County
Dale City, VA (cdp)	Prince William County
Daly City, CA (city)	San Mateo County
Danbury, CT (city)	Fairfield County
Danville, CA (town)	Contra Costa County
Darien, IL (city)	Du Page County
Davis, CA (city)	Yolo County
DeKalb, IL (city)	De Kalb County
Delano, CA (city)	Kern County
Denville, NJ (township)	Morris County
Derry, PA (township)	Dauphin County
Des Moines, WA (city)	King County
Des Plaines, IL (city)	Cook County
Diamond Bar, CA (city)	Los Angeles County
Dix Hills, NY (cdp)	Suffolk County
Dobbs Ferry, NY (village)	Westchester County
Doral, FL (cdp)	Miami-Dade County
Downers Grove, IL (village)	Du Page County
Downey, CA (city)	Los Angeles County
Drexel Hill, PA (cdp)	Delaware County
Druid Hills, GA (cdp)	De Kalb County
Duarte, CA (city)	Los Angeles County
Dublin, CA (city)	Alameda County
Dublin, OH (city)	Franklin County
Duluth, GA (city)	Gwinnett County
Dumont, NJ (borough)	Bergen County
Dunwoody, GA (cdp)	De Kalb County
Eagan, MN (city)	Dakota County
East Brunswick, NJ (township)	Middlesex County
East Hanover, NJ (township)	Morris County
East Hartford, CT (town)	Hartford County
East Hill-Meridian, WA (cdp)	King County
East Lansing, MI (city)	Ingham County
East Meadow, NY (cdp)	Nassau County
East Norriton, PA (township)	Montgomery County
East Palo Alto, CA (city)	San Mateo County
East San Gabriel, CA (cdp)	Los Angeles County
East Windsor, NJ (township)	Mercer County
Eastchester, NY (cdp)	Westchester County
Eastchester, NY (town)	Westchester County
Eatontown, NJ (borough)	Monmouth County
Echelon, NJ (cdp)	Camden County
Eden Prairie, MN (city)	Hennepin County
Edison, NJ (township)	Middlesex County
Edmonds, WA (city)	Snohomish County
Egg Harbor, NJ (township)	Atlantic County
El Cerrito, CA (city)	Contra Costa County
El Dorado Hills, CA (cdp)	El Dorado County
El Monte, CA (city)	Los Angeles County
El Segundo, CA (city)	Los Angeles County
El Sobrante, CA (cdp)	Contra Costa County
Elk Grove, CA (cdp)	Sacramento County
Elk Grove Village, IL (village)	Cook County
Elk Plain, WA (cdp)	Pierce County
Elkridge, MD (cdp)	Howard County
Ellicott City, MD (cdp)	Howard County
Elmont, NY (cdp)	Nassau County
Elmwood Park, NJ (borough)	Bergen County
Elwood, NY (cdp)	Suffolk County
Englewood, NJ (city)	Bergen County
Enterprise, NV (cdp)	Clark County
Escondido, CA (city)	San Diego County
Euless, TX (city)	Tarrant County
Evanston, IL (city)	Cook County

Everett, WA (city)	Snohomish County
Evesham, NJ (township)	Burlington County
Ewa Beach, HI (cdp)	Honolulu County
Fair Lawn, NJ (borough)	Bergen County
Fair Oaks, CA (cdp)	Sacramento County
Fairfax, VA (city)	Fairfax Independent City
Fairfield, CA (city)	Solano County
Fairland, MD (cdp)	Montgomery County
Fairview, NJ (borough)	Bergen County
Falls Church, VA (city)	Falls Church Independent City
Farmers Branch, TX (city)	Dallas County
Farmington Hills, MI (city)	Oakland County
Farmington, MI (city)	Oakland County
Farmington, CT (town)	Hartford County
Federal Heights, CO (city)	Adams County
Federal Way, WA (city)	King County
Ferguson, PA (township)	Centre County
Fitchburg, MA (city)	Worcester County
Five Corners, WA (cdp)	Clark County
Florin, CA (cdp)	Sacramento County
Folsom, CA (city)	Sacramento County
Fontana, CA (city)	San Bernardino County
Foothill Farms, CA (cdp)	Sacramento County
Foothill Ranch, CA (cdp)	Orange County
Fords, NJ (cdp)	Middlesex County
Forest Park, GA (city)	Clayton County
Forest Park, IL (village)	Cook County
Fort Lee, NJ (borough)	Bergen County
Fort Lewis, WA (cdp)	Pierce County
Fort Smith, AR (city)	Sebastian County
Fort Washington, MD (cdp)	Prince George's County
Foster City, CA (city)	San Mateo County
Fountain Valley, CA (city)	Orange County
Framingham, MA (town)	Middlesex County
Franconia, VA (cdp)	Fairfax County
Franklin Lakes, NJ (borough)	Bergen County
Franklin Square, NY (cdp)	Nassau County
Franklin, NJ (township)	Somerset County
Freehold, NJ (township)	Monmouth County
Fremont, CA (city)	Alameda County
Fresno, CA (city)	Fresno County
Friendly, MD (cdp)	Prince George's County
Fullerton, PA (cdp)	Lehigh County
Fullerton, CA (city)	Orange County
Gages Lake, IL (cdp)	Lake County
Gainesville, FL (city)	Alachua County
Gaithersburg, MD (city)	Montgomery County
Galloway, NJ (township)	Atlantic County
Garden Grove, CA (city)	Orange County
Gardena, CA (city)	Los Angeles County
Garland, TX (city)	Dallas County
Germantown, MD (cdp)	Montgomery County
Germantown, TN (city)	Shelby County
Gilbert, AZ (town)	Maricopa County
Gilroy, CA (city)	Santa Clara County
Glastonbury, CT (town)	Hartford County
Glen Allen, VA (cdp)	Henrico County
Glen Cove, NY (city)	Nassau County
Glen Ellyn, IL (village)	Du Page County
Glen Rock, NJ (borough)	Bergen County
Glendale Heights, IL (village)	Du Page County
Glendale, CA (city)	Los Angeles County
Glendora, CA (city)	Los Angeles County
Glenn Dale, MD (cdp)	Prince George's County
Glenview, IL (village)	Cook County
Goleta, CA (cdp)	Santa Barbara County
Grand Prairie, TX (city)	Dallas County
Grand Terrace, CA (city)	San Bernardino County
Grayslake, IL (village)	Lake County
Greenbelt, MD (city)	Prince George's County
Greenburgh, NY (town)	Westchester County
Greentree, NJ (cdp)	Camden County
Greenwich, CT (town)	Fairfield County
Gretna, LA (city)	Jefferson Parish
Grover Beach, CA (city)	San Luis Obispo County
Groveton, VA (cdp)	Fairfax County
Guilderland, NY (town)	Albany County
Gurnee, IL (village)	Lake County
Guttenberg, NJ (town)	Hudson County
Hacienda Heights, CA (cdp)	Los Angeles County
Hackensack, NJ (city)	Bergen County
Halawa, HI (cdp)	Honolulu County
Haltom City, TX (city)	Tarrant County
Hampden, PA (township)	Cumberland County
Hampton, VA (city)	Hampton Independent City
Hamtramck, MI (city)	Wayne County
Hanover Park, IL (village)	Cook County
Hanover, NH (town)	Grafton County
Hanover, NJ (township)	Morris County
Harrison, NJ (town)	Hudson County
Harrison, NY (village)	Westchester County
Harvey, LA (cdp)	Jefferson Parish
Hasbrouck Heights, NJ (borough)	Bergen County
Hatfield, PA (township)	Montgomery County
Hawaiian Gardens, CA (city)	Los Angeles County
Hawthorne, CA (city)	Los Angeles County
Hayward, CA (city)	Alameda County
Henderson, NV (city)	Clark County
Henrietta, NY (town)	Monroe County
Hercules, CA (city)	Contra Costa County
Hermosa Beach, CA (city)	Los Angeles County
Herndon, VA (town)	Fairfax County
Hershey, PA (cdp)	Dauphin County
Hickory, NC (city)	Catawba County
Hicksville, NY (cdp)	Nassau County
Highland Park, NJ (borough)	Middlesex County
Highland, CA (city)	San Bernardino County
Highlands Ranch, CO (cdp)	Douglas County
Hilliard, OH (city)	Franklin County
Hillsboro, OR (city)	Washington County
Hillsborough, CA (town)	San Mateo County
Hillsborough, NJ (township)	Somerset County
Hillsdale, NJ (borough)	Bergen County
Hilo, HI (cdp)	Hawaii County
Hinsdale, IL (village)	Du Page County
Hoboken, NJ (city)	Hudson County
Hockessin, DE (cdp)	New Castle County
Hoffman Estates, IL (village)	Cook County
Holland, MI (city)	Ottawa County
Holmdel, NJ (township)	Monmouth County
Honolulu, HI (cdp)	Honolulu County
Hopewell, NJ (township)	Mercer County
Hopkins, MN (city)	Hennepin County
Horsham, PA (township)	Montgomery County
Houston, TX (city)	Harris County
Howell, NJ (township)	Monmouth County
Huntington Beach, CA (city)	Orange County
Hyattsville, MD (city)	Prince George's County
Hybla Valley, VA (cdp)	Fairfax County
Idylwood, VA (cdp)	Fairfax County
Imperial Beach, CA (city)	San Diego County
Independence, MO (city)	Jackson County
Inglewood-Finn Hill, WA (cdp)	King County
Inkster, MI (city)	Wayne County
Iowa City, IA (city)	Johnson County
Irvine, CA (city)	Orange County
Irving, TX (city)	Dallas County
Iselin, NJ (cdp)	Middlesex County
Isla Vista, CA (cdp)	Santa Barbara County
Issaquah, WA (city)	King County

Ithaca, NY (city)	Tompkins County
Ives Estates, FL (cdp)	Miami-Dade County
Jefferson, VA (cdp)	Fairfax County
Jericho, NY (cdp)	Nassau County
Jersey City, NJ (city)	Hudson County
Johnson City, NY (village)	Broome County
Jollyville, TX (cdp)	Williamson County
Kahului, HI (cdp)	Maui County
Kailua, HI (cdp)	Honolulu County
Kaneohe, HI (cdp)	Honolulu County
Kaneohe Station, HI (cdp)	Honolulu County
Kearns, UT (cdp)	Salt Lake County
Kearny, NJ (town)	Hudson County
Kenmore, WA (city)	King County
Kent, WA (city)	King County
Kentwood, MI (city)	Kent County
Kihei, HI (cdp)	Maui County
Killeen, TX (city)	Bell County
King of Prussia, PA (cdp)	Montgomery County
Kingsgate, WA (cdp)	King County
Kirkland, WA (city)	King County
La Canada Flintridge, CA (city)	Los Angeles County
La Crescenta-Montrose, CA (cdp)	Los Angeles County
La Crosse, WI (city)	La Crosse County
La Habra, CA (city)	Orange County
La Mesa, CA (city)	San Diego County
La Mirada, CA (city)	Los Angeles County
La Palma, CA (city)	Orange County
La Presa, CA (cdp)	San Diego County
La Puente, CA (city)	Los Angeles County
La Riviera, CA (cdp)	Sacramento County
La Verne, CA (city)	Los Angeles County
Lacey, WA (city)	Thurston County
Lafayette, CA (city)	Contra Costa County
Lafayette, CO (city)	Boulder County
Laguna, CA (cdp)	Sacramento County
Laguna Hills, CA (city)	Orange County
Laguna Niguel, CA (city)	Orange County
Lake Forest Park, WA (city)	King County
Lake Forest, CA (city)	Orange County
Lake Grove, NY (village)	Suffolk County
Lake Oswego, OR (city)	Clackamas County
Lake Ridge, VA (cdp)	Prince William County
Lake Zurich, IL (village)	Lake County
Lakeland North, WA (cdp)	King County
Lakeland South, WA (cdp)	King County
Lakewood, CA (city)	Los Angeles County
Lakewood, WA (city)	Pierce County
Lancaster, CA (city)	Los Angeles County
Lanham-Seabrook, MD (cdp)	Prince George's County
Lansdale, PA (borough)	Montgomery County
Lansing, NY (town)	Tompkins County
Larkspur, CA (city)	Marin County
Las Vegas, NV (city)	Clark County
Lathrop, CA (city)	San Joaquin County
Laurel, VA (cdp)	Henrico County
Laurel, MD (city)	Prince George's County
Lawndale, CA (city)	Los Angeles County
Lawrence, KS (city)	Douglas County
Lawrence, NJ (township)	Mercer County
Lea Hill, WA (cdp)	King County
Lemon Grove, CA (city)	San Diego County
Lemoore, CA (city)	Kings County
Lewisville, TX (city)	Denton County
Lexington Park, MD (cdp)	Saint Mary's County
Lexington, MA (town)	Middlesex County
Libertyville, IL (village)	Lake County
Lilburn, GA (city)	Gwinnett County
Lincoln Park, NJ (borough)	Morris County
Lincolnia, VA (cdp)	Fairfax County
Lincolnwood, IL (village)	Cook County
Linda, CA (cdp)	Yuba County
Lisle, IL (village)	Du Page County
Little Falls, NJ (township)	Passaic County
Little Ferry, NJ (borough)	Bergen County
Livermore, CA (city)	Alameda County
Livingston, CA (city)	Merced County
Livingston, NJ (township)	Essex County
Lodi, NJ (borough)	Bergen County
Lodi, CA (city)	San Joaquin County
Loma Linda, CA (city)	San Bernardino County
Lombard, IL (village)	Du Page County
Lomita, CA (city)	Los Angeles County
Lompoc, CA (city)	Santa Barbara County
Long Beach, CA (city)	Los Angeles County
Lorton, VA (cdp)	Fairfax County
Los Alamitos, CA (city)	Orange County
Los Alamos, NM (cdp)	Los Alamos County
Los Altos, CA (city)	Santa Clara County
Los Angeles, CA (city)	Los Angeles County
Los Gatos, CA (town)	Santa Clara County
Lowell, MA (city)	Middlesex County
Lower Gwynedd, PA (township)	Montgomery County
Lower Macungie, PA (township)	Lehigh County
Lower Makefield, PA (township)	Bucks County
Lower Providence, PA (township)	Montgomery County
Lutherville-Timonium, MD (cdp)	Baltimore County
Lynchburg, VA (city)	Lynchburg Independent City
Lyndhurst, NJ (township)	Bergen County
Lynn, MA (city)	Essex County
Lynnwood, WA (city)	Snohomish County
Madison Heights, MI (city)	Oakland County
Madison, WI (city)	Dane County
Mahwah, NJ (township)	Bergen County
Makakilo City, HI (cdp)	Honolulu County
Malden, MA (city)	Middlesex County
Manalapan, NJ (township)	Monmouth County
Manassas Park, VA (city)	Manassas Park Independent City
Manchester, MO (city)	Saint Louis County
Manhattan Beach, CA (city)	Los Angeles County
Manhattan, KS (city)	Riley County
Manhattan, NY (borough)	New York County
Mansfield, CT (town)	Tolland County
Maple Shade, NJ (township)	Burlington County
Maplewood, MN (city)	Ramsey County
Marina, CA (city)	Monterey County
Marlboro, NJ (township)	Monmouth County
Marlborough, MA (city)	Middlesex County
Marlton, NJ (cdp)	Burlington County
Marple, PA (township)	Delaware County
Martha Lake, WA (cdp)	Snohomish County
Martin, TN (city)	Weakley County
Martinez, GA (cdp)	Columbia County
Martinez, CA (city)	Contra Costa County
Maryland Heights, MO (city)	Saint Louis County
Marysville, CA (city)	Yuba County
Marysville, WA (city)	Snohomish County
Mayfield Heights, OH (city)	Cuyahoga County
Mays Chapel, MD (cdp)	Baltimore County
McLean, VA (cdp)	Fairfax County
Medford, MA (city)	Middlesex County
Melville, NY (cdp)	Suffolk County
Menlo Park, CA (city)	San Mateo County
Merced, CA (city)	Merced County
Mercer Island, WA (city)	King County
Meridian charter, MI (township)	Ingham County
Merrifield, VA (cdp)	Fairfax County
Mesa, AZ (city)	Maricopa County
Mesquite, TX (city)	Dallas County
Metuchen, NJ (borough)	Middlesex County

Middlesex, NJ (borough)	Middlesex County
Mililani Town, HI (cdp)	Honolulu County
Mill Creek, WA (city)	Snohomish County
Millbrae, CA (city)	San Mateo County
Millburn, NJ (township)	Essex County
Milpitas, CA (city)	Santa Clara County
Mineola, NY (village)	Nassau County
Minneapolis, MN (city)	Hennepin County
Mission Bend, TX (cdp)	Fort Bend County
Mission Viejo, CA (city)	Orange County
Missouri City, TX (city)	Fort Bend County
Modesto, CA (city)	Stanislaus County
Monrovia, CA (city)	Los Angeles County
Montclair, CA (city)	San Bernardino County
Montebello, CA (city)	Los Angeles County
Monterey Park, CA (city)	Los Angeles County
Monterey, CA (city)	Monterey County
Montgomery Village, MD (cdp)	Montgomery County
Montgomery, NJ (township)	Somerset County
Montgomery, PA (township)	Montgomery County
Montgomeryville, PA (cdp)	Montgomery County
Montville, NJ (township)	Morris County
Moorpark, CA (city)	Ventura County
Moraga, CA (town)	Contra Costa County
Moreno Valley, CA (city)	Riverside County
Morgan Hill, CA (city)	Santa Clara County
Morganville, NJ (cdp)	Monmouth County
Morris, NJ (township)	Morris County
Morton Grove, IL (village)	Cook County
Mount Laurel, NJ (township)	Burlington County
Mount Olive, NJ (township)	Morris County
Mount Prospect, IL (village)	Cook County
Mount Vernon, VA (cdp)	Fairfax County
Mountain Park, GA (cdp)	Gwinnett County
Mountain View, CA (city)	Santa Clara County
Mountlake Terrace, WA (city)	Snohomish County
Mukilteo, WA (city)	Snohomish County
Mundelein, IL (village)	Lake County
Muni. of Monroeville, PA (borough)	Allegheny County
Munster, IN (town)	Lake County
Myrtle Grove, FL (cdp)	Escambia County
Nanakuli, HI (cdp)	Honolulu County
Nanuet, NY (cdp)	Rockland County
Naperville, IL (city)	Du Page County
Nashua, NH (city)	Hillsborough County
Natick, MA (town)	Middlesex County
National City, CA (city)	San Diego County
Needham, MA (town)	Norfolk County
New Brighton, MN (city)	Ramsey County
New Brunswick, NJ (city)	Middlesex County
New Carrollton, MD (city)	Prince George's County
New Castle, NY (town)	Westchester County
New City, NY (cdp)	Rockland County
New Haven, CT (city)	New Haven County
New Milford, NJ (borough)	Bergen County
New Paltz, NY (town)	Ulster County
New Providence, NJ (borough)	Union County
New Rochelle, NY (city)	Westchester County
New Territory, TX (cdp)	Fort Bend County
New York, NY (city)	New York City
Newark, CA (city)	Alameda County
Newark, DE (city)	New Castle County
Newington, VA (cdp)	Fairfax County
Newport Beach, CA (city)	Orange County
Newport News, VA (city)	Newport News Independent City
Newton, MA (city)	Middlesex County
Newtown, PA (township)	Bucks County
Niles, IL (village)	Cook County
Niskayuna, NY (town)	Schenectady County
Norfolk, VA (city)	Norfolk Independent City
North Andover, MA (town)	Essex County
North Arlington, NJ (borough)	Bergen County
North Atlanta, GA (cdp)	De Kalb County
North Bergen, NJ (township)	Hudson County
North Bethesda, MD (cdp)	Montgomery County
North Brunswick, NJ (township)	Middlesex County
North Castle, NY (town)	Westchester County
North Creek, WA (cdp)	Snohomish County
North Decatur, GA (cdp)	De Kalb County
North Druid Hills, GA (cdp)	De Kalb County
North Hempstead, NY (town)	Nassau County
North Highlands, CA (cdp)	Sacramento County
North Las Vegas, NV (city)	Clark County
North Laurel, MD (cdp)	Howard County
North Merrick, NY (cdp)	Nassau County
North Miami Beach, FL (city)	Miami-Dade County
North New Hyde Park, NY (cdp)	Nassau County
North Plainfield, NJ (borough)	Somerset County
North Potomac, MD (cdp)	Montgomery County
North Valley Stream, NY (cdp)	Nassau County
Northborough, MA (town)	Worcester County
Northbrook, IL (village)	Cook County
Northville, MI (township)	Wayne County
Norwalk, CA (city)	Los Angeles County
Norwood, MA (town)	Norfolk County
Novato, CA (city)	Marin County
Novi, MI (city)	Oakland County
Nutley, NJ (township)	Essex County
Oak Harbor, WA (city)	Island County
Oak Park, IL (village)	Cook County
Oak Ridge, FL (cdp)	Orange County
Oakland, CA (city)	Alameda County
Oakton, VA (cdp)	Fairfax County
Ocean, NJ (township)	Monmouth County
Oceanside, CA (city)	San Diego County
Okemos, MI (cdp)	Ingham County
Old Bridge, NJ (township)	Middlesex County
Olivehurst, CA (cdp)	Yuba County
Olney, MD (cdp)	Montgomery County
Olympia, WA (city)	Thurston County
Ontario, CA (city)	San Bernardino County
Orange, CA (city)	Orange County
Orangetown, NY (town)	Rockland County
Orchards, WA (cdp)	Clark County
Orcutt, CA (cdp)	Santa Barbara County
Orem, UT (city)	Utah County
Orinda, CA (city)	Contra Costa County
Orland Park, IL (village)	Cook County
Oroville, CA (city)	Butte County
Ossining, NY (town)	Westchester County
Ossining, NY (village)	Westchester County
Overland Park, KS (city)	Johnson County
Owings Mills, MD (cdp)	Baltimore County
Oxnard, CA (city)	Ventura County
Oyster Bay, NY (town)	Nassau County
Pacific Grove, CA (city)	Monterey County
Pacifica, CA (city)	San Mateo County
Paine Field-Lake Stickney, WA (cdp)	Snohomish County
Palatine, IL (village)	Cook County
Palisades Park, NJ (borough)	Bergen County
Palm Springs, CA (city)	Riverside County
Palmdale, CA (city)	Los Angeles County
Palo Alto, CA (city)	Santa Clara County
Palos Verdes Estates, CA (city)	Los Angeles County
Paradise, NV (cdp)	Clark County
Paramus, NJ (borough)	Bergen County
Parkland, WA (cdp)	Pierce County
Parkway-S. Sacramento, CA (cdp)	Sacramento County
Parsippany-Troy Hills, NJ (township)	Morris County
Pasadena, CA (city)	Los Angeles County

Passaic, NJ (city)	Passaic County
Patton, PA (township)	Centre County
Peachtree City, GA (city)	Fayette County
Pearl City, HI (cdp)	Honolulu County
Pedley, CA (cdp)	Riverside County
Pelham, NY (town)	Westchester County
Pembroke Pines, FL (city)	Broward County
Pennsauken, NJ (township)	Camden County
Perry Hall, MD (cdp)	Baltimore County
Petaluma, CA (city)	Sonoma County
Pflugerville, TX (city)	Travis County
Philadelphia, PA (city)	Philadelphia County
Phoenix, AZ (city)	Maricopa County
Picnic Point-N. Lynnwood, WA (cdp)	Snohomish County
Piedmont, CA (city)	Alameda County
Pike Creek, DE (cdp)	New Castle County
Pinecrest, FL (village)	Miami-Dade County
Pinellas Park, FL (city)	Pinellas County
Pinole, CA (city)	Contra Costa County
Piscataway, NJ (township)	Middlesex County
Pittsburg, CA (city)	Contra Costa County
Pittsfield charter, MI (township)	Washtenaw County
Pittsford, NY (town)	Monroe County
Placentia, CA (city)	Orange County
Plainsboro, NJ (township)	Middlesex County
Plainview, NY (cdp)	Nassau County
Plano, TX (city)	Collin County
Pleasant Hill, CA (city)	Contra Costa County
Pleasanton, CA (city)	Alameda County
Plymouth, MN (city)	Hennepin County
Plymouth, PA (township)	Montgomery County
Pomona, CA (city)	Los Angeles County
Port Arthur, TX (city)	Jefferson County
Port Hueneme, CA (city)	Ventura County
Port Lavaca, TX (city)	Calhoun County
Port Washington, NY (cdp)	Nassau County
Porterville, CA (city)	Tulare County
Portland, OR (city)	Multnomah County
Portsmouth, VA (city)	Portsmouth Independent City
Potomac, MD (cdp)	Montgomery County
Poughkeepsie, NY (town)	Dutchess County
Poway, CA (city)	San Diego County
Princeton Meadows, NJ (cdp)	Middlesex County
Princeton, NJ (borough)	Mercer County
Princeton, NJ (township)	Mercer County
Prospect Heights, IL (city)	Cook County
Providence, RI (city)	Providence County
Provo, UT (city)	Utah County
Pullman, WA (city)	Whitman County
Queens, NY (borough)	Queens County
Quincy, MA (city)	Norfolk County
Radcliff, KY (city)	Hardin County
Radnor, PA (township)	Delaware County
Rahway, NJ (city)	Union County
Ramapo, NY (town)	Rockland County
Ramsey, NJ (borough)	Bergen County
Rancho Cordova, CA (cdp)	Sacramento County
Rancho Cucamonga, CA (city)	San Bernardino County
Rancho Palos Verdes, CA (city)	Los Angeles County
Rancho San Diego, CA (cdp)	San Diego County
Rancho Santa Margarita, CA (city)	Orange County
Randolph, MA (town)	Norfolk County
Randolph, NJ (township)	Morris County
Redland, MD (cdp)	Montgomery County
Redlands, CA (city)	San Bernardino County
Redmond, WA (city)	King County
Redondo Beach, CA (city)	Los Angeles County
Redwood City, CA (city)	San Mateo County
Reedley, CA (city)	Fresno County
Reisterstown, MD (cdp)	Baltimore County
Reno, NV (city)	Washoe County
Renton, WA (city)	King County
Reston, VA (cdp)	Fairfax County
Revere, MA (city)	Suffolk County
Rialto, CA (city)	San Bernardino County
Richardson, TX (city)	Dallas County
Richfield, MN (city)	Hennepin County
Richland, WA (city)	Benton County
Richmond Heights, OH (city)	Cuyahoga County
Richmond, CA (city)	Contra Costa County
Richmond, VA (city)	Richmond Independent City
Ridgecrest, CA (city)	Kern County
Ridgefield Park, NJ (village)	Bergen County
Ridgefield, NJ (borough)	Bergen County
Ridgewood, NJ (village)	Bergen County
River Edge, NJ (borough)	Bergen County
Riverdale, GA (city)	Clayton County
Riverside, CA (city)	Riverside County
Riverton-Boulevard Park, WA (cdp)	King County
Roanoke, VA (city)	Roanoke Independent City
Rochester Hills, MI (city)	Oakland County
Rochester, MI (city)	Oakland County
Rochester, MN (city)	Olmsted County
Rockaway, NJ (township)	Morris County
Rocklin, CA (city)	Placer County
Rockville, MD (city)	Montgomery County
Rocky Hill, CT (town)	Hartford County
Rohnert Park, CA (city)	Sonoma County
Rolla, MO (city)	Phelps County
Rolling Meadows, IL (city)	Cook County
Rose Hill, VA (cdp)	Fairfax County
Roselle Park, NJ (borough)	Union County
Roselle, IL (village)	Du Page County
Rosemead, CA (city)	Los Angeles County
Rosemont, CA (cdp)	Sacramento County
Roseville, CA (city)	Placer County
Roseville, MN (city)	Ramsey County
Rossmoor, CA (cdp)	Orange County
Rossville, MD (cdp)	Baltimore County
Roswell, GA (city)	Fulton County
Rowland Heights, CA (cdp)	Los Angeles County
Rowlett, TX (city)	Dallas County
Roxbury, NJ (township)	Morris County
Rutherford, NJ (borough)	Bergen County
Rye, NY (city)	Westchester County
Sacramento, CA (city)	Sacramento County
Saddle Brook, NJ (township)	Bergen County
Saint George, UT (city)	Washington County
Saint Louis, MO (city)	Saint Louis Independent City
Saint Paul, MN (city)	Ramsey County
Salem, OR (city)	Marion County
Salida, CA (cdp)	Stanislaus County
Salinas, CA (city)	Monterey County
Salisbury, NY (cdp)	Nassau County
Salisbury, MD (city)	Wicomico County
Salt Lake City, UT (city)	Salt Lake County
Sammamish, WA (city)	King County
San Bernardino, CA (city)	San Bernardino County
San Bruno, CA (city)	San Mateo County
San Carlos, CA (city)	San Mateo County
San Diego, CA (city)	San Diego County
San Dimas, CA (city)	Los Angeles County
San Francisco, CA (city)	San Francisco County
San Gabriel, CA (city)	Los Angeles County
San Jose, CA (city)	Santa Clara County
San Leandro, CA (city)	Alameda County
San Lorenzo, CA (cdp)	Alameda County
San Luis Obispo, CA (city)	San Luis Obispo County
San Marcos, CA (city)	San Diego County
San Marino, CA (city)	Los Angeles County

San Mateo, CA (city)	San Mateo County
San Pablo, CA (city)	Contra Costa County
San Rafael, CA (city)	Marin County
San Ramon, CA (city)	Contra Costa County
Sandy, UT (city)	Salt Lake County
Santa Ana, CA (city)	Orange County
Santa Clara, CA (city)	Santa Clara County
Santa Clarita, CA (city)	Los Angeles County
Santa Cruz, CA (city)	Santa Cruz County
Santa Maria, CA (city)	Santa Barbara County
Santa Monica, CA (city)	Los Angeles County
Santa Rosa, CA (city)	Sonoma County
Saratoga, CA (city)	Santa Clara County
Savage, MN (city)	Scott County
Savage-Guilford, MD (cdp)	Howard County
Sayreville, NJ (borough)	Middlesex County
Scarsdale, NY (village)	Westchester County
Schaumburg, IL (village)	Cook County
Schiller Park, IL (village)	Cook County
Schofield Barracks, HI (cdp)	Honolulu County
Scio, MI (township)	Washtenaw County
Scotch Plains, NJ (township)	Union County
Scott Township, PA (cdp)	Allegheny County
Scott, PA (township)	Allegheny County
Scotts Valley, CA (city)	Santa Cruz County
SeaTac, WA (city)	King County
Seal Beach, CA (city)	Orange County
Seaside, CA (city)	Monterey County
Seattle Hill-Silver Firs, WA (cdp)	Snohomish County
Seattle, WA (city)	King County
Secaucus, NJ (town)	Hudson County
Setauket-East Setauket, NY (cdp)	Suffolk County
Severn, MD (cdp)	Anne Arundel County
Sharon, MA (town)	Norfolk County
Sharonville, OH (city)	Hamilton County
Sheboygan, WI (city)	Sheboygan County
Shoreline, WA (city)	King County
Shrewsbury, MA (town)	Worcester County
Sierra Madre, CA (city)	Los Angeles County
Silver Spring, MD (cdp)	Montgomery County
Silverdale, WA (cdp)	Kitsap County
Simi Valley, CA (city)	Ventura County
Skokie, IL (village)	Cook County
Smyrna, GA (city)	Cobb County
Solana Beach, CA (city)	San Diego County
Solon, OH (city)	Cuyahoga County
Somerset, NJ (cdp)	Somerset County
Somerville, NJ (borough)	Somerset County
Somerville, MA (city)	Middlesex County
South Brunswick, NJ (township)	Middlesex County
South El Monte, CA (city)	Los Angeles County
South Elgin, IL (village)	Kane County
South Gate, MD (cdp)	Anne Arundel County
South Lake Tahoe, CA (city)	El Dorado County
South Laurel, MD (cdp)	Prince George's County
South Pasadena, CA (city)	Los Angeles County
South Plainfield, NJ (borough)	Middlesex County
South San Francisco, CA (city)	San Mateo County
South San Jose Hills, CA (cdp)	Los Angeles County
South Windsor, CT (town)	Hartford County
South Yuba City, CA (cdp)	Sutter County
Spanaway, WA (cdp)	Pierce County
Sparks, NV (city)	Washoe County
Spokane, WA (city)	Spokane County
Spring Valley, CA (cdp)	San Diego County
Spring Valley, NV (cdp)	Clark County
Spring Valley, NY (village)	Rockland County
Springdale, NJ (cdp)	Camden County
Springdale, AR (city)	Washington County
Springfield, VA (cdp)	Fairfax County
Springfield, NJ (township)	Union County
Stafford, TX (city)	Fort Bend County
Stamford, CT (city)	Fairfield County
Stanford, CA (cdp)	Santa Clara County
Stanton, CA (city)	Orange County
Starkville, MS (city)	Oktibbeha County
State College, PA (borough)	Centre County
Staten Island, NY (borough)	Richmond County
Sterling Heights, MI (city)	Macomb County
Stevens Point, WI (city)	Portage County
Stillwater, OK (city)	Payne County
Stockton, CA (city)	San Joaquin County
Stony Brook, NY (cdp)	Suffolk County
Storm Lake, IA (city)	Buena Vista County
Storrs, CT (cdp)	Tolland County
Streamwood, IL (village)	Cook County
Succasunna-Kenvil, NJ (cdp)	Morris County
Sudbury, MA (town)	Middlesex County
Suffolk, VA (city)	Suffolk Independent City
Sugar Land, TX (city)	Fort Bend County
Suisun City, CA (city)	Solano County
Summit, NJ (city)	Union County
Sunnyvale, CA (city)	Santa Clara County
Sunrise Manor, NV (cdp)	Clark County
Syosset, NY (cdp)	Nassau County
Tacoma, WA (city)	Pierce County
Takoma Park, MD (city)	Montgomery County
Tamalpais-Homestead Vly, CA (cdp)	Marin County
Tarrytown, NY (village)	Westchester County
Taylorsville, UT (city)	Salt Lake County
Teaneck, NJ (township)	Bergen County
Temecula, CA (city)	Riverside County
Tempe, AZ (city)	Maricopa County
Temple City, CA (city)	Los Angeles County
Tenafly, NJ (borough)	Bergen County
Thousand Oaks, CA (city)	Ventura County
Tigard, OR (city)	Washington County
Timberlane, LA (cdp)	Jefferson Parish
Tinton Falls, NJ (borough)	Monmouth County
Torrance, CA (city)	Los Angeles County
Towamencin, PA (township)	Montgomery County
Town and Country, MO (city)	Saint Louis County
Towson, MD (cdp)	Baltimore County
Tracy, CA (city)	San Joaquin County
Tredyffrin, PA (township)	Chester County
Troy, MI (city)	Oakland County
Tualatin, OR (city)	Washington County
Tucker, GA (cdp)	De Kalb County
Tucson, AZ (city)	Pima County
Tukwila, WA (city)	King County
Tumwater, WA (city)	Thurston County
Turlock, CA (city)	Stanislaus County
Tustin Foothills, CA (cdp)	Orange County
Tustin, CA (city)	Orange County
Tysons Corner, VA (cdp)	Fairfax County
Union City, CA (city)	Alameda County
Union Hill-Novelty Hill, WA (cdp)	King County
Union, NJ (township)	Union County
University Place, WA (city)	Pierce County
Upland, CA (city)	San Bernardino County
Upper Darby, PA (township)	Delaware County
Upper Dublin, PA (township)	Montgomery County
Upper Gwynedd, PA (township)	Montgomery County
Upper Macungie, PA (township)	Lehigh County
Upper Merion, PA (township)	Montgomery County
Upper St. Clair, PA (township)	Allegheny County
Urbana, IL (city)	Champaign County
Vacaville, CA (city)	Solano County
Vadnais Heights, MN (city)	Ramsey County
Valinda, CA (cdp)	Los Angeles County

Vallejo, CA (city)	Solano County
Valley Stream, NY (village)	Nassau County
Vancouver, WA (city)	Clark County
Ventnor City, NJ (city)	Atlantic County
Vernon Hills, IL (village)	Lake County
Verona, NJ (township)	Essex County
Vestal, NY (town)	Broome County
Victorville, CA (city)	San Bernardino County
Vienna, VA (town)	Fairfax County
Villa Park, IL (village)	Du Page County
Vincent, CA (cdp)	Los Angeles County
Vineyard, CA (cdp)	Sacramento County
Virginia Beach, VA (city)	Virginia Beach Independent City
Visalia, CA (city)	Tulare County
Vista, CA (city)	San Diego County
Voorhees, NJ (township)	Camden County
Wahiawa, HI (cdp)	Honolulu County
Waianae, HI (cdp)	Honolulu County
Wailuku, HI (cdp)	Maui County
Waimalu, HI (cdp)	Honolulu County
Waipahu, HI (cdp)	Honolulu County
Waipio, HI (cdp)	Honolulu County
Wallington, NJ (borough)	Bergen County
Walnut Creek, CA (city)	Contra Costa County
Walnut, CA (city)	Los Angeles County
Waltham, MA (city)	Middlesex County
Wappinger, NY (town)	Dutchess County
Warren, NJ (township)	Somerset County
Warrenville, IL (city)	Du Page County
Wausau, WI (city)	Marathon County
Wayland, MA (town)	Middlesex County
Wayne, NJ (township)	Passaic County
Weehawken, NJ (township)	Hudson County
Wellesley, MA (town)	Norfolk County
Wells Branch, TX (cdp)	Travis County
West Bloomfield, MI (township)	Oakland County
West Caldwell, NJ (township)	Essex County
West Carson, CA (cdp)	Los Angeles County
West Covina, CA (city)	Los Angeles County
West Freehold, NJ (cdp)	Monmouth County
West Goshen, PA (township)	Chester County
West Hartford, CT (town)	Hartford County
West Hempstead, NY (cdp)	Nassau County
West Hollywood, CA (city)	Los Angeles County
West Jordan, UT (city)	Salt Lake County
West Lafayette, IN (city)	Tippecanoe County
West Orange, NJ (township)	Essex County
West Puente Valley, CA (cdp)	Los Angeles County
West Sacramento, CA (city)	Yolo County
West Springfield, VA (cdp)	Fairfax County
West University Place, TX (city)	Harris County
West Valley City, UT (city)	Salt Lake County
West Whiteland, PA (township)	Chester County
West Windsor, NJ (township)	Mercer County
Westborough, MA (town)	Worcester County
Westbury, NY (village)	Nassau County
Westchase, FL (cdp)	Hillsborough County
Westfield, NJ (town)	Union County
Westford, MA (town)	Middlesex County
Westlake, OH (city)	Cuyahoga County
Westminster, CA (city)	Orange County
Westminster, CO (city)	Adams County
Westmont, IL (village)	Du Page County
Weston, MA (town)	Middlesex County
Westwood, NJ (borough)	Bergen County
Wheaton, IL (city)	Du Page County
Wheaton-Glenmont, MD (cdp)	Montgomery County
Wheeling, IL (village)	Cook County
White Center, WA (cdp)	King County
White Oak, MD (cdp)	Montgomery County
White Plains, NY (city)	Westchester County
Whitpain, PA (township)	Montgomery County
Whittier, CA (city)	Los Angeles County
Wichita, KS (city)	Sedgwick County
Williamsburg, VA (city)	Williamsburg Independent City
Wilmette, IL (village)	Cook County
Winchester, NV (cdp)	Clark County
Winchester, MA (town)	Middlesex County
Winfield, KS (city)	Cowley County
Woburn, MA (city)	Middlesex County
Wolf Trap, VA (cdp)	Fairfax County
Woodbridge, VA (cdp)	Prince William County
Woodbridge, NJ (township)	Middlesex County
Woodbury, MN (city)	Washington County
Woodland, CA (city)	Yolo County
Woodlawn, MD (cdp)	Baltimore County
Woodmere, LA (cdp)	Jefferson Parish
Woodmere, NY (cdp)	Nassau County
Woodridge, IL (village)	Du Page County
Woonsocket, RI (city)	Providence County
Worcester, MA (city)	Worcester County
Worthington, MN (city)	Nobles County
Wright, FL (cdp)	Okaloosa County
Wyckoff, NJ (township)	Bergen County
Yonkers, NY (city)	Westchester County
Yorba Linda, CA (city)	Orange County
Yuba City, CA (city)	Sutter County

UNIVERSAL REFERENCE PUBLICATIONS

FREE CD-ROM

UNIVERSAL REFERENCE PUBLICATIONS

Universal Reference Publications/An Imprint of Grey House Publishing
PO Box 860 ◆ 185 Millerton Road ◆ Millerton, NY 12546
(800) 562-2139 ◆ (518) 789-8700 ◆ FAX (518) 789-0556 www.greyhouse.com ◆ e-mail: books@greyhouse.com

FREE CD-ROM WITH YOUR PURCHASE

The Asian Databook – Free Companion CD-ROM

This FREE companion CD-ROM contains data for over 3,400 places – **thousands more than the print version.** Data covers all states, counties and cities with Asian or Native Hawaiian and Other Pacific Islander residents. This easy-to-use CD-ROM allows users to view and print Statistics by Topic and Ranking Tables as ready-to-use resources – right from PDF files. Just attach this coupon to your payment and we'll ship your CD-ROM at no cost.

FREE CD-ROM COUPON

☐ I have enclosed payment for *The Asian Databook.* Send my FREE CD-Rom to the address below.

Name: ______________________ Invoice#: ____________

Company Name: ______________________

Address: ______________________

City: ____________ State: ____________ Zip Code: ____________

Telephone Number: ____________ Fax Number: ____________

Authorization Signature: ____________ Date: ____________

America's Top-Rated Cities, 2004

America's Top-Rated Cities provides current, comprehensive statistical information and other essential data in one easy-to-use source on the 100 "top" cities that have been cited as the best for business and living in the U.S. This handbook allows readers to see, at a glance, a concise social, business, economic, demographic and environmental profile of each city, including brief evaluative comments. In addition to detailed data on Cost of Living, Finances, Real Estate, Education, Major Employers, Media, Crime and Climate, city reports now include Housing Vacancies, Tax Audits, Bankruptcy, Presidential Election Results and more. This outstanding source of information will be widely used in any reference collection.

"The only source of its kind that brings together all of this information into one easy-to-use source. It will be beneficial to many business and public libraries." –ARBA

2,500 pages, 4 Volume Set; Softcover ISBN 1-59237-038-1, $195.00

America's Top-Rated Smaller Cities, 2004

A perfect companion to *America's Top-Rated Cities, America's Top-Rated Smaller Cities* provides current, comprehensive business and living profiles of smaller cities (population 25,000-99,999) that have been cited as the best for business and living in the United States. Sixty cities make up this 2004 edition of *America's Top-Rated Smaller Cities,* all are top-ranked by Population Growth, Median Income, Unemployment Rate and Crime Rate. City reports reflect the most current data available on a wide-range of statistics, including Employment & Earnings, Household Income, Unemployment Rate, Population Characteristics, Taxes, Cost of Living, Education, Health Care, Public Safety, Recreation, Media, Air & Water Quality and much more. Plus, each city report contains a Background of the City, and an Overview of the State Finances. *America's Top-Rated Smaller Cities* offers a reliable, one-stop source for statistical data that, before now, could only be found scattered in hundreds of sources. This volume is designed for a wide range of readers: individuals considering relocating a residence or business; professionals considering expanding their business or changing careers; general and market researchers; real estate consultants; human resource personnel; urban planners and investors.

"Provides current, comprehensive statistical information in one easy-to-use source... Recommended for public and academic libraries and specialized collections." –Library Journal

1,100 pages; Softcover ISBN 1-59237-043-8, $160.00

The American Tally, 2003/04 **Statistics & Comparative Rankings for U.S. Cities with Populations over 10,000**

This important statistical handbook compiles, all in one place, comparative statistics on all U.S. cities and towns with a 10,000+ population. *The American Tally* provides statistical details on over 4,000 cities and towns and profiles how they compare with one another in Population Characteristics, Education, Language & Immigration, Income & Employment and Housing. Each section begins with an alphabetical listing of cities by state, allowing for quick access to both the statistics and relative rankings of any city. Next, the highest and lowest cities are listed in each statistic. These important, informative lists provide quick reference to which cities are at both extremes of the spectrum for each statistic. Unlike any other reference, *The American Tally* provides quick, easy access to comparative statistics – a must-have for any reference collection.

"A solid library reference." -Bookwatch

500 pages; Softcover ISBN 1-930956-29-0, $125.00

The Comparative Guide to American Elementary & Secondary Schools, 2004/05

The only guide of its kind, this award winning compilation offers a snapshot profile of every public school district in the United States serving 1,500 or more students – more than 5,900 districts are covered. Organized alphabetically by district within state, each chapter begins with a Statistical Overview of the state. Each district listing includes contact information (name, address, phone number and web site) plus Grades Served, the Numbers of Students and Teachers and the Number of Regular, Special Education, Alternative and Vocational Schools in the district along with statistics on Student/Classroom Teacher Ratios, Drop Out Rates, Ethnicity, the Numbers of Librarians and Guidance Counselors and District Expenditures per student. As an added bonus, *The Comparative Guide to American Elementary and Secondary Schools* provides important ranking tables, both by state and nationally, for each data element. For easy navigation through this wealth of information, this handbook contains a useful City Index that lists all districts that operate schools within a city. These important comparative statistics are necessary for anyone considering relocation or doing comparative research on their own district and would be a perfect acquisition for any public library or school district library.

"This straightforward guide is an easy way to find general information. Valuable for academic and large public library collections." –ARBA

2,400 pages; Softcover ISBN 1-59237-047-0, $125.00

The Comparative Guide to American Suburbs, 2001

The Comparative Guide to American Suburbs is a one-stop source for Statistics on the 2,000+ suburban communities surrounding the 50 largest metropolitan areas – their population characteristics, income levels, economy, school system and important data on how they compare to one another. Organized into 50 Metropolitan Area chapters, each chapter contains an overview of the Metropolitan Area, a detailed Map followed by a comprehensive Statistical Profile of each Suburban Community, including Contact Information, Physical Characteristics, Population Characteristics, Income, Economy, Unemployment Rate, Cost of Living, Education, Chambers of Commerce and more. Next, statistical data is sorted into Ranking Tables that rank the suburbs by twenty different criteria, including Population, Per Capita Income, Unemployment Rate, Crime Rate, Cost of Living and more. *The Comparative Guide to American Suburbs* is the best source for locating data on suburbs. Those looking to relocate, as well as those doing preliminary market research, will find this an invaluable timesaving resource.

"Public and academic libraries will find this compilation useful... The work draws together figures from many sources and will be especially helpful for job relocation decisions." – Booklist

1,681 pages; Softcover ISBN 1-930956-42-8, $130.00

The Value of a Dollar 1860-2004, Third Edition

A guide to practical economy, *The Value of a Dollar* records the actual prices of thousands of items that consumers purchased from the Civil War to the present, along with facts about investment options and income opportunities. This brand new Third Edition boasts a brand new addition to each five-year chapter, a section on Trends. This informative section charts the change in price over time and provides added detail on the reasons prices changed within the time period, including industry developments, changes in consumer attitudes and important historical facts. Plus, a brand new chapter for 2000-2004 has been added. Each 5-year chapter includes a Historical Snapshot, Consumer Expenditures, Investments, Selected Income, Income/Standard Jobs, Food Basket, Standard Prices and Miscellany. This interesting and useful publication will be widely used in any reference collection.

"Recommended for high school, college and public libraries." –ARBA

600 pages; Hardcover ISBN 1-59237-074-8, $135.00

Working Americans 1880-1999
Volume I: The Working Class, Volume II: The Middle Class, Volume III: The Upper Class

Each of the volumes in the *Working Americans 1880-1999* series focuses on a particular class of Americans, The Working Class, The Middle Class and The Upper Class over the last 120 years. Chapters in each volume focus on one decade and profile three to five families. Family Profiles include real data on Income & Job Descriptions, Selected Prices of the Times, Annual Income, Annual Budgets, Family Finances, Life at Work, Life at Home, Life in the Community, Working Conditions, Cost of Living, Amusements and much more. Each chapter also contains an Economic Profile with Average Wages of other Professions, a selection of Typical Pricing, Key Events & Inventions, News Profiles, Articles from Local Media and Illustrations. The *Working Americans* series captures the lifestyles of each of the classes from the last twelve decades, covers a vast array of occupations and ethnic backgrounds and travels the entire nation. These interesting and useful compilations of portraits of the American Working, Middle and Upper Classes during the last 120 years will be an important addition to any high school, public or academic library reference collection.

"These interesting, unique compilations of economic and social facts, figures and graphs will support multiple research needs. They will engage and enlighten patrons in high school, public and academic library collections." –Booklist

Volume I: The Working Class ◆ 558 pages; Hardcover ISBN 1-891482-81-5, $145.00
Volume II: The Middle Class ◆ 591 pages; Hardcover ISBN 1-891482-72-6; $145.00
Volume III: The Upper Class ◆ 567 pages; Hardcover ISBN 1-930956-38-X, $145.00

Working Americans 1880-1999 Volume IV: Their Children

This Fourth Volume in the highly successful *Working Americans 1880-1999* series focuses on American children, decade by decade from 1880 to 1999. This interesting and useful volume introduces the reader to three children in each decade, one from each of the Working, Middle and Upper classes. Like the first three volumes in the series, the individual profiles are created from interviews, diaries, statistical studies, biographies and news reports. Profiles cover a broad range of ethnic backgrounds, geographic area and lifestyles – everything from an orphan in Memphis in 1882, following the Yellow Fever epidemic of 1878 to an eleven-year-old nephew of a beer baron and owner of the New York Yankees in New York City in 1921. Chapters also contain important supplementary materials including News Features as well as information on everything from Schools to Parks, Infectious Diseases to Childhood Fears along with Entertainment, Family Life and much more to provide an informative overview of the lifestyles of children from each decade. This interesting account of what life was like for Children in the Working, Middle and Upper Classes will be a welcome addition to the reference collection of any high school, public or academic library.

600 pages; Hardcover ISBN 1-930956-35-5, $145.00

Working Americans 1880-2003 Volume V: Americans At War

Working Americans 1880-2003 Volume V: Americans At War is divided into 11 chapters, each covering a decade from 1880-2003 and examines the lives of Americans during the time of war, including declared conflicts, one-time military actions, protests, and preparations for war. Each decade includes several personal profiles, whether on the battlefield or on the homefront, that tell the stories of civilians, soldiers, and officers during the decade. The profiles examine: Life at Home; Life at Work; and Life in the Community. Each decade also includes an Economic Profile with statistical comparisons, a Historical Snapshot, News Profiles, local News Articles, and Illustrations that provide a solid historical background to the decade being examined. Profiles range widely not only geographically, but also emotionally, from that of a girl whose leg was torn off in a blast during WWI, to the boredom of being stationed in the Dakotas as the Indian Wars were drawing to a close. As in previous volumes of the *Working Americans* series, information is presented in narrative form, but hard facts and real-life situations back up each story. The basis of the profiles come from diaries, private print books, personal interviews, family histories, estate documents and magazine articles. For easy reference, *Working Americans 1880-2003 Volume V: Americans At War* includes an in-depth Subject Index. The *Working Americans* series has become an important reference for public libraries, academic libraries and high school libraries. This fifth volume will be a welcome addition to all of these types of reference collections.

600 pages; Hardcover ISBN 1-59237-024-1; $145.00
Five Volume Set (Volumes I-V), Hardcover ISBN 1-59237-034-9, $675.00

Weather America, A Thirty-Year Summary of Statistical Weather Data and Rankings

This valuable resource provides extensive climatological data for over 4,000 National and Cooperative Weather Stations throughout the United States. *Weather America* begins with a new Major Storms section that details major storm events of the nation and a National Rankings section that details rankings for several data elements, such as Maximum Temperature and Precipitation. The main body of *Weather America* is organized into 50 state sections. Each section provides a Data Table on each Weather Station, organized alphabetically, that provides statistics on Maximum and Minimum Temperatures, Precipitation, Snowfall, Extreme Temperatures, Foggy Days, Humidity and more. State sections contain two brand new features in this edition – a City Index and a narrative Description of the climatic conditions of the state. Each section also includes a revised Map of the State that includes not only weather stations, but cities and towns.

"Best Reference Book of the Year." –Library Journal

2,013 pages; Softcover ISBN 1-891482-29-7, $175.00

The Environmental Resource Handbook, 2004

The Environmental Resource Handbook, now in its second edition, is the most up-to-date and comprehensive source for Environmental Resources and Statistics. Section I: Resources provides detailed contact information for thousands of information sources, including Associations & Organizations, Awards & Honors, Conferences, Foundations & Grants, Environmental Health, Government Agencies, National Parks & Wildlife Refuges, Publications, Research Centers, Educational Programs, Green Product Catalogs, Consultants and much more. Section II: Statistics, provides statistics and rankings on hundreds of important topics, including Children's Environmental Index, Municipal Finances, Toxic Chemicals, Recycling, Climate, Air & Water Quality and more. This kind of up-to-date environmental data, all in one place, is not available anywhere else on the market place today. This vast compilation of resources and statistics is a must-have for all public and academic libraries as well as any organization with a primary focus on the environment.

"…worth consideration by libraries with environmental collections and environmentally concerned users." –Booklist

1,000 pages; Softcover ISBN 1-59237-030-6, $155.00 ◆ Online Database $300.00

Education Directories

Educators Resource Directory, 2003/04

Educators Resource Directory is a comprehensive resource that provides the educational professional with thousands of resources and statistical data for professional development. This directory saves hours of research time by providing immediate access to Associations & Organizations, Conferences & Trade Shows, Educational Research Centers, Employment Opportunities & Teaching Abroad, School Library Services, Scholarships, Financial Resources, Professional Consultants, Computer Software & Testing Resources and much more. Plus, this comprehensive directory also includes a section on Statistics and Rankings with over 100 tables, including statistics on Average Teacher Salaries, SAT/ACT scores, Revenues & Expenditures and more. These important statistics will allow the user to see how their school rates among others, make relocation decisions and so much more. In addition to the Entry & Publisher Index, Geographic Index and Web Sites Index, our editors have added a Subject & Grade Index to this 2003/04 edition – so now it's even quicker and easier to locate information. *Educators Resource Directory* will be a well-used addition to the reference collection of any school district, education department or public library.

"Recommended for all collections that serve elementary and secondary school professionals." –Choice

1,000 pages; Softcover ISBN 1-59237-002-0, $145.00 ◆ Online Database $195.00 ◆ Online Database & Directory Combo $280.00

Sedgwick Press
Health Directories

The Complete Learning Disabilities Directory, 2004/05

The Complete Learning Disabilities Directory is the most comprehensive database of Programs, Services, Curriculum Materials, Professional Meetings & Resources, Camps, Newsletters and Support Groups for teachers, students and families concerned with learning disabilities. This information-packed directory includes information about Associations & Organizations, Schools, Colleges & Testing Materials, Government Agencies, Legal Resources and much more. For quick, easy access to information, this directory contains four indexes: Entry Name Index, Subject Index and Geographic Index. With every passing year, the field of learning disabilities attracts more attention and the network of caring, committed and knowledgeable professionals grows every day. This directory is an invaluable research tool for these parents, students and professionals.

"Due to its wealth and depth of coverage, parents, teachers and others… should find this an invaluable resource." -Booklist

900 pages; Softcover ISBN 1-59237-049-7, $145.00 ◆ Online Database $195.00 ◆ Online Database & Directory Combo $280.00

The Complete Directory for People with Disabilities, 2005

A wealth of information, now in one comprehensive sourcebook. Completely updated for 2005, this edition contains more information than ever before, including thousands of new entries and enhancements to existing entries and thousands of additional web sites and e-mail addresses. This up-to-date directory is the most comprehensive resource available for people with disabilities, detailing Independent Living Centers, Rehabilitation Facilities, State & Federal Agencies, Associations, Support Groups, Periodicals & Books, Assistive Devices, Employment & Education Programs, Camps and Travel Groups. Each year, more libraries, schools, colleges, hospitals, rehabilitation centers and individuals add *The Complete Directory for People with Disabilities* to their collections, making sure that this information is readily available to the families, individuals and professionals who can benefit most from the amazing wealth of resources cataloged here.

"No other reference tool exists to meet the special needs of the disabled in one convenient resource for information." –Library Journal

1,200 pages; Softcover ISBN 1-59237-054-3, $165.00 ◆ Online Database $215.00 ◆ Online Database & Directory Combo $300.00

The Complete Directory for People with Chronic Illness, 2003/04

Thousands of hours of research have gone into this completely updated 2003/04 edition – several new chapters have been added along with thousands of new entries and enhancements to existing entries. Plus, each chronic illness chapter has been reviewed by an medical expert in the field. This widely-hailed directory is structured around the 90 most prevalent chronic illnesses – from Asthma to Cancer to Wilson's Disease – and provides a comprehensive overview of the support services and information resources available for people diagnosed with a chronic illness. Each chronic illness has its own chapter and contains a brief description in layman's language, followed by important resources for National & Local Organizations, State Agencies, Newsletters, Books & Periodicals, Libraries & Research Centers, Support Groups & Hotlines, Web Sites and much more. This directory is an important resource for health care professionals, the collections of hospital and health care libraries, as well as an invaluable tool for people with a chronic illness and their support network.

"A must purchase for all hospital and health care libraries and is strongly recommended for all public library reference departments." –ARBA

1,200 pages; Softcover ISBN 1-930956-83-5, $165.00 ◆ Online Database $215.00 ◆ Online Database & Directory Combo $300.00

The Complete Mental Health Directory, 2004

This is the most comprehensive resource covering the field of behavioral health, with critical information for both the layman and the mental health professional. For the layman, this directory offers understandable descriptions of 25 Mental Health Disorders as well as detailed information on Associations, Media, Support Groups and Mental Health Facilities. For the professional, *The Complete Mental Health Directory* offers critical and comprehensive information on Managed Care Organizations, Information Systems, Government Agencies and Provider Organizations. This comprehensive volume of needed information will be widely used in any reference collection.

"… the strength of this directory is that it consolidates widely dispersed information into a single volume." –Booklist

800 pages; Softcover ISBN 1-59237-046-2, $165.00 ◆ Online Database $215.00 ◆ Online & Directory Combo $300.00

To preview any of our Directories Risk-Free for 30 days, call (800) 562-2139 or fax to (518) 789-0556

The Complete Directory for Pediatric Disorders, 2004/05

This important directory provides parents and caregivers with information about Pediatric Conditions, Disorders, Diseases and Disabilities, including Blood Disorders, Bone & Spinal Disorders, Brain Defects & Abnormalities, Chromosomal Disorders, Congenital Heart Defects, Movement Disorders, Neuromuscular Disorders and Pediatric Tumors & Cancers. This carefully written directory offers: understandable Descriptions of 15 major bodily systems; Descriptions of more than 200 Disorders and a Resources Section, detailing National Agencies & Associations, State Associations, Online Services, Libraries & Resource Centers, Research Centers, Support Groups & Hotlines, Camps, Books and Periodicals. This resource will provide immediate access to information crucial to families and caregivers when coping with children's illnesses.

"Recommended for public and consumer health libraries." –Library Journal

1,200 pages; Softcover ISBN 1-59237-045-4, $165.00 ◆ Online Database $215.00 ◆ Online Database & Directory Combo $300.00

Older Americans Information Directory, 2004/05

Completely updated for 2004/05, this Fifth Edition has been completely revised and now contains 1,000 new listings, over 8,000 updates to existing listings and over 3,000 brand new e-mail addresses and web sites. You'll find important resources for Older Americans including National, Regional, State & Local Organizations, Government Agencies, Research Centers, Libraries & Information Centers, Legal Resources, Discount Travel Information, Continuing Education Programs, Disability Aids & Assistive Devices, Health, Print Media and Electronic Media. Three indexes: Entry Index, Subject Index and Geographic Index make it easy to find just the right source of information. This comprehensive guide to resources for Older Americans will be a welcome addition to any reference collection.

"Highly recommended for academic, public, health science and consumer libraries…" –Choice

1,200 pages; Softcover ISBN 1-59237-037-3, $165.00 ◆ Online Database $215.00 ◆ Online Database & Directory Combo $300.00

The Complete Directory for People with Rare Disorders, 2002/03

This outstanding reference is produced in conjunction with the National Organization for Rare Disorders to provide comprehensive and needed access to important information on over 1,000 rare disorders, including Cancers and Muscular, Genetic and Blood Disorders. An informative Disorder Description is provided for each of the 1,100 disorders (rare Cancers and Muscular, Genetic and Blood Disorders) followed by information on National and State Organizations dealing with a particular disorder, Umbrella Organizations that cover a wide range of disorders, the Publications that can be useful when researching a disorder and the Government Agencies to contact. Detailed and up-to-date listings contain mailing address, phone and fax numbers, web sites and e-mail addresses along with a description. For quick, easy access to information, this directory contains two indexes: Entry Name Index and Acronym/Keyword Index along with an informative Guide for Rare Disorder Advocates. The Complete Directory for People with Rare Disorders will be an invaluable tool for the thousands of families that have been struck with a rare or "orphan" disease, who feel that they have no place to turn and will be a much-used addition to the reference collection of any public or academic library.

"Quick access to information… public libraries and hospital patient libraries will find this a useful resource in directing users to support groups or agencies dealing with a rare disorder." –Booklist

726 pages; Softcover ISBN 1-891482-18-1, $165.00

The Directory of Drug & Alcohol Residential Rehabilitation Facilities, 2004

This brand new directory is the first-ever resource to bring together, all in one place, data on the thousands of drug and alcohol residential rehabilitation facilities in the United States. *The Directory of Drug & Alcohol Residential Rehabilitation Facilities* covers over 1,000 facilities, with detailed contact information for each one, including mailing address, phone and fax numbers, email addresses and web sites, mission statement, type of treatment programs, cost, average length of stay, numbers of residents and counselors, accreditation, insurance plans accepted, type of environment, religious affiliation, education components and much more. It also contains a helpful chapter on General Resources that provides contact information for Associations, Print & Electronic Media, Support Groups and Conferences. Multiple indexes allow the user to pinpoint the facilities that meet very specific criteria. This time-saving tool is what so many counselors, parents and medical professionals have been asking for. *The Directory of Drug & Alcohol Residential Rehabilitation Facilities* will be a helpful tool in locating the right source for treatment for a wide range of individuals. This comprehensive directory will be an important acquisition for all reference collections: public and academic libraries, case managers, social workers, state agencies and many more.

"This is an excellent, much needed directory that fills an important gap…" –Booklist

300 pages; Softcover ISBN 1-59237-031-4, $135.00

To preview any of our Directories Risk-Free for 30 days, call (800) 562-2139 or fax to (518) 789-0556

The Directory of Venture Capital Firms, 2005

This edition has been extensively updated and broadly expanded to offer direct access to over 2,800 Domestic and International Venture Capital Firms, including address, phone & fax numbers, e-mail addresses and web sites for both primary and branch locations. Entries include details on the firm's Mission Statement, Industry Group Preferences, Geographic Preferences, Average and Minimum Investments and Investment Criteria. You'll also find details that are available nowhere else, including the Firm's Portfolio Companies and extensive information on each of the firm's Managing Partners, such as Education, Professional Background and Directorships held, along with the Partner's E-mail Address. *The Directory of Venture Capital Firms* offers five important indexes: Geographic Index, Executive Name Index, Portfolio Company Index, Industry Preference Index and College & University Index. With its comprehensive coverage and detailed, extensive information on each company, *The Directory of Venture Capital Firms* is an important addition to any finance collection.

"The sheer number of listings, the descriptive information provided and the outstanding indexing make this directory a better value than its principal competitor, Pratt's Guide to Venture Capital Sources. Recommended for business collections in large public, academic and business libraries." –Choice

1,300 pages; Softcover ISBN 1-59237-062-4, $450.00 ◆ Online Database (includes a free copy of the directory) $889.00

The Directory of Mail Order Catalogs, 2005

Published since 1981, this 2005 edition features 100% verification of data and is the premier source of information on the mail order catalog industry. Details over 12,000 consumer catalog companies with 44 different product chapters from Animals to Toys & Games. Contains detailed contact information including e-mail addresses and web sites along with important business details such as employee size, years in business, sales volume, catalog size, number of catalogs mailed and more. Four indexes provide quick access to information: Catalog & Company Name Index, Geographic Index, Product Index and Web Sites Index.

"This is a godsend for those looking for information." –Reference Book Review

1,700 pages; Softcover ISBN 1-59237-066-7 $250.00 ◆ Online Database (includes a free copy of the directory) $495.00

The Directory of Business to Business Catalogs, 2005

The completely updated 2005 *Directory of Business to Business Catalogs*, provides details on over 6,000 suppliers of everything from computers to laboratory supplies... office products to office design... marketing resources to safety equipment... landscaping to maintenance suppliers... building construction and much more. Detailed entries offer mailing address, phone & fax numbers, e-mail addresses, web sites, key contacts, sales volume, employee size, catalog printing information and more. Jut about every kind of product a business needs in its day-to-day operations is covered in this carefully-researched volume. Three indexes are provided for at-a-glance access to information: Catalog & Company Name Index, Geographic Index and Web Sites Index.

"An excellent choice for libraries... wishing to supplement their business supplier resources." –Booklist

800 pages; Softcover ISBN 1-59237-064-0, $165.00 ◆ Online Database (includes a free copy of the directory) $325.00

Thomas Food and Beverage Market Place, 2005

Thomas Food and Beverage Market Place is bigger and better than ever with thousands of new companies, thousands of updates to existing companies and two revised and enhanced product category indexes. This comprehensive directory profiles over 18,000 Food & Beverage Manufacturers, 12,000 Equipment & Supply Companies, 2,200 Transportation & Warehouse Companies, 2,000 Brokers & Wholesalers, 8,000 Importers & Exporters, 900 Industry Resources and hundreds of Mail Order Catalogs. Listings include detailed Contact Information, Sales Volumes, Key Contacts, Brand & Product Information, Packaging Details and much more. *Thomas Food and Beverage Market Place* is available as a three-volume printed set, a subscription-based Online Database via the Internet, on CD-ROM, as well as mailing lists and a licensable database.

"An essential purchase for those in the food industry but will also be useful in public libraries where needed. Much of the information will be difficult and time consuming to locate without this handy three-volume ready-reference source." –ARBA

8,500 pages, 3 Volume Set; Softcover ISBN 1-59237-058-6, $495.00 ◆ CD-ROM $695.00 ◆
CD-ROM & 3 Volume Set Combo $895.00 ◆ Online Database $695.00 ◆ Online Database & 3 Volume Set Combo, $895.00

To preview any of our Directories Risk-Free for 30 days, call (800) 562-2139 or fax to (518) 789-0556

Sedgwick Press
Hospital & Health Plan Directories

The Directory of Hospital Personnel, 2005

The Directory of Hospital Personnel is the best resource you can have at your fingertips when researching or marketing a product or service to the hospital market. A "Who's Who" of the hospital universe, this directory puts you in touch with over 150,000 key decision-makers. With 100% verification of data you can rest assured that you will reach the right person with just one call. Every hospital in the U.S. is profiled, listed alphabetically by city within state. Plus, three easy-to-use, cross-referenced indexes put the facts at your fingertips faster and more easily than any other directory: Hospital Name Index, Bed Size Index and Personnel Index. *The Directory of Hospital Personnel* is the only complete source for key hospital decision-makers by name. Whether you want to define or restructure sales territories… locate hospitals with the purchasing power to accept your proposals… keep track of important contacts or colleagues… or find information on which insurance plans are accepted, *The Directory of Hospital Personnel* gives you the information you need – easily, efficiently, effectively and accurately.

"Recommended for college, university and medical libraries." -ARBA

2,500 pages; Softcover ISBN 1-59237-065-9 $275.00 ◆ Online Database $545.00 ◆ Online Database & Directory Combo, $650.00

The Directory of Health Care Group Purchasing Organizations, 2004

This comprehensive directory provides the important data you need to get in touch with over 800 Group Purchasing Organizations. By providing in-depth information on this growing market and its members, *The Directory of Health Care Group Purchasing Organizations* fills a major need for the most accurate and comprehensive information on over 800 GPOs – Mailing Address, Phone & Fax Numbers, E-mail Addresses, Key Contacts, Purchasing Agents, Group Descriptions, Membership Categorization, Standard Vendor Proposal Requirements, Membership Fees & Terms, Expanded Services, Total Member Beds & Outpatient Visits represented and more. With its comprehensive and detailed information on each purchasing organization, *The Directory of Health Care Group Purchasing Organizations* is the go-to source for anyone looking to target this market.

"The information is clearly arranged and easy to access…recommended for those needing this very specialized information." –ARBA

1,000 pages; Softcover ISBN 1-59237-036-5, $325.00 ◆ Online Database, $650.00 ◆ Online Database & Directory Combo, $750.00

The HMO/PPO Directory, 2005

The HMO/PPO Directory is a comprehensive source that provides detailed information about Health Maintenance Organizations and Preferred Provider Organizations nationwide. This comprehensive directory details more information about more managed health care organizations than ever before. Over 1,100 HMOs, PPOs and affiliated companies are listed, arranged alphabetically by state. Detailed listings include Key Contact Information, Prescription Drug Benefits, Enrollment, Geographical Areas served, Affiliated Physicians & Hospitals, Federal Qualifications, Status, Year Founded, Managed Care Partners, Employer References, Fees & Payment Information and more. Plus, five years of historical information is included related to Revenues, Net Income, Medical Loss Ratios, Membership Enrollment and Number of Patient Complaints. *The HMO/PPO Directory* provides the most comprehensive information on the most companies available on the market place today.

"Helpful to individuals requesting certain HMO/PPO issues such as co-payment costs, subscription costs and patient complaints. Individuals concerned (or those with questions) about their insurance may find this text to be of use to them." -ARBA

600 pages; Softcover ISBN 1-59237-057-8, $275.00 ◆ Online Database, $495.00 ◆ Online Database & Directory Combo, $600.00

The Directory of Independent Ambulatory Care Centers, 2002/03

This first edition of *The Directory of Independent Ambulatory Care Centers* provides access to detailed information that, before now, could only be found scattered in hundreds of different sources. This comprehensive and up-to-date directory pulls together a vast array of contact information for over 7,200 Ambulatory Surgery Centers, Ambulatory General and Urgent Care Clinics, and Diagnostic Imaging Centers that are not affiliated with a hospital or major medical center. Detailed listings include Mailing Address, Phone & Fax Numbers, E-mail and Web Site addresses, Contact Name and Phone Numbers of the Medical Director and other Key Executives and Purchasing Agents, Specialties & Services Offered, Year Founded, Numbers of Employees and Surgeons, Number of Operating Rooms, Number of Cases seen per year, Overnight Options, Contracted Services and much more. Listings are arranged by State, by Center Category and then alphabetically by Organization Name. *The Directory of Independent Ambulatory Care Centers* is a must-have resource for anyone marketing a product or service to this important industry and will be an invaluable tool for those searching for a local care center that will meet their specific needs.

"Among the numerous hospital directories, no other provides information on independent ambulatory centers. A handy, well-organized resource that would be useful in medical center libraries and public libraries." –Choice

986 pages; Softcover ISBN 1-930956-90-8, $185.00 ◆ Online Database, $365.00 ◆ Online Database & Directory Combo, $450.00

To preview any of our Directories Risk-Free for 30 days, call (800) 562-2139 or fax to (518) 789-0556